KV-087-058

B79 208 414 6

DICTIONARY

OF

NATIONAL BIOGRAPHY

SUPPLEMENT

1901—1911

THE

DICTIONARY
of
NATIONAL BIOGRAPHY

Founded in 1882

by

GEORGE SMITH

SUPPLEMENT

January 1901 – December 1911

Edited by Sir Sidney Lee

VOL. I. *ABBEY–EYRE*

Now published by the

OXFORD UNIVERSITY PRESS

Printed by Spottiswoode & Co., Ltd.
and published 1912 by Smith, Elder & Co.
Plated from moulds of the first edition and reprinted
at the University Press, Oxford, 1920
Reprinted 1927, 1939, 1951, 1958, 1963, 1966, 1969, 1976

ISBN 0 19 865201 1

Printed in Great Britain
at the University Press, Oxford
by Vivian Ridler
Printer to the University

PREFATORY NOTE

The present Supplement has been undertaken by Mrs. George M. Smith, now the proprietor of the Dictionary of National Biography, and has been edited by Sir Sidney Lee. It furnishes biographies of noteworthy persons who died between 22 Jan. 1901 and 31 Dec. 1911. The former date was the day of Queen Victoria's death, and the First Supplement, which was published in the autumn of 1901, brought the record of national biography down to that limit. The bounds are now extended by nearly eleven years. The new volumes treat exclusively of those whom death has qualified for admission within the prescribed period.

When the present Supplement was planned the death of King Edward VII was not anticipated. Among the great names which the present volume includes, that of the late King is bound to attract chief attention. His memoir, like that of Queen Victoria in the First Supplement, is from the pen of the Editor.[1] It is an attempt—made it is believed for the first time—to co-ordinate the manifold activities of the sovereign in a just historic and biographic spirit. To the information which is already scattered through numerous published sketches and books of reminiscence at home and abroad much has been added, through the courtesy of those associated with the late King, from unpublished and unwritten sources. It is hoped that the result will be to remove some widely disseminated misapprehensions and to furnish some new and authentic elucidations. Although the article is shorter than that on Queen Victoria, it is on a larger scale than is habitual to the Dictionary. But the prominent place which the late King filled for half a century in the nation's public life, both before and after his accession, seemed, in the absence of a full record elsewhere, to compel a treatment which should be as exhaustive and authoritative as the writer's knowledge allowed, with due regard to the recent dates of the events.

The late King had a personal relation with the Dictionary which,

[1] Mr. Lionel Cust, F.S.A., M.V.O., has added to the article an account of the portraits.

apart from other considerations, calls in its pages for the tribute of an adequate memoir. On 25 May 1900, on the eve of the publication of the sixty-third and last volume of the substantive work, the late King, then Prince of Wales, honoured with his presence a private dinner-party given to congratulate the late Mr. George M. Smith, the public-spirited projector, proprietor, and publisher of the undertaking, on its completion.[1] He then spoke with his customary grace and charm of his interest in the Dictionary, and he afterwards expressed in a letter to the Editor the satisfaction which the meeting gave him. On 25 October 1901, the day of the publication of the last volume of the First Supplement, the King furthermore sent a letter of congratulation 'on the final completion of this great work.' Finality is no attribute of a record of national biography, but in the late King's lifetime the Dictionary came to a close with its First Supplement. It will now stand completed with its Second Supplement.

In February 1902 his late Majesty was pleased to accept from Mrs. George M. Smith a complete set of the volumes, which he placed in his private library at Sandringham. In acknowledging the gift the King's secretary wrote that His Majesty, who regarded the work as 'one of the highest interest and utility,' would 'always value Mrs. Smith's kind present as a memento' of the late George Smith, 'who did so much for literature, and whose acquaintance it was a satisfaction to His Majesty to remember to have made.

The number of names in the present Supplement reaches a total of 1660, of which 500 appear in this volume and the remainder fill two succeeding volumes. The contributors to this volume number 166.

The principles of selection and treatment are those with which students of the Dictionary are already familiar. Special care has been taken to make the genealogical data uniform and precise, and to give full particulars of memorial foundations, and of portraits whether painted or in sculpture.

[1] Of the twenty-nine persons who were present on the occasion twelve, including the King and the late Mr. George M. Smith, have since passed away. All are now commemorated in the Dictionary. Memoirs of Mr. George M. Smith and of Mandell Creighton, bishop of London, appeared in the First Supplement. The Second Supplement supplies notices of the rest, viz. King Edward VII, Lord Acton, Canon Ainger, Dr. Richard Garnett, Sir Richard Jebb, Mr. Joseph Knight, Mr W. E. H. Lecky, Sir Theodore Martin, Sir Leslie Stephen, and Sir Spencer Walpole.

The sources of biographical knowledge in the case of these whose careers have very recently closed differ from the sources in the case of those who belonged to more or less remote generations. In the interests of accuracy and completeness it has been necessary here to test and supplement previous notices—often inaccurate and incomplete—in the press or elsewhere, by application to living representatives and associates. The thanks of the Editor and contributors are due to the many hundred persons who have corrected current errors from private knowledge or have supplied information which has not hitherto been published. The readiness with which such co-operation has been given calls for very warm acknowledgment. The service has invariably been rendered without any conditions which might tend to impair the essential independence of the Dictionary. Officials of public institutions of every kind have also been most generous in their assistance, and have offered welcome proof of their anxiety to make the Dictionary authentic at all points.

In agreement with the principle of the Dictionary the memoirs embrace comprehensively all branches of the nation's and the empire's activity. In any endeavour to classify the vocations of the persons commemorated, allowance must be made for the circumstance that in a certain proportion of cases the same person has gained distinction in more fields than one. If the chief single claim to notice be alone admitted in each instance, the callings of those whose careers are described in this volume may be broadly catalogued under ten general headings thus:

	NAMES
Administration of Government at home, in India, and the colonies	53
Army and navy	44
Art (including architecture, music, and the stage)	70
Commerce and agriculture	17
Law	19
Literature (including journalism, philology, philosophy, printing, and lexicography)	115
Religion	54
Science (including engineering, medicine, surgery, and exploration)	86
Social Reform (including philanthropy and education)	34
Sport	8

The names of twenty-five women appear in this volume, on account of services rendered in art, literature, science, and social or educational reform.

Articles bear the initials of their writers save in a very few cases where material has been furnished to the Editor on an ampler scale than the purpose of the undertaking permitted him to use. In such instances the Editor and his staff are solely responsible for the shape which the article has taken, and no signature is appended.

In preparing this Supplement the Editor has enjoyed the advantage of the assistance of Mr. W. B. Owen, M.A., formerly scholar of St. Catharine's College, Cambridge, and of Mr. G. S. Woods, M.A., formerly exhibitioner of Exeter College, Oxford.

*** In the lists of authors' publications the date of issue is alone appended to the titles of works which were published in London in 8vo. In other cases the place of issue and the size are specifically indicated in addition.

Cross references are given thus: to names in the substantive work [q.v.]; to names in the First Supplement[1] [q.v. Suppl. I]; and to names in the present Supplement[2] [q.v. Suppl. II].

[1] i.e. Vol. XXII (of the thin paper edition). [2] i.e. 1901–1911.

LIST OF WRITERS

IN THE SUPPLEMENT 1901–1911

⁂ The names of deceased contributors are marked thus †.

J. P. A. .... J. P. ANDERSON.
W. R. A. .... †WILLIAM REYNELL ANSON.
A. L. A. .... ARTHUR L. ARMSTRONG.
W. A. .... †WALTER ARMSTRONG.
C. A. .... †CHEWTON ATCHLEY.
J. B. A–S. .. JOHN BLACK ATKINS.
J. B. A. .... †JAMES BERESFORD ATLAY.
R. B. .... †RONALD BAYNE.
T. B. .... †THOMAS WILSON BAYNE.
C. E. A. B... CYRIL EDWARD ALFRED BEDWELL.
M. B. .... †HENRY THOMAS MACKENZIE BELL.
F. L. B. .... FRANCIS L. BICKLEY.
L. B. .... LAURENCE BINYON.
W. A. B. .... WILLIAM ARTHUR BONE.
T. G. B. .... †THOMAS GEORGE BONNEY.
G. S. B. .... †GEORGE SIMONDS BOULGER.
G. C. B. .... †GILBERT CHARLES BOURNE.
C. W. B. .... †CHARLES WALTER BOYD.
J. C. B. .... †JOSEPH COX BRIDGE.
E. M. B. .... EDWARD MANSFIELD BROCKBANK.
A. A. B. .... †ARTHUR AIKIN BRODRIBB.
F. H. B. .... FRANK HERBERT BROWN.
P. H. B. .... †PETER HUME BROWN.
E. G. B. .... †EDWARD GRANVILLE BROWNE.
H. W. B. .... H. W. BRUTON.
A. R. B. .... AUGUSTUS ROBERT BUCKLAND.
W. W. B. .... WILLIAM WARWICK BUCKLAND.
J. B. .... †JOHN BURNET.
J. C. C. .... †JOHN CANNELL CAIN.
J. L. C. .... JAMES LEWIS CAW.
A. C–L. ..... ALGERNON CECIL.
H. H. C. .... HAROLD HANNYNGTON CHILD.
H. P. C. .... †HENRY PATRICK CHOLMELEY.
R. F. C. .... ROBERT FRANCIS CHOLMELEY.
A. C. .... †ANDREW CLARK.
E. C. .... †ERNEST CLARKE.
G. A. J. C... †GRENVILLE ARTHUR JAMES COLE.
S. C. .... †SIDNEY COLVIN.
E. T. C. .... †EDWARD TYAS COOK.
J. C. .... †JAMES COOPER.
F. C. .... †FREDERICK CORDER.
P. C. .... PERCY CORDER.
V. C. .... VAUGHAN CORNISH.
J. S. C. .... †JAMES SUTHERLAND COTTON.
W. C. .... WILLIAM CUBBON.
C. of K. .... †GEORGE NATHANIEL CURZON, EARL CURZON.
L. C. .... †LIONEL HENRY CUST.
G. H. D. .... †GEORGE HOWARD DARWIN.
H. D. .... †HENRY DAVEY.
J. D. H. D. . †JAMES DOUGLAS HAMILTON DICKSON.
A. D. .... †AUSTIN DOBSON.
C. D. .... CAMPBELL DODGSON.
P. E. D. .... PERCY ENFIELD DOWSON.
S. R. D. .... †SAMUEL ROLLES DRIVER.
J. D. D. .... JAMES DUFF DUFF.
W. B. D. .... WILLIAM BARTLETT DUFFIELD.
R. D. .... †ROBERT DUNLOP.
P. E. .... PELHAM EDGAR.
E. E. .... †EDWARD EDWARDS.
H. E. .... †HENRY ELLERSHAW.
A. R. D. E. . †ARTHUR RALPH DOUGLAS ELLIOT.
H. S. R. E. . HUGH SAMUEL ROGER ELLIOT.
M. E. .... †M. EPSTEIN.
A. L. F. .... ALFRED LAURENCE FELKIN.
W. G. F. .... W. G. FIELD.
J. N. F. .... †JOHN NEVILLE FIGGIS.
T. A. F. .... THOMAS ALOYSIUS FINLAY.
C. H. F. .... †CHARLES HARDING FIRTH.
H. A. L. F. . HERBERT ALBERT LAURENS FISHER.

D. F........ †David Fitzgerald.
J. F-K...... †James Fitzmaurice-Kelly.
W. G. D. F.. William George Dimock Fletcher.
W. H. G. F.. †William Henry Grattan Flood.
N. F........ †Nevill Forbes.
W. H. F.... Walter Howard Frere.
D. W. F.... †Douglas William Freshfield.
S. E. F..... S. E. Fryer.
F. W. G..... †Frederick William Gamble.
F. W. G–n.. Frank William Gibson.
G. A........ †George Alexander Gibson.
P. G........ †Peter Giles.
A. T. G..... Alfred Thomas Scrope Goodrick.
A. G........ †Alexander Gordon.
E. G........ †Edmund Gosse.
F. G........ †Francis Gotch.
E. G–m..... Eric Graham.
C. L. G..... Charles Larcom Graves.
R. E. G..... †Robert Edmund Graves.
W. F. G..... William Forbes Gray.
G. A. G–n... George Abraham Grierson.
F. Ll. G.... †Francis Llewellyn Griffith.
H. G....... Henry Guppy.
L. G........ †Leonard Guthrie.
J. C. H..... †James Cuthbert Hadden.
E. S. H..... Elizabeth Sanderson Haldane.
T. H........ †Thomas Hamilton.
D. H....... †David Hannay.
M. H....... Martin Hardie.
C. A. H..... Charles Alexander Harris.
F. H........ †Frederic Harrison.
P. J. H..... Philip Joseph Hartog.
F. J. H..... †Francis John Haverfield.
T. F. H..... †Thomas Finlayson Henderson.
J. A. H..... John Alexander Herbert.
H. H....... Henry Higgs.
A. P. H..... †Alfred Peter Hillier.
A. M. H..... Arthur Magyer Hind.
A. R. H..... Arthur Robert Hinks.
R. L. H..... Robert Lockhart Hobson.
D. G. H..... †David George Hogarth.
B. H. H..... †Bernard Henry Holland.
F. C. H..... Francis Caldwell Holland.
H. P. H..... Henry Park Hollis.
C. H........ †Charles Holroyd.
E. S. H–r... Edith S. Hooper.
J. H........ James Hooper.
W. W. H.... †Walter Wybergh How.
O. J. R. H.. Osbert John Radcliffe Howarth.
A. H–s...... Arthur Hughes.
T. C. H..... Thomas Cann Hughes.
W. H....... †William Hunt.
W. H. H.... †William Holden Hutton.
C. P. I..... †Courtenay Peregrine Ilbert.
E. im T..... †Everard Ferdinand im Thurn.
R. I........ †Roger Ingpen.
H. M'L. I... Hugh M'Leod Innes.
C. H. I..... †Clarke Huston Irwin.
A. V. W. J.. †Abraham Valentine Williams Jackson.
H. J........ †Henry Jackson.
W. S. J..... Wilfrid Scarborough Jackson.
M. R. J..... †Montague Rhodes James.
T. E. J..... T. E. James.
R. J........ Richard Jennings.
A. H. J..... †Arthur Henry Johnson.
C. J........ Claude Johnson.
J. K........ James Kennedy.
F. G. K..... Frederic George Kenyon.
D. R. K..... David Reid Keys.
C. L. K..... †Charles Lethbridge Kingsford.
P. G. K..... †Paul George Konody.
H. L........ †Horace Lamb.
J. N. L..... †John Newport Langley.
J. L........ Joseph Larmor.
D. C. L..... †Daniel Conner Lathbury.
J. K. L..... †John Knox Laughton.
L. G. C. L... Leonard George Carr Laughton.
W. J. L..... William John Lawrence.

W. R. M. L.. William Ralph Martin Leake.
E. L........ †Elizabeth Lee.
R. W. L. ... Robert Warden Lee.
S. L........ †Sidney Lee.
W. L-W..... †William Lee-Warner.
C. H. L..... Charles Herbert Lees.
R. C. L..... †Rudolph Chambers Lehmann.
J. H. L..... John Henry Leslie.
T. M. L..... †Thomas Martin Lindsay.
E. M. L..... †Ernest Marsh Lloyd.
J. E. L..... John Edward Lloyd.
B. F. L..... †Benjamin Fossett Lock.
B. S. L..... Basil Somerset Long.
J. H. L..... †Joseph Henry Longford.
H. L........ Henry Louis.
S. J. L...... †Sidney James Low.
C. P. L..... †Charles Prestwood Lucas.
E. V. L..... †Edward Verrall Lucas.
P. L........ Perceval Lucas.
R. L........ †Reginald Lucas.
J. R. M..... †James Ramsay Macdonald.
A. A. M..... †Arthur Anthony Macdonell.
C. D. M..... †Charles Donald Maclean.
G. A. M..... †George Augustin Macmillan.
W. G. M. ... †W. G. McNaught.
J. G. S. M... †John Gordon Swift Macneill.
A. M. .... Andrew Macphail.
F. M........ †Falconer Madan.
H. E. M..... †Henry Elliot Malden.
B. M. .... †Bernard Mallet.
J. M–t...... James Marchant.
J. M........ John Masefield.
A. M–n. .... †Annie Matheson.
D. S. M..... David Storrar Meldrum.
L. M........ †Lewis Melville.
E. M. ...... †Everard Meynell.
H. A. M..... Henry Alexander Miers.
A. H. M..... †Alexander Hastie Millar.
M. .... †Alfred Milner, Viscount Milner.
J. D. M..... †James Donald Milner.
H. C. M..... Harry Christopher Minchin.
J. E. G. de M. †James Edward Geoffrey de Montmorency.
W. F. M. ... †William Flavelle Monypenny.
N. M. ...... †Norman Moore.
E. M. ...... Edward Moorhouse.
S. M........ Sophia Morrison.
A. L. M..... †Arthur Lewis Mumm.
R. H. M. ... †Robert Henry Murray.
G. Le G. N.. Gerald Le Grys Norgate.
C. B. N..... C. B. Norman.
P. N........ †Philip Norman.
R. B. O'B... †Richard Barry O'Brien.
D. J. O'D... David James O'Donoghue.
G. W. T. O.. †George William Thomson Omond.
John Ossory †John Henry Bernard.
D. J. O..... David John Owen.
W. B. O. ... W. B. Owen.
T. E. P..... †Thomas Ethelbert Page.
S. P........ †Stephen Paget.
J. P........ John Parker.
E. A. P..... Edward Abbott Parry.
D. P........ †David Patrick.
E. H. P..... †Ernest Harold Pearce.
P. .... †John Sinclair, Lord Pentland.
L. R. P..... †Lancelot Ridley Phelps.
T. G. P..... †Theophilus Goldridge Pinches.
C. P........ †Charles Plummer.
A. W. P..... Alfred William Pollard.
D'A. P...... D'Arcy Power.
D. P–n. .... David Prain.
G. W. P..... †George Walter Prothero.
A. Q.-C. .... Arthur Thomas Quiller-Couch.
J. R........ †John Rae.
R. S. R. .... †Robert Sangster Rait.
G. S. A. R... †George Speirs Alexander Ranking.
C. H. R..... †Charles Hercules Read.
J. M. R..... †James McMullen Rigg.
V. R........ Vernon Horace Rendall.
W. R....... William Roberts.
L. R........ Lionel Robinson.

F. R........ Frederick Rogers.
H. D. R..... Humphry Davy Rolleston.
T. K. R..... Thomas Kirke Rose.
R. R. ...... †Robert Ross.
R. J. R..... Robert James Rowlette.
A. W. R. ... †Arthur William Rücker.
G. W. E. R.. †George William Erskine Russell.
M. E. S..... Michael Ernest Sadler.
F. S........ †Francis Sanders.
L. C. S...... †Lloyd Charles Sanders.
S........... †Thomas Henry Sanderson, Lord Sanderson.
J. E. S...... †John Edwin Sandys.
J. S. .... †John Sargeaunt.
T. S......... †Thomas Seccombe.
W. N. S..... William Napier Shaw.
C. S. S...... Charles Scott Sherrington.
E. S........ †Edith Sichel.
L. P. S...... L. P. Sidney.
A. F. S. .... Albert Forbes Sieveking.
F. S. S...... Francis Sheehy Skeffington.
A. H. S..... Arthur Hamilton Smith.
C. F. S...... Charlotte Fell-Smith.
G. S........ †George (Murray) Smith.
G. G. S. .... †George Gregory Smith.
J. G. S-C.... John George Snead-Cox.
W. R. S..... †William Ritchie Sorley.
W. F. S..... William Forbes Spear.
M. H. S..... Marion Harry Spielmann.
H. M. S..... Henry Maxwell Spooner.
V. H. S..... †Vincent Henry Stanton.
R. S........ Robert Steele.
H. S........ †Herbert Stephen.
J. A. S...... †John Alexander Stewart.
J. L. S.-D... †James Leigh Strachan-Davidson.
C. W. S..... †Charles William Sutton.
S. H. S. .... †Shapland Hugh Swinny.
H. T-S...... Harry Tapley-Soper.
J. T. .... James Taylor.
H. R. T..... †Henry Richard Tedder.
W. T. T-D. . †William Turner Thiselton-Dyer.
D. Ll. T.... Daniel Lleufer Thomas.
F. W. T..... Frederick William Thomas.
D'A. W. T. . D'Arcy Wentworth Thompson.
S. P. T...... †Silvanus Phillips Thompson.
B. T......... Basil Home Thomson.
T. H. T..... †Thomas Henry Thornton.
J. R. T. .... †James Richard Thursfield.
T. F. T. .... †Thomas Frederick Tout.
W. W. T..... †William Weir Tulloch.
R. Y. T..... †Robert Yelverton Tyrrell.
J. V......... †John Venn.
R. H. V..... †Robert Hamilton Veitch.
H. M. V..... †Henry Meredith Vibart.
E. W........ Ernest Walker.
P. M. W. ... Percy Maxwell Wallace.
R. W........ Robert Wallace.
W. S. W. ... William Stewart Wallace.
A. W. W.... †Adolphus William Ward.
P. W........ †Paul Waterhouse.
E. W. W.... †Edward William Watson.
F. W........ †Foster Watson.
J. C. W..... Josiah Clement Wedgwood.
C. W. ...... †Charles Welch.
H. B. W.... †Henry Benjamin Wheatley.
A. B. W. ... Amber Blanco White.
W. H. W.... †William Henry White.
E. T. W..... Edmund Taylor Whittaker.
A. W........ †Arthur Naylor Wollaston.
H. T. W. ... †Henry Trueman Wood.
G. S. W..... Gabriel S. Woods.
H. B. W. ... †Horace Bolingbroke Woodward.
W. W....... †Warwick William Wroth.

DICTIONARY

OF

NATIONAL BIOGRAPHY

1901–1911

ABBEY, EDWIN AUSTIN (1852–1911), painter and black-and-white and decorative artist, born on 1 April 1852 at 315 Race Street, Philadelphia, was eldest child in the family of two sons and a daughter of William Maxwell Abbey (1827–1897), a merchant of Philadelphia. His mother, Margery Ann (1825–1880), was daughter of Jacob Kipel, second son of Jacob Kypel (*d.* 1797), a farmer who emigrated to America from Freiburg, Baden, in 1760.

Abbey received his education in Philadelphia at the Randolph school (1862–4) and Dr. Gregory's school (1864–8), where he had drawing lessons from Isaac L. Williams of the Pennsylvania Academy, a landscape painter of local repute; for three months in 1868 he studied penmanship at Richard S. Dickson's writing-school. While there he contributed picture puzzles to Oliver Optic's 'Our Boys and Girls' under the pseudonym of 'Yorick.' In 1869 he entered the employ of Van Ingen and Snyder, wood-engravers of Philadelphia, who sent him to work in the antique and life classes at the Academy of Fine Arts. He was employed mainly on commercial and news illustrations. Soon afterwards he studied under Professor Christian Schuessèle at the Pennsylvania Academy and worked on historical compositions. The experience developed his power of imagination and faculty for design, while he applied himself to research in history and costume. In 1870 he sent drawings to the New York publishing house of Harper & Brothers for production in their 'Weekly.' In 1871 he went to New York, and after a month's probation in that firm's art department received a permanent position on the staff. He worked for Harpers continuously for twenty years.

In 1878 he came to England with a commission from Harpers to illustrate Herrick's poems. After two years he returned to New York for three months, and then settled permanently in England. He lived much in London, with country residences, first at Broadway, and then at Morgan Hall, Fairford, where he had a private cricket-ground. Latterly he purchased Woodcote Manor, previously occupied by Sir Francis Seymour Haden at Alresford, but did not live to occupy it. In London he acquired Chelsea Lodge, where he also worked much.

It was with his pen-and-ink illustrations that Abbey first conquered the English and American public. These appeared in editions of (among other works) Dickens's 'Christmas Stories' (1876); Herrick's poems ('Hesperides' and 'Noble Numbers') (1882); 'She Stoops to Conquer' (1887); 'The Good-Natured Man; Old Songs' (1889); 'The Comedies of Shakespeare' (1896)—132 illustrations which, by invitation, were exhibited at the Salon of the Société Nationale des Beaux-Arts, Paris, 1896—and 'The Tragedies of Shakespeare.' In 1885 a sketching tour in Holland with his friend George Henry Boughton [q. v. Suppl. II] was commemorated in 'Sketches and Rambles in Holland,' to which both artists contributed drawings. His first contribution to the Royal Academy was 'A Milkmaid' (1885), in black and white.

Meanwhile Abbey's power matured in water-colour, pastel, and oil. Although his delicate fancy lent itself admirably to water-colour painting, he executed not much more than a score of works in that medium; but they stand high in the list of his achievements. His first water-colour was 'Rustics Dancing in a Barn,' which was shown at the exhibition of the American Water-Colour Society of New York before 1876, and a few others followed in that and succeeding years. To the Royal Institute of Painters in Water-Colours he contributed 'The Widower' (1883); 'The Bible Reading' (1884); 'The Old Song' (1885); and 'The March Past' (1887); and to the Royal Society of Painters in Water-Colours, 'An Attention' (1893–4–5); and 'Quiet Conscience' (1896). On occasion Abbey would use pastel with brilliant effect, as in 'Good Friday Morning' (1884); his pastel sketches from Goldsmith's plays, exhibited in 1896, are masterly; but the examples of his work in this method are relatively few.

In 1890 he sent to the Royal Academy his first oil picture, 'A May-Day Morning,' which attracted wide attention for its originality, humour, truth, and joyousness. This was retouched and somewhat modified in 1904. He now embarked on a great commission for Boston, and not until 1894 did he send again to the Royal Academy. His second work seen there in oils, 'Fiammetta's Song,' created so deep an impression that he was immediately elected A.R.A. Many important historical and poetic compositions were now shown at the Academy: 'Richard, Duke of Gloucester and the Lady Anne' (1896), and 'King Lear, Act 1, Scene 1' (both in the McCulloch-Coutts Michie collection) and 'Hamlet' (1897). 'The Bridge' was shown in 1898, when Abbey was elected full member of the R.A. Subsequently came 'Who is Sylvia, what is she . . . ?' and 'O Mistress mine, where are you roaming?' (1899) (now in the Walker Art Gallery, Liverpool); 'A Lute Player' (diploma work), 'The Trial of Queen Katherine' (Senator W. A. Clarke's collection), and 'The Penance of Eleanor, Duchess of Gloucester, &c.' (1900); 'Crusaders sighting Jerusalem' (1901); 'Pot-Pourri' (1903 — signed '1899'); 'A Measure,' and a decoration, a triple panel reredos for the Holy Trinity Church, Paris (1904); 'Columbus in the New World' (1906), which startled the public by its decorative scheme; and in 1910, the last year of his career, an historical picture, 'The Camp of the Army at Valley Forge, Feb. 1778,' as well as a great upright decoration, 'Penn's Treaty with the Indians,' both for the state capitol of Pennsylvania. Meanwhile Abbey painted a few other pictures: 'The Poet,' his only contribution to the New Gallery (afterwards much altered and almost wholly re-painted); 'A Pavane' (1897) for Mr. Whitelaw Reid; 'Fair is my Love' (1906), in the gallery of the corporation of Preston; and the official picture of 'The Coronation of H.M. King Edward VII,' at Buckingham Palace, a work fifteen feet by nine feet, containing 120 excellent portraits and occupying the artist during 1903–4.

Abbey's mural decorations comprise the most ambitious part of his work. The great frieze for the delivery room of the public library of Boston, U.S.A., on which he was engaged between 1890 and 1901, is lofty in conception and original in plan and one of the most elaborate decorations produced by either American or British artist. Five of the paintings—90 feet in aggregate length—were shown at the Conduit Street Galleries, London, in January 1895, and the completed series at the Guildhall, October to November 1901—fifteen paintings in all. The dramatic presentation and artistic power of this great effort were recognised at once. For the Royal Exchange, London, he executed in 1904 a mural panel representing the ancient reconciliation of the two City companies, the Skinners and the Merchant Taylors, 1484. There followed a vast commission to decorate the state capitol of Pennsylvania at Harrisburg. In April 1908 eight large allegorical paintings, forming a portion for the dome, were exhibited in London at the Imperial Institute. At his death he had completed the immense composition 'The Apotheosis of Pennsylvania,' in which the whole history of the state is summarised, and the dome-ceiling 'The 24 Hours.' Other decorative work had occupied Abbey, especially the designs for Sir Henry Irving's contemplated but abandoned production of 'Richard II' (1898). At the request of the office of works Abbey superintended the decoration of the peers' corridor in the Houses of Parliament with historical pictures, approximating in sentiment to the Tudor style of the architecture, by a group of young artists working on an harmonious plan. These were completed in 1910.

Abbey died on 1 Aug. 1911 at Chelsea Lodge of an affection of the liver. After cremation he was buried at the old churchyard of Kingsbury, Neasden. On 22 April 1890 he had married Mary Gertrude (daughter of Frederick Mead, merchant, of New York). She survived him without issue.

Abbey's artistic and intellectual merits, which his personal charm and sympathetic and generous temperament enhanced, were widely acknowledged. He rapidly became a leading force in the English and American art of the day and founder of a school. Steeped in mediæval and seventeenth and eighteenth-century art and literature, he captivated the public by the charm, dignity, and dramatic ability which he brought to the rendering of his subjects. At the same time his artistic qualities, alike as to colour, draughtsmanship, composition, and invention, appealed on technical grounds to his fellow-artists, whether his medium were oil, water-colour, pen-and-ink, or pastel.

He was chosen member of many artistic societies in England and other countries, including the American Water-Colour Society of New York (elected 1876) and the Royal Institute of Painters in Water-Colours (London) (elected 1883 and resigned in 1893). In 1895, when he became one of the original incorporators of the American Academy at Rome, he was elected associate of the Royal Water-Colour Society. In 1901 he was made an associate and in 1902 a member of the (American) Academy of Design; and he was an original member of the American Academy of Arts and Letters. He was an hon. member of the American Institute of Architects (1895); hon. member of the Royal Bavarian Academy and of the Madrid Society of Artists; hon. associate of the Royal Institute of British Architects. After exhibiting his work in Paris in 1896 he was made chevalier of the legion of honour and corresponding member of the Institut de France, as well as of the Société Nationale des Beaux-Arts, Paris (1896). Yale University made him an hon. M.A. and the University of Pennsylvania an hon. LL.D. Among the awards won by Abbey were a second-class gold medal, Munich International Exhibition in 1883; a first-class gold medal, Exposition Universelle, Paris, in 1889; two gold medals, Chicago Exhibition, 1893; a gold medal of honour, Pennsylvania, 1897; and a first-class gold medal, Vienna Exhibition, 1898. In Jan.–March 1912 a memorial exhibition of Abbey's works, comprising 322 items, was included in the 'Old Masters' exhibition of the Royal Academy at Burlington House.

Abbey remained to the end an American citizen; but he deeply appreciated his reception in England, and he had a full faith in the beneficial influence and equitable organisation of the Royal Academy.

Among portraits of Abbey are a crayon drawing by J. S. Sargent, R.A.; an oil portrait by Sir W. Q. Orchardson, R.A. (1910, Orchardson's last work); a bronze bust by E. Onslow Ford, R.A. (1902); a sketch portrait by John H. Bacon, A.R.A.; drawings by Griyayédoff and Napoleon Sarony respectively, and a caricature and portrait by Leslie Ward ('Spy') in 'Vanity Fair' (1898).

[Private information and documents in the possession of Mrs. E. A. Abbey; Royal Academy Catalogues.] M. H. S.

ABBOTT, EVELYN (1843–1901), classical scholar, born at Epperstone, Nottinghamshire, on 10 March 1843, was third of the five sons of Evelyn Abbott, a farmer and landowner, by his wife Mary Lambe. Educated first at Lincoln grammar school and afterwards at the Somerset College, Bath, Abbott was elected in 1862 to an open exhibition at Balliol College, Oxford, and commenced his university residence in October. He established a high reputation among his contemporaries as a scholar, and was likewise distinguished in athletic sports. In 1864 he won the Gaisford prize for Greek verse and a first class in classical moderations. In the Easter vacation of 1866, just before he entered for his final examination, he fell in a hurdle race and injured his spine. Unhappily, he was so unaccustomed to illness that he did not recognise the serious nature of the accident, and continued his exertions, both at his books and at cricket, as if nothing had occurred. In the summer he obtained a first class in literæ humaniores. In the following autumn, when the mischief became manifest, it was too late for a cure; he became hopelessly paralysed in the lower limbs, and until his death never put foot to the ground. The inevitable effect of these unnatural conditions on his health and activity was held at bay for thirty-five years by a very strong natural constitution and by his admirable courage and patience. He soon began to take private pupils, sometimes near his birthplace in Sherwood Forest, sometimes at Filey. In 1870 he was appointed by Dr. Percival sixth form master at Clifton College. In 1873 Benjamin Jowett, Master of Balliol, invited him to return to Oxford, and until 1875 he took work at Corpus as well as at Balliol. In 1873 he graduated B.A. and M.A. In 1874 he was elected a fellow and tutor of Balliol. From that time till his resignation, only a few days before his death, he was a mainstay of the administration and teaching of his college. At first he taught mainly Latin and Greek scholarship; in his later years Greek history was his principal subject. He won the affection and confidence of his pupils by his unceasing efforts for their welfare and by the cheerfulness with which he bore his physical disabilities. He became Jowett lecturer in Greek in 1895, and was librarian of the college from 1881 to 1897, and in 1882 served as junior bursar.

Throughout his life Abbott was constantly engaged in writing in addition to his college work. He was well versed in German, and besides Curtius's 'Elucidations of the Students' Greek Grammar' (1870) he translated Max Duncker's 'History of Antiquity' (6 vols. 1877–81). He also assisted Miss Sarah Francis Alleyne (*d.* 1885) in English versions of Duncker's 'History of Greece' (2 vols. 1883–6) and Zeller's 'Outlines of Greek Philosophy' (1885). He was editor of 'Hellenica' (1880; 2nd edit. 1898), a collection of essays on Greek themes, and was general editor of the 'Heroes of the Nations' series, to which he contributed a life of Pericles (1891). Other works were 'Elements of Greek Accidence' (1874) and an index to Jowett's translation of Plato (1875). With Lewis Campbell [q. v. Suppl. II] he wrote the biography of his life-long friend, Benjamin Jowett, Master of Balliol (1897). His most important literary work is his 'History of Greece' in three volumes (1888–1900), admirable alike for its learning, sound judgment, and simple and lucid style. The sceptical view of the 'Iliad' and 'Odyssey,' which regards them as purely works of poetical imagination, has nowhere been more ably presented, and the presentation well illustrates Abbott's independent method in treating historical problems.

Abbott, who was made LL.D. of St. Andrews in 1879, maintained his activities till a few weeks before his death at Malvern on 3 Sept. 1901. He was buried at Redlands cemetery, near Cardiff.

[Personal knowledge; Foster's Alumni Oxon.]

J. L. S.-D.

À BECKETT, ARTHUR WILLIAM (1844–1909), humorist, third son of Gilbert Abbott à Beckett [q. v.], was born at Portland House, North End, Fulham, in October 1844. His godfather was William Gilbert [q. v.], the father of Sir William Schwenck Gilbert [q. v. Suppl. II]. Gilbert Arthur à Beckett [q. v. Suppl. I] was his elder brother. Arthur was educated first at Honiton and then at Felsted from January 1858 to December 1859 (Beevor, *Alumni Felsted.*). While at Felsted he contributed to the 'Braintree Times'; and later he was a favourite chairman of Old Felstedians. Palmerston nominated him in 1862 to a clerkship in the war office, but he soon migrated to the post office, and left the civil service in 1865 to engage in journalism. From 1871 to 1874 he was private secretary of the duke of Norfolk. Subsequently he became a student of Gray's Inn, 13 June 1877, and was called to the bar 3 May 1882, but he obtained no practice.

His vocation for the press showed itself early. At twenty he was assisting (Sir) Francis Burnand on the 'Glow-Worm,' a penny evening humorous paper, with which he was associated till 1868. He afterwards edited a satirical weekly, 'The Tomahawk.' At twenty-two, with the aid of his brother Gilbert, he wrote a 'Comic Guide to the Royal Academy' (1863–4). Good verbal spirits were the mainspring of his humour. Later he edited the 'Britannia' magazine (1868–70) and acted as special correspondent to the 'Standard' and the 'Globe' during the second period of the Franco-Prussian war in 1870, when he was arrested at Amiens and astonished a court of French officers by his jocularity. In 1871, after experience in the volunteers, he was given a company in the king's own light infantry militia, and for a short time in 1896 edited the 'Naval and Military Magazine.' From 1891 to 1895 he was also editor of the 'Sunday Times,' under the directorship of Sir Augustus Harris. His best work was done in connection with 'Punch,' of which he claimed that his father was part-originator and founder. Tom Taylor first invited him to contribute in May 1874; in August 1875 he was called to the table, and for the following twenty-seven years he was an ardent devotee. His 'Papers from Pump Handle Court, by A Briefless Junior' (in continuation of the *jeu d'esprit* of his father) were much quoted. After Burnand's promotion to the editorship in 1880 he occasionally acted as locum tenens. His withdrawal from 'Punch' under pressure in June 1902 left some resentment, and he projected and edited through 1902–3 a rival comic paper, 'John Bull,' which met with no success. Apart from his 'Punch' work he wrote 'About Town,' '£. *s. d.*,' and some melodramatic novels, one of which, 'Fallen among Thieves' (1876), he and John Palgrave Simpson [q.v.] dramatised as 'From Father to Son.' He was also author of 'Our Holiday in the Scottish Highlands' in conjunction with Linley Sambourne in 1876, and in his last years of several very loosely knit volumes of recollections, among them 'London at the End of the Century' (1900), 'The À Becketts of Punch' (1903), and 'Recollections of a Humourist' (1907). President of the Newspaper Society in 1895, of the Institute of Journalists in 1900, and British delegate of the press congress at Liège in 1905, he was universally liked in his profession. Irrepressible egotism in À Beckett lent an additional charm to a character simple, kindly, and genial to its foundation. His naiveté was well shown in his relations with Cardinal Manning, to whose church he became, like his friend Burnand, a convert in 1874. An accident necessitated the removal of À Beckett's leg at St. Thomas's Home on 11 Jan. 1909, and he died of collapse on 14 Jan. 1909. After a requiem mass at Westminster he was buried in Mortlake cemetery. He married in 1876 Susanna Francesca, daughter of Dr. Forbes Winslow, by whom he left two sons. His completion of his father's 'Comic History of England' is still unpublished.

[The Times, 12–15, 19 Jan. 1909; Illustrated London News, 18 Jan. 1909 (portrait); Men and Women of the Time, 1899; Foster's Men at the Bar, 1885; Burnand's Records and Reminiscences, 1904, ii. 230; Recollections of a Humourist, 1907 (portrait); Spielmann's Hist. of Punch (1895); Brit. Mus. Cat.; À Beckett's works; personal recollections.]

T. S.

ABEL, Sir FREDERICK AUGUSTUS, first baronet (1827–1902), chemist, born on 17 July 1827 at Woolwich, was son of Johann Leopold Abel (1795–1871), a music-master in Kennington, by his wife Louisa (*d.* 1864), daughter of Martin Hopkins of Walworth. His paternal grandfather, August Christian Andreas Abel (*b.* 12 Aug. 1751), was court miniature-painter to the Grand Duke of Mecklenburg-Schwerin.

Abel was attracted to a scientific career by a visit at the age of fourteen to an uncle in Hamburg, A. J. Abel, a mineralogist and a pupil of Berzelius. After a course of chemistry under Dr. Ryan at the Royal Polytechnic Institution, he entered the Royal College of Chemistry, founded in October 1845 under A. W. Hofmann; he was one of the twenty-six original students. Next year he became an assistant, holding the position for five years. In 1851 he was appointed demonstrator of chemistry at St. Bartholomew's Hospital to Dr. John Stenhouse [q. v.], and in March 1852 lecturer on chemistry at the Royal Military Academy at Woolwich in succession to Faraday [q. v.] In conjunction with Charles Loudon Bloxam (*d.* 1887), his assistant and successor there, he published a useful 'Handbook of Chemistry; Theoretical, Practical, and Technical' (1854; 2nd edit. 1858).

Abel became ordnance chemist at Woolwich on 24 July 1854, and he was made chemist to the war department there in January 1856. From 1854 till 1888, when he retired from Woolwich, Abel was the chief official authority on all matters connected with explosives. He was a member of the ordnance select committee, was expert for submarine defence and smokeless powder, and from 1888 until his death was president of the explosives committee. The transformation of arms and ammunition which took place during the thirty-four years of his service at Woolwich necessarily occupied the greater part of his scientific career, though almost every branch of technical science was enriched by his labours. The supersession of black by 'smokeless' powder was due to his researches on guncotton, founded on the attempts of Baron von Lenk to utilise this explosive in 1862. He developed the process of reducing guncotton to a fine pulp which enabled it to be worked and stored without danger. These results of his work were published in 1866 in his lectures 'Gun Cotton' and in 'The Modern History of Gunpowder.' Another important research, carried out in conjunction with Captain (afterwards Sir) Andrew Noble, aimed at determining the nature of the chemical changes produced on firing explosives. This work, carried out at great personal risk, is of the highest value and threw new light on the theory of explosives. The conclusions were published in various papers and lectures from 1871 to 1880 (cf. *On Explosive Agents*, a lecture, Edinburgh, 1871; *Researches on Explosives with Capt. Noble*, 1875 and 1880). The explosion in Seaham Colliery in 1881 led to the appointment of a royal commission on accidents in coal mines on which he served, and to Abel's researches on dangerous dusts (1882), in which he investigated the part played by dust in bringing about an explosion. In other directions Abel reached equally important results. As an expert in petroleum he devised the Abel open-test, with a flash-point of 100° Fahr., legalised in 1868, which was superseded in 1879 by the Abel close-test, with a flash-point of 73°. He also carried out many researches into the composition of alloyed metals with reference to their physical properties. His last piece of work, carried out in conjunction with Prof. (afterwards Sir) James Dewar, was the invention of cordite in 1889. The use of high explosives abroad forced the English government to seek for a better material than guncotton, and a committee was appointed in 1888, under Abel's presidency, to examine all the modern high explosives. None of them was exactly suitable to service requirements, and their inventors refusing to make the necessary modifications, Abel and Dewar devised and patented a compound of guncotton and nitroglycerine and assigned it to the secretary of war in 1890 (cf. *Hansard*, 11 Sept. 1893). Cordite is now the standard explosive of this country.

Abel's remarkable powers of organisation and his official position as scientific adviser to the government gave him a prominent position in the scientific world. He was elected F.R.S. in 1860, and received the royal medal in 1887. He was president of the Chemical Society (1875–7), of the Institute of Chemistry (1881–2), of the Society of Chemical Industry (1883), and of the Institute of Electrical Engineers. He was also president of the Iron and Steel Institute in 1891, and was awarded the Bessemer gold medal in 1897. He acted as chairman of the Society of Arts (1883–4) and received the Albert Medal in 1891. The Telford medal was bestowed on him by the Institution of Civil Engineers in 1879.

At Plymouth in 1877 he presided over the chemistry section of the British Association, and as president of the Association at Leeds in 1890 he gave an address on recent practical applications of science. When the foundation of the Imperial Institute was decided on in 1887, Abel was appointed organising secretary, remaining its honorary secretary and director from its opening in 1893 till it was handed over to the board of trade in 1901. He was made C.B. 1877, was knighted 1883, became K.C.B. 1891, a baronet 1893, G.C.V.O., 1901; he received the hon. D.C.L. (Oxford) 1883, and D.Sc. (Cambridge) 1888. In addition to the publications already cited, he contributed sixty-five papers to scientific publications and some important articles to the 9th edition of the 'Encyclopædia Britannica.'

Abel, who combined with his scientific capacity high accomplishments as a musician, died at his residence, 2 Whitehall Court, S.W., on 6 Sept. 1902, and was buried at Nunhead cemetery. He married (1) Sarah Selina (1854–1888), daughter of James Blanch of Bristol; (2) in 1889, Giulietta de la Feuillade (*d.* 1892). He had no children. His portrait, by Frank Bramley, was exhibited at the Royal Academy in 1901.

[War Office List; Burke's Baronetage; Nature, lxvi. 492; The Times, 8 Sept. 1902; Journal, Iron and Steel Institute, lxii. 1902; Journal, Soc. of Arts, Sept. 1902; Soc. Chem. Industry, xxi. 1902; Trans. Chem. Soc. 1905, i. 565; Oscar Guttmann's Manufacture of Explosives, 1895, i. 346–8.] R. S.

ABRAHAM, CHARLES JOHN (1814–1903), first bishop of Wellington, New Zealand, born on 17 June 1814 at the Royal Military College, Sandhurst, was second son of Captain Thomas Abraham of the 16th regiment, who was on the staff there. His mother was Louisa Susannah, daughter of Edward Carter of Portsmouth. After attending Dr. Arnold's school at Laleham, he went in 1826 to Eton as an oppidan, but to save expenses soon went into college, then half empty. He reached the sixth form, and played in the school cricket eleven. In 1833 Abraham went as a scholar to King's College, Cambridge. King's at that time had the privilege of giving its own degrees without university examination in a tripos. Abraham was a good and accurate scholar, with a special memory for Horace and Homer, which he retained through life. He graduated B.A. in 1837, and succeeded to a fellowship at King's, which he held until 1849. He proceeded M.A. in 1840 and D.D. in 1859, and took the *ad eundem* degree of M.A. at Oxford on 14 June 1849.

After being ordained deacon in 1838 and priest in 1839 and entering on parochial work as curate of Headley Down, Hampshire, he returned to Eton as a master. For thirteen years he threw himself heart and soul into Eton life. There were few masters and the classes were large and unwieldy; Abraham had more than ninety boys in his division. With George Augustus Selwyn [q. v.], who was private tutor to the earl of Powis's sons at Eton and curate of Windsor, Abraham now began the friendship which determined his career. When in 1841 Selwyn became bishop of New Zealand, Abraham was anxious to follow him, but for the present the calls of

Eton kept him at home. In 1846, in the interests of the reform of the school, he resigned the lucrative post of house-master to become assistant-master in college, and was largely responsible for the rapid improvement in the moral tone of the King's scholars. He helped to modify the system of fagging, and repressed the old college songs. As a teacher, Abraham widened the range of the curriculum, combining the teaching of history and geography and stimulating the boys' interest in history and literature. The collegers regarded him as a kind adviser and friend, and in 1850 gave a font and cover to the college chapel as a tribute of their regard. His pupils included Edward Henry Stanley, fifteenth earl of Derby [q. v.], to whom for a time he was private tutor at Knowsley, and Lord Robert Arthur Talbot Gascoyne Cecil, afterwards third marquis of Salisbury [q. v. Suppl. II], who visited him in New Zealand in 1852. In 1848 Abraham was appointed divinity lecturer of St. George's Chapel, Windsor, and next year, when he became B.D. at Cambridge, published his 'Festival and Lenten Lectures.'

He left Eton at Christmas 1849 to join Bishop Selwyn in New Zealand, and arrived in Auckland harbour in July 1850. Selwyn at once put him in charge, as chaplain and principal, of St. John's College, Auckland, a small training college for Maori and English youths. In 1853 he was made archdeacon of Waitemata, with the oversight of a large district. He took long tramps with Selwyn for months together through the native districts, visiting mission stations and schools. He returned to England in 1857 for surgical treatment of a broken arm. Whilst in England the new dioceses of Wellington and Nelson were constituted; Abraham was consecrated bishop of Wellington at Lambeth Palace on 29 Sept. 1858, and his friend, Edmund Hobhouse [q. v. Suppl. II], bishop of Nelson. For twelve years Abraham was fully occupied in creating the machinery of his new diocese, the chief town in which had just been made the seat of government. Three or four months in the year he spent in visiting outlying stations. During the Maori war in 1860 he powerfully urged just treatment of the natives.

In 1870 Abraham returned to England with Selwyn, who was appointed to the see of Lichfield, and owing to Selwyn's temporary failure of health became coadjutor bishop. In 1872 he was collated to the prebendal stall of Bobenhall in Lichfield Cathedral, and in 1876 was made a canon-residentiary and precentor. He assisted in the revision of the mediæval statutes of the cathedral, taught in the theological college, helped in beautifying and strengthening the fabric of the cathedral, of which he was the keeper, and although no musician was unremitting in devotion to the welfare of the choristers. In 1875–6 Abraham was also non-resident rector of Tatenhill, in Needwood Forest. A total abstainer, he was long a frequent speaker at meetings of the United Kingdom Alliance.

After Selwyn's death in April 1878, Abraham, with Bishop Edmund Hobhouse and Sir William Martin [q. v.], organised, by way of memorial, Selwyn College, Cambridge, which was opened in October 1882. He rendered the college much generous service, and as a chief benefactor he is mentioned annually in the chapel commemoration on 4 Feb. Abraham worked with William Dalrymple Maclagan [q. v. Suppl. II], Selwyn's successor at Lichfield, until 1890, when he resigned his canonry, thenceforth residing with his only son, the Rev. Charles Thomas Abraham, first at Christ Church, Lichfield, until 1897, and afterwards at Bakewell, Derbyshire. He died on 4 Feb. 1903 at Bakewell vicarage, and was buried at Over Haddon churchyard. A memorial service was held the same day in Eton College Chapel, where a marble slab and effigy have been placed. Abraham married on 17 Jan. 1850 Caroline Harriet (*d.* 1877), daughter of Sir Charles Thomas Palmer, second baronet, of Wanlip, Leicestershire. Charles Thomas Abraham, his son, is now bishop suffragan of Derby.

Besides the work mentioned Abraham was author of: 1. 'The Unity of History,' 1845; 2nd edit. 1846. 2. 'The Three Witnesses on Earth,' 1848. 3. 'Personal Religion and Cathedral Membership,' 1858. 4. 'Readings, Meditations, and Prayers on the Lord's Supper,' 2nd edit., 1858.

[Articles on Charles John Abraham, by A. L. Brown and C. T. Abraham, in the Selwyn College Calendar for 1903, 1904, 1905, 1906; W. H. Tucker, Bishop Selwyn's Life, 1879; G. H. Curteis, Life of G. A. Selwyn, 1889; Maxwell Lyte's History of Eton, 1875, p. 421; A. D. Coleridge's Eton in the Forties, 1896, p. 381; A. L. Brown's Selwyn College, 1906; The Times, 5, 9, and 13 Feb. 1903; Crockford's Clerical Directory; Lichfield Diocesan Magazine, March 1903; Foster's Peerage and Baronetage; original letters in the possession of Mr. Percy Simpson; private information.]

W. G. D. F.

ACTON, JOHN ADAMS (1830–1910), sculptor. [See ADAMS-ACTON, JOHN.]

ACTON, Sir JOHN EMERICH EDWARD DALBERG, first Baron Acton of Aldenham and eighth baronet (1834–1902), historian and moralist, born at Naples on 10 Jan. 1834, was the only child of Sir Ferdinand Richard Edward Acton, seventh baronet (1801–1835), by a German wife, Marie Louise Pellini de Dalberg, only child of Emeric Joseph Duc de Dalberg. After his father's early death his mother married (2 July 1840) Granville George Leveson-Gower, second Earl Granville [q. v.], the liberal statesman; she died 14 March 1860. The Acton family had long been settled in Shropshire, and the first baronet owed his title (conferred in 1643) to his loyalty to Charles I. Acton was descended from a cadet branch of the family. His great-grandfather, Edward Acton, was the youngest son of a younger son of the second baronet, and settled at Besançon as a doctor. From his marriage with a daughter of a Burgundian gentleman there issued Sir John Francis Edward Acton [q. v.], the friend of Queen Caroline and premier of the Two Sicilies at the time of Nelson. His career was not unstained, and Acton, it is said, refused to touch monies coming to him from that source. Acton, who although a Roman Catholic by race and training was deeply hostile to the arbitrary power of the Pope, owed his existence to a papal dispensation. In 1799 Sir John Acton (who eight years earlier succeeded to the title owing to the lapse of the elder branch of the family) obtained a dispensation to marry his brother's daughter. From this marriage issued Acton's father.

Of mingled race and bred amid cosmopolitan surroundings, Acton was never more than half an Englishman. His education was as varied as his antecedents. After a brief time at a school in Paris, he was sent in 1843 to the Roman Catholic College at Oscott, then under Dr. Wiseman, for whom he always retained affection in spite of later divergence of opinion. Thence he went for a short time to Edinburgh as a private pupil under Dr. Logan. There he found neither the teaching nor the companionship congenial. In 1848 began that experience which was to mould his mind more than any other influence. He went to Munich to study under Professor von Döllinger, and as his private pupil to live under the same roof. There he remained for six years in all, and not only laid the foundations of his vast erudition but also acquired his notions of the methods of historical study and the duty of applying fearless criticism to the history of the church. From this time he never wavered in his unflinching and austere liberalism, and very little in his dislike of the papal curia. A passionate sense of the value of truth, of the rights of the individual conscience, and of the iniquity of persecution, and hatred of all forms of absolutism, civil or ecclesiastical, were henceforth his distinctive qualities, and coupled with these was that desire to bring his co-religionists into line with modern intellectual developments and more particularly the science of Germany.

In 1855 he accompanied Lord Ellesmere to the United States; presence at the important constitutional debates at Philadelphia stimulated his interest in the question of state rights. In 1856 he accompanied his step-father, Lord Granville, to the coronation of the Czar Alexander II, and made a great impression on statesmen and men of intellectual eminence by a display of knowledge surprising in a youth. In 1857 he journeyed to Italy with Döllinger, and became versed in Italian affairs. Minghetti, the successor of Cavour, was a family connection and a frequent correspondent. (For evidence of Acton's insight into Italian matters, see articles in the *Chronicle*, 1867–8, and hitherto unpublished correspondence with T. F. Wetherell.)

On his return from Italy, Acton settled at the family seat at Aldenham, Shropshire, beginning to collect there the great library which reached a total of some 59,000 volumes. In 1859 he was elected to the House of Commons as whig M.P. for Carlow, and he sat for that constituency till 1865. He was then elected for Bridgnorth, in his own county, by a majority of one, and was unseated on a scrutiny. His parliamentary career was not successful. He was no debater; he only made a single short speech and put two questions while a member of the house. What he said of himself, 'I never had any contemporaries,' rendered him unfit for the rough and tumble of political life. The House of Commons proved a thoroughly uncongenial atmosphere, but it brought him the acquaintance of Gladstone, who soon inspired Acton with devotional reverence.

Acton proceeded to win intellectual and moral eminence at the expense of immediate practical influence. Even before he entered parliament he had actively joined those who were seeking to widen the horizons of English Roman Catholics. In 1858 he acquired an interest in a liberal catholic monthly periodical, called the 'Rambler,' which, having been started ten years before by an Oxford convert, John Moore Capes, had won the support of Newman. Acton's fellow proprietors were Richard Simpson [q.v.] and Frederick Capes, and Simpson was serving as editor. In 1859 Newman, whose aid was reckoned of great moment, succeeded Simpson as editor (cf. GASQUET, *Lord Acton and his Circle*, xxi), but the authorities urged his retirement within four months. Thereupon Acton became editor in name, although Simpson did most of the work. The periodical in its old shape came to an end in 1862, being converted into a quarterly, with the title 'The Home and Foreign Review.' This review represents the high-water mark of the liberal catholic movement. Probably no review of the reign of Queen Victoria maintained so high a standard of general excellence. Some of the strongest articles were written by Acton himself, though his style had neither the point nor the difficulty of his later writings. Many of them have since been republished in the two volumes entitled 'The History of Freedom' and 'Lectures and Essays on Modern History.' The amazing variety of his knowledge is better shown in the numerous shorter notices of books, which betrayed an intimate and detailed knowledge of documents and authorities. The new quarterly had, however, to run from the first the gauntlet of ecclesiastical criticism. Cardinal Wiseman publicly rebuked the editors in 1862. Acton in reply claimed for catholics the right to take 'a place in every movement that promotes the study of God's works and the advancement of mankind.'

Acton attended in March 1864 the Congress of Munich, when Döllinger pleaded on liberal grounds for a reunion of Christendom. Acton reported the proceedings in the 'Review.' His report awakened orthodox hostility, and when a papal brief addressed to the archbishop of Munich asserted that all Roman Catholic opinions were under the control of the Roman congregations, Acton stopped the review instead of waiting for the threatened veto. In withdrawing from this unequal contest, Acton, in a valedictory article called 'Conflicts with Rome' (April), which he signed as proprietor, declared once more in stately and dignified language his loyalty at once to the church and to the principles of freedom and scientific inquiry. At the end of the year Pope Pius IX promulgated the encyclical 'Quanta Cura' with the appended 'Syllabus Errorum,' which deliberately condemned all such efforts as those of Acton to make terms between the church and modern civilisation. At the time Acton informed his constituents at Bridgnorth that he belonged rather to the soul than the body of the catholic church. This expressed very clearly the distinction dominant in his mind between membership of the church of Rome and trust in the court of Rome.

The 'Review' was replaced to some extent by a weekly literary and political journal called the 'Chronicle,' which was started by T. F. Wetherell in 1867 with some pecuniary aid from Sir Rowland Blennerhassett [q. v. Suppl. II]. It ran for the most part on secular lines merely coloured by a Roman Catholic liberalism. Acton wrote regularly through 1867 and 1868. In some of his articles, notably in that on Sarpi and others on the Roman question, he was seen at his best. None of these contributions have been reprinted. On the stoppage of the 'Chronicle' at the end of 1868 he again interested himself in a journalistic venture of an earlier stamp. He helped Wetherell to launch in a new form and in the liberal catholic interest an old-established Scottish quarterly, the 'North British Review.' Acton eagerly suggested writers and themes, and was himself a weighty contributor until the periodical ceased in 1872. For the first number he wrote a learned article on 'The Massacre of St. Bartholomew,' wherein he sought to establish the complicity if not of the papacy, at least of the Popes in this great *auto da fé*. Acton subsequently modified his conclusions. The article, which was afterwards enlarged and translated into Italian by Signor Tommaso Gar, was doubtless designed as a piece of polemics as well as an historical inquiry.

Meanwhile, two lectures which Acton delivered at the Bridgnorth Literary and Scientific Institution—on the American Civil War (18 Jan. 1866) and on Mexico (10 March 1868)—illustrated his masterly insight alike into past history and current politics. In Nov. 1868 he stood unsuccessfully for his old constituency of Bridgnorth. By that time Acton's intimacy with Gladstone, now the liberal prime minister, had ripened into very close friendship. They were in Rome together in Dec. 1866, and Acton had guided Gladstone through the great library of Monte Cassino. Acton was Gladstone's junior by twenty-five years, and to the last he addressed the statesman with all the distant marks of respect due to a senior. But Acton influenced Gladstone more deeply than did any other single man. Gladstone had implicit faith in his learning and sagacity, and in such vital matters as home rule and disestablishment Acton's private influence was great if not decisive. Gladstone submitted to his criticism nearly everything he wrote. Acton was no admirer of Gladstone's biblical criticism, and endeavoured, not always with success, to widen the scope of Gladstone's reading. But from 1866 the fellowship between the two men grew steadily closer, and the older sought the guidance and advice of his junior on all kinds of matters. On 11 Dec. 1869, while Acton was in Rome, he was on Gladstone's recommendation raised to the peerage. He took the title of Baron Acton of Aldenham.

At the time a new general council was sitting at Rome to complete the work begun at Trent and to formulate the dogma of papal infallibility. Acton was in Rome to aid the small minority of prelates who were resisting the promulgation of the dogma. He worked hard to save the church from a position which in his view was not so much false as wicked. He urged the British government, of which Gladstone was the head, to interfere; but Archbishop Manning, whose interest was on the opposite side, neutralised Acton's influence with the prime minister through his friendship with Lord Odo Russell, the unofficial British agent at Rome. Acton's work at Rome was not confined to heartening the opposition or to sending home his views to Gladstone. To Döllinger at Munich, the centre of the German opposition, he wrote long accounts (with the names in cypher) of the various movements and counter-movements. These were combined with letters from two other persons in the series published in the 'Allgemeine Zeitung' from December 1869 under the name 'Quirinus.' They were republished at Munich in 1870 (4 pts.) and were translated into English as 'Letters from Rome on the Council' (London, 3 ser., 1870). Acton is only partially responsible for 'Quirinus's' deliverances. In some places the sympathies of the writer are strongly Gallican—a point of view which appealed to Döllinger but never to his pupil. Acton's difficulties at Rome were great. Many of the prelates who were opposing the infallibility dogma regarded it as true, and objected only to its being defined at that time and in existing conditions. Acton was an open assailant of the doctrine itself. Conscious of inevitable defeat, the opposition eventually withdrew from Rome, and the dogma was adopted by the council with unanimity. On 11 July 1870 Acton had already arrived at his house at Tegernsee, and there in August he completed his 'Sendschreiben an einen deutschen Bischof des vaticanischen Concils' (Nordlingen, 1870), in which he quoted from numerous anti-infallibilists, living or dead, and asked whether their words still held good. But the catholic world, to which Acton appealed, accepted the new law without demur. Döllinger refused, and was consequently excommunicated (1 April 1871), while a small body of opponents formed themselves at Munich in Sept. 1871 into the 'Old Catholic' communion, which Döllinger did not join.

Acton for the time stood aside and was unmolested. But when in 1874 Gladstone issued his pamphlet on 'The Vatican Decrees,' the publication of which Acton had not approved, he denied in letters to 'The Times' any such danger to the state as Gladstone anticipated from possible Roman Catholic sedition owing to their allegiance to a foreign bishop. Yet Acton, while defending his co-religionists in England, dealt subtle thrusts at the papacy. He made it clear that what preserved his allegiance and minimised his hostility to the Vatican Decrees was a sense that the church was holier than its officials, and the bonds of the Christian community were deeper than any dependent on the hierarchy. Acton was therefore able to speak of communion in the Roman church as 'dearer than life itself.' His present attitude, however, was suspected by the authorities. Archbishop Manning more than once invited an explanation. Acton replied adroitly that he relied on God's providential government of His church, and was no more disloyal to the Vatican council than to any of its predecessors. After more correspondence Manning said he must leave the matter to the pope. Acton made up his mind that he would be excommunicated, and wrote to Gladstone that the only question was, when the blow would fall. But it did not fall. Perhaps as a layman, perhaps as a peer, less probably as a scholar, he was left alone, and died in full communion with the Holy See.

With the letters to 'The Times' of Nov. to December 1874 Acton's polemical career closed. He admitted in a letter to Lady Blennerhassett that the explanations given by Newman in the 'Letter to the Duke of Norfolk' on Gladstone's expostulations (1875) would enable him to accept the decrees. But if he thought his fears of the decrees had been in some respects exaggerated, his hatred of ultramontanism was never appeased.

Through middle life Acton divided his time between Aldenham, the Dalberg seat at Herrnsheim on the Rhine, and a house at Prince's Gate in London. In 1879 financial difficulties drove him to sell Herrnsheim and to let Aldenham. He thenceforth spent the winter at Cannes and the autumn at the Arco Villa at Tegernsee, Bavaria, which belonged to his wife's family, and only parts of the spring or summer in London. He read more and wrote less than previously, but his historical writing lost nothing in depth. In the spring of 1877 he gave two lectures at Bridgnorth on the 'History of Freedom in Antiquity and in Christianity.' Two articles in the 'Quarterly' on 'Wolsey and the Divorce of Henry VIII' (Jan. 1877) and on Sir Erskine May's 'Democracy in Europe' (Jan. 1878) and an article on Cross's 'Life of George Eliot' in the 'Nineteenth Century' (March 1885) are exhaustive treatises. In 1886 he helped to set on foot the 'English Historical Review' and contributed to the first number a heavy but pregnant article on 'German Schools of History' (German transl. 1887). In London he saw much of Gladstone and encouraged him in his home rule propaganda. A member of Grillion's and The Club, he was in intimate relations with the best English intellectual society. Honours began to flow in. In 1872 the University at Munich had given him an honorary doctorate, and in 1888 he was made hon. LL.D. of Cambridge, and in 1887 hon. D.C.L. of Oxford. In 1891, on a hint from Gladstone, he was elected an honorary fellow of All Souls. When Gladstone formed his fourth administration in 1892, Acton was appointed a lord-in-waiting. Queen Victoria appreciated his facility of speech in German and his German sympathies, but the position was irksome. In 1895 came the great chance of Acton's life in his capacity of scholar. On Lord Rosebery's recommendation he became regius professor of modern history at Cambridge in succession to Sir John Seeley.

Acton was at once elected an honorary fellow of Trinity College, and took up his residence in Neville's Court. He threw himself with avidity into professorial work. His inaugural lecture on the study of history (11 June 1895) was a striking success; it contained a stimulating account of the development of modern historical methods and closed with an expression of that belief in the supremacy of the moral law in politics which was the dominant strain in Acton. It was published with a bulky appendix of illustrative quotations, illustrating at once the erudition and the weakness of the author, and was translated into German (Berlin, 1897).

Settled at Cambridge, Acton began almost at once to lecture on the 'French Revolution' for the historical tripos. His lectures were largely attended, both by students and by the general public. They were read almost verbatim from manuscript with very rare asides. The dignity of his delivery, his profound sense of the greatness of his task and of the paramount import of moral issues gave them a very impressive quality. Probably his half a dozen years at Cambridge were the happiest time in Acton's life. He loved to think of himself as a Cambridge man at last, and was as proud as a freshman of his rooms in College. He had the pleasure of finding eager pupils among some of the junior students. In 1899 and 1900 much of his energy was absorbed by the project of the 'Cambridge Modern History.' He did not originate it, but he warmly forwarded it, and acted as its first editor, with disastrous results to his health. On the business side he was never strong; and the effort of securing contributors, of directing them and of co-ordinating the work was a greater strain than he could bear. He regarded his editorial position very seriously; and although nothing was published while he was still alive, yet nearly the whole of the first volume and more than half the second were in type some two years before his death. The plan of the whole twelve volumes and the authorship of many even of the later chapters were his decision. Unfortunately Acton contributed nothing himself. The notes prepared for what should have been the first chapter on 'The Legacy of the Middle Ages' were not sufficiently advanced for publication. For all that the history remains a monument to his memory. In 1901 his final illness overtook him; suffering from a paralytic stroke, he withdrew to Tegernsee, and after lingering some months he died there on 19 June 1902. He was buried at Tegernsee.

Acton married on 1 Aug. 1865 the Countess Marie, daughter of Maximilian, Count Arco-Valley of Munich, a member of a distinguished and very ancient Bavarian house. His widow survived him with a son, Richard Maximilian, who succeeded him as second Baron Acton, and three daughters.

Of two pencil drawings done in 1876 by Henry Tanworth Wells [q.v. Suppl. II] one is at Grillion's Club, Hotel Cecil, London, and the other at Aldenham. He had become F.S.A. in 1876, and was made K.C.V.O. in 1897. Acton's valuable historical library at Aldenham, containing over 59,000 volumes, was bought immediately after his death by Mr. Andrew Carnegie, and was presented by him to John (afterwards Viscount) Morley. Lord Morley gave it in 1903 to the University of Cambridge. The whole collection is divided into 54 classes under the main headings of (1) ecclesiastical history, (2) political history, and (3) subjects not falling under these two heads. The first heading illustrates with rare completeness the internal and external history of the papacy; under the second heading works on Germany, France, and Switzerland are represented with exceptional fulness (cf. *Camb. Mod. Hist.* vol. iv. pp. viii, 802). Acton's books bear many traces of his method of reading. He was in the habit of drawing a fine ink line in the margin against passages which interested him, and of transcribing such passages on squares of paper, which he sorted into boxes or Solander cases.

Apart from his periodical writings Acton only published during his lifetime some separate lectures and letters, most of which have been already mentioned. The two on 'Liberty' delivered at Bridgnorth in 1877 appeared also in French translations (Paris, 1878). He edited Harpsfield's 'Narrative of the Divorce' (book ii.) and 'Letters of James II to the Abbot of La Trappe' (1872–6) for the Philobiblon Society, and 'Les Matinées Royales,' a hitherto unpublished work of Frederick the Great (London and Edinburgh, 1863). Since his death there have been issued his 'Lectures on Modern History,' edited with introduction by J. N. Figgis and R. V. Lawrence (1906); 'The History of Freedom, and other Essays,' introduction by the editors (1907); 'Historical Essays and Studies' (1907); and 'Lectures on the French Revolution' (1910). These four volumes, like his inaugural lecture, are fair evidence of his powers. The vast erudition, the passion for becoming intimately acquainted with many different periods, were a bar to production on a large scale. This was also hindered by a certain lack of organising power and a deficient sense of proportion. He abandoned his project for writing a 'History of Liberty,' which indeed was never more than a chimera displaying his lack of architectonic faculty. Nor did the notion of a history of the 'Council of Trent' fare any better, and of the projected biography of Döllinger we have nothing but a single article on 'Döllinger's Historical Works' from the 'English Historical Review' (1890). His essays are really monographs, and in many cases either said the final word on a topic or advanced the knowledge of it very definitely. As an historian Acton held very strongly to the ideal of impartiality, yet his writings illustrate the impossibility of attaining it. The 'Lectures on Modern History' are actually the development of the modern world as conceived by a convinced whig—and except in the actual investigation of bare facts no historian is less impartial and more personal in his judgments than Acton appears in the volume on the 'French Revolution.' His writing again has a note as distinctive as though very different from that of Macaulay. His style is difficult; it is epigrammatic, packed with allusions, dignified, but never flowing. He has been termed a 'Meredith turned historian'; but the most notable qualities are the passion for political righteousness that breathes in all his utterances, the sense of the supreme worth of the individual conscience and the inalienable desire for liberty alike in church and state.

[Personal knowledge; The Times, 20 June 1902; unpublished correspondence with Döllinger, Newman, Gladstone, Lady Blennerhassett, and others; editorial introductions to Lectures on Modern History (1906) and the History of Freedom (1907); Letters of Lord Acton to Mary Gladstone (with memoir by Herbert Paul), 1904; Gasquet, Lord Acton and his Circle, 1906; Edinburgh Review, April 1903; Independent Review, art. by John Pollock, October 1904; Bryce's Studies in Contemporary Biography, 1903; Morley's Life of Gladstone, 1904, ii. and iii.; Grant Duff's Notes from a Diary; Purcell's Life of Manning, 1896; Wilfrid Ward's Life of Cardinal Newman, 1912. A bibliography, edited by Dr. W. A. Shaw for the Royal Historical Society, 1903, gives most of Acton's writings whether in books or periodicals. Various sections of the catalogue of the Acton collection have been published in the Cambridge University Library Bulletin (extra series)].

J. N. F.

ADAM, JAMES (1860–1907), classical scholar and Platonist, born on 7 April 1860 at Kinmuck in the parish of Keithhall near Inverurie in Aberdeenshire, was second child and only son of James Adam and Barbara Anderson. The father owned the general store and tailor's shop which served the neighbouring countryside; he died of typhoid fever when his son was only eight. His mother (still living) by her own energy carried on the business, and brought up her six children. After varied scholastic experiences Adam made rapid progress at the parish school of Keithhall under George Kemp, M.A., and having spent some months at the grammar school of Old Aberdeen won the third bursary at Aberdeen University in Oct. 1876. Though chiefly interested in Greek, Adam took a good place in most of the classes of the arts course. His devotion to Greek was fostered by the professor, (Sir) William Geddes [q. v. Suppl. I]. In 1880 he graduated with first-class honours in classics and carried off the chief classical prizes and the Ferguson scholarship. Meanwhile in the spring of 1880 he had been elected classical scholar at Caius College, Cambridge. In the summer of 1882 he was placed in division i. of the first class in the classical tripos, part i. In 1883 he just missed the Craven scholarship, but in 1884 was awarded the first chancellor's medal and obtained a specially brilliant first class (only once equalled) in part ii. of the classical tripos with distinction in classics, ancient philosophy, and comparative philology. In Dec. 1884 he was elected a junior fellow and was soon appointed classical lecturer of Emmanuel College, where he settled down at once to his life's work as a teacher. During his undergraduate career at Cambridge Adam had devoted himself with increasing ardour to the study of Plato, and this author for the rest of his life generally furnished a subject (most frequently the 'Phaedo' or some books of the 'Republic') for one of the two courses of intercollegiate lectures which it was part of his college duty to deliver annually. Aristotle's 'Ethics,' Lucretius, Cicero's 'de Finibus,' and above all the Greek lyric poets were also frequent subjects. His lectures were full of wit as well as learning, and however mystical some might consider his philosophical views, there was no lack of precision in his scholarship. Throughout his teaching career Adam took classes with rare intermissions at Girton College, and was an ardent supporter of the claims of women to degrees, when the question came before the senate of the university in 1897. A knowledge of Greek he regarded as an essential part of university education, and he was a resolute opponent of all attempts to make Greek an optional subject of study. At Easter 1890 he visited Greece. In the same year he was appointed joint tutor of his college with Mr. W. N. Shaw (now director of the Meteorological Office), and in 1900, the number of tutors having been meantime increased, he succeeded Mr. Shaw as senior tutor. His relations with pupils and colleagues were kindly and affectionate, while his efficiency as a lecturer proved of great benefit to the college. The changes in the classical tripos, which came into force in 1903, emphasised the importance of ancient philosophy, and the college hall was barely able to hold the numbers that flocked to Adam's lectures on Plato and Aristotle. In 1887, inspired probably by his closest friend, Robert Alexander Neil [q. v. Suppl. II], he published his first edition of a Platonic dialogue, the 'Apology.' This was followed by the 'Crito' in 1888, the 'Euthyphro' in 1890, and (in conjunction with his wife) the 'Protagoras' in 1893. In 1890 he had announced an intention of preparing an edition of the 'Republic.' In 1897 he published a revised text. This, however, differs in many passages from the large edition in two volumes which appeared after many years of labour in 1902, and immediately took its place as the standard edition. Adam's notes and excursuses, which are very concise considering the difficulty of the subject, represent a judgement based upon a thorough knowledge of the vast work of his many predecessors. In textual matters as years went on he became steadily more conservative, believing that the tradition of the Platonic text was in the main quite sound. An investigation preliminary to his edition of the 'Republic' was a discussion of the 'Platonic Number' (Cambridge University Press, 1891). Adam's interpretation has been confirmed by Professor Hilprecht's discovery of the Babylonian perfect number. At Christmas 1902 he was nominated Gifford lecturer at Aberdeen. He chose for his subject 'The Religious Teachers of Greece,' and the lectures delivered in 1904 and 1905 were very successful.

In the spring of 1907, Adam, who, amid his unceasing work, retained his youthful appearance in middle age, was attacked by illness. He died in Aberdeen after an operation on 30 August 1907, and was buried at Woking. Adam married, on 22 July 1890, a former pupil, Adela Marion, youngest daughter of Arthur Kensington, formerly fellow and tutor of Trinity College, Oxford. His wife survives him with two sons and a daughter. An enlarged photograph hangs in the parlour of Emmanuel College.

The Gifford lectures, which were left complete, but not finally revised for publication, were edited with a short memoir by his widow and published in 1908 (2nd edit. 1909). A collection of his essays and lectures was edited by Mrs. Adam in 1911 under the title of 'The Vitality of Platonism, and other Essays.' These collected papers best illustrate the bent of Adam's mind in later life. For many years he had been deeply interested in the relationship between Greek philosophy and the New Testament. Though he would not have said with Westcott that 'the final cause of Greek was the New Testament,' he certainly tended to regard Greek philosophy pre-eminently as a 'Praeparatio Evangelica,' and his occasional lectures on such semi-religious topics at summer meetings in Cambridge found large and appreciative audiences. Witty and paradoxical in conversation, though with a vein of melancholy in his nature, Adam found fullest scope for his abilities as a teacher, and to education in the highest sense all his work as lecturer and writer was devoted.

[Information from the family; the Memoir by his wife quoted above; intimate personal knowledge for over twenty-five years.] P. G.

ADAMS, JAMES WILLIAMS (1839–1903), army chaplain in India, born on 24 Nov. 1839 in Cork, was only son of three children of James O'Brien Adams, magistrate of Cork (*d.* 1854), by his wife Elizabeth Williams. Educated at Hamlin and Porter's School, on the South Mall, Cork, he proceeded to Trinity College, Dublin, where he graduated B.A. in 1861. He always excelled in athletics, and was regarded as the strongest man in Ireland, vying with his friend Frederick Burnaby [q. v.] in gymnastic feats. He was ordained deacon 1863 and priest 1864 and served curacies at Hyde, Hampshire (1863–5), and at Shottesbrook, Berkshire (1865–6). In Oct. 1866 he became a chaplain on the Bengal establishment under Bishop Robert Milman [q. v.] at Calcutta. Here he had a severe attack of fever, and after sick leave to Ceylon was appointed to Peshawar. There he was indefatigable in visiting the out stations Naushahra and Kohat; he did much in restoring and beautifying the church and the cemetery at Peshawar, and received the thanks of government for his exertions in the cholera camps during two outbreaks. Save for some months at Allahabad (March to Dec. 1870) he remained at Peshawar till December 1872. He was then stationed at the camp of exercise at Hassan Abdul army headquarters till March 1873, and in 1874 he was sent to Kashmir on special duty. Here he built, in great part with his own hands, a church of pine logs, where services were frequently held for the numerous visitors to Gulmarg and Sonamarg; it was subsequently burnt down by accident.

In January 1876 Adams was appointed to Meerut, and in December took charge of the cavalry and artillery camp for the Delhi durbar on the visit of the Prince of Wales (afterwards King Edward VII).

Subsequently he had experience of much active warfare. In Nov. 1878 he joined the Kuram field force under Sir Frederick (afterwards Earl) Roberts, and was engaged in all the operations in the advance on Kabul. At Villa Kazi on 11 Dec. 1879 he risked his life in rescuing several men of the 9th lancers, who were in danger of drowning in a watercourse while the Afghans were near at hand. Lord Roberts witnessed Adams's exploit and recommended him for the Victoria Cross, which he received from Queen Victoria on 4 Aug. 1881. He also took part in the march of Lord Roberts from Kabul to Kandahar in August 1880, and was present at the battle of Kandahar on 1 Sept. 1880.

On returning to India after furlough in 1881 Adams spent a year at Lucknow. During three years (1883–5) at Naini Tal he was instrumental in the erection of an east window and reredos in memory of the victims of the great landslip. In 1885 he accompanied the field force under Lord Roberts up country in Burma, and he took part in the operations there. He had already received the bronze star for the Kabul - Kandahar march and the Afghan war medal with four clasps, Kandahar, Kabul, Charasiab, and Peiwar Kotal; he was now awarded the Burmah field force medal.

Through twenty years' service in India Adams was 'the idol of the soldiers.' In 1886 he settled in England, and from 1887 to 1894 he held the rectory of Postwick near Norwich. After two years' rest in Jersey he became in 1896 vicar of Stow Bardolph with Wimbotsham near Downham Market. He was appointed in 1900 honorary chaplain to Queen Victoria, and King Edward VII made him chaplain in ordinary in 1901. In 1902 he left Stow for the small living of Ashwell, near Oakham. There he died on 20 Oct. 1903. On 30 June 1903 Dublin University had conferred on him the honorary degree of M.A. While in England on furlough he married on 16 Aug. 1881 Alice Mary, daughter of General Sir Thomas Willshire [q. v.]

She survived him with an only daughter, Edith Juliet Mary.

Three brass tablets were erected to his memory—one by the patron, Sir Thomas Hare, in Stow Bardolph church; another by Lord Roberts in a little church in the fen district of Stow, built as a memorial; and the third in Peshawar Church, put up in 1910 by friends who had known 'Padre Adams' in Peshawar or during the Afghan war.

[Private information from his widow; Army Lists; The Times, October 1903; H. B. Hanna, The Second Afghan War, 1910, iii. 181; Lord Roberts, Forty-one Years in India, pp. 142, 143, and 275; Burke's Baronetage.] H. M. V.

ADAMS, WILLIAM DAVENPORT (1851–1904), journalist and compiler, born at Brixton on 25 Dec. 1851, was elder son of William Henry Davenport Adams (1828–1891) [q. v. Suppl. I] by his wife Sarah Esther Morgan. Entering Merchant Taylors' School in January 1863, he went to Edinburgh University, but ill-health precluded his securing any academic distinction. Becoming a journalist, he was appointed in 1875 leader-writer and literary and dramatic critic for the 'Glasgow Daily News,' and later he edited the evening and weekly editions. From 1878 to 1880 he was editor of the 'Greenock Advertiser'; from 1880 to 1882 acting-editor of the 'Nottingham Guardian'; from 1882 to 1885 editor of the 'Derby Mercury'; and from 1885 till his death literary editor and dramatic critic of the London 'Globe.'

Adams's main interest lay in the drama, and the leisure of twenty years was devoted to the compilation of 'A Dictionary of the Drama,' which was to be 'a guide to the plays, playwrights, players, and playhouses of the United Kingdom and America, from the earliest times to the present day.' Only the first of the two projected volumes (A–G) was completed at Adams's death at Putney on 27 July 1904. He was buried at Putney Vale cemetery. On 19 Oct. 1875 he married Caroline Estelle, daughter of John Körner, a Polish exile of noble family.

Besides the comprehensive but unfinished 'Dictionary of the Drama' (1904), Adams published: 1. 'A Dictionary of English Literature, being a comprehensive guide to English authors and their works,' 1878. 2. 'By-Ways in Book-Land,' 1888. 3. 'A Book of Burlesque,' 1891. 4. 'With Poet and Player: Essays on Literature and the Stage,' 1891.

[The Times and Globe, 28 July 1904; Theatre, 1894 (portrait); Reg. Merchant Taylors' School; private information.] L. M.

ADAMS-ACTON, JOHN (1830–1910), sculptor, born at Acton Hill, Middlesex, on 11 Dec. 1830, was the son of William Adams, a tailor, of Acton Hill by his wife Helen Elizabeth Humphreys (*Par. Reg.*). Two sons and three daughters survived the father. The second daughter, Clarissa, engaged in art and exhibited at the Royal Academy. To avoid confusion with other artists of the same name, Adams adopted in 1869 the additional surname of Acton from his birthplace.

Educated at Lady Byron's school, Ealing, he received his first tuition as a sculptor under Timothy Butler. He subsequently worked in the studio of Matthew Noble [q. v.], and during 1853–8 studied at the Royal Academy Schools, where his promise was liberally recognised. He won first medals in the antique and life classes, and the gold medal for an original sculpture group, 'Eve supplicating forgiveness at the feet of Adam,' in December 1855. As a student he exhibited a medallion of Dr. Chalton in 1854, and other medallions in 1855 and 1856. In 1858 he gained the Academy's travelling studentship, and was at Rome till 1865. There his success in portraiture, to which he devoted his main efforts, excited the admiration of John Gibson [q. v.], who sent many visitors to his studio.

After 1865 Acton settled in London, where he was soon busily employed. He executed the Wesley memorial in Westminster Abbey, the Cruikshank memorial in St. Paul's Cathedral, the statue of Wesley before the City Road chapel, and the memorial of Cardinal Manning in the new Roman Catholic Cathedral at Westminster. He also executed a colossal statue of Sir Titus Salt, erected near Bradford Town Hall in 1874, and statues of Queen Victoria for Kingston and the Bahamas, of Mr. Gladstone, a close friend and the godfather of his fourth son, for Blackburn and Liverpool, and of Bishop Waldegrave for Carlisle Cathedral. Edward VII, as Prince of Wales, sat to him many times, and the Emperor and Empress Frederick of Germany showed interest in his art. He exhibited regularly at the Royal Academy till 1892, sending there statues or busts of Gladstone (1865, 1868, 1869, 1873, 1879), Lord Brougham (1867, 1868) John Bright (1870), Charles Dickens (1871), Charles Spurgeon (1874), Earl Russell (1874), Archbishop Manning (1884), the earl of Beaconsfield (1885), and Leo XIII (1888). Others who sat to him were Canon Duckworth, Lord Shaftesbury, Dr. Parker, Mr. Fawcett, Lord Napier of Magdala, Cobden, Lord Roberts, Dean Farrar, Sir Wilfrid Lawson, Sir Isaac Holden, Sir Edwin Landseer, and many leading academicians. Of his ideal works the best were 'The First Sacrifice,' 'The Lady of the Lake,' 'Pharaoh's Daughter,' 'Zenobia,' and 'The Millennium.'

Acton's last work, which was left unfinished, was a small figure of 'The Angel of Peace.' He died at his wife's home, Ormidale, Brodick, in the Isle of Arran, which he visited every summer, on 28 Oct. 1910.

Acton married on 15 Aug. 1875, at St. Mark's Church, Hamilton Terrace, London, Marion Hamilton of the Isle of Arran, an authoress writing under the name 'Jeannie Hering.' He had four sons and three daughters. Two of his sons, Harold and Murray, practised their father's art.

[The Times, 29 Oct. 1910; Daily Telegraph and Morning Post, 1 Nov. 1910; Graves's Roy. Acad. Exhibitors; Art Journal, Nov. 1910; Studio, Nov. 1910; Hodgson and Eaton, The Royal Academy and its Members, 1905; information supplied by Mrs. Acton and others.]

S. E. F.

ADAMSON, ROBERT (1852–1902), philosopher, born at Edinburgh on 19 Jan. 1852, was fifth of the six children of Robert Adamson and Mary Agnes Buist. The father was a writer (*i.e.* solicitor) in Dunbar and afterwards at Coldstream, but had removed with his family to Edinburgh before the birth of his son Robert, and died when the latter was three years old. The boy passed from Daniel Stewart's Hospital, Edinburgh, to Edinburgh University in November 1866, and after obtaining first prizes in metaphysics and in English literature, graduated, in 1871, with first-class honours in philosophy and with a scholarship awarded to the best graduate in that subject. He spent the summer of 1871 at Heidelberg, and acted as assistant in the following winter to Henry Calderwood [q. v. Suppl. I], professor of moral philosophy at Edinburgh, and in 1872–4 to A. Campbell Fraser, professor of logic and metaphysics. During these years he read omnivorously in the Signet library and elsewhere, and gained other post-graduate scholarships or fellowships, including the Ferguson scholarship and the Shaw fellowship, both open to graduates of any Scottish university. In 1874 he was appointed additional examiner in philosophy in the university, and joined the editorial staff of the 'Encyclopædia Britannica' (9th edition). To the third and fourth volumes of that work he contributed a large number of articles on subjects of general literature, and in the third volume began a series of important philosophical articles. The article on Francis Bacon (which James Spedding [q. v.] had originally undertaken and had relinquished) first gave public proof of Adamson's powers as a philosophical critic and historian. There followed biographies of Hume, Kant, Fichte, and Schelling, and the very learned article on Logic.

In the summer of 1876 Adamson was appointed professor of philosophy and political economy at Owens College, Manchester, in succession to W. Stanley Jevons [q. v.] After six years he was relieved of the work of lecturing in economics; but he greatly extended the philosophical teaching, especially after 1880, when the creation of the Victoria University gave him freedom to plan the work in accordance with his own views. He was made hon. LL.D. of Glasgow in 1883.

In 1893 he was appointed by the crown to the chair of logic in the university of Aberdeen. He removed to Glasgow in 1895 on his election to the professorship of logic and rhetoric there. Between 1885 and 1901 he acted on six occasions as examiner for the moral science tripos at Cambridge. For five years (1887–91) he was one of the examiners in mental and moral science in the University of London. He was also the first external examiner in philosophy to the newly founded University of Wales (1896–9). On 5 Feb. 1902 he died of enteric fever at Glasgow; his body was cremated at the Western Necropolis. In 1881 he married Margaret, daughter of David Duncan, a Manchester merchant, who survived him with two sons and four daughters.

Adamson took an active part in academic business. At Manchester he supported warmly the admission of women students to college and university on equal terms with men; he threw himself zealously into the movement for an independent university, and when the Victoria University was created in 1880 he took a prominent part in its organisation. He acted as temporary registrar, was first secretary and afterwards chairman of the new board of studies, and gave important assistance to the institution of the university department for training elementary teachers. At

Glasgow he served on the court as well as on the senatus, and took a leading part in the early stages of the movement which afterwards resulted in substituting a three-term system for the unbroken session of the Scottish universities. He was also a keen politician, and gave active support to the advanced liberal party.

Adamson's literary activity, which was unusually great in youthful manhood, afterwards diminished, largely owing to the demands of lecturing work and academic business, and partly at any rate to a gradual change in his philosophical views. But his lectures to his students gave the results of his original thinking. The standpoint adopted in his earlier work was idealistic, and akin to the prevalent neo-Hegelianism. But he found increasing difficulties in working out a coherent interpretation of reality on these lines, and in adapting to such an interpretation the knowledge of nature, mind and history arrived at by modern science. In his later thinking his attitude to idealism changed, and he aimed at a constructive philosophy from a point of view which he did not refuse to describe as naturalism or realism. By this term, however, he did not mean that the external mechanism of things in space and time was equivalent to the sum-total of reality, but rather that truth in philosophy is to be reached by turning from abstract conceptions to concrete experience. Mind has indeed come into being, but it is not, on that account, less essential than, or inferior to, nature; each is a partial manifestation of reality. An outline of a theory of knowledge on these lines is given in the concluding part of his posthumously published lectures on 'Modern Philosophy'; but this theory was never worked out by him in detail, nor subjected to the same thorough criticism as idealistic philosophies received at his hands. Both in his earlier and in his later period his own views are developed by means of a critical study of the history of thought. Following the biological analogy of 'recapitulation' he found in the history of philosophy a treatment, only more elaborate and leisurely, of the same questions as those which face the individual inquirer. In general his work is distinguished by extensive and exact learning, by keen perception of the essential points in a problem, by great power of clear and sustained reasoning, by complete impartiality, and by rigid exclusion of metaphor and the imaginative factor.

In addition to articles in the 'Encyclopædia Britannica,' the 'Dictionary of National Biography,' 'Mind,' and elsewhere, Adamson was author of the following works: 1. 'Roger Bacon: the philosophy of science in the middle ages (an introductory address),' Manchester, 1876. 2. 'On the Philosophy of Kant' (Shaw Fellowship Lectures, 1879), Edinburgh, 1879 (translated into German by Professor C. Schaarschmidt, 'unter Mitwirkung des Verfassers,' Leipzig, 1880). 3. 'Fichte' (Philosophical Classics for English Readers), Edinburgh, 1881. After his death there appeared: 4. 'The Development of Modern Philosophy, with other Lectures and Essays,' ed. by W. R. Sorley, 2 vols., Edinburgh, 1903 (with complete bibliography). 5. 'The Development of Greek Philosophy,' ed. by W. R. Sorley and R. P. Hardie, Edinburgh, 1908. 6. 'A Short History of Logic,' ed. by W. R. Sorley, Edinburgh, 1911.

A medallion of Adamson, executed in 1903 by Mr. Gilbert Bayes, was presented by old students and other friends to the University of Glasgow in February 1904. Later in the same year, a replica of this medallion was presented by another body of subscribers to the University of Manchester, and the Adamson Lecture there was founded in his memory; at the same time his philosophical books, numbering about 4387 volumes, were presented to the Manchester University by Mrs. Adamson (see *Manchester Guardian*, 4 June 1904).

[Memorial introduction prefixed to Development of Modern Philosophy, 1903; Prof. (Sir) Henry Jones in Mind, July 1902; private information. For an account of his philosophy see Prof. G. Dawes Hicks, in Mind, January 1904, and Ueberweg-Heinze, Grundriss der Geschichte der Philosophie, 10th edit. 1909, part iv. pp. 535–7.] W. R. S.

ADDERLEY, Sir CHARLES BOWYER, first Baron Norton (1814–1905), statesman, born at Knighton House, Leicestershire, on 2 Aug. 1814, was eldest son of Charles Clement Adderley (1780–1818) by his wife Anna Maria (*d.* 1827), daughter of Sir Edmund Burney Cradock-Hartopp, first baronet, a descendant of Oliver Cromwell. On the death without issue of his great-uncle, Charles Bowyer Adderley of Hams Hall, Warwickshire, on 12 April 1826, Charles succeeded to the great family estates round Birmingham, and in Warwickshire and Staffordshire. Thereupon he was taken from school at Redland near Bristol, and placed under a clerical tutor of low church views, who deepened the evangelical convictions with which his parents had imbued him. In 1832 he became a gentleman-commoner at Christ Church, Oxford, where his piety suffered no diminution, while he acquired a knowledge of music and art and a love of horse riding and of tobacco. He rode daily till he was eighty-eight, and hunted for many years. At Christ Church he began, too, a life-long friendship with John Robert Godley [q. v.], who greatly influenced him. He took a pass degree in 1835.

From 1836 to 1841 Adderley mainly engaged in travel, study, and the management of his estates. He sought to develop his property on enlightened principles. When he came of age in 1835 the estate at Saltley near Birmingham supported a population of 400, which grew to 27,000 in his lifetime. Planning the streets of the town in 1837 so as to avoid the possibility of slums, he may be called the father of town-planning. In providing, endowing, and supporting places of worship in Saltley he spent 70,000*l*. He gave Adderley Park to Birmingham; in 1847 he promoted the foundation of the Saltley Church Training College (in which he was interested to the end) and in 1852 he founded the Saltley Reformatory on the model of that of Mettray in France.

The family residence at Hams Hall was not far from the home of Sir Robert Peel at Drayton Manor, Tamworth. Peel urged Adderley to enter Parliament and in June 1841 he was elected as a tory for the northern division of Staffordshire. He held the seat through eight elections, retiring in 1878. Adderley opposed Peel's free trade policy of 1846, although he formally abandoned protection at the general election of 1852. He took at first little part in debate, but wrote occasionally in 1848 on general topics in the 'Morning Chronicle' and on colonial subjects in the 'Spectator' in 1854.

Gradually colonial questions roused Adderley's enthusiasm, and he soon rendered services of the first importance to colonial development. In 1849 he joined his friends Godley, Edward Gibbon Wakefield [q. v.], and Lord Lyttelton in founding the Church of England colony of Canterbury in New Zealand. In the same year he strenuously resisted Lord Grey's proposal to transport convicts to the Cape, and elaborated his argument in a pamphlet, 'Transportation not necessary' (1851). To Adderley's advocacy the Cape colonists assigned the government's abandonment of its threat to send Irish political convicts among them, and by way of gratitude they named Adderley street after him. Penal colonial settlements were abrogated in 1852, partly owing to Adderley's activity.

Meanwhile Adderley helped Wakefield to found in 1849 the Colonial Reform Society for promoting colonial self-government, and of that society he became secretary. In 'The Australian Colonies Bill Discussed' (1849) he urged complete delegation of powers to the colony while throwing on it the cost of any imperial assistance. The independent constitution of New Zealand was drafted at Hams Hall in 1850 and the constitution of the other colonies followed this precedent. In 'Some Reflections on the Speech of Lord John Russell on Colonial Policy' (1850) Adderley declared that principles of self-government could alone yield 'thriving colonies, heartily and inseparably and usefully attached to England.' He powerfully developed his views in 'The Statement of the Present Cape Case' (1851); in his 'Remarks on Mr. Godley's Speech on Self-government for New Zealand' (1857); in his letter to Disraeli on 'The Present Relation of England with her Colonies' (1861; 2nd edit. 1862); and finally in his 'Review of "The Colonial Policy of Lord John Russell's Administration," by Earl Grey [1853], and of subsequent Colonial History' (1869, 3 pts.), a comprehensive survey of the progress of colonial freedom. At the age of ninety, in his 'Imperial Fellowship of Self-governed British Colonies' (1903), he enunciated anew his lifelong conviction that 'colonial self-administration and imperial fellowship' are 'co-ordinate elements' in 'true colonial relationship.'

In Lord Derby's first administration of 1852 Adderley refused the secretaryship of the board of control, and continued to advocate as a private member of the House of Commons social and educational as well as colonial reforms with an independence of party cries which earned him the epithet of liberal-conservative. In 1852 he introduced a reformatory schools bill, for bringing refractory children or young criminals under educational control. In 1853 he opposed with great foresight the abandonment of the Orange River sovereignty. In 1854 he was responsible for the Young Offenders Act (a part of his 'reformatory' policy), and he introduced the Manchester and Salford education bill, in which a local education rate was first proposed. In 'Punishment is not Education' (1856) and in his 'Tract on

Tickets of Leave' (1857), he pushed further his plea that education might cure crime more effectually than punishment.

On the formation of Lord Derby's second ministry in Feb. 1858 Adderley was appointed vice-president of the education committee of the privy council, and was admitted to the privy council. His office also constituted him president of the board of health, and a charity commissioner. The educational situation was peculiarly interesting. On 21 June 1858 Adderley in moving the education vote gave the first official estimate of the cost of a national system of elementary education: he put the amount at a million pounds per annum. At the same time he pointed out that that was the first day on which the University of Oxford was conducting its middle class examinations throughout the country, and was thereby inaugurating a new correlation of the universities to national life. Next day the first royal commission on elementary education was gazetted.

During his brief term of office Adderley consolidated the accumulated minutes of the council on education, prepared the way for the revised code, passed a Reformatory Act amending that of 1854, and (faithful to the principle of devolution) passed a first Local Government Act, the term 'local government' being his own invention.

In March 1859 Lord Derby's ministry was defeated on a second reading of its reform bill. A dissolution followed, leaving the conservatives in a minority. In the event Lord Palmerston became prime minister. The outbreak of the Maori war in New Zealand in 1860 moved Adderley deeply, but he advised the colonists to provide an army of their own, while urging that all parts of the Empire should give mutual help in case of need. In the same year he introduced without success an education bill which aimed at making education compulsory. In Lord Derby's third administration of 1866 Adderley became under-secretary for the colonies, and was immediately confronted by the difficult case of Governor Eyre [see EYRE, EDWARD JOHN, Suppl. II], whom he loyally defended from the attacks of John Stuart Mill (cf. FINLASON's *Hist. of the Jamaica Case*, 1869). In the same session he carried through the House of Commons the British North America Act (1867), which created the Dominion of Canada. Amid his parliamentary occupations, Adderley published 'Europe Incapable of American Democracy (1867), in which he sought to reconcile his conservative faith with advanced ideas of social freedom and progress.

Adderley continued in office when Disraeli succeeded Lord Derby as prime minister. He resigned with his colleagues in Dec. 1868, and was made K.C.M.G. next year by Gladstone, the new liberal prime minister, who was a personal friend. 'I am glad our opponents decorate our bench,' remarked Disraeli. Adderley was made chairman of the sanitary commission which reported in 1871 and led to the passing of the Public Health Acts of 1872 and 1875. He took a prominent part in opposing Irish disestablishment.

When Disraeli returned to office in February 1874, Adderley became president of the board of trade, but owing to his frank independence, which the prime minister feared, he was not admitted to the cabinet. 'Single-heartedness, unfailing temper, and unwearied zeal' characterised his departmental work. The amendment of the merchant shipping law was his first official concern in the House of Commons, and he was brought into painful conflict with Samuel Plimsoll [q. v. Suppl. I]. Adderley's bill of 1875 was assailed by Plimsoll and withdrawn. In 1876 another bill which legalised a 'loadline' usually named after Plimsoll, although Adderley claimed it as his own, was introduced and passed. On 8 March 1878 Adderley retired from office with a peerage, assuming the title of Baron Norton. In the same year he presided at the Cheltenham meeting of the Social Science Congress, and he was a frequent speaker in the House of Lords on education and colonial and social questions. In 1880 he refused an offer of the governorship of Bombay. In his speech in the upper house on the Education Code of May 1882 (reprinted as a pamphlet) he practically advocated free education and protested against the complexity of the code with its detailed system of payment by results. He sat on the reformatory and industrial schools commission (1883) and on the education commissions of 1883–4 and 1887. In 1884 he promoted the compromise between the two houses on the liberal government's reform bill.

Norton had long played an active part in religious affairs. As early as 1849 he had published a devotional 'Essay on Human Happiness' (rev. edit. 1854). In his 'Reflections on the Rev. Dr. Hook's Sermon on "the Lord's Day"' (1856) he dwelt on the need of popular parks, gardens, and reading-rooms for Sunday recreation and religious contemplation. A strong churchman, he yet advocated in 1889 a union between the Church of England and the Wesleyans, and he developed an aspiration to heal protestant schism and stay controversy in 'High and Low Church' (1892, 2nd ed. 1893). His hope of reconciling apparently opposing social as well as religious forces found expression in his 'Socialism' (1895), in which respect for manual labour and zeal in social service and social reform were shown to harmonise with conservative and Christian feeling. In his 'Reflections on the Course from the Goal' (1898, 2nd ed. 1899) Norton discussed the formation of character. His religious views kept him in touch with all classes of thinkers, and neither doctrinal nor political differences affected his private friendship. With Mr. Gladstone especially he was long on cordial terms. Cobden and Bright were among his political friends, and he reckoned Archbishop Benson, Cardinal Manning, Dr. Dale, and Edward King, bishop of Lincoln, among his intimate acquaintances. To the end of his life Norton wrote long letters to 'The Times' on his favourite themes of social reform, education, and colonial affairs. He was no brilliant writer nor speaker, and was reckoned by political colleagues to be tenacious and outspoken to the verge of obstinacy and bluntness, but his views were enlightened, generous, and far-seeing, and they influenced the progress of public opinion. A skilled musician and a competent art critic, Norton died at Hams Hall on 28 March 1905, and was buried in the family vault in Lea Marston Church. Adderley on 28 July 1842 married Julia Anne Eliza, daughter of Chandos, first Baron Leigh of Stoneleigh. There were ten children—five sons and five daughters. He was succeeded as second Baron Norton by his eldest son, Charles Leigh Adderley. His youngest son, James Granville, became vicar of Saltley in 1904. Lady Norton died on 8 May 1887.

A portrait was painted in 1890 by Jacomb Hood. George Richmond, R.A., made a drawing for Grillion's Club. A cartoon by 'Spy' appeared in 'Vanity Fair' 1892. The Norton Memorial Hall at Saltley was erected in Norton's memory.

[W. S. C. Pemberton's Life of Lord Norton, 1814–1905, Statesman and Philanthropist, 1909, contains autobiographic notes, with portraits; see also The Times, 29 March 1905; Hansard's Reports; Burke's Peerage; J. R. Godley's Letters edited by Adderley for private circulation; Adderley's works.]

J. E. G. de M.

ADLER, HERMANN (1839–1911), chief rabbi of the united Hebrew congregations of the British empire, born at Hanover on 30 May 1839, was second son of two sons and three daughters of Nathan Marcus Adler [q. v.], chief rabbi, by his first wife Henrietta Worms. Through his mother Adler was cousin of Henry de Worms, first Baron Pirbright [q. v. Suppl. II]. His elder brother, Marcus Nathan (1837–1910), was vice-president of the Institute of Actuaries and a founder of the Royal Statistical and London Mathematical Societies. Brought to London in June 1845, when his father became chief rabbi of England, Adler was sent to University College School and University College, London. After a brilliant career there he graduated B.A. at London University in 1859. He preached his first sermon at the consecration of the Swansea synagogue in September 1859. Next year he went to the University of Prague and continued his theological studies under Dr. Rapoport, chief rabbi there; from him in 1862 he received the rabbinical diploma. In December 1862 he obtained at Leipzig the degree of Ph.D. for a thesis on Druidism.

On his return to England he became in 1863 temporary principal of the Jews' Theological College, then in Finsbury Square, and he held that office until 1865; he subsequently acted as theological tutor until 1879, was chairman of council in 1887, and was president at his death. He was appointed in February 1864 first minister at the Bayswater Synagogue, Chichester Place, Harrow Road, where till 1891 he attracted large congregations by his cultivated preaching. While at Bayswater he helped to found Jewish schools there, and was instrumental in establishing religious classes for Jewish children at the board schools in the east of London. His vigorous replies in the 'Nineteenth Century' for April and July 1878 to Prof. Goldwin Smith's attack (in the February number) on the Jews for lack of civic patriotism brought him praise from Gladstone and made for him a general reputation as a Jewish apologist both in Europe and in America. Next year he became delegate chief rabbi for his father, then in declining health; and on his father's death he was installed as chief rabbi on 23 June 1891. Adler, who spared himself no labour in discharging his rabbinical duties, tenaciously upheld the spiritual authority of his office over his own community. Rigidly orthodox in ceremonial observances, he at the same time gained much influence in social spheres outside Jewish ranks by virtue of his tact and wide culture.

Adler's main and invariable endeavour was to serve the best interests of his co-religionists at home or abroad, and he actively identified himself with all movements or institutions, charitable, political, social, educational, and literary, which were likely to serve that end. In 1885 he joined the Mansion House committee for the relief of persecuted Jews in Russia. The same year he visited the Holy Land and inspected many of the colonies established there by Russo-Jewish refugees. He represented the Russo-Jewish community at the conferences of the Hebrew congregations of Europe and America, held at Berlin in 1882 and at Paris in 1890. He was president of the Jewish Historical Society of England (1897), and vice-president of the Anglo-Jewish Association. His other offices included those of vice-president of the Society for the Prevention of Cruelty to Children, and of the Mansion House Association for Improving the Dwellings of the Poor; he was a governor of University College, an administrator of the 'People's Palace,' Mile End, and an energetic member of the committees of the King Edward Hospital Fund and the Metropolitan Hospital Sunday Fund. He gave useful evidence before the select committee of the House of Lords on sweating in 1888; before the joint committee on Sunday closing in May 1907; and before the divorce commission in 1910.

Adler's seventieth birthday in 1909, which synchronised with the jubilee of his ministry, was publicly celebrated with general enthusiasm. A portrait in oils, executed by Mr. Meyer Klang, was hung in the council chamber of the United Synagogue, Aldgate. A replica was presented by the Jewish congregations to Mrs. Adler, and on her death passed to his elder daughter. He was also made hon. D.C.L. of Oxford, and he received the C.V.O. from King Edward VII. He had already been made honorary LL.D. of St. Andrews in 1899, and he was elected a member of the Athenæum Club under Rule II on the suggestion of Mandell Creighton, bishop of London, in 1900.

Adler died of heart failure on 18 July 1911 at his residence, 6 Craven Hill, London, and was buried at the Willesden Jewish cemetery. He married in September 1867 Rachel, elder daughter of Solomon Joseph, who survived him till 9 Jan. 1912. Of his two daughters, the elder, Nettie, was elected member of the London county council. His only son, Alfred, a minister, predeceased him in 1911. By his will he left the testimonials and addresses which had been presented to him to the Frederic David Mocatta [q. v. Suppl. II] library and museum at University College, as well as various sums to Jewish and other institutions (*The Times*, 11 Aug. 1911). Of two portraits in oils, besides that mentioned above, one painted by Mr. B. S. Marks, in 1887, belongs to Adler's younger daughter, Mrs. Ruth Eichholz; the other, executed by Mr. Solomon J. Solomon, R.A., in 1908, was presented by (Sir) Adolph Tuck to the Jews' College. A cartoon by 'Spy' appeared in 'Vanity Fair' in 1894.

His published works, besides sermons and pamphlets and reviews, include: 1. 'Ibn Gabirol, the Poet Philosopher, and his Relation to Scholastic Philosophy' (in University Coll. Essays), 1864. 2. 'A Jewish Reply to Bishop Colenso's Criticism on the Pentateuch,' 1865. 3. 'Sermons on the Biblical Passages adduced by Christian Theologians in support of the Dogmas of their Faith,' 1869. 4. 'Anglo-Jewish Memories, and other Sermons' (jubilee memorial volume), 1909. He also contributed a chapter to 'Immortality: a Clerical Symposium' (1885); and a paper on 'The Chief Rabbis of England' (in Anglo-Jewish Historical Exhib. volume, 1887) (1888).

[The Times, 19 July 1911; Jewish Chron. and Jewish World, 21 July (with portraits); Jewish Year Book, 1911; Who's Who, 1911; Jewish Encyclopædia; Men and Women of the Time, 1899.] W. B. O.

AGNEW, Sir JAMES WILLSON (1815–1901), prime minister of Tasmania, born at Ballyclare, co. Antrim, Ireland, on 2 Oct. 1815, was son of James William Agnew and Ellen Stewart of Larne, co. Antrim. Educated for the medical profession at University College, London, at Paris, and Glasgow, he qualified as M.R.C.S. in 1838 and graduated M.D. at Glasgow in 1839. He almost immediately started for Sydney, N.S.W., sailing on the Wilmot. He spent a few months practising in Sydney, and then tried for a time the rough station life of the western part of Victoria. Subsequently he reached Hobart, and there he was disappointed of the post of private secretary to Sir John Franklin, then governor of Tasmania. On 24 Dec. 1841 he became assistant surgeon on the agricultural establishment; in July 1842 he was removed to Saltwater Creek in the same capacity, and on 28 Feb. 1845 he was transferred to be colonial assistant surgeon at Hobart, with charge of the general hospital. With this work he combined a general practice which laid the foundation of his influence amongst the people of Hobart. Yet he found time for studies in science and art; one of the founders of the Tasmanian Royal Society, he joined the council in 1851, and became honorary secretary in 1860.

In 1877 Agnew gave up his practice and entered the legislative council as member for Hobart at the general election of July 1877. From 9 Aug. 1877 to 5 March 1878 he served with Philip Oakley Fysh as minister without a portfolio, and continued in the ministry as reconstructed under Giblin till 20 Dec. 1878. He was again in office with Giblin from 29 Oct. 1879 to 5 Feb. 1880, when he resigned in order to visit the Melbourne Exhibition, being president of the Tasmanian Commission; thence he proceeded to England (see Fenton's *Hist. Tasm.* p. 370, note).

Returning from England in 1881, Agnew re-entered the legislative council in 1884. On 8 March 1886 he formed a ministry in succession to (Sir) Adye Douglas [q. v. Suppl. II], and was premier till 29 March 1887; he was also chief secretary till 1 March. His tenure of office was marked by educational reform. In 1891 he left the colony for a long visit to England, returning to Tasmania in 1894, when he was made K.C.M.G. In 1899 he was disabled by illness, and died at Hobart on 8 Nov. 1901. He was accorded a public funeral and buried at the Cornelian Bay cemetery.

'Good doctor Agnew' left his mark on Tasmania alike in public life, science, and art. He was a contributor to the 'Journal' of the Tasmanian Royal Society, his chief papers (1843 and 1864) being on the poison of Tasmanian snakes. He was a liberal donor to the museum at Hobart, of which, as well as of the botanic garden, he was the first chairman. In 1888 he bore the cost of the last shipment of salmon ova to Tasmania. He was a member of the council of education and of the university till 1891, when he resigned on absence from the colony. He was also president of the racing club.

Agnew married: (1) in 1846, Louisa Mary, daughter of Major J. Fraser of the 78th highlanders; she died on 10 March 1868; by her he had eight children, of whom one married daughter survives; (2) in 1878, Blanche, daughter of William Legge, of Tipperary, widow of Rev. Dr. Parsons of Hobart; she died without issue on 16 Dec. 1891.

A portrait painted by Tennyson Cole is in the Art Gallery in Hobart.

[Tasmanian Mail, 9 and 16 Nov. 1901 (with portrait); Mennell's Dict. Australas. Biog.; Burke's Colonial Gentry, ii. 592; Tasmanian Blue Books; private information.]

C. A. H.

AGNEW, Sir WILLIAM, first baronet (1825–1910), art dealer, was born at Salford on 20 Oct. 1825. The family derive from the Sheuhan branch of Agnew of Lochnaw. William's grandfather, John Agnew (1751–94) of Culhorn, migrated to Liverpool. His father, Thomas Agnew (1794–1871), who in boyhood studied drawing and modelling there, became a partner in 1816 of Vittore Zanetti, a dealer in clocks and opticians' wares, of Market Street Lane, Manchester. The firm soon took up picture dealing. The elder Agnew was from 1835 sole proprietor of the concern, to which he added a print-selling and print-publishing branch. He served as mayor of Salford 1850–1. His portrait by J. P. Knight, R.A., is in the Peel Park Museum, Salford, to which he gave many pictures (cf. *The Intellectual Repository*, 1871, pp. 253–4; *Art Journal*, 1861, p. 319; *The Dawn*, 24 April 1884; Axon's *Annals of Manchester*, 1886, p. 327). He was a fervent Swedenborgian (Bayley's *New Church Worthies*, 1881). He married, on 17 Feb. 1823, Jane, daughter and coheir of William Lockett (*d.* 1856), first mayor of Salford; by her he had five sons, of whom William was the eldest, and four daughters.

Educated at the Rev. J. H. Smithson's Swedenborgian school, Salford, William and his younger brother Thomas (1827–1883), who adhered through life to their father's Swedenborgian faith, early joined their father's business, which rapidly developed under their control. They were partners from 1850, when the firm took the style of Thomas Agnew & Sons. Establishing branches in London (first at Waterloo Place and from 1876 at Old Bond Street), as well as in Liverpool, they had the chief share in the formation during the middle period of the century of the great art collections in the north of England and the Midlands—the Mendel, Gillott, and many others. Among the collections, chiefly of old masters, which they helped to form between 1870 and 1890, were those of Sir Charles Tennant and Lord Iveagh. From 1860 onwards they purchased largely at Christie's (see Redford's *Art Sales*, ii. *passim*), where William Agnew usually represented the firm. They dealt in works by old masters, or early English and modern artists, as well as in water-colour drawings. Agnew bought the collection *en bloc* of Marlborough Gems at 35,000 guineas in June 1875 for Mr. Bromilow of Bitteswell Hall (where it remained until dispersed at Christie's 26–29 June 1899). On 6 May 1876 he purchased at the Wynn Ellis sale for 10,100 guineas the Gainsborough portrait of the Duchess of Devonshire which, on the night of 26 May, was cut out of its frame and stolen from Agnew's Old Bond Street gallery; it was not recovered until March 1901, when it was bought by Mr. J. P. Morgan (see *Catalogue Raisonné of Mr. J. Pierpont Morgan's Pictures*, by T. H. WARD and W. ROBERTS, 1907, s.v. 'Gainsborough'). From 1867 onwards the firm held an annual exhibition of drawings at their London gallery.

Agnew came into business relations with the leading artists, which often developed into personal friendships. He was an early friend of Fred Walker (MARKS, *Life and Letters of Walker*, 1896, *passim*), with whom he visited Paris in May 1866; from Walker he purchased many pictures, notably 'Spring,' 'Vagrants,' and 'The Harbour of Refuge'; the last he presented to the National Gallery of British Art in 1893 (*Catalogue*, ed. 1910, p. 378; cf. *The Times*, 9 Feb. 1911). He was a promoter of the fund for making purchases for the nation at the Fountaine sale in 1884, and of the Royal Jubilee Exhibition at Manchester, 1887, when he was chairman of the fine art section. He was on the royal commissions of the Melbourne Centenary Exhibition, 1888, and of the Paris Exhibition of 1900; and was long president of the Printsellers' Association. He presented in 1883 Reynolds's portrait of Malone, and in 1890 Ballantyne's portrait of Landseer to the National Portrait Gallery, and in 1903 Reynolds's Mrs. Hartley and child to the National Gallery.

In 1870 Agnew undertook new business responsibilities. His sister Laura was wife of William Bradbury of the London printing firm of Bradbury & Evans (the proprietors of 'Punch'). On F. M. Evans's death in 1870 Agnew and his two brothers, Thomas and John Henry, joined their brother-in-law, and the firm became Bradbury & Agnew; William Agnew became chairman in 1890, when the firm was turned into a limited company. He took a keen interest in 'Punch,' was on terms of intimacy with members of the staff, and, as long as his health permitted, regularly attended the weekly dinner.

In politics a strong liberal, and a faithful follower of Gladstone, whom he came to know intimately, Agnew was elected M.P. for S.E. Lancashire, 1880–5, and for the Stretford division of Lancashire 1885–6. In 1885 he spoke in the House of Commons in support of the vote of 83,520*l.* for the purchase of the Ansidei Madonna by Raphael, and the portrait of Charles I by Van Dyck from the Duke of Marlborough for the National Gallery (*The Times*, 6 March 1885, report reprinted in REDFORD's *Art Sales*, i. 397; and *Pall Mall Gazette*, 23 July 1886). He supported Gladstone's home rule bill in the spring of 1886 and was defeated at the general election in the summer; he unsuccessfully contested the Prestwich division in 1892. Deeply identifying himself with the organisation of his party, he was one of the founders of the National Liberal Club, London, and was president of the Manchester Reform Club (where his portrait appears in the gallery of past presidents), which he also assisted to start. His interest in philanthropical and other enterprises, especially at Manchester, was wide and practical. He was also a patron of music. At one time he was fond of travelling and of yachting, and was a member of the Royal Clyde Yacht Club.

Agnew, who was created a baronet on 2 Sept. 1895 on the recommendation of Lord Rosebery, died at his London residence, Great Stanhope Street, on 31 Oct. 1910. His body was cremated at Golder's Green. The gross value of the personal and real estate was sworn at 1,353,592*l.* (for will, see *The Times*, 18 Feb. 1911). He married, on 25 March 1851, Mary, eldest daughter of George Pixton Kenworthy of Manchester and Peel Hall, Lancashire (she died in 1892). He had four sons and two daughters, his eldest son, George, succeeding him in the baronetcy.

A portrait by Frank Holl (1883) and a marble bust by E. Onslow Ford (1899), together with a painting of him in infancy with his mother by J. W. Reynolds, jr., belong to his eldest son. A portrait by Sir H. von Herkomer is the property of his second son, Mr. C. Morland Agnew; and a chalk drawing by G. F. Watts that of his fourth son, Mr. Philip Agnew. Agnew figures in 'A Picture Sale at Christie's,' in 'The Graphic' 10 Sept. 1887 (reproduced in REDFORD's *Art Sales*, ii., facing p. xxix), in T. W. Wilson's 'A Sale at Christie's' (*Mag. of Art*, May

1888, p. 229), and in 'The Old Masters Exhibition, 1888,' by H. Jermyn Brooks (reproduced in *Sphere*, 23 Oct. 1909).

[Manchester Guardian, The Times, and Daily Telegraph 1 Nov. 1910 (with portrait); Punch, 9 Nov. 1910 (with in memoriam verses by the Editor and notice by Sir Henry Lucy); Lucy's Sixty Years in the Wilderness, 1909; M. H. Spielmann's Hist. of Punch, 1895 (with portraits), p. 39; Mitchell's Newspaper Press Directory, 1911 (with portrait); Manchester Faces and Places, 10 July 1890 (with portrait); Heywood's Authentic Series of Press Biographies; information from Sir George W. Agnew and Mr. C. Morland Agnew.]

W. R.

AIDÉ, CHARLES HAMILTON (1826–1906), author and musician, born in rue St. Honoré, Paris, on 4 Nov. 1826, was younger son of George Aïdá, son of an Armenian merchant settled in Constantinople, by his wife Georgina, second daughter of Admiral Sir George Collier [q. v.] His father, who acquired in Vienna a complete knowledge of languages, travelled widely, was admitted to good society in the chief capitals of Europe, came to England during the regency, and was killed in Paris in a duel when Aidé was four years old. His elder brother, Frederick (*b.* July 1823), was killed by an accident at Boulogne in 1831. Brought by his mother to England, Charles was educated privately at East Sheen and at Greenwich till at the age of sixteen he was sent to the University of Bonn. Subsequently he obtained a commission in the British army, serving with the eighty-fifth light infantry until 1853, when he retired with the rank of captain. After a spell of foreign travel he settled in England, living chiefly at Lyndhurst in the New Forest with his mother, till her death at Southsea on 12 Oct. 1875. Subsequently he took rooms in Queen Anne's Gate, London, where he entertained largely, his guests including the chief figures in the social and artistic world of France as well as England. Many months each year were spent abroad, —in Egypt and every country in Europe except Russia. In after-life he shared with his cousins, Colonel and Mrs. Collier, Ascot Wood Cottage, Berkshire.

A man of versatile accomplishments and with abundant social gifts, Aidé, who spoke and wrote French as easily as English, devoted himself with equal success to society, music, art, and literature. From early youth he composed poetry; his first published volume appearing in 1856, under the title of 'Eleanore, and other Poems.' 'The Romance of the Scarlet Leaf' followed in 1865, and 'Songs without Music; Rhymes and Recitations' (2 edits. 1882; third enlarged edit. 1889). His last volume of poems, 'Past and Present,' appeared in 1903. Many of his poems and ballads, 'The Pilgrim,' 'Lost and Found,' and 'George Lee,' found their way into popular anthologies. Aidé was also a prolific musical composer, and set many of his own verses to music. 'The Danube River,' 'The Fisher,' 'The Spanish Boat Song,' and 'Brown Eyes and Blue Eyes' were among songs by him which won a general repute.

At the same time Aidé made some reputation as an amateur artist, exhibiting at many of the London galleries sketches which he made in foreign travel. But his chief energies were devoted to fiction, and novels came regularly from his pen for some fifty years. His first novel, 'Rita,' appeared anonymously in 1856 (French translation, 1862). Some eighteen others followed, the most popular being 'Confidences' (1859; 2nd edit. 1862, 16mo); 'Carr of Carlyon' (3 vols. 1862; new edit. 1869); 'Morals and Mysteries' (1872), short stories; and 'Passages in the Life of a Lady in 1814–1815–1816' (3 vols. 1887). 'The Chivalry of Harold' was published posthumously in 1907. Aidé's novels mainly dealt with fashionable society, and although they lacked originality or power, were simply written under French influence and enjoyed some vogue.

Meanwhile Aidé turned his attention to the stage. On 7 Feb. 1874 'Philip,' a romantic drama in four acts from his pen, was produced by (Sir) Henry Irving at the Lyceum theatre, Irving taking the title rôle. On 12 June 1875 (Sir) John Hare with Mr. and Mrs. Kendal produced at the Court theatre 'A Nine Days' Wonder,' a comedy, adapted from a simultaneously published novel (JOSEPH KNIGHT, *Theatrical Notes*, 1903, pp. 43–7). Aidé also published in 1902 seven miniature plays in a volume entitled 'We are Seven; Half Hours on the Stage; Grave and Gay'; the last, called 'A table d'hôte,' is in French. Aidé died in London, unmarried, on 13 Dec. 1906, and was buried in the churchyard of All Souls, South Ascot.

A portrait in oils, painted at Rome by Duke Sante della Rovera, and exhibited at the New Gallery in 1907, is in the possession of the artist.

[The Times, 17 and 21 Dec. 1906; Pratt, People of the Period, 1897; G. Vapereau, Dict. Univ. des contemporains, 1893; J. D. Brown, Biog. Dict. of Musicians, 1886; Biograph, March 1880; Biog. Mag. August 1887; Lord Ronald Gower's My Reminiscences,

1882, and Old Diaries, 1902; Allingham's Diary, 1907; Brit. Mus. Cat.; private information.]

AIKMAN, GEORGE (1830–1905), painter and engraver, born at the top of Warriston Close, in the High Street, Edinburgh, on 20 May 1830, was ninth child of George Aikman of Edinburgh by his wife Alison McKay. The father, after employment by William Home Lizars [q.v.] the engraver in St. James Square, Edinburgh, started business for himself about 1825 in Warriston Close, where he carried on the Lizars' tradition by producing all the plates and illustrations for the seventh edition of the 'Encyclopædia Britannica.' Many of these were drawn and engraved by his son George. From a private school the boy was sent to Edinburgh High School, where he was for three sessions in the class of Dr. James Boyd. He was then apprenticed to his father, who had removed his business to 29 North Bridge, and after a journeyman period, during which he worked in Manchester and London, he was admitted a partner.

While serving his apprenticeship he had attended the classes of the Trustees' Academy, then directed by Robert Scott Lauder [q. v.], and the Royal Scottish Academy life-class. As early as 1850 he was exhibiting at the Scottish Academy exhibitions, but it was not until 1870 that he abandoned business for painting. In 1880 he was elected an A.R.S.A. Between 1874 and 1904 he exhibited at nine of the Royal Academy exhibitions in London. Except for a few portraits and some canvases depicting humours of monastic life, Aikman's theme as a painter was landscape, chiefly that of the Perthshire Highlands and of Warwickshire. It was generally low in tone; his skies were sometimes very luminous, but in oils his colour tended to heaviness, which was avoided in his water-colours, in which medium, though he treated it lightly, he was more successful. He practised etching during the greater part of his life, and towards the end he engraved several mezzotints. Impressions of some of these were exhibited, but only a few of them were published. The engraved plates included 'Robert Burns' (etching), after A. Nasmyth, and 'Sir Douglas Maclagan' (etching), after Sir George Reid; while among his original plates were 'Carlyle in his Study' (etching); 'Sir Daniel Macnee, P.R.S.A.' (etching); 'Norham Castle' (etching); 'Coming Storm across the Moor' (mezzotint). An etching after his picture 'For the Good of the Church' (R.A., 1874) was purchased by the Association for the Promotion of the Fine Arts in Scotland. Aikman contributed to the 'Etcher' (1880, 1882), 'English Etchings' (1883–4), and 'Selected Etchings' (1885), and he illustrated 'A Round of the Links: Views of the Golf Greens of Scotland' (1893), with etchings after the drawings of John Smart, R.S.A., and 'The Midlothian Esks' (1895).

Aikman acquired through his father and through his own study and research an exceptionally full knowledge of the engravers and painters of earlier generations, and some contributions on this topic to the 'Art Journal' were of considerable value. Devotedly attached to Edinburgh, he made drawings of ancient houses doomed to demolition, and the City Museum possesses a collection of these memorials.

He died in Edinburgh on 8 Jan. 1905, and was buried in Warriston cemetery. On 2 Dec. 1859 Aikman married Elizabeth Barnett, who with three daughters and two sons survived him.

[Private information; Scotsman, 9 Jan. 1905; Graves, Royal Acad. Exhibitors, 1905; Catalogues of the Royal Scottish Academy.]

D. S. M.

AINGER, ALFRED (1837–1904), writer, humourist and divine, born at 10 Doughty Street, London, on 9 April 1837, was youngest of four children of Alfred Ainger by his first wife, Marianne Jagger, of Liverpool. The father, an architect of scientific tastes, who designed the first University College Hospital (demolished and rebuilt 1900–6) and the Palm House at Kew, was of French Huguenot stock and of unitarian belief. The mother, who was musically gifted, died two years after her son Alfred's birth; her husband soon married again, and had a second family. Alfred, after attending as a child University College School, went in 1849 to Joseph King's boarding-school at Carlton Hill, where he fell under the two potent influences of Charles Dickens and of Frederick Denison Maurice (for some account of schoolmaster King see FREDERIC HARRISON's *Memoirs*, i. 28 sq.). His schoolmaster took him to hear Maurice preach, and he turned from his father's unitarianism to the Church of England. Charles Dickens's sons were Alfred's schoolfellows at Mr. King's school, and with them he visited their father. Dickens early discovered the boy's dramatic gift, and for several years Alfred was his favourite dramatic pupil, acting with him and Mark Lemon in the amateur performances which Dickens organised at Tavistock House. Subsequently for a time he played with a fancy of making the stage his profession, and he was always an admirably dramatic reciter. At sixteen, Ainger passed to King's College, London, where Maurice was professor both of divinity and of English literature. Literature now absorbed Ainger. With Lamb and Crabbe, he discovered that he had many affinities. Devotion to Shakespeare manifested itself early and in 1855 he became first president of the college Shakespeare Society. A passionate love of music also developed into one of his chief resources. In October 1856 he matriculated at Trinity Hall, Cambridge, with a view to a legal career. Henry Latham and Leslie Stephen were tutors of his college, while Henry Fawcett—soon Ainger's intimate friend—was elected a fellow in the year of Ainger's entrance. At Cambridge Ainger became the leading spirit of a literary circle which included Hugh Reginald Haweis [q. v. Suppl. II], Mr. Horace Smith, and Dr. A. W. Ward. He was a foremost contributor to a short-lived undergraduate magazine (3 nos. 1857–8), called 'The Lion,' which Haweis edited. Ainger's skit there on Macaulay and his criticisms of Shakespeare bore witness to his literary gifts and brilliant humour. At Cambridge, too, he came to know Alexander Macmillan, then a bookseller in Trinity Street, afterwards the famous London publisher, and was admitted to Macmillan's family circle.

Ainger's health allowed him to do no more than take the ordinary law examination (in June 1859). He graduated B.A. in 1860 and M.A. in 1865. His father's death in November 1859 made a waiting profession impossible for him and, acting upon his own inclination and upon the advice of his friends, Leslie Stephen among them, he took holy orders. In 1860 he was ordained deacon, and soon after became curate to Richard Haslehurst, Vicar of Alrewas, in Staffordshire. In 1863 he was ordained priest, and from 1864 to 1866 was assistant master in the Collegiate School at Sheffield. In the autumn of 1865 he had competed successfully for the readership at the Temple. That post he held for twenty-seven years, and in that capacity won a wide reputation as reader and preacher.

Both Ainger's sisters married early, the younger, Marianne, to a German named Wiss, and the elder, Adeline, to Dr. Roscow of Sandgate, who died in 1865. Shortly after his resettlement in London (1867) he experienced the great sorrow of his life in the sudden death of his widowed sister, Mrs. Roscow. The shock aged Ainger prematurely and turned his hair white. He became the guardian of his sister's four children—two girls and two boys, and devoted himself to their care. In 1876 Ainger moved to Hampstead, where his two nieces, Ada and Margaret Roscow, lived with him, and where he formed an intimacy with the artist of 'Punch,' George du Maurier [q. v. Suppl. I]. That companionship provided Ainger with a definite field for his wit. He constantly suggested the jests which du Maurier illustrated.

He had an exceptional power of making friendships. When he came to the Temple, Dr. Thomas Robinson (1790–1873) [q. v.] was master; in 1869 Robinson was succeeded by Dr. Charles John Vaughan [q. v.], with whom Ainger formed close relations. The poet Tennyson was among his acquaintances (Lord Tennyson's *Life*, i. 117, ii. 327), and he was elected a member of the Literary Club which was founded by Dr. Johnson (Grant Duff's *Notes from a Diary*, passim). He was a copious correspondent, and his letters, always spontaneous, abounded, like his conversation, in sudden turns and airy quips.

Meanwhile Ainger made a position in literature. At twenty-two he contributed his first successful article, 'Books and their Uses,' to an early number of 'Macmillan's Magazine' (December 1859, i. 110). He took the whimsical pseudonym 'Doubleday' (Doubled A). Eleven other articles appeared under the same friendly auspices between 1871 and 1896. In the latest period of his life, 1900–4, he was a regular contributor to a weekly journal called the 'Pilot,' edited by Mr. D. C. Lathbury.

Ainger's chief writings dealt with the life and work of Charles Lamb, with whose genius he had native sympathy. His monograph on Lamb was published in 1882, in the 'English Men of Letters' series (revised and enlarged 1888). There followed editions of 'Lamb's Essays' (1883), 'Lamb's Poems, Plays, and Miscellaneous Essays' (1884), and 'Lamb's Letters' (1888, new ed. 1904), the only collection which could lay claim at the time of publication to completeness. Ainger's life of Lamb and his edition of Lamb's writings embody much patient and original research. But Ainger was somewhat fastidious in his editorial method, and occasionally omitted from the letters characteristic passages which clashed with his conception of their writer's character. His labour remains a memorial of the editor's personal feeling and delicate insight rather than a monument of scholarship, and it has been largely superseded by Mr. E. V. Lucas's fuller biography and edition of Lamb's works and letters (1903–5). To this Dictionary Ainger contributed the articles on Charles and Mary Lamb, on Tennyson, and on George du Maurier, and wittily summed up its principle of conciseness in the motto, 'No flowers, by request,' with which he made merry in a speech at a dinner of the contributors (8 July 1897).

As a lecturer on literary subjects Ainger was popular with cultivated audiences throughout the country, and from 1889 onwards he frequently lectured at the Royal Institution, his subjects including 'True and False Humour in Literature,' 'Euphuism, Past and Present,' and the 'Three Stages of Shakespeare's Art.' In 1885 the University of Glasgow conferred upon him the honorary degree of LL.D., and he was made honorary fellow of his college, Trinity Hall.

During his last twenty years Ainger's influence as a preacher grew steadily. In 1887 he became canon of Bristol, where he formed many new and agreeable ties. He was appointed select preacher of Oxford in 1893. In the same year bad health compelled him to resign his readership at the Temple. Thereupon he accepted the living of St. Edward's at Cambridge. Again illness speedily forced him to retire, and he spent two months in travel in Egypt and Greece. In June 1894 Ainger, on Lord Rosebery's recommendation, was appointed Master of the Temple in succession to Dr. Vaughan. Thenceforth his duties of preacher became the main concern of his life. In 1895 he was made honorary chaplain, in 1896 chaplain-in-ordinary to Queen Victoria, and in 1901 chaplain-in-ordinary to King Edward VII. His sermons in the Temple were marked by beauty of language, and by a quiet, practical piety, which was impatient of excess. Neither high church nor low church, Ainger professed an unaggressive, moderate evangelicalism.

In 1903 Ainger's health broke after an attack of influenza, and at the end of the year he resigned his canonry at Bristol. He died of pneumonia on 8 Feb. 1904 at Darley Abbey, near Derby, the home of his younger niece, Ada Roscow, who, in 1896, had married an old friend, Walter Evans. He was buried in the churchyard of Darley Abbey.

Apart from the works already mentioned and articles in periodicals, Ainger was author of a volume of sermons (1870), a selection of Tennyson for the young (1891), a biographical preface to an edition of Hood's poems (1893, 1897), an introduction to an edition of Galt's 'Annals of the Parish' (1895), and a monograph on Crabbe (1903, in 'English Men of Letters' series). After his death 'The Gospel of Human Life' (a volume of sermons, 1904) and 'Lectures and Essays' (2 vols. 1905) were edited by H. C. Beeching, dean of Norwich.

Of two portraits in oils by Hugh Goldwin Riviere, one, which was painted in 1897 and has been reproduced in photogravure, belongs to Ainger's nephew, the Rev. Bentley Roscow, at Flint House, Sandwich; the other, which is smaller and was painted in 1904 after Ainger's death, is at Trinity Hall. Of two portraits by George du Maurier, one in water-colour (about 1882) belongs to the artist's widow, and the other, in black and white, dated 1882, to Ainger's niece, Miss Roscow. Mrs. Alexander Macmillan owns a portrait in pastels by the Norwegian artist, C. M. Ross; and a sixth portrait by Sir Arthur Clay, done in oils in 1893, belongs to the Rev. Bentley Roscow. A cartoon by 'Spy' appeared in 'Vanity Fair' 1892.

[Life and Letters of Alfred Ainger, by Edith Sichel, 1906; Dean Beeching's prefaces to The Gospel of Human Life and Lectures and Essays; Dr. A. W. Ward in Macmillan's Mag., April 1904; Quarterly Review, Jan. 1905; Monthly Review, March 1904; The Times 9 Feb. 1904; Old and Odd Memories, by Lionel Tollemache, 1908.] E. S.

AIRD, Sir JOHN, first baronet (1833–1911), contractor, born in London on 3 Dec. 1833, was the only child of John Aird (1800–1876), by his wife Agnes (*d.* 29 July 1869), daughter of Charles Bennett of Lambeth, Surrey. His father, son of Robert Aird of Fortrose, Ross-shire, originally a mason at Bromley by Bow, was (for twenty years) superintendent of the Phœnix Gas Company's station at Greenwich, and started in 1848 a contracting business for himself, laying down mains for many gas and water companies in London.

After private education at Greenwich and Southgate, Aird joined on his eighteenth birthday his father's business, which was soon known as John Aird & Sons. He was entrusted with the removal of the 1851 exhibition buildings (erected by his father) and their reconstruction as the Crystal Palace at Sydenham. The firm now engaged in large enterprises both in this country and abroad. They constructed reservoirs at Hampton and Staines, and the Beckton plant of the Gas Light and Coke Company. Abroad their works included the first waterworks at Amsterdam, and others at Copenhagen and Berlin, as well as gasworks in Copenhagen, Moscow, and elsewhere in Russia, France, Italy, and Brazil. They were also associated with Brassey & Wythes in constructing the Calcutta waterworks, with Sir John Kirk in building the Millwall Docks, and with Peto, Brassey & Betts in civil engineering works in Sardinia.

In 1860 the firm was renamed Lucas & Aird. Ten years later the elder Aird died, and John became a chief partner. In 1895 the concern changed its designation to John Aird & Co. Meanwhile it had carried out much railway and dock work, including various extensions of the Metropolitan, District, and St. John's Wood railways, Royal Albert Docks, Tilbury Docks, East and West India Docks extension, and the West Highland railway. Aird's firm also completed the Manchester canal.

Aird is best known by his great work of damming the Nile; the necessity for this had long been recognised, but its execution was prevented by the poverty of the Egyptian exchequer. In February 1898 Aird offered to construct dams at Assuan and Assyût, payment being deferred until the completion of the contract, and then spread over a term of years. His offer was accepted by the Egyptian government, and the work, begun in April 1898, was finished in 1902, a year before the stipulated time [see Baker, Sir Benjamin, Suppl. II]. About one million tons of masonry were employed in its construction, and at one time 20,000 men (90 per cent. of them natives) were engaged. Aird received for his services the grand cordon of the Medjidieh in 1902. Later undertakings of the firm include the Royal Edward Dock at Avonmouth (1902–8), the Tanjong Pagar Dock works at Singapore, the barrage at Esneh (opened in 1909), and the elevation of the height of the Assuan dam.

Aird became an associate of the Institution of Civil Engineers in 1859 and a member of the Iron and Steel Institute in 1887. In 1886 he served on the royal commission on the depression of trade, and from 1887 to 1905 represented North Paddington in the conservative interest in the House of Commons, where he was well known and respected. He became in 1900 the first mayor of Paddington, and was re-elected in the following year. Aird was popular in City circles, and was in 1882 appointed on the commission of lieutenancy of the City of London. He was a liveryman of the Needlemakers' Company, and served as master in 1890–2 and 1897–8. For many years he was associated with the volunteer movement, and was major and honorary lieutenant-colonel of the engineer and railway volunteer staff corps. He was created a baronet on Lord Salisbury's recommendation on 5 March 1901.

Aird was an ardent collector of pictures from 1874, when he removed from Tunbridge Wells to his London residence, 14 Hyde Park Terrace. His collection was confined almost exclusively to modern British art, of which he was a judicious patron. His artistic treasures included some of the finest examples of Calderon, Dicksee, Fildes, Frith, Leighton, Marks, Orchardson, Noel Paton, Prinsep, Briton Riviere, Rossetti, Marcus Stone, Storey, Tadema, and F. Walker (cf. illustrated description by J. F. Boyes in *Art Journal*, xliii. 135–140; and a catalogue of the collection by Henry Blackburn, privately printed in June 1884, with miniature reproductions of each painting, water-colour drawing, and sculpture). He was a member of council of the Art Union of London from 1891 until death. An enthusiastic mason, Aird was senior grand deacon for the same period.

He died on 6 Jan. 1911 at his country residence, Wilton Park, Beaconsfield, Bucks, and was buried at Littleworth, near Beaconsfield. His estate under his will was sworn at 1,101,489*l.* gross.

Aird married on 6 Sept. 1855 Sarah (*d.* 4 April 1909), daughter of Benjamin Smith of Lewisham, Kent, by whom he had two sons and seven daughters. His elder son, John, succeeded to the baronetcy. Portraits of Aird were painted by (Sir) Luke Fildes in 1898 and by Sidney Paget in 1902; the latter is in Paddington Town Hall.

[Engineering (portrait), 13 Jan. 1911; the Times, 7 and 12 Jan. and 23 March 1911; Cassier's Mag. (portrait and sketch), Aug. 1901, xx. 266, 343–4; Pratt's People of the Period, p. 18; Burke's Peerage, 1910.]

C. W.

AIREDALE, first Baron. [See Kitson, James, 1835–1911.]

AITCHISON, GEORGE (1825–1910), architect, born in London on 7 Nov. 1825, was son of George Aitchison by his wife Maria Freeman. After education at Merchant Taylors' School (1835–41), he was articled in 1841 to his father, then architect to the St.

Katharine Dock Co. Entering the schools of the Royal Academy in 1847, he graduated B.A. at London University in 1851, and began in 1853 an architectural tour which led to his acquaintance in Rome with George Heming Mason [q. v.]. Mason introduced him to Frederic Leighton [q. v. Suppl. I]. Concluding the tour with William Burges [q. v.], he returned to London in 1855 and four years later was taken into partnership by his father, to whose practice and appointment he succeeded in 1861, becoming subsequently joint architect to the London and St. Katharine Docks Co. In 1865 Leighton, the friend of his lifetime, gave him the opportunity of designing his house and studio in Holland Road, South Kensington (now Leighton House), to which the Arab Hall was added at a later date. Aitchison's other principal works were the hall of the Founders Co. (1877); offices for the Royal Exchange Insurance Co., Pall Mall (1886); decorations for the apartments of the Princess Louise at Kensington Palace; and the board room for the Thames Conservancy (1868), with a frieze by Leighton. He was examiner in architecture and the principles of ornament at the Science and Art Department, South Kensington, and for many years district surveyor for East Wandsworth and Tooting. Aitchison was elected A.R.A. in 1881 and R.A. in 1898. He had already become professor of architecture to the Academy, a post which he resigned in 1905. From 1896 to 1899 he was president of the Royal Institute of British Architects, and during his presidency (1898) was awarded the royal gold medal. His work as an architect, always scholarly, is chiefly marked by his promotion of higher standards of internal decoration and by his collaboration with other artists in such work. He was a wide reader, a good talker, and the collector of an interesting library.

His numerous writings were mostly professional lectures, presidential addresses, or communications to architectural journals. He edited and wrote an introduction to Ward's 'Principles of Ornament' (1892), and was a contributor of several memoirs to this Dictionary, including those of Sir Charles Barry, Francis Hall, and George Heming Mason.

Aitchison resided and worked at 150 Harley Street, where he died, unmarried, on 16 May 1910. An excellent portrait by Sir L. Alma-Tadema, R.A., which was exhibited at the Academy in 1901, hangs in the room of the Royal Institute of British Architects.

[Journal Royal Inst. of Brit. Architects, xvii., 3rd series (1909–10), 581; The Times, 17 May 1910; personal knowledge.]

P. W.

ALDENHAM, first Baron. [See Gibbs, Henry Hucks, 1819–1907.]

ALDERSON, HENRY JAMES (1834–1909), major-general, born at Quebec, Canada, on 22 May 1834, was son of Lieut.-colonel Ralph Carr Alderson, royal engineers, by his wife Maria, daughter of Henry Thorold of Cuxwold, Lincolnshire. John Alderson (1757–1829) [q. v.] physician, of Sculcoates, Yorkshire, was his grandfather. Educated privately at Messrs. Stoton & Mayer's school at Wimbledon (1844–8), he entered the Royal Military Academy, Woolwich, as a cadet, in May 1848. He received a commission as second lieutenant in the royal artillery on 23 June 1852, and served in Canada until 1854, when, on promotion to the rank of lieutenant, he returned to England. Serving through the Crimean war, he was present at the battles of the Alma, Inkerman, and at the siege and fall of Sebastopol. He was mentioned in despatches, and received the medal with three clasps, the Turkish medal, and the légion d'honneur, third class. He was promoted to the rank of second captain on 1 April 1859 and from Feb. to June 1864 was attached on special mission to the headquarters of the federal army under General O. A. Gillmor during the civil war in the United States of America, and was present at the bombardment of Charleston.

On his return to England Alderson joined the experimental department of the school of gunnery, Shoeburyness, and became successively captain on 6 July 1867; major 3 July 1872; lieut.-colonel 1 Oct. 1877; colonel (by brevet) 1 Oct. 1881, and major-general 9 July 1892.

From 1871 he held various appointments in the department of the director of artillery at the war office, and in 1891 became president of the ordnance committee. This important office he held until his retirement from the army on 22 May 1896, on account of age. From 1897 until his death he was a director of Sir W. G. Armstrong, Whitworth & Co., the gunmaking firm at Elswick, Newcastle-on-Tyne.

He was made C.B. on 21 June 1887; a K.C.B. on 30 May 1891; and was appointed colonel commandant in the royal artillery on 4 Nov. 1905. He died at Durham on 10 Sept. 1909. He married in 1877 his second cousin, Florence, youngest daughter of Sir Edward Hall Alderson (1787–1857) [q. v.], baron of the exchequer, and had one son, Ralph Edward.

[The Times, 11 Sept. 1909; R.A. Institution Leaflet, October 1909.] J. H. L-E.

ALEXANDER, Mrs. (pseudonym) (1825–1902), novelist. [See Hector, Mrs. Annie French.]

ALEXANDER, BOYD (1873–1910), African traveller and ornithologist, born at Cranbrook, Kent, on 16 Jan. 1873, was a twin son (with Robert Alexander) of Colonel Boyd Francis Alexander, of an Ayrshire family, by his wife Mary Wilson. Boyd, after education at Radley College (1887–91), passed into the army in 1893, joining the 7th battalion rifle brigade. Devoting himself to travel and ornithology, he visited the Cape Verde Islands twice in 1897 to study their ornithology, and he went, in 1898, for the same purpose to the Zambesi river and its tributary the Kafue. In 1899 he joined the Gold Coast constabulary, and in 1900 he was present at the relief of Kumasi. For this service he received the medal and clasp, and on his return to England he was offered and accepted a commission in the rifle brigade. Keeping up his studies of bird life in West Africa, he visited Fernando Po in 1902, and made there not only ornithological but also ethnological investigations and a map, and gathered material for a review of Spanish missionary work. In 1904 he started on an expedition which was designed to survey northern Nigeria and to show that Africa could be crossed from west to east by means of its waterways. Accompanied by his younger brother, Captain Claud Alexander, Captain G. B. Gosling, Mr. P. A. Talbot, and his assistant and taxidermist José Lopes, Alexander left Lokoja on the Niger on 31 March, and travelled to Ibi on the Benue. There the party separated for a time. Gosling, a zoologist, went off to shoot big game. Claud Alexander and Talbot carried out a valuable survey of the Murchison mountains in spite of sickness, scarcity of food, and difficulties with carriers and hostile natives; they finally reached Maifoni, where Claud Alexander died of fever, after six weeks' illness, on 13 Nov. 1904, at the age of 26. Boyd Alexander meanwhile travelled alone by Loko on the Benue, Keffi, the Kachia and Panda Hills and Bauchi to Yo (26 Oct.), some thirty miles from Lake Chad. He succeeded in visiting his dying brother at Maifoni, and thence he (now with Talbot, Gosling and Lopes as companions) reached Lake Chad by way of Kukawa and Kaddai. Some months were spent in the difficult exploration of the lake. Their valuable surveys of the lake, when compared with other surveys, enabled geographers to form an idea of the remarkable periodic variations of level and other physical conditions to which the lake is liable in sympathy with periods of drought or heavy rainfall. On 26 May 1905 Alexander, Gosling and Lopes (Talbot having returned to the west) started up the Shari, making a detailed survey of the Bamingi tributary in September. They then traversed the watershed to the Ubangi, and proceeded across the centre of the continent, following that river and the Welle. At Niangara on the Welle Gosling died of blackwater fever. Alexander now travelled to N'Soro, turned north to the Lado country, and followed the Yei river and Bahr-el-Jebel downward through the Anglo-Egyptian Sudan. He surveyed the Kibali tributary of the Welle in July and the Yei in October 1906, besides carrying out important zoological studies. He reached the Nile in December 1906.

For his journey across the continent Alexander received the gold medal of the Geographical Society of Antwerp in 1907, and the founder's medal of the Royal Geographical Society of London in 1908, as well as the thanks of his colonel, the duke of Connaught, on behalf of his regiment. At the close of 1908 Alexander, with Lopes, left England again for West Africa. He visited the islands of São Thomé, Principe, and Annobom, and, in March 1909, the Kamerun mountain, whence he proceeded to Lake Chad by way of the upper Benue, intending thereafter to make for Egypt through Wadai and Darfur. The country was known to be in a disturbed condition, and Alexander, on reaching Nyeri, seventy miles north of Abeshr, the capital of Wadai, was murdered by the natives on 2 April 1910. He was buried at Maifoni, by the grave of his brother Claud. Lopes, who had accompanied him since his earliest journey to the Cape Verde Islands, escaped. There is a memorial to Boyd and his brother Claud at the parish church of Cranbrook, Kent, and his portrait as a boy, by Godbold, is preserved by his family.

Alexander published an account of his journey of 1904–7 in 'From the Niger to the Nile' (2 vols. 1907). He contributed a detailed account of Fernando Po to the 'Ibis' (1903), and a paper 'From the Niger, by Lake Chad, to the Nile,' to the 'Geographical Journal,' xxx. 119.

[Obit. notice, Geographical Journal, xxxvi. 108; private information.] O. J. R. H.

ALEXANDER, WILLIAM (1824–1911), archbishop of Armagh, was born in Derry on 13 April 1824. His father, Robert Alexander, rector of Aghadowey, was nephew of Nathanael Alexander, bishop of Meath, and a cousin of James Alexander, first earl of Caledon. His mother was Dorothea, daughter of Henry M'Clintock of Ballyarton, co. Donegal. William was the eldest son in a family of three sons and five daughters; of his two brothers, Henry became a rear admiral, and Robert was killed at the siege of Delhi. Educated at Tonbridge School, Kent, William matriculated at Exeter College, Oxford, in November 1841, afterwards migrating to Brasenose. Residence at the university during the last years of the Oxford movement permanently affected his life and his attitude towards religious questions. In later years he used to recall the spell of Newman's sermons. He graduated in classical honours (fourth class) in 1847, but in spite of the low class he had proved command of poetic and literary gifts. On 19 Sept. 1847 he was ordained deacon by Richard Ponsonby [q.v.], bishop of Derry, accepting the curacy of the cathedral parish. He received priest's orders on 16 June 1848, when the ordination sermon was preached by William Archer Butler [q.v.] Subsequently he held in turn the benefices of Termonamongan (1850), Fahan (1855), and Camus-juxta-Mourne (1860), and was appointed dean of Emly (a sinecure office) in 1864.

Meanwhile in 1850 Alexander won at Oxford the Denyer theological prize for an essay on the 'Divinity of Christ'; in 1853 he recited in the Sheldonian theatre a congratulatory ode to Lord Derby, then assuming the chancellorship of the university, and in 1860 he obtained the university prize for his sacred poem 'The Waters of Babylon.' In 1867 he was a candidate for the university professorship of poetry at Oxford, when Sir Francis Doyle [q.v. Suppl. I] was elected by a narrow majority.

In the same year Alexander became bishop of Derry, being consecrated in Armagh cathedral on 6 Oct. 1867, and proceeding D.D. at Oxford. At Derry he lived for the next twenty-nine years. The requirements of his episcopal office were exacting and he diligently discharged his pastoral duties, confirmations, ordinations, visitations and the like, gaining in a marked degree the affection of his clergy. He never cared for the routine work of committees or for the details of financial organisation. The disestablishment of the Irish church in 1869 was a blow to him, and he held that it had done serious injury to religion in Ireland. By conviction a high churchman, although with no leaning to what is called ritualism, Alexander was not in full sympathy with the party which became dominant for a time in the councils of the disestablished Irish church, and synodal controversy was distasteful to his spirit. On the death of Archbishop Robert Bent Knox [q.v. Suppl. I] in 1893 he was elected by the Irish bishops to the see of Armagh and the primacy of all Ireland. It was not until his succession to the primacy, with the full concurrence of all ecclesiastical parties, that he became the recipient of that full measure of honour and respect in Ireland which had already been accorded to him in England and in the colonial churches. 'I have been, perhaps,' said Alexander of himself in 1893, with modesty and some justice, 'enough of a writer to prevent me being a very good speaker. I have been enough of a speaker to prevent me being a thinker. And I have been enough of a writer and speaker and thinker to prevent me being a very good bishop for these troublous times.'

Poetry and literature were always the delight of Alexander's leisure, although not a chief occupation. Through life he wrote verses, which good critics recognised as genuine poetry. In 1886 he published 'St. Augustine's Holiday and other Poems' (with a preface of autobiographical interest), and in 1900 another edition of his poems appeared under the title of 'The Finding of the Book.' Many striking verses of his on occasions of public interest appeared in 'The Times' and the 'Spectator' during later years.

But from the early stages of his clerical career it was as an eloquent and accomplished speaker, preacher, and lecturer that he made his mark. In America his power was no less recognised than in England. Literary themes attracted him as well as religious or theological ones. A Dublin lecture on Matthew Arnold's poetry (1863) was full of suggestiveness and of nice critical discrimination. Another on Virgil and St. Augustine was printed in 1869 along with a spirited blank verse translation of part of the 'Æneid.' To the end of his days Alexander was under the spell of St. Augustine, and one of his most characteristic lectures, delivered in 1876 in St. James's, Piccadilly, dealt with St. Augustine's Confessions. Not only was he sensible of the merits of the African bishop as a theologian and a spiritual guide, but he was strongly attracted by his terse and epigrammatic style. The larger part of Alexander's writings and lectures, however, was on theological subjects and much of it was prepared for English pulpits. Not so powerful as Magee, he became, probably, the most brilliant Anglican preacher of his day. No one approached him as a master of felicitous and striking phrase. His sermons were not so closely reasoned as Liddon's, but their effectiveness was much enhanced by their delivery without manuscript, by a splendid and sympathetic voice and a dignified presence. 'My habit,' he wrote, 'is to prepare carefully and to take into the pulpit a complete skeleton of the discourse, and as much argumentative or illustrative matter as might occupy some minutes in delivery, trusting for the rest to the suggestions of the moment founded upon previous thought.' His sermons on great occasions were very numerous, two notable examples being his discourse at the enthronement of his old friend Magee as archbishop of York on 17 March 1891, and that before the Lambeth conference in Canterbury Cathedral on 4 July 1897.

Steeped in the writings of Pearson and the great Caroline divines, he wrote and spoke with a just sense of proportion, and knew how to distinguish things essential from things of secondary importance. His Oxford prize essay on the 'Divinity of Christ' was reprinted twice in a slightly modified form, in 1854, and again in one of his latest books, 'Primary Convictions' (1893, 2nd ed. 1898). This work also contains the substance of lectures delivered in America in 1892; it deals with the main topics of the Christian creed, and in picturesque and impassioned language dwells upon its beauty, its reasonableness and its response to the aspirations of the soul. His reasoned apologetic is reverent, telling, and brilliant; but he did not read German, and he took the critical labours of Germany at second hand. In 1876 he delivered at Oxford the Bampton lectures on the 'Witness of the Psalms to Christ and Christianity' (1876; 3rd edit. 1890). This contains much that is permanently valuable and suggestive, from the theological rather than the critical side. The same may be said of the 'Leading Ideas of the Gospels' (1872, 3rd edit. 1898), which grew out of Oxford sermons preached in 1871. His commentaries on the Johannine epistles (1881) in the 'Speaker's Commentary' and in the 'Expositor's Bible' (1889) abound in devout and beautiful thoughts and in proofs of a refined taste.

A convinced unionist in politics, Alexander showed his rhetorical power to advantage at the Albert Hall, London, in 1893, in his speech against the second home rule bill; but he had friends in all political camps. The most delightful of hosts, his conversation was full of interest and *esprit*, and even in extreme old age a literary problem or nice point of criticism would be eagerly taken up by him and discussed with his old fire. With the manners and the courtesy of a grand seigneur he combined the fatherly dignity of a prince of the church. He resigned the archbishopric on 30 Jan. 1911, and died in retirement at Torquay on 12 Sept. 1911. He was buried in Derry Cathedral cemetery beside his wife who had died on 15 Oct. 1895. Alexander was hon. D.C.L. Oxon (1876), hon. LL.D. Dublin (1892), hon. D.Litt. Oxon (1907), and he received the G.C.V.O. in 1911. On 15 Oct. 1850 he married Cecil Frances (daughter of John Humphreys, D.L.), well known as a hymn writer [see ALEXANDER, MRS. CECIL FRANCES, Suppl. I], by whom he had two sons and two daughters.

Alexander's portrait was thrice painted: (1) for his family, by C. N. Kennedy, when he had been twenty-five years bishop of Derry; (2) for the palace of Armagh, by Walter Osborne; and (3) by Harris Brown for presentation to the National Gallery of Ireland by friends, representing all religious denominations, on his resignation of the primacy. A synod hall at Armagh is being built (1912) in his memory, and in Derry also his name is to be associated with a monument. A cartoon by 'Spy' appeared in 'Vanity Fair' in 1895.

In addition to the works enumerated he published 'The Great Question and other Sermons' (1885; 2nd edit. 1887), and 'Verbum Crucis' (1892), and he edited Ephesians, Colossians, Thessalonians, and Philemon (1880) in the 'Speaker's Commentary.'

[The Times, 13 Sept. 1911, memoir by the present writer; Irish Times and Daily Express of same date; Sunday Mag. (August 1896), by S. L. Gwynn; Miles's Sacred Poets of the Nineteenth Century, 1907, pp. 59 sq.; family information; personal knowledge.] JOHN OSSORY.

ALGER, JOHN GOLDWORTH (1836–1907), journalist and author, born at Diss, Norfolk, and baptised on 7 Aug. 1836, was the only son of John Alger, a corn merchant of that town, by his wife Jemima, daughter of Salem Goldworth, yeoman, of Morning Thorpe, Norfolk. Educated at Diss, Alger became a journalist at the age of sixteen. At first he wrote for the 'Norfolk News,' and afterwards transferred his services to the 'Oxford Journal.' In 1866 he joined the parliamentary reporting staff of 'The Times,' and after eight years' work in that capacity was sent to Paris in 1874 to act as assistant to Henri Opper de Blowitz, 'The Times' Paris correspondent. There he remained for twenty-eight years. His leisure he chiefly devoted to historical research in the Bibliothèque Nationale and National Archives. He made himself thoroughly familiar with the topographical history of Paris, and threw new light on byways of the French revolution, investigating with especial thoroughness the part which Englishmen played in the great movement. His chief publications were: 1. 'Englishmen in the French Revolution,' 1889. 2. 'Glimpses of the French Revolution,' 1894. 3. 'Paris in 1789–94; Farewell Letters of Victims of the Guillotine,' 1902. 4 'Napoleon's British Visitors and Captives,' 1904. He also published 'The Paris Sketch Book' (a description of current Parisian life) (1887); contributed historical articles to several leading magazines, and was an occasional contributor to this Dictionary. In 1902 Alger retired from the service of 'The Times' on a pension, and settled in London. He died unmarried at 7 Holland Park Court, Addison Road, West Kensington, on 23 May 1907.

[The Times, 25 May 1907; Who's Who, 1907; M. de Blowitz, My Memoirs, 1903.]

S. E. F.

ALINGTON, first BARON. [See STURT, HENRY GERARD, 1825–1904.]

ALISON, SIR ARCHIBALD, second baronet (1826–1907), general, born at Edinburgh on 21 Jan. 1826, was eldest son of Sir Archibald Alison, first baronet [q. v.], the historian, by Elizabeth Glencairn, daughter of Lieut.-colonel Tytler. In 1835 Possil House, near Glasgow, became the family home. The father educated his son privately, till he went to Glasgow University. There, at the age of fifteen, he gained the first prize for an English essay on the character and times of Sulla, and reviewed Thierry's 'History of the Gauls' in 'Blackwood's Magazine.' Between Alison and his father there was always the closest intimacy. They shared the same tastes, and the son replied in 'Blackwood' (May 1850) to the criticisms in the 'Edinburgh Review' on the continuation of his father's history.

On 3 Nov. 1846 Alison was commissioned as ensign in the 72nd foot (afterwards Seaforth highlanders) and joined the depot at Nenagh. He was promoted lieutenant on 11 Sept. 1849, and joined the headquarters of the regiment in Barbados. Yellow fever was raging there, and his father had arranged for an exchange, but Alison refused to leave his regiment at such a time. He went with it to Nova Scotia in 1851, and came home with it in October 1854, having been promoted captain on 11 Nov. 1853.

After some months at Malta, the regiment went to the Crimea in May 1855, and having taken part in the expedition to Kertch, was placed in the highland brigade at the end of June. While serving with the regiment in the trenches before Sebastopol, Alison attracted the notice of Sir Colin Campbell [q. v.], by opportunely producing a sketch plan of the trenches, which he had drawn on the inside of an envelope, as well as by his coolness under fire during the assault of 8 Sept. He was mentioned in despatches, was made brevet-major on 6 June 1856, and received the Crimean medal with clasp and the Turkish medal. On 19 Dec. 1856 he left the 72nd for an unattached majority.

When Sir Colin Campbell left England at twenty-four hours' notice on 12 July 1857 to deal with the Indian Mutiny, he took Alison with him as his military secretary, and a younger brother, Frederick, as his aide-de-camp. In the second relief of Lucknow both brothers were wounded, the elder losing his left arm. He returned to duty early in 1858, but the stump inflamed, and he was invalided home (10 March). He had been mentioned in despatches (*Lond. Gaz.* 16 Jan. 1858), was made brevet lieut.-colonel and C.B. (28 Feb. 1861), and received the medal with clasp. On his arrival in England he dined with Queen Victoria. When entertained by the corporation of Glasgow, he explained Sir Colin Campbell's work, and wrote on 'Lord Clyde's Campaign in India' in 'Blackwood' (Oct. 1858).

Alison was unemployed for the next four years. From 17 March 1862 to 19 Oct. 1867 he was an assistant adjutant-general, first with the inspector-general of infantry at headquarters, and three years afterwards in the south-western district. He became brevet-colonel on 17 March 1867. On 1 Oct. 1870 he was placed on the staff at Aldershot as assistant adjutant-general. At the end of 1873 he went to the west coast of Africa in command of the British brigade sent out for the Ashanti war, with the local rank of brigadier-general. He took part in the battle of Amoaful, the capture of Bequah, the action at Ordashu, and the taking of Coomassie. At Amoaful the fire was very hot, and the dense growth made direction difficult, but his staff were struck by his self-possession and the precision of his orders. When abscesses in his only hand made him nearly helpless, he bore his suffering with 'sweet . . . serenity.' He was repeatedly mentioned in despatches (*Lond. Gaz.* 6, 7 and 17 March 1874), received the thanks of parliament and the medal with clasp, and was made K.C.B. on 31 March 1874. After a few months at Aldershot, Alison went to Ireland as deputy adjutant-general on 17 Oct. 1874. He received a reward for distinguished service on 6 Oct. 1876, and was promoted major-general on 1 Oct. 1877. After four months as commandant of the Staff College at Camberley, he was deputy quartermaster-general for intelligence, and helped at the headquarters staff (1878–82) to meet the Egyptian crisis of 1882.

On 6 July Alison left England to take command of a force which was assembled at Cyprus to secure the Suez Canal. The bombardment of Alexandria took place on the 11th, and Alison landed there on the 17th with two battalions which were soon reinforced. On the 24th he occupied Ramleh, and receiving instructions to 'keep Arabi constantly alarmed,' he made repeated demonstrations towards Kafr-ed-Dauar, especially on 5 Aug. Thus Arabi was led to expect that the British advance on Cairo would be from Alexandria, and not from Ismailia, as was intended. In that advance Alison commanded the highland brigade, consisting of the highland light infantry, Camerons, Gordons, and black watch. This was the leading brigade of the second (Hamley's) division in the storming of the intrenchments at Tel-el-Kebir; and Alison took a personal part, revolver in hand, in the confused fighting inside. After the surrender of Cairo he was sent to occupy Tanta with half a battalion of the Gordon highlanders (17 Sept.). He found there an Egyptian force of all arms disposed to resist; but by coolness and tact he induced them to lay down their arms (Maurice, p. 103). He was mentioned in despatches (*Lond. Gaz.* 29 July, 6 Oct., and 2 Nov.), received the thanks of parliament, and was promoted lieut.-general for distinguished service on 18 Nov. 1882. After Lord Wolseley's departure Alison was in command of the British force in Egypt till 17 May 1883. On his return to England a sword of honour was presented to him by the citizens of Glasgow, with a tiara for Lady Alison.

Alison held the command of the Aldershot division from 1 Aug. 1883 till the end of 1888, with the exception of part of 1885, when he acted as adjutant-general during Lord Wolseley's absence in Egypt. He received the G.C.B. on 21 June 1887, and was placed on the retired list under the age rules on 12 Jan. 1893. He was given the colonelcy of the Essex regiment on 24 Nov. 1896, and was transferred to his old regiment, the Seaforth highlanders, on 30 March 1897. He was also honorary colonel of the 1st volunteer battalion of the highland light infantry, 25 July 1883, and was made honorary LL.D. of Cambridge, Edinburgh, and Glasgow. In 1889 he was appointed a member of the Indian council, and remained on it for ten years. He died at 93 Eaton Place, London, on 5 Feb. 1907, and was buried at Edinburgh with military honours, the Seaforth highlanders taking part in the ceremony. On 18 Nov. 1858 he married Jane, daughter of James Black of Dalmonach, a Glasgow merchant. She died on 15 July 1909. She edited her father-in-law's autobiography, and was a woman of many gifts. They had two sons and four daughters. The eldest son, Archibald (the third baronet), was born on 20 May 1862. At his residence, Possil House, Copse Hill, Wimbledon, there are portraits of Alison by S. West (1865) and by Miss Munro (1900).

'Modest and self-effacing to the very verge of humility, he never asserted his individuality until duty summoned him to the front'; but he knew how to combine courtesy with insistence on duty. Among contributions to 'Blackwood,' besides those mentioned, were articles on the British army and its organisation (1869 and 1892) and on 'Armed Europe' (1893–4).

[Cornhill Magazine, March 1907; Blackwood's Magazine, March 1907; private information; The Times, 6 Feb. 1907; Autobiography of Sir Archibald Alison (first baronet), 1883; Major Brackenbury, The Ashanti War, 1874; Sir Frederick Maurice, The Campaign of 1882 in Egypt, 1908; Shand, Life of Sir E. Hamley, 1895.]

E. M. L.

ALLAN, Sir WILLIAM (1837–1903), engineer and politician, born at Dundee on 29 Nov. 1837, was third son of James Allan (*d.* 1883), machine maker and proprietor of Seabraes Foundry, Dundee, by his wife Margaret Dickson (*d.* 1879). Allan served his apprenticeship as an engineer at his father's foundry As a journeyman he removed to Glasgow, and shortly afterwards (1856) he went for a short time to Paterson, New Jersey. In 1857 he joined the royal navy as engineer, and spent the next three years mainly at foreign stations. In 1861, when the civil war broke out in America, Allan's love of adventure led him to take service as chief engineer on board a blockade-runner. He was in Charleston harbour when the Federals bombarded the city (21 Dec. 1861), and was captured and carried as a prisoner to the Capitol, Washington. Being released on parole, he returned to Dundee, resuming work at Seabraes Foundry. His varied experience had made him a competent workman, and when the North-Eastern Engineering Company was formed at Sunderland in 1866 he was engaged as foreman over one of the departments. The new venture was not at first successful. In 1868 the company was in difficulties and Allan became manager. Under his control the concern flourished, and after its removal to Wallsend, on the Tyne, enjoyed a high position in Tyneside engineering. In 1886 Allan started with great success on his own account the Scotia Engine Works at Sunderland, and remained active head of the firm till 1900. The business was then amalgamated with Messrs. Richardson, Westgarth & Co., Ltd. Allan became director, and was also until his death chairman of the Albyn Line, Ltd., shipowners of Sunderland.

From his youth Allan was an advanced radical, and showed practical sympathy with the working-classes. He was the first large employer to introduce an eight-hours day in his own works. At a bye-election at Gateshead on 24 Feb. 1893 Allan was returned in the liberal interest by a majority of 868 over his opponent, Mr. Pandeli Ralli. He represented Gateshead till his death. He spoke in the house with more force than elegance, but always with sincerity and common-sense. His practical knowledge led him to oppose strenuously the introduction of the Belleville type of boilers into the navy (*Hansard*, 25 June 1896; LUCY'S *Unionist Parliament*, 1895-1900, p. 78). On the occasion of King Edward VII's coronation in 1902 Allan was knighted. He died on 28 Dec. 1903 at Scotland House, Sunderland, and was buried in Ryhope Road cemetery, Sunderland. Allan was married to Jane, daughter of Walter Beattie of Lockerbie, who survived him.

In addition to his other activities Allan was a writer of Scottish songs—fluent, patriotic, fervid. From 1871 till his death he published so many volumes of verse that he was described as 'the most prolific poet of our time.' His poetic publications include: 1. 'Rough Castings in Scotch and English Metal,' 1872. 2. 'Hame-spun Lilts, or Poems and Songs chiefly Scottish,' 1874. 3. 'Heather-bells, or Poems and Songs,' 1875. 4. 'Ian Vor, a Drama,' 1876. 5. 'Roses and Thistles, Poems and Songs,' 1878. 6. 'A Life's Pursuit,' 1880. 7. 'After Toil Songs,' 1882. 8. 'Lays of Leisure,' 1883. 9. 'Northern Lights, or Poems and Songs,' 1889. 10. 'A Book of Songs in English and Scottish,' Sunderland, 1890, 4to. 11. 'A Book of Poems,' 1890. 12. 'Democratic Chants,' 1892. 13. 'The Rose of Methlic,' 1895. 14. 'Sunset Songs,' 1897. 15. 'Songs of Love and Labour,' 1903. Allan's only technical publication was 'The Shipowners' and Engineers' Guide to the Marine Engine' (Sunderland, 1880).

A cartoon portrait by 'Spy' appeared in 'Vanity Fair' in 1893.

[Dundee Year Book, 1903; Dundee Advertiser, 29 Dec. 1903; Cat. of Lamb Collection of Dundee Books, Dundee Reference Library; Reid's Bards of Angus and the Mearns; H. W. Lucy's Balfourian Parliament, 1906, p. 109 (with sketch portrait by Phil May); private information.]

A. H. M.

ALLEN, GEORGE (1832–1907), engraver and publisher, son of John and Rebecca Allen, was born on 26 March 1832 at Newark-on-Trent, and was educated at a private grammar school there. His father died in 1849, and in that year he was apprenticed for four years to an uncle (his mother's brother), a builder in Clerkenwell. He became a skilled joiner, and was employed for three and a half years in that capacity upon the woodwork of the interior of Dorchester House, Park Lane. A reference to this work occurs in Ruskin's 'Munera Pulveris' (§ 151). Upon one door in the house Allen and another workman were employed for seventy-nine days, and Ruskin used to show a model of this door to his friends as a specimen of English craftsmanship. Upon the foundation of the Working Men's College in 1854 he joined the drawing class, and became one of Ruskin's most promising pupils there. 'The transference to the pen and pencil of the fine qualities of finger that had been acquired by handling the carpenter's tools,' coupled with an 'innate disposition to art,' enabled Allen, says Ruskin, to attain rapidly great precision in drawing. Allen was brought further into connection with Ruskin by marrying (25 Dec. 1856) his mother's maid, Anne Eliza Hobbes. He was offered a post in Queen Victoria's household in connection with the furniture of the royal palaces; but this he declined in order to devote himself entirely to Ruskin's service, in which he remained successively as general assistant, engraver, and publisher for fifty years. For a few years he acted as an assistant drawing-master under Ruskin at the college. Ruskin then encouraged him to specialise in the art of engraving, which he studied under J. H. Le Keux, the engraver of many of the finest line plates in 'Modern Painters.' He also studied mezzotint under Lupton, who engraved some of the 'Liber' plates for Turner. Allen's knowledge of the two methods enabled him to produce the plates of mixed styles, which were included in Ruskin's later books. Of the original illustrations in 'Modern Painters,' three were from drawings by Allen; he engraved three plates for the edition of 1888; and in all executed ninety other plates for Ruskin. Some of Allen's drawings are included among the examples in the Ruskin school at Oxford; and he is one of three or four assistants whose work has often been mistaken for Ruskin's. In addition to engraving and copying, Allen was employed by Ruskin as general factotum. Many of his reminiscences were of distinguished visitors to Ruskin's house at Denmark Hill to whom he was instructed to show the collection of Turner drawings. It was he, too, with others, who assisted Ruskin in sorting and arranging the Turner drawings and sketches at the National Gallery. In 1862, when Ruskin thought of settling in Savoy, Allen with his family went out to Mornex. He was an excellent geologist, and Ruskin often trusted to his observations. Like Ruskin, he was an enthusiastic mineralogist; his collection of minerals was acquired after his death by the University of Oxford. He was a keen volunteer, and Ruskin took no offence when his assistant engaged in rifle-practice among the mountains. In 1871 Ruskin decided to set up a publisher of his own. At a week's notice, and without any previous experience of the trade, Allen started upon this enterprise. His publishing establishment was first his cottage at Keston, and afterwards an out-house in the garden of his villa at Orpington. Sarcastic reference was made in the public prints to Ruskin's idea of publishing 'in a field in Kent,' and the net-system, then a novelty in the trade, upon which Ruskin insisted, encountered much opposition. Ruskin, however, was able to create the demand for his publications, and the experiment prospered. The original idea of allowing no commission to the booksellers, but leaving them to charge it to the public, was, however, presently abandoned; and the expansion of the business necessitated the addition of premises in London. In 1890 Allen opened a London publishing house at 8 Bell Yard, Chancery Lane; and in 1894 he moved to larger premises at 156 Charing Cross Road. There he engaged in general publishing, though Ruskin's works remained the principal part of his business. Allen was one of the original 'Companions' of Ruskin's 'Guild of St. George,' and was a familiar figure at all Ruskinian gatherings. His unaffected simplicity and sterling character made him many friends. At his house at Orpington he took pleasure in flowers and bees, and he was a judicious buyer of water-colours and 'Martin' ware, as well as of minerals. Most of his collections—including many Ruskiniana—were privately disposed of after his death. His last enterprise was the library edition of Ruskin's works (1903–11), of which, however, he did not live to see the completion. He died, in his seventy-sixth year, on 5 Sept. 1907, at Orpington, and is buried in the parish churchyard there. His wife had died, in her eightieth year, eight months before him. They had four sons and four daughters. The eldest daughter, Miss Grace Allen, and the two eldest sons, William and Hugh, continued the business, which is now carried on at 44 Rathbone Place. A portrait of Allen (1890) was painted in oils by F. Yates; the chair in which he is shown as seated came from Ruskin's study at Denmark Hill, and is said to have been the one used by Ruskin when writing 'Modern Painters.'

[Library edition of Ruskin, vol. xxxvii. pp. lx-lxiii; the present writer's Life of Ruskin, 1911; private information.] E. T. C.

ALLEN, JOHN ROMILLY (1847–1907), archæologist, born in London on 9 June 1847, was the eldest son of George Baugh Allen (*d.* 1898), a special pleader of the Inner Temple, of Cilrhiw, near Narberth, by his wife Dorothea Hannah, third daughter of Roger Eaton of Parc Glas, Pembrokeshire. John was educated at King's College school (1857–60), Rugby school (1860–3), and King's College, London (1864–6). In 1867 he was articled to G. F. Lyster, engineer in chief to the Mersey Docks and Harbour Board, with whom he remained until 1870. He was next employed as resident engineer to the Persian railways of Baron de Reuter and afterwards in supervising the construction of docks at Leith and at Boston, Lincolnshire. Meanwhile he was interested in archæology, and to this pursuit, and particularly to the study of prehistoric antiquities and of pre-Norman art in Great Britain, he devoted the rest of his life. His earliest contribution to 'Archæologia Cambrensis' ('A description of some cairns on Barry Island') appeared in April 1873; he joined the Cambrian Archæological Association in 1875, was elected a member of the general committee in 1877, became one of two editors of the 'Journal' in 1889, and was sole editor from 1892 until his death. Having begun with the antiquities of Wales, Allen from 1880 gave special attention to those of Scotland also; in 1883 he was elected fellow of the Scottish Society of Antiquaries, and in 1885 was Rhind lecturer in archæology in the University of Edinburgh. In England, he became F.S.A. in 1896, editor of the 'Reliquary and Illustrated Archæologist' in 1893; and Yates lecturer in archæology in University College, London, for 1898.

Allen had in a high degree the patience, thoroughness, and insight of the scientific archæologist. Possessed of a certain sardonic humour, he was skilful in exposition and fertiie in illustration. In knowledge of early Celtic art and ability to unravel its history he was without a rival. He was unmarried, and during his later years made his home in London, where he died on 5 July 1907. In addition to his numerous contributions to archæological journals, Allen published: 1. 'Theory and Practice in the Designs and Construction of Dock Walls,' 1876. 2. 'Early Christian Symbolism in Great Britain and Ireland' (Rhind lectures), 1887. 3. 'The Monumental History of the Early British Church,' 1889. 4. 'The Early Christian Monuments of Scotland,' Edinburgh, 1903. 5. 'Celtic Art in Pagan and Christian Times,' 1904.

[Burke's Landed Gentry, 11th edit. (1906); Who's Who, 1907; The Times, 13 July 1907; Archæologia Cambrensis, sixth series, vii., Oct. 1907, 441–2.] J. E. L.

ALLEN, ROBERT CALDER (1812–1903), captain R.N., born on 8 Aug. 1812, was son of William Allen, a master in the navy and presumably a follower of Admiral Sir Robert Calder [q. v.]. He entered the navy as a second-class volunteer in July 1827. In that grade and as second master he served with credit, principally on the west coast of Africa and in China. In 1841 he was advanced to be master, and in 1842–4 was master of the Dido, with (Sir) Henry Keppel [q. v. Suppl. II], in her celebrated cruises against the Malay pirates of Borneo. In 1850–1 he was master of the Resolute in the Arctic, under Captain Austin, whom he followed from the Blenheim, and had charge of the magnetic observations. In 1854–5 he was master of the Hogue blockship in the Baltic, and rendered efficient service by his survey, often under fire, of the approaches to Bomarsund. In 1863 he was promoted to the then new rank of staff-commander, and in 1867 to that of staff-captain. In 1866–7 he was master-attendant and harbour-master at Malta; and in 1867 was appointed in the same capacity to Devonport, whence he was transferred to Deptford. When that dockyard was closed in October 1870, he retired with the rank of captain. He was a silent, thoughtful man, singularly modest and retiring. The subordinate position in which so much of his service was passed prevented his name from coming prominently before the public; but in the navy his reputation as a sound and skilful navigator and pilot stood very high, and was officially recognised in his nomination to a C.B. in 1877. He died in London on 28 Jan. 1903.

Allen was twice married. His first wife brought him a daughter and four sons, who all entered the public service, navy, army, or marines. The second wife survived him.

[Royal Navy Lists; The Times, 31 Jan. 1903; Keppel, Expedition of H.M.S. Dido to Borneo for the Suppression of Piracy, 1846; Markham, Life of Sir Leopold McClintock, 1909; private information.] J. K. L.

ALLIES, THOMAS WILLIAM (1813–1903), theologian, born at Midsomer Norton, Somerset, on 12 Feb. 1813, was son of Thomas Allies, then curate of Henbury and later rector of Wormington, by his wife Frances Elizabeth Fripp, daughter of a Bristol merchant. His mother died a week after his birth, and he was brought up by his father's second wife, Caroline Hillhouse. After education at Bristol grammar school he entered Eton in April 1827 under Edward Coleridge. There in 1829 he was the first to win the Newcastle scholarship. He matriculated at Wadham College, Oxford, in 1828, where he was exhibitioner from 1830–3, graduated B.A. with a first class in classics in 1832, proceeded M.A. in 1837, was fellow from 1833 till 1841, and humanity lecturer 1838–9.

Allies early came under the influence of

John Henry Newman, and with him and Pusey was soon in constant intercourse. His sympathy with the tractarians was strong, but his loyalty to the Anglican church was only shaken slowly. After a tour in France and Italy during 1836 he took holy orders in 1838, and assisted William Dodsworth [q. v.] at Christ Church, St. Pancras, in 1839. From 1840 to 1842 he was examining chaplain to Dr. Blomfield, bishop of London, who in June 1842 presented him to the living of Launton, Bicester, Oxfordshire. Travels in France in 1845 and 1847 with John Hungerford Pollen [q. v. Suppl. II] quickened doubt of the validity of the Anglican position, and a statement of his views in his 'Journal in France' (published February 1848) brought on him the censure of Samuel Wilberforce, bishop of Oxford. Study of the Fathers, and especially of Suarez's work, 'De Erroribus Sectæ Anglicanæ,' combined with the Gorham decision on baptismal regeneration in 1850, shattered his faith in the established church, and in his 'Royal Supremacy' (1850) he forcibly presented the Roman point of view (cf. LIDDON's *Life of E. B. Pusey*, iii. 257 seq.). In October 1850 he resigned his Launton living and joined the Roman communion. He removed to Golden Square, London, where he took pupils, and later for a time to the Priory, 21 North Bank, St. John's Wood, the house afterwards inhabited by George Eliot [q. v.]. From August 1853 until his retirement on a pension in 1890 he was secretary of the catholic poor school committee in John Street, Adelphi (instituted in 1847), and actively promoted catholic primary education. To his energy was due the foundation of the Training College of Notre Dame, Liverpool, in 1855, of the Training College for Women at the Convent of the Sacred Heart, Wandsworth, in 1874, and of the St. Mary's Training College for Men in Hammersmith. In March 1855 he became first professor of modern history at the new Catholic University of Ireland, Dublin, under Newman's rectorship. On his lectures there he based his voluminous 'The Formation of Christendom' (8 vols. 1865–95; popular edit. 1894 and following years). The work trenchantly expounds St. Peter's predominance in history. Among Allies's intimate friends in his last years were Lord Acton and Aubrey de Vere, who addressed a sonnet to him on the publication of his 'Holy See,' the sixth volume of his 'Formation of Christendom,' in 1888. In 1885 Pope Leo XIII created him knight commander of St. Gregory, and in 1893 he received through Cardinal Vaughan the pope's gold medal for merit. In 1897 his health declined, and he died at St. John's Wood on 17 June 1903, being buried at Mortlake by the side of his wife. He married on 1 Oct. 1840, at Marylebone parish church, Eliza Hall, sister of Thomas Harding Newman (an Oxford fellow student), and had issue five sons and two daughters. His wife, who joined the Roman catholic church five months before himself, predeceased him on 24 Jan. 1902. A portrait, painted by Mrs. Carpenter in 1830, is reproduced in the memoir by his daughter Mary (1907).

Allies, one of the most learned of the Oxford converts to Rome, traced the growth of his opinions in 'A Life's Decision' (1880; 2nd edit. 1894). Other works by Allies are: 1. 'The Church of England cleared from the Charge of Schism,' 1846; 2nd edit. 1848. 2. 'The Royal Supremacy,' 1850. 3. 'The See of St. Peter,' 1850; 4th edit. 1896. 4. 'St. Peter, his Name and Office,' 1852; 2nd edit. 1871; new edit. 1895. 5. 'Dr. Pusey and the Ancient Church,' 1866. The last four were reprinted with Allies's other controversial writings in 'Per Crucem ad lucem,' 2 vols. 1879.

[Thomas William Allies, by Mary Allies, 1907; art. in Catholic Encyclopædia, vol. i. 1907, by the same writer; The Times, 2 July 1903; Tablet, 20 June 1903; Liddon's Life of E. B. Pusey, 1894, vol. iii.; Life of J. H. Pollen, 1912; Wilfrid Ward, Life of J. H. Newman, 1912.] W. B. O.

ALLMAN, GEORGE JOHNSTON (1824–1904), mathematician, was born on 28 Sept. 1824 at Dublin. He was a younger son of William Allman, M.D. [q. v.], professor of botany in Trinity College, Dublin (1809–44). He entered Trinity College, and after a distinguished career graduated in 1844 as senior moderator and gold medallist in mathematics with Samuel Haughton [q. v. Suppl. I]. He was also Bishop Law's mathematical prize-man and graduated LL.B. in 1853 and LL.D. 1854.

Allman was elected professor of mathematics in Queen's College, Galway, in 1853, and remained in this post till he retired in 1893, having reached the age-limit fixed by civil service regulations. He was elected a member of the senate of Queen's University in 1877, and in 1880, when the Royal University of Ireland was founded, he was nominated by the Crown as a life senator. He was made F.R.S. in 1884, and hon. D.Sc. of Dublin in 1882. He contributed a few papers on mathematical subjects to scientific periodicals, besides an account of Prof. McCullagh's [q. v.] lectures on the 'Attraction of the Ellipsoid' which appears in the latter's collected works. He also wrote a number of articles in the 9th edition of the 'Encyclopædia Britannica' on Greek mathematicians. His chief contribution to science is his 'History of Greek Geometry from Thales to Euclid' (Dublin 1889), which first appeared as articles in 'Hermathena.' In this he traced the rise and progress of geometry and arithmetic, and threw new light on the history of the early development of mathematics. With his life-long friend, John Kells Ingram [q. v. Suppl. II], he was attracted to positivism, and entered into correspondence with Comte in 1852; in 1854 he went to Paris and made his personal aquaintance. His position at Galway prevented his taking any public part in the positivist movement, but his teaching was much influenced by Comte's mathematical work, the 'Synthèse Subjective,' and his general theory of historical development. Allman died of pneumonia on 9 May 1904 at Farnham House, Finglass, Dublin.

He married in 1853 Louisa (*d.* 1864), daughter of John Smith Taylor of Dublin and Corballis, co. Meath. A son and two daughters survived him.

[Proc. Roy. Soc. 78 A. (1907), p. xii; Positivist Review, July 1904, p. 149; The Times, 13 May 1904.] R. S.

ALMOND, HELY HUTCHINSON (1832–1903), headmaster of Loretto school, born in Glasgow on 12 Aug. 1832, was second son of George Almond, incumbent of St. Mary's Episcopal Chapel, Glasgow, by his second wife, Christiana Georgina, eldest daughter of Thomas Smith, barrister, of London. His paternal great-grandfather was headmaster of Derby school, and his maternal great-grandfather was John Hely-Hutchinson [q. v.], provost of Trinity College, Dublin. Precociously clever, he began to learn his letters at sixteen months, and at three years was struggling with the multiplication table. After attending the collegiate school, Glasgow, he entered in 1845 the University of Glasgow. At the end of the session he gained the Cowan gold medal in the Blackstone Latin examination, and he also specially distinguished himself in the Greek, mathematics and logic classes. Having been elected in 1850 to a Snell exhibition, he proceeded to Balliol College, Oxford. Here, contrary to the expectations of his tutors, who had the poorest opinions of his chances, he, in 1853, obtained a first class both in classical and mathematical moderations (a record for Balliol College); but, owing to ill-health and other causes, only a second in the final schools. Although he delighted in boating and won a place in the Balliol eight, he found little that was congenial in undergraduate life. In his later years he wrote, 'there is hardly a period of my life (since Oxford, which I hated) I would not gladly live over again.' He graduated B.A. in 1855 and M.A. in 1862. In 1855 he left Oxford for Torquay, where his father was living in retirement; and having failed to pass into the Indian civil service, he was induced by a friend, who had fallen ill, to assist him in his tutorial establishment. This led him to conceive a liking for teaching, and in 1857 he accepted the office of tutor in Loretto school, Musselburgh, then merely a preparatory for the English public schools. In the following year he became second master at Merchiston school, Edinburgh, where he took an active part in Rugby football, and did his utmost to foster a love of cricket, introducing an English professional to instruct the boys in the game. Already he had begun the strenuous advocacy of systematic physical exercise in schools, and of the cultivation of hardiness as essential to a thoroughly healthy boyhood, and of prime importance in the formation of proper habits of mind. These and other educational ideas he found opportunity to put into fuller practice, when, in 1862, he became proprietor of Loretto school—so called from its contiguity to the site of the old chapel and hermitage dedicated to Our Lady of Loretto.

Here he began with only fourteen boys, supplemented for the first two or three years with a few university pupils; and, as he himself put it, gradually built up a school out of nothing, though the numbers never reached 150. His early, almost insuperable, difficulties he met with perfect gaiety; and he was accustomed to refer to this period of his life as 'the happy early days when I was nearly bankrupt.' He closely pursued a special educational aim. The first duty of a headmaster he conceived to be the direction of a school so as to accomplish the purpose of training the individual character. It was his leading maxim to rule by persuasion, not by force, and to secure what he called 'behind-back obedience.' 'Relations between master and boys were thus unusually sincere, and the place had rather the aspect of a family than of a school' (MACKENZIE'S *Almond of Loretto*, p. 160). So far also as he could he sought to develop an independent interest in study and to diminish the evils of cram and competition, although hampering outside influences interfered here seriously with his ideals. But the main feature in which he may justly be regarded as a pioneer was 'the application of the best knowledge to the physical nurture of the young; the total elimination from our practice with regard to this nurture, of convention, tradition and rule of thumb' (*ib.* p. 391). He attached a cardinal importance to fresh air, personal cleanliness, proper and regular diet with the abolition of 'grubbing,' the regulation of the hours of sleep and study, physical exercise in all weathers, and the disuse 'of linen shirts and collars and suits of close material for ordinary school wear, in favour of tweed knickerbocker suits of loose texture and flannel shirts worn open at the neck without neckties'; with 'the practice of changing into flannels for all forms of violent exercise.' In regard to the question of fresh air he anticipated the methods now employed as a preventative and cure of consumption; and the coatless, flannelled, bare-headed athlete was also largely his creation. That the stamina of Loretto boys greatly exceeded the average was manifested, year by year, by the large proportion of them who won athletic distinction at the English universities; but the result was attained by a proper attention to physical health, not an over attention to physical exercise. Almond did not a little to revolutionise the school methods of Scotland.

After showing for a few years signs of failing health, he died of a bronchial affection on 7 March 1903. He was buried in Inveresk churchyard. He married in 1876 Eleanor Frances, daughter of Canon Tristram of Durham [q. v. Suppl. II], and had issue three sons and three daughters.

Besides various contributions to reviews and magazines, in which he expounded his educational principles, he was author of: 1. 'Health Lectures,' 1884. 2. 'Sermons by a Lay Head Master,' 2 series, Edinburgh, 1886 and 1892. 3. 'English Prose Extracts,' Edinburgh, 1895. 4. 'Christ the Protestant, and other Sermons,' Edinburgh, 1899.

[R. J. Mackenzie's Almond of Loretto, 1905; H. B. Tristram's Loretto School Past and Present, 1911.] T. F. H.

AMHERST, WILLIAM AMHURST TYSSEN-, first BARON AMHERST of HACKNEY (1835–1909), born at Narford Hall, Norfolk, on 25 April 1835, was eldest son of William George Daniel-Tyssen (1801–1855), whose surname was originally Daniel, by Mary, eldest daughter of Andrew Fountaine of Narford Hall, Norfolk. Together with his father, who represented a branch of the old Kentish family of Amherst and had inherited the Tyssen property in Hackney through his mother, he took by royal licence, 6 Aug. 1852, the name of Tyssen-Amhurst, for which he substituted, again by royal licence, that of Tyssen-Amherst on 16 Aug. 1877. He was educated at Eton and matriculated at Christ Church, Oxford, 19 May 1853. Inheriting large property in Norfolk and in Hackney, he was high sheriff for Norfolk in 1866. He was M.P. for West Norfolk in the conservative interest from 1880 to 1885, afterwards representing south-west Norfolk from 1885 to 1892. He was created Baron Amherst of Hackney on 26 Aug. 1892.

For more than fifty years Lord Amherst collected rare books and MSS., tapestries, antique furniture, and other works of art. One object was to illustrate the history of printing and bookbinding from the earliest times down to modern days. Another was to illustrate the history of the Reformation at home and abroad and of the Church of England by means of bibles, liturgies, and controversial tracts. A 'Handlist of the Books and MSS. belonging to Lord Amherst of Hackney' was compiled by Seymour de Ricci (privately printed, 1906). The compiler had also prepared an exhaustive *catalogue raisonné* of Lord Amherst's whole library. Owing to the dishonesty of a solicitor entrusted with the administration of estate and trust funds, Lord Amherst found himself in 1906 obliged to announce the sale of the finer portion of the magnificent library at Didlington Hall. A series of splendid 'Caxtons,' eleven out of the seventeen being perfect examples, were sold privately to Mr. J. Pierpont Morgan, and the other portions of the library, including many extremely rare printed books and fine Italian, Flemish, French, and English illuminated MSS., were disposed of by auction by Messrs. Sotheby, Wilkinson & Hodge in a sale which began on 3 Dec. 1908. The second portion of the library was sold 24 to 27 March 1909, and the total realised by both sales was 32,592*l.*, which does not include the 25,000*l.* understood to have been paid for the 'Caxtons.' Messrs. Christie disposed (11 Dec. 1908) of some fine examples of old Gobelins and other tapestry, old French and English furniture, Limoges enamels and old Italian majolica. The amount realised was 38,796*l.* The pictures sold for 1561*l.*; the engravings for about 2000*l.*

Lord Amherst travelled much in the East, and his collection of Egyptian curiosities was almost as well known as his books and china. Some of these were described in 'The Amherst Papyri, being an Account of the Egyptian Papyri in the Collection of Lord Amherst,' by P. E. Newberry (1899, 4to), and 'The Amherst Papyri, being an Account of the Greek Papyri in the Collection of Lord Amherst of Hackney,' by B. P. Grenfell and A. S. Hunt (1900, 4to).

He died after a few hours' illness at 23 Queen's Gate Gardens, London, S.W., on 16 Jan. 1909, in his seventy-fourth year, and was buried in the family vault in Didlington churchyard, Norfolk.

His portrait by the Hon. John Collier is now in the possession of Baroness Amherst of Hackney. It has been engraved. He married on 4 June 1856, at Hunmanby, co. York, Margaret Susan (*b.* 8 Jan. 1835), only child of Admiral Robert Mitford of Mitford Castle, Northumberland, and Hunmanby, Yorkshire. His widow and six daughters survived him. The eldest daughter, Mary Rothes Margaret, who married in 1885 Lord William Cecil, succeeded to the peerage by special limitation in default of male heirs. He bore the undifferenced arms of the family of Amherst, quartering Daniel and Tyssen. He was of middle height and sturdy appearance, of genial and unassuming manners, much interested in his literary, artistic, and antiquarian collections and the pursuance of the duties of country life in Norfolk, where he farmed on a large scale and was known as a breeder of Norfolk polled cattle. He was an excellent shot and fond of yachting. He presented a volume to the Roxburgh Club, of which he was a member, and one to the Scottish Text Society. He wrote: 1. (with Hamon Lestrange) 'History of Union Lodge, Norwich, No. 52,' privately printed, Norwich, 1898. 2. (with Basil Home Thomson) 'The Discovery of the Solomon Islands, by Alvaro de Mendaña, in 1568, translated from the original Spanish MSS., edited with introduction and notes,' 1901, 2 vols. small 4to, 100 copies on large paper (the translation was made by Amherst from the MSS. in his own collection; it was also issued by Hakluyt Soc.).

[Family information; Complete Peerage, by G. E. C., new edit. by Vicary Gibbs, 1910; The Times, 18 and 21 Jan. 1909; Alfred Austin's Autobiog. 1911, ii. 269–73.]

H. R. T.

ANDERSON, ALEXANDER (1845–1909), labour poet writing under the pseudonym of 'Surfaceman,' born on 30 April 1845, in the village of Kirkconnel in Upper Nithsdale, was sixth and youngest son of James Anderson, a Dumfriesshire quarryman, by his wife Isabella Cowan. When the boy was three, the household removed to Crocketford in Kirkcudbright, and at the village school there Anderson got all his schooling; there too he began to make rhymes. At sixteen he was back in his native village working in a quarry; some two years later (1862), he became a surfaceman or platelayer on the Glasgow and South-western railway there. While performing his long day's task on the line he found opportunity of an evening or at meal times on the embankment to read Shelley, Wordsworth, and Tennyson; and by help of 'Cassell's Educator' and an elementary grammar, acquired French enough to puzzle out Racine and Molière. Later he managed in like manner to read Goethe, Schiller, and Heine in German, learnt a little Italian, and acquired a smattering of Spanish and Latin. In 1870 he began to send verses to the 'People's Friend' of Dundee, whose sub-editor, Mr. A. Stewart, brought Anderson's work under the notice of George Gilfillan [q. v.] and advised the publication of a volume of collected pieces, 'A Song of Labour and other Poems' (1873). This Gilfillan reviewed very favourably; and to a second volume, 'The Two Angels and other Poems' (Dundee, 1875), the friendly critic prefixed an appreciative memoir of the 'Surfaceman,' whose verse now appeared from time to time in 'Good Words,' 'Chambers's Journal,' 'Cassell's Magazine,' and the 'Contemporary Review.' A wealthy Glasgow citizen, Mr. Thomas Corbett, sent Anderson to Italy with his son (Archibald Cameron Corbett, afterwards Lord Rowallan). But the sonnet series 'In Rome' does not record the impressions made by Italian experiences; they are the imaginings of the railway labourer who, when he published them (1875), had hardly been out of his native county. Before the surfaceman returned to his labours on the rail he had made personal acquaintance with Carlyle, Roden Noel, Lord Houghton, Miss Mulock (Mrs. Craik), and Alexander Macmillan. His next venture, 'Songs of the Rail' (1878; 3rd edit. 1881), was largely composed of railway poems from the two earlier collections. 'Ballads and Sonnets' (1879), published by Macmillan, also contained a selection from the earlier volumes with new pieces.

In 1896 all the volumes were out of print.

In October 1880 Anderson passed from the exhausting twelve hours a day with pick and shovel at 17*s.* a week to the lighter appointment of assistant librarian in Edinburgh University. Learned leisure failed to stimulate his poetic impulses; henceforward he wrote little but occasional verses, mainly when on holiday amongst old friends at Kirkconnel. For private circulation he printed some translations from Heine; and from time to time he revised, amended, or extended a long blank verse poem on the experiences of Lazarus of Bethany in the world of spirits, and after restoration to life. In 1883 he left the university to become secretary to the Edinburgh Philosophical Institution, a library and lecture society. But in 1886 he returned to the university library, where at his death on 11 July 1909, he had for five years been acting chief librarian. He was unmarried. In Edinburgh he conciliated respect and affection, not less by the native dignity and force of his character than by his geniality and social gifts, although in later years ill-health made him much of a recluse.

Anderson's poetical work shows lyrical power, generous feeling, and vivid vision, as well as a command of metre and a literary equipment that would be noteworthy in a writer of liberal education and in a cultured environment. He had no faculty for prose writing. His most characteristic achievement was as laureate of the rail (after the manner of the 'Pike County Ballads' or Bret Harte) and of child life in humble Scottish homes. In his best-known poems the vernacular of the south-west of Scotland is employed with verve and discretion. Few anthologies of Scots poems now lack one or two of Surfaceman's, and several of the railway and child poems are popular recitations.

In 1912 a modest memorial was erected in Anderson's native village; his scattered and unpublished pieces were collected for issue; and the publication of the Lazarus poem was contemplated.

[Dundee Advertiser, 6 Jan. 1896; Frank Miller, The Poets of Dumfriesshire, 1910; private information; personal knowledge.]
D. P.

ANDERSON, GEORGE (1826–1902), Yorkshire batsman, was born at Aiskew near Bedale, Yorkshire, on 20 Jan. 1826; he early showed athletic aptitude as a high and long jumper and as a cricketer; his cricket was greatly improved by the visit to Bedale of the eminent bowler William Clarke in 1848. Employed as a clerk in youth, he made the game his profession in early manhood. Anderson first appeared at Lord's in 1851, when he played for the North *v.* South, and for the Players *v.* Gentlemen in 1855. He was from 1857–64 a member of the All England XI captained by William Clarke and George Parr [q. v.]. He visited Australia with Parr's team in the winter of 1863, but met with little success. His most successful season was that of 1864, when in first-class matches he averaged 42 runs an innings, and scored 99 not out for Yorkshire *v.* Notts. He captained the Yorkshire team for a few seasons; in May 1869 a match was played for his benefit at Dewsbury between the All England XI and the United All England XI.

Anderson was a kindly, handsome man of fine physique; he was six feet high, weighed 14½ stone, and was of great strength. His style as a batsman was described as 'the model of manliness'; he had a good defence, and though he took time to get set, he was in his day the hardest and cleanest hitter of the best bowling. In 1862 he made a drive for eight runs at the Oval when playing for the North of England *v.* Surrey. Another hit by him off Bennett, the Kent slow bowler, was reputed to have pitched farther than any previously recorded at the Oval. On retiring from professional cricketing, Anderson became in 1873 actuary of the Bedale Savings Bank, and held the office until the bank's failure in 1894. He died at Bedale on 27 Nov. 1902.

[The Times, 28 Nov. 1902; Daft's Kings of Cricket (portrait, p. 61); W. Caffyn's 71 not out (portrait, p. 39); Wisden's Cricketers' Almanack, 1902, p. lxxx; Haygarth's Scores and Biographies, iv. 277, xiv. p. xxxi; R. S. Holmes, History of Yorkshire County Cricket, 1904; information from Mr. P. M. Thornton.]
W. B. O.

ANDERSON, Sir THOMAS McCALL (1836–1908), professor of practice of medicine in the University of Glasgow, born in Glasgow on 9 June 1836, was second of three sons of Alexander Dunlop Anderson, M.D., medical practitioner in Glasgow, who in 1852 was president of the faculty of physicians and surgeons of Glasgow, by his wife Sara, daughter of Thomas McCall of Craighead, Lanarkshire. His father's family was descended on the maternal side from William Dunlop [q. v.], principal of Glasgow University, 1690–1700; and in the male line from John Anderson (1668–1721) [q. v.], the stout defender of presbyterianism, and collaterally from John Anderson (1726–1796) [q. v.], founder of the Andersonian Institute, Glasgow.

After early education in Edinburgh Anderson entered Glasgow University to study medicine. There in April 1858 he graduated M.D. with honours, and became a licentiate and fellow of the faculty of physicians and surgeons of Glasgow. Two years were spent as resident physician in the Glasgow Royal Infirmary; two more in travel and medical study at Paris, Würzburg, Berlin, Vienna, and Dublin. On returning home he was speedily appointed lecturer on practice of medicine in the Andersonian Institute and, not long after, physician to the royal infirmary. There the lucidity and skill of his clinical teaching attracted large numbers of students.

In 1861 a hospital and dispensary were founded at Glasgow for diseases of the skin. Anderson and Dr. Andrew Buchanan were appointed the first two physicians. Buchanan died prematurely in 1865. For forty-seven years Anderson bore the main share of the duty. In 1909 the institute was absorbed by the western infirmary, and the dermatological teaching was provided for by the foundation of a lectureship at the university on which Anderson's name was conferred in recognition of his services. Meanwhile in 1874 Anderson was appointed to a newly founded chair of clinical medicine in Glasgow University. He held this post till 1900 in conjunction with that of physician to the western infirmary. His clear and systematic method of exposition and demonstration, his strict concentration on the subject in hand, and his organising power enabled him to fulfil his functions with admirable efficiency. From 1897 to 1901 he was examiner in medicine and pathology for the British and Indian medical services. In 1900 he succeeded Sir William Tennant Gairdner [q. v. Suppl. II] in the chair of practice of medicine, and removed from his house in Woodside Terrace to the official residence in the college square. The practical aspects of his subject chiefly appealed to him. The physician's business, he insisted, was to cure the sick. But he took a high view of the moral responsibilities of a medical adviser, and never suffered his pupils to forget that medicine is a liberal profession as well as a useful art.

For many years Anderson engaged in extensive consulting practice. His opinion was especially valued, not only in skin diseases, in which he long specialised and his eminence in which was recognised in England and on the Continent, but also in consumption, in the curability as well as in the prevention of which he was a believer, and in certain forms of paralysis.

In 1903 he was appointed university representative on the general medical council; he was knighted in 1905; in 1906 he was entertained at a public dinner by representatives of the medical profession in the west of Scotland, including many former pupils and assistants; in 1908 he was made honorary physician to the king in Scotland.

A conservative in politics, and in religion a member of the Church of Scotland, Anderson was genial in society and obliging in disposition. He died suddenly on 25 Jan. 1908, after speaking at the dinner of the Glasgow Ayrshire Society. He was honoured with a public funeral in the necropolis of Glasgow.

Anderson married on 20 July 1864 Margaret Richardson, daughter of Alexander Ronaldson, merchant, Glasgow, and left one son, Thomas, who is in medical practice at New York. There is a good portrait of Anderson in possession of his widow.

Anderson's chief publications were: 1. 'The Parasitic Affections of the Skin,' 1861; 2nd edit. 1868. 2. 'On Psoriasis and Lepra,' 1865. 3. 'On Eczema,' 1867, 3rd edit. 1874. 4. 'Treatment of the Diseases of the Skin, with an Analysis of 11,000 Consecutive Cases,' 1872. 5. 'Lectures on Clinical Medicine,' 1877. 6. 'Curability of Attacks of Tubercular Peritonitis and Acute Phthisis (Galloping Consumption),' 1877. 7. 'A Treatise on Diseases of the Skin,' 1887; 2nd edit. 1894. 8. 'On Syphilite Affections of the Nervous System, their Diagnosis and Treatment,' 1889.

[Private information; personal knowledge; obit. notices in Lancet, Brit. Med. Journal, Medical Times, Glasgow Herald, and The Times, 27 Jan. 1908; William Stewart, Glasgow University, 1891, p. 136 (with portrait).] J. C.

ANDREWS, THOMAS (1847–1907), metallurgical chemist and ironmaster, born at Sheffield on 16 Feb. 1847, was only son of Thomas Andrews, proprietor of the old-established Wortley Iron Works, near that town, by his wife Mary Bolsover. Educated at Broombank school, Sheffield, and afterwards a student of chemistry under Dr. James Allan of Sheffield, Andrews early developed a faculty for original scientific research, which was fostered by the practical advice and guidance of his father. On the latter's death in 1871 he became head at Wortley.

Andrews's researches in metallurgy proved

of great scientific and industrial value. After prolonged investigation on a large scale he determined the resistance of metals to sudden concussion at varying temperatures down to zero (0 deg. F.); and was one of the first to study metals by the aid of the microscope, following up the pioneer inquiries of Henry Clifton Sorby [q. v. Suppl. II]. In 1888 he was elected F.R.S. and was besides a fellow of the Royal Society of Edinburgh and of the Chemical Society, and member, respectively, of the Institution of Civil Engineers and Society of Engineers. To the publications of these societies and to technical periodicals he contributed some forty papers. The Society of Engineers awarded him two premiums for papers in their 'Transactions,' viz. 'On the Strength of Wrought-iron Railway Axles' (1879), and 'On the Effect of Strain on Railway Axles' (1895). In 1902 he received the society's gold medal for the memoir, 'Effect of Segregation on the Strength of Steel Rails.' In 1884 the Institution of Civil Engineers awarded him a Telford medal. An important paper on 'Wear of Steel Rails on Bridges' was published in the 'Journal of the Iron and Steel Institute' (1895).

From time to time Andrews acted as consultant to the admiralty and the board of trade on metallurgical questions. He paid special attention to the microscopic examination of metallic materials with a view to determining the cause of naval accidents, and he contributed a detailed series of observations on the subject to 'Engineering' (1904). In a paper on the microscopic effects of stress on platinum (*Roy. Soc. Proc.* 1902) he broke new ground. At Cambridge University he delivered lectures to engineering students. At Sheffield Andrews was a consistent advocate of technical education directed to industrial ends; and he actively assisted in founding and developing Sheffield University. He died at his home, 'Ravencrag,' near Sheffield, on 19 June 1907. He married in 1870 Mary Hannah, daughter of Charles Stanley of Rotherham, and had issue three sons (two died in childhood) and one daughter.

[Roy. Soc. Proc. vol. lxxxi. A.; The Times, 20 June 1907; Engineering, 28 June 1907; Industries and Iron (with portrait), 24 April 1896; private information.] T. E. J.

ANGUS, JOSEPH (1816–1902), baptist divine and biblical scholar, only son of John Angus, a farmer and later a leather merchant, by his wife Elizabeth Wanless, was born at Bolam, Northumberland, on 16 Jan. 1816. His first schooling was at Newcastle, under George Ferris Whidborne Mortimer [q. v.], who wanted to send him to Cambridge. As a nonconformist and a member of the baptist church under Thomas Pengilly at Newcastle, he preferred Edinburgh, where he entered in 1834, after passing a year at King's College, London. In 1835 he studied for the baptist ministry at Stepney College (instituted 1810), under W. H. Murch, D.D., a good scholar. Returning to Edinburgh with a scholarship under Dr. Ward's trust, he graduated M.A. with distinction on 27 April 1837, and gained the gold medal in moral philosophy and the university English essay prize. In 1838 he accepted a call to New Park Street chapel, Southwark, where subsequently Charles Haddon Spurgeon [q.v.] won his fame as a preacher. In 1840 he was appointed colleague to John Dyer in the secretaryship of the Baptist Missionary Society, and became sole secretary in 1841. He had much to do with the raising of the jubilee fund (32,000*l.*), by means of which, among other enterprises, the mission house in Moorgate Street was built. In 1849 he was placed at the head of Stepney College, which under his presidency largely increased in efficiency and importance, was removed to Regent's Park in 1856, and equipped with special chairs and scholarships by means of a 'professorial fund' (30,000*l.*), secured by his exertions. He held the presidency till 1893. In connection with his academic work he brought out some useful handbooks to the Bible (1853; 2nd imp. 1907), to the English language (1864), and to English literature (1866); and editions of Butler's 'Analogy and Sermons' (1855; 2nd edit. 1881) and Francis Wayland's 'Elements of Moral Science' (1858); all these were published by the Religious Tract Society. The degree of D.D. was conferred in 1852 by Brown University, Rhode Island. From 1859 he was for ten years examiner in English to the London University, and in 1865 to the civil service commissioners. In 1870 he was appointed on the New Testament company for the revision of the 'authorised' version of the Scriptures. He was elected in 1870 for Marylebone to the first London school board, held office for ten years, and was re-elected for the period 1894–7. In the bibliography of baptist authors of all classes, ancient and modern, he took the greatest interest; his own collection of such works was unsurpassed, and his privately printed lists of acquirements and desiderata were of no small service to students of the byways of religious history. His latest summary of results, 'Baptist Authors and History, 1527–1800,' was printed in the 'Baptist Handbook' in 1894, and issued separately in 1896. As a theologian his position was essentially conservative; in a controversy of 1870 he upheld the doctrine of eternal torments; he was not without mellowing influences in his later years. He died at Hampstead on 28 Aug. 1902, and was buried in Norwood cemetery.

Angus's portrait by Melville is in Regent's Park College, and has been engraved. He married on 3 March 1841 Amelia (*d.* 1893), fourth daughter of William Brodie Gurney. Of his family of four sons and six daughters, the second son, John Mortimer Angus, M.A., is registrar of the University of Wales.

In addition to the manuals indicated above and subsidiary pieces Angus published 1. 'The Voluntary System' (prize essay), 1839. 2. 'Four Lectures on the Advantages of a Classical Education as auxiliary to a Commercial,' 1846. 3. 'Christian Churches' (bicentenary prize essay), 1862; 1864. 4. 'Egypt and the Bible,' 1863. 5. 'Apostolic Missions,' &c., 1871; 2nd edit. 1892. 6. 'Man, a Witness for Christianity,' 1872. 7. 'Popular Commentary on the New Testament' (Hebrews to Jude), 1883. 8. 'Six Lectures on Regeneration' (the Angus Lectureship), 1897.

[The Times, 30 Aug. 1902; Baptist Handbook, 1903, p. 189 (with portrait); Cat. of Edin. Graduates, 1858, p. 225; information kindly supplied by Mr. Charles J. Angus.]

A. G.

ANNANDALE, THOMAS (1838–1907), surgeon, born at Newcastle-on-Tyne on 2 Feb. 1838, was second son of Thomas Annandale, surgeon, by his wife E. Johnstone. Annandale was educated at Bruce's academy in Newcastle, and was afterwards apprenticed to his father. Continuing his professional studies at the Newcastle Infirmary, he matriculated in 1856 at Edinburgh, and graduated M.D. in 1860 with the highest honours, receiving the gold medal for his thesis 'On the Injuries and Diseases of the Hip Joint.' He was appointed in 1860 house-surgeon to James Syme [q. v.] at the Edinburgh Royal Infirmary, and was Syme's private assistant from 1861 to 1870. In 1863 he was admitted F.R.C.S. Edinburgh, and became a junior demonstrator of anatomy in the university under Prof. John Goodsir [q. v.]. He was also appointed in 1863 a lecturer on the principles of surgery in the extramural school of medicine, and gave there a course of lectures yearly until 1871, when he began to lecture on clinical surgery at the Royal Infirmary.

Annandale was admitted a M.R.C.S., England, on 15 July 1859, and F.R.C.S. on 12 April 1888; in 1864 he won the Jacksonian prize for his dissertation on 'The malformations, diseases and injuries of the fingers and toes, with their surgical treatment' (Edinburgh 1865). Appointed assistant surgeon to the Royal Infirmary at Edinburgh in 1865, and acting surgeon there in 1871, he became regius professor of clinical surgery in the university of Edinburgh in 1877, in succession to (Lord) Lister, who then migrated to King's College, London. He was made honorary D.C.L. of Durham in April 1902, and was surgeon-general to the Royal Archers, his Majesty's bodyguard in Scotland, from 27 May 1900 until his death. He joined the corps as an archer in 1870.

Annandale died suddenly on 20 Dec. 1907, having operated as usual at the Royal Infirmary on the previous day. He was buried in the Dean cemetery, Edinburgh.

He married in 1874 Eveline, the eldest daughter of William Nelson, the publisher, of Edinburgh, and had a family of three sons and three daughters.

A bust, executed by W. G. Stevenson, R.S.A., is in the lecture theatre of the Edinburgh Royal Infirmary.

Annandale, who began to practise surgery when it was an art left it a science. He kept himself abreast of all the incidents of the change and combined the good points of each period. He was keenly interested in university matters and especially in the welfare of the students. He was prominent at the Students' Union and in the Athletic Club. 'The Annandale gold medal in clinical surgery' was founded in his memory at Edinburgh university.

Annandale published (all at Edinburgh), in addition to the work named and many separate papers in professional periodicals: 1. 'Surgical Appliances and Minor Operative Surgery,' 1866. 2. 'Abstracts of Surgical Principles,' 6 pts. 1868–70 (3rd ed. 1878). 3. 'Observations and Cases in Surgery,' 1875. 4. 'On the Pathology and Operative Treatment of Hip Disease,' 1876.

[Brit. Med. Journal, 1908, i. 60 (with portrait); Lancet, 1908, i. 70; Scottish Medical and Surgical Journal, vol. xxii. 1903, p. 68 (with portrait); Edinburgh Medical Journal, vol. xxiii. n.s., 1908, p. 1; information from Mr. J. W. Dowden, F.R.C.S. Edin.]

D'A. P.

ARBUTHNOT, Sir ALEXANDER JOHN (1822–1907), Anglo-Indian official and author, third son of Alexander Arbuthnot, Bishop of Killaloe, by his second wife, Margaret Phœbe, daughter of George Bingham, was born at Farmhill, co. Mayo, on 11 Oct. 1822, a younger brother (*b.* 1824) being General Sir Charles George Arbuthnot [q. v. Suppl. I]. Sir Alexander's great grand-uncle was Dr. John Arbuthnot [q. v.], poet and wit, and his father's brothers included Charles Arbuthnot [q. v.], General Sir Robert Arbuthnot [q. v.], and General Sir Thomas Arbuthnot [q. v.]. His father died suddenly towards the close of 1828, leaving his widow ill provided for. She settled at Rugby in order that her two boys might be educated under Dr. Arnold. Alexander entered Rugby as a foundationer in April 1832, his contemporaries and friends there including Arthur Stanley, Tom Hughes, and Matthew Arnold. His last two years were spent in the sixth form, and he retained through life the impressions made upon his mind by the great headmaster.

It was an unsolicited testimonial from Arnold which secured for him nomination to a writership for the East India Company. He accordingly studied at the East India College, Haileybury, from 23 Jan. 1840 to Christmas 1841, winning distinction in classics and Telugu. Leaving England on 24 May 1842, he sailed round the Cape and landed at Madras on 21 Sept. In the following June he earned the honorary reward of 1000 pagodas for proficiency in Telugu and Hindustani. After serving as assistant collector in Chingleput and then in Nellore, he was appointed early in 1845 head assistant to the registrar of the Sadr court and Foujdari Adalat, the forerunners of the chartered high court. In 1851 he completed the compilation of a selection of reports of criminal cases in the Sadr court between 1826 and 1850, with an historical preface. He similarly compiled and summarised the papers relating to public instruction in the Madras province from the time that Sir Thomas Munro [q. v.] took charge in 1822. With his Sadr court appointment he combined the secretaryship of the so-called university board, which had charge of what later became the presidency college.

The memorable education despatch of the court of directors in 1854 led to Arbuthnot's appointment in March 1855 as the first director of public instruction for Madras. In this capacity he established the education department on the basis still maintained, organising an inspecting staff, opening district schools, and introducing the grant-in-aid system. He also worked out the details of the scheme under which the university was incorporated in 1857. He was one of the original fellows, and was vice-chancellor in 1871–2, filling the same position in the Calcutta University in 1878–80. A warm supporter of the policy of fitting Indians for situations of trust and emolument in the public service, he always strongly defended from attack the government's educational system, which proved more successful in Madras than elsewhere in India, owing in part at any rate to Arbuthnot's wise control of its early years.

In October 1862 Arbuthnot was appointed chief secretary to the Madras government, becoming *ex officio* member of the local legislature. From October 1867 he was a member of the executive council, and as senior member he acted as governor from 19 Feb. to 15 May 1872, when on the assassination of Lord Mayo (8 Feb. 1872) Lord Napier of Merchiston went to Calcutta temporarily to assume the viceroyalty. He was created C.S.I., but with characteristic independence he declined the decoration, on the ground that it was an inadequate recognition of his office and services. Next year (24 May) he was gazetted K.C.S.I. At the close of his council term (28 Oct. 1872) he came home on furlough, and two years later, on expiry of leave, he resigned the service.

In the spring of 1875 he went back to India, on the invitation of Lord Salisbury, the secretary of state, as a member of the governor-general's council. He joined the council on 6 May, serving first with Lord Northbrook and then, from April 1876, with Lord Lytton. In September 1876 Lytton nominated him for the lieutenant-governorship of Bengal in succession to Sir Richard Temple [q. v. Suppl. II], but the law member of the India council, Sir H. S. Maine [q. v.], advised Lord Salisbury that, as Arbuthnot had resigned the civil service, he was statutorily ineligible, and to his severe disappointment he was passed over. Already in 1871 the same office, in the event of its being declined by Sir George Campbell [q. v. Suppl. I], had been destined for Arbuthnot (Buckland's *Bengal under the Lieutenant-Governors*, vol. i.).

As home member of the governor-general's council Arbuthnot was largely responsible for the measures dealing with the great southern India famine in 1877–8. He took part in the proclamation durbar at Delhi on 1 Jan. 1877, and his name headed the list of 'Counsellors of the Empress,' a new order intended but never actually constituted to form an Indian privy council. A year later he was created C.I.E.

Great as was Arbuthnot's attachment to Lytton, he never hesitated to exercise his independent judgment. In December 1877 he strongly dissented, in the gloomy financial circumstances, from the reduction of the duties on salt in Bengal and northern India. He was always opposed to proposals for the reduction of the cotton duties, proposals which he assigned to political pressure from Lancashire. In March 1879, when he voted with the majority of his colleagues against a reduction, Lord Lytton exercised the rarely used power of overruling his council. The governor-general's action was only confirmed by the council of India in London on the casting-vote of the secretary of state, Lord Cranbrook (*East India Cotton Duties*, white paper, 1879). Arbuthnot endeavoured to prevent Sir Louis Cavagnari [q. v.] from going to Kabul with a small escort, and on 22 Oct. 1879 he minuted against what he regarded as the unduly aggressive spirit of Lytton's Afghan policy. Arbuthnot had the unanimous support of his colleagues in his conduct of the Vernacular Press Act, 1878, and he viewed with great disfavour its repeal, after he had left India, by Lord Ripon's government (19 Jan. 1882).

Returning to England on the expiry of his term in May 1880, Arbuthnot settled at Newtown House, Hampshire, where the rest of his life was spent. He was a generous benefactor of the locality, building a parish room and handing over the ownership of the village school, after enlargement, to the National Society. A strong conservative and churchman, he was for many years a member of the Winchester diocesan conference and chairman of the Andover division conservative association. But India still held the foremost place in his thoughts. In the spring of 1883 he accepted the chairmanship of the London committee to resist the famous 'Ilbert Bill' of Lord Ripon's government, and both by speech and pen he brought the issues to the notice of the public. On the nomination of Lord Cross he joined the India council on 1 Nov. 1887, and there, during his ten years' term, showed his old strength and independence. In 1894–5 he steadfastly deprecated, as concessions to Lancashire interests, the opposition to the reimposition of cotton import duties in India. He was most assiduous in his attendance at the India office, and spoke very frequently in the council discussions. When he retired, on 31 Oct. 1897, his service of the Crown had extended over fifty-five years, throughout which he showed unusual administrative powers and combined tact and courtesy with a spirit naturally somewhat despotic and impatient of control. He died in London of heart failure on 10 June 1907, and was buried in the churchyard at Newtown.

While at the India office Arbuthnot largely suspended the journalistic and literary work in which he had engaged on leaving India. But he remained a regular contributor to this Dictionary from the first volume, published in January 1885, writing in all fifty-three articles, including those on Clive, Wellesley, Canning, and Sir Thomas Munro. In 1881 he compiled a selection of the minutes of Munro—whom in many points he resembled—and wrote an introductory memoir, which was republished separately in 1889. He also wrote a biography of Clive, published in 1898, for Mr. H. F. Wilson's 'Builders of Greater Britain' series. The recollections he was compiling at the time of his death were completed by his widow, and were published in 1910 under the title of 'Memories of Rugby and India.'

Arbuthnot married on 1 Feb. 1844 Frederica Eliza, daughter of General R. B. Fearon, C.B. She died in 1898, and on 6 June 1899 he married Constance, daughter of Sir William Milman, 3rd bart., niece of Robert Milman, bishop of Calcutta. There were no children of either union.

[Memories of Rugby and India, 1910; Lord Lytton's Indian Administration, 1899; The Times, 12 June 1907; Winchester Dioc. Chron., July 1907; Minutes of Dissent; unpublished sketches by Sir Charles Lawson, and private papers kindly lent by Lady Arbuthnot.]

F. H. B.

ARBUTHNOT, FORSTER FITZGERALD (1833–1901), orientalist, born at Belgaum, Bombay presidency, on 21 May 1833, was second son of Sir Robert Keith Arbuthnot, second baronet, by his wife Anne, daughter of Field-marshal Sir John Forster Fitzgerald [q. v.]. He was educated privately on the Continent, at Anhalt and Geneva. Receiving a nomination to Haileybury in 1851, he went out to India in the Bombay civil service in 1853, where his father had served before him, and retired in 1878. His last appointment was that of collector of Bombay city and island, in which capacity he fixed the existing assessment on what are known as *toka* lands. He is remembered for driving a four-in-hand, and for his seaside residence at Bandra, outside the island, where he entertained Sir Richard and Lady Burton in 1876. He had already been initiated into Oriental literature by Edward Rehatsek, an eccentric but learned Hungarian, who led the life of a *faqir* at Bombay. Shortly after his return to England Arbuthnot associated himself with Burton in founding the Kama Shastra Society, for the issue to private subscribers of unexpurgated translations of Oriental classics. He was himself active in procuring the translation of Jāmī's 'Behāristān' and of S'adi's 'Gulistān'; and to him Burton dedicated the fourth volume of his 'Arabian Nights,' commending his critical appreciation of Oriental literature, which enabled him 'to detect the pearl which lurks in the kitchen-midden.' Arbuthnot's own books were in the nature of popular compilations, the two most important being 'Persian Portraits' (1887), and 'Arabic Authors' (1890). A work of more permanent value was his inauguration, in 1891, of a new series of the 'Oriental Translation Fund,' which he started with some translations by Rehatsek, and which was continued after his death through his munificence. He was a member of council and also a trustee of the Royal Asiatic Society, and he took a prominent part in organising the reception of the International Congress of Orientalists that met in London in 1892. He was given to hospitality both at his town house in Park Lane and at his country residence near Guildford. He took a lively interest in his village neighbours, and his memory is preserved by the Arbuthnot Institute, Shemley Green, under the charge of the Wonersh parish council. He died in London on 25 May 1901. In 1879 he married Ellinor, daughter of Admiral Sir James Stirling [q. v.] and widow of James Alexander Guthrie of Craigie, Forfarshire, who survived him until 9 May 1911. There were no children of the marriage.

[The Times, 28 May 1901; personal knowledge.] J. S. C.

ARCHER, JAMES (1823–1904), painter, born in Edinburgh on 10 June 1823, was eldest child of Andrew Archer, dentist in Edinburgh, who married Ann Cunningham Gregory, and by her had two sons and two daughters. The younger son, Andrew, was the author of a history of Canada (1876), while the youngest child, Georgina, was the founder of the Victoria Institute, Berlin, and tutoress of the German Emperor William II, Prince Henry, and Princess Charlotte of Prussia. After education at Edinburgh High School, James studied art at the Trustees' Academy, while Sir William Allan [q. v.] was at its head, with Thomas Duncan [q. v.] as his assistant. Archer's generation thus immediately preceded that which studied under Scott Lauder [q. v.], although he outlived and outworked many of Lauder's pupils. He was elected an associate of the Royal Scottish Academy in 1850, and he became a full member in 1858. The life-class in that year passed from the Trustees' School to the control of the Scottish Academy, and (Sir) Joseph Noel Paton [q. v. Suppl. II], James Drummond [q. v.], and Archer were appointed visitors. Their report on the conduct of the life-class insisted on drawing as opposed to colour in the training, a recommendation which Lauder appears to have regarded as a reflection on his own methods (cf. HARDIE, *Life of Pettie*, p. 12).

While resident in Edinburgh, Archer showed his versatility in the many pictures which he exhibited at the Scottish Academy; these included 'The Child John in the Wilderness' (exhibited 1842); 'The Messiah' (1846); 'The Condemned Souls Crossing the River Acheron' and 'The Last Supper' (1849); 'Douglas Tragedy' and 'Mary Magdalene at the Sepulchre' (1850); 'The Mistletoe Bough' and 'Burger's Leonora' (1852); 'Hamlet' (1853); 'Rosalind and Celia,' his diploma work (1854); 'The Last Supper' (1856), and the first (1861) of several scenes from the 'Mort d'Arthur.' In these years he also painted many portraits in oils, and until his migration to London had a large practice in portraiture in chalks; among his sitters were Professor Aytoun and Alexander Smith.

In 1862–3 Archer gave up his Edinburgh studio, 2 York Place, and removed to London. He resigned at the time his lieutenancy in the artists' company of the city of Edinburgh artillery volunteers, in which, under the captaincy of Sir Noel Paton, with John Faed as first lieutenant, was enrolled every artist of note in Edinburgh at that time. He was also a member of the Smashers Sketching Club, which he helped to revive in London later under the name of the Auld Lang Syne Sketching Club (see *Chambers's Journal*, January 1906).

In London, settling first at 21 Phillimore Gardens, and after 1882 at 7 Cromwell Place, he diligently contributed to the Royal Academy, to which he had sent pictures since 1850, and where he continued to exhibit until 1900, missing one year only during the half-century. He had some difficulty in disentangling himself from the Arthurian legend, but was most successful with costume pictures and portraits of children, such as 'Playing at Queen with a Painter's Wardrobe' (R.A. 1861), 'How the Little Lady Stood to Velasquez' (R.A. 1864), 'Old Maid: Maggie, you 're cheatin'' (R.A. 1865), 'In the Time of Charles I: Portraits of the Children of W. Walkinshaw, Esq.' (R.A. 1867), 'Against Cromwell' (R.A. 1869), 'Colonel Sykes, M.P.' (R.A. 1871). A long series of portraits included several painted during prolonged visits between 1884 and 1887 both to the United States (Mr. James G. Blaine and Mr. Andrew Carnegie) and to India (Lady Dufferin and Lord Clandeboye, Lord Dalhousie, and a posthumous portrait of Sir Charles Macgregor). Among his chief sitters at home were Sir George Trevelyan (R.A. 1872), Professor Blackie, three times (the portrait of 1873 hangs in the library of the Scottish Academy), Sir Henry Irving in 'The Bells' (R.A. 1872), Dr. Ellicott (R.A. 1883), and Sir Edwin Arnold (R.A. 1890). In 1877 he painted for and presented to the Scottish Academy a portrait of Sir Daniel Macnee. Archer continued to the end of his life to produce large canvases, such as 'King Henry II and Fair Rosamund,' 'The Worship of Dionysus,' 'Peter the Hermit,' 'St. Agnes of the Early Christian Martyrs,' and 'In the Second Century—"You a Christian?"—'. He also painted a few landscapes. For the first number of 'Good Words' (1860) he did six drawings illustrating the serial story 'Lady Somerville's Maidens,' and he contributed two illustrations to 'Household Song' (1861).

During his last years he lived at Shian, Haslemere, where he died on 3 Sept. 1904; he was buried at Haslemere. Archer married, in 1853, Jane Clark, daughter of James Lawson, W.S., Edinburgh; a son and three daughters survived him.

Archer's work was always refined, and reflected his interest in literature and a certain sympathy with the Pre-Raphaelites; a lack of force may be attributed to what his friend Professor Blackie described as 'his thoughtful, evangelico-artistic mildness' (*Letters of John Stuart Blackie to his Wife*). Unluckily for his reputation he continued to work after his powers failed. He was at the time of his death the oldest member of the Royal Scottish Academy, and had been for ten years on its retired list.

A portrait painted by himself at an early age is in the possession of the widow of Henry Gregory Smith, Edinburgh.

[Private information; The Times, 6 Sept. 1904; Scotsman, 8 Sept. 1904; Graves's Royal Academy Exhibitors, 1905; Cat. Royal Scot. Academy.] D. S. M.

ARCHER-HIND, formerly HODGSON, RICHARD DACRE (1849–1910), Greek scholar and Platonist, born at Morris Hall, near Norham, on 18 Sept. 1849, came of an ancient Northumbrian family, being third and youngest son of Thomas Hodgson (*b.* 1814), who, on the death of a brother in 1869, succeeded to the estates of Stelling and Ovington and assumed the surname of Archer-Hind. The father, a learned horticulturist, graduated B.A. from Trinity College, Cambridge, in 1837 and M.A. in 1840. His wife was his first cousin, Mary Ann, second daughter of John Thomas Huntley, vicar of Kimbolton. Richard Dacre had from his father his early teaching in Latin and Greek, and even when he was at Shrewsbury school, whither he proceeded in 1862, and where he was the pupil of Dr. B. H. Kennedy and Dr. H. W. Moss, his father continued to assist his studies. In 1868 he won an open minor scholarship at Trinity College, Cambridge, and in the following October he went into residence at the university, living with his parents, who now established themselves at Cambridge, as they had formerly established themselves at Shrewsbury, that he might have the comforts of a home life. He was elected to a college foundation scholarship in 1869 and to a Craven University scholarship in 1871. In 1872 he was placed third in the first class of the classical tripos and won the first chancellor's medal for classical learning. He was elected to a fellowship in his college in October 1873 and was appointed assistant lecturer in April 1877 and assistant tutor in December 1878. At Easter 1899 he was made a senior lecturer, and in December 1903 he retired from the staff. During the last two years of his life Archer-Hind was an invalid. He died at Cambridge on 6 April 1910. The body was cremated at Golder's Green, and the ashes were buried at Cambridge. He married on 17 March 1888 Laura, youngest daughter of Lewis Pocock [q. v.]. He left one son, Laurence, born in 1895.

Both in Latin and in Greek the exceptional quality of Archer-Hind's scholarship was recognised from the beginning of his Cambridge career. But Greek came to interest him more than Latin. At a later time, while his love of Pindar,

Æschylus, and Sophocles never wavered, his admiration for Plato waxed exceedingly. In 1883 he published an admirable edition of the 'Phædo,' in which he investigated the argument of the dialogue, and traced its relations to the rest of Plato's writings. A second edition appeared in 1894. In 1888 he brought out his *magnum opus*, an original and complete edition of the difficult, important, and neglected 'Timæus,' which gave a new impetus to Platonic studies. The translation is exact and scholarly; the commentary is helpful, learned, many-sided; and in the introduction Archer-Hind sets out the results of his profound study of Plato's metaphysic. His aim is to 'show that in this dialogue we find, as it were, the focus to which the rays of Plato's thoughts converge, that in fact the "Timæus" and the "Timæus" alone enables us to recognise Platonism as a complete and consistent scheme of monistic idealism.'

Archer-Hind's conception of the theory of ideas as 'a thorough-going idealism' is the key at once to Platonic philosophy and to Platonic science. Papers in the 'Journal of Philology' (see especially xxiv. 49; xxix. 266; xxxi. 84) supplemented the editions of the 'Phædo' and the 'Timæus.' In 1905 Archer-Hind published a volume of admirable 'Translations into Greek Verse and Prose.'

An industrious teacher and a singularly efficient examiner, Archer-Hind took no prominent part in the affairs of the university; but his occasional allocutions at university discussions and college meetings were incisive and epigrammatic. He was always an earnest supporter of the movement for the education of women, and gave much time to the affairs of Newnham College and the instruction of its students. His literary interests were by no means limited to the classical tongues. He loved his garden, and kept an exact record of the rare plants which it contained. He took a passionate interest in music; his knowledge of certain favourite composers was intimate and minute. He had made a careful study of Greek music. His quiet, retiring manner covered strong convictions tenaciously held.

[Information from Mrs. Archer-Hind, Dr. J. W. L. Glaisher and Mr. R. D. Hicks; personal knowledge; school, college, and university records. See Cambridge University Review, 28 April 1910 (an article by the present writer); The Times, 8 April 1910 (obit. notice by Dr. S. H. Butcher); Burke's Landed Gentry, s.v. Hind.] H. J.

ARDAGH, Sir JOHN CHARLES (1840-1907), major-general, royal engineers, born at Comragh House on 9 Aug. 1840, was second son of William Johnson Ardagh, vicar of Rossmire, of Comragh House and Stradbally, co. Waterford, by his wife Sarah Cobbold, of Ipswich. After education at the endowed school in Waterford under Dr. Price, John entered Trinity College, Dublin, in 1857, with the intention of taking orders. He gained a prize in Hebrew and honours in mathematics. But deciding on a military career he passed first at the entrance examination to the Royal Military Academy at Woolwich in 1858, and was again first at the final examination, receiving a commission as lieutenant in the royal engineers on 1 April 1859. After the usual training at Chatham, Ardagh superintended the construction of Fort Popton, one of the new works of defence for Milford Haven, under the Defence Act of 1860. When a rupture with the United States, owing to the Trent affair, threatened in November 1861, Ardagh embarked at Queenstown in the transport Victoria (26 Dec. 1861) with the stores necessary to construct a line of telegraph through the colony of New Brunswick to the St. Lawrence river. The vessel, which was badly found, encountered tempestuous weather and was driven back to Queenstown; leaving port again on 13 Feb. 1862, she was only saved from foundering by Ardagh's and his sappers' ingenuity and exertions, which enabled her to reach Plymouth on 12 March. Ardagh's conduct was highly commended by the duke of Cambridge, commander-in-chief.

Ardagh, who remained at home, was charged with the construction of the new fort at Newhaven, and there invented an equilibrium drawbridge, which was used at Newhaven fort and elsewhere (cf. his description of it in *Royal Eng. Prof. Papers*, new series, vol. xvii.). After other employment on southern defences, he was appointed, in April 1868, secretary of Sir Frederick Grey's committee to report on the fortifications in course of construction under the Defence Act of 1860, and in September 1869 accompanied Sir William Jervois [q. v.] on a tour of inspection of the defence works at Halifax and Bermuda. Permitted to witness the entry of the German troops into Paris in February 1871, Ardagh visited the defences of the city, and went on to Belfort and Strassburg. After three months in Malta and a year at Chatham, he was promoted captain on

3 Aug. 1872, and joined the Staff College in February 1873, passing the final examinations in December 1874. In April 1875 he was attached to the intelligence branch of the war office, was in Holland on intelligence duty (10 Jan.–8 Feb. 1876), and became a deputy assistant quartermaster-general for intelligence (13 July).

In August 1876 Ardagh began important services in the Near East. He was then sent on special service to Nisch, the headquarters of the Turkish army operating against Servia. In October he was summoned to Constantinople to report on the defence of the city. In fifteen days he prepared sketch-surveys of nearly 150 square miles, and proved himself an expert in strategic geography. These surveys included the position of Buyuk-Chekmedje-Dere, with projects for the defence of the Dardanelles and the Bosphorus, the Bulair lines and Rodosto. The actual works were subsequently constructed by the Turks. Ardagh also reported for the foreign office on the operations in Herzegovina and Montenegro, and in December 1876 went to Tirnovo in Bulgaria to report on the state of the country. After an attack of fever, from which he recuperated in Egypt and Greece, he resumed his duties at the war office in April 1877, when he completed a report and survey begun in the previous year on the sea defences of the Lewes and Laughton levels.

From December 1877 to March 1878 Ardagh was in Italy on special foreign office service, and in the summer attended the congress of Berlin as technical military delegate under General Sir Lintorn Simmons [q. v. Suppl. II]. Ardagh's knowledge of the Turkish provinces proved of value, and in July he was created C.B. (civil). Between September 1878 and September 1879 he was employed on the international commission to delimitate the frontiers of the new principality of Bulgaria. On 30 Nov. 1878 he was gazetted a brevet-major, and was promoted regimental major on 22 Sept. 1880. On 14 June 1881, after much negotiation among the great powers, in which he played some part, he became British commissioner for the delimitation of the Turco-Greek frontier. In spite of obstacles the work was completed by the end of October.

In February 1882 Ardagh was appointed instructor in military history, law, and tactics at the School of Military Engineering at Chatham, but on 5 July he was sent suddenly to Egypt, where he was occupied almost continuously for nearly four years. His first duty was to place Alexandria in a state of defence after its bombardment by the British fleet and to take charge of the intelligence department there. Becoming on 21 Aug. deputy assistant adjutant-general, he was subsequently employed in the railway administration at Ismailia, and was present at the actions of Kassassin and Tel-el-Mahuta, and at the battle of Tel-el-Kebir. He was mentioned in Lord Wolseley's despatch at the end of the campaign and was promoted brevet lieutenant-colonel (18 Nov. 1882). He also received the British war medal with clasp for Tel-el-Kebir, the Khedive's bronze star, and the fourth class of the order of the Osmanieh.

Ardagh remained in Egypt as deputy assistant adjutant-general to the British army of occupation, and was largely employed in making surveys. In July 1883 he went home on leave, but returned to Egypt almost immediately on an outbreak of cholera, and laboured untiringly during the epidemic.

In February 1884 Ardagh, as commanding royal engineer and chief of the intelligence department, accompanied the British force under Sir Gerald Graham [q. v. Suppl. I], which was sent from Cairo to the Eastern Soudan. He was present at the battle of El Teb (29 Feb.), and at the relief of Tokar (1 March) he arranged the removal of 700 Egyptian inhabitants. By 8 March the change of base from Trinkitat to Suakin had been made, and on the 12th Ardagh reconnoitred with the mounted infantry the ground towards the hills. After the battle of Tamai (13 March) the road was open to Berber, and Ardagh shared his general's opinion that an advance should then have been made to Berber to reach out a hand to General Gordon at Khartoum. He afterwards wrote: 'Berber was then in the hands of an Egyptian garrison, and had we gone across, the subsequent operations for the attempted relief of General Gordon at Khartoum would not have been necessary.' Graham's force returned to Cairo in April, leaving a battalion to garrison Suakin. Ardagh was mentioned in despatches and was made C.B. (military).

In May 1884 he went home on leave. In the autumn an expedition to relieve Khartoum was organised. Ardagh favoured the Suakin-Berber route, but Lord Wolseley, who commanded, resolved to ascend the Nile. Ardagh was appointed commandant at the base (Cairo), with the grade of assistant adjutant-general. His energy, devotion, and quiet cheerfulness helped to expedite the fatal enterprise, and at the end of the disastrous campaign he was promoted to a brevet colonelcy (15 June 1885), receiving the third class of the order of the Medjidieh. On 30 Dec., as chief staff officer of a combined British and Egyptian force, he took part in the engagement at Giniss, when a large army of the Khalifa, which was endeavouring to invade Egyptian territory, after the abandonment of the Soudan, was defeated with great loss. For his services Ardagh was mentioned in despatches. On 17 Dec. 1886 he was promoted to a regimental lieutenant-colonelcy, and on 26 Jan. 1887 he was gazetted a colonel on the staff.

In Nov. 1887 Ardagh returned to London as assistant adjutant-general for defence and mobilisation at the war office, and he inaugurated schemes of mobilisation for over-sea service, and of local home defence. From April 1888 to 1893 he was aide-de-camp to the duke of Cambridge, commander-in-chief. In October 1888 he became, with war office sanction, private secretary to the marquis of Lansdowne, viceroy of India. Save for a period of absence through illness in 1892, he remained with Lord Lansdowne through his term of office. He returned to England in May 1894, after a short service with Lord Lansdowne's successor, Lord Elgin. He was made a C.I.E. in 1892, and K.C.I.E. in 1894.

Ardagh had spent less than a year as commandant of the School of Military Engineering at Chatham (from 16 April 1895), when he rejoined (27 March 1896) the war office for five years as director of military intelligence, with the temporary rank of major-general. He was promoted major-general on the establishment, on 14 March 1898. The South African war broke out in October 1899, and during the black days at the opening of the campaign an outcry was made that Ardagh's department had not kept the government informed of the number of men the Boers could put into the field, nor of the preparations they had made for the war. Yet Ardagh, in spite of a limited staff and inadequate funds, had performed his duty thoroughly. He compiled for the government a full statement of the number and military resources of the Boer forces, estimating that the defence of the British colonies alone would require 40,000 men, while to carry the war into the enemy's country would require 200,000. Copies of this paper were eventually laid on the tables of both houses of parliament at Ardagh's request. Meanwhile 'Military Notes on the Dutch Republic,' a secret work prepared under Ardagh's auspices in the intelligence branch, fell early in the campaign into the hands of the Boers after the action of Talana (20 Oct. 1899), and was published. These documents, which were corroborated by evidence before the royal commission on the war, relieved Ardagh of all blame.

In addition to his ordinary duties Sir John was a member of a committee on submarine telegraph cables, and in 1899 military technical adviser to the British delegates, Sir Julian (afterwards Lord) Pauncefote [q. v. Suppl. II] and Sir Henry Howard, at the first Hague peace conference. There he took a leading part in drawing up the 'Rules respecting the Laws and Customs of War on Land.' In 1900 he was awarded the distinguished service pension.

After leaving the war office in March 1901 he showed to advantage his tact and knowledge of international law as British agent before a commission to investigate the claims of foreign powers on account of the deportation to Europe of subjects of theirs domiciled in South Africa during the war. From December 1901 to June 1902 he was in South Africa settling miscellaneous claims in connection with the war, which was still going on. He returned to South Africa later in the year with the temporary rank of lieutenant-general as member of the royal commission for the revision of martial law sentences. In October he was a member of the British tribunal on the Chili-Argentina boundary arbitration and helped to draft the award. On 9 Aug. 1902, when sixty-two years of age, Ardagh retired from military service, but was still employed by the foreign office. He succeeded Lord Pauncefote on the permanent court of arbitration at the Hague, and became a British government director of the Suez Canal. In December 1902 he was created K.C.M.G.

Ardagh was deeply interested in the British Red Cross Society, of which he became a member of council in 1905. He represented the British army, being one of four delegates of the British government in June 1906, at the conference held by the Swiss government for the revision of the Geneva Convention of 1864. The new convention was signed in the following month. His last public duty was to act as a delegate of the central committee of the society at the eighth international conference in London in June 1907. On his deathbed he received from the Empress Marie Féodorovna of Russia the Red Cross commemoration medal for his services during the Russo-Japanese war. Ardagh died on 30 Sept. 1907 at Glynllivon Park, Carnarvon, and was buried at Broomfield Church, near Taunton. He married on 18 Feb. 1896 Susan, widow of the third earl of Malmesbury and daughter of John Hamilton of Fyne Court House, Somerset, who survived him without issue.

Ardagh served on the council of the Royal Geographical Society, was an associate of the Institution of Civil Engineers, and was a member of the Royal Society's geodetic arc committee in 1900. He was made hon. LL.D. of Trinity College, Dublin, in 1897. He wrote in the 'Quarterly Review' (October 1894) on British rule in Egypt, and contributed occasionally to other periodicals. He was a skilful artist. A collection of 140 water-colour drawings by him was presented by his widow to the Royal Engineers Institute at Chatham.

His portrait, painted in oils by Miss Merrick in 1896, and exhibited at the Royal Academy that year, was presented by his widow to the officers of the royal engineers, and now hangs in their mess room at Chatham. A replica is in Lady Malmesbury's possession.

[War Office Records; The Times, 2 Oct. 1907; Royal Engineers Journal, Nov. 1907; Life, by Susan, Countess of Malmesbury, 1909.]

R. H. V.

ARDITI, LUIGI (1822–1903), musical conductor and composer, born at Crescentino, in Piedmont, on 16 July 1822, was son of Maurizio Arditi by his wife Caterina Colombo. He was educated as a violinist at the Milan conservatoire, showing also some talent for composition. In 1840 an overture of his was produced in Milan, and during the carnival of the following year a light opera, 'I Briganti.' He made his first appearance as an operatic conductor at Vercelli in 1843, and became an honorary member of the Accademia Filarmonica there. From 1846 he frequently visited America, where he produced and conducted operas; he brought out his 'La Spia' at New York in 1856. The same year he toured through eastern Europe to Constantinople, and in 1858 settled in London as conductor to the opera at Her Majesty's theatre, retaining this appointment through the management of Lumley, E. T. Smith, and Mapleson until the destruction of the theatre by fire in 1867. Upon the resignation of Costa from Covent Garden, Arditi was engaged there for the single season of 1869. In the winters of 1871 and 1873 he conducted the Italian opera at St. Petersburg, and from 1870 onwards for several years did similar work every spring at Vienna. From 1874–7 he conducted the promenade concerts at Covent Garden, and in 1878 visited Madrid for a two months' season. Arditi was the favourite conductor of Madame Adelina Patti, and between 1882 and 1887 he went on operatic tours to America and through the United Kingdom with Mapleson's company, of which she was a leading member. He conducted the first performances of the following notable works amongst others: Gounod's 'Faust' (Her Majesty's, 11 June 1863); Wagner's 'Flying Dutchman' (Drury Lane, 25 July 1870); Mascagni's 'Cavalleria Rusticana' (Shaftesbury, 19 Oct. 1891); and Humperdinck's 'Hänsel and Gretel' (Daly's, 26 Dec. 1894). He retired shortly after 1894, and died at Hove on 1 May 1903. He married on 20 June 1856 Virginia, daughter of William S. Warwick, of Richmond, Virginia, U.S.A., and had issue one son and one daughter.

Arditi's vocal waltz, 'Il Bacio' (1860), has long been a favourite with vocalists; other songs of similar character and merit, such as 'L'Ardita' (1862), enjoyed a temporary vogue. In later life he wrote nothing of value. He published in 1896 'My Reminiscences' (ed. Baroness von Zedlitz). A caricature portrait by 'Ape' appeared in 'Vanity Fair' in 1885.

[Arditi's My Reminiscences, 1896; Musical World, May 1903; Grove's Dict. of Musicians; Benjamin Lumley's Reminiscences, 1864; The Mapleson Memoirs, 1888, passim; personal knowledge.]

F. C.

ARDWALL, LORD. [See JAMESON, ANDREW, 1845–1911.]

ARMES, PHILIP (1836–1908), organist and musical composer, born at Norwich on 15 Aug. 1836, was eldest son of Philip Armes (a bass singer) by Mary his wife. A chorister in Norwich Cathedral 1846–8, he joined the choir of Rochester Cathedral in 1848 on the appointment of his father as bass lay clerk there. Possessed of a beautiful voice, he achieved great success as solo boy, and on retiring from the choir in 1850 received a public testimonial. Determined to follow the profession of music, he was articled in 1850 to John Larkin Hopkins [q. v.], organist of Rochester Cathedral, and up to 1856 acted as his assistant, at the same time serving as organist of Milton Church, Gravesend. In 1857 he passed to St. Andrews, Wells Street, London, then to

Chichester Cathedral in 1861, and finally to Durham Cathedral in 1862, where he remained till his death. He had graduated Mus. Bac. Oxon. in 1858, and was admitted to the same degree *ad eundem* at Durham 1863. He proceeded Mus. Doc. at Oxford in 1864 and at Durham *ad eundem* in 1874. The honorary degree of M.A. was conferred on him by Durham University in 1891.

When the chair of music was founded at Durham University in 1897, Armes was appointed first professor. In 1890 he drew up the scheme of examinations for musical degrees which is still in use.

Armes's compositions comprise: oratorio, 'Hezekiah,' produced at Newcastle-on-Tyne (1877); cantatas, 'St. John the Evangelist,' produced at York Minster (1881); and 'St. Barnabas' produced at Durham (1891); services, anthems, hymn tunes, &c. He obtained the Molineux prize and gold medal offered by the Madrigal Society in 1897 for his madrigal 'Victoria.'

He died at Durham on 10 Feb. 1908, and was buried in the cemetery of St. Mary-le-bow there. He married in 1864 Emily Jane, daughter of Sir Henry Davison, chief justice of the supreme court, Madras, by whom he had two sons and two daughters.

[Private information; Grove's Dict. of Music.] J. C. B.

ARMOUR, JOHN DOUGLAS (1830–1903), judge of the supreme court of Canada, born on 4 May 1830, near Peterborough, Ontario, was youngest son of Samuel Armour, rector of Cavan, Canada, by his wife Margaret Douglas. The father, of Irish origin, graduated M.A. from Glasgow University in 1806, and emigrating to Canada about 1821, taught in a school in York (now Toronto) before taking orders in the Church of England. The son John, after early education at the local schools and at Upper Canada College, where he was head boy, entered the University of Toronto as a King's College exhibitioner, and graduated B.A. in 1850, gaining the gold medal in classics. He began the study of law under his brother, Robert Armour, and in the office of Chancellor Vankoughnet. Called to the bar in 1853, he practised in Cobourg in partnership with Sidney Smith, afterwards postmaster-general of Canada. He was appointed county crown attorney for Northumberland and Durham on 26 Mar. 1858, and clerk of the peace on 2 May 1861, and a queen's counsel by Lord Monck in 1867. He was elected warden of the counties in 1859-60. In the same year he was chosen a senator of the University of Toronto, and in 1871 became a bencher of the Law Society of Upper Canada. In 1874 he declined the liberal nomination for West Northumberland in the House of Commons. He was appointed a puisne judge of the court of queen's bench in 1877, and was promoted chief justice of the court in 1887. He was made commissioner to revise the Ontario statutes in 1896. In July 1900 he became chief justice of Ontario, and president of the court of appeal. He declined a knighthood more than once. In June 1902 he received an honorary LL.D. from his university. In November 1902 he was nominated a judge of the supreme court of Canada by Sir Wilfrid Laurier. In May 1902, as one of the 'distinguished jurists of repute,' he was chosen by the Canadian government to represent Canada on the international tribunal constituted to decide the Alaska boundary dispute. He died in London on 11 July 1903, whither he had gone to attend the sittings of the arbitration. A memorial service was held at the Temple Church. He was buried in St. Peter's cemetery, Cobourg, Ontario.

Armour was among the greatest jurists whom Canada has produced. Absolutely fearless and outspoken, he not infrequently aroused hostile prejudice. His alleged unfriendliness to corporations failed to affect his judgments, which were based on a thorough knowledge of the law and a profound insight into human nature.

He married on 28 April 1855 Eliza, daughter of Francis Schimerhorn Clench of Cobourg and Eliza Cory. Of eleven children of this marriage ten survive (1912). Several portraits exist. One by E. Wyly Grier is in the National Gallery, Ottawa, and three replicas of this are owned by the family. Another by G. T. Berthon is at Osgood Hall, Toronto. There is a bust by Lady Ross (Miss Peel) in the Normal School, Toronto.

[The Times, 13 July 1903; Canada Law Journal, xxxix. 458 *seq.*; Canadian Law Times, xxiii. 319.] P. E.

ARMSTEAD, HENRY HUGH (1828–1905), sculptor, born in Bloomsbury on 18 June 1828, was fourth and youngest son of John Armstead, an heraldic chaser, by his wife Ann, daughter of Hugh Dyer of Belfast. A wide reader from youth, he received little school education. At eleven he was working in his father's workshop, and at thirteen was sent to the old School of Design, Somerset House. While sketching at the British Museum he began a lifelong friendship with a fellow student,

William Holman-Hunt [q. v. Suppl. II]. Subsequently, at Mr. Leigh's Academy in Maddox Street, he came to know J. R. Clayton, designer of stained glass windows, and his future brother-in-law Henry Tanworth Wells [q. v. Suppl. II]. Later he was employed at Messrs. Hunt & Roskell's factory of gold and silver work, enjoyed the occasional tuition of E. H. Baily, R.A. [q. v.], and at the same time joined the Royal Academy schools. Finally he became designer in chief to Hunt & Roskell, and in that capacity did a great deal of work in and for metal: designing, modelling, and chasing in gold, silver, and bronze. His style was influenced by that of Vechté, the great French silver-chaser, who was then in England. Among Armstead's works in metal the most important are a 'Testimonial (the Shakespeare Cup) to Charles Kean,' the 'St. George's Vase,' the 'Tennyson Cup' (for which he was premiated at the Paris Exhibition of 1855), the 'Packington Shield,' and the 'Outram Shield,' now in the Victoria and Albert Museum. Save for a brief engagement by Hancock's firm of like character, he remained with Hunt & Roskell till 1863, when he left to devote himself exclusively to sculpture. Armstead had already practised that art in his leisure, and had won two Art Union prizes (for 'Satan Dismayed' and 'The Temptation of Eve'), besides designing external mural decoration for Evelyn Shirley's mansion at Ettington, Warwickshire. A short visit to Italy in 1863–4 was followed by an introduction to Sir Gilbert Scott. Scott soon employed Armstead on the Albert Memorial, and thenceforth his position was assured. From his early tutor, Bailey, he derived some of that over-suavity of style which marked the early Victorian school of modelling, of which John Gibson was perhaps the most typical exemplar. To a certain extent, however, Armstead now rose above the tradition in which he had been reared, and his later works show little of the fluid modelling and superficial elegance which characterised his master. He was industrious and business-like; one commission always led to another, and down nearly to the end of his life he was one of the best employed sculptors of his time. Armstead's most important works are the marble reliefs on the south and east sides of the podium to the Albert Memorial and four bronze statues—rhetoric, astronomy, chemistry, and medicine—on the same structure; the external sculpture on the colonial office, Whitehall; the reredos in Westminster Abbey; the fountain in the forecourt of King's College, Cambridge; the memorial to George Edmund Street [q. v.] in the central hall of the law courts, and the effigies of Bishop Wilberforce in Winchester Cathedral and of Bishop Ollivant in Llandaff Cathedral. Armstead executed a few imaginative works such as 'Ariel,' 'Hero and Leander,' 'The Ever-reigning Queen' (his diploma work), and 'Remorse.' The last named was bought by the Chantrey trustees and is now in the Tate Gallery.

Armstead was elected A.R.A. on 16 Jan. 1875, and R.A. on 18 Dec. 1879. He was a loyal and industrious servant of the Academy and extremely popular as a man. He taught in the Academy schools from 1875 till near his death. He gave proof of unusually fine taste as an arranger of works of art when it became his turn to place the sculpture in the annual exhibitions. He also arranged the British sculpture in the Paris Exhibition of 1900. He died at his house, 52 Circus Road, St. John's Wood, on 4 Dec. 1905.

Armstead married, on 9 Sept. 1857, Sarah, daughter of Henry Tanworth Wells, and sister of Henry Tanworth Wells, R.A. [q. v. Suppl. II]; he had issue three daughters and one son. A portrait, painted in 1878 by his brother-in-law Wells, is, with a bust executed by W. R. Colton, A.R.A., in 1902, in the possession of his son, Dr. H. W. Armstead. A second portrait, painted by Sir Hubert von Herkomer, R.A., in 1902, belongs to his daughter, Miss C. W. Armstead.

[Henry Hugh Armstead, R.A., by his daughter, Miss C. W. Armstead [1906]; The Times, 6 Dec. 1905; Men and Women of the Time, 1899; private information.] W. A.

ARMSTRONG, Sir GEORGE CARLYON HUGHES, first baronet (1836–1907), journalist and newspaper proprietor, younger son of Colonel George Craven Armstrong, of the East India Company's army, and of Georgianna, daughter of Captain Philip Hughes, was born at Lucknow on 20 July 1836. He was privately educated and was nominated to a military cadetship in the company's service .in the year 1855. During the Indian Mutiny he was attached to the 59th Bengal native infantry, and afterwards to Stokes's Pathan horse, a newly raised regiment of native irregulars. As second in command of the latter he was dangerously wounded in the course of the operations around Delhi. On the suppression of the mutiny he was appointed orderly officer at Addiscombe Military College, a post which he occupied till the closing of that institution in 1861, when he retired from the army with the rank of captain. In 1866 he took up the duties of secretary and registration agent to the Westminster Conservative Association, and his powers of work and organisation were largely responsible for the defeat of John Stuart Mill [q. v.] by W. H. Smith [q. v.] in November 1868. After acting for a short time as financial manager of Watney's brewery, he was offered in 1871 the editorship and management of the 'Globe' newspaper, then in the hands of a small conservative syndicate of which Mr. George Cubitt, afterwards Lord Ashcombe, was the leading member. The paper had been run for some years past at a heavy financial loss, but Captain Armstrong, though without any previous experience of journalism, was an excellent man of business with a keen political instinct. He rapidly raised the paper from the position of a mere derelict to that of a valuable property, and he made it one of the most thoroughgoing and influential supporters of Disraeli in the metropolitan press; down to his death it remained the typical organ of the militant conservative school. As an acknowledgment of his labours and success the sole property of the 'Globe' was made over to him by the owners in 1875, and in 1882 he acquired a large interest in the 'People,' a Sunday conservative paper with a large circulation among the working classes. Thanks to these joint ventures Armstrong acquired a handsome fortune, but he took no part in public or political affairs outside the columns of his paper. Perhaps the best remembered incident in connection with his editorship of the 'Globe' was the disclosure in its pages, on 30 May 1878, of the terms of the Salisbury-Schouvaloff Treaty. A summary of that document had been brought to the paper by an occasional contributor, Charles Marvin [q. v.], to whom the foreign office had given employment as an emergency 'writer.' The official denial of its correctness was followed by the publication in the same paper on 14 June of the full text, which completely vindicated Marvin's accuracy. Proceedings were instituted against the latter on the part of the government, but were speedily abandoned. In 1892 Armstrong received a baronetcy in recognition of his services to the unionist party; he had relinquished the editorship of the 'Globe' in 1889, and in 1899 the control of the paper passed to George Elliot, his second surviving son, who succeeded to the baronetcy. He died on 20 April 1907, after a long illness, and was buried at Woking. He married on 2 Feb. 1865 Alice Fitzroy, daughter of the Rev. Charles Joseph Furlong, who survived him. His eldest son, Arthur Reginald, lieutenant 19th Hussars, died at Secunderabad 1 Nov. 1898. A portrait in oils by Herkomer belongs to his widow. A cartoon portrait by 'Spy' appeared in 'Vanity Fair' in 1894.

[The Globe, 1 Jan. 1903 and 22 April 1907; personal knowledge.] J. B. A.

ARMSTRONG, THOMAS (1832–1911), artist, born at Fallowfield, Manchester, on 19 Oct. 1832, was eldest son of Thomas Armstrong. Educated at a private school at Tarvin, near Chester, he was originally intended for business in Manchester. His tastes, however, led him to take up drawing under Mr. Crazier, of the Manchester Fine Art Academy. Deciding to adopt painting as a profession, he went to Paris in 1853, contemporaneously with du Maurier, Poynter, Lamont, and Whistler. At first he worked in the Académie of Suisse, who had been for many years a prisoner of war at Dartmoor and on his release had set up an art class in Paris, which the principal painters of the Restoration period from Ingres onwards had frequented. Armstrong subsequently entered the *atelier* of Ary Scheffer, who greatly influenced his style and method of work. In the summer he joined Millet, Bodmer, and Charles Jacque at Barbizon, and from them learnt much of which he made profitable use in his work in Algiers (1858–9) and subsequently on the Riviera (1870–2). Meanwhile he had studied in the Académie Royale of Antwerp under Van Lerius (1855–6), and in 1860 he was joined by du Maurier at Düsseldorf. There Professor Eduard Bendemann had recently succeeded F. W. Schadow, who had brought from Rome to Germany the traditions of Renaissance art. On his return to England Armstrong devoted himself to decorative painting in houses in the north, and on more than one occasion associated with his work that of his friend Randolph Caldecott [q. v.], whom he was the means of bringing into public notice. In 1864 he definitely fixed himself in London, exhibited regularly at the Royal Academy from 1865 to 1877, and subsequently up to 1881 at the Grosvenor Gallery. His landscape painting was distinguished by its fidelity and poetic feeling, but in his figure pieces, to which he devoted much time and conscientious labour, the conflicting influences of his early training were often apparent.

In 1881 Armstrong was appointed director for art at the South Kensington (now Victoria and Albert) Museum in succession to Sir Edward J. Poynter, R.A., and he promptly made his influence felt on the methods of teaching. He held that so rarely were the talents of the craftsman and designer to be found united in the same pupil, that it was the duty of technical schools to recognise the independence of the two capacities, while applying art to industry in every branch of teaching. Before his appointment to South Kensington he had guided and instructed Miss Jekyll in her efforts to establish at Chelsea a school for art needlework for the first time in this country, efforts which were amply justified by the results. In his official capacity he continued to work on the same lines. He warmly supported the efforts of Walter Copland Perry [q. v. Suppl. II] to supply art students with an adequate representation of antique sculpture, and developed and carried out the plans of his predecessor (Sir) Edward Poynter, for a museum of casts. To his initiative also was due the revival of the art of English enamelling, under Professor Dalpeyrat in 1886. He was, too, a warm supporter of the School of Art Wood-carving, which, though not officially countenanced or aided by the department, received the active support of its chief, Sir John Donnelly [q. v. Suppl. II], to whose place as chairman of the committee Armstrong succeeded in 1902. But it was by the personal interest which he took in the pupils' work, scattered though it was all over the country, that Armstrong's services to art and its application to industry must be gauged. He made himself acquainted with the requirements of each district, the special aptitudes of the students and the lines on which they needed help and guidance. It was owing to Armstrong's insistence that the Victoria and Albert Museum possesses the reproduction to scale of the Camerino of Isabelle d'Este, the Appartamento Borgia in the Vatican, the dome of the Chapel of St. Peter Martyr at Milan, and the chief room of the Palazzio Madama at Rome and other works—works representing the highest period of the Italian renaissance and invaluable to students of decorative art. With the same object he applied himself to the acquisition of works of art for the museum having an educational value or bearing upon the development of artistic taste and feeling. His colloquial knowledge of foreign languages, combined with an attractive personality, behind which lay a shrewd sense of business, enabled him not only to purchase and acquire for the museum many important works, but to establish friendly relations with the directors and officials of similar museums on the continent, and to attract them to this country to compare and explain their methods. Armstrong retired from South Kensington in 1898, when he was made C.B. Thereupon he took up painting again, and devoted himself especially to the execution of a mural tablet in plaster and copper which was placed in the church at Abbots Langley to the memory of his only child—the subjects of the panels being a Riposo and Christ and the doctors.

Armstrong died suddenly at Abbots Langley on 24 April 1911, and was buried there. On 22 April 1881 he married Mary Alice, daughter of Colonel Brine of Shaldon, Devon.

[The Times, 26 April 1911; private information; Graves's Royal Academy Exhibitors; Art Journal 1891 with portrait.] L. R.

ARNOLD, Sir ARTHUR (1833–1902), radical politician and writer, born on 28 May 1833, at Gravesend, Kent, was third son of the three sons and three daughters of Robert Coles Arnold, J.P., of Whartons, Framfield, Sussex, by his wife Sarah, daughter of Daniel Pizzi of Clement's Hall, Rochford, Essex. Sir Edwin Arnold [q. v. Suppl. II] was an elder brother. Owing to delicate health, Arnold, whose full Christian names were Robert Arthur, was educated at home, and subsequently adopted the profession of surveyor and land agent. He was professionally engaged on proposals connected with the construction of the Thames embankment; and in 1861 he issued a pamphlet, entitled 'The Thames Embankment and the Wharf Holders,' in which he supported the adoption of the scheme of (Sir) Joseph William Bazalgette [q. v. Suppl. I]. Cherishing literary ambitions, he produced in his leisure two sensational novels, 'Ralph; or, St. Sepulchre's and St. Stephen's' (1861) and 'Hever Court' (1867), the latter appearing as a serial in 'Once a Week.'

In 1863, under the Public Works (Manufacturing Districts) Act, Arnold was appointed by Charles Pelham Villiers [q. v.], then president of the poor law board, assistant commissioner and subsequently government inspector of public works. For three years he was engaged on the difficult task of supervising the employment of the destitute cotton operatives of Lancashire on the making of roads and other public works, and he contributed some striking articles on the subject to the 'Daily Telegraph.' In 1864 he issued his popular 'History of the Cotton Famine from the fall of Sumter to the passing of the Public Works Act,' which reappeared in a cheap edition next year. In 1867 a tour in the south and east of Europe first aroused his philo-Hellenic sympathies, which were conspicuous in his descriptive letters 'From the Levant,' published in 1868, and to which he was constant through life. In the same year Arnold became first editor of the 'Echo,' a new evening paper, and one of the earliest to be sold for a halfpenny, which attained great success under his control. He resigned the post in 1875, soon after the purchase of the paper by Albert Grant, known as Baron Grant [q. v. Suppl. I], and immediately started on a journey through the East with his wife, riding the whole length of Persia, a distance of more than 1000 miles. His 'Through Persia by Caravan' (1877), dedicated to Earl and Countess Granville, gives a spirited account of his adventures.

Arnold's interests were divided between politics and journalism. A staunch radical, he studied with attention current social and agrarian problems, and contributed frequently to the leading reviews. Articles and pamphlets by him were collected into a volume, entitled 'Social Politics' (1878), in which he warmly advocated the reform of the land laws and the political enfranchisement of women. He was in sympathy with the movement in favour of the nationalisation of land, and in 1885 was elected chairman of the Free Land League.

Meanwhile Arnold's ambition to enter parliament had been gratified. After contesting unsuccessfully the borough of Huntingdon in the liberal interest in 1873, he was returned in 1880 as radical member for Salford. While acting with the radical wing of his party on questions of home politics, Arnold frequently criticised with vigour and independence the government's conduct of foreign affairs. In 1880 he became chairman of the Greek committee, in succession to Sir Charles Dilke, and he was active in urging the claims of the Hellenic kingdom to an extension of territory in accordance with the suggestion of the treaty of Berlin. In 1873 the King of Greece had conferred on him the golden cross of the Order of the Saviour. In the House of Commons he made his mark as an effective speaker in debates on the franchise. On 21 March 1882 his proposal of a uniform franchise and a redistribution of seats was approved by the house (*Hansard*, 3 S. cclxvii. 1443, 1532). In 1883 he moved for an elaborate return of electoral statistics, which influenced the reform bill of 1884. At the general election of 1885 Arnold was defeated in the newly formed division of North Salford. He stood again there in 1886 as a supporter of home rule, with the same result, and he was defeated in 1892 for North Dorset. He did not re-enter the House of Commons. As a liberal imperialist Arnold gradually lost sympathy with the official policy of the liberal party, and in 1900 he opposed the views of Sir Henry Campbell-Bannerman [q. v. Suppl. II] on the conduct of the South African war.

Abandoning party politics, Arnold devoted his energies to problems of municipal government. In 1889, on the formation of the London county council, he was elected an alderman for six years; he was re-elected in 1895 for three and again in 1898 for six years. On 12 March 1895 he was chosen chairman, and was re-elected on 10 March 1896, thus enjoying the unique distinction of holding the office for more than one year. On 18 July 1895 he was knighted, and Cambridge bestowed on him the hon. degree of LL.D. in 1897. He died at 45 Kensington Park Gardens on 20 May 1902, and was buried at Gravesend. In 1867 he married Amelia, only daughter of Captain H. B. Hyde, 96th regiment, of Castle Hyde, co. Cork, who survived him without issue. She founded a scholarship in his memory at Girton College, Cambridge, and a brass memorial tablet has been placed there.

[Times and Westminster Gazette, 21 May 1902; Tinsley, Random Recollections of an Old Publisher, 1900, ii. 67; T. H. S. Escott, Masters of English Journalism, 1911; Men and Women of the Time, 1899; private information from Miss Arnold.] G. S. W.

ARNOLD, Sir EDWIN (1832–1904), poet and journalist, born at Gravesend on 10 June 1832, was second son of Robert Coles Arnold of Whartons, Framfield, and elder brother of Sir Arthur Arnold [q. v. Suppl. II]. Educated at King's School, Rochester, and at King's College, London, where he was a friendly rival of F. W. (Dean) Farrar (1850–1), Edwin obtained a scholarship at University College, Oxford, in 1851 and graduated B.A. in 1854 and M.A. in 1856. Although he won only a third class in the final classical school, he read Greek poetry with enthusiasm, and in 1852 he obtained the Newdigate with an ornate poem on 'Belshazzar's Feast.' This was published separately (1852) and was also reissued to form next year the staple of an elegant volume, 'Poems Narrative and Lyrical' (Oxford, 1853). Dedicated to Lady Waldegrave, Arnold's 'Poems' obtained the distinction of a review, on 'The two Arnolds,' in 'Blackwood' (March 1854). In America, many years later, Matthew Arnold found himself credited to an embarrassing extent with the poetical baggage of his namesake. After a short period as second English master at King Edward's School, Birmingham, Arnold was in 1856 nominated principal of the government Deccan College at Poona. On settling there he was elected a fellow of Bombay University. He soon studied Eastern languages, and mastered not only those of India but also Turkish and Persian. A successful translation of 'The Book of Good Counsels. From the Sanskrit of the Hitopadésa,' with pleasing illustrations by Harrison Weir (1861), dedicated to his first wife, indicates his rapid attraction to Oriental study. He also wrote a pamphlet on education in India (1860), pleading for a more scientific grafting of Western knowledge upon the lore of the East, and a 'History of the Marquis of Dalhousie's Administration' (2 vols. 1862–5). His demeanour as principal during the trying times of the mutiny won him commendations from the Indian government.

During a visit to England in 1861 Arnold obtained through a chance advertisement the post of leader-writer on the 'Daily Telegraph,' which Joseph Moses Levy [q. v.] was just setting to work to regenerate. This appointment finally determined his career. His colleague George Augustus Sala describes in his 'Reminiscences' how in the early days of 1862 the Eastern aroma first began to make itself felt in the leading articles of the 'Daily Telegraph.' Arnold and Sala were responsible, perhaps, in about equal measure for the roaring tones in which the 'Telegraph' began about this time to answer back the thunder of 'The Times' newspaper (see MATTHEW ARNOLD'S *Friendship's Garland*, 1871). On Thornton Hunt's death in 1873 Arnold became a chief editor of the 'Daily Telegraph,' and with the proprietors was responsible for the despatch of some enterprising and important journalistic missions, that of George Smith [q. v.] to Assyria in 1874, that of H. M. Stanley (jointly with the 'New York Herald') to complete the discoveries of Livingstone in the same year, and that of Sir H. H. Johnston to Kilima-Njaro in 1884. Arnold's Oriental knowledge proved of vital influence on his editorial work, and as a champion of Turkey through the Russo-Turkish war and of Lord Lytton's forward policy in India he helped to mould public opinion. He was made C.S.I. when Queen Victoria was proclaimed Empress of India on 1 Jan. 1877. In 1879 he published the epic poem 'The Light of Asia,' to which he owed most of his fame. In blank verse, of Oriental luxuriance, in which colour and music were blended in the Tennysonian manner with heightened effects, Arnold here presented the picturesque and pathetic elements of the Buddhist legend and the life of Gautama. The moral doctrines were those to which Europeans had been accustomed all their lives, but the setting was new to English and American readers. The poem aroused the animosities of many pulpits, but there were sixty editions in England and eighty in America, and translations were numerous. A sequel appeared in 1891 as 'The Light of the World,' and proved a signal failure.

After twenty-eight successful years in the editorial room, where his staff of writers included Edward Dicey, James Macdonell, H. D. Traill, and others, Arnold, who was made K.C.I.E. in 1888, became a travelling commissioner of the paper. In August 1889 he started with his daughter, Katharine Lilian, upon a long ramble chiefly devoted to the Pacific coast and Japan. As a picturesque tourist in books like 'India Revisited' (1886), 'Seas and Lands' (1891), 'Wandering Words' (1894), and 'East and West' (1896) (studies of Egypt, India, and Japan), he has had few rivals. His first visit to Japan was often repeated, and he was fascinated by the artistic and social side of Japanese life. His writings on Japan helped to spread in England optimistic views of Japanese progress and culture. In 1891 he undertook a reading tour in America, and he received numerous foreign decorations from Turkey, Persia, Siam, and Japan.

During the last nine or ten years of his life his sight gradually failed, but in spite of infirmities he maintained a keen interest in contemporary affairs. In 1899 he dedicated to his third wife his interesting story of the wrongs of an Indian cultivator called 'The Queen's Justice,' and in 1895 he dedicated to the Duchess of York, afterwards Queen Mary, his 'Tenth Muse and Other Poems, including many Renderings of Japanese "uta."' He died at his house in Bolton Gardens, London, on 24 March 1904; he was cremated at Brookwood and his ashes bestowed in the chapel of his old college at Oxford. A portrait by James Archer was exhibited at the Royal Academy in 1890. He married (1) in 1854 Katharine Elizabeth (*d.* 1864), daughter of Rev. Theo. Biddulph of Bristol; (2) Fannie Maria Adelaide (*d.* 1889), daughter of Rev. W. H. Channing of Boston, U.S.A.; he issued 'In my Lady's Praise' in the year of her death; (3) Tama KuroKawa of Sendai, Japan, who survives him. He left issue Mr. Edwin Lester Arnold, the author, and four other children, two sons and two daughters.

Arnold was a copious and animated writer, and where he is describing actual events, often vivid and terse. Somewhat insensitive to the finer kinds of metrical effect, he is as a poet over-sensuous, and at times allows his glowing imagery to vitiate his taste. He confidently expected the reversion of the laureateship after Lord Tennyson's death.

Apart from those already enumerated, his original works include (chiefly in verse): 1. 'Griselda, a tragedy, and other poems,' 1856. 2. 'The Wreck of the Northern Belle,' 1857. 3. 'The Poets of Greece,' 1869. 4. 'Indian Poetry,' 1881. 5. 'Pearls of the Faith,' 1883. 6. 'The Secret of Death,' 1885. 7. 'Lotus and Jewel,' 1887. 8. 'With Sa'di in the Garden,' 1888. 9. 'Japonica' (papers from 'Scribner's Magazine'), 1892. 10. 'Potiphar's Wife,' 1892. 11. 'Adzuma' (a story of a Japanese marriage), 1893. 12. 'The Voyage of Ithobal,' 1901. Among his translations are 'Political Poems by Victor Hugo and Garibaldi' (under initials E. A.), 1868; 'Hero and Leander,' from Musæus, 1873; 'The Indian Song of Songs from the Jayadeva,' 1875; 'Indian Idylls from the Mahábhárata,' 1883 and 1885; 'The Chaura panchásika,' 1896; 'Sa'di's Gulistan,' parts i.–iv. 1899. He was also author of 'A Simple Transliteral Grammar of Turkish,' 1877. A collection of his poetical works came out in 1888. Selections appeared in the same year and 'The Edwin Arnold Birthday Book' in 1885.

[The Times, 26 March 1904; Daily Telegraph; Athenæum; Illustrated London News (portrait); Alfred Austin's Reminiscences, ii. 175; Hatton's Journalistic London; Arena, April 1904; Men of the Time; Bookman, 1901, xiii. p. 373 (caricature by Phil May); Brit. Mus. Cat.; private information.]

T. S.

ARNOLD, GEORGE BENJAMIN (1832–1902), organist and musical composer, born on 22 Dec. 1832 at Petworth, Sussex, was son of George Frederick Arnold, organist of the parish church there, by his wife Mary. He was articled to George William Chard [q. v.], the organist of Winchester Cathedral, in 1849, and on Chard's death the articles were transferred to his successor, Dr. Samuel Sebastian Wesley [q. v.]. Arnold was organist successively at St. Columba's College, Rathfarnham, near Dublin (1852), St. Mary's Church, Torquay (1856), and New College, Oxford (1860). He graduated Mus. Bac. at Oxford in 1853 and Mus. Doc. in 1860. In 1865 he succeeded Wesley at Winchester, retaining the post for the rest of his life. He was a fellow of the College of Organists, acting long as an examiner for that body. He died at Winchester on 31 Jan. 1902, and was buried there. He married on 6 June 1867 Mary Lucy Roberts, who survived him with three sons and a daughter. An alabaster tablet to his memory, with a quotation from one of his works, was placed in the north transept of the cathedral in 1904.

Arnold, whose sympathies were with Bach and his school, was a composer, chiefly of church music. His published compositions include a national song, 'Old England' (1854); an oratorio, 'Ahab,' produced by the National Choral Society at Exeter Hall (1864); 'Sennacherib,' a sacred cantata, produced at the Gloucester festival of 1883; 'The Song of the Redeemed,' written for and produced at St. James's Church, New York (1891); 'An orchestral introduction and chorus in praise of King Alfred,' performed at the inauguration of the Alfred Memorial at Winchester in 1901, besides two motets, two psalms, anthems, part songs, and two sonatas.

[Musical Times, Nov. 1901, March 1902 (with portrait), May 1902; Brown and Stratton, Musical Biog., 1897; Brit. Mus. Cat.; private information.]

F. C.

ARNOLD, WILLIAM THOMAS (1852–1904), author and journalist, born at Hobart, Tasmania, on 18 Sept. 1852, was eldest son and second child of Thomas Arnold [q. v. Suppl. I], nephew of Matthew Arnold [q. v. Suppl. I], and grandson of Dr. Arnold of Rugby [q. v.]. His mother was Julia, daughter of William Sorell, registrar of deeds, Hobart. His elder sister is the well-known novelist Mrs. Humphry Ward. On the return of his parents to England in 1856 Arnold lived mainly with his father's kindred at Fox How, Ambleside. From 1862 to 1865 he was at the Oratory School, Birmingham, where his father was classical master under

John Henry Newman [q. v.]. When Thomas Arnold left the Roman catholic church, his son was sent to Rugby, where he lived for a year with the headmaster, Frederick Temple [q. v. Suppl. II], and then in September 1866 entered Charles Arnold's house. He matriculated on 14 Oct. 1871 at University College, Oxford, then under the mastership of G. G. Bradley [q. v. Suppl. II], and was elected to a scholarship in 1872. He took a second class both in honour moderations (in 1873) and in lit. hum. (in 1875). After graduating B.A. in 1876 Arnold settled at Oxford, combining literary work with private coaching.

In 1879 he won the Arnold prize with an essay on 'The Roman System of Provincial Administration to the Accession of Constantine the Great.' The work, which was published in 1879, was a thorough digest of the literary and epigraphic sources, and is the chief English authority. A new edition, revised from the author's notes by E. S. Shuckburgh [q. v. Suppl. II], appeared posthumously in 1906.

In 1879 Arnold adopted the profession of a journalist, joining the staff of the 'Manchester Guardian' and settling at Manchester. As writer and sub-editor he devoted his versatile energy to the 'Manchester Guardian' for seventeen years. A Gladstonian liberal in politics, he fought with courage and consistency through the long home rule controversy of 1885–95. Subsequently, in 'German Ambitions as they affect Britain and the United States' (1903), a collection of letters originally contributed to the 'Spectator' under the signature 'Vigilans et Æquus,' Arnold proved his mastery of foreign contemporary literature and his ability to draw prudent deductions from it. But history, literature, and art continued to compete with politics for his interest. He helped to develop the literary section of the 'Manchester Guardian,' and he encouraged local artists, taking an active part in the establishment of the Manchester School of Art. His house at Manchester was the centre of an interesting political, literary, and artistic circle.

Arnold never ceased to devote his scanty leisure to Roman history. In 1886 he published a critical edition of the section on the Punic war in his grandfather's 'History of Rome'; and contributions between 1886 and 1895 to the 'English Historical Review' showed the strength of his interest in ancient history. As years went on Arnold grew fastidious over writing on his chosen subject; and though to the last he kept up with the latest research, eight chapters of an incomplete history of the early Roman empire, posthumously edited by E. Fiddes under the title of 'Studies in Roman Imperialism' (1906), are all that remain of his accumulated material. They bear witness to his width of knowledge, maturity of thought, and cautious temper.

Spinal disease compelled Arnold's retirement from the 'Manchester Guardian' in 1898, and next year he moved to London, where he was for a time still able to see friends and to write a little. Occasionally he travelled south. On his return from a visit to St. Jean-de-Luz he died at Carlyle Square, Chelsea, on 29 May 1904. He was buried at Little Shelford, near Cambridge. In 1877 Arnold married Henrietta, daughter of Charles Wale, J.P., of Little Shelford, and granddaughter of Archbishop Whately [q. v.]; she survived him without issue.

In addition to the publications already mentioned Arnold issued a scholarly edition of Keats (1884; new edit. 1907). He was a contributor to T. Humphry Ward's 'English Poets' (1880–2); and some penetrating dramatic reviews by him were published in 'The Manchester Stage, 1880–1900' (1900). He revised his father's edition of Dryden's 'Essay of Dramatic Poesy' in 1903.

[Memoir of William Thomas Arnold (with portrait) by his sister, Mrs. Humphry Ward, and his colleague of the Manchester Guardian, C. E. Montague, 1907; The Times, 30 May 1904; Manchester Guardian, 30 May 1904; Quarterly Review, Oct. 1905; Rugby School Register, 1842–1874, p. 266, 1902; Foster's Alumni Oxon. 1888.] G. S. W.

ARNOLD-FORSTER, HUGH OAKELEY (1855–1909), author and politician, born on 19 Aug. 1855 at Dawlish in Devonshire, was second son and third child in the family of two sons and two daughters of William Delafield Arnold [q. v.], sometime director of public instruction in the Punjab. His mother was Frances Anne, daughter of General John Anthony Hodgson. Thomas Arnold [q. v.], headmaster of Rugby, was his grandfather, and Matthew Arnold [q. v. Suppl. I] his uncle. His parents took him out to Kangra when he was four months old. There his mother died in 1858; next year the four children were sent home to England, and the father, who followed them, died at Gibraltar on 9 April 1859. The orphaned children were at once adopted by their father's eldest sister, Jane Martha, and her husband, William Edward Forster [q. v.], who had no children of their own. Perfect confidence and affection marked for life the relations between foster-parents and adopted children.

From a private school at Exmouth kept by his kinsman, John Penrose, Hugh passed in 1869 to Rugby, then under the headmastership of Frederick Temple; but when Temple was succeeded by Dr. Hayman [q. v. Suppl. II] Forster removed the boy and placed him under a private tutor. On 24 Jan. 1874 he matriculated at University College, Oxford. There he graduated B.A. in 1877 with a first class in modern history. He only proceeded M.A. in 1900. At the time of leaving Oxford he with his brother and sisters formally assumed the name of Arnold-Forster.

Settling in London, Arnold-Forster read for the bar in the chambers of Mr. R. A. M'Call (now K.C.) and was called to Lincoln's Inn on 5 Nov. 1879. There was early promise of a lucrative practice, but on Forster's appointment as chief secretary for Ireland in the second Gladstone administration in 1880, Arnold-Forster, his adopted son, became his private secretary, and he shared Forster's labours, anxieties, and incessant perils through the next two years. During this period, too, he gave first proof of his literary aptitudes. In 1881 he published anonymously 'The Truth about the Land League,' a damaging collection of facts, speeches, and documents, which ran through many editions and helped to discredit the nationalist cause in Great Britain. Thenceforth Arnold-Forster wrote much on political and social questions in the press or in independent books.

In 1885 he became a member of the publishing firm of Cassell & Co., and devoted himself with characteristic thoroughness to its affairs, until he became absorbed in politics. For Cassell's he prepared many educational handbooks designed to propagate a wise patriotism. These works included 'Citizen Reader' series (1886 and frequently re-issued), describing for children the principles and purposes of English institutions; 'The Laws of Every-day Life' (1889); 'This World of Ours,' lessons in geography (1891); 'Things New and Old' (1893, English History readers in seven volumes); 'History of England for Children' (1897); and 'Our Great City' (1900). He was also largely concerned as a member of the firm of Cassell's in the preparation of 'The Universal Atlas,' which subsequently became 'The Times Atlas.'

Meanwhile he was developing his political interests. In 1884, on the foundation of the Imperial Federation League with Forster for its president, he became its secretary, and thenceforward enthusiastically advocated a closer union of the empire, actively supporting the efforts of Mr. Joseph Chamberlain in that direction and ultimately accepting his policy of tariff reform and colonial preference. From boyhood he had devoted himself to the close study of naval affairs and of warships. His love of the sea was insatiable, and he spent many a holiday cruising in a Thames barge, which he fitted out in quite homely fashion. In 1884 he inspired the famous articles on 'The Truth about the Navy' (published by Mr. Stead in the 'Pall Mall Gazette'), which led to a large increase in the navy estimates under the Gladstone government and to endeavours of later governments to place the navy on a footing of adequate efficiency. In a forecast of a modern naval battle entitled 'In a Conning Tower' (1888, 8th edit. 1898) he showed a technical knowledge remarkable in a civilian.

As early as 1881 Arnold-Forster declined an invitation to stand for parliament as liberal candidate for Oxford. In 1883 a similar invitation from Devonport led him to make several speeches in that constituency; but before the election (of 1885) he followed Forster in dissent from the liberal policy, especially in Egypt, and he withdrew his candidature. He joined the newly formed liberal unionist party in 1886 on Gladstone's adoption of home rule, and was defeated as a unionist candidate in June 1886 for Darlington, and again at a bye-election in 1888 for Dewsbury. At the general election of 1892 he was elected for West Belfast, and retained that seat until 1906. As a private member of parliament he addressed himself with somewhat uncompromising independence chiefly to naval, military, and imperial questions. Pamphlets on 'Our Home Army' (1892), 'Army Letters' (1898), and 'The War Office, the Army, and the Empire' (1900) gave him some reputation as a critic of military affairs. Interesting himself during the early stages of the Boer war in land settlement in South Africa, he pressed the subject on the attention of Mr. Chamberlain, then colonial secretary, who in August 1900 sent out a commission of inquiry with Arnold-Forster as chairman. Amid many interruptions and impediments he completed his task in South Africa by November, when he received and accepted Lord Salisbury's offer of the office of secretary of the admiralty. After drafting the report of the South African land commission he entered on his new duties. His chief, Lord Selborne, who had just succeeded George Joachim (afterwards Lord) Goschen [q. v. Suppl. II] as first lord of the admiralty, sat in the House of Lords. Arnold-Forster consequently represented the admiralty in the House of Commons, and exercised there more authority than usually belongs to a subordinate minister. At the admiralty he actively helped to carry out the drastic reforms which Lord Selborne initiated, mainly on the inspiration of Sir John (afterwards Lord) Fisher. He was prominent in formulating the administrative measures required by the new scheme of naval training; he directed much administrative energy to the standardisation of dimensions and material in the navy, and to the higher organisation of defence with a view to the needful correlation of naval and military preparations of the kingdom and empire; he helped in the reconstruction of the committee of imperial defence.

In the autumn of 1903 secessions from the cabinet owing to Mr. Chamberlain's promulgation of the policy of tariff reform led to a reconstruction of Mr. Balfour's ministry [see CAVENDISH, SPENCER COMPTON, eighth DUKE OF DEVONSHIRE, Suppl. II; RITCHIE, CHARLES THOMSON, first BARON RITCHIE OF DUNDEE; Suppl. II]. Arnold-Forster, an ardent supporter of tariff reform, now entered the cabinet as secretary of state for war in succession to Mr. St. John Brodrick, now Viscount Midleton, who became secretary of state for India. He was thereupon admitted to the privy council. During his recent holidays a severe strain had permanently affected Arnold-Forster's heart, and he was thenceforth hampered by increasing debility, but he threw himself into the task of reorganising the war office and the military forces of the crown with indefatigable energy. The royal commission on the South African war had lately reported, and schemes of reform were rife. The government had already decided to appoint a small committee to advise on the reconstruction of the machinery of the war office. One of Arnold-Forster's first administrative acts was to appoint Viscount Esher, Sir John Fisher, and Sir George Sydenham Clarke as the sole members of this committee, whose report resulted in the constitution, on a new and established footing, of the committee of imperial defence, and in the reconstruction of the hierarchy of the war office more or less on the model of the board of admiralty. Other reforms were initiated by Arnold-Forster, but his definite views on problems of military organisation did not always find acceptance with colleagues, who were distracted by other political issues, and by the growing weakness of the government. Stiff in opinion, clear and incisive in expression, he was perhaps a little intolerant of the views of others equally entitled to be heard; nevertheless he secured the acceptance of the lines on which in his judgment the general staff of the army ought to be organised. But many of his general schemes were frustrated by Mr. Balfour's resignation on 4 December 1905, and his measures were not adopted by his successor.

In 1906, owing to the distance of the constituency and his decline of physical strength, he retired from the representation of West Belfast, and was returned for Croydon. In the same year he published 'The Army in 1906: a Policy and a Vindication,' his own estimate of the needs of the army and an account of his administration. In opposition he was energetic in his criticism of the military policy of Viscount Haldane, his successor at the war office. His last literary effort was 'Military Needs and Military Policy' (1908), with an introduction by Field-marshal Earl Roberts, an attempt to expose the defects which he saw in the liberal war minister's schemes.

In 1907, after recovering from a grave attack of illness, he went with his wife and a son to Jamaica on the invitation of Sir Alfred Jones [q. v. Suppl. II] in order to attend a conference of the Imperial Cotton-Growing Association. During his stay there a terrible earthquake devastated Kingston, and destroyed Port Royal. Thenceforth his health steadily failed, although he continued his political work with exemplary fortitude. He died suddenly at his London residence in South Kensington on 12 March 1909, and was buried at Wroughton, Wiltshire, the parish in which his father-in-law lived. In 1884 Arnold-Forster married Mary, eldest daughter of Mervyn Herbert Nevil Story-Maskelyne [q. v. Suppl. II]. She survived him with four sons.

With the shadow of death long hanging over him, no man, as Mr. Balfour remarked after his death, was 'more absolutely absorbed in a great and unselfish desire to carry out his own public duty.' His speeches in parliament were models of lucid exposition. He spoke, as he wrote, easily, fluently, and with an orderly evolution of his topics. He made no use of rhetorical ornament, but he seldom wearied his hearers, and never confused them by any slovenliness of preparation or obscurity of expression.

He proved his versatility by publishing, besides the works mentioned, 'What to do and how to do it' (1884), a manual of the laws affecting the housing and sanitation of London; 'The Coming of the Kilogram' (1898, 2nd edit. 1900), a defence of the metric system; and 'English Socialism of To-day' (1908, 3 edits.).

[A memoir by his wife, 1910, with a list of his more important writings; Hansard's Debates; The Times, 13 March 1909; personal knowledge; private information.] J. R. T.

ARTHUR, WILLIAM (1819–1901), Wesleyan divine, born at Glendun, co. Antrim, on 3 Feb. 1819, was son of James Arthur, whose ancestors belonged to the counties of Limerick and Clare, by his wife Margaret Kennedy, who was of Scottish and Ulster descent. Shortly after his birth his father removed to Westport, co. Mayo. Brought up as an Episcopalian, he became a Wesleyan methodist, and began to preach at the age of sixteen, when, coming to England, he entered Hoxton academy for the training of Wesleyan ministers. Resolving to engage in mission work, he sailed for India on 15 April 1839, under the auspices of the Wesleyan Missionary Society. In India he laboured at Gubbi, about eighty miles north-west of Bangalore; but his health gave way, and he returned to England in 1841. In 1842 he was stationed at Wesley's chapel, City Road, London. From 1846 to 1848 he laboured in France, first at Boulogne and then in Paris. In 1849 and 1850 his ministry was in London, at Hinde Street and Great Queen Street. From 1851 to 1868 he was one of the secretaries of the Wesleyan Missionary Society, and he was an honorary secretary 1888–91. From 1868 to 1871 he was principal of the Methodist College, Belfast.

Meanwhile he was elected a member of the legal hundred in 1856, and was president of the Wesleyan Conference in 1866. In 1888 he settled at Cannes, where he preached occasionally in the Presbyterian church. He died at Cannes on 9 March 1901. He married on 18 June 1850 Elizabeth Ellis Ogle of Leeds, who bore him six daughters.

Arthur rendered good services to his church in its foreign mission work, in its educational enterprise, and in its home mission. To him was due its Metropolitan Chapel Building Fund in 1862, and he sympathised with Hugh Price Hughes [q. v. Suppl. II] in his 'Forward movement,' especially in modifying the three-years' system of pastorate. His portrait by Gooch is in possession of his daughter, Miss Arthur.

Arthur's chief influence was exercised through his writings. 'The Tongue of Fire' (1856; 18th ed. 1859) sets forth in glowing language and with great wealth of illustration the importance of spiritual power in life. Three books treat of Italy and the Papacy; 'Italy in Transition' (1860; 6th ed. 1877) describes a visit in 1859; 'The Modern Jove' (1873) reviews the collected speeches of Pope Pius IX; 'The Pope, the Kings and the People' (1877, 2 vols.) is a history of the papacy from the issue of the 'Syllabus' in 1864 to the Vatican Council of 1870; Arthur consulted the best authorities in Italian and German, and criticised adversely Manning's 'True Story of the Vatican Council' (1877).

Besides the books mentioned and numerous sermons, lectures and pamphlets, Arthur's works include: 1. 'A Mission to the Mysore,' 1847. 2. 'The Successful Merchant; a Life of Samuel Budgett,' 1852. 3. 'The People's Day,' 1855; 11th ed. 1856; an appeal to Lord Stanley against the opening of Exhibitions on Sunday. 4. 'Life of Gideon Ouseley, the Irish Evangelist,' 1876.

[William Arthur: a biography, by Thos. B. Stephenson, D.D., 1907; Crookshank, History of Methodism in Ireland, 1885; private information.] C. H. I.

ASHBY, HENRY (1846–1908), physician, born at Carshalton, Surrey, on 8 March 1846, was the son of John and Charlotte Ashby, both members of the Society of Friends. Educated firstly at Ackworth School, near Pontefract, and from 1864 at the Flounder's Institute, Ackworth (belonging also to the Society of Friends), Ashby after some experience as a teacher entered Guy's Hospital. Winning the gold medal for clinical medicine, he was for two years assistant in the physiological laboratory and also resident obstetric and house physician. He was admitted M.R.C.S. in 1873 and graduated M.B. in 1874 and M.D. in 1878 with a gold medal in the University of London. In 1875 he was appointed demonstrator of anatomy and physiology in the Liverpool School of Medicine and assistant physician to the Liverpool Infirmary for Children. In 1878 he removed to Manchester to become honorary physician to the Manchester Hospital for Diseases of Children (known as Pendlebury Hospital). From 1880 to 1882 he was evening lecturer on animal physiology in the Owens College, and from 1880 till death lecturer on diseases of children, first in the Owens College and then in the Victoria University. He became a member in 1883 and a fellow in 1890 of the Royal College of Physicians. An active member of the medical societies of Manchester, he promoted the transformation of the microscopical section of the Medical Society into the Pathological Society (1885), of which he was the first president (1885–6). He also was president of the Medical Society and of the Medico-Ethical Association. In 1902, when the British Medical Association visited Manchester, he was president of the section on children's diseases.

Ashby, who rapidly acquired a very large practice as consultant on children's diseases, zealously devoted himself to the welfare of poor children. He was honorary consulting physician of the schools in and near Manchester for the crippled and deaf and dumb. When the Manchester education committee undertook the education of the feeble-minded children, he helped and reported on the work unofficially for two years (1902), and was special medical adviser to the committee from 1904. In 1904 he gave important evidence before the departmental committee on physical deterioration appointed by the lord president of the council. Of especial value was the medical advice and guidance which Ashby gave Miss Mary Dendy, who successfully founded in 1898 the Lancashire and Cheshire society for the permanent care of the feeble-minded; the object being not only to educate such persons but to take care of them *throughout their lives*, so as to prevent them transmitting their disability. Schools were opened, and a colony which was established at Sandlebridge in Cheshire (1902) provided in 1911 accommodation for 268 residents. A royal commission on the care and control of the feeble-minded, before which Ashby gave evidence of importance in 1905, was largely an outcome of Ashby's support of Miss Dendy's experiments. In 1905 on Ashby's advice the Manchester education committee inaugurated a residential school for cripple children at Swinton, the only one of its kind under municipal administration. Ashby enjoyed a world-wide reputation as an expert on diseases of children, and his wards at Pendlebury were visited by physicians from the Continent and America. In later life he closely studied the psychology of the child, and began a book on the subject which he did not live to complete. In 1905 he delivered the Wightman lecture on 'Some neuroses of early life.'

He died on 6 July 1908 at his residence, Didsbury, Manchester, and was cremated at the Manchester crematorium, his ashes being buried in St. James, Birch, churchyard. He married in 1879 Helen, daughter of the Rev. Francis Edward Tuke of Borden, Kent, and left two sons, one of whom entered the medical profession, and one daughter.

A memorial scholarship was founded by Ashby's friends in the Victoria University of Manchester, to be awarded triennially for the encouragement of the study of diseases of children. A tablet placed by the family at Pendlebury Hospital commemorates his services to the institution.

Apart from papers on diseases of children Ashby wrote with Mr. George Arthur Wright: 'Diseases of Children, Medical and Surgical' (1899; 5th ed. 1905), a standard text-book. His other books were: 'Notes on Physiology' (1878; 8th ed. 1910, edited by Ashby's son, Hugh) and 'Health in the Nursery' (1898; 3rd ed. 1908).

[Personal knowledge; information from Mrs. Ashby, Mr. Hugh Ashby, M.B. (Camb.), M.R.C.P., and Miss Dendy; Brit. Med. Journal, 25 July 1908; Lancet, 18 July 1908; Manchester Guardian, 7 July 1908 (with portrait).] E. M. B.

ASHER, ALEXANDER (1835–1905), solicitor-general for Scotland, born at Inveravon, Banffshire, in 1835, was son of William Asher, parish minister of Inveravon. After education at Elgin Academy and at King's College, Aberdeen, he entered Edinburgh University, where he was a member of the Speculative Society (president 1863–5), but did not graduate. Passing to the Scottish bar on 10 Dec. 1861, he gradually acquired a large practice, and became one of the most distinguished counsel of his day, his only rival being John Blair Balfour, first Baron Kinross [q. v. Suppl. II]. He took a leading part in numerous cases which attracted public attention, and he represented the United Free Church in litigation which ended in 1904 with the defeat of that body. A strong liberal in politics, he was appointed in 1870, during the Gladstone ministry of 1868–74, advocate-depute. At the general election of 1880 Asher was unsuccessful as liberal candidate for the Universities of

Glasgow and Aberdeen; but in 1881 he was elected for the Elgin district of boroughs (in succession to Sir M. E. Grant Duff) and retained this seat for the rest of his life. He made no great mark in the House of Commons, where he followed Gladstone in his support of home rule. Meanwhile in 1881 he became Q.C., and was solicitor-general for Scotland during Gladstone's later ministries in the years 1881–5, 1886, and 1892–4. He received the honorary degree of LL.D. from the Universities of Aberdeen (1883) and of Edinburgh (1891). In 1894 he resigned office, 'largely,' it was said, 'owing to the very inadequate remuneration then paid to the Scottish solicitor-general' (*The Times,* 7 Aug. 1905), and in the following year was elected dean of the faculty of advocates. Suddenly taken ill in London on 4 July 1905, he died at Beechwood, near Edinburgh, on 5 Aug. following, and was buried in the churchyard of Corstorphine. Asher, who married in 1870 Caroline, daughter of the Rev. C. H. Gregan Craufurd, left no family. There is a portrait of him in the Parliament House at Edinburgh, painted, at the request of the Scottish bar, by Sir William Quiller Orchardson, R.A. [q. v. Suppl. II], in 1902.

[Scotsman and The Times, 7 Aug. 1905; Roll of Alumni in Univ. and King's Coll., Aberdeen, 1596–1860, p. 170; Hist. Speculative Soc. p. 150; Rolls of the Faculty of Advocates.]

G. W. T. O.

ASHLEY, EVELYN (1836–1907), biographer of Lord Palmerston, born in London on 24 July 1836, was fourth son of Anthony Ashley Cooper, seventh earl of Shaftesbury [q. v.], by his wife Emily, daughter of Peter Leopold Cowper, fifth Earl Cowper; his maternal grandmother was sister of Lord Melbourne, and in 1839 married as her second husband Lord Palmerston.

Ashley, whose baptismal names were Anthony Evelyn Melbourne, was educated at Harrow and Trinity College, Cambridge, where he graduated M.A. in 1858. In the same year he became private secretary to Lord Palmerston, then prime minister. The government was on the eve of defeat, and on its fall (1858) Ashley paid a visit to America with Lord Frederick Cavendish [q. v.] and Lord Richard Grosvenor, afterwards Lord Stalbridge. Next year Lord Palmerston returned to office, and Ashley acted as his private secretary until the prime minister's death in 1865. Meanwhile he made more than one eventful excursion abroad. In 1860 he told Lord Palmerston that he was going to Italy to see what Garibaldi was doing and should take full advantage of his official position. Lord Palmerston replied that what his secretary did during his holiday was no business of his. With this implied permission, Ashley presented himself to Garibaldi in camp and was given ample facilities for watching the progress of the campaign. In 1863 he accompanied Laurence Oliphant [q. v.] on an expedition into the Russian province of Volhynia, where they were arrested on suspicion of being Polish insurgents (OLIPHANT, *Episodes in a Life of Adventure,* p. 333). In 1865 he was attached to the mission sent to convey the Order of the Garter to King Christian IX of Denmark, and was then created a commander of the Danish Order of the Dannebrog.

In 1864 Ashley joined Algernon Borthwick [q. v. Suppl. II] and others in producing 'The Owl,' the forerunner of society newspapers. The editors were intimately acquainted with current public and private affairs, and secured contributions of literary value. The publication attracted much attention during the six years of its existence. Ashley had become a student of Lincoln's Inn on 22 Nov. 1856, and was called to the bar in 1863. After Lord Palmerston's death (1865) he joined the Oxford circuit; he held the office of treasurer of county courts from 1863 until 1874. He devoted most of his time to the completion of 'The Life of Lord Palmerston,' which had been begun by Lord Dalling, but was interrupted by his death in 1872. Lord Dalling published in 1870 two volumes and had written part of a third. This Ashley finished in 1874, and he added two concluding volumes which he published in 1876. Though new material has since been published, the book still holds standard rank.

In 1874 Ashley entered parliament as a member of the liberal party. At the general election in February he had been defeated in the Isle of Wight, but he was returned for Poole, Dorset, at a bye-election on 26 May 1874. As a private member he persistently but unsuccessfully endeavoured to pass a bill to enable accused persons to give evidence. The principle was eventually sanctioned by Lord Halsbury's Act of 1898. In 1879 he distinguished himself by his defence of Sir Bartle Frere from an attack by members of his own party. At the general election of 1880 he was returned for the Isle of Wight and was appointed parliamentary secretary to the board of trade in Gladstone's second administration. The president,

Mr. Chamberlain, was also in the House of Commons, so that Ashley's parliamentary duties were light, but he presided over the railway rates committee (1881–2). In 1882 he was transferred to the colonial office; the secretary of state was Lord Derby, and Ashley represented his department in the House of Commons. To him fell the important task of explaining the conditions of service in which the Australian contingents were to proceed to the Soudan in 1885. From 1880 to 1885 he was one of the ecclesiastical commissioners.

At the general election of 1885 Ashley was beaten in the Isle of Wight by Sir Richard Webster (Lord Alverstone). When Gladstone announced his adoption of the principle of home rule, Ashley joined the liberal unionists. At the general election of 1886 he stood as a liberal unionist for North Dorset, and was beaten. Thenceforward he sustained a series of defeats—at Glasgow, Bridgeton division, in 1887, at the Ayr boroughs in 1888, and at Portsmouth in 1892 and 1895. Of statesmanlike temper, he was brought up in an older political school, and was untrained in modern electioneering methods; on the mass of voters his intellectual ability and attainments made small impression. Although his active interest in county politics never declined, he made no further attempt to renew his parliamentary career.

On the death in 1888 of his uncle, William Cowper-Temple, Lord Mount-Temple [q. v. Suppl. I], Ashley succeeded to the properties bequeathed to Mount-Temple by Lord Palmerston, his stepfather—Broadlands, Romsey and Classiebawn, co. Sligo. He was sworn of the privy council in 1891. He was D.L. Hampshire and J.P. Hampshire, Dorset, and Sligo, an alderman of the Hampshire county council, official verderer of the New Forest, and five times mayor of Romsey (1898–1902). He was also chairman of the Railway Passengers' Assurance Company. He died at Broadlands on 15 Nov. 1907, and was buried at Romsey.

Ashley married twice: (1) in 1866, Sybella, daughter of Sir Walter and Lady Mary Farquhar (*d.* 1886), by whom he left one son (Wilfrid, M.P. for the Blackpool division of Lancashire since 1906) and one daughter; (2) in 1891, Alice, daughter of William Willoughby Cole, third earl of Enniskillen, by whom he left one son. A portrait painted by Miss Emmett in 1899 is at Broadlands. A cartoon by 'Spy' appeared in 'Vanity Fair' in 1883.

[The Times, 16 Nov. 1907; Daily Telegraph 16 Nov. 1907; Blackpool Herald, 16 Nov' 1907; private sources; cf. Lucy's Disraeli Parliament, pp. 57 et seq.] R. L.

ASHMEAD BARTLETT, Sir ELLIS (1849–1902), politician. [See Bartlett, Sir Ellis Ashmead].

ASTON, WILLIAM GEORGE (1841–1911), Japanese scholar, born near Londonderry on 9 April 1841, was son of George Robert Aston, minister of the Unitarian Church of Ireland and schoolmaster. Receiving early education from his father, he matriculated at Queen's College, Belfast, 1859, and after a distinguished career as a student, graduated in the Queen's University of Ireland, B.A. in 1862 and M.A. in 1863, on both occasions being gold medallist in classics and taking honours also in modern languages and literature. In 1890 he was made by the Queen's University hon. D.Lit.

In 1864 Aston was appointed student interpreter in the British Consular Service in Japan, and in the autumn joined the staff of the British legation at Yedo (Tokio), where (Sir) Ernest Satow was already filling a like position.

Aston's official career extended over twenty-five highly interesting years in the history of Japan and Korea. Sir Harry Parkes [q. v.] became envoy at Yedo in 1865, and it was largely on the advice of Aston and Satow, based on the result of their historical researches, that Parkes supported the revolutionary movement in Japan in 1868, and unlike the diplomatic representatives of other western powers hastened to acknowledge the new government of the emperor. From 1875 to 1880 Aston was assistant Japanese secretary of the British Legation at Tokio, and from 1880 to 1883 consul at Hiogo. He prepared the way for the first British treaty with Korea, which was signed on 26 Nov. 1883, and from 1884 to 1886 was British consul-general in Korea. He was the first European consular officer to reside in Söul, and he was present through the early troubles that marked Korea's first entry into the world, including the sanguinary émeute at the capital in 1884. From 1886 to 1889 Aston was Japanese secretary of the British legation at Tokio.

From his first arrival in Japan Aston rapidly turned to advantage his linguistic aptitudes, which proved of value in his official work and eventually gave him a high reputation as a Japanese scholar. When he reached Japan, scarcely half a dozen Europeans had succeeded in acquiring a practical knowledge of the language. There was hardly a phrase book; there were no dictionaries, and no elementary grammar either for Europeans or for Japanese students, grammar being ignored in the Japanese school and college curriculum, and left entirely to philologists, whose works (few in number) were too abstruse for study by any but the most advanced students. Not until ten years after Aston's arrival was the first attempt at a grammar on European models published by the education department of the imperial government. Aston in the interval not only acquired a complete, accurate, and eloquent command of the spoken language, and a facility of using the written language, which is different from the spoken in essential characteristics, but he compiled grammars (1869 and 1872) of both the spoken and written Japanese languages on the European method, and on lines of scientific philology. Aston's grammars were superseded by the more comprehensive works of Professor Basil Hall Chamberlain on 'Colloquial Japanese' (1888) and 'The Study of Japanese Writing' (1899), but Aston led the way in the arduous task. Later he extended his studies into Chinese and Korean philology, and was the first among either European or Asiatic scholars to show the affinity of the Korean and Japanese languages.

At the same time Aston was an original and exhaustive investigator of the history, religion, political system, and literature of Japan. He was the first European to complete a literal translation of the Nihongi, the 'Ancient Chronicles of Japan' (1896); this work and Professor Chamberlain's translation of the Kojiki, the Ancient Records, form the original authorities for the mythology and history of ancient Japan. The original is written in the most abstruse style, and Aston for the purpose of his translation, which though literal is graceful and simple, had to consult hundreds of explanatory volumes by native commentators, as well as the Chinese classics.

His subsequent works on 'Japanese Literature' (1899) and on 'Shinto' (1905), the indigenous religion of Japan, became recognised text-books; they have been translated into Japanese and are used and quoted by leading native scholars in Japan. Aston also wrote on historical and philological subjects in the 'Transactions' of the Asiatic Society of Japan, the Japan Society, and the Royal Asiatic Society of London. According to Dr. Haga, professor of literature in Tokio University, Aston's literary exertions, combined with those of Satow and Chamberlain, generated that thorough understanding of the Japanese by the English which culminated in the Anglo-Japanese alliance of 1902.

On retiring from Japan on a pension in 1889, Aston was made C.M.G. Thenceforward he resided at Beer, South Devon, where he died on 22 Nov. 1911. He had long suffered from pulmonary trouble, but ill-health never diminished his geniality. He married in 1871 Janet, daughter of R. Smith of Belfast; she predeceased him, without issue. His unique collection of native Japanese books, numbering some 9500 volumes and including many rare block printed editions, was acquired for Cambridge University library in January 1912.

[The Times, 23 Nov. 1911, 2 Feb. 1912; Foreign Office List; Who's Who, 1911; personal knowledge.] J. H. L.

ATKINSON, ROBERT (1839–1908), philologist, born at Gateshead on 6 April 1839, was only child of John Atkinson, who was in business there, by his wife Ann. After education at the Anchorage grammar school close to his home from 1849 to 1856, he matriculated in Trinity College, Dublin, on 2 July 1856, but he spent the years 1857 and 1858 on the Continent, principally at Liège. There he laid the foundation of his knowledge of the Romance languages. On his return to Ireland he worked as a schoolmaster in Kilkenny till he won a Trinity College scholarship in 1862. Thenceforward his academic progress was rapid. He graduated B.A. on 16 Dec. 1863, M.A. in 1866, and LL.D. in 1869. In 1891 he received the honorary degree of D.Litt.

In 1869 Atkinson became university professor of the Romance languages, and from 1871 till near his death he filled at the same time the chair of Sanskrit and comparative philology. His masterly powers of linguistic analysis made him an admirable teacher, notably of composition in Latin and Romance tongues, while the immense range of his linguistic faculty enabled pupils of adequate capacity to learn in his classroom languages new to them, with almost magical rapidity and thoroughness.

Atkinson was both a linguist and a philologist of exceptional power and range. With equal facility he taught not only most of the Romance languages but also Sanskrit, Tamil, Telugu, and other Indian tongues. He was a brilliant Hebrew scholar, and Persian, Arabic, and several languages of Central and Western Asia were familiar to him. In all the many forms of speech that he studied he acquired a mastery of colloquial idiom and of pronunciation, as well as of the literary style. In his later years he devoted his leisure to Chinese, and at his death he had completed a dictionary of that tongue. The 'Key' which he intended to accompany it, and without which it could not be used, he did not live to complete. The MS. as it stands has been presented by his widow to the library of Trinity College, Dublin.

A scientific philologist, Atkinson was always intent upon analysis of the structure of a language rather than on its literature. His philological teaching impressed on his pupils the principle of law in language, as opposed to theories of 'sporadic changes.' Therein he long anticipated Brugmann and the new school of philologists.

The most important outcome of Atkinson's study of Romance languages was a scholarly edition of a Norman-French poem attributed to Matthew Paris, and entitled 'Vie de Seint Auban' (1876).

In Sanskrit learning Atkinson confined himself to the language of the Vedas and to Sanskrit grammar, planning and partially writing a Vedic dictionary, and learning by heart, as Pandits have done for twenty-four centuries, the whole of the intricate masterpiece of the great grammarian Pānini.

In addition, Atkinson was both an expert scholar in Celtic and an advanced scholar in Coptic, the Christian descendant of the ancient Egyptian language. In two communications dealing with the latter, and made by him to the Royal Irish Academy (*Proc.* 3rd series, iii. 24, 225) in 1893, he subjected to searching examination a series of Coptic texts published during the preceding ten years by Professor Rossi and M. Bouriant. It was not perhaps difficult to show the inferior character of these publications; but the service rendered by Atkinson was to enter a much-needed protest against a tendency to 'play hieroglyphics' with Coptic texts. In the decipherment of the ancient Egyptian language there is room, no doubt, for conjecture and hypothesis: in Coptic, as Atkinson showed once and for all, the rules of accidence and syntax are fully known, and editing and translation should proceed with the scientific regularity of any other better known Oriental language.

On 11 Jan. 1875 Atkinson was elected a member of the Royal Irish Academy, and in March became a member of its council. In 1876 he was chosen librarian. Secretary of council from 1878 to 1901, he was then elected president. Meanwhile in 1884 he was Todd professor of the Celtic languages in the academy, delivering an inaugural lecture on Irish lexicography on 13 April 1885. His connection with the Royal Irish Academy drew him to Celtic studies. His Celtic work was that of a pioneer, being undertaken before many fundamental principles of old Irish grammar were recognised. But he edited two documents which are of the utmost importance for the student of the history of the Irish language. Of these the first was 'The Passions and Homilies from the Leabhar Breac,' with translation and glossary (Dublin 1887; perhaps the most important source of information with regard to Middle Irish), to which he appended the 'Todd Introductory Lecture on Irish Lexicography.' His second Irish publication of great philological value was Keating's 'Three Shafts of Death' (Trí Bior-gaoithe an Bhàis, Dublin, 1890), with glossary and appendices on the linguistic forms. He also wrote valuable introductions and analyses of contents for several of the MS. facsimiles issued by the Royal Irish Academy, viz. 'The Book of Leinster' (1880), 'The Book of Ballymote' (1887), and 'The Yellow Book of Lecan' (1896). With Dr. John Bernard, now bishop of Ossory, he edited for the Henry Bradshaw Society in 1898 'The Irish Liber Hymnorum' (2 vols). A 'Glossary to the Ancient Laws of Ireland' which he prepared for the 'Rolls' series, 1901, was severely criticised by Whitley Stokes [q. v. Suppl. II]. To Irish, Atkinson added a knowledge of Welsh. To Welsh grammatical study he contributed a paper 'On the use of the Subjunctive Mood in Welsh' (*Trans. Royal Irish Acad.* 1894).

Atkinson's varied energies were by no means confined to philology, he being an accomplished botanist and a fine violinist. In 1907 his health failed. He died on 10 Jan. 1908 at his residence, Clareville, Rathmines, near Dublin, and was buried at Waltonwrays cemetery, Skipton, Yorkshire.

On 28 Dec. 1863 he married, at Gateshead, Hannah Maria, fourth daughter of Thomas and Elizabeth Whitehouse Harbutt of that town. The only child, Herbert Jefcoate Atkinson, became a civil engineer.

[Obituary notices in the Times, 13 Jan. 1908; Athenæum, 18 Jan. 1908; Journal of the Royal Asiatic Society, April 1908, and Proceedings of the Royal Irish Academy, July 1908; information received from Atkinson's family, and personal reminiscences of the writer, who has also to record his obligations to Professor W. Ridgeway, of Gonville and Caius College, Cambridge, for a note on Atkinson as an authority on the Romance languages, to Mr. E. C. Quiggin, Gonville and Caius College, and to Mr. Stephen Gaselee, Magdalene College, Cambridge, for similar notes dealing respectively with his studies in Celtic and Coptic.] G. A. G-N.

ATTHILL, LOMBE (1827-1910), obstetrician and gynæcologist, born on 3 Dec. 1827 at Ardess, Magheraculmoney, co. Fermanagh, was youngest of ten surviving children of William Atthill (1774-1847). The father, of a Norfolk family, after graduating in 1795 as second wrangler and Smith's prizeman, became fellow of Gonville and Caius College, Cambridge, acted as chaplain (1798-1804) to his relative, Dr. Porter, bishop of Clogher, and was thenceforth beneficed in Ireland. Atthill's mother was Henrietta Margaret Eyre, eldest daughter of George Maunsell, dean of Leighlin. Atthill's elder brother, John Henry Grey Atthill, became chief justice of St. Lucia.

After attending the grammar school, Maidstone, Kent (1839-41), he returned to Ireland to prepare for Trinity College, Dublin. In June 1844 he was apprenticed to Maurice Collis, a surgeon to the Meath Hospital, Dublin, and in July he entered Trinity. In July 1847, while under twenty, he obtained the licence of the Royal College of Surgeons in Ireland, and in 1849 he graduated B.A. and M.B. of Dublin University, and in 1865 M.D.

In 1847 he became honorary surgeon to a charitable dispensary in Fleet Street, Dublin, where he gained much experience of typhus, small-pox, and other infective fevers, and during the following winter was assistant demonstrator in the Park Street School of Medicine. From 1848 to 1850 he was dispensary doctor of the district of Geashill in King's County. In 1850 he settled in Dublin and was made assistant physician to the Rotunda Hospital in 1851. While in the Rotunda Hospital for the usual period of three years he endeavoured, without much success, to build up a private practice. A period of pecuniary struggle followed. In 1860 he was elected fellow of the King's and Queen's College of Physicians, and from that year to 1868 was registrar of the college. In 1868 there was a turn of fortune. He joined the staff of the Adelaide Hospital and was given charge of a ward for the treatment of diseases peculiar to women, the first appointment of the kind in any Dublin hospital. Gynæcology was practically a new study, and thenceforth Atthill, by his teaching and writings, did much for its development. He was one of the first in Ireland successfully to perform the operation of ovariotomy, his first two cases being successful. In November 1875 he was elected master of the Rotunda Hospital, and thus commanded the best field in the kingdom for obstetric and gynæcological experience. In the Rotunda Hospital he gave gynæcology a place almost as important as midwifery. He re-organised the working of that institution by the introduction of Listerian principles, and practically drove puerperal sepsis from the wards (JOHNSTON, *Proc. of the Dublin Obstetrical Society*, 1875-6, p. 28; SMYLY, *Trans. of the Royal Acad. of Med. in Ireland*, 1891). From 1874 to 1876 he was president of the Dublin Obstetrical Society. He was president of the obstetric section of the Royal Academy of Medicine in Ireland in 1884-5, and again in 1895-7, and was president of the Academy 1900-3. In 1888 he was elected president of the Irish College of Physicians, and from 1889 to 1903 represented the college on the General Medical Council. In 1898 he retired from practice, in which he finally achieved great success. He died suddenly on the platform of Strood railway station near Rochester on 14 September 1910. He was buried at Mount Jerome cemetery, Dublin. He married (1) in April 1850 Elizabeth (*d.* 1870), daughter of James Dudgeon of Dublin, by whom he had one son and nine daughters; and (2) on 1 June 1872 Mary, daughter of Robert Christie of Manchester, and widow of John Duffey of Dublin, mother of Sir George Duffey, a president of the Royal College of Physicians of Ireland.

Atthill published at Dublin in 1871 'Clinical Lectures on Diseases Peculiar to Women' (7th edit. 1883; reprinted in America, 5th edit. 1882; and translated into French 1882, and Spanish 1882). Consisting of lectures to students in the Adelaide Hospital, the book embodied the results of Atthill's own experience, and was for many years regarded as the best English text-book on the subject. In 1910 he published in the 'British Medical Journal' (1910, vol. i.) 'Recollections of a Long Professional Life,' afterwards reprinted for private circulation. Posthumously in 1911 there appeared his 'Recollections of an Irish Doctor,' an interesting reminiscence of Irish life prior to the famine, and a modest description of Atthill's early struggles. Atthill contributed much to professional journals.

[Atthill's Recollections, supra; Medical Press and Circular, 21 Sept. 1910; Burke's Landed Gentry; Todd's Dublin Graduates; MS. Entrance Book, Trin. Coll., Dublin; Proc. Dublin Obstetrical Soc.; Trans. Royal Acad. of Medicine in Ireland; private sources.]

R. J. R.

AUMONIER, JAMES (1832–1911), landscape painter, born in Camberwell on 9 April 1832, was son of Henry Collingwood Aumonier, a jeweller, by his wife, Nancy Frances, daughter of George Stacy. The family was of French descent. A younger brother did excellent work as an engraver, and a nephew, Stacy Aumonier, became a landscape painter and decorative designer. James's childhood was spent at Highgate and High Barnet, and at fourteen he was placed in a business which was little to his taste. For some time he attended the evening classes, first at the Birkbeck Institution, then known as the Mechanics' Institute, and subsequently at South Kensington, where he worked with such application that he soon found employment as a designer of calicoes in a London firm.

Meanwhile he used all his spare time to practise landscape painting out of doors, working in the early morning hours in the cloisters of Westminster and in Kensington Gardens, and later in Epping Forest. He exhibited for the first time at the Royal Academy in 1871, but continued his work in the factory until after 1873, when Sir Newton Mappin purchased a picture shown by Aumonier at the Royal Academy, 'An English Cottage Home.' The title is typical of the class of subject that appealed most forcibly to Aumonier. He devoted himself almost exclusively to the painting of the peaceful English countryside, and showed a special preference for the warm golden tints of autumn and of the late afternoon. A true lover of nature, he took her facts as he found them, without imposing upon her his own ideas of pictorial fitness. Aumonier never left England until 1891, when he visited Venice and the Venetian Alps, but he always preferred to find his subjects in his own country.

He became associate of the Royal Institute of Painters in Water-colours in 1876, and was one of the original members of the Institute of Oil Painters. In 1889 he was awarded a gold medal for water-colour in Paris, and a bronze medal for oil painting at Adelaide. He also received a silver medal at the Brussels exhibition in 1897. An exhibition of his water-colour drawings was held at the Leicester Galleries in 1908, and another of his work in oils as well at the Goupil Gallery in March 1912. Among his best pictures are 'When the Tide is Out,' 'The Silver Lining of the Cloud' (both in the Royal Academy of 1895), 'In the Fen Country,' 'The Old Sussex Farmstead,' 'Sunday Evening,' and, above all, 'Sheep Washing,' now in the Chantrey bequest collection at the Tate Gallery, which also owns his 'Black Mountains.' He is represented, too, in the municipal galleries of Manchester, Birmingham, Leeds, Liverpool, Sheffield, Oldham, Adelaide, and Perth (Western Australia).

Aumonier died in London on 4 Oct. 1911, and his remains were cremated at Woking. He married in 1863 Amelia Wright, and had two sons and two daughters. A sketch portrait in oils by James Charles [q. v. Suppl. II] was executed in 1900.

[Studio, vol. xx. 1900; Morning Post, 6 Oct. 1911; private information.] P. G. K.

AUSTEN, Sir WILLIAM CHANDLER ROBERTS- (1843–1902), metallurgist. [See Roberts-Austen.]

AUSTEN LEIGH, AUGUSTUS (1840–1905), thirty-second provost of King's College, Cambridge, born at Scarlets, Berkshire, on 17 July 1840, was sixth son of J. Edward Austen (after 1836 Austen Leigh, who died vicar of Bray (Berks) in 1874) and of Emma (*d.* 1876), daughter of Charles Smith, M.P., of Suttons in Essex.

Austen Leigh entered Eton as a colleger in 1852; in 1858–9 he played cricket for the school. In 1859 he entered King's College, Cambridge, as a scholar on the foundation, gained a Browne medal for Latin ode, and a members' prize for Latin essay in 1862, graduated as fourth classic in 1863, and proceeded M.A. in 1866. He became fellow of his college in 1862, was ordained deacon by the bishop of Lincoln (visitor of the college) in 1865, and from 1865 to 1867 was curate of Henley-on-Thames. He never proceeded to priest's orders.

In 1867 he returned to King's College, where he passed the rest of his life, taking an active part in teaching and administrative work. From 1868 to 1881 he was tutor, dean in 1871–3 and again in 1882–5, and from 1877 to 1889 vice-provost. On the death of Richard Okes [q. v.] he was elected provost (9 Feb. 1889). In 1876–80 and again in 1886–90 he was a member of the council of the senate, and in 1893–5 he served the office of vice-chancellor.

Austen Leigh's work was that of an administrator, and his leading characteristics were fair-mindedness, courtesy, and unsparing industry. In the year in which he entered King's College, the old privilege of the foundation, in virtue of which Kingsmen were admitted to the degree of B.A. without passing any university examination, had been surrendered. This was only the first of a long series of reforms, which took shape in two successive bodies of statutes, ratified in 1861 and 1882 respectively. Under these the college, hitherto a close corporation of Eton collegers, was thrown open to the world. In the furthering of these reforms and in guiding their progress with justice and moderation, lay the principal achievement of Austen Leigh's life. As provost, he presided over the college with striking success during a period of its history remarkable for intellectual growth. He was an active member of the governing body of Eton College from 1889, and from 1890 did equally good service as a governor of Winchester College. Others of his interests are indicated by the fact that he was president of the Cambridge University Musical Society (from 1883), and of the university cricket club (from 1886). On 20 Jan. 1905 he died suddenly in his house at Cambridge of angina pectoris, and was buried at Grantchester. On 9 July 1889 he had married Florence Emma, eldest daughter of G. B. Austen Lefroy, but left no issue.

A portrait by the Hon. John Collier is in possession of his college.

His only published work is a 'History of King's College' (in 'Cambridge University College Histories') 1899.

[Personal knowledge; Augustus Austen Leigh: a Record of College Reform, by W. Austen Leigh, 1906.] M. R. J.

AYERST, WILLIAM (1830–1904), divine, born at Dantzig on 16 March 1830, was eldest son of William Ayerst, vicar of Egerton, Kent. Educated at King's College, London (1847–9), he became in 1849 scholar and Lyon exhibitioner of Caius College, Cambridge, graduating B.A. with a third class in the classical tripos and junior optime in 1853, and M.A. in 1856. Ordained deacon in 1853 and priest in 1854, he served the curacies successively of All Saints, Gordon Square (1853–5), St. Paul's, Lisson Grove (1855–7), and St. Giles'-in-the-Fields (1857–9). Whilst working as a curate he won the Hulsean prize at Cambridge in 1855 and the Norrisian prize in 1858. In 1859 Ayerst went out to India as rector of St. Paul's School, Calcutta. In 1861 he was appointed to a chaplaincy on the Bengal ecclesiastical establishment; served as senior chaplain with the Khyber field force from 1879 to 1881, and received the Afghan medal. Returning to London, he was appointed by the London Society for Promoting Christianity amongst the Jews principal of its missionary college and minister of the Jews' Episcopal Chapel, Cambridge Heath; but accepted in 1882 the vicarage of Hungarton with Twyford and Thorpe Satchville, Leicestershire. In 1884 he opened at Cambridge a hostel, Ayerst Hall, designed to aid men of modest means in obtaining a university degree and theological training. He resigned his living in 1886, but served as curate of Newton, Cambridgeshire, from 1888 to 1890, and continued his work at Ayerst Hall until 1897.

In 1885 the church party in Natal, which had stood by Bishop Colenso after his deposition from the see of Natal, and continued after his death an independent ecclesiastical existence, formally applied to the English archbishops through the church council of Natal for the consecration of a successor to Colenso. The request was refused. After some delay, Ayerst accepted the offer of the bishopric, and again attempts were made to obtain consecration. This, in spite of Ayerst's persistency, was definitely refused by Archbishop Benson on 21 Oct. 1891. During his later years Ayerst lived quietly in London, where he died on 6 April 1904.

Ayerst married (1) in 1859 Helen Sarah Hough Drawbridge, by whom he had ten children, of whom three sons and a daughter survived him; and (2) in 1893 Annie Young Davidson. He published 'The Influence of Christianity on the Language of Modern Europe' (1856) and 'The Pentateuch its Own Witness' (1858).

[Guardian, 13 April 1904; A. C. Benson's Life of Edward White Benson, 1899, ii. 484–511; C. F. Pascoe, Two Hundred Years of the S.P.G., 1901, p. 334; Cambridge University Calendar; private information.] A. R. B.

AYRTON, WILLIAM EDWARD (1847–1908), electrical engineer and physicist, born in London on 14 Sept. 1847, was son of an able barrister, Edward Nugent Ayrton (1815–1873), and nephew of Acton Smee Ayrton [q. v.] [see for earlier relatives EDMUND AYRTON and WILLIAM AYRTON]. Ayrton's father, a distinguished linguist, had severe ideas of education, and tried, without much success, to enforce on his son the practice of speaking different languages (including Hebrew) on each day of the week. After attending University College school from 1859 to 1864, he entered University College London in 1864–5, and in July 1865 and July 1866 took the Andrews mathematical scholarships for first and second year students respectively.

In 1867 he passed the first B.A. examination of the University of London, with second-class honours in mathematics, and entered the Indian telegraph service, being sent by government on passing the entrance examination to Glasgow to study electricity under (Sir) William Thomson, afterwards Lord Kelvin [q. v. Suppl. II]. Of his work in Kelvin's laboratory he gave a vivid account in 'The Times,' 8 Jan. 1908. After some practical study at the works of the Telegraph Construction and Maintenance Company he went out to Bombay in 1868, his appointment as assistant-superintendent of the fourth grade dating from 1 Sept. 1868. With Mr. C. L. Schwendler, electrician on special duty, he soon worked out methods of detecting faults which revolutionised the Indian overland system of telegraphs. In 1871 Ayrton was moved to Alipur; returning on short leave, he married in London, on 21 Dec. 1871, his cousin, Matilda Chaplin [see AYRTON, MATILDA CHAPLIN]. In 1872–3 he again returned to England for special investigations; and was also placed in charge of the testing for the Great Western Railway telegraph factory under (Sir) William Thomson and Fleeming Jenkin [q. v.]. In 1873 the Japanese government founded the Imperial Engineering College at Tokio, which became for a time the largest technical university in the world. Ayrton accepted the chair of physics and telegraphy, and proceeding to Japan created a laboratory for teaching applied electricity. The first of its kind, this laboratory served as a model for those which Ayrton himself organised in England later, and through them for numerous other laboratories elsewhere. During the five years in Japan Ayrton with his colleague, Professor John Perry, carried out an extraordinarily large amount of experimental work; their joint researches include the first determinations of the dielectric constant of gases and an important memoir on the significance of this constant in the definition of the electrostatic unit of quantity; memoirs on the viscosity of dielectrics, the theory of terrestrial magnetism, on electrolytic polarisation, contact electricity, telegraphic tests, the thermal conductivity of stone, a remarkably ingenious solution of the mystery of Japanese 'magic' mirrors, and a paper interesting to the philosophy of æsthetics on 'The Music of Colour and Visible Motion.' In 1878 Ayrton returned home and acted as scientific adviser to Messrs. (Josiah) Latimer Clark [q. v.] and Muirhead. In 1879 Ayrton became a professor of the City and Guilds of London Institute for the Advancement of Technical Education, an institution founded by certain City companies. He delivered the inaugural address on 1 Nov., and began the institute's work in the basement of the Middle Class Schools, Cowper Street. He and Professor Henry Edward Armstrong, F.R.S., the chemist, were at first the sole professors, and his first class consisted of an old man and a boy of fourteen. Perry soon joined the small staff and the movement spread rapidly. In 1881 the governors of the institute laid the foundation of two colleges, the Finsbury Technical College and the Central Technical (now the City and Guilds) College, South Kensington. Ayrton acted as professor of applied physics at Finsbury from 1881 till 1884, and then became first professor of physics and electrical engineering in the Central Technical College, a post which he held till his death.

Ayrton and Perry continued till about 1891 their scientific partnership; in 1881 they invented the surface-contact system for electric railways with its truly absolute block system, which in 1882 they applied together with Fleeming Jenkin to 'telpherage,' a system of overhead transport used little in England, but to a greater extent in America.

In 1882 Ayrton and Perry brought out the first electric tricycle; they next invented in rapid succession a whole series of portable electrical measuring instruments, an ammeter (so named by the inventors), an electric power meter, various forms of voltmeter, and an instrument for measuring self and mutual induction. Great use is made in these instruments of an ingeniously devised flat spiral spring which yields a relatively great rotation for a small axial elongation. The instruments have served as prototypes for the measuring instruments which have come into use in all countries, as electric power has become generally employed for domestic and commercial purposes. Ayrton and Perry also invented a clock meter and motor meter which served as models for the meters now used, and would have brought them an immense fortune, had they not abandoned their patents at too early a date. Of the instruments other than electric invented by them about this time may be mentioned transmission and absorption dynamometers, and a dispersion photometer. Apart from specific inventions of apparatus and instruments the two men carried out investigations into almost every branch of electric engineering and the branches of mechanical engineering specially useful to the electrical engineer.

In 1891 Ayrton and Perry published their last joint paper, in which, together with one of Ayrton's pupils, Dr. W. E. Sumpner, they showed that the theoretical law previously worked out for quadrant electrometers was not valid. From 1891 onwards Ayrton worked mainly in collaboration with Mr. Thomas Mather, F.R.S. (first his assistant and later his successor), with Dr. Sumpner, and with others of his pupils, past and present. Among his later researches of importance are those on accumulators, on Clark cells, on galvanometer construction, on glow lamps, on non-inductive resistances, on the three voltmeter method of determining the power supplied to a circuit (devised jointly with Dr. Sumpner), on the very ingenious 'universal shunt box' and electrostatic voltmeters, invented jointly with Mr. Mather, work on alternate-current dynamos, on ampère-balances and on transformers, an elaborate determination of the ohm in conjunction with Principal John Viriamu Jones [q. v. Suppl. II], and an investigation of the phenomena of smell, dealt with in Ayrton's presidential address to the mathematical and physical section of the British Association in 1898.

An address on 'Electricity as a Motive Power' delivered to working men at the Sheffield meeting of the British Association, 23 Aug. 1879, put forward for the first time the important suggestion that power could be distributed at once most economically and safely by means of high tension currents of relatively small quantity 'transformed down' at the distant end of the transmission system. In the lecture delivered at the Johannesburg meeting of the British Association on 29 Aug. 1905, Ayrton pointed to the fulfilment of his prophecies; and at the same time discouraged the project for utilising the Victoria Falls on the Zambesi as a generating station, on the ground that the plan proposed was inefficient and that their beauty would be spoilt to no purpose.

Research work was only one side of Ayrton's many activities; he was employed as a consulting electrical engineer by government departments and by many private firms, and took part as an expert in many important patent cases. He invariably declined to act in legal cases unless a preliminary investigation had convinced him of the soundness of the cause for which he was to appear.

Ayrton was elected fellow of the Royal Society in 1881, and was awarded a royal medal in 1901. In the Institution of Electrical Engineers (founded in 1871 as the Society of Telegraph Engineers and Electricians) Ayrton took a special interest, and the development of the institution, which he joined in 1872, was largely due to his energetic support. From 1878 to 1885 he acted as chairman of the editorial committee and as honorary editor of the 'Journal.' In 1892 he was elected president and from 1897 to 1902 acted as honorary treasurer of the institution. He was president of the Physical Society from 1890 to 1892.

For the admiralty Ayrton carried out important investigations on the heating of cables used in the wiring of warships, on searchlights (in conjunction with his second wife), on sparking pressures, and other matters, and he was a member of the committee appointed in 1901 to consider and report upon 'the electrical equipment of His Majesty's ships.' He served on the committee appointed in 1889 to advise the board of trade on electrical standards, of which the report led to the formation of the present board of trade testing laboratory; and he also served on the general board of the national physical laboratory and on juries of several international exhibitions, including that of Chicago in 1893 and of Paris in 1900. He acted in 1903 as a member of the educational commission organised by Mr. Alfred Mosely, C.M.G., to visit the United States and report on American education.

Above all Ayrton threw himself heart and soul into his teaching. The laboratories, which he created at Finsbury and South Kensington, turned out hundreds of electrical engineers, and by his stirring addresses on technical education, he played an important part in the technical development of the country. His public lectures were elaborately prepared, abounded in striking illustration, and were delivered with the skill and fire of an accomplished advocate. In the laboratory he taught each student to carry out every experiment 'as if he were the first who had ever investigated the matter,' and criticised the work that came to his notice in the most minute detail, and on any indication of want of energy or thoroughness he was mercilessly severe.

He treated himself with the same severity; for years together he took no rest from work, and towards 1901 he developed weakness of the arterial system, from which he ultimately died on 8 Nov. 1908, at his house, 41 Norfolk Square, Hyde Park. He was buried at the Brompton cemetery without religious rites, but with a choral service of sacred music. His son-in-law, Mr. Israel Zangwill, and Professor Perry delivered addresses over the grave.

By his first marriage Ayrton had one daughter, Edith Chaplin Ayrton, who married the writer, Israel Zangwill, and is herself the author of several novels. On 6 May 1885 he married Miss Sarah (Hertha) Marks, a distinguished Girton student, who was in 1906 awarded the Hughes medal of the Royal Society for her researches on the electric arc and on sand ripples; by his second marriage he had one daughter, Barbara Bodichon, now married to Mr. Gerald Gould.

The list of Ayrton's papers, 151 in all, includes eleven published before 1876, independently; seventy published between 1876 and 1891 with Prof. Perry (of which two were in collaboration with other workers); and twelve in collaboration with Professor Mather. Ayrton published in 1887 a work on 'Practical Electricity,' which went through eleven editions in his lifetime and has since been reissued as a joint work with Professor Mather.

It is as a pioneer in electrical engineering and a great teacher and organiser of technical education that Ayrton will be remembered. He was a man of restless energy and of the most varied capacities, scientific, dramatic, and musical, and alive to problems of philosophy and religion to which he refrained from devoting his time only because he saw no possibility of immediate solutions. Like other members of his family he was an active and generous supporter of women's rights.

Ayrton was somewhat above the medium height, fair, with brown hair and blue eyes. A medallion in plaster by Miss Margaret Giles (Mrs. Bernard Jenkin) is in the possession of Mrs. Ayrton.

[A short account of the Families of Chaplin and Skinner and connected Families, privately printed, 1902, for Nugent Chaplin; Univ. Coll. School Register for 1831–1891; Univ. Coll. London, Calendars for 1865–6, pp. 55, 118; *ib.* for 1866–7, pp. 67, 116; *ib.* for 1867–8, pp. 109, 130; University of London Calendar; Government of India Telegraph Department, Classified Lists . . . and Distribution Returns for years ending 31 March 1869 (pp. 3, 50) and 1870–1873; article by P. J. Hartog in Cassier's Magazine, xxii. 541 (1902); obituary notice in The Central (Journal of the City and Guilds of London Central Technical College), vol. vii. (1910) (with portrait from photograph) by Maurice Solomon and Professor Thomas Mather, F.R.S., with a bibliography containing a 'fairly complete' list of papers, by F. E. Meade, as well as in Nature, 19 Nov. 1908, and in Proc. Roy. Soc. 85 A, p.i., by Professor John Perry; information from Mrs. Ayrton and personal knowledge.]

P. J. H.

B

BACON, JOHN MACKENZIE (1846–1904), scientific lecturer and aeronaut, born at Lambourn Woodlands, Berkshire, on 19 June 1846, was fourth son of John Bacon, vicar of Lambourn Woodlands, a friend and neighbour of Charles Kingsley and Tom Hughes, by his wife Mary Lousada, of Spanish ancestry. His great-grandfather was John Bacon, R.A. [q. v.], and his grandfather John Bacon (1777–1859), sculptor [q.v.]. After education at home and at a coaching establishment at Old Charlton, with a view to the army, he matriculated from Trinity College, Cambridge, in October 1865, gaining a foundation scholarship in 1869. Eye trouble compelled an 'ægrotat' degree in the mathematical tripos of 1869. His intimate friends at Cambridge included William Kingdon Clifford [q. v.], Francis Maitland Balfour [q. v.], and Edward Henry Palmer, the orientalist [q. v.].

From 1869 to 1875 he worked with a brother at Cambridge as a pass 'coach.' Taking holy orders in 1870, he was unpaid curate of Harston, Cambridge, until 1875, when he settled at Coldash, Berkshire. There he assisted in parochial work, was a poor law guardian, initiated cottage shows, and encouraged hand-bell ringing and agriculture. He acted as curate of Shaw, four miles from Coldash, from 1882 until 1889, when his 'The Curse of Conventionalism: a Remonstrance by a Priest of the Church of England,' boldly challenged the conventional clerical attitude to scientific questions, and brought on him the censure of the orthodox. Thereupon he abandoned clerical work, and devoted himself to scientific study.

Astronomy and aeronautics had interested him from boyhood, and much of his life was devoted to stimulating public interest in these subjects. On 10 Feb. 1888 he became a fellow of the Royal Astronomical Society, before which he read in 1898 a paper on 'Actinic qualities of light as affected by different conditions of atmosphere.' With the British Astronomical Association, which he joined in 1895, subsequently becoming a member of council and of the eclipse committees, he witnessed at Vadsö, in Norwegian Lapland, the total eclipse of the sun (9 Aug. 1896). In Dec. 1897 he led a party to Buxar in India for the solar eclipse of January 1898, and took the first animated photographs of the eclipse, but the films mysteriously disappeared on the voyage home. Of this eclipse Bacon gave an account in the 'Journal' of the association (viii. 264). Bacon, as special correspondent to 'The Times,' observed the solar eclipse of 28 May 1900 at Wadesborough, North Carolina, and made further experiments with the cinematograph.

From kite-flying Bacon early turned to ballooning and to the acoustic and meteorological researches for which it gave opportunity. His first balloon ascent was made from the Crystal Palace on 20 Aug. 1888 with Captain Dale. Experiments in 1899 proved that sound travelled through the air less rapidly upwards than downwards. In August of that year he successfully experimented from his balloon with wireless telegraphy. On 15 Nov. 1899 he and his daughter narrowly escaped a fatal accident when descending at Neath, South Wales, after a balloon journey of ten hours to examine the Leonid meteors (for account see *Journal Brit. Astr. Assoc.* x. 48). In November 1902 Bacon crossed the Irish Channel in a balloon, a feat accomplished only once before—in 1817. On the voyage he proved the theory that the sea bottom was visible and could be photographed from a great height. Bacon photographed from his balloon, at a height of 600 feet, the beds of sand and rock ten fathoms deep in the bottom of the Irish Channel. Bacon's photographs were exhibited at the Royal Society's soirée at Burlington House in the spring of 1903. With Mr. J. Nevil Maskelyne Bacon began experiments in the inflation of balloons with hot air by the vaporisation of petroleum, in place of coal gas, thereby greatly quickening the process and the better adapting balloons to military uses. Bacon also prosecuted inquiries into the causes and cure of London fog, insisting on the need of stronger currents of air through the streets, by widening thoroughfares and increasing the number of open spaces.

Bacon's investigations exhausted his slender resources, and from the winter of 1898 he was active and successful as a popular lecturer on his work and experiences and as a popular scientific writer in the press. On 15 Feb. 1899 and 22 Jan. 1902 he read before the Society of Arts papers on 'The Balloon as an Instrument of Scientific Research' (cf. *Journal Soc. of Arts*, 17 Feb. 1899), and 'Scientific Observations at High Altitudes' (*ib.* 24 Jan. 1902). In a paper at the Cambridge meeting of the British Association on 'Upper Air Currents and their Relation to the Far Travel of Sound' (1904) he summarised his more recent acoustic experiments in balloons. He died of pleurisy at Coldash on 26 Dec. 1904, and was buried in Swallowfield churchyard, near Reading.

Bacon married twice: (1) on 11 April 1871 Gertrude (*d.* 19 Jan. 1894), youngest daughter of Charles John Myers, fellow of Trinity College, Cambridge, and vicar of Flintham, Nottingham, and had issue two sons and one daughter, Gertrude; (2) on 7 Oct. 1903 Stella, youngest daughter of Captain T. B. H. Valintine of Goodwood, by whom he had one daughter. His elder daughter, Gertrude, who was his biographer, often accompanied him in his ascents and eclipse expeditions (see her accounts in *Journal Brit. Astron. Assoc.* x. 18, 288; xi. 149) and wrote on ballooning.

Bacon's separately published works were: 1. 'By Land and Sky,' 1900, a lucid account of the fascination of ballooning. 2. 'The Dominion of the Air,' 1902, a popular history of aeronautics.

[The Record of an Aeronaut, being the life of John M. Bacon, by Gertrude Bacon (with photogravure portrait), 1907; The Times, 27 and 28 Dec. 1904; Journal Brit. Astron. Assoc. 19 Jan. 1905; Roy. Astron. Soc.'s Monthly Notices, Feb. 1905; E. W. Maunder, The Indian Eclipse, 1898 (1899), and The Total Solar Eclipse, 1900 (1901).] W. B. O.

BADCOCK, Sir ALEXANDER ROBERT (1844–1907), general, Indian staff corps, born at Wheatleigh, Taunton, on 11 Jan. 1844, was third son of Henry Badcock, J.P., of Wheatleigh, by Georgina Jeffries. His father's family had long been connected with a bank in Taunton, now a branch of Parr's bank. Educated at Elstree and at Harrow School, he passed to Addiscombe, and obtaining his first commission as ensign on 1 Oct. 1861, was promoted lieutenant on 1 Oct. 1862 and captain on 1 Oct. 1873, brevet-colonel on 2 March 1885, major-general on 1 April 1897, lieutenant-general on 3 April 1900.

After a brief period of regimental duty with the 38th foot and then with the 29th Bengal native infantry, he entered in 1864 the commissariat department, in which he remained till 1895, achieving a remarkable success and rising to the highest post of commissary general-in-chief, December 1890. In his three earliest campaigns, Bhootan (1864–5), the Black Mountain expedition (1868), and Perak (1875–6) he attracted notice for his foresight and power of organisation, winning the thanks of government. His next service was rendered as principal commissariat officer under Sir Frederick (afterwards Earl) Roberts in the Kuram field force (1878–9), taking part in the forcing of the Peiwar Kotal and other actions. Returning from furlough when operations were resumed, he joined the Kabul field force, and owing to his admirable preparations Lord Roberts found in Sherpur when it was invested 'supplies for men stored for nearly four months and for animals for six weeks.' Badcock also assisted in recovering the guns abandoned near Bhagwana, and finally when the Kabul-Kandahar field force, consisting of 9986 men and eighteen guns with 8000 followers and 2300 horses and mules, started on 9 Aug. 1880 he relieved Roberts's 'greatest anxiety,' and the force reached Kandahar, 313 miles from Kabul, on 31 Aug., with a safe margin of supplies. For these services he received the medal and three clasps, the bronze star, brevets of major and lieutenant-colonel, and the C.B. Roberts reported to government that he knew of 'no officer so well qualified as Major Badcock to be placed at the head of the commissariat in the field.' In 1885 he collected transport for the Sudan, and in 1895 received the C.S.I. and the thanks of government for his services in connection with the Chitral relief force. He was appointed quartermaster-general in India on 7 Nov. 1895. Besides these appointments he acted as secretary in the military department 1890–1 and was president of a committee to consider the grant of compensation for dearness of provisions, October 1894. On his retirement at the expiration of his term of office as quartermaster-general in 1900, he took an active part in the organisation of the imperial yeomanry, and was appointed member of the council of India, receiving on 26 June 1902 the K.C.B. He died in London on 23 March 1907, while still holding that office, and was buried at Taunton.

He married in 1865 Theophila Lowther, daughter of John Shore Dumergue, I.C.S., judge of Aligarh, by whom he had four sons and a daughter. All his sons entered the army. Sir Alexander appears in the picture of officers who took part in the Kabul-Kandahar march published by Major Whitelock of Birmingham in 1911.

[The Times, 25 March 1907; Walford's County Families; Hart's and Official Army Lists; Roberts's Forty-one Years in India, 1898; H. B. Hanna's Second Afghan War, 3 vols. 1899–1910.]

BADDELEY, MOUNTFORD JOHN BYRDE (1843–1906), compiler of guide-books, born at Uttoxeter on 6 March 1843, was the second son of three children of Whieldon Baddeley, solicitor, of Rocester, Staffordshire, by his wife Frances Blurton Webb. His elder brother, Richard Whieldon Baddeley (1840–76), was the author of several novels and a volume of poems 'The Golden Lute' (1876), which was published posthumously. After education at King Edward's grammar school, Birmingham, Baddeley obtained a classical scholarship at Clare College, Cambridge, and matriculating in October 1864, graduated B.A. with a second class in the classical tripos in 1868. In 1869 he was appointed assistant master, and subsequently house master, at Somersetshire College, Bath. From 1880 to 1884 he was assistant master at Sheffield grammar school. Retiring from school work, Baddeley then settled at The Hollies, Windermere, and later removed to Lake View Villas, Bowness. Intimately acquainted with the Lake district and keenly interested in local affairs, he was chairman of the Bowness local board until its dissolution in 1894, and identified himself with movements for preserving footpaths and for popularising the Lake district as a pleasure resort. On his initiative sign posts were placed by the Lakes District Association on mountain paths, and a flying squadron of young members was organised to report periodically on the condition of the passes. The new road from Skelwith bridge to Langdale, and the drive along the west side of Thirlmere, which was completed by the Manchester corporation in 1894, were largely due to Baddeley's active intervention. He was opposed to the multiplication of railways or of local industries.

From 1884 to 1906 Baddeley, who was an untiring walker through most parts of England and a close observer of nature, mainly occupied himself with preparing the 'Thorough Guide' series of guide-books for Great Britain and Ireland. The series opened with the 'English Lake District' (1880; 11th ed. 1909). In 'South Wales' (1886; 4th ed. 1908), 'North Wales,' 2 parts (1895; 8th ed. 1909), and 'South Devon and South Cornwall' (1902; 3rd ed. 1908) he collaborated with the Rev. C. S. Ward. Remaining volumes include: 'Glasgow' (1888; 3rd ed. 1900); 'Yorkshire,' 2 parts (1893; 5th ed. 1909); 'Scotland,' 3 parts (1894): part i. 'The Highlands' (11th ed. 1908); part ii. 'The Northern Highlands' (7th ed. 1906); part iii. 'The Lowlands' (5th ed. 1908); 'The Isle of Man' (1896; 2nd ed. 1898); 'Ireland,' part i. (1897; 6th ed. 1909); 'The Peak District' (1899; 9th ed. 1908); 'Orkney and Shetland' (1900; 6th ed. 1908); 'Liverpool' (1900); 'Bath, Bristol and forty miles around' (1902; 2nd ed. 1908). Baddeley's guides were accurate, concise and practical. He had the gift not only of describing natural scenery but of forming a comparative estimate of its beauty. He paid special attention to the needs of the pedestrian. Though an enthusiastic mountaineer he deprecated hazardous adventure.

Baddeley died on 19 Nov. 1906, at his house at Bowness, of pneumonia, which he contracted on a visit to Selby while revising one of his Yorkshire volumes; he was buried at Bowness. In 1891 he married Millicent Satterthwaite, daughter of Robert Henry Machell Michaelson-Yeates of Olive Mount, Windermere, who survived him without issue. In 1907 a clock tower was erected at Bowness in his memory by public subscription from friends and admirers in all parts of the British Isles.

[The Lakes Chronicle, 28 Nov. 1906; Sheffield Daily Telegraph, 24 Nov. 1906; Brit. Mus. Cat.; Concerning Guide Books, by Claude E. Benson, art. in Cornhill Mag., September 1910; private information.]

G. S. W.

BAILEY, PHILIP JAMES (1816–1902), author of 'Festus,' only son of Thomas Bailey of Nottingham [q. v.], by his first wife, Mary Taylor, was born on 22 April 1816, at Nottingham, in a house, now demolished, on the Middle Pavement facing the town hall. He showed an early interest in his father's poetical tastes, which his father stimulated by taking him to see Byron's lying-in-state at the Old Blackamoor's Head in Nottingham High Street, and by encouraging him to learn by heart the whole of 'Childe Harold.' Educated in Nottingham, he was tutored in classics by Benjamin Carpenter, a unitarian minister. In his sixteenth year he matriculated at Glasgow University with a view to the presbyterian ministry; but quickly renouncing this ambition, he began in 1833 to study law in a solicitor's office in London. On 26 April 1834 he was entered a member of Lincoln's Inn, and was called to the bar on 7 May 1840, but never practised. Meanwhile his interest in legal studies had been interrupted by the reading of Goethe's 'Faust.' The German poem took possession of his whole mind and energy, but it failed to satisfy his moral ideals, especially in its treatment of the problem of evil. He felt under compulsion to produce his own version of the legend, and retired for that purpose in 1836 to the seclusion of his father's house at Old Basford, near Nottingham, where in three years' time the original version of his poem 'Festus' was written. It was printed in Manchester by W. H. Jones, and published without the author's name in London by William Pickering in 1839.

On the whole the reception of 'Festus' was enthusiastic. If the 'Athenæum' (21 Dec. 1839) pronounced the idea of the poem to be 'a mere plagiarism from the "Faust" of Goethe, with all its impiety and scarcely any of its poetry,' Bulwer Lytton, James Montgomery, Ebenezer Elliott, J. W. Marston, R. H. Horne, and Mary Howitt joined with other leading reviews in a chorus of praise (see press notices in 2nd edit.). Tennyson wrote to FitzGerald in 1846 that he had just bought the poem, and advised his friend: 'order it and read: you will most likely find it a great bore, but there are really very grand things in "Festus."' The Pre-Raphaelites discussed the work with much admiration, although Patmore complained that Bailey was 'painting on clouds' (*Pre-Raphaelite Diaries*, ed. W. M. Rossetti, 229, 262, 265).

In the second edition of 1845 Bailey made large additions, and processes of addition and recasting went on in later editions until, in the eleventh or jubilee edition of 1889, the work reached more than 40,000 lines. In that volume was incorporated the greater part of three volumes of poetry, which Bailey had meanwhile published separately. These were 'The Angel World, and other Poems' (1850), which attracted the attention of the Pre-Raphaelites, and was eagerly noted by W. M. Rossetti for review in 'The Germ'; 'The Mystic, and other Poems' (1855); and 'The Universal Hymn' (1867). Although the popularity of 'Festus' fluctuated, it was alive at the end of the nineteenth century. The 'Festus Birthday Book' appeared in 1882, and the 'Beauties of Festus' in 1884. A 'Festus Treasury' was edited by Albert Broadbent in 1901. In the United States thirty unauthorised editions of 'Festus' appeared before 1889.

Bailey's poetic power was never so fresh and concentrated as in the first edition of 'Festus.' His later additions turned the poem into a theological and metaphysical treatise, for which some critics claimed high philosophical merits, but beneath which the poetry was smothered. In 1876 W. M. Rossetti spoke of 'Festus' as 'but little read,' but by way of remonstrance Mr. Theodore Watts claimed that the poem contained 'lovely oases of poetry,' among 'wide tracts of ratiocinative writing' (*Athenæum*, 1 April 1876). Bailey prefixed to the jubilee edition an elaborate account of the aims of the poem in its final form and of the general principles of its arrangement. He was often regarded as the father of the 'spasmodic' school of poetry, and satirised as such along with Alexander Smith [q. v.] and Sydney Dobell [q. v.] by W. E. Aytoun [q. v.] in 'Firmilian' (1854); but in his last year he denied the imputation in a long letter in which he restated, with a self-satisfied seriousness, the intention of his work. He there claimed Browning as well as Tennyson among his admirers (see ROBERTSON NICOLL and T. J. WISE, *Lit. Anecdotes Nineteenth Century*, ii. 413–8).

Bailey wrote a play on the subject of Aurungzebe, which Talfourd admired. Talfourd introduced the author to Macready, but the play was not produced and was finally destroyed by Bailey in a fit of despondency. Besides the volumes afterwards incorporated in 'Festus,' he published in 1858 'The Age,' a colloquial satire; in 1861 a prose essay, 'The International Policy of the Great Powers'; in 1878 'Nottingham Castle, an Ode'; and in 1883 (undated, published at Ilfracombe) 'Causa Britannica, a Poem in Latin Hexameters with English Paraphrase.'

In 1856 Bailey received a civil list pension of 100*l.* in recognition of his literary work. In 1864 he settled in Jersey, whence he paid frequent visits to the continent. He witnessed the eruption of Vesuvius in 1872, impairing his health by exposure to heat. In 1876 he returned to England, settling first at Lee near Ilfracombe, and in 1885 at Blackheath. Finally he retired to a house in the Ropewalk of his native Nottingham, where he died after an attack of influenza on 6 September 1902. He was buried in Nottingham cemetery. He married twice. His first marriage was unhappy, and he was compelled to divorce his wife, by whom he had a son and daughter. His second wife was Anne Sophia, daughter of Alderman George Carey of Nottingham, whom he married in 1863. She devotedly watched over his later years, but died before him in 1896. In 1901 Glasgow University conferred upon him an hon. LL.D. degree in his absence. A bronze bust of Bailey executed by Albert Toft in 1901 is in the Nottingham Art Gallery. A marble bust by John Alexander MacBride, exhibited at the Royal Academy in 1848, is in the Scottish National Portrait Gallery, Edinburgh. A plaster cast of it, dated 1846, is in the Nottingham Art Gallery.

[Recollections of Philip James Bailey, by James Ward, Nottingham, 1905 (with portrait); Men and Women of the Time, 1899; Miles's Poets and Poetry of the Nineteenth Century, iv. 517 seq.; The Times, Daily Chronicle, and Daily News, 8 Sept. 1902; Athenæum, 13 Sept. 1902; Notes and Queries, 9th ser. x. 242, 1902. See also Eclectic Review, vi. 654; Academy, 1901, p. 447; 1902, pp. 248, 250; Sunday Mag., Jan. 1898; Session of Poets, by Caliban [i.e. Robert Buchanan]; Spectator, 18 Sept. 1866; and Fortnightly Rev., Nov. 1902 (art. by Mr. Edmund Gosse, giving careful account of the gradual growth of Bailey's Festus, with an excellent estimate of his worth and significance as a poet).]

R. B.

BAIN, ALEXANDER (1818–1903), psychologist, logician, and writer on education, born on 11 June 1818 in Aberdeen, was one of the eight children of George Bain, a man of energy and a strict Calvinist. Son of a small farmer, the father served as a soldier, and finally settled in Aberdeen as a weaver. Alexander's mother, Margaret Paul, active and industrious, but delicate in health, died young. Bain himself preserved his health by a carefully planned system of simple living. At eleven he left school to work for his living. Although occupied in weaving, he found time to study mathematics by himself, and at sixteen he attended first of all an evening school and afterwards a mutual instruction class connected with the Mechanics' Institution. John Murray, a minister in Aberdeen, helped him in acquiring Latin, and introduced him to Professor John Cruikshank, who assisted him greatly in his studies. After spending three months at the grammar school, Bain obtained a bursary at Marischal College at the age of eighteen; in 1840 he graduated at the head of the honours list, and in the same year he began to contribute to the 'Westminster Review,' while he also attended classes in chemistry and anatomy. In 1841 he became assistant to the professor of moral philosophy, Dr. Glennie, and in 1842 he visited London and made the acquaintance of John Stuart Mill, George Grote, George Henry Lewes, Edwin Chadwick, Thomas Carlyle, and other men of note. At Mill's request Bain revised the manuscript of his 'Logic' and later on he reviewed it in the 'Westminster Review'; he was likewise led by Mill to make a special study of the philosophy of George Combe [q. v.], and in 1861 he wrote 'The Study of Character, including an Estimate of Phrenology.' In 1844 Bain lost his post of assistant to Dr. Glennie owing to his having made some innovation in the teaching, but he was asked temporarily to take the place of the professor of natural philosophy, William Knight (1786–1844) [q. v.], though doubts of his religious orthodoxy prevented his becoming his successor. A like disappointment was experienced in regard to the logic chair at St. Andrews University, for which he was a candidate, and several further applications for vacant chairs proved futile, largely from the same cause. In 1845–6 Bain lectured in Glasgow in connection with the Andersonian University, and continued to write for magazines, besides publishing educational works on science for Messrs. Chambers. Through Edwin Chadwick's influence he came to London in 1848 to fill the post of assistant secretary to the metropolitan sanitary commission, and he was occupied in public health work in London until 1850. Subsequently he lectured at the Bedford College for Women while carrying on his literary labours. In 1852 he edited Paley's 'Moral Philosophy.' On his first marriage in 1855 he resigned his appointment at Bedford College and resided at Richmond for five years. During this period he held examinerships for the University of London and Indian civil service and occupied himself with writing; in 1855 he published 'The Senses and the Intellect' (4th edit. 1894), and in 1859 'The Emotions and the Will' (4th edit. 1899).

Bain was again defeated in his application for the logic chair at St. Andrews in 1860, but despite much opposition from the orthodox party, he was in the same year appointed by the crown to the newly created professorship of logic and English in the United University of Aberdeen on the recommendation of Sir George Cornewall Lewis, then home secretary. Bain set himself to improve the teaching of logic and English in Aberdeen University. For his English class he wrote an English grammar in 1863, which was followed three years later by a manual on 'English Composition and Rhetoric' (new edit. 1887) and then by 'English Extracts.' In 1872 and 1874 he issued two other English grammars. In 1868 he published his important work, 'Mental and Moral Science, a Compendium of Psychology and Ethics' (3rd edit. 1872), and in the following year he edited along with J. S. Mill, George Grote, and Andrew Findlater, James Mill's 'Analysis of the Phenomena of the Human Mind.' In 1870 appeared his 'Logic' and in 1872 there was published (in the 'International Scientific' series) his 'Mind and Body' (3rd edit. 1874; German trans. 1874; Spanish trans. 1881). He was accorded the degree of LL.D. by the University of Edinburgh in 1869.

Bain assisted his pupil and close friend, George Croom Robertson [q. v.] in editing 'Grote's Aristotle' (1872), and he also edited Grote's minor works in 1873. In 1876 there was issued on Bain's initiative and at his expense the first number of 'Mind,' the philosophical journal for which he frequently wrote. He appointed Croom Robertson editor, and was financially responsible for the periodical until 1891, when Croom Robertson resigned his editorship. Bain published another educational work, 'Education as a Science' also in the 'International Scientific' series, in 1879 (German trans. 1879). His health began at this time to flag, and in 1880 he resigned his chair; a year later he was elected Lord Rector of the Aberdeen University, an honour which was accorded him for two separate terms of three years each. His later works were 'James Mill: a biography' and 'John Stuart Mill: a Criticism with Personal Recollections' (1882); 'Practical Essays,' a collection of addresses and papers (1884); an edition of G. Croom Robertson's philosophical remains (1894); 'Dissertations on Leading Philosophical Topics' (1903), and finally his 'Autobiography,' published posthumously in 1904. In addition, he continued to write largely in periodicals. All through life he was keenly interested in public affairs, educational and other, and in university matters he led the progressive party. He received a civil list pension of 100*l*. on 18 June 1895. He died at Aberdeen on 18 Sept. 1903, and was buried there.

Bain was married twice: (1) in 1855 to Frances A. Wilkinson, who died in 1892; and (2) in 1893 to Barbara Forbes. He had no issue. His portrait by (Sir) George Reid was presented to him in 1883 and hangs in Marischal College. In 1892 his bust by Mr. Bain Smith was presented to the public library of Aberdeen.

Bain was an ardent promoter of education, advocating reform in methods of teaching natural science and the claims of modern languages to a larger place in the curriculum. But his chief claim to notice rests on his work as a psychologist and as an advocate of the application of 'physiology to the elucidation of mental states.' One of the first in this country to apply to psychology the results of physiological investigations, he greatly advanced and popularised the science as it is usually understood.

Bain was a conspicuous exponent of what is sometimes termed the *a posteriori* school of psychology, whose foundation was laid by Hobbes and Locke while its tenets were carried to their extreme consequences by David Hume. The so-called Scottish philosophy of Reid and Dugald Stewart (which was carried on alongside the idealistic system of the German philosophers whose origin may be traced to Descartes) represented a reaction against this school, and James Mill by way of a counter-reaction stoutly maintained that a return must be once more made to Locke. In this conviction he was supported by Bain, who developed more fully the ideas which Mill propounded. He felt that the old psychology which regarded the mind as though it were divided up into separate compartments must be discarded, and, like Mill, he argued that the laws of the human intellect necessarily correspond with the objective laws of nature from which they may be inferred.

Bain and his followers admit that there are certain notions such as extension, solidity, time, and space, which are constructed by the mind itself, the material alone being supplied to it, but they make it their work to trace the process by which the mind constructs its ideas, and believe that the laws by which it operates will be found not to be anything remote or inexplicable, but simply the actual working out of well-known principles. Thus Bain's conclusion is (1) that the phenomena of the mind which seem the more complicated are formed out of the simple and elementary; and (2) that the mental laws by means of which the formation takes place are the laws of association. Bain considers that these laws extend to everything, and he proceeds to inquire how much of the apparent variety of the mental phenomena they are capable of explaining. Then he endeavours to determine the ultimate elements that remain in the mind when everything that can be accounted for by the law or laws of association is deducted, and he proceeds by means of these elements to determine how the remainder of the mental phenomena can be built up with the aid of these same laws. It must not be forgotten, however, that in his later years he laid considerable stress on the part played by heredity in accounting for the facility with which the individual acquires knowledge.

Bain's system of philosophy has been termed materialistic because it endeavours to ascertain the material condition of our mental operations and the connection that exists between mind and body, and also to follow out the development of the higher mental states from the lower. He expounded the association psychology with which his name is connected with lucidity and in great detail, for he possessed an exceptional gift of methodical exposition. He applied natural history methods of classification to psychical phenomena in a manner which gave scientific value to his work, and a knowledge of the physical sciences unusual to a philosopher of his day, conjoined with remarkable analytic powers, enabled him to present his system with effect.

In ethics Bain was a utilitarian, and for the confirmation of his views his appeal was made frankly to experience. He claimed indeed in his psychology to have purged himself of metaphysics, of which, especially in its idealistic development, he had the greatest distrust, regarding metaphysics as having separated itself from the experimental test which he regarded as all-important.

[Autobiography, ed. W. L. Davidson, with bibliography by P. J. Anderson, 1904; Dissertations and Discussions, by John Stuart Mill, 1867; Th. Ribot, La Psychologie anglaise contemporaine, 1870; Blackwood's Mag., July 1904; Mind, April 1904, vol. xiii (new series) by W. L. Davidson; Encyclopædia Britannica, 11th edit.; and Hastings' Encyc. Religion and Ethics, ii.]

E. S. H.

BAIN, ROBERT NISBET (1854–1909), historical writer and linguist, born in London on 18 November 1854, was eldest son of David Bain, Cape and India merchant (still living in 1912), by his wife

Elizabeth, daughter of Robert Cowan of Liverpool.

After education at private schools, he was for some years a shorthand writer in the office of Messrs. Henry Kimber & Co., solicitors, of 79 Lombard Street. From boyhood Bain showed an aptitude for languages, with a preference for those of northern Europe, and although he was only out of England for four brief periods—in Denmark and Sweden in 1884, in Salies de Bearn and Pau in 1886, in Paris for a short time a few years later, and in Germany and Switzerland for some weeks in 1908 for health—he acquired, unaided, a high degree of proficiency in no less than twenty foreign tongues, including Russian, Swedish, Hungarian, Finnish, Polish and Ruthenian. In 1883 he entered the printed books department of the British Museum as a second-class assistant, easily heading the list of candidates in the examination. He became in due course a first-class assistant.

Bain did much besides his official work, where his linguistic talent proved of great service. After his visit to Denmark and Sweden in Aug.-Sept. 1884, he began writing on Scandinavian and Russian history. 'Gustavus III and his Contemporaries, 1746–92; an Overlooked Chapter of 18th Century History' (2 vols. 1894) was based on the best Swedish authorities. There soon followed four monographs on Russian history: 'The Pupils of Peter the Great' (1897), based largely on the collections of the Russian Imperial Historical Society; 'The Daughter of Peter the Great: a History of Russian Diplomacy and of the Russian Court under the Empress Elizabeth Petrovna, 1741–62' (1899), a capable survey of an obscure and difficult period; 'Peter III, Emperor of Russia: the Story of a Crisis and a Crime' (1902), in which Keith's dispatches and the Mitchell papers were utilised for the first time; and 'The First Romanovs, 1613–1725' (1905). 'The Last King of Poland and his Contemporaries,' presenting a new view of its subject, appeared in 1909.

Of equal value were two volumes in the 'Cambridge Historical' series (ed. G. W. Prothero), 'Scandinavia, 1513–1900' (1905), and 'Slavonic Europe' (1908), and a life of Charles XII (1895) for the 'Heroes of the Nations' series. He contributed to the 'Cambridge Modern History' seven chapters on the history and literature of eastern Europe (vols. iii. v. vi. and xi.); and historical and biographical articles relating to Hungary, Poland, Russia and Sweden to the 11th edition of the 'Encyclopædia Britannica.'

Bain's interests extended to literature as well as to history. In 1893 he issued a version of Andersen's 'The Little Mermaid and Other Stories,' and in 1895 a sympathetic 'Life of Hans Christian Andersen,' founded on Andersen's letters and itineraries. He was chiefly instrumental in introducing the Hungarian novelist, Maurus Jókai, to the English public, rendering into English ten of his stories, as well as a collection of 'Tales from Jókai' (1904). From the Russian he translated the Skazki of Polevoi as 'Russian Fairy Tales' (1893), as well as 'Tales' from Tolstoi (1901 and 1902) and Gorky (1902). From the Finnish he rendered Juhani Aho's 'Squire Hellmann and Other Stories' (1893). His 'Cossack Fairy Tales and Folk Tales' (1894; illustrated by E. W. Mitchell) was the first English translation from the Ruthenian. He also translated from the Danish J. L. I. Lie's 'Weird Tales from Northern Seas' (1893), and from the Hungarian Dr. Ignàcz Kunos's 'Turkish Fairy Tales and Folk Tales' (1896).

Bain, who was in early life a fairly good gymnast and light-weight boxer, injured his health by excessive hours of work. A zealous high-churchman, he was for some years a sidesman and a constant attendant at St. Alban's, Holborn. He died prematurely, at 7 Overstrand Mansions, Battersea Park, on 5 May 1909, and was buried in Brookwood cemetery. He married in 1896 his cousin, Caroline Margaret Boswell, daughter of Charles Cowan of Park Lodge, Teddington; she survived him only two months, dying on 10 July 1909.

[Private information; Mr. G. K. Fortescue and E. P. R., in St. Alban's, Holborn, Monthly, June 1909; The Times, 11 May 1909; Athenæum, 15 May, 1909; Who's Who, 1909; Brit. Mus. Cat.] G. Le G. N.

BAINES, FREDERICK EBENEZER (1832–1911), promoter of the post-office telegraph system, born on 10 Nov. 1832 and baptised at Chipping Barnet, Hertfordshire, on 19 Jan. 1834, was younger son of Edward May Baines, surgeon, of Hendon and Chipping Barnet, by Fanny, his wife.

Educated at private schools Baines early showed interest in practical applications of electricity, and helped by his uncle, Edward Cowper [q. v.], and an elder brother, G. L. Baines, mastered, when fourteen, the principles of telegraphy, constructing and manipulating telegraphic apparatus. Two years later, through the influence of Frederick Hill, an uncle by marriage, and Rowland, afterwards Sir Rowland Hill [q. v.], he obtained an appointment under the Electric Telegraph Company, in whose service he remained seven years, having charge for the first three years of a small office established by the company in 1848, within the buildings of the general post-office.

In April 1855, on the nomination of Rowland Hill, Baines was made a clerk in the general correspondence branch of the general post-office, being transferred after a few months, on account of his knowledge of railways, to the home mails branch. His leisure was devoted to schemes for telegraphic extension. He planned the laying of a cable to the Canary Islands, across the South Atlantic to Barbados, and along the chain of West India Islands; and he also proposed a cable to connect England with Australia by way of the Canary Islands, Ascension Islands, St. Helena, and the Cape of Good Hope. In a letter to 'The Times' (14 Sept. 1858) he further advocated the connection of the Atlantic and Pacific coasts by a line across Canada. His most important scheme, which he drew up in 1856, was for the government acquisition of existing telegraph systems. This proposal, with the permission of the duke of Argyll, then postmaster-general, he forwarded to the lords of the treasury. After a long interval, in 1865 Frank Ives Scudamore [q. v.], a post-office official, was instructed by Lord Stanley, then postmaster-general, to report on the advisability of post-office control of the telegraphic systems. In his report Scudamore acknowledged Baines's responsibility for the first practical suggestion. In the result, control of existing telegraph systems was transferred to the post-office on 5 Feb. 1870. Baines's knowledge of telegraphy was helpful in bringing the new public service into operation, and all the main features of his original scheme—free delivery within a mile, the creation of a legal monopoly, a uniform sixpenny rate irrespective of distance—are now in operation.

In 1875 Baines was made surveyor-general for telegraph business, and in 1878, with a view to decreasing the danger of invasion and increasing the efficiency of the coastguard service, he proposed the establishment of telegraphic communication around the sea-coast of the British Isles, to be worked by the coastguard under the control and supervision of the post-office. The proposal, renewed in 1881 and again in 1888, was adopted by the government in 1892.

In 1882 Baines was made inspector-general of mails and assistant secretary in the post-office under Sir Arthur Blackwood. He organised the parcel post service, introduced by Mr. Fawcett in 1883, extending the system subsequently to all British colonies and most European countries. Different views and systems of postal administration on the continent made his task difficult. He became C.B. in 1885 and retired through ill-health on 1 Aug. 1893.

Baines lived for the greater part of his life at Hampstead, where he took an active interest in parochial work. He assisted in the acquisition of Parliament Hill Fields for the public use, was a member of the Hampstead select vestry, and in 1890 edited 'Records of Hampstead.' He was also an enthusiastic volunteer, serving both as a non-commissioned and commissioned officer. His latter years he devoted to literature. His main work, 'Forty Years at the Post Office' (2 vols. 1895), reminiscences written in an agreeable style, contains valuable details of reforms at the post-office both before and during Baines's connection with it. He also published 'On the Track of the Mail Coach' (1896), and contributed an article on the post-office to J. Samuelson's 'The Civilisation of Our Day' (1896).

Baines died on 4 July 1911 at Hampstead, and was cremated at Golder's Green. He married in 1887 Laura, eldest daughter of Walter Baily, M.A., of Hampstead.

[The Times, 7 July 1911; Forty Years at the Post Office, 1895; Athenæum, 20 Jan. 1896, and 4 Feb. 1895; Frank Ives Scudamore, Reports on the Proposed Government Acquisition of Telegraphs, 1866 and 1868; Kelly's Handbook; St. Martin's-le-Grand, vols. iii. and xxi.]
S. E. F.

BAIRD, ANDREW WILSON (1842–1908), colonel, royal engineers, eldest son in a family of five sons and four daughters of Thomas Baird, of Woodlands, Cults, Aberdeen, and of Catherine Imray, his wife, was born at Aberdeen on 26 April 1842. Educated at the grammar school and at Marischal College, Aberdeen, Andrew entered the Military College of the East India Company at Addiscombe in June 1860, and was transferred to the Royal Military Academy at Woolwich in January 1861, owing to the amalgamation of the Indian with the royal army. He received a commission as lieutenant in the royal engineers on 18 Dec. 1861, and after instruction at Chatham sailed for India on

1 March 1864. Baird was employed as special assistant engineer of the Bombay harbour defence works, and had charge of the construction of the batteries at Oyster Rock and Middle Ground until the end of 1865. He was then appointed special assistant engineer in the government reclamations of the harbour foreshore. During 1868 he served as assistant field engineer in the Abyssinian expedition under Sir Robert Napier, afterwards Lord Napier of Magdala [q. v.]. For his work as traffic manager of the railway from the base he was mentioned in despatches (*Lond. Gaz.* 30 June 1868), and received the war medal.

In December 1869 Baird became assistant superintendent of the great trigonometrical survey of India. He was employed successively on the triangulation in Kathiawar and Gujarat. His health suffered from the extreme heat in this arid country, and he went on furlough to England in the spring of 1870. While he was at home, Colonel (afterwards General) James Thomas Walker [q. v.], the surveyor-general of India, chose him to study the practical details of tidal observations and their reduction by harmonic analysis as carried on under the supervision of Sir William Thomson, afterwards Lord Kelvin [q. v. Suppl. II], for the British Association.

Tidal observations were only undertaken by the survey of India, in the first instance, with the object of determining the mean sea level as a datum for the trigonometrical survey. But Baird, widening his aim, determined 'to investigate the relations between the levels of land and sea on the coasts of the gulf of Cutch, which were believed by geologists to be gradually changing. This necessitated a more exact determination of the mean sea level than had hitherto sufficed for the operations of the survey' (Baird, *Manual of Tidal Observations, and their Reduction by the Method of Harmonic Analysis*, 1886, pref.). It was decided to carry out observations at stations in the gulf of Cutch, in accordance with the recommendations of the tidal committee of the British Association, by self-registering gauges, set up for at least a year at a time. Having returned to India in December 1872, Baird selected three stations on the gulf of Cutch for his tidal observatories, one at the mouth, another at the head and as far into the 'Runn' as possible, and the third about the middle of the gulf. These observatories were inspected periodically by Baird and his assistant in turn, in circumstances involving severe privation.

Baird was promoted captain on 4 April 1874. In 1876 the governor-general in council commended Baird's labours, and in July 1877 instructions were issued for systematic tidal observations at all the principal Indian ports, and at other ports on the coast lines where the results would be of general scientific interest, apart from their usefulness for purpose of navigation. To Baird, who had become deputy superintendent in the great trigonometrical survey department, was entrusted the general superintendence.

Meanwhile, in 1876, Baird was at home, working out with assistance the results of his observations in the gulf of Cutch. In the autumn he read a paper on 'Tidal Operations in the Gulf of Cutch' before the British Association at Glasgow. On his return to India in June 1877 he organised a new department of the survey along the coast lines from Aden to Rangoon, with its centre at Poona, Bombay.

In July 1881 Baird was at Venice as one of the commissioners from India to the third international congress of geography, and there he exhibited a complete set of tidal and levelling apparatus in practical use in an adjoining canal. Baird was awarded the gold medal of the first class.

After some eighteen months on furlough in England, Baird, who had been promoted major on 18 Dec. 1881, resumed his tidal duties in India in March 1883, his field of operations including India, Burma, Ceylon, and the Andaman Islands. On 27 Aug. the great volcanic eruption of Krakatoa, in Java, caused a wave which was distinctly traceable in all the tidal diagrams, and Baird sent a paper on the subject to the Royal Society, of which he was elected a fellow in the following May (*Proc. Roy. Soc.* No. 229, 1884).

Between July 1885 and August 1889 Baird was temporarily employed as master of the mint at both Calcutta and Bombay, and also as both assistant and deputy surveyor-general of India. He was promoted brevet lieutenant-colonel on 18 Dec. 1888, and on 12 Aug. 1889 became permanent mint master at Calcutta. In that office he re-organised the manufacturing department. In 1895–6, in accordance with his proposals, the government withdrew from circulation worn and dirt-encrusted coinage.

Promoted regimental lieutenant-colonel on 9 April 1891, brevet colonel on 29 Sept. 1893, and substantive colonel on 9 April 1896, he retired from the mint owing to the age-limit on 20 April 1897, and received the special thanks of the governor-general for his varied services. He was created C.S.I. in June 1897. On his return home, he bought a small property at Palmers Cross, near Elgin. He died suddenly of heart failure in London, on 2 April 1908, and was buried at Highgate.

Sir George Darwin, who first made Baird's personal acquaintance at Lord Kelvin's house in 1882, wrote of Baird's tidal work on his death, 'In science he has left a permanent mark as the successful organiser of the first extensive operations in tidal observations by new methods. The treatment of tidal observations is now made by harmonic analysis in every part of the world, and this extensive international development is largely due to the ability with which he carried out the pioneer work in India.'

Baird married at Aberdeen, on 14 March 1872, Margaret Elizabeth, only daughter of Charles Davidson, of Forrester Hill, Aberdeen, and of Jane Ross. She survived him with a family of two sons and five daughters.

Besides the works cited, Baird was author of articles on the Gulf of Cutch, Little Runn, and Gulf of Cambay in the 'Bombay Gazetteer'; 'Notes on the Harmonic Analysis of Tidal Observations,' published by order of the secretary of state (1872); 'Auxiliary Tables to facilitate the Calculations of Harmonic Analysis of Tidal Observations' (1897); 'Account of the Spirit-Levelling Operations of the Great Trigonometrical Survey of India' (British Association, 1885). He was also joint author with Sir George Darwin of a report on the results of the 'Harmonic Analysis of Tidal Observations' (*Proc. Roy. Soc.* March 1885); and with Mr. Roberts of the Nautical Almanac Office of 'Annual Tidal Tables of Indian Ports.'

[War Office Records; India Office Records; The Times, 10 April 1908; Men and Women of the Time, 1899; Proc. Roy. Soc., 1908, Obit. by Prof. G. H. Darwin; Proc. Institution of Civil Engineers, vol. 172, part ii. 1908; Journal of the Asiatic Society of Bengal, vol. 47, part ii. 1878, account of the tidal observations in the Gulf of Cutch, compiled by Captain J. Waterhouse.] R. H. V.

BAKER, SIR BENJAMIN (1840–1907), civil engineer, born at Keyford, Frome, Somerset, on 31 March 1840, was son of Benjamin Baker and Sarah Hollis. His father, a native of county Carlow, became principal assistant at ironworks at Tondu, Glamorgan. After being educated at Cheltenham grammar school, Baker was for four years (1856–60) apprentice to H. H. Price, of the Neath Abbey ironworks. Coming to London in 1860, he served as assistant to W. Wilson on the construction of the Grosvenor Road railway bridge and Victoria station. In 1861 he joined the permanent staff of (Sir) John Fowler [q. v. Suppl. I], became his partner in 1875, and was associated with him until Fowler's death in 1898. As a consulting engineer he rapidly gained the highest reputation for skill and sagacity, and was consulted by the home and Egyptian governments, by the colonies, and by municipal and other corporations. The credit of the design and execution of the great constructional engineering achievements with which Baker's name is associated was necessarily shared by him with Fowler and many other colleagues, but Baker's judgment and resource were highly important factors in the success of these undertakings.

Baker early engaged on the underground communications of London. As assistant to Fowler, he was at the outset from 1861 employed on the construction of the Metropolitan (Inner Circle) railway and the St. John's Wood extension. In 1869 he became Fowler's chief assistant in the construction of the District railway from Westminster to the City. In a paper on 'The Actual Lateral Pressure of Earthwork,' for which he received in 1881 the George Stephenson medal of the Institution of Civil Engineers, he discussed some fruits of this experience (*Proc. Inst. C. E.* lxv. 140), and described the work itself in 1885 (*ib.* lxxxi. 1). Subsequently Fowler and Baker acted as consulting engineers for the first 'tube' railway (the City and South London line, opened in 1890), and with J. H. Greathead were the joint engineers for the Central London (tube) railway, opened in 1900. In the construction of this line Baker carried out the plan suggested by him five-and-twenty years earlier, of making the line dip down between the stations in order to reduce the required tractive effort (see his articles on urban railways in *Engineering*, xvii. 1 *et seq.*). After Greathead's death in 1896 Baker also acted as joint engineer with Mr. W. R. Galbraith for the Baker Street and Waterloo (tube) railway.

From the early years of his career Baker studied deeply the theory of construction and the resistance of materials. For 'Engineering' he wrote a series of articles on 'Long Span Bridges' in 1867, and another, 'On the Strength of Beams,

Columns, and Arches,' in 1868. Both series were published in book form, the first in 1867 (2nd edit. 1873) and the second in 1870. A third series, 'On the Strength of Brickwork,' was written in 1872. In the work on long span bridges he reached the conclusion that the maximum possible span would necessitate the adoption of cantilevers supporting an independent girder—the system adopted later for the Forth bridge. To his early training in the Neath Abbey ironworks he owed the foundation of his thorough knowledge of the properties and strength of metals, on which he wrote many masterly papers (cf. 'Railway Springs,' *Proc. Inst. Civ. Eng.* lxvi. 238; 'Steel for Tires and Axles,' *ibid.* lxvii. 353, and 'The Working Stress of Iron and Steel,' *Trans. Am. Soc. Mech. Eng.* viii. 157). Baker's special equipment thus enabled him to play a foremost part in association with Fowler in the designing of the Forth bridge on cantilever principles. This great work, begun in 1883, was completed in 1890, and Baker's services were rewarded by the honour of K.C.M.G. (17 April 1890) and the Prix Poncelet of the Institute of France.

From 1869 Baker was also associated with Fowler in investigating and advising upon engineering projects in Egypt. One of these was for a railway between Wady Halfa and Shendy and a ship incline at Assuan, and another (about 1875) was a project for a sweet-water canal between Alexandria and Cairo, which was intended to be used for both irrigation and navigation but was not carried out. Thenceforward Baker played a prominent part in the engineering work which has promoted the material development of the country. He was consulted by the Egyptian government on various occasions as to the repair of the Delta barrage (see Sir Hanbury Brown's paper in *Proc. Inst. Civ. Eng.* clviii. 1); and when, after several years' investigation, schemes were prepared by Sir William Willcocks (*Report on Perennial Irrigation and Flood Protection for Egypt*, Cairo, 1894) for the storage of the waters of the Nile for irrigation purposes, a commission appointed by Lord Cromer, of which Baker was a member, approved the project for a reservoir at Assuan and chose a site for the dam. To meet the objection of one of the commissioners, Mr. Boulé, to the partial submergence by this plan of the temples at Philæ, the height of the proposed dam was reduced from 85 to 65 feet. The work, for which Baker was consulting engineer, was commenced in 1898 and was completed in 1902, when Baker was made K.C.B. and received the order of the Medjidieh. The dam is 6400 feet in length, 1800 feet of it being solid and the other 4600 feet pierced by 180 sluice-openings at different levels, which can be closed by means of iron sluices working on free rollers on the Stoney principle (cf. Maurice Fitzmaurice's description in *Proc. Inst. Civ. Eng.* clii. 71). For a subsidiary dam which was built at the same time at Assyût, below Assuan, Baker was also consulting engineer. When the contractors, Messrs. Aird, had this work well in hand, with a large part of their contract time to run, Baker, realising the advantages of early completion of the dam, advised the Egyptian government to cancel the contract and to instruct the contractors to finish the work at the earliest possible moment, regardless of cost, leaving the question of contractors' profit to be settled by him. His advice was followed, the work was completed a year before the contract time, and the gain to the country from the extra year's supply of water was estimated to be 600,000*l.* (G. H. Stephens, 'The Barrage across the Nile at Assyût,' *Proc. Inst. Civ. Eng.* clviii. 26). The vast benefits conferred upon Egypt by the Assuan reservoir rendered further schemes for storage inevitable, and as no suitable site could be found for another reservoir above Assuan, it was decided to raise the dam there to about the height originally proposed by Sir William Willcocks. Baker solved the difficult problem of uniting new to old masonry so as to form a solid structure, in the conditions obtaining in the Assuan dam, by building the upper portion of the dam as an independent structure which could be united to the lower by grouting with cement when it had ceased to settle and contract. Just before his death Baker went to Egypt to settle the plans and contract for this work (since completed), as well as preliminary plans for a bridge across the Nile at Boulac.

Smaller but important works which Baker also undertook include the vessel which he designed with Mr. John Dixon in 1877 for the conveyance of Cleopatra's Needle from Egypt to England (see his 'Cleopatra's Needle,' *Min. Proc. Inst. Civ. Eng.* lxi. 233, for which, and for a paper on 'The River Nile,' he received a Telford medal from Inst. Civil Eng.); the Chignecto ship railway, for which Fowler and Baker were consulting engineers, and which was commenced in 1888 and abandoned in 1891 owing to financial difficulties;

the Avonmouth docks (in association with Sir John Wolfe Barry, 1902–8); the Rosslare and Waterford railway; the widening of the Buccleuch dock entrance at Barrow, and the construction of the bascule bridges at Walney (Barrow-in-Furness) and across the Swale near Queenborough.

Baker gave much professional advice in regard to important structures at home and abroad. When the roof of Charing Cross railway station collapsed on 5 Dec. 1905 he at once examined it, at some personal danger, and gave serviceable counsel. He was also consulted by Captain J. B. Eads in connection with the design of the St. Louis bridge across the Mississippi, and in regard to the first Hudson river tunnel. When the latter undertaking threatened failure, he designed a pneumatic shield which enabled the work to be extended 2000 ft., about three-fourths of the way across the river (1888–91). Nowhere were his abilities appreciated more highly than in Canada and the United States. He was an honorary member of both the Canadian and the American Society of Civil Engineers and of the American Society of Mechanical Engineers.

Baker served from 1888 until his death on the ordnance committee, of which he became the senior civil member on the death of Sir Frederick Bramwell [q. v. Suppl. II] in 1903. He was active in many government inquiries. He was a member of a committee on light railways in 1895, and of the committee appointed by the board of trade in 1900 to inquire into the loss of strength in steel rails. To the London county council he reported in 1891, with (Sir) Alexander Binnie, on the main drainage of London, and in 1897, with George Frederick Deacon [q. v. Suppl. II], on the water-supply of London from Wales.

Baker was elected an associate of the Institution of Civil Engineers in 1867, a member in 1877, a member of council in 1882, and president in 1895, remaining on the council till his death. His services to the institution were very valuable. During his presidency the governing body was enlarged with a view to giving the chief colonies and the principal industrial districts at home representation on the council, and the system of election of the council was modified.

Baker became a fellow of the Royal Society in 1890 and a member of its council in 1892–3, and was one of its vice-presidents from 1896 until his death.

Of the British Association, Baker was president of the mechanical science section at Aberdeen in 1885. He was also actively interested in the Royal Institution, in the Institution of Mechanical Engineers (on the council of which he sat from 1899 until death), in the (Royal) Society of Arts, and in the Iron and Steel Institute. He was an associate of the Institution of Naval Architects and an honorary associate of the Royal Institute of British Architects. Honorary degrees were conferred upon him by the Universities of Cambridge (D.Sc. 1900), Edinburgh (LL.D. 1890), and Dublin (M.Eng. 1892).

Baker died suddenly from syncope at his residence, Bowden Green, Pangbourne, on 19 May 1907, and was buried at Idbury, near Chipping Norton. He was unmarried.

His portrait in oils, by J. C. Michie, is in the possession of the Institution of Civil Engineers, and an excellent photograph forms the frontispiece of vol. clviii. of that society's 'Proceedings.'

A memorial window, designed by Mr. J. N. Comper, was unveiled by Earl Cromer on 3 Dec. 1909 in the north aisle of the nave of Westminster Abbey.

[Proc. Roy. Soc., vol. lxxxiv.; Min. Proc. Inst. Civ. Eng., clxx. 377; The Times, 20 May 1907; Engineering, lxxiii. 685, lxxviii. 791; the Engineer, ciii. 524; see art. FOWLER, Sir JOHN, Suppl. I.] W. F. S.

BAKER, SHIRLEY WALDEMAR (1835–1903), Wesleyan missionary and premier of Tonga, born at Brimscombe near Stroud, Gloucestershire, in 1835, was son of George Baker by his wife Jane Woolmer. He emigrated to Australia about 1853, where, after acquiring a knowledge of pharmacy, he studied for the Wesleyan ministry. In 1860 he was sent as a missionary to the island of Tonga in the South Pacific. In consequence of the cession of Fiji to England in 1874 the Tongans became seriously alarmed for their independence, and Baker, at the request of King George of Tonga, negotiated a treaty with Germany recognising Tonga as an independent kingdom in return for the perpetual lease of a coaling-station in Vavau. In reward for his good offices Baker received a German decoration. In 1879 the Wesleyan conference in Sydney, at the request of Sir Arthur Gordon (afterwards Lord Stanmore), British high commissioner of the Western Pacific, appointed a commission to inquire into various charges preferred against Baker by the British vice-consul in connection with his method of collecting money from the natives, and Baker was recalled to a circuit in Australia. But he did not obey the order. In January

1881 he severed his connection with the Wesleyan mission, and was immediately appointed premier by King George. Under his guidance the constitution was revised, and the little kingdom of 20,000 people was loaded with a cabinet, privy council, and two houses of Parliament. In 1885 a Wesleyan Free Church was set up by Baker in opposition to the conference in Sydney. Unfortunately Baker's government attempted to coerce members of the old church by persecution, and in January 1887 the discontent culminated in a determined attempt on Baker's life, in which his son and daughter were injured. Four natives were executed and others sentenced to imprisonment for this attempt. Secure in the confidence of the king, Baker was now all-powerful; he had taught the people to acquire many of the externals of prosperity and civilisation. But he had failed to conciliate the powerful chiefs, whose position as the king's advisers he had usurped. In 1890 they appealed against him to Sir John Thurston, the British high commissioner, who removed him from the islands for two years. When he returned in 1893 King George was dead, and his political influence was at an end. Disappointed in his hope of preferment among Wesleyan adherents, he proceeded to set up a branch of the Church of England, which gained a good many followers. He died at Haapai on 30 Nov. 1903. He was married, and had one son and four daughters.

[The present writer's Diversions of a Prime Minister, 1894, and his Savage Island, 1902, which embody personal observation of Baker's career in Tonga; Résumé of Inquiry, Tonga Mission Affairs, Auckland, 1879; Reports, by Sir Charles Mitchell, Bluebook, 1887, and by Rev. G. Brown, Sydney, 1890; The Times, 29 and 30 Dec. 1903, 2 Jan. 1904; Blackwood's Mag., Feb. 1904.]

B. H. T.

BALFOUR, GEORGE WILLIAM (1823–1903), physician, born at the Manse of Sorn, Ayrshire, on 2 June 1823, was sixth son and eighth of the thirteen children of Lewis Balfour, D.D., by his wife Henrietta Scott, third daughter of George Smith, D.D., minister of Galston, who is satirised by Burns in 'The Holy Fair.' The father was grandson, on his father's side, of James Balfour (1705–1795) [q. v.] of Pilrig, professor of moral philosophy and of public law at Edinburgh, and on his mother's side of Robert Whytt [q. v.], professor of medicine at Edinburgh. Of George William's brothers the eldest, John Balfour (*d.* 1887), surgeon to the East India Company, served throughout the second Burmese war and the Mutiny, and finally practised his profession at Leven, in Fife. Another brother, Mackintosh, who spent his life in India, became manager of the Agra bank. A sister, Margaret Isabella, married Thomas Stevenson [q. v.], the lighthouse engineer, and was mother of Robert Louis Stevenson [q. v.].

George William, after education at Colinton, to which parish his father was transferred in the boy's infancy, began the study of veterinary science with a view to settling in Australia; but soon resolving to join the medical profession, he entered the Medical School of Edinburgh. In 1845 he graduated M.D. at St. Andrews, and became L.R.C.S. Edinburgh. After acting as house surgeon to the Maternity Hospital of Edinburgh, he in 1846 proceeded to Vienna, where he studied the clinical methods of Skoda, the pathological researches of Sigmund, and the homœopathic treatment of Fleischmann. On his return from Austria, in 1846, he published papers on 'The Treatment of Pneumonia as practised by Skoda' (*Northern Journal of Medicine*, Jan. 1846, p. 55); on 'Necrosis of the Jaw induced by Phosphorus as taught by Sigmund' (*ibid.* May 1846, p. 284); and on 'The Homœopathic Treatment of Acute Diseases by Fleischmann' (*British and Foreign Medico-Chirurgical Review*, Oct. 1846, p. 567), which at once placed him in the front rank of the younger medical inquirers. Thenceforth Balfour contributed largely to medical literature.

Balfour was a general practitioner in the county of Midlothian from 1846 till 1857, when he removed to Edinburgh, and practised as a physician on becoming F.R.C.P. Edinburgh in 1861. In 1866 he was appointed physician to the Royal Hospital for Sick Children, and from 1867 he was physician to the Royal Infirmary, being appointed consulting physician in 1882, on the expiry of his term of office. At the infirmary Balfour won general recognition as a clinical teacher of the first eminence, alike in the lecture theatre, at the bedside, and through his writings. For the New Sydenham Society he translated (1861–5) the 'Hand-book of the Practice of Forensic Medicine,' by Johann Ludwig Casper. In 1865 he published 'An Introduction to the Study of Medicine'—a work which well illustrated his philosophic temper, independent judgement, and historical sense, as well as the literary grace which was a family heritage.

In 1868, following out a suggestion of his father-in-law, Dr. James Craig of Ratho, he wrote two able papers on 'The Treatment of Aneurysm by Iodide of Potassium,' and thenceforth mainly concentrated his attention on diseases of the heart. 'Clinical Lectures on Diseases of the Heart and Aorta,' which appeared in 1876, greatly enhanced his reputation, and 'The Senile Heart,' which was issued in 1894, at once took rank as a classic. With Sir William Tennant Gairdner [q. v. Suppl. II] in Glasgow, and Charles Hilton Fagge [q. v.] in London, Balfour shared the credit of making the most important contributions of his generation to the clinical study of affections of the circulation.

Balfour, who was interested in bibliography, was librarian to the College of Physicians of Edinburgh from 1873 to 1882 and from 1887 to 1899. He was president of the college 1882–4, and was a member of the University Court of St. Andrews for many years. He received the honorary degree of LL.D. at Edinburgh in 1884, and at St. Andrews in 1896. He was appointed physician in ordinary to Queen Victoria in 1900 and honorary physician to King Edward VII in 1901.

In 1899 Balfour retired from Edinburgh to Colinton, the home of his youth, where he died on 9 Aug. 1903. Of impassive demeanour, he charmed his friends by his quaint humour and culture. Although probably the best auscultator of his time, he lacked all appreciation of music. A portrait, by R. H. Campbell, hangs in the Royal College of Physicians of Edinburgh.

Balfour was thrice married: (1) in 1848 to Agnes (*d.* 1851), daughter of George Thomson, by whom he had one son, Lewis; (2) in 1854 to Margaret Bethune (*d.* 1879), eldest daughter of Dr. James Craig, of Ratho, by whom he had eight sons and three daughters; and (3) in 1881 to Henrietta, daughter of John Usher, who survived him.

[Lancet, 22 Aug. 1903; Brit. Med. Journal, 22 Aug. 1903; Edinb. Med. Journal, September 1903; Scottish Med. and Surg. Journal, September 1903; The Balfours of Pilrig, by Miss Balfour Melville of Pilrig, 1907; R. L. Stevenson, Memories and Portraits, 1887; private information.] G. A. G.

BALFOUR, JOHN BLAIR, first BARON KINROSS OF GLASCLUNE (1837–1905), lord president of the court of session in Scotland, born at Clackmannan on 11 July 1837, was second son (in a family of two sons and a daughter) of Peter Balfour (1794–1862), parish minister of that place, by his wife Jane Ramsay (*d.* 1871), daughter of Peter Blair of Perth. Educated at Edinburgh Academy, of which he was 'dux,' or head boy, he passed to the University of Edinburgh, where he had a distinguished career, but did not graduate. Passing to the Scottish bar on 26 Nov. 1861, he rose with almost unexampled rapidity to be the foremost advocate in Scotland, his only rival being Alexander Asher [q. v. Suppl. II]. He first engaged prominently in politics at the general election of April 1880, when he contested North Ayrshire, as a liberal, against Robert William Cochran-Patrick [q. v. Suppl. I], afterwards permanent under-secretary for Scotland. Balfour was defeated by fifty-five votes, but was returned unopposed on 1 Dec. 1880 for Clackmannan and Kinross when William Patrick Adam [q. v.], the sitting member, was appointed governor of Madras. Appointed immediately solicitor-general for Scotland in Gladstone's second ministry, he in 1881 succeeded John (afterwards Lord) McLaren [q. v. Suppl. II] as lord advocate. He was made honorary LL.D. of Edinburgh University in 1882, and became a privy councillor in 1883. He remained in office till the liberals went out in 1885. For nearly 150 years prior to 1885 the lord advocates were practically ministers for Scotland; but during Lord Salisbury's short-lived administration of 1885–6 the ancient office of secretary of state for Scotland, which had been abolished at the close of the rebellion of 1745–6, was revived. Balfour was thus the last of the old line of lord advocates, and though he was always stronger as a lawyer than as a politician, managed the affairs of Scotland with ability in the face of considerable difficulties caused by the crofter question and the movement in favour of 'home rule' for Scotland. In 1886 he was again lord advocate, but went out when the Gladstone government was defeated on the Irish question. In 1885–6 he was dean of the faculty of advocates, and again in 1889–92. From 1892 to 1895 he was once more lord advocate under Gladstone and Lord Rosebery, and, during that period, took a prominent part in carrying through the House of Commons the Local Government Act for Scotland (1894), by which parish councils, framed on the model of the English Act, were established. The defeat of the Rosebery government in June 1895 was the end of Balfour's official career; but at the ensuing general election he was again returned by his old constituency, and remained in parliament till 1899. In that year the lord president of the court of session, James Patrick Bannerman (afterwards Lord) Robertson [q. v. Suppl. II], became a lord of appeal, on the death of William Watson (Lord Watson) [q. v. Suppl. I], and so high was the estimation in which Balfour was held that the conservative government bestowed on him the vacant office. 'I have never in my life known an appointment which gave such universal pleasure,' Lord Rosebery said at a banquet given by the Scottish Liberal Club in honour of Balfour's appointment. In 1902 Balfour was raised to the peerage as Baron Kinross of Glasclune. His health, which had begun to fail before he left the bar, broke down rapidly after he became a judge. On 22 Jan. 1905 he died at Rothsay Terrace, Edinburgh, and was buried in the Dean cemetery there.

Balfour married twice: (1) in 1869, Lilias, daughter of the Hon. Lord Mackenzie (Scottish judge) by whom he had one son, Patrick Balfour, second Baron Kinross (*b.* 23 April 1870); (2) in 1877, Marianne Elizabeth, daughter of the first Baron Moncreiff [q. v.], by whom he had four sons and one daughter.

There are two portraits of Balfour: one, painted by John Callcott Horsley, R.A., was presented to him by his supporters in Ayrshire; the other, by Sir George Reid, president of the Royal Scottish Academy, was presented to him by the counties of Clackmannan and Kinross on the occasion of his becoming lord president. Both paintings are in the possession of his widow. A cartoon portrait by 'Spy' appeared in 'Vanity Fair' 1887.

[Scotsman, 23 Jan. 1905; The Times, 23 Jan. 1905; Roll of Faculty of Advocates; Records of Juridical Society 1859–63; History of Speculative Society, p. 152; personal knowledge.] G. W. T. O.

BANKS, Sir JOHN THOMAS (1815?–1908), physician, was grandson of Percival Banks, surgeon in good practice in Ennis, co. Clare, who came of an English family settled in Ardee, co. Louth, in comfortable circumstances, from the middle of the seventeenth century. His father, also Percival Banks (*d.* 1848), the youngest of twenty-four children, after much foreign travel, and both naval and military service, succeeded to his father's practice at Ennis, and was later surgeon to the co. Clare Infirmary. John was the second son. His mother, Mary, was sister of Capt. Thomas Ramsay of the 89th regiment. The elder son, Percival Weldon Banks (*d.* 1850), a graduate of Trinity College, Dublin, and a barrister of Gray's Inn, took to literature in London, writing as 'Morgan Rattler' in 'Fraser's Magazine' and elsewhere.

John was born in London on 14 Oct., probably in 1815. The year is doubtful, but on entering Trinity College on 6 Feb. 1833 he gave his age as seventeen (*MS. Entrance Book*, Trinity College, Dublin). According to his insurance policy, however, he was ninety-five at the time of his death; if this be correct, he was born in 1812. After attending the grammar school of Ennis he began his medical studies in the school of the Royal College of Surgeons in Ireland as a pupil of (Sir) Henry Marsh [q. v.], professor of the practice of medicine there. Banks obtained the licence of the college in 1836.

Meanwhile he had in 1833 entered Trinity College, where in 1837 he graduated B.A. and M.B., and in 1843 proceeded M.D. In 1841 he became a licentiate, and in 1844 a fellow, of the King's and Queen's (now Royal) College of Physicians in Ireland. Professional promotion was rapid. In 1842 he was appointed lecturer in medicine in the Carmichael School of Medicine in Dublin, and in 1843 physician to the House of Industry Hospital; this position he held till his death. In 1847 and 1848 he was censor of the College of Physicians in Ireland. In 1849 he was elected king's professor of the practice of medicine in the school of physic, Trinity College, a post which carried with it duties as physician to Sir Patrick Dun's Hospital. He resigned both these appointments in 1868, but he was afterwards consulting physician to the hospital. In 1851 he became assistant physician, and in 1854 physician, to the Richmond Lunatic Asylum. Among the many Dublin charities at which Banks filled the position of consulting physician in his later years was the Royal City of Dublin Hospital.

Banks was president of the College of Physicians 1869–71. From 1880 to 1898 he was regius professor of physic in the University of Dublin, and from 1880 to his death physician in Ireland successively to Queen Victoria and to King Edward VII.

In 1861 Banks became president of the Dublin Pathological Society, and in 1882, when the Royal Academy of Medicine in Ireland was formed, Banks was chosen its first president. In 1887 the British Medical Association met in Dublin, with Banks in the office of president.

For many years Banks enjoyed a large

practice, and his professional and social position alike made him the virtual head of the medical profession of Dublin and Ireland. Papers which he wrote in his younger days gave a promise of valuable scientific work, which he failed to fulfil. But his article on 'Typhus Fever' in Quain's 'Dictionary of Medicine' (1882) was long regarded as an authority. He was recognised as an expert in mental disease, and he so effectually urged the importance of psychological study for medical students and physicians, that to his influence may be partly assigned the inclusion of mental disease in the medical curriculum. In 1868 he published (*Dublin Journal of Medical Science*, vol. xxxi.) a note on the writ 'De Lunatico Inquirendo' in the case of Dean Swift, which had fallen into his hands.

Banks was always interested in medical education. He represented from 1880 to 1898 at first the Queen's University and then the new Royal University (of both of which he was a senator) on the General Medical Council, where he pleaded for a high standard of general preliminary education. He urged the lengthening of the medical curriculum from four to five years, and he added a medal and a second prize to the medical travelling prize in the school of physic, Trinity College. Banks's culture, old-fashioned courtesy, and handsome person gave him a high place in social life, and his social engagements probably impaired his devotion to scientific research. He numbered among his friends the leading professional men of Dublin. He was a polished and convincing speaker, an admirable talker, and a writer of clear, scholarly English. In 1883 Banks declined the offer of a knighthood (cf. comment in *Punch*, 28 July 1883), but in 1889 he accepted the honour of K.C.B. He was made hon. D.Sc. of the Royal University (1882) and hon. LL.D. of Glasgow (1888). Connected by marriage and property with the co. Monaghan, he was a magistrate and deputy-lieutenant of that county, and served as high sheriff in 1891. Banks, whose eyesight failed in later life without impairing his social activity, died on 16 July 1908 at his residence, 45 Merrion Square, Dublin, and was buried in Mount Jerome cemetery, Dublin.

Banks married in 1848 Alice (*d.* 1899), youngest daughter of Captain Wood Wright of Golagh, co. Monaghan. Their only child, Mary, in 1873 married the Hon. Willoughby Burrell, son of the fourth Baron Gwydyr, and died in 1898, leaving an only surviving child, Catharine Mary Sermonda, wife of John Henniker Heaton the younger.

A portrait by Miss Sara Purser, Hon. R.H.A., painted in 1888, hangs in the Royal College of Physicians, having been presented to the college by the Dublin branch of the British Medical Association. A portrait medal was engraved by Mr. Oliver Sheppard, R.H.A., in 1906 for award to the winner of the travelling medical prize at Trinity, and a medallion from the same design is in the medical school of Trinity College.

[Irish Times, 17 July 1908; Medical Press and Circular (notice by Sir F. R. Cruise), 29 July 1908; Cameron's Hist. of Royal Coll. of Surgeons in Ireland; Todd's Cat. of Graduates in Dublin University; private sources.] R. J. R.

BANKS, Sir WILLIAM MITCHELL (1842–1904), surgeon, born at Edinburgh on 1 Nov. 1842, was son of Peter S. Banks, writer to the signet. He received his early education at the Edinburgh Academy, whence he passed to the university. After a brilliant career in medicine he graduated M.D. with honours and the gold medal for his thesis on the Wolffian bodies (1864). During his university career he acted as prosector to Professor John Goodsir [q. v.]. Whilst at the Infirmary he acted as dresser and as house surgeon to James Syme [q. v.]. After graduating he was demonstrator of anatomy for a short time to Professor Allen Thomson [q. v.] at the University of Glasgow. Afterwards he went to Paraguay, where he acted as surgeon to the Republican government. He settled at Liverpool in 1868 as assistant to Mr. E. R. Bickersteth in succession to Reginald Harrison [q. v. Suppl. II], and joined the staff of the Infirmary school of medicine, first as demonstrator and afterwards as lecturer on anatomy. This post he retained, with the title of professor, when the Infirmary school was merged in University College. He resigned the chair in 1894, when he became emeritus professor of anatomy.

Meanwhile, having served the offices of pathologist and curator of the museum, he succeeded Reginald Harrison as assistant surgeon to the Royal Infirmary at Liverpool in 1875, and was full surgeon from 1877 till November 1902, when, on being appointed consulting surgeon, the committee paid him the unique compliment of assigning him ten beds in his former wards.

Banks was admitted F.R.C.S. England on 9 Dec. 1869 without having taken the examinations for the diploma of member. He served as a member of the council from 1890 to 1896. He was the first representative of the Victoria University on the General Medical Council. In 1885 he was one of the founders of the Liverpool Biological Association and was elected the first president; in 1890 he was president of the Medical Institution. In 1892 he was made J.P. of Liverpool, and in 1899 was knighted and was made hon. LL.D. of Edinburgh.

He died suddenly at Aix-la-Chapelle on 9 Aug. 1904 whilst on his way home from Homburg, and was buried in the Smithdown Road cemetery, Liverpool.

He married in 1874 Elizabeth Rathbone, daughter of John Elliott, a merchant of Liverpool; by her he had two sons, one of whom survived him.

Mitchell Banks deserves recognition as a surgeon and as a great organiser. To his advocacy is largely due the modern operation for removal of cancer of the breast. He practised and recommended in the face of strenuous opposition an extensive operation with removal of the axillary glands when most surgeons were contented with the older method of partial removal. He made this subject the topic of his Lettsomian lectures at the Medical Society of London in 1900. As an organiser he formed one of the band who built up the fortunes of the medical school at Liverpool. Finding it a provincial school and at a very low ebb Banks and his associates raised it by dint of hard work first to the rank of a medical college and finally to that of a well-equipped medical faculty of a modern university. The plan involved the rebuilding of the infirmary, and Banks was a member of the medical deputation which, with characteristic thoroughness, visited many continental hospitals for the purpose of studying their design and equipment before the foundation stone of the Liverpool building was laid in 1887.

Mitchell Banks had a good knowledge of the history of medicine. His collection of early medical works was sold in seventy-eight lots by Messrs. Sotheby, Wilkinson & Hodge in June 1906. He was a frequent contributor to the scientific journals. 'The Gentle Doctor,' a scholarly address to the students of the Yorkshire College at Leeds in October 1892, and 'Physic and Letters,' the annual oration delivered before the Medical Society of London in May 1893, are good examples of his style and methods. These two addresses were reprinted at Liverpool in 1893.

His portrait by the Hon. John Collier was presented to him on his retirement from active duties at University College, Liverpool, by his colleagues and students.

The William Mitchell Banks lectureship in the Liverpool University was founded and endowed by his fellow-citizens in his memory in 1905.

[Lancet, 1904, ii. 566 (with portrait); Brit. Med. Journal, 1906, ii. 409; Liverpool Medico-Chirurgical Journal, Jan. 1906, p. 2; information kindly given by R. A. Bickersteth, Esq., F.R.C.S. Eng.; personal knowledge.]

D'A. P.

BANNERMAN, SIR HENRY CAMPBELL- (1836–1908), prime minister. [See CAMPBELL-BANNERMAN.]

BARDSLEY, JOHN WAREING (1835–1904), bishop of Carlisle, born at Keighley on 29 March 1835, was eldest son of James Bardsley, hon. canon of Manchester, and Sarah, daughter of John Wareing of Oldham. He had six brothers, all in holy orders. Educated at Burnley and afterwards at Manchester grammar school, he entered Trinity College, Dublin, where he graduated B.A. on 8 March 1859, proceeding M.A. in 1865, and receiving the Lambeth degree of D.D. in 1887. He was ordained deacon in 1859, becoming priest in 1860. Bardsley's sympathies were with the evangelical party, and he shared the views of the Islington Protestant Association, of which he was secretary (1861–4). He served curacies at Sale, Cheshire (1859–60), at St. Luke's, Liverpool (1860–4) and at St. John's, Bootle (1864–71). In 1871 he accepted the perpetual curacy of St. Saviour's, Liverpool, where he acquired the reputation of an industrious organiser and a fluent preacher. On the formation of the new see of Liverpool in 1880, bishop John Charles Ryle [q. v. Suppl. I] appointed Bardsley one of his chaplains and archdeacon of Warrington. In 1886 he was transferred to the archdeaconry of Liverpool. Although a party man, Bardsley was no bigot. He performed his archidiaconal visitations with tact and vigour; and in more than one instance he enforced clerical discipline by coercive measures.

In 1887 Bardsley was nominated by Lord Salisbury to the bishopric of Sodor and Man in succession to Dr. Rowley Hill [q. v.] and was consecrated in York Minster on 24 Aug. 1887. His evangelical views were in accordance with the traditions of the Manx church; and the main feature of his episcopate was the development of the Bishop Wilson Theological College. On the death of Harvey Goodwin [q. v. Suppl. I] Bardsley was translated to the see of Carlisle, and at his enthronement on 22 April

1892 he publicly declared his intention of being the bishop not of a party, but of the whole church. He was helpful and sympathetic to all his clergy, who trusted him implicitly, and by prudent administration he left little scope for extreme propaganda on either side. He was especially active in supporting the Diocesan Society and in organising in his diocese a systematised clergy sustentation fund. He died at Rose Castle, Carlisle, on 14 Sept. 1904, and was buried at Raughton Head.

In 1862 he married Elizabeth, daughter of Rev. Benjamin Powell of Bellingham Lodge, Wigan, and sister of Sir Francis Sharp Powell, first baronet. He left two sons and three daughters.

Although no profound nor exact scholar, Bardsley was a thorough and capable administrator. He travelled much in the East, especially in Palestine.

Besides sermons Bardsley published: 1. 'Counsels to Candidates for Confirmation,' 1882. 2. 'Apostolic Succession,' 1883.

[The Times, 15 and 19 Sept. 1904; Guardian, 21 Sept. 1904; Dublin University Calendar, 1860; Crockford, Clerical Directory, 1902.]

G. S. W.

BARING, THOMAS GEORGE, first Earl of Northbrook (1826–1904), statesman, born at 16 Cumberland Street, London, on 22 Jan. 1826, was eldest son of Sir Francis Thornhill Baring, first Baron Northbrook [q. v.], and great-grandson of Sir Francis Baring, first baronet [q. v.]. His mother was Jane, daughter of Sir George Grey, first baronet, and sister of Sir George Grey, second baronet [q. v.], the whig statesman, to whose character that of his nephew bore much resemblance.

Thomas George Baring was educated privately and went at the age of seventeen to Oxford, where he entered as a gentleman commoner at Christ Church in 1843, graduating B.A. in 1846 with a second class in the final classical school. Nurtured in an atmosphere of whig politics and high official position, he was early drawn to public life. On leaving Oxford he served a political apprenticeship in a variety of private secretaryships—to Henry Labouchere (afterwards Lord Taunton) [q. v.] at Dublin and the board of trade, to his uncle, Sir George Grey [q. v.] at the home office, and to Sir Charles Wood (afterwards Viscount Halifax) [q. v.] at the board of control. In 1848, the year of his marriage, his father succeeded to the family baronetcy and estates, including Stratton in Hampshire, a place destined to be his own home for forty years. In 1857 Baring entered the House of Commons as whig member for Penryn and Falmouth. The liberal party had long been in power, and Baring served the government in a succession of subordinate posts. In 1857, in Lord Palmerston's government, he became civil lord of the admiralty, and on Lord Palmerston's return to power in 1859 was under secretary in the newly constituted India office under Sir Charles Wood until 1864, with a brief interlude in 1861 as under-secretary at the war office. In 1864 he went in the same capacity to the home office under his uncle, Sir George Grey, and in April 1866 he was appointed secretary to the admiralty, going out of office with Lord Russell's administration in June of the same year. In Sept. 1866 he succeeded his father as second Lord Northbrook, and leaving the House of Commons devoted himself to the business of his estate and local affairs in Hampshire.

In 1868 Northbrook was again recalled to office as under-secretary of state for war in Gladstone's first administration, and he took a leading share, under Edward (afterwards Viscount) Cardwell, in the reform and reorganisation of the army. In this capacity it fell to his lot to pilot the regulation of the forces bill through the House of Lords and to be an interested witness of the exciting struggle which ended in the abolition of the purchase system by royal warrant.

Lord Northbrook was now marked out for high office, and in February 1872, on the assassination of Lord Mayo [q. v.], he accepted the governor-generalship of India, a country with which he had some hereditary connection, his great-grandfather, Sir Francis Baring, first baronet, having been chairman of the court of directors of the East India Company, while his own service at the India office had familiarised him with Indian problems. Lord Northbrook's term of office gained for him the reputation of one of the best and most successful of modern viceroys. He found in India a situation of considerable unrest, caused principally by the energy with which necessary reforms both in legislation and in finance and administration had been carried out since the mutiny, and notably by his predecessor, Lord Mayo. It was fortunate for India that Lord Northbrook at once realised the necessity of what he called 'steady government,' in respect of both foreign and home policy. His first acts were intended to remove the discontent which had been aroused by the increase of imperial and local taxation; and it was in the teeth of much expert opinion that he decided on the non-renewal of the income-tax, the disallowance of the Bengal municipalities bill, and the modification of certain local imposts. Finance indeed he took under his special charge, and exercised a rigid and effective control over expenditure on public works, civil and military, with the result that during his four years' administration there was a surplus of ordinary revenue over expenditure of not less than a million sterling without the imposition of new taxation, notwithstanding an expenditure of 6,306,673*l*. for famine, which had been charged against revenue.

The Bengal famine was the most noteworthy occurrence of Northbrook's viceroyalty, for not only was it the worst famine which had arisen in India for at least a hundred years, but it was the first in which the state was able, by vast but well-designed measures of relief, to save the lives of the population. These measures, taken under the direct supervision of the viceroy, who for eighteen months hardly left Calcutta, were (wrote Sir Evelyn Baring, afterwards Lord Cromer, then private secretary to Northbrook, his second cousin) 'fully successful'; and 'The Times' gave expression to the general feeling, when it stated that to Lord Northbrook belonged the high honour of commanding one of the greatest and noblest campaigns ever fought in India. As in his financial measures, so on this occasion he showed his strength of character by resisting the universal outcry for regulating prices, stopping the operations of private traders, and preventing the export of rice.

The only other incident which aroused much excitement or controversy was the deposition in 1875 of the Gaekwar of Baroda following upon the rare procedure of a commission of investigation, partly British and partly native, in connection with his alleged attempt to poison the resident, Colonel (afterwards Sir Robert) Phayre [q. v.] and the subsequent restoration of the native administration of the state in pursuance of the non-annexation policy always cordially adhered to by Lord Northbrook.

The close of Lord Northbrook's term was marked by a certain amount of friction between the government of India and Lord Salisbury [q. v. Suppl. II], who had taken the place of the duke of Argyll as secretary of state for India upon the fall of Gladstone's administration in 1874. Lord Salisbury, contrary to Northbrook's views and wishes, was inclined to exercise a more vigilant control from home than his predecessor. The increasing use of the telegraph was in fact beginning to revolutionise the relations between the two governments. On the question of Afghanistan, Lord Salisbury, influenced by the Russophobist views of Sir Bartle Frere [q. v.] and Sir Henry Rawlinson [q. v.], put forward a proposal in his despatch of 22 Jan. 1875 for placing British agents at Herat and possibly at Kandahar, for the purpose of supplying the British government with information. Lord Northbrook, who deprecated the alarmist views put forward from home, and was firmly opposed to anything like external aggression, more especially in the direction of Afghanistan, remained as usual open-minded as to this suggestion until he had satisfied himself by careful inquiries from the best qualified sources; he finally came to the conclusion that the proposed action would be impolitic except with the full consent of the Ameer, which he had reason to believe would not be given. No further steps were taken in this direction, until Lord Lytton [q. v.] succeeded Lord Northbrook as viceroy. Meanwhile another question, that connected with the tariff and the cotton duties, led to a more serious collision of opinion, in which Lord Northbrook, though a convinced freetrader in principle, stood out as a champion of Indian interests against the pressure from Lord Salisbury and the home government in favour of a remission of the duties against Lancashire goods. By this time Lord Northbrook had decided on private grounds to resign his office, and he only remained in India until the conclusion of the visit of King Edward VII, then Prince of Wales, in the winter of 1875–6, a fitting climax to his viceroyalty. He left India on 15 April 1876.

The distinguishing mark of Lord Northbrook's rule was, apart from his administrative capacity, his determination to guide himself by the wishes of the population at large so far as he could ascertain them. His genuine feeling for the natives, to whom his strict impartiality and the sympathy which underlay his reserve strongly appealed, procured him the title of 'The just Northbrook.'

An earldom was conferred on him in recognition of his work in India on 10 June 1876. On his return home, Lord Northbrook's first care, having inherited a large fortune, a house in Hamilton Place, and a great collection of pictures from his uncle, Thomas Baring (1799–1873), M.P. for Huntingdon, was to reorganise his private life both in London and at Stratton. While his own party remained in opposition, he was again able to attend to the duties and occupation of a country gentleman. Much as he deprecated party conflict on Indian questions, the development of the Afghan imbroglio under his successor, Lord Lytton, forced him by degrees to take a prominent part in the controversy; and even if it be admitted that the Lawrence policy of complete non-interference had practically broken down before Lord Northbrook left India, the disastrous results of the counter-policy as actually pursued completely vindicated Northbrook's foresight and courage in the line he took on this question.

On the accession to office of Gladstone in 1880, Lord Northbrook was appointed first lord of the admiralty. At the same time he became the principal adviser of the cabinet on Indian questions, and later on, when Sir Evelyn Baring, his cousin, was consul-general at Cairo, on Egyptian policy also. He was one of the four ministers—Lord Granville, Lord Kimberley, and Sir Charles Dilke were the other three—who were directly responsible for the despatch of General Gordon [q. v.] to the Soudan, a step which he afterwards admitted to have been a 'terrible mistake.' In Sept. 1884 he went to Cairo as a special commissioner to advise the government on the 'present situation in Egypt,' and especially on the 'present exigencies of Egyptian finance,' and in the reports brought home by him in the following November he definitely ranged himself on the side of single British control, with all which that conclusion implied. His colleagues, however, did not accept his plan of reorganisation, and though he remained a member of the government for the short remainder of its term, his relations with Gladstone became from that time markedly less cordial. He had returned from Egypt to find himself the object of serious attack on account of the agitation started in the 'Pall Mall Gazette' by Mr. Stead's articles on 'The Truth about the Navy,' which resulted in the decision of the government, in Lord Northbrook's absence, to introduce a programme of expenditure on ship-building. As a matter of fact the board, headed by Lord Northbrook and advised by Sir Cooper Key [q. v.], had, as Admiral Colomb, the biographer of the latter, wrote, taken more decided steps in reorganising the navy 'than perhaps any board which preceded it,' and technical opinion has long since vindicated Lord Northbrook from any suspicion of neglect or supineness. The fall of Gladstone's administration in June 1885 marked the close of Lord Northbrook's official career, although he refused high office in the cabinet on two subsequent occasions. In February 1886 Gladstone offered him the choice of the lord-lieutenancy of Ireland or the lord-presidentship of the council, but his Egyptian experience had decided him never again to serve under Gladstone, and though he retained an open mind on the Irish question longer than many of his old colleagues, he was already moving towards the liberal unionist position of strong hostility to the home rule solution, which he adopted on the production of Gladstone's bill in 1886. In December 1886, upon Lord Randolph Churchill's resignation, he declined a suggestion that he should join Lord Salisbury's cabinet with George Joachim (afterwards Viscount) Goschen [q. v. Suppl. II], preferring with the rest of his old colleagues to support the government from without. When the time arrived, in 1895, for a unionist coalition, it was too late for him to re-enter the political arena and take office with the leader with whom throughout his political career he was much in sympathy, the Duke of Devonshire [q. v. Suppl. II]. He retained, moreover, strong liberal sympathies, which he showed at the close of his life by withdrawing his support from the unionist party in 1903 at the commencement of the agitation in favour of tariff reform.

After the break-up of the liberal party in 1886, Lord Northbrook, living much at Stratton, found himself increasingly involved in the business of local administration. As a member of the committee of quarter sessions he took a leading part in the arrangements for the transfer of authority to the new Hampshire county council under the Local Government Act of 1888; he became chairman of the finance committee of the county council, and in 1894, on Lord Basing's death, he yielded, though with reluctance, to the unanimous wish of his colleagues that he should accept the chairmanship of the council which he held until his death. In 1889 he had been elected to the ancient office of high steward of Winchester, and in the following year he succeeded Lord Carnarvon as lord-lieutenant of Hampshire. In these various capacities, his courteous dignity, his force of character, his known impartiality, his complete mastery of detail, and his financial ability enabled him to render conspicuous service. Lord Northbrook died after a short illness at Stratton on 15 Nov. 1904, and was buried at Micheldever church.

Lord Northbrook belonged to the best type of whig statesmanship. Trained from boyhood to political life he had, like other men of position and fortune in his generation, a high ideal of citizenship and public spirit, and both as a statesman and country gentleman left an example of energy and capacity expended in the service of his fellow-men. He had a remarkable aptitude for official business and especially for finance. His judgment was sound, and though naturally quick and vivacious in temperament he was eminently fairminded and impartial, and took the utmost pains to inform himself by exhaustive study and inquiry on the merits of any political or administrative question with which he had to deal. He had little power of speaking and was shy and reserved in manner, but he had great self-reliance, wide sympathies, and much natural dignity. Travelling, sketching, fishing, and in earlier life hunting, were his favourite recreations; he was a lover of books and reading and of art and pictures, of which he was a highly competent judge.

Lord Northbrook married in September 1848 Elizabeth Harriet, daughter of Henry Charles Sturt of Crichel, who died on 3 June 1867. There were three children of the marriage, two sons, of whom the elder succeeded as second Earl of Northbrook in 1904, and the second, Arthur, was drowned when serving as a midshipman on board H.M.S. Captain in 1870, and one daughter, Lady Jane Emma, who from her thirteenth year was her father's constant companion. She accompanied him to India, where at a very early age she acted as hostess for the viceroy with tact and success, and her marriage in 1890 to Col. the Hon. Henry George Lewis, third son of John Crichton, third earl of Erne, caused little interruption to their lifelong intercourse.

The principal portraits are a water-colour drawing of Lord Northbrook as a young man, by George Richmond, R.A., at Netley Castle, Hampshire, a drawing by H. T. Wells, R.A., for Grillion's Club, a portrait in peer's robes by W. W. Ouless, R.A., at Government House, Calcutta (a copy at Stratton), and a portrait painted in 1903 by A. S. Cope, R.A., in the County Hall at Winchester (copy at Stratton). There is also at Calcutta a bronze statue of Lord Northbrook in the robes of a G.C.S.I., by Sir Edgar Boehm. Cartoon portraits are in 'Vanity Fair' 1876 and 1882.

[Memoir by the present writer with the aid of Lord Northbrook's family, and based on private papers and official documents, 1908; see also Sir Henry Cotton, Indian and Home Memories, 1911.] B. M.

BARKER, THOMAS (1838–1907), professor of mathematics, born on 9 Sept. 1838, was son of Thomas Barker, farmer, of Murcar, Balgonie, near Aberdeen, and of his wife Margaret. Three other children died in infancy. He was educated at the grammar school, Aberdeen, and at King's College in the same town, where he graduated in 1857 with great distinction in mathematics. He entered Trinity College, Cambridge, as minor scholar and subsizar in 1858, became foundation scholar in 1860, Sheepshanks astronomical exhibitioner in 1861, and came out in the mathematical tripos of 1862 as senior wrangler; he was also first Smith's prizeman. He was elected to a fellowship in the autumn of 1862, and was assistant tutor of Trinity till 1865, when he was appointed professor of pure mathematics in the Owens College, Manchester. He held this post for twenty years, during which the college advanced greatly both in resources and in public estimation. To this progress Barker's high repute as a teacher greatly contributed.

Barker's ideals as a mathematician differed much from those that were current in most colleges and universities of the country at the time. He was a follower of De Morgan and Boole; like them he was interested in the logical basis rather than in the applications of mathematics, and he endeavoured to set forth the processes of mathematical reasoning as a connected system from their foundation. His presentment of the subject was consequently not attractive to ordinary students, but on the more gifted minds which came under his influence it made a deep impression. His severely critical habit made him diffident of publication, but his success as a teacher is attested by the number of distinguished pupils on whom he exercised a great and possibly a determining influence. These include John Hopkinson, [q. v. Suppl. I], J. H. Poynting, A. Schuster, and Sir Joseph John Thomson.

After resignation of his chair in 1885 he lived in tranquil retirement, first at Whaley Bridge and afterwards at Buxton. His mathematical interests were varied by an almost passionate study of cryptogamic botany. He died unmarried at Buxton on 20 Nov. 1907, and was buried in the Manchester southern cemetery. By his will he provided for the foundation in the University of Manchester of a professorship of cryptogamic botany, and for the endowment of bursaries for poor students in mathematics and botany.

[The Times, 22 Nov. 1907, 7 Dec. (will); Manchester Guardian, 23 Nov. 1907; Manchester Univ. Mag., Dec. 1907.] H. L-B.

BARLOW, WILLIAM HAGGER (1833–1908), dean of Peterborough, born at Matlock on 5 May 1833, was younger son (of five children) of Henry Barlow, curate in charge of Dethick, near Matlock, and afterwards vicar of Pittsmoor, Sheffield, by his wife Elizabeth, only daughter of John Hagger, of Sheffield. William, sent first to the grammar school and then to the collegiate school at Sheffield, won a school exhibition and a scholarship in classics at St. John's College, Cambridge, where he matriculated in October 1853. He took honours in four triposes—a rare achievement (16th junior optime and third in second class, classical tripos, 1857; second in first class, moral sciences tripos, and second class in theological examinations, 1858). He also won the Carus Greek Testament (bachelors') prize, 1858. He proceeded M.A. 1860, and B.D. 1875. Incorporated M.A. of Oxford through Christ Church (1874), he proceeded B.D. and D.D. there in 1895.

Barlow was ordained deacon on 30 May 1858 and priest on 10 June 1859, serving the curacy of St. James, Bristol. When the new ecclesiastical district of St. Bartholomew was formed out of this poor parish and a church built in 1861, he was the first vicar (1861–73). After a brief incumbency of St. Ebbe's, Oxford (1873–5), he was appointed in 1875 by the committee of the Church Missionary Society principal of their college, in Upper Street, Islington, for the training of missionaries. Barlow quickly succeeded in improving the numbers and course of training. In 1883 he helped to collect 18,000*l.* for the enlargement of the society's headquarters in Salisbury Square.

In 1882 Barlow was appointed vicar of St. James, Clapham, and in 1887 was promoted by the trustees at the wish of the evangelical leaders to the vicarage of Islington, the 'blue ribbon' of their patronage. Barlow's tenure of this important benefice greatly strengthened his influence as an evangelical leader. He was made trustee of the Peache, the Aston, and the Sellwood Church Patronage Trusts, which governed about 200 English and Welsh benefices. The annual Islington Clerical Meeting, founded in a small way at the vicarage by Bishop Daniel Wilson [q. v.] in 1827, greatly expanded after Barlow took the management of it in 1888, and it became the rallying-point of the evangelicals. From 1887 to 1894 he was official chairman of the Islington Vestry, and when the local government act, 1894, took away the right of the vicar, the vestry continued to elect him to the chair 1895–1899, entitling him to be J.P. for London.

Barlow, who was made a prebendary in St. Paul's cathedral by Bishop Creighton in 1898, accepted in May 1901 Lord Salisbury's offer of the deanery of Peterborough. Though a convinced evangelical, he attempted no changes in the manner of service at the cathedral, contenting himself with taking the 'north-end' position at Holy Communion. He raised money for further repairs in the north transept and the clerestory of the choir.

While actively engaged in the management of the chief evangelical, missionary, and educational institutions, he was a member of Bishop Creighton's round-table conference at Fulham Palace on the Holy Communion (1900); served on the prayer-book revision committee of the lower house of Canterbury convocation which was appointed on 15 February 1907; was examining chaplain (1883–1900) to Dr. J. C. Ryle [q. v. Suppl. I], bishop of Liverpool, and select preacher both at Oxford and Cambridge. He mainly owed his wide influence to his shrewdness in counsel, his knowledge of men, and his ability to draw out opinions from others without parading his own. He died at Peterborough on 10 May 1908, and was buried beside his wife on the south side of the cathedral. A portrait in oils is at the deanery.

Barlow married on 15 Aug. 1861 Eliza Mary, eldest daughter of Edward Pote Williams, of Upton Park, Slough. She died at Peterborough on 4 Oct. 1905. They had three sons and three daughters. The eldest son, Henry Theodore Edward Barlow (1862–1906), was honorary canon of Carlisle, and rector of Lawford, Essex. The second son, Clement Anderson Montagu, LL.D., was elected unionist M.P. for South Salford in December 1910.

[Life of W. H. Barlow, by Margaret Barlow (with portraits), 1910; E. Stock, History of Church Missionary Society, 1899, vol. iii.; E. Stock, My Recollections, 1909, pp. 75–6, &c.; The Times, 11 May 1908; The Times Literary Supplement, 17 November 1910, p. 447; Record, 15 May 1908; Crockford, 1908; private information.] E. H. P.

BARLOW, WILLIAM HENRY (1812–1902), civil engineer, born at Woolwich on 10 May 1812, was younger son of Peter Barlow [q. v.] and brother of Peter William Barlow [q. v. Suppl. I]. After education at home by his father he received three years' practical training, at first in the machinery department of Woolwich dockyard, and then at the London Docks under Henry Robinson Palmer, the engineer-in-chief. At twenty he was sent by Messrs. Maudslay and Field to Constantinople, where he spent six years on the erection of machinery and buildings for the manufacture of ordnance for the Turkish government. For the Porte he also reported on the lighthouses at the mouth of the Bosporus in the Black Sea, and the work suggested a paper, which he communicated to the Royal Society, on the adaptation of different modes of illuminating lighthouses (*Phil. Trans.* 1837, p. 211). For his services in Turkey he was decorated with the order of the Nischan-el-Iftikar. On returning to England in 1838 he became assistant engineer on the construction of the Manchester and Birmingham railway, in 1842 resident engineer on the Midland Counties railway, and in 1844 resident engineer to the North Midland and the other lines which were amalgamated during that year to form the Midland railway. Of the Midland railway he became principal engineer-in-charge, and in 1857 he removed as the company's consulting engineer from Derby to London. The saddleback form of rail which bears his name was invented by him during this period (cf. his patent No. 12438 of 1849); and between 1844 and 1886 he took out, either alone or in conjunction with others, several other patents relating to permanent way. In 1862–9 Barlow, who carried out many improvements of the Midland railway, laid out and constructed the southern portion of the London and Bedford line, including St. Pancras Station with its fine roof (opened 1 Oct. 1868; cf. *Proc. Inst. Civ. Eng* xxx. 78). Meanwhile in 1860 he designed, with Sir John Hawkshaw [q. v. Suppl. I], the completion of the Clifton suspension bridge (cf. *ib.* xxvi. 243).

Concurrently with his constructional work Barlow carried on many scientific researches. In 1847 he observed certain spontaneous diurnal deflections of the needles of railway telegraph-instruments, as well as spasmodic movements corresponding with magnetic storms. These he attributed to electric currents on the earth's surface (cf. his paper in *Phil. Trans.* 1849, p. 61). Another communication to the Royal Society in 1874 (*Proc.* xxii. 277) describes the 'logograph,' an instrument which he devised for recording graphically the sound waves caused by the human voice, and which was a forerunner of the telephone and phonograph. But his chief scientific inquiries concerned the theory of structures. In 1846 he presented to the Institution of Civil Engineers (*Proc.* v. 162) a paper 'On the Existence (practically) of the Line of Equal Horizontal Thrust in Arches, and the Mode of determining it by Geometrical Construction.' Later he investigated practically the strength of beams (cf. three papers in *Phil. Trans.* 1855, p. 225; *ib.* 1857, p. 463; and *Proc. R.S.* xviii. 345). In 1859 he made experiments on continuous beams, which indicated the advantages of increasing the depth of such beams over the points of support (cf. his patent No. 908 of 1859).

Barlow was often consulted on engineering principles, as well as on large structural designs. He was a member of a committee of engineers formed in 1868 to investigate the applicability of steel to structures, and after he had urged the advantages of steel in his address to the mechanical science section of the British Association in 1873, the board of trade appointed a committee of inquiry (on which he served) which recommended (1877) the 6½ tons limit of working-stress for steel. Barlow was a member of the court of inquiry into the Tay bridge disaster (1879) which counselled a precise calculation of the stresses due to wind-pressure, and he served on the board of trade committee which defined an allowance of 56 lbs. per square foot for such pressure.

Consulted by the directors of the North British railway in regard to reconstruction of the Tay bridge, he recommended an independent viaduct, which was commenced in 1882 and opened for traffic 20 June 1887 (for a description by Barlow's son, Crawford, see *Proc. Inst. Civil Eng.* 1888, xciv. 87).

Barlow was one of three consulting engineers to whom the railway companies concerned referred the question of bridging the Forth after the collapse of the Tay bridge [cf. art. FOWLER, SIR JOHN, Suppl. I], and he submitted two designs (suspension bridges with braced chains); but the type of bridge proposed by (Sir) Benjamin Baker [q. v. Suppl. II] was adopted, with certain modifications in the piers to meet objections taken by Barlow.

Barlow attained a chief place in his

profession. Of the Institution of Civil Engineers he became a member on 1 April 1845; he was elected to the council in 1863, and was president in 1879–80 (*Address* in *Proc. Inst. Civ. Eng.* lx. 2). He received in 1849 a Telford medal for a paper 'On the Construction of the Permanent Way of Railways, &c.' (*Proc. Inst. Civ. Eng.* ix. 387). He was elected a fellow of the Royal Society on 6 June 1850, and was a vice-president in 1880–1. In 1889 he was elected an honorary member of the Société des Ingénieurs civils de France. In 1881 he and Sir Frederick Bramwell [q. v. Suppl. II] were appointed the first civil members of the ordnance committee. He was one of the judges of the centennial exhibition at Philadelphia in 1875; was elected a member of the Athenæum club *honoris causa* in 1881; and was a lieut.-colonel in the engineer and railway volunteer staff corps.

Barlow practised from 1857 to 1866 at 19 Great George Street, Westminster, and from 1866 onwards at 2 Old Palace Yard. In 1874 he took into partnership his second son, Crawford, and his assistant, Mr. C. B. Baker.

He died on 12 Nov. 1902 at his residence, High Combe, Old Charlton. He married Selina Crawford, daughter of W. Caffin, of the Royal Arsenal, by whom he had four sons and two daughters. His portrait in oils, by the Hon. John Collier, is at the Institution of Civil Engineers.

[Proc. Inst. Civ. Eng., vol. cli.; Men and Women of the Time, 1899.] W. F. S.

BARNARDO, THOMAS JOHN (1845–1905), philanthropist, born in Dublin on 4 July 1845, was younger son of John Michaelis Barnardo, who, born at Hamburg in 1800, had settled in Dublin as a wholesale furrier and had become a naturalised British subject. The Barnardo family, of Spanish origin, left Spain for Germany in the eighteenth century on account of religious persecution by the catholic church. Thomas John's mother was the daughter of Andrew Drinkwater, who belonged to an old quaker family, long settled in Ireland. She was a woman of strong religious convictions and exercised abiding influence upon her family. The son, after attending private schools in Dublin kept by the Rev. A. Andrews and the Rev. J. Dundas, became at fourteen a clerk in a wine merchant's office in his native city, but he subsequently gave up the employment on growing convinced of the evils of intemperance. During the protestant religious revival in Dublin of 1862 he was 'converted,' the date of conversion being, according to an entry in his Bible, 26 May 1862. Soon after, he devoted his spare time to preaching and evangelising work in Dublin slums, until the call came to him to go as a missionary to China.

With a view to that work, he came to London in April 1866 and settled in Coburn Street, Stepney, under the guidance of the Rev. Hudson Taylor, the founder of the China Inland Mission, and of Henry Grattan Guinness [q. v. Suppl. II]. In Oct. 1866 he entered the London Hospital as a missionary medical student, becoming a licentiate of the Royal College of Surgeons Edinburgh on 31 March 1876 and a fellow on 16 April 1879. Whilst pursuing his studies in East London he joined the Ernest Street ragged school and became superintendent. He preached in the open air, visited common lodging-houses and slums, and volunteered for service in the district during the cholera epidemic of 1866–7. Whilst thus engaged he was impressed by the number of homeless and necessitous children in the East End, and he gave up his intention of going to China in order to devote himself to their interests. On 15 July 1867 he founded the East End Juvenile Mission for the care of friendless and destitute children. The work rapidly developed, and in December 1870, under the patronage of Lord Shaftesbury, he opened a boys' home at 18 Stepney Causeway to provide for destitute lads. This institution developed into the immense organisation known as 'Dr. Barnardo's Homes.' His next step was to purchase, in 1873, a notorious public-house known as 'Edinburgh Castle,' Limehouse, and to convert it into a mission church and coffee palace for working-men, which became the centre of his evangelistic work. The 'Dublin Castle,' Mile End, was similarly treated in 1876. In 1874 Barnardo opened a receiving house for girls, and on 9 July 1876 he started the Girls' Village Home, Barkingside, Essex, with church and schools. On 20 Aug. 1882 he sent for the first time a party of boys, and a year later a party of girls, to Canada for training and settlement there. In 1887 he established offices in Toronto, Canada, with distributing homes and an industrial farm. In 1886 he adopted in England the boarding-out system as an integral part of his scheme. In the same year he opened the Babies' Castle at Hawkhurst, Kent, for 100 infants (9 Aug.).

Barnardo's work grew with amazing rapidity, both at home and in Canada, until the waif and destitute children in his daily charge numbered about 8000. Before his death in 1905 he had rescued and trained 59,384 destitute children and had otherwise assisted as many as 250,000 children in want. Over ninety homes and agencies were founded and maintained by him. The Young Helpers' League which he formed in 1891, under the patronage of Princess Mary Adelaide, Duchess of Teck, who became the first president, and later of Queen Alexandra, aimed at banding together the children of the rich in the service of the sick and suffering poor. The income of the homes was wholly drawn from voluntary sources, and rose from 214*l.* 15*s.* in 1866 to 196,286*l.* 11*s.* in 1905, making a total of nearly 3,500,000*l.*

In 1877 charges reflecting on Barnardo's disinterestedness and good management were submitted to arbitration and fully refuted. He then conveyed the property to trustees. On 20 April 1899 the homes were incorporated under the Companies Act, and became known as 'The National Incorporated Association for the Reclamation of Destitute Waif Children, otherwise known as "Dr. Barnardo's Homes."' In 1903 Queen Alexandra accepted the office of patron. The cardinal principle of Barnardo's homes, 'No destitute child ever refused admission,' was never forsaken even when his financial resources were temporarily exhausted. The religious teaching of the homes was stated in the title-deeds to be protestant, and every child admitted into the homes was to be brought up in the protestant faith. Barnardo frequently came into conflict in the law courts with Roman catholic authorities, who claimed to recover from the homes children of catholic parentage. Between 1889 and 1891 Barnardo was involved in much litigation on such grounds. Ultimately an equitable agreement was reached without prejudice to the protestant character of the homes.

Barnardo died at Surbiton on 19 Sept. 1905 from heart failure. In a message of condolence from King Edward VII and Queen Alexandra he was called 'that great philanthropist.' A public funeral was accorded him at his Girls' Village Home, Barkingside. There a memorial room was opened on 30 June 1906, and on Founder's Day, 1908, a beautiful monument fashioned by Sir George Frampton, R.A., who gave his services gratuitously, was erected over his tomb. A national memorial was organised to free his homes from debt, and their prosperity is now firmly established.

On 17 June 1873 he married Syrie Louise, only daughter of William Elmslie of Lloyds and Richmond, Surrey, who survives him with two sons and two daughters. Three sons predeceased him.

[Memoirs of the late Dr. Barnardo, by Mrs. Barnardo and Rev. James Marchant, secretary of the National Memorial Council, 1907; original books and documents in Dr. Barnardo's Homes; private sources.] J. M-T.

BARNES, ROBERT (1817–1907), obstetric physician, born at Norwich on 4 Sept. 1817, was second son and second child of the six children of Philip Barnes, an architect and one of the founders of the Royal Botanic Society of London, by his wife Harriet Futter, daughter of a Norfolk squire. The father, also of an old Norfolk family, claimed descent from Robert Barnes [q. v.], the Marian martyr. Educated at Bruges from 1826 to 1830 and at home, where one of his tutors was George Borrow, author of 'The Bible in Spain,' Barnes began his medical career in 1832 as an apprentice in Norwich to Dr. Richard Griffin, founder of an association of poor-law medical men. When his family moved to London he continued his medical work at University College, the Windmill Street school, and at St. George's Hospital. After becoming M.R.C.S. in 1842 he spent a year in Paris, where he paid much attention to mental diseases; on his return to London after unsuccessfully competing for the post of resident physician at Bethlehem Royal Hospital, he settled in general practice in Notting Hill and engaged in literary work on the 'Lancet.' His ambition was to become a medical teacher. He soon lectured at the Hunterian School of Medicine and on forensic medicine at Dermott's School, and was obstetric surgeon to the Western general dispensary. He graduated M.D. London in 1848, and in 1853 became L.R.C.P. and in 1859 F.R.C.P.

On 1 April 1859 Barnes was elected assistant obstetric physician, and on 14 July 1863 obstetric physician, to the London Hospital. From the London Hospital he passed on 24 April 1865 to a like post at St. Thomas's Hospital, where he had lectured on midwifery since April 1862. In 1875 he left St. Thomas's Hospital, where he was dean of the medical school, to become obstetric physician at St. George's Hospital; there he was elected consulting obstetric physician in 1885. He thus had the rare distinction of lecturing on midwifery at three great medical schools in London. He had also acted as physician to the Seamen's Hospital, the East London

Hospital for Children, and the Royal Maternity Hospital.

Barnes took a prominent part in founding the Obstetrical Society of London in 1858 and was president in 1865–6. But a dispute with the council of this society led him in 1884 to establish the British Gynæcological Society, of which he was honorary president until his death. The justification of the schism was the antagonism of the old society to the performance of ovariotomy and other important operations by obstetricians. Barnes was one of the pioneers of operative gynæcology, and the cause he advocated gained the day. The two societies were united in the obstetrical and gynæcological section of the Royal Society of Medicine in 1907.

At the College of Physicians Barnes delivered the Lumleian lectures 'On Convulsive Diseases in Women' in 1873 and was censor (1877–8). He was elected honorary fellow of the Royal College of Surgeons in 1883; of the Medical Society of London in 1893 (he had given the Lettsomian lectures in 1858), and of the Royal Medical and Chirurgical Society at the centenary meeting of 1905.

A leading teacher and gynæcologist in London, Barnes was a rival of James Matthews Duncan [q. v. Suppl. I] both in debates at the Obstetrical Society and in practice. One of the first to work at the minute pathology of obstetrics, he influenced the progress of obstetric medicine. His name has been attached to an obstetric instrument and to a curve of the pelvis. He expressed with decision his very definite opinions, and his mental and physical vigour was shown by his learning Spanish when over eighty-five and by rowing out to sea and bathing from the boat until he was eighty-nine. He was a director of the Prudential Assurance Company (1848–9; 1884–1907), amassed a considerable fortune, and gave liberally to medical institutions, among others to the medical school of St. George's Hospital, where the pathological laboratory is called after him. He died at Eastbourne on 12 May 1907, and was buried there. A portrait by Horsburgh is in possession of his family.

Barnes married: (1) Eliza Fawkener, daughter of a London solicitor; (2) Alice Maria, daughter of Captain W. G. Hughes, of Carmarthenshire, D.L. and J.P. for that county. By his first wife he had one son, Dr. R. S. Fancourt Barnes, and two daughters, and by his second wife one son and one daughter.

Besides thirty-two papers in the 'Transactions of the Obstetrical Society,' and an official report on scurvy at the Seamen's Hospital, 1864, Barnes was author of: 1. 'Obstetrical Operations,' 1870; 3rd ed. 1876; translated into French. 2. 'Medical and Surgical Diseases of Women,' 1873; translated into French. 3. 'Obstetric Medicine and Surgery,' 2 vols. (with his son, Fancourt Barnes), 1884. 4. 'Causes of Puerperal Fever,' 1887.

[Brit. Med. Journ., 1907, ii. 1221; information from his son-in-law, H. Robinson, M.D.]

H. D. R.

BARRETT, WILSON [originally WILLIAM HENRY] (1846–1904), actor and dramatist, born at the Manor House Farm, near Chelmsford, Essex, on 18 Feb. 1846, was eldest son of George Barrett, a farmer, by his wife and cousin Charlotte Mary Wood. The family was of old Hertfordshire descent. Two brothers, George Edward (1848–1894), an excellent low comedian, and Robert Reville (*d.* 1893), with a sister, Mary Brunell, were also on the stage, and the three were in 1872 members of Barrett's travelling company.

Owing to family reverses, Barrett began life as a printer in London, but in 1864 made his first appearance on the stage at the Theatre Royal, Halifax, where he was engaged for 'general utility.' He was seen three months later at the Adelphi theatre, Liverpool, and shortly afterwards, purchasing a 'fit-up' theatre, he started management at Burnley in Lancashire with disastrous results. Returning to stock work, he played 'the heavy business' at Nottingham, under Mrs. Saville. At Aberdeen he met on a starring visit Caroline Heath (1835–1887), actress and reader to the Queen, and after a short wooing he married her at Brechin on 31 July 1866. For many years he lent support to his wife's leading rôles, and her reputation overshadowed his.

On 26 June 1867, at the Surrey theatre, London, Barrett played at very short notice Tom Robinson in 'It's never too late to mend,' in place of Richard Shepherd, the actor-manager, who had lost his voice. On 29 June he performed Archibald Carlyle to Miss Heath's Lady Isabelle in 'East Lynne.' In this rôle he was welcomed by the press as a painstaking newcomer to the London stage. For the autumn season of 1867 he joined F. B Chatterton's company at Drury Lane, and subsequently travelled in the provinces with Miss Heath and a company of his own.

He was at the Queen's, Dublin, in May 1869, and for the rest of the year at the Princess's, Edinburgh, playing Mephistopheles in 'Faust' on 9 Oct., Master Ford in 'The Merry Wives of Windsor,' and Triplet to Miss Heath's Peg Woffington on 10 Dec.

In 1874 Barrett became lessee and manager of the Amphitheatre, Leeds, and on 8 March 1875 first produced there W. G. Wills's drama 'Jane Shore,' with himself as Henry Shore and Miss Heath in the title character. Husband and wife toured in these characters with great success. The Amphitheatre, Leeds, was soon burnt down, to Barrett's loss, but in 1878 the Grand Theatre was built at Leeds by a syndicate, and Barrett becoming lessee opened the new house on 18 Nov. as Benedick in 'Much Ado.' Meanwhile in 1877 he had assumed control of the Theatre Royal, Hull, and both the theatres remained under his control during his career in London.

Barrett first became manager in London on 20 Sept. 1879, when he opened the Court Theatre, with his wife as chief actress. On 13 Oct. he created there the part of the Rev. Richard Capel in 'A Clerical Error,' the earliest play by Mr. Henry Arthur Jones to be produced in London. Barrett's wife soon withdrew from the stage owing to failing health (she died in retirement on 26 July 1887). Under Barrett's auspices at the Court, Madame Modjeska made her first appearance in London, playing Constance in 'Heartsease' on 1 May 1880, and speedily winning popularity. Barrett was Mercutio to her Juliet at the Court (26 March 1881) and Friar John to her Juana Esteban in Wills's tragedy 'Juana' (7 May). He had appeared as Romeo to her Juliet at the Alexandra, Liverpool (1 Sept. 1880).

On 4 June 1881 Barrett began his notable management of the Princess's Theatre with Madame Modjeska still in his company. His first conspicuous successes were achieved with Mr. G. R. Sims's melodramas 'The Lights o' London' (10 Sept.) and 'The Romany Rye' (10 June 1882). In both Barrett played the leading part with good effect, the first piece running for 286 nights. On 16 November Messrs. H. A. Jones and Henry Herman's excellent melodrama 'The Silver King' was first produced, and Barrett scored a triumph as Wilfred Denver, the piece running for 300 nights. W. G. Wills and Henry Herman's poetic drama 'Claudian,' with Barrett in the title-character, followed on 6 Dec. 1883 and maintained the tradition of success. The mounting of this play, with a sensational earthquake scene, was applauded by Ruskin, who wrote: 'With scene-painting like that, this Princess's Theatre might do more for art-teaching than all the galleries and professors of Christendom.' Barrett gave a striking impersonation of the boy-poet in Messrs. Jones and Herman's new one-act drama 'Chatterton' (22 May 1884). He revived 'Hamlet' (16 Oct.), and by his new readings and his youthful interpretation of the Prince provoked controversy; but he failed to satisfy rigorous critical standards. The production was repeated for 117 nights, by way of forcing a rivalry with (Sir) Henry Irving at the Lyceum (for analyses of Barrett's Hamlet see CLEMENT SCOTT'S *Some Notable Hamlets* and WILLIAM WINTER'S *Shadows of the Stage*, second series (1893), chap. xxvii.). With the revival of 'Hamlet' Barrett's fortunes at the Princess's declined, and although his tenancy lasted another eighteen months, he thenceforth enjoyed few successes.

From an early period in his career he had essayed playwriting in addition to acting, and during his later sojourn at the Princess's and throughout his subsequent career he relied largely on his own pen for his plays, either in collaboration or alone. In 1885 he wrote, with Mr. H. A. Jones, 'Hoodman Blind,' a melodrama which ran for 171 nights (produced 18 August 1885), and also a romantic drama, 'The Lord Harry,' which he produced without success 18 Feb. 1886. With Mr. Sydney Grundy he wrote a blank verse tragedy, 'Clito,' which, though splendidly mounted, again failed to attract (produced 1 May 1886).

In the summer of 1886 Barrett left the Princess's heavily in debt, and went to America with his entire company and accessories. After producing 'Claudian' with success at the Star Theatre, New York, on 11 Oct. 1886, he made a profitable six months' tour. He revisited America five times: in 1890, 1893, 1894, 1895, and 1897, often for only a month or two, and producing there some new pieces from his own pen.

On 22 December 1887 Barrett began a brief management of the Globe Theatre in London. The venture began well with 'The Golden Ladder,' a drama by himself and Mr. George R. Sims. Morning performances of old plays were given early in 1888, and on 22 Feb. Barrett played Claude Melnotte for the first time in London. On 17 May he went back to the Princess's, opening there with 'Ben-my-Chree,' an adaptation of Mr. T. Hall Caine's novel 'The Deemster' by himself and the novelist.

This was the beginning of a somewhat extended collaboration. Small success attended the production at the Princess's of 'The Good Old Times,' a play from the same pens (12 Feb. 1889), or of Barrett's own drama, 'Now-a-days: a Tale of the Turf' (28 Feb.).

On 4 December 1890, after his second American tour, he opened the new Olympic Theatre, London, with 'The People's Idol,' by himself and Victor Widnell. An impersonation of the Stranger in Thompson's old play of that title was followed on 21 April 1891 by 'The Acrobat,' Barrett's version of Dennery and Fournier's 'Le Paillasse' (1850). During a provincial tour he first played Othello at the Court Theatre, Liverpool, on 22 Oct. 1891. Barrett still retained control of the Grand Theatre, Leeds, and there he now brought out three new pieces of his own, 'Pharaoh' (29 Sept. 1892); his first, and best, version of Hall Caine's novel 'The Manxman' (22 August 1894), in which his Pete was probably the best of his later characterisations; and for the first time in England 'The Sign of the Cross,' an adroit amalgam of popular religion and crude melodrama (26 Aug. 1895), which had been originally produced at the Grand Opera House, St. Louis, on 27 March 1895.

On 4 January 1896 Barrett opened management of the Lyric Theatre, London, with 'The Sign of the Cross,' which ran prosperously for a year and restored his long precarious fortunes. There followed at the Lyric 'The Daughters of Babylon,' by himself (6 Feb. 1897). In May he was seen there as Virginius and Othello. After a last visit to America, and a first visit in 1898 to Australia, Barrett in 1899 succeeded Irving as manager of the Lyceum, but the experiment was a failure. A new drama by himself and Mr. L. N. Parker, 'Man and His Makers' (produced 7 Oct.), was unfavourably received, and revivals of 'The Sign of the Cross,' 'Hamlet,' and 'Othello' attracted small audiences.

Meanwhile he continued to bring out new pieces by himself at provincial houses. During 1902 he also paid a second visit to Australia, and on his return he brought out at the Adelphi in London (on 18 Dec.) 'The Christian King,' a piece of his own which was first seen at the Prince's, Bristol, 6 Nov. In this he played Alfred of Engleland. Next year he toured in 'In the Middle of June,' yet another of his dramas, first produced at Middlesbrough (11 June 1903). On 9 June 1904 he paid a three weeks' visit to the Shakespeare theatre, Liverpool, and after producing his last new play, 'Lucky Durham,' made his final appearance on the stage as Wilfred Denver. He died in a private hospital in London on 22 July after an operation for cancer, and was buried in Hampstead cemetery. He was survived by two sons, Frank and Alfred, and by a daughter, Dollie.

Barrett's features were cast in a classic mould and his presence was manly and graceful. Hence his predilection for classical impersonations. But his articulation suffered either from a defect in his utterance or from an affectation of delivery, and his method of acting was usually stilted. In melodrama he presented heroic fortitude with effect. His dramas made no pretence to literature. They aimed at stage effect and boldly picturesque characterisation without logical sequence or psychological consistency. His portrait as Hamlet was painted by Frank Holl, R.A.

Besides the pieces by himself already mentioned he wrote (among many others) 'Sister Mary,' with Clement Scott (produced at Brighton 8 March 1886); and a dramatic version of Mr. Hall Caine's novel 'The Bondman' (produced at the Chestnut Street Theatre, Philadelphia, Dec. 1893). He also published one or two novels, based on his own plays.

[Arthur Goddard's Players of the Period, 1891; Boyle Lawrence's Celebrities of the Stage, 1899; J. C. Dibdin's Annals of the Edinburgh Stage, 1888; Notes and Queries, 11th ser. iii. 225 and 276; Broadbent's Annals of the Liverpool Stage; Dramatic Notes, 1881–1885; Theatre Magazine, Dec. 1891; Dramatic Year Book for 1892; Col. T. Allston Brown's History of the New York Stage, 1903; William Archer's Theatrical World for 1895; Daily Telegraph, 23 July 1904; New York Dramatic Mirror, 30 July 1904; private information.]

BARRY, ALFRED (1826–1910), primate of Australia and canon of Windsor, born at Ely Place, Holborn, on 15 Jan. 1826, was second son of Sir Charles Barry [q. v.], architect, whose 'Life and Works' he published (1867; 2nd ed. 1870), and elder brother of Edward Middleton Barry [q. v.], whose Royal Academy lectures on architecture he edited with a memoir in 1881. His mother was Sarah, daughter of Samuel Rowsell. His youngest brother is Sir John Wolfe Wolfe Barry, K.C.B., the civil engineer. Educated at King's College, London, from 1841 to 1844, Barry proceeded in 1844 to Trinity College, Cambridge; in 1848 he was placed fourth among the wranglers, Isaac Todhunter [q. v.] being senior, and seventh in the first class of classical tripos, C. B. Scott and Brooke Foss Westcott [q. v. Suppl. II] being bracketed senior. He also won the second Smith's prize, the first going to Todhunter. Barry was elected a fellow of Trinity the same year. He graduated B.A. in 1848, proceeding M.A. in 1851, B.D. in 1860, and D.D. in 1866.

Ordained deacon in 1850 on the title of his fellowship, and priest in 1853, Barry became in 1849 vice-principal of Trinity College, Glenalmond, the seminary of the Scottish Episcopal church. In 1854 he became headmaster of Leeds grammar school. From 1862 to 1868 he was principal of Cheltenham College, and during his tenure of office there were built the gymnasium (1864), the junior school (1865), and five of the boarding houses. He was made a life member of the council in 1893 (*Cheltonian*, May 1910).

In 1868 Barry was appointed, in succession to Richard William Jelf [q. v.], principal of King's College, London, of which he had been a fellow since 1849. Here Barry arranged that students for the theological associateship could attend evening classes for two years, without sacrificing their employment by day, devoting their whole time to their college course only in their third year. He encouraged the establishment of a ladies' branch of the college at Kensington, a scheme carried out in 1881. From 1871 to 1877 he served on the London School Board.

In 1871 Gladstone made him a residentiary canon at Worcester, and in 1881 transferred him to a similar office in Westminster Abbey. Appointed honorary chaplain to Queen Victoria in 1875 and chaplain in ordinary 1879, he also held the Boyle lectureship 1876–8. He published the first series as 'What is Natural Theology?' (1877) and the second series as 'The Manifold Witness for Christ' (1880). He was made D.C.L. of Oxford in 1870 and of Durham in 1888.

After refusing the see of Calcutta in 1876, Barry in 1883 accepted the see of Sydney, Australia. With the office went the metropolitanate of New South Wales and the primacy of Australia and Tasmania. He was thus head of 'a general synod embracing all the dioceses of Australia and Tasmania' (BARRY, *Ecclesiastical Expansion*, 1895, p. 255; *Digest of S.P.G. Records*, 1895, pp. 761, 766). He was consecrated in Westminster Abbey on 1 Jan. 1884, Westcott preaching the sermon (*Life and Letters of B. F. Westcott*, 1903, ii. 1, 2; E. STOCK, *History of C.M.S.*, 1899, iii. 311–312). Misfortune attended his departure. He sent on his entire library, lectures, and manuscripts in a vessel which was lost by shipwreck. Queen Victoria and others showed their sympathy by endeavouring to replace the books.

Barry's vigour of intellect adapted itself to the unfamiliar conditions and conceptions of colonial life, and his good judgment and clearness of utterance stood him in good stead, when he presided over the provincial or the general synod. He successfully urged the Australian church to accept in 1886 missionary responsibility for New Guinea. Barry's residence in Sydney was not prolonged enough to give his abilities their full opportunity there. For private reasons he constantly revisited England during the five years of his Australian episcopate. He vacated his office in 1889.

Having been vainly recommended for various English sees, e.g. Chester in 1884 (J. C. MACDONNELL, *Life and Correspondence of W. C. Magee*, 1896, ii. 255), Barry devoted himself to helping bishops at home. From 1889 to 1891 he was assistant to A. W. Thorold [q. v.], bishop of Rochester, and in 1891 he took charge of the diocese of Exeter during the absence in Japan of Bishop Edward Henry Bickersteth [q. v. Suppl. II]. From 1891 till his death he was canon of St. George's Chapel, Windsor. In 1892 he was chosen Bampton lecturer at Oxford, taking as his subject 'Some Lights of Science on Faith.' He was Hulsean lecturer at Cambridge for 1894, and gave a masterly review of the 'Ecclesiastical Expansion of England in the Growth of the Anglican Communion.' From 1895 to 1900 he held the rectory of St. James, Piccadilly, rendering episcopal assistance in central London to Frederick Temple [q. v. Suppl. II], bishop of London. After 1900 he confined himself to his canonry at Windsor. He represented the chapter in the lower house of convocation from 1893 until 1908. He died in his sleep at his residence in the cloisters, Windsor Castle, on 1 April 1910, and was buried in the cloisters at Worcester Cathedral, beside his only daughter, Mary Louisa (*d.* 1880). He married, on 13 Aug. 1851, Louisa Victoria, daughter of T. S. Hughes (*d.* 1847), canon of Peterborough. She survived him with two sons. A portrait painted by Sir Edward Poynter, P.R.A., was presented to Mrs. Barry by his King's College friends in 1883.

Of fine presence and with a sonorous

voice, Barry was an effective speaker and preacher. A broad churchman, he avoided enthusiasm, and his manner seemed distant and unsympathetic save to his intimates. His chief works, apart from separate sermons and the lectures already mentioned, were: 1. 'Introduction to the Study of the Old Testament,' 1856 (incomplete). 2. 'Sermons preached in the Chapel of Cheltenham College,' 1865. 3. 'Sermons for Boys or Memorials of Cheltenham Sundays,' 1869. 4. 'The Architect of the New Palace at Westminster,' a reply to a pamphlet by E. W. Pugin, 2 edits. 1868. 5. 'The Atonement of Christ,' 1871. 6. 'Sermons preached at Westminster Abbey,' 1884. 7. 'First Words in Australia,' 1884. 8. 'Lectures on Christianity and Socialism,' 1890. 9. 'The Teacher's Prayer-Book,' 1884; 16th edit. 1898, a popular handbook. 10. 'England's Mission to India,' 1895. 11. 'The Position of the Laity in the Church,' 1895. 12. 'The Christian Sunday; its Sacredness and its Blessing,' 1905. 13. 'Do we Believe? The Law of Faith perfected in Christ,' 1908.

[The Times, 2 April 1910; Guardian, 8 April 1910; Crockford, Clerical Directory, 1909; Burke's Family Records; private information.]

E. H. P.

BARTLETT, Sir ELLIS ASHMEAD (1849-1902), politician, born in Brooklyn, New York, on 24 August 1849, was eldest son of Ellis Bartlett of Plymouth, Massachusetts, a graduate of Amherst, and a good classical scholar, who died in 1852. His mother was Sophia, daughter of John King Ashmead of Philadelphia. On the father's side he was directly descended from Robert Bartlett or Bartelot, of Sussex, who landed on Plymouth Rock from the ship Ann in 1623 and married in 1628 Mary, daughter of Richard Warren, who had sailed in the Mayflower in 1620. On his mother's side he derived through her father from John Ashmead of Cheltenham, who settled in Philadelphia in 1682, and through her mother from Theodore Lehman, secretary to William Penn, first governor of Pennsylvania.

Ellis and his younger brother, William Lehman Ashmead, now Mr. Burdett-Coutts, were brought to England in early boyhood by their widowed mother, and were educated at a private school, The Braddons, at Torquay. Ellis showed precocity in classics; but illness interrupted his studies, except in history, of which—aided by an admirable memory—he early gained a wide knowledge. On 16 Feb. 1867 he matriculated from St. Mary Hall, Oxford, but soon migrated to Christ Church. A taste for politics asserted itself at Oxford. Becoming the recognised leader of the conservative party in the Union, and an ardent champion of Disraeli, he was elected president in Easter term 1873, defeating Mr. Asquith by a large majority. He was also prominent in athletics. He graduated B.A. at Christ Church in 1872 with first-class honours in law and history, and proceeded M.A. 1874. After leaving Oxford he became an inspector of schools 1874–7, and an examiner in the privy council office (education department) 1877–80. On 13 June 1877 he was called to the bar from the Inner Temple.

With a view to ascertaining the truth regarding the reported 'Bulgarian atrocities' of 1876, Ashmead Bartlett visited Servia, Bulgaria, and Roumelia in 1877-8, and was a witness of barbarous outrages committed by Bulgarians and Russians on the Turkish inhabitants in Roumelia. He conceived the strongest distrust of Russia, and returning to England began a vigorous campaign against that power by speech and pen. In 1880 Lord Beaconsfield assigned to him what was practically the 'pocket borough' of Eye, in Suffolk. He held the seat until it was disfranchised under the redistribution bill of 1884. In 1885 he was elected for the more popular constituency of the Ecclesall division of Sheffield, for which he sat until his death. Energetic in his loyalty to the conservative party, he chiefly devoted himself both inside and outside the House of Commons to advocacy of British imperialism. In the House he was untiring in attack on liberal foreign policy and, notably in his first parliament, proved a constant torment to Gladstone. But a tendency to grandiloquence excited in parliament the impatient ridicule of his opponents. Outside the House he quickly gained an exceptional reputation as a platform speaker which he maintained throughout his public life. He was probably in greater demand among conservative organisers of great popular meetings than any other speaker, and invariably roused the enthusiasm of his audiences to the highest pitch. His organising capacity was also of much service to his party. He was chairman of the National Union of Conservative Associations for three years, 1886–7–8, and he carried on a ceaseless propaganda on behalf of his principles and his party by pamphlets, articles, and letters to the press. In March 1880, too, he started 'England, the first conservative penny weekly newspaper. This venture, which rendered great service to the conservative cause, he conducted in its original form until June 1886. Continued in a somewhat different shape until 28 May 1898, it was a constant drain on his resources, and helped to involve him in financial embarrassments which clouded the closing years of his life.

On the accession of conservatives to power in June 1885 Ashmead Bartlett became civil lord of the admiralty, and he returned to the office in July 1886 on the formation of Lord Salisbury's second administration. He showed himself an industrious official. He retired on the fall of the government in Aug. 1892, when he was knighted. On the outbreak of war between Turkey and Greece in 1897 Sir Ellis proceeded to Constantinople, where the Sultan conferred on him the grand cordon of the Medjidieh, and he joined the Turkish army in the field. He was present at the defeat of the Greeks at Mati and was among the first noncombatants to enter Tyrnavo and Larissa. He was afterwards taken prisoner by the commander of a Greek warship and carried to Athens, but was soon released. When the Boer war broke out in South Africa in Oct. 1899 Sir Ellis went to the front and witnessed some early stages of the campaign, in which two of his sons took part. He died in London, after an operation for appendicitis, on 18 Jan. 1902, and was buried at Tunbridge Wells.

He married in 1874 Frances Christina, daughter of Henry Edward Walsh, and had issue five sons and three daughters. His eldest son, Ellis Ashmead Bartlett, is well known as a war correspondent.

Ashmead Bartlett's published works included 'Shall England keep India?' (1886); 'Union or Separation' (1893); 'British, Natives and Boers in the Transvaal; the Appeal of the Swazi People' (1894); 'The Transvaal Crisis; the Case for the Uitlander Residents' (1896); 'The Battlefields of Thessaly' (1897).

A portrait by Ernest Moore of Sheffield, painted in 1895, belongs to the family. A cartoon by 'Spy' appeared in 'Vanity Fair' in 1882.

[The Times, 20 Jan. 1902; Foster's Alumni Oxon., and Men at the Bar; private information; cf. Lucy's Gladstone Parliament, 1880–5, pp. 150 seq.; and Unionist Parliament, 1895–1900, pp. 145 seq.] J. P. A.

BARTLEY, Sir GEORGE CHRISTOPHER TROUT (1842–1910), founder of the National Penny Bank, born at Rectory Place, Hackney, on 22 Nov. 1842, was son by his second wife, Julia Anna Lucas, of Robert Bartley of Hackney, of the war office. After early education at Blackheath, at Clapton, and at University College school, he entered in 1860, as science examiner, the science and art department at South Kensington, of the education branch of which Sir Henry Cole [q. v.], father of his chief school friend, was the head. In 1866 he was made official examiner, and remained there until 1880 as assistant director of the science division, which was responsible for the establishment of science schools through the country.

Since 1870 Bartley had written several pamphlets on social questions, especially on thrift and poor law and on education. His first published work, 'The Educational Condition and Requirements of One Square Mile in the East End of London' (1870; 2nd edit. 1870), was quoted by William Edward Forster during the discussion of the education bill of 1870. In 1871 followed 'Schools for the People,' which treated of the historical development and methods of schools for the working classes in England. From 1873 to 1882 he edited with Miss Emily Shirreff [q. v.] the journal of the Women's Educational Union, which aimed at the general improvement of women's education.

Poverty and its remedy also claimed his attention. In 1872 he read a paper before the Society of Arts on old age pensions, urging that help should be given in old age to those who had made some provision for themselves. Twenty-one years later he laid before the House of Commons a bill for old age pensions, which embodied his earlier principles (Booth, *Pauperism and the Endowment of Old Age*, 1892, p. 350). For the encouragement of thrift among the masses he published in 1872 twelve penny 'Provident Knowledge Papers,' which he supplemented in 1878 with his 'Domestic Economy: Thrift in Everyday Life.' In 1872 he started the instalment club at 77 Church Street, Edgware Road, which enabled workmen to buy tools or clothes by regular weekly payments. The foundation of the Middlesex Penny Bank at the same address followed the same year. In 1875, in conjunction with Sir Henry Cole (whose daughter he had married in 1864) and others, Bartley established the National Penny Bank; its main object was to encourage thrift among the working classes on a purely business basis. The scheme met with rapid success, and since its foundation over 2,900,000 accounts have been opened, and more than 22,000,000 deposits have been made; 180,000 depositors hold over 3¼ million pounds, and 26 million pounds have passed through the bank, while fourteen district branches have been established in London. Meanwhile Bartley had devoted himself to the question of poor law reform. In 'The Poor Law in its Effects on Thrift' (1873) he urged improvement of the system of out-door relief. Other works, 'The Village Net' (1874) and 'The Seven Ages of a Village Pauper' (1875), give dark pictures of the existing poor law system; in 1876 appeared his 'Handy Book for Guardians of the Poor.'

In 1880 Bartley resigned his post at South Kensington to stand for parliament in the conservative interest. He unsuccessfully opposed Henry Fawcett [q. v.] at Hackney in March of that year. From 1883 to 1885 he was chief agent to the conservative party. In 1885 he was returned for North Islington, and retained that seat till 1906. He was narrowly defeated in November 1907 at a by-election in West Hull. In the House of Commons Bartley, although a fluent speaker, strenuously advocated the curtailment of parliamentary speeches; in 1891 he voted against his party in opposition to the free education bill brought in by the Salisbury government and played a prominent part in obstructing the chief measures of the liberal government (1892–5). Bartley was created K.C.B. in November 1902, and was long J.P. for London and Middlesex.

He died in London on 13 Sept. 1910 after an operation, and was buried in Holtye Churchyard, near Shovelstrode Manor, East Grinstead, his country house. He married in 1864 Mary Charlotte, third daughter of Sir Henry Cole, K.C.B., and had issue four sons and one daughter, who with his widow survived him. His second son, Douglas Cole Bartley (*b.* 2 Oct. 1870), barrister, succeeded him as managing director of the National Penny Bank. A bust of Bartley by Mr. Basil Gotto is in possession of Lady Bartley at Shovelstrode Manor, East Grinstead; a replica was placed in 1911 at the head office of the National Penny Bank, 59 Victoria Street, Westminster.

Bartley published, besides the works already mentioned: 1. 'A Catalogue of Modern Works on Science and Technology,' 1872. 2. 'Toys' ('British Manufacturing Industries'), 1876; 2nd edit. 1877. 3. 'The Rhine from its Source to the Sea,' translated from the German, 1877.

[Information supplied by Douglas C. Bartley, Esq.; The Times, 15 Sept. 1910; H. W. Lucy, Diary of the Salisbury Parliament, 1886–1892, pp. 288–9; Diary of Home Rule Parliament, 1892–5, pp. 259–261. Charity Organisation Review, Sept. 1892.]

W. B. O.

BARTON, JOHN (1836–1908), missionary, born at Eastleigh, Hampshire, on 31 Dec. 1836, was sixth child of John Barton (1798–1852) by his wife Fanny, daughter of James Rickman. His ancestors were Cumberland quakers. Bernard Barton [q. v.] was his uncle. His mother died in 1841, and her only sister, Josephina, brought up her family.

After education at schools at Bishop Waltham and Highgate, John matriculated from Christ's College, Cambridge, at Michaelmas 1855. He soon decided to enter the mission field, and founded the Cambridge University Church Missionary Union. Graduating B.A. in Jan. 1859 (M.A. in 1863), he was ordained in September 1860 and sailed in October for Calcutta. After receiving priest's orders, he proceeded to Agra. There he helped in superintending the missionary college with an attendance of 260 students, and the orphanage at Secundra (five miles away) with 300 children. He was transferred to Amritsar in May 1863, and was appointed in 1865 principal of a new cathedral missionary college at Calcutta. From 1871 to 1875 he was secretary of the Madras mission, twice visiting the missions in South India. During 1870–1 and again during 1876–7 he did secretarial work at the Church Missionary House in London. From 1877 to 1893 he was vicar of Holy Trinity Church, Cambridge, but was absent in Ceylon for four months in 1884, and during 1889, after refusing offers of the bishoprics of both Travancore and Tinnevelly, was in charge of the latter district. In 1893 he refused the call to a bishopric in Japan, and left Cambridge for London to become chief secretary of the Church Pastoral-Aid Society, whose 'forward movement' he organised with immense vigour. Of massive build, Barton was a born organiser, and 'a giant for work'; he was a keen botanist, geologist, and mountaineer. He died at Weybridge on 26 Nov. 1908, and was there buried, a tablet and memorial window being placed in Holy Trinity Church, Cambridge.

He married twice: (1) in May 1859, Catherine Wigram (*d.* 1860); and (2) in October 1863, Emily Eugenia, daughter of Charles Boileau Elliott. His second wife, six sons, and two daughters survived him.

A son, Cecil Edward Barton (*d.* 1909), missionary in the Punjab, was rector of Rousdon, Devonshire, and joint author of 'A Handy Atlas of Church and Empire . . . showing British Possessions' (1908).

Barton published 'Remarks on the Orthography of Indian Geographical Names,' reprinted from 'Friend of India '(1871); 'Missionary Conference Report' (1873), and 'Memorial Sketch of Major-General Edward Lake, Commissioner of Jalundhur' (2nd edit. 1878). A map of India, made largely by him while in Calcutta, was published in 1873, and is still in use.

[Life, by his son, Cecil Edward Barton (1911); The Times, 1 Dec. 1908; private information.]

C. F. S.

BASS, Sir MICHAEL ARTHUR, first Baron Burton (1837–1909), brewer and benefactor, born in Burton-on-Trent on 12 Nov. 1837, was elder son of Michael Thomas Bass, brewer [q. v.], by his wife Eliza Jane, daughter of Major Samuel Arden of Longcroft Hall, Staffordshire. Educated at Harrow and Trinity College, Cambridge, he graduated B.A. in 1860, M.A. in 1864. Bass on leaving the university at once entered his father's brewing business, and was soon well versed in all branches of the industry. By his energy he did much to extend its operations, became head of the firm on the death of his father in 1884, and to the end of his life never relaxed his interest in the active management. The firm, which was reconstructed in 1888 under the style of Bass, Ratcliff & Gretton, Ltd., has buildings covering over 160 acres of land, employs over 3000 men, pays over 300,000*l.* a year in duty, and has a revenue of over 5,000,000*l.* per annum.

Bass entered parliament in 1865 as liberal member for Stafford, represented East Staffordshire 1868–85, and the Burton division of Staffordshire 1885–6. He proved a popular member of the house, and was a personal friend of Gladstone. His father having refused both a baronetcy and a peerage, Bass was made a baronet *in vita patris* in 1882, with remainder to his brother, Hamar Alfred Bass, and his heirs male; Hamar Bass died in 1898, leaving his son, William Arthur Hamar Bass, heir to the baronetcy. Bass was opposed to Gladstone's home rule policy in 1886, but on other great questions he remained for the time a consistent liberal, and presided on 9 March 1887 when Francis Schnadhorst, the liberal party organiser, was presented with a testimonial of 10,000 guineas. He was raised to the peerage on Gladstone's recommendation on 13 Aug. 1886 as Baron Burton of Rangemore and Burton-on-Trent, both in co. Stafford.

The growing hostility of the liberal party to the brewing interest as shown in their licensing policy and the widening of the breach on the Irish question led Burton to a final secession from the liberals, and he became a liberal unionist under Lord Hartington and Mr. Chamberlain. After 1903 he warmly supported the latter's policy of tariff reform, and he led the opposition to Mr. Asquith's licensing bill in 1908, which was rejected by the House of Lords.

Always genial, outspoken, and good-humoured, Burton was a personal friend of King Edward VII, both before and after his accession. The king frequently visited him at his London house, Chesterfield House, Mayfair, at his Scottish seat, Glen Quoich, and at Rangemore, his stately home on the borders of Needwood Forest, near Burton. The king conferred upon him the decoration of K.C.V.O. when he visited Balmoral in 1904.

He was a deputy-lieutenant and a J.P. for Staffordshire, and a director of the South Eastern Railway Company. An excellent shot, he was long in command of the 2nd volunteer battalion of the North Staffordshire regiment, retiring in August 1881 with the rank of hon. colonel. He built and presented to the regiment the spacious drill-hall at Burton, and gave for competition at Bisley the Bass charity vase and a cup for ambulance work.

Burton's gifts and benefactions to the town of Burton were, like those of his father, munificent; together they presented the town hall, which cost over 65,000*l.* He gave club buildings to both the liberal and the conservative parties in succession; he constructed, at a cost of about 20,000*l.*, the ferry bridge which spans the valley at the south end of Burton, and afterwards freed the bridge from toll at a cost of 12,950*l.* and added an approach to it over the marshy ground known as the Fleet Green Viaduct in 1890. As an acknowledgment he accepted a piece of silver plate, but he declined the proposed erection of a public statue. As a loyal churchman he generously contributed towards all diocesan funds, but will chiefly be remembered as a builder of churches. St. Paul's Church at Burton, built by him and his father, is a miniature cathedral; its cost in first outlay was 120,000*l.*, a sum of 40,000*l.* was provided for its endowment.

and large sums in addition for improvements and embellishments. Another fine church, St. Margaret's, Burton, was also built by father and son, and they erected St. Paul's Church Institute at a cost of over 30,000*l*.

Burton had a cultivated taste as an art collector, and Chesterfield House, his residence in Mayfair, which he bought of Mr. Magniac, was furnished in the style of the eighteenth century and contained a choice collection of pictures by English artists of that period, which became widely known owing to his generosity in lending them to public exhibitions; Gainsborough, Reynolds, and Romney were represented both numerously and by masterpieces. His more modern pictures were at Rangemore, and included some of the best works of Stanfield, Creswick, and their contemporaries.

Burton died after an operation on 1 Feb. 1909, and was buried at Rangemore church. He married on 28 Oct. 1869 Harriet Georgiana, daughter of Edward Thornewill of Dove Cliff, Staffordshire, by whom he had issue an only child, Nellie Lisa, born on 27 Dec. 1873, who married in 1894 James Evan Bruce Baillie, formerly M.P. for Inverness-shire. In default of male issue, the peerage, by a second patent of 29 Nov. 1897, descended to his daughter.

By his will he strictly entailed the bulk of his property to his wife for life, then to his daughter, then to her descendants. The gross value exceeded 1,000,000*l*. He requested that every person and the husband of every person in the entail should assume the surname and arms of Bass, and reside at Rangemore for at least four months in every year.

A portrait by Herkomer, painted in 1883, is at Rangemore. Another (also by Herkomer), painted in 1896, and presented by Lord Burton to the Corporation, is in Burton Town Hall, a replica being at Rangemore.

A memorial statue of Lord Burton in King Edward Place, by Mr. F. W. Pomeroy, A.R.A., was unveiled on 13 May 1911 (*Burton Chronicle*, 18 May 1911). At Rangemore there is a bust, by the same artist, presented by public subscription to Lady Burton.

[G.E.C., Complete Peerage, 1889; Burton Evening Gaz., 2 Feb. 1909; The Times, 2, 6, and 8 Feb., 16, 18 March 1909; Fortunes made in Business, 1887, ii. 409 seq.; Who's Who, 1907; Debrett's Peerage and Baronetage; Sir Wilfred Lawson and F. C. Gould's Cartoons in Rhyme and Line, 1905, p. 31 (caricature portrait).] C. W.

BATES, CADWALLADER JOHN (1853-1902), antiquary, born on 14 Jan. 1853 at Kensington Gate, London, was eldest son of Thomas Bates, barrister and fellow of Jesus College, Cambridge (1834–49), by his first wife, Emily, daughter of John Batten of Thorn Falcon, Somerset. The Bates family had been established in Northumberland since the fourteenth century, but their connection with the Blayneys of Gregynog, Montgomeryshire, introduced a strain of Celtic blood, and Cadwallader himself was named after a cousin, the twelfth and last Lord Blayney (*d.* 1874). His great-uncle was Thomas Bates [q. v. Suppl. I], stockbreeder, whom he commemorated in an elaborate biography, entitled 'Thomas Bates and the Kirklevington Shorthorns' (Newcastle-upon Tyne, 1897). Entering Eton in 1866, he left two years later owing to serious weakness of eyesight. In 1869 he proceeded to Jesus College, Cambridge; but the same cause compelled him to take an ægrotat degree in the moral science tripos of 1871. He proceeded M.A. in 1875. After leaving Cambridge, Bates, who was an accomplished linguist, travelled much in Poland and the Carpathians, paying frequent visits to his uncle, Edward Bates, who resided at Schloss Clöden, Brandenburg, Prussia. In 1882 he succeeded on his father's death to the family estates of Aydon White House, Heddon, Kirklevington, having already inherited his uncle's Prussian property. Although his interests were mainly antiquarian, he had practical knowledge of farming, and was partially successful in building up again the famous herd of Kirklevington shorthorns, which had been dispersed in 1850 [see BATES, THOMAS, Suppl. I]. In 1882 he purchased from the Greenwich Hospital commissioners Langley Castle near Haydon Bridge, and spent large sums on its restoration. As a magistrate and deputy-lieutenant Bates took his full share of county business, and in 1890 served the office of high sheriff of Northumberland. In later years he developed a taste for hagiography, and in 1893, while on a visit to Austrian Poland, he was received into the Roman catholic church. His indefatigable historical labours told on his health. He died of heart failure at Langley Castle on 18 March 1902, and was buried in the castle grounds. On 3 Sept. 1895 he married Josephine, daughter of François d'Echarvine, of Talloires, Savoy, who survived him without issue. The representation of the family devolved on his eldest half-brother, Edward H. Bates, now Bates Harbin.

Bates was a recognised authority on the medieval history of Northumbria. In

'Border Holds' (1891), a minute study of Northumbrian castles, he showed thoroughness of research and sedulous accuracy. His design of completing the work in a second volume was unfulfilled. His popular 'History of Northumberland' (1895) suffered somewhat from compression, but remains a standard work. Bates also assisted both as critic and contributor in the compilation of the first six volumes of a 'History of Northumberland' (Newcastle-on-Tyne, 1893–1902), designed to complete the work of John Hodgson [q. v.]. He was a vice-president of the Newcastle Society of Antiquaries, and from 1880 a frequent contributor to 'Archæologia Æliana.' He left some unfinished studies on the lives of St. Patrick and St. Gildas, 'The Three Pentecosts of St. Colomb and Kille,' and 'The Early Paschal Cycle.' A collection of his letters, chiefly on antiquarian subjects, was published in 1906.

[The Times, 20 March 1902; Ushaw Mag., July 1902; Letters of C. J. Bates ed. Rev. Matthew Culley, Kendal, 1906; Archæologia Æliana, 1903, xxiv. 178 seq., memoir by Dr. Thomas Hodgkin; private information from the family.] G. S. W.

BATESON, MARY (1865–1906), historian, born at Ings House, Robin Hood's Bay, near Whitby, on 12 Sept. 1865, was the daughter of William Henry Bateson [q. v.], Master of St. John's College, Cambridge, by his wife Anna, daughter of James Aikin. She spent practically all her life at Cambridge. Educated first privately, then at the Misses Thornton's school, Bateman Street, Cambridge, afterwards at the Institut Friedländer, Karlsruhe, Baden, 1880–1, and finally at the Perse school for girls, Cambridge, she became in October 1884 a student of Newnham College, of which her parents had been among the first promoters. She won a first class in the Cambridge historical tripos in 1887, being placed second in 'an exceptionally good year.' Next year she began to teach at her own college, of which she was an associate, and was long a member of the council and a liberal contributor to its funds. With occasional interruptions she continued to lecture there for the rest of her life. She furthered the interests of Newnham in every way in her power, and was popular among students and teachers, although her zeal for historical investigation made routine teaching or educational discipline secondary interests with her. She disliked and sought to amend the system of historical study prescribed by the Cambridge tripos, and was at her best in helping post-graduate students. She took a prominent part in procuring the establishment of research fellowships at Newnham. In 1903 she accepted one of these recently founded fellowships, and when it lapsed three years later resumed her teaching. Her historical work often required her to travel to libraries and archives, and when she was at home she lived, surrounded by her books, in her own house in the Huntingdon Road. She left her library and all her property to Newnham at her death. Her memory has been appropriately commemorated there by the foundation of a fellowship which bears her name.

Mandell Creighton [q. v. Suppl. I], when professor of ecclesiastical history at Cambridge, first awoke in Miss Bateson a zeal for historical scholarship. At his suggestion she wrote as a student a dissertation on 'Monastic Civilisation in the Fens,' which gained the college historical essay prize. By aphorisms of good counsel, Creighton checked a tendency to dissipate her energy in public agitation on the platform or in the press in the cause of political liberalism and women's enfranchisement, of which she was always a thorough-going advocate (see CREIGHTON, *Life and Letters*, i. 108–9). He persuaded her that her main business in life was to 'write true history' and pursue a scholar's career.

She proved an indefatigable worker, and made herself a fully trained mediævalist. Continuing her study of monastic history, she published in 1889 her first work, 'The Register of Crabhouse Nunnery,' for the Norfolk and Norwich Archæological Society. In 1890 she first contributed to the 'English Historical Review' (v. 330–352, and 550–573), of which Creighton was then editor; she wrote on the 'Pilgrimage of Grace.' The most solid result of her monastic studies was her article on the 'Origin and Early History of Double Monasteries,' published in 'Transactions of the Royal Historical Society' (new series, xiii. 137–198, 1899).

Miss Bateson in 1899 turned to municipal history. The corporation of Leicester, the chief town of Creighton's diocese, entrusted to her the editing of extracts from its archives. In her municipal research she received much help from the writings and advice of Frederic William Maitland [q. v. Suppl. II], whose whole-hearted disciple she soon became. Her work at Leicester resulted in the three stout volumes called 'Records of the

Borough of Leicester,' vol. i. 1103–1327 (1899); vol. ii. 1327–1509 (1901); vol. iii. 1509–1603 (1905). It was not only a scholarly edition of an important series of texts, but the elaborate introductions showed real insight and grasp of her stubborn material. She pursued her study of local history in editing 'The Charters of the Borough of Cambridge' with Prof. Maitland (1901) and 'The Cambridge Gild Records' (Cambridge Antiquarian Society, 1903). For the same society she issued, in 1903 and 1905, two volumes of 'Grace Book B,' containing proctors' accounts, 1488–1511 ('Luard Memorial' series, vols. ii. and iii.). This was her chief contribution to Cambridge University history. Cambridge libraries, especially the manuscript collections at Corpus, often provided her with material. From them came the texts for an edition of the hitherto unprinted poems of George Ashby [q. v.], a fifteenth-century poet (Early English Text Society, extra series, pt. lxxvi. 1899), and 'The Scottish King's Household and other Fragments' (*Scottish History Soc. Miscellany*, ii. 1–43, 1904). Her interest in mediæval bibliography, a fruit of her monastic studies, she illustrated in her edition of a sixteenth-century 'Catalogue of the Library of Syon Monastery, Isleworth, 1898' and in her collaboration with Mr. R. L. Poole in editing from a Bodleian manuscript the note-book which contains the materials collected by Bishop Bale for his second edition of his 'Catalogue of British Writers' (*Index Britanniæ Scriptorum quos ex variis bibliothecis non parvo labore collegit Ioannes Baleus. Anecdota Oxoniensia*, 1902; for her share see preface, pp. xxv–xxvi). She contributed the bibliography of British and Irish mediæval history to the 'Jahresberichte der Geschichtswissenschaft' for 1904 and 1905 (xxvii. iii. 186–234, in German, 1906; and in *ib.* xxviii. iii. 79–107, in English, 1907). Her conjoint interest in municipal and monastic history is well brought out in one of her latest articles on the topography and antiquities of the borough and abbey of Peterborough in 'Victoria County Hist., Northamptonshire,' ii. 424–60 (1906). Yet she seriously studied periods of history besides the Middle Ages. She published a 'Narrative of the changes of the Ministry, 1765–7,' told by unpublished letters of the Duke of Newcastle (Royal Historical Society, 'Camden' series, 1898), and in 1893 she edited 'A Collection of Original Letters from the Bishops to the Privy Council,' 1564 (pp. 6–84) (*Camden Miscellany*, 1893, vol. xi.).

Unduly modest in postponing continuous literary composition, Miss Bateson spent many years in editing, calendaring, and compiling. But gradually the full extent of her powers was revealed. Her papers on the 'Laws of Breteuil,' in the 'English Historical Review' (vols. xv. and xvi. 1900–1), showed that she was a scholar of the first rank, able to grapple with the hardest problems, and possessed of rare clearness and excellent method. Here she gave the death-blow to the ancient error that a large number of English towns base their institutions on the laws of Bristol, whereas the little town of Breteuil in Normandy is the true origin. Her last and in some ways her most masterly contribution to early municipal history was her two volumes of 'Borough Customs,' edited by her for the Selden Society, with very elaborate introductions (vol. i. 1904; vol. ii. 1906). Her method of arranging extracts of the custumals according to their subject-matter was only possible to one who had complete command of her extensive material. Maitland anticipated that the book would fill a permanent place 'on the same shelf with the "History of the Exchequer," and the "History of Tithes." Neither Thomas Madox nor yet John Selden will resent the presence of Mary Bateson' (*Collected Papers*, iii. 542–3).

The freshness and individuality of Mary Bateson's work showed to advantage in her occasional efforts at popularising knowledge. Her 'Mediæval England, 1066–1350' ('Story of the Nations,' 1903), is an original and brightly written survey of mediæval social life. She contributed much social history of modern times to 'Social England' (1895–7), and gave a striking instance of her versatility by writing on 'The French in America (1608–1744)' in the 'Cambridge Modern History,' vii. 70–113. To this Dictionary she contributed 109 articles between 1893 and 1900, chiefly on minor mediæval personages, but showing thoroughness of research and sedulous accuracy.

In 1905 Miss Bateson was Warburton lecturer in the University of Manchester. In 1906 she accepted the appointment as one of the three editors of the projected 'Cambridge Mediæval History,' of which vol. i. appeared in 1911. In spite of her fine physique and vigour, she died on 30 Nov. 1906, after a brief illness, and after a funeral service in St. John's College chapel was buried at the Cambridge cemetery, Histon Road.

Miss Bateson had an immense variety of interests. High-spirited, good-humoured, and frank, she was innocent of academic stiffness, provincialism, or pedantry. She delighted in society, in exercise, in travel, in the theatre, in music, and in making friends with men and women of very different types. Outside her work, what interested her most was the emancipation of women and the abolition of imposed restrictions which cripple the development of their powers.

[Personal knowledge and private information; article by her Newnham colleague, Miss Alice Gardner, in Newnham College Letter, 1906, pp. 32–39, reprinted for private circulation; notice by Miss E. A. McArthur of Girton College in the Queen, 8 Dec.; The Times, 1 Dec. 1906; Manchester Guardian, 3 Dec., by the present writer; Athenæum, by Prof. F. W. Maitland, reprinted in his Collected Papers, iii. 541-3, 1911, a masterly appreciation.] T. F. T.

BAUERMAN, HILARY (1835–1909), metallurgist, mineralogist and geologist, born in London on 16 March 1835, was younger son, in the family of two sons and one daughter, of Hilary John Bauerman by his wife Anna Hudina Rosetta, daughter of Dr. Wychers. His parents migrated from Emden, in Hesse Cassel, to London in August 1829. On 6 Nov. 1851 Hilary was entered as one of the seven original students of the Government School of Mines at Jermyn Street. This school became in 1862 the 'Royal School of Mines,' and the degree of associate of the Royal School of Mines was then conferred on Bauerman. In 1853 he went to the Bergakademie at Freiburg in Saxony to complete his studies, and on his return to England in 1855 he was appointed an assistant geologist to the Geological Survey of the United Kingdom. In 1858 he went to Canada as geologist to the North American boundary commission, and after the completion of its labours in 1863 he was intermittently engaged for many years in searching for mineral deposits and surveying mining properties in various parts of the world, chiefly by private persons or by companies, but also by the Indian and Egyptian governments (1867–9). This exploratory work carried him to the following countries: Sweden and Lapland in 1864, Michigan in 1865, Labrador in 1866, Arabia, the shores of the Red Sea and the Gulf of Aden in 1867–9, Savoy in 1870, Missouri in 1871, Bengal, Borar and Kumaon in 1872–3, Northern Peru in 1874, Murcia and Granada in 1876, Asia Minor in 1878, N. and S. Carolina, Colorado and Mexico in 1881, Brazil in 1883, Arizona in 1884, Cyprus and Portugal in 1888.

Meanwhile he was also engaged in making his chief contributions to technical and scientific literature. His well-known work on the 'Metallurgy of Iron' was published in 1868, and reached its sixth and last edition in 1890. Of his two text-books on mineralogy, 'Systematic Mineralogy' came out in 1881 and 'Descriptive Mineralogy' in 1884. Lastly, in 1887 he collaborated with J. A. Phillips in revising and enlarging the latter's 'Elements of Metallurgy,' which was originally published in 1874 (3rd edit. 1891).

In his later years Bauerman devoted himself mainly to teaching. In 1874 he first acted as an examiner of the science and art department. In 1883 he was lecturer in metallurgy at Firth College, Sheffield. In 1888 he succeeded Dr. John Percy [q. v.] as professor of metallurgy at the Ordnance College, Woolwich. He retired from the post in 1906, keenly interesting himself until his death in the developments of metallurgy and mining. Despite partial deafness, which increased with his years, his prodigious memory and his genial manner made him a highly successful teacher. He was an indefatigable and versatile worker, his favourite hobbies in later years being crystallography and geometry. He died, unmarried, at Balham on 5 Dec. 1909, and was cremated at Brookwood. By his will, after payment of bequests and subject to the lapse of two lives, the income from the residue of his property of 12,000*l.* was devoted to the encouragement of the study of mineralogical science in connection with the Royal School of Mines.

Bauerman wrote much for the technical journals, and occasionally contributed papers to the transactions of the Geological Society, the Iron and Steel Institute, and other learned societies. He was a fellow, and for some time a vice-president, of the Geological Society; an associate member of the Institute of Civil Engineers, by which he was awarded the Howard prize in 1897; an honorary member of the Iron and Steel Institute, and also of the Institution of Mining and Metallurgy, which awarded him its gold medal in 1906 in recognition of his many services in the advancement of metallurgical science.

[Engineer, 10 Dec. 1909, p. 604; Mining Journal, 18 Dec. 1909; Journ. Iron and Steel Inst. 1909, pt. ii. p. 305; Nature, 16 Dec. 1909; Geol. Mag., Jan. 1910; The Times,

10 Dec. 1909; Register of Associates of the Royal School of Mines, London, 1897; Who's Who in Mining and Metallurgy, 1908; private information supplied by Bedford McNeill, one of the executors.] T. K. R.

BAXTER, LUCY (1837–1902), writer on art, chiefly under the pseudonym of LEADER SCOTT, born at Dorchester on 21 Jan. 1837, was third daughter of William Barnes [q. v.], the Dorsetshire poet, by his wife Julia Miles.

Lucy Barnes began writing at eighteen, and from the small profits of stories and magazine articles saved enough to visit Italy, a cherished ambition. There she met and in 1867 married Samuel Thomas Baxter, a member of a family long settled in Florence, which then became her home. For thirty-five years she was a well-known figure in the literary and artistic life of the city, and in 1882 was elected an honorary member of the Accademia delle Belle Arti. For thirteen years her residence was the Villa Bianca, outside Florence, in the direction of Vincigliata and Settignano. Among those with whom she was associated in literary research was John Temple Leader [q. v. Suppl. II], a wealthy English resident at Florence, who owned the castle of Vincigliata. Her literary pseudonym of 'Leader Scott' combined the maiden surnames of her two grandmothers, Isabel Leader being her mother's mother and Grace Scott the mother of her father.

Leader Scott's principal publication was 'The Cathedral Builders' (1899 and 1900), an important examination of the whole field of Romanesque architecture in relation to the Comacine masons. Though necessarily based on Merzario's 'I Maestri Comacini,' 'The Cathedral Builders' shows much original observation and research and, if its arguments are not always conclusive, the international scope of the work and its wealth of illustration render it a storehouse of information and a useful introduction to an unfrequented field of speculation. The intention of the work is to attribute the entire genesis of mediæval architecture to masonic guilds derived, so it is supposed, from the Roman Collegia.

Apart from this work and numerous magazine articles, Leader Scott published: 1. 'A Nook in the Apennines,' 1879. 2. 'Fra Bartolommeo and Andrea del Sarto,' 1881. 3. 'Ghiberti and Donatello,' 1882. 4. 'Luca della Robbia,' 1883 (these three volumes in the 'Great Artists' series). 5. 'Messer Agnolo's Household,' 1883. 6. 'Renaissance of Art in Italy,' 1883. 7. 'A Bunch of Berries,' Bungay, 1885. 8. 'Sculpture, Renaissance and Modern,' 1886. 9. 'Life of William Barnes,' 1887. 10. 'Tuscan Studies and Sketches,' 1887. 11. 'Vincigliata and Maiano,' Florence and London, 1891. 12. 'The Orti Oricellari,' Florence, 1893. 13. 'Echoes of Old Florence,' Florence and London, 1894. 14. 'The Renunciation of Helen,' 1898. 15. 'Filippo di Ser Brunellesco' ('Great Masters' series), 1901. 16. 'Correggio' (Bell's 'Miniature Series of Painters'), 1902. She translated from the Italian 'Sir John Hawkwood,' by John Temple Leader and G. Marcotti (1889).

Lucy Baxter died at the Villa Bianca near Florence on 10 Nov. 1902; she was survived by her husband, a son, and two daughters.

[Athenæum, 22 Nov. 1902; information from Miss Grace Baxter.] P. W.

BAYLIS, THOMAS HENRY (1817–1908), lawyer and author, born in London on 22 June 1817, was second son of Edward Baylis, D.L. and J.P. for Middlesex. Sent to Harrow school, near which his father was then living, in 1825, at the early age of seven, he spent nine years there, leaving as a monitor in 1834. In 1835 he matriculated as a scholar at Brasenose College, Oxford, graduating B.A. in 1838 and proceeding M.A. in 1841. In 1834 he had already entered as a student of the Inner Temple; but he practised for some time as a special pleader before being called to the bar in 1856, when he joined the northern circuit. He became Q.C. in 1875, and two years later a bencher of his inn. From 1876 to 1903 he was judge of the court of passage at Liverpool, an ancient court of record with local jurisdiction wider than that of a county court. He was an active volunteer, retiring in 1882 with the V.D. as lieutenant-colonel of the 18th Middlesex rifles. Retaining his health and vigour almost to the last, he died at Bournemouth on 4 Oct. 1908, and was buried in the cemetery there. He married on 14 Aug. 1841 Louisa Lord, youngest daughter of John Ingle, D.L. and J.P. for Devon. His third son, Thomas Erskine, was called to the bar in 1874.

Baylis published in 1893 'The Temple Church and Chapel of St. Anne,' an historical record and guide, which reached a third edition in 1900, and is still in use as a standard guide-book. A man of wide interests and great mental activity, Baylis was a vice-president of the Royal United Service Institution, to the museum of which he presented an autograph letter from the signal officer on board the Victory at Trafalgar, explaining the substitution of 'expects' for 'confides' in

Nelson's famous signal. In his pamphlet on the subject, 'The True Account of Nelson's Famous Signal' (1905), he dealt with the question whether Nelson permanently lost the sight of one eye. He was one of the founders of the Egypt Exploration Fund, drafting the original articles of association, and attending the committee meetings with regularity.

As a lawyer, Baylis is chiefly known for a treatise on domestic servants, 'The Rights, Duties, and Relations of Domestic Servants and their Masters and Mistresses' (1857; 6th edit. 1906). Other works were: 'Fire Hints' (1884); 'Introductory Address on the Office of Reader or Lector and Lecture on Treasure Trove, delivered in the Inner Temple Hall, Michaelmas 1898' (1901), and 'Workmen's Compensation Act' (1902; 7th edit. 1907).

[Personal knowledge; Brit. Mus. Cat.]

J. S. C.

BAYLISS, Sir WYKE (1835–1906), painter and writer, born at Madeley, Shropshire, on 21 Oct. 1835, was second son of John Cox Bayliss of Prior's Leigh and Anne Wyke. His maternal grandfather was Dr. Wyke of Shrewsbury, to whom Darwin was articled as a pupil. His father was a railway engineer and a successful teacher of military and mathematical drawing. At an early age Bayliss showed an aptitude for drawing, and studied under his father, from whom he obtained the sound knowledge of perspective and architecture which influenced his later career as a painter. He worked also in the Royal Academy schools and at the School of Design, Somerset House. From the first his interest lay entirely with architecture, and his whole life as an artist was spent in painting, in oil and water-colour, all the beauties of the Gothic style in the interior of cathedrals and churches. In an exceptionally narrow range of subjects he was a sincere and accomplished executant, painting with sound draughtsmanship and strong colour 'not merely architecture but the poetry of architecture.' At the Royal Academy he exhibited twice, sending 'La Sainte Chapelle' in 1865, 'Treves Cathedral' and 'Strasbourg Cathedral' in 1879. His best work was given to the Royal Society of British Artists, of which he was elected a member in 1865. In 1888 he became president of the society in succession to James McNeill Whistler [q. v. Suppl. II], and till the close of his life held this office, for which his geniality, wide artistic sympathies, and energy were well adapted. Among the pictures which he himself selected as his most important works are: 'La Sainte Chapelle' (R.A. 1865), 'St. Laurence, Nuremberg' (Liverpool, 1889), 'St. Mark's, Venice' (Nottingham, 1880), 'St. Peter's, Rome' (R.B.A. 1888), and 'The Cathedral, Amiens' (R.B.A. 1900).

Bayliss also won reputation as an author. The best known of his books is 'Rex Regum' (1898; library edit. revised, 1902), an elaborate study of the traditional likenesses of Christ. In his 'Seven Angels of the Renascence' (1905), a blending of fact and sentiment, he gives his views upon seven selected great masters and their influence upon the art of the Middle Ages. Among his other publications were 'The Elements of Aerial Perspective' (1885); 'The Witness of Art' (1876; 2nd edit. 1878); 'The Higher Life in Art' (1879; 2nd edit. 1888); 'The Enchanted Island' (1888); and 'Five Great Painters of the Victorian Era' (1902; 2nd edit. 1904). Bayliss also published a short volume of poems, entitled 'Sæcula Tria, an Allegory of Life' (1857), and contributed to 'Literature' in 1889 (v. 387, 414), 'Shakespeare in Relation to his Contemporaries in the Fine Arts.' Before his death he completed 'Olives, the Reminiscences of a President,' which was edited by his wife and published, with a preface by Frederick Wedmore, in 1906.

Bayliss, who was elected F.S.A. in 1870, was knighted by Queen Victoria in 1897. He died at his residence, 7 North Road, Clapham Park, on 5 April 1906, and was buried at Streatham cemetery. A memorial is in the church of Madeley, Shropshire, his birthplace. He married in 1858 Elise, daughter of the Rev. J. Broade of Longton, Staffordshire, but left no issue. Two portraits of him, by John Burr and by T. F. M. Sheard, R.B.A., belong to Lady Bayliss.

[The Times, 7 April 1906; Who's Who, 1906; Contemp. Review, Aug. 1898; Graves's Royal Acad. Exhibitors; 'Olives,' his own reminiscences; private information.] M. H.

BAYLY, ADA ELLEN (1857–1903), novelist under the pseudonym of Edna Lyall, born at 5 Montpelier Villas, Brighton, on 25 March 1857, was youngest of the three daughters and son of Robert Bayly, barrister of the Inner Temple, by his wife, Mary Winter. Her father died when she was eleven and her mother three years later. A delicate child, she was first educated at home, then in the house of her uncle and guardian, T. B. Winter of Caterham, and finally at private schools at Brighton (cf. *The Burges Letters*,

1902, a record of her youthful days). After leaving school she lived successively with her two married sisters. Until 1880 she resided at Lincoln with her elder sister, who had married John Henchman Crowfoot, canon of the cathedral. From 1880 till death her home was with her younger sister, wife of the Rev. Humphrey Gurney Jameson—in London until 1881, in Lincoln 1881–4, and after 1884 at Eastbourne, where she devoted much time and money to charitable and religious causes. With strong religious feeling she combined through life an earnest faith in political and social liberalism. She was a secretary of the Eastbourne branch of the Women's Liberal Association, and a warm supporter of women's suffrage.

Under the appellation of EDNA LYALL, which she formed by transposing nine letters of her three names and made her permanent pseudonym, Miss Bayly published in 1879 her first book, 'Won by Waiting,' a juvenile story of a girl's life, which attracted at the time no attention, but was reissued, to her annoyance, in 1886, after she became known, and by 1894 was in a 13th edition. There followed in 1882 her second novel, 'Donovan' (3 vols.), which dealt with her religious beliefs and spiritual experiences. Although only 320 copies were sold, the book won the admiration of Gladstone, who wrote to Miss Bayly in 1883 of its first volume as 'a very delicate and refined work of art.' An intelligent review in the 'National Reformer' led to a correspondence with Charles Bradlaugh [q. v.], many of whose political convictions she shared. In spite of her dissent from his religious views, her liberal sentiments resented his exclusion on religious grounds from the House of Commons (1880–5). She thrice subscribed to the fund for defraying his electoral expenses. After his death on 30 Jan. 1891, she wrote for the press (in June) the appeal for a memorial fund, and subscribed to it her royalties for the half-year, amounting to 200*l*. With Bradlaugh's daughter, Mrs. Bradlaugh Bonner, she formed a lasting friendship. Meanwhile, on some notes supplied by Bradlaugh Miss Bayly based her novel 'We Two' (1884, 3 vols.), a sequel to 'Donovan.' The career of the secularist hero, Luke Raeburn, vaguely reflects that of Bradlaugh, although the main theme is the conversion of Erica Raeburn, the secularist's daughter, to Christianity. 'We Two' established the author's reputation, and drew 'Donovan' from its threatened oblivion. For the copyright of these two books she received no more than 50*l*. But with the publication in 1885 of 'In the Golden Days,' an able historical novel of the seventeenth century, her profits grew substantial. 'In the Golden Days' was the last book read to Ruskin on his deathbed (COLLINGWOOD, *Life of John Ruskin*, 1900, p. 403). It was dramatised later by Edwin Gilbert, but had no success on the stage. 'Donovan,' 'We Two,' and 'In the Golden Days' are Miss Bayly's best books.

Miss Bayly's popularity was thenceforth secure. In 1886 a stranger falsely claimed in public to be 'Edna Lyall,' and a report also circulated that the authoress was in a lunatic asylum. Miss Bayly met the falsehood by announcing her identity, and the experience suggested her 'Autobiography of a Slander' (1887), a brief study of the evil wrought by false gossip, which enjoyed an immense vogue and was translated into French, German, and Norwegian.

Two of her succeeding works expounded anew her political convictions. An ardent home ruler, she in 'Doreen,' an Irish novel (1894) which was first published in the 'Christian World,' presented the Irish revolutionary leader, Michael Davitt [q. v. Suppl. II], in the guise of her hero, Donal Moore. Gladstone, writing to her 25 Nov. 1894, commended 'the singular courage with which you stake your wide public reputation upon the Irish cause.' In 1896 she championed the Armenians against their Turkish oppressors in her comparatively unimpressive 'The Autobiography of a Truth' (1896), the profits of which she gave to the Armenian Relief Fund. Strongly opposed to the South African war, she spoke out with customary frankness in her last novel, 'The Hinderers' (1902).

An attack of pericarditis in 1889 had left permanent ill effects. Miss Bayly died on 8 Feb. 1903 at 6 College Road, Eastbourne. The body was cremated and the ashes buried at the foot of the old cross in Bosbury churchyard, near Bosbury Hill, Herefordshire, a place which figures in her novel 'In Spite of All' (1901), and of which her brother, the Rev. R. Burges Bayly, was vicar.

Slight in build and of medium height, with dark brown hair and dark grey-blue eyes, Miss Bayly was fond of music and of travelling, and described her tours in vivacious letters. Her style is always clear and pleasant. She developed a genuine faculty of constructing a plot, and she was especially happy in the characterisation of young girls. But her earnest political purpose, which came of her native horror of oppression and injustice, militated against her mastery of the whole art of fiction.

In 1906 a memorial window by Kempe was placed in St. Peter's Church, Eastbourne (built 1896), where Miss Bayly had worshipped and to which she had presented the seats. She had given in 1887 a peal of three bells to St. Saviour's Church, named Donovan, Erica, and Hugo, after leading characters in her three chief books.

Other works by Miss Bayly are: 1. 'Their Happiest Christmas,' 1886. 2. 'Knight Errant,' 1887 (a story of the life of a public singer, suggested by her acquaintance with Miss Mary Davies, formed while travelling in Norway). 3. 'Derrick Vaughan, Novelist,' 1889, dedicated to Miss Mary Davies, an embodiment of Miss Bayly's literary experiences, first published periodically in 'Murray's Magazine.' 4. 'A Hardy Norseman,' 1889. 5. 'Max Hereford's Dream,' 1891 (new edit. 1900). 6. 'To Right the Wrong,' 1892, an historical seventeenth-century novel, first published in 'Good Words.' 7. 'How the Children raised the Wind,' 1895. 8. 'Wayfaring Men,' 1897, a story of the stage. 9. 'Hope the Hermit,' 1898, a Cumberland tale of the days of William and Mary, which had run through the 'Christian World,' of which 9000 copies were sold on the day of separate publication. 10. 'In Spite of All,' 1901, an historical tale of the seventeenth century, originally written as a drama and produced without success at Eastbourne by the Ben Greet company, 4 Jan. 1900, then at Cambridge, and finally at the Comedy Theatre, London, 5 Feb. 1900. She also wrote a preface to 'The Story of an African Chief' by Mr. Wyndham Knight-Bruce, 1893, and on Mrs. Gaskell in 'Women Novelists of Queen Victoria's Reign,' 1897.

[J. M. Escreet, Life of Edna Lyall, 1904; The Times, 10 Feb. 1903; Athenæum, 14 Feb. 1903; G. A. Payne, Edna Lyall, 1903; H. C. Black, Notable Women Authors of the Day, 1893, with portrait; private information.] E. L.

BEALE, DOROTHEA (1831–1906), principal of Cheltenham Ladies' College, born on 21 March 1831 at 41 Bishopsgate Street Within, London, was fourth child and third daughter of the eleven children of Miles Beale, a surgeon, of a Gloucestershire family, who took an active interest in educational and social questions. His wife, Dorothea Margaret Complin, of Huguenot extraction, was first cousin to Caroline Frances Cornwallis [q. v.], to early intercourse with whom Dorothea owed much. Educated till the age of thirteen partly at home and partly at a school at Stratford, Essex, Dorothea then attended lectures at Gresham College and at the Crosby Hall Literary Institution, and developed an aptitude for mathematics. In 1847 she went with two older sisters to Mrs. Bray's fashionable school for English girls in Paris, where she remained till the revolution of 1848 brought the school to an end. In 1848 Dorothea and her sisters were among the earliest students at the newly opened Queen's College, Harley Street. Their companions included Miss Buss and Adelaide Procter [q. v.]. In 1849 Miss Beale was appointed mathematical tutor at Queen's College, and in 1854 she became head teacher in the school attached to the college, under Miss Parry. During her holidays she visited schools in Switzerland and Germany. At the end of 1856 she left Queen's College owing to dissatisfaction with its administration, and in January 1857 became head teacher of the Clergy Daughters' School, Casterton, Westmorland (founded in 1823 by Carus Wilson at Cowan Bridge, the Lowood of Charlotte Brontë's 'Jane Eyre'; cf. DOROTHEA BEALE, *Girls' Schools Past and Present*, in *Nineteenth Century*, xxiii.). At Casterton Miss Beale's insistence on the need of reforms led to her resignation in December following; many changes in the management of the school were made next year. In 1906 Miss Beale established a scholarship from Casterton School to Cheltenham.

While seeking fresh work Miss Beale taught mathematics and Latin at Miss Elwall's school at Barnes, and compiled her 'Students' Text-Book of English and General History from B.C. 100 to the Present Time,' for the use of teachers (published Aug. 1858; 5th edit. 1862).

On 16 June 1858 Miss Beale was chosen out of fifty candidates principal of the Ladies' College, Cheltenham, the earliest proprietary girls' school in England, which had been opened on 13 Feb. 1854 with eighty-two pupils on a capital of 2000*l.* With Cheltenham the rest of Miss Beale's career was identified. When she entered on her duties there were sixty-nine pupils and only 400*l.* of the original capital remained. For the next two years the college had a hard struggle. In 1860 the financial arrangements were reorganised, and by 1863 the numbers had risen to 126. Thenceforward the success of the college was assured. In 1873 it was first installed in buildings of its own, which were enlarged three years later, when there were 310 names on the books. In 1880 the college was incorporated as a company. The numbers then had reached 500. Numerous additions were made to the buildings between 1882 and 1905. In the present year (1912) there are over 1000 pupils and 120 teachers, fourteen boarding houses, a secondary and a kindergarten teachers' training department, a library of over 7000 volumes, and fifteen acres of playing-fields.

As early as 1864 Miss Beale's success as a head-mistress was acknowledged, and in 1865 she gave evidence before the endowed schools inquiry commission, the seven other lady witnesses including Miss Buss and Miss Emily Davies. The evidence, published in 1868, gave an immense impetus to the education of girls in England [see GREY, MARIA, Suppl. II, and SHIRREFF, EMILY, Suppl. I]. In 1869 Miss Beale published, with a preface by herself, the commissioners' 'Reports on the Education of Girls. With Extracts from the Evidence.' It is a remarkable exposure of the low average standard of the teaching in girls' secondary schools before 1870.

Miss Beale perceived that the absence of all means of training teachers was a main obstacle to improvement. A modest endeavour to meet the need was made by a friend at Cheltenham in 1876. Next year, on her friend's death, Miss Beale undertook to carry on the work. The progress was rapid; a residential training college for secondary women teachers, the first in this country, called St. Hilda's College, was built in Cheltenham, and opened in 1885. It was enlarged in 1890, and incorporated under the Companies Act in 1895. In order to give teachers in training the benefit of a year at Oxford, Miss Beale purchased in 1892 for 5000*l.* Cowley House, Oxford, which was opened as St. Hilda's hall of residence for women in 1893, and was in 1901 incorporated with the Cheltenham training college as 'St. Hilda's Incorporated College.' The students at St. Hilda's Hall, Oxford, are mainly but not exclusively old Cheltonians. A kindergarten class was also started by Miss Beale at Cheltenham in 1876, and a department for the training of kindergarten teachers soon followed, and became an integral part of the college work.

In 1880, mainly with a view to supplying a link between past and present pupils, Miss Beale founded 'The Cheltenham Ladies' College Magazine,' and remained its editor until her death. With the same aim, she established in 1884 'The Guild of the Ladies' Cheltenham College,' which now (1912) numbers 2500 members. On 26 Oct. 1889 the guild started in Bethnal Green the Cheltenham settlement, which is now carried on as St. Hilda's East, a house built by past and present pupils and opened on 26 April 1898. An earnest churchwoman of high church principles, Miss Beale, who was guided through life by deep religious feeling, instituted at Cheltenham in 1884 Quiet Days—devotional meetings for teachers—generally at the end of the summer term, when addresses were given by distinguished churchmen.

Outside her college work Miss Beale associated herself with nearly every effort for educational progress, and with local philanthropic institutions. She was president of the Headmistresses' Association from 1895 to 1897, and was a member of numerous educational societies. In 1894 she gave evidence before the royal commission on secondary education, of which Mr. James Bryce was chairman. In collaboration with Miss Soulsby and Miss Dove she embodied her matured views on girls' education in 'Work and Play in Girls' Schools' (1898). She identified herself with the movement for women's suffrage, being a vice-president of the central society.

Miss Beale's activities remained unimpaired in her later years, despite deafness and signs of cancer, which became apparent in 1900. On 21 Oct. 1901 the freedom of the borough of Cheltenham was conferred on her. On 11 April 1902 the university of Edinburgh awarded her the honorary degree of LL.D., in recognition of her services to education. Eleanor Anne Ormerod [q. v. Suppl. II], the entomologist, was the only woman on whom the degree had been previously conferred. The staff at Cheltenham presented her with the academic robes.

Miss Beale died after an operation for cancer in a nursing home in Cheltenham, 9 Nov. 1906. The body was cremated at Perry Barr, Birmingham, and the ashes buried in a small vault on the south side of the Lady chapel of Gloucester Cathedral.

From the time of her appointment to Cheltenham until her death Miss Beale devoted her life to the welfare of the college and to the improvement of girls' education. Living frugally, she spent large sums of her own money on the college, and at her death made it her residuary legatee, her residuary estate amounting to 55,000*l.* As a teacher Miss Beale's main object was to kindle a thirst for knowledge rather than merely to impart information (cf. for her method in teaching English literature her *Literary Studies of Poems New and Old*, 1902). She herself taught literature and the exact sciences equally well, and she attached chief importance to the teacher's personality and character and mental outlook (cf. *Addresses to Teachers*, 1909). The most original features of her organisation of the college were the rule of silence among the pupils, the absence of prizes, the weekly hearing of marks in every class by the principal herself, whereby she gained knowledge of the progress of every girl in the college, and the placing of the boarding-houses—there are now fourteen—under the direct supervision of the college authorities. A benevolent despot in her government of the college, she allowed large liberty of procedure to those members of her staff who showed capability. Open-minded and willing to experiment in new methods, she combined business ability with the enthusiasm of a reformer and shrewdness with a mystical idealism.

Miss Beale was of short stature, with an expressive face and a beautiful voice. Her bearing was somewhat cold, shy, and reserved, but to her intimate friends she was tender and sympathetic. A portrait in academic robes by J. J. Shannon, R.A., presented to her by old pupils on her jubilee, 8 Nov. 1904, hangs in the college library. Another portrait, also in the college, was painted in 1893 by Mrs. Lea Merritt at the request of the council. A miniature painted by Florence Meyer was bequeathed to the college by Miss Mary Holmes Gore in February 1907, and a marble bust by J. E. Hyett was presented to the college in May 1905. Another bust in white plaster—a better likeness than Mr. Hyett's—modelled by Miss Evangeline Stirling in 1893, was presented by the artist to St. Hilda's Hall, Oxford, in May 1905. A bronze tablet to her memory, with medallion portrait by Alfred Drury, A.R.A., is in the Lady chapel of Gloucester Cathedral; a stone tablet by L. Macdonald Gill, with an inscription, is in the college, and a memorial fund has been formed for the benefit of the staff past and present, and of old pupils who may be in special need.

[Raikes, Dorothea Beale of Cheltenham (with reproduction of Shannon's portrait), 1908; History of the Cheltenham Ladies' College, 1904; The Times, 10, 17, 19 Nov., 4 Dec. 1906; Journal of Education, Dec. 1906, Jan. 1907; Cheltenham Ladies' College Magazine, Memorial Number, 1906; private information.]

E. L.

BEALE, LIONEL SMITH (1828–1906), physician and microscopist, born at Bedford Street, Covent Garden, London, on 5 Feb. 1828, was son of Lionel John Beale (1796–1871), surgeon, who wrote on physical deformities (1830–1) and on the laws of health (1857) and was the first medical officer of health for St. Martin's in the Fields. His mother was Frances Smith (1800–1849), third daughter of James Frost Sheppard. Of his three sisters, Ellen Brooker (1831–1900) married William Watkiss Lloyd [q. v. Suppl. I], author of 'Essays on Shakespeare,' and Miss Sophia Beale is a painter and author.

Educated first at a private school and then at King's College School, Lionel became a medical student at King's College, London, and at King's College Hospital. In 1841 he was apprenticed to an apothecary and surgeon at Islington. In 1847, after matriculating at the University of London with honours in chemistry and zoology, he went to Oxford as anatomical assistant to Sir Henry Wentworth Acland (1815–1900) [q. v. Suppl. I], then Lee's reader in anatomy at Christ Church. In 1849 he obtained the licence of the Society of Apothecaries, and at the request of the government board of health made a house to house visitation at Windsor during the cholera epidemic. In 1850-1 he was resident physician at King's College Hospital and graduated M.B. Lond. (1851). He never proceeded to the degree of M.D. In 1852 he taught the use of the microscope in normal and morbid histology and physiological chemistry in a private laboratory at 27 Carey Street, and next year at the early age of twenty-five he succeeded Robert Bentley Todd [q. v.], to whose teaching he always acknowledged a deep debt, in the professorship of physiology and general and morbid anatomy in King's College; Thomas Henry Huxley was an unsuccessful candidate. Beale shared the duties for two years with (Sir) William Bowman (1816–1892) [q. v. Suppl. I], who had been Todd's assistant. In 1869 he gave up the chair to become professor of pathological anatomy, and was made at the same time honorary physician to the hospital. Although an energetic lecturer and teacher, he continued to pursue enthusiastically histological and physiological research by aid of the microscope.

In 1876 he was promoted to the professorship of medicine. A slight attack of cerebral thrombosis which scarcely impaired his vigour led to his retirement from the professorship as well as from the acting staff of the hospital in 1896. He was thereupon nominated emeritus professor and honorary consulting physician. His lectures on medicine, although they included a useful series 'On Slight Ailments, their Nature and Treatment' (1880; new edit. 1887), did not as a rule supply teaching for examination purposes; but if the audience was small, it was stimulated by Beale's scientific insight.

At the Royal College of Physicians Beale became a member in 1856 and a fellow in 1859. In 1871 he was awarded the biennial Baly gold medal for his physiological work in relation to medicine. He delivered the Lumleian lectures in 1875 on 'Life and Vital Action in Health and Disease.' He was frequently examiner to the college, a member of the council in 1877–8, censor 1881–2, and curator of the museum 1876–88.

From early life Beale was a voluminous writer, reading over 100 papers on medical subjects between 1851 and 1858 before scientific and medical societies. Of his many separately published books, the earliest, 'The Microscope and its Application to Clinical Medicine' (1854), came out when he was twenty-nine and foretold his ultimate position as one of the most brilliant of English microscopists, who not only introduced new methods of microscopic research but also showed the value of the microscope to diagnosis in clinical medicine. The word 'practical' replaced 'clinical' in subsequent editions of this work, the fourth and last of which appeared in 1870. There followed in 1857 'The Use of the Microscope in Clinical Medicine'; in later editions, the fifth and last of which appeared in 1880, the title was changed to 'How to Work with the Microscope.'

In 1858 he published a small book, 'Illustrations of the Constituents of the Urine, Urinary Deposits and Calculi' (2nd edit. 1869), and in 1861 a larger work 'On Urine, Urinary Deposits, and Calculi, their Microscopical and Chemical Examination' (12mo; 2nd edit. 1864, with 'and Treatment, &c.' added to the title; American edit. 1885). Other important early works were 'On the Structure of the Simple Tissues of the Human Body' (1861; German trans. 1862) and 'The Structure and Growth of the Tissues, and on Life' (1865).

Beale's scientific promise was acknowledged in 1865 by his election as fellow of the Royal Society, where he delivered the Croonian lectures in the same year on 'The Ultimate Nerve Fibres distributed to the Muscles and to some other Tissues.' In 1868–9 he lectured at Oxford for the Radcliffe trustees on 'Disease Germs.' He embodied his conclusions in two books: 'Disease Germs, their Supposed Nature' (1870), and 'Disease Germs, their Real Nature, an Original Investigation' (1870). Both were reissued in 'Disease Germs, their Nature and Origin' (1872). In 1870 there appeared his 'Protoplasm, or Life and Matter' (4th edit. 1892), and in 1872 his 'Bioplasm, an Introduction to the Study of Physiology and Medicine.' In his works on germs Beale foreshadowed by virtue of his microscopic methods of investigation some of the most modern conceptions of bacterial disease, anticipating by fully five years the microbic theory of disease and also Pasteur's doctrine of 'immunisation.'

Beale was the first physiological investigator to practise the method of fixing tissues by injections and so prevent the alterations which result in them from uncontrolled post-mortem changes. He also treated tissues with dilute acetic acid, which enabled him to see delicate nerve fibres almost as well as they are seen by modern *intra vitam* staining methods, and he introduced carmine in ammoniacal solution as a stain for differentiating between the component parts of the tissues. By means of the staining effects of carmine he was able, after a close study of tissues in various conditions, to draw a distinction between the 'germinal' matter or 'bioplasm,' as he called it, and the 'formed' matter of the tissues. Beale's discoveries also included the pyriform nerve ganglion cells, called 'Beale's cells,' and he showed the peculiar arrangement of the two fibres which he thought (incorrectly, as later inquiry shows) were prolonged from them. An unusually good draughtsman, Beale illustrated his books profusely with graphic drawings by himself, many of which were coloured, and all were drawn strictly to scale. He made the drawings direct upon the boxwood blocks, and even engraved many with his own hand. Beale's drawings of Beale's cells are still reproduced in standard works on histology. All his microscopic specimens are in the possession of his son and are still improving in clearness.

In later life Beale was president of the Microscopical Society (1879–1880) and fellow or member of numerous European and American medical or scientific societies. He also acted from 1891 to 1904 as physician to the pensions commutation board and as government medical referee for

England. To the close of his life he speculated much on philosophical and religious themes. His mental attitude is disclosed in his 'Life Theories' (1870); 'Life Theories; their Influence on Religious Thought' (1871), and 'Our Morality, and the Moral Question, chiefly from the Medical Side' (1887). In discussing 'vitality and vital action' (cf. *Lancet*, 1898) he pronounced strongly against 'atheism,' 'materialism,' 'agnosticism,' 'monism,' and 'free thought.' His religious point of view was that of a broad churchman. He treated the differences between man and animals as absolute, but he failed to defend his scientific position quite clearly, or to draw into controversy as he hoped fellow men of science.

Beale's intimate friends included Edward Thring (1821–1887) [q. v.], headmaster of Uppingham, Sir Henry Acland, Victor Carus of Leipzig, Sir William Bowman, and Henry Wace, dean of Canterbury. An indefatigable worker, he took no real holiday after 1858. He eschewed alcohol and ate little meat. An enthusiastic and skilful gardener, he made his country home at Weybridge known amongst horticulturists, chiefly by his culture of palms and Japanese plants, and in a small greenhouse at 61 Grosvenor Street, where he lived for forty-five years, he successfully grew orchids and other hothouse plants. In 1900 he suffered from a second attack of cerebral hæmorrhage. In 1904 he left Weybridge, where he had been living since 1885, for Bentinck Street, the house of his only surviving child, Peyton Todd Bowman Beale, F.R.C.S. He died there from pontine hæmorrhage on 28 March 1906. He was buried in Weybridge cemetery. He married in 1859 Frances, only daughter of the Rev. Peyton Blakiston, M.D., F.R.S., of St. Leonards, formerly of Birmingham; she died in 1892.

Beale was of moderate height and of sturdy build, with remarkably abundant hair, which retained its brown colour up to the age of seventy. A portrait by H. T. Wells, R.A., exhibited in the Royal Academy (1876) and the Paris exhibition (1878), belongs to his son, and a memorial tablet in bronze, designed, worked and erected by his son, is in King's College Hospital.

Besides the works cited and contributions to periodicals Beale's publications include: 1. 'On Some Points in the Anatomy of the Liver of Man and Vertebrate Animals,' 1856. 2. 'Tables for the Chemical and Microscopical Examination of Urine in Health and Disease,' 1856. 3. 'On Deficiency of Vital Power in Disease,' 1863. 4. 'New Observations upon the Structure and Formation of Certain Nervous Centres,' 1864. 5. 'The Liver,' 1889.

[Information from Mr. Peyton Todd Bowman Beale, F.R.C.S., and Miss Sophia Beale; Lancet, 7 April 1906 (with portrait from photograph) and 16 Oct. 1909; Brit. Med. Journal, 7 April 1906; Index Catalogue, Surgeon General's Office, Washington; Beale's own books; Proc. Roy. Soc., 1907, 77 B.]

E. M. B.

BEATTIE-BROWN, WILLIAM (1831–1909), Scottish landscape painter, born in the parish of Haddington in 1831, was son of Adam Brown, farmer, and Ann Beattie. He removed at an early age to Edinburgh and was educated at Leith High School. Having early shown a taste for art, he was apprenticed as a glass-stainer to the well-known firm of Messrs. Ballantine, and here his artistic tastes were so rapidly developed that before his apprenticeship was completed he entered the Trustees' Art Academy, then under the charge of Robert Scott Lauder [q. v.]. Among his fellow-students of this period and companions of a later time were William Bell Scott [q. v.], Horatio MacCulloch, Sam Bough, and George Paul Chalmers [q. v.]. In 1848, when seventeen years of age, he exhibited a picture, 'On the Forth,' at the Royal Scottish Academy, and from that time till his death he was always represented at the annual exhibitions. His skill and accuracy as a draughtsman led to his being employed to make illustrations for several medical works; and his care and discretion as an artist brought him much employment in restoring pictures for Henry Doig, art-dealer, Edinburgh, whose daughter he married in 1858. To extend his experience he studied for a long time in Belgium, there using water-colour as his principal medium, though his chief work was done in oil-colour. He found English subjects for his pictures in Surrey, Kent, and Yorkshire, but his main themes were Scottish highland landscapes. He was a pioneer among the Scottish 'out-of-door' artists, frequently completing his pictures directly from nature—a practice which explains his vigour and realism. In 1871 he was elected an associate of the Royal Scottish Academy, and in 1884 an academician. His diploma picture, dated 1883, is a characteristic highland landscape, 'Coire-na-Faireamh.' now in the Scottish National Gallery,

Edinburgh. Representative works by him are in the public galleries at Liverpool, Manchester, Oldham, and Bolton. He was a frequent exhibitor at the Royal Academy, London, and also at Glasgow and other Scottish exhibitions. In his later years he adopted a more glowing scheme of colour than in his earlier work; but his pictures were always noticeable for their realistic line and tone, and for their technical excellence. Beattie-Brown died at Edinburgh on 31 March 1909.

By his wife, Esther Love Doig, he had three sons and six daughters. The eldest son, H. W. Jennings Brown (1862–1898), showed promise as a portrait and figure-painter.

[Cat. Nat. Gall. of Scotland (42nd edit.); Scotsman, 1 April 1909; Graves's Royal Acad. Exhibitors; private information.] A. H. M.

BECKETT, Sir EDMUND, first Baron Grimthorpe (1816–1905), lawyer, mechanician and controversialist, born at Carlton Hall, near Newark, on 12 May 1816, was eldest son of Sir Edmund Beckett, fourth baronet (1787–1874), who assumed the additional surname of Denison by royal letters patent in 1816 and resumed his original surname by the same process on succeeding to the baronetcy in 1872. The elder Sir Edmund was conservative M.P. for the West Riding in 1841 and again from 1848 to 1859. Beckett's mother, who died on 27 March 1874, was Maria, daughter of William Beverley of Beverley, and great-niece and heiress of Anne, daughter of Roundell Smithson of Millfield, near Harewood, and widow of Sir Thomas Denison, judge of the king's bench.

Educated at Doncaster grammar school, Eton, and Trinity College, Cambridge, Beckett Denison graduated B.A. as thirtieth wrangler in 1838 (M.A. 1841, LL.D. 1863). He was called to the bar at Lincoln's Inn in 1841, became a Q.C. in 1854, a bencher of his inn in the same year, and its treasurer in 1876. He soon acquired a large practice, chiefly in connection with railway bills, becoming famous for his severe cross-examination and retentive memory. Advancing rapidly in his profession, Beckett Denison had by 1860 become recognised as the leader of the parliamentary bar, though his powers of sarcasm and assertive manner stood him in better stead with committees and rival counsel than his knowledge of law. He was very tenacious of the rights of the inns of court, and strongly resented any attempt to interfere with them. Keeping a keen eye on his fees, he accumulated a large fortune. He ceased to practise regularly after 1880, though he still accepted an occasional brief. Succeeding his father in the baronetcy on 24 May 1874, Beckett Denison followed his example by discarding the second surname. As Sir Edmund Beckett he was appointed chancellor and vicar-general of the province of York in 1877, an office which he held until 1900. Beckett was created a peer by the title of Baron Grimthorpe of Grimthorpe, Yorkshire, on 17 Feb. 1886, with remainder to the issue male of his father.

Meanwhile Grimthorpe showed an exceptional versatility of interest in matters outside the law, and conducted numerous controversies on ecclesiastical, architectural, scientific, and other topics with vigour and acrimony. His earliest energies were engaged in theological warfare. In 1848 he published 'Six Letters on Dr. Todd's Discourses on the Prophecies relating to the Apocalypse,' a strenuous polemic. The controversy on marriage with a deceased wife's sister then engaged his attention, and between 1849 and 1851 he produced four pamphlets in favour of that cause, the most important of which was 'A Short Letter on the Bishop of Exeter's [Dr. Phillpotts'] Speech on the Marriage Bill.' To the end of his life he supported a measure of relief.

As chancellor of York he became the attached friend of the archbishop, William Thomson [q. v.], but did not hesitate to criticise episcopal proceedings with freedom, when he disagreed with them. A strong advocate of reform in church discipline, he gave evidence before the royal commission of 1883, and drafted a disciplinary bill of his own with racy notes, which he sent to the commissioners. There followed an outspoken 'Letter to the Archbishop of York on the Report of the Commission on Ecclesiastical Courts.' Together with Dean Burgon [q. v. Suppl. I], he took exception to the revised version of the New Testament, publishing in 1882 'Should the Revised New Testament be Authorised?' and a rejoinder to Dr. Farrar's answer to that criticism [see Farrar, Frederick William, Suppl. II]. Much alarmed by the spread of ritualism in the Church of England, he became president of the Protestant Churchmen's Alliance, which held its inaugural meeting in Exeter Hall in 1889. The Lincoln judgment of 1890 [see King, Edward, Suppl. II] stirred him to write what Archbishop Benson called a 'furious letter,' entitled 'A Review of the Lambeth Judgment in Read *v.* the Bishop of

Lincoln' (A. C. BENSON'S *Edward White Benson*, ii. 373). Benson acknowledged Grimthorpe's assistance on the church patronage bill of 1893, when he produced 'a set of amendments really helpful.' The measure was reintroduced and passed its second reading two years afterwards with Grimthorpe's approval. When, later, in 1895, Lord Halifax moved the second reading of a divorce bill, amending the Act by which the clergy were compelled to lend their churches for the remarriage of those guiltily divorced, Grimthorpe 'treated this relief as an attempt to secure the "supremacy of the clergy," and vituperated the archbishop of York as a Solon and Janus.' 'I never,' wrote Benson, 'saw spite so open in the house before' (*ibid.* ii. 641). Not long before his death, Grimthorpe eagerly supported Sir William Harcourt [q. v. Suppl. II], who was denouncing ritualistic practices in a series of letters to 'The Times.' His standpoint through all his disputes was strongly erastian and orthodox, as he understood orthodoxy.

Architecture, especially on its ecclesiastical side, also long occupied Grimthorpe's mind. In 1855 he published 'Lectures on Gothic Architecture, chiefly in relation to St. George's Church at Doncaster.' This parish church, having been burnt down, was rebuilt by Sir George Gilbert Scott [q. v.], with suggestions from Grimthorpe, who contributed liberally to the funds. Grimthorpe, while expressing admiration of Scott's work, was mercilessly sarcastic at the expense of Scott's rivals; Scott on his side admitted Grimthorpe's generosity and strenuous support of sound architecture, but ungraciously added that 'he has an unpleasant way of doing things, which makes one hate one's best work' (SCOTT'S *Personal and Professional Recollections*, 173). Grimthorpe next published 'A Book on Building, Civil and Ecclesiastical, with the Theory of Domes and of the Great Pyramid' (1876; 2nd edit., enlarged, 1880), which again contained many shrewd hits at the architectural profession. In it are enumerated the buildings which he himself had 'substantially designed,' including the Church of St. James, Doncaster, in which Scott had a hand (*ib.*); St. Chad's Church, Headingley; Cliffe parish church in the East Riding; St. Paul's, Burton-on-Trent; the tower-top of Worcester Cathedral; Doncaster grammar school, and the extension of Lincoln's Inn library. His influence is also to be traced in the injudicious restoration of Lincoln's Inn chapel in 1882, but his contemplated demolition of Sir Thomas Lovell's gate-house in Chancery Lane was happily frustrated.

The architectural enterprise with which his name is inseparably connected came later. Living in a house at Batch Wood, St. Albans, designed by himself, 'the only architect with whom I have never quarrelled,' he was much interested in the unsound condition of St. Albans Abbey, and the endeavour of the St. Albans reparation committee to fit it for cathedral and parochial service. He subscribed generously to the funds, contributing, from first to last, some 130,000*l.*, and interfered freely with Scott the architect. 'The leader,' wrote Scott in 1877, 'among those who wish me to do what I ought not to do is Sir Edmund Beckett' (*ib.* 357). In 1880, various parts of the building being in danger of falling down, and the committee having exhausted its funds and being 3000*l.* in debt, Grimthorpe obtained a faculty to 'restore, repair and refit' the church at his own expense. He set to work with characteristic zeal, and by 1885 the nave was finished. But his arbitrary treatment of the roof and new west front and his insertion of windows in the terminations of the transepts excited the fiercest criticism, and he returned blow for blow. In favouring a high-pitched roof, instead of the existing flat roof, he found himself at sharp issue with George Edmund Street [q. v. Suppl. I], but nothing could divert him from his purpose (A. E. STREET'S *Memoir of George Edmund Street*, 242–7). Meanwhile Henry Hucks Gibbs, afterwards Lord Aldenham [q. v. Suppl. II], had obtained a concurrent faculty to restore the high altar screen, and a conflict of authorities ensued. In 1889 the case came before Sir Francis Jeune [q. v. Suppl. II], chancellor of the diocese, the point really at issue being Gibbs's right to fill up the central place on the high altar with a crucifix. Grimthorpe conducted his own case against Sir Walter Phillimore and Mr. C. A. Cripps, Q.C. Neither side was completely successful, but Gibbs was eventually allowed to erect the crucifix. Grimthorpe described his part in the St. Albans controversies in 'St. Albans Cathedral and its Restoration' (1885; 2nd edit., revised and enlarged, 1890), which, though purporting to be a guide-book, is also a somewhat vehement review of old arguments with 'Street and Co.,' 'sham critics of shams,' and others.

Through his long life Grimthorpe was further busy over mechanical inventions, working at them with his own hands. In 1850 he published a clearly written and instructive work, 'A Rudimentary Treatise on Clock and Watchmaking.' It passed through eight editions, with some changes of title, becoming in 1903 'A Rudimentary Treatise on Clocks, Watches and Bells, with a new preface and a new list of great bells and an appendix on weathercocks.' His articles on clocks, watches and bells in the 'Encyclopædia Britannica,' which were reprinted separately, were based on this work. He designed the great clock for the International Exhibition of 1851, made by Edward John Dent [q. v.]; it is now at King's Cross railway station. In the same year he undertook, in conjunction with (Sir) George Biddell Airy [q. v. Suppl. I] and Dent, the construction of the great clock for the clock-tower in the Houses of Parliament, Westminster. The design was his, as an inscription records, and it included his new gravity escapement, in which a pendulum weighing 6 cwt. is kept going by a scape wheel weighing little more than a quarter of an ounce; this is known as the 'double three-legged gravity escapement,' and was inserted in 1859. Grimthorpe also prepared the specifications for the bell commonly called 'Big Ben,' after Sir Benjamin Hall, commissioner of public works. The clock and 'Big Ben,' like most of Grimthorpe's undertakings, involved him in fierce controversies, and he waged battle for sixteen years with the office of public works, with Sir Charles Barry [q. v.] the architect, with Sir George Airy, who withdrew from the undertaking, and others. In the libel action, Stainbank *v.* Beckett, turning on the soundness of the bell, he was cast in 200*l.* damages (1859). (For an excellent, if disputatious account of the Westminster clock, see BECKETT's *Rudimentary Treatise*, 8th edit.; also the *Journal of the Soc. of Arts*, 13 Jan. 1854, and the *Horological Journal*, xv.). Grimthorpe was elected president of the Horological Institute in 1868, on condition that he should not attend dinners, and was annually re-elected, though not always without opposition. In the preface to the eighth edition of the 'Rudimentary Treatise' he stated that he had 'either directly or indirectly' designed over forty clocks, 'including those at Westminster and St. Paul's (with the great peal of bells), and in many other cathedrals and churches, as well as town-halls, railways stations and others in several of our colonies.' The new clock at St. Paul's Cathedral, which was constructed after his specifications, was finished in 1893; he said of its makers, Messrs. John Smith of Derby, that they 'would clock you in the best way and as near eternity as possible' (SINCLAIR'S *Memorials of St. Paul's Cathedral*, 430–4). Grimthorpe's services and advice were always gratuitously given, and no municipal council or country clergyman, who approached him with due deference on the subject of clocks or bells, ever appealed to him in vain.

In 1852 Grimthorpe invented an ingenious lock, but it proved to be too elaborate for commercial success; it does not appear to have been patented. The wide scope of his scientific knowledge was further proved by a clever little handbook, 'Astronomy without Mathematics' (1865).

He died at Batch Wood, St. Albans, on 29 April 1905, after a short illness, aggravated by a fall. He was interred by his wife's side in the north-west side of the burial-ground of St. Albans Cathedral. His personal estate was valued at 1,562,500*l.*, and he left a complicated will with many codicils which was the cause of prolonged litigation. He had married on 7 Oct. 1845 Fanny Catherine (*d.* 1901), daughter of Dr. John Lonsdale [q. v.], bishop of Lichfield. Leaving no issue, he was succeeded in the baronetcy and in the peerage (by special remainder) by his nephew, Ernest William Beckett, born 25 Nov. 1856, who had been M.P. for the Whitby division of Yorkshire since 1885.

Lord Grimthorpe, who owed his peerage to his activity in ecclesiastical matters, combined with his architectural skill and mechanical genius, possessed a manly intellect and varied talents. If he won his position at the bar by his self-assertive personality rather than by learning, his knowledge of horology was unquestioned, and he had a genuine grasp of architectural principles, though he was inclined to be ruthless in carrying them out. His mind, unfortunately, was given to cavil, and, troubled by no doubts on any subject, he rushed into print, often without provocation. In his ecclesiastical controversies he at times appeared in an unamiable light. His faults were, however, outweighed by the strength of his friendships, the largeness of his generosity, and his kindness towards those who stood in need of help. He was tall and stern of aspect and was always faithful to early Victorian costume.

Besides the works cited Grimthorpe wrote his father-in-law's biography, 'The Life of John Lonsdale, Bishop of Lichfield, with some of his Writings' (1868); and

'A Review of Hume and Huxley on Miracles' (S.P.C.K. 1883), which Bishop Harold Browne considered one of the best books in defence of the Christian faith. Of kindred purpose was his volume 'On the Origin of the Laws of Nature' (1879). His masculine common sense appeared in 'Trade Unionism and its Results' (1878), a hostile criticism which he originally wrote as letters in 'The Times.' A cartoon portrait by 'Spy' appeared in 'Vanity Fair' in 1889.

[The Times, 1 May 1905; Guardian, 3 May 1905; Law Times, 6 May 1905; Horological Journal, June 1905, art. by F. J. Britten (with portraits).] L. C. S.

BEDDOE, JOHN (1826–1911), physician and anthropologist, born at Bewdley, Worcestershire, on 21 Sept. 1826, was son of John Beddoe by his wife Emma, only daughter of Henry Barrer Child of Bewdley.

Educated at Bridgnorth School, he read for the law, but soon entered University College, London, where he began the study of medicine. After graduating B.A. at London in 1851, he pursued his medical studies at Edinburgh University, qualifying M.D. in 1853. For some time he was house physician at the Edinburgh Royal Infirmary. During the Crimean war Beddoe served at Renkioi on the medical staff of a civil hospital, afterwards proceeding to Vienna to complete his medical training. He subsequently made an extended continental tour, and then in 1857 began practice as a physician at Clifton. He was physician to the Bristol Royal Infirmary (1862–73), and consulting physician to the Children's Hospital there (1866–1911). He was elected F.R.C.P. in 1873. Retiring from practice in Bristol (1891), he settled at Bradford-on-Avon, Wiltshire.

Beddoe began active researches in ethnology during his early wanderings in Austria, Hungary, Italy, France, and other countries, and ultimately he became an authority on the physical characteristics of living European races. Much of his work was pioneer, and was carried on when researches of the kind were little valued. But Beddoe's unflagging industry and stimulating zeal influenced profoundly the development of anthropological science at home and abroad.

In 1846, when twenty years old, he began observations on hair and eye colours in the West of England, continuing these in Orkney (1852), with amended methods. There followed a long series of kindred observations, as time and areas served. In 1853 he published 'Contributions to Scottish Ethnology,' and fifty-five years afterwards, in 'A Last Contribution to Scottish Ethnology,' a paper before the Royal Anthropological Institute, he surveyed the intervening progress (*Journ. Roy. Anthrop. Inst.* xxxviii.). In 1867 he received from the Welsh National Eisteddfod a prize of 100 guineas for the best essay on the origin of the English nation, subsequently embodied in 'The Races of Britain' (1885). His racial data on 'Stature and Bulk of Man in the British Isles' appeared with critical observations and deductions in 1870 (*Memoirs Anthrop. Soc. Lond.* iii.). A paper, 'De l'Évaluation et de la Signification de la Capacité cranienne,' which he communicated in 1903 to 'L'Anthropologie' (vol. xiv.), met with hostile criticism from Mr. M. A. Lewenz and Prof. Karl Pearson, F.R.S., in a joint paper in 'Biometrika' (vol. iii. 1904). Beddoe replied in the 'Journal of the Royal Anthropological Institute' (vol. xxxiv. 1904) at the same time as he published there 'The Somatology of Eight Hundred Boys in Training for the Royal Navy,' a series of detailed colour-observations and head-measurements. Later (*ibid.* xxxvii. 1907) he sent a paper 'On a Series of Skulls collected by John E. Pritchard from a Carmelite Burying-ground in Bristol.'

Beddoe was a foundation member (1857) of the Ethnological Society, president of the Anthropological Society, 1869–70, and of the (Royal) Anthropological Institute, 1889–91. In 1905 he delivered the Huxley lecture of the institute on 'Colour and Race' (*Journ. Roy. Anthrop. Inst.* xxxv.), and received on that occasion the Huxley memorial medal. He served on the council of the British Association 1870–5, and as chairman of the anthropological department of Section D, at the Bradford meeting in 1873, delivered an address on the 'Anthropology of Yorkshire.' He was joint author of the association's 'Anthropological Instructions for Travellers.'

He was elected F.R.S. on 12 June 1873. In 1891 the University of Edinburgh conferred the honorary degree of LL.D., and he delivered there the Rhind lectures in archæology, on 'The Anthropological History of Europe,' of which the substance appeared in the 'Scottish Review' in 1892. Shortly before his death Beddoe expanded the MS. of the lectures for issue in volume form. Beddoe was made Officier (1re classe) de l'Instruction Publique, France, in 1890, and he was a member of the chief continental anthropological societies. In 1908 the

University of Bristol elected him honorary professor of anthropology.

One of the founders in 1875 of the Bristol and Gloucestershire Archæological Society, he was president in 1890; in 1909 president of the Wiltshire Archæological and Natural History Society, and at the time of his death president of the British Kyrle Society.

Beddoe's 'Memories of Eighty Years' appeared in 1910. He died at Bradford-on-Avon on 19 July 1911. In 1858 he married Agnes Montgomerie Cameron, daughter of Rev. A. Christison and niece of Sir Robert Christison, first baronet [q. v.], and had issue one son, who predeceased him, and one daughter.

A portrait of Beddoe, painted by Miss E. B. Warne, and purchased by private subscription in 1907, was presented to the Municipal Art Gallery, Bristol.

[Beddoe's Memories of Eighty Years, 1910; Proc. Roy. Soc., Anniv. Address, 30 Nov. 1911; Nature, 27 July 1911; The Times, 20 July 1911; Man (with portrait), Oct. 1911; Brit. Med. Journal (with portrait), 5 Aug. 1911; Lancet, 29 July 1911; Men and Women of the Time, 1899; Trans. Bristol and Gloucestershire Archæol. Soc. xxxiii.; Rept. Bristol Kyrle Soc. (with portrait), Oct. 1911.] T. E. J.

BEDFORD, WILLIAM KIRKPATRICK RILAND (1826–1905), antiquary and genealogist, born at Sutton Coldfield rectory on 12 July 1826, was eldest of five sons of William Riland Bedford, rector of Sutton Coldfield, Warwickshire (*d.* 1843), by his wife Grace Campbell, daughter of Charles Sharpe of Hoddam, Dumfriesshire. Charles Kirkpatrick Sharpe [q. v.] was his mother's brother. After education at Sutton Coldfield grammar school, Bedford won a Queen's scholarship at Westminster school in 1840, and passing head of the list qualified for a studentship at Christ Church, Oxford. An attack of scarlet fever denied him the advantage of his success, and on 5 June 1844 he matriculated as a commoner at Brasenose College. In 1847 he was secretary of the Union Society when Lord Dufferin [q. v. Suppl. II] was president. He graduated B.A. in 1848 and proceeded M.A. in 1852. In 1849 he was ordained to the curacy of Southwell, Nottinghamshire, and in 1850 he succeeded his uncle, Dr. Williamson, as rector of Sutton Coldfield. He held the post for forty-two years, and was rural dean for twenty-five.

Bedford was an acknowledged authority on the antiquities of Sutton Coldfield, which he described in 'Three Hundred Years of a Family Living, being a History of the Rilands of Sutton Coldfield' (1889), and 'The Manor of Sutton, Feudal and Municipal' (1901). He was well versed in heraldry and genealogies, and was a frequent contributor to 'Notes and Queries.' From 1878 to 1902 he was chaplain of the order of St. John of Jerusalem, and in his capacity of official genealogist he compiled many works dealing with the history and regulations of the knights hospitallers, including 'Malta and the Knights' (1870; 2nd edit. 1894), 'Notes on the Old Hospitals of the Order of St. John of Jerusalem' (1881), and a history of the English Hospitallers (1902) in collaboration with R. Holbeche.

Bedford was a keen cricketer in the early days of the game. On 20 July 1856 he founded 'The Free Foresters,' an amateur wandering club with headquarters at Sutton Coldfield, and he recorded the fortunes of the club in his 'Annals of the Free Foresters from 1856' (1895). He was also an expert archer and frequently attended the meetings of the Woodmen of Arden at Meriden, Warwickshire, winning the Arden medal on 16 July 1857. In 1885 he published 'Records of the Woodmen of Arden from 1785,' and contributed to the volume on 'Archery' in the Badminton series (1894). In addition to the works already mentioned his chief publications were a 'Memoir of C. K. Sharpe,' his uncle, written from family papers (1888), 'The Blazon of Episcopacy' (1858; 2nd edit. 1897), and 'Outcomes of Old Oxford' (1899).

Bedford died at Cricklewood on 23 Jan. 1905; his ashes were buried after cremation at Golder's Green. He married: (1) on 18 Sept. 1851, Maria Amy, youngest daughter of Joseph Houson (*d.* 1890) of Southwell, Nottinghamshire; (2) in 1900, Margaret, daughter of Denis Browne. He had by his first wife seven sons and three daughters.

[Westminster School Register, 1764–1883, p. 19; The Times, 25 January 1905; Wisden's Cricketer's Almanack, 1906; Annals of the Free Foresters, 1895 (with portrait); Memories of Dean Hole, p. 7; Notes and Queries, 10th s. iii. 120; Brit. Mus. Cat.; Brasenose College Register, 1509–1909, i. 532.] G. S. W.

BEECHAM, THOMAS (1820–1907), patent medicine vendor, was born at Witney, Oxfordshire, on 3 Dec. 1820, being the son of Joseph and Mary Beecham. About 1845 he opened a chemist's shop in Wigan, South Lancashire, and there invented a formula for pills, his first patent-medicine licence being dated Liverpool, 8 July 1847. In 1846 he married. In 1859 he removed his business, still quite small, to the then new township of St. Helens, half-way between Wigan and Liverpool. At St. Helens he picked up, from the chance remark of a lady who purchased his pills, the phrase 'worth a guinea a box,' which he made the advertising motto of his concern. In 1866 his elder son, Joseph, joined the business, and infused into it a highly enterprising spirit. In 1885 the present head-factory and office-buildings in Westfield Street, St. Helens, were built at an initial cost of 30,000*l*. Joseph Beecham then visited the United States, and established a factory in New York, since followed by factories and agencies in several other countries. In 1887 the father bought an estate, Mursley Hall, near Winslow, Buckinghamshire, where he farmed till 1893. In 1895 he retired from active work in favour of his son Joseph. After an extended tour in the United States he built a house, Wychwood, Northwood Avenue, Southport, Lancashire, where he died on 6 April 1907, leaving a large personal fortune, and his share in an immense business. In South Lancashire he was well known as an eccentric public benefactor. By religion he was a congregationalist. Besides his son Joseph (*b*. 1848), mayor of St. Helens in 1889–99 and 1910–12, who was knighted in 1912, he had a second son, William Eardley Beecham (*b*. 1855), a doctor practising in London.

[The Times, 8 April and 5 June (will), 1907; Chemist and Druggist, 13 April 1907; private information.] C. M–N.

BEEVOR, CHARLES EDWARD (1854–1908), neurologist, born in London on 12 June 1854, was eldest son of Charles Beevor, F.R.C.S., and Elizabeth, daughter of Thomas Burrell. He received his early education at Blackheath proprietary school and at University College, London. Pursuing medical study at University College Hospital, he proceeded M.R.C.S. in 1878, M.B. London in 1879, M.D. London in 1881. In 1882 he became M.R.C.P. London, and in 1888 F.R.C.P. After holding the appointments of house physician at University College Hospital, and resident medical officer at the National Hospital for the Paralysed and Epileptic, Queen Square, W.C., he went abroad in 1882–3, and studied under the great teachers, including Obersteiner, Weigert, Cohnheim, and Erb, at Vienna, Leipzig, Berlin, and Paris. On his return in 1883 he was appointed assistant physician to Queen Square Hospital, and to the Great Northern Hospital in 1885. In course of time he became full physician to both institutions, offices which he held until his death.

From 1883 to 1887 Beevor was engaged with (Sir) Victor Horsley in experimental research on the localisation of cerebral functions, especially with regard to the course and origin of the motor tracts. This work crystallised the truth of the results obtained by previous investigators, and established the reputation of the authors (*Phil. Trans.* clxxxi. 1890; also 1887–9). In 1903 Beevor delivered the Croonian lectures before the Royal College of Physicians, on 'Muscular Movements and their Representation in the Central Nervous System' (published in 1904), a classical piece of work entailing prodigious labour and painstaking observation. In 1907 he delivered before the Medical Society of London the Lettsomian lectures on 'The Diagnosis and Localisation of Cerebral Tumours.' He contributed many papers on subjects connected with neurology to 'Brain' and other medical journals, and in 1898 he published a 'Handbook on Diseases of the Nervous System,' which became a leading text-book. His most important work, however, was embodied in a paper on 'The Distribution of the Different Arteries supplying the Brain,' which was published in the 'Philosophical Transactions of the Royal Society' in 1908. After many attempts, he succeeded in injecting simultaneously the five arteries of the brain with different coloured substances held in solution in gelatin. By this means he determined exactly the blood supply to different parts of the brain, and showed that the distribution of blood is purely anatomical, and does not vary according to the physiological action of the parts. Until this work was published, no book contained an accurate description of the cerebral arterial circulation. The importance of Beevor's discovery was not only from the anatomical side but also from the pathological, for it enables the physician to know the exact portions of the brain which are liable to undergo softening when any particular artery is blocked by a clot of blood.

In May 1908 he went by invitation to America. There his lectures on his own subjects were received with enthusiasm at Philadelphia, New York, Chicago, and Boston by the members of the American Neurological Society, and by those of the

American Medical Association at their fifty-ninth annual session. In 1907–8 he was president of the Neurological Society, and on its amalgamation with the Royal Society of Medicine he became the first president of the corresponding section, and died in office. For ten years he was hon. secretary to the Association for the Advancement of Medicine by Research.

He died from sudden cardiac failure, on 5 Dec. 1908, at his residence in Wimpole Street. He married on 7 Feb. 1882 Blanche Adine, daughter of Dr. Thomas Robinson Leadam, who with a son and daughter survive him. He was buried at Hampstead cemetery.

An enlarged photograph hangs in the committee-room of the medical board of the National Hospital, Queen Square, Bloomsbury.

Beevor ranks amongst the great authorities on the anatomy and diseases of the nervous system. He possessed great intellectual power, energy and industry, and was unsurpassed in accuracy of observation. As a recorder of facts he was conscientious and precise. Yet he was so imbued with scientific caution, that he often hesitated to publish his own observations when they seemed at variance with tradition and accepted teaching.

[Lancet, 19 Dec. 1908; Brit. Med. Journal, 12 Dec. 1908; Presidential Address, Royal College of Physicians, 1909.] L. G.

BEIT, ALFRED (1853–1906), financier and benefactor, born at Hamburg on 15 Feb. 1853, was eldest son of Siegfried and Laura Beit. The father was a merchant belonging to a well-known Hamburg family, Jewish by race, Lutheran by religion. 'I was one of the poor Beits of Hamburg,' the son once said, implying that another branch was better off than his own. Beit was educated privately, and at seventeen entered the Hamburg office of a firm of South African merchants, D. Lippert & Co., his kinsmen. With a view to qualifying to act as a representative of the branch of this firm, just extended from Port Elizabeth to Kimberley at the diamond mining centre in Griqualand West, Cape Colony, Beit spent 1874 at Amsterdam, where he obtained a knowledge of the diamond trade at first hand. Early in September 1875 he sailed for Cape Town, and proceeding to Kimberley by waggon was one of Lippert's representatives there until 1878, when he revisited Hamburg. His Amsterdam training enabled him to see that Cape diamonds, so far from deserving their current repute of being an inferior product, were generally as good as any in the world, and were being sold in Africa at a price far below their worth in Europe. Accordingly borrowing 2000*l.* from his father by way of capital, he returned to Kimberley in the same year, and set up under his own name as a diamond merchant. Foreseeing the growth of Kimberley, he is said to have invested most of his capital in purchasing ground on which he put up a number of corrugated iron offices. For twelve of these the rent ultimately received by him was estimated at 1800*l.* a month, and later he is believed to have sold the ground for 260,000*l.*

In 1882 he became associated in the diamond business at Kimberley with J. Porges and Julius Wernher. The latter, who was created a baronet in 1905, was a young Hessian who, having fought in the Franco-German war, had come out to South Africa as a qualified architect and surveyor. In 1884 Porges and Wernher returned to England and constituted the London firm of J. Porges & Co. dealing in diamonds and diamond shares, and after 1888 in gold mines as well. Beit was sole representative of this firm at Kimberley until July 1888, when he made London his headquarters, although his subsequent visits to Africa were frequent. On 1 Jan. 1890 the firm of Wernher, Beit & Co. replaced J. Porges & Co., in the same line of business.

When settled at Kimberley, Beit made the acquaintance of Cecil John Rhodes [q. v. Suppl. II], and while close business relations followed he felt the full force of Rhodes's personality. Yielding to its fascination, he became his intimate friend, accepting his ideas and aspirations with enthusiasm. He soon joined Rhodes on the board of the original De Beers Diamond Company (founded in 1880) and played an important part in Rhodes's great scheme of the amalgamation of the chief diamond mines of Kimberley as De Beers Consolidated Mines. The scheme took effect in 1888 after Beit had advanced to Rhodes without security a sum of 250,000*l.* Under Rhodes's influence, Beit, who had become a naturalised British subject, thoroughly assimilated, despite his foreign birth, the patriotic spirit of British imperialism, and was in politics as all else a strenuous supporter of Rhodes. His association with Rhodes became the chief interest of his life. The two men rendered each other the best kind of mutual assistance. Without Beit, Rhodes was puzzled, or at least wearied, with the details of business. Without Rhodes, Beit might have been a mere successful gold and diamond merchant.

Meanwhile the gold-mining activity in the Transvaal Republic, which first began at Barberton in 1884, had spread to the conglomerate formation of Witwatersrand, familiarly known as the Rand, where Johannesburg now stands. The Rand was declared a public gold-field on 20 September 1886. Early in 1888 Beit paid it a visit, and before leaving Kimberley he arranged provisionally that Hermann Eckstein should establish a branch of his firm on the Rand, trading as H. Eckstein—later H. Eckstein & Co. To the development of the Transvaal gold-mines Beit signally contributed. Perceiving the possibilities of the Witwatersrand, he acquired a large interest in the best of the outcrop mines, which soon became valuable properties. But his chief stroke was made in 1891, when he revisited South Africa and illustrated his characteristic perception of possibilities. Adopting the suggestion, in face of much expert scepticism, that it might be possible not only to work the outcrop but to strike the slanting reef by deep level shafts, at some distance away from the outcrop, he evolved, and devoted capital to testing, the Great Deep Level scheme. Beit was the first to recognise the importance of employing first-class mining engineers. With their aid he proved the scheme to be practicable, and to its success the subsequent prosperity of the Rand is chiefly due. In the whole deep level system Beit's firm were forerunners and creators; other firms followed later in their footsteps.

Beit was deeply interested in the scheme of northern expansion which Rhodes had formed early in his South African career. On the formation (24 Oct. 1889) of the British South Africa Company for the administration of the extensive territory afterwards known as Rhodesia, Beit became an original director. He first visited the country in 1891, entering the country by the old Tuli route, and travelling by Victoria to Hartley. He joined later the boards of the various Rhodesian railway companies. His loyal support of Rhodes had its penalties. Like all who had a great stake in the Transvaal, he sympathised with the reform movement in Johannesburg of 1895 and shared the general impatience with the rule of President Kruger. Beit was concerned with Rhodes in placing Dr. (later Sir) Starr Jameson with an armed force on the Transvaal border (Dec. 1895). After nebulous intrigue with Johannesburg there followed the raid into the Transvaal. Beit's share in this blunder cost him 200,000*l*. Censured for his part in the transaction by the British South Africa committee of the House of Commons in 1897, he resigned his directorship of the Chartered Company, although the committee relieved him of any suspicion that he acted from an unworthy financial motive. During the South African war of 1899–1902 he spent immense sums on the imperial light horse and on the equipment of the imperial yeomanry, and before and after the war he poured money into land settlement, immigration, and kindred schemes for the development of South Africa.

Meanwhile Beit pursued other interests than politics or commerce. With a genuine love of beautiful things he formed from 1888 onwards, under the guidance of Dr. Bode, director of the Berlin Museum, a fine collection of pictures and works of art, including Italian Renaissance bronzes. He finally housed these treasures in a mansion in Park Lane, which Eustace Balfour built for him in 1895. Of painting he had a thorough knowledge, and among his pictures were the 'Prodigal Son' series of Murillo, six pictures acquired from Lord Dudley's Gallery, and many of the finest examples of the Dutch and English schools.

On Rhodes's death in March 1902 Beit succeeded to much of his friend's position. He became the chief figure on the boards of the De Beers Company and of the Chartered Company, which he rejoined in that year. He was also one of Rhodes's trustees under his will. In all these capacities he faithfully endeavoured to do what Rhodes would have done. His health had long been feeble, and in the autumn of 1902, when he visited South Africa for the purpose of examining—with admirable results in the future—the organisation of Rhodesia, he had a stroke of paralysis at Johannesburg. Through Dr. Jameson's skill he rallied, but never recovered. But his interests were unslackened. He identified himself with the movements for a better understanding with Germany and for tariff reform. He bore witness to his enlightened colonial interests by founding at Oxford in 1905 the Beit professorship of colonial history and the Beit assistant lectureship in colonial history, besides giving a sum of money to the Bodleian Library for additions to its collections of books on colonial history.

In the early spring of 1906 he was sent to Wiesbaden on account of heart trouble. By his own wish he was brought home to England, a dying man, and passed away at his country residence, Tewin Water in Hertfordshire, on 16 July. He was buried in the churchyard there.

Beit, who was unmarried, was survived by his mother, two sisters, and his younger brother Otto, and while providing liberally for various relatives and friends he left the residue of his fortune to his brother. At the same time his public benefactions, amounting in value to 2,000,000*l.*, were impressive alike by their generosity to England and Germany, and by their breadth of view. To the Imperial College of Technology, London, was allotted 50,000*l.* in cash and De Beers shares, valued at the testator's death at 84,843*l.* 15*s.* To Rhodesia, for purposes of education and charity, 200,000*l.* was bequeathed to be administered by trustees. King Edward's Hospital Fund and the trustees of Guy's Hospital were left 20,000*l.* each. Rhodes University at Grahamstown received 25,000*l.*, Rhodes Memorial Fund 10,000*l.*, and the Union Jack Club, London, 10,000*l.* Funds for benefactions in the Transvaal, in Kimberley, and the Cape Colony were also established. Two sums of 20,000*l.* were left to his executors for distribution to the charities of London and Hamburg respectively. Finally 1,200,000*l.* passed to trustees for the extension of railway and telegraph communication in South Africa, with a view to forwarding the enterprise known as the Cape to Cairo railway. With admirable sagacity Beit made his public bequests elastic. Thus, while bequeathing an estate at Hamburg as a pleasure-ground to the people of that city, he provided that twenty years later Hamburg might realise the estate and apply the proceeds to such other public objects as might seem desirable. Two of the bequests—200,000*l.* for a university at Johannesburg and 50,000*l.* destined for an Institute of Medical Sciences—lapsed into the residuary estate owing to the schemes in question being abandoned, but Mr. Otto Beit intimated his intention of devoting the 200,000*l.* to university education in South Africa, and the 50,000*l.* was made by him the nucleus of a fund of 215,000*l.*, with which he founded in 1909 thirty Alfred Beit fellowships for medical research in memory of the testator. Beit also left to the National Gallery the picture known as 'Lady Cockburn and her Children,' by Sir Joshua Reynolds; and to the Kaiserliche Museum in Berlin another by Sir Joshua, 'Mrs. Boone and her Daughter,' together with his bronze statue 'Hercules' by Pollaiuolo. His large Majolica plate from the service of Isabella d'Este was bequeathed to the Hamburg Museum.

A wealthy financier of abnormal intuition and power of memory, combined with German thoroughness of method, Beit had nothing in common with the financial magnate. He was no speculator in any ordinary sense, acquiring property whether on the Rand or elsewhere solely with the object of seriously developing it. He did not gamble, and advice on speculative investments which he always gave reluctantly was far from infallible. Shy and retiring to excess, he was devoid of social ambition, and was little known beyond a small circle of intimates who included men in the high position of Lord Rosebery and Lord Haldane. An active sympathy with every form of suffering and an ardent belief in great causes led him to distribute vast sums of money, but his benefactions were always made privately with rare self-effacement. He was the target through life for much undeserved abuse. The terms of the will give the true measure of his character.

A statue was unveiled at Salisbury, Rhodesia, on 11 May 1911.

[Personal knowledge; private information from, among others, Mr. Otto Beit, Sir Julius Wernher, Bart., and Sir Starr Jameson; Sir Lewis Michell, Life of Cecil Rhodes; The Times, 17 July and 21 July 1906 (account of will).] C. W. B.

BELL, CHARLES FREDERIC MOBERLY (1847–1911), manager of 'The Times,' born in Alexandria on 2 April 1847, was youngest child of Thomas Bell, of a firm of Egyptian merchants, who was on his mother's side first cousin of George Moberly [q. v.], bishop of Salisbury. Moberly Bell's mother was Hester Louisa, daughter of one David, by a sister of the Miss Williams who accompanied Lady Hester Stanhope [q. v.] on her sojourn in the East. The two Misses Williams were, it is said, wards of William Pitt. Lady Hester was Mrs. Bell's godmother. An accomplished musician and above the average of her time and sex in general cultivation, Mrs. Bell first married a naval chaplain named Dodd, and by him had a son who became a general in the Indian army. By her second marriage with Thomas Bell she had four children who grew to maturity, but only the youngest displayed striking ability.

Both Bell's parents died when he was a child, and he was sent to England to be brought up by an aunt who lived in Clapham. He attended for a time a little day school in Stockwell, and afterwards went to a school kept by the Rev. William Clayton Greene at Wallasey in Cheshire, where he was chiefly distinguished by his aptitude for mathematics. He was engaged in preparation for the Indian civil service when he developed a tendency to consumption and was sent back to Egypt in 1865. There he entered the service of his father's old firm, Peel & Co., in Alexandria, and in 1873 he was admitted as a partner.

But his heart was never in business, and a taste and aptitude for journalism had already asserted themselves. Even in his schooldays he had been in the habit, it is said, of writing to the newspapers; and having succeeded immediately after his arrival in Egypt in 1865 in establishing an informal connection with 'The Times,' he lost no opportunity of practising his pen as an occasional correspondent. He left the firm of Peel & Co. in 1875, and thenceforth devoted his main energies to journalism. Always an omnivorous reader, he had continued his education during the years he spent in business and with practice had acquired a fluent and vivacious style. With the opening of the Suez Canal and the adventurous finance of Ismail, the Khedive, Egypt was now becoming a subject of international interest, and Bell's ready and incisive pen and access to 'The Times,' coupled with his political insight and his knowledge of all the actors on the stage of Egyptian politics, soon made him a power. In company with two friends he founded the 'Egyptian Gazette' (1880), long the only successful English newspaper in Egypt. His great opportunity came with the Arabi revolt of 1882 and the subsequent British occupation. He had now been recognised by 'The Times' as 'Our own correspondent,' and one of his greatest achievements in that capacity was his telegraphic description of the bombardment of Alexandria, at which he was present on board the Condor with Lord Charles Beresford. In 1884, when he was about to start with the Gordon relief expedition, he met with a serious accident, which detained him in hospital to his intense chagrin and left him slightly lamed for life. He continued, however, at Cairo to play a prominent part in the events by which the Egyptian question was gradually unravelled. 'He was an ideal correspondent,' 'The Times' wrote of him after his death, 'alert in observation, quick and sagacious in judgment, prompt in execution, rapid and yet never slovenly in composition, never sparing himself and never letting an opportunity slip. He knew everyone worth knowing in Egypt, and enjoyed the confidence of all who knew him. It is no secret that Lord Cromer had a warm personal regard for him and always entertained a high opinion of his sagacity, regarding his judgment on Egyptian affairs as pre-eminently sound and exceptionally well informed.' His interest in Egyptian politics embraced the welfare of the Egyptian people as well as the international relation. He published in these years 'Khedives and Pashas,' an appreciation of the leading Egyptian personalities of the time, in 1884; a pamphlet on 'Egyptian Finance' in 1887; and 'From Pharaoh to Fellah,' a series of historical and descriptive sketches, in 1888.

In 1890 he was summoned to England by the chief proprietor of 'The Times' to take up the post of manager in succession to John Cameron MacDonald, who had recently died. The moment was critical in the history of the paper, for it had suffered a heavy loss of money and a serious blow to its prestige during the proceedings, then just concluded, of the Parnell commission. Bell threw himself into the task of repairing the damage, financial and other, with the energy of a giant. Devotion to the interests of 'The Times' soon grew with him to be a religion. He was proud of its power and influence and of its long record of public service, and he had a deep conviction of the importance of upholding its best traditions and so maintaining its efficiency as a regulating force in English public life. He brought to his new task, at which he toiled with little rest for the remainder of his life, an acute and ingenious mind, great quickness of apprehension, insight into character, unfailing resource, and executive ability of a high order. He laboured incessantly to improve its business organisation. During his management an independent literary organ, 'Literature,' ran in association with the newspaper from 1897 to 1901, when it was replaced by a weekly 'Literary Supplement' to 'The Times'; other supplements, 'Financial and Commercial' and 'Engineering,' were subsequently added. Bell was the first to establish a system of wireless press messages across the Atlantic. His interest in foreign affairs was always especially keen, and he was able to effect many notable improvements in the organisation of 'The Times' service in that field. He was an ardent imperialist, and by his creation or improvement of news services as well as by his personal influence he did no little to further that cause.

Bell's overflowing energies prompted him to utilise the resources of 'The Times' for many enterprises that were strictly beyond the bounds of journalism. He acquired for the newspaper in 1895 the MS. and copyright of Dr. Moritz Busch's 'Bismarck: Some Secret Pages of his History' which he published through Macmillans in 1898 (3 vols.). But 'The Times' itself undertook an ambitious series of publications, including 'The Times Atlas' (1895), a reprint of the ninth edition of the 'Encyclopædia Britannica' (1898) with supplementary volumes (1902–3), and the well-known 'History of the South African War.' (7 vols., 1900–9). Another of Bell's enterprises was 'The Times' Book Club, established in September 1905, which provided a circulating library gratuitously for subscribers to the newspaper, frankly with a view to increasing its circulation. A furious conflict followed with publishers and booksellers, who deemed their interests injured by the club's practice of selling off second-hand copies soon after publication. Bell defended the club's position unflinchingly, and gave way only after two years' stubborn resistance. In the course of the struggle he attacked many publishing methods, and one result of his strenuous polemic was a general reduction in the selling price of books.

Down to 1908 'The Times' was owned by a large number of proprietors without definite liability, but legal proceedings arising out of conflicting rights compelled in that year a reconstitution on the principle of limited liability, and it was mainly owing to Bell's diplomacy and exertions that the transition was smoothly effected. When 'The Times' publishing company was formed in 1908 he became managing director.

Of a commanding personality Bell was for many years a well-known figure in London life and society. In person he was tall and massive of frame and of a constitution that seemed never to know illness or fatigue. But unsparing labour eventually weakened his heart, and he died suddenly in 'The Times' office, while writing a letter on some question of newspaper copyright on 5 April 1911. He was buried in Brompton cemetery.

He married in 1875 Ethel, eldest daughter of Rev. James Chataway, by whom he had two sons and four daughters; the eldest daughter died before him.

A portrait painted by Mr. Emile Fuchs in 1904 is in the possession of Bell's widow.

[The Times, 6 April 1911; Encycl. Brit., 11th edit., s.v. Newspapers and Publishing; family information and personal knowledge.]

W. F. M.

BELL, HORACE (1839–1903), civil engineer, born in London on 17 June 1839, was son of George Bell, merchant, of Harley Street, London, by his wife Frances Dade, of Norfolk. Educated in France and at Louth, Lincolnshire, he began engineering at fifteen, under Mr. John Wilson, in Westminster, served as apprentice to Messrs. D. Cook & Company of Glasgow, and spent some time later in the workshops of the Caledonian railway. After employment on the London, Chatham and Dover railway he entered the Indian public works department as a probationary assistant engineer on 1 July 1862. At first he was employed on the Grand Trunk road in the Central Provinces (1862–70). On 1 April 1866 he became an executive engineer, and in that capacity, after a few months on the Chanda railway survey, served on the Indore (1870), the Punjab Northern (1874), the Rajputana (1875), and Neemuch (1878) state railways. On the opening of the Punjab Northern in 1883 he was mentioned in the list of officers employed, and was congratulated by the viceroy. Promoted a superintending engineer on 1 Jan. 1880 and a chief engineer, third class, on 22 Oct. 1890, and first class on 31 Jan. 1892, he was successively (1881–4) chief engineer of the Dacca-Mymensingh railway surveys, and (1884–7) chief engineer to the Tirhoot state railway, of which for a time he was also manager. He received in 1887 the thanks of the government of India for services in connection with the completion of the Gunduck bridge on that railway. His next employment was as engineer-in-chief on the surveys for the Great Western of India and the Mogal-Serai railways. From 8 Aug. 1892 until his retirement in June 1894 he was consulting engineer to the government of India for state railways, acting for a short time as director-general of railways.

Bell published 'Railway Policy in India' (1894), which dealt with constructional, financial, and administrative matters. A paper by him, 'Recent Railway Policy in India' (1900), was reprinted from the 'Journal' of the Society of Arts. For natives of India he published at Calcutta a 'Primer on the Government of India' (3rd edit. 1893) and 'Laws of Wealth' (1883); both were adopted in government schools.

On leaving India he established himself as a consulting engineer in London, and under his guidance were carried out the Southern Punjab railway (5 feet 6 inches gauge), 1897, and the Nilgiri mountain railway, a rack railway of metre gauge opened in 1899 (*Minutes of Proceedings Inst. Civ. Eng.* cxlv. 1). He was elected an associate of the Institution of Civil Engineers 5 March 1867, and a member 30 Jan. 1892. In 1897 he was elected to the council, on which he served until his death. He died at 114 Lexham Gardens, W., on 10 April 1903, and was buried in Brompton cemetery. By his wife Marcia Napier Ogilvy he had issue four sons and five daughters. One son and three daughters survived him.

[Min. Proc. Inst. Civ. Eng. cliii. 319; The Times, 11 April 1903; History of Services of the Indian Public Works Department.]

W. F. S.

BELL, Sir ISAAC LOWTHIAN, first baronet (1816–1904), metallurgical chemist and pioneer in industrial enterprise, born at Newcastle-on-Tyne on 15 Feb. 1816, was eldest son (in a family of four sons and three daughters) of Thomas Bell (1774–1845), a native of Lowhurst, Cumberland, by his wife Catherine (*d.* 1875), daughter of Isaac Lowthian of Newbiggin near Carlisle. Of his brothers, Thomas (1817–1894), who followed him in the management of the Walker works, took an active part in the early development of the Cleveland salt deposits, whilst John (1818–1888), a practical geologist, gave valuable advice to Lowthian in connection with mining properties. His sister Mary Grace (*d.* 1898) married George Routledge [q. v.], the publisher, and Katherine (*d.* 1905) married William Henry Porter (*d.* 1895), to whom the original idea of the patent anchor is due.

His father removed to Newcastle in 1808 to enter the service of Messrs. Losh & Co., merchants, who were then launching out into the manufacture of both alkali and iron. In after years he joined the firm, which became known as Messrs. Losh, Wilson & Bell, of the Walker Ironworks, Tyneside. The family of Bell's mother had long been tenants of the Loshes of Woodside, near Carlisle. To his parents' association with the Losh family (one of whose members in conjunction with Lord Dundonald had pioneered the Leblanc soda process in this country) Lowthian Bell owed his early introduction to chemical and metallurgical technology, then on the eve of a period of remarkable development and advance. His father, who early discerned the important bearing of physical science upon industrial problems, gave his son an adequate training in physics and chemistry. After completing his school education at Bruce's Academy, Newcastle, Bell spent some time in Germany, in Denmark, at Edinburgh University, and at the Sorbonne in Paris; finally he went to Marseilles to study a new process for the manufacture of alkali.

In 1835, at the age of nineteen, Lowthian Bell entered, under his father, the office of Messrs. Losh, Wilson & Bell, in Newcastle, and a year later joined his father at the firm's ironworks at Walker. In 1827 there had been erected at these works what was considered then to be a very powerful rolling mill capable of turning out 100 tons per week of bar iron; the puddling process was installed in 1833, and five years later there was added a second mill for rolling rails. John Vaughan, the superintendent of this mill, by virtue of his character and practical knowledge about iron, exercised on the young man a powerful directing influence. In 1842, owing to a shortage of pig iron, the firm decided to put down a blast furnace plant, the erection of which was carried out under Bell's superintendence. The first furnace was designed for smelting mill cinder, but on the addition of a second furnace in 1844 experiments were made, extending over twelve months, with Cleveland ironstone from the neighbourhood of Grosmont. The use of Cleveland ore was for the time abandoned, but these initial experiments at Walker prepared the way for the opening-up of the Cleveland iron industry some six years later.

In 1842 Bell married Margaret, second daughter of Hugh Lee Pattinson [q. v.], the chemical manufacturer. In 1850, in partnership with his father-in-law, he started chemical works at Washington near Gateshead, where he built a house and resided for nearly twenty years.

About 1866 a single blast furnace adjoining the chemical works was built by Bell in partnership with others, and the exhaust steam from the blowing engines was utilised for heating water to be used in Pattinson's white lead process. The furnace was blown out in 1875. There was also established about 1860, at Washington, a manufactory of aluminium under a very ingenious process discovered by the distinguished French chemist St. Claire Deville. This was the earliest and for many years the only source of aluminium in this country. Improvements in manufacture rendered Deville's process obsolete, and the works were abandoned before 1880. In 1874 Bell sold his interest in the Washington business to his partners, who included Robert Stirling Newall [q. v.], husband of his wife's sister.

Meanwhile Bell's main energies were occupied elsewhere. On 1 Aug. 1844 he and his two brothers, Thomas and John, leased a blast furnace at Wylam-on-Tyne from Christopher Blackett, thus inaugurating the firm of Bell Brothers, and next year, on the death of his father, Lowthian Bell also assumed the chief direction of the Walker works. The furnace at Wylam had been built in 1836 on lines typical of its epoch, and it continued in working until 1863, when it was finally blown out.

At Wylam the trials of Cleveland ore which Bell had begun at Walker continued under his direction. Before long Messrs. Bolckow & Vaughan, at their Witton Park furnaces (county Durham), commenced to smelt Cleveland ore with such success that they decided to erect three blast furnaces near Middlesbrough in close proximity to the new ore supplies. Bell was not slow to profit by this example. In 1852 his firm acquired a lease, from the Ward-Jackson family, of important ore supplies at Normanby, and ultimately, in 1854, they started their Clarence works, with three blast furnaces, on the north bank of the Tees opposite Middlesbrough, then a very small and newly incorporated borough. The only rival works in the district were those of Messrs. Bolckow, Vaughan & Company and of Messrs. Cochrane & Company. These three firms were the pioneers of the Cleveland industry.

Early difficulties arose over the carriage of the ore. Messrs. Bolckow & Vaughan supported the endeavour of the Stockton and Darlington Railway Company, an undertaking in which Messrs. Joseph and Henry Pease had a very large interest [see PEASE, EDWARD], to monopolise the carriage of the whole of the Cleveland ironstone. In becoming lessees of the Normanby royalty and in building the works at Clarence the Bells had associated themselves with Ralph Ward Jackson, the younger brother of the tenant for life of the Normanby estate. Jackson had taken an active part in the development of the West Hartlepool Harbour and Railway Company, which had acquired collieries in the county of Durham. In the result Messrs. Bell joined Jackson in promoting the construction of another railway, the Cleveland Railway, to bring the ironstone to the banks of the Tees. The first portion of this railway, seven miles in length, ran from Normanby through the Jackson estate to the Normanby jetty on the river Tees, where the ironstone was shipped in barges to a wharf at Clarence on the Durham side. Parliamentary sanction was only obtained after repeated severe and expensive contests. It is said that the seven miles of railway cost the builders 35,000*l.* in Parliamentary expenses alone. A proposed extension of the railway from Normanby to Skelton and then to Loftus with a view to developing other property was again the subject of very severe Parliamentary contests. The result, however, was commensurate with the expenditure, for the great field of ironstone lying to the south and east of Guisborough was thereby opened. The Skelton extension of the railway enabled Bell Brothers to obtain in 1858 an important tract of ironstone on the Skelton estate. There the little-known bed of ironstone, ten feet thick, had been reckoned so far from any railway that it would ruin anyone who undertook to work it. Limestone quarries were also acquired in Weardale, until ultimately the firm owned all the supplies of raw material required for their Clarence works.

A great depression of trade followed the Cleveland developments. Jackson's speculative enterprises were ruined, and the West Hartlepool Harbour and Railway Company went into liquidation. Bell Brothers acquired certain of the company's colliery properties and these the firm subsequently developed largely and added others to them. The North Eastern Railway Company took over the railway and harbour, and also purchased by negotiation the Cleveland railway. As a part of the transaction Lowthian Bell became a director of the North Eastern in 1865, and held the office till death.

Subsequently Bell's firm turned its attention to the manufacture of steel. As a result of experiments on a large scale for the utilisation of Cleveland pig iron in the manufacture of steel, open hearth furnaces were erected at Clarence, and steel was first made there in Jan. 1889. After carrying on the manufacture for two years, Bell and his partners satisfied themselves of the feasibility of their plan, and entering into negotiation with Messrs. Dorman, Long & Co., a leading firm of manufacturers who were among the first to manufacture rolled steel girders in this country, they formed in

1899 an amalgamation, and important steel works were built at Clarence. The Clarence works are now producing about 1000 tons of pig iron daily, and 4000 tons of ingots and 2400 tons of finished steel weekly.

Yet another industry was added later to the wide range of the firm's activities. The discovery (during boring operations for water) of rock salt at a depth of 1200 feet below the surface on the south side of the river Tees by Messrs. Bolckow & Vaughan in 1862 induced Messrs. Bell Bros., in 1874, to sink a bore-hole near their Clarence works. The result was that salt was encountered at a depth of 1127 feet below the surface; the salt bed at this point being about eighty feet thick and estimated to contain about 200,000 tons to the acre. It was not, however, until 1881, when Thomas Bell suggested (after independent thought) the adoption of a special mode of winning the salt, which (as he subsequently found) had been long practised near Nancy, that the firm proceeded to realise this new asset. Two years later they were making 320 tons of salt per week.

The firm of Bell Brothers in all its branches became in Lowthian Bell's lifetime a gigantic concern employing in its mines, collieries, and ironworks some 6000 workpeople. Bell was always active in numerous directions beyond the immediate and varied calls of business. He constantly travelled abroad, and closely studied the conditions of iron manufacture in foreign countries, especially in America. His work in applied science almost excelled in importance his labours as an industrial pioneer. In both capacities his eminence was soon universally acknowledged. Taking an active part in the establishment of the Iron and Steel Institute in 1869, he filled the office of president during 1873–5, and was the first recipient of the Bessemer gold medal in 1874. He helped to found in 1888 the Institution of Mining Engineers, of which he was president in 1904. He was also president of the Institution of Mechanical Engineers (1884), of the British Iron Trade Association in 1886 and of the Society of Chemical Industry (1889). In 1895 he was awarded the Albert medal of the Society of Arts, and in 1900 the George Stephenson medal from the Institution of Civil Engineers, as well as a Telford premium for a paper on rails in Great Britain.

Bell's scientific attainments rank very high. 'For the last fifty years of his life he had few superiors in general knowledge of chemical metallurgy and he was an unrivalled authority on the blast furnace and the scientific processes of its operation' (cf. *Roy. Soc. Proc.* 1907, p. xvii). Between 1869 and 1894 he embodied in papers in the Iron and Steel Institute's 'Journal' the results of exhaustive experimental researches. Among the most important were: 'The Development of Heat and its Appropriation in Blast Furnaces of Different Dimensions' (1869); 'Chemical Phenomena of Iron Smelting' (1871 and 1872); 'The Sum of Heat utilised in smelting Cleveland Ironstone' (1875); 'The Separation of Carbon, Silicon, Sulphur, and Phosphorus, in the Refining and Puddling Furnace, and in the Bessemer Converter' (1877); 'The Separation of Phosphorus from Pig Iron' (1878); and 'On the Value of Excessive Addition to the Temperature of the Air used in Smelting Iron' (1883).

The outcome of Bell's experimental researches upon blast furnace practice, in which he was assisted by Dr. C. R. A. Wright, was published in 1872 in his classical 'Chemical Phenomena of Iron Smelting; an experimental and practical examination of the circumstances which determine the capacity of the blast furnace, the temperature of the air and the proper condition of the materials to be operated upon' (translated into French, German and Swedish). In his research on the blast furnace he had taken full advantage of contemporary research and invention and advanced beyond them. He explained the economy of hot blast which James Beaumont Neilson [q. v.] demonstrated in 1828, and indicated the limits beyond which it could not be pushed in practice; Bunsen and Playfair, by the analysis of the gases at various levels of the furnace, had proved the main source of avoidable loss in current blast practice, and had elucidated the chemistry of the process; Bell amplified and completed their work both by establishing a true basis for estimating the 'heat balance' of the furnace, and by determining once and for all the main sequence of the chemical changes as the descending charge of ore, fuel, and flux met the ascending furnace gases; finally he supplemented the inventions of regenerative stoves made during 1860–5 by Edward Alfred Cowper (*d.* 1895) and Thomas Whitwell, which rendered high blast temperatures possible and led to the construction of much larger furnaces; Bell demonstrated on scientific grounds how far the furnace dimension could be increased in the interest of fuel economy, apart from any purely mechanical difficulties. In his book he fully expounded the various laws which regulate the process of iron-smelting. He showed that no advantage can possibly accrue from an increase in height or capacity of the furnace beyond the limits which would permit of the gases leaving the throat at a temperature of about 300° centigrade. The accumulated experience of the forty years since Bell wrote has abundantly confirmed the general validity of his conclusions.

Bell's next separate publications were the fruit of his study of the American iron industry. Their titles were 'Notes of a Visit to Coal and Iron Mines and Works in the United States' (1875), and 'Report on the Iron Manufacture of the United States of America, and a Comparison of it with that of Great Britain' (1877). To a volume on the American industry, published by the Iron and Steel Institute in 1890, he contributed a paper, 'On the American Iron Trade and its Progress during Sixteen Years.'

In 1884 was published, in London and New York, Bell's second great scientific treatise, 'The Principles of the Manufacture of Iron and Steel,' for which he received in 1892 the Howard quinquennial prize of the Institution of Civil Engineers. He had acted as a juror at the Paris Exhibition of 1878, when he received the legion of honour, and this work was his report made at the request of the board of management of the British Iron Trade Association, on the condition of the manufacture of iron and steel, as illustrated by the Paris exhibits. The book reviewed the economic condition of the industry as well as the scientific aspects of the actual manufacturing processes. At the close he made an authoritative comparison of the economic conditions of the principal iron-producing countries, a favourite subject of his study, while a suggestive review of the problems connected with the elimination of impurities from pig iron included an account of his own experiments on the phosphorus elimination in the manufacture of steel in the Bessemer converter [see THOMAS, SIDNEY GILCHRIST]. Bell evolved a method of elimination which was for a time used at Woolwich, at Krupp's works in Essen (where, however, it had been independently invented), and also in the United States. But it was superseded by the final development of the basic Bessemer process patented by Messrs. Thomas & Gilchrist in 1879.

Bell also found time for many offices in public life. He was twice mayor of Newcastle-on-Tyne, in 1854–5 and again in 1862–3, and deputy lieutenant and high sheriff for the county of Durham in 1884. In 1868 he contested in the liberal interest without success the constituency of North Durham, but was returned with (Sir) Charles Mark Palmer [q. v. Suppl. II] on 14 Feb. 1874. This election was declared void on petition, and Bell was defeated at the following bye-election. On 29 July 1875 he was, however, returned for the Hartlepools, and he sat in parliament for that constituency till the dissolution of 1880, but took little part in its proceedings. In recognition of his many services to science and industry, he was elected F.R.S. in 1875, and on 21 July 1885, on the nomination of Gladstone, he received a baronetcy. He was made an hon. D.C.L. of Durham (1882), LL.D. of Edinburgh (1893) and Dublin, and D.Sc. of Leeds University (1904). He was an active promoter and supporter of the Armstrong College at Newcastle, and a tower which he gave to the building is called by his name.

His intellectual vigour was unimpaired to the end of his long life; he died on 20 Dec. 1904 at his residence, Rounton Grange, Northallerton, and was buried at Rounton.

Bell's wife died in 1886, and in her memory he dedicated to public uses his house, Washington Hall, and its grounds; it is now used as a home for waifs and strays of that city under the name of Dame Margaret's Home. Of his two sons and three daughters his eldest son, Hugh Bell, succeeded him both in the baronetcy and in the direction of the firm. His second son, Charles Lowthian, *b.* 24 March 1853, died on 8 Feb. 1906. His second daughter married the Hon. Edward Lyulph Stanley, now Lord Sheffield.

Bell's portrait was twice painted by Henry Tanworth Wells—in 1865 and in 1894; the earlier picture now belongs to Lord Sheffield, and the later picture was presented by 'friends in Great Britain, Europe and America' to the corporation of Middlesbrough. Sir Hugh Bell possesses a replica of the second portrait, together with a painting by Sir William Richmond, R.A., which was presented to Bell by the electors of the Hartlepools. A fifth portrait, by Frank Bramley, A.R.A., was painted for the North Eastern Railway Company, and is in the company's offices at York.

[Proc. Roy. Soc., 1907, A. xv; Journ. Iron and Steel Inst., 1904, ii. 426; Trans. Inst. Min. Eng., 1905; Engineering, 23 Dec. 1904; also Mr. Greville Jones's papers, Messrs. Bell Bros. Blast Furnaces from 1844 to 1908 in Journ. Iron and Steel Inst., 1908, iii. 59; Burke's Baronetage; private information.]

W. A. B.

BELL, JAMES (1824–1908), chemist, born in co. Armagh in 1824, was educated privately and at University College, London, where he studied mathematics and chemistry, the latter under Dr. Alexander William Williamson [q. v. Suppl. II]. In 1846 he became an assistant in the Inland Revenue Laboratory at Somerset House, which had been established to carry out the provisions of the Tobacco Act of 1842, and was successively deputy principal from 1867 to 1874, and principal from 1874 till his resignation in 1894. The work of the laboratory was not long restricted to the examination of tobacco, but was extended to the value of brewing materials, the denaturing of alcohol for use in manufacture, and other matters affecting the excise. When the Food and Drugs Act of 1872 was amended in 1875, Bell was made chemical referee when disputed analyses of food were brought before the magistrates. In this capacity he elaborated methods for analysing chemically such articles of food as came within the operation of the Act, and in this work he made a high scientific reputation. Bell was also consulting chemist to the Indian government, 1869–94. His researches into the grape and malt ferments were published in the 'Excise Officers' Manual' (1865) and in the 'Journal of the Chemical Society' in 1870. Many of his general results were embodied in his work on 'The Analysis and Adulteration of Foods' (3 pts. 1881–3; German transl., Berlin, 1882–5). His 'Chemistry of Tobacco' (1887) is another valuable scientific study. Bell's work was recognised in 1884 by his election as F.R.S., and he obtained the degree of Ph.D. from Erlangen in 1882 and received the hon. D.Sc. from the Royal University of Ireland (1886). He was made C.B. in 1889. He was a member of the Playfair committee on British and foreign spirits, and served as president of the Institute of Chemistry 1888–91. Bell died at Hove on 31 March 1908, and was buried at Ewell. He married in 1858 Ellen (*d.* 1900), daughter of W. Reece of Chester, and left issue one son, Sir William James Bell, alderman of the London county council (1903–7), who possesses a portrait in oils of his father, painted by W. V. Herbert in 1886.

[Proc. Roy. Soc., 82A 1909, p. v; Analyst, xxxiii. 157; Nature, lxxvii. 539; The Times, 2 April 1908.] R. S.

BELL, VALENTINE GRAEME (1839–1908), civil engineer, born in London on 27 June 1839, was youngest son of William Bell, merchant, of Aldersgate Street, London, who was subsequently official assignee in bankruptcy. Educated at private schools, and apprenticed in 1855 to Messrs. Wren & Hopkinson, engineers, of Manchester, he became in 1859 a pupil of (Sir) James Brunlees [q. v. Suppl. I]. For Brunlees he was resident engineer in 1863–5 on the Cleveland railway in Yorkshire, and in 1866–8 on the Mont Cenis railway (on the Fell system), for which he superintended the construction of special locomotives in Paris in 1869–70. While in charge of the Mont Cenis line he rebuilt for the French government the *route impériale* between St. Jean de Maurienne and Lanslebourg after its destruction by flood. He was elected a member of the Institution of Civil Engineers on 4 May 1869. In 1871 he set up in private practice in London. In 1872–5 he carried out waterworks at Cadiz for a company which failed and involved him pecuniarily. With Sir George Barclay Bruce [q. v. Suppl. II] he constructed, during the same period, a railway for the Compagnie du chemin de fer du vieux port de Marseille.

In 1880 Bell took service under the colonial office in Jamaica, where his chief professional work was done. Until 1883 he was engaged in reconstructing the government railway in Jamaica between Kingston and Spanish Town, extending the line to Ewarton and Porus, and later to Montego Bay and Port Antonio. The governor, Sir Henry Norman, who recognised Bell's capacity and energy, appointed him in 1886 a member of the legislative council. Next year he became director of public works and held the office for nearly twenty-one years with admirable results. Under his direction the mileage of good roads was extended from 800 to near 2000; 110 bridges and most of the modern public buildings were built, and works for water-supply, drainage, and lighting were carried out. He unsuccessfully opposed with characteristic frankness the transfer, in 1889, of the government railways to an American syndicate, which proved a failure, the government resuming possession in 1900. He was made C.M.G in 1903. Bell resigned his appointment in March 1908, and returned to England in failing health. He died in London on 29 May 1908.

He married (1) in 1864 Rebecca (*d.* 1868), daughter of Alexander Bell Filson, M.D.; and (2) in 1882 Emilie Georgina, daughter of Frances Robertson Lynch, clerk of the legislative council of Jamaica. By his first marriage he had a daughter and a son, Archibald Graeme, now director of public works in Trinidad, and by his second marriage he had two daughters and a son.

[Min. Proc. Inst. Civ. Eng. clxxii.; The Times, 1 June 1908.] W. F. S.

BELLAMY, JAMES (1819–1909), President of St. John's College, Oxford, born on 31 Jan. 1819 in the school house of Merchant Taylors' School, then in Suffolk Lane, was elder son in the family of two sons and three daughters of James William Bellamy, B.D. The father (of an old Huguenot family settled in Norfolk and Lincolnshire) was headmaster of Merchant Taylors' School from 1819 to 1845. His mother was Mary, daughter of Thomas Cherry, B.D., headmaster of Merchant Taylors' School, London, from 1795 to 1819. In 1822 the father, while still headmaster, became vicar of Sellinge, Kent, a living which he held till his death in 1874. The son James entered Merchant Taylors' School in June 1826. 'The Merchant Taylors' Magazine' 1833–4 contains three poems by him. On 11 June 1836 he was elected scholar (leading to a fellowship) at St. John's College, Oxford, matriculating on 27 June. In 1841 Bellamy graduated B.A., with a second class in classics and a first class in mathematics. He proceeded M.A. in 1845, B.D. in 1850, and D.D. in 1872; was ordained deacon in 1842 and priest in 1843, and settled down to the ordinary life of a college 'don.' He held the college offices in turn, made a very efficient bursar in his year of office, was a successful tutor (but had no belief in supplying his pupils with knowledge ready made), and until 1871 was precentor, with charge of the choristers, the college having a foundation for choral service [see PADDY, SIR WILLIAM]. He was a keen and capable musician, a devoted admirer of Handel, and a friend of John Hullah [q. v.] and other musicians. His fine collection of music was given in trust, after his death, by his sister, Mrs. Tylden, to form the nucleus of an historical library of music in Oxford.

Bellamy took a prominent part from the first in the general life of Oxford. He was librarian of the Union Society in 1841, and became an important member of the conservative party in the university. Without professing full sympathy with the tractarians, he was an admirer of J. H. Newman, whose sermons at St. Mary's he attended, and was intimate with Charles Marriott, Dr. Pusey, and their friends, and he supported them by his vote in congregation. He was in later years regarded as Dr. Pusey's adviser in academic matters. He examined for the university, and occasionally took private pupils. One of these was Robert Gascoyne Cecil, afterwards Marquis of Salisbury [q. v. Suppl. II], with whom he remained on cordial terms till his death. During the vacations he occasionally visited Germany, where he studied music, but his home was with his father in Kent.

Shortly before the death, on 4 Nov. 1871, of Dr. Wynter, the President of St. John's, he accepted the college living of Crick, Northamptonshire; but he never entered upon the duties, being elected President of his college on 7 Dec. 1871. In that capacity he actively controlled its business for over thirty years. Serious financial embarrassments from time to time threatened its prosperity, but his coolness helped to surmount the difficulties. When in 1888 it was necessary to reduce the emoluments of all members of the foundation by 22 per cent., Bellamy made good the deficiency, out of his own purse, to all the open scholars of the college, and, in conjunction with the Merchant Taylors' Company, to those from Merchant Taylors' School. This benefaction was continued until the need ceased.

With the Merchant Taylors' Company the old-standing relations of the college were especially cordial during Bellamy's presidentship. He delighted in his annual visit to the school on 'Election Day' (11 June), and at the dinner with the company in the evening he always spoke both thoughtfully and wittily. On 25 June 1894 the court bestowed on him the honorary freedom of the company. He was admitted on 14 July.

Meanwhile at Oxford Bellamy won an influential position, mainly due to his determined and straightforward character, his capacity for business, and his entire absence of self-assertion and self-seeking. He was a member of the university commission 1877–9, and a constant attendant at its sessions, criticising the proposed reforms with acuteness, and presenting a bold front to any change which he regarded as revolutionary in the statutes either of his own college or of the university. A scheme presented by the college in December 1877, which proposed to retain the clerical restriction for the presidentship and for one-third of the fellowships, was rejected, but the connection made by Sir Thomas White [q. v.], 1555, with certain schools, was retained. From 1874 till 1907 Bellamy was a member of the hebdomadal council. From 1886 to 1890 he was vice-chancellor in succession to Benjamin Jowett, whom he had known from childhood but with whom he disagreed on almost every subject. In both positions he exercised sound judgment, clearly and trenchantly expressed. From 1895 to 1907 he held the sinecure rectory of Leckford, Hampshire, paying the income into the college funds. For many years he was leader of the conservative political party in Oxford, and meetings at the times of contested elections were held in his house. Till extreme old age, Bellamy retained his powers. An admirable *raconteur*, with a great fund of reminiscence, he was a genial host, and a pointed speaker at college gatherings, whose sharp criticism and wit were never tinged with ill-nature. Up to his ninetieth year he sang the service in the college chapel on stated days, in perfect tune and with remarkable power of voice. Failing health led him to resign the presidentship on 24 June 1909. Retiring to Ingoldisthorpe Manor, the Norfolk property which he had inherited from an uncle, and where he had proved himself an admirable landlord, he died there on 25 Aug. 1909. He was buried in the churchyard adjoining his garden. His estate was sworn at over 300,000*l*. His portrait, painted by Frank Holl, R.A., presented in 1887, is in the hall of St. John's College, Oxford, and a drawing by W. Strang, A.R.A., executed in 1907, is in the common room. A mural tablet is in the college chapel.

[W. H. Hutton, History of St. John Baptist College; The Times, 28 August 1909; Court Minutes of the Merchant Taylors' Company; Register of St. John's College, Oxford; private information.] W. H. H.

BELLEW, HAROLD KYRLE (1855–1911), actor, was youngest son of John Chippendall Montesquieu Bellew [q. v.]. Born at Prescot, Lancashire, on 28 March 1855, he was educated at the Royal Grammar School, Lancaster, and though originally intended for the army, he drifted into the navy, and for some time served on the training ship Conway under Sir Digby Murray, leaving it for the merchant service, in which he remained intermittently for several years. Subsequently he went to Australia, and during a four years' sojourn amid very varied employment made his first appearance as an actor, appearing at Solferino, New South Wales, in 1874, as Eglinton Roseleaf in T. J. Williams's old farce 'Turn Him Out.' He returned to England in August 1875, and almost immediately secured an engagement with Helen Barry, making his first appearance on the English stage at the Theatre Royal, Brighton, on 30 Aug. 1875, as Lord Woodstock in Tom Taylor's 'Lady Clancarty,' performing under the name of Harold Kyrle, by which he was known until the end of 1878. Coming to London, he made his London *début* at the old Park Theatre, Camden Town, on 16 Oct. 1875, as Roseleaf in 'Turn Him Out,' and was next engaged at the Haymarket Theatre, where he first appeared on 17 Jan. 1876 as Paris in 'Romeo and Juliet,' with Adelaide Neilson [q. v.]. He was then engaged by the Bancrofts for the old Prince of Wales's theatre in Tottenham Street. Returning to the Haymarket, he made his first notable success there on 3 Feb. 1877, when he played Belvawney in Gilbert's comedy 'Engaged.' The following year he supported Adelaide Neilson as leading man in 'Measure for Measure,' 'Twelfth Night,' and other plays.

In Dec. 1878 he was engaged by (Sir) Henry Irving for the opening of his Lyceum management, and there he played Osric in 'Hamlet,' Glavis in 'The Lady of Lyons,' and De Beringhen in 'Richelieu.' In Sept. 1879 he joined Marie Litton's company at the old Imperial Theatre, achieving success as Frederick in George Colman's comedy 'The Poor Gentleman' and Jack Absolute in 'The Rivals,' while his Orlando in 'As You Like It' was universally regarded as one of his best efforts. Subsequently he was seen to advantage in London as Charles Surface in 'The School for Scandal' and in less important parts, while in the provinces he achieved success with his own company as Fabien and Louis in 'The Corsican Brothers' and as Romeo. Leaving for New York in 1885, he played at Wallack's Theatre there, chiefly in old comedy parts.

After his return to London in 1887 he commenced at the Gaiety Theatre, on 27 June, a long artistic association with Mrs. Brown-Potter. Forming a company in the autumn, they toured for ten years through England, Australia, America, South Africa, and the Far East, their repertory including such plays as 'Antony and Cleopatra,' 'Romeo and Juliet,' 'Camille,' 'She Stoops to Conquer,' 'As You Like It,' 'La Tosca,' and 'David Garrick.' Brief appearances in London during this period were made in three plays of his own composition: 'Hero and Leander,' at the Shaftesbury, June 1902; 'Francillon,' at the Duke of York's, Sept.

1897; and Marat in 'Charlotte Corday,' as well as in Sims and Buchanan's 'The Lights of Home,' at the Adelphi, July 1892, and Claude Melnotte in 'The Lady of Lyons,' at the Adelphi, Jan.–Feb. 1898.

At the termination of his partnership with Mrs. Brown-Potter he appeared at the Criterion, Nov. 1898, with (Sir) Charles Wyndham, in 'The Jest,' but soon rejoined Irving at the Lyceum (April 1899), where he appeared as Olivier in Sardou's 'Robespierre.' Later in the year he returned to Australia, and interested himself in mining ventures, which proved profitable. From Jan. 1902, when he reappeared at Wallack's Theatre, New York, until his death he was entirely associated with the American stage. His new parts, which were few, included Raffles, in the play of that name (1903), Brigadier Gerard (1906), and Richard Voysin in 'The Thief' (1907).

Bellew was an actor of ease and distinction, with a beautiful voice, handsome, clear-cut features, and a courtly bearing. He died of pneumonia while on tour at Salt Lake City, Utah, on 2 Nov. 1911, and was buried in a cemetery on the Boston Post Road, New York. He was unmarried.

[Personal recollections; private correspondence; The Theatre, Nov. 1882 and Dec. 1897 (with photographs); M.A.P., 13 Sept. 1902; The Green Room Book, 1909; The Bancrofts' Recollections, 1909; New York Dramatic Mirror, 8 Nov. 1911 (with portrait); The Stage, 9 Nov. 1911; New York Dramatic News, 18 Nov. 1911 (with portrait).]

J. P.

BELLOWS, JOHN (1831–1902), printer and lexicographer, born at Liskeard, Cornwall, on 18 Jan. 1831, was elder son of William Lamb Bellows by his wife Hannah, daughter of John Stickland, a Wesleyan preacher. The father, of nonconformist stock, joined the Society of Friends soon after his marriage, and started a school in 1841 at Camborne, Cornwall, from which he retired in 1858; removing to Gloucester, he died there in December 1877; he published a memoir of his father-in-law (1838; 3rd edit. 1855), educational treatises, and pamphlets on quaker principles.

After education by his father, John was apprenticed to a printer at Camborne at fourteen. In 1851 he became foreman of a small printing business in Gloucester, and in 1858 started for himself, introducing the first steam engine in the town. His business prospered and grew to large dimensions. Meanwhile he studied philology, mastered French, soon made the acquaintance of Max Müller [q. v.], and opened a correspondence with Oliver Wendell Holmes, which lasted twenty-five years, and with Prince Lucien Bonaparte, the philologist. A rapid journey abroad in 1863 impressed Bellows with the need of extending the supply of dictionaries in a portable form. In 1867 he compiled and printed on strong thin paper, made by a Scots firm for Confederate banknotes which had failed to run the Charleston blockade, his 'Outline Dictionary for Missionaries, Explorers, and Students of Language.' Max Müller compiled a key alphabet and an introduction. There followed an 'English Outline Vocabulary of Chinese, Japanese and other Languages' (1868), and 'Tous les Verbes, French and English' (5th thousand 1869).

In 1870 he helped to distribute in France a fund raised by the Friends for non-combatant sufferers at the seat of the Franco-German war, and described his experience in letters to his wife published as 'The Track of the War round Metz' (1871). He was already (since 1861) working hard with the aid of French friends on a pocket 'French-English Dictionary.' The first edition of 6000, printed entirely by hand in 12mo, mostly in diamond type, appeared in 1872. It was dedicated to Prince Lucien Bonaparte. French-English and English-French vocabularies were both printed on the same page. The title ran 'The Bonâ Fide Pocket Dictionary, Le Vrai Dictionnaire de Poche, on an entirely new System, revised and corrected by Auguste Beljame, B.A., Alexandre Beljame, M.A., and John Sibree, M.A., 1872.' The issue was exhausted in twelve months; a second edition with many new features was published in 1876, and an enlarged edition was issued by Bellows's son, William Bellows, with the assistance of MM. Marrot and Friteau, in 1911.

Bellows studied archæology as well as philology, interesting himself in Palestine exploration as well as in that of Roman Britain. When making excavations for building new business premises at Eastgate House, Gloucester, in 1873, he discovered traces of the Roman city wall (see his papers in *Proc. Cotteswold Naturalists' Field Club* 1875, and *Trans. Bristol and Gloucester Archæol. Soc.* 1876, i. 153–6). In 1892 he and a Friend, J. J. Neave, went on a mission to the persecuted dissenters, the Dukhobortsi (spirit-wrestlers), in Russia, who had refused to bear arms. Bellows travelled through the Caucasus nearly to the Persian frontier, and paid two visits to Count Tolstoi, with whom he corresponded to the end of his life. Four years later he again visited Tolstoi while making plans on behalf of a committee of Friends for the transportation to Cyprus and Canada of the Dukhobortsi. In May 1901 he visited New England, where his friends were numerous, and he received from Harvard University in June the honorary degree of M.A.

He died at his house on the Cotteswold Hills on 5 May 1902, and was buried at Painswick. Bellows wore to the end the quaker dress, and used the simple language in vogue in his youth. He was a teetotaller, and a vegetarian from 1890. He married in January 1869, at Clitheroe, Lancashire, Elizabeth, daughter of Mark Earnshaw, surgeon, of that place. His wife, four sons, and five daughters survived him.

Besides works already mentioned and papers in antiquarian periodicals, Bellows published: 1. 'A Winter Journey from Gloucester to Norway in 1863,' 1867. 2. 'Two Days' Excursion to Llanthony Abbey and the Black Mountains,' 1868. 3. 'Ritualism or Quakerism? and Who sent thee to baptise?' 1870. 4. 'A Week's Holiday in the Forest of Dean,' 1881, many times reprinted. 5. 'Chapters of Irish History,' 1886. 6. 'William Lucy and his Friends of the Cotteswold Club Thirty-five Years Ago,' 1894. 7. 'Evolution in the Monastic Orders, and Survivals of Roman Architecture in Britain' ('Proc. Cotteswold Naturalists' Field Club'), 1898. 8. 'The Truth about the Transvaal War and the Truth about War,' 1900, translated into French and German.

He was the inventor of a cylindrical calculator for rapid and accurate reckoning of workmen's wages, and compiled a series of concentric calculators for converting the metric system into English equivalents and *vice versa*.

[Life and Letters, by his wife, 1904; Morse's Life of O. W. Holmes, 1896; Life of Max Müller, 1902, vol. i.; Hoar's Autobiography, ii. 449; Nature, 1902, lxvi. 113; Elkinton's Doukhobors in Russia, 1903; The Times, 6 May 1902; Boase and Courtney, Bibliotheca Cornubiensis, i. 20; Smith's Catalogue of Friends' Books.] C. F. S.

BEMROSE, WILLIAM (1831–1908), writer on wood-carving, born at Derby on 30 Dec. 1831, was second son in a family of three sons and one daughter of William Bemrose of Derby, founder in 1827 of the printing and publishing firm of William Bemrose & Sons of Derby and London. His mother was Elizabeth Ride of Lichfield. His elder brother, Henry Howe Bemrose (1827–1912), was conservative member of parliament for Derby from 1895 to 1900 and was knighted in 1897.

After education at King William's College in the Isle of Man, Bemrose, like his brother Henry, joined his father's business. The business, which passed to the management of the two brothers on their father's retirement in 1857, grew rapidly in all directions. A publishing house was established in London, with branch offices at Leeds and Manchester, and the printing works were repeatedly extended. Bemrose, although always active in the printing business, pursued many other interests. In middle life he became a director of the Royal Crown Derby Porcelain Works, and thus helped to revive an important local industry.

Bemrose chiefly devoted his leisure to travel and to a study of varied forms of art, on which he wrote with much success. Practising in early life artistic pastimes like wood-carving, fret-cutting, and modelling in clay, he compiled useful manuals concerning them for the instruction of amateurs which were well illustrated and circulated widely. The chief of these was his 'Manual of Wood-carving' (1862), the first work of its kind in England, which attained standard rank, reaching a twenty-second edition in 1906. There followed 'Fret-cutting and Perforated Carving' (Derby, 1868); 'Buhl Work and Marquetry' (1872); 'Paper Rosette Work and how to Make it' (1873); 'Instructions in Fret-cutting with Designs' (1875); and 'Mosaicon: or Paper Mosaic and how to Make it' (1875).

Meanwhile Bemrose's association with the local pottery led him to publish three authoritative works on china. The first, 'The Pottery and Porcelain of Derbyshire' (1870), he wrote in collaboration with A. Wallis. But 'Bow, Chelsea and Derby Porcelain' (1898) and 'Longton Hall Porcelain' (1906) were solely his own.

Bemrose was also a clever amateur painter in oils and water-colours and collected pictures, china, and articles of 'vertu,' especially rare specimens of Egyptian art, which he acquired on visits to the East. In 1885 he published a sumptuously illustrated and finely printed 'Life and Work of Joseph Wright, A.R.A., commonly called Wright of Derby.' He also wrote on technical education and archæological and ceramic subjects.

Bemrose, who was elected a F.S.A. in 1905, played an active part in local affairs of Derby. He was chairman of the Derby Art Gallery Committee, a member of the Derbyshire Archæological Society, and vice-president of the Derby Sketching Club. A member of the Derby school board from 1879, he was its chairman from 1886 to 1902, and was a founder and for many years chairman of the Railway Servants' Orphanage. A pioneer of the volunteer movement, he retired as lieutenant in the 1st Derby volunteers in 1874 after seventeen years' service. He died at Bridlington, while on a short holiday, on 6 Aug. 1908, and was buried at the new cemetery, Derby.

Bemrose married (1) in 1858 Margaret Romana (*d.* 1901), only daughter of Edward Lloyd Simpson of Spondon, by whom he had five sons and one daughter; (2) in 1903 Lilian, daughter of William John Cumming, M.R.C.S., of Matlock, and widow of Alderman William Hobson of Derby, proprietor of the 'Derbyshire Advertiser.' His second wife survived him.

[The Times, 8 Aug. 1908; the Derby Express, 8 Aug. 1908; private information.]

S. E. F.

BENDALL, CECIL (1856–1906), professor of Sanskrit at Cambridge, born at Islington on 1 July 1856, was youngest son in a family of six sons and three daughters of Robert Smith Bendall, a tradesman in London, by his wife Elizabeth Kay, daughter of William Holmes. A precocious child, he attended the City of London School from 1869 to 1875, under Dr. Edwin Abbott Abbott. There he gained a Carpenter scholarship in 1871. As a boy he developed a keen taste, which he retained through life, for ecclesiastical architecture and monumental brasses, as well as for music, especially the work of Bach and Palestrina. From 1873 onwards he was taught Sanskrit at school, his teacher being Mr. George Frederick Nicholl, afterwards professor of Arabic at Oxford, who offered to instruct a few of the more promising classical scholars. Bendall made rapid strides in the language. In October 1875 he went to Cambridge as minor scholar in classics and Sanskrit exhibitioner of Trinity College. During seven years' residence in the university he read Sanskrit with Prof. Edward Byles Cowell [q. v. Suppl. II], whose influence decided the direction of his career. In October 1877 he migrated as a scholar to Caius College, graduating B.A. as fifth in the first class in the classical tripos in 1879. He was fellow of Caius from 1879 to 1886. Meanwhile in the summer of 1879 he attended Prof. Benfey's lectures at Göttingen on the Veda and on Zend, and in 1881 gained a first class in the Indian languages tripos at Cambridge. He had already in 1880 contributed an annotated abridgment of 'The Megha-Sutra,' with translation, to the 'Journal of the Royal Asiatic Society' (n.s. xii. 286 seq.). In the October term of 1881 he gave lectures in Sanskrit to classical students and to Indian civil service candidates studying at the university, and he completed in 1883 at Mr. Henry Bradshaw's suggestion a still indispensable 'Catalogue of the Buddhist Sanskrit MSS. in the University Library of Cambridge,' which had been initiated by Prof. Cowell. In the introduction, Bendall for the first time showed systematically how palæography determined the age of Sanskrit MSS. In 1882 he left Cambridge to become senior assistant in the department of Oriental MSS. and printed books in the British Museum, and he held the post till his retirement, through ill-health, in 1898. While at the museum he published for the trustees catalogues of the Sanskrit and Pali books (1893) and of the Sanskrit manuscripts (1902).

He also engaged in professorial work, holding the chair of Sanskrit at University College, London, from 1885 to 1903.

With the aid of grants from the Worts fund at Cambridge he twice visited Nepal and Northern India for the acquisition of MSS. for the Cambridge University library. On his first visit (1884–5) he obtained some 500 Sanskrit MSS. and nine inscribed tablets (cf. J. F. Fleet, *Inscriptions of the Gupta Dynasty*, p. 184). Of this visit he gave an account in his 'Journey of Literary and Archæological Research in Nepal and Northern India' (1886). To the Royal Asiatic Society's 'Journal' (1888, pp. 465–501) he contributed extracts from the Sanskrit text, with translation and notes, of 'The Tantrākhyāna,' a collection of Indian folklore, which he had discovered in a unique palm-leaf MS. during this visit to Nepal. A second visit followed his withdrawal from the British Museum (1898–9) and resulted in the acquisition of some ninety MSS. (see *Roy. Asiat. Soc. Journal,* 1900, p. 162). Elected in 1883 a member of the Royal Asiatic Society, he was from 1884 a member of its council. He frequently read papers at the meetings of the International Congress of Orientalists, and was delegate for his university in 1899 and 1902.

In 1901 he succeeded Robert Alexander Neil [q.v. Suppl. II] as university lecturer and lecturer to the Indian civil service board at Cambridge. In 1902 he became curator of Oriental literature in the university library. Next year, on the death of his old teacher, Prof. Cowell, he was elected professor of Sanskrit in the university, delivering on 24 Oct. his inaugural address on 'Some of the aims and methods of recent Indian research.' He was made honorary fellow of his college in 1905.

Bendall, who combined a lifelong devotion to music with many other social gifts, died on 14 March 1906 at Liverpool after a long illness, and was buried at the Huntingdon Road cemetery, Cambridge. He married at Esher on 19 July 1898 a French lady, Georgette, daughter of Georges Joseph Ignace Jung, and widow of G. Mosse of Cowley Hall, Middlesex, but had no issue. She became a member of the Royal Asiatic Society in 1901, was author of 'Practical Lessons in Cookery for Small Households' (1905), and died on 24 Dec. 1910 at her sister's residence in Paris.

Bendall was a sound textual critic, an expert in Indian palæography and epigraphy, and an inspiring teacher. The Tibetan language was within his range of knowledge. His most important published works dealt with the Sanskrit Buddhist literature of the Mahāyāna, which he made his special study. They were: 1. 'Çikṣāsamuccaya' (an important compendium of Buddhist doctrine), Sanskrit text with critical notes published in 'Bibliotheca Buddhica' by the Imperial Academy of Sciences at St. Petersburg, 1897–1902. Bendall, who had discovered the work in Nepal, was engaged with Dr. W. H. D. Rouse on its translation at his death. 2. 'Subhāṣita-saṃgraha,' text with notes, Louvain, 1903. 3. (with Louis de la Vallée Poussin) 'Bodhisattvabhūmi,' Louvain, 1905.

By his will he left his Oriental palm-leaf MSS. and printed books to Cambridge University (for description see *Journal Royal Asiatic Soc.* 1900, p. 345, and April 1907). His residuary estate after Mrs. Bendall's death was assigned to the foundation of a prize for Sanskrit at Caius College, a small sum being allotted to the formation there of an Oriental library for junior students (*The Times*, 18 June 1906). Part of his valuable musical collection was acquired by the Fitzwilliam Museum.

[The Times, 15 March 1906; will, 18 June 1906; Who's Who, 1906; Journal, Roy. Asiat. Soc. n.s. 1906, xx. 527 seq. (notice by Prof. E. J. Rapson); In Memoriam Cecil Bendall, by H. T. Francis (privately printed), 1906; Cambridge Review, 26 April 1906; private information.] W. B. O.

BENHAM, WILLIAM (1831–1910), hon. canon of Canterbury and author, was born on 15 Jan. 1831 at West Meon near Petersfield, Hampshire, where his grandfather and his father, James Benham, successively held the position of village postmaster. He was educated at the village school, built by the rector, Henry Vincent Bayley [q. v.], who made him his secretary, and taught him Greek and Latin. At his death Bayley left instructions that the boy's education should be continued, and he was sent in 1844 to St. Mark's College, Chelsea, recently established under the headmastership of Derwent Coleridge [q.v.], to be trained as a schoolmaster. On completing his course he taught in a rural school, and was tutor to Sir John Sebright between 1849 and 1852. Then by his own exertions and the help of Archdeacon Bayley's family he was enabled to attend the theological department of King's College, London, where the influence of F. D. Maurice permanently affected his religious position. In 1857 he was ordained deacon and priest in 1858. Appointed divinity tutor and lecturer in English literature at St. Mark's, Chelsea, still under Derwent Coleridge, he then first exhibited his gift as a teacher and his power of stimulating character He remained at Chelsea until in 1865 he became editorial secretary to the Society for Promoting Christian Knowledge. At the same time he engaged in Sunday ministerial work as curate of St. Lawrence Jewry, under Benjamin Morgan Cowie [q. v. Suppl. I]. From 1866 to 1871 he was also professor of modern history at Queen's College, Harley Street, in succession to F. D. Maurice.

Meanwhile his preaching attracted the attention of Archbishop Longley, who made him in 1867 first vicar of the newly formed parish of Addington, where the archbishop resided. The health of the primate was giving way. Benham assisted him as his private secretary during the anxious period of the first Lambeth Conference in 1867, and was with him at his death in 1868. Comparative leisure at Addington enabled Benham to increase his literary work. He produced an edition of Cowper's poetry in 1870, worked on a commentary on the New Testament, and published in 1873 his well-known 'Companion to the Lectionary' (new edit. 1884). With Tait, Longley's successor in the Archbishopric, Benham's relations at Addington grew very intimate. Tait gave him the Lambeth degree of B.D, made him one of the six preachers of Canterbury.

and in 1872 bestowed on him the important vicarage of Margate. Here Benham restored the parish church, was chairman of the first school board of the town, and made the Church Institute a centre of intellectual and spiritual life. But he found time to edit the memoirs of Catherine and Craufurd Tait, the wife and son of the archbishop (1879; abridged edit. 1882). In 1880 Tait made him vicar of Marden, and in 1882 he was appointed rector of St. Edmund the King with St. Nicholas Acons, Lombard Street. That benefice he held for life.

He made St. Edmund's Church a preaching centre of exceptional intellectual force and impartiality; 'Lombard Street in Lent' (1894), the title of a course of addresses by various preachers, presented the kind of sermon which he thought a City church should supply, in order to attract the business man in the luncheon hour. In 1888 Archbishop Benson made him hon. canon of Canterbury, and in 1898 Hartford University, U.S.A., granted him the degree of D.D. He was Boyle lecturer in 1897, and rural dean of East City from 1903 till his death.

Benham's literary activity was always great. His collaboration with Dr. Davidson in the writing of the 'Life of Archbishop Tait' (1891) was the most important of his later works. His editorship of the long series of cheap reprints entitled the 'Ancient and Modern Library of Theological Literature' was a laborious and laudable effort to popularise good literature. But the characteristic work of the last twenty years of his life was the lightly written series of miscellaneous paragraphs which he contributed to the 'Church Times' week by week under the heading 'Varia' and with the signature of 'Peter Lombard.' He died of heart failure on 30 July 1910, and was buried at Addington. Benham was twice married: (1) to Louisa, daughter of Lewis Engelbach, by whom he had three daughters; (2) to Caroline, daughter of Joseph Sandell of Old Basing, Hampshire, who survived him.

Besides the works mentioned, and a translation of 'The Imitatio' (1874; new ed. 1905), Benham's chief works were: 1. 'The Gospel according to St. Matthew . . . with Notes,' 1862. 2. 'The Epistles for the Christian Year with Notes,' 1865. 3. 'The Church of the Patriarchs,' 1867. 4. 'A short History of the Episcopal Church in the United States,' 1884. 5. 'Winchester' (in 'Diocesan Histories'), 1884. 6. 'Sermons for the Church's Year, original and selected,' 2 vols. 1883–4. 7. 'The Dictionary of Religion; an Encyclopædia of Christian and other Religious Doctrines, . . . Terms, History, Biography,' 1887; reissued 1891, begun by J. H. Blunt. 8. 'Winchester Cathedral,' 1893; illustrated, 1897. 9. 'Rochester Cathedral,' 1900 (both in 'English Cathedrals'). 10. 'Mediæval London,' 1901 and 1911, with Charles Welch. 11. 'Old St. Paul's Cathedral,' 1902. 12. 'The Tower of London,' 1906 (all three in the 'Portfolio Monographs'). 13. 'St. John and his Work' ('Temple' series of Bible handbooks), 1904. 14. 'Old London Churches,' 1908. 15 'Letters of Peter Lombard,' 1911, posthumous, with a preface by Archbishop Davidson.

[Memoir by his daughter, Mrs. Dudley Baxter, prefixed to the Letters of Peter Lombard, 1911; The Times, 1 Aug. 1910; Treasury, Oct. 1902; Men and Women of the Time, 1899; Crockford's Clerical Directory.]

R. B.

BENNETT, ALFRED WILLIAM (1833–1902), botanist, born at Clapham, Surrey, on 24 June 1833, was second son of William Bennett (*d.* 1873), a tea-dealer. Like his parents, he was a member of the Society of Friends. The father, a good field botanist, was intimate with the naturalists Edward Newman [q. v.] and Edward and Henry Doubleday [q. v.]; he published 'A Narrative of a Journey in Ireland in 1847' and 'Joint-stock Companies' in 1861, and in 1851 retired to Brockham Lodge, Betchworth, Surrey, where it is said that he bred emus to the third generation. His mother, Elizabeth (*d.* 1891), wrote some religious books (JOSEPH SMITH, *Friends' Books*, supplement, p. 56). Bennett's elder brother, Edward Trusted (1831–1908), at one time edited the 'Crusade,' a temperance magazine. Save for some months in 1841–2 at the Pestalozzian School at Appenzell, Bennett was educated at home. Long walking tours in Wales, the west of England, and the lake district, undertaken by Bennett with his father and brother, were reported by them in the 'Phytologist' (iv. (1851), 312, 439 and (1852), 757–8). On the last occasion they called upon Wordsworth at Rydal Mount, and he accompanied them up Fairfield to show them *Silene acaulis.*

Bennett attended classes at University College, London, and graduated B.A. from the University of London in 1853, with honours in chemistry and botany, proceeding M.A. in 1855 and B.Sc. in 1868. After leaving college he acted for a short time as tutor in the family of Gurney Barclay, the banker. In 1858 he started business as a bookseller and publisher at

5 Bishopsgate Street Within, London. Besides works by his father and mother he issued the early poems of the Hon. John Leicester Warren, afterwards third Baron de Tabley [q. v.], a fellow botanist. In 1868 Bennett gave up business, was elected a fellow of the Linnean Society, and became lecturer on botany at Bedford College and at St. Thomas's Hospital. From 1870 to 1874 he was biological assistant to Dr. (now Sir) Norman Lockyer, while editing the newly established paper 'Nature.' After writing on pollination and the Order *Polygalaceæ* for Sir Joseph Hooker's 'Flora of British India' (vol. i. 1872), and for Martius's 'Flora Brasiliensis' (1874), Bennett, who knew German well, performed what was, perhaps, his greatest service to British botanical students, by translating and editing, with the assistance of Mr. (now Sir William) Thiselton-Dyer, the third edition of Julius Sachs's 'Lehrbuch der Botanik' (1875). He also translated and edited Professor Otto Thomé's 'Lehrbuch,' as 'Text-book of Structural and Physiological Botany,' in 1877.

On Alpine plants Bennett published three works: 'Alpine Plants,' translated from the 'Alpenpflanzen' of J. Seboth, in four volumes, with 100 plates in each (1879–84); 'The Tourist's Guide to the Flora of the Austrian Alps,' from the German of K. W. von Dalla Torre (1882), with better illustrations; and 'The Flora of the Alps . . . descriptive of all the species of flowering plants indigenous to Switzerland and of the Alpine species of the adjacent mountain districts . . . including the Pyrenees' (2 vols. 1896–7), with 120 coloured plates from David Wooster's 'Alpine Plants.'

In 1879 Bennett became a fellow of the Royal Microscopical Society, and thenceforth mainly confined his researches to cryptogamic plants, especially the freshwater algæ. He re-wrote the section on cryptogams for Henfrey's 'Elementary Botany' (4th edit., by Maxwell Masters, 1884); and in the 'Handbook of Cryptogamic Botany,' an original work, which he undertook with George Robert Milne Murray [q. v. Suppl. II] in 1889, he wrote of all groups containing chlorophyll. From 1897 he edited the 'Journal of the Royal Microscopical Society.' He died suddenly from heart disease, on his way home from the Savile Club, on 23 Jan. 1902, and was buried in the Friends' burial-ground at Isleworth. He married in 1858 Katherine, daughter of William Richardson of Sunderland, who predeceased him, leaving no children.

Described by Professor Vines, in his presidential address to the Linnean Society for 1902, as 'a laborious student and a conscientious teacher of botany,' Bennett was a contributor to the 'Journal of Botany,' 'The Popular Science Review,' the 'Reports' of the British Association, and other scientific periodicals. Among his minor publications were: 1. 'Mycological Illustrations,' with W. Wilson Saunders and Worthington G. Smith, 1871. 2. 'Introduction to the Study of Flowerless Plants,' 1891. 3. 'Pre-Foxite Quakerism,' reprinted, with additions, from the 'Friends' Quarterly Examiner,' 1894.

[Journal of the Royal Microscopical Society, 1902, 155–7 (with photographic portrait); Journal of Botany, 1902, 113; Proceedings of the Linnean Society, 1901–2, 26; Nature, lxv. 34; Gardeners' Chronicle, 1902, i. 85.]

G. S. B.

BENNETT, EDWARD HALLARAN (1837–1907), surgeon, born at Charlotte Quay, Cork, on 9 April 1837, was youngest child in the family of five sons of Robert Bennett, recorder of Cork, by his wife Jane, daughter of William Saunders Hallaran, M.D., of Cork, who made some reputation as a writer on insanity (Cork, 1810 and 1818). His grandfather, James Bennett, was also a physician in Cork. A kinsman, James Richard Bennett, was a distinguished teacher of anatomy in Paris about 1825. An elder brother, Robert Bennett, served all through the Crimean war, and retired in 1886 with the rank of major-general. After education at Hamblin's school in Cork, and at the Academical Institute, Harcourt Street, Dublin, he entered Trinity College, Dublin, in 1854, and in 1859 graduated B.A. and M.B., also receiving the new degree of M.Ch., which was then conferred for the first time. He pursued his professional studies in the school of physic, Trinity College, and in Dr. Steevens', the Meath, the Richmond, and Sir Patrick Dun's Hospitals. In 1863 he became a fellow of the Royal College of Surgeons in Ireland, without having become a licentiate. In 1864 he proceeded M.D., and was appointed university anatomist in Dublin University, the post carrying with it the office of surgeon to Sir Patrick Dun's Hospital. In 1873 he became professor of surgery in Trinity College, and curator of the pathological museum. These posts, with the surgeoncy to Sir Patrick Dun's, he held till 1906. In 1880 he was president of the Pathological Society of Dublin. From 1884 to 1886 he was president of the Royal College of Surgeons in Ireland; from 1894 to 1897 he was president of the Royal Academy of Medicine in Ireland; and from 1897 to 1906 he represented the University of Dublin on the General Medical Council. During the viceroyalty of the Earl of Dudley (1902–5) he was surgeon to the lord-lieutenant, and in 1900 he was made honorary fellow of the Royal College of Surgeons of England.

Bennett was an authority on fractures of bones. His best work is the collection of fractures and dislocations in the pathological museum of Trinity College. This was begun by R. W. Smith, whom he succeeded as curator in 1873, and was formed by Bennett into one of the most important collections of the kind in the kingdom. He spent years in compiling a catalogue furnished with notes and clinical histories, but it remained unfinished. He frequently published communications and reports dealing with the surgery and pathology of bones. In 1881 he described before the Dublin Pathological Society a form of fracture of the base of the metacarpal bone of the thumb previously unrecognised (*Dublin Journal of Medical Science*, lxxiii.). It closely simulates dislocation and is now universally known as 'Bennett's fracture' (Miles and Struthers, *Edin. Medical Journal*, April 1904). As an operating surgeon he was one of the earliest in Ireland to apply Listerian methods. As a teacher, he was forcible and practical, and he enlightened the driest subject with touches of humour.

Bennett died on 21 June 1907 at his residence, 26 Lower FitzWilliam Street, Dublin, and was buried at Mount Jerome cemetery, Dublin. On 20 Dec. 1870 he married Frances, daughter of Conolly Norman of Fahan, co. Donegal, and first cousin of Conolly Norman [q. v. Suppl. II]. He had two daughters, of whom one, Norah Mary, survived him. Two bronze portrait medallions by Mr. Oliver Sheppard, R.H.A., were placed respectively in the school of physic, Trinity College, and in Sir Patrick Dun's Hospital by subscription of his pupils. A bronze medal, to be awarded biennially to the winner of the surgical travelling prize in the school of physic, also bears on one side Mr. Sheppard's portrait of Bennett, and on the other a metacarpal bone showing 'Bennett's fracture.'

[Obituary notice in Dublin Journal of Medical Science (by Sir J. W. Moore), July 1907; Cameron's History of the Royal College of Surgeons in Ireland; Todd's Catalogue of Graduates in Dublin University; Dublin University Calendars; MS. Entrance Book, Trinity College, Dublin; private sources and personal knowledge.] R. J. R.

BENT, Sir THOMAS (1838–1909), prime minister of Victoria, born at Penrith in New South Wales on 7 Dec. 1838, was the eldest son in a family of four sons and two daughters. His father, having lost money in Sydney, came to Victoria in 1849 and began life again, first as a contractor in a small way of business, then as a market gardener, near McKinnon in the Brighton suburb of Melbourne; here he soon managed to build and run an inn called the Gardeners' Arms. From the age of eleven Bent worked with his father, and for education depended on his own efforts. Characterised from youth by cheery 'push' and enterprise, he started a small market garden in 1859, taking his own produce weekly to market in a rough cart. In 1861 he became rate-collector for Brighton.

In 1862 Bent made his entry into public life by becoming a member of the Moorabbin shire council, of which he was afterwards president on twelve occasions. In 1871 he entered the Victoria parliament for Brighton, defeating, to general surprise, George Higinbotham [q. v. Suppl. I], one of the greatest public figures in Australia. He represented the constituency with one short interval throughout his career. In 1874 he resigned his position as rate-collector on being also elected to the Brighton borough council, to the business of which he devoted himself despite political calls. Gradually he made his way in parliament and became the life and soul of the attack on (Sir) Graham Berry [q. v. Suppl. II], and a leader of the 'party of combat.' As whip for the opposition in 1877 Bent prevented the Berry government from getting a majority for their reform bill, and eventually in January 1880 brought about the fall of that ministry.

In March 1880 Bent joined the ministry of James Service as vice-president of the board of public works, but went out with his colleagues in August of the same year. In July 1881 he resumed the same position under the title of commissioner of railways and president of the board of land and works in the ministry of Sir Bryan O'Loghlen. In this capacity he was connected with the 'octopus' railway bill; and he was to some extent discredited by his tendency to over-sanguine advertisement. O'Loghlen's government lasted till March 1883, when for a time Bent led the opposition, but his temperament was little suited to such a task and he was displaced by a more conciliatory leader. In October 1887 he was defeated by one vote as candidate for the office of speaker of the assembly. Almost immediately afterwards he was elected chairman of the first railways standing committee, and in that capacity for two years did much solid work. In 1892 he was elected speaker, and held the office, for which he had few qualifications, for nearly two years. During these years 1887–94 he with six others was engaged in the 'land boom,' which at first seemed likely to give him a huge fortune and in 1893 left him practically a ruined man. Thrown out of the assembly in 1894, Bent retired to Port Fairy, and devoted himself for the next six years to dairy farming. During that period he was defeated ignominiously at South Melbourne. But in 1900 he was elected for his old constituency, Brighton. On 10 June 1902 he joined William Hill Irvine's ministry as minister for railways and works, and though on 6 Feb. 1903 he parted with the railway work to another minister he bore the brunt of the great railway strike of May 1903. On Irvine's retirement Bent became prime minister (16 Feb. 1904). His ministry lasted over four years, and in that period passed many measures aimed at improving the conditions of life amongst manual workers and their economic position.

In 1907, after a serious illness, Bent paid a long visit to England, where he completed the arrangements for the new Victoria agency building, Melbourne House, Strand. Returning in August 1907, he still held the reins for over a year; but on 1 Dec. 1908 was defeated on a vote of want of confidence. At his request the governor, Sir T. G. Carmichael, dissolved parliament. Bent was defeated at the polls, and a commission was appointed by the new government to investigate charges made against him on the hustings. Out of this ordeal he emerged with general credit. But the strain of work proved fatal. He died on 17 Sept. 1909. A state funeral was accorded him; he was buried at Brighton cemetery.

Bent was made a K.C.M.G. in 1908. Rough and uncultivated, shrewd and strong, Bent was 'one of the most interesting and remarkable figures in the public life of Australia.' At his public meetings he would break off an argument to sing or recite, indulging in 'execrable songs, purely Bentian jokes, extraordinary reminiscences'—all prepared to serve as 'impromptus.' In parliament he displayed unusual power in gauging the temper and feelings of members. The keynote of his policy as premier was opposition to the labour party. Unorthodox and even unprincipled in his methods, and apt to take the shortest road to his end, he always boldly accepted the responsibility for his actions. He showed courage in all concerns of life.

Bent married twice. His first wife (born Hall) died childless. His second wife (born Huntley) died in 1893, leaving one daughter.

Bent Street in Sydney appears to have been named after the father as owner of a corner lot (*Melbourne Argus*, 18 Sept. 1909).

[Melbourne Age, Melbourne Argus, 18 Sept. 1909 (both of these papers have a rough portrait); The Times, 18 Sept. 1909; Mennell's Dict. of Australasian Biog.; John's Notable Australians.] C. A. H.

BENTLEY, JOHN FRANCIS (1839–1902), architect, born at Doncaster on 30 Jan. 1839, was third surviving son of Charles Bentley by his wife Ann, daughter of John Bachus of that town, and received his education at a private school there. In boyhood he made a model of St. George's Church, Doncaster, from notes and measurements taken before its destruction by fire in 1853, and when Sir George Gilbert Scott [q. v.] began the rebuilding in 1854, Bentley frequented the fabric and rendered some services to the clerk of works. In 1855 he acted as voluntary superintendent in the restoration of Loversall Church, and there tried his hand at carving. Meanwhile his father, who deprecated an artistic career, placed him for a short time with Sharp, Stewart & Co., a firm of mechanical engineers at Manchester; but in August 1855 Bentley entered on a five years' indenture with the building establishment of Winsland & Holland in London. Next year his father died, and Richard Holland, a partner of this firm, recognising his promise, placed him (1858) in the office of Henry Clutton, an architect in extensive domestic and ecclesiastical practice, who had joined the Church of Rome. Bentley took the same step in 1862, and in the same year, though invited by Clutton to join him in partnership, preferred the risks of independence and took chambers at 14 Southampton Street, Covent Garden.

While waiting for commissions Bentley continued the sketching and modelling which had already occupied his evening leisure, and often made for other architects designs for work in metal, stained glass, and embroidery. He submitted designs at the exhibitions of London (1862) and Paris (1867). For St. Francis's Church, Notting Hill (the scene of his own baptism by Cardinal Wiseman), he designed the stone groined baptistery, font, and porch, as well as the altars of St. John and the Blessed Virgin (with paintings by his friend, N. H. J. Westlake), a jewelled monstrance, and at a later date the high altar. In 1866 he undertook for the poet Coventry Patmore [q. v.] the adaptation of an old Sussex House, Heron's Ghyll, near Uckfield. His work betrayed from the first conscientious anxiety for perfection in detail and soundness of construction. He regarded architectural competitions as inimical to art.

In 1868 he transferred his office to 13 John Street, Adelphi, began the Seminary of St. Thomas at Hammersmith (now the Convent of the Sacred Heart), at the time his best work, and designed the altar and reredos of the Church of St. Charles, Ogle Street, Marylebone. In 1884 Bentley built in the style of the Renaissance the large preparatory school (St. John's) in connection with Beaumont College at Old Windsor. For some years (beginning in 1874) he spent much thought and labour on the internal decoration and furniture of Carlton Towers, Selby, for Lord Beaumont.

For thirty years he was engaged at intervals on the Church of St. Mary of the Angels, Westmorland Road, Bayswater, where he designed additional aisles, a baptistery, and various chapels. The Church and Presbytery of Our Lady at Cadogan Street (1875) and the Church of St. Mary and the Holy Souls at Bosworth Road, Kensal New Town (1881) are simple examples of Bentley's brick construction. In 1885 he built the unfinished portion of Corpus Christi Church, Brixton, in Early Decorated style.

For the Redemptorist Fathers he did varied work at Bishop Eton, Liverpool, and Clapham. To the Church of Our Lady of Victories at Clapham he added a fine Lady chapel (1883), a transept, stained glass windows, and a monastery completed in 1894. For the Church of St. James, Spanish Place, London, he designed several altars and some glass. His fine Church of the Holy Rood at Watford was with its schools and presbytery in hand from 1887 to 1892. Other works were a house (Glenmuire) for E. Maxwell-Steuart at Ascot and a private chapel in the neighbourhood for C. J. Stonor (1885–90). In 1897 he built with stone and red-brick in the early fifteenth-century style the Convent of the Immaculate Conception for Franciscan nuns at Bocking Bridge, near Braintree. The screen and organ case of St. Etheldreda's, Ely Place, Holborn, are from his designs.

Bentley also had commissions from the Church of England. In 1893–4 the two City churches of St. Botolph came under his care. For St. Botolph, Bishopsgate, he provided external repair as well as internal decoration, and for that at Aldgate he designed numerous interior embellishments, notably the fine cornice of angels bearing the shields of the City companies. Similar works were done at Holy Trinity, Minories, and St. Mark's, North Audley Street. For St. John's Church, Hammersmith (designed by William Butterfield [q. v. Suppl. I]) he schemed a morning chapel, organ case, sacristy, and general decorations. In 1899 he built a new church at Chiddington, Penshurst.

In 1894 came the great opportunity of his life. Cardinal Vaughan [q. v. Suppl. II] called upon him to design the Roman catholic cathedral of Westminster. The conditions laid upon the architect were that the church should have a nave of vast extent giving an uninterrupted view of the high altar, and that the methods of construction should not be such as to involve undue initial expenditure of either time or money. On this account a strong preference was expressed in favour of Byzantine style.

Bentley perceived that his design should be preceded by special foreign study, and though not in robust health set out in November of the same year for a tour of Italy. Visiting Milan (especially for Sant' Ambrogio), Pavia, and Florence, Rome (where the work of the Renaissance disappointed him), Perugia (which with Assisi delighted him), and Ravenna, he came at last to Venice, where cold and fatigue compelled him to rest before he could study St. Mark's.

His natural wish to proceed to Constantinople was frustrated by the prevalence there of cholera, and returning to London in March 1895 he was ready by St. Peter's and St. Paul's Day (29 June) for the laying of the foundation stone.

The cathedral is outwardly remarkable for its tall campanile and its bold use of brick and stone (for description see *Architectural Review*, xi. 3, by W. R. Lethaby, and *Builder*, 6 July 1895, 25 Feb. 1899, 23 June 1900). The design is throughout marked by the greatest simplicity, largeness of scale and avoidance of trivial ornament. Internally the vast nave consists of three bays measuring 60 feet square and each surmounted by a concrete dome. A fourth bay nearest the nominal east forms the sanctuary and beyond it is an apse. The nave is flanked on each side by an aisle; outside the aisles are the many chapels. When first opened for worship, and before any progress had been made with the marble decorations, the interior effect was a triumph of pure form. The construction was remarkable, Bentley having set himself to avoid any structural materials but brick-work, masonry, and concrete. 'I have broken,' he said, 'the back of that terrible superstition that iron is necessary to large spans' (Memoir by CHARLES HADFIELD in *Architectural Review*, xi. 115).

In 1898 Bentley was summoned to the United States to advise on the design and construction of the Roman catholic cathedral at Brooklyn, for which he prepared a scheme.

Seized in November 1898 with paralytic symptoms, which in June 1900 affected his speech, he died on 2 March 1902 at his residence, The Sweep, Old Town, Clapham Common, the day before his name was to be submitted to the Royal Institute of British Architects for the royal gold medal (*R.I.B.A. Journal*, ix. 219). He was buried at Mortlake.

Bentley had married in 1874 Margaret Annie, daughter of Henry J. Fleuss, a painter, of Düsseldorf, and had four sons and seven daughters, of whom one son and one daughter died in infancy, and the remainder survived him. His third son, Osmond, succeeds, in partnership with Mr. J. A. Marshall, to the architectural practice, and his eldest daughter, Mrs. Winifred Mary de l'Hôpital, is engaged on her father's biography. There is in the possession of the family a portrait in oils by W. Christian Symons.

[R.I.B.A. Journ., 3rd series, 1901–2, ix. 437 (memoir by T. J. Willson); Architectural Review, 1902, xi. 155, and xxi. 18 (art. by Halsey Ricardo); Builder, 1902, lxxxii. 243; Building News, 1902, lxxxii. 339; information from Mr. Osmond Bentley.]

P. W.

BERGNE, SIR JOHN HENRY GIBBS (1842–1908), diplomatist, born in London on 12 Aug. 1842, and descended from a French family originally resident in Auvergne, which settled in England after the French revolution, was elder son of John Brodribb Bergne, a valued member of the foreign office for fifty-six years (1817–1873), who acquired a high reputation both at home and abroad as an authority on matters connected with treaties and diplomatic precedent. Educated at schools at Brighton and Enfield and at London University, where he passed the first B.A. examination, John Henry entered the foreign office as a clerk on the diplomatic establishment after passing a competitive examination in 1861, was appointed an assistant clerk in 1880, and promoted to be superintendent of the treaty department in 1881. He held that office until 1894, when he became superintendent of the commercial department and examiner of treaties. This position he held for eight years, doing much valuable work in the development of the commercial department and particularly in the arrangement of its relations with the board of trade, and in introducing a more regular and complete system of reports on commercial and industrial subjects from diplomatic and consular officers in foreign countries. He was occasionally employed abroad on business which came within the sphere of his permanent work, and on which he was possessed of special knowledge. In 1875 he assisted the British agent before the international commission, which sat under Article XXII of the treaty of Washington, to assess the amount to be paid by the United States to Great Britain in return for the fishery privileges accorded to the citizens of the United States under Article XVIII of that treaty, and on the meeting of the commission at Halifax in 1877 he acted as secretary and protocolist to it. In September 1887 he was appointed secretary to Mr. Joseph Chamberlain's special mission to Washington to adjust certain questions relating to the North American fisheries. For his services he received the K.C.M.G. in 1888, having been made C.M.G. in 1886. In 1885 he had been second British delegate at the international copyright conference held at Berne, and signed the convention which was there agreed upon (9 Sept. 1886). While at Washington in 1887 he was deputed to discuss the copyright question with the United States department of state. In May 1896 he signed at Paris as British delegate the additional act to the international copyright convention of 1886. He was appointed a member of the departmental committee on trade marks in 1888, and was sent as British delegate to the conference on industrial property held at Rome in 1888, at Madrid in 1890, and at Brussels in November 1897 and again in 1900. From 1898 onwards he was constantly employed in the negotiations for the abolition of bounties on the export of sugar, was one of the British delegates at the conferences held in Brussels on this question in 1899 and 1901, and signed the convention concluded on the latter occasion 5 March 1902. In 1903 he was appointed the British delegate on the permanent commission established under Article VII. of that convention, and attended the various meetings of the commission, furnishing reports which were laid before parliament and which were marked by his usual power of terse, lucid explanation. He served as a member on the royal commission for the Paris exhibition of 1900. He retired from the foreign office on a pension on 1 Oct. 1902, but his employment on the special subjects of which he had an intimate acquaintance continued. He received the C.B. in 1902 and the K.C.B. in the following year. In November 1908 he served as British delegate at the international copyright conference at Berlin, and died there of a chill on 15 Nov.

Though scarcely an author in the ordinary sense of the term, Bergne rendered important services to the Authors' Society, of which he became a member in 1890, and after his retirement from the foreign office served on the committee of management, and copyright sub-committee, acting as chairman of the general committee (1905–7). He contributed to the 'Quarterly Review,' 'Blackwood's Magazine,' 'The Spectator,' and other periodicals articles on subjects with which he was professionally well acquainted (including the 'Halifax Fishery Commission,' the 'Law of Extradition,' 'Anglo-American Copyright,' and 'Queen's Messengers'). He was also an accomplished mountaineer and well-known member of the Alpine Club from 1878 to death. His father had been known as an expert numismatist; he was himself a collector of Oriental china.

He married in 1878 Mary à Court, daughter of Rev. S. B. Bergne, and had two sons, the elder of whom was killed in an accident near Saas Fee in Switzerland in January 1908; the younger, Evelyn, survives.

[The Times, 16 Nov. 1908; Author, 1 Dec. 1908; Alpine Journal, xxiv. 499–501; Foreign Office List, 1909, p. 397.] S.

BERKELEY, Sir GEORGE (1819–1905), colonial governor, born in the Island of Barbados, West Indies, on 2 Nov. 1819, was eldest son of General Sackville Hamilton Berkeley, colonel of the 16th regiment of foot. The father, who descended from a branch of the family of the earls of Berkeley, served at the capture of Surinam in 1804, of the Danish Islands of St. Thomas, St. John and St. Croix in 1807, and of Martinique in 1809. Sir George's mother was Elizabeth Pilgrim, daughter of William Murray of Bruce Vale Estate, Barbados. Educated at Trinity College, Dublin, which he entered on 3 July 1837, he graduated B.A. in 1842, and soon returned to the West Indies, where his active life was almost wholly passed. On 11 Feb. 1845 he was appointed colonial secretary and controller of customs of British Honduras and ex-officio member of the executive and legislative councils. While still serving in that colony he was chosen in 1860–1 to administer temporarily the government of Dominica, and on 8 July 1864 was appointed lieutenant-governor of the Island of St. Vincent. During his tenure of office in 1867 an Act to amend and simplify the legislature substituted a single legislative chamber for the two houses which had been in existence since 1763. He was acting administrator of Lagos from December 1872 to October 1873, when he was appointed governor in chief of the West Africa settlements (Sierra Leone, Gambia, Gold Coast, and Lagos). The Gold Coast and Lagos were soon erected into a separate colony (24 July 1874), and Berkeley was recalled, so as to allow of a new governor (of Sierra Leone and Gambia) being appointed at a reduced salary. While on his way home in June 1874 he was offered, and accepted, the government of Western Australia, but did not take up the appointment, being sent instead to the Leeward Islands as governor in chief. There he remained until 27 June 1881, when he retired on a pension. He was created C.M.G. on 20 Feb. 1874, and K.C.M.G. 24 May 1881.

Berkeley died unmarried in London on 29 Sept. 1905, and was buried in Kensal Green cemetery.

[Colonial Office List, 1905; The Times, 2 Oct. 1905; Oliver's Hist. of the Island of Antigua, 1899, iii. 319; Hart's Army List, 1863; Dublin Univ. Matric. Book, 1837; Colonial Office Records.] C. A.

BERNARD, Sir CHARLES EDWARD (1837–1901), Anglo-Indian administrator, born at Bristol on 21 Dec. 1837, was son of James Fogo Bernard, M.D., of 16 The Crescent, Clifton, by his wife Marianne Amelia, sister of John, first Lord Lawrence [q. v.]. He was educated at Rugby, which he entered in 1851, in company with his cousin, Alexander Hutchinson, eldest son of Sir Henry Montgomery Lawrence [q. v.], and C. H. Tawney, whose sister he afterwards married. In 1855 he accepted a cadetship at Addiscombe; but in the following year he received a nomination to Haileybury in the last batch of students at that college. After gaining prizes in mathematics, Persian, Hindustani, and Hindi, he passed out in 1857 at the head of the list for Bengal. His early service was in the Punjab, and afterwards in the Central Provinces, where he was secretary under two chief commissioners, Sir Richard Temple [q. v. Suppl. II] and Sir George Campbell [q. v. Suppl. I]. The latter appointed him his secretary in 1871, when he became lieutenant-governor of Bengal; and he accompanied the former as secretary in his famine tour through Madras and Bombay in 1877. In the following year he became secretary to the government of India in the home department. In 1880 he officiated as chief commissioner of British Burma, being confirmed in 1882. Except for a short interval, he held that office until his retirement in 1887. This long period included anxious negotiations with Thibaw, king of independent Burma, the brief war that ended in Thibaw's deposition, the annexation of the upper province, and the tedious process of pacification. Sir Charles Bernard came back to England in 1887, in order to take up the appointment of secretary at the India office in the department of revenue, statistics, and commerce. He finally retired in 1901, after a continuous service of forty-three years. He died on a visit to Chamonix, on 19 Sept. 1901, and there he was buried. He was created C.S.I. in 1875, and K.C.S.I. in 1886. He married at Calcutta, on 23 Oct. 1862, Susan Capel, daughter of Richard Tawney, rector of Willoughby, Warwickshire. His eight children survived him. The eldest son, James Henry, after following his father into the Indian civil service, died of cholera, together with his wife and other members of his household, at Chinsura, Bengal, in November 1907.

Bernard was possessed of inexhaustible energy in both body and mind. At Rugby he was prominent in the football field, and at Calcutta he won a cup for single rackets. In India he had the reputation of being the hardest worker in a hardworking secretariat; and at the India office it was said of him that he undertook the duties of every subordinate in his department, including those of the messenger. In 1887 he delivered an address before the Royal Scottish Geographical Society at Edinburgh on 'Burma: the New British Province.' In 1889 he compiled a valuable report on Indian administration during the past thirty years of British rule, which was laid before Parliament. In 1891 he wrote a confidential minute on opium, in view of a debate in the House of Commons in April of that year. In 1893 he saw through the press the posthumous memoirs of his friend, Sir George Campbell. In politics he was a liberal. The Bernard Free Library was built as a memorial to him at Rangoon.

[Personal knowledge; Sir Richard Temple, Men and Events of my Time in India, 1882; J. H. Rivett-Carnac, Many Memories, 1910; Sir Henry Cotton, Indian and Home Memories, 1911; Sir Charles Crosthwaite, The Pacification of Burma, 1912.] J. S. C.

BERNARD, THOMAS DEHANY (1815–1904), divine, second son of Charles Bernard of Eden Estate, Jamaica, the descendant of a Huguenot family, by Margaret, daughter of John Baker of Waresley House, Worcestershire, was born at Clifton on 11 Nov. 1815. Mountague Bernard [q. v.] was his brother. After private education he matriculated in December 1833 from Exeter College, Oxford, and in 1837 was placed in the second class of the final classical school. He graduated B.A. in 1838, when he won the Ellerton theological prize with an essay 'On the Conduct and Character of St. Peter.' In 1839 he was awarded the chancellor's prize for an English essay on 'The Classical Taste and Character compared with the Romantic.' In 1840 he was ordained deacon and licensed to the curacy of Great Baddow, Essex. Ordained priest in 1841, he succeeded to the vicarage of Great Baddow, where he remained until 1846. After working for a short time as curate of Harrow-on-the-Hill, he became in 1848 vicar of Terling, Essex. He showed a keener interest in the cause of foreign missions than was usual at that time. He was thrice select preacher at Oxford —in 1858, 1862, and 1882. In 1864 he delivered the Bampton lectures on 'The Progress of Doctrine in the New Testament' (5th edit. 1900).

Of strong evangelical sympathies, Bernard was appointed by Simeon's trustees to the rectory of Walcot, Bath, in 1864. There Bernard's gifts of organisation were called into play. He increased the church accommodation and built St. Andrew's church and schools. In 1867 the bishop of Bath and Wells collated him to a prebendal stall in Wells Cathedral; and next year the dean and chapter elected him to a residentiary canonry. He succeeded to the chancellorship of the cathedral in 1879, and from 1880 to 1895 represented the chapter in convocation.

Bernard was as zealous a cathedral dignitary as he was an energetic town rector. He revived the cathedral grammar school, at his own cost provided buildings for it, established a high school for girls, and interested himself in the general parochial life of Wells. An evangelical whom all trusted, though unfettered by party conventions, Bernard was a frequent speaker at the Islington clerical meeting, He resigned Walcot in 1886, and went to live at Wimborne. In 1901 he retired from his canonry, retaining only the unpaid office of chancellor. He died at High Hall, Wimborne, on 7 Dec. 1904. Bernard combined the qualities of the student and the man of affairs, of the wise counsellor in private and the clear, cogent teacher in public. He married in 1841 Caroline, daughter of Benjamin Linthorne, of High Hall, Wimborne; she died in 1881, leaving two sons and seven daughters.

Besides the works noticed, Bernard published: 1. 'Before His Presence with a Song,' 1885; 2nd edit. 1887. 2. 'The Central Teaching of Jesus Christ,' 1892. 3. 'Songs of the Holy Nativity,' 1895. 4. 'The Word and Sacraments,' 1904.

[Guardian, 14 Dec. 1904; Record, 9 Dec. 1904; The Times, 8 Dec. 1904; Foster's Alumni Oxon.; E. Stock, History of the C.M.S., 1899, ii. 359, 387 and iii. 10; private information.]

A. R. B.

BERRY, Sir GRAHAM (1822–1904), prime minister of Victoria, born at Twickenham, England, on 28 Aug. 1822, was son of Benjamin Berry, a retired tradesman, by his wife Clara Graham. After education at Chelsea he was apprenticed to a draper and silk mercer there, and subsequently in 1848 or 1849 opened a small shop in the King's Road. Emigrating to Victoria in 1852, he went into business as a general storekeeper and wine and spirit merchant at South Yarra, Prahran. In 1856 he revisited England on business connected with his father's will.

In 1860 he purchased in Victoria a newspaper called the 'Collingwood Observer,' and in the next year entered the legislative assembly of Victoria as member for East Melbourne. At the general election in August 1861 he was returned for Collingwood as an advanced liberal protectionist. He supported the ministry of Sir James McCulloch [q. v.] in its struggle with the legislative council, which refused to sanction the assembly's imposition of protectionist duties (1863–6). But when McCulloch failed in his plan of 'tacking' the customs bill to the appropriation bill, and sought to borrow from a bank in order to meet the public expenditure, Berry withdrew his support. In the ensuing election (1865) McCulloch routed all opponents, and Berry, losing his seat, was out of parliament for three years.

In 1866 Berry purchased the 'Geelong Register,' amalgamated it with the 'Geelong Advertiser,' and settled in Geelong to edit his new venture. He shortly stood for South Grant and was beaten; in 1868 he became member for Geelong West. On 12 Jan. 1870 he became treasurer in the government of John Alexander Macpherson, but the ministry fell almost immediately after his first budget speech. On 19 June 1871 he entered the ministry of Sir Charles Gavan Duffy [q.v. Suppl. II] as treasurer, but resigned on 21 May 1872: a private member attacked him in the house for having appointed his father-in-law to a local post of some emolument, and to avoid embarrassing the government he resumed the status of a private member. The charge was investigated by a select committee which never reported (see *Victorian Parl. Deb.* 1872, xiv.). Six months later the ministry went out of office.

In August 1875 Berry for the first time became prime minister and chief secretary. Introducing a land tax bill which was intended to strike at the undue accumulations of large holders, he was defeated, and on the refusal of his application for a dissolution Sir James McCulloch (20 Oct. 1875) returned to power. A great fight in the assembly followed; the 'stonewallers,' as Berry's followers were called, were met by what was known as McCulloch's 'iron hand.' In the intervals of parliamentary attendance Berry stumped the country, denouncing McCulloch's government and making a good impression. At the general election in May 1877 Berry obtained an overwhelming majority. He failed to form a coalition with James Service and the prominent opponents of McCulloch, and with a less representative cabinet set to work on a series of highly controversial measures. He revived the main features of his old land bill, and endeavoured to carry the payment of members, first by tacking a resolution to the appropriation bill and then by framing a separate bill to authorise the payment. A stern fight with the upper house produced an administrative deadlock, which lasted from May 1877 to April 1878. On 'Black Wednesday,' 8 Jan. 1878, money to pay the services failed, and Berry, consistent with his previous views, preferred the dismissal of public servants to borrowing. This strong measure, though generally condemned, had the effect of weeding the overcrowded departments. In April 1878 a compromise was effected, and Berry sought anew to strengthen the power of the lower house. But the other chamber offered uncompromising resistance. At the very end of the year he came to England with Charles Henry Pearson [q. v.] in the hope of inducing the central government to pass an Act for amending the Constitution of Victoria. His mission is locally known as 'the embassy.' He was recommended to try other methods. On his return in June 1879 he introduced a reform bill, and early in 1880 appealed to the constituencies. He incurred defeat, and on 5 March 1880 Mr. Service took office for less than six months. On 3 August 1880 Berry was once more prime minister and reached a working compromise with the upper chamber, whereby the franchise qualifications for the upper chamber were reduced. On 9 July 1881 he was defeated in parliament and resigned.

The political passion roused by Berry's policy had paralysed administration and became known as the 'Berry blight.' Rest was sorely needed and a sort of sufferance government carried on the administration till 1883. Then at a general election Berry and Service found themselves at the head of equal numbers in the house. On 8 March 1883 a coalition government was formed with great benefit to the colony; a new Public Service Act and a Railways Management Act, both aimed at the evils of patronage, were amongst its achievements. In May 1883 Berry represented the colony at the general postal conference at Sydney, and won golden opinions.

In February 1886 Berry resigned office and proceeded to London as agent general for the colony. In June 1886 he was made K.C.M.G. He represented Victoria at the colonial conference of 1887.

Returning to Melbourne in 1891, Berry represented Victoria at the federal convention of that year; he re-entered parliament in April of 1892 as member for East Bourke Boroughs, and joined William Shiel's ministry as treasurer. In 1894 he was elected speaker in succession to (Sir) Thomas Bent [q. v. Suppl. II], and held that office with success till 1897, when he lost his seat. An annuity of 500*l.* a year was voted by the new house of assembly.

Save that in 1897 and 1898 he represented his colony at federal conventions at Sydney and Adelaide, Berry thenceforth lived in retirement until his death at Balaclava on 25 Jan. 1904; a public funeral at Boroondara cemetery was accorded him.

A self-made man, without education, a democratic leader with a fervent belief in democratic principles, and a fluent speaker, he was no violent demagogue. According to Mr. Alfred Deakin, afterwards prime minister of the Australian commonwealth, 'he had the pronounced gift of generalship both in the house and in the country; was a resolute and far-seeing premier and a fighting chieftain, conspicuously able, earnest, and consistent' (JOHN'S *Notable Australians;* cf. *Victorian Parliamentary Debates,* lxxxvii. 763).

Among his other honours was the cross of the legion of honour, which he received as commissioner of Victoria at the Paris Exhibition of 1889.

Berry was twice married: (1) in 1846, to Harriet Anne Blencowe, who died in 1866, leaving eight children; (2) in 1869, to Rebecca Madge, daughter of J. B. Evans of Victoria, who survived him; by her he left seven children.

[Heaton's Australian Dict. of Dates; Mennell's Dict. of Australasian Biog.; Blair's Cyclopædia of Australasia; Melbourne Age, 26 Jan. 1904, and Argus of same date; Leader 30 Jan. 1904; The Times, 26 Jan. 1904; Who's Who, 1901; private information.] C. A. H.

BESANT, SIR WALTER (1836–1901), novelist, born on 14 Aug. 1836 at 3 St. George's Square, Portsea, was fifth child and third son in a family of six sons and four daughters of William Besant (*d.* 1879), merchant, of Portsmouth, by his wife Sarah Ediss (*d.* 1890), daughter of a builder and architect, of Dibden near Hythe. His eldest brother, William Henry Besant, F.R.S. (*b.* 1828), senior wrangler (1850) and fellow of St. John's College, Cambridge (1853), became a mathematician of repute. Mrs. Annie Besant (*b.* 1847), theosophical lecturer and author, was wife of his brother Frank, vicar of Sibsey, Lincolnshire, from 1871. Much of Walter's boyhood is described by him in his novel 'By Celia's Arbour.' As a boy he devoured his father's small but representative library of the English classics. After education at home, he was sent in 1848 to St. Paul's grammar school, Portsea (now a Wesleyan chapel), where his eldest brother had been captain. After the closing of the school, Besant was at home again for eighteen months, and in 1851 went to Stockwell grammar school, which was affiliated to King's College, London. While there he made, on half-holidays, short excursions into the City, studying its streets and buildings and developing a love of London archæology and history which absorbed him in later life. Having spent three terms at King's College, London (1854–5), where Dean Wace and Canon Ainger [q. v. Suppl. II] were among his contemporaries, he matriculated at Christ's College, Cambridge, in 1856. At Christ's his undergraduate friends included his seniors, Charles Stuart Calverley, W. W. Skeat, (Sir) Walter Joseph Sendall [q. v. Suppl. II], and (Sir) John Robert Seeley, as well as John Peile [q. v. Suppl. II], who was of his own age. He was bracketed with Calverley for the gold medal for English essay at Christ's in 1856, and won the prize offered by Calverley for an examination in the 'Pickwick Papers' at Christmas 1857, Skeat being second. After graduating B.A. as 18th wrangler in 1859, Besant gained the special bachelor's theological prize, made some unsuccessful attempts at journalism in London, and then was appointed a mathematical master of Leamington College, with the intention of taking holy orders and becoming chaplain there. In 1860 he enjoyed a first experience of continental travel, on a walking tour in Tyrol with Calverley, Peile, and Samuel Walton. Rejecting thoughts of holy orders, he accepted in 1861 the senior professorship at the Royal College, Mauritius. Among his colleagues was Frederick Guthrie, F.R.S., with whom he was on very intimate terms until Guthrie's death in 1886. Friends on the island also numbered Charles Meldrum [q. v. Suppl. II], whom he succeeded at the college, and James Dykes Campbell [q. v. Suppl. I]. He proceeded M.A. at Cambridge in 1863. His vacations were devoted to the study of French, both old and modern, and to essay writing. At the end of six and a half years he was offered the rectorship of the college, but he refused it on the ground of ill-health. He finally left Mauritius for England in June 1867, visiting Cape Town and St. Helena on his way home.

Thereupon Besant settled in London with a view to a literary career. Next year he was engaged to write leading articles on social topics in the 'Daily News,' and published 'Early French Poetry,' his first book, the fruit of recreations in Mauritius. Though loosely constructed, the work presents much valuable information in a readable style. Encouraged by the book's reception, he contributed articles on French literature to the 'British Quarterly Review' and the 'Daily News,' besides a paper on 'Rabelais' to 'Macmillan's Magazine' (1871). These were collected in 'The French Humourists from the Twelfth to the Nineteenth Century' (1873). Later French studies were 'Montaigne' (1875); 'Rabelais' (in Blackwood's foreign classics, 1879; new edit. 1885); 'Gaspard de Coligny' (1879; new edit. 1894, in the 'New Plutarch' series of biographies, of which Besant was general editor 1879–81); and 'Readings in Rabelais' (1883). He was author also of 'A Book of French: Grammatical Exercises, History of the Language' (12mo, 1877). Besant especially helped to popularise Rabelais in England. Joining the Savile Club in 1873, he formed in 1879, chiefly among its members, a Rabelais Club for the discussion of Rabelais's work. The club lasted ten years, and to its three volumes of 'Recreations' (3 vols. 1881–8) Besant was a frequent contributor.

Meanwhile Besant identified himself with other interests. In June 1868 he became secretary of the Palestine Exploration Fund, a society founded in 1864 for the systematic exploration of Palestine. The salary was 200*l.* a year, afterwards raised to 300*l.* Besant held the office till 1886, when pressure of literary work compelled his retirement; but he remained honorary secretary till his death. He devoted his pen to the interests of the fund with characteristic energy. In collaboration with E. H. Palmer [q. v.], professor of Arabic at Cambridge, with whom in his secretarial capacity he grew intimate, he wrote in 1871 'Jerusalem: the City of Herod and Saladin' (4th edit. 1899; fine paper edit. 1908), and he edited the 'Survey of Western Palestine' (1881). On Palmer's death in 1882 Besant wrote a sympathetic but uncritical 'Life' of him. He also gave an account of the society's activities in 'Twenty-one Years' Work, 1865–86' (1886), which was revised in 'Thirty Years' Work, 1865–95' (1895). Of the subsidiary Palestine Pilgrims Text Society for the translation of narratives of ancient pilgrimages in Palestine, which was founded in 1884 with Sir Charles Wilson as director, Besant was likewise secretary.

An accident diverted Besant's energy to novel writing. He sent early in 1869 an article on the Island of Reunion, which he had visited from Mauritius, to 'Once a Week.' No acknowledgment was received. By chance Besant discovered at the end of the year that the paper was published with many misprints in the issues of 16 and 23 Oct. Besant expostulated in a letter to the editor, who proved to be James Rice [q. v.]. Rice offered a satisfactory explanation, and courteously requested further contributions. Besant wrote a short Christmas story, 'Titania's Farewell,' for the Christmas number of the journal (1870). Friendly relations with the editor followed, and in 1871 Rice asked Besant to collaborate in a novel, the plot of which he had already drafted. The result was 'Ready Money Mortiboy,' which first appeared as a serial in 'Once a Week' and was published in three volumes in 1872. The book was welcomed by the public with enthusiasm. The partnership was pursued till Rice's disablement through illness in 1881. The fruits were 'My Little Girl' (1874), 'With Harp and Crown' (1874), 'This Son of Vulcan' (1875), 'The Golden Butterfly,' a triumphant success (1876), 'The Monks of Thelema' (1877), 'By Celia's Arbour' (1878), 'The Chaplain of the Fleet' (1879), and 'The Seamy Side' (1881). Besant and Rice also wrote jointly the Christmas number for 'All the Year Round' from 1872 till 1882. The division of labour made Rice mainly responsible for the plot and its development, and Besant mainly responsible for the literary form (see RICE, JAMES, preface to Library edit. of *Ready Money Mortiboy*, 1887, and *Idler*, 1892). With Rice Besant further wrote an historical biography, 'Sir Richard Whittington' (1879; new edit. 1894), and made his first attempt as a playwright, composing jointly 'Such a Good Man,' a comedy, produced by John Hollingshead at the Olympic Theatre in Dec. 1879 (HOLLINGSHEAD, *My Lifetime*, i. 38–9). Besant made a few other dramatic experiments in collaboration with Mr. Walter Herries Pollock. In 1887 they adapted for an amateur theatrical company which played at Lord Monkswell's house at Chelsea, De Banville's drama 'Gringoire' under the title of 'The Balladmonger.' It was subsequently performed by (Sir) H. Beerbohm Tree at the Haymarket Theatre (Sept. 1887) and at His Majesty's Theatre (June 1903). With Pollock, too, Besant published 'The Charm, and other Drawing-room Plays' in 1896.

While Rice lived, Besant made only one independent effort in fiction, producing in 1872 an historical novel, 'When George the Third was King.' On Rice's death, he continued novel-writing single-handed, producing a work of fiction of the regulation length each year for twenty years, besides writing the Christmas number for 'All the Year Round' between 1882 and 1887 and many other short stories. The plots of Besant's sole invention are far looser in texture than those of the partnership, and he relied to a larger extent than before on historical incident. In 'Dorothy Forster' (3 vols. 1884), which Besant considered his best work, he showed ingenuity in placing a graceful love story in an historical setting. 'The World went very well then' (1887), 'For Faith and Freedom' (1888), 'The Holy Rose' (1890), and 'St. Katharine's by the Tower' (1891) deal effectively with English life in the seventeenth and eighteenth centuries. Besant's treatment of current society is for the most part less satisfactory. But two of his pieces of modern fiction, 'All Sorts and Conditions of Men' (1882) and 'Children of Gibeon' (1886), achieved a popularity in excess of anything else from his pen, but on other than purely literary grounds.

Besant, in whom philanthropic interest was always strong, had made personal inquiry into the problems of poverty in East London, and in these two novels he enforced definite proposals for their solution. The second book dwelt on the evils of sweating, and helped forward the movement for the trades-organisation of working women. The first book, 'All Sorts and Conditions of Men,' which was mainly a strenuous plea for the social regeneration of East London, greatly stimulated the personal sympathy of the well-to-do with the East End poor. In this novel Besant depicted a fictitious 'Palace of Delight,' which should cure the joyless monotony of East End life. Besant helped moreover to give his fancy material shape. A bequest of 13,000*l.* left in 1841 by John Thomas Barber Beaumont [q. v.], with the object of providing 'intellectual improvement and rational recreation and amusement for people living at the East End of London,' was made the nucleus of a large public fund amounting to 75,000*l*, which was collected under the direction of Sir Edmund Hay Currie, with Besant's active co-operation, for the foundation of an institution on the lines which Besant had laid down. The Drapers' Company added 20,000*l.* for technical schools. Ultimately, Besant's 'People's Palace' was erected in Mile End Road, and was opened by Queen Victoria on 14 May 1887. The Palace contained a hall—the Queen's hall—capable of holding 4000 people for cheap concerts and lectures. There were soon added a swimming-bath, library, technical schools, winter garden, gymnasium, art schools, lecture rooms, and rooms for social recreation. Besant actively engaged in the management, was leader of the literary circle, and edited a 'Palace Journal.' But the effort failed, to Besant's regret, to realise his chief hope. Under the increased patronage and control of the Drapers' Company, the educational side encroached on the social and recreative side until the scheme developed into the East London Technical College, and finally into the East London College, which was in 1908 recognised as a branch of London University. A portion of the People's Palace was maintained under that title for social and recreative purposes, but it became a subsidiary feature of the institution (see article by SIR EDMUND HAY CURRIE in *Nineteenth Century*, Feb. 1890; cf. *Century Magazine*, June 1890, and *Guide to the People's Palace*, 1900).

At C. G. Leland's suggestion Besant took, in 1884, another step in promoting beneficial recreation. He initiated 'The Home Arts and Industries Association,' which established evening schools through the country for the voluntary teaching and practice of the minor arts, such as wood-carving, leather-work, fretwork, weaving, and embroidery. There are now some 500 schools, and annual exhibitions of work are held. Besant also suggested in 1897 the Women's Central Bureau for the employment of women, in connection with the National Union of Women Workers.

At the same time much of Besant's public spirit was absorbed by an effort to improve the financial status of his own profession of author. In 1884 he and some dozen other authors formed the Society of Authors, with Lord Tennyson as president and leaders in all branches of literature as vice-presidents. The society's object was threefold, viz. the maintenance, definition, and defence of literary property; the consolidation and amendment of laws of domestic copyright; and the promotion of international copyright. Besant, who organised the first committee of management and was chairman of committee from 1889 till 1892, was the life and soul of the movement throughout its initial stages. On 15 May 1890 he started, with himself as editor, 'The Author,' a monthly organ of propaganda. He represented the society at an authors' congress at Chicago (with Mr. S. Squire Sprigge) in 1893 and gave an account of its early struggles and growth. In his lifetime the original membership of sixty-eight grew to nearly 2000. The society's endeavour to secure copyright reform under his direction proved substantially successful and influenced new copyright legislation in America in 1891, in Canada in 1900 and in Great Britain in 1911. But Besant's chief aim was to strengthen the author's right in his literary property and to relieve him of traditional financial disabilities, which Besant ascribed in part to veteran customs of the publishing trade, in part to publishing devices which savoured of dishonesty, and in part to the unbusinesslike habits of authors. His agitation brought him into conflict with publishers of high standing, who justly resented some of his sweeping generalisations concerning the character of publishing operations. Like other earnest controversialists Besant tended to exaggerate his case, which in the main was sound. The leading results of his propaganda were advantageous to authors. He practically established through the country the principle that author's accounts with publishers should be subject to audit. He exposed many fraudulent practices on the part of disreputable publishers, both here and in America, and gave injured authors a ready means of redressing their grievances. At Besant's instigation the society's pension fund for impoverished authors was started in 1901. In 1892 he established an Authors' Club in connection with the society, and in 1899, in his 'The Pen and the Book,' he gave his final estimate of the authors' financial and legal position. In George Meredith's words, Besant was 'a valorous, alert, persistent advocate' of the authors' cause and sought 'to establish a system of fair dealing between the sagacious publishers of books and the inexperienced, often heedless, producers' (*Author*, July 1901). In 1895 Besant, who had already advocated the more frequent bestowal on authors of titles of honour, was knighted on Lord Rosebery's recommendation. He had been elected in 1887 a member of the Athenæum under Rule II.

In Oct. 1894 Besant entered on what he considered his greatest work, which was inspired conjointly by his literary and public interests. He resolved to prepare a survey of modern London on the lines on which Stow had dealt with Tudor London. With the aid of experts, he arranged to describe the changing aspects of London from the earliest times till the end of the nineteenth century. Preliminary studies of general London history he embodied in 'London' (1892; new edit. 1894), 'Westminster' (1895), 'South London' (1899), 'East London' (1901), and 'The Thames' (1902). He was also general editor from 1897 of 'The Fascination of London,' a series of handbooks to London topography. But the great survey was not completed at his death, and, finished by other hands, it appeared in ten comprehensively illustrated volumes after his death, viz.: 'Early London' (1908), 'Mediæval London' (2 vols. 1906), 'London in the Time of the Tudors' (1904), 'London in the Time of the Stuarts' (1903), 'London in the Eighteenth Century' (1902), 'London in the Nineteenth Century' (1909), 'London City' (1910), 'London North' (1911) and 'London South' (1912). He also originated in 1900, with (Sir) A. Conan Doyle, Lord Coleridge, and others, the 'Atlantic Union,' a society for entertaining in England American and British colonial visitors. Becoming a Freemason in 1862, he was hon. sec. of the small society, the Masonic Archæological Institute. Some eighteen years later he was member of a small Archæological Lodge, which, originally consisting of nine members, now has 2000 corresponding members scattered over the globe. He long resided at Hampstead, where he was president of the Antiquarian Historical Society, and vice-president of the Art Society. He was elected F.S.A. in 1894.

Besant died at his residence, Frognal End, Hampstead, on 9 June 1901, and was buried in the burial ground in Church Row attached to Hampstead parish church. He married in Oct. 1874 Mary Garrett (*d.* 1904), daughter of Eustace Forster Barham of Bridgwater, and left issue two sons and two daughters. His library was sold at Sotheby's on 24 March 1902. Bronze busts by (Sir) George Frampton, R.A., were set up in the crypt of St. Paul's Cathedral in 1901 and on the Victoria Embankment, near Waterloo Bridge, in 1902. A portrait, painted by John Pettie, R.A., and exhibited at the Royal Academy in 1887, now belongs to his elder son. A portrait was also painted by Emslie.

Besant was of a thick-set figure, with bushy beard, somewhat brusque in manner, but genial among intimate friends, generous in help to struggling literary aspirants, and imbued with a high sense of public duty. His methodical habits of mind and work, which were due in part to his mathematical training, rendered his incessant labour effective in very varied fields. In his own business of authorship his practice did not always cohere with his principle; by selling outright the copyrights of his novels he contradicted the settled maxim of the Authors' Society that authors should never part with their copyrights. He had no love of priests and religious dogma, and tended to depreciate the religious work of the church in the East End of London (see *Nineteenth Century*, 1887), but he admired and energetically supported the social work of the Salvation Army.

Of Besant's novels written alone after Rice's death fifteen appeared in the three-volume form (at 31*s.* 6*d.*), and were soon reissued in cheap single volumes. These works were: 1. 'All Sorts and Conditions of Men,' 1882. 2. 'The Revolt of Man,' 1882. 3. 'All in a Garden Fair,' 1883. 4. 'The Captain's Room,' 1883. 5. 'Dorothy Forster,' 1884. 6. 'Uncle Jack,' 1885. 7. 'Children of Gibeon,' 1886. 8. 'The World went very well then,' 1887. 9. 'Herr Paulus,' 1888. 10. 'For Faith and Freedom,' 1888. 11. 'The Bell of St. Paul's,' 1889. 12. 'Armorel of Lyonesse,' 1890. 13. 'St. Katharine's by the Tower,' 1891. 14. 'The Ivory Gate,' 1892. 15. 'The Rebel Queen,' 1893; Dutch trans. 1895. There followed, with two exceptions, in single volumes at six shillings, 16. 'Beyond the Dreams of Avarice,' 1895. 17. 'In Deacon's Orders,' 1895. 18. 'The Master Craftsman,' 2 vols. 1896. 19. 'The City of Refuge,' 3 vols. 1896. 20. 'A Fountain Sealed,' 1897. 21. 'The Changeling,' 1898. 22. 'The Orange Girl,' 1899. 23. 'The Fourth Generation,' 1900 24. 'The Lady of Lynn,' 1901. 25. 'No Other Way,' 1902. 'The Holy Rose,' 1890, and 'A Five Years' Tryst,' 1902, were collections of short stories in single volumes. 'Katharine Regina' (1887; Russian trans. 1888) and 'The Inner House' (1888) appeared in Arrowsmith's Shilling Library.

He was also author of 'The Eulogy of Richard Jefferies' (1888), 'Captain Cook' (1889), 'The Rise of the Empire' (1897), and 'The Story of King Alfred' (1901). In 1879 he wrote 'Constantinople,' with William Jackson Brodribb [q. v. Suppl. II]. There appeared posthumously 'Essays and Historiettes' and 'As we are and as we may be' in 1903, and his 'Autobiography,' edited by S. Squire Sprigge, in 1902.

[Autobiography of Sir Walter Besant, ed. by S. Squire Sprigge, 1902; The Author, 1901, and passim; The Times, 11, 13, and 17 June 1901; Athenæum, 15 June 1901;

Palestine Exploration Fund, Quarterly Statement, 1901, pp. 207–9; Forum, July 1902; Review of Reviews, Sept. 1893 (art. by John Underhill); Nineteenth Cent., Sept. 1887; private information.] W. B. O.

BEVAN, WILLIAM LATHAM (1821–1908), archdeacon of Brecon, born on 1 May 1821 at Beaufort, Breconshire, was eldest of three sons of William Hibbs Bevan (1788–1846), then of Beaufort, but later of Glannant, Crickhowell (high sheriff for Breconshire 1841), by Margaret, daughter of Joseph Latham, also of Beaufort, but originally from Boughton-in-Furness. With a stepbrother, Edward Kendall, the father carried on the Beaufort Iron Works, trading as Kendall & Bevan, until 1833 (J. Lloyd, *Old S. Wales Iron Works*, 178–189). The youngest brother, George Phillips Bevan (1829–1889), wrote popular tourists' guides for Hampshire, Surrey, Kent, the three Ridings of Yorkshire, Warwickshire, the Wye Valley, and the Channel Islands (between 1877 and 1887, and repeatedly reprinted); industrial geographies of Great Britain and Ireland, France, and the United States (London 1880); and in conjunction with Sir John Stainer a handbook to St. Paul's Cathedral (1882) (see *The Times*, 10 August 1889).

After Bevan's education at Rugby under Dr. Arnold, he matriculated from Balliol College, Oxford, on 14 Dec. 1838; but he almost immediately removed to Magdalen Hall (now Hertford College) on being elected Lusby scholar there. He graduated B.A. in 1842, with a second class in the final classical school, and M.A. in 1845. In 1844 he was ordained deacon, and in 1845, after a short curacy at Stepney, he was admitted priest and presented to the living of Hay, Breconshire, by Sir Joseph Bailey, who was married to his mother's sister. This living, though a very poor one without a parsonage, he held for fifty-six years, his private means enabling him to contribute largely to the restoration of the church, the erection of British schools and of a town clock and tower, besides building a parish hall at his own expense. He was also prebendary of Llanddewi-Aberarth in St. David's Cathedral, 1876–9; canon residentiary of St. David's, 1879–93; archdeacon of Brecon from 1895 till 1907 (when at his resignation his son Edward Latham was appointed in his place); proctor for the diocese of St. David's, 1880–95; examining chaplain to the bishop, 1881–97; and chaplain of Hay Union, 1850–95. He was offered, but declined, the deaneries of Llandaff (in 1897), St. David's (in 1903), and St. Asaph. On resigning the living of Hay in Nov. 1901 Bevan retired to Ely Tower, Brecon, where he died on 24 Aug. 1908; he was buried at Hay, where his widow, who died on 23 Oct. 1909, was also buried. He is commemorated in Hay Church by carved oak choir stalls and a marble chancel pavement, given by his family in August 1910. The St. David's diocesan conference in 1908 resolved on founding a diocesan memorial to him.

Bevan married on 19 June 1849, at Whitney Church, Herefordshire, Louisa, fourth daughter of Tomkyns Dew of Whitney Court, by whom he had three sons and four daughters.

Bevan was a moderate churchman, who believed in enlarging the powers of the laity. He was a great linguist, and had a literary knowledge of Welsh, though he never preached in it. His general attitude to Welsh questions was that of a critical, scholarly anglican. He is best known for various pamphlets or printed essays and sermons in defence of the Welsh Church, which include: 'The Church Defence Handy Volume' (1892) and 'Notes on the Church in Wales' (1905). During the last twenty years of his life he was regarded as an authority on the history of the Welsh Church, but probably his only work of permanent value on the subject is his 'History of St. David's' in the S.P.C.K. series of diocesan histories (1888).

Besides contributing numerous articles to Smith's 'Dictionary of the Bible,' Bevan was also author of three works on ancient geography — 'A Manual' (1852); 'A Student's Manual,' based on [Dr. Smith's] 'Dictionary of Greek and Roman Geography' (1861, 12mo); and 'A Smaller Manual' (1872, 12mo)—as well as of 'A Student's Manual of Modern Geography, Mathematical, Physical and Descriptive' (2 vols. 1868, 12mo; 7th edit. 1884), which was translated into Italian and Japanese.

[Western Mail, 25 and 28 Aug. 1908; Guardian, 26 Aug. 1908; Church Times, 28 Aug. 1908; an excellent Welsh notice in Ceninen Gwyl Dewi, 1909; private information from his eldest daughter, Mrs. Dawson of Hartlington Hall, Yorkshire.] D. Ll. T.

BEWLEY, Sir EDMUND THOMAS (1837–1908), Irish lawyer and genealogist, born in Dublin on 11 Jan. 1837, was son of Edward Bewley (1806–1876), licentiate of the Royal Colleges of Surgeons and Physicians, Ireland, by his wife Mary, daughter of Thomas Mulock of Kilnagarna, King's County (1791–1857). Entering Trinity College, Dublin, in 1855, he obtained a classical scholarship in 1857, and a first senior moderatorship and gold medal in experimental science in 1859. In 1860 he graduated B.A. and in 1863 M.A. Subsequently (1885) he proceeded LL.D. In 1861 he obtained the degree of B.A., *ad eundem*, and also that of M.A., with honours and first gold medal in experimental science, in the Queen's (afterwards Royal) University of Ireland. Called to the Irish bar in 1862, he practised successfully for some years, and in 1882 took silk. From 1884 to 1890 he was regius professor of feudal and English law in Dublin University, and in 1890 became a judge of the supreme court of judicature of Ireland, and judicial commissioner of the Irish Land Commission. Owing to declining health he retired in 1898, when he was knighted. He was elected F.S.A. 10 Jan. 1908, and died at Dublin on 27 June following.

Bewley married in 1866 Anna Sophie Stewart, daughter of Henry Colles, a member of the Irish bar, and by her had two sons and one daughter.

Bewley spent his leisure in genealogical pursuits. He was a frequent contributor to the 'Genealogist,' 'Ancestor,' and other genealogical periodicals. His most important researches were privately printed. His three books, 'The Bewleys of Cumberland' (1902); 'The Family of Mulock' (1905); and 'The Family of Poe' (1906), are sound and patient investigations into family history; in the monograph on the Poe family he proved that Edgar Allan Poe was descended from a family of Powell, for generations tenant-farmers in co. Cavan. Bewley was also author of 'The Law and Practice of Taxation of Costs' (1867); 'A Treatise on the Common Law Procedure Acts' (1871); and joint-author of 'A Treatise on the Chancery (Ireland) Act, 1867' (1868).

[The Bewleys of Cumberland, 1902; The Times, 29 June 1908; Dublin Nat. Libr. Cat.; Irish Times, 28 June 1908.] D. J. O'D.

BICKERSTETH, EDWARD HENRY (1825–1906), bishop of Exeter, only son of the Rev. Edward Bickersteth (1786–1850) [q. v.] by his wife Sarah, eldest daughter of Thomas Bignold of Norwich, was born at Barnsbury Park, Islington, on 25 Jan. 1825, when his father was assistant secretary to the Church Missionary Society. Edward Bickersteth (1814–1892) [q. v.], dean of Lichfield, and Robert Bickersteth [q. v.], bishop of Ripon, were his cousins. Brought up at the rectory of Watton, Hertfordshire, which his father accepted in 1830, Edward remained faithful through life to the earnest evangelical piety of his family. At fourteen he determined to take holy orders. Educated entirely at home, his tutor was Thomas Rawson Birks [q. v.], his father's curate, and subsequently his son-in-law. In 1843 he matriculated from Trinity College, Cambridge. In 1847 he graduated B.A. as a senior optime and third classman in classics. He proceeded M.A. in 1850, and hon. D.D. in 1885. His comparatively low place in the class lists was atoned for by his unique success in winning the chancellor's medal for English verse in three successive years, 1844–5–6 (a volume of 'Poems' collected these and other verses in 1849). Later, in 1854, he won the Seatonian prize for an English sacred poem on 'Ezekiel,' which was also published. Ordained deacon in 1848 and priest in 1849 by Bishop Stanley, Bickersteth was licensed as curate-in-charge of Banningham near Aylsham. On a failure of health in 1851 he became curate to Christ Church, Tunbridge Wells. In 1853 he was appointed by Lord Ashley, afterwards earl of Shaftesbury, to the rectory of Hinton Martell near Wimborne, Dorset, and in 1855 he accepted the important vicarage of Christ Church, Hampstead.

Bickersteth remained vicar of Christ Church, Hampstead, for thirty years. His incumbency furnishes a typical example of the pastoral ideals of current evangelical piety. He insisted on the value of retreats and quiet days. In 1879 he established daily services in his parish and recommended the open church. His devotion to the Church Missionary Society was hereditary. Throughout his Hampstead incumbency he was a member of the committee, and the yearly contribution of his congregation ultimately reached 1000*l*. He paid two long visits to the East, mainly to encourage missionary work, in 1880–1, when he visited India and Palestine, and in 1891, when he went to Japan. When he was a deacon he composed for the jubilee of the Church Missionary Society the well-known hymn 'O Brothers, lift your voices,' and fifty years later he composed another for use when he presided over the centenary of the society. He also impartially supported many church and diocesan societies which lacked earlier evangelical sanction.

While at Hampstead Bickersteth won a wide recognition as a religious writer in both verse and prose. In 1866 he published 'Yesterday, To-day, and For Ever; a poem in twelve books,' which achieved remarkable popularity among religious people. It was estimated that 27,000 copies were sold in England and 50,000 in America; the seventeenth English edition appeared in 1885. The poem embodied in copious flowing blank verse the account of heaven and the last things given in the Apocalypse. It supplied evangelicals with poetry that did not offend their piety, and took for them the place held by Keble's 'Christian Year' among another school of churchmen. As literature it has the weakness of nearly all imitations of Milton. Bickersteth was a voluminous writer of hymns. In 1858 he brought out 'Psalms and Hymns,' based on his father's 'Christian Psalmody' (new edit. 1860). A second effort, to which he gave the title 'The Hymnal Companion to the Book of Common Prayer,' soon superseded in evangelical parishes all other compilations; there were two editions, one with and one without annotation (1870; revised and enlarged 1876, and 1880). About thirty of Bickersteth's own hymns are in common use, the best-known being 'Peace, perfect peace,' which appeared in 'From Year to Year' (1883; 3rd edit. 1896), his best collection of scattered verse (JULIAN, *Dictionary of Hymnology*, pp. 141, 342). Bickersteth's religious writing in prose includes a 'Practical and Expository Commentary on the New Testament' (1864), intended especially for family use, of which more than 40,000 copies were sold. Of his devotional works 'The Master's Home Call, or, Brief Memorials of [his daughter] Alice Frances Bickersteth, by her Father' (1872; 3rd edit. in the same year) circulated most widely.

In January 1885 Bickersteth was appointed dean of Gloucester, but immediately after his institution the prime minister, Gladstone, pressed upon him the bishopric of Exeter, in succession to Frederick Temple [q. v. Suppl. II], who was translated to London. Bickersteth's appointment was probably intended as a counterpoise to the nomination of Edward King [q. v. Suppl. II] to the see of Lincoln. Both bishops were consecrated in St. Paul's Cathedral on St. Mark's Day, 25 April 1885, when Canon Liddon preached on the episcopal office. Bickersteth carried forward many reforms in the diocese which Temple had initiated, notably the employment of the canons of the cathedral in diocesan work. Despite his gentleness, Bickersteth's spiritual gifts as a pastor made him a potent influence. His hospitality was comprehensive. For five months in 1891 he was in Japan and Bishop Barry officiated in his absence. In 1894 he presided over the Church Congress at Exeter, and in an opening address advocated compulsory retirement from clerical work at seventy unless a medical certificate of efficiency could be produced. The death of his son Edward, the bishop of South Tokyo [q. v.], in 1897, was a heavy blow, and after a serious attack of influenza in the spring of 1900 he resigned his see. After five years of illness, he died on 16 May 1906, at his residence in Westbourne Terrace, London, and was buried at Watton.

In 1898 his portrait, a three-quarter length in oils, was painted by A. S. Cope, and given to the bishop to be kept in the Palace, with a replica for Mrs. Bickersteth. A memorial monument was placed in Exeter cathedral.

Bickersteth married twice: (1) in February 1848 his cousin Rosa, daughter of Sir Samuel Bignold of Norwich; she died in 1873, having borne him six sons and ten daughters; (2) in 1876 his cousin Ellen Susanna, daughter of Robert Bickersteth of Liverpool, who was the devoted companion of his later life and survived him without issue.

Besides the poetical works already mentioned Bickersteth published 'Nineveh, a poem' (1851), and 'The Two Brothers and other Poems' (1871; 2nd edit. 1872).

His prose work included, besides charges, sermons and the works cited, 1. 'Water from the Well-Spring . . . being Meditations for every Sunday,' 1852; revised and reissued 1885. 2. 'The Rock of Ages; or Scripture Testimony to the one Eternal Godhead of the Father and of the Son and of the Holy Ghost,' 1859, 1860; new edit. 1888. 3. 'The Blessed Dead: what does Scripture reveal of their State before the Resurrection?' 2nd edit. 1863. 4. 'The Second Death; or the Certainty of Everlasting Punishment, &c.' 1869. 5. 'The Reef and other Parables,' 1874; 2nd edit. 1885. 6. 'The Lord's Table,' 1884; reissued as 'The Feast of Divine Love; or The Lord's Table,' 1896. 7. 'Thoughts in Past Years,' 1901, a volume of 18 selected sermons.

[F. K. Aglionby, Life of E. H. Bickersteth, 1907; The Times, 17 May 1906; information from son, Dr. Samuel Bickersteth, vicar of Leeds.] R. B.

BIDDULPH, SIR MICHAEL ANTHONY SHRAPNEL (1823–1904), general and colonel commandant royal artillery, born on 30 July 1823 at Cleeve Court, Somerset, was eldest surviving son of Thomas Shrapnel Biddulph of Amroth Castle, Pembrokeshire, prebendary of

Brecon, by his wife Charlotte, daughter of James Stillingfleet, prebendary of Worcester and great-grandson of Edward Stillingfleet [q. v.], bishop of Worcester. His paternal grandmother was Rachel, sister of Lieut.-general Henry Shrapnel [q. v.], whose surname he added to his Christian names in 1843.

Destined for the church and with expectation of a considerable fortune, Biddulph was being educated under a private tutor, when speculations in South Wales coal mines brought about such serious reverses that the family seat was sold and his career was changed. He entered the Royal Military Academy at Woolwich on 19 Nov. 1840, and while a gentleman cadet was awarded the Royal Humane Society's silver medal for saving a comrade from drowning in the canal at the Royal Arsenal on 25 Aug. 1842. Becoming second lieutenant in the royal artillery on 17 June 1843, and first lieutenant on 26 April 1844, Biddulph served for three years in Bermuda, and then at various home stations until 1853, being promoted second captain on 4 Oct. 1850. When war was declared with Russia in the spring of 1854 he was ordered to Turkey with the British army as adjutant of the royal artillery.

From Varna, in September, Biddulph accompanied the army to the Crimea, where he took part in the battles of the Alma, Balaklava, Inkerman, and the Tchernaya. He served in the trenches during the siege of Sebastopol as assistant engineer, and was present at the repulse of the Russian sortie on 26 Oct. 1854, and in the three bombardments. After the final assault of the Malakoff by the French, he was sent by Lord Raglan to ascertain from the French commander whether he could retain the position, and received the laconic and well-known answer 'J'y suis, j'y reste.' Biddulph was afterwards attached to the quartermaster-general's staff, and became director of submarine telegraphs in the Black Sea. As a sportsman in the Crimea he won the grand point-to-point race of the allied army in front of Sebastopol. For his services Biddulph was mentioned in despatches, given a brevet majority on 12 Dec. 1854 and a brevet lieutenant-colonelcy on 6 June 1856, and received the British war medal with four clasps, the Turkish medal, the French legion of honour, and the Turkish medjidie, fifth class.

When the war was over he was employed on special telegraph construction service in Asia Minor until 1859, and on his return to England was on the committee of the first Atlantic cable. After serving in Corfu until 1861 he went to India on the amalgamation of the royal and Indian armies, was promoted brevet colonel on 14 Aug. 1863 and regimental lieutenant-colonel on 10 Aug. 1864. On 20 Feb. 1868 he was appointed deputy adjutant-general for royal artillery in India, on 30 March 1869 was promoted major-general, and on relinquishing his staff appointment at the end of five years was created a C.B., military division, on 24 May 1873. After a visit home on furlough, Biddulph returned to India in Sept. 1875 to take up the command of the Rohilkhand district. Two years later he was given the command of the Quetta field force in the Afghan war, 1878–9, and he held successively the command of the second division of the Kandahar field force, and of the Thal Chotiali field force. He was present at the occupation of Kandahar and the action of Khusk-i-Nakhud. His march with the Thal Chotiali field force on his return to India in 1879 was made through a country which had never been visited by British troops, or even by any European traveller. In spite of preliminary negotiations the force was not allowed to make a peaceful progress, although Biddulph carefully observed his orders to avoid irritating the tribes on the route. Repeated acts of hostility were threatened by the natives, and at Baghao the first column was seriously assailed by 2000 Kakars under Shah Jehan of Zhob and other chiefs. But Biddulph surmounted all difficulties, and took farewell of the force in a general order dated Mian Mir, 16 May 1879. For his services in this war he was mentioned in despatches, received the thanks of both houses of parliament and the medal, and was promoted to be K.C.B. on 25 July 1879.

In 1880 Biddulph was given the command of the Rawal Pindi district in India, and during his command entertained the Amir of Afghanistan at the grand durbar of 1884 and the Duke of Connaught on his tour of inspection in 1885. Biddulph was promoted lieut.-general on 13 Feb. 1881, colonel commandant of royal artillery on 14 July 1885, and general on 1 Nov. 1886, when he left India for good. On his return to England he was for three years president of the ordnance committee.

Biddulph retired from the service under the age regulation on 30 July 1890. He was offered but refused a colonial governorship. From 1879 to 1895 he had been groom-in-waiting to Queen Victoria and from 1895 an extra groom-in-waiting successively to Queen Victoria and King Edward VII. From 1891 to 1896 he was keeper of the regalia at the Tower of London. On 25 May 1895 he was made G.C.B., and in the following year was appointed gentleman usher of the black rod. That office he held until his death. An all-round and enthusiastic sportsman, he was also an accomplished painter of landscape in water-colour.

Biddulph died at his residence, 2 Whitehall Court, on 23 July 1904, and was buried at Kensal Green cemetery. He married in 1857 Katherine Stepan, daughter and coheiress of Captain Stepan Stamati of Karani, Balaklava, commandant of Balaklava, by Helen, daughter and heiress of Paul Mavromichalis of Greece. Lady Biddulph died on 27 Sept. 1908, and was buried beside her husband at Kensal Green. Biddulph's five sons, all of the military service, survived him, together with two of his five daughters.

An oil portrait by Sylvester was painted in 1887, and another by A. Fletcher, which was exhibited at the Royal Academy in 1904, attracted the attention of King Edward VII, who caused a copy to be made for Buckingham Palace. Both originals are in possession of Sir Michael's daughter, Miss Biddulph, at 15 Hanover Square, London.

[The Times, 25 July 1904; Men and Women of the Time, 1891; Royal Artillery Record; Royal Artillery Institution leaflet, August 1904; H. B. Hanna, The Second Afghan War, 3 vols. 1899–1910; private information.]

R. H. V.

BIDWELL, SHELFORD (1848–1909), pioneer of telephotography, born at Thetford, Norfolk, on 6 March 1848, was eldest son of Shelford Clarke Bidwell, brewer, of Thetford, who married his first cousin, Georgina, daughter of George Bidwell, rector of Stanton, Norfolk. Educated privately at a preparatory school in Norfolk, and then at a private school at Winchester, Bidwell entered Caius College, Cambridge, where he graduated B.A. (as a junior optime in the mathematical tripos) in 1870, LL.B. (with a second class in the law and history tripos) and M.A. in 1873. Called to the bar at Lincoln's Inn on 27 Jan. 1873, he joined the south-eastern circuit, and practised for some years, but finally devoted himself to scientific study, specialising with success in electricity and magnetism and physiological optics. To friendships formed among members of the Physical Society of London, which he joined in 1877, he traced the beginning of his scientific interests (see his *Presidential Address,* 1898). Obscure and apparently paradoxical phenomena fascinated him, and he showed exceptional subtlety and ingenuity in endeavours to account for them. About 1880 he began investigations into the photo-electric properties of the substance selenium, which led to an important practical application. On 11 March 1881 he lectured at the Royal Institution on 'Selenium and its Applications to the Photophone and Telephotography,' and described an instrument which he had devised for electrically transmitting pictures of natural objects to a distance along a wire. 'It is so far successful' (he said) 'that although the pictures hitherto transmitted are of a very rudimentary character, I think there can be no doubt that further elaboration of the instrument would render it far more effective. Should there ever be a demand for telephotography, it may in time turn out to be useful' (see also *Nature,* 10 Feb. 1881). A paper 'On Telegraphic Photography,' read at the York meeting of the British Association in 1881, further described the invention. The character of other of Bidwell's scientific inquiries is indicated by the titles of the following papers: 'The Influence of Friction upon the Generation of a Voltaic Current' (*Proc. Phys. Soc.* iv.); 'On the Electrical Resistance of Carbon Contacts' (*Proc. Roy. Soc.* xxxv.); 'The Electrical Resistance of Selenium Cells' (*Proc. Phys. Soc.* v.); 'On a Method of Measuring Electrical Resistances with a Constant Current' (*Proc. Phys. Soc.* v.); 'On the Sensitiveness of Selenium to Light, and the Development of a Similar Property in Sulphur' (*Proc. Phys. Soc.* vi.); 'On an Effect of Light upon Magnetism' (*Proc. Roy. Soc.* xlv.); 'On the Changes produced by Magnetisation in the Dimensions of Rings and Rods of Iron and of some other Metals' (*Phil. Trans.* clxxix. A.); and 'On the Formation of Multiple Images in the Normal Eye' (*Proc. Roy. Soc.* lxiv.).

Bidwell's interests extended to meteorology, and in 1893 he lectured at the Royal Institution on 'Fogs, Clouds, and Lightning,' and before the Royal Meteorological Society, of which he was a fellow, on 'Some Meteorological Problems.'

Another of his Royal Institution discourses, 'Some Curiosities of Vision' (1897), appeared in an enlarged shape as 'Curiosities of Light and Vision' (1899). Bidwell, who was a skilful lecturer, was also a clear and sound writer. Many papers on physics appeared in 'Nature' and the chief scientific periodicals, and for the 'Encyclopædia Britannica' (tenth and eleventh editions) he wrote the article 'Magnetism.'

Elected F.R.S. on 4 June 1886, he served on the council 1904–6. He was president of the Physical Society 1897–9, and a member of the Institution of Electrical Engineers. In 1900 he obtained the degree of Sc.D. from the University of Cambridge.

He died at his house, Beechmead, Oatlands Chase, Weybridge, on 18 Dec. 1909, and was buried at Walton cemetery. He married in 1874 Wilhelmina Evelyn, daughter of Edward Firmstone, rector of Wyke, near Winchester, and had issue one son and two daughters.

[Proc. Phys. Soc. xxii.; Journ. Inst. Elect. Eng. xlv.; Quart. Journ. Roy. Meteorol. Soc. xxxvi.; Roy. Soc. Catal. Sci. Papers; Nature, 30 Dec. 1909; Foster's Men at the Bar; The Times, 25 Dec. 1909: will, 3 Feb. 1910; Electrical Review, 31 Dec. 1909; Engineering, 24 Dec. 1909; Men of the Time, 1899.] T. E. J.

BIGG, CHARLES (1840–1908), classical scholar and theologian, born on 12 Sept. 1840, at Higher Broughton, near Manchester, was second son of Thomas Bigg, a Manchester merchant, by his wife Sarah, daughter of Charles Elden. Educated at Manchester grammar school, Bigg was elected to a scholarship at Corpus Christi College, Oxford, 26 March 1858. He had a brilliant academical career, obtaining first-class honours in classics in moderations in Michaelmas term, 1859, and in the final schools in Easter term, 1862, and carrying off the Hertford scholarship for Latin in 1860, the Gaisford prize for Greek prose composition, with a Platonic dialogue, in 1861 (printed in that year), and the Ellerton theological essay in 1864. The appointed subject for this essay, 'The Life and Character of St. Chrysostom,' directed him to the field of study which he was to make his own. He graduated B.A. in 1862, M.A. in 1864, and D.D. in 1876, being ordained deacon in 1863 and priest in 1864. Becoming a senior student and classical tutor of Christ Church, Oxford, in 1863, he acted as one of the classical moderators from 1862 to 1865. In 1866 he left Oxford to become second classical master at Cheltenham College, whence he passed in 1871 to the headmastership of Brighton College. To this period of his life belong school editions of portions of Thucydides, books i. and ii. (1868), and of Xenophon's 'Cyropædeia' (1884, 1888).

Resigning his post at Brighton in 1881, he returned to Oxford to serve as chaplain to his old college, Corpus Christi, and to devote himself to severe study of the early history of the Christian church, and its relations to pagan writers and especially to pagan philosophers. The fruit of these researches appeared in his Bampton lectures on 'The Christian Platonists of Alexandria,' delivered and published in 1886. These at once won him recognition as an exact scholar and an acute philosopher and theologian.

In 1887, on the presentation of Corpus Christi College, he became rector of Fenny Compton, in Warwickshire. His diocesan, Henry Philpott, bishop of Worcester, made him his examining chaplain in 1889, and honorary canon of Worcester, 1889–1901. In 1891 he became examining chaplain to Mandell Creighton [q. v. Suppl. I], bishop of Peterborough. At Oxford he was a select preacher in 1891, and again in 1900, and a theological examiner in 1891–3 and again in 1897–9. When Dr. Creighton was translated to London in 1897, he asked Dr. Bigg to continue acting as his examining chaplain, and assigned to him, in October 1900, a leading part in the Fulham Palace conference. To this period of his life belong editions, with thoughtful introductions, of various standard devotional works, such as 'The Confessions of St. Augustine' (1898), 'The Imitation of Christ' (1898; new edit. 1905), and William Law's 'Serious Call' (1899; new edit. 1906), and a strongly conservative edition of, and commentary on, 'The Epistles of St. Peter and St. Jude' (1901).

Bigg found his true sphere of work in 1901, when he succeeded Dr. William Bright [q. v. Suppl. II] in the regius professorship of ecclesiastical history at Oxford, with which was associated a canonry of Christ Church. His professorial lectures were exhaustive expositions of historical biography. A frequent preacher in the University church and in the cathedral, he enlisted the attention of widely different classes of hearers (Dr. Francis Paget, bishop of Oxford, in his preface to *The Spirit of Christ in Common Life*, p. vi). Both as lecturer and preacher he was distinguished by quaint simplicity of thought, originality of expression, and dry humour. He was also proctor for the chapter of Christ Church in the lower house of convocation. He was taken ill suddenly at Christ Church on 13 July 1908, having just sent to press the most important of his works, 'The Origins of Christianity.' He died on 15 July, and was buried in the Christ Church portion of Osney cemetery, near Oxford. Bigg married on 2 Jan. 1867, at Kersal Moor, Manchester, Millicent, daughter of William Sale, a Manchester solicitor, and had issue three sons and a daughter.

Besides the works already noticed, Bigg's chief publications were: 1. 'Neoplatonism,' 1895, in the popular series of 'Ancient Philosophies.' 2. 'The Doctrine of the Twelve Apostles' (Early Church Classics), 1898. 3. 'Wayside Sketches in Ecclesiastical History,' 1906, nine lectures on Latin writers of the fourth and fifth centuries. 4. 'The Spirit of Christ in Common Life,' 1909, a collection of addresses and sermons. 5. 'The Origins of Christianity,' 1909, a summary of the history and thought of the church in the first three centuries.

[Foster, Oxford Men; Crockford, Clerical Directory; The Times, 16 July 1908; Oxford Mag. xxvii. 7; Guardian, 1908, p. 1230; Oxford Times, 18 and 25 July 1908; appreciation by W. R. Inge, since Dean of St. Paul's, in Journal of Theological Studies, Oct. 1908; Life of Mandell Creighton, 1904, vol. ii.] A. C.

BIRCH, GEORGE HENRY (1842–1904), architect and archæologist, fourth son of Charles Birch by his wife Emma Eliza Cope, was born at Canonbury on 2 Jan. 1842, and educated at Darnell's private school, Islington. At the age of sixteen he was articled to Charles Gray, architect, and was afterwards (about 1859–60) with an architect in Worcester, and then with Sir M. Digby Wyatt and Mr. Ewan Christian. For a time in active practice as an architect (in Chancery Lane and in Devereux Court, Temple), he designed amongst other works the interior of Acton Reynald Hall, Shrewsbury, for Sir Walter Corbet, baronet, and in 1884 the scheme of redecoration for the church of St. Nicholas Cole Abbey, London. For several years he devoted much of his leisure to the re-arrangement of J. E. Gardner's well-known collection illustrating the topographical history of London (now the property of Major Coates). In 1884 he designed for the Health Exhibition at South Kensington the picturesque and accurate Old London street, the first attempt ever made to reproduce old London on such a scale. His original water-colour drawing of the street was exhibited at the Royal Academy in 1886. The street itself, with its church tower, gates, wall, &c., cost nearly 14,000*l.*, and contained shops of the Elizabethan period fitted up at the expense of the City Livery Companies (Welch, *Mod. Hist. of the City of London*, p. 367). It formed a highly popular exhibit, and was afterwards shown in America.

Elected an associate of the Royal Institute of British Architects in 1875, Birch served as vice-president of the Architectural Association from 1871 to 1873, and as president in 1874–5; was hon. secretary of the London and Middlesex Archæological Society from 1877 to 1883, and Cantor lecturer to the Society of Arts in 1883. He became F.S.A. in 1885, and in 1894 was appointed curator of Sir John Soane's Museum. For many years he took a leading part in the affairs of the St. Paul's Ecclesiological Society, many papers by him being printed in its 'Transactions.' He was one of the original members of the Architectural Company, formed in 1869, of the Artists' Volunteer Corps.

Birch is best known as an author by his 'London Churches of the Seventeenth and Eighteenth Centuries,' a splendid folio published in 1896. He also published: 1. 'Illustrations of an Old House in Lime Street' (with R. Phenè Spiers), folio, 1875. 2. 'London on Thames in bygone Days,' 1903.

Birch died unmarried on 10 May 1904, at Soane's Museum, and was buried in Islington cemetery, Finchley.

[Builder, 17 May 1884, 21 May 1904; Journal of Royal Inst. of Brit. Arch., ser. 3, xi. 396–7; Proc. Soc. Antiq., series 2, xx. 296–7; private information.] C. W.

BIRD, HENRY EDWARD (1830–1908), chess player, born at Portsea, Hampshire, on 14 July 1830, was son of Henry Bird, of a Somerset family, by his wife Mary. His father afterwards kept a shop in south London. Bird's schooling was scanty, but he educated himself and as a boy developed notable powers of memory. In 1846 he became clerk to an accountant in London, and was afterwards partner in the firm of Coleman, Turquand, Young & Co. During the financial crises of 1847, 1857, and 1867 Bird was greatly occupied in professional business, and between 1860 and 1870 he paid four visits to Canada and America. To railway finance and management he devoted his special attention, giving evidence before the parliamentary committee on amalgamations of home railways in 1868 and framing the statistical tables which still govern the Great Eastern railway. He wrote pamphlets on railway accounts, a comprehensive 'Analysis of Railways in the United Kingdom' (1868 fol.) and 'A Caution to Investors' (1873).

But Bird's serious interest through life lay in chess. He learned the moves by watching the games at Raymond's coffee house near the City Road Gate in 1844, moved thence to Goode's, Ludgate Hill, and so to Simpson's, in the Strand, where the professionals at first gave him the odds of queen. Buckle, the historian, who was considered the first amateur in England and who did not mind hard work, soon found Bird too much for him at the odds of pawn and move. In 1851 in the great international tournament he played eighteen games with the great Anderssen with an even result, and later played Boden, Harrwitz, Lowenthal, Falkbeer, Wisker, Mason and others. With the dignified Howard Staunton [q. v.] he only played two games on even terms and won both, but this at a date when Staunton's best days were over. In 1866 he played a match of twenty games against Steinitz and was only beaten by seven to six (seven being drawn). He was a friend of Steinitz's rival, John Hermann Zukertort [q. v.], who lived near him in Heygate Street, Walworth Road. In 1879 he won first prize in the Lowenthal tourney against Blackburne, Mason, and McDonnell, and in the same year took the first prize at Gouda, winning nine and a half out of ten games and first prize in the B.C.A. tournament (1889), not losing a single game. At Venice in 1873, Paris in 1878, Nuremberg in 1883, Hereford in 1885, and Manchester 1890 he was among the prizewinners. His last appearance as a public player was at the London tournament in 1899, where, however, he took a low place.

Bird had long since retired from professional work and his resources failed. Members of the St. George's Chess Club purchased an annuity for him, which enabled him to spend his last days in comfort. He died at Tooting on 11 April 1908. He married young and was left a widower in 1869.

Well known for his rapidity (R. J. Buckley says he once played three games in ten minutes at Simpson's, scoring one and a half), dash, and eccentric openings (KBP2 is often called Bird's opening), Bird was the most popular referee of his time and answered more questions about chess than any man living. In chivalry and enthusiasm for chess as a pastime, in pluck, and in readiness to play at a moment's notice for stakes or no stakes, Bird had no equal. After Staunton, Blackburne, and Burn he probably ranks next among English masters of the last sixty years. Unfortunately his patience and judgment were very inferior to his power of combination. As a problem composer he was not great. His books, discursive compilations of mediocre value, include: 1. 'Chess Masterpieces,' 1875. 2. 'Chess Openings,' 1878 (reviewed by Steinitz in 'Field,' Dec. 1879). 3. 'Chess Practice,' 1882. 4. 'Modern Chess,' 1887 and 1889. 5. 'Chess History and Reminiscences,' 1893. 6. 'Chess Novelties,' 1895. These last two were dedicated to his favourite opponent and patron, W. J. Evelyn of Wotton. Among his opponents at the chess clubs and divans were Buckle, Bradlaugh, Isaac Butt, Lord Randolph Churchill, Ruskin, and Prince Leopold. For a time he was chess correspondent of 'The Times.'

[Who's Who, 1908; The Times, 16 April 1908; Chess Mag., 1908, 211, 248, 303; Chess Monthly, March 1889 (portrait); McDonnell's Knights and Kings of Chess; Lee and Gossip's Chess Player's Mentor; Fortnightly Rev., Dec. 1886; Bird's Chess History (portrait), and Chess Novelties, 1895; Sketch, 21 Aug. 1895.] T. S.

BIRD, ISABELLA LUCY (1831–1904), traveller. [See BISHOP.]

BIRDWOOD, HERBERT MILLS (1837–1907), Anglo-Indian judge, born at Belgaum, Western India, on 29 May 1837, was third son of fourteen children of General Christopher Birdwood, deputy commissary general of the Bombay army (of an old Devonshire family), by his wife Lydia, eldest daughter of the Rev. Joseph Taylor, agent of the London Missionary Society in the southern Mahratta country. His great-grandfather, Richard Birdwood, mayor of Plymouth in 1796, and his grandfather, Peter Birdwood, were both agents at Plymouth of the East India Company. His eldest brother is Sir George Birdwood (*b.* 1832).

Educated successively at the Plymouth new grammar school and at Mount Radford school, Exeter, he matriculated at Edinburgh University in 1851, and distinguished himself in mathematics. In October 1854 he entered Peterhouse, Cambridge, and graduated B.A. in 1858 as twenty-third wrangler in the mathematical tripos and with a second class in the natural science tripos. At once elected to a fellowship at his college, he took eighteenth place in the Indian civil service examination. He proceeded M.A. in 1863, LL.M. in 1879, and LL.D. in 1890, being called to the bar at Lincoln's Inn in 1889. In Oct. 1901 he was elected an honorary fellow of Peterhouse.

Arriving in Bombay on 26 Jan. 1859, he served successively in Thana, Broach, Surat and Ahmedabad as assistant collector. In 1863 he became under-secretary in the judicial, political and educational departments and secretary to the Bombay legislative council. In June 1866 he went to Kathiawar as first political assistant, but in 1867 returned to Bombay as acting registrar of the high court. In Dec. 1871 he was appointed judge of the Ratnagiri district, being subsequently transferred to Thana and then to Surat. In Ratnagiri he won a reputation for independence, by deciding against the government cases challenging the legality of the operations of the revenue survey department.

In February 1881 Birdwood went to Karachi as judicial commissioner and judge of the Sadr court in Sind. He effected steady improvement in the work of the subordinate courts in the province. He also laid out on a new design the Karachi public gardens, some forty acres in extent, establishing there a fine zoological collection. He stimulated the volunteer movement by serving in the local corps. From Jan. 1885 to April 1892 he was judge of the Bombay high court, and from April 1892 to April 1897 was judicial and political member of the Bombay council. His term of office coincided with the outbreak of the plague epidemic, the great famine of 1897, and the political unrest leading to murderous outrage at Poona. In June 1893 he was created a C.S.I. He was acting governor of the presidency in the brief interval between Lord Harris's departure and Lord Sandhurst's arrival (16 to 18 Feb. 1895). While efficiently performing his judicial and political duties he actively interested himself in educational and scientific movements. He had been a fellow of the Bombay University since 1863 and dean in arts in 1868, 1880, and 1888. He was vice-chancellor in 1891–2. He was president of the botanical section of the Bombay Natural History Society, and compiled for its 'Journal' (1886, vols. i. and ii.) a comprehensive catalogue of the flora of the Matheran and Mahabaleshwar hill-stations (reprinted separately, Bombay, 1897). He was for many years president of the Agri-Horticultural Society of Western India. Between 1871 and 1890 Birdwood ably edited, either solely or in collaboration with Mr. Justice Henry J. Parsons, vols. iv. to xi. of the Acts and Regulations in force in the Bombay presidency, commonly known as West's code.

After his return to England in April 1897 he collaborated with Mr. Justice Wood Renton and E. G. Phillimore in a revised edition of Burge's 'Commentaries on Colonial and Foreign Laws' (1907; vol. i.), editing the Indian portion. He practised before the privy council on Indian appeals, and in the important case of the Taluka of Kota Sangani *v.* the State of Gondal (No. 58 of 1904) he, with Sir Edward Clarke as his leader, obtained a judgment upholding the sovereignty of the Kathiawar chiefs, and sustained the contention that their courts are outside the appellate jurisdiction of the British courts. To the 'Journal of the Royal Society of Arts' he contributed (1898) valuable sketches of the history of plague in western India. At Twickenham, where he finally settled, he was active in local affairs and did much philanthropic work.

He died of pneumonia at his residence, Dalkeith House, Twickenham, on 21 Feb. 1907, and was buried at Twickenham cemetery. He married on 29 Jan. 1861 Edith Marion Sidonie, eldest daughter of Surgeon-major Elijah G. H. Impey of the Bombay horse artillery and postmaster-General of the Bombay presidency; by her he had a daughter, wife of General R. C. O. Stuart, inspector-general of ordnance in India, and five sons, all of whom served in the army in India; the eldest son, Capt. H. C. T. Birdwood, R.E., died at Umballa in 1894 and the second son, Brigadier-general William Riddel Birdwood (*b.* 1865), was military secretary to Lord Kitchener while commander-in-chief in India (1905–10). An engraved portrait by Walton & Co. is in Mrs. Birdwood's possession.

[Representative Men of India, Bombay, 1889; India List; The Times, 23 Feb. 1907; personal knowledge; information kindly supplied by Sir George Birdwood.]

F. H. B.

BIRRELL, JOHN, D.D. (1836–1901), orientalist, elder of two sons of Hugh Birrell, architect, by his wife Margaret Smith, was born at Drumeldrie, Newburn parish, Fife, on 21 Oct. 1836. His only brother, George, an architect, died in 1876 at the age of thirty-seven. After attending the parish school and Madras College, St. Andrews, Birrell entered St. Andrews University as first bursar in 1851, and after a brilliant course graduated M.A. in 1855. The next two years, with thoughts of the Indian civil service, he passed at Halle, sojourning with the orientalist, Prof. Roediger. The Indian Mutiny altered his plans, and, returning to St. Andrews, he completed in 1861 at St. Mary's College the training for the ministry of the Church of Scotland.

Licensed as a preacher in 1861 by St. Andrews Presbytery, Birrell for two years held the post of tutor at the College Hall

St. Andrews. In 1863 he became assistant to Dr. Robertson at Glasgow Cathedral, and in 1864 he was presented by the senatus of St. Andrews, then patrons of the living, to the parish of Dunino adjoining that of St. Andrews. He was there able to maintain his hold on academic life. He was examiner in classics in the United College, St. Andrews, in 1862–6, for some years assisted Dr. John Cook, professor of church history, and was clerk to the Senatus Academicus In 1871 he was appointed by the crown to the chair of Hebrew and Oriental languages in St. Mary's College, St. Andrews, and proved himself a painstaking, broad-minded, and lucid teacher. His abilities were widely recognised. He received the degree of D.D. from Edinburgh University in 1878, and he was a member of the Old Testament revision committee, 1874–84. He was the first chairman of the St. Andrews school board, and held the position for sixteen years. Examiner of secondary schools in Scotland from 1876 to 1888, he originated and carried out with great success the scheme (afterwards superseded by the system of leaving certificates) of university local examinations at St. Andrews.

Birrell died at St. John's, St. Andrews, on 31 December 1901, and was buried in the cathedral burying-ground of the city. On 3 June 1874 he married Elizabeth, daughter of James Wallace of The Brake, Dunino, and had by her three sons and two daughters.

[Private information; personal knowledge; St. Andrews Citizen, 4 and 11 Jan. 1902:]

T. B.

BISHOP, Mrs. ISABELLA LUCY (born Bird) (1831–1904), traveller and authoress, born on 15 Oct. 1831 at Boroughbridge Hall, Yorkshire, the home of her maternal grandmother, was eldest child of the Rev. Edward Bird (*d.* 1858). The Bird family was long settled at Barton-on-the-Heath, Warwickshire, and William Wilberforce [q. v.] and John Bird Sumner [q. v.], archbishop of Canterbury, were kinsmen. Miss Bird's mother, Dora, second daughter of the Rev. Marmaduke Lawson of Boroughbridge, was her father's second wife. Both parents were strongly religious, and Isabella inherited pronounced evangelical views. Her childhood was passed in her father's successive benefices, Tattenhall in Cheshire from 1834 to 1842, St. Thomas's, Birmingham, from 1842 to 1848, and from 1848 onwards at Wyton, Huntingdonshire. At Tattenhall, Isabella, who suffered through life from a spinal complaint, lived much in the open air, learnt riding, becoming in after years an expert and fearless horsewoman, and was trained to observe objects of country life. At Birmingham she began to help in Sunday school work, and started her literary career by writing in 1847 an essay in favour of fiscal protection which was printed for private circulation at Huntingdon. At Wyton she learnt rowing on the Ouse. In 1850 she underwent an operation for spinal trouble; and in the summer of 1854, when she was twenty-two, being recommended a sea voyage for her health, she visited a cousin in Prince Edward Island. Seven months were spent on this trip, which extended to Canada and the United States. It was the first of her travels, and she recorded her experience in 'The Englishwoman in America,' published in January 1856 by John Murray the third (1808–1892) [q. v.], who became at once her publisher and her personal friend for life.

In 1857–8 she revisited America for the sake of health. At the suggestion of her father she studied the current religious revival in the United States, and described it in serial articles in 'The Patriot,' which were collected in 1859 as 'The Aspects of Religion in the United States of America.'

Meanwhile Miss Bird paid, with her family, constant visits to Scotland, and on her father's death in 1858 she, her mother, and only sister, Henrietta, made their home in Edinburgh. For her sister she cherished the closest affection, and after her mother died they continued to live together, when Isabella was resting from travel, and letters to her sister from distant parts formed material for many of her books. Her sister had a cottage, too, at Tobermory, in the Island of Mull. Miss Bird grew to be especially interested in the social and spiritual welfare of the people in the West Highlands; she co-operated with Lady Gordon Cathcart in crofter emigration to Canada (1862–6), and in 1866 personally visited the settlers in Canada. She also wrote much for magazines, including papers on hymns in the 'Sunday Magazine' (1865–7), and in the 'Leisure Hour' she described in 1867 a tour to the Outer Hebrides in 1860. In 1869 she attacked the slums and poverty of Edinburgh in 'Notes on Old Edinburgh.'

Miss Bird's health was still bad; much of her writing was done while she lay on her back, and she failed to benefit by a trip to New York and the Mediterranean in 1871. In July 1872 she started for

Australia and New Zealand, and recovering her health went on in 1873 to the Sandwich Islands. There she stayed for six to seven months, and then spent the autumn and early winter of 1873 in America, mainly in the Rocky Mountains, where her riding powers came into play. This tour lasted in all eighteen months, and the outcome of it was two notable volumes—'The Hawaiian Archipelago. Six Months among the Palm Groves, Coral Reefs and Volcanoes of the Sandwich Islands' (1875), a book of interest to men of science as well as to the general reader, and 'A Lady's Life in the Rocky Mountains' (1879), a collection of letters originally published in 1878 in the 'Leisure Hour,' which was subsequently translated into French.

While at home at Edinburgh in 1876–7 she closely studied the microscope, and engaged in the promotion of the national Livingstone memorial, to take the form of a college for the training of medical missionaries. These interests brought her the acquaintance of her future husband, Dr. John Bishop, who was her sister's medical adviser. In April 1878 she set out for Japan, where she spent seven months travelling through the interior and visiting the country of the hairy Ainos in the island of Yezo. After five weeks in the Malay Peninsula (January and February 1879), she reached England in May 1879 by way of Cairo and the Sinai Peninsula, where she contracted typhoid fever. This tour supplied material for 'Unbeaten Tracks in Japan' (1880) and 'The Golden Chersonnese and the Way thither' (1883). In June 1880 her sister died, and on 8 March 1881 she married Dr. Bishop, ten years her junior, at St. Lawrence's Church at Barton-on-the-Heath, the Warwickshire home of her father's family. Her husband died after a long illness at Cannes in March 1886.

Thenceforth Mrs. Bishop largely devoted herself to the cause of medical missions, which she considered 'the most effective pioneers of Christianity' (STODDART, p. 325). In 1887 she studied medicine at St. Mary's hospital, London, and in 1888 was baptised by Spurgeon by way of consecration to the missionary cause, not as joining the baptist denomination. At the end of 1887 she was in Ireland while the 'Plan of Campaign' was in operation, and described the episode in 'Murray's Magazine' in the summer of 1888. She left for India in February 1889. Proceeding to Cashmere, where she came into close touch with the Church Missionary Society, she went on to Lesser Tibet, and described it in 'Among the Tibetans,' published by the Religious Tract Society in 1894. She was back at Simla in October, and soon travelled from Karachi to Bushire, thence to Bagdad and Teheran, an 'awful journey'; and through the Bakhtiari country, Western Persia, Kurdistan, and Armenia to Trebizond on the Black Sea. She reached London again in December 1890. An intention to establish a hospital at Nazareth was frustrated by the opposition of the Turkish government. Instead, she founded in the early stages of this long and adventurous journey the John Bishop Memorial Hospital in Cashmere, and the Henrietta Bird Hospital for Women near Amritsar in the Punjab. In 1891 she published 'Journeys in Persia and Kurdistan,' as well as two articles in the 'Contemporary Review' on the persecution of the Christians in Asiatic Turkey, entitled 'The Shadow of the Kurd.' Her meetings with the Nestorian Christians on her difficult tour added to her zeal for mission work. In a missionary address given by her in 1893 on 'Heathen Claims and Christian Duty' (published in 1905 by the Church Missionary Society as 'A Traveller's Testimony') she said that she had 'been made a convert to missions, not by missionary successes, but by seeing in four and a half years of Asiatic travelling the desperate needs of the un-Christianised world.'

By 1890 Mrs. Bishop's fame was fully established as a traveller and a missionary advocate. She addressed the British Association in 1891, 1892, and 1898, was made in 1891 a fellow of the Royal Scottish Geographical Society, and in 1892 a fellow of the Royal Geographical Society, to which no lady had previously been admitted.

In January 1894 she left England once more, and was absent for three years and two months, till March 1897. Through Canada she passed to Japan, Corea and China. Four visits were paid to Corea; on the first she explored the Han river and crossed the Diamond Mountains to the east coast of the peninsula. After a visit to Chinese Manchuria, she went up the Yangtze and into the interior of China, through the province of Szechuan to the borders of Tibet, thus spending fifteen months and travelling 8000 miles in China alone. On her way she founded three hospitals as memorials to her husband, parents, and sister, one in Corea and two in China, as well as an orphanage in Japan. On her return to England she published 'Korea and her Neighbours' (Jan. 1898) and 'The Yangtze Valley and Beyond' (November 1899) dedicated to Lord Salisbury.

Mrs. Bishop was a keen photographer, and in 1900 published a collection of 'Chinese Pictures,' notes on photographs made in China. In December 1900, though nearly seventy years of age, she went to Morocco for six months, but illness prevented her from writing more than an article in the 'Monthly Review' on her experiences. Another visit to China was contemplated, but her health entirely gave way, and after many months of illness she died at Edinburgh on 7 Oct. 1904; she was buried at the Dean cemetery. In 1905 a memorial clock to her sister's memory, the 'Henrietta Amelia Bird' memorial clock, was erected at Tobermory from funds bequeathed by her for the purpose.

Mrs. Bishop was small in stature, quiet in speech and manner, and was a traveller of extraordinary courage. Fearless on horseback, she explored alone the most dangerous and barbarous countries. A keen observer with a retentive memory, she was a fluent speaker and had great power of vivid narrative. A restless disposition led her, even when not travelling, constantly to change her home in England and Scotland. Her love of travel was stimulated by chronic ill-health, the repeated losses in her family, which produced a sense of loneliness, and above all by her missionary enthusiasm. 'A critical but warm supporter of missions, especially of medical missions,' she held that Christianity should be presented to natives as far as possible through native teaching. She combined with a sympathetic interest in native races love of adventure and zeal for scientific study. Her valuable records of travel and the extent of her wanderings give her a place among the most accomplished travellers of her time (*Geographical Journal*, July to December, 1904, p. 596).

[Life of Isabella Bird (Mrs. Bishop), by Anna M. Stoddart, 1906; Women of Worth, by Jennie Campbell, 1908—the Adventures of a Lady Traveller; The Story of Isabella Bird Bishop, by Constance Williams, Sunday School Union, 1909; Annual Register, 1904; The Times, 10 Oct. 1904; Geographical Journal (Roy. Geog. Soc.), July to Dec. 1904.]

C. P. L.

BLACKBURN, HELEN (1842–1903), pioneer of woman's suffrage, born at Knightstown, Valencia Island, co. Kerry, on 25 May 1842, was only surviving daughter of Bewicke Blackburn, civil engineer, manager of the Knight of Kerry's slate quarries on Valencia from 1837. Her mother was Isabella, youngest daughter of Humble Lamb of Ryton Hall, co. Durham.

The father (1811–1897), who left Ireland for London about 1859, was an ingenious inventor (cf. *Indexes*, 1854–63, *Patent Office Library*). The Blackburn steam car which he patented 1877 was an early anticipation of the motor-car (see *Field*, 23 Nov. 1878, p. 660; W. W. BEAUMONT's *Cantor Lectures*, 1896, p. 29; his *Motor Vehicles*, 1900, i. 41, 320; and RHYS JENKINS's *Motor Cars*, 1902, p. 116). Blackburn also patented improvements in velocipedes; his death at the age of eighty-five resulted from an accident while riding near Tunbridge Wells, on 13 Jan. 1897. Some relics of Charles I which he inherited were sold subsequently to King Edward VII.

Miss Blackburn, who early developed literary and artistic tastes, soon interested herself in the woman's suffrage movement. From 1874 to 1895 she acted in London as secretary to the central committee of the National Society, which was founded in 1867. But she frequently visited Bristol, and from 1880 to 1895 was also secretary of the Bristol and West of England Suffrage Society. A series of historical portraits of notable women which she formed for the International Exhibition at Chicago of 1893 she presented to the women's hall of University College, Bristol. She was sole editor of the 'Englishwoman's Review' from 1881 to 1890; from that year Miss Ann Mackenzie was joint editor with her. In 1895 Miss Blackburn gave up most of her public work to look after her father. She was well versed in the history of the suffrage movement, and her 'Women's Suffrage: a Record of the Movement in the British Isles' (1902) remains the standard work.

She died at Greycoat Gardens, Westminster, on 11 Jan. 1903, and was buried at Brompton cemetery. A crayon portrait by Miss Guinness, on her retirement from the Bristol secretaryship, was presented to University College there, and hangs in the women students' room. By her will she bequeathed her excellent library of books upon women's interests to Girton College, Cambridge. A loan fund for training young women, established in her memory in 1905, is administered by the Society for Promoting the Employment of Gentlewomen.

Besides the books cited, Miss Blackburn wrote: 1. 'A Handbook for Women engaged in Social and Political Work,' Bristol, 1881; new edit. enlarged, with two charts, 1895. 2. 'Because: Reasons why Parliamentary Franchise should be no longer denied to Women,' 1888. 3. (with E. J. Boucherett [q.v. Suppl. II]) 'The Condition of Working Women,' 1896. 4. 'Words of a Leader,' 1897. 5. (with N. Vynne) 'Women under the Factory Acts,' 1903.

[The Times, 12 Jan. 1903; Englishwoman's Review, xxxiv. 1, 73; information from Miss FitzGerald, Valencia Island; personal knowledge.] C. F. S.

BLACKLEY, WILLIAM LEWERY (1830–1902), divine and social reformer, born at Dundalk on 30 Dec. 1830, was second son of Travers Robert Blackley, of Ashtown Lodge, co. Dublin, and Bohogh, co. Roscommon. His maternal grandfather was Travers Hartley, M.P. for Dublin city 1776–1790, and governor of the Bank of Ireland. Blackley's mother was Eliza, daughter of Colonel Lewery, who was taken prisoner by the French at Verdun. In boyhood (1843–5) Blackley was sent with his brother John to a school at Brussels kept by Dr. Carl Martin Friedländer, a Polish political refugee, whose daughter he subsequently married. There he acquired proficiency in French, German, and other foreign languages. In 1847 he returned to Ireland, entered Trinity College, Dublin, graduated B.A. in 1850, M.A. in 1854, and took holy orders. In 1854 he became curate of St. Peter's, Southwark; but an attack of cholera compelled his retirement from London. From 1855 to 1867 he had charge of two churches at Frensham, near Farnham, Surrey. He was rector of North Waltham, Hampshire (1867–83), and from 1883 to 1889 of King's Somborne with Little Somborne (to which was added Upper Eldon in 1885). In 1883 he was made honorary canon of Winchester.

Meanwhile Blackley, who was an energetic parish priest and was keenly interested in social questions, carefully elaborated a scheme for the cure of pauperism by a statutory enforcement of thrift which had far-reaching results at home and abroad. In November 1878 he contributed to the 'Nineteenth Century' an essay entitled 'National Insurance a Cheap, Practical, and Popular Way of Preventing Pauperism,' and thenceforth strenuously advocated a scheme of compulsory insurance, which the National Providence League, with the earl of Shaftesbury as president, was formed in 1880 to carry into effect. Blackley at the same time recommended temperance as a means of social regeneration. His views reached a wide public through his writings, which included 'How to teach Domestic Economy' (1879), 'Collected Essays on the Prevention of Pauperism' (1880), 'Social Economy Reading Book, adapted to the New Code' (1881), 'Thrift and Independence; a Word for Working-men' (1884).

Blackley's scheme provided that all persons between eighteen and twenty should subscribe 10*l.* to a national fund, and should receive in return 8*s.* a week in time of sickness, and 4*s.* a week after the age of seventy. The plan was urged on the House of Lords by the earl of Carnarvon in 1880 (*Hansard*, cclii. 1180), and was the subject of inquiry by a select committee of the House of Commons from 1885 to 1887. The majority of the boards of guardians in England and Wales supported the proposals; but the commons' committee, while acknowledging Blackley's ingenuity and knowledge, reported adversely on administrative and actuarial grounds (2 Aug. 1887). At the same time the friendly societies, which Blackley had censured in his 'Thrift and Independence' (pp. 75 and 80), regarded the principle of compulsion as a menace to their own growth, and their historian and champion, the Rev. John Frome Wilkinson, sharply criticised Blackley's plan in 'The Blackley National Providence Insurance Scheme; a Protest and Appeal' (1887). Blackley's plan, although rejected for the time, stimulated kindred movements in the colonies and in foreign countries, and led directly to the adoption of old age pensions in England by legislation in 1908, while the national insurance scheme which received parliamentary sanction in 1911 bears some trace of Blackley's persistent agitation (*Quarterly Review*, July 1908; HERBERT PAUL, *Modern England*, iv. 372).

In 1887 Blackley, who was director of the Clergy Mutual Insurance Company, made proposals to the church congress which led to the formation of the 'Clergy Pension Scheme' and of a society for 'ecclesiastical fire insurance.' In the autumn of 1889 Blackley, whose active propagandism brought him constantly to London, became vicar of St. James the Less, Vauxhall Bridge Road. There he enlarged the schools, and built a parish hall and a vicarage. He died after a brief illness at 79 St. George's Square, on 25 July 1902. He married on 24 July 1855 Amelia Jeanne Josephine, second daughter of his Brussels tutor, Dr. Carl Martin Friedländer, by whom he had issue one son, who died in infancy, and two daughters, who with his widow survived him. Brasses were put up in Blackley's memory in the churches of St. James the Less, North Waltham, and Frensham.

Blackley, whose Irish humour and eloquence made him an attractive platform speaker, was an accomplished linguist and a capable parochial organiser. His published writings, besides sermons, review articles, short stories, and the works mentioned in the text, are: 1. 'The Frithiof Saga, or Lay of Frithiof,' a translation in original metre from the Swedish of Esaias Tegnér, bp. of Wexio, Dublin, 1857; American edit. New York, 1867; illustr. edit. 1880. 2. (with Dr. Friedländer) 'A practical dictionary of the German and English languages,' 1866 (pocket edition, 1876). 3. 'Word Gossip,' 1869, a series of familiar essays on words and their peculiarities. He was also editor (with James Hawes) of the 'Critical English [New] Testament,' an adaptation of Bengel's 'Gnomon,' 1866, 3 vols. His 'Collected Essays' (1880) was re-issued in 1906, under the title of 'Thrift and National Insurance as a Security against Pauperism,' with a prefatory memoir by his widow, who zealously aided in propagating his views of social reform.

[Memoir by widow prefixed to re-issue of Collected Essays, 1906; The Times, 26 July 1902; Charles Booth, Pauperism and the Endowment of Old Age, 1892, pp. 182–7; Charity Organization Review, Sept. 1892; Journal of Institute of Actuaries, Oct. 1887, xxvi. 480–8; Frank W. Lewis, State Insurance, a Social and Industrial Need, 1909; private information.] W. B. O.

BLACKWELL, ELIZABETH (1821–1910), the first woman doctor of medicine, born at Counterslip, Bristol, on 3 Feb. 1821, was third daughter of Samuel Blackwell, a Bristol sugar refiner. The father, a well-to-do Independent, emigrated with seven children in August 1832 to New York. Here Elizabeth and her sisters continued their education and became intimate with William Lloyd Garrison and other anti-slavery friends. When Elizabeth was seventeen they removed to Cincinnati, where her father died suddenly, leaving his family of nine unprovided for. In order to support their mother and younger brothers, Elizabeth and her two sisters started a day and boarding school. They joined the Church of England, and became enthusiastic politicians and keen supporters of the movement for a wider education of women. They were intimate with Dr. Channing and studied the writings of Emerson, Fourier, and Carlyle. In 1842 the school was relinquished. Elizabeth became head of a girls' school in Western Kentucky, which she left after a term owing to her dislike of slavery. Resolving to become a doctor in spite of the discouragement of friends, she studied medicine privately while continuing to teach in North Carolina and in Charleston. After three years she vainly applied for admission to medical schools at Philadelphia and in New York. In October 1847 she formally applied for entry to the medical class at a small university town, Geneva, in Western New York State. The entire class, on the invitation of the faculty, unanimously resolved that 'every branch of scientific education should be open to all.' Outside her class she was regarded as 'either mad or bad.' She refused to assent, save by the wish of the class, to the professor's request to absent herself from a particular dissection or demonstration. No further obstacle was offered to her pursuit of the medical course. She graduated M.D. (as 'Domina' at Geneva, N.Y.) in January 1849, the first woman to be admitted to the degree (cf. gratulatory verses to 'Doctrix Blackwell,' 'An M.D. in a Gown,' in *Punch* (1849), xvi. 226).

In the following April she came to England, was courteously received by the profession on the whole, and shown over hospitals in Birmingham and London. In May, with 'a very slender purse and few introductions of value,' she reached Paris, and on 30 June entered La Maternité, a school for midwives, determined to become an obstetrician. After six months' hard work she contracted purulent ophthalmia from a patient and lost the sight of one eye. Thus obliged to abandon her hope of becoming a surgeon, she, on returning to London, obtained (through her cousin, Kenyon Blackwell) from James (afterwards Sir James) Paget, dean of St. Bartholomew's Hospital, permission to study there. She was admitted to every department except that of women's and children's diseases, and received the congratulations of Mrs. Jameson, Lady (Noel) Byron, Miss Rayner (Mdme. Belloc), Miss Leigh Smith (Madame Bodichon), the Herschells, Faraday, and Florence Nightingale.

Meanwhile her sister Emily was studying for a doctor at Cleveland, Ohio, and in 1854 acted as assistant to Sir James Simpson [q. v.] in Edinburgh, but declined an urgent request to go to the Crimea.

Elizabeth went back to America in 1850

and was refused the post of physician to the women's department of a dispensary in New York. She spent her leisure in preparing some excellent lectures on the physical education of girls ('Laws of Life,' New York, 1852). In 1853 she opened a dispensary of her own, which was incorporated in 1854 as an institution of women physicians for the poor, and developed into the New York Infirmary and College for Women. Joined in 1856 by her sister Emily, who had now also qualified at Cleveland, and by Marie Zackrzewska (a Cleveland student in whose education she had taken much interest and the third woman to qualify), she opened in New York in May 1857 a hospital entirely conducted by women. Opposition was great, but the quakers of New York gave valuable support from the first. In 1858 Elizabeth revisited England and gave lectures at the Marylebone Literary Institution on the value of physiological and medical knowledge to women and on the medical work already done in America. Liverpool, Manchester, and Birmingham welcomed her, and she issued an English edition of 'Laws of Life' (1859; 3rd edit. 1871). A proposal was made to establish a hospital for women's diseases, to which the Comtesse de Noailles, the Hon. Russell Gurney, and others contributed handsomely. Dr. Elizabeth Blackwell's name was placed upon the British medical register on 1 Jan. 1859, ten years after she had qualified.

Again in America, Elizabeth joined her sister in a rapidly growing hospital practice. Students came to them from Philadelphia. At the outbreak of the American civil war they established the Ladies Sanitary Aid Institute and the National Sanitary Aid Association, and organised a plan for selecting, and training for the field, nurses whose services did much to win sympathy for the entire movement. In 1865 the trustees of the infirmary obtained a charter. The Blackwells would have preferred to secure the benefits of joint medical instruction, but, failing this, they organised a full course of college instruction, with hygiene as one of the principal chairs, an independent examination board, and a four years' course of study. Elizabeth delivered the opening address on 2 Nov. 1868, and held the first professorship of hygiene. Dr. Sophia Jex-Blake (*d.* 1912) was among her first students. In twenty years free and equal entrance of women into the profession of medicine was secured in America.

Elizabeth returned to England with a view to the same end. She settled in Burwood Place, Marylebone, where in 1871, at a drawing-room meeting, the National Health Society was formed. She lectured to the Working Women's College on 'How to keep a Household in Health' (published 1870), and on 'The Religion of Health' (3rd edit. 1889) to the Sunday Lecture Society, but in 1873 her health gave way and she travelled abroad. At the London School of Medicine for Women, opened in 1875, she accepted the chair of gynæcology. She took an active part in the agitation against the Contagious Diseases Act. During a winter at Bordighera she wrote 'The Moral Education of the Young considered under Medical and Social Aspects,' which under its original title, 'Counsel to Parents on the Moral Education of their Children,' was refused by twelve publishers, and at last appeared through the intervention of Jane Ellice Hopkins [q. v. Suppl. II] (2nd edit. 1879). She also contributed an article on 'Medicine and Morality' to the 'Modern Review' (1881). Miss Blackwell delivered the opening address at the London School of Medicine for Women in October 1889, and revisited America in 1906; but an accident in Scotland enfeebled her in 1907, and she died at her home, Rock House, Hastings, on 31 May 1910, in her ninetieth year. She was buried at Kilmun, Argyll. A portrait from a sketch by the Comtesse de Charnacée, Paris, 1859, hangs at the London School of Medicine for Women.

Her other writings are: 1. 'The Human Element in Sex,' 1884; new edit. 1894. 2. 'Purchase of Women; a Great Economic Blunder,' 1887. 3. 'Decay of Municipal Representative Government,' 1888. 4. 'Influence of Women in Medicine,' 1889. 5. 'Erroneous Method in Medical Education,' 1891. 6. 'Christian Duty in Regard to Vice,' 1891. 7. 'Christianity in Medicine,' 1891. 8. 'Why Hygienic Congresses Fail,' 1892. 9. 'Pioneer Work. Autobiographical Sketches,' 1895. 10. 'Scientific Method in Biology,' 1898. Many of these were republished with additions in 'Essays in Medical Sociology' (2 vols. 1902).

[The Times, 2 June 1910; Medical Times, May and June 1849, pp. 560, 613, 633 ('Domina Blackwell'); Mesnard, Miss E. Blackwell et les femmes médecins, 1889; Miss Blackwell's works; Hays, Women of the Day, 1885.]

C. F. S.

BLACKWOOD, FREDERICK TEMPLE HAMILTON-TEMPLE, first MARQUIS OF DUFFERIN AND AVA (1826–1902), diplomatist and administrator, was born at Florence on 21 June 1826. Vice-admiral Sir Henry Blackwood [q. v.] was his uncle. His father, Price Blackwood, fourth Baron Dufferin and Clandeboye in the Irish peerage, at one time captain R.N., married Helen Selina, one of the three famous daughters of Thomas (Tom) Sheridan [q. v.], her sisters being Jane Georgina, wife of Edward Adolphus Seymour, twelfth duke of Somerset, and Caroline Elizabeth Sarah Norton, the Hon. Mrs. Norton [q. v.]. Dying on 21 July 1841, he entrusted his son, then at Eton, to the guardianship of Sir James Graham. The boy's mother [see SHERIDAN, HELEN SELINA] exercised a potent influence on him. After leaving Eton in April 1843 he spent eighteen months with her at home before he went up to Christ Church, Oxford, 1844–6. On finishing his residence at Oxford he spent the next ten years in managing his Irish estates, widening his circle of friends, and acquiring by travel a first-hand acquaintance with the near East. At the same time he identified himself with the liberal party, and being advanced to the English peerage took his seat as Baron Clandeboye, 31 Jan. 1850, in the House of Lords. He became lord-in-waiting to Queen Victoria during the ministry of Lord John Russell, 26 June 1849 to 1852, and again under Lord Aberdeen, 28 November 1854 to 1858. He also established his reputation as a speaker, supporting (18 April 1853) Lord Aberdeen's motion for an inquiry into the management of Maynooth College, and speaking to an attentive house at considerable length (28 Feb. 1854) on landlord and tenant right in Ireland. His favourite recreation was yachting, and the Foam, which carried him to the Baltic in August 1854, gave him an opportunity of proving not only his seamanship but his presence of mind and courage. He got on board H.M.S. Penelope and the Hecla during the siege of Bomarsund; and not satisfied with his experiences of a naval action he advanced on foot into the French trenches, where he displayed notable strength of nerve. In February 1855 he made his first start in the field of diplomacy as attaché to Lord John Russell's mission at the conference convoked at Vienna for the purpose of bringing the Crimean war to an end. The conference proved abortive. At the end of seven weeks Lord Dufferin returned to his yacht and achieved reputation as a brilliant writer by his account in 'Letters from High Latitudes' of his voyage in 1856 to Iceland, Jan Mayen, and Spitzbergen. His only other publication was 'Mr. Mill's Plan for the Pacification of Ireland examined' (published in 1868). He otherwise reserved his marked literary powers for official use. Tours which followed to Egypt, Constantinople, and Syria added fresh knowledge and experience and prepared him for his official career.

On 30 July 1860, at the age of thirty-four, he was appointed British commissioner to assist Sir Henry Lytton Bulwer, Lord Dalling [q. v.], the British ambassador at the Porte, in inquiring into the massacres in the Levant and other districts of Syria with a view to preventing their recurrence. Great Britain, Austria, France, Prussia, and Russia named representatives to assist the Sultan in establishing order. But when it came to devising practical measures, French ambitions, the Sultan's insistence on his sovereign powers, popular feeling in Russia, the implacable blood feuds between Christian Maronites and Mussalman Druses, and the attempts of guilty Turkish officials to make scapegoats of the Druses interposed difficulties which seemed interminable. Lord Dufferin by his tact, firmness, and political sagacity found a way out of the labyrinth. His proposal to appoint an independent governor selected by the Porte and approved by the Powers was finally adopted—the Syrian population being brought under a Christian governor nominated by the Porte with administrative councils appointed by the several communities. French hopes were disappointed to an extent which Lord Dufferin had occasion to realise during the concluding part of his diplomatic career, but his government (May 1861) conveyed to him 'the Queen's gracious approval of all his conduct,' and other Powers warmly recognised his ability, judgment, and temper. He was made a civil K.C.B. on 18 June 1861.

For the next few years Lord Dufferin engaged in political work at home. On 6 Feb. 1862 he moved in the House of Lords the address in answer to the Queen's speech and referred to the death of the Prince Consort in terms which touched Queen Victoria's heart. He received the riband of St. Patrick on 17 June 1863, and in the following year was made lord-lieutenant of co. Down. On 16 Nov. 1864 he obtained in Lord Palmerston's administration his first ministerial appointment as under-secretary for India, and in 1866 was transferred to the war office in a like capacity. In 1868 Gladstone became prime minister, and Dufferin was included in the new liberal ministry as chancellor of the Duchy of Lancaster without a seat in the cabinet.

On the other hand he was advanced in the peerage to an earldom on 13 Nov. 1871, and he rendered useful service as chairman of a royal commission on military education. In 1872, on the retirement of Sir John Young, Lord Lisgar [q. v.], the second governor-general of confederated Canada, Lord Dufferin was nominated his successor, and entered on duties calculated to give full play to his talents.

Lord Dufferin was installed in office on 25 June 1872. It was a critical period of Canadian history. The federal union which was inaugurated in 1867 was completed after the arrival of Lord Dufferin by the admission to the dominion of Prince Edward Island on 1 July 1873. What was needed was to kindle the imagination of the population thus brought together, and inspire the several provinces with the true spirit of confederation, familiarising both them and the United Kingdom with the conception of a great nation within the empire. Some angry controversies had fanned into flame passions which tended to disunion rather than consolidation. The rebellion in Manitoba of Louis Riel [q. v.] against the new constitution had been quelled in 1870, but Riel and his lieutenant, Lepine, had escaped. Under Lord Dufferin's rule Riel was returned to parliament in Oct. 1873 as member for a constituency in Manitoba and evaded arrest, while fanning fresh resistance. Lepine, however, was captured and sentenced to be hanged in 1875, a sentence which Lord Dufferin commuted to one of short imprisonment. Another source of disturbance of a different character was the delay in completing the Canadian Pacific railway. After the opening of the second parliament of the united dominion at Ottawa in March 1873, a storm was raised over alleged fraudulent practices of Sir Hugh Allan, to whom the contract had been granted. The 'great Pacific scandal' led to the prorogation of parliament, a commission of inquiry, and the retirement of the conservative premier, Sir John Alexander Macdonald [q. v.], in favour of his liberal rival, Alexander Mackenzie [q. v.], who remained premier from November 1873 to October 1878. Yet, despite the angry turmoil, Lord Dufferin, by his personal influence and stirring speeches, pacified the agitators, filled the minds of Canadians with pride in their dominion, and impressed his own countrymen at home with a new conception of a Greater Britain. A speech of his at Toronto was described by the 'Spectator' (26 Sept. 1874) as restoring to politics their 'glow and spring.' On 26 May 1876 he was made G.C.M.G. In his farewell address to Canada in Sept. 1878 he boasted with truth that he left Canadians 'the truest-hearted subjects of her Majesty's dominions.' He infected them with his own visions of a glorious future, and at the time no greater service could have been rendered to the dominion and the Empire. In June 1879 he received the hon. degree of D.C.L. from Oxford.

Meanwhile in Feb. 1879 Dufferin became the British ambassador at St. Petersburg. The appointment was made by Lord Beaconsfield, the conservative prime minister, but it involved no severance from the liberal party. To maintain friendly relations with Russia while insisting upon unwelcome restrictions imposed by the Treaty of Berlin, and upon the complete observance of engagements undertaken in regard to central Asia and Afghanistan, was no easy task. The political situation was overshadowed by the prevalence of nihilism, which was already manifesting itself in attempts on the Emperor's life. It must therefore have been a relief to Lord Dufferin when in June 1881 his own party, which had returned to office, transferred him as Ambassador to the Porte. Dufferin's first important task at Constantinople was connected with the demarcation of the frontier of Greece, and the introduction of reforms into Armenia.

In September 1881 the revolt at Cairo of Ahmed Arabi Bey against the Khedive Tewfik Pasha laid on Dufferin difficult and delicate responsibilities. The Sultan professed readiness to despatch his troops to restore order and Turkish control, but neither England nor France was prepared to agree to that course without imposing strict conditions and limitations. Recourse was had to a conference which was willing to accept the Sultan's intervention with a proviso which he deprecated. The long negotiations led to little result. In the summer of 1882 England took forcible action single-handed, after France declined co-operation. Arabi Bey was defeated at Tel-el-Kebir on 15 Sept. 1882, and the process of reorganising the Khedive's administration under British auspices was commenced. Throughout the negotiations at Constantinople Lord Dufferin by his tact and quiet resolution secured for his country liberty of action without unnecessarily provoking the susceptibilities of foreign governments, and prevented any attempt on the part of the Porte to ignore its engagements to the protecting Powers. He became consequently the central figure in the transactions at the Turkish capital. In October 1882 Gladstone's government sent him to Cairo to complete the work he had begun. He was directed to reconstruct the Egyptian administration 'on a basis which will afford satisfactory guarantees for the maintenance of peace, order, and prosperity in Egypt, for the stability of the Khedive's authority, for the judicious development of self-government, and the fulfilment of obligations towards foreign powers.' His notable Report of February 1883 was the outcome of these instructions. At the same time he recognised the possibility that Turkish authority would be restored, and it was in order to provide 'a barrier' against that intolerable tyranny that he advocated a generous policy 'of representative institutions, of municipal and communal self-government, and of a political existence untrammelled by external importunity.' He called into being the legislative council and the assembly. Experience has since suggested that Egypt was not ripe for representative institutions even of the limited character which Dufferin devised, but Lord Dufferin's aims and motives were in the circumstances quite intelligible. He received on 15 May 1883 the cordial thanks of the British government, and on 15 June promotion to the G.C.B. Disappointment followed. As Dufferin admitted, the Hicks disaster in the Soudan in Nov. 1883, and Gordon's fateful mission to Khartoum next year, which he was not in a position to foresee, 'let in the deluge.'

On the retirement of George Frederick Samuel Robinson, Lord Ripon [q. v. Suppl. II], from the governor-generalship of India on 13 Dec. 1884 Dufferin was nominated to succeed him. The post was far more responsible and onerous than any he had previously held. But his special gifts of tact and conciliation and his interest in land questions were the precise qualities that were needed at the outset. When Lord Ripon left India it was distracted by angry controversy over the Ilbert bill, and by Ripon's unfinished schemes of self-government. The Indian press and congress party were agitating for constitutional changes, while in Bengal, Oudh, and the Punjab the relations of landlord and tenant were strained, and beyond the frontiers the Amir of Afghanistan was uncertain regarding British intentions and the position of his boundaries on the side of Russia. In this condition of unrest Lord Dufferin's personal magnetism and tact were at once called into play. By natural disposition and political profession favourable to reform and self-government, he had not forgotten his experiences in Egypt. In his speeches and published 'Resolutions' he enjoined on all sections of the population 'the need of unity, concord, and fellowship,' and 'the community of their interests.' Inviting the co-operation of educated Indians, and promising them a larger share in provincial affairs, he condemned incendiary speechifying, and refused to relax his grasp on the supreme administration. The 'parliamentary system' he put on one side as impossible. But he sanctioned a legislative council and a university at Allahabad for the North-west Provinces, and advocated the enlargement of the legislative councils elsewhere, with powers of interpellation and the right of discussing the provincial budget of each year. His dealing with the land question was equally reasonable, and he held the balance true between landlord and tenant. By Act VIII., 1885, which Lord Ripon had advanced to its penultimate stage, the Bengal landowners were obliged to concede occupancy rights to their tenants who had cultivated their lands in a village for twelve years, and to accept certain limitations on their right of enhancing the rent. On the other hand the landowner's right to a fair share in the increased value of land was affirmed, facilities were created for settling disputes, and provision made for a survey and record of rights. In Oudh, by the Rent Act XXII. of 1886, tenants at will secured compensation for improvements, and were guaranteed possession for seven years in conditions which placed the landlords' rights on a just basis. By the Punjab Act XVI. of 1887, the rights of occupancy and profits of agriculture were judiciously divided without undue opposition.

At the same time the Amir of Afghanistan was charmed with his reception by Dufferin at Rawal Pindi in April 1885, and was so completely reassured as to the nature of the assistance he would receive if an unprovoked attack were made on him, that neither the Panjdeh conflict (1885) with Russia, nor in 1888 the rebellion of his cousin Ishak Khan, shook his confidence. Sindhia, the leading Mahratta sovereign in India, was gratified by the restoration of the Gwalior fortress in 1886, and cordial relations were established with all the native princes. While Lord Dufferin successfully pursued his work as conciliator Lady Dufferin in August 1885 instituted the 'National Association for Supplying Female Medical Aid to the Women of India.' The scheme touched the heart of the people, and its value was recognised by Queen Victoria, who bestowed on Lady Dufferin the royal order of Victoria and Albert as well as the imperial order of the Crown of India.

Lord Dufferin's policy included measures for strengthening British rule. He improved railway communications with Quetta and the Afghan border; he increased the army by 10,600 British and 20,000 Indian soldiers, introduced the linked battalion and reserve system into the native army, and constituted a new force of Burma military police. By the annexation of Upper Burma he completed the work of consolidation begun by Lord Dalhousie. King Thibaw having murdered most of his father's house, and refused to redress the wrongs inflicted on a British trading company, assumed a defiant attitude. Recourse to war became imperative. Mandalay was occupied on 28 Nov. 1885 by General Prendergast, and after his kingdom was annexed on 1 Jan. 1886 Sir Charles Bernard [q. v. Suppl. II] established a British administration. Other military operations during Dufferin's rule were in 1888 the expulsion of the Tibetans from a position which, taking advantage of the British policy of non-interference, they had seized at Lingtu within the protectorate of Sikkim, and expeditions against various clans of the Black Mountain on the North-west frontier.

Lord Dufferin retired from India in December 1888. For his Indian services he received advancement to a marquisate in 1888, and on 29 May 1889 the city of London made him an honorary freeman. Early in 1889 he resumed his diplomatic career as ambassador at Rome. Italy, encouraged by her position as a member of the triple alliance, and stimulated by her past traditions, was then seeking compensation for her exclusion from Tunis in a policy of adventure in East Africa, thus dissipating her economic energies and courting disaster. On 24 March 1891 Dufferin concluded with the Marchese di Rudini the protocol which defined the respective spheres of British and Italian influence in East Africa. Apart from the work of the embassy his leisure time was passed pleasantly in visiting the scenes of his father's closing years and places of family interest. Proof of his high reputation at home was given by his election as lord rector of St. Andrews University in April 1890, when he delivered an address to the students full of admirable and practical advice. On the death of Lord Lytton, British ambassador in Paris, in 1891, he was transferred in December to the British embassy in Paris, where he remained until 13 Oct. 1896. Lord Dufferin's earlier exploits in the Lebanon, Egypt, and Burma, in which he was deemed to have ignored French interests, led a party in France to assail the new British ambassador with criticism and quite unmerited suspicion. The French nation was passing at the time through a disturbing series of events—the Panama canal scandals in 1892, the funeral of Marshal MacMahon in 1893, the assassination of President Carnot in June 1894, and the abdication of his successor, M. Casimir Perier, in the following year. The British ambassador defended himself with vigour against the imputation of hostile designs which were entirely foreign to his character, and though perhaps he never attained in Paris the full amount of popularity which he commanded elsewhere, he succeeded in gaining the confidence and regard of the French government. By the part which he took in the discussion of the Siamese question he contributed to the satisfactory settlement of a possible cause of conflict with France. Siam was a near neighbour of Burma and of the Malay states, and a line of British Indian frontier as far as the Mekong had been traced. On the east, however, the kingdom was exposed to peaceful penetration and even hostile attack from the possessions of France in Cochin China. The agreement signed by Lord Salisbury and the French ambassador on 15 Jan. 1896 secured the independence of the central part of Siam, fixed the 'Thalweg' of the Mekong as the limit of the possessions and spheres of influence of the two powers, and included a provision for delimitation in Nigeria. Other differences with France in the Congo and elsewhere were adjusted, and when Lord Dufferin, having completed his seventieth year, retired from official life he left Paris in 1896 with every public assurance that he had rendered excellent service towards the improvement of relations between the two countries.

Lord Dufferin had become warden of the Cinque Ports in 1891, but he resigned the office in 1895 in order that he might spend the rest of his days at Clandeboye in quiet attention to his own affairs. Civic and academic honours still flowed upon him in a constant stream. He was made hon. LL.D. of Cambridge in 1891, was given the freedom of Edinburgh in 1898, and was elected lord rector of its university in 1899. But misfortune put the finishing touch to a career of previously unbroken success. Through an error of judgment he was induced in 1897 to accept the chairmanship of the London and Globe Finance Corporation, a financial company connected with the mining markets, of whose affairs no one except the managing director, Whitaker Wright [q. v. Suppl. II], had any knowledge. In Dec. 1900 he resigned his position in order to attend the bedside of his youngest son, Frederic, of the 9th lancers, who was severely wounded in South Africa but recovered. Dufferin, however, soon learned that the corporation was in difficulties, and at once resumed his position, courageously facing the storm. The mischief was widespread. On 9 Jan. 1901 (see *The Times*, 10 Jan.) Lord Dufferin explained his position to a meeting of shareholders in a 'manly and touching address,' and his own honour and spirit were unimpeached. But he had associated himself with a speculative business which he could not control, and thus ruined others, while bringing heavy losses upon his own family.

This disaster, together with the death of his eldest son, Lord Ava, who had been wounded in the South African war on Waggon Hill in Jan. 1900, clouded the close of a brilliant life. He delivered his rectorial address to the Edinburgh students on 14 Nov. 1901, and soon after his return to Clandeboye broke down in health. He died there on 12 Feb. 1902, and there he was buried.

Dufferin married on 23 Oct. 1862 Harriot, daughter of Archibald Rowan Hamilton, at Killyleagh Castle, co. Down. His wife survived him with three sons and three daughters. He was succeeded in the title by his son Terence Temple, a clerk in the foreign office.

A statue of him by Sir Edgar Boehm, R.A., was erected by public subscription in Calcutta, and another by F. W. Pomeroy, A.R.A., in Belfast. Several portraits of him by Swinton and Ary Scheffer as a young man, and by Frank Holl, Benjamin Constant, and Henrietta Rae in later life, are at Clandeboye, in addition to a bust by Marochetti. A painting by G. F. Watts is in the National Portrait Gallery.

[Life of the Marquis of Dufferin and Ava, by Sir Alfred Lyall, 2 vols. 1905; The Marquess of Dufferin and Ava, by C. E. D. Black, 1903; Lord Cromer, Modern Egypt, 2 vols. 1908; Lord Milner, England in Egypt, 11th edit. 1904; Speeches in India by Lord Dufferin, 1890; L. Fraser, India under Curzon and after, 1911; Hansard's Parliamentary Debates; Parliamentary Blue Books on India and Egypt; The Times, 13 Feb. 1902; Annual Register, 1902.] W. L-W.

BLANDFORD, GEORGE FIELDING (1829–1911), physician, born at Hindon, Wiltshire, on 7 March 1829, was only son of George Blandford, a medical practitioner who practised successively at Hindon, Hadlow in Kent, and Rugby. After education at Tonbridge school (1840–1) and at Rugby under Dr. Arnold (1841–8) Blandford matriculated at Oxford from Wadham College on 10 May 1848; he graduated B.A. in 1852, M.A. and M.B. in 1857, and M.D. in 1867. He began his medical studies at St. George's Hospital, London, in October 1852, was admitted a licentiate of the Society of Apothecaries in 1857, and M.R.C.S. England in 1858. In 1865 he delivered his first course of lectures on insanity at St. George's Hospital, and remained lecturer on psychological medicine until May 1902. At the Royal College of Physicians of London he became a member in 1860 and was elected a fellow in 1869; he acted as a councillor in 1897–9, and delivered the Lumleian lectures in 1895, taking as the subject 'The Diagnosis, Prognosis, and Prophylaxis of Insanity.'

Early in Blandford's career he became acquainted with Dr. A. J. Sutherland, like himself an Oxford medical graduate, who was physician to St. Luke's Hospital. Blandford often visited the hospital with Sutherland and took the holiday duty of the medical superintendent, Henry Stevens (cf. *Minute of Committee*, October 1857). From 1859 to 1863 he was resident medical officer at Blacklands House, a private asylum for gentlemen, owned by Dr. Sutherland. In 1863 he began to practise in lunacy privately, first in Clarges Street, then in Grosvenor Street, and finally in Wimpole Street, and acquired rapidly a large connection. He was appointed visiting physician to Blacklands House and its successor, Newlands House, Tooting, as well as to Otto House, posts which he retained until he retired from London in 1909. He was also for many years visiting physician to Featherstone Hall, Southall, and to Clarence Lodge, Clapham Park, both private asylums for ladies. From 1874 to 1895 he was the principal proprietor of the asylum at Munster House, Fulham, and when the premises became unsuitable, owing to the growth of London, Blandford pulled them down and converted the property into a building estate.

For forty-four years from 1857, when he

became a member, he identified himself prominently with the Medico-Psychological Association of Great Britain and Ireland. A member of the council and of the educational and parliamentary committees, he gave as president in 1877 an important address on lunacy legislation, in which he described the evolution of the lunacy laws in this country down to the Acts of 1845, 1853, and 1862 which were then in force. In 1894, as president of the psychological section of the British Medical Association, he delivered an address on the prevention of insanity, in which he made an important pronouncement on the development of neurotic affections attributable to the increased demands of modern life on the nervous system; he was of opinion that no man or woman should marry who has had an attack of insanity. From 1898 until his death he took an active part in the 'After Care Association' established to help poor patients who have been discharged from asylums for the insane. At the time of his death he was president of the Society for the Relief of the Widows and Orphans of Medical Men.

After his retirement from London he settled at Tunbridge Wells, where he died on 18 Aug. 1911 and was buried. In 1864 he married Louisa, only daughter of the Rev. George Holloway, by whom he had two sons and two daughters. Blandford was athletic in early life, and belonged for several years to the 2nd (South) Middlesex volunteers. He was also interested in art, literature, and music, showing skill in water-colour sketching and collecting from an early period Whistler's etchings, besides contributing a few unsigned articles to the 'Cornhill Magazine.'

Blandford's chief work was an admirably practical and comprehensive text-book, 'Insanity and its Treatment; Lectures on the Treatment, Medical and Legal, of Insane Patients' (Edinburgh 1871; 4th edit. 1892). The book was reissued in America, with a summary of the laws in force in the United States on the confinement of the insane, by Isaac Ray (Philadelphia 1871; 3rd edit. with the Types of Insanity, an illustrated guide in the physical diagnosis of mental disease, by Allan McLane Hamilton, New York 1886). A German translation by Dr. H. Kornfeld appeared at Berlin in 1878. Blandford also wrote valuable articles on 'Insanity' in the second (1894) and third (1902) editions of 'Quain's Dictionary of Medicine'; 'Prevention of Insanity' and 'Prognosis of Insanity' in 'Tuke's Dictionary of Psychological Medicine' (1892); and 'Insanity' in the 'Twentieth Century Practice of Medicine' (1897). He was a frequent contributor to the 'Journal of Mental Science,' to the first twenty-four volumes of which he prepared an index.

[Journal of Mental Science, 1911, lvii. 753; Lancet, 1911, ii. 733; Brit. Med. Journal, 1911, ii. 524; private information.] D'A. P.

BLANEY, THOMAS (1823–1903), physician and philanthropist, of Bombay, was born at Caherconlish, Pallas-green, co. Limerick, on 24 May 1823. Of humble origin, he went out to Bombay with his parents when only three. Ten years later (1836) he was apprenticed to the subordinate medical department of the East India Company. He served 'up-country' for eight years, but returning to Bombay in 1847 entered the Grant medical college as a government student in 1851, and attended classes there for four years. After reaching the post of apothecary at the European general hospital on Rs. 100 per mensem, he was invalided from the service in 1860. He rapidly founded a large private practice among all classes and races in the city. In 1867 he published a pamphlet on 'Fevers as connected with the Sanitation of Bombay'; during the prevalence of famine in southern Indian in 1878 he identified relapsing fever. When plague betrayed its presence in 1896, he was foremost in detecting its true nature, and realised the gravity of the situation, which was much under-estimated by the health department of the municipality. Known as 'the jury-wallah doctor,' because he served as coroner from 1876 to 1893, he was held in great local repute professionally, and grateful native patients often remembered him in their wills. All his large earnings, save the small amount needed for his simple style of life, were given to the poor and to causes which won his sympathy. He made it a rule to take no professional fee from a widow. For many months he provided in his own home free tuition and a midday meal for children of 'poor whites.' More than seventy children were thus cared for, and ultimately, under the name of the Blaney school, the institution was taken over and maintained for a time by a representative committee.

In civic affairs Blaney first came into notice by the vigour with which he condemned in the local press, under the pseudonym of 'Q in the Corner,' the wild speculation of the period (1861–5). In 1868 he was appointed to the bench of justices, which had restricted powers of municipal administration, and when a municipal corporation at Bombay was established in 1872 he was one of the original members, retaining office until his retirement from public life. He was elected to the chair on four occasions between 1877 and 1893. A member of the municipality's statutory standing committee responsible for the civic expenditure for nine years, and its chairman from 1890 to 1894, he refused the fees payable for attendance, and thus saved the rates about 1000*l.* An eloquent speaker and an ardent but always fair fighter, he exercised a wise and salutary influence on civic polity. He successfully resisted the efforts of a powerful English syndicate to obtain control of the water supply, the adequacy and efficiency of which under municipal management were his special care. He was chairman of the joint schools committee, a member of the city improvement trust, and a fellow of the university. The government of India appointed him sheriff of Bombay in 1875 and 1888. He was created a C.I.E. in May 1894, and on 2 June of the same year a statue of him in Carrara marble, by Signor Valla of Genoa, for which upwards of Rs. 22,000 (1460*l.*) were subscribed by his fellow-citizens, was unveiled, opposite the Bombay municipal buildings, by Mr. H. A. Acworth, I.C.S., then municipal commissioner. Four years later the infirmities of age compelled Blaney's relinquishment of both civic and professional work. His liberality had deprived him of means of support, but a few fellow-townsmen provided for his simple needs. He died unmarried on 1 April 1903, and was buried at Sewri cemetery next day.

[Times of India, 3 June 1894 and 2 April 1903; Bombay Gazette, 2 April 1903; Maclean's Guide to Bombay: personal knowledge.] F. H. B.

BLANFORD, WILLIAM THOMAS (1832–1905), geologist and zoologist, born on 7 Oct. 1832 at 27 Bouverie Street, London, was eldest of four sons of William Blanford by his wife, Elizabeth Simpson. Henry Francis Blanford [q. v. Suppl. I] was a younger brother. At fourteen he left a private school at Brighton for Paris, where he remained till March 1848. After a serious illness he spent two years in a mercantile house at Civita Vecchia, returning to England in 1851, when he joined his father's business of carver and guilder, studying at the school of design, Somerset House. Next year he followed his brother Henry to the Royal School of Mines, gaining at the end of the two years' course the duke of Cornwall's and the council's scholarships. In 1854 he studied at the mining school of Freiberg in Saxony, and late in the autumn both brothers left England for India with appointments on its geological survey.

Their first work was to examine a coalfield near Talchir, about 60 miles N.W. of Cuttack in Orissa. The chief results were the separation of the coal measures into an upper and lower division and the discovery of boulders in the fine silt of the Talchir strata which Blanford rightly concluded bore marks of ice action. At the outbreak of the mutiny he was busy surveying, and had a narrow escape in returning to Calcutta where he joined the volunteer guards. The danger ended, he resumed work in the field, and was engaged in 1858–9 on the Rariganj coalfield. After November 1860 he spent two years in investigating the geology of Burma, discovering an extinct volcano near Pagan, and making extensive zoological collections.

In November 1862, on returning from leave in England, he was raised to the post of deputy superintendent, and employed during the next four years in the survey of the Bombay presidency, determining among other things the age of the Deccan traps. Late in 1867 he was attached to the Abyssinian expedition and accompanied the troops to Magdala, making large collections, both geological and zoological. Work on these occupied much time after his return to India in October 1868, and brought him to England on six months' service leave; the outcome was his valuable book, 'Observations on the Geology and the Zoology of Abyssinia' (1870).

He resumed field work in India, and by the end of the season of 1871 had traversed nearly the whole peninsula on foot or horseback. Attached to the Persian Boundary commission, he went to Teheran, visited the Elburz Mountains, and returned to England from the Caspian by Moscow, arriving home in September 1872. The hardships of this expedition affected his health, and during two years' enforced leave he prepared a volume for the report of the boundary commission (published in 1876). Some important work on the geology of Sind was done after his return to India in 1874, but his time was chiefly occupied by office duties in Calcutta. Here he joined with his chief, Henry Benedict Medlicott [q. v. Suppl. II], in writing a 'Manual of the Geology of India' (1879), fully one-half of which was Blanford's work. He was again home on furlough from 1879 to 1881, during which he attended the geological congress at Bologna. After he returned to India in October 1881, field work brought on an attack of fever which rendered retirement from the service prudent. Settling in London he recovered his health and took an active part in scientific societies, writing numerous papers, and editing for the government of India a series of books on the fauna of British India. To this series he contributed two volumes on the mammals (1888 and 1891) and two on birds (vols. iii. and iv., 1895 and 1898); he was engaged at his death on a volume on the land and fresh-water molluscs, which was completed by Lieut.-colonel H. H. Godwin-Austen, and published in 1908. At the Montreal meeting of the British Association in 1884 he was president of the geological section; he also took part in the Toronto meeting and visited Vancouver Island in 1897. He was secretary, member of council, vice-president, and treasurer, as well as president, of the Geological Society (1888–90), delivering addresses on the nomenclature and classification of geological formations and on the permanence of ocean basins, to which he gave a guarded adherence. The society awarded him the Wollaston medal in 1882. He was elected F.R.S. in 1874, receiving a royal medal in 1901. The degree of LL.D. was conferred upon him by Montreal University in 1884, the Italian order of St. Maurice and St. Lazarus in 1881; and he was made C.I.E. in 1904. His published papers are nearly 170 in number, and embrace a great variety of subjects. 'His many-sided accomplishments gave him a notable place among geologists, geographers, palæontologists, and zoologists.' He was master of the Cordwainers' Company 1900–1. He shot well, and on the whole enjoyed good health till near the end. He died in London on 23 June 1905. He married in February 1883 Ida Gertrude, daughter of Mr. R. T. Bellhouse, an artist. His widow survived him with two sons and a daughter.

[Nature, lxxii.; Geol. Mag. (with portrait), 1905; Quarterly Journal of Geological Soc., 1906; Proc. Roy. Soc. lxxix. B, 1907; information from T. Blanford, Esq. (brother); personal knowledge.] T. G. B.

BLAYDES, FREDERICK HENRY MARVELL (1818–1908), classical scholar, born at Hampton Court Green on 29 Sept. 1818, was third son of Hugh Blaydes (1777–1829) of High Paull, Yorkshire, and of Ranby Hall, Nottinghamshire, J.P. and high sheriff for the latter county; his mother was Delia Maria, second daughter of Colonel Richard Wood of Hollin Hall, Yorkshire. James Blaides of Hull, who married on 25 March 1615 Anne, sister of the poet Andrew Marvell, was a direct ancestor.

After his father's death in 1829, Blaydes was sent to a private school at Boulogne, and thence, on 14 Sept. 1831, to St. Peter's School, York, where he became a free scholar in June 1832 and gained an exhibition before matriculating at Oxford, 20 Oct. 1836, as a commoner of Christ Church. John Ruskin, about five months his junior, was already a gentleman commoner there, and Thomas Gaisford [q. v.] was dean (cf. RUSKIN, *Præterita*, 1900, i. 371). In 1838 Blaydes was elected Hertford scholar and a student of Christ Church, and in Easter term 1840 was placed in the second class in literæ humaniores along with (Sir) George Webbe Dasent [q. v. Suppl. I] and James Anthony Froude [q. v. Suppl. I]. He graduated B.A. in 1840, proceeding M.A. in 1843.

After a long tour (which he described in family letters) through France and Italy in 1840–1, finally spending a week in Athens, he returned to Oxford in Aug. 1841, and issued an edition of Aristophanes' 'Birds' (1842), with short Latin notes. Ordained deacon in 1842 and priest in 1843, he accepted the college living of Harringworth, Northamptonshire. Harringworth was Blaydes' home for forty-three years (1843-86). A staunch 'protestant,' he joined on 10 Dec. 1850 the deputation from his university which, headed by the Chancellor, the Duke of Wellington, presented an address to Queen Victoria against the 'papal aggression' (*The Times*, 11 Dec. 1850).

But Blaydes' interest and ample leisure were mainly absorbed by classical study. In 1845 he published an edition of a second play of Aristophanes—the 'Acharnians.' In 1859 he published in the 'Bibliotheca classica' three plays of Sophocles. The reception of the book was not altogether favourable, and a difference with the publishers (Bell & Daldy) led him to issue separately the four remaining plays with Williams & Norgate. He reckoned that he gave more than twenty years to Sophocles, and, with intervals, more than fifty to Aristophanes.

Blaydes resigned his benefice in 1884, and from 1886 lived at Brighton. In 1907 he moved to Southsea, where he died, retaining his vigour till near the end, on 7 Sept. 1908; he was buried in Brighton cemetery.

Scholarship meant for Blaydes what it

had meant for Elmsley at Oxford, for Porson and Dobree at Cambridge. With the later and more literary school of Sir Richard Jebb in England and von Wilamowitz-Moellendorff in Germany he had small sympathy. Verbal criticism and the discovery of corrupt passages mainly occupied him, and his fertile and venturesome habit of emendation exposed his work to disparagement (N. WECKLEIN in *Berliner philologische Wochenschrift,* 28 Jahrgang, 1908, No. 20). Yet not a few of his emendations have been approved by later editors (S. G. OWEN in BURSIAN'S *Jahresbericht über die Fortschritte der classischen Altertumswissenschaft,* 1909; *Biographisches Jb.* pp. 37 ff.). His own views on the editing of classical texts will be found in the introduction to his 'Sophocles,' vol. i., and in the preface to 'The Philoctetes of Sophocles,' 1870. The University of Dublin made him hon. LL.D. on 6 July 1892; he was also a Ph.D. of Budapest, and a fellow of the Royal Society of Letters at Athens.

Blaydes made a hobby of homœopathy and delighted in music, being an accomplished singer and naming his third son, George Frederick Handel, after the composer. To St. Paul's school, where his eldest son was a pupil, he was a munificent benefactor. In 1901 he presented to it the greater part of his classical library, amounting to 1300 volumes, with many framed engravings, principally of Italian scenery, now hung in the dining hall. In following years he gave many specimens of marble from the Mediterranean basin, together with more pictures, books, and a large collection of curios. The ample fortune which his first wife brought him he spent to the amount of 30,000*l.* on his studies, collections, and the printing of his books.

Blaydes married firstly, in 1843, Fanny Maria, eldest daughter and eventually (on the death in 1874 of her only brother, Sir Edward Henry Page-Turner, 6th baronet) one of the co-heiresses of Sir Edward George Thomas Page-Turner, of Ambrosden, Oxfordshire, and Battlesden, Bedfordshire; she was killed in a carriage accident, 21 Aug. 1884, leaving issue three sons and four daughters. Blaydes' second wife was Emma, daughter of Mr. H. R. Nichols.

Blaydes' principal publications were: 1. 'Aristophanis Aves,' 1842. 2. 'Aristophanis Acharnenses,' 1845. 3. 'Sophocles,' 1859 (vol. i. of the 'Bibliotheca classica' edition). 4. The 'Philoctetes,' 'Trachiniæ,' 'Electra,' and 'Ajax' of Sophocles, 1870–5. 5. 'Aristophanis quatuor fabulæ,' a collection subdated 1873–8. 6. 'Aristophanis comici quæ supersunt opera,' 1886. 7. 'Aristophanis comœdiæ'—his best work; in 12 pts. dated 1882–1893. 8. Nine sets of 'Adversaria' on various authors, 1890–1903. 9. 'Æschyli Agamemnon,' 1898; 'Choephoroi,' 1899; 'Eumenides,' 1900. 10. 'Spicilegium Aristophaneum,' 1902; 'Spicilegium Tragicum,' 1902; 'Spicilegium Sophocleum,' 1903. 11. 'Sophoclis Œdipus Rex,' 1904; 'Œdipus Coloneus,' 1904; 'Antigone,' 1905; 'Electra,' 1906; 'Ajax,' 1908; 'Philoctetes,' 1908. 12. 'Analecta Comica Græca,' 1905; 'Analecta Tragica Græca,' 1906. 13. 'Miscellanea Critica,' 1907.

[The Pauline, No. 170, pp. 172 ff. (with portrait); Oxford Magazine, 29 Oct. 1908; private information; Foster's Alumni Oxon.]

W. G. F.

BLENNERHASSETT, SIR ROWLAND, fourth baronet (1839–1909), political writer, born at Blennerville, co. Kerry, on 5 Sept. 1839, was only son of Sir Arthur Blennerhassett, third baronet (1794–1849), whose ancestors had settled in Kerry under Queen Elizabeth, by his wife Sarah, daughter of John Mahony. An only sister, Rosanna (*d.* 1907), became a sister of the Red Cross, and described her arduous labours in South Africa in 'Adventures in Mashonaland' (with L. Gleeman, 1893). Both parents were Roman catholics. Rowland succeeded to the baronetcy on the death of his father in 1849. After being educated first at Downside, under the Benedictines, and then at Stonyhurst, under the Jesuits, he matriculated at Christ Church, Oxford, but left without a degree for the University of Louvain. There he took a doctor's degree in political and administrative science, 'with special distinction.' He afterwards, in 1864, studied at Munich, where he formed a lifelong friendship with Döllinger. Finally he proceeded to Berlin, where he became acquainted with many leading politicians, including Prince Bismarck. A frequent visitor to France in later years, he came to know the chief men of all parties under the second empire.

About 1862 Blennerhassett became intimate with Sir John Dalberg (afterwards Lord) Acton [q. v. Suppl. II], with whose stand against later developments of ultramontanism he had a strong sympathy. The discontinuance by Acton in December 1863 of the 'Home and Foreign Review,' a Roman catholic organ of liberal tendencies, suggested the possibility of establishing a journal the main objects of which should be political and literary; and Blennerhassett found the money for starting the 'Chronicle,' a political and literary organ of liberal catholicism, under the direction of Mr. T. F. Wetherell. Blennerhassett and Acton were of great service in searching for competent foreign correspondents. The first number appeared on 23 March 1867, and the last on 13 Feb. 1868. As Gladstone predicted, it proved too Roman catholic for liberals, and too liberal for Roman catholics, and its early support of home rule for Ireland further prejudiced its chances of success. Save on ecclesiastical questions, the paper seldom expressed Blennerhassett's opinions. The 'Chronicle' lacked sympathy with the reasoned imperialism which developed out of Blennerhassett's early admiration of Bismarck and engendered a faith in the superiority of German to English methods of progress. His early desire that England should learn from Germany passed into a strong desire that she should prepare herself for the rivalry which the new German ambitions were making inevitable. Thus with him foreign policy grew to be an absorbing interest.

Meanwhile Blennerhassett took an active part in Irish politics. In 1865 he became liberal M.P. for Galway City, retaining the seat until 1874. But he lost the confidence of the priesthood owing to his association with Döllinger and Acton, although he declined to join the new community of Old Catholics. From 1880 to 1885 he represented Kerry, his native county. In that interval his attitude on the home rule controversy completely changed. A lukewarm supporter of home rule as a parliamentary movement under Butt and Shaw, he actively opposed it as a national movement under Parnell. Defeated in the Harbour division of Dublin city at the general election of Nov. 1885, he did not re-enter the House of Commons.

During his parliamentary career Blennerhassett was mainly concerned with Irish university education and the Irish land question. His speeches on Fawcett's Irish university bill in 1871, and on Gladstone's Irish university bill of 1873, which he supported, showed an intimate knowledge of continental universities. He regretted Gladstone's exclusion of modern history and moral philosophy from the curriculum, and pressed the system—borrowed from Germany—of duplicate faculties in the same university. In 1872 he moved the second reading of a bill for the purchase of Irish railways. In regard to the land question he anticipated the legislation of 1903 in a confidential memorandum, dated April 1884 (afterwards printed), suggesting the appointment of a commission to convert large tracts of Irish land into peasant properties, by buying the estates of landlords willing to sell, at twenty-two years' purchase of the judicial rent.

After his retirement from the House of Commons he continued to play a part in Irish public life. He was a commissioner of national education and a member of the senate of the Royal University. From 1890 to 1897 he was an inspector of reformatory and industrial schools; from 1897 to 1904 he was president of Queen's College, Cork; and in 1905 he was made a member of the Irish privy council. During these years he constantly wrote with fulness of knowledge on political subjects in 'The Times,' the 'Daily Telegraph,' the 'Nineteenth Century,' the 'Fortnightly Review,' the 'Deutsche Rundschau,' and, especially at the end of his life, in the 'National Review.' He deeply regretted the change in the papal policy on the election of Pius X, and the retirement of Cardinal Rampolla, though he admitted the provocation given by the French government, and the difference between the modernism of the Abbé Loisy and the liberal catholicism of his youth. A ready talker as well as writer, he died on 22 March 1909, at 54 Rutland Gate, the house of his daughter, and was buried at Downside. On 9 June 1870 he married the Countess Charlotte von Leyden, only daughter of Count von Leyden, of an old Bavarian family, whom he first met in Rome four months earlier; she survived him. He left two sons, of whom Arthur Charles Francis Bernard succeeded to the baronetcy; an only daughter, Marie Carola Franciska Roselyne, married Baron Raphael d'Erlanger (*d.* 1897).

Blennerhassett published several of his speeches in parliament and his inaugural address on 'University Education' at Queen's College, Cork, 1898. He edited Ringhoffer's 'Bernstorff Memoirs' in 1908.

[The Times, 24 March 1909; the Home and Foreign Review; Acton and his Circle, by Abbot Gasquet, 1907. The publication of some of Blennerhasset's scattered papers, under the editorship of Lady Blennerhassett, is in contemplation.] D. C. L.

BLIND, KARL (1826–1907), political refugee and author, was born of middle-class parents in Mannheim, in the grand duchy of Baden, Germany, on 4 Sept. 1826. Educated at the Lyceum, Mannheim, and then at Karlsruhe, where he won gold and silver medals, he proceeded in 1845 with a scholarship to Heidelberg University, and there studied jurisprudence, literature, archæology, and philosophy. At Mannheim, the centre of the German radical movement, he had imbibed revolutionary principles, attaching himself to the extreme party which aimed at a united Germany under a republican government. At Heidelberg he actively engaged in political agitation, helping to form democratic clubs among undergraduates, soldiers, and citizens, and contributing to the advanced nationalist press of Baden, Bavaria, and Prussia. For writing an article in 1846 in which he hotly denounced the punishment of a freethinking soldier, Blind was arrested on a charge of treason. He was acquitted on trial through the eloquence of his advocate, Friedrich Hecker, leader of the advanced liberal group in the Baden Reichstag, but he was dismissed from Heidelberg University shortly afterwards, and lost his scholarship. He continued his studies at Bonn, and pursued his violent propaganda there. He repeatedly revisited Heidelberg in disguise to take part in political meetings of the students. For the secret distribution at Dürkheim, near Neustadt, in 1847 of a treasonable pamphlet entitled 'Deutscher Hunger und Deutsche Fürsten' he was arrested for the third time, and with the lady who became his wife was condemned to imprisonment.

In March 1848—the year of revolution throughout Europe—Blind took part in the democratic risings in Karlsruhe and other towns in Baden. He was present at Frankfort during the meetings of the Vorparlament, the gathering of advanced liberals, and with Hecker, Gustav von Struve, and other leaders of the republican party, agitated for the body's continuance as a permanent national assembly. He was wounded slightly in a street riot in a conflict with the police, and in April joined Hecker in the republican rising near Lake Constance. Proscribed by the Baden government, he took refuge in Alsace, but was there accused of complicity in the June rising in Paris. Imprisoned at Strassburg by order of General Cavaignac, who was trying to repress the revolutionary movement in France, he was taken in chains to the Swiss frontier. Re-entering Baden, he was prominent in the rising under Struve at Staufen (24 Sept. 1848), and was with Struve taken prisoner at Wehr by some members of the 'city guard' soon afterwards. Sentenced to eight years' imprisonment, he was placed in the underground casemates at Rostatt, and ultimately, in May 1849, removed to Bruchsal. The revolutionary movement spread thither, and Blind was released by a party of armed citizens. The revolutionists soon established at Offenburg under Brentano, on 1 June 1849, a provisional government for Baden and Rhenish Bavaria, and Blind was sent as its representative on a political mission to Paris. Implicated there in Ledru-Rollin's movement against Louis Napoleon, the president of the new French republic, he was arrested on 13 June, sentenced to perpetual exile from France, and, after arbitrary imprisonment for two months in La Force, was conducted to the Belgian frontier. He was there joined by his wife and children. In 1852 he was in turn exiled from Belgium, owing to pressure from Louis Napoleon's government, and coming to England, settled with his family at Hampstead.

Blind, though never naturalised, thenceforth made England his permanent home, and for more than half a century devoted himself without intermission to literary support of 'nationalism' and democratic progress in Germany and elsewhere. His house at Hampstead became a rendezvous for political refugees from Europe, and filled a prominent place in the history of all advanced political movements. He welcomed to England Mazzini, who became an intimate friend, and whom he introduced to Swinburne. At Garibaldi's reception in London in 1864 he spoke on behalf of the German community. He entertained Ledru-Rollin, Louis Blanc, Karl Marx, Kinkel, and Freiligrath. It was his especial aim to enlist and educate English public opinion on behalf of the German revolutionary cause. In 1863–4, as head of a London committee to promote the independence of Schleswig-Holstein, he acted as intermediary between the leaders of the Schleswig Diet and the English foreign office. An ardent champion of Polish freedom, he was in communication with the revolutionary government at Warsaw during 1863, and in lectures which he delivered throughout England and Scotland denounced Russia's oppression of the Poles. His pen was active in support of the North during the American civil war, of Germany during the Franco-German war, 1870–1, of Greece in her various disputes with Turkey, and of Japan in her war with Russia in 1904. For his services to Greece he was decorated by King George of Greece with the order of St. Andrew. He also strenuously advocated the claims to independence of the Egyptian nationalists from 1882 onwards, and of the Transvaal Boers from 1878 till his death.

Apart from current politics, Blind wrote much on history and on German and Indian mythology, contributing to leading reviews in England, Germany, America, and Italy. Among his better known articles were biographical studies of Freiligrath, Ledru-Rollin, and the Hungarian statesman, Francis Deak, 'Zur Geschichte der republikanischen Partei in England' (Berlin, 1873), and 'Fire-Burial among our Germanic Forefathers' (1875), which were reprinted in pamphlet form. To his advocacy was due the foundation of a memorial to Feuerbach the philosopher at Landshut, and the erection of monuments to Hans Sachs, the cobbler bard of Nuremberg, and to Walther von der Vogelweide at Bozen in 1877.

Blind died at Hampstead on 31 May 1907, and was cremated at Golder's Green. He married about 1849 Friederike Ettlinger, the widow of a merchant named Cohen, by whom he had one son, Rudolf Blind, an artist, and one daughter. Mathilde Blind [q. v. Suppl. I] was his step-daughter; Ferdinand Cohen Blind, who attempted Bismarck's life in Unter den Linden on 7 May 1866, and then committed suicide in prison, was his step-son.

A bust of Karl Blind is in the possession of his daughter, Mrs. Ottilie Hancock.

[The Times, 1 June 1907; Illustrierte Zeitung, 6 Sept. 1906 (with portrait); Vapereau, Dictionnaire des Contemporains; Men and Women of the Time, 1899; Eugene Oswald, Reminiscences of a Busy Life, 1911; Hans Blum, Die Deutsche Revolution; Brockhaus, Conversations-Lexicon; autobiographical articles on the years 1848–9 by Blind in the Cornhill Magazine, 1898–9.]

S. E. F.

BLOOMFIELD, GEORGIANA, Lady (1822–1905), author, born on 13 April 1822 at 51 Portland Place, London, was sixteenth and youngest child of Thomas Henry Liddell, first Baron Ravensworth, by his wife Marion Susannah, daughter of John Simpson of Bradley Hall, co. Durham. She was educated at home, and in December 1841 became maid of honour to Queen Victoria, resigning in July 1845. On 4 Sept. 1845, at Lanesley church, co. Durham, she married John Arthur Douglas, second Baron Bloomfield [q. v.], and accompanied her husband on his diplomatic missions, going at first to St. Petersburg, thence to Berlin (1851–60), and to Vienna (1861–71). There were no children of the marriage, and after her husband's death at his residence, Newport, co. Tipperary, in 1879, Lady Bloomfield settled at Shrivenham, in Berkshire, to be near her sister, Jane Elizabeth, widow of the sixth Viscount Barrington. When Lady Barrington died on 22 March 1883, Lady Bloomfield removed to Bramfield House, about two miles from Hertford. Here she exercised much hospitality and interested herself in the affairs of the village.

In 1883 she published 'Reminiscences of Court and Diplomatic Life' (2 vols.), 'a constant ripple of interesting anecdote,' as Augustus J. C. Hare described Lady Bloomfield's conversation (cf. *Story of My Life*, 1900, vol. vi.). She edited in 1884 a 'Memoir of Benjamin, Lord Bloomfield' [q. v.], her father-in-law, in 2 volumes. Her last work, 'Gleanings of a Long Life' (1902), collected extracts from her favourite books.

Lady Bloomfield, a 'grand dame' of an old school, kept up her friendship with Queen Victoria and her family, and delighted in social intercourse with all classes. While deeply religious on old, low church lines, she was tolerant and charitable. She founded in 1874 the Trained Nurses' Annuity Fund, and built and endowed almshouses on her husband's estate near Newport, co. Tipperary. She sketched well in water-colours, and her sketches formed a sort of diary of her journeys. She was an accomplished musician, playing the organ; was a good billiard player, and an excellent gardener.

She died, after a long illness, at Bramfield House on 21 May 1905, and was buried in the family mausoleum beside her husband in the churchyard of Borrisnafarney, King's County, Ireland.

[Lady Bloomfield's Reminiscences of Court and Diplomatic Life, 1883; The Times, 23 May 1905; Allibone, Dict. of Eng. Lit., Suppl. I; Burke's Peerage, 1907; private information.]

E. L.

BLOUET, LÉON PAUL ('Max O'Rell') (1848–1903), humorous writer, born in Brittany on 2 March 1848 and educated in Paris, served as a cavalry officer in the Franco-German war, was captured at Sedan, set at liberty early in 1871, and severely wounded in the second siege of Paris. In 1872 (having been retired on account of his wound) he came to England as correspondent to several French papers, and four years later became French master at St. Paul's school, wrote several manuals and edited texts. In 1887, under the pseudonym of 'Max O'Rell,' which he permanently adopted, he dedicated to John Bull his 'John Bull et son Île,' a vivacious picture of English eccentricities and racial characteristics. It was translated by his English wife (born Bartlett) and achieved a success so rapid as to determine the writer to abandon his teaching career, successful as it had hitherto proved, for one of popular writing and lecturing. There flowed from his pen in rapid succession 'John Bull's Womankind' (1884), 'The Dear Neighbours' (1885), 'Friend Macdonald' (1887), 'Drat the Boys' (1886), in collaboration with Georges Petilleau, 'John Bull, Junior' (1889), 'Jonathan and his Continent' (1889), 'A Frenchman in America' (1891), 'John Bull and Co.' (1894), 'Woman and Artist' (dedicated to his wife, 1900), 'Her Royal Highness Woman' (dedicated 'to the nicest little woman in the world,' 1901), 'Between Ourselves' (1902), and 'Rambles in Womanland' (1903). All of these were written originally in French and were produced almost simultaneously in English. Many were translated into other languages. In 1887 and 1890 he lectured in America; in 1893 with his wife and daughter he made a round of the English colonies, his readiness as a speaker and lecturer ensuring him a welcome everywhere from people who like to see their foibles presented in a humorous light. In 1902 he settled in the Champs Elysées quarter of Paris as correspondent of the 'New York Journal' and wrote in the French 'Figaro' in support of the *entente cordiale* between England and France. He died of cancer in the stomach at 9 Rue Freycinet on 25 May 1903, and was buried in the church of St. Pierre de Chaillot. A tolerant, shrewd, and on the whole impartial observer, on lines inherited from Voltaire, About, Taine, and Jules Verne, Blouet mixed a good deal of flattery with his smart and witty banter, and with the leverage thus gained was able now and again to tell an unpalatable truth, not entirely without effect.

[The Times, 26 May 1903; Illustr. Lond. News, 30 May 1903 (portrait); Nouveau Larousse; Men and Women of the Time; Blouet's works.] T. S.

BLOUNT, Sir EDWARD CHARLES, K.C.B. (1809–1905), Paris banker and promoter of French railways, born on 16 March 1809 at the family seat, Bellamour, near Rugeley, Staffordshire, was second son of Edward Blount (1769–1843) by his wife Frances (*d.* 1859), daughter of Francis Wright of Fitzwalters, Essex. The Blount family, the head of which was settled at Sodington, Worcestershire, and at Mawley, Shropshire, was a staunchly catholic house of ancient lineage. The father, who was second son of Sir Edward Blount, sixth baronet, of Mawley Hall, was active in the agitation for catholic emancipation, was secretary of the Catholic Association, joined with Daniel O'Connell in founding the Provincial Bank of Ireland, and was whig M.P. for Steyning, Sussex, in the unreformed parliaments of 1830 and 1831.

Of Edward Blount's four brothers, none of whom married, Walter Aston, the eldest (1807–1894), was Clarenceux king of arms.

In spite of the catholic fervour of the family, Blount was sent as a child to the neighbouring grammar school of Rugeley, of which the vicar was master. At home at Bellamour he gained a useful knowledge of French from Father Malvoisin, an *émigré* priest. In 1819 he went to St. Mary's College at Oscott near Birmingham. There he stayed until 1827

After a short experience of commercial life in the London office of the Provincial Bank of Ireland, he entered the home office. Through his father's influence he went much in youth into whig society, and occasionally attended the breakfast parties at Holland House. In the autumn of 1829, the first Lord Granville, British ambassador in Paris, appointed him an attaché to the Paris embassy. Next year he was transferred to the consulate at Rome. At Rome he made the acquaintance of Cardinals Weld and Wiseman; and at the palace of Queen Hortense he first met her son, the future Napoleon III. In 1831 he left Rome to join the Paris banking firm of Callaghan & Co. With his father's help, he soon started the bank of Edward Blount, Père et Fils, at No. 7 Rue Laffitte. The business proved successful, and he afterwards joined Charles Laffitte (nephew of the financier and statesman, Jacques Laffitte) in forming the new firm of Charles Laffitte, Blount & Co., Rue Basse du Rempart.

Meanwhile Blount mainly devoted his energies to the promotion of railway enterprise in France. In 1836 France had only one short line between Strassburg and Bâle. In 1838 the French government's bill for the construction of seven great trunk-lines under the control of the state was defeated, and the way thrown open to private enterprise. Blount offered M. Dufaure, then minister of public works, to construct a line from Paris to Rouen, proposing to raise 600,000*l*. in England and the same amount in France, on the minister's undertaking to give a guarantee for the third 600,000*l*. The proposal was accepted, and a company (the Chemin de fer de l'Ouest) was formed by Blount, who became chairman. The directors were half French and half English; capitalists who aided the venture included Baron James Rothschild and Lord Overstone. The law authorising Blount's firm to construct the railway from Paris to Rouen was signed by King Louis Philippe on 15 July 1840. The line, which was designed by Joseph Locke [q. v.], with Thomas Brassey as contractor, was opened on 9 May 1843. To gain a thorough knowledge of railway management, Blount learned engine-driving, spending four months on the London and North Western railway. Mr. Buddicom, the locomotive manager of the L. and N.W.R. at Liverpool, brought over fifty English drivers for the French railway, which prospered from the first. Blount remained chairman for thirty years, With his partner, Laffitte, Blount next constructed in 1845 the line from Amiens to Boulogne by way of Abbeville and Neufchâtel, and subsequently (1852–3) he was administrator of the lines from Lyons to Avignon, and between Lyons, Mâcon and Geneva.

To King Louis Philippe, who gave Blount every encouragement, he professed deep attachment, and on the outbreak of the revolution of 1848, he helped members of the royal family to escape to England. The revolution caused the failure of his bank, and, though the creditors were eventually paid in full, he had to retire to St. Germains to economise. With the aid of Brassey and other wealthy friends he started in the autumn of 1852 a third banking business under the style of Edward Blount & Company at No. 7 Rue de la Paix. The venture prospered. Blount acted as banker to the Papal government. After the war of Italian independence of 1859, and the annexation of the Papal States to the new kingdom of Italy, he had the delicate task of arranging the transfer of the financial liabilities of the Papal States to the new Italian government, and the conversion of the papal debt.

On the outbreak of the revolution in Paris on 4 Sept. 1870, he wound up the affairs of his bank and transferred the business to the Société Générale of Paris, of which he became president. When the Prussians threatened to besiege Paris, he sent his wife and family to England, but remained in the capital with his son Aston through the siege. His letters to his wife give a vivid picture of its horrors. Lord Lyons, the British ambassador, left for Tours on 17 Nov. and in the absence of all the officials of the English embassy Blount took charge of British interests, being on 24 Jan. 1871 formally appointed British consul. During the siege, and especially at its close, he with (Sir) Richard Wallace and Dr. Alan Herbert distributed the money and food contributed in England to relieve the besieged. He dined with Bismarck at Versailles after the fall of the city, and left for London at the end of March 1871. He was convinced that England should have come to the rescue of France, and he expressed his views with frankness, when on his arrival in England he breakfasted with Gladstone, the prime minister, Lord Granville, the foreign minister, being a fellow guest (cf. *The Times*, 16 March 1905). For his services he was made C.B. on 13 March 1871, becoming K.C.B. (civil) on 2 June 1878. He was also a commander of the legion of honour.

In 1894 Blount resigned the chairmanship of the Chemin de fer de l'Ouest. A popular agitation condemned as a military peril the control by a foreigner of the railways of the country. The French government handsomely acknowledged Blount's services, and his fellow directors elected him honorary president. He long maintained his position in English and French society in Paris, and was for many years president of the British chamber of commerce there. His financial interests extended beyond France. He was a director among other ventures of the General Credit and Finance Company (afterwards the Union Discount Company of London) and of the London Joint Stock Bank. Devoted to the turf, he was largely interested in the stable of the Comte de Lagrange, on whose death in 1883 he kept a small stable of his own. He was a member of the French Jockey Club, and was reputed a good whip.

In June 1901, owing to his advanced age, he retired from the presidency of his banking concern, the Société Générale of Paris, and leaving France, was made honorary president. He then settled at his Sussex home, Imberhorne, East Grinstead. He dictated his interesting recollections to a neighbour, Dr. Stuart J. Reid, who published them in 1902.

He died at East Grinstead on 15 March

1905, aged ninety-six, and was buried in the family vault at the cemetery of St. Francis, Crawley, Sussex. He was a staunch adherent of the Roman catholic church, for which community he built a school near Birmingham, and a church at East Grinstead.

On 18 Nov. 1834 he married Gertrude Frances, third daughter of William Charles Jerningham. She died on 9 Nov. 1907. Of his two sons and three daughters, he was survived only by his younger son, Henry Edmund Blount.

Two paintings of Blount, one by Ricart of Paris (*circ.* 1850–60), and the other by J. A. Vinter (1866), are at Imberhorne.

[Recollections of Sir Edward Blount, ed. Dr. Stuart J. Reid, 1902 (portrait); Debrett's Peerage; The Times, 16 and 20 March 1905; Men of Note in Finance and Commerce, 1900–1; Athenæum, 4 Oct. 1902.] C. W.

BLUMENTHAL, JACQUES [JACOB] (1829–1908), composer of songs, born at Hamburg on 4 Oct. 1829, was son of Abraham Lucas Blumenthal. Destined from youth for the musical profession, he studied under F. W. Grund in Hamburg and under C. M. von Bocklet and Sechter in Vienna. He entered the Paris Conservatoire in 1846, studying the piano under Herz, and also under Halévy. In 1848 he settled in London, becoming pianist to Queen Victoria and a fashionable teacher, and was naturalised as a British subject. He published numerous fugitive piano pieces and a very large number of songs, some of which, such as 'The Message' and 'The Requital' (1864) and 'We Two' (1879), achieved a lasting popularity. His more ambitious attempts at composition attracted no attention. A pianoforte trio and a 'Morceau de Concert for Piano,' both early works, were printed; but his published 'Albums of Songs' alone represented his characteristic work.

He died on 17 May 1908 in Cheyne Walk, Chelsea. He married in 1868 Léonie Souvoroff Gore, leaving no issue. In accordance with his wish, his widow assigned the valuable copyrights of his songs to the Royal Society of Musicians. His portrait, painted in 1878 by G. F. Watts, R.A., was presented by his widow to the Royal College of Music.

[Grove's Dict.; Musical World, June 1908; Musical Times, June 1908; personal inquiry.] F. C.

BLYTHSWOOD, first BARON. [See CAMPBELL, SIR ARCHIBALD (1835–1908).]

BODDA PYNE, MRS. LOUISA FANNY (1832–1904), soprano vocalist, born in London on 27 Aug. 1832, was youngest daughter of George Pyne, alto singer (1790–1877), and niece of James Kendrick Pyne, tenor singer (*d.* 1857). She studied singing from a very early age under (Sir) George Smart, and in 1842, at the age of ten, made a successful appearance in public with her elder sister Susan at the Queen's Concert Rooms, Hanover Square. In 1847 the sisters performed in Paris, and in August 1849 Louisa made her début on the stage at Boulogne as Amina in 'La Sonnambula.' Lablache offered to take her to St. Petersburg and Moscow, but she declined because the engagement would have involved her singing on Sunday, to which she had a strong objection. Some years later Auber made her an advantageous offer to appear at the Opéra Comique in Paris, which she refused on the same grounds. Her first original part was Fanny in Macfarren's 'Charles II,' produced at the Princess's Theatre on 27 Oct. 1849. On 14 Aug. 1851 she performed the Queen of Night in Mozart's 'Il Flauto magico' at Covent Garden, and during the season fulfilled many important oratorio and concert engagements. In August 1854 she went to America with William Harrison (1813–1868) [q. v.], and was received there with great enthusiasm, staying through three seasons. On her return to England in 1857 she went into partnership with Harrison, lessee of the Lyceum and Drury Lane Theatres, for the performance of English opera. The Harrison-Pyne enterprise was inaugurated with success at the Lyceum on 21 Sept. 1857, and was transferred to Covent Garden next year, where the performances continued each winter till 19 March 1862. No other undertaking of the kind lasted so long. Nearly a dozen new operas, by Balfe, Benedict, Glover, Mellon and Wallace were produced, but the success of the venture was not maintained. Pungent, not to say derisive, notices in 'The Musical World' finally assisted to kill the enterprise. Subsequently Miss Pyne transferred her services to Her Majesty's Opera House and the Haymarket. In 1868 she married Frank Bodda, the baritone singer. She then retired from public life and successfully engaged in teaching in London. Her husband died on 14 March 1892, aged sixty-nine. She received a civil list pension of 70*l.* in 1896, and died without issue in London on 24 March 1904. Her sister Susan, who married Frank H. Standing, a baritone vocalist known as F. H. Celli, died in 1886.

[Grove's Dict. of Music; Brown and Stratton's

Dict. of Musicians; Musical World, 1857; Athenæum, 26 March 1904; Musical Times, April 1904; Kuhe's Reminiscences; H. Saxe-Wyndham, Annals of Covent Garden; Hays' Women of the Day, 1885.] F. C.

BODINGTON, Sir NATHAN (1848–1911), vice-chancellor of Leeds University, born at Aston, Birmingham, on 29 May 1848, was only son in a family of one son and one daughter of Jonathan Bodington (1794–1875), miller, by his wife Anne Redfern (1818–1894). He entered King Edward's School, Birmingham, in 1860, and thence proceeded to Oxford as a scholar of Wadham College in 1867. He won the Hody exhibition for Greek in 1870, and in the following year a first class in the final classical school. Graduating B.A. in 1872, he proceeded M.A. in 1874. After holding successively assistant masterships at Manchester grammar school and Westminster school, Bodington was elected in 1875 fellow and tutor of Lincoln College, Oxford, and lecturer at Oriel College. His fellowship was of the old kind which lapsed unless its holder took holy orders within a fixed period. Bodington, who remained a layman, ceased to be a fellow of Lincoln in 1885; the college elected him to an honorary fellowship in 1898.

Meanwhile he had left Oxford in 1881 to become the first professor of Greek at Mason College, Birmingham. He only retained the chair for one session, being appointed in 1882 professor of Greek and principal of the Yorkshire College, Leeds. With the steady growth of the Yorkshire College Bodington's life was thenceforth identified. Founded in 1874, the college was exclusively concerned with science till 1878, when an arts course was added to the curriculum and the college became a place of education in all branches. In 1884 it was united with the Leeds school of medicine, and in 1887 was admitted as a constituent member of the Victoria University, a federation of Owens College, Manchester, and University College, Liverpool, which had been established in 1880. From 1896 to 1900 Bodington served as vice-chancellor of the Victoria University, and when in 1903 Manchester and Liverpool obtained charters for separate universities, he actively promoted the foundation of an independent University of Leeds. With the help of Lord Ripon [q. v. Suppl. II], afterwards first chancellor of the university, he was successful in raising a fund of over 100,000*l.*, which it was stipulated should be subscribed before the royal charter was granted. On the inauguration of the newly constituted university (18 Aug. 1904) Bodington resigned his chair of Greek, and was nominated vice-chancellor. In this capacity he did much to bring the university into touch with the typical industries of Leeds, by providing the appropriate scientific and technical instruction. At the same time he always strove hard to secure a wider appreciation of art and literature as an integral part of the university course of study. His administrative ability was generally recognised in the county, and he took an active interest in the educational development of the West Riding and in archæological discovery. He was a zealous member of the territorial association, a magistrate of the West Riding from 1906, and president of the Leeds Literary and Philosophical Society (1898–1900). Victoria University conferred on him the hon. degree of Litt.D. in 1895, and Aberdeen that of LL.D. in 1906. King Edward VII opened the new university buildings at Leeds in June 1908, and in the following November conferred the honour of knighthood on Bodington. He died after a short illness at Headingley, Leeds, on 12 May 1911, and was buried there. He married on 8 Aug. 1907 Eliza, daughter of Sir John Barran, first baronet, of Chapel Allerton Hall, Leeds. She survived him without issue.

[The Times, and Yorkshire Post, 13 May 1911; the Gryphon, the Journal of the University of Leeds, May 1911; private information from Lady Bodington.] G. S. W.

BODLEY, GEORGE FREDERICK (1827–1907), architect, born at Hull on 14 March 1827, was youngest son of William Hulme Bodley, M.D. of Edinburgh, who practised as a physician at Hull, by his wife Mary Anne Hamilton. The father, who traced his descent to the family of Sir Thomas Bodley [q. v.], and derived the surname from Budleigh (Bodley) Salterton in Devon, removed his practice from Hull to Brighton in his son's youth. At Brighton young Bodley met as a boy George Gilbert Scott [q. v.], then a rising architect. One of Bodley's sisters married Scott's brother. A study of Bloxam's 'Gothic Architecture' roused Bodley's interest in the subject, and with his father's permission he became Scott's first pupil and went (1845–6) to reside with his master in Avenue Road, Regent's Park. The pupilage lasted five years and later brought him into association with Thomas Garner [q. v. Suppl. II], afterwards his partner. But Garner only joined Scott's office in 1856, when Bodley was twenty-nine years of age, and they were not, as is sometimes supposed, contemporary fellow pupils.

Bodley, who first exhibited at the Royal Academy in 1854, had little opportunity of independent practice before 1860. He lived in Harley Street with his mother, and conducted his work, which he carried out almost single-handed, at home. His first work was the addition of an aisle to a church at Bussage in Gloucestershire for Thomas Keble [q. v.], brother of John Keble [q. v.]. This was rapidly followed by other commissions, of which the chief were the churches of St. Michael and All Angels, Brighton; of Stanley End, Gloucestershire; of France Lynch; St. Martin on the Hill, Scarborough (consecrated 1863); All Saints' in the same town; All Saints', Cambridge; St. Michael, Folkestone, and St. John the Baptist, Tue Brook, Liverpool (1869). Bodley also designed in 1869 a number of villas at Malvern and many parsonages.

The representative ecclesiastical buildings which Bodley produced in the decade 1860–70 may be classed as his first period, though in certain points of style and development they differ vastly from one another. The Brighton church (St. Michael) shows the first revolt of a strong genius against its teacher. 'Tired of mouldings' in his pupilage, he here sets himself to avoid their use and obtains an effect with flat bands and unchamfered arches which is surprising in its vigour. The church has since been altered by another hand. St. Michael's, Scarborough, comes nearer to the method of other English Gothic designers. It shows the influence of the French examples of the thirteenth century, but its details are original and by no means simple copies.

In 1869 Bodley and Garner formed a partnership which lasted until 1898. The offices of the partnership were in Gray's Inn, first in South Square, later in Gray's Inn Square, but both Bodley and Garner for many years personally worked out their own detail drawings each in his own house at Church Row, Hampstead. Between 1869 and 1884 the collaboration was as a rule so complete that it is impossible to differentiate the authorship of individual works. But in the later years of the union the two architects adopted methods of divided labour and gave individual control to separate works. On joining Garner, Bodley, by a spontaneous impulse and not by the prompting of his partner, developed in his work a freer and richer style which was later in its mediæval prototypes. The two churches most typical of their style at this epoch are those of the Holy Angels, Hoar Cross, and of St. Augustine, Pendlebury. Outwardly the latter church (1874) owes its effect to its giant simplicity. It is constructed on the principle of internal buttresses, the narrow aisles being simply formed by piercings or archways in stout walls which connect the nave piers with the outer wall. The tracery of the rich east window is an original development of fourteenth-century models. The church at Hoar Cross is an example of generous profusion in a small compass. It was built for the Hon. Mrs. Meynell Ingram, a patron who left the architects an unstinted field for the display of genius. Other churches of this period were St. Salvador's at Dundee, All Saints', Cambridge (opposite Jesus College), which is said to be the first fruits of the combination with Garner, and St. Michael's, Camden Town, a church which returns once more to earlier Gothic inspirations.

To Bodley's personal activity belonged subsequently the churches at Clumber and Eccleston, built respectively for the dukes of Newcastle and Westminster on the same munificent conditions as those prevailing at Hoar Cross. These churches Bodley claimed as his favourite works. To the same category belong the Community Church and other buildings for the Society of St. John the Evangelist, Cowley, Oxford; the church of the Eton Mission at Hackney Wick; Chapel Allerton, Holbeck near Leeds; St. Aidan's, Bristol; St. Faith's, Brentford; churches at Homington and Warrington, and that of the Holy Trinity in Prince Consort Road, South Kensington.

Bodley rarely submitted designs in competition. In 1878, to his great disappointment, he failed to secure the building of Truro Cathedral, which fell to John Loughborough Pearson [q. v. Suppl. I]. Similarly he competed in the practically abortive (first) competition for the cathedral at Liverpool. An award was indeed made, the design of (Sir) William Emerson being premiated; but the site and scheme were abandoned till 1903, when a new competition was instituted and Bodley was appointed one of the assessors. He had the satisfaction of joining in the selection of Mr. G. Gilbert Scott (grandson of his former master), with whom he was subsequently associated as consulting architect.

On both Oxford and Cambridge Bodley left his mark. He competed in vain for the Oxford 'Schools,' which were entrusted to Mr. T. G. Jackson, but the successful work done by Bodley & Garner (chiefly the latter) at Magdalen College, Oxford, was also the outcome of a limited competition, George Edmund Street [q.v.], Mr. Basil Champneys, and Wilkinson of Oxford being the rivals. With his partner, too, he built the tower at the S.E. angle of 'Tom quad' at Christ Church, and the master's lodge at University College, designing also the reredos at Christ Church. At Cambridge he had the rare distinction of adding to King's College a group of buildings to which his name has been attached, and he built the chapel at Queens' College. Bodley & Garner's ecclesiastical building and decoration also included the cathedral of Hobart Town, Tasmania; the churches of St. Germain and St. Saviour at Cardiff; All Saints', Danehill; All Saints', Leicester; the Wayside Chapel at Woodlands, Dorset, and churches at Eckenswell, Horbury, Skelmanthorpe, Norwood, Branksome, and Epping. The firm engaged at the same time in some domestic and official work, which included River House, Tite Street, Chelsea (1879), and the school board offices on the Thames Embankment (since added to).

The dissolution of partnership in 1898 was a perfectly friendly separation not perhaps unconnected with Garner's reception into the Roman church. Subsequently in 1906 Bodley, who held several advisory appointments to cathedral chapters—at York from 1882, Peterborough from 1898, as well as at Exeter and Manchester—and was also diocesan architect for Leicestershire, was invited to prepare in conjunction with Mr. Henry Vaughan of Boston (Mass.) plans for the episcopal cathedral of SS. Peter and Paul, Washington, a monster church to seat 27,000 persons and to cost from ten to fifteen million dollars. Bodley was already well advanced in his scheme when his death took place.

In 1882 Bodley became A.R.A., and R.A. in 1902. For many years he held aloof from the Royal Institute of British Architects, but in 1899 he received the royal gold medal, was elected a fellow, and served for two years on its council. In the same year he was appointed British representative on a jury to adjudicate on designs for the Francis Joseph Jubilee Memorial Church at Vienna.

Bodley, who in early life was energetic, even athletic, a good walker, a keen angler, and a passable cricketer, was struck down in middle age by a serious illness, due to blood poisoning contracted in the professional examination of some infected vaults, with the result that through later life he was troubled with lameness. This disability had little effect on his energy.

From Hampstead he moved in 1885 to Park Crescent, thence (about 1890) to 41 Gloucester Place; about five years later he took as a country home Bridgefoot House, Iver, Bucks, which he forsook in 1906 for the Manor House of Water Eaton on the banks of the Upper Thames, where on 21 Oct. 1907 he died.

In 1872 Bodley married Minna Frances, daughter of Thomas Reaveley of Kinnersley Castle, Herefordshire, and had one son, George Hamilton Bodley, who survived him.

Bodley fills an important position in the history of English ecclesiastical architecture. If Pugin, Scott and Street were the pioneers whose work went hand in hand with the Oxford movement in its early days, Bodley is their counterpart in the last quarter of the nineteenth century. Between 1870 and 1880 he and his partner stood alone as experts in the propriety of internal church decoration, and thence to the end of his life Bodley was justly looked upon as combining ecclesiological knowledge with sound taste (especially in colour decoration) to a degree which few rivals could approach. A friend of William Morris, Burne Jones, Madox Brown and Dante Gabriel Rossetti, he secured their collaboration (as at St. Martin's, Scarborough) and imbibed their spirit. C. E. Kempe was started by Bodley in his career of glass staining, and the depot for the sale of fabrics and decorative materials opened in Baker Street under the name of 'Watts' was in great measure Bodley's own enterprise. Many a church designed by other architects gained its decorative completion from Bodley's taste.

Among his pupils were Henry Skipworth, Prof. Frederick M. Simpson, and Messrs. Edward Warren, J. N. Comper, C. R. Ashbee, F. Inigo Thomas, and Walter Tapper. Sir Robert Stoddart Lorimer, the Edinburgh architect, was also for eighteen months (1892–3) in Bodley's office.

Impatient of ceremonies, avoiding when possible even the stone-layings of his own buildings, he was yet a gracious prime warden (1901–2) of the Fishmongers Company. Singularly deficient in ordinary business habits, he nevertheless contrived to complete in the most intricate detail a large number of important buildings, and though he observed his engagements punctually, he never kept a written list of appointments. Stories, mostly true, are told of sketches pencilled on cheques, and even of architectural drawings in a bank pass-book. Some of his apparent negligences in correspondence were intentional. Bodley would always have his own way in architecture, and if a client's letters were importunate, they would receive no answer. His drawings, excellent in their results, were not very beautiful in themselves, and he was no great sketcher; but he had an unrivalled power of absorbing and retaining in memory the features and details of any building he admired. Bodley published in 1899 a volume of verse, largely sonnets, neat in diction but of small poetic power. He was elected F.S.A. in 1885, and received the honorary degree of D.C.L. at Oxford at Lord Curzon's installation as chancellor in 1907.

[R.I.B.A. Journal, xv. 3rd series, 13, 145, and xvii. 305; Builder, xciii. (1907) 447–8 (with full list of buildings); Graves's Royal Academy Exhibitors; private information from Mr. Edward Warren, F.S.A.] P. W.

BODY, GEORGE (1840–1911), canon of Durham, born at Cheriton Fitzpaine, Devonshire, on 7 Jan. 1840, was son of Josiah Body, surgeon, by his wife Mary Snell. He was educated at Blundell's school, Tiverton, from 1849 to 1857, and subsequently entered St. Augustine's Missionary College, Canterbury. But his intention of undertaking missionary work abroad had to be abandoned owing to ill-health. In 1859 he matriculated from St. John's College, Cambridge, and graduated B.A. in 1862, proceeding M.A. in 1876. Subsequently he received from Durham University the degree of M.A. *ad eundem* (1884) and that of hon. D.D. (1885). Ordained deacon in 1863 and priest the following year, he served successively the curacies of St. James, Wednesbury (1863–5), of Sedgeley (1865–7), and of Christ Church, Wolverhampton (1867–70). In these places he sought to bring the teaching of the tractarian movement home to the working classes and rapidly made a reputation as a mission preacher. Nominated rector of Kirby Misperton, Yorkshire, in 1870, he took an active part in the parochial mission movement. In 1883 he was appointed 'canon-missioner' of Durham by Bishop Lightfoot, and for twenty-eight years carried on fruitful mission work among the Durham miners.

Body's varied activities covered a wide area. He was proctor in convocation for Cleveland from 1880 to 1885, and for Durham in 1906, vice-president of the Society for the Propagation of the Gospel (1890), and warden of the Community of the Epiphany, Truro (1891–1905). His sermons were remarkable for the directness and sincerity of their appeal, and he collected large sums for mission work. He was select preacher at Cambridge (1892–4–6 and 1900–4–6), and lecturer in pastoral theology at King's College, London, in 1909. He also acted as examining chaplain to the bishop of St. Andrews from 1893 to 1908. He died at the College, Durham, on 5 June 1911. He married on 25 Sept. 1864 Louisa, daughter of William Lewis, vicar of Sedgeley, who survived him with three sons and four daughters. A miniature painted by Mrs. Boyd is in the possession of Mrs. Hutchings, 11 Filey Road, Scarborough, and a black-and-white drawing by Lady Jane Lindsey belongs to his son, Mr. L. A. Body, of the College, Durham. In 1911 a memorial fund was raised for the maintenance of the diocesan mission house and of a home of rest for mission workers among Durham miners.

Body combined evangelical fervour with tractarian principles. Although he was a member of the English Church Union, his sympathies were broad, and his conciliatory attitude during the church crisis concerning ritualism in 1898–9 exercised a moderating influence on the militant section of the high church party. In addition to many separate sermons his published works, which were mainly devotional, included: 1. 'The Life of Justification,' 1871; 6th edit. 1884. 2. 'The Life of Temptation,' 1873; 6th edit. 1885. 3. 'The Present State of the Departed,' 1873; 9th edit. 1888. 4. 'The Appearances of the Risen Lord,' 1889. 5. 'The School of Calvary,' 1891. 6. 'The Guided Life,' 1893; new edit. 1899. 7. 'The Life of Love,' 1893. 8. 'The Work of Grace in Paradise,' 1896. 9. 'The Soul's Pilgrimage,' 1901. 10. 'The Good Shepherd,' 1910.

[The Times, 6 June 1911; Guardian, 9 June 1911; Blundellian, June 1911; Eagle, Dec. 1911; private information.] G. S. W.

BOMPAS, WILLIAM CARPENTER (1834–1906), bishop of Selkirk, born on 20 Jan. 1834, at No. 11 Park Road, Regent's Park, N.W., was fourth son of Charles Carpenter Bompas by his wife Mary Steele Tomkins of Broughton, Hampshire. The father, whose family was of French origin, was serjeant-at-law and leader of the western circuit, and is said to have been the original of Dickens's 'Mr. Serjeant Buzfuz.' He died suddenly on 29 Feb. 1844, leaving his widow with five sons and three daughters poorly provided for.

Educated privately, William received strong religious impressions, his parents being strict though not narrow Baptists.

On 7 July 1850 he was publicly baptised by immersion at John Street chapel by Baptist Wriothesley Noel [q. v.]. Having been articled in 1852 to the solicitors' firm of his brother, George Cox Bompas, and being employed during 1857 by Messrs. Ashurst, Morris & Co., he studied in his leisure for orders in the church of England. He was confirmed in 1858, ordained deacon in 1859, and licensed to curacies at Sutton-in-the-Marsh, 1859–1862, New Radford, Nottingham, 1862–3, Holy Trinity, Louth, Lincolnshire, 1863–4, and Alford, 1864–5.

Bompas was accepted by the Church Missionary Society on 1 May 1865, to relieve Robert (afterwards archdeacon) McDonald, who had broken down at Fort Yukon on the Arctic circle (cf. STOCK, *Hist. Church Missionary Society*, 1899, ii. 394). He was ordained priest in St. Paul's, Covent Garden, on 25 June 1865, by Robert Machray [q. v. Suppl. II], who was consecrated bishop of Rupert's Land the day before.

After a journey of 177 days he reached Fort Simpson on the Mackenzie river on Christmas morning 1865. In due time he arrived at Fort Yukon in July 1869. Thenceforth his life was a ceaseless round of journeys from station to station—Forts Norman, Rae, Vermilion, Chipewyan, Simpson, and Yukon—teaching the Indian and Esquimaux children, systematising various Indian dialects, and sometimes acting as 'public vaccinator' (CODY, p. 131).

In 1872 Bishop Machray created three new sees out of Rupert's Land. Bompas was consecrated bishop of one of them, Athabasca, in Lambeth parish church on 3 May 1874, by Archbishop Tait. On 4 Sept. 1876 he held a synod of his new diocese, consisting of one archdeacon, two other clergymen, two catechists, and a servant of the Hudson Bay Company. In 1884 there was a further subdivision of Bompas's diocese into 'Athabasca,' i.e. the southern part, with the Peace river district, and 'Mackenzie River,' i.e. the northern and less civilised portion, stretching from the sixtieth parallel to the Arctic circle. Bompas chose the latter. In August 1886 he held the first synod of his new diocese at Fort Simpson. Once more, in 1890, there was a division of Bompas's diocese. The eastern portion, stretching to Hudson Bay eastward and to the Arctic regions northward, became 'Mackenzie River,' while to the western portion, which as the more remote he again chose for himself, Bompas gave the name of 'Selkirk,' subsequently altered to 'Yukon.'

The discovery of gold on the Klondyke and the creation of Dawson City in 1897 changed the character of his see. Bompas, who preferred itinerating among Indians, passed his closing years at Caribou Crossing, an important railroad centre, whose name was changed to 'Carcross.' There he carried on a school for Indian children and built a church which he consecrated on 8 Aug. 1904. In 1905 he resigned his bishopric and welcomed his successor (I. O. Stringer). Declining a pension, he desired to start a mission on Little Salmon river, but died suddenly at Carcross on 9 June 1906. With the exception of his visit to England for consecration in 1874 he remained continuously in Canada for over forty years.

On 7 May 1874 he married his first cousin, Charlotte Selina, daughter of Joseph Cox, M.D., of Fishponds, Bristol, for many years in practice at Naples. They had no children.

Bompas was author of 'The Diocese of Mackenzie River' (1888) and 'Northern Lights on the Bible' (1892), both embodying his experiences and observations of travel. More important publications were his primers and translations of portions of the Bible, the Prayer Book, hymns, prayers, &c., in Slavi (for Indians on Mackenzie river), in Chipewyan, in Beaver (for Indians on the Peace river), and in Tukudh (for the Loucheux Indians). These were published by the S.P.C.K. and the Bible Society.

HENRY MASON BOMPAS (1836–1909), county court judge, the bishop's youngest brother, born on 6 April 1836, studied at University College, London (B.A. London University, 1855; M.A. 1857, mathematical gold medal; LL.B. 1862), proceeded to St. John's College, Cambridge (5th wrangler, 1858), and was called to the Bar by the Inner Temple, 1863 (bencher, 1881; treasurer, 1905). Like his father he joined the western circuit, becoming recorder of Poole in 1882 and of Plymouth and Devonport in 1884. In 1891 he was appointed commissioner of assize for South Wales, and in 1896 county court judge (circuit No. 11), with his centre at Bradford. He resigned shortly before his death, which took place in London on 5 March 1909. Judge Bompas, who was for many years an active volunteer, remained through life a Baptist, and took a keen part in denominational affairs. He married, at Westminster chapel, Rachel Henrietta, eldest daughter of Rev. Edward White, on 20 Sept. 1867, and left three sons and four daughters (*The Times*, 6 March 1909).

[H. A. Cody, An Apostle of the North, Memoirs of W. C. Bompas, 1908; Robert Machray, Life of Robert Machray, D.D., 1909; E. Stock, History of Church Missionary Society, vols. ii. iii., 1899; private information.] E. H. P.

BOND, WILLIAM BENNETT (1815–1906), primate of all Canada, born at Truro on 15 Sept. 1815, was son of John Bond, grocer, of that town, by his wife Nanny Bennett. He received his early education at Truro and in London. Subsequently emigrating to Newfoundland, he became a lay reader there, and after studying at Bishop's College, Lennoxville, was ordained deacon at Quebec in 1840 and priest in 1841. For two years he acted as a travelling missionary in the region between the southern shores of the St. Lawrence and the American frontier, his headquarters being at Russeltown Flats and Napierville. Under instructions from George Mountain [q. v.], bishop of Quebec, he organised missions in the district, and founded schools in connection with the Newfoundland school society. In 1842 he settled as a missionary at Lachine and in 1848 was appointed curate of St. George's, Montreal.

Bond's connection with this church remained unbroken for thirty years. He succeeded to the rectory in 1860, and during his incumbency the church buildings in Dominion Square were erected together with the school house and rectory. In the inauguration of Christ Church cathedral chapter and the diocesan synod he played a prominent part. In 1863 he was nominated rural dean and in 1866 canon of Christ Church. During the campaigns of 1866 and 1870 against the Fenian raiders Bond served as chaplain to the 1st Prince of Wales's rifles. He became archdeacon of Hochelaga in 1870, and dean of Montreal in 1872. In 1878 the synod, recognising his organising capacity, elected him bishop of Montreal in succession to Ashton Oxenden [q. v.]. Bond waived his claim to the title of metropolitan of Canada, which had previously been associated with the bishopric. The higher rank passed with his assent to the senior bishop, John Medley [q. v.] of Fredericton. In 1901 Bond's bishopric was raised to the dignity of an archbishopric, and he then assumed the title of metropolitan of Canada. In 1904, on the death of Robert Machray [q. v. Suppl. II], archbishop of Rupertsland, he succeeded to his dignity of primate of all Canada.

Bond lived to see a rapid expansion of the Anglican church in Canada, and during his long episcopate seven new bishoprics were created. In his dealings with his clergy he showed broad sympathies and sound business qualities. Without learning or eloquence, he rose to eminence through sheer force of character. A pronounced low churchman, he actively co-operated with nonconformists, but his conscientious devotion to evangelical principles did not prevent his living on cordial terms with the Roman catholic population. Good relations with other denominations were fostered by his strenuous advocacy of temperance. In Montreal he strongly supported the cause of municipal reform and helped to found the Citizens' League. He served as secretary of the Colonial and Continental Church Society Schools in Ontario (1848–1872) and was active in promoting the welfare of the Montreal Diocesan College. He was also president of Bishop's College, Lennoxville, which conferred upon him the honorary degree of M.A. in 1854 and subsequently that of D.D. and D.C.L. He was made LL.D. of McGill University in 1870. He retained his vigour till the end, and died at Bishop's Court, Montreal, on 9 Oct. 1906. He was buried there in the Mount Royal cemetery. In 1841 he married Eliza Langley (*d.* 1879) of St. John's, Newfoundland. He left one son, Col. Frank Bond, and a daughter; two sons and one daughter predeceased him. In his memory the Archbishop Bond chair of New Testament literature was endowed at Montreal Diocesan College, where there is a portrait in oils by R. Harris, C.M.G. (1890). Another painting by E. Dyonnet (1892) is in Verdun protestant hospital.

[The Times, and Montreal Gazette, 10 Oct. 1906; Montreal Daily Witness, 9 Oct. 1906; Guardian, 17 Oct. 1906; Dent, Canadian Portrait Gallery, iii. 454; F. S. Lowndes, Bishops of the Day, 1897; R. Machray, Life of Robert Machray, 1909.] G. S. W.

BONWICK, JAMES (1817–1906), Australian author and archivist, born in London on 8 July 1817, was eldest son of James and Mary Ann Bonwick. His grandfather was a farmer and maltster at Lingfield, Surrey. Educated at the Borough Road school, Southwark (cf. BONWICK's account in *An Octogenarian's Reminiscences*, 1902), he was appointed master of the British School at Hemel Hempstead, Hertfordshire, in June 1834, when not quite 17, and showed efficiency as a teacher. During 1836 he was master in a large boarding-school at Bexley. In June 1837 he was appointed to the British School at Liverpool. In 1840 he and his wife—he married in this year—were chosen by the Borough Road school committee, acting on behalf of the government of Van Diemen's Land (now Tasmania), to conduct the Model School of Hobart Town, where they arrived on 10 October 1841.

Bonwick, resigning this appointment in 1843, opened a school on his own account. After eight years in Van Diemen's Land, he removed to Adelaide in 1849 and started a school at North Adelaide. From Adelaide he joined in the rush to the Victorian goldfields in February 1852, and returning to Melbourne published the 'Life of a Gold Digger,' and started in October 1852 the 'Gold Diggers' Magazine,' which proved a failure. For a time he was an unsuccessful land agent.

From July 1856 to the end of 1860 he was an efficient inspector of denominational schools in the colony of Victoria. Partial paralysis due to a coach accident on one of his tours of inspection led to his resignation. He then took up lecturing, and opened a school at St. Kilda, near Melbourne, which he carried on until his permanent return to England in 1884. Then he was soon appointed archivist to the government of New South Wales, and until midsummer 1902 he was actively employed in collecting material for the official history of the colony. Two volumes were completed and issued (1889–94). After 1894 a change of plan was effected and the documents were printed in extenso under the title of 'Historical Records of New South Wales.' Seven volumes appeared between 1893 and 1901, bringing the record down to the opening years of Governor Macquarie's term of office.

Bonwick died at Norwood on 6 February 1906, and was buried in the Crystal Palace district cemetery, Beckenham, Kent. He married on 17 April 1840 Esther, daughter of Barnabas Beddow, a baptist minister of Exeter, and had three sons and two daughters.

Bonwick was a voluminous writer on many subjects, but his contributions to early Australian history are alone of permanent value. The most noteworthy of these are 'The Last of the Tasmanians' (1870); 'Daily Life of the Tasmanians' (1870); 'Curious Facts of Old Colonial Days' (1870); 'First Twenty Years of Australia' (1882); 'Port Phillip Settlement' (1883); 'Romance of the Wool Trade' (1887); and 'Early Struggles of the Australian Press' (1890). 'An Octogenarian's Reminiscences' (1902) gives a complete list of his works.

[The Times, 8 Feb. 1906; Geographical Journal, xxvii. 1906; Mennell's Dict. of Australasian Biog., 1892; An Octogenarian's Reminiscences, 1902; personal knowledge.]

C. A.

BOOTHBY, GUY NEWELL (1867–1905), novelist, born at Glenosmond, Adelaide, South Australia, on 13 Oct. 1867, was eldest of three sons of Thomas Wilde Boothby, member of the South Australian house of assembly, by his wife Mary Agnes, daughter of Edward Hodding of Odstock, Salisbury, Wiltshire. His grandfather, Benjamin Boothby (1803–1868), a native of Doncaster, emigrated with his family to South Australia in 1853 on being appointed second judge of the supreme court of South Australia, and was removed from office in 1867 by the South Australian parliament owing to his objections to the Real Property (Torrens) Act. His uncle, Josiah Boothby, C.M.G., born at Nottingham, was permanent under secretary for the government of South Australia from 1868 to 1880.

About 1874 Boothby was sent to England, and received his education at Salisbury. In 1883 he returned to South Australia, and in 1890 became private secretary to the mayor of Adelaide. During this period he devoted himself to writing plays without success. In October 1888 he produced a melodrama at the Albert Hall, Adelaide, entitled 'Falsely Accused,' and in August 1891 at the Theatre Royal 'The Jonquille,' a piece founded upon incidents connected with the French revolution. Of a roving disposition, he made in 1891–2 a journey across Australia from north to south; and in 1894 published 'On the Wallaby,' in which he described in a lively style his travelling experiences. In the same year he settled in England, first at Champion Hill and afterwards near Bournemouth, where he devoted himself to novel-writing and occupied his leisure in collecting live fish and breeding horses, cattle, and prize dogs. He died unexpectedly of influenza at his house in Boscombe on 26 Feb. 1905, and was buried in Bournemouth cemetery.

The many stories which Boothby wrote at an exceptionally rapid rate during his last ten years were crowded with sensation, showed an eye for a dramatic situation, and enjoyed a wide vogue, but he had small faculty for characterisation or literary style. He produced in all fifty-five volumes. He was at his best in his earlier studies of Australian life in 'A Lost Endeavour' (1895), 'Bushigrams' (1897), and 'Billy Binks, Hero, and other Stories' (1898). His best known novel, 'A Bid for Fortune, or Dr. Nikola's Vendetta' (1895; 2nd edit. 1900), first appeared as a serial in the 'Windsor Magazine.' Its success led Boothby to prolong his hero's mysterious adventures through many subsequent volumes, including 'Dr. Nikola' (1896), 'Dr. Nikola's Experiment' (1899), and 'Farewell Nikola' (1901).

On 8 Oct. 1895 Boothby married Rose Alice, third daughter of William Bristowe of Champion Hill. She survived him with two daughters and one son.

[The Times, 28 Feb. 1905; Athenæum, 4 March 1905; Adelaide Chronicle, 4 March 1905; Adelaide Advertiser, 28 March 1905; Bournemouth Guardian, 4 March 1905; Brit. Mus. Cat.; private information.] G. S. W.

BORTHWICK, Sir ALGERNON, first Baron Glenesk (1830–1908), proprietor of the 'Morning Post,' born at Cambridge on 27 Dec. 1830, was elder son in the family of two sons and a daughter of Peter Borthwick [q. v.], editor of the 'Morning Post,' who belonged to a Midlothian branch of the ancient Borthwick family of Selkirkshire. His mother was Margaret (*d.* 1864), daughter of John Colville of Ewart, Northumberland. After education at a school in Paris and at King's College School, London, Algernon in Sept. 1850, before he was twenty, was sent to Paris as foreign correspondent of the 'Morning Post.' The finances of the paper were at a low ebb and compelled the utmost economy. Algernon's work was controlled by his father, but he quickly proved himself a journalist of ability and resource. He witnessed the *coup d'état* of 1851, and gained access to the Emperor Napoleon III and the leading public men in Paris. His later letters were warmly praised by Lord Palmerston, whose intimate connection with the 'Morning Post' was a matter of common knowledge and who, after reading one of Algernon's letters, declared that the young correspondent was the only man—besides himself—fit to be foreign secretary. On the death of Algernon's father on 18 Dec. 1852 the proprietor, Mr. Crompton, appointed Algernon, then twenty-two, his father's successor as editor. The ensuing years were full of labour and anxiety. Great efforts were needed to render the paper secure and profitable: and upon Algernon devolved the care of his mother and her younger children. In 1858, on Crompton's death, the ownership of the paper passed to Mr. Rideout, Crompton's nephew. Borthwick made an offer of purchase, which was not accepted, and he remained editor, with a share in the profits and the promise of first offer in the event of a sale at Rideout's death. Borthwick quickly acquired full control of the paper. Foreign affairs specially interested him. He kept in close communication with ministers and diplomatists whose acquaintance he had made in Paris, and he maintained the intimacy with Palmerston which his father had begun. In 1864 Borthwick varied his serious editorial work by joining Evelyn Ashley [q. v. Suppl. II], Lord Wharncliffe, and James Stuart Wortley in producing a periodical called the 'Owl.' The experiment, which ran on somewhat frivolous lines, was a forerunner of 'society' journalism. The writers dealt freely and anonymously with private and personal matters. Amongst the many regular or occasional contributors were Lord Houghton, Bernal Osborne, Sir Henry Drummond Wolff, Sir George Trevelyan, and Mr. Gibson Bowles. The paper only appeared when the editors found it convenient—usually once a fortnight during the summer, and the profits were spent mainly on dinners. In an early number an imaginary letter from M. Mocquard, secretary to Napoleon III, drew from him an official repudiation. The comments on foreign politics usually mingled gravity with caricature. The 'Owl,' which proved unexpectedly successful, lived for six years, and only died in 1870, when Borthwick was deprived of the leisure necessary to its conduct.

In 1872 Borthwick, while retaining full direction of the 'Morning Post' and maintaining and extending in the paper's interest his interviews with leading men at home and abroad, installed Sir William Hardman (*d.* 1890) in his place of working editor of the 'Morning Post.' In 1876, on the death of Rideout the proprietor, with the aid of a loan which he was able in a few years to repay, he became the owner. Although the paper was producing a good income, he in 1881, against the advice of his friends and with personal misgivings, reduced the price from 3*d.* to 1*d.* In the event he was amply justified. At the end of seven years the revenue had been multiplied tenfold.

Meanwhile Borthwick was playing a prominent part in public life. With the family of Napoleon III, Borthwick continued intimate relations after the fall of the Empire, and he was a very active promoter in 1879 of the scheme to erect a statue in Westminster Abbey as a memorial to the Prince Imperial. Owing to opposition in Parliament the statue was eventually placed in St. George's Chapel, Windsor. At the general election of 1880 he stood unsuccessfully as a conservative for his father's former constituency at Evesham. He was knighted on the resignation of Lord Beaconsfield's government in April 1880.

On 19 April 1883, on the occasion of unveiling Lord Beaconsfield's statue at Westminster on the second anniversary of his death, an article in the 'Morning Post' inaugurated the devotion of that day to an annual national celebration of the statesman's memory. Borthwick also claimed that the Primrose League, the details of which Sir Henry Drummond Wolff [q. v. Suppl. II.] devised, owed its first suggestion to the 'Morning Post.' Borthwick never ceased to take a prominent part in the conduct of the league. When the constituencies were rearranged after the Redistribution Act (1885), Borthwick, who had paid special attention to conservative organisation in Chelsea, became conservative candidate for South Kensington, and was returned by a majority of over 2000 in November. His majority was increased next year, and he was unopposed in 1892. In the House of Commons he played no conspicuous part. His most successful achievement was in 1888, when he carried a measure amending the law of libel in the interest of newspaper editors. The political question to which he attached most importance was that of tariff reform, which was known while he was in the House of Commons as 'fair trade.' The 'Morning Post' had always opposed free trade from the days when it supported Lord George Bentinck in 1846, and Borthwick never wavered in his convictions. He attached himself closely to Lord Randolph Churchill, whose fortunes he never forsook, and whose fall he always deplored. But he had entered Parliament at a time of life (fifty-five) when it was hardly possible to succeed. In 1887 he was created a baronet on the occasion of Queen Victoria's Jubilee, and in 1895 he retired from the House of Commons on being raised to the peerage as Baron Glenesk. At the same time he made over the control of the 'Morning Post' to his only son, Oliver.

Glenesk's social position grew with the prosperity of his paper. In 1870 he had married Alice, younger daughter of Thomas Henry Lister [q. v.] of Armitage Park, Staffordshire. Her mother, Lady Maria Theresa, was daughter of George Villiers and sister of George William Villiers, fourth earl of Clarendon [q. v.]; she married after Lister's death Sir George Cornewall Lewis [q. v.] [see Lewis, Lady Maria Theresa]. Her two daughters were brought up among prominent and interesting people, and the elder, Maria Theresa, was first wife of Sir William Harcourt [q. v. Suppl. II], who was thus Borthwick's brother-in-law and became a close friend. Borthwick's wife proved, in spite of bad health, a celebrated hostess. Their first house was in Eaton Place (1871–84). In 1884 they moved to 139 Piccadilly (rebuilt on the site of what was once Lord Byron's house). Two years later they bought a house on Hampstead Heath; and they long rented Invercauld and Glen Muick in Scotland, where in the autumn they came into close relations with Queen Victoria at Balmoral and exchanged visits with her and other members of the royal family. Finally they bought the Château St. Michel at Cannes. In 1898 Lady Glenesk died at Cannes, and Lord Glenesk's activity was afterwards much diminished. A further calamity befell him in the death on 23 March 1905 of his son Oliver (1873–1905), who had controlled the 'Morning Post' since 1895, had temporarily edited it Jan.–June 1895, and had exhibited remarkable ability as a journalist and great powers of initiative and organisation. On his son's death Lord Glenesk, then in his seventy-fifth year, went back to work in the office for his few remaining years. He died in his house in Piccadilly on 24 Nov. 1908, and was buried near his wife at Hampstead. His only other child, Lilias Margaret Frances, married in 1893 Seymour Henry Bathurst, seventh Earl Bathurst, and to her was bequeathed, with his other property, the possession of the 'Morning Post.' A portrait in oils of Borthwick before his elevation to the peerage was painted by Carlo Pellegrini [q. v.], 'Ape' of 'Vanity Fair.'

Glenesk was always keenly interested in theatrical matters, and had a wide acquaintance amongst actors and actresses (cf. *The Bancrofts*, 1909, pp. 312 sq.). He was a prominent member of the Garrick Club. He was closely associated, too, with many public and charitable institutions. In 1885 he succeeded Lord Houghton as president of the Newspaper Press Fund, to which he was a generous benefactor. He was also a liberal supporter of the Newspaper Benevolent Association, the

Press Club, the Institute of Journalists, and the Gallery Lodge of Freemasons. He raised the Chelsea Hospital for Women out of difficulty and debt, and became president of the institution in 1905, after serving on the board for twenty-two years, during half of which he was chairman. His son Oliver founded in 1897, with the help of readers of the 'Morning Post,' the 'Morning Post' Embankment Home in Milbank Street for the relief of destitute men willing to work but out of employment. In 1903 the institution was moved to new premises in New Kent Road. Glenesk gave much aid to the charity, which after its founder's death was continued as a memorial of him and was named the Oliver Borthwick Memorial 'Morning Post' Embankment Home.

[Lord Glenesk and the Morning Post, by the present writer, 1910.] R. L.

BOSWELL, JOHN JAMES (1835–1908), major-general, son of Dr. John James Boswell of the East India Company's Bengal medical service by his wife Anna Mary, daughter of Andrew Moffat Wellwood, was born at Edinburgh on 27 Sept. 1835. He was educated at the West Academy, Jedburgh, and at the Academy, Edinburgh. Boswell entered the Bengal army as ensign on 10 Aug. 1852, and becoming lieutenant on 23 Nov. 1856, joined the 3rd Punjab infantry on field service in the Meeranzai Valley in Dec. 1856. In June 1857, on the outbreak of the Indian Mutiny, he proceeded in command of a detachment of the 3rd and 6th Punjab infantry to join the movable column under John Nicholson [q. v.] at Amritsar. Accompanying the column on its forced march of forty-four miles to Gurdaspore, he commanded the native infantry in the actions with Sialkot mutineers on 12 and 16 July at Trimmu Ghat, and for his service there he received the medal. With his regiment he joined General Sir Sydney John Cotton's field force in 1858 in the expedition to Sittana over the Eusofzai border in the north-west to root out a colony of fanatics and rebel sepoys, Promoted captain on 10 Aug. 1864, he took part in the Hazara campaign of 1868, and was engaged with Colonel Keyes's force against the Bezotis in Feb. 1869, receiving the North-West frontier medal with clasp. He became major on 10 Aug. 1872, and lieut.-colonel on 10 Aug. 1878. Boswell attended the Delhi durbar (1 Jan. 1877), when Queen Victoria was proclaimed Empress of India, and received the Kaiser-i-Hind medal. Throughout the Afghan war of 1878–80 he commanded the 2nd Sikh infantry, and was present in the battle of Ahmed Khel (19 April 1880), being mentioned in despatches. He was also at the engagement at Ursu near Ghazni (23 April) under Sir Donald Stewart [q. v. Suppl. I]. Subsequently he accompanied Sir Frederick (afterwards Lord) Roberts on the march to Kandahar and was present at the battle of Kandahar, being mentioned in despatches and receiving the medal with two clasps and bronze decoration. He was made C.B. on 28 Feb. 1881, and colonel on 10 Aug. 1882. He retired as honorary major-general, 1 May 1885, and was appointed J.P. for Roxburghshire. He died at Darnlee, Melrose, on 9 Oct. 1908, and was buried at Greyfriars, Edinburgh. He married in 1860 Esther, daughter of John Elliot, solicitor, Jedburgh. She survived him without issue.

[The Times, 19 Oct. 1908; Hart's Army List; H. B. Hanna, The Second Afghan War, 1910, vol. iii.; Sydney John Cotton's Nine Years on the North-West Frontier, 1868; private information.] H. M. V.

BOSWORTH SMITH, REGINALD (1839–1908), biographer and schoolmaster. [See SMITH, REGINALD BOSWORTH.]

BOUCHERETT, EMILIA JESSIE (1825–1905), advocate of women's progress, born in November 1825 at Willingham, near Market Rasen, Lincolnshire, was youngest child of Ayscoghe Boucherett (1791–1857) (third of the name) by his wife Louisa, daughter of Frederick John Pigou of Dartford, Kent. The father, who was high sheriff of Lincolnshire in 1820, and published 'A Few Observations on Corn, Currency, &c., with a Plan for promoting the Interests of Agriculture' (1840), descended from Mathew Boucheret, a Frenchman who was naturalised in this country in 1644 and became lord of the manor at Willingham. That property remained in the possession of his issue until its extinction. An elder sister, Louisa (1821–1895), a pioneer of the movement for boarding out pauper children, succeeded to the family estates on the death unmarried in 1877 of her only surviving brother, Henry Robert, high sheriff of Lincolnshire in 1866. On Louisa's death in 1895 the property passed to Emilia Jessie, the last of the family.

Jessie was educated at the school of the four Miss Byerleys (daughters of Josiah Wedgwood's relative and partner, Thomas Byerley) at Avonbank, Stratford-on-Avon, where Mrs. Gaskell had been a pupil. A lover of the country and a bold rider to hounds, Miss Boucherett at the same time read widely. An early study of the 'Englishwoman's Journal' (founded March 1858) led her to consider means of providing profitable employment for educated women. Coming to London in June 1859, she, in partnership with Adelaide Ann Procter [q. v.] and Barbara Leigh Smith (Madame Bodichon) [q. v. Suppl. I], founded in 1860 the Society for the Promotion of Employment of Women. When John Stuart Mill entered parliament in 1865, and urged the extension of the franchise to women, Jessie Boucherett organised a committee of which Harriet Martineau, Frances Power Cobbe, Mary Somerville, and others were members, to present the first petition on the subject to parliament in 1866. The same year she founded and edited the 'Englishwoman's Review' (with which the earlier 'Journal' was amalgamated). She retired from the editorship in January 1871, but continued to support it until her death.

A strong conservative, and one of the founders of the Freedom of Labour Defence League, she urged the return of the people to the land, and advocated poultry and pig farming as occupations for educated women. She also started a middle-class school in London for training young women as bookkeepers, clerks, and cashiers. She died on 18 Oct. 1905 at North Willingham, and was buried there.

Besides contributions on manorial history and on women's work and culture to the 'Englishwoman's Review,' she wrote articles on industrial women for the 'Edinburgh Review' (1859); on the condition of women in France for the 'Contemporary Review' (May 1867; republished 1868); and on 'Provision for Superfluous Women' for Josephine Butler's 'Essays' (1868).

[The Times, 21 Oct. 1905; Burke's Landed Gentry; Englishwoman's Review, passim; Helen Blackburn's Woman's Suffrage (with portrait); Madame Belloc's Essays on Woman's Work, 1865; Hays, Women of the Day, 1885.]

C. F. S.

BOUGHTON, GEORGE HENRY (1833-1905), painter and illustrator, was born on 4 Dec. 1833, at a village near Norwich where his father, William Boughton, was occupied in farming. Taken by his parents to America in 1834, he was educated at the High School, Albany, New York. At an early age he began painting without any regular teacher, and won success by the exhibition of his picture 'The Wayfarer' at the American Art Union Exhibition in New York. In 1856 he spent some months in travelling, sketching, and studying art in the British Isles; and returning to New York made his next success with 'Winter Twilight,' exhibited in 1858 at the New York Academy of Design. In 1860 he went to Paris, not entering on any regular course of study, but receiving much help from Edward May, a pupil of Couture, and afterwards from Edouard Frère. After working for two years in France, he started on his homeward journey, but made a halt in London, and finally settled there for the rest of his career. In 1862 and 1863 he exhibited two pictures each year at the British Institution. To the Royal Academy in 1863 he contributed 'Through the Fields' and 'Hop-pickers returning'; and from this year till his death never failed to exhibit annually, sending eighty-seven pictures in all. He became an associate of the Royal Academy in 1879, and a full member in 1896. In 1879 he was elected a member of the Royal Institute of Painters in Water-colour. Never attempting anything beyond his range, Boughton brought his freshness of imagination to bear on a variety of themes, noteworthy always for their delicate poetry and touch of sentiment. Whether grave or gay, imaginative or seriously didactic, he stamped his work with a personal and original touch. Two classes of subject he made peculiarly his own: the one, scenes of peasant life and quaint costume in Brittany and Holland; the other, New England history and romance in the puritan days of Evangeline and Hester Prynne. His 'Weeding the Pavement' (1882) is in the Tate Gallery; 'The Road to Camelot' (1898) in the Walker Art Gallery, Liverpool; and 'A Dutch Ferry' (1883) in the Whitworth Institute, Manchester. Other of his more important works are 'The Waning of the Honeymoon' (1878); 'Hester Prynne' (1881); 'Muiden, N. Holland'; 'An Exchange of Greetings' (1882); 'Milton visited by Andrew Marvell' (1885); 'Golden Afternoon, the Isle of Wight' (1888, now in the Metropolitan Museum, New York); 'After Midnight Mass, 15th Century' (1897); and 'When the Dead Leaves Fall' (1898, Municipal Gallery, Rome).

Boughton also made a name as an illustrator; and his water-colours, pastels, and black-and-white drawings were remarkable for their fine quality. Among books which he illustrated were 'Rip Van Winkle' (1893), and, for the Grolier Club of New York, Irving's 'Knickerbocker History' (1886) and Hawthorne's 'Scarlet Letter.' His 'Sketching Rambles in Holland' (1885) is noteworthy not only for its illustrations, by Boughton and his fellow-traveller,

Edwin Austin Abbey [q. v. Suppl. II], but for the vividness and charm of its narrative. Boughton also contributed short stories, from time to time, to 'Harper's Magazine' and the 'Pall Mall Magazine,' and for the 'Studio' (xxx. 1904) he wrote an interesting article on his friend Whistler, under the title of 'A Few of the Various Whistlers I have known.'

Boughton died on 19 Jan. 1905, from heart disease, at his residence, West House, Campden Hill, which had been built for him by his friend, Mr. Norman Shaw. He was cremated at Golder's Green, where his ashes are deposited. An exhibition of his remaining works was held at the Leicester Galleries in 1905 (*Catalogue* with prefatory note by A. L. Baldry).

On 9 Feb. 1865 he married Katherine Louisa, daughter of Thomas Cullen, M.D. A portrait of him by John Pettie [q. v.] is in the Metropolitan Museum, New York.

[The Portfolio, 1871, art. by Sir Sidney Colvin; G. H. Boughton, R.A., his Life and Work, by A. L. Baldry (Art Journal, Christmas Art Annual, 1904); The Times, 21 Jan. 1905; Who's Who, 1905; Graves' British Institution and Royal Acad. Exhibitors; private information.] M. H.

BOURINOT, Sir JOHN GEORGE (1837–1902), writer on Canadian constitutional history, born at Sydney, Cape Breton, on 24 Oct. 1837, was eldest son in the family of five sons and two daughters of John Bourinot, a member of the Canadian senate, by his wife Mary Jane, daughter of Judge John Marshall, well known as a temperance advocate of Nova Scotia. The father, of Huguenot extraction, came to America from Jersey. After private education, Bourinot entered in 1854 Trinity College, Toronto, where he graduated B.A. with distinction in 1857. Next year he joined the staff of the 'Toronto Leader.' In 1860 he founded the 'Halifax Herald,' and for several years he was its editor-in-chief. He was long a voluminous contributor to the English and American, as well as to the Canadian press. In 1861 he was appointed chief reporter of the Nova Scotia Assembly, and thus commenced his long career as a parliamentary official. In 1868, after Confederation, he joined the Hansard staff in the Canadian Senate. He became in 1873 second assistant clerk of the Canadian House of Commons; in 1879 first assistant clerk; and in 1880 chief clerk, a position which he held until his death. In that capacity he devoted himself to a study of the constitutional law and history of Canada, and acquired a high reputation by his writings on those subjects.

His useful 'Parliamentary Procedure and Practice in Canada' (1884; new edit. 1892) was the fruit of sound learning and long experience. His 'Manual of the Constitutional History of Canada' (1888; new and revised edit. 1901) became a standard text-book, although the constitutional lawyer's point of view is unduly obtruded. As an historian, Bourinot, although accurate and painstaking, seldom penetrated the surface of events, and his method was formal and unimaginative. His 'Canada under British Rule' (1900) and 'Story of Canada' ('Story of the Nations' series, 1897) show his characteristic defects, but these are less apparent in 'Lord Elgin' (published posthumously in 1903 in the 'Makers of Canada' series). Other works are: 'The Intellectual Development of the Canadian People' (1881); 'Local Government in Canada' (1887); 'Federal Government in Canada' (1889); 'How Canada is Governed' (1895); and 'Builders of Nova Scotia' (1900).

In his later life Bourinot was also much occupied with the Royal Society of Canada, of which he became the first secretary in 1882; was president in 1892; and from 1893 to 1902 honorary secretary. To his efforts the society largely owed its success, and to its 'Transactions' he contributed many important papers.

Bourinot received numerous honours. In 1883 he was elected an honorary member of the American Antiquarian Society. He was made hon. LL.D. of Queen's University, Kingston (1887), and of Trinity College, Toronto (1889); hon. D.C.L. of King's College, New Brunswick (1890), and Bishop's College, Lennoxville (1895); and, although a protestant English-Canadian, hon. docteur-ès-lettres of the Roman catholic French-Canadian University of Laval (1893). In 1890 he was created a C.M.G., and in 1898 K.C.M.G.

He died at Ottawa on 13 Oct. 1902, and was buried in Beechwood cemetery, Ottawa.

Bourinot married three times: (1) in 1858 Delia, daughter of John Hawke; (2) in 1865 Emily Alden, daughter of Albert Pilsbury, the American consul in Halifax; and (3) in 1889 Isabelle, daughter of John Cameron of Toronto. He had one daughter and four sons.

[Obituary notices in the Globe and the Mail and Empire, Toronto; Rose, Cyclopædia of Representative Canadians; Trans. Royal Soc. of Canada, 1894 (bibliography) and 1903.] W. S. W.

BOURKE, ROBERT, BARON CONNEMARA (1827–1902), governor of Madras, born at Hayes, co. Meath, on 11 June 1827, was third son of Robert Bourke, fifth earl of Mayo, by his wife Annie Charlotte, only child of John Jocelyn, fourth son of the first earl of Roden. Richard Southwell Bourke, sixth earl of Mayo [q. v.], governor-general of India, to whom he bore striking physical resemblance, was his elder brother. Educated at Enniskillen Royal School, at Hall Place, Kent, and at Trinity College, Dublin, he settled in London, being called to the bar at the Inner Temple on 17 Nov. 1852. Besides joining the South Wales circuit and attending the Knutsford sessions for twelve years, he acquired a large practice at the parliamentary bar, and he embodied the decisions of Speaker Shaw-Lefevre, afterwards Viscount Eversley [q. v.], in a volume of 'Parliamentary Precedents' (London, 1857).

Returned as conservative member for King's Lynn at the general election of December 1868, he retained the seat for eighteen years. Known as 'Bobby' Bourke (cf. H. W. LUCY's *Diary of the Salisbury Parliament*, 1886–1892, p. 17), he won popularity in the house by his modest and unassuming manner, and without shining in debate held his own in argument. On Disraeli's accession to power in February 1874 Bourke was appointed under-secretary for foreign affairs. Bourke's successive chiefs, Lords Derby and Salisbury, were peers, and the task of representing them in the Commons was no light one at a time when the Eastern question in most of its phases was acute, and when Gladstone was rousing the country over the Bulgarian atrocities and the Afghan war. The drudgery of question-time and debate was not altogether agreeable to Bourke's easy good-nature, but he combined urbanity with discretion, to his chiefs' satisfaction. He was a member of the royal commission on copyright laws appointed in October 1875, and was one of the unsuccessful candidates when Sir William Thomas Charley [q. v. Suppl. II] became common serjeant of the City in 1878. On the retirement of the ministry in April 1880 he was admitted to the privy council. He was a severe critic of the foreign policy of the Gladstone government of 1880–5, and in Lord Salisbury's brief 'stop-gap' administration (June 1885-February 1886) he again held the foreign under-secretaryship.

When the conservatives returned to power after the elections of July 1886, Lord Salisbury, the prime minister, nominated him in September to the governorship of Madras in succession to Sir M. E. Grant-Duff [q. v. Suppl. II]. He assumed the office on 8 Dec. 1886. On 12 May 1887 he was created a baron in recognition of his foreign office service, and chose the title of Connemara, in memory of descent from ancestors who once resided there. On 21 June he was made a G.C.I.E.

Bourke was the brother of one former governor-general of India (Lord Mayo), and the son-in-law of another (Lord Dalhousie), for he had married, on 21 Nov. 1863, Lady Susan Georgiana Broun Ramsay of Coalstoun, eldest daughter and co-heir of James Andrew, first and last marquis of Dalhousie [q. v.] (cf. Sir W. LEE-WARNER's *Life* of her father, 1904). He thus carried to Madras a reflected prestige. Just before his arrival there had been unpleasant revelations and parliamentary discussions of administrative irregularities in the presidency (cf. *Annual Register*, 1886, pp. 431–4), and 'blunder had followed blunder' (*Madras Weekly Mail*, 4 Dec. 1890). He soon improved the situation, and his tenure of office was untroubled, largely owing to his tact and kindliness, his industry and caution. Frequent and strenuous tours made him familiar with the presidency and its peoples. His versatile private secretary (Sir) J. D. Rees, afterwards well known in English political life, compiled full records of these journeys, and they were published after the governor's retirement, under the title of 'Narrative of Tours in India made by Lord Connemara' (Madras, 1891). In the midsummer of 1889 he travelled to Ganjam, a then famine-stricken district on the extreme north of the presidency, which was extremely difficult of access, and he ordered relief measures which were of great advantage to the people; but the malarious region had prejudicial effect upon his health, and was fatal to the medical member of the staff (Dr. MacNally). Connemara improved the sanitation of the presidency city, and strengthened and reorganised the sanitary department of government. He pressed forward railway communications, particularly the important east coast line linking Madras with Calcutta. A volume of his 'Minutes,' mostly written during his tours (Madras, 1890), and another of his 'Speeches' (Madras, 1891), both edited by Sir J. D. Rees, show terseness and penetration, and his administration was held to form 'a bright epoch in the annals of Madras' (*Madras Weekly Mail*, 4 Dec. 1890).

But the governorship ended abruptly a year before its normal term under a dark cloud, which closed Connemara's public life. It was announced from India on 8 Nov. 1890 that he had tendered his resignation, to take effect from the following March. Soon afterwards (27 Nov.) the divorce court in London heard the petition of his wife for dissolution of marriage on charges of cruelty and adultery going back to 1875. Though Bourke's pleadings denied the charge and made a counter-charge of adultery against his wife and Dr. Briggs, a former member of his staff, he was not represented at the hearing. A decree nisi was pronounced, and was made absolute on 9 June 1891. Lady Connemara and Dr. Briggs denied the counter-charge in court; they were subsequently married, and she died on 22 Jan. 1898.

Connemara handed over acting charge of the governorship to a civilian colleague on 1 Dec. 1890, and embarked for England on the 7th. He married a second wife on 22 Oct. 1894, Gertrude, widow of Edward Coleman of Stoke Park, a lady of considerable wealth; she died on 23 Nov. 1898. He died at his London residence, Grosvenor Street, after long illness, on 3 Sept. 1902, and was buried at Kensal Green cemetery. There being no issue by either marriage, the barony became extinct with his death. There is a portrait at Government House, Madras, and the chief hotel there is named after him. A caricature by 'Spy' is in '"Vanity Fair" Album' (1877, plate 250).

[Burke's Peerage, 1902; Men and Women of the Time, 1899; J. D. Rees's Narrative of Tours in India, Madras, 1891; India List, 1902; The Times, 10, 25 and 28 Nov. 1890, 10 June 1891, 4 and 6 Sept. 1902; Madras Weekly Mail, 13 Nov. and 4 Dec. 1890.]

F. H. B.

BOURNE, HENRY RICHARD FOX (1837–1909), social reformer and author, born at Grecian Regale, Blue Mountains, Jamaica, on 24 Dec. 1837, was one of eight children of Stephen Bourne, magistrate and advocate of the abolition of slavery, and of Elizabeth Quirk. His father had founded in Dec. 1826 the 'World,' the first nonconformist and exclusively religious journal in England. His parents left Jamaica in 1841 for British Guiana, and moved to London in 1848, where, after attending a private school, Henry entered London University in 1856, and joined classes at King's College and the City of London College. He also attended, at University College, lectures on English literature and history by Henry Morley [q. v.], whose intimate friend and assistant he afterwards became. In 1855 he entered the war office as a clerk, devoting his leisure to literary and journalistic work. He regularly contributed to the 'Examiner,' an organ of advanced radical thought, of which Henry Morley was editor, and wrote for Charles Dickens in 'Household Words.'

In 1862 Fox Bourne made some reputation by his first independently published work, 'A Memoir of Sir Philip Sidney,' which showed painstaking research and critical insight, and remains a standard biography. There followed 'English Merchants' (1866); 'Famous London Merchants' (1869), written for younger readers; 'The Romance of Trade' (1871); 'English Seamen under the Tudors' (1868), and 'The Story of Our Colonies' (1869). In these books Fox Bourne traced in a popular style the rise of England's commerce and colonial expansion.

In 1870 Fox Bourne retired from the war office, and with the money granted him in lieu of a pension purchased the copyright and control of the 'Examiner.' Although John Stuart Mill, Herbert Spencer, and Frederic Harrison were still among the contributors, the paper proved in Bourne's hands a financial failure, and he disposed of it in 1873 (see F. HARRISON'S *Reminiscences*, 1911).

The next two years he mainly spent on a 'Life of John Locke,' which he published in 1876. From 1876 to 1887 he was editor of the 'Weekly Dispatch,' which under his auspices well maintained its radical independence. Fox Bourne freely criticised the Gladstonian administration of 1880–5, and his hostility to Gladstone's home rule bill of 1886 led to his retirement from the editorship.

Thenceforth Fox Bourne devoted almost all his energies to the work of the Aborigines Protection Society, of which he became secretary on 4 Jan. 1889. He edited its journal, the 'Aborigines' Friend,' and pressed on public attention the need of protecting native races, especially in Africa. One of the first to denounce publicly the cruel treatment of natives in the Congo Free State in 1890, he used all efforts to secure the enforcement of the provisions of the Brussels convention of 1889–90 for the protection of the natives in Central Africa. He forcibly stated his views in 'The Other Side of the Emin Pasha Expedition' (1891) and in 'Civilisation in Congo Land' (1893). To his advocacy was largely due the ultimate improvement in native conditions in the Belgian Congo.

Although he failed in his attempts to secure the franchise for natives in the Transvaal and Orange River colonies in 1906, his strong protests against the slave traffic in Angola and the cocoa-growing islands of San Thomé and Principe compelled the Portuguese government to admit the necessity of reform. In a series of six pamphlets (1906–8) on Egyptian affairs he denounced alleged abuses of the English military occupation, and advocated Egyptian self-government. Fox Bourne's pertinacious patience in investigation and his clearness of exposition gave his views on native questions wide influence.

Fox Bourne died suddenly at Torquay, from bronchitis contracted on his holiday, on 2 Feb. 1909, and was cremated at Woking. A memorial service was held at Araromi chapel, Lagos. He married on 1 May 1862 Emma Deane, daughter of Henry Bleckly, a Warrington ironmaster. His widow, with two sons and a daughter, survived him.

Besides the works mentioned, Fox Bourne published: 1. (with the Earl of Dundonald) 'Life of Thomas, Lord Cochrane,' 1869. 2. 'Foreign Rivalries in Industrial Products,' 1877. 3. 'English Newspapers,' 2 vols. 1887, a serviceable chronicle of journalistic history. 4. 'The Aborigines Protection Society; Chapters in its History,' 1899.

[The Times, 5, 6, 8, 11 Feb. 1909; The Aborigines' Friend, May 1909; Lagos Weekly Record, 13 Feb. 1909; Memorial Discourse by J. M. Robertson, M.P., 28 Feb. 1909.]

W. B. O.

BOUSFIELD, HENRY BROUGHAM (1832–1902), first bishop of Pretoria, born on 27 March 1832, was son of William Cheele Bousfield, barrister-at-law. Entering Merchant Taylors' School in 1840, he passed to Caius College, Cambridge, where he was exhibitioner, and graduated B.A. as junior optime in 1855 and M.A. in 1858. Ordained deacon in 1855 and priest in 1856, he was licensed to the curacy of All Saints', Braishfield, Hampshire, and became incumbent of the parish in 1856. From 1861 to 1870 he was rector of St. Maurice with St. Mary Kalendre and St. Peter Colebrook, Winchester, and in 1870 became vicar of Andover with Foxcote. In 1873 he was made rural dean of West Andover. From early boyhood Bousfield had been interested in missionary work, more especially in British colonies. After the Transvaal was separated in 1877 from the diocese of Bloemfontein, Bousfield accepted after a first refusal an offer of the new see from the Society for the Propagation of the Gospel. On 2 Feb. 1878 he was consecrated at St. Paul's, bishop of Pretoria, and landed at Durban on 17 Sept. He trekked to Pretoria, where he found about 3000 inhabitants, of whom 1500 were whites, and the church organisation only in embryo, the clergy numbering five. Bousfield's work was hindered by the Zulu war of 1879, and by the Boer war of 1880–1; but under the Boer republic Bousfield, avoiding political entanglement, continued the organisation of his diocese. He sought to meet the needs of the white population drawn by the goldfields, and extended missionary work amongst the natives. New difficulties from the Jameson raid arose in 1896; but when war with Great Britain broke out in 1899, the clergy of the diocese numbered thirty-two, and the white church members exceeded 18,000. From October 1899 to April 1901 Bousfield was a refugee in Natal, acting for a time as military chaplain, and rendering aid to distressed refugees. Despite failing health he attended the episcopal synod of South Africa (3–5 Feb.), but died suddenly at Capetown of heart disease on 9 Feb. 1902.

Bousfield was a man of high devotion; but extreme candour and his view of episcopal power sometimes strained his relations with his clergy. He married twice: (1) in 1861 Charlotte Elizabeth, daughter of Jonathan Higginson of Rock Ferry, Liverpool, who died in 1886; and (2) in 1888 Ellen, daughter of Thomas Lamb of Andover. He described his first six years of episcopal work in 'Six Years in the Transvaal' (1886).

[Guardian, 12 March 1902; Record, 14 Feb. 1902; Register of Merchant Taylors' School, 1883, ii. 278; Taylorian, April 1902; Lowndes, Bishops of the Day, 1897; Two Hundred Years of the S.P.G.]

A. R. B.

BOWEN, EDWARD ERNEST (1836–1901), schoolmaster and song writer, born at Woolaston, near Chepstow, on 30 March 1836, was second of three sons of Christopher Bowen of Hollymount, co. Mayo, an evangelical clergyman who was successively curate of Woolaston and of Bath Abbey church, and perpetual curate of St. Mary Magdalene's, Southwark. His mother, who died on 1 Feb. 1902, at the age of 94, having survived all her three sons and husband, was Catherine Emily, daughter of Sir Richard Steele, 4th baronet, of Hampstead, co. Dublin. Charles, afterwards Lord Bowen [q. v. Suppl. I], was

Edward's elder brother. Edward was at school at Lille and at the Rev. E. J. Selwyn's school, Blackheath, and after two years at King's College, London, went up to Trinity College, Cambridge, in the autumn of 1854. He was made a scholar of his college, and won the Bell University scholarship in 1855, the Carus Greek Testament (undergraduates') prize in 1856, and a prize for an English essay, which was published with the title 'The Force of Habit considered as an Argument to prove the Moral Government of Man by God' (Cambridge, 1858). He graduated B.A. in 1858 as fourth in the first class of the classical tripos, and next year was elected to a fellowship at Trinity. He proceeded M.A. in 1861.

After one term's work as an assistant master at Marlborough, Bowen became in January 1859 a master at Harrow under Dr. Vaughan. He remained at Harrow for life, and from the outset threw himself with ardour into the various activities of the place. As a schoolmaster he was mainly guided by two principles—that the boy must be interested in his lessons and at ease with the teacher. While other teachers were grave and distant, Bowen was always cheerful, vivacious, and familiar, abounding in genial irony and ingenious fancy. Although order and discipline were necessities of his existence, he held that 'boys ought hardly ever to be punished against their will.' 'Punishments, rewards, and marks' his fantastic humour defined as 'the three great drawbacks to education.' Teaching he regarded as an individual gift, and when giving evidence before the secondary education commission of 1894 he deprecated any systematic training of teachers for secondary schools. Delighting in form-teaching, he accepted in 1863 a 'small' house, from a sense of duty rather than from choice, and he found it 'a nuisance.' In 1881 he became head of 'The Grove,' one of the 'large' houses, and there his wise and strong guidance of boys was best felt.

Meanwhile, in order to widen the methods and scope of education, he had recommended the creation of the modern side at Harrow. This department was started in 1869, to rank as far as possible on an equality with the classical side, with himself as its head. In 1881 he wrote, at the wish of Dr. Henry Montagu Butler, the headmaster, an exhaustive memorandum on the principles, character, and thoroughly successful results of the new development. Bowen continued the management of the modern side till 1893, when, feeling that under Dr. Butler's successor, Dr. Welldon, the modern side was silently becoming 'a refuge for the destitute,' he resigned his leadership, but he continued to teach the two highest forms.

Bowen's versatile capacity embraced much literary power and insight, and his interests travelled far beyond his school work. He was, like his elder brother, a constant contributor to the 'Saturday Review' in its early days, and there chiefly distinguished himself by his wit. Although he was an ardent lover of peace, he was deeply interested in military tactics, and visited wellnigh all the battlefields of Europe. He taught military history admirably, and published with notes Thiers's account of the Waterloo campaign (1872). Two articles in the 'National Review' (Jan. and Oct. 1863) attest his religious feeling and theological position: they deal in a liberal spirit with 'Bishop Colenso on the Pentateuch' and 'The Recent Criticism of the Old Testament.' At school he organised Shakespeare readings, but for school purposes his literary gift was turned to best advantage as a writer of school songs. His 'Forty Years On,' which he penned in 1872, became 'the national anthem of Harrow' (cf. *Harrow School*, 1898, with facsimile of Bowen's MS., pp. 212–3), and many other songs followed of almost equal merit and influence. Set to stirring music by John Farmer [q. v. Suppl. II], they greatly increased the sense of corporate union among the boys. Bowen collected his poetic work in 'Harrow Songs and other Verses' in 1886.

Bowen was the first master at Harrow to identify himself thoroughly with sports and games, most of which he played himself. He was a cricketer and a pioneer of football, which he still played with his boys in the last year of his life. He contributed a chapter on 'Harrow Football' to 'Harrow School' (ed. Howson and Warner, 1898). He was also an accomplished skater and a skilful mountaineer. From youth, too, he was a pedestrian of exceptional endurance and enthusiasm. As an undergraduate he walked from Cambridge to Oxford in twenty-six hours; in after life he walked all over England and over many of the battlefields of Europe. His summer holiday of 1870 was spent in the track of the Prussian army, and his Christmas in Paris, when the Commune was besieged there by the republican army. Always a staunch liberal in politics, he unsuccessfully contested Hertford against Mr. Arthur Balfour in 1880.

Bowen died suddenly near Moux on 8 April 1901, while on a bicycle tour in the Côte d'Or with his friend Mr. James Bryce. He was buried at Harrow. The bulk of his property he bequeathed to the school. He had previously added two acres to the playing fields at his own expense. He was unmarried. Dr. Wood, the fourth and last headmaster under whom Bowen served at Harrow, credited him with 'Attic versatility and Spartan simplicity.'

[Memoir by his nephew, the Rev. the Hon. W. E. Bowen 1903, with many of his essays and songs, together with his evidence before the Royal Commission on Secondary Education in 1894; Mr. James Bryce's admirable sketch in his Studies in Contemporary Biography 1903, pp. 343–63; Harrow School, ed. E. W. Howson and G. Townsend Warner, 1898, passim.]

BOWLER, HENRY ALEXANDER (1824–1903), painter, son of Charles and Frances Anne Bowler, was born in Kensington on 30 Nov. 1824. After being educated at private schools he studied art at Leigh's School and the Government School of Design at Somerset House. In 1851 he was appointed headmaster of the Stourbridge School of Art, but was soon transferred to a teaching appointment in the school at Somerset House, where he had received his training. In 1855 he was appointed an inspector in the science and art department, and in 1876 became assistant director for art at South Kensington. From 1861 to 1899 he was teacher of perspective at the Royal Academy. He also held important posts in organising the international exhibitions of 1862 and subsequent years. From 1847 to 1871 he exhibited ten pictures, mostly landscapes, at the Royal Academy, and others at the British Institution and elsewhere. A water-colour by him, 'Luccombe Chine, Isle of Wight,' is in the Victoria and Albert Museum, and the figure of Jean Goujon, among the mosaic decorations of the south court of the museum, was executed from his design. He retired from the science and art department in 1891. He died on 6 Aug. 1903, and was buried at Kensal Green. On 4 Aug. 1853 he married Ellen Archer Archer, daughter of Thomas Archer, J.P., vicar of Whitchurch, Bucks, and had three sons and one daughter.

[Victoria and Albert Museum, Catalogue of Water-Colour Paintings, 1908; Graves's Royal Academy and British Institution Exhibitors; private information.] M. H.

BOYCE, Sir RUBERT WILLIAM (1863–1911), pathologist and hygienist, born on 22 April 1863 at Osborne Terrace, Clapham Road, London, was second son of Robert Henry Boyce, originally of Carlow, Ireland, an engineer who was at one time principal surveyor of British diplomatic and consular buildings in China, by his wife Louisa, daughter of Dr. Neligan, a medical practitioner in Athlone.

After attending a preparatory school at Rugby, and then a school in Paris, where an aunt, Henrietta Boyce, resided, Rubert began the study of medicine at University College, London. He graduated M.B. in 1889 at London University, and in 1892 was appointed assistant professor of pathology at University College. In the same year he published 'A Text-book of Morbid Histology' and made important contributions to the research work of the laboratory. In 1894 he was appointed to the newly endowed chair of pathology in University College, Liverpool, then a constituent of the Victoria University, Manchester. At Liverpool he quickly organised a laboratory of scientific pathology on modern lines. In 1898 his department of pathology was installed in a fine building erected for it, and at the same time he was appointed bacteriologist to the Liverpool corporation.

Meanwhile in the senate of the college he powerfully advocated the development and expansion of the college into a fully equipped and self-centred university. As an officer both of the college and of the municipality he was able in the double capacity effectually to promote the early success of Liverpool University, which was finally established in 1902. Four endowed chairs in the new university owed their creation mainly to him, namely, those of bio-chemistry, of tropical medicine, of comparative pathology, and of medical entomology, as well as the university lectureship on tropical medicine.

In 1897 Boyce visited Canada with the British Association as a secretary to the section of physiology. Thenceforth he cherished the ideal of bringing the dominion and the home country into closer relations. By his influence a fellowship for young medical graduates from the colonies was endowed in the Liverpool University. In 1898 Mr. Joseph Chamberlain, then secretary of state for the colonies, urged the school of medicine at Liverpool to establish a department for the special study of tropical diseases. Accordingly Boyce, in conjunction with (Sir) Alfred Jones [q. v. Suppl. II], founded the Liverpool School of Tropical Medicine, of which (Sir) Ronald Ross became director, a post which was soon associated with an endowed chair at the university. In 1901 Boyce took the lead in organising with an unfailing optimism a series of expeditions sent by the school to the tropics to investigate diseases in their habitat there. In six years there were despatched seventeen expeditions, which, though costly in life and money, were rich in fruitful knowledge. In 1905 Boyce went himself to New Orleans and British Honduras to examine epidemics of yellow fever.

Boyce's zealous efforts were generally recognised. He was made a fellow of University College, London. In 1902 he was elected F.R.S. In 1906 he was knighted. He became a member of the African advisory board of the colonial office, and served on the royal commissions on sewage disposal and on tuberculosis.

In September 1906, after a spell of exceptionally heavy work, he suffered a stroke of paralysis, but after a year partially resumed his university work, although he was permanently crippled. In 1909 he visited the West Indies to report at the instance of the government on yellow fever, and in 1910 he went to West Africa for the like purpose. In his enforced withdrawal from laboratory work he sought to arouse sympathy with the problems of tropical sanitation by writing for the general reader accounts of the bearing of recent biological discoveries on the health and prosperity of tropical communities. His 'Mosquito or Man' (1909; 3rd edit. 1910), 'Health Progress and Administration in the West Indies' (1910; 2nd edit. 1910), and 'Yellow Fever and its Prevention' (1911) all influenced public opinion. The latest of his projects was the formation at Liverpool of a bureau of yellow fever. The first number of its bulletin was sent to press just before his death. He died of an apoplectic seizure on 16 June 1911, at Park Lodge, Croxteth Road, Liverpool, and was buried at Bebington cemetery, Wirral, Cheshire.

Boyce married in 1901 Kate Ethel, (*d.* 1902), daughter of William Johnston, a Liverpool shipowner, of Woodslee, Bromborough, Cheshire, and left issue one daughter.

The success of the Liverpool School of Tropical Medicine was the aim and reward of Boyce's later life. Besides the works mentioned, Boyce wrote many papers on pathology and tropical sanitation from 1892 onwards for the Royal Pathological and other scientific societies, and he was joint author with Dr. J. H. Abram of 'Handbook of Anatomical Pathology,' published in 1895.

[The Times, 19 June 1911; Proc. Royal Soc. obit. notices, 1911; private information.]

C. S. S.

BOYD, Sir THOMAS JAMIESON (1818–1902), lord provost of Edinburgh, born on 22 Feb. 1818, was son of John Boyd, merchant, of Edinburgh, by his wife Anne, daughter of Thomas Jamieson. At an early age he entered the publishing house of Oliver & Boyd, of which his uncle, George Boyd, was a partner; when he retired from business in 1898 he had been head of the firm for a quarter of a century. Long a prominent member of the Merchant Company of Edinburgh, he was elected master in 1869, and held the office twice subsequently. In this capacity he was chiefly responsible for the scheme by which the educational foundations of the corporation were reformed. The reforming scheme, which was described in a paper read by Boyd before the British Association in Edinburgh in 1871 and subsequently published, provided for the conversion of the buildings of the four hospitals (George Watson's, James Gillespie's, Daniel Stewart's, and the Merchant Maiden Hospital) into day schools; opened to competition presentations to the foundation; established bursaries and travelling scholarships, as well as industrial schools for neglected Edinburgh children; and endowed a chair in Edinburgh University to complete the commercial side of the education given in the Merchant schools. The scheme was approved by the government, and a provisional order was issued in July 1870, under the recent Scottish Educational Endowment Act, bringing it into operation. It worked efficiently and was taken as a model by the English endowed school commissioners. In recognition of his services a marble bust of Boyd, by William Brodie, R.S.A. [q. v.], was presented to his wife in July 1872, and a portrait by Otto Leyde, R.S.A., was placed in the Merchant Hall. Boyd was also instrumental in promoting another great Edinburgh institution, the building of the New Royal Infirmary on the west side of the Meadow Walk, the largest and best equipped hospital in Europe. He was chairman of the committee which raised for the purpose 320,000*l.*, a larger sum than had ever been subscribed in the city for a benevolent purpose. The foundation stone was laid by King

Edward VII, when Prince of Wales, in the autumn of 1870, and the buildings were formally opened on 29 Oct. 1879. Boyd's notable services were acknowledged by the presentation, at a public meeting on 11 Oct. 1880, of a marble bust by Brodie (now standing in the vestibule of the building opposite that of Provost Drummond, founder of the old infirmary of 1741), with an inscription by Sir Robert Christison.

Boyd was elected lord provost of Edinburgh in 1877, was re-elected in 1880, and held office till the end of 1882. During his provostship the new Edinburgh dock, Leith, was opened by the Duke of Edinburgh on 26 July 1881. In the following month, when Queen Victoria held a review of Scottish volunteers, Boyd, who was hon. colonel of the Queen's Edinburgh regiment, was knighted by her (25 Aug.). As a curator of Edinburgh University from 1879 to 1885, as a commissioner for northern lighthouses, 1877–82, a commissioner for Scottish Educational Endowments, 1882–9, and as chairman for ten years of the Scottish Fishery Board, he also did useful work. After relinquishing all other public duties, he continued to act as director of the Union Bank of Scotland and of the Scottish Provident Institution till within a few months of his death. Boyd was F.R.S. of Edinburgh and a D.L. and J.P. He died at 41 Moray Place, Edinburgh, on 22 Aug. 1902, and received a public funeral at the Dean cemetery. He married on 6 June 1844 Mary Ann, daughter of John Ferguson, surgeon, of Edinburgh. She died on 21 Feb. 1900, leaving two sons and six daughters.

[Foster's Baronetage and Knightage; Burke's Peerage; Who's Who, 1902; The Times, 23 Aug. 1902; Scotsman, 30 Oct. 1879, 12 Oct. 1880, 23 and 27 Aug. 1902; Educational Hospital Reform: the Scheme of the Edinburgh Merchant Company, 1871; James Grant's Old and New Edinburgh, iii. 288 seq.; Ill. Lond. News, 27 July 1872 (with reproduction of bust); Graphic, 10 Sept. 1881 (portrait).] G. Le G. N.

BOYLE, Sir COURTENAY EDMUND (1845–1901), permanent secretary of the board of trade, born on 21 Oct. 1845 in Jamaica, where his father was then stationed, was elder son of Captain Cavendish Spencer Boyle, 72nd regiment. His mother was Rose Susan, daughter of Col. C. C. Alexander, R.E. Vice-admiral Sir Courtenay Boyle (1770–1844) was his grandfather, and Edward Boyle, seventh earl of Cork, his great-grandfather. His younger brother is Sir Cavendish Boyle, K.C.M.G., at one time governor of Newfoundland and Mauritius. He was educated at Charterhouse, where he was at once a good classical scholar and captain of the cricket XI. A Latin speech which he made at school before leaving for Oxford attracted the notice of Thackeray, who was present on the occasion as an old Carthusian. Boyle gained in 1863 an open junior studentship at Christ Church, Oxford, which was supplemented by an exhibition from his school. Although well read in classics, with an extraordinary memory for quotation, he only took a second class in moderations in 1865 and a third class in lit. hum. in 1868 (B.A. and M.A., 1887). He cherished interests outside the schools. He played in the University cricket XI against Cambridge in 1865–7, proving himself 'a splendid field at point,' 'a pretty useful bat,' and 'an excellent wicket keeper' (Haygarth). He was also a fine racquet player, representing Oxford against Cambridge in tennis in 1866–7, and he held the silver racquet for tennis for some years. Soon after leaving Oxford, Lord Spencer, to whom he was related and who was viceroy of Ireland in Gladstone's first administration, 1868–1874, took him on his staff in Dublin, first as assistant private secretary and then as private secretary. After acting as assistant inspector of the English local government board from 1873, he was appointed in 1876 inspector for the eastern counties. In 1882, when Lord Spencer went back to Ireland as viceroy, Boyle, still holding his inspectorship, again became his private secretary, and was on the scene of the Phœnix Park murders almost immediately after they had taken place. In 1885 he received the C.B. and was made assistant secretary to the local government board. In the following year he was appointed by Mr. Mundella, then president of the board of trade, to be assistant secretary in charge of the railway department, which, under his superintendence, engaged in much important work. As the result of prolonged inquiry there was a complete revision of railway rates and tolls, and the Railway and Canal Traffic Act of 1888 and the Regulation of Railways Act of 1889 were passed. The regulation of electric lighting and traction also dates from this period and, advised by Lord Kelvin, Boyle was responsible officially for settling the standards of measurement in electricity and for preparing the requisite legislation. Another important matter with which he was concerned and in which he took great interest was the establishment of the National Physical

Laboratory. In 1892 he was made a K.C.B. and in 1893 he was promoted to be permanent secretary of the board of trade. That post he held till his sudden death at his London residence, 11 Granville Place, on 19 May 1901. While he was head of the board of trade the present commercial intelligence branch first came into existence; he was chairman of the inter-departmental committee which was appointed to consider the subject.

As an official Boyle was a very hard worker, coming to his office at abnormally early hours. He was clear and practical and a great believer in method, as is shown by his little books, 'Hints on the Conduct of Business, Public and Private' (1900) and 'Method and Organisation in Business' (1901). He made a very good chairman of a committee. His Irish descent may account for his versatility. He was not only a strong and capable official but a scholar with much aptitude for writing in prose and verse, a man of society with a great gift for after-dinner speaking, and a sportsman. He kept up his interest in cricket in later life, advocating cricket reform in 'The Times' under the pseudonym of 'An Old Blue.' Fishing was his favourite sport in later life, and when at the board of trade he worked hard for the improvement of the salmon fishing laws and was largely responsible for a royal commission on the subject. He edited in 1901 'Mary Boyle, her Book,' autobiographical sketches by an aunt. He married in 1876 Lady Muriel Campbell, daughter of the second earl of Cawdor, but left no children. He was buried at Hampton, Middlesex.

[The Times, 21 May 1901; Wisden's Cricketer's Almanack, 1902, p. lviii; Haygarth's Scores and Biographies, ix. 99; Ann. Reg. 1901, obituary; private information.]

C. P. L.

BOYLE, Sir EDWARD, first baronet (1848–1909), legal writer, born in London on 6 Sept. 1848, was elder son of Edward O'Boyle, civil engineer, of London, by his wife Eliza, daughter of James Gurney of Culloden, Norfolk. He was educated privately for the army, but finally became a surveyor, and was elected a fellow of the Surveyors' Institution in 1878. After some twenty years' practice of that profession, he forsook it for the bar, to which he was called at the Inner Temple on 17 Nov. 1887. He rapidly acquired a lucrative practice as an expert in rating and compensation cases, utilising the experience gained in his former profession, and took silk in 1898. Interesting himself in politics, he contested as a conservative Hastings in 1900 and Rye in 1903 unsuccessfully. He was created a baronet on 14 Dec. 1904. In the arbitration as to the purchase by the Straits Settlements government of the Tanjong Pagar Dock Company in 1905 Boyle acted as the arbitrator nominated by the company under the authority of a special ordinance (Straits Settlements Ordinance vii. of 1905, s. ii.). At the general election in Jan. 1906 he was returned M.P. for Taunton. Ill-health compelled his retirement from parliament in 1909. He travelled widely and was a F.R.G.S. He died at his London residence, 63 Queen's Gate, on 19 March 1909. Portraits by the Hon. John Collier and in the robes of a K.C. by Herbert Olivier are in the possession of his son, who presented a replica of the latter picture to the Surveyors' Institution.

Boyle married on 18 March 1874 Constance Jane, younger daughter of William Knight, J.P., of Kensington Park Gardens, senior partner of Knight & Sons, soap manufacturers, of Silvertown, E., and had issue a son, Edward (*b.* 12 June 1878), who succeeded him in the baronetcy, and a daughter.

Boyle was joint author of three important legal treatises: 1. 'Principles of Rating,' with G. Humphreys Davies, 1900; 2nd edit. 1905. 2. 'Railway and Canal Traffic,' with Thomas Waghorn (*d.* 1 Dec. 1911), 3 vols. 1901. 3. 'The Law and Practice of Compensation,' with Thomas Waghorn, 1903.

[The Times, 20 March 1909; Burke's Peerage, 1909; Law List, 1908; Dod's Parliamentary Companion, 1907; private information.]

C. E. A. B.

BOYLE, GEORGE DAVID (1828–1901), dean of Salisbury, born at Edinburgh, on 17 May 1828, was eldest child of David Boyle, Lord Boyle [q. v.], Scottish judge, by his second wife, Camilla Catherine, eldest daughter of David Smythe of Methven, Lord Methven. As 'a small, shy child' he saw Sir Walter Scott in his father's study (*Recollections*, p. 2). Educated first at Edinburgh Academy and by a private tutor, he went in 1843 to Charterhouse. In June 1846 he matriculated at Exeter College, Oxford, went into residence in April 1847, and graduated B.A. in 1851, M.A. in 1853. In London, as at Edinburgh, family connections brought him, while a schoolboy, the acquaintance of persons of literary distinction and he developed a precocious interest in the Oxford movement; but the influence of John Campbell Shairp [q. v.], whom he met first in 1838, and who became a lifelong friend, preserved him from partisanship (cf. his recollections of Shairp in *Principal Shairp and his Friends*, 1888). Ordained deacon in 1853 and priest in 1854, Boyle was from 1853 till 1857 curate of Kidderminster under Thomas Legh Claughton [q. v. Suppl. I], and from 1857 to 1860 of Hagley. In 1860 he 'had three offers of new work at once' and he chose the incumbency of St. Michael's, Handsworth, Birmingham (*Recollections*, p. 203). He entered into the public life of Birmingham, especially on its educational side, was a governor of King Edward VI's school, and numbered amongst his friends men differing as widely as John Henry Newman, George Dawson, and Robert William Dale. In 1867 Boyle became vicar of Kidderminster, where he won universal confidence. He was chairman of the first school board for Kidderminster, acted as arbitrator in an industrial dispute, promoted the building of an infirmary, and greatly developed the church schools.

In 1880 Boyle was appointed dean of Salisbury. A sum of 14,000*l*. was spent on the cathedral under his direction. His love of literature and his acquaintance with men of affairs continued to widen his interests (cf. GRANT-DUFF, *Notes from a Diary*, 1886–8, i. 119–21). On ecclesiastical controversy, in which he took no active part, he exercised a moderating influence. He died suddenly of heart failure at Salisbury on 21 March 1901. He married, in 1861, Mary Christiana, daughter of William Robins of Hagley, and left no issue. A mural tablet and a window to his memory are in Salisbury Cathedral, and a portrait in oils in the Church House, Salisbury.

Boyle edited with notes 'Characters and Episodes of the Great Rebellion, selected from the History and Autobiography of Edward Earl of Clarendon' (1889), and also published a small volume on 'Salisbury Cathedral' (1897). In his 'Recollections' (1895, with portrait) he gives a full account of his intercourse with men of letters and affairs.

[Boyle's Recollections, 1895; The Times, 22 March 1901; Guardian, 27 March 1901, 12 Nov. 1902; Foster's Alumni Oxon.; private information.] A. R. B.

BOYLE, RICHARD VICARS (1822–1908), civil engineer, born in Dublin on 14 March 1822, was third son of Vicars Armstrong Boyle of that city, a descendant of a branch of the Boyles of Kelburn, Ayrshire, who had migrated to the north of Ireland in the seventeenth century. His mother was Sophia, eldest daughter of David Courtney of Dublin. After education at a private school and two years' service on the trigonometrical survey of Ireland he became a pupil to Charles Blacker Vignoles [q. v.]. On the expiration of his articles he was engaged on railway construction in Ireland, at first as assistant to William Dargan [q. v.], who employed him on the Belfast and Armagh and Dublin and Drogheda railways. In 1845, under Sir John Benjamin Macneill [q. v.], he surveyed and laid out part of the Great Southern and Western railway, and in 1846–7 was chief engineer for the Longford and Sligo railway. In the autumn of 1852 he laid out railways and waterworks in Spain as chief assistant to George Willoughby Hemans (son of the poetess).

In 1853 he was appointed a district engineer on the East Indian railway. At first he was stationed at Patna, and was thence transferred to Arrah (Shahabad). At the outbreak of the Indian mutiny, Boyle honourably distinguished himself. When, towards the end of July 1857, the native troops in the cantonments at Dinapore, about twenty-five miles from Arrah, mutinied and deserted, Boyle fortified a detached two-story house fifty feet square standing in the same compound as his own private residence, and provisioned it to withstand a siege. Here on Sunday, 26 July, sixteen Europeans and about forty Sikhs took refuge, and the following morning the mutineers, having crossed the river Son and taken possession of Arrah, besieged the little garrison. But, thanks to the courage and fidelity of the Sikhs, the inmates defended the house successfully against about 3000 men until sunset on 2 August, when the approach of the relieving force, under Major (Sir) Vincent Eyre [q. v.], from Buxar drew off the rebels and left the besieged free. Boyle was thereupon appointed field-officer to Eyre's force, and was engaged in restoring broken communications and bridges. A few days later he was disabled by a kick from a horse. When somewhat recovered he was summoned to Calcutta, and travelling down the Ganges in the steamer River Bird was wrecked on the Sunderbunds. After a sea-trip to Penang and Singapore to recruit his health, he returned to Arrah early in 1858. For his services Boyle received the mutiny medal and a grant of land near Arrah. In 1868, after leaving the East Indian railway company, he became a first-class executive engineer in the Indian public works department, but was soon recalled to England by private affairs. He was made C.S.I. in

1869. From 1872 to 1877 he was in Japan as engineer-in-chief for the imperial Japanese railways. With English assistants he laid out an extensive system of railways in Japan and left about seventy miles of completed line in full working order.

To the Institution of Civil Engineers, of which he became an associate on 10 Jan. 1854 and member on 14 Feb. 1860, he presented in 1882 a paper on the Rokugo river bridge, Japan (*Proc. Inst. C.E.* lxviii. 216). He joined the Institution of Electrical Engineers in 1874. On retiring in 1877 from professional work he spent much time in travelling. He died at 3 Stanhope Terrace, Hyde Park, on 3 Jan. 1908, and was buried at Kensal Green. He married in 1853 Eleonore Anne, daughter of W. Hack of Dieppe, and had issue one son who died in infancy.

[Min. Proc. Inst. Civ. Eng. clxxiv.; Biographer, May 1898; C. Ball, History of the Indian Mutiny, ii.; G. B. Malleson's Recreations of an Indian Official, 1892.]

W. F. S.

BRABAZON, HERCULES BRABAZON (1821–1906), painter, born in Paris on 27 Nov. 1821, was younger son of Hercules Sharpe, of Blackhalls, Durham, and of Oaklands, Battle, Sussex. His mother was Ann, daughter of Sir Anthony Brabazon, first baronet, of New Park, co. Mayo; Sir Capel Molyneux, fourth baronet, was her uncle. His childhood was passed at Domons, Northiam, and he was educated first at Dr. Hooker's private school. From 1835 to 1837 he was at Harrow, and after pursuing his education abroad, mostly at Geneva, proceeded in 1840 to Trinity College, Cambridge, where he graduated B.A. in 1844 and M.A. in 1848. In 1847 he succeeded his elder brother, William, in the Brabazon estates, Ballinasloe, co. Galway and Roscommon, and Brabazon Park, co. Mayo, and, under the will of his mother's brother, Sir William John Brabazon, second baronet (*d.* 24 Oct. 1840), took the surname of Brabazon. On the death of his father in 1858 he inherited the Sussex property at Oaklands.

From 1844 to 1847 Brabazon studied art in Rome. At a later period he received some lessons in painting from J. H. D'Egville and from Alfred Fripp, to whom he attributed much of his facility in handling colour. His chief training, however, was acquired from his practice of copying water-colours by the earlier masters of the British school and from the habit, continued throughout his life, of making rapid colour notes, transcripts into his own language rather than copies, of his favourite paintings in public and private collections by Velasquez, Turner, Rembrandt, Hals, Guardi, Tintoretto, Watteau, Delacroix, and other artists. His earlier and careful sketches from nature show the influence of Cox, De Wint, and Muller, and sometimes of Ruskin, with whom he travelled and painted in France; but as he gained in confidence and colour sense, he worked more and more in the manner of Turner's later sketches, making a free use of body colour. He was a keen traveller, and from frequent tours in Italy, France, Spain, Switzerland, Egypt, and from a visit to India in 1876, brought back stores of sketches in which he aimed always at freshness of impression, handling his colour with directness and with an entire avoidance of elaboration.

Brabazon always set a high value on his own work, but it was not till he reached the age of seventy that he was induced to exhibit or sell his drawings. In November 1891 he was elected a member of the New English Art Club, and from that year till his death was a constant exhibitor. His work appeared also at the exhibitions of the Pastel Society and the International Society. In December 1892 he yielded to Mr. J. S. Sargent's persuasion, and held an exhibition of his paintings at the Goupil Gallery. In a prefatory note to the catalogue Mr. Sargent said 'The gift of colour, together with an exquisite sensitiveness to impressions of Nature, has here been the constant incentive, and the immunity from "picture making" has gone far to keep perception delicate and execution convincing.'

Brabazon was also an ardent pianist, with a rare facility for reading and rendering the most difficult music at sight. In his village of Sedlescombe (to the north of Hastings) he was a model landlord, and to his friends in private life was unfailing in deeds of kindness and goodwill. During his last two years he was confined to his rooms at Oaklands, where he died, unmarried, on 14 May 1906. He was buried in Sedlescombe churchyard. Examples of his water-colours are in the Tate Gallery, the British Museum, the public galleries at Dublin and Edinburgh, and the Metropolitan Museum, New York. Memorial exhibitions of his work were held at the Goupil Gallery in November 1906 and at the Hastings Museum in February 1907, the latter exhibition being under the auspices of the Hastings and St. Leonards Museum Association, of which

Brabazon was an active vice-president for fifteen years.

Brabazon's folios, containing over two thousand drawings, were bequeathed to his niece, Mrs. Harvey Brabazon Combe, who has converted an old tithebarn at Sedlescombe into a Brabazon Gallery open daily to the public. An oil portrait of Brabazon and a charcoal sketch of his head, both by Mr. J. S. Sargent, R.A., are in the possession of Mr. Harvey Combe.

[Goupil Gall. Exhib. Cat. (with prefatory note by J. S. Sargent, R.A.), 1892; Goupil Gall. Memorial Exhib. (with an essay by F. Wedmore), 1906; biographical notice in Cat. of Nat. Gall. of Brit. Art; The Studio, xxxv. 95, 1905; Art Journal, 1906, pp. 58, 209; Sussex Daily News (memorial notice by Lord Brassey), 1 June 1906; Whitechapel Art Gall. Exhib. Cat. 1908; Notes on the Life of H. B. Brabazon, by Mrs. H. B. Combe (Handbook to the Brabazon Gallery, Sedlescombe); Hastings and St. Leonards Observer, 22 April 1911 (Lecture on Brabazon to the East Sussex Art Club, by T. Parkin); private information from Mrs. Harvey Combe and from Mr. C. Lewis Hind, author of a volume on Brabazon to be published in 1912.]

M. H.

BRADDON, Sir EDWARD NICHOLAS COVENTRY (1829–1904), premier of Tasmania, born at Skisdone Lodge, Cornwall, on 11 June 1829, was third and only surviving son of Henry Braddon, solicitor, of an old Cornish family, by his wife Fanny, daughter of Patrick White of Limerick. Miss Braddon, the novelist, is his younger sister. Educated at a private school at Greenwich and at University College, London, he joined in 1847 the mercantile firm of Bagshaw & Co., his cousins, in Calcutta; but left them in 1854 for employment as an assistant on the government railways. It was the employés of the railway at Pir Pointi who met the first shock of the Sonthal rising in July 1855. Braddon's cousin, an assistant engineer, was killed, and he successfully brought the insurgents to justice. His vigorous action attracted attention, and on 19 Oct. 1857 he was appointed an assistant commissioner for Deoghur in the Sonthal district. He was, however, actually sent to Purneah to act against the mutineers, and raised a regiment of Sonthals with which he served under Sir George Adney Yule through the Indian Mutiny, receiving the mutiny medal and favourable mention in despatches.

On 1 May 1862 Braddon became superintendent of excise and stamps in Oudh, and subsequently superintendent of trade statistics (1868). He was appointed in 1868 to inquire into the operation of the salt tax in Oudh and the North-west Provinces; from Oct. 1869 to 30 June 1871 he combined with his substantive duties those of personal assistant to the financial commissioner. On 1 July 1871 he was made inspector-general of registration. In March 1875 he was the delegate for Oudh to the trade conference at Allahabad. Two years later the decision of the Indian government to abolish his appointment came as a great blow to him, and as no other employment was offered him he retired on a pension in 1878, and went to live in Tasmania.

Here in 1879 Braddon entered the House of Assembly as member for West Devon, and made his mark as a stalwart free-trader in opposition to the ministries of (Sir) Adye Douglas [q.v. Suppl. II] and (Sir) James Willson Agnew [q.v. Suppl. II] during 1885 and 1886. On 30 March 1887 he joined an administration in which Philip Oakley Fysh became premier while he led the assembly as minister of lands and works and also of education. In January 1888 he represented Tasmania at the federal council held at Hobart. On 29 Oct. 1888 he resigned office to become agent-general for the colony in London. In 1891 he was made K.C.M.G.

Braddon was recalled to Tasmania in 1893, and on 19 Dec., having re-entered the assembly as member for West Devon, turned out the government which had recalled him. On 14 April 1894 he became premier, and in this capacity in 1897 he represented Tasmania at Queen Victoria's Diamond Jubilee and was made a privy councillor. In that year he also received the hon. degree of LL.D. at Cambridge. In 1898, at the federal conference at Sydney, he carried a clause in the constitution bill which became known as the 'Braddon blot.' His term of office, during the latter part of which he was treasurer as well as premier, came to an end on 12 Oct. 1899.

In 1901 Braddon was elected by a large majority senior member for Tasmania in the first parliament of the Commonwealth of Australia, and on 16 Dec. 1903 he was elected to the second parliament in the interest of free trade. He died on 2 Feb. 1904 at his residence, Treglith, Leith, where he was buried privately, though a state funeral was offered. He twice married: first, on 24 Oct. 1857, Amy Georgina, daughter of William Palmer of Purneah (she died in 1864, leaving six children); secondly, on 16 Oct. 1876, Alice Harriet, daughter of John H. Smith, by whom he had one daughter.

Braddon was an enthusiastic sportsman. He was hardly popular; his bluff manner of speech was too often touched with sarcasm. He was author of 'Life in India' (1872) and 'Thirty Years of Shikar' (1895).

[Buckland's Indian Biog., s.v.; The Times, 3 Feb. 1904; Mennell's Dict. of Australasian Biog.; Tasmanian Mail, 6 Feb. 1904, p. 32; Who's Who, 1903; Burke's Colonial Gentry, i. 331; India Office Records; for appreciation of his work see Austral. Commonw. Parly. Debates, 1904, xviii. 14; private information.]
C. A. H.

BRADFORD, SIR EDWARD RIDLEY COLBORNE, first baronet (1836–1911), Anglo-Indian administrator and commissioner of the metropolitan police, London, born on 27 July 1836 at Hambleden Cottage, Buckinghamshire, was second son (in a family of three sons and five daughters) of William Mussage Kirkwall Bradford (1806–1872), who was rector successively of Rotherfield Greys, Oxfordshire, Weeke, Hampshire, and finally from 1844 of West Meon, Hampshire. His mother, Mary (1810–1894), was elder daughter of Henry Colborne Ridley, rector of Hambleden, who was younger brother of Sir Matthew White Ridley, third baronet. His eldest brother, Henry William (1835–1907), was a bencher of the Middle Temple and a county councillor for Westminster. Edward attended a private school at Henley on Thames, and at the age of ten joined his eldest brother at Marlborough; but a dangerous illness cut short his career there, and after studying with a tutor at Blackheath he accepted a cadetship in the service of the East India Company from one of the directors, Butterworth Bayley. He sailed for India on 13 Nov. 1853 and joined the 2nd Madras light cavalry at Jalna. For the next ten years he gave abundant promise of a brilliant military career, winning the confidence of his men by his peculiar charm of manner and being distinguished for his horsemanship and quick perception of character. In 1855 he became lieutenant and joined the 6th Madras cavalry at Mhow. Throughout his service in Central India it was said of him that 'the good sowars (troopers) loved him, while the bad instinctively feared him.'

On the outbreak of the war with Persia General John Jacob [q. v.] selected him for the duty of organising a corps of irregular cavalry in Persia. But the project was abandoned, and Bradford was attached to a troop of 14th light dragoons, serving at the capture of Muhammara, and receiving the medal and the clasp. The progress of the mutiny hastened his return to India, where he was soon engaged in three fields of operations, near Jabalpur, in the Sagar and Nerbudda districts, and in the pursuit of Tantia Topi. The mutiny of the 52nd Bengal native infantry on 18 Sept. 1857 and the rebellion of local chiefs led to frequent skirmishes, in which Bradford, as adjutant of the left wing 6th Madras cavalry, took part. More serious operations followed after his transfer to the famous corps of irregular cavalry, Mayne's horse, of which he became adjutant, and on 25 Oct. 1858 second in command. He was engaged on 19 October in the brilliant charge of seventy sabres on the rear of Tantia Topi's force, as they retired from Sindwah before General Sir John Michel [q. v.]. He was again to the front on 25 October at Korai, where, after covering sixty-four miles of difficult country in sixty hours, the British cavalry separated one wing of Tantia's force from the other and cut it to pieces. He was specially mentioned in despatches for 'his great influence over the native soldiery, his excellent tact and judgment,' and Lord Canning commended his 'spirit and gallantry.' He won fresh laurels at Rajgarh, having acted as commandant of 1st regiment Mayne's horse as well as political agent at Goona in 1859. Captain Mayne (8 June 1860) recommended him to the special notice of government for his constant 'gallantry, discretion and energy.' Broken down by the strain of these operations, Bradford was ordered home in September 1860, and on his return to duty he was appointed political assistant in West Malwa in addition to his military duties.

On 10 May 1863 Bradford suffered a calamity which changed the course of his career. He joined a party of officers from Goona on a shooting expedition. After eighteen tigers were killed without casualty Bradford and Captain Curtis, Inniskilling dragoons, having exhausted their leave, left for Agar. On their way near Dilanpur they heard of a tiger, and they and a trooper went in pursuit. The tiger, twice wounded, charged Bradford, whose second gun failed to fire. Bradford dropped into an adjoining pool, whence the tiger dragged and played with him 'just as a cat does with a mouse, occasionally taking his arm in its mouth and giving him a crunch.' A change of position enabled Bradford's companion Curtis to fire without risk to his friend, and the tiger, driven off, was despatched by the trooper. Then followed a painful journey to Agar, and at a point thirty-five miles from the station Dr. Beaumont amputated the arm without chloroform. The patient's quiet courage saved his life. As soon as Bradford's health was restored, he gradually resumed his former pursuits, hunting, shooting, and even spearing boars with his reins held between his teeth. He met in after life with frequent falls, yet his nerve never deserted him up to his death.

Returning to duty, he filled various political offices, where his magnetic influence attracted to him the ruling chiefs and nobles of the native states under his supervision. After serving as political agent in Jaipur, Baghelkand, Bhartpur, and Meywar he was selected by the viceroy, Lord Northbrook, to be general superintendent of thagi and dakaiti (8 May 1874), an office which controlled cases of sedition as well as organised crime, and called for much tact in his relations with the various local governments and the ruling chiefs responsible for crime within their several jurisdictions. The viceroy, Lord Lytton, promoted him on 8 March 1878 to the supreme control of relations with the Rajput chiefs and the office of chief commissioner of Ajmir. There he smoothed over difficulties with the native states in the early days of railway construction, encouraged social reforms, and introduced municipal government into Ajmir. His influence with Indians was so well recognised, that he was attached to the staff of the duke of Edinburgh on his visit to India in 1870, to that of Edward VII when Prince of Wales on his visit in 1875, while in 1889 he accompanied Prince Albert Victor on his Indian tour. In June 1885 he was made K.C.S.I., and two years later was on the point of becoming resident at Hyderabad, when Lord Cross summoned him to the India office, London, as secretary in the political and secret departments. He refused the offer, 14 Feb. 1889, of the post of governor and high commissioner at the Cape, and was thus available when, later on, a grave crisis in London demanded the appointment of a commissioner of police endowed with sympathy and high moral courage. In June 1890 symptoms of disaffection in the ranks of the metropolitan police force were aggravated by the public announcement of grave differences between the commissioner, Mr. Monro, and the home secretary, Mr. Matthews, regarding police administration and in particular the rules of superannuation. After Monro's resignation thirty-nine men refused to go on duty (5 July), and a general strike of the men threatened unless their pay was increased and other concessions granted. Bradford had accepted the vacant office with hesitation on 20 June 1890. But he now acted with vigour, dismissing the thirty-nine men for insubordination, and sternly enforcing discipline; then he devoted himself to remedial measures. He visited every one of his police stations, which extended fifteen miles on every side from Hyde Park Corner, and listened to all complaints. He paid the greatest attention to recruitment and the physical and moral welfare of his men. Labour was economised by a judicious increase of stations, signal boxes, and fixed points for concentration. In their sports and recreations he took a constant interest, knowing his subordinates and being known and trusted by them. The term of his office included the diamond jubilee and the funeral of Queen Victoria, the coronation of King Edward VII, the wild excitement over the relief of Ladysmith and Mafeking, and several disorderly meetings and processions of the unemployed. When he retired on 4 March 1903, he left a contented force of 14,470 effective men, excluding those on special duty at dockyards, maintaining law and order over a population of 6,700,000 souls. He was made A.D.C. to the Queen in 1889, G.C.B. on 22 June 1897, G.C.V.O. on 9 Nov. 1902, a baronet on 24 July 1902, extra equerry to King Edward VII in 1903, and to King George V in 1910.

After his retirement from the public service he acted as chairman of a committee to inquire into the wages of postal servants, but his chief interest lay in hunting and shooting. He hunted several days a week with the Bicester, Warwickshire, Heythrop, and Whaddon chase hounds. He died suddenly in London on 13 May 1911, and was buried in the churchyard at Chawton, Hampshire, beside his first wife. Eight police sergeants bore him to the grave. Bradford was married twice: (1) on 17 June 1866 to Elizabeth, third daughter of Edward Knight of Chawton House, Hampshire, a nephew of Jane Austen; by her (*d.* 21 May 1896) he had six children, of whom three died in India; and (2) on 25 Oct. 1898 to Edith Mary, daughter of William Nicholson of Basing Park, Hampshire, formerly high sheriff of the county and M.P. for Petersfield. She survived him with a daughter and two sons of the first marriage. His eldest surviving son, Major Evelyn Ridley Bradford, who served with distinction in the Egyptian and South African wars, succeeded him in the baronetcy. A portrait of Sir Edward, subscribed for by friends and painted by W. W. Ouless, R.A., hangs in the Mayo

College at Ajmir, while another, painted by M. Benjamin Constant in 1901, is in the possession of the family. A drawing by H. T. Wells, R.A. (1900), belongs to Grillion's Club.

[The Times, 15 May 1911; Strand Mag. (portraits), Feb. 1896; Visitation of England and Wales, vol. 16, by F. Arthur Crisp; Kaye and Malleson's History of the Indian Mutiny, 1888; Sir Evelyn Wood, From Midshipman to Field-Marshal, 1906; official reports.]

W. L-W.

BRADLEY, GEORGE GRANVILLE (1821–1903), dean of Westminster and schoolmaster, born at High Wycombe on 11 Dec. 1821, was fourth son of Charles Bradley [q. v.]. In 1829 the family moved to Clapham, Surrey, where in 1834 Bradley became a pupil at the grammar school under Charles Pritchard [q. v.]. In August 1837 he was admitted to Rugby under Arnold and placed in the upper fifth form. On 20 March 1840 he was admitted a scholar of University College, Oxford, where his tutors were (Sir) Travers Twiss [q. v.] and Piers Calverley Claughton [q. v. Suppl. I], but he was more influenced by a younger fellow, Arthur Penrhyn Stanley [q. v.]. In 1844 he was one of four in the first class in classics and in October was elected fellow of his college. In 1845 he won the Latin essay prize. He did not reside on his fellowship but went as a master to Rugby under Archibald Campbell Tait [q. v.]. There he soon won renown both as a teacher and as a housemaster. When in 1849 Edward Meyrick Goulburn [q. v. Suppl. I] succeeded Tait there was trouble at Rugby, and Bradley, in conjunction with his colleague, T. S. Evans, saved the school from disaster. On 18 Dec. 1849 he married Marian, fourth daughter of Benjamin Philpot, vicar general and archdeacon of Sodor and Man.

In 1858 the headmastership of Marlborough was vacated by George Edward Lynch Cotton [q. v.], who till 1852 had been one of Bradley's colleagues at Rugby, and by Cotton's desire Bradley succeeded him. He took orders on his appointment. He had no easy post. Though Cotton had begun to relieve the school of its money troubles, and introduced a public-school spirit, there was still a heavy debt, and memories of disorder were not extinct. By good management, by raising the fees, and by increasing the numbers, Bradley not only removed the debt but was able to add greatly to the school buildings. Disorder he quelled by 'inspired invective' (S. H. BUTCHER), and though the sixth form, accustomed to Cotton's gravity, was at first 'inclined to disparage the little man who had succeeded the tall and dignified head, they soon found out their mistake, and were all roused and stimulated as they had never been before by contact with an active, vigorous mind and extraordinary power of teaching' [T. L. PAPILLON]. When in 1859 both the Balliol scholarships went to Marlburians, T. L. Papillon and C. P. Ilbert, Bradley's success was established. He kept most of the teaching of the sixth form in his own hands, and was especially successful in teaching Latin prose, while he widened the old curriculum by reading with his boys Butler's 'Analogy' and modern historical works. The general teaching he supervised by a monthly 'review' of each form; in presence of the master he took the boys through some of the work which they had been doing, and spared neither boy nor master. At the same time by the gentler side of his nature he made the boys his friends. To both sides Tennyson bore witness by sending his son Hallam 'not to Marlborough but to Bradley.' Bradley had first met Tennyson in 1841, when they were both on a visit to Edmund L. Lushington [q. v. Suppl. I] at Park House near Maidstone, and when in 1860 Bradley took a house near Farringford, Tennyson's residence in the Isle of Wight, the acquaintance was renewed and soon ripened into the closest friendship. At this time Marlborough won more scholarships at Oxford than any other school, Rugby alone coming at all near it. The fame of Marlborough crossed the Channel, and when in 1866 the French government sent Demogeot to study the English public-school system, he had instructions to visit Marlborough, and was warmly welcomed by Bradley.

Among Bradley's earlier buildings had been a sanatorium. The increase in numbers now made it necessary to build afresh. Instead of adding to the hostel Bradley chose to create houses and thereby modify the Spartan simplicity of the first foundation. The school had been liable to epidemics, due in part to overcrowding, and the change greatly improved both its health and its general well-being.

In 1870 Bradley left Marlborough for Oxford, succeeding as Master of University college Frederick C. Plumptre, a head of the old school with a modified interest in learning. The college had never lacked men of ability among its scholars, but most of the commoners were passmen with the reputation of a 'rackety mirth-loving' set. Bradley was determined to raise the standard of industry and insisted that every commoner should read for an honour school. Some consequent unpopularity was increased by an edict banishing dogs from the college, but he had his way, and he strengthened his position by bringing back James Franck Bright from Marlborough as tutor in history, and importing from Cambridge his old Marlborough pupil, Samuel Henry Butcher [q. v. Suppl. II], as a tutor in classics. Moreover, contrary to the practice of heads of houses, he took an active part in the teaching. His lectures on Sophocles, Cicero, and Latin prose attracted many undergraduates from other colleges. Entrance to his own college became competitive, and of the commoners of this period four have since been cabinet ministers and many distinguished in other lines. In 1880 Bradley was nominated in succession to Lord Selborne a member of the University Commission, and his services were rewarded by a canonry of Worcester. In 1881 the death of his old friend Stanley vacated the deanery of Westminster, and Bradley was chosen by Gladstone to take his place.

Once more Bradley found himself in a difficult situation. Stanley was no man of business, and his devotion to the abbey church had not extended to the care of the masonry. There was 'a ruinous fabric and a bankrupt chapter.' After long negotiations and much opposition Bradley induced the government to act. The ecclesiastical commissioners were empowered to provide a sum for immediate repairs and an income for the future, but one so small that it had to be supplemented by the proceeds of a suppressed canonry. Thus the building was saved. In 1889, at Bradley's instigation, a parliamentary commission was appointed to consider the question of space for future monuments and interments. As a substitute for interments Bradley extended the system of memorial services. The chief actual burials in his time were those of Darwin, Browning, Tennyson and Gladstone. The chief ceremonials were the jubilee service of Queen Victoria on 21 June 1887 and the coronation of Edward VII on 9 Aug. 1902. After Stanley's example Bradley used to take parties of working men round the abbey weekly in spring and summer. In the proceedings of convocation he took some part, and though he left the liberal party on the home rule question, his ecclesiastical liberalism was never shaken. After the coronation he resigned the deanery on 29 September 1902, and retired to Queen Anne's Gate, where he died on 13 March 1903. He was buried in the south aisle of the nave of the abbey by the grave of Atterbury.

Bradley, whose wife survived him till 27 Nov. 1910, had two sons and five daughters. The elder son, Arthur Granville, is known as an author of historical and topographical works, the second daughter, Mrs. Margaret L. Woods, as a poet and novelist, and the fourth, Mrs. Alexander Murray Smith, as an historian of Westminster Abbey. There are portraits of him at Rugby by Lowes Dickinson, at Marlborough by W. W. Ouless, and at the deanery of Westminster by Reginald Higgins (posthumous).

Bradley published several sermons and some schoolbooks, one of which, 'A Practical Introduction to Latin Prose Composition' (1881; new impression 1910) is still in great demand. He also wrote: 1. 'Recollections of Arthur Penrhyn Stanley,' three lectures delivered in 1882 at Edinburgh, 1883. 2. 'Lectures on Ecclesiastes,' 1885. 3. 'Lectures on the Book of Job,' 1887. He co-operated in writing R. E. Prothero's 'Life and Correspondence of Dean Stanley,' 2 vols. 1883.

[History of Marlborough College, by A. G. Bradley and others, 1893, pp. 156 seq.; The Times, 13, 16 March 1903; Fortnightly Review, July 1903 (S. H. Butcher); Life of Tennyson, 1897, i. 204–207, 467–469; ii. 35–57, 273–274; F. D. How's Six Great Schoolmasters, 1904, pp. 226–269; Tennyson and his Friends, ed. by Lord Tennyson, 1911; private information; personal knowledge.] J. S.

BRAMPTON, Baron. [See Hawkins, Sir Henry, 1817–1907.]

BRAMWELL, Sir FREDERICK JOSEPH (1818–1903), engineer, born on 7 March 1818 in Finch Lane, Cornhill, was younger son of George Bramwell, a partner in the firm of Dorrien & Co., bankers, of Finch Lane, afterwards amalgamated with Glyn, Mills, Currie & Co. His mother was Elizabeth Frith. His elder brother, George, Lord Bramwell [q. v. Suppl. I], attained eminence at the bar and on the bench. After attending the Palace School, Enfield, Frederick was apprenticed in 1834 to John Hague, a mechanical engineer, whose works in Cable Street, Wellclose Square, were afterwards bought up by the Blackwall Rope railway. Hague invented a system for propelling railway trains by means of atmospheric pressure, which was adopted with some success on a short railway in Devonshire. Bramwell, impressed by the contrivance, joined about 1845 another of Hague's pupils, Samuel Collett Homersham (afterwards a surveyor), in projecting a scheme for an atmospheric railway in a low-level tunnel from the Bank viâ Charing Cross to Hyde Park Corner. The details of the scheme (including hydraulic lifts to raise the passengers) were worked out, but nothing came of it (cf. a paper by Bramwell before the Institution of Mechanical Engineers at Plymouth in 1899, reprinted in *Engineering*, lxviii. 246–280). Equally abortive was a more modest proposal to construct an experimental atmospheric railway from Waterloo station over Hungerford suspension bridge to Hungerford Market. In Hague's engineering works Bramwell also studied methods of steam propulsion on common roads, and while still an apprentice came to know Walter Hancock [q. v.], who first constructed a successful road locomotive. In later life Bramwell was sole survivor of those associated with the first experiments in steam-carriages, which the development of railroads killed. A paper which he read before the British Association in 1894 (reprinted in *Engineering*, lviii. 222) on 'Steam Locomotion on Common Roads' is a valuable contemporary record of this phase of the history of locomotion.

At the expiration of his indentures Bramwell became chief draughtsman and afterwards manager in Hague's office. Under his supervision in 1843 a locomotive of 10 tons weight was constructed for the Stockton and Darlington railway. The engine was taken to Middlesbrough by sea, and Bramwell drove it between Stockton and Darlington. On leaving Hague's employ he became manager of an engineering factory in the Isle of Dogs, and was connected with the Fairfield railway works, Bow, then under the management of William Bridges Adams [q. v.].

In 1853 Bramwell set up in business on his own account, and sharing some of his brother's aptitude for advocacy, soon left the constructive side of his profession almost exclusively for the legal and consultative side. He early showed great facility of exposition and a gift for describing complicated mechanical details in clear and simple language. A quick intelligence, a power of rapidly assimilating information, a ready wit, and a handsome presence, to which in after years age lent dignity, rendered him an invaluable witness in scientific and especially in patent cases. Yet it was not till he was over forty that he made 400*l*. in any one year. In 1860 he took with hesitation an office at No. 35A Great George Street. Thenceforth his practice as a consultant rapidly increased, and within ten years his income grew very large.

Bramwell was perhaps the first to practise regularly as a scientific witness or technical advocate, and the legal cast of his mind and his alertness of wit made him the ablest and most skilful scientific witness of his time. His information was always sound and in accord with the best scientific knowledge of the day, although he did not profess that it was unbiassed. A keen mechanical instinct enabled him to contrive ingenious models for the illustration of his evidence. In parliamentary committee-rooms, where he dealt almost entirely with questions of civil engineering, Bramwell soon gained as great a reputation as in the law courts. His authority on questions relating to municipal and water-works engineering especially became so high that he was permanently retained by all the eight water companies of London. In his later life he was chiefly in request as an arbitrator, where his forensic capacity and judicial temper found full scope. Although he was not responsible for any important engineering works, he as chairman of both the East Surrey Water Company from 1882 until his death and of the Kensington and Knightsbridge Electric Lighting Company supervised the construction of much of the two companies' works. Among the few constructive undertakings which may be put to his credit was the designing and execution of a sewage disposal scheme for Portsmouth, which had certain original features from the low levels of parts of the district.

Bramwell, whose only relaxation was in variety of work, was indefatigable in honorary service to the various societies and institutions of which he was a member. Here he showed to advantage his exceptional gifts of speech and his powers of historical survey. He joined the Institution of Mechanical Engineers in 1854, was elected to the council in 1864, and became president in 1874, when he reviewed the history and progress of mechanical engineering. To the interests of the Institution of Civil Engineers, which was 'born in the year' of his own birth, and which he joined in 1856, being elected to the council in 1867 and becoming president in 1884, he was especially devoted; his presidential address in 1885 summarised the course of invention since 1862. He was a vice-president of the Institution of Naval Architects, and served many years on its council. He became a member of the British Association in 1865 and he regularly attended the annual meetings for many years. He was president of section 'G' (mechanical science, afterwards engineering) in 1872 at Brighton, and again in 1884, when the association met at Montreal. In 1888 he was elected president of the Association at the Bath meeting, and in his address brilliantly vindicated the claims of applied science and technology. He was always a leading spirit at the convivial 'Red Lion' dinner, with which the more serious labours of the association were lightened. In 1874 he joined the Society of Arts, and for twenty-eight years he served continuously on its council, of which he was chairman in 1881 and 1882, giving an address on the first occasion on the industrial applications of science, and on the second occasion on the law of patents. He was president in the interval between King Edward VII's resignation of the office on his accession in 1901 and the election of the Prince of Wales (King George V). In 1885 he became honorary secretary of the Royal Institution, and held the office till 1900, discharging its duties with the utmost regularity.

Bramwell was a liveryman of the Goldsmiths' Company, having being apprenticed to his father 'to learn his art of a banker.' He was prime warden of the company 1877–8. As representative of the company on the council of the City and Guilds Institute for the promotion of technical education (established in 1878) he became the first chairman, and filled the post with energy and efficiency until his death. He was knighted on 18 July 1881 on the occasion of the laying of the first stone of the City and Guilds Institute by the Prince of Wales at South Kensington. He was also chairman of the Inventions Exhibition in 1885, the second of the successful series organised at South Kensington by Sir Francis Philip Cunliffe-Owen [q. v.].

In later life Bramwell was constantly employed by government on various departmental committees. When the ordnance committee was appointed in 1881 he was made one of its two lay members, and he continued in the post for life. Many honorary distinctions were accorded him. He was elected to the fellowship of the Royal Society in 1873, and in 1877–8 served on its council. In 1875 he was elected a member of the Société des Ingénieurs Civils de France. He was made D.C.L. of Oxford in 1886 and of Durham in 1889; LL.D. of McGill (Montreal) University in 1884, and of Cambridge in 1892. He was created a baronet in 1889.

Active to the last, Bramwell attended meetings at the Society of Arts and at the Institution of Civil Engineers within a month of his death, and was at work in his office on 10 Nov. 1903. He died on 30 Nov. 1903 at his residence, 1A, Hyde Park Gate, from cerebral hæmorrhage, and was buried at Hever in Kent, where he possessed a small property.

Despite his devotion to the cause of scientific and technical education, Bramwell's intellect was not cast in the scientific mould, and his interests were mainly confined to the practical applications of science, the developments of which he eagerly watched in his own time, and anticipated with something like prophetic insight. When, at the jubilee meeting of the British Association at York in 1881, he described the previous fifty years' progress in mechanical engineering, he predicted that in 1931, after another half-century, the internal combustion engine would have superseded the steam-engine, which by that time (he added with humorous exaggeration) would be looked upon as merely 'a curiosity to be found in a museum.' In 1903, realising that the rapid development of the new form of motor was confirming his prophecy, he sent to the president of the association, (Sir) James Dewar, 50*l.*, to be invested so as to produce about 100*l.* by 1931, when that sum should be awarded for a paper which, taking as its text his utterances in 1881, should deal with the relation between steam engines and internal combustion engines in 1931.

Besides numerous contributions to the proceedings of societies, Sir Frederick was author of the article on James Watt in this Dictionary and of many letters to 'The Times,' sometimes in his own name, sometimes (after the death of his brother, who used the same initial) signed R.

Bramwell married in 1847 his first cousin, Harriet Leonora, daughter of Joseph Frith. She died in 1907, aged ninety-two. There were three daughters. The second daughter, Eldred, married Sir Victor Horsley, F.R.C.S. The baronetcy became extinct on Bramwell's death.

The Institution of Civil Engineers possesses a portrait by Frank Holl, R.A., painted when he was president, and the Society of Arts one by Seymour Lucas, R.A., painted after his death. There is a marble bust executed in 1901 by Onslow Ford, R.A., at the Royal Institution.

[Personal knowledge; Proc. Inst. C.E. clvi. 426; Proc. Inst. Mech. Eng. Dec. 1903, pp. 3–4, 913; Engineer, 4 Dec. 1903; Engineering, 4 Dec. 1903; Journal Soc. Arts, lii. 67; The Times, 1 Dec. 1903.] H. T. W.

BRAND, HENRY ROBERT, second VISCOUNT HAMPDEN and twenty-fourth BARON DACRE (1841–1906), governor of New South Wales, born at Devonport on 2 May 1841, was eldest son of Sir Henry Bouverie William Brand, first viscount [q. v. Suppl. I], by his wife Eliza, daughter of General Robert Ellice, who was brother of Edward Ellice [q. v.].

Educated at Rugby, Brand served in the Coldstream guards from December 1858 to October 1865, retiring with the rank of captain. From October 1861 to October 1862 he was attached to the staff of Viscount Monck [q. v. Suppl. I], governor-general of Canada. In 1868 Brand was returned as junior member for Hertfordshire, as a liberal, together with the Hon. Henry Cowper; but at the general election of February 1874 both were defeated. At Stroud, where two successive petitions against sitting members had been successful in April and May, Brand stood and defeated a conservative candidate in July, but was himself unseated on petition. In 1880 he contested the seat again, and was returned. From 1883 to 1885 he held the office of surveyor-general of ordnance in Gladstone's second administration. After the Redistribution Act of 1885 he sat for the Stroud division of Gloucestershire, but in 1886 he dissociated himself from the home rule policy of his party, and with W. S. Caine [q. v. Suppl. II] was a teller for the hostile majority (343–313) in the division on the second reading of the home rule bill (7 June 1886). At the ensuing general election he stood for Cardiff as a liberal unionist, but was beaten by Sir E. J. Reed.

Brand did not return to the House of Commons. He inclined to reunion with the followers of Gladstone. On the death of his father in 1892 he became second Viscount Hampden and twenty-fourth Baron Dacre, and inherited the Dacre property of The Hoo, Hertfordshire. In 1895 Lord Hampden was appointed governor of New South Wales, where he arrived in Nov. He acted as a constitutional governor. At the same time questions which required the exercise of influence and discretion arose during his term of office. In Oct. 1896 a conference of colonial premiers at Sydney took the first effective step in the direction of union. In September 1897 the federal convention met at Sydney; and in March 1898, at Melbourne, the commonwealth bill was accepted. Royal assent was not given to the imperial measure until 1900, after Lord Hampden's return; but the crisis of the constitutional movement was met and passed while he was governor. In 1897 he celebrated with fitting ceremony the Diamond Jubilee of Queen Victoria. He resigned in 1899, a year before his appointment lapsed, owing to private affairs. He was made G.C.M.G., and took no further part in public life. He died at 5 Grosvenor Gardens, London, on 22 Nov. 1906, and was buried at Kimpton. Hampden married twice: (1) in 1864, Victoria, daughter of Silvian van de Weyer, the Belgian minister in London; she died in the following year without issue; (2) in 1868, Susan Henrietta, daughter of Lord George Henry Cavendish, M.P.; by her he had six sons and three daughters. The eldest son, Thomas Walter, succeeded as third Viscount Hampden and twenty-fifth Baron Dacre. A portrait, painted by the Hon. John Collier, is at The Hoo, Welwyn.

[The Times, 23 Nov. 1906; private sources.] R. L.

BRAND, HERBERT CHARLES ALEXANDER (1839–1901), commander R.N., born on 10 July 1839 at Bathwick, Somersetshire, was son of Charles Brand by his wife Caroline Julia Sanders. He entered the navy in December 1851, and as a midshipman served on the Britannia flagship in the Black Sea in 1854, and in the Colossus in the Baltic in 1855, thus getting the Baltic medal in addition to the Crimean, with the Sebastopol clasp, and the Turkish. He was appointed in 1856 to the Calcutta, going out to China as the flagship of Sir Michael Seymour (1802–87) [q. v.]. While in her he was present at the destruction of the junks in Fatshan Creek, at the capture of Canton, and at the capture of the Taku forts in 1858. Afterwards, as a sub-lieutenant of the Cruiser, he took part in the unsuccessful attack on the Taku forts (25 June 1859) [see HOPE, Sir JAMES], and the next day received from the commander-in-chief his promotion to the rank of lieutenant. In 1865, still a lieutenant, he commanded the Onyx gun-vessel on the West Indian station, and gave efficient support to the military in suppressing the revolt of the negroes in Morant Bay [see EYRE, EDWARD JOHN, Suppl. II; NELSON, Sir ALEXANDER ABERCROMBY], and sat as president of the court-martial held, by order of the general in command, on the ringleaders. For this service he was officially thanked by the governor, the general and the assembly; but at home the humanitarians, unable to realise the urgency of a danger to which themselves and their families had not been exposed, preferred charges of murder against both Nelson and Brand, which were inquired into by the magistrate at Bow Street in February 1867. On 10 April they were brought up for trial at the Old Bailey, when Lord Justice Cockburn ended his very full charge to the grand jury with the statement that, 'if ever there were circumstances which justified the application of martial law, in his judgment they were to be found in this case.' As a result, the grand jury found 'no true bill,' and the prisoners were discharged. If, in addition to the stern resolution which had made his services valuable in Jamaica, Brand had possessed the useful quality of discretion, he would probably have been rewarded for his good and disagreeable services; but he permitted his temper to rule his action and to dictate several ill-judged letters to his principal accusers, who promptly published them, and thus held him up to public opprobrium as a quarrelsome bully. These letters forced the admiralty to the conclusion that he could not be promoted, and thus, though employed for some little time in the command of a gun vessel on the coast of Ireland during the Fenian troubles, he was virtually shelved some time before his retirement with the nominal rank of commander in July 1883. He died at Bath early in June 1901.

[Royal Navy Lists; Annual Registers; Irving, Annals of our Time (see Index, s. vv. Brand, Eyre, Nelson, Jamaica); Hamilton Hume, Life of Edward John Eyre, 1867; The Times, 11 June 1901.] J. K. L.

BRANDIS, Sir DIETRICH (1824–1907), forest administrator and botanist, born at Bonn on 31 Mar. 1824, was eldest son of Christian August Brandis (1790–1867) by his wife Caroline Hausmann, of a good Hanoverian family, who was a pioneer in social work. His father, son of the court physician at Copenhagen, after studying at Göttingen and Kiel, was privatdocent at Copenhagen and Berlin, secretary to the Roman historian Niebuhr, when ambassador at Rome (1816–1821), and from 1822 to his death in 1867 was, save for three years' absence in Greece (1837–9), professor of philosophy at Bonn. Appointed kabinetsrat by Otho, King of Greece, in 1837, the elder Brandis spent that and the two following years with his family at Athens, where the archæologist Ernst Curtius acted as their tutor. Of Dietrich's younger brothers Bernhard (1826–1911), geheimer-sanitätsrat, obtained a reputation as a physician, while Johannes, kabinetsrat, was private secretary to Augusta, the German Empress.

Dietrich, after early education at Bonn, commenced botanical pursuits at Athens, studying under Fraas and accompanying Link on excursions. Returning to Bonn in August 1839, he attended the royal high school and university there. Subsequently he studied botany at Copenhagen under Schouw, at Göttingen under Grisebach and Lantzius-Beninga, and again at Bonn with Treviranus. He became Ph.D. Bonn on 28 Aug. 1848, and privatdocent in 1849.

In 1854 he married Rachel, daughter of Joshua Marshman [q. v.], Indian scholar and missionary, and widow of Voigt (1798–1843), Danish surgeon and botanist. This marriage determined his career. His wife's sister was wife of General Sir Henry Havelock [q. v.]. When Pegu in Burma was annexed in 1852, the valuable teak forests were being depleted by unscrupulous adventurers: strong control was essential to their preservation. In 1855 General Havelock was consulted; on his suggestion the governor-general, Lord Dalhousie, put Brandis in charge of the threatened forests on 16 Jan. 1856. Next year his commission was extended to include all Burmese forests. So thoroughly did Brandis perform his task that by 1861 the Burmese forests were saved. His professional duties precluded much scientific study, but his interest in botany was maintained, and on 5 May 1860 he was elected F.L.S. In 1862 Brandis was summoned to Simla to advise the government of India on general forest policy. The problem was difficult because rights of public user everywhere prevailed. Brandis, overcoming official and popular opposition, devised a just and successful system of eliminating or adequately curtailing these rights; he provided for the co-ordination and ultimately for the strengthening of the provincial departments which had control of the forests, and on 1 April 1864 was appointed inspector-general of Indian forests.

During 1863–5 and 1868–70 he toured extensively, establishing sound forest management in Northern India. While on furlough in 1866 he arranged for the continental training of candidates for employment in forestry work.

Invalided on 4 Feb. 1871, Brandis was on duty in England from 12 April 1872 till 22 May 1873, completing 'The Forest Flora of North-west and Central India,' commenced by Dr. John Lindsay Stewart. Prepared at Kew, this work, published in March 1874, established Brandis's botanical reputation; he was elected F.R.S. on 3 June 1875, and appointed C.I.E. on 1 Jan. 1878. After his return to India he founded in 1878 at Dehra Dun a school for native foresters. During 1881–3 he inaugurated a sound system of forest management in Madras. On 24 April 1883 he retired from Indian service, with a special honorarium and valedictory notice. As administrator and as professional forester he had proved himself equally eminent.

Settling in Bonn, Brandis, who inherited his mother's social interests, instituted a workmen's club. At the same time he resumed his botanical studies, working on specimens collected by himself or communicated from Calcutta. While Brandis had been absent from Simla on duty at Madras during 1881–3, it had been proposed to substitute an English for a continental training of forestry officers in India. Accordingly in 1885 a forestry school was established at Coopers Hill, and although Brandis thought the step to be premature, he joined the board of visitors. On 16 Feb. 1887 he was promoted K.C.I.E. On 10 Oct. following Brandis agreed to supervise the practical continental training of English students. He performed this duty from 1888 to 1896, not only for English students but also for the young foresters of the U.S.A. forest department. His services and expert knowledge were recognised by the honorary degree of LL.D. from Edinburgh in 1889, and the grade of a Prussian 'professor' in 1890. In 1898 his university gave him a jubilee diploma; on 22 Nov. 1905 he received a message of thanks from Theodore Roosevelt, the president of the United States.

After 1896 Brandis again confined his attention to botanical work, dividing his time from 1897 to 1900 between London and Bonn. In 1901 he settled in Kew in order to prepare a botanical forest manual. There he resided till November 1906, when he finally returned to Bonn.

His great work, 'Indian Trees,' which he completed while suffering from a painful malady, was issued in London in November 1906. It is a model of botanical exactitude and a monument of enthusiasm and perseverance.

Brandis died at Bonn on 29 May 1907, and was buried in the family grave in the old cemetery.

His first wife had died at Simla in 1863, and in 1867 he married secondly, at Bonn, Katharine, daughter of Dr. Rudolph Hasse. By his second marriage Brandis had four sons and three daughters; three children died young. The eldest, Joachim, is a civil engineer; Bernhard is judge in the higher court of Elberfeld; Caroline is a sister in the Evangelische Diakonie Verein. A pastel portrait, made in 1867 by G. H. Siebert of Godesberg, is now at Elberfeld.

[Meyer, Konversations-Lexikon, iii. 384 Brandis, Forest Flora of North-west and Central India, preface, pp. xiv, xvi; Eardley-Wilmot, Indian Forester, xxxiii. 305; B. D. J[ackson], Proc. Linn. Soc. Lond. 1907–8, p. 46; Pinchot, Proc. Soc. Amer. For. iii. 54; W. S[chlich], Proc. Roy. Soc. lxxx. obit. not. p. iii; India Office Records; Letters of Lady Brandis.] D. P–n.

BRAY, Mrs. CAROLINE (1814–1905), friend of George Eliot and author, eighth and youngest child of James Hennell (*d.* 1816), traveller and afterwards partner in the mercantile house of Fazy & Co., Manchester, and his wife Elizabeth, daughter of Joel Marshall of Loughborough, was born at 2 St. Thomas's Square, Hackney, London, on 4 June 1814. Her brother Charles Christian [q. v.] and her sisters Mary [q.v.] and Sara [see below] won distinction as writers. Caroline was educated at home, and her home life probably suggested to George Eliot that of the Meyrick family in 'Daniel Deronda.' Caroline was for a short time a governess, and the experience was helpful to her later in writing schoolbooks. She married on 26 April 1836 Charles Bray [q.v.], a ribbon manufacturer of Coventry. The Hennells were unitarians of the school of Priestley, but Bray, like her own brothers and sisters, held more advanced views, which Mrs. Bray never wholly shared.

In 1841 Mrs. Bray and her sister Sara were introduced to Mary Anne Evans (to be known later as George Eliot the novelist), and the acquaintance quickly ripened into close friendship. Portraits of Miss Evans and of her father, drawn by Mrs. Bray in 1842, were presented by the artist to the National Portrait Gallery in 1899. The correspondence with George Eliot, which began in 1842, only ceased with life, and on it Mr. J. W. Cross's biography of George Eliot is largely based.

In 1840 Charles Bray bought a small property near Coventry known as Rosehill, and there entertained many interesting visitors. Emerson stayed there in 1848 (cf. M. D. Conway, *Emerson at Home and Abroad*, 1882, pp. 273–5); Herbert Spencer in 1852, 1853, 1856, and 1862 (cf. Herbert Spencer, *An Autobiography*, 1904). Bray retired from business in 1856. Between 1859 and 1881 he and his wife resided for part of each year at Sydenham. After Bray's death in 1884 Mrs. Bray lived at Ivy Cottage, St. Nicholas Street, Coventry, where she died of heart failure on 22 Feb. 1905. She was buried in Coventry cemetery.

Mrs. Bray, an accomplished woman, of gentle temper and sound judgment, wrote many educational books notable for their clearness and simplicity. The most important are 'Physiology and the Laws of Health, in Easy Lessons for Schools' (1860), and 'The Elements of Morality, in Easy Lessons for Home and School Teaching' (1882). About 15,000 copies of the former were sold. It was translated into French, and at Dr. Colenso's desire into Zulu. The latter, an excellent little book, was translated into Italian, Dutch, and Hindustani. 'Our Duty to Animals' (1871), for a long period a class book in the schools of the midland counties, 'Richard Barton' (1871), 'Paul Bradley' (1876), and 'Little Mop' (1886), impressed on the young the duty of kindness to animals. The establishment of the Coventry Society for the Prevention of Cruelty to Animals in 1874 was due to Mrs. Bray's initiative, and she acted as its honorary secretary until 1895.

SARA HENNELL (1812–1899), author, Mrs. Bray's elder sister, born at Hackney on 23 Nov. 1812, was educated at home, and from 1832 to 1841 was employed as a governess. In 1841 she settled at home at Hackney, and ten years later moved with her mother to Coventry. During 1844–6 she supervised George Eliot's translation of Strauss' 'Life of Jesus' (CROSS, *George Eliot's Life*, i. chap. 2). George Baillie of Glasgow having offered and awarded a prize for the best layman's essay against infidelity, in 1854 offered a second prize of 'twenty sovereigns' for the best discussion of 'both sides of the subject.' Sharing the religious views of her brother Charles and brother-in-law, Charles Bray, Miss Hennell won the second prize with her severely impartial 'Christianity and Infidelity: an Exposition of the Arguments on Both Sides' (1857). George Eliot credited it with 'very high and rare qualities of mind' (CROSS, *George Eliot's Life*, i. 35). In 1859 appeared Miss Hennell's 'Essay on the Sceptical Tendency of Butler's "Analogy,"' which ranks as a classical commentary on Butler's work. Gladstone, who refers to Miss Hennell as 'a member of a family of distinguished talents which is known to have exercised a powerful influence on the mind and career of George Eliot,' wrote that 'No critic can surpass her either in reverence or in candour' (*Nineteenth Century*, Nov. 1895). 'Thoughts in Aid of Faith' (1860) is an attempt to reconcile religious feeling with philosophy and 'the higher criticism.' Her most ambitious work, 'Present Religion as a Faith owning Fellowship with Thought' (3 vols. 1865, 1873, and 1887), is marred by a laboured and involved style. Her object is 'to present a philosophical theism in consistence with scientific thought by the help of a doctrine of evolution' (cf. LESLIE STEPHEN, *George Eliot*, pp. 23–4). After Charles Bray's death in 1884 she lived with Mrs. Bray at Ivy Cottage, St. Nicholas Street, Coventry. She died there on 7 March 1899, and was buried in Coventry cemetery.

[Sara S. Hennell, A Memoir of Charles Christian Hennell, 1899; J. W. Cross, George Eliot's Life as related in her Letters and Journals, 3 vols., 1885; Coventry Herald, 25 Feb. 1905; Charles Bray, Phases of Opinion, 1884; private information. For SARA HENNELL see also Coventry Herald, 10 March 1899, reprinted in Memoir of Charles Christian Hennell, pp. 127–131.] E. L.

BRERETON, JOSEPH LLOYD (1822–1901), educational reformer, born on 19 Oct. 1822 at Little Massingham Rectory, King's Lynn, was third son of eleven children of Charles David Brereton (*d.* 1868), for forty-seven years rector of Little Massingham, by his wife Frances (*d.* 1880), daughter of Joseph Wilson of Highbury Hill, Middlesex, and Stowlangtoft Hall, Suffolk. His father was an influential writer on poor law and agricultural questions between 1825 and 1828. Brereton was educated at Islington proprietary school under Dr. John Jackson [q. v.], afterwards bishop of London, and at Rugby under Dr. Arnold (1838–41). He gained a scholarship at University College, Oxford, in 1842, obtained the Newdigate prize for a poem on the 'Battle of the Nile' in 1844, and graduated B.A. in 1846 and M.A. in 1857.

Taking holy orders, Brereton held curacies at St. Edmund's, Norwich, St. Martin's-in-the-Fields, London, and St. James's, Paddington (1847–50). From 1852 to 1867 he was rector of West Buckland, North Devon, and from 1867 till death rector, in succession to his father, of Little Massingham. In 1882 Brereton, with his brother, General John Alfred Brereton, was severely injured in a railway accident between

Cambridge and Ely, which interrupted for some years his public work.

Brereton's interest in educational reform among the agricultural and middle classes was early stimulated by his father's example and by the influence of Dr. Arnold at Rugby. While rector of West Buckland he, with Hugh Fortescue, second Earl Fortescue, lord-lieutenant of Devonshire, and his son, afterwards third earl [see FORTESCUE, HUGH, Suppl. II], established in 1858 at West Buckland the farm and county school (now the Devon county school), to supply education suitable for farmers' sons. The object was to provide public boarding-schools, with liberal and religious education, at fees large enough to cover the cost of board and tuition and to return a fair interest on capital invested. The main feature of the scheme was that the county rather than the diocese should be the unit of the area of organisation, and that upon the county basis the whole scheme of national education should be co-ordinated. In recognition of his efforts Brereton was made, in 1858, prebendary of Exeter Cathedral.

His removal to Little Massingham in 1867 as rector led in 1871 to the foundation there of the Norfolk county school, which was transferred in 1874 to Elmham. His next step was to connect the county school system with the universities. After an unsuccessful attempt at Oxford he founded at Cambridge in 1873 a 'county' college, which was named Cavendish College, after the chancellor of the university, the duke of Devonshire [q. v. Suppl. II]. Brereton described his scheme in his 'County Education: a Contribution of Experiments, Estimates and Suggestions' (1874). Cavendish College was instituted as a 'public hostel' of the university, students in residence being eligible for a university degree. The undergraduates were younger than was customary, and the cost of board and tuition, which was covered by an inclusive charge of eighty guineas a year, was lower. The venture received educational and ecclesiastical support; but the proprietary principle excited distrust; and the public schools withheld their recognition (*Pall Mall Gazette*, 30 July 1874). The scheme proved financially unsuccessful, and the college was dissolved in 1892, being used since 1895 as a training college—Homerton College—for women teachers. Subsequently in 1881 Brereton formed the Graduated County Schools Association, whose aim was the establishment of self-supporting schools and colleges for girls and women—the last step in his practical scheme for a national system of county education.

Brereton was interested in agricultural questions, and while in Devon founded in 1854 the Barnstaple Farmers' Club, of which he was president. Later he was president of the west Norfolk chamber of agriculture. In north Devon his interest in rural prosperity was marked by many permanent works of reform and improvement, and by his efforts he helped to bring the railway from Taunton to Barnstaple, a line afterwards absorbed in the Great Western railway; similar efforts in west Norfolk led to the Lynn and Fakenham railway, which was subsequently extended to Norwich, Cromer, and Yarmouth.

Brereton died on 15 Aug. 1901, and was buried in Little Massingham churchyard. He married on 25 June 1852 Frances, daughter of William Martin, rector of Staverton, south Devon, and had issue five sons and six daughters. His wife died on 13 May 1891. A portrait of Brereton as a boy with his maternal grandfather, Joseph Wilson, painted by Sir David Wilkie, is now in the possession of Arthur Wilson, of Stowlangtoft Hall, Suffolk. A second portrait, by George Richmond, R.A., with a companion portrait of his wife, was exhibited at the Royal Academy in 1868; both are now at Little Massingham Rectory. A bust of Brereton was placed in 1861 in the Devon county school, West Buckland, by Hugh, Earl Fortescue; there are memorials to him in Little Massingham church, where there is also a carved oak reredos in memory of his wife. His writings, beside his works on county education, pamphlets, and sermons, include: 1. 'The Higher Life,' 1874, a blank verse exposition of New Testament teaching. 2. 'Musings in Faith and other Poems,' 1885.

[The Times, 17 Aug. 1901; Brereton's County Education, 1874; private information from sons.] W. B. O.

BRETT, JOHN (1831–1902), landscape painter, born at Bletchingley, Surrey, on 8 Dec. 1831, was eldest son of Captain Charles Curtis Brett of the 12th lancers by his wife Ann Philbrick. At an early age he attended drawing classes at Dublin, and then had passing thoughts of joining the army. He entered the schools of the Royal Academy in 1854, and soon afterwards became deeply affected by the work of the Pre-Raphaelite Brotherhood. In

1858 he sent to the Academy exhibition a picture entitled 'The Stone-breaker,' which was enthusiastically welcomed by Ruskin. Brett was with Ruskin in Italy next year, and there he painted the 'Val d'Aosta,' in which Pre-Raphaelite principles were carried still further. Ruskin bought the picture, and it remained his property till his death, when it was purchased by Mr. R. P. Cooper. A photogravure appears as frontispiece to Ruskin's 'Works' (library edition, vol. xiv.). In his 'Academy Notes' for 1859 Ruskin described the painting as 'historical' and even 'meteorological' landscape, toilsomely and delicately handled. From this time onward Brett worked unswervingly on the same lines, producing a series of landscapes which would demand a very high place in the world's esteem, if the object of painting were the closest possible imitation of natural phenomena. After 1870 his subjects were almost always taken from the southern coasts of England, especially the rocky shores of Cornwall. Among his better works were 'Spires and Steeples of the Channel Islands' (1875), 'Mounts Bay' (1877), 'Cornish Lions' (1878), and 'The Sere and Yellow Leaf' (1895). Two examples of his work, 'From the Dorsetshire Cliffs' (1871) and 'Britannia's Realm' (1880), are in the Tate Gallery, the latter purchased by the Chantrey trustees. The 'Norman Archipelago' is in the Manchester Gallery and 'North-west Gale off the Longships Lighthouse' in the Birmingham Gallery.

Brett painted in a scientific rather than an artistic spirit, caring more for detailed veracity of record than for the creation of beauty. In other ways he showed that his heart was more with science than with art. He was elected a fellow of the Royal Astronomical Society on 9 June 1871, and devoted a considerable part of the strange house which he built in Keswick Road, Putney, to the purposes of astronomical observation. On the roof were mounted an equatorial telescope, resting on a solid brick pier going down to the foundation level of the house, and an azimuth reflector. In an introductory essay to the catalogue of a collection of his sketches, shown by the Fine Art Society in 1886, he devoted most of his space to scientific polemics. His Putney house was designed entirely on utilitarian principles. The floors and flat roofs were of asphalte, the ceilings brick vaults, the heating done by hot water pipes, everything to minimise human labour and avoid dirt. The house was electrically protected against burglars and other uninvited intruders.

Brett was elected A.R.A. in 1881, but never attained the rank of R.A. He died in his house at Putney on 8 Jan. 1902. He married in 1870, and had four sons and three daughters who survived him. A portrait in oils by himself, painted about 1865, belongs to his son, Mr. Michael Brett. A bust in bronze, executed in 1888 by Thomas Stirling Lee, is in the possession of the Art Workers' Guild, London, of which Brett was at one time master.

[The Times, 9 Jan. 1902; Cat. of Nat. Gall. of Brit. Art (Tate Gallery); Bryan's Dict.; Percy Bate's English Pre-Raphaelite Painters, 1899; Art Journal for 1882, p. 57; Roy. Astr. Soc. Notices, 1902, lxii. 238–40; private information.] W. A.

BREWTNALL, EDWARD FREDERICK (1846–1902), painter, born in London on 13 Oct. 1846, was eldest son of Edward Brewtnall, headmaster of the People's College, Warrington, Lancashire. Coming to London about 1868 with Edward John Gregory [q. v. Suppl. II], he studied at the Lambeth School of Art. As a painter in water-colours he made his first appearance at the Royal Society of British Artists in 1868 with a picture entitled 'Post Time,' and from 1882 to 1886, when he resigned, he was a member of the Society. In 1875 he became an associate of the Royal Water Colour Society, and a full member in 1883. His pictures there exhibited include 'When Love was Young' (1878); 'The Honeymoon' (1880); 'The Visit to the Witch' (1882); 'Bluebeard's Wife' (1884); 'The Ravens' (1885); 'Where to next?' (1886); 'On the Wing' (1888); 'The Red Fisherman' (1891); 'The Shell' (1894); 'The Fisherman and the Genie' (1897), and 'La Vie de Bohème' (1900). He painted also in oils, and was a member of the Institute of Oil Painters. From 1872 to 1900 he exhibited eighteen pictures at the Royal Academy, most of them in oils, among his later contributions being 'Merely Players' (1898); 'On the Embankment' (1899); and 'The Inn by the Sea' (1900). His picture of 'The Model's Luncheon' is in the Mappin Art Gallery, Sheffield, and two of his water colours, 'At Cley-next-the-Sea, Norfolk,' and 'Near St. Mawgan, Cornwall,' are in the Victoria and Albert Museum. He died on 13 Nov. 1902 at his residence at Bedford Park, and was buried in the old churchyard, Chiswick. On 17 Sept. 1884 he married Ellen Faraday, sister of Alice Faraday, the wife of Frederick

Barnard [q. v. Suppl. I], and had three daughters.

[Bryan's Dictionary of Painters and Engravers; Graves's Royal Academy Exhibitors; private information.] M. H.

BRIDGE, THOMAS WILLIAM (1848–1909), zoologist, born at Birmingham on 5 Nov. 1848, was eldest son of Thomas Bridge, a boot and shoe maker, and Lucy, daughter of Thomas Crosbee, both of Birmingham. After attending a private school he studied at the Birmingham and Midland Institute, and in 1870 went to Cambridge as private assistant to John Willis Clark [q. v. Suppl. II], then superintendent of the University Museum of Zoology. Two years later he entered Trinity College as a foundation scholar, and whilst an undergraduate was appointed university demonstrator in comparative anatomy. Coming out first in the second class of the natural science tripos of 1875, he graduated B.A. in 1876 and M.A. in 1880. In 1879 Bridge was elected professor of zoology at the Dublin Royal College of Science, but after a year, on the institution of Mason College, Birmingham, he returned to his native place as professsor of biology. Subsequently the chair was divided into a botanical and a zoological professorship, and Bridge held the latter appointment to the time of his death.

Both as teacher and as organiser, Bridge contributed much to the success of the Mason College and of the new Birmingham University, being chairman of the academic board in the former and devoting himself unstintingly to the welfare of his college and department.

As an investigator Bridge was distinguished for his researches into the anatomy of fish, and in particular for his work upon the swim or air-bladder. His most important contribution upon this subject was published in the 'Philosophical Transactions of the Royal Society' in 1893; whilst his article on 'Fishes' in the 'Cambridge Natural History' (vol. vii. 1904) is a good example of his careful, lucid, and accurate method. He was made Sc.D. at Cambridge in 1896 and was elected F.R.S. in 1903. He died at Birmingham, unmarried, on 29 June 1909.

[Proc. Roy. Soc. lxxxii. B., 1910; Birmingham Daily Post, 1 July 1909.] F. W. G.

BRIDGES, JOHN HENRY (1832–1906), positivist philosopher, second son of Charles Bridges [q. v.] by Harriet Torlesse, his wife, was born on 11 Oct. 1832, at Old Newton, Suffolk, where his father was then vicar. Brought up in the strictest system of evangelical orthodoxy, he was at first educated at private schools. Entering Rugby in August 1845, under Dr. Tait, he left the school with a scholarship from the sixth form at midsummer, 1851, the head master then being Dr. Goulburn. He became senior scholar at Wadham College, Oxford, in Oct. 1851; was placed in the second class in classical moderations in 1853, and in the third class in the final examination in 1854. He was *proxime accessit* for the Hertford University scholarship in 1852, and gained the Arnold prize in 1856 for an essay on 'The Jews in Europe in the Middle Ages,' which was published in 'Oxford Essays,' 1857. On 1 Feb. 1855 he graduated B.A. and in March won a fellowship at Oriel. Thereupon Bridges took up the study of medicine; and after attending St. George's Hospital, London, and working in Paris, he graduated M.B. at Oxford in 1859.

In 1860 he married his cousin Susan, fifth daughter of C. Torlesse, vicar of Stoke-by-Nayland, and immediately (February 1860) emigrated to Melbourne in Australia, with high testimonials to his professional skill. The death of his wife followed soon after their arrival. Bridges at once returned to England and began practice in Bradford, Yorkshire, where he was appointed physician to the infirmary in 1861. In 1867 he was elected F.R.C.P., and in 1869 he became a factory inspector for the North Riding. Next year he was appointed a metropolitan medical inspector to the local government board, and until his resignation in 1898 he resided in London, occupied with his official work at Whitehall. After his retirement he worked on the metropolitan asylums board and took part in movements for the improvement of the public health. He died at Tunbridge Wells on 15 June 1906, being buried there in the churchyard of St. Barnabas (for service of commemoration see *Positivist Review*, xiv. 179).

Bridges married secondly, in 1869, Mary Alice, eldest daughter of George Hadwen, of Kebroyde, a silk manufacturer of Halifax. Mrs. Bridges survived her husband. A life-sized portrait in oils was painted by Frederick Yates in 1906.

Bridges impressed his associates through life 'not merely with his ability but with his courageous pursuit of truth at all hazards.' At Wadham College he had come under the influence of Dr. Richard Congreve [q. v. Suppl. I], who was then fellow and tutor; and during the next thirty years he maintained a close friendship with him. Under Congreve's influence Bridges devoted himself, on leaving Oxford, to the study of the works of Auguste Comte. His friends at Wadham, Professor E. S. Beesly and Mr. Frederic Harrison, shared the faith which he developed in positivism. Bridges became one of the foremost leaders of the positivist movement in England. When an English positivist committee was nominated by Pierre Laffitte, Comte's successor in Paris, in 1879, Bridges was chosen the first president. From 1870 until his retirement in 1900 he constantly lectured to the Positivist Society in London and elsewhere. He had great familiarity with French language, society, and literature, and enjoyed the intimacy of all French positivists. He translated into English Comte's 'Politique Positive I.' (1865 and 1875) and published 'The Unity of Comte's Life and Doctrine—a reply to J. S. Mill' (1866; reprinted 1911), as well as 'Five Discourses on Positive Religion' (1882). To the 'Positivist Review' (1893–1906) he contributed a hundred articles. For the 'New Calendar of Great Men' (1892) Bridges wrote 194 biographies of very varied range, and also the general 'Introductions' on philosophy and science.

At the same time history, science, and social reform also occupied his pen. In 1866 he delivered before the Philosophical Institution of Edinburgh a course of lectures on 'Richelieu and Colbert' which were published, and obtained high praise from J. A. Cotter Morison [q. v.] and Mr. James Bryce. In 1869 he lectured to the Royal Institution of London on 'Health,' a subject on which he wrote and discoursed incessantly, publishing: 'Influence of Civilization on Health,' 1869; 'A Catechism of Health for Primary Schools,' 1870; and 'Moral and Social Aspects of Health,' 1877. In 1892 he delivered and published the annual Harveian oration before the Royal College of Physicians.

In 1897 Bridges edited for the Clarendon Press the text of Roger Bacon's 'Opus Majus' in two volumes. This work, of great importance to the history of science, occupied Bridges from 1893, but on its publication critics detected errors in the text due to Bridges' misreading of the MSS. and to his dependence on Samuel Jebb's edition of 1733. He had also overlooked an important MS. at the Vatican. The volumes were withdrawn from circulation by the Clarendon Press, stock and copyright being transferred to Bridges, who reissued them in 1900 through Messrs. Williams & Norgate, with a new third volume, which presents parts i. and iii. of the 'Opus Majus' from a photographic copy of the Vatican MS. and a full list of corrections and emendations of the previously issued text with additional notes.

Bridges published, in addition to the works cited: 1. 'History an Instrument of Political Education,' 1882. 2. 'Centenary of the French Revolution,' 1890. 3. 'Harvey and Vivisection,' 1896. For a volume called 'International Policy' (1866) he wrote 'England and China,' and for Mr. Bryce's 'Two Centuries of Irish History,' 1888, a chapter called 'Ireland from the Union to Catholic Emancipation, 1801–1829.' He was a contributor to the 'Fortnightly Review,' 'La Revue Occidentale,' and the 'Sociological Review,' 1905–6. In 1907 Professor L. T. Hobhouse, his brother-in-law, collected, with biographical 'Introduction' by Mr. Frederic Harrison, a selection of his 'Essays and Addresses,' including a commemorative address on Roger Bacon. Mrs. Bridges also issued in 1908 a collection of friends' 'Recollections' of her husband.

[Mrs. Bridges' collected Recollections of J. H. Bridges, 1908; introduction to Bridges' Essays and Addresses, 1907; the present writer's Autobiographic Recollections, 1911; personal knowledge from 1851 to 1906.]

F. H.

BRIGGS, JOHN (1862–1902), Lancashire cricketer, was born at Sutton-in-Ashfield, Nottinghamshire, on 3 Oct. 1862. His elder brother Joseph (1860–1902) played in a few Nottinghamshire matches in 1888. The family moved to Lancashire in his childhood. Briggs showed an aptitude for cricket as a boy, and at seventeen was a professional member of the Lancashire county team, showing promise as a fieldsman and batsman. Subsequently he developed a high reputation as a bowler. At Lord's in 1886, when playing for England *v.* Australia, he became famous by taking 5 wickets for 29 runs. Thenceforth his position as a first-rate bowler was assured. In 1890 he took 158 wickets for 12½ runs apiece. Briggs paid six visits to Australia, thrice with Shaw and Shrewsbury's teams in the winters of 1884, 1886 and 1887, with Lord Sheffield's team in 1891–2, and twice with Mr. A. E. Stoddart's teams of 1894 and 1897. Briggs was the best all-round Lancashire player of his time, and for some twelve seasons (1883–1894) was a tower of strength to the team. Short and stout of build, he made himself popular on the cricket field by his humour, nonchalance and energy (cf. C. B. FRY in *Giants of the Game*, p. 134). A slow left-hand bowler, with an easy action and plenty of spin, he was most misleading to batsmen; he was especially destructive on 'dead' wickets. Against Australia his most memorable performances were those at Sydney, when in December 1894 he and Peel dismissed the last eight Australian batsmen on a wet wicket for 53 runs, and snatched a victory for England by 10 runs; in the 1887–8 tour, when he with George Lohmann [q. v. Suppl. II] bowled unchanged through the test match; and in February 1892, when he accomplished the 'hat trick' for England, a very rare feat in test matches. In May 1900, when playing for Lancashire *v.* Worcestershire, he took all ten wickets.

In June 1899 an epileptic seizure after the match England *v.* Australia, at Leeds, interrupted his career, and he spent several months in Cheadle Asylum. On his recovery in 1900 he played again for Lancashire; but a fresh seizure in 1901 compelled his return to Cheadle Asylum, where he died on 11 Jan. 1902.

[The Times, 13 Jan. 1902; Wisden's Cricketers' Almanack, 1903, p. lxx; Daft's Kings of Cricket (portrait, p. 153); W. G. Grace's Cricketing Reminiscences 1889, pp. 330–3; Giants of the Game, ed. Hon. R. H. Lyttelton, pp. 134–6.] W. B. O.

BRIGHT, WILLIAM (1824–1901), church historian, born at Doncaster on 14 Dec. 1824, was only son of William Bright, town-clerk of Doncaster, Yorkshire. Sent first to a preparatory school at Southwell, and thence, in 1837, to Rugby, he there reached the sixth form at the time of Dr. Thomas Arnold's death. Gaining a scholarship at University College, Oxford, he matriculated on 20 March 1843; obtained first-class honours in classics in 1846; was awarded the Johnson theological scholarship in 1847, and the Ellerton theological essay in 1848, the subject being 'The Prophetic Office under the Mosaic Dispensation.' He graduated B.A. in 1846, proceeding M.A. in 1849, and D.D. in 1869. He was ordained deacon in 1848 and priest in 1850.

Elected fellow of University College in 1847, he retained his fellowship till 1868. He became tutor of his college in 1848, but in 1851 accepted the theological tutorship at Trinity College, Glenalmond, under the wardenship of Dr. Charles Wordsworth [q. v.], afterwards bishop of St. Andrews. The Scottish bishops also appointed him to the Bell lectureship in ecclesiastical history, an office which entailed the custodianship of a mass of important documents illustrating the church history of Great Britain, which had been accumulated by the founder for the use of his lecturer. Bright was thus encouraged to pursue the historical studies to which he came to devote his best powers. In 1858 the bishop of Glasgow, Walter John Trower, took umbrage at a casual, but not unjust, remark of Bright as to the imperfection of the church settlement effected by Henry VIII, and procured his ejection from both Glenalmond tutorship and Bell lectureship. Bright protested in a pamphlet, 'A Statement of the Facts as to Certain Proceedings of the Bishop of Glasgow' (1858). Later on, the injustice of the proceedings was acknowledged, and Bright was honorary canon of Cumbrae cathedral from 1865 to 1893.

Returning to Oxford in 1858, and resuming his tutorship at University College, he was appointed in 1868 regius professor of ecclesiastical history at Oxford and canon of Christ Church in succession to Henry Longueville Mansel [q. v.]. In his new office he proved himself a student of unwearied industry. His 'Sylva,' his set of manuscript note-books of matter bearing on lectures from 1870 to 1880, amounts to over sixty large and methodical volumes (W. LOCK, *The Age of the Fathers*, p. vi). He was a most forcible lecturer, full of fire, contagious energy, and quaint humour (H. S. HOLLAND, *Personal Studies*, p. 298). He preached effectively in the university church and in the cathedral, and was always ready to help any Oxford clergyman by a sermon, or by taking the chair at church meetings. Anxious to make provision for the rapidly growing suburbs of Oxford, he earnestly advocated, and liberally contributed to, the building of the fine church of St. Margaret in the north suburb.

He was proctor in convocation for the chapter of Christ Church from 1878; examining chaplain to Edward King [q. v. Suppl. II], bishop of Lincoln, from 1885; and sub-dean of Christ Church from 1895. He died unmarried at Christ Church on 6 March 1901, and was buried in the Christ Church portion of Osney cemetery, by Oxford.

Bright's chief historical works were: 1. 'A History of the Church, A.D. 313–451,' Oxford, 1860; 5th edit. 1888, a summary of his Glenalmond lectures: accepted as the standard treatise for Anglican theological students. 2. 'Chapters of Early English Church History,' Oxford, 1878; 3rd edit.

1897, the substance of lectures on Bede. 3. 'Lessons from the Lives of Three Great Fathers [Athanasius, Chrysostom, and Augustine],' 1890. 4. 'Waymarks of Church History,' 1894, papers on the Arian and Pelagian controversies, on Papal claims, and William Laud's ideals. 5. 'The Roman See in the Early Church,' 1896. 6. 'The Age of the Fathers' (posthumous), 1903, 2 vols., a substantial treatise founded on lectures on the history of the church in the fourth and fifth centuries.

Besides other devotional treatises, sermons, and tracts, Bright also published: 7. 'Ancient Collects and other Prayers for the Use of Clergy and Laity,' London, 1857; Oxford, 1862. 8. 'Faith and Hope: Readings for the greater Holy-days and Sundays from Advent to Trinity,' 1864. 9. 'Liber Precum Publicarum,' 1865, a Latin version of the Anglican liturgy, jointly with Peter Goldsmith Medd [q. v. Suppl. II], 1852–7. 10. 'The Cathedral Church of Christ in Oxford,' Oxford, 1880. 11. 'Iona and other Verses,' 1886. 12. 'The Seven Sayings from the Cross,' 1887, meditations for the Good Friday Three Hours' Service. 13. 'The Incarnation as a Motive Power,' 1889, a volume of sermons. 14. 'Morality in Doctrine,' 1892, twenty-eight characteristic sermons.

Bright was also a hymn-writer of the first rank. He was author of 'We know Thee who Thou art, Lord Jesus, Mary's Son,' of the noble communion hymn 'And now, O Father, mindful of the love,' and of the evening hymn 'And now the wants are told.' His 'Hymns and other Poems' were published in 1866, and again in 1874.

[Bright, Selected Letters, 1903; Foster, Oxford Men; The Times, 7 March 1901; Guardian, 1901, p. 346; Oxford Times, 9 March 1901; Oxford Mag. xix. 276, appreciation by Canon Driver.] A. C.

BRIGHTWEN, Mrs. ELIZA (1830–1906), naturalist, born at Banff on 30 Oct. 1830, was fourth child of George and Margaret Elder. On the death of her mother in 1837 she was adopted by her uncle, Alexander Elder, one of the founders of the publishing house of Smith, Elder & Co. He had no children, and Eliza Elder ('Lizzie' as she was called throughout her life) was brought up in his country house, Sparrow Hall, Streatham, and afterwards at Stoke Newington. From infancy she took an absorbing interest in natural history, and read much, but had no regular education. In 1847 Mr. Elder retired from business; in 1855 Miss Elder married George Brightwen (1820–1883), who was then in the banking firm of Messrs. Overend & Gurney, but left it before the smash in 1867, to start for himself in the discount business, where he made a considerable fortune. They settled in Stanmore, where Mrs. Brightwen resided for the remainder of her life. Her health had been always uncertain, and in 1872 her nervous system broke down completely. For ten years she was almost wholly excluded from books, from nature, and from her friends. The death of her husband in 1883 roused her from her lethargy and suffering, and though she was liable to violent attacks of pain until the end of her life, they interfered no longer with her intellectual activity.

She had no children, and was left in sole possession of a very beautiful and secluded estate, The Grove, Stanmore, where the woods and shrubberies, a lake and a large garden offered a field for her zoological observations. It was not, however, until her sixtieth year that she began to be a writer. Her notes on animal life seemed so copious and fresh that she was induced to put them together, and a volume called 'Wild Nature Won by Kindness' (1890) was the result. This enjoyed a very wide and prolonged success, and Mrs. Brightwen became recognised as one of the most popular naturalists of her day. She published 'More about Wild Nature' in 1892; 'Inmates of my House and Garden,' perhaps the best of her books, in 1895; 'Glimpses into Plant Life' in 1898; 'Rambles with Nature Students,' 1899; and 'Quiet Hours with Nature,' 1903. She continued to live at Stanmore, corresponding with a very wide circle of persons interested in natural history, but seldom quitting the bounds of her own estate. She died there on 5 May 1906, and was buried in the churchyard of Stanmore. Mrs. Brightwen was an artless writer; but she had boundless patience, great perseverance and humour, and a sort of natural magic in dealing with wild creatures. Her books are storehouses of personal notes, in which nothing is borrowed from other authors, or accepted on any other authority than that of her own eyes. She enjoyed in later years the friendship of several of the leading men of science of the day, and in particular of Philip Henry Gosse (whose second wife was her husband's sister), of Sir William Flower, of Sir William Hooker, and of Sir James Paget, all of whom encouraged her efforts. After her death were published another volume of essays, 'Last Hours with Nature,' edited by W. H. Chesson (1908), and fragments of an autobiography, with introduction and epilogue by her nephew, Edmund Gosse, entitled 'Eliza Brightwen: the Life and Thoughts of a Naturalist' (1909). She was an evangelical churchwoman and much concerned with philanthropy.

[Personal knowledge; Eliza Brightwen: the Life and Thoughts of a Naturalist, 1909.]

E. G.

BROADBENT, SIR WILLIAM HENRY, first baronet (1835–1907), physician, born at Lindley on 23 Jan. 1835, was eldest son (in a family of five sons and two daughters) of John Broadbent (*d.* 1880) of Lindley, near Huddersfield, woollen manufacturer and a prominent Wesleyan, who married Esther (*d.* 1879), daughter of Benjamin Butterworth of Holmforth. Col. John Edward Broadbent, R.E., C.B. (*b.* 1848), is his younger brother. Brought up as a Wesleyan, William joined the Church of England in 1860. After early education at a day school at Longwood, near Lindley, and at Huddersfield College, William left school at fifteen for his father's factory, where he spent two years in learning the processes of manufacture. Resolving on a medical career, he, in 1852, when seventeen, was apprenticed to a surgeon in Manchester and entered the Owens College, then in Quay Street. At the Owens College and at the Manchester Royal School of Medicine (Pine Street) he gained medals in chemistry, botany, materia medica, anatomy, physiology, midwifery, surgery, and operative surgery. In 1856 he carried off the gold medals in anatomy, physiology, and chemistry at the first M.B. London examination. Next year he became a member of the Royal College of Surgeons and licentiate of the Society of Apothecaries, London. After failing in an application for the post of house surgeon at the Manchester Royal Infirmary he went, in 1857, to Paris, where he studied under Trousseau, Ricord, Reyer, and other eminent masters in medicine. Living with a French family, he acquired a first-rate knowledge of the French language and an excellent accent. Returning to England in 1858, he passed the final M.B. (London) examination, taking the gold medal in obstetric medicine and first-class honours in medicine. Soon afterwards he obtained the post of obstetric officer at St. Mary's Hospital, London, and became resident medical officer in 1859. In 1860 he was appointed pathologist and lecturer on physiology and zoology in the medical school of St. Mary's Hospital, and curator of the museum. The same year he proceeded to the degree of M.D. (London). He was physician to the London Fever Hospital from 1860 until 1879, when he became consulting physician. In 1861 he was appointed lecturer in comparative anatomy in St. Mary's Hospital medical school, and in 1863 physician to the Western General Dispensary. But despite his many offices, Broadbent's practice was not lucrative. Residing at 23 Upper Seymour Street, he could only meet his household expenses by coaching and by taking resident students. With hesitation he refused an offer of a professorship of anatomy and physiology at Melbourne University at 1000*l.* a year.

With St. Mary's Hospital his association lasted long. In 1865 he was elected physician to the out-patients and in 1871 was promoted to the charge of the in-patients, with a lectureship in medicine, which he held for seventeen years. He remained on the active staff of St. Mary's until 1896, his retirement being deferred for five years by special resolution. He then became honorary consulting physician. Broadbent proved one of the finest clinical teachers of the London schools, especially at the bedside.

Meanwhile his practice and his reputation, both as an investigator of medical problems and as an expert on the treatment of specific diseases, steadily grew. In 1866 he published a book 'On Cancer,' describing his treatment of some cases by the injection of acetic acid into the tumour, but although some good results were at first obtained, later experience was unsatisfactory, and Broadbent discontinued the treatment. An early paper on 'Sensori-motor Ganglia and Association of Nerve Nuclei' (*Brit. and Foreign Med. Clin. Review*, April 1866) also attracted attention. There he explained the immunity from paralysis of bilaterally associated muscles in hemiplegia, and advanced the theory which is generally known as 'Broadbent's hypothesis' to explain the unequal distribution of paralysis in face, trunk, arm and leg, in the ordinary form of hemiplegia. The essential principle has not been invalidated in the forty years since it was originally promulgated, and it is widely applicable to neurological questions, and to the solution of problems in physiology, pathology, and psychology.

Broadbent also did valuable work on aphasia, both in reporting important cases and in suggesting explanations of the working of the cerebral mechanism of speech and thought. In an important memoir 'On the Cerebral Mechanism of Speech and Thought' (*Trans. Roy. Med. Chir. Soc.* 1872) he was the first authoritative propounder of the notion of an altogether separate centre for conception of ideation, which although subsequently adopted by Charcot and others has been rejected by Charlton Bastian and others. In a later paper (*Brain*, i. 1878) Broadbent developed his views and termed the centre for concepts the 'naming centre,' whilst a related higher motor centre was postulated as a 'propositionising centre' in which words other than nouns were supposed to be registered and where sentences were formulated preparatory to their utterance through the instrumentality of Broca's centre. Here, too, Broadbent located the more strictly mental faculties in those parts of the human cerebrum which differentiate it from that of the quadrumana and which are the latest to develop in man. This location was re-advanced with modifications but partly through a similar process of reasoning by Flechsig in 1895, and recent opinion somewhat hesitatingly supports Broadbent's views. At his death he was engaged on a treatise on aphasia. Other important papers concerned the scientific study of therapeutics. Of these the first was 'An Attempt to apply Chemical Principles in Explanation of the Action of Remedies and Poisons' (*Proc. Roy. Soc.* 1868; *Brit. Med. Journ.* ii.). Later themes were the remote effects of remedies (1886) and on 'The Relation of Pathology and Therapeutics to Clinical Medicine' (*Brit. Med. Journ.* 1887).

At the Royal College of Physicians, Broadbent, who had become a member in 1861 and a fellow in 1869, was examiner in 1876–7 and in 1883–4, a member of the council in 1885–6, censor in 1888–9, and senior censor in 1895. In 1887 he delivered the Croonian lectures 'On the Pulse,' which he made the subject of a book (1890), and in 1891 he gave the Lumleian lectures 'On Structural Diseases of the Heart from the Point of View of Prognosis.'

In 1874 he also delivered the Lettsomian lectures before the Medical Society of London 'On Syphilitic Affections of the Nervous System'; in 1884 the Harveian lectures before the Harveian Society on 'Prognosis in Valvular Disease'; and in 1894 the Cavendish lecture 'On some Points in the Treatment of Typhoid Fever,' before the West London Medico-Chirurgical Society. He was examiner in medicine to London (1883) and Cambridge (1888) Universities. In 1881 he served as a member of the royal commission on fever hospitals.

On heart disease Broadbent became a leading authority. In conjunction with his elder son he published, in 1897, a valuable treatise on it which was founded on a large, acutely observed, clinical experience; the book reached a fourth edition in 1906. To typhoid fever he likewise devoted special attention, strongly deprecating the 'expectant' or 'do-nothing' treatment, and enforcing careful dieting and nursing and suitable hydro-therapeutic and other measures.

From 1872, when Broadbent removed to 34 Seymour Street, to 1892, when he went into a larger house at 84 Brook Street, his private consultant practice was expanding, chiefly among the upper classes of society, and it finally reached vast proportions. In 1891 his income from this source far exceeded 13,000*l.*, and he refused twice as much work as he could undertake. His patients soon included the royal family. In 1891 he attended King George V when Duke of York, during an attack of typhoid fever, and in 1892 was in constant attendance on the Duke of Clarence during his fatal illness of acute pneumonia. In the same year (1892) he was appointed physician in ordinary to King Edward VII, then Prince of Wales, and in 1896 physician extraordinary to Queen Victoria. On the death of the Queen he was appointed physician in ordinary to King Edward VII and to the Prince of Wales (King George V). He was created a baronet in 1893 and K.C.V.O. in 1901.

Broadbent played a prominent part in many public movements affecting the cure or prevention of disease. In 1898 he became chairman of the organising committee for promoting the National Association for the Prevention of Consumption, which was formally registered under the board of trade regulations in 1899 with King Edward VII, then Prince of Wales, as president. The object of the association was to instruct the general public in the methods by which the spread of tuberculosis could best be prevented or arrested. He was chairman of the organising council of the British Congress on Tuberculosis which met in London in July 1901, when Prof. Koch of Berlin threw doubt on the intercommunicability of human and bovine tuberculosis, a view which a royal commission at once investigated and disputed. Broadbent was also chairman of the advisory committee of King Edward VII's Sanatorium at Midhurst and was consulting physician to this institution and to the King Edward VII Hospital for Officers.

Broadbent was secretary (1864–1872), treasurer (1872–1900), and subsequently president (1900) of the British Medical Benevolent Fund, to which he was a generous subscriber. An honorary member of many foreign medical societies, he was in 1904 a chief organiser of and first president of the Entente Cordiale Médicale, and at the banquet given at Paris in honour of the English physicians was invested with the grand cross and insignia of a commander of the legion of honour. He was elected F.R.S. in 1897. He received the hon. degree of LL.D. from the Universities of Edinburgh (1898), St. Andrews (1899), Montreal (1906), Toronto (1906), and that of D.Sc. from the University of Leeds (1904). He was president of the Harveian (1875), Medical (1881), Clinical (1887), and Neurological (1896) Societies; vice-president of the Imperial Cancer Fund; consulting physician to the New Hospital for Women, and to the Victoria Hospital for Sick Children (1896).

An acute clinical observer, sound and accurate in diagnosis, resourceful in his methods of treating disease, Broadbent was frank and outspoken in speech, and of resolute will, with business-like powers of concentration. Of robust constitution, he met the exacting requirements of his practice and public work with comparative ease. He died in London on 10 July 1907 from influenza, and was buried in the parish churchyard, Wendover, where he had a country house.

He married in 1863 Eliza, daughter of John Harpin of Holmforth, Yorks, who survived him with two sons, both members of the medical profession, and three daughters. The elder son, John Francis Harpin, succeeded to the baronetcy. A portrait by Scholderer is in the possession of the family.

In addition to the work already cited, Broadbent also revised Tanner's 'Practice of Medicine' (7th edit. 1875). His more important contributions to medical journals have been collected and published by Dr. Walter Broadbent, the second son, with a full bibliography (1908).

[Life of Sir William Broadbent, by Mary Ethel Broadbent (daughter), 1909; notices in the British Medical Journal, 20 July 1907 (portrait); Lancet, 13 July 1907; Practitioner, Aug. 1907 (portrait); Collected Papers by Dr. Walter Broadbent (son) with bibliography, 1908; Index Catalogue, Surgeon-General's Office, Washington; Proc. Roy. Soc. Med., series B., vol. lxxx.] E. M. B.

BROADHURST, HENRY (1840–1911), labour leader, born in the parish of Littlemore, Oxfordshire, on 13 April 1840, was fourth son and 'eleventh or twelfth child,' as he says in his autobiography, of Thomas Broadhurst, stonemason, and his wife Sarah. He was educated at a village school near Littlemore, and at the age of twelve he left to do miscellaneous jobs about the village, and soon afterwards was regularly employed by its blacksmith. In 1853 he was apprenticed to his father's trade in Oxford, and was soon working as a stonemason in Buckingham and Banbury. Coming to London, he felt so country-sick that he left in a month, and, after ill-fortune compelled him to return, he immediately obtained an engagement in Norwich, whither he went by sea. During the depressed time of 1858–9 he tramped twelve hundred miles in the south of England without finding employment. When at Portsmouth on this fruitless search, he attempted to enlist in the army, but was rejected. In 1865 he came finally to London, and shortly afterwards was employed by the contractor who was building the clock tower and its adjoining corridor of the houses of parliament. The mallet and chisels then used by him are preserved in the library of the House of Commons.

In 1872 an agitation for increased pay in the London building trade came to a head by the employers locking out their men. Broadhurst was elected chairman of the masons' committee and was its chief spokesman. The result of the contest was an immediate increase of pay by a halfpenny per hour, a reduction of hours by four per week in summer, and a full half-holiday on Saturdays. Thenceforth he ceased to work at his trade. He had become a leader in his trade union and was active in political agitations conducted by the Reform League, of which he was a member. He had succeeded in changing the character of his trade union by inducing it to offer superannuation and unemployment benefits, and he led it to fix its headquarters in London, and cease moving them every third year. For the first time, in consequence, the central committee became a real executive with power to negotiate on behalf of the whole membership. This establishment of representative democracy in trade unions is an historic event. In 1872 he was sent to represent his trade union at congress, and was elected a member of the parliamentary committee. The labour unrest of the time brought into being a renewed political agitation in favour of labour legislation, such as the removal of objectionable provisions in the conspiracy and master and servant laws, and in that agitation Broadhurst was prominent. In 1873 he was elected secretary to the Labour Representation League, formed to send trade unionists to parliament. That year he tried to enter the London School Board for Greenwich, but failed. Workmen had been candidates for parliament before the league's days, but it produced the first list of labour candidates at any election—that of 1874—and succeeded in returning two of them, Alexander MacDonald for Stafford and Thomas Burt for Morpeth. Broadhurst himself stood for High Wycombe on a day's notice, but only polled 113 votes. In 1875 the trade union congress elected him secretary of its parliamentary committee.

At this time the leading members of the parliamentary committee were prominent supporters of programmes of radical reform, like the extension of the franchise, the abolition of property qualifications for office on local governing bodies—the first subject upon which Broadhurst had to draft a bill (1876)—and the Plimsoll merchant shipping bill [see PLIMSOLL, SAMUEL, Suppl. I]. Above all the committee had begun to lobby in parliament, to send deputations to ministers and leading politicians on labour questions, and to interfere in parliamentary elections. The agitations for the repeal of what the trade unionists considered the unjust laws relating to conspiracy, masters and servants, and the legal status of trade unions had been so far successful [see HOWELL, GEORGE, Suppl. II], but Broadhurst and his friends brought within the scope of their urgent activity questions like employers' liability and workmen's compensation for industrial injuries and amendments to the Factory Acts. Broadhurst was also the secretary of the workmen's committee of the Eastern Question Association, which stimulated public opinion in England against the conduct of the Turks in Bulgaria (1875–1880). He promoted international trade union conferences, like that of Paris in 1883, which was one of the beginnings of the present International Socialist Congresses.

After the general election of 1874 the Labour Representation League ceased to move the interest of trade unionists, and gradually collapsed. Broadhurst thenceforth identified himself with the liberal party, and in 1878 was chosen one of the two liberal candidates for Stoke-on-Trent. He was elected in 1880 with a poll of 11,379 votes. In the House of Commons Broadhurst at once engaged in miscellaneous but most useful work. He supported employers' liability bills (1880–1) and proposed amendments in factory legislation. He investigated the hardships attending the employment of women and children in the heavy industries of the Black Country (producing in the House of Commons in 1883 one of the nail-making machines to illustrate his speech on the subject). In 1884 he moved for the first time the appointment of working-men to the bench of justices and in 1885 the inclusion of a fair wages clause in government contracts. At that time all his income, which came to him as secretary of the trade union congress parliamentary committee, was 150*l.* a year, from which he had to pay for clerical help at his office; he could only afford clothes made by his wife.

From 1882 Broadhurst took an active interest in leasehold enfranchisement, which rapidly became a popular radical demand, and was the subject of a memorandum attached to the report of the royal commission on the housing of the working classes (1884). Of that commission he was a member. In 1882 he was offered an assistant factory inspectorship, and in 1884 an inspectorship of canal boats, but declined both.

In 1884 Broadhurst, as secretary of the trade union congress parliamentary committee, became the leading spirit on the workmen's side in the final phase of the agitation for an extension of the franchise. At the election, which followed the Franchise and Redistribution Acts of 1885, Broadhurst declined to contest either of the new Pottery constituencies, into which Stoke-on-Trent had been divided, and stood for the Bordesley division of Birmingham, which he won with 5362 votes. On the formation of Gladstone's liberal ministry in February 1886 he accepted office as under-secretary in the home department. This necessitated his resignation of the secretaryship of the parliamentary committee. Queen Victoria agreed to excuse him from attending levees, and he was the first minister to whom such permission was granted.

On the defeat of the liberal government in the autumn, Broadhurst retired from Bordesley, and contested West Nottingham, which he won, polling 5458 votes, and in September 1886 he again was elected secretary to the trade union congress parliamentary committee. A steady drift towards an independent political position had set in within trade unionism, and Broadhurst's official connection with the liberal party was bitterly resented by growing sections of the congress. About 1885 the trade union congress embarked anew on the interrupted agitation for sending working-men to Parliament. A demand for a legal eight hours' day was also put forward by trade unionists, and Broadhurst's difficulties were further increased by his opposition to this proposal. At the congresses of Swansea (1887), Bradford (1888) and particularly at that of Dundee (1889) Broadhurst had to defend his political position against attacks, which were too personal to be successful; consequently the overwhelming votes which were cast in his support obscured the changes in opinion which were taking place. Next year at Liverpool the attack was more prudently directed, and on the issue of a general eight hours' bill Broadhurst's policy was defeated by 193 votes to 155. Owing partly to this defeat and partly to ill-health Broadhurst resigned his secretaryship. The dock strike in 1889 confirmed the new development of trade unionism. Broadhurst continued to be the object of bitter attack, and the defeat of his parliamentary candidatures at West Nottingham in 1892, when he polled 5309 votes, and at Grimsby in 1893, when he polled 3463 votes, was undoubtedly helped by the opposition of the advanced section of trade unionists. At West Nottingham he agreed in a lukewarm way to support the miners' eight hours bill, but the earnestness of his pledge was questioned. In 1892 he was appointed a member of the royal commission to inquire into the condition of the aged poor. In 1894 he stood for Leicester, and was elected with 9464 votes, and this constituency he retained, till he retired in 1906 owing to ill-health. He was an alderman and J.P. of the county of Norfolk. He died at Cromer on 11 October 1911, and was buried at Overstrand.

He married in 1860 Eliza, daughter of Edward Olley of Norwich. She died on 24 May 1905, leaving no children. A bust of Broadhurst is in the art gallery of the Leicester corporation.

He wrote: 1. 'Leasehold Enfranchisement,' in collaboration with Sir Robert Reid (Lord Loreburn), 1885. 2. 'Henry Broadhurst, M.P.: the Story of his Life from the Stonemason's Bench to the Treasury Bench,' 1901.

[The Times, 12 Oct. 1911; Autobiography; Webb's History of Trade Unionism, 1894; Howell, Labour Legislation, Labour Leaders, and Labour Movements, 1902, Humphrey, The History of Labour Representation; Trade Union Congress Annual Reports]. J. R. M.

BRODRIBB, WILLIAM JACKSON (1829–1905), translator, only son of William Perrin Brodribb, M.R.C.S., by his first wife, Maria Louisa Jackson, was born at Warminster on 1 March 1829. On his father's removal to a practice in Bloomsbury Square, he was educated first at a neighbouring private school and afterwards at King's College, London. From King's College he was elected in 1848 to a classical scholarship at St. John's College, Cambridge. In 1852 he was bracketed sixth in the classical tripos, was a junior optime in the mathematical tripos, and graduated B.A. Elected a fellow of his college in 1856, he was ordained in 1858, and was presented in 1860 to the college living of Wootton Rivers, Wilts. This preferment he held for life. Devoted to classical study, Brodribb joined his cousin, Alfred John Church, in translating the works of Tacitus; the History appeared in 1862, Germania and Agricola in 1868, the Annals in 1876, and De Oratoribus in 1877. The useful work is competently done and gained general recognition. The two translators also edited the Latin text of Germania and Agricola in 1869, and of select letters of Pliny in 1871; a translation of Livy, books 21–24, followed in 1883.

Brodribb died at his rectory on 24 Sept. 1905, and was buried in the churchyard. He married in 1880 Elizabeth Sarah Juliana, only daughter of David Llewellyn, vicar of Easton Royal, Wilts, but was left a widower, without children, in 1894.

Among works by Brodribb not already noticed are 'Demosthenes' in 'Ancient Classics for English Readers' (1877), 'A Short History of Constantinople' (1879), in collaboration with Sir Walter Besant, and classical contributions to the 'Encyclopædia Britannica' and scholarly periodicals.

[Private information.] A. A. B.

BRODRICK, GEORGE CHARLES (1831–1903), warden of Merton College, Oxford, born on 5 May 1831, at his father's rectory, Castle Rising in Norfolk, was second of four sons of William John Brodrick (1798–1870), rector of Bath (1839–54), canon of Wells (1855–61), dean of Exeter (1861–7), and seventh Viscount Midleton (1863–70). His mother, Harriet (1804–1893), third daughter of George Brodrick, fourth Viscount Midleton, was his father's second wife and first cousin. From 1843 to 1848 Brodrick was an oppidan in Goodford's house at Eton, but in 1848 he broke down under the strain of reading for the Newcastle examination, and was sent on a voyage to India for his health. Returning next year, Brodrick became a commoner of Balliol in March 1850, at a time when Richard Jenkyns [q. v.] was Master and Benjamin Jowett [q. v. Suppl. I] was the leading tutor. He had a distinguished university career, obtaining first classes in moderations in 1852 and in literæ humaniores in 1853, in company with his lifelong friend, George Joachim Goschen, first Viscount Goschen [q. v. Suppl. II]. He also took a first class in law and history in 1854, was president and librarian of the Union (1854–5), won the English essay and Arnold prizes in 1855, and was elected a fellow of Merton College on 30 May 1855. He graduated B.A. in 1854, M.A. in 1856, and D.C.L. in 1886.

In 1856 Brodrick left Oxford for London, and there passed the next twenty-five years of his life. In 1858 he took the degree of LL.B. with a law scholarship at the University of London. He was called to the bar at Lincoln's Inn in 1859, and went the western circuit (1859–62), but in 1860 turned from law to journalism, joining the staff of 'The Times.' During the next thirteen years he contributed some 1600 leading articles to that newspaper, chiefly on political themes. Journalism was in his case intended to be the prelude to a political career. But in his parliamentary ambitions Brodrick was disappointed. He fought a good fight for the liberals at Woodstock in 1868, and again in 1874, when Lord Randolph Churchill was the successful candidate. A third defeat in 1880 in Monmouthshire led him to abandon the quest of a seat in parliament. More successful as a writer than as a candidate, he gave lucid and forcible expression to the old liberal or 'philosophical radical' doctrines of reform, which formed his creed through life. His political views are chiefly expounded in his 'Political Studies' (1879), which included articles on primogeniture and local government in England, and in his 'English Land and English Landlords' (published by the Cobden Club, 1881).

Though his earlier ambitions were anything but academic, Brodrick was elected warden of Merton College, Oxford, on 17 Feb. 1881, and made his chief reputation in that capacity. The only definitely educational position Brodrick had previously held was membership of the London School Board (1877–9), he being the first member who was co-opted to fill a vacancy caused by death. He had also promoted the University Tests Act of 1870, and he served on the council of the London Society for university extension. In the administration and government of the reformed Oxford University, to which he now returned, he took little active part. But for many years (1887–1903) he served on the governing body of Eton, and as a member of the council of the Geographical Society he zealously promoted the foundation in 1899 of the school of geography in Oxford. He likewise endeavoured to make college and university history popular in his 'Memorials of Merton College' (1885) and a short 'History of the University of Oxford' (1886). As warden he did much to prevent university society from becoming narrow and provincial. His week-end parties kept Oxford in touch with the wider world of politics and letters to which he never ceased to belong. His unfailing flow of conversation and anecdote and old-world courtesy of manner gave him a place of distinction in society, while his fairness, loyalty, and unaffected kindliness won him the love and respect of his college and university.

Brodrick by no means lost all interest in politics when he returned to Oxford. Both with tongue and pen he fought against the socialistic tendencies of modern democracy, the Irish land legislation of Gladstone's government, and above all against home rule. For an incautious expression in a speech at Oxford he was summoned before the Parnell commission for alleged contempt of court (14 Jan. 1889). But his later years were given in the main to the duties of his office and to literary work. He published a volume of 'Memories and Impressions' (1900), and wrote the greater part of 'The History of England 1801–1837,' which, after being completed and recast by J. K. Fotheringham, forms vol. xi. of the 'Political History of England' (ed. W. Hunt and R. L. Poole, 1906). He resigned the wardenship on 14 Sept. 1903, and died unmarried in the warden's house on 8 Nov. 1903, being buried at Peper Harrow in Surrey.

A good portrait in the hall of Merton College by William Carter (1899) has been engraved. Brodrick's writings include, besides those already cited, an edition of 'Ecclesiastical Judgments of the Judicial Committee of the Privy Council' (with W. H. Fremantle, 1865) and 'Literary Fragments' (articles from magazines, lectures, speeches, &c.), printed but not published, 1891.

[Memories and Impressions, 1900; The Times, 9 Nov. 1903; personal knowledge and private information.] W. W. H

BROMBY, CHARLES HENRY (1814–1907), second bishop of Tasmania, born at Hull on 11 July 1814, was son of John Healey Bromby, vicar of Holy Trinity, Hull. He entered Uppingham school in August 1829, became captain of the school, and left it with an exhibition in October 1833. Elected to a scholarship at St. John's College, Cambridge, he graduated B.A. as junior optime and with a third class in the classical tripos in 1837, proceeding M.A. in 1840 and D.D. in 1864. Ordained deacon in 1838 and priest in 1839, he was licensed in 1838 to the curacy of Chesterfield. In 1843 he became vicar of St. Paul's, Cheltenham, and first principal of the Cheltenham training college for school masters and mistresses, which he organised with marked success. He was also one of the founders of the Ladies' College, Cheltenham, and helped to form a large Working Men's Club, one of the first institutions of its kind.

On the resignation of Francis Russell Nixon [q. v.] in 1864, Bromby was appointed by the Crown to the bishopric of Tasmania, being the last colonial prelate appointed by letters patent. He was consecrated in Canterbury Cathedral on 29 June 1864. Bromby worked for eighteen years in the colony. He managed with tact and skill the financial reorganisation of the church on its disestablishment in Tasmania, and it was largely owing to his influence that a Commutation Act was passed, which supplied the church with the nucleus of the diocesan church fund. He took an active part in the movement which led to the formation in 1872 of a general synod of the dioceses of Australia and Tasmania, and in 1874 saw a cathedral for the diocese consecrated at Hobart. A high churchman, and opposed to erastianism, Bromby enjoyed the general confidence of the colonists. Advancing years led him to resign in 1882.

Returning to England, Bromby was, from 1882 to 1887, assistant bishop in the diocese of Lichfield and rector of Shrawardine with Montford, Shropshire. He resigned the living in 1887 on appointment as warden of St. John's Hospital, Lichfield, but remained assistant bishop until 1891. He then filled the like office in the diocese of Bath and Wells until 1900. Bromby died at All Saints' Vicarage, Clifton, on 14 April 1907. He married Mary Ann (*d.* 1885), daughter of Dr. Bodley of Brighton and sister of George Frederick Bodley [q. v. Suppl. II]. A son and daughter survived him. A Bishop Bromby memorial studentship was founded by the Synod of Tasmania in 1910. Bromby published three pamphlets on education, in 1861, 1862 and 1895.

Bromby's second son, CHARLES HAMILTON BROMBY (1843–1904), born on 17 June 1843 and educated at Cheltenham College, matriculated at St. Edmund Hall, Oxford, on 3 May 1862, and graduated B.A. (New Inn Hall) in 1867. He was called to the bar at the Inner Temple on 18 Nov. 1867. Joining the New South Wales bar and practising in Tasmania, he became a member of the executive council and attorney-general of Tasmania (1876–8). Returning to England, he practised at the English bar. Of artistic temperament and a keen student of Italian literature, he published a translation, with introduction and notes, of Dante's 'Quæstio de Aqua et Terra' (1897). After his death (on 24 July 1904) there appeared 'Alkibiades, a Tale of the great Athenian War' (1905), edited by Mary Hamilton Bromby.

[Lowndes, Bishops of the Day; Uppingham School Roll (1894–1899); E. Stock, History of the C.M.S. 1899, ii. 455, 456; Brit. Mus. Cat.; private information.] A. R. B.

BROOKING ROWE, JOSHUA (1837–1908), Devonshire antiquary. [See ROWE, JOSHUA BROOKING.]

BROTHERHOOD, PETER (1838–1902), civil engineer, born at Maidenhead on 22 April 1838, was the son of Rowland Brotherhood, a railway contractor, of Chippenham. After four years' study of applied science at King's College, London (1852–6), and practical training in his father's works and in the Great Western railway works at Swindon, he entered, at twenty-one, the drawing-office of Messrs. Maudslay, Sons & Field, then at the height of their fame in marine engineering practice. In 1867 he became a partner in the Compton Street engine works, Goswell Road, London, at first with Mr. H. Kitto, and after Kitto's retirement successively with Mr. Hardingham and Mr. G. B. Oughterson. The firm was mainly engaged in producing machines and engines of Brotherhood's invention. In 1872 he introduced the Brotherhood engine, in which three single-acting cylinders are arranged at angles of 120° around a central chamber. In this chamber is a single crankshaft acted upon by three connecting-rods, the other ends of which are attached to the inner sides of their respective pistons. The engine can be used with steam, water, or compressed air as the working medium.

Among the many purposes to which it has been applied is that of driving torpedoes by means of compressed air. In 1876 he designed his air-compressor, with the object of simplifying the type of compressor then in use for torpedoes. He succeeded in obtaining four stages of expansion while using only two cylinders, by means of a combined piston and plunger, to which motion was imparted by a cross-head worked by a pair of reciprocating double-acting steam-cylinders, their valves being again actuated from a crankshaft fitted with a flywheel. Later on he devised a three-stage pump worked from a single rod, and in 1876 a servo-motor for torpedoes. He also had a share in the introduction of the high-speed engine. His first ordinary double-acting engines—designed, constructed, and under steam within twenty-seven working days—were used in Queen Victoria's yacht Victoria and Albert for electric lighting, being directly coupled to the dynamo.

In 1881 the works were transferred to Belvedere Road, Lambeth, where Brotherhood designed and built a model engineering workshop of moderate size.

Brotherhood was elected an associate member of the Institution of Civil Engineers on 5 May 1868, and a full member on 4 Feb. 1879. He was elected a member of the Institution of Mechanical Engineers in 1874, and of the Iron and Steel Institute in 1877.

He died at his residence, 15 Hyde Park Gardens, W., on 13 Oct. 1902, and was buried at Kensal Green. He married on 19 April 1866 Eliza Pinniger, eldest daughter of James Hunt of Kensington and Brighton; she survived him with three sons and two daughters.

[Min. Proc. Inst. Civ. Eng. cli. 405; Engineering, 17 Oct. 1902; Proc. Inst. Mech. Eng. 1902, p. 1023.] W. F. S.

BROUGH, BENNETT HOOPER (1860–1908), mining expert, born at Clapham on 20 Sept. 1860, was elder son of John Cargill Brough, F.C.S., librarian of the London Institution in Finsbury Circus, and nephew of Robert Barnabas Brough [q. v.], William Brough [q. v.], and Lionel Brough [q. v. Suppl. II]. His father died when he was twelve. With the aid of funds raised by friends, Bennett was sent to the City of London School. Thence he passed in 1878 to the Royal School of Mines, of which he became an associate in 1881. The following year was spent at the Royal Prussian Mining Academy at Clausthal in the Harz. In 1882 Brough was appointed assistant to Sir Warington W. Smyth [q. v.], professor of mining at the Royal School of Mines, and in 1886 he started at the school a course in mine surveying, which proved a great success. His 'Treatise on Mine Surveying,' of which the first edition appeared in 1888, reached its thirteenth edition in 1907. From 1883 to 1893 he was co-editor of the 'Journal of the Iron and Steel Institute,' and in 1893 became secretary of that institute, a post which he retained till his death. His services were constantly in request as abstractor, writer, lecturer, and juror on mining subjects. He contributed to 'Chambers's Encyclopædia' the article on 'Mining,' and to the 'Dictionary of Applied Chemistry' the article on 'Fuel.' The 'Journals' of the Iron and Steel Institute, Institution of Mining Engineers, Society of Arts, and other publications contain numerous articles from his prolific pen. He was on the governing bodies of the Institute of Chemistry, Chemical Society, and Institute of Secretaries. He was also a knight of the Swedish Order of Vasa. On 1 Oct. 1908, whilst at Middlesbrough for a meeting of the Iron and Steel Institute, Brough was suddenly taken ill and died at a nursing home at Newcastle two days later, being buried in the Surbiton and Kingston cemetery. He married in 1895 Barbara, daughter of Edward Lloyd, barrister at law (who was assassinated near Athens in 1870), and had by her one son and one daughter.

[Journal of the Iron and Steel Institute, 1908, lxxviii. 462–3 (with portrait); Trans. Chemical Soc. xcv. 1909; family information.] E. C.

BROUGH, LIONEL (1836–1909), actor, born at Pontypool, Monmouthshire, on 10 March 1836, was youngest of the four children (all sons) of Barnabas Brough, a brewer and wine merchant, of tory principles, who fell into reduced circumstances through political persecution, and, late in life, wrote plays under the pseudonym of Barnard de Burgh (*d.* 1854). Lionel's brothers, William [q. v.], Robert Barnabas [q. v.], and John Cargill (1834–1872), all won some literary distinction.

Brough was educated at Manchester grammar school and at Williams's private academy in London, but when about twelve was compelled by family necessities to start life as an errand-boy in the editorial offices of the 'Illustrated London News.' On 26 Dec. 1854 he made his first appearance on the stage at the Lyceum Theatre, under Madame Vestris and Charles Mathews, in his brother William's extravaganza

'Prince Pretty Pet and the Butterfly.' Six months later he withdrew from the stage to become assistant publisher to the 'Daily Telegraph' on its establishment, and in that position originated the custom of selling newspapers on the streets, by organising a staff of 240 boys for the purpose. In 1858 he again returned to the theatre, appearing at the Lyceum on 27 December under the name of 'Lionel Porter,' in Robert Brough's extravaganza 'The Siege of Troy.' But he soon left the stage to fill for some three years a commercial position on the staff of the 'Morning Star.' In 1862 he began giving monologue entertainments in the Polytechnic Institution in Regent Street, and in 1863 introduced to the provinces the spectral illusion known as 'Pepper's Ghost' [see PEPPER, JOHN HENRY]. Late in 1863 he visited Liverpool with other members of the Garrick Club to give a dramatic performance on behalf of the Lancashire famine relief fund. Struck by his abilities, Alexander Henderson, the manager of the local Prince of Wales's Theatre, offered him an engagement. In Feb. 1864 he seriously entered at Liverpool on the profession of an actor. Remaining at the Prince of Wales's for over two years, he was seen there on 8 May 1865 as the original John Chodd, jun., in T. W. Robertson's 'School,' and on Whit-Monday, 1866, as Castor to the Œnone of Henry Irving in Burnand's extravaganza 'Paris.'

Brough reappeared in London on 24 Oct. 1867, on the opening of the new Queen's Theatre, Long Acre, when he was the original Dard in Charles Reade's 'The Double Marriage.' But it was not until the production of H. J. Byron's 'Dearer than Life,' on 8 Jan. 1868, that his ability became recognised. His acting as the old reprobate, Ben Garner, was marked by both power and finish. At Christmas he appeared with John Lawrence Toole [q. v. Suppl. II], and Henrietta Hodson [q. v. Suppl. II] in William Brough's extravaganza 'The Gnome King.' In October 1869 when Mrs. John Wood opened the St. James's Theatre with a revival of 'She Stoops to Conquer,' Brough played Tony Lumpkin for close on two hundred nights. Thenceforth he was the accepted representative of the character, and played it in all 777 times. Subsequently at the St. James's he gave a droll impersonation of Paul Pry, which proved popular. On 16 Jan. 1871 he was in the original cast of T. W. Robertson's 'War,' a play which failed to attract. On 7 March he played Sir Kidd Parkhouse in Albery's new comedy 'Two Thorns.'

In March 1872 Brough, although he was no trained singer, joined Mr. Fell at the Holborn Theatre to sustain prominent parts in 'La Vie Parisienne' and other light musical pieces. On 29 Aug. he appeared at Covent Garden in Boucicault and Planché's fantastic spectacle of 'Babil and Bijou,' an elaborate production which he was engaged to superintend. In April 1873 he became principal low comedian at the Gaiety Theatre under John Hollingshead [q. v. Suppl. II]. In 1874 he transferred his services to the Globe. At the Charing Cross Theatre (afterwards the Folly and Toole's) on 19 Sept. of that year he played the title character in Farnie's extravaganza of 'Blue Beard' (originally produced in America), and by his ample comic invention materially contributed to the great success of an indifferent production.

Brough was at this period an uncertain and unequal actor, but was steadily outgrowing a curious habit of bleating in his speech as well as a tendency towards excessive noise and extravagant gesture. On 23 April 1879 he joined the company of Marie Litton [q. v.] at the Imperial Theatre, Westminster, as 'first low comedian,' appearing on that date as Claude Melnotte in Younge's burlesque of 'The Lady of Lyons.' Subsequently he gave a number of excellent old comedy characterisations, his Tony Lumpkin and his Croaker in Goldsmith's 'Good-natured Man' being especially commended. On 25 Feb. 1880 he appeared as Touchstone.

On 13 June 1881 Brough returned to the Alexandra, Liverpool, to play Dromio of Ephesus in a revival of 'The Comedy of Errors.' On 19 Sept. he appeared at the Theatre Royal, Brighton, as Laurent XVII in the first English performance of Audran's opera comique 'La Mascotte'; he played the part for the first time in London on 15 Oct. at the opening of the new Royal Comedy Theatre. In May 1884 he played Bob Acres in the Haymarket revival of 'The Rivals,' and on 9 Sept. became joint lessee with Willie Edouin [q. v. Suppl. II] of Toole's Theatre (formerly the Folly). The opening bill presented Paulton's burlesque 'The Babes,' which, with Brough as Bill Booty, ran 100 nights. In 1886 Brough went to America with the Violet Cameron company, playing in opera bouffe. Returning to England early in 1887, he appeared with Kate Vaughan [q. v Suppl. II] at the Opera Comique in the spring, in a round of old comedies.

Subsequently he paid a visit to South Africa, playing there in all the principal towns in a repertory of thirty-eight pieces. Returning to London, he reappeared at the Lyric on 9 Oct. 1890 in Audran's comic opera 'La Cigale.' In 1894 he joined (Sir) Herbert Beerbohm Tree's company, with which he remained associated, with slight intermissions, down to his death. Among the parts played by him during Tree's management of the Haymarket were the Laird in 'Trilby' (1895) and Bardolph in 'King Henry IV, Pt. I' (1896). After an interval, he rejoined Sir Herbert Tree at Her Majesty's, playing such parts as Picolet in Robert Buchanan's adaptation 'A Man's Shadow' (1897), Sir Toby Belch in 'Twelfth Night' (1901), Brunno Rocco in Hall Caine's 'The Eternal City' (1902), and Trinculo in 'The Tempest' (1904). On 15 June 1905 his stage jubilee was celebrated at His Majesty's by a testimonial performance in his honour. Here, too, he made his last appearance on the stage, in 1909, as Moses in 'The School for Scandal.'

Brough had little capacity for interpreting character, and obtained his effects mainly by simple drollery. Early in his career his gifts of improvisation and theatrical resourcefulness, allied to a rich sense of humour, gained him pre-eminence in burlesque. His most striking effects were procured by an assumption of blank stolidity.

Brough died on 8 Nov. 1909 at Percy Villa, South Lambeth, where he had long resided. He married on 12 July 1862 Margaret Rose Simpson (*d.* 1901), who was not connected with the profession, and had four children, Mary, Sydney, Percy, and Margaret, all of whom took to the stage. Mary and Sydney survived him, the latter dying in April 1911.

A crayon portrait of Brough by J. Macbeth was shown at the Grafton Galleries in 1897. An oil-painting of Brough and Toole in 'Dearer than Life' was sold at the Toole sale in November 1906.

[Pascoe's Dramatic List; W. Davenport Adams's Dict. of the Drama; Bancroft Memoirs; Dutton Cook's Nights at the Play; Mowbray Morris's Essays in Theatrical Criticism; John Hollingshead's My Lifetime, 1895, and Gaiety Chronicles 1898; Dramatic Notes for 1881; Tatler, 10 July 1901; Green Room Book. 1909; private information; personal knowledge.]

BROUGH, ROBERT (1872–1905), painter, born at Invergordon, Ross-shire, in 1872, was educated at Aberdeen. There he was apprenticed to Andrew Gibb, engraver and lithographer, with whom Sir George Reid, president of the Royal Scottish Academy, also began his artistic career. Brough studied at the Aberdeen Art School, and at the close of his apprenticeship he removed to Edinburgh, pursuing his art education there. He entered the Royal Scottish Academy life-school in 1891, and distinguished himself as a student, gaining the Chalmers bursary and the Maclaine-Waters medal and other prizes. From Edinburgh he went to Paris, continuing his studies under Jullien and Constant, and attracting much notice by his vigorous style. Returning to Aberdeen in 1894, he began practice there as a portrait painter, contributing also lithographic pictures to the local illustrated journals, 'The Scottish Figaro' and 'Bon-Accord.' His first notable picture was the portrait of Mr. W. D. Ross of Aberdeen (afterwards editor of 'Black and White,' London), which was painted in 1893, and was presented in 1907 to the National Gallery of Scotland, Edinburgh. In 1897 Brough moved to London, taking a studio in Tite Street, Chelsea, where he became the friend and protégé of Mr. John Singer Sargent, R.A., exhibiting regularly at the Royal Academy, the New Gallery the Royal Scottish Academy, and the International Society Exhibitions. In December 1904 he was elected an associate of the Royal Scottish Academy, but his brilliant and promising career was suddenly terminated before he painted his diploma picture. He had been painting the portraits of the daughter-in-law and grandson of Sir Charles Tennant of The Glen, Peeblesshire, and was on the return journey to London when he was fatally injured in a railway accident at Storrs Mill, near Cudworth Junction, between Leeds and Sheffield, on 20 Jan. 1905. He died unmarried in Sheffield Hospital next day, and was buried at Old Machar, Aberdeenshire.

Brough gave promise of becoming one of the most notable of Scottish portrait-painters. His style was both powerful and original, uniting simplicity with breadth of treatment. While his study at Paris had served to develop his style, he retained his originality, and his portraits are remarkable alike for their richness of colour and virility of draughtsmanship. Among his most notable portraits are 'Miss Julie Opp, actress'; 'The Viscountess Encombe' (1898); 'Master Philip Fleming' (a work which attracted attention at the

New Gallery in 1900); 'Surgeon-Colonel Gallway, C.B.'; 'Mrs. Milne of Kinaldie' and 'Richard Myddleton of Chirk Castle' (1901); 'Rev. James Geddie'; 'Sir Herbert Maxwell, Bart.' (1902); 'The Marquess of Linlithgow'; 'Dr. Alexander Ogilvie' (headmaster of Gordon's College, which is in the permanent collection at Aberdeen), and the portrait-group of 'Sir Charles Tennant's family,' which was his last work. His fanciful picture entitled 'Fantasie en Folie,' shown at the Royal Academy in 1897, won a gold medal at the Paris Exhibition of 1900. He is represented in the Royal Scottish Academy by the portrait of Mr. W. D. Ross.

[Scotsman, 23 Jan. 1905; Cat. of Nat. Gall. of Scotland, 42nd edit.; Dundee Advertiser, 23 Jan. 1905; private information.]

A. H. M.

BROWN, GEORGE DOUGLAS (1869–1902), novelist, born at Ochiltree, in Ayrshire, on 26 Jan. 1869, was son of George Douglas Brown (*d.* 1897), farmer, of Muirsmudden, in Ochiltree parish, by Sarah Gemmell (*d.* 1895), of Irish parentage. Brown at first went to the schools in his native village and the parish of Colyton, and when his family moved to Crofthead near Ayr in 1883 he attended the academy at Ayr. In 1887 he matriculated at the university of Glasgow, and in 1890 graduated M.A. with first-class honours. He won at the same time the Eglinton fellowship, but relinquished it the following year on carrying off the Snell exhibition, with which in the autumn of 1891 he proceeded to Balliol College, Oxford. There, though he never enjoyed good health or perfect ease, he took a first class in classical moderations in 1893. Absence in Scotland in solicitous attendance on his mother's deathbed accounts for his only obtaining a third class in the final classical school in 1895. On leaving Oxford in 1895 Brown settled in London, where he earned a living by his pen and by private tuition. In July 1896 he contributed a centenary paper on Burns to 'Blackwood's.' He wrote a boy's book, 'Love and a Sword' (1899), under the pseudonym of Kennedy King. He 'read' for the publishing firm of John Macqueen, and reviewed books and wrote fiction anonymously or pseudonymously for the 'Speaker,' 'Chapman's Magazine,' and other periodicals.

In the autumn of 1900 he rented for a few months a cottage at Hindhead, and there he wrote, after long deliberation, the novel 'The House with the Green Shutters.' Published in the autumn of 1901 under the pseudonym of George Douglas, the book achieved at home and in the United States a popular success, and was recognised by good critics to be a notable piece of fiction. A well-constructed story, it vigorously fused a rich store of vivid and first-hand impressions, some of them already embodied in earlier studies which Brown had not troubled to get printed. Brown avowed impatience with the complacent temper of contemporary Scottish novelists, and painted Scottish character in sombre colours.

Brown next planned further works, including an historical romance of the Cromwellian period, and a metaphysical study of 'Hamlet,' of which fragments remain. But nothing had been completed when he died unexpectedly while on a visit to a friend, Mr. Andrew Melrose, at Muswell Hill, on 28 Aug. 1902. He was buried in his mother's grave in the cemetery at Ayr.

Mr. William Strang, A.R.A., etched a portrait.

[Cuthbert Lennox's memoir, with introduction by Mr. Andrew Lang and an appreciation by Mr. Andrew Melrose, 1902; private information.]

BROWN, SIR GEORGE THOMAS (1827–1906), veterinary surgeon, born in London on 30 Dec. 1827, was elder son of Thomas Brown of Notting Hill Terrace, London, by his wife Grace Bryant. Colonel Sir William James Brown, K.C.B. (*b.* 1832), is his younger brother. George, after being educated privately, entered in 1846 the Royal Veterinary College. On 15 May 1847 he obtained his diploma and commenced veterinary practice in London. In 1850, when only twenty-three, he was appointed professor of veterinary science at the Royal Agricultural College at Cirencester, where he remained for thirteen years. A change in the administration of the college brought him back to London in 1863, though he continued to the end his association with the college as honorary professor. On the outbreak of cattle-plague in June 1865 he was appointed by the government to assist John Beart Simonds [q. v. Suppl. II] in stamping out the disease, and he remained associated with the veterinary department of the privy council until 1872, when he succeeded as chief veterinary officer. Under various titles he remained in charge of veterinary matters at the privy council office and (after 1889) at the board of agriculture until his retirement under the age clause at the end of 1893. He was made C.B. in 1887, at Queen Victoria's Jubilee, and was knighted at Osborne on 23 January 1898.

In addition to his official labours, Brown was from 1881 professor of cattle pathology at the Royal Veterinary College, and from 1888 to 1894 was principal. He was also an examiner of the Royal College of Veterinary Surgeons (the examining body), and became president in 1893. In December 1862 he joined the Royal Agricultural Society of England, of which he was elected an honorary member on 1 May 1878, and was consulting veterinary surgeon.

Brown edited in 1862 'Harley and Brown's Histology,' and in 1885 published 'Animal Life in the Farm.' Otherwise his contributions to professional literature mainly consisted of reports to his department and of articles in the 'Journals' of the Royal and Bath and West of England agricultural societies, bodies which he greatly assisted with his sound and clearly expressed advice. His addresses to the students of the Royal Veterinary College were models of style. He was a fluent and forcible speaker, and a strong and fearless administrator. Successive presidents of his department bore testimony to his merits as an official at times of outbreak of animal disease.

After his resignation from the board of agriculture he lived in retirement at Stanmore, where he died on 24 June 1906, and was buried. He married in 1860 Margaret, daughter of James Smith of Stroud, by whom he had two sons and three daughters.

[Veterinarian, October 1894 and February 1898, and Veterinary Journal, August 1906 (all with portrait); Journal Roy. Agr. Soc. 1906, lxvii. 215; personal knowledge; information from family.] E. C.

BROWN, JOSEPH (1809–1902), barrister, born at Walworth on 4 April 1809, was second son of Joseph Brown, wine merchant, of the Cumberland family of Scales near Kirk Oswald. Educated by his uncle, the Rev. John Whitridge of Carlisle, at Camberwell grammar school, and at a private school at Wimbledon, he entered at eighteen the office of Armstrong & Co., a London firm of West India merchants, but after two years commenced to study law with Peter Turner, a solicitor in the City of London. Meanwhile he matriculated at Queens' College, Cambridge, where he graduated B.A. in 1830 and M.A. 1833. He was admitted to the Middle Temple on 12 Jan. 1832, and under Sir William Henry Watson [q. v.] and Sir John Bayley [q. v.] he learnt the art of special pleading, becoming a pleader under the bar in 1834. Called to the bar on 7 Nov. 1845, he soon acquired a large commercial practice and was engaged in several important actions, including the trial of the Royal British Bank directors before Lord Campbell in 1858. In 1865 he took silk and was made a bencher of the Middle Temple, of which he was treasurer 1878–9. Brown played a prominent part in the steps taken to supersede the old law reports, which were entirely due to private initiative. He was largely responsible for the preparation and publication in 1865 of the 'Law Reports,' which began the new departure. He was chosen to represent the Middle Temple on the Council of Law Reporting in 1872, and from 1875 to 1892 was chairman of the council. Created C.B. upon his retirement, he largely contributed by his energy and practical ability to the success of the council's publications. He died at his residence, 54 Avenue Road, N.W., on 9 June 1902.

Brown was a fellow of the Geological Society and a skilled numismatist and antiquary. He contributed to the 'Proceedings' of the Social Science Congress, and wrote several pamphlets, including two urging reform of the system of trial by jury. He married in 1840 Mary (*d.* 1891), daughter of Thomas Smith of Winchcomb, Gloucestershire, by whom he had three sons and two daughters.

[The Times, 10 June 1902; Law Journal, 14 June 1902; Who's Who, 1901.] C. E. A. B.

BROWN, WILLIAM HAIG (1823–1907), master of Charterhouse. [See Haig Brown, William.]

BROWNE, Sir JAMES FRANKFORT MANNERS (1823–1910), general, colonel-commandant royal engineers, born in Dublin on 24 April 1823, was eldest son of Henry Montague Browne (1799–1884), dean of Lismore, second son of James Caulfeild Browne, second Lord Kilmaine. His mother was Catherine Penelope (*d.* 1858), daughter of Lodge Evans Morres, first Viscount Frankfort de Montmorency. Educated at Epsom and at Mr. Miller's at Woolwich, he became a gentleman cadet of the Royal Military Academy on 15 May 1838. On 1 Jan. 1842 he received a commission as second lieutenant in the royal engineers. After serving at Woolwich and in Ireland, he embarked for Halifax, Nova Scotia, in March 1845, and on 1 April was promoted lieutenant. In Nov. 1846 he was transferred to Quebec.

In June 1847 Browne was sent on special

service to Fort Garry in the Red River Settlement, Hudson's Bay territory (now Manitoba), where a detachment of royal artillery, another of royal sappers and miners, and three companies of the 6th foot had been quartered since the summer of 1846 in connection with the Oregon boundary settlement. Browne took two months to reach the inaccessible spot now known as Winnipeg, and was engaged in surveying, superintending the clearance of forest, and pioneer work generally. In August 1848 the force was withdrawn, and Browne went back to Quebec.

In the autumn of 1851 he was in Ireland, doing duty first at Clonmel, and then at Kilkenny. Promoted second captain on 7 Feb. 1854, he went to Chatham in July to take command of the 1st company of royal sappers and miners. He put it through a course of field work instruction, and on 5 Jan. 1855 embarked with it for the Crimea. On reaching Balaclava on 5 Feb., Browne and his company were soon moved to the trenches of the British right attack on Sevastopol, and remained there until near the end of August.

On 22 March 1855, and again on 5 April, Browne took part in the repulse of sorties made in force by the Russians. He was promoted first captain on 1 June and was the senior executive officer of engineers on 7 June, when he rendered conspicuous service in the successful attack on the quarry outworks covering the Redan. The execution of the arrangements as well as the general superintendence of the work was in his hands. Captain (now Field-marshal Viscount) Wolseley of the 90th foot was his assistant engineer, and Browne reported in high terms of his conduct. Browne was mentioned in the despatches both of Sir Harry Jones (8 June) and of Lord Raglan (9 June). On 17 July he received a brevet majority.

When Lieutenant-colonel Richard Tylden, R.E. [q. v.], director of the right attack, was fatally wounded on 18 June 1855, his duties devolved on Browne. But on 24 Aug. Browne was severely wounded, and on 18 Nov. was invalided home. He was mentioned in Sir Harry Jones's despatch of 9 Sept. 1855. For his services in the Crimea he was created C.B. (military division) and a knight of the legion of honour; he received the war medal with clasp for Sevastopol, the Sardinian and Turkish medals, the order of the Medjidieh (5th class), and a second brevet, that of lieutenant-colonel, was gazetted on 26 Dec. 1856. A pension of 200*l.* a year, awarded him for three years, was afterwards made permanent.

Recovering his health at the end of 1856, Browne was quartered in Dublin until July 1859, when he went out to India to command the engineers in the Bombay presidency, with headquarters at Poona; in March 1860 he went on to Mauritius as commanding royal engineer, and in Aug. 1861 he returned home to become superintendent of military discipline (now called assistant-commandant) at Chatham, where he was second in command. He was promoted brevet-colonel on 26 Dec. 1864, and regimental lieutenant-colonel on 2 May 1865.

On 1 Jan. 1866 Browne was moved to headquarters at the war office, as assistant adjutant-general for royal engineers, on the staff of the commander-in-chief, and five years later he was appointed deputy adjutant-general. In July 1870 he was a member of the committee on the pay of officers of the royal artillery and royal engineers, and in January 1873 on the admission of university men to the scientific corps. He was awarded a distinguished service pension in Oct. 1871.

On 1 Jan. 1876 Browne was appointed colonel on the staff, and commanding royal engineer of the south-eastern district, with his headquarters at Dover; but his promotion to be major-general on 2 Oct. 1877 (afterwards antedated to 22 Feb. 1870) placed him on the half-pay list. For seven years from 2 June 1880 he was governor of the Royal Military Academy at Woolwich; was promoted lieutenant-general on 13 Aug. 1881; was placed on the unemployed list in 1887, and was promoted general on 12 Feb. 1888.

Browne retired on a pension on 5 May 1888. On 6 April 1890 he was made a colonel-commandant of royal engineers, and on 26 May 1894 was created K.C.B. He died at his residence, 19 Roland Gardens, London, on 6 Dec. 1910, and was buried in Brompton cemetery.

On 24 April 1850 Browne married, at Quebec, Mary (*d.* 1888), daughter of James Hunt of Quebec, by whom he had two daughters, both unmarried. A portrait in oils, painted by Mr. Charles Lutyens, is in the possession of his daughters.

[War Office Records; Porter, History of the Royal Engineers, 1889, 2 vols.; Connolly, Royal Sappers and Miners; The Times, 9 Dec. 1910; Royal Engineers' Records; private information.] R. H. V.

BROWNE, Sir SAMUEL JAMES (1824–1901), general, born on 3 Oct. 1842 in India, was son of John Browne of the East India Company's medical service, by his wife Charlotte Isabella, daughter of Captain S. Swinton, R.N. After education in England he returned to India in 1840, on receiving a commission as ensign in the 46th Bengal native infantry. He spent the early years of his career in Lower Bengal, where he first showed an aptitude for sport. During the second Sikh war Browne was present at the cavalry skirmish at Ramnagar on 22 Nov. 1848, at the passage of the river Chenab on 1 Dec. by Sir Joseph Thackwell [q. v.], and at the battle of Sadulapur on 3 Dec., subsequently taking part in the victories of Sir Hugh (afterwards first viscount) Gough [q. v.] at Chillianwallah on 13 Jan. 1849 and at Gujarat on 21 Feb. He received the medal and clasp for his services, and after the campaign was selected by Sir Henry Lawrence [q. v.] for employment in the newly raised Punjab force. He was promoted captain on 10 Feb. 1855, and from 1851 to 1863 he acted as adjutant and commanding officer of the 2nd Punjab cavalry. During this period he served mainly on the Derajat and Peshawar frontier, and was engaged in the operations against the Umarzai Waziris in 1851–2, in the expedition to the Bozdar hills in March 1857, and in the attacks on Narinji in July and August of the same year. He received the medal with clasp.

During the Indian Mutiny Browne commanded the 2nd Punjab cavalry at the siege of Lucknow in 1858, and after the capture of the city formed part of the movable column, under Sir James Hope Grant [q. v.], which inflicted a severe blow on the rebels near Kursi on 22 March 1858. He was in the actions at Ruyah, Aligunge, and at the capture of Bareli on 6 May; and he was in command of a field force which defeated the mutineers at Mohunpur. With 230 sabres of his regiment and 350 native infantry Browne made a surprise attack on the rebels at Sirpura at daybreak on 31 Aug. 1858. Pushing forward to the rear of the enemy's position, he charged the gunners almost single-handed and prevented them from reloading and firing on the advancing infantry. In this desperate hand to hand fight his left arm was severed, and he was also twice wounded in the knee. A tourniquet promptly applied to the injured limb by Dr. Maxwell prevented him from bleeding to death. For this act of gallantry he was awarded the V.C. in 1861. Browne, who was thrice mentioned in despatches, received the thanks of the commander-in-chief and the government of India as well as the war medal with two clasps. He had already been given the brevet rank of major on 20 July 1858, and on 26 April 1859 he was promoted lieutenant-colonel. On 17 Nov. 1864 Browne attained the rank of colonel, and was given the command of the Guides. On 6 Feb. 1870 he was promoted major-general, and in 1875 was chosen to represent the Anglo-Indian army during the Indian tour of Edward VII when Prince of Wales. At the close of the tour in 1876 he was nominated K.C.S.I., and became lieut.-general on 1 Oct. 1877.

From 9 Aug. to 5 Nov. 1878 Browne was military member of the governor-general's council, and in this capacity was actively concerned with the preparations for the Afghan war in 1878–9. He knew well from his experience of the north-west frontier the independent character of the Afghans, and he pointed out to the viceroy, Lord Lytton [q.v.], the immense difficulties which a British invasion of Afghanistan involved. His advice, however, was disregarded, and it was only with reluctance that the viceroy acceded to the insistent demands of Browne and Sir Frederick Haines [q. v. Suppl. II], the commander-in-chief in India, for additional reinforcements for the Kandahar field force. Browne himself received the command of the 1st division of the Peshawar field force, and had orders to force the Khyber pass, which was strongly held by the Afghans. His progress was much retarded by the inefficiency of the commissariat, transport and hospital arrangements; but on 21 Nov. 1878, by a skilful turning movement, he captured with trifling loss the fortress of Ali Masjid, together with thirty-two guns. Little opposition was offered to his subsequent advance, and Jellalabad was occupied on 20 Dec. Browne however met with considerable difficulty in keeping his communications open, and was compelled to send for further reinforcements. The magnitude of his task was increased by his ignorance of Lord Lytton's policy; nor was he allowed to exercise, in fact, the political power with which he had been invested. Further advance was hindered by the threatening attitude of the Khyber tribes. After consultation with Sir Frederick Haines, Browne was ordered to prepare a scheme for an advance on Kabul. This report, which was sent to the viceroy in April 1879, amounted to a demonstration of the impossibility of the undertaking, but did not shake Lord Lytton's determination to bring the war to an end by the capture of Kabul. Meanwhile the victory of general Sir Charles Gough at Fatehabad on 2 April 1879 enabled Browne to occupy Gandamak. In the subsequent political negotiations which led to the signature of the treaty of Gandamak on 26 May with Yakub Khan, the son of the dispossessed Ameer Shere Ali, Browne had no share. On the withdrawal of British troops from Afghanistan Lord Lytton, despite the protests of Sir Frederick Haines, visited on Browne the discredit of the failure of his transport service, a result which was mainly due to the dilatory preparations of the government. Browne was not reappointed military member of the council, and was relegated to the command of the Lahore district. Nevertheless his services did not pass altogether unrewarded. He was created a K.C.B. in 1879, and received the thanks of the government of India and both houses of parliament. Shortly after he retired from active service, and when the massacre of the Cavagnari mission at Kabul on 3 Sept. 1879 reopened the Afghan war he was no longer eligible for a command.

Browne was promoted general on 1 Dec. 1888, and made a G.C.B. in 1891. He was well known in military circles as the inventor of the sword-belt which was universally adopted in the army. After his retirement he resided at The Wood, Ryde, Isle of Wight, where he died on 14 March 1901. After cremation his remains were buried at Ryde. In 1860 he married Lucy, daughter of R. C. Sherwood, M.D., of the East India Company's medical service. A portrait by Consley Vivian is at the East India United Service Club, St. James's Square, London, S.W. A memorial tablet has been erected in the crypt of St. Paul's Cathedral.

[The Times, 15 and 19 March 1901; Army and Navy Gazette, 16 March 1901; W. H. Paget, A Record of the Expeditions against the North-West Frontier Tribes, 1884, p. 86; Kaye and Malleson, History of the Indian Mutiny, 1889, vols. iv. and v.; Lord Roberts, Forty-one Years in India, 1898; W. H. Russell, The Prince of Wales's Tour, 1877; G. J. Younghusband, The Story of the Guides, 1908; H. B. Hanna, The Second Afghan War, 1899–1910, 3 vols.; The Official History of the Second Afghan War, 1908; Lady Betty Balfour, History of Lord Lytton's Indian Administration, 1899; R. S. Rait, Life of Field-marshal Sir Frederick Haines, 1911.]

BROWNE, THOMAS (1870–1910), painter and black-and-white artist, born at Nottingham on 8 Dec. 1870, was son of Francis and Maria Browne. He was educated at St. Mary's national school in his native place, and at the age of eleven became an errand boy, first at a milliner's, and then in the lace-market. When fourteen he was apprenticed to a firm of lithographic printers, and served the full period of seven years. In the meantime he began to practise as a black-and-white artist, and had his first humorous drawings accepted by the periodical called 'Scraps.' In 1895 he came to London, which remained his headquarters till his death. He quickly found a ready market for his work in such papers as 'Cycling,' the 'Tatler,' the 'Illustrated Sporting and Dramatic News,' 'Punch,' the 'Sketch,' and the 'Graphic.' He paid more than one visit to America, and there published many sketches and cartoons in the 'New York Herald,' the 'New York Times,' and the 'Chicago Tribune.' His illustrations were characterised not only by their ready wit but by their admirable quality of line and fluency of draughtsmanship. By his contemporaries 'Tom Browne' will perhaps be best remembered for his creation of those comic types of American illustrated journalism, Weary Willie and Tired Tim. Among special volumes which he illustrated were 'Tom Browne's Cycle Sketch Book' (1897), 'The Khaki Alphabet Book' (1901), 'The Night Side of London' (1902), and 'Tom Browne's Comic Annual' (1904–5). He also won considerable success as a designer of posters, and in 1897 was one of the founders of the lithographic colour-printing firm of Tom Browne & Co. at Nottingham.

Though Browne was best known as a humorous draughtsman, his work as a painter in water-colour showed in its refinement of colour and design highly artistic gifts. For many of his paintings he found subjects in Holland and Spain, and in 1909 brought back much material from a tour in China and Japan. In 1898 he was elected a member of the Royal Society of British Artists, and in 1901 a member of the Royal Institute of Painters in Water-colour, while from 1898 to 1901 he exhibited each year at the Royal Academy, sending seven pictures in all. He was a member of the London Sketch Club from its foundation in 1897, and president in 1907. An active freemason, he was a past master of the Pen and Brush Lodge. The happy geniality which distinguished his life as well as his pictures won him hosts of friends.

On 1 Jan. 1910 Browne was operated on for an internal malady, and died on

16 March 1910. He had been a lance-corporal in the City of London roughriders, and then held a commission in the Woolwich company of the army service corps (territorial). He was buried with military honours at Shooter's Hill cemetery. In 1892 he married Lucy Pares, and left one son and two daughters. His portrait in oils, by Kay Robertson, belongs to the Savage Club.

[The Times, 17 and 21 March, 1910; Who's Who, 1910; A. E. Johnson, Tom Browne, R.I., 1909; private information.] M. H.

BRUCE, Sir GEORGE BARCLAY (1821-1908), civil engineer, born at Newcastle-on-Tyne on 1 Oct. 1821, was younger son of John Bruce, founder of the Percy Street Academy. John Collingwood Bruce [q. v. Suppl. I] was his eldest brother. Robert Stephenson [q. v.] was among his father's pupils, and Bruce, who was educated in his father's school, served five years' apprenticeship (1836–41) in the locomotive works of Messrs. Robert Stephenson & Company. After two years' experience on the construction of the Newcastle and Darlington railway, he spent a term as resident engineer on the Northampton and Peterborough line, and then was appointed, at the age of twenty-four, by the engineers-in-chief, Messrs. Robert Stephenson and Thomas Elliott Harrison [q. v.], resident engineer of the Royal Border bridge, one of the largest stone bridges in Great Britain, which carries the North Eastern railway across the Tweed at Berwick, on twenty-eight semicircular arches, each of sixty-one feet six inches span. It was opened by Queen Victoria in August 1850, and in 1851 Bruce presented an account of it to the Institution of Civil Engineers (*Proc.* x. 219), for which he was awarded a Telford medal. While next engaged on the construction of the Haltwhistle and Alston Moor branch of the Newcastle and Carlisle railway, Bruce was called to India, and was thenceforth largely concerned with Indian railways. After working on the Calcutta section of the East Indian railway until 1853, he served as chief engineer of the Madras railway until 1856, when ill-health compelled his return home. He had then laid out and partly constructed about 500 miles of the Madras railway, employing free native labourers under proper supervision instead of depending on contractors. On 5 Dec. 1857 Robert Stephenson presided at a dinner in London, when Bruce was presented by his associates on the Madras Railway Company with an address and with plate to the value of 515*l.* In 1857 he wrote a paper, 'Description of the Method of Building Bridges upon Brick Wells in Sandy Foundations, illustrated by the Viaduct over the River Poiney, on the Line of the Madras Railway' (*Proc. Inst. Civ. Eng.* xvi. 449).

From 1856 Bruce was established as a consulting engineer in Westminster, from 1888 in partnership with Mr. Robert White. He was consulting engineer for fifty years to the metre-gauge South Indian railway, and from 1894 to the Great Indian Peninsula and Indian Midland railways of five feet six inches gauge—the broader gauge which Bruce preferred.

Bruce's work included the Kettering, Thrapston and Huntingdon, the Peterborough, Wisbech and Sutton, the Whitehaven, Cleator and Egremont, and the Stonehouse and Nailsworth railway lines. Abroad he constructed the Tilsit-Intersburg, East Prussian, and Berlin-Gorlitz lines. During 1873–6 he constructed works for the shipment of ore from the Rio Tinto copper-mines at Huelva in Spain, including a railway and a pier of considerable magnitude and novel construction. He also did engineering work for the East Argentine railway, the Buenos Ayres Grand National tramways, and the Beira railway in South Africa.

Bruce was elected a member of the Institution of Civil Engineers in 1850, became a member of council in 1871, and was president in the Jubilee year 1887 (*Address* in *Minutes of Proceedings*, xci. 1). He served a second term as president in 1888, when he was knighted. In 1883, while vice-president, he represented the institution in Canada at the opening of the Northern Pacific railway (cf. *Proc.* lxxv. 1). In 1889 he was created an officer of the legion of honour of France. He became a member of the Institution of Mechanical Engineers in 1874, and served on the royal commissions on the water-supply of London of 1892 and 1897.

Outside his professional work Bruce was deeply interested in the Presbyterian church in England and public education. To the extension of the Presbyterian church at home and abroad he gave time and money liberally, and he actively promoted the union of presbyterians in England, which was effected in 1876. At Wark-on-Tyne he built a church and manse. His chief services to the cause of public education were rendered as a member of the school board for London, on which he represented Marylebone from 1882 to 1885.

Bruce died at his residence, 64 Boundary

Road, St. John's Wood, on 25 Aug. 1908. He married in 1849 Helen Norah, daughter of Alexander H. Simpson, solicitor, of Paisley, by whom he had one son and four daughters.

His portrait in oils by W. M. Palin was presented to the Institution of Civil Engineers by members in 1889.

[Proc. Inst. Civ. Eng. clxxiv.; The Times, 26 Aug. 1908; Morning Herald, 7 Dec. 1857.]

W. F. S.

BRUSHFIELD, THOMAS NADAULD (1828–1910), lunacy specialist and antiquary, born in London on 10 Dec. 1828, was son of Thomas Brushfield, of an ancient Derbyshire family, J.P. and D.L. of the Tower of London, by his wife Susannah Shepley. His grandfather, George Brushfield, married Ann Nadauld, great granddaughter of Henri Nadauld, a Huguenot who, settling in England after the revocation of the Edict of Nantes, became a sculptor and in 1698 decorated Chatsworth House with statuary and friezes.

Brushfield was educated at a private boarding school at Buckhurst Hill, Essex, and matriculated with honours at the London University in 1848. He studied medicine and surgery at the London Hospital, which he entered in 1845, and won three gold medals—for chemistry in 1847, and for medicine and physiology in 1849—besides other honours. He became M.R.C.S. in 1850 and graduated M.D. at St. Andrews University in 1862. After serving as house surgeon at the London Hospital he joined Dr. Millar at Bethnal House Asylum, London, and acquired there his first experience of lunacy. He was appointed house surgeon to Chester County Lunatic Asylum in 1852, and was first resident medical superintendent from 1854 until 1865. In 1865 he was appointed medical superintendent of the then projected Surrey County Asylum at Brookwood. The buildings at Brookwood were planned in accordance with his suggestions, and later on he helped to design the Cottage Hospital there. He retired on a pension in 1882. Brushfield was a pioneer of the 'non-restraint' treatment of lunatics. He sought to lighten the patients' life in asylums by making the wards cheerful and by organising entertainments. His contribution to the literature of lunacy includes 'Medical Certificates of Insanity' (*Lancet*, 1880) and 'Practical Hints on the Symptoms, Treatment and Medico-Legal Aspects of Insanity,' which was read before the Chester Medical Society in 1890.

On his retirement from professional work in 1882 Dr. Brushfield settled at Budleigh Salterton, on the east Devon coast, near Hayes Barton, the birthplace of Sir Walter Ralegh. Brushfield made the career of Ralegh his main study for the rest of his life. He became a member of the Devonshire Association in 1882, was elected to the council in 1883, and was president in 1893–4. A paper, 'Notes on the Ralegh Family,' which he read before the 1883 meeting of the Association (*Trans.* xv. 1883), proved the first of a long series of papers called 'Raleghana,' embodying minutest research into Ralegh's life and literary work, which were published in the same 'Transactions' between 1896 and 1907. 'Ralegh Miscellanea' (pts. i. and ii.) followed in 1909–10. He contributed many other papers on the same and cognate themes to other archæological journals. He was a reader for the 'New English Dictionary,' and contributed over 72,000 slips (see preface, vol. i.). His bibliography of Ralegh, which was published in book form in 1886 (2nd edit. 1908, with photographic portrait), first appeared serially in the 'Western Antiquary,' vol. 5, 1885–6.

Brushfield was a freemason, was elected F.S.A. in 1899 and was a founder of the Devon and Cornwall Record Society. He was a popular lecturer in the west country, and his lantern slides are now in the Exeter Public Library, together with the more important 'Ralegh' items from his library. The rest of his library of about 10,000 volumes and manuscripts, many of local interest, was dispersed after his death. He died at Budleigh Salterton on 28 Nov. 1910, and was buried there. He married, on 5 Aug. 1852, Hannah, daughter of John Davis of London, who survived him with three sons and three daughters.

[Devon and Cornwall Notes and Queries, 1910–11, vi. 161; private information; personal knowledge.]

H. T-S.

BRYDON, JOHN McKEAN (1840–1901), architect, born at Dunfermline in 1840, was son of John Brydon, tailor and draper of that place, by his wife, whose maiden surname was McKean. He was educated at the Commercial Academy in Dunfermline. After receiving his early architectural training in Liverpool from 1856 and studying in Italy, he served under David Bryce [q. v.] in Edinburgh. In 1866 he became managing assistant at Glasgow to Campbell Douglas and John James Stevenson [q. v. Suppl. II], and subsequently for two or three years worked in the London offices of William Eden Nesfield [q. v.] and Mr. Norman Shaw,

R.A. After establishing with Wallace & Cottier, two fellow architects, a decorating and furnishing business in Langham Place, Brydon returned to architectural practice, and in 1883–4 was engaged in building St. Peter's Hospital, Henrietta Street, Covent Garden. In 1885 he won the competition for the Chelsea vestry hall and subsequently built (1889) the neighbouring free library and the South-West London Polytechnic. Brydon was frequently successful in competitions, securing in 1891 the commission to build the municipal buildings at Bath (opened 1895), an important engagement followed by the erection of the Technical Schools (1895–6), the Victoria Art Gallery and Library (opened 1901), and the pump room extensions, all in the same city. The last undertaking, obtained in competition (1894), involved the covering-in of the scholæ of the Roman bath [see DAVIS, CHARLES EDWARD, Suppl. II]. In 1889 Brydon carried out the New Hospital for Women in the Euston Road, London, and in 1896 the London School of Medicine for Women in Handel Street, W.C. (1897–9). Other of his works were the village hall, Forest Row, Sussex (1892) (which after destruction by fire he rebuilt); the private residences, Lewins in Kent for Joseph Robinson, Bournemead at Bushey, and Pickhurst, Surrey; residential chambers for ladies in Chenies Street, W.C.; and for J. J. Tissot, the French artist, a studio and certain alterations at the Château de Buillon.

Brydon was selected in 1898 from a limited number of first-rate architects as the designer of the offices in Whitehall for the local government board and the education department. His style for domestic and hospital work had been generally of a Georgian type of English renaissance, but in the designs at Bath he had shown a command of orthodox classicism. Brydon, before designing the great buildings now entrusted to him, paid a special visit to Italy. His design was worthy of its important site and purpose, but he died before the work was finished, leaving the completion of the buildings in the hands of the office of works. He became a fellow of the Royal Institute of British Architects in 1881, a vice-president in 1899 and 1901, and served for several years on its council. Brydon died at his residence 31 Steele's Road, Haverstock Hill, on 25 May 1901, and was buried in Highgate Cemetery.

[Journal Royal Inst. of Brit. Architects, 3rd series, 1901, viii. 381, 400; Builder, 1901, lxxx. 340.] P. W.

BUCHAN, ALEXANDER (1829–1907), meteorologist, born at Kinnesswood, Kinross-shire, on 11 April 1829, was the youngest of four children of Alexander Buchan, weaver, by his wife Margaret Kay Hill. At an early age he took a practical interest in field botany. Educated at the Free Church Training College, Edinburgh, he passed to the University of Edinburgh, where he graduated M.A. in 1848. He was schoolmaster or 'public teacher' at Banchory and Blackford, and subsequently became headmaster of the Free Church School at Dunblane. At Christmas 1860, owing to an affection of the throat which hampered his school work, he abandoned the teaching profession and was appointed secretary of the Scottish Meteorological Society, which had been founded in 1855 through the instrumentality of Dr. James Stark, head of the statistical department of the office of the Scottish registrar-general. Buchan devoted his life to the work of this office and to meteorological research or discussion. The mainstay of the society, he superintended a network of stations with a view to the compilation of meteorological statistics for the registrar-general for Scotland. To such duties was added the supervision of the weather journals of the lighthouses of the Board of Northern Lights, and of a separate series of rainfall stations. Except the lighthouses the Scottish stations were maintained by voluntary observers, generally noblemen and country gentlemen, to whom Buchan periodically paid visits of inspection. Under Buchan's direction the society inaugurated an observatory at the summit of Ben Nevis, which was in active operation from November 1883 till its abandonment for lack of funds in September 1904. In 1887 Buchan was appointed by the Royal Society of London a member of the meteorological council, which from 1877 to 1905 administered the parliamentary grant for meteorology and directed the operations of the meteorological office in London.

From 1878 to 1906 he was librarian and curator of the museum of the Royal Society of Edinburgh, and thus came into constant relations with the chief Scottish men of science. He was secretary of the Royal Society Club, a social coterie of the fellows. Thomas Stevenson [q. v.], the lighthouse engineer, who was Buchan's colleague at the Meteorological Society as honorary secretary in 1871, became an intimate associate, while Stevenson's son,

Robert Louis, was long another close friend.

In 1867 Buchan published in Edinburgh 'The Handy Book of Meteorology' (2nd edit. 1868), which became a recognised text-book all over the world. There followed in 1871 'Introductory Text-book of Meteorology.' Buchan and Dr. A. J. Herbertson prepared the comprehensive volume on meteorology for 'Bartholomew's Physical Atlas' (1899). But it was as the chief contributor to the 'Journal of the Scottish Meteorological Society' (in which appeared 66 papers) and as a frequent contributor to the 'Transactions of the Royal Society of Edinburgh' that Buchan's most valuable work, which touched every phase of climatology and meteorology, was done. His paper on 'Mean Pressure and Prevailing Winds of the Globe' (*Roy. Soc. Edin. Trans.* 1869)—of which the Austrian meteorologist von Hann wrote 'It is even more important than ['The Distribution of Heat over the Surface of the Earth' (Berlin, 1852)] the celebrated work of Dove'—fully justifies Buchan's claim in behalf of meteorology that it should be regarded as the youngest of the sciences. The subject is developed further in his 'Report on Atmospheric Circulation, based on Observations made on Board H.M.S. Challenger and other Meteorological Observations' (*Challenger Reports,* 'Physics and Chemistry,' vol. ii. part 5, 1889). The numerous tables in the text co-ordinate a vast mass of data, and the fifty-two coloured maps show the mean temperature, isobaric lines, and prevailing winds over the globe, for each month of the year and for the year, while two plates of curves indicate the deviations at different hours of the day from the mean daily temperature, mean daily atmospheric pressure, wind velocity, and the like. Buchan's 'Report on Oceanic Circulation, based on Observations made on Board H.M.S. Challenger and other Observations,' which appeared in 1895, illustrates with equal thoroughness the mean annual specific gravity and the mean annual temperature at the surface of the ocean, as well as the temperature at various depths beneath the surface and at the bottom. These subjects are dealt with again in a paper on 'Specific Gravities and Oceanic Circulation' (*Trans. Roy. Soc. Edinburgh,* 1896, with nine maps), showing the specific gravities observed at the surface, and at various depths beneath the surface, of the ocean.

Of scarcely less value are the papers written for the Royal Society in conjunction with Sir Arthur Mitchell [q. v. Suppl. II] on the 'Influence of Weather on Mortality from different Diseases and at different Ages' and on 'Influenza and Weather in London.' According to Dr. von Hann other papers by Buchan on the relations between the distribution of atmospheric pressure and long continued weather-anomalies broke 'new ground for a sound advance of meteorology in central Europe.'

Buchan's merits were widely recognised in many ways. From the Royal Society of Edinburgh he received the Makdougall Brisbane medal in 1876 and the Gunning prize in 1893; Glasgow conferred upon him the honorary degree of LL.D. in 1887; he was elected F.R.S. in 1898, and in 1902 he was the first recipient of the medal founded by the Royal Meteorological Society of London in commemoration of George James Symons [q. v. Suppl. I].

Buchan's interests were varied. A skilled botanist, he was president of the Edinburgh Botanical Society in 1870–1. He had a profound appreciation for and knowledge of literature, particularly old English poets, dramatists, and historians. He was also an elder of St. George's United Free Church in Edinburgh. Buchan died on 13 May 1907 at 2 Dean Terrace, Edinburgh, and was buried at the Warriston cemetery. He married in 1864 Sarah, daughter of David Ritchie of Musselburgh; she died on 13 May 1900, leaving a son, A. Hill Buchan, who took up the profession of medicine.

[Contributions towards a Memorial Notice of Alexander Buchan, M.A., LL.D., F.R.S.; Journal of the Scottish Meteorological Society, 3rd series, vol. xiv. No. xxiv. 1907; Men and Women of the Time, 15th edition, 1899; Who's Who, 1907; Nature, 1907, lxxvi. 83.]

W. N. S.

BUCHANAN, GEORGE (1827–1905) surgeon, born at Glasgow on 29 March 1827 was son of Moses Steven Buchanan (1796–1860) and Agnes Leechman, his wife. The father, who was surgeon to the Royal Infirmary and lecturer on anatomy in the Portland Street Medical School from 1836 to 1841, was appointed in the latter year professor of anatomy in the Andersonian University.

George was educated at the University of Glasgow, where he graduated M.A. in 1846. Three years later, after studying under his father and others at the Andersonian University, he became M.D. St. Andrews and L.R.C.S. Edinburgh, and in 1852 fellow of the Royal Faculty of Physicians and Surgeons of Glasgow. In early life he allowed the advantages of chloroform anæsthesia to be demonstrated upon himself, his father being the operator. He began to practise in Glasgow, but in 1856 went to the Crimea as a civil surgeon. He returned to Glasgow at the end of the war, and was one of the first to practise there purely as a consulting surgeon. In 1860, when he succeeded his father as professor of anatomy in the Andersonian University, he was also appointed surgeon to the Glasgow Royal Infirmary. There he had as a colleague Joseph (afterwards Lord) Lister, who was led by the prevalence of septic diseases in the wards to the great work of his life—the introduction of the antiseptic method of wound treatment. Buchanan thus had the earliest opportunity of becoming acquainted with methods whereby the practice of surgery was revolutionised. He soon became known as a bold and skilful operator and as a good teacher. He first pointed out (1865 and 1867) the possibility and safety of removing half the tongue in cases of cancer. He was amongst the earlier surgeons to remove the upper jaw (1864 and 1869). He gave reasons for preferring lithotrity to lithotomy in operating for stone in the adult male (1868) and he was the first (1863) to perform ovariotomy successfully in the west of Scotland. When the Western Infirmary was opened he was transferred thither, and held the post of professor of clinical surgery from 1874 until 1900, when he retired with the title of emeritus professor of clinical surgery in the University of Glasgow and settled at Stirling. There he died on 19 April 1905.

He married Jessie, daughter of Patrick Blair of Irvine, and left one son, Dr. G. Burnside Buchanan, assistant surgeon to the Western Infirmary, Glasgow.

Buchanan published 'Camp Life as seen by a Civilian' (Glasgow, 1871), and he re-edited and largely rewrote (Sir) Erasmus Wilson's 'Anatomist's Vade Mecum' (London, 1873; 2nd edit. 1880).

[Glasgow Med. Journal, 1906, lxv. 354; Brit. Med. Journal, 1906, i. 1078; additional information kindly given by his son.]

D'A. P.

BUCHANAN, ROBERT WILLIAMS (1841–1901), poet and novelist, born at Caverswall, Staffordshire, on 18 August 1841, was only surviving child of Robert Buchanan (1813–1886) by his wife Margaret Williams (*d.* 1894), daughter of a socialistic lawyer of Stoke-upon-Trent. The father, originally a tailor of Ayr, was at the time of his son's birth an itinerant lecturer in support of Robert Owen's socialist scheme, and soon took to journalism in London. Buchanan went early to schools at Hampton Wick and Merton. At home he saw and heard his father's socialist friends, who included Louis Blanc, Caussidière, and the Chartist champion of co-operation, Lloyd Jones [q. v.]. His father, on principle, denied him all religious training and inculcated hostility to religion.

About 1850 the family went to Glasgow, where the father for several years owned and edited the 'Sentinel,' the 'Glasgow Times,' and the 'Penny Post,' journals expounding his socialistic views. After attending a preparatory school, Buchanan went successively to a Rothesay boarding-school, to Glasgow Academy, and to Glasgow high school. In 1857–8 he completed his education by joining the junior classes of Greek and Latin at Glasgow University. An ardent devotee of the theatre, he revelled as a boy in Vandenhoff's presentation of King Lear, and made the acquaintance of various actors, among them the youthful Henry Irving, 'a quiet, studious young man.' A fellow-student at the university, David Gray [q. v.], became a close friend, and together they read Anderson's 'British Poets.'

Owing to his father's financial embarrassments, Buchanan went to London in 1860, being presently followed by Gray, who died next year. Their experiences of hardship and Gray's brief career are vividly delineated by Buchanan in 'David Gray and other Essays' (1868). In 1863 William Black [q. v. Suppl. I], the novelist, who was an early Glasgow friend, stayed in Buchanan's lodgings in Camden Town on first coming to London (Wemyss Reid, *William Black*, pp. 38–41). Buchanan had already made some contributions to Glasgow newspapers. In London he obtained employment on the 'Athenæum' and other periodicals, and formed many literary acquaintances. Dickens accepted some contributions to 'All the Year Round,' and gave him helpful introductions to Edmund Yates and others. He sought the acquaintance of T. L. Peacock, G. H. Lewes—who gave him practical advice—George Eliot, Browning, and other prominent writers. Under Peacock's influence he produced what he calls his 'pseudo-classic poems,' 'Undertones' (1863) (Miss Jay's *Robert Buchanan*, p. 103; Van Doren, *Life of Peacock*, 1911, pp. 164–5). After a weary and exacting struggle his work gradually won recognition. At length, in 1865, he published 'Idyls and Legends of Inverburn,' which strongly appealed to Alexander Strahan the publisher and Roden Noel [q. v.], thenceforth two valued friends. His 'London Poems' (1866) established his reputation as a graphic writer of narrative poetry whose sympathies with humble life were deep.

With improved prospects, Buchanan settled near Oban, 1866–74, living as a country gentleman and writing steadily, both verse, chiefly narrative, and prose sketches and criticisms. 'Ballad Stories of the Affections' (translated from Danish) appeared in 1866, 'North Coast and other Poems' in 1867, 'The Book of Orm,' a mystical study, in 1870, 'Napoleon Fallen,' a lyrical drama (2 edits.) and 'The Drama of Kings' in 1871, 'St. Abe and his Seven Wives,' a tale in verse of Salt Lake City (anonymously), in 1872, and 'White Rose and Red,' a love story in verse, in 1873. Vivacious ballads like 'The Starling' (in 'London Poems'), 'Phil Blood's Leap,' and the 'Wedding of Shon McLean' (in 'Ballads of Life, Love, and Humour,' 1882) powerfully impressed the general reader. The 'Wedding' originally appeared in the 'Gentleman's Magazine' (July 1874). In prose his best efforts of this period were 'The Land of Lorne,' vivid sketches of a yachting tour to the Hebrides (1871), and critical essays on contemporary authors collected from magazines entitled 'Master Spirits' (1874). The poet soon outran his income, and in order to retrieve his position he gave at the rooms in Hanover Square, London, in 1869, two readings from his works; but the physical strain prevented him from continuing them. In 1870 Gladstone granted him a civil list pension of 100*l*.

In the 'Spectator' on 15 Sept. 1866 Buchanan had published under the pseudonym 'Caliban' a poem called 'The Session of the Poets,' in which he wrote insolently of Swinburne, and satirically of other leading poets of the day. In a pamphlet on Swinburne's 'Poems and Ballads' (1867), W. M. Rossetti retorted by calling Buchanan 'a poor but pretentious poetaster.' Reviewing Matthew Arnold's 'New Poems' (1867) Swinburne attacked David Gray's 'poor little book' in a merciless foot-note (*Essays and Studies*, p. 153). Buchanan now retaliated with vehemence. In October 1871 Buchanan, under the pseudonym of Thomas Maitland, contributed to the 'Contemporary Review' an article entitled 'The Fleshly School of Poetry,' severely handling the Pre-Raphaelites and especially Dante Gabriel Rossetti. A bitter controversy followed (ROSSETTI'S *Family Letters*, ii. 249). Rossetti protested in the 'Athenæum' against 'The Stealthy School of Criticism' (16 Dec. 1871), while Swinburne, with biting causticity, denounced Buchanan in 'Under the Microscope' (1872). Having revised and amplified his attack, Buchanan in 1872 issued it as a pamphlet with his name and the title 'The Fleshly School of Poetry and other Phenomena of the Day.' The warfare was long continued. Swinburne, under the mocking signature of 'Thomas Maitland St. Kilda,' renewed his attack on Buchanan in a letter entitled 'The Devil's Due,' published in the 'Examiner' on 28 Dec. 1875. Buchanan brought an action for libel against the proprietor of the newspaper, Peter Taylor, and after three days' trial (29 June–1 July 1876) won 150*l*. damages. Subsequently Buchanan acknowledged the extravagance of his assault, and sought to make reparation by dedicating to his 'old enemy,' i.e. Rossetti, his novel 'God and the Man' (1881). He wrote in the 'Academy' on 1 July 1882, 'Mr. Rossetti, I freely admit now, never was a Fleshly Poet at all,' and he eulogised Rossetti's work in 'A Look round Literature' (1887).

Leaving Oban in 1874, Buchanan in search of health settled at Rossport, co. Mayo. A collection of his poems in three volumes appeared that year, and although it was censured for its irregularities, improved his position. 'Balder the Beautiful,' an ambitious but heavy poem, followed in 1877, and was received with indifference. Meanwhile, Buchanan turned to prose fiction. In 1876 came out his first novel, 'The Shadow of the Sword' (new edit. 1902), which proved thoroughly readable, and was the forerunner of a long series, two of which, 'A Child of Nature' (1881) and 'Father Anthony' (not issued till 1898), were coloured by his Irish experience. Wearying of Irish life after 1877, Buchanan presently settled in London, which thenceforth remained his headquarters. His literary activity was now at its height. His most powerful novel, 'God and the Man,' a vivid study of a family feud, appeared in 1881, and hardly a year passed till near his death without the issue of a new book of fiction from his pen. He did not abandon poetry, but published less. For the opening of the Glasgow International Exhibition in May 1888 he composed a patriotic ode, which was set to music by Sir Alexander Mackenzie. 'The City of Dream,' an epic poem (1888), the chief poem of his latter years, illustrates his mystical vein and love of mythology.

While a boy at Glasgow Buchanan wrote

a fairly successful pantomime, and comparatively early in his literary career he thought of writing for the stage. After some preliminary trials he wrote and produced successfully at the Connaught Theatre, London, in 1880 a drama called 'A Nine Days' Queen.' From that time till 1897 he was independently or conjointly responsible for a long series of plays, which showed theatrical skill and won the public ear. He also engaged in theatrical management from time to time. He dramatised his two novels, 'The Shadow of the Sword' (1881) and 'God and the Man' (with the title 'Stormbeaten') (1883), the latter venture proving profitable. In 1883 he became lessee of the Globe Theatre for the purpose of producing 'Lady Clare,' his version of Georges Ohnet's 'Le Maître de Forges.' He secured a run of over a hundred nights. In 1884 he visited America, and there staged in Philadelphia the melodrama 'Alone in London,' a composite work by himself and his sister-in-law, Harriett Jay, which was triumphantly produced at the Olympic Theatre in London in 1885. Two plays, 'Sophia' (1886) and 'Joseph's Sweetheart' (1888), which were produced by Thomas Thorne and his company at the Vaudeville Theatre, were based respectively on Fielding's 'Tom Jones' and 'Joseph Andrews.' An adaptation of 'Roger La Honte,' entitled 'A Man's Shadow,' was very popular at the Haymarket Theatre, 1889-90, with (Sir) Herbert Beerbohm Tree in the chief character. In co-operation with Mr. G. R. Sims he wrote for the Adelphi, during 1890-3, a series of melodramas, including 'The English Rose,' 'The Trumpet Call,' 'The White Rose,' 'The Lights of Home,' and 'The Black Domino.' Meanwhile Buchanan's 'Clarissa Harlowe' and 'Miss Tomboy' (adapted from Vanbrugh's 'Relapse') both appeared at the Vaudeville in 1890, Winifred Emery being heroine in each. In the same year 'The Bride of Love,' a rendering of the story of Cupid and Psyche, was produced at the Adelphi. During the same season Buchanan leased the Lyric Theatre, where he brought out 'Sweet Nancy,' a dramatic version of Miss Rhoda Broughton's novel 'Nancy.' On Dostoievski's 'Crime and Punishment' he based 'The Sixth Commandment' (1890). 'The Charlatan' (1894) was one of his later successes, with (Sir) Herbert Beerbohm Tree as chief exponent. There followed in 1895 'The Strange Adventures of Miss Brown.' His last dramatic experiment was 'Two Little Maids from School,' adapted from 'Les Demoiselles de St. Cyr' (1898).

Although his literary and dramatic profits were substantial, Buchanan, who was generous in his gifts to less successful writers, was always improvident, and he lost late in life all his fortune in disastrous speculation. In 1900 he was made bankrupt. An attack of paralysis disabled him late in that year, and he died in poverty at Streatham on 10 June 1901, being buried at Southend-on-Sea, Essex. On 2 Sept. 1861 Buchanan married Mary, daughter of Richard Jay, an engineer. She died without issue after a long illness in Nov. 1882. Just after her death Buchanan wrote a touching dedication to her for the 'Selected Poems' (1882). In his latter years he depended largely on the care of his sister-in-law, Miss Harriett Jay, who aided him in his dramatic work both as actress and as collaborator in authorship and management.

Buchanan wrote too much and too variously to achieve the highest results, but his lyric gift was strong, and there was abundant, if often ill-regulated, force in his novels and plays. He was loyal through life to the anti-religious tradition in which he was bred. In criticism his polemical spirit distorted his judgment, and his combative temperament precluded his making many friends. But with a few men, including Charles Reade, Roden Noel, and Mr. William Canton, his good relations were uninterrupted, and his work found a warm admirer in Mr. Lecky.

Besides the poetical work already mentioned he published: 1. 'Ballads of Life, Love, and Humour,' 1882. 2. 'The Earthquake,' 1885. 3. 'The Outcast,' 1891. 4. 'Buchanan's Poems for the People,' 1892. 5. 'The Wandering Jew,' 1893. 6. 'Red and White Heather' (a miscellany), 1894. 7. 'The Devil's Case,' 1896 (bitter but virile). 8. 'The Ballad of Mary the Mother,' 1897. 9. 'The New Rome,' 1900. The author published a collected edition of his 'Poems' (3 vols.) 1874, and a selection in 1882. His 'Poetical Works' appeared in 1884 and 1901. His prose work included, beside the volumes already mentioned, two characteristic miscellanies, 'A Look round Literature' (1887), and 'The Coming Terror and other Essays' (1891); and the following novels: 1. 'The Martyrdom of Madeline'; 2. 'Love Me for Ever'; and 3. 'Annan Water,' 1883. 4. 'Foxglove Manor,' and 5. 'The New Abelard,' 1884. 6. 'The Master of the Mine'; 7. 'Matt,' and 8. 'Stormy Waters,' 1885. 9. 'That Winter Night,' 1886. 10. 'The Heir of Linne,' 1887. 11. 'The Moment After,' 1890. 12. 'Come Live with

Me and be My Love,' 1891. 13. 'Woman and the Man,' 1893. 14. 'Lady Kilpatrick' and 15. 'The Charlatan,' 1895. 16. 'Diana's Hunting.' 17. 'Marriage by Capture'; and 18. 'Effie Hetherington,' 1896. 19. 'The Rev. Annabel Lee,' 1898. 20. 'Andromeda,' 1900.

[Harriett Jay's Robert Buchanan: Some Account of his Life, 1903; A. S. Walker's Robert Buchanan, 1901; Miles's Poets and Poetry of the Nineteenth Century, vol. vi.; Stedman's Victorian Poets; Grant Wilson's Poets and Poetry of Scotland; Chambers's Cyclopædia of Eng. Lit.; Dante Gabriel Rossetti: Family Letters and Memoir, by W. M. Rossetti; Lives of Rossetti, by Joseph Knight (Great Writers) and A. C. Benson (English Men of Letters); W. Bell Scott's Autobiographical Notes, ii. 161 seq.; The Times, Scotsman, Glasgow Herald, 11 June 1901; Athenæum, 15 June 1901; information from Miss Harriett Jay and Dr. A. H. Millar, Dundee; Stage Cyclopædia, 1909.] T. B.

BUCKTON, GEORGE BOWDLER (1818–1905), entomologist, born at Hornsey on 24 May 1818, was eldest son of George Buckton, a proctor of the prerogative court of Canterbury, of Doctors Commons and Oakfield, Hornsey, by his wife Eliza, daughter of Richard Merricks, D.L., of Runcton, Cheshire. An accident at the age of five crippled him for life, and deprived him of a public school and university career.

Buckton early became interested in natural history and astronomy, and after the death of his father removed to London and became a student at the Royal College of Chemistry in 1848 under A. W. Hofmann. There he remained seven years, being for part of the time research assistant to Hofmann. His first researches dealt with platinum compounds; the most important of a series dating from 1852 to 1865 described his discovery and isolation of mercuric methyl. On his marriage in 1865 and settlement at Weycombe, Haslemere, he abandoned the study of chemistry and took up again the thread of an early interest in entomology.

His first important research in natural history was a study of parthenogenesis in aphides, which led to his 'Monograph of British Aphides' (Ray Society, 4 vols. 1876–1883). This was followed by a 'Monograph of British Cicadæ or Tettigiidæ' (2 vols. 1890–1), the 'Natural History of Eristalis Tenax or the Drone Fly' (1895), and a 'Monograph of the Membracidæ of the World' (1901–3). Meanwhile he pursued astronomical study in a private observatory until 1882, when he fell in trying to reach the long focus of a Newtonian telescope, fracturing his leg in two places, and lying for some hours undiscovered. He was elected F.R.S. in 1857, and contributed fourteen papers to scientific periodicals, two of them in conjunction with Prof. Hofmann, and one with Dr. Odling. He died from the effects of a chill on 25 Sept. 1905. In 1865 he married Mary Ann, daughter of George Odling of Croydon and sister of Prof. William Odling of Oxford. His wife survived him with a son and five daughters. His bust, by R. Hope-Pinker, was exhibited in the Royal Academy of 1904.

[Proc. Roy. Soc. lxxix. B. (1907), p. xlv; Nature, 1905, 587; Trans. Chem. Soc. lxxii. 1907, i. 663; Allingham's Diary, 1910.] R. S.

BULLER, Sir REDVERS HENRY (1839–1908), general, born at Downes, Crediton, co. Devon, on 7 Dec. 1839, was second son of James Wentworth Buller of Downes by Charlotte Juliana Jane, third daughter of Lord Henry Thomas Howard-Molyneux-Howard, a younger brother of Bernard Edward, twelfth Duke of Norfolk [q. v.]. His father, who graduated B.A. from Oriel College, Oxford, in 1819 and B.C.L. in 1824, and D.C.L. in 1829 from All Souls' College, was M.P. for Exeter and for North Devon, and died on 13 March 1865. His mother died on 15 Dec. 1855. The Bullers had been settled in the west country for three centuries. Redvers Buller succeeded to the family manor of Downes on the death of his elder brother, James Howard Buller, on 13 Oct. 1874.

Buller was educated mainly at Eton, where he was fag to the present provost, Dr. Warre, who found him very solid and sturdy, with a will of his own. He was fond of outdoor pursuits, a bold rider, and very observant, but did not make his mark in games or scholarship. He was commissioned as ensign in the 60th (the king's royal rifle corps) on 23 May 1858, and after six months at the depôt joined the second battalion at Benares. At the end of February 1860 it embarked for China, and in August it landed at Pehtang with the rest of the force under Sir James Hope Grant [q. v.], and took part in the occupation of Peking. Buller received the medal and clasp, but saw little fighting.

He was promoted lieutenant on 9 Dec. 1862, and joined the fourth battalion at Quebec. It was commanded by Colonel Robert Hawley, to whom, Buller afterwards said, he owed all that he knew of soldiering. Hawley persuaded him to act as adjutant in 1868. The battalion returned to England in 1869; but on promotion to captain on 28 May 1870, Buller was posted to the first battalion, and went back to Canada, in time to take part with it in the Red River expedition. The troops had to make their way in boats from Lake Superior to Fort Garry, 600 miles, with dangerous navigation and frequent portages. Buller soon attracted the notice of Colonel Wolseley, the commander of the expedition. 'He was a thorough soldier, a practised woodman, a skilful boatman in the most terrifying of rapids, and a man of great physical strength and endurance' (WOLSELEY, ii. 279).

He returned to England in the autumn of 1870, and at the end of 1871 he entered the Staff College. In August 1873, before he had finished the course, he was invited by Sir Garnet Wolseley to go with him to Ashanti as chief intelligence officer. During the advance through the bush he was always in front, and was slightly wounded at Ordashu. He was appointed prize agent after the capture of Coomassie. He was repeatedly mentioned in despatches, received the medal with clasp, and was made brevet-major and C.B. on 31 March 1874.

He served in the adjutant-general's department of the headquarters staff from 1 April 1874 to 30 Jan. 1878, and then went to South Africa with General Thesiger (afterwards Lord Chelmsford) [q. v. Suppl. II], as a special service officer. The sixth Kaffir war was in progress. A corps, known as the frontier light horse, had been raised locally by Lieutenant Frederick Carrington, a medley of many tongues and types, which needed a strong hand to control it. Buller was placed in command of it, and under him it rendered good service against the Gaikas in the Perie bush near King William's Town (WOOD, i. 319 seq.). The campaign was over by June, and its success was due, as Thesiger wrote, to Evelyn Wood's untiring energy and Buller's dogged perseverance (VERNER, ii. 146). He was mentioned in despatches (*Lond. Gaz.* 11 and 18 June 1878) and was made brevet lieutenant-colonel on 11 Nov.

The frontier light horse accompanied Colonel Wood's force to Natal, which was threatened with a Zulu invasion; and it formed part of Wood's flying column, when Lord Chelmsford entered Zululand in January 1879. Wood's advance was arrested by news of the disaster of Isandhlwana, but he encamped at Kambula, and made diversions. On 29 March the camp was attacked by a Zulu army from Ulundi, which was repulsed with heavy loss after four hours' fighting. On the previous day Buller had been sent out with his horsemen and two native battalions, to seize the Inhlobana mountains and capture cattle. He succeeded, but the approach of the Zulu army obliged him to make a hasty retreat. The ground was very rough and steep, and many of his men were cut off; out of 400 Europeans, 92 were killed. At great personal risk Buller rescued two officers and a trooper, and on Wood's recommendation he received the Victoria Cross on 17 June 1879. He was present at the battle of Ulundi, fought on ground which he had reconnoitred the day before. He then went home, as his health had suffered from fatigue and exposure. He had been repeatedly mentioned in despatches (*Lond. Gaz.* 5, 15, 28 March, 7 May and 21 Aug.). He received the medal with clasp, was made aide-de-camp to the Queen with the rank of colonel on 27 Sept., and C.M.G. on 19 Dec. Regimentally he was still a captain, but he was given a half-pay majority on 13 March 1880. Sir Bartle Frere [q. v.] remarked in a despatch, dated 15 Aug. 1879, that 'the action of General Wood and Buller had destroyed the prejudice of the colonists against the strict discipline of regular military service and their distrust of the ability of Her Majesty's officers generally to conduct operations against the Kaffirs' (WOOD, i. 307).

In April 1880 Buller was appointed to the staff in Scotland, and in July he was transferred to Aldershot. In February 1881 he went back to South Africa, and was appointed chief of the staff to Sir Evelyn Wood, who was commanding the troops, and was also acting governor of Natal. The first Boer war had practically ended at Majuba; but Wood was engaged in negotiations, and most of the military work was left to Buller. He received the local rank of major-general on 29 March 1881. He returned to England at the end of the year.

Before the end of August 1882 Buller was on his way to Egypt, having been chosen by Sir Garnet Wolseley as chief of his intelligence staff. He reconnoitred the Egyptian position at Tel-el-Kebir, and was present at the battle. He was mentioned in despatches (*Lond. Gaz.* 2 Nov.), and received the medal with clasp, the bronze star, and the Osmanieh (3rd class). He was made K.C.M.G. on 24 Nov.

He was appointed to the headquarters staff as assistant adjutant-general on 22 July 1883. In February 1884 he returned to Egypt to command the first infantry brigade of the force sent to Suakim under Sir Gerald Graham [q. v. Suppl. I], to deal with Osman Digna. He led his brigade at El Teb and Tamai. In the latter action the two brigades formed separate squares, and the second brigade, which was in advance, was broken and driven back in disorder by a sudden charge of the tribesmen. It was soon rallied owing to the firm attitude of the first brigade, which moved forward, and covered the burning of the Mahdist camp. Graham in his final despatch bore witness to Buller's 'coolness in action, his knowledge of soldiers, and experience in the field, combined with his personal ascendancy over officers and men' (*Lond. Gaz.* 6 May). He was promoted major-general for distinguished service on 21 May, and received two clasps.

In the expedition for the relief of Khartoum Buller was appointed chief of the staff on 26 Aug. 1884. Lord Wolseley wrote of him as invaluable in that capacity owing to his rare instinct for war (Verner, ii. 270). He was sent forward to take command of the desert column, when Sir Herbert Stewart [q. v.] was fatally wounded. He joined it at Gubat on 11 Feb. 1885, with instructions to take Metemmeh; but the strength of its garrison and the approach of the Mahdist forces from Khartoum made him decide on a retreat across the desert to Korti. The skill with which this retreat was carried out averted what might have been a disaster. His services were noted in despatches (*Lond. Gaz.* 27 March, 25 Aug.), he was made K.C.B., and received an additional clasp.

He remained in Egypt till October, and on 1 Nov. he became deputy adjutant-general at headquarters. In August 1886 he went to Ireland for civil employment, to restore law and order in Kerry. The Salisbury administration, on taking office, thought that a 'fresh, vigorous mind, accustomed to strict discipline,' would be useful in overhauling the police arrangements in Ireland (Verner, ii. 328). Buller succeeded so well, that in November he was made under-secretary for Ireland, and called to the Irish Privy Council. He soon found this position irksome. His sympathy with the Irish peasantry made the enforcement of evictions distasteful, and he was not always in accord with ministers. On 15 Oct. 1887 he returned to military duty as quartermaster-general, and on 1 Oct. 1890 he succeeded Lord Wolseley as adjutant-general. He held this office till 30 Sept. 1897.

The ten years thus spent at the war office were a period of unusual activity there; and Buller took a leading part in the changes made to improve the condition of the soldier, and prepare the army for war. The question with which he was specially identified was the reorganisation of supply and transport, combining these two services, and adapting them to the regimental system. He showed a regard for the public purse which was rare among soldiers, and successive secretaries of state, conservative and liberal, thought highly of him as an administrator. Sir Henry Campbell-Bannerman [q. v. Suppl. II] meant him to succeed George, second Duke of Cambridge [q. v. Suppl. II], as commander-in-chief in 1895; but a change of ministry interfered with that arrangement, and Lord Wolseley was appointed. In 1893 Buller had been offered, but had declined, the post of commander-in-chief in India. He became lieut.-general on 1 April 1891, and general on 24 June 1896. He received a reward for distinguished service on 10 March 1892 and the G.C.B. on 26 May 1894. He was made a colonel commandant of the king's royal rifle corps on 13 July 1895, and he became honorary colonel of the 1st volunteer battalion of the Devonshire regiment on 4 May 1892.

On 9 Oct. 1898 Buller succeeded the Duke of Connaught in the command of the troops at Aldershot, but remained there only a year. On 14 Oct. 1899 he embarked for South Africa to enforce the British demands on the Transvaal republic, at the head of 70,000 men, the largest army which England had ever sent abroad. His knowledge of the country and the people, combined with his reputation as a soldier and administrator, justified the selection. He was informed of it in June, but it was not till the end of September that he could form a plan of operations, owing to the doubtful attitude of the Orange Free State. When it became clear that the Free State would be hostile, his plan was to advance on Bloemfontein with 45,000 men from Cape Town, Port Elizabeth, and East London, while 15,000 men should defend Natal, and 7000 should guard Kimberley and other points in Cape Colony. But the whole of the British force could not reach South Africa before December, so that the Boers had the advantage of the initiative.

They declared war on 11 Oct., and invaded Natal with 23,000 men. When Buller arrived at Cape Town at the end of the month, he learnt that Sir George White not only had been unable to drive them back, but was shut up in Ladysmith. The situation was of the gravest, and Buller decided to sacrifice the organisation of his army corps, to send most of the regiments on to Natal as the transports came in, and to go there himself. He hoped to return to Cape Colony and resume his plan of advance, after relieving Ladysmith; and in the meanwhile Lord Methuen was to relieve Kimberley, which was also invested, and Generals French and Gatacre [q. v. Suppl. II] were to cover Cape Colony. His decision was much criticised, but in the circumstances he 'had absolutely no alternative but to attempt to relieve both garrisons simultaneously' (HENDERSON, *Science of War*, p. 368).

On 15 December, having assembled 18,000 men, he moved on Colenso, and made a frontal attack on the Boer position behind the Tugela. There were only 6000 Boers, but they were well hidden, and their fire was so heavy that the attack was not pressed. It cost the British 1100 men and 10 guns. Three days before, Buller had reported that a direct assault on this position would be too costly, and that he meant to turn it by a flank march westward. News of the checks met with by General Gatacre at Stormberg and Lord Methuen at Magersfontein led him to change his mind; he did not like to expose his communications to an enemy elated by success.

In the battle of Colenso he was himself under fire, and was hit by a shrapnel bullet, while he was trying to save the guns. In the evening he reported that he was not strong enough to relieve White, adding—'My view is that I ought to let Ladysmith go, and occupy good positions for the defence of South Natal.' Next day he sent a cipher message to White, asking how long he could hold out, and suggesting that he should make the best terms he could. The reply of the Government was, that the abandonment of White's force would be a national disaster of the greatest magnitude. They urged him to devise another attempt to relieve it, and promised reinforcements. They also decided to send out Lord Roberts as commander-in-chief in South Africa, leaving Buller to devote himself exclusively to the operations in Natal.

Lord Roberts arrived at Cape Town on 10 Jan. 1900. Buller, having been joined by a fresh division under Sir Charles Warren, had just begun an attempt to reach Ladysmith by a wide sweep westward. But the Boers had ample time to shift their ground, and the attempt ended in failure at Spion Kop on 24 January. Warren was in immediate command of the principal force engaged, but Buller was often present, and exercised some control. There was divided responsibility, and Warren's report, forwarded with Buller's comments and those of Lord Roberts, led to much subsequent recrimination. Buller was invited to write a fresh despatch better suited for publication, but this he flatly refused to do. The papers were at first published with large omissions, but ultimately in full (Cd. 968, 17 April 1902).

A third attempt to penetrate the Boer positions, by way of Vaal Krantz, had no better success; but in the middle of February the British began to get possession of the Hlangwane heights, east of Colenso, and after a fortnight of obstinate fighting they entered Ladysmith on 28 February. It was the day after the surrender of Cronje at Paardeberg, and Lord Roberts's progress in the Free State had drawn away some of the Boers from Natal. The relief of Ladysmith had taken nearly three months, and cost 5000 men.

Buller's leadership was severely criticised at the time and afterwards. He showed instability of view and purpose. His care for his men, which was incessant, made him shrink from staking heavily for success. 'The men are splendid,' he reported during the fight at Spion Kop; and they remained staunch to him in spite of failures, recognising the extreme difficulty of his task, and regarding disparagement of him as a slur on themselves.

Two months were spent in recuperation and re-equipment. In April a division was sent to join the main army, leaving three divisions in Natal. In May, after much discussion with Lord Roberts as to his line of advance, Buller moved on the Biggarsberg; and skilfully turning the Boer positions, which were not strongly held, he entered Dundee on 15 May. At the end of the month he opened negotiations with Christian Botha, who was in command of the Boers at Laing's Nek, but they came to nothing. Instead of a direct attack on the Nek, Buller turned it by way of

Botha's pass, and after a sharp action at Alleman's Nek on 11 June reached Volksrust in the Transvaal. Lord Roberts had entered Pretoria on 5 June.

As soon as the railway was repaired Buller advanced to Standerton, and by 4 July the Natal army came in touch with the main army. A combined movement on Belfast was arranged, and on 7 Aug. Buller marched north with 11,000 men. On the 21st he came into collision with the left flank of the Boer forces under Louis Botha, which were opposing the advance of Roberts eastward, along the Delagoa Bay railway. On the 27th the Boers were defeated in the battle of Bergendal, so called from an intrenched kopje on the Boer left which was stormed by Buller's troops. As Lord Roberts reported on 10 Oct.: 'The success of this attack was decisive. It was carried out in view of the main Boer position, and the effect of it was such, that the enemy gave way at all points, flying in confusion to the north and east.' Thus it fell to Buller to give the *coup de grâce* to the resistance of the Boer republics in the way of regular warfare. Their operations from that time onward were of a guerilla character.

While part of the army went on to Komati Poort, Buller marched north to Lydenburg, and made a circuit through that mountainous district, dislodging the Boers from some very strong positions and dispersing their bands. On 2 Oct. he was back at Lydenburg, and took farewell of his troops, for the Natal army was to be broken up. He went to Pretoria on the 10th, and in a special army order of that date Lord Roberts thanked him for the great services he had rendered to his country. He returned to England by Natal, and was presented with a sword of honour at Maritzburg. He landed at Southampton on 9 Nov. He was warmly welcomed and received the freedom of the borough, an example soon followed by Exeter and Plymouth. He was the guest of Queen Victoria at Windsor on the 17th. His services were mentioned in Lord Roberts's despatches of 28 March, 3 and 10 July 1900, and 2 April 1901. He received the G.C.M.G. and the Queen's medal with six clasps.

In January 1901 he resumed command of the Aldershot division, and on 1 Oct. this was merged in the 1st army corps, under a new organisation. Buller had still two years of his five years' term to complete, and he was given command of the corps for that period. But it had been announced that the new army corps would be commanded in peace by the men who would lead them in war, and his appointment was sharply criticised in the press. He was aggrieved that the war office did not defend him or allow him to defend himself. At a public luncheon at the Queen's Hall, Westminster, on 10 Oct. he made a speech which his friends admitted to be a grave indiscretion, and which the government held to be a breach of the King's Regulations. On the 21st he was removed from his command, and was not employed again, though he remained on the active list five years longer. A motion in the House of Commons by Sir Edward Grey, on 17 July 1902, blaming the action of the government, was defeated by 236 votes to 98.

He spent the rest of his life as a country gentleman, regarded locally as one of the foremost worthies of Devon, and meeting a hearty reception at Birmingham and Liverpool, when he visited them in 1903. An equestrian statue of him by Captain Adrian Jones was erected at Exeter in 1905, near Hele's school, by 'his countrymen at home and beyond the seas,' bearing the inscription 'He saved Natal.' In February 1903 he gave very full evidence before the royal commission on the war, which was reprinted in pamphlet form (pp. 160). He was prime warden of the goldsmiths' company in 1907–8. But his health was beginning to fail, and he died at his home near Crediton on 2 June 1908. He was buried at Crediton with military honours, the escort consisting of a battalion of rifles and a battalion of the Devonshire regiment, which alike laid claim to him. The depôt of the rifles is at Winchester, and in the north transept of Winchester cathedral a memorial of him, a recumbent figure in bronze on a tomb, by Mr. Bertram Mackennal, A.R.A., was unveiled by Lord Grenfell on 28 Oct. 1911. There is also a memorial in Crediton church. H. Tanworth Wells [q. v. Suppl. II] painted a portrait in 1889. There is a cartoon by 'Spy' in 'Vanity Fair' (1900).

On 10 Aug. 1882 he married Lady Audrey Jane Charlotte, daughter of the 4th Marquis Townshend, and widow of Greville Howard, son of the 17th earl of Suffolk. They had one daughter.

[His life has yet to be written, but there is a good sketch by Captain Lewis Butler, of his regiment (pp. 120), 1909. In 1900 Mr. Edmund Gosse contributed to the North American Review a character study of him as 'a genial country gentleman and a man of refined intellectual culture.' See The Times, 3 June 1908, and for special campaigns, Huyshe, Red River Expedition, 1871; Brackenbury, Ashanti War, 1874; official narrative of the Zulu War, 1881; Maurice, Campaign in Egypt, 1887; H. E. Colville, Sudan Campaign, 1889; Sir Evelyn Wood, From Midshipman to Field-marshal, 1906; Wolseley, Story of a Soldier's Life, 1903; Willoughby C. Verner, Military Life of the Duke of Cambridge, 1905; Maurice, War in South Africa, 1906–8; Royal Commission on the War in South Africa, Evidence, ii. 169–223, and appendix J, 1904; South African Despatches, 2 vols., 1901; Knox, Buller's Campaign in Natal, 1902; Chron. King's Royal Rifle Corps, 1903–1909.]

E. M. L.

BULLER, Sir WALTER LAWRY (1838–1906), ornithologist, born on 9 Oct. 1838, at Newark, Bay of Islands, New Zealand, was eldest surviving son of the Rev. James Buller, who, born in Cornwall in December 1812, went out to New Zealand as a Wesleyan missionary in 1835, was successively president of the Australasian and of the New Zealand Wesleyan Methodist Conferences, and wrote 'Forty Years in New Zealand' (1878) and 'New Zealand, Past and Present' (1880), dying at Christchurch, N.Z., on 6 Nov. 1884.

Buller was educated at Wesley College, Auckland, and received scientific instruction from William Swainson [q.v.] the naturalist. Having learnt the Maori language, he was appointed government interpreter at Wellington in 1855, and started a weekly Maori paper. In 1861 he was made editor-in-chief of the 'Maori Messenger,' a bilingual journal; in 1862 he became a resident magistrate, and in 1865 a judge of the native land court. In the same year he engaged in the Maori war as a volunteer on the staff of Sir George Grey, and received the New Zealand war medal for his gallantry in carrying without escort Grey's despatches by night through forty miles of the enemy's country. In 1871 he came to England as secretary to the agent-general for New Zealand, and was called to the bar at the Inner Temple on 6 June 1874. He then returned to New Zealand, and practised in the Supreme Court till 1886. In 1875 he was made C.M.G., in recognition of his work on New Zealand ornithology, being elected F.R.S. for the same reason in 1876. He was already a fellow of the Linnean, Geological, and other scientific societies. In 1886 he came back to England as a commissioner for the Colonial and Indian Exhibition, and was made K.C.M.G. He was a member of the Mansion House committee for the Paris Exhibition of 1889, and was given the legion of honour. On his return to New Zealand he was involved in some land transactions concerning the Horowhenna block which were made the subject of serious charges in the house of representatives by the Hon. J. McKenzie, minister of lands in October 1895. An action in the supreme court in August 1897 vindicated Buller, though Mr. McKenzie persisted in his charges. On another visit to England in 1900 Buller was made hon. Sc.D. of Cambridge. He had already received the same degree from the university of Tübingen and had been awarded many foreign decorations.

Buller's principal claim to notice is his complete study of the ornithology of New Zealand, on which he contributed sixty-one papers to scientific periodicals. His chief works were the 'History of the Birds of New Zealand' (1873; 2nd and enlarged edition 1888), and a 'Manual of the Birds of New Zealand' (1882). He was engaged on a supplement to his 'History' when he died. His work, at once accurate, complete, and well illustrated, ranks among the most magnificent contributions to ornithological literature.

He died at Pontdail Lodge, Fleet, Hampshire, on 19 July 1906, and was buried at Fleet. He married in 1862 Charlotte (*d.* 1 Nov. 1891), third daughter of Gilbert Mair, J.P., of Auckland, N.Z., and left two sons and a daughter. There is a bronze tablet to his memory in the St. Michael and St. George chapel in St. Paul's Cathedral.

[Mennell, Dict. of Australasian Biog.; Nature, lxxiv. 354; The Times, 23 July 1906.]

R. S.

BULWER, Sir EDWARD EARLE GASCOYNE (1829–1910), general, colonel of the royal Welsh fusiliers, born on 22 Dec. 1829 at Heydon in Norfolk, was second of the three children, all sons, of William Earle Lytton Bulwer of Heydon Hall, who married on 11 Dec. 1827 Emily (*d.* 1836), daughter of General Isaac Gascoyne, M.P. for Liverpool. The eldest son, William, born on 1 Jan. 1829, of the Scots guards, was severely wounded in the Crimea, and subsequently took an active part in the volunteer movement, becoming brigadier-general in command of the Norfolk volunteer infantry. The third son is Sir Henry Ernest Gascoyne Bulwer, G.C.M.G., late colonial governor. Their father was elder brother of Sir William Henry Lytton Earle

Bulwer, Lord Dalling and Bulwer [q. v.], and of Edward George Earle Lytton Bulwer-Lytton, first Baron Lytton, the novelist. [For early descent, see article on the first LORD LYTTON.]

Edward was privately educated, partly at Putney. Then, like his brothers, he went to Trinity College, Cambridge; but after a year there made up his mind to enter the army. On 21 Aug. 1849 he joined at Winchester the 23rd royal Welsh fusiliers. Before he was of age he gained by purchase on 13 Dec. 1850 the step of lieutenant, and he spent the next few years partly in Canada and partly at home stations. On 4 April 1854 he embarked on the Trent with his regiment for Scutari, where it was formed, with the 7th fusiliers, the 33rd regiment, and the 2nd battalion of the rifle brigade, into the 1st brigade of the light division. A company of his regiment were the first British soldiers who landed in the Crimea on 14 Sept. On 20 Sept., on which day his eldest brother was severely wounded, Edward Bulwer took part in the crossing of the Alma and the storming of the redoubt, which added lustre to the past services of the royal Welsh fusiliers. On the following day Bulwer was promoted to be captain. The regiment endured great hardships afterwards in the trenches, losing ninety-six men in January 1855, was severely handled on 8 Sept. in the attack on the Redan, and maintained its reputation for valour, until the news of the armistice signed in March 1856 reached the allied forces in the middle of April. It left Sevastopol 14 June, arriving 21 July at Gosport, and proceeded to Aldershot, where it was inspected by Queen Victoria. Bulwer received the Crimean medal with two clasps and the Turkish medal, and then for six months served as A.D.C. to the major-general commanding the eastern district.

Under article 23 of the treaty which was signed at Paris on 30 March and ratified on 27 April 1856, it was necessary to investigate the condition of the Danubian principalities. Bulwer was attached to the commission under his uncle, Sir Henry (afterwards Lord Dalling), and he served on this special duty from September 1856 to September 1857. In May and June 1857 his regiment had sailed for service in China, but on news of the Indian Mutiny was diverted to India. Bulwer rejoined the colours while the royal Welsh fusiliers were proceeding from Calcutta to serve under Sir Colin Campbell at Lucknow. The 23rd regiment was engaged in constant fighting at the relief of Lucknow on 22 Nov. 1857, and at the operations which followed until the advance on Lucknow in March 1858, when the 23rd formed part of the attacking force under Sir James Outram. Bulwer, who had obtained his majority by purchase on 26 Jan. 1858, marched in September, in the temporary absence of Colonel Pratt, with his regimental headquarters and six companies out of Lucknow to join Colonel Purnell's force. The final capture of Lucknow had dispersed many thousands of armed rebels, whom it was necessary to reduce to order before it was possible to re-establish the civil government. In this work Bulwer especially distinguished himself on three occasions in command of a detached column, of which 180 men of his own regiment formed a part. On 23 Sept. he encountered the rebels entrenched near Selimpore on the river Gumti behind an outer and inner ditch with rampart. His men, after a hot march of twenty miles, carried the entrenchments and scattered the enemy, killing 700 of them. Then occupying the fort of Gosainganj, he cleared the neighbourhood of mutineers, and, in the words of Brigadier-general Chute's despatch, 'established confidence and tranquillity.' 'Every credit,' wrote the brigadier on 26 Sept. 1858, 'is due to Major Bulwer for the zeal and ability evinced in the performance of this most important duty.' Lord Clyde reported to the governor-general on 5 Oct. his 'high opinion of the brilliant manner in which these operations were conducted.' Again, at Jabrowli on 23 Oct. and at Purwa on 29 Oct., Bulwer won victories over vastly superior forces, leaving on the latter occasion 600 sepoys dead or wounded on the field and carrying off two guns (cf. THOMAS HENRY KAVANAGH, *How I won the V.C.*). For these and other mutiny services Bulwer received a brevet lieutenant-colonelcy dated 26 April, and the C.B. in 1859.

Despite Bulwer's prowess in the field, it was in staff employ and not in active service that he was henceforth employed. He served as assistant inspector of reserve forces in Scotland (1865–70), and then as assistant adjutant-general for recruiting there in 1870. From 1873 to 1879 he was assistant adjutant-general, at headquarters, for auxiliary forces. The period was a critical one in British military history. Lord Cardwell's new short-service system made it necessary to re-organise the infantry regiments and weld into a homogeneous whole the regular and auxiliary forces, as far as possible, as a county organisation. During Bulwer's term of office and in the teeth of much opposition a commencement was made of this localisation. His experience taught him that 'in an army raised by voluntary enlistment it is not wise to have too many compulsory clauses,' that young men still growing and immature are of great value as soldiers, that the reserves may be trusted when called on, and that 'the interest of the man and the interest of the state should be made identical' (cf. his article on the British army in the *National Review*, March 1898). On 1 Oct. 1877 he was promoted to the rank of major-general, and on 10 March 1879 was given command of the Chatham district; but in the following year he was back at headquarters as inspector-general of recruiting (1880–6), taking active part in the supply of troops for the Egyptian and Sudan wars and in carrying out the reforms of H. C. E. Childers, the secretary of state for war [q. v. Suppl. I]. In 1886 he received the K.C.B., and became deputy adjutant-general to the forces (1886–7), being promoted to the rank of lieutenant-general on 10 March 1887. He was also deputed in 1886 to serve on the commission of inquiry into the Belfast riots. From 1889 to 1894 he was lieutenant-governor and commander of the troops in Guernsey, serving also as a member of Lord Wantage's committee to inquire into the conditions of service in the army in 1891, and being promoted to be general on 1 April 1892. He retired from the active list in 1896. Honours still awaited him. He was honorary colonel of the 3rd battalion Norfolk regiment 1896–1905, and on 31 March 1898 he received the distinction, which he valued above all others, of colonel of the royal Welsh fusiliers. He was made G.C.B. in 1905. To the end of his life he took a deep interest in the Duke of York's Royal Military School, Chelsea, of which he was for many years a commissioner. He died after a long illness in London on 8 Dec. 1910.

In July 1863 he married Isabella, daughter of Sir J. Jacob Buxton, baronet, of Shadwell Court, Norfolk, who, dying in 1883, left one son and four daughters.

[The Times, 10 Dec. 1910; Kinglake, Invasion of the Crimea; T. H. Kavanagh, How I won the Victoria Cross, 1860; Major Broughton Mainwaring, Historical Record of the Royal Welsh Fusiliers; Reports on annual recruiting presented to Parliament.]

W. L-W.

BUNSEN, ERNEST DE (1819–1903), theologian, was second son in the family of five sons and five daughters of Christian Charles Josias, Baron von Bunsen, Prussian diplomatist, who was Prussian minister at the court of St. James's from 1841 to 1854, by his wife Frances, daughter of Benjamin Waddington of Dunston Park, Berkshire. Of his brothers, Henry (1818–1855) became a naturalised Englishman and was rector of Donnington, Wolverhampton; George (1824–1896) was an active politician in Germany; and Karl (1821–1887) and Theodor (1832–1892) passed their careers in the Prussian and German diplomatic service.

Ernest was born on 11 Aug. 1819 at the Villa Caffarelli, Rome, while his father was the Prussian representative at the Vatican. Educated at home by his parents till 1834, and afterwards at the school for cadets at Berlin, Bunsen in 1837 became an officer in the Kaiser Franz regiment of grenadier guards. He subsequently served in the regiment of the Emperor Alexander at Berlin, and after a severe illness joined his parents in England in 1843 on long leave. He served under his father as secretary of the Prussian legation in London, and in 1848 joined the suite of the Prince of Prussia, afterwards William I, first German Emperor, during his visit to England. In 1849 he returned to Germany and served during the Baden campaign on the staff of the Prince of Prussia, by whom he was decorated for distinguished service at the battle of Sedenburg. He left the German army shortly afterwards. Settling in England, he made his home at Abbey Lodge, Regent's Park, London, a house which he acquired on his marriage in 1845. While his father lived he paid annual visits to Baden, and was also frequently in Italy. During the Franco-German war he helped in the hospitals on the Rhine (1870–1), and in 1871 was made chamberlain at the court of William I. But his main interests lay in literary study. In 1854 he published a free German rendering of Hepworth Dixon's biography as 'William Penn oder die Zustände Englands 1644–1718.' Following his father's example, he made laborious researches into biblical history and comparative religion among Oriental peoples. His chief work, 'Biblical Chronology' (1874), was an attempt to fix the dates of Hebrew history by a comparison with contemporary history of Egypt, Babylon, and Assyria. Later research has questioned his conclusions, but he continued to write much on the same theme in both German and English. His last years were absorbed by a work never finished called 'The Transmission,' which he hoped would ultimately unite the catholic churches of east and west and the various branches of the Protestant church.

Bunsen, who had unusual musical talents, died at Abbey Lodge on 13 May 1903, and was buried at Leytonstone churchyard. He married on 5 August 1845, at West Ham church, Elizabeth (*d.* Jan. 1903), daughter of Samuel Gurney [q. v.] and niece of Elizabeth Fry [q. v.]. His eldest son, Fritz, died in 1870; a second son, Sir Maurice de Bunsen, who became British minister at Lisbon in 1905, survived him with two daughters.

A water-colour drawing of Bunsen as a child by his grandmother is in the possession of his daughter, Baroness Deichmann, and an oil painting of him as a German officer is in the possession of the second daughter, Miss Marie de Bunsen.

Besides the works mentioned, Bunsen published: 1. 'Hidden Wisdom of Christ,' 1865. 2. 'The Keys of St. Peter,' 1867. 3. 'Die Einheit der Religionen in Zusammanhange mit den Völkerwanderungen der Urzeit und der Geheimlehre,' Berlin, 1870. 4. 'Das Symbol des Kreuzes bei Allen Nationen,' Berlin, 1876. 5. 'Die Plejaden und der Thierkreis,' Berlin, 1879. 6. 'The Angel-Messiah of the Buddhists, Essenes, and Christians,' 1880. 7. 'Die Ueberlieferung. Ihre Entstehung und Entwicklung,' 2 vols., Leipzig, 1889. 8. 'Essays on Church History,' 1889. 9. 'Die Rekonstruktion der Kirchlichen Autorität,' Leipzig, 1892.

[The Times, 15 and 18 May 1903; Hare, Life and Letters of Baroness Bunsen, 1879; Encyc. Brit., 11th ed., s.v. Baron von Bunsen; Brockhaus's Conversations-Lexicon; Meyer's Conversations-Lexicon; unpublished Memoir by the Baroness Deichmann.]

S. E. F.

BUNTING, Sir PERCY WILLIAM (1836–1911), social reformer and editor of the 'Contemporary Review,' born at Ratcliffe, near Manchester, on 1 February 1836, was only son of Thomas Percival Bunting by his wife Eliza Bealey, whose mother carried on the family business of bleachers at Ratcliffe. Bunting's father, third son of Jabez Bunting [q. v.], was a solicitor in Manchester. His sister, Sarah Maclardie (*d.* 1908), who married Sheldon Amos [q. v. Suppl. I], joined Mrs. Josephine Butler [q. v. Suppl. II] in her strenuous agitation against the state regulation of vice.

After education at home he became in 1851 an original student at the newly founded Owens College, Manchester, and survived all of his companions save one, graduating there as an associate in 1859. Meanwhile he obtained a scholarship at Pembroke College, Cambridge, and graduated B.A. as twenty-first wrangler in 1859, developing during his university career unusual musical gifts. Called to the bar in 1862 at Lincoln's Inn, he gradually acquired a large practice as a conveyancer and at the chancery bar. After 1882 he grew less active in his profession in the presence of new interests, and finally retired from practice about 1895.

From an early age Bunting devoted himself to social reform, political liberalism, and the welfare of modern methodism. He was an active promoter of the forward movement in methodism, and he aimed at the organisation of nonconformity as a national religious force. In 1892 the National Free Church Council was founded at his house, and he was long the lay secretary of the committee of privileges for methodism. He sought to stimulate the educational and social as well as the religious activity of the free churches, and was a founder in 1873 and thenceforth a governor of the Leys School at Cambridge. With Hugh Price Hughes [q. v. Suppl. II] he was a projector and founder in 1887 of the West London Mission, of which he acted as treasurer.

The promotion of moral purity was the social reform which engaged much of his adult energy. He frequently visited the Continent in the cause, becoming an apt French and a moderately good German scholar. The repeal of the Contagious Diseases Acts was finally achieved in 1886. From 1883 until his death Bunting was also chairman of the National Vigilance Association, which he helped to found, employing his continental influence to extend its operations to every capital in Europe.

In politics Bunting was a zealous liberal and admirer of Gladstone, serving on the executive committee of the National Liberal Federation from about 1880 till his death, and interesting himself in the National Liberal Club; in 1892 he unsuccessfully contested East Islington as a Gladstonian liberal.

Meanwhile in 1882 Bunting became editor of the 'Contemporary Review,' founded in 1862 by the publisher, Alexander Strahan, and first edited by Dean Alford [q. v.], and subsequently from 1870 to 1877 by Sir James Knowles [q. v. Suppl. II]. Bunting remained editor until his death, conducting the 'Review' on liberal lines. He enlisted the services of foreign contributors with whom his endeavours in social reform had brought him into touch, and he encouraged all writers, whether or no of established fame, who could adequately present salient phases of contemporary theology, science, art, literature and politics. He maintained in the 'Review' a moderately advanced religious tone and gave topics of social reform a prominent place in its pages.

In 1902 Bunting succeeded Hughes as editor of the 'Methodist Times' and carried on the work concurrently with the 'Review' until 1907.

A firm believer in international amity, he joined in 1907 the journalists, and in 1909 the representatives of the churches, on visits to Germany, and he aided in the formation in the summer of 1911 of the Anglo-German Friendship Society. He was knighted in 1908. Subsequently his physical powers slowly failed, and he died somewhat unexpectedly on 22 July 1911 at 11 Endsleigh Gardens, N.W. Bunting married on 21 June 1869 Mary Hyett, daughter of John Lidgett of Hull, a London shipowner, and aunt of the Rev. John Scott Lidgett, president of the Wesleyan Conference 1908–9. Lady Bunting, who survived her husband with two sons and two daughters, was a co-worker with him in many of his activities.

Bunting contributed to the volumes entitled 'The Citizen of To-morrow' (1906) and 'Christ and Civilisation' (1910), and wrote many pamphlets concerning the movements in which he was engaged. To the 'Contemporary Review' he was an occasional contributor, his articles including 'Reminiscences of Cardinal Manning' (1892), 'Nonconformists and the Education Bill' (1902), 'The White Slave Trade' (1902), 'The Journalistic Tour in Germany' (1907), 'Convocation and the Bishop of Hereford' (1911).

[Information from relations; personal knowledge; The Times, 24 July 1911; Contemporary Review, August 1911; Manchester Guardian, 24 July 1911; Methodist Times, 27 July and 3 Aug. 1911.] J. E. G. de M.

BURBIDGE, EDWARD (1839-1903), liturgiologist, born on 9 Aug. 1839 at Laura Place, Upper Clapton, London, was younger son in the family of two sons and two daughters of William Smith Burbidge, distiller, of London, by his wife Sarah Jane Peacock. Privately educated owing to delicate health, he was on 26 May 1858 admitted to Emmanuel College, Cambridge. In 1859 he was elected to a Whichcote scholarship and to an Ash and Browne exhibition. In 1860 he won a Thorpe scholarship, and graduated B.A. in 1862 with a second class in the classical tripos, proceeding M.A. in 1865. He was ordained deacon in 1863 and priest in 1864. After serving curacies at Aldbourne, Wiltshire (1863-8) and at Warminster (1868-73), he became in 1873 rector, and in 1882 vicar of Backwell, Somerset. In 1887 he was appointed to a prebendal stall in Wells cathedral. On resigning his living in October 1902, he retired to Weston-super-mare. There he died on 7 Feb. 1903, and was buried at Backwell. He married on 21 April 1869 Susan Mary, youngest daughter of William Topley Humphrey, vicar of East Stockwith, Lincolnshire, who survived him with four sons and three daughters.

Burbidge took an active interest in education, especially in the improvement of voluntary schools, and for many years he acted as diocesan inspector. But he was chiefly known as a zealous student of ancient liturgies. His valuable 'Liturgies and Offices of the Church' (1885), to which was prefixed a catalogue of the remains of Archbishop Cranmer's library, formed a scholarly commentary on the original sources of the Book of Common Prayer. It was generally recognised as a standard work, and was quoted as authoritative on 21 Nov. 1890 by archbishop E. W. Benson [q. v. Suppl. I] in delivering judgment in the bishop of Lincoln case. Burbidge also published: 1. 'The Parish Priest's Book of Offices and Instructions for the Sick,' 1871. 2. 'A Plain Manual of Holy Communion,' 1878; 2nd edit. 1882. 3. 'Peace with God,' a manual for the sick, 1880.

[The Times, 10 Feb. 1903; Brit. Mus. Cat.; information from Mrs. Burbidge.] G. S. W.

BURBIDGE, FREDERICK WILLIAM (1847–1905), botanist, born at Wymeswold, Leicestershire, on 21 March 1847, was son of Thomas Burbidge, a farmer and fruit-grower. He entered the gardens of the Royal Horticultural Society at Chiswick as a student in 1868, and proceeded in the same year to the Royal Gardens, Kew. Here he showed skill as a draughtsman and was partly employed in making drawings of plants in the herbarium. Leaving Kew in 1870, he was on the staff of the 'Garden' from that year until 1877.

During this period he published 'The Art of Botanical Drawing' (1872); 'Cool Orchids and how to grow them, with a Descriptive List of all the Best Species' (1874); 'Domestic Floriculture, Window Gardening and Floral Decorations' (1874), one of the best books of the kind; 'The Narcissus: its History and Culture' (1875), with coloured plates drawn by himself and a scientific review of the genus by Mr. John Gilbert Baker; the volume on 'Horticulture' (1877) in G. P. Bevan's 'British Industries' series; and 'Cultivated Plants, their Propagation and Improvement' (1877), an excellent text-book for young gardeners, which won public appreciation from Gladstone.

In 1877 Burbidge was sent by Messrs. Veitch as a collector to Borneo. He was absent two years, during which he also visited Johore, Brunei, and the Sulu Islands. He brought back many remarkable plants, especially pitcher-plants, such as 'Nepenthes Rajah' and 'N. bicalcarata'; orchids, such as 'Cypripedium Laurenceanum,' 'Dendrobium Burbidgei' and 'Aërides Burbidgei'; and ferns, such as 'Alsophila Burbidgei' and 'Polypodium Burbidgei.' The chronicle of his journey was published in 1880 as 'The Gardens of the Sun, or a Naturalist's Journal on the Mountains and in the Forests and Swamps of Borneo and the Sulu Archipelago.' The first set of the dried specimens brought back by him numbered nearly a thousand species, and was presented by Messrs. Veitch to the Kew herbarium. Sir Joseph Hooker in describing the Scitamineous 'Burbidgea nitida' (*Botanical Magazine* 1879 t. 6403) names it 'in recognition of Burbidge's eminent services to horticulture, whether as a collector in Borneo, or as author of "Cultivated Plants, their Propagation and Improvement," a work which should be in every gardener's library.'

In 1880 Burbidge was appointed curator of the botanical gardens of Trinity College, Dublin, at Glasnevin. There he did much to encourage gardening in Ireland (*Gardeners' Chronicle*, 1901, ii. 460). In 1889 Dublin University conferred on him the honorary degree of M.A., and in 1894 he became keeper of the college park as well as curator of the botanical gardens. While at Dublin he published 'The Chrysanthemum: its History, Culture, Classification and Nomenclature' (1883) and 'The Book of the Scented Garden' (1905). On the establishment of the Victoria medal of honour by the Royal Horticultural Society, in 1897, Burbidge was one of the first recipients, and he was also a member of the Royal Irish Academy.

Burbidge died from heart-disease on Christmas Eve 1905, and was buried in Dublin. He married in 1876 Mary Wade, who died, without issue, six months before him. Although no scientific botanist, nor very skilful as a cultivator, Burbidge did admirable service as a horticultural writer.

[Journal of Botany, 1906, 80; Gardeners' Chronicle, xxxviii. (1905) 460, and xxxix. 10 (with portrait); Kew Bulletin, 1906, 392; Journal of the Kew Guild, 1906, 326 (with portrait); and 'Hortus Veitchii' (1906) 75, 399.] G. S. B.

BURBURY, SAMUEL HAWKSLEY (1831–1911), mathematician, born on 18 May 1831 at Kenilworth, was only son of Samuel Burbury of Clarendon Square, Leamington, by Helen his wife.

He was educated at Shrewsbury (1848–1850), where he was head boy, and at St. John's College, Cambridge. At the university he won exceptional distinction in both classics and mathematics. He was twice Porson prizeman (1852 and 1853), Craven university scholar (1853), and chancellor's classical medallist (1854). He graduated B.A. as fifteenth wrangler and second classic in 1854, becoming fellow of his college in the same year; he proceeded M.A. in 1857. On 6 Oct. 1855 he entered as a student at Lincoln's Inn, and was called to the bar on 7 June 1858. From 1860 he practised at the parliamentary bar; but increasing deafness compelled him to take chamber practice only, from which he retired in 1908. While engaged in legal work Burbury pursued with much success advanced mathematical study, chiefly in collaboration with his Cambridge friend, Henry William Watson [q. v. Suppl. II]. Together they wrote the treatises, 'The Application of Generalised Co-ordinates to the Kinetics of a Material System' (Oxford, 1879) and 'The Mathematical Theory of Electricity and Magnetism' (2 vols. Oxford, 1885–9), in which the endeavour was made to carry on the researches of Clerk Maxwell and to place electrostatics and electromagnetism on a more formal mathematical basis. Among many papers which Burbury contributed independently to the 'Philosophical Magazine' were those 'On the Second Law of Thermodynamics, in Connection with the Kinetic Theory of Gases' (1876) and 'On a Theorem in the Dissipation of Energy' (1882). He was elected F.R.S. in 1890. He died on 18 Aug. 1911 at his residence, 15 Melbury Road, London, W., and was buried at Kensal Green.

Burbury married on 12 April 1860 Alice Ann, eldest daughter of Thomas Edward Taylor, J.P., of Dodworth Hall, Barnsley, Yorkshire, and had issue four sons and two daughters. A portrait of Burbury by William E. Miller (1884) is in the possession of his widow.

[The Times, 23 Aug. 1911; Nature, 31 Aug. 1911; Proc. Roy. Soc. A. 584, p. 81; Proc. Lond. Math. Soc. vol. x.; Men of the Time, 1899; private information; see art. WATSON, HENRY WILLIAM.] D. J. O.

BURDETT-COUTTS, ANGELA GEORGINA, BARONESS BURDETT-COUTTS (1814–1906), philanthropist, born at the residence of her maternal grandfather, 80 Piccadilly, London, 21 April 1814, was youngest of the six children—a son and five daughters—of Sir Francis Burdett (1770–1844) [q. v.], politician. Her mother was Sophia, third and youngest daughter of Thomas Coutts [q. v.], the banker, by his first wife, Susan Starkie. Thomas Coutts very soon after the death of his first wife in 1815 married Harriot Mellon [q. v.], the actress, to whom, at his death on 24 Feb. 1822, he bequeathed unconditionally his entire fortune, including his interest in his bank.

Miss Burdett's childhood was passed with her parents at their country residences, Ramsbury, Wiltshire, and Foremark, Derbyshire, with occasional visits to Bath. Later she spent most of her time at her father's town house in St. James's Place. The house was frequented by leading politicians and literary men, including Disraeli, Tom Moore, and Samuel Rogers, all of whom became the girl's lifelong friends. She inherited many of her father's broad views, and among other qualities his natural and persuasive power of public speaking. While still young she made a prolonged tour abroad with her mother, lasting some three years. She studied under foreign masters and mistresses in each country where a stay was made. Her maternal grandfather's banking connection with European royalty and nobility, and her father's wide acquaintance with leaders of advanced opinion on the continent, introduced her to a wide social foreign circle which liberalised her interests and sympathies. She never considered her education ended, and amongst those whom she looked on almost as tutors in later years were William Pengelly [q. v.], the geologist, Faraday, and Wheatstone, all of whom stirred in her scientific interests.

Meanwhile Angela had attracted the favourable notice of the widow and heiress of her grandfather Coutts, who on 16 June 1827 married as her second husband William Aubrey de Vere Beauclerk, ninth duke of St. Albans. The duchess took a great liking to the girl, and on her death on 6 Aug. 1837 she made Angela heiress to her vast property. After providing for an annuity of 10,000*l.* a year to the duke, together with the occupancy of No. 80 Piccadilly and Holly Lodge, Highgate, during his life, the duchess left to Angela the reversion of those properties, and the whole of her remaining possessions, including her dominant share in Coutts's bank, and her leasehold interest in the town mansion, No. 1 Stratton Street. The duke her second husband died on 27 May 1849, when the duchess's testamentary disposition took full effect.

The duchess's selection of Angela, the youngest of her five step-granddaughters, to succeed to her first husband's fortune was kept secret to the end, and came as a surprise to the family. The duchess at first devised her bequest to Angela absolutely, but under pressure of the partners in Coutts's bank, which had become a financial institution of great importance, she modified her intention by devising the bank property in remainder to Angela's elder sisters on Angela's death without issue. The rest of the fortune remained free of restriction.

On her succession to her fortune, Miss Burdett assumed the additional surname of Coutts by royal licence, and added the Coutts arms to those of the Burdett family.

In the autumn of 1837 Miss Burdett-Coutts removed from her father's house to 1 Stratton Street, taking there as her companion Hannah Meredith, her former governess. Miss Meredith married in 1844 William Brown, a medical practitioner, who died on 23 Oct. 1855, but Mrs. Brown remained the inseparable friend and chief companion of Miss Burdett-Coutts until her death on 21 Dec. 1878. Both Miss Burdett-Coutts's parents died within a few days of each other in January 1844, but since reaching her majority she had depended little on family counsel. From the outset Miss Burdett-Coutts, as 'the richest heiress in all England' (cf. RAIKES, *Journal*, iv. 345), enjoyed a fame through the country second only to Queen Victoria. Her appearance in Westminster Abbey at Queen Victoria's Coronation (28 June 1838) excited enormous curiosity. Barham in his 'Mr. Barney Maguire's Account of the

Coronation' in the 'Ingoldsby Legends' called special attention to the presence of

'that swate charmer,
The famale heiress, Miss Anjā-ly Coutts.'

Suitors were soon numerous and speculation as to her choice of a husband greatly exercised the public mind. No young man of good family is said to have abstained from a proposal, and exaggerated rumour included the duke of Wellington and Prince Louis Napoleon among aspirants to her hand. But she declined all advances, and devoted herself exclusively to social entertainment and philanthropy, both of which she practised at her sole discretion on a comprehensive scale and on the highest and most disinterested principles.

To her house, No 1 Stratton Street, she annexed the adjoining house, No. 80 Piccadilly, which reverted to her when the duke of St. Albans died in 1849, and there as well as at Holly Lodge, of which the duke's death also put her in possession, she extended hospitality to everybody of rank or any sort of distinction, whether English or foreign, for nearly sixty years. Her intimates were not many, but were of varied interests. She travelled little away from London, but from 1860 to 1877 she had a winter residence at Torquay. Her father's literary associates, Tom Moore and Samuel Rogers, were among her earliest friends. To the former she showed her tiara of Marie Antoinette and other famous jewels in 1845. The duke of Wellington was also soon one of her frequent guests. In May 1850 a grand entertainment which she gave in the duke's honour provoked much public notice. To her inner circle there were at the same time admitted Sir Robert Peel and Samuel Wilberforce, bishop of Winchester, while both Disraeli and Gladstone were well known to her. With the royal family, many of whom were clients of Coutts's bank, she was from the first in close social relations. She was on very cordial terms with the first duke and duchess of Cambridge, and the intimacy was maintained with their son, the second duke of Cambridge, and especially with their daughter, the duchess of Teck. The latter's son, Prince Francis of Teck, was her godson, and to the duchess of Teck's daughter Mary, afterwards Queen Mary, she was always attached. French acquaintances were numerous. She visited the Emperor Napoleon III and the Empress Eugénie at Compiègne, and she numbered the Duc d'Aumale among her friends till his death. For Americans the baroness cherished a regard. Her guests included from time to time the American ministers—Motley, Bancroft, J. R. Lowell, Phelps, as well as statesmen of distinction, like Daniel Webster, Everett, and Robert Winthrop.

In literature, science, art, and the stage she was always interested. Shakespeare was an early hero, and she acquired by the advice of her friend William Harness [q. v.] the finest known copy of the first folio in 1864 at the then record price of 716*l.* [see art. DANIEL, GEORGE]. Queen Victoria wrote her a letter of congratulation on the acquisition, and sent her a piece of Herne's oak from Windsor forest to make a casket to contain the book. At the sale of Samuel Rogers's pictures in 1855 she was a liberal purchaser. With Charles Dickens she formed a close friendship. The novelist aided her in many of her schemes of beneficence, and she took charge of his eldest son's education. To her Dickens dedicated his novel 'Martin Chuzzlewit' in 1844. 'She is a most excellent creature,' he wrote in 1843, 'and I have a most perfect affection and respect for her.' Her scientific friends included Sir William Hooker and his son Sir Joseph, whom she often visited at Kew, as well as Faraday and Tyndall. To leading actors she extended a generous hospitality. She was well acquainted with Macready, and when Henry Irving made his first success at the Lyceum Theatre in 1870 she became one of his most loyal admirers. Though she did not interest herself financially in his theatrical ventures, she freely used her social influence on his behalf, and commissioned Edwin Long to paint several portraits of him. She never missed any of his great revivals, and after the first performance of 'Richard III,' on 29 Jan. 1877, she presented him with Garrick's ring. In 1879 he was one of her yachting party in the Mediterranean and Adriatic, where he studied the costumes and scenic effects for his production of 'The Merchant of Venice.'

But Miss Burdett-Coutts's aim and chief occupation in life did not lie in social hospitality or recreation, although she never neglected either. Her business capacity was very great, and she personally administered her vast wealth. In the affairs of the bank, in which she held the largest share, she played an active part. Yet her energies were mainly spent in applying her fortune to purposes of private and public beneficence. Her relief of private suffering was catholic and discriminating; she personally studied each case, and her sturdy commonsense duly restrained her lively sense of pity and protected her from imposture. Her private beneficiaries were chiefly the very poor, but she was always accessible to the appeal of struggling professional men, and all victims of sudden calamity. Doing little vicariously, she devised and developed for herself her schemes of philanthropy. Dickens was her almoner for a time, and on his recommendation William Henry Wills [q. v.] acted in that capacity from 1855 to 1871, when he was succeeded by Sir John Hassard. But all her charities were carried on under her own supervision, and her house at Stratton Street was often the meeting-place of the administrative committees. She was fertile in suggestion of method, and sought to turn to practical use existing agencies before instituting new ones. At the same time she was a pioneer in creating new modes of dealing with the problems of poverty, many of which were subsequently adopted well-nigh universally. Her public benevolence embraced an exceptional range, and knew no distinction of race or creed. The welfare of the Church of England, the housing of the poor, elementary and scientific and technical education, the care of neglected children, the extension of women's industrial opportunities, the protection of dumb animals, colonial expansion, female emigration, the exploration of Africa, the civilisation of native races, the care of the wounded in war, were all causes in which she took an originating part and expended, virtually with her own hand, vast sums of money. Those who could help her in the distribution of her wealth on her own lines were among her most welcome guests at Stratton Street or Holly Lodge.

A strong protestant, but no doctrinal partisan, she first gave play to her philanthropic instinct by munificent benefactions to the Church of England, which she regarded as the best of all philanthropic organisations. William Howitt, in his 'Northern Heights of London' (1869), wrote, 'I suppose no other woman under the rank of a queen ever did so much for the established church; had she done it for the catholic church she would undoubtedly be canonised as St. Angela.' The beautiful church of St. Stephen in Rochester Row, Westminster, which with the schools and vicarage form a striking and important architectural group in the Gothic style, designed by Benjamin Ferrey [q. v.], was built and endowed by Miss Burdett-Coutts, at a cost of more than 90,000*l.*, in memory of her father, who represented the city of Westminster in parliament for thirty years. The foundation stone was laid on 20 July 1847, and the consecration followed on 24 June 1850. The duke of Wellington presented an altar cloth and a silk curtain taken from Tippoo Sahib's tent at the storming of Seringapatam. There lie buried William Brown and his wife, Mrs. Hannah Brown, the baroness's lifelong friend. The district was poor, and Miss Burdett-Coutts, besides building the church, the patronage of which she retained, created a new and complete parochial organisation, including guilds, working and friendly societies, temperance societies, Bible classes, soup kitchens, self-help club, and the like.

Three other churches in London—St. John's, Limehouse, in 1853; St. James', Hatcham, in 1854; and St. John's, Deptford, in 1855—were built by the assistance of Miss Burdett-Coutts, who placed in the hands of Charles James Blomfield [q. v.], the bishop of London, a sum of 15,000*l.* to be applied to the erection of churches at his discretion. In 1877 she joined with the Turners' Company in giving four of the peal of twelve bells to St. Paul's Cathedral. In the poorest district of Carlisle, too, she built at her entire cost another St. Stephen's church, which was consecrated on 31 May 1865. In 1872 she acquired the right of presentation to the vicarage of Ramsbury on her father's Wiltshire estate, and subsequently restored the church, while she acquired the living of the adjoining parish of Baydon, repaired the church, and increased the value of the living in perpetuity.

Religious feeling at first coloured her interest in colonial expansion, which grew steadily with her years. In 1847 she endowed the bishoprics of Capetown, South Africa, and Adelaide, South Australia, both of which were strictly modelled on the English diocesan system. Ten years later she founded the bishopric of British Columbia, providing 25,000*l.* for the endowment of the church, 15,000*l.* for the bishopric, and 10,000*l.* towards the maintenance of the clergy. She intended that her colonial bishoprics should remain in dependence on the Anglican church at home. In 1866, however, Robert Gray [q. v.], bishop of Capetown, in the course of his dispute with Bishop Colenso of Natal, declared his see to be an independent South African church. Miss Burdett-Coutts petitioned Queen Victoria to maintain the existing tie, but her action was without avail, and her colonial bishoprics became independent of the Church of England (cf. LEAR, *Life of Gray*, ii. 263 seq.; Cox, *Life of Colenso*, i. 269, ii. 36 seq.).

Miss Burdett-Coutts's first endeavour to enlarge the scope and opportunities of elementary and technical education formed part of her church work. In 1849 she built and established schools in connection with her church of St. Stephen's, Westminster, and in 1876 she enlarged her scheme by founding and endowing the Townshend School, partly from her own resources, and partly from a bequest left at her entire discretion by Chauncey Hare Townshend [q. v.]. The two schools were amalgamated in 1901, under the title of the Burdett-Coutts and Townshend Foundation Schools, and enjoy a high reputation. To complete her educational scheme for the district the baroness founded in 1893 the Westminster Technical Institute, which was handed over to the London County Council in 1901. In regard to the curriculum and administration of these foundations she was fertile in independent suggestion. She was the first to introduce sewing and cookery into elementary schools. At Whitelands (Church of England) Training College, in which she took a personal interest, she insisted on the importance of household economy, and gave prizes for essays in 'Household Work,' 'Country Matters,' 'Thrift,' and 'Household Management.' In 1865, while living at Torquay, she devised a scheme of grouping schools in the rural districts of Devonshire which was adopted by the authorities. She continued her father's interest in the Birkbeck Literary and Scientific Institute. In 1879 she founded an Art Students' Home in Brunswick Square for girls, the first of its kind in London.

By way of advancing higher scientific education, she endowed at Oxford in 1861 two scholarships for 'the study of geology and of natural science as bearing on geology,' each of the annual value of about 115*l.* and tenable for two years. They were accompanied by the gift to the university of the valuable Pengelly collection of Devonshire fossils, which she purchased of her scientific teacher, William Pengelly. For Kew Gardens she bought the rare and extensive Griffiths collection of seaweed and Schimper's great herbarium of mosses.

Poor and neglected children were always Miss Burdett-Coutts's especial care. Dickens had encouraged her to subsidise the Ragged School Union, started in 1844, and in his company she examined for herself the squalid poverty of child-waifs in London. Besides liberally supporting ragged schools, she actively aided the shoeblack brigades established about 1851 to provide employment for lads rescued by the ragged schools. In 1874 she made a first contribution of 5000*l.* to the scheme for training poor boys for a sailor's life on the ships Chichester, Arethusa, and Goliath. With a particularly attentive eye to the physical needs of poor children, she became president of the Destitute Children's Dinner Society, which was founded in 1866. Of a 'small society' for the defence and protection of children she was for a time trustee, and by directing the attention of the home secretary to its work in 1883 helped in the foundation of the National Society for the Prevention of Cruelty to Children from which she withdrew when its operations were extended from London to the whole country [see WAUGH, BENJAMIN, and STRETTON, HESBA, Suppl. II]. Urania Cottage, in Shepherd's Bush, a home and shelter for fallen women, was inaugurated by her in 1847 with the aid of Charles Dickens. The rescued women were enabled to begin life anew; situations were found for them at home, and some were sent under safe guidance to the colonies.

The reform of the humble industries, especially in the East End of London, always appealed to her. About 1860 she started a 'sewing school' in Brown's Lane, Spitalfields, where adult women were taught the profitable and improved use of the needle during their spare hours. They were fed and housed for the time, and an organisation created which was able to undertake large government contracts. Medical comforts were at the same time dispensed under the same roof. Professional nurses were engaged to visit the sick poor of the district, and especially to relieve the dangers and privations of childbirth in poor homes. In 1860, when the treaty with France, by encouraging increased importation of French silks, destroyed the occupation of the handloom weavers, Miss Burdett-Coutts by forming the East End Weavers' Aid Association helped the operatives to meet the difficulty of finding other employments. Many families were installed in small shops, and the young girls were trained for service. Her enthusiasm for the colonies led her to send other East End weavers to Queensland or to Halifax, Nova Scotia (1863). In 1869 she sent some 1200 weavers of Girvan, in Ayrshire, to Australia. In 1879 she instituted a Flower Girls' Brigade for flower-sellers between thirteen and fifteen years of age, and simultaneously established a factory in Clerkenwell with the object of teaching crippled girls the art of artificial flower-making, while others were trained for domestic service and other work.

But the hard-working East End labouring poor, especially in Shoreditch and Bethnal Green, were always her foremost consideration. A night school which she established in Shoreditch in 1875 was converted into the Burdett-Coutts Club for young men and boys of the working-class, one of the first of its kind in London. A gymnasium was added in 1891, and the club is still carried on by Mr. Burdett-Coutts. At Bethnal Green she took a life-long interest in the costermonger class, and organised a club for them, and on the Columbia estate provided healthy and extensive stables for their donkeys. She was the first to institute donkey shows, with prizes for the humane treatment and good condition of the donkeys. She valued as much as anything in her great art collection a donkey in silver presented by the Costermongers' Club in 1875.

The baroness's love of animals was intense. She was long the acknowledged leader of the Royal Society for the Prevention of Cruelty to Animals. As president of the ladies' committee she instituted the great scheme of essays for which many thousands of children throughout the country competed annually. She contributed largely to the prize fund, and her annual speeches to the vast audiences of children in the transept of the Crystal Palace were full of inspiration and pathos. She spoke at meetings in all parts of the country on the subject. 'Life whether in man or beast is sacred' was one of her oft-quoted sayings. Her pen was always at the service of the cause, and her letter to the Scottish Society (*The Times*, 5 Dec. 1873), on the ill-treatment of the Edinburgh tram-horses, is an eloquent indictment of cruelty. In 1872 she erected a handsome fountain at the corner of George IV Bridge, Edinburgh, in memory of 'Grey Friars Bobby,' the dog who refused to leave his master's grave. She provided other beautiful fountains and drinking-troughs, of which the best-known are those in Victoria Park at a cost of 5000*l.* in 1862, in the Zoological Gardens in London, and in Ancoats, Manchester. She encouraged the breeding of goats largely for the benefit of poor cottagers. She became president of the British Goat Society, and her goats were famous at all shows. She distributed the young stock in distant parts of the country; the milk was sent to hospitals.

With characteristic energy and prescience she faced the housing problem in the poorer districts of London almost for the first time. On the site of Nova Scotia Gardens in Bethnal Green, a plague spot and den of crime, she erected before the close of 1862 four blocks of model tenements, affording accommodation for over 1000 persons. The place was renamed Columbia Square. The Peabody dwelling-houses were built later on the same plan. On another plane of the housing problem, the baroness originated and carried out the idea of a garden city on her Holly Lodge estate, where she built 'Holly Village,' which provides separate residences for middle-class occupiers with the common enjoyment of open space and flower gardens.

In order to cheapen the food supply in the East End of London, Miss Burdett-Coutts embarked in 1864 on a great scheme of a market for fish and vegetables which should be free of the tolls of existing London markets. Columbia market was built at her expense on a site adjoining Columbia Square, after a private Act of Parliament was secured in 1866. The fine Gothic design had been prepared by Henry Ashley Darbishire. The cost exceeded 200,000*l.*, and the opening ceremony was performed on 28 April 1869 (*The Times*, 29 April 1869). The venture proved one of Miss Burdett-Coutts's few philanthropic failures, owing to the antagonism of vested interests, but it directed attention to the public disadvantages of the pre-existing market monopolies. After vainly seeking to work the market as a wholesale fish store, she transferred it to the corporation of London on 3 Nov. 1871; but no better success followed, and the corporation retransferred it to her in 1874. It was reopened again in 1875 under an arrangement with three of the great railway companies, but the opposition of Billingsgate was again too strong. Later an effort was made to carry it on (1884–6) with a fleet of fishing-boats and steam carriers, and subsequently to constitute it a railway market served by all the great trunk lines, for which a new Act of Parliament was obtained. But further obstacles arose and the fine building was turned to other uses. The results of this protracted effort were at the same time far-reaching, and the methods of food distribution greatly improved both in London and in the country.

But Miss Burdett-Coutts's philanthropic efforts were not limited to England. Ireland early attracted her. There she characteristically sought to combine with relief of distress a permanent improvement of the conditions of life and industry amongst the poor. In 1862 Father Davis, the parish priest of Rathmore, co. Cork (now Baltimore), appealed to her for aid on behalf of the people of the south-west of Ireland, especially in the district of Skibbereen, Crookhaven, and the 'Islands' (Cape Clear, Sherkin, Hare, and the Calves), which had never recovered from the sufferings of the famine years 1848 and 1849. She established large relief stores at Cape Clear and Sherkin. In 1863 she sent a party of emigrants from the district to Canada, and later on two other parties. She sought to create a demand in England for Irish embroidery and other cottage industries. Her chief work, however, was to revive and extend the fishing industry of the south-west coast. She advanced large sums of money, on a well-devised scheme of repayment out of profits, to provide the fishermen of Baltimore and the Islands with the best fishing-boats that could be built, and fitted them with modern and suitable gear. In the course of five years the new fishing fleet of Baltimore was valued at 50,000*l*. Much of the capital was in time repaid; and Father Davis used all his influence to keep his parishioners scrupulously to their engagements. In 1884 she paid her first visit to the district and was everywhere welcomed with enthusiasm. With the assistance of Sir Thomas Brady she soon afterwards helped to inaugurate a fishery training school for 400 boys at Baltimore. The school was opened by her on 16 Aug. 1887, when she was received with bonfires on the wild hill-sides, and flags flew from every cottage down the coast from Queenstown to Baltimore. In the distressed 'congested' districts of the west of Ireland she also took a keen interest. In 1880 she offered to advance no less a sum than 250,000*l*. to the English government for the supply of seed potatoes, on the failure of the potato crop. The government after some hesitation decided to take the matter up themselves.

An ardent desire to spread civilisation and enlightenment led her to support liberally many schemes for the extension of British rule over savage lands. She largely aided the enterprise of her friend, Sir James Brooke [q. v.], who founded the kingdom of Sarawak, in Borneo, in 1842, long maintaining there a model farm for native training in agriculture; she gave generous aid to Robert Moffat and David Livingstone in their African exploration, and extended like support to (Sir) Henry Morton Stanley, who rescued Livingstone in 1871. From the doubts at first cast on Stanley's veracity in his accounts of his African experiences she defended him with spirit, and he became a devoted friend. In 1887 she actively encouraged Stanley's expedition in search of Emin Pasha, which led to the foundation of a new East African empire.

On the Guinea coast she also exerted her beneficence from early life. She learned that the cotton industry was retarded there by want of appliances, and she introduced cotton-gins into Abeokuta (Southern Nigeria). There followed a large increase in both cotton culture and trade, which were mainly in the hands of the natives. The Alake of Abeokuta visited England in 1904, and thanked his father's benefactress personally for her gift. Other of her foreign benefactions included the provision of lifeboats for the coast of Brittany and the supplying of funds for the ordnance survey of Jerusalem. An offer to restore the aqueducts of Solomon, and so secure a regular supply of water for the poor population of the sacred city, was not accepted.

Meanwhile in 1871 Queen Victoria gave signal expression to the gratitude of the nation to Miss Burdett-Coutts for her many services by conferring a peerage on her under the title of Baroness Burdett-Coutts of Highgate and Brookfield, Middlesex. This is the only instance of a woman being raised to the peerage in recognition of her personal worth and public achievement. An honour no less unique for a woman proceeded from the City of London, which conferred its honorary freedom on her on 18 July 1872. The freedom of the city of Edinburgh followed on 15 Jan. 1874. Various City companies paid her the same tribute, the Turners on 10 Jan. 1872, the Clothworkers on 16 July 1873, the Haberdashers on 1 Nov. 1880, and the Coachmakers in 1894.

In 1877, during the Russo-Turkish war, the baroness made a strenuous effort to help the Turkish peasantry who were swept from their native villages in Roumelia and Bulgaria by the Russian advance. An eloquent appeal from her in the 'Daily Telegraph' of 13 Aug. 1877 led to the formation of the Turkish Compassionate Fund, to which she subscribed 2000*l*. Large contributions both in money, amounting to 50,000*l.*, and in kind were received, mainly from the working classes. Mr. Burdett-Coutts (then Mr. Ashmead-Bartlett), as special commissioner to the fund, undertook with great efficiency the difficult task of organisation and administration. Eventually the refugees were drafted to Asia Minor. This generous help from England produced a lasting impression on the Turkish people, and endeared the baroness's name to the Moslem world. On the conclusion of peace at the close of the Russo-Turkish war in March 1878 the Sultan conferred on the baroness the diamond star and first class of the order of the Medjidie, which was given to no other woman save Queen Victoria. To this he subsequently added the grand cross and cordon of the Chafakat (Mercy), an order specially established in honour of ladies assisting in the work of relief. She was made a lady of grace of the order of St. John of Jerusalem on 17 Dec. 1888.

In 1879 the baroness in a like spirit served as president of a ladies' committee to aid the sick and wounded in the Zulu war, and she sent out a hospital equipment, trained women nurses forming a special feature of the staff. The voluntary hospitals in the South African war of 1899–1902, where women nurses were reluctantly sanctioned by military authorities, were largely modelled on the Zulu experiment of 1879.

On 12 Feb. 1881 the baroness was married at Christ Church, Down Street, to Mr. William Lehman Ashmead-Bartlett, who assumed by royal licence the names of Burdett-Coutts and has been unionist M.P. for Westminster from 1885. He was of American birth, his grandparents on both sides having been British subjects [see BARTLETT, SIR ELLIS ASHMEAD, Suppl. II], and he had lived in England and been known to the baroness since boyhood. He was already associated in a voluntary capacity with many of her philanthropic schemes, notably in Ireland and Turkey. The difference of ages caused much gossip at the time; but by common consent the alliance ensured the baroness's happiness and prolonged her useful work to the end of her life. Her friend, Lady St. Helier, who was well qualified to judge, writes: 'The last years of her life were happy ones, and only those who knew her intimately perhaps realised how much her husband helped her' (*Memories of Fifty Years*).

The baroness's marriage did not slacken her philanthropic energies and interests. The war in the Soudan in 1884 greatly moved her, and she warmly admired Gordon's character and aims. On 18 Jan. 1884 he paid her a farewell visit at Stratton Street an hour before he left England for the last time. On his asking for some personal memento, she handed him a small letter-case which she always carried, and which was with him to the last. On 10 May 1884, in a letter to 'The Times,' she eloquently expressed the national sentiment, and appealed for his rescue from Khartoum.

In 1889 she opened a pleasure ground which had been made out of the Old St. Pancras cemetery, and she erected there a memorial sun-dial, with a record of famous persons buried there. One of these was Pascal Paoli, the Corsican patriot and refugee. His remains she restored at her own expense, with the approval of the French government, to Corsica, greatly to the Corsicans' satisfaction. In 1896, on her first visit to Corsica, the baroness received a popular ovation.

For the Chicago Exhibition in 1893 she compiled and edited a book describing 'Woman's Work in England,' from which she excluded all mention of herself. The omission was supplied by the duchess of Teck, who arranged for the separate publication at Chicago of a special memoir of the baroness's own work. In a preliminary letter the duchess wrote of the baroness, 'Great as have been the intrinsic benefits that the baroness has conferred on others, the most signal of all has been the power of example—an incalculable quantity which no record of events can measure. She has ever sought, also, to increase the usefulness of women in their homes, to extend their opportunities of self-improvement, and to deepen the sources of influence which they derive from moral worth and Christian life.'

The baroness died on 30 Dec. 1906 in her ninety-second year, of acute bronchitis, at 1 Stratton Street. For two days the body lay in state there surrounded by innumerable tributes, while nearly 30,000 persons, rich and poor, paid her their last respects. She was accorded burial in Westminster Abbey on 5 Jan. 1907, and was laid there in the nave near the west door, amidst notable demonstrations of popular grief and in the presence of a vast congregation representing nearly all the interests she had lived to serve, from the crown down to the humblest of its subjects.

The baroness's character and career gave philanthropy a new model. In the breadth and sincerity of her sympathies and in the variety of her social and intellectual interests she had no rival among contemporary or past philanthropists. She became in her time a great and honoured 'English institution,' and most of her enterprises bore lasting fruit. Her example not only gave an immense stimulus to charitable work among the rich and fashionable but suggested solutions of many social problems.

In person the baroness was tall and slender, stately yet gentle and graceful in manner, and habitually wearing an expression of gravity and quiet composure, which was often brightened by subtle play of humour. She kept under stern control a highly strung nervous system, and until her closing years her physical strength enabled her to endure enormous labour without undue strain. There are portraits of the baroness by Stump about 1840 (head); by J. Jacob about 1846; two by J. J. Masquerier; by J. R. Swinton in 1863, engraved by George Zobel in 1874; by Edwin Long, R.A., in 1883. She was also painted with Mrs. Brown by James Drummond in 1874. There are also miniatures, by Stewart when four years old, by Jagger in 1826, and by Sir W. C. Ross, R.A., in 1847; and marble busts by William Brodie in 1874, and by G. C. Adams. All these are in the collection of Mr. Burdett-Coutts at 1 Stratton Street. A cartoon appeared in 'Vanity Fair' in 1883.

[The Times, 31 Dec. 1906 and 7 Jan. 1907; Thomas Moore's Memoirs, edited by Lord John Russell, 1853–6; Henry Crabb Robinson's Diary, 1869; William Howitt's Northern Heights of London, 1869; Julian Charles Young's Journal, 1871; John Forster's Life of Charles Dickens, 1872–4; Sir T. W. Reid's Life, Letters and Friendships of R. M. Milnes, first Lord Houghton, 1890; Baroness Burdett-Coutts: a sketch of her public life and work, prepared for the Lady Managers of the World's Columbian Exposition, by command of Princess Mary Adelaide, Duchess of Teck, 1893; Woman's Mission: a series of Congress Papers on the philanthropic work of women, by eminent writers, 1893; George A. Sala's Life, 1895; A. J. C. Hare's Story of My Life, 1900; C. Kinloch Cooke's Memoir of the Duchess of Teck, 1900; Prebendary F. Meyrick's Memories, 1905; Bram Stoker's Personal Reminiscences of Henry Irving, 1906; Lady St. Helier's Memories of Fifty Years, 1909; R. C. Lehmann's Charles Dickens as Editor, 1912.] J. P. A.

BURDON, JOHN SHAW (1826–1907), missionary, bishop of Victoria, Hongkong, and Chinese scholar, only son of James Burdon, by Isabella his second wife, was born at Auchterarder in Perthshire on 12 Dec. 1826. On his father's early death he was brought up by an uncle, who kept a school at Liverpool, where he was overworked. From Liverpool he went to Glasgow. In 1850 he was accepted as a missionary by the Church Missionary Society, and spent two years at their training college at Islington. He was ordained deacon by the bishop of London on 19 Dec. 1852.

He sailed for Shanghai on 20 July 1853, and was ordained priest by the bishop of Victoria, Hongkong, on 8 Oct. 1854. Meanwhile the T'ai-p'ing rebels were menacing the whole empire. Shanghai was taken by them just before Burdon's arrival, and he occupied himself with long and very hazardous journeys into the surrounding country. There he preached, interviewed the iconoclastic and professedly half-Christian rebel leaders, and opened new mission stations. From Jan. to July 1859 he stayed at Hang-chow; but the people proved inaccessible, and he returned to the coast. In 1860 he made a second attempt on Hang-chow, but was obliged to fall back on Shaohsing, where he worked until late in 1861. In December 1861 he was in Ningpo with Mr. and Mrs. Russell, G. E. Moule, and others when that city was captured by the rebels. Early in 1862 he went to Peking as pioneer of the Church of England at the capital, and after eleven years of hard work and domestic sorrow he returned to England on 22 May 1864.

In September 1865 he was again in Peking, where he added to his other work the duties of chaplain to the British legation (1865–1872). In 1864 he had been appointed one of a committee of five eminent Chinese scholars to translate the New Testament into the vernacular of North China. The work, with which his name will be always associated, appeared in 1872, and has been the foundation of all subsequent revisions. In 1872 appeared also a version of the Book of Common Prayer by Burdon and (Bishop) Schereschewsky, which likewise forms the basis of all the Prayer-books since printed for the North China missions. Subsequently he prepared other editions of the Prayer-book (1879, 1890, 1893), issued a revision of the New Testament translation with H. Blodget (1889), and from 1891 to 1901 was a member of a committee for revision of the Chinese Bible.

On his election as bishop of Victoria, Hongkong, he returned to England on 25 Oct. 1873, and early next year received the degree of D.D. from the archbishop of Canterbury. On 15 March 1874 he was consecrated third bishop of Victoria, a diocese which until 1883 included Japan as well as all South China. At his own request his name was kept on the roll of C.M.S. missionaries, and he had sometimes to insist on the fact that he was a missionary, as well as a colonial, bishop. His episcopate was marked by ceaseless if unobtrusive work and boundless hospitality at Hongkong and by arduous visitations in Fukien and elsewhere. He enjoyed the regard alike of the merchants of Hongkong and the missionaries in Fukien. He resigned the bishopric on 26 Jan. 1897, and retired to Pakhoi, where his missionary life closed. He left China in 1901, and his last years of failing health were spent with his youngest son in England. He died at Bedford on 5 Jan. 1907, and was buried at Royston.

Burdon was married thrice: (1) on 30 March 1853 to Harriet Anne Forshaw who died at Shanghai on 26 Sept. 1854; (2) on 11 Nov. 1857 to Burella Hunter Dyer, who died on 16 Aug. 1858; (3) on 14 June 1865 to Phœbe Esther, daughter of E. T. Alder, vicar of Bungay; she died on 14 June 1898. By his third wife he had three sons.

[MS. notes and documents supplied by his youngest son, Edward Russell Burdon; MS. Register of C.M.S. Missionaries; Church Missionary Review, April 1907, pp. 227-236; E. Stock, History of the C.M.S., 3 vols., 1899; Notes on Hangchow Past and Present, by G. E. Moule, 1907.]

BURDON-SANDERSON, Sir JOHN SCOTT, first baronet (1828–1905), regius professor of medicine at Oxford, born at Jesmond, near Newcastle-on-Tyne, on 21 Dec. 1828, was second son and fourth child of Richard Burdon (1791-1865), at one time fellow of Oriel College, Oxford, who took the additional surname of Sanderson on his marriage in 1815 to Elizabeth, only daughter of Sir James Sanderson, first baronet, M.P. His father's mother, Jane, daughter of William Scott of Newcastle-on-Tyne, was sister of Lord Eldon and Lord Stowell. His sister Mary Elizabeth married Robert Haldane of Cloanden, and Viscount Haldane is her son. As a boy Burdon-Sanderson was educated at home and was intended by his father for the law, in which two great-uncles had won distinction. But the youth's strong interest in natural science pointed to medicine as a more appropriate profession, and entering the university of Edinburgh in 1847 he graduated M.D. in 1851, with the gold medal for his thesis on the metamorphosis of the coloured blood corpuscles. Proceeding to Paris, he first studied chemistry under Gerhardt and Wurtz, and later devoted himself to physiology under the celebrated Claude Bernard and to hospital work.

In 1853 he settled in London as a practising physician, was soon appointed medical registrar of St. Mary's Hospital, Paddington, and in 1854 served the medical school there as lecturer, first in botany and then in medical jurisprudence. In 1856 he was appointed medical officer of health for Paddington, and during the eleven years of his tenure of the post gave the first proofs of eminence. Two outbreaks of cholera rendered reforms in the sanitation of the district imperative. Food adulteration and insanitary dwelling-houses were evils which his efforts greatly diminished. Dr. (afterwards Sir) John Simon [q. v. Suppl. II], the chief medical officer of the privy council, recognised his ability and scientific acumen, and in 1860 Burdon-Sanderson was made an inspector under the council. Official reports by him dealt with the etiology of various contagious and infectious diseases, and inaugurated the successful experimental study of them in this country. A laborious inquiry into the contagium of cattle plague (1865–6) and a report on the conditions determining tuberculosis were particularly illuminating. In 1869 he investigated an epidemic of cerebro-spinal meningitis in North Germany. In an article 'On the Intimate Pathology of Contagion,' forming an appendix to the report of the council for 1869, Burdon-Sanderson gave prophetic intimation of the causal relationship of specific micro-organisms to disease.

In 1860 he became physician at the Brompton Hospital for Consumption, and also at the Middlesex Hospital, and there pursued his investigations.

In 1867 he was elected fellow of the Royal Society and Croonian lecturer, taking for his subject the influence of respiratory movements on the circulation. The lecture embodied results of experimental study which, though strictly physiological, was suggested by his numerous sphygmographic and stethographic observations at Brompton Hospital (*Phil. Trans.* clvii.).

In 1870 he gave up his hospital appointments and private practice in order to devote himself exclusively to scientific research. He had retired from the privy council in 1865, and from Paddington in 1867. His opportunity of research was increased by his appointments as professor superintendent (1871) of the Brown Institution (London University) and as professor of practical physiology and histology (1870) at University College, London, in succession to (Sir) Michael Foster [q. v. Suppl. II]. In 1874 he succeeded William Sharpey [q. v.] as Jodrell professor of physiology at University College. The courses of practical teaching which he organised in that capacity served as models for instruction in the medical curriculum of the country. Until 1878 he retained in addition his post in the Brown Institution. He had become F.R.C.P. in 1871, was Harveian orator at the College of Physicians in 1878, was awarded the Baly medal in 1880, and gave the Croonian lectures there on the progress of discovery relating to the origin of infectious diseases in 1891.

In 1882 he was invited to Oxford as first Waynflete professor of physiology, a fellowship at Magdalen College being attached to the chair. The degree of M.A. was conferred on him in 1883, and that of D.M. in 1895. He remained Waynflete professor until 1895, when he was appointed regius professor of medicine in the university. He was elected at the same time an honorary fellow of Magdalen College, Oxford. At Oxford he steadily pursued his researches in physiology and pathology, until his resignation of the regius professorship at the close of 1903. In pathology he powerfully enforced the truth that experimental investigations are essential for the elucidation of pathological problems, and that sound pathology must rest upon an accurate physiological basis.

In physiology his experimental activity was particularly identified with the investigation of the fundamental physical characteristics of living tissues when these are thrown into the active excitatory state. In this investigation, which largely occupied him for twenty-five years, he devoted himself to the precise determination of the comparatively small electrical changes presented by active tissues. The tissues selected included plants like Dionæa (*Phil. Trans.* 1877, 1882, and 1888), the heart (*Journal of Physiology*, 1880, 1883), muscle (*ibid.* 1895, and *Proc. Roy. Soc.* 1899), and the electrical organs of the skate (*Journal of Physiology*, 1888, 1889). He employed for this purpose a modified form of Lippmann's capillary electrometer, which was brought to a state of great perfection in the Oxford laboratory. The value of his work in this field of research was recognised by his being chosen in 1877 for the second time to give the Croonian lecture at the Royal Society on the excitatory changes in the leaf of Dionæa (*Proc. Roy. Soc.* xxv.), and by the award of a royal medal in 1883 by the Royal Society. In 1889 he was for the third time selected by the society as Croonian lecturer, taking as his subject 'The Relation of Motion in Animals and Plants to the Associated Electrical Phenomena' (*Proc. Roy. Soc.* lxv.).

To large audiences throughout the country Burdon-Sanderson frequently gave suggestive addresses, biological, physiological, and pathological. He was president of the biological section of the British Association at Newcastle in 1889, where he delivered an address on 'Elementary Problems in Physiology.' In 1893 he was president of the association at Nottingham, and in his presidential address he set forth his intellectual attitude to the general nature of the physiological problems presented by the living organism. The most noteworthy of his addresses are appended to the memoir commenced by his widow and completed by his nephew and niece, Dr. J. S. Haldane and Miss E. S. Haldane (Oxford, 1911).

Burdon-Sanderson served on three important royal commissions—on hospitals for infectious diseases in 1883, on the consumption of tuberculous meat and milk in 1891, and on the University of London in 1892. On 10 Aug. 1899 he was created a baronet. Many other honours fell to him. He was hon. LL.D. of Edinburgh, hon. D.Sc. of Dublin, corresponding member of the Institute of France and of the Academy of Science, Berlin. After several months of increasing physical weakness, he died at Oxford on 23 Nov. 1905, and was buried at Wolvercote cemetery. He married, on 9 August 1853, Ghetal, eldest daughter of Ridley Haim Herschell [q. v.] and sister of Farrer, afterwards Lord Herschell, lord chancellor [q. v. Suppl. I]. His widow survived him until 5 July 1909. He had no children, and the baronetcy became extinct at his death.

He bequeathed the sum of 2000*l.* 'for the support of the pathological department of the University of Oxford and especially to provide for the expenses of research in pathology conducted in the said laboratory or elsewhere.' Of fine presence and striking features, Burdon-Sanderson had rare charm of manner. A portrait (1883) by the Hon. John Collier is in the lecture theatre of the Oxford Physiological Laboratory, and another by Charles Wellington Furse

(1901) is in the hall of Magdalen College, Oxford. A marble bust by Hope Pinker is in the Oxford university museum. A pencil sketch was made by Rudolf Lehmann in 1893 and a cartoon by 'Spy' for 'Vanity Fair' in 1894.

Burdon-Sanderson took part in the great modern advance in pathology. In physiology he was an acknowledged master in his own somewhat recondite branch of experimental research; he founded an English school of exact experimental work, and initiated new methods of teaching. Always interested in the work of others, he was a venerated leader to the younger generation of physiologists and pathologists. The University of Oxford owes him a special debt of gratitude, as the virtual founder of her medical school.

He edited in 1873 'Handbook for the Physiological Laboratory,' writing himself on circulation, respiration, &c. He wrote on 'Inflammation' in Holmes' 'System of Surgery' (1883), on 'Fever' in Allbutt's 'System of Medicine' (1896), and many papers for the Royal Society's Transactions and Proceedings (1877–1889); the 'Journal of Physiology' from 1880 to 1900; and 'Reports of the British Association,' 1872, 1881, 1889, 1893. His address to the thirteenth International Medical Congress (Paris) on 'Cellular Pathology' appeared in the 'Lancet,' 25 Aug. 1900.

[Memoir of Sir J. Burdon-Sanderson, with a selection from his papers and addresses, by Lady Burdon-Sanderson, J. S. Haldane and E. S. Haldane, Oxford, 1911; Privy Council Reports, 1861 to 1870; Burke's Landed Gentry and Baronetage; Nature, lxxiii. (1905–6); Brit. Med. Journal, 2 Dec. 1905; Oxford Mag. 29 Nov. 1905; Proc. Roy. Soc. lxxix. B, 1907.] F. G.

BURN, ROBERT (1829–1904), scholar and archæologist, born at Kynnersley, Shropshire, on 22 Oct. 1829, was second son of Andrew Burn, rector of Kynnersley, by his second wife. His elder brother, George, fourth classic and chancellor's medallist at Cambridge in 1851, was fellow of Trinity College. Robert entered Shrewsbury school under Benjamin Hall Kennedy [q. v.] in 1843 and Trinity College, Cambridge, in 1849. He had remarkable skill in the writing of Latin hexameter verse. He was senior classic in 1852, and took a second class in natural science in 1853. He was elected a fellow of Trinity in 1854, and spent the rest of his life at Cambridge. He was ordained deacon in 1860 and priest in 1862. For many years he lectured on classical subjects; from 1862 to 1872 he was a tutor of Trinity, and discharged the duties of that office with conspicuous success. He vacated his fellowship on his marriage in 1873, but was re-elected next year, and was also appointed prælector in Roman archæology.

Burn, who frequently visited Rome and its neighbourhood during his vacations, was one of the first Englishmen to study the archæology of the city and the Campagna, and he published several important works dealing with it, viz.: 1. 'Rome and the Campagna,' Cambridge and London, 1871; new edit. 1874. 2. 'Old Rome,' an epitome of the former work, 1880. 3. 'Roman Literature in Relation to Roman Art,' 1888. 4. 'Ancient Rome and its Neighbourhood,' 1895. He received an honorary degree from Glasgow University in 1883.

Burn was a distinguished athlete in his youth and a good tennis player up to middle age; but for the last twenty years of his life, though his intellectual interests were unabated, he was an invalid confined to a bath-chair. He died on 30 April 1904 and was buried in St. Giles's cemetery at Cambridge. There is a brass to his memory in the ante-chapel of Trinity College.

He married in 1873 Augusta Sophia Prescott, a descendant of Oliver Cromwell; he left no issue.

[Private information; personal knowledge.] J. D. D.

BURN-MURDOCH, JOHN (1852–1909), lieutenant-colonel, born at Edinburgh on 17 June 1852, was eldest son of William Burn-Murdoch (1822–1878), M.D. Edinburgh, second son of John Burn-Murdoch (1793–1862), of Garlincaber, co. Perth. His mother was Jessie Cecilia, daughter of William Mack. The father's younger brother, James M'Gibbon Burn-Murdoch, was father of Colonel John Francis Burn-Murdoch, C.B., a distinguished cavalry officer. Educated at the Edinburgh Academy, at Nice for a year, and afterwards in London, Burn-Murdoch entered the royal engineers from Woolwich on 2 May 1872. He served in the Afghan war of 1878–80, and was present in the engagement of Charasiab on 6 Oct. 1879 and in the operations round Kabul in December 1879, including the storming of the Asmai Heights, when he was severely wounded while employed in blowing up one of the Afghan forts (HANNA, *Second Afghan War*, iii. 250). He was mentioned in despatches, 4 May 1880, and received the medal with two clasps.

Burn-Murdoch took part in the Egyptian

war of 1882 with the contingent from India under Major-general (Sir) Herbert Taylor Macpherson [q. v.]. The engineers were commanded by Sir James Browne, known as 'Buster Browne' (1839–1896), and Burn-Murdoch and (Sir) William Gustavus Nicholson were the two field engineers. Reaching Bombay with his companions on 6 Aug., Burn-Murdoch aided Browne in preparing all the requisite material, and arrived at Suez, where they repaired the roads, local canals, and railways. From Ismailia they reached Kassassin on 11 Sept., and were present at the battle of Tel-el-Kebir on the 13th. Immediately afterwards Burn-Murdoch, with the Indian force, pushed on for some thirty miles to Zagazig, and took a foremost part in seizing the railway there, and General Browne sent a captured train back under Burn-Murdoch to help in the 72nd regiment, six miles off. The brilliant seizure of Zagazig, in which Burn-Murdoch did useful service, deprived the rebels of command of the railway and facilitated the capture of Cairo. He was mentioned in despatches and received the medal with clasp, fifth class of the Medjidieh, and Khedive's star.

Burn-Murdoch was promoted captain on 2 May 1884, major on 6 Aug. 1891, and lieut.-colonel on 1 March 1900. Meanwhile he served in India on the state railways, and in 1893 became officer commanding engineer of state railways and subsequently was chief engineer of the Southern Mahratta railways. He retired on an Indian pension on 28 May 1900. He died at Bridge of Leith Cottage, Doune, Perthshire, on 30 Jan. 1909, and was buried in Old Kilmadoch burial ground. He married in August 1889 Maud (*d.* 1893), widow of William Forster. Burn-Murdoch left no issue. His wife had by her former husband three sons and a daughter.

[Burke's Landed Gentry; Hart's Army List; Official Army List; W. Porter, History of the Corps of Royal Engineers, 1889, ii. 45, 66; J. J. McLeod Innes's Life and Times of General Sir James Browne, 1905, p. 22; Sir J. F. Maurice, The Campaign of 1882 in Egypt, 1908, p. 105; private information.]

H. M. V.

BURNE, Sir OWEN TUDOR (1837–1909), major-general, born at Plymouth on 12 April 1837, was eleventh child in a family of nineteen children of the Rev. Henry Thomas Burne (1799–1865), M.A., of Trinity College, Cambridge, by his wife Knightley Goodman (1805–1878), daughter of Captain Marriott, royal horse guards (blue). The father resigned orders in the Church of England in 1835 to join the 'Holy Catholic Apostolic Church,' founded by Edward Irving [q. v.]. To that church his children adhered. Owen's eldest brother was Col. Henry Burne, and another brother, Douglas (*d.* 1899), was manager of the bank of Bengal.

Educated at home by his father and at the Royal Military College at Sandhurst, Owen received a commission in the 20th East Devonshire regiment (now the Lancashire fusiliers) on 15 May 1855. After some months at the depôt at Parkhurst, Isle of Wight, Burne joined his regiment in the Crimea, in charge of a draft of 200 recruits, on 3 April 1856. Peace had just been proclaimed in London, and he returned home in July. After a year at Aldershot, he embarked with his regiment for India to assist in the suppression of the mutiny. On the voyage he studied Hindustani to good purpose.

On reaching Calcutta in November 1857 the regiment was ordered to Oudh to clear away the mutineers between Benares and Lucknow. Owing to his knowledge of Hindustani, Burne, who had been appointed adjutant of his regiment, was made brigade-major to Brigadier Evelegh, commanding a brigade in the 4th infantry division under Brigadier Franks. His first brush with the rebels was on 19 Feb. 1858 at Chunda, where guns were captured. After some hard fighting his division joined Sir Colin Campbell's army before Lucknow on 4 March, and established itself in outworks near the Dilkusha on the outskirts of the city, where it was exposed to a heavy fire. On 11 March Burne performed a feat of gallantry, for which he was recommended without result for promotion and the Victoria Cross. Communication was interrupted between the right and left attacks, and Burne, who was sent to ascertain the cause, found that the Nepalese troops had retired in a panic from their intermediate position, which had been occupied by the enemy; after bringing them back to the front as best he could, he made in safety a most perilous return journey. On 14 March, when Franks's division attacked the Kaisar Bagh and Imambara, the keys of the enemy's position, he was brigade-major of the column of attack, and was one of the first to get through the gate of the Kaisar Bagh. He was actively engaged until Lucknow fell on 21 March. Promoted lieutenant on 10 April 1858, he continued on the staff of Evelegh's brigade in the vicinity of Lucknow, and was busy in clearing the country round of rebels in spite of sickness and the hot weather. Later Burne re-joined as adjutant the 20th regiment, which took part with a field force under Sir John Campbell in operations in Northern Oudh. He next acted as staff officer to a column under Brigadier Holdich in the final operations in Oudh under Sir James Hope Grant [q. v.] in 1859. Several times mentioned in despatches, he received the medal with clasp for Lucknow, and being promoted captain on 9 Aug. 1864, was made brevet-major for his services in the mutiny (Jan. 1865).

Meanwhile Burne's efficient work as adjutant, while his regiment was quartered at Goudah, some sixty miles from Lucknow, had greatly impressed Sir Hugh Rose, the commander-in-chief in India, who inspected the regiment on 14 Dec. 1860. In the following spring Rose unexpectedly appointed him, in spite of his junior rank, military secretary. The choice, though confirmed from home, caused friction between the commander-in-chief there and Rose. As a result, at the end of 1862 Burne resigned the post, becoming private secretary to Sir Hugh. In 1865 Burne went with Sir Hugh to England, and when Rose took the Irish command, he became one of his aides-de-camp. For his aid in suppressing the Fenian conspiracy of 1867 Burne received the thanks of government.

At the end of 1868 he returned to India as private secretary to Lord Mayo, the newly appointed governor-general. Burne not only was the confidential friend and companion of the viceroy but was in complete political accord with his views (see BURNE'S *Letters on the Indian Administration of Lord Mayo*, 1872). He was with his chief at the Andaman Islands on 6 Feb. 1872, when the viceroy was assassinated. He remained at Calcutta as private secretary to Lord Napier and Ettrick, governor of Madras, who temporarily assumed the office of viceroy, but left on the arrival of Lord Northbrook, the new viceroy, in May 1872, when the five secretaries to the government of India, home, foreign, public works, finance, and commerce, presented him with a silver vase accompanied by a warmly appreciative letter. On 19 June 1872 Burne reported in person to Queen Victoria at Osborne the details of Lord Mayo's death, and was created C.S.I.

In August he was appointed to the newly instituted post of political aide-de-camp to the duke of Argyll, secretary of state for India. The duties were to take charge of all native embassies and chiefs visiting England, and to assist the India office generally on native questions. In the summer of 1873 he took part in the entertainment of the Shah of Persia. In April 1874 he became assistant secretary to the political and secret department of the India office, and being promoted lieutenant-colonel on 16 July, he succeeded Sir John Kaye [q. v.] as secretary and head of the political and secret department in October. In that capacity he was in continual personal consultation with the marquis of Salisbury, secretary of state, on the Central Asian and the Afghanistan questions.

In April 1876 Burne arrived once more in India as private secretary for a two years' term to the new viceroy, Lord Lytton [q. v.]. To Burne was largely due the success of the ceremonial proclamation at Delhi of Queen Victoria as Empress of India, which he described in the 'Asiatic Quarterly' (January 1887), but Afghan policy was among the principal matters which occupied his attention. When he left India in the beginning of 1878 Lytton wrote to him: 'You have done for me, and been to me, all that one man could have done or been.' Created C.I.E. on 1 Jan. 1878, he returned to the India office in February, was promoted K.C.S.I. in July 1879, and became colonel in the army. In 1880 he ably negotiated with the Nawab Nazim of Bengal a settlement highly satisfactory to the Indian exchequer, and the affairs of Maharaja Duleep Singh were placed under his supervision. In December 1886 he joined the council of India, filling the vice-presidency in 1895 and 1896, and retiring on 31 Dec. 1896, when he was made G.C.I.E. He had been promoted major-general in 1889.

Burne had literary aptitude, and from 1879 was a regular contributor to 'The Times' on Eastern questions and an occasional contributor to magazines. He wrote 'Clyde and Strathnairn' for the Oxford series of 'Rulers of India' in 1891; and an autobiography entitled 'Memories' (1907). He was a royal commissioner for numerous international exhibitions, and was member of the international congress of hygiene and demography (1894). After his retirement from the India office he busily engaged in philanthropic, mercantile, and other public work, acting as chairman of the council of the Society of Arts (1896–1897) and as member of the advisory committee of the board of trade (1903). He died after a long illness at his house in Sutherland Avenue, Maida Vale, on 3 Feb. 1909

He was buried with military honours at Christchurch Priory, Hampshire.

A portrait, painted by Mrs. Leslie Melville, is in the possession of the family.

Sir Owen was twice married: (1) on 20 Nov. 1867, at Dublin, to Evelyne, daughter of Francis William Browne, fourth Baron Kilmaine; she died on 22 April 1878; (2) on 9 Aug. 1883, in London, to Lady Agnes Charlotte, youngest daughter of Douglas, the nineteenth earl of Morton, who survived him. By his first wife Sir Owen left three sons, two of whom joined the army and the other the navy, and two daughters.

[Kaye and Malleson's History of the Indian Mutiny; India Office Records; The Times, 4, 9, and 10 Feb. 1909; Memories by Sir O. T. Burne, 1907; Lord Lytton's Correspondence, ed. Lady Betty Balfour, 1899.] R. H. V.

BURNS, DAWSON (1828-1909), temperance reformer, born at Southwark on 22 Jan. 1828, was younger son of Jabez Burns, D.D. (1805-1876), baptist minister of New Church Street Chapel, Edgware Road, for forty-one years, and a popular religious writer and temperance advocate from 1836. His mother was Jane, daughter of George Dawson of Keighley. At twelve Dawson Burns took the pledge and addressed the young members of his father's congregation in New Church Street. He wrote 'A Plea for Youths' Temperance Societies' at the same age, held a public discussion soon after, and contributed articles to the 'Weekly Temperance Journal' and the 'National Temperance Advocate.' In Feb. 1845 he became assistant secretary to the National Temperance Society, and a year later joint secretary, besides conducting its monthly organ, the 'Temperance Chronicle.' He was official reporter of the World's Convention held in August 1846, in which his father took a prominent part. From September 1847 to 1850 he studied at the General Baptist College, then at Leicester, becoming pastor of the baptist chapel at Salford in September 1851. In 1853 he helped Nathaniel Card, a quaker, to found in Manchester the United Kingdom Alliance with a view to influencing the licensing laws. He was in London in March 1853 as metropolitan superintendent, and was enrolled the sixth member on 1 June 1853.

Residing in North London, he worked energetically for the cause with pen and speech. From March 1856 he wrote a 'London Letter' for the 'Alliance News' (weekly) and constantly published books and pamphlets. He was made an hon. M.A. of Bates College, Maine, U.S.A., in 1869 and afterwards D.D. He edited 'Graham's Annual Temperance Guide' from 1867 to 1876. At his father's death in 1876 he took over the pastorate of New Church Street Chapel, where he had lately assisted, but resigned it in 1881, to devote himself wholly to temperance work.

He represented the Baptist New Connexion at the centennial conference in America in 1880, acted as secretary to the Temperance Hospital opened in 1881, and was president of the Association of General Baptists held at Norwich in the same year. He was active in promoting temperance legislation, holding that the law should protect the public and not the liquor trade. In a series of annual letters to 'The Times' (1886–1909), on the 'National Drink Bill,' he showed a notable grasp of facts and statistics. Burns was a director of the Liberator Building Society, which his brother-in-law, Jabez Balfour, founded in 1868 and of which Balfour was chairman. Owing to disapproval of the increase of directors' fees, Burns resigned before the society's failure in October 1892. Subsequently Balfour and other directors were convicted of fraud and sentenced to long terms of imprisonment.

Burns died at Battersea on 22 Aug. 1909, and was buried at Paddington. On 22 Dec. 1853 he married Cecile, only daughter of James and Clara Lucas Balfour [q. v.]. His wife died at Battersea on 27 March 1897; of his five sons and a daughter, only two sons survived him. Burns wrote memoirs of his wife and of his third son, EDWARD SPENSER BURNS (1861–1885), who died on 1 March 1885 at Leopoldville, Stanley Pool, on the Lower Congo, after performing much valuable exploring work for the International African Association in the Congo district, opening up a new route towards the Niadi river, and constructing charts (see *Memorials*, privately printed 1886; STANLEY's *Congo Free State*, 1885, vol. ii. 212, 225, 272, 274).

Among Burns's numerous publications are: 1. 'Mormonism Exposed,' 1853. 2. 'Scripture Light on Intoxicating Liquors,' 1859. 3. 'The Temperance Dictionary,' Nos. 1–34, 1861. 4. (with F. R. Lees) 'The Temperance Bible Commentary,' 1868; other editions, 1872, 1876, 1880, 1894. 5. 'Statistics of the Liquor Traffic,' 1872. 6. 'Temperance Ballads,' 1884, 7. 'Local Option,' 1885, 3rd edit. 1896; new standard edit. 1909. 7. 'Temperance History,' 2 vols. 1889–91. 8. 'The Bible and Temperance Reform: the Lees and Raper

Memorial Lecture,' 1906. 9. 'Country Walks and Temperance Talks,' 1901.

[Burns's Temperance Dictionary, 1861; biographical sketch affixed to Temperance Ballads, 1884; Graham's Temperance Guide, 1877, pp. 63–5 (with portrait); works above cited; The Times, 23 and 27 Aug. 1909.]

C. F. S.

BURROUGHS [afterwards TRAILL-BURROUGHS], SIR FREDERICK WILLIAM (1831–1905), lieutenant-general, born on 1 Feb 1831, was eldest of the seven children of Major-general Frederick William Burroughs (*d.* 1879), of the Bengal army. His grandfather, Sir William Burroughs of Castle Bagshaw, co. Cavan, was advocate-general of Bengal under Marquis Cornwallis. His mother, Caroline (*d.* 1863), only daughter of Captain Charles Adolphus Marie de Peyron, of the Bengal light cavalry, was grand-daughter of Chevalier Charles Adrien de Peyron, who was killed in a duel in Paris in 1777 by the Comte de la Marck.

After education at Kensington grammar school, at Blackheath proprietary school, and in Switzerland, Burroughs was gazetted ensign in the 93rd highlanders on 31 March 1848. Promoted lieutenant on 23rd Sept. 1851, he became captain on 10 Nov. 1854 and major on 20 July 1858. On his twenty-first birthday (1 Feb. 1852) Burroughs succeeded to the Scottish estates of his grand-uncle, George William Traill, of Viera, Orkney, and assumed the surname of Traill-Burroughs. He served with the 93rd highlanders under Sir Colin Campbell (afterwards Lord Clyde) [q. v.] throughout the Crimean war of 1854–5, and was present at the battle of the Alma and at Balaklava, when he commanded the left centre company of his regiment, on which Howard Russell bestowed the name of 'the thin red line' (cf. KINGLAKE, *Crimea*, v. 80). Burroughs took part in the expedition to Kertch and Yenikhale, the siege and fall of Sevastopol, and assaults of 18 June and 8 Sept. He was awarded for his services the medal with three clasps, the Turkish medal, and the fifth class of the order of the Medjidieh. During the Indian Mutiny of 1857–8 Burroughs was engaged again under Lord Clyde in the fighting that preceded the relief of Lucknow, in the storming of the Secunderabagh and of Shah Najaf. He was the first through the breach at the Secunderabagh, and with some dozen men overpowered the gate guard. For this service, in which he received a slight wound, he was recommended for, but was not awarded, the Victoria Cross. For his subsequent conduct at the battle of Cawnpore on 6 Dec., and the pursuit to Serai Ghat at the action of Khodagunge, the storming of the Begum Kotee and the siege and capture of Lucknow, Burroughs was mentioned in despatches, and received a brevet majority (29 July 1858) and the medal with two clasps. The wounds he received during the mutiny campaign disabled him for two years, and it was not till 1860 that he rejoined his regiment. In 1862 he succeeded to the temporary command of the 93rd highlanders, which had lost two commanding officers owing to an outbreak of cholera.

He accompanied the Eusofzai field force, under Sir Neville Chamberlain [q. v. Suppl. II], in the campaign against the Hindustani fanatics and other tribes on the North-west frontier in December 1863, and commanded the 93rd highlanders in the action at Ambela. He was mentioned in despatches (*Lond. Gaz.* 19 March 1864) and received the medal with clasp.

Promoted lieutenant-colonel on 10 Aug. 1864, he became full colonel on 10 Aug. 1869. Retiring from the command of the 93rd highlanders in 1873, he was promoted major-general on 16 March 1880 and lieutenant-general on 1 July 1881. In 1904 he was transferred from the colonelcy of the Royal Warwickshire regiment, which he had held since 1897, to that of the Argyll and Sutherland highlanders. He was appointed C.B. on 24 May 1873 and K.C.B. in 1904. He died in London on 9 April 1905 and was buried at Brompton. His seat was Trumland House, Island of Rousay, Orkney, and he was vice-lieutenant of Orkney and Shetland. On 4 June 1870 he married Eliza D'Oyly, youngest daughter of Colonel William Geddes, C.B., Bengal horse artillery, J.P. and D.L. of Midlothian (*d.* 1879), by Emma, daughter of Edward D'Oyly, of Zion Hill, Yorkshire; he had no issue.

[The Thin Red Line, the regimental paper of 93rd Sutherland Highlanders, May 1905; Kaye and Malleson, History of the Indian Mutiny, 1889, iv. 129; W. H. Paget, A Record of the Expeditions against the North-West Frontier Tribes, revised by A. H. Mason, 1884, 150; P. Groves, History of the 93rd Sutherland Highlanders, 1895; W. Munro, Reminiscences of Service with the 93rd Sutherland Highlanders, 1883; Burke's Landed Gentry; Walford's County Families; Hart's Army List and Official Army List.]

H. M. V.

BURROWS, MONTAGU (1819–1905), Chichele professor of modern history at Oxford, born at Hadley, Middlesex, on

27 Oct. 1819, was third son of lieutenant-general Montagu Burrows (1775–1848), by his wife Mary Anne Pafford, eldest daughter of Joseph Larcom, captain R.N., and sister of Sir Thomas Aiskew Larcom [q. v.]. Amongst the five other sons were the Rev. H. W. Burrows, canon of Rochester, and Major-general A. G. Burrows. The grandfather, John Burrows (1733–1786), the pluralist incumbent of the livings of Hadley in Middlesex, St. Clement Danes in London, and Christ Church in Southwark, preached to Dr. Johnson at St. Clement Danes and stood high in the estimation of literary ladies, including Hannah More and Mrs. Elizabeth Montagu; the latter, an intimate friend, stood godmother to his eldest son, Montagu, father of the Chichele professor.

The younger Montagu entered the Royal Naval College as a cadet in August 1832. Two years later, in October 1834, at the age of fifteen he joined the Andromache as a midshipman and passed through the college as a mate in 1842. During his period of active service (1834–46) on this and other ships he was present at one engagement of importance, the bombardment of Acre, in November 1840, which brought Mehemet Ali, the rebellious Pasha of Egypt, to terms. For this he received the English and Turkish medals and clasp. For the rest of his time at sea he was engaged under (Sir) Henry Ducie Chads [q. v.] in suppressing piracy in the Straits Settlements and slavers on the west coast of Africa.

In November 1846 he was appointed gunnery lieutenant on the training-ship Excellent, and in 1852 he became commander. Immediately on his promotion he resolved to study at Oxford, till he should be called to active service. He had married in 1849, and early in 1853 entered Magdalen Hall, one of the few societies that then admitted married men. Rapidly passing responsions and pass moderations, he was left undisturbed by the Crimean war, for owing to a mistake his acceptance of a post, which had been offered him, came too late. In Michaelmas term, 1856, he was placed in the first class of literæ humaniores, and after little more than four months' further reading took a first class in the newly created honour school of law and modern history (Easter term, 1857). Of the professors' lectures in his undergraduate days Burrows spoke with praise, more especially of those of Mansel for logic and classical philosophy, Rawlinson for ancient history, Wall for logic, and Wilson for modern philosophy. The college tutors proved in his opinion incompetent, and he mainly depended on private tuition.

After graduating, Burrows engaged with much success in private teaching, mainly in law and modern history. In 1860 he published 'Pass and Class,' a useful handbook to all the Oxford schools (3rd edit. 1866). In 1862 he became a retired post-captain, and gave up the navy. His shortsightedness and slight deafness would have seriously interfered with his effectiveness as a captain of a ship.

At Oxford he attached himself to the party of moderate churchmen and political conservatives, and was always active in both church and political affairs. He contributed to the 'Guardian' till that paper adopted views too high for him in church matters and too liberal in politics. Afterwards he started new papers to enforce his views, the 'Church and State Review' in 1861 and the 'Churchman' in 1866, both of which soon failed. He was an original member of the English Church Union, acting as chairman of the Oxford branch till 1866, when its 'ritualistic' tendencies led him to retire; he was secretary to the Oxford branch of the Universities' Mission to Central Africa on its foundation in 1859, and acted as joint secretary of the Church Congress, which held its second meeting at Oxford in 1862. He materially assisted in the building, during the same year, of SS. Philip and James' church in North Oxford. Later he actively fought the cause of church denominational schools in Oxford, was for many years president of the Church Schools Managers and Teachers Association, and had much to do with the establishment of the Oxford diocesan conference. He was a member of the committee which founded Keble College in 1870.

Meanwhile in 1862 Burrows was elected to the Chichele professorship of modern history, which had been founded by the royal commission of 1852. His election was a surprise to himself and others. Stubbs, Freeman, and Froude, all three destined eventually to hold the chair of regius professor of modern history, and Pearson, the author of a 'History of Medieval England,' were among the candidates. Three of the five electors were liberals. But his candidature was warmly supported by Samuel Wilberforce, bishop of Oxford, and apparently by Gladstone, who was still burgess for the University of Oxford. The school of law and modern history was new; none of the other more formidable candidates had had any experience of teaching, and Burrows's reputation as a teacher and as the author of 'Pass and Class' carried weight. Thus, probably for the first time in the annals of Oxford, a naval officer sat in a professorial chair. Three years later Burrows was elected a fellow of All Souls College. As professor, Burrows lectured with exemplary regularity, but the attendance of undergraduates somewhat fell off as college lectures improved and the exigencies of the examination system increased.

Burrows published several courses of lectures, contributed to the 'Quarterly,' and made some reputation as an historical writer. Of his books the most important were: 'The Worthies of All Souls' (1874); 'The Cinque Ports' (1888; 4th edit. 1895); and 'The History of the Brocas Family of Beaurepaire and Roche Court' (1886), with which his wife's family was connected. In writing the last work he studied the Gascon rolls, and was created Officier de l'instruction publique by the French government for the help he gave in inducing the English government to cooperate with them in publishing these rolls in 1885. Meanwhile, he examined in the school of law and modern history in 1867–8, and was chairman of the modern history board from January 1889 to March 1893. In earlier years he had served on the Oxford extension committee which led to the foundation of the society of non-collegiate students in 1868. Owing to increasing deafness he transferred his professorial work to a deputy in the summer of 1900, but took as active an interest as ever in university, college, and city affairs until his death at Oxford on 10 July 1905. Burrows married on 13 September 1849 Mary Anna (*d.* 3 June 1906), third daughter of Sir James Whalley Smythe Gardiner, third baronet, of Roche Court, Fareham, a descendant of the Brocas family. Of six children three sons survived him. His eldest son, Edward Henry Burrows, born in 1851, was inspector of schools until his death in 1910. A pastel by Miss Nelly Erichsen is in the possession of his son, Mr. S. M. Burrows, at 9 Norham Gardens, Oxford.

Besides the works mentioned Burrows published: 1. 'The Relations of Church and State, historically considered,' 1866. 2. 'Memoir of Admiral Sir Henry Ducie Chads, K.C.B.,' 1869. 3. 'Constitutional Progress,' 1869; 2nd edit. 1872. 4. 'Parliament and the Church of England,' 1875. 5. 'Imperial England,' 1880. 6. 'Wiclif's Place in History,' 1882; 2nd edit. 1884. 7. 'The Life of Lord Hawke,' 1883; 3rd edit. 1904. 8. 'Commentaries on the History of Great Britain,' 1893. 9. 'History of the Foreign Policy of Great Britain,' 1895. 10. 'The History of the Family of Burrows of Sydenham and Long Crendon' (printed for private circulation), 1877. 11. 'The Families of Larcom, Hollis, and McKinley,' 1883. He edited vols. ii. and iii. of 'Collectanea' (Oxford Historical Society), 1890, 1896; and wrote a few articles for this Dictionary. He was English correspondent of the 'American Churchman,' the organ of the American episcopal church.

[History of the Family of Burrows, by Montagu Burrows, printed for private circulation; the Autobiography of Montagu Burrows, edited by his son, S. M. Burrows, 1908; personal knowledge.] A. H. J.

BURTON, first Lord. [See Bass, Sir Michael Arthur (1837–1909).]

BUSHELL, STEPHEN WOOTTON (1844–1908), physician and Chinese archæologist, born at his father's house on 28 July 1844, was third son of William Bushell of the Moat, Ash-next-Sandwich, Kent, by his wife Sarah Francis Wootton. After education at Tunbridge Wells school and Grange Court, Chigwell, he studied medicine at Guy's Hospital, and in 1866 graduated as M.B. of the University of London, where he won a scholarship and the gold medal in organic chemistry in 1864, a scholarship in biology and first-class honours in geology and palæontology in 1865, and first-class honours in medicine and gold medal in forensic medicine in 1866. Appointed house surgeon at Guy's Hospital in 1866, and resident medical officer to Bethlehem Royal Hospital in 1867, he in 1868 went out to Peking to fill the post of physician to the British legation there. He retired owing to ill-health in 1900. The services which he rendered to the Tsungli Yamen and other Chinese government departments received formal acknowledgement in 1894. In 1897 he was created C.M.G. On returning to England he devoted himself to the study of Chinese art and archæology. He died on 19 Sept. 1908 at his residence, Ravensholt, Harrow-on-the-Hill. He married in 1874 Florence, daughter of Dr. R. N. B. Mathews, of Bickley, Kent, and left one son.

Bushell won general recognition as the highest authority in his day on Chinese ceramics. He brought to bear upon the subject scientific training and practical connoisseurship as well as an adequate knowledge of the Chinese language, which enabled him to study, and in many cases to publish in translation, the best Chinese works on the arts and handicrafts. He himself formed extensive collections of Chinese porcelain, pottery, coins and books, and was a frequent contributor to the journals of the Royal Asiatic Society and of the Royal Numismatic Society, of which he joined the councils. He was also a corresponding member of the Zoological and Numismatic Societies of Vienna.

His chief works are: 1. 'Oriental Ceramic Art,' being a description of the W. T. Walters collection in Baltimore, published in ten richly illustrated volumes in 1897, followed by a separate edition of the text in 1899; though this work might be supplemented in regard to the earlier wares, it remains the classic on Chinese wares of the Ming and Ch'ing dynasties. 2. 'Chinese Art' (Victoria and Albert Museum Handbook), 1904, 2 vols., dealing briefly with all branches of Chinese art; a valuable work, and full of information, though necessarily summary in its treatment of controversial points. 3. 'Porcelain of Different Dynasties,' 1908, a reproduction with translation of a sixteenth-century Chinese collector's album with coloured illustrations; the original by Hsiang Yüan-p'ien, was unfortunately destroyed by fire in 1887, and the illustrations in Dr. Bushell's publication are taken from a copy of the original and are consequently of uncertain value; of the text, which is of great interest, a translation had been previously published by Bushell in 'Chinese Porcelain before the Present Dynasty' in the 'Journal of the Peking Oriental Society' in 1886. 4. 'Chinese Pottery and Porcelain, being a translation of the T'ao Shuo,' prepared in 1891, and published posthumously in 1910, an extremely valuable work, ranking with (and in many points above) Stanislas Julien's translation of the 'Ching-tê-chên T'ao Lu' (1856). The 'T'ao Shuo' itself ranks higher as a Chinese work on porcelain than the 'T'ao Lu,' and Bushell's translation, though not as precise as Julien's, is made with a practical knowledge of the subject which Julien did not possess. 5. 'Jade in China' (1906), an illustrated work on the Bishop collection, including translations of the 'Yü Shuo' (discussion of Jade) by T'ang Jung-tso, and of the 'Yü tso t'ou' (illustrations of the manufacture of jade) by Li Shih-chü'an.

Bushell also edited Cosmo Monkhouse's book on 'Chinese Porcelain' in 1901; and with W. M. Laffan prepared the catalogue of the Morgan collection of Chinese porcelain in the Metropolitan Museum, New York (1907).

[Royal Asiatic Soc. Journal, 1909, p. 239; Who's Who, 1908; Brit. Mus. Cat.; private information.] R. L. H.

BUSK, RACHEL HARRIETTE (1831–1907), writer on folk-lore, born in 1831, in London, was the youngest of five daughters of Hans Busk the elder [q. v.] by his wife Maria, daughter of Joseph Green. An elder sister was Mrs. Julia (Pitt) Byrne [q. v.], and Hans Busk the younger [q. v.] was the elder of her two brothers. Miss Busk was well educated by her father, and from an early age she spent much time in foreign travel, becoming an excellent linguist. Brought up as a protestant, she joined the Roman catholic church in 1858, and her example was followed subsequently by her four sisters and younger brother. She lived much at Rome from 1862 onwards, and gained an intimate knowledge of the city and of society there in days of papal independence. Her wide sympathies gave her a wide circle of friends, among them Cardinal Giacchino Pecci, afterwards Pope Leo XIII (in 1878). In 1867 and 1868 she contributed a series of letters to the 'Westminster Gazette' (a weekly Roman catholic paper that ran from February 1859 till April 1879) on Roman politics and society, some of which were reprinted in 1870 in a volume entitled 'Contemporary Annals of Rome, Notes Political, Archæological and Social, with a Preface by Monsignor Capel.' Travelling in outlying parts of Italy, Spain, and Austria, Miss Busk specially interested herself in folk-lore, collecting thousands of folk-tales and songs by word of mouth from the people. She published anonymously 'Patrañas or Spanish Stories' (1870); 'Household Stories from the Land of Hofer, or Popular Myths of Tirol' (1871); and 'Sagas from the Far East: Kalmouk and Mongol Tales' (1873). Under her own name she issued 'The Folk-lore of Rome' (1874); 'The Valleys of Tirol' (1874); and 'The Folk-Songs of Italy' (1887): a well-edited selection, giving a specimen from each province with a line-for-line translation and notes. In 1898 she edited and published in 2 vols. her sister Mrs. Pitt Byrne's 'Social Hours with Celebrities.' She died at Members' Mansions, Westminster, on 1 March 1907, and was buried in the family vault at Frant, near Tunbridge Wells.

[The Times, 8 March 1907; Brit. Mus. Cat.] E. L.

BUTCHER, SAMUEL HENRY (1850–1910), scholar and man of letters, was born in Dublin on 16 April 1850. His father, Samuel Butcher [q. v.], was then professor of ecclesiastical history in Trinity College. His mother was Mary Leahy, a member of a Kerry family. His early years were spent in Dublin, or at Ballymoney, co. Cork, where his father held a college living, and after 1866, when his father became bishop of Meath, at Ardbraccan, near Navan. His only brother, John George (*b.* 1853), is now a K.C. and M.P. for the city of York. His eldest sister, Elizabeth, became Lady Monteagle (*d.* 1908). He had three younger sisters—Mary Frances (Mrs. G. W. Prothero), Augusta (Mrs. Charles Crawley, *d.* 1899), and Eleanor, who died unmarried in 1894. Butcher was educated at home till the age of fourteen, when he went to Marlborough. His progress was rapid. In 1865 he won a senior scholarship. He also carried off many prizes for Latin and Greek composition, and ultimately became senior prefect. In later life he often acknowledged the debt he owed to the teaching of George Granville Bradley [q.v. Suppl. II], then headmaster. He also showed keenness in games, was a fair cricketer, and became captain of football. In 1869 he won an open scholarship for classics at Trinity College, Cambridge, and began residence at the university in the autumn of that year. His undergraduate career at Cambridge was one of unbroken success. In 1870 he won the Bell scholarship, in 1871 the Waddington scholarship, in 1871 and 1872 the Powis medal. In 1873 he graduated as senior classic, and was awarded a chancellor's medal. As an undergraduate he was the centre of a brilliant group of friends, and a member of the select society known as 'The Apostles.' In 1874 he was elected to a fellowship at Trinity.

Shortly after taking his degree he accepted from Dr. Hornby the offer of an assistant-mastership at Eton, and remained there for a year (1873–4). He then returned to Cambridge, and took up the post of lecturer in classics at his own college. There he might have remained, but for his engagement in 1875 to Rose, youngest daughter of Archbishop Trench [q. v.]. Under the existing statutes, a fellowship was forfeited by marriage. In this dilemma Dr. Bradley, then Master of University College, Oxford, offered him a tutorship at University, to the tenure of which a 'married' fellowship was attached. He therefore migrated to Oxford, and in 1876 married. At Oxford his teaching rapidly made its mark. His scholarship, at once brilliant and solid, his enthusiasm for the classics, his interest in the matter as well as the language of his authors, made his lectures both attractive and profitable. Among his pupils were J. W. Mackail, (Sir) Cecil Spring-Rice, and other men who later won distinction in various lines, and to whom he was a friend as well as a teacher. A university commission was appointed in 1877, and Butcher gained an acquaintance with academical problems which was highly useful to him in later years. In the promotion of female education he showed an active interest, and he was honorary secretary to the council of the association for the higher education of women at Oxford (1879–82). He also began to distinguish himself as an author. In 1879 he published, with Mr. Andrew Lang, a translation of the 'Odyssey,' which was at once recognised as the most successful prose reproduction of the original that had yet appeared. It combines great literary charm with delicate feeling for the subtleties of Greek; it is correct without being slavish; and has just enough archaic flavour, without an affectation of archaism. In the same year Butcher published an admirable little book on Demosthenes, which gives, in brief compass, the political conditions of the day and the peculiar methods and excellences of the orator's rhetoric.

These works, and his growing reputation as a scholar and a teacher, procured for him, in 1882, his appointment to the chair of Greek in the University of Edinburgh, rendered vacant by the retirement of Professor Blackie [q. v. Suppl. I]. He met at first some opposition as a southerner; but the charm of his character and the ability of his teaching soon overcame all obstacles. Popular among his students, with whom he was on much more intimate terms than is usual in Scottish universities, he speedily gained a leading rank in the senatus. In 1889 the Scottish universities bill became law; and a royal commission was nominated to draw up new statutes and reform the whole academical system in Scotland. The chairman of the commission was Lord Kinnear; and Butcher was chosen to represent the professorial body. The work of the commission, which was an executive and not merely (as usual) an advisory body, was peculiarly difficult and onerous, for two reasons. In the first place, the duty of the commissioners was to draw up for all the four Scottish universities not only statutes but ordinances or regulations. In the second place, the constitutions of the four universities had to be harmonised and, so far as possible, made identical. This laborious task lasted nearly eleven years, during which the commission held 251 meetings. Its general report was not issued until April 1900. It was generally recognised by the commissioners and by the academical body that Butcher's wide experience and varied culture, his industry, tact, and temper, were of the greatest value in determining the principles and working out the multitudinous details of a beneficent and far-reaching reform.

Meanwhile Butcher not only continued to discharge his professorial duties with energy and success but took an active part in Edinburgh society; and his house, graced by the social gifts and conversational powers of his wife, became a brilliant social centre. Among his closest friends were Professor and Mrs. W. Sellar (cf. MRS. SELLAR'S *Recollections, passim*). In 1891 Butcher published a volume of essays and addresses, entitled 'Some Aspects of the Greek Genius,' mostly written or delivered during his residence in Edinburgh. These essays set forth, lucidly and attractively, the nature of the Greek mind, in some of its most striking and important aspects. From the point of view of scholarship, the most notable essay in the volume is that which analyses Aristotle's conception of fine art and poetry. This essay was the germ out of which grew Butcher's most important work, 'Aristotle's Theory of Poetry and Fine Art' (1895). It contains a critical text and translation of the 'Poetics,' with a commentary which analyses and judges Aristotle's views on poetry and art, in the light of modern philosophy and achievement.

It was during his residence in Edinburgh that Butcher was first drawn into active connection with politics. The question of home rule became pressing, and he threw himself with decision and energy into the conflict. A man of liberal views but strong conservative instincts, he at once took a leading share in organising the unionist party in Edinburgh. Six years later, when, with Gladstone's return to power in 1892, the danger of home rule reappeared, he actively promoted the election of his friend Lord Wolmer (now second earl of Selborne) for West Edinburgh. In these contests he first showed his capacity for politics, and at once tested and improved his powers of speech.

In 1902 Mrs. Butcher died after a brief illness. This event loosened the ties which bound him to Edinburgh; and, having held his professorship long enough to earn a pension, he resigned in the following year. At a farewell dinner in January 1904 Mr. Arthur Balfour presided, and many speeches, made by distinguished persons, testified to the esteem and affection which he had won. He removed to London, taking a house (No. 6) in Tavistock Square, where he passed the remainder of his life. In 1904 he accepted an invitation to lecture at Harvard University and elsewhere in the United States. Some of his addresses he subsequently published in a volume entitled 'Harvard Lectures on Greek Subjects' (1904), a sort of sequel to 'Some Aspects of the Greek Genius.' Such leisure for literary work as Butcher subsequently enjoyed he spent on a critical edition of the speeches of Demosthenes, two volumes of which were published (1903, 1907), and in correcting and improving successive editions of the 'Poetics.'

Before leaving Edinburgh he had been nominated a member of the Royal Commission on University Education in Ireland (1901), of which Lord Robertson was chairman. In its discussions Butcher took a prominent part. Believing in the justice of the catholic demands, he aimed at satisfying the catholic authorities, without infringing the independence of Trinity College. He therefore aided the chairman in excluding that foundation from the discussion, while doing his utmost to elicit the exact views of catholic witnesses as to the extent of ecclesiastical control which they considered advisable. He also endeavoured to secure the attendance of the students of Maynooth in the new university. When, in 1903, the report appeared, it was found to be accompanied by eight 'reservations'; and the chairman himself dissented from the scheme. The report, therefore, produced no result.

Another royal commission was appointed to deal with the same subject in June 1906. Sir Edward Fry was chairman. Butcher was the only person who served on both this and the former commission. This time, Trinity College was expressly included in the purview of the commissioners, and its financial and other conditions were carefully examined; but in their report (January 1907) the commissioners declared that, in their opinion, it was impossible to make that foundation available for the higher education of catholics. They therefore recommended the establishment in Dublin of a separate college. When Mr. Birrell's bill for the creation of a new university was introduced in parliament (31 March 1908), Butcher opposed the granting of indefinite powers of affiliation to the senate, but in vain. Although the scheme differed in many ways from what he desired, he accepted a place in the senate of the new university, and thenceforward took an active part in its proceedings.

In 1906, on the death of his old friend Sir Richard Jebb [q. v. Suppl. II], Butcher was chosen in his place to represent the University of Cambridge in parliament. His first speech was made on the Irish university bill, and produced a marked effect. It was an impassioned appeal to substitute for the existing royal university a real teaching university where the catholic Irish layman could obtain the education he desired. He spoke in the House of Commons comparatively seldom, and confined himself chiefly to educational and Irish questions; but he always displayed mastery of his subject, and the elegance and lucidity of his language, his clear voice and conciliatory manner, combined with deep feeling and evident sincerity of purpose, gained him a notable position.

In other directions also the last years of his life were full of activity. In 1903 he had been one of the principal founders of the English Classical Association. He acted as chairman of its council from that date onwards, and as president in 1907. He was specially instrumental in bringing about, through the agency of the association, a reform in the pronunciation of Latin which is now generally accepted in this country. Of the Irish Classical Association he was also the first president. He was a prominent member of the Hellenic Society and of the committee for the British school at Athens. He opposed the abolition of compulsory Greek at the older universities, but was willing to make certain concessions in favour of students specialising in other subjects. When the British Academy was founded in 1902 he was one of its original members, and became its president in 1909. In July 1908 he was appointed a trustee of the British Museum, and six months later became a member of the standing committee. On educational questions and appointments he was continually consulted, general confidence being placed in his judgment. Honours fell thick upon him. He received honorary degrees from the universities of Oxford, Dublin, St. Andrews, Edinburgh, Glasgow, Manchester, and Harvard. He was a corresponding member of the American Academy. He received from the King of Greece, in 1910, the Order of the Redeemer. He was an honorary fellow both of University College, Oxford, and of Trinity College, Cambridge.

The multifarious labours in which he was engaged told eventually upon his health. Although naturally somewhat delicate in constitution, he generally bore all the appearance of a healthy man. He spent the summer vacation of 1910 at Danesfort, near Killarney, on a little property inherited from his father, where he loved to spend his holidays among his own people. His last public appearance was at the dinner in celebration of the completion of the eleventh edition of the 'Encyclopædia Britannica' on 21 Oct. 1910. Shortly afterwards he had an attack of internal hæmorrhage, which led to suffusion of blood on the brain. He died without issue in a nursing home in London on 29 Dec. 1910, and was buried in the Dean cemetery, Edinburgh, by the side of his wife.

Of middle height, well but rather slightly built, Butcher was remarkably handsome. His eyes were large, of a deep brown, and very brilliant. His hair was black and abundant, slightly grizzled towards the end of his life. His conversation was fluent, vivacious and energetic, but playful as well as vigorous, argumentative on occasion, but never overbearing. Generous to others, he was capable of fiery indignation against public or private wrongs. Withal he had a strong sense of humour, delighting especially in the sometimes unconscious wit of his countrymen. His character, like his descent, was a happy blend of what is best in the two nations to which he belonged—of Irish charm, vivacity, and eloquence, with English energy, courage, and resolution. A portrait of him, in oils, by Mr. Sholto Douglas, is in the possession of Lord Monteagle.

His most important publications are: 1. 'The Odyssey of Homer done into English Prose' (with Andrew Lang), 1879. 2. 'Demosthenes' ('Classical Writers' series), 1881. 3. 'Some Aspects of the Greek Genius,' 1891; republished with an additional chapter, 1893. 4. 'Aristotle's Theory of Poetry and Fine Art, with a critical text and a translation of the Poetics,' 1895; revised editions, 1897, 1902: the text of the 'Poetics,' with notes and translations, was published separately in 1898. 5. 'Greek Idealism in the Common Things of Life' (reprinted from the *Journal of Education*), 1901.

6. 'Demosthenis Orationes' (Scriptorum classicorum Bibliotheca Oxoniensis), 2 vols. Oxford, 1903, 1907. 7. 'Harvard Lectures on Greek Subjects,' 1904; republished in 1911 with the title 'Harvard Lectures on the Originality of Greece.' With his brother, Mr. J. G. Butcher, he edited (1877) his father's 'Ecclesiastical Calendar.' His published speeches comprise 'Irish Land Acts and their Operation' (Glasgow, 1887), and 'The Reign of Terror or the Rule of Law in Ireland' (1908).

[Obituary notices by Professor A. W. Verrall in the Classical Review (February 1911) and Professor W. Rhys Roberts in the Gryphon (February 1911); address by Lord Reay before the British Academy, 18 Jan. 1911; paper by Professor Verrall (Proceedings of the British Academy, vol. iv.); address by Professor Gilbert Murray before the Acad. Committee of the Royal Soc. of Literature, 10 April 1911; private information.]

G. W. P.

BUTLER, ARTHUR GRAY (1831–1909), headmaster of Haileybury, born at Gayton Rectory, Northamptonshire, on 19 Aug. 1831, was third son of George Butler [q. v.], dean of Peterborough, by his wife Sarah Maria, eldest daughter of John Gray of Wembley Park, Middlesex. His youngest brother, Henry Montagu, became Master of Trinity College, Cambridge, in 1886. Arthur entered Rugby under A. C. Tait in August 1844, and was admitted as a scholar of University College, Oxford, in March 1850. At school and college he was distinguished in both work and games, and 'Butler's Leap' at Rugby still recalls a juvenile athletic feat. At Oxford he was an original member of the Essay Club founded in 1852 by his friend George Joachim (afterwards Lord) Goschen [q. v. Suppl. II], and was president of the Union in 1853. In the same year he won the Ireland scholarship, and graduated B.A. with a first class in the final classical school. He was elected a fellow of Oriel in 1856, proceeding M.A. in the following year. He did not reside on his fellowship. Returning to Rugby in 1858, he served as assistant master under Frederick Temple [q. v. Suppl. II], and was ordained deacon in 1861 and priest in 1862.

On the reconstitution of Haileybury College in 1862 Butler was appointed the first headmaster. In September the school took over the buildings of the East India Company's college near Hertford, which had been founded in 1805 for the training of its civil servants. Butler at once proved his capacity as an organiser despite initial difficulties. Haileybury had no endowment, and from the outset he was hampered by inconvenient buildings and lack of modern appliances. Nevertheless he set himself to infuse into the school something of the strenuous vitality of the Rugby system. He himself served as chaplain. He provided racquet and fives courts. He encouraged the growth of corporate feeling in the dormitories, and maintained the continuity of associations by naming the various houses after prominent Anglo-Indian civilians. Butler's labours bore fruit, and, thanks to his energy, the numbers rose rapidly in a few years from fifty-four to 360. His attractive personality, his contagious enthusiasm, his persuasive eloquence, and downright thoroughness exercised a marked influence over boys and masters. Although never a profound scholar, he was a stimulating classical teacher, and had the faculty of throwing new light on familiar passages. A breakdown in health compelled his resignation in December 1867. He had then raised Haileybury to a recognised place among great English public schools.

On resuming active work in 1874 Butler served as chaplain of the Royal Indian Civil Engineering College, which was established at Coopers Hill near Egham in 1871. Returning to Oxford in 1875, he settled down to the more congenial duties of dean and tutor of Oriel. He was select preacher before the university in 1885 as well as Whitehall preacher. Butler, who was a strong liberal in politics, actively promoted movements for the better housing of the poor and the higher education of women in Oxford. After resigning his official position in 1895 he maintained the closest relations with his college, and it was partly due to his suggestions that both Oriel and Oxford benefited by the will of Cecil Rhodes [q. v. Suppl. II]. He was elected to an honorary fellowship at Oriel in 1907. He died at Torquay on 16 Jan. 1909, and was buried in Holywell cemetery, Oxford. On 4 April 1877 he married Harriet Jessie, daughter of Michael Pakenham Edgeworth and niece of Maria Edgeworth [q. v.], who survived him with one son and three daughters. His son, Harold Edgeworth, became professor of Latin at University College, London, in 1911. At Haileybury his name is commemorated by the Butler prizes for English literature. In 1910 a fund was raised by old pupils to found a Butler scholarship, and a tablet was erected to his memory in the chapel. A portrait by George Richmond, R.A., hangs in the library.

Butler cherished through life strong literary instincts, which found expression mainly in verse. His poetry made no claim to be original, but was marked by sound scholarship and feeling. He published two dramas, 'Charles I' (1874; 2nd edit. 1907) and 'Harold' (1892; 2nd edit. 1906), and two volumes of verse entitled 'The Choice of Achilles' (1900) and 'Hodge and the Land' (1907). In 'The Three Friends: a Story of Rugby in the Forties' (1900), he recorded the effect produced on his contemporaries by the early poems of Tennyson.

[The Times, 17 Jan. 1909; Haileyburian, 16 Feb. 1909; L. S. Milford, Haileybury College, Past and Present, 1909; Oxford Magazine, 21 Jan. 1909; A. D. Elliot, Life of G. J. Goschen, 1911; private information.]

G. S. W.

BUTLER, ARTHUR JOHN (1844–1910), Italian scholar, born at Putney on 21 June 1844, was eldest of six children of William John Butler [q. v.], at that time curate of Puttenham, near Guildford. His mother was Emma, daughter of George Henry Barnett, banker, of Glympton Park, Woodstock. On both parents' sides he was connected with Stratford Canning [q. v.], first cousin of George Canning—Stratford being maternal grandfather of his mother, and great-grand-uncle (by marriage) of his father.

After a childhood at Wantage, affectionately dominated by parents of strong if differing characters, both devoted pioneers of the tractarian movement, Arthur went in 1852 with a scholarship to St. Andrew's College, Bradfield. From Bradfield he proceeded at Easter 1857 to Eton, where he was Newcastle select (1861–3), Tomline prizeman (1862), and captain of oppidans (Michaelmas 1862–Easter 1863). From Eton he passed to Trinity College, Cambridge, where he obtained a scholarship. He won the Bell university scholarship in 1864, and graduated eighth classic in the tripos of 1867, and as a junior optime in mathematics. He was elected a fellow of Trinity in 1869. In the following year he reluctantly left Cambridge on accepting a post as examiner under the board of education. He worked in the education office, Whitehall, until 1887, when an invitation to become salaried partner in the publishing firm of Rivington tempted him from a routine which had never been congenial. After the amalgamation of Messrs. Rivington with the firm of Longmans he transferred his services to Messrs. Cassell & Co. as chief editor. In 1894 he relinquished business, and was appointed an assistant commissioner on secondary education. Subsequently from 1899 until death he was engaged at the Public Record Office in editing 'Calendars of Foreign State Papers' from 1577 onwards, of which he published four volumes between 1901 and 1909. In 1898 he became professor of Italian language and literature at University College, London, and also filled that office till the end.

Butler, who 'had a Roman integrity of character but no Roman pride,' was an accomplished scholar, owing his reputation to activities lying outside his official or business services. His most important work was his contribution to the study of Dante, under whose spell he came first during his time at Cambridge. He was in point of time the first Englishman to replace the old dilettante enjoyment of the 'Divine Comedy' by exact and disciplined study, and (obedient to Cambridge tradition) to treat it as Porson or Shilleto would have treated a Greek or Latin classic. His 'Purgatory of Dante,' a prose translation with notes, appeared in 1880 (2nd edit. 1892); his 'Paradise' in 1885 (2nd edit. 1891); his 'Hell' in 1892. In 1890 he edited the Italian text. In 1893 he put forth a translation of Scartazzini's 'Companion to Dante'; in 1895 a small work on 'Dante, his Times and his Work' (2nd edit. 1897). 'The Forerunners of Dante' (1910), an annotated selection from the Italian poets before 1300, was finished a few days before his death. Other scholars have followed and may have outstripped him, but Butler was 'the breaker of the road.' Much leisure was also devoted to translating French and German works, of which the chief were 'Memoirs of Baron de Marbot' (1892); 'Letters of Count Cavour and Mme. de Circourt' (Count Nigra's edit. 1894); 'Select Essays of Sainte-Beuve' (1895); 'Memoirs of Baron Thiébault' (1896), and 'The History of Mankind,' by Prof. Friedrich Ratzel (1896). He edited the English version of 'Bismarck, the Man and the Statesman' (1898). At the same time for thirty-five years Butler wrote for the 'Athenæum,' and was an occasional contributor to magazines on his favourite topics—Dante, mountaineering, Eton, the Napoleonic campaigns; but much of his most characteristic writing was spent in fugitive contributions to the press, which were always trenchant, original, humorous, and exhibited an unusual blend of inborn churchmanship with an outspoken and militant liberalism.

From school days Butler was also a mountaineer, delighting in Alpine expeditions off the beaten track. In a prefatory note to the 'Alpine Journal' (vol. xv. 1892), he wrote that the 'centres' were from various causes almost totally unknown to him, that his acquaintance with the chain of Mont Blanc was founded on dim schoolboy recollections of a walk round the lower cols in days when the Alpine Club itself did not exist; that he had not seen Zermatt for nearly a quarter of a century, while Grindelwald remained to him merely a place on the map. In 1886, when he became a member of the Alpine Club, he brought to it an intimate knowledge—beyond challenge by any mountaineer in Europe—of the Oetzthal Alps, which he first attacked in 1874, and revisited many times, with an ardour that was almost a passion, up to 1890. His attitude towards climbing for mere display may be gathered from a single sentence in a note of this last expedition, in which he and his companion were badly baffled by fogs. On one occasion they missed the peak of their assault and wandered on in a mist until 'We found ourselves on the top of something.' The mist lifted and 'it became clear that we had strayed on to the top of the highest and most northerly of the Hennesiegelköpfe. When we got back, Praximarer (the landlord), who is probably as good an authority as anyone, said that he knew of no previous ascent, nor can I conceive any reason why there should ever have been one.' Butler became editor of the 'Alpine Journal' in 1890, and supervised it until the close of 1893 (vols. xv. and xvi.). He delighted in the dinners of the A.D.C. (Alpine Dining Club). He was a member of the band of 'Sunday Tramps' which (Sir) Leslie Stephen organised in 1882, ranking number ten on the original list (cf. MAITLAND's *Life of Stephen*).

Butler died at Weybridge on 26 Feb. 1910, and was buried at Wantage. He married on 6 April 1875, Mary, daughter of William Gilson Humphrey, vicar of St. Martin's-in-the-Fields, and left issue one son and six daughters.

A small oil portrait by Lady Holroyd belongs to Mrs. Butler.

[Life and Letters of William John Butler, ed. A. J. Butler, 1897; Alpine Journal, vols. xv. xvi. and to 1890 *passim*; Maitland, Life of Sir Leslie Stephen; The Times, 28 Feb. and 8 March 1910; Athenæum, 5 March 1910; Cambridge Review, notice by Sir Frederick Pollock, March 1910; Eton College Chronicle and Eton Register; private letters and records.] A. Q-C.

BUTLER, MRS. JOSEPHINE ELIZABETH (1828–1906), social reformer, born on 13 April 1828 at Millfield Hill, Glendale, Northumberland, was fourth daughter of John Grey of Dilston [q. v.] by his wife Hannah Annett, whose family was of Huguenot extraction. Much influenced in girlhood by her father's strong religious and ethical convictions, she was educated at home, save for a short period at the boarding-school of a Miss Tydey at Newcastle-on-Tyne. She studied in girlhood much Italian and English literature, and read translations of the fathers. On 8 Jan. 1852 she married George Butler [q. v. Suppl. I], then engaged in tuition at Oxford. The first five years of her married life were spent in Oxford, whence she moved successively to Cheltenham, Liverpool, and Winchester, where her husband held in turn educational or ecclesiastical appointments.

From an early period Mrs. Butler, moved by what she believed to be a divine call, devoted her energies to the moral elevation of her sex. She supported in its early stages the movement for the higher education of women (cf. her introduction to *Woman's Work and Woman's Culture*, 1869), but after the accidental death by a fall before her eyes of her youngest child and only daughter, she concentrated her efforts on the protection and reclamation of women subjected to vicious influences. Having settled in Liverpool in 1866, she visited women in the workhouse and helped to establish homes and refuges for the drifting population of workgirls and fallen women. Many of the latter were with her husband's assent received into their home. At the end of 1869 she engaged in the agitation then just begun for the repeal of the Contagious Diseases Acts of 1864, 1866, and 1869, which gave a legal sanction to vice by placing women living immoral lives under police supervision while exposing them to cruel injustice. These measures only applied to seaports and garrison towns, but their extension to the whole country was recommended by their more extreme advocates. After an agitation for repeal of the Acts had been begun by Daniel Cooper, secretary of the Rescue Society, the Ladies' National Association for Repeal was formed in 1869, with Mrs. Butler as hon. secretary, and it gained influential support not only from Englishwomen like Florence Nightingale [q. v. Suppl. II], Harriet Martineau [q. v.], and Lydia Becker [q. v. Suppl. I] (*Daily News*, 31 Dec. 1869), but from foreigners like Mazzini and Victor Hugo. For sixteen years Mrs. Butler was indefatigable in the cause with pen and speech. At a by-election at Colchester (October-November 1870), when the government candidate, Sir Henry Storks [q. v.], championed the Acts, Mrs. Butler actively opposed him, and was rewarded by his defeat. She similarly intervened in 1872 with smaller success when a member of the government, H. C. E. Childers [q.v. Suppl. I], offered himself for re-election at Pontefract. In March 1871 she gave evidence before the royal commission which was appointed in deference to the agitation; and next year opposed a bill introduced by the home secretary, Henry Austin Bruce, afterwards Lord Aberdare [q. v. Suppl. I], which substituted for the Acts provisions under the Vagrancy Act. She was equally energetic in denouncing the working of the offending law in India. At length in May 1883 the English Acts were repealed in part, mainly through the exertion of (Sir) James Stansfeld [q. v. Suppl. I]; and in 1886 they were totally repealed. In 1896 Mrs. Butler published an account of the conflict in 'Personal Reminiscences of a Great Crusade.'

Meanwhile Mrs. Butler had extended the agitation to the continent, where her zeal evoked much active sympathy. After urging continental action at a meeting at York on 25 June 1874, she visited France, Italy, and Switzerland (1874–5). At Brussels in 1880 she exposed in the newspaper 'Le National' the treatment of English girls, under age, who were detained, it was alleged, in licensed houses with the connivance of the 'police des mœurs,' of whom the chief and his subordinate were in consequence dismissed. To meet the evil she formed in London a committee for the suppression of 'the white slave traffic.' It was largely through her influence that the law affecting the state regulation of vice was reformed in Switzerland, Holland, Norway, France, and Italy.

In 1886 the serious illness of her husband, who fully sympathised with her aims, prevented further public activity. After her husband's death at Winchester in 1890 she lived near the residence of George Grey Butler, her eldest son, at Wooler, Northumberland, where she died on 30 Dec. 1906. She was buried at Kirknewton. Her three sons survived her.

A crayon drawing of Mrs. Butler in youth, by George Richmond, and an oil painting by Jacobs are in the possession of her son, George Grey Butler, Ewart Park, Wooler. The former is reproduced, with the inscription 'Josephine Butler and all brave champions of purity,' in the atrium of the Lady chapel, Liverpool cathedral. An oil-painting by G. F. Watts, begun in 1895, was intended by the artist to be placed in the National Portrait Gallery at his death, and is in the possession of his widow, at Guildford. A pencil drawing made by Emily Ford in 1903 was reproduced for the subscribers to a presentation to Mrs. Butler in 1906. Of two marble busts by Alexander Munro, who also produced a medallion in profile, one is at Ewart Park, and the other belongs to Mrs. Butler's brother-in-law, Dr. H. M. Butler, Master of Trinity College, Cambridge.

Besides numerous pamphlets and the memoirs of her father (1869), her husband (1892), and her sister, Madame Meuricoffre (1901), Josephine Butler wrote a 'Life of St. Catherine of Siena' (1898), which Gladstone praised, and a 'Life of Pastor Oberlin' (1882). 'The Hour before the Dawn' (1876) was probably the most widely read of her very numerous writings upon abolition. 'Rebecca Jarrett' (1886) was a reasonable defence of the witness whose evidence was discredited at the trial of W. T. Stead in that year. In 'Native Races and the War' (1900) she defended the government against pro-Boer criticism during the South African war.

[G. W. and L. A. Johnson, Josephine E. Butler, 1909 (with bibliography); W. T. Stead, Josephine Butler, 1888; The Times, 2 Jan. 1907; A Rough Record of Events connected . . . with Repeal. Compiled by H. J. Wilson; the Shield, January and May 1907; Benjamin Scott, A State Iniquity, 1890; private information.] E. S. H–r.

BUTLER, SAMUEL (1835–1902), philosophical writer, born at his father's rectory of Langar, near Bingham, Nottinghamshire, on 4 Dec. 1835, was eldest son of Thomas Butler (1806–86), who graduated B.A. from St. John's College, Cambridge, in 1829; was collated to the rectory of Langar in 1834; revised his father's 'Antient Geography,' 1851 and 1855; and subsequently became canon of Lincoln (Baker, *St. John's College*, 1869, p. 901). His grandfather, Dr. Samuel Butler [q. v.], was headmaster of Shrewsbury, and afterwards bishop of Lichfield and Coventry. His aunt Mary, elder daughter of the bishop, was the second wife of Archdeacon Bather [q. v.]. His mother was Fanny (*m.* 1831), daughter of Philip John Worsley (1769–1811), a sugar refiner, of Arno's Vale, Bristol, and a connection of the Taylors of Norwich; she died at Mentone in 1873.

After a grand tour with his parents at a time when European railways were in their infancy (1843), an expedition which impressed Butler profoundly, he in 1848 was placed under Benjamin Hall Kennedy, his grandfather's successor at Shrewsbury. In October 1854 'Sam' went up to Cambridge and graduated from the family college (St. John's), as twelfth in the classical tripos in 1858. He was grounded in Homer and Thucydides by Shilleto, and while still an undergraduate wrote among other trifles 'The Shield of Achilles, an Homeric Picture of Cambridge Life,' which skilfully burlesques a typical Homer 'crib' of the period (reprinted in *The Eagle*, December 1902). Paternal influence exercised with unsparing hand constrained Butler into the priestly path, which he traversed far enough to become a lay reader to the curate of St. James's, Piccadilly, (Sir) Philip Perrin. At Cambridge he had come under Simeon's influence. But doubt first assailed him in connection with the question of the efficacy of infant baptism. An angry correspondence ensued with his father (upon whom he was pecuniarily dependent), and Samuel remained unconvinced.

Early attempts at becoming a painter were sternly deprecated by the family, and Butler resolved to emigrate to New Zealand. Taking passage in the ill-fated Burmah, he changed his berth at the last moment to the Roman Emperor, and sailed from Gravesend on 30 Sept. 1859. His success in the colony, mainly as a sheep-breeder in the Rangitata district of the middle (Canterbury) Island, is detailed in long letters home, which—supplemented by two chapters contributed to the St. John's College 'Eagle'—formed the basis of his first book 'A First Year in Canterbury Settlement,' published by Longmans, and edited by his father, with a preface dated 'Langar Rectory, 29 June 1863.' The work is full of Butler's quasi-humorous detail, sub-acid in flavour, and plain almost to aridity in point of style. In the same vein are the contributions which Butler made to the 'Christchurch Press,' among them the witty speculation entitled 'Darwin among the Machines,' which formed the nucleus of 'Erewhon,' the book which first brought him recognition. His sheep run was successful, and selling out at a fortunate moment he practically doubled what money his father had given him (approximately four thousand pounds).

In 1864–5 Butler returned to England, and established himself in chambers, consisting of three rooms and a pantry, on the second floor at 15 Clifford's Inn. After a brief course at South Kensington he studied painting at F. S. Cary's (the son of Lamb's friend), and then at Heatherley's school in Newman Street. In the course of the next few years he exhibited as many as eleven pictures in the Royal Academy. In 1865 he printed the anonymous pamphlet (drafted in New Zealand) 'The Evidence for the Resurrection of Jesus Christ as given by the Four Evangelists critically examined,' the product of the doubts which had assailed him since 1859, and which he subsequently incorporated in 'The Fair Haven.' In 1872 he produced the brilliant, if somewhat fragmentary, 'Erewhon,' a jeu d'esprit which recalled the vein of Swift. The trial of a man for the offence of suffering from consumption (as an illustration of the analogy of crime and disease), and the view of machines—as representing and eventually dominating the functions of man—are strongly suggestive of a new Gulliver, but the book also contains the most original of Butler's conceptions—his preference for physical over moral health, his derision of earnestness and of the solemn pretences of parenthood, his conviction of the unconscious transmission of habit and memory from one generation to another, the superior importance of manners to beliefs, the antennæ of art to the sledge-hammers of science. All the more from the fact that they were quite unfathomable by his own age, Butler clung to his ideas with grim and humorous tenacity. 'Erewhon' was published anonymously, like its successor—a far more elaborate exercise in irony—'The Fair Haven' (1873). This volume pretended to be a defence of the miraculous element in our Lord's ministry upon earth, both as against rationalist impugners and certain orthodox defenders, and was put forth as by the late John Pickard Owen and as edited by William Bickersteth Owen, with a memoir of the author (published by Trübner, with preface dated 'Brighton, 10 March 1873'). Incredible as it seems, in view of the ubiquitous mockery and fictitious titles, 'The Fair Haven' was accepted as seriously as Defoe's 'Shortest Way with the Dissenters' by the ultra-Protestant press. Butler's anonymity was due in part to Swift's Bickerstaff tradition of mystification, and partly to his unwillingness to provoke further controversy with his father, but he affixed his name to subsequent editions both of this book and of 'Erewhon.' The profits which he had made in New Zealand were at this time imperilled by unsound investments; some of these were Canadian, and it was during a series of distracting visits to the Dominion, in an attempt to save the wreck of his invested capital, that Butler produced one of his most original and argumentative works, entitled 'Life and Habit,' dedicated to Charles Paine-Pauli, a New Zealand acquaintance (Dec. 1877). The line of argument which he there took up against the tyranny of natural selection was completed in 'Evolution, Old and New' (1879), 'Unconscious Memory' (1880), 'Luck or Cunning' (1886), 'The Deadlock in Darwinism' (*Universal Review*, 1890), and 'Notes,' afterwards reprinted in the 'New Quarterly Review' of 1910. These books and papers were a revolt against what Butler considered as a conspiracy of the Darwins to banish mind from the universe, and the scientific controversy was complicated by a grievance —partly justified even now, wholly justified as far as Butler could possibly then have seen—against Charles Darwin's method of interpreting a private communication (see FESTING JONES, *Darwin and Butler: a Step towards Reconciliation*, 1911). Butler brought to the subject in dispute tenacity, memory, and power of concentration, which enabled him to discover certain defects in the armour of natural selection. A Prague professor, Ewald Hering, had formulated a theory connecting heredity with memory a few years before. Butler knew nothing of this until his 'Life and Habit' was on the eve of publication, but when he looked at Hering's lecture he found the kernel of Hering's theory was practically identical with his own. His object was to show that variation was due less to chance and environment, and more to cunning and effort, design, or memory—whether conscious or unconscious—than Darwin had supposed. As a guiding principle, however, his views though highly suggestive have not proved of direct service, save as a stimulus to fresh hypotheses.

Butler was now at the parting of the ways; his most successful picture, 'Mr. Heatherley's Holiday' (the drawing master mending the studio skeleton), now in the Tate Gallery, had appeared at the Royal Academy in 1874, but the influence of literature had triumphed, and Butler eventually surrendered himself to a succession of controversies, which have not in the main greatly enhanced his reputation. Meanwhile as a topographer of Italian Switzerland and critic of Italian art he did creative work in 'Alps and Sanctuaries of Piedmont and the Canton Ticino' (1881). Butler's headquarters in north Italy were primarily at Faido and then at Varallo, where he stayed repeatedly from 1871 to 1901. 'Alps and Sanctuaries' omitted Varallo, to which he promised to devote a separate book. The town gave Butler a civic dinner in August 1887, and he redeemed his pledge next year with his 'Ex Voto,' an account of the Sacro Monte or New Jerusalem at Varallo-Sesia, with some notes of Tabachetti's remaining work at the Sanctuary of Crea. Archæologically speaking, this is a far more elaborate study than its predecessor; it is a revelation of the highly original art of Tabachetti and Gaudenzio Ferrari. An article 'Art in the Valley of Saas' followed in the 'Universal Review' (1890).

In 1886 Butler's financial position, which had become a good deal involved, was relieved by the death of his father (29 Dec.). He now spent most of the summer abroad, but lived habitually at his chambers in Clifford's Inn, London, working steadily at the British Museum. In 1886 he was an unsuccessful candidate for the Slade professorship at Cambridge. Every evening when in London he was wont to visit his friend, Mr. H. Festing Jones, at Staple Inn, mainly for the purpose of musical study. Together they began to compose at first Handelian minuets and gavottes. They next wrote and issued an oratorio buffo, 'Narcissus' (1888), about shepherds losing money in Capel Court, studied counterpoint with W. S. Rockstro and designed a Ulysses oratorio (published in 1904). Butler committed much of the 'Odyssey' to memory, and he was so impressed by the peculiar mental attitude of certain portions of the narrative, that he conceived the theory that the epic was written by a woman, while he identified the dwelling-place of the writer as Trapani in Sicily (see his 'On the Trapanese Origin of the Odyssey,' 1893). He embodied this view in 'The Authoress of the Odyssey,' published in 1897, after a visit to the Troad and a careful study of the Sicilian coast. He translated the 'Iliad' in 1898, and the 'Odyssey' in 1900 into colloquial prose. Other works produced in his lifetime were 'The Life of Samuel Butler, bishop of Lichfield and Coventry' (2 vols. 1896), published from family papers which had come to him in 1886; 'Shakespeare's Sonnets Reconsidered' (1899), upholding the view that the sonnets were addressed to a man of humble birth, a speculation which has found extremely few adherents; and

'Erewhon Revisited' (1901), an examination of the religion which had come into existence among the Erewhonians after the ascension of their first explorer in a balloon. This last was the most rapidly written of any of his books, and is perhaps more consecutive than its predecessor, though it lacks something of its eccentric charm. Butler's health was indifferent when he set out for Sicily on Good Friday, 1902. He returned to Clifford's Inn, but soon left for the nursing home in which he died on 18 June 1902. His body was cremated at Woking, in accordance with his instructions, and the ashes dispersed.

Two of his most seminal books, an autobiographical novel entitled 'The Way of All Flesh' (1903) and 'Essays on Life, Art and Science,' were published posthumously, with introductions by Mr. Streatfeild, and have since been reprinted. A selection from his ironic 'Notebooks' was edited by Mr. Festing Jones in 1912.

Church and state man, or advanced member of the broad church party, as he whimsically described himself, Butler, the most versatile of iconoclasts, attacked received opinion in religion, science, painting, archæology, literary criticism, and music; but his most determined onslaught was on the canting, conventional morality in which the genteel children of his age were reared. Commenced by 'Erewhon,' this work was carried to its conclusion in his posthumous novel, imperishably graven out of the flint of life. A spiritual autobiography, the incentive to which was supplied by a lady, Miss Savage, who appears in the book as Alethea, whom he first met in 1871, 'The Way of All Flesh' was touched and retouched down to her death in 1885, though published only in 1903. Through 'Erewhon,' 'The Way of All Flesh,' and the posthumous 'Essays' (each a masterpiece of idiosyncrasy), Butler chiefly influenced contemporary thought. His style was framed with the object of attaining the maximum of terseness, consistent with absolute lucidity.

Butler's outwardly conventional aspect, with his brick-dust complexion and bushy eyebrows, is well represented by portraits. Of those by himself there is one at Christchurch, N.Z., one at Shrewsbury School, and one at St. John's College, Cambridge. A good likeness by Charles Gogin is in the National Portrait Gallery. An excellent photograph in 'Ex Voto' represents Butler standing by the side of one of Gaudenzio Ferrari's terra-cotta figures. A satirical picture by Butler, 'Family Prayers,' belongs to Mr. Festing Jones, who has many of the artist's delicate and highly finished water-colour drawings of the Ticino region. Other of his drawings are in the British Museum.

[The Times, 20 June 1902; Athenæum, 28 June 1902; Monthly Review, Sept. 1902; Eagle, Dec. 1902; Streatfeild's Records and Memorials, 1903 (portrait); H. Festing Jones' Italian Journey; Mr. Streatfeild's Introductions to the re-issue of Butler's Works; Marcus Hartog's preface to Unconscious Memory; Fortnightly Review, June 1912; Salter's Two Moderns, 1911; Independent Rev., Sept. 1904; Mercure de France, July 1910; Brit. Mus. Cat.; information kindly given by Mr. H. Festing Jones.] T. S.

BUTLER, Sir WILLIAM FRANCIS (1838–1910), lieut.-general and author, born on 31 Oct. 1838 at Suirville, co. Tipperary, was the seventh child of Richard and Ellen Butler of Suirville. He was of the stock of Thomas Butler, tenth earl of Ormonde [q. v.]. Among the recollections of his childhood were the great famine, the evictions, and Daniel O'Connell; while as a Roman catholic he heard much of the penal laws and English misrule. These things made a lasting impression on him. In 1847 he was sent to a Jesuit school at Tullabeg, in King's County, and afterwards to Dr. James Quinn's school in Dublin.

He obtained a commission as ensign in the 69th foot on 17 Sept. 1858, and after serving nearly two years at the depôt at Fermoy he joined the headquarters of the regiment at Tonghoo in Burmah. In the spring of 1862 the regiment was moved to Madras, and in 1863 Butler spent two months' leave in a visit to the western coast, from Calicut to Cape Comorin. He also went to Vellore, and by his efforts a monument was erected there to the men of the 69th who were killed there in 1806. He was promoted lieutenant on 17 Nov. 1863. The regiment went home in the spring of 1864, and on the voyage Butler spent two days at St. Helena —days 'steeped in thoughts of glory and of grief,' for he worshipped Napoleon. At first stationed at Gosport, Butler removed with the regiment to Aldershot early in 1865, and there began 'A Narrative of the Historical Events connected with the 69th Regiment,' which was published in 1870. In the summer of 1866 the regiment went to the Channel Islands, where Butler saw much of Victor Hugo, who recognised him as an *enfant terrible*. After five months' sojourn at the Curragh, the regiment embarked in August 1867 for

Canada on account of threatened Fenian raids. It was stationed at Brantford, north of lake Erie. Butler got three months' leave in September, went off to Nebraska, and made his first acquaintance with buffalo and 'the glorious prairies.'

In the spring of 1868 he succeeded lieutenant Redvers Buller [q. v. Suppl. II] as look-out officer on the frontier, and had to travel 1500 miles a month to visit the posts placed to intercept deserters. In September 1869 he went home on leave, in the hope of finding some way of escape from being purchased over in his regiment, but he was disappointed. His father died in March 1870, and was buried at Killardrigh; his mother had died in 1849. He returned to Canada; but before he left Ireland he learnt that Colonel Wolseley, whom he had met two years before, was organising an expedition to the Red River. He telegraphed 'Remember Butler 69th regiment.' There were no vacant berths on the staff, when he reached Toronto, but he was sent independently on a special mission to the Red River settlement, to find out what was the state of affairs there, and what the rising of the half-breeds really meant. He set out on 8 June. Travelling through the United States, he descended the Red River to Winnipeg, had an interview with Louis Riel [q. v.], and met the expedition on 4 August about halfway on its route. He accompanied it to Fort Garry, from which Riel had fled; and he remained there when the expedition went back.

On 24 Oct. he set out on a new mission, to investigate the situation in Saskatchewan and report on the need for troops, the Indians, and the fur trade. Striking the north Saskatchewan at Carlton, he followed it up to the base of the Rocky Mountains, and then descended it, reaching Fort Garry on 20 Feb. 1871, after a winter journey of 2700 miles. He told the story of this journey and of his earlier mission in 'The Great Lone Land,' which was published in 1872 and reached a fourth edition in 1873. His report to the lieut.-governor of Manitoba was printed as an appendix to that book, and was a most able paper. There was in fact a rare combination in Butler of the qualities needed for such work. Tall, strong, and active, he was quick of observation and full of resource; genial, yet with much force of character, he was a ready writer, and had the gift of style. He was also a good draughtsman. Lord Wolseley has said that he was pre-eminent in imagination, 'that quality so much above the other gifts required for excellence in military leaders' (WOLSELEY, ii. 202).

His work brought him praise but no more substantial recognition, and it was not till 13 April 1872 that he succeeded in obtaining an unattached company. A lucky land-venture had given him the means to travel, and returning to Canada he went to lake Athabasca, where he had 'movement, sport, travel, and adventure sufficient to satisfy the longings of anybody,' and found material for another book, 'The Wild North Land,' 1873 (new edit. 1904). He was back at Ottawa at the end of August 1873, and learning that Sir Garnet Wolseley was leading an expedition to Ashanti, he hurried to England, sending a telegram ahead of him. On his arrival he found instructions that he should follow Wolseley to West Africa, and he reached Cape Coast Castle on 22 October.

He was sent to Accra to make his way inland to Western Akim, muster its fighting men, and intercept the Ashanti army as it retreated across the Prah. This proved impossible; with the utmost difficulty he persuaded the Akims to move forward towards Coomassie eastward of the main line of advance. By the end of January 1874 he was within 20 miles of it with 1400 men; then they took alarm and hurried home. But Butler had done his work. As Wolseley reported: 'He has effected a most important diversion in favour of the main body, and has detained before him all the forces of one of the most powerful Ashanti chiefs' (*Lond. Gaz.* 7 March 1874). He had been struck down several times with fever, and was in Netley Hospital for two months on his return to England. He was promoted major, and received the C.B. and the medal with clasp. He described his share of the campaign in 'Akim-Foo: the History of a Failure,' published in 1875.

While he was engaged on this book, and was regaining health in Ireland, he was called upon for special service in Natal. In Feb. 1875 Sir Garnet Wolseley went there as temporary governor, to put things straight. Butler accompanied him, and was made protector of Indian immigrants, with a seat in the council and assembly. He was sent on a mission to the Orange Free State, to Kimberley, and to Basutoland, and made many acquaintances, British and Boer. He returned to England in Oct., and on 30 Nov. he was placed on the headquarters staff as deputy assistant quartermaster-general. He remained on it till the end of Feb. 1879, when he went back to South Africa for the Zulu war

He remained there till the end of the year, with plenty of hard work but no fighting, for he was in charge of the base at Durban. He was mentioned in despatches, and was made brevet lieut.-colonel on 21 April 1880.

He was chief staff officer at Devonport from 1 July 1880 till the end of August 1884, with the exception of three months (Aug.–Oct. 1882), when he was serving on Sir Garnet Wolseley's staff in Egypt. He was present at Tel-el-Kebir, was mentioned in despatches (*Lond. Gaz.* 2 Nov. 1882), and received the medal with clasp, the bronze star, and the Medjidieh (3rd class). He was made aide-de-camp to the Queen, with the rank of colonel, on 18 Nov. 1882.

In 1884, when the relief of Gordon became a practical question, Butler was consulted by Lord Wolseley, and threw himself heartily into the plan of ascending the Nile in boats, such as had been used in the Red River expedition. He had met Gordon some years before, and had been deeply impressed by him. He regarded the relief expedition as 'the very first war during the Victorian era in which the object was entirely noble and worthy.' On 12 August he was charged with the provision of 400 boats, and in a month they were ready and some of them on their way. Butler went to Egypt in September, and during the next three months he worked superhumanly to get boats and troops up the cataracts. This having been accomplished, he joined headquarters at Korti, and was sent on with the river column under General Earle. The victory at Kirbekan on 10 Feb. 1885 was largely due to him; for he had examined the ground on which the Mahdists were posted, and persuaded Earle to turn their position instead of attacking it in front. When the expedition returned down the Nile, Butler was put in command of the small force left behind at Meroë. In June he brought this force to Dongola, and went home. His services were mentioned in despatches (*Lond. Gaz.* 10 April and 25 Aug. 1885) and he received two clasps.

In September he was back at Wady Halfa. He had been given command of the troops on the new frontier of Egypt, after the abandonment of the Sudan, with the local rank of brigadier-general on 1 July 1885. In December the Mahdists advanced in force from Dongola, and attacked him near Kosheh. He had four battalions, two of them British, and some cavalry and mounted infantry, and he had built some forts. The Mahdists tore up the railway, but could effect nothing more; and at the end of the month, when reinforcements had come up from Cairo, they were decisively beaten at Giniss. Butler commanded one of the two brigades of General Stephenson's force in this action, and was mentioned in despatches (*Lond. Gaz.* 6 Feb. 1886). Four British battalions were left at Wady Halfa under his command, but they suffered greatly from the heat; they were replaced by Egyptian troops in May, and Butler himself was invalided at the end of June.

He came home embittered. He had had no reward for his exertions, his warnings and remonstrances had given offence, and there was no immediate employment for him. On 25 Nov. he was made K.C.B. He spent the next two years in Brittany and in Ireland. He wrote 'The Campaign of the Cataracts,' published in 1887, and he became intimate with Charles Stewart Parnell [q. v.], being himself a strong home-ruler. In the autumn of 1888 he was associated with Colonel Macgregor in an inquiry into the ordnance store department. Their report, which he drafted, gave so much offence to the civil side of the war office that it was suppressed. During 1889 he was employed in negotiations for the purchase of sites for defensible storehouses on the south and east sides of London.

He returned to Egypt in February 1890, to command the garrison of Alexandria. In 1877 he had married Elizabeth Southerden, daughter of T. J. Thompson, and already distinguished as the painter of 'The Roll Call.' He and his wife now paid a visit to Palestine, which had for him a twofold interest, religious and Napoleonic. He was promoted major-general on 7 Dec. 1892, and on 11 Nov. 1893 he was appointed to the command of a brigade at Aldershot. He was transferred to the command of the S.E. district on 24 Feb. 1896. He had received a reward for distinguished service on 12 Dec. 1894.

In October 1898 he was offered and accepted the command of the troops in South Africa, vacant by the death of General Goodenough. It was not a happy choice at such a time, for he was predisposed to sympathise with people who came in collision with England. He landed at Cape Town on 30 Nov., and in the absence of Sir Alfred Milner he was sworn in as high commissioner. He found himself in 'the central stormspot of the world,' having received no directions to guide him on leaving England. The ill-treatment of 'outlanders' in the Transvaal was exciting indignation, but in the clamour that arose he saw only the action of 'a colossal syndicate for the spread of systematic misrepresentation,' with the object of embittering the relations between the races. He refused to forward the petition of the outlanders asking for British intervention. He had already declared in a speech at Grahamstown on 17 Dec. that South Africa did not need a surgical operation.

Sir Alfred Milner returned from England in February 1899, and Butler was relieved of civil administration. He had been called upon to prepare a scheme of defence for Cape Colony and Natal in case of a sudden outbreak of hostilities. He paid a visit to Natal and formed his plans, but believing that they would not find favour at the war office, he kept them to himself, till there was a peremptory call for them in June. His relations with the high commissioner became strained owing to their widely different views of the situation. Butler could only see in it 'a plot to force war on the Transvaal,' which he did his best to balk. At length a reproof from the war office led him to tender his resignation on 4 July. It was accepted, and he handed over the command on 23 Aug. He returned to England, and on 8 Sept. assumed command of the western district.

He held this command for six years, with the exception of four months spent at Aldershot at the end of 1900. On 9 Oct. in that year he was promoted lieut.-general. In February 1903 he gave evidence before the royal commission on the war in South Africa. In the spring of 1905 he presided over a committee on the disposal of the war stores in South Africa. His report (dated 22 May) led to the appointment of a royal commission with Sir George Farwell as president, which toned down his strictures to some extent. On 31 Oct. 1905 he was placed on the retired list, having reached the age of 67. He received the G.C.B. in June 1906, and was called to the privy council (Ireland) in 1909. He was made a governor of the Royal Hibernian Military School, a member of the senate of the National University of Ireland, and a commissioner of the board of national education in Ireland. He took keen interest in educational questions, sympathised with the Gaelic League, and gave many striking addresses on aspects of Irish life and character. He died on 7 June 1910 at Bansha Castle, co. Tipperary, where he had lived since his retirement. He was buried with military honours at Killardrigh, the resting-place of his forefathers.

His wife survived him. They had issue three sons and two daughters. The younger daughter, Eileen, married Viscount Gormanston in 1912.

A portrait of him as a general officer on horseback, painted by Lady Butler in 1899, is at Bansha Castle.

Besides the works already mentioned describing his own experiences, Butler wrote: 1. 'Far out: Rovings retold,' 1880. 2. 'Red Cloud, the Solitary Sioux,' 1882. 3. 'Charles George Gordon,' 1889, and 4. 'Sir Charles Napier,' 1890, both in the 'Men of Action' series. 5. 'Sir George Pomeroy Colley,' 1899. 6. 'From Naboth's Vineyard: being Impressions formed during a Fourth Visit to South Africa,' 1907. 7. 'The Light of the West, with some other Wayside Thoughts,' 1909. His autobiography, which he began in March 1909 and worked on till his death, was edited by his elder daughter, and published in 1911. He also wrote much which is unpublished on Napoleon and the St. Helena captivity.

[Sir William Butler: an autobiography, 1911, with reproduction of Lady Butler's portrait; Report of the Royal Commission on the War in South Africa (pp. 201–7) and Evidence, ii. 72–92, 1904; The Times, 8 June 1910; Lord Wolseley, Story of a Soldier's Life, 1903; H. E. Colville, History of the Sudan Campaign, 1889.] E. M. L.

BYRNE, Sir EDMUND WIDDRINGTON (1844–1904), judge, born at Islington on 30 June 1844, was eldest son of Edmund Byrne of Whitehall Place, Westminster, solicitor, by his wife Mary Elizabeth Cowell. Educated at King's College, London, he entered as student at Lincoln's Inn on 5 Nov. 1863, was a pupil in the chambers of (Sir) George Osborne Morgan [q. v. Suppl. I], and was called to the bar on 26 Jan. 1867. Starting his career with a family connection among solicitors, he soon made for himself a large business as a conveyancer and equity draftsman, while his powers of clear and concise statement in court gave him a position among the leading juniors of the chancery bar; a place in his pupil room in Lincoln's Inn was much sought after. He took silk in 1888 and became a bencher of his inn in 1892. Attaching himself to the court of Mr. Justice Chitty [q. v. Suppl. I], he quickly obtained the lion's share of the work there in conjunction with Robert Romer, Q.C., destined to be his colleague on the bench. A well-grounded lawyer and pleasant speaker, he was an admirable leader in routine chancery cases, and the care with which he got up his briefs and the pertinacity with which he plied his arguments made him an especial favourite among clients professional and lay. He was essentially the advocate for a court of first instance, and his appearances in the higher tribunals were rare, except when following to the court of appeal cases in which he had appeared at the former hearing. In July 1892 he successfully contested the Walthamstow division of Essex as a conservative. The Finance Act of 1894 and the abortive employers' liability bill of the following year provided ample opportunity for a fluent and careful lawyer's intervention in debate. Byrne surprised his friends by the facility with which he acquired the parliamentary manner, and he was bracketed by the ministerial press with Mr. J. G. Butcher, K.C., and Mr. T. Gibson Bowles as 'the busy bees.' In July 1895 he was again returned for Walthamstow by a largely increased majority, and on 18 Jan. 1897, on the promotion of Chitty to a lord-justiceship, the vacant judgeship in the chancery division was given to Byrne. He was knighted in due course. On the bench he was accurate, painstaking, courteous, and patient to all comers, and his judgments, which included an unusual number of patent cases, were, with hardly an exception, affirmed upon appeal. On the other hand he was morbidly conscientious, apt to be too dependent on authority, and extremely slow; arrears accumulated in his court and in his chambers. He died after a very short illness on 4 April 1904, at his house, 33 Lancaster Gate, Hyde Park. He was buried at Brookwood cemetery.

Byrne married on 13 Aug. 1874 Henrietta Johnstone, daughter of James Gulland of Newton, of Wemyss, Fifeshire, by whom he left a family. A portrait by Edmund Brock is in the possession of Lady Byrne.

[The Times, 6 April 1905; personal knowledge and private information.] J. B. A.

C

CAINE, WILLIAM SPROSTON (1842–1903), politician and temperance advocate, born at Egremont, Wallasey, Cheshire, on 26 March 1842, was eldest surviving son of Nathaniel Caine, J.P. (*d.* 1877), metal merchant, by his wife Hannah (*d.* 1861), daughter of William Rushton of Liverpool. Educated privately at Gibson's school, Egremont, and the Rev. Richard Wall's school at Birkenhead, Caine in 1861 entered his father's business at Egremont, and in 1864 he was taken into partnership. He removed to Liverpool in 1871. Public affairs soon occupied much of his attention, and he retired from the firm in 1878. He retained, however, the directorship of the Hodbarrow Mining Co., Ltd., Millom, and he secured the controlling interest in the Shaw's Brow Iron Co., Liverpool, leaving the management of the concern in the hands of his partner, Arthur S. Cox. The collapse of this business in 1893 involved Caine in heavy liabilities, which he honourably discharged. Thenceforth his resources were largely devoted to paying off the mortgage which he raised to meet the firm's losses.

Brought up as a baptist under the influence of Hugh Stowell Brown [q. v. Suppl. I], he developed early a bent for preaching and philanthropic work. In later life in London he was from 1884 to 1903 the unprofessional pastor of a mission church known as the Wheatsheaf in Stockwell, S.W. But the temperance movement mainly absorbed him, and at Liverpool he found his first scope for propagandist zeal. As president of the Liverpool Temperance and Band of Hope Union, he formed and became chairman of a 'Popular Control and License Reform Association,' with a monthly organ, the 'Liverpool Social Reformer.' In 1873 he was elected vice-president of the United Kingdom Alliance. He was also president of the Baptist Total Abstinence Society, of the Congregational Temperance Society, of the British Temperance League, and of the National Temperance Federation.

In 1873 Caine first sought election to parliament, mainly with a view to enforcing his temperance views. He was in general agreement with the radical wing of the liberal party, and unsuccessfully contested Liverpool in the liberal interest in both that and the next year. In 1880 he was returned as radical member for Scarborough, and without delay he urged on the House of Commons his advanced temperance opinions. In a maiden speech on 18 June 1880 he supported the successful motion of his friend, Sir Wilfrid Lawson [q. v. Suppl. II], in favour of local option. Identifying himself with the extreme radical section of the party, he seconded Henry Labouchere's motion of dissent from Gladstone's proposal for a national monument to Lord Beaconsfield (12 May 1881). His activity was officially recognised by Gladstone on 17 Nov. 1884 by his appointment as civil lord of the admiralty in succession to Sir Thomas (afterwards Lord) Brassey. Although he retained his seat at the necessary by-election, he failed in an attempt at the general election of Nov. 1885 to capture the Tottenham division of Middlesex for the liberals. He soon however returned to the house as M.P. for Barrow-in-Furness at a by-election on 6 April following.

Caine declined to accept Gladstone's home rule policy, and took an active part in organising under Mr. Chamberlain's direction the dissentient liberals into a new party of 'liberal unionists.' In the division on the second reading of Gladstone's home rule bill (7 June) Caine and Henry Robert Brand, afterwards second Viscount Hampden [q. v. Suppl. II], acted as tellers for the liberal unionists, who, numbering 93, voted with the conservatives and defeated the measure. The home rulers gave the new party the sobriquet of the 'Brand of Caine.' At the ensuing general election Caine was again returned for Barrow, and was appointed chief liberal unionist whip. But Caine's radical convictions and extreme temperance views, which were unaltered, soon rendered the alliance with the conservatives distasteful. Although the scheme of G. J. Goschen [q. v. Suppl. II] in 1890 for compensating holders of extinguished public-house licences was modified under pressure from Caine, he marked his dislike of it not only by resigning his post of whip but by vacating his seat in the house. On seeking re-election at Barrow as an independent liberal he was defeated. Within the same year he rejoined the liberal fold, and in 1892 re-entered the house for East Bradford as a Gladstonian liberal. He voted for Gladstone's amended home rule bill of 1893. At the general election of 1895 he lost his seat, and only re-entered the house in 1900 as liberal member for Camborne. In the interval he sat on Lord Peel's royal commission on the liquor licensing laws (1896–9), and signed the minority report and the addendum in favour of direct local veto.

The native population of India also engaged Caine's sympathies, and he criticised severely British methods of government, especially the encouragement for fiscal purposes of the liquor and opium trade. In 1890 he visited India as a delegate to the Indian National Congress at Calcutta, and contributed to the 'Pall Mall Gazette' a series of letters called 'Young India' which ably advocated large measures of self-government. He sat on the royal commission of 1895–6 on the administration of Indian expenditure, and signed the minority report recommending a diminution of civil and military expenditure.

Caine's activities exhausted his strength. A voyage to South America in 1902 failed to restore his health, and he died of heart failure on 17 March 1903 at 42 Grosvenor Road, S.W. He was buried in Woking cemetery.

Caine was a puritan in politics and religion, whose moral courage and philanthropic instincts were superior to his intellectual gifts. Abrupt in manner, downright in speech, but of imperturbable good-humour, he was dubbed by political associates the 'genial ruffian.'

Caine married on 24 March 1868 Alice, eldest daughter of Hugh Stowell Brown [q. v. Suppl. I], by whom he had issue two sons and three daughters. The eldest daughter, Hannah Rushton, married in 1893 Mr. J. Herbert Roberts, M.P. The youngest daughter, Ruth, is wife of Mr. J. Herbert Lewis, M.P.

Caine's chief published works included: 1. 'Tables for use in the Tin Plate Trade,' 1877. 2. 'Local Option,' 1885. 3. 'Hugh Stowell Brown: a Memorial Volume,' 1887. 4. 'A Trip round the World in 1887–8,' 1888. 5. 'Picturesque India, a Handbook for European Travellers,' 1891.

[W. S. Caine: a memoir by John Newton (with photographs); The Times, 18 March 1903, and Lit. Suppl., 19 April 1907; Annual Reg., 1886, 1889, 1890; Athenæum, 13 April 1907; P. W. Clayden, England under the Coalition, 1892; G. W. E. Russell, Sir Wilfrid Lawson, Bart., 1909.] G. S. W.

CAIRD, EDWARD (1835–1908), Master of Balliol College, Oxford, and philosopher, born in Greenock on 22 March 1835, was fifth of the seven sons, one of whom died in infancy, of John Caird, partner and manager of a firm of engineers (Caird & Co.) in Greenock. John Caird [q. v. Suppl. I], principal of Glasgow University, by whom Edward was greatly influenced, was the eldest son. Four sons went into business and prospered there. Their mother, Janet, daughter of

Roderick Young of Paisley, was left a widow in September 1838, when the eldest son was not eighteen years old and the youngest hardly more than an infant. With limited though not straitened means, she faced her maternal responsibilities with placid optimism.

Edward lived in early childhood with his aunt, Miss Jane Caird, 'a woman of strong mind, and most deeply religious,' whose devotion to the boy did not spare him attendance at frequent and long religious services—'four hours at a yoking.' Passing to Greenock Academy in boyhood, he was repelled by the rough methods of Dr. Brown, his first headmaster; but a new rector, David Duff, only twenty-three years old, a fellow-student of Caird's eldest brother John, and afterwards professor of church history in Edinburgh, awoke his intellectual zeal and proved the kindest friend and counsellor. Caird left Greenock Academy to enter the University of Glasgow in the winter session of 1850–1. He attended the classes first in the faculty of arts and afterwards in the faculty of divinity till the end of session 1855–6. He won many distinctions, mainly in the classical department. His intimate circle of classmates included John Nichol [q. v. Suppl. I], two years his senior, and George Rankine Luke. Caird ranked among them as their 'philosopher in chief.'

Owing to weak health he left Glasgow after the session of 1856 for the sea-air of St. Andrews, under the care of his aunt. He was a student in St. Andrews University in 1856–7. Thence he removed in the spring of 1857 to the house of his brother John, who was then minister of the parish of Errol in Perthshire. At Errol Edward's health was re-established. At the same time an intention of entering the ministry of the Church of Scotland was reconsidered and abandoned. His brother's gifts as a preacher, acting on his modest estimate of himself, may have helped to alter his purpose. His reading exerted a more potent influence. Through Carlyle, whose work was eagerly studied by Scottish undergraduates, Caird was led to Goethe and to German literature, whose poetic and philosophical idealism encouraged dissatisfaction with current theology. On his return, however, to Glasgow in 1857 he resumed attendance at classes in divinity in the winter session.

Caird's mind had already turned towards Oxford and the life of a scholar and teacher. On 28 April 1860 he was elected Snell exhibitioner, and in October he matriculated at Balliol College. There he soon made for himself a high reputation. He gained the Pusey and Ellerton scholarship in Hebrew in the university in 1861, and the Jenkyns exhibition in the college next year, being placed in the same year in the first class in classical moderations. In 1863 he obtained a first class in the final classical school. Considerably older than his fellow-undergraduates and with a 'maturity of mind' beyond their reach, Caird found his intimate associates at Oxford amongst graduates of his own age, who welcomed him as one of themselves; such were John Nichol and Luke, his Glasgow friends, and David Binning Monro, Mr. James Bryce, Mr. A. V. Dicey, and, above all, Thomas Hill Green. With Green, Caird was from the first in closest sympathy, alike in thought and practical aim. Jowett was Caird's tutor, 'watchful and exigent,' but at that time 'eager to direct students to the new sources of thought opened by the German philosophy and theology.' The most powerful of all the educative forces that played upon Caird in Oxford was, however, the 'Old Mortality Club,' formed of young graduates by John Nichol in 1857, and called by that name because 'every member was, or lately had been, in a weak or precarious state of bodily health.' Amongst its original members were Prof. A. V. Dicey, Luke, T. H. Green, Swinburne, and Mr. James Bryce. Caird had the unique honour of being elected when he was still an undergraduate. Many years afterwards Caird spoke of the meetings of the club as 'the very salt of their university life for some of its members,' with its 'free discussion of everything in heaven or earth, the fresh enjoyment of intellectual sympathy, the fearless intercommunion of spirits.' Caird, Green, and Luke were, according to Prof. Dicey, regarded by the club as 'the most remarkable [of its members] both morally and intellectually.'

Friends noted how little in later life Caird's outward aspect changed after his early Oxford days. His mental and spiritual convictions and his attitude to life's problems took at the same period, largely under the club's stimulus, a form which, while it ripened, remained essentially what it had been. He was a 'radical,' like his friend Green, not only in politics, but in religion and philosophy. In his youth he tried to persuade his brother Stuart to join the 'red-shirts' of Garibaldi. Abraham Lincoln was the political hero of his youth and in his later years he wrote of him as the 'greatest statesman of the English-speaking race since the elder Pitt.' He did not take up many social causes, or excite himself over the daily barometrical changes in politics; but there were principles, fundamental in their character and vital alike to his political, religious, and philosophical convictions, by which he stood all his life with firmness and steadiness, and with a complete absence of concern as to ridicule or obloquy. Having graduated B.A. in 1863, Caird remained at Oxford, teaching philosophy privately. In 1864 he was elected to an open fellowship at Merton and was appointed tutor. After lecturing and teaching there for two years, he was elected professor of moral philosophy at Glasgow on 28 May 1866. With characteristic magnanimity he had declined to stand when he heard that his friend Nichol was candidate, but Nichol with no smaller loyalty retired in his favour, and supported his candidature. There was an unexampled field of candidates, amongst them Henry Calderwood, John Cunningham, Robert Flint, Simon S. Laurie, John Campbell Shairp, and James Hutchison Stirling, of all of whom memoirs appear in this Dictionary. Caird's election was unanimous. He held the post for twenty-seven years. At the close of his introductory lecture in Nov. 1866 he said that his highest ambition had been 'to teach philosophy in a Scottish university, and above all,' he added, 'in this university to which I owe so much; and now there is almost nothing I would not give for the assurance that I should be able to teach it well.' Twenty years afterwards, on the presentation of his portrait to the university, he struck the same note: 'If fortune had given me the power of choosing my place and work in life, I do not think I should have chosen any other than that which has fallen to me.'

Caird put all his energies into his work as professor. His classes were large, and he read with conscientious thoroughness, night by night, during the winter session, the weekly and fortnightly essays of his many pupils. The main endeavour, he said of his teaching, was to plant a few 'germinative ideas' in his pupils' minds. But at the same time he connected his ideas into a system of thought with characteristic passion for synthesis and construction. He excited the interest of his hearers by insisting 'that what was true could be reasoned,' and 'that what was reasoned must be true.' Some critics urged that he was prone to repetition in both lectures and books. But 'having laboriously worked his way to central coherent convictions he could not avoid repeating them in all their manifold applications' (Prof. McCunn). A buoyant optimism, too, which was yet allied with an active sympathy with suffering (cf. 'Optimism and Pessimism' in *Evolution of Religion*), and a resolute adherence to what he called 'the speculative attitude,' enabled him thoroughly to impress and stimulate youthful thought of the best kind.

At the same time Caird interested himself in many matters outside his classroom. In the earliest years of his Glasgow professorship he advocated the higher education of women, when there was no member of the senate to support him save his brother; but he persisted till he persuaded. Meanwhile Caird, in the phrase of Prof. Bosanquet, was 'punctuating his laborious life at almost regular intervals with philosophical treatises, any one of which by itself would have sufficed to found a philosopher's reputation.' 'A Critical Account of the Philosophy of Kant, with an historical introduction,' appeared at Glasgow in 1877, and a further volume on the same theme in 1889 (2nd edit. 1909, 2 vols.); in 1883 he published a monograph on Hegel (in 'Philosophical Classics for English Readers,' Edinburgh); and in 1885 'The Social Philosophy and Religion of Comte' (Glasgow). In these works Caird critically interpreted other thinkers on lines of his own. In his great volumes on Kant he sought 'to display in the very argument of the great metaphysician, who was supposed to have cut the world in two with a hatchet, an almost involuntary but continuous and inevitable regression towards objective organic unity.' Notably in his treatment of Kant as of Comte his purpose was to show that there is a centre of unity to which the mind must come back out of all differences, however varied and alien in appearance. The analysis was preliminary to reconstruction. Caird's way of criticism differed indeed from that of other philosophical writers. It was consistently and even obtrusively constructive. He seized upon the truths contained in the authors with whom he dealt, and was only incidentally concerned with their errors, if he were concerned at all. He constrained the truths to expose their one-sidedness and abstractness, and to exhibit their need of their opposites. The like originality and continuity of thought is visible in Caird's two treatises on the philosophy of religion, 'The Evolution of Religion'

(1893) and 'The Evolution of Theology in the Greek Philosophy' (1904, 2 vols.). The books were based on two courses of Gifford lectures, the first delivered before the University of St. Andrews in 1891–2 and the second before the University of Glasgow in 1900. In the first work he exhibits the spiritual sense of mankind as at first dominated by the object, but constrained by its own abstractions to swing round so as to fall under the sway of the subject. In the second work there is the same exhibition of spiritual continuity and evolution. The story of Greek philosophy, which Caird considered mainly in its relation to theology, was carried from Plato to Plotinus and St. Augustine; and was told 'with a thoroughness and mastery of detail, a soundness of judgment, and a lucidity of expression, which makes it the best complete text-book on the subject.' Two volumes of 'Essays on Literature and Philosophy' (1892) bore further witness to the breadth and depth of his interests. In literature Goethe and Carlyle divided his allegiance with Dante and Wordsworth.

On the death of Jowett, Master of Balliol, on 1 Oct. 1893, Caird was elected to the mastership by the fellows. He returned to Oxford after much grave reflection and only because he felt that to follow Green and Jowett was to continue his Glasgow work in a situation in which, as he said to a friend, 'he could have his hand on the heart of England.' He found himself face to face with a new kind of task in conditions that were very different from those of the Oxford of his Merton days, but he adapted himself to the situation. 'Where it was necessary,' wrote one of his Balliol colleagues, 'Caird acquainted himself with the often trivial details of college business; took his full share, both by lecturing and personal tuition, in its teaching work; showed the liveliest interest in all sides of the college life; made himself readily accessible to all members of the college, and always found time to listen to those who wished to consult him; was lavishly generous in his estimate of the knowledge and work of others and loyally trustful of his colleagues.' In general university affairs 'he was deeply interested in the movement for the extension of university education to women and was chosen to propose to the university the motion for granting degrees to them. When that motion was defeated he continued to help the movement in other ways.' He supported the university settlement at Toynbee Hall, London, and the Ruskin College for the education of working-men at Oxford. In politics, as in all else, he remained steadfast to his early beliefs and stoutly opposed the Boer war. He therefore resisted the bestowal of the honorary degree by the university on Cecil Rhodes [q. v. Suppl. II] in 1899. But his devotion to philosophic speculation was his main interest. He was a candidate in 1897 for the Whyte professorship of moral philosophy on the vacancy caused by the death of his friend William Wallace [q. v.], and the failure of his candidature was an unwelcome rebuff, but his activity as a college lecturer on philosophy was undiminished. Throughout his career as Master, too, he delivered impressive lay-sermons on social problems in the College Hall, and occasionally at Toynbee Hall, and he wrote many articles on literature and philosophy in the reviews. He collected into a volume 'Lay Sermons and Addresses delivered in the Hall of Balliol College, Oxford' (1907). In 1907 serious illness compelled him to resign the mastership of Balliol, and he removed from the college to a residence in Oxford, where he died on 1 Nov. 1908. He was buried in St. Sepulchre's cemetery beside Green and Jowett.

Caird married on 8 May 1867 Caroline Frances, eldest daughter of John Wylie, minister of the parish of Carluke in Lanarkshire. She survived him without issue.

Caird was made hon. LL.D. of St. Andrews in 1883, of Glasgow in 1894; hon. D.C.L. of Oxford in 1891, and D.Lit. of Cambridge in 1898 and of the University of Wales on 9 May 1902. He became in 1902 one of the original fellows of the British Academy, before which he read on 24 May 1903 a paper on 'Idealism and the Theory of Knowledge.' He was also elected a corresponding member to the French Académie des Sciences morales et politiques. Besides the works cited, Caird wrote the article 'Cartesianism' in the 'Encyclopædia Britannica' (11th edit.) and on Anselm's argument for the being of God in 'Journal of Theological Studies' (Oct. 1899).

Of singularly tranquil and passive temperament and of simple, frank nature, Caird must be credited with genuinely great intellectual and moral stature. His life was devoted to what was for him the only 'one reasonable controversy'—the controversy not as to the existence but as 'to the Nature of the all-embracing unity on which every intelligible experience must rest, and on the other hand, as to the nature of the differences which it equally involves.' He would probably have admitted that the total effect of his labour, sustained through so many years of heroic speculative industry, was to state the problem anew; and that his whole exposition of the movement of thought in the great philosophers, and of the movement of the world as caught up in their thought, was only the illustration and exemplification of an hypothesis rather than philosophic proof. If there is one sense in which he could not admit that the rationality of the Universe, or what to him was the same thing, the omnipresence and utter sovereignty of the Divine, was not a debatable question, there was another sense in which it was a 'Grand Perhaps.' 'It is involved in the very idea of a developing consciousness such as ours,' he wrote late in life, 'that while, as an intelligence, it presupposes the idea of the whole, and, both in thought and action, must continually strive to realise that idea, yet what it deals with is necessarily a partial and limited experience, and its actual attainments can never, either in theory or practice, be more than provisional. . . . If in one sense we must call this idea a faith, we must remember that it is in no sense an arbitrary assumption; rather it is the essential faith of reason, the presupposition and bases of all that reason has achieved or can achieve.'

A portrait painted by the Hon. John Collier hangs in the hall of Balliol College, and a tablet is designed for the College chapel. In 1886, after Caird had been twenty years professor at Glasgow, his pupils presented to the university his portrait by Sir George Reid; a bronze medallion by David MacGill was placed in the moral philosophy class room there in 1910. There is a caricature portrait by 'Spy' in 'Vanity Fair' (1895).

[Personal knowledge; Mr. Bernard Bosanquet's memoir in Proc. Brit. Acad. 1907–8, pp. 379 sq.; The Times, 3 Nov. 1908; James Addison's Snell Exhibitions, 1911; Prof. Knight's Life of Nichol; memorial address by J. L. Strachan-Davidson, Master of Balliol College, 1908; speeches by Prof. MacCunn and others at unveiling of memorial tablet at Glasgow Univ. 1910; reminiscences of Prof. A. V. Dicey, Prof. Saintsbury and Prof. Wenley; for an examination of Caird's theology see A. W. Benn's English Rationalism in the Nineteenth Century, 1906.]

CAIRNES, WILLIAM ELLIOT (1862–1902), captain, military writer, born at Galway on 18 Sept. 1862, was son of John Elliot Cairnes [q. v.], the economist, by Eliza Charlotte, daughter of George Henry Minto Alexander. After education at Blackheath proprietary school, University College school, and the International College, Isleworth, he was commissioned as lieutenant in the militia (royal Irish rifles) on 16 Sept. 1882. From the militia he obtained a commission as lieutenant in the 3rd dragoon guards on 14 May 1884, was transferred to the South Staffordshire regiment a week later, and to the royal Irish fusiliers on 16 July 1884. He served with the second battalion of that regiment at several home stations. Promoted captain on 21 May 1890, he became on 31 March 1897 adjutant of the 1st volunteer battalion of the Yorkshire light infantry. This appointment prevented his going to South Africa with his regiment, both battalions of which served in the Boer war. He found scope however for his abilities and military knowledge at home, by writing on military subjects. Though stationed at Wakefield, he joined the staff of the 'Westminster Gazette' in November 1899, and till April 1901 he wrote a daily article on the war in progress as 'military correspondent.' His articles were among the best of their kind. In 1900 he published anonymously 'An Absent-minded War,' which was widely read for its pungent and well-informed criticism. Its sarcasm, if not always just, fell in with the public mood; and the epigrams were often happy. Other books by Cairnes, dealing with military questions in a more constructive way, did not find so much favour, though they showed more solid qualities. In April 1901 a committee was appointed to consider the education and training of officers of the army, with Mr. Akers-Douglas as chairman, and Cairnes as secretary. In their report, in March 1902, the committee stated that Cairnes's knowledge, tact and ability had greatly facilitated their inquiry. He was also secretary to the military court of inquiry into the remount department. These duties and his literary activity taxed his strength. He died of pneumonia in London on 19 April 1902. He married in June 1884 Mamie, daughter of M. McClelland of Glendarragh, co. Londonderry. She survived him, with one daughter.

In addition to 'An Absent-minded War' he published anonymously 'The Army from within' (1901) and 'A Commonsense Army' (1901); also under his own name, 'The Coming Waterloo' (1901) and 'Lord Roberts as a Soldier in Peace and War' (1901). He wrote in the 'National' and 'Contemporary' Reviews, in 'Harper's Magazine,' and occasionally in 'The Times.' He was a clever draughtsman, able to illustrate his articles, and he took out several patents for inventions.

[Army and Navy Gazette, 26 April 1902; The Times, 22 April 1902; private information.] E. M. L.

CALKIN, JOHN BAPTISTE (1827–1905), organist and composer, born in London on 16 March 1827, was son of James Calkin (1786–1862), composer and pianist. Reared in a musical atmosphere, he studied music under his father, and his three brothers, Joseph, James, and George, also adopted the profession. When nineteen he was appointed organist, precentor, and choirmaster of St. Columba's College, Rathfarnham, co. Dublin, in succession to Edwin George Monk. St. Columba's College was a school mainly for the boys of the upper classes and for candidates for the ministry of the Church of Ireland; music and the Irish language were prominent features in the curriculum. From 1846 to 1853 Calkin zealously maintained a high standard of choral music at St. Columba's, and he cultivated composition. From 1853 to 1863 he was organist and choirmaster of Woburn Chapel, London; from 1863 to 1868 organist of Camden Road Chapel; and from 1870 to 1884 organist at St. Thomas's Church, Camden Town. In 1883 he became professor at the Guildhall School of Music under Mr. Weist Hill, and thenceforth devoted himself to teaching and composing. He was on the council of Trinity College, London, a member of the Philharmonic Society (1862), and a fellow of the College of Organists, incorporated in 1893.

As a composer, Calkin essayed many forms, but his sacred music is best known, especially his morning and evening services in B flat, G, and D. His communion service in C is marked Op. 134, a sufficient proof of his fertility. He wrote much for the organ, including numerous transcriptions, and he scored many string arrangements, as well as original sonatas, duos, &c. A few of his anthems are still heard, while his hymn tunes, though not to be found in 'Hymns Ancient and Modern,' are in many other collections. His setting of 'Fling out the Banner' (by Bishop G. W. Doane) has a great vogue in America and the colonies, and is included in the Canadian 'Book of Common Praise,' edited by Sir George Martin in 1909. His 'Agape' was composed specially for the 'Church Hymnary' of Scotland in 1871, to the words 'Jesu, most loving God,' and was inserted in the 'Church Hymnal' of Ireland in 1874.

Calkin died at Hornsey Rise Gardens on 15 April 1905, and was buried in Highgate cemetery.

[Personal knowledge; Brown and Stratton's Brit. Musical Biog. 1897; Cowan and Love's Music of the Church Hymnary, 1901; Musical Times, May 1905.] W. H. G. F.

CALLOW, WILLIAM (1812–1908), water-colour painter, was born at Greenwich on 28 July 1812. Descended from an old family of the eastern counties, his grandfather, John Callow (1730–1786), was an artist engaged in the decoration of porcelain at the Lowestoft factory, while his father, Robert Callow, was employed in the supervision of building works at Greenwich and elsewhere. William was an elder brother and the instructor of John Callow (1822–1878) [q. v.]. At a very early age he developed a love for drawing, and in 1823 he was engaged by Theodore Fielding, an elder brother of Copley Fielding, to assist him in colouring prints and engraving in aquatint. Subsequently, in 1825, he was articled for eight years to Theodore and Thales Fielding as a pupil for instruction in water-colour painting and aquatint engraving. He worked with them and their brother Newton in London, and from 1829 with the latter in Paris. There Charles Bentley was his fellow-pupil, and he and Thomas Shotter Bays much influenced his style. In 1831 he sent to the Salon a 'View of Richmond' which attracted so much attention that he was invited to give lessons to the family of King Louis Philippe, whose daughter, the Princess Clémentine, became his pupil for some years. At the same period he took long walking tours in France, as well as in the Pyrenees, Switzerland, and Italy, for the purpose of sketching. He also sent drawings to various provincial exhibitions, at some of which he obtained medals, and he received a gold medal at the Paris Salon of 1840.

In 1841 he left Paris and settled in London, where in 1838 he had been elected an associate of the Society of Painters in Water Colours, of which in 1848 he became a full member, contributing during his long life to the exhibitions of that body upwards of 1400 drawings. He acted as its secretary from 1866 to 1870, and he was presented with an illuminated address of congratulation from the president and his fellow-members on completing his ninetieth year in 1902.

About 1848 he took to oil-painting, and he contributed thirty-seven works to the exhibitions of the British Institution from that year until its close in 1867. From

1850 to 1876 he sent twenty-nine oil-pictures to the Royal Academy.

Early in 1855 he left London for Great Missenden, where he afterwards built a house and resided for the rest of his life. He made frequent journeys to town to give lessons until 1882, when he abandoned teaching. He numbered among his pupils the Empress Frederick of Germany, Lord Dufferin, Lord Northbrook, the ladies of the Rothschild family, and Lady Amherst of Hackney and her six daughters. Meanwhile he continued his sketching tours in Scotland and on the continent, visiting France, Italy, and Germany. His work became somewhat mannered and after a time it ceased to attract. About two years before his death, however, he began to turn out his portfolios of early works, and these sold so well that in the autumn of 1907 he was induced to open an exhibition of them at the Leicester Galleries, which was a great success. After his death an exhibition of his remaining drawings and sketches was held at the same place in 1909.

Callow died at The Firs, Great Missenden, Buckinghamshire, on 20 Feb. 1908, from influenza, followed by pleurisy, and was buried in the churchyard there. He possessed a remarkably strong physique and had an intense love for good music. He was married twice: (1) in 1846 to Harriet Anne (*d.* 1883), daughter of Henry Smart, the violinist [q. v.]; (2) in 1884 to Mary Louisa Jefferay.

Among water-colour drawings by Callow in the Victoria and Albert Museum are those of 'Easby Abbey, Yorkshire,' 'The Town Hall, Bruges,' 'The Market Place, Frankfort,' 'Old Houses, Berncastel, on the Moselle,' and 'The Leaning Tower, Bologna.' An interior of 'St. Mary's Church, Richmond, Yorkshire,' is in the possession of the Royal Society of Painters in Water Colours.

[William Callow, R.W.S., F.R.G.S. An Autobiography, ed. H. M. Cundall, 1908 (with portrait of Callow, aged 86, and plates in colour from his drawings); The Times, 24 Feb. 1908; Art Journal, April 1908; the Parish Registers of Lowestoft, Suffolk [1751–1812], privately printed by F. A. Crisp, 1904; Exhibition Catalogues of the Royal Academy, British Institution, and Royal Society of Painters in Water Colours, 1838–1908.]

R. E. G.

CALTHORPE, sixth BARON. [See GOUGH-CALTHORPE, SIR AUGUSTUS CHOLMONDELEY (1829–1910).]

CAMBRIDGE, second DUKE OF. [See GEORGE WILLIAM FREDERICK CHARLES (1819–1904).]

CAMPBELL, SIR ARCHIBALD CAMPBELL, first BARON BLYTHSWOOD (1835–1908), amateur of science, born at Florence on 22 Feb. 1835, was eldest of nine children of Archibald Douglas (1809–1868), 17th laird of Mains, Dumbartonshire, who assumed the name of Campbell in 1838 on succeeding his cousin, Archibald Campbell, as 12th laird of Blythswood. His father claimed descent from Sir Duncan Campbell (created Lord Campbell in 1445), ancestor of the dukes of Argyll [see CAMPBELL, COLIN, *d.* 1493], and from William de Douglas (*fl.* 1174), ancestor of the earls of Douglas, Hamilton and Morton. His mother was Caroline Agnes, daughter of Mungo Dick of Pitkerrow, co. Fife. After private education for the army, he joined in 1854 the 79th highlanders; next year he was transferred to the Scots guards, and served in the Crimea (where he was severely wounded in the trenches before Sevastopol), retiring from the army in 1868. Thenceforth his interests lay in politics, the auxiliary forces, and in science. A wealthy landowner and a strong conservative, he was active in organising the party in Scotland and sat in the House of Commons for Renfrewshire 1873–4, and for West Renfrewshire 1885–92. On 4 May 1880 he was made a baronet, and on 24 Aug. 1892 was raised to the peerage as Baron Blythswood. He commanded the 4th battalion of the Argyll and Sutherland highlanders from 1874 to 1904, and was aide-de-camp to Queen Victoria and King Edward VII from 1894. At Blythswood House, Renfrewshire, he entertained King Edward VII and Queen Alexandra (when Prince and Princess of Wales) in 1870 and Queen Victoria in 1888.

Lord Blythswood, who enjoyed the intimate friendship of Lord Kelvin and other notable men of science, rendered important services to astronomical and physical science. He maintained at Blythswood House a splendidly equipped laboratory, the resources of which he placed freely at the disposal of scientific friends. He obtained photographic action through various opaque substances before Röntgen announced his results in 1895, and came near, according to Prof. Andrew Gray, F.R.S., to the discovery of the X-rays. Much of his time and labour was devoted to the construction of instruments of precision; foremost amongst these is his great dividing engine for ruling diffraction gratings. After his death Lady Blythswood placed this instrument and other apparatus connected therewith on loan at the National Physical Laboratory at

Teddington, to be kept together and known as the 'Blythswood Collection.' At the end of his life Blythswood was among the first to make experiments in the mechanics of aerial propulsion (see *Engineering*, 25 Dec. 1908). Blythswood, who was made hon. LL.D. of Glasgow in April 1907 and was elected F.R.S. on 2 May 1907, died at Blythswood House on 8 July 1908. He married on 7 July 1864 Augusta Clementina Carrington, daughter of Robert John, second baron Carrington, but left no issue. The peerage passed by special remainder to his brother, the Rev. Sholto Douglas Campbell-Douglas. A portrait of Blythswood by Sir Hubert von Herkomer was exhibited at the Royal Academy in 1887. A replica is in the Conservative Club, Glasgow.

[Nature, lxxviii.; The Times, 9 July 1908; Glasgow Herald, 9 July 1908 (portrait); Nat. Phys. Lab. Reports, 1908, 1909.]

T. E. J.

CAMPBELL, FREDERICK ARCHIBALD VAUGHAN, third EARL CAWDOR (1847–1911), first lord of the admiralty, the eldest son of John Frederick Vaughan, second earl, by his first wife, Sarah Mary, second daughter of Henry Compton-Cavendish, was born on 13 Feb. 1847 at St. Leonard's Hill, Windsor. Known before his accession to the earldom as Viscount Emlyn, he was educated at Eton and Christ Church, Oxford. From 1874 to 1885 he sat as a conservative for Carnarvonshire, and was active in promoting Welsh interests. In 1892 he unsuccessfully contested South Manchester against Sir Henry Roscoe, and in 1898 he was defeated in the Cricklade division of Wilts by Lord Edmond (afterwards Lord) Fitzmaurice. He succeeded to the peerage on the death of his father on 29 March 1898.

Lord Emlyn was a man of various employments. In 1880 he became an ecclesiastical commissioner and he was an unpaid commissioner in lunacy from 1886 to 1893. In 1896 he was appointed lord-lieutenant of Pembrokeshire, becoming twelve years later president of the Territorial Force Association. He had earlier shown his interest in local defence by commanding the Carmarthen artillery militia for ten years. He was also deputy-lieutenant of the counties of Nairn and Inverness, a county councillor for Carmarthenshire after 1888, and a justice of the peace for Carmarthenshire and Pembrokeshire. Becoming early an energetic member of the Royal Agricultural Society, he was chosen a member of the council in 1882, chairman of the chemical committee in 1889, a trustee in 1892, and (as Lord Cawdor) a vice-president in 1900. He was president of the society in 1901, when the show was held at Cardiff.

Railway work brought Emlyn more prominently before the public. He became a director of the Great Western railway in 1890, and deputy-chairman in the following year. In July 1895 he accepted the chairmanship of the company in succession to Mr. F. G. Saunders, and held that post until he became a member of Mr. Balfour's cabinet in 1905. Under his guidance a bold policy was adopted. The ten minutes' stop at Swindon was abolished on the payment of 100,000*l.* in compensation to the refreshment contractor, and routes were shortened by the creation of the Stert and Westbury, Langport and Castle Cary, and the South Wales and Bristol direct lines; while by the Acton and High Wycombe line quicker access was gained to Birmingham. After his resignation, Fishguard harbour was opened at much expense as the starting-point of a new route for south Ireland and a port of call for Atlantic steamers. Long-distance runs, the reduction of second-class fares, and the institution of motor-trains and road-motors were other features of Lord Cawdor's chairmanship. Under him the gross annual receipts of the line rose from just over 9,000,000*l.* to 12,342,000*l.*

The announcement on 6 March 1905 of Lord Cawdor's appointment as first lord of the admiralty, in succession to Lord Selborne, who went to South Africa as high commissioner, came as a general surprise, but the desire for business men was understood to be the cause. Carrying on his predecessor's policy, he authorised the redistribution of the fleet recommended by the first sea lord, Sir John Fisher (afterwards Lord Fisher of Kelverstone), and the Dreadnought and Invincible, the first ships of a new class, were laid down. On 30 Nov. 1905, just before the resignation of the ministry, the admiralty issued a memorandum surveying the reforms of three years, and stating that 'at the present time strategic requirements necessitate the output of four large armoured ships annually' (*Naval Annual*, 1906).

The abandonment of the Cawdor programme by the government of Sir Henry Campbell-Bannerman [q. v. Suppl. II] called forth vigorous protests from its author on 30 July 1906 (*Hansard*, clxii. cols. 291–9) and 24 Nov. 1908 (*ibid.* clxxxxvii. cols. 25–31). He had become one of the most effective debaters on the front opposition bench, and powerful in unionist councils. It was on his motion that the select committee to consider suggestions for increasing the efficiency of the House of Lords was appointed in 1907; he was a member of the committee and concurred in the paragraph of the report stating that 'it was undesirable that the possession of a peerage should of itself give the right to sit and vote in the House of Lords.' He was strenuous in recommending the upper house to refuse to accept the budget of 1909 until it had been referred to the country. On 30 Nov. 1909 he concluded the debate on Lord Lansdowne's amendment to that effect, vigorously accusing the government of 'denying socialism in words, but putting socialism into their budget' (*Lords Debates*, vol. iv. cols. 1310–24). The amendment was carried. Cawdor was one of the four unionist statesmen who took part in the conference with four members of the liberal government which, sitting from 17 June to 10 Nov. 1910, made an ineffectual attempt to settle the constitutional question, and he was consulted in the drafting of Lord Lansdowne's resolutions for the reform of the House of Lords produced in November of that year.

Soon after leaving office in 1905 Cawdor accepted the presidency of the Institution of Naval Architects, and in 1908 he was chosen a member of the council of the Prince of Wales. He died at Stackpole Court, Pembrokeshire, after an illness of some months on 8 Feb. 1911, and was buried at Cheriton, Pembrokeshire. On the day after his death conspicuous tributes were paid to his memory by Lords Crewe and Lansdowne in the House of Lords. Lord Crewe declared that his case was almost unique, since after a long absence from political life he had been accepted as one of the best ministers that had ever been at the admiralty, and subsequently had obtained a position in the public esteem 'only very little short of the highest.' He was a most formidable antagonist, but 'though his weapons were sharp, they were never barbed.' Lord Lansdowne, after dwelling on Lord Cawdor's merits as a debater and administrator, said that ever since his school days he had been surrounded by troops of friends. He managed his great estates in Scotland and Wales with businesslike ability. He married on 16 Sept. 1868 Edith Georgiana, eldest daughter of Sir Christopher Turnor, by whom he had eight sons and five daughters, and was succeeded by his eldest son, Hugh Frederick Vaughan, Viscount Emlyn, who was born on 21 June 1870.

Two portraits in oils are at Stackpole Court, one by Sir Hubert von Herkomer, R.A., painted in 1883, and the second by Mr. W. W. Ouless, R.A., in 1903.

[The Times, and Engineering, 9 Feb. 1911; Engineer, 16 Dec. 1910 (art. Great Western Railway) and 9 Feb. 1911; Naval Annual, 1905–6.] L. C. S.

CAMPBELL, Sir JAMES MACNABB (1846–1903), Indian official and compiler of the 'Bombay Gazetteer,' born at Partick, Lanarkshire, on 4 Oct. 1846, was a younger son of six children of John McLeod Campbell [q. v.] by his wife Mary Campbell. Of three brothers, the eldest, Donald (*d.* 1909), was rector of Oakford, Devonshire, and rural dean of Tiverton. His other brothers lived with him in Bombay, John McLeod (*d.* 1888) being a member of the Bombay civil service, and Robert Story a merchant.

Campbell was educated at Glasgow, first at the academy and then at the university, graduating M.A. in 1866, with the highest honours in logic, philosophy, and English literature. Passing the Indian civil service examination in 1867, he went out to Bombay in November 1869, and served as an assistant collector. Quickly winning repute for interest in the history and customs of the people, he was in June 1873, when only twenty-seven, entrusted with the compilation of the provincial 'Gazetteer' of Bombay. At the same time he discharged some other duties. From April to August 1877 he was on famine work in the Bijapur (then the Kaladgi) district; and from April 1880 till near the close of 1881 he held successively the posts of municipal commissioner of Bombay, under-secretary to government in the political, judicial, and educational departments, and collector of Bombay. Yet to the 'Gazetteer' he devoted every spare moment. By August 1884 the statistical accounts alone occupied twenty-seven volumes averaging 500 pages each. The government, while then terminating Campbell's formal appointment as compiler, eulogised his work as 'a record as complete perhaps as ever was produced on behalf of any government.' Sir W. W. Hunter, the editor of the 'Imperial Gazetteer of India' (1881; 2nd edit. 1885–7), largely based the Bombay portions upon Campbell's work, and spoke of his compilation as 'perhaps unequalled and certainly unsurpassed' (*Bombay* 1885 *to* 1890). Campbell was made C.I.E. in January 1885, and going home on his first furlough in that year was created hon. LL.D. of his university (Glasgow). Campbell completed his 'Bombay Gazetteer' at the close of 1901, when it consisted of thirty-four volumes, embracing twenty-six sections, he himself writing much in those dealing with ethnology. In 1904 Mr. R. E. Enthoven added an index volume, and brought down to date some of Campbell's earlier statistics, while in 1910 Mr. S. M. Edwards added three further volumes on the history of the town and island of Bombay.

After serving as collector of various districts, Campbell was from November 1891 stationed at Bombay as collector of land revenue, customs, and opium. In 1895 and 1897 he acted also there as commissioner of customs, salt, opium, and abkari. Occasionally he served too as chairman of the port trust. In 1894 he arranged for the additional work cast on the Bombay customs house by the general re-imposition of import duties.

Campbell was recalled from furlough early in 1897 to aid in measures against the great outbreak of plague. In June 1897 he succeeded General Sir William Gatacre [q. v. Suppl. II] as chairman of a new and independent plague committee at Bombay. The committee's compulsory measures of sanitation provoked rioting and murderous outrage against officers on plague duty (22 June 1897). The difficulties of the situation were soon multiplied by the appearance of famine in the country and the return to Bombay of thousands of refugees. Campbell's resourcefulness, and the personal regard in which the masses held him—the 'Murani Collector-Saheb' (the collector with the divinely lighted face) —greatly improved the popular attitude and encouraged voluntary co-operation in inspection and other work. Largely under his influence, in June 1898 the plague administration was restored to the municipality.

In June 1897 Campbell was made K.C.I.E., and on 29 April 1898 he left Bombay in broken health, resigning, on the expiry of his furlough, in April 1900. The Bombay government placed on record a resolution of appreciation of his work and character. Residing with his brother Robert at his father's old home, Achnashie, Rosneath, Dumbartonshire, he found his main recreation in gardening. He died unmarried at Achnashie on 26 May 1903, and was buried in Roseneath churchyard, beside his parents. A memorial tablet on the ruined wall of the old church, in which his father had often preached when minister of the adjoining parish of Row, pays tribute to 'the noble example set by him during the great plague in Bombay, which led to his premature and deeply lamented death.' His friends also founded a gold medal, conferred triennially by the Bombay branch of the Royal Asiatic Society, for the best original work on Indian folklore, history, or ethnology. The first medal was presented on 1 March 1909 to Dr. A. M. Stein, the explorer, for his 'Ancient Khotan.'

Campbell collected masses of material on Indian history and folklore, but, apart from his 'Gazetteer,' only published the history of Mandogarh in the 'Journal of the Bombay Branch, Royal Asiatic Society' (vol. xix. 1895–7), some papers in the proceedings of the Bombay Anthropological Society, and studies of demonology, under the title of 'Notes on the Spirit Basis of Belief and Custom,' in the 'Indian Antiquary' (1894 *et seq.*).

[Bombay Gazetteer; Times of India, 30 April 1898, 12 April 1902, 3 June 1903, 2 March 1909; Jour. of Roy. Asiat. Soc., July 1903; Rept. Indian Plague Comm., 1901, cd. 810; personal knowledge.] F. H. B.

CAMPBELL, LEWIS (1830–1908), classical scholar, born at Edinburgh on 3 Sept. 1830, was son of Commander Robert Campbell, R.N., first cousin to Thomas Campbell the poet, by his wife Eliza Constantia, eldest daughter of Richard Pryce of Gunley, Montgomeryshire. Educated at Edinburgh Academy, he was 'Dux' there in 1847, when he entered Glasgow University. There his principal teachers were Edmund Lushington, to whom he ascribed his love of Greek literature, and William Ramsay. He won the Blackstone medal in Greek, the highest distinction in the subject. In 1849 Campbell matriculated as a scholar at Trinity College, Oxford; but on winning the Snell exhibition at Glasgow he migrated to Balliol, where that exhibition is tenable. He was deeply influenced by Benjamin Jowett, who was his tutor, and whom he regarded with devotion all his life. In 1853 he graduated B.A. with first-class honours in classics, and was elected to a fellowship at Queen's College in 1855. From 1856 to 1858 he was tutor of his college, and always kept in close touch with his pupils. In 1858 he resigned his fellowship on marriage, and having been ordained deacon in 1857 and priest in 1858, was presented to the vicarage of Milford, Hampshire. He held the benefice for five years. This was his only active ministry in the Church of England, but he remained an ardent champion of the liberal theology which he had learned from Jowett. His position is fully explained in a volume of sermons entitled 'The Christian Ideal' (1877) and in his 'Nationalisation of the Old English Universities' (1900).

In 1863 Campbell was elected to the Greek chair at St. Andrews, vacated by the translation of William Young Sellar [q. v.] to Edinburgh. His academic life was occasionally troubled by the students' impatience of discipline. But his relations with his own classes were always friendly. He founded a Shakespearean and dramatic society, and successfully directed it along with his wife. With his wife, too, he took an active part in raising the standard of girls' secondary education through the country.

From the first he held that a professor's duty was not confined to his classroom. Jowett had planned a series of editions of the Platonic dialogues, of which the 'Theætetus,' 'Sophistes,' and 'Politicus' were assigned to Campbell. The 'Theætetus' appeared in 1861 (2nd edit. 1883), the 'Sophistes' and 'Politicus' in 1867. To the problem of the chronology of Plato's dialogues Campbell here applied linguistic tests, of which he learned the value from his Shakespearean studies, distinguished between Plato's earlier and later work, and identified a later group of dialogues which might be presumed to represent Plato's maturer thought. The discovery passed almost unnoticed, and even Jowett, to Campbell's keen disappointment, was sceptical, but Campbell lived to see his conclusions, after a quarter of a century, generally adopted.

Campbell next turned his attention to Sophocles, of whose tragedies he produced a complete edition (vol. i. 1875; 2nd edit. 1879; vol. ii. 1881). This edition was severely criticised by Benjamin Hall Kennedy [q. v.], and was overshadowed by the popularity of Jebb's edition; but Campbell excelled most of his competitors in poetic and dramatic insight. At a later date he returned to the subject, and discussed the main differences between Jebb and himself (*Paralipomena Sophoclea*, 1907). He translated into English verse Sophocles (completed 1883; 2nd edit. 1896) and Æschylus (1890), and edited the text of Æschylus in the 'Parnassus' series (1897).

From Sophocles Campbell turned to Plato again, and completed the edition of the 'Republic' which Jowett had undertaken for his series of Plato's works. Jowett finished the commentary and prepared some introductory matter; Campbell was responsible for the text and for the greater part of the essays. The edition appeared in 1894 (3 vols.).

In 1889 a parliamentary commission was appointed to reform the Scottish universities, and the consequent discussions to which this gave rise greatly tried Campbell's sensitive nature. In 1891–2 ill-health compelled a long absence, and in the summer of 1892 he resigned his chair. He retired to Alassio, where he built a house, and, acquiring a new lease of life, engaged with greater vigour than before in literary labour. He collaborated with Evelyn Abbott [q. v. Suppl. II] in the 'Life of Jowett' (1897). In 1894 he returned to St. Andrews as Gifford lecturer, during the winters of 1894 and 1895, and he published his lectures under the title of 'Religion in Greek Literature' (1898). He also issued an edition of Thomas Campbell's poems (1904) and 'Tragic Drama in Æschylus, Sophocles and Shakespeare' (1904), with minor works and articles. At the age of seventy he planned a 'Lexicon Platonicum' on a large scale, and did a great deal of the work, completely revising and rearranging Ast's 'Lexicon,' and verifying all the quotations. The work is still being carried on with a view to publication.

Campbell, who was elected an honorary fellow of Balliol in 1894, and was made an hon. D.Litt. of the university on Lord Goschen's installation as chancellor in 1904, died at Brissago, Lago Maggiore, after a short illness, on 25 Oct. 1908. He married in 1858 Frances Pitt, daughter of Thomas Andrews, serjeant-at-law, who survived him without issue; her practical temperament efficiently balanced Campbell's more nervous and excitable character. The only adequate portrait of Campbell is a medal, by Roty, for which his pupils at St. Andrews subscribed after his resignation in 1892.

Besides the works mentioned, he published a 'Life of James Clerk Maxwell,' in collaboration with W. Garnett (1882; 2nd edit. 1884), and a 'Guide to Greek Tragedy' (1891). He also edited Jowett's 'Letters' (1889) and 'Theological Essays' (1906).

[Personal recollections; communications from Mrs. Campbell; Who's Who, 1908.]

J. B.

CAMPBELL, WILLIAM HOWARD (1859-1910), missionary and entomologist, was born on 30 Sept. 1859 at Londonderry, where his father, Thomas Callender

Campbell, was in business. Of his six brothers Mr. Sidney George Campbell became fellow of Christ's College, Cambridge.

Educated at the Academical Institution, Londonderry, he took both his arts and divinity courses at Edinburgh University, being a first prizeman in the divinity class and in church history, and graduating M.A. in 1880 and B.D. in 1882. At Edinburgh he also studied Sanskrit for two years, and attended some medical classes. His services being accepted by the London Missionary Society, he was ordained on 12 Sept. 1884 at the congregational church, Londonderry, and reached Cuddapah, South India, in November 1884. In 1895 he settled at Jammulamadugu, and in 1900 he was appointed to the training institution at Gooty. In 1907 he acted as secretary of the South India district committee.

Campbell was a great missionary. Journeying from village to village, he established scores of Christian churches during his seventeen years of labour. A pioneer in the cause of union among missions, he helped to form the united church of South India, in which presbyterians, congregationalists, and baptists united for ecclesiastical purposes, forming a Christian community of upwards of 150,000 people, about one-fourth of the protestants of South India (cf. his art. *L.M.S. Chronicle*, November 1908). Economic and social problems interested him. While he sympathised with socialist ideals, he fully admitted the beneficent effects of British rule in India (cf. letter in *Labour Leader*, 25 Nov. 1905). Articles which he contributed to the 'Madras Mail' during the famine of 1897 led to the establishment of relief works.

His linguistic gifts and scholarly attainments made him a leading authority on the Telugu language. In that tongue he published 'Grounds for Belief in a Personal God' (1893). 'Christian Evidences' (1898), 'Christian Theology' (1905), and a short work on Hinduism. The first three of these became text-books in theological institutions. In conjunction with Veerasalingam Pantalu he by order of the Madras government revised Browne's 'Telugu-English Dictionary' (1906) and Arden's 'Telugu Grammar' (1908), and he was a member of the revision committee of the Telugu Bible (1898-1903).

Campbell, who acted as examiner in philosophy to the university of Madras, was a close student of science, especially of entomology and ornithology. In his home in Ireland he and his brothers had made one of the best private collections of Irish moths and butterflies. In India he formed a fine collection of moths of that country, adding sixty or seventy species that were new to science. This collection is now at Gooty, in the Madras presidency.

Campbell returned to England under medical advice in 1909, before taking up the principalship of the new union theological college at Bangalore, to which he had been nominated. He died on 18 Feb. 1910 at Bordighera, and was buried there.

On 7 Dec. 1885 he married at Madras Elizabeth Nevin, daughter of David Boyd of Drukendult, Ballymoney, co. Antrim. They had four sons.

[Private information; L.M.S. Chronicle, Nov. 1908, April 1910; British Weekly, 24 Feb. 1910.] C. H. I.

CAMPBELL-BANNERMAN, Sir HENRY (1836–1908), prime minister, born at Kelvinside House, Glasgow, on 7 Sept. 1836, was second son, and youngest of the six children of Sir James Campbell, Knt., of Stracathro, co. Forfar, by his wife Janet, daughter of Henry Bannerman, a Manchester manufacturer; her mother's brother was William Motherwell [q. v.], the Scottish poet. The future prime minister assumed the additional name and arms of Bannerman in 1872 under the will of his maternal uncle, Henry Bannerman, of Hunton Court, near Maidstone, Kent.

Sir Henry's grandfather, James Campbell, came from Inchanoch, in Menteith, to Glasgow in 1805, and began business as a yarn merchant; his second son James (the prime minister's father), then a lad of fifteen, becoming a tailor, and William, his fourth son (afterwards of Tullichewan, co. Dumbarton), a draper. In 1817 these two brothers founded the great Glasgow firm of J. & W. Campbell, wholesale drapers and warehousemen. The father was a strong conservative, stood in that interest as parliamentary candidate for Glasgow in 1837 and in 1841, without success, and as lord provost of Glasgow (1840–3) was knighted on the birth of prince Albert Edward, afterwards King Edward VII (9 Nov. 1841). He bought the estate of Stracathro in 1848.

The elder son, James Alexander Campbell of Stracathro (1825–1908), conservative M.P. for the universities of Glasgow and Aberdeen (1880–1906), succeeded his father in 1876, and was made a privy councillor in 1898. He died on 10 May 1908.

Sir Henry was educated at Glasgow High School, and then at Glasgow University (1851–3), where in 1853, the same year in which Edward Caird [q. v. Suppl. II], afterwards Master of Balliol, won the Latin medal, he won, among other things, the Cowan gold medal for the best examination in Greek. In 1883 his university, on the installation of John Bright as lord rector, conferred upon him the honorary degree of LL.D., and at the time of his death in 1908 he was liberal nominee for the lord rectorship. From Glasgow he went to Trinity College, Cambridge, where, taking a double degree—as twenty-second senior optime in the mathematical tripos, with a third class in the classical tripos—he graduated B.A. in 1858 and M.A. in 1861. He took no part in the debates at the union. After leaving Cambridge he joined his father and uncle's prosperous business in Glasgow, in which he became and remained a partner until 1868. He was one of the original members of the first Lanarkshire rifle volunteers, and commanded his company (M company, known as 'Campbell's Corps,' the members being drawn exclusively from the employees of Messrs. J. & W. Campbell & Co.) at the royal review at Edinburgh on 7 Feb. 1860.

In April 1868 he contested the Stirling Burghs against John Ramsay of Kildalton. Both candidates were liberal, Campbell the more advanced of the two. He declared himself 'a warm adherent of the party of progress,' advocating national education, the repeal of university tests, administrative reform of the army and navy, Irish church disestablishment, and land reform. Ramsay defeated him by 565 to 494 votes. He fought Ramsay again at the general election which followed the 1868 Reform Act, and won the seat on 19 November, polling 2192 votes against Ramsay's 1670. He sat for the Stirling Burghs uninterruptedly until his death. His opponent subsequently sat for the Falkirk Burghs from 1874 to 1886.

In the new parliament of 1868 Campbell soon identified himself with the more independent and advanced supporters of Gladstone's first administration, advocating the reform of endowed schools in Scotland, compulsory attendance at parochial schools, the abolition of university tests, the application of the representative principle to county government, the infusion of new blood into Oxford and Cambridge, the abolition of hypothec, and the cause of the tenant farmer. His political ability was recognised by his appointment, in November 1871, as financial secretary to the war office, of which Cardwell was then the head. He retained the post until the fall of the administration in February 1874.

During the years of liberal opposition, from 1874 to 1880, Campbell-Bannerman took little part in general debate, but intervened regularly in the discussion of army votes and the affairs of Scotland. He characterised the bill for the abolition of patronage (1875) as a political device to strengthen the established church at the cost of the other presbyterian churches.

In March 1880 parliament was dissolved, Lord Beaconsfield's government was defeated, and in April Gladstone formed his second administration. Campbell-Bannerman returned to his former post at the war office, of which Childers was then the chief, and he held the office till May 1882. Then, in succession to Sir George Trevelyan, who was transferred to the Irish chief secretaryship on the murder of Lord Frederick Cavendish, he became secretary to the admiralty. Lord Northbrook, the first lord, was in the House of Lords, and Campbell-Bannerman represented the department in the House of Commons. In October 1884, again in succession to Sir George Trevelyan, he was appointed chief secretary for Ireland (without a seat in the cabinet), while Lord Spencer was still lord-lieutenant. The office was one of danger and difficulty, and Campbell-Bannerman was held at the time to be the only man who ever actually enhanced his political reputation by its tenure. He discharged his duties with imperturbability and good-humour, and Ireland grew more peaceful. Parnell wrote of him 'as an Irish secretary he left things alone—a sensible thing for an Irish secretary' (see Barry O'Brien's *Life of Parnell*). According to Mr. Tim Healy he 'governed Ireland with Scotch jokes'; Mr. T. P. O'Connor likened him to a 'sandbag.' During his short tenure of the Irish secretaryship it was announced that some provisions of the Crimes Act would be re-enacted, and an Irish land purchase bill was promised; but the life of the government came to an end in June 1885, and Campbell-Bannerman retired from his Irish office after holding it for only eight months.

In February 1886, on the fall of Lord Salisbury's first administration, Campbell-Bannerman became secretary of state for war in Gladstone's third government, entering the cabinet for the first time, together with Lord Herschell, Mr. John, afterwards Viscount, Morley, and Mr. Mundella. Home rule for Ireland, which was the chief measure before the cabinet, met with Campbell-Bannerman's approval. On 8 June the proposals of the government were defeated in the House of Commons by 343 to 313, ninety-three liberals voting against the bill (MORLEY'S *Gladstone*, iii. 341). Gladstone dissolved parliament, was defeated at the polls, and Lord Salisbury accepted office for a second time. For six years (1886–92) the liberal party remained in opposition. During the period Campbell-Bannerman actively supported Gladstone in fighting the cause of Ireland and home rule. In 1887 he moved an amendment to Mr. A. J. Balfour's Irish land bill, to the effect that no bill of the kind was satisfactory which did not provide for revision of the judicial rents. In the course of the Irish controversy he described the process of adopting home rule as 'finding salvation,' and he invented the term 'Ulsteria' for the peculiar blend of Orange bigotry and Irish toryism which he imputed to the Irish opponents of home rule.

During the agitation for improved national defence in 1888–9 he maintained a critical attitude, strongly opposing any diminution of civilian control of the army, and any attempt to place that control entirely in the hands of military advisers. In June 1888 he served with Lord Randolph Churchill, W. H. Smith, and others, under the chairmanship of Lord Hartington (afterwards eighth duke of Devonshire [q. v. Suppl. II]), upon the royal commission appointed to inquire into the civil and professional administration of the naval and military departments. The commission reported finally in February 1890 (C. 5979 of 1890), when Campbell-Bannerman, who had been unable to take part in the consideration of the second portion of the report, added a memorandum expressing his general acquiescence in its tenour and his cordial concurrence in its principal recommendation, 'that the secretary of state should be advised by a council of military officers, who should be the heads of several military departments.' He at the same time strongly dissented 'from the further proposal to create a new department—that, namely, of chief of the staff.' He reasoned that the innovation was unnecessary, and likely to re-introduce the evils incidental to the office of commander-in-chief which the new council of general officers was designed to replace (10 Feb. 1890).

Lord Salisbury dissolved parliament in 1892, and his government was defeated at the polls. Thereupon Gladstone formed his fourth administration (July 1892), and Campbell-Bannerman joined the cabinet in his former post of secretary of state for war. He was a member of the cabinet committee which drafted the second home rule bill, which passed the House of Commons, but was decisively rejected by the House of Lords. When Lord Rosebery succeeded Gladstone as prime minister on 3 March 1894, Campbell-Bannerman retained his office. He was an active administrator. Under his régime at Pall Mall there was established a forty-eight hours week (or an average of eight hours a day) in the ordnance factories at Woolwich Arsenal and he justly anticipated no necessity for 'a reduction in wages' (see *Hansard*, 5 Jan. 1894). He also arranged for the delicate matter of the retirement of the duke of Cambridge from the office of commander-in-chief, and tactfully effected the step without disturbing the good relations which had always existed between the duke and himself. But he doubted the wisdom of offering the duke a special pension which was offered him later by the conservative government, and the duke declined the offer on the ground of this difference of view. On the day of Campbell-Bannerman's announcement of the duke's retirement (21 June 1895) Mr. St. John Brodrick (afterwards secretary of state for war and Viscount Midleton) moved a reduction of Campbell-Bannerman's salary on the ground that the reserves of cordite and other smallarm ammunition were inadequate. Campbell-Bannerman admitted that the reserves did not exceed 100,000,000 cartridges. The government was defeated by seven votes in a small house, 132 against 125; Lord Rosebery, the prime minister, resigned next day. A lack of harmony between Lord Rosebery and some of his colleagues partly prompted so serious a treatment of the adverse division. Harcourt, in announcing to the House of Commons Lord Rosebery's resignation and the queen's acceptance of it, said: 'The division of last Friday night upon the army vote for the war office was a direct vote of censure upon the secretary of state for the war department, than whom I will take on me to say there is no more able, more respected, or more popular minister.' Campbell-Bannerman received the G.C.B. on leaving office. The adverse vote had little positive justification. As Campbell-Bannerman subsequently explained (cf. speech at Newport, 30 Nov. 1903), expert opinion proved it inexpedient to keep in stock any large supply of cordite.

then a new explosive in an experimental stage, which was easily and rapidly manufactured as the need for it arose.

Meanwhile in 1895, when Mr. Peel resigned the speakership of the House of Commons, Campbell-Bannerman frankly confessed to a wish to succeed him. The conservatives were prepared to acquiesce in his selection, in view of his fairness and impartiality. But his colleagues were unwilling to lose him, and he was persuaded to concur in the selection of William Court Gully, Viscount Selby [q. v. Suppl. II].

Lord Salisbury accepted office on 23 June 1895 and formed an administration. Parliament was dissolved on 8 July, and a majority of 152 was returned to support the new conservative government. Campbell-Bannerman, speaking at Blairgowrie on 12 Dec. as one of the liberal leaders, announced that so long as the Irish declared by constitutional methods that they were in favour of self-government, liberals would be bound to support their demand.

Before the end of the year South African affairs became a predominant political interest. Dr. Jameson's abortive raid into the territory of the Transvaal Republic, and his surrender after two days' fighting at Krugersdorp (1 Jan. 1896), roused in the more advanced section of the liberal party a suspicion that Mr. Chamberlain, the colonial secretary, was implicated in the affair. Campbell-Bannerman, Sir Michael Hicks-Beach, then chancellor of the exchequer, Sir William Harcourt, Henry Labouchere, John Ellis, and others, were, on 14 Aug. 1896, appointed members of a select committee of inquiry into the circumstances of the raid. This South African committee sat to take evidence from January to June 1897. The majority report of 14 July, which was signed by both Campbell-Bannerman and Harcourt, while condemning Cecil Rhodes and two of his associates in general terms, exonerated the imperial and South African governments of all complicity. In the House of Commons both Campbell-Bannerman and Harcourt frankly defended the report when it was impugned by a member of their own party, Mr. Philip Stanhope (afterwards Lord Weardale), whose amendment of dissent was rejected by 333 to seventy-four. A bitter feeling against both Rhodes and Mr. Chamberlain ran high in the left wing of the liberal party, but no other conclusion than that which Campbell-Bannerman and his colleagues reached was justified on a temperate review of the material evidence.

As far back as 1894, when the resignation of Gladstone disclosed differences of opinion within the liberal party, Campbell-Bannerman was named by competent observers as a probable future leader. He had enjoyed much administrative experience, and held alike the peculiar confidence of his colleagues and the esteem and goodwill of the House of Commons. But he had made no impression on the public outside the house, and many of his colleagues stood far higher in popular favour. A continuance of personal dissensions among the leaders of his party during the long unionist régime gradually brought him to the first place. On 6 Oct. 1896 Lord Rosebery resigned his leadership on the ground of 'internal difficulties,' the want of 'explicit support' from any quarter, and 'apparent difference with a considerable mass of the party on the Eastern question' (Turkey and Armenia). Thereupon Harcourt naturally succeeded to the leadership. But Lord Rosebery still had his followers in the House of Commons, and Harcourt's authority was often called in question. On 14 Dec. 1898 Harcourt retired from the leadership of a party which he described as 'rent by sectional disputes and personal interests.' Mr. John Morley approved Harcourt's action, and declared 'that he, too, could no longer take an active and responsible part in the formal councils of the heads of the liberal party' (17 Jan. 1899). There seemed to be fundamental divergences of view within the party touching the whole field of foreign, colonial, and Irish politics. In this critical embarrassment the liberal party elected Campbell-Bannerman as its leader in the House of Commons. Lord Kimberley now led the liberals in the House of Lords since the withdrawal of Lord Rosebery. At a meeting held at the Reform Club on 6 Feb. 1899, which was attended by 143 members of parliament, the choice of Campbell-Bannerman was unanimously adopted. The names of Sir Henry Fowler and Mr. Asquith had been previously suggested and had been withdrawn. The new leader promised 'to bring all his powers to his task' and to give 'the government a watchful and active, and not a violent and reckless, opposition.' He still adhered to his home rule convictions, but laid on them a qualified stress. On 21 March, at the meeting of the National Liberal Federation at Hull, he declared that it was impossible to make home rule the first item of the liberal programme, but added 'we will remain true to the Irish people as long as the Irish remain true to themselves.'

The South African policy of Mr. Chamberlain, which culminated in war at the end of 1899, was the first great question with which Campbell-Bannerman in his new capacity had actively to deal. His attitude was from the outset clear and firm; it did not, however, succeed in winning the support of the whole party. On 17 June 1899, in a speech delivered at Ilford, before hostilities broke out, he declared that 'he could see nothing in what had occurred to justify either warlike action or military preparation.' With this view Lord Kimberley, the liberal leader in the House of Lords, associated himself (*Hansard*, 28 July). At the opening of the autumn session (17 Oct.), when the war had just begun, Campbell-Bannerman at once offered to facilitate the grant of supplies 'for the prosecution of the war.' But in speeches at Manchester (14 Nov.) and Birmingham (24 Nov.) he continued to criticise the conduct of the government before the war in mixing up negotiations with military preparations 'in such a manner as to prejudice greatly the chances of a peaceful solution.' After the grave reverses at Stormberg (10 Dec.), Magersfontein (12 Dec.), and Colenso (15 Dec.), Campbell-Bannerman, speaking at Aberdeen (19 Dec.), deprecated 'doubt or despondency,' and urged the nation to brace itself 'more earnestly to the task before us.' At the same time he repeated that 'Mr. Chamberlain is mainly answerable for this war.' When the military situation improved next summer, he laid it down as England's first duty to aim, 'after the security of the imperial power,' at 'the conciliation and the harmonious co-operation of the two European races in South Africa, and to restore as early as possible' to the conquered states the 'rights of self-government' (Glasgow, 7 Jan. 1900). From this aim he never swerved.

On 25 Sept. 1900 parliament was dissolved, and the country returned Lord Salisbury's government again to power with a majority of 132. The 'khaki' election, as it was called, was won on the plea that the war was finished, and that the government responsible for it should finish their task and be responsible for the settlement after the war. Yet the war dragged on for another twenty months. Throughout this period Campbell-Bannerman consistently advocated conciliatory and definite terms of peace. On 10 Dec. 1901 Lord Rosebery (at Chesterfield) expressed concurrence with him on this point, and Campbell-Bannerman thereupon invited Lord Rosebery anew to co-operate with his former colleagues; but Lord Rosebery preferred an attitude of detachment, and Campbell-Bannerman thenceforth pursued his own line, even at the risk of prolonging existing party dissensions.

On the methods which were adopted in the field during the later stages of the difficult warfare, Campbell-Bannerman declared his views without shrinking. On 6 Dec. 1900, in the House of Commons, he extolled the humanity and the generosity of the British soldier and the British officer, expressing his entire disbelief 'in the stories that have been told on both sides of discreditable, irregular, and cruel outrages.' Subsequently he urged (at Peckham, 7 Aug. 1901) the need of making 'even the stern necessities of war minister to conciliation,' and both denounced and promised to 'continue to denounce all this stupid policy of farm-burning, devastation, and the sweeping of women and children into camps.' To this promise he remained faithful, with the emphatic approval of one important section of liberal opinion, and with the no less emphatic disapproval of another important section.

On 31 May 1901, at a liberal meeting in Edinburgh, he had acknowledged the existence of differences in the opposition ranks about the war, but claimed that at any rate they were united, with a few insignificant exceptions, against 'the most unwise as well as the most unworthy policy of enforcing unconditional surrender upon those who were to be their loyal and contented subjects in the new colonies.' A fortnight later (14 June), at a National Reform Union banquet given to Harcourt and himself, he used a phrase which obtained much currency and moved applause and resentment in almost equal measure. The government had lately described the war as 'not yet entirely terminated.' Campbell-Bannerman added the comment, 'A phrase often used is that war is war: but when one came to ask about it one was told that no war was going on—that it was not war. When was a war not a war? When it was carried on by *methods of barbarism* in South Africa.' Three days later (17 June) in the House of Commons he supported Mr. Lloyd George's motion for the adjournment of the house in order to call attention to the concentration camps in South Africa, and while he deprecated the 'imputation of cruelty, or even indifference, to officers or men,' he repeated his application to 'the whole system' of the term 'barbarous.' Renewed signs of party discontent followed these deliverances. Mr. Haldane refused to support the motion, and with Mr. Asquith, Sir Edward Grey, Mr. Lawson Walton (afterwards attorney-general), Mr. Robson (afterwards solicitor-general), and nearly fifty liberals, walked out of the house before the division. There seemed a likelihood of an open breach on the part of the dissentient section of the party. On 2 July, speaking at Southampton, Campbell-Bannerman described the position of the party as 'critical.' But on 9 July, at the Reform Club, 163 liberal members of the House of Commons, of all sections, including Sir William Harcourt, Mr. Asquith, and Sir Edward Grey, expressed unanimously continued confidence in Campbell-Bannerman's leadership. Later in the year (25 Oct. 1901) Campbell-Bannerman hopefully appealed to true liberals throughout the country for unity. Passing to another controverted topic, on which there was not universal consent in the liberal ranks, he declared that he was 'as strongly as ever in favour of giving self-government to Ireland.' 'There is no actual alliance,' he added, with the Irish party, but he hoped for a cordial co-operation. The declaration checked for a time the movement towards unity. A liberal imperial council had been in existence to maintain within the party the views of Lord Rosebery on imperial and Irish questions. On 27 Feb. 1902 it was decided to reconstitute the council with its old aims as the Liberal League. Campbell-Bannerman saw no reason for such a step (speech, National Liberal Club, 5 March). He denied that there were personal differences among the leaders. The war was a transient interlude, and the only final solution of either the South African or the Irish question lay in the liberal principle of assent. In Lord Spencer, who spoke at Eastbourne on the same day, Campbell-Bannerman found a whole-hearted adherent.

The terms of peace in South Africa were announced on 2 June. On 11 July Lord Salisbury, prime minister, resigned, and on 14 July Campbell-Bannerman in the House of Commons, on behalf of the house as a whole, congratulated Mr. Balfour on filling the vacant place. Through the session he steadily opposed the government's chief measure, the education bill, which he called the bill of the church party. It was finally passed in an autumn session (December 1902), in spite of nonconformist opposition and some dissatisfaction among liberal-unionist supporters of the government. Next year the liberal party's position was immensely improved by a schism which rent the government and its supporters. The healing of internal differences among the liberals was greatly facilitated by the perplexity and division which Mr. Chamberlain's announcement at Birmingham of his new fiscal programme (May 1903) created in the unionist ranks. Without delay Campbell-Bannerman made strategic use of his new opportunity. On the adjournment for the Whitsuntide recess (28 May) he denounced the government for their 'cuttle-fish' policy in raising a new issue, which he characterised on 9 June as a proposal to tax anew the food of the people. He laid stress on Mr. Chamberlain's statement that it was the question on which the next general election was to be fought. In the autumn the resignations of Mr. Chamberlain, Mr. Ritchie, the duke of Devonshire, and other prominent members of the government illustrated practically the disintegrating tendency of the fiscal policy. At Glasgow, on 6 October, Mr. Chamberlain explained his proposals at length, and Campbell-Bannerman, at Bolton (15 Oct.), retorted by denouncing as a wicked slander on the mother country and the colonies alike the assertion that the empire could only be saved from dissolution by a revolution in fiscal policy. On the new free trade issue Lord Rosebery declared that all liberals were united (7 Nov.). Thereupon Campbell-Bannerman renewed his former advances; but Rosebery's reply was very cautious, and no further attempt was made to close the breach between the two.

The reconstructed government's difficulties grew rapidly. At the end of 1903 resolutions were adopted by the Transvaal legislative council for the importation of Chinese indentured labour, and they were sanctioned by the home government. Liberals at once contended that slavery was revived, and the plea found support in the constituencies. Yet henceforth, both in parliament and outside, the paramount political issue was fiscal reform. On that theme Campbell-Bannerman and his colleagues concentrated most of their energy. On 1 Aug. 1904 he moved a vote of censure upon the government, because three members of the government had accepted office in the Tariff Reform League, which advocated preferential duties and therefore the taxation of food. Next year his position was strengthened when the National Union of Conservative and Constitutional Associations at Newcastle formally adopted fiscal reform as a plank in the party platform, and Mr. Balfour's appeal to the party on the same evening to unite on a practical fiscal policy failed to conciliate unionist free traders. Meanwhile on all political topics Campbell-Bannerman was now sedulously defining his position and developing a programme, with a view to the increasing likelihood of the party's return to power. He criticised Arnold-Forster's army reforms (14 July 1904); he advocated the encouragement of small holdings, better security for the farmer, and the provision of cottages (26 Oct.); he urged the payment of members and of election expenses (17 Nov.), and in a speech at Dunfermline (8 Dec.) he discussed comprehensively education, licensing, housing, rating, and the poor law. On two questions he pronounced himself with growing precision and emphasis inside and outside the house, viz. the extravagance of the government and the need of retrenchment in public expenditure, and the curbing of the veto of the House of Lords. He still adhered to 'the policy of thorough and fundamental alteration in the whole system of Irish government'; he was there treading on slippery ground, even on the eve of victory. Differences in the unionist cabinet over Irish administration had given new life to the home rule controversy (March 1905), and the uncompromising restatement by Campbell-Bannerman of his views seemed to threaten a renewal of the old liberal schism. On 23 Nov. 1905 he made at Stirling a plain declaration in favour of home rule. Two days later, on 25 Nov., Lord Rosebery, at Bodmin, said he would not fight under that banner. On 27 Nov. Sir Edward Grey, at Newcastle-under-Lyme, expressed the view that if a liberal majority were obtained at the next general election it would be obtained on other issues than home rule, and it would not be fair to use the votes to reverse the anti-home rule verdict of 1895. This view was assented to by two other prominent liberal leaders, by Mr. Asquith on 28 Nov. and on 30 Nov. by Mr. James Bryce. An accommodation was reached on these lines. For the sake of the unity of the party, Campbell-Bannerman tacitly accepted the understanding that the consideration of home rule was postponed for the present. The proper solution of the Irish question was, Campbell-Bannerman finally declared (12 Jan. 1906), to refer purely Irish affairs to an Irish parliament; but he did not believe there would be any opportunity for such a scheme in the near future.

On Monday, 4 Dec. 1905, Mr. Balfour resigned, and on the following day Campbell-Bannerman was invited to form a government. Lord Kimberley had died in 1902, Harcourt on 1 Oct. 1904. Lord Spencer, Kimberley's successor as leader of the liberal party in the House of Lords, had been generally designated as the next liberal prime minister, but he had fallen seriously ill on 13 Oct. 1905. Campbell-Bannerman's claim as leader of the party in the House of Commons was therefore unquestioned. He brought to the great office imperturbable good temper, a strong sense of humour, personal popularity, much administrative experience and earnest convictions of the advanced liberal stamp. Campbell-Bannerman formed a ministry which was representative of all sections of the party. Mr. Asquith became chancellor of the exchequer and Mr. John Burns was chosen to be president of the local government board, being the first labour member of parliament to receive cabinet rank. In accordance with the rule observed by the liberal government of 1892–5, but discarded by Lord Salisbury and his successor, Mr. Balfour, Campbell-Bannerman made acceptance of office by those invited to join the government conditional on the resignation of all public directorships held by them. Mr. Balfour had already arranged that any new prime minister should be accorded by royal warrant a high place of precedency in ceremonial functions. Hitherto the office had not been formally recognised in the official table of precedency. Accordingly Campbell-Bannerman was the first prime minister to receive this formal recognition, and he was admitted to the fourth place among the king's subjects, the archbishops of Canterbury and York and the lord chancellor alone preceding him.

The new government at once dissolved parliament, and the general election followed in January 1906. Campbell-Bannerman's seat was not contested, owing to his opponent's illness, and he was free to speak elsewhere during the campaign. The main issues which he placed before the electors were free trade and the stopping of Chinese labour, which he had already promised in a speech at the Albert Hall on 21 Dec. 1905. He also undertook to revise drastically the Education and Licensing Acts of the late government. The result of the general election was startling. The unionists suffered a net loss of 214 seats—213 to the liberal and labour parties, and one to the nationalists. Wales did not return a single unionist. Scotland only returned twelve, out of a total of seventy-two members. London (including north and south West Ham and London University—sixty-two seats in all) returned twenty unionists, as compared with fifty-four in 1900. The rout of unionism was complete.

The liberals numbered 377, the labour members 53, and the nationalists 83, while the conservatives were only 132 and the liberal unionists 25. Independently of the Irish party the liberal and labour parties had a majority of 273 over the unionists. Not since the election of 1832, after the first reform bill, when the liberals numbered 486 against 172 conservatives, were the liberals in so strong a position. The first king's speech of Campbell-Bannerman's administration (19 Feb.) promised legislation on most of the lines to which the recent declarations of himself and his colleagues committed them. They pledged themselves at once to a policy of retrenchment and to a new education bill for England and Wales. Without directly raising the home rule issue, they announced undefined plans for associating the people of Ireland with the conduct of Irish affairs. Throughout the session Campbell-Bannerman took an active part in debate. At the outset the procedure of the House of Commons was revised with a view to economising the time of the house, and a Scottish grand committee was set up to deal with Scottish business (9 April). In South African affairs Campbell-Bannerman showed special resolution. While bringing Chinese labour to an end, he boldly insisted on establishing without delay full responsible government in the newly conquered Transvaal and Orange Free State colonies and on revoking the plan of the late government for giving a preliminary trial to a very modified scheme of representative government. The opposition declared this step unduly venturesome, but Campbell-Bannerman carried with him his colleagues and his party. After a committee had gone out to South Africa and had reported on the electoral basis of the constitution to be granted to the two new colonies, he announced the main provisions of the new responsible constitution on 31 July. The three domestic measures which mainly occupied the time of parliament were the education bill for the public control of all public money spent on education and for the abolition of religious tests for teachers, the trades disputes bill for extending the rights of trades unions in trades disputes, and the plural voting bill for disallowing more votes than one to any voter. The discussion of these bills was prolonged through an autumn session. All passed the House of Commons by great majorities, although the trades disputes bill excited misgivings among some supporters who thought the prime minister making unwise concessions to his labour allies. 'C.-B. seems,' wrote the duke of Devonshire, 'prepared to go any lengths.' In the House of Lords all three bills were strongly opposed. The trades disputes bill was freely amended by the lords, but somewhat ironically they abstained from insisting on their amendments, and the bill became law. The plural voting bill was summarily rejected. Much negotiation took place over the lords' amendments to the education bill, but no compromise was reached, and the bill was dropped on the final adherence of the lords to their demand that in all non-provided schools denominational teaching should continue independently of the local authority. In the House of Lords the duke of Devonshire and the bishop of Hereford supported the government. Campbell-Bannerman on 20 Dec. laid the blame for the failure of the bill on Mr. Balfour, and argued that the lords' amendments would perpetuate and extend the very system which the bill was designed to abrogate.

But the action of the lords raised far larger issues than details of the education question. Campbell-Bannerman at the same time as he announced the withdrawal of the education bill charged the upper house with neutralising and thwarting and distorting 'the policy which the electors have shown they approve.' He warned the lords that the resources neither of the British constitution nor of the House of Commons were exhausted, and 'that a way must be found, by which the will of the people, expressed through their elected representatives in this house, will be made to prevail.'

In matters of foreign policy Campbell-Bannerman devoted his efforts to advocating arbitration for the settlement of international disputes, to urging the policy of limiting armaments by negotiation with rival powers, and to encouraging liberal sentiment in foreign countries. On 23 July 1906 there assembled in London the fourteenth inter-parliamentary conference, which was attended by members of the Russian duma, the newly instituted Russian parliament. Before the opening of the conference the duma was dissolved by the Tsar. Campbell-Bannerman, who was present to welcome the conference, referred to the incident in the memorable words 'La duma est morte: vive la duma!' Speaking in the house (5 March 1906), he favoured the two-power naval standard, with the qualification that close alliances with the greatest naval powers might make its maintenance needless. His hopes of reducing armaments were not realised.

In the vacation of 1906 Lady Campbell-Bannerman died at Marienbad, and although the prime-minister's political energy seemed unimpaired during the following autumn session and at the opening of the new session, he never recovered the blow. The anxiety in which her ill-health had long involved him had intensified the strain of public life. But his sense of public duty was high. When parliament met on 12 Feb. 1907, he repeated his determination to bring the conflict with the lords to a decisive end. The king's speech contained the sentence: 'Serious differences affecting the working of our parliamentary system have arisen from unfortunate differences between the two houses. My ministers have this important subject under consideration with a view to a solution of the difficulty.' A final handling of the problem was, however, postponed. The government prepared to devote their strength to Ireland—to 'measures for further associating the people of Ireland with the management of their domestic affairs.' These words were identical with those used in the former king's speech. The government's hope was to conciliate by a moderate policy those of their party who distrusted a thorough-going policy of home rule. The effort failed. A plan of creating a series of Irish councils was rejected by the Irish members, and was consequently dropped. The prime minister pointed with greater pride to a reduction of nearly 2,000,000*l.* on the navy estimates (5 March). On the eve of the Hague peace conference of May 1907 he contributed to the 'Nation' newspaper an article entitled 'The Hague Conference and the Limitation of Armaments' (*Nation,* 7 March 1907), in which he urged his favourite plea. But the pronouncement excited mistrust in Germany, and on 30 May the German chancellor, Prinz von Bülow, announced that Germany would refuse to discuss at the conference the arrest of armaments.

The session of 1907 bore fruit in Mr. Haldane's army scheme, the Criminal Appeal Act, the Deceased Wife's Sister's Marriage Act, and the Small Holdings Act for England and Wales. Two government bills adopted by the commons, the land values (Scotland) bill and the small landholders (Scotland) bill, were rejected by the lords in August. Meanwhile, Campbell-Bannerman, after three days' debate, carried by 434 to 149 the motion 'That in order to give effect to the will of the people as expressed by their elected representatives, it is necessary that the power of the other house to alter or reject bills passed by this house should be so restricted by law as to secure that within the limits of a single parliament the final decision of the commons shall prevail' (26 June).

There was no autumn session, but Campbell-Bannerman was not free from public business. Speaking in Edinburgh (5 Oct.) he said that the dominant political fact of the day was that the government, though powerful in the House of Commons and in the country, lived on sufferance; and he recapitulated the serious grievances of the commons against the lords. In November the German emperor and empress paid a state visit to King Edward VII, which required Campbell-Bannerman's constant attendance. He left Windsor early on 13 Nov. for a luncheon at the Guildhall in honour of their imperial majesties, and the same evening spoke at the Colston banquet at Bristol. An attack of heart failure took place in the night. Recovery seemed rapid. He presided at several meetings of the cabinet before the end of the month; but acting on medical advice, he spent the next eight weeks at Biarritz (27 Nov. 1907 to 20 Jan. 1908).

On his return journey Campbell-Bannerman stayed a few days in Paris, and had interviews with the prime minister, M. Clemenceau, and M. Pichon, the French foreign minister. He was not in his place in parliament when the session opened on 29 Jan. In the king's speech an announcement of the re-introduction of the two Scottish bills rejected by the House of Lords was the only reminder of the constitutional struggle with the lords. A promise of old age pensions and of an Irish universities bill was the most important item in the government's programme. Campbell-Bannerman came to the house on 4 Feb. to move in vigorous language an address to the king on the assassination of King Carlos and the duke of Braganza, and to express sympathy with the royal family of Portugal. On 12 Feb. he moved the 'guillotine,' or an 'allocation of time' motion, providing for the rapid passage through the House of Commons of the two Scottish bills. He did not reappear in parliament. He had become 'father of the House of Commons' on 22 May 1907, when George Henry Finch, M.P. for Rutland (since 1867), died. He had sat nearly forty years continuously for the Stirling Burghs when his parliamentary career ended.

Campbell-Bannerman stayed at home on 13 and 14 Feb. on grounds of fatigue. On 15 Feb. a sharp attack of influenza supervened, and he never recovered his strength. On 4 March King Edward VII, whose relations with him during his period of office had been very cordial, called to see him before leaving for Biarritz and saw him alone for some time. On 4 April he resigned his office, and was succeeded by Mr. Asquith. He died of heart failure at 9.15 a.m. on 22 April at his official residence, 10 Downing Street. By his own desire he was buried at Meigle, by the side of his wife (28 April), the first part of the service taking place on 27 April in Westminster Abbey. On the same day the House of Commons re-assembled after the Easter vacation, and it adjourned out of respect for him, after impressive tributes had been paid to his memory. Mr. Asquith, his successor, called attention to his modest estimate of himself, to his sensitiveness to human suffering and wrong-doing, to his contempt for victories won in any sphere by mere brute force, and to his almost passionate love of peace, combined with personal courage—'not of a defiant and aggressive type, but calm, patient, persistent, indomitable.' 'He was,' Mr. Asquith continued, 'the least cynical of mankind, but no one had a keener eye for the humours and ironies of the political situation. He was a strenuous and uncompromising fighter, a strong party man, but he harboured no resentment. He met both good and evil fortune with the same unclouded brow, the same unruffled temper, the same unshakable confidence in the justice and righteousness of his cause.'

Campbell-Bannerman's career as leader lasted rather more than nine years. At the outset his opportunity, unsought by himself, was due to the withdrawal of senior and more prominent colleagues. He was twice unanimously elected leader.

For seven years in opposition he led his party fearlessly and cheerfully through its darkest days; restoring confidence by his sagacity and determination; turning to good account the errors of his opponents; developing a frankly progressive programme; and finally undertaking without hesitation to form a government in which he successfully combined all the elements of strength in his party. When the time came, his original selection as leader as well as his authority as prime minister were emphatically ratified at the polls by the liberal victory of 1906, which Gladstone's greatest triumphs never approached. The new House of Commons revealed his strong personal popularity with his party; and though his term of office as prime minister ended in little more than two years, it will be memorable for the grant of self-government to South Africa and for his House of Lords policy subsequently embodied in the Parliament Act of 1911.

A man of ample means and many social interests, a good linguist and a born raconteur, he found his chief recreation in European travel, in his books, and in entertaining his friends. It was his habit for many years to spend a portion of the autumn recess at Marienbad for his wife's health. He was not an orator. But as a widely read scholar he was scrupulous and even fastidious in the choice of language, and his speeches, which he carefully prepared, were admirable in form. As a rule he spoke from copious notes. Though this somewhat marred his delivery, he was effective and ready in debate, and a strong and successful platform speaker. His shrewd wit, which was always good humoured, his courage, and sincerity never failed. He was a warm supporter of women's suffrage.

In 1880 he purchased Belmont Castle, near Meigle, which had been the abode of James Steuart Mackenzie, and known as Kirkhill where the bishop of Dunkeld occasionally resided. Campbell-Bannerman thoroughly restored the house, which had been greatly injured by fire while in possession of Lord Wharncliffe, of whom Campbell-Bannerman bought it. In 1907 he was made both hon. D.C.L. of Oxford and hon. LL.D. of Cambridge. He was known familiarly both inside and outside the House of Commons as 'C.-B.'

In 1860 he married Sarah Charlotte, daughter of Major-general Sir Charles Bruce, K.C.B. Lady Campbell-Bannerman died at Marienbad on 30 Aug. 1906, without issue. She was a woman of great spirit and of fine feeling and discernment, was the constant companion of her husband, and shared all his interests. For many years before her death her health was indifferent, and she lived much in retirement. Campbell-Bannerman's heir was James Hugh

Campbell (*b.* 1889), grandson of his elder brother.

There are portraits of Campbell-Bannerman in the National Liberal Club, by Mr. John Colin Forbes; in the Reform Club, by Mr. J. H. F. Bacon, A.R.A.; and in the National Portrait Gallery, Edinburgh, by Sir James Guthrie, P.R.S.A.; all were painted while he was prime minister.

A monument to him was voted by parliament. It was placed in Westminster Abbey in 1912; the design includes a bust by Mr. Paul Raphael Montford, who has since been commissioned to execute a full-length statue, to be erected at Stirling.

[Private information; personal knowledge; The Times, 23 April 1908; Lucy's Diaries of Parliament; Holland's Duke of Devonshire, 1911; Hansard's Debates.] P.

CANNING, Sir SAMUEL (1823–1908), a pioneer of submarine telegraphy, born at Ogbourne St. Andrew, Wiltshire, on 21 July 1823, was son of Robert Canning of that place by his wife Frances Hyde. Educated at Salisbury, he gained his first engineering experience (1844–9) as assistant to Messrs. Locke & Errington on the Great Western railway extensions, and as resident engineer on the Liverpool, Ormskirk and Preston railway. From railway work he turned in 1852 to submarine telegraphy, and entering the service of Messrs. Glass & Elliot, laid in 1855–6 his first cable—that connecting Cape Breton Island with Newfoundland.

In 1857 he assisted (Sir) Charles Bright [q.v. Suppl. I] in the construction and laying of the first Atlantic cable, and he was on board H.M.S. Agamemnon during the submergence of the cable in 1857 and 1858. Subsequently until 1865 he laid, while in the service of Messrs Glass, Elliot & Company, cables in the deep waters of the Mediterranean and other seas.

When the Telegraph Construction and Maintenance Company was formed in 1865, Canning was appointed its chief engineer, and in that capacity had charge of the manufacture and laying of the Atlantic cables of 1865 and 1866, for which the company were the contractors. This work involved the preparation and fitting-out of the Great Eastern. On 2 Aug. 1865 the cable broke in 2000 fathoms of water. After a second cable had been successfully laid by the Great Eastern (13–27 July 1866) Canning set to work to recover the broken cable, using special grappling machinery, which he devised for the purpose. After several failures the cable was eventually recovered on 2 Sept. 1866. For these services he was knighted in 1866; the King of Portugal conferred upon him the Order of St. Jago d'Espada, and the Liverpool chamber of commerce presented him with a gold medal. In 1869 he laid the French Atlantic cable between Brest and Duxbury, Massachusetts.

After his retirement from the service of the Telegraph Construction Company, he practised as a consulting engineer in matters connected with telegraphy, and, among other work, superintended the laying of the Marseilles-Algiers and other cables for the India Rubber, Gutta Percha and Telegraph Works Company, acting later as adviser to the West Indian and Panama and other telegraph companies. He was a member both of the Institution of Civil Engineers (from 1 Feb. 1876) and of that of Electrical Engineers. He died at 1 Inverness Gardens, Kensington, on 24 Sept. 1908, and was buried in Kensal Green cemetery. He married in 1859 Elizabeth Anne (*d.* 1909), daughter of W. H. Gale of Grately, Hampshire, by whom he had three sons and three daughters.

His portrait in oils, by Miss B. Bright, is in the possession of his only surviving daughter, Mrs. Morris.

[The Times, 26 Sept. 1908; Minutes of Proc. Inst. Civ. Eng. clxxv. 316; C. Bright, Submarine Telegraphs, 1898; private information.] W. F. S.

CAPEL, THOMAS JOHN (1836–1911), Roman catholic prelate, born at Ardmore, county Waterford, on 28 Oct. 1836, was eldest son and second child in a family of two sons and four daughters of John Capel by his wife Mary Fitzgerald, daughter of an Irish farmer. Both parents were rigid catholics and cultivated exclusively a catholic circle of friends. The father after some years in the royal navy joined the coastguard service, and was long stationed at Hastings. There the son Thomas was educated by a priest on duty in the town, who noticed his promise. At the priest's suggestion the boy passed into the charge of Father John Melville Glenie, who conducted a school for catholics at Hammersmith. There Capel took part in 1854 in the foundation of St. Mary's Normal College, Hammersmith, of which in 1856 he was made vice-principal. In 1860 he was ordained by Cardinal Wiseman, but owing to delicate health he went in the same year to reside at Pau, in the south of France. There he established a mission for English-speaking catholics, of which he became chaplain, and he formed friendly relations with many English visitors. He lectured with effect on Bishop Colenso's works, and acquired a high reputation as a preacher, while he proved very successful in making converts of his protestant fellow-countrymen and fellow-countrywomen. In 1868 he returned to England, and soon achieved his greatest success in proselytism by receiving into the catholic church on 8 Dec. 1868, at the chapel of the Sisters of Notre Dame, Southwark, John Patrick Crichton-Stuart, third marquis of Bute [q. v.]. In 1868 Capel was named private chamberlain to Pope Pius IX, with the title of monsignor, and in 1873 became domestic prelate. In Disraeli's 'Lothair' (1870), of which the hero is a portrait of Lord Bute, Capel figures as 'Monsignor Catesby,' and once, by mistake, under his own name. Disraeli emphasises Capel's winning manners and his knowledge alike of the ways of the world and the works of the casuists. Capel acted for some years as the marquis of Bute's chaplain, and with him visited the Holy Land. Meanwhile Capel, who was attached to the pro-cathedral, Kensington, was a prominent figure in London society, and a popular preacher. He also paid several visits to Rome, where, by Pope Pius's express wish, he lectured to English and American visitors.

In February 1873 Capel founded the catholic public school at Kensington. In 1874 he was elected by the unanimous vote of the catholic bishops, rector of another newly formed institution, the College of Higher Studies, also at Kensington. Intended to be the nucleus of a Roman catholic university, the college became heavily involved in debt; and in 1878 the bishops requested Capel to resign (cf. PURCELL, *Life of Cardinal Manning*, ii. 503). He claimed and received compensation for money spent by him on the college. Shortly afterwards his school also became bankrupt for 28,000*l*. On the ground of general mismanagement of his scholastic offices, he was suspended in 1882 by Cardinal Manning from his office of priest in the diocese of Westminster, but on appeal to Rome, the charges preferred against him were found to be not proven. Even so Cardinal Manning was opposed to Capel again working in London, and after lecturing at Florence by the wish of Leo XIII on the doctrines of the Roman catholic church, he migrated in 1883 to the United States, furnished by the Pope with commendatory letters to the bishops of that country. He resumed work there, preaching and lecturing in the more important cities. He finally settled in California, at first as tutor at Arno in the McAulay Valensin family, and ultimately becoming the prelate in charge of the Roman catholic church for the district of northern California. Long the guest of Thomas Grace, bishop of Sacramento, he died suddenly of heart failure at the bishop's residence on 23 Oct. 1911. A cartoon of Capel appeared in 'Vanity Fair' in 1872.

A keen controversialist, Capel wrote many religious pamphlets, including: 1. 'A Reply to Gladstone's "Vaticanism,"' 1874 (3rd ed. 1875), which attracted notice. 2. 'Ought the Queen of England to hold Diplomatic Relations with the Pope?' 1882. 3. 'Catholic: an Essential Attribute of the True Church,' New York, 1884. 4. 'The Pope the Vicar of Christ,' San Francisco, 1885.

[The Times, 25 Oct. 1911; Tablet, 28 Oct. 1911; Galaxy, vol. x. (with portrait); Men of Mark, 1876 (with portrait); Pratt, People of the Period, 1897; Men and Women of the Time, 1899; New Internat. Encyclop. 1910; E. S. Purcell, Life of Cardinal Manning, 1895; private information.]

S. E. F.

CARDEW, PHILIP (1851–1910), major R.E., born at Oakshade, near Leatherhead, Surrey, on 24 Sept. 1851, was eldest son in a family of four sons and four daughters of Captain Christopher Baldock Cardew, 74th highlanders, of East Hill, Liss (son of Lieut.-general George Cardew, colonel commandant royal engineers), by his wife Eliza Jane, second daughter of Sir Richard Bethell, first Baron Westbury [q. v.]. Educated at Guildford grammar-school, he passed first into the Royal Military Academy, Woolwich, in 1868, and left it at the head of his batch. He was awarded the Pollock medal and the sword of honour, and received a commission as lieutenant in the royal engineers on 4 Jan. 1871. After two years at Chatham, Cardew was sent to Aldershot and Portsmouth; from September 1873 to April 1874 he was employed at the war office on defences; and, after a year at Glasgow, went to Bermuda in May 1875. He was placed in charge of military telegraphs, and joined the submarine mining service, engaging in the application of electricity to military purposes, which was to be the pursuit of his life. At the end of 1876 he was transferred to Chatham, where the headquarters of the submarine mining was on board

H.M.S. Hood, which lay in the Medway off Gillingham. In 1878 he was acting adjutant of the submarine miners at Portsmouth, and became in the same year (1 April) assistant instructor in electricity at Chatham.

In addition to his work of instruction Cardew assisted in carrying out some important experiments with electric search-light apparatus for the royal engineers committee, at a time when the subject was in its infancy. The need of better instruments for such work led him to design a galvanometer for measuring large currents of electricity (cf. description in paper, read before Institution of Electrical Engineers, 25 May 1882). He next evolved the idea of the hot-wire galvanometer, or voltmeter, the value of which was universally recognised among electricians. He was awarded the gold medal for this invention at the Inventions Exhibition in London of 1885. He also originated a method of finding the efficiency of a dynamo.

Cardew's invention of the vibratory transmitter for telegraphy was perhaps his most important discovery, and in the case of faulty lines proved most useful, not only on active service in the Nile expedition and in India, but also during heavy snowstorms at home. Cardew received a money reward for this invention, half from the imperial and half from the Indian government. The utility of the invention was much extended by Cardew's further invention of 'separators,' consisting of a combination of 'choking coil' and two condensers. These instruments enable a vibrating telegraph circuit to be superimposed on an ordinary Morse circuit without interference between the two, thus doubling the message-carrying capability of the line. His apparatus for testing lightning conductors was adopted by the war department for service.

Promoted captain on 4 Jan. 1883, and major on 12 April 1889, Cardew was from 1 April 1882 instructor in electricity at Chatham. On 1 April 1889 he was appointed the first electrical adviser to the board of trade. He held a long inquiry into the various proposals for the electric lighting of London, and drew up valuable regulations concerning the supply of electricity for power and for light. Cardew retired from the royal engineers on 24 Oct. 1894, and from the board of trade in 1898. He then entered into partnership with Sir William Preece & Sons, consulting engineers, and was actively engaged on large admiralty orders, involving an expenditure of 1,500,000*l.* He joined the board of the London, Brighton and South Coast railway in 1902. Cardew paid two visits to Sydney, New South Wales, in connection with the city's electrical installations. Soon after his return home from the second visit in 1909, by way of Japan and Siberia, he died on 17 May 1910 at his residence, Crownpits House, Godalming.

In 1881 Cardew wrote a paper on 'The application of dynamo electric machines to railway rolling stock'; in 1894 he contributed a paper to the Royal Society on 'Uni-directional currents to earth from alternate current systems'; and in 1901 he delivered the Cantor lecture before the Society of Arts on 'Electric railways.' He contributed several papers to the Institution of Electrical Engineers, on whose council he served for many years, and was vice-president in 1901–2.

Cardew married in London, on 19 June 1879, his first cousin, Mary Annunziata, daughter of Mansfield Parkyns [q. v.], the Abyssinian traveller. She survived him with three sons and two daughters.

[War Office Records; R. E. Records; Memoirs in Royal Engineers Journal, 1910, by Major L. Darwin and others; Porter, History of the Corps of Royal Engineers, 1889, 2 vols.; Brown, History of Submarine Mining in the British Army, 1910.]

R. H. V.

CAREY, ROSA NOUCHETTE (1840–1909), novelist, eighth child and fourth daughter of William Henry Carey, ship-broker, by his wife Maria Jane, daughter of Edward J. Wooddill, was born at Stratford-le-Bow, London, on 24 Sept. 1840. Her childhood was spent at Hackney. She was educated first at home and later at the Ladies' Institute, St. John's Wood, where Mathilde Blind was a school-fellow. The friendship then formed was interrupted later by the divergence of their religious opinions. As a child she wrote little plays for her brothers and sisters to act, and invented stories for their amusement. Her first novel, 'Nellie's Memories,' told verbally in this way when in her teens, was published in 1868, and was immediately successful. Henceforward her career as a writer was assured. More than 52,000 copies of this book have been sold. Between 1868 and the year of her death Miss Carey published thirty-nine novels. The large sales, varying between 41,000 and 14,000 copies, testify to their popularity. Those which enjoyed the widest vogue were 'Wee Wifie' (1869); 'Wooed and Married' (1875); 'Not like other Girls' (1884); 'Uncle Max' (1887) and 'Only the Governess' (1888). Her last novel, 'The Sunny Side of the Hill,' appeared in 1908. Besides novels Miss Carey wrote short stories, many of which were issued by the Religious Tract Society, and a volume of brief biographies, 'Twelve Notable Good Women of the Nineteenth Century' (1899). Miss Carey held orthodox and conservative views of life, and like that of Charlotte Mary Yonge [q. v. Suppl. II] and Elizabeth Missing Sewell [q. v. Suppl. II] her fiction favoured high church principles. Her plots closely resemble one another, and her style lacks distinction. But her sentiment was well adapted to girls, who were her most numerous and appreciative readers. She mainly depicts women of a generation whose education and sphere of action were restricted by a convention which no longer prevails.

Miss Carey led a retired life, but formed many close and enduring friendships. Her most intimate friends were Mrs. Henry Wood [q. v.], her son, Charles Wood, and Miss H. M. Burnside. She resided for about thirty-nine years at Hampstead, and then for about twenty years at Putney, where she died on 19 July 1909, at Sandilands, Keswick Road. She was buried in the West Hampstead cemetery.

[The Times, 20 July 1909; Helen C. Black, Notable Women Authors of the Day, 1893; Pratt, People of the Period, 1897; private information.] E. L.

CARLISLE, ninth Earl of. [See Howard, George James (1843–1911).]

CARNEGIE, JAMES, sixth de facto and ninth de jure Earl of Southesk (1827–1905), poet and antiquary, born at Edinburgh on 16 Nov. 1827, was eldest son in a family of three sons and two daughters of Sir James Carnegie, fifth baronet of Pittarow, by his wife Charlotte, daughter of Daniel Lysons [q. v.] of Hempstead Court, Gloucester. The father, who was fifth in descent from Alexander, fourth son of David Carnegie, first earl of Southesk, laid claim without success to the family earldom which had been forfeited in 1715 on the attainder of James Carnegie, fifth earl, for his share in the Jacobite rebellion of that year.

Educated at Edinburgh Academy and Sandhurst, young Carnegie obtained a commission in the Gordon highlanders in 1845, was transferred in 1846 to the grenadier guards, and retired on succeeding his father as sixth baronet in 1849. A man of cultivated taste, he practically rebuilt the family residence, Kinnaird Castle, Brechin, in 1854, and collected there with much zest antique gems, mainly intaglios (from 1879), pictures by the old masters, books, and some hundred and fifty cylinders—Assyrian, Hittite, Babylonian, Persian, and Accadian. But he disposed of much of the extensive family property elsewhere, selling his estate of Glendye to Sir Thomas Gladstone, baronet. Renewing his father's claim to the earldom of Southesk in 1855, he obtained on 2 July an Act of Parliament reversing the attainder of 1715, and was confirmed in the title by the House of Lords on 24 July. In 1869, on Gladstone's recommendation, he was made a knight of the thistle, and on 7 Dec. of the same year a peer of the United Kingdom, with the title Baron Balinhard of Farnell.

In 1859 Southesk undertook in search of health a prolonged hunting expedition in Western Canada. He traversed some of the wildest and least known parts of the Rockies about the sources of the rivers Athabasca and Saskatchewan. He returned home in 1860, and was made a fellow of the Geographical Society. After a long interval he published 'Saskatchewan and the Rocky Mountains' (1875), a spirited account of his experiences in diary form. Meanwhile he had engaged in other forms of literature. 'Herminius, a romance' (1862), was followed by an essay on art criticism, 'Britain's Art Paradise: or Notes on some of the Pictures of the Royal Academy of 1871' (1871). In 1875 he published anonymously his first poetical work, 'Jonas Fisher: a Poem in Brown and White,' a rather crude effort at satire on current extravagances in art, poetry of the Rossetti type, and emotional religion. On its publication the book was assigned in a hostile review in the 'Examiner' to Robert Buchanan [q. v. Suppl. II]. Buchanan deemed this erroneous attribution one of the grounds for a successful action of libel against Peter A. Taylor, the proprietor of the 'Examiner.' Other verse from Southesk's pen often presented scenes of adventure in vigorous and simple metre; it included 'Lurida Lumina' (1876), 'Greenwood's Farewell and other Poems' (1876), 'The Meda Maiden and other Poems' (1877) (inspired by Longfellow's 'Hiawatha'), and 'The Burial of Isis and other Poems' (1884). 'Suomira, a fantasy,' privately printed in 1893, was a curious experiment in metre printed as prose.

Southesk devoted his later years to recondite antiquarian research, which he pursued with thoroughness and judgment. A prominent member of the Society of

Antiquaries of Scotland, he read before the society papers on 'The Newton Stone' (1884) and 'The Ogham Inscriptions of Scotland' (1885), while in 1893 he discussed 'The Origin of Pictish Symbolism.' The papers were published separately. He was made hon. LL.D. of St. Andrews in 1872, and of Aberdeen University in 1875. He died at Kinnaird Castle on 21 Feb. 1905.

Southesk married (1), on 19 June 1849, Lady Catharine Hamilton (*d.* 1855), third daughter of Charles Noel, first earl of Gainsborough, by whom he had one son, Charles Noel, who succeeded as tenth earl of Southesk, and three daughters; (2) on 29 Nov. 1860, Lady Susan Catharine Mary Murray, daughter of Alexander Edward, sixth earl of Dunmore, by whom he had three sons and four daughters. The youngest son, David Winford (1871–1900), distinguished himself as a traveller in Australia and Nigeria.

There are at Kinnaird Castle portraits in oils by Sir John Watson-Gordon [q. v.] (1861) and by Miss A. Dove Wilson (1899), and a chalk drawing (1861) by James Rannie Swinton [q. v.].

[The Times, 22 Feb. 1905; Athenæum, 18 March 1905, by (Sir) John Rhys; Who's Who, 1905; Burke's Peerage; Paul's Scots Peerage, 1910.] S. E. F.

CARPENTER, GEORGE ALFRED (1859–1910), physician, born at Lambeth, Surrey, on 25 Dec. 1859, was son of John William Carpenter, M.D. (*d.* 1903), by his wife Mary, daughter of George Butler, of New Shoreham, Sussex, of Kilkenny descent. His father was son of John William Carpenter, surgeon, of Rothwell, Northamptonshire, and was brother of Dr. Alfred Carpenter [q. v.] of Croydon.

George received his early education at King's College School and at Epsom College, and pursued medical study at St. Thomas's Hospital and at Guy's Hospital. At St. Thomas's Hospital he won the third college prize for 1880–1, and the first college prize for 1881. As second year's student he gained the third college prize and the prosector's prize. He was prosector to the Royal College of Surgeons, and in 1885 became M.R.C.S. and L.S.A. In 1886 he graduated M.B. and in 1890 M.D. at London, having become M.R.C.P., London, in 1889.

He at first engaged in lunacy work, and after holding a residential appointment at The Coppice, Nottingham, a private asylum, he returned to London in 1885, and began a close study of children's diseases, to which his professional energies were afterwards almost entirely devoted. Having served as house surgeon, registrar and chloroformist, he was elected physician to the Evelina Hospital, Southwark, and at the time of his death he was physician to the Queen's Hospital for Children, Hackney. He died suddenly at Coldharbour, Waddon, Surrey, on 27 March 1910, and was buried in Old Sanderstead churchyard. He married on 21 April 1908 Hélène Jeanne, daughter of Henry, Baron d'Este.

Carpenter's work in connection with diseases of children was voluminous and valuable. In 1896 he acted as English editor to an Anglo-American journal entitled 'Pediatrics,' which soon succumbed so far as the English edition was concerned. But in 1904 he founded, and edited with conspicuous ability until he died, the 'British Journal of Children's Diseases.'

In 1900 he took an active part with Dr. A. Ernest Sansom, Dr. Henry Ashby [q. v. Suppl. II], and others in founding the 'Society for the Study of Disease in Children,' the first of its kind in this, though not in other countries. The society was a success from the first, and Carpenter's interest in its welfare never flagged. He acted as one of its secretaries for three years, as editor of its 'Transactions' for eight years, and when the society was incorporated in the Royal Society of Medicine in 1908, and became the section for the study of disease in children, he was elected its president. The eight volumes of 'Reports' of the original society which he edited are admirably compiled and illustrate the current progress in the study of children's diseases. He contributed many papers to various medical journals in this country and in France; he was a Membre Correspondant de la Société de Pédiatrie de Paris, and also a member and contributor to La Société Française d'Ophtalmologie. His most noteworthy publications were on congenital malformations of the heart, which was also the subject of his Wightman lecture delivered in 1909 before the section for the study of disease in children, Royal Society of Medicine, and published in the 'British Journal of Children's Diseases,' Aug., Sept., Oct. 1909.

In 1901 he published an instructive and well-written book on 'The Syphilis of Children in Every-day Practice.' A small work, 'Golden Rules for Diseases of Infants and Children,' published in 1901, reached a fourth and revised edition in 1911.

Two portraits in oils, one by William Nicholson, are in the possession of his family.

[Lancet, 9 April 1910; Brit. Med. Journal, 9 April 1910; British Journal of Children's Diseases, April 1910.] L. G.

CARPENTER, ROBERT (1830–1901), cricketer, was born at Mill Road, Cambridge, on 18 Nov. 1830. His elder brother George (1818–1849), a butcher, played cricket for the Cambridge town club about 1839. Originally a bootcloser by trade, Robert early became a professional cricketer in a humble way, having engagements at Godmanchester (1854), at Ipswich (1855–7), at Birkenhead (1858), and at Marlborough College (1859–60). Subsequently at Cambridge, where he was known as the 'Old Gardener,' he was custodian of Parker's Piece, a position which he resigned on 9 Nov. 1881. Carpenter appeared late in first-class cricket, first taking part in it in June 1858, when he scored 45 for the United XI against the All England XI at Lord's. His performance brought him immediate fame. The following year he first appeared for the Players *v.* Gentlemen, and played for them in eighteen matches from 1859 to 1873; his chief scores were 119 in 1860 and 106 in 1861 at Kennington Oval. In the famous match between Surrey and England in 1862, when John Lillywhite no-balled Willsher for illegal bowling, Carpenter scored 94. Other noteworthy performances were 100 for Cambridgeshire *v.* Surrey at Kennington Oval in 1861 and 134 for the All England XI *v.* Yorkshire at Sheffield in July 1865. Carpenter's name is especially associated with that of Tom Hayward (1835–1876), also of Cambridgeshire. They were the two best batsmen in England for a few seasons from 1860, and with the bowler George Tarrant (1838–1870) raised Cambridgeshire for several seasons to a leading position among cricketing counties. They went together to America in 1859 with the English XI, and to Australia in George Parr's team in the winter of 1863–4. Through the greater part of his career Carpenter toured with the United XI throughout the country, playing against local teams of 18 or 22 players.

Carpenter, a strong man of medium height, batted in elegant style, standing up at the wicket 'to his full height in a commanding attitude like a man' (PYCROFT'S *Cricketana*, p. 237). He was the champion back player of the nineteenth century, a fine lofty square leg hitter, and a brilliant fieldsman at point.

He died on 13 July 1901 at his home in Cambridge. He was married. One of his sons, Harry Carpenter (*b.* 1869), is the Essex batsman.

[The Times, 15 July 1901; Wisden's Cricketers' Almanack, 1902, p. lix; Pycroft's Cricketana, 1865 (portrait with T. Hayward, p. 176); Daft's Kings of Cricket (portrait with T. Hayward, p. 69); Haygarth's Cricket Scores and Biographies, vi. 30; viii. 374; W. Caffyn's Seventy-one Not Out, 1899, pp. 123–41 *passim* (portrait with Diver and Hayward, p. 164); information from Mr. P. M. Thornton.] W. B. O.

CARTE, RICHARD D'OYLY (1844–1901), promoter of English opera, born on 3 May 1844 in Greek Street, Soho, was elder son, in a family of six children, of Richard Carte by his wife Eliza, daughter of the Rev. Thomas Jones of the Chapel Royal, Whitehall, who traced her descent to the D'Oyly family. The father, a well-known flautist, was a partner in the firm of Rudall, Carte & Co., of Berners Street, London, army musical instrument makers, and the founder of the 'Musical Directory.' Carte's grandfather, also Richard, served at Waterloo as quartermaster of the Blues. The Carte family, originally of Leicestershire, claimed Norman origin.

At the age of twelve Richard went to University College, where he remained for four years. Having matriculated at London University in 1861, he entered his father's business. In his leisure hours he studied music and composed with some success one-act operettas. Among these were 'Dr. Ambrosius—his Secret,' which was produced at St. George's Hall (Aug. 1868), and 'Marie,' which was produced at the Opéra Comique (Aug. 1871). Leaving his father's firm during 1870, he set up as a concert agent in Craig's Court. His first clients included Mario, whose farewell tour in 1870 he organised. The agency proved a permanent success, and later under its auspices Archibald Forbes, Oscar Wilde, Sir Henry Morton Stanley, and many others made popular lecture tours. Meanwhile, theatrical management absorbed most of Carte's energies. In 1875 he was manager for Selina Dolaro, who played 'La Périchole' at the Royalty Theatre. By way of successor D'Oyly Carte produced on 25 March 1875 'Trial by Jury,' a comic opera by (Sir) Arthur Sullivan [q. v. Suppl. I] and (Sir) William Schwenck Gilbert [q. v. Suppl. II]. Owing to the success of this piece Carte formed a small syndicate of music publishers and private capitalists to rent the Opéra Comique theatre for the presentation of other light operas by the same author and composer. 'The Sorcerer,' produced on 17 Nov. 1877, ran for one hundred and seventy-five nights, and 'H.M.S. Pinafore,' produced on 25 May 1878, for seven hundred nights. The syndicate was then dissolved, and D'Oyly Carte became the responsible manager of the venture, with Gilbert and Sullivan as partners. The triumph was well maintained by 'The Pirates of Penzance' (produced on 3 April 1880) and 'Patience' (produced on 23 April 1881). The profits of the triumvirate soon reached a total of 60,000*l*. a year.

Carte invested a portion of his gains in the erection of a more commodious theatre, which, being situated within the precincts of the Savoy, was called by that name. He also formed a company for the erection of an adjoining hotel to be designated similarly. The Savoy Theatre was the first public building in the world to be lighted by electricity, and D'Oyly Carte first applied in England the principle of the queue to the crowds awaiting admission to the pit and gallery (29 Dec. 1882).

The new theatre was opened on 10 Oct. 1881 with 'Patience,' which was transferred from the Opéra Comique, and succeeding pieces from the same author and composer were 'Iolanthe' (25 Nov. 1882), 'Princess Ida' (5 Jan. 1884), 'The Mikado' (14 March 1885), 'Ruddigore' (22 Jan. 1887), 'The Yeomen of the Guard' (3 Oct. 1888), and 'The Gondoliers' (7 Dec. 1889). A financial quarrel between Gilbert and himself interrupted the partnership, when 'The Gondoliers' was last performed on 20 June 1891. Other collaborations, 'The Nautch Girl,' by George Dance and Edward Solomon (produced on 30 June 1891), 'Haddon Hall,' by Sydney Grundy and Sullivan (24 Sept. 1892), and 'Jane Annie, or The Good Conduct Prize,' by J. M. Barrie, Conan Doyle, and Ernest Ford (13 May 1893), were only partially successful. But D'Oyly Carte, having made up his disagreement with Gilbert, produced on 7 Oct. 1893 the Gilbert and Sullivan new opera, 'Utopia, Limited.' 'Mirette,' by Carré and Messager (3 July 1894), and 'The Chieftain,' by Burnand and Sullivan (12 Dec. 1894), preceded 'The Grand Duke' (7 March 1896), which was the last work in which Gilbert and Sullivan collaborated. Subsequently Carte depended on revivals of earlier pieces or on fresh combinations in authorship. His latest productions were 'His Majesty,' by Burnand, Lehmann, and Mackenzie (20 Feb. 1897), a new version of Offenbach's 'The Grand Duchess' (4 Dec. 1897), 'The Beauty Stone,' by Pinero, Carr, and Sullivan (28 May 1898), 'The Lucky Star,' by C. H. E. Brookfield and Ivan Caryll (7 Jan. 1899), and 'The Rose of Persia,' by Basil Hood and Sullivan (29 Nov. 1899).

Carte's activity as a light-opera impresario extended to the United States. There he often had five touring companies performing the Gilbert and Sullivan operas. While at the Savoy, Carte, in partnership with John Hollingshead and Michael Gunn, also managed for several seasons leading theatres in Liverpool, Manchester, and elsewhere.

Carte's speculative energy was not exhausted by his work for light English opera. He sought to provide London with a theatre which should be devoted to grand English opera. Here his efforts failed. In the heart of London, at Cambridge Circus, Shaftesbury Avenue, he erected a magnificent Royal English Opera House, which he opened on 31 Jan. 1891 with 'Ivanhoe,' a grand opera by Sullivan with libretto by Julian Sturgis. The best singers were engaged, and the orchestra and mounting were both excellent. 'Ivanhoe' ran till 31 July 1891, a longer period than any previous grand opera, but it failed to yield a profit. An English version of Messager's 'La Basoche,' which followed after an interval in November, also proved unremunerative, and in Jan. 1892 the house was temporarily closed. Madame Sarah Bernhardt played Sardou's 'Cleopatra' there (28 May–23 July 1892). By that time D'Oyly Carte had reached the conclusion that his venture was impracticable. Had the repertory system been attempted, the result might have been different. Later in 1892 the theatre was sold to Sir Augustus Harris [q. v. Suppl. I] and a syndicate, and, under the new name of the Palace Theatre of Varieties, began a flourishing career as a music-hall on 10 Dec. 1892.

In the course of 1900 Carte's health failed. The death of Sullivan (Nov. 1900) proved a great blow. Carte died on 3 April 1901, and was buried at Fairlight church, Hastings. A cartoon of Carte by 'Spy' appeared in 'Vanity Fair' in 1891.

Carte deserves the main credit of rescuing the light opera stage in England from the slough of French opéra-bouffe, and of raising the standard of musical taste in the theatre. Carte also did excellent work by enlisting in his service cultured young singers whose status would not have allowed them to join an opéra-bouffe chorus. Many members of the Savoy chorus who began their artistic career under Carte's management became leading artists on the operatic stage. A keen man of business, D'Oyly Carte was a generous employer and a good friend.

D'Oyly Carte married twice. By his first wife, Blanche Prowse, daughter of a piano manufacturer, he had two sons, Lucas, a barrister (*d.* 1907), and Rupert, now chairman of the Savoy Hotel, Ltd. His second wife, Helen Couper-Black, daughter of the procurator-fiscal of Wigtownshire, matriculated at London University with high honours and was at one time D'Oyly Carte's secretary; she took an active part in the management of his ventures, and after his death revived the Gilbert and Sullivan operas, occasionally at the Savoy Theatre, and continuously in the provinces. She married in 1902 Mr. Stanley Carr Boulter, and died 5 May 1913.

[The Times, Daily Telegraph, and Daily News, 4 April 1901; Era, 6 April 1901; University Coll. and London Univ. Registers; Lawrence's Sir Arthur Sullivan, Life-Story, 1899; John Hollingshead's My Life Time, 1895; Grove's Dict. of Musicians; private information.] L. M.

CARTER, HUGH (1837–1903), painter, was born in Birmingham on 4 March 1837. His father, Samuel Carter, was solicitor to the London and North Western and Midland railway companies, and was at one time M.P. for Coventry. Coming to London, Carter studied for a short time at Heatherley's Art School, and afterwards with J. W. Bottomley, Alexander Johnson, Topham, and John Phillip. He also worked at Düsseldorf under K. F. von Gebhardt. From 1859 to 1902 Carter exhibited twenty-four pictures at the Royal Academy, mostly subject paintings of domestic interest, together with portraits of 'Alexander Blair, LL.D.' (1873 and 1898), 'Sir Joshua Staples, F.S.A.' (1887), and 'Mrs. Worsley Taylor' (1890). Two of his most successful exhibits were 'Music hath Charms' (1872) and 'Card Players' (1873), both representing scenes from Westphalian peasant life. His work was distinguished throughout by delicacy of colour and subtle expression of human character. Much of his best work was done in water-colour and pastel. In those mediums he painted a number of landscapes which displayed a fine sense of colour and atmospheric effect. As a water-colour painter he was a frequent exhibitor at the Royal Institute, of which he became an associate in 1871 and a member in 1875. He was also a member of the Institute of Oil Painters from its start in 1883, and latterly of the New English Art Club. At the Tate Gallery he is represented by an oil painting, 'The Last Ray' (1878); in the permanent collection at the Guildhall by 'Hard Times'; and at the Victoria and Albert Museum by two water-colours, 'Buildings and Gondolas at Venice' and 'Interior of the Capuchin Convent at Albano.' His portrait of his uncle, Sir Francis Ronalds [q. v.], the inventor of the first working electric telegraph, is in the National Portrait Gallery. Carter died on 27 Sept. 1903, and was buried at Kensal Green. A memorial exhibition of his works was held at Leighton House in October 1904.

On 7 July 1866 Carter married Maria, daughter of J. W. Bottomley, and had four daughters and two sons, one of whom, Mr. Frank W. Carter, is well known as an artist.

[Graves's Royal Acad. Exhibitors; Catalogue of the National Gallery of British Art; private information.] M. H.

CARTER, THOMAS THELLUSSON (1808–1901), tractarian divine, born at Eton on 19 March 1808, was the younger son of the Rev. Thomas Carter, then lower master and afterwards vice-provost of Eton, by Mary, daughter of Henry Proctor. He entered Eton when 'just six years old,' and spent twelve years of school life under his father's roof. He left Eton captain of the oppidans, matriculated at Christ Church, Oxford, on 8 Dec. 1825, and went into residence in 1827. E. B. Pusey, one of his father's pupils, who in 1828 became regius professor of Hebrew, was from the first 'kind' to him, though Carter 'was unconscious at that time of any such influence as afterwards so affected' him (*Life*, pp. 8, 9). He graduated with a first class in classics in 1831, sat unsuccessfully for an Oriel fellowship, and left Oxford before the tractarian movement had developed. In 1832 he was ordained deacon by the bishop of Salisbury and was licensed to St. Mary's, Reading, of which H. H. Milman, afterwards dean of St. Paul's, was vicar. He was ordained priest in 1833, and went to Burnham, Buckinghamshire, as curate for his father. There the 'Tracts for the Times' vitally influenced Carter, who 'in reading them . . . felt a sense of interest and earnestness in religious doctrines one had not known before' (*Life*, p. 14). In 1838 he became rector of Piddlehinton near Dorchester, and in 1844 rector of Clewer, near Windsor, a parish with which his family had associations.

Clewer found in Carter a zealous incumbent bent on social as well as ecclesiastical reform. He restored the services and the fabric of the church, steadily developing the ritual used and the doctrine taught. Though his zeal and personal charm won over most of the people, his ritual changes bred opposition, which in time produced appeals to the law. In March 1849, moved by the example of John Armstrong, bishop of Grahamstown, and by facts observed in his own parish, Carter founded the House of Mercy at Clewer for the rescue of fallen women. The work, conducted on clearly defined ecclesiastical lines, led to many extensions, directly or indirectly connected with Clewer, reaching even to India and the colonies. To meet the needs of the House of Mercy, he founded in 1852 a sisterhood, the Community of St. John the Baptist, Clewer. The movement was viewed by many with alarm, provoked controversy, and caused Samuel Wilberforce [q. v.], bishop of Oxford, much anxiety (*Life*, iii. 328). Owing to the nature of Carter's work, and his part in the revival of the religious life, requests for spiritual direction came to him from all sides, and he discharged the task with conviction and sympathy. The bishop of Oxford acknowledged his parochial work by making him in 1870 hon. canon of Christ Church.

Prominent in most movements of the advanced high churchmen, Carter signed in 1856 the protest against the Bath judgment in the case of Archdeacon Denison, which was a considered statement on the doctrine of the Real Presence. In 1870 he sent to A. C. Tait [q. v.], archbishop of Canterbury, the memorial of 1529 clergy against the admission to Holy Communion in Westminster Abbey of 'teachers of various sects' in the company of New Testament revisers. When, in 1873, a petition for 'the education, selection and licensing of duly qualified confessors' was read in Canterbury convocation, and led to some public excitement, Carter with W. Bright, H. P. Liddon, and E. B. Pusey drew up a declaration in defence of confession, published in 'The Times,' 6 Dec. 1873. In the organisation of his party Carter was also conspicuous. He was a founder and long vice-president of the English Church Union, a founder and superior general of the Confraternity of the Blessed Sacrament, and master of the Society of the Holy Cross.

Three times the law was set in motion against Carter on the score of ritual excesses, and three times J. F. Mackarness [q. v.], bishop of Oxford, vetoed proceedings. On the third occasion Dr. Julius, a parishioner of Clewer, obtained from the Queen's Bench a mandamus against the bishop; but the decision was reversed on appeal and the appeal upheld by the Lords. Carter knew, however, that the bishop disapproved of his policy, and whilst the case was pending placed his resignation at the bishop's disposal on 11 July 1878. When the House of Lords delivered their judgment on 22 March 1880 he definitely resigned the rectory of Clewer.

Carter retired to St. John's Lodge, Clewer, and continued the active supervision of the House of Mercy and the Clewer sisterhood. On the issue of 'Lux Mundi' (1889) he signed the declaration on inspiration put forth by eighteen clergy. As late as 1893 he spoke at the Birmingham church congress. He died after a few days' illness on 28 Oct. 1901.

Carter's piety, spiritual insight, and zeal in good works, combined with his courage and skill in organisation, gave him for many years an almost unequalled influence amongst advanced high churchmen, an influence much extended by his fecundity as an author. He married on 26 Nov. 1835, Mary Anne, daughter of John Gould of Amberd, near Torquay, by whom he had one son, who died in 1899. There is a mural table with a bronze figure in Clewer church, a life-size effigy in the chapel of the Clewer community, and a memorial window in Piddlehinton church. A presentation portrait, painted by Frank Holl, was exhibited at the Royal Academy in 1883.

Carter's first publication, 'Eton System of Education Vindicated,' appeared in 1834; his last, 'The Spirit of Watchfulness and other Sermons,' in 1899. Of his more important books, 'The First Five Years of the House of Mercy, Clewer' (1855), 'The First Ten Years of the House of Mercy, Clewer' (1861), and 'Harriet Monsell: a Memoir' (1884; 3rd edit. 1890), deal with the Clewer organisations. The 'Memoir of J. Armstrong, D.D., Bishop of Grahamstown' (1857) also reflects Carter's interest in penitentiaries. Much of his best homiletical work is in the volume of 'Sermons' (1862); and his controversial manner is well shown in 'The Doctrine of Confession in the Church of England' (1865). Between 1860 and 1866 he published four volumes of Lent Lectures; and from 1870 to 1891 six volumes of 'Spiritual Instructions.' In addition, Carter appeared as the editor of many works, some of which were of his own devising, amongst them the 'Treasury of Devotion' (1869; 8th ed. 1885), perhaps his most widely used book.

[W. H. Hutchings, Life and Letters of T. T. Carter, 1903; H. M. Luckock, The Beautiful Life of an Ideal Priest, 1902; The Times, 29 Oct. 1901; Guardian, 30 Oct. 1901; Foster, Alumni Oxon.; J. C. Macdonnell, Life and Correspondence of W. C. Magee, 1896, ii. 64, 99–106; Davidson and Benham, Life of A. C. Tait, 1891, i. chap. xvi.; ii. chaps. xx. xxii.; G. A. Denison, Notes of My Life, 1878, cap. viii.; Liddon, Life of E. B. Pusey, 1894, iii. cap. xvii.; F. W. Cornish, The English Church in the Nineteenth Century, 1910, part ii. caps. iv. and vi.]

A. R. B.

CARVER, ALFRED JAMES (1826–1909), master of Dulwich College, born at King's Lynn on 22 March 1826, was only son of James Carver, an evangelical clergyman of an old Norfolk family, by his wife Anne Spurling. The father, after graduating at Corpus Christi College, Cambridge (B.A. 1812, M.A. 1815), devoted himself in London to the spiritual welfare of prisoners for crime or debt in Newgate and other prisons. On 20 Feb. 1836 the son was admitted to St. Paul's School, London, whence he proceeded to Trinity College, Cambridge, as a scholar in 1845. At Cambridge he was elected Bell University scholar in 1846, and he won the Burney University prize essay in 1849. He graduated B.A. with a first class in classics and as a senior optime in 1849. Next year he became classical lecturer and fellow of Queens' College, Cambridge, and was ordained. On his marriage in 1853 his fellowship lapsed, and his active connection with his university ceased after he served as examiner in the classical tripos in 1857–8.

Meanwhile, in 1852, Carver became surmaster of St. Paul's, his old school. In 1858 he was appointed master of Alleyn's College of God's Gift at Dulwich. A new scheme for the development of Alleyn's educational foundation had just been sanctioned by a private act of parliament. Although Alleyn by statutes drawn up in 1626 had intended to found a public school of the high grade, his educational endowment was until 1858 applied solely to the instruction of 'twelve poor scholars.' The new act, which Carver was first to administer, created two schools of different types. The upper school, for public-school education of the highest kind, was soon known as Dulwich College, and the lower school, for middle-class secondary education, was named Alleyn's School. Both schools were under Carver's control and prospered greatly. The houses which were first employed soon proved inadequate, and were replaced by new buildings. The upper school or Dulwich College moved to a building designed by Sir Charles Barry, which was formally opened by King Edward VII when Prince of Wales on 21 June 1870. Carver's energy created Dulwich College, and made it one of the great public schools of England; its pupils numbered when he left in 1883 some 600 boys. The lower-grade school, Alleyn's School, also moved into new buildings under his guidance, and its numbers soon after rose from 250 to 650. Carver gave effect to broad-minded and sagacious views on education. He saw that every subject can offer educational facilities, and that education based on one rigid formula was bad. His object was to develop a boy's faculties on lines most congenial to his natural aptitude. He encouraged the study of modern languages and paid much attention to the drawing classes, and he was the first headmaster to pass boys direct from school into the India civil service. His ideal of education was high, and his energy and perseverance indomitable.

On the passing of the act of 1882 Dulwich College and Alleyn's School became two distinct schools under separate masters. Carver retired next year with a pension after twenty-five years' service. His interest in his school and in education was maintained until his death. He never missed the annual dinner of the Alleyn Club, the old boys' club, which was founded at his instigation in 1873. The archbishop of Canterbury had made him D.D. of Lambeth in 1861, and in 1882 he was appointed an honorary canon of Rochester. In later life he was chairman of the governors of James Allen's Girls' Schools at Dulwich, and vice-president and member of the council of the Royal Naval School, Eltham (closed in 1909). Carver died at Tynnhurst, Streatham, on 25 July 1909, and was buried in West Norwood cemetery, the first part of the funeral service being held in the college chapel. In 1853 he married Eliza (*d.* 1907), youngest daughter of William Peek, of Peek, Winch & Co., tea merchants. By her he had issue three sons and five daughters.

Carver himself founded at Dulwich College the Carver memorial prize for efficiency in modern languages. A fine organ in the college hall also commemorates his mastership. Posthumous memorials are a wing to the school library and a reredos in the college chapel. A portrait by Eden Upton Eddis, presented to Carver in 1867, is now in the possession of his son Arthur

Wellington Carter, vicar of Langton, Wragby. Another portrait, painted by S. Melton Fisher, a pupil of the school, hangs in the masters' common room.

[The Times, 26 July 1909; R. B. Gardiner's Reg. St. Paul's School, 1884; R. Hovenden's History of Dulwich College, 1873; W. H. Blanch's Dulwich College, 1877; A. M. Gater's Norwood and Dulwich, 1890; personal knowledge.]

W. R. M. L.

CASSELS, WALTER RICHARD (1826–1907), theological critic, fourth son of Robert Cassels, for many years British consul at Honfleur, by his wife Jean, daughter of John Scougall of Leith, was born in London on 4 Sept. 1826. The family, whose pedigree has been traced to Alfred the Great, and through alliance with the Gibson stock to William the Conqueror, was of mercantile capacity.

Walter, who early showed literary aptitude, became partner with his brothers Andrew and John in the firm of Peel, Cassels & Co. at Bombay. That position he held until 1865. From 1863 to 1865 he was an active member of the legislative council of Bombay. Referring to a debate in the council on 8 Sept. 1864, the 'Bombay Gazette' distinguished Sir William Rose Mansfield (afterwards Lord Sandhurst) [q. v.] and Cassels as 'men known not only throughout India but in England for the knowledge and ability they have shown in discussing the most important questions of commercial law and practice.' Returning to England, Cassels lived in London, save for an interval spent in the neighbourhood of Manchester.

In 1874 he published anonymously two volumes entitled 'Supernatural Religion; an Inquiry into the Reality of Divine Revelation,' in which he impugned the credibility of miracles and the authenticity of the New Testament. This publication, which was calculated to provoke antagonism, aroused instant attention, both by its display of minute learning and by its trenchant conclusions. The wildest conjectures as to its author were rife; it was attributed among others to a nephew of Dr. Pusey and, as Lightfoot says, to 'a learned and venerable prelate' (Thirlwall, who had just resigned his bishopric). Early reviewers agreed in taking for granted the soundness of the scholarship; deeper critics came later. In December 1874 Joseph Barber Lightfoot [q. v.], moved by what he deemed its 'cruel and unjustifiable assault . . . on a very dear friend' (Westcott), began in the 'Contemporary Review' a series of nine articles entitled 'Supernatural Religion,' which appeared at intervals up to May 1877; though left unfinished, these articles materially reduced the anonymous writer's pretensions to scholarship, and were regarded as giving new strength to the defence of the New Testament canon; they were collected into a volume of 'Essays' in 1889. Meanwhile Cassels's book passed through six editions by 1875; in 1877 a third volume was added; a revised edition of the complete work appeared in 1879; popular editions in one volume, after compression and further revision, were issued in 1902 and 1905. To Lightfoot's first 'essay' the author had replied in the 'Fortnightly Review' (Jan. 1875); to subsequent ones in prefaces and notes to the various editions of his work; these rejoinders he collected in 'A Reply to Dr. Lightfoot's Essays. By the Author of "Supernatural Religion"' (1889). Lightfoot reverted to the controversy in a paper in the 'Academy,' the last he wrote (21 Sept. 1889), to which Cassels replied anonymously in the 'Academy' (28 Sept.). In 1894 appeared 'The Gospel according to Peter. A Study. By the Author of "Supernatural Religion."' The secret of this authorship was marvellously well kept. Lightfoot in 1889 wrote that he knew neither his name nor 'whether he is living or dead.' On the appearance in the 'Nineteenth Century' (April 1895) of an article on the 'Diatessaron of Tatian,' signed Walter R. Cassels, the statement was made in the 'Manchester City News' (20 April 1895) that Cassels (described as 'a Manchester poet') 'has now avowed himself the author of "Supernatural Religion."' There was no public avowal. Further articles appeared in the 'Nineteenth Century' on the 'Virgin Birth of Jesus' (January 1903) and on the 'Present Position of Apologetics' (October 1903), signed Walter R. Cassels, yet the public was slow to connect them with the author of 'Supernatural Religion.'

Cassels was long a collector of pictures. Five of his pictures were sold at Christie's on 30 June 1906; they had cost him 1685*l.* 5*s.*, and they realised 8547*l.* Among them Turner's 'Rape of Europa,' which he had bought in 1871 for 295 guineas, sold for 6400 guineas, and the portrait of John Wesley, by Romney, which had cost him 530 guineas, fetched 720 guineas. He died unmarried at 43 Harrington Gardens, South Kensington, on 10 June 1907.

In addition to the theological publications above enumerated, he was the author of the following: 1. 'Eidolon, or the Course of a Soul; and other Poems,' 1850. 2. 'Poems,' 1856. 3. 'Cotton. An Account of its Culture in the Bombay Presidency,' Bombay, 1862, 4to.

[R. Cassels, Records of the Family of Cassels, 1870; The Times, 1 July 1906, 20 June 1907; Annual Register, 1906, 1907; private information.] A. G.

CATES, ARTHUR (1829-1901), architect, son of James Cates by his wife Susan, daughter of John Rose, was born at 38 Alfred Street, Bedford Square, London, on 29 April 1829. After education at King's College School he entered as pupil the office of Sydney Smirke, R.A. [q. v.], in 1846. Cates's executed works were few, but in 1870 he succeeded Sir James Pennethorne [q. v.] as architect to the land revenues of the crown under the commissioners of woods and forests. In that capacity and as a promoter of architectural education he rendered English architecture important services. As architect to the commissioners Cates exercised large powers of critical censorship, and though on occasion his brother architects may have resented æsthetic interference, his artistic control over the architecture of the crown estates in London was advantageous.

Cates, who joined the Architectural Association in 1847, became an associate of the Royal Institute of British Architects in 1856, a fellow in 1874, and a member of the council in 1879; he served as vice-president from 1888 to 1892. Cates long controlled the examination system of the institute. From 1882 to 1896 he was chairman of its board of examiners, and under his guidance the progressive examinations (preliminary, intermediate, and final) were initiated and carried into effect. He made a point of coming personally into contact with the candidates. He bequeathed an annual prize bearing his name, which has, since his death, been awarded in connection with these examinations. He was also a fellow of the Surveyors' Institution. From 1859 to 1892 Cates acted as hon. secretary of the Architectural Publication Society, and assisted in the compilation of the 'Architectural Dictionary,' which his friend Wyatt Papworth [q. v.] edited. He wrote for the Dictionary of National Biography memoirs of Wyatt Papworth, his father and brother. As surveyor to the Honourable Society of the Inner Temple he designed in 1887 the archway and gatehouse leading from Tudor Street to King's Bench Walk. When in 1894 the tribunal of appeal under the London Building Act was appointed, Cates was elected the first chairman, and was re-elected in 1900 for a further term of five years. He formed a good architectural library, and many of his books were given or bequeathed to the library of the Royal Institute of British Architects. He died at his residence, 12 York Terrace, Regent's Park, on 15 May 1901, and was buried at Woking.

Cates married in 1881 Rosa, daughter of William Rose, who survived him. There was no issue of the marriage.

[Journal R.I.B.A., 3rd series, viii. 353; the Builder, 1901, lxxx. 494; information from Mrs. Cates.] P. W.

CAVENDISH, SPENCER COMPTON, MARQUIS OF HARTINGTON and eighth DUKE OF DEVONSHIRE (1833–1908), statesman, born on 23 July 1833 at Holker Hall, Lancashire, was eldest of three sons of William Cavendish, second earl of Burlington, and afterwards seventh duke of Devonshire [q. v. Suppl. I], by his wife, Lady Blanche Georgiana, daughter of George Howard, sixth earl of Carlisle [q. v.]. She died on 27 April 1840, leaving four children, three sons and a daughter. The second son was Lord Frederick Cavendish [q. v.]. The third son, Edward (1838–1891), was father of Victor Christian William Cavendish, ninth duke of Devonshire. The daughter, Louisa Caroline, married Admiral Francis Egerton (1824–1895), second son of Francis Egerton, first earl of Ellesmere [q. v.], and died 21 Sept. 1907.

The sons were educated at home, chiefly by their father, whose attainments in both mathematics and classics were high. The eldest son, known at first as Lord Cavendish, was sent to Trinity College, Cambridge, at eighteen, in 1851. Without much reading he gained a second class in the mathematical tripos of 1854, graduating M.A. in the same year. During the following three years he led the life of a young man of high social position, hunted a good deal, and was an officer first in the Lancashire Yeomanry, and then in the Derbyshire militia. In 1856 he went to Russia attached to the staff of his cousin, Granville George Leveson-Gower, second Earl Granville [q. v.], who had been sent as a special ambassador to represent Queen Victoria at the coronation of the Tsar Alexander II.

In the spring of 1857, at the age of twenty-four, Cavendish was returned to Parliament for North Lancashire as a liberal and a supporter of Lord Palmerston. In January 1858 his cousin, the sixth duke of Devonshire, died. Cavendish's father, the earl of Burlington, succeeded to the dukedom and estates, and he himself became marquis of Hartington, under which name he made his political position. In June 1859, after a general election, Lord Palmerston, having effected a reconciliation of the sections whose divergence had led to his fall from office in 1858, was prepared to displace Lord Derby's government, and to resume power. He commissioned Lord Hartington to move a motion of want of confidence intended to effect this object. The speech (7 June) was very successful, the motion was carried on 10 June by 323 to 310, and the resignation of the Derby government followed. The speaker, John Evelyn Denison [q. v.], wrote to the duke of Devonshire that his son possessed 'a power of speaking rarely shown by persons who have had so little practice.' In 1862, when his father was installed as chancellor of Cambridge University, he was created hon. LL.D.

In August 1862 Lord Hartington made a holiday tour through the United States of America, where the civil war was now at its height. He visited the headquarters of both the northern and southern armies, and had an interview both with Abraham Lincoln and with Jefferson Davis. Lincoln was struck by his visitor, and predicted to Sir John Rose, of Canada, that Lord Hartington would have a distinguished political career in his own country. Hartington's sympathies were, on the whole, at this time on the side of the south.

After his return to England (Feb. 1863) Hartington was appointed by Lord Palmerston junior lord of the admiralty (23 March) and in May under-secretary at the war office. In the last capacity he helped in promoting the organisation of the new volunteer force. In Feb. 1866 he succeeded George Frederick Samuel Robinson (afterwards first Marquis of Ripon) [q. v. Suppl. II] as secretary of state for war during the few months of Lord Russell's government, thus entering the cabinet in his thirty-fourth year. When Lord Russell's government fell in June, Hartington visited Germany, saw the entry into Berlin of the Prussian army after the seven weeks' war, talked to Bismarck, and inspected the battlefield of Sadowa. In April 1868 he supported in the House of Commons Gladstone's resolutions in favour of the disestablishment of the Irish church. This policy was unpopular in the county divisions of Lancashire, and Hartington, like Gladstone himself, lost his seat there at the general election of December. Three months later, however, he obtained a new seat from the Radnor Boroughs, in Wales. Gladstone, on forming his administration, offered Lord Hartington the post of lord-lieutenant of Ireland. This he declined, but accepted the office of postmaster-general, with a seat in the cabinet. His chief work in this office was the nationalisation of the telegraphs. He also had charge of the measure which established voting by ballot. This bill was first introduced in 1870, but was not passed into law until 1872.

At the end of 1870 Lord Hartington, much against his will, became chief secretary for Ireland. One of his first duties in this capacity was to pass through the House of Commons a special 'coercion bill,' on the principle of suspension of habeas corpus, for the county of Westmeath and some adjoining districts, which were disturbed by a powerful 'Ribbon Society.' Hartington was not in sympathy with Gladstone's scheme of 1873 for settling the Irish University question, which, as he foresaw, would satisfy no party, and he felt no surprise when it was defeated in the House of Commons on 11 March. His own wish was to carry through the nationalisation of the Irish railways, a measure which he believed 'would do more good to Ireland than anything else,' but this desire was thwarted by the prime minister's want either of time or of inclination.

Soon after the defeat of the liberal party at the elections of 1874 and the accession of Disraeli to power, Gladstone at the beginning of 1875 formally announced his intention to resign the leadership, and at a party meeting held under John Bright's presidency at the Reform Club, London, on 3 Feb., Hartington reluctantly agreed, at the request of the party, to fill the vacant place. In 1876 Disraeli began to develop his forward imperial policy by the purchase of the Suez Canal shares, and the bestowal on the Queen of the title of Empress of India. Hartington approved, on the whole, of the first of these steps, and felt no great objection to the second, and his speeches on these occasions were confined within the limits of moderate criticism. During the following two years the great subject of party controversy was that of the attitude of England to the Turkish question, and the Russo-Turkish war. Hartington, while he maintained that the British government might have prevented the war and secured a pacific reform in the administration of the Turkish provinces by a cordial co-operation from the beginning with Russia and the other continental powers, was by no means disposed to go so far as Gladstone, who was, he thought, far too violent in his denunciations of the policy of the government, and too oblivious of the extent to which British interests were involved in the maintenance, to some degree, of the Turkish dominion, and the preservation of Constantinople from the hands of a stronger and more dangerous power. Hartington was, however, a more severe critic of the government in the matter of the policy which led to the Afghan war in 1878, and publicly stated his opinion that Lord Lytton [q. v.], the viceroy of India, ought to be recalled.

Hartington's position in the country was growing in importance. The city of Glasgow bestowed on him the freedom of the city on 5 Nov. 1877, and on 31 Jan. 1879 he was installed as lord rector of Edinburgh University. Meanwhile Gladstone had been recalled by the Eastern question to the fighting line; his speeches had an immense effect in destroying the government of Lord Beaconsfield, and after the liberal victory at the elections of 1880 it became evident that no one save Gladstone could successfully discharge the function of prime minister. In April 1880 Queen Victoria invited Lord Hartington, who had been returned M.P. for North-East Lancashire, to form a government, and showed herself extremely anxious that he should be prime minister, but he declared himself, in view of the position which Gladstone had reassumed in the liberal party, unable to meet her wishes (MORLEY'S *Life of Gladstone*, ii. 621–4).

Gladstone became prime minister on 23 April, and Lord Hartington was appointed secretary of state for India, a post to which the Afghan question now gave special importance. In the previous September the war, which had seemed to be ended by the treaty of Gandamak, was rekindled by the massacre at Kabul of Sir Louis Cavagnari [q. v.], the British envoy, with his staff and escort. Kabul, after some fighting, had been occupied, the Amir Yakub had been deported to India, negotiations were in progress with the exiled Prince Abdurrahman for the succession to the vacant throne, and a plan had been devised by Lord Lytton to separate the province of Kandahar from the rest of Afghanistan and to place it under a distinct native ruler, supported by a British garrison. This policy the new government, with the co-operation of the new viceroy, the Marquis of Ripon [q. v. Suppl. II], decided to reverse, and Hartington explained the reasons in a speech in parliament (25 March 1881) which Gladstone said was the most powerful that he had ever made. After the defeat of the pretender Ayub by Sir Frederick (afterwards Lord) Roberts (Aug.–Oct. 1880), Amir Abdurrahman was installed in power and all the British forces were withdrawn from Afghanistan, except from the Sibi and Pishin frontier districts, which with Quettah were permanently added to the Empire.

On 16 Dec. 1882 Lord Hartington was transferred to the war office, and was secretary of state for war until Gladstone's government fell in the summer of 1885. He entered upon this office soon after the battle of Tel-el-Kebir in Egypt (13 Sept. 1882) and the virtual establishment of the British protectorate over Egypt. On 3 Nov. 1883 the Egyptian army, commanded by General Hicks [q. v.], was totally destroyed at El Obeid in the Soudan by the dervish host which followed the Mahdi, and in the following January the British Government decided to compel that of Egypt to withdraw altogether from the Soudan, and sent General Gordon to carry out the evacuation. Lord Hartington was one of the four ministers, the others being Lord Granville, Lord Northbrook, and Sir Charles Dilke, who were virtually responsible, in the first instance, for this step. When it became apparent in March that Gordon had failed, and that Khartoum and Berber would be taken by the Arabs unless they received military assistance, Hartington, supported by strong memorandums by Lord Wolseley, the adjutant-general, repeatedly urged the prime minister and the cabinet as strongly as he could to come to a decision on the subject. He was not, however, able to induce the cabinet to agree to any preparations until the end of July 1884, and then only by a threat of resignation. Consequently Lord Wolseley's Nile expedition arrived near Khartoum just too late to save that city from capture and Gordon from death on 26 Jan. 1885. The Government decided at first to retake Khartoum, and Hartington pledged himself in Parliament (25 Feb. 1885) to this policy in the strongest terms. But the feeling died away; the momentary probability of a war with Russia in connection with the Afghan frontier enabled Gladstone to withdraw from the undertaking, which he had never liked, and Hartington had the mortification of seeing the complete abandonment of the Soudan, even including the province of Dongola which had not as yet fallen into the power of the Mahdi.

In internal affairs during this period Hartington was the recognised leader of the whigs or moderate liberals, and came into frequent collision, both within and without the cabinet, with Mr. Chamberlain and Sir Charles Dilke [q. v. Suppl. II], who led the radical section. He acquiesced reluctantly in the great extension of the franchise carried out in 1884–5, especially with regard to Ireland, and with difficulty was persuaded to remain in the cabinet, when it was proposed to pass the extension at once, and a redistribution bill, separately, at a later indefinite date. Chiefly to him and to his consultations with Sir Michael Hicks Beach (afterwards Lord St. Aldwyn), at the instance of Queen Victoria, was due the pacific settlement of the conflict upon this point between the government and the House of Lords in the autumn of 1884, when it was arranged to pass the redistribution bill at the same time as the franchise bill. The scheme of redistribution was settled at a conference between Gladstone, Lord Salisbury, Lord Hartington, Sir Charles Dilke, Sir Michael Hicks Beach, and other leading men of both parties. From the time when the 'home rule for Ireland' movement began, about 1872, he had always uncompromisingly opposed any plan of altering the 'legislative union' of Great Britain and Ireland, and had publicly predicted in the House of Commons on 30 June 1874 that if any liberal statesman were rash enough to embark upon this policy, he would break up the liberal party. He had also been a strong supporter of measures necessary for preserving order and resisting the wave of agrarian crime and supersession of law by the edicts of the Land League, which swept over Ireland after 1880. This *régime* of violence culminated in the assassination of his brother, Lord Frederick Cavendish [q. v.], when chief secretary of Ireland, on 6 May 1882. In all these Irish questions the views of Hartington diverged widely from those of Gladstone, especially after the latter inaugurated negotiations with the Irish leader, Charles Stewart Parnell [q. v.], in April 1882.

Gladstone's administration fell in June 1885, and was succeeded by that of Lord Salisbury. The general election at the end of the year resulted in a return of conservatives and Irish nationalists about equal in number, when added together, to the liberals. Hartington stood and was elected for the new electoral division of Rossendale, in Lancashire, for which he sat henceforth, while he remained in the House of Commons. Gladstone's determination to embark upon a home rule policy was first made known in December 1885 after the election. Most of the members of the last liberal cabinet, despairing of further resistance to home rule, decided to follow Gladstone. A minority, however, led by Hartington, declined to accept office in the government, which Gladstone formed on the defeat of Lord Salisbury's government in the debate on the address in February 1886. Chamberlain and (Sir) George Trevelyan joined the new government provisionally, but on ascertaining the character of the measure proposed, left it, and made common cause with Hartington. On the introduction of the home rule bill (8 April), Hartington declared his opposition to it. He also addressed outside meetings, of which the most famous was that at the Opera House in the Haymarket (14 April), when he appeared upon the same platform with Lord Salisbury [q. v. Suppl. II], thus laying the foundation of the unionist alliance between the conservatives and dissentient liberals. The great difficulty urged by Lord Hartington in his speeches was that there could be no guarantee that the supremacy of the imperial parliament over Ireland would be in practice maintained as Gladstone asserted. 'Mr. Gladstone and I,' he said, 'do not mean the same thing by the word "supremacy."' Hartington on the second reading of the home rule bill, on 10 May 1886, moved the rejection of the measure in a very powerful speech, which made a great impression upon the House of Commons and the country. Over ninety liberal members of Parliament followed Hartington and Chamberlain, and on 8 June 1886 the bill was defeated on a second reading by a majority of 30. Gladstone at once obtained a dissolution of parliament, and, in consequence of the recent addition of two million voters to the electorate there was some doubt as to the result. Hartington fought in the country the most strenuous campaign of his life. The elections gave a sufficient majority to the combined conservatives and the liberal unionists, who now were a distinct organised party under the presidency and leadership of Hartington. The conservatives numbered 316, the liberal unionists 78, Gladstone's followers 191, and the Irish nationalists 85.

Salisbury, with Queen Victoria's consent, asked Hartington to form a government, in which he would serve, or to take office in a government which he (Salisbury) should form. Hartington declined, for he considered that such a step would break up the liberal party and probably lead to a reversion of part of it, in time, to the Gladstonian standard, thus imperilling the legislative union. Salisbury renewed the proposal in January 1887, after the crisis due to the sudden resignation of Lord Randolph Churchill, then leader of the House of Commons; but Hartington again, for the same reasons, declined. Thus he three times declined to be prime minister, in 1880, in 1886, and in 1887. During the next five years he sat upon the front opposition bench, giving an independent support to the government, who were largely kept in power by the aid of the liberal unionists. His breach with Gladstone continued to widen under the influence of events in Irish history, and of the policy and tone adopted by that statesman. During this period Hartington presided over two royal commissions, one, constituted in 1890, upon the 'civil and professional administration of the naval and military departments, and their relation to each other, and to the treasury'; the other, constituted in 1891, upon the 'relations between employers and employed, the combination of employers and employed, and the conditions of labour.'

On 21 Dec. 1891 Lord Hartington, now aged fifty-eight, became eighth duke of Devonshire on his father's death and left the House of Commons after thirty-four years of service there. The elections of 1892 produced a small majority of forty for the liberal-Irish alliance. Gladstone, now in his eighty-third year, once more took office, and in 1893 introduced a second home rule bill, differing in some respects from the first (notably in its retention of the existing mumber of Irish members in the House of Commons), but not more acceptable to the duke. The bill passed its third reading in the House of Commons on 29 July, but the duke on 5 Sept. moved its rejection in the House of Lords in a lucid and able speech, and it was thrown out on 8 Sept. by 419 to 41. On 21 June 1895 Lord Rosebery, who had succeeded Gladstone as prime minister in March 1894, resigned upon a defeat in the House of Commons, and Lord Salisbury, called upon to form his third administration, invited the liberal-unionist leaders to accept office. A coalition government was formed. The duke of Devonshire became president of the council, to which office at that time the educational departments were attached. He showed interest in the development of technical education, but had small acquaintance with educational duties. He also presided over the cabinet 'defence committee' as it then existed. This government, which lasted till 11 July 1902, was remarkably strong and upon most points harmonious, and under it the limits of the Empire in north-east, west, and south Africa were widely extended.

When Lord Salisbury resigned on 11 July 1902 and Mr. Balfour became prime minister, the duke continued to hold the office of president of the council, but surrendered his functions in connection with the education departments, which were now placed under a distinct board and a minister of education. The duke also succeeded Lord Salisbury as government leader in the House of Lords. But his connection with Mr. Balfour's government was a short one. In the session of 1902, Sir Michael Hicks Beach, then chancellor of the exchequer, with the assent of the cabinet, had imposed a small duty on all corn stuffs imported, partly with a view to the expenditure due to the war, but chiefly, he explained, as a permanent source of revenue. Mr. Chamberlain, in the autumn of 1902, proposed to the Cabinet that advantage should be taken of this tax to give to the colonies the preference in British markets, for which they had asked at the conferences of 1887 and 1897. He left for Africa, thinking that the cabinet had accepted his proposal, but on his return, early in 1903, he found that the new chancellor of the exchequer, Charles Thomson Ritchie (afterwards Baron Ritchie of Dundee) [q. v. Suppl. II], proposed to repeal this unpopular tax. Mr. Chamberlain, then, in speeches, publicly declared his views in favour of duties for the sake of preference; his movement was supported by a majority of the unionist party and opposed by a minority. The government at first set on foot an inquiry into statistics, and the duke of Devonshire supported this course in a speech on 15 June 1903 in the House of Lords. It was, however, found to be impossible to stave off a schism later than September 1903. On 14 Sept. took place a cabinet meeting, the result of which was the resignation of three cabinet ministers, Mr. Ritchie, Lord Balfour of Burleigh, and Lord George Hamilton, who took strongly the free-trade view. The duke was acting in unison with these ministers, and would have resigned at the same moment, had not Mr. Balfour informed him that Mr. Chamberlain had also resigned in order to carry on independently the propaganda of tariff reform, and that his resignation had been accepted. The duke continued to hold his place in the cabinet till 1 October, when he resigned in consequence of the strong expressions in favour of a change in fiscal policy which were used by the prime minister in a speech at Sheffield. The duke's own explanation of his conduct in this matter was given in a speech which he made in the House of Lords on 19 Feb. 1904. During the remaining years of his life the duke opposed the new policy of tariff reform in the House of Lords (especially in speeches of 19 Feb. 1904 and 22 July 1905). In the spring of 1904 he resigned, after a meeting held on 18 May 1904, his chairmanship of, and connection with, the Liberal Unionist Association, over which he had presided since its formation in 1886. The majority of its members followed Mr. Chamberlain, and it was remodelled upon new lines. Upon other matters of policy the duke still sympathised with Mr. Balfour as prime minister, or, as he became in December 1905, leader of the opposition. But in debates on the new liberal government's education bill of 1906 he accepted, in opposition to the unionist point of view, the final position taken by the government.

The last speech in parliament made by the duke was on 7 May 1907, when he defined and defended the powers and functions of the House of Lords. His last public appearance was as chancellor at Cambridge, at a conferring of degrees, on 12 June 1907. A few days later he suffered a sudden collapse of health through weakness of the heart. Recovering to some degree, he left England on 24 October, and went to Egypt for the winter. On his way home, on 24 March 1908 he died almost suddenly at an hotel at Cannes. His body was brought to Derbyshire and buried at Edensor, close to Chatsworth.

The duke succeeded his father in 1892 as lord-lieutenant of Derbyshire, and the same year he was made K.G. by Queen Victoria. He also succeeded his father as chancellor of Cambridge University. He discharged his duties with energy, and did his best to raise a large fund for the better endowment of the university, towards which he himself gave 10,000*l.* He took special interest in the promotion of the teaching of applied science in the university. In 1895 he became lord-lieutenant of county Waterford. In the summer of 1892 the duke married Louise, daughter of Count von Alten of Hanover, and widow of William Montague, seventh duke of Manchester. After his marriage he entertained freely at Devonshire House, Chatsworth, and his other seats, and was, as Lord Rosebery said in his speech in the House of Lords upon the occasion of his death, the 'most magnificent of hosts.' One of the most famous festivities was the historic fancy dress ball given at Devonshire House in 1897, the year of the 'diamond jubilee,' when the duke himself appeared as the Emperor Charles V, there being a certain resemblance of type between the houses of Hapsburg and Cavendish. With Edward VII, both as Prince of Wales and as King, he was long on intimate terms of friendship. On several occasions the duke and duchess entertained King Edward VII and Queen Alexandra at Chatsworth, and once at Lismore Castle in Ireland. Annually during this reign there was a ball on Derby Day at Devonshire House which was attended by the King and Queen and other members of the royal family. In the control and management of his large estates in England and Ireland the duke was recognised as an excellent landlord and public-spirited benefactor. He encouraged the development of his property at Eastbourne with great effect, and he was actively interested in the industrial progress of Barrow, where he owned much property. No man had a stronger sense of duty or of all that is implied in the maxim 'Noblesse oblige.' His chief recreation in earlier days was hunting, though he also liked shooting and fishing, and throughout life he was addicted to the turf. He built himself a house at Newmarket, and was, perhaps, never happier than when he was there. His success in racing was, however, hardly equal to his zeal for it and expenditure upon it. He never won the Derby, though in 1898 a horse of his, Dieudonné, was the favourite for that race. His best horses at different times were Belphœbe—who won the One Thousand Guineas in 1877 and was second to Placida for the Oaks—Morion, Marvel, Cheers, and Dieudonné.

The duke of Devonshire at no time in his life had much taste or leisure for either literature or the fine arts, though after his accession he took care that the library at Chatsworth should be kept up to date, and the sculptures and pictures carefully looked after. Sandford Arthur Strong [q. v. Suppl. II] was his capable librarian and keeper of art collections from 1895 to his death in 1904. His tastes were mainly those of a country gentleman. His favourite resort in London was the Turf Club and, after that, the Travellers and Brooks's Clubs. His speeches were not marked by brilliancy, rhetoric or imaginative wit, but they were well-constructed, logical, massive, most sincere, and effective. A lethargic manner gave rise to the story that he yawned during one of his early orations. But an American orator, after hearing the foremost speakers in England, said that he thought the duke was the most effective of all, and likened the way in which he laid down his arguments to the operation of 'driving in piles.' But the weight which he carried in the country was due to the character revealed through the speeches. Mr. Balfour, when speaking in the House of Commons on the announcement of his death, ascribed the great political influence which the duke possessed not only to his abilities but 'to that transparent honesty and simplicity of purpose . . . obvious to every man with whom he came into personal contact.' He said that of all the great statesmen he had known the duke was the most persuasive speaker, and that 'because he never attempted to conceal the strength of the case against him' and because he 'brought before the public in absolutely clear, transparent and unmistakable terms the very arguments he had been going through patiently and honestly before he arrived at his conclusion.' Mr. Asquith said of the duke that 'in the closing years of his life he commanded in a greater degree than perhaps any other public man the respect and confidence of men of every shade of opinion in this kingdom' by virtue of simplicity of nature, sincerity of conviction, directness of purpose, intuitive 'insight into practical conditions, quiet and inflexible courage, and, above all, tranquil indifference to praise and blame, and by absolute disinterestedness.'

The duke left no children, and the title and estates passed to his nephew, Victor, son of the late Lord Edward Cavendish. The duchess survived him, dying suddenly at Esher Place on 15 July 1911, and being buried at Edensor. The present duke has two younger brothers, Lord Richard Cavendish and Lord John Cavendish, and two sons, the present marquis of Hartington and Lord Charles Cavendish.

There is a portrait of the eighth duke (as marquis of Hartington) by Sir John Millais at Chatsworth. His portrait was also painted by G. F. Watts, R.A. (1882), and by A. S. Cope (1889). In the National Portrait Gallery there are two portraits, one painted by Lady Abercromby in 1888, and one by Sir Hubert von Herkomer, R.A., in 1892. The last-mentioned is by far the most exact and life-like picture of the five. Statues were erected by public subscription in both London and Eastbourne. The former, which is by Mr. Herbert Hampton, is in Whitehall Avenue, beside the war office.

[Life of the Eighth Duke of Devonshire, by Bernard Holland, C.B., 1911; Election Speeches, 1879–80, by the Marquis of Hartington, M.P., 1880; see also Morley, Life of Gladstone; Lord (Edmond) Fitzmaurice, Life of Lord Granville, 1905, 2 vols.; Wemyss Reid, Life of W. E. Forster, 1888; Earl Selborne's Memorials, 1898, 2 vols.; B. Mallet, Life of Lord Northbrook, 1908; Hansard's Reports; Proc. Royal Soc. 82a, 1909, by Prof. G. D. Liveing; Sir Wilfrid Lawson and F. C. Gould, Cartoons in Rhyme and Line, No. 53, 1904.] B. H. H.

CAWDOR, third Earl. [See Campbell, Frederick Archibald Vaughan, (1847–1911).]

CECIL, ROBERT ARTHUR TALBOT GASCOYNE-, third Marquis of Salisbury (1830–1903), prime minister, the lineal descendant of Robert Cecil, first earl of Salisbury [q. v.], was born at Hatfield on 3 Feb. 1830. His father, James Brownlow William Gascoyne-Cecil, second marquis (1791–1868), held the offices of lord privy seal and lord president of the council in the conservative administrations of 1852 and 1858 respectively, and assumed by royal licence the surname of Gascoyne before that of Cecil in 1821 on his marriage to Frances Mary, only child and heiress of Bamber Gascoyne (1758–1828), M.P. for Liverpool 1780–96, whose grandfather, Sir Crisp Gascoyne [q. v.], was lord mayor of London in 1753. Cecil's mother was the friend and frequent correspondent of the first duke of Wellington. Of Cecil's brothers, the elder, James, Viscount Cranborne (1821–1865), who became blind at an early age, was an historical essayist of some power and a member of the Société de l'histoire de France and corresponding member of the Société de l'histoire de Belgique and of the Institut Génevois; and the younger, Lt.-col. Lord Eustace Cecil (*b.* 1834), was surveyor-general of the ordnance (M. P. 1865–85) in the conservative administration (1874–80). His elder sister, Lady Mildred, married Alexander Beresford-Hope [q. v.], member for Cambridge University; the younger, Lady Blanche, married James Maitland Balfour of Whittinghame and was the mother of Mr. Arthur James Balfour, Salisbury's successor in the premiership, of Francis Maitland Balfour [q. v.], and of Mr. Gerald William Balfour.

Cecil was at Eton from 1840 to 1845, and at Christ Church, Oxford, from 1847 to 1849. At Oxford he obtained the honorary distinction of a fourth class in mathematics. During Michaelmas term 1848 he was secretary and during Easter term 1849 treasurer of the Oxford Union. Subsequently in 1853 he was elected to a fellowship at All Souls College. Private memoranda show that he experienced the impact of the Oxford movement (e.g. 'Every virtue is a narrow mountain ridge with a valley of sin on each side'), though in these notes on religious and ethical subjects (written *c.* 1853–4) he maintains throughout a critical and sometimes hostile independence of judgment. After leaving the university he went between July 1851 and May 1853 to Australia—at the time considerably agitated by the recent gold discoveries—and visited the mines near Melbourne. On his return in 1853 he was elected in the conservative interest M.P. for Stamford, which he continued to represent until his succession to the peerage. His election address exhibits the readiness to abide by the *fait accompli* (in this case the abolition of the corn laws) which was one of his most salient characteristics. He made his maiden speech in Parliament on 7 April 1854, opposing the second reading of the Oxford University Bill (which embodied the recommendations of the recent commission) on the ground that endowments ought either to continue to be applied to those purposes for which they had been bestowed or else to revert to the donor's heirs. This speech in defence of property was followed within the year by speeches on religious education and foreign affairs. It was along these three lines of political thought that his mind was principally to travel.

The ability which he had shown led to his being selected on 17 July 1855 on behalf of the opposition to second the previous question after John Arthur Roebuck [q. v.] had moved his famous vote of censure upon the late ministry of Lord Aberdeen, which had been responsible for the conduct of the Crimean war. The previous question was carried. On this occasion Cecil gave indirect support to Palmerston's government. Three years later he was amongst those who combined to defeat the same administration upon its Chinese policy. Palmerston was however returned at the ensuing general election of 1857. In the new parliament Cecil introduced a bill to substitute the use of voting-papers for personal attendance at the polling booths, urging that such a measure would prevent both disorder and intimidation, but the proposal had no success. He also entered upon a vigorous resistance to the abolition of compulsory church rates, which was prolonged until 1868, when, seeing that further opposition was hopeless, he supported the measure in a moderate form (speech, 19 Feb. 1868).

On 11 July 1857 he married Georgina Caroline, the eldest daughter of Sir Edward Hall Alderson [q. v.], baron of the exchequer, and a woman of great ability. Owing to his father's disapproval of the union, his married life was started on a very limited income, and he was at this time partly dependent upon his pen. He wrote for 'Bentley's Quarterly Review' (1859) and for the 'Saturday Review' (the property of his brother-in-law, Alexander Beresford-Hope) between 1857 and 1865, and in 1860 he began the long series of articles in the 'Quarterly Review'—thirty-three in all—which are perhaps the best mirror of his mind. In 1858 he contributed an article called 'Theories of Parliamentary Reform' to the volume of 'Oxford Essays' for that year. It is remarkable (i.) for its frank recognition of the utilitarian as the only genuine standpoint in modern politics; (ii.) for its definite abandonment of the feudal basis of the older toryism; and (iii.) for the selection of persons of substance as the class whose position and privileges it was the particular business of the conservative party, in the interest of equity, to defend. His distrust of democracy was in fact laid not in any distrust of the poorer classes as such—he regarded them as neither better nor worse than other men (speech in the House of Commons, 27 April 1866)—but in the belief that the law ought not to expose them to predatory temptations, which poverty encouraged and wisdom was not present to resist, nor to strip their more fortunate neighbours of that influence which was the 'single bulwark' of wealth against the weight of numbers. The conclusion therefore was, that 'we must either change enormously or not at all.' Since symmetrical constitutions like that of Sieyès were opposed to human nature, since an educational franchise could not be constructed so as to embody any logical principle, since a wide or 'geographical' franchise imperilled property, the writer expressed himself in favour of leaving things where they were. Reform, however, was in the air, and as soon as Derby took office on the fall of the Palmerston administration in 1858 a reform bill was adumbrated, which Disraeli introduced in the following year with a view to settling the question on conservative lines. Cecil spoke on 21 March 1859 in favour of the clause depriving the forty-shilling freeholder, who voted in a borough, of the vote for the county which he had possessed as well. But the new government fell without being able to carry the measure, and from July 1859 to 1866 the conservatives were once more in opposition.

This period was 'the most interesting stage in Cecil's career' (Traill). Inside Parliament he was making a name by incisive attacks upon the liberal government. He crossed swords with Gladstone both by supporting the action of the House of Lords in refusing to repeal the paper duties (1860–1) and by opposing the taxation of charitable corporations (1863), and it was his motion charging the vice-president of the council with the mutilation of the reports of school-inspectors, which brought about the resignation of Robert Lowe (afterwards Viscount Sherbrooke) [q. v.] in 1864. By his speech of 8 Feb. 1861 on Villiers's motion for a committee to inquire into the relief of the poor he revealed an interest in and knowledge of social problems, and by that of 7 April 1862 a considerable mastery over finance. Outside Parliament his articles in the 'Quarterly Review' were making an effect upon a public opinion still responsive to such influences. Their trenchancy was such that both Russell and Gladstone paid them the compliment of uncomplimentary references (see *Quarterly Review*, July 1860, p. 292, and July 1866, p. 266), and they still constitute a formidable and independent criticism of the conduct of the leaders of both parties during the period as well as a lively review of the problems and politics of the time. Singularly free of literary artifice as well as of literary allusion, seldom if ever attaining any great height of eloquence, their style has long been recognised as a rare model of restrained, pungent, and vigorous English.

The Russell ministry fell in June 1866 owing to the opposition of the whigs and conservatives to their reform bill, and Cecil (who by the death of his elder brother on 14 June 1865 had become Viscount Cranborne and his father's heir) was appointed to the Indian secretaryship in the Derby government and sworn of the privy council (6 July 1866). Within a week of taking office it fell to his lot to bring in the Indian budget, and the ability which he displayed added considerably to his credit. Otherwise his nine months' administration was uneventful. In the counsels of the cabinet, however, he played an important part. The July riot in Hyde Park converted the parliamentary agitation for a reform bill into a popular movement, and Disraeli resolved to anticipate his opponents in giving effect to it. He hoped to do so without losing the support of his more conservative colleagues, and two bills, one to establish in the boroughs a conditional household suffrage, the other a 6*l.* rating franchise, were submitted to the cabinet. On 23 Feb. 1867 Disraeli contrived by a judicious manipulation of statistics to get the more radical measure for household suffrage provisionally accepted by the whole cabinet. During the following day, however, which was Sunday, Cranborne had leisure to examine the figures more particularly, and by the evening had reached the conclusion that he could not support the measure. On the Monday morning he tendered his resignation to Derby, who was to address a party meeting the same afternoon. Peel and Carnarvon followed suit. To avoid a schism the ministry fell back, at the last minute, on the less violent project. But this manœuvre had no success with the House of Commons, and ten days later (4 March) Derby allowed his dissentient colleagues to withdraw, and proceeded with the household suffrage reform bill, which in due course became law, though not until it had been shorn of all its anti-democratic checks. Its passage was the occasion of some of Cranborne's most biting oratory and of the most famous of his 'Quarterly Review' articles—'The Conservative Surrender'—in which he pressed home the great outrage upon political morality committed by the conservative leaders. A private letter (printed in the *Life of Lord Coleridge*, ii. 156) shows that he was near abandoning public life on the ground that his 'opinions were of the past,' and that the new constitution should be worked by those who believed in it. In any case the scene of his activities was bound to change, for the death of his father on 12 April 1868 had made him a member of the House of Lords. His last speech in the lower house was delivered on 30 March in opposition to Gladstone's motion for the disestablishment of the Irish Church.

He continued his defence of that church establishment in the upper house, and counselled the lords to reject Gladstone's bill which temporarily suspended the exercise of the Irish crown patronage. This course was taken, and the question referred to the constituencies, which returned a substantial liberal majority. A bill to disestablish the Irish Church was then sent up to the lords. Prior to the general election (speech in House of Lords, 26 June 1868) Salisbury had laid down, in words often quoted since, what he conceived to be the function of the peers in the modern state. They must secure for the country, he said, an opportunity of expressing its 'firm, deliberate, and sustained conviction,' whenever that opportunity was denied to it by the lower house. After that opportunity had once been secured, they must abide by the result whichever way it might go. He re-affirmed this doctrine after the general election in an impressive speech, advising them to pass the second reading of the bill (17 June 1869). 'It is no courage,' he said, 'it is no dignity to withstand the real opinion of the nation. All that you are doing thereby is to delay an inevitable issue—for all history teaches us that no nation was ever thus induced to revoke its decision—and to invite besides a period of disturbance, discontent, and possibly of worse than discontent.' In the ensuing division he went so far as to vote for the bill, which was passed. Difficulties, however, arose between the two houses in respect to the lords' amendments, but these were eventually overcome, mainly by the exertions of Archbishop Tait, but to some extent by his own (*Life of Tait*, chap. 19).

Towards the two other great Acts of this Parliament—the Irish Land Act and the Education Act of 1870—he showed a spirit of benevolent criticism and amendment, and his severest language was reserved for Gladstone's arbitrary abolition of army purchase. That step would produce, he said characteristically, not (as Cardwell had claimed) 'seniority tempered by selection' but 'stagnation tempered by jobbery.' His other activities included the introduction of a measure in March 1869 to carry over into the succeeding session bills which had been passed in one house and had lacked time to reach the other, as well as of a limited owners improvements bill, designed, in the interest of cottagers, to shift the financial burdens of administering an estate from the life-tenant to the corpus of the property. He failed, however, to carry either of them; nor did Russell's life peerage bill, which he supported, fare any better. He was equally unsuccessful in his resistance to the Universities Tests Abolition Act in 1871, and the lords, who on his advice had inserted in the bill a clause imposing a pledge on tutors, deans, and divinity lecturers to teach nothing contrary to the teaching of the Old and New Testaments, did not insist upon this amendment. A special importance attached to his opinion, as on 12 Nov. 1869 he had been elected to the chancellorship of Oxford University, vacant through Derby's death. He held that dignified office for his life, but took little active part in the university's affairs. In 1876 he made an unsuccessful attempt to get rid of 'idle fellowships.' At his instigation the universities' commissions were appointed in 1877, and on their recommendation important changes were introduced into academic organisation. One reform limited the tenure of prize fellowships to seven years. Salisbury, however, though he approved the report of the commissioners, held aloof from university contentions.

His activities were, indeed, by no means confined to politics. On 16 Jan. 1868 he had been elected to the chairmanship of the Great Eastern railway, which he retained until 1872, and under a special act of parliament he became during part of 1871–2, in conjunction with Lord Cairns (who afterwards bore witness to the admirable character of his work), arbitrator of the disordered affairs of the London, Chatham and Dover Railway Co. But in spite of his political pessimism and discouragement, political interests remained dominant in his nature. In October 1869 he had contributed a striking article to the 'Quarterly' on 'The Past and the Future of Conservative Policy.' He started from the thesis that the religious motive in politics, which has hitherto repressed the class motive, had passed away with the struggle over the Irish Church. The contest of the future would be a contest about material things. The new electorate was incontestably liberal. The conservatives therefore could not look for power at all and only for office on the same ignoble terms as those upon which they had obtained it for three short periods during the previous twenty years—that is to say, by allying themselves with the radicals to the discomfiture of the whigs. They would do better to look to nothing but their character and be guided by no rule except that 'of strict fidelity to conviction.'

The diagnosis seemed plausible, but it was nevertheless to prove false. The liberal ascendancy could not survive five years of drastic legislation, and Disraeli returned to office in Feb. 1874. Salisbury resumed his place at the India office—an event which caused some surprise, as his relations with the leader of his party had long been of the coldest nature. In the later years of the administration these became, however, much more cordial, and Salisbury paid a sympathetic tribute to Beaconsfield on the occasion of the latter's death on 19 April 1881. His conviction and commonsense had, meanwhile, been brought once more into contrast with the opportunism of the prime minister on the introduction of the public worship regulation bill (1874), when Disraeli played upon the protestant sentiment of the country and took occasion to describe his colleague, who had shown a just appreciation of the futility of the proposed measure, as 'a great master of gibes and flouts and jeers.' It was in criticising this bill that Salisbury defined his conception of the Church of England, over whose establishment and privileges he was ever on the guard. 'There are,' he said, 'three schools in the church, which I might designate by other names, but which I prefer to call the sacramental, the emotional, and the philosophical. . . . They arise, not from any difference in the truth itself, but because the truth must necessarily assume different tints as it is refracted through the different media of various minds. But it is upon the frank and loyal tolerance of these schools that the existence of your establishment depends.'

At the India office Salisbury's administration was marked by his refusal to check the export of corn during the famine in Bengal, contrary to the advice of the lieut.-governor, Sir George Campbell [q. v. Suppl. I]. 'The difficulty,' he told the House of Lords, was 'not to procure grain but to bring the supplies to the houses of the starving population.' The event justified his policy. In this case Lord Northbrook [q. v. Suppl. II], the governor-general, had seen eye to eye with him, but there was a difference of opinion between them about the advisability of appointing a mixed commission to try the Gaikwar of Baroda, which Northbrook aggravated by altering some of the customs duties without reference to the secretary of state. Afghan frontier policy proved a more serious source of friction. Northbrook belonged to the old 'Lawrence' school of administrators, who were satisfied with the existing north-west frontier, and desired to avoid interference with the Amir. Salisbury, on the other hand, was of opinion that 'a diplomatic invasion' of Afghanistan by Russia was taking place, and must be resisted by the establishment of a British agent at Herat. This 'forward policy' was inaugurated by Lytton, who replaced Northbrook in April 1876. Salisbury defended it, as well as his personal integrity in respect of it, in a speech in the House of Lords on 10 Dec. 1878. Of a Russian military invasion of India he made light, advising one who feared it 'to use large maps' (11 June 1877). But he maintained that, unless we took our precautions, there was a danger that the Russians might at some convenient moment prompt the Afghans to embarrass us upon the frontier:—'Russia can offer to the Afghans the loot of India; we, if we desired to make a competing offer, can promise nothing—because there is nothing in Turkestan to loot' (*Quarterly Review*, April 1881, p. 548).

It was not, however, from the India office that he was principally to oppose Russian designs and to win in the Tsar's eyes the character of being 'l'ennemi acharné de la Russie' (*Life of Lord Randolph Churchill*, p. 719). The Eastern question, owing to a rebellion attended by Turkish atrocities in Bulgaria and the adjacent provinces, had become acute in 1876, and a conference between the great powers was arranged to meet in Constantinople. Salisbury was sent out in December as British plenipotentiary. His purpose was to secure so far as possible both the integrity of Turkey and the safety of its Christian subjects. Instead of any occupation of Bulgaria by Russia he brought the Powers to agree upon the appointment of an international commission to re-organise the territory with the support of six thousand Belgian troops, in the intention of placing it, together with Bosnia and the Herzegovina, under the control of governors nominated by the Sultan and approved by the Concert. To these terms, however, the Porte obstinately and unexpectedly refused its assent, and Salisbury returned to England in the end of Jan. 1877. War between Russia and Turkey followed in April, and the Russians were within reach of Constantinople by the end of the year. On 6 Dec. Cranbrook records in his diary, 'Salisbury is bent upon England having a share, if there should be a break up in the East, and evidently has no desire that Turkey should stand.' The treaty of San Stefano (3 March 1878), however, put Russia clearly in the wrong, inasmuch as it was a violation of the integrity of Turkey, guaranteed by England, France, and Austria in 1856. The British government accordingly required all the terms of that armistice to be submitted to a European conference. The Russian reply reserved to Russia the right of excluding from discussion whatever clauses of the treaty it chose. This brought the two Powers to the brink of war, and Derby, who was constitutionally unprepared for that contingency, resigned the foreign secretaryship, under some misapprehension, however, as to the exact intentions of his colleagues, which resulted in a regrettable passage at arms in the House of Lords with his successor (see *Life of Lord Cranbrook*, ii. 77). Salisbury was appointed to the vacant office on 1 April 1878. His qualifications for filling it included, besides his recent mission to Constantinople, a prolonged study of foreign affairs, of which the evidence is to be found as well in early speeches (e.g. House of Commons, 7 June 1855) as in some of his articles contributed to the 'Quarterly Review' ['Lord Castlereagh' (Jan. 1862); 'Poland' (April 1863); 'The Danish Duchies' (Jan. 1864); 'Foreign Policy' (April 1864)]. He brought to his work a clear conception both of the character and aim of English diplomacy, which is best stated in his own language. 'In our foreign policy,' he said at Stamford in 1865, 'what we have to do is simply to perform our own part with honour; to abstain from a meddling diplomacy; to uphold England's honour steadily and fearlessly and always to be rather prone to let action go along with words than to let it lag behind them' (PULLING'S *Life and Speeches of Lord Salisbury*, i. 68). Five years before (*Quarterly Review*, April 1860, p. 528) he had approved (in contrast to the then existing policy of non-interference) the 'traditional' part which England had played in Europe—'England did not meddle with other nations' doings when they concerned her not. But she recognised the necessity of an equilibrium and the value of a public law among the states of Europe. When a great Power abused its superiority by encroaching on the frontier of its weaker neighbours, she looked on their cause as her cause and on their danger as the forerunner of her own.'

It was in accordance with these precepts that a day after (2 April 1878) he took over the foreign office he issued the 'Salisbury Circular,' requiring that all the articles of the treaty of San Stefano should be submitted to the proposed conference, declaring emphatically against the creation of a 'big' Bulgaria, and arguing that, even though the Turkish concessions to Russia might be tolerated individually, taken together they constituted a serious menace to Europe. One of Salisbury's successors at the foreign office has pointed to this despatch as the masterpiece of Salisbury's diplomatic work (LORD ROSEBERY, speech at the Oxford Union, 14 Nov. 1904). It is at any rate remarkable for its promptitude, its lucidity, and its firmness, and it undoubtedly secured for the government a large measure of public support. England was clearly in earnest, and subsequent secret negotiations between Salisbury and Shuvalov, the Russian ambassador, resulted in an agreement to divide the proposed province into two parts—that south of the Balkans to be administered by a Christian governor, nominated by the Sultan. Through the treachery of Charles Thomas Marvin [q. v.], a foreign office copyist, the terms of this agreement appeared in the 'Globe' newspaper, and Salisbury's denial in the House of Lords of the authenticity of the statements, thus disclosed at a momentous diplomatic crisis, is the most debatable incident in a singularly honourable career. The secret convention with Russia, balanced by the 'Cyprus' convention with Turkey, secured the semblance of a diplomatic success for England at Berlin, and Salisbury, who in company with Lord Beaconsfield, the prime minister, represented this country at the congress (13 June–13 July 1878), returned bringing in the famous phrase 'peace with honour.' His services were rewarded with the garter, almost the only distinction which he was ever induced to accept (30 July 1878). A well-known epigram of Bismarck—'The old Jew means business, but his colleague is lath painted to look like iron'—may have strengthened the idea that Salisbury was at this time something of a tool in the hands of his chief. It is unlikely, however, that, when the diplomatic history of this period comes to be more fully told, this verdict will be endorsed.

The principal provisions of the treaty of Berlin were that the Slavonic settlement of the Eastern question, embodied in the idea of a 'big Bulgaria,' should be abandoned; that Austria, for which Salisbury, like his diplomatic model, Castlereagh, entertained a peculiar regard, should be entrusted—and this was done at his particular instance—with the administration of Bosnia and the Herzegovina; that Russia, who obtained Batum (together with Kars and Ardahan), should make of it 'a free port, essentially commercial.' The

Cyprus convention transferred to England the protectorate of that island, so long as Russia retained the cities just named and on the understanding that if the Porte carried out the reforms desired in Armenia England should guarantee its Asiatic dominions. It is evident, therefore, if the history of the last thirty years be interrogated, that the diplomacy of 1878, whatever its immediate merit, has produced no lasting triumph. The cession of Cyprus did not result in any immunity of the Armenians from Turkish misgovernment, nor even, as was perhaps dreamed of, in the creation of an English sphere of influence in the Euphrates valley: the Russian port of Batum has been closed and fortified: Bosnia and the Herzegovina were annexed by Austria with the utmost cynicism when at length in 1908 the opportunity offered: and Bulgaria and Eastern Roumelia were united by Prince Alexander in 1885, if not actually with Salisbury's *post factum* approval, at least without any active resistance on his part; though, as he was careful to point out (Newport speech, 7 Oct. 1885), the Bulgaria thus formed was not the 'big Bulgaria' of the San Stefano treaty, nor was it evolved under Russian influences. About the underlying principle of the English policy—the maintenance of Turkey—he was himself eighteen years later, in the height of the Armenian atrocities, to encourage the gravest doubt. The defence of the Berlin Treaty, he told the House of Lords on 19 Jan. 1897, lay in its traditional character, not in its inherent excellence. 'The parting of the ways was in 1853, when the Emperor Nicholas's proposals were rejected. Many members of this house will keenly feel the nature of the mistake that was made, when I say that we put all our money upon the wrong horse. It may be in the experience of those that have done the same thing, that it is not very easy to withdraw from a step of this kind, when it has once been taken, and that you are practically obliged to go on. All that Lord Beaconsfield did was to carry out the policy which his predecessors had laid down. I am acquainted with Lord Beaconsfield's thoughts at that time; he was not free from misgiving; but he felt that the unity of the policy in this great country was something so essential, and that the danger of shifting from one policy to another without perfectly seeing all the results to which you would come was so paramount, that he always said that the policy of Lord Palmerston must be upheld. He still entertained hopes, which I did not entertain in quite the same degree. But those hopes have not been justified.'

The brilliant effect of the Berlin Congress was even more evanescent than its provisions. Two years later the conservatives were put in a minority by the election of 1880. Beaconsfield only survived his defeat by about a year, and at his death (19 April 1881) Salisbury was chosen (9 May) to lead the opposition in the House of Lords, Sir Stafford Northcote [q. v.] continuing to do so in the House of Commons, and the party being left without any recognised leader in the country. The years of this 'dual control' are perhaps the least effective of Salisbury's life. His great ability was not yet fully realised, and he had still to make himself a name for sagacity and moderation. Irish questions, involving the larger issue of interference with the established rights of property, were dominant, and much of his activity was devoted to opposing the Irish legislation of the government, represented by the land bill of 1881 and the arrears bill of 1882, which he did with partial success by means of amendments instead of open resistance. To the bill of 1884 introducing household suffrage in the counties he only offered opposition contingent on the refusal of the government to make public the complementary redistribution of seats bill. A compromise, which involved a constitutional innovation, was however eventually arrived at. Salisbury and Northcote were taken into counsel by the ministry, and, to the profound indignation of some members of the conservative party, their leaders privately negotiated the provisions of a redistribution bill, on the understanding that the House of Lords would pass the franchise bill (extending the vote to nearly twice as many persons as was done in 1867), without forcing an appeal to the country.

The domestic policy of the liberals was not easy to attack from any popular standpoint, but their conduct of affairs in the Sudan, in Egypt, in Afghanistan, and in Ireland gave Salisbury the opportunity for trenchant criticism. Northcote, on the other hand, as Lord Randolph Churchill [q.v. Suppl. I] was at pains to show, possessed little aptitude for turning occasion to advantage, and when the government fell on 12 June 1885, Salisbury, who had been Beaconsfield's choice (*Life of Lord Cranbrook*, ii. 149), and during the last year had been more and more taking the lead (*ibid.* p. 215) was summoned by the queen. With reluctance he accepted office on 23 June. He was embarrassed as well by his unwillingness to take precedence of Northcote as by Churchill's refusal to serve, if Northcote retained the leadership in the commons, but the pressure put on him by the queen, by the party itself (*Life of Lord Randolph Churchill*, p. 332), and by the exigencies of the political situation (*Life of Sir Stafford Northcote*, ii. 210) overcame his disinclination. He decided to take the foreign office himself, thus associating it with the premiership for the first time since it had been a distinct office. To Northcote, who went to the House of Lords as earl of Iddesleigh, he made over the post of first lord of the treasury, which had hitherto gone with that of prime minister. Sir Michael Hicks Beach became leader of the House of Commons.

With the assistance of Lord Dufferin, the Indian viceroy, Salisbury carried forward the Afghan frontier negotiations, which had been interrupted by the Penjdeh incident. All danger of war with Russia was removed by the protocol of 10 Sept. 1885, securing the Zulfikar pass to the Amir, though the final delimitation of the boundary between the Hari Rud and the Oxus was not completed until the treaty of St. Petersburg in July 1887. The eastern frontier of India was similarly secured against French influences by the annexation of Burmah. Other activities included the raising of a long-delayed Egyptian loan and, by a curious irony, the diplomatic support of Prince Alexander's action in uniting Eastern Roumelia to Bulgaria. Salisbury's foreign policy appeared very able to his contemporaries. Cranbrook thought it had secured a European reputation to its author, and Gladstone said that he could not object to one item in it (*Life of Lord Cranbrook*, ii. 239).

In Parliament Salisbury promoted and passed a bill for the housing of the working classes (based upon the report of a commission for which he had moved on 22 Feb. 1884), by which landlords were penalised for letting insanitary tenements and the local government board empowered to pull down dwellings unfit for habitation. It was a type of the only kind of ordinary legislation in which he really believed [. . . 'Those matters on which parties do not contend we hold . . . to be so far from objectionable that they and they alone are the proper work of Parliament, and that it is detained from its normal labours by the perpetual intrusion of revolutionary projects' (*Quarterly Review*, Oct. 1873, p. 556)]. There is no dispute as to its salutary effect upon urban slums.

More sensational matter, however, occupied the public mind, as Ireland continued to be in a state of unrest. Salisbury dealt with the question at some length on 7 Oct. 1885 at Newport, and from the elaborate disquisition on local government which the speech contains it has been argued that his mind was at this time oscillating towards a home rule policy. This passage of the speech is, however, followed by an explicit repudiation of the federative principle in connection with Ireland, and in his private correspondence there is nothing to show that he ever contemplated anything more than the measure of Irish local government which in fact he afterwards granted. Any shadow of plausibility which the charge possesses is derived solely from the fact that Carnarvon, the lord-lieutenant of Ireland, had (with his previous assent and subsequent approval, but without the knowledge of the cabinet) held a secret conversation with Parnell in which, according to Parnell's but not Carnarvon's account, Carnarvon used words favourable to an extensive measure of home rule [see Herbert, Henry Howard Molyneux, fourth Earl of Carnarvon]. The general election of December 1885 left the Irish the real masters of the field, since neither side could retain office without their aid. In the course of the next month Gladstone matured his home rule convictions, thus attracting the Irish vote at the same time that the conservatives, contrary to the wishes of Carnarvon, whose resignation was, however, made in accordance with a previous understanding on grounds of health, were repelling it by the project of a coercion bill. The government was defeated on 27 Jan. 1886 and Salisbury resigned on the 28th. Gladstone resumed office, and introduced his first home rule bill in the following April, but the conservatives, materially aided by the secession of Hartington, John Bright, and Mr. Joseph Chamberlain, effected its defeat on 8 June. Parliament was dissolved, and the question referred to the country. In strong contrast to Gladstone's sentimental appeal for justice to Ireland Salisbury had declared (15 May 1886, speech at Union of Conservative Associations) for 'twenty years of resolute government,' introducing this statement of policy with the ill-judged remark, not to be forgotten or forgiven, that some races, like the Hottentots and the Hindus, were unfit for self-government. The electorate returned a majority of 118 for the maintenance of the union. In the hope of including liberal-unionists in the administration, Salisbury expressed his readiness to leave the premiership to Hartington, but the offer was declined. He therefore took office on 26 July 1886, and formed a conservative ministry dependent on a unionist majority. He himself became first lord of the treasury; Iddesleigh foreign secretary under his supervision; and Lord Randolph Churchill, chancellor of the exchequer and, through Sir Michael Hicks Beach's self-abnegation, leader of the House of Commons. Churchill, whose speeches were perfectly attuned to the ear of the new electorate, and who by virtue of them had become the best known of the unionist leaders, was not slow to try conclusions with the premier. He had already, in 1884, made a vigorous though, on the whole, unsuccessful attack upon his chiefs with the view of democratising the party organisation, and his attitude had facilitated the passage of the franchise bill through the commons. In the next year he had made his power felt by compelling the withdrawal of Northcote to the House of Lords, and he now took exception to Iddesleigh's foreign policy, threatening to resign unless the military estimates which that policy necessitated were reduced. Deeper differences lay in the antagonism between the spirit of the new tory democracy, of which Churchill was the exponent, and that of the old conservatism of opinion and method, which Salisbury represented. The prime minister made no effort to retain his rebellious lieutenant at the price of concession, and Churchill left the government in December 1886. Salisbury, after again ineffectually offering to serve under Hartington, induced George Joachim (afterwards Lord) Goschen [q. v. Suppl. II] to fill the breach and take the exchequer, and in the ensuing shuffle of places, necessitated by the transfer to W. H. Smith of the treasury with the leadership of the house (*Life of Lord Cranbrook*, ii. 273), himself took the foreign office, a little brusquely, out of Iddesleigh's hands into his own. It must be remembered, however, that Iddesleigh had volunteered to resign, and had refused any other office.

Subsequent events showed that the cabinet had disliked Churchill's dictation more than his policy. Not only the service estimates of Goschen's budget, but the greatest legislative achievement of the administration (the Local Government Act, 1888) and the new Closure Act regulating parliamentary procedure were framed in accordance with his ideas. But the prime minister, even though he had in his own department been content with less interference in the Near East than had commended itself to Iddesleigh, could never be induced to recall him (*Life of Lord Randolph Churchill*, p. 776).

More lasting interest attaches to Salisbury's African policy. By granting a royal charter to the British East Africa Co. (1888), lately founded by Sir William Mackinnon [q. v. Suppl. I], he recovered for England the hold over the upper sources of the Nile which Iddesleigh by an agreement with Germany in 1886 had nearly lost. It was not, however, until 1890 that, after the fall of Bismarck, the Kaiser relinquished any claim to this region and to Uganda, and acknowledged a British protectorate over Zanzibar. In return for this Salisbury gave up Heligoland and, to the dismay of constitutional theorists, invited the consent of parliament to the surrender (see Anson's *Law and Custom*, ii. 299). It was characteristic of his diplomacy that he never regarded concessions—'graceful concessions,' as his critics called them—as a heavy price to pay for a good understanding, and there is little doubt that, in the belief that the Triple Alliance furnished the best guarantee for European peace, his policy was at this time governed by the idea of a good understanding with Germany. But beyond a good understanding he was not disposed to go. Like all the great English foreign ministers from Wolsey downwards, he saw that England's true function and strength consisted in maintaining the balance of power. The charter granted to the British East Africa Company was followed in 1889 by one in favour of the British South Africa Company which, under the guidance of Cecil Rhodes, was to colonise what is now Rhodesia. This occasioned trouble with the Portuguese, who raised a shadowy claim to Matabeleland. Salisbury sent an ultimatum to Lisbon, requiring their withdrawal from the British sphere of influence. Portugal was obliged to yield, and shortly afterwards a treaty delimiting the frontiers of Rhodesia was concluded. Trouble had also arisen with France in the same region in 1888, but in 1890 the French protectorate in Madagascar was acknowledged by England in return for a recognition of the English protectorate in Zanzibar. At the same time the British sphere of influence in Bornu was admitted and the French were compensated with the sands of the Sahara. It is plain that here, as well as in respect of the agreements with Germany and Portugal, British diplomacy had got the best of the bargain, and these bloodless African settlements are probably the most enduring monument of Salisbury's skill.

To return to home affairs. In 1888 the prime minister himself introduced in the House of Lords a life peerage bill, empowering the crown to create fifty peers for life, selected from the superior ranks of judges, officers in the army and navy, civil servants, and diplomatists as well as from among ex-colonial governors. The bill passed its second reading, but was then withdrawn. In 1891 the government passed a Free Education Act, which Salisbury had foreshadowed in 1885 (Newport speech), when he argued that since the state had made education compulsory, it was not fair that the very poor should have to find the money for it. But it was neither by this non-controversial act nor by that introducing local government in 1888 that the government was judged. It had been constituted upon the Irish issue, and Irish affairs played a conspicuous part in its history. The appointment of the Parnell commission Salisbury supported on the ground that it was most nearly analogous to the practice adopted by the House of Commons in respect of exceptional cases of bribery and some other matters (speech in the House of Lords, 10 August 1888). The discretion which Mr. Balfour showed in defending the Crimes Act of 1887, and the indiscretion which brought Parnell into the divorce court in 1890, enabled the ministry to fulfil its natural term of office.

At the general election of 1892, however, Gladstone was returned with a coalition majority of forty, and Salisbury gave place to the liberal leader. Gladstone introduced his second home rule bill, which, on Salisbury's advice, was rejected by the House of Lords. The new government retained office, however, under Lord Rosebery's leadership, until its defeat in 1895, when Salisbury formed a coalition ministry with Devonshire and Mr. Chamberlain (June 1895). At the ensuing general election he secured a majority of 152, and the country, in accordance with his ideas, entered upon a seven-year period of singularly unobtrusive but not unimportant legislation, which included such measures as the Workmen's Compensation Act (1897), the Criminal Evidence Act (1898), and the Inebriates Act (1898) (see for a useful list of laws passed MEE, *Lord Salisbury*, Appendix II). His special activities, however, lay at the foreign office, which he again combined with the premiership. Between 1895 and 1900 England found herself on the brink of war with each of the four great powers of the world, but no war occurred. The first crisis was produced by President Cleveland, who in his message to the United States Congress on 17 Dec. 1895 declared that Salisbury's refusal to agree to arbitration in the matter of the boundary between British Guiana and Venezuela amounted to a violation of the Monroe doctrine, and asked leave to appoint a boundary commission, whose finding should be enforced by the Republic. Salisbury took no immediate notice of this intemperate action, which roused American feeling to fever-point, but, when the clamour began to subside, supplied to the United States Commission, without prejudice, papers setting out the British case. That case was in fact so strong that the international tribunal, which in the end determined the dispute, decided almost wholly in its favour. A reaction in favour of England had meanwhile set in in America. Salisbury was careful to encourage it, by refusing to consent to European intervention in the Spanish-American war of 1898; thus reversing the traditional English policy of keeping Cuba out of the hands of a first-class power. He spared no effort to bring about a good understanding between the two Anglo-Saxon communities. Even though his project of a general treaty of arbitration was thrown out by the United States Senate in 1897, he continued to manifest goodwill by the surrender of the British rights in Samoa, including the harbour of Pago-Pago in 1899, while by the abrogation (Hay-Pauncefote treaty, 1901) of that part of the Clayton-Bulwer treaty of 1850 which stood in the way of a canal at Panama under American control, he allowed the United States to strengthen further their dominant influence over Central America.

The crisis in Anglo-German relations was destined to leave more durable memories. Within three weeks of Cleveland's message (on 3 Jan. 1896) the German Emperor despatched a telegram to President Kruger of the South African Republic congratulating him in imprudent language on the suppression of the Jameson Raid. English feeling rose high, but Salisbury contented himself with a naval demonstration in home waters which was probably so calculated as to produce an effect also in America.

At the close of the next year he suffered in the Far East what were perhaps the only considerable diplomatic reverses in his career. He was not able to prevent either the Germans from acquiring from China the lease of Kiao-Chau or Russia that of Port Arthur in 1897; nor was he prepared to resent the Russian representation that the presence of two British ships at the latter harbour, where they had a treaty right to be, had 'produced a bad impression at St. Petersburg.' Wei-hai-wei, which he secured for England as a set-off against these cessions to Russia and Germany, has admittedly proved to be a place of no strategic value. On the commercial side, however, his policy was successful. He checked the attempt of Russia to secure exclusive trading rights—in violation of the Treaty of Tientsin (1858)—within her recognised sphere of influence in Manchuria, and he obtained an undertaking from China not to alienate the Valley of the Yangtse, where British interests pre-eminently lay. This insistence upon the policy of the open door was followed by a very remarkable development of British enterprise in China.

His Far-Eastern policy, besides, must not be viewed alone. A dispute with France was already on the horizon. Early in 1897 a French expedition under Major Marchand had left the Congo, and the French flag was planted at Fashoda on the Upper Nile in July 1898. From this place Sir Herbert (Lord) Kitchener dislodged it shortly after the battle of Omdurman. The action was deeply resented in France, but Salisbury declined any compromise, and boldly faced the likelihood of war. The French eventually gave way, and relinquished any claims in the Sudan by the declaration of 21 March 1899. It is significant of Salisbury's far-sightedness that a secret agreement with Germany about Portuguese Africa was being concluded, when Marchand was discovered at Fashoda.

His most characteristic work is however to be found in his Near-Eastern policy. In 1897 the Armenian massacres had aroused great indignation, which was fostered by Gladstone. Salisbury, however, was not to be moved. He fully admitted the legitimacy of the feeling against Turkish rule; he solemnly warned the Sultan of the ultimate fate of misgoverned countries; but he steadily maintained that to endanger the peace of Europe for the sake of avenging the Armenians was not to be thought of. Hence he declined to act without the approval of the greater Powers—of the 'Concert of Europe,' an expression which in his time became very familiar. And though nothing was effected in Armenia, the use of this cumbrous instrument of diplomacy was vindicated in Crete, where, after the Greco-Turkish war of 1897, an autonomous constitution was established in 1899 by the pressure which the Concert under his leadership brought to bear upon the Porte. His support of arbitration was of a piece with his support of the Concert, and the English deputation to the Hague Conference, which followed upon the Tsar's Rescript (1899), proved perhaps the most efficient of those sent to it.

Meanwhile events in South Africa had brought England into open war with the Boer republics there, as a result of long pending disputes between the Boer rulers and British settlers. It was something of an irony that the largest army England had ever assembled should have been put into the field under the administration of a man who so earnestly laboured for peace. But to the charge that he ever wavered in his belief in the justice and necessity of the South African war he returned an indignant denial (speech at Albert Hall, 7 May 1902). He firmly refused to entertain any idea of foreign mediation (statement in the House of Lords, 15 March 1900), and his diplomacy was probably never more skilful than during that period of acute European Anglophobia. But his pre-occupation with foreign affairs had necessarily restricted his activity as prime minister, and at the reconstitution of the ministry in Nov. 1900, after the 'khaki' election of that year had confirmed him in power by a majority of 134, he took the sinecure post of lord privy seal and resigned the foreign office to Lord Lansdowne, retaining, however, a special supervision over its business so that the Anglo-Japanese Treaty of 1902 was concluded under his eye. His health had been failing for some time, but he regarded it as a matter of duty to retain the premiership until the war was finished. During that interval Queen Victoria died on 22 Jan. 1901. His personal devotion to her had been one of the deepest springs of his energy, and she had compared him with Peel and spoken of him as a greater man than Disraeli (BOYD-CARPENTER, *Some Pages of my Life*, p. 236). He was closely associated with some of the leading events in the great movement which gave lustre to the latter part of her reign. The Royal Titles Act making her Empress of India had been carried during his tenure of the India office. Both her jubilees fell within his premierships. The first Colonial Conference in 1887 was inaugurated under his administration. The ideal of pacific imperialism was one which he endeavoured to impress upon his countrymen, and with which he believed the future of his country to be closely bound up, though with characteristic caution he deprecated any factitious attempt to quicken or consolidate imperial sentiment. Almost his last public utterance (Albert Hall, 7 May 1902) was a warning not to hurry the affections of the mother-country and her daughter states. 'They will go on,' he told his audience, with a touch of mysticism very seldom to be found in his language, 'in their own power, in their own irresistible power, and I have no doubt they will leave combinations behind them which will cast into the shade all the glories that the British Empire has hitherto displayed. But we cannot safely interfere by legislative action with the natural development of our relations with our daughter countries. . . . There is nothing more dangerous than to force a decision before a decision is ready, and therefore to produce feelings of discontent, feelings of difficulty, which, if we will only wait, will of themselves bring about the results we desire.'

Peace was concluded with the Boers on 31 May 1902, and on 11 July he tendered his resignation. He had regarded it as a matter of public duty to see the war ended, and would thus, but for King Edward's illness, have attended the coronation ceremony of that year. His premiership had lasted through a total period of thirteen years and ten months, a tenure exceeding in duration by sixteen months that of Gladstone. On his recommendation his place as prime minister was filled by his nephew, Mr. A. J. Balfour, already first lord of the treasury and leader of the House of Commons. Salisbury died at Hatfield, a year after his retirement, on 22 Aug. 1903. In accordance with his wishes he was buried beside his wife (*d.* 20 Nov. 1899) to the east of Hatfield church; in this last point, as throughout his life, avoiding publicity so far as he was able. Parliament voted a monument to him in Westminster Abbey.

Owing to his great reserve, his character, so lovable to those few who knew him well, remained to the end something of an enigma to his countrymen. They were sensible of a sort of massive wisdom in his presence, and they came to trust him completely, because he was so evidently indifferent to all the baser allurements of place and power. But they hardly realised either the large simplicity of his nature or the profundity of his religion. His life, it was said, had been 'a consecrated one.' Each day at Hatfield was in fact begun in the chapel. The very deep belief in the greatness of goodness, which appears in his tribute to Dr. Pusey (speech at Arlington Street, 17 Nov. 1882), and in his constant insistence upon the superiority of character over intellect, was fortified as well as balanced by a very keen perception of the impenetrable mystery of the universe. He was to the end of his life, as his library and laboratory bore witness, a close student of science as well as of theology. These, though dominant and, as it sometimes seemed during his lifetime, conflicting interests, were curiously blended in the address on 'Evolution' which, as president of the British Association, he delivered at Oxford in 1894. He shows himself there as jealous for the honour of science that no guesses, however plausible, should be taken for solid proof of the theory of natural selection, as, for the honour of theology, that nothing should be allowed to overthrow the argument from design. The address (although one at least of its principal arguments—that correlating the antiquity of man with the rate of the cooling of the earth's crust—is no longer in date) exhibits a wide range of reading and reflection just as the brilliant article on 'Photography' (*Quarterly Rev.* Oct. 1864) exhibits great power of lucid exposition and of practical foresight, but it must nevertheless remain doubtful whether he possessed any real talent for original scientific work. The article 'On Spectral Lines of Low Temperature' (*Philos. Mag.* xlv. 1873, pp. 241–5) does not make for an affirmative conclusion. His early bent was towards chemistry, but he became much interested in electricity later in life.

Theology, science, and history filled his leisure moments. There seemed to be no inclination for any of the thousand forms of recreation which men ordinarily affect. He was accustomed to pass part of the year near the sea, sometimes at Walmer, which came to him in 1895 with the lord wardenship of the Cinque Ports, more usually at his villa in France, first at Puys near Dieppe and afterwards at Beaulieu on the Riviera. He was an interested observer of French developments and a careful student of French thought; his keen taste in literature made him a reader of the finely cut work of Mérimée and Feuillet. Yet no man was less of a doctrinaire. He considered questions on their merits, not in the light of *a priori* ideas. Politics, as he said, speaking on the question of hostile tariffs, were no exact science (speech at Dumfries, 21 Oct. 1884). He was all in favour of promising experiments, provided they were undertaken with caution. His mind was, indeed, of the broad English pattern; he enjoyed the poetry of Pope; he possessed an English contempt for the impracticable. The unfailing resolve to keep within the limits of the actual and the possible was, it has been said, at the root of the most familiar of his characteristics—his so-called cynicism—if cynicism be 'the parching-up of a subject by the application to it of a wit so dry as to be bitter' (LORD ROSEBERY, speech at the Oxford Union, 14 Nov. 1904). But also his cynicism was a continual protest against sentiment, for he dreaded more than all things the least touch of cant.

It is of a piece with this that the note of passion is wanting in his eloquence, for his emotion, instinctively repressed, seldom stirs the polished surface of his language. No great passage of oratory, no vivid imaginative phrase, keeps green the memory of his speeches. It is something of a satire upon this master of satire, that he is best remembered by certain casual and caustic comments, which criticism denominated 'blazing indiscretions.' His diplomatic caution and his extreme courtesy seemed to slacken in his public speeches, and he occasionally expressed himself before popular audiences with a humour as reckless as it was shrewd; not that he was, as was sometimes alleged, a blue-blooded aristocrat of the traditional type, but that he cordially detested all the plausible manœuvres by which party-managers set themselves to catch the vote of an electorate. He regarded democracy as inimical to individual freedom. A belief in letting men alone to develop their own thoughts and characters was native to his nature and at the heart of his creed. His relations with his colleagues, like his relations with his children, were characterised by this intense dislike of interfering with others. His conservatism itself rested upon the old conviction that by means of well-contrived checks and balances our ancestors had provided for the utmost possible freedom of the subject compatible with the maintenance of society. He desired to see the state just and not generous. And though his mind was too tenacious of experience, too intensely practical to allow of his making any very original contribution to conservative theory, his presentment of that theory was singularly penetrating. Whilst he saw 'the test-point of conservatism' in the maintenance of an hereditary second chamber (*Quarterly Rev.* July 1860, p. 281) he found 'the central doctrine of conservatism' in the belief 'that it is better to endure almost any political evil than to risk a breach of the historic continuity of government' (*ib.* Oct. 1873, p. 544). In regulating the franchise, he maintained that only a material and not any spiritual nor philosophic conception of the state was in point, and he vindicated the analogy between the state and a joint-stock company with singular ingenuity by an appeal to 'natural rights.' 'The best test of natural right is the right which mankind, left to themselves to regulate their own concerns, naturally admit' (*ib.* April 1864, p. 266). He was thus the inveterate enemy of the alliance of 'philosophy and poverty' against 'property.' He believed that the remedy for existing discontents—so far as they were susceptible of remedy at all—lay in the encouragement of forces diametrically opposed to free thought and legislative confiscation—that is in dogmatic religion and in production stimulated by security. He was a merciless querist of the radical idea of progress (*ib.* 'Disintegration,' Oct. 1883, p. 575). After the more definite conservatism of his youth had become a lost cause, he urged the need of restoring 'not laws or arrangements that have passed away, but the earlier spirit of our institutions, which modern theory and crotchet have driven out. . . . The object of our party is not and ought not to be simply to keep things as they are. In the first place the enterprise is impossible. In the next place there is much in our present mode of thought and action which it is highly undesirable to conserve. What we require in the administration of public affairs, whether in the executive or legislative department, is that spirit of the old constitution which held the nation together as a whole, and levelled its united force at objects of national import instead of splitting it into a bundle of unfriendly and distrustful fragments.'

Above all things, then, he was a patriot. His conservatism, trenchant and thorough as it was, merged in a larger devotion to his country. The bitterest moment of his career (1867), when public life seemed to be slipping from his grasp, evoked the loftiest of his utterances: 'It is the duty of every Englishman and of every English party to accept a political defeat cordially and to lend their best endeavours to secure the success, or to neutralise the evil, of the principles to which they have been forced to succumb. England has committed many mistakes as a nation in the course of her history; but their mischief has often been more than corrected by the heartiness with which after each great struggle victors and vanquished have forgotten their former battles, and have combined together to lead the new policy to its best results' (*ib.* Oct. 1867, p. 535). Here was the secret spring of his greatness, and it enabled him to hold back the forces he feared for a full decade. For, though his special talent lay in the sphere of foreign affairs, he ranks with the greatest of prime ministers. He thrice led his party to decisive victory at the polls, and held the first place in the state for a longer period than any prime minister of the nineteenth century save one, Lord Liverpool. He retired in the enjoyment of the unabated confidence of the country. For seven years he held a coalition together in office, though the combination had shown symptoms of splitting before his ministry was formed (*Life of the Duke of Devonshire*, ii. 267–9), and a split at once followed the withdrawal of his influence. In all his nearly fourteen years of office only one member of his cabinets resigned on principle, and this was a man constitutionally unfit for cabinet government. Curiously enough it is Lord Randolph Churchill's son who has drawn attention to Salisbury's exceptional capacity for managing that machine (WINSTON CHURCHILL'S *Life of Lord Randolph Churchill*, p. 602).

In his relations with the rank and file of his party Salisbury was perhaps less successful. Though he was a most considerate host, society bored him; the ready word, the genial interest in unknown men's endeavour were not his to give; and he was frequently charged with availing himself too exclusively of the ability that lay close at hand. For all that something akin to reverence was felt for his person and his opinion. Like Pitt, one of the two statesmen on whom he formed himself, he seemed towards the end to move in an atmosphere of splendid aloofness from common cares and aims. Yet it is rather to the character which he drew of Castlereagh that the student of his life and work will turn for a concluding sentence: 'He was that rare phenomenon—a practical man of the highest order, who yet did not by that fact forfeit his title to be considered a man of genius.'

Among the honours bestowed on him he received, besides the Garter, the G.C.V.O. from King Edward VII on 22 July 1902. He was lord warden of the Cinque Ports and constable of Dover Castle from 1895 (installed 15 Aug. 1896); one of the Elder Brethren of Trinity House; high steward of Westminster and Great Yarmouth; and from 1868 to 1876 chairman of the Hertfordshire quarter sessions. Academic distinctions included a D.C.L. at Oxford (1869), a LL.D. at Cambridge (1888), and an hon. studentship of Christ Church (1894).

There are portraits of him (1) by G. Richmond (1872) at Hatfield, of which there is a replica at All Souls' College, Oxford; and (2) by the same artist (1887) at Windsor; (3) by Millais (1882) in the possession of the Hon. W. F. D. Smith; (4) by Watts (1884) at the National Portrait Gallery; (5) by Sir H. von Herkomer (1893) at the Carlton Club; and (6) by Anton von Werner as a study for the head in the picture of the Berlin Congress painted for the German Emperor. This portrait is in the possession of the present marquis of Salisbury. There is also in Lord Salisbury's possession a well-known crayon head by Richmond, which was done between 1865 and 1868. A statue of him by Sir G. Frampton stands just outside Hatfield Park gates, and another by Mr. H. Hampton at the foreign office. Both of these are posthumous. In the last year of his life he sat for the bust, by Sir G. Frampton, now in the debating hall of the Oxford Union Society. There is also a bust of him by W. Theed, jun. (1875), at Hatfield House. The monument near the west door of Westminster Abbey was designed by Mr. Goscombe John, who is now (1912) executing one for Hatfield church.

Of his sons, the present Lord Salisbury, who succeeded to the title, has been under-secretary of state for foreign affairs (1900–3), lord privy seal (1903–5), and president of the board of trade (1905); Lord William, the rector of Hatfield, is an hon. canon of St. Albans and chaplain to the King; Lord Robert, a K.C. and M.P. (1906–10 and 1911); Lord Edward, D.S.O., is under-secretary for finance in Egypt; Lord Hugh has been M.P. for Oxford University since 1910.

[Pending the appearance of the authoritative Life of Salisbury by Lady Gwendolen Cecil, that by H. D. Traill (1890), though it closes in 1886, remains the best. S. H. Jeyes's Life and Times of the Marquis of Salisbury (4 vols. 1895–6) carries the story up to 1895.

F. S. Pulling's Life and Speeches of the Marquis of Salisbury (2 vols. 1885) and H. W. Lucy's Speeches of the Marquis of Salisbury (1885) will also be found useful. The Third Salisbury Administration, by H. Whates (1900), gives a full account of the activities of his government between 1895 and 1900. There are numerous other lives of him of no great value, among which that by F. D. How (1902) may be mentioned. Scattered references to his work and character appear in the biographies of his colleagues and contemporaries, viz. in those of Lord Cranbrook (Hon. A. E. Gathorne-Hardy), Lord Iddesleigh (Andrew Lang), Lord Randolph Churchill (W. S. Churchill), Bishop Wilberforce (R. Wilberforce), Duke of Devonshire (B. Holland), and Mr. Alfred Austin's Autobiography.

The two most suggestive things that have appeared about him are Lord Rosebery's tribute at the unveiling of his bust at the Oxford Union (14 Nov. 1904) and an anonymous article signed 'X' in the Monthly Review, Oct. 1903. The latter, which is of an intimate character, was written by Lord Robert Cecil, K.C. In the Quarterly Review Oct. 1902 and Jan. 1904 are articles dealing respectively with his foreign policy and with his connection with the Review. The student will, however, find in Salisbury's own contributions to that periodical, of which a complete list is subjoined, the most valuable of all the sources of information about him. These contributions were:—1860: April, The Budget and the Reform Bill; July, The Conservative Reaction; Oct., Competitive Examinations. 1861: Jan., The Income Tax and its Rivals; April, Lord Stanhope's Life of Pitt, i. and ii.; July, Democracy on its Trial; Oct., Church Rates. 1862: Jan., Lord Castlereagh; April, Lord Stanhope's Life of Pitt, iii. and iv.; July, The Bicentenary; Oct., The Confederate Struggle and Recognition. 1863: Jan., Four Years of a Reforming Administration; * April, Poland. 1864: * Jan., The Danish Duchies; * April, The Foreign Policy of England; July, The House of Commons; Oct., Photography. 1865: Jan., The United States as an Example; April, Parliamentary Reform; July, The Church in her Relations to Political Parties; The Elections. 1866: Jan., The Coming Session; April, The Reform Bill; July, The Change of Ministry. 1867: Oct., The Conservative Surrender. 1869: Oct., The Past and the Future of Conservative Policy. 1870: Oct., The Terms of Peace. 1871: Jan., Political Lessons of the War; Oct., The Commune and the Internationale. 1872: Oct., The Position of Parties. 1873: Oct., The Programme of the Radicals. 1881: April, Ministerial Embarrassments. 1883: Oct., Disintegration.

The three articles marked * were republished in 1905 in a volume as 'Essays: Foreign Politics.'] A. C-l.

CHADS, Sir HENRY (1819–1906), admiral, born at Fareham, Hampshire, on 29 Oct. 1819, was son of Admiral Sir Henry Ducie Chads [q. v.] by his wife Elizabeth, daughter of John Pook of Fareham. Major-general William John Chads, C.B., is his younger brother. After two years at the Royal Naval College at Portsmouth, Henry entered the navy in 1834, and served with his father in the Andromache, in the East Indies and against Malay pirates in the straits of Malacca. In June 1841 he was promoted lieutenant, and as lieutenant of the Harlequin was, in 1844, severely wounded in an attack on the pirate settlements in Sumatra. For this service he was specially promoted to commander on 31 Jan. 1845. From 1846 to 1848 he commanded the Styx on the west coast of Africa with considerable success, and on 5 June 1848 was advanced to post rank. As captain he served with credit but without distinction; in 1863 he was appointed superintendent of Deptford dock and victualling yards, from which, in April 1866, he was promoted to his flag. In 1869–70 he was second-in-command of the Channel fleet; was promoted rear-admiral in October 1872; was commander-in-chief at the Nore 1876 to Sept. 1877, when he reached the rank of admiral. On 27 Oct. 1884, having attained the age of sixty-five, he was placed on the retired list. He was made K.C.B. in 1887. Settling at Southsea, he largely devoted himself there to the care and organisation of charities in connection with the navy, and especially the Seamen and Marines' Orphanage, the committee of which he joined in 1868 in succession to his father. He died unmarried at Southsea on 30 June 1906.

[Royal Navy Lists; The Times, 2 July 1906; Clowes, Royal Navy, vols. vi. and vii. 1901–3.] J. K. L.

CHALMERS, JAMES (1841–1901), missionary and explorer, born at Ardrishaig, Argyllshire, on 4 Aug. 1841, was son of a stonemason near Peterhead. His mother, also of highland blood, came from Luss on Loch Lomond. His early years were mainly spent at Ardrishaig, Lochgilphead, and Glenaray, near Inverary, and he was educated at the village schools. At ten he saved a schoolfellow from drowning. Before he was fifteen he entered the office of a firm of lawyers at Inverary. A letter from a Fiji missionary, read in a Sunday-school class, led him in 1856, at the age of fifteen, to determine on being a missionary (*Autobiog.* p. 27). Chalmers at once began religious work, and in 1861 was for eight months in the service of the Glasgow City Mission. Offering himself to the London Missionary Society, the work of which in the South Seas had already appealed to him, Chalmers was accepted for training, entered Cheshunt College in September 1862, and remained here until June 1864; he then spent a year at Highgate in a home for missionary students, and for another year worked at Plumstead in mastering the Rarotongan language. He was ordained to the congregationalist ministry in October 1865, and on 4 January 1866 sailed for Rarotonga, the largest island of the Hervey group, which was reached after much adventure on 20 May 1867.

Chalmers spent ten years in this comparatively quiet field of work. Soon in charge of the mission, he pursued a policy of moral reform, cultivated a missionary spirit amongst the more devoted natives, and was diligent in work at the institution for the training of native teachers. His methods, characteristic and unconventional, drew some criticism from his colleagues, but endeared him to the people. His bold spirit sought, however, severer experience. In 1876 Chalmers was appointed to New Guinea, where work amongst the savages had been begun in 1871. In May 1877 Chalmers left Rarotonga, reaching Port Moresby, New Guinea, in October. The new duty contrasted strongly with that he had left. The land was little known, and the savages were of evil repute. There was need of incessant travel, mainly by water, and there was constant peril of death. Such work suited Chalmers. In 1878 he visited 105 villages, at ninety of which he was the first white man ever seen. He went unarmed, firmly resisted extortion by chiefs, and diligently sought out stations for his South Sea teachers. From 1879 to 1886 Chalmers did much exploration work of general value. He began a systematic examination of the Gulf of Papua, visiting the entire coast from Yule Island to Bald Head. In 1879 he discovered the mouths of the Purari river, which he revisited in 1883. By 1881 he thought he knew 'more of the country and the people than any other foreigner' (*Autobiog.* p. 201). He was not a scholar, but in that year he translated the synoptic gospels into Motu, a language spoken east and west of Port Moresby (*Hist. of the British and Foreign Bible Society*, v. 244). At home some hesitation was felt as to Chalmers's rough-and-ready methods: he freely used tobacco as currency; but he worked well with his fellow missionary, William George Lawes [q. v. Suppl. II]. By 1884 Chalmers had placed out nine New Guinea evangelists, and thought that the mission might prove 'one of the greatest . . . that ever yet has been worked' (*Autobiog.* pp. 228–9). He succeeded, indeed, in planting a line of mission posts from the Papuan Gulf to the Louisiade Archipelago.

Chalmers regretted the policy under which Mr. Chester, police magistrate of Thursday Island, in 1883 took formal possession of south-east New Guinea as a kind of appendage to Queensland. The reputation of the colony in dealing with native labour was not good; and Chalmers went to Australia in the hope of serving the interests of his people. Opponents called him the 'tyrant missionary,' but his visit had good effect. A protectorate was proclaimed by Commodore Erskine at Port Moresby in November 1884, Chalmers and Lawes helping to bring the New Guinea chiefs together for the ceremony there and at other points. The commodore warmly acknowledged the 'invaluable services' of the two missionaries, a commendation repeated later by Admiral Bridge (*The Times*, 4 May 1901) and by another official, H. H. Romilly (*The Western Pacific and New Guinea*, pp. 241–2).

Chalmers came home on furlough in 1886; declined overtures to enter government service; read papers on New Guinea before the Colonial Institute (*Proceedings*, xviii. pp. 88–122) and before the Royal Geographical Society (*Proceedings*, n.s., ix. 71–86); saw a book through the press, and addressed many meetings. In June 1887 he sailed again for New Guinea, and spent two years in visiting stations up and down the coast. In 1890 he crossed to Australia, and visited Samoa, where he met Robert Louis Stevenson, who wrote of him as 'a man I love' (*Letters*, ii. 212, *cf.* ii. 220), and one for whom he felt a 'kind of hero-worship' (*Life of R. L. Stevenson*, ii. 127).

From 1892 to 1894 Chalmers undertook work in the Fly river and western district of the mission, making his centre at Saguane amidst the mangrove swamps of the Fly delta. The dangers from the natives were even greater than those already met, and Chalmers prophetically regarded the work as his last. It was interrupted by another visit to England, but he was at Saguane again in January 1896. His hope was to establish a base from which to reach the little known tribes of the interior. In

1900 he was joined by the Rev. O. C. Tomkins. The end came, in the way so often feared and so often nearly reached, in 1901. On 4 April Chalmers and Tomkins, with some South Sea mission boys and a teacher, sailed for Goaribari Island. They reached Risk Point on 7 April and anchored off the village of Dopima. Crowds boarded the boat and would not leave. In the hope of drawing them off, Chalmers and Tomkins landed with their party. They never returned. Invited into a native house, the missionaries were knocked on the head, killed, and eaten.

Chalmers was twice married: (1) to Jane, daughter of Peter Hercus, who died at Sydney on 20 Feb. 1879; and (2) to Elizabeth Harrison, a widow who, as Elizabeth Large of Leeds, had been a friend of his first wife. She died on the island of Daru on 5 Oct. 1900. There were no children.

Chalmers was a man of simple, unquestioning faith and overflowing zeal, of sanguine temperament, restless spirit, and dauntless courage; in manner unconventional, and possessing singular powers of winning the confidence alike of white men and of the wildest savages. He was an excellent speaker, and had some command of vivid, picturesque narrative. He left three records of his experiences: 'Work and Adventure in New Guinea' (jointly with W. Wyatt Gill, 1885; new edit. 1902); 'Pioneering in New Guinea' (1887; new edit. 1902); and 'Pioneer Life and Work in New Guinea' (1895). His autobiography is incorporated in the Life by Lovett (1902).

[Lovett's James Chalmers: his Autobiography and Letters (with portraits), 1902; Lovett's History of the London Missionary Society, vol. i. (1899); King's W. G. Lawes of Savage Island and New Guinea.]

A. R. B.

CHAMBERLAIN, Sir CRAWFORD TROTTER (1821-1902), general, born in London on 9 May 1821, was third son of Sir Henry Chamberlain, first baronet, sometime consul-general and chargé d'affaires in Brazil, by his second wife. Sir Neville Bowles Chamberlain [q. v. Suppl. II] was an elder brother.

After education at private schools and under tutors Crawford obtained a cadetship in the Bengal army in 1837, and was posted to the 28th Bengal native infantry. From this corps he was transferred to the 16th Bengal native infantry, and with the outbreak of the Afghan war in 1839 his active service began. He was present at the siege of Ghazni (23 July 1839) and at the operations around Kandahar. In Sept. 1841 he was appointed to the command of the 5th Janbaz cavalry, and in the following month he became adjutant of Christie's horse. Until the end of the Afghan campaign he was engaged in constant and severe fighting. In 1843 he was sent to Scinde with two squadrons of Christie's horse as an independent command, to be known as Chamberlain's horse. In 1845 he was invalided to the Cape, where he married. Next year he returned to India as second in command of the 9th irregular cavalry, into which his own corps had been absorbed. During the Sikh war (1845–9) he was constantly in action. He was at the battle of Chillianwalla on 13 Jan. 1849, receiving the medal and clasp. On 30 Jan. he was again engaged in the neighbourhood; here he was wounded, and was made the subject of a special despatch by Lord Gough (31 Jan.) (Forrest, *Sir Neville Chamberlain*, pp. 236–7). At the battle of Gujarat on 21 Feb., he had to be lifted into the saddle, where he remained throughout the day. He was awarded the clasp, was mentioned in despatches, and, being promoted to captain and brevet major in Nov. 1849, was given the command of the 1st irregular cavalry, formerly Skinner's horse. He served with them in the Momund expedition of 1854 and received a medal and clasp.

With 1857 came more serious work. On the outbreak of the mutiny Chamberlain displayed the utmost courage and resolution. The force of his influence and the fine state of discipline in his regiment were made manifest when his men, in the midst of mutiny, suspected and overt, volunteered to shoot condemned rebels at Jullundur (4 June 1857). Stronger proof still was forthcoming, when Chamberlain, although not the senior officer on the spot, was entrusted with the dangerous duty of disarming the 62nd and 69th regiments at Mooltan. He executed this commission on 11 June with what was described as 'an extraordinary mixture of audacity and skill.' Sir John Lawrence in his report declared that 'the disarming at Mooltan was a turning-point in the Punjab crisis second only in importance to the disarming at Lahore and Peshawur.' At Cheechawutnee (Sept.) Chamberlain was attacked by an overwhelming force of the enemy, and was compelled to take the unusual course of housing his cavalry in a caravanserai. The situation required great promptness and the firmest exercise of discipline. Chamberlain himself was sick, but he succeeded in maintaining the defence, until he was relieved three days later.

For his services in the mutiny he was promoted to be lieutenant-colonel, a reward which was generally regarded as inadequate. The oversight was admitted and rectified long afterwards. In April 1862 he was made colonel, in 1864 he was appointed honorary A.D.C. to the governor-general, and two years later was made C.S.I., and was included in the first list of twelve officers for good service pension. In 1866, too, he was transferred to the command of the central Indian horse, and next year to the command of the Gwalior district with the rank of brigadier-general. In 1869 he was officiating political agent at Gwalior, and received the thanks of government for his services. From Oct. 1869 to Feb. 1870 he was acting political agent at the court of Scindia until his promotion to major-general. During his unemployed time as major-general he served on various commissions and courts of inquiry; and from 1874 to 1879 he commanded the Oudh division. He became lieutenant-general in Oct. 1877 and general in Jan. 1880. In 1880 he returned to England for the first time since 1837; with the exception of his visit to the Cape, he had never left India in the interval. In 1884 he was retired from the active list. In 1897, on the occasion of Queen Victoria's diamond jubilee, he was made G.C.I.E. Sir Crawford, who retained his splendid physique till near the end, died at his residence, Lordswood, Southampton, on 13 Dec. 1902, and was buried at Rownhams. He was married twice: (1) in 1845, at the Cape, to Elizabeth, daughter of J. de Witt; she died on 19 Jan. 1894; and (2) in 1896 to Augusta Margaret, daughter of Major-general John Christie, C.B., who survived him. There was no issue by either marriage.

[Broad Arrow, 20 Dec. 1902; Nav. & Mil. Gazette, 15 Feb. 1896 and 20 Dec. 1902; Major-gen. O. Wilkinson and Major-gen. J. Wilkinson, Memoirs of the Gemini Generals, 2nd edit. 1896; Lord Roberts, Forty-one Years in India, 30th edit. 1898, p. 70 seq.; R. Bosworth Smith, Life of Lord Lawrence, 1901, i. 538; T. Rice Holmes, History of the Indian Mutiny, 5th edit. 1898; G. W. Forrest, Life of Sir Neville Chamberlain, 1909.] R. L.

CHAMBERLAIN, Sir NEVILLE BOWLES (1820–1902), field-marshal, born at Rio de Janeiro on 10 Jan. 1820, was second son of Henry Chamberlain, consul-general and chargé d'affaires in Brazil, by his second wife, Anne Eugenia (*d.* 1867), daughter of William Morgan of London. His father was created a baronet in 1828, on account of the negotiation of a treaty of commerce with Brazil, and died in London on 31 July 1829, when he was about to go to Lisbon as minister (*Gent. Mag.* 1829, ii. 274). He was succeeded in the baronetcy by Henry, the elder son of his first marriage (with Elizabeth Harrod of Exeter), which had been dissolved in 1813. By his second marriage he had five sons and three daughters. The eldest of these sons, William Charles (1818–1878), became an admiral; the other four entered the East India Company's service and distinguished themselves as soldiers. The third son, Sir Crawford Trotter [q. v. Suppl. II], was closely associated with Neville throughout his military career. The fourth son, Thomas Hardy (1822–1879), was major-general, Bombay staff corps. The fifth son, Charles Francis Falcon, C.B.(1826–1879), was colonel in the Indian army, Bombay staff corps.

At thirteen Neville entered the Royal Military Academy as a cadet; but he proved more combative than studious, and was withdrawn at the end of his probationary year. On 24 Feb. 1837 he was commissioned as ensign in the East India Company's army. He reached Calcutta in June, and after being temporarily attached to other regiments, he was posted to the 55th Bengal native infantry, and joined it at Lucknow early in 1838. On 28 Aug. he was transferred to the 16th Bengal native infantry, which was at Delhi, and his brother Crawford was attached to the same regiment. Sir Henry Fane [q. v.], the commander-in-chief in India, had been a friend of his father, and wished the two sons to take part in the expedition to Afghanistan, which was then in preparation.

The 16th formed part of the Bengal column of the army of the Indus, which reached Kandahar on 27 April 1839, and was joined there by the Bombay column. At the end of June the army marched on Kabul and on 23 July Ghazni was stormed. Chamberlain distinguished himself in the fighting which preceded the assault. His regiment was left at Ghazni as a garrison when the army moved on to Kabul. In the autumn of 1840 some of the sons of Dost Mahomed (including Shere Ali, the future Ameer) were sent to Ghazni as prisoners on parole, and the Chamberlain brothers became intimate with them. In June 1841 the 16th was relieved of its garrison duty by the 27th, in which John Nicholson [q. v.] was a subaltern. He and

Neville Chamberlain at once became warm friends.

On 25 Aug. the 16th arrived at Kandahar, and on 8 Nov. it set out on its march back to India; but the outbreak at Kabul led to its immediate recall to Kandahar. During the next nine months the force there under General (Sir) William Nott [q. v.] had repeated encounters with the Afghan levies, and Chamberlain took a prominent part in these actions. He was temporarily appointed to the 1st cavalry of Shah Sujah's force, and soon made himself a name as a skilful swordsman and a daring leader of irregular horse. In the action of the Urghundab (12 Jan. 1842) he was wounded in the knee, but nevertheless took part in the pursuit. In March his men failed him, and he had to fight hard for his life (FORREST, p. 106). On 29 May he was again wounded, being stabbed in the thigh by a Ghazi, who sprang upon his horse. He was given a gratuity of twelve months' pay on account of his wounds.

In August 1842 Nott's force marched from Kandahar on Kabul. Chamberlain went with it, and took part afterwards in the capture and burning of Istaliffe on 28 Sept., which made him 'disgusted with myself, the world, and, above all, with my cruel profession' (FORREST, p. 149). The combined forces of Nott and Pollock left Kabul on 12 Oct. They were harassed by the Afghans on their homeward march as far as Peshawar, and Chamberlain, who was with the rear-guard, was twice wounded —by a bullet near the spine on 16 Oct. and a bullet in the leg on 6 Nov. He had been nearly four years in Afghanistan and had been wounded six times. He had earned the 1839 medal for Ghazni and the 1842 medal for Kandahar, Ghazni, and Kabul. General Nott spoke so highly of him that on 2 Jan. 1843 he was appointed to the governor-general's bodyguard. This did not remove him from his regiment (the 16th), in which he had become lieutenant on 16 July 1842.

Though still suffering from his last wound, he took part in the Gwalior campaign and in the battle of Maharajpore on 29 Dec. 1843, for which a bronze star was awarded. On 20 Feb. 1845 he left Calcutta for England, very reluctantly, for the first Sikh war was imminent, but as his only chance of cure. He returned to India at the end of 1846, having partially recovered the use of his leg. He was military secretary to the governor of Bombay till May 1848, and was then employed for a few months under the resident at Indore; but on the outbreak of the second Sikh war he applied for active service, and was appointed brigade-major of the 4th cavalry brigade (irregulars).

In the operations preceding the passage of the Chenab Lord Gough [q. v.] called for a volunteer to swim the river and reconnoitre the right bank. Death was certain, if the Sikhs were still there; but Chamberlain swam across with a few men of the 9th lancers, found that the Sikhs had gone, and was greeted by Gough on his return as 'the bravest of the brave.' At Chillianwalla his brigade was left to protect the baggage, but at Gujarat it was actively engaged. Chamberlain distinguished himself in the pursuit, and Gough promised him the command of the first regiment of irregular cavalry that might be in his gift. He received the Punjab medal with two clasps, and when he became captain in his regiment on 1 Nov. 1849, he was given a brevet-majority.

In May 1849 he was appointed assistant adjutant-general of the Sirhind division, but he soon tired of office routine. He asked for civil employment, and in December he was made assistant commissioner in the Rawul Pindi district, whence he was transferred to Hazara in June 1850. He was entrusted with the organisation of the military police for the Punjab, and at the beginning of 1852 he was appointed military secretary to the board of government at Lahore, which supervised the police. Within three months he wished to throw up this post in order to take part in the expedition to Burmah, but Lord Dalhousie objected that such volunteering would be to the detriment of the government he was serving (FORREST, p. 255).

In the autumn his health broke down, from malarial fever caught in Hazara. He went to South Africa on sick leave and spent a year and a half hunting lions north and south of the Vaal. He returned to India at the end of 1854 to take up the command of the Punjab irregular force, which Lord Dalhousie had reserved for him. This force, modelled upon the Guide corps raised in 1846 by (Sir) Harry Burnett Lumsden [q. v. Suppl. I], numbered 11,000 men and had to guard 700 miles of frontier against turbulent tribes. Chamberlain was only a captain in his regiment, but he was made brevet lieutenant-colonel (28 Nov. 1854) and was given the local rank of brigadier. In April 1855 he led an expedition into Meeranzie, and in August against the Orakzais, for which he received the thanks of the governor-general. In the autumn of 1856 he had to go again to Meeranzie, and in March 1857 it became necessary to penetrate the Bozdar country, which no European had visited. By skilful handling he maintained a certain degree of order on the frontier with a minimum of bloodshed and exasperation.

In May 1857 came the Indian Mutiny. On the first news of it a movable column was formed to crush any outbreak in the Punjab, and Chamberlain was given command of it, with lieutenant (now Earl, Roberts as his staff-officer. But he soon handed over this command to John Nicholson, being appointed adjutant-general of the Bengal army, and he joined the force before Delhi on 24 June. He took a leading part in repulsing the attacks of the mutineers on 9 and 14 July. In the latter action, seeing that the men hesitated before an enclosure wall which was lined by the enemy, he set them an example by leaping his horse over it. They followed him, but he got a ball in his shoulder which partially disabled him for the rest of the siege. He helped, however, to stiffen the wavering purpose of the British commander during the storming of the city, and on 16 Sept. he took temporary command of the force, to allow General (Sir) Archdale Wilson [q. v.] some much needed rest. He received the thanks of the governor-general and the mutiny medal with Delhi clasp, and was made C.B. on 11 Nov. 1857.

Chamberlain was disabled by his wound from taking part in the relief of Lucknow, and was obliged to decline Sir Colin Campbell's offer of command of the cavalry in the Rohilla campaign of 1858. He resigned the post of adjutant-general and was re-appointed to the command of the Punjab irregular force with the rank of brevet-colonel on 27 Nov. 1857, and the local rank of brigadier-general. In August 1858 he nipped in the bud a dangerous conspiracy among the Sikh troops at Dera Ismail Khan, and received the thanks of the secretary of state. In December 1859 he led an expedition against the Kabul Khel Waziris, and another in April 1860 against the Mahsuds, forcing his way to Kaniguram, which they boasted that hostile eyes had never seen. His force was composed entirely of native troops, and included tribesmen under their own chiefs. The India medal with a clasp for north-west frontier was afterwards granted to the men who took part in these expeditions or in those to Meeranzie and the Bozdar country. On 11 April 1863 Chamberlain was made K.C.B.

In the autumn of 1863 he was called upon to lead a force of 5000 men against the Wahabi fanatics, who had found shelter at Sitana and had been persistently troublesome. He decided to take one column from Peshawur over the Ambela pass into the Chamla valley, while another column co-operated from Hazara. He reached the top of the pass on 20 Oct., but found that the Bunerwals meant to dispute his advance and that other tribesmen were gathering from all the country between the Indus and the Afghan frontier. His force was not strong enough to overcome such opposition, and pending reinforcement he took up a defensive position on the top of the pass, with outlying picket posts on commanding heights. These posts were assailed again and again, taken and retaken. On 20 Nov. Chamberlain himself led three regiments (the Highland light infantry, 5th Gurkhas, and 5th Punjab infantry) to recover the Crag picket; he succeeded, but received a wound in the forearm, which obliged him to hand over command. The governor-general, Lord Elgin, died on the same day, and his council decided to withdraw the expedition. Chamberlain thought such a step most inadvisable; eventually reinforcements were sent up, and under General Garvock the Yusafzai field force completed its task. Those who served in it received the India medal with clasp for Ambela.

Chamberlain went home as soon as he was fit to travel, and joined his mother and sisters at Versailles in July 1864. His mother died there on 28 Dec. 1867. He was promoted major-general on 5 Aug. 1864, and was made K.C.S.I. on 24 May 1866. Towards the end of 1869 he accompanied the Duke of Edinburgh, by Queen Victoria's wish, on his visit to India. He was promoted lieutenant-general on 1 May 1872, G.C.S.I. on 24 May 1873, and G.C.B. on 29 May 1875.

Chamberlain returned to India in February 1876, to take command of the Madras army. When it was decided, in August 1878, to send a British mission to Kabul, he consented to go as envoy, being personally known to Shere Ali; but the mission was stopped at Ali Musjid on 21 Sept. by the Ameer's orders. Chamberlain agreed with Lord Lytton that it must be shown 'that the British government loses no time in resenting a gross and unprovoked insult,' and he acted for some months as military member of council. But he did not wholly approve of the treaty of Gandamak; still less of the policy of disintegration which Lord Lytton adopted after the second occupation of Kabul. In July 1879 he wrote: 'I have lived sufficiently long on the frontier to know that a time *does* come when one feels the benefit of not being committed to a single outpost more than is indispensable for internal security' (FORREST, p. 492). He strongly deprecated the retention of Kandahar in 1880.

His term of command at Madras came to an end on 3 Feb. 1881, and he bade farewell to India. He spent the rest of his life at Lordswood near Southampton. He had become general on 1 Oct. 1877, was placed on the unemployed supernumerary list on 3 Feb. 1886, and was made field-marshal on 25 April 1900. He died at Lordswood on 18 Feb. 1902, and was buried beside his wife at Rownhams near Southampton. Sir Charles Napier called him 'Cœur de Lion.' He was 'the very soul of chivalry.'

On 26 June 1873 Chamberlain married Charlotte Cuyler, sixth daughter of Major-general Sir William Reid [q. v.]; she died on 26 Dec. 1896 without children.

[G. W. Forrest, Life of Chamberlain, 1909; The Times, 19 Feb. 1902; W. H. Paget, Record of Expeditions against the North-west Frontier Tribes, 1884; Daly, The Punjab Frontier Force, in United Service Institution Journal, 1884; Lord Roberts, Forty-one Years in India, 1897; Adye, Sitana, 1867; Lady B. Balfour, Lord Lytton's Indian Administration, 1899.]

E. M. L.

CHAMIER, STEPHEN HENRY EDWARD (1834–1910), lieutenant-general, royal (Madras) artillery, born in Madras on 17 Aug. 1834, of Huguenot descent [see CHAMIER, ANTHONY], was fifth son of Henry Chamier, chief secretary to the Madras government and afterwards member of council, 1843–8, by his wife Marie Antoinette Evelina, daughter of Thomas Thursby, H.E.I.C.S. His grandfather, Jean Ezéchiel Deschamps Chamier, was also member of the Madras council. Captain Frederick Chamier [q. v.] was an uncle.

Educated at Cheltenham College and Addiscombe, Chamier was appointed on 11 June 1853 second lieutenant in the Madras artillery, and joined artillery headquarters at St. Thomas Mount, on 8 Oct. 1853. Posted to the first battery in March 1854, he proceeded to Burmah in July 1854. After commanding an outpost of artillery at Sittang on 3 Aug. 1854, he was appointed station staff officer there on 16 Nov. 1854. On 11 April 1856 he proceeded on field service to Kareen Hills in command of a mountain train of howitzers and rockets, and was engaged with hill Kareens on 22 April. For driving the enemy from their position on the Zoungzalen river and dispersing them, Chamier received the thanks of the government of India. After commanding B battery horse artillery for a few months at Bangalore, he proceeded in May 1857 to Madras *en route* for Burmah, but the news of the Sepoy mutiny at Meerut led to a change of plans, and he went with Major Cotter's horse battery to Calcutta and thence to Benares and Allahabad. Detached to Gopigunge with two guns and some infantry, he disarmed a part of the Bengal native infantry. Proceeding to Mirzapur and on towards Rewa, he held the Kattra Pass, where he was joined by a Madras regiment and C battery Madras artillery, and received the command of a battery. Ordered to Cawnpore to aid General Windham's operations against the Gwalior contingent, the force was continuously engaged for three days, with heavy loss; out of thirty-six men with Chamier's guns seventeen were killed or wounded. For his splendid handling of his guns Chamier was complimented by General Dupuis Ple on the field, and thanked in public despatches. Chamier also took part on 8 Dec. 1857 in the utter rout of the Gwalior contingent mutineers by Sir Colin Campbell [q. v.] in the vicinity of Cawnpore. At his own request he, in February 1858, rejoined Major Cotter's horse battery and marched with General Franks from Benares through Oude to Lucknow, engaging on the way in the actions of Chanda, Ameerapur, Sultanpur, and the different skirmishes. At Lucknow Chamier joined the fifth division of the army under Lord Clyde, and took part in the operations before and during the siege and capture of the city. After its fall Chamier's battery joined the force which went under Major-General Lugard to the relief of Azimgurh, being engaged against Koer Singh's rebel force and against other rebels near Jagdispur and Arrah. In June 1858 the campaign, during which, according to artillery orders, Chamier was engaged in nineteen actions, came to a close (*Lond. Gaz.* 25 May and 29 June 1858).

In Sept. 1858 Lord Canning, the governor-general, appointed Chamier, in consideration of his recent service, to be commandant of the first battery artillery, Hyderabad contingent. He was promoted to second captain on 29 Feb. 1864 and received a brevet-majority on 11 Oct. 1864 for his actions in the field, together with the medal for the Indian Mutiny campaign and the clasp for Lucknow. After commanding a battery of horse artillery at home from 1872 to 1876, he was, on promotion to regimental lieutenant-colonel, put in command of two batteries at Barrackpur. From 1877 to 1881 he was deputy inspector-general and from 1881 to 1886 inspector-general of ordnance, Madras. During his tenure of these posts expeditions were sent to Malta, Afghanistan, and Upper Burmah, and he received the thanks of the Madras government, which were endorsed by the viceroy. He retired in October 1886 with the rank of lieutenant-general, being made C.B. for his services during the Indian Mutiny and receiving the reward for distinguished service. All under whom he served, including Sir James Outram [q. v.], Sir Harry Lumsden [q. v. Suppl. I], and Sir Thomas Harte Franks [q. v.], eulogised his soldierly qualities.

Chamier was a good musician and played the violincello. He graduated Mus. Bac. of Trinity College, Dublin, in 1874. He died after a long illness at his residence, Brooke House, Camberley, on 9 June 1910.

On 4 Sept. 1858 he married, at Dinapore, Dora Louisa, daughter of George Tyrrell, Esq., M.D., county Down, and by her had six daughters and three sons. His widow survived him with two daughters and one son, George Daniel, C.M.G., lieutenant-colonel of the royal artillery.

[The Times, 11 June 1910; Army Lists; private records and correspondence; G. B. Malleson, Hist. of Indian Mutiny, 1880, ii. 244 seq.; G. W. Forrest, Indian Mutiny, 1904, vol. ii.] H. M. V.

CHANCE, Sir JAMES TIMMINS, first baronet (1814–1902), manufacturer and lighthouse engineer, born at Birmingham on 22 March 1814, was the eldest of the six sons of William Chance (1788–1856), merchant and glass manufacturer, of Spring Grove, Birmingham (high bailiff 1829–30), by his wife Phoebe (*d.* 1865), fourth daughter of James Timmins of Birmingham. From a private school at Totteridge James passed to University College, London, where he gained high honours in languages, mathematics, and science. At seventeen he entered his father's mercantile business, but finding the work distasteful began to study for holy orders. In 1833 he matriculated from Trinity College, Cambridge, where he made mathematics his chief study, won a foundation scholarship, and graduated B.A. as seventh wrangler in 1838, after losing a year through insomnia brought on by overwork; he proceeded M.A. in 1841, and M.A. *ad eundem* at Oxford in 1848. Changing his views as to a profession, he became a student at Lincoln's Inn, but he ultimately joined his uncle and father in their glass works at Spon Lane near Birmingham. Here he devoted himself to the manufacturing side of the business and to its scientific developments.

Whilst still at Cambridge he had invented a process for polishing sheet glass so as to produce 'patent plate,' the machinery for which still remains in use. But it was the manufacture and perfection of dioptric apparatus for lighthouses which came to absorb Chance's attention. This difficult manufacture, originally a French invention, was first carried on in England by Messrs. Cookson & Co. of South Shields from 1831 to 1845, when it became again the monopoly of two firms in Paris. About 1850 the manufacture was taken up by Chance's firm. M. Tabouret, a French expert, was engaged for its superintendence, but he left the Chances' service in 1853. Two years later the manufacture began in earnest under James Chance's direction. Royal commissioners had been appointed in 1858 to inquire into the state of the lights, buoys, and beacons of the United Kingdom, and had soon detected grave defects in the existing dioptric apparatus. On 23 Dec. 1859 the commissioners thoroughly examined the works at Spon Lane, under the guidance of James Chance, who placed his mathematical and technical knowledge at their disposal. At the request of the commissioners, Sir George Airy, the astronomer royal, consulted with Chance and examined at Spon Lane, on 2 and 3 April 1860, a large apparatus under construction for the government of Victoria. New principles formulated by Airy were first tried upon an apparatus which the firm was constructing for the Russian government. In the autumn of 1860 Chance joined Professor Faraday, acting for the Trinity House, in experimenting with the firm's apparatus at the Whitby southern lighthouse. Faraday acknowledged deep indebtedness to Chance 'for the earnest and intelligent manner in which he has wrought with me in the experiments, working and thinking every point out,' and he announced that the manufacturer could henceforth be relied upon to adjust the apparatus perfectly. One thing that Chance discovered at Whitby was that for the adjustment by 'internal observation' it was not necessary to see the horizon itself, but that a graduated staff at a short distance from the lighthouse might represent its direction. This important discovery enabled the apparatus to be adjusted accurately before it left the manufactory.

Chance effected permanent alterations in the Whitby light on the newly formulated scientific principles. An elaborate paper on all the questions at issue which he sent to the commissioners in January 1861 is printed in their report. In May 1861, by request of the Trinity House, Chance took part in an examination of all the dioptric apparatus in their charge. Most of the lights were of French manufacture, and in several cases Chance could only remedy the defects by entire reconstruction, in which he made the final adjustments mostly with his own hands. The old system of requiring the firm to make the light in conformity with prescribed specifications was abandoned, and Chance with rare exceptions was left to design the light himself. He personally superintended every detail of the work, and from a sense of patriotism declined to patent improvements but made them public property. At the Paris Exhibition of 1867 the instruments of his design were proved by scientific tests to be superior in efficiency to similar apparatus of French manufacture. On 7 May in the same year he read before the Institution of Civil Engineers a paper on 'Optical Apparatus used in Lighthouses' (*Proc. Inst. of Civ. Eng.* xxvi. 477–506), which became a classic, and for which he was awarded a Telford medal and premium. He was also elected (21 May) an associate of the institution. On 22 April 1879 he read before the institution a second important paper on 'Dioptric Apparatus in Lighthouses for the Electric Light' (*ib.* lvii. 168–183.) Meanwhile in 1872, he relinquished to Dr. John Hopkinson [q. v. Suppl. I], whose services the firm then secured, the direction of the lighthouse works, and gradually retired from the management of the firm.

Chance was actively engaged in local and county affairs, and was prominent in directing the chief religious, educational, and philanthropic institutions in Birmingham. At a cost, including the endowment, of 30,000*l.* he gave the town in 1895 West Smethwick Park. He was high sheriff of Staffordshire in 1868, and was mainly instrumental in forming the Handsworth Volunteer Rifle Corps, the first corps in the Midlands. He was a director of the London and North Western railway from 1863 to 1874. In 1900 he endowed, at a cost of 50,000*l.*, the Chance School of Engineering in the university of Birmingham. He was created a baronet on 19 June 1900. He lived at Brown's Green, Handsworth (1845–69), Four Oaks Park, Sutton Coldfield (1870–9), and afterwards at 51 Prince's Gate, London, and 1 Grand Avenue, Hove, where he died on 6 Jan. 1902. He was buried, after cremation at Woking, in the Church of England cemetery, Warstone Lane, Birmingham. By his will, dated 16 Oct. 1897, with codicils (1898–1901), he left an estate of the gross value of 252,629*l.* 19*s.* 5*d.*

He married, on 26 June 1845, Elizabeth, fourth daughter of George Ferguson of Houghton Hall, Carlisle; she died on 27 Aug. 1887, leaving three sons and five daughters. William, the eldest son, a barrister of the Inner Temple, succeeded as second baronet.

A portrait by J. C. Horsley, R.A. (1854), is in the possession of Mr. George F. Chance, of Clent Grove near Stourbridge. Another by Roden of Birmingham (*circ.* 1874) is in the possession of Sir William Chance, Orchards, near Godalming. A posthumous portrait by Joseph Gibbs, of Smethwick, was presented on 16 Dec. 1902 to the borough of Smethwick, and hangs in the town hall. A successful bust in bronze by Hamo Thornycroft, R.A. (1894), is the property of Sir William Chance; there is a replica in West Smethwick Park, and another (in marble) in the possession of Mr. George F. Chance.

[The Lighthouse Work of Sir James Chance, Baronet, by James Frederick Chance, M.A. (with preface by James Kenward, C.E., F.S.A., manager of the lighthouse works), 1902; Proceedings of Inst. of Civil Engineers, cxlix. 361-6; Birmingham Daily Post, 8 Jan. 1902; Birmingham Weekly Post, 11 Jan. 1902; Debrett; information kindly supplied by J. F. Chance, Esq.] C. W.

CHANNER, GEORGE NICHOLAS (1842–1905), general, Indian staff corps, born at Allahabad on 7 Jan. 1842, was eldest surviving son of eight children of George Girdwood Channer, colonel, Bengal artillery (1811–95). His mother was Susan (*d.* 1895), eldest daughter of Nicholas Kendall, J.P., vicar of Talland and Lanlivery, Cornwall. Educated at Truro grammar school and Cheltenham college (1856–9), he passed direct on 4 Sept. 1859 into the Indian army, but served with the 89th and 95th regiments till 7 Aug. 1866, when he entered the Bengal staff corps. He was first employed on active service in the north-west frontier of India campaign in 1863–4. He served in the Ambela campaign, and was present at the actions of 16 and 17 December 1863 against the Sitana fanatics. He afterwards was with General Wilde's column in Jadur country in 1864. He also shared in the Lushai operations in 1871–2. He next served, when a captain, with the 1st Gurkhas in the Malay peninsula in 1875–6, and when with the Malacca column in operations in Sungei Ujong, Terrachi and Sri-Mentani, won the Victoria Cross on 20 Dec. 1875. Channer was sent forward in command of a party of his Gurkhas to reconnoitre the road across the Burkit Putus Pass, which was known to be occupied by the enemy, though owing to the contour of the country and the density of the jungle it was impossible to ascertain without close approach either the number of the foe or the strength of his defences. Selecting two men only to support him, and leaving his company in the rear, Channer pushed on into the jungle. Discovering a native, to act as his unwitting guide, he reached the stockade, within which the enemy were in force. He and his two men leaped the stockade, which was formidably constructed, and rushed on the enemy, who were at a meal. Shots were exchanged, but under the impression that a large force was at hand the natives bolted. A signal brought up the remainder of the Gurkhas, who occupied the captured position. In his despatch describing the operations Colonel Clay, commanding the column, assigned to Channer's foresight and intrepidity prevention of great loss of life (*Lond. Gaz.* 29 Feb. 1876). The gallant deed practically brought the campaign to a close. Channer was mentioned in despatches, and obtained the brevet of major on 12 April 1876. He next served with the expedition against the Jowaki Afridis in 1877 (clasp); was with the 29th Punjab infantry in the Afghan war of 1878–80, and with the Kuram field force, and was present in command of the regiment at the attack and capture of the Peiwar Kotal; he was mentioned in despatches (*Lond. Gaz.* 7 Nov. 1879), and received medal with clasp and the brevet of lieutenant-colonel on 22 Nov. 1879. He attained the rank of colonel in the army on 22 Nov. 1883, at the early age of forty-one. In 1888 he commanded the 1st brigade of the Hazara field force, under General (Sir) John McQueen, in the expedition to the Black Mountain which was undertaken to punish the tribes for an attack on British troops in British territory. Active operations were commenced on 3 Oct., and by 18 Nov. the troops had returned to British territory. Channer was the moving spirit of the campaign, and earned universal approval by his splendid energy and the inexhaustible fertility of his resources in every emergency. He was mentioned in despatches and was nominated C.B. on 10 April 1889.

Channer returned to his command, at Jalandhar, and received the reward for distinguished service on 9 Sept. 1892. He was colonel on the Bengal staff from 19 Nov. 1888 to 17 Aug. 1890, and brigadier-general from 22 April 1892 to 11 Dec. 1896, in command of the Assam district. He attained the rank of major-general on 27 April 1893, and was promoted lieutenant-general on 9 Nov. 1896, and general on 12 Jan. 1899. In November 1901 he was placed on the unemployed supernumerary list.

He died on 13 Dec. 1905 at Buckleigh, Westward Ho! Devonshire. He married in June 1872 Annie Isabella, daughter of John William Watson. His widow survived him, and of his four surviving sons two served in the army.

[Army Lists; The Times, 16 Dec. 1905; Daily Telegraph and Western Daily Mercury, 14 Dec. 1905; Lt. Rich, Campaign in Malay Peninsula; private information.] H. M. V.

CHAPMAN, EDWARD JOHN (1821–1904), mineralogist, was born in London on 22 Feb. 1821, and educated in France and Germany, where he gave special attention to chemistry and mineralogy. He was professor of mineralogy in University College, London, from 1849 to 1853, and professor of mineralogy and geology at the University of Toronto from 1853 to 1895.

His earlier researches, dealing mostly with analyses of minerals, were published in the 'Philosophical Magazine,' 'Chemical Gazette,' &c. He also described some artesian wells near Silsoe, in Bedfordshire (*Phil. Mag.* 1852); and made experiments on the absorption of water by chalk (*ibid.* 1853), the mean results indicating that certain strata in that formation could absorb two and a half gallons of water per cubic foot.

After settling in Canada he acted as general editor (1856–66) of the 'Canadian Journal: a Repertory of Industry, Science, and Art,' published at Toronto. His researches now widened. He studied the minerals, rocks, and fossils of Canada, published analyses of coal and iron-ore, wrote on fossil brachiopods, on crinoids and their classification, on trilobites, and on certain fossil tracks termed 'Protichnites' and 'Climactichnites,' which he regarded as impressions of fucoids. In 1864 he issued 'A Popular and Practical

Exposition of the Minerals and Geology of Canada' (2nd edit. 1871; 3rd edit. 1888, re-named 'The Minerals and Geology of Central Canada').

Chapman became Ph.D. in 1860, and the degree of LL.D. was subsequently conferred on him. He died at the Pines, Hampton Wick, Middlesex, on 28 Jan. 1904.

His works include: 1. 'Practical Mineralogy,' 1843. 2. 'A Brief Description of the Characters of Minerals,' 1844. 3. 'An Outline of the Geology of Canada,' Toronto, 1876. 4. 'Blowpipe Practice,' Toronto, 1880. 5. 'Mineral-Systems: a Review, with Outline of an attempted Classification of Minerals in Natural Groups' (posthumous), 1904. He also published 'A Drama of Two Lives,' a volume of verse, in 1899.

[Mineralogical Mag. xiv. 1904, p. 65; Geol. Mag., 1904, p. 144.] H. B. W.

CHARLES, JAMES (1851–1906), portrait and landscape painter, born at Warrington, Lancashire, in January 1851, came of a family, originally French, who were long settled in Carnarvon, and owned fishing and cargo boats trading with Anglesey. His father, Richard Charles, was a draughtsman and cabinet maker, who designed the mayor of Carnarvon's chair of office, now in the town hall, where also hangs his portrait painted by his son. As a lad of fourteen, James Charles accompanied his father to London, where he received a desultory education while working in his father's office. He was for some time employed at a lithographer's, then studied at Heatherley's school of art in Newman Street, and finally entered the Royal Academy School in 1872. Marrying and settling in 1875 at 15 Halsey Street, Chelsea, he exhibited his first picture at the Royal Academy, 'An Italian Youth in Armour,' and sold it on the opening day. In 1876 he had four pictures in the Academy, including his father's portrait, and in 1877 three portraits, one being of Victor Cavendish the present duke of Devonshire, and his brother as children; from this date to 1904 he was yearly represented by from one to four pictures. He also exhibited at the Grosvenor Gallery. In 1879 he was introduced to a picture collector of Bradford, Mr. John Maddocks, who appreciated his work, and henceforward not only purchased many of his canvases himself (see *Sale Cat.* of Maddocks' collection, 30 April 1910) but made him known in Bradford and the north of England, where he established a lasting and profitable connection. From 1877 onwards he painted a good deal, first at Thorpacre near Loughborough, Leicestershire, and subsequently at South Harting, Petersfield, Sussex, where his subject pictures included 'Christening Sunday' (R.A. 1887), now in the Manchester Corporation Art Gallery; the landscape 'The Lost Cap' (McCulloch collection); 'The Village Post Office' (Johannesburg Gallery); and 'Will it Rain?' (Tate Gallery). Between 1889 and 1895 he lived at Colnor House, Bosham, Chichester, where he painted 'Milking Time,' a sunny landscape with cattle (now in the Melbourne Art Gallery). and 'Signing the Marriage Register' (R.A. 1895; now in Bradford Gallery). In 1896 he moved to East Ashling House, Chichester, and engaged in pictures of rustic life.

Charles, who had spent two previous seasons in the Paris studios, visited Venice in 1891, and in the same year was elected an associate of the Société Nationale des Beaux Arts in Paris. In 1896 he produced 'The Chalk Pit,' and a year or two later 'Souvenir of Watteau,' a fine work in chiaroscuro (now in the Johannesburg Gallery), 'In Spring Time,' and many landscapes. The two darkest months of every year he now devoted to Yorkshire, where he undertook many family and presentation portraits. The summer months of 1902 and 1904 were passed at Montreuil-sur-Mer, where some of his most charming coast- and sea-scapes were painted. During the winter of 1905 he was at Capri. Appointed judge at the Carnarvon Eisteddfod in August 1906, he underwent an operation for appendicitis whilst staying at Plas Bennett, Denbigh, in the vale of Clwyd, and died there on 27 Aug. 1906; he was buried in Fulham cemetery.

His friend George Clausen wrote of his sincerity, his enthusiasm, and of his devotion to his ideal of colour and atmosphere. 'His work is marked by restraint and delicacy of perception, as well as by freedom from affectation and mannerism and striving for effect. He had a strong perception of character akin to that of Charles Keene.... The thing he most loved to express—the beauty of sunlight—he has painted better than any other of our time. He was a rapid and tireless worker and had attained such mastery and control of his means that in his later years he could render his subject in the simplest way, with the instinctive directness of a master' (cf. *Leicester Gallery Cat.* pref., 1907).

In 1907, after his death, some of his work was shown in the winter exhibition of the

Royal Academy, and the sale of seventy-six of his remaining works at the Leicester Gallery produced about 3000*l*. In addition to the art galleries named, those of Warrington and Dublin also possess examples of his work. In January 1875 he married at the pro-cathedral, Kensington, Ellen Agnes Williams (*d.* 1909) by whom he had five sons and seven daughters. In 1908 a civil list pension of 70*l*. was granted to his widow.

[Private information from his daughter, Miss Nina Charles, and from Mr. John Maddocks; The Times, 30 Aug., 5 Sept. 1906; Mr. George Clausen, R.A. (Preface to Leicester Gallery Catalogue, portrait as frontispiece); Athenæum, 8 Sept. 1906, 16 Feb. 1907; Algernon Graves, Royal Academy Exhibitors (in which much of Charles's work is erroneously attributed to *John* Charles); Christie's Sale Cat. 30 April 1910; Royal Academy Winter Exhibition Cat. 1907.]

A. F. S.

CHARLEY, Sir WILLIAM THOMAS (1833–1904), lawyer, born at Woodbourne, co. Antrim, on 5 March 1833, was youngest son of Matthew Charley (1788–1846) of Finaghy House, Belfast, by his wife Mary Anne, daughter of Walter Roberts of Collin House. He received his education at Elstree House School, Lee, Kent, and at St. John's College, Oxford, where he matriculated on 28 June 1856, graduating B.A. in 1856 and proceeding B.C.L. and D.C.L. by accumulation in 1868. Entering as a student at the Inner Temple on 3 June 1857, he was called to the bar on 9 June 1865. Though a fair lawyer and the editor of several text-books, Charley never obtained more than a moderate practice, for the most part carried on in Liverpool and Salford.

Charley was an active politician in the conservative interest all his life, and he took a prominent part in the reorganisation of the conservative party in the metropolis and Lancashire which accompanied the extension of the franchise in 1867. At the general election of Dec. 1868 he was returned as one of the conservative members for Salford, and he retained his seat in Feb. 1874. At the general election, however, of April 1880 he was defeated, and he was an unsuccessful candidate at Ipswich in 1883 and 1885. While in Parliament Charley was a constant speaker, and an out-and-out supporter of Disraeli, taking an especial interest in social and ecclesiastical questions, on which latter he held strong protestant views; he was the author of some useful measures, one of which, the Offences against the Persons Act of 1875, was the forerunner of the celebrated Criminal Law Amendment Act of 1885 for the better protection of young women and girls.

Charley's election as common serjeant in April 1878 against a strong field of competitors occasioned, in view of his modest legal qualifications, general surprise in the profession. The result was the abolition in the Local Government Act of 1888 of 'the right claimed by the court of common council to appoint to the office of common serjeant,' which was thereby vested in the crown (51 & 52 Vict. c. 41, s. 42). Though he was knighted on 18 March 1880, and was made a Q.C. in the same year, his performance of his official duties was the cause of dissatisfaction, and he retired on a liberal pension of 1500*l*. in 1892.

Charley was a vigorous defender of the Church of England and trustee of numerous church societies. His later years were largely devoted to lecturing on 'the higher criticism,' a subject for which his studies had imperfectly qualified him. An enthusiastic volunteer from the early days of the movement, he commanded the 3rd volunteer battalion of the royal fusiliers, the City of London regiment, retiring in 1889 with the rank of honorary colonel. He rode at the head of his old regiment at the annual inspection in Hyde Park a few weeks before his death, which took place suddenly in the Literary Institute at East Grinstead, Sussex, on 8 July 1904. He was buried at East Grinstead cemetery.

Charley married in April 1890 Clara, daughter of F. G. Harbord of Kirby Park, Cheshire; there was no issue.

Charley edited reports of cases determined in the Supreme Court of Judicature, 1876, and was author of a treatise on the 'Real Property Acts, 1874–5' (3rd edit. 1876); 'The New System of Practice and Pleading' (1877); 'The Crusade against the Constitution, an Historical Vindication of the House of Lords' (1895); 'Mending and Ending the House of Lords' (1900); and 'The Holy City, Athens, and Egypt' (1902).

[Men and Women of the Time; Foster's Baronetcy; Foster's Men at the Bar; The Times, 9 July 1904; private information.]

J. B. A.

CHARTERIS, ARCHIBALD HAMILTON (1835–1908), biblical critic, born at Wamphray, Dumfriesshire, on 13 Dec. 1835, was eldest son of John Charteris, parish schoolmaster, by his wife Jean Hamilton. From his parish school he passed to Edinburgh University, where he took honours in Latin, mathematics.

moral philosophy, natural philosophy, and logic, and graduated B.A. in 1852 and M.A. in 1853.

Entering the Church of Scotland ministry, he was presented in 1858 to the parish of St. Quivox, Ayrshire, but in the following year became minister of New Abbey parish in Galloway, of which James Hamilton, his maternal uncle, had been minister from 1813 to 1858. While there he wrote the biography of James Robertson (1803–1860) [q. v.], founder of the endowment scheme of the Church of Scotland (Edinburgh, 1863; abridged as 'A Faithful Churchman,' in 'Church of Scotland Guild Library' series, 1897). In 1863 he succeeded John Caird [q. v. Suppl. I] as minister of Park Church, Glasgow, where his preaching and his work among the young attracted attention.

After some time spent abroad on account of ill-health, he became, in 1868, professor of biblical criticism in Edinburgh University and retained the post till 1898. He was a conservative theologian, his most notable theological work being 'Canonicity: a Collection of Early Testimonies to the Canonical Books of the New Testament' (Edinburgh, 1880). The book, which is based on Kirchhofer's 'Quellensammlung,' was commended by Hilgenfeld, Godet, and Professor Sanday. He also published 'The New Testament Scriptures: their Claims, History, and Authority' (Croall lecture, 1882), and 'The Church of Christ: its Life and Work' (Baird lecture, 1887, published 1905).

Charteris was mainly responsible for a marked revival of practical Christian effort within the Church of Scotland. He was the founder, and from 1871 to 1894 convener, of the general assembly's Christian life and work committee, which inaugurated many new forms of Christian enterprise. Under his guidance there were originated the Young Men's Guild and the Young Women's Guild. He also revived the order of deaconesses, took a lead in founding at Edinburgh the Deaconess Institution and Training Home, and the Deaconess Hospital. He started (January 1879), and for many years edited, 'Life and Work,' the monthly magazine of the Church of Scotland, which has now an average circulation of 120,000 copies. He also originated and successfully promoted the scheme of 'Advance' in connection with the foreign missions of his church, and rendered conspicuous service as vice-convener of the general assembly's committee for the abolition of patronage and of the endowment committee. He was moderator of the general assembly in 1892.

Charteris was one of the royal chaplains in Scotland from 1870. From Edinburgh University he received the hon. degrees of D.D. (1868) and LL.D. (1898). After some years of ill-health he died on 24 April 1908 at his residence in Edinburgh, and was buried at Wamphray. In 1863 he married Catherine Morice, daughter of Sir Alexander Anderson, Aberdeen; she survived him without issue. His portrait, painted by J. H. Lorimer, R.S.A., was presented to the Church of Scotland, and now hangs in the offices of the church, 22 Queen Street, Edinburgh.

[Scotsman, 25 April 1908; Scottish Review (weekly), 30 April 1908; My Life, by Very Rev. William Mair, D.D., 1911, pp. 134–5, 214, 281, 304; private information; personal knowledge. A biography by the Hon. and Rev. Arthur Gordon is in preparation.]

W. F. G.

CHASE, DRUMMOND PERCY (1820–1902), last principal of St. Mary Hall, Oxford, born on 14 Sept. 1820 at Château de Saulruit, near St. Omer, was second son of John Woodford Chase of Cosgrave, Northamptonshire. Matriculating at Pembroke College, Oxford on 15 Feb. 1839, he became scholar of Oriel College on 22 May 1839, and was one of four who obtained first-class honours in classics in Michaelmas term, 1841. He graduated B.A. on 25 Nov. 1841, proceeding M.A. on 14 June 1844 and D.D. in 1880, and was ordained deacon in 1844 and priest in 1849. Elected fellow of Oriel College on 1 April 1842, just when the question of John Henry Newman's relation to the Anglican church was at its acutest phase, he retained his fellowship till his death, sixty years afterwards. He was tutor of Oriel from 1847 to 1849 and again from 1860 to 1866. He was senior proctor of the University in 1853, and printed his Latin speech on going out of office on 26 April 1854. He was a select preacher before the university in 1860, and was vicar of St. Mary's, Oxford, from 1855 to 1863 and again from 1876 to 1878.

When he began his duties as college tutor, he took the unusual step of printing the substance of his principal course of lectures for the use of his pupils and other Oxford passmen. This was an edition, with translation and notes, of Aristotle's 'Nicomachean Ethics' (1847; 4th edit. 1877). The translation has been twice reprinted alone, in 1890 and again in 1906. He also issued 'A First Logic Book' in 1875, and 'An Analysis of St. Paul's Epistle to the Romans' in 1886.

In 1848 Chase became vice-principal of

St. Mary Hall, Oxford, the principal being Philip Bliss [q. v.]. In 1857 he was appointed principal on Bliss's death, and set himself vigorously to reform the place. He would admit no idle or extravagant candidate who was seeking to migrate from a college. But he welcomed diligent and frugal men, whose poverty excluded them from expensive colleges. The institution of the non-collegiate body in 1868, and the foundation of Keble College in 1870, made other and better provision in the university for poor undergraduates. Chase therefore advised the university commissioners of 1877 to merge, on his death, St. Mary Hall in Oriel College, with which it was connected both locally and personally. This suggestion was embodied in the Commissioners' Statutes in 1881, and accordingly, on Chase's death in 1902, St. Mary Hall ceased, after an independent existence of nearly six hundred years.

Chase, between 1854 and 1881, published frequent pamphlets on academic questions, and many occasional sermons preached before the university. In speeches and pamphlets he resisted in 1854, in the interests of poor professional men in country places, the abolition by the university commission of all local and other special qualifications for scholarships and fellowships. A don of the old school, courteous, gentle, and kindly, brimming over with quiet fun and quaint Oxford anecdotes, he died at St. Mary Hall on 27 June 1902. He was buried in Holywell cemetery, Oxford.

He married on 28 June 1859 Caroline Northcote, who died without children in 1904.

[Macleane, Pembroke College, 1897, p. 240; Shadwell's Registrum Orielense, 1902, ii. 438; The Times, 30 June 1902; Guardian, 1902, p. 954; Oxford Times, 5 July 1902; Appreciations by Rev. L. R. Phelps in Oxford Magazine, xxi. 10, and by Rev. R. S. Mylne in Oxford Times, 7 July 1902.]

A. C.

CHASE, MARIAN EMMA (1844–1905), water-colour painter, born on 18 April 1844 at 62 Upper Charlotte Street, Fitzroy Square, London, was the second of the three daughters of John Chase (1810–1879) by his second wife Georgiana Ann Harris. Miss Chase was educated at a private school at Ham, near Richmond. Her father, a member of the New Water Colour Society (now the Royal Institute of Painters in Water Colours), taught her perspective and water-colour painting; Margaret Gillies [q. v.] gave her instruction in drawing from the life; and she enjoyed the friendship and advice of Henry Warren, president of the New Water Colour Society, E. H. Wehnert [q. v.], Henry Tidey [q. v.], and other artists. In early life she devoted a good deal of time to illuminating, but it was as a painter in water-colour of flowers, fruit, and still-life that she made her mark, by virtue of her truthful colouring and delicate treatment. She painted in the same medium interiors, a few landscapes, and, towards the close of her life, studies of flower-gardens; in her figure subjects she was less successful. She also occasionally worked in oil. She exhibited from 1866 to 1905 at the Royal Academy, the Royal Society of British Artists, the Royal Institute, the Dudley Gallery, the Grosvenor Gallery, the International Exhibition of 1871 and various provincial, colonial, and foreign exhibitions. On 22 March 1875 she was elected an associate of the Institute of Painters in Water Colours (now the Royal Institute), and in 1879 she became a full member. In 1888 the Royal Botanical Society awarded her a silver medal. Save for a tour abroad with her father about 1876, Miss Chase, who resided in later life at Brondesbury, worked entirely in England. She died from heart-failure after an operation on 15 March 1905, and was buried in St. Pancras Cemetery, Finchley.

At the Bethnal Green Museum is a water-colour drawing, 'Wild Flowers,' by her. Miss M. C. Matthison of Temple Fortune House has a collection of her works, as well as a pastel portrait of her as a child, and a miniature portrait painted shortly before her death by Miss Luie Chadwick.

[Information kindly supplied by Miss M. C. Matthison; E. C. Clayton, English Female Artists, ii. 183–5; Men and Women of the Time, 1899; Graves, Dictionary of Artists; Cat. Royal Institute of Painters in Water Colours (with some reproductions); Cat. Water Colours, Victoria and Albert Museum; W. S. Sparrow, Women Painters of the World, 1905, p. 130 (reproduction); Standard, 18 April 1878; Queen, 15 Feb. 1890 (portrait); St. John's Wood, Kilburn and Hampstead Advertiser, 29 Aug. 1901 and 23 March 1905 (portrait).]

B. S. L.

CHASE, WILLIAM ST. LUCIAN (1856–1908), lieut.-colonel, eldest son of Captain Richard Henry Chase of the control department of the war office, was born in St. Lucia, West Indies, on 21 Aug. 1856. He was educated at the Royal Military College, Sandhurst, and entered the army as sub-lieutenant in the 15th foot on 10 Sept. 1875, becoming lieutenant and joining the Bombay staff corps on 31 May 1878. He served in the Afghan war of 1879 to 1880, taking part in the defence of Kandahar. With Private James Ashford of the royal fusiliers he showed conspicuous gallantry on the occasion of the sortie from Kandahar on 16 Aug. 1880 against the village of Deh Kwaja. Chase and Ashford then rescued a wounded soldier, Private Massey of the royal fusiliers, who had taken shelter in a blockhouse, and brought him to a place of safety, carrying him over 200 yards under the fire of the enemy. For this service both Chase and Ashford were awarded the Victoria Cross (4 Oct. 1881) and were mentioned in despatches.

Chase served with the Zhob Valley expedition in 1884 as deputy assistant quartermaster-general, and was again mentioned in despatches. From 1 Nov. 1882 to 10 Dec. 1887 he was deputy assistant adjutant-general, Bombay. Promoted captain on 10 Sept. 1886, he was appointed on 28 Aug. 1889 wing commander of the 28th Bombay native infantry (pioneers). He took part in the Lushai expeditionary force in 1889–90, and was again mentioned in despatches, receiving also the medal with clasp. In 1893 he officiated as second in command of the regiment. Promoted major on 10 Sept. 1895, he served on the N.W. frontier in 1897–8 against the Mohmands (*Lond. Gaz.* 11 Jan. 1898), receiving the medal with clasp, and was also present in the Tirah campaign of 1897–8, taking part in the capture of the Sampagha Pass, in the operations at and around Datoi, in the action of 24 Nov. 1897, and in the operations in the Bara Valley, 7 to 11 Dec. 1897 (*Despatches, Lond. Gaz.* 5 April 1898).

On 10 June 1899 he became regimental commandant of the 28th Bombay native infantry, with the temporary rank of lieut.-colonel. He was nominated C.B. in 1903. Later he became assistant adjutant-general Quetta division, and was on leave when promoted to command the Fyzabad brigade. He returned to Quetta, where he died of brain disease on 30 June 1908.

He was a fellow of the Royal Asiatic Society and of the Royal Geographical Society. He married in 1901 Dorothy, daughter of Charles Edward Steele, district magistrate of Hyderabad.

[Hart's and Official Army Lists; The Times, 20 July 1908; H. B. Hanna, The Second Afghan War, 1910, iii. 456.] H. M. V.

CHEADLE, WALTER BUTLER (1835–1910), physician, born at Colne on 15 Oct. 1835, was son of James Cheadle, thirteenth wrangler at Cambridge in 1831, who was vicar of Christ Church, Colne, Lancashire. His mother was Eliza, daughter of John Butler of Ruddington, Nottinghamshire. Educated at the grammar school of Bingley, Yorkshire, of which town his father became vicar in 1837, he proceeded in 1855 to Cambridge as a scholar of Gonville and Caius College. In 1859, when a family bereavement prevented him from rowing in the university eight, he graduated B.A. In 1861 he took the M.B. degree, having studied medicine both at Cambridge and at St. George's Hospital, London.

In June 1862 he started with William Fitzwilliam, Viscount Milton (1839–1877), to explore the then little known western parts of Canada. After their return in 1864 they published in their joint names a successful account of their travels as 'The North-West Passage by Land' (1865), which soon ran through eight editions. A ninth and last edition appeared in 1891. The book was written by Cheadle, and narrates a notable series of hardships faced with indomitable courage in mountainous and untracked country. The expedition conducted by Sir Sandford Fleming in 1892 through the Rocky mountains to plan the Canadian Pacific railway was guided largely by the track of Cheadle and his companion (cf. SANDFORD FLEMING, *Ocean to Ocean*, p. 251).

In 1865 he proceeded M.A. and M.D. at Cambridge, and, becoming a member of the Royal College of Physicians in 1865, was elected a fellow in 1870; he was subsequently councillor (1889–91), censor (1892–3) and senior censor in 1898; he acted as examiner in medicine in the college (1885–8). He delivered in 1900 the Lumleian lectures before the college 'On some Cirrhoses of the Liver.' Meanwhile elected physician to the Western General Dispensary in 1865, and assistant physician to St. Mary's Hospital in 1867, he was dean of the medical school of the hospital (1869–73). He held this last post at a critical period of the school's existence, but under his guidance the school more than doubled the number of its students. He became physician to in-patients in 1885, and remained on the active staff until 1904, when he was appointed honorary consulting physician. For sixteen years of his connection with the hospital he acted as dermatologist. He also acted as lecturer on materia medica and therapeutics for five years, on pathology for ten years, on medicine jointly with Sir William Broadbent [q. v. Suppl. II] and Dr. David Bridge Lees for ten years, and on clinical medicine for twelve years. For St. Mary's medical school he did much good service, helping to found scholarships and encouraging the athletic clubs. In 1898 he gave over 1000*l.* to endow a Cheadle prize (value 20*l.*) and a gold medal for an essay on clinical medicine. As a teacher he was best at the bedside with senior students and qualified men. In treatment he relied on experience and intuition, and while always careful to ease his patients in their suffering, put faith in nature and time as healing agents. In 1869 he had also been appointed assistant physician to the Hospital for Sick Children, Great Ormond Street, where his active work on the staff terminated in 1892, when he became honorary consulting physician. During his twenty-three years' service at the Children's Hospital he endowed the 'Cheadle' cot in memory of his first wife. It was among children that his private practice mainly lay, and his chief writings dealt with children's health and ailments.

Cheadle was the first (1877) to define the nature of a then mysterious disease in childhood characterised by pain and tenderness of the limbs, hæmorrhages, and swelling of the gums. He ascribed the disease to artificial foods that possessed no antiscorbutic properties, giving it the name of 'infantile scurvy.' The pathology of the disease was afterwards worked out by Sir Thomas Barlow (*Lancet*, 1878, ii.). A valuable series of lectures on the proper way to feed infants, in the post-graduate course at St. Mary's Hospital and at the Hospital for Sick Children, Great Ormond Street, were published under the title 'On the Principles and Exact Conditions to be observed in the Artificial Feeding of Infants; the Properties of Artificial Foods; and the Diseases which arise from Faults of Diet in Early Life' (1889; 5th edit., ed. by Dr. F. J. Poynton, 1902). Cheadle also published 'The Various Manifestations of the Rheumatic State as exemplified in Childhood and Early Life' (1889). It contained the Harveian lectures delivered before the Medical Society in 1888. Cheadle maintained that the true type of acute rheumatism is that which occurs with manifold and serious symptoms and complications in childhood, and not the less severe affection of adult life.

A radical in politics, Cheadle was one of the early supporters in face of much professional opposition of the claims of medical women, and was one of the first to lecture at the London School of Medicine for Women. He visited Canada with the British Association in 1884, and contracted dysentery which permanently injured his health. He died on 25 March 1910 at 19 Portman Street, London, and was buried in Ocklynge cemetery, Eastbourne.

He was married twice: (1) on 31 Jan. 1866, to Anne, youngest daughter of William Murgatroyd of Bankfield, near Bingley, Yorkshire; and (2) on 4 Aug. 1892, to Emily, daughter of Robert Mansel, of Rothbury, Northumberland, inspector of Queen Victoria's Jubilee Institute for Nurses. Both wives predeceased him. Four sons by his first wife survive him.

Tall and of heavy build, he was dignified and reserved in manner, but won the confidence of his many child patients. A portrait painted by George Henry, R.S.A., presented to Cheadle on his retiring from the active staff of St. Mary's Hospital, now hangs in the library of St. Mary's Hospital Medical School, to which it was bequeathed. There is also a portrait on china in the possession of Cheadle's son Walter.

[Information from Mr. Walter W. Cheadle; Lancet, 2 April 1910 (portrait); Brit. Med. Journal, 9 April 1910; St. Mary's Hosp. Gaz., Dec. 1904 (portrait) and Feb. 1907.]

E. M. B.

CHEETHAM, SAMUEL (1827–1908), archdeacon of Rochester, was the son, by Emma Mary Woolston his wife, of Samuel Cheetham, farmer, of Hambleton, Rutland, where he was born on 3 March 1827. Educated at the neighbouring grammar school of Oakham, he matriculated at Christ's College, Cambridge, in 1846. He graduated B.A. in 1850, being a senior optime and eighth in the first class of the classical tripos, and was elected to a fellowship at his college. He proceeded M.A. in 1853 and D.D. in 1880. Meanwhile in 1851 he became vice-principal of the Collegiate Institute, Liverpool, and, being ordained deacon in 1851 and priest in 1852, was licensed to the curacy of St. Mary, Edgehill. In 1853 he returned to Cambridge to serve as tutor of Christ's College till 1858. He was curate of Hitchin, Hertfordshire (1858–61), and was vice-principal of the Theological College at Chichester (1861–3), at the same time acting as curate of St. Bartholomew's. In 1863 he was appointed professor of pastoral theology at King's College, London, where for nineteen years he did excellent work.

Cheetham was associated with Sir William Smith [q. v.] as editor of the 'Dictionary of Christian Antiquities' (vol. i. 1875; vol. ii. 1880), doing practically all the editorial work after the letter C was passed, besides writing many of the articles, and betraying an exceptional combination of laborious erudition and sound judgment. In 1866, on his marriage, his fellowship lapsed, but he added to his professorship the post of chaplain to Dulwich College, which he held till 1884. His work at Dulwich brought him into touch with the south London diocese of Rochester, and led to his appointment by Bishop Thorold as examining chaplain and honorary canon of Rochester in 1878. In the next year he was made archdeacon of Southwark, and the rest of his life was largely filled with diocesan activities in south London. He was transferred in 1882 as archdeacon from Southwark to Rochester, and was made a canon residentiary of Rochester in 1883. He remained examining chaplain to the bishop of Rochester until 1897. He was Hulsean lecturer at Cambridge for 1896–7, and published his lectures, 'The Mysteries, Pagan and Christian' (1897). Cheetham, who was elected F.S.A. in 1890, devoted all his leisure to work on church history. He completed the sketch of Church history which Charles Hardwick [q. v.], archdeacon of Ely, in 1859 left unfinished at his death. In 1894 Cheetham published 'A History of the Christian Church during the First Six Centuries,' and in the year before his death 'A History of the Christian Church since the Reformation.' These volumes are introductory or supplemental to Hardwick's work, and with it 'form a complete history of the Christian church on a small scale . . . written with constant reference to original authorities.'

He died without issue at Rochester on 19 July 1908, and is buried in the cathedral. He was twice married: (1) in 1866 to Hannah, daughter of Frederick Hawkins, M.D., who died in 1876; and (2) in 1896 to Ada Mary, eldest daughter of S. Barker Booth of Bickley, who survives him. A portrait painted by H. W. Pickersgill was exhibited at the Royal Academy in 1872.

In addition to works already mentioned, he published occasional sermons; articles in the 'Quarterly' and 'Contemporary' reviews; 'An Essay on John Pearson' in 'Masters in English Theology,' edited by Alfred Barry (1877); and 'A Sketch of Mediæval Church History' (1899).

[The Times, 20 July 1908; New Schaff-Herzog Encyclopædia of Religious Knowledge, vol. iii.; Athenæum. 25 July and 7 Nov. 1908; Spectator, 3 April 1909; Guardian, 10 Feb. 1909; Crockford's Clerical Directory.] R. B.

CHELMSFORD, second Baron. [See Thesiger, Frederic Augustus (1827–1905).]

CHEYLESMORE, second Baron. [See Eaton, William Meriton (1843–1902).]

CHILD, THOMAS (1839–1906), minister of the 'new church,' son of John Child, heckle-comb maker, and his wife Grace M'Kay, was born at Arbroath on 10 Dec. 1839, and brought up in connection with the Free Church of Scotland. He was put under a relative at Darlington to learn tanning, but ran away. After serving apprenticeship to a chemist he was employed by manufacturing chemists at Horncastle; here, as there was no presbyterian congregation, he joined the congregational body and, with a view to its ministry, studied at Airedale College (1862–7). As a congregational minister he settled successively at Castleford, West Riding (1867–8), and Sittingbourne, Kent (1870). His perusal of the 'Appeal' by Samuel Noble [q. v.] led him to accept the doctrines of Emanuel Swedenborg. As a preacher in connection with the 'new church,' he officiated at Newcastle-on-Tyne (1872), removing to Lowestoft (1874) and to Bath (1876), where he was ordained on 15 Oct. 1878. In March 1886 he became assistant at the chapel in Palace Gardens Terrace, Kensington, to Jonathan Bayley, who died on 12 May following, when Child became his successor. He died on 23 March. 1906. He married in October 1870 Louisa Hadkinson.

Child's writings in support of 'new church' principles, for the publication of which Sir Isaac Pitman [q. v. Suppl. I] was responsible, enjoyed considerable vogue. His chief work was 'Root Principles in Rational and Spiritual Things' (1905; 2nd edit. 1907), a reasoned reply to Haeckel's 'Riddle of the Universe,' which was commended by Dr. A. R. Wallace. He also wrote: 1. 'Are New Churchmen Christians?' 1882. 2. 'The Key of Life,' 1887 (sermons at Kensington, with forms of prayer). 3. 'Is there an Unseen World?' 1888–9. 4. 'The Church and Science,' 1892. 5. 'The Glorification of the Lord's Humanity,' 1906; lectures delivered in 1894, with biographical sketch by William Alfred Presland and James Speirs, and portrait (posthumous). 6. 'The Bible: its Rational Principle of Interpretation,' 1907 (posthumous).

[Presland and Speirs, biographical sketch, 1906.] A. G.

CHRYSTAL, GEORGE (1851–1911), mathematician, born at Mill of Kingoodie in the parish of Bourtie near Old Meldrum, Aberdeenshire, on 8 March 1851, was the son of William Chrystal, first a grain merchant and afterwards a farmer and landed proprietor, by his wife Margaret, daughter of James Burr of Mains of Glack, Aberdeenshire. After education at Aberdeen grammar school and university (1867) he proceeded in 1872 to Peterhouse, Cambridge. There he won the member's prize for an English essay in 1873, and graduated B.A. in 1875 as second wrangler and Smith's prizeman, proceeding M.A. in 1878. He was elected to a fellowship of Corpus Christi College in 1875, and was appointed a lecturer there; in later life he was made an honorary fellow. While an undergraduate at Cambridge, Chrystal not only read mathematics but studied experimental physics under Prof. Clerk-Maxwell [q. v.], and at Maxwell's suggestion engaged in a series of investigations for verifying 'Ohm's law' respecting the relation between the current and the electromotive force in a wire. To the report of these experiments which Clerk Maxwell presented to the British Association at Glasgow in 1876 Chrystal added a brief account of another series of experiments which he had undertaken on the deflection of a galvanometer (published in *Philos. Mag.* 1876; cf. CAMPBELL and GARNETT, *Life of J. C. Maxwell*, 1882, p. 365).

In 1877 Chrystal left Cambridge to become professor of mathematics at St. Andrews university, and two years later he was elected to the chair of mathematics at Edinburgh (Nov. 1879). There he greatly stimulated interest in mathematics in the university through the clearness and conciseness of his expositions of mathematical theory. At the same time he actively interested himself in the general academic organisation. Elected dean of the faculty of arts in 1891, he rendered valuable service in reorganising the arts curriculum. He was also first chairman of the provincial committee for the training of teachers, and for many years served on a committee appointed by the war office to advise the army council on the education of officers. In addition to his professorial duties, Chrystal pursued experimental researches which he had begun at Cambridge, working in the laboratory of his colleague, Peter Guthrie Tait [q. v. Suppl. II], and he took an active part in the affairs of the Royal Society of Edinburgh. He was elected a fellow of the society in 1880 and became vice-president in 1887, at the early age of thirty-six. He served in this capacity for two terms of six years, and in 1901, on Professor Tait's death, he was chosen general secretary. He was largely instrumental in the movement which led to the transfer of the society's premises from the Mound to George Street. To the society's 'Transactions' (xxix. 609 seq.) he contributed in 1880 the result of his inquiries into the differential telephone, for which he was awarded the society's Keith prize. Photography was another of Chrystal's interests, and his photographic studies produced an account of the properties of lenses and doublets (*Trans. Edin. Math. Soc.* 1895, vol. xiv.).

During his later years he was engaged in investigating theories on the oscillations in lakes, and invented instruments and obtained results which shed a new light on the whole set of phenomena. These are embodied in his papers 'On the Hydrodynamical Theory of Seiches,' with a bibliographical sketch (*Trans. Roy. Soc. Edin.* 1905, xli. 599 seq.; cf. *Proc. Roy. Soc. Edin.* xxv. 328 and 637); 'Calculation of the Periods and Nodes of Lochs Earn and Treig, from the Bathymetric Data of the Scottish Lake Survey' (*Trans.* xli. 823 seq.; 'An Investigation of the Seiches of Loch Earn' (*ibid.* xlv. 362 seq., 1907–8); and 'Seiches and other Oscillations of Lake Surfaces, observed by the Scottish Lake Survey' (in *Bathymetrical Survey of the Scottish Freshwater Lochs*, edit. by Murray and Pullar, Edinburgh, 1910, i. 29 seq.). For these researches he was awarded a royal medal by the Royal Society of London in 1911. He read a paper on the subject before the Royal Institution in London on 17 May 1907. He was made hon. LL.D. of Aberdeen University in March 1887 and of Glasgow in Oct. 1911.

Chrystal wrote many articles for the 9th edition of the 'Encyclopædia Britannica,' the chief being those on 'Electricity' and 'Magnetism' (1883), which compress into a small compass a very complete account of those sciences at that date. His 'Algebra, an Elementary Textbook for the Higher Classes of Secondary Schools' (Edinburgh, 2 pts. 1886–9), became a standard book, and was notable for the lucidity of its reasoning. The first part reached a fifth edition in 1904, and a second edition of part ii. was published in 1900. He also published 'Introduction to Algebra' (1898; 3rd edit. 1902) and 'Non-Euclidean Geometry' (in *Proc. Roy. Soc. Edin.* 1880).

Chrystal died on 3 Nov. 1911 at his residence, 5 Belgrave Crescent, Edinburgh, and was buried at Foveran, Aberdeenshire. He married on 26 June 1879 Margaret Anne (*d.* 22 Sept. 1903), daughter of William Balfour, and left surviving issue four sons and two daughters.

[The Times, and Scotsman, 4 Nov. 1911; Nature, 9 Nov. 1911; private information.]

D. J. O.

CLANWILLIAM, fourth EARL OF. [See MEADE, RICHARD JAMES (1832–1907).]

CLARK, JOHN WILLIS (1833–1910), man of science and archæologist, born at Cambridge on 24 June 1833, was only child of Dr. William Clark [q. v.], professor of anatomy at Cambridge, and of Mary Willis, sister of Robert Willis [q. v.], Jacksonian professor.

In 1847 he entered Eton as an oppidan. His tutor was William Johnson (afterwards Cory) [q. v. Suppl. I]. In 1852 he entered Trinity College, Cambridge, of which he became a scholar in April 1855, and a fellow in October 1858, having graduated B.A. in 1856 as thirteenth in the first class of the classical tripos. During parts of the years 1860–1 he acted as tutor to Viscount Milton, eldest son of Earl Fitzwilliam, at Wentworth; but a considerable portion of his leisure in these and in the following years was spent in foreign travel. Thus, the Faroe Islands and Iceland were visited in 1860, Italy and Germany in 1861 and 1864 respectively, Norway and Denmark in 1866. Accounts of some of these expeditions were among Clark's earliest publications. While residing at Cambridge he assisted his father in the work of his professorship. Dr. Clark resigned that post in 1865, and in 1866 his son was appointed superintendent of the museum of zoology and secretary to the museums and lecture rooms syndicate. These posts he retained until his election as registrary in 1891. His energy and exceptional talent for methodical arrangement and organisation enabled him to effect great improvements in the classification and exhibition of the specimens in the museum, as well as to increase the collections. He contributed a good many papers to scientific journals, principally on the marine mammalia, and it seemed likely at this time that natural science would become the main subject of his studies. This, however, was not to be the case. In 1875 Professor Willis died, and bequeathed to Clark the unfinished manuscript of his 'Architectural History of the University and Colleges of Cambridge.' The completion of this monumental work entailed a vast amount of research among college records and a close study of existing buildings. A very large proportion of the book was rewritten, and all Willis's conclusions verified. The book finally appeared in four volumes in 1886, and must rank as Clark's most considerable achievement. In addition to the history of the Cambridge buildings, it includes an architectural history of Eton College, and also a number of essays on the constituent parts of a college—chapel, hall, library, &c., and an admirable series of plans, showing the development of each collegiate site.

A part of 1874 was spent in an expedition to Algiers. In 1877–80 Clark acted as deputy for Dr. H. R. Luard, registrary of the university; in 1887 he was a candidate for the Disney professorship of archæology, and in 1889 for the post of university librarian. He was elected F.S.A. on 26 May 1887. In 1891, at the death of Luard, he was chosen registrary, and continued in the office until a few days before his death. The work of this post was in many ways congenial; it brought Clark into contact with the whole *personnel* of the university, and it gave him a voice in the arrangement of ceremonies and 'functions,' which appealed to his instinct for stage-management. Much was also required of him in the way of codifying university regulations and investigation of records. Of the numerous publications issued by Clark as registrary the most important is probably an edition of the 'University Endowments,' which appeared in 1904.

During these years Clark was one of the best-known personalities in Cambridge, alike in his private and in his public capacity. In university politics he was a liberal, and a fiery supporter of every cause which he took up. His quickness of temper and freedom of expression involved him in many somewhat acute personal controversies; but the geniality which was his leading characteristic seldom allowed a quarrel to develop into an enmity. No university institution benefited more largely by his efforts than the library. For many years he was an active member of the syndicate which governed it; in 1905 he initiated a movement for procuring further endowment for it; and the appeal which he then first issued has resulted in contributions to the value of over 20,000*l.*

Clark's relations with the younger members of the university were always of the happiest. He wholly ignored, and did much to break down, any barriers established by university convention between dons and undergraduates, and he had a genius for making friends of his juniors. In one branch of undergraduate activities—the dramatic—he was specially helpful. In 1861 he became an honorary member of the Amateur Dramatic Club (A.D.C.); for many years he acted as its treasurer, and was finally elected perpetual vice-president of it. He also took a large part in the production of Greek plays at Cambridge from their inception in 1882. Always an enthusiastic student of English and French drama, he hardly allowed a year to pass without paying a visit to the Paris theatres. He was the author of some dramatic adaptations, and in earlier years of a considerable mass of theatrical *critiques*.

The bulk of his published work, however, naturally centred round Cambridge, where his whole life was passed. Besides the 'Architectural History' (cited above) and 'Cambridge: Brief Historical and Descriptive Notes' (illustrated, 1880; re-issues, 1890 and 1908), he produced a very large number of less considerable books and papers dealing with all sides of Cambridge life. Many of these will be found in the 'Transactions' of the Cambridge Antiquarian Society. Of his contributions to Cambridge biography this Dictionary includes many; others were collected from various journals and republished in 1900; but the most important is the 'Life of Professor Sedgwick,' written in collaboration with Professor T. McKenny Hughes (2 vols. 1890).

Closely connected with Cambridge history were the two volumes of Barnwell Priory documents which Clark issued in 1897 and 1907 under the titles respectively of 'The Observances in use at the Augustinian Priory of S. Giles and S. Andrew' and 'Liber Memorandorum Ecclesie de Bernwelle.' His excellent monograph on the externals of ancient libraries ('The Care of Books'), which first appeared in 1901 (2nd edit. 1902), grew directly out of the essay on college libraries which is appended to the 'Architectural History.' A 'Concise Guide to Cambridge' (1898; 4th edit. 1910), an edition of Loggan's seventeenth-century engravings of the colleges ('Cantabrigia Illustrata,' 1905), and 'Old Friends at Cambridge and Elsewhere' (1900), an unfinished series of reminiscences of social life at Cambridge, were among the more noteworthy writings of his later years.

The variety of his interests is strikingly exemplified in a 'Festschrift' ('Fasciculus Joanni Willis Clark dicatus') presented to him by a number of friends on his seventy-sixth birthday (June 1909). To this volume a bibliography of his published work is appended.

In 1873 Clark married Frances Matilda, daughter of Sir Andrew Buchanan, G.C.B. [q. v.], by whom he had two sons. The death of his wife in December 1908 inflicted a shock from which he never recovered; during considerable portions of the years 1909 and 1910 he was away from Cambridge, or prostrated by illness. In 1909 he resigned the auditorship of Trinity College, which he had held for twenty-seven years; on 1 Oct. 1910 he gave up the post of registrary, and on 10 Oct. he died at his home, Scroope House, in Cambridge. He was buried in the Mill Road cemetery.

He bequeathed his valuable collections of Cambridge books and pamphlets to the university library.

A portrait by C. M. Newton is in possession of the Amateur Dramatic Club.

[Personal knowledge; information derived from his mother's diaries; 'J': a memoir of John Willis Clark, by A. E. Shipley, 1913.

M. R. J.

CLARKE, Sir ANDREW (1824–1902), lieutenant-general, colonel commandant royal engineers, and colonial official, born at Southsea on 27 July 1824, was eldest son of Lieutenant-colonel Andrew Clarke, K.H. (1793–1847), 46th South Devonshire regiment, governor of Western Australia, by his wife Frances, widow of the Rev. Edward Jackson, and daughter of Philip Lardner of Devonshire. Young Clarke was educated at the King's School, Canterbury, at Portora School, Enniskillen, and at the Royal Military Academy, Woolwich. He left Woolwich at the head of his batch and was commissioned as second lieutenant in the royal engineers on 19 June 1844.

After professional instruction at Chatham, he was employed at Fermoy during the worst period of the Irish famine. Promoted lieutenant on 1 April 1846, he was despatched at his own wish to Van Diemen's Land, now Tasmania, next year. Making fast friends on the way out with the newly appointed governor, Sir William Denison [q. v.], who travelled in the same ship, Clarke spent a year and a half in pioneering work in the colony with the aid of convict labour. Clarke was transferred to New Zealand in September 1848, to help in making the road from Keri-Keri to Okaihou. He was also sent on a mission to the Maori chiefs at Heki and the Bay of

Islands with a view to reconciling them to British rule, and on his advice the proposed Church of England (Canterbury) settlement, which was at first designed for the Bay of Islands, was formed instead at Port Cooper on Middle Island, where natives were fewer. At the end of August Clarke returned to Van Diemen's Land to become private secretary to Sir William Denison, the governor. In 1851 he took his seat on the new legislative council, and was put in charge of some government measures.

In May 1853 Clarke moved to Melbourne to become surveyor-general of Victoria, with a seat on the legislative council. Promoted second captain on 17 Feb. 1854, he drafted the bill for a new constitution for the colony, on a representative basis. This was carried in the council early in 1854. At the same time he took a prominent part in organising the Melbourne Exhibition of 1854, and in founding the Royal Philosophical Society of Victoria, of which he was the first president. In the autumn he carried a useful bill (known as Clarke's Act) to enable the inhabitants of any locality, not less than a hundred in number and not spread over a greater area than thirty-six square miles, to institute automatically a municipality for their district with full municipal powers. The new constitution for Victoria, which was proclaimed in November 1855, relieved Clarke of his appointments on the old terms and provided him with a pension of 800*l.* a year in case he returned to Europe. Remaining in the colony, Clarke stood and was returned for the constituency of South Melbourne, and entered the cabinet of Mr. Haines as surveyor-general and commissioner of lands. In these capacities he was associated with the inauguration of railways in the colony, starting with 185 miles of trunk road in 1857. It was soon arranged that Clarke as head of the land department, with Captain Charles Pasley [q. v.], the chief of the public works department, should become permanent heads of their departments, retiring from the cabinet, but retaining their parliamentary seats. In the session 1857–8 Clarke, always a strong radical, urged universal suffrage in opposition to the premier, and defeated the government. Being refused a dissolution, he declined the governor's invitation to form a new administration.

After promotion to first captain on 19 March 1857, Clarke decided to return to England for military duty. In January 1859 he was accordingly appointed to the command of the royal engineers at Colchester. While there he gave the war office and the government valuable advice on colonial matters. In 1862 he was transferred to the Birmingham command. Towards the end of 1863 he was sent with the local rank of major to the Gold Coast of Africa, where a state of war existed with the King of Ashanti. He gave varied assistance, acting temporarily as chief justice. At Lagos, where he suffered seriously from fever, he wrote a valuable report on the Gold Coast. His information proved useful ten years later to Sir Garnet Wolseley's Ashanti punitive expedition, the despatch of which he strongly deprecated.

After serving in London temporarily in 1864 as agent-general of Victoria in place of his former colleague in the Victorian government, Hugh C. E. Childers [q. v. Suppl. I], who now became a lord of the admiralty, Clarke was made in August director of engineering works at the admiralty. He was reappointed for a second term of five years in 1869, when he was awarded the C.B. (civil). In this post he thoroughly proved his efficiency. To meet the needs of the new ironclad fleet and the rapid increase in the size of battleships, he devised large extensions to the docks at Chatham and Portsmouth, and new docks at Queenstown, Keyham, Malta, and Bermuda, at a cost of many millions sterling.

In January 1870 he and the hydrographer of the navy, Captain G. H. Evans, officially visited the new Suez Canal and reported that the carrying capacity of the canal only excluded large ironclads and transports, which with increased width of waterway could readily pass through. Clarke recommended the purchase of the canal by an English company to be formed for the purpose. Promoted regimental lieut.-colonel on 6 July 1867, and full colonel in the army on 6 July 1872, he was created a K.C.M.G. in April 1873.

On leaving the admiralty Clarke became governor of the Straits Settlements. He arrived at Singapore on 4 Nov. 1873, and during his eighteen months' stay there put down piracy, which was rampant on his arrival, made settlements with the native states by which British residents were appointed to advise the rajahs and sultans, placed the secret Chinese societies under effective control, cultivated the friendship of his neighbour the Maharaja of Johore, and visited Chululonkorn, the King of Siam, at his request. His policy made for peace and laid the foundation of the present prosperity and security of the whole peninsula.

On 4 June 1875 Clarke arrived in India, having been appointed member of the council and head of the public works department for the purpose of constructing productive public works, such as railways and irrigation. Famine, frontier wars, and depreciation of silver left no money to spend on public works, and Clarke found little scope for his special work during his five years in India. But he was of service in other directions. On the occasion of the durbar at Delhi for the proclamation of Queen Victoria as Empress of India on 1 Jan. 1877, when he was made C.I.E., he in a long letter to Montagu Corry (afterwards Lord Rowton) sagaciously suggested the creation of an imperial senate for India on which the princes and chiefs should sit as well as the great officers of the paramount power. In the same year he succeeded in establishing the useful Indian Defence Committee.

During the subsequent invasion of Afghanistan he did his best to assist the military commanders in the field, although his urgent advocacy of the immediate construction of frontier railroads led to friction with the viceroy (Lord Lytton). In February 1880 Sir Andrew went home on short leave of absence, and was wrecked off Otranto with great peril in the P. & O. steamer Travancore, sailing from Alexandria. He travelled back to India with the newly appointed liberal viceroy, the marquis of Ripon, so as to advise him on current Indian affairs; but his term of office expired soon after they reached Simla, and he was in England again at the end of July.

In June 1882, after serving a year as commandant of the School of Military Engineering at Chatham, Clarke was appointed by Mr. Childers, then secretary of state for war, to be inspector-general of fortifications. Being only a colonel, he was given the temporary rank of major-general. The pending Egyptian campaign at once occupied him. He organised a railway corps, showing admirable discretion in the choice of men [see Wallace, William Arthur James, Suppl. II]. For the general work of his office he secured both naval and artillery advisers, and welcomed every proposal of promise. He took up warmly the Brennan torpedo, the dirigible balloon, and even the submarine boat, which at that time found no support at the admiralty. To the defences of coaling stations and commercial harbours, which had been long deferred, he paid close attention, and he also found time to advise the government on many other questions. He sat on Lord Granville's committee, which recommended the permanent neutralisation of the Suez Canal, and on a visit to Egypt on business of military buildings at the end of 1882 he, after re-examining the canal, strongly advocated its widening in preference to a proposed second canal. In 1884 he was one of the British representatives on the international committee, and was chosen its vice-president. The committee's decision accorded with his views.

In 1884, during the difficult warfare with Osman Digna in the Eastern Soudan, Clarke urged the construction of a railway from Suakin to Berber, and subsequently supported the Suakin-Berber route for the relief of Khartoum, in opposition to Lord Wolseley's suggested Nile expedition. In 1885, when it was too late, Clark's advice was taken. He then worked out the engineering details of a railway from Suakin to Berber, but the contract was not carried out owing to the menace of war with Russia and the abandonment of the Soudan. On 6 June 1885 Sir Andrew was made G.C.M.G. In March 1886 he was permitted to act temporarily as agent-general for Victoria. The question of the cession of the New Hebrides to France was under discussion, and he induced the British government to recognise the right of Australia to forbid any such arrangement.

Always an ardent liberal politician, Clarke resolved early in 1886 to stand for the representation of Chatham at the next vacancy. His term of active service was expiring in the summer under the age regulation. But on dissolution of parliament in June, after Gladstone's defeat on home rule, Clarke, on 27 July 1886, anticipated by a few weeks the obligatory date of his retirement from the army, and offered himself for Chatham in the liberal interest. He was given the honorary rank of lieutenant-general. Defeated in the parliamentary contest, he experienced the same fate in 1892, and he then abandoned his parliamentary ambitions. He found much to occupy him elsewhere. For acting without pay as consulting engineer in connection with the stability of the dam of the Vyrnwy waterworks, he received in January 1887 the honorary freedom of the city of Liverpool. After visits to Siam and Singapore (December 1887), he was busily engaged as director of Palmers Shipbuilding Company at Jarrow-on-Tyne, of the

Colonial Mutual Life Assurance Society, of the Maxim Nordenfelt Gun Company, and of the British North Borneo Company. The last company commemorated his services by naming after him Clarke Province in that country. He was also chairman of the Delhi-Umballa Railway Company.

Once more from 1891 to 1894, save for a few months' interval, and continuously from 1 Jan. 1897 till his death, he served as agent-general for Victoria, occasionally acting also as agent-general for Tasmania. He was of great service to Victoria in 1893, during the financial crisis. In 1899 he was one of the Australian representatives at the International Commercial Congress at Philadelphia. He interested himself in the 'all red' line of telegraph which was to connect the scattered parts of the empire without entering foreign territory, and he was one of two Australian representatives on the board of directors of the Pacific Telegraph Cable. In 1900 Clarke took the place of the delegate for Victoria, who was disabled by illness, in the final deliberations with the colonial office over the Australian commonwealth bill. He thus shared in the settlement of Australian federation. On 8 Jan. 1902 he was appointed a colonel commandant of the corps of royal engineers.

Clarke's outlook was wide and his views prescient. Untiring in energy and pertinacious in purpose, he showed distinction in all his varied employments. He died at his residence, 31 Portland Place, on 29 March 1902. On 17 Sept. 1867 he was married at St. George's, Hanover Square, to Mary Margaret, elder daughter of Charles William MacKillop, formerly of the Indian civil service. Lady Clarke died on 8 Nov. 1895, and was buried in the Locksbrook cemetery at Bath. Over her grave Sir Andrew erected a monument designed by E. Onslow Ford, R.A. [q. v. Suppl. II], one of the sculptor's last commissions. Sir Andrew's remains were laid beside those of his wife. His only child, Elinor Mary de Winton, married Captain M. F. Sueter, R.N.

Clarke's portrait by Lowes Dickinson was exhibited at the Royal Academy in 1891. A life-size bust in bronze by E. Onslow Ford, R.A., was presented by his brother officers to the royal engineers' mess at Chatham. Another bust, colossal size, by the same artist, was after exhibition at the Melbourne Exhibition placed in the Singapore Chamber of Commerce as a memorial of Clarke's government of the Straits Settlements.

[War Office and Colonial Office Records; R.E. Records; the present writer's Life of Lieut.-general Sir Andrew Clarke, 1905.]

R. H. V.

CLARKE, Sir CASPAR PURDON (1846–1911), architect, archæologist, and museum director, born at Richmond, co. Dublin, on 21 Dec. 1846, was second son of Edward Marmaduke Clarke, of an old Somerset family, who married Mary Agnes, daughter of James Close of Armagh. Caspar was educated at Gaultier's School, Sydenham, and at a private school in Boulogne. In 1862 he entered the National Art Training Schools at South Kensington, and was trained for the profession of an architect. Leaving the schools in 1865, he entered H.M. office of works, where he distinguished himself in work connected with the Houses of Parliament. Two years later he was transferred to the works department of the South Kensington Museum. In 1869 he was sent by the museum to superintend the reproduction of mosaics in Venice, Florence, and Rome, and in 1872 he went to Alexandria to supervise the decorative work at St. Mark's Church. In 1874 he was appointed H.M. superintendent of works for the consular buildings in Teheran, where he spent the following two years, completing during this time the Roman catholic church of St. Mary's.

Having returned to London in 1876, he was sent on a purchasing tour through Turkey, Syria, and Greece, where he acquired many valuable objects for the South Kensington Museum. A similar mission took him in 1879 to Spain, Italy, and Germany, after having acted in the preceding year as architect of the Indian section and commercial agent to the Indian government at the Paris Exhibition. In 1880 he arranged the Indian collections at South Kensington, and after spending two years as special commissioner in India, became keeper of the India Museum at South Kensington in 1883. In that capacity he displayed splendid gifts as an organiser, and was consequently appointed keeper of the art collections at South Kensington Museum in 1892, assistant director in 1893, and director in 1896. He also filled the posts of royal commissioner at the Paris Exhibition in 1900, and at St. Louis in 1904. In 1905 he resigned his directorship of the South Kensington Museum (renamed in 1899 Victoria and Albert Museum) and accepted the post of director of the Metropolitan Museum, New York, from which he retired on a year's leave of absence on account of ill-health in 1909, when he returned to England. He resigned his directorship in 1910, but remained European correspondent of the museum. He died in London on 29 Mar. 1911, and was buried at Kensal Green.

Clarke's strenuous official duties did not prevent him from notable work in other directions. He organised and conducted evening art classes for artisans in Soho, Lambeth, and Clerkenwell in 1870; and among the buildings which he designed and built were Cotherstone Church, Durham, (1876); Alexandra House, Kensington (for students at the Royal College of Music) (1886); the National School of Cookery (1887); Lord Brassey's Indian Museum, Park Lane (1887); and the Indian Palace, Paris Exhibition (1889). He visited America to study the housing of female students at Boston in 1884; edited a work on Oriental carpets for the Austrian government in 1892; and besides lecturing, contributed numerous papers on architecture, Eastern arts and crafts, and arms and armour to the 'Society of Arts Journal,' the 'Journal of Indian Art,' the 'Journal of the Royal Institute of British Architects,' and other publications. He was made chevalier of the Legion of Honour in 1878, in which year he also received silver and bronze medals at the Paris Exhibition, which were followed by a gold medal in 1889. He was elected F.S.A. on 4 May 1893. He was created C.I.E. in 1883, and knighted in 1902. He was also given the commander's cross of the Order of the Crown of Germany.

Clarke married on 20 Nov. 1866 Frances Susannah, daughter of Charles Collins. Of their eight children—three sons and five daughters—the eldest son, C. Stanley Clarke, became assistant-keeper of the Indian section of the Victoria and Albert Museum, which owes its present form to his father's organising genius.

A portrait of Clarke by George Burroughes Torry was presented by the trustees of the Metropolitan Museum, New York, to the Victoria and Albert Museum, London. Another portrait was painted in New York by Wilhelm Funk.

[The Critic and Literary World, Sept. 1905; Sir Caspar Purdon Clarke, with a Note on the Arts and Crafts of America by John Lane, 1905; private information.] P. G. K.

CLARKE, CHARLES BARON (1832–1906), botanist, born at Andover, Hampshire, on 17 June 1832, was eldest son of Turner Poulter Clarke, J.P., by his wife Elizabeth, daughter of James Parker and Elizabeth Ward. He inherited botanical tastes from his father's mother, Elizabeth Baron, whose brother Charles founded the Agricultural Society of Saffron Walden and was an enthusiastic gardener (*Journal of Botany*, 1890, p. 84).

Clarke was at a preparatory school at Salisbury (1840–6), and at King's College school, London (1846–52). He entered Trinity College, Cambridge, in 1852. At the university he became the close friend of Henry Fawcett, of Leslie (afterwards Sir Leslie) Stephen (F. W. MAITLAND, *Life and Letters of Leslie Stephen*, p. 73), and of John (afterwards Sir John) Rigby [q. v. Suppl. II]. All held what were then considered advanced political and social views. In 1856, when Clarke was bracketed third, Rigby came out second wrangler, and Fawcett seventh. After graduating B.A. in 1856, Clarke was elected fellow of Queens' College, and from 1858 to 1865 was lecturer in mathematics there. He proceeded M.A. in 1859 and was called to the bar at Lincoln's Inn in 1860. Clarke, who was through life a tireless walker, spent most of his Easter vacations in the Lake district, and on his last visit in 1865 he and Leslie Stephen climbed together the Pillar Rock, Wastdale. In Switzerland, too, he combined Alpine climbing with plant-collecting. Meanwhile he actively helped Fawcett in his candidature for parliament at Cambridge in 1863 and at Brighton in 1864, and aided him in his studies in political economy.

In 1865 Clarke entered the uncovenanted civil service of Bengal. He joined the staff of the Presidency College at Calcutta, and was subsequently inspector of schools in eastern Bengal, with his headquarters at Dacca. He had already collected with care the plants of his native place; and he published at Calcutta in 1866, in a threepenny pamphlet, 'A List of the Flowering Plants . . . of Andover' (cf. *Journal of Botany*, 1867, pp. 51–9). Clarke continued to collect in India with Spartan zeal. Within two and a half years in Eastern Bengal he got together 7000 specimens, which were lost in the wreck of a boat in 1868. His existing collections date from May 1868. His knowledge of the Indian country soon equalled that of Hamilton, Wallich, or Hooker, and was second only to that of William Griffith [q. v.]. To his specimens he attached full field notes made on the spot. He generally neglected trees, and concentrated his attention for several years together upon single natural orders.

From 1869 to 1871 Clarke acted as superintendent of the Calcutta botanical gardens and of cinchona cultivation in Bengal. Returning to his work as an inspector in 1871, Clarke studied in 1872 the Eastern Sundarbans, and in the following year he visited Chittagong. Transferred to Calcutta in 1874, he published there his second work, 'Commelinaceæ et Cyrtandraceæ Bengalenses,' and reprinted Roxburgh's 'Flora Indica' of 1832 at his own expense. In 1876 he issued a monograph on the Compositæ, to which and to the Gentianaceæ his interest was now directed. In 1875 he was transferred to Darjeeling, and explored the Nipal frontier and British Bhutan. Next year, during a three months' furlough, he visited Kashmir, ascending 17,000 feet in the Karakoram range.

In 1877 Clarke came home on two years' furlough, and presented his herbarium, some 25,000 specimens, representing 5000 species, to the Kew herbarium. Settling down to voluntary botanical work for Sir Joseph Hooker's 'Flora of British India,' he was placed on special duty at Kew on the expiration of his leave in 1879, and described, between 1879 and 1883, more than fifty natural orders for the second, third, and fourth volumes of Hooker's work. Returning to India in 1883, Clarke was temporarily appointed director of public instruction in Bengal in 1884, and went in 1885 as inspector to Shillong in Assam, when he studied the flora of the Khasia, Naga, and Manipur hills.

Retiring from India in 1887, Clarke settled at Kew with his brother, Poulter Clarke, to work mainly at Cyperaceæ, on which his authority was soon recognised. In the Linnean Society's 'Transactions' he described the Cyperaceæ of the Malay peninsula in 1893–4, those of Mt. Kinabalu in 1894, those of Matto Grosso in 1895, of Madagascar in 1883, those of India in 1884 and 1898, and those of China in 1903–4. In Engler's 'Jahrbücher' he described those of Chile; and after his death his descriptions of those of the Philippines appeared in the 'Philippine Journal of Science,' and those of the African species in the 'Bulletin of the French Botanical Society'; whilst 144 plates prepared under his supervision were published, and his monumental monograph of the entire group, although unpublished, was practically completed.

Clarke became a fellow of the Linnean Society in 1867, and of the Geological Society in 1868; from 1880 he served on the council of the former, being a vice-president from 1881 and president from 1894 to 1896. He was elected F.R.S. in 1882, and served on the council from 1888 to 1890. He joined the Geologists' Association in 1897, and constantly engaged in its excursions. In his later years he took to bicycling, riding long distances by day only, without lamp, brake, or bell. He died at Kew, unmarried, of internal inflammation, mainly brought on by excessive bicycling, on 25 Aug. 1906, and was buried at Andover.

To Clarke, Sir Joseph Hooker dedicated in 1880 the Rubiaceous genus Clarkella. His exceptionally versatile interests found expression in 'Speculations from Political Economy' (1886); in a 'Class-book of Geography' (1889); in an ethnological paper, 'On the Stone Monuments of the Khasi Hills,' in the 'Journal of the Anthropological Institute' for 1874; in a musico-mathematical note on 'Equal temperament of the scale' in 'Nature' (1883); and in an unpublished history of England down to the reign of James I. His botanical works, besides those cited and many scattered papers in scientific journals, included monographs on the Commelinaceæ (1881) and on the Cyrtandraceæ (1883) for the continuation of De Candolle's 'Prodromus,' and an account of the ferns of British India in the Linnean Society's 'Transactions' (1879). He described the Acanthaceæ, Gesneraceæ, and Commelinaceæ for Sir William Thiselton-Dyer's 'Flora Capensis,' and for Professor Daniel Oliver's 'Flora of Tropical Africa'; and several orders for Schmidt's 'Flora of Koh Chang' and for Sir George King's 'Malayan Flora.'

[Journal of Botany, 1906, pp. 370–377, by Colonel Prain and the Rev. W. H. Bliss (with an excellent portrait from a photograph); Kew Bulletin, 1906, pp. 271–281, with full bibliography; Nature, 1906, lxxiv. 495; Proceedings of the Linnean Society, 1906–7, pp. 38–42; Proceedings of the Royal Society, lxxix. series B, pp. xlix–lvi.] G. S. B.

CLARKE, HENRY BUTLER (1863–1904), historian of Spain, born on 9 Nov. 1863 at Marchington, Staffordshire, of which parish his father was incumbent, was elder son of Henry Clarke by his wife Helen, daughter of John Leech of Etwall, near Derby. In 1867 his father became rector of Rokeby. Henry was educated successively at a small school at Whorlton, near Rokeby, at a preparatory school at Richmond, Yorkshire, and finally (1879–83), owing to delicate health, at Jean-de-Luz, where he read with the Basque scholar

Wentworth Webster [q. v. Suppl. II], and where his father was British chaplain in 1882–3. Spanish history and literature thus came to attract him, and during early visits to Spain he became intimate with many social and political leaders, including Cánovas de Castillo. In 1883 he went for a time to Germany with a pupil. Improved health enabled him to matriculate at Wadham College, Oxford, in October 1885, and although with little or no previous knowledge of Greek, he obtained a good second class in honour moderations in 1887. In 1888 he won the Taylorian scholarship for Spanish. An attack of neurasthenia obliged him to content himself with a pass degree next year. From 1890 to 1892 he was Taylorian teacher of Spanish at Oxford, and in 1894 was elected, after examination in the subjects of the literæ humaniores school, to a Fereday fellowship (open to natives of Staffordshire) at St. John's College. Thenceforth till his death he usually resided for a term every year in college. An annual tour, chiefly on the Continent in company with his father or Oxford friends, extended on one occasion to Syria and in 1900–1 to India. A keen fisherman and a fair shot, he was a collector of ancient brass work, tiles and MSS., became keenly interested in art, and painted very happily in water-colours. But his main interest for the last twenty years of his life was in Spain, her history and literature. In 1891 he built for himself a house at St. Jean-de-Luz, just across the Spanish border, and there the greater part of his time was spent reading and writing on Spanish themes. After completing some smaller studies he resolved to concentrate himself for twenty years on the early history of Spanish civilisation. He acquired a thorough knowledge of Arabic and collected a fine library for the purpose. But in 1904, when ready to set to work seriously, he suffered a severe return of illness, and while he was recruiting at Torquay his brain gave way, and he shot himself on 10 Sept. 1904. He was buried in Torquay cemetery. He was unmarried.

Clarke was author of: 1. 'A Spanish Reader,' 1891. 2. 'A Spanish Grammar,' 1892. 3. 'History of Spanish Literature,' 1893, a valuable critical work. 4. 'The Cid Campeador' ('Heroes of the Nations' series), 1897, an historical study based on an intimate knowledge of the sources, Arabic, Latin and Spanish. 5. 'Modern Spain, 1815–1898,' a history, published posthumously with a memoir in 1906, which has established itself as by far the best work on the subject.

He also published two interesting papers on Andorra in the (London) 'Guardian,' July 1902, a chapter on the Catholic Kings in the 'Cambridge Modern History' (vol. i. 1902); and his Lecture on the Spanish Rogue-Story in 'Taylorian Lectures, Oxford' (1900). A careful edition of the 'Spanish Gypsy,' by the Elizabethan dramatist, Thomas Middleton, is still unpublished.

The greater part of Clarke's fine library was presented by his family to St. John's College and a catalogue of it was printed. A portrait in water-colour by his friend Mrs. Lilburn and Henri de Meurville is in the possession of the writer of this notice. Strikingly handsome, Clarke had remarkable personal charm. His stimulating talk was both humorous and profound.

[Memoir prefixed to his Modern Spain, Cambridge, 1906; Revue Hispanique, 1904, pp. 575–6; private information.] W. H. H.

CLARKE, Sir MARSHAL JAMES (1841–1909), South African administrator, born at Shronell, co. Tipperary, on 18 Oct. 1841, was eldest son of the Rev. Mark Clarke of Shronell. After being educated at a private school in Dublin and later at Trinity College, Dublin, he went to Woolwich in 1860 and obtained a commission in the royal artillery on 22 Feb. 1863, retiring in 1883 with the rank of lieut.-colonel. He spent the greater part of his career in South Africa, serving in a civil more often than in a military capacity. In 1874 he became resident magistrate of Pietermaritzburg in Natal. In 1876 he was A.D.C. to Sir Theophilus Shepstone [q.v.], then appointed special commissioner for South Africa. In 1877 he was sent on a mission to Sekukuni, who had been at war with the Boers on the northern frontier of the Transvaal near the Lydenburg goldfields, and he was in that year political officer and special commissioner at Lydenburg. He served in the Transvaal war of 1880–1, was twice mentioned in despatches, and was present at Potchefstroom as special commissioner. He was in charge of the Landdrost's office there when it was attacked and compelled to surrender by the insurgent Boers in December 1880. In 1881 he became resident magistrate at Quthing in Basutoland, and in 1882 commissioner of Cape police at King William's Town in the Cape Colony. In the same year he was sent to Egypt and appointed colonel commanding the Turkish regiment of Egyptian gendarmerie, receiving the third class of the order of the Medjidie. On 13 March 1884 Basutoland was taken over by the crown from the Cape government, and Clarke, who had now retired from the army, was appointed resident commissioner. He held that post till 1893, when he was made resident commissioner and chief magistrate of Zululand. After Zululand had been annexed to Natal, he was in 1898 appointed imperial resident commissioner of Rhodesia, under the southern Rhodesia order in council of that year, and held that appointment until he retired in 1905. Clarke, who had lost his left arm through a shooting accident, showed great capacity in native administration. Basutoland, which under the Cape government had been in a constant state of ferment, made marked progress in peace, contentment, and prosperity under his guidance. Constantly selected to fill difficult positions in South Africa, he was conspicuous among the men who won the confidence and respect of the natives of South Africa. He was created C.M.G. in 1880 and K.C.M.G. in 1886. He died at The Lodge, Enniskerry, co. Wicklow, on 1 April 1909, and was buried at Mount Jerome, Dublin.

He married in 1880 Anne Stacy, daughter of Major-general Bannastre Lloyd, and left two sons and one daughter.

[Colonial Office List; Blue Books; Who's Who; The Times, 5 April 1909; South Africa, 3 April 1909.] C. P. L.

CLASPER, JOHN HAWKS (1836–1908), boat-builder and oarsman, born at Newcastle-on-Tyne on 13 Oct. 1836, was eldest son of Henry Clasper (1812–1870), oarsman and boat-builder of that place.

The father took to rowing about 1830, while working at the Garesfield coke ovens. He became a practical waterman, and his mechanical skill enabled him to devise for the first time boats of a racing build, those of ordinary traffic having hitherto served for racing purposes. His chief invention was the outrigger, which permitted diminution of beam in the boat without loss of leverage in the oar. His outrigger was first applied to a four-oar in 1844, and was adopted for eights in the university race of 1846. His improvements in boats, combined with his skill in rowing and sculling, brought him numerous aquatic successes. In 1842 he was already undisputed champion of the Tyne, and between 1842 and 1870 he appeared in 120 first-class races. Of thirty-one skiff races he won eighteen; and fourteen pair-oar races out of twenty-five. As stroke in a four he was without equal, being beaten only thirteen times in sixty-three engagements.

The son John began his aquatic career as a coxswain at the age of ten, and in 1852 started rowing and sculling at regattas. In 1854 he was apprenticed to a London waterman and won a sculling race at Richmond. In 1855 he gained a four-oar victory at Wandsworth. In 1856 he twice defeated John Carrol in matches on the Clyde. 1857 was a year full of successes at the regattas of Durham, Thames, Lancaster and the Northern Rowing Club. In 1858 Clasper and his father (they began racing together two years before) beat with Richard and Thomas Clasper (his uncles) the brothers Taylor for 100*l.* with the championship of the Tyne. Next day (15 June) the success was repeated over the same crew at Durham, where father and son also won the prize for pair-oars. In the winter the son beat George Francis on the Putney to Mortlake course for 40*l.* In the Durham regatta of 1859 he not only won the open boat sculling race but was in the crew which after winning the Patrons' plate also secured the champion prize at Thames regatta and the Pomona cup at Manchester. 1860 was another year of successes; as a sculler Clasper won at Durham and at Talkin Tarn; with his father he won the pair-oared races at the Manchester regatta and at the Newcastle and Gateshead regatta. He beat Tom Pocock in sculling twice in 1861 on the Thames. Clasper's performance at Manchester regatta in the same year was remarkable as a feat of endurance. He won the Pomona prize, and though beaten in the sculling handicap was only defeated by M. Scott, to whom he gave eleven lengths' start; in the preliminary heat he had beaten a rival whose handicap was six lengths. On 26 May 1861 he beat George Drewitt (for 200*l.*) on the Tyne.

His triumphs of 1861 mark the climax of his athletic life, but in six subsequent seasons he was still a winner. His four in which his father rowed at the age of fifty won the Durham race in 1862 and the Thames regatta champion prize. As late as 1876 (his fortieth year) he stroked, and won a prize in, a scratch eight at the Oxford regatta.

Clasper had already established himself as an expert trainer of crews and 'pilot' of scullers when he began in 1868 to take seriously to boat building at his father's works on the Tyne. He was the inventor neither of the sliding seat, which was an American invention first used by a four-oar on the Tyne in 1871, nor of the keel-less boat, which was due to Mat. Taylor, the professional of the Royal Chester Rowing Club, in 1856. But both inventions owed improvements to Clasper. Like one or two other oarsmen he early discovered the advantage to be derived from allowing the body to slide on a fixed seat. Clasper subsequently devoted much time to perfecting the mechanical slide, and experimented with brass slides, glass, and rollers. In regard to the keel-less boats, Clasper worked out and perfected two radical changes of value: one was a lessening of the depth or draught of the boat, thereby reducing the water friction, and the other was the formation, after the analogy of a fish, of what may be called the 'shoulder.' In other words he placed the maximum width not in the centre of the length, but somewhat in advance. He also invented the countervail to obviate the steering difficulty caused by side wind.

John, whose father had never built eight-oared boats, greatly developed his business during the period (1870–4) when Cambridge were enjoying a run of victories over Oxford, and he built the 'eights' which were successful in 1870, 1871, 1872, and 1873. Continuous orders from both universities followed, and Clasper transferred a branch of his building business to the river at Oxford. About 1880 the supremacy in successful construction of racing boats was divided between Swaddle & Winship (a Tyneside firm) and Clasper. One of his best boats was that in which Oxford rowed in 1883. After training in a Swaddle & Winship craft the crew took to a new 'Clasper,' and won with the odds at three to one on Cambridge.

Clasper, whose integrity was recognised among all classes of oarsmen, was long a well-known figure at aquatic meetings, and in middle age was remarkable for his youthful appearance. His rowing weight when stripped was only 8 stone 3 lbs. and his height 5 feet 5½ inches. He died on 15 Sept. 1908 at his residence, Lower Richmond Road, Putney. Clasper married in 1871 Elizabeth, daughter of George Rough of Wandsworth Common, and sister of Frederick Rough, boat-builder, of Oxford. His boat-building business is now carried on by his widow, assisted by his younger brother, Henry.

[Field, 1908, cxii. 528, 562; Newcastle Daily Chronicle, 13 July 1870; notes supplied by J. H. Clasper & Co.] P. W.

CLAYDEN, PETER WILLIAM (1827–1902), journalist and author, eldest son (of four children) of Peter Clayden (*d.* 1865), ironmonger, and Eliza Greene (*d.* 1873), was born at Wallingford on 20 October 1827. He was educated at a private school in Wallingford, and early went into business. Brought up among congregationalists, he was led by the writings of Dr. James Martineau [q. v. Suppl. I] to unitarian views, and was admitted to the unitarian ministry. For thirteen years —from 1855 to 1868—he was an active unitarian minister. He was in charge successively of unitarian churches at Boston (1855–9), at Rochdale (1859–60), and at Nottingham (1860–8). In 1865 Clayden appealed to Dr. James Martineau to act as leader in a movement for the union of all congregations that rested on a spiritual and not on a dogmatic basis; and on 14 March 1866 the Free Church Union was formed, of which Clayden became secretary (*Life and Letters of James Martineau*, i. 418). Meanwhile he was also devoting himself to journalism. While at Boston he edited for a time the 'Boston Guardian'; while at Nottingham he wrote chiefly on political and social questions for the 'Edinburgh Review,' the 'Fortnightly,' and the 'Cornhill Magazine.' He strongly advocated the cause of the north during the American civil war. He had already become acquainted with Miss Harriet Martineau [q. v.], and she, in 1866, introduced him to Thomas Walker [q. v.], editor of the 'Daily News,' who engaged him at once as an occasional writer in his paper. A thirty years' association with the 'Daily News' was thus inaugurated. In 1868, when the 'Daily News' was reduced to 1*d.*, Clayden resigned his ministry and joined the regular staff in London as leader writer and assistant editor. In 1887 he became night editor, a post he retained till 1896.

Clayden, an ardent liberal of strong nonconformist leanings, greatly increased the influence of the 'Daily News' as an organ of liberal nonconformist opinion. He was especially active in support of Gladstone's anti-Turkish views of the Eastern question, and in hostility to the pro-Turkish policy of Lord Beaconsfield and his successors.

Clayden thrice sought in vain to enter parliament in the liberal interest, unsuccessfully contesting Nottingham in 1868, Norwood in 1885, and North Islington in 1886. He was a member of the executive committee of the National Liberal Federation and an alderman of St. Pancras. Clayden's journalistic efficiency and honesty of purpose were well recognised by professional colleagues. In 1893 he was elected president of the Institute of Journalists, and in 1894 president of the International Congress of the Press at Antwerp. In 1896, when freed from regular journalistic work, he advocated the cause of the Armenians, whom Turkey was persecuting anew. As honorary secretary of the committee which was formed to press the question in parliament, Clayden organised meetings, and in 1897 published 'Armenia, the Case against Lord Salisbury.' He died suddenly on 19 Feb. 1902 at 1 Upper Woburn Place, and was buried in Highgate cemetery.

He married (1) in 1853, Jane, daughter of Charles Fowle, of Dorchester, Oxfordshire (*d.* 1870); (2) in 1887, Ellen, daughter of Henry Sharpe, of Hampstead (*d.* 1897). His second wife was grandniece of Samuel Rogers [q. v.], the poet, and a niece of Samuel Sharpe [q. v.], the Egyptologist; of the latter, Clayden published a biography in 1883, while of Samuel Rogers he wrote two memoirs from family papers, 'The Early Life of Samuel Rogers' (1887); and 'Rogers and his Contemporaries' (2 vols. 1889). His eldest son by his first wife, Arthur William Clayden, became principal of University College, Exeter.

In addition to separately published pamphlets and the works already mentioned, Clayden's chief publications were: 1. 'The Religious Value of the Doctrine of Continuity,' 1866. 2. 'Scientific Men and Religious Teachers,' 1874. 3. 'England under Lord Beaconsfield,' 1880. 4. 'Five Years of Liberal and Six Years of Conservative Government,' 1880.

[The Times, 20 Feb. 1902; Daily News, 20 Feb. 1902; F. M. Thomas, Recollections of Sir John Robinson, 1904; Letters to William Allingham, 1911; Athenæum, 22 Feb. 1902; private information.] G. S. W.

CLERKE, AGNES MARY (1842–1907), historian of astronomy, born at Skibbereen, co. Cork, on 10 Feb. 1842, was younger daughter of John William Clerke (1814–1890), by his wife Catherine, daughter of Rickard Deasy of Clonakilty, co. Cork, and sister of Rickard Deasy [q. v.], an Irish judge. Her elder sister, Ellen Mary, is noticed below. Her only brother, Aubrey St. John Clerke, became a chancery barrister in London. The father, a classical scholar and graduate of Trinity College, Dublin, was manager until 1861 of a bank at Skibbereen, owned land in the district, and practised astronomy as a recreation.

Interested as a child by her father in astronomy, Agnes Clerke was highly educated at home. In 1861 she and her family moved to Dublin, and in 1863 to Queenstown. The years 1867–77 were spent in Italy, chiefly in Florence, where Agnes studied in the libraries and wrote an article, 'Copernicus in Italy,' which was published in the 'Edinburgh Review' in April 1877. Numerous articles on both astronomical and literary themes appeared in the 'Review' between that date and her death. In 1877 the family settled in London, which was thenceforth Agnes Clerke's home. A paper in the 'Edinburgh' on 'The Chemistry of the Stars' in 1880 was followed in 1885 by her first book, 'A Popular History of Astronomy during the Nineteenth Century' (4th edit. 1902). Nothing of the kind had appeared since 1852, when the 'History of Physical Astronomy' was published by Professor Robert Grant (1814–1892) [q. v. Suppl. I]. In the interval the spectroscope had been applied to astronomy and the science of astronomical physics inaugurated. Miss Clerke's work, which at once took standard rank, was especially valuable for its wealth of references. In 1888 she had the opportunity of practical astronomical work during a three months' visit to Sir David and Lady Gill at the observatory at the Cape of Good Hope. In 1890 her second book, 'The System of the Stars' (2nd edit. 1905), maintained her reputation. The third and last of her larger works, 'Problems in Astrophysics,' came out in 1903. Smaller volumes were 'The Herschels and Modern Astronomy,' in 'Century Science' series, edited by Sir Henry Roscoe (1895), 'Astronomy,' in 'Concise Knowledge' series (1898), and 'Modern Cosmogonies' (1905). Each annual volume of the 'Observatory Magazine' from 1886 until her death contained reviews by her of books or descriptions of new advances in astronomy. She contributed many astronomical articles, including 'Laplace,' to the 'Encyclopædia Britannica' (9th edit.). In this Dictionary she wrote almost all the lives of astronomers from the first volume to the supplementary volumes in 1901. In 1892 the governors of the Royal Institution awarded to Miss Agnes Clerke the Actonian prize of 100*l.*, and in 1903 she was elected an honorary member of the Royal Astronomical Society, a rare distinction among women, shared at the time with Lady Huggins; it had been accorded previously only to Mrs. Somerville, Caroline Herschel, and Ann Sheepshanks.

Miss Clerke's devotion to astronomy never lessened her interest in general literature, on which she wrote constantly in the 'Edinburgh.' In 1892 she published

'Familiar Studies in Homer,' which well illustrated her width of culture. An accomplished musician, she died of pneumonia at her residence in South Kensington on 20 Jan. 1907.

The elder sister, Ellen Mary Clerke (1840–1906), born at Skibbereen on 26 Sept. 1840, was her sister's companion through life, and shared her taste for music, literature, and science. In 1881 she published a collection of English verses, 'The Flying Dutchman and other Poems.' Residence in Italy (1867–77) gave her a complete command of the Italian language, which she wrote and spoke with facility, and she devoted much time to verse translations of Italian poetry. Some specimens appear in Garnett's 'History of Italian Literature' (1898) and in her own book, 'Fable and Song in Italy' (1899). 'Flowers of Fire,' a novel which graphically describes an eruption of Vesuvius, appeared in 1902. A regular contributor to periodicals, she wrote a weekly leader for twenty years for the 'Tablet.' Like her sister she interested herself in astronomy. Small monographs on 'Jupiter' and on 'Venus' from her pen appeared in 1892 and 1893; her short note on 'Algol' in the 'Observatory Magazine' for June 1892 gives evidence of acquaintance with the Arabic language. Miss Ellen Clerke died after a short illness at her home in South Kensington on 2 March 1906.

[An Appreciation of Agnes Mary and Ellen Mary Clerke, by Lady Huggins, with Foreword by Aubrey St. John Clerke, 1907 (printed for private circulation); Roy. Astr. Soc.'s Journ., Feb. 1907; Observatory Mag., Feb. 1907; The Times, 21 Jan. 1907.] H. P. H.

CLEWORTH, THOMAS EBENEZER (1854–1909), advocate of religious teaching in public elementary schools, eldest survivor of the seven sons and five daughters of Enoch Cleworth of Tyldesley, near Manchester, and Mary Sykes of Heywood, was born at Westminster on 2 April 1854, his father at that date being a London city missionary. Cleworth was educated at the West Ham Pelly Memorial School, and was for some years a teacher there. About 1871 he began mission work under the Evangelisation Society and attached himself to the American missioner, D. L. Moody, for whom he addressed meetings in Dublin and Cork. In 1874 his health broke down. In 1879 he entered St. John's College, Cambridge, whence he graduated as a passman in 1882. He was stroke of one of the college boats. Ordained deacon and priest (1881), he served in the Cambridge long vacations as curate of Kirk German, Isle of Man. In 1882 he joined the staff of the Church Parochial Mission Society under Canon Hay Aitken, in 1884 became on the nomination of the trustees vicar of St. Thomas, Nottingham, and in 1888 rector of Middleton, Lancashire, on the presentation of his father-in-law, Mr. Alfred Butterworth. In 1899 Dr. James Moorhouse, bishop of Manchester, created him rural dean of Middleton and Prestwich, and in 1902 an honorary canon of Manchester. At Middleton he organised many missions and 'instruction services' held after the Sunday evening service in Lent. His parochial schools, on which he spent much time as well as money, were of unusual efficiency. Cleworth did much for the renovation of the parish church, of which the chancel has since his death been restored in his memory.

Convinced that the efficiency of church life ultimately depended on the schools, Cleworth actively devoted himself to educational controversy, especially resisting, during the discussion of the education bill of 1902, every proposal to diminish the absolute control of the church over the religious teaching of its schools [see Kenyon-Slaney, William Slaney, Suppl. II]. In November 1903 Cleworth formed the Church Schools Emergency League, for the maintenance of church schools as such and of religious education by church teachers and clergy in school and church during school hours. Cleworth acted as secretary and treasurer of the league, which opposed with effect much of the board of education's policy touching church schools, and attacked the passive attitude of the National Society. Ultimately Cleworth's policy, while maintaining the *status quo* of the church schools, claimed that church teaching should be given in council schools by a church teacher on the staff, with parallel rights for nonconformists. He was a member of the Middleton local education authority, a member of the standing committee of the National Society, and a leader of the 'no surrender' party in 1906, when he was largely responsible for the great demonstrations in Lancashire and London against the liberal government's education bill of 1906, which the House of Lords rejected. Speaking incessantly through the country, he compiled the first eighty-four leaflets of the Emergency League, afterwards bound in seven volumes, besides contributing largely to the Manchester and London press, including 'The Times' and the 'Church Family Newspaper.' He published a volume on the education crisis in 1906 jointly with the Rev. John Wakeford. Cleworth died on 5 April 1909 at Middleton Rectory. 'In days of fluid convictions and wavering beliefs Canon Cleworth was pre-eminently "justus ac tenax propositi vir"' (Dr. Knox, bishop of Manchester, in *Manchester Diocesan Magazine*, May 1909). In 1884 he married Edith, daughter of Alfred Butterworth, J.P., of Oldham and Andover. He was survived by his wife, two sons and two daughters.

[Family information; Rev. A. Aspin, curate 1903–9; Emergency Leaflet (No. lxxxv.); The Times, 7 April 1909; Treasury (with portrait), March 1905.] J. E. G. de M.

CLIFFORD, FREDERICK (1828–1904), journalist and legal writer, born at Gillingham, Kent, on 22 June 1828, was fifth son of Jesse Clifford, of a north-country family, by his wife Mary Pearse. After private schooling, he engaged before he was twenty in provincial journalism. In 1852 he settled in London and joined the parliamentary staff of 'The Times,' of which his elder brother George was already a member. This employment he long combined with much other work. He retained his connection with the provinces by acting as London correspondent of the 'Sheffield Daily Telegraph,' a conservative journal, and in 1863 he became joint proprietor of that newspaper with (Sir) William Christopher Leng [q. v. Suppl. II]. In 1866 he went to Jamaica to report for 'The Times' the royal commission of inquiry into the conduct of Governor Eyre. He helped in 1868 to found the Press Association, an institution formed to supply newspaper proprietors of London and the provinces with home and foreign news, and he acted as chairman of the committee of management during two periods of five years each, finally retiring in 1880. In 1877, owing to the failing health of the editor, John Thaddeus Delane [q. v.], Clifford was transferred by 'The Times' from the reporters' gallery of the House of Commons to Printing House Square, and he acted as assistant editor until his health obliged him to resign in 1883.

Meanwhile Clifford had made a position as a legal writer. He was admitted to the Middle Temple on 3 Nov. 1856, and was called to the bar on 10 June 1859. In 1870 he, with his lifelong friend, Mr. Pembroke S. Stephens, K.C., published 'The Practice of the Court of Referees on Private Bills in Parliament.' This standard textbook on private bill practice first embodied important alterations in the procedure of the court of referees made by act of parliament (30 & 31 Vict. c. 136) and by standing orders of the House of Commons in 1867, and it contained the decisions as to the *locus standi* of petitioners during the sessions 1867–9. Clifford continued to act as joint editor of the 'Locus Standi Reports' to the end of the session of 1884. Clifford's 'Practice' brought him work at the parliamentary bar. The historical aspect of the practice especially interested him, and he published later 'The History of Private Bill Legislation' (2 vols. 1885–1887), a compilation of permanent value. He took silk in 1894, and was elected a bencher of his inn on 18 May 1900.

In early life Clifford co-operated with Edward Bulwer, the first Lord Lytton [q. v.], Charles Dickens, and other men of letters and artists in forming the Guild of Literature and Art, which was incorporated by private act of parliament in 1858. Clifford was a member of the council. The guild failed of its purposes, and Clifford and Sir John Richard Robinson [q. v. Suppl. II], the last surviving members of the council, wound up its affairs in 1897 by means of an Act (60 & 61 Vict. c. xciii.) drafted by Clifford, and they distributed the funds and landed property (at Knebworth) between the Royal Literary Fund and the Artists' General Benevolent Institution. Clifford was a student of agricultural questions and an active member of the Royal Botanic Society. He died at his residence, 24 Collingham Gardens, Earl's Court, on 30 Dec. 1904. A portrait by Miss Ethel Mortwell belongs to the family. His library formed a three days' sale at Sotheby's (5–7 May 1905). He was a collector of fans and other works of art.

Clifford married in 1853 Caroline, third daughter of Thomas Mason of Hull; she died in 1900. His second son, Philip Henry Clifford (1856–1895), graduated B.A. in 1878 from Christ's College, Cambridge, and proceeded M.A. in 1881. His surviving family of four sons and two daughters presented in his memory a silver-gilt claret jug to the Middle Temple (*Master Worsley's Book*, ed. by A. R. Ingpen, K.C., p. 324).

In addition to the books above mentioned, Clifford was author of 'The Steamboat Powers of Railway Companies' (1865); 'The Agricultural Lockout of 1874, with notes upon Farming and Farm Labour in the Eastern Counties' (1875), founded upon letters in 'The Times'; and a small treatise on the Agricultural Holdings Act,

1875, reprinted from the Royal Agricultural Society's 'Journal,' 1876.

[The Times, 31 Dec. 1904, 2 Jan. 1905; Sheffield Telegraph, 31 Dec. 1904; Men and Women of the Time, 15th edit. 1899; Foster, Men at the Bar; Brit. Mus. Cat.; private information.] C. E. A. B.

CLOSE, MAXWELL HENRY (1822–1903), geologist, born in Merrion Square, Dublin, on 23 Oct. 1822, was eldest of eleven children of Henry Samuel Close, a partner in Balls' Bank, Dublin, by his wife Jane, daughter of Holt Waring, dean of Dromore. Sir Barry Close [q. v.] was his grand-uncle. A brother, Major George Close, was distinguished in the Abyssinian war of 1868.

After education at a school at Weymouth, where his mathematical tastes developed, he entered Trinity College, Dublin, and graduated B.A. in 1846 and proceeded M.A. in 1867. He was ordained in the Church of Ireland in 1848, and was rector of Shangton in Leicestershire from 1849 to 1857. Resigning his living owing to scruples as to the propriety of holding a benefice under lay patronage, he acted as curate at Waltham-on-the-Wolds until 1861. Shortly afterwards he returned to Dublin, and did occasional clerical work there. Science had already engaged his interest, and thence forth he devoted himself to geology. He closely studied the features impressed upon Ireland by the glaciers and ice-sheets of the ice age, keenly observing phenomena during long traverses in the field, and publishing his results in the 'Journal of the Geological Society of Dublin,' in its successor the 'Journal of the Royal Geological Society of Ireland,' and in the 'Geological Magazine.' In a paper modestly entitled 'Notes on the General Glaciation of Ireland' (1867) he embodied powerful arguments for the former presence of an ice-cap over Ireland, and for the movement of ice outward towards the edges of the country from a region somewhere about Fermanagh. Another important contribution to glacial geology, written in collaboration with George Henry Kinahan [q. v. Suppl. II], was 'The General Glaciation of Iar-Connaught,' separately issued in 1872. Close's work proved beyond question that the main glacial features of Ireland must be ascribed to land-ice, though he regarded the glacial gravels with marine shells as formed by floating icebergs during a temporary submergence.

Close was president of the Royal Geological Society of Ireland in 1878 and 1879; and was treasurer of the Royal Irish Academy from 1878 until his resignation in 1903. He was for many years a member of the Council of the Royal Dublin Society. He possessed considerable archæological as well as scientific knowledge, and quietly supported the study of the Irish language when few other scholars had entered the field. Unobtrusively he did much to promote in Ireland research and intellectual progress.

He died unmarried, in rooms long occupied by him at 39 Lower Baggot Street, Dublin, on 12 Sept. 1903. He was buried in Dean's Grange cemetery, co. Dublin.

Close published two works on physics and astronomy under assumed names: 'Ausa dynamica: Force, Impulsion, and Energy' (by John O'Toole) in 1884 (2nd edit. 1886), and 'A Few Chapters in Astronomy' (by Claudius Kennedy) in 1894.

[Abstract of Minutes, Roy. Irish Acad., 16 March 1904; Irish Naturalist, 1903, p. 301 (with bibliography and a portrait from a photograph taken in 1867); Quarterly Journ. Geol. Soc. London, lx. 1904; Proceedings, p. lxxi; personal knowledge.] G. A. J. C.

CLOWES, Sir WILLIAM LAIRD (1856–1905), naval writer, born at Hampstead on 1 Feb. 1856, was the eldest son of William Clowes, sometime registrar in chancery and part editor of the 5th edition (1891) of Seton's 'Forms and Judgments.' Educated at Aldenham school and King's College, London, he entered as a student of Lincoln's Inn on 16 April 1877. He had already, in 1876, published 'Meroë,' an Egyptian love tale in verse, and on 11 March 1879 he left Lincoln's Inn for the profession of journalism. Employed at first in the provinces, he returned to London in 1882 and gained his first insight into naval affairs on the staff of the 'Army and Navy Gazette.' Concentrating his attention on naval questions, Clowes accompanied the home fleets during the manœuvres as special naval correspondent successively of the 'Daily News' (1885), the 'Standard' (1887–90), and 'The Times' (1890–5). His reputation for expert naval knowledge was soon established. Articles by him, some under the pseudonym 'Nauticus,' on topics like the mission of torpedo-boats in time of war, the gunning of battleships, and the use of the ram, were widely translated and influenced expert opinion in all countries. His series of anonymous articles on 'The Needs of the Navy,' in the 'Daily Graphic' in 1893 (Clowes, *Royal Navy*, vii. 83), was credited with substantially affecting the naval estimates.

Naval interests did not monopolise his attention. In the autumn of 1890 he paid one of many visits to America, commissioned by 'The Times' to study racial difficulties in the southern states. The results appeared first in a series of ten letters to 'The Times' (November and December 1890), and then in 1891 in 'Black America: A Study of the Ex-slave and his Master.' In view of the growing birth-rate and exclusion from political power of the black, Clowes foretold a race war incomparably terrible between black and white in America.

Clowes gradually gave up journalism for research in naval history. Between 1897 and 1903 he compiled 'The Royal Navy: its History from the Earliest Times' (7 vols.) in collaboration with Sir Clements Markham, K.C.B., Captain A. T. Mahan, W. H. Wilson, and others. The value of this work was generally recognised. He was knighted in 1902, but owing to ill-health was compelled to live abroad, settling for some years at Davos. He was granted, in 1904, a civil list pension of 150*l.* He was awarded the gold medal of the United States Naval Institute in 1892, was an associate of the Institute of Naval Architects, and in 1896 was elected an honorary member of the Royal United Service Institution, where he gave several lectures. In 1895 he was elected a fellow of King's College. He died at Eversleigh Gardens, St. Leonards-on-Sea, on 14 Aug. 1905.

Clowes married in 1882 Ethel Mary Louise, second daughter of Lewis F. Edwards of Mitcham, by whom he had one son, Geoffrey S. Laird (*b.* 1883). A civil list pension of 100*l.* was granted to his widow, 30 Nov. 1905.

An excellent linguist, Clowes contributed frequently in his later years to reviews in England, France and Germany. Besides his historical and technical books he wrote many tales, mainly of the sea, and some verse. He was part-author of 'Social England' (6 vols. 1892–7), and founded in 1896, and for some years edited, the 'Naval Pocket Book.' He also edited Cassell's 'Miniature Encyclopædia' (16mo, 1898), and did much to promote the issue of cheap reprints of standard literature, being advisory editor of the 'Unit Library,' 1901.

Besides the works cited, Clowes's long list of publications includes: 1. 'The Great Peril, and how it was Averted,' a tale, 1893. 2. 'The Naval Campaign of Lissa,' 1901. 3. 'The Mercantile Marine in War Time,' 1902. 4. 'Four Modern Naval Campaigns,' 1902.

[Who's Who, 1905; The Times, 16 Aug. 1905; Standard, 15 Aug. 1905; Army and Navy Gazette, 18 Aug. 1905; Men and Women of the Time, 15th edit. 1899; the New International Encyclopædia, 1910.]

S. E. F.

CLUNIES-ROSS, GEORGE (1842–1910), owner of Cocos and Keeling Islands, born on 20 June 1842, in the Cocos Islands, was eldest son in the family of six sons and three daughters of John George Clunies-Ross by his wife S'pia Dupong, a Malay lady of high rank. His grandfather, John Clunies-Ross, born in the Shetland Islands, of a family which had taken refuge there after 'being out in 1715,' landed in 1825, after many adventures as captain of an East Indiaman during the English occupation of Java, on Direction Island, one of the Cocos or Cocos-Keeling Islands; there he settled with his whole family.

In 1823 an English adventurer, Alexander Hare, had settled on another of the islands with some runaway slaves. The islands, till then uninhabited, had been first sighted and named in 1609 by Captain William Keeling [q. v.]. Hare soon departed, and Clunies-Ross alone obtained permanent rights by settlement. Although the Dutch government professed a vague and informal supremacy, Clunies-Ross regarded himself, and was apparently regarded by others, as not merely the owner of the soil but as also possessed of sovereign authority over the islands. These Cocos Islands—the name is now commonly applied to the whole group, but should, strictly speaking, be reserved for the more southern islands, the name of Keeling being correspondingly reserved for the more northern—are a tiny group of very small coral islets, some twenty in number, 'extraordinary rings of land which rise out of the ocean' (DARWIN, *Voyage of the Beagle,* iii. 539), strangely isolated in the Indian Ocean about 700 miles S.W. from Sumatra and 1200 from Singapore. Clunies-Ross's original intention was to form a depôt on the islands whence the spices collected from the surrounding East Indies might be dispersed to the markets of the old world. This scheme failed; but the coconut palm, almost the only plant which really flourishes on the bare coral atolls of the tropics, yielded sufficient oil and other products to maintain the fortunes of the family. In 1857, in the time of John George, the first settler's son, the islands were first declared a British possession, and subjected to British sovereignty—but without detriment to the Ross family's ownership of the land. The head of the family was until 1878 treated by the British Government as governor as well as landowner.

George, the grandson of the first settler, was, like the rest of his brothers, sent to Scotland for education. In 1862, when studying engineering at Glasgow, he was recalled to the Cocos Islands to help in re-establishing the then somewhat decadent fortunes of the family there. In 1872 he succeeded to his father's interests in the Cocos Islands and married Inin, a Malayan who, like her mother-in-law, S'pia Dupong, was of high rank and resolute temper. Clunies-Ross resembled his grandfather in strength of character, business capacity, and attractiveness of personality. By the introduction into the islands of modern machinery and of scientific methods, by planting coconut palms where these had before been chiefly self-planted, and by devising new markets for the produce, he not merely restored the family fortunes but transformed the industry, on which these depended, from the moderate state of prosperity which the favourable natural conditions had hitherto allowed into a well-paying concern.

Under George Clunies-Ross's rule the authority implied in the governorship of the islands was definitely transferred, by letters patent, first (in 1878) to the governor of Ceylon and next (in 1886) to the governor of the Straits Settlements—still, of course, without detriment to the family's ownership of the land. A further change took place in 1903, when the islands were actually annexed to the Straits Settlements and incorporated as part of the settlement of Singapore. But none of these administrative changes in any way affected George Clunies-Ross's interest as owner of the land. Meanwhile he steadily pursued his business and improved his island estates. From time to time he was in England, attending to his affairs and to the education of his children.

He died at Ventnor, in the Isle of Wight, on 7 July 1910, and was buried in Bonchurch churchyard. His property, which was considerable even outside that in the Cocos Islands, was devised to his wife and his family of four sons and five daughters; but his eldest son, John Sydney, was recognised as, by primogeniture, 'chief' of the island estate.

[The Times, 8 July 1910; H. B. Guppy's The Cocos-Keeling Islands, Scottish Geog. Soc., v. 1889; H. O. Forbes, A Naturalist's Wanderings in the Eastern Archipelago, 1884; Law Reports, and public records.]

E. IM T.

CLUTTON, HENRY HUGH (1850–1909), surgeon, born on 12 July 1850 at Saffron Walden, was third son of Ralph Clutton, B.D., vicar of that parish. He was educated at Marlborough college from 1864 to 1866, but left prematurely on account of ill-health. He entered Clare College, Cambridge, in 1869, and graduated B.A. in 1873, proceeding M.A. and M.B. in 1879 and M.C. in 1897. He entered St. Thomas's Hospital in 1872, and was appointed resident assistant surgeon in 1876, assistant surgeon in 1878, and full surgeon in 1891. Whilst assistant surgeon he had charge of the department for diseases of the ear. He was surgeon to the Victoria Hospital for Children at Chelsea from 1887 to 1893.

At the Royal College of Surgeons of England he was admitted a member in 1875 and a fellow in 1876; he served on the council from 1902 until his death, and sat on the senate of the University of London as representative of the college. He was also consulting surgeon at Osborne, and in 1905 was president of the Clinical Society.

Clutton died at his house, 2 Portland Place, after a long illness, on 9 Nov. 1909, and was buried in Brompton cemetery. He married in 1896 Margaret Alice, third daughter of Canon Young, rector of Whitnash, Warwickshire, and left one daughter.

Clutton was imbued with the modern spirit which bases surgery on pathology and not merely on anatomy. Diseases of the bones and joints more especially interested him, and he was one of the earliest surgeons to recognise the importance of the active treatment of middle-ear disease. His powers as a clinical teacher were of the highest order. Not only had he a wide knowledge of surgical literature but his practical and original mind lent to his teaching a rare vivacity. He disregarded tradition, unless it could justify itself on its merits. His health and his active devotion to St. Thomas's Hospital and medical school prevented him from writing much. But he published an important paper in the 'Lancet' (1886, i. 516), describing an affection of the knee occurring in children who are the subjects of congenital syphilis. His description was generally accepted, the condition becoming known as 'Clutton's joints.'

He wrote on 'Disease of Bones' in Treves' 'System of Surgery' (1895), and he was co-editor of the St. Thomas's Hospital Reports, 1885.

[Lancet, 1909, ii. 1552 (with portrait); Brit. Med. Journal, 1909, ii. 1504; information kindly given by Mrs. H. H. Clutton and by Dr. H. G. Turney; personal knowledge.]

D'A. P.

COBB, GERARD FRANCIS (1838–1904), musician, born at Nettlestead, Kent, on 15 Oct. 1838, was younger son of William Francis Cobb, rector of Nettlestead, by his wife Mary Blackburn. Educated at Marlborough College from 1849 to 1857, he matriculated in 1857 from Trinity College, Cambridge, where he won a scholarship in 1860. He graduated B.A. in 1861 with a first class both in the classical and the moral science triposes. Interested in music from an early date, Cobb thereupon went for a short time to Dresden to study music. Elected a fellow of Trinity in 1863, he proceeded M.A. next year, and was appointed junior bursar in 1869. That post, in which he showed great business capacity, he held for twenty-five years.

In sympathy with the advanced tractarian movement, Cobb at one time contemplated, but finally declined, holy orders. He actively advocated reunion between the Roman and Anglican communions, and published in 1867 an elaborate treatise, 'The Kiss of Peace, or England and Rome at one on the Doctrine of the Holy Eucharist' (2nd edit. 1868). Two short tracts, 'A Few Words on Reunion' and 'Separation not Schism,' appeared in 1869.

Resigning his offices at Trinity College after his marriage in 1893, Cobb continued to reside in Cambridge, and devoted himself mainly to musical composition and the encouragement of musical study, which had already engaged much of his interest. He was president of the Cambridge University Musical Society from 1874 to 1883, and as chairman of the University Board of Musical Studies from 1877 to 1892 gave Sir George Macfarren valuable help in the reform of that faculty. He was a prolific composer of songs, wrote much church music, including Psalm lxii. for the festival of the North Eastern Choir Association at Ripon Cathedral in 1892, church services, and anthems. His most ambitious work was 'A Song of Trafalgar,' ballad for chorus and orchestra, Op. 41 (1900); his most popular compositions were settings of twenty of Rudyard Kipling's 'Barrack Room Ballads,' which were collected in 1904, and songs called 'The Last Farewell,' 'Love among the Roses,' and 'A Spanish Lament.' He also published a quintet in C (Op. 22) for pianoforte and strings (1892) and a quartet (1898).

Cobb was an enthusiastic cyclist, and was first president in 1878 of the National Cyclists' Union, originally the Bicycle Union, and was president of the Cambridge University Cycling Club. For the International Health Exhibition in 1884 he contributed a chapter on 'Cycling' to the handbook on athletics, part ii. He took part in the municipal life of Cambridge, and addressed to the district council in 1878 a pamphlet on 'Road Paving,' in which he urged improvement of the roads.

Cobb died at Cambridge on 31 March 1904, and was cremated at Woking. He married in 1893 Elizabeth Lucy, daughter of John Welchman Whateley, of Birmingham and widow of Stephen Parkinson [q. v.], tutor of St. John's College, Cambridge; she survived him without issue.

[The Times, 1 April 1904; Musical News, 9 April 1904 (notice by Dr. L. T. Southgate); Musical Times, May 1904; Brown and Stratton, British Musical Biog. 1897; Marlborough Coll. Reg.]

COBBE, FRANCES POWER (1822–1904), philanthropist and religious writer, born at Dublin on 4 Dec. 1822, was only daughter of Charles Cobbe (*d.* 1857) of Newbridge House, co. Dublin, by his wife Frances (*d.* 1847), daughter of Captain Thomas Conway. Her father, great-grandson of Charles Cobbe [q. v.], archbishop of Dublin, was a man of strong opinions but a good landlord and magistrate, who on occasion sold some of his pictures to build cottages for his tenants. Frances was educated first at home, next spent two years (1836–8) in a school at Brighton, at a cost of 1000*l.*, then learned a little Greek and geometry from the parish clergyman of Donabate. Not fond of society, though she spent holidays in London, she read a great deal, using Marsh's library (see Marsh, Narcissus), giving attention to history, astronomy, architecture, and heraldry, writing small essays and stories, and tabulating Greek philosophers and early heretics. The household was strict in its evangelical observances; Frances became the first heretic in a family which counted five archbishops and a bishop among its connections. Having doubted the miracle of the loaves and fishes in her fourteenth year, she experienced conversion in her seventeenth, and was confirmed by Archbishop Richard Whately [q. v.] at Malahide. She drifted into agnosticism, but soon recovered, and never again lost faith in God. She continued attendance at church till her mother's death in 1847, after which her father sent her to live with her brother on a farm in the wilds of Donegal; when recalled, after nine or ten months, she gave up attendance at church and at family prayers, retaining, however, the habit of solitary prayer. Books which helped her were the 'Life of Joseph Blanco White' [q. v.], 'The Soul,' by Francis William Newman [q. v.], with whom she corresponded, and works by Theodore Parker, of Boston, Massachusetts, who sent her his sermon on the immortal life. One New Year's day she ventured to the unitarian meeting-house in Eustace Street, Dublin, but got no refreshment from a learned discourse on the theological force of the Greek article. As a distraction from ill-health (bronchitis) she resolved to write. Kant's 'Metaphysic of Ethics,' put in her way by a friend, Felicia Skene, suggested a theme; between 1852 and 1855 she wrote her essay on 'The Theory of Intuitive Morals' (4th edit. 1902), which she published anonymously lest it should cause her father annoyance. The essay was meant as one of a series to deal with personal duty and social duty. Her father's death left her with 100*l.* and an income of 200*l.* a year. She set out on foreign travel in Italy, Greece, and the East as far as Baalbec, taking a keen interest in all she saw, and impressed with 'the enormous amount of pure human good-nature which is to be found almost everywhere.' In November 1858 began her association with Mary Carpenter [q. v.], whose 'Juvenile Delinquents' she had read, and with whom for a time she lived in Park Row, Bristol, co-operating in the work of the Red Lodge reformatory and the ragged schools. Finding the conditions too trying, for Mary Carpenter had no idea of creature comforts, she removed in 1859 to Durdham Down, and engaged in workhouse philanthropy and the care of sick and workless girls, in conjunction with Miss Elliot, daughter of the dean of Bristol. To this mission she devoted her first money earned by magazine work, 14*l.* for sketches in 'Macmillan's Magazine.' Her love of travel continued; by 1879 she had paid six visits to Italy, spending several seasons in Rome and in Florence, and a winter at Pisa. Her 'Italics' (1864), notes of Italian travel, was written at Nervi, Riviera di Levante. She acted as Italian correspondent for the 'Daily News.'

Mazzini failed to convert her to his scheme of an Italian republic. At Florence she met Theodore Parker a few days before his death there on 10 May 1860. Subsequently she edited his works, in fourteen volumes (1863–71). In 1862 she read before the Social Science Congress a paper advocating the admission of women to university degrees: a proposal, as she says, received then with 'universal ridicule.' Her crusade against vivisection, originating in her love of animal life, began in 1863, and continued till her death. Philanthropy inspired much of her journalistic work. From December 1868 to March 1875 she was on the staff of the 'Echo,' under its first editor, Sir Arthur Arnold [q. v. Suppl. II], and made a speciality of investigating cases of misery and death by destitution. For a considerable time she wrote for the 'Standard,' till she thought it unsound on vivisection; for some time (till 1884) she edited the 'Zoophilist'; and she now contributed to most of the current periodicals. She interested herself in the promotion of the Matrimonial Causes Act of 1878, whereby separation orders may be obtained by wives whose husbands have been convicted of aggravated assaults upon them; the movement for conferring the parliamentary franchise on women had her warm support. Her lectures on the duties of women were twice delivered (1880–1) to audiences of her own sex. In 1884 she removed from South Kensington, with her friend Miss Lloyd, to Hengwrt, near Dolgelly. An annuity of 100*l.* was presented to her by her anti-vivisectionist friends in February 1885. In 1898 she left the National Anti-Vivisection Society, of which she was a founder in 1875 and had been joint secretary (till 1884), to form a more thorough-going body, the British Union for the Abolition of Vivisection. She was left residuary legatee by the widow (*d.* 1 Oct. 1901) of Richard Vaughan Yates of Liverpool [see under Yates, Joseph Brooks]. She died at Hengwrt on 5 April 1904, and in dread of premature burial left special instructions for precluding its possibility in her case. The interment took place in Llanelltyd churchyard.

In person Miss Cobbe was of ample proportions, with an open and genial countenance. Frankness and lucidity marked all her writing and gave her social charm. She met 'nearly all the more gifted Englishwomen' of her time, except George Eliot and Harriet Martineau. Fanny Kemble [q. v. Suppl. I] she regarded as the most remarkable woman she had known. Her advocacy of women's rights was born of her association with Mary Carpenter, from whom also she derived her interest in progressive movements in India. As an exponent of theism Keshub Chunder Sen took a place in her estimate beside Theodore Parker. She attended the ministry of James Martineau [q. v. Suppl. I], and occasionally conducted services in unitarian chapels. In detaching unitarians from the older supernaturalism her influence was considerable. It may be safely said that she made no enemies and many friends, quite irrespective of agreement with her special views, in the course of 'a long, combative and in many ways useful career' (*Athenæum*, 9 April 1904). Among her publications (which include numerous pamphlets on vivisection, 1875–98), the following may be noted: 1. 'Friendless Girls, and How to Help them,' 1861, 16mo. 2. 'Female Education and . . . University Examinations,' 3rd edit. 1862. 3. 'Essays on the Pursuits of Women,' 1863 (reprinted from magazines). 4. 'Thanksgiving,' 1863 (embodied in No. 6). 5. 'Religious Duty,' 1864; new edit. 1894. 6. 'Broken Lights: an Inquiry into the Present Conditions and Future Prospects of Religious Faith,' 1864; 2nd edit. 1865 (one of the most influential of her religious writings). 7. 'The Cities of the Past,' 1864 (reprinted from 'Fraser'). 8. 'Studies . . . of Ethical and Social Subjects,' 1865. 9. 'Hours of Work and Play,' 1867. 10. 'The Confessions of a Lost Dog,' 1867. 11. 'Dawning Lights, . . . Secular Results of the New Reformation,' 1868; new edit. 1894. 12. 'Criminals, Idiots, Women and Minors,' Manchester, 1869 (on the property laws). 13. 'The Final Cause of Woman,' 1869, 16mo. 14. 'Alone to the Alone: Prayers for Theists,' 1871; 4th edit. 1894. 15. 'Auricular Confession in the Church of England,' 1872; 4th edit. 1898. 16. 'Darwinism in Morals and other Essays,' 1872 (reprinted from magazines). 17. 'Doomed to be Saved,' 1874. 18. 'The Hopes of the Human Race,' 1874; 2nd edit. 1894. 19. 'False Beasts and True,' 1876 (in 'Country House Library'). 20. 'Re-echoes,' 1876 (from the 'Echo'). 21. 'Why Women desire the Franchise,' 1877. 22. 'The Duties of Women,' 1881; posthumous edit. by Blanche Atkinson, 1905. 23. 'The Peak in Darien,' 1882; 1894 (on personal immortality). 24. 'A Faithless World,' 1885; 3rd edit. 1894 (reprint from the 'Contemporary'; reply to Sir Fitzjames Stephen). 25. 'The Scientific Spirit of the Age,' 1888. 26. 'The Friend of Man; and his Friends, the Poets,' 1889. 27. 'Health and Holiness,' 1891. 28. 'Life,' by herself, 1894, 2 vols.; 1904 (edit. by Blanche Atkinson).

[Life by herself (ed. B. Atkinson), 1904 (with portrait); The Times, 7 and 11 April 1904; J. Chappell, Women of Worth, 1908; Men and Women of the Time, 1899; Letters of Matthew Arnold (1843–83), 1903, iii. 91.] A. G.

COILLARD, FRANÇOIS (1834–1904), protestant missionary under the Paris Missionary Society in the Zambesi region, born at Asnières-les-Bourges, Cher, France, on 17 July 1834, was youngest of the seven children of François Coillard, at one time a prosperous yeoman, who also had a considerable dowry with his wife, Madeleine Dautry. Both parents were of Huguenot descent. The boy was baptised in the Temple at Asnières on 5 Oct. 1834. Two years later his mother was left a nearly destitute widow.

After attending the protestant school at Asnières, and passing under revivalist influences, Coillard offered himself in 1854 to the Société des Missions Évangéliques de Paris, and was trained for missionary work, partly at the University of Strassburg (1855) and partly in Paris. In 1857, having been ordained at the Oratoire, Paris, he was sent to Basutoland, which had been the society's sphere since 1833. On his arrival at Cape Town on 6 Nov. 1857, he found Basutoland disturbed by war, and it was not until 12 Feb. 1859 that he reached Leribé. There he worked for twenty years. His activities are graphically described in his journal and in letters which he wrote in large characters to his aged mother until her death in 1875. Early difficulties arose, partly from the witchcraft, animism, and polygamy of the Basutos, and partly from the hostility of the chief Molapo, son of Moshesh, who had been baptised and had apostatised.

At an interview at Witzie's Hoek in July 1865 between Sir Theophilus Shepstone [q. v.] and the Basuto chief Makotoko, Molapo's cousin, who was threatened by the Boers, Coillard acted as interpreter and peacemaker, rôles which he invariably filled. In April 1866, by order of the Orange Free State government, the missionaries evacuated Leribé, and Coillard perforce spent some time in Natal. In 1868, when the British protectorate was established over Basutoland, he visited Motito and Kuruman in Bechuanaland at the request of the Paris Evangelical Mission, and at Kuruman had his first meeting with Robert Moffat [q. v.]. In 1869 he returned to Leribé, and the next six years showed how fruitful Coillard's devotion to the Basutos was becoming. On 27 July 1868 he had baptised Makotoko; in 1870 came the conversion and baptism of Moshesh; and in May 1871 the church at Leribé was completed. Coillard's twenty years' work for Basutoland made him, involuntarily, a political power and a civilising and educative influence. He translated into Sesuto some hymns and certain of La Fontaine's fables.

In April 1877 Coillard, with his wife and niece Élise, undertook an expedition to the wild and majestic Banyai territory, north of the Limpopo river. By December 1877 the party found themselves at Buluwayo as Lobengula's prisoners. They had partially evangelised the Banyai on the way, and Lobengula refused his sanction for further effort. They turned southward to Shoshong in the territory of the friendly Khama, who commended them to the Barotsi chief and set them on their way from Mangwato across the Makarikari desert. By August 1878 they had reached Sesheke, the chief town on the Lower Zambesi, and were cordially greeted by the subordinate Barotsi chiefs, finding everywhere the traces and the influence of David Livingstone [q. v.]; but they failed to obtain an interview with the Barotsi king, Lewanika.

After a visit to Europe (1880–2) and a meeting at Leribé with General Gordon on 21 Sept. 1882, they started again for Barotsiland. In March 1886 Coillard was received by Lewanika at Lealui, and from that time till 1891 was engaged in establishing strong mission stations at Sesheke, Lealui and Sefula, promoting industrial work, and urging Lewanika to develop cattle-rearing and agriculture. In 1890 and following years Coillard engaged somewhat unwillingly in the negotiations between Lewanika and the British South Africa Company, and in a letter to Cecil Rhodes [q. v. Suppl. II] on 8 April 1890 agreed, while he could 'not serve two masters,' to be a medium of communication. In bringing about the signature of the first treaty between Lewanika and the Company on 27 June 1890, he acted on the belief that for the Barotsis 'this will prove the one plank of safety' (cf. COILLARD'S *On the Threshold of Central Africa*, p. 388). But the missionary had great difficulty in keeping the king from violating the treaty. (On Coillard's whole attitude towards British influence, see an appreciative letter by Mr. P. LYTTELTON GELL, in *The Times*, 5 July 1904.)

After a serious illness in 1895, Coillard spent 1896–8 in Europe; but by 21 Feb. 1899 he was again at Leribé on his way back to the Zambesi. The Barotsi country, now styled North-west Rhodesia, was being peaceably administered. But great mortality ensued among the missionary recruits of 1897 and onwards, eight out of twenty-four dying and eleven returning home. Coillard's last years were clouded by an outbreak in 1903 of Ethiopianism under Willie Mokalapa, who drew away for a time many Barotsi converts. He was still engaged in preaching at the Upper Zambesi stations, when hæmaturic fever carried him off, at Lealui, on 27 May 1904; he was buried under 'the great tree' at Sefula, near his wife, who had died on 28 Oct. 1891.

On 26 Feb. 1861 Coillard married in Union Church, Cape Town, Christina, daughter of Lachlan Mackintosh, a Scottish baptist minister, who was a friend and co-worker of James Alexander Haldane [q. v.] and of Robert Haldane [q. v.]. Coillard's wife accompanied him in all his African travel.

Coillard's right to recognition rests not so much on the number of his converts as on his steady exercise of a civilising influence over Basutos, Matabeles, and Barotsis many years before their territory came within the British sphere, and on the consistency with which 'this single-hearted and indomitable Frenchman' created an atmosphere of trust in British administration. A short, keen-eyed, white-bearded man, he was a notable figure in modern South African history. His religious position was that of English evangelical nonconformity. In 1889 Coillard published 'Sur le Haut Zambèze' (2nd edit. 1898), which appeared in an English translation by his niece, Catherine Winkworth Mackintosh, entitled 'On the Threshold of Central Africa' (1897).

[C. W. Mackintosh, Coillard of the Zambesi, 1907; É. Favre, François Coillard; enfance et jeunesse, 1908. See also F. Coillard's preface to H. Dieterlen's Adolphe Mabille, missionnaire, 1898; and the Journal des Missions Évangéliques during his period.]

E. H. P.

COKAYNE, GEORGE EDWARD (1825–1911), genealogist, born in Russell Square, London, on 29 April 1825, was fourth son and youngest child (in a family of eight) of William Adams, LL.D., of Thorpe, Surrey, advocate in Doctors' Commons, by his wife the Hon. Mary Anne (*d.* 1873), daughter of William Cockayne and niece and co-heiress of Borlase Cockayne, sixth and last Viscount Cullen. His mother belonged to the well-known family of Cokayne of Rushton Hall,

Northamptonshire. On 15 Aug. 1873 he assumed the name and arms of Cokayne by royal warrant in accordance with his mother's testamentary directions. After private education owing to delicate health, he went to Oxford, matriculating from Exeter College on 6 June 1844. He graduated B.A. in 1848 and proceeded M.A. in 1852. He was admitted a student of Lincoln's Inn on 16 Jan. 1850, and was called to the bar on 30 April 1853. Entering the Royal College of Heralds six years later, he held successively the offices of rouge dragon pursuivant-of-arms (1859–70) and Lancaster herald (1870–82). In his heraldic capacity he was attached to the garter missions to Portugal in 1865, to Russia in 1867, to Italy in 1868, to Spain in 1881, and to Saxony in 1882. Appointed Norroy king-of-arms in the latter year, Cokayne succeeded to the post of Clarenceux king-of-arms in 1894. He was an active member of the Society of Antiquaries, being elected fellow on 22 Feb. 1866. He died at his residence, Exeter House, Roehampton, on 6 Aug. 1911, and was buried at Putney Vale. On 2 Dec. 1856 he married Mary Dorothea, second daughter of George Henry Gibbs of Aldenham Park, Hertfordshire, and sister of Henry Hucks Gibbs (afterwards Lord Aldenham) [q. v. Suppl. II]. He had issue eight children, of whom two sons and two daughters survived him. A portrait by Kay Robertson is at Exeter House, Roehampton.

Industrious and scholarly, Cokayne published 'G. E. C.'s Complete Peerage' (8 vols. 1887–98; new edit. 1910), and 'G. E. C.'s Complete Baronetage' (5 vols., Exeter, 1900–6). These works won him general recognition as a genealogist of the first authority. To this Dictionary he contributed a memoir of Sir Aston Cokayne (1608–1684).

[The Times, 8 Aug. 1911; Foster, Men at the Bar; G. E. C.'s Complete Peerage, 1889, ii. 437; A. E. Cockayne, Cokayne Memoranda, 1873; private information.] G. S. W.

COKE, THOMAS WILLIAM, second EARL OF LEICESTER (1822–1909), agriculturist, born at Holkham, the family seat in Norfolk, on 26 Dec. 1822, was eldest son of Thomas William Coke, 'Coke of Norfolk,' afterwards first earl of Leicester [q. v.], by his second wife, Lady Anne Amelia, third daughter of William Charles Keppel, fourth earl of Albemarle, whom he married when sixty-eight years old (STIRLING, *Coke of Norfolk*, ii. 284). Educated at Eton and Winchester, Coke received the courtesy title of Viscount Coke on his father becoming earl of Leicester at the accession of Queen Victoria in 1837. He was a minor when his father died on 30 June 1842.

Taking no prominent part in politics, sport or in public affairs, he was an ardent agriculturist and a skilful forester; and devoted himself to the management and improvement of his vast estate. A table appended to Mr. R. H. Rew's report on the agriculture of Norfolk, made to the second Royal Commission of Agriculture of 1893, gives some instructive details as to the expenditure of money by the earl and his father in keeping up and improving the Holkham agricultural estate of 39,612 acres. The first earl spent in buildings and repairs 536,992*l.*, the second earl spent 575,048*l.* up to 1894—in buildings, drainage and cottages, 377,771*l.*, and in the purchase of land for the improvement of the estate, 197,277*l.*—or a total by both owners of 1,112,040*l.* The gross rents of the farms, which in 1878 were 52,682*l.*, were only 28,701*l.* in 1894, or a shrinkage of 23,981*l.* (45·5 per cent.). In the year ending Michaelmas 1894 the disbursements on the estate were 12,311*l.*, despite the earl's personal supervision over all the details (App. C. 2 and C. 3 of *Parly. Paper* C. 7915 of session 1895).

The earl was appointed on 1 Aug. 1846 lord-lieutenant of the county of Norfolk, and held this appointment for sixty years, retiring in 1906, when he was succeeded by his eldest son. In 1866 he was made a member of the council of the Prince of Wales, and in 1870 keeper of the privy seal of the duchy of Cornwall, retiring in 1901 on the accession of King Edward VII. On 30 June 1873 he was made K.G. on the recommendation of Gladstone. He was in politics a whig of the old school, and became at the end of his days the 'father' of the House of Lords.

He maintained his health till 1905. He died at Holkham of heart failure on 24 Jan. 1909, and was buried there.

Leicester married twice: (1) on 20 April 1843, before he was of age, at Cardington, Bedfordshire, Juliana (*d.* 1870), eldest daughter of Samuel Charles Whitbread, of Southill, Bedfordshire, by whom he had four sons and seven daughters; (2) on 26 Aug. 1875, at Latimer, Buckinghamshire, Georgiana Caroline, eldest daughter of William George Cavendish, second Lord Chesham, by whom he had six sons and one daughter.

A portrait of him by George Richmond, R.A., was presented to Lady Leicester by his tenantry on 22 Sept. 1858, and hangs at Holkham. The earl is represented as a young man on one of the bas-reliefs ('Granting a Lease') of the monument erected in the park by public subscription in 1845–50 as a memorial to his father.

[The Times, 25, 29 Jan., 1 March 1909; Mrs. A. M. W. Stirling's Coke of Norfolk and his Friends, 2 vols. 1908.] E. C.

COLEMAN, WILLIAM STEPHEN (1829–1904), book illustrator and painter, born at Horsham in 1829, was one of the twelve children of a physician practising there. His mother, whose maiden surname was Dendy, belonged to an artistic family. Four of her children evinced a talent for drawing. The fifth daughter, Helen Cordelia Coleman (1847–1884), acquired a high reputation as a flower painter and assisted her brother William in ceramic decoration; she married in 1875 Thomas William Angell, postmaster of the south-western district of London; two flower-pieces by her belong to the Victoria and Albert Museum (cf. *Art Journal*, 1884, p. 127; *The Times*, 12 March 1884; *Athenæum*, 15 March 1884).

Coleman was destined for a surgeon, but beyond giving very occasional assistance to his father, he saw no practice. He early developed a keen interest in natural history, and in 1859 he published 'Our Woodlands. Heaths, and Hedges,' and in 1860 'British Butterflies,' both books running through several editions. He drew his own illustrations, and at the same time collaborated with Harrison Weir, Joseph Wolf, and other well-known artists in illustrating books from other pens, chiefly on natural history. In the preparation of the wood-blocks he was assisted by his sister Rebecca. The books which he illustrated included: 'Common Objects of the Country' (1858), 'Our Garden Friends' (1864), and 'Common Moths' (1870), by the Rev. J. G. Wood; 'Playhours and Half-holidays' (1860), 'Sketches in Natural History' (1861), and 'British Birds' Eggs and Nests' (1861), by J. C. Atkinson; 'British Ferns' (1861), by T. Moore; 'A Treasury of New Favourite Tales' (1861), by Mary Howitt; 'Philip and his Garden' (1861), by Charlotte Elizabeth [Tonna]; 'Hymns in Prose for Children' (1864), by Mrs. Barbauld; 'The Illustrated London Almanack' and 'Cassell's Natural History'; and he designed the heading of the 'Field' newspaper. At the same time he executed numerous water-colour drawings, chiefly landscapes with figures, somewhat after the manner of Birket Foster, and pretty semi-classical figure subjects. He also executed some etchings, occasionally worked in pastel, and painted in oil. He was a member of the original committee of management of the Dudley Gallery, contributing to the first exhibition in 1865. He continued to exhibit till 1879, and remained on the committee till 1881.

In 1869 he began to experiment in pottery decoration; Minton's Art Pottery Studio in Kensington Gore was established under his direction in 1871, and he executed figure designs for Minton's ceramic ware. He died after a prolonged illness at 11 Hamilton Gardens, St. John's Wood, on 22 March 1904. His widow survived him.

At the Bethnal Green Museum is a water-colour drawing of a girl with basket of coral by him, and an oil painting, 'A Naiad,' is at the Glasgow Art Gallery. An exhibition of figure subjects, landscapes, and decorative panels by Coleman was held at the Modern Gallery, 61 New Bond Street, Oct.–Nov. 1904. His portrait was painted by F. C. King.

[Roget, Old Water Colour Society, ii. 424; Graves, Dict. of Artists; Brit. Mus. Cat.; E. C. Clayton, English Female Artists, ii. 47–67; Coleman's autograph letter of 2 March 1880 in copy of his British Butterflies in Kensington Public Library; Cat. Dudley Gallery, Glasgow Art Gallery, and Victoria and Albert Museum (water-colours); Art Journal, 1904, pp. 170 and 393; The Times, 28 March 1904; Lloyd's Weekly Newspaper, 9 Oct. 1904; Queen, 22 Oct. 1904.] B. S. L.

COLERIDGE, MARY ELIZABETH (1861–1907), poet, novelist and essayist, born at Hyde Park Square, London, on 23 Sept. 1861, was daughter of Arthur Duke Coleridge, clerk of the crown on the midland circuit. Her grandfather, Francis George Coleridge (1794–1854), was son of James Coleridge (1759–1836), elder brother of Samuel Taylor Coleridge, the poet. Her mother was Mary Anne, eldest daughter of James Jameson of Montrose, Donnybrook, Dublin. Mary Coleridge was educated at home and early showed signs of literary gifts. As a child she wrote verse of individual quality and stories of mystical romance. Her father's friend, William Johnson Cory [q. v. Suppl. I], taught her and influenced her development. At twenty she began to write essays for the 'Monthly Packet,' 'Merry England,' and other periodicals. In 1893 appeared her first novel, 'The Seven Sleepers of Ephesus,' a fantastic romance praised by R. L. Stevenson, but otherwise achieving scant success. Her first volume of poems,

'Fancy's Following,' which appeared in 1896, was published at the instigation of the poet Robert Bridges, by the Oxford University Press. In 1897 a selection from these was issued with additions. But it was the appearance in that year of 'The King with Two Faces' (10th. edit. 1908), an historical romance centering round Gustavus III of Sweden, which established her reputation. Its atmosphere of adventure tinged with mysticism lent it immediate success.

In 1900 'Non Sequitur' appeared, a volume of essays, literary and personal; in 1901 'The Fiery Dawn,' a story dealing with the Duchesse de Berri; in 1904 'The Shadow on the Wall,' and in 1906 'The Lady on the Drawing-room Floor.' Meanwhile she contributed reviews and articles regularly to the 'Monthly Review,' the 'Guardian,' and, from 1902 onwards, to 'The Times Literary Supplement,' as well as three short stories to the 'Cornhill Magazine.' She also wrote a critical preface to Canon Dixon's 'Last Poems' (1905). Her literary work did not absorb her. She devoted much time to teaching working-women in her own home and gave lessons on English literature at the Working Women's College.

She died at Harrogate, unmarried, on 25 Aug. 1907, after a sudden illness. She had just finished a short 'Life of Holman Hunt' ('Masterpieces in Colour' series), undertaken at that painter's request and printed soon after her death. Her 'Poems, New and Old' were collected at the end of 1907 under the editorship of Mr. Henry Newbolt, and 'Gathered Leaves,' a volume of stories and essays hitherto unpublished or little known, and of extracts from letters and diaries, came out in May 1910, with a preface by the present writer.

Two portraits belong to her father, Mr. A. D. Coleridge, 12 Cromwell Place, S.W.—one at about twenty by Miss Skidmore; the other painted after her death, by Mr. Frank Carter.

[Prefaces to collected Poems, 1907; Gathered Leaves, 1910; art. in Cornhill, by Mr. Robert Bridges, Nov. 1907.] E. S.

COLLEN, Sir EDWIN HENRY HAYTER (1843–1911), lieutenant-general, born on 17 June 1843 at Somerset Street, London, was son of Henry Collen, miniature painter, of Holywell Hill, St. Albans, by his wife Helen Dyson. Educated at University College School, Collen passed to Woolwich, and was gazetted lieutenant in the royal artillery on 1 July 1863. He first served in the Abyssinian war of 1867–8, for which he received the medal. After passing through the Staff College with honours, he was transferred to the Indian army in 1873, and attained the rank of captain on 1 July 1875. The efficient manner in which he discharged the duties of secretary of the Indian ordnance commission of 1874 led to his entering the military department of the government of India as assistant-secretary in 1876. The next year Collen acted as deputy assistant quartermaster-general at the Delhi durbar (1 Jan. 1877) when Queen Victoria was proclaimed empress of India, and in 1878 he was nominated secretary of the Indian army organisation commission. His administrative talents were recognised in the later phases of the second Afghan war of 1880, when as assistant controller-general he was mainly responsible for the smooth and efficient working of the supply and transport system. He was mentioned in despatches and was awarded the medal.

Collen's routine work in the military department was interrupted by a short spell of active service. Promoted major on 1 July 1883, he joined the Eastern Soudan expedition of 1885, and served with distinction in the intelligence department and as assistant military secretary to General Sir Gerald Graham [q. v. Suppl. I]. He took part in the actions at Tamai (2 April 1885) and Thakul (5 May); he was mentioned in despatches and received the medal with clasp, the bronze star, and the brevet of lieutenant-colonel (15 June 1885).

On his return to India Collen was appointed successively accountant-general in 1886, and in the following year military secretary to the government of India—a post he retained for the unusual period of nine years. On 15 June 1889 he became full colonel and in April 1896 succeeded Sir Henry Brackenbury as military member of the governor-general's council. During his administration many improvements were effected in the composition of commands and regiments, in military equipment and mobilisation. The defects in army administration revealed by the South African war of 1899–1902 gave fresh impetus to Collen's activities, but many desirable reforms had to be postponed owing to financial difficulties. In the debate on the budget in the legislative council on 27 March 1901 Collen summarised the measures of army improvements with which he had been connected. The Indian army was being rearmed with the latest weapons; the building of factories for the manufacture of war material had already been begun at Wellington, Kirki and Jabalpur; a scheme for decentralisation had been drawn up and a remount commission established. Fresh drafts of officers were added to the native army and staff corps, and the supply and transport corps thoroughly reorganised. The record showed that 'Collen had left an enduring mark on the personnel, the organisation and the equipment of the Indian army' (*Speeches of Lord Curzon*, 1902, ii. 265). The reforms inaugurated by Collen were subsequently completed by Lord Kitchener, commander-in-chief in India (1902–9).

Collen was raised to the rank of major-general on 18 Jan. 1900 and of lieutenant-general on 3 April 1905. He was made C.I.E. in 1889, C.B. in 1897, and K.C.I.E. in 1893; he was nominated G.C.I.E. on his retirement in April 1901. In the following May he represented India at the opening of the first parliament of the Australian commonwealth by the duke of Cornwall, now King George V. On his return to England he served as member of the war office regulations committee (1901–4) and as chairman of the Staff College committee of 1904. When the controversy between Lord Curzon and Lord Kitchener on questions of army administration broke out in 1905, Collen actively supported the views of the viceroy as to the wisdom of keeping a military member on the council. A zealous member of the National Service League and of the Essex Territorial Association, he was a frequent speaker and contributor to the press on military subjects. He died on 10 July 1911 at his residence, the Cedars, Kelvedon, Essex.

He married in 1873 Blanche Marie, daughter of Charles Rigby, J.P., of Soldier's Point, Anglesey. She survived him with three sons and a daughter.

In addition to many articles in periodicals Collen published: 1. 'The British Army and its Reserves,' 1870. 2. 'The Indian Army: a Sketch of its History and Organisation,' published separately and in 'The Imperial Gazetteer: the Indian Empire,' vol. iv. chap. ix., Oxford, 1907.

[The Times, 12 July 1911; British Empire Review, Sept. 1911; R. H. Vetch, Life of Sir Gerald Graham, 1901, p. 465; L. Fraser, India under Lord Curzon and After, 1911, p. 411 seq.; The Imperial Gazetteer, vol. iv. chap. ix., 1907; Speeches of Lord Curzon, 2 vols., 1900–2.] G. S. W.

COLLETT, Sir HENRY (1836–1901), colonel Indian staff corps, born on 6 March 1836 at Thetford, Norfolk, was fourth son of the Rev. W. Collett, incumbent of St. Mary's, Thetford, Norfolk, by his second wife, Ellen Clarke, daughter of Leonard Shelford Bidwell of Thetford. Educated at Tonbridge school and at Addiscombe, he entered the Bengal army on 8 June 1855, and joined the 51st Bengal native infantry on 6 Aug. 1855 at Peshawar. He served with the expeditions under Sir Sydney Cotton [q. v.] on the Eusofzai frontier in 1858, being present at the affairs of Chingli and Sittana and receiving the medal with clasp. He next saw service in Oude during the campaign of the Indian Mutiny there, 1858–9, and was at the storm and capture of the fort of Rampur Kussia by Sir Edward Robert Wetherall [q.v.] on 3 Nov. 1858, for which he received the medal. During the rebellion of 1862–3 in the Khási and Jaintia Hills, Assam, he was present at the storm and capture of Oomkoi, Nungarai and at Oomkrong, where he was severely wounded in the ankle. He was mentioned in despatches. Promoted captain in 1867, he served in the Abyssinian campaign of 1868, was again mentioned in despatches (*Lond. Gaz.* 30 June and 10 July 1868), and received the medal. He became major in 1875 and lieutenant-colonel in 1879. In the Afghan war of 1878–80 he acted as quartermaster-general on the staff of Sir Frederick (afterwards Lord) Roberts, and was present at the capture of the Peiwar Kotal, in the operations in Khost Valley and round Kabul in Dec. 1879. Subsequently he accompanied General Roberts on the march from Kabul to Kandahar (Aug. 1880) and commanded the 23rd pioneers at the battle of Kandahar on 1 Sept. 1880. In the course of these operations he was further mentioned in despatches and was made C.B. on 22 Feb. 1881 and received the medal with three clasps and the bronze decoration (*Lond. Gaz.* 4 Feb. 1879, 4 May, 30 July, and 3 Dec. 1880). He was promoted colonel in 1884. During 1886–8 he was in command of the 3rd brigade in the expedition to Burma. He took part in the Karenni expedition in 1888 and commanded the eastern frontier district during the Chin Lushai expedition in 1889–90, receiving for his services the thanks of the government of India (*Lond. Gaz.* 2 Sept. 1887, 15 Nov. 1889, 12 Sept. 1890).

In 1891 he played a prominent part in the expedition to Manipur [see Quinton, James Wallace], and was left in command when the rebellion of the Manipuris was suppressed, acting there temporarily as chief commissioner of Assam and showing much resolution. He received the thanks of the government of India (*Lond. Gaz.* 14 Aug. 1891) and was promoted K.C.B. on 19 Nov. 1891. From 1892-3 he commanded the Peshawar district with the rank of major-general. He was given the reward for distinguished service and was placed by his own wish on the unemployed list on 8 June 1893. His military reputation stood at the time very high, but increasing deafness unfitted him in his opinion for active duty.

Collett was a keen student of botany. He first became interested in this subject in 1878 during the Kuram Valley expedition at the opening of the Afghan war. He published the results of his botanical work in the southern Shan States, Burma, in the 'Journal of the Linnean Society' (*Botany*, xxviii. 1-150). He was an original member of the Simla Naturalists' Society. After his retirement he worked assiduously at Kew, and at his death was preparing a handbook of the flora of Simla, which appeared posthumously, edited by W. B. Hemsley, F.R.S., as 'Flora Simlensis' (Calcutta and Simla, 1902). He died, unmarried, at his residence, 21 Cranley Gardens, South Kensington, on 21 Dec. 1901, and was buried in Charlton cemetery, Blackheath. His herbarium was presented by his family to Kew.

[Memoir by Sir W. T. Thiselton-Dyer prefixed to Flora Simlensis, 1902; Dod's Knightage; The Times, 24 Dec. 1901; Hart's and Official Army Lists; Official Account of the Second Afghan War, 1908; Lord Roberts, Forty-one Years in India, 30th edit. 1898; Sir James Willcocks, From Kabul to Kumassi, 1904, p. 120 seq.; Parl. Papers, C. 6353 and 392, correspondence relating to Manipur, 1891; E. St. C. Grimwood, My Three Years in Manipur, 1891, p. 315; private information.]

H. M. V.

COLLINGWOOD, CUTHBERT (1826–1908), naturalist, born at Greenwich on 25 Dec. 1826, was fifth of six sons of Samuel Collingwood, architect and contractor, of Wellington Grove, Greenwich, by his wife Frances, daughter of Samuel Collingwood, printer to Oxford University. Educated at King's College School, he matriculated from Christ Church, Oxford, on 8 April 1845, and graduated B.A. in 1849, proceeding M.A. in 1852 and M.B. in 1854. He subsequently studied at Edinburgh University and at Guy's Hospital, and spent some time in the medical schools of Paris and Vienna. From 1858 to 1866 he held the appointment of lecturer on botany to the Royal Infirmary Medical School at Liverpool. Elected F.L.S. in 1853, he served on the council in 1868. He also lectured on biology at the Liverpool School of Science. In 1865 he issued 'Twenty-one Essays on Various Subjects, Scientific and Literary.' In 1866–7 he served as surgeon and naturalist on H.M.S. Rifleman and Serpent on voyages of exploration in the China Seas, and made interesting researches in marine zoology. One result of the expedition was his 'Rambles of a Naturalist on the Shores and Waters of the China Seas' (1868). Returning to Liverpool he became senior physician of the Northern Hospital and took a leading part in the intellectual life of the city. In 1876–7 he travelled in Palestine and Egypt. Collingwood was through life a prominent member of the New Church (Swedenborgian). Besides 'The Travelling Birds' (1872) and forty papers on natural history in scientific periodicals he published many expositions of his religious beliefs, of which the chief were: 'A Vision of Creation,' a poem with an introduction, critical and geological (1872); 'New Studies in Christian Theology' (Anon. 1883); and 'The Bible and the Age, Principles of Consistent Interpretation' (1886). For the last years of his life he resided in Paris, where he died on 20 Oct. 1908. He married Clara (*d.* 1871), daughter of Lieut.-col. Sir Robert Mowbray of Cockavine, N.B.; he had no issue.

[The Times, 22 Oct. 1908; New Church Mag., 1908, p. 575; Who's Who, 1908.]

R. S.

COLLINS, JOHN CHURTON (1848–1908), author and professor of English literature, born at Bourton-on-the-Water, Gloucestershire, on 26 March 1848, was eldest of three children, all sons, of Henry Ramsay Collins, a medical practitioner, by his wife Maria Churton (*d.* 1898) of Chester. The father died of consumption on 6 June 1858 at Melbourne while on a voyage for his health. John was looked after by his mother's brother, John Churton (*d.* 1884) of Chester. After some preliminary schooling at King's School, Chester, he entered in 1863 King Edward's School, Birmingham, where at the first speechday (July 1866) he distinguished himself by his declamation of English poetry. On 20 April 1868 he matriculated as a commoner from Balliol College, Oxford. Although he was already well read in the classics and in English literature, he made no mark in pure scholarship. After obtaining a third class in classical moderations he graduated with a second class in the school of law and modern history. His undergraduate companions included Mr. H. H. Asquith,

Dr. T. H. Warren, and Canon Rawnsley, and they delighted in his spirited talk and in his capacious memory, which enabled him to recite with a rare facility and enthusiasm long extracts from great prose as well as from great poetry in Latin, Greek, and English. This faculty he retained through life. From his undergraduate days he cherished an abiding affection for his university. Through life he spent most of his vacations in literary work at Oxford.

His comparative failure in the Oxford schools and an unwillingness to entertain the clerical profession disappointed his uncle, and Collins had thenceforth to depend solely on his own efforts for a livelihood. A period of struggle followed. For three years he divided his time between coaching in classics at Oxford and writing for the press in London. From 1872 he contributed miscellaneous articles, many on Old London, to the 'Globe' newspaper. In the autumn of 1873, when his resources were low, he accepted the offer of W. Baptiste Scoones, the proprietor of a London coaching establishment, to prepare candidates for the public service in classics and English literature, and this occupation was long the mainstay of his income. But he was always ambitious of literary fame, and in the same year (1873) he designed an edition of the plays of Cyril Tourneur, the Elizabethan dramatist.

Swinburne had recently published a high commendation of Tourneur's work, and Collins, an ardent admirer of Swinburne's genius, wrote to him of his scheme. The result was a close intimacy with the poet, which lasted thirteen years. Swinburne was fascinated by his new acquaintance's literary zeal, frequently entertained him, read to him unpublished poems, and showed confidence in his literary judgment. Subsequently Collins sought with a youthful naïveté introductions to other prominent men of letters. He met and corresponded with Mark Pattison. He had long interviews with Carlyle, Robert Browning (1886), and Froude, confiding to his full diaries records of these experiences.

Although Collins's edition of Tourneur's writings did not appear till 1878, he made in the interval progress as an author. His earliest volume, 'Sir Joshua Reynolds as a Portrait Painter' (1874), was mere letterpress for illustrations. An edition of the 'Poems of Lord Herbert of Cherbury' (1881) was eagerly welcomed by Swinburne. At the same time his literary connections extended. He edited Milton's 'Samson Agonistes' for the Clarendon Press (1883), the first volume in a long series of school editions of English classical poetry. (Sir) Leslie Stephen, then editor of the 'Cornhill,' accepted an article on Aulus Gellius (March 1878). In three subsequent articles in the 'Cornhill' called 'A New Study of Tennyson' (Jan., July 1880 and July 1881) Collins directed attention to parallels between Tennyson's poetry and that of earlier poets with an emphasis which, while displeasing the poet, provoked curiosity. In Oct. 1878, to Collins's intense satisfaction, an essay by him on Dryden appeared in the 'Quarterly Review.' Regular relations with the 'Quarterly' were thus established and increased his repute. Three articles there on Lord Bolingbroke (Jan. 1880 and Jan. and April 1881), together with another essay on 'Voltaire in England' (from the 'Cornhill,' Oct. and Dec. 1882), were collected into a volume in 1886; while in 1893 two articles on Swift were similarly reissued from the 'Quarterly' of April 1882 and July 1883. Collins's contributions to the 'Quarterly' reached a total of sixteen, and all showed a faculty for research and were marked by a trenchancy of style which recalled Macaulay.

In 1880 Collins inaugurated an additional occupation in which he won great success. He then lectured for the first time for the London University Extension Society, delivering a course on English literature in the Lent term at Brixton. He pursued this work, with missionary fervour, for twenty-seven years, lecturing for the Oxford Extension Society as well as for the London society in all parts of England. His extension lectures owed much of their effect to his powers of memory, and they stirred in his hearers something of his own literary enthusiasm. He also lectured with like result at many ladies' schools in or near London; gave an extension course to the English community at Hamburg; early in 1894 lectured in Philadelphia for the American University Extension Society, also addressing audiences in New York and many towns in New England; and thrice —in 1897, 1901 and 1905—delivered short literary courses at the Royal Institution in London.

From an early stage of his career as a lecturer he sought to bring home to his university the need of repairing the neglect which English literature suffered in the academic curriculum. He argued that the conjoint study of classical and English literature was essential to an efficient education. Ambitious to give effect to his principles from a chair of English literature at Oxford, he was disappointed by the failure of his candidature for the newly established Merton professorship of English in 1885, when Professor A. S. Napier, an eminent philologist, was elected. Thereby literature in Collins's view was left unprovided for. In an article in the 'Quarterly' (October 1886) on 'English Literature at the Universities' Collins showed a certain sense of neglect while denouncing with pugnacity some English teaching lately given at Cambridge. The article roused a personal controversy which incidentally suspended his intimacy with Swinburne. He had already in an anonymous 'Quarterly' article on 'The Predecessors of Shakespeare' (Oct. 1885) attacked Swinburne's prose essays, and when defending himself from a charge of exceeding the limits of fair criticism in his new article he incautiously cited his friend Swinburne as tacitly approving his critical frankness. But Collins's censure had hitherto escaped Swinburne's notice, and the critic's confession drew on his head the poet's wrath (*Athenæum*, Oct.–Nov. 1886). The breach with Swinburne was partially healed later. Swinburne agreed to meet Collins on 18 Feb. 1900, and although the poet then greeted his critic 'with a stiff courtesy,' something of the old cordiality was subsequently renewed.

Collins pursued undaunted his crusade for the recognition of English literature at Oxford. He collected the views of leading public men, and published them in the 'Pall Mall Gazette' (Dec. 1886). He re-stated his case in a 'Quarterly' article, 'A School of English Literature' (January 1887), in an essay in the 'Nineteenth Century' (Nov. 1887) on 'Can English Literature be taught?' and in a volume 'The Study of English Literature' (1891). While his strenuous temper excited much hostility, Collins won his point. In 1893 a final honours school in English was established at Oxford largely owing to his agitation. In 1901 the philanthropist, John Passmore Edwards [q. v. Suppl. II], gave, at Collins's personal persuasion, the sum of 1675*l.* to found at Oxford a scholarship for the encouragement of the study of English literature in connection with the classical literatures of Greece and Rome. The scholarship was first awarded at Michaelmas 1902. A chair in English literature was established in 1903. Collins's victory brought him no personal reward. He applied for the new chair at Oxford without result.

Collins was always extending his journalistic and teaching work at the risk of his health. From 24 Nov. 1894 to 17 Feb. 1906 he was a constant writer in the 'Saturday Review,' and was allowed a free hand in censure of what he deemed incompetence. The titles of his first and last articles—'A Specimen of Oxford Editing' and 'Twaddle from a Great Scholar'—suggest his attitude to established reputations. In the spring of 1898, when threatened with a nervous breakdown, he made his only foreign tour, visiting Rome by way of Paris. In 1901, during which year he suffered an exceptionally severe attack of melancholia, he illustrated his critical severity in 'Ephemera Critica; or Plain Truths about Current Literature' (1901), while in an edition of the early poems of Tennyson (1899, 1900 and 1901), he continued the minute examination of what he deemed to be the sources of Tennyson's inspiration which he had inaugurated in the 'Cornhill' in 1880.

At length in 1904 Collins received some practical recognition of his energies. He was then appointed to the chair of English literature at the new University of Birmingham. Though he did not abandon all his lecturing engagements in London, he devoted himself with customary ardour to the duties of his new post, which he retained till his death. In 1905 he received the hon. degree of Litt.D. at Durham. In June 1907 he planned a school of journalism at Birmingham University, drawing up a scheme which was approved by the governing body but was abandoned on his death.

Collins's interests were not wholly confined to literature. His intellectual curiosity was always active and versatile. Spiritualism long attracted him, and he was a close student of criminology. In later life he investigated for himself many crimes which were reported in the press, visiting the scenes, interviewing witnesses, and describing his views and experiences in magazines or newspapers (cf. *National Review*, Dec. 1905, Jan. 1906). In 1906 he joined Sir Arthur Conan Doyle in establishing the innocence of a young solicitor, Mr. George Edalji, who had been wrongfully convicted of cattle maiming outrages at Wyrley, in Staffordshire, and had suffered a long imprisonment.

Collins died in somewhat mysterious circumstances. He left Birmingham in July 1908, and subsequently made his habitual autumn sojourn in Oxford. Suffering from severe depression, he arrived on 21 August at Oulton Broad, near

Lowestoft, on a visit to an intimate friend, Dr. Daniel, who was his medical adviser. On 12 September he met his death by drowning in a shallow dyke on a farm at Carlton Colville, in the neighbourhood. At the inquest the jury returned a verdict of accidental death. The evidence showed that Collins had been taking drugs to procure sleep, and while resting on a bank had fallen into the dyke in a somnolent condition. He was buried in Oulton churchyard. He married on 11 April 1878 Pauline Mary, daughter of Thomas Henry Strangways, by whom he had issue seven children, three sons and four daughters. A civil list pension of 100*l.* was awarded to Mrs. Churton Collins in 1909.

By way of a memorial, Collins's friends and pupils founded Churton Collins prizes for the encouragement of English and classical study among university extension students of Oxford, Cambridge, and London. A Churton Collins memorial prize for the same subjects was also founded in the University of Birmingham. A portrait in oils by Mr. Thomas W. Holgate was placed in the Bodleian Library, and a water-colour portrait head by Mr. George Phoenix in the upper library of Balliol College, Oxford, together with a brass memorial tablet with Latin inscription by Dr. T. H. Warren. A brass memorial tablet was set up in Oulton church.

Collins's genuine love and wide knowledge of literature showed to best advantage in his lectures and in private talk, where his vivacious powers of memory never flagged. His incisive style and wide reading gave real merit to some of his 'Quarterly' articles; but his learning was broad rather than deep, and he suffered his combative temper and personal resentments often to cloud his critical judgment. For most of his life he overworked in order to make an adequate income, and his long exclusion from professional posts at times embittered a kindly and generous nature. Yet his vehement denunciation by speech and pen of what he had convinced himself to be injustice or imposture was invariably sincere. Excessive toil strained his nerves and fostered some morbid mental traits.

An enthusiastic student of Shakespeare, he did service by fighting in lectures and essays some popular misconceptions, but he tended to exaggerate Shakespeare's debt to classical and more especially Greek writers. Although he dwelt with effect on the debt of English poetry to the classics, he was inclined to overstate his case. He was not successful as a textual critic. An edition of the 'Plays and Poems of Robert Greene' (Clarendon Press, 1905), on which he was long engaged, brought together in the introduction and notes a mass of interesting information, but the text was severely censured for inaccuracy (cf. W. W. Greg in *Modern Lang. Rev.* 1906). Besides those cited, his works included: 1. 'Studies in Shakespeare,' 1904. 2. 'Studies in Poetry and Criticism,' 1905. 3. 'Voltaire, Montesquieu, and Rousseau in England,' 1905 (partly based on 'Quarterly' articles, Oct. 1898 and April 1903); translated into French by Pierre Deseille, 1911. 4. 'Greek Influence on English Poetry,' ed. by Prof. Macmillan, posthumous, 1910. 5. 'Posthumous Essays,' ed. by his son, L. Churton Collins, including essays on Shakespeare, Johnson, Burke, Matthew Arnold, and Browning, 1912. He also edited for educational purposes numerous English classics as well as a series of English translations of Greek drama (Clarendon Press, 1906–7).

[Life and Memoirs of John Churton Collins by his son, L. C. Collins, 1911; Letters from Algernon Charles Swinburne to John Churton Collins, 1873–1886, privately printed, 1910; The Times, 16–18 Sept. 1908; William Watson's Poems, 1906, ii., a sonnet commending Collins's stimulating conversational powers; personal knowledge.] S. L.

COLLINS, RICHARD HENN, Baron Collins, of Kensington (1842–1911), judge, born in Dublin on 1 January 1842, was third son of Stephen Collins, Q.C., of the Irish bar, by his wife Frances, daughter of William Henn, a master-in-chancery. Entering Trinity College, Dublin, in 1860, he was elected scholar in 1861, and passed his final examinations in 1863 with honours in classics and moral science. He left Dublin without graduating, receiving, however, the honorary degree of LL.D. in 1902. From Dublin he migrated in 1863 to Downing College, Cambridge. At Cambridge he was bracketed fourth in the classical tripos of 1865, and the same year was elected to a fellowship at Downing, becoming an honorary fellow in 1885. Having entered as a student at the Middle Temple on 8 May 1862, and after reading in the chambers of John Welch and R. C. Williams, he was called to the bar by that society on 18 Nov. 1867. Collins joined the northern circuit, then still undivided, and it was some little time before he got into practice; his attainments were not showy, and to the end of his career at the bar he was less successful with juries than men who in all other respects were his inferiors; his strength lay in other directions. Gradually his industry together with his wide and accurate knowledge of the common law brought him fame and work. In 1876 he was chosen, in conjunction with G. Arbuthnot, to edit the seventh edition of 'Smith's Leading Cases' [see SMITH, JOHN WILLIAM], a task which had hitherto been carried on by Mr. Justice Willes and Mr. Justice Keating; he was also jointly responsible for the eighth edition (1879) and the ninth edition (1887) of the same work. To the experience thus acquired he owed the reputation which he enjoyed as a case lawyer both at the bar and on the bench, but he was no mere accumulator and classifier of cases; any that he took in hand had to undergo a careful process of crushing and probing until the essence and principle were extracted. He was made a Q.C. on 27 Oct. 1883, and his success as a leader was never in doubt. His services were in the greatest demand where complicated business transactions were involved and in litigation between rival municipalities or railway companies.

Collins did not possess either in voice or manner the external graces of an advocate, but he had scarcely a rival at the bar in the power of presenting his case or framing his arguments. Propositions of law were developed by him with all the lucidity and exactitude of a legal treatise into which his facts fitted with minute precision. Lord Esher, master of the rolls, then the dominating spirit in the court of appeal, was invariably impressed by his arguments, and the fact materially enhanced Collins's reputation among solicitors. He was regularly employed in the heaviest cases in the court of appeal and in the House of Lords, and he was one of the very few common law counsel who were imported to argue in the chancery courts.

Collins was appointed a judge of the queen's bench division of the high court of justice on 11 April 1891, on the resignation of Sir James Fitzjames Stephen [q. v.], and his exceptional learning and acuteness were at once recognised on the bench. He possessed the gift of combining in his judgments clear arrangement and logical accuracy with an unusual insight into modern commercial methods and ways of business. Owing to the grasp which his practice at the bar had given him of the law affecting traffic and locomotion he was appropriately chosen in 1894 to succeed Sir Alfred Wills as judicial member and chairman of the railway and canal commission. At the same time he showed himself thoroughly at home in the ordinary routine of nisi prius and circuit work. He was an excellent criminal judge, and during an emergency, due to the ill-health of the president, he sat for two or three months in the divorce court. On the retirement of Lord Esher in November 1897 he was appointed to fill the vacancy in the court of appeal and was sworn of the privy council. In 1901 he succeeded Sir Archibald Levin Smith [q. v. Suppl. II] as master of the rolls, and on the death of Horace, Lord Davey [q. v. Suppl. II], in 1907 he was made a lord of appeal, being granted a life peerage under the title of Lord Collins of Kensington. In the court of appeal his judgments were marked by breadth of view and by a courageous logic which never shrank from its legitimate conclusions, and he showed no inclination to enlarge the construction of statutes of which he disapproved, such as the Workmen's Compensation Act of 1897 (60 & 61 Vict. c. 37). As a consequence his judgments were not unfrequently reversed by the House of Lords in the numerous cases arising out of that Act, and a growing tendency to undue subtlety and over-refinement brought down upon him more than one rebuff from the same tribunal.

During these years Collins took much external public work upon his shoulders. As master of the rolls he was chairman of the Historical MSS. Commission from 1901 to 1907. He played a leading part in the management of the Patriotic Fund. In 1899 he represented Great Britain on the arbitral tribunal appointed to determine the boundaries between British Guiana and Venezuela. The inquiry which was held at Paris for some weeks during the summer resulted in a unanimous decision in favour of Great Britain. In 1904 he was appointed chairman of a commission consisting of Sir Spencer Walpole [q. v. Suppl. II], Sir John Edge, and himself, which was entrusted with the investigation of the case of Adolf Beck, a Swede resident in London who had been twice (in 1896 and 1904) wrongfully convicted at the central criminal court on charges of defrauding and robbing prostitutes. The report of the commissioners helped to give a final impetus to the passing of the Criminal Appeal Act of 1907 (7 Ed. 7, c. 23).

During his last years in the court of appeal his health had shown signs of failure, and he was a broken man when he was promoted to the House of Lords. He resigned his office as lord of appeal on 7 Oct. 1910, being succeeded by the attorney-general, Sir William (afterwards Lord) Robson. He died at Hove on 3 Jan. 1911. In private life

Collins was of most unassuming and sympathetic manner, with a strong undercurrent of humour which found vent in after-dinner speeches. When at the bar his contributions in prose and verse to the grand court of the northern circuit won him the honorary title of poet laureate. He maintained his interest in literature and the classics to the end, and was the first president of the Classical Association (1903). Collins took no part in politics. He married in September 1868 Jane, daughter of O. W. Moore, dean of Clogher, who survived him with three sons and two daughters. A portrait in oils by Charles Furse is in the possession of Lady Collins.

[The Times, 4 Jan. 1911; Annual Register, 1904; private information.] J. B. A.

COLLINS, WILLIAM EDWARD (1867–1911), bishop of Gibraltar, born in London on 18 Feb. 1867, was second son in a family of five sons and four daughters of Joseph Henry Collins, mining engineer and writer on geology, by his wife Frances Miriam Denny (*d.* 1888). After education at Mr. Nuttall's collegiate school, Truro, he passed to the Chancellor's School, which was closely connected with Truro Cathedral. Here his early association with Canon Arthur James Mason, now Master of Pembroke College, Cambridge, proved a determining factor in his career. After a short interval spent in a solicitor's office in London and in frequent visits to Spain, whither his family had removed, Collins decided to study with a view to holy orders. In 1884 he was able, thanks to the generosity of friends, to proceed to Selwyn College, Cambridge, and graduated B.A. as junior optime in the mathematical tripos of 1887, proceeding M.A. in 1891 and D.D. in 1903. The more congenial study of church history next engaged his attention, and the rapid development of his powers was mainly due to the stimulating teaching of Mandell Creighton [q. v. Suppl. I], then Dixie professor of ecclesiastical history. In 1889 Collins won the Lightfoot scholarship in ecclesiastical history, and in 1890 the Prince Consort's prize. In the same year he was ordained deacon, and priest in 1891, serving his first curacy under Canon Mason, who invited him to become a mission preacher at All Hallows Barking. He continued to combine historical study with the holding of missions and retreats, and in 1891 returned to Cambridge as lecturer at St. John's College on international law and at Selwyn on divinity.

In 1893, at the age of twenty-six, Collins was appointed professor of ecclesiastical history at King's College, London. His sympathetic methods of teaching, fortified by wide reading and strong convictions, served to establish close relations with his pupils. Meanwhile he was active in church work outside his official sphere. In 1894 he organised the missionary conference at St. James's Hall, and in the same year helped Mandell Creighton, then bishop of Peterborough, to start the Church Historical Society. In his capacity of vice-president Collins was responsible for preparing the society's publications for the press, and himself issued numerous historical studies, based on original authorities, including 'The Authority of General Councils' (1896), 'The English Reformation and its Consequences' (1898), and 'Church and State in England before the Conquest' (1903). In 1894 he renewed his connection with All Hallows Barking, where he took part in the celebration of the 250th anniversary of Archbishop Laud's execution (10 Jan. 1895), subsequently editing a commemorative volume of lectures on Laud (published in the same year). His reputation as a student of documents steadily grew, and his advice on church questions was frequently sought. In May 1899, when the archbishops heard at Lambeth arguments for and against the liturgical use of incense, Collins adduced early and mediæval authorities in disproof of the allegation of lawfulness. This evidence largely influenced the decision of Archbishop Temple [q. v. Suppl. II], prohibiting the use of incense as contrary to the second act of uniformity of 1559.

In 1904 Collins, despite delicate health, accepted the see of Gibraltar in succession to Dr. Charles Waldegrave Sandford. His earnest preaching, his linguistic attainments, and his cordial relations with the leaders of the orthodox Greek Church gave him special qualifications for the post. His duties, which included not only the administration of the diocese of Gibraltar and Malta but also the supervision of the English chaplaincies and congregations in southern Europe, involved constant travelling. In 1907 he visited Persia and Asiatic Turkey in the interests of the archbishop of Canterbury's Assyrian Mission, and on his return published his journal, 'Notes of a Journey to Kurdistan' (1908). At the same time he still rendered service to the church at home. During the meetings of the Pan-Anglican Congress (15–24 June 1908) his encyclopædic knowledge was frequently in evidence, and he presided with ability over the debates on the Anglican communion. Subsequently he assisted Dr. Randall Davidson, archbishop of Canterbury, in drafting the encyclical letter which was issued on behalf of the Lambeth Conference (7 Aug. 1908). The strain of his unceasing activities produced a serious breakdown in 1909, when lung and throat trouble developed. By the autumn of 1910 he recovered sufficiently to resume his episcopal visits, but fell ill shortly after at the British embassy, Constantinople, and died at sea on 22 March 1911 on his way to Smyrna; he was buried in St. John's Church, Smyrna. A memorial service was held at Lambeth Palace. Collins was married on 26 Jan. 1904 to Mary Brewin Sterland, who died on 15 July 1909 without issue. A posthumous volume, 'Hours of Insight and other Sermons,' appeared in 1912 with a preface by Dr. Randall Davidson, archbishop of Canterbury.

[A memoir of the bishop is being prepared by Canon A. J. Mason; The Times, 25 March 1911; Guardian, 31 March 1911; Truro Diocesan Magazine, April 1911; L. Creighton, Life of Mandell Creighton, 1904, vol. ii.; private information.] G. S. W.

COLNAGHI, MARTIN HENRY (1821–1908), picture dealer and collector (who was christened MARTINO ENRICO LUIGI GAETANO), was eldest son of Martin Lewis Gaetano Colnaghi, printseller, of 23 Cockspur Street, Charing Cross, where he was born on 16 Nov. 1821; his mother's maiden name was Fanny Boyce Clarke. The original firm of Colnaghi was established by the grandfather, Paul Colnaghi [q. v.], about 1750, and was for many years carried on at 23 Cockspur Street by his sons, Dominic Paul Colnaghi [q. v.], Martin's uncle, and Martin's father. In 1826 the grandfather and uncle set up the new firm of Colnaghi, Son & Co. (afterwards known as P. & D. Colnaghi & Co.) in Pall Mall East (where it still exists). Martin's father remained in Cockspur Street, and traded at first as Colnaghi & Co., and from 1840 as Colnaghi & Puckle. In 1845 this business passed to Edward Puckle. In the interval, owing to an unfortunate speculation, Martin's father was gazetted bankrupt on 22 Aug. 1843; he died in Piccadilly in May 1851 (*Gent. Mag.*). The business misfortunes of the father thwarted young Martin's intention of entering the army, and his early manhood was a struggle. He was for two or three years the most active organiser of the system of railway advertising which was afterwards taken over by W. H. Smith, a small City stationer, who developed out of it the gigantic business of W. H. Smith & Son (*The Times*, 29 June 1908). About 1860 Colnaghi turned his attention to art, for which he had an hereditary taste. For some years he travelled as an expert and buyer for his uncle's firm of P. & D. Colnaghi & Co. (in which he was never a partner), then for Henry Graves, and then on his own account. He helped to form many important collections, notably that of Albert Levy (dispersed at Christie's in March 1876), and in later years the three existing collections (among others) of Mrs. Stephenson Clarke, Mr. Charles Crews, and Mr. William Asch.

In 1877 he took Flatou's Gallery at No. 11 Haymarket, and called it the Guardi Gallery in honour of two fine pictures by that master which he had purchased. Hitherto his business had been conducted from his private residence in Pimlico. His important purchases in the auction room date from 1875, when he gave 4100 guineas at the Bredel sale for F. Mieris's 'Enamoured Cavalier,' and shortly afterwards 4500 guineas at the Lucy sale for a classical subject by Jan Both. Colnaghi remained in the Haymarket until 1888, when he took over the galleries of the Royal Institute of Painters in Water-Colours (originally called the New Society of Painters in Water-Colours) at 53 Pall Mall, which he named the Marlborough Gallery At each place he held, at irregular intervals, exhibitions of ancient and modern pictures, including works by the Barbizon and other continental schools; in 1892 he held one of the embroideries of Madame Henriette Mankiewicz, and in 1895 he exhibited the colossal canvas (330 square feet) of 'The Triumph of Ariadne' by Hans Makart. This he had bought at Christie's (9 Feb. 1895) for the emperor of Austria, who conferred upon him the Austrian Goldene Verdienst Kreuz mit der Krone.

His remarkable knowledge of the old masters of every school was acquired not through study of books but by direct examination of pictures at home and abroad. His 'eye' for a picture rarely led him into an error. He was more particularly an authority on the Dutch and Flemish schools; he claimed to have had quite 100 works of Franz Hals through his hands at prices which varied from 5*l.* to 100*l.*, long before the subsequent rise in values. Van Goyen was one of the many old masters he 'discovered,' and his last important public purchase at Christie's was on 9 Dec. 1905, when he gave 2100 guineas for an example by P. de Koninck. Chief among his private purchases was the Colonna or Ripaldi Raphael, which had been on loan at the South Kensington Museum for many years, after being offered to the nation, and refused, for 40,000*l.* It was then in a dirty and repainted condition. In his private diary, under date 15 June 1896, Martin Colnaghi recorded the purchase of this picture from the earl of Ashburnham for 17,000*l.*, whilst a further 500*l.* was paid as commission to an intermediary (see also *The Times*, 27 July 1896). He disposed of it to Mr. C. Sedelmeyer of Paris, who sold it to Mr. John Pierpont Morgan, of New York, not, as generally stated, for 100,000*l.* but for 80,000*l.* (two million francs). Among other private purchases was the beautiful Hoppner group of the Frankland sisters, for which he paid Lady Frankland 8000*l.* He frequently lent pictures to the Old Masters at Burlington House from 1885 and to other exhibitions. He was a member of the Printsellers' Association from 1879, but published only a few engravings.

Martin Colnaghi outlived all his brothers and sisters. He died at the Marlborough Galleries, Pall Mall, on 27 June 1908, and was buried in the family grave at Highgate. He bequeathed a number of pictures to the National Gallery (*The Times*, 15 July 1908, and *Connoisseur*, October 1908, pp. 126–7), and, subject to his widow's life interest, left the whole of the residue of his fortune, amounting to about 80,000*l.*, to the trustees of the National Gallery for the purchase of pictures, annually or otherwise, at their discretion, such pictures to be grouped and known as the Martin Colnaghi Bequest (*The Times*, 5 Aug. 1908). In his will he is described as of Pall Mall and Arkley Cottage, Chipping Barnet, Hertfordshire.

He was married three times: (1) to Sarah Nash; (2) to Elizabeth Maxwell Howard, who died in 1888; (3) in 1889 to Amy, daughter of George Smith, the artist, but left no children.

His portrait was painted by R. L. Alldridge, by J. C. Horsley, R.A., by his father-in-law, George Smith, and by G. Marchetti. The first portrait was exhibited at the Royal Academy in 1870, and the second, which was exhibited at the same place in 1889, was presented by Colnaghi's widow to the National Gallery. A bust in marble was sculptured by Adams-Acton.

Colnaghi's stock of pictures was sold at Robinson Fisher & Co.'s in six portions from 22 Oct. 1908 to 7 Jan. 1909, and realised upwards of 15,000*l.*

[The Times, 29 June 1908; Redford's Art Sales, ii. p. xxix, reproducing plate of a picture sale at Christie's from Graphic, 10 Sept. 1887, including figure of Colnaghi; Art Journal, 1896, p. 126, with portrait from photograph; information kindly supplied by Mrs. Martin Colnaghi; personal knowledge.]

W. R.

COLOMB, Sir JOHN CHARLES READY (1838–1909), writer on imperial defence, born in the Isle of Man on 1 May 1838, was fourth son of General George Thomas Colomb (*d.* 1874) by his wife Mary, daughter of Sir Abraham Bradley King, first baronet. Vice-admiral Philip Howard Colomb [q. v. Suppl. I] was his elder brother.

John Colomb was educated privately. He entered the royal marines in June 1854, and after a year of probation at the Royal Naval College, Portsmouth, was promoted to a lieutenancy in the R.M. artillery in August 1855. He retired with the rank of captain in August 1869. He was afterwards adjutant of the Cork artillery militia till May 1872. His mixed naval and military service, creditable but undistinguished, turned his mind to the consideration of our needs as the centre of a vast and far-spreading empire, and enabled him to realise, with a force then little understood, how the navy was the connecting chain of the whole. As early as 1867 he published an anonymous pamphlet on 'The Protection of our Commerce and Distribution of our Naval Forces'; and from the date of his retirement (1869) onwards he devoted himself largely to the attempt to induce the public to study these questions seriously and imperially. By addresses and papers at the Royal United Service Institution and Royal Colonial Institute, by pamphlets and by occasional volumes, he never ceased from his task, publishing in 'The Times' (17 April 1909), a month before his death, a long letter addressed to the chairman of the parliamentary labour party. He has been spoken of as the originator and apostle of 'the Blue Water School,' whose doctrines, in fact, travesty or parody his teaching. Contrary to those doctrines, he urged throughout the necessity of military preparation, and of an army for garrison at home, for field defence, and for expeditions; but he insisted as strongly that, in the face of a navy of sufficient strength, properly organised, any attempt to invade these islands must be on a very limited scale; and that the idea of preparing an army to defend the country, on the assumption that it had no navy, had smaller justification than the idea of a navy acting without the support of an army. He joined William Edward Forster [q. v.] in forming the Imperial Federation. He urged his views in the House of Commons, where he sat in the conservative interest as member for the Bow and Bromley division of the Tower Hamlets from 1886 to 1892, and for Great Yarmouth from 1895 to 1906. He was a member of the royal commission on the supply of food and raw materials in time of war, in 1905, and on the congestion of Ireland, in 1906–7. Having inherited the estate of Dromquinna, Kenmare, co. Kerry, he took part in Irish local government, and acted as chairman of appeals under the Local Government Act in 1898. He was nominated C.M.G. in 1887, K.C.M.G. in the following year, and privy councillor in 1903. He died, after an operation, at his residence, Belgrave Road, London, on 27 May 1909. Colomb married on 1 Jan. 1866 Emily Anna, daughter of Robert Samuel Palmer, and widow of Charles Augustus Francis Paret, lieutenant R.N.; she died in 1907, leaving a son and two daughters.

Colomb's chief publications are: 1. 'The Defence of Great and Greater Britain,' 1879. 2. 'Naval Intelligence and Protection of Commerce,' 1881. 3. 'Imperial Federation, Naval and Military,' 1886.

[Royal Navy Lists; Who's Who; The Times, 28 May 1909; Library Cat., R.U.S. Institution; information from the family.] J. K. L.

COLTON, Sir JOHN (1823–1902), Australian statesman and premier of South Australia, son of William Colton, a Devonshire farmer, afterwards of McLaren Vale, South Australia, and Elizabeth his wife, was born in Devonshire on 23 Sept. 1823, and went to Australia with his father when sixteen years of age. Left early to his own resources, he began business in a humble way in Adelaide, but soon won a leading position in commercial life there. For many years senior partner in the mercantile firm of Colton & Co., he retired in 1883.

He first entered public life in 1859 as an alderman of the city of Adelaide, and was mayor in 1874–5. He was elected to the House of Assembly in March 1865 as member for Noarlunga, and, with short intervals, he represented that place throughout his public life. A staunch liberal, he took office for the first time on 3 Nov. 1868 as commissioner of public works in the Strangways ministry, from which he retired on 12 May 1870. He was treasurer under Sir James Boucaut from 3 June 1875 to 25 March 1876, when the cabinet was reconstructed. On 6 June 1876, having carried a vote of no confidence against the Boucaut ministry, Colton became premier and commissioner of public works. His government lasted till October 1877, when Boucaut in his turn moved a vote of no confidence, which was carried by the casting vote of the Speaker.

Colton resigned his seat for Noarlunga on 29 Aug. 1878 on account of ill-health, and did not re-enter parliament till 6 Jan. 1880. In June 1881, on the fall of the Morgan ministry, he declined, owing to the state of his health, an appeal to form a government. In June 1884, however, he again became premier and chief secretary, with a strong cabinet, including Mr. C. C. Kingston, Mr. W. B. Rounsevell, and Sir R. Baker. His government, which carried a bill embodying the principle of land and income taxation, lasted exactly one year. Colton led the opposition for a time, but at the close of the parliament he withdrew from public life and visited England. Colton made up in commonsense and energy for what he lacked in eloquence. The strength of the cabinets which he formed proved that he was quick to recognise ability. The political antagonism which he aroused did not survive his retirement.

A staunch Wesleyan and an earnest advocate of temperance, Colton took great interest in education, and was a leading supporter of Prince Alfred College, of which he long was treasurer. He was made a K.C.M.G. on 1 Jan. 1891. He died at his residence in Adelaide on 6 Feb. 1902, and was buried in the West-terrace cemetery in that city.

Colton married on 4 Dec. 1844 Mary, daughter of Samuel Cutting of London, and had four sons and one daughter.

[Burke's Colonial Gentry, ii. 613; The Times, 7 Feb. 1902; Adelaide Advertiser, 7 Feb. 1902; Year Book of Australia, 1903; Hodder's History of South Australia, vol. ii.; Colonial Office Records.] C. A.

COLVILE, Sir HENRY EDWARD (1852–1907), lieutenant-general, born at Kirkby Mallory, Leicestershire, on 10 July 1852, was only son of Colonel Charles Robert Colvile of Lullington, Derbyshire, M.P. for South Derbyshire 1841–9 and 1865–8, by his wife Katharine Sarah Georgina, eldest daughter of Captain John Russell, R.N., and of Sophia, twenty-third Baroness de

Clifford in her own right. His father was fifth in descent from Richard Colvile, of Newton Colvile, who succeeded his uncle, Sir William Colvile (*d.* 1680), a staunch royalist. His mother's father was grandson of John Russell, fourth duke of Bedford [q. v.]. Educated at Eton, he entered the army as lieutenant in the grenadier guards on 1 Oct. 1870, and was promoted captain on 15 March 1872. From 1876 to 1880 he was instructor of musketry; from 1880 to 1883 he was A.D.C. to the Hon. Leicester Smyth, the general commanding the troops at the Cape of Good Hope, and in 1884 he obtained employment in the intelligence department in the Soudan. He was present at the battles of El-Teb (29 Feb. 1884) and Tamai (13 March) under Sir Gerald Graham [q.v. Suppl. I], was mentioned in despatches (*Lond. Gaz.* 27 March and 6 May 1884), and received the medal with clasp and bronze star. Later in the same year he was specially employed in the Soudan expedition on the Nile which was designed to rescue General Gordon at Khartoum. Attached to the intelligence department, he was present at the action of Abu Klea in January 1885 (despatches, *Lond. Gaz.* 25 Aug. 1885). He was made C.B. on 25 Aug. 1885 and received the clasp. From 1885 to 1888 he was on the staff in Egypt, and during that period was employed with the frontier field force, being present at the action of Giniss on 30 Dec. 1885 (despatches, *Lond. Gaz.* 9 Feb. 1886).

Repeatedly mentioned in despatches, Colvile achieved a solid reputation as one of the best intelligence officers in the army, and becoming lieutenant-colonel on 1 Nov. 1882, was promoted colonel on 2 Jan. 1886 for his services in the Soudan. In 1893 he was sent to the Uganda protectorate as acting commissioner, and next year he commanded the expedition against Kabarega, king of Unyoro, the slave raider, which proved a conspicuous success. For these services he received the central African medal and the brilliant star of Zanzibar and was nominated C.M.G. on 3 Jan. 1895. Forced to retire from Uganda by ill-health, he came home, and on 5 July 1895 was promoted to K.C.M.G., and on 10 March 1898 became major-general.

After a short time in command of a brigade at Gibraltar, Colvile was in 1899 given the command of the guards brigade in the war with the Boers of South Africa, which was declared on 12 Oct. 1899. He was with the force, under Lord Methuen, which was ordered to relieve Kimberley (besieged since 15 Oct.), and took part in the successful actions at Belmont (23 Nov. 1899) and Modder River (28 Nov.), and the defeat of Magersfontein (10–11 Dec.) (despatches, *Lond. Gaz.* 26 Jan. and 16 March 1900; medal with clasps). When the South African field force was reorganised on the arrival of Lord Roberts as commander-in-chief (10 Jan. 1900), Colvile was placed in command of the new ninth division, and marched with the main army to attack General Cronje's force. Colvile's and General Kelly-Kenny's division hemmed in Cronje at Paardeberg after desperate fighting (18 Feb.); Colvile took part with Lord Roberts in the occupation of Bloemfontein (13 March), after engagements at Poplar Grove and Driefontein (10 March). While at Bloemfontein he became entangled in events which ruined his military career. Colvile failed in his attempt to relieve General Broadwood's column, after it had been ambushed by General De Wet at Sanna's Post (30–31 March 1900), and his failure was assigned by Lord Roberts to a reprehensible lack of vigour. A further disaster befell Colvile later. Lord Roberts, on his advance from Bloemfontein to Pretoria in May, left Colvile, who was still nominally in command of the division, on the line of communication, with orders to press on to Heilbron. At the end of May, Colonel Spragge, in command of a detachment of Irish imperial yeomanry, which had been directed to join Colvile's division, was surrounded at Lindley by De Wet's force. Appeals for help reached Colvile, who disregarded them, and arrived at Heilbron, after severe fighting, according to his orders, on 29 May. Spragge's force was captured by the Boers, with heavy casualties, on 31 May. Colvile's position was difficult; on the one hand he had been led to believe that his presence at Heilbron by a certain date was essential to Lord Roberts's plans; on the other there was a definite appeal for help from a part of the force assigned to him, the absence of which increased the difficulty of his march to Heilbron and diminished his usefulness when he arrived there. Colvile failed to realise that an officer in his responsible position must, in exceptional circumstances, take the risk of acting even contrary to orders.

After the disaster at Lindley the ninth division was broken up, and Colvile being sent home reverted to the command of a brigade at Gibraltar. But when Lord Roberts became commander-in-chief of the army on 30 Nov. 1900, he insisted that Colvile should be recalled. Colvile returned to England, and on landing at Dover on

31 Dec. stated his own view of his case to a representative of Reuter's agency. On 19 Jan. 1901 he was placed on retired pay as a lieutenant-general. He skilfully elaborated his defence and complained of his treatment by Lord Roberts in 'The Work of the Ninth Division' (1901).

Settling at Bagshot, Colvile, on 24 Nov. 1907, while riding a motor-bicycle, came into collision at Frimley with a motor-car, and died almost immediately of his injuries at Brompton Sanatorium. He was buried at Lullington, near Burton-on-Trent, where his ancestral estates lay.

He was twice married: (1) on 6 Aug. 1878 to Alice Rosa (*d.* 1882), eldest daughter of Robert Daly and granddaughter of John Daly, second Baron Dunsandle; (2) in 1886 to Zélie Isabelle, daughter of Pierre Richard de Préville of Château des Mondrans, Basses Pyrénées, France, by whom he had one son.

Colvile was a skilful writer and effectively narrated his experiences as a traveller in little known lands as well as a soldier. He published, besides the work cited: 1. 'A Ride in Petticoats and Slippers,' relating to Morocco, 1880. 2. 'The Accursed Land,' a description of the land of Edom near the Dead Sea, 1884. 3. 'The History of the Soudan Campaign,' for the war office, 3 parts, 1889. 4. 'The Land of the Nile Springs,' 1895, chiefly an account of the fight against Kabarega in Uganda. 5. 'The Allies, England and Japan,' 1907.

[Burke's Peerage; Hart's and Official Army Lists; Celebrities of the Army, edited by Commander Charles N. Robinson, R.N.; R. H. Vetch, Lieut.-General Sir Gerald Graham, 1901; The Scapegoat, a selection from articles in The Review of the Week, 1901; Journal, Roy. Geog. Soc., Jan. 1908; The Times, 26 Nov. 1907; The Times History of War in South Africa, vols. iii. and iv.; Sir F. Maurice, Official History of War in South Africa, vols. i. and ii.] H. M. V.

COLVIN, Sir AUCKLAND (1838–1908), Anglo-Indian and Egyptian administrator, born at Calcutta on 8 March 1838, was third son of the ten children of John Russell Colvin [q. v.], lieutenant-governor of the North-Western Provinces, by his wife Emma Sophia, daughter of Wetenhall Sneyd, vicar of Newchurch, Isle of Wight. Three of his brothers, Bazett Wetenhall Colvin, Elliott Graham Colvin, and Sir Walter Mytton Colvin (see below), all passed distinguished careers in India, and a fourth, Clement Sneyd, C.S.I., was secretary of the public works department of the India office in London.

Educated at Eton from 1850, Auckland went in 1854 to the East India College, Haileybury, and arriving in India on 17 Jan. 1858, he was posted to the Agra provinces. After serving the usual district novitiate, Auckland went to headquarters in May 1864 as under secretary in the home, and afterwards in the foreign department of the government of India. He returned to his own province in July 1869 as a settlement officer, and did good work in the revision of the Allahabad district settlement. He officiated as secretary to the government of the North-West Provinces in April 1873, and from the following June as commissioner of excise and stamps. The lieutenant-governor, Sir George Couper [q. v. Suppl. II], resented some brilliant criticism of the local government in the 'Pioneer' (Allahabad), which was attributed to Colvin's pen or inspiration. In the spring of 1877 Couper sent Colvin back to district work as collector of Basti. From November 1877 he officiated for a short period as commissioner of inland customs under the government of India, and he was afterwards collector of Bijnaur.

Colvin's opportunity came when in January 1878 he was transferred for employment in Egypt, serving first as head of the cadastral survey, and then from 24 May as British commissioner of the debt, in place of Major Evelyn Baring (now Lord Cromer). Again in June 1880 he succeeded Major Baring as English controller of Egyptian finance, with M. de Blignières as his French colleague. From time to time he acted as British consul-general in Sir Edward Malet's absence, and he was acting for Malet when the mutiny of 9 Sept. 1881 broke out. By his advice and persuasion the timorous Khedive Tewfik confronted Arabi, the rebel leader, in the square of the Abdin palace, and succeeded in postponing the insurrection (cf. Colvin's official minute, 19 Sept.; Cromer, *Modern Egypt*, i. 206–8). In various ways, and not least by his work as Egyptian correspondent of the 'Pall Mall Gazette,' he influenced public opinion at home, and forced the reluctant hands of Gladstone's government towards acceptance of responsibility in Egypt. Mr. Wilfrid Scawen Blunt, Colvin's bitterest opponent, in his 'Secret History of the English Occupation' (1907), pays unwilling homage to the resource with which Colvin conducted the struggle. After the British occupation Colvin became financial adviser to the Khedive, who conferred on him the grand cordons of

Osmanieh and Medjidie. He was created K.C.M.G. in 1881.

When Lord Cromer became British agent in Egypt, Colvin succeeded him as financial member of the viceroy's council in India in Aug. 1883. Financial difficulties faced him. The war in Upper Burma and the danger of hostilities with Russia, consequent upon the Penjdeh incident, were not only costly in themselves, but were followed by great capital outlay on improving the strategic position on the north-west frontier, and by increases of the British and native armies. With Sir Courtenay Ilbert, then legal member, Colvin minuted against this increase, and after retirement he complained that the military element in the council was disproportionately strong (*Final Report of Ind. Expend. Comm.* 1900, Cd. 131). The finances were also disturbed by the continued decline in the sterling value of the rupee, while suggestions made by the governor-general in council, at Colvin's instance, for seeking an international acceptance of bimetallism were treated by the cabinet at home, Colvin thought, with scant respect.

Although he caused a committee to be appointed under Sir Charles Elliott [q. v. Suppl. II] to recommend economies, he was compelled not only to suspend the Famine Insurance Fund, and to take toll of the provincial governments, but to increase taxation. In January 1886 he converted some annual licence duties in certain provinces into a general tax on non-agricultural incomes in excess of Rs. 500 per annum. This unpopular proceeding was immortalised in Kipling's 'Departmental Ditties' by 'The Rupaiyat of Omar Kal'vin,' which represents the finance member as plying the begging-bowl among his European countrymen. In his last budget (1887–8) he increased the salt duty by twenty-five per cent. and imposed an export duty on petroleum.

Colvin welcomed his transfer on 21 Nov. 1887 to Allahabad as lieutenant-governor of the North-West Provinces and chief commissioner of Oudh, in succession to Sir Alfred Comyn Lyall [q. v. Suppl. II]. His father had been charged with 'over-governing' the same provinces thirty years before, and the son resembled him in his personal attention to detail. To his influence were due good water supplies and drainage systems in the larger towns of what are now the United Provinces, several new hospitals, and the Colvin Taluqdars' school at Lucknow.

Towards the Indian National Congress he declared himself uncompromisingly hostile, both in allocutions at divisional durbars and in a published correspondence with Mr. A. O. Hume, formerly of his own service, the 'father' of the new movement (1885). Colvin resolutely rallied loyalist opinion against the congress.

Created C.I.E. in Oct. 1883, he was gazetted a K.C.S.I. in May 1892, six months before retirement. In England, Colvin settled at Earl Soham, Framlingham, and took an active part in local affairs and charities. He mainly occupied himself with literature. He wrote the life of his father for the 'Rulers of India' series (1895), warmly defending him against contemporary criticism. His 'Making of Modern Egypt' (1906), while dealing generously with the work of other Englishmen, says nothing of his own part in surmounting the crises of 1881 and 1882. The book was soon overshadowed by Lord Cromer's 'Modern Egypt' (1908). From 1896 onward he was chairman of the Burma railways, the Egyptian Delta railway, and the Khedivial Mail Steamship Company, and was on the boards of other companies. He died at Sutton House, Surbiton, the residence of his eldest daughter, on 24 March 1908. He was buried at Earl Soham.

He married on 4 Aug. 1859 Charlotte Elizabeth (*d.* 1865), daughter of Lieut.-general Charles Herbert, C.B., and had a son, who died in infancy, and three daughters.

COLVIN, SIR WALTER MYTTON (1847–1908), Sir Auckland's youngest brother, born at Moulmain, Burma, on 13 Sept. 1847, was educated at Rugby and Trinity College, Cambridge, where he was captain of the boats. He was called to the bar at the Middle Temple in 1871, went out to Allahabad in the following year, and built up a vast practice as a criminal lawyer. He served for several biennial terms as a nominated member of the provincial legislature. His insight into the manners, customs, and thoughts of the people was of great value to the police commission of 1902–3, of which he was a member. Mainly for this service he was knighted in 1904. He died at Allahabad on 16 Dec. 1908, and was buried in the European cemetery there. There is a tablet to his memory in Milland Church, Hampshire. He married in 1873 Annie, daughter of Wigram E. Money, and had a family of three daughters.

[John Russell Colvin, Rulers of India series; Debrett's Peerage; the India List; Annual Registers for various years from 1882; Lord Cromer's Modern Egypt; Audi Alteram

Partem, being two letters on Ind. Nat. Congress Movement, Simla, 1888; Sir A. Lyall, Marquis of Dufferin and Ava; The Times, 26 March 1908; Times of India, 28 March 1908; Pioneer Mail, 3 April and 25 Dec. 1908; family details supplied by Lady Bindon Blood, daughter of Sir Auckland.] F. H. B.

COMMERELL, Sir JOHN EDMUND (1829–1901), admiral of the fleet, born in London on 13 Jan. 1829, was second son of John William Commerell of Strood Park, Horsham, by his wife Sophia, daughter of William Bosanquet. Entering the navy in February 1842, he was at once sent out to China and initiated in the realities of war. Later on he was in the Firebrand with Captain (afterwards Sir) James Hope [q. v.], and took part in the several operations in the Parana, including the engagement with the batteries at Obligado on 20 Nov. 1845, when the chain was cut by the boats of the Firebrand, a most gallant piece of work, which passed without official recognition. As lieutenant of the Vulture he was in the Baltic in 1854, and took part in the operations in the Gulf of Bothnia, the next year in the Black Sea and Sea of Azoff, and on 29 Sept. was promoted to be commander of the Weser gun vessel, employed in the Sea of Azoff. A few days later, on 11 Oct., he landed with a small party, made a hazardous march inland, and set fire to a large store of forage and corn. The service was both important and dangerous, in acknowledgement of which the Victoria Cross was given to Commerell and two seamen of his party. In 1859 he was in China in the Fury, and commanded a division of the seamen landed for the unsuccessful attack on the Taku forts. Although repulsed, the determined courage in the face of insurmountable difficulties was everywhere recognised, and Commerell was promoted to the rank of captain. In 1866 his services while in command of the Terrible, employed for laying the Atlantic cable, were rewarded with a civil C.B. In 1869 he commanded the Monarch, which in December carried across the Atlantic the remains of George Peabody [q. v.]. In 1870 he received the military C.B., and in February 1871, with a broad pennant in the Rattlesnake, was appointed commander-in-chief on the west coast of Africa. In August 1873, while reconnoitring up the river Prah, he was dangerously wounded by a musket shot in the lungs, which compelled him to invalid. In March 1874 he was created a K.C.B., and attained his flag on 12 Nov. 1876. In the following year he was sent out to the Mediterranean as second in command, at the special request of Sir Geoffrey Hornby [q. v. Suppl. I], with whom his relations were throughout most cordial and who highly commended his ability and loyalty while he served with him. In November 1882 he went out as commander-in-chief on the North American station, where he remained for nearly three years, returning in the autumn of 1885. At the general election of that year, and again in the following, he was returned as conservative member for Southampton, and zealously for the next two years endeavoured to awaken the country to the necessity of strengthening the navy. He was thus largely instrumental in bringing about the Naval Defence Act of 1889, though he was not then in parliament, having resigned his seat in July 1888 on being appointed commander-in-chief at Portsmouth. He had already been promoted to admiral in April 1886, and had been made a G.C.B. on the occasion of Queen Victoria's Jubilee in June 1887. At Portsmouth it fell to his lot in 1889 to command at the naval review, and to receive the German emperor, who afterwards wrote him an autograph letter on presenting him with a sword. At court he had always been a *persona grata*; and on the death of Sir Provo Wallis [q. v.], on 13 Feb. 1892, was by special desire of Queen Victoria promoted to the high rank of admiral of the fleet, although not the senior admiral. In January 1899, at the age of seventy, he was placed on the retired list, and died in London on 21 May 1901. He married in 1853 Mathilda Maria, daughter of Joseph Bushby.

[Royal Navy Lists; Annual Register; Sir Evelyn Wood, from Midshipman to Field-marshal, 1907, p. 255; M. A. Egerton, Life of Sir Geoffrey Hornby, 1896; Times, 22 May 1901.] J. K. L.

COMMON, ANDREW AINSLIE (1841–1903), astronomer, born at Newcastle-on-Tyne on 7 Aug. 1841, was son of Thomas Common, surgeon, a descendant of a Scottish Border family, the name being a variant of Comyn. Owing to his father's premature death, Andrew was mainly self-taught. In early manhood he joined his uncle in the firm of Matthew Hall & Co., sanitary engineers, Wigmore Street, London, and was long prominent in the management of the business. As a boy of ten he had shown an interest in astronomy, and in London he resumed the study, setting up in 1874 at Ealing a refracting telescope with an object-glass of 5½ inches aperture. He joined the Royal Astronomical Society in June

1876, and in January 1878 contributed to the society's 'Monthly Notices' a note on the satellites of Mars and Saturn, depending on observations made with a silver-on-glass mirror of 18 inches diameter made by Mr. Calver. With this type of astronomical instrument the name of Common will be always associated. A note on large telescopes, and a suggestion of the desirability of photographing the planets Saturn and Mars (*Monthly Notices,* March 1879) indicated his foresight as a practical astronomer, before large telescopes and photography were in general use. Insisting on the superior merits of silver-on-glass mirrors over metal specula, he mounted a silver-on-glass mirror of 3 feet diameter, obtained from Mr. Calver; adopting a plan of his own, he supported the weight of the instrument by partially floating the polar axis in mercury, and with this instrument Common made experiments in astronomical photography which were subsequently acknowledged to have opened a new field for astronomers. With this 3-foot mirror Common was able after much experimental work to photograph on 24 June 1881 the great comet of that year, the first successful photograph on record of a comet, though a second was obtained on the same night by Dr. Draper, in America. On 17 March 1882 Common photographed the great nebula in Orion. After some improvement of his instrument and further trials, a more successful photograph of the same object was obtained on 30 Jan. 1883. By way of recognition of this pioneer work in a branch of astronomy now very much practised, the gold medal of the Royal Astronomical Society was awarded to Common in February 1884. The 3-foot mirror was ultimately sold to Mr. Crossley of Halifax, who presented it to the Lick Observatory, where, after refiguring and alterations, it is in efficient use.

The successful performance of the 18-inch and the 3-foot silver-on-glass mirror induced Common to attempt the construction of a larger telescope of the same kind. With characteristic confidence he made his first essay in mirror-grinding with a disc of 5 feet diameter, which was begun in the workshop adjoining his house at Ealing in 1886, and after five years of hard work and anxious experiment, a successful 5-foot equatorial reflecting telescope was completed (see memoir presented to Royal Astron. Soc. 11 Dec. 1891). Common made little use personally of this telescope, which is now in the Harvard College Observatory, U.S.A. Subsequently Common found the construction of small mirrors an easy task, and of these he made many. He generously presented to the Royal Society mirrors for observing eclipses. He not only made the plane mirror but constructed the mechanical parts of cœlostats for use by the official expeditions for the solar eclipse of 1896, while 30-inch mirrors now at the Solar Physics Observatory, South Kensington, at the Khedivial Observatory, Helwan, and one which forms part of the Thompson equatorial at Greenwich, were all from his workshop. There are also smaller flat mirrors by him at the National Physical Laboratory and at the Cambridge University Observatory.

Apart from his mechanical skill, Common made various noteworthy observations. Specially memorable is his observation in daylight on 17 Sept. 1882 of the great comet of that year, when it was quite close to the sun. Common was unaware of an earlier discovery of this comet in the southern hemisphere, when he made his observations in accordance with a plan of searching for comets near the sun that he had been following for some time.

Common was somewhat distracted in later years from scientific pursuits by his association with the British Aluminium Company, of which he was one of the first directors, and in connection with this he was interested in the adaptation of the water power of the Falls of Foyer in Scotland. After severing connection with this enterprise he invented a telescopic gun-sight for use in the army and navy, working out a suggestion which he had read in youth in an early manual on astronomy. His telescopic gun-sight, when properly used, has been estimated as quadrupling the fighting efficiency of battleships.

Common was elected a fellow of the Royal Society in 1885, and served on its council in 1893–5. He was treasurer of the Royal Astronomical Society from 1884 to 1895, and its president from 1895 to 1897. In 1891 he was made hon. LL.D. of St. Andrews. He was a member of the board of visitors of the Royal Observatory, Greenwich, from 1894 until his death. In 1900, as president of the astronomical section at the British Association, he delivered an address on the development of astronomical instruments and the application of photography to astronomy. For some years he was joint editor with Professor H. H. Turner of the 'Observatory Magazine.'

Of resolute temperament, and strong both physically and intellectually, Common was a clubbable man with many friends.

He died suddenly from heart failure at his house, 63 Eaton Rise, Ealing, on 2 June 1903, and was cremated at Golder's Green. He married in 1867 Ann Matthews of Gayton in Norfolk, who, with a son and three daughters, survived him. A portrait is in the meeting room of the Royal Astronomical Society at Burlington House.

[Monthly Notes, Royal Astronomical Soc., Feb. 1904, vol. lxxv.; Proc. Roy. Soc.; The Times, 4, 6 and 8 June 1903.] H. P. H.

COMPTON, LORD ALWYNE FREDERICK (1825–1906), bishop of Ely, born at Castle Ashby on 18 July 1825, was fourth son of Spencer Joshua Alwyne Compton, second marquis of Northampton [q. v.], by his wife Margaret, daughter of Major-general Douglas Maclean Clephane of Torloisk. He was educated at Eton and Trinity College, Cambridge, whence he graduated as fourteenth wrangler in 1848. He was ordained deacon in 1850 and priest in 1851.

After serving as curate of Horsham he was appointed in 1852 by his brother, who had recently become third marquis, to the rectory of Castle Ashby, the chief family seat. He held this benefice for twenty-six years.

In 1857 he was elected one of the proctors in Convocation for the diocese of Peterborough, and was re-elected on four successive occasions till he became an ex-officio member of the Lower House, through his appointment in 1875 by William Connor Magee, bishop of Peterborough, to the archdeaconry of Oakham. From the first he took an active interest in the business of Convocation, and became after a few years one of its leading members, was elected prolocutor on 30 April 1880, and held the office for nearly six years. Meanwhile, in the year 1879, Compton was nominated by Lord Beaconsfield to the deanery of Worcester. At Worcester he promoted the common good of the city and county, and entered into the friendliest relations with his neighbours of all classes. He also effected changes in the arrangements for the triennial musical festivals in the cathedral with a view to securing greater reverence in the performances. After seven years at Worcester he was appointed by Lord Salisbury to the see of Ely on the death of James Russell Woodford [q. v.]. He was consecrated on 2 Feb. 1886. In 1882 he had been made Lord High Almoner, and he retained this office till his death.

Lord Alwyne increasingly won the respect and affection both of the clergy and the laity of his diocese during his episcopate of nearly twenty years, by his unostentatious liberality, his frankness and indifference to mere popularity, his unaffected modesty, and his unflagging zeal and industry in his episcopal work. Although his sermons made no pretensions to oratory either in form or delivery, or to originality of thought, they were often impressive from their simplicity, directness, and sincerity.

In his theological views he was an old-fashioned high churchman. At his primary and second visitations he expressed disapproval of the practice of evening communions on the ground that it was a departure from the long-received custom of the Church. But there was no diminution in the cordiality of his relations with the incumbents, whom he sought vainly to persuade to discontinue the practice. He felt that men of an opposite school, whose views were more advanced than his own, had likewise a place in the Church of England, and he was ready to protect them fearlessly, so far as they seemed to him to be within their rights, at the same time as he discountenanced excesses in ritual.

Compton's chief intellectual interest outside his clerical duties lay in the study of architecture and archæology, and he was a good draughtsman, especially of the details of architecture. He rendered a valuable service to historical students by collecting all the documents connected with the see which had been stored in different places, and causing them to be arranged and catalogued by an expert, and publishing the catalogue. He finally placed them in a building, once the gaol of the bishops of Ely in the days when they had civil jurisdiction, which he turned into a diocesan registry and muniment rooms.

In July 1905, on the completion of his eightieth year, he resigned his see and settled at Canterbury. He died there on 4 April 1906, and was buried in the churchyard of St. Martin's, which his garden bordered.

On 28 Aug. 1850 he married Florence Caroline, eldest daughter of Robert Anderson, a Brighton clergyman, by Caroline Dorothea, daughter of John Shore, first Lord Teignmouth [q. v.]. He left no issue. A portrait painted in middle age by Edward Clifford belongs to his widow.

[Chronicles of the Lower House of Convocation, 1857–86; the bishop published his Charges in 1889, 1893, 1897, and 1903; The Times, 5 April 1906; Guardian, 11 April 1906; personal knowledge.] V. H. S.

CONDER, CHARLES (1868-1909), artist, born in London in 1868, was son of James Conder, a civil engineer, and cousin of Claude Reignier Conder [q. v. Suppl. II]. He was a direct descendant in the female line of the sculptor, Roubiliac. His mother died shortly after his birth, and in infancy he was taken to India by his father, who held an engineering appointment there. Brought back at nine to England for schooling, he was educated at a private school at Eastbourne. At sixteen he was sent to Sydney, New South Wales, where he entered the lands department of the colonial civil service with a view to the profession of a trigonometrical land surveyor. He disliked the work and soon abandoned it. His predilection was for art, and from an early age he drew and painted from nature. He obtained what art education he could by drawing from the life at night classes in Sydney, by studying at the National Gallery, Melbourne, and by painting in the country with other Australian artists. During August 1889, he, with Arthur Streeton and Tom Roberts, contributed to a small exhibition in Melbourne, called 'Sketches and Impressions.' Next year, 1890, he showed at the Society of Victorian Artists several paintings, most of which were realistic, but among them an imaginative work, 'The Hot Wind,' which attracted notice; it showed a nude female figure in the foreground of a sun-baked landscape, vigorously blowing into flame the ashes of a fire. Another of his pictures at this exhibition, 'Departure of the ss. Orient,' was purchased for the National Gallery, Sydney. An uncle thereupon provided the artist with the means of studying painting, and in 1890 Conder returned to England.

Proceeding to Paris, he worked intermittently in Cormon's studio. Always impatient of school routine, he followed his own lines, and studied the work of artists around him. The art of Anquetin especially influenced him, and he derived something from Toulouse Lautrec and perhaps from Daumier. In March 1891 Conder and Mr. William Rothenstein had an exhibition together at the gallery of a Paris dealer called Thomas, 43 Boulevard Malesherbes; both artists' work was reproduced in 'L'Art français.' In 1896 an exhibition of Conder's work at the gallery of Bing, another Paris dealer, consisted chiefly of panels on silk for a boudoir and a few designs for fans, which inaugurated his most original contributions to art. His first design for a fan was in oils on a wooden panel, executed about 1895. Elected an associate member of the Société Nationale des Beaux-Arts in 1893, he quickly won a reputation by the originality and charm of the work which he exhibited at the Société's salon.

Marrying and settling at 91 Cheyne Walk, Chelsea, in 1901, he there did his finest work, which he exhibited chiefly at the New English Art Club and the International Society of Painters; at the same time holding single exhibitions at the Carfax, at Van Wisselinghs, and the Leicester Galleries. Early in 1907 he contracted brain disease, of which he died on 9 Feb. 1909 at the Virginia Water Asylum. He was buried at the cemetery there. His widow, Stella Maris Bedford, a Canadian, whom he met in Paris, died on 18 April 1912.

Conder drew entirely from memory, rarely from life. He was quite careless about materials, brushes, or colours, and his work seemed to develop without method or scheme. Of a few lithographs, which he designed at night, the best are six dated 1899, of which four are scenes from Balzac and two are fanciful subjects. A single etching by Conder is known, a dry point, of which Mr. Rothenstein owns a print. Conder painted a good deal in oils, his subjects being chiefly landscapes more or less romantically treated, seashore scenes, modern watering places with gaily dressed crowds, and an occasional portrait, in a decorative style. But Conder's most characteristic works are the dainty water-colour drawings which date between 1895 and 1905, painted after a fashion of his own on panels of white silk, many shaped for fans. The delicate tones of their colour agree perfectly with the frail texture of the material. The subjects are dreamlike fancies which, while they are far removed from reality, reflect modern life. The colour and general character of his landscape backgrounds were derived entirely from the scenery at Chartamelle on the Seine, but the scenery of Normandy also influenced his designs. Conder's art has been compared with that of Watteau, but it is never constructive like that of the French master, and is usually more elusive in subject. Conder exerted much influence on contemporary art.

Conder painted a fine head of himself which belongs to Mr. Rothenstein, who also painted portraits of the artist.

[The Studio, May 1898 (Charles Conder's paintings on Silk, by D. S. MacColl); Burlington Mag., April 1909, vol. xv. (art. by Charles Ricketts); Modern Art, by J. Meier-Graefe; Art Journal, vol. ii. March 1909;

private information. Mr. Rothenstein owns Conder's first sketch-book.] F. W. G-N.

CONDER, CLAUDE REIGNIER (1848–1910), colonel royal engineers, Altaic scholar, and Palestine explorer, born at Cheltenham on 29 Dec. 1848, was the son of Francis Roubiliac Conder (1815–1889), civil engineer and a writer in the 'Edinburgh Review,' by his wife Anne Matilda Colt (1823–1890). Josiah Conder [q. v.], his grandfather, married a granddaughter of Louis François Roubiliac [q. v.], the sculptor.

After spending eight years of his youth in Italy, Conder passed from University College, London, to the Royal Military Academy at Woolwich, where he distinguished himself in surveying and geometrical and freehand drawing. He received a commission as lieutenant in the royal engineers on 8 Jan. 1870, and after a two years' professional course at Chatham was selected with the assent of the military authorities to continue a scientific survey of Western Palestine, which had been begun by engineer officers under the auspices of the Palestine Exploration Fund some seven years earlier [see under WILSON, SIR CHARLES WILLIAM, Suppl. II].

In July 1872 Conder took charge of the survey party at Nablus in Samaria. Work was begun by the measurement of a base line, about four miles in length, near Ramleh on the road from Jaffa to Jerusalem, and the triangulation was carried gradually over the whole country. In the course of three years the greater part of the country west of the Jordan had been surveyed and, in addition to actual mapping, a mass of information regarding the topography and archæology of the country had been collected, while many places mentioned in the Bible and previously unknown had been identified. Conder also devoted himself to the languages of the country and to the decipherment of ancient inscriptions, to which he brought abundant ingenuity. C. F. Tyrwhitt Drake [q. v.] at first assisted Conder, and on his death of fever at Jerusalem in June 1874 his place was filled by Lieut. Kitchener, R.E., now Field-marshal Viscount Kitchener of Khartoum.

A murderous attack on Conder and his party by the inhabitants of Safed, a town in the hills north-west of the Sea of Galilee (July 1875), in which Conder and Kitchener with others of the party were seriously injured, temporarily suspended the survey. Conder was sufficiently recovered to return to England in October 1875, after having surveyed 4700 square miles of Western Palestine. Plotting of the maps and preparation of the 'Memoirs' were then taken in hand. In 1877 the unfinished portion of the survey was completed by Lieut. Kitchener, and the whole survey was plotted and the 'Memoirs' finished in April 1878. The map, on a scale of one inch to the mile, was printed at the Ordnance Survey Office, Southampton, and, with seven volumes of 'Memoirs,' was issued by the committee of the Palestine Exploration Fund in 1880. For his work Lieut. Conder received the thanks of the committee and the commendation of the secretary of state for war. 'It may fairly be claimed,' wrote Sir Walter Besant, 'that nothing has ever been done for the illustration and right understanding of the historical portions of the Old and New Testaments since the translations into the vulgar tongue which can be compared with this great work. The officer whose name is especially associated with it has made himself a name which will last as long as there are found men and women to read and study the sacred books.'

Returning to regimental duty in May 1878, Conder was employed for three years on the new defences of the Forth and stationed in Edinburgh. In his leisure hours he continued his studies of the history and archæology of the Holy Land and adjacent countries. In 1878 he published his first book 'Tent Work in Palestine,' illustrated with his own drawings. It gives a popular account of the survey operations and of the customs of the inhabitants of Palestine, of various Bible sites, and the topography of Jerusalem. In 1879 he published 'Judas Maccabæus and the Jewish War of Independence,' and in collaboration with his father 'Handbook to the Bible.' These works were popular, and went through several editions.

In the spring of 1881 Conder resumed his labours for the Palestine Exploration Fund in the country east of the Jordan. Near the lake of Homs in the valley of the Orontes, he discovered the remains of the ancient city of Kadesh; then going south and crossing the Jordan, a base line was measured between Heshbon and Medeba. Conder devoted especial attention to the description of the rude prehistoric stone monuments which abounded in the district; he photographed and made plans of many stone circles, cromlechs and menhirs, and other relics of bygone ages. Turkish obstruction impeded Conder's progress, but he acted with great discretion, and managed to complete the survey of about 500 square miles.

On 8 Jan. 1882 he was promoted to be captain, and in March and April conducted Princes Albert Victor and George of Wales (now King George V) on a tour through the Holy Land. He wrote a report on the sacred Haram at Hebron and another on the Palestine tour for the information of the princes' father, King Edward VII, then Prince of Wales (printed in the *Palestine Exploration Fund Quarterly Statement,* 1882).

After his return home in June 1882, Conder joined the expedition to Egypt, under Sir Garnet Wolseley, to suppress the rebellion of Arabi Pasha. He was appointed a deputy assistant adjutant and quartermaster-general on the staff of the intelligence department. In Egypt his perfect knowledge of Arabic and of Eastern people proved most useful. He was present at the action of Kassassin, the battle of Tel-el-Kebir, and the advance to Cairo, but then, seized with typhoid fever, he was invalided home. For his services he received the war medal with clasp for Tel-el-Kebir, the Khedive's bronze star and the fourth class of the Order of the Medjidie. On recovering his health, Captain Conder devoted himself to plotting the survey and preparing the Memoir of Eastern Palestine. He published in 1883 'Heth and Moab,' a popular account of his second expedition to Palestine.

On 10 Nov. 1883 he took command of a depôt company at Chatham. A year later, graded as deputy assistant adjutant and quartermaster-general in the intelligence department, he joined the staff of Major-general Sir Charles Warren in the Bechuanaland expedition to South Africa, and the topographical work was entrusted to him. He was mentioned in despatches and recommended for 'some recognition of good services.' Declining an offer of a land commissionership in South Africa, he returned to the command of his company at Chatham in October 1885. While there he published some important works: 'Syrian Stone Lore' (1886); 'The Canaanites' (1887); and 'Altaic Hieroglyphs and Hittite Inscriptions' (1887), where he proved his philological acumen and ingenuity.

On 1 July 1887 Conder went to Plymouth to work on the ordnance survey, and was transferred in the following April to Southampton to take charge of the engraving department. He remained there for seven years, receiving the thanks of the board of works for his introduction of double printing on copper plates. He assisted Sir Charles Wilson, then director-general of the ordnance survey, with the publications of the Palestine Pilgrims Text Society, of which Sir Charles was the director. In 1891 he published 'Palestine,' a *résumé* of the history and geography of the country, and in 1893 he wrote 'The Tell Amarna Tablets,' a translation and description of letters in cuneiform character, written about 1480 B.C. from Palestine and Syria to the King of Egypt; they throw a flood of light on the connection between the countries.

Conder had been promoted major on 1 July 1888. After superintending the construction of the new defences for the naval base of Berehaven in 1894, he was engaged during 1895 in directing public works for the relief of distress in the congested districts of Ireland; and being promoted lieutenant-colonel on 12 Aug. 1895, was appointed commanding royal engineer at Weymouth. There he remained for five years and wrote some of his most important works. At Weymouth he was occupied with defence work in connection with the great naval base at Portland; fortifications, barracks, submarine mining, and electric searchlights all claimed his attention. He was promoted brevet colonel on 12 Aug. 1899, and a year later was placed on half pay. He was afterwards employed on the ordnance survey in the west of Ireland with headquarters at Ennis, co. Clare, until his retirement from the service on 2 Nov. 1904. Thenceforth he lived at Cheltenham, where he died on 16 Feb. 1910.

Conder married on 12 June 1877, at Guildford, Surrey, Myra Rachel, eldest daughter of Lieutenant-general Edward Archibald Foord (*d.* 1899) of the royal (Madras) engineers. She survived him with a daughter and a son.

Conder led a busy life, and although his services were invariably commended by those under whom he served he received little reward. In 1891, however, the University of Edinburgh made him honorary LL.D. A great Palestine explorer, he was one of several differing authorities on the Hittite and on the Altaic language. In 1893 he announced to the Royal Asiatic Society a discovery of what he claimed to be the clue to the Hittite inscriptions, but his claim was contested, and it is maintained that all suggested interpretations are based upon hypotheses at present incapable of verification.

Conder's industry as a writer was untiring, but his modesty deterred him from controversy with his critics. Apart from the works already mentioned, Conder proved his learning in: 1. 'The Latin Kingdom of Jerusalem,' 1897. 2. 'The Hittites and their Language,' 1898. 3. 'The First Bible,' 1902. 4. 'The Rise of Man,' 1908. 5. 'The City of Jerusalem,' 1909. His minor works are: 1. 'Primer of Bible Geography,' 1883. 2. 'Eastern Palestine,' 1892. 3. 'The Bible in the East,' 1896. 4. 'The Hebrew Tragedy,' 1900. 5. 'Critics and the Law,' 1907. Conder, a prolific writer for magazines and reviews, particularly 'Blackwood's Magazine' and the 'Edinburgh Review,' contributed very largely to Smith's 'New Bible Dictionary,' to the publications of the Palestine Pilgrims Text Society, and from 1872 to 'The Quarterly Statement of the Palestine Exploration Fund,' where his last article on 'Recent Hittite Discoveries' appeared in January 1910. He was a competent artist and drew the illustrations in 'Pictorial Scenes from Bunyan's Pilgrim's Progress' (4to, 1869).

[War Office Records; Porter's History of the Corps of Royal Engineers 1889; Besant's Twenty-one Years' Work in the Holy Land 1886; The Times, 17 Feb. 1910; Royal Engineers Journal, April 1910; Geographical Journal, April 1910; Quarterly Statement of the Palestine Exploration Fund, April 1910.]

R. H. V.

CONNEMARA, first Baron. [See Bourke, Robert (1827–1902).]

CONQUEST, GEORGE (AUGUSTUS), whose real surname was Oliver (1837–1901), actor and manager, born at the house adjoining the old Garrick Theatre, Leman Street, Goodman's Fields, on 8 May 1837, was eldest son of Benjamin Oliver (1805–72), actor and theatrical manager, who used professionally the surname of Conquest, and was then manager of the old Garrick Theatre. There in 1837, as a child in arms, in the farce 'Mr. and Mrs. White,' George made his first appearance on the stage. He played there, while a child, in such pieces as 'Peter the Waggoner,' 'Isabella, or the Fatal Marriage,' and 'The Stranger.' Educated at the collège communal, Boulogne, he was a contemporary there of Benoît Coquelin, the eminent French actor, and acquired a full command of the French language. He was intended for a violinist, but from his earliest years he resolved on the profession of acrobatic pantomimist. Before he left school he made numerous adaptations from the French for his father, who in 1851 became manager of the Grecian Theatre in City Road. His first play, 'Woman's Secret, or Richelieu's Wager,' was produced at the Grecian on 17 Oct. 1853. In 1855 he adopted the stage as his vocation, and long combined acting at the Grecian with dramatic authorship on a prolific scale. On 3 Sept. 1855 he was highly successful as the Artful Dodger in a version of Dickens' 'Oliver Twist.' At Christmas 1855 he first appeared as a pantomimist, in his own pantomime, 'Harlequin Sun, Moon, and the Seven Sisters'; and at Easter 1857 he made his first notable success in this class of work as Hassarac, in 'The Forty Thieves.' At Christmas 1857 he appeared as Pastrano Nonsuch, a 'flying pantomimist,' in 'Peter Wilkins and the Flying Indians.' Subsequently he effectively adapted Charles Reade's novel, 'It is never too late to mend,' which ran for six months at his father's theatre, and in which he appeared as Peter Crawley. In 1861 he distinguished himself as Prince Pigmy in 'The Blue Bird in Paradise.'

Conquest became manager of the Grecian in 1872, on the death of his father, continuing to fill leading parts there. In 1881 he joined Paul Merritt as co-lessee and manager of the Surrey Theatre, of which he was sole lessee and manager from 1885. His only appearances in the west end of London were at the Gaiety Theatre, in 1873, in 'The Snaefell,' and at the Globe, in 1882, in 'Mankind'; but he once visited America, performing in 'The Grim Goblin' at Wallack's Theatre, New York, on 5 Aug. 1880, when he sustained severe injuries through the breaking of trapeze ropes, caused, it was stated, through the treachery of a rival. He retired from the stage in 1894.

Conquest was best known as an acrobatic pantomimist. He produced no fewer than forty-five pantomimes, and played in as many as twenty-seven. He impersonated animals with much popular approval, and is said to have invented the modern method of 'flying' by means of 'invisible' wires. It was his boast that as a pantomimist he had broken every bone in his face and body. In his performance of the title rôle in 'The Devil on Two Sticks' he employed no fewer than twenty-nine 'traps'—one 'vampire' and twenty-eight ordinary.

Of the hundred and more plays, for the most part original melodramas or adaptations from the French, of which he was author, several were written in collaboration, and of these the more successful were 'Velvet and Rags' (with Paul Merritt, 1874); 'Sentenced to Death' (with Henry Pettitt, 1875); 'Queen's Evidence' (with Pettitt, 1876); 'The Green Lanes of England' (with Pettitt, 1878); 'Mankind' (with Merritt, 1881); 'For Ever' (with Merritt, 1882); 'The Crimes of Paris' (with Merritt, 1883). His last play, 'The Fighting Fifth,' written with Herbert Leonard, was produced at the Surrey Theatre in October 1900. He showed his melodramatic power to good effect in such parts as Daniel Groodge in 'Mankind,' Zacky Pastrana, the Man Monkey in 'For Ever,' Simmonet and Jagon in 'The Strangers of Paris,' Ezra Lazareck in 'The New Babylon,' and Coupeau in 'Drink.' Off the stage he suffered from an impediment in his speech, which disappeared when he was acting.

Conquest died at his residence in Brixton on 14 May 1901, and was buried at Norwood cemetery. He left a fortune of over 64,000*l*. He married in 1857 Elizabeth Ozmond, and his three sons, George, Fred, and Arthur, all successfully adopted their father's calling, both as actors and acrobatic pantomimists. Engraved portraits of Conquest appeared in 'The Theatre,' Sept. 1895, and in 'The Era,' 18 May 1901.

[Personal recollections; Clement Scott, Thirty Years at the Play, 1890; Scott and Howard's Life of E. L. Blanchard, 1891; Daily Telegraph, 15 May 1901; Era, 18 and 25 May 1901.] J. P.

COOK, SIR FRANCIS, first baronet (1817–1901), merchant and art collector, born at Clapham on 3 Jan. 1817, was second son (in a family of seven children) of William Cook (1784–1869) of Roydon Hall, Kent, by his wife Mary Ann (*d.* 1862), daughter of John Lainson (1779–1844), alderman of London (1835–43), and of Silchester, Hants. The father, descended from a family settled at Wymondham, Norfolk, started in business as a retail linendraper at 7 Great Warner Street, Clerkenwell; he traded with a partner as Cook & Martin from 1807 to 1812, and continued this business there and at Fish Street Hill in his own name until 1830. By 1819 he had opened a wholesale warehouse at 89 Cheapside, where he took into partnership his brother James in 1822 and a Mr. Gladstones in 1825. The wholesale firm removed to 21–3 St. Paul's Churchyard in 1834, when the style became Cook, Son, & Gladstones, the last-named partner disappearing in 1843. The concern became one of the largest of its kind in the country, both as a manufacturing and distributing house, doing an immense trade with Great Britain and the colonies in all classes of silk, linen, woollen, and cotton goods. The founder, William Cook, left a fortune of over 2,000,000*l*.

Educated at Totteridge and Frankfort, young Cook started in the print department of the firm in 1833, and in 1843 became a partner, the style of the firm being altered to Cook, Sons & Co. On the death of his eldest brother, William, in 1852 the firm assumed its present style of Cook, Son & Co., and Francis on his father's death in 1869 became its head, greatly contributing to its prosperity by his business capacity and tact in the selection of his assistants. Despite other interests he actively superintended his business till the end of his life.

In 1841 Cook paid a first visit to Portugal, where his first wife's father was settled, and he subsequently spent there parts of the spring and autumn of each year. In 1856 he bought for his residence the palace of Monserrate at Cintra near Lisbon, renowned both in history and in literature. He entered with enthusiasm on a complete restoration of the building and the formation of its world-famous gardens. By gradual purchase he acquired much land near Cintra, many square miles in extent, and renewed the prosperity of the district, where villages and gardens had fallen into decay. In recognition of these services and of his benevolence to the Portuguese poor Cook was created Viscount Monserrate in 1864 by Dom Luiz, King of Portugal.

About 1860 Cook acquired for his residence Doughty House, Richmond Hill, and there formed one of the finest collections of pictures of his time. His most important purchases were made between 1860 and his death, from Italian, Spanish, and English collections, under the advice of (Sir) J. C. Robinson. All schools were well represented, including the early Flemish masters (especially Van Eyck), Rubens and his successors, Rembrandt, the Dutch landscape and genre painters, the French, Spanish, and Italian schools, and (by fewer examples) the English school. Italian majolica, bronzes, ivories, tapestries, and antique statuary also formed part of the collections. A generous owner, the Doughty House gallery was always freely open to genuine students, and many of the pictures were lent to various exhibitions here and abroad.

Cook was elected F.S.A. on 16 Jan. 1873, and in 1885 he established at a cost of about 80,000*l*., as a tribute to Queen Alexandra, then Princess of Wales, Alexandra House, South Kensington, a home for lady students of music and other branches of art. He was created a baronet on 10 March 1886.

Cook, who continued his almost daily attendance in the City until within ten days of his death, died at Doughty House,

Richmond Hill, on 17 Feb. 1901, and was buried in Norwood cemetery. He left a personal estate valued at 1,500,000*l.* net. The picture and art collection was divided, part passing by will to his younger son, Wyndham Francis (*d.* 1905); this is now in Cadogan Square in trust for the latter's son, Humphrey. The main portion, including the pictures and statuary, was entailed on his elder son, the present baronet.

Busts executed by lady students at Queen Alexandra's House are preserved there, at Monserrate, and at Doughty House.

Cook married (1) on 1 Aug. 1841, Emily Martha (*d.* 12 Aug. 1884), daughter of Robert Lucas of Lisbon; (2) on 1 Oct. 1885, Tennessee, daughter of Reuben Buckman Claflin of New York, a prominent advocate of women's rights. By his first wife he had surviving issue two sons and a daughter; the elder son, Frederick Lucas, at one time M.P. for the Kennington division of Lambeth, succeeded to the baronetcy.

[The Times, 19 Feb., 13 Mar. 1901; Drapers' Record, 23 Feb. 1901; Thames Valley Times, 20 Feb. 1901; Richmond and Twickenham Times, 23 Feb. 1901; P.O. London Directories, 1807–38; Lodge's Peerage and Baronetage, 1911; Register and Mag. of Biog. vol. 1, 1869; private information.] C. W.

COOPER, Sir ALFRED (1838–1908), surgeon, born at Norwich on 28 Dec. 1838, was son of William Cooper, at one time recorder of Ipswich, by his wife Anna Marsh. Cooper entered Merchant Taylors' School, then in Suffolk Lane, London, in April 1850, and was afterwards apprenticed to W. Peter Nichols, surgeon to the Norfolk and Norwich Hospital, and some time mayor of Norwich. In 1858 Cooper entered as a student at St. Bartholomew's Hospital. He was admitted M.R.C.S. England on 29 June 1861, and in the same year he obtained the licence of the Society of Apothecaries. He then went to Paris in company with (Sir) Thomas Smith [q. v. Suppl. II] to improve his anatomical knowledge, and on his return was appointed a prosector to the examiners at the Royal College of Surgeons.

Cooper started practice in Jermyn Street. After an interval of waiting he acquired a fashionable private practice. But his social success rather stimulated than retarded his ardour for surgery. He was surgeon to St. Mark's Hospital for Fistula, City Road, from April 1864 till 1897; surgeon to the West London Hospital (1867–1884); to the Royal Hospital for Diseases of the Chest, City Road, and to the Lock Hospital, Soho. At the last institution he gained that sound knowledge of syphilis with which his name is chiefly associated. He was admitted F.R.C.S. Edinburgh in 1868, and F.R.C.S. England on 9 June 1870. Cooper had early won the friendship of William Alexander, twelfth duke of Hamilton, and the duke presented him with Cooper-Angus Lodge, Whiting Bay, in the Isle of Arran, which he made his home when he retired from London.

Cooper visited St. Petersburg as medical attendant of Edward VII, when Prince of Wales, on the marriage of Alfred Ernest Albert, duke of Edinburgh, in 1874, and he received from the Tsar the knighthood of St. Stanislas. He was appointed in 1893 Surgeon-in-Ordinary to the duke of Edinburgh when he became duke of Saxe-Coburg. Cooper was knighted at King Edward VII's coronation in 1902.

Cooper, whose social qualities were linked with fine traits of character and breadth of view, gained a wide knowledge of the world, partly at courts, partly in the out-patient rooms of hospitals, and partly in the exercise of a branch of his profession which more than any other reveals the frailty of mankind.

Although the possession of a competence limited his professional activity, he was twice elected to the Council of the Royal College of Surgeons of England, on one occasion at the top of the poll, and was co-opted vice-president. Appointed in early life surgeon to the Inns of Court Rifle Volunteers, 'The Devil's Own,' he cherished a deep interest in the reserve forces throughout life. He obtained the volunteer decoration for long service, and was latterly surgeon-colonel to the Duke of York's Loyal Suffolk Hussars. Freemasonry appealed to him. He held high office in the United Grand Lodge of England, and was instrumental in founding the Rahere Lodge, which was the first masonic body to be associated with a hospital.

Cooper died at Mentone on 3 March 1908, and was buried in the English cemetery there. He married in 1882 Lady Agnes Cecil Emmeline Duff, third daughter of James, fifth earl of Fife, and sister of Alexander, the first duke; her first husband was Herbert Flower; by her Cooper had three daughters and a son.

Cooper's works are: 1. 'Syphilis and Pseudo-Syphilis,' 1884; 2nd edit. 1895. 2. 'A Practical Treatise on Disease of the

Rectum,' 1887; 2nd edit., with Mr. F. Swinford Edwards, entitled 'Diseases of the Rectum and Anus,' 1892.

[St. Bartholomew's Hospital Journal, xv. 1908, p. 105; Lancet, 1908, i. 901; Brit. Med. Journal, 1908, i. 660; personal knowledge.]

D'A. P.

COOPER, Sir DANIEL, first baronet (1821–1902), Australian merchant, was second son of Thomas Cooper and Jane, daughter of Nathaniel Ramsden, being one of a family of five sons and four daughters. He was born at Bolton-le-Moors, Lancashire, on 1 July 1821, but went out quite young with his father to Sydney, New South Wales. In 1833 he returned to England for his education in schools near London and at University College; in 1841 he entered a mercantile house at Havre, partly for general training, and in 1843 returned to Sydney to take his place in the firm of Holt & Cooper, which several years later became Cooper & Co.

In 1849 Cooper decided to enter public life, and was elected to the old legislative council of New South Wales. His most prominent public action, however, in the ensuing period was his part in raising funds for the relief of the sufferers from the Crimean campaign; he himself subscribed 1000*l.* to start the fund in Australia, and promised 500*l.* a year for each year the war might continue. He also visited England more than once in these years, partly in connection with this charitable work.

In 1856, on the grant of responsible government to New South Wales, Cooper was elected member for Sydney Hamlets in the new council, and on 22 May 1856 was made the speaker. In the following year he was knighted by patent. On 31 Aug. 1859 he decided to resign office and settle anew in England, and, though pressed to form a ministry in succession to Mr. Forster, he adhered to his decision.

He returned to England shortly before the long period of distress in Lancashire caused by the American civil war, which cut off the cotton supplies. His active sympathy and competent organisation were readily placed at the disposal of the sufferers, and it was mainly for his services in this crisis that he was created a baronet (26 Jan. 1863) as of Woollahra, New South Wales.

Though he now resided permanently in London, Cooper was always ready to render assistance in the development of New South Wales, with the interests of which he was constantly identified. He did good work in regulating the trade in Australian wool. He acted as agent-general for the colony (1897–9) and looked after its interests at numerous exhibitions, both on the Continent and in London. He was president of the bank of New South Wales (1855–61) and a member of the council of Sydney University, where he founded in 1857 the Cooper scholarship.

Cooper was made a K.C.M.G. in 1880, and G.C.M.G. in 1888. He died on 5 June 1902 at 6 De Vere Gardens, Kensington.

He married, on 3 Sept. 1846, Elizabeth, third daughter of William Hill of Sydney, and left two sons and five daughters. He was succeeded as second baronet by his eldest son, Daniel, a deputy-lieutenant of Cambridgeshire.

[Heaton's Austral. Dict. of Dates; Mennell's Dict. of Australas. Biog.; Burke's Peerage and Baronetage, 1902; The Times, 6 June 1902.]

C. A. H.

COOPER, EDWARD HERBERT (1867–1910), novelist, born at Trentham on 6 Oct. 1867, was eldest son of Samuel Herbert Cooper of New Park, Trentham, and Newcastle-under-Lyme, Staffordshire, by his wife Katharine, daughter of the Rev. Edward James Justinian George Edwards and grand-daughter of James Edwards [q. v.] the bibliographer.

Whilst at a preparatory school at Hoddesdon, Hertfordshire, he contracted a chill, which led to a seven years' illness and made him a cripple for life. Prepared for Oxford by a private tutor, he matriculated at University College on 18 Oct. 1886, took third-class honours in history in 1889, and graduated B.A. in 1890. On leaving the university he was for a short time in the office of a firm of chartered accountants in London. He also engaged in political work as secretary of the Suffolk liberal unionist association at the general election of 1892, and of the Ulster Convention League in 1893. Soon adopting journalism as his profession, he joined in Paris the staff of 'Galignani's Messenger' in 1896, and acted as Paris correspondent of the 'New York World.' In 1901 he visited Finland and afterwards wrote in the London press on her constitutional struggle, and assisted in the preparation of the English version of N. C. Fredericksen's 'Finland: its Public and Private Economy' (1902). In 1903 he returned to London, and was for three years special reporter on the 'Daily Mail.' Meanwhile he attained some distinction both as a novelist and as a writer for children. His first novels, 'Richard Escott' (1893) and 'Geoffrey Hamilton' (1893), showed promise, and were followed by The

Enemies' (1896), a semi-political story. In 1897 he first proved his strength in 'Mr. Blake of Newmarket' (new edit. 1904), an excellent sporting novel, and in 'The Marchioness against the County,' a social satire.

Through life Cooper delighted in the companionship of children, whose psychology he carefully studied. He aided Benjamin Waugh [q. v. Suppl. II], the philanthropist, in practical efforts to protect children from cruelty or corruption. In 1899 he began a series of imaginative stories for children with 'Wyemark and the Sea Fairies' (a special edition, illustrated by Dudley Hardy), which was succeeded by 'Wyemark and the Mountain Fairies' (illustrated by Jacomb Hood, 1900); 'Wyemark's Mother' (1903); 'Sent to the Rescue: or Wyemark's Adventures in South America' (1903); and 'My Brother the King' (posthumous, 1910). The tales owed much to the suggestion of Lewis Carroll, but there was originality in their execution.

Cooper, whose features were marked by a rare refinement, bore his physical disabilities with courage and cheerfulness. In 1898, supported by two sticks, he made the new ascent of Mont Blanc, as far as the Col du Goûter. He died suddenly at Newmarket, from an apoplectic seizure, on 26 April 1910, and was buried in Kensal Green cemetery. He was unmarried.

Besides the works named, Cooper wrote: 1. 'Resolved to be Rich,' 1899. 2. 'Children, Racehorses, and Ghosts' (a collection of sketches), 1899. 3. 'The Monk Wins,' 1900. 4. 'The Eternal Choice,' 1901 (a more serious study). 5. 'A Fool's Year' (another sporting story), 1901. 6. 'George and Son,' 1902. 7. 'The Gentleman from Goodwood,' 1902; 3rd edit. 1909. 8. 'The Viscountess Normanhurst,' 1903 (a study of mother and child). 9. 'Lord and Lady Aston,' 1904. 10. 'The Twentieth-Century Child,' 1905 (a collection of essays). 11. 'The Marquis and Pamela,' 1908. 12. 'The End of the Journey,' 1908 (both pictures of smart society). 13. 'A Newmarket Squire,' 1910 (a novel of sport and child life).

[Private information and letters; Brit. Mus. Cat.; Foster's Alumni Oxonienses; Hist. Register of Oxf. University; The Times, and Daily Telegraph, 2 May 1910; Athenæum, and Staffordshire Sentinel, 7 May 1910; engraved portraits are in Lady's Pictorial, the Playgoer, and Society Illustrated—all 7 May 1910.] G. Le G. N.

COOPER, JAMES DAVIS (1823-1904), wood-engraver, born at Pratt's Place, Lambeth, on 18 Nov. 1823, was son of George and Emily Cooper. He belonged to a family of musicians who from father to son were organists at St. Sepulchre's, Snow Hill, for over one hundred years. His father, George Cooper, besides being organist at St. Sepulchre's, was assistant organist at St. Paul's Cathedral, under Thomas Attwood [q. v.] as well as at the Chapel Royal, St. James's, under Sir George Smart [q. v.]. George Cooper, elder brother to James Davis, succeeded his father, on his death in 1832, in all these posts, and was at one time organist at Christ's Hospital, Newgate Street. James Davis entered the City of London School in Feb. 1837, as one of the original scholars, and leaving in December of the same year passed into the studio of Josiah Whymper [q. v. Suppl. II], the wood-engraver, in Canterbury Road, Lambeth. During his apprenticeship he rapidly developed the talent which made him one of the most successful engravers of the period known as 'the 'sixties,' when the art of wood-engraving enjoyed a noteworthy revival. From 1848 he lived in Ely Place, Holborn, then in Camberwell till 1854, when he moved to 26 Great James Street, Bedford Row. His office was here till about 1860, when he established his business at 188 Strand.

Among Cooper's earlier works were the engraved illustrations to 'Favourite English Poems' (1859), Mrs. Barbauld's 'Hymns in Prose' (1863), and Robert Barnes' 'Pictures of English Life' (n.d., c. 1865). Later, he worked with Randolph Caldecott [q. v.] on the well-known illustrations for the Macmillan edition of Washington Irving's 'Old Christmas' (1876) and 'Bracebridge Hall' (1877). The excellence of his craftsmanship may be judged by a comparison of his engravings for Caldecott's 'Breton Folk' (text by H. Blackburn, 1880) with the original drawings, which are in the Victoria and Albert Museum. Many illustrated books, like the first four mentioned above, were entirely planned by Cooper; and whilst seeking suitable artists to carry out his ideas, he discovered and encouraged the talent of such men as Robert Barnes, Caldecott, E. M. Wimperis, and William Small. Cooper also engraved the illustrations for works by many eminent authors. His handiwork appears in Queen Victoria's 'Our Life in the Highlands' (1868) and in 'The Prince of Wales' Tour in India' (by Sir W. H. Russell, 1877). He was responsible for the illustrations to books by Darwin,

Huxley, Tyndall, Owen, Livingstone and others. In his engravings for Stanley's 'How I found Livingstone' (1872) and 'In Darkest Africa' (1890) he showed remarkable skill and intuition as an interpreter of the hints for landscape, groups of natives, animals or weapons, given in Stanley's rough but suggestive sketches. Among his later work were the engravings for 'Pictures from Shelley' (1892) after designs by Etheline E. Dell.

Cooper lived to see the art of wood-engraving superseded by photographic processes. Owing to this and failing eyesight he retired from active work some years before his death. Jovial and breezy in manner, full of kindness and geniality, the old 'wood-pecker,' as he described himself, died at his residence, Rothesay, North Road, Highgate, on 27 Feb. 1904, and was buried at the Great Northern cemetery. On 20 July 1848 he married Jane Eleanor, daughter of Benjamin Ovington, a clerk in the Bank of England. He had three sons and four daughters. The latter were each awarded in 1905 a civil list pension of 25*l.*

[The Times, 4 March 1904; Builder, 5 March 1904; Publishers' Circular, 12 and 19 March 1904; private information.] M. H.

COOPER, THOMAS SIDNEY (1803–1902), animal painter, was born in St. Peter's Street, Canterbury, on 26 Sept. 1803. His mother was left to bring up her family of two sons and three daughters entirely by her own exertions. After a very slender school education Cooper was engaged in 1815 by a coach-builder, the uncle of a school friend named William Burgess, to learn and practise coach-painting. As a child he was seen by George Cattermole [q. v.] sketching the cathedral on his slate, and received from him a gift of the first pencils and paper that he used. His sketching of the cathedral was also noticed by Archbishop Manners Sutton, who encouraged him and gave him his first commissions for drawings. He was also helped and instructed by a scene-painter, Doyle, who had noticed him at his work; and as the coach-builder no longer wanted his services, he took seriously to scene-painting, being engaged by the manager of a company which played in Faversham, Folkestone, and Hastings. Returning to Canterbury after the company broke up, he again turned to coach-painting, and between this and occasional work as a scene-painter and draughtsman earned his living until he was twenty.

About 1823 he was invited by an uncle, a dissenting minister named Elvey, to London. He at once got permission to copy in the British Museum, and there made the acquaintance of Stephen Catterson Smith [q. v.] and George Richmond [q. v.], then students like himself. He obtained his recommendation to the council of the Royal Academy through Abraham Cooper, R.A. [q. v.] (no relative), and submitted drawings which secured his admission to the Academy schools at the same time as Smith and Richmond. He also received marked encouragement from Sir Thomas Lawrence. But at this critical moment his uncle proved unable to keep him, and he had no resource but to return to Canterbury. For three or four years he earned a living as a drawing-master in Canterbury, Dover, Margate, and Herne Bay. In 1827 he crossed the Channel with his old school friend Burgess, and by dint of drawing the portraits of his hosts at the various inns on his road managed to pay his way to Brussels. Here he soon secured a large number of pupils, and what was even more fortunate, the friendship of the Belgian animal painter Verboekhoven, who greatly influenced the formation of Cooper's style. But both painters found their chief models in Cuyp and Potter and the Dutch school of the seventeenth century, and made up for the lack of originality by the thoroughness of their methods and the faithfulness of their renderings of nature. Cooper took to painting in oil about this period; hitherto he had done little except water-colour and pencil drawings. Up till the last he was most careful in his use of the pencil in outlining the main features of even his largest paintings in oil.

While in Brussels he also produced two lithographs after pictures in Prince d'Aremberg's collection (Paul Potter and A. van de Velde). Another lithograph (a view of Dover) is dated 1825, while practically all his other drawings on stone were produced before 1840 (*e.g.* a series of rustic figures, dated 1833, and published by Dickinson in 1834; another similar series published by F. G. Moon in 1837; a series illustrating hop-growing; studies of cattle, two series, published by S. and J. Fuller, about 1835 and 1837; thirty-four subjects of cattle, published by T. McLean in 1837; groups of cattle drawn from nature, twenty-six lithographs, published by Ackerman, 1839).

He also did a large line-engraving after Landseer (interior of a Scottish cotter's home), which does not seem to have been published (impression in collection of Mr. Neville Cooper). The revolution of 1830 meant the loss of many of his patrons, who had left Brussels at the crisis. Returning to England, he settled in London early in 1831, and for some time earned his living by doing drawings and lithographs for box lids, &c., for Ackerman and others, continuing to practise his painting of sheep and cattle in Regent's Park. His first exhibit at Suffolk Street in 1833 at once brought him into notice, and secured him a patron in Robert Vernon. He exhibited forty-eight pictures in all at the British Institution between 1833 and 1863. He also had occasional exhibits at the Society of British Artists, the New Water Colour Society, the Royal Institute of Painters in Oil-colours, and at exhibitions of the Liverpool Academy and Royal Manchester Institution.

A picture, 'Landscape and Cattle,' was hung in the Royal Academy in 1833. It now belongs to Lord Northbrook. It was the first of a series of 266 exhibits which were shown without the interruption of a single year down to 1902. His Royal Academy pictures in 1843-5 ('Watering Cattle, Evening'; 'Repose'; 'Going to Pasture') greatly increased his popularity, and in 1845 he was elected A.R.A. Studies of sheep or cattle were his constant subjects, but in 1846 he attempted a large historical painting, the 'Defeat of Kellermann's Cuirassiers at Waterloo' (the half-past one o'clock charge), which was exhibited with the 'Cartoons' in Westminster Hall in 1847. This picture and a 'Hunting Scene' (R.A. 1890) were isolated examples of an endeavour to depict vigorous action; he cannot be said to have succeeded in excursions outside the somewhat narrow field of his art.

Between 1848 and 1856 he painted the cattle in numerous landscapes by Frederick Lee, R.A. (examples being preserved in South Kensington and the Tate Gallery). Fifteen of these were shown at the Academy and four at the British Institution between 1849 and 1855. He also painted animals in several of Creswick's landscapes. This middle period probably contains the best of his work. After about 1870 commissions were so constant and so lucrative that he was tempted to yield to facile repetition of his favourite themes, seldom developing new subjects or giving the requisite thought to those that he repeated.

Among the best pictures may be mentioned 'Drovers crossing Newbigging Muir in a Snowdrift, East Cumberland' (R.A. 1860); 'Drovers collecting their Flocks under the Fells, East Cumberland' (R.A. 1861; for the earl of Ellesmere); 'Catching Wild Goats on Moel Siabod, North Wales' (Brit. Inst. 1863); 'The Shepherd's Sabbath' (R.A. 1866). He was elected R.A. in 1867, presenting 'Milking Time in the Meadows' for the diploma gallery in 1869. In 1873 and 1874 he exhibited two pictures of bulls, 'The Monarch of the Meadows' (sold in 1873 to Mr. J. D. Allcroft for 2500*l.*) and 'Separated, but not Divorced.' His largest picture, 'Pushing off for Tilbury Fort, on the Thames,' painted when he was eighty, was exhibited at the Academy in 1884.

In 1848 he purchased land at Harbledown near Canterbury, calling the house which he had built 'Vernon Holme,' after his early patron. He still kept on his London house and studio, but 'Vernon Holme' remained his retreat until his death, in his ninety-ninth year, on 7 Feb. 1902. He published his autobiography under the title 'My Life' (2 vols. 1890). His activity continued to the last, and he was engaged on pictures intended for the Royal Academy of 1902 within a few weeks of his death. In 1901 he was made C.V.O. by King Edward VII.

Soon after the death of his mother in 1865 he had bought her house in St. Peter's Street, Canterbury, and an adjacent block, converting it into a school of art and picture gallery, with the purpose of giving free tuition to poor boys. In 1882 he presented the gallery (to be known as the 'Sidney Cooper Gallery of Art') to the town of Canterbury, making the condition that only a nominal fee should be charged for tuition to the artisan classes. On the acceptance of the gift, the corporation decided to convert the gallery into a regular school of art, and affiliate it with South Kensington.

The following public galleries possess one or more of his pictures: National Gallery (two pictures from the Vernon collection, 'Milking Time,' exhibited R.A. 1834, and 'Cattle, Morning,' R.A. 1847, now on loan to the Albert Museum, Exeter, and to the Laing Art Gallery, Newcastle, respectively); National Gallery of British Art (the Tate Gallery) (three pictures, one done in collaboration with Frederick Lee, R.A.); Victoria and Albert Museum (three pictures, one in collaboration with Frederick Lee); Wallace collection; Royal Academy, Diploma Gallery; Cambridge, Fitzwilliam Museum; Birmingham Art Gallery;

Sheffield, Mappin Art Gallery; Manchester Art Gallery; Glasgow Art Gallery; Canterbury, Royal Museum (Beaney Institute); Canterbury, Sidney Cooper School of Art; public galleries at Melbourne, Sydney, and Adelaide. Two pictures are in the royal collection, the 'Pasture, Osborne' (done at Queen Victoria's invitation in 1848), and 'Carisbrook Castle' (painted in 1837, and presented by the artist to the Queen in 1887).

The following are some of his pictures that have been engraved: 'Milking Time' (R.A. 1834; Vernon Coll., Nat. Gall.; engraved by J. Godfrey); 'Cattle, Morning' (R.A. 1847; Vernon Coll., Nat. Gall.; engraved by J. Cousen); 'The Pasture, Osborne' (1848, Royal Collection; engraved by C. Cousen); 'Goatherd of Snowdon' (mezzotint by J. Harris, 1850); 'Kentish Farmyard' (mezzotint by R. B. Parkes, 1864); 'The Sheep Farm' (mixed mezzotint by C. C. Hollyer, 1872); 'Summer Evening' (mixed mezzotint by H. Sedcole, 1903); 'Landscape and Cattle' (1855, reproduced in 'Pictures in the Collection of J. Pierpont Morgan,' 1907).

He married (1) on 1 Oct. 1829, Charlotte Pearson (*d.* 1842), the daughter of an English resident in Brussels, having issue three daughters and one son, Thomas George (1835–1901), who followed his father as an animal painter, and exhibited at the British Institution and Royal Academy 1861–96; (2) in 1863, Mary, daughter of W. Cameron of Canterbury, and had issue Neville Louis (*b.* 1864).

The following oil portraits are known: (1) by himself, 1832; (2) by Walter Scott, 1841; (3) by W. W. Ouless, R.A., 1889 (all three in the collection of Mr. Neville Cooper); (4) another by Walter Scott, 1841 (exhibited R.A. 1842), was formerly in the possession of his daughter Lucy (Mrs. Coxon), and now belongs to his granddaughter, Mrs. Alfred Earle. Thomas George Cooper exhibited an etched portrait of his father at the Royal Academy in 1884.

[My Life, by T. Sidney Cooper, 2 vols., 1890; Graves, Royal Acad. Exhibitors, and Exhibitors at the British Institution; Lists of the Printsellers' Association; The Times, 8 Feb. 1902; information supplied by Mr. Neville Cooper.] A. M. H.

COOPER, THOMPSON (1837–1904), biographer and journalist, born at Cambridge on 8 Jan. 1837, was eldest son of Charles Henry Cooper [q. v.] the Cambridge antiquary, by his wife Jane, youngest daughter of John Thompson of Prickwillow, Cambridgeshire.

A younger brother, John William Cooper (1845–1906), graduated from Trinity Hall, Cambridge, LL.B. in 1866, LL.M. in 1869, and LL.D. in 1880; was called to the bar from Lincoln's Inn in 1868, but resided in Cambridge almost all his life, taking a prominent part in municipal affairs, becoming revising barrister for the county, and acting as local correspondent for 'The Times'; he died at Cambridge on 10 Nov. 1906. He added a fifth volume (posthumously published, 1908) to his father's 'Annals of Cambridge,' and revised the four previous volumes of the work.

Thompson Cooper, educated at a private school kept at Cambridge by the Rev. John Orman, was articled to his father, who became a solicitor in 1840, and was admitted in due time to the profession. But the law was only nominally his vocation, and he took no part in his father's considerable business. His real inheritance was a love of biographical and antiquarian research. He was elected a fellow of the Society of Antiquaries at the early age of 23, and never ceased, while he lived, to investigate antiquarian bye-ways of literature.

Biography was his principal interest. Cooper collected, while still a boy, materials for a work that should rival the 'Athenæ Oxonienses' of Anthony à Wood. His father joined in the project, with the result that in 1858 appeared the first volume of 'Athenæ Cantabrigienses,' containing memoirs of the authors and other eminent men, being alumni of Cambridge, who died between 1500 and 1585. A second volume, published in 1861, carried the work forward to 1609. A part of the third volume was printed, but not published, when the father died in 1866; and, though the university offered to defray the cost of printing the manuscript, neither Thompson Cooper nor his younger brother, John William Cooper, [see above] had leisure to complete the undertaking.

From 1861 onwards Cooper was a working journalist, his first engagement being that of a sub-editor of the 'Daily Telegraph.' In 1862 he became a parliamentary reporter of that paper. He had learned shorthand, the Mason-Gurney system, and, besides putting it to practical purposes, published a manual of the system, 'Parliamentary Shorthand,' as early as 1858. Later, he became a recognised authority on the history of the art. A long connection with 'The Times' began in 1866, and ended only with his death. He was a parliamentary reporter from 1866 to 1886, when he was appointed to write the daily summary of the debates in the House of Commons; an arduous post, requiring accuracy, conciseness, and familiarity with parliamentary and public affairs. In 1898 he became summary-writer in the House of Lords, and performed the less exacting duties of that office until the short illness that preceded his death.

Cooper's work for 'The Times' left him leisure which he filled industriously. In the compilation of this Dictionary, almost from its inception in 1884 to the publication of the first supplement in 1901, he took a useful and important part. From 1884 to 1891 he prepared from his vast collection of biographical data the successive preliminary lists of names (Baalun-Meyrig) which were distributed at half yearly intervals among the contributors. As a writer of memoirs his work continued longer. No less than 1422 articles from his pen were published in the 63 original volumes (1885-1901). His chief subjects were Roman catholic divines and writers. But he was also responsible for many Cambridge graduates of early date and modern journalists and shorthand writers. His literary and historical insight was not profound, but he had a rare faculty for gathering from obscure sources biographical facts, and his eagerness to acquire new knowledge never lost a youthful zest.

In 1869 Cooper projected a new periodical, the 'Register and Magazine of Biography,' but it ceased with the completion of one volume. His most important independent work was his 'Biographical Dictionary,' mainly of Englishmen, which first appeared in 1873, and to which a supplement was added ten years later. This incorporates the materials of the unpublished third volume of 'Athenæ Cantabrigienses,' and contains much that, at the time of its publication, was not elsewhere accessible. He also wrote biographies published under the title of 'The Hundred Greatest Men,' and the letterpress to a series of photographic reproductions of portraits called 'Men of Mark' (1876–1883). He was responsible for four editions of 'Men of the Time,' 1872, 1875, 1879, and 1884. He was a frequent contributor to 'Notes and Queries' for fifty years, his first contribution appearing on 29 Jan. 1853, and his last on 21 April 1903.

He died at his house in Brixton on 5 March 1904, and was buried, with the rites of the Roman catholic church, in Norwood cemetery. He had become a Roman catholic in early life. He married at a youthful age, his wife being a widow with children. He had no issue.

[The Times, 6 March 1904; the Journalist, March 1903; private information.]

A. A. B.

COPELAND, RALPH (1837–1905), astronomer, born on 3 Sept. 1837 at Moorside Farm near Woodplumpton, Lancashire, was son of Robert Copeland, yeoman, by his wife Elizabeth Milner. After education at the grammar school of Kirkham, he went to Australia in 1853, and divided five years in the colony of Victoria between work on a sheep run and at the gold diggings.

Being much interested in astronomy, he on his voyage home in 1858 observed the great comet (Donati) of that year. Entering the works of Beyer, Peacock & Co., locomotive engineers, of Manchester, as a volunteer apprentice, he continued his astronomical studies, and with some fellow-apprentices fitted up a small observatory for a 5-inch refractor by Cooke at West Gorton near Manchester. Copeland's first recorded observation was of a non-instantaneous occultation of κ Cancri by the moon on 26 April 1863, which the well-known observer the Rev. W. R. Dawes communicated to the Royal Astronomical Society. Resolved to devote himself exclusively to astronomy, Copeland in 1865 matriculated at the University of Göttingen, and attended the lectures of Klinkerfues, who was in charge of the observatory, and of other professors. With Börgen, a fellow-student, Copeland undertook the observation with the meridian circle of the Göttingen observatory of the position of all the stars down to the ninth magnitude, in the zone two degrees wide immediately south of the celestial equator. The intention was to contribute the result of the observation to a larger scheme then being organised by the Astronomische Gesellschaft, but the work when completed was declined by the Gesellschaft, because the computation did not conform to their plan. Copeland and Börgen's catalogue was published independently in 1869 as the 'First Göttingen Catalogue of Stars.'

In 1869 Copeland took the degree of Ph.D. with a dissertation on the orbital motion of α Centauri. On 15 June of the same year he and Börgen sailed as members of a German Arctic expedition for the exploration of the east coast of Greenland, their special object being to measure an arc of the meridian in this neighbourhood. They wintered in latitude 74° 32′. Copeland's training in mechanical engineering and his skill with a rifle rendered him a useful member of the expedition. By the beginning of May in the next year a base 709 metres long was measured close to the ship, the Germania, and later the geodetic operations were continued to latitude 75° 11·5′ N. The results were published in 'Die Zweite Deutsche Nordpolarfahrt' (vol. ii. Leipzig, 1872).

In Jan. 1871 Copeland became assistant astronomer at Lord Rosse's observatory at Birr Castle, Parsonstown. There he was for the next two years chiefly occupied with the observations on the moon's radiant heat (see Lord Rosse's paper in *Phil. Trans.* 1873). In 1874 he was elected a fellow of the Royal Astronomical Society, and in the same year was appointed assistant in the Dublin University observatory at Dunsink, but was allowed to accompany Lord Lindsay to Mauritius to observe the transit of Venus in December of that year. The journey was made on the yacht Venus, and during a call at the uninhabited island of Trinidad in the South Atlantic Copeland was fortunate enough to discover a great tree fern (*Cyathea Copelandi*), groves of which are found only in the loftiest and nearly inaccessible parts of the island. The observation of the transit was only partially successful, but Copeland was thenceforth associated with Lord Lindsay (now the earl of Crawford and Balcarres), and left Dunsink in 1876 to take charge of his observatory at Dun Echt, Aberdeen, in succession to (Sir) David Gill. At first Copeland was much occupied in preparing for publication the 'Dun Echt Observatory Publications,' vol. iii., containing computations relating to the observations made at Mauritius. At the end of 1876 the temporary star known as Nova Cygni was discovered. Observing this star on 2 Sept. 1877, Copeland made the noteworthy discovery that its spectrum had become reduced to a bright line. In pursuit of Lord Crawford's plan of rendering Dun Echt a centre for the dissemination of astronomical information, it was Copeland's business to announce to the astronomical public all cometary discoveries in circulars giving the orbits and ephemerides, these being in many cases computed by him from his own observations. For ten years he observed every comet as it appeared, both for position and spectroscopically, and made noteworthy observations of the spectra of nebulæ and stars, which he recorded in the 'Monthly Notices.' In 1882 he went to Jamaica and successfully observed the transit of Venus, continuing his journey westward through Lord Crawford's liberality in order to test the suitability of the slopes of the Andes for observation.

Subsequently Copeland prepared the catalogue (1890) of Lord Crawford's valuable library of astronomical literature, which he had helped to arrange, began a spectroscopic study of nebulæ which was not completed, and in 1887 journeyed to Russia to observe the total solar eclipse of that year, when his purpose was frustrated by bad weather.

Meanwhile he edited with his friend, Dr. Dreyer of Armagh, 'Copernicus, a Journal of Astronomy,' an organ of the Dun Echt observatory, of which three volumes appeared in Dublin (1881–4). They contain much of Copeland's writing, including his 'Account of some Recent Astronomical Experiments at High Elevations in the Andes,' with other incidents of his expedition to America in 1882 (vol. iii.).

In 1889 Lord Crawford presented the instrumental equipment of his observatory at Dun Echt, together with his astronomical library, to the Edinburgh observatory, on condition that it should be maintained as a Royal Observatory. On the acceptance of the offer by the nation Copeland was made Astronomer Royal for Scotland, on 29 Jan. 1889, in succession to Charles Piazzi Smyth [q. v. Suppl. I]. To this office was attached the professorship of astronomy in Edinburgh University. Copeland's first task in his new capacity was to remove the observatory from Calton Hill and to rebuild it on Blackford Hill. This work was not completed until 1895, and in the interval he began a new reduction of the meridian observations of one of his predecessors, Henderson (published posthumously). Next year he journeyed to Vadsö in a fruitless effort to observe the total solar eclipse of that year; but in India in 1898 (as a member of the official expedition), and at Santa Pola, on the south-east coast of Spain, in May 1900, he successfully observed eclipses of the sun. At Blackford Hill, Copeland continued by the issue of 'Edinburgh Circulars' the announcements of astronomical events, which he had begun at Dun Echt; his last circular (No. 54) referred to the appearance of the Nova in Perseus at the beginning of 1900, the spectroscopic observation of which was his last astronomical work. In 1901 he had an attack of influenza, and from this time his health gradually failed. He ceased his professorial lectures in 1902, and died at Edinburgh on 27 Oct. 1905.

Copeland married twice: (1) in 1859 Susannah Milner, his first cousin (*d.* 1866), by whom he had issue one son and one daughter; and (2) in Dec. 1871 Theodora, daughter of the orientalist, Professor Benfey of Göttingen, by whom he had three daughters and a son.

[Notice by Dr. J. L. E. Dreyer in the Monthly Notices of the Royal Astronomical Society for February 1906; Macpherson's Astronomers of To-day, 1905 (with portrait).]

H. P. H.

COPINGER, WALTER ARTHUR (1847–1910), professor of law, antiquary and bibliographer, born on 14 April 1847 at Clapham, was second son of Charles Louis George Emanuel Copinger and his wife Mary, relict of George James, and daughter of Thomas Pearson of Shepperton, Surrey. Educated at the private school of John Andrews at Wellesley House, Brighton, he passed to University College, Durham, but left Durham without completing his course to enter the office of a relative who was a solicitor in London. He did not remain there long. In 1866 he was admitted a student of the Middle Temple, and after spending a short time in the chambers of T. Bourdillon, a well-known conveyancing counsel, he was called to the bar on 26 Jan. 1869. He had mastered the principal treatises of law, and especially the law of real property. After his call he turned his attention to the law of copyright, and in 1870 he published a work on the 'Law of Copyright in Works of Literature and Art' (4th edit. 1904).

Meanwhile in 1870 Copinger settled in Manchester, and commenced practice as an equity draughtsman and conveyancer, and in the chancery court of the county palatine of Lancaster. His work as a conveyancer increased so rapidly that he soon ceased to take court work and became the leading conveyancer out of London. At the same time he was widely consulted on questions of copyright. He owed his success to his complete grasp of the intricacies of the law, especially that relating to real property, to his mental acuteness, his memory, his power of concentration, and his easy style of draughtsmanship. Pupils found his chambers an admirable school of training, for he had the power of making law live.

Amid his heavy professional work Copinger continued to write on legal subjects, more particularly on conveyancing. In 1872 appeared an exhaustive 'Index to Precedents in Conveyancing'; and in 1875 'Title Deeds, their Custody and Production of other Documentary Evidence at Law and Equity.' His 'Law of Rents with special Reference to the Sale of Land in Consideration of a Rent Charge,' which was written many years before, was published in 1886, in collaboration with Professor Munro. In 1876 he published 'An Essay on the Abolition of Capital Punishment,' which, to his amusement, was so enthusiastically received by the abolitionists that his intention to publish another pamphlet demolishing all the arguments in the first was abandoned.

In 1888 Copinger was appointed lecturer in law in the Owens College, Manchester, and in 1892, upon the resignation of Professor Munro, he became professor of law, and finally dean of the faculty of law in the Victoria University. He received the Lambeth degree of doctor of laws from Archbishop Benson in 1889, and that of M.A. from the Victoria University in 1905, He was president of the Manchester Law Society's Library, and of the East Anglians of Manchester and district.

Copinger pursued versatile interests with untiring industry. Besides being an expert in old property law, he was also a keen bibliographer and antiquary, and took a deep interest in theology. Unfortunately all his bibliographical and historical work lacks the essential quality of minute accuracy. Largely owing to his efforts, supported by Richard Copley Christie [q. v. Suppl. I], the Bibliographical Society was founded in London in 1892; he was the society's first president, and held the office for four years, doing much to establish the society on a firm basis. Between 1895 and 1898 he published his most important bibliographical work, the 'Supplement to Hain's Repertorium bibliographicum,' comprising 7000 corrections of and additions to the collations of fifteenth-century works described or mentioned by Hain, and a list of nearly 6000 works not referred to by Hain. This work extends to upwards of 1630 closely printed double-column pages, and is of great value for reference, but it must be used with caution. He contributed several papers to the 'Transactions of the Bibliographical Society,' including an exhaustive monograph on the fifteenth-century printed editions of Virgil. In 1892 he published a fine folio volume on 'Incunabula Biblica,' being a bibliographical account of 124 editions of the Latin Bible printed between 1450 and 1500. At his Manchester residence, The Priory, Greenheys, he set up a small press, at which he printed for private circulation four volumes: 1. 'Catalogue of the Copinger Collection of Editions of the Latin Bible,' 1893. 2. 'Corrections and Additions to the Catalogue of Incunabula in the Mazarin Library,' 1893. 3. Reprint of Leland's 'New Year's Gift to Henry VIII,' 1895. 4. 'On the Authorship of the First Hundred numbers of the "Edinburgh Review,"' 1895. Nos. 3 and 4 bear the serial title 'Bibliographiana.'

Copinger was quite as keenly interested in genealogy, heraldry, and manorial history. In 1882 he published his 'History of the Copingers or Coppingers' (new enlarged edit. 1884), in which he traces the descent of his family from the Danes in the tenth century, when they appear to have settled in Suffolk and in the south of Ireland. The energies of his last years were devoted almost exclusively to the history of Suffolk. In 1902 he issued the 'History of the Parish of Buxhall,' of which he was lord of the manor. Between 1904 and 1907 the 'History of Suffolk as described by Existing Records' (in 5 vols.) made its appearance together with the 'Manors of Suffolk: Notes on their History and Devolution' (7 vols. 1905–11). He also found time to compile the 'History of the Smith-Carrington Family' (2 vols. 1907), and to write 'Heraldry Simplified,' which appeared in the year of his death.

In religion Copinger was an Irvingite, and for a number of years was the angel of the Catholic Apostolic church in Manchester. His interest in theology was wide and deep. The work which he valued most among his writings was a huge treatise from his pen on 'Predestination, Election, and Grace' (1889). His other theological writings were: 'Testimony of Antiquity . . . being a Reprint of the Homily by Elfric,' edited by himself, 1877; 'Thoughts on Holiness, Doctrinal and Practical,' 1883; 'Contributions to Hymnody,' 1886; 'The Bible and its Transmission,' 1897; A new translation of 'Imitatio Christi,' 1900; and Law's 'Serious Call adapted to the Requirements of the Present Day,' 1905.

Copinger mainly found all the relaxation which he allowed himself in a change of work; but music always attracted him. He played several instruments, including the pianoforte and violin, and found time to compose a number of musical pieces, amongst which is a collection of seventy-five original hymn tunes.

Copinger was an ardent book-collector, and accumulated a considerable library. It was rich in early printed books, Bibles, manuscripts, and printed editions of the 'Imitatio Christi,' hymn books, Elzevirs, and general works of reference. Genial and affable with every one, he was always ready to place not only the rich stores of his knowledge but the resources of his library at the disposal of any student.

He died at his residence in Manchester on 13 March 1910 from pneumonia following an attack of influenza. He was buried at Birch, Rusholme, Manchester. On 3 Sept. 1873 Copinger married Caroline Agnes, eldest daughter of Thomas Inglis Stewart, vicar of Landscove, Devon. She predeceased him, leaving two sons and three daughters.

[Manchester Faces and Places, viii. 8–12 (portrait); Manchester Univ. Mag., vii. 182–4; Copinger's History of the Copingers, 1884; Manchester Guardian, 14 March 1910; Athenæum, 26 March 1910; Dr. Copinger's own and other notes communicated by Mr. C. W. Sutton; private information and personal knowledge.] H. G.

COPPIN, GEORGE SELTH (1819–1906), actor and Australian politician, born at Steyning, Sussex, on 8 April 1819, was only child of George Selth Coppin (1794–1854) and his wife, Mrs. Elizabeth Jane Jackson. His father, of a Norwich family, gave up medical practice for the stage and became a theatrical manager.

As a child the son showed proficiency on the violin, became a musical prodigy at the age of four, and played juvenile characters on the stage a year or two later. At seventeen he took to his profession seriously, and in November 1837 he was a minor member of the Sheffield stock company, playing at that period Osric to the Hamlet of the young starring tragedian Gustavus Vaughan Brooke [q.v.]. Developing into a capable low comedian, he was engaged at the Queen's Theatre, Manchester, early in 1841, and on 7 August in that year (when he was described as 'from the Strand Theatre') began an engagement at the Abbey Street Theatre, Dublin. For a time he sang comic songs nightly between the pieces, accompanying himself on the violin. Here he met a fascinating American actress, Mrs. Watkins Burroughs, the wife of a provincial actor-manager, with whom he eloped to Australia, landing at Sydney on 10 March 1843. There Coppin acted on sharing terms at the Victoria Theatre, and frequently made 50*l.* a night. But the money thus amassed was lost in commercial enterprises, and he left Sydney in debt. On 5 January 1845 Coppin began a starring engagement at Hobart Town, and on 3 March commenced theatrical management at Launceston, where he had a prosperous season. Three months later he took his company to Melbourne, where he rented the Queen's Theatre, making his first appearance there on 21 June, when he played Glavis in 'The Lady of Lyons' and Crack in 'The Turnpike Gate.' Subsequently Coppin removed to Adelaide, where he built a theatre in five weeks, and opened it on 2 Nov. 1846. Here within three or four years he made a fortune, only to lose it in copper mining. After passing through the insolvency court in 1851, he returned to Melbourne and spent a fortnight at the gold diggings without benefit. After a short starring engagement in Melbourne, he in 1852 commenced management at the Great Malop Street theatre, Geelong, where he rapidly made another fortune. Returning to Adelaide he paid his creditors in full, and sailing for England in January 1854 made his first appearance at the Haymarket, in London, on 26 June. Subsequently he fulfilled engagements at Birmingham, Manchester, Edinburgh, and Dublin. While at Birmingham in August he induced G. V. Brooke to sign articles to star under his management for 200 nights in Australia and New Zealand.

Returning to Melbourne, Coppin reappeared at the Queen'sTheatre on 18 Dec.,and next month began a successful engagement at the Victoria Theatre, Sydney. In June 1855 he opened the new Olympic theatre, Melbourne, familiarly known as 'The Iron Pot,' under his own management, on 30 July, playing Colonel Damas in 'The Lady of Lyons' and Mr. Trotter Southdown in 'To Oblige Benson.' Meanwhile Brooke's tour proved highly prosperous. Thereupon Coppin joined Brooke in purchasing the new Theatre Royal,Melbourne, for 23,000*l.*,opening that house on 9 June 1856. About the same period they also acquired the freehold of the Cremorne Gardens, upon which they spent much. At the Theatre Royal they organised the first grand opera season in the Australian colonies. The partnership was dissolved in Feb. 1859, Brooke continuing the management. Coppin then built the Pantheon Theatre; but owing to Brooke's difficulties, he resumed control of the Theatre Royal on 20 Dec. 1860. On 15 Sept. 1862 he completed a new theatre, the Haymarket. A second bankruptcy followed, but he brought out Mr. and Mrs. Charles Kean to Melbourne in Oct. 1863, and then took them to Sydney, with the result that he paid his creditors in full. After touring with the Keans in America (1864–5), he reappeared at the Haymarket, Melbourne (Jan. 1866), in a variety of characters, including Daniel White in Craven's 'Milky White.'

In 1871 he went into partnership with Messrs. Harwood, Stewart, and Hennings in the management of the Melbourne Theatre Royal, but suffered a considerable loss through the burning of the uninsured building on 19 March 1872. At once taking a ninety-nine years' lease of the site, he rebuilt the theatre, subsequently transferring the property to the Theatre Royal Proprietary Association, Limited, of which he remained managing director till his death. At this house in Nov. and Dec. 1881 he gave farewell performances for twelve nights. His last appearance was on 9 Dec., as Bob Acres and Crack.

Meanwhile Coppin engaged in politics. In 1858 he was elected to the legislative council of Victoria for the south-western province, but resigned his seat on leaving the colony in 1864 for an American tour. During this period he helped to pass the Transfer of Real Property Act, and to secure the adoption of the English principle of the Post Office Savings Bank. He advocated the federation of the colonies and intercolonial free trade, and opposed the payment of members. Subsequently, from 1874 to 1889 he was member of the legislative assembly for East Melbourne. He was then returned to the Upper House, unopposed, for Melbourne province. He was twice elected chairman of the Richmond municipality, and for two years was chairman of magistrates in that district.

A man of immense energies and extraordinarily diverse interests, Coppin left the impress of his talents upon the colony of Victoria. As early as 1870 he advocated acclimatisation, and was the first to import camels and English thrushes into Australia. About 1861, in association with (Sir) Charles Gavan Duffy [q. v. Suppl. II], he founded the beautiful watering place, Sorrento on the Sea, forty miles S.E. of Melbourne, where Mount Coppin is called after him, and where till his death he had a charming seat. In 1868 he built a magnificent residence, Pine Grove, Richmond Hill, Melbourne (cf. J. B. Howe, *A Cosmopolitan Actor*, p. 191).

Coppin died at Melbourne on 12 March 1906. He was twice married: (1) in 1855, to Harriet Bray (*d.* 1859) of Birmingham, a sister of Mrs. G. V. Brooke; and (2) in 1861 to Lucy Hilsden. He left issue, by his first wife, two daughters, and by his second wife, two sons and five daughters.

[Burke's Colonial Gentry, 1897; R. M. Sillard, Barry Sullivan; Theatrical Journal (London), vol. xvi. No. 801, 1855; J. B. Howe, A Cosmopolitan Actor; Illustrated Australian News, 10 Sept. 1872; Melbourne Punch, 16 May 1861; Melbourne Age, 2 Nov. 1889; W. J. Lawrence's Life of G. V. Brooke, 1890; Heaton, Australian Dict. of Dates (1879), where Coppin's early career is confused with that of his father; private information.]

COPPINGER, RICHARD WILLIAM (1847–1910), naval surgeon and naturalist, born on 11 Oct. 1847 in Dublin, was youngest of the six sons of Joseph William Coppinger, a solicitor of Farmley, Dundrum, co. Dublin, by his wife Agnes Mary, only daughter of William Lalor Cooke, landed proprietor of Fortwilliam, co. Tipperary. The father's family was long settled at Ballyvolane and Barryscourt, co. Cork, and was said to descend from the first Danish settlers in Cork city. Coppinger received his medical education in Dublin, graduating M.D. at the Queen's University in 1870. Entering the medical department of the navy, he was appointed surgeon to H.M.S. Alert, which, with H.M.S. Discovery, left Portsmouth on 29 May 1875 under the command of captain (afterwards Sir) George S. Nares on a voyage of exploration towards the North Pole. The Alert reached a higher latitude than had ever been touched before, and Coppinger distinguished himself as the naturalist in charge of one of the sledging parties. On the return of the Alert to England in October 1876 he was specially promoted staff-surgeon and awarded the Arctic medal. Coppinger again served as naturalist in the Alert on her four years' exploring cruise in Patagonian, Polynesian and Mascarene waters from 1878 to 1882.

In 1889 he was appointed instructor in hygiene at the Haslar naval hospital at Gosport, where he was a most successful teacher, his knowledge of bacteriology being in advance of the time. On 13 March 1901 he was appointed inspector-general of hospitals and fleets, and was for three years in charge at Haslar. On 15 May 1904 he was placed on half-pay, and being disappointed in not being made director-general of the medical department of the navy, he retired in 1906.

He died at his residence, Wallington House, Fareham, on 2 April 1910, and was buried at Fareham cemetery. He married, on 8 Jan. 1884, Matilda Mary, daughter of Thomas Harvey Browne, landed proprietor of Sydney, N.S.W., and had issue three sons and one daughter.

Coppinger was author of 'The Cruise of the Alert, 1878–82' (1883). He also wrote 'Some Experiments on the Conductive Properties of Ice made in Discovery Bay, 1875–6' (*Proc. Roy. Soc.* 1878, xxvi.); and 'Account of the Zoological Collections made in the Years 1878–1881, during the Survey of H.M.S. Alert in the Straits of Magellan and the Coast of Patagonia' (*Proc. Zoolog. Soc.*, 1881). He contributed to the parliamentary paper containing the report of the committee (1877) on 'Scurvy in the Arctic Expedition, 1875–6,' and to the 'Report on the Zoological Collections of H.M.S. Alert made in 1881–2' (British Museum, Nat. Hist., 1884).

[Brit. Med. Journ., 1910, i. 1090; private information.] H. D. R.

CORBET, MATTHEW RIDLEY (1850–1902), painter, born on 20 May 1850 at South Willingham, Lincolnshire, was son of the Rev. Andrew Corbet by his wife Marianne Ridley. He was educated at Cheltenham College, and coming to London entered the Royal Academy schools. His first exhibits at the Royal Academy were portraits, among them those of Lady Slade (1875), Mrs. Heneage Wynne-Finch (1877), and Lady Clay (1879). Though he continued to paint occasional portraits, such as those of Lord Northbourne (1886), Mrs. Stuart (afterwards Lady) Rendel (1891), the Hon. Walter James (1892), Lady Morpeth (1895), and Lady Cecilia Roberts (1897), he was concerned from 1883 onwards almost entirely with landscape. Between 1875 and 1902 he exhibited thirty-eight works in all at the Royal Academy, of which he was elected an associate in 1902. After 1880 he also sent several of his important works to the Grosvenor Gallery, and later to the New Gallery. His 'Sunrise' gained a bronze medal at the Paris Exhibition of 1889; and his 'Morning Glory' (1894) and 'Val d'Arno—Evening' (1901), bought under the terms of the Chantrey bequest, are now in the Tate Gallery.

As a pupil and devoted follower of Giovanni Costa, Corbet was steeped in the beauty of Italian landscape, and though he found the subject of his 'Morning Glory' near the Severn, he was, as a rule, at his best when painting under Italian skies. The title that he chose from Keats for one of his exhibits in 1890—'A land of fragrance, quietness, and trees and flowers'—suggests the spirit of the Italian scenes which inspired his brush. In his work there was always a fine sensitiveness to the poetic beauties of nature, and a restful harmony of colour. His sense of beauty was too refined and cultivated to win the masses, and his distinguished talent was just beginning to win appreciation at the time of his death. Among his more important works, besides those already mentioned, are 'Passing Storm' (1896), 'Autumn Rains' (1896), and 'Florence in Spring' (1898).

Corbet died on 25 June 1902 at his residence, 54 Circus Road, St. John's Wood, from an attack of pneumonia, and after cremation his ashes were laid behind a tablet in the wall of South Willingham church. On 17 March 1891 he married Mrs. Arthur Murch (born Edith Edenborough), herself a landscape painter, whose vision and methods were in close sympathy with his own. A bust portrait of Corbet, sculptured by E. Onslow Ford, R.A., and medallion portrait by Alfred Gilbert, R.A., are now in the possession of his widow.

[The Times, 27 June 1902; Mag. of Art, xxvi. 236, 1902; Graves's Academy Exhibitors; private information.] M. H.

CORBETT, JOHN (1817–1901), promoter of the salt industry in Worcestershire and benefactor, born at Brierley Hill, Staffordshire, on 12 June 1817, was eldest son in a family of five sons and one daughter of Joseph Corbett by his wife Hannah. The father, originally a Shropshire farmer, migrated to Staffordshire to become a carrier of merchandise by canal boats. John, after attending as a child Mr. Gurney's school at Brierley Hill, helped on his father's boats from the age of ten to that of three and twenty. He devoted his leisure to an unaided study of mechanical problems; and in 1840, at the mature age of twenty-three, was apprenticed for five years to W. Lester, chief engineer of Messrs. Hunt & Brown of the Leys ironworks, Stourbridge. In 1846 he reluctantly abandoned the career of an engineer to become his father's partner, and under the name of Corbett & Son a prosperous business was carried on, a large fleet of boats being maintained between the Staffordshire district and London, Liverpool, Manchester, and other commercial centres. In 1852 the business was sold, the advent of railways threatening to decrease canal traffic, and Corbett then bought the Stoke Prior salt works near Droitwich.

Corbett's new venture was unpromising. Salt had been discovered at Stoke Prior by a Cheshire 'brine-smeller' in 1828. Vast sums had since been expended in the sinking of brine pits and the erection of salt-works. But the great depth of the brine springs and the weakening of the brine within the pits by an inflow from neighbouring fresh-water springs made production costly. Six private owners in turn became bankrupt, and then the property was divided between two rival joint-stock companies with no better result. Corbett acquired in 1852 the premises of both the companies, which stood respectively on opposite banks of the Worcester and Birmingham canal. Within a few years the enterprise was completely transformed. New brine pits lined with cast-iron cylinders to prevent the inflow of fresh water were sunk to a depth of 1000 feet, and by the introduction of a patent process whereby a system of pipes doubled the intensity of both the fire-heat and steam, a whiter, more finely grained salt was produced than was obtainable elsewhere, the size of the grain or crystal depending on the temperature at which the brine was evaporated. Other changes were the acquisition of fifty canal boats, the cutting of tributaries from the canal to the lofts in which the salt was stored, the building of a railway—the property of Corbett—which traversed the works, carrying coal to and salt from such places as could not be reached by water, and the establishment of a wagon factory, a foundry, fitting shops, sawmills, and a brickyard. As many as seven depôts were established in London. Corbett himself supervised all details. Within twenty-five years he converted an annual output of 26,000 tons of salt into one of 200,000 tons, and built up the most perfect system of salt-manufacture in the world. For his workpeople he built model houses, gardens, schools, a club-house, lecture-room, and dispensary. In 1859 he abolished female labour on the works, a step now commemorated by a window placed by public subscription in Stoke Prior church. He sold the works in 1889 to the Salt Union.

Corbett was interested in politics on the liberal side. In 1868 he contested unsuccessfully Droitwich against the conservative candidate, Sir John Pakington [q. v.]; but Droitwich reversed its decision in 1874, when Corbett defeated Pakington and was elected. He kept the seat in 1880; in 1885, when the old borough was merged in the mid-Worcestershire division, he was returned unopposed for that constituency. In the house, though never prominent in debate, he showed interest in questions of local taxation, advocated alterations in the laws of land tenure, and was an early advocate of woman suffrage. Opposed to home rule, he joined the ranks of the liberal unionists in 1886 and was returned by a large majority in that interest in July 1886. He retired at the dissolution of 1892.

Corbett acquired from Lord Somers a large estate at Impney near Droitwich and from Athelston Corbet (no relation) a second estate near Towyn in Wales. On the Impney property he erected a residence in the style of a French château of the time of Francis I. A generous supporter of philanthropic institutions in the Midlands, Corbett presented Corbett Hospital to Stourbridge and Salters' Hall, a building capable of holding 1500 people, to Droitwich. He also contributed generously to the funds of Birmingham University, of which he was a governor, and of the Bromsgrove Cottage Hospital; he helped in the development of Droitwich as a health-resort by the erection of St. Andrew's Brine Baths (1889), and by the restoration of the old Raven Hotel and the building of the Worcester Hotel; he presented a church clock to Brierley Hill and placed memorial windows in the church there to his father and mother. To the development of Towyn he contributed by the erection of a fine esplanade and a massive sea-wall.

Corbett, who was an associate of the Institute of Civil Engineers, died at Impney on 22 April 1901.

Corbett married in April 1856 Anna Eliza, daughter of John O'Meara of county Tipperary, and had issue two sons and four daughters.

A bust was executed by E. Onslow Ford, R.A., and a presentation portrait by H. T. Wells, R.A., was exhibited at the Royal Academy in 1895.

[The Times, 24 April 1901; Mining World, 27 April 1901; John Corbett of Impney: a Sketch of his Career, Stourbridge; Handbook to Droitwich, by L. D. B.; John Murray's Worcestershire; Soc. of Arts Journal, 1901; Oil Trade Review, 4 Jan. 1868; History of Worcestershire in Victoria County History; Journal of the Institute of Civil Engineers, 1901.] S. E. F.

CORBOULD, EDWARD HENRY (1815–1905), water-colour painter, born in London on 5 Dec. 1815, was son of Henry Corbould [q. v.], historical painter and draughtsman, and grandson of Richard Corbould [q. v.], portrait, landscape, and historical painter, and designer of book illustrations. He was a pupil of Henry Sass, and a student of the Royal Academy. In 1834, 1835 and 1836 he won gold medals of the Society of Arts, in 1834 with a water-colour of the 'Fall of Phaethon,' and in the last two years with models of 'St. George and the Dragon' (collection of Dr. Victor Corbould) and a 'Chariot Race, from Homer' (now in the possession of Mrs. G. H. Heywood). His first exhibits in the Royal Academy in 1835 included a model ('Cyllarus and Hylonome'), but he did not pursue the art of sculpture for long. It is interesting, however, to note that in 1889, when the London corporation invited various artists to submit designs for four pieces of sculpture for Blackfriars bridge (a project never carried out), he produced four drawings of colossal groups, which are still in the possession of Dr. Victor Corbould. The main work of his life was in water-colour, in which he produced a large number of subjects illustrating literature (chiefly Chaucer, Spenser, and Shakespeare), history, and daily life. He continued to the end even in his larger subjects to paint in the careful stippled manner that is more adapted to miniature portrait and illustration; and only a small proportion of his pictures are in oil (*e.g.* 'The Canterbury Pilgrims,' R.A. 1874, in the possession of Dr. Victor Corbould). He started exhibiting at the New Water Colour Society (later the Royal Institute of Painters in Water Colours) in 1837, becoming a member of that body in the same year. One of the most important of his early exhibits at this society, 'The Canterbury Pilgrims assembled at the old Tabard Inn' (1840), is now at Norbury Park, Dorking. In 1842 his water-colour of 'The Woman taken in Adultery' was purchased by the Prince Consort, and nine years later he was appointed 'instructor of historical painting to the royal family.' He continued for twenty-one years teaching various members of the royal family, and many of his best works were acquired by Queen Victoria, Prince Albert, and his royal pupils, *e.g.* an illustration of Tennyson's 'Morte d'Arthur' (now in Kensington Palace), presented by Queen Victoria to Princess Louise, and 'Henry VI welcomed to London after his Coronation in Paris,' and 'The Iconoclasts of Basle,' acquired by the Empress Frederick and still in the imperial collection, Berlin. Apart from the royal collections, one of the largest collections of his works was that of George Strutt of Belper. Corbould exhibited in all about 250 drawings at the Royal Institute, only retiring from active membership in 1898. He also produced a large number of designs (chiefly subjects of fancy and romance) for book illustration, *e.g.* in the Abbotsford edition of the 'Waverley Novels' (Cadell, 1841–6), and in Black's edition of the same (1852–3), Spenser's 'Faerie Queen' and Chaucer's 'Canterbury Tales' (Routledge, 1853), Tupper's 'Proverbial Philosophy' (1854), Willmott's 'Poets of the Nineteenth Century' (1857), 'Merrie Days of England' (1858–9), and in periodicals such as 'London Society,' the 'Churchman's Family Magazine,' 'Cassell's Magazine,' and the 'Illustrated London News.' He died at Kensington on 18 Jan. 1905.

He was thrice married: (1) on 28 Sept. 1839 to Fanny Jemima (*d.* 1850), daughter of the engraver Charles Heath [q. v.], by whom he had three daughters, one of whom, Isabel Fanny (Mrs. G. H. Heywood), has two daughters who are artists, Mrs. Eveline Corbould-Ellis and Mrs. Weatherley; (2) on 7 Aug. 1851 to Anne Middleton Wilson (*d.* 1866), by whom he had two sons, Ridley Edward Arthur Lamothe (1854–1887) and Victor Albert Louis Edward (*b.* 1866); (3) on 15 Jan. 1868 to Anne Melis Sanders, by whom he had one son and one daughter.

The only painting preserved in a public gallery is a water-colour of 'Lady Godiva' in the National Gallery of New South Wales. The following are among the more important prints after his paintings: 'The Canterbury Pilgrims assembled at the old Tabard Inn' (mezzotint by C. E. Wagstaff, 1843); 'Henry VI welcomed to London after his Coronation' (engraved by E. Webb, 1847; the original now in Berlin); 'My Chickens for Sale' (1847), 'Maid of the Mill' (1849), and 'Valentine's Eve' (1850) (mezzotints by Samuel Bellin); 'Happy as a Queen' (1852), and 'The Wood Nymph' (mezzotints by W. H. Egleton, 1855); 'The Fairy Well' (mezzotint by J. E. Coombs, 1855); 'Lady Godiva' (mezzotint by J. J. Chant, 1860); 'The Queen of the Tournament' (mezzotint by T. W. Huffam); 'The Plague of London' (one of the Westminster Hall Cartoons, lithograph by Frank Howard); portrait of the Prince Consort (lithograph by R. J. Lane, 1862).

A miniature portrait of Corbould by his grand-daughter, Mrs. Weatherley, is in the possession of Dr. Victor Corbould.

[The Biograph and Review, vol. iii. no. 16 (April 1880); M. H. Spielmann in the Daily Graphic, 19 Jan. 1905; Daily Chronicle, 21 Jan. 1905; A. Graves, Dictionary of Artists (1895) and Royal Academy Exhibitors; Lists of the Printsellers' Association; Gleeson White, English Illustration: The Sixties, 1897; The Brothers Dalziel, 1901; information supplied by Dr. Victor Corbould.]

A. M. H.

CORFIELD, WILLIAM HENRY (1843–1903), professor of hygiene and public health, born on 14 Dec. 1843 at Shrewsbury, was eldest son of Thomas Corfield, a chemist of that town, by his wife Jane Brown, of a Gloucestershire family. Educated at Cheltenham grammar school, he gained a demyship in natural science at Magdalen College, Oxford, matriculating on 12 Oct. 1861, and gaining a first class in mathematical moderations in 1863. He was then selected by Prof. C. G. B. Daubeny [q. v.] to accompany him to Auvergne, where he investigated the volcanic appearances in the Montbrison district. Returning to Oxford, he gained a first class in the final school of mathematics and physics in Michaelmas term 1864, and graduated B.A. From 1865 to 1875 he held, after open competition, the Sheppard medical fellowship at Pembroke College. In Michaelmas term 1865 he won a first class in the natural science school, in which he acted as examiner during 1873–4. He entered University College, London, as a medical student in 1865, in 1866 won the Burdett-Coutts scholarship at Oxford for geology, and next year was elected Radcliffe travelling fellow.

Influenced by Sir Henry W. Acland [q. v. Suppl. I] and by George Rolleston [q. v.], Corfield had by this time directed his attention more particularly to hygiene and sanitary science. A portion of his foreign travel was spent in Paris, where he attended Bouchardat's lectures and studied hygiene under Berthelot at the Collège de France. He proceeded afterwards to Lyons, worked at clinical medicine and surgery, and made a special study of the remains of the remarkable aqueducts of ancient Lugdunum. He also visited some of the medical schools in Italy and Sicily. He graduated M.B. at Oxford in 1868, and M.D. in 1872. In 1869 he was admitted M.R.C.P. London, and in 1875 he was elected F.R.C.P. He became a fellow of the Institute of Chemistry in 1877.

Meanwhile in 1869 Corfield was appointed professor of hygiene and public health at University College, London, and in 1875 he opened the first laboratory in London for the practical teaching of hygiene. In 1876 Corfield actively helped to found a museum of practical hygiene in memory of E. A. Parkes [q. v.], which was placed first at University College, afterwards at Margaret Street, Cavendish Square, and since 1909 at Buckingham Palace Road, Westminster, being now maintained by the Royal Sanitary Institute. Medical officer of health for Islington (1871–2), and for St. George's, Hanover Square (1872–1900), Corfield was at one time president of the Society of Medical Officers of Health.

A member of the committee appointed in 1869 by the British Association to inquire into the treatment and utilisation of sewage, Corfield worked as reporter to the committee until 1875, and be became an ardent advocate of land filtration and sewage farms. He delivered at the Royal Society of Arts in 1879 the Cantor lectures on 'Dwelling houses, their sanitary construction and arrangements'; in 1893 the Harveian lecture before the Harveian Society of London, on 'Disease and defective house sanitation,' and in 1902 the Milroy lectures at the Royal College of Physicians of London, 'On the ætiology of typhoid fever and its prevention' (1902).

Corfield shares with Rogers Field the honour of being a pioneer in house sanitation and of being the first to enunciate the true principles of a healthy home. Public attention was called to the topic in 1871 by the attack of enteric contracted by the Prince of Wales (afterwards King Edward VII) at Londesborough Lodge, Scarborough. Corfield was called upon to make a careful inspection of Lord Londesborough's house. In a letter to 'The Times' on 22 Jan. 1872 he pointed out that the disease had not been conveyed by sewer air as had been suggested. For the next thirty years Corfield enjoyed a large consulting practice throughout England in connection with the sanitation of public and private buildings. In 1899 he was the first holder of the newly established office of consulting sanitary adviser to the office of works.

Corfield acted conjointly with Dr. John Netten Radcliffe [q. v.] as secretary of the Epidemiological Society (1870–2), and was president (1902–3). President of the public health section of the British Medical Association held at Bristol in 1894, and of a section of the sanitary congress of the Sanitary Institute held at Newcastle-on-Tyne in 1896, Corfield originated the successful International Congress of Hygiene held in London in 1891. He represented the office of works at the International Congress of Hygiene and Demography, of which he was honorary president, at Paris in 1900; and presided at the conference held by the Sanitary Institute at Paris in August 1900 under the auspices of the Société Française d'Hygiène.

Corfield died at Marstrand in Sweden, on a visit for his health, on 26 Aug. 1903. He married in 1876 Emily Madelina, youngest daughter of John Pike, F.S.A., and left a family of six children, two of whom are carrying on his work, one, Dr. Walter Francis Corfield, as medical officer of health for Colchester, the other, Frederick John Arthur Corfield, as a sanitary adviser.

Corfield belongs to the second generation of sanitary reformers in England. Entering professional life after a first-rate general education, he took up the subject of public health where it had been left by Chadwick, Simon, Buchanan, Netten Radcliffe, Thorne-Thorne and others, and carried it forward until it became a highly specialised science.

Corfield, who had wide interests outside his profession, was a collector of rare books and a connoisseur in binding. His library was especially rich in works on fishing, for he was an ardent angler. He was also a lover of prints, and made a fine collection of Bewick's woodcuts. For more than twenty years he was chairman of the committee of the Sunday Society, which has for its object the opening of museums, picture galleries, and public libraries on Sunday.

Corfield's chief works are: 1. 'A Digest of Facts relating to the Treatment and Utilisation of Sewage,' 1870; 3rd edit. 1887. 2. 'Water and Water Supply,' Part 1; and 'Sewerage and Sewerage Utilisation,' Part 2, New York, 1875. 3. 'Dwelling Houses: their Sanitary Construction and Arrangements,' 1880; 4th edit. 1898; translated into French from 2nd edit. by P. Jardet, Paris, 1889. 4. 'Laws of Health,' 1880; 9th edit. 1896. 5. 'Disease and Defective House Sanitation,' 1896; translated into French, Italian and Hungarian. 6. 'Public Health Laboratory Work,' 1884 (jointly with W. W. Cheyne and C. E. Cassal).

[Lancet, 1903, ii. 778 (with portrait); Brit. Med. Journal, 1903, ii. 627 (with portrait); Journal of the Sanitary Institute, 1903, vol. xxiv. part iii. p. 530 (with portrait); the Medico-Chirurgical Trans., 1904, lxxxvii. p. cxxxi; Trans. Epidemiological Society of London, New Series, xxii. 160; information from Mr. F. J. A. Corfield.] D'A. P.

CORNISH, CHARLES JOHN (1858–1906), naturalist, born on 28 Sept. 1858 at Salcombe House, near Sidmouth, the residence of his grandfather, Charles John Cornish, J.P., D.L., was eldest son of Charles John Cornish, then curate of Sidbury, Devonshire, by his first wife, Anne Charlotte Western (*d.* 1887). He was brought up at Debenham, Suffolk, where his father became vicar in 1859. In 1872 he entered Charterhouse as a gownboy, and left in 1876. After engaging in private tuition, he entered Hertford College, Oxford, as a commoner in 1881, was elected Brunsell exhibitioner in 1882 and Lusby scholar in 1883. In the same year he obtained his 'blue' in association football, a second class in classical moderations in 1883, and a second class in literæ humaniores in 1885. He was then appointed assistant classical master at St. Paul's School, and held the post until his death. He was the founder in 1896 of the school field club. Soon after coming to London he wrote occasional articles on natural history and country life, and in 1890 became a regular contributor to the 'Spectator,' and, later, to 'Country Life.' Many of his articles re-appeared in book form. Cornish's country tastes and love of shooting and fishing were fostered by his father, in whose family they were traditional. His artistic and literary gifts he inherited from his mother. His powers of observation were unusually keen and rapid, his memory remarkably good, and he had powers of vivid expression. His literary energy, which continued through twenty years, stimulated public interest in natural history and country life, and helped to give these subjects an assured place in English journalism. He died at Worthing on 30 Jan. 1906, from an illness originating in an accident incurred many years before when shooting. After cremation his ashes were interred at Salcombe Regis, near Sidmouth, and a mural tablet to his memory was placed in the parish church. He married in 1893 Edith, eldest daughter of Sir John I. Thornycroft, C.E., F.R.S., by whom he had one daughter.

Cornish was author of the following books: 1. 'The New Forest,' 1894. 2. 'The Isle of Wight,' 1895. 3. 'Life at the Zoo,' 1895 (the work which made him generally known). 4. 'Wild England of To-day, and the Wild Life in it,' 1895. 5. 'Animals at Work and Play,' 1896. 6. 'Nights with an Old Gunner,' 1897. 7. 'Animals of To-day,' 1898. 8. 'The Naturalist on the Thames,' 1902. 9. 'Sir William Henry Flower, a Personal Memoir,' 1904. He co-operated with others in 'Living Animals of the World' (2 vols. 1901–2). 'Animal Artisans and other Studies of Birds and Beasts,' with a prefatory memoir by his widow, was published in 1907.

[Memoir by his widow, 1907; The Times, 31 Jan. and 5 Feb. 1906; personal knowledge.]

V. C.

CORNWELL, JAMES (1812–1902), writer of school books, born in East London on 4 August 1812, was one of nine children of James Cornwell, silk manufacturer, and his wife Mary Blake. Up to the age of fifteen he was mainly self-taught. He then studied at the model school of the Borough Road Training College of the British and Foreign School Society, and by August 1829 was a full-fledged student. In the early part of 1830 he was sent as a teacher on supply to the society's schools at Brighton and Chelmsford, and in October to Lindfield in Sussex. He returned to the college in January 1833 for a short period of training.

In April 1835 the society appointed him organiser of country schools, his duty being to 'organise new schools' and assist newly appointed masters in obtaining 'good discipline by moral means.' In October 1839 he was appointed normal school teacher and inspector, and from 1835 worked both in the training college and as an inspector outside. In 1846, when the training department of the institution in the Borough Road became recognised by the privy council as a grant-earning normal college, Cornwell was appointed by the British and Foreign School Society its head teacher or principal. Under his care the institution greatly developed and took a high position among the normal colleges of the country. His lectures were clear, pertinent, and accurate, and he showed much ability in practical teaching. In principles and methods of school management he anticipated many later results of educational science and experience.

In 1841 Cornwell began to publish school-books which in simplicity of style and practical usefulness were far in advance of the text-books of their day and deservedly enjoyed a universal vogue. He shares with J. T. Crossley, (Sir) Joshua Girling Fitch [q. v. Suppl. II), and Henry Dunn the merit of having devised the modern school-book. In collaboration with Dr. Allen he issued 'A New English Grammar' (1841, 12mo), 'An English School Grammar' (18mo), and 'Grammar for Beginners' (1855, 12mo; 90th edit. 1904). His popular 'School Geography,' first published in 1847, passed through ninety editions. Memorial editions of the 'Grammar for Beginners' and of the 'Geography' were published in 1904.

After his resignation of the principalship at Borough Road in 1885, Cornwell devoted his leisure to writing new educational works or revising former ones. He was fond of music and of the study of nature. For sixteen years he resided at a house he built for himself, Loughborough Park Villa, Brixton, and then removed to Purbrook, Crescent Wood Road, Sydenham, where he died on 12 Dec. 1902. He was buried in Norwood cemetery.

Cornwell received the degree of Ph.D. from a German university in 1847, and in 1860 he became a fellow of the Royal Geographical Society. A portrait, painted by J. R. Dicksee, was presented by the artist to the Borough Road Training College in Nov. 1903, and is now at the College, Isleworth (cf. reproduction in the *Educational Record*, Feb. 1904).

Cornwell married on 19 Nov. 1840 Mary Ann Wilson of Besthorpe, Nottinghamshire. There was one daughter of the marriage.

Other works not mentioned above are: 1. 'The Young Composer, or Progressive Exercises in Composition,' 1844, 12mo; 17th edit. 1855. 2. 'Complete Guide to English Composition,' founded on the above; 49th edit. 1904. 3. 'Geography for Beginners,' 1858, 12mo; 70th edit. 1904. In collaboration with Sir Joshua Fitch he published 'The Science of Arithmetic' (1855, 12mo; new edit. 1878) and 'Arithmetic for Beginners' (1858, 12mo; another edit. 1872).

[The Times, 15 Dec. 1902; Educational Record, xvi.; private information.] E. L.

CORRY, MONTAGU WILLIAM LOWRY, first Baron Rowton (1838–1903), politician and philanthropist, born in London on 8 Oct. 1838, was second son of the four children—two sons and two daughters—of Henry Thomas Lowry Corry [q. v.], a prominent member of the conservative party, by his wife Lady Harriet Ashley (*d.* 1868), second daughter of Cropley Ashley Cooper, sixth earl of Shaftesbury.

Educated at Harrow and Trinity College, Cambridge, where he graduated in 1861, Corry was called to the bar at Lincoln's Inn in 1863 and joined the Oxford circuit. He made some progress in his profession, but his personal charm and social accomplishments rendered him popular in society and social diversions occupied much of his time. He was an occasional contributor to (Sir) Algernon Borthwick's society journal called the 'Owl,' and was especially well known in fashionable conservative circles. In 1865, while a guest of the duke of Cleveland at Raby Castle, he met for the first time Disraeli, who was impressed by Corry's ingenuity and resource in saving the fortunes of what threatened to be a dull party. When Disraeli became chancellor of the exchequer in June 1866 Corry wrote reminding the statesman of their meeting, and asking his help to some political post. Disraeli replied by inviting Corry to become his private secretary. He served Disraeli in that capacity until the statesman's death. Disraeli succeeded Lord Derby as prime minister in February 1868. On his chief's retirement from office in the following December, Corry refused other offers of employment and remained with him without salary. During Disraeli's second administration, from 1874 to 1880, Corry played a prominent part in public life as the inseparable companion of his chief, who became Lord Beaconsfield in 1876. Corry attended him at the Congress of Berlin in 1878, when he acted as secretary of the special embassy and was made on his return C.B. Although other private secretaries of Lord Beaconsfield fully shared his responsibilities, Corry enjoyed a far closer intimacy with the prime minister than they. He sought no political reputation for himself. On his fall from power in 1880 Lord Beaconsfield acknowledged Corry's personal devotion by recommending him for a peerage. On 6 May 1880 he was created Baron Rowton. Corry took his title from Rowton Castle in Shropshire, the property of his aunt, Lady Charlotte Ashley, who had become possessed of it on the death of her husband, Henry Lyster, on 12 Dec. 1863. Lady Charlotte, who was childless, had already designated her nephew her heir. Lord Rowton succeeded to the estate on his aunt's death on 11 Dec. 1889. Lord Beaconsfield gave a final proof of his confidence in his secretary, who was recalled from a holiday in Algiers to his deathbed in April 1881, by leaving by will to Corry's unfettered discretion the sole responsibility for the use, treatment, and publication of his correspondence and papers. Corry examined the papers, but in private he always deprecated the writing of a life of the statesman. At any rate he felt himself unequal to the task. Although reports to the contrary were occasionally circulated, he made no attempt to grapple with it. After Rowton's death, when his responsibilities passed to Lord Beaconsfield's trustee, Lord Rothschild, the material at Lord Rowton's disposal was placed in the hands of Mr. W. F. Monypenny, and a biography of Lord Beaconsfield was prepared (vol. i. 1910, vol. ii. 1912).

Rowton after Lord Beaconsfield's death remained a prominent figure in London society and in conservative political circles, although he held no official position. Queen Victoria, whose acquaintance he made in Lord Beaconsfield's service, long consulted him confidentially on public affairs, and he was her frequent guest.

Rowton, who combined vivacity and exceptional sociability with tact, formed friendships among all classes. A serious philanthropic endeavour occupied much of his attention in his last years. In November 1889 he accepted the invitation of Sir Edward Cecil Guinness, afterwards Lord Iveagh, to become a trustee of the Guinness Trust Fund of 250,000*l.* for the provision of artisans' dwellings, 200,000*l.* to be allotted to London and 50,000*l.* to Dublin. While examining as a Guinness trustee the conditions of life in the poor districts of London, Rowton, impressed by the unhealthy and squalid character of the common lodging-houses, resolved to provide a new form of poor man's hotel, where lodging, catering, and the advantages of a club should be offered at the lowest price. The scheme lay outside the scope of the Guinness Trust, which Rowton actively administered. After consultation with his cousin, Mr. Cecil Ashley, and Sir Richard Farrant, directors of the Artisans' Dwellings Company, who warned Rowton that the hotel scheme could not prove a safe investment, he himself undertook to devote 30,000*l.* of his own money to the experiment. A site was secured in Bond Street, Vauxhall, and building was begun. Lord Rowton made himself responsible for every detail. The Vauxhall house, accommodating 447 persons, was opened on 31 Dec. 1892, and in the face of many difficulties and discouragements was organised on a satisfactory basis. The success of this first 'Rowton House' justified the extension of the enterprise, and in March 1894 a company, Rowton Houses, Limited, was incorporated with a subscribed capital of 75,000*l.*, of which 30,000*l.* in shares was allotted to Lord Rowton in return for the money he had advanced. Lord Rowton became chairman, with Sir Richard Farrant, Mr. Cecil Ashley, and Mr. Walter Long, M.P., as directors. The capital was subsequently raised to 450,000*l.* Rowton Houses were erected in King's Cross (1896), Newington Butts (1897), Hammersmith (1899), Whitechapel (1902), and Arlington Road, Camden Town (1905). The last contained 1087 beds. The total number in the six Rowton Houses exceeded 5000. The catering produced little profit, but the income derived from lodging accommodation provided a dividend. Rowton approached the problem without thought of gain, but the realisation of a profit is a tribute to his sagacity and no disparagement of his benevolent intention. Since his death the company's prosperity has been uninterrupted and Rowton Houses have been imitated in the great towns of Great Britain and in Europe and America.

Rowton was made K.C.V.O. in 1897, and was sworn of the privy council in 1900. He suffered frequent attacks of illness, and died of pneumonia at his residence in Berkeley Square, London, on 9 Nov. 1903. He was buried at Kensal Green. He was unmarried, and the peerage became extinct at his death. He left his property to Lieut.-colonel Noel Corry, grenadier guards, son of his elder brother, Armar Corry, at one time in the foreign office, who died in 1893.

Cartoon portraits by 'Spy' appeared in 'Vanity Fair' in 1877 and in 1880 (with Lord Beaconsfield).

[The Times, Daily Telegraph, and Daily News, 10 Nov. 1903; Vanity Fair, 12 Nov.; Reports of Rowton Houses, Ltd., 1895–1903; E. R. Dewsnup, The Housing Problem in England, 1907; R. H. Vetch, General Sir Andrew Clarke, 1905; private sources.]

R. L.

CORY, JOHN (1828–1910), philanthropist, coal-owner, and ship-owner, born on 28 March 1828, at Bideford, Devonshire, was eldest of five sons of Richard Cory (1799–1882) by Sarah (*d.* 5 Oct. 1868), daughter of John Woollacott, both of Bideford. The family traces descent through Walter Cory (*d.* 1530) of Cory in West Putford, Devonshire, to Sir Walter de Cory, who in the reign of King John married the eventual co-heiress of the Levingtons in Cumberland (Burke's *Peerage*, 1910, s.v. Cory). After trading for years with Cardiff in coasters, Richard Cory settled in the town about 1831, opening a ship-chandler's store, to which he soon added a shipbroking business. About 1835 he began exporting coal, first as agent and later on his own account. In 1844 his two eldest sons, John and Richard (*b.* 1830), joined him in the business, thence carried on under the name of Richard Cory & Sons, and from 1859, when the father retired, as Cory Brothers. The firm's shipping and coal-exporting business steadily increased, and the universal demand for South Wales steam coal for navigation led John Cory to conceive the idea of establishing foreign depôts in all parts, one of the earliest being established at Port Said on the opening of the Suez Canal in 1869. At the time of his death the firm had in all about eighty such depôts on the shipping routes to India, China, South Africa, and South America. About 1868 the firm had acquired its first colliery, that of Pentre, Rhondda, to which others in the same valley, and in the Ogmore and Neath valleys, were from time to time added. Large colliery interests were also acquired elsewhere. In 1883 Cory became associated with other Rhondda coal-owners in the promotion of the Barry dock and railway, in which he afterwards held a large interest, and became vice-chairman of its company. In 1888 Cory's firm was converted into a limited company, but its entire control remained in the hands of members of the family, his three sons becoming directors, and Cory himself chairman of the board.

When in 1836 teetotalism was first advocated in Cardiff, Cory's father is reputed to have been the first to sign the pledge, and he soon became the recognised leader of the movement in the town, his co-workers being nicknamed 'Coryites' (JENKINS and JAMES, *Nonconformity in Cardiff*, p. 212). Though a churchman, and for a time a churchwarden, he was led by his zeal for total abstinence to associate himself with one of the minor methodist bodies (*ibid.* p. 192), while his second son, Richard, became a baptist, and the eldest, John, a Wesleyan methodist, all three being noted for their interest in temperance and evangelical work (*ibid.* pp. 110, 150).

John Cory was one of the earliest supporters of 'General' Booth, and besides many other generous contributions to the Salvation Army, he gave it Maendy Hall at Ton Pentre, with thirty acres of land, as a home of rest. Among the many other institutions to which he gave liberally were the Band of Hope Union and Dr. Barnardo's Homes. In many seaports he established soldiers' and sailors' rests (*e.g.* at Cardiff, Barry, Milford Haven), one of the best known, built for the British and Foreign Sailors' Society (of which he was president), being the John Cory Hall in Poplar. In Cardiff he gave the police institute at a cost of 3000*l.* (besides contributing annually to its maintenance), the original Y.M.C.A. building, 6500*l.* to the University College, and gifts to Aberdare Hall (women students' hostel), 2000*l.* to the Seamen's Hospital, and large sums to the infirmary. For many years before his death his benefactions amounted to nearly 50,000*l.* a year. He was a member of the Cardiff school board for twenty-three years, and gave annually a large number of prizes for proficiency in Bible knowledge. In politics he was a liberal.

After living for some years at Vaendre Hall, near Cardiff, he acquired the manor of Dyffryn, St. Nicholas, near Cowbridge, and in 1907 began laying out part of the estate, near Peterston, as a garden village under the name of Glyn-Cory. He also converted the inn at St. Nicholas into a temperance house, with reading-rooms and mission hall. He died at Dyffryn on 27 Jan. 1910, and was buried at St. Nicholas, a memorial service, presided over by the bishop of Llandaff, being simultaneously held at Park Hall, Cardiff. By his will he left (including his reversionary bequests) about a quarter of a million sterling for charitable purposes, of which 20,000*l.* was given to the Salvation Army, one half of it to be applied to its foreign work, the other half to its home and rescue work. He also gave 5000*l.* each to the Cardiff Infirmary, the Bible Society, Spezzia Mission, and Müller's Orphanage.

In June 1906 a statue in bronze of Cory, by (Sir) W. Goscombe John, was placed in Cathays Park, Cardiff.

On 19 Sept. 1854, at St. Paul's Church, Newport, he married Anna Maria, daughter of John Beynon, colliery proprietor, of Newport, Monmouthshire. She died in August 1909, leaving by him one daughter and three sons, of whom the second, Clifford John Cory, of Llantarnam Abbey, Monmouthshire, has been liberal M.P. for the St. Ives division of Cornwall since 1906, and was made a baronet in 1907.

[South Wales Daily News, 28 Jan. 1910; The Times, 28 and 31 Jan., 2 and 4 Feb., 24 and 25 March, and 4 April 1910; for his work for sailors see the Chart and Compass (the official organ of the Brit. and For. Sailors' Society), especially the issues for Aug. 1906, p. 234, and for March and May 1910, pp. 39 and 84.] D. LL. T.

COUCH, SIR RICHARD (1817–1905), judge, only son of Richard Couch of Bermondsey, was born on 17 May 1817. After being educated privately, he entered as a student of the Middle Temple on 10 Jan. 1838, and was called to the bar on 15 Jan. 1841. In 1844 he assisted in editing Blackstone's 'Commentaries' (21st edit.). For some years he practised on what was then the Norfolk circuit, and he was recorder of Bedford from 1858 to 1862. In the last year he became a puisne judge of the high court of Bombay upon its re-establishment under the charter of 1862. Upon the retirement of Sir Matthew Sausse in 1866 he succeeded to the chief justiceship of the court and was knighted. In 1870 he succeeded Sir Barnes Peacock [q. v.] as chief justice of the high court of Calcutta. In 1875 Couch was appointed president of the commission of inquiry into the charge brought against the Gaekwar of Baroda of conspiring to poison Colonel (afterwards Sir) Robert Phayre [q. v. Suppl. I]. The Gaekwar was defended by Serjeant Ballantine [q. v. Suppl. I]. Couch and the other English commissioners found the Gaekwar guilty of instigating the crime, but the native commissioners gave in effect a verdict of 'not proven.' In the same year Couch resigned the chief justiceship. Returning to England, he was made a member of the privy council, and in January 1881 he was appointed to the judicial committee as one of the two members enjoying judicial experience in India or the colonies (Act 3 & 4 Will. IV c. 41). In that capacity Couch did valuable work for twenty years. He was not a brilliant judge, but his judgements were invariably clear and his grasp of principles enabled him to deal efficiently even with appeals from South Africa and other parts of the empire where the prevailing system of law is not English. He was elected a bencher of his inn in March 1881. He died at his residence, 25 Linden Gardens, London, W., on 29 Nov. 1905, and was buried at Paddington cemetery.

Couch married on 1 Feb. 1845 Anne (*d.* 1898), eldest daughter of Richard Thomas Beck of Combs, Suffolk, and had one son, Richard Edward, also a barrister of the Middle Temple, who predeceased him.

[The Times, 30 Nov. 1905; Men and Women of the Time, 1899; Who's Who, 1904; Foster, Men at the Bar; Law Journal, 2 Dec. 1905.] C. E. A. B.

COUPER, Sir GEORGE EBENEZER WILSON, second baronet (1824-1908), Anglo-Indian administrator, born at Halifax, Nova Scotia, on 29 April 1824, was eldest of six children of Sir George Couper, first baronet (1788-1861), then military secretary to Sir James Kempt [q. v.], the governor there, by his wife Elizabeth, daughter of Sir John Wilson [q. v.], judge of common pleas. The father was subsequently comptroller of the household and equerry to the duchess of Kent. The second son, Major-general George Kempt Couper (1827-1901), served in the Indian staff corps, and the fifth son, Henry Edward, captain 70th regiment (1835-1876), saw service in the mutiny.

After education at Sherborne and at Coombe, Surrey, Couper entered, in 1839, the Royal Military College, Sandhurst. Passing out with distinction in 1842, he was gazetted to the 15th regiment as ensign. But receiving nomination to a 'writership' in India, he went to the East India College, Haileybury, early in 1844, and joined the Bengal civil service at the close of 1846. After being stationed at Dinajpur, Eastern Bengal, he was included in the first commission sent to the Punjab upon its annexation in 1849. When only twenty-five he was assistant commissioner at Jehlam, with the powers of a collector.

Dalhousie, the 'oldest and dearest friend' of Couper's father, took a keen interest in him, and the governor-general's 'Private Letters' to the elder Couper (1910) make frequent reference to the young man's progress. In 1853 Couper went to headquarters as under-secretary to the government of India, first in the home and finance, and then in the foreign departments. On the annexation of Oudh in February 1856 he was appointed secretary at Lucknow to the chief commissioner, Sir James Outram [q. v.], whose place was taken in March 1857 by Sir Henry Lawrence [q. v.]. Through the mutiny he was with Lawrence in all encounters with the rebels up to and including the battle of Chinhut on 30 June, when his horse was wounded. He was A.D.C. as well as chief secretary to Lawrence until his death at the residency on 4 July, then to Sir John Inglis [q. v.], and finally, after the relief, to Outram. During the siege of Lucknow Couper showed tireless energy, courage, and sagacity, which were liberally acknowledged in the despatches of his chiefs (cf. Kaye's *History*; Hutchinson's *Narrative of Events in Oudh*; Dr. George Smith's *Physician and Friend*). He was the author, save for the mentions of himself, of Inglis's celebrated despatch of 26 Sept. 1857, which he reprinted with selections from his own speeches on the mutiny, for private circulation, with characteristic omission of Inglis's references to himself (1896). He also wrote the letterpress to Captain Mecham's 'Illustrations of the Siege of Lucknow' (1858). He received the medal with two clasps, and was made C.B. (civil division) in May 1860.

The governor-general, Canning, declined Outram's emphatic recommendation of Couper as his successor in the chief commissionership of Oudh (6 Jan. 1858) on the ground that Couper had been only twelve years in the service. After furlough home he went to Allahabad, in 1859, as chief secretary of the north-west provinces government. Sir Evelyn Wood, then a young officer, who visited Allahabad at the time, regarded him as the cleverest man in India (*From Midshipman to Field-Marshal*). He succeeded to the baronetcy in February 1861, and went back to Oudh as judicial commissioner in 1863. From April 1871 he acted as chief commissioner of the province, and was confirmed in the appointment in December 1873. In that office he carefully revised the land assessments, which had been hurriedly settled, and created a separate establishment to administer encumbered taluqdari estates.

On the retirement of Sir John Strachey [q. v. Suppl. II] in July 1876, Couper was made acting lieutenant-governor of the north-western provinces, while retaining his control of Oudh. The long-pending reform of partial amalgamation of Oudh with the larger province under a single head was thereby accomplished. On 17 Jan. 1877 Couper became the first 'lieutenant-governor of the north-western province and chief commissioner of Oudh.' The change was unwelcome to the taluqdars; but Couper's tact rendered the new union thoroughly successful.

Couper handled a widespread famine in 1877–8 with strict business-like efficiency. By careful conservation of provincial resources, which was occasionally censured as parsimony, he was able to initiate a policy of canal and light railway construction, and to leave accumulated balances of about a million sterling for its development by his successor, Sir Alfred Comyn Lyall [q. v. Suppl. II]. Owing to the decision of the government of India not to allow the railways to be 'provincial' undertakings, the united provinces of Agra and Oudh, as they have been named since 1901, did not reap full financial benefit from Couper's economy. But his programme of construction was closely followed. Material progress was the keynote of his policy; he developed the agricultural department, so that it became a model for other provinces; and he heartily encouraged Indian industrial enterprises, such as the 'Couper' paper mills at Lucknow. He was created K.C.S.I. and a councillor of the empire in January 1877, and C.I.E. a year later. On his retirement in April 1882 he declined, with characteristic modesty, the proposal of the Husainabad Endowment Trustees, Lucknow, to erect a statue in his memory, and as an alternative they built a clock tower.

After residing at Cheltenham for a few years Sir George settled at Camberley, where he died on 5 March 1908, being buried in St. Michael's churchyard there.

Couper married on 29 April 1852 Caroline Penelope, granddaughter of Sir Henry Every, ninth baronet, of Eggington Hall, Burton-on-Trent; she died on 28 Nov. 1910, and was buried beside her husband. By her Couper had a family of five sons and four daughters; one of the latter, who died young, was born in the Lucknow residency during the siege. The eldest son, Sir Ramsay George Henry, succeeded as third baronet.

[Kaye, Hist. of Sepoy War and other mutiny literature; minute of governor-general on services of civil officers during mutiny, 2 July 1859; Pioneer (Allahabad), 17 April 1882, 13 March 1908; The Times, 7 March 1908; Burke's Peerage; India Office List; private papers kindly lent by Sir George Couper's eldest daughter, Lady Benson, who is preparing a brief biography of her father.]

F. H. B.

COUSIN, Mrs. ANNE ROSS (1824–1906), hymn-writer, only child of David Ross Cundell, M.D., an assistant surgeon of the 33rd regiment at Waterloo, was born in Hull on 27 April 1824, her family removing soon after to Leith. Educated privately, she became an expert pianist under John Muir Wood. In 1847 she married William Cousin, minister of Chelsea presbyterian church, who was subsequently called to the Free church at Irvine, Ayrshire, and thence in 1859 to Melrose. He retired to Edinburgh in 1878 and died there in 1883. Mrs. Cousin survived him for twenty-three years, dying in Edinburgh on 6 Dec. 1906. In 1910 a stained-glass window to her memory was placed in St. Aidan's United Free church, Melrose. She had four sons and two daughters. A son, John W. Cousin, who died in December 1910, compiled 'A Biographical Dictionary of English Literature,' published in Dent's 'Everyman's Library.'

Mrs. Cousin is best known by her hymn 'The sands of time are sinking,' written at Irvine in 1854. 'I wrote it,' she said, 'as I sat at work one Saturday evening, and though I threw it off at that time, it was the result of long familiarity with the writings of Samuel Rutherford, especially his Letters.' The original was in nineteen stanzas, and appeared first in 'The Christian Treasury' in 1857, under the heading 'Last Words of Samuel Rutherford.' It did not become generally known until the Rev. Dr. J. Hood Wilson, of the Barclay church, Edinburgh, introduced a shortened version of five verses (only the fourth and fifth of which correspond with the now popular version) into a hymn book, 'Service of Praise,' prepared for his congregation in 1865. The refrain of the hymn gave the leading title to Mrs. Cousin's 'Immanuel's Land and other Pieces' (1876; second edition, revised, 1896). Next in popularity among her hymns are 'O Christ, what burdens bowed Thy head,' which Mr. Sankey eulogised as a 'Gospel hymn' that had been 'very much blessed,' and 'King Eternal! King Immortal,' which has been frequently set to music and sung at great choral festivals.

[Information from her daughter, Miss Anne P. Cousin; Julian's Dict. of Hymnology; Life of Dr. J. Hood Wilson; Duncan Campbell's Hymns and Hymn Makers; Musical Times, Jan. 1907, specially as to the tune of 'The sands of time.'] J. C. H.

COWELL, EDWARD BYLES (1826–1903), scholar and man of letters, born at Ipswich on 23 Jan. 1826, was eldest son (in a family of three sons and one daughter) of Charles Cowell, who had inherited a successful business of merchant and maltster, and as a cultured liberal was active in local affairs. His mother was Marianne, elder daughter of Nathaniel Byles Byles of the Hill House, Ipswich, also a successful merchant of that town. Cowell developed early an appetite for study. From his eighth year he attended the Ipswich grammar school. In 1841 he compiled a few numbers of 'The Ipswich Radical Magazine and Review,' in which he showed sympathy with his father's politics, combined with a singularly wide reading in classical literature. To Oriental literature he was first drawn by finding (1841) in the public library of Ipswich a copy of Sir William Jones's works, including the 'Persian Grammar' and the translation of Kālidāsa's 'Śakuntalā.' In the same year Macaulay's essay on Warren Hastings made him aware of Wilson's 'Sanskrit Grammar,' a copy of which he promptly acquired. Meanwhile he took his first steps in Persian, at first by himself, but soon with the aid of a retired Bombay officer, Major Hockley, who probably also initiated him into Arabic. As early as 1842, while still at school, he contributed to the 'Asiatic Journal' a number of verse renderings from the Persian.

On his father's death in 1842 Cowell was taken from school to be trained for the management of the business. But during the next eight years, while engaged in commerce, he read in his spare hours with extraordinary zeal and variety. Of his scholarship and width of knowledge he soon gave proof in a series of contributions to the 'Westminster Review,' writing on Oriental and Spanish literature. At the same time he formed the acquaintance of many who shared his interests, among them the Arabic and Persian scholar, William Hook Morley [q. v. Suppl. I], and Duncan Forbes [q. v.], the Persian scholar and he also called upon Carlyle in London. In 1846 he sought an introduction to 'the great professor,' Horace Hayman Wilson [q. v.], and four years later he read in the East India library and obtained a loan of a Prākrit MS. (Vararuci's 'Prākṛta-Prakāśa'), his edition of which was destined (1854) to establish his reputation as a Sanskrit scholar. Through John Charlesworth, rector of Flowton near Ipswich, whose daughter he married in 1845, he came to know Edward FitzGerald [q. v.], the most interesting of his many friends and correspondents. Their correspondence at first related chiefly to classical literature.

In 1850, the next brother being now of an age to carry on the Ipswich business, Cowell matriculated at Magdalen Hall, Oxford, going with his wife into lodgings. 'I went there [to Oxford],' he wrote later, 'a solitary student, mainly self-taught; and I learned there the method of study.' During the six years of his university life he greatly widened his social circle, receiving visits not only from FitzGerald, who now read Persian with him, but from Tennyson and Thackeray, to whom FitzGerald introduced him. He saw much of Jowett, Morfill, Max Müller, and Theodor Aufrecht, and was greatly aided by the lectures and tuition of the Sanskrit professor, H. H. Wilson. In 1854 he took a first class in literæ humaniores and an honorary fourth in mathematics. While missing the scholarship in Hebrew, he was awarded a special prize of books. The next two years were spent in coaching, chiefly in Aristotle's 'Ethics.' He also catalogued Persian and other Oriental MSS. for the Bodleian Library.

As an undergraduate he had made a reputation by his Oriental publications. A translation of Kālidāsa's 'Vikramorvaśī,' though finished earlier, was published in 1851. His admirable edition of Vararuci's 'Prākṛta-Prakāśa' followed in 1854. On taking his degree he wrote on the Persian poets for 'Fraser's Magazine,' besides contributing to 'Oxford Essays' (1855) an essay on 'Persian Literature.'

In June 1856 Cowell was appointed

professor of English history in the re-formed Presidency College, Calcutta. His post involved him in arduous work. He soon instituted an M.A. course in the Calcutta University, and extended the themes of his lectures to political economy and philosophy. In 1857 Cowell became secretary of a Vernacular Literature Society, founded with the object of providing the natives with translations of good English literature. At the same time he was more and more attracted to missionary work. He held Bible readings in his house on Sundays, and latterly a number of conversions resulted, not without some risk of offence to his Hindu connections. One of his chief Calcutta friends was William Kay [q. v.], principal of Bishop's College. Meanwhile he pursued Oriental studies untiringly. Persian continued to fascinate him. Of two copies which he procured of the MS. of Omar Khayyam belonging to the Asiatic Society at Calcutta, he sent one to FitzGerald. His own important article on Omar Khayyam appeared in the 'Calcutta Review' in March 1858. Having passed the government examinations in Hindustani and Bengali, he undertook in 1858 an additional office at Calcutta, that of principal of the Sanskrit College, a foundation of Warren Hastings. Cowell's predecessor was a native. His relations with the pundits of the college were soon intimate and affectionate. By their aid he acquired a profound familiarity with the scholastic Sanskrit literature in rhetoric and philosophy, while he stimulated the pundits' scholarly activity, and often gratified them with a prepared speech in Bengali and a Sanskrit 'Śloka.' Many native editions of works on rhetoric and poetry which were published in the 'Bibliotheca Indica,' a series issued by the Asiatic Society of Bengal, of which he became early in 1858 a joint philological secretary, express their indebtedness to Cowell. Cowell's own Sanskrit publications during this period also appeared chiefly in the 'Bibliotheca Indica.' With Dr. Roer he continued the edition of the 'Black Yajur Veda' (1858–64, vols. i. and ii.), which he afterwards carried on alone—it was ultimately finished by its fifth editor in 1899; and singly he edited two Upaniṣads, the 'Kauṣītaki' (1861) and the 'Maitrī' (1863; translation added 1870). The most important of his works at this time was his edition and translation of the 'Kusumāñjali' with the commentary of Haridāsa (Calcutta, 1864). The book, which in respect of difficulty might be compared with the 'Metaphysics' of Aristotle, supplies the Hindu proof of the existence of God. Cowell read it with Maheśa Candra, whose name he associated with his own on the title-page, and the edition was dedicated to Max Müller. He made a close study of the 'Siddhānta-Muktāvalī,' a philosophical work, which he used as a college manual and examination text-book, and of the 'Sarvadarṣanasaṃgraha,' of which he translated one chapter, relating to the Cārvāka system (*Journal of the Asiatic Society of Bengal*, 1862). He contemplated full translations of both books.

One of his last official duties in India was to visit the Tols (native quasi-colleges) at Nuddea, which were homes of pundit research and had last been inspected by Wilson in 1829. His report, published in the 'Proceedings of the Asiatic Society of Bengal' for 1867, supplies interesting details concerning the methods of this pundit university.

By the spring of 1864 the state of Cowell's health demanded a furlough. With his Oriental scholarship immensely strengthened he revisited England. His original intention of returning to India was not carried out. In the summer of 1865 he became examiner in Oriental subjects to the Civil Service Commission; in the same year he refused a curatorship at the Bodleian and in 1866 a similar position at the British Museum. Occupying himself in varied literary work, he recommenced his general reading and his epistolary and personal intercourse with FitzGerald.

In 1867 the University of Cambridge bestowed on Cowell the newly founded professorship of Sanskrit. Theodor Aufrecht was another candidate, but Cowell was warmly supported by Max Müller and many eminent scholars and friends. He was elected on a general vote of the university by ninety-six votes to thirty-seven. He published his inaugural lecture on the Sanskrit language and literature in 1867. The remainder of his life was spent at Cambridge in complete content. In 1874 he became fellow of Corpus Christi College. He retained the professorship and the fellowship until his death in 1903. During those thirty-six years his time was unstintingly given to his duties. He announced each term a formidable list of lectures, generally delivered at his own house. In accordance with a life-long habit, his private literary work occupied him before breakfast. At first he lectured not only on

Sanskrit but also on comparative philology; but of that subject he was soon relieved. As a philological lecturer he became one of the founders of the Cambridge Philological Society, with which he was connected as auditor until the close of his life, and he contributed to the early numbers of the 'Journal of Philology' (1868 seq.). In 1884 a lecturer was appointed to take charge of the more elementary Sanskrit teaching. Nevertheless, the pupils who read with Cowell were of all grades of proficiency, ranging from undergraduates grappling with their first Sanskrit play to eminent scholars (both English and foreign) eager to elucidate the various Indian philosophies, the Vedic hymns, the 'Zendavesta,' or the Pali 'Jātaka.' Alone or with his pupils Cowell issued an imposing series of Sanskrit texts and translations, of which the most important are 'The Sarva-Darśana-Saṃgraha' (translated with A. E. Gough in Trübner's 'Oriental' series, 1882); 'Divyāvadāna' (edited with R. A. Neil, Cambridge, 1886); 'The Buddha Karita of Aśvaghosha' ('Anecdota Oxoniensia,' Aryan ser. vii. 1893), with translation in 'Sacred Books of the East,' xlix. 1894; 'The Jātaka,' translated under Cowell's editorship (6 vols., Cambridge, 1895); 'The Harṣacarita of Bāna' (translated with F. W. Thomas, Oriental Translation Fund, n.s., ii. 1897).

Outside Sanskrit, Cowell still prosecuted other interests. Persian he resumed as opportunity offered. Spanish he always kept up, reading 'Don Quixote,' at first with FitzGerald, and after his death with other friends in Cambridge. His Hebrew notes were utilised by Dr. Kay in 1869 for the second edition of a translation of the Psalter, and later he studied the 'Talmud.' About 1877 he took up archæology and architecture, a new study which led him to render into English Michael Angelo's sonnets, two of which were published in the 'Life.' Welsh poetry and the science of botany had been passing fancies of Cowell's youth. During 1870–80 they were cultivated simultaneously in vacations spent in Wales, sometimes in company with the Cambridge professor of botany, C. C. Babington. The Welsh studies, which were inspired by Borrow's 'Wild Wales,' culminated in a masterly paper on the poet Dafydd ap Gwilym, read before the Cymmrodorion Society in 1878, and published in 'Y Cymmrodor' (July 1878). Cowell's MS. translation of this poet's work is in the University Library at Cambridge. Botany remained one of the chief delights of his later life, and his scientific interests extended to geology. He collected a complete flora of Cambridgeshire, and gave expression to his botanical enthusiasm in some charming sonnets.

In 1892 Cowell was prevailed upon to accept the presidency of the Arian section of the International Congress of Orientalists held in London. His inaugural address (comparing Rabbinical and Brahmanical learning) and his charming Sanskrit 'Śloka' made a very favourable impression. In 1895 he was made an honorary member of the German Oriental Society. In 1898 he was awarded the gold medal of the Royal Asiatic Society, then bestowed for the first time. Among Cowell's other distinctions were the hon. LL.D. of Edinburgh University in 1875 and the hon. D.C.L. of Oxford in 1896. In 1902 he was chosen as one of the original members of the British Academy.

Cowell's last publication was a verse translation, revised after thirty years, of some episodes from an old Bengali poem 'Candi,' which he had read at Calcutta and subsequently with Bengali students at Cambridge (*Journal As. Soc. Bengal*, 1903). Although he continued to lecture, he had long been conscious of failing powers when he died at his residence, 10 Scroope Terrace, Cambridge, on 9 Feb. 1903. He was buried at Bramford beside his wife, who was fourteen years his senior and predeceased him on 29 Sept. 1899, after fifty-five years of married life. There was no issue of the marriage. His wife's sister, Maria Louisa Charlesworth, is already noticed in this Dictionary.

During his lifetime Cowell founded a scholarship in Sanskrit at the Sanskrit College in Calcutta (1878), and endowed a prize for classics at his old school in Ipswich; by his will he devised to Corpus Christi College the sum of 1500*l.* for a scholarship in classics or mathematics, besides leaving his library for distribution between that college, the University Library, the Fitzwilliam Museum, and Girton College.

Cowell's portrait by C. E. Brock, presented to him by his friends and pupils in 1896, is in the hall of Corpus Christi College. Another painting made by a native artist from a photograph is in the library of the Sanskrit College at Calcutta.

Cowell was remarkable for the versatility of his knowledge of language and literature and for the breadth of his scholarly interests. Primarily a modest, patient, and serious savant, he was at the same time an accomplished man of letters, who excelled as an essayist, a familiar correspondent, and could write charming and thoughtful verse. An unusual tenacity and subtlety of intellect appears in his mastery of Sanskrit logic and metaphysics (Nyāya and Vedānta).

In addition to the works cited and many other contributions to periodicals and separate lectures, Cowell published: 'The Chárváka System of Philosophy' ('Journ. Asiat. Soc. Bengal,' 1862); 'The Rig-Veda Sanhitá' ('Quarterly Rev.' July 1870); Introduction to Boyd's translation of the 'Nāgānanda' (1872); 'A Short Introduction to the Ordinary Prakrit of The Sanskrit Dramas' (1875); 'A Catalogue of Buddhist Sanskrit MSS. in the possession of the Royal Asiatic Society' (with Prof. J. Eggeling, 'Journ. Roy. Asiat. Soc.' 1876); 'The Aphorisms of Śáṇḏilya, with the commentary of Swapneśwara' ('Bibliotheca Indica' 1878); 'The Tattva-muktāvalî . . . edited and translated' ('Journ. Roy. Asiat. Soc.' 1882); 'The Cātaka: Two Short Bengali Poems translated . . .' (ib. 1891).

[Life and Letters of Edward Byles Cowell, by George Cowell, 1904 (with engraved portraits and bibliography), in spite of numerous mis-spellings, a valuable biography; Edward FitzGerald's Life and Letters; The Pilot, art. by Sir Frederick Pollock, 21 Feb. 1903; memoirs in Athenæum, 14 Feb. 1903, by Cecil Bendall, reprinted in Journal Roy. Asiat. Soc. 1903, pp. 419–24; and in Proc. Brit. Acad. 1903–4, by T. W. Rhys Davids.]

F. W. T.

COWIE, WILLIAM GARDEN (1831–1902), bishop of Auckland, born in London on 8 Jan. 1831 was second son of Alexander Cowie of St. John's Wood, London, by his wife Elizabeth, daughter of Alexander Garden. Both parents came from Aberdeenshire. Admitted a pensioner of Trinity Hall, Cambridge, on 20 May 1852, and elected scholar in the following October, he was second in the first class of the law tripos in 1854 and graduated B.A. in 1855, M.A. in 1865, and D.D. in 1869. Ordained deacon in 1854 and priest in 1855, he served the curacies of St. Clement's, Cambridge (1854), and Moulton, Suffolk (1855–7). Appointed in 1857 chaplain to the forces in India, he was present at the capture of Lucknow (receiving medal and clasp) and at the battles of Aliganj, Rooyah, and Bareli; he accompanied Sir Neville Chamberlain's column in the Afghan campaign of 1863–4 (medal and clasp), and in 1864 acted as domestic and examining chaplain to G. E. L. Cotton [q. v.], bishop of Calcutta. In 1865 he was chaplain in Kashmir, and warmly supported the work of the Church Missionary Society at Srinagar. In 1867 he returned home and became rector of Stafford. In 1868 bishop G. A. Selwyn [q. v.], on his translation from the see of New Zealand to that of Lichfield, was empowered by the diocesan synod of Auckland to choose a successor for the diocese of Auckland (the title of New Zealand expiring). He nominated Cowie, who was, in 1869, consecrated bishop of Auckland in Westminster Abbey.

Cowie readily won the confidence of the settlers, diligently visiting all parts of his diocese. He fostered St. John's college, Auckland, for ordination candidates, of which he was visitor and governor, and in 1880 was made a fell w of the University of New Zealand. He found many of the Maoris alienated by the war, but conciliated these, encouraged the native ministry, and established native church boards in his northern archdeaconries. He came home for the Lambeth Conference of 1888, and in a small book, 'Our Last Year in New Zealand' (1888), he explained the conditions of his diocese and his mode of life. In 1895 he was made primate of New Zealand. He came home again for the Diamond Jubilee of Queen Victoria and the Lambeth Conference of 1897, receiving in that year the D.D. degree at Oxford. His strength failing, he resigned his see in 1902, and died shortly afterwards at Wellington, New Zealand, on 21 June.

He married in 1869 Eliza Jane, eldest daughter of William Webber of Moulton, Suffolk, and granddaughter of Sir Thomas Preston, Bart., of Beeston Hill, Norfolk. She died in New Zealand on 18 Aug. 1902.

Cowie published, in addition to the work mentioned, 'Notes on the Temples of Cashmir,' and 'A Visit to Norfolk Island.'

[The Times, 27 June 1902; Guardian, 1 Oct. 1902; E. Stock, History of the Church Missionary Society, 1899, ii. 575; Two Hundred Years of the S.P.G., p. 442; Jacob, Colonial Church Histories: New Zealand, pp. 340–1; Lowndes, Bishops of the Day; private information.]

A. R. B.

COWPER, FRANCIS THOMAS DE GREY, seventh Earl Cowper (1834–1905), lord-lieutenant of Ireland, born in Berkeley Square, London, on 11 June 1834, was eldest son of George Augustus Frederick, sixth Earl Cowper, lord-lieutenant of Kent, and of Anne Florence, elder daughter and co-heiress of Thomas Philip, second Earl de Grey and fifth Baron Lucas. Lord Cowper's mother succeeded her father as Baroness Lucas on his death in 1859. Many of his family attained distinction. His father's mother was sister of William, second Viscount Melbourne, and married Viscount Palmerston as her second husband. His uncle was William Francis Cowper (afterwards Cowper-Temple, Baron Mount-Temple) [q. v. Suppl. I]. His younger brother, Henry Frederick (1836–1887), well known for his humour and sagacity, was M.P. for Hertfordshire (1865–85). Three of his sisters married respectively Auberon Edward William Molyneux Herbert [q. v. Suppl. II]; Julian Henry Charles Fane [q. v.]; and Admiral Lord Walter Kerr.

From a preparatory school at Bembridge, Viscount Fordwich (as Lord Cowper was then called) was sent to Harrow in Sept. 1847. But the strenuous and somewhat inflexible life of a public school was not altogether suited to a boy who neither was very strong nor cared for games, and was, moreover, of a sensitive temperament; and accordingly after one and a half years he was removed by his parents and placed in a private school kept by the rector of Silsoe just outside Wrest Park, which belonged to his maternal grandfather. There he read to his heart's content, and passed on to a happy university career at Christ Church, Oxford, in 1851. He did not row or play cricket at Oxford, but was addicted to riding and shooting, and such study as 'the House' encouraged any young nobleman at that date to pursue. Early in 1855 he paid a visit to Rome with Lord Mount Edgcumbe; and, profiting by the solid historical reading which he managed to combine with social distractions there, he went in for honours on his return to the university, and obtained with ease a first class in law and history in December 1855.

He was destined for a parliamentary career; but the death of his father in 1856 deprived him of the chance of entering the House of Commons, and diverted his attention for a number of years to the less showy but useful routine of county work. In this he rendered admirable service, whether as colonel of his volunteer regiment (in which movement he was, along with Lord Elcho, afterwards Earl Wemyss, one of the original pioneers), as chairman of quarter sessions, or as lord-lieutenant of Bedfordshire—duties which he varied with sport in England and Scotland and the making of many friends. His numerous possessions also gave him wide territorial interests; for while he had inherited from his father the fine domain of Panshanger in Hertfordshire, and many titles, in 1869 he succeeded, on the death of his grandmother, Lady Palmerston, to the adjoining park and property of Brocket and a large estate in Nottinghamshire. At a later date, in 1880, the death of his own mother brought him the barony of Lucas, the Craven property in North Lancashire, a fine house in St. James's Square, and the splendid 'chateau' of Wrest in Bedfordshire. In the comparative leisure of this part of his life he also developed the taste for reading which was his main recreation, and along with it a memory which came to be the admiration of his contemporaries. In October 1870 he married Katrine Cecilia, eldest daughter of William Compton, fourth marquis of Northampton, and of Eliza, third daughter of Admiral the Hon. Sir George Elliot, and entered upon a period of domestic and social happiness. Few men possessed greater social gifts or practised them with more unselfish enjoyment.

A liberal in politics, he was made K.G. by Lord Palmerston (5 Aug. 1865). In 1871 he accepted on the recommendation of Gladstone the household office of captain of the gentlemen-at-arms, coupled with the duty of answering for the board of trade in the House of Lords. These incongruous and rather unsatisfying responsibilities he fulfilled till the end of the session in 1873. In May 1880, on Gladstone's return to power, a larger horizon opened when he accepted the prime minister's offer of the lord-lieutenancy of Ireland, with William Edward Forster [q. v.] as his chief secretary in the cabinet. Already the outlook in Ireland was clouded, and, when it was decided not to renew the Peace Preservation Act, which expired on 1 June, it speedily became worse, Parnell utilising the Land League for an agitation that speedily took effect in boycotting, in political terrorism, and presently in agrarian crime. Lord Cowper, who viewed the situation throughout with an insight and courage that were to be painfully justified by the results, was strongly in favour of an autumn session and a renewal of the Coercion Act, and Forster went over to England to press upon the cabinet the calling of parliament and the grant of extra powers. These appeals were refused by the government, and Lord Cowper, who felt more strongly on the matter than his chief secretary, and hardly thought that the latter had done full justice to his case, was only deterred from resigning by the gravity of the crisis and the persuasion of his political allies. At the beginning of the next session (Feb. 1881) the need for legislation could no longer be evaded or denied, and in March the protection of property bill and the arms bill, after parliamentary scenes of great tumult, became law. In spite of the 'message of peace' offered by Gladstone in his land bill of the same session, the ensuing autumn showed no improvement in the condition of Ireland. Parnell and several of his colleagues were arrested and imprisoned, and the Land League was suppressed (Oct.). In the course of the winter the rift between the lord-lieutenant, who had the nominal responsibility without the power of control, and his chief secretary imperceptibly widened, although in the public interest a scrupulous silence was observed; and Lord Cowper, feeling that he could no longer remain in office with satisfaction to his conscience, insisted upon resignation, which on this occasion was accepted by Gladstone (April 1882). Lord Spencer [q. v. Suppl. II] was appointed to succeed him, with a seat in the cabinet, the absence of which had been the chief stumbling-block to his predecessor. Then came the Kilmainham treaty and the release of Parnell, to which Lord Cowper's signature was appended under protest and when he was really *functus officio*. To Parnell's release Forster was not privy, and the event brought about his resignation. Lord Cowper left Dublin on 4 May, and two days later Lord Frederick Cavendish [q. v.], the new chief secretary, and Mr. Burke, the permanent under-secretary, were murdered in Phœnix Park (6 May 1882). The need for a strong Coercion Act, which had been so often and ineffectually pressed by the retiring viceroy, was universally admitted; and the draft bill prepared by him was accepted by the government and passed at once into law. Thus Lord Cowper had the melancholy satisfaction of seeing conceded to his successor the powers which had been persistently denied to himself.

Returning to England, he resumed the happy domestic existence, the local obligations, and the more tranquil public duties, for which two years of Irish tumult had given him if possible a greater zest. In his county he devoted himself to his functions as lord-lieutenant of Bedfordshire, and later on became chairman of the Hertfordshire county council. He was a frequent and facile contributor to the magazines: notably the 'Nineteenth Century,' in which a number of his articles may be found between 1883 and 1887, and to 'The Times,' which in 1885 and subsequent years printed many of his letters on public events. He spoke in the House of Lords on a great variety of subjects, but perhaps with less ease and distinction than he wrote. Among his literary contributions was the preface to the volume of Lord Melbourne's Letters edited by Mr. L. C. Sanders (1889). In 1885 he joined the Naval Volunteer Association, and spoke in the House of Lords and attended public meetings on the necessity of providing for the defence of our national harbours.

But it was when Gladstone announced his conversion to home rule and introduced the first home rule bill of 1886 that Lord Cowper's strong convictions, fortified by an exceptional experience, brought him again into the fighting line, and drew from him a series of letters and public speeches that lasted throughout the controversy, until it faded away in the defeat of the second home rule bill in 1893. He was chosen by virtue of his character quite as much as his previous official position to preside at the famous meeting at Her Majesty's Theatre in the Haymarket, London, on 14 April 1886, where he was supported on the one side by Lord Salisbury, W. H. Smith, and Mr. D. Plunket, and on the other by Lord Hartington (afterwards duke of Devonshire), George Joachim (afterwards Lord) Goschen, and the duke of Fife. In another respect his high character and personal charm enabled him to render conspicuous public service. In 1885 he presided over the Manchester Ship Canal commission. In 1886 he was asked by Lord Salisbury to undertake the chairmanship of the royal commission on the working of the Irish Land Acts of 1881 and 1885, which, after six months' hard work, reported in February 1887. He was also chairman in 1892 of the commission to create a teaching university for London.

In such capacities he continued to serve his country, although becoming, as time went on, an increasing martyr to gout, which caused him intervals of excruciating pain. Amid the ordered gardens and canals of Wrest, or in the more purely English surroundings of Panshanger, where the beauties of nature were rivalled by the masterpieces of art collected by his ancestors, he dispensed a hospitality free from ostentation, and surveyed the world with kindly but critical eye. When he passed away at Panshanger on 19 July 1905 there lingered in the minds of his contemporaries a picture of a vanishing type—the great English nobleman of high lineage and broad possessions, of chivalrous manners and noble mien, who played, without effort and with instinctive humility, an eminent part in things great and small, and moulded himself to the responsibilities of an illustrious station and name. He lies buried in Hertingfordbury churchyard outside the gates of Panshanger. A beautiful recumbent effigy was erected in the church by his widow, who survived him till 23 March 1913. There are portraits of an earlier period painted (kitcat size) by G. F. Watts, R.A., at Panshanger; by Lord Leighton, P.R.A., at Wrest Park; and by Ellis Roberts (three-quarters length) at Panshanger.

Lord Cowper left no children, and his numerous estates were divided upon his death. Of his many titles the earldom of Cowper with the viscounty of Fordwich, the barony of Cowper, and the baronetcy became extinct. He had been declared on 15 Aug. 1871 to have inherited as heir general to Thomas Butler, earl of Ossory, whose attainder of 1715 was reversed in July 1871, the English barony of Butler and the Scottish barony of Dingwall. The barony of Butler went into abeyance between Lord Cowper's sisters and their heirs. The barony of Lucas, which he derived from his mother, passed together with the Scottish barony of Dingwall to his nephew and heir-general, Auberon Thomas Herbert, son of his second sister.

[Hansard's Debates; Morley's Life of Gladstone, 1903, vol. iii.; Herbert Paul's History of Modern England, 1905, vols. iv. and v.; personal recollections; The Times, 20 July 1905 and passim.] C. of K.

COX, GEORGE (called Sir GEORGE) WILLIAM (1827–1902), historical writer, born at Benares on 10 Jan. 1827, was eldest son of the six children of Captain George Hamilton Cox (*d.* 1841), of the East India Company's service, and Eliza Kearton, daughter of John Horne, planter, of St. Vincent in the West Indies. A brother, Colonel Edmund Henry Cox of the royal marine artillery, fired the first shot against Sevastopol in the Crimean war. Sent to England in 1836, Cox attended a preparatory school at Bath and the grammar school, Ilminster. In August 1842 he was admitted to Rugby under A. C. Tait [q. v.]. In 1843 Cox won the senior school scholarship at Rugby, and in 1845 he was elected scholar of Trinity College, Oxford. Although he obtained only a second class in the final classical school in 1848, his scholarship was commended by the examiners. He both graduated B.A. and proceeded M.A. in 1859. The Oxford movement excited Cox's sympathy, and in 1850 he was ordained by Dr. Wilberforce, bishop of Oxford. After serving a curacy at Salcombe Regis, he resigned owing to ill-health, and in 1851 accepted the post of English chaplain at Gibraltar. But Cox's high church views, which coloured his 'Life of Boniface' in 1853, met with the disapproval of his bishop, Dr. Tomlinson, and he gladly embraced the opportunity of accompanying John William Colenso [q. v.] on his first visit to South Africa as bishop of Natal (1853–4). On his return to England he became curate of St. Paul's, Exeter, in 1854 and for a year (1859–60) he was a master at Cheltenham.

Meanwhile Cox's religious principles completely changed, largely under the influence of historical study. An article in the 'Edinburgh Review' (January 1858) on Milman's 'History of Latin Christianity' illustrates the development of his views on broad church lines. He ardently supported Bishop Colenso in his stand for liberal criticism of the scriptures and in his struggle over his episcopal status in South Africa. He defended Colenso in a long correspondence with F. D. Maurice [q. v.], and warmly supported the bishop during his sojourn in England (1863–5). Cox's association with Colenso gave him abundant material for his life of the bishop, which he published in 1888. In the same year he issued a last vindication of Colenso, in 'The Church of England and the Teaching of Bishop Colenso,' maintaining Colenso's loyalty to the church.

Throughout his life Cox was largely occupied by literary or historical work of varied kinds. His earliest volume, 'Poems Legendary and Historical' (1850), was written in collaboration with his friend E. A. Freeman [q. v. Suppl. I]. From 1861 to 1885 he was literary adviser to Messrs. Longmans & Co., and for many years he was engaged in writing historical works of popular character. These included 'The Great Persian War' (1861), 'Latin and Teutonic Christendom' (1870), 'The Crusades' (1874), 'The Greeks and the Persians' (1876), 'The Athenian Empire' (1876), 'History of the Establishment of British Rule in India' (1881), 'Lives of Greek Statesmen' (2 vols. 1886), 'A Concise History of England' (1887). His most elaborate work was a well-written 'History of Greece' (2 vols. 1874), which, largely based on Grote, has long since been superseded. He showed to best advantage in the study of mythology, where he followed Max Müller with some independence. His 'Tales from Greek Mythology' (1861), 'A Manual of Mythology' (1867), 'The Mythology of the Aryan Nations' (1870; new edit. 1882), and 'An Introduction to the Science of Comparative Mythology' (1881), all enjoyed a wide vogue, although they pressed to extravagant limits the solar and nebular theory of the origin of myths. He was a frequent contributor to the leading reviews, and joint editor with William Thomas Brande [q. v.] of the 'Dictionary of Science, Literature, and Art' (3 vols. 1865–7; new edit. 1875).

In 1877 Cox claimed to succeed to the baronetcy of Cox of Dunmanway, which had been granted to Sir Richard Cox [q. v.] in 1706. He believed himself to be the heir male of William the eighth son of the first baronet. On the death in 1873 of a distant cousin, Sir Francis Hawtrey Cox, the twelfth baronet, the title had been treated by the Ulster office of arms as extinct. Nevertheless it was then assumed by Cox's uncle, Colonel (Sir) Edmund Cox, on whose death in 1877 Cox adopted the titular prefix. His right to the dignity was disallowed after his death by a committee of the privy council on 9 Nov. 1911, when his son and heir, Mr. Edmund Charles Cox, petitioned for recognition as a baronet. The petition was opposed by one who asserted descent from the eldest son of the first baronet.

In 1880 Cox was appointed vicar of Bekesbourne by A. C. Tait, archbishop of Canterbury, and from 1881 to 1897 he was rector of the crown living of Scrayingham, Yorkshire. In 1886 he was chosen bishop of Natal by the adherents of Colenso, but was refused consecration by Archbishop Benson owing to his election being unacceptable to the high church party (A. C. Benson, *Life of Edward White Benson*, 1899, p. 500). On 18 May 1896 he received a civil list pension of 120*l*. He died at Ivy House, Walmer, on 9 Feb. 1902. His ashes were buried after cremation at Long Cross, Chertsey. Cox married in 1850 Emily Maria, daughter of Lieutenant-colonel W. Stirling (*d.* 1898) of the East India Company's service. He had five sons and two daughters. His eldest surviving son, Edmund Charles Cox, at the time district superintendent of police at Poona, was the unsuccessful claimant to the baronetcy.

[The Times, 11 Feb. 1902; Sir Frederick Maurice, Life of F. D. Maurice, 1884, ii. 449; Dean Stephens, Life of Edward A. Freeman, 1895, i. 84, 128; Men of the Time, 1899; Foster's Baronetage, Chaos, 1882; Public Men at Home and Abroad; private information.]

G. S. W.

CRAIG, ISA, poetical writer. [See Knox, Mrs. Isa (1831–1903).]

CRAIG, WILLIAM JAMES (1843–1906), editor of Shakespeare, born on 6 Nov. 1843 at Camus juxta Bann, known also as Macosquin, co. Derry, was second son of George Craig (1800–1888), who was then curate of that place and from 1853 till his retirement in 1880 was rector of Aghanloo in the same county. Craig's mother was Mary Catherine Sandys (1803–1879), daughter of Charles Brett of Belfast and of Charleville, co. Down.

After attending Portora School, Enniskillen, Craig entered Trinity College, Dublin, as a pensioner on 1 July 1861, and graduated B.A. in 1865 as junior moderator with silver medal in history and English literature, proceeding M.A. in 1870. From his undergraduate days he devoted himself with enthusiasm to English study, and was a pedestrian of unusual endurance. After graduating, he acted as private tutor in history and literature at Trinity, and in 1874 he migrated to London to engage in private coaching for the army and civil service. In 1876 he was appointed professor of English language and literature at University College, Aberystwyth. A Shakespeare reading class, which he instituted there, did much to stimulate a knowledge of the dramatist's work, and he infected his pupils, who included Thomas Edward Ellis (afterwards M.P. for Merionethshire) and Sir Samuel Evans (afterwards president of the probate and divorce division of the high court), with something of his own eager literary zeal. He resigned his professorship in 1879 to resume coaching in London. Save during 1884, when he was tutor at Hatfield to Lord Hugh Cecil, youngest son of the marquis of Salisbury, he was continuously employed in private tuition in London till 1898.

From that year till his death Craig confined his energies to philological and literary research, frequently reading at the British Museum. He had already published in 1883, for the New Shakspere Society, a minute collation of the first folio text of 'Cymbeline' with the later folios. There followed in 1894 a one-volume edition of Shakespeare's complete works with a brief glossary for the Clarendon Press at Oxford. This edition, known as 'The Oxford Shakespeare,' has since been reprinted in many forms. While still engaged in teaching he had been collecting materials for a comprehensive glossary of Shakespeare, and after his retirement he added to his material a vast mass of illustrative quotations from Elizabethan authors. But he left his collections in too incomplete a condition to allow of publication. He succeeded, however, in completing, for Messrs. Methuen & Co., 'The Little Quarto Shakespeare' with introductions and foot-notes (40 vols. 1901–1904), and from 1901 he acted as general editor in succession to his friend, Professor Edward Dowden, of the 'Arden Shakespeare,' also in 40 vols., an edition fully annotated by various scholars. To the 'Arden Shakespeare' Craig contributed the volume on 'King Lear' (1901), an admirably thorough piece of work, and he was preparing the volume on 'Coriolanus' at his death.

Craig, who was a popular member of the Savage Club, combined broad sympathies with his scholarly interests and his love of poetry. To the last he was a sturdy walker, and although an unmethodical worker spared himself no pains in his editorial efforts. He died, unmarried, in a nursing home in London, after an operation, on 12 Dec. 1906, and was buried in Reigate churchyard. Several hundred volumes from his library were presented by his sister, Mrs. Merrick Head, to the public library at Stratford-on-Avon, where they are kept together in a suitably inscribed bookcase. His portrait was painted in 1904 by Alfred Wolmark.

[The Times, 18 Dec. 1906, by present writer; Spectator, 5 Jan. 1907, by S. L. Gwynn, M.P.; Shakespeare Jahrbuch (Weimar), 1907; private information and personal knowledge.]

S. L.

CRAIGIE, Mrs. PEARL MARY TERESA (1867–1906), novelist and dramatist, writing under the pseudonym of John Oliver Hobbes, born at Chelsea, near Boston, Massachusetts, on 3 Nov. 1867, was eldest child in a family of three sons and two daughters of Mr. John Morgan Richards, a merchant of New York. Her mother was Laura Hortense, fourth daughter of Seth Harris Arnold of Chelsea, Massachusetts. The father was summoned to London within a week of the child's birth to conduct a manufacturing chemist's business there. Mother and daughter joined him in February 1868. London remained Pearl's home for life, though she was proud of her American origin and often revisited America. In London her parents resided successively at Kennington, Bloomsbury, and Bayswater. From 1872 she chiefly spent the summer with her parents in the Isle of Wight, at Ventnor, whither she constantly retired for purposes of work in later years.

Pearl was educated at the Misses Godwin's boarding school at Newbury, Berkshire (1876–7), and subsequently at private day schools in London. A lively child, fond of story-telling and story-writing, she read widely for herself. Her parents regularly attended the services at the City Temple of the congregational preacher Joseph Parker [q. v. Suppl. II], and Parker, who became a close family friend, first encouraged the girl to pursue literary composition. He accepted stories from her at the age of nine for his newspaper 'The Fountain.' During 1885 she studied music in Paris and became an accomplished pianist. In November 1886 she visited America, and on her return in February 1887 she married in London, when little more than nineteen, Mr. Reginald Walpole Craigie.

The unhappiness of her wedded life profoundly affected her career and temperament. A son, John Churchill Craigie, was born to her at Rock Cottage, Ventnor, on 15 Aug. 1890, but in the following spring she left her husband for good. Emotional suffering working on a mind of a mystical cast impelled her after due reflection to join the Roman catholic church. She was admitted in London on 5 July 1892, taking the additional Christian names of 'Mary Teresa.' She was regular in the observances of her new faith, in which she found spiritual solace, although it failed to silence all spiritual questionings. In July 1895 she was granted on her petition a divorce from Mr. Craigie with the exclusive custody of their child. The public trial occasioned her acute distress.

During her early married life Mrs. Craigie decided to adopt the literary profession. For a weekly periodical, 'Life,' she wrote the dramatic and art criticism as well as a series of articles 'The Note-book of a Diner-out, by Diogenes Pessimus,' which showed a cynical vein of humour. But as her domestic sorrows increased, she grew ambitious of accomplishing more serious work and began a varied preliminary course of study. With a private tutor she worked at mathematics, and then on her separation from her husband she entered University College, London, chiefly devoting herself to Greek, Latin, and English literature. Her teachers were impressed by her promise and eager interest.

In 1891 she published in Mr. Fisher Unwin's 'Pseudonym Library' her first book, 'Some Emotions and a Moral.' The epigrammatic style and lightly cynical flavour ensured a popular success. In England alone 6000 copies were sold within a year, and over 40,000 in her lifetime. In this volume Mrs. Craigie first adopted the pseudonym of John Oliver Hobbes, to which she adhered throughout her career. It was a combination of her father and son's name of John, of Cromwell's Christian name, and of the homely surname of the great philosopher whose severe dialectic she admired. In May 1892 there followed her second book of like texture, 'The Sinner's Comedy,' which was sketched, she wrote, 'under the strain of unspeakable grief and anxiety.' Thenceforth Mrs. Craigie wrote incessantly. 'A Study in Temptations' (1893), 'A Bundle of Life' (1894), and 'The Gods, Some Mortals, and Lord Wickenham' (1895), which ran serially through the 'Pall Mall Budget,' failed to win the popularity of her first volume, whilst 'The Herb Moon: a Fantasia' (1896) was a comparative failure. Yet collectively these novels established her position as a brilliant observer and critic of current social life.

At her father's house she gathered round her a large literary and musical circle, and was a welcome figure in fashionable London society. She frequented theatres and concert rooms and took an active part in philanthropic and literary movements, serving as president of the Society of Women Journalists in 1895–6. Despite weak health her energy seemed inexhaustible, but her occasional withdrawal for religious meditation to the Convent of the Assumption in Kensington Square apparently provided her with adequate rest.

Friends encouraged a wish to try her fortune in drama, and under the influence of the modern French theatre she assiduously sought the suffrages of English playgoers with varying results. Her 'Journeys end in Lovers meeting,' a 'one-act proverb,' was produced at Daly's Theatre (June 1895) with Miss Ellen Terry, Mr. Forbes Robertson, and William Terriss in the three parts; it was first printed in 'Tales about Temperaments' (1901). The theme of a comedy which she next planned for Sir Henry Irving failed to attract the actor, and she converted the draft into a novel, 'The School for Saints' (1897), which proved a more serious effort in psychology than she had yet essayed. But her zeal for drama was undiminished. To her gratification, 'The Ambassador,' a comedy by her in four acts, was produced by (Sir) George Alexander at St. James's Theatre on 2 June 1898, and ran through the season. Witty dialogue atoned for the slenderness and some incoherence in the plot and characterisation. In the same year she finished a more serious dramatic effort, 'Osbern and Ursyne,' a tragedy in verse, which was first published in Lady Randolph Churchill's 'Anglo-Saxon Review.' In 1899 (Sir) George Alexander produced 'A Repentance,' a vague dramatic study of character which was based on an incident in the Carlist wars, and was ill received. Another rebuff attended the production of her comedy 'The Wisdom of the Wise,' which came out at St. James's Theatre on 22 Nov. 1900. Her next effort, 'The Bishop's Move,' in which Murray Carson collaborated, was produced with popular acceptance at the Garrick Theatre (1902), Mr. Arthur Bourchier and Miss Violet Vanbrugh assuming the chief rôles. But the success proved fleeting. A fanciful drama in four acts, 'The Flute of Pan,' after successful production by Miss Olga Nethersole at the Queen's Theatre, Manchester, on 21 April 1904, was unfavourably received at the first London performance at the Shaftesbury Theatre on 12 Nov. 1904. The play was quickly withdrawn and Mrs. Craigie converted it into a novel.

Meanwhile Mrs. Craigie was very busy in many other directions. She pursued her earlier path in fiction in 'The Serious Wooing' (1901) and 'Love and the Soul Hunters' (1902). In 'Robert Orange,' a novel which appeared in July 1902, she ingeniously elaborated the psychological study which she began in 'The School for Saints.' The hero, Robert Orange, was a deliberately idealised portrait of Disraeli, in whose career and character she developed an intense interest. The statesman also figured in the book under his own name in his historical guise. 'The Vineyard,' her penultimate novel, ran serially through the 'Pall Mall Magazine' and was issued independently in 1904. She was then at work on her final novel, 'The Dream and the Business' (issued in August 1906), in which she contrasted the Roman catholic with the nonconformist temper of mind.

Requests for sketches or essays at the same time were growing. Travelling constantly for pleasure, rest, or the local colour of her novels and plays, she repeatedly described such experiences in the press. Among her most intimate friends was Miss Mary Leiter of Washington, who married Lord Curzon in 1895. At the Delhi durbar in January 1903 she was the guest of Lord and Lady Curzon, and she narrated the incidents of the pageantry in letters to the London 'Daily Graphic' and 'Collier's Weekly' of New York, which were collected as 'Imperial India' in 1903. To the 'Academy,' the ownership of which her father acquired in 1896, she contributed in a very different style during 1903 a series of thoughtful essays, 'Letters from a Silent Study' (republished in 1904). Her critical power was seen to best advantage in an admirable notice of George Eliot written in 1901 for the 10th edition of the 'Encyclopædia Britannica,' and in a critical essay on George Sand prepared for a series of English translations of French novels edited by Mr. Edmund Gosse (1902). At the end of 1905 she undertook a lecture tour in America, where her popularity ran high, but she overtaxed her strength and abandoned the tour in Feb. 1906.

In England, where she lately found her chief recreation in motor tours, she mainly divided her time between her father's residences, 56 Lancaster Gate, London, and Steephill Castle, Ventnor. Since 1900 she rented near Steephill Castle a small house, St. Lawrence Lodge, where she wrote much. On Sunday 12 Aug. 1906 she left Ventnor for her London home. The next morning she was found dead in bed of cardiac failure. Her will directed that her body should be cremated; but cremation was forbidden by the Roman church, and she was buried in St. Mary's cemetery, Kensal Green, after a requiem mass at the church of the Jesuit fathers in Farm Street. Her gross personalty was proved at 24,502*l.* 8*s.*, but the net personalty only amounted to 975*l.* 3*s.* 11*d.* (*The Times*, 26 Sept. 1906).

Mrs. Craigie wrote that she lived two lives in one. Her worldly delight in social pleasures and activities seemed to be combined with a mystical conviction of their hollowness and futility. In spite of marked business aptitudes and a capacity to make money, she spent more than she could afford, and failed to husband her resources. With her sincere devotion to the creed of her adoption, there went a deep despondency which colours much of her intimate correspondence and is in painful contrast with her vivacity in social intercourse. Her sensitiveness to criticism and her eagerness to defend her work at all hazards against public censure are hard to reconcile with her claim to be treated as an idealist. Such inconsistencies were doubtless due in part to uncertain health and the shock of her unhappy marriage, but mainly to intellectual instability and impulsive emotion. Well acquainted with French and Italian, and widely read in philosophy and theology as well as in fiction and belles lettres, she was more ambitious of the reputation of a serious thinker than of a witty novelist. Her philosophic ideas are, however, too dim and elusive to be quite intelligible; her psychological insight, although fitfully luminous, lacked a steady glow, while her plots were too often without adequate coherence. But her command of epigram—humorous, caustic, and cynical—gives her work high value, and her style, which owes much to her literary heroes, Newman, Disraeli, George Meredith, and George Eliot, is notable for its vivid picturesqueness.

An oil painting by Miss L. Stacpoole in 1885, which is reproduced in the 'Life' (1911), belongs to her family. A portrait plaque in bronze was placed by her friends in University College, London, being unveiled by Lord Curzon of Kedleston on 2 July 1908. A replica was presented to Barnard College, New York. A John Oliver Hobbes scholarship for English literature was founded at University College at the same time. After her death her house at Ventnor was purchased by her father and renamed 'Craigie Lodge.'

[The Life of John Oliver Hobbes, told in her correspondence, with biogr. sketch by her father, John Morgan Richards, and introd. by Bishop Welldon (with portraits), 1911; The Times, 14 Aug. 1906; William Archer, Real Conversations, 1904; personal knowledge.]

S. L.

CRANBROOK, first Earl of. [See Gathorne-Hardy, Gathorne (1814–1906).]

CRAVEN, HAWES (1837–1910), scene-painter, whose full name was Henry Hawes Craven Green, was born at Kirkgate, Leeds, on 3 July 1837. His father, James Green (*d.* 1881), at first a publican of Leeds and amateur pugilist, became known as a comedian and pantomimist. His mother, Elizabeth Craven, was an actress, who left the stage, and published several volumes of prose and verse. As a boy young Craven acted with his father on tour, but early evincing an artistic bent, attended the school of design at Marlborough House (1851–3), where he won numerous prizes. Apprenticed in 1853 to John Gray, scene-painter of the Britannia Theatre, Hoxton, he passed with him to the Olympic Theatre, and provided in his absence through illness the scenery for Wilkie Collins's drama 'The Lighthouse' (23 July 1857). His work won the approval of Clarkson Stanfield [q. v.], who had painted the scenery, when the piece was originally produced by Charles Dickens and other amateurs. Subsequently Craven worked with William Roxby Beverley [q. v. Suppl. I] at Drury Lane and Covent Garden. From 1862 to 1864 he was principal scene-painter at the Theatre Royal, Dublin, where, according to Mr. Percy Fitzgerald, an eye-witness, his work possessed all 'the breadth and effect of rich water-colour drawings somewhat of the Prout school.' In the summer vacation of 1863 and again in 1864 he worked for Fechter at the Lyceum on some elaborate set scenes, after the new mode of mounting plays which Fechter inaugurated.

From Dublin Craven passed successively to the Olympic (under Horace Wigan), where he distinguished himself by his scenery for 'The Frozen Deep' (October 1864), and to the Adelphi (under Benjamin Webster). He soon increased his reputation by his work for 'Play' and 'School,' both produced at the Prince of Wales's Theatre (15 Feb. 1868, and Jan. 1869), and by 'The Enchanted Isle' in the Covent Garden pantomime of 'Robinson Crusoe' (December 1868).

In 1871 Craven joined H. L. Bateman [q. v.] at the Lyceum, but his opportunities were restricted, until Henry Irving became lessee and manager in 1878. Inexpensive as Irving's opening production of 'Hamlet' (30 December 1878) was, Craven's scenery was notable for its construction and deft mechanical arrangement. In succeeding years Craven, harmoniously co-operating with Irving, carried scenic realism and stage illusion to the full limit of legitimate artistic expression, and he turned to advantage the newly introduced electric lighting, which compelled a readjustment of old methods of distemper painting. Among his early triumphs at the Lyceum was his grandiose interior of the Temple of Artemis in 'The Cup' (3 Jan. 1881), from a design by Sir James Knowles. In 'Romeo and Juliet' (8 March 1882) he gave the effect of the clear blue Italian sky by using a new pigment of his own invention. For his scenes in Irving's production of 'Faust' (19 Dec. 1886) he visited Nuremberg and the Hartz mountains with admirable results. Sound work followed for 'Macbeth' (December 1888), 'King Henry VIII' (January 1892), 'King Lear' (10 Nov.), Tennyson's 'Becket' (February 1893), 'King Arthur' under Burne-Jones's direction (January 1895), and finally for 'Coriolanus' from the designs of Sir Lawrence Alma-Tadema (15 April 1902), when Craven's long association with Irving closed.

Meanwhile London scene-painters had ceased to be salaried employés of the theatre, and Craven worked on contract for Irving, who employed other scenic artists along with him. But he rented the Lyceum scene-loft for his studio, and there he painted for many managers in addition. For the Savoy Theatre he worked on the 'Mikado' (14 March 1885) and 'Utopia, Limited' (7 Oct. 1893). For (Sir) Herbert Beerbohm Tree at Her Majesty's he provided scenes for 'King John' (29 Sept. 1899), 'Twelfth Night' (February 1901), and Mr. Stephen Phillips's 'Ulysses' (February 1902). In September 1902 he painted two scenes for the revival of 'As you Like It' at the Prince's Theatre, Manchester. His last work of note was done for Mr. Bourchier's revival of 'The Merchant of Venice' at the Garrick (October 1905). In the same year he was elected president of the Scenic Artists' Association.

Craven died at his residence, Fairlight, 246 Brockley Road, S.E., on 22 July 1910, and was buried at Brockley. By his marriage in 1866 with Maria Elizabeth Watson Lees (1838–1891), a première danseuse, he left three sons and three daughters. Mr. Alfred E. Craven, the second eldest surviving son, was for sixteen years his father's pupil-assistant and partner.

Craven was probably the greatest scene-painter of his century. The equal of Stanfield and Beverley in craftsmanship and imagination, he excelled both in the capacity to adapt his knowledge to the needs of the stage. As scenic innovator he ranks with Loutherbourg. He was the first to demonstrate that tones thrown upon the scene by phantasmagoric lights are subtler in atmospheric effect than tones wholly expressed by paint on canvas. He painted his Lyceum scenery with a view to the particular kind of light it was to bear. He excelled in landscape, and, in Ellen Terry's words, 'could paint the flicker of golden sunshine for the stage better than anyone.'

[The Bancroft Memoirs, 1909; Percy Fitzgerald's Sir Henry Irving, 1895; Alfred Darbyshire's The Art of the Victorian Stage, 1907; Joseph Hatton's The Lyceum Faust, 1886; Journal of the Society of Arts, 1887, vol. xxxv. No. 1791; Bram Stoker's Sir Henry Irving, 1907; Magazine of Art, Jan. 1889; Scottish Art Review, Feb. 1889; Idler, March 1893; Architectural Review, July

1901; Era, 8 Oct. 1904; Manchester Guardian, 27 July 1910; Stage and Dublin Evening Telegraph, 28 July 1910; private information.]

CRAVEN, HENRY THORNTON, whose real name was HENRY THORNTON, (1818–1905), dramatist and actor, born in Great Poland Street, London, on 26 Feb. 1818, was son of Robert Thornton, a schoolmaster in Holborn. Starting life as a publisher's clerk in Paternoster Row, Henry subsequently acted as amanuensis to Bulwer Lytton, and began writing for 'Bentley's Miscellany.' Ambitious to become a dramatist, he took to the stage, making his first appearance at York in 1840 and his London début soon after at Fanny Kelly's theatre, Dean Street, Soho. In 1841 he was acting on the Sunderland circuit, and in 1842 his first play, 'Bertram the Avenger,' was produced at North Shields. Craven produced his second play, 'Miserrimus,' at Portsmouth late in 1843. In the spring of 1844 he joined the Keeleys at the Lyceum, and after both acting and writing for the stage of the smaller theatres he was in 1850 engaged at Drury Lane, where, on the occasion of Macready's farewell on 28 Feb. 1851, he played Malcolm to the tragedian's Macbeth. On 12 June following his operetta, 'The Village Nightingale' was produced at the Strand, with himself in one of the characters. Eliza (1827–1908), daughter of Sydney Nelson [q. v.], the composer, took the leading female rôle. In November 1851 the two were engaged by Lloyd of Edinburgh for the Theatre Royal stock company, Craven as principal stage director. In that city they were married on 12 May 1852 and simultaneously transferred their services to the Adelphi.

In October 1854 Mr. and Mrs. Craven landed at Sydney, where they fulfilled a successful engagement at the Victoria Theatre. In partnership with the actor W. H. Stephens, Craven then built the little Lyceum Theatre in the same city, which they opened in 1855. In April 1857 Mr. and Mrs. Craven appeared at the Theatre Royal, Melbourne, in several of Craven's own pieces. No marked success either as dramatist or actor attended his reappearance in London. His first notable success as a dramatist came when Robson produced and played in Craven's domestic drama, 'The Chimney Corner,' at the Olympic on 21 Feb. 1861. For Robson, Craven also designed the title-character in 'Milky White,' which was first produced at the Prince of Wales's, Liverpool, on 20 June 1864. Robson's sudden death altered Craven's plans (6 Aug. 1864), and he himself sustained the title-rôle when the piece was brought out at the Strand on 28 Sept. following. 'Milky White' enjoyed a run and a revival at the Strand and was subsequently popular in the provinces. In the dual rôle of actor and dramatist Craven scored again at the new Royalty on 17 Oct. 1866, when 'Meg's Diversion' was produced, with himself as Jasper, the play running 330 nights. In 1873 he made his last provincial tour. His last play, an historical drama, 'Too True,' was produced at the Duke's on 22 Jan. 1876, and in this he made his final appearance on the stage.

Craven was a capable writer of rural domestic drama, but his incident was illogically theatrical, and like most actor-playwrights he relied on puns and catch-phrases to raise a laugh. As an actor he imitated Robson. Many of his numerous plays were published by Duncombe, Lacy, and French. In 1876 he published a novel, 'The Old Tune.'

Craven died at his residence, Thorntonville, Clapham Park, on 13 April 1905, and his widow at Eastbourne on 20 March 1908. Both are buried in Norwood cemetery. Two of their four children survived them, a daughter and a son, Mr. Tom Sidney Craven (*b.* 1864), dramatist and actor.

[Pascoe's Dramatic List; Dibdin's Annals of the Edinburgh Stage; W. Davenport Adams's Dict. of the Drama; Henry Morley's Journal of a London Playgoer; Lawrence's Life of G. V. Brooke; Brit. Mus. Cat.; Michael Williams's Some London Theatres; Dramatists of the Present Day, 1871; Joseph Knight's Theatrical Notes; Daily Telegraph, 14 April 1905; private information.]

CRAWFURD, OSWALD JOHN FREDERICK (1834–1909), author, born at Wilton Crescent, London, on 18 March 1834, was son of John Crawfurd [q. v.], diplomatist, by his wife Horatia Ann (*d.* 1855), daughter of James Perry, editor of the 'Morning Chronicle,' and god-daughter of Lord Nelson. Educated at Eton, he matriculated at Merton College, Oxford, in 1854, but left the university without a degree. Nominated on 12 Jan., and appointed, after examination, on 23 Jan. 1857, to a junior clerkship in the foreign office, he was sent in April 1866 as acting consul to Oporto. He became consul there on 13 Jan. 1867, and filled the post efficiently for the next twenty-four years. On 1 Jan. 1890 he was made C.M.G. While at Oporto he spent his leisure in sport and literary work. In addition to several novels he published three sympathetic but sketchy studies of Portuguese life, which are of interest for their accounts of the Portuguese rustic and of country sports in Portugal: 'Travels in Portugal,' under the pseudonym John Latouche (1875; 3rd edit. 1878), 'Portugal Old and New' (1880; 2nd edit. 1882), and 'Round the Calendar in Portugal' (1890). Crawfurd's last two years (1890–1) in Portugal were of exceptional difficulty. An ultimatum from Lord Salisbury (Jan. 1890), the result of the occupation by Portuguese troops of British territory in East Africa, led to an outburst of anti-British feeling, more violent in Oporto than in other Portuguese towns. Crawfurd's house was stoned, but he carried on his duties till the trouble subsided, and then on 17 June 1891 resigned. Returning to England, he devoted himself entirely to literature. He died at Montreux on 31 Jan. 1909.

Crawfurd married (1) Margaret (*d.* 1899), younger daughter of Richard Ford [q. v.], author of the 'Handbook to Spain,' by whom he had one son who died in infancy; (2) in 1902, Lita Browne, daughter of Hermann von Flesch Brunningen. His second wife survived him.

Although literature was for Crawfurd merely a recreation, his literary activity was many-sided. A novelist, an essayist, a poet, and an anthologist, he was also a frequent contributor under his own name and under pseudonyms to 'The Times' and leading reviews; he edited for some years the 'New Quarterly Magazine' (1873) and 'Chapman's Magazine of Fiction' (1895, &c.), and had some experience of publishing, being an original director of 'Black and White,' founded in 1891, and, through his friendship with Frederic Chapman [q. v. Suppl. I], a director and then managing director of Chapman & Hall, Limited—a post for which he lacked qualification. Of his novels 'Sylvia Arden' (1877) was the best known. In others like 'The World we Live In' (1884), 'In Green Fields' (1906), and 'The Mystery of Myrtle Cottage' (1908), he discussed political and social questions. His plays, 'Two Masques' (1902) and 'The Sin of Prince Eladane' (1903), are marked by a studied choice of diction and some capacity for verse, but lack dramatic quality. Crawfurd also compiled 'Laws of Opposition Bridge' (1906).

[The Times, 2 Feb. 1909; Athenæum, 4 Feb. 1909; Allibone's Dict. of Eng. Lit., 1891; Foreign Office List, 1900; Black and White, 5 Feb. 1909; Who's Who, 1908; private information.] S. E. F.

CREAGH, WILLIAM (1828–1901), major-general and administrator, born at Newry, co. Down, on 1 June 1828, was second son of the seven children of General Sir Michael Creagh, K.H. (1787–1860), and Elizabeth, only daughter of Charles Osborne, judge of the King's Bench, Ireland, and niece of Sir Thomas Osborne, eighth baronet, of Newtown Anner, co. Tipperary. He came of an old Roman catholic family, and his father, who entered the army at the age of fourteen, saw much service with the 86th regiment, and was at his death in 1860 colonel commandant of the 73rd regiment; he was the first to become a protestant. His eldest brother, General Charles Creagh-Osborne, C.B. (*d.* 1892), after service in India, was commandant of the staff college, Camberley, 1878–86; his youngest brother, Major James Henry Creagh (*d.* 1900), served in the 27th regiment during the mutiny, and retired owing to illness then contracted.

William Creagh attended for six years Mr. Flynn's private school in Dublin. After instruction at Sandhurst (Jan. 1842–Dec. 1844) he became a cadet in the East India Company's service, and joined his regiment, the 19th Bombay infantry, in June 1845. In 1847, being then stationed at Karachi, he was placed by Gen. Walter Scott, R.E., in charge of an extensive district in upper Sindh (subdued in 1843 by Sir Charles Napier). Short of ordering the death-sentence and imprisonment for life, his powers were practically unlimited and strangely varied. Recalled from administrative duties by the outbreak of war in the Punjab (April 1848), he served with his regiment through the campaign of 1848–9. For his services he received the Punjab medal, with two clasps for Mooltan and Gujarat; his regiment, now the 119th, bears the title of 'The Mooltan Regiment.'

Coming home early in 1856, he married next year. Learning on his wedding trip at Killarney of the mutiny, he returned to duty, but sailing round the Cape, did not reach India until Delhi had fallen. He took part, however, with his regiment, under Sir Hugh Rose in Central India, in the pursuit of Tantia Topi, Nana Sahib's right-hand man, and was present at Tantia's defeat near Jhansi on 1 April 1858, and, a year later, at his capture.

Gazetted captain on 3 Feb. 1860, he successfully administered, by commission from Sir Richmond Shakespeare, resident at Indore, the native state of Dhar, during the minority of its Rajah (1861–2). Promoted major in 1865, lieutenant-colonel in 1871, and colonel in 1876, he was in command of his regiment when the second Afghan war broke out in 1878. From the first he had shown an aptitude for engineering and had made the earliest road up to the hill station of Matheran, near Bombay. His talent was now to stand him in good stead. From 16 Dec. 1878 to 26 Feb. 1879 he was employed with his men in making a military road from Jacobabad to Dhadar, a distance of 109 miles. On 27 Feb. the regiment thence began to ascend the Bolan Pass, making in its progress a further roadway, accessible to heavy guns and transport. At Dozan (half-way through the pass), which was reached in June, the workers were attacked by cholera, and more than fifty succumbed. During this outbreak Col. Creagh visited the hospital twice daily, and on one occasion a sepoy died holding his hand. On 31 July he was put in command of the Bombay troops in line of communication, with the rank of brigadier-general. By September the road was carried to Darwaza, a distance of 63 miles from Dhadar. Sir Richard Temple described the long road as 'a signal example of what may be accomplished by a small body of troops with their trained followers.'

Owing to urgent private business, Creagh retired from the service in December, with the rank of major-general. He was mentioned in despatches and received the Afghan medal. Returning to England early in 1880, he passed the remainder of his life at St. Leonards-on-Sea. A churchman and conservative, he took an active though unostentatious part in religious, philanthropic, and political affairs. He died at St. Leonards on 23 May 1901, and is buried in the Hastings borough cemetery. Two small oil paintings of him at the ages of twenty-eight and forty respectively belong to his widow.

General Creagh was twice married: (1) on 29 April 1857 to Haidée Sarah Rose, daughter of John Dopping, of Derrycassan, co. Longford, by whom he had five sons and two daughters; (2) on 10 November 1877 to Dora, younger daughter of Edwin Sturge of Gloucester, by whom he had one son and two daughters. The four sons who reached manhood all entered the army. The eldest, Ralph Charles Osborne, served with distinction in Burmah, in Manipur, at the relief of Chitral, in the Kurram Valley, and in South Africa, and died at Netley on 27 Jan 1904.

[Historical Record of the 86th Regiment; The Afghan Campaigns of 1878–80, by Sydney H. Shadbolt, 1882, 2 vols.; private information.] H. C. M.

CREMER, Sir WILLIAM RANDAL (1838–1908), peace advocate, born on 18 March 1838 at Fareham, Wiltshire, was son of George Cremer, a coach-painter, by his wife Harriet Tutte, daughter of a local builder. Soon after his birth his father deserted his family, and the child was brought up in great poverty. At twelve years of age he went to work as a pitchboy in a shipyard. Three years afterwards he was apprenticed to a carpenter. Then he went to Brighton, where he came under the influence of Frederick William Robertson [q. v.], and in 1852 found his way to London, where he soon mixed in politics and trade unionism. A good speaker, he represented his fellow workmen on the committee in charge of the nine hours' movement of 1858, which involved the lock-out of 70,000 men in 1859–60. From this arose the Amalgamated Society of Carpenters and Joiners (4 June 1860), Cremer being one of the promoters. He was secretary to the workmen's committee, formed to maintain sympathy with the Northern states of America, after the outbreak of the civil war in 1861, and he organised the meeting in St. James's Hall addressed by John Bright, to protest against the British government having allowed the privateering Alabama to escape.

When the International Working-men's Association was formed in 1865, Cremer was the secretary of the British section, and next year he was a delegate to the conference at Geneva, when wide divergence was discovered between the English and some of the continental representatives. Cremer and his friends pleaded for a practical programme, the others for a revolutionary propaganda. Thereupon Cremer severed his connection with the association. But he was steadily extending his international friendships. He knew Mazzini, and was active in the receptions given in London to Garibaldi. At length in 1870 he formed a committee of working men to try to keep Great Britain neutral during the Franco-German War. This committee became in 1871 the Workmen's Peace Association, of which Cremer was secretary till his death, and on behalf of which he journeyed repeatedly to America and the continent, bearing petitions and appeals for international arbitration. He thus became an international figure whose name was known everywhere, especially among workmen. In 1889 the Inter-parliamentary Union was formed, and Cremer became British secretary until his death. For his unwearying service in the cause of international arbitration he was awarded by the Swedish government in 1903 the Nobel prize of 8000*l.*, 7000*l.* of which he handed over in trust to the International Arbitration League. For his work in the cause of peace he was made commander of the Norwegian Order of St. Olaf in 1904, and was knighted in 1907. He had received the cross of the legion of honour in 1890.

In politics Cremer was a radical. He was a member of the Reform League from its commencement in 1864, and he always claimed that he proposed 'that it would be for the health of the reformers if they should take an airing in Hyde Park on 23 July 1866,' the suggestion which led to the demolition of the Hyde Park railings. In 1868 he addressed a meeting in Warwick, and accepted an invitation to stand as radical candidate. He was defeated with only 260 votes to his credit. He fought the same constituency in 1874, and found only 183 supporters. Twice he failed in his candidature for the London School Board, in 1870 and 1873; but in 1884 he was elected to the St. Pancras vestry. The reform bill of 1885 increased the representation of London, and Cremer contested the Haggerston division of Shoreditch with success. In the elections of 1886 and 1892 he retained his seat, but was defeated in 1895. He recovered it in spite of the South African war fever in 1900, and kept it till his death. In the controversies which arose inside trade unionism when the labour party came into existence, Cremer stoutly opposed the new independent labour movement and remained with the liberal party.

He died at 11 Lincoln's Inn Fields, London, on 22 July 1908, and was bureid in Hampstead cemetery after cremation. He was twice married: (1) in 1860, to Charlotte, daughter of J. Wilson of Spalding; she died in August 1876; (2) to Lucy Coombes of Oxford, who died on 8 Aug. 1884. He had no children.

He intended to write his autobiography, but only left some notes behind him. His literary work is confined to the pages of the 'Arbitrator,' a monthly peace journal which he edited from its appearance in 1889. On 7 Dec. 1911 a bust executed by Mr. Paul Montford for the International Arbitration Society was unveiled by Mr. J. W. Lowther, the Speaker, in the library of the House of Commons; the bust is intended ultimately for the Palace of Peace at the Hague.

[Howard Evans, Sir Randal Cremer; his Life and Work, 1911; Sidney Webb's History of Trade Unionism; Dr. Eugene Oswald, Reminiscences of a Busy Life, 1911; The Times, 23 July 1908.] J. R. M.

CRIPPS, WILFRED JOSEPH (1841–1903), writer on plate, was descended from an ancient Cirencester family, members of which took a prominent part in the affairs of the town from the time of Elizabeth, and gained their wealth from the great wool trade of the Cotswolds. His grandfather, Joseph Cripps, sat for Cirencester in parliament, with one short interruption, from 1806 until his death in 1841, when he was succeeded in the representation by his son, William Cripps. The latter, a barrister on the Oxford circuit, became a whip of the Peelite party and a junior lord of the treasury in August 1845, and married his cousin, Mary Anne, daughter of Benjamin Harrison, a descendant of 'Parson Harrison' who held the living of Cirencester for sixty-three years (1690–1753). Wilfred Joseph Cripps, the eldest surviving issue of this marriage, was born in London on 8 June 1841, and was educated at Kensington grammar school, King's College, London, and Trinity College, Oxford, where he graduated B.A. in 1863, proceeding M.A. in 1866. He took an active part in the volunteer movement, frequently attending the rifle competitions at Wimbledon. In May 1865 he was called to the bar in the Middle Temple, practising for a few years on the Oxford circuit.

About 1871 or 1872 he began his researches into old English plate, and three or four years later, on the introduction of William Lord Bathurst, Charles Octavius Swinnerton Morgan [q. v.] entrusted Cripps with his notes on the subject, with a view to completing the inquiry. Cripps published in 1878 his scholarly treatise, 'Old English Plate.' The foundations of the research had been laid by Sir A. W. Franks, Morgan, and others, but Cripps gave earlier researches a wider vogue. Nine editions of his manual, which greatly stimulated the demand for antique silver, appeared between 1878 and 1906, and each new edition embodied fresh discoveries. Cripps's labours covered a wide field. In April 1892 he read a paper on the old church plate of Northumberland and Durham before the Society of Antiquaries of Newcastle-on-Tyne (*Arch. Ael.* ser. 1. xvi. 249–267). In 1880 he published a volume on 'Old French Plate,' which stirred a keen interest in Europe and America (2nd edit. 1893). For the Science and Art Department at South Kensington he prepared in 1881 a handbook dealing with college and corporation plate.

Cripps's expert authority was universally recognised. In October 1880, associated with Sir Philip Cunliffe Owen, he examined by the request of the Russian government the magnificent imperial collection of plate in Russia, and in 1881 he was similarly employed in Sweden and Denmark and at Berlin. In 1880 he was a member of the English sub-commission connected with the Exhibition of Gold and Silver Work at Amsterdam (*Athenæum*, 28 Feb. 1880, p. 289). Through his efforts valuable replicas of famous objects of artistic workmanship were obtained for the national collections at South Kensington and elsewhere.

Cripps interested himself in the archæology of his native town, and unearthed about the site of the forum of Roman Cirencester remains of the basilica and other principal buildings. His discoveries were communicated to the Society of Antiquaries in two papers, 'Roman basilica of Corinium at Cirencester' (*Proc. Soc. Ant.* new ser. xvii. 201–8), and 'Roman Altar and other Sculptured Stones found at Cirencester in April 1899' (*ib.* xviii. 177–184). He served many years in the royal North Gloucester militia, retiring with the rank of major; he completed in 1875 a history of the regiment which had been begun by Captain Sir J. Maxwell Steele-Graves. He was elected a fellow of the Society of Antiquaries in June 1880, and became local secretary for Gloucestershire, was made a C.B. in 1889, and in 1894 received the honorary freedom of the Goldsmiths' Company. Deputy-lieutenant of the county of Gloucester, and J.P. for the counties of Gloucester and Kent, he took a very active share in all local, especially educational, affairs. He keenly interested himself in the local welfare of the conservative cause.

Cripps died at his residence, Cripps Mead, Cirencester, on 26 Oct. 1903, and was buried at Cirencester cemetery. He was twice married: (1) on 31 May 1870 to Maria Harriet Arabella (*d.* 1881), second daughter of John Robert Daniel-Tyssen; (2) on 2 Dec. 1884 to Helena Augusta Wilhelmine, Countess Bismarck, daughter of Count Bismarck, of Schierstein, Prussia, a relative of the German chancellor. He had no issue.

Cripps also wrote, among many other papers and articles: 1. 'Notes on Ancient Plate of the Merchant Taylors' Company' (privately printed), 1877. 2. 'English and Foreign Silverwork' (*Journ. of Soc. of Arts*, 11 May 1883). 3. 'Report on the Plate at Welbeck Abbey,' 1883. 4. 'Church Plate and how to describe it' (*Trans. Bristol and Glouc. Arch. Society*, 27 Apr. 1893).

[Proc. Soc. Ant., ser. 2, xx. 110; Archæologia Aeliana, ser. 2, xxv. 188–191; Wilts. and Gloucestershire Standard, 31 Oct. 1903; Burke's Peerage, s.v. Amherst; private information.] C. W.

CROCKER, HENRY RADCLIFFE (1845–1909), dermatologist. [See RADCLIFFE-CROCKER, HENRY.]

CROFT, JOHN (1833–1905), surgeon, born on 4 Aug. 1833 at Pettinghoe near Newhaven, in Sussex, was son of Hugh Croft, who at the age of nineteen married his first wife Maria, aged sixteen. His grandfather, Gilmore Croft, a successful medical practitioner in the City of London, left Hugh Croft a competence, much of which was spent in farming. Hugh's first wife died in 1842, and marrying again he moved to Lower Clapton. John Croft was educated at the Hackney Church of England school, and through life held earnest religious views. He served a short apprenticeship with Thomas Evans of Burwash in Sussex, and entered St. Thomas's Hospital in 1850. Admitted M.R.C.S., and a licentiate of the Society of Apothecaries in 1854, he served as house surgeon at St. Thomas's Hospital. After spending five years (1855–60) as surgeon to the Dreadnought seamen's hospital ship, he returned to St. Thomas's to become demonstrator of anatomy and surgical registrar. He was successively resident assistant surgeon (Dec. 1863), assistant surgeon (1 Jan. 1871), and surgeon (1 July 1871), when the new buildings of the hospital were opened on the Albert Embankment. In the medical school he was in succession demonstrator of anatomy, lecturer on practical surgery, and lecturer on clinical surgery. He resigned his appointments in July 1891, when he was elected consulting surgeon. He was also surgeon to the Surrey dispensary; to the National Truss Society; to the Magdalen Hospital at Streatham, and to the National Provident Assurance Society. He was elected F.R.C.S. in 1859; was a member of the council (1882–90); vice-president in 1889, and a member of the court of examiners (1881–6).

Croft was one of the earlier hospital

surgeons in London to adopt the improved methods advocated by Lister. His name is chiefly associated with the introduction of 'Croft's splints,' which were plaster of Paris cases made with scrubbing flannel and shaped to the limb. They were employed in place of the ordinary splints and the 'gum and chalk' bandages which had previously been used in the treatment of fractures of the leg. Croft was a strong advocate for early excision of the joint in cases of hip disease.

He died on 21 Nov. 1905, and was buried in Kensal Green cemetery. He married in 1864 Annie, daughter of Alexander Douglas Douglas, but left no issue.

Croft contributed to the 'St. Thomas's Hospital Reports,' Holmes's 'System of Surgery,' the 'Transactions' of the Royal Medical and Chirurgical Society, the Clinical, and other medical societies.

[St. Thomas's Hosp. Reports, xxxiv. 505; private information; personal knowledge.]

D'A. P.

CROFTS, ERNEST (1847–1911), historical painter, born at Leeds, Yorkshire, on 15 Sept. 1847, was second son of John Crofts, J.P., a manufacturer. His mother, Ellen Wordsworth, was a descendant of the poet Wordsworth.

Ernest received his general education at Rugby and Berlin, and subsequently studied art at Düsseldorf under Horace Vernet's pupil, Professor Hünten, and in London under Alfred Borron Clay [q. v.]. In 1874 he first exhibited at the Royal Academy, the subject of his picture being 'A Retreat: Episode in the Franco-German War.' From that time to the year before his death he was rarely absent from the annual exhibitions at Burlington House. He was elected A.R.A. in 1878, R.A. in 1896, and keeper and trustee of the Royal Academy, in succession to P. H. Calderon [q. v. Suppl. I], in 1898.

Crofts devoted himself almost exclusively to the military historical subject, and was particularly interested in the Napoleonic war and in the struggles between Cavalier and Roundhead. His draughtsmanship was as impeccable as his accuracy in the minutest details of costumes, accoutrements, and accessories. He had all the qualifications to make him a great pictorial illustrator. He had the gift to represent the stirring episodes of past history in dramatic intensity, but was rather deficient, especially towards the end of his career, in the sensuous appreciation of colour.

His most ambitious work as regards scale is the panel in the ambulatory of the Royal Exchange, 'Queen Elizabeth opening the first Royal Exchange.' The Diploma Gallery at Burlington House owns his 'To the Rescue.' 'The Funeral of Charles I' is at the Bristol Art Gallery, and 'On the Evening of the Battle of Waterloo' (R.A. 1879) at the Walker Art Gallery, Liverpool. Among his other notable pictures are 'Marlborough after Ramillies' (1880), 'Charles I on the Way to Execution' (1883), 'Wallenstein' (1884), 'Gunpowder Plot: the Conspirators' last Stand at Holbeach House' (1892), 'Napoleon and the Old Guard at Waterloo' (R.A. 1895), 'Oliver Cromwell at the Storming of Basing House' (1900), 'The Capture of a French Battery at Waterloo,' 'King Edward VII distributing South African War Medals,' 'The Funeral of Queen Victoria' (1903), 'Prince Rupert and his Staff at Marston Moor' (1904). Crofts was elected F.S.A. on 1 March 1900.

He died at Burlington House on 19 March 1911, and was buried at Kensal Green. He married in 1872 Elizabeth Wüsthofen, of Düsseldorf, and had one daughter. His portrait is included in Sir Hubert von Herkomer's large group of the Royal Academy Council, at the National (Tate) Gallery of British Art. The works and sketches remaining in his possession were sold at Christie's after his death on 19 Dec. 1911.

[Windsor Mag., March 1909; Graves, Royal Acad. Exhibitors; private information.]

P. G. K.

CROKE, THOMAS WILLIAM (1824–1902), Roman catholic archbishop of Cashel, born on 19 May 1824 at Castlebar, in the parish of Ballyclough, co. Cork, was son of William Croke by his wife Isabella Plummer. His father, who died young, was a catholic, but his mother was a protestant till four years before her death. Seven members of Croke's family were priests. A great-uncle, Dr. McKenna, was bishop of Cloyne, and an uncle was vicar-general there. Two sisters were nuns; one brother, William, died while a young curate, and another, James, died a priest in America in 1889.

Thomas Croke was taken charge of in boyhood by his uncle, vicar-general of Cloyne, who sent him to the endowed school at Charleville, where he gained a reputation for athleticism rather than for learning. Encouraged to adopt the priestly vocation, he studied from 1839 to 1845, mainly at the Irish College in Paris, but spending one of these years at the college of Menin, in Belgium, where he acted as professor of rhetoric. In 1845 he went to the Irish College at Rome, of which Dr. (afterwards Cardinal) Cullen was then rector. Here he carried off several distinctions, including two gold medals, in 1846. In 1847 he received the degree of doctor of divinity. In 1848, according to an uncombated statement of William O'Brien M.P. (*Recollections*, p. 49), he was again in Paris, and took part in the fighting at the barricades during the revolution. After ordination he returned to Ireland in 1849 to take for a short time the place of his brother William as curate of Charleville. He was subsequently professor of rhetoric at Carlow College, teacher of theology at the Irish College, Paris, curate in Ireland for a second time, and professor of ecclesiastical history at the Catholic University in Dublin when John Henry Newman was rector. From 1858 to 1868 he was president of St. Colman's College, Fermoy. In 1865 he was made chancellor of the diocese of Cloyne and parish priest of Doneraile. As a theologian he attended Dr. William Delany, the bishop of Cork, at the Vatican Council in 1870, where he met Archbishop, afterwards Cardinal, Manning, and formed a lifelong friendship with him.

From 1870 to 1875 Croke was catholic bishop of Auckland, New Zealand, and his administration of the diocese was a triumphant success, to which his business ability largely contributed. In 1875 he succeeded Patrick Leahy [q. v.] as archbishop of Cashel, largely through the influence of Cardinal Cullen and possibly that of Manning. His first public appearance as archbishop was at the O'Connell centenary in Dublin in 1875, when he preached the centennial sermon in the pro-cathedral. In his diocese he warmly encouraged athletic pastimes, and was a powerful advocate of temperance. Mainly through his influence the Gaelic Athletic Association became a great force in the rural life of Ireland. He was a stern and exacting administrator and an admirable manager of diocesan affairs. A strong nationalist, holding advanced views on the agrarian problem, Croke threw himself with ardour into the land agitation which broke out in 1878, soon after his arrival in Cashel. His unvarying support of the land agitation and of the Irish nationalist party powerfully aided the advance of the nationalist cause. Although Cardinal Cullen was wholly at variance with him in political and agrarian questions, their affectionate relations were undisturbed. Croke, however, dissented from some of the Land League's procedure, and strongly objected to the no-rent manifesto of 1881. When, a little later, Pope Leo XIII requested him to take a less active part in the land war, he obeyed, but his sympathies underwent no change. He was in favour of Parnell's retirement after the divorce proceedings in November 1890.

Croke celebrated his silver jubilee as bishop in 1895 amid great rejoicings. He died at his palace in Cashel on 22 July 1902, and was buried in the grounds of his cathedral at Thurles.

Although a rigid disciplinarian, and ascetic in his personal tastes, Croke was on occasion a noted raconteur. His generosity and hospitality were unbounded, and Cardinal Manning, 'who loved him as a brother,' regarded him as a saint. Of commanding presence, he wielded an immense influence among the Irish people, and his high personal character, combined with his austerity and deep conviction, was of immense service to the nationalist cause. No other prelate in Ireland possessed the same weight in public affairs. He was the most notable figure of his day in the Irish catholic church. His only publications were a few pastorals, though he had written a few poems for the 'Nation' newspaper while a curate in Charleville.

[Men of the Time, 1899; William O'Brien's Recollections; T. P. O'Connor's Parnell Movement, p. 514; Barry O'Brien's Parnell Movement; Irish Ecclesiastical Record, 1902, pp. 301–311 (which suggested the publication of a full biography of Croke); Purcell's Life of Cardinal Manning, 1896; Morley's Life of Gladstone, 1903; D'Alton's History of Ireland, iii. 29, 379; A Roll of Honour, Dublin, 1905; Freeman's Journal, 23 July 1902.]

D. J. O' D.

CROMPTON, HENRY (1836–1904), positivist and advocate of trade unions, born at Liverpool on 27 Aug. 1836, was second of five sons of Sir Charles Crompton [q. v.], judge of the queen's bench, by Caroline Fletcher, his wife. The eldest son, Charles Crompton (1833–1890), Q.C., was M.P. for Staffordshire (Leek division), and the fourth son, Albert, was founder of the positivist church at Liverpool. Of his three sisters, the eldest, Mary, married the Rev. J. Llewelyn Davies, the second, Caroline Anna, married Prof. George Croom Robertson [q. v.], and the third, Emily, married Prof. E. S. Beesly. Educated at University College school, London, in a private school at Bonn, and at Trinity College, Cambridge, where he graduated B.A. as junior optime in 1858, Crompton afterwards studied medicine at

St. Mary's Hospital, Paddington. In 1858 he was appointed clerk of assize on the Chester and North Wales circuit, a post which he held for forty-three years, rendering the judges during that long period valuable aid in their criminal work by virtue of his experience and judgment. He was called to the bar at the Inner Temple on 6 June 1863. He died on 15 March 1904 at Churt near Farnham, and is buried there. He married on 8 Nov. 1870 Lucy Henrietta, daughter of John Romilly, first Lord Romilly [q. v.], and had two sons.

During a long illness (1858–9), Crompton read Comte's 'Philosophie Positive' and became an ardent positivist. He met Professor Beesly in 1864, and thenceforward took an active part in the positivist movement. In his later life he was chief assistant to Dr. Richard Congreve [q. v. Suppl. I] at the Church of Humanity, Chapel Street, becoming leader after Congreve's death in 1899. There he gave many addresses on religion, philosophy, history, and public affairs. Some were published as pamphlets. A paper on Rabelais (*Positivist Review*, June 1910) is a good example of the range and breadth of his thought.

Crompton sedulously applied his principles to public questions. He was always active to protest against international injustice and the oppression of weaker races. He served on the Jamaica committee, formed to prosecute Governor Eyre in 1867; worked for the admission of women to the lectures at University College; was untiring in efforts for the improvement and just administration of the criminal law; and gave a strenuous and useful support to the trade unions in their struggle to reform the labour laws. When bills affecting trade unions were before parliament, 'his technical knowledge and skill were invaluable and were ever placed unstintedly and disinterestedly at the service of labour' (Thomas Burt, *Northumberland Miners' Monthly Circular* for March 1904). In recognition of his services he was made in 1868 a member of the Amalgamated Society of Carpenters and Joiners. In 1876, being at that time referee to the board of arbitration and conciliation for the Nottingham lace trade, he published 'Industrial Conciliation,' to which Mr. and Mrs. Webb refer as 'the classic work' on the subject (*Industrial Democracy*, p. 223, note). It was translated into French. Crompton's 'Letters on Social and Political Subjects,' reprinted from the 'Sheffield Independent,' were published in book form in 1870, and after his death some papers by him were collected under the title 'Our Criminal Justice,' with an introduction by Sir Kenelm Digby (1905); the book gives an accurate account of the English system of criminal procedure. A volume of 'Selections of Prose and Poetry by Henry Crompton' was issued by his widow in 1910.

[Professor Beesly in Positivist Review, May 1904; private information; personal knowledge.] S. H. S.

CROSSMAN, SIR WILLIAM (1830–1901), major-general, royal engineers, born at Isleworth, Middlesex, on 30 June 1830, was eldest son of Robert Crossman of Cheswick House, Beal, and Holy Island, Northumberland, by his wife Sarah, daughter of E. Douglas of Kingston-on-Thames. After education at Berwick-on-Tweed grammar school and Mr. Jeffery's at Woolwich, he entered the Royal Military Academy at the head of his batch in January 1847. He received a commission in the royal engineers as second lieutenant on 19 Dec. 1848. After professional instruction at Chatham and duty at Woolwich, Crossman was employed on the organisation of the Great Exhibition of 1851, and next year was sent to Western Australia, to superintend the construction of public works by the convicts [see Du Cane, Sir Edmund Frederick, Suppl. II]. He was a police magistrate for the colony and a visiting magistrate for the ticket-of-leave stations, being stationed principally at Albany in King George's Sound and at Perth, the capital of the colony. He was promoted first lieutenant on 17 Feb. 1854. His services were commended by the governor, but the exigencies of the Crimean war necessitated his recall in February 1856.

After employment at Aldershot and Chatham he joined the war office for special duty under the inspector-general of fortifications, and was engaged in surveys and designs for new defences of dockyards and naval bases, for which parliament had just sanctioned a loan. Several of the sea defences of Portsmouth and the Isle of Wight, of Hilsea lines and the detached forts of the Gosport advanced line, of the Verne Citadel at Portland, and Scraesdon and Tregantle Forts at Plymouth, were subsequently his work. Meanwhile he was promoted second captain on 12 Aug. 1858 and first captain on 5 Feb. 1864; was a member of the committee on the equipment of coast batteries (Jan. 1860); went to Canada (Dec. 1861) to aid in preparing quarters for troops from England in view of the menace of war with the United States of America over the Trent affair; and afterwards acted as secretary to the royal commission, of which Sir J. W. Gordon [q. v.] was president, on the defences of Canada, visiting every post on the frontier.

Between 1866 and 1870 Crossman was engaged by the treasury to report on the legation and consular buildings in Japan and China and to arrange for new buildings where necessary. In the course of his mission he secured for the admiralty the site for a new dockyard at Shanghai; and he accompanied both the naval expedition to Nanking and Yung Chow in 1869 and the force of sailors and marines which was landed in Formosa and at Swatow in 1868 and 1869. Varied service occupied him after his return to England. Promoted regimental major on 5 July 1872 and lieutenant-colonel on 11 Dec. 1873, he became assistant director of works for fortifications at the war office on 1 April 1875, but on 6 Sept. following he joined a special commission appointed by the colonial office to inquire into the resources and finances of Griqualand West. In recognition of his services he was made C.M.G. (May 1877). From 1876 to 1881 he served as the first inspector of submarine mining defences and as member of the royal engineers committee for submarine experiments and stores, visiting all the defended harbours at home and also at Halifax (Nova Scotia), Bermuda, and Jamaica abroad. Under his auspices submarine mining became a valuable part of harbour defence. During 1879 and 1880 he was also president of an important committee on siege operations, which conducted many practical experiments with a view to remodelling siege operations to meet improved artillery. In 1881–2 he visited Esquimalt, Fiji, Hong-kong, Singapore, Penang and Labuan and the Australian colonies, making full reports on their defences and requirements. On his return (July 1882) he was commanding royal engineer of the southern military district with headquarters at Portsmouth, but was absent in 1883 on a commission of inquiry with Sir George Smyth Baden-Powell [q. v.] into the financial condition of Jamaica and other West India islands. He was made K.C.M.G. on rendering the final report (March 1884).

Crossman, who was promoted brevet colonel on 11 Dec. 1878 and regimental colonel on 6 May 1885, resigned his command at Portsmouth in order to stand for parliament. He was returned in June 1885 as liberal M.P. for Portsmouth. Refusing to accept Gladstone's home rule policy, he joined the liberal unionists and retained the seat till 1892. He had retired from the army with the honorary rank of major-general (6 Jan. 1886), and in Jan. 1883 had succeeded to his father's estate in Northumberland. He was a J.P. for the county, alderman of the county council, and served as sheriff in 1894–5. He was for many years chairman of the River Tweed commission and president of the Berwick Naturalists' Club. He was also an associate member of the Institution of Civil Engineers. He died at the Hotel Belgravia, in London, on 19 April 1901.

Crossman was twice married: (1) at Albany, King George's Sound, Western Australia, on 3 March 1855 to Catherine Josephine (*d.* 1898), daughter of John Lawrence Morley of Albany; and (2) in London, on 29 June 1899, to Annie, eldest daughter of Lieut.-general R. Richards, Bombay staff corps, who survived him. By his first wife he had two sons and three daughters.

[War Office Records; Royal Engineers Records; Blue Books; W. Porter's History of the Royal Engineers, 2 vols. 1889; The Times, 22 April 1901; Royal Engineers Journal (notice by General Sir E. F. Du Cane), Oct. 1901.] R. H. V.

CROWE, EYRE (1824–1910), artist, eldest son of Eyre Evans Crowe [q. v.] by his first wife Margaret, daughter of Capt. Archer of Kiltimon, co. Wicklow, was born in London on 3 Oct. 1824. Sir Joseph Archer Crowe [q. v. Suppl. I] was his younger brother. His sister Amy Mary Anne (*d.* 1865) married in 1862, as his first wife, Col. (Sir) Edward Thackeray, V.C., a cousin of the novelist. During his childhood Eyre's father removed with his family to France, where they remained till 1844. In Paris Eyre and his brother Joseph learnt drawing as boys of M. Brasseur and in 1839 Eyre became a pupil of the great painter Paul Delaroche. In 1844 Crowe accompanied his master and his fellow pupils to Rome. With one of them, the distinguished French painter and sculptor Jean Léon Gérôme (1824–1904), Crowe enjoyed a lifelong friendship, and they corresponded with one another till Gérôme's death.

In 1844 Crowe's family resumed residence in London, where he joined them and spent most of his remaining life

He continued his art education at the Royal Academy schools, and first exhibited at the Academy in 1846, sending the picture 'Master Prynne searching Archbishop Laud's pocket in the Tower.' Next year he engaged in the competition for the decoration of the Houses of Parliament, taking for his subject 'The Battle of Agincourt.'

Meanwhile his relations with Thackeray, whose acquaintance he made in Paris, grew closer. In 1845 he drew a caricature of the novelist in Turkish dress, and transferred to wood the sketches which Thackeray drew for 'Notes of a Journey from Cornhill to Grand Cairo' (1846). In April 1851 he became Thackeray's secretary and amanuensis and spent much time with him at the British Museum in preparing material for 'Esmond.' Crowe was Thackeray's companion in his lecturing tour to the United States (Nov. 1852 to April 1853), and he vividly described the experience in 'With Thackeray in America' (1893, illustrated), while he gave many glimpses of the intimacy in his 'Haunts and Homes of Thackeray' (1897, with illustrations).

After returning from America Crowe worked zealously at his art, mainly occupying himself with historical and genre themes, which caught the popular taste and were treated with precision and delicacy if without distinctive power. A few of his subjects were suggested by tours in France. He exhibited at the Academy from 1848 to 1904 with small interruption. His last exhibits there were 'Shelley at Marlow' and 'John Bright at the Reform Club, 1883.' His best work was done between 1860 and 1881; it included 'Brick Court, Middle Temple, April 1774,' depicting the morning after Goldsmith's death (1863); 'Mary Stuart, Feb. 8, 1586' (1868); 'Old Mortality' (1871); 'The Rehearsal' (1876); 'The Queen of the May' (1879); and 'Sir Roger de Coverley and the Spectator at Westminster Abbey' (1881). He was elected A.R.A. in 1875 and was after Frith's death in 1909 the Academy's oldest member. He also exhibited at the British Institution in 1850 and 1861. Several of Crowe's works are in public galleries. Mosaics of William Hogarth and Sir Christopher Wren, from his designs in oils, as well as a lunette, 'A Sculptor with a Nude Model and two Pupils,' and a chalk drawing, 'A Dead Stork on the Bank of a Stream' (1860) are in the Victoria and Albert Museum, South Kensington; 'The Founder of English Astronomy, Jeremiah Horrocks' (R.A. 1891), is in the Walker Art Gallery, Liverpool; 'Nelson's Last Farewell to England' (R.A. 1888) was purchased for the Castle Museum, Norwich, in 1905; and an example of his work is at Bristol Art Gallery.

In later life he acted as an inspector and examiner under the science and art department, South Kensington. Outliving his contemporaries and spending his last years in much seclusion, he was long an habitué of the Reform Club, which he joined in 1866. He died, unmarried, in London on 12 Dec. 1910, and was buried at Kensal Green cemetery. He owned a water-colour portrait of himself (10 in. by 7 in.) by Thackeray, which was sold at Sotheby's on 27 July 1911 for 31*l*. (*The Times*, 28 July 1911). A portrait in oils of Crowe as a young man by himself belongs to his half-sister in Paris.

[The Times, 13 and 14 Dec. 1910; Crowe's works cited; Melville's Life of Thackeray; Sir Joseph Crowe's Reminiscences, 1895; J. G. Wilson, Thackeray in the United States, 2 vols. 1904; Graves, Royal Acad. Exhibitors, 1905; Brit. Instit. Exhibitors, 1908; private information.]

CRUTTWELL, CHARLES THOMAS (1847–1911), historian of Roman literature, born in London on 30 July 1847, eldest son of Charles James Cruttwell, barrister-at-law, of the Inner Temple, by his wife Elizabeth Anne, daughter of Admiral Thomas Sanders Educated under James Augustus Hessey [q. v.] at Merchant Taylors' School (1861–6), he proceeded with a foundation scholarship to St. John's College, Oxford, in 1866. There he greatly distinguished himself. Placed in the first class in classical moderations in 1868 and in literæ humaniores in 1870, he obtained the Pusey and Ellerton Hebrew scholarship in 1869, won the Craven scholarship for classics in 1871, and the Kennicott Hebrew scholarship in 1872. He graduated B.A. in 1871, proceeding M.A. in 1874, and was classical moderator (1873–5). Meanwhile he was elected fellow of Merton College in 1870, and was tutor there 1874–7. Ordained deacon by the bishop of Oxford in 1875 and priest in 1876, he was curate of St. Giles's, Oxford, from 1875 till 1877.

In 1877 Cruttwell left Oxford for Bradfield College, where he was headmaster till 1880. In that year he passed to the headmastership of Malvern College. But despite his efficient scholarship he showed little aptitude for public school administration, and resigned in 1885 to become rector of Sutton, Surrey. A few months later he was appointed rector of Denton,

Norfolk, and in 1891 he accepted from Merton College the benefice of Kibworth-Beauchamp in succession to Dr. Knox, afterwards bishop of Manchester. While at Kibworth he was also rector of Smeeton-Westerby, Leicestershire (1891–4), rural dean of Gartree (1892–1902), examining chaplain to the bishop of Peterborough (1900), and proctor in convocation (1900). In 1901 he was nominated by Lord Salisbury to the crown benefice of Ewelme, near Wallingford, and in 1903 he was collated by the bishop of Peterborough to a residential canonry, which being of small value could be held with a benefice. Cruttwell was also select preacher to Oxford University in 1896–8, and again in 1903–5. In 1909 he joined the party of bishops and clergy who visited Germany in the cause of international peace. He died at Ewelme on 4 April 1911.

Deeply read in ancient and modern literature, Cruttwell published little. The best of his books, 'A History of Roman Literature' (London and Edinburgh, 1877), was a concise yet satisfying account of the development of Roman literature from the earliest times till the death of Marcus Aurelius. Other contributions to Latin literary history were 'Specimens of Roman Literature' (Glasgow, 1879, in collaboration with the Rev. Peake Banton), and 'A Literary History of Early Christianity' (2 vols. 1893). He also published 'The Saxon Church and Norman Conquest' (1909) and 'Six Lectures on the Oxford Movement' (1899).

Cruttwell married on 5 Aug. 1884 Anne Maude, eldest daughter of Sir John Robert Mowbray, first baronet [q. v. Suppl. I], by whom he had three sons and one daughter.

[Who's Who, 1911; Crockford's Clerical Directory, 1911; The Times, 5 April 1911; Lodge's Peerage, Baronetage and Knightage, 1911.] S. E. F.

CUBITT, WILLIAM GEORGE (1835–1903), colonel, Indian staff corps, born in Calcutta on 19 Oct. 1835, was son of Major William Cubitt of the Bengal native infantry, third son of George Cubitt of Catfield, Norfolk. His mother was Harriet Harcourt. His sister, Selena Fitzgerald, married in 1859 Julian (afterwards Lord) Pauncefote [q. v. Suppl. II]. Educated privately at Latham, Yorkshire, he entered the Indian army as ensign in the 13th regiment Bengal native infantry on 26 July 1853. He served against the Santhal rebels in 1855, and joined the Indian staff corps in 1861.

Promoted lieutenant on 23 Nov. 1856, he was at Lucknow with his regiment in 1857, when the Indian Mutiny broke out and his regiment revolted. With the volunteer cavalry he was engaged at the action of Chinhut near Lucknow on 30 June 1857, and was awarded the Victoria Cross for having on the retreat from Chinhut saved, at great risk to himself, the lives of three men of the 32nd regiment (duke of Cornwall's light infantry). He was afterwards present throughout the defence of the residency at Lucknow. His gallant conduct was commended during the capture of the Tehri Koti on 25–26 September and in a successful attack on a barricaded gateway held by the enemy on 12 Nov. 1857, when he was wounded. He received the medal with clasp and was granted a year's extra service (*Lond. Gaz.* 17 Feb. 1858).

Cubitt, who was promoted captain on 26 July 1865, major on 26 July 1873, lieutenant-colonel on 27 July 1879, and colonel on 26 July 1883, served with the Duffla expedition on the north-west frontier in 1874–5, when he was mentioned in despatches; was with the Khyber line force in the Afghan war in 1880, when he received a medal; was present with the Akha expedition in 1883–4, when he was mentioned in despatches, and with the Burmese expedition in 1886–7, when he obtained the distinguished service order and was awarded the medal with clasp (*Lond. Gaz.* 2 Sept. 1887). At the time of his retirement in 1892 he was in command of the 43rd Gurkhas.

Accomplished in all outdoor games, especially racquets and cricket, Cubitt after retirement resided at Collingwood House, Camberley, Surrey, where he died on 25 Jan. 1903. He married at Fort church, Calcutta, on 19 May 1863, Charlotte Isabella, second daughter of James Hills of Nichindapur, Bengal, and sister of Lieutenant-general Sir James Hills-Johnes, V.C., G.C.B. She survived him with three sons and two daughters. The third son, Lewis, died of blood poisoning while assistant commissioner in Uganda on 31 July 1911. A painted portrait of Cubitt is in the Victoria Cross Gallery; a replica belongs to the widow.

[The Times, 27 Jan. and 7 Feb. 1903; Indian Mutiny, 1857–8, Selections from State Papers in the Military Department, edited by G. W. Forrest, 1902, ii. 257, 275; Hart's Army List.] H. M. V.

CULLINGWORTH, CHARLES JAMES (1841–1908), gynæcologist and obstetrician, son of Griffith Cullingworth, bookseller, by his wife Sarah Gledhill of Eddercliff, was born on 3 June 1841 at Leeds. Of Wesleyan stock, although he afterwards joined the Church of England, he was educated at Wesley College, Sheffield. On leaving school he was employed in his father's business, but on the latter's death in 1860 entered the Leeds School of Medicine (1861), and there took many prizes in anatomy and physiology, surgery and medicine. Whilst studying he served four years as an apprentice to a general practitioner in Leeds. He became M.R.C.S. in 1865, and licentiate of the Society of Apothecaries in 1866. After eighteen months as assistant in a country practice at Bawtry, near Doncaster, he entered the Manchester Royal Infirmary in 1867 as resident physician's assistant, and later was appointed resident medical officer. In 1869 he commenced private practice in Manchester, and from 1872 to 1882 was police surgeon. In 1873 he began his special work, on being appointed honorary surgeon to the St. Mary's Hospital for Women and Children at Manchester. In 1881 he graduated M.D. at Durham University, and then gradually relinquished private practice and became a consultant only.

Meanwhile, appointed lecturer in medical jurisprudence at the Owens College in 1879, he made a pronounced success as a teacher. His lectures were invariably clear and comprehensive and were delivered with elocutionary power. In 1885 he was appointed to the chair of obstetrics and gynæcology in the Owens College. He was secretary to the board of studies in medicine at Victoria University, Manchester, from 1883, when the university obtained in its supplemental charter power to confer degrees in medicine.

Cullingworth worked hard for the Manchester Medical Society for nineteen years. He was honorary librarian (1872–8) and honorary secretary (1879–84). Actively interested in literature generally, he devoted much of his spare time to the library of the society and to the cataloguing of the books. At Manchester, too, he helped to found the 'Medical Chronicle,' a monthly magazine, still published, which provides abstracts of good work appearing in medical journals.

In 1888 he gave up his posts at Manchester to become obstetric physician at St. Thomas's Hospital, London. He remained on the active staff until 1904, staying on for three years beyond the usual age limit. He was then appointed consulting obstetric physician and made a governor of the hospital. On removing to London he was appointed visiting physician to the General Lying-in Hospital, York Road.

In 1879 Cullingworth became a member of the Royal College of Physicians. In 1887 he was elected a fellow, and in 1902 he was the first obstetric physician to read the Bradshawe lecture, his subject being 'Intraperitoneal hæmorrhage incident to ectopic gestation.' For many years he was active in the proceedings of the Obstetrical Society of London and contributed his best papers on strictly obstetrical and gynæcological topics to its 'Transactions.' He was one of the founders, and always an active member of the committee which published the 'Journal of Obstetrics and Gynæcology of the British Empire,' and he contributed some papers to it. During the last two years of his life he was editor.

Cullingworth was prominent in the movement for securing the legal registration of midwives. In 1902 the midwives bill became law, and he was appointed to represent the Incorporated Midwives Institute on the Central Midwives Board which was instituted for the proper working of the Act. He received the honorary degrees of D.C.L. from Durham in 1893 and LL.D. from Aberdeen in 1904; he was a member of numerous gynæcological societies at home and abroad.

Never of a robust type, he suffered during his later years from angina pectoris, but continued his work till his death in London on 11 May 1908. He was buried in the Marylebone cemetery at Finchley. He married in April 1882 Emily Mary, daughter of Richard and Harriet Freeman of London, and left one daughter. An enlarged photographic portrait is in the board room at St. Thomas's Hospital.

Cullingworth was a great pioneer of gynæcology. He did his best professional work on the causation of pelvic peritonitis, which he was one of the first in England to maintain was secondary to other conditions, and not a primary disease. His most original and valuable book was on this subject: 'Clinical Illustrations of the Diseases of the Fallopian Tubes and of Tubal Gestation,' a series of excellent and lifelike drawings with descriptive text and histories of the cases (1895; 3rd edit. 1902). Cullingworth also published 'The Nurse's Companion, a Manual of General and Monthly Nursing,' 1876; 'A Manual of Nursing, Medical and Surgical' (1883; 3rd edit. 1889); 'A Short Manual for Monthly Nurses' (1884; 6th edit. 1907); and he wrote an important article on pelvic inflammation for Allbutt, Playfair and Eden's 'System of Gynæcology' and many papers for medical periodicals. A paper read before the Obstetrical Society in 1892, entitled 'The value of abdominal section in certain cases of recurrent peritonitis, based on a personal experience of fifty cases,' gave rise to discussion in which all the leading gynæcologists in England joined, but Cullingworth's views are now generally accepted.

[Personal knowledge; information from Mrs. Cullingworth; Brit. Med. Journal, 23 May 1908; Journal of Obstetrics and Gynæcology, June and July 1908]. E. M. B.

CUNINGHAM, JAMES McNABB (1829–1905), surgeon-general, born on 2 June 1829, was son of Major William Cunningham, of the 54th Bengal infantry, who entered the service in 1804 and retired on 18 May 1833. Cuningham, who modified the spelling of his surname, was born at the Cape of Good Hope, when his father was on leave from 1827 to 1829. He received his medical education at Edinburgh University, where he graduated M.D. in 1851, his thesis on the medical conditions of the aorta being commended. In 1892 he was made hon. LL.D. of Edinburgh.

Cuningham joined the Bengal medical service as an assistant surgeon on 20 Nov. 1851; was promoted surgeon on 12 March 1864; surgeon-major on 20 Nov. 1871, and surgeon-general on 29 March 1880, retiring on 31 March 1885. His first important charge in India was as superintendent of the central prison at Bareilly in 1861; he afterwards held a similar position at Meerut, and was appointed superintendent of the government press, north-west provinces, in 1863.

Cuningham was secretary of the sanitary commission appointed in 1866 under Sir John Strachey [q. v. Suppl. II], first president, to report and advise on the health of European troops and on the sanitary state of India generally. He was made professor of hygiene at the Calcutta medical college in 1866; in 1869, sanitary commissioner for the Bengal presidency, and from 1875 until his retirement for the whole Indian empire. In 1880 he became in addition head of the Bengal medical department, with the rank of surgeon-general.

Cuningham's administrative faculties rather than scientific knowledge enabled him to carry through a great sanitary work. He wrote and spoke well, although his habit of mind tended to scientific agnosticism, and he doubted the value of bacteriological research. In the reorganisation of medical administration in India in 1880 Cuningham played a chief part. With Surgeon-general (afterwards Sir Thomas) Crawford, principal medical officer of the British forces in India, he drew up a report, known as the Crawford-Cuningham commission, for the complete amalgamation of the army medical department and the Indian medical service, which, issued in August 1881, was rejected by the war office. Cuningham left India on 4 April 1885, and on 16 June 1885 he was made C.S.I. He was appointed honorary surgeon to Queen Victoria on 15 Aug. 1888, and from 1891 to 1896 was on the army sanitary committee, representing India in 1894 at the international sanitary conference at Paris.

He died in London on 26 June 1905. He was twice married: (1) on 2 March 1854, to Mary, only daughter of James McRae, and (2) to Georgina Euphemia, daughter of Robert Reid Macredie, on 11 April 1889. He left two sons and a daughter by the first marriage.

Cuningham was author of, besides official sanitary reports: 1. 'A Sanitary Primer for Indian Schools,' Calcutta, 1879. 2. 'Cholera; What the State can do to prevent it,' Calcutta, 1884, translated into German with a preface by Dr. Max von Pettenkofer, Brunswick, 1885.

[Brit. Med. Journal, 1905, ii. 164; information kindly given by Surgeon-General Branfoot, C.I.E., I.M.S., and Lieut.-Col. D. G. Crawford, I.M.S.] D'A. P.

CUNNINGHAM, DANIEL JOHN (1850–1909), professor of anatomy at Dublin and Edinburgh, born at the Manse of Crieff, in Strathearn, on 15 April 1850, was younger son of John Cunningham (1819–1893) [q. v. Suppl. I]. His mother was Susan Porteous, daughter of William Murray of Crieff, by his wife Susan Porteous, a relative of Captain John Porteous [q. v.]. After education at Crieff Academy, Cunningham spent some three years in a large mercantile house in Glasgow. But his inclination was for medical study, and in 1870 he entered the University of Edinburgh as a medical student. From the first he took a high place amongst his contemporaries, and he graduated in 1874 with the highest honours. For a few months he engaged in practice in Glasgow; but he returned in 1876 to become demonstrator of anatomy in the University of Edinburgh, and for a time held, with this post, the chair of physiology in the Edinburgh Veterinary College. In 1882 he became professor of anatomy in the school of the Royal College of Surgeons of Ireland, and next year was appointed professor of anatomy in Trinity College, Dublin. Here, for twenty years, he was the most popular teacher in the university. In 1903 he succeeded Sir William Turner as professor of anatomy in the University of Edinburgh where he laboured with enthusiasm and success until his premature death on 23 June 1909. He married in 1878 Elizabeth Cumming, eldest daughter of Andrew Browne, minister of the parish of Beith in Ayrshire, and had by her three sons and two daughters.

As a lecturer Cunningham had the faculty of illuminating all scientific subjects by illustrations drawn from every field of science. His enthusiasm and perseverance were contagious, and roused the latent powers of both colleagues and pupils. He published much original research in human and comparative anatomy, as well as in the wider field of anthropology. In addition to numerous papers in the 'Journal of Anatomy and Physiology,' of which he was the acting editor, and in other scientific publications, he issued 'Report on the Marsupialia brought home by H.M.S. Challenger' (1878), and 'The Dissector's Guide' for students (1879), which subsequently developed into his 'Manual of Practical Anatomy' (2 vols. 1893–4; 4th edit. revised, 1910). A 'Cunningham Fund,' founded in memory of Timothy Cunningham [q. v.], for the publication of work of special merit connected with the Royal Irish Academy, issued two papers by Cunningham: 'On the Lumbar Curve in Man and the Apes' (1886), and 'On the Surface Anatomy of the Cerebral Hemispheres' (1892). To the 'Transactions' of the same academy he contributed a 'Memoir on Cornelius Magrath, the Irish Giant; a Research into the Connection which exists between Giantism and Acromegaly' (1891); and to the 'Transactions of the Royal Dublin Society' a 'Memoir on the Microcephalic Idiot' (1895). He delivered before the Anthropological Institute in 1902 the third Huxley memorial lecture, on 'Right-Handedness and Left-Brainedness,' for which he was awarded a memorial medal. In conjunction with Edward Hallaran Bennett [q. v. Suppl. II] he wrote 'The Sectional Anatomy of Congenital Cæcal Hernia' (1888). Of the 'Textbook of Anatomy,' published in 1902 (3rd edit. 1909) by the pupils of Sir William Turner, he acted as editor and joint-author.

As a man of affairs, he exercised great influence in the councils of the universities and of the learned societies with which he was connected, and he played a chief part in the establishment of post-graduate instruction at Edinburgh. He was a member of the commission to inquire into the management of the sick and wounded in the South African war, of the war office committee on the standard of candidates and recruits for the army, and of the viceregal commission on the inland fisheries of Ireland. He was largely responsible for inaugurating the medical department of the territorial army in Scotland. He received many honorary degrees—M.D. and D.Sc. Dublin, LL.D. St. Andrews and Glasgow, and D.C.L. Oxford in 1892, on the celebration of the tercentenary of Trinity College, Dublin. He was elected F.R.S. on 4 June 1891, and was president of the Royal Zoological Society of Ireland, and vice-president of the Royal Dublin Society. A memorial bronze bas-relief has been placed, in duplicate, on the walls of the anatomical departments of the University of Edinburgh and of the University of Dublin.

[Lancet, 1 July 1909; Brit. Med. Jour., 1 July 1909; Edin. Med. Jour., July 1909; Dublin Med. Jour., July 1909.] G. A. G.

CURRIE, Sir DONALD (1825–1909), founder of the Castle Steamship Company, born at Greenock on 17 Sept. 1825, was third son of ten children of James Currie (1797–1851) and Elizabeth (1798–1839), daughter of Donald Martin, all of Greenock. His parents removed to Belfast in 1826, and Currie was sent at seven to the Belfast Academy, and subsequently to the Royal Belfast Academical Institution; at both schools he distinguished himself.

As a boy he interested himself in the sea and shipping, and at fourteen entered the shipping office of a relative in Greenock. After four years there, he joined in 1844 the Cunard Steamship Company, Liverpool, owners of the only regular line of steamers sailing between Europe and America, which numbered no more than three—the Caledonia, the Arcadia, and the Britannia, all of small tonnage. Currie became head of the company's cargo department. In 1849, in order to take advantage of the abolition of the navigation laws, the company sent him to establish branch houses at Havre and Paris, and in a short time they had a steamer running between Havre and America viâ Liverpool. He also established branch offices at Bremen and Antwerp, returning to Liverpool in 1854.

In 1862, determining to start for himself, he established the 'Castle' shipping company, which consisted at first of sailing ships plying between Liverpool and Calcutta, owned by a circle of personal friends. Currie first introduced the plan of despatching sailing ships on fixed dates.

In 1865 he made London the port of departure of his vessels and took up his residence there. The line grew steadily in strength and importance, and he resolved on a line of steamers from England to Cape Town, the first of which, the Iceland, a vessel of 946 tons, started on her outward trip on 23 Jan. 1872. At the time the Union Steamship Company, founded in 1853, carried on the principal trade between England and South Africa and had the contract for the mail service. In 1876 the Cape parliament resolved to divide this service equally between the old company and the new. Ultimately in 1900 the two were amalgamated under the name of the Union-Castle Mail Steamship Company, Limited, the joint concern being managed by Messrs. Donald Currie & Co. Before Sir Donald's death the fleet of the united company consisted of forty-seven steamers, with a gross tonnage of 295,411 tons. The enormous improvement of communication between England and South Africa was largely due to Sir Donald and his ships.

Currie soon became recognised as one of the highest authorities on shipping. In 1875 he was elected chairman of a committee of shipowners to consider proposed changes in laws affecting the mercantile marine, and he was responsible for important amendments of the Merchant Shipping Act of 1876.

His knowledge of South African affairs often proved of advantage to the British government. In 1875 Lord Carnarvon, the colonial secretary, entrusted him with the conduct of negotiations with President Brand of the Orange Free State and President Burgers of the Transvaal Republic regarding the occupation of the Kimberley diamond fields. Currie defined the boundaries, and arranged the terms of agreement. Currie supplied the home government with the first news of the disaster of Isandhlwana during the Zulu war in January 1879. There was at that time no telegraphic connection between England and South Africa; the despatch announcing the calamity was sent from Cape Town by a Castle liner to St. Vincent, and thence telegraphed to Currie in London. Within forty-eight hours one of the Castle liners started for South Africa with reinforcements. In 1883, on Currie's representations, the British flag was hoisted at St. Lucia Bay in Zululand, which the Germans would have captured a few days later.

In 1877 Paul Kruger and two others came to England as a deputation from the Transvaal Boers to the British government, begging for self-government. They sought Currie's aid. He introduced them to Lord Carnarvon, supporting their appeal; but his advice was not taken. When the South African war broke out in 1899, Currie's services were of great value in the conveyance of troops. His ships carried altogether 172,835 men to and from South Africa, together with thousands of tons of stores, and this without an accident. At the critical juncture in Dec. 1899, when Lord Roberts and Lord Kitchener were ordered to the seat of war, he arranged that the Castle liner which conveyed Lord Roberts from England should be so timed as to meet Lord Kitchener at Gibraltar on his arrival there from Egypt, so that the two generals might travel together to Cape Town.

In 1880 Currie had entered parliament in the liberal interest as one of the members for Perthshire. This seat he held until 1885, when, on the division of the constituency, he was elected for West Perthshire. In 1886 he broke on the home rule question with Gladstone, whom he had hitherto followed. He represented West Perthshire as a liberal unionist from 1886 until his retirement from parliament in 1900. He remained on intimate social terms with Gladstone, who was on several occasions between 1883 and 1895 his guest with other distinguished persons on one or other of his ships for summer cruises (cf. MORLEY's *Gladstone*, iii. 115, 517).

In 1880 Currie purchased the Garth estate in Perthshire. In 1884 he added to this great property the adjoining Glen Lyon estate, and in 1903 that of Chesthill. He also purchased from Lord Macdonald the island of Scalpay, beside Skye, and the adjacent islands of Longa, Guillamon, and Paba. To his tenantry on all these properties Currie proved a generous landlord. New breeds of cattle and sheep were introduced, and large sums expended on the erection and improvement of churches, schools, and cottages. He delighted in sport in his deer-forests, on his grouse moors, and salmon rivers.

In his later years Currie was munificent in public gifts. In 1904 he gave to University College Hospital, London, 80,000*l.* for a school of final medical studies, and 20,000*l.* for a nurses' home and a maternity students' house. To the University of Edinburgh he gave 25,000*l.* for 'The Donald Currie Lectureship Endowment Fund,' and 6000*l.* for the enlargement of the Students' Union. He also bestowed numerous benefactions on the United Free church of Scotland (he had 'come out' with his minister at the disruption of 1843) and the presbyterian church of England. He restored at a large cost the choir of Dunkeld cathedral. To Belfast, where he spent his boyhood, he was especially generous. To the 'Better Equipment Fund' of Queen's College there he gave 20,000*l.*, a gift which 'The Donald Currie Laboratories' there commemorate. He contributed a fourth of the cost of an athletic field for the Belfast students. In the Belfast Royal Academy, his first school, he founded scholarships at a cost of 2000*l.*, and scholarships in the Royal Belfast Academical Institution at an expense of 1000*l.* He helped, too, to pay off the debt of Fisherwick presbyterian church, Belfast, of which his father had been a member.

Sir Donald's tall, manly figure was singularly striking, especially in old age. A man of shrewdness and sagacity, of large and broad ideas, energetic, tenacious of purpose, and pious, he was a staunch friend and a genial companion. He died on 13 April 1909 at the Manor House, Sidmouth, Devonshire, and was buried in the churchyard of Fortingal, beside his Highland home. A sculptured Iona cross of granite, ten feet in height, was placed above the grave in 1910.

Currie was married in 1851 to Margaret, daughter of John Miller of Liverpool and Ardencraig, Bute, who survived him. He left three daughters, who are erecting at a cost of 25,000*l.* a university hall to their father's memory in the University of Cape Town, of which the foundation stone was laid by the duke of Connaught in 1910.

Currie was awarded many honours. In 1880 he received the Fothergill gold medal of the Royal Society of Arts in recognition of 'the improvements which he had introduced into his passenger steamers.' In 1877 he was created C.M.G., in 1881 K.C.M.G., and in 1897 G.C.M.G. In 1906 he was made LL.D. at Edinburgh, and received the freedom of the city of Belfast.

A lifelike portrait was painted in 1908 by Walter W. Ouless, R.A., and hangs in the dining-room at Garth. Two others by the same artist hang respectively in the library of the medical school of University College, London, and in his town house, 4 Hyde Park Place, London. A cartoon portrait by 'Ape' appeared in 'Vanity Fair' in 1884.

Currie had a fine taste in pictures. In his London residence he formed one of the best collections of Turner's works, containing eighteen oil paintings, seventy-two water-colours, and three pen-and-ink sketches.

[Personal knowledge; private information; obituary notices in The Times, Scotsman, Belfast News Letter, and African World.]

T. H.

CURRIE, MARY MONTGOMERIE, Lady Currie (1843–1905), author under the pseudonym of Violet Fane, born at Beauport, Littlehampton, Sussex, on 24 Feb. 1843, was eldest daughter of Charles James Saville Montgomerie Lamb by his wife Anna Charlotte, daughter of Arthur Hopwood Grey of Bersted, Sussex. Her grandfather, Sir Charles Montolieu Lamb, second baronet, of Beauport, Sussex, married Mary, daughter and heiress of Archibald Montgomerie, eleventh earl of Eglinton [q. v.]; her great-grandfather was Sir James Bland Burges, afterwards Lamb [q. v.]. Her ancestors both English and French numbered among them many literary amateurs. Brought up at Beauport, she early showed a love of nature and of poetry, and from a youthful age tried her hand, in spite of her family's stern discouragement, at verse-making and story-writing. She etched illustrations for a reprint of Tennyson's 'Mariana' (Worthing, 1863). She married on 27 Feb. 1864 Henry Sydenham Singleton of Mell, co. Louth, and Hazely Heath, Hampshire, an Irish landowner.

Her first publication was a volume of verse entitled 'From Dawn to Noon' (1872), written under the pseudonym of 'Violet Fane,' which she chose at random, and retained in permanence in order to conceal her identity from her family. (It is the name of a character in Disraeli's 'Vivian Grey.') In 1875 appeared 'Denzil Place: a Story in Verse,' an interesting love-tale, never rising to high passion, but showing much feeling. 'The Queen of the Fairies and other Poems' appeared in 1876, and in 1877 'Anthony Babington,' a drama in prose and verse. In 1880 she issued her 'Collected Verses.'

Meanwhile, Mrs. Singleton became well known in London society. Possessed of great personal beauty and charm of manner, she was an original and witty talker. Mr. W. H. Mallock dedicated to her his 'New Republic' (1877) in which she figures prominently as Mrs. Sinclair, 'who has published a volume of poems, and is a sort of fashionable London Sappho.'

Mrs. Singleton also wrote prose, beginning with the witty social sketches entitled 'Edwin and Angelina Papers' (1878). Three novels, 'Sophy, or the Adventures of a Savage' (1881); 'Thro' Love and War' (1886); and 'The Story of Helen

Davenant' (1889), were followed by further poems, 'Autumn Songs' (1889). In 1892 her poems were again collected, now in two handsome volumes.

Mr. Singleton, by whom she had two sons and two daughters, died on 10 March 1893. On 24 Jan. 1894 Mrs. Singleton married secondly Sir Philip Henry Wodehouse Currie, G.C.B., afterwards Baron Currie of Hawley [q. v. Suppl. II]. She accompanied him to Constantinople, where he was ambassador. While there she produced two volumes of poems, 'Under Cross and Crescent' (1896) and 'Betwixt two Seas: . . . Ballads written at Constantinople and Therapia' (1900). In 1898 her husband was transferred to Rome, and there she lived until his retirement in 1903. Settling at Hawley, Hampshire, Lady Currie took keen interest in gardening. She died of heart failure on 13 Oct. 1905, at the Grand Hotel, Harrogate, and was buried at Mattingley Church, Hampshire.

Her poems, generally in a minor key and slightly sentimental, show command of metrical technique and a gift of melody. Some of them were set to music, notably 'For Ever and for Ever,' by Sir Paolo Tosti. Her novels, while they take original views of life and show careful delineation of character, are somewhat dull and over-long. Her best prose is to be found in her light essays, contributed to periodicals and afterwards republished in volume form (cf. 'Edwin and Angelina Papers,' 1878; 'Two Moods of a Man,' 1901; and 'Collected Essays,' 1902). A prose work of a different character was 'Memoirs of Marguerite of Valois, Queen of Navarre' (1892). First editions of her early poetical volumes are valued by collectors.

A portrait engraved by Stodart forms the frontispiece of 'Poems' (2 vols. 1892).

[Burke's Peerage, 1910; The Times, 16 Oct. 1905; Lady, 29 Dec. 1904; Men and Women of the Time, 1899; private information.]

E. L.

CURRIE, PHILIP HENRY WODEHOUSE, first Baron Currie of Hawley (1834–1906), diplomatist, born in London on 13 Oct. 1834, was fourth son of Raikes Currie (1805–1881) of Bush Hill, Middlesex, and Minley Manor, Hampshire, M.P. for Northampton 1837–57, by his wife Laura Sophia (*d.* 1869), eldest daughter of John, second Baron Wodehouse. After education at Eton, he entered the foreign office at the age of twenty, and served in that department for forty years, passing through the various grades of the political staff until his selection to be assistant under-secretary of state for foreign affairs in 1882 and permanent under-secretary of state in 1889. He was précis writer to the earl of Clarendon during his tenure of office as foreign secretary in 1857–8, and was temporarily attached to the British legation at St. Petersburg in 1856 and 1857 during Lord Wodehouse's special mission to that capital on the conclusion of the Crimean war. He assisted Julian Fane [q. v.] in his duties as protocolist to the conferences on the affairs of Luxemburg in May 1867. When Lord Salisbury was sent to Constantinople in 1876 to act as British plenipotentiary in the conferences held there on the Eastern question, Currie was appointed secretary to the special mission, and Lord Salisbury formed on that occasion a high estimate of his ability. On Lord Salisbury's accession to the office of foreign secretary in April 1878 he appointed Currie to be his private secretary, and when Lord Beaconsfield and Lord Salisbury went as the British plenipotentiaries to the congress of Berlin in June following, Currie and Montagu Corry (afterwards Lord Rowton) accompanied them as joint-secretaries to the special mission. He received the C.B. in recognition of his services at the close of the congress, and on his return to England in addition to his work as private secretary was entrusted by Lord Salisbury with the correspondence respecting Cyprus, which had been leased from the sultan under the convention of 4 June 1878.

On Lord Salisbury's resignation in 1880 Currie resumed his work as a senior clerk in charge of the Eastern department. He was attached as secretary to the marquis of Northampton's special mission to invest King Alfonso XII of Spain with the garter in 1881, and in October 1882 was appointed assistant under-secretary of state by earl Granville, who succeeded Lord Salisbury as foreign secretary. In June to August 1884 Currie acted as joint protocolist to the conferences held in London on the finances of Egypt. In 1885 he received the K.C.B., and in December 1888 he was promoted permanent under-secretary of state in succession to Lord Pauncefote, who had become British envoy at Washington.

After five years' service as permanent under-secretary, during which he was made G.C.B. in 1892, he was appointed by Lord Rosebery in December 1893 British ambassador at Constantinople, being sworn as usual a privy councillor. This post he held for four and a half years.

The period of his service was one of exceptional difficulty. The continued misrule and oppression of the Christian subjects of the Porte in Asia Minor drove the Armenians into an active and widespread conspiracy of revolt, which was repressed by the authorities and the Mussulman population with savage severity. In May 1895 the representatives of the great European powers made a collective demand for reforms in the administration. This was met by the Porte with the usual dilatory pleas, and by the eventual announcement of inadequate concessions in September and October following. Riots broke out in the latter month at Constantinople, in which a considerable number of Armenians lost their lives, and terrible massacres shortly afterwards took place at Trebizond and in other places in Asia Minor. Collective demands were again made by the representatives of the great powers in November for investigation of the circumstances and punishment of those responsible, but were again met by evasive answers; there was, however, some amendment of the situation, and a formidable rising in the district of Zeitoun north of Aleppo was pacified by the mediation of the powers in 1896. But on 1 August of that year a sanguinary massacre of Armenians was perpetrated in Constantinople itself by a Mahomedan mob which had received arms from the Turkish authorities. Fresh remonstrances were made by the embassies and met by fresh excuses on the part of the Turkish government. More effective precautions were however taken against further outbreaks, and the troubles gradually subsided.

Throughout this period the British ambassador, under the instructions first of Lord Kimberley and later of Lord Salisbury, who became foreign secretary in 1895, was taking a leading part in the efforts of the European representatives to secure protection and redress for the sufferers. British policy was greatly hampered by a frank declaration from the Russian government that the tsar had an invincible repugnance to the employment of coercive measures against the sultan, but there was a moment after the massacres at Constantinople, when it seemed possible that the British government might decide on intervention even at the risk of ulterior complications. The objections to this course were considered to be too serious to permit of its adoption, and subsequently a sporadic recrudescence of disorders made it clear that the sultan's authority and goodwill were in fact the only means, however imperfect and untrustworthy, of keeping Mahomedan fanaticism in check. The relations of the British ambassador with the Turkish sovereign could hardly in such circumstances be altogether cordial, and a certain impulsiveness of energy and directness of speech which were among Currie's characteristics were not qualities likely to win favour with an Oriental autocrat. It was no secret that the sultan would have been glad that he should be replaced, and that Lord Salisbury turned a deaf ear to intimations to that effect. A personal episode of a somewhat unusual character, which occurred in the autumn of 1895, added to the difficulties of the ambassador's position. Said Pasha, a former grand vizier, having refused the request of the sultan to resume that office, was imprisoned in the grounds of Yildiz Kiosk, but succeeded in making his escape, and took refuge late at night in the British embassy, which he positively declined to leave, until after five days of negotiation the sultan had given full assurances to the ambassador that the recalcitrant ex-minister should not be molested in any way. In 1897 the troubles in Asia Minor were succeeded by the revolt of Crete, the despatch to the island of a Greek force, the consequent outbreak of war between Turkey and Greece, resulting in the disastrous defeat of the Greek army, the intervention of the powers to secure favourable terms of peace for the Hellenic kingdom, and the autonomy of Crete under Turkish suzerainty. In all these matters the British embassy necessarily took an active part, and Currie who, though physically strong, was not possessed of a very robust constitution, found his health giving way under the strain, and was glad to succeed Sir Clare Ford at the embassy at Rome in July 1898.

His period of service in Italy was marked by the assassination of King Humbert and the accession of King Victor Emmanuel III on 30 July 1900. No very critical diplomatic work devolved on him, the principal questions for discussion between the two countries being connected with Italian claims and interests in Africa, which were not unsympathetically regarded by Great Britain. He was one of the British delegates at the international conference held at Rome in the winter of 1898 to consider the means of dealing with anarchism, a matter in which this country was unable entirely to associate itself with the methods agreed upon by other powers. In January 1899 he was raised to the peerage as Baron Currie of Hawley, and retired on pension on 17 Jan. 1903. He passed the rest of his life in England until his death at his country place, Hawley, on 12 May 1906.

Currie was an admirable official, rapid in his work, clear in judgment, and wanting in neither courage nor decision. As a diplomatist he was somewhat lacking in power to appreciate and make allowance for the susceptibilities of those with whom he had to deal. In social life he was a warm friend, kindly, hospitable, and good-naturedly sarcastic, not universally popular but greatly liked by the majority of those with whom he was closely associated.

He married on 24 Jan. 1894 [see CURRIE, MARY MONTGOMERIE, Suppl. II], but had no children.

[The Times, 14 May 1906; Foreign Office List 1907, p. 397; correspondence laid before Parliament.] S.

CURZON-HOWE, SIR ASSHETON GORE (1850–1911), admiral, born at Gopsall, Leicestershire, on 10 August 1850, was ninth son of Richard William Penn Howe, first Earl Howe of the present creation, being second son of his second wife, Anne (*d.* 1877), second daughter of Admiral Sir John Gore. He was a great-grandson of Richard, first Earl Howe [q. v.], the great admiral, whose daughter and heir, Sophia Charlotte, Baroness Howe, married Penn, eldest son of Assheton Curzon, first Viscount Curzon. Curzon-Howe entered the navy on board the Britannia in Dec. 1863, and from 1868 to 1871 served in the frigate Galatea, Captain the duke of Edinburgh, which went round the world during that commission. He was promoted to sub-lieutenant on 18 March 1870, and served in that rank on board the Bellerophon in the Channel squadron. His commission as lieutenant was dated 18 Sept. 1872, and in Nov. 1873 he was appointed to the sloop Eclipse on the North American station. A year later he was transferred to the Bellerophon, flagship on the same station, and in Feb. 1876 was appointed to the Sultan in the Mediterranean, commanded by the duke of Edinburgh, whom two years later he followed into the Black Prince. In July 1879, when the Bacchante was commissioned by Captain Lord Charles Scott for a cruise round the world, and to give Albert Edward, duke of Clarence, and Prince George of Wales, afterwards King George V, their sea training as cadets, Curzon-Howe was chosen to be her first lieutenant, and was directly responsible for the seamanship instruction of the princes. On the return of the ship to England he was promoted to commander on 31 August 1882.

In Jan. 1883 he became executive officer of the sultan in the Channel squadron, and two years later was appointed in the same capacity to the Raleigh, flagship on the Cape station. In July 1886 he was given the command of the royal yacht Osborne, from which on 6 Jan. 1888 he was promoted to captain. Shortly afterwards Curzon-Howe commissioned the Boadicea for the East Indies station, where, in Aug. 1888, she relieved the Bacchante as flagship of Sir Edmund Fremantle. As flag-captain and chief of the staff he took part in the Vitu expedition of Oct. 1890, for which he received the C.B. and the medal. From August 1891 he served for a year at the admiralty as assistant-director of naval intelligence, and then went to the North American station in command of the Cleopatra, and as commodore during the Newfoundland fishing season. In this ship he was present at Bluefields, Nicaragua, during the disturbances of 1894, and by his prompt action in landing a party of seamen and marines averted a civil war. In Jan. 1896 he was awarded the C.M.G. for his services in Newfoundland, and in the same month became flag-captain to Rear-Admiral A. T. Dale in the Revenge, flagship of the flying squadron which was put in commission shortly after the publication of the German emperor's telegram to President Kruger. In April 1897 he was appointed to command the cadets' training-ship Britannia at Dartmouth, and afterwards, from Feb. 1900, he commanded the battleship Ocean on the China station. In July 1899 Curzon-Howe was appointed an aide-de-camp to Queen Victoria, and held this post until promoted to flag rank on 23 July 1901.

In June 1902 he hoisted his flag in the Magnificent as second in command in the Channel, and from that time his employment was practically continuous. In June 1903 he became second in command on the China station with his flag in the Albion. On 30 June 1905 he was awarded the K.C.B., and on 12 Sept. he was promoted to vice-admiral. In Dec. following he returned to the Channel fleet, now greatly enlarged, as second in command, with his flag on board the Cæsar. In Feb. 1907 he was appointed commander in chief of the Atlantic fleet, whence in Nov. 1908 he was transferred in the same capacity, but with acting rank as admiral, to the Mediterranean, his flagship during both commands being the Exmouth. The disastrous earthquake at Messina in Dec. 1908 called the commander-in-chief with part of his squadron to the spot to aid in the relief work, and the crisis which accompanied the revolution in Turkey made the Mediterranean for the time the centre of interest. On 2 Jan. 1909 he was advanced to the rank of admiral, and in July of that year received the G.C.V.O. Sir Assheton was relieved in April 1910, and immediately hoisted his flag at the main of the Victory as commander-in-chief at Portsmouth. He died suddenly at Admiralty House there on 1 March 1911. He was buried with naval honours at Highcliffe, near Christchurch. A memorial tablet was placed in Portsmouth dockyard church. 'Holding strong opinions on some points, he constantly stood aloof from all controversies of public character. Few flag-officers who have held such important appointments have ever been so little in the public eye as he.'

Curzon-Howe married on 25 Feb. 1892 Alice Ann, eldest daughter of General Sir John Cowell, P.C., K.C.B., and had issue two sons (the elder is in the navy) and three daughters. His eldest daughter, Victoria Alexandrina, to whom Queen Victoria stood sponsor, died at Malta on 3 Feb. 1910.

[The Times, 2 March 1911.] L. G. C. L.

CUST, ROBERT NEEDHAM (1821–1909), orientalist, born at Cockayne Hatley, Bedfordshire, on 24 Feb. 1821, was second son of Henry Cockayne Cust (1780–1861), canon of Windsor, by his wife Lady Anna Maria Elizabeth, eldest daughter of Francis Needham, first earl of Kilmorey. His father was second son of Sir Brownlow Cust, first baron Brownlow (1744–1807). Educated at Eton, Robert was intended for the bar, but accepting a nomination for the Indian civil service, he passed to Haileybury College, where he greatly distinguished himself in Sanskrit, Persian, Arabic and Hindūstāni. At Calcutta in 1843 he completed his studies in the college of Fort William, receiving medals and a degree of honour besides qualifying in Bengāli.

His first appointment in the public service was as assistant to the magistrate of Ambala, then the headquarters of the political administration of Northern India. He next became personal assistant to Major George Broadfoot [q. v.], newly appointed agent to the governor-general for the then north-western frontier. While he was marching with his chief through the domains of the Cis Satlaj protected chiefs, news of the Sikh invasion took them to the front and he engaged in the great battles on the Satlaj in 1845—at Mudki, Ferozeshah, and Sobraon. At Ferozeshah (21–2 Dec. 1845) Major Broadfoot was killed in action, and Cust, albeit a junior officer, carried on for a time the duties of governor-general's agent. His services were mentioned in the governor-general's despatch, and he was appointed by Lord Hardinge to the charge of a district in the newly formed province of the Punjab, that of Hoshiarpur. He had little experience to guide him; but under the inspiration of his new chief, John (afterwards Lord) Lawrence [q. v.], he organised the district on a 'non-regulation' system of firmness and kindness; living alone amongst the people, without soldiers or policemen—the court held under the green mango trees in the presence of hundreds. Here Cust developed an intense love for India and its people. 'The experience of half a century,' he remarked later, 'has given the stamp of approval to our strong but benevolent, rigorous but sympathetic system.'

From Hoshiarpur he was moved to his old district of Ambala, and took its administration vigorously in hand. Cust, if lacking in magnetic power, showed himself a masterly organiser and administrator, and an indefatigable and methodical worker. After the second Sikh war, which ended decisively in March 1849 with the annexation of the Punjab, the government commissioned Cust to report on the country and its capabilities. He visited every district in the newly acquired territory, and after nearly two years' immense labour he presented his report in 1851. Cust then proceeded to England on a brief furlough. Returning to India, he was appointed magistrate of Benares, and afterwards to the more important charge of Banda in Bundelkand, and in three years he put the district, which was in a most unsatisfactory condition, into perfect order. In recognition of his services he was offered the more important post of magistrate and collector of Delhi, but fortunately for himself declined it. The officer who accepted the post was a victim of the Delhi massacre.

Cust was in England at the outbreak of the mutiny of 1857, being called to the bar at Lincoln's Inn on 13 Aug. 1857. Returning to India in February 1858, he was immediately appointed at the special request of Sir John Lawrence to be commissioner of the Lahore division of the Punjab, and when that division was found too large and was subdivided, he chose the moiety forming the division of Amritsar. For a time he acted as financial commissioner of the province, and in 1861 as judicial commissioner. The death of his first wife on 17 Jan. 1864 brought him back to England, but he returned to India in October to join the legislative council, and to act temporarily as home secretary to the supreme government (1864–5). From another visit to England he was recalled to fill the important post of member of the board of revenue in the North-west Provinces, but the death at Allahabad after childbirth in August 1867 of his second wife determined Cust to retire altogether from the Indian service just nine months before completing his service for a full pension.

In England Cust gradually recovered his energies. He studied Hebrew and completed the draft of a code of revenue law for Northern India. For a time he helped in the preparation of the Oxford 'Dictionary of the English Language' edited by Sir James Murray. Although he had rowed at Eton, he cared nothing for sports or games, and henceforth found recreation in foreign travel, while devoting himself at home to Oriental and religious studies, which he pursued with characteristic industry and method. Without being a profound scholar he had some acquaintance with Hebrew, Arabic, Persian, Sanskrit, Hindī, Ūrdū or Hindūstāni, Panjābi, Bengālī, as well as with the chief European languages. Between 1870 and 1909 he published more than sixty volumes chiefly on Oriental philology or phases of religious belief. His 'Modern Languages of the East Indies' (1878) was followed by a scholarly description of the 'Modern Languages of Africa' (1883), which was translated into Italian (1885), 'Oceania' (1887), 'The Caucasian Group' (1887), 'The Turki Branch of the Ural-Altaic Family' (1889). 'Linguistic and Oriental Essays,' in seven series, were issued between 1880 and 1904. Less laborious works included, apart from translations into French, Italian and Greek, 'Poems of Many Years and Places' (2 ser. 1887, 1897), 'Clouds on the Horizon or Forms of Religious Error' (1890); 'Common Features which appear in all Religions of the World' (1895); 'Five Essays on Religious Conceptions' (1897), and 'Life Memoir' (1899). Cust was prominent in the proceedings of many literary societies. With the Royal Asiatic Society, which he joined in 1851, his association was especially long and active; he was appointed member of council and honorary librarian in 1872, and from 1878 to 1899 was honorary secretary; he was also a vice-president, and read many papers at its meetings. Making annual tours abroad through Europe, West Africa, and Western Asia, and coming to know numerous foreign scholars, Cust represented the Asiatic Society at the Oriental Congresses of London, St. Petersburg, Florence, Berlin, Leyden, Vienna, and Stockholm. He was interested in missionary enterprise and philanthropic work, and served on the committees of the Church Missionary Society and the Society for the Propagation of the Gospel. He was made honorary LL.D. of Edinburgh in 1885.

Cust, who had attended the coronation of William IV in 1831, and that of Queen Victoria in 1838, was also present at that of Edward VII in 1902. In 1904 his sight failed, but he pursued his studies with assistance until 1908, when his strength gave way. He died on 28 Oct. 1909 at his residence, Campden Hill Road, Kensington, and was buried at Putney Vale.

Cust was thrice married: (1) on 10 May 1856 to Maria Adelaide, second daughter of Henry Lewis Hobart, dean of Windsor; she died on 17 Jan. 1864, leaving two sons and three daughters; (2) on 28 Dec. 1865 to Emma, eldest daughter of E. Carlyon, rector of Debden, Hampshire; she died on 10 Aug. 1867; (3) on 11 Nov. 1868 to Elizabeth Dewar, only daughter of J. Mathews; by her he had a daughter, Anna Maria Elizabeth. His son, Robert Henry Hobart Cust, is a well-known writer on art, and his daughters showed literary aptitude.

A portrait was painted by Miss Carpenter in 1840, of which three copies were made: one is at the Provost's Lodge, Eton; a second belongs to Sir Reginald Cust, and a third to Cust's son, Mr. Robert Cust. He also appears as a child in a large group by Samuel William Reynolds, now in the possession of Mr. Henry Cust. A native painting, executed in Calcutta (c. 1843), also belongs to Mr. Robert Cust.

[Cust's Life Memoir, 1899; The Times, 29 Oct. 1909; Royal Asiatic Society's Journal, 1910. i. 255; private information.] T. H. T.

CUSTANCE, HENRY (1842–1908), jockey, born at Peterborough on 27 Feb. 1842, was son of Samuel Custance, a postboy, by his wife Elizabeth Carpenter. Devoted to horses and to riding from childhood, he rode at thirteen in a pony race at Ramsey, in Huntingdonshire, and afterwards won a contest for a saddle when he weighed four stone. Vainly seeking employment at Newmarket, he spent three years at Epsom, where he had 'a jolly, though rough, time' in the employment of Mr. Edward Smith of South Hatch, who was associated with 'Bell's Life,' and raced his horses in the name of Mellish.

Custance's first important victory was gained on Rocket in 1858 in the Cesarewitch, which he won again in 1861 on Audrey. The following year he attached himself to the Russley stable, then under the management of Matthew Dawson, and that season rode over forty winners. In 1860 he rode Thormanby to victory in the Derby. This was the first of three successes he scored in that race, the others being on Lord Lyon in 1866 and on George Frederick in 1874. In the Derby of 1861 he rode Dundee, who, breaking down during the race, was second to Kettledrum. He had a mount in the Derby for twenty consecutive years. Custance won the One Thousand Guineas on Achievement in 1867, and his solitary success in the St. Leger was gained on Lord Lyon in 1866. His last winning mount was on Lollypop in the All-Aged Stakes at the Newmarket Houghton meeting in 1879. As a jockey he was bold and resolute, had good hands, and was a fine judge of pace. After his retirement from the saddle he long remained a familiar figure on the racecourse. He held for many years a licence as deputy starter to the Jockey Club, and was also official starter to the Belgian Jockey Club. Living at Oakham, he regularly hunted with the Quorn and Cottesmore packs. He was always a cheerful and amusing companion, and published 'Riding Recollections and Turf Stories' in 1894, with a dedication to the duke of Hamilton, a good patron during his riding career. He died of a paralytic seizure at 53 New Walk, Leicester, on 19 April 1908. His will was proved for 8081*l.*

[Sporting Life and The Times, 20 April 1908; Ruff's Guide to the Turf; Custance's Riding Recollections, 1894.] E. M.

CUTTS, EDWARD LEWES (1824–1901), antiquary, born on 2 March 1824, at Sheffield, was son of John Priston Cutts, optician, by Mary, daughter of Robert Waterhouse. He was educated at Sheffield Collegiate School and graduated B.A. at Queens' College, Cambridge, in 1848. Being ordained in the same year, he was curate successively of Ide Hill, Kent, until 1850, of Coggeshall, Essex, until 1857, and of Kelvedon until 1859, and was perpetual curate of Billericay until 1865. He had already acted also as local organising secretary of the Additional Curates Society, and on leaving Billericay became general secretary of the society in London, resigning in 1871, on presentation to the vicarage of Holy Trinity, Haverstock Hill.

In 1876 Cutts was selected by the Archbishops of Canterbury and York to visit the East and inquire into the position of the Syrian and Chaldean churches; his report resulted in the formation of the Archbishop's Mission to the Assyrian Christians. He described his travels in 'Christians under the Crescent in Asia' (1887). Although accepting the ecclesiastical views of the high church party, he was sympathetic with every school of thought within the church. He received the degree of D.D. from the University of the South, U.S.A.

Cutts long devoted himself to archæology and the study of ecclesiastical history. In 1849 he published 'A Manual for the Study of the Sepulchral Slabs and Crosses of the Middle Ages.' This was followed in 1853 by 'Colchester Castle not a Roman Temple,' and in 1872 by 'Scenes and Characters of the Middle Ages,' a series of articles contributed originally to the 'Art Journal'; in 1888 by 'Colchester,' in Freeman and Hunt's series of 'Historic Towns'; in 1893 by 'History of Early Christian Art'; and in 1898 by 'Parish Priests and their People in the Middle Ages in England.' Among his works on Church history are 'Turning Points of English Church History' (1874); 'Turning Points of General Church History' (1877); 'A Dictionary of the Church of England' (1887); 'A Handy Book of the Church of England' (1892); and 'Augustine of Canterbury' (1895) in Methuen's 'English Leaders of Religion.' The most notable of his religious works are 'A Devotional History of Our Lord' (1882) and 'Some Chief Truths of Religion' (1875), which was translated into Swahili and printed at the Universities Mission Press at Zanzibar in 1895. From 1852 to 1866 he was honorary secretary of the Essex Archæological Society and editor of its 'Transactions.'

Cutts died at Holy Trinity Vicarage, Haverstock Hill, on 2 Sept. 1901, and was buried at Brookwood cemetery, Woking. He married on 23 April 1846 Marian, daughter of Robert Knight of Nottingham, and by her had ten children, seven of whom survived him. Mrs. Cutts died on 14 Dec. 1889.

[The Times, 4 and 6 Sept. 1901; Guardian, 11 Sept. 1901; Athenæum, 7 Sept. 1901 information from his son, John E. K. Cutts F.R.I.B.A.] R. E. G.

D

DALE, Sir DAVID, first baronet (1829–1906), ironmaster, born on 11 Dec. 1829 at Moorshedabad, Bengal, was younger of two sons (in the family of three children) of David Dale (of the East India Company's service), judge of the city court there, by his wife Ann Elizabeth, daughter of the Rev. George Douglas of Aberdeen, who was married at Calcutta on her seventeenth birthday. His great-uncle was David Dale [q. v.], the Glasgow banker and philanthropist, whose daughter married the socialist Robert Owen [q. v.] and was mother of Robert Dale Owen [q. v.]. David's elder brother, James Douglas (1820–1865), joined the Indian army on the Madras establishment, and became lieutenant-colonel. The father died on board the Providence on 23 June 1830, during a voyage home with his wife and children. Mrs. Dale, while on a journey with her children to New Lanark to visit her kindred, was detained at Darlington by an accident to the mail coach, and received such kindness from members of the Society of Friends of that town that she returned and made the place her home. After four years' probation she was in 1841 received into the Friends' community. She died in 1879.

Dale was educated privately at Edinburgh, Durham, and Stockton. Brought up among Friends, he early displayed unusual steadfastness of purpose and sobriety of judgment. His adult career began in the office of the Stockton and Darlington Railway Company, and at the age of twenty-three he was appointed secretary to the Middlesbrough and Guisborough section of the line. After six years in that position he entered in 1858 into partnership with Mr. W. Bouch and became lessee of the Shildon Locomotive Works. Henceforth his activities rapidly expanded. He was concerned with the formation of the Consett Iron Co., of which he subsequently became managing director and chairman. In 1866 he embarked on extensive shipbuilding enterprises in co-operation with Richardson, Denton, Duck & Co. of Stockton, Denton, Grey & Co. of Hartlepool, and Thomas Richardson & Sons, Hartlepool, who combined together with a view to amalgamation. Dale became vice-chairman of this ambitious undertaking, but the union was not successful, and the companies reverted shortly afterwards to their former independent positions. Dale retained an interest in the two first-named concerns. He was also managing partner of J. W. Pease & Co., later Pease & Partners Ltd., and chairman of companies working iron ore mines near Bilbao. In 1881 he became a director of the North Eastern Railway Company, having previously served as director of the Stockton and Darlington railway, and on the formation of the Dunderland Iron Ore Company in 1902 he was appointed chairman. He was an active member of the Durham Coal Owners' Association and of the Cleveland Mine Owners' Association.

Dale owes his main distinction to his work as pioneer in applying the principle of arbitration to industrial disputes. The first board of arbitration was formed in connection with the iron trade of the north of England in March 1869, and Dale was its first president. The success of the experiment was chiefly due to the tact, firmness, and discrimination of its president. 'Its inauguration ushered in a millennium of peace and goodwill between employers and employed compared with the chaotic and demoralising state of matters that previously existed' (Jeans, *Pioneers of the Cleveland Iron Trade*, p. 211). In recognition of Dale's services to the board he was publicly presented in 1881 with an address and a portrait painted at a cost of 500 guineas by W. W. Ouless. This is now in the possession of his son at Park Close, Englefield Green, Surrey. His high position and influence in the industrial world of the north led to his appointment on several royal commissions, amongst which were those on trade depression (1885–6); on mining royalties (1889–93); and on labour (1891–4). At the Berlin labour conference of 1890, convened at the instance of the German emperor, he was one of the representatives of Great Britain, and during the sittings he received marked attention from the emperor and from Bismarck. He had helped to found the Iron and Steel Institute in 1869, and acted as hon. treasurer from that date until 1895, when he was elected president. He was created a baronet in the same year.

In politics Sir David was a liberal. His business interests monopolised his attention, and he declined to contest a seat in parliament. The University of Durham made him hon. D.C.L. in 1895. In 1888 he became high sheriff for Durham. He died at York on 28 April 1906, and was buried at Darlington. In his honour the 'Sir David Dale chair of economics' was instituted at Armstrong University, Newcastle-on-Tyne, in 1909, as well as a memorial lectureship on labour problems at Darlington; the first lecture was delivered by Sir Edward Grey on 28 Oct. 1910. Dale was twice married: (1) on 27 Jan. 1853 to Annie Backhouse (*d.* 1886), only daughter and heiress of Edward Robson and widow of Henry Whitwell of Kendal, by her he had a son, James Backhouse, who succeeded him in the baronetcy, and one daughter; and (2) on 2 Aug. 1888 to Alice Frederica, (*d.* 1902), daughter of Sir Frederick Acclom Milbank, Bart.

[Pioneers of the Cleveland Iron Trade, by J. S. Jeans, Middlesbrough, 1875; Journal of the Iron and Steel Institute, lxix.; Sir David Dale, inaugural lecture by Sir Edward Grey, with a Memoir by Howard Pease, 1910; Biographical Mag., June 1889; The Times, 30 April 1906; private information.]

L. P. S.

DALLINGER, WILLIAM HENRY (1842–1909), Wesleyan minister and biologist, born in Devonport on 5 July 1842, was son of Joseph Stephen Dallinger, artist and engraver. He was educated privately. In boyhood he showed a bent towards natural science, but his religious instinct led him to qualify for the Wesleyan ministry in 1861. After serving Wesleyan churches in Faversham, Cardiff, and Bristol, he passed to Liverpool, where he remained twelve years (1868–80). There in 1870 he began microscopic researches into minute septic organisms, which he pursued for ten years. In 1880 he was appointed governor and president of Wesley College, Sheffield, and had held the post for eight years, when the Wesleyan conference, recognising his scientific attainments, allowed him to retire from the position whilst retaining the status and privilege of a Wesleyan minister without pastoral charge. In addition to his work as minister and governor, Dallinger was a successful public lecturer on microscopical subjects. For thirty years he lectured for the Gilchrist Educational Trust.

Dallinger's contributions to science are of two kinds—his classical investigations into the life-history of certain micro-organisms, and his improvements in microscopical technique. The organisms he worked at in collaboration with Dr. John James Drysdale of Liverpool were 'flagellates' or 'monads,' about the life-history of which little was known. Dallinger showed not only unwearied patience and application but a mastery of manipulation. By using a binocular instrument an individual monad was kept under observation first by one and then by the other of the two students for a considerable time; on one occasion for thirty-two hours. By such means the transformations of these obscure animals were established. In addition to these important investigations, Dallinger and his colleague contributed valuable evidence in regard to the then controverted question of abiogenesis. They were able to show that by acclimatising these monads to an increasingly high temperature, they acquired a power of living freely in a temperature far above the normal, and one which is lethal to unacclimatised specimens. Further, they proved that though the temperature of boiling water was fatal to all such monads in an active state, yet that their spores were extraordinarily resistant, enduring a temperature of 268° in water and 300° or more in a dry state. These discoveries showed that the ordinary precautions (such as boiling) by which organic solutions are sought to be sterilised are insufficient, and they also explain the origin of life in experiments where spontaneous generation had been supposed to occur.

As an expert microscopist, Dallinger enjoyed the highest reputation. He occupied the post of president of the Royal Microscopical Society four times (1884–7) and that of the Quekett Club (1890–2). He was elected F.R.S. in 1880; hon. LL.D. of Toronto in 1884; D.Sc. of Dublin in 1892, and D.C.L. of Durham in 1896. In 1879 he delivered the Rede lecture at Cambridge on 'The Origin of Life,' illustrated by the life-histories of the least and lowest organisms in nature. His chief papers are published in the 'Monthly Microscopical Journal' (1873–6). He rendered students a great service by editing and rewriting Carpenter's classical book, 'The Microscope and its Revelations' (1890; new edit. 1901). He was also author of a theologico-scientific work, 'The Creator and what we may know of the Method of Creation' (1887). A good portrait of him was published in the 'Journal of the Royal Microscopical Society' for 1909.

He died at his residence, Ingleside, Lee, Kent, on 7 Nov. 1909. He married Emma, daughter of David Goldsmith of Bury St. Edmunds, and had one son.

[Nature, 1909, lxxxii. 71; Proc. Roy. Soc. 1910, lxxxii. B. iv; personal knowledge.]

F. W. G.

DALZIEL, EDWARD (1817–1905), draughtsman and wood-engraver, second of the Brothers Dalziel [see DALZIEL, GEORGE, and DALZIEL, THOMAS BOLTON GILCHRIST SEPTIMUS, Suppl. II], was fifth son of Alexander Dalziel by his wife Elizabeth Hills. Born at Wooler, Northumberland, on 5 Dec. 1817, he was educated at Newcastle-on-Tyne. Brought up at first for business, he followed his brother George to London in 1839 and entered into a partnership with him as engraver, and afterwards as publisher and printer, which lasted till 1893. He is said to have taken the leading part in extending the operations of the firm, and is credited with the faculty of discerning and fostering a talent for illustration in artists hitherto untried. He himself studied, after coming to London, at the Clipstone Street life school, where he was a contemporary of Sir John Tenniel and of Charles Keene; he painted in his leisure time both in oils and water-colours, and exhibited occasionally at the Royal Academy. As an illustrator he was less gifted and prolific than his brother Thomas. No book was illustrated entirely by him, but woodcuts from his designs appear in the following: 'Poetical Works of William Cullen Bryant' (New York, 1857); 'Home Affections with the Poets' (1858); Dalziel's 'Arabian Nights' (1864); 'A Round of Days' (1865); 'Poems' by Jean Ingelow (1867); Robert Buchanan's 'Ballad Stories of the Affections' (1866) and 'North Coast' (1868); Novello's 'Our National Nursery Rhymes' (1871); Dalziel's 'Bible Gallery' (1880). Thirty illustrations to Parnell's 'Hermit' from drawings made by Edward Dalziel in 1855 were privately printed at the Camden Press in 1904. Dalziel died on 25 March 1905 at 107 Fellows Road, South Hampstead, where he had resided since 1900, and was buried in old Highgate cemetery. Portraits of Edward Dalziel, from a painting by his brother Robert about 1841, and from a photograph of 1901, appear in 'The Brothers Dalziel,' the book of memoirs of which he was joint author with his brother George.

By his marriage in 1847 with Jane Gurden, who died in 1873, Edward Dalziel had five sons and four daughters. The eldest, Edward Gurden, born in London on 7 Feb. 1849, died on 27 April 1888; a painter and draughtsman of some merit (see GRAVES, *Dict. of Artists*), he illustrated 'Christmas Stories,' 'The Uncommercial Traveller,' and the tales published with 'Edwin Drood,' in Chapman & Hall's 'Household' edition of Charles Dickens (1871–9). The second son, Gilbert, artist and journalist, born on 25 June 1853, a pupil of the Brothers Dalziel as wood-engraver, and a student at the Slade School of Art under Sir Edward Poynter, P.R.A., became proprietor and editor of 'Judy' and other comic papers and annuals. The third and fourth sons, Harvey Robert, born on 13 March 1855, and Charles Davison, born on 16 Jan. 1857, carried on the Camden Press, the printing business of the Brothers Dalziel, under the name of Dalziel & Co., Limited, from 1893 till 1905, when the press was closed.

[The Brothers Dalziel, 1901; Gleeson White's English Illustration: The Sixties, 1897; The Times, 27 March 1905; information from Mr. Gilbert Dalziel.]

C. D.

DALZIEL, GEORGE (1815–1902), draughtsman and wood-engraver, the senior of the Brothers Dalziel [see DALZIEL, EDWARD, and DALZIEL, THOMAS BOLTON GILCHRIST SEPTIMUS, Suppl. II], was born at Wooler, Northumberland, on 1 Dec. 1815, and educated at Newcastle-on-Tyne. His father, Alexander Dalziel (1781–1832), was something of an artist, and seven of his eight sons by Elizabeth Hills (1785–1853) became artists by profession, four of them, George, Edward, John, and Thomas, constituting the firm which produced, as engravers, draughtsmen, and publishers, a large proportion of the English woodcut illustrations issued between 1840 and 1880.

Of the elder sons, William (1805–1873) was a painter of still life and heraldic decoration, Robert (1810–1842) a portrait and landscape painter, and Alexander John (1814–1836) a promising draughtsman in black and white. The two sons of Robert Dalziel, Alexander Aitcheson and John Sanderson, became pupils of the Brothers Dalziel in wood-engraving, but did not persevere in their profession.

John, the sixth son of Alexander Dalziel (born at Wooler on 1 Jan. 1822, died at Drigg, Cumberland, on 21 May 1869), the most notable member of the family after George, Edward, and Thomas, became associated with his brothers' firm in 1852, and was a highly accomplished engraver on wood, but failing health compelled him in 1868 to abandon artistic work and retire to Cumberland. He was twice married: in 1846 to Harriet Carter, by whom he had a son and two daughters, and in 1863 to Elizabeth Wells, who was childless. The eighth son of Alexander Dalziel, Davison Octavian, born at Newcastle on 30 Oct. 1825, devoted himself to commerce.

A daughter, Margaret Jane Dalziel (born at Wooler on 3 Nov. 1819, died unmarried on 12 July 1894), was a skilful wood-engraver and aided her brothers from 1851 onwards.

George Dalziel came from Newcastle to London early in 1835 as pupil to the wood-engraver Charles Gray, with whom he remained four years. He then set up independently, but was soon joined by his brother Edward [q. v. Suppl. II], who entered into partnership with him as joint founder of 'The Brothers Dalziel.' John joined the firm in 1852 and Thomas [q. v. Suppl. II] in 1860. The work of the firm was done from 1857 onwards at 53 (afterwards 110) High Street, Camden Town, where John Dalziel lived, while his brothers resided at various addresses in Camden Town, Primrose Hill, and Hampstead. In their memoirs George and Edward Dalziel give 1840 as the opening date of their combined career. Some of their early wood-engravings are signed with their respective initials, but they soon adopted the common signature, 'Dalziel sc.,' and their individual work was thenceforth merged in the joint production of the firm. George Dalziel produced few original designs. Between 1840 and 1850 the brothers worked much in association with Ebenezer Landells [q. v.], through whose introduction they obtained the engraving of blocks for the early numbers of 'Punch' and the 'Illustrated London News.' Their Tyneside connection brought them into relations with Bewick's pupil, William Harvey [q. v.], many of whose drawings they engraved from 1839 to 1866. Harvey introduced them to the publisher Charles Knight, for whose Shakespeare and 'The Land we live in' (1854–6) they engraved many blocks. They were also employed by T. Cadell of Edinburgh for the Abbotsford edition of the 'Waverley Novels.' About 1850 they entered into business relations with George Routledge, which continued for forty years; they were on similar friendly terms with the firm of Frederick Warne & Co., till 1865 partners of Routledge. Though the brothers Dalziel worked for many other publishers, including Cundall, Chapman & Hall, Longmans, Macmillan, Smith & Elder, Strahan, and Ward & Lock, it was mainly through Routledge and Warne that they were enabled to begin the issue of the long series of illustrated books by which their name became famous in a generation which had grown tired of steel engravings. For these 'fine art' books, often issued in the name of other firms, the Dalziels made all arrangements and undertook the financial risk, commissioning artists on their own responsibility to design the woodcuts, contributing part of the designs themselves, and engraving the blocks by their own hands or those of pupils.

Much of their early work was done after artists whose popularity was already established, such as George Cruikshank, John Leech, Richard Doyle, Kenny Meadows, F. R. Pickersgill, and Sir John Gilbert. Their connection with the pre-Raphaelites began in 1855, when Millais was advised by Doyle to employ the Dalziels to cut one of the blocks which he was then preparing for Moxon's edition of Tennyson's poems (1857). Their first engravings after Millais, Rossetti, and Arthur Hughes were made for William Allingham's 'The Music Master and Day and Night Songs' (1855). Most of the illustrations of Rossetti and Holman Hunt passed through their hands, while Ford Madox Brown and Burne-Jones were contributors to their 'Bible Gallery.' They engraved a large proportion of Millais's black-and-white work, the most famous set of illustrations from his pen being the 'Parables of Our Lord,' commissioned in 1857 and completed in 1864. Other illustrators who owed much to the zeal and enterprise of the firm were Birket Foster, George du Maurier, Sir John Tenniel, and Harrison Weir. They cut the illustrations to the nursery classics, Edward Lear's 'Book of Nonsense' (1862) and Lewis Carroll's 'Alice in Wonderland' (1866) and 'Through the Looking-glass' (1872).

On the foundation of the 'Cornhill Magazine' in 1859 they were entrusted with the engraving of all the illustrations, and in 1862 they undertook, at the request of Alexander Strahan, the engraving and entire control of the illustrations to 'Good Words.' Such a commission gave them ample opportunities of enlisting new forces, and they deserve especial credit for discovering original talent for illustration in the cases of Frederick Walker, George John Pinwell, Arthur Boyd Houghton, Matthew James Lawless, John Dawson Watson, Frederick Barnard, and Mr. John W. North, A.R.A. The merit of English illustration during 1855–70 is due in no small measure to the co-operation of this distinguished band of draughtsmen on wood, and others, with such conscientious and artistic interpreters as the Dalziels. Their aim was to preserve each line intact when the drawings were made, as Gilbert and Tenniel made them, by a pure line method, but they often had the more difficult task of reproducing in facsimile a mixture of line and brush work, touched on the block with Chinese white, a practice habitual with later illustrators, such as Pinwell and Small. During the latter part of this period Joseph Swain [q. v. Suppl. II] and other engravers were doing interpretative work of equal merit, but no other firm combined technical skill with initiative to the same degree as the Dalziels. The most important books for the illustration of which they were wholly or in large part responsible are Staunton's Shakespeare, illustrated by Gilbert (1858–61), 'Lalla Rookh' illustrated by Sir John Tenniel (1861), Birket Foster's 'Pictures of English Landscape' (1862), John Dawson Watson's 'Pilgrim's Progress' (1863), Millais's 'Parables' (1864), 'The Arabian Nights' Entertainments' (1864), illustrated largely by Houghton and Thomas Dalziel, Goldsmith's works, illustrated by Pinwell (1865), and Dalziel's 'Bible Gallery' (1880). Complete sets of India proofs of the woodcuts to all these books, except the 'Arabian Nights' and 'Bible Gallery,' are in the print room of the British Museum. The Dalziels' work is also well represented in the Victoria and Albert Museum, and a framed collection of 226 India proofs was presented by Mr. Gilbert Dalziel in 1909 to the Hampstead Central Library. A complete illustrated record of the brothers' work in chronological sequence remains in Mr. Gilbert Dalziel's possession.

The 'Bible Gallery,' completed in 1880 after many years of preparation, was the last important undertaking of the Dalziels on the artistic side. In the next decade the photo-mechanical processes were already beginning to prevail in competition with the slower and more expensive methods of the wood-engraver. The Dalziels' energies were thenceforth more devoted to the business of printing and the production of illustrated newspapers, chiefly comic. In 1870 they had become proprietors of 'Fun,' which they continued to publish until 1893, and in 1871 they acquired 'Hood's Comic Annual,' to which George Dalziel frequently contributed poems and stories; he also wrote much in 'Fun.' Several volumes of stories and three volumes of verse from his pen were published by the firm. In 1872 the Brothers Dalziel acquired another comic paper, 'Judy,' which they sold to Mr. Gilbert Dalziel in 1888. George Dalziel and his brother Edward were joint authors of a volume of reminiscences, 'The Brothers Dalziel, a Record of Fifty Years' Work . . . 1840–90,' published in 1901.

George Dalziel had no issue by his marriage, in 1846, to Mary Ann, daughter of Josiah Rumball, of Wisbech. After his wife's death he resided with his brother Edward at Hampstead, removing with him in 1900 to 107 Fellows Road, South Hampstead, where he died on 4 Aug. 1902; he was buried in old Highgate cemetery.

[The Brothers Dalziel, 1901 (with full list of books); Gleeson White's English Illustration of the Sixties, 1897; The Times, 8 Aug. 1902; information from Mr. Gilbert Dalziel.]

C. D.

DALZIEL, THOMAS BOLTON GILCHRIST SEPTIMUS (1823–1906), draughtsman, youngest and last surviving member of the firm of the Brothers Dalziel [see Dalziel, Edward, and Dalziel, George], was seventh son of Alexander Dalziel by his wife Elizabeth Hills. Born at Wooler, Northumberland, on 9 May 1823, he was educated at Newcastle-on-Tyne. Unlike his brothers, he was brought up as a copperplate engraver, but did not pursue that vocation after completing his apprenticeship. He came to London in 1843, and worked as an independent illustrator for the Dalziels among others, until he joined the firm in 1860. He did not take part in the engraving of blocks, but devoted himself to drawing on wood. He also undertook the important improvements to be carried out before a finished proof was submitted to the artist. He also painted both landscape and figure subjects in water-colour, and made drawings of coast scenery in charcoal. As an illustrator Thomas Dalziel holds a higher rank than any of his brothers. The hundred illustrations to the 'Pilgrim's Progress' (Ward & Lock, 1865) are entirely by him, and he contributed eighty-nine illustrations to the 'Arabian Nights' (1864), twenty to Jean Ingelow's 'Poems' (1867), twenty-five to Robert Buchanan's 'North Coast' (1868), fourteen to the 'Bible Gallery' (1880), and a smaller number to several anthologies, illustrated by various artists and produced by the Brothers Dalziel. In designing the illustrations to the 'Arabian Nights' he profited by the oriental costumes and objects of art in the collection of his collaborator, Arthur Boyd Houghton, with whom, as with Pinwell and Walker, he was on terms of intimate friendship. Thomas Dalziel died at Herne Bay, Kent, where he had chiefly resided since 1893, on 17 March 1906, and was buried in old Highgate cemetery. By his marriage in 1856 with Louisa, daughter of Charles Gurden, who survived him, he had five sons and three daughters. His two elder sons, Herbert, born on 8 Dec. 1858, and Owen, born on 24 July 1860, are painters.

[The Brothers Dalziel, 1901; Gleeson White's English Illustration: The Sixties, 1897; Hampstead Express, 22 March 1906; information from Mr. Gilbert Dalziel.] C. D.

DANIEL, EVAN (1837–1904), writer on the Prayer-book, born at Pontypool on 4 Sept. 1837, was second son of Evan Daniel of Pontypool, builder and architect, by his wife Sarah Beach. After education at the national school, Pontypool, he entered St. John's Training College, Battersea, in 1856. He became lecturer in English literature at the college in 1859 and vice-principal in 1863. In the same year he was ordained deacon, and priest in 1864. He was appointed principal in 1866, a post which he held for 28 years. On assuming the office of principal he began reading for a degree at Trinity College, Dublin; and both in 1868 and 1870 he won there the vice-chancellor's prize for English verse, and in 1869 the prize for English prose. He graduated B.A. in 1870 as senior moderator and gold medallist in English literature, history, and political science, and proceeded M.A. in 1874.

Daniel was generally recognised as an educational expert. From 1873 to 1879 he served on the second London school board, and in 1881 he was appointed practical lecturer on education at Cambridge. In 1879 Anthony Wilson Thorold [q. v.], bishop of Rochester, made him an hon. canon of his cathedral; and from 1892 he was proctor in convocation for the dean and chapter of Rochester. On his resignation of the principalship of St. John's Training College in 1894, Archbishop E. W. Benson [q. v. Suppl. I] nominated him to the vicarage of Horsham, and in 1902 he became rural dean of Storrington. Daniel, who held broad church views, was esteemed a powerful preacher. He died at Horsham vicarage on 27 May 1904, and was buried in the churchyard there. He married in 1863 Elizabeth Mosell of Pontypool, who died in 1901. He had issue six daughters and three sons.

A portrait of Daniel, painted after his death by P. Keelan, is in the hall of St. John's College, Battersea, where he is also commemorated by the establishment of the Daniel Library. A stained glass window to his memory is in Horsham parish church.

Daniel was best known for his valuable and popular work 'The Prayer-book, its History and Contents' (1877; 20th edit. 1901); this has been largely supplemented since, but not altogether superseded. He also published several educational books, including 'Outlines of English History' (1863; 2nd edit. 1872); 'The Grammar, History, and Derivation of the English Language' (1881); 'How to teach the Church Catechism' (1882); 'How to teach the Prayer-book' (1882); 'Elementary Algebra' (1st pt. 1883, 2nd pt. 1885); he edited Locke's 'Some Thoughts on Education' (1880).

[The Times, 28 May 1904; Guardian, 1 June 1904; Horsham Times, and Schoolmaster, 4 June 1904; Brit. Mus. Cat.; private information from Miss Daniel.] G. S. W.

DANVERS, FREDERIC CHARLES (1833–1906), writer on engineering, born at Hornsey on 1 July 1833, was second son of Frederick Samuel Danvers of Hornsey, an officer in the East India Company's service, by his wife Mary Matilda, daughter of H. Middleton of Wanstead, Essex. After education at the Merchant Taylors' School, King's College, London, and Addiscombe, he studied for two years as a civil and mechanical engineer. Then, adopting his father's career, he became, on 26 Jan. 1853, a writer in the old East India House. On the creation of the India office he was, in September 1858, made a junior clerk in its public and ecclesiastical department, and after being deputed in 1859 to Liverpool and Manchester to report on the fitness of traction engines for use in India, where railway construction was in its infancy, he was transferred on account of his technical knowledge to the public works department of the India office in 1861. He there rose to be senior clerk in June 1867, and assistant secretary in February 1875. Plans by him for a tunnel under the Hugli to continue the East India railway into Calcutta were forwarded by Sir Stafford Northcote [q. v.] to India in 1868. In addition to his official duties, he engaged in literary work, mainly of a technical character. He contributed articles on public works in India to 'Engineering' (1866–75), and an article on 'India' to Spon's 'Information for Colonial Engineers' (1877), besides compiling memoranda on Indian coal, coal washing, and artificial fuel (1867–9), and publishing 'Statistical Papers relating to India' (parliamentary paper, 1869), 'Coal Economy' (1872), and 'A Century of Famines, 1770–1870' (1877).

In 1877 Danvers was transferred as assistant secretary to the revenue department of the India office, and was in January 1884 made registrar and superintendent of records. Marked efficiency in this capacity led to his being sent to Lisbon in 1891 to study records of Portuguese rule in the East. His report, based on research in the Torre do Tombo archives and the public libraries in Lisbon and Evora, was published in 1892. There followed his 'History of the Portuguese in India' (2 vols. 1894). This, his most ambitious work, was marred by want of perspective and incomplete reference to authorities. In 1893–5 Danvers studied at the Hague records of Dutch power in the East, but published nothing on the subject. He retired from the India office in July 1898.

Danvers read papers before the Society of Arts on 'Agriculture in India' (1878), 'Famines in India' (1886), and 'The India Office Records' (1889). The first and third of these papers gained the society's silver medal. He was elected a fellow of the Royal Statistical Society in 1880, subsequently served on its council, and read papers before it on 'Agriculture in Essex' (1897; *Stat. Soc. Journal,* lx. 251–69) and 'A Review of Indian Statistics' (1901; *ib.* lxiv. 31–65).

He died on 17 May 1906 at Broad Oaks, Addlestone, Surrey, and was buried at All Saints' Church, Benhilton.

Danvers married in 1860, at Hove, Louisa (*b.* 2 Nov. 1837), daughter of Elias Mocatta. She died at Sutton, Surrey, on 29 May 1909, and was buried beside her husband. There was issue three sons and five daughters.

Danvers also wrote: 1. 'The Covenant of Jacob's Heritage,' 1877. 2. 'Bengal, its Chiefs, Agents and Governors,' 1888. 3. 'The Second Borgian Map,' 1889. 4. 'Israel Redivivus,' 1905 (an endeavour to identify the ten tribes with the English people). He edited 'Memorials of Old Haileybury College' (1894), and wrote introductions to 'Letters received by the East India Company from its Servants in the East' (1896); 'List of Factory Records of the late East India Company' (1897); and 'List of Marine Records of the late East India Company' (1897).

[The Times, 21 May 1906; the Engineer, 25 May 1906; Soc. of Arts Journal, 1906; India Office List, 1905; private information.]

S. E. F.

DARBYSHIRE, ALFRED (1839–1908), architect, son of William Darbyshire, manager of a dyeworks, by his wife Mary Bancroft, and nephew of George Bradshaw [q. v.], originator of the railway guide, was born at 8 Peru Street, Salford, on 20 June 1839. Of an old Quaker stock, he went to Quaker schools, first to that of Charles Cumber at Manchester, then to Ackworth school near Pontefract (1851–4), and finally to Dr. Satterthwaite's school at Alderley, Cheshire. After serving his articles in the office of Peter B. Alley, architect, Manchester, he began at the age of twenty-three to practise for himself, and was elected associate of the Royal Institute of British Architects in 1864 (fellow in 1870, and vice-president, 1902–5). His first commission was to carry out additions at Lyme Hall, Cheshire. Among other buildings he designed the Pendleton town hall, Alston Hall, near Preston, St. Cyprian's and St. Ignatius' churches, Salford, and he enlarged Galtee Castle, co. Cork. His reputation, however, was chiefly that of a theatrical architect. In Manchester he built the Comedy Theatre (afterwards called the Gaiety) and the Palace of Varieties, and carried out alterations at the Theatre Royal and the Prince's. He also designed a theatre at Rawtenstall and one at Exeter. In London he altered and decorated the Lyceum Theatre for (Sir) Henry Irving in 1878. For some years much of his time was occupied in designing and modelling on artistic plans temporary exhibitions, including a military bazaar at Manchester in 1884, a great Shakespearean show in the Royal Albert Hall, London, in the same year, and the Old Manchester section of the Royal Jubilee exhibition at Manchester in 1887.

Darbyshire had a strong leaning towards the stage, and was an amateur actor and a friend of actors. Charles Calvert [q. v.] received material artistic aid from him in the production of his Shakespearean revivals at the Prince's Theatre, Manchester (1864–74), and he was on intimate terms with (Sir) Henry Irving from about 1864 onwards. Irving was at that date a stock actor at the Theatre Royal, Manchester, and when he took leave of Lancashire in 1865, Darbyshire played the part of Polonius to his Hamlet. In the Calvert memorial performances at Manchester in October 1879 he was instrumental in obtaining the assistance of Tom Taylor, Herman Merivale, Lewis Wingfield, and Helen Faucit, who gave her last performance of Rosalind, Darbyshire acting the part of Jacques.

He was one of the original members of the Brasenose Club, Manchester, and wrote two volumes of reminiscences of that resort of literary and artistic bohemians. From 1901 to 1903 he was president of the Manchester Society of Architects, and did much to encourage the foundation of a chair of architecture at Manchester University. He was elected F.S.A. in 1894. An expert student of heraldry, he made a fine collection of books on that subject which was acquired by the John Rylands library.

Dying at Manchester on 5 July 1908, he was buried at Flixton church near that city. He married on 10 August 1870 Sarah, daughter of William Marshall of Westmoreland, and had one son and three daughters.

Besides several pamphlets and lectures, he wrote: 1. 'A Booke about Olde Manchester and Salford,' 1887. 2. 'A Chronicle of the Brasenose Club, Manchester,' 2 vols. 1892–1900. 3. 'An Architect's Experiences, Professional, Artistic, and Theatrical,' 1897 (with portraits). 4. 'The Art of the Victorian Stage,' 1907.

[Works cited; J. H. Nodal's Bibliography of Ackworth School, 1889; Manchester Guardian, 6 July 1908; Manchester City News, 11 July 1908; private information.]

C. W. S.

DAUBENEY, Sir HENRY CHARLES BARNSTON (1810–1903), general, born at Ripon, Yorkshire, on 19 Dec. 1810, was eldest son of lieut.-general Henry Daubeney, K. H., by his first cousin, Elizabeth, daughter of Charles Daubeny [q. v.], archdeacon of Sarum. Educated at Sandhurst, he entered the army as ensign of the 55th foot (later 2nd battalion Border regiment) in 1829. He served in that corps for thirty years until he attained the rank of colonel. In the Coorg campaign, in South India (1832–4), he served with his regiment with the northern column under Colonel Waugh; he was present at the assault and capture of the stockade of Kissenhully, and at the attack on that of Soamwarpettah. There he was in charge of one of the two guns attached to the column, and by his perseverance saved it from capture during the retreat. The British losses amounted to three officers and forty-five men killed and 118 men wounded, but the Rajah of Coorg, who was opposing the British advance, was defeated and deposed on 5 April 1834. Daubeney served with his regiment during the Chinese war of 1841–2, and as a captain commanded the light company at the repulse of the enemy's night attack at Chinhae, and at the storm and capture of Chapou (18 May 1842). He was on the staff as major of brigade to Sir James Schoedde at Woosung, Shanghai, and Chin-Kiang, and was twice mentioned in despatches. He received the medal, was promoted brevet major on 23 Dec. 1842, and was made C.B. on 24 Dec. 1842. Becoming major (25 Nov. 1845) he went through the Crimean campaign of 1854. On 26 Oct. 1854 he helped to repulse the sortie of the Russians from Sevastopol. At Inkerman, on 5 Nov. 1854, Daubeney, at the head of thirty men of his regiment, executed a flank charge; without firing a shot he forced his way through the attacking Russian column, and by this manœuvre compelled the enemy's battalions to fall back in confusion. He was commended in despatches and was gazetted to a substantive lieut.-colonelcy on 12 Dec. 1854 for his services at Inkerman, but he declined a promotion which would have removed him from the seat of war and placed him on half pay, while his regiment was serving in the field. General Sir John Pennefather recommended him for the Victoria Cross, but being a regimental field officer he was held to be ineligible according to existing rules. He received next year the reward for distinguished service, the medal with three clasps, the legion of honour, and the fourth class of the order of the Medjidie. From 1858 to 1869 he was inspector of army clothing. Promoted major-general on 6 March 1868 and lieut.-general on 1 Oct. 1877, he was nominated K.C.B. on 30 May 1871, was appointed colonel of his regiment on 3 Feb. 1879, became general on 4 March 1880, and was promoted G.C.B. on 24 March 1884.

On his retirement from active service in 1880 Daubeney resided at Osterley Lodge, Spring Grove, Isleworth, where he died on 17 Jan. 1903. He was thrice married: (1) in 1840, to Amelia (*d.* 1857), only child of Samuel Davy Liptrap of Southampton, by whom he had two sons; (2) in 1859 to Henrietta Anne (*d.* 1876), only daughter of Charles Jacomb of Upper Clapton, Middlesex; and (3) in 1878 to Eliza, second daughter of Charles Carpenter of Brunswick Square, Brighton.

[Burke's Landed Gentry, s.v. Daubeney of Cote; A. W. Kinglake, The Invasion of the Crimea, 6th edit. 1877, vi. 336–49; Dod's Knightage; Hart's and Official Army Lists.]

H. M. V.

DAVENPORT-HILL, ROSAMOND (1825–1902), educational administrator. [See Hill, Rosamond Davenport-.]

DAVEY, HORACE, BARON DAVEY (1833–1907), judge, born at Horton, Buckinghamshire, on 29 August 1833, was second son of Peter Davey (1792–1879) of that place by his wife Caroline Emma, daughter of William Pace, rector of Rampisham-cum-Wraxall, Dorset. He was educated at Rugby and at University College, Oxford, where he won an open scholarship in 1852, matriculating on 20 March of that year. He gained a double first class in classics and mathematics, both in moderations in 1854 and in the final schools in 1856. He was chosen a fellow of his college in 1854. In 1857 he was elected Johnson's (now the junior) mathematical scholar of the university, and senior mathematical scholar in the following year; in 1859 he obtained the Eldon law scholarship. He graduated B.A. in 1856 and proceeded M.A. in 1859.

Davey was admitted a student of Lincoln's Inn on 19 Jan. 1857, and was called to the bar on 26 Jan. 1861, having read in the chambers of John Wickens [q. v.], then regarded as the most distinguished school of equity pleading. Lord Macnaghten, afterwards Davey's rival at the bar, but slightly his senior in standing, relates how Wickens announced to him one morning that in the person of Davey he had at last found a pupil of whose success he felt assured. From the first Davey acquired an extensive junior practice in the chancery courts, running neck and neck with Montagu Cookson, now Montagu Crackanthorpe, K.C., who had come down from Oxford with identical distinctions in the class lists. In 1865 Davey collaborated with (Sir) George Osborne Morgan [q. v. Suppl. I] in a standard work upon costs in Chancery (1865) and helped Morgan in 'The New Reports' (1863–5). On the appointment of Wickens as vice-chancellor in 1871 Davey became his secretary, and filled the same office under Vice-chancellor Hall, who succeeded Wickens in 1873. He took silk on 23 June 1875 'with strange misgivings,' says Lord Macnaghten, 'and much hesitation.' As a leader his success was instantaneous. He practised in the court of the master of the rolls, Sir George Jessel [q. v.], and soon divided the business there with J. W. Chitty [q. v. Suppl. I], afterwards lord justice. Davey's legal judgment was intuitive and almost infallible, and his wide acquaintance with foreign law systems gave him a marked advantage over his competitors, leading to constant employment in the privy council and in Scottish cases in the House of Lords. Before long he succeeded to the solid reputation which Wickens had held as an unrivalled 'case lawyer,' so that at last his 'opinions' came to be regarded as equivalent to judgments and from time to time were accepted as decisions by mutual consent of the parties. His argument delivered in the court of appeal in 1876 on behalf of one of the interveners in the St. Leonards will case, shortly after he had become a Q.C., created a deep impression on the court and the bar. On the elevation of Sir Edward Fry to the bench in 1877 Davey became a 'special,' and was henceforward retained largely in the superior tribunals, his chief rivals being (Sir) John Rigby [q. v. Suppl. II], Montagu Cookson, and Edward (now Lord) Macnaghten. 'He was never dull or tedious,' writes the latter; 'he always knew his case thoroughly, nothing came amiss to him, nothing was too small for his attention, nothing was too great for his powers.' From his boyhood he had been remarkable for his clear-cut phrases and admirably constructed sentences. When his argument at Lambeth in the proceedings instituted against Bishop King of Lincoln in 1890 was praised for its style to Archbishop Benson, the archbishop remarked 'It was exactly in the same way that he used to construe Thucydides to me when I was school-house tutor at Rugby.'

In politics Davey was an advanced liberal, and he was returned to parliament in that interest for Christchurch in April 1880, but he lost his seat at the general election of November 1885. Following Gladstone in his home rule policy, he received the post of solicitor-general on 16 Feb. 1886, and was knighted on 8 March. His efforts to recover his place in the House of Commons involved him in a long series of electoral misfortunes. He was beaten in a bye-election at Ipswich in April, and at Stockport in the general election of July 1886, going out of office with his party a week or two later. At a bye-election in Dec. 1888 he was successful at Stockton-on-Tees, only to be defeated at the general election of July 1892. Owing to his exclusion from the house, Sir John Rigby became solicitor-general in his stead when Gladstone resumed office in August. Davey failed as a candidate because he could not adopt an ingratiating manner or suit his oratory to the requirements of an uncultivated audience. On the platform he provoked irritation owing to his intensely judicial habit of mind forcing him to qualify and guard every statement. Nor, though listened to with respect, did he ever succeed in winning the ear of the

House of Commons. While possessed of all the qualities of an advocate, he could never accommodate himself to any tribunal that was not purely forensic.

On 15 August 1893 he was appointed lord justice of appeal in the place of his lifelong friend, Lord Bowen, and was sworn of the privy council; in July 1894 he succeeded Lord Russell of Killowen as lord of appeal in ordinary, being created a life peer with the title of Lord Davey of Fernhurst. During his short sojourn in the court of appeal he created a most favourable impression, not only by the admirable judicial qualities which he displayed but by his patience and urbanity to all who appeared before him, whereas at the bar he had been admired rather than liked by those who were not admitted to his intimacy. In the House of Lords and on the judicial committee of the privy council, where the last thirteen years of his life were spent, Davey found himself in a position well adapted for the exercise of his highest faculties. As an old member of the equity bar he restored to that side of the profession the share of representation in the final court of appeal which it had lost since the withdrawal of Lord Selborne. Sitting with Lords Herschell, Watson, and Macnaghten he helped to give it a reputation for strength and originality which it has not always sustained, and he not unfrequently found himself in conflict with the vigorous personality and strongly conservative instincts of Lord Halsbury. His judgments in the cases relating to trades unionism, which occupied much of the time of the house during his latter years, were generally in favour of the men, but accident rendered him absent on the occasions when Allen *v.* Flood and the Taff Vale case were argued. In the case of the Earl and Countess Russell in 1896 he was one of the majority which held that the conduct of the latter in making vile and unfounded charges against her husband did not constitute cruelty such as the law could relieve. But he was in a minority of two who held, on a very different subject, that the 'ring' on the racecourse was 'a place within the meaning of the Act' for the suppression of betting places (16 & 17 Vict. c. 119). Davey had very decided views on the evils of gambling, and was largely responsible for the Street Betting Act of 1906 (6 Edward VII c. 43). The last reported case in which he delivered judgment was that of the Attorney-General *v.* the West Riding County Council, 14 Dec. 1906, when the House of Lords unanimously overruled the decision of Richard Henn Collins, master of the rolls [q. v. Suppl. II], and Lord Justice Farwell, and held that the local education authority is bound to pay what is reasonable for denominational religious education in lawful hours in non-provided schools. Davey's judgments lacked the literary finish of Bowen, but they were conspicuous for conciseness, for lucid statement and clear arrangement, and for a mastery of legal principle. As well equipped with regard to the common law as in matters of pure equity and conveyancing, he was especially at home when it was necessary to construe the complicated Income Tax Acts. His death, after a short illness, at his house in London, on 20 Feb. 1907, was an almost irreparable loss both to the House of Lords and to the judicial committee of the privy council; his presence on the committee had been acknowledged by lawyers from every part of the empire as a chief element in its strength and prestige. Davey has been not unjustly described as the most accomplished lawyer of his day.

Through life Davey was handicapped in public by cold and ungenial manners, and by more than a touch of Oxford donnishness. Among congenial friends he was a delightful companion, and he was idolised by his family. Mr. Frederic Harrison in his 'Autobiographic Memoirs' (ii. 78) speaks of the 'unerring judgment and inexhaustible culture of Horace Davey.' And in an unpublished communication to the writer of this article he adds that, 'in spite of his intensely laborious professional life—for he constantly began work at five before rising, and in earlier days would light his own fire at four—he always kept up a keen interest in literature, especially in French current works, of which he was an omnivorous reader. He had an almost unrivalled familiarity with modern European romances in various languages, and with classical literature, which he continued to read to the last.' He was a man of refined artistic taste and formed a small but choice collection of modern paintings which was dispersed at his death.

Davey was made an honorary fellow of his college in 1884, and received an honorary D.C.L. degree in 1894; he was standing counsel to the University of Oxford from 1877 to 1893. In 1898 he was appointed chairman of the royal commission appointed to make statutes for the reconstituted University of London. and therein showed himself a strenuous champion of a more scientific study of law.

He was elected a fellow of the British Academy in 1905. He interested himself in the work of the Society of Comparative Legislation; and wrote on legal reforms of the past thirty years in the 'Encyclopædia Britannica' (10th edit. 1902).

Davey married on 5 Aug. 1862 Louisa Hawes, daughter of John Donkin, civil engineer, who survived him. Of his family of two sons and four daughters, the two youngest daughters, Beatrix Wickens and Margaret Bowen (twins), married respectively Major-General Sir William Gatacre [q. v. Suppl. II] and F. W. Pember, son of Edward Henry Pember, K.C. [q. v. Suppl. II].

An oil painting of Davey by G. F. Watts, R.A., is in the possession of his widow. Another portrait, by Mr. S. J. Solomon, R.A., is at University College, Oxford; a replica of the latter by the artist belongs to the benchers of Lincoln's Inn.

[The Times, 22 Feb. 1907; Journal Soc. of Comparative Legislation, n.s. viii. 10 (Lord Macnaghten); Proc. Brit. Acad. 1907–8, pp. 371 seq. (by Sir Courtenay Ilbert); Oxford Historical Reg.; the Law Reports; private information; personal knowledge.]

J. B. A.

DAVIDSON, ANDREW BRUCE (1831–1902), Hebraist and theologian, born in 1831 at Ellon, North Aberdeenshire, was son of Andrew Davidson, a sturdy farmer who was keenly interested in the pending controversy respecting church government; his mother, Helen Bruce, was strongly attracted by the evangelical revival of the day. At his mother's wish he was sent in 1845 to the grammar school of Aberdeen, where James Melvin [q. v.] was headmaster; and in 1846 he gained a small bursary in what was then the Marischal University, Aberdeen. There in 1849 he graduated M.A. From 1849 to 1852 he was teacher at the Free church school in Ellon, and during those three years mastered not only Hebrew but various modern languages. In 1852 he entered the Divinity Hall of the Free church in Edinburgh, called the New College; and at the end of the four years' course was licensed in 1856 to become a preacher, but did little preaching or other parochial work. In 1858 he was appointed assistant to John Duncan (1796–1870) [q. v.], professor of Hebrew at the New College, who exerted upon him a stimulating influence. In 1863 he became Duncan's successor in the chair of Hebrew and Oriental languages, and held the post until his death, exerting from the first, partly by his writings, but chiefly by his personality, a commanding influence. Of a small and spare figure, quiet and unpretending in speech and manner, retiring in disposition, he riveted in the lecture-room the admiration and affection of his pupils. 'Easy mastery of his subject, lucid and attractive discourse, the faculty of training men in scientific method, the power of making them think out things for themselves, were united in him with the capacity of holding their minds, quickening their ideas, and commanding their imaginations.' He had a keen sense of humour, and a power of quiet but effective sarcasm. He preached rarely, but his sermons show freshness, independence, religious sympathy, and penetration. He was an influential member of the Old Testament revision company (1870–1884), and was made hon. LL.D. of Aberdeen (1868), hon. D.D. of Edinburgh (1868) and Glasgow, and hon. Litt.D. of Cambridge (1900). He died unmarried at Edinburgh on 20 Jan. 1902.

Davidson devoted his life to the study of the Old Testament, its language, its exegesis, its theology. Whatever aspect of it he touched, his treatment was always masterly, sympathetic, and judicial. In his exegetical works one feels that, whatever opinion he puts forth upon a difficult subject, it is the result of long and mature study and represents the best conclusion which the circumstances of the case permit, and he excelled in the analysis of moral feeling and in the delineation of character.

At the time when he began to lecture, the Old Testament was mostly studied uncritically and superficially, and solely with a view to the dogmatic statements to be found in it. Davidson taught his pupils to realise its *historical* significance, to understand what its different writings meant to those who first heard them uttered, or read them, to trace the historical progress of religious ideas, to cultivate, in a word *historical* exegesis. Some of his pupils have left on record, what a revelation it was to them to find that the prophets, for instance, were men of flesh and blood like themselves, interested in the political and social movements of their times, eager to influence for good their own contemporaries. Davidson initiated in this country that *historical* view of the Old Testament which was afterwards more fully developed by his pupil William Robertson Smith [q.v.], and is now generally accepted among scholars. Davidson also gave valuable help in other directions. He was the power which lay behind W. R. Smith; and though he took hardly any personal part in the struggle of

1876–82 for liberty of biblical criticism, he by his moral weight was recognised as the real author of the victory which, at the cost of his own chair, Smith won for Scotland. Davidson supplied influence and guidance at a time when opinions which had come to be regarded by many as axiomatic were being rudely disturbed. He was equally alive to the historical and the religious importance of the Old Testament; and he was the first leader of thought in this country who taught successfully the reality of both.

Apart from numerous articles in theological periodicals and in Hastings' 'Dictionary of the Bible,' Davidson's chief publications were: 1. A grammatical and exegetical 'Commentary on Job,' 1862, unhappily never completed. 2. 'An Introductory Hebrew Grammar,' 1874; 9th edit. 1888, very largely used as a class-book (now in its 18th edit.). 3. 'A Hebrew Syntax,' 1894, intended for more advanced students, and remarkably thorough and complete. 4. Commentaries on the 'Epistle to the Hebrews,' 1882. 5. 'Job,' 1884; 6. 'Ezekiel,' 1892; 7. 'Nahum, Habakkuk, Zephaniah,' 1896: the last three in the 'Cambridge Bible.' There were published posthumously 'Biblical and Literary Essays' (1902); two volumes of sermons, 'The Called of God' (1902) and 'Waiting upon God' (1904); and two volumes based upon his lectures, 'Old Testament Prophecy' (1903) and 'The Theology of the Old Testament' (1904). There is a portrait by Sir George Reid in the New College, Edinburgh.

[British Weekly, 30 Jan. 1902; Expositor, Jan. 1888, p. 29 ff. (with portrait); Expos. Times, July 1897, p. 441 ff. (with portrait—the best); Biblical World (Chicago), Sept. 1902, pp. 167 seq., and Oct. 1902, pp. 288 seq. (by G. A. Smith); Introd. to The Called of God (with portrait), pp. 3–58; complete list of publications in Expos. Times, July 1904, pp. 450 seq.] S. R. D.

DAVIDSON, CHARLES (1824–1902), water-colour painter, born in London, of Scottish parents, on 30 July 1824, was left an orphan at an early age. After education at a school in Chelsea, he apprenticed himself to a seedsman and market-gardener at Brompton. At the end of a year he forfeited his premium in order to study music, but finally decided on painting, and worked for some years under John Absolon, a member of the New Water Colour Society (now the Royal Institute of Painters in Water Colours). Of that society he was himself elected an associate in 1847 and a member in 1849. He resigned his membership in 1853, and on 12 Feb. 1855 was elected an associate of the Old Water Colour Society (now the Royal Society of Painters in Water Colours); he became a full member on 14 June 1858 and an honorary retired member in 1897. A friend of John Linnell, Samuel Palmer, and the Varleys, he soon established a high reputation. He exhibited from 1844 to 1902 at the Old Water Colour Society (where over 800 of his works appeared), at the New Water Colour Society, the Royal Academy, the British Institution, the Royal Society of British Artists, and elsewhere. His subjects were chiefly typical English landscapes, and he was skilful in depicting the homely scenes of the countryside. He worked a good deal in Wales. A few of his paintings were chromolithographed by Messrs. Day & Son.

Davidson resided for about twenty-eight years at Redhill, Surrey, and from 1882 at Trevena, Falmouth, where he died on 19 April 1902. About 1843 he married a sister of Francis William Topham [q. v.]; he had two sons and four daughters, the eldest of whom became the wife of Frank Holl, R.A. [q. v.]. The Victoria and Albert Museum owns six water-colour drawings by Davidson; four of them are at the Bethnal Green Museum.

[Private information; Graves, Dict. of Artists; A. M. Reynolds, Life of Frank Holl, 1912, pp. 36–40; Cat. of Water Colours, Victoria and Albert Museum; The Year's Art, 1890, p. 32 (portrait); W. J. Stillman, Autobiog. of a Journalist, 1901, pp. 110–2; The Times, 22 April 1902.] B. S. L.

DAVIDSON, JOHN (1857–1909), poet, son of Alexander Davidson, minister of the Evangelical Union, by his wife Helen, daughter of Alexander Crockett of Elgin, was born at Barrhead, Renfrewshire, on 11 April 1857. Put to school at the Highlanders' Academy, Greenock, his education was soon interrupted. At the age of thirteen he entered the chemical laboratory of Walker's sugar house at Greenock (1870), and in 1871 became assistant to the town analyst there. In these employments he developed an interest in science which became an important characteristic of his poetry. In 1872 he returned for four years to the Highlanders' Academy as a pupil-teacher, and, after a year at Edinburgh University (1876–7), received in 1877 his first scholastic employment at Alexander's Charity, Glasgow. During the next six years he held positions in the following schools:

Perth Academy (1878–81), Kelvinside Academy, Glasgow (1881–2), and Hutchinson's Charity, Paisley (1883–4). He varied his career by spending a year as clerk in a Glasgow thread firm (1884–5), and subsequently taught in Morrison's Academy, Crieff (1885–8), and in a private school at Greenock (1888–9).

Davidson's first published work was 'Bruce,' a chronicle play in the Elizabethan manner, which appeared with a Glasgow imprint in 1886. Four other plays, 'Smith, a Tragic Farce' (1888), 'An Unhistorical Pastoral' (1889), 'A Romantic Farce' (1889), and the brilliant 'Scaramouch in Naxos' (1889) were also published while he was in Scotland. In 1889 Davidson abandoned schoolwork, and next year went to London to seek his literary fortune. Besides writing for the 'Speaker,' the 'Glasgow Herald,' and other papers, he produced several novels and tales, of which the best was 'Perfervid' (1890). But these prose works were written for a livelihood. Davidson's true medium was verse. 'In a Music Hall and other Poems' (1891) suggested what 'Fleet Street Eclogues' (1893) proved, that Davidson possessed a genuine and distinctive poetic gift. The second collection established his reputation among the discerning few. His early plays were republished in one volume in 1894, and henceforward he turned his attention more and more completely to verse. A volume of vigorous 'Ballads and Songs' (1894), his most popular work, was followed in turn by a second series of 'Fleet Street Eclogues' (1896) and by 'New Ballads' (1897) and 'The Last Ballad' (1899). For a time he abandoned lyric for the drama, writing several original plays which have not been staged and translating with success Coppée's 'Pour la Couronne' in 1896 and Victor Hugo's 'Ruy Blas' in 1904, the former being produced as 'For the Crown' at the Lyceum Theatre in 1896, the latter as 'A Queen's Romance' at the Imperial Theatre. Finally Davidson engaged on a series of 'Testaments,' in which he gave definite expression to his philosophy. These volumes were entitled 'The Testament of a Vivisector' (1901), 'The Testament of a Man Forbid' (1901), 'The Testament of an Empire Builder' (1902), and 'The Testament of John Davidson' (1908). Though he disclaimed the title of philosopher, he expounded an original philosophy which was at once materialistic and aristocratic. The cosmic process, as interpreted by evolution, was for him a fruitful source of inspiration. His later verse, which is often fine rhetoric rather than poetry, expressed the belief which is summed up in the last words that he wrote, 'Men are the universe become conscious; the simplest man should consider himself too great to be called after any name.' The corollary was that every man was to be himself to the utmost of his power, and the strongest was to rule. Davidson professed to reject all existing philosophies, including that of Nietzsche, the German philosopher, as inadequate, but Nietzsche's influence is traceable in his argument. The poet planned ultimately to embody his revolutionary creed in a trilogy entitled 'God and Mammon.' Only two plays, however, were written, 'The Triumph of Mammon' (1907) and 'Mammon and his Message' (1908).

In 1906 he was awarded a civil list pension of 100*l.*; but poverty and ill-health made life burdensome. Late in 1908 Davidson left London to reside at Penzance. On 23 March 1909 he disappeared from his house at Penzance. He had committed suicide by drowning in a fit of depression. His body, which was discovered by some fishermen in Mount's Bay on 18 Sept., was, in accordance with his known wishes, buried at sea. In his will he desired that no biography should be written, none of his unpublished works published, and 'no word except of my writing is ever to appear in any book of mine as long as the copyright endures.' In 1885 Davidson married Margaret, daughter of John M'Arthur of Perth. She survived him with two sons, Alexander and Menzies.

Davidson was a prolific writer. Besides the works cited, he wrote: 1. 'The Great Men, and a Practical Novelist,' 1891. 2. 'Laura Ruthven's Widowhood,' a novel (with C. J. Wills), 1892. 3. 'Sentences and Paragraphs,' 1893. 4. 'Baptist Lake,' a novel, 1894. 5. 'A Random Itinerary,' 1894. 6. 'The Wonderful Mission of Earl Lavender,' a novel, 1895. 7. 'Miss Armstrong's Circumstances,' a novel, 1896. 8. 'Godfrida,' a play, 1898. 9. 'Self's the Man,' a tragi-comedy, 1901. 10. 'The Knight of the Maypole,' 1903. 11. 'A Rosary,' 1903. 12. 'The Theatrocrat: a Tragic Play of Church and State,' 1905. 13. 'Holiday and other Poems,' 1906. 14. 'Fleet Street and other Poems,' 1909. He translated Montesquieu's 'Lettres Persanes' (1892) and contributed to Shakespeare's 'Sonnets' (Renaissance edition, 1908) an introduction which, like his various prefaces and essays, shows him a subtle literary critic. Davidson's portrait was drawn by Walter Sickert and by Robert

Bryden. A caricature by Max Beerbohm appeared in 'The Chapbook,' 1907.

[The Times, 27 and 30 March, 1 and 19 April, 20 and 22 Sept. 1909; Encyclopædia Britannica, 11th edit.] F. L. B.

DAVIDSON, JOHN THAIN (1833–1904), presbyterian minister, born on 25 April 1833 at Broughty Ferry, near Dundee, was a twin son of David Davidson, parish minister of Broughty Ferry, who seceded from the established church at the disruption of 1843 and died a few months later. His grandfather, Dr. David Davidson of Dundee, and his great grandfather were also ministers of the church of Scotland. His mother, daughter of Dr. Ireland of Leith, removed to Edinburgh on her husband's death, and at her house the boy John met Drs. Guthrie, Candlish, Cunningham, and other religious leaders. Educated successively at Edinburgh High School and at Edinburgh University, he studied for the ministry at the Free Church Theological College. After a few months in charge of a mission station at Craigmill in Perthshire, and as a probationer in Free St. George's, Montrose, he was ordained on 19 Feb. 1857 a minister of the Free church at Maryton, near Montrose, and remained there until 1859, when he was inducted minister of the presbyterian church at Salford. Thenceforth his life was spent in England.

After three years in Salford, he removed on 5 August 1862 to the presbyterian church, Colebrooke Row, Islington. There he achieved a memorable success, He not only converted a decaying congregation into a large and growing one, but his influence spread beyond his own denomination. On 4 Oct. 1868 he inaugurated in the Agricultural Hall, and continued every Sunday for nearly twenty-three years, the novel enterprise of services on Sunday afternoons for non-churchgoing people. The services, held at first in the smaller hall, which seated about 1000, were soon transferred to the great hall, where about 4000 persons were regularly present. The meetings were catholic in spirit. The speakers included the earls of Shaftesbury, Aberdeen, and Kintore, the bishops of Ballarat and Bedford, Canon Fleming, the vicars of Islington, Holloway, and Clerkenwell, Dr. Guthrie and Dr. Talmage.

In 1872 he was elected moderator of the synod of the presbyterian church of England. Subsequently he received the degree of D.D. from Montgomery College, Alabama. After nearly thirty years' work at Islington, he removed in 1891 to Ealing, where he became on 16 Sept. minister of St. Andrew's presbyterian church. In 1903 he obtained as colleague W. S. Herbert Wylie, M.A., who succeeded him. Dr. Davidson died on 7 November 1904 and is buried in the churchyard of Gray's 'Elegy' at Stoke Poges.

He married on 4 Oct. 1859 Isabella, daughter of M. M'Callum of Glasgow, by whom he had two sons and six daughters.

Davidson's varied powers as a preacher were, perhaps, seen to best advantage in his monthly sermons to young men, commenced at Islington in 1878 and continued through the rest of his ministry. The main points in these addresses were published in 'Talks with Young Men' (1884); 'Forewarned, Forearmed' (1885); 'The City Youth' (1886); 'Sure to Succeed' (1888); 'A Good Start' (1890); and 'Thoroughness' (1892).

[John Thain Davidson: Reminiscences, by his daughter Mrs. Newson, 1906; British Weekly, 9 July and 17 Sept. 1891; private information.] C. H. I.

DAVIES, CHARLES MAURICE (1828–1910), author, born in 1828, was of Welsh origin. He entered Durham University as a scholar of University College in 1845, and graduated B.A. in 1848 with a second class in classical and general literature. He proceeded M.A. in 1852 and D.D. in 1864. Elected a fellow of the university on 1 Nov. 1849, he was ordained deacon in 1851 and priest in 1852. After serving various curacies Davies settled down to educational work in London. Meanwhile his religious views underwent a change. Once an active supporter of the tractarian movement, Davies soon adopted broad church principles, and published anonymously a series of sensational novels, attacking high church practices, among them being 'Philip Paternoster' (1858), 'Shadow Land' (1860), and 'Verts, or the Three Creeds' (3 vols. 1876). After holding the headmastership of the West London Collegiate School (1861–8) he devoted himself mainly to journalism. In 1870 he represented the 'Daily Telegraph' in France on the outbreak of the Franco-Prussian war, and was arrested as a suspected spy, while he was searching Metz for his colleague, George Augustus Sala [q. v.]. Amongst other contributions to the 'Daily Telegraph' was a series of independent studies of religious parties in the metropolis, which attracted attention. His articles were collected into a volume entitled 'Unorthodox London' (1873; 2nd edit. 1875). There followed on the same lines, 'Heterodox London, or Phases of Free Thought in the Metropolis' (2 vols. 1874), 'Orthodox London, or Phases of Religious Life in the Church of England' (2 vols. 1874–5), and 'Mystic London, or Phases of Occult Life in the Metropolis' (1875). On quitting the service of the 'Daily Telegraph,' Davies went out to Natal to work under Bishop J. W. Colenso [q. v.]. After 1882, however, he abandoned holy orders. On his resettling in London, he was employed after 1893 in superintending a series of translations, undertaken at the instance of Cecil Rhodes [q. v. Suppl. II], of the original authorities used by Gibbon in his 'Decline and Fall of the Roman Empire.' Davies retired from active work in 1901, and died at Harlesden on 6 Sept. 1910.

[The Times, 9 Sept. 1910; Durham University Calendar, 1850; Brit. Mus. Cat.; Sir T. Fuller, Life of Cecil Rhodes, 1910, p. 133 seq.; private information from Mr. A. L. Humphreys.] G. S. W.

DAVIES, ROBERT (1816–1905), philanthropist, born at Llangefni, Anglesey, on 1 April 1816, was second son of Richard Davies (1778–1849) by Anne, daughter of Owen Jones of Coedhowel near Llangefni. The father (son of a yeoman at Capel Farm, Llangristiolus) was a general store-keeper at Llangefni and a Calvinistic methodist.

Robert was educated at the national school, Llangefni, and at a private school at Chester. As he and his brothers grew up, their father extended his business, opening a branch for importing timber and iron at Menai Bridge, which he placed under the management of his eldest son, John, who died unmarried in 1848 and to whose business ability the successful development of the family firm was largely due. A foundry at Carnarvon was put under Robert's charge, while a store at Redwharf Bay was entrusted to the youngest son, Richard. From purchasing ships to carry their own timber the firm came to confine itself to shipowning, with headquarters at Menai Bridge (where the three brothers settled), and the other businesses were disposed of. While at Carnarvon, Robert took an active part in the work of a ragged school there, and in subsequent years he had charge of a class of children in a Sunday school of which he was for a short time superintendent. With these exceptions, and that of serving as high sheriff for Anglesey for 1862, he took no part in public work. About 1856 he settled at Bodlondeb, a house overlooking the Menai Straits, near Bangor, and here he led a somewhat eccentric and parsimonious life, letting his share of the profits of the business accumulate. After 1885 he began giving money, generally anonymously or under assumed names, towards liquidating the debts of Calvinistic methodist chapels. He was popularly credited with giving half a million sterling towards chapel debts, but most probably it did not much exceed 150,000*l.* His other benefactions were 177,000*l.* to endow the Welsh Methodist Mission in India, 10,000*l.* to an orphanage (of the same connexion) at Bontnewydd, Carnarvon, and 10,000*l.* to the British and Foreign Bible Society (of which he was a vice-president). At a cost of 5000*l.* he built an English chapel for his connexion at Menai Bridge (where he is commemorated by a window and tablet), and gave 1200*l.* towards restoring the Welsh chapel at the same place, to the erection of which he and his brother had contributed largely. His gifts to educational objects, comparatively few and small, included 1000*l.* to the founding of the Normal College at Bangor in 1856, 1000*l.* to the University College at the same place in 1884, besides assistance in establishing and maintaining a British school at Menai Bridge. His almsgiving took the eccentric form of a weekly distribution for many years of twelve lbs. of flour to from seventy to a hundred persons, presumably poor, but not a few of them undeserving. It was a condition that each recipient should personally fetch this dole from Bodlondeb on Tuesday in each week.

Davies died unmarried and intestate at Bodlondeb on 29 Dec. 1905, and was buried in the parish churchyard of Llangefni. His estate was valued at under 500,000*l.*

His younger brother, RICHARD DAVIES (1818–1896), possessed business and public qualities of a high order. A liberal in politics, he unsuccessfully contested Carnarvon Boroughs in 1852, but in 1868 he was returned unopposed for his native county of Anglesey, for which he sat till 1886. He was high sheriff of Anglesey in 1858, and was appointed its lord-lieutenant by Gladstone on 27 April 1884, being probably the first nonconformist to hold those offices in Wales. He died at his residence, Treborth, near Bangor, on 27 Oct. 1896. He married in 1855 Annie, only child of the Rev. Henry Rees, a nonconformist divine, of Liverpool, and left issue (MARDY REES, *Notable Welshmen*, p. 445).

[The most trustworthy account of Robert Davies is by the Rev. T. Charles Williams, M.A., of Menai Bridge in Y Drysorfa (in

Welsh), 1906; reprinted in a volume of gossiping and often inaccurate reminiscences concerning Davies by the Rev. John Jones, Pwllheli—Adgofion am Mr. Robert Davies (Pwllheli, 1906). Cf. T. R. Roberts, Eminent Welshmen, p. 57. Private information has also been furnished by Mr. J. R. Davies (Richard Davies's son), Ceris, Bangor.] D. Ll. T.

DAVIS, CHARLES EDWARD (1827–1902), architect and antiquary, born near Bath on 29 Aug. 1827, was son of Edward Davis by his wife Dorothy (widow of Captain Johnston of the Madras cavalry), whose maiden name was Walker. The father, an architect of Bath, had been a pupil of Sir John Soane [q. v.], restored Prior Bird's Chantry in Bath Abbey, the 'Gothic ornaments' of which he described in a volume (1834), designed several houses, and laid out the Victoria Park at Bath, opened in 1830. Charles Edward began the study of architecture as his father's pupil, and in 1863, having recently won a competition for the cemetery buildings on the lower Bristol Road, was appointed city architect and surveyor to the corporation of Bath. He held these offices for forty years. In 1863 he designed an escritoire, Bath's wedding gift to Queen Alexandra, presented in 1869 and costing 700*l*.

Davis carefully examined the mineral baths from both the antiquarian and the therapeutic points of view, with important results. Exploring in 1869 the site of the hot springs of the old King's bath, he found extensive remains of Roman thermal work and published a descriptive account. In 1877–8 he was successful in exposing the Roman well beneath the King's bath. This discovery was foreshadowed by Alexander Sutherland, M.D. ('An attempt to ascertain and extend the virtues of Bath and Bristol waters, &c.,' 2nd edit. 1764), who followed the researches made by Dr. Lucas in 1755 (cf. R. E. M. Peach, *Bath Old and New*, pp. 35–6). In 1880–1 Davis found the Great bath and in 1884–6 the Circular bath, both Roman. With a view to collecting information on the nature and management of spas, Davis in 1885 made a tour of the chief continental springs. He applied his knowledge to various improvements at Bath, and was consulted by English corporations owning natural baths, such as Harrogate and Droitwich.

The old Queen's bath, constructed in 1597 and named after Anne, wife of James I, was removed in the course of the Roman discoveries of 1885. Davis's principal original design in connection with the baths was the new Queen's bath, begun in 1886, completed in 1889, and costing something less than the contract piece of 20,000*l*. This work and the incidental restoration met with criticism on structural as well as archæological grounds. Reports were made on behalf of the Society of Antiquaries by Professor J. H. Middleton [q. v. Suppl. I] and Mr. W. H. St. John Hope. Controversy in Bath grew warm, and an independent opinion was sought from Alfred Waterhouse, R.A. [q. v. Suppl. II], whose report, dated 14 Jan. 1887, decided (1) that the new works though somewhat slender in construction were not such as to cause apprehension on grounds of stability; (2) that on the whole Davis had judiciously compromised between the utility of the baths and their antiquarian value. Difficulties with the corporation regarding his official duties led in 1900 to the transfer to another of the supervision of the corporate property. But the baths and the provision markets were left in Davis's charge at a fixed salary of 400*l*.

Besides his work for the corporation Davis had an extensive private practice. He designed the church of St. Peter and schools at Twerton, restored several churches, including Northstoke (1888) and that of St. Thomas à Becket at Widcombe, and was architect of the Imperial Hotel, Bath, opened in 1901 and costing 50,000*l*. He was elected a fellow of the Society of Antiquaries in 1850, and published 'Mineral Baths of Bath; the Bath of Bathes Ayde in the Reign of Charles II' (4to, Bath, 1883), besides several pamphlets on the same subject.

The rank of major by which Davis was generally designated was due to his commission in the Worcestershire militia; he had also been a member of the Bath volunteer rifles.

Davis died at his residence, Bathwick Hill, on 10 May 1902. He married in 1858 Selina Anne, eldest daughter of Captain Howarth, who survived him without issue. A portrait by Leonard Skeates is in the Grand Pump Room at Bath.

[Builder, 1902, lxxxii. 504; Building News, lxxxiii. 696; Bath Herald, 10 and 12 May 1902; Keene's Bath Journal, 17 May 1902; Peach, Bath Old and New.] P. W.

DAVITT, MICHAEL (1846–1906), Irish revolutionary and labour agitator, born on 25 March 1846, at Straide, co. Mayo, came of a Roman catholic peasant stock, originally from Donegal. His father, who subsisted with his family on a small holding, was head of an agrarian secret society in his youth, and was evicted in 1852 during the clearances that followed the great Irish famine. He emigrated with his wife and children to Lancashire, and settled at Haslingden. Here the boy Michael, as soon as he was able to work, was sent to a cotton mill. Forced in 1857 to mind a machine ordinarily attended by a youth of eighteen, he was caught in the machinery, and his mangled right arm had to be amputated. Thus disabled before he was twelve, he was removed from the factory and sent to a Wesleyan school. While still a lad, he organised a band of youths to defend catholic churches at Rochdale, Bacup, and Haslingden, which were threatened with destruction in anti-catholic riots. On leaving school, at about fifteen, he became in 1861 printer's devil and newsboy with a printer, who was also postmaster at Haslingden; afterwards he worked as book-keeper and assistant letter-carrier in the same employment. In 1865 he joined the Fenian organisation, and soon became 'centre' of the local (Rossendale) 'circle.' In February 1867 he was one of those told off to attack Chester Castle and seize the arms there. He first showed his abilities in extricating himself and his comrades from this fiasco. In 1868 he was appointed organising secretary of the Irish Republican Brotherhood for England and Scotland, and left his employment at Haslingden to assume the rôle of a commercial traveller in firearms, as a cloak for his revolutionary work—buying firearms and shipping them to Ireland. On 14 May 1870 he was arrested at Paddington while awaiting a consignment of arms from Birmingham. Tried at the Old Bailey by Lord Chief Justice Cockburn, he was sentenced to fifteen years' penal servitude for treason-felony. The principal evidence against him was a letter which he had written to prevent a young Fenian (whose name Davitt never would reveal) from assassinating a supposed spy, but which bore on the face of it (as Davitt's aim in writing was to gain time for the interference of the heads of the organisation) an apparent approval of the deed. He spent over seven years in prison—ten months in Millbank, and the remainder (except one month at Portsmouth in 1872) in Dartmoor. A pamphlet prepared by him in 1878, as the basis of his evidence (20 June 1878) before the royal commission on the working of the Penal Servitude Acts, gives a full account of what he endured, and how every prison rule was strained against him. On 19 Dec. 1877 he was released on ticket-of-leave, as a result of the exertions of Isaac Butt [q. v.] and the Amnesty Association. In prison he had thought out his plans for an Irish movement of a new kind, to blend revolutionary and constitutional methods, while abandoning secret conspiracy. He at once rejoined the Fenian movement, with the view of converting its heads to this plan. After lecturing for some months in Great Britain on behalf of the amnesty movement, he went in August 1878 to America, whither his family had emigrated. Here he met not only all the leaders of the constitutional and extreme Nationalists but also Henry George. The latter's land programme harmonised with and developed the views which Davitt had already formed independently in prison. Before leaving America, he made a speech at Boston, on 8 Dec. 1878, in which he outlined the new departure in Irish agitation. The essence of his suggestion was to bring the movement for Irish independence into close touch with the realities of life in Ireland by linking it up with the agrarian agitation, and to give the latter a wider scope by demanding the complete abolition of landlordism. On his return to Ireland he laid his plan before the supreme council of the Irish Republican Brotherhood, which rejected it. Davitt proceeded with the work on his own responsibility, enlisting the sympathy of most of the rank and file Fenians. He organised a meeting at Irishtown, Mayo, on 20 April 1879, when the new land programme was put forward. A second meeting, at Westport on 8 June, was attended by Charles Stewart Parnell [q. v.], whom Davitt had convinced of the possibilities of the new movement. The agitation rapidly spread through the west; in August Davitt grouped the various local committees into the 'Land League of Mayo.' The 'Land League of Ireland,' in which Parnell's influence was soon to clash with Davitt's, came into being in October. In November Davitt and others were arrested and tried at Sligo for their share in the movement; but the prosecutions were dropped early in 1880. After the general election of 1880, in which Davitt assisted to procure the successes of Parnell's party, he was expelled from the supreme council of the Irish Republican Brotherhood; he remained an ordinary member of the body till 1882. In May 1880 Davitt went to America to organise the American Land League, and to raise funds. On his return he founded the Ladies' Land League, and devoted himself to the task of preventing outrages in connection with the policy of 'boycotting.' He also penetrated into Ulster, and addressed an enthusiastic meeting of Orangemen at Armagh on the land question. He urged the issue of the 'No Rent' manifesto in Feb. 1881 instead of later, but the Parliamentary section of the movement postponed its publication till Oct., when the liberal government retorted by suppressing the Land League. Meanwhile Davitt had been arrested as a ticket-of-leave man on 3 Feb. 1881, and endured a second but milder term of penal servitude in Portland. While in prison he was elected to parliament for co. Meath (24 Feb. 1882), but was disqualified as a treason-felony prisoner. He was released on 6 May 1882, and forthwith learned from Parnell that he had concluded the 'Kilmainham Treaty' with the government, that the agitation was to be mitigated, and that the Ladies' Land League had been suppressed by Parnell for declining to accept the compromise. Davitt at once prepared to fight Parnell in favour of a resumption of the agitation; but the assassination of Lord Frederick Cavendish, which took place on the day of Davitt's release, threw him back into alliance with Parnell, whose proposed co-operation with liberalism was necessarily for the time at an end.

After another visit to America, in June 1882, Davitt induced Parnell to found the National League, successor of the suppressed Land League; the programme of the new organisation, however, marked the triumph of parliamentarianism over the more revolutionary ideas of Davitt. He declined office in the National League, but spoke regularly on its platforms. In 1883 (Jan. to May) he was imprisoned on a charge of sedition for a further period of four months in Richmond Bridewell, Dublin. Between 1882 and 1885 he devoted much of his time to advocating land nationalisation, lecturing throughout Great Britain, either alone or in company with Henry George, who was touring in the United Kingdom. He brought George to Ireland, and spoke with him at a meeting in Dublin, on 9 April 1884. This brought on him a categorical repudiation of land nationalisation by Parnell. In 1885, his health having broken down, Davitt visited Italy, Palestine, and Egypt. He opposed the policy adopted by Parnell at the general election of that year, of throwing the Irish vote in England for the conservatives. In 1886 he again visited America, and married Miss Mary Yore, of Michigan. As a token of national regard, his wife was presented with a house, known as Land League Cottage, at Ballybrack, co. Dublin. This was the only occasion on which Davitt accepted any material gift from the Irish people; he always refused to assent to any public testimonial, supporting himself, often with great difficulty, by his labours as a journalist. It was not till near the close of his life (1901) that a legacy from a relative of his wife relieved him of financial anxiety.

In 1887–8–9 Davitt was engrossed in the work involved by 'The Times' commission [see Parnell, Charles Stewart], which was appointed to investigate the charges brought by 'The Times' against Parnell and others, namely, that their real aim was to bring about the total independence of Ireland, that they had instigated assassination and other outrages, and that they had accepted money and other assistance from open advocates of crime and dynamite. Davitt was not originally included in these charges, but on his presenting himself before the tribunal, 'The Times' repeated the same charges against him, with two additional ones, namely, that he had been a convicted Fenian, and that he had brought about the alliance between the Parnellite home rule party in Ireland and the party of violence in America—both of which were undenied facts. The chief labour of the defence fell on him, as the link between the constitutional and extreme nationalists, between the Irish and American branches of the movement. It was Davitt who first suspected Richard Pigott [q. v.], and he, by the aid of a volunteer secret service, countered every move of 'The Times' in the collection of evidence (*Fall of Feudalism*, ch. 44–49). When Parnell and the other Nationalists withdrew from the proceedings of the commission, as a protest against the refusal of the judges to order the production of the books of the 'Loyal and Patriotic Union,' Davitt dissented from this course, and continued to appear. Conducting his own case, he made a five-days' speech before the tribunal (Oct. 24–31, 1889), afterwards published as 'The Defence of the Land League,' a book which contains the best record of Davitt's life and work up to that time. In the report of the commission, the chief findings relating to Davitt were that he had entered the agrarian movement with the intention of bringing about the absolute independence of Ireland, and that he had in a special manner denounced crime and outrage. Immediately after the commission's attack had failed, came the proceedings in the divorce court against Parnell. Davitt had been led by Parnell to believe that the suit brought by William Henry O'Shea [q. v. Suppl. II] was another conspiracy, destined to the same collapse as the Pigott forgeries. He resented Parnell's mis-representation, and immediately flung himself into the campaign against Parnell's leadership. He had just started 'The Labour World' (first number, 21 Sept. 1890) to be the organ of the labour movement in Great Britain, which was on a fair way to success, but was ruined by Davitt's attitude towards Parnell, and by his personal absorption in the political struggle. The paper lived only till May 1891. Davitt had many times declined a seat in parliament, but he now yielded to the urgencies and needs of the anti-Parnellite party, and in the end of 1891 contested Waterford City against Mr. John Redmond, the leader of the Parnellites after Parnell's death. Defeated here, he was elected for North Meath at the general election of 1892, and was unseated on petition, owing to the use in his favour of clerical influences which he had done his best to stop. He was returned unopposed for North-East Cork at the bye-election of Feb. 1893, but having been declared bankrupt was unseated next June. In 1895 he went lecturing in Australia, and returned home to find himself M.P. for two constituencies, East Kerry and South Mayo; he chose to sit for South Mayo. He was not a parliamentary success, but was always listened to with respect, especially on prison reform, a subject he had long made his own. In 1897 he visited the United States to stop the projected Anglo-American Alliance; his active work was mainly responsible for the rejection of that year's Anglo-American Arbitration Treaty by the United States Senate. In 1898 he helped Mr. William O'Brien to found the United Irish League, an organisation which brought about the reunion of the Parnellite and anti-Parnellite sections. On 25 Oct. 1899 he dramatically withdrew from parliament as a protest against the Boer War. Early in 1900 he went to South Africa in a capacity partly journalistic and partly diplomatic; he held the threads of a plot to bring about European intervention on behalf of the Boers—a plot which broke down because of the hesitancy at a critical moment, and the subsequent death, of Colonel de Villebois Mareuil, who was to have led the French contingent. Davitt fiercely attacked the Dunraven conference report on the land question (1903) and the Wyndham Land Purchase Act of the same year, the purchase terms of which he regarded as a surrender of much that had been gained by the twenty-five years' agitation that he had started. Temporarily overborne by Mr. William O'Brien, he had the satisfaction of seeing, in little over a year, a complete revulsion of feeling in the Nationalist party with regard to Mr. O'Brien's policy. In 1903–4–5 he paid, mainly as the representative of American journals, three visits to Russia, where his sympathies were with the revolutionary party. At the general election of 1906 he devoted himself to supporting the labour party in England, and helped to secure many of their notable victories. The last months of his life were occupied with a struggle over the English education bill, on which he fell foul of the catholic clergy. The Irish Press having been closed to his letters advocating secular education, he was contemplating the establishment of a weekly paper, to express strongly democratic as well as nationalist views, when he caught cold after a dental operation. Blood poisoning set in, and he died in Dublin on 31 May 1906. He was buried in Straide, co. Mayo, where the 'Davitt Memorial Church' has been erected. His wife survived him with five sons and one daughter. A portrait by William Orpen is in the Dublin Gallery of Modern Art. Another was painted by Mr. H. J. Thaddeus.

Davitt stood for the reconciliation of extreme and constitutional nationalism; although he never wavered, as his latest writings show, from the ultimate idea of an independent Ireland he abandoned at an early stage all belief in those methods of secret conspiracy and armed rebellion which are generally associated with the separatist ideal. His notions of constitutional agitation were, however, always permeated by the vigour of his early revolutionary plans. He also stood for the harmonising of democracy and nationality. With his whole-hearted nationalism he combined from early life a growing conviction that any thoroughgoing regeneration of government and society in Ireland, and indeed throughout the world, must rest on a socialistic basis. In his collectivist, as in his anti-clerical, views he differed from most of the Irishmen with whom he was politically associated. His political affinities inclined to industrial and secularist democracy. His strength of character, disinterestedness, and steadiness of purpose won him the personal respect even of those who held his doctrines to be erroneous or pernicious.

Davitt's principal published works are: 1. 'Leaves from a Prison Diary,' 1884 (to be distinguished from the pamphlet on his experiences in Dartmoor, mentioned above). 2. 'The Defence of the Land League,' 1891. 3. 'Life and Progress in Australasia,' 1898. 4. 'The Boer Fight for Freedom,' 1902. 5. 'Within the Pale' (a study of anti-semitism in Russia), 1903. 6. 'The Fall of Feudalism in Ireland' (a history of the land agitation), 1904. He also wrote many pamphlets and a mass of uncollected journalistic work.

[Davitt's own books, especially The Defence of the Land League and The Fall of Feudalism; Michael Davitt: Revolutionary, Agitator, and Labour Leader, by F. Sheehy Skeffington, 1908; see also Cashman's Life, 1882; R. Barry O'Brien's Life of Parnell, 1898; Life of Henry George, 1900; D'Alton, History of Ireland, vol. iii. 1910.] F. S. S.

DAWSON, GEORGE MERCER (1849–1901), geologist, eldest surviving son of Sir John William Dawson [q. v. Suppl. I] by his wife Margaret Mercer, was born on 2 Aug. 1849 at Pictou, Nova Scotia, but was taken to Montreal in 1855, when his father became president of McGill College. At ten he went to the high school in that city, but was soon removed because of weak health, and studied under tutors at home. He joined McGill College for the session of 1868–9, spending the summer of the latter year at Gaspe in dredging for foraminifera, the results of which were described in his first scientific paper. In 1870 he began work at the Royal School of Mines in London. He went through the full course, obtained the associateship, the Duke of Cornwall's scholarship, the Edward Forbes medal and prize in palæontology, and the Murchison medal in geology, and in his summer holidays worked in the Lake district with James Clifton Ward [q. v.]. Dawson returned to Canada in 1872, and next year, after reporting on some mining properties in Nova Scotia and giving lectures at Morrin College, Quebec, was appointed geologist and botanist to the commission for drawing the boundary line between Canada and the United States from the Lake of the Woods to British Columbia. Facing without flinching much toil and hardship, he made a large collection of natural history specimens, now preserved partly at Kew and partly in the British Museum, and his excellent report, published in 1875, described a section over 800 miles in length, of which some 300 were previously unknown even to geographers. Dawson was next appointed to the Canadian geological survey, and made a long and important series of exploratory investigations in the North West and British Columbia. His reports deal with both economic and scientific geology, and contain many valuable notes on other branches of natural history and on ethnology. He showed the relation of the laramie and cretaceous formations, the occurrence of a fresh-water episode in the latter, the existence of archæan and early palæozoic rocks in the plateau region of British Columbia, and of metamorphosed volcanic rocks in the Cordilleran region of that province and on the Lake of the Woods. Dawson also pointed out that an ice-sheet had once had its centre in British Columbia; believing, however, that the northern part of the great plain had been submerged. The prescience of his remarks on economic questions has been thankfully acknowledged by those engaged in developing the resources of this great territory. After 1884 Dawson took a leading part in a committee formed by the British Association for studying the north-western tribes of Canada, and subsequently engaged in the ethnological survey of the dominion. With W. F. Tolmie he published in 1884 'Comparative Vocabularies of the Indian Tribes of British Columbia.' In 1883 he was made assistant-director of the geological survey and succeeded Dr. A. R. C. Selwyn as director in 1895.

He was appointed one of the Behring Sea Commissioners in 1891 to investigate the conditions of seal life in the North Pacific, making a long cruise in that region (the scientific results of which were published by the Geological Society of America in 1894). Afterwards he took part in the conference at Washington and helped in preparing the British case for the arbitration at Paris in 1893. Sir Richard Webster (now Lord Alverstone) spoke in the highest terms of the value of Dawson's services.

Dawson was elected a fellow of the Geological Society in 1875 and of the Royal Society in 1891. He was also a fellow of the Royal Society of Canada, its president in 1894, and president also of the Geological Society of America in 1900. He received the degree of D.Sc. from Princetown University in 1887, of LL.D. from the Queen's University in 1890, from McGill University in 1891, and from Toronto University in 1897. He was awarded the Bigsby medal of the Geological Society of London in 1891 and the gold medal of the Royal Geographical Society in 1897. He was created C.M.G. for his services in the Behring Sea arbitration.

Though rather small in stature, frail in aspect, and slightly deformed in consequence of an accident in childhood, Dawson was capable of prolonged physical and mental labour, was an excellent talker, and wrote with facility in prose and verse, the latter both grave and gay. His contributions to science were about 130 in number. He died unmarried at Ottawa of bronchitis, after a two days' illness, on 2 March 1901.

[Geol. Mag. 1897 (with portrait) and 1901; Quarterly Journal of Geol. Soc. 1902; Proc. and Trans. Roy. Soc. of Canada (memoir by Prof. Harrington, with portrait and list of publications), 1902.] T. G. B.

DAWSON, JOHN (1827–1903), trainer of racehorses, born at Gullane, Haddingtonshire, on 16 Dec. 1827, was a younger son in the family of seventeen children of George Dawson, who had previously trained horses at Bogside, in Ayrshire, by his wife Jean Alison. Three brothers who survived infancy, Thomas (*d.* 1880), Joseph (*d.* 1880), and Matthew [q. v. Suppl. I], also became expert trainers. All were brought up about their father's training stable at Gullane. Thomas, the eldest, left Gullane in 1830, and settled at Middleham, in Yorkshire, where he trained for Lord Eglinton. In 1838 he was joined by his brother Matthew as 'head lad,' and later Joseph and John also served apprenticeships at Middleham. In 1853, Joseph went to Ilsley. Thomas trained Ellington and Pretender, who won the Derbys of 1856 and 1869; Matthew prepared Thormanby (1860), Kingcraft (1870), Silvio (1877), and Melton (1885). Joseph alone of the brothers failed to saddle a Derby winner, but he trained winners of the Two Thousand, One Thousand, and St. Leger.

In 1857 John left his eldest brother's stable at Middleham, and took Hamilton House, at Compton, Berkshire, a village which adjoins Ilsley. At Compton he trained Bel Esperanza, the first of four winners of the Lincolnshire Handicap which he saddled. In 1861 he removed to Warren House, Newmarket, where he lived for the remainder of his life. Shortly after settling there he was appointed private trainer to Prince Batthyany and General Peel, and in 1863 Lord Vivian became a patron of the stable. In later years horses belonging to Mr. R. C. Naylor and Sir Robert Jardine [q. v. Suppl. II] were trained at Warren House. The Lincolnshire Handicap was won for Prince Batthyany by Suburban in 1862, and by Vandervelde in 1867; and for Sir Robert Jardine by Wise Man in 1889. For Mr. Naylor, Dawson won the Cesarewitch with Jester in 1878. In 1875 he won the Derby with Galopin. Dawson had four other successes in classic events. He trained Petrarch to win the Two Thousand Guineas and the St. Leger in 1876 for Lord Dupplin; Elizabeth the One Thousand Guineas in 1880 for Mr. T. E. Walker; and Disraeli the Two Thousand in 1898 for Mr. Wallace Johnstone. Other patrons included General Owen Williams, Mr. E. Loder, Mr. Renfrew, and Mr. C. Alexander.

Dawson's triumphant career was checked by the sudden death, in 1883, of Prince Batthyany. One of the two-year-olds belonging at that time to the prince was St. Simon, who won all the races for which he started, and afterwards had a most distinguished career at the stud. Immediately after Prince Batthyany's death, St. Simon was sold to the duke of Portland, and went into Matthew Dawson's stable. Perdita II, who, when mated with St. Simon, produced Florizel II, Persimmon, and Diamond Jubilee, bearers of Edward VII's colours, was for a time trained at Warren House. Dawson gave up training in 1900. He died on 13 May 1903, and was interred in Newmarket cemetery.

In 1855 Dawson married Miss Grant Peddie. Of his five children, George and John enjoyed a reputation as trainers. A daughter, Ellen Rose (*d.* 1884), married Fred Archer [q. v. Suppl. I], the jockey.

A cartoon portrait appeared in 'Vanity Fair' in 1896.

[Notes from Mr. John A. Dawson, of St. Albans House, Newmarket; Baily's Mag. liv. 235–7; Sportsman and Sporting Life, 14 May 1903; Ashgill, Life of John Osborne, p. 32; Ruff's Guide to the Turf.] E. M.

DAY, Sir JOHN CHARLES FREDERIC SIGISMUND (1826–1908), judge, son of Captain John Day of the 49th foot, of Englishbatch, near Bath, by his wife Emily, daughter of Jan Caspar Hartsinck, was born at the Hague on 20 June 1826. His parents were Roman catholics, and he received his education at Freiburg and at the Benedictine College of St. Gregory at Downside, near Bath. In 1845 he graduated B.A. at London and entered at the Middle Temple (29 Oct.). Called to the bar by that society on 26 Jan. 1849, he chose the home circuit, and early made his mark by becoming joint editor of Roscoe's 'Evidence at Nisi Prius,' and by bringing out the first annotated edition of the Common Law Procedure Act of 1852

(4th edit. 1872), thus acquiring the reputation of an authority on the new methods of pleading and practice. He soon enjoyed a lucrative and substantial business as a junior, owing no small part of his success in advocacy to his whimsical countenance and his variety of facial expression. To the end of his life he retained the whiskers which were fashionable in his early manhood, and his dry humour, aided by much natural shrewdness and a wide acquaintance with human nature, made him irresistible to juries in breach of promise and libel cases. He was also largely employed in election petitions. He took silk in 1872 and was made a bencher of his inn next year; he served as treasurer in 1896. In June 1882 he was made a judge of the Queen's Bench Division, receiving the honour of knighthood. Though he occupied a seat on the bench for nearly twenty years, the reputation he acquired there never equalled that which he enjoyed at the bar; while a sound and capable lawyer, he showed little interest in the problems of law which came before him when sitting in banc, and his apparent inattention, combined with his habit of never taking notes, made him very unpopular with civil litigants. In reality his retentive memory and native commonsense seldom failed him. When administering the criminal law, especially on circuit, he showed a sternness and upheld a standard of conduct which belonged to another age. The severity with which he punished the young roughs locally known as the 'High Rip gang' at Liverpool in 1887 was long remembered with gratitude in the north of England. He was a firm believer in the lash, and by perambulating the worst streets of Liverpool at night accompanied by his marshal and a single detective he got a first-hand acquaintance with the conditions of life in that city. But the sentences which he habitually dealt out in cases of minor crimes or indiscretions were extraordinary as coming from a man who was remarkably tender-hearted in private life; and where sexual immorality was concerned he knew no compassion, and seemed lost to all sense of proportion. Here the intensity of his religious convictions swayed him to the prejudice of judicial calmness. But his punishments were inflicted on a system of his own after careful inquiry, which led to the now universal practice of furnishing the judge with a complete *dossier* of the prisoner, an innovation which in practice does not always conduce to the impartial administration of justice.

The fact of his being a very devout Roman catholic led to the only two incidents in Day's career which brought him prominently before the public at large. In October 1886, as representing his co-religionists, he was appointed chairman of the royal commission to inquire into the Belfast riots of the preceding summer, and his refusal to allow counsel for the incriminated parties to cross-examine the witnesses involved him in an acute controversy with some of the leaders of the Irish bar. In July 1888 he was nominated, with Sir James Hannen [q. v. Suppl. I] and Sir A. L. Smith [q. v. Suppl. II], one of the three members of what was known as the Parnell commission appointed by Act of Parliament to investigate the allegations against certain Irish members contained in the pamphlet entitled 'Parnellism and Crime.' Like his two colleagues Day had never taken any part in politics, but he had a year or two previously made some ill-judged or probably mis-reported remarks about Irishmen at the Liverpool assizes, and his appointment was bitterly assailed by the nationalist members. In the course of debate in the House of Commons (30 July) Mr. John (afterwards Viscount) Morley quoted a private letter from one of the Belfast commissioners, Judge Adams, who wrote that 'Mr. Justice Day is a man of the seventeenth century in his views, a catholic as strong as Torquemada, a tory of the old high flier and non-juror type.' Day was vigorously defended from the ministerial benches. During the protracted proceedings of the Parnell commission he maintained an almost unbroken silence, and his cadaverous features were expressive of profound boredom; but it was gossip in the Temple that it was his insistence on early proof being tendered of the authenticity of the letters attributed to Parnell which forced Pigott into the box and led to the collapse of that part of the case. Day resigned at the beginning of the Michaelmas sittings of 1901, and was sworn of the privy council.

Day's catholicism was of the continental rather than the English type, and he had small sympathy with modern thought or manners. But his convictions did not debar him from warm friendship with those who were his opposites from every point of view, and his constant travelling companion at home and abroad was a fervent baptist and radical, William Willis [q. v. Suppl. II], county court judge. Though no great horseman, he was fond when it was practicable of preserving the old custom of riding round the circuit. From his early years he had been a keen and discriminating patron of contemporary painting; his collection, comprising some of the choicest works of Millet and Corot, fetched 95,000*l.* when sold by auction (13 May 1909) after his death. He died on 13 June 1908 at his residence, Falkland Lodge, Newbury, and was buried at the Roman catholic cemetery, Kensal Green. He was twice married: (1) on 1 Oct. 1846 to Henrietta (*d.* 26 March 1893), daughter of Joseph Henry Brown, by whom he had six sons and three daughters; (2) on 19 May 1900 to Edith, daughter of Edmund Westby; she survived him. A portrait in oils by Prince Troubetzkoy belongs to his widow. A cartoon portrait by 'Spy' appeared in 'Vanity Fair' in 1888.

[The Times, 14 June 1908; Men of the Time; Hansard, 3rd ser. cccxxix. 806; Sir John Day, by William Willis, K.C. (privately printed), 1909; personal knowledge; private information.] J. B. A.

DAY, LEWIS FOREMAN (1845–1910), decorative artist, born at Peckham Rye on 29 Jan. 1845, was son of Samuel Hulme Day, wine merchant in the City of London, of an old Quaker family of Essex, which claimed descent from John Day (1522–1584) [q. v.], the Elizabethan printer. His mother was Mary Ann Lewis. After attending a school in France, he entered Merchant Taylors' School in January 1858, and on leaving continued his education in Germany for eighteen months. He then after a short time as a clerk went at the age of twenty into the works of Lavers & Barraud, glass painters and designers. Thence he moved to the workshops of Clayton & Bell, makers of stained glass, and there he remained for two years, his principal work being to design the cartoons. In 1870 he worked for Heaton, Butler & Bayne on the decoration of Eaton Hall, Cheshire, and in the same year he started for himself in London. He took from his early training special interest in stained glass, gradually acquiring a wide reputation as a designer for textiles, pottery, carpets, wall-papers, and many other branches of manufacture. His designs were always carefully adapted to the material in which they were to be carried out, and to the processes of manufacture which had to be employed. He belonged to the same school of art-craftsmen as William Morris and Walter Crane, and his influence on contemporary ornament, if not so fully recognised as that of those two artists, was considerable. Many of the best-known designers of his day were taught by him.

One of the first promoters of the Arts and Crafts Society and a founder of the Art Workers Guild, of which he was at one time master, Day was from 1897 to his death almost continuously a member of the council of the Royal Society of Arts, before which society he delivered four courses of Cantor lectures. To the government department, originally that of science and art, and afterwards the board of education, he rendered important and well-appreciated service. From 1890 onwards he examined in painting and ornament, and later was, in addition, associated with William Morris, Walter Crane, and other decorative artists, in examining works sent in by schools of art for national competition. Shortly before 1900 he gave courses of lectures on ornamental art at the Royal College of Art at South Kensington, and he also inspected and reported on provincial schools of art where ornamental work was studied and practised.

When the Victoria and Albert Museum was established in its new building (1909) he was a member of the committee appointed to report upon the arrangement of the collections, and he greatly influenced the scheme which was eventually adopted.

A course of Cantor lectures at the Royal Society of Arts in 1886 on 'Ornamental Design' was followed by the publication of many important volumes on ornament and decoration. On his Cantor lectures were founded: 'Anatomy of Pattern' (1887) and 'The Planning of Ornament' (1887). The work which he esteemed his best was 'Windows' (1897; 3rd edit. 1909), the fruit of an exhaustive study of continental stained glass pursued in holiday tours of twenty years. He was also author of 'Instances of Accessory Art' (fol. 1880), 'Every Day Art' (1882; 2nd edit. 1894; Dutch trans. 1886); 'Alphabets Old and New' (1898; 3rd enlarged edit. 1910); (with Mary Buckle) 'Art in Needlework' (1900; 3rd edit. 1908); 'Lettering in Ornament' (1902); 'Pattern Design' (1903); the South Kensington handbook on 'Stained Glass' (1903); 'Ornament and its Application' (1904); 'Enamelling' (1907); and 'Nature and Ornament' (2 vols. 1908–9).

Day died at his house, 15 Taviton Street, W.C., on 18 April 1910, and was buried in Highgate cemetery. He married Ruth Emma Morrish in 1873, and had one daughter, Ruth.

[Personal knowledge; information from Mrs. Day; Merchant Taylors' School Reg. ii. 330; Manchester Guardian and Glasgow Herald, 19 April 1910; Journal Soc. of Arts, lviii. 560.] H. T. W.

DAY, WILLIAM [HENRY] (1823–1908), trainer and breeder of racehorses, born on 9 Aug. 1823 at Danebury, Hampshire, was younger son of John Barham Day by an Irish lady whose surname was Goddard. His father, known as 'Honest John,' founded the famous Danebury racing stable, where he had for patrons the duke of Grafton, Lord George Bentinck, and Lord Palmerston, among many others. His grandfather, John Day of Houghton Down Farm, Stockbridge, was racing adviser to the Prince of Wales, afterwards George IV, and acquired the reputation of being able to drink two more bottles of wine than any of his companions. He was the 'Gloomy Day' of Deighton's caricature, made on the Steyne at Brighton in 1801.

William was educated privately with his cousin, the Rev. Russell Day, afterwards a master at Eton, by his uncle, Henry Thomas Day, LL.D., rector of Mendlesham, Suffolk. Entering his father's stable at Danebury, he acquired some fame as a jockey, and rode Lord George Bentinck's horse, Grey Momus, when it won the Ascot Cup. His eldest brother, John, was to succeed the father at Danebury; consequently William started training at Woodyates, by Cranborne Chase, Dorset. There on the splendid downs he trained many good winners, including Mr. James Merry's Lord of the Isles and his own Promised Land, who carried off the Two Thousand Guineas in 1855 and 1859 respectively; Sir F. Johnstone's Brigantine, who won the Oaks and the Ascot Cup in 1869, and many good handicap horses. His brother Alfred, a most elegant rider, often rode his horses. Day also won in 1859 the Goodwood Cup with Promised Land, who finished fourth in the Derby. Day's patrons included Lord Ribblesdale, the marquis of Anglesey, Lord Coventry, and Lord Westmorland.

In 1873 Day gave up training and sold off his stud, which realised upwards of 25,000*l.*, but resumed operations in 1881, when Mr. J. R. Keene sent him some horses to train, including Foxhall, who won the Grand Prix, the Cesarewitch and the Cambridgeshire in 1881, and the Ascot Cup in 1882. Day afterwards trained a few horses at Salisbury, but finally retired in 1892. Meanwhile he formed a large breeding stud at Alvediston, near Salisbury, in 1873, and to it he devoted much attention. At that establishment there were over sixty thoroughbred brood mares. Cast-Off, the dam of Robert-the-Devil, winner of the St. Leger (1880), was bred there, and for a time Flying Duchess, the dam of Galopin, the Derby winner of 1875, was also at Alvediston.

Day, who had literary aptitude, wrote several articles on turf politics in the 'Fortnightly Review.' He published 'The Racehorse in Training' (1880), which was translated into French, and was universally regarded as valuable; 'Reminiscences of William Day, of Woodyates' (1886); and 'The Horse: How to Breed and Rear him' (1888).

Of medium height, and possessed of an iron will, Day was a model man of business. Like his father, who, on Sunday evenings, used to read Blair's sermons to the stable lads until they fell asleep, he was most punctilious in the discharge of his religious duties. For his patrons he won stakes to the value of over 200,000*l.* At one time a comparatively rich man, he lost the bulk of his fortune by speculating in poor land.

Day died at Shirley, Southampton, on 29 Aug. 1908, and was buried by the side of his wife at the parish church, Pentridge, near Cranborne, Dorset. He married his cousin, Ellen, daughter of James Day, veterinary surgeon, of Kenford, Devonshire. They celebrated their golden wedding in 1896. Mrs. Day died shortly afterwards. Of five sons, Alfred James, the youngest, formerly lieutenant in the Middlesex yeomanry, and now a captain of cavalry in the national reserve, alone maintained the family associations with the turf, carrying on a training and breeding establishment near Arundel, Sussex.

[Notes supplied by Mr. Alfred James Day; Ruff's Guide to the Turf; Reminiscences of William Day, of Woodyates; Sporting Life, 31 Aug. 1908.] E. M.

DEACON, GEORGE FREDERICK (1843–1909), civil engineer, born at Bridgwater, Somerset, on 26 July 1843, was eldest son of Frederick Deacon, a solicitor of that town, who afterwards practised in Preston and was at one time sheriff of the county palatine. His mother was Katharine, third daughter of William H. Charlton, vicar of St. Mary's, Bryanston Square, London. Educated at Heversham grammar school, he was apprenticed at seventeen to Messrs. Robert Napier & Sons of Glasgow. During his apprenticeship he studied at Glasgow University under Professors Rankine [q. v.] and Thomson (Lord Kelvin) [q. v. Suppl. II].

On the recommendation of Lord Kelvin he was appointed assistant to Cromwell Fleetwood Varley [q. v.], the engineer to the Atlantic Telegraph Company, and under him he took part in 1865 in the laying of the second Atlantic cable by the Great Eastern steamship. From 1865 to 1871 he practised at Liverpool as a consulting engineer, making so special a study of the Mersey estuary as to become a recognised authority in regard to it. He also lectured on civil engineering and mechanics at Queen's College, Liverpool. From 1871 to 1880 he was borough and water engineer of Liverpool.

As borough engineer he was responsible for the construction or reconstruction of about seventy miles of sewerage; and he laid the inner-circle tramway-rails in 1877, on a system of his own, besides introducing wood pavement into Liverpool and improving the method of set paving by adopting a solid concrete foundation for the wearing surface. His paper on 'Street Carriage-Way Pavements,' which he contributed to the 'Proceedings of the Institution of Civil Engineers' (lviii. 1) in 1879, was awarded a Watt medal and a Telford premium.

As water engineer his work was of even greater importance. In 1873 he invented the well-known waste-water meter which bears his name. The adoption of this meter throughout the corporation's district of supply satisfactorily economised the existing sources, which were becoming inadequate, largely owing to loss through leaky pipes and fittings. In 1875 he presented a paper on the subject to the Institution of Civil Engineers (*Proc.* xlii. 129), and was awarded a Telford medal and premium. In 1880 new sources of water-supply had become necessary, and Deacon projected a scheme, which was adopted, for the utilisation of the river Vyrnwy in North Wales. Thereupon he resigned the duties of borough engineer in order to devote himself entirely to those of water engineer, which he discharged until 1890. The works which Deacon designed, in conjunction with Thomas Hawksley [q. v. Suppl. I], included the fine masonry dam in the valley of the Vyrnwy, forming a lake 1121 acres in extent and having an average depth of seventy feet—the first reservoir in Great Britain in which a high masonry dam was employed. The dam has a maximum height to the overflow level of 144 feet, and impounds about 13,000 million gallons of water. From this lake the water is conveyed to Liverpool by an aqueduct seventy-six miles in length, which traverses three mountain tunnels and crosses under or over several railways and beneath a number of canals and rivers, including the Mersey. Messrs. Hawksley and Deacon were joint engineers of the undertaking until 1885, when Hawksley retired and the undivided responsibility fell upon Deacon. The works were opened by the duke of Connaught in July 1892. A description of them was presented by Deacon to the Institution of Civil Engineers (*Proc.* cxxvi. 24) and gained for him a George Stephenson medal and a Telford premium.

In both branches of his work in Liverpool Deacon won for himself a high reputation. Every question or problem was studied with the scientific thoroughness with which his former teacher and lifelong friend, Lord Kelvin, had imbued him. He regarded no practical detail as too small for earnest study and attention. He recognised, too, the æsthetic claims of constructional work.

In 1890 Deacon established a consulting practice in Westminster. In that capacity he constructed waterworks for Kendal, Merthyr Tydfil, Todmorden, Biggleswade, Milton (Kent), and other places. At his death he was engaged upon the plans of works, now in course of construction, for supplying Birkenhead from the river Alwen, and of new works for Ebbw Vale. He reported in 1890 to the International Niagara Commissioners on the utilisation of the Falls; in 1897, in conjunction with Sir Benjamin Baker [q. v. Suppl. II], to the London county council on the water-supply of London; and in the same year, in conjunction with Dr. W. C. Unwin and Mr. John Carruthers, on the Coolgardie water-supply scheme.

Deacon was elected an associate of the Institution of Civil Engineers on 3 Dec. 1872, became a full member on 6 Jan. 1874, and was a member of the council from November 1900 until his death. He was also a member of the Institution of Mechanical Engineers and a fellow of the Royal Meteorological Society. He was president of the mechanical science section of the British Association in 1897, as well as of many professional societies. In 1902 the University of Glasgow conferred upon him the honorary degree of LL.D.

He died suddenly at his office, 16 Great George Street, Westminster, on 17 June 1909, and was buried at Addington. In 1910 two memorial windows were placed in Llanwddyn Church, near Lake Vyrnwy, one by members and officials of the corporation of Liverpool, and the other by his family. He married twice: (1) Emily Zoë, eldest daughter of Peter Thomson, of Bombay; and (2) Ada Emma (*d.* 1912), eldest daughter of Robert Pearce of Bury

St. Edmunds. By his first wife he had one son and three daughters.

Deacon read papers before the Society of Arts, the British Association, and provincial societies, and he wrote the article 'Water-supply' in the 'Encyclopædia Britannica' (10th edit.).

[Min. Proc. Inst. Civ. Eng. clxxvii. 284; Men and Women of the Time, 1899.]

W. F. S.

DEANE, Sir JAMES PARKER (1812–1902), judge, born at Hurst Grove, Berkshire, on 25 June 1812, was second son of Henry Boyle Deane by his wife Elizabeth, daughter of James Wyborn of Hull House, Shelden, Kent. He went to Winchester as a colleger in 1824, and matriculated at St. John's College, Oxford, on 29 June 1829, as a law fellow of founder's kin. In 1833 he obtained a second class in the final classical school and a third in the final mathematical school. He graduated B.C.L. on 28 May 1834, and proceeded D.C.L. on 10 April 1839, being admitted on 2 Nov. following a member of the College of Advocates. He had previously, on 8 Nov. 1837, entered as a student at the Inner Temple, and on 29 Jan. 1841 he was called to the bar by that society. He was made a Q.C. on 16 Jan. 1858, and became bencher of his inn in the same year, serving the office of treasurer in 1878.

In 1854 Deane was appointed legal adviser to Admiral Sir Charles Napier [q. v.] commanding the British fleet in the Baltic: he was present on board H.M.S. Duke of Wellington at the bombardment of Bomarsund, and formed one of the landing party. On the abolition of Doctors' Commons in 1858 Deane transferred himself to the courts of probate and divorce, where he obtained a large practice. An effective speaker and a vigorous advocate, he adapted himself to juries and to the *viva voce* examination of witnesses more readily than some of his old colleagues and rivals. His most conspicuous appearances, however, were in the ecclesiastical courts, in which the practice and the traditions of 'The Commons' still flourished, and for a quarter of a century there were few ecclesiastical cases of interest or importance in which Deane was not retained, the most celebrated of them, perhaps, being those of Boyd *v.* Phillpotts, in which the legality of the Exeter reredos was challenged, and of Martin *v.* the Rev. A. H. Mackonochie [q. v.], which dragged on in one shape or another from 1867 to 1882, and in the earlier stages of which he appeared on behalf of the defendant. In 1872 he was appointed vicar-general of the province and diocese of Canterbury on the resignation of Sir Travers Twiss [q. v.]; he had already (in 1868) been made Chancellor of the diocese of Salisbury by Bishop Hamilton. In 1868 he became admiralty advocate-general. He also discharged from 1872 to 1886, under the title of legal adviser to the foreign office, the duties of the now obsolete office of Queen's advocate. In this capacity he prepared the British case in the arbitration between Great Britain and Portugal over the territory south of Delagoa Bay, and he advised his government throughout the long disputes arising from the action of the Alabama and her consorts in the American civil war. On 1 Aug. 1885 he received the honour of knighthood, and in 1892 was sworn a member of the privy council. His duties as vicar-general did not interfere with his forensic work, and he held the leading brief in the famous case of the missing will of the first Lord St. Leonards [q. v.], tried in 1876. He continued to practise at the bar until increasing deafness forced him to retire. His picturesque figure was one of the most striking features in the proceedings against Bishop King of Lincoln in the library at Lambeth Palace, when he sat as vicar-general in full-bottomed wig and doctor's robes beside Archbishop Benson and his episcopal assessors. On the occasion of the confirmation of Bishop Winnington Ingram as Bishop of London at Bow Church on 17 April 1901, the turbulent conduct of the 'opposers' got beyond his power of control. His last public appearance was at the confirmation of Dr. Paget as Bishop of Oxford a few months later; he was then in his ninetieth year, the greatest age at which any Englishman since Serjeant Maynard is believed to have exercised judicial functions.

He and Dr. T. H. Tristram, Q.C., who survived him until 1912, were the last of the 'civilians' trained in 'The Commons' and described in Dickens's 'David Copperfield' and Warren's 'Ten Thousand a Year.' He died at his house in Westbourne Terrace on 3 Jan. 1902, having resigned his offices a few days previously. He was buried at Brackwood cemetery.

Deane was a strong conservative in politics, and in the general election of Nov. 1868 he contested the city of Oxford against Edward (afterwards Viscount) Cardwell [q.v.] and (Sir) William Vernon Harcourt [q. v. Suppl. II], but was heavily defeated.

He married in 1841 Isabella Frances (*d.* 1894), daughter of Bargrave Wyborn.

His only surviving son is Sir Henry Bargrave Deane, a judge of the probate, admiralty and divorce division of the high court of justice.

[Foster's Alumni Oxonienses; Foster's Men at the Bar; The Times, 18 April 1901, 4 Jan. 1902; private information.] J. B. A.

DE LA RAMÉE, MARIE LOUISE, 'OUIDA' (1839–1908), novelist, born on 1 Jan. 1839 at 1 Union Terrace, Bury St. Edmunds, was daughter of Louis Ramé and his wife Susan Sutton. She owed all her education to her father, a teacher of French, whose mental power was exceptional. She expanded her surname of 'Ramé' into 'De la Ramée' at an early age. A diary of girlhood from April 1850 to May 1853 (HUNTINGTON, *Memories*, 1911, pp. 228–96) proves her precocity, love of reading, and eagerness to learn. She visited Boulogne with her parents in 1850, and accompanied them to London in 1851 to see the Great Exhibition. In 1859 she was living in London at Bessborough House, Ravenscourt Park, Hammersmith, and her neighbour and medical adviser, Dr. Francis W. Ainsworth, introduced her to his cousin, William Harrison Ainsworth [q. v.]. She began her literary career under Harrison Ainsworth's auspices, publishing in 'Bentley's Miscellany' a short story entitled 'Dashwood's Drag; or, the Derby and what came of it' (1859). Ainsworth, convinced of her ability, accepted and published by the end of 1860 seventeen tales by her, none of which she reprinted, although they brought her into notice. Like her later novels they dealt with dubious phases of military and fashionable life. Her first long novel, 'Granville de Vigne,' appeared in the same magazine in 1863. Tinsley published it in three volumes, changing the title with her consent to 'Held in Bondage' and paying her 80*l.* On the title-page Miss Ramé first adopted the pseudonym of 'Ouida,' a childish mispronunciation of her name Louise, by which she was henceforth exclusively known as a writer. 'Strathmore' followed in 1865, and 'Idalia,' written when she was sixteen, in 1867. 'Strathmore' was parodied as 'Strapmore! a romance by "Weeder"' in 'Punch' by (Sir) Francis Burnand in 1878. Ouida's vogue, thenceforth established, was assisted by an attack which Lord Strangford made on her novels in the 'Pall Mall Gazette.'

From 1860 onwards 'Ouida' spent much time in Italy. When in London she stayed at the Langham Hotel, and attracted attention—which was not always flattering—in literary society. William Allingham met her at a dinner in London in December 1868; he describes her as dressed in green silk, with a sinister clever face, her hair down, small hands and feet, and a voice like a carving-knife (H. ALLINGHAM and D. RADFORD, *William Allingham, a Diary*, 1907, pp. 193–4). She made a more favourable impression on Shirley Brooks in 1870 (LAYARD, *Shirley Brooks*, 1907). Bulwer Lytton greatly admired her work, and in 1871 on the publication of 'Folle-Farine' he wrote her an eight-page letter in which he hailed the book as a triumph of modern English romance. In 1874 she settled permanently with her mother in Florence, and there long pursued her work as a novelist. At first she rented an 'apartment' at the Palazzo Vagnonville. Later she removed to the Villa Farinola at Scandicci, three miles from Florence, where she lived in great style, entertained largely, collected *objets d'art*, dressed expensively but not tastefully, drove good horses, and kept many dogs, to which she was deeply attached. She declared that she never received from her publishers more than 1600*l.* for any one novel, but that she found America 'a mine of wealth.' In 'The Massarenes' (1897) she gave a lurid picture of the parvenu millionaire in smart London society. This book was greatly prized by Ouida, but it failed to sustain her popularity, which waned after 1890. Thenceforth she chiefly wrote for the leading magazines essays on social questions or literary criticisms, which were not remunerative.

Unpractical, and not very scrupulous in money matters, Ouida fell into debt when her literary profits declined, and gradually became a prey to acute poverty. Her mother, who died in 1893, was buried in the Allori cemetery at Florence as a pauper. From 1894 to 1904 Ouida lived, often in a state bordering on destitution, at the Villa Massoni, at Sant' Alessio near Lucca. From 1904 to 1908 she made her home at Viareggio, where a rough peasant woman looked after her, and her tenement was shared with dogs which she brought in from the street. A civil list pension of 150*l.* a year offered her by the prime minister, Sir Henry Campbell-Bannerman, on the application of Alfred Austin, George Wyndham, and Lady Paget, was at first declined on the score of the humiliation (AUSTIN, *Autobiography*, 1835–1910, 1911, ii. 105–6), but her scruples were overcome by her old friend, Lady Howard of Glossop, and Ouida accepted the recognition on 16 July 1906. The pension was granted her in August to date from the previous 1 April. An appeal made to her admirers to subscribe for her relief was met by Ouida's indignant denial that she was in want. She died on 25 Jan. 1908, at 70 Via Zanardelli, Viareggio, of the effects of pneumonia, and was buried in the English cemetery at the Bagnì di Lucca. An anonymous lady admirer erected over the grave a monument representing the recumbent figure of Ouida with a dog at her feet.

Ouida had an artificial and affected manner, and although amiable to her friends was rude to strangers. Cynical, petulant, and prejudiced, she was quick at repartee. She was fond of painting, for which she believed she had more talent than for writing, and she was through life in the habit of making gifts of her sketches to her friends. She knew little at first hand of the Bohemians or of the wealthy men and women who are her chief dramatis personæ. She described love like a precocious schoolgirl, and with an exuberance which, if it arrested the attention of young readers, moved the amusement of their elders (cf. G. S. STREET in *Yellow Book*, 1895, vi. 167–176). Yet she wrote of the Italian peasants with knowledge and sympathy and of dogs with an admirable fidelity. Her affection for dumb animals grew into a craze, but it came of her horror of injustice. Her faith in all humanitarian causes was earnest and sincere. She strongly sympathised with the Boers through the South African war.

Slightly built, fair, with an oval face, she had large dark blue eyes, and golden brown hair. A portrait in red chalk, drawn in September 1904 by Visconde Giorgio de Moraes Sarmento, was presented by the artist to the National Portrait Gallery, London, in 1908. He presented another drawing, made also in her declining years, to the Moyses Hall Museum, Bury St. Edmunds. A memorial drinking fountain (with trough), designed by Ernest G. Gillick, with a medallion portrait, was erected by public subscription at Bury St. Edmunds (unveiled on 2 Nov. 1909); the inscription is by Earl Curzon of Kedleston.

Ouida published forty-four works of fiction—either separate novels or volumes of collected short stories. The most popular were 'Held in Bondage' (1863, 1870, 1900); 'Strathmore' (1865); 'Idalia' (1867); 'Under Two Flags' (1867); 'Tricotrin' (1869); 'Puck' (1870); 'A Dog of Flanders and other Stories' (1872); 'Two Little Wooden Shoes' (1874); 'Moths' (1880); and 'Bimbi, Stories for Children' (1882), which was translated into French for the 'Bibliothèque Rose.' Her books were constantly reprinted in cheap editions, and some of them translated into French, or Italian, or Hungarian. Many of her later essays in the 'Fortnightly Review,' the 'Nineteenth Century,' and the 'North American Review' were republished in 'Views and Opinions' (1895) and 'Critical Studies' (1900). There she proclaimed her hostility to woman's suffrage and to vivisection, or proved her critical insight into English, French, and Italian literature. Her uncompleted last novel, 'Helianthus' (1908), was published after her death.

Ouida tried to write a play for the Bancrofts, but did not get far beyond the title, 'A House Party' (cf. *The Bancrofts*, 1909, p. 293); a novel of that name appeared in 1887. An opera by G. A. à Beckett and H. A. Rudall was founded in 1893 on her novel 'Signa' (1875), and the light opera 'Muguette' by Carré and Hartmann on 'Two Little Wooden Shoes.' Plays based on 'Moths' (by Henry Hamilton, produced at the Globe Theatre 25 March 1883) and on 'Under Two Flags' had much success.

[The Times, 27 Jan. 1908; S. M. Ellis, William Harrison Ainsworth and his Friends, 1911, ii. 234–236; W. G. Huntington, Memories, 1911, pp. 190–296, with diary of Ouida, April 1850 to May 1853; Tinsley, Random Recollections, i. 82–85; Edmund Yates, Celebrities at Home, first ser. 1877; private information.] E. L.

DE LA RUE, SIR THOMAS ANDROS, first baronet (1849–1911), printer, born in London on 26 May 1849, was second of the four sons of Warren de la Rue [see RUE, WARREN DE LA], astronomer and inventor, by his wife Georgiana, third daughter of Thomas Bowles of Guernsey. Thomas de la Rue [q. v.] was his grandfather. He entered Rugby in Feb. 1864, and matriculating in 1868 from St. John's College, Cambridge, graduated B.A. in 1871 and proceeded M.A. in 1874. In 1871 he joined the family printing business established by his grandfather, which was celebrated for its playing cards and printed stamps. By his enterprise he helped to increase the firm's reputation for artistic quality and convenience in the production of the postage-stamp, contracts for the manufacture of which the firm held not only for the United Kingdom but for most of the colonies and for many foreign countries. On the death of his father in 1889, and the retirement of his elder brother, Warren, Thomas became head of the business, and retained that position until 1896, when the firm became a limited company, of which his three sons subsequently became directors. De la Rue was created a baronet on 17 June 1898. He took a generous interest in the Royal Hospital for Diseases of the Chest, City Road, much of his spare time being devoted to its service. He died at his residence, 52 Cadogan Square, on 10 April 1911, and was buried at Golder's Green.

De la Rue married, on 1 Feb. 1876, Emily Maria (*d.* 11 Oct. 1904), daughter of William Speed, Q.C., by whom he had three sons, of whom Evelyn Andros, the eldest, succeeded to the baronetcy, and a daughter.

[Stationery World, xxxix. 232; Stationery Trades Journal (portrait), xxxii. 236; Lodge's Peerage and Baronetage; Rugby School Register, 1886, ii. 115; Book of Matriculations and Degrees, Univ. of Cambridge, 1851 to 1900, p. 165; The Times, 10 and 15 April 1911, Athenæum, 15 April 1911.] C. W.

DE MONTMORENCY, RAYMOND HARVEY, third Viscount Frankfort de Montmorency (1835–1902), major-general, born at Theydon Bower, Epping, Essex, on 21 Sept. 1835, was only son of Lodge Raymond, second viscount (1806–1889), by his wife Georgina Frederica (*d.* 1885), daughter of Peter Fitzgibbon Henchy, Q.C., LL.D., of Dublin. Educated at Eton and at the Royal Military College, Sandhurst, he was commissioned as ensign in the 33rd duke of Wellington's regiment on 18 Aug. 1854, promoted lieutenant on 12 Jan. 1855, and served with his regiment during that year in the Crimea in the war with Russia. He did duty in the trenches at the siege of Sevastopol, and took part in the storming of the Redan on 8 Sept., when Sevastopol fell. For his gallantry at the assault he was recommended for the Victoria Cross, but he did not receive it. For his services during the campaign he was given the British medal with clasp for Sevastopol and the Turkish and Sardinian medals.

De Montmorency accompanied his regiment to India. During the Indian Mutiny in 1857-8 he was in charge of a detachment against the mutineers in central India, and for his services he received the Indian Mutiny medal.

Promoted captain on 29 March 1861, de Montmorency exchanged into the 32nd duke of Cornwall's light infantry, and from 6 Dec. 1861 to 31 Dec. 1864 was aide-de-camp to his uncle by marriage, Major-general Edward Basil Brooke, commanding the troops in the Windward and Leeward Islands.

From 4 June 1865 de Montmorency was aide-de-camp to Lieut.-general (afterwards Field-marshal) Sir John Michel [q. v.], commanding the troops in British North America, and next year took part in the repulse of the Fenians, receiving the British medal for his services.

While travelling in Abyssinia, he volunteered under Sir Robert Napier, afterwards Lord Napier of Magdala [q. v.], in the hostilities against King Theodore (Oct. 1867). He accompanied the expedition to the gates of Magdala, when all volunteers were recalled. For his service he received the war medal.

De Montmorency commanded the frontier force during the operations in the Sudan in 1886–7, and received the Khedive's bronze star. In 1887 while commanding the troops at Alexandria with the local rank of major-general, he directed the operations of the British field column of the frontier force during the operations on the Nile, and was mentioned in despatches. He was promoted major-general on the establishment on 30 Nov. 1889, and succeeded to the peerage on the death of his father on 25 December.

From 1890 to 1895 Lord Frankfort commanded a first-class district in Bengal, and from 1895 to 1897 the Dublin district. He retired from the service on 21 Sept. 1897, on attaining 62 years of age. A keen soldier, a strict disciplinarian, and a master of the art of drill, kind-hearted and open-handed, he died suddenly of apoplexy at Bury Street, St. James's, London, on 7 May 1902, and was buried on the 12th in the village churchyard of Dewlish, Dorsetshire, with military honours.

De Montmorency married on 25 April 1866, at Montreal, Canada, Rachel Mary Lumley Godolphin, eldest daughter of Sir John Michel [q. v.]. She survived him. By her he had two sons and three daughters. The eldest son, Raymond Harvey de Montmorency (1867–1900), captain of the 21st lancers, distinguished himself in the charge of his regiment at Omdurman in 1898 and was awarded the Victoria Cross for his gallantry. He served in the South African war and was killed in action in February 1900 at Molteno, in Cape Colony, at the head of the corps of scouts which he had organised and which bore his name.

[The Times, 8 May 1902; regimental records; private information.] R. H. V.

DERBY, sixteenth Earl of. [See Stanley, Sir Frederick Arthur, 1841–1908.]

DE SAULLES, GEORGE WILLIAM (1862–1903), medallist, was born on 4 Feb. 1862 at Villa Street, Aston Manor, Birmingham. His grandfather was a Frenchman, but his father, William Henry de Saulles, was settled in Birmingham as a glass merchant. At an early age he began his art training at the Birmingham School of Art, under the master, Mr. Taylor, and there he gained several prizes. He was apprenticed to Mr. Wilcox, die-sinker, in Birmingham, under whom he had varied practice, which included the execution of large labels for Manchester goods, at that time not inartistic in design. He came to London in 1884, and worked for Mr. John H. Pinches, the die-engraver, then in Oxenden Street, Haymarket. In 1888 he returned to Birmingham and worked for Joseph Moore [q. v.], the medallist.

During 1892 De Saulles was employed in London at the Royal Mint, on the death of Leonard Charles Wyon [q. v.], the chief engraver. In January 1893 he was gazetted 'engraver to the mint' (*Ann. Report of Deputy-Master of the Mint* for 1893, p. 30), and from that time till his death was actively engaged in the production of dies for English and colonial coins and for official medals. He was a skilful craftsman who worked with great rapidity, and he designed, modelled and engraved most of his dies. He was in some degree influenced by the French school of Roty and Chaplain, but in his official work there was no great scope for innovation and the play of fancy. He was a man of kindly disposition, entirely devoted to his craft. He was engaged in the preparation of the new seal of Edward VII when he died at Chiswick, after a few days' illness, on 21 July 1903. He was buried in Chiswick churchyard. He was married, but had no children.

His medallic work between 1894 and 1903 includes at least thirty medals and three plaques, among which may be mentioned the following medals: Sir George Buchanan (Royal Society Medal), 1894; Professor Stokes, 1899; Samuel Carnegie, 1901; coronation medal of Edward VII, 1902; Royal Society of British Architects, 1902; National Lifeboat Institution, 1903. Besides these he engraved and designed a number of official medals such as the South Africa medal, 1899–1902; the Ashanti medal, 1900; the Transport Service medal, 1902. A fuller list is given by J. H. Pinches in the 'Numismatic Chronicle,' 1903, pp. 312, 313, and by Hocking, 'Catal. of Coins in Royal Mint,' ii. p. 301. He executed the dies for the new issue of coins of Queen Victoria in 1893, designed by Thomas Brock. He designed the Britannia reverse of the English bronze coins of 1895, and the issue of English coins made in 1902 after the accession of Edward VII. His signature on the coins is 'De S.' He also designed and engraved the dies for various colonial coins, such as the British East Africa copper coins, 1897; the British Honduras coins 1894; the British dollar for India, 1895, and the Straits Settlements dollar, 1903. He made the last great seal of Queen Victoria (1899), and many designs for official seals for the colonies. At the time of his death he was preparing the models for the great seals of the United Kingdom and those of Ireland and Scotland, subsequently executed by F. Bowcher. He was an exhibitor at the Royal Academy, 1898–1903.

[Memoir in Numismatic Chronicle, 1903, pp. 311–313, by Mr. John H. Pinches and private information supplied by him; Hocking's Catal. of Coins in Royal Mint, 2 vols. 1906–10; Forrer's Biog. Dict. of Medallists, 1904; Annual Reports of Deputy-Master of the Mint.] W. W.

DES VŒUX, Sir (GEORGE) WILLIAM (1834–1909), colonial governor, born at Baden on 22 Sept. 1834, was eighth of the nine children of Henry Des Vœux (1786–1857), who had given up clerical duty at home for foreign travel. The father was third son of Sir Charles Des Vœux (*d.* 1814), of Huguenot descent, who had held high office in the government of India and was created a baronet in 1787. His mother, his father's second wife, Fanny Elizabeth, eldest daughter of George Hutton—afterwards Hutton-Riddell—of Carlton, Nottinghamshire, died when William was two years old, and the father married in 1839, as third wife, Julia, daughter of John Denison of Ossington, and sister of Speaker John Evelyn Denison, first Viscount Ossington [q. v.]. Des Vœux always spoke with affection of his stepmother.

The family had returned to England from the continent in 1839, settling first in London and then at Leamington.

From a preparatory school William passed to Charterhouse (1845–1853) as a foundationer, and thence to Balliol College, Oxford, in 1854, but, unable to comply with his father's wish that he should take orders, he left Oxford in his third year without graduating. He went to Canada in 1856, originally intending to farm, but instead settled at Toronto, graduating B.A. at the university there, and also passing in law. After a brief practice at the Canadian bar, he in 1863 became a stipendiary magistrate and superintendent of rivers and creeks in an up-river district of British Guiana. Transferred to a coast district including extensive sugar estates, which were worked largely by means of East Indian and Chinese 'coolie' labourers, imported under a careful system of indenture and under close government supervision, Des Vœux, new to the conditions, and a somewhat ardent liberal, conceived that the 'coolies' were grievously oppressed by the planters. He was reluctant, as magistrate, to enforce 'the Draconic laws against the coolie indentured labourers,' and rather demonstratively took the part of the labourer against the employer, thereby incurring—though not to the extent which he imagined—the hostility of the planters and the distrust of the government. Relations became so strained that he asked for a transfer to another colony, and was sent as administrator to St. Lucia in 1869. From his new post he at once wrote to Lord Granville of what he regarded as the grievances of the 'coolies' in Guiana. He himself afterwards characterised his letter as 'defective,' 'written in great haste,' and 'without notes to refresh his memory.' 'The Times' described it as 'the severest indictment of public officers since Hastings was impeached.' A royal commission of inquiry was appointed and Des Vœux was recalled to Guiana to prove his case. The commission corrected certain genuine abuses in the labour system, but Des Vœux failed to prove what he afterwards admitted to have been an exaggerated view.

Des Vœux returned to his duties in St. Lucia, 'depressed,' as he says, 'by a sense of personal failure,' although the colonial office did not condemn him. At St. Lucia he reorganised and codified the old French system of law in force there, put right the island finances, and started a central sugar factory.

In 1878 he left St. Lucia and acted for about a year as governor of Fiji during the absence on leave of Sir Arthur Gordon (afterwards Lord Stanmore). Des Vœux carried on with success Sir Arthur's task of creating the first British crown colony in the South Sea Islands, and after a visit home, during which he was appointed governor of the Bahamas (1880) but did not take up the post, he, on the retirement of Sir Arthur Gordon in 1880, returned to Fiji as actual governor and as high commissioner of the Western Pacific. These posts he filled with credit till 1885. He was governor of Newfoundland in 1886 and of Hongkong from 1887 till his final retirement from the service in 1891.

Thenceforth Des Vœux lived quietly in England, chiefly in London. He published his autobiography, 'My Colonial Service,' in 1903, a pleasant, gossipy book, containing much of interest on colonial administration. He had been made G.C.M.G. in 1893. He died in London on 15 Dec. 1909.

Des Vœux, while on sick leave, married, on 24 July 1875, Marion Denison, daughter of Sir John Pender [q. v. Suppl. I], by whom he had two surviving sons and two daughters.

[Des Vœux, My Colonial Service, 1903; public records; personal knowledge.]

E. IM T.

DETMOLD, CHARLES MAURICE (1883–1908), animal painter and etcher, son of Edward Detmold, electrical engineer, by his wife Mary Agnes Luck, was born at Putney on 21 Nov. 1883. Together with his twin brother, Edward Julius, who shared in every stage of his artistic development, he was distinguished by extreme precocity. The two began as children, living at Hampstead, to draw and study animals in the Zoological Gardens and Natural History Museum, and they exhibited at the Royal Academy while still in their fourteenth year. On the advice of Burne-Jones they were not sent to any art school. They were profoundly influenced by Japanese art, and developed a style in which a searching study of natural forms, especially of the plumage of birds, was always subordinated to decorative arrangement. In 1897 both brothers began to etch, and in 1898 had made sufficient progress to issue jointly a portfolio of eight etchings of birds and animals. In 1899 a volume of coloured reproductions of their drawings was published by Dent under the title 'Pictures from Birdland.' In the same year appeared the first of a series of etchings executed jointly by the two brothers, each working on the same plate, which continued at intervals till 1906. Maurice produced in all ten etchings and two woodcuts in collaboration with Edward, and twenty-five etchings executed entirely by himself, though in part from drawings by his brother. Many of the brothers' etchings are immature, but the technical ability displayed in the best of them, especially in the latest of the joint works, is very remarkable. In 1900 the Detmolds held an exhibition of their prints and water-colours at the Fine Art Society's galleries. In 1904 they contributed a joint etching to 'The Artist Engraver,' and on 12 Jan. 1905 they were elected associates of the Royal Society of Painter Etchers; they contributed some of their best work to the 1905 exhibition, but afterwards resigned their membership; two plates produced late in that year were Maurice's last etched works. Jointly with his brother he painted large illustrations in water-colour to Rudyard Kipling's 'Jungle Book,' which were published in 1903. For several years the two Detmolds, who continued to reside at Hampstead, spent part of the year at Ditchling, Sussex. On 9 April 1908, when about to leave Hampstead for the country, Maurice committed suicide by inhaling chloroform; his twin brother survives him.

[M. H. Spielmann in Mag. of Art, Jan. 1900 (portrait); A. Graves, Royal Acad. Exhibitors; Cat. of Royal Soc. of Painter Etchers, 1905; The Times, 14 April 1908; art. by C. Dodgson in Die Graphischen Künste, Vienna, 1910, xxxiii. 16, with complete catalogue of the etchings; private information.] C. D.

DE VERE, AUBREY THOMAS (1814–1902), poet and author, born at Curragh Chase, Adare, co. Limerick, Ireland, on 10 Jan. 1814, was the third son of a family of five sons and three daughters of Aubrey Thomas Hunt, afterwards Sir Aubrey de Vere, second baronet [q. v.], by his wife Mary (*d.* 1856), eldest daughter of Stephen Edward Rice of Mount Trenchard, co. Limerick, and sister of Thomas Spring-Rice, first Lord Monteagle [q. v.]. His elder brothers Vere and Stephen de Vere [q. v. Suppl. II] successively inherited their father's baronetcy. Save for a three years' visit to England between 1821 and 1824, Aubrey's boyhood was spent at his Irish home, where he was educated privately. While he was a boy a tutor encouraged an enthusiasm for English poetry, especially that of Wordsworth. In October 1832 he entered Trinity College, Dublin. 'Almost all the university course' was uncongenial and he devoted himself to metaphysics. In 1837 he won the 'first Downes premium' for theological essay-writing. He left college next year. To his father's wish that he should take orders in the established church he offered no objection and the idea was present to his mind for many years, but no active step was taken. His time was spent in travel or in literary and philosophical study. In 1838 he visited Oxford and there first met Newman, who after Wordsworth's death filled the supreme place in De Vere's regard, and Sir Henry Taylor [q. v.], who became his lifelong friend. Next year he visited Cambridge and Rome. He was introduced at London or Cambridge to the circle which his eldest brother Vere and his cousin, Stephen Spring Rice, had formed at the university; of this company Tennyson was the chief, but it included Monckton Milnes, Spedding, Brookfield, and Whewell. In 1841 De Vere, whose admiration of Wordsworth's work steadily grew, made in London the poet's acquaintance. In 1843 he stayed at Rydal. He regarded the invitation as 'the greatest honour' of his life, and the visit was often repeated. He came to know Miss Fenwick, Wordsworth's neighbour and friend, and he began a warm friendship, also in 1841, with the poet Coleridge's daughter, Sara Coleridge [q. v.]. In 1843-4 De Vere travelled in Europe, chiefly in Italy, with Sir Henry Taylor and his wife. In 1845 he was in London, seeing much of Tennyson, and in the same year he made Carlyle's acquaintance at Lord Ashburton's house. Later friends included Robert Browning and R. H. Hutton. After visits to Scotland and the Lakes, De Vere returned to Ireland at the beginning of 1846 to find the country in the grip of the famine. He threw himself into the work of the relief committees with unexpected practical energy.

De Vere had already begun his career as a poet by publishing in 1842 'The Waldenses and other Poems,' a volume containing some sonnets and lyrics which now have a place in modern anthologies. 'The Search after Proserpine and other Poems' came out in 1843, the title-poem winning Landor's praise. Now in a poem 'A Year of Sorrow' he voiced the horrors of the winter 1846–7. Turning to prose, in which he showed no smaller capacity than in verse, he published in 1848 'English Misrule and Irish Misdeeds.' There he supported the union and loyalty to the crown, but betrayed intense Irish sympathy, criticised methods of English rule, and deprecated all catholic disabilities. Through all the critical events in Irish history of his time he maintained the same point of view. He always opposed concession to violent agitation, but when, after the Phœnix Park murders in 1882, he wrote a pamphlet on 'Constitutional and Unconstitutional Political Action,' he admitted no weakening in his love of his country.

Meanwhile the death of his father in July 1846 and the experience of the Irish famine deepened De Vere's religious feeling, and from 1848 his sentiment inclined towards the Roman catholic church. Carlyle and other friends warned him in vain against the bondage which he was inviting. But in Nov. 1851 he set out for Rome in company with Henry Edward Manning, and on 15 Nov. was received into the Roman catholic church on the way in the archbishop's chapel at Avignon (see his explanatory letter to Mrs. Coleridge written the same day in WILFRID WARD, *Aubrey de Vere*, 1904, pp. 198, 199; and his own *Religious Problems of the 19th Century*, 1893).

In 1854 he was appointed by the rector, Newman, to be professor of political and social science in the new Dublin catholic university (cf. WILFRID WARD, *Cardinal Newman*, **i.** 359, 1912). He discharged no duties in connection with the post, but he held it in name until Newman's retirement in 1858. At Pope Pius IX's suggestion he wrote 'May Carols,' hymns to the Virgin and saints (1857; 3rd edit. 1881), with an introduction explaining his conversion.

Thenceforth he lived chiefly in his beautiful Irish home, exchanging visits and corresponding with his friends and publishing much verse and prose. Tennyson had spent five weeks with De Vere at Curragh in 1848, and De Vere from 1854 onwards constantly visited Tennyson at Farringford and Aldworth. Always interested in Irish legend and history, De Vere published in 1862 'Inisfail, a Lyrical Chronicle of Ireland,' illustrating the Irish annals of six centuries, and after another visit to Rome in 1870 set to work on 'The Legends of St. Patrick,' his most important work of the kind, which appeared in 1872. He made a first attempt at poetic drama in 'Alexander the Great' (1874), which was followed by 'St. Thomas of Canterbury' in 1876. The two dramas were designed to contrast pagan and Christian heroism.

Death of friends saddened his closing years. He published a volume of 'Recollections' in 1897, and next year he revisited the Lakes and other of his early English haunts. He died unmarried at Curragh Chase on 21 Jan. 1902, and was buried in the churchyard at Askeaton, co. Limerick.

A coloured drawing of De Vere at twenty, showing a handsome countenance, and an oil portrait also done in youth by Samuel Laurence, are at Curragh Chase. An oil painting by Elinor M. Monsell (now Mrs. Bernard Darwin) when De Vere was eighty-seven is in her possession.

De Vere was a charming conversationalist; his grace of thought and expression was said to shed 'a moral sunshine' over the company of hearers, and he told humorous Irish stories delightfully. His verse is intellectual, dignified, and imaginative, but somewhat too removed from familiar thought and feeling to win wide acceptance. A disciple of Wordsworth from the outset, he had a predilection for picturesque and romantic themes. He was at his best in the poems on old Irish subjects, and in his sonnets some of which like 'The Sun-God' and 'Sorrow' reach a high standard of accomplishment. Sara Coleridge said of him that he had more entirely a poet's nature than even her own father or any of the poets she had known. His poetry enjoyed much vogue in America. An accomplished writer of prose, De Vere was judged by R. H. Hutton to be a better critic than poet. His critical powers are seen to advantage throughout his 'Critical Essays' (3 vols. 1887–9), but his correspondence with Sir Henry Taylor contains his best literary criticism.

Besides the volumes of verse cited De Vere wrote: 1. 'The Infant Bridal and Other Poems,' 1864; 1876. 2. 'Antar and Zara, an Eastern Romance,' 1877. 3. 'The Foray of Queen Meave,' 1882. 4. 'Legends and Records of the Church and Empire,' 1887. 5. 'St. Peter's Chains, or Rome and the Italian Revolution,' 1888. 6. 'Mediæval Records and Sonnets,' 1893. Other prose works are: 1. 'Picturesque Sketches of Greece and Turkey,' 2 vols., 1850. 2. 'The Church Settlement of Ireland,' 1866. 3. 'Ireland's Church Property and the Right Use of it,' 1867. 4. 'Pleas for Secularization,' 1867. 5. 'Ireland's Church Question,' 1868. 6. 'Proteus and Amadeus: a Correspondence about National Theology,' 1878. 7. 'Ireland and Proportional Representation,' 1885.

[Wilfrid Ward, Aubrey de Vere, a memoir based on his unpublished diaries and correspondence, 1904 (with two portraits—in youth and age); Recollections of Aubrey de Vere, 1897; The Times, 22 Jan. 1902; Stopford A. Brooke and T. W. Rolleston, A Treasury of Irish Poetry, 1900, pp. 311–14; Hallam, Lord Tennyson's Alfred Lord Tennyson, 1897, and his Tennyson and his Friends, 1911; Sir Henry Taylor, Autobiography, 1885; Mary Anderson, a Few Memories, 1896; private information.]

E. L.

DE VERE, Sir STEPHEN EDWARD, fourth baronet (1812–1904), translator of Horace, and elder brother of the above, was born at Curragh Chase, Adare, co. Limerick, on 26 July 1812. He was educated at Trinity College, Dublin, and shared through life the literary tastes of his family. After reading at Lincoln's Inn, he was called to the Irish bar in 1836. His life was dedicated to the service of his fellow-countrymen, and he worked hard for the relief of the distress during the Irish famine. He believed emigration to be the only panacea, and encouraged the young men to go out to Canada. Hearing of the terrible sufferings of the emigrants on the voyage, in May 1847 he went himself as a steerage passenger to Canada. The emigrant ships were sailing vessels, and the voyage took six weeks or more. He returned to England in the autumn of 1848. His letter describing the voyage was read in the House of Lords by Lord Grey, with the result that the Passengers Act was amended, and proper accommodation provided for emigrants. His admiration of the Irish catholic peasants led him to embrace the Roman catholic religion, and his reception into that church took place during his visit to Canada in 1848.

De Vere was member of parliament for Limerick (1854–9). He was a liberal, but, though opposed to home rule, approved Gladstone's Land Act. He succeeded his brother Vere as fourth baronet in 1880. He died unmarried on 10 Nov. 1904 at Foynes, co. Limerick, an island in the river Shannon, and was buried there, by the door of the Roman catholic church, which was built mainly by his exertions. A fountain was erected in the village during his lifetime to commemorate his work in the district. His kindness to his tenants was remarkable; they were suffered to help themselves to wood from the park, and even, it is said, to the deer. The baronetcy became extinct at his death.

De Vere published 'Translations from Horace' in 1886, together with some original verse. The renderings of Horace are vigorous and are often finely turned, but he expands freely. He wrote also a few pamphlets, including 'Is the Hierarchy an Aggression?' in 1851 (two edits.).

[The Times, 11 Nov. 1904; Wilfrid Ward, Aubrey de Vere, pp. 183–4; Aubrey de Vere, Recollections, 1897, pp. 252–4; private information.] E. L.

DEVONSHIRE, eighth **Duke of.** [See Cavendish, Spencer Compton, 1833–1908.]

DE WINTON, Sir FRANCIS WALTER (1835–1901), major-general and South African administrator, born at Pittsford, Northamptonshire, on 21 June 1835, was second son of Walter de Winton (1809–1840), of Maesllwch Castle, Radnorshire, whose surname was changed from Wilkins to De Winton by royal licence in 1839. His mother was Julia Cecilia, second daughter of Richard John Collinson, rector of Gateshead.

Educated at the Royal Military Academy, Woolwich, he entered the royal artillery as second lieutenant on 11 April 1854. Serving in the Crimean war, he was present at the siege and fall of Sevastopol, and received the medal with one clasp, Turkish medal, and the légion d'honneur, 5th class. Becoming captain in 1861, he acted as A.D.C. to Sir W. Fenwick Williams [q. v.] when commanding the forces in British North America, and was again on his staff when he was lieutenant-governor of Nova Scotia from 1864 to 1867 and when he was governor of Gibraltar in 1870–5. From 1877 to 1878 De Winton was military attaché at Constantinople, and from 1878 to 1883 he was secretary to the marquis of Lorne (afterwards ninth duke of Argyll) when governor-general of Canada. Promoted lieut.-colonel in 1880, he became brevet-colonel in 1884, and was made C.M.G. in 1882 and K.C.M.G. in Feb. 1884.

In 1885 he was appointed administrator-general of the Congo under the Belgian government, just before it was raised to the rank of a state. He held this office only until 1886, when he was created a commander of the Order of Leopold. In 1887 he acted as secretary of the Emin Pasha relief committee, and assisted (Sir) H. M. Stanley [q. v. Suppl. II] in his preparations for the relief expedition (H. M. Stanley, *In Darkest Africa*, i. 40). Subsequently Sir Francis, who became a substantive colonel in 1887, commanded the expedition against the Yonnies on the West Coast of Africa. Robarrie, the stronghold of the insurgents, was captured on 21 Nov. 1887, and the rebellion suppressed. For his services De Winton was made a C.B. in March 1888, receiving the medal and clasp, and on his return home he was appointed assistant quartermaster-general at headquarters. The end of 1889, however, found him once more in Africa. Repeated requests had been made by the King of Swaziland that his country should be taken under the protection of the British government, owing to the aggressive attitude of the Boers, but the government had declined to interfere. Left to themselves, the Boers gained virtual possession of the pastoral resources of Swaziland, In 1889 De Winton was sent as a commissioner to Swaziland, with instructions to hold an inquiry into its affairs in conjunction with a commissioner of the South African republic. He reached Pretoria in Nov. 1889, and after several interviews with President Kruger left for Swaziland, accompanied by Generals Joubert and Smit. The joint commissioners held a meeting of the native chiefs and head-men, and, amongst other things, promised them that the independence of the Swazis should be maintained by both governments; but, according to the report which De Winton subsequently made respecting his mission, the Swazis had already parted 'not only with all their actual territory but with rights which should only belong to the government of a country, to a lot of adventurers whose sole object was to make money by them.' He therefore considered a British protectorate inadvisable and impracticable. Not until the close of the South African war was the position of the Swazis improved. In May 1890 Sir Francis, who retired from the army on 21 June of that year with the honorary rank of major-general, was appointed governor of the Imperial East African Association's possessions; but he resigned in June 1891. In January 1892 he was appointed controller and treasurer of the household of the duke of Clarence, after whose death in January 1892 he continued to act in the same capacity in the household of the duke of York, now King George V. He was promoted G.C.M.G. in 1893. He was hon. sec. of the Royal Geographical Society in 1888–9. He was made hon. LL.D. of Cambridge in 1892, and was also hon. LL.D. of Durham. He died at Llanstephan, Llyswen, South Wales, on 16 Dec. 1901, and was buried at Glasbury, Breconshire.

He married in 1864 Evelyn, daughter of Christopher Rawson of Lennoxville, Canada, and had issue two sons and two daughters. One son predeceased him in 1892.

[Burke's Landed Gentry; The Times, 18, 19, and 21 Dec. 1901; G. Schweitzer, Life and Work of Emin Pasha, 1898, i. 309; H. M. Stanley, Autobiography, 1909, p. 338.]

J. H. L–E.

DE WORMS, HENRY, first Baron Pirbright (1840–1903), politician, born in London on 20 Oct. 1840, was third and youngest child of Baron Solomon Benedict de Worms (1801–82), by his wife Henrietta, eldest daughter of Samuel Moses Samuel of London. The father, Solomon de Worms, was son of Benedict de Worms of Frankfort-on-the-Maine, by his wife Jeanette, eldest daughter of Meyer Amschel Rothschild of the same city, and sister of Nathan Meyer Rothschild [q. v.], the first of the Rothschild family to settle in England. Solomon de Worms and his two brothers came to England in 1815 and formed a banking and colonial business in London. Becoming interested in coffee-planting in Ceylon, they did much to further the economic development of the island (Sir J. Emerson Tennent, *Ceylon*, 5th edit. ii. p. 250). Solomon de Worms was created hereditary baron of the Austrian empire in 1871, and in 1874 Queen Victoria gave him and his descendants permission to use the title in England, in recognition of the services rendered by the family to Ceylon.

Henry was educated at King's College, London, of which he became a fellow in 1873. He originally intended to devote himself to medicine (Montagu Williams, *Reminiscences*, i. p. 64), but in 1860 he entered the Inner Temple as a student, and in 1863 was called to the bar, joining the old home circuit and practising at the Kent sessions. Later he engaged with his eldest brother, George, in the management of the family business in Austin Friars, until it was dissolved in 1879.

From early manhood De Worms was interested in public affairs both at home and abroad. A frequent visitor to Austria, he formed a close acquaintance with the Austrian statesman Count von Beust, which grew more intimate during Beust's tenure of the Austrian embassy in London (1871–8). After Beust's death in 1886 De Worms edited with an introduction an English translation of the count's memoirs (1887, 2 vols.). Meanwhile De Worms had become an active politician in England on the conservative side. Beust had introduced him by letter to Disraeli in 1867, with the result that he contested the borough of Sandwich in Nov. 1868, when he was defeated. He was returned at the general election of 1880 as the conservative member for Greenwich, in succession to Gladstone, and was made parliamentary secretary to the board of trade in Lord Salisbury's first administration (June 1885–Jan. 1886). In Nov. 1885 he was elected for the East Toxteth division of Liverpool and was re-elected in June 1886. He resumed office at the board of trade in Lord Salisbury's second administration, and retained that position until February 1888, when he was appointed under-secretary for the colonies (1888–92) and a member of the privy council, being the first Jew upon whom this honour was conferred. On 24 Nov. 1887 an international conference on sugar bounties met in London in the interest of the sugar-growing colonies. The United States was not represented. De Worms was chosen president. As one of the British plenipotentiaries he signed a protocol with a convention (19 Dec. 1887), wherein all the representatives of sugar producing or manufacturing countries condemned in principle the bounty system, and recommended legislation for its abolition. De Worms early next year visited the chief European capitals to urge practical effect being given to the convention. All countries, save France, Denmark, and Sweden, signed (30 Aug. 1888) a final convention, but this was not ratified by the English parliament. De Worms, despite the failure of his efforts, continued to denounce the bounty system in the interest of the sugar-growing colonies. On 15 Nov. 1895 he was raised to the peerage as Baron Pirbright, taking the title from the village of Pirbright, Surrey, where he had acquired an estate.

In the Jewish community he was long a prominent worker, serving as president of the Anglo-Jewish Association (1872–86). In 1886, on the marriage of his daughter Alice to John Henry Boyer Warner of Quorn Hall, Leicestershire, a union contrary to Jewish observance, he severed his connection with the Jewish community. He died on 9 Jan. 1903, and was buried in the churchyard of Wyke St. Mark, near Guildford.

De Worms, who was elected a fellow of the Royal Society, published: 1. 'The Earth and its Mechanism,' 1862. 2. 'The Austro-Hungarian Empire,' 1870; 2nd edit. 1872. 3. 'England's Policy in the East,' 1877.

He married: (1) in 1864 Fanny, eldest daughter of Baron von Todesco, of Vienna, by whom he had three daughters, and whom he divorced in 1886; and (2) in 1887 Sarah, then Mrs. Barnett, only daughter of Sir Benjamin Samuel Phillips. He left no heir.

A portrait of Lord Pirbright in his peer's robes, painted by Sir Luke Fildes, R.A., is in possession of Lady Pirbright. A cartoon portrait by 'Ape' appeared in 'Vanity Fair' in 1880. A public hall and recreation ground commemorate him at Pirbright.

[Jewish Chronicle, 16 Jan. 1903; Hansard's Debates; private information.] M. E.

DIBBS, SIR GEORGE RICHARD (1834–1904), premier of New South Wales, born in Sydney on 12 Oct. 1834, was youngest son of Capt. John Dibbs, formerly of the East India Co.'s service, by his wife Sophia Elizabeth Allwright. He was educated in Sydney at St. Philip's Church of England school and at Dr. Lang's Australian College. In 1857 he joined his father-in-law in a sugar refinery which passed into other hands. In 1859 he formed a shipping business (joined by his brother next year) in Sydney and Newcastle (New South Wales), and started a successful branch at Valparaiso. In 1866 the firm became bankrupt on the failure of the Agra bank. Later the creditors were paid in full, and Dibbs & Co. became one of the foremost firms in Sydney. In 1868 he toured through Europe and the British Isles. In 1871 he was cast in a libel suit and spent a year in Darlinghurst debtors' prison rather than pay damages.

At forty years of age he began his political career, advocating republicanism and free trade. He was one of the leading members of the Public Schools League, which championed free compulsory and secular education in state primary schools. In 1874 he was elected one of the members for West Sydney of the legislative assembly of New South Wales. In 1877 he was defeated, but in 1882 was returned for St. Leonards. In January 1883 he became treasurer and colonial secretary in the ministry of Sir Alexander Stuart [q.v.]. At this time, owing to enormous sales of crown land, the state coffers were overflowing with money. The Stuart-Dibbs government passed a law stopping these sales. On 7 Oct. 1885 Sir George Dibbs succeeded Sir Alexander Stuart as premier, first holding the office of colonial secretary, then that of treasurer. His ministry was defeated on 22 Dec. 1885. From 26 Feb. 1886 to January 1887 he was colonial secretary in the Jennings ministry. In 1887 he lost his seat at St. Leonards to Sir Henry Parkes [q. v. Suppl. I], but was immediately returned by the Murrumbidgee. From 17 Jan. to 6 March 1889 he was again premier and colonial secretary. During his new term of office he declared his conversion from free trade to protection and succeeded in carrying a tariff. His republican views had undergone modification, and in March 1891 he was appointed a delegate to the federation convention held in Sydney, in spite of Sir Henry Parkes's objection on the ground of his republican sympathies. On 23 Oct. 1891, on the defeat of Sir Henry Parkes's ministry, Sir George Dibbs became, for a third time, premier and colonial secretary. In June 1892 he visited England as premier of his colony and on a special mission to reassure London capitalists of the financial stability not only of New South Wales but of Victoria, South Australia, Tasmania, and New Zealand. He was largely successful in his mission, and was created K.C.M.G. on 23 July 1892. In 1893 a financial crisis followed, many banks closed their doors, and the panic was stopped only by the prompt action of Sir George Dibbs's government in giving the banks a state guarantee. His popularity was thereby immensely increased, but he himself became bankrupt. He resigned his seat, while retaining the premiership, and was at once re-elected. At the elections in July 1894 he was defeated, and resigned office. He retired from political life in July 1897 and from that date was managing trustee of the savings banks of New South Wales till his death at Sydney on 5 Aug. 1904.

He married in 1857 Annie Maria, daughter of Ralph Meyer Robey, of the legislative council of New South Wales. Two sons and nine daughters survived him.

[Mennell's Dict. of Australas. Biog.; British Australasian, 18 Aug. 1904; Sydney Mail, 10 Aug. 1904.] A. B. W.

DICEY, EDWARD JAMES STEPHEN (1832–1911), author and journalist, born on 15 May 1832 at Claybrook near Lutterworth, Leicestershire, was second son of Thomas Edward Dicey, of an old Leicestershire family, who was senior wrangler in 1811, was a pioneer of the Midland Railway, and owned the 'Northampton Mercury.' His mother Anne Mary, sister of Sir James Stephen [q.v.], was aunt of Sir James Fitzjames Stephen [q. v.] and Sir Leslie Stephen [q. v. Suppl. II]. His younger brother is Professor Albert Venn Dicey.

Educated at home and, for about two years, at King's College, London, Edward went up to Trinity College, Cambridge, in 1850, was president of the Cambridge Union, and graduated B.A. in 1854 with a third class in the classical tripos, and as a senior optime in mathematics. After leaving Cambridge he went for a short time into business without success, and then took to writing, for which he had inherited from his mother and her family a singular facility. He travelled abroad and interested himself in foreign politics. In 1861 he published both 'Rome in 1860' and 'Cavour—a Memoir,' thereby establishing his position as a writer on public matters (GRAVES's *Life and Letters of Alexander Macmillan*, p. 180). In 1862 Dicey visited America, and wrote on the American civil war in 'Macmillan's Magazine' and the 'Spectator' with 'admirable honesty of style and thought,' and in a 'quiet judicial tone' (*ibid.*). There followed in 1863 'Six Months in the Federal States,' which 'met with a somewhat lukewarm reception,' on account of the northern sympathies of the author (*ibid.*).

In 1861 Dicey became connected with the 'Daily Telegraph,' and his style and knowledge of foreign questions led to his being made a permanent member of the staff in 1862. Among his colleagues were Sir Edwin Arnold [q. v. Suppl. II], an old school friend, Francis Lawley [q. v. Suppl. II], and George Augustus Sala [q. v.]. He was a leader-writer for the paper, and also acted as special correspondent in the Schleswig-Holstein war of 1864, and the Seven Weeks' war of 1866. He embodied these experiences in the volumes 'The Schleswig-Holstein War' (1864), and 'The Battle-fields of 1866' (1866). He afterwards described other foreign excursions in 'A Month in Russia during the Marriage of the Czarevitch' (1867), and in 'The Morning Land, being Sketches of Turkey, the Holy Land, and Egypt' (1870), the result of three months' tour in the East.

While in the East in 1869 he accepted an offer of the editorship of the 'Daily News,' and held this post for three months in 1870. On leaving it he at once became editor of the 'Observer,' and filled that office for nineteen years (1870–89), continuing to write for the paper for some time after he ceased to edit it.

Subsequently he was a constant contributor to the 'Nineteenth Century,' the 'Empire Review,' and other periodicals. His interest in foreign politics remained keen, especially in the affairs of Eastern Europe. He was a frequent visitor to Egypt, and formed at first hand well-defined views of England's position there, at one time advocating the annexation of the country by Great Britain. He was a strong supporter of friendly relations between England and Germany, and closely studied South African matters in later years.

His latest books, which indicate the range of his interest, were: 1. 'England and Egypt,' mainly papers republished from the 'Nineteenth Century,' 1881. 2. 'Victor Emmanuel' in the 'New Plutarch' series, 1882. 3. 'The Peasant State, an Account of Bulgaria in 1894,' 1894. 4. 'The Story of the Khedivate,' 1902. 5. 'The Egypt of the Future,' 1907.

Dicey had entered at Gray's Inn as a student in 1865, and was called to the bar in 1875, but did not practise. During his later life he made his home in chambers in the Inn, of which he became a bencher in

1896, and treasurer in 1903 and 1904. In 1886 he was made a C.B. He was a familiar figure at the Athenæum and Garrick clubs. He died at his chambers in Gray's Inn on 7 July 1911, and was buried in the Brompton cemetery, the first part of the funeral service taking place in Gray's Inn Chapel. He married in 1867 Anne Greene Chapman of Weymouth, Massachusetts; she died in 1878. He had one son, who died in his father's lifetime. A portrait of him by a French artist, M. Laugée, is in the possession of his cousin, Godfrey Clark, Talygarn Pontyclun, Glamorganshire.

Dicey was by nature a singularly good observer; he had a great store of knowledge, much dry humour, a cool judgment, and a sound and vivid style. Though in a sense reserved and indifferent to outward appearances, he associated easily and genially with men around him, especially with foreigners, while he possessed a rare capacity for easy and clear description of scenes and events which were passing before his eyes. Being neither didactic nor controversial, nor in the ordinary sense professional, he exercised by his writings alike in books and newspapers considerable influence on public opinion.

[Authorities cited; The Times, 8 July 1911; Daily Telegraph, 8 July 1911; Observer, 9 July 1911; Men of the Time, 1899; Who's Who; Life of Sir James Fitzjames Stephen, by Sir Leslie Stephen, 1895; Life and Letters of Alexander Macmillan, by Charles L. Graves, 1910; Letters of Alexander Macmillan, edited by his son, George A. Macmillan, and printed for private circulation, 1908; private sources.] C. P. L.

DICKINSON, HERCULES HENRY (1827–1905), dean of the Chapel Royal, Dublin, youngest son of Charles Dickinson, afterwards bishop of Meath, by his wife Elizabeth, daughter of Abraham Russell, of Limerick, was born at Dublin on 14 Sept. 1827. Two brothers, Charles and John Abraham, were in holy orders, and the eldest of his four sisters, Elizabeth, married John West, afterwards dean of St. Patrick's. Dickinson was educated at Dr. Flynn's school, Harcourt St., Dublin, and at Trinity College, Dublin, where he obtained a classical scholarship in 1848, graduating as senior moderator in logic and ethics in 1849. He was auditor of the College Historical Society in 1850. In the same year he gained Archbishop King's divinity prize, and the divinity testimonium (1st class) in 1851, when he was ordained deacon by his father's old friend, Archbishop Whately [q. v.], receiving priest's orders in 1852. Becoming curate of St. Ann's on his ordination, he was appointed by Whately vicar of this important parish in 1855, and ministered there for forty-seven years. Dickinson, who proceeded D.D. in 1866, was appointed dean of the Chapel Royal, Dublin, by the Crown in 1868. He entered the chapter of St. Patrick's cathedral as treasurer in 1869, on the nomination of Archbishop Trench [q. v.], and became precentor in 1876. He was elected to the chair of pastoral theology in Dublin University in 1894 by the Irish bishops—a post for which his delight in the society of young men and his long pastoral experience specially qualified him. For many years he was a prominent figure in Dublin clerical life; and as examining chaplain to successive archbishops, as the most active supporter of the Association for Promoting Christian Knowledge, and as chairman of the Dublin Clerical Association, he rendered services of value to the church. He was also a member of the Representative Church Body; and at the annual meetings of the General Synod he was a frequent speaker, his ready and genial wit enlivening many debates. The dean was an ardent advocate of the temperance cause, and he served on the royal commission for licensing reform (1896–9). He was, besides, one of the commissioners of charitable donations and bequests, and few philanthropic enterprises in Dublin were carried on without his co-operation. As dean of the Chapel Royal he was also almoner to many viceroys. A pioneer in the movement for the higher education of women, he aided Archbishop Trench in the foundation in 1866 of Alexandra College, Dublin, of which he was warden for thirty-six years.

A disciple of Whately in theological matters, Dickinson was opposed to the tractarian movement, while he was a strong supporter of the Society for the Propagation of the Gospel at a time when it was not popular in Ireland. Of fearless honesty, chivalrous spirit, and unfailing wit, he had friends among all classes. Failing health obliged him to resign his offices in 1902, when he retired from active life. He died in Dublin on 17 May 1905, and was buried in Mount Jerome cemetery. As a memorial of his pastoral work, three decorated panels have been placed in the chancel of St. Ann's Church, Dublin.

Dickinson married, 2 Oct. 1867, Mary, daughter of Dr. Evory Kennedy of Belgard, co. Dublin, by whom he had nine children, of whom five sons and a daughter survived him.

He was author of 'Lectures on the Book of Common Prayer' (1859), and 'Scripture and Science' (1879), besides occasional sermons and papers.

[Dublin University Calendars; obituary notices in Irish newspapers; personal knowledge.] JOHN OSSORY.

DICKINSON, LOWES [CATO] (1819–1908), portrait painter, born at Kilburn on 27 Nov. 1819, was one of the family of seven sons and four daughters of Joseph Dickinson by his wife Anne Carter of Topsham, Devonshire, whose kinsmen were officers in the navy. His paternal grandfather was a farmer in Northumberland, and his father started business in Bond Street as a stationer and publisher of lithographs. Educated at Topsham school and Dr. Lord's school, Tooting, Lowes Dickinson worked with his father at lithography, and was earning his own living from the age of sixteen. By the help of (Sir) Robert Michael Laffan [q. v.] he was enabled to visit Italy and Sicily, where he resided from Nov. 1850 to June 1853. Diary letters in the hands of his family give a vivid picture of artist life in Rome, Naples, and elsewhere during that period, and already reveal the strong sympathy both for man and nature which became characteristic. On returning to England he took a studio in Langham Chambers, where Millais then also had a studio. He was well acquainted with the Pre-Raphaelites, and about 1854 came into contact with Frederic Denison Maurice, and together with Charles Kingsley, Tom Hughes, John Malcolm Ludlow [q. v. Suppl. II], Llewelyn Davies, and others was one of the band of Christian socialists who, under Maurice's banner, strove to infuse Christian ideals into the budding movement for social reform. An important and permanent outcome of the movement was the foundation of the Working Men's College, where in early days Lowes Dickinson taught drawing with Ruskin and Dante Gabriel Rossetti, and in which, until his death, he maintained as one of the longest lived of the founders a warm interest, testified by the admirable portraits of Maurice, Kingsley, and Hughes which he painted for the college walls. In 1858 he painted portraits of the same three fellow-workers for his friend, Alexander Macmillan, the publisher, of whom in later life he made a most characteristic crayon drawing (GRAVES'S *Life and Letters of A. Macmillan*, 1910).

In 1860 he took an active part in the formation of the 'Artists' volunteer rifle corps, of which he was treasurer.

Dickinson regularly exhibited portraits at the Royal Academy from 1848 to 1891, missing only the years 1849, 1853, and 1884. Among his numerous subjects were Queen Victoria, the Prince of Wales (afterwards Edward VII), Princess Alice, Lord Kelvin, * Richard Cobden (in the Reform Club), the duke of Argyll, * Lord Napier of Magdala, Sir Henry Norman, George Grote, Viscount Goschen, * Sir Henry Maine, Prof. Edmund Lushington, Sir Arthur Helps, Professor Cayley, Sir George Gabriel Stokes, Professor Clerk Maxwell, Dean Stanley (now at Rugby), Mr. Gladstone's cabinet in 1872 (now in the Devonshire club), Mr. Gladstone, Lord Cairns, Lord Palmerston, * Lord Granville, * John Bright, and Quintin Hogg. His striking posthumous portrait of * General Gordon at Khartoum hangs in the dining-hall of the Gordon Boys' Home. Many of his portraits hang in college halls at Cambridge, and those marked with an asterisk have been engraved. He had an almost unique gift for posthumous portraiture in crayons.

Shortly after his marriage he took a cottage at Hanwell, where he lived from 1864 to 1879, still retaining his studio in Langham Chambers. In 1879 he built the house close by, known as All Souls' Place, where he died on 15 Dec. 1908. He was buried at Kensal Green cemetery.

He married, on 15 Oct. 1857, Margaret Ellen, daughter of William Smith Williams, who, as reader to Messrs. Smith, Elder & Co., discovered the genius of the Brontës. Mrs. Dickinson died in 1882. Her sister, Anna Williams, was the well-known singer. He had a family of two sons and five daughters, who founded in his memory in 1909 the 'Lowes Dickinson Memorial Studentship' at the Working Men's College for the study of art abroad. His younger son, Goldsworthy Lowes Dickinson, fellow of King's College, Cambridge, has achieved distinction as an essayist and writer on political and social subjects.

[The Times, 21 Dec. 1908; Athenæum, 2 Jan. 1909; Working Men's Coll. Journal, Jan. and Feb. 1909; The Working Men's College, ed. J. Ll. Davies, 1904, with private information.] G. A. M.

DICKSON, SIR COLLINGWOOD (1817–1904), general, born at Valenciennes on 20 Nov. 1817, was third son of Major-general Sir Alexander Dickson [q. v.] and Eulalia, daughter of Don Stefano Brionès of Minorca. Educated at the Royal Military Academy, Woolwich, he was commissioned as second-lieutenant in the royal artillery on 18 Dec. 1835, and was promoted first-lieutenant on 29 Nov. 1837. In February of that year he had gone to

Spain with the artillery detachment, which formed part of the British legion under Sir George De Lacy Evans [q. v.], co-operating with the Christinist army against the Carlists. He served with this force on the north coast, distinguishing himself in the operations in front of San Sebastian, and being present at the capture of Hernani. In August 1839 he went to Catalonia as assistant to Colonel Edward Thomas Michell [q. v.], British commissioner with the Spanish army there. He was present at the actions of Andoain and Solsona. In the spring of 1840 he accompanied Michell to the headquarters of Espartero, and was present at the capture of Morella and the defeat of the Carlists near Berga. He was made a knight of Charles III, of San Fernando (1st class), and of Isabella the Catholic.

In March 1841 he went to Constantinople to instruct the Turkish artillery, and remained there till June 1845, being employed under the British foreign office. In the spring of 1846 he attended Ibrahim Pasha during his visit to England. He was promoted second-captain on 1 April 1846, and was given a brevet majority on 22 May. He became first-captain on 2 Sept. 1851, and was inspector of gunpowder at Waltham Abbey from 1 July 1852 to 14 Feb. 1854.

He served in the Crimea from June 1854 to July 1855. At the battle of the Alma he was on Lord Raglan's staff; and when Raglan rode forward to a knoll on the Russian flank, and asked for guns there, Dickson brought up two 9-pounders, and helped to serve them. Their fire was so effective that the Russian batteries guarding the post-road retired. He was made brevet lieut.-colonel from that date, 20 June 1854. He commanded the siege train of the right attack during the siege of Sevastopol up to 21 July 1855. In the first bombardment on 17 Oct. 1854 the siege batteries ran short of powder, and under Dickson's direction several field-battery wagons were brought up under a heavy fire to supply the want, and he took a personal part in unloading them. For this he afterwards received the Victoria Cross, on 23 June 1855.

At the battle of Inkerman Dickson, after Colonel Gambier was wounded, brought up the two 18-pounders which dominated the Russian guns. He chose the site for them, and maintained them there, though he was urged by French officers to withdraw them. When the Russians retreated, Lord Raglan said to him—'You have covered yourself with glory' (KINGLAKE, v. 372, 439). He was wounded on 4 Feb., but took part in the bombardments of 9 April and 17 June and in the expedition to Kertch. He was mentioned in despatches (*Lond. Gaz.* 2 Dec. 1854, 20 Feb. 1855, and 15 Feb. 1856), was made aide-de-camp to the Queen on 29 June 1855, and received the Crimean medal with four clasps, the Legion of Honour (officer), the Medjidie (2nd class), and the Turkish medal.

From September 1855 till the end of the war he was employed with the Turkish contingent, first as brigadier-general, and latterly with the temporary rank of major-general (15 Feb. 1856). After the war he was assistant adjutant-general for artillery in Ireland for six years from 4 Nov. 1856, and was then at Leith Fort for five years in command of the royal artillery. He was promoted regimental lieut.-colonel on 23 February 1856, and regimental colonel on 5 April 1866. Four months later he became major-general. He had been made C.B. on 5 July 1855. In 1868–9 he served on the fortifications committee, which examined into the work done under the Palmerston loan for defences, and enlivened its proceedings by his boundless store of anecdote and humour.

From April 1870 till 1875 Dickson was inspector-general of artillery. The adoption of rifled guns had caused great changes in artillery material, and to qualify himself for his new duties he went through courses at Woolwich Arsenal and at Shoeburyness. His inspections were thorough, and he was punctilious on points of duty, but everyone felt the charm of his personality. He was made K.C.B. on 20 May 1871, and he became colonel commandant on 17 Nov. 1875, lieut.-general on 8 June 1876, and general on 1 Oct. 1877. In May of that year he went to Constantinople as military attaché, his old friend Sir Austen Henry Layard [q. v.] being at that time British ambassador there. He remained in Turkey till 9 Sept. 1879, thus covering the whole period of the Russo-Turkish war. He was president of the ordnance committee (1881–5), though he was placed on the retired list under the age rules on 20 Nov. 1884. On 24 May in that year he received the G.C.B.

He married on 14 Jan. 1847 Harriet (*d.* Feb. 1894), daughter of Thomas Burnaby, vicar of Blakesley, Northamptonshire. After her death he lived a retired life at 79 Claverton Street till his death on 28 Nov. 1904. He was buried at Kensal Green. He had three sons, of whom two predeceased him. He was a good linguist, speaking French, Spanish, and Turkish fluently, a ready writer, and a man of 'downright commonsense.' Dickson closely and affectionately studied the traditions of his regiment. He left a portrait of himself to it, and presented to the Royal Artillery Institution the Dickson MSS. written or collected by his father. These are now in course of publication under the editorship of Major J. H. Leslie, R.A., and supply valuable material for the history of the Peninsular war.

[The Times, 30 Nov. 1904; Duncan, The English in Spain, 1877; Kinglake, Invasion of the Crimea, 1863–87; materials furnished by Major J. H. Leslie, R.A.] E. M. L.

DICKSON, WILLIAM PURDIE (1823–1901), professor of divinity and translator, third son of George Dickson, parish minister of Pettinain, and afterwards of Kilrenny, Fifeshire, by his first wife, Mary Lockhart, was born at Pettinain manse, Lanarkshire, on 22 Oct. 1823. After attending Pettinain parish school and the grammar school, Lanark, he studied at St. Andrews (1837–44) for the ministry of the Church of Scotland. A high prizeman in Greek, at the Divinity Hall he gained in 1843 the Gray prize for an English essay. On 5 May 1845 he was licensed as a preacher by St. Andrews presbytery, and he retained his first charge at Grangemouth, Stirlingshire, from 1846 to 1851. On 9 Sept. 1851 Dickson was ordained minister of Cameron parish, St. Andrews. There brought into touch with his university and its interests, he frequently lectured for Principal Tulloch and other professors, successfully helped to put the university library in order, and was classical examiner (1861–2). Meanwhile he proved a strong preacher and a diligent pastor.

From 1863 to 1873 Dickson filled with success the new chair of biblical criticism in Glasgow University, and from 1873 until his retirement in 1895 he was in succession to John Caird [q. v. Suppl. I] professor of divinity. From 1866 to his death he was curator of the Glasgow University library, the post having been created for him in recognition of his special fitness. He was president of the Library Association in 1888, when he delivered a scholarly and characteristically humorous address. From 1875 to 1888 he was the convener of the education committee of the Church of Scotland, but he twice declined nomination as moderator of the general assembly. He was made D.D. by both St. Andrews in 1864 and Glasgow University in 1896 and hon. LL.D. by Edinburgh in 1885.

While minister of Cameron, Dickson began the translation of Mommsen's 'History of Rome,' at first practising only to improve his German knowledge. Duly verifying the numerous quotations, he completed a wholly admirable version, which was published with the author's approval (4 vols. 1862–7). A second and revised edition appeared in 1895. His translation of Mommsen's 'Roman Provinces' followed in 1887. Dickson edited the translation of Meyer's 'Commentary on the New Testament' (10 vols. 1873–80). As the Church of Scotland Baird lecturer in 1883 he discussed with learning and discrimination from the orthodox standpoint 'St. Paul's Use of the Terms Flesh and Spirit.'

Dickson died at 16 Victoria Crescent, Partick, on 9 March 1901, and was interred in Glasgow Necropolis. By way of memorial friends presented to the university library, which he reorganised, Migne's 'Patrologia' (388 vols.) in an oak bookcase.

On 7 Dec. 1853 Dickson married Tassie Wardlaw, daughter of John Small [q. v.], the Edinburgh University librarian, and had issue two daughters and a son, George, M.D. Glasgow.

[Information from Dr. George Dickson and Mr. J. J. Smith, University Library, St. Andrews; The Curator of Glasgow University, by Mr. James L. Galbraith; Mrs. Oliphant, Memoir of Principal Tulloch, 1888; Glasgow Herald, and Scotsman, 11 March 1901; personal knowledge.] T. B.

DIGBY, WILLIAM (1849–1904), Anglo-Indian publicist, third son of William Digby of Walsoken, Wisbech, by his wife Ann Drake, was born there on 1 May 1849. Scantily educated at the British schools, Wisbech, he studied for himself, and from 1864 to 1871 was apprentice in the office of the 'Isle of Ely and Wisbech Advertiser.' In 1871 he went out to Colombo as sub-editor of the 'Ceylon Observer.' There he advocated temperance and free trade, proved successful in his effort to abolish revenue farming, and publishing 'The Food Taxes of Ceylon' (1875) was elected in March 1878 an honorary member of the Cobden Club. As official shorthand-writer for the legislative council, he prepared six volumes of the Ceylon 'Hansard' (1871–6).

In 1877 he became editor of the 'Madras Times,' and persistently urged the need of alleviating the great Southern Indian famine. Largely owing to his representations a relief fund was opened at the Mansion House in London, and 820,000*l.* was subscribed. He was active as honorary secretary in India of the executive committee, which distributed relief through 120 local committees. He was made C.I.E. on 1 Jan. 1878, and in his 'Famine Campaign in Southern India' (1878, 2 vols.) faithfully described the visitation.

Returning to England in 1879 for domestic reasons, Digby edited the 'Liverpool and Southport Daily News' for a few months in 1880, and from that year to 1882 was editor of the 'Western Daily Mercury' at Plymouth. From Nov. 1882 till 1887 he was the energetic secretary of the newly founded National Liberal Club in London, and eagerly flung himself into political work. He contested unsuccessfully in the liberal interest North Paddington in 1885 and South Islington in 1892.

In 1887 he established, and became senior partner of, the firm of William Hutchinson & Co., East India agents and merchants. Meanwhile he pursued in the press and on the platform with almost fanatical warmth the agitation for extending self-government among the natives of India. In 1885 he published 'India for the Indians—and for England,' a book praised by John Bright in a speech at St. James's Hall on 25 Feb. 1885. In 1887 he founded, and until 1892 he directed, the Indian political agency, which distributed information about India to the English public. In 1889 he became secretary to the newly constituted British committee of the Indian national congress, and he edited the committee's organ, 'India' (1890–2). In 'Prosperous British India' (1901) he claimed to prove a steady growth of poverty among the Indian masses under British rule.

Digby died from nervous exhaustion at his home, Dorset Square, London, N.W., on 24 Sept. 1904, and was buried by the side of his second wife at Bromley cemetery. An oil-painting of him by John Colin Forbes, R.C.A., was presented to the National Liberal Club by friends and admirers on 19 Dec. 1905.

He married (1) in 1874, Ellen Amelia, only daughter of Captain Little of Wisbech; she died in June 1878, leaving one son, William Pollard Digby, electrical engineer; and (2) in December 1879, Sarah Maria, eldest daughter of William Hutchinson, some time mayor of Wisbech; she died in January 1899, leaving a daughter and three sons, the eldest of whom, Everard, has been editor of the 'Indian Daily News,' Calcutta.

Besides many pamphlets and the works cited, Digby published 'Forty Years of Official and Unofficial Life in a Crown Colony' (Madras, 1879, 2 vols.), being a biography of Sir Richard F. Morgan, acting chief justice in Ceylon.

[Digby's books and pamphlets; Biographical Mag., July 1885; Isle of Ely and Wisbech Advertiser, 24 and 27 Sept. 1904, and 20 Dec. 1905; personal knowledge.]

F. H. B.

DILKE, Sir CHARLES WENTWORTH, second baronet (1843–1911), politician and author, born on 4 Sept. 1843 in the house in Sloane Street, London (No. 76), which his father had occupied and in which he himself lived and died, was elder son of Sir Charles Wentworth Dilke, first baronet [q. v.]. Charles Wentworth Dilke [q. v.], the antiquary and critic, was his grandfather. His mother, Mary, daughter of William Chatfield, captain in the Madras cavalry, died on 16 Sept. 1853. His younger brother was Ashton Wentworth Dilke [q. v.], M.P. for Newcastle-on-Tyne from 1880 until his death in 1883.

Dilke, after being educated privately, became in 1862 a scholar of Trinity Hall, Cambridge—his father's college. There (Sir) Leslie Stephen was his tutor. He graduated LL.B. as senior legalist, i.e. head of the law tripos, in 1866, and proceeded LL.M. in 1869. He was an active member of the Cambridge Union, serving twice as vice-president and twice as president. He was an enthusiastic oarsman and rowed in his college boat when it was head of the river. That recreation he pursued all his life. In later years he built himself a bungalow at Dockett Eddy near Shepperton and spent much of his time on the water. He was also a keen and capable fencer and frequently invited his friends to a bout with the foils at his house in Sloane Street. He was called to the bar at the Middle Temple on 30 April 1866, but never practised.

In 1866 Dilke left England for a tour round the world, beginning with a visit to the United States. Here he travelled alone for some months, but was subsequently joined by William Hepworth Dixon [q. v.], editor of the 'Athenæum,' the paper of which his father was proprietor. The two travelled together for some time, visiting the Mormon cities of Utah, but they parted at Salt Lake City, Dixon returning to England and Dilke continuing his journey westward, visiting San Francisco on his way to Panama. Thence he crossed the Pacific and visited all the Australasian colonies in turn. He returned home by way of Ceylon, India, and Egypt, reaching England at the end of 1867. In the following year he published the results of his studies and explorations in English-speaking and English-governed lands in a work entitled 'Greater Britain: a Record of Travel in English-speaking Countries during 1866 and 1867.' The book immediately achieved an immense success, and passed through four editions. The title, a novel and taking one, was Dilke's invention (see MURRAY'S *New Eng. Dict.*), and the whole subject as treated by Dilke was as new as its title. 'The idea,' wrote Dilke in the Preface, 'which in all the length of my travels has been at once my fellow and my guide—a key wherewith to unlock the hidden things of strange new lands—is a conception, however imperfect, of the grandeur of our race, already girdling the earth, which it is destined, perhaps, to overspread.' Thus, while Dilke was an advanced radical through life, he was also from first to last a convinced and well-informed imperialist.

In 1868 the first general election took place under the Reform Act of the previous year. Dilke was selected by the radical party in the newly constituted borough of Chelsea, to which two members were allotted, as one of its two candidates. His colleague was Sir Henry Hoare, and their opponents were (Sir) William H. Russell [q. v. Suppl. II] and C. J. Freake. Dilke headed the poll on 17 Nov. with 7374 votes, Hoare receiving 7183, and Russell only 4177. He at once attracted the favourable notice of the party leaders and was chosen to second the address at the opening of the session of 1870. He joined the extreme nonconformists in opposition to Mr. Forster's education bill, and moved the amendment which the government accepted for the substitution of directly elected schoolboards in place of committees of boards of guardians. To the normal articles of the radical creed, Dilke added republican predilections, and he frankly challenged the monarchical form of government on many public platforms. He questioned whether monarchy was worth its cost. His statement at Newcastle on 6 Nov. 1871, in the course of an elaborate republican plea, that Queen Victoria paid no income tax excited a bitter controversy. At Bristol, Bolton, Derby, and Birmingham he pursued the propaganda, often amid scenes of disturbance. Heated protests against his attitude were raised in the House of Commons, where he moved on 19 March 1872 for a full inquiry into Queen Victoria's expenditure. His confession of republican faith was then echoed by Auberon Herbert [q. v. Suppl. II], who seconded his motion. A passionate retort followed from Gladstone, the prime minister. Sir Wilfrid Lawson and another were the only members who voted in support of Dilke's motion, for which he and Herbert told. Sharply opposed at Chelsea on the score of his advanced opinions at the next election in 1874, he yet was the only one of three liberal candidates who was elected. He polled 7217 votes, and the conservative candidate was returned as his colleague.

In 1869, on the death of his father, Dilke succeeded to the baronetcy and also to the then lucrative proprietorship of the 'Athenæum' and of 'Notes and Queries'—the former purchased and edited by his grandfather and the latter established by him in 1849—and to a part proprietorship of the 'Gardeners' Chronicle.' He always took an active interest in the conduct of the 'Athenæum' and frequently contributed to its columns, though except during the occasional absence of the responsible editor he never edited it himself. He collected for the press his grandfather's 'Papers of a Critic' (1875), chiefly contributions to the 'Athenæum.' In 1872 he married Katherine Mary Eliza, only daughter of Captain Arthur Gore Sheil.

Meanwhile he was a frequent visitor to Paris, where he became intimate with Gambetta and other republican leaders. He spoke French fluently, though not perhaps quite with the accent of a Parisian. French influence was apparent in his second literary venture, which was published anonymously in 1874. A thin brochure bound in white, it was entitled 'The Fall of Prince Florestan of Monaco.' It told the story of a light-hearted prince, educated at Eton and Cambridge, who was unexpectedly called to the sovereignty of Monaco. He at once set to work to put in action the liberal and reforming ideas he had imbibed at Cambridge, and soon found himself at loggerheads with his subjects, who were all catholics and led by a Jesuit priest. Foiled in his projects of reform, he abdicated and returned to Cambridge. The story was brightly written and displayed no little satiric humour—which spared neither Dilke himself nor his radical contemporaries. It showed in Dilke a mood of genial banter and shrewd detachment from popular shibboleths which was otherwise so little in evidence that few suspected its existence. The book passed through three editions and was translated into French. Perhaps it was better appreciated in France than in England.

In 1874 Dilke's first wife died after giving birth to an only son, Charles Wentworth Dilke, subsequently the third baronet. Next year Dilke made a second tour round the world, now visiting China and Japan, and thenceforth for many years he spent much leisure at a modest villa which he purchased near Toulon. At the same time during his second parliament (1874–80) he greatly improved his position. He became an effective speaker, and won the ear of the House of Commons (Lucy's *Diary of Parliament*, 1874–80, pp. 307–10). His radicalism lost nothing of its strength on shedding its republican features. He made an annual attack on unreformed corporations. On 4 March 1879 he seconded (Sir) George Trevelyan's resolution for extending the county franchise to the agricultural labourer, and on 31 March he moved on behalf of the liberal party a vote of censure on the government's South African policy. To the cause of Greece he proved himself a warm friend. At the general election of April 1880, Dilke for the third time headed the poll at Chelsea with 12,408 votes, carrying the second liberal candidate (Mr. J. B. Firth) in with him with 12,040 votes.

Before Gladstone returned to power in 1880, Dilke was an acknowledged leader of the radical section of his party. Mr. Joseph Chamberlain, M.P. for Birmingham since June 1876, was his chief colleague. Gladstone, however, was very slowly persuaded of the importance of the radical leaders. At first 'he never dreamed of them for his cabinet.' When at length he sent for Dilke while forming his administration, he was annoyed by Dilke's refusal 'to serve unless either himself or Mr. Chamberlain were in the cabinet.' In the end, despite Dilke's superior position in public esteem, Mr. Chamberlain entered the cabinet as president of the board of trade, and Dilke remained outside as under-secretary to the foreign office (cf. Morley, *Life of Gladstone*, ii. 630).

Dilke's knowledge of foreign affairs was exceptional, and as representing the foreign office in the commons with his chief, Lord Granville, in the lords, he enjoyed an influence little short of that of a cabinet minister not yet of the first rank. Of prodigious industry, he conducted the parliamentary business of his department with assiduity, courtesy, and discretion. In 1881–2 he served as chairman of a royal commission for the negotiation of a commercial treaty with France in conjunction with commissioners of the French government. He spent many months over this business, which was conducted in London and in Paris. Early in 1880 his growing reputation had led the Prince of Wales (afterwards Edward VII) to seek his acquaintance and a close intimacy between them lasted through the next four years. They met in Paris as well as at home, and at Paris, by the prince's request, while the commercial negotiations were in progress, Dilke invited his close friend Gambetta to join them at breakfast (24 Oct. 1881).

On Forster's retirement from the Irish secretaryship in April 1882 Dilke was offered the post, but he declined it on the ground that it did not carry with it a seat in the cabinet. Towards the close of the year the cabinet was partially reconstructed, and Dilke at last obtained a place in it as president of the local government board (8 Dec.). At the statutory election at Chelsea he was returned without a contest. There were rumours of reluctance on Queen Victoria's part to assent to Dilke's appointment, which great firmness on the part of the prime minister was needed to dispel (*Annual Register*, 1882, p. 180). In the House of Commons there was now a general belief that he was destined before long to lead his party (cf. Acton's *Letters to Mary Gladstone*). An indication of the public confidence which he commanded was shown by the bestowal on him of the freedom of the borough of Paisley (1 Nov. 1883). He had long given close attention to the problems of local government, and his tenure of office as president of the board was marked by much important legislation. In 1884 he presided as chairman over the royal commission on the housing of the working classes, of which the Prince of Wales, Lord Salisbury, and Cardinal Manning were members. He also took an active part in the negotiations which were initiated in that year by Queen Victoria between government and the opposition in the controversy over the Franchise Act of 1884 and the attendant redistribution of seats. By virtue of his office and by reason of what Lord Morley in his 'Life of Gladstone' called his 'unrivalled mastery of the intricate details' of the whole question of redistribution, he took charge of the redistribution bill and conducted it through the House of Commons with exceptional skill.

On 18 Jan. 1884 Dilke, Lord Granville, and Lord Northbrook met General Gordon with Lord Hartington and Lord Wolseley at the war office and they decided on behalf of the cabinet to send Gordon to the Soudan.

In 1885 the Gladstone ministry, externally weakened by the miscarriages of its Egyptian policy, and discredited by its failure to rescue Gordon, was also distracted almost to dissolution by internal dissensions arising out of its Irish policy. New bills for a partial renewal of the expiring Coercion Act, for land purchase and for local government in Ireland were before the cabinet early in 1885. Dilke and Mr. Chamberlain recommended a central administrative board, and resisted the other proposals without effect. On 19 May Gladstone announced in the House of Commons a land purchase bill. Thereupon Dilke and Mr. Chamberlain tendered their resignations. They were requested to reconsider them (MORLEY'S *Gladstone*, iii. 194). But that necessity was spared them. An unexpected defeat on a proposed increase in the beer duties under the budget gave the whole cabinet an opportunity, which they eagerly welcomed, of resigning (8 June 1885). Neither Dilke nor Mr. Chamberlain had favoured the increase of the beer duties. He and Mr. Chamberlain projected under Parnell's auspices a tour in Ireland for the autumn. But Parnell's negotiations with the new conservative lord-lieutenant, the earl of Carnarvon, led him to withdraw his support, and the visit was abandoned. Dilke never again held office under the crown.

Dilke's fall was sudden and tragical. In August 1885 Mr. Donald Crawford, liberal M.P. for Lanark, filed a petition for divorce against his wife on the ground of her alleged adultery with Dilke. Mrs. Crawford was a sister of the wife of Dilke's only brother Ashton, and with her family he was on intimate terms. On the announcement of the charge, Dilke denied its truth in an open letter to the liberal association of Chelsea. The association accepted his disclaimer. He stood for the constituency —now a single member division—at the general election in Dec. 1885 and was returned by 4291 votes against 4116 cast for the conservative candidate. The divorce suit was heard on 12 Feb. 1886, when Mr. Crawford obtained a decree nisi against his wife, solely on the evidence of her confession. Dilke offered to deny on oath in the witness-box Mrs. Crawford's story, but his counsel declined to call him and his friends unwisely dissuaded him from insisting on being called. The outcome of the suit was equivocal. The case against Dilke was dismissed, but Mrs. Crawford's guilt was declared proven on her own evidence, which inculpated none but him. In public opinion Dilke was not cleared of the allegations against him.

Meanwhile Dilke was not included in Gladstone's third administration (Feb. 1886), but he attended parliament as usual, and voted for Gladstone's home rule bill (7 June). His liberal friends at Chelsea expressed sympathy with him, and he stood again at the general election of July 1886. But he was defeated by 176 votes. His connection with the constituency was thus severed after eighteen years. Mainly owing to Dilke's representations to the queen's proctor, the divorce case was re-opened before the decree nisi was made absolute. The queen's proctor did not intervene directly on Dilke's behalf, and the application of both Dilke and Mrs. Crawford to plead in the suit was refused— in Dilke's case on the ground that he had not given evidence at the first hearing (30 June). The second hearing began on 16 July 1886. Dilke and Mrs. Crawford both gave evidence at length and sustained a searching cross-examination. Mrs. Crawford acknowledged that she had committed adultery with a man not mentioned in her original confession, but withdrew none of her former charges against Dilke, and added odious details which were regarded by believers in Dilke's innocence to be inventions directed solely to prejudice. Dilke absolutely denied all the accusations. Finally the jury found that the original 'decree was obtained not contrary to the facts of the case and not by reason of material facts not having been brought before the court.' Public opinion for the most part took this finding as a verdict against Dilke and regarded it as just. Dilke, however, maintained from the first and through the rest of his life the attitude and demeanour of an innocent man, and many, though not all, of his friends avowed and manifested their unshaken confidence in his honour and veracity.

Dilke bowed at once to the decision. To the electors of Chelsea he announced his withdrawal from public life; he pointed out the legal disadvantages under which he laboured at the second trial in being denied the status of a party to the proceedings, and at the same time he reasserted his innocence.

At the opening of these difficulties, on 3 Oct. 1885, Dilke married at Chelsea Emilia

Francis, widow of Mark Pattison [q. v.; see DILKE, EMILIA FRANCIS, LADY, Suppl. II]. The marriage was singularly happy, and Dilke owed much to her affection and belief in his innocence. Although saddened, he was not soured nor corrupted by his political and social eclipse.

On his retirement from parliament in 1886 Dilke returned with great zeal and industry to the study of those larger English and imperial problems which had engaged his attention at the outset of his career. In 1887 he published 'The Present Position of European Politics' (translated into French) and in 1888 'The British Army.' In 1890 appeared his 'Problems of Greater Britain' in two volumes, designed as a sequel to his earlier work on 'Greater Britain.' It was a treatise on the present position of Greater Britain in which special attention was given to the relations of the English-speaking countries with one another and to the comparative politics of the countries under British government. Foreign travel varied his occupation. He paid at least one annual visit to Paris, where his French friends always welcomed him with enthusiasm. In the autumn of 1887 he made a journey through the Near East, visiting Greece, the cause of which he had always championed, and Constantinople, where he was entertained by the Sultan. In the winter of 1888-9 he was the guest of Lord Roberts, commander of the forces in India, and attended with his host the military manœuvres of the season.

In 1892 Dilke returned to public life as member of parliament for the Forest of Dean. The electors had convinced themselves of his innocence. He beat his conservative opponent after a contest by a large majority. He represented that constituency till his death, fighting the elections of 1900 and Jan. and Dec. 1910, but being returned without a contest in 1895 and 1906. Henceforth a private member, he did not speak frequently in the House of Commons. He confined himself almost entirely to industrial questions, to foreign and imperial affairs, and to the larger questions of policy involved in the navy and army estimates. On these subjects his authority was recognised, but his position in the house remained one of some aloofness. He enjoyed, however, the complete confidence of the labour party. He continued his literary work, publishing in 1898 a little volume on 'Imperial Defence' in co-operation with Mr. (now Professor) Spenser Wilkinson; and yet another work on the British Empire in the same year. Although he hospitably entertained his friends, he continued to be little seen in society. In Oct. 1904 the death of his wife gravely disabled him, and he prefixed a touching memoir to a work of hers, 'The Book of the Spiritual Life,' which appeared in 1905. In 1906 he served as chairman of the select committee on the income tax and drafted its report, some of the recommendations of which were subsequently embodied in legislation. In 1910 his health began to fail. After the exhausting session of that year he fought with success the general election of Dec. 1910 in the Forest of Dean. But he was unequal to the effort. He returned in Jan. 1911 from a brief vacation in the South of France only to die. He died of heart failure at his house in Sloane Street on 26 Jan. 1911, and his remains were cremated at Golder's Green. He was succeeded in the baronetcy by his only son.

A portrait of Dilke by G. F. Watts was left to his trustees for presentation to a public institution. It is now on loan at the National Portrait Gallery. A caricature portrait appeared in 'Vanity Fair' in 1871.

Dilke owned a valuable collection of works of art, and he dedicated those which were of historic interest to public uses. He left by will the portrait by Watts of John Stuart Mill to the Westminster city council; the portrait by Madox Brown of Mr. and Mrs. Fawcett, and the portrait by Frank Holl of Mr. Joseph Chamberlain, to the National Portrait Gallery; the portrait of Gambetta by Alphonse Legros went to the Luxemburg Museum in Paris. Most of the relics of Keats, which he inherited from his grandfather, were bequeathed to the Hampstead public library. His literary executor, Miss Gertrude Tuckwell, his second wife's niece, was warned, in preparing his political papers for the press, against seeking the assistance of 'anyone closely connected with either the liberal or conservative party.' His pictures by old masters, water-colour drawings, tapestries, and miniatures were sold by auction at Christie's on 7–8 April 1911. The 'Athenæum' and 'Notes and Queries' were, in accordance with the powers given by the trustees under Dilke's will, transferred in 1911 to the printer and publisher, Mr. John Collins Francis.

[Authorities mentioned in the text; obituary notices in the press, especially The Times, 27 Jan. 1911; Dilke's publications; Herbert Paul's History of Modern England; personal knowledge and private information.]

J. R. T.

DILKE, EMILIA FRANCIS STRONG, Lady Dilke (1840–1904), historian of French art, born at Ilfracombe on 2 Sept. 1840, was fourth daughter of Major Henry Strong of the Indian army, by his wife Emily, daughter of Edward Chandler Weedon. Her grandfather, Samuel S. Strong (*d.* 1816), was settled at Augusta, Georgia, and was deputy surveyor-general of the state before the outbreak of the war of independence, during which he remained loyal to the British crown. Lady Dilke's father, who was educated at Addiscombe, served in India from 1809 till 1825; he ultimately became manager of the Oxfordshire branch of the London and County Bank, residing at Iffley. A friend of his, Francis Whiting, who was his daughter's godfather, gave her her second Christian name.

Educated at Oxford by a governess, who was sister of the African traveller, Thomas Edward Bowdich [q. v.], she made while a girl the acquaintance of leading professors at Oxford, including Goldwin Smith, Dr. Ince, and Dr. Henry Acland. From childhood she showed a taste for art, and on the recommendation of Ruskin, to whom Acland showed some of her drawings, she went to London in 1859 to study at South Kensington. She worked hard at the Art School there from March 1859 to Feb. 1861, and saw much artistic society. Her drawing showed promise, but her interests covered a wider field. She studied Dante and the 'Imitatio,' and developed a mystical sense of religion. At the same time her youthful spirits ran high and her outlook on life betrayed independence.

In September 1861 she married, at Iffley church, Mark Pattison, rector of Lincoln College, Oxford, her senior by twenty-one years. Thereupon she settled down to a life of literary study under her husband's direction. She devoted much time to the classics and to modern languages and acquired an exceptional facility in speaking French. Nor did she neglect academic society. She formed among her husband's friends a sort of salon at Lincoln College. Her circle soon included Robert Browning, with whom she long corresponded, Richard Congreve, Emanuel Deutsch, Prince Leopold, (Sir) Charles Newton (of the British Museum), and (Sir) Edgar Boehm (the sculptor). But the guest who attracted her most deeply was George Eliot (Marian Lewes). There is no doubt that Mrs. Mark Pattison suggested to George Eliot the character of Dorothea in her work 'Middlemarch' (1871), and that the novelist's conception of Casaubon was based on Mark Pattison. But in neither case was the fictitious study realistic portraiture. Travel with her husband at home and abroad during her early married life widened Mrs. Pattison's interests and acquaintances. Nervous illness which constantly recurred from 1867 onwards led her to spend an increasing part of each of the next seventeen years abroad. She tried medical treatment at Wildbad and Aix, but after 1875 she was a constant visitor to Nice and Grasse, and permanently hired rooms at a villa at Draguignan, near Cannes.

Abandoning her practice of art, she soon concentrated her energies on its history and criticism. She sent notes on art to the 'Westminster Review,' and regularly reviewed books on art in the 'Saturday Review,' the 'Portfolio,' and from 1869 in the newly founded 'Academy.' In 1872, moved by the conviction that one ought to become an authority on a special subject, she began researches in the renaissance of art in France. From time to time she studied at the archives in Paris; corresponded with and entertained Eugène Muntz, the historian of French art; became intimate with many French artists, including Dalou and Legros; and visited galleries and collections in Rome, Vienna, and other European capitals. The organisation of the arts in France, as well as the practical development of them in all branches, came within her design. The results of her inquiries filled many volumes; the first appeared in 1879 under the title, 'Renaissance of Art in France' (1879). As an historian of art she was very thorough and painstaking. But her critical powers were inferior to her industry. A critical biography of Lord Leighton followed in 1881 in Dumas' 'Modern Artists,' and a life of Claude in French, largely from unpublished materials, in 1884.

Meanwhile such time as she spent in England was in part absorbed by zeal for social reform, especially for the improvement of the social and industrial condition of working women. She joined in 1876 the Women's Provident and Protective League, now the Women's Trades Union League, which had been founded in 1874 by Mrs. Paterson [q. v.], with the aim of organising women workers. She spoke at annual meetings of the league in London in July 1877 and in 1880, when she urged the need of technical education for women, and was supported by William Morris and Professor Bryce. She founded a branch at Oxford, and showed immense enthusiasm for the cause. She also advocated the political enfranchisement of women, and joined the Woman's Suffrage Society at Oxford.

On 30 July 1884 Mark Pattison died at Oxford after a long illness. His widow, to whom he left his fortune, settled in the autumn at Headington Lodge and edited his early 'Memoirs,' which were published in 1885. In the spring of that year she paid a visit to her friend, Sir Mountstuart Elphinstone Grant-Duff [q. v. Suppl. II], then governor of Madras. An attack of typhoid fever delayed her return to England till the autumn. Meanwhile, in July she publicly announced her engagement to Sir Charles Wentworth Dilke [q. v. Suppl. II], with whom her relations had been friendly from youth. At the moment Sir Charles's brilliant political career was prejudiced by charges of immorality, which had been laid against him in the divorce court. The marriage took place at Chelsea on 3 Oct. 1885, and thenceforth her career was largely moulded by that of her second husband. She fully believed in his innocence, and when the verdict of the second trial (July 1886) was assumed by a large section of the public to imply his guilt, she resolved to consecrate her life to his rehabilitation in public esteem. At the same time she continued with undiminished ardour her pursuits as historian of French art and reformer of women's industrial status. She and her husband continued to travel much; they spent part of each year in Paris; in 1887 they extended their tour to Greece and Turkey, and late in 1888 they visited India. No opportunity was lost of inspecting art treasures abroad. At the same time her literary industry bore fruit in the elaborate treatises: 'Art in the Modern State, or the Age of Louis XIV' (1888); 'French Painters of the Eighteenth Century' (1889); 'French Architects and Sculptors of the Eighteenth Century' (1900), and 'French Engravers and Draughtsmen of the Eighteenth Century' (1902). She also attempted short stories of a mystical or allegorical temper. These were collected in her lifetime as 'The Shrine of Death, and other Stories' (1886) and 'The Shrine of Love, and other Stories' (1891). A posthumous collection was called 'The Book of the Spiritual Life' (1905). Her style in these tales shows an individuality which is wanting in her writings on art.

Meanwhile Lady Dilke's activity in the women's trades union movement knew no intermission. The committee of the Women's Trades Union League was largely guided by her counsel. From 1889 to 1904 she attended each September the trades union congress as representative of the women's league. She thus was brought into constant touch with labour leaders, and she frequently spoke at meetings throughout the country on labour questions affecting women. She spared no pains to promote co-operation between the sexes in the field of manual labour, and championed with especial fervour the cause of unskilled workers in dangerous trades.

She died after a brief illness on 24 Oct. 1904 at Pyrford Rough, Woking, a house which was her personal property. Her remains were cremated at Golder's Green after a funeral service at Holy Trinity Church, Sloane Square. She had no issue.

In accordance with her direction some valuable jewels in her possession passed on her death to the Victoria and Albert Museum, South Kensington, together with her collection of art books, Aldines and Elzevirs. An early portrait by her friend, Pauline, Lady Trevelyan, of Cambo, Northumberland (reproduced in Sir Charles Dilke's 'Memoir,' p. 24), was left by Sir Charles Dilke, together with a miniature by Camino, to the National Portrait Gallery, but the trustees have, according to their rule, postponed the consideration of acceptance till the expiration of ten years from death. She was also painted by William Bell Scott and by J. Portaels in Paris in 1864.

[The Book of the Spiritual Life, with a memoir by Sir Charles W. Dilke, 1905; Athenæum, 30 Oct. 1904; The Times, 25 Oct. 1904, 2 Dec. (will); Cornhill, Feb. 1912 (letter from Lady Dilke to Sir Henry Lucy); private information.] S. L.

DILLON, FRANK (1823–1909), landscape painter, born in London on 24 Feb. 1823, was the youngest son of John Dillon, of the firm of Morrison, Dillon & Co., silk mercers, of Fore Street, London, and the owner of a fine collection of water-colour drawings which was sold by auction in 1869.

After having been educated at Bruce Castle School, Tottenham, he entered the schools of the Royal Academy, and subsequently became a pupil of James Holland, the water-colour painter. He there began painting in oil-colours, and in 1850 sent to the Royal Academy a view 'On the Tagus, Lisbon,' and until 1907 was a fairly regular contributor to its exhibitions, as well as to those of the British Institution until its close in 1867. He was one of the original members of the Dudley Gallery, and after it ceased to exist he, in 1882, became a member of the Royal Institute of Painters in Water Colours. He travelled much, and as early as 1850 he published a folio volume of 'Sketches in the Island of Madeira.' He visited Egypt first in 1854, and many of his works were the outcome of this and subsequent visits to that country. Among these were: 'Rising of the Nile: Philæ,' 'The Nile Raft,' 'Luxor, on the Nile,' 'The Sphinx at Midnight,' 'The Great Pyramid,' 'The Pyramids from Gizeh,' 'The Date Harvest, Egypt,' and 'The Granite Quarries of Syene.' He took a keen interest in the preservation of the Arab monuments of Cairo, and was active in opposition to the destruction of Philæ. He also studied appreciatively the arts of Japan, spending a year in that country in 1876–7, and writing an introduction to the catalogue of the 'Exhibition of Japanese and Chinese Works of Art,' held at the Burlington Fine Arts Club in 1878.

In early life he was in full sympathy with the liberal movement of 1848, when he formed a lifelong friendship with Mazzini. He was intimate also with many of the leaders of the Hungarian revolution, and assisted them when in exile. Dillon died unmarried at 13 Upper Phillimore Gardens, Kensington, on 2 May 1909.

Eleven drawings by him of interiors of houses in Cairo are in the Victoria and Albert Museum.

[The Times, 5 and 8 May 1909; Athenæum, 8 May 1909; Art Journal, July 1909; Exhibition Catalogues of the Royal Academy, British Institution, Dudley Gallery, and Royal Institute of Painters in Water-colours, 1850–1907.] R. E. G.

DIMOCK, NATHANIEL (1825–1909), theologian, born at Stonehouse, Gloucestershire, on 8 July 1825, was son of John Dimock of Bridge-end, Stonehouse, and afterwards of Rylands, Randwick, Gloucestershire, by his wife Emma Rook, daughter of Dr. James Parkinson of Hoxton. Educated at two private schools, he matriculated from St. John's College, Oxford, on 31 May 1843, and in 1846 obtained a fourth class in the final classical school, graduating B.A. in 1847, and proceeding M.A. in 1850. He was ordained deacon in 1848, and priest in 1850. From 1848 to 1872 he was curate of East Malling, Kent. There he devoted himself to patristic and mediæval theology, began a series of 'Papers on the Doctrine of the English Church,' and wrote, under the pseudonym of 'An English Presbyter,' numerous books and pamphlets, which attracted notice. In 1872 Dimock was appointed to the vicarage of Wymynswold, Kent, and in 1876 to St. Paul's, Maidstone. In 1887 he resigned his benefice owing to ill-health, and resided abroad, acting as English chaplain at San Remo (1887–8). Subsequently he lived at Eastbourne, and from 1896 until death at Redhill, Surrey.

In 1900 Dimock joined Bishop Creighton's 'Round Table Conference' at Fulham Palace, on the doctrine and ritual of the Holy Communion, and the deliberations largely turned on a statement of his views, which by request he printed for the use of the conference. He afterwards published 'Notes on the Round Table Conference.' He died at his residence, Hemstede, Redhill, on 3 March 1909, and was buried at Reigate. His valuable library was sold by Sotheby, Wilkinson, & Hodge on 26 May 1909. Dimock married at East Malling, on 31 March 1853, Georgiana, daughter of John Alfred Wigan of Clare House, Kent, and sister of Sir Frederick Wigan, first baronet. His wife died shortly after marriage, on 14 July 1853.

A profound student of sacramental questions from the evangelical standpoint, Dimock had an unrivalled knowledge of liturgiology. His style was not attractive, and his pages are often too heavily weighted with footnotes and references, but his erudition was profound, his judgment sound, and his attitude to opponents absolutely fair. His most important works are: 1. 'Conversion, Six Plain Sermons,' 1855. 2. 'A Word for Warning and Defence of the Church of England against Ritualism and Romanism,' 1868. 3. 'The Real Objective Presence: Questions suggested by the Judgment of Sir Robert Phillimore,' 1870. 4. 'The Doctrine of the Sacraments in relation to the Doctrine of Grace,' 1871; new edit. 1908. 5. 'Essays on the Principles of the Reformation,' 1872. 6. 'The Romish Mass and the English Church,' 1874. 7. 'Eucharistic Worship in the Church of England,' 1876. 8. 'The Eucharist considered in its Sacrificial Aspect,' 1884. 9. 'The Apostolic Fathers and the Christian Ministry,' 1887. 10. 'Questions suggested by so much of the Lambeth Judgment as deals with the North Side Rubric,' parts i. and ii., 1891. 11. 'Curiosities of Patristic and Mediæval Literature,' parts i., ii., and iii., 1891, 1892, 1895. 12. 'The Doctrine of the Death of Christ,' 1890; 2nd edit. 1903.

13. 'Dangerous Deceits,' 1895. 14. 'Missarum Sacrificia,' 1896. 15. 'Vox Liturgiæ Anglicanæ,' 1897. 16. 'The Christian Doctrine of Sacerdotism,' 2 edits. 1897. 17. 'The Crisis in the Church of England,' 1899. 18. 'Light from History on Christian Ritual,' 1900. 19. 'The Bennett Judgment cleared from Misconception,' 1900. 20. 'The History of the Book of Common Prayer in its bearing on present Eucharistic Controversies.' A 'Memorial Edition' of his chief works was published in 1910–11.

[The Times, 4 March 1909; Record, 5 March 1909; Guardian, 10 March 1909; English Churchman, 11 March 1909; Church Family Newspaper, 12 March 1909; Foster's Alumni Oxonienses; Crockford's Clerical Directory; Gloucestershire Notes and Queries, v. 245; Phillimore's County Pedigrees, Nottinghamshire, i. 65–71; private information, and personal knowledge.] W. G. D. F.

DIXIE, Lady FLORENCE CAROLINE (1857–1905), authoress and traveller, born in London on 24 May 1857, was youngest of six children of Archibald William Douglas, seventh marquis of Queensberry, by his wife Caroline Margaret, daughter of General Sir William Robert Clayton. Sir John Sholto Douglas, eighth marquis [q. v. Suppl. I], was her eldest brother. She was educated for the most part at home, and showed in youth literary talents. Verses from her pen were published when she was ten. Of impulsive, adventurous temper, she in early life developed a zeal for sport and travel. A first-rate rider, a good shot and swimmer, she became, while a girl, a huntress of big game; one of the first women to take up this form of sport in recent years, she visited Africa, Arabia, and the Rocky Mountains in its pursuit.

In 1875 she married Sir Alexander Beaumont Churchill Dixie, eleventh baronet (*b.* 1851), and had two sons, George Douglas (*b.* 1876) and Albert Edward Wolston Beaumont (*b.* 1878), a godson of King Edward VII when Prince of Wales.

Her marriage did not check her energies as a traveller. In 1878–9 she made an exploratory journey in Patagonia, and published her experiences in 'Across Patagonia' (1880). In 1879 she was war correspondent for the 'Morning Post,' during the Zulu war in South Africa. She advocated Cetewayo's release and restoration to Zululand (a course which was ultimately adopted); her views of Zulu affairs and her experiences she described in 'A Defence of Zululand and its King' (1882) and 'In the Land of Misfortune' (1882).

Soon afterwards home politics attracted her attention. While professing advanced liberalism, including home rule all round, she vehemently denounced in letters to newspapers the tyranny of the land league agitation in Ireland of 1880–3. On 17 March 1883, when fenian outrages were exciting London, Lady Florence announced that, while she was walking by the Thames near Windsor, two men disguised as women, whom she inferred to be fenian emissaries, vainly attempted her assassination. Her statement attracted worldwide attention, but Sir William Harcourt, the home secretary, declared in the House of Commons that Lady Florence's story was unconfirmed, and nothing further followed.

Her discursive interests were thenceforth mainly concentrated on the advocacy of complete sex-equality. Her aims ranged from the reform of female attire to that of the royal succession law, which, she held, should prescribe the accession of the eldest child, of whichever sex, to the throne. She desired the emendation of the marriage service and of the divorce laws so as to place man and woman on the same level. She formulated such views in 'Gloriana, or the Revolution of 1900' (1890); her stories for children, 'The Young Castaways, or the Child Hunters of Patagonia' (1890), and 'Aniwee, or the Warrior Queen' (1890), had a like purpose. In later life she convinced herself of the cruelty of sport, which she denounced in 'Horrors of Sport' (1891; new edit. 1905) and the 'Mercilessness of Sport' (1901). Lady Dixie died at Glen Stuart, Annan, on 7 Nov. 1905, and was buried in the family grave at Kinmount.

Besides the works mentioned, she published: 1. 'Abel Avenged,' a dramatic tragedy, 1877. 2. 'Waifs and Strays, or the Pilgrimage of a Bohemian Abroad,' 1884. 3. 'Redeemed in Blood,' 1889. 4. 'Little Chérie, or the Trainer's Daughter,' 1901. 5. 'Songs of a Child,' under the pseudonym of 'Darling,' pt. i. 1902; pt. ii. 1903. 6. 'Ijain, or the Evolution of a Mind,' 1903. 7. 'Isola, or the Disinherited,' a drama, 1903. 8. 'Izra, or a Child of Solitude,' published posthumously, 1906.

A cartoon portrait appeared in 'Vanity Fair' in 1884.

[The Times, 8 Nov. 1905; Who's Who, 1902.] O. J. R. H.

DODS, MARCUS (1834–1909), presbyterian divine and biblical scholar, born in Belford Vicarage, Northumberland, on 11 April 1834, was youngest son of Marcus

Dods [q. v.] by his wife Sarah Palliser. On the father's death in 1838 the family removed to Edinburgh, where Dods first attended a preparatory school and, later, Edinburgh Academy (1843–1848). After spending two years in the head office of the National Bank in Edinburgh, he resolved in 1850 to study for the ministry of the Free church of Scotland. In 1854 he graduated M.A. at Edinburgh University and began his theological course at New College, Edinburgh. During his university career he was assistant in the Signet Library. On 7 Sept. 1858 he was licensed to preach by the presbytery of Edinburgh.

Dods had a long probationership. Although he preached in twenty-three vacancies, he failed for six years to get a church. During these years of enforced leisure he edited the complete works of Augustine (1871); translated Lange's 'Life of Christ' (Edinburgh, 1864, 6 vols.); and wrote his 'Prayer that Teaches to Pray' (1863; 5th edit. 1885) and 'Epistles to the Seven Churches' (Edinburgh, 1865).

On 4 Aug. 1864 he was inducted minister of Renfield Free church, Glasgow, and from its pulpit for exactly twenty-five years he exercised a notable influence, especially on young men of culture, chief among whom was Henry Drummond [q. v. Suppl. I] (George Adam Smith, *Life of Henry Drummond*, 7th edit. p. 132). The sermons at Renfield formed the substance of his popular volumes, 'Israel's Iron Age, or Sketches from the Period of the Judges' (1874; 4th edit. 1880), 'The Parables of our Lord' (first series, Matthew, 1883; second series, Luke, 1885), and they provided material for his editions of 'Genesis' (Expositor's Bible, 1888); of '1 Corinthians' (Expositor's Bible, 1889); and of 'St. John's Gospel' (Expositor's Greek Test. 1897).

Though not a theologian in the technical sense, Dods brought wide and exact scholarship and an expository gift to the popularising of modern critical views about the Bible. In 1877 Dods published a sermon on 'Revelation and Inspiration,' which questioned verbal inspiration. The presbytery of Glasgow, while declining to enter on a process, advised withdrawal of the sermon with a view to some modification. Dods assented on conditions; the matter was brought in 1878 before the general assembly, which declined by a majority to intervene.

Dods refused in 1869 an invitation to become colleague to Dr. Robert Smith Candlish [q. v.] at St. George's Free church, Edinburgh, the most influential congregation in the denomination. In 1889, when he celebrated the semi-jubilee of his ordination, he was appointed to the chair of New Testament criticism and exegesis in New College, Edinburgh. The appointment implied that the Free church of Scotland was prepared to tolerate critical views of the Bible for which Robertson Smith [q. v.] had been removed from his chair only eight years before. At the general assembly of 1890 Dods was libelled, along with Professor Alexander Balmain Bruce [q. v. Suppl. I], owing to his views on inspiration, which he had discussed anew in a paper read before the pan-presbyterian council in London. The general assembly, after a protracted debate, while exhorting Dods to teach the faith held by his church, declined to institute a process. In 1891 he received the honorary degree of D.D. from Edinburgh University, and in 1901 he declined nomination for the moderatorship of the general assembly of the United Free church of Scotland (formed in the previous year by the union of the Free and United Presbyterian churches). Appointed in May 1907, on the death of Dr. Robert Rainy [q. v. Suppl. II], principal of New College, Edinburgh, he was prevented by ill-health from entering on the duties of the office. He died at Edinburgh on 26 April 1909, and was buried in the Dean cemetery there.

In 1871 he married Catherine, daughter of James Swanston of Marshall Meadows, Berwickshire, by whom he had three sons and one daughter. His eldest son, Marcus Dods, M.A., is the author of 'Forerunners of Dante.'

A portrait in oils by Sir James Guthrie, P.R.S.A., presented by his friends to the United Free church, now hangs in the Rainy Hall, New College.

Dods' chief writings, besides those already mentioned and contributions to religious periodicals, were: 1. 'Mohammed, Buddha, and Christ' (four lectures on natural and revealed religion, delivered at the English Presbyterian College), 1877. 2. 'Isaac Jacob, and Joseph,' 1880. 3. 'Erasmus and other essays,' 1891; 2nd edit. 1892. 4. 'An Introduction to the New Testament' ('Theological Educator' series), 1891. 5. 'The Visions of a Prophet: Studies in Zechariah' ('Little Books on Religion' series), 1895. 6. 'Why be a Christian?' (the same series), 1896. 7. 'How to become like Christ, and other papers,' 1897. 8. 'The Bible: its Nature and Origin' (Bross Lectures), 1905, a full account of his views on inspiration. Two volumes,

'Footsteps in the Path of Life' and 'Christ and Man' (sermons), were posthumously published in 1909, while two volumes of Dods' letters were edited by his son in 1910 and 1911 respectively.

[Dods' Early Letters 1910 (with memoir); his Later Letters, 1911; British Monthly, March 1904; British Weekly, 6 May 1909; Patrick Carnegie Simpson, Life of Principal Rainy (2 vols.), 1909; George Adam Smith, Life of Henry Drummond, 1898; personal knowledge.]

W. F. G.

DOLLING, ROBERT WILLIAM RADCLYFFE, 'FATHER DOLLING' (1851–1902), divine and social reformer, born on 10 Feb. 1851 in the old rectory, Magheralin, co. Down, was the sixth of nine children and the elder son of Robert Holbeach Dolling, a landlord in co. Down, and at one time high sheriff of Londonderry, by his wife Eliza, third daughter of Josias Du Pré Alexander, M.P., a nephew of James Alexander, first earl of Caledon. Dolling's childhood was spent at Kilrea, co. Derry. After education at a private school, the Grange, Stevenage, Hertfordshire (1861–4), and at Harrow (1864–8), he matriculated in 1868 from Trinity College, Cambridge; but bad health and ophthalmia compelled his withdrawal in the spring of 1869, and he spent the next twelve months in foreign travel, mostly in Italy and Florence. His mother's death in 1870 recalled him to Ireland, where he assisted his father in land agency work. His spare time in Kilrea was devoted to Bible-classes and night schools for young men and clubs for working men, and he similarly occupied himself in Dublin, whither his family soon removed. On his father's death on 28 Sept. 1878, he made London his permanent home; there he became intimate with 'Father' Stanton and Alexander Heriot Mackonochie [q. v.], whom he had met at Cambridge. The two men were then engaged in stubbornly defending the ritualistic services which they were conducting at St. Alban's, Holborn. Through their influence he became in 1879 warden of the south London branch of the St. Martin's Postman's League, and in that capacity did much social and religious work. But 'Brother Bob,' as he was called by the postmen, found more congenial work among the poorest classes in Southwark, and exerted a magnetic influence over not only the respectable but also the disreputable poor. Early in 1882 he entered Salisbury theological college, where his Bohemian temperament revolted against both social and theological convention. Ordained on 23 May 1883, Dolling became curate of Corscombe, Dorset, and then missionary deacon of St. Martin's Mission at Holy Trinity, Stepney. Failing health and difficulties on questions of ritual with Frederick Temple, bishop of London [q. v. Suppl. II], led to Dolling's retirement from Stepney (1 July 1885). After a short stay at St. Leonards-on-Sea, Dolling became in 1885 vicar of the Winchester College Mission of St. Agatha's, Landport, where for ten years he did much to mitigate the evils of slum life, and was in frequent controversy with his diocesan concerning ritual observances. In 1895 the church of St. Agatha was rebuilt through Dolling's exertions. Fresh disagreements in regard to ritual with the newly appointed bishop (Randall Davidson) caused Dolling's resignation of his living on 8 Dec. 1895. In his enforced leisure he wrote 'Ten Years in a Portsmouth Slum' (1896), which gave a full account of his work and experiences at Landport.

During 1896–7 Dolling stayed in London with his sister at Earl's Court, giving occasional addresses in various parts of England. In May 1897 he went to America, visiting many of the cities there. At Chicago in March 1898 he was offered the deanery of the cathedral by Bishop McLaren; but meanwhile he had accepted the living of St. Saviour's, Poplar, and returned to England in July 1898. At Poplar, as at Landport, he sought to solve the social and municipal problems of the district; the East London water famine of 1898, the evils of overcrowding, and the small-pox epidemic of 1901 roused all his energies and he fiercely denounced those responsible for the scandals.

In March 1901 Dolling's health failed, and after vainly travelling abroad in hope of relief he died unmarried on 15 May 1902 at his sister's house, South Kensington; he was buried at Woking cemetery. In June 1902 a government annuity was purchased in his memory for his two sisters, Elise and Geraldine, who had helped him in his work, and the Dolling memorial home of rest for the working girls of Poplar and Landport was opened at Worthing under their management in 1903.

Dolling's missionary zeal curiously blended evangelical fervour with advanced ritual. Impatient of ecclesiastical authority, he was an unconventional and emotional preacher who appealed potently to the very poor. A radical in politics, he strongly advocated home rule, church disestablishment, and the labour movement. He had a liking for the theatre, and was a frequent play-goer.

A portrait of Dolling, painted from a photograph after death, is at the Dolling memorial home, Worthing, Sussex.

[The Life of Father Dolling, by Charles E. Osborne, 1903; Father Dolling, a memoir, by Joseph Clayton, with preface by Canon Scott Holland, 1902; Robert Dolling, et blad af den Engelske Statskirkes historie 1 Bet. 19 Aarhundrede, by Richard Thomsen, Copenhagen, 1908; The Times, 16, 19, 21, 22 May, 10 June 1902; British Weekly, 22 May 1902 (with engraving of portrait taken in America); Lord Ronald Gower, Old Diaries, 1902.]

W. B. O.

DONKIN, BRYAN (1835–1902), civil engineer, born at 88 Blackfriars Road, London, on 29 Aug. 1835, was eldest son in a family of four sons and three daughters of John Donkin (1802–1854), civil engineer, and grandson of Bryan Donkin, F.R.S. [q. v.]. His mother was Caroline, daughter of Benjamin Hawes. He was educated at private schools and at University College, London, and then pursued for two years an engineering course at the École centrale des Arts et Métiers in Paris. From 1856 to 1859 he served three years' apprenticeship in the Bermondsey engineering works of Bryan Donkin & Company, which his grandfather established in 1803. He was then engaged in St. Petersburg on some very large mills, which his firm were erecting for the Russian government for the production of paper for making banknotes and other purposes. He returned to the Bermondsey works in 1862, and became a partner in 1868. The firm was formed into a limited liability company in 1889 with Donkin as chairman. In 1900 there was an amalgamation with Messrs. Clench & Company of Chesterfield. He remained chairman for a time, though he ceased to take an active part in the management.

Donkin devoted much time and labour to scientific research, and proved to be an able, indefatigable, and accurate investigator. His researches were especially directed to the design and construction of heat-engines and steam-boilers and to the application to them of scientific tests. One of the first to practise systematic testing of the efficiency of steam-engines, he introduced a method of determining steam-consumption by measuring the condensed water flowing over a tumbling bay or weir. His researches into the action and behaviour of steam in the cylinders of steam-engines, and the advantages of jacketing, formed the subject of four papers presented to the Institution of Civil Engineers (*Minutes of Proceedings*, xcviii. 250; c. 347; cvi. 264, and cxv. 263), and two to the Institution of Mechanical Engineers (*Proc.* 1893, p. 480; 1895, p. 90). In the course of these experiments he perfected his 'revealer,' an apparatus of glass which, attached to the cylinder of a steam-engine, rendered visible the condensation effects taking place within the cylinder. Meanwhile, after close study of internal-combustion engines, he published 'A Text-Book on Gas, Oil and Air Engines,' 1894 (5th edit. 1911), and in 1894 he also translated Rudolf Diesel's 'Theory and Construction of a Rational Heat Motor.'

His latest inquiry was into the practicability of working gas-engines with the gases produced in blast-furnaces, and a few weeks before his death he contributed to the 'Proceedings of the Institution of Civil Engineers' an important paper on 'Motive Power from Blast-Furnace Gases' (cxlviii. 1). He was a member of committees appointed by the Institution to report upon standards of thermal efficiency for steam-engines and on the tabulation of results of steam-engine and boiler trials. He was also a member of research committees of the Institution of Mechanical Engineers on the steam-jacket, on marine engines, on gas-engines, and on steam-engines. In conjunction with (Sir) Alexander Kennedy he made exhaustive tests of different types of boilers, the results of which were published in 'Engineering' from 1890 onwards, and he was author of 'The Heat Efficiency of Steam Boilers' (1898). Fuel calorimeters (*Proc. Inst. Civ. Eng.* cii. 292), centrifugal fans (*ibid.* cxxii. 265), the velocity of air through pipes (*ibid.* cxi. 345), the Perret system of forced draught (*Proc. North of Eng. Inst. Min. and Mech. Eng.* xlii. 32), and heat-transmission (*Proc. Inst. Mech. Eng.* 1896, p. 501) were among the other subjects of his investigation.

He was elected a member of the Institution of Civil Engineers on 5 Feb. 1884, and received its Watt medal in 1894, Telford premiums in 1889 and 1891, and a Manby premium in 1896, in recognition of the value of papers contributed to the Institution's 'Proceedings.' He was also, from 1873, a member of the Institution of Mechanical Engineers, and became a member of council in 1895 and a vice-president in 1901. He died suddenly at the Grand Hotel, Brussels, on 4 March 1902, and was buried at

Bromley, Kent. He married twice: (1) in 1869, Georgina, daughter of Frank Dillon, by whom he had issue one daughter and one son; (2) Edith Marshman Dunn (born Edith Marshman), by whom he had a daughter.

[Minutes of Proc. Inst. Civ. Eng. cl. 428; Proc. Inst. Mech. Eng. 1902, p. 378; Engineering, lxxiii. 320.] W. F. S.

DONNELLY, Sir JOHN FRETCHEVILLE DYKES (1834–1902), major-general, royal engineers, born in the Bay of Bombay on 2 July 1834, was only child of Lieutenant-colonel Thomas Donnelly (1802–1881), at one time deputy adjutant-general of the Bombay army, and from 1851 staff captain and afterwards staff officer at the East India Company's military college at Addiscombe until the closing of the college in 1861 (see Vibart's *Addiscombe*, with portrait). His mother was Jane Christiana, second daughter of Joseph Ballantine Dykes of Dovenby Hall, Cumberland. Educated at Highgate School (1843–8), he entered the Royal Military Academy at Woolwich at the head of the list after a year's private tuition in August 1849, passed out first, and received a commission as second-lieutenant in the royal engineers on 23 June 1853, and after professional instruction at Chatham was promoted first-lieutenant on 17 February 1854. Going out to the Crimea in June, Donnelly joined his corps on its march to Balaklava on 23 September, and next month was detailed for duty with the left attack on Sevastopol. He was present at the battle of Inkerman on 5 November, and subsequently worked in the trenches before Sevastopol with an energy to which Sir John Burgoyne called Lord Raglan's attention (21 Nov.). Through the severe weather of the winter of 1854–5 he was on duty in the trenches forty-one times by day and forty-three times by night. On the day after the abortive assault on the Redan (18 June), when he was with the second column, he by his promptitude and zeal obtained a substantial lodgment in the Russian rifle pits at the Little Mamelon. Donnelly was mentioned in Lord Raglan's despatches for this service. Soon after the fall of Sevastopol in September 1855, during which he was thrice in all mentioned in despatches (*London Gazette*, 18 Dec.), he was appointed aide-de-camp to Colonel E. T. Lloyd on 12 Nov. 1855, the commanding royal engineer in the Crimea, and accompanied him home in June 1856. He received the Crimea medal with clasps for Inkerman and Sevastopol, the Turkish medal, and the 5th class of the legion ot honour. He had been recommended for the Victoria Cross without result, and received no promotion nor British distinction.

Joining the London military district in 1856, he was placed in command of a detachment of royal sappers and miners employed in preparing for building purposes the ground purchased at South Kensington out of the surplus funds of the Great Exhibition of 1851. It was intended to erect there a permanent museum and centre of science and art. Sir Henry Cole [q. v.], the director of the scheme, secured Donnelly's services on 1 April 1858 in reorganising at South Kensington the science and art department, which was controlled by the privy council's committee of education. On 1 Oct. 1859 he was appointed inspector for science in connection with the department. He had been promoted second captain on 1 April 1859, and was now seconded in his corps for ten years. But he did not return to regimental duty, and the rest of his career was identified with South Kensington. In 1869 he was allowed two and a half years' special leave, and in 1872 was placed on the reserve list. His promotion continued, as he was still liable for emergency service, and he became lieutenant-colonel on 1 Oct. 1877 and brevet-colonel on 1 Oct. 1881, retiring with the honorary rank of major-general on 31 Dec. 1887.

The success of the scheme for national instruction in science and art was largely due to Donnelly, although some of his methods came to be reckoned reactionary. In agreement with a much controverted principle he arranged (by minute of 1859) that grants should be made to certificated teachers on the results of the examinations of their pupils. Prizes were at the same time to be awarded to successful students, whether trained in recognised schools or otherwise. He obtained due recognition for drawing and manual training as class subjects, and having induced the Society of Arts, which he joined in 1860, to form a class in wood-carving, he procured from City companies and other sources funds to carry it on as the School of Art Wood-carving, which is now located in Thurloe Place, South Kensington.

In 1874 his title at South Kensington became 'Director of Science,' and his duties included the supervision not only of the science schools and classes throughout the country but of other important scientific institutions like the Government School of Mines, the Museum of Practical Geology, the Royal College of Chemistry, the Edinburgh Museum of Science and Art, and the Museum of Irish Industry, which developed into the Royal College of Science for Ireland. In 1868, as a member of a commission appointed to consider the question, he had drafted a report adverse to the establishment of a separate department of science and art for Ireland. In 1881 he was appointed in addition assistant secretary of the science and art department, and in 1884 secretary and permanent head of the department.

Joining the council of the Society of Arts in 1870, he was mainly responsible in 1871 for the society's scheme of technological examinations, out of which by his advice the City Guilds Institute for technical education was developed. As chairman of the council of the Society of Arts in 1894 and 1895, he led the society to organise the International Congress on Technical Education in 1897.

For many years the museums of science and art at Kensington had been housed in temporary and straggling make-shift galleries and sheds, and Donnelly was untiring in his efforts to secure parliamentary grants for the erection of permanent buildings. In 1896 the House of Commons appointed a select committee on whose report in 1899 a sum of 800,000*l.* was voted to complete the museums. In the course of the inquiry Donnelly's administration was called in question (see *Report and Evidence of Committee of House of Commons on the Museums of the Science and Art Department,* 1899). Whatever the defects of the educational policy pursued, the study of science grew immensely under Donnelly's direction. In 1859 the total number of science students was under 400; ten years later there were over 1400 classes comprising 25,000 students, while at the time of Donnelly's death these numbers were increased eight-fold. In accordance with the civil service rule he retired on 2 July 1899 on attaining the age of sixty-five. A minute of the privy council dated the following day animadverted on the committee's Report, stating that the sole responsibility lay on their lordships for the administration of the Science and Art Department, which had been loyally carried out by Colonel Donnelly and his staff, in whom they retained the fullest confidence. Sir John Gorst, vice-president of the committee of council on education, when presenting Donnelly with a testimonial from 500 of the South Kensington staff (29 November), warmly defended him from adverse criticism, and Sir John presided at a complimentary dinner given by his old colleagues (12 December).

Donnelly was made C.B. in 1886 and K.C.B. (civil) in 1893. In 1888 he was elected a member of the Athenæum under Rule II. He was no mean artist, and from 1888 to 1901 he exhibited water-colour paintings and etchings at the Royal Academy or the New Gallery. In 1888 he took part in the formation of the committee for the preservation of the monuments of ancient Egypt. He wrote two pamphlets, on 'The Employment of Iron Shields in Siege Operations' (1868), and on 'Army Organisation' (1869) in which he advocated personal service.

He died on 5 April 1902 at his residence, 59 Onslow Gardens, London, and was buried at Brompton cemetery.

A portrait in oils by H. T. Wells, R.A. (exhibited at the Royal Academy in 1901), and a charcoal head by Sir E. J. Poynter, P.R.A., are in Lady Donnelly's possession.

Donnelly was twice married: (1) at Bridekirk, Cumberland, on 5 Jan. 1871, to his first cousin Adeliza (*d.* 1873), second daughter of Fretcheville Lawson Ballantine Dykes of Dovenby Hall, Cumberland; by her he had two daughters; (2) at Neuchatel, Switzerland, on 17 Dec. 1881, to his first wife's elder sister, Mary Frances Dykes, who survives him; by her he had two sons, Thomas and Gordon Harvey, both lieutenants in the royal garrison artillery, and a daughter.

[Nature, 10 April 1902; Journ. of the Soc. of Arts, 11 April 1902; The Manual Training Teacher, April 1902; The Times, 7 April 1902; Standard, 12 April 1902; Daily Chronicle, 8 April 1902; Royal Engineers Records; Connolly's History of the Royal Sappers and Miners, 1855; Porter's History of the Corps of Royal Engineers, 1889; Russell's Letters from the Crimea; Report and Evidence of the Select Committee on the Museums of the Science and Art Department, 1899; Minute of 3 July 1899, of the Lords of the Committee of the Privy Council on Education.] R. H. V.

DONNET, Sir JAMES JOHN LOUIS (1816–1905), inspector-general of hospitals and fleets, born at Gibraltar in 1816, was son of Henry Donnet, surgeon, R.N. After studying at the University of Paris, where he graduated B. ès L., and Anderson College, Glasgow, he became L.S.A. of London in 1838, L.R.C.S. of Edinburgh in 1840, and M.D. at St.

Andrews in 1857. He entered the navy as assistant-surgeon in 1840. He was at once appointed to the Vesuvius and sent out to the Mediterranean, where, on the coast of Syria, he had his first experience of the realities of war, and where, after the capture of Acre, he was placed in charge of the wounded in a temporary hospital established on shore. Four years later he was medical officer and secretary of an embassy to the emperor of Morocco under (Sir) John Hay Drummond-Hay [q. v. Suppl. I], appointed in 1845 consul-general. Donnet was promoted to be surgeon, and in 1849 was in the Calypso in the West Indies during a violent outbreak of yellow fever. In 1850–1 he was surgeon of the Assistance in the Arctic with Captain (Sir) Erasmus Ommanney [q.v. Suppl. II], and helped to break the tedium of the long winter by editing 'an excellent periodical, entitled the "Aurora Borealis," to which the men as well as the officers contributed' (Markham, 113). In 1854 he was surgeon of the President, flag-ship in the Pacific, and in her was present at the disastrous attacks on Petropaulowski, on 29 Aug. and 7 Sept. (Clowes, vi. 429–32). In May 1867 he was promoted deputy inspector-general, and for the next two years was in medical charge of the hospital at Jamaica, years marked by an epidemic of yellow fever. In 1870 he was appointed honorary surgeon to the queen, and in 1873–4 was placed in charge of the medical wards of Haslar, crowded with cases of smallpox, enteric fever, and dysentery after the Ashanti war. On 14 April 1875 he was promoted inspector-general. He was after this employed on various committees and commissions, including one in 1876 to select a site for a college for naval cadets and one in 1877 to inquire into the causes of the outbreak of scurvy in Sir George Nares' Arctic expedition (1875–6). He was awarded a good-service pension in 1878, and was nominated K.C.B. at the Queen's Diamond Jubilee. During his last years he resided at Bognor, where he died on 11 Jan. 1905. He married in 1852 Eliza, daughter of James Meyer, who died in 1903 without issue. He published 'Notes on Yellow Fever.'

[Royal Navy Lists; Who's Who; The Times, 12 Jan. 1905; Markham, Life of Sir Leopold McClintock, 1909; Clowes, Royal Navy, vol. vi. 1901.] J. K. L.

DOUGLAS, Sir ADYE (1815–1906), premier of Tasmania, son of an officer in the army, was born at Thorpe near Norwich on 30 May 1815, and was intended for the navy. He was sent to school in Hampshire, and then to Caen, Normandy, for two years. Returning to England, he was articled tc a firm of solicitors in Southampton, and in 1838 was admitted to practice. He emigrated to Tasmania in 1839, and in the same year was admitted to the bar at Hobart. He was, however, soon (1840) tempted to try a squatter's life in Victoria, and there spent two years. Returning to Tasmania in 1842, he founded the legal firm of Douglas & Collins at Launceston, and became one of the leading lawyers in the colony.

In 1853, on the introduction of a regular municipal administration for Launceston, Douglas became an alderman of the town, of which he was subsequently five times mayor. It was about this time he made a name by his vigorous opposition to the system of transportation. He was defeated at his first attempt to enter the council, but in July 1855 he took his seat in the old legislative council as member for Launceston. He was from the first forward in urging the claims of Tasmania to a constitution of greater responsibility. In 1857 he revisited England for a time, and came back to Tasmania full of projects for introducing railways into the colony. In 1862, under the new constitution, he represented Westbury in the assembly. In 1863 he was delegate for Tasmania to the conference on intercolonial tariffs. In 1871 he was elected member for Norfolk plains and in 1872 for Fingal.

On 15 Aug. 1884, Douglas became premier and chief secretary of Tasmania, and after a somewhat uneventful period of office resigned on 8 March 1886 to go to England as first agent-general for the colony. He represented Tasmania at the Colonial Conference of 1887, but in October 1887 resigned his agency and returned to Tasmania.

In 1890 Douglas re-entered the political life of the colony as member for Launceston in the legislative council, and represented Tasmania at the Federal Convention at Sydney in 1891. He served in the Dobson ministry as chief secretary from 17 Aug. 1892 to 14 April 1894, when he became president of the legislative council; this position he held for ten years, being knighted at the coronation of Edward VII in 1902. In May 1904 he was defeated at the elections for Launceston, and retired from public life. He died on 10 April 1906 at Hobart, where he had come to reside ten years before; he was buried at the Cornelian Bay cemetery.

Of striking personality, he gave the impression of being brusque and unsympathetic, until he was more intimately known.

He was a good fighting leader, acute and tenacious in debate. He was married three times and left issue.

[Tasmanian Mercury and Examiner, 11 April 1906; John's Notable Australians; information checked by the agent-general for Tasmania.] C. A. H.

DOUGLAS, GEORGE (1869–1902), novelist. [See Brown, George Douglas.]

DOUGLAS, GEORGE CUNNINGHAME MONTEATH (1826–1904), Hebraist, born on 2 March 1826, in the manse of Kilbarchan, West Renfrewshire, was fourth son in the family of five sons and one daughter of Robert Douglas, minister of the parish, by his wife Janet, daughter of John Monteath, minister of Houston. The fifth son, Carstairs Douglas (1830–1877), became a missionary, and was a Chinese scholar of repute. George was educated at home by his father with such success that he entered the University of Glasgow in 1837 at the early age of eleven, and took a distinguished place in the classes of languages and philosophy. He graduated B.A. in 1843, the year of the disruption. Throwing in his lot with the Free church, he took the prescribed four years' training in theology at the theological college in Edinburgh, which the Free church had erected with Dr. Thomas Chalmers [q. v.] at its head. He was duly 'licensed to preach' by his presbytery, and, after some years spent in 'assistantships,' was ordained in 1852 minister of Bridge-of-Weir in Renfrewshire. In 1856 the Free church erected a third theological college, at Glasgow, and Douglas was appointed tutor of the Hebrew classes. The year after (26 May 1857) he became professor, and held this position until his retirement on 23 May 1892. On the death of Dr. Patrick Fairbairn, Douglas succeeded him as principal (22 May 1875), and held office till 26 May 1902. His whole public life was spent in Glasgow in close connection with its university and with its educational and social activities. He took a keen interest in the establishment of the system of national education, which now exists in Scotland, was chairman of the Free church committee on the matter, and was sent to London in 1869 to watch the progress of the education bill through parliament. He was member of the first two Glasgow school boards, and for several years an active member of Hutcheson's educational trust. He was also chairman of the university council's committee on university reform. He received the degree of D.D. in 1867. Douglas was an early member of the Old Testament company for the revision of the authorised version, and served till the completion of the work in 1884; his accurate acquaintance with the Hebrew text rendered him a valuable coadjutor. He died at Woodcliffe, Bridge-of-Allan, on 24 May 1904, and is buried in the Necropolis, Glasgow. A full-length portrait by G. Sherwood Calvert hangs on the walls of the Free Church College at Glasgow.

As a Hebraist Dr. Douglas belonged to the older school of scholars. He had an exact and minute acquaintance with the Massoretic text of the Old Testament and with extra-canonic Hebrew literature. He read widely and had at his command the results of Hebrew scholarship, German, French, and English. But he had a profound distrust of what he called 'the hasty generalisations' of the higher criticism, and was always ready to defend his conservative position. His writings fail to do justice to his genuine and extensive scholarship. He published: 'Why I still believe that Moses wrote Deuteronomy' (1878); 'Handbooks on Judges' (1881), and on 'Joshua' (1882); 'A Short Analysis of the Old Testament' (1889); 'The Six Intermediate Minor Prophets' (1889); 'Isaiah one and his Book one' (1895); 'Samuel and his Age' (1901); 'The Old Testament and its Critics' (1902); 'The Story of Job' (1905).

[Private information.] T. M. L.

DOUGLAS-PENNANT, GEORGE SHOLTO GORDON, second Baron Penrhyn (1836–1907), born at Linton Springs, Yorkshire, on 30 Sept. 1836, was elder son of Edward Gordon Douglas (1800–1886), third son of John Douglas, second son of James Douglas, sixteenth earl of Morton. His mother, his father's first wife, was Juliana Isabella Mary (*d.* 1842), eldest daughter and co-heiress of George Hay Dawkins-Pennant of Penrhyn Castle. In 1841 the father, whose wife inherited vast property in North Wales, assumed the additional surname of Pennant by royal licence, and was raised to the peerage as Baron Penrhyn on 3 Aug. 1866. George was educated at Eton and Christ Church, Oxford. A project of entering the army was abandoned in deference to his father's wishes, but he always interested himself in military affairs. He was major of the Carnarvonshire rifles and honorary colonel of the 4th battalion of royal Welsh fusiliers. In 1866 he was elected conservative M.P. for Carnarvonshire, and held the seat until 1868. He was again elected in 1874, but was defeated in 1880 by Watkin Williams, Q.C. He succeeded to the peerage on his father's death in 1886. Thenceforth he devoted the greater part of his time and energies to the management of the large property which came to the family through his mother. The Penrhyn estate contained no less than 26,278 acres, with a rent-roll of 67,000*l.*, and the family owned the Bethesda slate quarries which, when fully employed and in former times of good trade, were estimated to produce 150,000*l.* a year.

In his later years his father had allowed much of the management of the Bethesda slate quarries to pass into the hands of an elective committee of the men, with the result that they were in 1885 on the verge of bankruptcy. In that year the son George had been entrusted with full powers to reform their administration. One of his first actions was to repudiate the authority of the workmen's committee. Under fresh and strenuous management the quarries once again became busy and prosperous. But a section of the quarrymen, incited by outside interference and agitation, cherished deep resentment at their exclusion from control, and a great strike began in 1897. Lord Penrhyn replied by closing the quarries, and an angry debate took place in the House of Commons. But Lord Penrhyn would abate none of his conditions, and the men capitulated. Lord Penrhyn as a champion of free labour refused to allow the intervention of outsiders in dealings with his men, and late in 1900 a second strike of great extent broke out. The quarries were again closed, but were reopened after a prolonged stoppage with 600 of the former non-union workmen. Penrhyn refused to re-engage the ringleaders of the agitation or to recognise any trades union officials. On 9 Aug. 1901 William Jones, M.P. for Carnarvonshire, raised a discussion as a matter of urgent public importance on the conduct of the local magistrates in requisitioning cavalry for maintaining peace in the district, but Penrhyn's position was unaffected. On 13 March 1903 he brought an action for libel against W. J. Parry, in respect of an article in the 'Clarion,' accusing him of cruelty to his workmen; he received 500*l.* damages and costs. Penrhyn acted throughout in accordance with what he believed to be stern equity and from a wish to obtain justice for non-union men. In 1907 he generously accorded the workmen a bonus of 10 per cent. on their wages, owing to a spell of bad weather which had interrupted work at the quarries.

Fond of horse-racing and breeding, he was elected to the Jockey Club in 1887, but was not very fortunate on the turf. In 1898, however, he won the Goodwood Cup with King's Messenger, which both in 1899 and 1900 carried his master's colours to the post for the Great Metropolitan Stakes at Epsom. With another horse, Quaesitum, in 1894 he won both the Chester cup and the Ascot gold vase. He was an excellent shot, but derived his chief enjoyment from fishing, in which he was exceptionally skilled. He was master of the Grafton hounds from 1882 to 1891.

Lord Penrhyn, who was a deputy-lieutenant for Carnarvonshire and was a county councillor for the Llandegai division of the county, was a man of strong and original character. A tory of the old school, he managed his estates in the feudal spirit, and with implicit justice and generosity. Though a thorough churchman he always insisted on equality of treatment for nonconformists both as tenants and quarrymen.

He scorned popularity, and played a detached part in public affairs. He was a founder of the North Wales Property Defence Association, of which he was chairman; in the course of his comprehensive evidence before the Welsh land commissioners in 1893, he stated that for many years he received from his land no income in excess of his expenditure upon it.

He died on 10 March 1907 at his town residence, Mortimer House, Halkin Street, S.W., and was buried near one of his country residences, Wicken, Stony Stratford. A portrait in oils, painted in 1907, after his death, by Miss Barbara Leighton, is at 37 Lennox Gardens, S.W.

He married twice: (1) in 1860 Blanche (*d.* 1869), daughter of Sir Charles Rushout Rushout; and (2) in 1875 Gertrude Jessy, daughter of Henry Glynne, rector of Hawarden. By his first wife he had a son, Edward Sholto, who succeeded as third Baron Penrhyn, and six daughters, and by his second wife two sons and six daughters.

[The Times, 12 March 1907; Burke's Peerage; Lucy's Balfourian Parliament, 1906, pp. 108 seq.; private information.] L. P. S.

DOWDEN, JOHN (1840–1910), bishop of Edinburgh, born in Cork on 29 June 1840, was elder son of John Wheeler Dowden, 'a staunch presbyterian,' and his wife Alicia Bennett, 'a devout churchwoman.' His younger brother, Edward Dowden (1843–1913), was professor of English literature in Dublin University. The family came from the south of England in the seventeenth century. John was educated at Cork, and at sixteen gained a classical scholarship at Queen's College in that town, whence he proceeded in 1858 to Trinity College, Dublin. His tutor was his cousin, George Salmon [q. v. Suppl. II]. His college career was distinguished; he graduated B.A. in 1861, being senior moderator in ethics and logic, and in 1864 he passed through the divinity school with first classes in all the examinations. He was ordained deacon in 1864 by Dr. Verschoyle, bishop of Kilmore, and priest next year. He married and for three years he was curate of St. John's, Sligo, until in 1867 he was appointed perpetual curate of Calry church, near Sligo, where he remained for eight years through the period of the disestablishment of the Irish church. From 1870 he also acted as chaplain to Earl Spencer, the lord-lieutenant of Ireland, and from 1872 was assistant minister of St. Stephen's church, Dublin.

A friend, the Rev. Percy Robinson, then headmaster of the boys' school at Glenalmond, to which was attached the theological college of the episcopal church of Scotland, was responsible for Dowden's association with the Scottish episcopal church. In 1874 he accepted the post of Pantonian professor of theology at Glenalmond. At the outset there was only one student, and the comparative leisure enabled Dowden to apply himself especially to ecclesiastical history and liturgiology. A fire in 1875 led to the removal of the few students to rooms in Edinburgh, until in 1880 the theological hall of the Scottish episcopal church was established, and Dowden became principal. At the same time he was made a canon of St. Mary's Cathedral, Edinburgh; in 1876 Dublin University had conferred upon him the degree of D.D. The success of the hall was largely due to Dowden, whose attractive personality and erudition won the loyal admiration of his students. The subsequent expansion and growth of the episcopal church owed much to the hall's prosperity under Dowden's guidance. On the death of Henry Cotterill, bishop of Edinburgh, in 1886 Dowden was as a consequence chosen to be his successor, after Canon Liddon's refusal. Dowden was consecrated on 21 Sept., when Dr. Salmon in a remarkable sermon on episcopacy in relation to unity defined generally the new bishop's theological position. The respect and affection in which the bishop was held by all sections of Edinburgh society was strikingly shown in 1904, when the degree of LL.D. was conferred upon him by Edinburgh University, and his portrait by Mr. John Bowie, A.R.S.A., presented to him by a large committee of his laymen. Under Dowden's leadership his church and diocese prospered. Declining to regard the Scottish episcopal church as a mere appendage of the Church of England, he was a keen promoter of the movement which in 1904 established the consultative council on church legislation. In 1905 the council undertook the revision of the canons, and on an appendix to the new code of proposals for revision of the services Dowden worked till death.

While he was bishop Dowden continued his liturgical and historical studies and retained the post of Bell lecturer at the theological hall, lecturing there once a week to keep himself in touch with the students. In the annotated Scottish communion office which appeared in 1884 he illustrated his happy faculty of combining exact scholarship with literary style. It was the precursor of 'The Workmanship of the Prayer Book' (1899; 2nd enlarged edit. 1902), which quickly became a classic of liturgical criticism. A supplementary volume, 'Further Studies in the Prayer Book,' appeared in 1908 and 'The Church Year and Calendar' for the 'Cambridge Handbooks of Liturgical Study' in 1910. In 1885–6 the bishop delivered the Donnellan lectures in the University of Dublin. He was select preacher at Dublin in 1886–7 and at Cambridge in 1888. In 1886 a committee under Dowden's convenership founded the Scottish History Society, and for the society Dowden edited in 1893 'The Correspondence of the Lauderdale Family with Archbishop Sharp,' 'The Chartulary of the Abbey of Lindores' in 1903, and in 1908, assisted by W. A. Lindsay, K.C., and Dr. J. Maitland Thomson, 'Charters, Bulls, and other Documents relating to the Abbey of Inchaffray.' A more popular result of his historical inquiries was 'The Celtic Church in Scotland,' published in 1894. In 1896 he went to America to lecture before the General Theological Seminary in New York. The lectures were published in 1897 as 'Outlines of the History of the Theological Literature of the Church of England from the Reformation to the close of the Eighteenth Century.' In 1901 he delivered the six Rhind lectures before the Society of Antiquaries of Scotland, which with revision and additions were published after the author's death in 1910 as 'The Mediæval Church in Scotland; its Constitution, Organisation, and Law.'

In 1890 Dowden's health failed, but a complete recovery followed. He died suddenly on 30 Jan. 1910, and is buried in the Dean cemetery, Edinburgh. A memorial tablet in bronze, giving a full figure of Dowden in episcopal robes, designed by Sir Robert Lorimer, and modelled by Mr. Deuchars, with a Latin inscription, was placed in the floor of the north side of the choir in Edinburgh Cathedral on 27 Oct. 1911. His library was bought by public subscription after his death and placed in the chapter house of the cathedral (*Scottish Chronicle*, 3 Nov. 1911).

Dowden married in 1864 Louisa, only daughter of Francis Jones, civil engineer. His widow, two sons, and four daughters survive him.

In addition to the works mentioned, Dowden printed various charges, sermons, and pamphlets, and at his death was engaged in rewriting 'Keith's Catalogue of Scottish Bishops,' of which portions appeared in the 'Scottish Historical Review'; this was completed by Dr. J. Maitland Thomson and published in 1912.

[A biographical sketch of Bishop Dowden by his daughter, Alice Dowden, is prefixed to The Mediæval Church in Scotland, 1910; The Times, 1 Feb. 1910; Guardian, 14 Jan. and 4 Feb. 1910; Men and Women of the Time, 1899; a life by Antony Mitchell, bishop of Aberdeen, is in preparation (1912).]

R. B.

DOWIE, JOHN ALEXANDER (1847–1907), religious fanatic, was born in Leith Street Terrace, Edinburgh, on 25 May 1847. At a school in Arthur Street he gained a silver medal at the age of fourteen (1861). His parents emigrated to Adelaide, South Australia, in 1860; he followed them, but in 1868 returned to Scotland, and with a view to the congregational ministry attended the Edinburgh University for two sessions, 1869–71. His first place of ministry was the congregational church at Alma, near Adelaide, whence he soon moved to the charge of Manly church, Sydney, New South Wales, and later to a church at Newton, a suburb of Sydney. At this period he was prominent as a social reformer, a temperance advocate, and a pleader for free, compulsory, and undenominational education. It is stated that Sir Henry Parkes [q. v. Suppl. I] offered him a seat in his cabinet. In 1878 he declared himself against a paid ministry. Two lectures, which he delivered in the Victoria Theatre, Sydney, in 1879, on 'The Drama, the Press, and the Pulpit,' attracted attention and were published. In 1882 he built a tabernacle at Melbourne, Victoria, in connection with an association for 'divine healing.' Healing was to be in answer to prayer. Dr. Dowie, as he was now styled, claimed that in ten years he laid hands on eighteen thousand sick persons, and healed most of them. He made expeditions to New Zealand, San Francisco (1888), Nebraska (1890), and in July 1890 made Chicago his headquarters, though extending his travels to Canada. In May 1893 he opened Zion's tabernacle, at Chicago, as a centre for the 'Divine Healing Association.' A move for the independent organisation of a new religious community in November 1895 led to trouble in the law courts. However, on 22 Jan. 1896 he succeeded in organising the 'Christian Catholic Church in Zion,' with a hierarchy of overseers, evangelists, deacons, and deaconesses. On 22 Feb. Dowie was made general overseer; his wife, Jane Dowie, was the only woman overseer; the wives of overseers were usually made elders; no unmarried man could be more than deacon. Zion City, on Lake Michigan, forty-two miles north of Chicago, was projected on 22 Feb. 1899; on 1 Jan. 1900, 6500 acres of land were secured, the title-deeds being held by Dowie as 'proprietor' and 'general overseer.' If Dowie is to be believed, his following had by 29 April 1900 increased from 500 to 50,000; his critics say that he never had more than half that number. The site of Zion temple was consecrated on 14 July 1900. Dowie now announced himself as 'Elijah the restorer,' otherwise 'the prophet Elijah,' and 'the third Elijah.' The gates of Zion City were opened on 15 July 1901; by 2 Aug. the first residence was ready. The religious organisation of the community, completed on 7 April 1902, was supplemented on 21 Sept. by the formation of a body of picked men, known as 'Zion restoration host.' The city was planned with great ostentation, and included both winter and summer residences for its inhabitants. Dowie distinguished himself by a showy costume of oriental appearance. On 18 Sept. 1904 he consecrated himself 'first apostle,' with authority to elect eleven others; the title of the body was now enlarged to 'Christian, Catholic, Apostolic Church in Zion,' and its purpose, frankly avowed by Dowie, was 'to smash every other church in existence.' Its members were bound to minute particulars of personal and ceremonial observance, alcohol and tobacco being prohibited. The leading motive was evidently the establishment of a sheer autocracy, wielded by Dowie. The publications of this body, including their organ, 'Leaves of Healing,' were translated into German and French, some of them into Danish, Norwegian, and Dutch, and some even into Chinese and Japanese. Dowie twice visited England, where a congregation of disciples had been formed in London; in 1903 he was not well received in London and Manchester; in 1904 some disrespectful allusions to King Edward, uttered in Australia, caused an uproar at the Zionist tabernacle in Euston road, London. In April 1906, while Dowie was in Mexico for his health, came a revolt in Zion against his sway. He was charged with having advocated polygamy in private, and was deposed by the officers of his church, who, with the concurrence of his wife and son, put Deacon Granger in possession, not only of the church property, but even of Dowie's private belongings. Dowie instituted a suit in the United States District Court for reinstatement, estimating the property at two millions sterling. The court decided that, as the property had been made by contributions to Dowie in his representative capacity, it passed to his successor in the office of general overseer. In the course of the suit it was stated that Dowie's account in Zion City bank was overdrawn more than 480,000 dollars, that he had been drawing for his personal use at the rate of 84,000 dollars a year, and had lost 1,200,000 dollars in Wall Street in the 1903–4 'slump.' Dowie was now a broken man. He was afflicted with partial paralysis, and with strange illusions as to the importance of his intervention in international politics. He died on 9 March 1907 at Shiloh House, Zion City, Illinois.

Dowie was an attractive personality, a man of fine build, though obese and bow-legged, with brilliant, sparkling eyes and a flowing white beard; a turban veiled his baldness, and his fancy dress was tasteful and picturesque. He did not shine as a speaker, being long-winded and dull. After his death a rival fanatic, Mirza Ghulam Ahmad, 'the promised Messiah,' published a pamphlet (*n.d.*, but written in April 1907), in which the fate of Dowie was treated as a 'divine judgment' on his opposition to Islâm.

[R. Harlan, J. A. Dowie, and the Christian Catholic Apostolic Church in Zion, 1906 (three portraits); The Times, 11 March 1907; Annual Register, 1907; sundry pamphlets and leaflets emanating from Zion city.]

A. G.

DOYLE, JOHN ANDREW (1844–1907), historian, born on 14 May 1844, was son of Andrew Doyle (*d.* 1888), for some time editor of the 'Morning Chronicle,' and afterwards a poor law inspector. His mother (*d.* Dec. 1896) was the youngest of three daughters of Sir John Easthope, baronet [q. v.], through whom he inherited property which made him independent of a profession. At Eton from 1853 to 1862, Doyle, after a year of private tuition, matriculated at Balliol College, Oxford, in October 1863. He graduated B.A. in 1867, with a first class in the school of literæ humaniores, but continued to reside in Oxford for several terms in order to study history. In the spring of 1869 he obtained the Arnold prize for an essay on 'The English Colonies in America before the Declaration of Independence'; and in November of the same year he was elected to a fellowship at All Souls, which he retained until his death. Though he was not a continuous resident in Oxford, he spent much time in the college, and took a large part in college affairs, helping in the framing of the statutes made by the commissioners of 1887, in the management of the college library, of which he was librarian from 1881 to 1888, and in the work of general administration.

His home was with his parents at Plasdulas in Denbighshire until 1880, when they moved to a property on which they built a house at Pendarren near Crickhowell in Breconshire. There Doyle continued to live after his parents' death. He took an active interest in local affairs, more especially in what concerned the higher education in Wales. He served as high sheriff of Breconshire in 1892–3, and was an alderman of the county council from 1889 until his last illness. He was a member of the joint committee for Breconshire under the Welsh Intermediate Education Act, 1889, of the Breconshire education committee under the Act of 1902, and of the council and agricultural committee of Aberystwyth College. He paid much attention to the development of agriculture in his own neighbourhood, which profited from his knowledge and interest in the breeding of stock and poultry.

The main literary work of his life was the 'History of the American Colonies down to the War of Independence,' an outcome of his studies for the Arnold essay. His aim was 'to describe and explain the process, by which a few scattered colonies along the Atlantic seaboard grew into that vast confederate republic, the United States of America.' After publishing in 1875 a 'Summary History of America' ('Historical Course for Schools') there followed the volumes 'The English in America' (1882), 'The Puritan Colonies' (2 vols. 1887), 'The Middle Colonies' (1907), and 'The Colonies under the House of Hanover' (1907). These books constitute the most complete authoritative account of the English colonies in America down to the conquest of Canada. The subject does not lend itself to continuous narrative or dramatic literary treatment; it is broken up by the necessary transition from the affairs of one colony to those of another. But the history is set forth in clear, vigorous style, with fulness of detail and judicial temper.

Doyle's literary work left him leisure for other interests besides those of local administration. He was a volunteer from the commencement of the volunteer movement; he was in the rifle corps as a boy at Eton and as an undergraduate at Oxford, and he took up rifle shooting with enthusiasm. He accompanied the Irish team which visited America in 1874; he shot in the Irish eight for the Elcho shield in 1875, and made the top score for the team, (147 out of a possible 180), and he was for many years adjutant of the Irish eight. He did much to encourage long-range rifle shooting at Oxford by getting up competitions with Cambridge teams, by offering and contributing to prizes, and by readiness to help with advice which was much valued. Though he was never very successful as a rifle shot, his knowledge was extensive and his judgment sound, as is apparent from an article on modern rifle shooting in the 'Quarterly Review' (1895). He was a constant attendant at Wimbledon and Bisley and was a member of the council of the National Rifle Association from 1889 to his death.

Doyle was also an authority on the breeding of dogs and of racehorses. He was one of the earliest members of the Kennel Club, founded in 1873, and was specially famous as a breeder and judge of fox-terriers. His knowledge of the pedigrees of racehorses was great and his judgment as to their breeding of recognised value. His own experiments in this line were not on a large scale, but Rosedrop, a filly foal, bred by him and sold with the rest of his stock after his death, was the winner of the Oaks in 1910. Doyle died, unmarried, at his house at Pendarren on 5 Aug. 1907.

Besides the literary work already mentioned, Doyle contributed chapters on American history to the 'Cambridge Modern History' and many memoirs of early colonists in America to this Dictionary. He also edited the 'Memoir and Correspondence (1782–1854) of Susan Ferrier' (1898) and 'Papers of Sir Charles Vaughan' (1902). A collection of his essays on various subjects (from the 'Quarterly,' the 'English Historical Review,' 'Baily's Magazine,' and the 'Kennel Encyclopædia') was published in 1911, being edited by Prof. W. P. Ker with an introduction by the present writer.

[Doyle's Essays on Various Subjects, 1911, introd.; personal knowledge; The Times, 7 Aug. 1907.] W. R. A.

DREDGE, JAMES (1840–1906), civil engineer and journalist, born in Bath on 29 July 1840, was younger son, by his wife Anne Vine, of James Dredge of that place, an engineer who designed and patented a form of suspension bridge with inclined suspension rods carrying the roadway. His elder brother, William, under whom he served articles, was also an engineer. After education at Bath grammar school Dredge spent three years (1858–61) in the office of D. K. Clark; in 1862 he entered the office of Sir John Fowler [q. v. Suppl. I], and was engaged for several years on work connected with the Metropolitan District railway. But Dredge soon gave up practical engineering for engineering journalism. From the start in Jan. 1866 of the weekly periodical 'Engineering,' which was founded by Zerah Colburn on his retirement from the editorship of the 'Engineer' in 1865, Dredge helped in illustrating and occasionally wrote for the paper. On Colburn's death in 1870 Dredge and W. H. Maw, the sub-editor, became joint editors and proprietors. Dredge helped actively in the management until May 1903, when he was disabled by paralysis.

Dredge was keenly interested in international exhibitions. He described for his journal those at Vienna (1873), Philadelphia (1876), and Paris (1878 and 1889), publishing his reports of the first and last in book form. He was also officially connected as a British commissioner with exhibitions at Chicago (1893), the transportation exhibits at which he described in a volume (1894), at Antwerp (1894), at Brussels (1897) and at Milan (1906). For services at Paris in 1889 he was appointed an officer of the Legion of Honour, and for his work at Brussels he was made C.M.G. in 1898.

As a close friend of the American engineer, Alexander Lyman Holley, he delivered an address in Chickering Hall, New York, on 2 Oct. 1890, at the installation of a bronze bust of Holley in Washington Square, New York (*Engineering*, l. 433). For the American Society of Mechanical Engineers, of which he was elected an honorary member in 1886, he prepared a special memoir of Sir Henry Bessemer [q. v. Suppl. I]. He also wrote the article on Bessemer for this Dictionary. He was elected a member of the Institution of Civil Engineers on 4 Feb. 1896, and of the Institution of Mechanical Engineers in 1874, and was a member of the council of the Society of Arts (1890–3). In 1901 he founded, as a monthly supplement to 'Engineering,' a journal called 'Traction and Transmission,' which he edited with much care until it ceased in 1904. Dredge died at Pinner on 15 August 1906. He was long a widower; an only child, Marie Louise, survived him. With Mr. Maw, Dredge published in 1872 'Modern Examples of Road and Railway Bridges.' Other of his publications, which were largely based on contributions to 'Engineering,' were: 'History of the Pennsylvania Railroad' (1879); 'Electric Illumination' (2 vols. 1882); 'Modern French Artillery' (1892), for which he received a second decoration from the French government, and 'The Thames Bridges from the Tower to the Source,' part i. (1897).

[Engineering (with portrait), 24 Aug. 1906; Min. Proc. Inst. Civ. Eng. clxvi. 382.]

W. F. S.

DRESCHFELD, JULIUS (1846–1907), physician and pathologist, born at Niederwären, near Bamberg, Bavaria, in 1846, was youngest son in the family of five sons and five daughters of Samuel Dreschfeld, a well-to-do merchant, by his wife Giedel (Elizabeth), a well-educated woman who had been acquainted with Napoleon I. The parents were orthodox Jews who were highly respected in their neighbourhood. The father lived till ninety-two and the mother till ninety-seven. After early education at Bamberg, Julius went with his mother to Manchester in 1861. Entering the Owens College, he took prizes in the English language, mathematics, and science. In 1863 he gained the Dalton chemical prize with an essay on 'The Chemical and Physical Properties of Water,' and in 1864 the Dalton junior mathematical scholarship. His medical education was received at the Manchester Royal School of Medicine (Pine Street). In 1864 he returned to Bavaria and continued his medical study at the university of Würzburg, where he graduated M.D. and acted for a time as assistant to von Bezold, professor of physiology. In 1866 he saw active service as an assistant army surgeon in the Bavarian army during the Austro-Prussian war. Whilst at Würzburg he paid special attention, under Virchow, to pathology, the branch of medical science to which he devoted himself in later years. In 1869 he returned to England, and after becoming licentiate of the Royal College of Physicians in London settled down in practice in Manchester. In 1872 he was appointed honorary physician to the Hulme Dispensary, Manchester. Next year he became an honorary assistant physician at the Manchester Royal Infirmary; in 1883, on the resignation of Sir William Roberts, [q. v. Suppl. I], honorary physician, and in due course senior honorary physician in 1899. His association with the active staff of the infirmary lasted until October 1905, when, on reaching the age limit, he became an honorary consulting physician. Even then he was granted the unique privilege of having a few beds in the infirmary allotted to him and was asked to continue his clinical teaching there.

Meanwhile Dreschfeld was pursuing the study of pathology. In 1875 he supervised the pathological section of the medical museum at Owens College and classified and catalogued the specimens. In 1876 he began to lecture in pathology, and the efficiency with which he conducted his department led in 1881 to his appointment as professor of general pathology and morbid anatomy and also of morbid histology, the first chairs in these subjects in England. His pathological laboratory was said to be the first of its kind in England. The number of Dreschfeld's students rose from three in 1873 to 110 in 1891. His lectures were models of clearness, conciseness, and completeness. Through his influence pathology and morbid anatomy was made a special subject in the medical examinations of the Victoria University and not part of the medicine and surgery papers. This reform was soon followed by other examining bodies throughout the kingdom. In 1891 Dreschfeld withdrew from his pathological chair to become professor of medicine on the resignation of Dr. John Edward Morgan, and he retained that post till death.

Dreschfeld read widely the work of German clinicians and pathologists, and tested it in his own wards or laboratories. He was near forestalling Pasteur in the latter's classical researches on hydrophobia. In 1882–3, when Pasteur had just published his researches on 'intensification' and 'diminution' of the poison of anthrax, which led to his results on 'immunisation,' Dreschfeld, in view of the presence of hydrophobia in Manchester, worked on hydrophobia poison on Pasteur's lines. He was apparently approaching success in attenuating its virulence sufficiently to use it for purposes of immunisation when the Vivisection Act stopped his work, no record of which was published. At the same time Dreschfeld was long the best-known consulting physician in the north of England, being specially in demand as a neurologist. At the Royal College of Physicians, of which he became a member in 1875 and a fellow in 1883, he delivered the Bradshawe lecture—'on diabetic coma'—in 1887. He was preparing the Lumleian lectures on a subject connected with food and digestion at his death.

Dreschfeld took a prominent part in many local medical, scientific, and philanthropic societies. A slowly progressing disease of the spinal cord from which he suffered since 1897 scarcely affected his varied industry. He died suddenly from angina pectoris on 13 June 1907. He was buried in Holy Trinity churchyard, Hoghton Street, Southport.

He was married twice: (1) in 1888 to Selina, daughter of Felix Gaspari of Berlin, by whom he had two sons and two daughters, who survive him; and (2) in 1905, to Ethel, daughter of Dr. James Harvey Lilley of Leamington, who survives him.

Dreschfeld wrote no book, but published over 120 papers in English and German journals, besides contributing admirable articles on infective endocarditis, ulcer of the stomach and duodenum, and typhoid fever to Sir Clifford Allbutt's 'System of Medicine.' He was the first to recommend the now widely used dye eosin in watery solution as a stain for animal tissues; he recorded the first post-mortem in a case of primary lateral sclerosis, previously described clinically by Erb and Charcot; he described creeping pneumonia, now known as influenzal pneumonia, alcoholic paralysis, a disease which he worked out with James Ross, and the lung complications of diabetes.

With strong and impressive Jewish features, Dreschfeld spoke English readily with a rather guttural and foreign intonation. A portrait in oils, painted posthumously by George Harcourt, hangs in the medical school of the Victoria University. The Dreschfeld memorial volume, which contains a biography, portrait, and bibliography, with scientific papers written by his former colleagues and students, was published in 1908.

A scholarship to his memory was founded in the Victoria University, to be awarded on the results of the entrance examination for medical students of the university.

[Personal knowledge; private information; Medical Chronicle, Nov. 1907 (with portrait); Dreschfeld Memorial Volume, ed. by Dr. E. M. Brockbank, 1908 (with collotype portrait); Brit. Med. Journal, 22 June 1907 (portrait); Lancet, 29 June 1907; Manchester Guardian, 14 June 1907 (portrait).]

E. M. B.

DREW, Sir THOMAS (1838–1910), architect, born at Victoria Place, Belfast, on 18 Sept. 1838, came of a good Limerick family. His father, Thomas Drew, D.D. (*d.* 1870), a militant Orange divine, was long rector of Christ Church, Belfast, subsequently becoming rector of Seaforde, co. Down, and precentor of Down cathedral. A sister Catherine (*d.* Aug. 1901) was a well-known journalist in London. Thomas was educated in his native town, and in 1854 was articled to (Sir) Charles Lanyon, C.E. [q. v.], and showed great aptitude for architectural design. In 1862 he entered the office, in Dublin, of William George Murray, R.H.A. Next year he began to write for the 'Dublin Builder,' and subsequently acted for a time as editor, introducing antiquarian features. In 1864 he was awarded a special silver medal by the Royal Institute of the Architects of Ireland for his set of measured drawings of the Portlester chapel in St. Audoen's Church, Dublin. In 1870 he was elected associate of the Royal Hibernian Academy and full member next year. In 1875 he began independent practice in North Frederick Street, Dublin, subsequently removing to Upper Sackville Street, and again to No. 6 St. Stephen's Green, a house designed by himself. His office was latterly at 22 Clare Street. In 1889 Drew was elected fellow of the Royal Institute of British Architects, and in 1892 president of the Royal Institute of Architects of Ireland. A fluent and witty speaker, he delivered from 1891 an annual lecture on St. Stephen's Day, in Christ Church cathedral, on its history and fabric. He was also instrumental in establishing in the crypt a museum of Irish antiquities. In 1895–7 he was president of the Royal Society of the Antiquaries of Ireland.

Drew was elected tenth president of the Royal Hibernian Academy on 18 Oct. 1900, on the death of Sir Thomas Farrell, the sculptor, and was knighted by the lord-lieutenant of Ireland, Earl Cadogan. In 1905 Dublin University gave him the honorary degree of LL.D.

Drew died in Dublin on 13 March 1910, and was buried in Dean's Grange cemetery, co. Dublin. He married in 1871 Adelaide Anne, daughter of William Murray, formerly architect of the board of works, Ireland, and a collateral descendant of Francis Johnston [q. v.], founder of the Royal Hibernian Academy. She survived him.

Among the chief buildings designed by Drew were the Rathmines town hall, the law library at the Four Courts, Dublin, and Clontarf presbyterian church in 1889, the Ulster bank, College Green, Dublin, in 1891, and Belfast cathedral in 1899. He was consulting architect to the three principal cathedrals of Ireland, and also restored Waterford cathedral. In ecclesiastical design he was noted for 'a robust and virile Gothic.' He built for himself a noble residence, Gortnadrew, near Monkstown, where he formed a good collection of miniatures, Waterford glass, and Georgian mantels.

[Irish Builder and Engineer, Jubilee issue, 1909, and 19 March and 2 April 1910; Belfast Newsletter, Irish Times, 14 March 1910.]

DRUMMOND, Sir GEORGE ALEXANDER (1829–1910), senator in the parliament of Canada, and president of the bank of Montreal, born in Edinburgh on 11 Oct. 1829, was son of George Drummond, a member of the city council, by his wife Margaret Pringle. Educated at the Edinburgh High School and attending the university for several terms, he emigrated in 1854 to Canada, and became manager for John Redpath & Son of Montreal, pioneers of the sugar refining industry. In 1879 he founded the Canada Sugar Refining Company, and became the first president. At the same time he interested himself in many other enterprises and was president of the Cumberland Railway Co., the Canada Jute Co., and the Intercolonial Coal Co. While president of the Montreal Board of Trade, a semi-official organisation of business men (1886–8), he induced the government to assume the cost of deepening the ship channel from Montreal to Quebec, so as to make it navigable by large ocean-going steamers. In 1882 he was elected director of the bank of Montreal, vice-president in 1887, and president in 1905, the position of highest distinction open in Canada to men engaged in finance.

Drummond began a political career in 1872, when he contested unsuccessfully the constituency of Montreal West. From 1880 until his death he was senator in the parliament of Canada. He was created K.C.M.G. in 1904 and C.V.O. in 1908.

As philanthropist, he was best known as president of the Royal Edward Institute for the prevention of tuberculosis, and he endowed the home for incurables conducted by the sisters of St. Margaret.

Deeply interested in art, Drummond was president of the Art Association of Montreal 1896–9, and was a discriminating and successful collector of pictures. His collection includes first-rate examples of the work of Constable, Corot, Cuyp, Daubigny, Franz Hals, De Hooge, Israels, Jacob Maris, Matthew Maris, William Maris, Mauve, Troyon, Vandyck, Velasquez, Watts, Lorraine, and Rubens. He was owner of five pictures by Turner, namely, 'Port of Ruysdael,' 'Sun of Venice,' 'Zurich,' 'Dudley Castle,' and 'Chepstow.' The collection is maintained intact in Montreal by his widow, and is easily accessible by visitors.

In later years he spent a large part of his time at Huntleywood, his country place near Montreal, where he was a successful breeder of cattle and sheep. He was devoted to golf, and was president of the Canadian Golf Association. He died in Montreal on 2 Feb. 1910, and was buried in Mount Royal cemetery.

Sir George Drummond was twice married: (1) in 1857 to Helen, daughter of John Redpath of Montreal, having by her two daughters and five sons; and (2) in 1884 to Grace Julia, daughter of A. D. Parker, of Montreal, having by her two sons.

Portraits by Sir George Reid, Troubetski, and Robert Harris are in possession of the family; a fourth, by Joliffe Walker, is owned by the Mount Royal Club, Montreal.

[Private information.] A. M.

DRUMMOND, WILLIAM HENRY (1854–1907), Canadian physician and poet, born on 13 April 1854 at Currawn, co. Leitrim, Ireland, was eldest of four sons of George Drummond, an officer in the Royal Irish constabulary, who was then stationed at Currawn. His mother was Elizabeth Morris Soden. In 1856 the family moved to Tawley, co. Donegal, where Paddy McNulty, one of the hereditary scholars of Ireland, gave the boy the rudiments of his education, and on the river Duff he first learned to cast a fly.

In 1865 the family went out to Canada, where the father soon died, and the mother and her four children were reduced to the slenderest resources. After a few terms at a private school in Montreal, William Drummond studied telegraphy, and by 1869 was an operator at the village of Bord-à-Plouffe on the Rivière des Prairies. Here he first came in contact with the *habitant* and *voyageur* French-speaking backwoodsmen, whose simple tales and legends he was later to turn to literary account.

In 1876 Drummond, having saved sufficient money, resumed his studies, first in the High School, Montreal, then at McGill University, and finally at Bishop's College, Montreal, where he graduated in medicine in 1884. He practised his profession for two years at the village of Stornoway, near Lake Megantic, and then bought a practice at Knowlton in the township of Brome. Towards the close of 1888 he returned to Montreal. There he became professor of medical jurisprudence at Bishop's College in 1895, and soon made a literary reputation. He received the hon. degree of LL.D. from Toronto in 1902 and of D.C.L. from Bishop's College, Lennoxville in 1905. In the summer of 1905 Drummond and his brothers acquired property in the silver region of Cobalt, in northern Ontario, and most of his time until his death was spent in superintending the valuable Drummond mines. He acted as vice-president of the company. In the spring of 1907 he hurried from Montreal to his camp on hearing that small-pox had broken out there. Within a week of his arrival he died at Cobalt of cerebral hæmorrhage, on 6 April. He was buried in Mount Royal cemetery, Montreal.

In 1894 he married May Isabel Harvey of Savanna la Mar, Jamaica. Of four children, a son, Charles Barclay, and a daughter, Moira, survive.

It was after his marriage in 1894 that Drummond transcribed for publication the broken *patois* verse in which he had embodied his memories of the *habitant*, and which raised the dialect to the level of a literary language of unspoiled freshness and humour. 'The Wreck of the Julie Plante,' composed at Bord-à-Plouffe, the first piece of his to circulate widely, showed something of his whimsical fancy and droll powers of exaggeration. His mingled tenderness and mirth were revealed later. Three collections of Drummond's verse appeared in his lifetime: 'The Habitant' (1897); 'Johnny Courteau' (1901); and 'The Voyageur' (1905). There appeared posthumously 'The Great Fight' (1908), with a memoir by his wife. All these volumes have been many times reprinted. In a preface to 'The Habitant' (1897) Louis Fréchette [q. v. Suppl. II] justly and generously transferred to Drummond a phrase which had been bestowed upon himself by Longfellow in 1863—'the pathfinder of a new land of song.' Few dialect poets have succeeded in equal measure with Drummond in capturing at once the salient and concealed characteristics of the persons whom they portray. Drummond's *habitant*, although using an alien speech, faithfully presents a highly interesting racial type. His humorous exaggeration of eccentricities never passes into unkindly caricature. Drummond had, too, at his command an admirable faculty of telling a story.

[Mrs. Drummond's memoir prefixed to The Great Fight, 1908; information from Drummond's brother, Mr. George E. Drummond.]

P. E.

DRURY-LOWE, Sir DRURY CURZON (1830–1908), lieutenant-general, born at Locko Park, Denby, Derbyshire, on 3 Jan. 1830, was second of the five sons (in a family of eight children) of William Drury-Lowe (1802–1877) of Locko Park, by his wife Caroline Esther (*d.* 1886), third daughter of Nathaniel Curzon, second Baron Scarsdale. His father, son of Robert Holden of Darley Abbey, Derbyshire, by his wife Mary Anne, only daughter and heiress of William Drury-Lowe (*d.* 1827), assumed the surname of Drury-Lowe in 1849 on his maternal grandmother's death. Educated privately and at Corpus Christi College, Oxford, Drury-Lowe graduated B.A. in 1853. Resolving on a military career at a comparatively late age, he obtained a commission in the 17th lancers (the Duke of Cambridge's own, 'Death or Glory Boys') on 28 July 1854, and was promoted lieutenant on 7 Nov. 1854, and captain on 19 Nov. 1856. With the 17th lancers he was associated throughout his active service. He accompanied his regiment to the Crimea (18 June 1855), and took part in the battle of the Tchernaya, and the siege and fall of Sevastopol, receiving the medal with clasp and the Turkish medal. Ordered to Bombay, he took part in the concluding episodes of the war of the Indian Mutiny, including the pursuit of the rebel force under Tantia Topi during 1858 and the action of Zerapore, when Evelyn Wood, who had just exchanged into the 17th lancers, was for the first time in action with him. Both won distinction. Drury-Lowe received the medal with clasp for Central India, having been mentioned in despatches (*Lond. Gaz.* 17 July 1860). He became major on 10 June 1862, lieut.-colonel on 15 June 1866, and colonel on 15 June 1871. In the Zulu war of 1879–1880 he commanded the 17th lancers and the cavalry of the second division, and was present at the battle of Ulundi, where he was slightly wounded, being awarded the medal and clasp, and being made C.B. on 27 Nov. 1879 (*Lond. Gaz.* 21 Aug. 1879). He returned to South Africa to engage under Sir Evelyn Wood in the Transvaal campaign of 1881, serving in command of the cavalry brigade; but the operations were early suspended and peace followed.

It was in the Egyptian war of 1882 that Drury-Lowe, who became major-general on 9 Dec. 1881, made his reputation as a commander of cavalry in the field. He was in action throughout the campaign in command of a cavalry brigade, and afterwards of the cavalry division. After taking part in the action at Tel-el-Maskhuta, and the capture of Mahsama (25 Aug. 1882), he made a cavalry charge by moonlight at the first action of Kassasin (28 Aug.), which effectually assured the British forces their victory under Sir Gerald Graham [q. v. Suppl. I]. In the night march preceding the battle of Tel-el-Kebir and during the battle itself, Drury-Lowe's energy proved most useful. From the battle-field he pursued the enemy to Belbeis, and thence pushed on and occupied Cairo, where he received the surrender of Arabi Pasha (Sir Charles M. Watson, *Life of Sir Charles Wilson*, 1909, p. 208). To Drury-Lowe's rapid movement was due the preservation of Cairo from destruction. Four times mentioned in despatches (*Lond. Gaz.* 8 Sept., 19 Sept., 6 Oct., and 2 Nov. 1882), he was afterwards thanked by both houses of parliament, received the second class of the Osmanieh, a medal with clasp, and the bronze star. On 18 Nov. 1882 he was made K.C.B.

In 1884 Drury-Lowe was put in command of a cavalry brigade at Aldershot, and from 1885 to 1890 was inspector-general of cavalry there. He made no innovations on the routine of his office and at Aldershot added little to his reputation. Promoted lieutenant-general on 1 April 1890, he was during 1890–1 inspector-general of cavalry at the Horse Guards. On 24 Jan. 1892 he was appointed colonel of the 17th lancers, his old regiment. He received the reward for distinguished service and on 25 May 1895 was nominated G.C.B. On his retirement he resided at Key Dell, Horndean, Hampshire. He died at Bath on 6 April 1908 and was buried at Denby, Derbyshire. He married in 1876 Elizabeth, daughter of Thomas Smith, but had no issue. His portrait was painted by Henry Tanworth Wells in 1892.

[The Times, 7 April 1908; Burke's Peerage; Burke's Landed Gentry; Walford's County Families; Hart's and Official Army Lists; F. E. Colenso, History of the Zulu War, 1880, p. 438; R. H. Vetch, Life of Sir Gerald Graham, 1901; Sir Frederick Maurice, The Campaign of 1882 in Egypt, 1908; Celebrities of the Army, by Commander Chas. N. Robinson, R.N.] H. M. V.

DRYSDALE, LEARMONT (1866–1909), musical composer, born in Edinburgh on 3 Oct. 1866, was younger son of Andrew Drysdale, and was descended on his mother's side from the Border poet, Thomas the Rhymer. Educated at the High School, Edinburgh, he afterwards studied architecture, but abandoned it in 1888 and entered the Royal Academy of Music, London, where he remained until 1892. He had a brilliant career as a student, winning in 1891 the academy's highest honour in composition, the Charles Lucas medal, with his 'Overture to a Comedy.' During this period he appeared frequently as a solo pianist at the students' concerts, and wrote several works which elicited high praise, notably an orchestral ballade, 'The Spirit of the Glen' (1889), an orchestral prelude, 'Thomas the Rhymer' (1890), and a dramatic scena for soprano and orchestra, 'The Lay of Thora' (1891). In 1891 a picturesque overture, 'Tam o' Shanter,' written within a week, gained the prize of thirty guineas offered by the Glasgow Society of Musicians for the best concert overture. This was produced, with marked success, by (Sir) August Manns, first in Glasgow, and afterwards at the Crystal Palace. In 1894 a dramatic cantata, 'The Kelpie,' was performed in Edinburgh; and in the same year, in London, the fine overture 'Herondean,' exemplifying anew 'his command of flowing melody, skilful and effective workmanship, and highly coloured instrumentation' (Kuhe). A mystic musical play, 'The Plague,' created a strong impression when produced by Mr. Forbes-Robertson at Edinburgh in 1896. Two years later, a romantic light opera, 'The Red Spider,' libretto by Mr. Baring Gould, was enthusiastically received when first produced at Plymouth, and toured the provinces for twenty weeks. His 'Border Romance,' an orchestral poem, was given at Queen's Hall, London, in 1904. That year he became theoretical master at the Athenæum

School of Music, Glasgow; later he was conductor of the Glasgow Select Choir, for which he wrote, among other things, the choral ballade, 'Barbara Allan.' When Professor Gilbert Murray's 'Hippolytus' was staged at Glasgow in 1905 he composed special music for it of great beauty and appropriateness. This was followed by a dramatic cantata, 'Tamlane,' a sublimation of the old Border spirit. His original settings of Scots lyrics and his arrangements of folk-songs show a true insight into the spirit of national song. Many arrangements are included in the 'Dunedin Collection of Scots Songs' (1908), which he edited. In 1907 he collaborated with the duke of Argyll in 'The Scottish Tribute to France,' not as yet (1912) performed, for chorus and orchestra; and at his death he had practically finished a grand opera provisionally entitled 'Fionn and Tera,' to a libretto by the duke; the orchestration was completed by Mr. David Stephen. Many other works were left in MS., including 'The Oracle' and other light operas, a romantic opera, 'Flora Macdonald,' several cantatas, orchestral, piano and violin pieces, and songs. He died prematurely, unmarried, at Edinburgh on 18 June 1909. Imbued with the national sentiment, he showed much originality, versatility, and inspiration.

[Private information; personal knowledge; Musical Herald, July 1909 (with portrait); Ernest Kuhe in Scottish Musical Monthly, July 1894 (with portrait).] J. C. H.

DU CANE, Sir EDMUND FREDERICK (1830–1903), major-general, R.E., and prison reformer, born at Colchester, Essex, on 23 March 1830, was youngest child in a family of four sons and two daughters of Major Richard Du Cane (1788–1832), 20th light dragoons, of Huguenot descent, who served in the Peninsular war. His mother was Eliza, daughter of Thomas Ware of Woodfort, Mallow, co. Cork.

Du Cane, after education at the grammar school, Dedham, Essex, until 1843, and at a private coaching establishment at Wimbledon (1843–6), entered the Royal Military Academy at Woolwich in November 1846, and passed out at the head of his batch at the end of 1848, having taken first place in mathematics and fortification, and receiving a commission as second lieutenant in the royal engineers on 19 Dec. 1848. He joined at Chatham, and in December 1850 was posted to a company of royal sappers and miners commanded by Captain Henry Charles Cunliffe-Owen [q. v.] at Woolwich. Du Cane was assistant superintendent of the foreign side of the International Exhibition of 1851 and assistant secretary to the juries of awards, and with the rest of the staff was the guest in Paris of the prince president, Louis Napoleon. From 1851 to 1856 Du Cane was employed in organising convict labour on public works in the colony of Swan River or Western Australia, which was then first devoted to penal purposes under the command of Captain (afterwards Sir) Edmund Henderson [q. v. Suppl. I]. Promoted first lieutenant on 17 Feb. 1854, he was stationed at Guildford in charge of the works in the eastern district of the colony. He was made a magistrate of the colony and a visiting magistrate of convict stations. Although recalled early in 1856 by the requirements of the Crimean war, Du Cane arrived home on 21 June to find the war at an end, and joined for duty at the war office, under the inspector-general of fortification, in August 1856. He was soon employed upon the designs and estimates for the new defences proposed for the dockyards and naval bases of the United Kingdom. Promoted second captain on 16 April 1858, he during the next five years designed most of the new land works at Dover, and the chain of land forts at Plymouth extending for five miles from Fort Staddon, in the east, across the Plym, by Laira, to Ernsettle on the Tamar.

In 1863, on the recommendation of Lieutenant-colonel Henderson, who had become chairman of the board of directors of convict prisons, Du Cane was appointed director of convict prisons, as well as an inspector of military prisons. He administered the system of penal servitude as it was reformed by the Prisons Act of 1865, and made the arrangements for additional prison accommodation consequent on the abolition of transportation in 1867. In 1869 Du Cane succeeded Henderson as chairman of the board of directors of convict prisons, surveyor-general of prisons, and inspector-general of military prisons. On 5 Feb. 1864 he was promoted first captain in his corps; on 5 July 1872 major; on 11 Dec. 1873 lieut.-colonel; and four years later brevet-colonel. He was placed on the supernumerary list in August 1877.

The charge of the colonial convict prisons was transferred to Du Cane in 1869. A strong advocate of the devotion of prison labour to works of national utility, on which he read a paper before the Society of Arts in 1871, Du Cane provided for the carrying out by convicts of the breakwater and works of defence at Portland, the docks at Portsmouth and Chatham, and additional prison accommodation. At the International Prison Congress in London in 1872 Du Cane fully described the British system of penal servitude.

Du Cane's main triumph as prison administrator was the reorganisation of county and borough prisons, which had long been mismanaged by some 2000 local justices and largely maintained by local funds. Du Cane in 1873 submitted to the secretary of state a comprehensive scheme for the transfer to the government of all local prisons and the whole cost of their maintenance. The much needed reform was legalised by the Prison Act of July 1877, when Du Cane, who had been made C.B., civil division, on 27 March 1873, was promoted K.C.B., civil division, and became chairman of the (three) prison commissioners under the new act to reorganise and administer the county and borough prisons. On 1 April 1878 these prisons came under government control. Their number was soon reduced by one-half, the rules made uniform, the progressive system of discipline adopted, the staff co-ordinated into a single service with a regular system of promotion, structural and other improvements introduced, and the cost of maintenance largely reduced. Useful employment of prisoners was developed and the discharged prisoner was assisted to earn his living honestly.

Du Cane also successfully inaugurated the registration of criminals. In 1877 he produced the first 'Black Book' list, printed by convict labour, of over 12,000 habitual criminals with their aliases and full descriptions. A register followed of criminals having distinctive marks on their bodies. Du Cane's suggestion to Sir Francis Galton that types of feature in different kinds of criminality were worthy of scientific study first prompted Galton to attempt composite portraiture (*Memories of My Life*, 1908). Du Cane encouraged the use of Galton's finger-print system in the identification of criminals. He retired from the army with the honorary rank of major-general on 31 Dec. 1887, and from the civil service on 23 March 1895. An accomplished man of wide interests, embracing archæology, architecture, and Napoleonic literature, he was a clever painter in water-colours. A set of his sketches of Peninsular battlefields was exhibited at the Royal Military Exhibition at Chelsea in 1890. He died at his residence, 10 Portman Square, London, on 7 June 1903, and was buried in Great Braxted churchyard, Essex.

He was twice married: (1) at St. John's Church, Fremantle, Western Australia, on 18 July 1855, to Mary Dorothea, daughter of Lieut.-colonel John Molloy, a Peninsula and Waterloo veteran of the rifle brigade, of Fairlawn, The Vasse, Western Australia; she died on 13 May 1881; (2) at St. Margaret's, Westminster, on 2 Jan. 1883, to Florence Victoria, widow of Colonel M. J. Grimston, of Grimston Garth and Kilnwick, Yorkshire, and daughter of Colonel Hardress Robert Saunderson. By his first wife Sir Edmund had a family of three sons and five daughters. A crayon drawing, done in 1851, is in Lady Du Cane's possession at 10 Portman Square.

Sir Edmund contributed largely to periodical literature, chiefly on penology, and frequently wrote to 'The Times' on military and other subjects. To the 'Royal Engineers Journal' he sent memoirs of several of his brother officers. In 1885 he published in Macmillan's 'Citizen' series 'The Punishment and Prevention of Crime,' an historical sketch of British prisons and the treatment of crime up to that date.

[War Office Records; R.E. Records; Men and Women of the Time, 1899; Biograph, 1883; The Times, 8 June 1903; Porter, History of the Royal Engineers, 1889, 2 vols.; private information.] R. H. V.

DUCKETT, Sir GEORGE FLOYD, third baronet (1811–1902), archæologist and lexicographer, born at 15 Spring Gardens, Westminster, on 27 March 1811, was eldest child of Sir George Duckett, second baronet (1777–1856), M.P. for Lymington 1807–12, by his first wife, Isabella (1781–1844), daughter of Stainbank Floyd of Barnard Castle, co. Durham. His grandfather Sir George Jackson, first baronet (1725–1822) [q. v.], assumed in 1797 the surname of Duckett, having married the heiress of the Duckett family. After attending private schools at Putney and Wimbledon Common, young Duckett was at Harrow from 1820 to 1823, when he was placed with a private tutor in Bedfordshire. In 1827–8 he gained a thorough knowledge of German at Gotha and Dresden. Matriculating on 13 Dec. 1828 as a gentleman commoner of Christ Church, Oxford, he devoted himself chiefly to hunting, and left the university without a degree.

Joining the West Essex yeomanry, Duckett on 4 May 1832 was commissioned a sub-lieutenant in the second regiment of life guards. On his coming of age in 1832, his father, whose means had been large, was ruined by wild speculations. Faced by beggary, Duckett began his economy by exchanging from the guards in 1834 into the 15th hussars, and subsequently into the 82nd regiment, in which he remained until 1839. Having obtained his company, he exchanged in 1839 into the 87th fusiliers, then on service at the Isle of France, and joined its depôt in Dublin.

Meanwhile Duckett concentrated himself on the compilation of a 'Technological Military Dictionary' in German, English, and French. To make the work accurate, he obtained leave to visit the arsenals of Woolwich, Paris, Brussels, and Berlin. To complete his task he retired on half-pay. The important work was published in the autumn of 1848, and its merits were recognised abroad. He received gold medals from the emperor of Austria in 1850, Frederick William IV of Prussia, and Napoleon III. At home the book was for the most part ignored. On resuming his commission on full pay he was placed at the bottom of the captains' list of the reserve battalion of the 69th regiment, and thirty-two years later, in 1890, he was awarded 200*l.* (DUCKETT, *Anecdotal Reminiscences*, p. 131).

On the death of his father on 15 June 1856 he became third baronet. He abandoned interest in military matters, and thenceforth devoted himself to archæological and genealogical studies, to which he brought immense industry but small judgment or historical scholarship. In 1869 he published his exhaustive 'Duchetiana, or Historical and Genealogical Memoirs of the Family of Duket, from the Conquest to the Present Time' (enlarged edit. 1874). Here he claimed descent from Gundrada de Warenne [q. v.] and a title to a dormant barony of Wyndesore. In 'Observations on the Parentage of Gundreda' (1877; Lewes, 1878) he vainly sought to confirm his belief that Gundrada was daughter of William the Conqueror. Pursuing his research, he investigated in the Bibliothèque Nationale at Paris the history of the first Cluniac monastery in England at Lewes in 1077, which Gundrada was reputed to have founded. He privately printed 'Record Evidences among the Archives of the Ancient Abbey of Cluni from 1077 to 1534' (1886); and a monumental compilation, 'Monasticon Cluniacense Anglicanum, Charters and Records among the Archives of the Ancient Abbey of Cluni from 1077 to 1534' (2 vols., privately printed, Lewes, 1888). There followed 'Visitations of English Cluniac Foundations, 1262–1279' (1890, 4to); and 'Visitations and Chapters-General of the Order of Cluni' (1893). For the 'Monasticon Cluniacense' he received in 1888 the decoration of an officer of public instruction in France. Duckett continued his literary pursuits until 1895, when he published his 'Anecdotal Reminiscences of an Octo-nonagenarian.' Subsequently blindness put an end to his literary activities. He was elected F.S.A. on 11 Feb. 1869. He died at Cleeve House, Cleeve, Somerset, on 13 May 1902, at the advanced age of ninety-one, and was buried in the cemetery at Wells.

He was the last of the ancient line of the Dukets. He married on 21 June 1845 Isabella (*d.* 31 Dec. 1901), daughter of Lieutenant-general Sir Lionel Smith, first baronet [q. v.], but had no issue, and the baronetcy became extinct.

Besides the works already mentioned, and numerous contributions to local archæological societies, Duckett's published works include: 1. 'The Marches of Wales' (Arch. Cambrensis), 1881. 2. 'Manorbeer Castle and its Early Owners' (Arch. Cambrensis), 1882. 3. 'Brief Notices on Monastic and Ecclesiastical Costume,' 1890. He edited 'Original Letters of the Duke of Monmouth,' in the Bodleian Library (Camden Soc.), 1879; 'The Sheriffs of Westmorland' (Cumb. and Westm. Ant. and Arch. Soc.), 1879; 'Evidences of Harewood Castle in Yorkshire' (Yorksh. Arch. Jo.), 1881; 'Description of the County of Westmorland, by Sir Daniel Fleming of Rydal, A.D. 1671' (Cumb. and Westm. Ant. and Arch. Soc.), 1882; 'Penal Laws and Test Act under James II' (original returns to the commissioners' inquiries of 1687–8), 3 vols., privately printed, 1882–3; 'Naval Commissioners, from 12 Charles II to 1 George III, 1660–1760,' 1890; 'Evidences of the Barri Family of Manorbeer and Olethan' (Arch. Cambrensis), 1891. He also translated from the German 'Mariolatry, Worship of the Virgin; the Doctrine refuted by Scripture' (1892).

Authorities cited; Burke's Peerage and Baronetage; The Times, 16 May 1902; Standard, 14 May 1902; Athenæum, 31 Aug. 1895, pp. 285–6; Brit. Mus. Cat.; private information.] C. W.

DUDGEON, ROBERT ELLIS (1820–1904), homœopath, born at Leith on 17 March 1820, was younger son of a timber merchant and shipowner in that town. After attending a private school he received his medical education at Edinburgh, partly in the university and partly in the extra-academical medical school. Having received the licence of the Royal College of Surgeons of Edinburgh in 1839, he attended the lectures of Velpeau, Andral, Louis, and others in Paris, graduated M.D. at Edinburgh on 1 Aug. 1841, and spent a semester at Vienna under Skoda, Rokitansky, Hebra, and Jaeger. At Vienna his fellow students John Drysdale and Rutherfurd Russell were attending the homœopathic practice which, invented by Hahnemann some forty years before, was then at its height in the city. Dudgeon was not at the time attracted by Hahnemann's system. From Vienna he went to Berlin to study diseases of the eye under Juengken, of the ear under Kramer, and organic chemistry under Simon; finally he passed to Dublin to benefit by the instruction of Graves, Stokes, Corrigan, and Marsh. Having started practice in Liverpool, in 1843 he was there persuaded by Drysdale to study homœopathy. The 'British Journal of Homœopathy' was first issued in this year, and Dudgeon translated for it German articles. After a second sojourn in Vienna to follow the homœopathic practice of Fleischmann in the Gumpendorf hospital, he began to practise in London in 1845. He was editor of the 'British Journal of Homœopathy' conjointly with Drysdale and Russell from 1846 until 1884, when the Journal ceased. In 1847 he published the 'Homœopathic Treatment and Prevention of Asiatic Cholera,' and devoted himself during the next three years to making a good English translation of Hahnemann's writings, of which the 'Organon' appeared in 1849 and the 'Materia Medica Pura' in 1880. In 1850 he helped to found the Hahnemann Hospital and school of homœopathy in Bloomsbury Square, with which was connected the Hahnemann Medical Society. Dudgeon lectured in the school on the theory and practice of homœopathy and published his lectures in 1854. In 1869 he was for a short time assistant physician to the homœopathic hospital. He was secretary of the British Homœopathic Society in 1848, vice-president in 1874-5, and president in 1878 and 1890. Although elected president of the International Homœopathic Congress which met in Atlantic City in 1904 he did not attend owing to ill-health.

In 1870–1 he was much interested in the study of optics, writing notes on the 'Dioptrics of Vision' (1871). He invented spectacles for use under water. The method adopted was to enclose a lens of air hermetically sealed between two concave glasses, the curvature being so arranged as to correct the refraction of the water. Original but unaccepted views which he held on the mechanism of accommodation of the eye, and described to the International Medical Congress were published in 'The Human Eye: its Optical Construction popularly explained' in 1878.

In 1878 he obtained a Pond's sphygmograph, and with the help of a young watchmaker from the Black Forest he made the pocket instrument for registering the pulse which is now known by his name. He published an account of it in 'The Sphygmograph: its history and use as an aid to diagnosis in ordinary practice' (1882).

He died at 22 Carlton Hill, N.W., on 8 Sept. 1904 and was cremated at Golder's Hill, his ashes being buried in Willesden cemetery. Dudgeon was twice married, and had a family of two sons and three daughters.

Dudgeon edited several volumes for the Hahnemann Publications Society of Liverpool, amongst others the 'Pathogenetic Cyclopædia' (1850). Besides the works mentioned, he published 'Lectures on the Theory and Practice of Homœopathy' (1854), and 'The Influence of Homœopathy on General Medicine since the Death of Hahnemann' (1874).

He also translated Professor Fuchs' 'Causes and Prevention of Blindness' (1885) and François Sarcey's 'Mind Your Eyes' (1886), and wrote on 'The Swimming Baths of London' (1870). In 1890, at the age of seventy, he published 'On the Prolongation of Life,' which reached a second edition.

[Monthly Homœopathic Rev. 1904, xlviii. 577 (with portrait); Journal Brit. Homœopathic Soc. (1905) xiii. 55; Homœopathic World, 1904, pp. 433, 464 (with portrait).]

D'A. P.

DUFF, Sir **MOUNTSTUART ELPHINSTONE GRANT** (1829–1906), governor of Madras. [See Grant Duff.]

DUFFERIN AND AVA, first Marquis of. [See Blackwood, Frederick Temple Hamilton-Temple, 1826–1902.]

DUFFY, Sir **CHARLES GAVAN** (1816–1903), Irish nationalist and colonial politician, born in the town of Monaghan on 12 April 1816, was son of John Duffy, a shopkeeper, by his wife, who was the daughter of a gentleman farmer, Patrick Gavan. Save for a few months at a presbyterian academy in Monaghan, where there were then no catholic schools, he was self-educated; but a passion for reading was born in him; he devoured all the books on which he could lay his youthful hands, and early developed a talent for journalism. When he was nearly eighteen he began to contribute to the 'Northern Herald,' a Belfast paper, whose founder, Charles Hamilton Teeling, an old United Irishman, had visited Monaghan for the purpose of promoting the interests of the journal. The 'Herald' urged the union of Irishmen of all creeds and classes in the cause of Irish nationality. Among the contributors was Thomas O'Hagan [q. v.], Duffy's lifelong friend, afterwards the first catholic lord chancellor of Ireland since the revolution. In 1836 Duffy left Monaghan for Dublin, where he joined the staff of the 'Morning Register' (founded by the Catholic Association); of this journal he finally became sub-editor. About the same time he became Dublin correspondent of Whittle Harvey's 'True Son' and wrote occasional articles for the 'Pilot.' In 1839 he left Dublin to edit the 'Vindicator,' a bi-weekly newspaper established in the interests of the northern catholics in Belfast. In the same year, while still editing the 'Vindicator,' he entered as a law student at the King's Inns, Dublin. In the autumn of 1841, while keeping his term in Dublin, he first met John Blake Dillon [q. v.], then a writer on the 'Morning Register.' Dillon introduced him to Thomas Davis [q. v.], also a writer on the 'Morning Register,' and the friendship which ultimately bound the three men together was soon cemented. Duffy suggested to his friends a new weekly journal, which should impart to the people sound political education based on historical study. The result was the 'Nation,' of which Duffy was proprietor and editor. The first number appeared on 15 Oct. 1842. Its motto was 'to create and foster public opinion in Ireland and to make it racy of the soil.' The creed of the Young Irelanders (as the writers of the 'Nation' came to be called) was to unite all Irishmen for the purpose of re-establishing the Irish parliament, by force of arms, if necessary.

Duffy gathered round him a brilliant staff, including Thomas Davis, Clarence Mangan, Denis Florence McCarthy, John Cornelius O'Callaghan, John Mitchell, John O'Hagan, and Lady Wilde. The articles in both verse and prose revealed a fervent, well-informed, and high-minded patriotism which captivated Ireland. They recalled memories which made the people proud of their country and filled them with detestation of the power which had destroyed its freedom. Liberal and tory publicists in both islands recognised that a new force had entered politics. Lecky wrote later: 'What the "Nation" was when Gavan Duffy edited it, when Davis, McCarthy, and their brilliant associates contributed to it, and when its columns maintained with unqualified zeal the cause of liberty and nationality in every land, Irishmen can never forget. Seldom has any journal of the kind exhibited a more splendid combination of eloquence, of poetry, and of reasoning.' The Young Irelanders supplemented the newspaper propaganda by publishing books in prose and verse, to instruct and inspire the people. 'Their first experiment' (made in 1843), Duffy tells us, 'was a little sixpenny brochure printed at the "Nation" office, and sold by the "Nation" agents—a collection of the songs and ballads, published during three months, entitled "The Spirit of the Nation." Its success was a marvel. The conservatives set the example of applauding its ability, while they condemned its aim and spirit.' The next scheme was a collection of the speeches of the orators of Ireland. But the speeches of Curran, edited with a brilliant memoir by Davis, alone appeared. To the same series belonged popular editions of Macgeoghegan's 'History of Ireland' (1844), MacNevin's 'Lives and Trials of A. H. Rowan and other Eminent Irishmen' (1846), Barrington's 'Rise and Fall of the Irish Nation' (1853), and Forman's 'Defence of the Courage, Honour and Loyalty of the Irish,' edited by Davis. Duffy also produced 'The Library of Ireland,' a series of shilling volumes of biography, poetry, and criticism, which included among other anthologies Duffy's 'Ballad Poetry of Ireland' (1845, fifty editions). No effort was spared to base political agitation on historical knowledge.

In the beginning the Young Irelanders were the devoted adherents of O'Connell. When in January 1844 O'Connell was indicted for seditious conspiracy, Duffy (with others) stood by his side in the dock. The prisoner's conviction by a packed jury on 30 May 1844 was quashed by the House of Lords [see O'Connell, Daniel]. Afterwards the relations between O'Connell and the Young Irelanders became strained. In 1844 the leader showed some disposition to substitute a federal plan for simple repeal of the union. Duffy attacked the plan in the 'Nation,' and O'Connell ultimately returned to repeal; but the controversy left some bitterness behind. In 1845 there were more serious causes of difference. O'Connell resisted, and the Young Irelanders approved, Peel's proposed new Queen's University in Ireland with affiliated colleges in Galway, Cork, and Belfast, which were to be open to both catholics and protestants.

In Michaelmas term, 1845, Duffy was called to the Irish bar, but he never practised. In the same year he made the acquaintance of Thomas Carlyle, to whom he was introduced by Frederick Lucas [q. v.]. An intimacy sprang up between them which lasted until Carlyle's death. Carlyle took some interest in the doings of the 'Young Ireland' party. He welcomed Duffy's gift of copies of the 'Nation,' and expressed sympathy with the cry 'Justice to Ireland—justice to all lands, and to Ireland first as the land that needs it most.' In 1846 Carlyle visited Ireland and spent some time with Duffy and his friends.

In the same year there was a final breach between O'Connell and the young men. O'Connell supported a resolution adopted by the Repeal Association to the effect that moral force furnished a sufficient remedy for public wrong in all times and in all countries, and that physical force must be abhorred. The young men declined to admit that physical force could never be justifiable. Open war followed between O'Connell and the 'Nation.'

Duffy and his associates formed a new association—the Irish Confederation—which disclaimed alliances with English parties and repelled O'Connell's moral force theory. In January 1847 the first meeting of the confederation was held. O'Connell's death in May and the outbreak of the famine caused fresh divisions in the national ranks. Mitchel, assistant editor of the 'Nation,' accepted Fenton Lalor's view that the direct demand for repeal of the union should be suspended, and that there should be a general strike against the payment of rent. Duffy allowed discussion of the proposal in the journal; but he declined to adopt it as the policy of the party. Mitchel then, towards the end of 1847, left the 'Nation' and started a new weekly paper, the 'United Irishman.' A report prepared by Duffy for the confederation in 1848 suggested that an independent Irish party should be sent to the English House of Commons—independent of English parties and governments, and pledged not to accept office from any government until repeal was conceded. The report was adopted by 317 to 188. Mitchel, who had no faith in a parliamentary agitation, opposed it, and leaving the confederation preached insurrection in the 'United Irishman.' The revolution in Paris in February 1848 inspired the leaders of the confederation with revolutionary projects, to which Duffy in the 'Nation' lent support. Many of his associates were at once arrested.

The confederates began preparations for a rising in August. But before anything effective was done the government intervened. On 9 July Duffy was arrested. On the 28th the 'Nation' was suppressed. Between July 1848 and April 1849 Duffy was arraigned five times. On three occasions the trial was postponed for one reason or another. On two occasions the juries disagreed. Finally in April 1849 Duffy was discharged.

On regaining freedom he revived the 'Nation,' which finally ceased many years later. Suspending the demand for repeal, which at the moment he believed to be inopportune, he flung himself heart and soul into the question of land reform. The evictions and calamities following famine and pestilence had made land reform urgent. The Irish Tenant League, which Duffy joined, was now founded to secure reform on the basis of parliamentary enforcement of the three F's—fixity of tenure, fair rents, and free sale. In the summer of 1849 Carlyle again visited Ireland, and he and Duffy spent some weeks together travelling throughout the country. At the general election of 1852 Duffy was elected parliamentary representative of New Ross, and the party of independent opposition (which he had proposed in 1847) was formed to oppose every government which would not pledge themselves to grant the demands of the Tenant League. This party consisted of some fifty members. In November 1852 Lord Derby's government introduced a land bill to secure to Irish tenants on eviction, in accordance with the principles of the Tenant League, compensation for improvements—prospective and retrospective—made by them in the land. The bill passed the House of Commons in 1853 and 1854, but in both years failed to pass the House of Lords. In 1855 the cause of the Irish tenants, and indeed of Ireland generally, seemed to Duffy more hopeless than ever. Broken in health and spirit, he published in 1855 a farewell address to his constituency, declaring that he had resolved to retire from parliament, as it was no longer possible to accomplish the task for which he had solicited their votes.

On 8 Oct. 1855 he sailed for Australia, where he was received with great enthusiasm by his fellow-countrymen, and began life anew as a barrister in Melbourne. But he soon glided into politics, and his admirers in the colony presented him with property valued at 5000*l.* to give him a qualification to enter the parliament of Victoria. In 1856 he became a member of the House of Assembly, quickly distinguished himself, and in 1857 was made minister of land and works, but resigned office in 1859 owing to a difference with the chief secretary, Mr. O'Shanassy, in respect of the management of public estates. It was Duffy's ambition to prove that one whose public life in Ireland had led to an indictment for treason could rise to the highest position in the state in a self-governing colony of England. After some years in opposition, he again became minister of land and works in 1862. He carried an important land bill which was known as Duffy's Land Act. Its main object practically was to facilitate the acquisition of the land by industrious inhabitants of the colony and by deserving immigrants, and to check the monopoly of the squatters. In 1865 he returned to Europe, visited England and Ireland (where he was fêted by his friends), and spent some months on the continent. On going back to Victoria he took up the question of the federation of the colonies and obtained the appointment of a royal commission to consider the question, anticipating in his action subsequent events. In 1871 he became chief secretary or prime minister of the colony; in 1872 he resigned on an adverse vote which left him in a minority of five. He advised the governor, Viscount Canterbury, to dissolve, but the governor refused. The refusal was regarded as a departure from constitutional usage, and was discussed in the imperial parliament.

In 1873 Duffy was knighted in recognition of his services to the colony. In 1874 he again returned to Europe, spending some time in England, Ireland, and the continent. He went back to the colony in 1876, and was unanimously elected speaker of the House of Assembly next year, when he was made K.C.M.G. During the early days of his speakership, he was an interested but independent observer of the struggle between the two branches of the legislature in 1877–8 over the question of payment of members [see Berry, Sir Graham, Suppl. II]. The legislative assembly, which supported the payment, appealed to the home government against the council, which resisted the payment, and the prime minister, Sir Graham Berry, named Duffy as the representative of the assembly in the mission sent to London to lay its case before the imperial government; but objection was taken to Duffy's appointment on the ground of his position as speaker, and he resigned his place to Charles Henry Pearson [q. v.].

In 1880 Duffy resigned the office of speaker and left the colony for good. He spent the remainder of his life mainly in the south of Europe. During this period he devoted himself to literary work, and took the keenest interest in all that went on in Ireland. He published valuable accounts of his own experiences in 'Young Ireland, a Fragment of Irish History, 1840–50' (2 vols. 1880–3; revised edit. 1896); 'The League of North and South: an episode in Irish History, 1850–4' (1886); 'The Life of Thomas Davis' (1890; abridged edit. 1896); 'Conversations with Thomas Carlyle' (1892; new edit. 1896); and 'My Life in Two Hemispheres' (1898). He also projected and edited 'A New Irish Library,' based on the principles of the old. He died at Nice on 9 Feb. 1903, and was buried in Glasnevin cemetery, Dublin. He was married thrice: (1) in 1842 to Emily (*d.* 1845), daughter of Francis McLaughlin, of Belfast; (2) in 1846 to Susan (*d.* 1878), daughter of Philip Hughes of Newry; and (3) in 1881 to Louise, eldest daughter of George Hall of Rock Ferry, Cheshire (who died in 1890). Ten children survive him—six sons and four daughters.

A small portrait in oils from a daguerreotype is in the National Gallery of Ireland, together with a terra-cotta plaque with a life-sized head in profile.

[Duffy's works; The Times, 11, 16, 17 Feb., 9 March 1903; Heaton's Dict. Austral. Dates; private information.] R. B. O'B.

DUFFY, PATRICK VINCENT (1836–1909), landscape painter, born on 17 March 1836, at Cullenswood, near Dublin, was son of James Duffy, a jeweller and dealer in works of art in Dublin. Patrick studied in the schools of the Royal Dublin Society, where he was often premiated. While still a student he was elected an associate of the Royal Hibernian Academy, and promoted three months later to be a full member. In 1871 he was elected keeper of the academy, a post he retained for thirty-eight years, until his death at Dublin on 22 Nov. 1909. His pictures are very unequal in merit. His better works show that under favourable conditions he might have taken a high place as a painter of landscape. A good example of his art, 'A Wicklow Common,' is in the Irish National Gallery. He married Elizabeth, daughter of James Malone, by whom he had one daughter.

[Private information.] W. A.

DUNMORE, seventh Earl of. [See Murray, Charles Adolphus, 1841–1907.]

DUNPHIE, CHARLES JAMES (1820–1908), art critic and essayist, born at Rathdowney on 4 Nov. 1820, was elder son of Michael Dunphy of Rathdowney House, Rathdowney, Queen's County, Ireland, and of Fleet Street, Dublin, merchant, by his wife Kate Woodroffe. His younger brother, Henry Michael Dunphy (*d.* 1889), who retained the early spelling of the name, was called to the bar at the Middle Temple on 26 Jan. 1861, but became a journalist and critic, being for many years chief of the 'Morning Post's' reporting staff in the House of Commons. Charles Dunphie was educated at Trinity College, Dublin. Coming to London, he studied medicine at King's College Hospital, where he was a favourite pupil of Sir William Fergusson, but soon took to literature and journalism. For some years he was on 'The Times' staff, and when the Crimean war broke out in 1853 he was offered (according to family tradition) the post of its special correspondent. But having lately married he persuaded his colleague and countryman, (Sir) William Howard Russell [q. v. Suppl. II], to go in his stead.

During the war he was one of the founders of the 'Patriotic Fund Journal' (1854–55), a weekly miscellany of general literature, to which he contributed prose and verse under the pseudonym of 'Melopoyn,' the profits being devoted to the Patriotic Fund. In 1856 he left 'The Times' to become art and dramatic critic to the 'Morning Post.' Those offices he continued to combine till 1895. From that date until near his death he only wrote in the paper on art. He thus spent over fifty years in the service of the 'Morning Post.' As a dramatic critic he belonged to the school of John Oxenford and E. L. Blanchard. His knowledge of art was wide and he had much literary power. A graceful writer of Latin, Greek, and English verse, and a semi-cynical essayist, Dunphie had something of the metrical dexterity of Father Prout and the egotistic fluency of Leigh Hunt. While serving the 'Morning Post' he contributed poems to 'Cornhill' and 'Belgravia,' and wrote essays for the 'Observer' (signed 'Rambler') and the 'Sunday Times.' Collected volumes of his essays appeared under the titles: 'Wildfire: a Collection of Erratic Essays' (1876), 'Sweet Sleep' (1879), 'The Chameleon: Fugitive Fancies on Many-Coloured Matters' (1888). In 'Freelance: Tiltings in many Lists' (1880) he collaborated with Albert King.

Of handsome presence and polished manners, Dunphie died at his house, 54 Finchley Road, on 7 July 1908, and was buried at Putney Vale cemetery. He married on 31 March 1853 Jane, daughter of Luke Miller, governor of Ilford gaol. Besides two sons, he left a daughter, Agnes Anne, wife of Sir George Anderson Critchett, first baronet.

[Private information; Foster's Men at the Bar, 1885; The Times, and Morning Post, 10 July 1908.] A. F. S.

DUPRÉ, AUGUST (1835–1907), chemist, born at Mainz, Germany, on 6 Sept. 1835, was second son of F. Dupré, merchant, of Frankfurt-am-Main. Both father and mother were of Huguenot descent. Migrating to London in 1843, the elder Dupré resided at Warrington until 1845, when, returning to Germany, he settled at Giessen. There and at Darmstadt August received his early schooling. In 1852, when seventeen years old, he, with his brother Friedrich Wilhelm (*d.* 1908), entered the University of Giessen, where they studied chemistry under Liebig and Will. In 1854 both proceeded to Heidelberg University, where they continued their chemical studies with Bunsen and Kirchhoff. After August had graduated Ph.D. at Heidelberg in 1855, he and his brother came to London, where he acted as assistant to Dr. W. Odling, then demonstrator of Practical Chemistry in the medical school of Guy's Hospital. In collaboration with Odling he discovered the almost universal presence of copper in vegetable and animal tissues (see *On the Presence of Copper in the Tissues of Plants and Animals*, *Report Brit. Assoc.* 1857; *On the Existence of Copper in Organic Tissues*, *Reports Guy's Hosp.* 1858). Friedrich meanwhile became lecturer in chemistry and toxicology at Westminster Hospital Medical School. In 1863 August succeeded Friedrich in the latter office, which he held till 1897. In 1866 he became a naturalised British subject. From 1874 to 1901 he was lecturer in toxicology at the London School of Medicine for Women.

With his hospital appointment Dupré soon held many responsible offices in which he turned his mastery of chemical analysis to signal public advantage. From 1873 to 1901 he was public analyst to the city of Westminster. Meanwhile in 1871 he was appointed chemical referee to the medical department of the local government board, and for the board conducted (1884-5, 1887) special inquiries respecting potable waters and the contamination and self-purification of rivers (see official *Reports*). Subsequently with W. J. Dibdin, Sir Frederick Abel [q. v. Suppl. II], and other chemists, he made a series of investigations, on behalf of the metropolitan board of works, on the condition of the river Thames, and on sewage treatment and purification methods (for details see *Report of the Royal Commission* (1884) *on Metropolitan Sewage Discharge* and paper by DIBDIN, *The Purification of the Thames*, with remarks by DUPRÉ, *Proc. Inst. Civil Eng.* cxxix.). 'Dupré was foremost' (wrote Otto Hehner) 'in giving the now orthodox modes of water analysis their present form; and contributed to the analytical methods of the examination of alkaloidal and other drugs. He was the first to observe (with H. Bence Jones) the formation of alkaloidal substances or "ptomaines" by the decomposition of animal matters' (see *On a Fluorescent Substance resembling Quinine in Animals, Proc. Roy. Soc.* 1866; *On the Existence of Quinoidine in Animals, Proc. Roy. Inst.* 1866).

Dupré was long officially engaged in researches on explosives. From 1873 he was consulting chemist to the explosives department of the home office; in 1888 he was nominated a member of the war office explosives committee, of which Sir Frederick Abel was chairman; and in 1906 he became a member of the ordnance research board. During thirty-six years he examined 'nearly four hundred entirely new explosives of the most varied composition, and further examined, at frequent intervals, all explosives imported into England, as to safety. He had often to evolve original methods of analysis or of testing for safety, and therein especially rendered important services' (H. WILSON HAKE). At the time of the Fenian outrages in 1882–3 he discharged dangerous duties in the examination of 'infernal machines' and especially in connection with the detection (1883) of the man Whitehead, at Birmingham, who had been secretly engaged there in the manufacture of nitro-glycerine (see *Eighth Annual Report of the Inspectors of Explosives*, 1883, and SIR WILLIAM HARCOURT, home secretary, in the House of Commons, *Hansard*, 16 April 1883).

The treasury was also among the government departments which sought Dupré's opinion in matters of applied chemistry, and he was often a witness in medico-legal cases in the law courts. At the Lamson poisoning trial in 1881 he gave notable evidence for the crown.

Dupré was elected a fellow of the Chemical Society in 1860, and served on the council (1871–5). He was president of the Society of Public Analysts (1877–8); was an original member of the Institute of Chemistry (1877), and a member of the first and four later councils. He was an original member of the Society of Chemical Industry, serving on the council (1894–7). Dupré was elected F.R.S. on 3 June 1875.

Dupré died at his home, Mount Edgcumbe, Sutton, Surrey, on 15 July 1907, and was buried at Benhilton, Sutton. He married in 1876 Florence Marie, daughter of H. T. Robberds, of Manchester, and had issue four sons and one daughter.

Dupré was joint author with Dr. Thudichum of a work, 'On the Origin, Nature, and Varieties of Wine' (1872); and with Dr. H. Wilson Hake, of 'A Short Manual of Inorganic Chemistry' (1886; 3rd edit. 1901). From 1855 he communicated many scientific papers to the publications of the Royal Society, the Chemical Society, the Society of Public Analysts, and the Society of Chemical Industry, at times in collaboration with his brother, Prof. Odling, H. Bence Jones, F. J. M. Page, H. Wilson Hake, and Otto Hehner. He also contributed much to the 'Analyst,' 'Chemical News,' 'Philosophical Magazine,' and foreign periodicals.

[Proc. Roy. Soc., vol. lxxx., A.; The Analyst (with portrait), vol. xxxii.; Trans. Chem. Soc., vol. xciii. (2); Journ. Soc. Chem. Industry, vol. xxvi.; Proc. Inst. Chemistry, 1907, pt. 4; Journ. Soc. Arts, vol. lv.; Roy. Soc. Catal. Sci. Papers; Nature, 1 Aug. 1907; Lancet, 20 July 1907; The Times, 17 July 1907; Men of the Time, 1899; 'The Rise and Progress of the British Explosives Industry,' 1909, published under the auspices of the VIIth Internat. Congress of Applied Chemistry; O. Guttman, The Manufacture of Explosives, 1909.] T. E. J.

DUTT, ROMESH CHUNDER (1848–1909), Indian official, author and politician, born in Calcutta on 13 Aug. 1848, was son of Isan Chunder Dutt, a Kayasth, who was one of the first Indians to become a deputy collector in Bengal. Romesh's great-uncle, Rasamoy Dutt, was the first Indian to be secretary to the Sanskrit College, Calcutta, and to be made a judge of the court of small causes. His female cousins, Aru and Toru Dutt, accomplished French and English scholars, both gave great poetic promise at the time of their early deaths from consumption in 1874 and 1877 respectively. Losing his father when he was thirteen, Romesh came under the guardianship of his uncle, Sasi Chunder Dutt, registrar of the Bengali secretariat, and a voluminous writer on Indian life and history. Educated at Hare's school and at the presidency college, Calcutta, Romesh took second place in the first examination in arts of the university in 1866. Some two years later, he, with his lifelong friend Mr. Behari Lal Gupta (afterwards judge of the Bengal high court), ran away from home, and the two, joined by Mr. Surendranath Banerjee, (afterwards famous as a Bengal political leader), set sail for England on 3 March 1868. The practice of studying in England was then rare among Indian youths and was deprecated by the orthodox. Entering University College, London, the three friends studied with diligence, and were all successful in the 1869 examination for the Indian civil service, Dutt taking third place. He also studied for the bar at the Middle Temple, and was called on 7 June 1871.

Joining the Bengal service at the close of 1871, Dutt went through the usual novitiate of district work. Devoting all his leisure through life to literary pursuits, he described in his first book his 'Three Years in Europe' (Calcutta, 1872; 4th edit. with additional matter, 1896). In 1874, in 'The Peasantry of Bengal,' a collection of articles which he had contributed serially to the 'Bengal Magazine,' he urged that the permanent settlement was unwise and ill-conceived, unfairly benefiting the zamindars at the cost both of the cultivators and of the state. His biographical and critical 'History of Bengali Literature' (Calcutta, 1877), issued under the pseudonym of Ar. Cy. Dae, reappeared under his own name in 1895. At the persuasion of Bunkim Chandra Chatterji, a vernacular Bengali writer of repute, he wrote six historical and social romances in his mother tongue, three of which were translated into English—'Shivajee, or the Morning of Maratha Life' (Broach, 1899); 'The Lake of Palms' (London, 1902; 2nd edit. 1903); and 'The Slave Girl of Agra' (London, 1909).

In April 1883 Dutt was appointed collector of Backerganj, being the first Indian to receive executive charge of a district since the establishment of British rule. The experiment was justified by the peace of this difficult district during his two years' tenure. Taking long furlough in 1885, he devoted the first portion to a Bengali translation of the 'Rig Veda.' The vernacular press contended with heat, that Brahman pundits alone could deal with the sacred text. But Dutt persevered, and published in 1886 the first, and still the only complete, Bengali translation of the ancient hymns. He never completely broke with orthodox Hinduism; and though in later years he showed strong leanings to the Brahmo Samaj, founded by Keshub Chunder Sen, he did not join that movement. On return to duty in 1887 he held charge successively of the Pabna, Mymensingh, Dinajpur, and Midnapur districts. While at Mymensingh he wrote an able 'History of Civilisation in Ancient India' based on Sanskrit literature (Calcutta, 3 vols., 1888–90; London, 2 vols., 1893), and also prepared school primers of Bengal and Indian history.

On 25 May 1892 Dutt was created a C.I.E. and in April 1894 he was appointed acting commissioner of Burdwan, being the only Indian to rise to executive charge of a division in the nineteenth century. He served on the Bengal legislative council from January to October 1895, when he was transferred to the commissionership of Orissa, with ex-officio superintendence of the twenty tributary mahals, or native states, of the province. In October 1897, after twenty-six years' work, he resigned the civil service, moved by a twofold desire to pursue his literary labour and to take part freely in Indian politics.

Settling in London, he published there 'England and India: a Record of Progress during 100 Years' (1897). It was a plea for extending the popular share in legislation and administration. At the close of 1899 he went to India to preside at the fifteenth annual national congress at Lucknow. India was then suffering from a severe famine, and he mainly devoted his presidential address to a condemnation of the land revenue policy of the government. Lord Curzon of Kedleston, the viceroy, gave him a long audience, and Dutt published 'Famines in India' (London, 1900), a series of open letters to Lord Curzon, setting forth in detail his views of agrarian policy and attributing famine to high assessments. The provincial governments were directed to examine his statements, and upon their replies was based the elaborate resolution of Lord Curzon's government (dated 16 Jan. 1902) on land revenue administration, which was presented to parliament (Cd. 1089). The official papers convicted Dutt's information of much inaccuracy (cf. S. M. MITRA, *Indian Problems*, London, 1908). Dutt sought to vindicate his conclusions in a new and exhaustive criticism of British agrarian and economic policy in India in two substantial volumes: 'Economic History of British India, 1757–1837' (1902), and 'India in the Victorian Age' (1904). They were brought out in a second edition under the uniform title of 'India under Early British Rule' (1906). A series of minor, yet cumulatively important, changes in land revenue administration, designed to protect the cultivators, were partly attributable to Dutt's representations. Prejudice disqualified him from becoming a safe guide on agrarian history, but the historian of Lord Curzon's viceroyalty admits that on the whole Dutt's agitation had beneficial results (L. FRASER'S *India under Curzon and After*, i. pp. 154–7).

Dutt acted as lecturer on Indian history at University College, London, from 1898 to 1904, and he found time to continue his Sanskrit studies. He translated into English metre large extracts of the two great epics, the 'Mahabharata' and the 'Ramayana,' linking the excerpts together by short explanatory notes (published in the 'Temple Classics' 1899–1900 and subsequently in Dent's 'Everyman's Library'). Max Müller acknowledged the value of Dutt's scheme. His versatile interests were illustrated by a volume of original poetry, 'Reminiscences of a Workman's Life' (Calcutta, 1896; privately printed).

While on a visit to India in 1904 Dutt was appointed revenue minister of the independent state of Baroda, and during his three years' active tenure (August 1904–July 1907) he helped on the reforms of the enlightened Gaekwar (Sayaji Rao). He was the Indian member of the royal commission on Indian decentralisation, which travelled through the country from November 1907 to the following April. He signed the report, but noted his dissent on many points of detail. With Mr. G. K. Gokhale he was unofficially consulted by Lord Morley respecting the scheme of political reforms which were promulgated in 1908–9. Returning to Baroda as prime minister in March 1909, he died there of a heart affection on 30 Nov. of that year, and was accorded a public funeral by order of the Gaekwar.

Dutt married in 1864 a daughter of Nobo Gopal Bose; a son is a barrister in practice in Calcutta, and of five daughters, three are married to native officials in government service.

[Biography by Dutt's son-in-law, J. N. Gupta, I.C.S., 1911; sketch of Dutt's career, a 4-anna (4*d.*) pamphlet pub. by Natesan, Madras, 1909; Indian National Congress, Natesan, Madras, 1907; Papers regarding Land Rev. System of Brit. India, 1902, Cd. 1089; Dutt's works; L. Fraser, India under Lord Curzon and After, 1911; The Times, 1 Dec. 1909; Indian Daily Telegraph, 2 Jan. 1903; Times of India Weekly, 4 Dec. 1909; personal knowledge.] F. H. B.

DUTTON, JOSEPH EVERETT (1874–1905), biologist, born on 9 Sept. 1874 at New Chester Road, Higher Bebington, Cheshire, was fifth son of John Dutton, a retired chemist of Brookdale, Banbury, by his wife Sarah Ellen Moore. After education at King's School, Chester, from January 1888 till May 1892, he entered the University of Liverpool, where he gained the gold medal in anatomy and physiology, and the medal in materia medica in 1895. At the Victoria University he won the medal in pathology in 1896, graduated M.B., C.M. in 1897, and was elected Holt fellow in pathology. He then acted as house surgeon to Prof. Rushton Parker and house physician to Dr. R. Caton at the Liverpool Royal Infirmary. In 1901 he gained the Walter Myers fellowship in tropical medicine.

In 1900 he accompanied Dr. H. E. Annett and Dr. J. H. Elliott of Toronto on the third expedition of the Liverpool school of tropical medicine to southern and northern Nigeria to study the life-history and surroundings of the mosquito and generally to take measures for the prevention of malaria. Two reports were issued as a result of this expedition, one dealing with anti-malaria sanitation, the other a very complete monograph upon filariasis. In 1901 Dutton proceeded alone to Gambia on the sixth expedition of the Liverpool school of tropical medicine, and drew up a most comprehensive and useful report on the prevention of malaria. During this expedition he identified in the blood of a patient at Bathurst a trypanosome belonging to a group of animal parasites which had hitherto been found only in animals. He described it accurately and named it Trypanosoma Gambiense. He found the same organism subsequently in numerous other cases in Gambia and elsewhere. Dutton's discovery of the first trypanosome in man was an important factor in determining the cause of sleeping sickness, which was afterwards shown by other observers to be due to the same parasite. In addition to this Trypanosoma

Gambiense he also described several other trypanosomes new to science. In 1902 he proceeded to the Senegambia with Dr. J. L. Todd and drew up a report on sanitation which was presented to the French government; he also published further papers on trypanosomiasis. His last expedition was made to the Congo in charge of the twelfth expedition of the Liverpool school of tropical medicine. He started in August 1903, accompanied by Dr. J. L. Todd and Dr. C. Christie. The expedition reached Stanley Falls about the end of 1904 and discovered independently the cause of tick fever in man, a discovery which had been anticipated by a few weeks by Major (Sir) Ronald Ross and Dr. Milne in the Uganda protectorate. Dutton was able to show the transference of the disease from man to monkeys. During the investigation Dutton and Christie contracted the disease. Dutton died of spirillum fever on 27 Feb. 1905 at Kosongo in the Congo territory. His burial was attended by more than 1000 persons, mostly natives to whom he had endeared himself and whose maladies he had treated.

Dutton's cheering enthusiasm made him a welcome comrade in every field of work. The skill and ability which he brought to the science of tropical medicine were of the highest order, and his work gave promise of future fruit.

[Brit. Med. Journal, 1905, i. 1020; Lancet, 1905, i. 1239; information kindly obtained by Professor H. E. Annett, M.D.] D'A. P.

DUVEEN, Sir JOSEPH JOEL (1843–1908), art dealer and benefactor, born at Meppel in Holland on 8 May 1843, was elder son in a family of two sons and two daughters of Joseph Duveen of that place by his wife Eva, daughter of Henry van Minden of Zwolle. His grandfather, Henry Duveen, who had first settled at Meppel during the Napoleonic wars, was youngest son of Joseph Duveen of Giessen, army contractor to the King of Saxony; Napoleon's repudiation of the debts of the Saxon forces ruined this Duveen, whose twelve sons were then driven to seek their fortunes in different countries.

Joseph left Meppel in 1866 and settled at Hull, starting as a general dealer on a site now partly covered by the Public Art Gallery built in 1910. He possessed a good knowledge of Nankin procelain, then coming into fashion, and of which cargo loads had been brought to Holland by the early Dutch traders with China; he purchased large quantities of this in various parts of his native country, shipped it to Hull, and found a ready market for it in London. In partnership with his younger brother Henry he soon secured the chief American trade in Oriental porcelain, and in 1877 opened a branch house at Fifth Avenue, New York. They formed many fine collections in America, among others that of Garland, which they bought back *en bloc* in March 1902, selling it at once to Mr. Pierpont Morgan. They also largely helped in the formation of the Taft, Widener, Gould, Altmann and Morgan art collections.

In 1879 the brothers erected fine art galleries adjoining the Pantheon in Oxford Street, London, and at once took an important share in the fine art trade, extending their interests in nearly every branch, particularly in that of old tapestry, of which they became the largest purchasers. When Robinson & Fisher vacated their auction rooms at 21 Old Bond Street the Duveens secured the additional premises and built spacious art galleries in the spring of 1894. From 1890 onwards they purchased pictures and were large buyers at the Mulgrave Castle sale of 1890 and at the Murrieta sale two years later. They purchased the whole of the Hainauer collection of renaissance objects of art for about 250,000*l.* in June 1906, and in 1907 the Rodolphe Kann collection of pictures and objects of art and vertu in Paris, for nearly three quarters of a million sterling (*The Times*, 7 Aug. 1907; *The Year's Art*, 1908, 367–72).

Duveen, whose fortune grew large, was generous in public benefaction. He was a subscriber to the public purchase of the 'Venus' of Velasquez for the National Gallery in 1906, in which year also he presented J. S. Sargent's whole-length portrait of Miss Ellen Terry as Lady Macbeth (bought in at the Irving sale at Christie's, 16 Dec. 1905, for 1200*l.*) to the National (Tate) Gallery of British Art, Millbank. In May 1908 he undertook the cost (about 35,000*l.*) of an addition of five rooms, known as 'The Turner Wing,' to that gallery (*The Times*, 7 May 1908; *Cat. of Nat. Gall. of Brit. Art*, 1911, pp. vi–vii). He was knighted on 26 June 1908.

He died at Hyères, France, on 9 Nov. 1908, and was buried at the Jewish cemetery, Willesden. He left a fortune tentatively valued at 540,409*l.*, with personalty of the net value of 486,675*l.* (*The Times*, 7 Dec. 1908; *Morning Post*, with fuller details, of same date). In 1869 he married Rosetta, daughter of Abraham

Barnett of Carr Lane, Hull, who survived him, and by whom he had a family of ten sons and four daughters.

His portrait by Emil Fuchs, M.V.O., is in the Turner wing of the gallery at Millbank. His eldest son, Joseph, who made additions to his father's benefaction to the Tate Gallery, presented to the new Public Art Gallery of Hull, as a memorial of his father's association with the town of Hull, 'The Good Samaritan,' by Edward Stott, A.R.A.

[Private information from the family and Mr. A. C. R. Carter; The Year's Art, 1908, (with portrait).] W. R.

E

EARLE, JOHN (1824–1903), philologist, born on 29 Jan. 1824 at Elston in the parish of Churchstowe near Kingsbridge, South Devon, was only son of John Earle, a small landed proprietor who cultivated his own property, by his wife Anne Hamlyn. Their other child, a daughter, married George Buckle, afterwards canon of Wells, and was mother of Mr. George Earle Buckle, editor of 'The Times.' John Earle received his earliest education in the house of Orlando Manley, then incumbent of Plymstock, whence he passed to the Plymouth new grammar school. He spent the year 1840–1 at the grammar school of Kingsbridge, and matriculated at Magdalen Hall, Oxford, in October 1841, graduating B.A. in 1845 with a first class in literæ humaniores. In 1848 he won a fellowship at Oriel College, then one of the chief distinctions in the university. The colleagues with whom Earle was brought into contact at Oriel included Charles Marriott, Fraser (afterwards bishop of Manchester), Clough, Matthew Arnold, Henry Coleridge, Alexander Grant, Sellar, and Burgon—men of very varied schools of thought. In ecclesiastical matters Earle was never a partisan, though his historical sense made him value whatever illustrated the continuity of the English church or conduced to the seemliness of public worship. In 1849 he proceeded M.A., was ordained deacon, and was elected to the professorship of Anglo-Saxon, then tenable only for five years. At the time the chair was little more than an elegant sinecure, but Earle raised it to a position of real usefulness before his retirement in 1854. Thenceforth he assiduously pursued his Anglo-Saxon studies. Meanwhile in 1852 he became tutor of Oriel in succession to his future brother-in-law, George Buckle. In 1857, when he took priest's orders, he was presented by his college to the rectory of Swanswick, near Bath, which he retained till death. In 1871 he was appointed to the prebend of Wanstrow in Wells cathedral, and from 1873 to 1877 he was rural dean of Bath.

In 1876 he was re-elected professor of Anglo-Saxon by convocation; his competitor was Thomas Arnold [q. v. Suppl. I]. The tenure of this chair had then been made permanent, and he held the post for the rest of his life. His inaugural lecture, 'A Word for the Mother Tongue,' was one of many published pleas for the bestowal of a place in the university curriculum on English philological study.

Earle was an industrious writer, and combined devotion to research with a power of popularising its fruits. His earliest published work was 'Gloucester Fragments, Legends of St. Swithun and Sancta Maria Ægyptiaca' (1861, 4to). In 1865 appeared 'Two of the Saxon Chronicles Parallel, with Supplementary Extracts from the Others, edited with Introduction, Notes, and a Glossarial Index.' This was in many ways his most important work, and was the first attempt to give a rational and connected account of the growth of the chronicle, and the relations of the different MSS. It was recast by the present writer in two volumes (1892, 1899). In 1866 appeared both 'A Book for the Beginner in Anglo-Saxon' (4th edit. 1902) and 'The Philology of the English Tongue' (5th edit. 1892). The latter volume was Earle's most popular work; it largely helped to popularise the results of the new science of comparative philology, as applied to the English language. With the later developments of comparative philology Earle hardly kept pace. He was always more interested in tracing the development of language as an instrument of thought, and in analysing the various elements which had contributed to the formation of English, than in purely philological science. In 1863 an abortive scheme was proposed for a 'final and complete critical edition' of 'Chaucer' to be published by the Clarendon Press, with Earle as general editor (*Letters of Alexander Macmillan*, 1908, pp. 160–1). Apart from English philology, Earle was an efficient Italian scholar. He wrote an introduction to Dr. Shadwell's translation of Dante's 'Purgatorio' (1892), and a remarkable essay on Dante's 'Vita Nuova' in the 'Quarterly Review' (1896).

A man of varied intellectual interests and of generous enthusiasms, Earle died on 31 Jan. 1903, at Oxford, and was buried in Holywell cemetery. A brass tablet was erected to his memory in Swanswick Church. In 1863 he married Jane, daughter of George Rolleston, vicar of Maltby, and sister of George Rolleston [q. v.], Linacre professor of anatomy at Oxford. By her Earle had three sons and four daughters. His second daughter, Beatrice Anne Earle, married her first cousin, Mr. George Earle Buckle. Earle's widow survived till 13 May 1911.

Besides the works cited, Earle's chief publications were: 1. 'Guide to Bath, Ancient and Modern,' 1864. 2. 'Rhymes and Reasons, Essays by J. E.,' 1871. 3. 'English Plant Names,' 1880. 4. 'Anglo-Saxon Literature,' 1884. 5. 'A Handbook to the Land Charters and other Saxonic Documents,' 1888. 6. 'English Prose, its Elements, History and Usage,' 1890. 7. 'The Deeds of Beowulf, done into Modern Prose, with an Introduction and Notes,' 1892. 8. 'The Psalter of 1539, a Landmark in English Literature,' 1894. 9. 'Bath during British Independence,' 1895. 10. 'A Simple Grammar of English now in Use,' 1898. 11. 'The Alfred Jewel,' 4to, 1901. To a volume on Alfred the Great (ed. Alfred Bowker, 1899) he contributed an article 'Alfred as a Writer,' and to an English miscellany presented to Dr. Furnivall (1901) an essay on 'The Place of English in Education.'

[The Times, 2 Feb. 1903 (by his brother-in-law, Canon Buckle); Oxford Mag. 11 Feb. 1903, by present writer; Men and Women of the Time, 1899; personal knowledge; private information.] C. P.

EAST, Sir CECIL JAMES (1837–1908), general, born at Herne Hill, London, on 10 July 1837, was son of Charles James East, merchant, of London, by his wife Eliza Frederica Bowman. After private education he entered the army on 18 Aug. 1854 as ensign in the 82nd regt., and became lieutenant on 5 June 1855. He served with his regiment in the Crimea from 2 Sept. 1855, and was present at the siege and fall of Sevastopol, for which he received the medal with clasp and Turkish medal. Subsequently he took part in the war of the Indian Mutiny in 1857 and was severely wounded at Cawnpore on 26 Nov. 1857, when he was awarded the medal. Promoted captain on 17 Nov. 1863, he joined the 41st regiment, and served as assistant quartermaster-general with the Chittagong column of the Lushai expeditionary force in 1871–2; he was mentioned in despatches and received the thanks of the governor-general in council as well as the medal with clasp and brevet of major (*Lond. Gaz.* 21 June 1872). Through the latter part of the Zulu war of 1879 he acted as deputy adjutant and quartermaster-general, and was present at the engagement at Ulundi, receiving the medal with clasp and brevet of colonel (*Lond. Gaz.* 21 August 1879). During the Burmese expedition in 1886–7 he commanded the first brigade after the capture of Mandalay and was mentioned in despatches by the government of India (*Lond. Gaz.* 2 Sept. 1887), receiving two clasps and being made C.B. on 1 July 1887. From 1883 to 1888 he commanded a second-class district in Bengal and Burma, and a first-class district in Madras from 1889 to 1893, having been made major-general on 23 Jan. 1889. Leaving India in 1893, he was till 1898 governor of Royal Military College at Sandhurst. He was nominated K.C.B. on 22 June 1897. He became lieut.-general on 28 May 1896, and general in 1902, retiring next year. After 1898 he resided at Fairhaven, Winchester, where he died on 14 March 1908, being buried at King's Worthy.

He married (1) in 1863 Jane Catharine (*d.* 1871), eldest daughter of Charles Case Smith, M.D., of Bury St. Edmunds, Suffolk, by whom he had issue one son and a daughter; (2) in 1875 Frances Elizabeth, daughter of Rev. Arthur Mogg of Chilcompton, Somerset, and widow of Edward H. Watts, by whom he had a daughter.

[The Times, 16 March 1908; selections from State Papers in Military Dept., 1857–8, ed. G. W. Forrest, 1902, ii. 383; Dod's Knightage; Hart's and Official Army Lists; Walford's County Families.] H. M. V.

EASTLAKE, CHARLES LOCKE (1836–1906), keeper of the National Gallery, London, born on 11 March 1836 at Plymouth, was fourth son of George Eastlake, who was admiralty law agent and deputy judge advocate of the fleet. His father's brother was Sir Charles Eastlake [q. v.], president of the Royal Academy. He was educated at Westminster School, where he became Queen's scholar in 1846. He maintained through life his interest in the school and in later years joined the governing body. Showing a taste for architecture, he became a pupil of Philip Hardwick, R.A. [q. v.], and then entered the Royal Academy Schools. There in 1854 he gained a silver medal for architectural drawings, and he exhibited two designs at the Academy in 1855–6. Developing some skill in water-colours, he gave up architectural work and for three years studied art abroad. On his return to England his interest again changed, and he devoted himself to literary work and design in various branches of industrial art.

From 1866 to 1877 he was secretary of the Royal Institute of British Architects. In 1878 Lord Beaconsfield appointed him keeper and secretary of the National Gallery, and he performed efficiently the duties of this post till 1898. During that period he rearranged and classified all the paintings at Trafalgar Square under the different schools to which they belonged, and had them placed under glass to protect them from the London atmosphere. He opened several rooms for the exhibition of Turner's sketches and water-colour drawings, and increased the accommodation for art students and copyists. He was greatly disappointed that he did not succeed Sir Frederic Burton [q. v. Supp. I], who retired in 1894, as director of the gallery. The post then fell to Sir Edward Poynter, and four years later Eastlake retired from the keepership.

Eastlake made a substantial reputation as a writer on art, publishing several books and occasionally contributing to the leading magazines. His earliest and best-known book, 'Hints on Household Taste in Furniture, Upholstery, and Other Details' (1868), shows strong Gothic bias; it at once became popular in England and America; it reached its fourth London edition in 1887. The sixth American edition (New York, 1881) has notes by Mr. C. C. Perkins. 'A History of the Gothic Revival' followed in 1871. In 1876 he issued 'Lectures on Decorative Art and Art Workmanship,' which he had delivered at the Social Science Congress. A series of illustrated 'Notes on the Principal Pictures' in foreign galleries dealt with the Brera Gallery at Milan (1883), the Louvre at Paris (1883), the old Pinakothek at Munich (1884), and the Royal Gallery at Venice (1888). In 1895, under the pseudonym of Jack Easel, he published 'Our Square and Circle,' a series of social essays.

Eastlake died on 20 Nov. 1906 at his house in Leinster Square, Bayswater, and was buried at Kensal Green. He married on 1 Oct. 1856 Eliza, youngest daughter of George Bailey; she survived him without issue until 2 Nov. 1911.

An oil painting by Mr. Shirley Fox belonged to Mrs. Eastlake.

[Art Journ. 1906; The Times, 22 Nov. 1906; Who's Who, 1906; Lady Eastlake, Memoirs of Sir Charles Eastlake.] F. W. G–n.

EATON, WILLIAM MERITON, second Baron Cheylesmore (1843–1902), mezzotint collector, second son in a family of three sons and two daughters of Henry William Eaton, first Baron Cheylesmore (*d.* 1891), by his wife Charlotte Gorham (*d.* 1877), daughter of Thomas Leader Harman of New Orleans, was born at 9 Gloucester Place, Regent's Park, London, on 15 Jan. 1843. His father founded the prosperous firm of H. W. Eaton & Son, silk brokers, represented Coventry in parliament as a conservative from 1865 to 1880 and from 1881 to 1887, and was raised to the peerage at Queen Victoria's jubilee in 1887 as first Baron Cheylesmore. He was an authority on fine arts and an enthusiastic collector; among his treasures was Landseer's 'Monarch of the Glen,' which, at the sale of his collection at Christie's in April 1892, fetched 6900 guineas.

After education at Eton, William entered his father's firm and subsequently became partner. He took, however, little part in the business, and from 1866 onward devoted himself to politics in the conservative interest with little success. He failed in his attempts to enter parliament for Macclesfield in 1868, 1874, and 1880. He succeeded to the peerage on his father's death in 1891.

Like his father, Cheylesmore had artistic tastes. In 1869 he started a collection of English mezzotint engravings, by way of illustrating each item in the catalogue compiled by John Chaloner Smith [q. v.]. Eaton gave Chaloner Smith much assistance in preparing his work. Although his collection was fully representative, only a small percentage of it was in the choicest condition. The prints which crowded his residence at Prince's Gate formed the largest and best private mezzotint collection ever formed; it included, with the work of all the best practitioners, examples of Ludwig von Siegen (*fl.* 1650), the inventor of the art of mezzotint, and was especially rich in the engravings of James MacArdell (1729–1765) [q. v.]. Thirty-nine of Cheylesmore's mezzotints, including the valuable 'Miranda,' engraved by W. Ward, after Hoppner, which he had bought from Mr. Herbert Percy Horne for 40*l.*, were shown at the exhibition in 1902 of English mezzotint portraits (1750–1830) of the Burlington Fine Arts Club, of whose committee Cheylesmore was a member. Cheylesmore died unmarried at his residence, 16 Prince's Gate, on 10 July 1902, and was buried at Highgate cemetery. He was succeeded in the peerage by his younger brother, Herbert Francis (*b.* 25 Jan. 1848), to whom passed his collection of mezzotints other than portraits. The portraits —some 11,000—were bequeathed to the British Museum, where a small portion was exhibited from 1905 to 1910. The acquisition filled many gaps in the national collection.

[The Times, 11 and 12 July and 5 Aug. 1902; Daily Telegraph, 7 July 1905; Burke's Peerage; British Museum Guide to an Exhibition of Mezzotint Engravings, chiefly from the Cheylesmore Collection, compiled by Freeman M. O'Donoghue, with preface by Sidney Colvin, 1905; Cat. of Exhibition of English Mezzotint portraits, Burlington Fine Arts Club, 1902; Connoisseur, Jan. 1902, illustr. art. on Lord Cheylesmore's mezzotints (with portrait); private information.]

W. B. O.

EBSWORTH, JOSEPH WOODFALL (1824–1908), editor of ballads, born on 2 Sept. 1824 at 3 Gray's Walk, Lambeth, was younger son (in the family of thirteen children) of Joseph Ebsworth [q. v.], dramatist and musician, by his wife Mary Emma Ebsworth [q. v.], writer for the stage. Thomas Woodfall of Westminster, son of Henry Sampson Woodfall [q. v.], the printer of Junius's letters, was the boy's godfather. In 1828 the family removed to Edinburgh, where the father opened a bookshop, and Joseph made good use of his opportunities of reading. At fourteen he entered the board of trustees' school of art, where he studied successively under Charles Heath Wilson, Sir William Allan, and David Scott. For the last he cherished a lifelong affection. In 1848 he went to Manchester to serve as chief artist to Faulkner Bros., lithographers, who were busy with railway plans during the railway mania, but he soon left for Glasgow, where he became a master at the school of design. In 1849 he exhibited for the first time at the Scottish Academy, sending four large water-colour views of Edinburgh. One of these pictures (the north view) he engraved privately. In 1850 he sent a picture illustrating Tennyson's 'Locksley Hall.' In July 1853 he started on a solitary pedestrian tour through central Europe and Italy. He returned to Edinburgh in 1854, and busied himself until 1860 with painting, engraving, and writing prose and verse for the press. Then his plans changed and he matriculated at St. John's College, Cambridge. He graduated B.A. in 1864 and M.A. in 1867. On 31 July 1864 he was ordained deacon, and in 1868 priest. He was successively curate of Market Weighton (1864–5), of St. Stephen's, Bowling, near Bradford (1866–7), and of All Saints (1868–9) and Christ Church (1870–1), both in Bradford.

In January 1871 Ebsworth became vicar of Molash near Ashford. The parishioners were few and of small means, and he raised outside the parish 1600*l.* wherewith to build a vicarage. A practical and genial sort of piety and an affectionate disposition enabled Ebsworth to discharge his clerical duties efficiently, although the bohemian strain in his nature made him impatient of much clerical convention. But the chief part of his time at Molash was devoted to literary work at home or to researches which he pursued in the British Museum. He had published at Edinburgh two collections of miscellaneous prose and verse, 'Karl's Legacy' (2 vols. 1867) and 'Literary Essays and Poems' (1868). Concentrating his interest on the amatory and humorous poems and ballads of the seventeenth century, he now produced a notable series of reprints of light or popular poetic literature. In 1875 he published editions of 'The Westminster Drolleries' of 1671 and 1672, and 'The Merry Drolleries' of 1661 and 1670. 'The Choyce Drolleries' of 1656 followed next year. The 'Ballad Society,' which had been founded in 1868, soon enlisted his services, and he became its ablest and most industrious supporter. For that society he edited the 'Bagford Ballads' from the British Museum (2 pts. 1876–8), together with the 'Amanda Group of Bagford Poems' (1880). His main labour for the Ballad Society was the completion of its edition of the Roxburghe collection of ballads in the British Museum. William Chappell [q. v. Suppl. I] edited three volumes (1869–79). From 1879 onwards Ebsworth continued Chappell's work and published volumes iv. to ix. of the Roxburghe collections between 1883 and 1899. The separate pieces numbered 1400, and Ebsworth classified them under historical and other headings, bringing together, for example, 'Early Naval Ballads' (1887), 'Early Legendary Ballads' (1888), 'Robin Hood Ballads' (1896), and 'Restoration Ballads' (1899). Ebsworth, who transcribed the texts which he reprinted, supplied exhaustive introductions, notes, and indices.

At the same time he interspersed his editorial contributions with original verse, and also executed with his own hand woodcuts after the original illustrations. A sturdy champion of the seventeenth century royalists, and a hearty hater of puritanism, he freely enlivened his editorial comments with the free expression of his personal prejudices, and with scornful references to current political and religious views from which he dissented. But despite editorial eccentricities his work forms a serious and invaluable contribution to the history of English ballad literature. Ebsworth was elected F.S.A. in 1881.

In 1894 he retired from Molash vicarage to live privately at Ashford. There he died on Whitsunday, 7 June 1908; he was buried in Ashford cemetery. His library was sold in 1907. On 29 May 1865 he married Margaret, eldest daughter of William Blore, rector of Goodmanham, East Yorkshire. She died on 18 April 1906, leaving no issue.

A portrait in early life was painted by Thomas Duncan [q. v.] of Edinburgh. Another portrait was taken in 1873 for the collection of portraits of the Canterbury clergy formed by Mrs. Tait, wife of the archbishop.

Besides the works mentioned, Ebsworth printed in 1887, for private circulation, a hundred and fifty copies of 'Cavalier Lyrics for Church and Crown.' Many of the poems were scattered through his reprints of the 'drolleries' and ballads. All reflect the manner of Suckling or Carew, and more or less genially expound the thorough-going toryism which was part of Ebsworth's nature. He also edited Shakespeare's 'Midsummer Night's Dream' of 1600 (Furnivall's 'Facsimile Texts,' 1880); 'Poems by Thomas Carew' (1892); 'Poems of Robert Southwell' (1892); and Butler's 'Hudibras' (1892, 3 vols.). With Miss Julia H. L. De Vaynes he edited 'The Kentish Garland' (2 vols. 1881–2), and for the early volumes of this Dictionary he wrote lives of his father and mother and of Charles and Thomas John Dibdin.

[J. C. Francis, Notes by the Way, 1909; Notes and Queries, 27 June 1908; Crockford's Clerical Directory, 1908.] S. L.

EDDIS, EDEN UPTON (1812–1901), portrait-painter, was the eldest son of Eden Eddis, a clerk in Somerset House, by his wife Clementia Parker. His grandfather, William Eddis, was secretary to Sir Robert Eden, governor of Maryland. Born on 9 May 1812, in London, he showed as a boy a talent for drawing, and became a pupil in the art school of Henry Sass. In 1828 he entered the painting school of the Royal Academy, and in 1837 won the silver medal. He first exhibited at the Academy in 1834, and then annually from 1837 to 1881. He also exhibited occasionally at the British Institution and at Suffolk Street.

While a young man, Eddis travelled and sketched on the continent with his friend James Holland [q. v.]. In 1848 he settled in Harley Street, where most of his professional life was passed.

Some portrait-drawings in chalk of members of the Athenæum, made when he was still quite young, were very successful and procured him many commissions. Though he had cherished wider ambitions, he determined to embrace the opportunity thus afforded by portrait-painting, chiefly from a generous desire to help his family. In 1838 he exhibited a portrait of Lord John Beresford, archbishop of Armagh, and in the following year one of Viscount Ebrington, lord-lieutenant of Ireland, together with a sketch of Chantrey, the sculptor. These were the first of a long list of distinguished sitters, men eminent in politics, law, the army, and the church, and women celebrated in the society of the day. The painter's social gifts made him a delightful companion; and many of his sitters became lifelong friends. Among the closest and most intimate of his friends were Samuel Jones Loyd, Lord Overstone [q. v.], and his family. Eddis exhibited a portrait of Lord Overstone in 1851; and thirteen of his pictures (not all portraits) are in the collection of Lady Wantage, Lord Overstone's daughter. Between 1840 and 1850 he painted, in addition to portraits, 'Naomi,' other biblical subjects, and two pictures illustrating a poem of Keble's. After 1860 the portraits were increasingly varied by subjects of rustic genre and pictures of children. Several of these were engraved by Every, Joubert, and others, and had great popularity as prints. Macaulay (1850), Archbishop Sumner (1851), Bishop Blomfield (1851), George Dallas, the American Minister (1857), Sir Erasmus Wilson (1859), Lord Coleridge (1878), and Sydney Smith were among those who sat to Eddis. His portrait of Theodore Hook is in the National Portrait Gallery. A series of his portrait-drawings in chalk was lithographed by Gauci.

In 1883 Eddis's health threatened to give way; he determined to exhibit no more after that year, and retired to Shalford, near Guildford. The trouble passed, and he lived, hale and strong, till 1901, continuing to paint for his own pleasure portraits of his friends and delicate studies of flowers. His personality and conversation charmed all who knew him, and to the last he was the centre of a large and devoted circle, and an especial favourite with the young. He died at Shalford on 7 April 1901, and is buried there.

He married Elizabeth Brown, who predeceased him, and had one son and one daughter.

[Graves's Royal Academy Exhibitors, 1905–1906; private information.] L. B.

EDOUIN, WILLIE, whose real name was WILLIAM FREDERICK BRYER (1846–1908), comedian, born at Brighton on 1 Jan. 1846, was son of John Edwin Bryer, a dancing master, by his wife Sarah Elizabeth May. He was the youngest member of a family of five clever children, all of whom took early to the stage. He first appeared in public in the summer of 1852 (with two sisters and others) in a juvenile troupe of 'Living Marionettes' at the Théâtre des Variétés, Linwood Gallery, Leicester Square, in farces, ballets d'action, and extravaganzas. At Christmas in 1852 and 1854 the Edouin children acted in pantomime at the Strand Theatre. In 1857 'The Celebrated Edouin Family' were taken by their parents on a prolonged tour of Australia, India, China, and Japan. In 1863, after the disbandment of the troupe, Willie and his sister Rose (afterwards Mrs. G. B. Lewis, of the Maidan Theatre, Calcutta) were both members of Fawcett's stock company at the Princess's Theatre, Melbourne, playing in burlesque. Subsequently Willie made a long stay in California. On 2 June 1870 he first appeared in New York, at Bryant's Minstrel Hall, as Mr. Murphy in 'Handy Andy.' Shortly afterwards he began a notable association with Lydia Thompson [q. v. Suppl. II], playing with her burlesque troupe at Wood's Museum, New York, in October and November. In the company was Alice Atherton, whom Edouin subsequently married. At Wallack's Theatre, New York, in August 1871 he was first seen in his droll impersonation of Washee-Washee the Chinaman, in Farnie's burlesque of 'Bluebeard.' In this character he made his first adult appearance in London at the Charing Cross Theatre on 19 Sept. 1874. In 1877 Edouin returned with the Lydia Thompson troupe to New York, where pantomime or burlesque largely occupied him for the next six years.

On 9 Sept. 1884 Edouin made his first experiment in London management by opening Toole's Theatre with 'The Babes, or Whines from the Wood,' which, with himself and his wife in the principal characters, ran 100 nights [see BROUGH, LIONEL, Suppl. II]. On 31 July 1886 he commenced a six weeks' season at the Comedy as Carraway Bones in the farcical comedy 'Turned Up,' which proved so successful that he transferred it, under his own management, to the Royalty Theatre, where it ran over 100 nights. On 25 Feb. 1888 Edouin began his first managerial period at the Strand by producing 'Katti, the Family Help,' with himself and his wife (Alice Atherton) in the principal characters. On 13 June 1889, at the Prince of Wales's Theatre, he proved very successful as Nathaniel Glover (an amiable caricature of Sir Augustus Harris [q. v. Suppl. I]) in 'Our Flat.' A fortnight later he transferred the play to the Opera Comique, under his own management, where it had a run of close on 600 nights. During 1891 and 1893 he resumed management of the Strand, appearing there in light pieces suiting his idiosyncrasy. On 18 June 1894 he had a congenial part in Jeremiah Grubb in Mark Melford's 'The Jerry Builder,' a farcical comedy in which, as Mattie Pollard, his daughter May made a promising début. On 24 Feb. 1897 he won great success at the Prince of Wales's with his quaint embodiment of Hilarius in 'La Poupée.' On 4 Feb. 1899 his wife, who had long acted with him, died. In 1900 he went to America for a brief period, In June 1901 he created Samuel Twanks in 'The Silver Slipper' at the Lyric. Subsequently he performed in sketches in South Africa. On his return he originated the rôle of Hoggenheimer in 'The Girl from Kay's' at the Apollo (15 Nov. 1902). Afterwards his acting showed a serious falling off, notably in 'The Little Michus' at Daly's in April 1905. In 1907 he was playing in vaudeville in the United States, but developed symptoms of mental failure. Returning home, he died in London on 14 April 1908. He was buried at Kensal Green. Two daughters survived him. A coloured portrait of the comedian as Hilarius in 'La Poupée' accompanies his memoir in 'Players of the Day' (1902).

In parts of grotesquerie and whim Edouin was an admirable comedian. As a manager he showed little business aptitude. He made large sums of money but died poor.

[W. Davenport Adams's Dict. of the Drama; Theatrical Journal, 1852 and 1854; Illustr. London News, 1852 (advts.); Col. T. Allston Brown's Hist. of the New York Theatres; William Archer's The Theatrical World of 1894; Players of the Day (Newnes), 1902, pt. xi.; Daily Telegraph, 15 April 1908; Green Room Book, 1909; personal knowledge.]

EDWARD VII (1841–1910), KING OF GREAT BRITAIN AND IRELAND AND OF THE BRITISH DOMINIONS BEYOND THE SEAS, EMPEROR OF INDIA, was eldest son and second child of Queen Victoria and her husband Prince Albert. Their first-born child, Victoria, Princess Royal [q. v. Suppl. II], was born on 21 Nov. 1840.

I

The prince was born at Buckingham Palace at 10.48 a.m. on Tuesday 9 Nov. 1841, and the birth was duly recorded in the parish register of St. George's, Hanover Square. The conservative prime minister, Sir Robert Peel, who had just come into office, with the duke of Wellington, the archbishop of Canterbury (William Howley), and other high officers of state, attended the palace to attest the birth. No heir had been born to the reigning sovereign since the birth of George IV in 1762, and the event was the signal for immense national rejoicings. The annual feast of the lord mayor of London took place the same evening, and the infant's health was drunk with abundant enthusiasm. A special thanksgiving service was arranged for the churches by the archbishop of Canterbury, and the birth was set as the theme of the English poem at Cambridge University for the next year, when the successful competitor was Sir Henry Maine. The child was named Albert Edward—Albert after his father, and Edward after his mother's father, the duke of Kent. In the family circle he was always called 'Bertie,' and until his accession his signature was invariably 'Albert Edward.' He inherited according to precedent the titles of Duke of Cornwall and Rothsay, Earl of Carrick, Baron of Renfrew, Lord of the Isles, and Great Steward of Scotland, but by his parents' wish he was gazetted in addition as Duke of Saxony, his father's German title. The innovation was adversely criticised by Lord Palmerston and his friends, who disliked the German leanings of the court. On 4 Dec. 1841 he was further created, in accordance with precedent, by patent under the great seal, Prince of Wales and Earl of Chester.

Birth, 9 Nov. 1841.

From the outset it was his mother's earnest hope that in career and character her son should be a copy of his father. On 29 Nov. 1841 she wrote to her uncle, King Leopold of Belgium, 'Our little boy is a wonderfully strong and large child. I hope and pray he may be like his dearest papa' (*Letters*, i. 456). A week later she repeated her aspirations to her kinsman: 'You will understand how fervent are my prayers, and I am sure everybody's must be, to see him resemble his father in *every, every* respect both in body and mind' (MARTIN, *Life of Prince Consort*). From the boy's infancy to his manhood Queen Victoria clung tenaciously to this wifely wish.

The prince was baptised by the archbishop of Canterbury on 25 Jan. 1842 at St. George's Chapel, Windsor. The boy's grand-uncle, the duke of Cambridge, seventh son of George III, and his great-aunt, Princess Sophia, daughter of George III, were the English sponsors. The princess's place was filled through her illness by the duke of Cambridge's daughter Augusta, afterwards grand duchess of Mecklenburg-Strelitz. The other sponsors were members of German reigning families. At their head came Frederick William IV, king of Prussia, who was present in person with Baron Alexander von Humboldt, the naturalist, in attendance upon him. The king much appreciated the office of godfather. He was chosen instead of the queen's beloved counsellor and maternal uncle, King Leopold of Belgium, for fear of giving offence to her difficult-tempered uncle, King Ernest of Hanover, but the plan hardly produced the desired effect of conciliation. The other German sponsors were absent. They were Prince Albert's stepmother, the duchess of Saxe-Coburg, who was represented by Queen Victoria's mother, the duchess of Kent; Prince Albert's widowed kinswoman, the duchess of Saxe-Gotha, who was represented by the duchess of Cambridge; and Prince Albert's uncle, Duke Ferdinand of Saxe-Coburg, who was represented by Princess Augusta of Cambridge. The Queen specially asked the duke of Wellington to bear at the ceremony the sword of state.

Baptism and sponsors, 25 Jan. 1842.

Gifts and orders, which were always congenial to the prince, were showered on his cradle by foreign royalty. The king of Prussia, whose baptismal offering was an elaborate gold shield adorned with figures cut in onyx, conferred on him the Order of the Black Eagle. The Emperor Ferdinand I of Austria, Emperor Francis Joseph's uncle, made the infant 'quite proud' with his present of the Grand Cross of St. Andrew on 18 June 1844. Louis Philippe sent him a little gun on his third birthday.

The lines which the education of the heir-apparent should follow became his parents' anxious concern very soon after he was born. Baron Stockmar, Prince Albert's mentor, whose somewhat pedantic counsel carried great weight in the royal circle, was from the first persistent in advice. Before the boy was six months old, the baron in detailed memoranda defined his parents' heavy responsibilities. He warned them of the need of imbuing the child with a 'truly moral and truly English sentiment,' and of entrusting him to the care of 'persons morally good, intelligent, well-informed, and experienced, who fully enjoyed the parental confidence' (6 March 1842). After due consultation and deliberation Lady Lyttelton was installed as head of Queen Victoria's nursery establishment in April 1842. Her responsibilities grew with the rapid increase of the queen's family. She held the post till 1851, and inspired the prince with the warmest affection.

Views of his education.

In 1843 an anonymous pamphlet—'Who shall educate the Prince of Wales?'—which was dedicated to Queen Victoria, bore witness to the importance generally attached to the character of the prince's training. The anonymous counsellor restated Stockmar's unexceptionable principles, and Prince Albert sent a copy to the sententious baron. An opinion was also invited from Lord Melbourne, the late prime minister, in whom the queen placed the fullest confidence (19 Feb. 1843). He laid stress on the 'real position' and 'duties' which attached to the rank of heir-apparent and on 'the political temptations and seductions' to which previous heirs-apparent, notably George III's eldest son, the prince regent (afterwards George IV), had succumbed. Melbourne recalled the tendency of English heirs-apparent to incur the jealousy of the reigning sovereign and to favour the party in opposition to the sovereign's ministers. Without Lord Melbourne's reminder Queen Victoria was well aware that her uncle George IV was a signal object-lesson of the evil propensities to which heirs-apparent were liable. Nor did she forget that she herself, while heir-presumptive to the crown, had suffered from the jealous ill-will of King William IV (*Queen's Letters,* i. 580).

Melbourne's advice.

In the result Lord Melbourne's hints and Stockmar's admonitions decided Queen Victoria and her consort's educational policy. Stockmar, tackling the question afresh, on 28 July 1846 deduced from the spirit of revolution abroad the imperative need of endowing the child with a sense of the sacred character of all existing institutions, a sound faith in the Church of England, a capacity to hold the balance true between conservative and progressive forces, and a sympathy with healthful social movements. With the utmost earnestness the boy's parents thereupon addressed themselves in Stockmar's spirit to the task of making their son a model of morality, of piety, of deportment, and of intellectual accomplishment, at the same time as they secluded him from any active political interest. Their effort was not wholly beneficial to his development. Yet, whether or no the result were due to his parents' precautions, the country was spared in his case, despite occasional private threatenings, any scandalous manifestation of the traditional rivalry between the sovereign and the next heir to the throne.

English, French, and German governesses soon joined the royal household. German the prince spoke from infancy with his father and mother, and he habitually conversed in it with his brothers and sisters (BUNSEN'S *Memoirs,* ii. 120). He always retained through life a full mastery of all the complexities of the language. To his many German relations he spoke in no other tongue, and to his grand-uncle, King Leopold I of Belgium, and to that monarch's son and successor, King Leopold II, with both of whom he was through youth and manhood in constant intercourse, he talked in German preferably to French. Yet French, too, he learned easily, and acquired in due time an excellence of accent and a width of vocabulary which very few Englishmen have equalled.

Early familiarity with German.

Childhood and boyhood were wholly passed with his parents, sisters, and brothers in an atmosphere of strong family affection. His eldest sister, Victoria, whose intellectual alertness was in childhood greatly in excess of his own, was his inseparable companion, and his devotion to her was lifelong. His next sister, Alice (*b.* 25 April 1843), and next brother, Alfred (*b.* 6 Aug. 1844), soon joined in the pursuits of the two elder children, but the tie between the prince and Princess Victoria was closer than that between him and any of his juniors. The children's time was chiefly spent at Buckingham Palace or Windsor Castle, but there were frequent sojourns at Claremont, Esher, the residence of King Leopold, and at seaside resorts. The prince stayed as a baby with the duke of Wellington at

Episodes of childhood.

Walmer Castle (Nov. 1842), and several times in infancy at the Brighton Pavilion, the royal residence which was abandoned by the queen in 1845, owing to the pertinacity of sight-seers. In the same year Osborne House in the Isle of Wight became the regular seaside home of the royal family, and was thenceforth constantly visited by the prince.

In 1846 he and the rest of the family made a first yachting excursion from Osborne, paying a first visit to Cornwall, which was his own appanage. Next year he made a tour through Wales, the principality which gave him his chief title. In the autumn of 1848 he paid his first visit to Scotland, staying at Balmoral House, then a hired shooting lodge. The Scottish visit was thenceforth an annual experience. the future Archbishop Benson saw the royal party at their first Braemar gathering (15 Sept. 1848), and described the little prince as 'a fair little lad of rather a slender make with an intelligent expression.' A like impression was made on all observers. 'Pretty but delicate looking' was Macaulay's description of him when the child caught the historian's eye as he stood shyly holding the middle finger of his father's hand at the christening of his third sister, Princess Helena, at Windsor on 26 July 1846 (Lord Broughton's *Recollections*, vi. 181).

In 1849 he made his first acquaintance with another part of his future dominions. He accompanied his parents on their first visit to Ireland. Queen Victoria on her return commemorated the Irish people's friendly reception of her and her family by creating her eldest son by letters patent under the great seal, Earl of Dublin (10 Sept. 1849). Her father had borne the same title, and its revival in the person of the heir-apparent was a politic compliment to the Irish capital. The visit to Ireland was repeated four years later, when the royal family went to Dublin to inspect an exhibition of Irish industries (Aug. 1853). In later life no member of the royal family crossed the Irish Channel more frequently than the prince.

First visits to Ireland, 1849-53.

Meanwhile his education was progressing on strict lines. In the spring of 1849 Henry Birch, an under-master of Eton, 'a young, good-looking, amiable man,' according to Prince Albert, was after careful inquiry appointed his first tutor. Birch held office for two years, and was succeeded by Frederick W. Gibbs, a barrister, who was recommended to Prince Albert by Sir James Stephen, then professor of history at Cambridge. Gibbs filled his post till 1858. Other instructors taught special subjects, and with M. Brasseur, his French teacher, the prince long maintained a cordial intimacy.

A tutor appointed, 1819.

Endowed with an affectionate disposition, which was readily moved by those about him, he formed with most of his associates in youth of whatever age or position attachments which lasted for life. Very typical of his fidelity to his earliest acquaintances in all ranks was his lifelong relation with (Sir) David Welch (1820–1912), captain of the Fairy and Alberta, Queen Victoria's earliest royal yachts. The prince made his first sea voyage in Welch's charge when little more than seven, and thenceforth until the prince's death Welch belonged to his inner circle of friends. They constantly exchanged hospitalities until the last year of the prince's life, nearly sixty years after their first meeting.

The prince's chief tutors performed their functions under the close surveillance of Prince Albert, who not only drafted elaborate regulations for their guidance and made almost daily comments on their action, but in the name of the queen and himself directly addressed to his son long written exhortations on minutest matters of conduct. To his religious training especial care was attached, and a sense of religion, if of a rather formal strain, soon developed in permanence. But to his father's disappointment, it was early apparent that the prince was not studious, that books bored him, and that, apart from progress in speaking French and German, he was slow to learn. It was difficult to interest him in his lessons. The narrow range of books at his disposal may partly explain the defect. History, the chief subject of study, was carefully confined to bare facts and dates. Fiction was withheld as demoralising, and even Sir Walter Scott came under the parental ban. In the result the prince never acquired a habit of reading. Apart from the newspapers he practically read nothing in mature years. He wrote with facility and soon corresponded voluminously in a simple style. By his parents' orders he kept a diary from an early age, and maintained the habit till his death, but the entries were invariably brief and bald. At the same time he was as a boy observant, was quick at gathering information from talk, and developed a retentive memory for facts outside school study.

Prince Albert's vigilance.

Impatience of study.

His parents meanwhile regarded the drama, art, and music as legitimate amusements for their children. The prince showed some liking for drawing, elocution, and music, and was soon introduced to the theatre, visiting Astley's pantomime as early as 24 March 1846. From 1848 to 1858 he attended all the annual winter performances at Windsor, where Charles Kean and his company provided the chief items of the performance. As a boy he saw at Windsor, too, the younger Charles Mathews in 'Used up' and the farce of 'Box and Cox' (4 Jan. 1849). To the London theatres he paid frequent visits. In 1852 he heard Meyerbeer's 'Huguenots' at the Opera House in Covent Garden. In the spring of 1853 he witnessed more than once Charles Kean's revival of 'Macbeth' at the Princess's Theatre. In 1855 he witnessed at Drury Lane a pantomime acted by amateurs for the benefit of Wellington College, in which his father was deeply interested, and he showed the utmost appreciation of the fun. In 1856 he saw Mme. Celeste in pantomime at the Adelphi, and was a delighted spectator of some old farces at the same house. The early taste for drama and opera never left him.

Youthful amusements.

The royal children were encouraged by their father to act and recite, and George Bartley the actor was engaged to give the prince lessons in elocution. He made sufficient progress to take part in dramatic entertainments for his parents' amusement. In Jan. 1853 he played the part of Abner to the Princess Royal's Athalie in some scenes from Racine's tragedy. Next month he played Max in a German piece, 'Die Tafelbirnen,' his sisters and brother supporting him, and on 10 Feb. 1854 he in the costume of 'Winter' recited lines from Thomson's 'Seasons.'

Amateur acting.

As a draughtsman he showed for a time some skill. Edward Henry Corbould [q. v. Suppl. II] gave him instruction. For an art exhibition in the spring of 1855 in aid of the Patriotic Fund for the benefit of soldiers' families during the Crimean war, he prepared a drawing called 'The Knight,' which sold for fifty-five guineas. Opportunities for experiment in other mechanical arts were provided at Osborne. There a Swiss cottage was erected in 1854 as a workshop for the prince and his brothers. The prince and his brother Alfred during the Crimean war were busy over miniature fortifications in the grounds.

Progress in drawing.

The gravest defect in Prince Albert's deliberate scheme of education was the practical isolation which it imposed on the prince from boys of his own age. Prince Albert to a greater extent than the queen held that members of the royal family and especially the heir-apparent should keep aloof from their subjects, and deprecated intercourse save in ceremonial fashion. He had a nervous fear of the contaminating influence of boys less carefully trained than his own sons. There were always advisers who questioned the wisdom of the royal policy of exclusiveness, and Prince Albert so far relented, when his eldest son was a child of six or seven, as to invite a few boys whose parents were of high character and good position to play with the prince in the gardens of Buckingham Palace. Among these child associates were Charles Carington (afterwards first Earl Carrington and Marquis of Lincolnshire) and Charles Lindley Wood (afterwards second Viscount Halifax). Some seven years later the practice was continued at Windsor, whither a few carefully chosen Eton boys were summoned to spend an occasional afternoon. Besides Charles Wood, there now came among others George Cadogan (afterwards fifth Earl Cadogan) and Lord Hinchingbrooke (afterwards eighth earl of Sandwich); but the opportunities of intercourse were restricted. Prince Albert, who was often present, inspired the boy-visitors with a feeling of dread. The young prince's good-humour and charm of manner endeared him to them and made most of them his friends for life, but owing to his seclusion from boys' society he was ignorant of ordinary outdoor games, and showed small anxiety to attempt them. This want was never supplied. Subsequently he showed some interest in croquet, but ordinary games made no appeal to him, and he betrayed no aptitude for them. The only outdoor recreation which his parents urged on him was riding. He was taught to ride as a boy, and as a young man rode well and hard, possessing 'good hands' and an admirable nerve, while at the same time he developed a genuine love of horses and dogs.

Companions of youth.

Meanwhile the prince's presence at public ceremonies brought him into prominent notice. On 30 Oct. 1849 he attended for the first time a public function. He then accompanied Prince Albert to the City to open the Coal Exchange. His sister, princess royal, accompanied him, but the queen was absent

Early public functions.

through illness. The royal party travelled in the royal barge from Westminster to London Bridge. On 1 May 1851 he was at the opening of the Great Exhibition, and was much impressed by the stateliness of the scene. With his tutor and his brother Alfred he frequently visited the place in the next few months, and in June 1854 he attended the inauguration at Sydenham of the Crystal Palace, into which the exhibition building was converted. He accompanied his parents to the art treasures exhibition at Manchester, staying at Worsley Hall with Lord Ellesmere (29 June–2 July 1857). He was twice at Eton (4 June 1853 and 1855) and once at Harrow (29 June 1854) for the speech days, but solely as an onlooker. More important was his first visit to the opening, on 12 Dec. 1854, of a new session of parliament, which was called in view of public anxiety over the Crimean war. That anxiety was fully alive in the royal circle. With his parents the prince visited the wounded soldiers in Brompton Hospital, and was at his mother's side when she first presented the V.C. decoration in Hyde Park (July 1857).

To the Crimean war, which brought his mother into alliance with Napoleon III, emperor of the French, the youth owed a new and more interesting experience than any that had yet befallen him. In August 1855 he and his eldest sister accompanied their parents on their glorious visit to Napoleon III and the Empress Eugénie at the Tuileries. It was the boy's first arrival on foreign soil. At once he won the hearts of the French people. His amiability and his delight in the attentions paid him captivated everybody. Prince Albert wrote to Stockmar with unusual lightness of heart how his son, 'qui est si gentil,' had made himself a general favourite. The impression proved imperishable. Frenchmen of every class and political creed acknowledged his boyish fascination. 'Le petit bonhomme est vraiment charmant,' wrote Louis Blanc, a French exile in England, who as he wandered about London caught frequent sight of the boy; 'il a je ne sais quoi qui plaît et, aux côtés de ses parents, il apparaît comme un vrai personnage de féerie.' This early friendship between the prince and France lasted through his life, and defied all vicissitudes of his own or of French fortunes.

First visit to Paris, 1855.

While the prince's general demeanour gratified his parents, they were not well satisfied with his progress. He was reported to be wanting in enthusiasm and imagination, and to be subject to fits of ill-temper, which although brief were easily provoked. Prince Albert earnestly sought new means of quickening his intelligence. The curriculum was widened. In January 1856 the prince and his brother Alfred attended Faraday's lectures on metals at the Royal Institution; and William Ellis was summoned to the palace to teach the prince and his eldest sister political economy. Ellis, like all the royal tutors, noted the superior quickness of the girl, and failed to move much interest in the boy. At the end of August 1856, a fortnight's walking tour was made with his tutor Gibbs and Col. William Henry Cavendish, groom-in-waiting to Queen Victoria and a first cousin of the duke of Devonshire. Starting from Osborne, the party slowly travelled incognito through Dorset, for the most part on foot, putting up at inns without ceremony. But the secret of the prince's identity leaked out, and the experiment was spoilt by public curiosity.

Faraday's lectures, 1856.

Prince Albert did not conceal his anxiety over his son's backwardness. He invited the counsel of Lord Granville (22 Jan. 1857). Granville frankly advised 'his being mixed up with others of his own age away from home.' He ridiculed as futile 'the visits of Eton boys to the Castle for a couple of hours.' Never out of the sight of tutors or elderly attendants, he was not likely to develop the best boyish characteristics. A foreign tour with boys of his own age was suggested, and at some future date a voyage through the colonies and even to India.

Lord Granville's protest against mode of education.

In a modified fashion the advice was at once taken. In the spring of 1857 a second tour was made to the English lakes in the company of certain of the Eton boys who had been already occasional visitors to Windsor. Among them were Charles Wood, Mr. Gladstone's son, W. H. Gladstone, and Frederick Stanley, afterwards earl of Derby. Dr. Alexander Armstrong went as medical attendant and Col. Cavendish and Gibbs were in general charge. Lancaster, Bowness, Grasmere, and Helvellyn were all visited. But on the prince's return Prince Albert examined his son's diary and was distressed by its scantiness. A foreign tour followed in the summer. It was designed to combine study, especially of German, with the pleasures of sightseeing. On 26 July 1857 the prince left England to spend a month at

Königswinter near Bonn on the Rhine. The same company of boys went with him and the suite was joined by Prince Albert's equerries, Col. Grey and Col. Ponsonby, as well as Charles Tarver, afterwards canon of Chester, who was appointed to act as classical tutor. No very serious study was pursued, but the experiences were varied. On the journey down the Rhine, the party met the ill-fated Archduke and Archduchess Maximilian of Austria, who were on their honeymoon. From Germany the prince and his companions went on to Switzerland. At Chamonix Albert Smith acted as guide. The prince walked over the Great Scheidegg, and Roundell Palmer (afterwards Earl Selborne), who was traversing the same pass, wrote with enthusiasm in his diary of 'the slender fair boy' and of his 'frank open countenance,' judging him to be 'everything which we could have wished the heir to the British throne at that age to be' (Selborne, *Memorials*, ii. 327). The prince also visited at the castle of Johannisburg the old statesman Prince Metternich, who reported to Guizot that 'le jeune prince plaisait à tout le monde, mais avait l'air embarrassé et très triste' (Reid, *Life of Lord Houghton*).

At Königswinter, 1857.

Home again at the end of October, he enjoyed in the winter his first experience of hunting, going out with the royal buckhounds near Windsor. He found the sport exhilarating, and soon afterwards tried his hand at deer-stalking in Scotland. In January 1858 the festivities in honour of his elder sister's marriage with Prince Frederick of Prussia absorbed the attention of his family. The prince attended the ceremony at St. James's Palace dressed in highland costume (25 Jan.). He felt the parting with the chief companion of his childhood, but corresponded incessantly with his sister and paid her repeated visits in her new home. The close relations with the Prussian royal family which had begun with his baptism were thus greatly strengthened. On 1 April 1858 he was confirmed at Windsor by the archbishop of Canterbury, John Bird Sumner. 'Bertie,' wrote his father, 'acquitted himself extremely well,' in the preliminary examination by Gerald Wellesley, dean of Windsor. His mother described 'his whole manner' as 'gentle, good and proper,' epithets which well expressed his attitude towards religion through life. A few days later he made a short pleasure tour with his tutor to Ireland. It was his third visit to that country. He now extended his knowledge of it by going south to Killarney and leaving by way of Cork.

The Princess Royal's marriage, 25 Jan. 1858.

Confirmation, 1 April 1858.

A further trial of the effect of absence from home was made in May. It was decided that he should join the army, and on 5 May 1858, with a view to preparing him for military service, he was sent to stay at White Lodge in Richmond Park, the unoccupied residence of the ranger, the duke of Cambridge. A sort of independent household was there first provided for him. In view of the approach of manhood, his parents redoubled their precautions against undesirable acquaintances, but after careful investigation three young officers, Lord Valletort (the earl of Mount Edgcumbe's son), Major Christopher Teesdale [q. v.], and Major Lindsay, afterwards Lord Wantage [q. v. Suppl. II], were appointed to be the prince's first equerries. For their confidential instruction, Prince Albert elaborated rules whereby they might encourage in the prince minute care of his 'appearance, deportment, and dress,' and foster in him good 'manners and conduct towards others' and the 'power to acquit himself creditably in conversation or whatever may be the occupation of society.'

In residence at White Lodge, 1858.

Already at fifteen he had been given a small allowance for the purchase of hats and ties, for which he carefully accounted to his mother. Now he was advanced to the privilege of choosing his own dress, and the queen sent him a formal minute on the sober principles which should govern his choice of material. To neatness of dress he always attached importance, and he insisted on a reasonable adherence to laws of fashion on the part of those about him. To the formalities of official costume he paid through life an almost exexaggerated attention. This quality was partly inherited from his grandfather, the duke of Kent, but was greatly stimulated by his parents' counsel. Gibbs was in chief charge at White Lodge, and intellectual society was encouraged. Richard Owen the naturalist was several times invited to dine, and Lord John Russell, who was residing at Pembroke Lodge, was an occasional guest. The talk ranged over many topics, but was hardly calculated to interest very deeply a boy under seventeen (*Life of R. Owen*). He spent some time rowing on the river, and attended his first dinner-party at Cambridge Cottage, Kew, the residence of his great-aunt, the duchess of Cambridge, but all was too strictly regulated to give a youth much satisfaction. His sojourn at White Lodge was interrupted in August, when he went with his parents to Cherbourg, and renewed his acquaintance with the emperor and empress of the French. On 9 Nov. 1858, his seventeenth birthday, one purpose of his retirement to Richmond was fulfilled. He was made a colonel in the army unattached and at the same time was nominated K.G., though the installation was postponed. The date was regarded by his parents as marking his entry on manhood. Among their gifts was a memorandum signed by themselves solemnly warning him of his duties as a Christian gentleman. Gibbs, too, retired from the prince's service, and his precise post was allowed to lapse.

Parental admonition on seventeenth birthday, 9 Nov. 1858.

But there was no real change in the situation. His parents relaxed none of their vigilance, and a more complete control of the prince's affairs and conduct than Gibbs had exercised was now entrusted to a governor, Colonel Robert Bruce. The colonel fully enjoyed Prince Albert's confidence; his sister, Lady Augusta, was a close friend of the queen and was lady-in-waiting of his grandmother, the duchess of Kent. At the same time Charles Tarver was formally installed as instructor in classics.

Col. Bruce governor, 10 Nov. 1858.

For the next four years the prince and Col. Bruce were rarely parted, and Col. Bruce's wife, Catherine Mary, daughter of Sir Michael Shaw Stewart, usually assisted her husband in the strict discharge of his tutorial functions. The first incident in the new régime was a second foreign expedition of more imposing extent than the first. Travel was proving attractive, and his parents wisely encouraged his taste for it. During December a short visit, the first of many, was paid to his married sister at Potsdam (December 1858). Next month he with Colonel and Mrs. Bruce started from Dover on an Italian tour. Stringent injunctions were laid on Bruce by his parents to protect the prince from any chance intercourse with strangers and to anticipate any unprincipled attempt of journalists to get into conversation with him. The prince was to encounter much that was new. He travelled for the first time under a formal incognito, and took the title of Baron of Renfrew. On leaving England he presented colours to the Prince of Wales's royal (100th) Canadian regiment, which was in camp at Shorncliffe (10 Jan. 1859), and delivered to the soldiers his first speech in public. The duke of Cambridge was present and pronounced it excellent. From Dover he crossed to Ostend to pay at the palace of Laeken, near Brussels, a first visit to his grand-uncle, King Leopold I. The king's influence over him was hardly less than that which he exerted on the boy's mother and father. Passing through Germany, the party made a short stay at Berlin, where Lord Bloomfield gave a ball in his honour. It was the first entertainment of the kind he had attended, and he was 'very much amused' with his first cotillon. He reached Rome near the end of January and settled down for a long stay. King Victor Emanuel was anxious to offer him hospitality at Turin. But Queen Victoria deemed King Victor's rough habit of speech, of which she had some experience at Windsor in 1855, an example to be avoided, and the invitation, somewhat to Cavour's embarrassment, was declined. At Rome the prince was soon busily engaged in seeing places and persons of interest. Attended by Bruce, he called on the Pope, Pius IX, and talked with him in French. The interview 'went off extremely well,' Queen Victoria wrote to King Leopold (15 Feb. 1859), and the pope interested himself in the endeavour to make the visit to Rome 'useful and pleasant' (*Queen's Letters*, iii. 411). Of duly approved English sojourners the prince saw many. He impressed Robert Browning as 'a gentle, refined boy'; he was often in the studio of the sculptor John Gibson, and an introduction there to Frederic Leighton led to a lifelong intimacy.

Visit to Rome, Jan.-April 1859.

The outbreak of war between Italy and Austria in April hastened the prince's departure at the end of three months. H.M.S. Scourge carried him from Civita Vecchia to Gibraltar, where he was met by the royal yacht Osborne. From Gibraltar he passed to Lisbon, where he was entertained by Pedro V, king of Portugal. Queen Victoria and Prince Albert were attached to the Portuguese royal house by lineal ties and sentiments of affection. King Pedro's mother, Queen Maria, had been a playmate of Queen Victoria, and his father, Prince Ferdinand of Saxe-Coburg, was a first cousin of both Queen Victoria and her consort. With Portugal's successive monarchs the Prince of Wales was always on friendliest terms. The prince only reached home in June, after six months' absence, and was then formally invested K.G. with full ceremony. On 26 June Prince Hohenlohe, the future chancellor of Germany, dined at Buckingham Palace, and learned from the prince's lips something of his travels. The young man gave the German visitor an impression of good breeding, short stature, and nervous awe of his father.

Prince Albert was not willing to allow his son's educational course to end prematurely. An academic training was at once devised on comprehensive lines, which included attendance at three universities in succession. A beginning was made at Edinburgh in the summer of 1859. Holyrood Palace was prepared for his residence. His chief instruction was in science under the guidance of Lyon Playfair, whose lectures at the university on the composition and working of iron-ore the prince attended regularly. He showed interest in Playfair's teaching, visiting with him many factories to inspect chemical processes, and proved his courage and obedient temper by dipping at Playfair's bidding in one of the workshops his bare arm into a hissing cauldron of molten iron by way of illustrating that the experiment could be made with impunity (GRANT DUFF, *Notes from a Diary*, 1877–86, ii. 27). At the same time Leonhard Schmitz taught him Roman history, Italian, German, and French. For exercise he paraded with the 16th lancers, who were stationed in the city, and made excursions to the Trossachs and the Scottish lakes. But the stay in Edinburgh was brief.

At Edinburgh, 1859.

On 3 Sept. the prince consort held a conference there with the youth's professors and tutors to decide on his future curriculum. The Edinburgh experience was proving tedious and cheerless. The prince mixed with none but serious men advanced in years. The public at large was inclined to protest that now when it seemed time to terminate the state of pupilage, there were visible signs of an almost indefinite extension. 'Punch' voiced the general sentiment in a poem entitled 'A Prince at High Pressure' (24 Sept. 1859). But Prince Albert was relentless, and in October the prince migrated to Oxford on conditions as restrictive as any that went before. The prince matriculated as a nobleman from Christ Church, of which Dr. Liddell was dean, on 17 Oct.

At Oxford, Oct. 1859.

It was the first recorded occasion on which a Prince of Wales had become an undergraduate of the University of Oxford. Tradition alone vouches for the story of the matriculation in 1398 of Prince Henry, afterwards Henry V—Prince Hal, with whom the new undergraduate was occasionally to be linked in satire hereafter. No other preceding Prince of Wales was in any way associated with Oxford. But Prince Albert's son was not to enjoy any of an undergraduate's liberty. A special residence, Frewen Hall, a house in the town, was taken for him. Col. Bruce accompanied him and rarely left him. Prince Albert impressed on Bruce the boy's need of close application to study, and of resistance to social calls, as well as the undesirability of any free mingling with undergraduates. Herbert Fisher, a student of Christ Church, was on the recommendation of Dean Liddell appointed his tutor in law and constitutional history. He did not attend the college lectures, but Goldwin Smith, professor of modern history, with three or four chosen undergraduates, waited on him at his residence and gave him a private course in history. The text-book was the 'Annals of England,' by W. E. Flaherty (1855), and the professor only partially compensated by epigram for the dryness of the work. By Prince Albert's wish, Arthur Penrhyn Stanley, then professor of ecclesiastical history, gave him some religious instruction, while Dr. Henry Acland, his medical attendant, occasionally invited him to social gatherings at his house. With both Stanley and Acland the prince formed very friendly relations. He saw comparatively little of the undergraduates. He confirmed his acquaintance with Mr. Charles Wood. At the same time fox-hunting was one of his permitted indulgences, and the recreation brought him into touch with some young men of sporting tastes, to a few of whom, like Mr. Henry Chaplin and Sir Frederick Johnstone, he formed a lifelong attachment. He hunted with the South Oxfordshire hounds, of which Lord Macclesfield was master, and he saw his first fox killed near Garsington on 27 Feb. 1860, when he was presented with the brush. Hunting was his favourite sport till middle age. The discipline which Col. Bruce enforced prohibited smoking. But the prince made surreptitious experiments with tobacco, which soon induced a fixed habit.

The prince remained in residence at Oxford with few interruptions during term time until the end of the summer term 1860. He was summoned to Windsor on

9 Nov. 1859 for the celebration of his eighteenth birthday, which was reckoned in royal circles a virtual coming of age. His parents again presented him with a carefully penned exhortation in which they warned him that he would henceforth be exempted from parental authority, but that they would always be ready with their counsel at his request. As he read the document the sense of his parents' solicitude for his welfare and his new responsibilities moved him to tears. But the assurance of personal independence lacked genuine significance. In the Easter vacation of 1860 he paid a first visit to his father's home at Coburg, and made 'a very good impression.' He pleased his parents by the good account he brought them of 'dear' Stockmar's state of health (*Letters of Queen Victoria,* iii. 5; 25 April 1860). On his return home he found (Sir) Richard Owen lecturing his brothers and sisters on natural history, and he attended once (23 April 1860). In London at the opening of the long vacation he enjoyed the first of his many experiences of laying foundation stones. He performed the ceremony for the School of Art at Lambeth.

A formidable journey was to interrupt his Oxford undergraduate career. In July 1860 he carried out a scheme long in his parents' minds, which exerted on his development a far more beneficial effect than any likely to come of his academic training. During the Crimean war the Canadian government, which had equipped a regiment of infantry for active service, had requested the queen to visit Canada. She declined the invitation, but promised that the Prince of Wales should go there as soon as he was old enough. When that decision was announced, the president of the United States, James Buchanan, and the corporation of New York, both sent the queen requests that he should visit America. The queen very gradually overcame maternal misgivings of the safety of an English prince among American republicans. The American invitations were at length accepted, with the proviso that the American visit was to be treated as a private one. In any case the projected tour acquired something more than a merely colonial interest. An impressive introduction to public life was thus designed for the heir to the English throne. A large and dignified suite was collected. The prince was accompanied by the duke of Newcastle, secretary of state for the colonies, by the earl of St. Germans, lord steward of the royal household, and by Col. Bruce, his governor. Major Teesdale and Capt. Grey (*d.* 1874), son of Sir George Grey, went as equerries, and Dr. Acland as physician. Young Lord Hinchingbrooke, one of the Eton associates, was to join the party in America.

In Canada, July–Sept. 1860.

Leaving Southampton on 9 July 1860 in H.M.S. Hero, with H.M.S. Ariadne in attendance, the prince reached Newfoundland on the 23rd. The colonial progress opened at St. John's with processions, presentations of addresses, reviews of volunteers, levees, and banquets, which were constant features of the tour. Thence they passed to Halifax and Nova Scotia (30 July). On 9 Aug. he landed on Prince Edward Island, and on the 12th, near the mouth of the St. Lawrence, the governor-general of the Canadas, Sir Edmund Head, boarded the royal vessel. On the 20th the prince made a state entry into Quebec, the capital of French Canada. He stayed at Parliament House, which had been elaborately fitted up for his residence, and a guard of honour of 100 men was appointed to form his escort through the colony. At Montreal on 1 Sept. he opened the great railway bridge across the St. Lawrence; and passing thence to Ottawa, he there laid the foundation stone of the Parliament building. On the way to Toronto, the capital of upper Canada, the only untoward incident took place. Strong protestant feeling in the upper colony resented the enthusiasm with which the French Roman catholics of lower Canada had welcomed the prince, and the Orange lodges resolved to emphasise their principles by forcing on the prince's notice in their street decorations the emblems of their faith. At Kingston on Lake Ontario the townsfolk refused to obey the duke of Newcastle's direction to remove the orange colours and portraits of William III from the triumphal arches before the royal party entered the town. Consequently the royal party struck the place out of their itinerary and proceeded to Toronto, where a like difficulty threatened. Happily the Orangemen there yielded to persuasion, and the reception at Toronto proved as hearty as could be wished.

Leaving Canada for the United States, the prince made an excursion to Niagara Falls (17 Sept.), where, somewhat to his alarm, he saw Blondin perform on the tight rope, and at the neighbouring village of Queenstown (18 Sept.) he laid the crowning stone on the great monument erected to the memory of Major-general Sir Isaac Brock [q. v.], who was slain in the American war of 1812. Crossing Detroit river, he touched United States soil at Detroit on 19 Sept.; there he was met by Lord Lyons, minister at Washington. At once scenes of extravagant enthusiasm belied all fears of a cool reception. Short stays in Chicago, St. Louis, Cincinnati, and Pittsburg preceded his arrival at Washington (3 Oct.), where President Buchanan (an old man of seventy-seven) received him at the White House with friendliest cordiality. A crowded levee at White House was given in his honour. With the president he visited on 5 Oct. Mount Vernon, Washington's home and burial place, and planted a chestnut by the side of the tomb. Such a tribute from the great-grandson of George III was greeted by the American people with loud acclamations of joy, and England was hardly less impressed. 'The Prince of Wales at the Tomb of Washington' was the subject set for the English poem at Cambridge University in 1861, and the prize was won by Frederic W. H. Myers. Going northwards, the prince stayed at Philadelphia (7 Oct.), where he heard Madame Patti sing for the first time. At New York (11 Oct.) he remained three days. A visit was paid later to the military school at West Point, and proceeding to Boston he went over to Cambridge to inspect Harvard University. At Boston he met Longfellow, Emerson, and Oliver Wendell Holmes. He embarked for home in H.M.S. Hero from Portland in Maine on 20 Oct. and arrived after a bad passage at Plymouth on 15 Nov., six days after completing his nineteenth year.

At Washington, 5 Oct. 1860.

Everywhere the prince's good-humour, courteous bearing, and simple delight in novel experiences won the hearts of his hosts. 'Dignified, frank, and affable,' wrote the president to Queen Victoria (6 Oct. 1860), 'he has conciliated, wherever he has been, the kindness and respect of a sensitive and discriminating people.' The tour differed in every regard from his previous trips abroad. It was originally planned as a ceremonial compliment to the oldest and most important of English colonies on the part of the heir to the throne travelling as the reigning sovereign's official representative. No British colony had previously received a like attention. Canada accorded the prince all the honours due to his royal station. In the United States, too, where it was stipulated by Queen Victoria that he should travel as a private person under his incognito of Baron of Renfrew, the fiction went for nothing, and he was greeted as England's heir-apparent no less emphatically than in British North America. The result satisfied every sanguine hope. It tightened the bond of affection between Canada and the mother country at the moment when a tide of public sentiment seemed setting in another direction, and it reinforced the sense of unity among the British American colonies, which found expression in their internal union of 1867. On the relations of the United States and England the effect was of the happiest. On 29 Nov. 1860 Sir Charles Phipps, who was high in the confidence of Queen Victoria and Prince Albert, gave expression to the general verdict in a letter to Dr. Acland. 'The success of the expedition has been beyond all expectation; it may be reckoned as one of the most important and valuable state measures of the present age, and whether we look to the excitement and encouragement of loyalty and affection to the mother country in Canada, or to the soothing of prejudice and the increase of good feeling between the United States and Great Britain, it seems to me impossible to overrate the importance of the good results which the visit promises for the future.'

Effect of the American tour.

The general verdict.

On the youth himself the tour exerted a wholly beneficial influence. The duke of Newcastle noticed in the prince a perceptible intellectual development. The journey left a lasting impression on his mind. If at times in later reminiscence he associated Canadian life with some want of material comfort, he always cherished gratitude for the colonial hospitality, and never lost a sense of attachment to the American people. His parents felt pride in the American welcome, and a year later, when Motley, then American minister at Vienna, was passing through England, he was invited to Balmoral, to receive from Queen Victoria and Prince Albert expressions of their satisfaction. Some American publicists were inclined to attribute to the heartiness of the prince's reception Prince Albert's momentous diplomatic intervention in behalf of the north over the affair of the Trent. When the American civil war broke out next year, Prince Albert on the eve of his death powerfully discouraged English sympathy with the revolt against the authority of the government at Washington, which had given his son an ovation.

The prince's career in England pursued its normal course. He returned to Oxford in November for the rest of the Michaelmas term, and in December the queen paid him a visit there. At the end of the year he left Oxford for good. Next month his protracted education was continued at Cambridge. As at Oxford, a private residence, Madingley Hall, was hired for him. The Cambridge house was of more inspiring character then Frewen Hall; it was an old and spacious country mansion, four miles from the town, 'with large grounds and capital stables.' Col. Bruce and his wife took domestic control, and under their eyes the prince was free to entertain his friends. He entered Trinity College, while Dr. Whewell was Master, on 18 Jan. 1861. A set of rooms in the college was placed at his disposal, but he did not regularly occupy them. Joseph Barber Lightfoot [q. v.] was his college tutor, and when in 1897 the prince visited Durham, of which Lightfoot was then bishop, he recalled the admiration and regard with which Lightfoot inspired him. History remained his main study and was directed by the professor of history, Charles Kingsley. The prince attended Kingsley's lectures at the professor's own house, together with some half-dozen carefully selected undergraduates, who included the present Viscount Cobham, and George Howard, ninth earl of Carlisle [q. v. Suppl. II]. The prince rode over thrice a week to the professor's house and each Saturday Kingsley recapitulated the week's work with the prince alone. He was examined at the end of each term; the course finally brought English history up to the reign of George IV. Kingsley was impressed by his pupil's attention and courtesy, and like all who came into contact with him, bore him thenceforth deep affection.

At Cambridge, Jan. 1861.

Kingsley's lectures.

In 1861 there began for the court a period of gloom, which long oppressed it. On 16 March the prince's grandmother, the duchess of Kent, died; and he met his first experience of death at close quarters. He first attended a drawing-room on 24 June 1861 in the sombre conditions of official mourning. But more joyful experience intervened, before there fell on him the great blow of his father's premature death. In the summer vacation he went for a fourth time to Ireland, at first as the guest of the lord-lieutenant, the eighth Earl of Carlisle; but his chief purpose was to join in camp at the Curragh the second battalion, grenadier guards. For the first time in his life he was freed from the strict and punctilious supervision of his veteran guardians and mentors. The pleasures of liberty which he tasted were new to him. A breach of discipline exposed him to punishment, and he grew impatient of the severe restrictions of his previous career. His mother and father came over in August to a review of the troops in which he took part. 'Bertie,' she wrote, 'marched past with his company, and did not look at all so very small' (*Letters*, 26 Aug. 1861). With his parents he spent a short holiday in Killarney, and then for a second time he crossed the Channel to visit his sister, the Princess Royal, at Berlin (Sept. 1861). After accompanying her and her husband on a tour through the Rhenish provinces, he witnessed at Coblenz the military manœuvres of the German army of the Rhine.

At the Curragh, Aug. 1861.

This German tour had been designed with an object of greater importance than mere pleasure or change. The prince was reaching a marriageable age, and the choice of a wife was in the eyes of King Leopold, of Stockmar, and of the youth's parents a matter of momentous concern. It was inevitable that selection should be made from among princely families of Germany. Seven young German princesses were reported to be under the English court's consideration as early as the summer of 1858 (*The Times*, 5 July 1858). Fifth on this list was Princess Alexandra, eldest daughter of Prince Christian of Schleswig-Holstein-Sonderburg-Glucksburg, next heir to the throne of Denmark, which he ascended on 15 Nov. 1863 as Christian IX. She was barely seventeen, nearly three years the prince's junior. Her mother, Louise of Hesse-Cassel, was sole heiress of the old Danish royal family, and the princess was born and brought up at Copenhagen. Though her kinship was with Germany, her life was identified with Denmark. King Leopold, who discussed the choice of a bride with Queen Victoria, reported favourably of her beauty and character. But the prince's parents acknowledged his right of selection, and a meeting between him and Princess Alexandra was arranged, while he was in Germany in the summer of 1861. The princess was staying near at hand with her mother's father, the Landgrave of Hesse-Cassel, at the castle of Rumpenheim. The prince saw her for the first time in the cathedral at Speier (24 Sept. 1861). Next day they met again at Heidelberg.

Prospects of marriage.

First meeting with Princess Alexandra at Speier, 24 Sept. 1861.

Each made a favourable impression on the other. On 4 Oct. Prince Albert writes; 'We hear nothing but excellent accounts of the Princess Alexandra; the young people seem to have taken a warm liking to one another.' Again, when the Prince of Wales returned to England a few days later, his father writes to Stockmar: 'He has come back greatly pleased with his interview with the princess at Speier.'

For the present nothing further followed. The prince resumed his residence at Cambridge. He was in London on 31 Oct., when he was called to the bar at the Middle Temple, was elected a bencher, and opened the new library at the Inn. But his studies at Cambridge went forward during the Michaelmas term. The stringent discipline was proving irksome, and he was involuntarily coming to the conclusion, which future experience confirmed, that his sojourns at the two English universities were mistakes. On 25 Nov. Prince Albert arrived to offer him good counsel. He stayed the night at Madingley Hall. A chill caught on the journey developed into what unhappily proved to be a fatal illness. On 13 Dec. the prince was summoned from Cambridge to Windsor to attend his father's deathbed. Prince Albert died next day.

Prince Albert's death, 14 Dec. 1861.

At his father's funeral in St. George's Chapel on 23 Dec. the prince was chief mourner, in his mother's absence. He joined her the same day at Osborne. At the queen's request he wrote a day or two later a letter publicly identifying himself with her overwhelming anxiety to pay her husband's memory all public honour. On the 28th he offered to place, at his own expense, in the gardens of the Royal Horticultural Society, a statue of the prince instead of one of the queen which had already been cast for erection there, by way of memorial of the Great Exhibition of 1851.

II

The sudden death of his father, when the prince was just turned twenty years of age, was a momentous incident in his career. The strict discipline, to which his father had subjected him, had restrained in him every sense of independence and had fostered a sentiment of filial awe. He wholly shared his mother's faith in the character and attainments of the dead prince. In her husband's lifetime the queen had acknowledged his superior right to control her sons. But after his death she regarded herself to be under a solemn obligation to fill his place in the family circle and to regulate all her household precisely on the lines which he had followed. To all arrangements which the prince consort had made for her sons and daughters she resolved loyally to give effect and to devise others in the like spirit. The notion of consulting their views or wishes was foreign to her conception of duty. Abounding in maternal solicitude, she never ceased to think of the Prince of Wales as a boy to whom she owed parental guidance, the more so because he was fatherless. A main effect of his father's death was consequently to place him, in his mother's view, almost in permanence 'in statu pupillari.' She claimed to regulate his actions in almost all relations of life.

Queen Victoria's parental control.

Earlier signs were apparent, even in Prince Albert's lifetime, of an uneasy fear on the queen's part that her eldest son might, on reaching manhood, check the predominance which it was her wish that her husband should enjoy as her chief counsellor. In 1857 she had urged on ministers a parliamentary enactment for securing Prince Albert's formal precedence in the state next to herself. Stockmar was asked to press upon her the imprudence of her proposal, and it was with reluctance dropped (FITZMAURICE, *Lord Granville*). But the episode suggests the limitations which threatened the Prince of Wales's adult public activity. In his mother's sight he was disqualified by his filial relation from filling the place which her husband had held in affairs of state or from relieving her of any political duties. His mother accurately described her lasting attitude alike to her husband's memory and to her children in a letter to King Leopold (24 Dec. 1861): 'And *no human power* will make me swerve from *what he* decided and wished. I apply this particularly as regards our children—Bertie, &c.—for whose future he had traced everything *so* carefully. I am *also determined* that *no one* person, may *he* be ever so good, ever so devoted among my servants—is to lead or guide or dictate to *me*' (*Letters*, iii. 606).

The Prince of Wales always treated his mother with affectionate deference and considerate courtesy. Naturally docile, he in his frequent letters to her addressed her up to her death in simple filial style, beginning 'Dear Mama' and ending 'Your affectionate and dutiful son.' To the queen the formula had a literal significance. But on reaching man's estate the prince's views of life broadened. He travelled far from the rigid traditions in which he had been brought up. Difference of view regarding his official privileges became with the prolongation of his mother's reign inevitable. The queen was very ready to delegate to him formal and ceremonial labours which were distasteful to her, but she never ceased to ignore his title to any function of government. His place in the royal succession soon seemed to him inconsistent with that perpetual tutelage, from which Queen Victoria deemed it wrong for him to escape in her lifetime. Open conflict was averted mainly by the prince's placable temper, which made ebullitions of anger of brief duration; but it was a serious disadvantage for him to be denied by the queen any acknowledged responsibility in public affairs for the long period of nearly forty years, which intervened between his father's death and his own accession to the throne.

As soon as the first shock of bereavement passed, Queen Victoria set herself to carry out with scrupulous fidelity two plans which her husband devised for his eldest son's welfare, another foreign tour and his marriage.

Tour in the Holy Land, Feb.-May 1862.

The tour to the Holy Land which was to conclude his educational travel had been arranged by Prince Albert in consultation with Arthur Penrhyn Stanley. The suite included Gen. Bruce, Major Teesdale, Col. Keppel, Robert Meade, who had been associated with Lord Dufferin on his mission to Syria in 1860, and Dr. Minter as physician. The queen's confidence in Stanley was a legacy from her husband, and at her persuasion he somewhat reluctantly agreed to join the party. The prince travelled incognito, and owing to the family mourning it was the queen's wish that ceremonial receptions should as far as possible be dispensed with. Leaving Osborne on 6 Feb. 1862, the prince and his companions journeyed through Germany and Austria. At Darmstadt he was welcomed by the Grand Duke, whose son was to marry his second sister, Alice; thence he passed to Munich, where he inspected the museums and the galleries and saw the king of Bavaria. At Vienna he met for the first time the Emperor Francis Joseph, who formed a favourable impression of him, and thenceforth cherished a genuine affection for him. At Vienna he was introduced to Laurence Oliphant [q. v.], who was well acquainted with the Adriatic coast of the Mediterranean. Oliphant readily agreed to act as guide for that part of the expedition. From Trieste, where Stanley joined the party, the royal yacht Osborne brought the prince to Venice, to Corfu, and other places of interest on the passage to Egypt. Oliphant, who served as cicerone for ten days, wrote that the prince 'was not studious nor highly intellectual, but up to the average and beyond it in so far as quickness of observation and general intelligence go.' He recognised the charm of his 'temper and disposition' and deemed travelling the best sort of education for him. His defects he ascribed to a 'position which never allows him responsibility or forces him into action' (MRS. OLIPHANT'S *Life of L. Oliphant*, i. 269). The prince was on his side attracted by Oliphant, and many years later not only entertained him at Abergeldie but took him to dine at Balmoral with Queen Victoria, who shared her son's appreciation of his exhilarating talk.

In Egypt.

The prince disembarked at Alexandria on 24 Feb. Passing to Cairo, he lodged in the palace of Kasr-en-nil, and every attention was paid him by the viceroy Said. A three weeks' tour was made through upper Egypt. He climbed the summit of the Great Pyramid without assistance and with exceptional alacrity; he voyaged up the Nile to Assouan (12 March), and explored the temple of Carnac at Luxor. At length on 31 March he arrived in the Holy Land, where no English prince had set foot since Edward I, more than six hundred years before.

At Jerusalem.

Jerusalem was thoroughly explored, and the diplomacy of General Bruce gained admission to the mosque of Hebron, into which no European was known to have penetrated since 1187. 'High station,' remarked the prince, 'has after all some merits, some advantages.' Easter Sunday (20 April 1862) was spent on the shores of Lake Tiberias and at Galilee. Through Damascus the party reached Beyrout and thence went by sea to Tyre, Sidon, and Tripoli (in Syria). During the tour Stanley succeeded in interesting the prince in the historic traditions of Palestine. While he was easily amused, he was amenable to good advice, and readily agreed that sporting should be suspended on Sundays. 'It is impossible not to like him,' Stanley wrote. 'His astonishing memory of names and persons' and his 'amiable and endearing qualities' impressed all the party.

On 15 May the Osborne anchored at the isle of Rhodes. Thence the prince passed to Constantinople, where he stayed at the embassy with Sir Henry Bulwer, ambassador, and was formally entertained in his rank of Prince of Wales by the sultan. He saw the sights of the city. His host reported favourably of his tact and manner, and while he did not anticipate that he would learn much from books, he discerned powers of observation which would well supply the place of study. But he detected a certain danger in an ease of demeanour which at times challenged his dignity and in the desire for amusement. A first sojourn in Athens, where he was to be a frequent visitor, and a landing at Cephallonia brought him to Marseilles. At Fontainebleau he was welcomed hospitably by the Emperor Napoleon III and the Empress Eugénie, and on 13 June he rejoined his mother at Windsor. One unhappy incident of the highly interesting journey was the serious illness contracted by General Bruce in the marshes of the upper Jordan. He managed with difficulty to reach London, but there he died on 27 June 1862. The prince was thus deprived finally of the close surveillance which his father had deemed needful to his welfare.

At Constantinople.

While the court was still in deep mourning the marriage of his second sister, Princess Alice, to Prince Louis of Hesse-Darmstadt took place at Windsor on 1 July 1862.

The International Exhibition of 1862, which the prince consort had designed, had been duly opened in May by the duke of Cambridge, to whom much court ceremonial was for the time delegated by Queen Victoria. The prince inspected the exhibition in the summer and received with charming grace the foreign visitors—to one of whom, General de Galliffet, he formed a lifelong attachment. But the queen's chief preoccupation was the scheme for the prince's marriage which King Leopold and the prince consort had inaugurated the previous year. In the summer the queen wrote to Prince Christian, formally soliciting the hand of his daughter, Princess Alexandra, for her eldest son. Assent was readily given. At the end of August Queen Victoria left England to revisit Coburg, her late husband's home. On the journey she stayed with her uncle Leopold at his palace of Laeken, near Brussels. Her future daughter-in-law was with her father on a visit to Ostend, and Princess Alexandra came over to Laeken to meet Queen Victoria for the first time. The queen left for Coburg on 4 Sept. On the same date the prince set out to meet his mother and to begin what proved another long continental tour. On the 7th he arrived at Brussels, and paid his respects to Princess Alexandra at Ostend. Both were summoned by King Leopold to the palace of Laeken, and there on 9 Sept. 1862 they were formally betrothed. Next day they went over the battlefield of Waterloo together, and in the evening they attended a court banquet which King Leopold gave in their honour. They travelled together to Cologne, where they parted, and the prince joined his mother at Coburg.

The coming marriage.

The betrothal at Laeken, 9 Sept. 1862.

The engagement was made public on 16 Sept. in a communication to the press drafted by Queen Victoria. It was stated that the marriage 'privately settled at Brussels' was 'based entirely upon mutual affection and the personal merits of the princess,' and was 'in no way connected with political considerations.' 'The revered Prince Consort, whose sole object was the education and welfare of his children, had,' the message continued, 'been long convinced that this was a most desirable marriage.' On 1 Nov. 1862 the queen gave her formal assent to the union at a meeting of the privy council. The announcement was received in England with enthusiasm. The youth and beauty of the princess and her association with Denmark appealed to popular sympathies. 'I like the idea of the Danish connection; we have had too much of Germany and Berlin and Coburgs,' wrote Lady Palmerston (REID, *Lord Houghton*, ii. 83). In spite of the queen's warning, a political colour was given to the match in diplomatic circles. Prussia and Austria were steadily pushing forward their designs on the Schleswig-Holstein provinces which Denmark claimed. Public feeling in England, which favoured the Danish pretensions, was stimulated. In Germany it was openly argued that the queen and prince consort had betrayed the German cause.

Although the match was wholly arranged by their kindred, it roused a mutual affection in the prince and princess. But they saw little of each other before their marriage. On 8 Nov. Princess Alexandra paid her first visit to England, coming with her father to Osborne as the guest of the queen. There and at Windsor she remained three weeks, spending much of her time alone with the queen.

Princess Alexandra in England, Nov. 1862.

By Queen Victoria's wish the prince was out of the country during his bride's stay. On leaving Coburg he had invited his sister and her husband, the crown prince and princess of Prussia, to accompany him on a Mediterranean tour on the yacht Osborne. They embarked at Marseilles on 22 Oct. 1862. A most interesting itinerary was followed. A first experience of the Riviera was obtained by a landing at Hyères. Palermo, the capital of Sicily, was visited, and thence a passage was made to Tunis, where the ruins of Carthage were explored. Owing to an accident to the paddle-wheel of the royal yacht, the vessel was towed by the frigate Doris from the African coast to Malta. On 5 Nov. the party reached Naples, and there the prince's twenty-first birthday was passed without ceremony. There was some incongruity in celebrating so interesting an anniversary in a foreign country. Yet the experience was not out of harmony with the zest for travel and for foreign society which was born of the extended and varied wanderings of his youth. Before leaving southern Italy he ascended Vesuvius, and on the return journey to England he revisited Rome. From Florence he made his way through Germany by slow stages. At Lille on 3 Dec. he met Princess Alexandra on her way from England. He reached home on 13 Dec. By far the greater part of the year had been spent abroad on three continents—America, Asia, and Europe. Although he was barely turned one and twenty, the prince was probably the best travelled man in the world. There was small chance that he should cultivate in adult life any narrow insularity.

The prince's foreign tour, Nov. 1862.

A separate establishment was already in course of formation at home. On reaching his majority he had come into a substantial fortune. The duchy of Cornwall was his appanage, and provided a large revenue. Owing to the careful administration of the prince consort the income of the duchy had risen from 16,000*l.* a year at the time of his son's birth to 60,000*l.* in 1862. The receipts had been allowed to accumulate during his minority, and these were now reckoned to amount to 700,000*l.* Out of these savings, the sum of 220,000*l.* was bestowed with the prince consort's approval on the purchase for his son from Spencer Cowper of the country residence and estate of Sandringham in Norfolk. The transaction was carried out in 1861. The estate covered 7000 acres, which the prince subsequently extended to 11,000; and the rental was estimated at 7000*l.* a year. The existing house proved unsuitable and was soon rebuilt. A London house was provided officially. Marlborough House had reverted to the crown in 1817 on the lapse of the great duke of Marlborough's long lease. It had since been lent to the Dowager Queen Adelaide, widow of William IV, on whose death in 1849 it was employed as a government art school and picture gallery. In 1859 it was decided to fit it up as a residence for the Prince of Wales. During 1861 it was thoroughly remodelled, and in 1862 was ready for his occupation.

The prince's income.

For the next three months preparations for his marriage absorbed his own and the country's attention. Simultaneously with his return to England the 'London Gazette' published an official list of his first household. General Sir William Knollys, the prince consort's close friend, became comptroller and treasurer and practically chief of the establishment; Earl Spencer was made groom of the stole; the Earl of Mount Edgcumbe and Lord Alfred Hervey lords of the bedchamber; Robert Henry Meade and Charles Wood, afterwards Lord Halifax, grooms of the bedchamber; and Major Teesdale, Captain G. H. Grey, and Lieut.-colonel Keppel equerries. Herbert Fisher, his Oxford tutor, who had resumed his work at the bar, was recalled to act as private secretary, and he held the office till 1870. Mr. Wood was a very early companion, and all save Earl Spencer, General Knollys, and Lord Alfred Hervey had been closely associated with the prince already.

The first household.

On 14 Dec. 1862 the prince was at Windsor, celebrating with his mother the first anniversary of his father's death. The queen refused to relax her habit of seclusion, and on 25 Feb. 1863 the prince took her place for the first time at a ceremonial function. He held a levee in her behalf at St. James's Palace. The presentations exceeded 1000, and severely tested his capacity for the fatigue of court routine. At a drawing-room which followed at Buckingham Palace (28 Feb.) the prince was again present; but his sister, the crown princess of Prussia, represented the sovereign.

Parliament opened on 5 Feb. 1863, and the prince took his seat for the first time in the House of Lords with due formality as a peer of the realm. He was introduced by the dukes of Cambridge and Newcastle. He showed his interest in the proceedings by staying till half-past nine at night to listen to the debate, which chiefly dealt with the cession of the Ionian islands to Greece.

In the House of Lords, 5 Feb. 1863.

The queen was absent. Her speech from the throne, which had been read by the lord chancellor at the opening of the session, announced the conclusion of her son's marriage treaty, which had been signed at Copenhagen on 10 Jan. 1863, and ratified in London the day before. The prime minister, Lord Palmerston, informed the House of Commons that the marriage might 'in the fullest sense of the word be called a love match' and was free of any political intention (HANSARD, *Commons Report*, 5 Feb. 1863). A few days later a message from the queen invited the House of Commons to make pecuniary provision for the bridegroom. Parliament on the motion of Palmerston granted him an annuity of 40,000*l.*, which with the revenues of the duchy of Cornwall brought his annual income up to 100,000*l.* At the same time an annuity of 10,000*l.* was bestowed on Princess Alexandra, with a prospective annuity of 30,000*l.* in case of widowhood. Advanced liberals raised the issue that the revenues of the duchy of Cornwall supplied the prince with an adequate income, and that parliament was under no obligation to make addition to it. It was complained, too, that public money had been voted to the prince on his creation as K.G. and for the expenses of his American tour. But Gladstone defended the government's proposal, and the resolutions giving it effect were carried *nem. con.* The grant finally passed the House of Commons without a division. No other of Queen Victoria's appeals to parliament for pecuniary grants to her children enjoyed the same good fortune.

Pecuniary provision.

The marriage was fixed for 10 March. The princess left Copenhagen on 26 Feb. and spent three days (2–5 March) on the journey in Brussels as the guest of King Leopold, who was a chief sponsor of the union. On 7 March the prince met his bride on her arrival at Gravesend. Travelling by railway to the Bricklayers' Arms, Southwark, they made a triumphal progress through the City of London to Paddington. The six carriages, headed by a detachment of life-guards, seemed to many onlookers a mean pageant, but a surging mass of people greeted the couple with boundless delight (cf. LOUIS BLANC's *Lettres sur l'Angleterre*, 2nd ser. i. 13 seq.). At times the pressure of the enthusiastic mob caused the princess alarm. From Paddington they went by railway to Slough, and drove thence to Windsor. The poet laureate, Tennyson, summed up the national exultation in a Danish alliance when in his poetic 'Welcome,' 7 March 1863, he greeted the princess, with some poetic licence, as

The Princess's entry into London, 7 March.

> 'Sea-kings' daughter as happy as fair,
> Blissful bride of a blissful heir,
> Bride of the heir of the kings of the sea.'

The wedding took place on 10 March in St. George's Chapel, Windsor. The prince was in the uniform of a general and wore the robes of the Garter. Queen Victoria in widow's weeds overlooked the proceedings from a gallery. 'A fine affair, a thing to remember,' wrote Disraeli of the ceremony. Kingsley, who attended as royal chaplain, admired 'the serious, reverent dignity of my dear young master, whose manner was perfect.' The crown princess brought her little son, Prince William (afterwards the German Emperor William II), who wore highland dress. The short honeymoon was spent at Osborne.

The wedding, 10 March.

On 17 March the prince and princess were back at Windsor, and on the 20th they held a court at St. James's Palace in honour of the event. At Marlborough House they received an almost endless series of congratulatory addresses. Numerous festivities and entertainments followed, and the prince's social experience widened. On 2 May he attended for the first time the banquet of the Royal Academy. He had hardly spoken in public before, and he had learnt by heart a short speech. His memory momentarily failed him and he nearly broke down. The accident led him to rely henceforth in his public utterances on the inspiration of the moment. He mastered the general idea beforehand but not the words. His tact and native kindliness stood him in good stead, and he soon showed as an occasional speaker a readiness of delivery and a grace of compliment which few of his contemporaries excelled. Lord Houghton, who was a pastmaster in the same art, judged the prince to be only second to himself.

Public engagements.

The corporation of the City of London presented the prince with the freedom on 7 June, and gave a ball in honour of himself and his bride on the same evening at the Guildhall. He had already identified himself with civic life by accepting the freedom of the Fishmongers' Company on 12 Feb., which his father had enjoyed. A second City company, the Merchant Taylors', paid him a like compliment on 11 June. In this busy month of June the prince and princess went, too, to Oxford to take part in the pleasures of Commemoration. They stayed with Dean Liddell at the prince's college, Christ Church (16–18 June), and at the encænia he received from the chancellor, Lord Derby, the honorary degree of D.C.L. A year later similar experiences awaited the prince and princess at Cambridge during May week. They stayed in the royal apartments at Trinity College, and the prince received the honorary degree of LL.D. Meanwhile a sumptuous ball given by the guards regiment in the exhibition building at South Kensington on 26 June 1863 brought the gaieties of their first season to an end.

The prince's married life was mainly spent at Marlborough House. But Sandringham constantly drew him from London; he visited friends in all parts of the country for sport or society, and was in Scotland every autumn. Nor was his habit of foreign travel long interrupted. Part of the early spring was soon regularly devoted to Cannes or Nice in the Riviera, and part of the early autumn to Homburg, while tours on a larger scale were not infrequent.

Outside London his career for the most part resembled that of any man of wealth and high station. At Sandringham the prince until his death spent seven or eight weeks each year, living the life of a private country gentleman. The first Easter after his marriage was spent at Sandringham, but the old house was then condemned as inadequate, and a new mansion was completed in 1870. The hospitality at Sandringham was easy and unconstrained; and the prince's guests were drawn from all ranks and professions. He interested himself in his tenants, and maintained his cottages in admirable repair. On every detail in the management of the estate he kept a watchful eye. The furniture and decorations of the house, the gardens, the farm, the stables, the kennels, were all under his personal care. For his horses and dogs he always cherished affection. The stables were always well filled. In the kennels at Sandringham were representatives of almost every breed. He was an exhibitor of dogs at shows from 27 May 1864, and was patron of the Kennel Club from its formation in April 1873. He actively identified himself with the sport of the county. For some twelve years he hunted with the West Norfolk hounds, at times with the princess for his companion, but after 1880 he abandoned hunting, both at home and on visits to friends. Shooting at Sandringham gradually took its place as the prince's main sport. To his shooting parties were invited his Norfolk neighbours as well as his intimate circle of associates. He reared pheasants and partridges assiduously, profiting by useful advice from his neighbour, Thomas William Coke, earl of Leicester, of Holkham. Partridge-driving grew to be his favourite sporting recreation. He was a variable and no first-rate shot, but was successful with high pheasants.

Sandringham rebuilt, 1870.

His love of animals.

For his autumnal vacation at Scotland during September and October Queen Victoria lent him Abergeldie Castle, on Deeside near Balmoral, which she had leased in 1862 for sixty years. He varied his sojourn there by visits to Scottish noblemen, with one of whom, the duke of Sutherland, he formed an intimate friendship. The duke's mother was a beloved associate of Queen Victoria, and at the ducal seat, Dunrobin Castle, the prince was a frequent guest. In Scotland the prince's chief sports were grouse-shooting and deerstalking. He had killed his first stag on 21 Sept. 1858; on 30 Aug. 1866 he killed as many as seven, and for years he was no less successful. Fishing never attracted him. But he was always fond of the sea, and his early life on the Isle of Wight made him an eager yachtsman. Succeeding his father as patron of the Royal Yacht Squadron at Cowes, he became a member on 8 July 1865, commodore in 1882, and finally admiral in 1901. He was soon a regular witness of the Cowes regatta in August, and as early as 1866 was owner of a small yacht, the Dagmar. But neither horse-racing nor yacht-racing occupied much of his interest till he reached middle life.

Autumn holidays in Scotland.

But while country life had no lack of attraction for the prince, London, which Queen Victoria had practically abandoned for Osborne, Balmoral, or Windsor, was the chief centre of his mature activities. In the capital city he rapidly became the leader of fashionable life. The queen's withdrawal left him without a rival as ruler and lawgiver of the world of fashion, and his countenance was sedulously sought by all aspirants to social eminence. With manhood he developed increasingly an accessibility and charm of manner, a curiosity about persons, a quickness of observation, and a love of hearing promptly the

Place in London society.

current news. He took genuine pleasure in the lighter social amusements and gave them every encouragement. Consequently society in almost all its phases appealed to him, and the conventions of royal exclusiveness, to which he had been trained, gave way to his versatile human interests. There was a democratic and a cosmopolitan breadth about his circle of companions. He did not suffer his rank to exclude him from gatherings to which royalty rarely sought admission. He attended the reunions of the Cosmopolitan Club as a private member, or dined with friends at the Garrick Club, or attended the more bohemian entertainments of the Savage Club. In 1869 there was formed under his immediate auspices and guidance a new club called the Marlborough Club, with a house in Pall Mall almost overlooking Marlborough House. The members were drawn from the wide range of his personal acquaintances, and he joined them at the Marlborough Club without ceremony. A chance meeting at the Cosmopolitan Club in 1867 with the Hungarian traveller, Arminius Vambéry, made the stranger thenceforth a favoured associate. The experience was typical of his easy catholicity of intercourse.

His mother, while denying his title to political responsibility, was well content that the prince should carry on in her behalf her husband's works of charity and public utility. He readily obeyed her wish in this regard. No public institution or social movement, which his father had favoured, sought his countenance in vain. Of the Society of Arts he was soon elected president (22 Oct. 1863) in succession to the prince consort. He always took an active part in the choice of the recipient of the Albert medal, which was founded by the society in 1862 in his father's memory to reward conspicuous service in the arts, manufactures, and commerce. When on his accession to the throne he exchanged the post of president for that of patron, he accepted with much satisfaction the award of the Albert medal to himself. But he went far beyond his father in his personal association with great public institutions. He created a new precedent by accepting the presidency of St. Bartholomew's Hospital on 20 March 1867, an office which he also held till his accession. His public energy in any genuine cause of social improvement, education, or philanthropy knew indeed no slackening till his death. In every part of the country he was busy pronouncing benedictions on good works. Among his early engagements of this kind were the opening of the British Orphan Asylum at Slough (24 June 1863); the opening of the new town hall at Halifax (August 1863); the laying of foundation stones of the new west wing of the London Hospital (June 1864), of the British and Foreign Bible Society (11 June 1866), and of new buildings at Glasgow University (8 Oct. 1868); and the unveiling of the statue of Peabody, the American philanthropist, in the City of London (23 July 1869). He presided at innumerable charity festivals, beginning on 18 May 1864 with the Royal Literary Fund dinner, and he repeated that experience at the centenary celebration of the Fund in 1890. Like his father, too, he was especially active, when the opportunity offered, in organising exhibitions at home and abroad.

His philanthropic energy.

Early visits to Ireland had brought that country well within the scope of his interest, and although political agitation came to limit his Irish sojourns, he lost few opportunities in manhood of manifesting sympathy with efforts for the country's industrial progress. As guest of the viceroy, Lord Kimberley, on 8 May 1865, he opened the Grand International Exhibition at Dublin. It was thus in Ireland that he first identified himself in an authoritative way with the system of exhibitions. He returned to Dublin in the spring of 1868 on a visit of greater ceremony, and the princess came with him to pay her first visit to the country. The lord-lieutenant was the marquis (afterwards first duke) of Abercorn, whose eldest son, Lord Hamilton, had joined the prince's household in 1866 and was a very intimate associate. The prince was now invested on 18 April with the order of St. Patrick; he was made honorary LL.D. of Trinity College, Dublin, witnessed the unveiling of Burke's statue outside the college, attended Punchestown races, and reviewed the troops in Phœnix Park. It was the period of the Fenian outbreak, and there were threats of disturbance, but they came to little, and the prince and princess were received with enthusiasm. The lord mayor of Dublin in an address of welcome expressed a hope that the prince would acquire a royal residence in Ireland. Before and since the recommendation was pressed on the English government and it was assumed that it had the prince's acquiescence. A third visit was paid to Ireland during the prince's adult career, in August 1871, when he opened the Royal

Visits to Ireland.

Agricultural Exhibition at Dublin. Earl Spencer, the lord-lieutenant, and Lord Hartington, the chief secretary, were his personal friends, and under their auspices he enjoyed a week of brilliant festivity. Unluckily at its close (Sunday, 7 Aug.), while he was staying at the Viceregal Lodge in Phœnix Park, a proposed meeting in the park of sympathisers with Fenian prisoners in England was prohibited. A riot broke out by way of demonstrating that 'patriots are dearer to [Irish] hearts than princes.' The political disaffection, although it did not prejudice the prince's relations with the Irish masses, was not easily silenced, and fourteen years passed before the prince sought a new experience of Irish hospitality.

III

His mother's desire to exclude the prince from all political counsels was not altogether fulfilled. Her ministers at the outset of his adult career questioned her prudence in keeping him in complete ignorance of political affairs. From 1864 onwards the prince, stirred in part by the princess's anxiety for the fortunes of her family, was deeply interested in the wars which disturbed central Europe. Prussia and Austria continued their endeavours to deprive Denmark of all hold on Schleswig-Holstein. The prince's Danish sentiment was in accord with popular English feeling. But it caused embarrassment to Queen Victoria, who in spite of her private German leanings was resolved on the maintenance of England's neutrality. Her relations with her son were often strained by his warm support of the Danes.

Attitude to foreign politics.

In 1865 Lord Russell, the prime minister, avowed sympathy with the prince's request for access to those foreign despatches which were regularly placed at the disposal of all cabinet ministers. The queen reluctantly so far gave way as to sanction the communication to the prince of carefully selected specimens of the confidential foreign correspondence. The restrictions which guarded the privilege dissatisfied the prince, and his endeavours to secure their diminution or removal formed a constant theme of debate with the sovereign and ministers till near the end of his mother's reign. The queen's oft-repeated justification for her restraints was the prince's alleged lack of discretion and his inability to keep a secret from his intimates. Resigning himself with some impatience to the maternal interdict, the prince sought other than official means of information and influence in foreign matters. To foreign ambassadors he offered abundant hospitality, and with them he always cherished frank and cordial intercourse.

The prince's relations with the French ambassador in London, Prince de la Tour d'Auvergne, during the Danish crisis of 1864 show him in a characteristic light. On 8 Jan. 1864 a first child, a boy, had been born to the prince and princess at Frogmore. There were many festive celebrations, and the prince's guests were influential. But the rejoicings over the new experience of fatherhood did not lessen the prince's excitement regarding the foreign situation. On 10 March the christening took place at Buckingham Palace. At a concert in the evening the French ambassador was present. Napoleon III was making proposals for arbitration between Denmark and the German powers. The prince at once questioned his French guest on the subject with what the latter described to his government as the prince's customary indifference to rules of etiquette. The prince warned the ambassador with heat that the Danes were a brave people, who were ready to meet death rather than any kind of humiliation (10 March 1864). King Leopold, who was staying with Queen Victoria, sought to moderate the prince's energy. Twelve days later the ambassador dined at Marlborough House, and was surprised by signs of greater prudence and moderation in the prince's talk, which he attributed to the influence of King Leopold. The prince now agreed that Denmark would be wise in assenting to a pacification. He also spoke in favour of the idea of Scandinavian unity. The ambassador in reporting fully to his government the prince's deliverances, pointed out that the views of the heir to the English throne needed consideration, and that it would be wise for France, in view of the prince's opinion, to do what was practicable in support of Danish interests (*Les origines diplomatiques de la guerre de 1870–1*, Paris 1910, tom. ii. pp. 109 seq.). Thus while Queen Victoria and her ministers held that the prince's opinions counted for nothing, he contrived privately to give foreign ambassadors quite a different impression. The discrepancy between the home and foreign verdicts on his relations with foreign policy grew steadily.

Birth of an heir, 8 Jan. 1864.

Danish sympathies.

The prince's tact always more or less controlled his personal feelings. Gladstone detected only 'a little Danism' in the prince's conversation. If the prince was careful to prevent Count von Beust, the Austrian ambassador, whose hostility to Denmark was admitted, from even approaching the princess, he succeeded in establishing the best social relations between himself and the count. A passion for direct personal intercourse with all who dominated great events tended to override personal sentiment and prejudice. In April 1864 he drew on himself a severe rebuke in the royal circle by visiting Garibaldi, who was staying with the prince's friend, the duke of Sutherland, at Stafford House. He sought out first-hand intelligence of all that was passing abroad. In July of the same year, when he dined with Lord Palmerston, Sir Horace Rumbold, who was then secretary of legation at Athens, was of the company. The prince at once sent for him to learn the exact position of affairs in Greece, where his wife's brother, Prince William of Denmark, had just been elected king as George I.

It was, too, never his practice to depend for his knowledge of foreign complications on those whom he met at home. Scarcely a year passed without a foreign tour which combined amusement with political discussions. In September 1864 the prince paid a visit to his wife's family in Denmark, crossing from Dundee to Copenhagen. He extended his tour to Stockholm, where he was entertained by King Charles XV and had a first experience of elk-shooting. He freely discussed the political situation from various points of view. The expedition extended his intimacy among the royal families of Europe. Not only did he make a lasting acquaintance with the cultured Swedish ruler, King Charles XV, who as the grandson of General Bernadotte had a warm affection for France and a keen suspicion of Prussia, but he then inaugurated a long and cordial intimacy with the Russian dynasty. During his visit to Copenhagen the Princess of Wales's sister Dagmar was betrothed to the Grand Duke Nicholas of Russia, the heir of the Tsar Alexander II. The grand duke's death next year annulled the match, but the princess transferred her hand to the grand duke's next brother, Alexander, afterwards Tsar Alexander III, and a first link between the royal families of England and Russia was thereby forged.

In Denmark and Sweden, Sept. 1864.

From Denmark the prince proceeded to Hanover and thence visited his sister Alice in Darmstadt. On the return journey he was the guest at Brussels of his grand-uncle King Leopold, who was fertile in political counsel. The prince was home again on 6 Nov. The visit to Germany was repeated in 1865, when Queen Victoria unveiled a statue of the prince consort at Coburg. The prince there saw much of his German and Prussian relatives, with some of whom he stalked and shot bustards.

His foreign engagements in 1866 brought him for the first time to Russia. On the journey he stayed for a few days at Berlin, where his sister and her husband gave in his honour a banquet which the king of Prussia attended. On 9 Nov., his twenty-fifth birthday, he reached St. Petersburg to attend the wedding of his wife's sister Dagmar with the tsarevitch Alexander. The ceremony took place at the Winter palace. A visit to Moscow preceded his return to Berlin on the way home. On the Russian court he exerted all his habitual charm. Indeed throughout Europe his personal fascination was already acknowledged. Lord Augustus Loftus, the English ambassador in Berlin, noted on his leaving Berlin that the golden opinions he was winning in every country and every court of Europe had an 'intrinsic value' in England's international relations. On the affection of Parisians he had long since established a hold. France welcomed him with marked cordiality when, as the guest of Napoleon III, he visited the International Exhibition in Paris in June 1867. He served on the royal commission for the British section—a first taste of a common later experience. A fellow guest in Paris was Abdul Aziz, the sultan of Turkey, whose acquaintance he had made at Constantinople in 1862. The sultan reached England next month, and the prince was active in hospitalities on the queen's behalf.

A first visit to Russia, Nov. 1866.

The prince's family was growing. A second son, George, who ultimately succeeded him on the throne as George V, was born to him at Marlborough House on 3 June 1865. Their first daughter, Princess Louise (afterwards Princess Royal), was born at Marlborough House on 20 Feb. 1867. A second daughter, Princess Victoria, was born on 6 July 1868, and a third daughter, Princess Maud, on 26 Nov. 1869. Visitors at Sandringham or Marlborough House were invariably introduced to the children without ceremony and with parental pride. After the birth of Prince George in 1865, the princess accompanied the prince on a yachting cruise off Devonshire and Cornwall, in the course of which they visited the Scilly Islands and descended the

The prince's children.

Botallack tin mine near St. Just. For the greater part of 1867, after the birth of Princess Louise, the Princess of Wales was disabled by severe rheumatism, and in the autumn her husband accompanied her to Wiesbaden for a six weeks' cure.

A year later a foreign trip of the comprehensive type, to which the prince was well accustomed, was accomplished for the first time with his wife. In November 1868 they left England for seven months' travel. At Paris they stayed at the Hotel Bristol, which was the prince's favourite stopping place in Paris through life. They visited the emperor at Compiègne, and the prince took part in a stag hunt in the park. Thence they passed to Copenhagen. The prince paid another visit to the king of Sweden at Stockholm, and there his host initiated him into the Masonic order, in which he subsequently found a new interest. Christmas was celebrated at the Danish court. Another sojourn at Berlin with the crown prince and princess (15–20 Jan. 1869) was attended by elaborate festivities. The king of Prussia formally invested the prince with the collar and mantle of the order of the Black Eagle. He had been knight of the order since his birth, but the full investiture could be performed only in the Prussian capital. The collar was the one which the prince consort had worn. In the evening there was a state banquet in the prince's honour, and then he had his first opportunity of conversing with Prince Bismarck, who with rare amiability wore, by command of his master, the Danish order of the Dannebrog in compliment to the guests. From Berlin the prince and princess passed to the Hofburg palace at Vienna, where the Emperor Francis Joseph was their host, and renewed an earlier acquaintance with the prince. They offered their consolation to the exiled king and queen of Hanover before leaving for Trieste.

A seven months' tour, Nov. 1868–May 1869.

Prince Bismarck.

There they embarked on H.M.S. Ariadne, which was fitted up as a yacht, and travel began in earnest. The duke of Sutherland was chief organiser of the expedition, and he enlisted in the company Sir Samuel Baker the African explorer, Richard Owen the naturalist, (Sir) William Howard Russell the war correspondent, and (Sir) John Fowler the engineer, who were all capable of instructive guidance. The ultimate aim was to inspect the great enterprise of the Suez Canal, which was nearing completion, but by way of prelude a voyage was made up the Nile. The itinerary followed the same route as the prince had taken eight years before. At Cairo the party saw much of the viceroy Ismail Pasha. On the Nile, Baker arranged for the prince's sport, Owen gave lectures on geology, and Fowler described the wonders of the Suez venture. The prince was in the gayest spirits, playing on his guests harmless practical jokes, and putting all at their ease.

On the Nile.

On 25 March the prince and his party reached Ismailia to visit the Suez Canal works. The Khedive was awaiting them, but a more interesting figure, M. de Lesseps, conducted them over the newly excavated waterway. The prince opened the sluice of a completed dam, allowing the Mediterranean to flow into an empty basin connecting with the Bitter Lakes. Before the Khedive parted with his English friends at Ismailia he invited Baker to take command of an expedition against the slavers on the White Nile. The prince took an active part in the negotiation and suggested the terms of service, which Baker finally accepted with good result (W. H. Russell's *Diary*).

At the Suez Canal.

The prince was deeply impressed by the proofs he witnessed of M. de Lesseps' engineering skill. The Suez Canal was opened on 16 Nov. following, and next summer Lesseps paid a visit to London. On 4 July 1870 the prince, as president of the Society of Arts, formally presented to him the Albert gold medal founded in his father's memory for conspicuous service. In an admirable French speech he greeted Lesseps as his personal friend, whose attendance on him at Suez he reckoned an inestimable advantage.

On the return journey from Alexandria on 1 April 1869, the royal party paused at Constantinople, where the Sultan Abdul Aziz was their host. But the prince interrupted his stay there to make a tour of the Crimean battle-fields and cemeteries. Subsequently they went to Athens, to stay with the Princess of Wales's brother, King George of Greece, and to visit the country's historic monuments. Paris was reached by way of Corfu, Brindisi, and Turin. For a week Napoleon III offered them splendid entertainment at the Tuileries. Not until 12 May 1869 were they home again at Marlborough House.

In Turkey and Greece.

A year later France was exposed to external and internal perils, and the prince's generous host fell from his high estate. The whole tragedy moved the prince; it stimulated his political interests and thirst for political news. It was at a dinner-party at Marlborough House that Delane, the editor of 'The Times,' who was one of the guests, received the first intelligence in England of the outbreak of the Franco-German war on 15 July 1870 (MORIER, *Memoirs*). Throughout the conflict the prince's sympathies inclined to France. His mother's hopes lay with the other side. But the queen was no less anxious than her son to alleviate the sufferings of the emperor and empress of the French, when they sought an asylum in England from their own country. The empress arrived at Chislehurst in September 1870, and the emperor on release from his German prison in March 1871. The prince and princess were assiduous in their attention to the exiles. To the young Prince Imperial especially he extended a fatherly kindness, and when in 1879 the French youth met his death in the Zulu war in South Africa, the prince personally made arrangements for the funeral at Chislehurst, and was himself a pall-bearer. He was a moving spirit of the committee which was formed for erecting a monument to the French prince's memory in Westminster Abbey in 1880, and when the House of Commons refused to sanction that project, he urged the transfer of the memorial to St. George's Chapel, Windsor. He was present, too, when a statue of the French prince was unveiled at Woolwich (13 Jan. 1883). But the downfall of the French empire and the misfortunes of the French imperial family in no wise diminished the cordiality of the prince's relations with France under her new rulers. No sooner was the republican form of government recognised than he sought the acquaintance of the republican leaders, and he left no stone unturned to maintain friendly relations with them as well as with his older friends in the French capital. The perfect quality of his social charm enabled him to keep on good terms with all political parties in France without forfeiting the esteem of any. The prince showed his lively curiosity about the incidents of the Franco-German war by exploring in August 1871 the battle-fields round Sedan and Metz in the company of Prince de Ligne and of his equerry, Major Teesdale. He travelled incognito as Baron of Renfrew. From Alsace he passed on to join the princess once again at Kissingen. His strong French leanings were kept well under control in German company. A certain coolness towards the Prussian royal family was popularly imputed to him during the course of the recent war. But when the crown prince of Prussia visited London in Sept. 1871 the prince greeted him with a geniality which caused surprise in Germany. His courtesies led Bismarck's circle to imagine some diminution of his affection for France. But his conduct merely testified to his natural complacency of manner in social life.

The Franco-German war, 1870.

The Prince Imperial.

While performing with admirable grace the ceremonial and social functions attaching to his station, and while keenly studying current political events from a detached and irresponsible point of view, the prince somewhat suffered in moral robustness through the denial to him of genuine political responsibility, and his exclusion from settled and solid occupation. The love of pleasure in his nature which had been carefully repressed in boyhood sought in adult life free scope amid the ambiguities of his public position. The gloom of his mother's court helped to provoke reaction against conventional strictness. From the early years of his married life reports spread abroad that he was a centre of fashionable frivolity, favouring company of low rank, and involving himself in heavy debt. There was gross exaggeration in the rumours. But they seemed in many eyes to receive unwelcome confirmation, when a member of fashionable London society, Sir Charles Mordaunt, brought an action for divorce against his wife, and made in his petition, solely on his wife's confession, a serious allegation against the Prince of Wales. The prince was not made a party to the suit, but the co-respondents, Viscount Cole, afterwards earl of Enniskillen, and Sir Frederick Johnstone, were among his social allies. The case opened before Lord Penzance on 16 Feb. 1870, and the prince volunteered evidence. Amid great public excitement he denied the charge in the witness-box (23 Feb.), and the court held him guiltless. Apart from the prince's intervention, the case presented legal difficulties which riveted on it public attention. Lady Mordaunt was proved to have become hopelessly insane before the hearing, and on that ground the court in the first instance refused the petitioner relief, but after five years' litigation the divorce was granted (11 March 1875).

Allegations against the prince.

The Mordaunt case, Feb. 1870.

Public feeling was roused by the proceedings, and the prince's popularity was for a time in peril with the austere classes of the nation. The sensational press abounded in offensive scandal, and during the spring of 1870 the prince's presence at the theatre, and even on Derby racecourse, occasioned more or less inimical demonstrations. He faced the situation with characteristic courage and coolness. The public censure was reinforced by a wave of hostility to the principle of monarchy which, partly owing to the republican triumph in France, was temporarily sweeping over the country. Enterprising writers sought to drive the moral home. At the end of 1870 there was published a clever parody of Tennyson's 'Idylls of the King' called 'The Coming K——,' which with much insolence purported to draw the veil from the prince's private life. The assault was pursued next year by the same authors in 'The Siliad,' and the series was continued in 'The Fijiad' (1873), 'Faust and 'Phisto' (1874), 'Jon Duan' (1875), and finally in a prophetically named brochure, 'Edward VII; a play on the past and present times with a view to the future' (1876). All current politics and society came under the satirists' lash. But the burden of the indictment, phrased in various keys of scurrility, was that the prince's conduct was unfitting him for succession to the throne. The recrudescence of Queen Victoria's popularity and the manifest good-nature and public spirit of the prince soon dissipated for the most part the satiric censure. Yet an undercurrent of resentment against reputed indulgences of the prince's private life never wholly disappeared.

Public criticism.

There was never any serious ground for doubting the prince's desire to serve the public interest. On 13 July 1870 the queen's dread of public ceremonies imposed on him the important task of opening the Thames Embankment. The queen had promised to perform the ceremony, and her absence exposed her to adverse criticism. Three days later the prince illustrated his fixed resolve to conciliate democratic feeling and to encourage industrial progress by inaugurating the Workmen's International Exhibition at the Agricultural Hall. His attendance proved his native tolerance and broad-minded indifference to social prejudice. The trades-union leaders who were the organisers existed on sufferance in the eye of the capitalist public, and Auberon Herbert [q. v. Suppl. II], who received the prince on behalf of the promoters, was a leading advocate of republicanism. But it was the sturdy faith in the virtue of exhibitions which he had inherited from his father that chiefly brought him to the Agricultural Hall. Already on 4 April 1870 he had placed himself at the head of a movement for the organisation of annual international exhibitions at South Kensington in modest imitation of former efforts. He played an active part in preliminary arrangements, and he opened the first of the series on 1 May 1870. The experiment was not a success, but it was continued for four years. The prince was undaunted by the failure, and a few years later revived the scheme on a different plan.

The Thames Embankment, 13 July 1870.

The year 1871 was one of sadness in the prince's household. On 6 April his last child, a son, was born to the princess and died next day. In the autumn he went into camp with his regiment, the 10th hussars, at Bramshill, and commanded the cavalry division in manœuvres in Hampshire. A private visit which he paid from the camp to his Cambridge lecturer Kingsley at Eversley illustrates his kindly memory for his early associates. Subsequently in October he stayed with the earl and countess of Londesborough at Londesborough Lodge near Scarborough. On returning to Sandringham early in November typhoid fever developed (19 Nov.), and a critical illness followed. Two of his companions at Londesborough Lodge, the eighth earl of Chesterfield and his own groom, Blegge, were also attacked, and both died, the earl on 1 Dec. and Blegge on 14 Dec. (cf. *The Times* 22 Jan. 1872). The gravest fears were entertained for the prince. His second sister, Alice, was staying at Sandringham, and she and the Princess of Wales were indefatigable in their attendance in the sick chamber. On 29 Nov. Queen Victoria arrived for a few days, and a serious relapse on 6 Dec. brought her back on an eleven days' visit (8–19 Dec.). Sunday 10 Dec. was appointed as a day of intercession in the churches with a special form of prayer. Four days later, on the tenth anniversary of the prince consort's death, there were signs of recovery which proved true. The date was long thankfully remembered. Princess Alexandra presented to Sandringham church a brass eagle lectern inscribed 'A thanksgiving for His mercy, 14 Dec. 1871.'

Serious illness, Nov.-Dec. 1871.

By Christmas the danger was past, and rejoicing succeeded to sorrow. There was an elaborate national thanksgiving at St. Paul's Cathedral on 27 Feb. 1872, when the prince accompanied the queen and the princess in public procession. The queen privately demurred to 'this public show' on the ground of 'the dreadful fatigue' for the prince, and of the incongruity of making religion 'a vehicle' for a display of popular feeling. But the whole nation had shared the anxiety of the royal family, and claimed a share in their elation.

A visit to the Riviera completed the prince's convalescence. He left on a yachting expedition to Nice on 11 March, and afterwards voyaged down the coast to Italy. Before coming home he repeated an early experience which always interested him. In full state he paid a third visit to Pope Pius IX. He was home again on 1 June ready for his public work. In the interests of health he made his headquarters at Chiswick House, which the duke of Devonshire lent him. There he gave garden parties, which surprised many by the number and range of invited guests. His chief public engagement in London was a rare visit to the East End in behalf of the queen. On 24 June he opened the Bethnal Green Museum, to which Sir Richard Wallace [q. v.] had lent a portion of his great collection. The prince's appearance at Ascot in the same month was the occasion of a highly popular greeting.

A third visit to Pope Pius.

IV

The prince's illness evoked a new enthusiasm for the monarchy. The duke of Cambridge voiced the general sentiment, when he wrote to his mother that it had 'routed' the recent republican agitation. 'The republicans say their chances are up—thank God for this! Heaven has sent this dispensation to save us' (SHEPPARD's *Duke of Cambridge*, i. 310). Yet the mighty outbreak of popular sympathy, though it discredited and discouraged criticism of the prince, had not wholly silenced it, nor was the anti-monarchical agitation altogether extinguished. On 19 March 1872 Sir Charles Dilke [q. v. Suppl. II], then a rising liberal politician, who had lately preached through the country republican doctrine, moved in the House of Commons for a full inquiry into Queen Victoria's expenditure, and the motion was seconded by Auberon Herbert, who shared Dilke's republican views. Gladstone, the prime minister, who strenuously resisted the motion, impressively confessed his firm faith in the monarchy, amid the applause of the whole house. But at the same time Gladstone in private admitted the moment to be opportune to improve the prince's public position. With the prince Gladstone's relations were uninterruptedly happy. He often spoke with him on politics, thought well of his intelligence and pleasant manners, and treated him with punctilious courtesy. On 25 Jan. 1870 Gladstone spent an hour explaining to the prince the Irish land bill, and was gratified by the prince's patience. The prince was no party politician, and he cherished no rigid political principles. His interest lay in men rather than in measures, and his native tact enabled him to maintain the best personal terms with statesmen whose policy he viewed with indifference or disapproval. Gladstone's considerate treatment of him conciliated his self-esteem without affecting materially his political opinions. The personal tie between the political leader and the heir-apparent was involuntarily strengthened, too, by the comprehensive differences which separated Queen Victoria from the liberal statesman.

Gladstone and the prince's position, 1872.

In the summer of 1872, to Queen Victoria's barely concealed chagrin, Gladstone invited her attention to the delicate question of the prince's official status. The welfare of the prince and the strength and dignity of the crown required, Gladstone urged, that he should be regularly employed. At great length and with pertinacity Gladstone pressed his views in writing on the sovereign. He offered various suggestions. The prince might be associated with the rule of India and join the Indian council. With somewhat greater emphasis Ireland was recommended as a fit field for the prince's energies. Some of the duties of the lord-lieutenant might be delegated to him, and a royal residence might be purchased for his occupation for several weeks each year. The Irish secretary, Lord Hartington, the prince's intimate friend, favoured the proposed Irish palace. But the queen was unconvinced. She doubted whether the duties of the Indian council were onerous enough to keep the prince employed. In Ireland the prince's intimacy with the family of the duke of Abercorn imbued him with Orangeism. She evasively allowed that increased occupation would be advantageous to the prince, and she gave vague

The Queen and the prince's official employment.

assurances of assent to Gladstone's general proposition. But her unwillingness to pursue the matter in detail brought the negotiation to an end.

The prince's career underwent no essential change, although there was a steady widening of experience on the accepted lines. New titular honours were from time to time bestowed on him. On 29 June 1875 he was, much to his satisfaction, made a field-marshal. The distinction stimulated his interest in the army, which was in name at least his profession. Foreign tours abroad became more frequent, alike in France, Germany, and Austria. The great International Exhibition at Vienna in 1873 gave him opportunity of assiduous work. He was president of the royal commission for the British section, and took an active share in its organisation. At the opening ceremonies in Vienna in May he was the guest of the Emperor Francis Joseph, and played his part with his accustomed grace. At the beginning of 1874 he went for a second time to St. Petersburg, again as a wedding guest, now to attend the marriage of his next brother, Alfred, the duke of Edinburgh, to the Duchess Marie. The bride was Tsar Alexander II's daughter, and her sister-in-law, the tsarevna, was the Princess of Wales's sister. The prince's amiability won him fresh laurels at the Russian court. On his way home he stayed once more in Berlin with the old German Emperor William I, and then with the crown prince and princess at Potsdam, joining his brother-in-law in a boar-hunt. In July 1874 the prince and princess gave evidence of their earnest wish to play with brilliance their part at home at the head of London society. They then gave at Marlborough House a fancy dress ball on a more splendid scale of entertainment than any they had yet attempted. The prince wore a Van Dyck costume, with doublet cloak of light maroon satin embroidered in gold. The only guests who were excused fancy dress were the duke of Cambridge and Disraeli. Two days later the duke of Wellington acknowledged the force of the example by offering the prince a similar festivity at Apsley House, where the prince appeared in the same dress.

In Russia, Jan. 1874.

An experience a few months later illustrated the good-humour and cool conciliatory temper in which the prince faced public affairs. The prince and princess decided to pay a first visit to the city of Birmingham. The mayor, Mr. Joseph Chamberlain, a friend of Sir Charles Dilke, was acquiring a general reputation as an advocate of extreme radicalism, and had in articles in the 'Fortnightly Review' shown republican leanings. The programme included a procession of the royal party through the streets of the city, the reception of an address in the town hall, an entertainment at lunch by the mayor, and visits to leading manufactories. All anticipations of constraint or unpleasantness between the prince and the mayor were belied. With a tact which the prince himself could not excel, Mr. Chamberlain proposed his guest's health in the words: 'Here in England the throne is recognised and respected as the symbol of all constituted authority and settled government.' The prince was as discreet in reply (3 Nov.). (Sir) John Tenniel's cartoon in 'Punch' (14 Nov. 1874), entitled 'A Brummagem Lion,' showed Mr. Chamberlain as a lion gently kneeling before the prince and princess, and the accompanying verses congratulated him on concealing his 'red republican claws and teeth,' and on comporting himself as 'a gentleman' in the glare of the princely sun. The episode merely served to illustrate the natural felicity with which both the chief actors in it could adapt themselves to circumstance.

At Birmingham, 3 Nov. 1874.

In spite of the queen's qualms a more important public duty was laid on the prince than had yet been assigned him. Even in his father's lifetime a tour in India had been suggested, and Gladstone had considered a plan for associating the prince with the government of India at home. Early in 1875 Disraeli's government decided that the prince should make a tour through India, with a view to proving the sovereign's interest in her Indian subjects' welfare (20 March). The unrest from which native India was never wholly free seemed to involve the project in some peril, and at the outset controversial issues were raised by politicians at home. The expenses were estimated at a sum approaching 200,000*l.*, although in the result they did not exceed 112,000*l.* The government decided to debit the amount to the Indian exchequer, and radical members of parliament raised a cry of injustice. The prince's status in India also raised a perplexing problem of a more academic kind. The unofficial position of the prince in England seemed to the queen and her advisers a just ground for denying him in India the formal rank

Tour in India.

of her official representative. That position was already held by the viceroy, and his temporary suspension was deemed impolitic. Consequently the prince went nominally as the guest of the viceroy. The distinction was a fine one, and made little practical difference to the character of his reception. But the precedence of the viceroy was left in form unquestioned, and the queen's exclusive title to supremacy was freed of any apparent risk of qualification for the time being. The prince's suite was large. It included the chief officers of his household, Lord Suffield, Colonel (Sir) Arthur Ellis, and Mr. Francis (now Lord) Knollys, who had become private secretary on Herbert Fisher's retirement in 1870, and held that office till his master's death. Other members of the company were Sir Bartle Frere and General (Sir) Dighton Probyn, both of whom had seen much service in India; Frere took with him Albert Grey (now Earl Grey) as his private secretary. Colonel (later General) Owen Williams and Lieutenant (now Admiral) Lord Charles Beresford acted as aides-de-camp; Canon Duckworth went as chaplain; (Sir) Joseph Fayrer as physician; (Sir) W. H. Russell as honorary private secretary (to write an account of the tour), and Sydney P. Hall as artist to sketch the chief incidents. Lord Alfred Paget, clerk marshal to Queen Victoria, was commissioned to go as her representative. Private friends invited by the Prince of Wales to be his guests were the duke of Sutherland, the earl of Aylesford, and Lord Carrington. The tour was so planned as to combine a political demonstration of amity on the part of the English crown with opportunity of sport and recreation for the prince. In both regards the result was thoroughly successful. The prince showed keenness and courage as a big game sportsman, bearing easily and cheerfully the fatigue, while he performed all the ceremonial functions with unvarying bonhomie.

The prince's precedence in India.

The prince started from London on 11 Oct. 1875, and embarked at Brindisi on H.M.S. Serapis, an Indian troopship, which had been converted into a royal convoy. He stayed at Athens with King George of Greece, visited the khedive and Cairo, and after passing through the Suez Canal landed for a few hours at Aden. He arrived off Bombay on 8 Nov., was received by the viceroy, Lord Northbrook, and was welcomed by the reigning princes. At Bombay he stayed with the governor, Sir Philip Wodehouse, at Government House, where his birthday was celebrated next day. Having laid the foundation stone of the Elphinstone dock on 11 Nov. he picnicked at the caves of Elephanta (12 Nov.), and left on the 18th on a visit to the Gaekwar of Baroda. The Gaekwar provided him with his first opportunity of big game hunting. By his own special wish he came back to Bombay before the end of the month in order to proceed to Ceylon, where he engaged in some venturesome elephant shooting. Returning to the mainland, he reached Madras on 13 Dec., laid the first stone of a new harbour, and attended many festivities. Sailing for Calcutta on 18 Dec., he arrived on the 23rd. There the viceroy became his host, and he spent Christmas at the viceroy's suburban residence at Barakpore. On New Year's Day 1876 he held a chapter of the order of the Star of India, and unveiled a statue of Lord Mayo, the viceroy who had been assassinated in 1872. After receiving the honorary degree of D.C.L. from Calcutta University, he proceeded to North India, where he inspected scenes of the mutiny, and laid at Lucknow the first stone of a memorial to Sir Henry Lawrence and to those who fell in the defence of the city. On 11 Jan. he entered Delhi in formal procession. Passing thence to Lahore, he later in the month went into camp in Cashmere as the guest of the Maharajah of the state. At Agra on 25 Jan. he visited the Taj Mahal. February was mainly devoted to big game shooting, chiefly tigers, at Moradabad and in Nepal. A visit to Allahabad early in March and to Jabalpur as a guest of the Maharajah preceded his embarkation at Bombay on the Serapis (13 March). Smallpox was raging in the town and his departure was hurried. In a farewell letter to the viceroy he bore testimony to the satisfaction with which he had realised a long cherished hope of seeing India and its historic monuments, and of becoming more intimately acquainted with the queen's Indian subjects.

At Bombay, 8 Nov. 1875.

At Calcutta, 1 Jan. 1876.

On the return journey he showed many tactful attentions. At Suez he received Lord Lytton, who was on his way out to succeed Lord Northbrook as viceroy. At Cairo he was again the guest of the khedive at the Ghezireh Palace. After leaving Alexandria he paused at two English possessions—Malta, where he met his brother, the duke of Connaught, and at Gibraltar. Subsequently he landed at Cadiz for the purpose of visiting Alfonso XII, the new king of Spain, at Madrid. Thence he passed by rail to Lisbon to enjoy the hospitality of Luis I, king of Portugal.

On 5 May the Serapis reached Portsmouth, and the prince was met there by the princess and their children. The English people welcomed him with enthusiasm, and at the public luncheon at the Guildhall on 19 May he expressed anew his delight with the great experience. The Indian tour conspicuously broadened the precedent which the prince had set in boyhood by his visit to Canada. The personal tie between the princes of India and English royalty was greatly strengthened by his presence among them in their own country. In future years the prince's two sons successively followed his Indian example. His elder son, the duke of Clarence, in 1889–90, and his younger son and successor, George (when Prince of Wales), in 1905–6, both made tours through India in their father's footsteps. When King George visited India for the second time in the winter of 1911–2 after his coronation he went over much of the same ground and observed many of the same ceremonies as his father had done thirty-six years before.

Reception in London, 19 May 1876.

The prince at once resumed his usual activities at home and on the European continent. The fascination which France exerted on him from boyhood had fully ripened, and in 1878 the popularity, which came of his repeated presence in Paris, acquired a signal strength. His position there was based on ever broadening foundations. Even when he was a favoured guest of the imperial court, he had not limited his French acquaintance to imperial circles. Louis Philippe and most of his large family, into whom the prince consort's kindred had married, had been exiles in England since 1848, and the prince from boyhood shared his parents' intimacy with them and their partisans. Thoroughly at home in Paris, he always succeeded in the difficult task of maintaining the friendliest intercourse with persons who were wholly alienated from one another by political sentiment or social rank. He enjoyed visits to the duc and duchesse de la Rochefoucauld-Bisaccia (15 Oct. 1874) and to the duc d'Aumale at Chantilly (22 Oct. 1874). La comtesse Edouard de Pourtalès, le comte La Grange, le marquis de Breteuil, and all the royalist members of the French Jockey Club who stood outside the political sphere, were among the most intimate of his French associates, and with them he exchanged frequent hospitalities. The marquis de Galliffet, one of Napoleon's generals, who afterwards served the republic, was many times a guest at Sandringham. At the same time the prince was on equally good terms with republican politicians of all views and antecedents. On private visits to Paris the prince gained, too, admission to theatrical and artistic society. Freeing himself of all official etiquette, he indeed so thoroughly explored Parisian life that he was in person as familiar to the public of Paris as to that of London. To the French journalists and caricaturists he was a 'bon garçon,' an arbiter of fashions in dress, 'le plus parisien des anglais,' even 'plus parisien que les parisiens.' If the press made somewhat insolent comment on his supposed debts, his patronage of fashionable restaurants, his pupilage to his mother, and his alleged intimacies with popular favourites of the stage, the journalistic portrayal of him as a jovial Prince Hal was rarely ungenial (cf. Jean Grand Carteret, *L'Oncle de l'Europe*, 1906, passim).

Growth of interest in France.

The International Exhibition in Paris of 1878 gave the prince an opportunity of publicly proving his identity with French interests in all their variety. The prince presided over the royal commission which was formed to organise the British section, and he impressed its members, among whom were the leaders of British commerce, with his business capacity as well as his courtesy. He spared no effort in promoting the success of the movement, which was intended to give the world assurance of France's recovery from the late war, and of the permanence of the new republican form of government. The prince entertained the members of the English commission at the Café de la Paix on 29 April before the exhibition opened. In the days that followed he together with the princess took part in Paris in an imposing series of public celebrations, and his presence deeply impressed the French people. On 13 May he attended in state the opening ceremony, which was performed by Marshal MacMahon, the French president. With the marshal and his ministers he was at once on the friendliest terms and lost no opportunity of avowing his affection for their country, and his strong desire for a good understanding between her and England. He was the president's guest at the Elysée, and Lord Lyons, the English ambassador, whose acquaintance he had made at Washington, gave in his honour a brilliant

At the Paris Exhibition, 1878.

ball, which was attended by the president and the chieftains of political and diplomatic society. At an entertainment provided by M. Waddington, minister for foreign affairs, the prince met for the first time Gambetta, whose career had interested him and whose oratory he had admired as a chance visitor to the Chambre des Députés. Lord Lyons undertook the introduction. Gambetta thanked the prince for his frank expression of sympathy with France, and the prince assured the republican statesman that he had never at any time been other than France's warm friend. The interview lasted three quarters of an hour. Before they parted the prince expressed the hope of seeing Gambetta in England. Though that hope was not fulfilled, the prince sought further intercourse with Gambetta in Paris. Later in the year (22 Oct.) the prince met the English exhibitors at the British embassy, and gracefully spoke of his wish to unite France and England permanently in bonds of amity. Nearly a quarter of a century later he was to repeat as king in the same place almost the identical words, with the effect of arresting the attention of the world.

V

The prince was less curious about domestic than about foreign policy, but his lively interest in every influential personality led him to cultivate the acquaintance of all who controlled either. It was still the queen's wish that her ministers should treat him with official aloofness, and habits of reticence were easy to Lord Beaconsfield, her favourite prime minister. Assiduously courting his royal mistress's favour, he tacitly accepted her modest estimate of her son's political discretion. Yet Lord Beaconsfield's forward foreign policy in opposition to Russia was quite as congenial to the prince as to his mother, and he made many professions of his agreement. In all companies he announced his anti-Russian sentiment, and he talked of applying for a command in the field, if war broke out between Russia and England (cf. RUMBOLD, *Further Recollections*, 1903, p. 126). He sedulously cultivated the conservative leader's society. In January 1880, when Lord Beaconsfield's political position speciously looked as strong as ever, the prince went by his own invitation on a visit to Hughenden, the prime minister's country residence (12 Jan.). The old statesman was somewhat embarrassed by the compliment.

The prince and Lord Beaconsfield.

After his fall from power, the prince's attentions continued, and Lord Beaconsfield dined with the prince at Marlborough House on 19 March 1881. It was the last time Lord Beaconsfield dined from home. Exactly a month later he died. The prince represented Queen Victoria at the funeral, and laid on the coffin a wreath with a card on which he wrote 'A tribute of friendship and affection.'

With a complete freedom from party prepossessions, the prince was at the same time seeking to extend his personal knowledge of the liberal leaders. The advanced radical wing of the liberal party won before the dissolution of 1880, both in parliament and the country, a prominent place which roused high expectations. Sir Charles Dilke was the radical chief, and Mr. Chamberlain, whom the prince met at Birmingham in 1874, was Dilke's first lieutenant. An invitation to Mr. Chamberlain to dine at Marlborough House in 1879 caused the group surprise, and when on 12 March 1880 Lord Fife, a member of the prince's inner circle, invited Dilke to dinner to meet the Prince of Wales, 'who would be very happy to make your acquaintance,' the situation looked to the radical protagonist a little puzzling. But the prince's only purpose was to keep in personal touch with the promoters of every rising cause. To Dilke the prince 'laid himself out to be pleasant.' They talked nearly all the evening, chiefly on French politics and the Greek question.

The prince and the radicals.

From an early period the prince had occasionally attended debates in both houses of parliament, seated in the upper chamber on the cross benches and in the House of Commons in the peers' gallery in the place over the clock. He rarely missed the introduction of the budget or a great political measure. On 6 May 1879 he personally engaged in the parliamentary conflict. He voted for the second reading of the deceased wife's sister bill, which, in spite of his support, was rejected by 101 to 81. Lord Houghton seems to have persuaded him to take the step, which challenged the constitutional tradition of the heir-apparent's insensibility in public to controversial issues. With the accession of Gladstone and the liberals to power in the spring of 1880 he set himself to follow the course of politics with a keener zest. He took the oath in the House of Lords at the opening of the new parliament with a view to regular attendance. The prime minister was willing

His vote in parliament, 6 May 1879.

to gratify his request for the regular communication to him of the confidential despatches, but Queen Victoria was still unwilling to assent, save on terms of rigorous selection by herself, which the prince deemed humiliating. He let it be known that he asked for all the confidential papers or none. But Gladstone encouraged his thirst for political knowledge, although it could only be partially and informally satisfied.

With Dilke, who became under-secretary for foreign affairs in Gladstone's administration in May 1880, the prince rapidly developed a close intimacy, and through him apparently hoped to play a part on the political stage. The prince anxiously appealed to the under-secretary 'to be kept informed of foreign affairs.' Dilke perceived that the prince's views of modern history were somewhat vitiated by the habitual refusal to him of official knowledge. But in Feb. 1881 Dilke willingly assented to the prince's proposal that while in Paris next month he should see M. Jules Ferry, the premier, and endeavour to overcome his unreadiness to negotiate promptly a new Anglo-French treaty of commerce. Dilke prepared a note of what the prince should say. In March he satisfactorily performed his mission, which was a new and pleasing experience. Gambetta, who was Dilke's personal friend, wrote that the prince 'had made some impression.' But the general negotiation moved forward slowly. In the autumn Dilke arrived in Paris. The prince was there again at the time, and once more offered to use his influence, both with M. Ferry and with M. Tirard, minister of commerce. The prince showed himself anxious to become better acquainted with Gambetta, and Dilke invited the two to meet at 'déjeuner' (24 Oct. 1881). A day or two later (on a suggestion from the prince made through Dilke) Gambetta sent him his photograph, which he signed thus: 'Au plus aimable des princes. L. Gambetta, un ami de l'Angleterre.'

Intimacy with Sir Charles Dilke.

The cordiality of the relations between Gambetta and the prince forms an interesting episode in the career of both men. Gambetta was clearly impressed by the width of the prince's interest in European affairs. The prince in the Frenchman's eyes was far more than 'un festoyeur'; he loved France 'à la fois gaîment et sérieusement,' and his dream was of an Anglo-French entente. According to Madame Adam, Gambetta's confidante, the prince, by disclosing to the statesman at an early meeting secret negotiations between Bismarck and Lord Beaconsfield, led Gambetta to qualify the encouragement which he was proposing to offer Greek ambitions for territorial expansion. But Madame Adam seems here to exaggerate the influence of the prince (ADAM, *Mes Souvenirs*, vii. 15 seq.).

In March 1881 the royal family was greatly shocked by the assassination of the Tsar Alexander II in St. Petersburg. Lord Dufferin, the English ambassador, promptly advised, on grounds of humanity and policy, that the prince and princess, whose sister was the tsarevitch's wife, should come to Russia for the funeral of the murdered sovereign. Queen Victoria deemed the risk almost prohibitive, and warned Lord Dufferin that the responsibility for any untoward result would rest on him (LYALL'S *Life of Lord Dufferin*). But neither prince nor princess hesitated for a moment. They attended the funeral, and the prince invested the new tsar with the order of the Garter. Their presence proved an immense consolation to the Russian royal family and lightened the heavy gloom of the Russian court and capital. Courage was never lacking in the prince. In the summer of 1882 the outbreak of rebellion in Egypt, and the resolve of the English government to suppress it by force of arms, deeply stirred his patriotic feeling. He at once offered to serve in the campaign. The duke of Cambridge, the commander-in-chief, to whom he addressed his proposal, forwarded it to the government, and Lord Granville, the foreign minister, replied to the duke on 30 July 1882, 'It is highly creditable to the pluck and spirit of the prince to wish to run the risks, both to health and to life, which the campaign offers, but it is clearly undesirable H.R.H. should go' (VERNER, *Duke of Cambridge*, 1901, ii. 234–5). Precedents for the appearance of the heir-apparent on the field of battle abounded in English and foreign history, but they were held to be inapplicable.

In St. Petersburg, March 1881.

Volunteers for the war in Egypt, July 1882.

A desire to be useful to the state, in spite of his lack of official position, repeatedly found expression during Gladstone's second administration. In the struggle between the two houses over the franchise bill (November 1884), the prince offered his services in negotiating a settlement. He asked Lord Rowton to let it be known that he was willing to act as intermediary

The franchise bill, Nov. 1884.

between Gladstone and Lord Salisbury, the leader of the opposition. But the friendly suggestion was not seriously entertained. The prince shared the queen's habitual anxiety concerning warfare between lords and commons, but his proffered intervention probably reflected nothing beyond a wish to figure in political affairs.

Friendliness with members of the liberal government did not always imply acquiescence in their policy. Of the liberal government's attitude to many of the problems which South Africa and Egypt presented, the prince openly disapproved. He was frank in private expression of dissatisfaction alike with the recall from the Cape in 1880 of Sir Bartle Frere, his companion in India, and with the treaty of peace made with the Boers after the defeat of Majuba in 1881. He was president of the committee for erecting a statue of Frere on his death, and unveiled it on the Thames Embankment on 5 June 1888, when he called Frere 'a highly esteemed and dear friend of myself.' Next year (1 Aug. 1889), when he presided at the Guildhall over a memorable meeting to celebrate the jubilee of the abolition of slavery in the British colonies, he paid in a stirring speech a further tribute to the services of his friend Sir Bartle Frere. Of the pusillanimity which seemed to him to characterise the liberal party's treatment of the Soudan in 1884 he spoke with impatience, and he earnestly deplored the sacrifice of General Gordon. When Lord Salisbury moved a vote of censure on the government for their vacillating policy he was in his place in the House of Lords on 25 Feb. 1885. He was present at the memorial service in St. Paul's Cathedral on the day of mourning for Gordon's death (13 March 1885). He actively interested himself in the movement for commemorating Gordon's heroism. He attended the first meeting for the purpose at the Mansion House on 30 May 1885, and moved the first resolution. He summoned another meeting at Marlborough House on 12 Jan. 1886, when the scheme of the Gordon boys' memorial home (now at Chobham) was inaugurated. On 19 May 1890 he unveiled Gordon's statue at Chatham.

Dissent from the liberal government, 1881-4.

Sir Bartle Frere.

On 8 Feb. 1884 the government decided to appoint a commission on the housing of the working classes. The prince's friend Dilke, now president of the local government board, was made chairman, and the prince expressed a desire to serve. Gladstone at once acceded to his request. The matter was referred to the queen, who raised no objection (13 Feb.). The subject interested him deeply. As duke of Cornwall he was owner of many small houses in south London, and as the leases fell in he was proposing to retain the buildings in his own hands, with a view to converting them into better habitations. The change in tenure improved the profits of the estate as well as the character of the dwellings. On 22 Feb. 1884 Lord Salisbury moved an address to the crown for the appointment of the commission. The prince supported the motion, making on the occasion his first and only speech as a peer in the House of Lords. 'I take the keenest and liveliest interest in this great question,' he said. He was flattered at having been appointed a member of the commission. He had greatly improved the dwellings on his Sandringham estate; he had 'visited a few days ago two of the poorest courts in the district of St. Pancras and Holborn, and had found the conditions perfectly disgraceful.' He hoped measures of a drastic kind would follow the inquiry.

A royal commission on housing, 8 Feb. 1884.

The commissioners formed an interesting but hardly homogeneous assembly. Cardinal Manning had accepted a seat, and difficulties arose as to his precedence. The prince's opinion was invited. He thought that Manning, being a cardinal, ranked as a foreign prince next to himself. Among the other members of the commission, the marquis of Salisbury held highest rank. The queen with certain qualifications took the prince's view, which was finally adopted, but not without some heart-burnings. The commissioners included, too, Henry Broadhurst, a labour member of parliament, and Mr. Joseph Arch, a leader of agricultural labourers. The prince attended the meetings with regularity, and abridged his holiday at Royat in May 1884 in order to be present at one of the early sittings. On 16 Nov. he entertained many of the members at Sandringham. With all his colleagues he established very cordial relations. With Mr. Arch, who lived in Warwickshire, at Barford Cottage, he was especially friendly, and the liking for him never waned. When Mr. Arch sat in the House of Commons (1885–6, 1892–1900) for the division of North West Norfolk in which Sandringham stands, the prince greeted him as his own representative and visited him at his home in the summer of 1898.

Friendliness with Mr. Joseph Arch.

The commission decided to take evidence at both Edinburgh and Dublin (January 1885). It was deemed politic for the prince, if he travelled with the commission at all, to go to Dublin if he went to Edinburgh. The final decision was that he should go to Dublin independently of the commission and study the housing question there privately. In spite of the political agitation that was raging in the country, both the queen and Lord Spencer, the lord-lieutenant, saw some advantage in such an expedition. The prince had not been to Ireland for fourteen years. It was now settled that he and the princess should revisit the country in April. The conditions admitted of his inspecting the crowded slums of Dublin and at the same time of his testing anew the loyalty of the Irish people.

Visit to Ireland, April 1885.

The experiment was not without its dangers, but the threats of opposition came to little. The nationalist leaders issued a manifesto urging on their followers an attitude of reserve. The lord mayor and corporation of Dublin refused to present an address of welcome, but a city reception committee well filled their place (9 April). The prince visited without protection the poor districts of the city and was heartily received. On 10 April he laid the foundation stone of the New Museum of Science and of the national library; at the Royal University he received the hon. degree of LL.D. and the princess that of Mus.Doc. Next day he opened the new dock at the extremity of North Wall, and named it the Alexandra basin. He paid a visit to Trinity College, Dublin, and presented in the gardens of Dublin Castle new colours to the duke of Cornwall's light infantry.

Nationalist attitude.

On 13 April the royal party started for Cork. The home rulers of the south urged the people to resent the visit as a degradation. On the road hostile demonstrations were made. But the prince was undisturbed. From Cork he passed to Limerick, where no jarring notes were struck, and thence went by way of Dublin to Belfast, where there was abundant enthusiasm (23 April). After a day at Londonderry (26 April), he left Larne for Holyhead (27 April). The nationalists' endeavour to prove the disloyalty of Ireland met with no genuine success.

VI

One of the interests which grew upon the prince in middle life was freemasonry, which powerfully appealed to his fraternal and philanthropic instincts. He lent his patronage to the craft in all parts of the British empire. Initiated into the order in Sweden in December 1868, he received the rank of Past Grand Master of England at a meeting of Grand Lodge on 1 Sept. 1869. In Sept. 1875, after the resignation of the marquis of Ripon, he was installed in great splendour at the Albert Hall as Grand Master of the order.

As freemason.

During the twenty-six years that the Prince of Wales filled the office he performed with full masonic rites the many ceremonies of laying foundation stones in which he took part. He did what he could to promote the welfare of the three great charitable institutions of freemasons, the Boys' School, the Girls' School, and the Benevolent Institution. He presided at festival dinners of all the charities, twice at the first (1870 and 1898) and the second (1871 and 1888), and once at the third (1873). On his accession to the throne he relinquished the grand mastership and assumed the title of protector of the craft in England. His interest in freemasonry never slackened.

Meanwhile Gladstone remained faithful to his resolve to provide the prince with useful and agreeable employment. One office which Lord Beaconsfield's death rendered vacant was filled on the prime minister's recommendation by the prince, with the result that he entered on a new if minor sphere of interest which proved very congenial. On 6 May 1881 he was appointed a trustee of the British Museum, and eight days later joined the standing committee, again in succession to Lord Beaconsfield. Until the prince's accession to the throne he constantly attended the committee's meetings, kept himself well informed of all matters of importance in the administration of the museum, and warmly supported the action of the director whenever it was called in question. It was with reluctance that he retired from the management of the museum at his accession, on learning that a sovereign could not be member of a body which was liable to be sued in a court of law. One of the prince's services to the museum was the election, through his influence, of his friend Baron Ferdinand de Rothschild [q. v. Suppl. I] as fellow trustee; the baron's Waddesdon bequest was an important addition to the museum's treasures. In the capacity of trustee the prince received on 9 June 1885 the statue of Darwin, which was erected at the

A trustee of the British Museum, 6 May 1881.

entrance of the Natural History Museum, South Kensington, and was unveiled by Professor Huxley.

Association with the British Museum stimulated his earlier interest in new educational institutions, especially those which developed technical or artistic instruction. In music he delighted from childhood, and to efforts for the expansion of musical teaching he long lent his influence. As early as 15 June 1875 he had presided at a conference at Marlborough House to consider the establishment of a National Training School for Music. Three years later he accepted a proposal to institute a National College of Music. On 28 Feb. 1882 he presided at a representative meeting at St. James's Palace, and in an elaborate speech practically called into being the Royal College of Music. He formally inaugurated the college on 7 May 1883 in temporary premises, with Sir George Grove as director. Six years later he personally accepted from Samson Fox [q. v. Suppl. II] a sum of 30,000*l.* (increased to 40,000*l.*) for the provision of a special building, the foundation stone of which he laid on 8 July 1890. He opened the edifice in May 1894 and never lost his enthusiasm for the venture.

Foundation of the Royal College of Music.

In no part of the country did he fail to encourage cognate enterprises with a readiness altogether exceeding that of his father, in whose steps in these regards he was proud to follow. In every town of England he became a familiar figure, opening colleges, libraries, art galleries, hospitals, parks, municipal halls, and docks. On 2 May 1883 he was at Oxford laying the foundation stone of the Indian Institute. On 28 April 1886 he visited Liverpool to inaugurate the working of the great Mersey tunnel. Very readily he went on like errands to places which no member of the royal family had hitherto visited. The centres of industry of every magnitude, Sheffield, Leeds, Wigan, Bolton, Hull, Newcastle, Portsmouth, Blackburn, Middlesbrough, Great Grimsby, and Swansea, as well as Birmingham, Liverpool, and Manchester, all possess public buildings which were first dedicated to public uses by the prince. One of the most memorable of his provincial engagements was his laying the foundation stone of the new cathedral at Truro on 20 May 1880. It was the first cathedral erected in England since St. Paul's was rebuilt in 1697. The bishop, Edward White Benson, was well known to the prince in his earlier capacity of headmaster of Wellington College. By the prince's wish the ceremony was performed, despite clerical misgivings, with full masonic rites. Some seven years later (3 Nov. 1887) the prince returned to attend the consecration of the eastern portion of the building, the first portion to be used for divine worship. Dr. Benson, then archbishop of Canterbury, was his companion.

His philanthropic activities in the country.

The new Truro Cathedral.

The development of his property at Sandringham stirred in him an active interest in agriculture, and his provincial visits were often associated with the shows of the Royal Agricultural Society, of which he was elected a life governor on 3 Feb. 1864, and subsequently became an active member. He was four times president, for the first time in 1869, when the show was held at Manchester, afterwards in 1878 at Kilburn, in 1885 at Preston, and in 1900 at York. He rarely failed to attend the shows in other years, being present at Gloucester in the year before his death; he subsequently accepted the presidency for the meeting at Norwich in 1911, which he did not live to see. In 1889, the jubilee year of the society, he acted at Windsor for the queen, who was president, and presided the same year at the state banquet given in St. James's Palace to the council and chief officers of the society. He showed minute interest in the details of the society's work.

His relations with the Royal Agricultural Society.

At the same time, there was no district of London to which he was a stranger. He not only laid the foundation stone of the Tower Bridge on 21 June 1886 but opened the complete structure on 30 June 1894. He showed interest in the East End by opening a recreation ground in Whitechapel on 24 June 1880. He laid the foundation stone of the People's Palace on 28 June 1886, and on 21 June 1887 he opened for a second time new buildings at the London Hospital. His educational engagements in the metropolis were always varied. They included during this period the formal installation of the Merchant Taylors' School in the old buildings of Charterhouse on 6 April 1878, the opening of the new buildings of the City of London School on 12 Dec. 1882, and of the City of London College in Moorfields on 8 July 1883, together with the new foundation of the City and Guilds of London Institute on 25 June 1884. On 21 Dec. 1885 he went to Sir Henry Doulton's works at Lambeth in order to present

Public engagements in London from 1878.

Doulton with the Albert gold medal of the Society of Arts in recognition of his services to the manufacture of pottery.

His faith in the advantage of exhibitions was not shaken by the inauspicious experiments of 1871–4, and he actively aided in 1883 a revival on a more limited scale of the old scheme. His neighbour in Norfolk, Sir Edward Birkbeck, had interested him in his attempts to improve the fishing industry of the country, and under the prince's direct auspices a National Fisheries Exhibition at Norwich in April 1881 developed in 1883 into an International Fisheries Exhibition at South Kensington, which the prince ceremonially opened and closed (14 May–31 Oct.). The success of the undertaking justified sequels at the same place, in the International Health Exhibition next year, and in the International Inventions and Music Exhibition in 1885. There followed a far more ambitious enterprise in 1886, when the prince with exceptional vigour helped to organise an exhibition of the manufactures and arts of India and the colonies. It was the only one of these ventures which was controlled by a royal commission, and the prince was president of the commissioners. Queen Victoria, on her son's representations, showed an unwonted activity by opening this exhibition in person (4 May 1886). Great popular interest was shown in the enterprise, and a handsome profit was realised.

His enthusiasm for London exhibitions, 1883-7.

The prince was anxious to set on a permanent basis the scheme which had made so powerful an appeal to the public not only of Great Britain but of India and the colonies. Queen Victoria's jubilee was approaching, and many suggestions for a national celebration were under consideration. In the autumn of 1886 the prince proposed to the lord mayor of London that a permanent institute in London, to form a meeting-place for colonial and Indian visitors, and a building for the exhibition of colonial and Indian products, should be erected as a memorial of the queen's long reign. The prince professed anxiety to pursue his efforts to strengthen the good feeling between the mother country, India, and the colonies. At a meeting which he called at St. James's Palace on 12 Jan. 1887, the project of an Imperial Institute at South Kensington was adopted and a fund was started with 25,000*l.* out of the profits of the recent Indian and colonial Exhibition. Large donations were received from India and the colonies. All promised well. Queen Victoria laid the foundation stone on 4 July 1887, and on 28 April 1891 the prince was formally constituted president of the corporation. The completed building was opened by Queen Victoria on 10 May 1893. A week later the Prince of Wales gave a great reception to all who had shown interest in the movement. Some interesting functions took place there under his guidance. On 28 July 1895 he presided when Dr. Jameson lectured on Rhodesia, and he attended a banquet to the colonial premiers on the occasion of the queen's diamond jubilee on 18 June 1897. But in spite of his active support the Institute failed to enjoy public favour. It satisfied no public need, and evoked no general enthusiasm. The prince reluctantly recognised the failure, and in 1899 assented to the transfer of the greater part of the building to the newly constituted London University. The operations of the Institute were thenceforth confined to very modest dimensions. Despite its chequered career, the venture gave the prince a valuable opportunity of identifying himself with the growing pride in the colonial empire, with that newborn imperialism which was a chief feature of the national sentiment during the close of his mother's reign.

The Imperial Institute. 1887.

Punctuality and a methodical distribution of his time enabled the prince to combine with his many public engagements due attention to domestic affairs, and at the same time he enjoyed ample leisure wherein to indulge his love of recreation at home and abroad. The education of his two sons, Albert Victor and George, called for consideration. In 1877 they were respectively thirteen and twelve years old. The prince had little wish to subject them to a repetition of his own strict and elaborate discipline. Nor had he much faith in a literary education for boys in their station. A suggestion that they should go to a public school, to Wellington College, met with Queen Victoria's approval; but the prince finally decided to send them as naval cadets to the Britannia training-ship at Dartmouth. He met his mother's criticism by assuring her that the step was experimental. But the prince was satisfied with the result, and in 1879 he pursued his plan of a naval training by sending the boys on a three years' cruise in H.M.S. Bacchante to the Mediterranean and the British colonies. The plan had the recom-

His sons' education.

mendation of novelty. In providing for the youths' further instruction, the prince followed less original lines. The younger boy, George, like his uncle Alfred, Queen Victoria's second son, made the navy his profession, and he passed through all the stages of nautical preparation. The elder son, Albert Victor, who was in the direct line of succession, spent some time at Trinity College, Cambridge, in 1883, according to precedent. He then proceeded to Aldershot to join the army. In all important episodes in his elder son's career his father's presence testified his parental concern. When Albert Victor, on coming of age, received the freedom of the City of London (29 June 1885), his father was the chief guest at the luncheon in the Guildhall which the corporation gave in honour of the occasion. The prince was with his son at Cambridge not only when he matriculated at Trinity in 1883 but when he received the honorary degree of LL.D. in 1888. A few years later the young man, pursuing most of his father's experiences, set out for an Indian tour, and his father accompanied him as far as Ismailia (October 1891).

His elder son's career.

Family rejoicings attended the celebration of the prince and princess's silver wedding on 10 March 1888, when Queen Victoria dined with them at Marlborough House for the first time. The old German emperor, William I, died the day before. With him the prince was always on affectionate terms and he had repeatedly accepted the emperor's hospitality in Berlin. He had visited him on 18 March 1885 to congratulate him on his eighty-eighth birthday. Queen Victoria was especially anxious to show his memory due respect, but she assented to the suspension of court mourning for the prince's silver wedding. The number of congratulations and presents bore striking witness to the prince's popularity.

Silver wedding, 10 March 1888.

The royal family was bound to experience many episodes of sorrow as well as joy. The prince was pained by the death in 1878 of his second sister, Alice, princess of Hesse-Darmstadt, who had helped to nurse him through his illness of 1871. To his acute distress, too, his youngest brother, Leopold, duke of Albany, died suddenly while on holiday at Cannes (24 March 1884), and the prince at once went thither on the melancholy errand of bringing the remains home. Subsequently he unveiled with much public ceremony a statue of the duke at Cannes. But the prince and all his domestic circle were perhaps more deeply affected by the tragic death of his brother-in-law, the crown prince of Prussia, who after a three months' reign as Frederick III had succumbed to the painful disease of cancer of the throat (15 June 1888). The tragedy gave the prince many grounds for anxiety. His lifelong affection for the Empress Frederick, his eldest sister, was quickened by her misfortune. He showed her every brotherly attention. On her first visit to England during her widowhood the prince crossed over to Flushing to escort her to her native country (19 March 1889). In Germany her position was difficult. Her English predilections and her masterful disposition often roused hostility. Bismarck and his son Herbert had treated her and her husband with scant respect. The prince's sympathies lay with his sister in her struggles abroad, and not unfrequently was he moved to anger by what seemed to him the cruel indifference of the Bismarcks to her feelings. The complexity of the situation was increased by the conduct of her eldest son, the prince's nephew, who now became, as William II, German emperor in succession to his father. His uncompliant attitude to his mother often wounded his uncle and threatened alienation. Yet the native amiability of the prince did not suffer any lasting breach between himself and those whose conduct roused his disapproval. In his family circle there were some whose dislike of the young ruler was far more firmly rooted than his own. But the prince sought paths of peace and conciliation. The new emperor was his mother's favourite grandson and had at command a social charm which equalled his uncle's. When in 1890 the emperor dismissed Bismarck from his service and he became politically his own master, the outer world came to attribute to uncle and nephew a personal and political rivalry which hampered the good relations of the two peoples. This allegation was without foundation in fact. On occasion the kinsmen caused each other irritation, but there was no real estrangement. The mutual resentments which at times ruffled their tempers were harboured solely when they were absent from one another. The ill-feeling disappeared when they met. The prince's unconcealed leanings to France barely touched the personal relation with his nephew. The prince's good-nature was comprehensive. The younger Bismarck's manner was even less

Accession of his nephew, Emperor William II.

complacent than that of his rough-spoken father, but the prince's social tact enabled him to meet the older man with a perfect grace and to extend a courteous greeting to Count Herbert Bismarck on his private visits to England.

No lack of cordiality marked the first meetings of uncle and nephew after the emperor's accession. The emperor arrived at Spithead on 2 Aug. 1889 in order to present himself to his grandmother in his new dignity; the prince met him on landing and welcomed him with warmth. Next year the prince and his second son, George, were the emperor's guests at Berlin (April 1890), just after Bismarck's dismissal. The emperor attested his friendly inclinations by investing Prince George with the distinguished order of the Black Eagle.

In 1889 a new factor was introduced into the prince's domestic history. The first marriage in his family took place. On 27 July 1889 his eldest daughter, Princess Louise, married the sixth earl of Fife, then created first duke. The prince's son-in-law, who was eighteen years senior to his wife, belonged to his most intimate circle of friends. Objection was raised in some quarters on the ground of the bridegroom's age and of his place in the prince's social coterie, and in other quarters owing to his lack of royal status. But the union proved thoroughly happy, and it made opportune a review of the financial provision for the prince's children. The prince's family was growing up, and his domestic expenses caused him some anxiety. His income had undergone no change since his marriage, and he deemed it fitting to raise the question of parliamentary grants to his children. The prince's income was not exorbitant in view of the position that he had long been called on to fill, now that Queen Victoria had ceased to play her part in society.

His eldest daughter's marriage, 27 July 1889.

Early in 1885, when his elder son came of age, the prince discussed the matter with the queen with the knowledge of the liberal ministry. There was no unwillingness on any side to treat his wishes considerately, but neither the queen nor her ministers showed undue haste in coming to close quarters with the delicate issue.

Pecuniary provision for the prince's family.

Lord Salisbury was now prime minister, but the conservative government was as reluctant as any liberal government to lay a large fresh burden on the revenues of the state in the interests of the royal family. The queen sent a message to the House of Commons, asking provision for the prince's two eldest children (July 1889). A committee of inquiry representative of all parties in the House of Commons was thereupon appointed. Mr. Bradlaugh opposed the appointment on the ground that the queen should make the necessary provision out of her savings. The government proposed, with the approval of the queen, that the eldest son of the Prince of Wales should receive an annuity of 10,000*l.*, to be increased to 15,000*l.* on his marriage. The second son was to receive, on coming of age, an annuity of 8000*l.*, to be increased on his marriage to 15,000*l.* Each of the three daughters was to receive on coming of age an annuity of 3000*l.*, with a dowry of 10,000*l.* on marriage. There would thus fall due immediately 21,000*l.* a year, with 10,000*l.* for Princess Louise. But signs of discontent were apparent in the committee, and Gladstone, who deprecated any weakening of the monarchy by a prolonged controversy over its cost, recommended the compromise that the prince should receive a fixed additional annual sum of 36,000*l.* for his children's support, and that the new provision should terminate six months' after Queen Victoria's death. The proposal was adopted by the committee, but was severely criticised in the House of Commons. Henry Labouchere bluntly moved a peremptory refusal of any grant to the queen's grandchildren. His motion was rejected by 398 votes to 116. Mr. John Morley moved an amendment complaining that room was left for future applications from the crown for further grants to the queen's grandchildren, and that the proposed arrangement ought to be made final. Most of Gladstone's colleagues supported Mr. Morley; but his amendment was defeated by 355 votes to 134 and the grant of 36,000*l.* a year was secured.

On 17 May 1891 the prince enjoyed the new experience of becoming a grandfather on the birth of the duchess of Fife's first daughter. But a severe blow was to befall his domestic circle within a year. In December his second son, George, fell ill of enteric fever, from which he recovered; but early in the next year Albert Victor, his elder son, who had been created duke of Clarence (24 May 1890), was seized by influenza, which turned to pneumonia and proved fatal (14 Jan. 1892). The calamity was for the moment crushing to both parents. But the sympathy of the nation was abundant,

First grandchild, 17 May 1891.

Death of elder son, 14 Jan. 1892.

and in a published letter of thanks the prince and princess gratefully acknowledged the national condolence. The duke's death was the more distressing owing to his approaching marriage to Princess Mary (May) of Teck. Next year, after the shock of mourning had passed away, Princess May was betrothed to the second son, Prince George, who filled his brother's place in the succession to the throne and was created duke of York on 24 May 1892. The marriage took place on 6 July 1893, and the succession to the throne was safely provided for when a first child, Prince Edward of Wales, was born on 23 June 1894.

The prince's recreations.

Amid all his domestic responsibilities and his other engagements the prince always found ample leisure for sport and amusement. Of the theatre and the opera he was from boyhood an ardent admirer, and both in London and Paris he enjoyed the society of the dramatic and musical professions. The lighter forms of dramatic and musical entertainment chiefly attracted him. But his patronage was comprehensive. Wagner's operas he attended with regularity, and Irving's Shakespearean productions at the Lyceum Theatre from 1872 onwards stirred his enthusiasm. With Irving, the leader of the dramatic profession through a great part of the prince's career, his social relations were of the friendliest. He supped on the stage of the Lyceum with Irving and a few of his friends after the performance of 'Much Ado about Nothing' (8 May 1883), and when Queen Victoria was on a visit to Sandringham (26 April 1889), he invited Irving to perform in her presence 'The Bells' and the trial scene from 'The Merchant of Venice.' With the comic actor J. L. Toole he was on like cordial terms, and thrice at the prince's request Toole appeared in characteristic parts on visits to Sandringham. Toole was there at the celebration of Prince Albert Victor's coming of age on 8 Jan. 1885. (Sir) Charles Wyndham, (Sir) Squire Bancroft, (Sir) John Hare, and many other actors in addition to Irving and Toole were the prince's guests on occasion at Marlborough House. The dramatic profession generally acknowledged his sympathetic patronage by combining to present him on his fiftieth birthday (9 Nov. 1891) with a gold cigar box. To the prince's influence is attributable the bestowal of official honours on leading actors, a practice which was inaugurated by the grant of a knighthood to Henry Irving in 1895.

The theatre.

The prince and the turf.

But the recreation to which the prince mainly devoted himself from middle life onwards with unremitting delight was horse-racing. He joined the Jockey Club on 13 April 1864. But it was not for at least ten years that he played any part on the turf. His colours were first seen at the July meeting at Newmarket in 1877. In 1883 he leased a few horses at John Porter's Kingsclere stable, and two years later he inaugurated a breeding stud at Sandringham. In 1893 he left John Porter's stable at Kingsclere, and thenceforward trained horses at Newmarket under Richard Marsh, usually having at least eleven horses in training. By that date he was a regular visitor at Newmarket, occupying a set of rooms at the Jockey Club. That practice he continued to the end of his life. He was a fair judge of horses, though hardly an expert. His luck as an owner was variable, and signal successes came late in his racing career. His main triumphs were due to the merits of the three horses Florizel II, Persimmon, and Diamond Jubilee, which he bred in 1891, 1893 and 1897 respectively out of the dam Perdita II by the sire St. Simon. With Persimmon, the best thoroughbred of his era, the prince won for the first time the classic races of the Derby and the St. Leger in 1896, and the Eclipse Stakes and the Gold Cup at Ascot in 1897. In 1900, when his winning stakes reached a total of 29,585*l.*, he first headed the list of winning owners. In that year his racing triumphs reached their zenith, when Persimmon's brother, Diamond Jubilee, won five great races, the Two Thousand Guineas, the Derby, Newmarket Stakes, Eclipse, and St. Leger. He had played a modest part in steeplechasing since 1878. But his only conspicuous success in that sport was also achieved in 1900, when his Ambush II won the Grand National at Liverpool. So imposing a series of victories for an owner in one year was without precedent. No conspicuous prosperity attended his racing during the early years of his reign. But in 1909 he was for a third time winner of the Derby with the horse Minoru, and was in the same year third in the list of winning owners. At the time of his death he had twenty-two horses in training, and his winning stakes since 1886 then amounted to 146,344*l.* 10*s.* 1*d.* The pastime proved profitable. He sold Diamond Jubilee to an Argentine breeder for 31,500*l.* The skeleton of Persimmon he presented to

His racing successes.

the South Kensington Museum (5 Feb. 1910).

With fellow patrons of the turf the prince always maintained cordial intimacy. The members of the Jockey Club included his closest friends. For twenty years he entertained to dinner all the members at Marlborough House and afterwards at Buckingham Palace on Derby night. Rarely missing an important race meeting, he was regularly the guest of Lord Sefton at Sefton Park or of Lord Derby at Knowsley for the Grand National, of Lord Savile at Rufford Abbey for the St. Leger at Doncaster, and of the duke of Richmond at Goodwood for the meeting in the park there.

In yacht racing also for a brief period he was only a little less prominent than on the turf. In 1876 he first purchased a racing schooner yacht, Hildegarde, which won the first queen's cup at Cowes in 1877. In 1879 he acquired the well-known cutter Formosa, and in 1881 the schooner Aline, both of which enjoyed racing reputations. But it was not till 1892 that the prince had a racing yacht built for him. The vessel known as the Britannia was designed by George Lennox Watson [q. v. Suppl. II], and was constantly seen not only in the Solent, on the Thames, and on the Clyde, but also at Cannes. For five years the yacht enjoyed a prosperous career, winning many races in strong competitions, often with the prince on board. In 1893 prizes were won on the Thames (25–26 May), and the Victoria gold challenge cup at Ryde (11 Sept.). Twice at Cannes the Britannia won international matches (13 March 1894 and 23 Feb. 1895); and on 5 July 1894 it defeated on the Clyde the American yacht Vigilant; but that result was reversed in a race between the two on the Solent on 4 Aug. 1895. In 1895 the German emperor first sent out his yacht Meteor to meet his uncle's Britannia, and for three years interesting contests were waged between the two vessels. Thrice in English waters during 1896 was the German yacht successful—at Gravesend (4 June), at Cowes (11 June), and at Ryde (13 Aug.). But after several victories over other competitors the Britannia won the race for the queen's cup against the Meteor at Cowes (3 Aug. 1897), and three days later the emperor's Meteor shield was awarded his uncle's vessel.

His career in yacht-racing.

The prince's open indulgence in sport, especially in horse-racing, attracted much public attention, and contributed to the general growth of his popularity. But in 1891 there was some recrudescence of public impatience with his avowed devotion to amusement. An imputation of cheating against a guest at a country house when the prince was of the company led to a libel action, at the hearing of which the prince for a second time appeared as a witness in a court of law (5 June 1891). The host was Mr. Arthur Wilson, a rich shipowner of Hull, and the scene of the occurrence was his residence at Tranby Croft. The evidence showed that the prince had played baccarat for high stakes. A wave of somewhat reckless gambling had lately enveloped English society, and the prince had occasionally yielded to the perilous fascination. Cards had always formed some part of his recreation. From early youth he had played whist for moderate stakes, and he impressed Gladstone in a homely rubber at Sandringham with his 'whist memory.' On his tours abroad at Cannes and Homburg he had at times indulged in high play, usually with fortunate results. The revelations in the Tranby Croft case shocked middle-class opinion in England, and there was a loud outburst of censure. In a private letter (13 Aug. 1891) to Dr. Benson, archbishop of Canterbury, long on intimate terms with the royal family, the prince expressed 'deep pain and annoyance' at the 'most bitter and unjust attacks' made on him not only 'by the press' but 'by the low church and especially the nonconformists.' 'I am not sure,' he wrote, 'that politics were not mixed up in it.' His genuine attitude he expressed in the following sentences: 'I have a horror of gambling, and should always do my utmost to discourage others who have an inclination for it, as I consider that gambling, like intemperance, is one of the greatest curses which a country could be afflicted with.' The scandal opened the prince's eyes to the perils of the recent gambling vogue, and he set himself to discourage its continuance. He gradually abandoned other games of cards for bridge, in which, though he played regularly and successfully, he developed only a moderate skill.

The Tranby Croft case, 1891.

VII

During Lord Salisbury's ministry (1886–1892) the prince's relations to home and foreign politics remained as they had been. Queen Victoria's veto on the submission of official intelligence was in no way relaxed. The prince was socially on pleasant terms with Lord Salisbury, who was foreign secretary as well as prime minister. The prince visited him at Hatfield, but they exchanged no confidences. Independently however of ministerial authority and quite irresponsibly, the prince with increasing freedom discussed foreign affairs with friends at home and abroad. At Biarritz, where he stayed in 1879, at Cannes, or at Paris he emphatically declared in all circles his love of France, his hope of a perpetual peace between her and England, and his dread of another Franco-German war. Nor did he qualify such sentiments when he travelled in Germany. He showed his open-mindedness as to the Channel tunnel scheme by inspecting the works at Dover (March 1882). In the spring of 1887 he was at Cannes during an alarming earthquake, and his cool and courageous behaviour during the peril enhanced his reputation in southern France. In the same year M. Taine, the historian, attached value to a rumour which credited the prince with meddling in internal French politics in order to keep the peace between France and Germany. The French prime minister, M. Rouvier, was threatened with defeat in the chamber of deputies at the hands of M. Floquet and M. Boulanger, who were reputed to be pledged to an immediate breach with Germany. The prince was reported to have persuaded the Comte de Paris to detach his supporters in the chamber from the war-faction and to protect with their votes the ministry of peace. M. Taine's rumour doubtless misinterpreted the prince's cordial relations with the Orleanist princes, but it bears witness to the sort of political influence which was fancifully assigned to the prince in France. It was rare, however, that his good-will to France incurred suspicion of undue interference. The monarchs of Europe looked askance on the French International Exhibition of 1889, which was designed to commemorate the revolution of 1789, and the prince abstained from joining the British commission, of which he had been a member in 1867 and president in 1878. But he had no scruples in visiting the exhibition together with the princess and his sons. They ascended under M. Eiffel's guidance to the top of the Eiffel Tower, which was a chief feature of the exhibition buildings. Before leaving the French capital, the prince exchanged visits with President Carnot, went over the new Pasteur Institute, took part in a meet of the French Four-in-Hand Club, and attended the races at Auteuil. A few years later (March 1894), when diplomatic friction was arising between France and England over events in northern Africa, Lord Dufferin, the English ambassador in France, addressed the British Chamber of Commerce, and denounced popular exaggeration of the disagreement. The prince, who was at Cannes, at once wrote to the ambassador, eagerly congratulating him on his prudent handling of his theme and reporting to him the commendations of German and Russian royal personages whom he was meeting on the Riviera. In Germany he was less suave in pronouncing his opinions. He complained to Prince von Hohenlohe at Berlin in May 1888 of the folly of the new and irritating system of passports which had lately been devised to discourage Frenchmen from travelling in Germany. But Bismarck ridiculed the notion that any importance attached to his political views. In Germany he was rarely regarded by publicists as other than a votary of Parisian gaiety.

His continued interest in foreign affairs.

A few months later, in Oct. 1888, he illustrated his love of adventure and his real detachment from current diplomatic controversy by extending his travels further east, where political conflict was rife among most of the great powers. He spent a week with the king of Roumania at his country palace of Sinaïa, engaging in a bear hunt in the neighbourhood, and attending military manœuvres. Thence he proceeded to Hungary to join the ill-starred crown prince Rudolph (*d.* 30 Jan. 1889) in bear-hunting at Görgény and elsewhere, finally accompanying him to Vienna (16 Oct.). No political significance attached to the tour. Subsequently he more than once boldly challenged the patrician prejudices of the German and Austrian courts by passing through Germany and Austria in order to shoot in Hungary as the guest of his friend Baron Hirsch, a Jewish millionaire, who was excluded from the highest Austrian social circles. In the autumn of 1894 he spent no less than four weeks with the baron at his seat of St. Johann. The sport was on a princely scale. The head of game shot during the visit numbered 37,654, of which 22,996 were partridges. According to German and Austrian strict social codes, the prince's public avowal of friendship with Baron Hirsch was a breach of royal etiquette. But he allowed neither social nor diplomatic punctilio to qualify the pleasures of foreign travel. His cosmopolitan sympathies ignored fine distinctions of caste.

Visits to Roumania and Hungary, 1888–94.

Russia throughout this period was the diplomatic foe of England, and the prince vaguely harboured the common English suspicion of Russian intrigues. But he lost no opportunity of confirming his knowledge of the country. Substantially Russia meant to him the home of close connections of his wife and of the wife of his brother Alfred. He signally proved how closely he was drawn to the land by ties of kindred in 1894, when he twice within a few months visited it at the call of family duty. In July 1894 he went to St. Petersburg to attend the wedding at Peterhof of the Grand Duchess Xenia, the daughter of Tsar Alexander III (the Princess of Wales's niece), to the Grand Duke Alexander Michaïlovitch. At the end of October 1894 he hurried to Livadia to the deathbed of his wife's brother-in-law, Tsar Alexander III. He arrived when all was over, but he attended the funeral ceremonies and greeted the accession of his wife's nephew, Tsar Nicholas II, who soon married a niece of his own. The old link between the prince and the Russian throne was thereby strengthened, but its strength owed nothing to diplomatic influences or to considerations of policy.

In Russia, 1894.

When Gladstone became prime minister in 1892, the problem of the prince's access to state business received a more promising solution than before. Gladstone sought to gratify the prince's wish that information of the cabinet's proceedings should be placed at his disposal. The queen's assent was not given very readily. She suggested that she herself should decide what official news should be passed on to her son. She deprecated the discussion of national secrets over country-house dinner-tables. But she finally yielded, and thenceforth the prince was regularly supplied by the prime minister's confidential secretary, Sir Algernon West, with much private intelligence. The privilege which the prince had long sought was thus granted on somewhat exceptional terms. The prince freely commented in writing on what was communicated to him. His interest was chiefly in persons, and he frankly criticised appointments or honours, and made recommendations of his own. He avoided intricate matters of general policy, but on minor issues he offered constant remark. Of the common prejudice of rank he gave no sign. Royal commissions of inquiry into social reforms continued to appeal to him. In 1891 he had sought Lord Salisbury's permission to serve on the labour commission, but his presence was deemed impolitic. When the agricultural commission was in process of formation in 1893, he urged the nomination of Mr. Joseph Arch, his colleague on the housing commission. The queen protested, but Arch owed to the prince an invitation to sit. In the same year another royal commission was constituted to inquire into the question of old age pensions, under the chairmanship of Lord Aberdare. Of this body the prince was a member; he attended regularly, put pertinent questions to witnesses, and showed sympathy with the principle at stake. Gladstone informed the prince of his impending resignation in February 1894, and thanked him for unbounded kindness. The prince replied that he valued their long friendship. When Lord Rosebery formed a government in succession to Gladstone, the prince had for the only time in his life a close personal ally in the prime minister. But his influence on public business saw no increase. Lord Rosebery's administration chiefly impressed him by the internal dissensions which made its life precarious.

Confidential relations with Gladstone's ministry, 1892–4.

Gladstone and the prince continued to the last to exchange marks of mutual deference. When on 26 June 1896 the prince opened at Aberystwyth the new University of Wales, of which he had become chancellor, Gladstone in spite of his infirmities came over from Hawarden to attend the ceremony, and at the lunch which followed it the old statesman proposed the prince's health. They met again at Cimiez next year, when Gladstone took his last farewell of Queen Victoria. On 25 May 1898 the prince and his son George acted as pall-bearers at the funeral of Gladstone in Westminster Abbey. So emphatic an attention caused among conservatives some resentment, which was hardly dissipated by the prince's acceptance of the place of president of the committee formed to erect a national memorial to Gladstone (1 July 1898). But it was not in a spirit of political partisanship that the prince publicly avowed his admiration of Gladstone. The prince acknowledged Gladstone's abilities, but he was chiefly grateful for the cordial confidence which had distinguished Gladstone's relations with him. Gladstone, who respected his royal station and deemed him the superior in tact and charm of any other royal personage within his

Final relations with Gladstone, 1896–7.

range of knowledge, saw imprudence in Queen Victoria's denial to him of all political responsibility.

On the fall of Lord Rosebery's ministry and the accession to office of Lord Salisbury, the prince illustrated his attitude to the party strife by inviting the out-going and the in-coming ministers to meet at dinner at Marlborough House. Other men of distinction were there, including the shahzada, second son of the amir of Afghanistan, who was visiting this country. The entertainment proved thoroughly harmonious under the cheerful influence of the prince. A little later, when Lord Salisbury's administration was firmly installed, the prince's right to receive as matter of course all foreign despatches was at length formally conceded. Like the members of the cabinet he was now invested with a 'cabinet' key to the official pouches in which private information is daily circulated among ministers by the foreign office. The privilege came too tardily to have much educational effect, but it gave the prince a better opportunity than he had yet enjoyed of observing the inner routine of government, and it diminished a veteran grievance. Yet his main energies were, even more conspicuously than of old, distributed over society, sport, and philanthropy, and in spite of his new privileges he remained an unofficial onlooker in the political arena.

The concession of the 'cabinet' key, 1895.

In some directions his philanthropic interest seemed to widen. The ardour and energy with which at the end of the nineteenth century the problems of disease were pursued caught his alert attention, and he gave many proofs of his care for medical research. He regularly performed the duties of president of St. Bartholomew's Hospital, and learned much of hospital management there and elsewhere. He did what he could to encourage the study of consumption, and the investigation of cancer interested him. When he laid the foundation stone of the new wing of Brompton Consumption Hospital in 1881, he asked, if the disease were preventable, why it was not prevented. On 21 Dec. 1888 he called a meeting at Marlborough House to found the National Society for the Prevention of Consumption. It was, too, under his personal auspices that the fund was formed on 18 June 1889 to commemorate the heroism of Father Damien, the Belgian missionary who heroically sacrified his life to the lepers of the Sandwich Islands. A statue of Father Damien which was set up at Kalawayo was one result of the movement. Another was the National Leprosy Fund for the treatment and study of the disease, especially in India. On 13 Jan. 1890 the prince presided at a subscription dinner in London in support of this fund, and to his activity was in part attributable the foundation of the Albert Victor Hospital for leprosy at Calcutta. He was always on good terms with doctors. Through his friendship with Sir Joseph Fayrer, who had accompanied him to India, he was offered and accepted the unusual compliment of being made honorary fellow of the Royal College of Physicians on 19 July 1897. He received not only the diploma but a model of the goldheaded cane in possession of the college, whose line of successive owners included Radcliffe and the chief physicians of the eighteenth century.

Interest in medical science.

In the summer of 1897 the prince took an active part in the celebration of Queen Victoria's diamond jubilee. The queen gave public expression of her maternal regard, which no differences on political or private matters effectually diminished, by creating in his behalf a new dignity—that of Grand Master and Principal Grand Cross of the Order of the Bath. In all the public festivities the prince filled a chief part. Among the most elaborate private entertainments which he attended was a fancy dress ball given by his friends the duke and duchess of Devonshire at Devonshire House, where the splendours recalled the prince's own effort of the same kind at Marlborough House in 1874.

Queen Victoria's diamond jubilee, 1897.

But the prince was responsible for a lasting memorial of Queen Victoria's diamond jubilee in the form of a scheme for permanently helping the London hospitals to lessen their burden of debt. On 5 Feb. 1897 the prince in honour of the jubilee inaugurated a fund for the support of London hospitals to which would be received subscriptions from a shilling upwards. The prince became president of the general council, and a meeting at Marlborough House christened the fund 'The Prince of Wales's Hospital Fund for London.' Success was at once achieved. Within a year the donations amounted to 187,000*l.*, and the annual subscriptions to 22,050*l.* The fund continued to flourish under the prince's and his friends' guidance until his accession to the throne, when it was renamed 'King Edward VII Hospital Fund,' and his son took his place as president. The effort has

The prince's hospital fund.

conspicuously relieved the pecuniary strain on the chief London hospitals.

VIII

Three years and a half were to pass between the celebration of Queen Victoria's sixty years of rule and the end of her prolonged reign. French caricaturists insolently depicted the extreme senility which would distinguish the prince when his time for kingship would arrive. But the prince as yet showed no loss of activity and no narrowing of interest. As soon as the diamond jubilee festivities ended the prince and princess proved their liking for modern music by attending the Wagner festival at Baireuth (Aug. 1897). Thence the prince went on his customary holiday to Homburg, and on his way home visited his sister the Empress Frederick at Cronberg. One of those recurring seasons of coolness was dividing his nephew the German emperor and himself. Private and public events alike contributed to the disagreement. There was a renewal of differences between the emperor and his mother, and the emperor had imprudently expressed by telegram his sympathy with President Kruger of the Transvaal Republic, who was resisting the demands of the British government in South Africa. The emperor disclaimed any intention of wounding English susceptibilities. He deemed himself misunderstood. The prince, however, for the time absented himself from Berlin on his foreign travels, and did not recommend himself to German public favour by an emphatic declaration of unalterable personal devotion to France, at the moment that a period of estrangement menaced that country and England. In the spring of 1898, when the two governments were about to engage in a sharp diplomatic duel over their relations in north Africa, the prince laid the foundation stone of a new jetty at Cannes and pleaded in public the cause of peace.

Difficulties with the German emperor.

Varied anxieties and annoyances were accumulating. The ambiguity of his position at home was brought home to him in April, when he was requested to preside, for the first and only time in his career of heir-apparent, over the privy council. Since 1880, when Queen Victoria had made it her practice to spend the spring in the Riviera, a commission had been privately drafted empowering the prince and some of the ministers to act, in cases of extreme urgency, on her behalf in her absence from the council. Hitherto the commission had lain dormant, and the prince merely learnt by accident that such a commission existed and that his name was included in it. The concealment caused him annoyance. Now in April 1898, on the outbreak of the Spanish-American war, it was necessary to issue a proclamation of neutrality, and he was called upon to fill the queen's place in the transaction.

The prince and the privy council.

In the summer an accidental fall while staying at Waddesdon with his friend Baron Ferdinand de Rothschild caused a fracture of his kneecap (18 July 1898), and disabled him for two months. The illness of his next brother, Alfred, now become duke of Saxe-Coburg, was a serious grief. His relations with the duke, who died on 30 July 1900, had been close from boyhood, and the wrench with the past was severe. At the end of 1899 the gloom had been lightened by the arrival, after a four years' absence, of the German emperor on a friendly visit to Queen Victoria and the prince. The episode was an eloquent proof that there was no enduring enmity between the emperor and either his uncle or his uncle's country, whatever were the passing ebullitions of irritation. The emperor arrived just after the outbreak of the South African war, in the course of which the prince was to learn that even in France there were limits to the effective exercise of his personal charm.

The German emperor's visit, Nov. 1899.

During 1899 and 1900 misrepresentations of England's aim in the war excited throughout Europe popular rancour which involved the prince, equally with his mother and the English ministers, in scurrilous attack. The war was denounced as a gross oppression on England's part of a weak and innocent people. The emperor's presence in England when the storm was breaking was a welcome disclaimer of approval of the abusive campaign. But in the spring of 1900 the prince suffered practical experience of the danger which lurked in the continental outcry. On his way to Denmark, while he and the princess were seated in their train at the Gare du Nord, Brussels, a youth, Sipido, aged fifteen, fired two shots at them (4 April). They were unhurt, and the prince showed the utmost coolness. The act was an outcome of the attacks on England which were prompted by the Boer war. It was the only occasion on which any nefarious attempt was made on the prince's life. The sequel was not reassuring to British feeling. Sipido and three alleged accomplices were put on their trial at Brussels

Attempt on the prince's life, 4 April 1900.

on 1 July. The three associates were acquitted, and Sipido was held irresponsible for his conduct. Ordered to be kept under government supervision till he reached the age of twenty-one, he soon escaped to France, whence he was only extradited by the Belgian government after a protest by British ministers. There was much cause for friction at the time between England and Belgium. Not only had the Boer war alienated the Belgian populace like the other peoples of Europe, but the old cordiality between the royal houses had declined. The close intimacy which had bound Queen Victoria to her uncle the late king, Leopold I, had been echoed in the relations between his successor King Leopold II and the prince. But the queen's sense of propriety was offended by reports of her royal cousin's private life, and the charges of cynical cruelty to which his policy in the Congo gave rise in England stimulated the impatience of the English royal family. After the outrage at Brussels, the prince and King Leopold II maintained only the formalities of social intercourse. The hostile sentiment which prevailed in Europe deterred the prince from attending the Paris International Exhibition of 1900. This was the only French venture of the kind in the long series of the century which he failed to grace with his presence. As in the case of 1878 he was president of the royal commission for the British section, and he was active in the preliminary organisation. During 1899 he watched in Paris the beginnings of the exhibition buildings. But the temper of France denied him the opportunity of seeing them in their final shape.

Strained relations with Leopold II, king of the Belgians.

IX

Early in 1901 the prince's destiny was at length realised. For some months Queen Victoria's strength had been slowly failing. In the middle of January 1901 physical prostration rapidly grew, and on 20 Jan. her state was critical. The Prince of Wales arrived at Osborne on that day, and was with his mother as life ebbed away. Her last articulate words were an affectionate mention of his name. Whatever had occasioned passing friction between them, her maternal love never knew any diminution. The presence of his nephew, the German emperor, at the death-bed was grateful to the prince and to all members of his family. Queen Victoria died at Osborne at half-past six on the evening of Tuesday, 22 Jan. 1901.

Queen Victoria's death, 22 Jan. 1901.

Next morning the new king travelled to London, and at a meeting of the privy council at St. James's Palace took the oaths of sovereignty under the style of Edward VII. 'I am fully determined,' he said, 'to be a constitutional sovereign in the strictest sense of the word, and as long as there is breath in my body to work for the good and amelioration of my people.' He explained that he had resolved to be known by the name of Edward, which had been borne by six of his ancestors, not that he undervalued the name of Albert, but that he desired his father's name to stand alone.

King Edward's first speech as sovereign, deliberately and impressively spoken, was made without any notes and without consultation with any minister. According to his habit, he had thought it over during his journey, and when he had delivered it he embarrassed the officials by his inability to supply them with a written copy. He had expected a report to be taken, he explained. The published words were put together from memory by some of the councillors and their draft was endorsed by the king. The episode, while it suggested a certain unfamiliarity on his part with the formal procedure of the council, showed an independent sense of his new responsibilities. A few days later (29 Jan. 1901) the king issued appropriate addresses to the army and the navy, to his people of the United Kingdom, to the colonies, and to India.

The new king and his council, 23 Jan. 1901.

In the ceremonies of Queen Victoria's funeral (2–4 Feb.) the king acted as chief mourner, riding through London behind the bier from Victoria station to Paddington, and walking through the streets of Windsor to St. George's Chapel, where the coffin was first laid. On Monday he again walked in procession from the Albert Memorial Chapel at Windsor to the burial place at the Royal Mausoleum at Frogmore. His nephew, the German emperor, was at his side throughout the funeral ceremonies. The emperor's brother, Prince Henry of Prussia, and his son the crown prince were also in the mourning company. Almost the first act of the king's reign was to give public proof of his good relations with his royal kinsmen of Germany. It had been Queen Victoria's intention to invest the crown prince her great-grandson with the order of the Garter. This intention the king now carried out; at the same time he made the

Queen Victoria's funeral.

emperor a field-marshal and Prince Henry a vice-admiral of the fleet. By way of marking his chivalric resolve to associate his wife with all the honour of his new status, he devised at the same time a new distinction in her behalf, appointing her Lady of the Garter (12 Feb. 1901).

His first public function as sovereign was to open in state the new session of parliament on 14 Feb. 1901. This royal duty, which the queen had only performed seven times in the concluding forty years of her reign and for the last time in 1886, chiefly brought the sovereign into public relation with the government of the country. The king during his nine years of rule never omitted the annual ceremony, and he read for himself the speech from the throne. That practice had been dropped by the queen in 1861, and had not been resumed by her.

Queen Victoria had been created Empress of India in 1876, and King Edward was the first British sovereign to succeed to the dignity of Emperor of India. By Act of Parliament (1 Edw. VII, cap. 15) another addition was now made to the royal titles with a view to associating the crown for the first time directly with the colonial empire. He was declared by statute to be King not only of Great Britain and Ireland but of 'the British dominions beyond the seas.' On the new coinage he was styled 'Britt. Omn. Rex,' in addition to the old designations.

His new style.

Queen Victoria left the new king her private residences of Osborne and Balmoral, but her pecuniary fortune was distributed among the younger members of her family. The king was stated on his accession to have no debts and no capital. Gossip which erroneously credited him with an immense indebtedness ignored his business instincts and the good financial advice which he invariably had at his disposal in the inner circle of his friends. Like Queen Victoria he relinquished on his accession the chief hereditary revenues of the crown, which had grown in value during her reign from 245,000*l.* to 425,000*l.* As in 1837, the duchies of Lancaster and Cornwall were held, despite radical misgivings, to stand on another footing and to be royal appanages in the personal control of the royal family. The duchy of Lancaster, which produced 60,000*l.* a year, was reckoned to be the sovereign's private property, and the duchy of Cornwall, which was of like value, that of the heir-apparent. On his ceasing to be Prince of Wales the parliamentary grant to him of 40,000*l.* lapsed, while the duchy of Cornwall passed to his son. The king's income, in the absence of a new parliamentary grant, was thus solely the 60,000*l.* from the duchy of Lancaster. The Act of 1889, which provided 36,000*l.* a year for his children, became void six months after the late sovereign's death.

His pecuniary position.

On 5 March a royal message invited the House of Commons to make pecuniary provision for the king and his family. A select committee of twenty-one was appointed on 11 March 1901 to consider the king's financial position. The Irish nationalists declined to serve, but Henry Labouchere represented the radical and labour sections, to whom the cost of the monarchy was a standing grievance. The committee was chiefly constituted of the leaders of the two chief parties in the state. It was finally decided to recommend an annual grant of 470,000*l.*, a sum which was 85,000*l.* in excess of the income allowed to the late queen. The increase was justified on the ground that a larger sum would be needed for the hospitalities of the court. No special grant was made to Queen Alexandra, but it was understood that 33,000*l.* would be paid her out of that portion (110,000*l.*) of the total grant allotted to the privy purse; 70,000*l.* was secured to her in case of widowhood. The king's son and heir, George, duke of York, who now became duke of Cornwall and York, received an annuity of 20,000*l.*, and his wife, the duchess, received one of 10,000*l.*, with an additional 20,000*l.* in case of widowhood; the three daughters of the king were given a joint annual income of 18,000*l.* Some other expenses, like the repair of the royal palaces (18,000*l.*) and the maintenance of royal yachts (23,000*l.*), were provided for independently from the Consolidated Fund. The resolutions to these effects were adopted by 250 to 62. They were resisted by the Irish nationalists and by a few advanced radicals, including Henry Labouchere, Mr. Keir Hardie, and Mr. John Burns. Mr. Burns warmly deprecated a royal income which should be comparable with the annual revenues of Barney Barnato [q. v. Suppl. I], Alfred Beit [q. v. Suppl. II], or Mr. Andrew Carnegie. The civil list bill which embodied the resolutions was finally read a third time on 11 June 1901 by 370 against 60, and it became law on 2 July (1 Edw. VII, cap. 4). The generous terms were accepted by the nation with an enthusiasm which proved the sureness of the crown's popularity and augured well for the new reign. The Irish opposition was mainly due to a feeling of resentment at the refusal of the government to alter the old terms of the sovereign's accession oath, in which while declaring himself a protestant he cast, in the view of Roman catholics, insult on their faith. Nowhere was there any sign of personal hostility to the new ruler.

The king came to the throne in his sixtieth year endowed with a personality of singular charm and geniality, large worldly experience, wide acquaintance with men and women, versatile interests in society and philanthropy, enthusiasm for sport, business habits, and a resolve to serve his people to the best of his ability. Among the king's friends there were fears that he would prove himself unequal to his new station, but the anticipations were signally belied. His mother's deliberate exclusion of him from political work placed him under some disadvantages. He was a stranger to the administrative details of his great office and he was too old to repair the neglect of a political training. Nor was he of an age at which it was easy to alter his general mode of life. He cherished a high regard for his mother's statesmanship and political acumen, but he had no full knowledge of the precise manner in which they had been exercised. At the outset there were slight indications that he over-estimated the sovereign's power. In consultation over a king's speech he seemed in some peril of misinterpreting the royal function. But his action was due to inexperience and to no impatience of ministerial advice. Despite his share in two royal commissions he had never studied deeply domestic legislation, and about it he held no well-defined views. He had watched more closely the course of foreign politics. His constant habit of travel, his careful maintenance of good relations with his large foreign kindred, his passion for making the personal acquaintance of interesting men and women on the continent, gave him much knowledge of foreign affairs both political and social. Yet the diplomatic details of foreign policy lay outside his range of study. While he was desirous of full information from his ministers, he soon came to view them as responsible experts whose procedure was rarely matter for much personal comment. The minutes of each cabinet meeting, with which the prime minister supplied the sovereign, usually provoked from Queen Victoria's pen voluminous criticism. King Edward VII usually accepted the prime minister's notes without remark, or if he was moved to avowal of acquiescence or remonstrance, he resorted to a short personal interview. The immense correspondence between the sovereign and the prime minister which continued during Queen Victoria's reign almost ceased, and its place, so far as it was filled at all, was taken by verbal intercourse, of which the king took no note. To appointments and the bestowal of honours he paid closer attention than to legislative measures or details of policy, and he was never neglectful of the interests of his personal friends, but even there he easily and as a rule gracefully yielded his wishes to ministerial counsel. His punctual habits enabled him to do all the formal business that was required of him with despatch. In signing papers and in dealing with urgent correspondence he was a model of promptitude. No arrears accumulated, and although the routine tried his patience, he performed it with exemplary regularity. He encouraged more modern technical methods than his mother had approved. He accepted type-written memoranda from ministers, instead of obliging them as in the late reign to write out everything in their own hands. He communicated with ministers through his chief secretary more frequently than had been customary before. Although he was for most of his life a voluminous letter writer, his penmanship greatly deteriorated in his last years and grew difficult to decipher. When the situation did not admit of an oral communication, he preferred to use a secretary's pen.

The king's conduct in his new station.

His relations with ministers.

It was inevitable that his place in the sphere of government should differ from that of his mother. Queen Victoria for the greater part of her reign was a widow and a recluse, who divided all her thought with unremitting application between politics and family affairs. The new king had wider interests. Without his mother's power of concentration or her tenacity of purpose, he distributed his energies over a more extended field. On acceding to his new dignity there was no lessening of his earlier devotion to sport, society, and other forms of amusement. He was faithful to his old circle of intimate friends and neither reduced nor extended it. His new official duties failed to absorb his whole attention. But it was in the revived splendours and developments of royal ceremonial that to the public eye

Contrasts between his rule and that of his mother.

the new reign chiefly differed from the old. Though Queen Victoria had modified her seclusion in her latest years, her age and her dislike of ceremonial functions had combined to maintain the court in much of the gloom in which the prince consort's death had involved it. The new king had a natural gift for the exercise of brilliant hospitality, and he sought to indulge his taste with liberality. London became the headquarters of the court for the first time for forty years. No effort was spared to make it a prominent feature of the nation's social life. Over the ceremonial and hospitable duties of sovereignty the king exercised a full personal control, and there he suffered no invasion of his authority.

The first year of the new reign was a year of mourning for the old. In its course it dealt the royal family another sorrowful blow. The king's eldest sister, the Empress Frederick, was suffering from cancer. On 23 Feb., within a month of his accession, the king left England for the first time during the reign to pay her a visit at Friedrichshof, her residence near Cronberg. They did not meet again. She died on 5 Aug. following. The king with the queen now crossed the Channel again to attend the funeral at Potsdam. Then the king went, according to his custom of thirty years' standing, to a German watering place, Homburg. No change was apparent there in his old habits which ignored strict rules of royal etiquette. Subsequently he joined the queen at Copenhagen, where he met his wife's nephew, the Tsar Nicholas of Russia, and the tsar's mother, the dowager empress, sister of Queen Alexandra. It was a family gathering of the kind which the king had long since been accustomed to attend periodically. As of old, it was wholly innocent of diplomatic intention. But the increased publicity attaching to the king's movements in his exalted station misled some domestic and many foreign observers into the error of scenting a subtle diplomatic purpose in his established practice of exchanging at intervals visits of courtesy with his royal kindred on the European continent. With his insatiable curiosity about men and things, he always liked frank discussion of European politics with foreign statesmen, and he continued the practice till his death. But such debate was scarcely to any greater degree than in earlier years the primary aim of his foreign tours.

Death of the Empress Frederick.

Meanwhile the king accepted without change the arrangements already made for a colonial tour of his son and his daughter-in-law. On 17 March he took leave of the duke and duchess of Cornwall and York on their setting out for Australia in the Ophir in order to open the new commonwealth parliament at Melbourne. On their return journey they visited Natal and Cape Colony, and thence traversed the whole of Canada. The king after a first visit as sovereign to Scotland met them on their arrival at Portsmouth on 1 Nov., and declared the tour to be a new link in the chain which bound the colonial empire to the throne. A few days later he created by letters patent the duke of Cornwall Prince of Wales. It was not easy, suddenly, to break the long association of that title with himself.

The duke of Cornwall and York's colonial tour, 17 March–1 Nov. 1901.

On 22 Jan. 1902 the year of mourning for the late queen ended, and court festivities began on a brilliant scale. Buckingham Palace and Windsor Castle had been thoroughly overhauled and newly decorated, the former becoming the chief residence of the court. Windsor saw comparatively little of the new king. Sandringham remained his country residence, and he spent a few weeks each autumn at Balmoral, but Osborne he abandoned, giving it over to the nation as a convalescent home for army and navy officers (9 Aug. 1902). Although little of his time was spent at Windsor or Balmoral, he greatly improved the facilities of sport in both places in the interests of his guests.

The first levee of the new reign was held on 11 Feb. at St. James's Palace, and the first evening court on 14 March at Buckingham Palace. The court initiated a new form of royal entertainment; it was held at night amid great magnificence, and replaced the afternoon drawing-rooms of Queen Victoria's reign. A tour in the west of England during March gave the king and queen an opportunity of showing their interest in the navy. At Dartmouth the foundation stone of the new Britannia Naval College was laid, while the queen launched the new battleship Queen at Devonport and the king laid the first plate of the new battleship Edward VII. A few weeks later he made a yachting tour off the west coast, paying a visit to the Scilly Isles on 7 April. The expedition followed a course with which he had familiarised himself in early youth.

The end of mourning.

Throughout the early period of the reign the nation's political horizon was clouded. Not only was the war in South Africa still in progress, but the alienation of foreign public opinion, which was a fruit of the conflict, continued to embarrass England's foreign relations. Neither in France nor Germany had scurrilous caricature of the king ceased. The king had always shown the liveliest sympathy with the British army in the field, and he did not conceal his resentment at the attacks made in England by members of the liberal party during 1901 on the methods of the military operations. On 12 June he presented medals to South African soldiers, and then conferred the same distinction on both Lord Roberts and Lord Milner, who was on leave in England discussing the situation. The king, though he did not interfere with the negotiations, was frank in his expressions of anxiety for peace. It was therefore with immense relief that he received the news that the pacification was signed in South Africa on 31 May 1902. He at once sent messages of thanks to the English plenipotentiaries, Lord Milner, high commissioner for South Africa, and Lord Kitchener, who had lately been in chief military command, and to all the forces who had been actively engaged in the war. On 8 June the king and queen attended a thanksgiving service in St. Paul's.

The close of the South African war, 31 May 1902.

X

The peace seemed an auspicious prelude to the solemn function of the coronation, which had been appointed for 26 June 1902. The king warmly approved proposals to give the formality exceptional magnificence. Since the last coronation sixty-four years ago the conception of the monarchy had broadened with the growth of the colonial empire. The strength of the crown now lay in its symbolic representation of the idea of imperial unity. There were anachronisms in the ritual, but the central purpose well served the present and the future. Representatives were invited not only from all the colonies but, for the first time, from all manner of administrative institutions—county councils, borough councils, learned societies, friendly societies, and railway companies. The king desired to render the event memorable for the poor no less than for the well-to-do. He gave the sum of 30,000*l.* for a commemorative dinner to 500,000 poor persons of London, while the queen undertook to entertain the humble class of general servants in the metropolis. Two other episodes lent fresh grace to the ceremony. The king announced his gift of Osborne House to the nation, and he instituted a new order of merit to be bestowed on men of high distinction in the army, navy, science, literature, and art. The order was fashioned on the lines of the Prussian 'pour le mérite' and was a more comprehensive recognition of ability than was known officially in England before. The total official cost of the coronation amounted to the large sum of 359,289*l.* 5*s.*, a sum greatly in excess of the 200,000*l.* voted by parliament for Queen Victoria's coronation (cf. *Blue Book* (382), 1909).

Plans for coronation.

A few days before the date appointed for the great ceremony rumours of the king's ill-health gained currency and were denied. But on 24 June, two days before Coronation Day, it was announced, to the public consternation, that the king was suffering from perityphlitis. An operation was performed the same morning with happy results, and during the next few weeks the king made a steady recovery.

The king's illness, 24 June 1902.

While still convalescent he had his first experience of a change of ministry. Lord Salisbury, whose failing health counselled retirement from the office of prime minister, had long since decided to resign as soon as peace in South Africa was proclaimed. But when that happy incident arrived, he looked forward to retaining his post for the six weeks which intervened before the coronation. The somewhat indefinite postponement of the ceremony led him to carry out his original purpose on 11 July 1902. On his recommendation his place was taken by Lord Salisbury's nephew, Mr. Balfour, who was already leader of the House of Commons. There was no immediate change in the complexion or the policy of the government, and no call for the sovereign's exertion. Although there was little in common between the temperament and training of the king and his first prime minister, the king was sensible of the value of Lord Salisbury's experience and wisdom, and the minister, whose faith in the monarchical principle was strong, showed him on his part a personal deference which he appreciated. The intellectual brillance of Lord Salisbury's successor often dazzled the king, but a thoroughly constitutional conception on each side of their respective responsibilities kept a good understanding alive between them.

Lord Salisbury's resignation, 11 July 1902. Mr. Balfour prime minister.

On 9 August the postponed coronation took place in Westminster Abbey. The ritual was somewhat abbreviated, but the splendour scarcely diminished. Although many of the foreign guests had left London, the scene lost little of its impressiveness. The crown was placed on the king's head by Frederick Temple, archbishop of Canterbury. Queen Alexandra was crowned at the same time by W. D. Maclagan, archbishop of York. There followed a series of public functions which aimed at associating with the ceremony various sources of imperial strength. An investiture and parade of colonial troops took place on 12 Aug., a review of Indian troops on 13 Aug., and a naval review at Spithead on 16 Aug. Next day at Cowes the king received visits from the Boer generals Delarey, De Wet, and Botha, who had greatly distinguished themselves in the late war and had come to England to plead on behalf of their conquered country for considerate treatment. The shah of Persia arrived to pay the king his respects three days later. On 22 Aug. the king and queen started for Scotland in the royal yacht Victoria and Albert; they went by the west coast, and visited on the passage the Isle of Man. On the return of the court to the metropolis, the king made a royal progress through south London (24 Oct.), and lunched with the lord mayor and corporation at the Guildhall. Two days later he attended at St. Paul's Cathedral a service of thanksgiving for his complete restoration to health.

The postponed coronation, 9 Aug.

With the close of the South African war England began to emerge from the cloud of animosity in which the popular sentiment of a great part of Europe had enveloped her. There was therefore every reason why the king should now gratify his cosmopolitan sympathies and his lively interest in his large circle of kinsmen and friends abroad by renewing his habit of foreign travel. Save during the pro-Boer outbreak of ill-will, he had always been a familiar and welcome figure among all classes on the continent. His cheering presence invariably encouraged sentiments of good-will, and it was congenial to him to make show of a personal contribution to an improvement of England's relations with her neighbours, and to a strengthening of the general concord. He acknowledged the obligation that lay on rulers and statesmen of preserving European peace; and he wished England, subject to a fit recognition of her rights, to stand well with the world. At the same time his constitutional position and his personal training disqualified him from exerting substantive influence on the foreign policy which his ministers alone could control. He repeatedly gave abroad graceful expression of general approval of his ministers' aims, and his benevolent assurances fostered a friendly atmosphere, but always without prejudice to his ministers' responsibilities. He cannot be credited with broad diplomatic views, or aptitude for technical negotiation. While he loved conversation with foreign statesmen, his interest in foreign lands ranged far beyond politics. In the intimacies of private intercourse he may have at times advanced a personal opinion on a diplomatic theme which lacked official sanction. But to his unguarded utterances no real weight attached in official circles either at home or abroad. His embodiment in foreign eyes of English aspirations inevitably exaggerated the popular importance of his public activities abroad. The foreign press and public often made during his reign the error of assuming that in his frequent interviews with foreign rulers and statesmen he was personally working out a diplomatic policy of his own devising. Foreign statesmen and rulers knew that no subtler aim really underlay his movements than a wish for friendly social intercourse with them and the enjoyment of life under foreign skies, quite unencumbered by the burden of diplomatic anxieties.

The king's foreign tours.

In his eyes all rulers of state were bound together by ties of affinity, and these ties were strengthened for him by many bonds of actual kinship. At his accession the rulers of Germany, Russia, Greece, and Portugal were related to him in one or other degree, and two additions were made to his large circle of royal relatives while he was king. In October 1905 his son-in-law, Prince Charles of Denmark, who had married his youngest daughter, Maud, in 1896, was elected king of Norway (as Haakon VII) when that country severed its union with Sweden; while on 31 May 1906 Alfonso XIII, king of Spain, married Princess Ena of Battenberg, daughter of the king's youngest sister, Princess Beatrice. There was good justification for the title which the wits of Paris bestowed on him of 'l'oncle de l'Europe.' Most of the European courts were the homes of his kinsfolk, whose domestic hospitality was always in readiness for him. In return it gratified his hospitable instinct to

His kinship with foreign rulers.

welcome his royal relatives beneath his own roof.

To no country of Europe did his attitude as king differ from that which he had adopted while he was prince. To France his devotion was always pronounced. He had delighted in visiting Italy, Russia, Austria, and Portugal. His relations with Germany had always stood on a somewhat peculiar footing, and they, too, underwent small change. They had been coloured to a larger extent than his other foreign connections by the personal conditions of family kinship. Since the Danish war, owing to the influence of his wife and her kindred, he had never professed in private much sympathy with German political ambitions. The brusque speech and manner, too, with which Bismarck invariably treated the English royal family had made German policy uncongenial to them. Despite the king's affection for his nephew, the German emperor, short seasons of domestic variance between the two were bound to recur, and the private differences encouraged the old-standing coolness in political sentiment. But the king was never long estranged from his nephew. He was thoroughly at home with Germans and when he went among them evoked their friendly regard. No deliberate and systematic hostility to the German people could be truthfully put to the king's credit. His personal feeling was very superficially affected by the mutual jealousy which, from causes far beyond his control, grew during his reign between the two nations.

Personal relations with Germany.

While ambitious to confirm as king the old footing which he had enjoyed on the European continent as prince, his conservative instinct generated involuntary misgivings of England's friendship with peoples outside the scope of his earlier experience. He was startled by so novel a diplomatic step as the alliance with Japan, which was concluded during the first year of his reign (12 Feb. 1902) and was expanded later (27 Sept. 1905). But he was reassured on learning of the age and dignity of the reigning Japanese dynasty. When the Anglo-Japanese arrangement was once effected he lent it all the advantage of his loyal personal support. He entertained the Japanese Prince and Princess Arisugawa on their visit to London, and conferred on the prince the distinction of G.C.B. (27 June 1905). In 1906, too, after the Russo-Japanese war, he admitted to the Order of Merit the Japanese heroes of the conflict, Field-marshals Yamagata and Oyama, and Admiral Togo.

His attitude to Japan.

XI

Family feeling solely guided the king's first steps in the foreign arena. After his eldest sister's death the king and emperor made open avowal of mutual affection. On 26 Jan. 1902 the Prince of Wales was the emperor's guest at Berlin for his birthday, and on the king's coronation the emperor made him an admiral of the German fleet. At the end of the year, on 8 Nov. 1902, the emperor arrived at Sandringham to attend the celebration of his uncle's sixty-first birthday. He remained in England twelve days, and had interviews with the prime minister and the foreign secretary. Details of diplomacy were not the theme of the uncle and nephew's confidences. Rumours to a contrary effect were current early next year, when the two countries made a combined naval demonstration in order to coerce the recalcitrant president of the Venezuelan republic, who had defied the just claims of both England and Germany. It was imagined in some quarters that the king on his own initiative had committed his ministers to the joint movement in an informal conversation with the emperor at Sandringham. Much wrangling had passed between the statesmen and the press of the two countries. But the apparently sudden exchange of a campaign of altercation for concerted action to meet a special emergency was no exceptional diplomatic incident.

The German emperor at Sandringham, Nov. 1902.

The spring of 1903 saw the first foreign tour of the king's reign and his personal introduction to the continent in his new rôle. On 31 March 1903 he left Portsmouth harbour on board the royal yacht the Victoria and Albert, on a five weeks' cruise, in the course of which he visited among other places Lisbon, Rome, and Paris. The expedition was a vacation exercise, which gave him the opportunity of showing friendly courtesy to foreign rulers and peoples. He went on his own initiative. His travelling companions were members of his own household, who were personal friends. There was also in his retinue a member of the permanent staff of the foreign office, the Hon. Charles Hardinge, assistant under-secretary there. Mr. Hardinge, who was made K.C.V.O. and K.C.M.G. in 1904, and Baron Hardinge of

The tour of 1903.

The status in his suite of Mr. Charles Hardinge.

Penshurst in 1910, served as British ambassador at St. Petersburg from 1904 to 1906 and was permanent under-secretary at the foreign office from 1906 till the king's death. While he was attached to the foreign office, he usually accompanied the king on his foreign tours, and the precise capacity in which he travelled with the sovereign occasionally raised a constitutional controversy, which the true facts deprived of genuine substance. The presence of the foreign minister or at any rate of a cabinet minister was necessary to bring any effective diplomatic negotiation within the range of the king's intercourse with his foreign hosts. Mr. Hardinge was personally agreeable to the king. He was well fitted to offer advice or information which might be of service in those talks with foreign rulers or statesmen on political themes in which the sovereign occasionally indulged. He could also record suggestions if the need arose for the perusal of the foreign minister. In debates in the House of Commons some ambiguity and constitutional irregularity were imputed to Mr. Hardinge's status in the king's suite, but it was made clear that no ministerial responsibilities devolved either on the king or on him during the foreign tours, and that the foreign policy of the country was unaffected by the royal progresses (*Hansard*, 23 July 1903 and 4 June 1908).

The king's route of 1903 was one with which he was familiar. His first landing-place was Lisbon, where he was the guest of King Carlos. The two monarchs complimented each other on their lineal ties and on the ancient alliance between their two countries. After short visits to Gibraltar and Malta, the king disembarked at Naples on 23 April, and four days later reached Rome. The good relations which had always subsisted between England and Italy had been little disturbed by pro-Boer prejudice. The Roman populace received King Edward with enthusiasm, and he exchanged with King Victor Emanuel professions of warm friendship. With characteristic tact the king visited Pope Leo XIII at the Vatican, where he had thrice before greeted Pope Pius IX. From Rome the king passed with no small gratification to his favourite city of Paris for the first time after more than three years. He came at an opportune moment. The French foreign minister, M. Delcassé, had for some time been seeking a diplomatic understanding with England, which should remove the numerous points of friction between the two countries in Egypt, Morocco, and elsewhere. The king's ministers were responsive, and his visit to Paris, although it was paid independently of the diplomatic issue, was well calculated to conciliate French public opinion, which was slow in shedding its pro-Boer venom. On the king's arrival the temper of the Parisian populace looked doubtful (1 May), but the king's demeanour had the best effect, and in his reply to an address from the British chamber of commerce on his first morning in Paris he spoke so aptly of the importance of developing good relations between the two countries that there was an immediate renewal of the traditional friendliness which had linked him to the Parisians for near half a century. The president, M. Loubet, and M. Delcassé did everything to enhance the cordiality of the welcome. The president entertained the king at a state banquet at the Elysée and the speeches of both host and guest gave voice to every harmonious sentiment. The king accompanied the president to the Théâtre Français, to a military review at Vincennes, and to the races at Longchamps. He did not neglect friends of the old régime, and everywhere he declared his happiness in strengthening old ties. His words and actions closely resembled those which marked his visit to Paris under Marshal MacMahon's auspices in 1878. But, in view of his new rank and the recent political discord, the episode was generally regarded as the propitious heralding of a new departure. On 5 May he returned to London and was warmly received.

The king lost no time in returning the hospitalities of his foreign hosts. On 6 July President Loubet came to London to stay at St. James's Palace as the king's guest, and M. Delcassé was his companion. Friendly negotiations between the two governments took a step forward. On 17 Nov. the king and queen of Italy were royal guests at Windsor, and were followed just a year later by the king and queen of Portugal. There was nothing in the visits of the foreign sovereigns to distinguish them from the ordinary routine of courtesy. The visit of the president of the French republic was unprecedented. It was proof of the desire of France to make friends with England and of the king's sympathy

At Lisbon.

At Rome.

At Paris.

England's diplomatic relations with France.

The king and President Loubet.

President Loubet in London, 6 July 1903.

The king's royal guests.

with the aspiration. M. Delcassé's policy soon bore practical fruit; on 14 Oct. 1903 an arbitration treaty was signed by the two governments. Its provisions did not go far, but it indicated a new spirit in the international relation. The Anglo-French agreement, which was concluded on 8 April 1904 between M. Delcassé and Lord Lansdowne, the English foreign secretary, was an instrument of genuine consequence. It formally terminated the long series of difficulties which had divided England and France in many parts of the world, and was a guarantee against their recurrence. The king's grace of manner both as guest and host of President Loubet helped to create a temper favourable to the 'entente cordiale.' But no direct responsibility for its initiation or conclusion belonged to him. Some French journalists who were oblivious of his aloofness from the detail of state business placed the understanding to his credit, and bestowed on him the title of 'le roi pacificateur.' The title is symbolically just but is misleading if it be taken to imply any personal control of diplomacy.

The entente cordiale, 8 April 1904.

'Le roi pacificateur.'

It was not the king's wish to withhold from Germany and the German emperor, whatever the difficulties between the two governments, those attentions which it had been his habit to exchange with his nephew from the opening of the emperor's reign. On 29 June 1904 the king sailed for Kiel in his yacht Victoria and Albert, attended by an escort of naval vessels. He was received by the emperor with much cordiality, visited under his nephew's guidance the German dockyards, attended a regatta off Kiel, and lunched at Hamburg with the burgomaster. In his intercourse with the German emperor it flattered the king's pride to give to their meetings every show of dignity, and contrary to his usual practice a cabinet minister now joined his suite. The presence of Lord Selborne, first lord of the admiralty, gave the expedition something of the formal character of a friendly naval demonstration, but no political significance attached to the interchange of civilities. An arbitration treaty with Germany of the same tenour as that with France was signed on 12 July 1904, but such a negotiation was outside the king's sphere of action. The failure of the Kiel visit to excite any ill-feeling in France indicated the purely external part which his charm of manner and speech was known to play in international affairs.

At Kiel, 29 June 1904.

The king's habitual appetite for foreign tours was whetted by his experience in the spring of 1903. While constant movement characterised his life at home, and a business-like distribution of his time enabled him to engage in an unending round of work and pleasure through the greater part of his reign, he spent on an average some three months of each year out of his dominions. His comprehensive travels did not embrace the colonies or dependencies outside Europe, but his son and heir, who had visited the colonies in 1901, made a tour through India (Nov. 1905–May 1906), and the king thus kept vicariously in touch with his Indian as well as with his colonial subjects. His travelling energy was freely lavished on countries nearer at hand. Five or six weeks each spring were spent at Biarritz, and a similar period each autumn at Marienbad. These sojourns were mainly designed in the interests of health. But with them were combined four cruises in the Mediterranean (1905, 6, 7, and 1909) and one cruise in the North Sea (1908), all of which afforded opportunities of pleasurable recreation, and of meetings with foreign rulers. In addition, he paid in the winter of 1907 a visit to Prussia and in the summer of 1908 one to Russia. Such frequent wanderings from home greatly increased the king's foreign reputation. It was only occasionally that he paid visits to foreign courts in the panoply of state. He travelled for the most part incognito. Few episodes, however, of his migrations escaped the notice of the journalists, who sought persistently to confirm the erroneous impression that he was invariably engaged on a diplomatic mission.

Range of the king's foreign travel.

In Paris he resumed his old career. Each year, on his way to or from the south, he revisited the city, seeing old friends and indulging in old amusements. In meetings with the president of the French republic and his ministers he repeated his former assurances of amity. When M. Loubet retired in January 1906, he showed equal warmth of feeling for his successor, M. Fallières, to whom he paid the courtesy of a state visit (3 May). In the summer of 1908 he had the satisfaction of entertaining the new president in London with the same ceremony as was accorded to his predecessor in 1904. He was loyal to all his French acquaintances new and old. On M. Delcassé's

His social circle in Paris.

fall from power in June 1905 he continued to exchange friendly visits with him during his later sojourns in the French capital. M. Clemenceau, who became prime minister in October 1906, and held office for nearly three years, was reared in Gambetta's political school, members of which had always interested the king since his pleasant meetings with their chief. M. Clemenceau was the king's guest at Marienbad on 15 Aug. 1909. Political principles counted for little in his social intercourse. He was still welcomed with the same cordiality by representatives of the fashionable royalist noblesse as by republican statesmen. A modest estimate was set on his political acumen when in informal talk he travelled beyond safe generalities. An irresponsible suggestion at a private party in Paris that the entente ought to be converted into a military alliance met with no response. Nor was much heed paid to some vague comment which fell from his lips on the intricate problem of the relations of the European powers on the north coast of Africa. But everyone in France appreciated his French sympathies and acknowledged his personal fascination.

Mediterranean cruises, 1905, 1906, 1907, and 1909.

His cruises to the Mediterranean during these years took him to Algiers in 1905, and to Athens and the Greek archipelago in April 1906; at Athens, where he was the guest of his brother-in-law, King George I, he witnessed the Olympic games. In 1907 he landed from his yacht at Cartagena to meet the young king of Spain, who had married his niece the year before. Twice in the course of the same journey he also met the king of Italy, first at Gaeta (18 April), and secondly on the return journey by rail outside Rome (30 April). Two years later (1909) he enjoyed similar experiences, meeting the king of Spain at San Sebastian and Biarritz, and the king of Italy at Baiae; then he also visited Malta and Sicily, besides Pompeii and other environs of Naples. In April 1908 he cruised in the North Sea, and he visited in state the three northern courts of Denmark, Sweden, and Norway, In Denmark he was a familiar figure. To the new kingdom of Norway, where his son-in-law reigned, he went for the first time. At Stockholm he had been the frequent guest of earlier Swedish kings while he was Prince of Wales.

In the Baltic.

During a single year, 1905, the German emperor and the king failed to exchange hospitalities. Germany lay outside the ubiquitous route of his pleasure cruises, and circumstances deterred the king from deliberately seeking personal intercourse with his nephew. For the continued friction between Germany and England the king had no sort of responsibility. But the emperor was for the moment inclined to credit his uncle with want of sympathy, and there followed one of those short seasons of estrangement to which their intimacy was always liable. Reports of unguarded remarks from the royal lips in the course of 1905 which reached the emperor from Paris had for him an unfriendly sound. Meanwhile the German press lost no opportunity of treating the king as a declared enemy of Germany. The king's voyages were held to be shrewd moves in a diplomatic game which sought German humiliation. The meetings of the king with the king of Italy were misconstrued into a personal attempt on the king's part to detach Italy from the triple alliance. The interview at Gaeta in April 1907 was especially denounced as part of the king's Machiavellian design of an elaborate coalition from which Germany was to be excluded. Adverse comment was passed on his apparent desire to avoid a meeting with the emperor. He was represented as drawing a cordon round Germany in the wake of his foreign journeys, and there were even German politicians who professed to regard him as a sort of Bismarck who used the velvet glove instead of the iron hand. He was deemed capable of acts of conciliation to suit his dark purposes. It was pretended that, with a view to soothing German irritation for his own objects, he by his own hand excised from the official instructions to the English delegates at the Hague conference (June 1907) his ministers' orders to raise the question of a general reduction of armaments. Serious French publicists well knew the king to be innocent of any such wiles. French caricaturists, who made merry over his 'fièvre voyageuse,' only echoed the German note in a satiric key. They pictured the king as a 'polype Européen' which was clutching in its tentacles all the sovereigns of Europe save the German emperor, without prejudice to the international situation.

Temporary estrangement from the German emperor.

Misapprehensions in Germany.

The German fancies were complete delusions. The king had no conception of any readjustment of the balance of European power. There was no serious quarrel between emperor and king. The passing cloud dispersed. On 15 Aug. 1906 the king visited the emperor at Friedrichshof near Cronberg on his journey to Marienbad, and a general conversation which only dealt in part with politics put matters on a right footing. Sir Frank Lascelles, the English ambassador at Berlin, who had accompanied the king from Frankfort, was present at the interview. Just a year later (14 Aug. 1907) a like meeting at Wilhelmshöhe renewed the friendly intercourse, and in the same year the German emperor and empress paid a state visit to Windsor (11–18 Nov.). The emperor exerted all his charm on his host and his fellow guests. The formal speeches of both emperor and king abounded in felicitous assurances of good-will. During the emperor's stay at Windsor the king gathered about him as imposing an array of royal personages as ever assembled there. On 17 November he entertained at luncheon twenty-four men and women of royal rank, including the king and queen of Spain, Queen Amélie of Portugal, and many members of the Orleans and Bourbon families, who had met in England to celebrate the marriage of Prince Charles of Bourbon to Princess Louise of Orleans. The entertainment showed the king at the head of the royal caste of Europe, and attested his social power of reconciling discordant elements. The emperor remained in England till 11 December, sojourning privately at Highcliffe near Bournemouth on leaving Windsor. Again on his way to Marienbad the king spent another pleasant day with the emperor at Friedrichshof (11 August 1908). King Edward returned the German emperor's formal visit to Windsor in February 1909, when he and the queen stayed in Berlin. For the second time during his reign a cabinet minister bore him company on a foreign expedition. At Kiel some four years earlier the first lord of the admiralty, Lord Selborne, had been in the king's suite when he met his nephew. The king was now attended by the earl of Crewe, secretary for the colonies. On neither of the only two occasions when a cabinet minister attended the king abroad did the foreign minister go. In both instances the minister's presence was of complimentary rather than of diplomatic significance, and was a royal concession to the German emperor's love of ceremonial observance. The king's Berlin expedition did not differ from his visits of courtesy to other foreign capitals.

At Friedrichshof, 15 Aug. 1906.

At Berlin, Feb. 1909.

With the aged emperor of Austria, whom he had known and liked from boyhood, and in whose dominions he had often sojourned, the king was equally desirous of repeating friendly greetings in person. He paid the emperor a visit at Gmünden on his way out to Marienbad in August 1905, and on each of the two meetings with the German emperor at Cronberg, in August 1907 and August 1908, he went the next day to Ischl to offer salutations to Emperor Francis Joseph. All these meetings fell within the period of the king's usual autumn holiday. But on his second visit to Ischl the emperor of Austria entertained him to a state banquet, and Baron von Aerenthal, who was in attendance on his master, had some political conversation on affairs in Turkey and the Balkan provinces with Sir Charles Hardinge, who was in King Edward's retinue. But the king's concern with the diplomatic problem was remote. He was once more illustrating his zeal for ratifying by personal intercourse the wide bounds of his friendships with European sovereigns.

Meetings with the emperor of Austria, 1905–8.

On the same footing stood the only visit which the king paid to the tsar of Russia during his reign. He made with the queen a special journey (9 June 1908) to Reval. It was the first visit ever paid to Russia by a British sovereign. It followed his cruise round the other northern capitals, and the king regarded as overdue the personal civility to the tsar, who was nephew of his wife, and to whom he was deeply attached. The tsar had been driven from his capital by revolutionary agitation and was in his yacht off Reval. The interview proved thoroughly cordial. French journalists hailed it with satisfaction; Germans scented in it a new menace, but the journey was innocent of diplomatic purpose. Objection was raised in the House of Commons that the king's visit showed sympathy with the tsar's alleged oppression of his revolutionary subjects. The suggestion moved the king's resentment. He acknowledged no connection between a visit to a royal kinsman and any phase of current political agitation. The unrest in Russia was no concern of his, and only awoke in him sympathy with the ruler whose life it oppressed. Unwisely the king took notice of the parliamentary criticism of his action, and cancelled the invitation to a royal garden party

The visit to Russia, 9 June 1908.

(20 June) of three members of parliament, who had questioned his prudence. His irritation soon passed away, but his mode of avowing annoyance was denounced by the labour party 'as an attempt by the court to influence members of parliament.' It was the only occasion during the reign on which the king invited any public suspicion of misinterpreting his constitutional position. The criticism to which he was subjected was due to a misunderstanding of the character of his foreign tours, but the interpellation was no infringement of public right.

He was hardly conscious of the deep-seated feeling which the alleged tyranny of the Russian government had excited in many quarters in England. When in the customary course of etiquette the king received the tsar as his guest at Cowes in August 1909 a fresh protest against his friendly attitude took the form of an influentially signed letter to the foreign secretary. But politics did not influence the king's relations with the tsar. The tsar was accompanied at Cowes by his foreign minister, M. Isvolsky; but as far as the king was concerned, the visit was solely a confirmation of old personal ties with the Russian sovereign, and lengthened impressively the roll of European rulers whom he sought to embrace in his comprehensive hospitality.

Protest against the king's friendliness with the tsar.

With the perilous vicissitudes of royalty the king naturally had a lively sympathy, and he suffered a severe shock on learning of the assassination of his friend and cousin and recent guest, King Carlos of Portugal, and of his son the crown prince in Lisbon on 2 Feb. 1908. Queen Amélie of Portugal had been a prominent figure in the great assembly of royal personages at Windsor less than three months before. By way of emphasising their intense sorrow the king and queen and other members of the royal family defied precedent by attending a requiem mass at St. James's church, Spanish Place, near Manchester Square, on 8 Feb. in memory of the murdered monarch. It was the first time that an English sovereign had attended a Roman catholic service in Great Britain since the Reformation. By the king's wish, too, a memorial service was held next day in St. Paul's cathedral, which he and his family also attended. Both houses of parliament presented an address to the crown expressing indignation and deep concern at the outrages. The king's heartfelt sympathy went out to the new king of Portugal, the late king's younger son, Manoel, and in November next year he entertained the young monarch at Windsor, investing him with the order of the Garter, and greeting him at a state banquet on 16 Nov. as 'the heir of our oldest ally in history.' King Manoel was King Edward's last royal guest. There was some irony in the circumstance. King Manoel's royal career was destined to be brief, and within five months of King Edward's death his subjects established a republic and drove him from his throne to seek an asylum in England.

The assassination of the king of Portugal, 2 Feb. 1908.

XII

Although so substantial a part of his reign was passed abroad, the king manifested activity in numberless directions when he was at home. From London, which was his headquarters, he made repeated expeditions into the country. As of old he was regular in attendance at Newmarket and other race meetings. Although he did not repeat during the reign his early triumphs on the turf, the successes of his horse Minoru, who won the Derby in 1909, greatly delighted the sporting public. He encouraged the opera and the theatres by frequent attendance. He was lavish in entertainment at Buckingham Palace and freely accepted hospitalities at the London houses of his friends. He was indefatigable in paying attention to foreign visitors to the capital, especially those of royal rank. When the duke of Abruzzi came at the end of 1906 to lecture to the Royal Geographical Society on his explorations of the Ruwenzori mountains in east Africa, the king was present and with impromptu grace and manifest desire to prove his interest in foreign policy moved a vote of thanks to the lecturer, whom he hailed as a kinsman of his ally the king of Italy (2 Jan. 1907). At stated seasons he was the guest for shooting or merely social recreation at many country houses, where he met at ease his unchanging social circle. From 1904 to 1907 he spent a week each January with the duke of Devonshire at Chatsworth. In the autumn he went a round of Scottish mansions.

The king's life at home.

While unremitting in his devotion to social pleasures, he neglected few of the philanthropic or other public movements with which he had already identified himself. Occasionally his foreign tours withdrew him from functions which could only be performed effectively at home. During the colonial conference of 1907 he was away from England, but he returned in time to entertain the colonial premiers at dinner on 8 May. On his birthday later in the year (9 Nov.) he received as a gift from the Transvaal people the Cullinan diamond, the largest diamond known, which was a notable tribute to the efficiency of the new settlement of south Africa. Two sections of the magnificent stone were set in the royal crown.

Every summer the king was at work both in London and the provinces, laying foundation stones and opening new public institutions. In London and the neighbourhood his varied engagements included the inaugurations of St. Saviour's cathedral, Southwark (3 July 1905); of the new streets Kingsway and Aldwych (18 Oct. 1905); of the new Victoria and Albert Museum, South Kensington (22 June 1909), and the laying of the first stone of the new buildings of the Imperial College of Science and Technology, South Kensington (8 July 1909).

Public engagements in London and neighbourhood, 1905–9.

To his earlier interests in medicine and therapeutics he was always faithful. On 3 Nov. 1903 he laid the foundation stone of the King Edward Sanatorium for Consumption at Midhurst, and he opened the building on 13 June 1906. He gave abundant proofs of his care for general hospitals; he opened a new wing of the London Hospital (11 June 1903) and laid foundation stones of the new King's College Hospital, Denmark Hill (20 July 1909), and of the new King Edward Hospital at Windsor (22 June 1908). His broad sympathies with philanthropic agencies he illustrated by receiving at Buckingham Palace 'General' Booth of the Salvation Army (22 June 1904) and Prebendary Carlile, head of the Church Army (13 Jan. 1905). His veteran interest in the housing of the poor led him to pay a visit (18 Feb. 1903) to the L.C.C. model dwellings at Millbank, and he showed a characteristic anxiety to relieve the sufferings of poverty by giving 2000 guineas to Queen Alexandra's Unemployment Fund (17 Nov. 1905).

In the country his public labours were year by year even more conspicuous. On 19 July 1904 he laid the foundation stone of the new Liverpool cathedral; and inaugurated the new King's Dock at Swansea (20 July) and the new water supply for Birmingham at Rhayader (21 July). A year later he visited Sheffield to instal the new university, and he went to Manchester to open a new dock of the Manchester Ship Canal and to unveil the war memorial at Salford. On 10 July 1906 he opened the high-level bridge at Newcastle, and later new buildings at Marischal College, Aberdeen (28 Sept.). In 1907 he laid the foundation stones of new buildings of University College of Wales at Bangor (9 July) and opened Alexandra Dock at Cardiff (13 July). In 1908 he opened the new university buildings at Leeds (7 July) and the new dock at Avonmouth, Bristol (9 July). In 1909 he returned to Manchester to open the new infirmary (6 July), and then passed on to Birmingham to inaugurate the new university buildings. His last public philanthropic function was to lay the corner stone of a new wing of the Norfolk and Norwich Hospital at Norwich (25 Oct. 1909).

Public engagements in the provinces, 1904–9.

To the public schools he showed as before many marks of favour. He twice visited Eton, on 13 June 1904, and again on 18 Nov. 1908, when he opened the hall and library, which formed the South African war memorial there. He was at Harrow School on 30 June 1905, and he opened the new buildings of University College School, Hampstead, on 26 July 1907, and a new speech room at Rugby on 3 July 1909. To Wellington College, founded by his father, he remained a frequent visitor, and on 21 June 1909 he attended the celebration of the college's jubilee. He proved his friendly intimacy with the headmaster, Dr. Bertram Pollock, by nominating him, as his personal choice, just before his death in 1910, to the bishopric of Norwich. It was the diocese in which lay his country seat.

Visits to public schools.

To Ireland, where, in spite of political disaffection, the prince's personal charm had always won for him a popular welcome, he gave as king evidence of the kindliest feeling. In July 1903 he and the queen paid their first visit in their capacity of sovereigns soon after his first foreign tour. They landed at Kingstown on 31 July. Although the Dublin corporation refused by forty votes to thirty-seven to present an address, the people showed no lack of cordiality. The king with customary tact spoke of the very recent death of Pope Leo XIII whom he had lately visited, and he bestowed his favours impartially on protestant and Roman catholic. The catholic archbishop of Dublin, Dr. Walsh, attended a levee, and the king visited Maynooth College. He subsequently went north to stay with Lord Londonderry at Mount Stewart, and after a visit to Belfast made a yachting tour

The king in Ireland.

round the west coast, making inland excursions by motor. Coming south, he inspected the exhibition at Cork, and on leaving Queenstown on 1 August issued an address of thanks to the Irish people for his reception. He expressed a sanguine belief that a brighter day was dawning upon Ireland. There was good ground for the anticipation, for the Land Purchase Act which was passed during the year gave promise of increased prosperity.

A second visit to Ireland of a more private character followed in the spring of 1904 and confirmed the good impression of the first visit. Two visits of the sovereign in such rapid succession were unknown to recent Irish history. The king was now the guest of the duke of Devonshire at Lismore Castle, and of the marquis of Ormonde at Kilkenny Castle, and he attended both the Punchestown and Leopardstown races. His chief public engagement was the laying the foundation stone of the new buildings of the Royal College of Science at Dublin (25 April–4 May). A third and last visit to Ireland took place in July 1907, when the king and queen opened at Dublin the International Exhibition (10 July). The popular reception was as enthusiastic as before.

Relations with the army and navy.

In his relations with the army and the navy he did all that was required of their titular head. Like his mother he was prouder of his association with the army than with the navy, but he acknowledged the need of efficiency in both services, and attached vast importance to details of etiquette and costume. He was an annual visitor at Aldershot, and was indefatigable in the distribution of war medals and new regimental colours. He did not study closely the principles or practice of army or navy organisation and he deprecated breaches with tradition. But he put no real obstacles in the way of the effective application of expert advice. He received daily reports of the army commission inquiry at the close of the South African war (1902–3), which led to extensive changes. The chief military reform of his reign was the formation in 1907 by Mr. (afterwards Viscount) Haldane of a territorial army. The king shared Queen Victoria's dislike of any plan that recalled Cromwell's régime, and he mildly demurred to the employment of Cromwell's term, 'County Association,' in the territorial scheme. But he was flattered by the request to inaugurate personally the new system. On 26 Oct. 1907 he summoned the lord-lieutenants of the United Kingdom to Buckingham Palace, and addressed them on the new duties that had been imposed on them as officers of the new territorial army. Twice in 1909—on 19 June at Windsor and on 5 July at Knowsley—he presented colours to territorial regiments. His attitude to measures was always conditioned to a large extent by his interest in the men who framed them, and his liking for Mr. Haldane, the war minister who created the territorial army, mainly inspired his personal patronage of the movement.

The territorial army.

His faith in Lord Fisher.

In the navy the same sentiment was at work. His faith in Lord Fisher, who played a leading part in the re-organisation of the navy during the reign, reconciled him to alterations which often conflicted with his conservative predilections. A large increase in the navy took place while he was king, and one of his last public acts was to review in the Solent on 31 July 1909 an imposing assembly of naval vessels by way of a royal benediction on recent naval policy.

His position in home politics.

In home politics the king was for the most part content with the rôle of onlooker. He realised early that the constitution afforded him mere formalities of supervision which required no close application. He failed to persuade his ministers to deal with the housing question. Few other problems of domestic legislation interested him deeply, and he accepted without searching comment his ministers' proposals. To complicated legislative details he paid small heed, and although he could offer shrewd criticism on a subsidiary point which casually caught his eye or ear, he did not invite elaborate explanation. His conservative instinct enabled him to detect intuitively the dangers underlying political innovations, but he viewed detachedly the programmes of all parties.

When the tariff reform controversy arose in 1903 he read in the press the chief pleas of the tariff reformers, and remarked that it would be difficult to obtain popular assent to a tax on bread. He deprecated licensing reform which pressed unduly on the brewer and he was displeased with political oratory which appealed to class prejudice and excited in the poor unwarranted hopes. He was unmoved by the outcry against Chinese labour in south Africa. He was not in favour of woman's suffrage.

Disapproval of political action usually took the shape of a general warning addressed to the prime minister. In filling all offices he claimed to be consulted, and freely placed his knowledge and judgment of persons at his minister's disposal. But, save occasionally where he wished to serve a friend in a military, naval, colonial, diplomatic, or ecclesiastical promotion, the minister's choice was practically unfettered. The personal machinery of government interested him, however, more than its legislative work or policy, but he effected little of importance even in that direction. When in 1904 resignations rent asunder Mr. Balfour's ministry and reconstruction became necessary, the king made some endeavour to repair the breaches. He sought to overcome in a powerful quarter hesitation to co-operate with Mr. Balfour. But to the king's disappointment nothing came of his effort. It was one of many illustrations of his virtual powerlessness to influence political events.

On 5 Dec. 1905 the king accepted Mr. Balfour's resignation, and admitted to office his third prime minister, Sir Henry Campbell-Bannerman [q. v. Suppl. II], the leader of the liberal party. The change of ministry was emphatically ratified by the general election of January 1906, and the liberals remained in power till the king's death. The fall of the conservatives caused the king little disquiet. The return of the liberals to office after a ten years' exclusion seemed to him to be quite fair, and to maintain a just equilibrium between opposing forces in the state. His relations with Gladstone had shown that a distrust of the trend of liberal policy need be no bar to friendly intimacy with liberal leaders. He had slightly known Campbell-Bannerman as minister of war in the last liberal administration of 1892–5. But the politician's severe strictures on military operations in south Africa during 1901 had displeased the king. Early in the reign he had hesitated to meet him at a private dinner party, but he suppressed his scruples and the meeting convinced him of Campbell-Bannerman's sincere anxiety to preserve the peace of Europe, while his Scottish humour attracted him.

Sir Henry Campbell-Bannerman prime minister 5 Dec. 1905.

With constitutional correctness the king abstained from interference in the construction of the new cabinet, and he received the new ministers with open-minded serenity. The innovation of including among them a labour member, Mr. John Burns, was not uncongenial to him. His earlier relations with Mr. Broadhurst and Mr. Arch taught him the prudence of bestowing responsible positions on representatives of labour. Mr. Burns personally interested him, and he was soon on cordial terms with him. With another of the liberal ministers, Lord Carrington, afterwards marquis of Lincolnshire, minister for agriculture, he had been intimate since boyhood. Mr. Herbert Gladstone, home secretary, was a son of his old friend. Mr. Haldane, secretary for war, whose genial temper and grasp of German life and learning appealed to him, quickly became a *persona grata*. With the ministers in other posts he found less in common, and he came into little contact with them, save in ceremonial functions.

The liberal ministry of 1905.

The grant by the new ministry of self-government to the newly conquered provinces of south Africa excited the king's serious misgivings, and he feared a surrender of the fruits of the late war. But he contented himself with a remonstrance, and there was no diminution of his good relations with the liberal prime minister. After little more than two years of power Campbell-Bannerman fell ill, and from February 1908 his strength slowly failed. Just before setting out on his annual visit to Biarritz the king took farewell of the statesman at his official residence in Downing Street (4 March 1908). The king manifested the kindliest sympathy with his dying servant. A month later the prime minister forwarded his resignation, and recommended as his successor Mr. Asquith, the chancellor of the exchequer. The king was still at Biarritz, and thither Mr. Asquith travelled to surrender his old place and to be admitted to the headship of the government. There was a murmur of dissatisfaction that so important a function of state as the installation of a new prime minister should be performed by the king in a foreign hotel. Nothing of the kind had happened before in English history. The king's health was held to justify the breach of etiquette. But the episode brought into strong relief the king's aloofness from the working of politics and a certain disinclination hastily to adapt his private plans to political emergencies.

Mr. Asquith prime minister, 8 April 1908.

Mr. Asquith's administration was rapidly formed without the king's assistance. It mainly differed from that of his predecessor by the elevation of Mr. Lloyd George to the chancellorship of the exchequer and the admission of Mr. Winston Churchill to the cabinet. Neither appointment evoked

Mr. Asquith's ministry.

royal enthusiasm. Mr. Lloyd George's speeches in the country often seemed to the king reckless and irresponsible. Mr. Churchill's father, Lord Randolph, had long been a close friend. Knowing the son from his cradle, the king found it difficult to reconcile himself to the fact that he was a grown man fitted for high office. With his new prime minister he was at once in easy intercourse, frankly and briefly expressing to him his views on current business, and suggesting or criticising appointments. While he abstained from examining closely legislative details, and while he continued to regard his ministers' actions as matters for their own discretion, he found little in the ministerial proposals to command his personal approval. Especially did Mr. Lloyd George's budget of 1909, which imposed new burdens on landed and other property, cause him searchings of heart. But his tact did not permit him to forgo social courtesies to ministers whose policy seemed to him dangerous. In society he often gave those of them whose political conduct he least approved the fullest benefit of his charm of manner.

Attitude to the budget of 1909.

XIII

Domestic politics in the last part of his reign brought the king face to face with a constitutional problem for which he had an involuntary distaste. All disturbance of the existing constitution was repugnant to him. In view of the active hostility of the upper chamber to liberal legislation, the liberal government was long committed to a revision of the powers of the House of Lords. The king demurred to any alteration in the status or composition of the upper house, which in his view, as in that of his mother, was a bulwark of the hereditary principle of monarchy. A proposal on the part of conservative peers to meet the outcry against the House of Lords by converting it partly or wholly into an elective body conflicted as directly with the king's predilection as the scheme for restricting its veto. The king deprecated the raising of the question in any form.

Conflict with the House of Lords.

In the autumn of 1909 a very practical turn was given to the controversy by the lords' threats to carry their antagonism to the year's budget to the length of rejecting it. Despite his dislike of the budget, the king believed the lords were herein meditating a tactical error. He resolved for the first time to exert his personal influence to prevent what he judged to be a political disaster. He hoped to exert the reconciling power which his mother employed in 1869 and again in 1884, when the two houses of parliament were in collision: in the first year over the Irish church disestablishment bill, in the second year over the extension of the franchise. The circumstances differed. In neither of the earlier crises was the commons' control of finance in question. Nor was the king's habit of mind as well fitted as his mother's for the persuasive patience essential to success in a difficult arbitration. The conservative peers felt that the king was in no position, whatever happened, to give their house protection from attack, and that he was prone by temperament to unquestioning assent to ministerial advice, which was the path of least resistance. Early in October 1909 he invited to Balmoral Lord Cawdor, one of the most strenuous champions of the uncompromising policy of the peers. The interview produced no result. A like fate attended the king's conversation, on his arrival at Buckingham Palace later in the month (12 Oct.), with the leaders of the conservative opposition in the two houses, Lord Lansdowne and Mr. Balfour. Although these negotiations could only be strictly justified by the emergency, there was no overstepping of the limits of the royal power. Mr. Asquith was willing that the interviews should take place. The conversations were in each case immediately communicated by the king to the prime minister in personal audience.

The king's desire for a peaceful solution.

The king's proved inability to qualify the course of events was a disappointment. The finance bill, which finally passed the House of Commons on 5 November by a majority of 379 to 149, was rejected by the lords on 30 November by 350 to 75. War to the knife was thereupon inevitable between the liberal party and the House of Lords, and the king at once acquiesced in the first steps of his government's plan of campaign. On 15 Dec. by the prime minister's advice he dissolved parliament, for the second time in his reign. The general election gave the government a majority which was quite adequate for their purpose. They lost on the balance seventy-five seats, and their former numerical superiority to any combination of other parties disappeared. But with nationalists and labour members they still were 124 in excess of their unionist oppo-

Passive acquiescence in the government's plans.

nents, and their efficient power to challenge the House of Lords' veto was unmodified. Mr. Asquith continued in office. The king was in no way involved in Mr. Asquith's declaration at the Albert Hall on the eve of the general election (10 Dec. 1909) that he would not again assume or hold office without the safeguards necessary to give legislative effect to the decisions of the majority in the House of Commons. Before the new parliament opened Mr. Asquith saw the king when he was staying privately at Brighton on 13 Feb. 1910. The king offered no impediment to the government's immediate procedure, which was publicly proclaimed eight days later when the king opened parliament and read his ministers' words: 'Proposals will be laid before you, with all convenient speed, to define the relations between the houses of parliament, so as to secure the undivided authority of the House of Commons over finance and its predominance in legislation. These measures, in the opinion of my advisers, should provide that this House [of Lords] should be so constituted and empowered as to exercise impartially, in regard to proposed legislation, the functions of initiation, revision, and, subject to proper safeguards, of delay.'

The king's speech. Feb. 1910.

The presence in the second sentence of the phrase 'in the opinion of my advisers' gave rise to the misconception that the words were the king's interpolation, and were intended to express his personal unwillingness to identify himself with his ministers' policy. As a matter of fact the phrase was, like the rest of the paragraph, from the prime minister's pen, and the king made no comment on it when the draft was submitted to him. A similar formula had appeared previously in the speeches of sovereigns to parliament when they were under the formal obligation of announcing a warmly controverted policy of their ministers' devising. The king's personal misgivings of the constitutional change were well known, and it was courteous to absolve him of any possible implication of a personal responsibility.

In March the cabinet drafted resolutions (with a view to a future bill) which should disable the lords from rejecting or amending a money bill, and which should provide that a bill being passed by the commons in three successive sessions and being thrice rejected by the lords should become law in spite of the lords' dissent. The terms of the resolutions were laid before the king, and he abstained from remonstrance. The resolutions were duly carried on 12 April, and the bill which embodied them was formally introduced into the commons. Meanwhile Lord Rosebery on 14 March moved that the House of Lords resolve itself into committee to consider the best means of reforming its constitution so as to make it strong and efficient, and on 16 March the lords agreed to Lord Rosebery's motion. For such a solution of the difficulty the king had no more zest than for the commons' scheme. On 25 April parliament adjourned for Easter, and next day the text of the commons' veto bill was circulated. The controversy went no further in the king's lifetime.

The commons' resolution on the lords' veto. March 1910.

The ministers were resolved in case of the peers' continued obduracy to advise the king to employ his prerogative so as to give their policy statutory effect. Should the majority of peers decline to pass the bill for the limitation of their veto, the ministers determined on a resort to Lord Grey's proposed plan of 1832, whereby a sufficient number of peers favourable to the government's purpose would be formally created in the king's name to outvote the dissentients. But the time had not arrived when it was necessary directly to invite the king's approval or disapproval of such a course of action. The king for his part did not believe that the matter would be pressed to the last extremity, and was content to watch the passage of events without looking beyond the need of the moment.

The political difficulty caused the king an anxiety and irritation which domestic policy had not previously occasioned him. He found no comfort in the action of any of the parties to the strife. The blank refusal of the conservative leaders to entertain his warnings was unwelcome to his *amour propre*. The prospect of straining his prerogative by creating peers solely for voting purposes could not be other than uncongenial. But while he tacitly recognised his inability to decline the advice of his responsible ministers, he had before him no plan for the creation of peers to call for an expression of opinion. To the last he privately cherished the conviction that peace would be reached by some less violent means. His natural buoyancy of disposition and his numerous social pleasures and interests outside the political sphere effectually counteracted the depressing influence of public affairs. While the last battle of his reign was waging in the houses

The king's personal attitude.

of parliament he was spending his annual spring holiday at Biarritz, where his time was mainly devoted to cheerful recreation. He returned to England on 27 April, just when the Easter vacation called a parliamentary armistice. Within nine days he was dead.

Return from Biarritz, 27 April 1910.

On the political situation the effect of his death was a prolongation of the truce. A conference of representatives of the two parties met in the endeavour to adjust amicably the differences between the two houses. The effort failed (15 Nov. 1910), and after another dissolution of parliament (28 Nov.) the liberal government's plan, in which King Edward had tacitly acquiesced, was carried into law, with the consent of a majority of the upper chamber and without the threatened special creation of peers (10 Aug. 1911).

The lords controversy 1910-11.

XIV

Since his severe illness of 1902 the king's physical condition, though not robust, had borne satisfactorily the strain of a busy life. He benefited greatly by his annual visits to Biarritz and Marienbad and by his yachting cruises, and he usually bore the appearance of good health. A somewhat corpulent habit of body rendered exercise increasingly difficult. He walked little and ate and smoked much. On the shooting expeditions in which he still took part he was invariably mounted, and his movements were slow. There were occasionally disquieting symptoms, and the king was not very ready in obeying medical directions when they interfered with his ordinary habits. But his general health was normal for his age.

The king's health.

For the past few years he was subject to sudden paroxysms of coughing, which indicated bronchial trouble. A seizure of the kind took place at the banquet at the British Embassy in Berlin on 8 Feb. 1909. On the outward journey to Biarritz early in March 1910 he stayed two days in Paris. A cold caught in the Théâtre Porte St. Martin, where he witnessed the performance of M. Rostand's 'Chantecler,' developed rapidly on the way south. A severe attack of bronchitis followed and caused his physician in attendance (Sir James Reid) much anxiety. The news of the illness was not divulged, and at the end of ten days recovery was rapid. A motor tour through the Pyrenees as far as Pau preceded his return home.

Bronchial trouble.

The king arrived in London from the continent on 27 April in good spirits. The same evening he went to the opera at Covent Garden. Queen Alexandra was absent on a Mediterranean cruise, sojourning for the time at Corfu. Next day the king paid his customary visit to the Royal Academy exhibition. On 29 April he entertained at lunch Viscount Gladstone on his departure for south Africa, where he had been appointed governor-general. Sunday, 1 May, was spent at Sandringham, where the king inspected some planting operations. There he contracted a chill. He reached Buckingham Palace next afternoon, and imprudently dined out in private the same evening. On reaching Buckingham Palace late that night his breathing became difficult, and a severe bronchial malady set in. Next morning his physicians regarded his condition as somewhat serious, but no early crisis was anticipated. The king rose as usual and transacted business, making arrangements for his reception the following week of Mr. Theodore Roosevelt, the late president of the United States of America, who had announced a visit to England. He spoke regretfully of the superiority of the climate of Biarritz to that of London. During the two following days the symptoms underwent little change. The king continued to transact business, receiving each morning in formal audience one or more representatives of the colonies. On Thursday, 5 May, he received Sir John Dickson-Poynder, Lord Islington, who had been appointed governor of New Zealand, and he considered details of the welcome to be accorded to a royal visitor from Japan, Prince Fushimi. He sat up and was dressed with his customary spruceness, but he was counselled against conversation. The breathing difficulty fluctuated and did not yield to treatment. Meanwhile Queen Alexandra had been informed of the king's illness and was returning from Corfu. The king was reluctant for any public announcement of his condition to be made. But on the Thursday evening (5 May) he was persuaded to assent to the issue of a bulletin on the ground that his enforced inability to meet the queen, according to custom on her arrival at the railway station, called for explanation. He modified the draft with his own hand. Queen Alexandra reached the palace that night, and next morning (6 May) the news of the king's condition appeared in the press. That day proved his last. He rose as usual, and in

Last illness, 2 May 1910.

the morning saw his friend, Sir Ernest Cassel. As the day advanced, signs of coma developed. In the evening his state was seen to be hopeless. About ten o'clock at night he was put to bed. He died just before midnight.

Death, 6 May 1910.

The shock of grief was great at home and abroad. The public sorrow exceeded that mighty outburst which his mother's death awoke in 1901. Yet the king may fairly be judged to be 'felix opportunitate mortis.' To the last he was able to conduct his life much as he pleased. In the course of the illness he had faced without repining the thought of death. He was spared any long seclusion from society or that enforced inactivity of slowly dwindling strength of which he cherished a dread. His popularity had steadily grown through his reign of nine years and three and a half months. There had been no conflicts with public opinion. Practically all his actions, as far as they were known, had evoked the enthusiasm of the mass of his subjects. There was a bare possibility of his injuring, there was no possibility of his improving, his position, in which he had successfully reconciled pursuit of private pleasure with the due performance of public duty.

The king's reputation.

On 7 May the king's only surviving son met the privy council at St. James's Palace, and was proclaimed as King George V on 9 May. On 11 May the new monarch formally announced his bereavement in messages to both houses of parliament, which had been in recess and were hastily summoned to meet. Addresses of condolence were impressively moved by the leaders of the two great parties in both houses of parliament—in the House of Lords by the earl of Crewe and Lord Lansdowne, and by Mr. Asquith and Mr. Balfour in the House of Commons. Mr. Enoch Edwards, on behalf of the labouring population, also gave voice in the lower house to the general sentiment of admiration and grief.

Fitting funeral ceremonies followed. For two days (14–15 May) the coffin lay in state in the throne room at Buckingham Palace, and there it was visited privately by relatives, friends, and acquaintances. On 16 May the coffin was removed in ceremonial procession to Westminster Hall, and there it lay publicly in state for four days. Some 350,000 persons attended. The interment took place on 20 May. The procession passed from Westminster Hall to Paddington station, and thence by train to Windsor. After the funeral service in St. George's Chapel, the coffin was lowered to the vault below. Besides the members of the king's family the chief mourners included the German emperor (the king's nephew), the king of Norway (his son-in-law), and the kings of Denmark and Greece (his brothers-in-law). Four other kings were present, those of Spain, Bulgaria, Portugal, and Belgium, together with the heirs to the thrones of Austria, Turkey, Roumania, Servia, and Montenegro. There were also kinsmen of other rulers, the prince consort of the Netherlands, Grand Duke Michael of Russia, and the duke of Aosta. The American republic had a special envoy in Mr. Roosevelt, lately president, and the French republic in M. Pichon, minister for foreign affairs. No more representative assembly of the sovereignty of Europe had yet gathered in one place. The exclusively military character of the ceremonial excited some adverse comment, but all classes took part in memorial services and demonstrations of mourning, not only in London and the provinces but throughout the empire and the world. In India, Hindus and Mohammedans formally celebrated funeral rites.

The funeral ceremonies.

The royal mourners.

XV

Edward VII eminently satisfied contemporary conditions of kingship. He inherited the immense popularity which belonged to the crown at the close of his mother's reign, and his personality greatly strengthened the hold of royalty on public affection. The cosmopolitan temperament, the charm of manner, the social tact, fitted him admirably for the representative or symbolic function of his great station. A perfect command of the three languages, English, French, and German, in all of which he could speak in public on the inspiration of the moment with no less grace than facility, gave him the ear of Europe. Probably no king won so effectually the good-will at once of foreign peoples and of his own subjects. He was a citizen of the world, gifted with abounding humanity which evoked a universal sympathy and regard.

His universal popularity.

The outward forms of rule were congenial to him. He deemed public ceremony essential to the royal state, and attached high value to formal dignity. Spacious splendour appealed to him. By all the minutiæ of etiquette he set great store, and he exerted his authority in securing

The king and royal state.

their observance. For any defect in costume or uniform he had an eagle eye and was plainspoken in rebuke.

King Edward cannot be credited with the greatness that comes of statesmanship and makes for the moulding of history. **His relations with politics.** Neither the constitutional checks on his power nor his discursive tastes and training left him much opportunity of influencing effectually political affairs. No originating political faculty can be assigned him. For the most part he stood with constitutional correctness aloof from the political arena at home. On questions involving large principles he held no very definite views. He preferred things to remain as they were. But he regarded all party programmes with a cheerful optimism, sanguinely believing that sweeping proposals for reform would not go very far. From youth he followed with close attention the course of foreign politics, and it was not only during his reign that he sought in tours abroad and in hospitalities at home to keep in personal touch with foreign rulers and statesmen. His main aim as a traveller was pleasurable recreation and the exchange of social courtesies. **His love of peace** But he rarely missed an occasion of attesting his love of peace among the nations. Not that he was averse from strong measures, if he thought them necessary to the due assertion of his country's rights. But in his later years he grew keenly alive to the sinfulness of provoking war lightly, and to the obligation that lay on rulers of only appealing to its arbitrament in the last resort. He was a peacemaker, not through the exercise of any diplomatic initiative or ingenuity, but by force of his faith in the blessing of peace and by virtue of the influence which passively attached to his high station and to his temperament. His frequent absences from his dominions remotely involved his position in a certain element of danger. There was a specious ground for the suggestion that in home affairs he did too little and in foreign affairs too much. The external show of personal control which belongs to the crown at home seemed at times to be obscured by his long sojourns in foreign countries. The impression was at times encouraged, too, that the king was exerting abroad diplomatic powers which under the constitution belonged to his ministers alone. He grew conscious of the exaggerated importance which the foreign public attached to his foreign movements, and he confessed at times to some embarrassment. But he fully realised the futility of encroaching on ministerial responsibilities, and in his intercourse with foreign rulers and diplomatists, so far as politics came within the range of the conversation, he confined himself to general avowals of loyal support of ministerial policy.

His sociability, his love of pleasure, and the breadth of his human interests stood him in good stead in all relations **His social instincts.** of life. He had an unaffected desire for others' happiness, and the sport and amusements in which he openly indulged were such as the mass of his subjects could appreciate and share. The austere looked askance on his recreations or deemed that the attention he paid them was excessive. But his readiness to support actively causes of philanthropy and social beneficence almost silenced articulate criticism. His compassion for suffering was never in question. He valued his people's approbation, and welcomed suggestions for giving every class opportunities of greeting him in person. Many times he cheerfully responded to a schoolmaster's request that in passing a schoolhouse on a private or public journey he should pause and exchange salutations with the schoolchildren. With the promptitude of an expert man of business, he was able to distribute his energies over a very wide field with small detriment to any of the individual calls on his time. He had a passion for punctuality. The clocks at Sandringham were always kept half an hour fast. He gave every encouragement to the progress of mechanical invention for the economising of time which distinguished his reign. He became an ardent devotee of motoring, in which he first experimented in 1899, and which during his last years formed his ordinary mode of locomotion at home and abroad. In the development of wireless telegraphy he also showed much interest, exchanging some of the earliest wireless messages across the Atlantic with Lord Minto, governor-general of Canada (21 Dec. 1902), and with President Roosevelt (19 Jan. 1903).

He had a strong sense of ownership and was proud of his possessions. Though his attitude to art was largely that of a rich owner of a great collection, he had a keen eye for the fit arrangement of his treasures, and knew much of their history. He disliked wasteful expenditure, but personally made careful provision for his own and his friends' comfort. No pride of rank limited his acquaintance, and he always **His hospitality.** practised hospitality on a generous scale. If he had a predilection for men of wealth, his catholic favour embraced every kind of faculty and fortune.

He rejoiced to escape from the constraints of public life into the unconventional ease of privacy. At times he enjoyed practical joking at the expense of close friends. But while encouraging unembarrassed social intercourse, he tacitly made plain the limits of familiarity which might not be overstepped with impunity. He loved the old fashions of domesticity. His own and his relatives' birthdays he kept religiously, and he set high value on birthday congratulations and gifts.

While he derived ample amusement from music and the drama, chiefly from the theatre's more frivolous phases, he showed small capacity for dramatic criticism. A man of the world, he lacked the intellectual equipment of a thinker, and showed on occasion an unwillingness to exert his mental powers. He was no reader of books. He could not concentrate his mind on them. Yet he was always eager for information, and he gathered orally very varied stores of knowledge. A rare aptitude for rapidly assimilating the outlines of a topic enabled him to hold his own in brief talk with experts in every subject. He did not sustain a conversation with much power or brilliance; but his grace and charm of manner atoned for any deficiency of matter. If his interest lay more in persons than in things, he remembered personal details with singular accuracy. He illustrated his curiosity about persons by subjecting all his guests at Sandringham to the test of a weighing machine, and by keeping the record himself. At the same time he deprecated malicious gossip, and his highest praise of anyone was that he spoke no ill-natured word. He was never happy save with a companion who could talk freely and cheerfully. Solitude and silence were abhorrent to him.

His gift of assimilation.

His love of conversation.

A loyal friend, he was never unmindful of a friendly service, and he was always faithful to the associates of his early days. He was fond of offering his friends good advice, and was annoyed by its neglect. He could be at times hasty and irritable; but his anger was short-lived, and he bore no lasting ill-will against those who excited it. His alert memory enabled him from boyhood to death to recognise persons with sureness, and many stories are told how instantaneously he greeted those to whom he had been once casually introduced when meeting them years afterwards in a wholly unexpected environment. His circle of acquaintances at home and abroad was probably wider than that of any man of his time. But he never seems to have forgotten a face.

His loyalty in friendship.

Physical courage was an enduring characteristic. By bodily peril or adverse criticism he was wholly unmoved. If his native shrewdness stimulated an instinct of self-preservation, he never showed any sign of flinching in the face of danger. He admired every manifestation of heroism, and in 1907 he instituted the Edward medal to reward heroic acts performed by miners and quarrymen. Two years later a like recognition was designed for brave service on the part of policemen and firemen. While religion played no dominant part in his life, he was strict in religious observances, and required those in his employment at Sandringham to attend church regularly. He had a perfect tolerance for all creeds, and treated with punctilious courtesy ministers of every religious persuasion. He was greatly attached to dumb animals, and his love for dogs excelled even that for horses. A favoured dog was always his companion at home and abroad. On tombstones in the canine graveyard at Sandringham there are many inscriptions bearing witness to the king's affection for his dog companions. The latest of these favourites, his terrier, 'Caesar,' was led behind his coffin in the funeral procession.

His physical courage.

XVI

As the heir to the crown, the eldest son of Queen Victoria and Prince Albert was the subject of portraiture from his infancy. The earliest portrait apparently is the large chalk drawing by Sir George Hayter in 1842. As a child the Prince of Wales was painted several times by Winterhalter, the court painter, and was also drawn and painted in miniature by Sir William C. Ross. Most of these early portraits, some of which are familiar from engravings or lithographs, remain in the royal collection at Buckingham Palace or Windsor Castle. The prince was painted in groups with his parents and brothers and sisters by Sir Edwin Landseer and Robert Thorburn, as well as by Winterhalter. A portrait by W. Hensel was painted in 1844 for King Frederick William of Prussia, one of the prince's godfathers. Other portraits were also drawn by R. J. Lane and artists who enjoyed the queen's confidence. As the youth of the Prince of Wales happened to synchronise with the invention and great development of portrait

Portraits.

photography, his portraits during boyhood up to the time of his marriage were for the most part based on photography, several excellent engravings being made from them. When about sixteen the prince was drawn and painted by George Richmond, R.A., and in 1862 a portrait in academical robes was painted by command for the University of Oxford by Sir J. Watson Gordon. Portraits of the prince in plain clothes were painted by S. Walton (1863) and Henry Weigall (1865). After the prince entered the army and joined the 10th hussars, he was painted in uniform several times by Winterhalter (1858), by Lowes C. Dickinson (1868), by H. Weigall (1870), and by H. von Angeli (1876). At the time of his marriage to Princess Alexandra of Denmark in 1863 a pair of portraits of the bridal couple were painted by Winterhalter. Among foreign artists who painted the Prince of Wales were Karl Sohn and Theodor Jentzen, but perhaps the most interesting was J. Bastien-Lepage, to whom the prince sat in Paris in 1880. During his later years as Prince of Wales the prince was not very frequently painted, except for official purposes, such as the portraits by Frank Holl, painted in 1884 for the Middle Temple and in 1888 for the Trinity House. A full-length portrait, painted by G. F. Watts, R.A., for Lincoln's Inn, was not considered successful, and was therefore withdrawn by the painter; it is now in the Watts Gallery at Compton in Surrey. The most successful of official pictures was the full-length standing portrait by A. Stuart-Wortley, painted in 1893 for the United Service Club. W. W. Ouless's painting of the prince as commodore of the Royal Yacht Squadron was executed in 1900. After the accession of King Edward VII to the throne in 1901, portraits of his majesty became more in demand. The official state portrait was entrusted to Mr. (afterwards Sir) Luke Fildes, R.A., and was exhibited at the Royal Academy in 1902. The design for the portrait of the king on the coinage, postage-stamps, and certain medals was entrusted to Mr. Emil Fuchs. Subsequent portraits of the king were painted by H. Weigall (for Wellington College), Harold Speed (for Belfast), Colin Forbes (for the Canadian Houses of Parliament at Ottawa), A. S. Cope, A.R.A. (in Garter robes; for Sir Ernest Cassel), P. Tennyson-Cole (for the Liverpool Chamber of Commerce, by whom it was presented to the king; a replica is in the possession of the Grocers' Company), James Mordecai (now in St. James's Palace), and Sir E. J. Poynter P.R.A. (for the Royal Academy). During the reign and after the king's death the number of pictorial presentments of every description increased to an indefinite extent. The king sat to more than one foreign painter. The greater number of the portraits mentioned here were exhibited at the Royal Academy.

Portraits in sculpture of King Edward VII as Prince of Wales or as king are also very numerous, whether busts or statues, from his childhood to his death, while posthumous busts continue in demand. He sat to both English and foreign sculptors, including Canonica, the Italian. A colossal bronze equestrian statue of the Prince of Wales as colonel of the 10th hussars, by Sir J. Edgar Boehm, was presented to the city of Bombay by Sir Albert Sassoon in 1878.

Pictures of public events.

The pictures of public events in which the king played the chief part are very many, including his baptism in 1842, painted by Sir George Hayter, Louis Haghe, George Baxter, and others; his marriage in 1863, painted by W. P. Frith, R.A., and G. H. Thomas; the paintings of the jubilee ceremonies in 1887 and 1897; the marriages of his brothers, sisters, and children; ceremonies at Windsor Castle, such as 'The Visit of Louis Philippe' and 'The Emperor of the French receiving the Order of the Garter'; leading up to the events of his own reign, 'The King opening his First Parliament' by Max Cowper; 'The King receiving the Moorish Embassy in St. James's Palace' by J. Seymour Lucas, R.A.; 'The Coronation of King Edward VII' by E. A. Abbey, R.A., and like events. During the Indian tour of 1875 a number of incidents were recorded in drawings by Sydney P. Hall, W. Simpson, and other artists. Most of these remain in the royal collection. A valuable collection of original drawings for illustrated periodicals, depicting scenes in his majesty's reign, is in possession of Queen Alexandra.

King Edward was a good and willing sitter, but a difficult subject. Hardly any portrait gives a satisfactory idea of a personality in which so much depended upon the vivacity of the likeness. One of the best likenesses is considered to be that in the group of the Prince of Wales and the duke of Connaught at Aldershot, painted by Edouard Détaille, and presented to Queen Victoria by the royal family at the Diamond Jubilee in 1897. Another good portrait is that in the group of Queen Victoria with her son, grandson, and great-grandson, painted by (Sir) W. Q.

Orchardson, R.A., in 1900 for the Royal Agricultural Society.

Memorials of the king were planned after his death in all parts of the world. In England it was decided that there should be independent local memorials rather than a single national memorial. In London it is proposed to erect a statue in the Green Park, and to create a park at Shadwell, a poor and crowded district of east London. In many other cities a statue is to be combined with some benevolent purpose, such as a hospital or a fund for fighting disease. Statues have been designed for Montreal, Calcutta, and Rangoon, and hospitals are also in course of erection at Lahore, Calcutta, Bombay, Madras, Secunderabad, Cashmere, Bornu, Bassein, and Poona. Memorial tablets have been placed in the English churches at Homburg, Marienbad, and Copenhagen. A statue by M. Denys Puech was unveiled at Cannes on 13 April 1912 by M. Poincaré, prime minister of France, amid an imposing naval and military demonstration. A new street and a 'place' in the heart of Paris are to be named after 'Edouard VII.' At Lisbon a public park was named after him in memory of the visit of 1903. At Cambridge University Sir Harold Harmsworth endowed in 1911 'The King Edward VII chair of English literature.'

Memorials.

[No attempt at a full biography has yet been made. The outward facts are summarised somewhat hastily and imperfectly in the obituary notices of the press (7 May 1910), but they are satisfactorily recorded, with increasing detail as the years progressed, in The Times, to which the indexes are a more or less useful guide. The fullest account of the external course of his life from his birth to his accession is given in W. H. Wilkins's Our King and Queen (1903), republished in 1910 with slight additions as Edward the Peacemaker. Various periods and episodes of his career have been treated either independently or in the biographies of persons who were for the time associated with him. A good account of the king's education from private documents at Windsor by Lord Esher appeared anonymously in the Quarterly Review, July 1910. The main facts of his youth are detailed in A. M. Broadley's The Boyhood of a Great King (1906); Queen Victoria's Letters 1837–61 (ed. Esher and Benson, 1907); Sir Theodore Martin's Life of Prince Consort (1874–80). The Greville Memoirs and the memoirs of Baron Stockmar are also useful. For his early manhood and middle age Sidney Whitman's Life of the Emperor Frederick (1901) is of value. For the Canadian and American tour of 1860 see N. A. Woods, The Prince of Wales in Canada and the United States (1861), Bunbury Gooch's The King's visit to Canada, 1860 (1910), and J. B. Atlay's Life of Sir Henry Acland (1903). For the tour in the Holy Land of 1862 see Prothero and Bradley's Life of Dean Stanley (1883), who published Sermons before the Prince during the Tour (1863). For the tour of 1869 see Mrs. William Grey's Journal of a Visit to Egypt, Constantinople, the Crimea, Greece, &c., in the Suite of the Prince and Princess of Wales (1869), and (Sir) W. H. Russell, A Diary in the East during the Tour of the Prince and Princess of Wales (1869). The chief account of the Indian tour is W. H. Russell's Diary (1877). Sir Joseph Fayrer, who privately printed Notes of the Indian Tour, gives very many particulars in Recollections of my Life (1900). The prince's philanthropic work can be followed in Sir H. C. Burdett's An Account of the Social Progress and Development of our own Times, as illustrated by the Public Life and Work of the Prince and Princess of Wales (1889), with The Speeches and Addresses of the Prince of Wales, 1863–1888, ed. by James Macaulay (1889), and The Golden Book of King Edward VII (1910), which collects many of his public utterances. References of varying interest appear in Lady Bloomfield's Reminiscences of Diplomatic Life (1883); Lord Augustus Loftus's Reminiscences (1892–4); Lord Malmesbury's Memoirs (1884); Sir Henry Keppel's A Sailor's Life under Four Sovereigns (1899); Col. R. S. Liddell's Memoirs of the 10th Royal (Prince of Wales's own) Hussars (1891); Arminius Vambéry's Memoirs (1904); Morley's Life of Gladstone; Sir Alfred Lyall's Life of Lord Dufferin (1905); Sir Horace Rumbold's Recollections of a Diplomatist (2 vols. 1902), Further Recollections (1903), and Final Recollections (1909); Edgar Sheppard's George, Duke of Cambridge, a Memoir of his Private Life (chiefly extracts from his diary), 2 vols. 1906; Sir C. Kinloch-Cooke's Mary Adelaide, Duchess of Teck (1900); as well as in Lives of Charles Kingsley, (Sir) Richard Owen, Laurence Oliphant, Sir Richard Burton, Lord Houghton, and Sir Samuel Baker. Some hints on the social side of his career are given in The Private Life of King Edward VII (1903); Society in the New Reign, by a foreign resident (i.e. T. H. S. Escott) (1904); Paoli's My Royal Clients (1911), gossip of a detective courier, and more authentically in Lady Dorothy Nevill's Reminiscences (1906) and Mme. Waddington's Letters of a Diplomat's Wife (1903). His chief residences are described in Mrs. Herbert Jones's Sandringham (1873) and A. H. Beavan's Marlborough House and its Occupants (1896); A full account of The Coronation of King Edward VII, by J. E. C. Bodley, appeared in 1903. Edward VII as a Sportsman (1911), by Alfred E. T. Watson, with introd. by Capt. Sir Seymour Fortescue, and contributions by various friends, gives an adequate account of the king's sporting life. Of foreign estimates of the king, which are for the most part misleading, the most interesting are Louis Blanc's Lettres sur l'Angleterre (1867); J. H. Aubry's Edward VII Intime (Paris, 1902), a favourable but outspoken estimate; Jean Grand-Carteret's L'oncle de l'Europe (1906), a study of the king in French and other caricature; M. Henri Daragon's Voyage à Paris de S.M. Édouard VII (1903), a detailed journal of the visit; Émile Flourens' La France Conquise: Édouard VII et Clemenceau (1906), an indictment of the policy of the 'entente cordiale,' and an allegation that King Edward was personally moved by a Machiavellian design of holding France in subjection to English interests; and Jacques Bardoux, Victoria I; Édouard VII; Georges V (Paris, 2nd ed. 1911, pp. 149 seq.). The German view may be gleaned from Austin Harrison's England and Germany (1909) and Max Harden's Köpfe (part ii., Berlin, 1912). Some hints of the king's relations with the successive rulers of Germany are given in: Memoirs of Prince Chlodwig of Hohenlohe-Schillingsfürst (trans., 2 vols. 1906); Moritz Busch's Bismarck, Some Secret Pages from his History (trans., 3 vols. 1898); Bismarck, His Reflections and Reminiscences (trans., 1898); untranslated Supplement ('Anhang') to latter work, in 2 vols. respectively entitled Kaiser Wilhelm und Bismarck and Aus Bismarcks Briefwechsel, ed. Horst Kohl (Stuttgart, 1901). The account of the portraits has been supplied by Mr. Lionel Cust. In preparing this article the writer has had the benefit of much private information, but he is solely responsible for the use to which the material has been put.] S. L.

EDWARD OF SAXE-WEIMAR, PRINCE (1823–1902), field-marshal, was eldest son of Duke Bernard (1792–1862) of Saxe-Weimar-Eisenach by his wife Princess Ida (1794–1852), daughter of George duke of Saxe-Meiningen. His father was younger son of Charles Augustus, grand duke of Saxe-Weimar, well known as Goethe's patron. His mother was younger sister of Princess (afterwards Queen) Adelaide [q. v.], wife of the duke of Clarence, afterwards King William IV. His parents were frequent visitors at the royal residence in Bushey Park, while the duke and duchess of Clarence were its occupants, and there Prince Edward, whose full names were William Augustus Edward, was born on 11 Oct. 1823. Brought up chiefly in England by his aunt, Queen Adelaide, the young prince was one of Queen Victoria's playfellows and was always on affectionate terms with her and her family. Another of his boyish associates, George, second duke of Cambridge [q. v. Suppl. II], became one of his closest friends. Having been duly naturalised, he passed through Sandhurst and entered the army as an ensign on 1 June 1841. His long career was wholly identified with British military service. Originally attached to the 67th foot, he was shortly afterwards transferred as ensign and lieutenant to the grenadier guards, became a captain on 19 May 1846, and was adjutant from November 1850 to December 1851. Prince Edward accompanied the 3rd battalion of grenadier guards to the Crimea, where he served with distinction as major (brevet major 20 June 1854) at Alma, Balaklava, and the siege of Sevastopol. He was wounded in the leg in the trenches on 19 Oct. and was mentioned in despatches (*Lond. Gaz.* 7 Nov. 1854). At Inkerman Prince Edward, who was on picket duty with his company at Quarter-guard Point, successfully repelled the attack of a Russian column on the flank of the British lines (KINGLAKE'S *Invasion of the Crimea*, vi. 107; *Letters of Queen Victoria*, 1837–1861, iii. 69:—*Prince Edward's Report of his experiences to the Queen*). On 15 June 1855 he was appointed A.D.C. to Lord Raglan, and three days later engaged in the desperate but unsuccessful attack on the Malakoff and the Redan. He was appointed A.D.C. to Queen Victoria on 5 Oct. 1855, and retained the position till 22 Feb. 1869, when he was promoted major-general. For his services he received the C.B., the Crimean medal, Turkish medal, legion of honour, and fourth class of Medjidie. From 1 April 1870 to 31 July 1876 he held command of the home district. On 6 July 1877 he became lieutenant-general, and from 1 Oct. 1878 till 30 April 1881 he commanded the southern district (Portsmouth). In 1878 he was appointed colonel of the Lincoln regiment, and on 14 Nov. 1879 became general. On relinquishing the southern district in 1881, he was unemployed for four years. In October 1885 he was given the command of the forces in Ireland, which he retained till 30 Sept. 1890, when he was succeeded by Viscount Wolseley. The Irish command carried with it the position of privy councillor of Ireland. On 24 May 1881 he was made K.C.B., and on 21 June 1887 G.C.B. In 1888 he held the command of the 1st life guards as colonel-in-chief till his death, and in that capacity filled the office of gold stick-in-waiting to the Queen. He was placed on the retired list on 11 Oct. 1890. In 1891 Dublin University conferred on him the honorary degree of LL.D., and on 22 June

1897 Queen Victoria made him a field-marshal. In addition to these honours he was created a knight of St. Patrick in 1890, and on 8 March 1901 G.C.V.O.

An excellent soldier who was popular with all ranks, he cherished the cultured traditions of his family. He exercised a wide hospitality at his London house, and his guests included representatives of literature, art, and science, as well as soldiers and men in public life. He was always on cordial terms with King Edward VII. He died at 16 Portland Place on 16 Nov. 1902, and was buried in Chichester Cathedral with military honours.

A portrait of Prince Edward by F. Marks is in the possession of the duke of Richmond and Gordon at Goodwood. On 27 Nov. 1851 he married in London Lady Augusta Katherine, second daughter of Charles Gordon-Lennox, fifth duke of Richmond and Gordon. The marriage was morganatic and the princess was given in Germany the title of countess of Dornburg; but she was later on granted the title of princess in Great Britain by royal decree in 1866. She died without issue on 3 April 1904.

[The Times, 17 Nov. 1902; Army and Navy Gazette, 22 Nov. 1902; Army List; Kinglake's Invasion of the Crimea, 6th edit. 1877, vols. iii. iv. and vi.; Edgar Sheppard, Duke of Cambridge, 1906; Willoughby Verner, Military Life of the Duke of Cambridge, 1905; Sir C. Kinloch-Cooke, Life of the Duchess of Teck, 2 vols. 1900.] H. M. V.

EDWARDS, Sir FLEETWOOD ISHAM (1842–1910), lieutenant-colonel, royal engineers, second son of Thomas Edwards of Woodside, Harrow-on-the-Hill, by his wife Hester, daughter of the Rev. William Wilson, of Knowle Hall, Warwickshire, was born at Harrow on 21 April 1842. Educated at Uppingham and at Harrow, he entered the Royal Military Academy in 1861, and on 30 June 1863 received a commission as lieutenant in the royal engineers. After professional instruction at Chatham, where he was captain of the cricket eleven, Edwards was acting adjutant at Dover. From 1867 to 1869 he accompanied General Sir Frederick Chapman [q.v.], governor, to Bermuda as private secretary and aide-de-camp. After serving at Fermoy, Ireland, he was appointed assistant inspector of works at the Royal Arsenal, Woolwich (Nov. 1870), and became aide-de-camp to General Sir John Lintorn Simmons [q. v. Suppl. II], inspector-general of fortifications (1 Aug. 1875). Promoted captain on 5 July 1877, he accompanied, in 1878, his chief to the Berlin Congress, where he came under the notice of Lords Beaconsfield and Salisbury. Appointed assistant privy purse and assistant private secretary to Queen Victoria in Oct. 1878, he became also groom-in-waiting in 1880, an extra equerry in Oct. 1888, and keeper of the privy purse and head of H.M.'s personal household in May 1895 in succession to Sir Henry Ponsonby [q. v.]. Promoted major (30 June 1883), lieutenant-colonel (22 Oct. 1890), he was made C.B. in 1882 and K.C.B. in 1887 and a privy councillor on his retirement from the army on 12 Oct. 1895.

From May 1895 Edwards was one of the most trusted and intimate advisers of the Queen until her death in 1901, and was one of the executors of her will. Retiring in demeanour, he was a man of remarkable charm and of strong moral fibre. Edward VII in 1901 made him a G.C.V.O., serjeant-at-arms of the House of Lords, and an extra equerry to himself, granting him a pension. George V appointed him paymaster to the household and an extra equerry. He died at his residence, the Manor House, Lindfield, Sussex, on 14 Aug. 1910, and was buried in Cuckfield cemetery.

Edwards married (1) on 19 April 1871, Edith (*d.* 1873), daughter of the Rev. Allan Smith-Masters of Camer, Kent; (2) on 20 May 1880, Mary, daughter of Major John Routledge Majendie, 92nd highlanders; she survived him.

[R.E. Records; Memoirs in the Royal Engineer Journal, by General Sir Richard Harrison; Porter, History of the Corps of Royal Engineers, 1889, 2 vols.; The Times, 15 August 1910.] R. H. V.

EDWARDS, HENRY SUTHERLAND (1828–1906), author and journalist, born at Hendon on 5 Sept. 1828, was eldest child in the family of three sons and three daughters of John Edwards, of independent means, by his wife Harriet Exton Teale Morris. After education at the Brompton grammar school and in France, where he acquired a full command of the language, Edwards engaged at a very early age in London journalism. He contributed to 'Pasquin,' a small weekly rival of 'Punch,' which lasted only from August to October 1847. To another short-lived rival of 'Punch,' 'The Puppet Show,' which the firm of Vizetelly [see Vizetelly, Henry] started in March 1848, Edwards also contributed, and on the recommendation of Gilbert à Beckett he, in 1848, joined the staff of 'Punch.' That engagement proved brief, although in 1880 he renewed his association with 'Punch' as an occasional contributor. He early collaborated with

Robert Barnabas Brough [q. v.] in writing for the London stage 'Mephistopheles, or an Ambassador from Below,' an extravaganza, and he also joined in 1851 and at later dates Augustus Septimus Mayhew [q. v.] in light dramatic pieces, including 'The Goose with the Golden Eggs,' a farce (Strand Theatre, February 1859), and 'The Four Cousins,' a comic drama (Globe, May 1871). Edwards meanwhile found active employment in varied branches of serious journalism. He was in Paris during the coup d'état of 1852, and in 1856 he went to Russia as correspondent of the 'Illustrated Times' to describe the coronation of the Tsar Alexander II. He remained at Moscow for some time to study the language, and was soon well versed in Russian politics and literature.

Returning to England he published 'The Russians at Home,' sketches of Russian life (1861). In 1862 and again in 1863 he was correspondent for 'The Times' in Poland and witnessed the insurrection until his friendly relations with the insurgents led to his expulsion. After revisiting Moscow and St. Petersburg he produced 'Polish Captivity, an Account of the Present Position of the Poles in Austria, Prussia and Russia' (2 vols. 1863), and he embodied his experiences in his 'Private History of a Polish Insurrection' (2 vols. 1865). 'The Times' sent him to Luxemburg in 1867, and for the same paper he accompanied the German army during the Franco-German war of 1870–1. His observations were collected as 'The Germans in France, Notes on the Method and Conduct of the Invasion.' A close student of the affairs of the Balkan Peninsula, he republished in 1876 a series of papers contributed to the 'Pall Mall Gazette' under the general title 'The Sclavonian Provinces of Turkey.' In 1885 appeared his 'Russian Projects against India from the Czar Peter the Great to Skobeleff.' Foreign politics was only one of many themes of Edwards's fertile pen. He wrote much on musical history and criticism. A 'History of Opera' (2 vols.) appeared in 1862; 'The Lyrical Drama,' a collection of papers, in 1881; and 'Rossini and his School,' 1881; together with lives of Rossini (1869) and Sims Reeves (1881).

Edwards was the first editor of the 'Graphic' (1869), and in 1877 he undertook an unfortunate venture, the 'Portrait,' photographs and biographical notices of notable persons, which ran to fifteen numbers. Edwards also tried his hand at fiction. His first novel, 'The Three Louisas,' appeared in 1866, and six others followed, the last, 'The Dramatist's Dilemma' (1898), being written in collaboration with Mrs. Church (Florence Marryat [q. v.]). His later years were largely devoted to translations from the French or Russian. A busy compiler to the end, Edwards brought out 'The Romanoffs, Tzars of Moscow and Emperors of Russia' in 1890, 'Personal Recollections' in 1900, and in 1902 a life of Sir William White, English ambassador at Constantinople. He died at his house, 9 Westbourne Terrace Road, London, on 21 Jan. 1906, being buried at St. John's cemetery, Woking.

On 2 Feb. 1857 he married in the English church, Moscow, Margaret, daughter of Thomas Watson, a Scottish engineer settled in Russia. She survived him with one son, Mr. Gilbert Sutherland Edwards.

Besides the works mentioned, Edwards published: 1. 'Famous First Representations,' 1886. 2. 'The Faust Legend,' 1886. 3. 'The Prima Donna,' 2 vols. 1888. 4. 'Idols of the French Stage,' 2 vols. 1889. 5. 'Old and New Paris,' 2 vols. 1892–4.

[Edwards's Personal Recollections, 1900, Lacy's British Theatre, vols. 25, 44, and 92; Brit. Mus. Cat.; private information; H. Vizetelly's Glances Back through Seventy Years, 1893; Spielmann's History of Punch.]

EDWARDS, JOHN PASSMORE (1823–1911), editor and philanthropist, born at Blackwater, near Truro, on 24 March 1823, was second son in a family of four sons of William Edwards by his wife Susan Passmore of Newton Abbot, Devonshire. His father, a carpenter by trade, kept a small public-house, to which was attached a large fruit garden; he was a calvinistic methodist, and his wife an orthodox baptist. John, after a very rudimentary education at the village school, helped his father from the age of twelve in brewing or gardening, continuing his attendance at the school of an evening, and reading, with the help of a dictionary, the 'Penny Magazine' and such cheap books as he was able to purchase. At fifteen he made futile experiments in verse and as a lecturer. Afterwards he helped to found and run a free evening school with good results.

In 1843 Edwards became at a salary of 10*l.* a year clerk to Henry Sewell Stokes [q. v.], a lawyer in Truro, and a poet. He had already interested himself in the Anti-Corn Law League agitation, and had distributed pamphlets for which he had applied to the league's secretary. At the end of eighteen months he left Stokes's employment and some months later became representative in Manchester of the 'Sentinel,' a new London weekly newspaper started in the interest of the Anti-Corn Law League. The paper failed, and Edwards received only 10*l.* for fifteen months' service. He met a debt to his landlord by lecturing for temperance societies at one shilling a lecture. At Manchester he heard Cobden and Bright at public meetings, and became a staunch adherent of the Manchester political school.

In 1845 Edwards went to London, and while maintaining himself by lecturing and journalism developed his interest in political and social reform. He actively promoted the Early Closing Association, and he suggested the invitation which led Emerson in 1848 to lecture on behalf of the association at Exeter Hall on 'Montaigne,' 'Napoleon,' and 'Shakespeare.' He showed sympathy with the Chartist movement but deprecated the use of physical force. The London Peace Society sent him as a delegate to the Peace Conference at Brussels in Sept. 1848, and he was at Paris and Frankfort-on-the-Maine on the like errand in 1849 and 1850.

In 1850 Edwards with savings of some 50*l.* started 'The Public Good,' a weekly newspaper, which he wrote, printed, and published single-handed in a small room where he lived in Paternoster Row. The paper, though widely sold, did not pay, and Edwards started others, the 'Biographical Magazine,' the 'Peace Advocate,' and the 'Poetic Magazine,' in the vain hope that they would advertise and so support each other. After a three years' struggle his health broke down and he became bankrupt, paying five shillings in the pound to his creditors. Engaging strenuously in journalistic work, he so far recovered his position as to be able to purchase at a nominal price in 1862 the 'Building News.' By careful management the paper was brought to a flourishing condition, and in 1866 Edwards paid in full his old debts, from which he was legally absolved. An inscription on a watch and chain presented by his former creditors on 29 Aug. 1866 at a banquet given in his honour at the Albion Tavern, Aldersgate Street, testified to their appreciation of 'his integrity and honour.' In 1869 he also acquired for a small sum the 'Mechanics' Magazine,' which rapidly returned substantial profits.

Edwards's next venture was the purchase in 1876 of the 'Echo,' the first halfpenny newspaper. He bought it from Baron Albert Grant [q. v.], who in 1875 had acquired it from Cassell, Petter & Galpin, its founders in 1868. Edwards became his own editor, and under his control the paper gained greatly in popularity. Its politics were liberal and it advocated the causes of social reform in which Edwards interested himself. After some years he excluded betting news, a step by which the paper gained commercially rather than lost. In 1884 he sold a two-thirds share of the paper to Andrew Carnegie and Samuel Storey for, it is said, 50,000*l.*, but, difficulties of management arising, he rebought it almost immediately at double the price. He retained control of the paper till 1896, when it was sold at a high figure to a syndicate specially formed for its purchase. The 'Echo' collapsed in 1905. Together with the 'Echo' Edwards also ran for many years the 'Weekly Times,' a periodical acquired from Sir John Hutton.

To all progressive movements Edwards accorded active and continuous support. From 1845 onwards he was on the committee of societies for the abolition of capital punishment, of taxes on knowledge and of flogging in the army and navy. He helped to direct the Political and Reform Association, the Ballot Society, and the Society for the Suppression of the Opium Trade. He became president (in 1894) of the London Reform Union, formed to stimulate progressive municipal legislation in London, and of the Anti-gambling League. He pressed his views on the public in pamphlets like 'The Triple Curse' (1858), which dealt with the effects of the opium trade on England, China, and India, and 'Intellectual Tollbars' (1854), a protest against taxes on paper and newspapers. An almost fanatical member of the Peace Society, he protested in 'The War: a Blunder and a Crime' (1855) against the Crimean war, and in later years strongly advocated the Transvaal's claim to independence. He was president of the Transvaal Independence Committee (1881) and of the Transvaal Committee (1901).

At the general election of 1868 Edwards was an unsuccessful candidate in the liberal interest for Truro, but made no further attempt to enter parliament till 1880, when he was returned with William Henry Grenfell (now Lord Desborough) for Salisbury. An unsupported charge of bribery led to a petition against Edwards's election, but it was contemptuously dismissed by the court. Edwards was disappointed at the lack of opportunity for useful work which the House of Commons offered, and he withdrew at the dissolution of 1885.

His later years Edwards mainly devoted to generous yet discriminate philanthropy, his public gifts generally taking the form of free libraries and hospitals. In all some seventy public institutions bear his name as founder. The first institution founded by him was a lecture and reading room at his native village, Blackwater, in 1889, followed in the same year by a school and meeting-room at St. Day, a literary institute at Chacewater, and a mechanics' institute at St. Agnes, all small villages in Cornwall within three miles of his birthplace. Among the hospitals which he afterwards established were those at Falmouth, Liskeard, Willesden, Wood Green, Acton, Tilbury, East Ham, and Sutton in Surrey. He also founded convalescent homes at Limpsfield, Cranbrook, Perranworth, Herne Bay, and Pegwell Bay. At Chalfont St. Peter, Buckinghamshire, he established separate epileptic homes for men, boys, women, and girls; and at Swanley, Bournemouth, and Sydenham 'homes for boys.' He erected free libraries at Whitechapel, Shoreditch, Hoxton, Edmonton, Walworth, Hammersmith, East Dulwich, St. George's in the East, Acton, Poplar, Limehouse, Nunhead, East Ham, Plaistow, North Camberwell, Newton Abbot, Truro, Falmouth, Camborne, Redruth, St. Ives, Bodmin, Liskeard, and Launceston. He also founded an art gallery for the Newlyn colony of artists, near Penzance, and technical schools at Truro, and contributed to the foundation of art galleries at Whitechapel and Camberwell. To him were also due the erection of the West Ham Museum; the Passmore Edwards Settlement, Tavistock Place, with Mrs. Humphry Ward as honorary secretary; University Hall, Clare Market, and the Sailors' Palace, Commercial Road. He erected drinking fountains in various places, presented over 80,000 volumes to libraries and reading-rooms, and placed thirty-two memorial busts of Lamb, Keats, Ruskin, Hogarth, Elizabeth Fry, Emerson, Dickens, and other well-known men in public institutions through the country. At Oxford in 1902, on the suggestion of John Churton Collins [q. v. Suppl. II], he endowed a Passmore Edwards scholarship for the conjoint study of English and classical literature, and he presented a lifeboat to Broughty Ferry, near Dundee, and a public garden to Woolwich.

Edwards declined offers of knighthood from both Queen Victoria and Edward VII. He accepted the honorary freedom of the five boroughs West Ham, Liskeard, Falmouth, Truro, and East Ham.

In 1905 Edwards printed privately 'A Few Footprints,' a rough autobiography (2nd edit. published 1906). He died at his residence, 51 Netherhall Gardens, Hampstead, on 22 April 1911, and was buried at Kensal Green cemetery. His net personalty was sworn at 47,411*l.* He made no public bequests. Edwards married Eleanor, daughter of Henry Vickers Humphreys, artist. One son and one daughter survived him.

A bust by Sir George Frampton was presented to Mrs. Edwards in 1897 and exhibited at the Royal Academy in 1898. Replicas were made and presented to various institutions in Cornwall. A portrait was painted by G. F. Watts for the National Portrait Gallery. A cartoon portrait by 'Ape' appeared in 'Vanity Fair' in 1885.

[Daily Telegraph, and The Times, 24 April 1911; A Few Footprints; J. J. Macdonald, Passmore Edwards Institutions, 1900; E. H. Burrage, J. Passmore Edwards, philanthropist, 1902; J. J. Ogle, The Free Library, 1897; Life and Memoirs of John Churton Collins, 1911.] S. E. F.

ELGAR, FRANCIS (1845–1909), naval architect, born at Portsmouth on 24 April 1845, was eldest son of nine children of Francis Ancell Elgar, who was employed at Portsmouth dockyard, by his wife Susanna Chalkley. At fourteen Elgar was apprenticed as a shipwright in Portsmouth dockyard, where his general education was continued at an excellent school for apprentices maintained by the admiralty. There he won a scholarship entitling him to advanced instruction. In 1864, when the admiralty, with the science and art department, established the Royal School of Naval Architecture and Marine Engineering at South Kensington, Elgar was appointed, after a competitive examination among shipwright apprentices in the dockyards, one of eight students of naval architecture. After the three years' course, he in May 1867 graduated as a first-class fellow, the highest class of diploma. Of much literary ability, he long helped as an old student in the publication of the school's 'Annual.' From 1867 to 1871 Elgar was a junior officer of the shipbuilding department of the royal navy, and was employed at the dockyards and in private establishments.

Leaving the public service in 1871,

Elgar became chief professional assistant to Sir Edward James Reed [q.v. Suppl. II], who was practising in London as a consulting naval architect. At the same time he helped Reed in the production of the quarterly review entitled 'Naval Science.' General manager of Earle's shipbuilding and engineering company at Hull (1874–6), he practised as a naval architect in London (1876–9). From 1879 to 1881 he was in Japan as adviser upon naval construction to the Japanese government, and from 1881 to 1886 resumed private practice in London, advising leading steamship companies on designs of new ships, but specially investigating the causes of loss of, or accident to, important vessels. His reports on the Austral, which foundered in Sydney harbour in 1881, and the Daphne, which capsized when being launched on the Clyde in 1883, made him a leading authority on the stability of merchant ships. Elgar also served in 1883 on a departmental committee of the board of trade whose report formed the basis of subsequent legislation and of the regulations for fixing the maximum load-line for seagoing merchant ships of all classes and of most nationalities.

In 1883 Elgar was appointed to the first professorship of naval architecture to be established in a university; it was founded at Glasgow by the widow of John Elder [q. v.], the marine engineer. Although permitted to continue private practice, Elgar during the next three years mainly devoted himself to the organisation of the new school. His personal reputation secured the sympathy of shipowners and shipbuilders, and attracted many students. In 1886 Elgar on the invitation of the admiralty re-entered the public service as director of dockyards—a newly created office. During his six years' control, work in the dockyards was done more economically and rapidly than before. Resigning this appointment in 1892, he was until 1907 consulting naval architect and director of the Fairfield shipbuilding and engineering company of Glasgow. The company, founded by John Elder and developed by Sir William Pearce, fully maintained its position during Elgar's management. The works were enlarged and improved, and their productive capacity increased. Novel types of vessels were designed and built, including torpedo-boat destroyers and cross-Channel steamers of high speed. Steam turbines and water-tube boilers were employed at an early date, with satisfactory results.

In 1908, after voluntarily retiring from Fairfield with a view to rest, Elgar, at the request of friends interested in the business, undertook as chairman the reorganisation of the firm of Cammell, Laird & Co. of Maryport, Cumberland, whose operations embraced steel and armour manufacture as well as shipbuilding and engineering. Soon after he became in addition chairman of the Fairfield company, which had intimate relations with Cammell, Laird & Co. Elgar's efforts proved successful, but the strain told on his health.

Combining a wide range of scientific knowledge with practical and commercial capacity, Elgar was made hon. LL.D. of Glasgow University in 1885; F.R.S. Edinburgh soon after, and F.R.S. London in 1895. To the Royal Society's 'Proceedings' he contributed important papers on problems of stability and strength of ships. Of the Institution of Naval Architects, of which he was a member from the outset of his career, he served on the council for twenty-six years, was treasurer for seven years, and finally was an honorary vice-president. His chief contributions to technical literature are in the 'Transactions' of the institution, and include valuable papers on 'Losses of Ships at Sea,' 'Fast Ocean Steamships,' 'The Cost and Relative Power of Warships,' and problems of strength and stability of ships. A member of the Institution of Civil Engineers for twenty-five years, Elgar sat on the council for six years, and as 'James Forrest Lecturer' in 1907 delivered an address on 'Unsolved Problems in the Design and Propulsion of Ships.' He also served on the council of the Royal Society of Arts and was a royal commissioner for the international exhibitions at Paris (1889) and Chicago (1894). His interests were wide outside professional matters. Literature always attracted him. He was elected F.S.A. in 1896, and from 1904 he served as a member of the Tariff Commission.

He died suddenly at Monte Carlo on 17 Jan. 1909, and was buried at Highgate cemetery. He married in 1889 Ethel, daughter of John Howard Colls of London, who survived him, but left no issue.

Elgar founded a scholarship for students of naval architecture at the Institution of Naval Architects, and provided for its future maintenance by his will. He also made large bequests to the Institution of Naval Architects and the department of naval architecture in Glasgow University.

He published in 1875 an admirably illustrated book on 'The Ships of the Royal

Navy,' and as president of the London dining club called the 'Sette of Odd Volumes' (1894–5) he privately printed an interesting paper on the earlier history of shipbuilding.

[Proc. Roy. Soc. lxxxiiiA, 1910, and Inst. Civil Engineers Proc. clxxv. (1908–9), memoirs by the present writer; Stewart's University of Glasgow, 1891 (portrait).]

W. H. W.

ELIOT, SIR JOHN (1839–1908), meteorologist, born at Lamesley in Durham on 25 May 1839, was son of Peter Elliott of Lamesley, schoolmaster, by his wife Margaret. He changed the spelling of his surname to Eliot. Matriculating at the rather late age of twenty-six at St. John's College, Cambridge, in 1865, he graduated B.A. in 1869 as second wrangler and first Smith's prizeman.

Soon elected to a fellowship, he accepted, owing to weak health and with a view to avoiding the climate of England, the professorship of mathematics at the Engineering College at Roorkee in the North-West Provinces, under the Indian government. In 1872 he was transferred to the regular Indian Educational Service as professor of mathematics at the Muir Central College, Allahabad. With that office was combined that of superintendent of the Meteorological Observatory. In 1874 he migrated to Calcutta as professor of physical science in the Presidency College and meteorological reporter to the government of Bengal. In 1886 he succeeded Henry Francis Blanford [q. v. Suppl. I] as meteorological reporter to the government of India and was appointed in addition director-general of Indian observatories in 1899. Eliot completed the organisation of meteorological work which Blanford began. 'The number of observatories working under or in connection with the department was increased from 135 to 240 (including two at an elevation of over 11,000 ft.) and the co-operation of the larger native states was secured. Under Sir John Eliot's superintendence the diffusion of weather information was extended by the issue of frequent reports at various centres. Methods of giving warnings of storms at sea were developed and telegraphic intimations of impending floods to engineers on large works under construction or in charge of railway canals and bridges saved the state from heavy losses. Vast improvement was effected in the mode of announcing . . . prospective drought and consequent danger of famine over greater or lesser areas.'

Eliot was elected fellow of the Royal Society in 1895, and was made C.I.E. in 1897. His last official step in India was to secure for his successor the increase of the scientific staff of which he had himself felt the need. He retired from India in 1903 and was created K.C.I.E. On his return to England he actively pursued his meteorological work. He joined the committee of management of the Solar Physics Observatory at South Kensington under the board of education. He was a member of the International Meteorological Committee from 1896 till his death. He was also secretary of the solar commission, suggested by Sir Norman Lockyer to the International Meteorological Committee which met at Southport in 1903. The purpose of the committee was to collect comparable meteorological data from all parts of the world and solar data for comparison with them. At the British Association meeting at Cambridge in 1904 he presided over the subsection for astronomy and cosmical physics, and there advocated the organisation of meteorological work upon an imperial basis and an imperial provision 'for organised observations from areas too wide to be within the control of any single government.' He died suddenly of apoplexy on 18 March 1908 at Bon Porto, the estate which he had acquired on account of his wife's health at Var in the south of France. He was buried within his own estate. An accomplished musician, he played well on both the organ and the piano. He married in 1877 Mary, daughter of William Nevill, F.G.S., of Godalming, who survived him with three sons.

Eliot's contributions to meteorological science are chiefly to be found in the long and important series of Indian meteorological memoirs published by his department. Of special value is a short paper on Indian famines contributed to the Congress of Meteorologists at Chicago in 1893.

Of his separate publications the chief are: 1. 'Report of the Vizingapatam and Backergunge Cyclones of October 1876,' with charts (Calcutta, 1877, fol.), a copy of which was ordered to be laid on the table of the House of Commons. 2. 'Report on the Madras Cyclone of May 1877,' with charts (Calcutta, 1879, fol.). 3. 'Handbook of Cyclonic Storms in the Bay of Bengal' (Calcutta, 1890; 2nd edit. 1900), a work of the highest service to navigation by its warnings and counsel. 4. 'Climatological Atlas of India,' 1906, Indian Meteorological Department, 120 plates (published by authority of the government of India), a wonderful pictorial representation of patient and painstaking work combined with skilful and stringent organisation.

[The Times, 20 March 1908; Nature, lxxvii. 490; Who's Who, 1907; Brit. Mus. Cat.]

W. N. S.

ELLERY, ROBERT LEWIS JOHN (1827–1908), government astronomer of Victoria, Australia, born at Cranleigh, Surrey, on 14 July 1827, was son of John Ellery, surgeon, of that place. After education at the local grammar school he was trained for the medical profession; but attracted by the goldfields of Australia he left England for Melbourne in 1851. He had already interested himself in astronomy and meteorology, and a suggestion made, apparently by Ellery, in the colonial press as to the growing need of an authoritative means of testing ships' chronometers and adjusting nautical instruments for purposes of navigation in Australian waters led the colonial government of Victoria to establish an observatory at Williamstown, four miles from Melbourne, in 1853. Ellery was appointed to organise the observatory and became its superintendent. At the outset the observatory consisted of a time ball on Gellibrand's Point, Williamstown, the ball being dropped at one o'clock local time, which was ascertained by Ellery from sextant observations. A few months later a small transit instrument and an astronomical clock were added, and the arrangement for the time signal made more complete, a night-signal being added by eclipsing the light of the lighthouse at two minutes to eight and suddenly exposing it exactly at eight o'clock; but for some years Ellery's work was confined to the determination of local time, the finding of the longitude and latitude of the place, and the keeping of a 'Journal of Meteorological Observations.' Meanwhile he was placed in charge for a short time of the electric telegraph line between Williamstown and Melbourne, and in 1858, when the Victorian government resolved to undertake a geodetic survey of the colony, Ellery was entrusted with the post of director. He retained the office till 1874.

In January 1860 a board of visitors was appointed to improve the organisation of the observatory, and Ellery induced the board to remove it from the town of Williamstown, whose growth made that place an unsuitable site, to an appropriate building and location to the south of Melbourne. The new observatory, begun in October 1861, was finished early in 1863. Ellery remained director of the new observatory and government astronomer of Victoria until 1895. As director he was responsible for three catalogues of star places, the first a small catalogue of 546 stars made at the original observatory at Williamstown, and the first and second Melbourne general catalogues published respectively in 1874 and 1890. With a view to examining the nebulæ that can only be seen in the southern hemisphere a large telescope was needed, and a new four-foot reflecting telescope ordered in 1865 from the firm of Grubb in Dublin, which took three years to complete, proved on arrival disappointing in its performance.

Ellery thereupon learned the art of figuring and polishing mirrors and put the Melbourne great reflector into order with his own hands. Photographs of the moon were taken with the reflector, and it was used for a systematic revision of all the southern nebulæ and for examination of comets as they arrived. Ellery observed the transits of Venus in 1874 and 1882. Under Ellery's control, the magnetic and meteorological work at the observatory grew heavy, and other work was added. He joined in 1887 in the great co-operative scheme of making a photographic chart of the whole sky, and a photographic catalogue of all the stars down to the eleventh magnitude (see *Report of Melbourne Observatory* for 1891, *Monthly Notices*, lii. 265).

Ellery was one of the founders of the Royal Society of Victoria, was its president from 1856 to 1884, and contributed many papers to its 'Proceedings.' He identified himself fully with public life in Australia, not alone on the scientific side. In 1873 he organised the Victorian torpedo corps which subsequently became the submarine mining engineers, and he was lieutenant-colonel of the corps. He was elected on 8 July 1859 a fellow of the Royal Astronomical Society, to whose 'Monthly Notices' he was a contributor from 1855 to 1884, and he became F.R.S. in 1873. In 1874 he was entrusted with an exploring expedition to northern Australia, but bad weather cut the scheme short. He was absent in England on a year's leave in 1875. He was created C.M.G. in 1889. After his resignation of his office of government astronomer in 1895, he joined the board of visitors, and lived in his house in the observatory domain until his death there on 14 Jan. 1908. Ellery married twice: (1) in 1853 a daughter of Dr. John Shields of Launceston, Tasmania (*d.* 1856); and (2) in 1858 his first wife's sister Margaret, who survived him.

Ellery's work is mainly recorded in the 'Astronomical Results of the Melbourne Observatory,' vols. i. to viii. (1869–88), in the 'First Melbourne General Catalogue' (1874), the 'Second Melbourne General Catalogue' (1890), and in various papers and Reports of the Melbourne Observatory by him in the 'Monthly Notices, R.A.S.' vols. xv. to lv. A 'Third Melbourne General Catalogue' was in preparation at his death.

[Melbourne Observatory Publications, i. p. vi; Proc. Roy. Soc. lxxxii.; Heaton's Austral. Dict. of Dates.] H. P. H.

ELLICOTT, CHARLES JOHN (1819–1905), bishop of Gloucester, was born on 25 April 1819 at Whitwell, near Stamford, where his father, Charles Spencer Ellicott, was rector. His mother was a Welsh lady, Ellen, daughter of John Jones. His grandfather was also a clergyman beneficed in Rutland, and was grandson of John Ellicott [q. v.], clock-maker to King George III and man of science. Ellicott was educated at the grammar schools of Oakham and Stamford, and proceeded in 1837 to St. John's College, Cambridge, where he won in 1838 the Bell University scholarship. At his tripos examinations he only passed as a senior optime and as second in the second class of the classical tripos; but he won the members' prize for a Latin essay in 1842 and the Hulsean prize for an essay on the Sabbath in 1843 (published the following year), and was elected to a Platt fellowship at St. John's College in 1845. He graduated B.A. in 1841 and M.A. in 1844, and was ordained deacon in 1846 and priest in 1847. After taking his degree he engaged in tutorial work. His fellowship lapsed on his marriage in 1848, and he accepted the small living of Pilton, Rutlandshire, where he pursued mathematical studies, publishing in 1851 'A Treatise on Analytical Statics.' He also began a series of commentaries on St. Paul's Epistles, and contributed an essay on the apocryphal gospels to 'Cambridge Essays' (1856). Until Bishop Lightfoot's works began to appear, Ellicott's commentaries on St. Paul's Epistles were recognised as the best in the English language for scholarship and breadth of view. His commentary on Galatians came out in 1854 (5th edit. 1884); that on Ephesians, on the pastoral epistles, on Philippians, Colossians, and Philemon, and on Thessalonians, followed successively in 1855–6–7–8; all reached four editions. The commentary on 1 Corinthians was not published until 1887, and those on Romans and on 2 Corinthians he never completed. In 1851 Ellicott reviewed the first volume of Henry Alford's New Testament in the 'Christian Remembrancer,' complaining of his reliance upon German commentators. Alford issued a pamphlet in reply, but his cordial appreciation of Ellicott's 'Galatians' in 1854 led to a close friendship. Alford helped to broaden Ellicott's intellectual and religious views. In 1858 Ellicott left Pilton to succeed Trench as professor of New Testament exegesis at King's College, London. In 1859 he was Hulsean lecturer at Cambridge, and delivered the 'Historical Lectures on the Life of our Lord Jesus Christ' (1860; 6th edit. 1876), which proved one of his most popular books. Next year he became Hulsean professor, holding the post for some time with his King's College professorship and residing in Cambridge. On 19 Feb. 1860 he was seriously injured in a railway accident at Tottenham, while travelling from Cambridge to London; his gallantry in ministering spiritually to his fellow sufferers attracted public admiration. Despite a permanent limp (he could never wear episcopal gaiters), he continued to skate and enjoyed mountaineering. He joined the Alpine Club in 1871 and remained a member till 1904.

In 1861 Ellicott was made dean of Exeter, and also undertook the task of organising a diocesan training college. In the same year he contributed to 'Aids to Faith,' a volume designed as a counterblast to 'Essays and Reviews'; his essay dealt with Jowett's article on the 'Interpretation of Scripture.' In 1863 he was called to the united sees of Gloucester and Bristol, and was consecrated in Canterbury Cathedral on 25 March 1863.

Ellicott's episcopate lasted for forty-two years. He threw himself vigorously into diocesan work, improving the efficiency of his clergy, showing himself sympathetic to all schools of thought, helping the establishment of the Gloucester Theological College, and raising in Bristol 85,000*l.* for the restoration of the 'truncated and naveless' cathedral. He promoted the work of church extension, forming in Bristol in 1867 the Church Aid Society, and encouraging the Bristol Church Extension Fund. Outside his own diocese his activity and influence were so conspicuous that in 1868, on Archbishop Longley's death, he was recommended by Disraeli for the vacant see of Canterbury; but Queen Victoria chose Archibald Campbell Tait [q. v.]. Ellicott was secretary of the first Lambeth conference in 1867, and of its successors in 1878 and 1888; at the conference of 1898 he was made registrar, and was the only English prelate who attended the four conferences. In 1867 he was a member of the royal commission on ritual and the rubrics (1867–70). Samuel Wilberforce (*Life*, iii. 216) described Ellicott as 'hot and intemperate in trying to force on condemnation of chasuble.' As a result of the fourth report of the commission, Ellicott formed one of a committee of bishops to consider the question of retranslation of the Athanasian creed, and in February 1872 read a proposed revision in Convocation, delivering one of the 'four great speeches' (*Life of Tait*, ii. 140) on the subject. In 1873 a committee of the upper house of Convocation drew up a report on confession. Magee, Ellicott's friend and ally, tells us that 'it was mine and Gloucester and Bristol's' (*Life of Magee*, 296). This declaration was in the main adopted by the Lambeth conference of 1878.

Among all Ellicott's activities he was proudest of his share in the revision of the Bible. As early as 1856, in the preface to his edition of 'St. Paul's Pastoral Epistles,' he had advocated revision, as against a new translation; and he was one of the 'five clergymen' who in 1857 published a revision of the Gospel of St. John (3rd edit., with notes, 1862), which was followed by revisions of Romans and Corinthians in 1858 and other epistles in 1861. In 1870 he brought the whole subject before the public in a volume of 'Considerations.' He was the chairman of the company which revised the New Testament, missing only two out of the 407 sittings, and in 1881 he presented the completed work to Convocation. He then attached himself to the company revising the Apocrypha, and presented the result of their labours to Convocation in 1896. Finally, in 1899, he presented the marginal references. A sharp controversy arose on the publication of the revised New Testament with regard to Ellicott's conduct as chairman. He was accused of allowing more changes in the text than his instructions permitted, but he defended himself with learning and good temper, and his 'Addresses on the Revised Version' of Holy Scripture (1901) remains the best popular account of the undertaking. His most important literary labour in the later part of his life was 'The Old and New Testaments for English Readers,' which he began to edit in 1878. He collected a strong band of collaborators, including Plumptre and Dr. Sanday. In scholarship and breadth of view the work was much in advance of any previous commentary for general use. 'A New Testament Commentary for English Readers' appeared in 3 vols. 1878–9; 3rd edit. 2 vols. 1892–6. 'An Old Testament Commentary' in 5 vols. 1882–4; reissued 1884–92. An abridgement of the 'New Testament Commentary,' 'for the use of schools,' followed in 14 vols. (1878–83), and was succeeded by 'The Complete Bible Commentary for English Readers,' 7 vols. 1897 (new edit. 1905, with 48 plates).

In 1891 the publication of 'Lux Mundi' stirred Ellicott to challenge the soundness of 'the analytical view' of the Old Testament. In his 'Christus Comprobator' (1891) he insisted that fresh views of doctrine as well as of history were involved in the new views. Although in his most popular volumes he might seem to stem the tide of modern thought, Ellicott's influence was not reactionary. His courage and honesty forced him continually to the task of correlating old and new views, and his conspicuous candour and courtesy always raised the tone of controversy. His last charge (1903) was a final proof that his mind to the end was open to new truth.

In 1897, with Ellicott's concurrence, the united sees of Gloucester and Bristol were divided. He remained bishop of Gloucester, surrendering 900*l*. of his income. As a memorial of his thirty-four years' connection with Bristol, a reredos from the designs of J. L. Pearson was dedicated in the cathedral on 19 Oct. 1899. In 1903 the fortieth anniversary of his consecration was celebrated in the chapter house of Gloucester Cathedral. He resigned on Lady day 1905, and died on 15 Oct. 1905 at Birchington-on-Sea, where he was buried. A recumbent effigy was erected to his memory in Gloucester Cathedral. A portrait in oils by Holl, which was presented to the see, is in the Palace, Gloucester. A replica belongs to the widow. A cartoon portrait by 'Spy' appeared in 'Vanity Fair' in 1885.

On 13 Aug. 1848 he married Constantia Annie, daughter of Admiral Alexander Becher, and had by her a son and two daughters. In addition to the works mentioned above, he published numerous annual reviews of 'diocesan progress,' charges, collections of addresses, and sermons and prefaces to books.

[Eagle, xxvii. No. 138, 84–106, and No. 139, 253–6; The Times, 16 Oct. 1905; Alpine Journal, xxiii. 171.] R. B.

ELLIOT, Sir GEORGE AUGUSTUS (1813–1901), admiral, born at Calcutta on 25 Sept. 1813, was the eldest son of Admiral Sir George Elliot [q. v.] by his wife

Eliza Cecilia, daughter of James Ness of Osgodby, Yorkshire. Entering the navy in November 1827, he was made lieutenant on 12 Nov. 1834. For the next three years he was in the Astræa with Lord Edward Russell [q. v.] on the South American station, and on 15 Jan. 1838 was promoted to the command of the Columbine brig, in which he served on the Cape and West Coast station, under the orders of his father, for two years, with remarkable success, capturing six slavers, two of them sixty miles up the Congo. In February 1840 he went on to China in company with his father, and on 3 June was promoted, on a death vacancy, to be captain of the Volage, in which in the following year he returned to England, his father, who was invalided, going with him as a passenger. From 1843 to 1846 he commanded the Eurydice frigate on the North American station, and after a prolonged spell of half-pay was appointed in December 1849 to the Phaeton frigate, which under his command attained a reputation as one of the smartest frigates in the service, and is even now remembered by the prints of the Channel fleet with the commodore in command making the signal 'Well done, Phaeton!' in commendation of a particularly smart piece of work in picking up a man who had fallen overboard (11 Aug. 1850). Early in 1853 the Phaeton was paid off, and in January 1854 Elliot commissioned the James Watt, one of the first of the screw line-of-battle ships, which he commanded in the Baltic during the campaigns of 1854 and 1855. On 24 Feb. 1858 he became rear-admiral, and was then captain of the fleet to Sir Charles Fremantle, commanding the Channel squadron. In 1861 he was a member of a royal commission on national defences, and from 1863 to 1865 was superintendent of Portsmouth dockyard. On 12 Sept. he became vice-admiral, and in the following year was repeatedly on royal commissions on naval questions, gunnery, tactics, boilers, ship-design, &c. In 1870 he reached the rank of admiral; and in 1874 was elected conservative M.P. for Chatham; but he resigned his seat in the following year on being appointed commander-in-chief at Portsmouth. On 2 June 1877 he was nominated a K.C.B., and the following year, 26 Sept., he was placed on the retired list. Continuing to occupy himself with the study of naval questions, he published in 1885 'A Treatise on Future Naval Battles and how to fight them.' He died in London on 13 December 1901. He married in 1842 Hersey, only daughter of Colonel Wauchope of Niddrie, Midlothian, and left issue.

[Royal Navy Lists; O'Byrne's Naval Biographical Dictionary; Who's Who; The Times, 14 Dec. 1901; information from the family.] J. K. L.

ELLIOT, Sir HENRY GEORGE (1817–1907), diplomatist, born at Geneva on 30 June 1817, was second son of Gilbert Elliot, second earl of Minto [q. v.], by his wife Mary, eldest daughter of Patrick Brydone of Coldstream, Berwickshire. His eldest sister, Lady Mary, married on 18 September 1838 Sir Ralph Abercromby, who was British minister at Turin and the Hague. Another sister, Lady Frances, on 20 July 1841 became the second wife of Lord John Russell [q. v.]. Educated at Eton and Trinity College, Cambridge, where he took no degree, Elliot served as aide-de-camp and private secretary to Sir John Franklin [q. v.] in Tasmania from 1836 to 1839, and as précis writer to Lord Palmerston at the foreign office in 1840. Entering the diplomatic service in 1841 as attaché at St. Petersburg, he was promoted to be secretary of legation at the Hague 1848, was transferred to Vienna in 1853, and in 1858 was appointed British envoy at Copenhagen. On the accession of Francis II to the throne of the Two Sicilies on 22 May 1859, the British government decided on resuming diplomatic relations with the court of Naples. These had been broken off by Lord Palmerston's government in 1856, in consequence of the arbitrary and oppressive character of the administration and the refusal of the government of King Ferdinand II to pay any attention to the joint representations of England and France. Elliot was in England on a short leave of absence early in 1859, and Lord Malmesbury, then foreign secretary, despatched him on a special mission to congratulate King Francis II on his accession, with instructions to hold out the expectation of the re-establishment of a permanent legation, if a more liberal and humane policy were pursued in the new reign, and also to dissuade the king from allying himself with Victor Emanuel in the war which had broken out between Piedmont and France on one side and Austria on the other. Elliot's brother-in-law, Lord John Russell [q.v.], who succeeded Lord Malmesbury at the foreign office in June, instructed Elliot to remain on at Naples, and eventually on 9 July appointed him permanent minister. In regard to neutrality, he was instructed not to press that course, if the public opinion of Naples so strongly favoured alliance with Piedmont as to render neutrality dangerous to the dynasty. Elliot's efforts to obtain constitutional reform and abandonment of the arbitrary methods of the previous reign were approved and supported, but had no substantial result. Francis II after some faint signs of a disposition to improve the methods of rule returned to the old methods. Elliot's representations seem on one occasion to have been instrumental in obtaining the release of a certain number of prisoners, who were being detained indefinitely without trial, but generally speaking the advice and the warnings given by him partly on his own initiative and partly under instructions from his government were neglected. The result was not slow in coming. Early in 1860 Garibaldi, with a force of 1000 volunteers, seized Sicily in the name of King Victor Emanuel. In August he advanced on Naples, and handed over the fleet, which surrendered to him, to the Piedmontese admiral. The British government decided on maintaining an attitude of non-intervention, despite the appeals of France to oppose Garibaldi. The favourable disposition which the British government manifested towards the progress of Italian unity was largely attributable to the reports of Sir James Hudson [q. v.], the envoy at Turin, and of Elliot regarding the condition of public feeling in Italy. On 10 Sept. Elliot, in pursuance of instructions from Lord John Russell, had an interview with Garibaldi in the cabin of Admiral Munday on board H.M.S. Hannibal, which was then stationed in the Bay of Naples. Elliot stated that he was instructed to remain at Naples for the present, and endeavoured to dissuade Garibaldi from any ulterior intention of attacking Venice (cf. WALPOLE's *Life of Lord John Russell*, ii. 322 seq.). Garibaldi was not much impressed by the arguments of the British minister. But the resistance offered by Francis II's forces at Capua hampered Garibaldi's plans. In October a portion of the Piedmontese army under King Victor Emanuel joined the Garibaldian forces, and finally drove King Francis and his troops into Gaeta, which surrendered after a three months' siege. On 21 October a plébiscite in Sicily and Naples gave an enormous majority of votes for Italian unity under King Victor Emanuel. The formal ceremony of annexation took place at Naples on 8 Nov. Thenceforward the British legation had no *raison d'être*, and Elliot left for England a few days later. For some time he was without active employment.

On the death of Sir Thomas Wyse [q. v.], British minister at Athens, in April 1862, he was sent on a special mission to Greece, where discontent against the rule of King Otho was assuming dangerous proportions, and had manifested itself in a mutiny of the garrison of Nauplia. Here again his instructions were to urge the necessity of a more liberal system of administration and of the observance of the rules of constitutional government. He was also to make it clear that the British government would not countenance aggressive designs against Turkey. He returned in July, Peter Campbell Scarlett [q. v.] having received the appointment of minister. During his short residence at Athens he had been greatly impressed with the unpopularity of the king, and his forebodings were soon justified. In October a provisional government deposed the king. The British government declined the offer of the crown to Prince Alfred, but promised, if a suitable candidate were chosen, and if the constitutional form of government were preserved and all attempt at aggression against Turkey were abandoned, to cede the Ionian Islands. Elliot was sent back to Athens on special mission to arrange matters with the provisional government on this basis. Prince William, second son of King Christian of Denmark, was on 30 March 1863 unanimously elected as King George I. Elliot returned to England in the following month. In September of the same year he succeeded Sir James Hudson as British envoy to the king of Italy, taking up his residence at Turin. The foreign secretary, Lord John Russell, was freely charged, both in private correspondence and in the press, with unjustly superseding Hudson to make a place for Elliot, his own brother-in-law. 'The Times' had already suggested (13 March 1860) such an intention on Lord John's part, and a warm political controversy, which Hudson did much to fan, followed the announcement in 1863 of Elliot's appointment. But the imputation of jobbery has no justification. Hudson's retirement was quite voluntary, and he in the first instance warmly approved the choice of his successor (WALPOLE's *Lord John Russell*, ii. 423 seq.; G. ELLIOT's *Sir James Hudson and Lord Russell*, 1886). In May 1865 Elliot moved from Turin to Florence, which had been made the capital of the kingdom, and there his sister and

Lord John Russell visited him in November 1866. In July 1867 he was appointed ambassador at Constantinople and sworn a privy councillor. At his new post he was almost at once engaged in the discussion over the troubles in Crete in 1868–9, and the consequent rupture of diplomatic relations between Turkey and Greece. In the winter of 1869 he was British representative at the opening of the Suez Canal, and was made G.C.B.

On 6 June 1870 a great fire broke out in Pera, in which the British embassy house was almost completely destroyed. Lady Elliot and her children narrowly escaped with their lives, and all the ambassador's private property was destroyed. though he and the staff succeeded in saving the government archives and much of the furniture of the state rooms. With the Russian ambassador at Constantinople, General Ignatieff, Elliot was often in conflict, and was held by the aggressive party in England to be no match for Russian ambition, but in the view of Lord Granville, the foreign secretary, Elliot by his 'quiet firmness' well held his own against all Russian intrigue in the sultan's court (Fitzmaurice, *Lord Granville*, ii. 412–3).

In 1875 an insurrection in Herzegovina which rapidly spread to Bosnia commenced the series of events issuing successively in the outbreak of war between Russia and Turkey in April 1877, the treaty of San Stefano, and the congress of Berlin in 1878. In 1876 Servia and Montenegro declared war against Turkey, and an insurrectionary movement commenced in Bulgaria. The Turkish authorities, being insufficiently provided with regular troops, proceeded to enrol irregulars and 'Bashi-Bazuks,' who resorted at once to savage massacres, which became notorious under the term of 'the Bulgarian atrocities.' The British embassy at Constantinople and the consular officers in the vicinity were at the time much criticised for their delay in reporting these events, which first became known through the public press. There was, in fact, no British consular officer very close to the spot, but it was not till January 1876 that the fact became known that a despatch from the British consul at Adrianople to the consul-general at Constantinople, which mentioned the receipt of reports of appalling massacres, had not been communicated to either the ambassador or the foreign office by the consul-general, who was at the time suffering from a mortal illness. As soon as it appeared that there was solid foundation for the rumours, both the consul at Adrianople and a secretary of the British embassy were sent to investigate the facts, and on receipt of their reports the ambassador was instructed to protest in the strongest manner against the barbarities perpetrated, and to demand the arrest and punishment of those responsible. In reply to attacks which were made on him, as not having been sufficiently alive to the danger of such occurrences, Elliot was able to show that he had constantly and urgently warned both the Porte and his own government of the consequences which were certain to attend the employment of irregular forces. Negotiations for the conclusion of peace between Turkey, Servia, and Montenegro were carried on by the ambassador under instructions from the British government in September 1876, and as these proved unsuccessful, he was instructed on 5 Oct. as a last resource to demand the conclusion of an armistice for at least a month, at the end of which a conference was to be called at Constantinople to consider the whole question. Failing compliance with this request, he was instructed to withdraw from Constantinople. The reply of the Porte was as usual unsatisfactory, but a Russian ultimatum delivered in October procured an armistice of two months, and on the proposal of Great Britain a conference met at Constantinople in December, to which the marquis of Salisbury, then secretary of state for India, was sent as first British plenipotentiary, Elliot being associated with him. In the meanwhile the supreme authority in the Turkish empire had twice changed hands. On 29 May 1876 the Sultan Abdul Aziz was deposed in pursuance of a fetvah obtained from the Sheikh-ul-Islam, and shortly afterwards he committed suicide or was assassinated. He was succeeded by his nephew Murad, who was in his turn removed as incompetent on 31 Aug., and replaced by his brother Abd-ul-Hamid II. The deliberations of the conference resulted in the presentation to the Turkish government in January 1877 of proposals for the pacification of the disturbed provinces, including supervision of these measures by an international commission supported by a force of 6000 Belgian and Swiss gendarmes. After ten years' experience of Turkish ways Elliot entertained little hope that the scheme would be accepted by the Porte, or that if accepted it would be found practicable in execution. He had moreover considerable faith in the sincerity and capacity of the new grand vizier, Midhat

Pasha, and in his power to carry through the measures of reform which he was introducing. But the suggestion, which was made in some organs of the press, that he failed to give Lord Salisbury, the senior British plenipotentiary, full and loyal support, or that he encouraged the Turkish government to resist the demands of the powers, was warmly repudiated by him, and must be dismissed at once by all who had any knowledge of his character. The proposals of the conference were refused by the Turkish government, who simultaneously with the opening of the conference had proclaimed the grant of a constitution to the empire, with representative institutions. The conference consequently separated without result. A further conference held in London in March 1877 presented demands which were again refused, and war was declared by Russia on 24 April. Elliot, whose health had suffered much during the continued strain, was granted leave of absence at the end of February, being replaced by the appointment of Sir A. H. Layard [q. v. Suppl. I] as special ambassador *ad interim*. At the close of the year Elliot was appointed ambassador at Vienna, where he took part in the critical negotiations which ensued between the conclusion of the treaty of San Stefano and the meeting of the congress at Berlin. In March 1880 he reported to his government the resentment caused in Vienna by Gladstone's attack, during his Midlothian campaign, on the Austrian government, and their desire for some disavowal, which Gladstone subsequently made (FITZMAURICE, *Life of Lord Granville*, ii. 200–3). Elliot remained at Vienna till his retirement on pension in January 1884. The rest of his life was passed mainly in England. In February 1888 he caused general surprise by publishing in the 'Nineteenth Century' his recollections of the events connected with the deposition and death of Sultan Abdul Aziz, and the efforts made for constitutional reform by Midhat Pasha. The article gave great umbrage to the reigning Sultan, whose subsequent policy he severely criticised. He died at Ardington House, Wantage, on 30 March 1907. His portrait by von Angeli is at Minto House, Hawick. A good photogravure is in 'The British Museum of Portraits'; a set is in the art library of the Victoria and Albert Museum. A cartoon portrait by 'Spy' appeared in 'Vanity Fair' in 1877.

He married on 9 Dec. 1847 Anne (*d.* 1899), second daughter of Sir Edmund Antrobus. By her he had one son, Sir Francis Edmund Hugh Elliot, G.C.V.O., K.C.M.G., British minister at Athens, and one daughter.

[The Times, 1 April 1907, which contains some inaccuracies; Foreign Office List, 1908, p. 397; Cambridge Modern History, xi. 390, 611, xvi. 381; papers laid before Parliament; Nineteenth Century, February 1888. Elliot printed for private circulation a volume of Diplomatic Recollections, which is cited in Mr. G. M. Trevelyan's Garibaldi and the Thousand, and his Garibaldi and the Making of Italy, together with letters from Elliot to Lord John Russell.] S.

ELLIOTT, SIR CHARLES ALFRED (1835–1911), lieutenant-governor of Bengal, born on 8 Dec. 1835 at Brighton, was son of Henry Venn Elliott [q. v.], vicar of St. Mary's, Brighton, by his wife Julia, daughter of John Marshall of Hallsteads, Ulleswater, who was elected M.P. for Leeds with Thomas Babington Macaulay in 1832. After some education at Brighton College, Charles was sent to Harrow, and in 1854 won a scholarship at Trinity College, Cambridge. In 1856 the civil service of India was thrown open to public competition. Elliott, abandoning his Cambridge career, was appointed by the directors, under the provisions of the Act 16 & 17 Vict. c. 97, one of fifteen members of the civil service of the East India Company (*Despatch*, 1 Oct. 1856). He was learning his work unattached to any district, when the mutiny broke out at Meerut, and he was then posted on 12 June 1857 as assistant magistrate to Mirzapur in the Benares division of the N.W. Provinces. That large district of 5238 sq. miles was the scene of fierce conflicts with the rebels. Elliott led several small expeditions from headquarters to quell disturbances, was favourably mentioned in despatches, and received the mutiny medal.

In the following year he became an assistant-commissioner in Oudh, where he served in Unao, Cawnpore, and other districts until 1863. In Unao he gave early proof of his industry by collecting information about its history, its folklore, and its families. He published in 1862 at Allahabad for private circulation 'Chronicles of Oonao,' believing 'that a knowledge of the popular traditions and ballads gives to its possessor both influence over the people and the key to their hearts.' When this treatise was printed he was serving in the N.W. Provinces, and in the following year (Sir) Richard Temple [q. v. Suppl. II], wishing to strengthen the administrative staff of the Central Provinces, then under his control, secured Elliott's transfer, entrusting to him the settlement of the Hoshangabad district. This task, which greatly raised his reputation, was completed in 1865, being regarded as a most successful operation, which has stood the test of time. Taking furlough, Elliott returned to duty in the N.W. Provinces, and was entrusted with the settlement of the Farukhabad district. He had assessed the whole district except the Tahwatahsil, when in 1870 he was chosen by Sir William Muir [q. v. Suppl. II] to be secretary to government. The final report, drawn up by H. F. Evans, 22 July 1875, included the rent rate reports written by Elliott 'in that elaborate and careful manner which,' according to Sir Charles Crosthwaite, 'has become the model for similar reports.' The cost of the settlement exceeded five lakhs, and although the rates charged were moderate, government received additional revenue of 22 per cent. on the expenditure, while the records were a permanent gain to the people. Settlement work, to which Elliott had thus devoted his best years, was in those days the most important and most coveted employment in the civil service, and it gave Elliott a thorough acquaintance with the needs of the people and the administrative machinery.

From 1870 to 1877 he held the post of secretary to the government of the N.W. Provinces, being concerned chiefly with settlement and revenue questions, with measures for suppressing infanticide in certain Rajput communities, and municipal administrations. Knowing every detail, he was inclined to interfere too much with subordinate authorities. After Sir John Strachey [q. v. Suppl. II] had succeeded to the government of Sir William Muir, he went to Meerut as commissioner. Thence he was summoned by Lord Lytton to visit Madras, and subsequently to apply to Mysore the famine policy of the paramount power. As Lord Lytton wrote in Nov. 1878, when reviewing his famine report on Mysore, 'he organised and directed relief operations with a patience and good sense which overcame all difficulties, and with the fullest tenderness to the people in dire calamity.' Elliott did not minimise the human suffering and the administrative shortcomings which he witnessed, and his experience and report indicated him as the best secretary possible to the royal commission on Indian famines (16 May 1878). Other commissions in 1898 and 1901 have built on the foundation laid by the famous report of 7 July 1878, but it will always remain a landmark in Indian history; for from that date the British government determined to fight with all its resources recurring and inevitable droughts, which had previously entailed heavy loss of life. For the planning of the requisite organisation no knowledge of detail was superfluous, and no better secretary could have been found for guiding and assisting the commissioners.

This work completed, Elliott became for a few months census commissioner for the first decennial census for 1881 which followed the imperfect enumeration of 1872. In March 1881 he became chief commissioner of Assam, and in Feb. 1886 was entrusted with the unpopular task of presiding over a committee appointed to inquire into public expenditure throughout India, and report on economies. A falling exchange and a heavy bill for war operations compelled Lord Dufferin to apply the shears to provincial expenditure, and while the committee inevitably withdrew funds needed by the local governments, it was generally recognised that immense pains were taken by Elliott and his colleagues. Elliott, who had been made C.S.I. in 1878, was promoted K.C.S.I. in 1887, and from 6 Jan. 1888 to 17 Dec. 1890 he was a member successively of Lord Dufferin's and then of Lord Lansdowne's executive councils. On the retirement of Sir Steuart Bayley, Elliott, although he had never served in Bengal, became lieutenant-governor of that province, holding the post, save for a short leave in 1893, until 18 Dec. 1895. The greatest service which Elliott rendered to Bengal was the prosecution of the survey and the compilation of the record of rights in Bihar, carried out in spite of much opposition from the zemindars, opposition that received some support from Lord Randolph Churchill. Sir Antony MacDonnell's views as to the maintenance of the record were not in harmony with those of Elliott, but Lord Lansdowne intervened to reduce the controversy to its proper dimensions. Public opinion has finally endorsed the opinion expressed by Mr. C. E. Buckland in 'Bengal under the Lieutenant-Governors' (1901), that 'there was not another man in India who could have done the settlement work he did in Bihar and Bengal, so much of it and so well.' In his zeal for the public service Elliott courageously faced unpopularity. Economy as well as efficiency were his principles of government. Towards the native press he took a firm attitude, prosecuting the editor and manager of the 'Bangobasi' for sedition in the teeth of hostile criticism. He was inclined to establish a press bureau, but Lord Lansdowne's government did not sanction his proposals. With the distressed Eurasian community he showed generous sympathy, and, always on the watch for the well-being of the masses he pushed on sanitary and medical measures, being largely instrumental in the widespread distribution of quinine as a remedy against fever. In foreign affairs he was impatient of Chinese delays in the delimitation of the frontiers of Tibet and Sikkim, and urged Lord Elgin to occupy the Chambi valley (19 Nov. 1895), and even to annex it.

After a strenuous service of forty years he retired in December 1895, and was soon afterwards co-opted a member of the London school board as a member of the moderate party, being elected for the Tower Hamlets division in 1897 and 1900. In 1904 he was co-opted a member of the education committee of the London county council, serving till 1906. From 1897 to 1904 he was chairman of the finance committee of the school board, and his annual estimates were remarkable for their exceptional agreement with the actual expenditure. A strong churchman, he took active part in the work of missionary and charitable societies; he was a member of the House of Laymen as well as of the Representative Church Council. He was also chairman of Toynbee Hall. He died at Wimbledon on 28 May 1911. He married twice: (1) on 20 June 1866 Louisa Jane (*d.* 1877), daughter of G. W. Dumbell of Belmont, Isle of Man, by whom he had three sons and one daughter; and (2) on 22 Sept. 1887 Alice Louisa, daughter of Thomas Gaussen of Hauteville, Guernsey, and widow of T. J. Murray of the I.C.S., by whom he had one son, Claude, now fellow of Jesus College, Cambridge. His eldest son by his first marriage, Henry Venn Elliott, is vicar of St. Mark's, Brighton. In his possession is a portrait of his father by Hugh Rivière. As a memorial to Elliott it is proposed to add a wing to St. Mary's Hall, Brighton, a church school in which he was especially interested.

Elliott's contributions to Indian literature were mainly official. They included, besides the 'Chronicles of Oonao,' 'Report on the Hoshangabad Settlement' (1866); 'Report on the Mysore Famine' (1878); 'Report on the Famine Commission' (1879); and 'Report on the Finance Commission' (1887).

[The Times, 29 May 1911; C. E. Buckland, Bengal under the Lt.-Governors, 1901; Lady Betty Balfour, Lord Lytton's Administration, 1899; Kaye's Sepoy War; Sir Henry Cotton, Indian and Home Memories, 1911; official reports.] W. L-W.

ELLIS, FREDERICK STARTRIDGE (1830–1901), bookseller and author, the sixth son of Joseph Ellis, hotel-keeper, of Richmond, was born there on 7 June 1830. He entered, at the age of sixteen, the house of Edward Lumley of Chancery Lane, and afterwards became assistant to C. J. Stewart, the well-known bookseller of King William Street, Strand, from whom he acquired his knowledge of books. In 1860 he went into business for himself at 33 King Street, Covent Garden, and in 1871 took into partnership G. M. Green (1841–1872), who had enjoyed the same training. After the death of Green in 1872 Ellis took the premises, 29 New Bond Street, previously occupied by T. & W. Boone, and carried on a large and successful business, chiefly in old books and MSS. His next partner was David White, who retired in 1884. For many years Ellis was official buyer for the British Museum, which brought him into rivalry with trade opponents in the auction rooms. Mr. Henry Huth entrusted to him the editing of the catalogue of his famous library, which was printed in 1880 (5 vols., large 8vo). The English books were catalogued by W. C. Hazlitt, those in other languages by Ellis. Another excellent catalogue compiled by Ellis was 'Descriptive Catalogue of a Collection of Drawings and Etchings by Charles Meryon, formed by the Rev. J. J. Heywood' (1880, 4to, privately printed). He also produced 'Horæ Pembrochianæ: some account of an illuminated MS. of the Hours of the B.V.M., written for William Herbert, first earl of Pembroke, about 1440' (1880), and a biographical notice appended to an account of 'The Hours of Albert of Brandenburg,' by W. H. J. Weale (1883, 4to). In 1885 he retired from business, and his stock of rarities was sold by Messrs. Sotheby for about 16,000*l.* He was succeeded in business by Mr. G. I. Ellis, a nephew.

Ellis was a publisher on a limited scale, and brought out the works of William Morris and Dante Gabriel Rossetti, with whom he formed a close personal intimacy. Among other friends were A. C. Swinburne, Sir Edward Burne-Jones, and John Ruskin, whose 'Stray Letters to a London Bibliopole' were addressed to Ellis and republished by him (1892). Ruskin called him 'Papa Ellis' (E. T. Cook, *Life of John Ruskin*, 1911, i. 371). It was in 1864 that Morris was first introduced by Swinburne to Ellis. They remained close friends to the end of

Morris's life, and Ellis was one of the poet's executors (J. W. Mackail, *Life of W. Morris*, 1899, i. 193).

After his retirement from business he gave himself up to a literary life. The firstfruits of his labours on Shelley was 'An Alphabetical Table of Contents to Shelley's Poetical Works,' drawn up for the Shelley Society in 1888. He devoted six years to compiling 'A Lexical Concordance to the Poetical Works of P. B. Shelley; an attempt to classify every word found therein according to its signification' (1892, 4to), an excellent piece of work on which his reputation must largely rest. He was an enthusiastic supporter of Morris's Kelmscott Press, and read the proofs of the folio edition of Chaucer's 'Works' (1896), Morris's masterpiece of printing, and edited many other productions of that press, including Cavendish's 'Life of Wolsey' (1893); Caxton's 'Golden Legend' (1892), which also appeared in the 'Temple Classics' (1899 and 1900). He further edited Guillaume de Lorris's 'Romance of the Rose,' 'englished' (1900, 'Temple Classics'), and 'H. Pengelly's Memoir,' with a preface (1897), and contributed some memoirs to Quaritch's 'Dictionary of English Book Collectors.'

He died at Sidmouth on 26 Feb. 1901, after a short illness, in his seventy-first year. He was a widely read and accomplished man, tall of stature and handsome in appearance, warm-hearted and good-natured, of genial manners, with a wide circle of literary and artistic friends.

His portrait was painted by H. S. Tuke, A.R.A.

He married in 1860 Caroline Augusta Flora, daughter of William Moates of Epsom, and left issue two sons and a daughter, who with his wife survived him.

[Family information; The Times, 1 March 1901; Athenæum, 2, 9, and 16 March 1901; Bookseller, 7 March 1901; Note by W. Morris on the Kelmscott Press, with a description by S. C. Cockerell, 1898. See also J. W. Mackail's Life of W. Morris, 1899, 2 vols.; D. G. Rossetti, his family-letters, 1895, 2 vols.; Letters of D. G. Rossetti to W. Allingham, by G. B. Hill, 1897; D. G. Rossetti as designer and writer, notes by W. M. Rossetti, 1889, passim; W. Roberts, The Book-Hunter in London, 1895, p. 245 (portrait).] H. R. T.

ELLIS, JOHN DEVONSHIRE (1824–1906), civil engineer and metallurgist, born at Handsworth on 20 April 1824, was son of Charles Ellis, a Birmingham brass manufacturer. Educated at King Edward VI's School, Birmingham, he obtained a practical knowledge of the manufacture and working of brass in his father's works, and in 1848 became a partner in the firm. In 1854 he purchased with (Sir) John Brown [q. v. Suppl. I] and William Bragge the Atlas engineering works at Sheffield, then a modest establishment covering about three acres and employing about 250 persons. Shortly after the partners took over the works the adoption of armour by the French for warships (1858) led Messrs. Brown and Ellis to produce iron plates by a new and cheaper process of rolling and welding them. Four-inch plates made by this process were fitted to the Black Prince and Warrior, the earliest ironclads of the British navy. For several years Ellis was occupied in devising appliances for the manufacture of thicker and thicker plates for guns and projectiles. Steel was tried, but was not found to have the necessary toughness under the impact of shot. After many experiments Ellis perfected a process for uniting a hard steel face with a wrought-iron backing. Such compound armour was used down to about 1893, the Royal Sovereign class of battleships being protected with an 18-inch belt of it on the water-line. Meanwhile, as early as 1871, Ellis had turned his attention to the process of cementation, and in that year he took out a patent relating to it; but it was not until the chilling process devised by Captain T. J. Tresidder, in which the heated surface of a plate was chilled by means of water under pressure, was applied in conjunction with cementation, that satisfactory results were obtained. The first Ellis-Tresidder chilled compound plate was tried with success at Shoeburyness in 1891.

Ellis was largely instrumental in promoting the success of the Bessemer system. Sir Henry Bessemer [q. v. Suppl. I] established works close to the Atlas works, and Ellis, adopting at an early stage the new process, at once put up at the Atlas works the first plant in England outside the inventor's own works. In conjunction with William Eaves he introduced the Ellis-Eaves system of induced draught, and he devised a mill for rolling the ribbed boiler-flues of the Purves and other types, and also in connection with the manufacture of Serve tubes.

The Atlas works soon acquired a world-wide reputation for mechanical engineering of all kinds. The concern was formed into a limited liability company in 1864. The capital rose to nearly three millions sterling; about 16,000 men were employed at Ellis's death, and the output exceeded 100,000 tons of steel per annum. Ellis was managing director from 1864 until 1905, when he became chairman of the company. Brown retired in 1870 and Bragge died in 1884, when Ellis acquired sole charge. In 1899 the Clydebank Shipbuilding and Engineering Works, employing 8000 men, were taken over by the concern.

In 1867 Ellis was decorated with the Cross of the Order of Vasa in recognition of his aid in certain fortifications in Sweden. From the Iron and Steel Institute, of which he was a member from 1875, a member of council in 1888, and a vice-president in 1901, he received the Bessemer gold medal in 1889, when Sir Henry Bessemer acknowledged Ellis's services in establishing the process. He was elected a member of the Institution of Civil Engineers on 8 Jan. 1884. For many years he was a member of the Cutlers' Company. He took little part in the public affairs of Sheffield, but was a magistrate for the West Riding, and was for ten years chairman of the South Yorkshire Coalowners' Association. He died at his residence, Sparken, Worksop, on 11 Nov. 1906, and was buried at Carlton in Lindrick.

He married on 5 Dec. 1848 Elizabeth Parsons Bourne of Childs Ercall, Shropshire, by whom he had five sons and one daughter.

A portrait by A. S. Cope, R.A., is at the Atlas Works, Sheffield.

[Journal Iron and Steel Institute, 1906, pt. iv. p. 706; Minutes of Proceedings Inst. Civ. Eng. clxviii. 340; The Engineer, 16 Nov. 1906; Engineering, 16 Nov. 1906; Cassier's Mag., Dec. 1903, pp. 194 seq.] W. F. S.

ELSMIE, GEORGE ROBERT (1838–1909), Anglo-Indian civilian and author, born at Aberdeen on 31 Oct. 1838, was only child of George Elsmie, shipowner, of Aberdeen, and from 1843 on the Southampton staff of the Royal Mail Steam Packet Company. His mother was Anne, daughter of Robert Shepherd, parish minister of Daviot, Aberdeenshire, whose family had been parish ministers in that county for several generations. Educated at private schools at Southampton and from 1852 to 1855 at the Marischal College, Aberdeen, Elsmie was studying German at Canstatt near Stuttgart in August 1855, when he was nominated to a writership in India by his maternal uncle, John Shepherd (1796–1859), for many years director and thrice chairman of the East India Company, and on the transfer of India to the crown member of the Council of India. Elsmie was among the last batch of men to enter, at the close of 1855, the East India College at Haileybury, and to pass out on the eve of its abolition in Dec. 1857.

Arriving in India on 12 Feb. 1858, he was appointed assistant commissioner in the Punjab, and served in various districts until 1863, when he acted as a judge of the small causes courts at Lahore, Delhi, and Simla. Meanwhile he prepared a useful 'Epitome of Correspondence regarding our Relations with Afghanistan and Herat, 1854–63' (Lahore, 1863). In March 1865 he became deputy commissioner (magistrate and collector) of Jullundur, and in October 1868 under-secretary to the government of India in the home department. Taking furlough in the spring of 1869, he entered Lincoln's Inn as a student, and was called to the bar on 27 Jan. 1871.

Returning to India immediately afterwards, he was appointed additional commissioner of the Amritsar and Jullundur divisions, his duties being almost entirely judicial. In October 1872 he was transferred to Peshawur to perform like functions, the lieutenant-governor being anxious to improve the judicial administration and reduce crimes of violence in the district. Elsmie's firmness and good sense in dealing with the Pathans had the desired effect at some personal risk. His suggestions to the government and his detailed examination of the subject in 'Crime and Criminals on the Peshawur Frontier' (Lahore, 1884) largely contributed to the promulgation in 1887 of the 'Frontier Criminal Regulations,' which were specially adapted to borderland conditions.

Elsmie left Peshawur in January 1878 to officiate as judge of the Punjab chief court for a year. After furlough in December 1880 he became commissioner of Lahore, and in April 1882 was appointed permanently to the chief court bench. In the same year he served on the Punjab reorganisation committee. In agreement with its recommendations the Lahore commissionership was greatly enlarged in area and relieved of judicial appellate work, and was bestowed anew on Elsmie in February 1885. He was on special duty for the Rawal Pindi durbar for Lord Dufferin to meet the Ameer Abdur Rahman (April 1885) and was vice-chancellor of the Punjab University (1885–7). He was made second financial commissioner in April 1887, a member of the governor-general's legislative council in May 1888, and first financial commissioner from March 1889.

He thus attained the highest positions in the province, short of the lieutenant-governorship, on both the judicial and executive sides. He was re-appointed to the governor-general's legislative council in June 1892, and was made C.S.I. in Jan. 1893. He left India on 4 Feb. 1894.

On 20 July 1904 Elsmie received from Aberdeen University the hon. degree of LL.D. He mainly devoted himself in his retirement to literary work. With General Sir Peter Lumsden he wrote Sir Harry Lumsden's biography, 'Lumsden of the Guides' (1899). On material collected by Sir Henry Cunningham he based the authorised life of Field-marshal Sir Donald Stewart [q. v. Suppl. I] (1903), and he edited letters of his mother (1804–1879) under the title of 'Anne Shepherd or Elsmie: a Character Sketch of a Scottish Lady of the Nineteenth Century as disclosed by her Letters' (Aberdeen, 1904). In his pleasant 'Thirty-Five Years in the Punjab' (Edinburgh, 1908) Elsmie threw much light on the contemporary history of his province; the book is dedicated to his university.

Elsmie died at Torquay on 26 March 1909, and was buried at Deeside cemetery, Aberdeen. He married at Southampton, on 27 Oct. 1861, Elizabeth, youngest daughter of Thomas Spears of Kirkcaldy, who survived him. Of a family of three sons and eight daughters, two sons became officers in the Indian army, four daughters married Indian civil servants (Sir Thomas W. Holderness, now revenue secretary, India office, being one of Elsmie's sons-in-law), and two daughters married officers in the army.

[Elsmie's Works; The Times, 28 March 1909; family details kindly given by Sir T. W. Holderness.] F. H. B.

ELWORTHY, FREDERICK THOMAS (1830–1907), philologist and antiquary, eldest son of Thomas Elworthy, woollen manufacturer, of Wellington, Somerset, by his wife Jane, daughter of William Chorley of Quarm, near Dunster, was born at Wellington on 10 Jan. 1830, and was educated at a private school at Denmark Hill. Though studious from boyhood, he did not enter on authorship until middle life. He became eminent first as a philologist and later as a writer on folk-lore. His two books on the evil eye and kindred superstitions contain much curious information gathered during travels in Spain, Italy, and other countries, in the course of which he made perhaps the finest collection of charms, amulets, and such-like trinkets in existence; this collection, at present in the possession of his widow, is destined for the Somersetshire Archæological Society's museum at Taunton. He contributed to 'Archæologia,' was on the council of the Philological Society, and in 1891–6 was editorial secretary of the Somersetshire Archæological Society, for whose 'Proceedings,' as well as for those of the Devonshire Association, he wrote some valuable papers. He was elected F.S.A. on 14 June 1900. He was a good linguist and possessed considerable skill as a draughtsman and as an artist in water-colours. He was a prominent churchman, and the erection of All Saints' Church, Wellington, was largely due to his liberality and exertions. He was a magistrate, a churchwarden, an active member of the Wellington school board, and a prominent freemason. After an illness which began in the summer of 1906 he died at his residence, Foxdown, Wellington, on 13 Dec. 1907, and was buried in the churchyard of the parish church there.

By his marriage with Maria, daughter of James Kershaw, M.P., on 17 Aug. 1854, he had three sons, who all predeceased him, and three daughters, two of whom survived him.

Elworthy prepared for publication by the English Dialect Society: 1. 'The Dialect of West Somerset,' 1875 (a paper read before the Philological Soc.). 2. 'An Outline of the Grammar of the Dialect of West Somerset,' 1877 (papers read before the Philolog. Soc. in 1876 and 1877); this work was described by Sir James A. H. Murray, editor of the 'New English Dictionary,' as 'the first grammar of an English dialect of any scientific value.' 3. 'An edition of 'An Exmoor Scolding and an Exmoor Courtship, with a Somersetshire Man's Complaint,' 1879. 4. 'The West Somerset Word-book, a Glossary,' 1886. Elworthy also published: 5. 'Canonsleigh,' 1892, reprinted from the 'Transactions of the Devonshire Association.' 6. 'Some Notes on the History of Wellington,' 4to, 1892. 7. 'The Evil Eye,' 1895. 8. 'Horns of Honour and other Studies in the By-ways of Archæology,' 1900. From the inception of the 'New English Dictionary' to his death Elworthy gave much voluntary help both in supplying quotations and in assisting in arrangement.

[Wellington Weekly News, 18 Dec. 1907, with an appreciation by Sir James Murray; Athenæum, 21 Dec. 1907; Somerset Archæol. Soc. Proc., 3rd ser. vol. xiii. 1908 (with good portrait); information supplied by Mr. C. Tite of Taunton; personal recollection.] W. H.

EMERY, WILLIAM (1825–1910), archdeacon of Ely, born in St. Martin's Lane, London, on 2 Feb. 1825, was son of William Emery of Hungerford Market, feltmaker and Master of the Feltmakers' Company in 1848, who married Mary Ann Thompson. He was the first boy to enter, in 1837, the new City of London School, then erected on the site of Honey Lane Market in accordance with a reformed scheme for employing the ancient charity of John Carpenter [q. v.]. At the school he was a favourite pupil of the headmaster, G. F. W. Mortimer [q. v.], and was the first holder of the newly founded 'Times' scholarship [see Walter, John, 1776–1847]. Admitted at Corpus Christi College, Cambridge, on 29 March 1843, he was elected Mawson scholar in May 1844; was fifth wrangler in 1847, graduating B.A., and proceeding M.A. in 1850 and B.D. in 1858. In March 1847 he became fellow of Corpus, retaining his fellowship till 1865; he was dean of the college (1853–5); bursar 1855–60; and tutor, along with E. H. Perowne [q. v. Suppl. II] (1855–65). He was made honorary fellow in 1905. Ordained deacon in 1849 and priest in 1853, he never confined himself to academic concerns. Among his interests in Cambridge was the volunteer movement. At a meeting in his college rooms on 2 May 1859, 'a volunteer corps for the university, town and county of Cambridge' was set on foot. In 1859, too, he helped to form in Cambridge a branch affiliated to the central Church Defence Institution. In October 1861 the Cambridge committee invited individual churchmen and the secretaries of church defence associations to join in a Church Congress on the pattern of 'annual meetings of societies for the advancement of science, archæology, &c.' (cf. *Preface to First Report*, p. iii). The first Church Congress met in the hall of King's College, Cambridge (27–29 Nov. 1861), when Emery was senior proctor, the chair being taken by the archdeacon of Ely, Francis France. Emery spoke on free seats in church, on diocesan associations for increasing the endowment of poor benefices, and on church rates. He became permanent secretary of the Church Congress in 1869, and with the exception of the meeting in Dublin in 1867 was present at every congress from the first to the forty-seventh at Great Yarmouth in 1907, being the most familiar feature and the chief organiser of every meeting. In 1864 Lord Palmerston nominated him to the archdeaconry of Ely, and he became residentiary canon of Ely in 1870. As archdeacon, he soon organised a diocesan conference, the first in the country, remaining its honorary secretary till 1906. In 1881, when the institution had spread widely, he helped to establish a central council of diocesan conferences, of which he was honorary secretary till 1906. He was also instrumental in founding the Hunstanton Convalescent Home (of which he was chairman 1872–1908) and the Church Schools Company for the promotion of the religious secondary education of the middle classes (of which he was chairman 1883–1903).

Owing to failing powers he resigned his archdeaconry in 1907. He retained his canonry till his death at the college, Ely, on 14 Dec. 1910. He was buried in the precincts of Ely Cathedral. On 6 July 1865, at St. John's, Stratford, London, he married Fanny Maria, eldest daughter of Sir Antonio Brady [q. v.]. He had six children, of whom two daughters and three sons survive.

Emery was a man of affairs, energetic and tactful, rather than a teacher. The Church Congress is his monument. Among his publications were his charges on 'Church Organisation and Efficient Ministry' (1866), and on 'The New Church Rate Act' (1869), and a popular explanation of the 'Free Education Act, 1891.'

[The Times, 15 Dec. 1910; Guardian, 16 Dec. 1910; Record, 16 Dec. 1910; Reports (annual) of Church Congresses, especially 1861 and 1910; the latter contains good portrait.] E. H. P.

ETHERIDGE, ROBERT (1819–1903), palæontologist, born at Ross, Herefordshire, on 3 Dec. 1819, was elder of two sons of Thomas Etheridge, shipper, of Gloucester, by his wife Hannah Pardoe, of a Worcestershire family. Through his mother he was cousin to Dr. John Beddoe [q. v. Suppl. II]. His paternal grandfather, formerly a seaman, and later harbour-master at Bristol, gave Robert shells and other natural objects or 'curiosities' from various countries, and stimulated the boy to form a museum of local plants, fossils, and other geological specimens. Educated at the grammar school at Ross, he served as usher there and at a school at Bristol, and after filling a post in a business house in that city, in 1850 he was made curator of the museum of the Bristol Philosophical Institution. All his leisure had been devoted to natural science. He worked hard at the museum till 1857, acting for five of the seven years as lecturer in vegetable physiology and botany in the Bristol

Medical School. In 1857 he gave a course of lectures at the Bristol Mining School on 'Geology: its Relation and Bearing upon Mining,' published in 1859. An active member of the Cotteswold Naturalists' Club, Etheridge in 1856, while on a visit to the earl of Ducie at Tortworth Court, was introduced to Sir Roderick Impey Murchison [q. v.], then director-general of the geological survey. This led to his appointment in 1857 as assistant palæontologist to the geological survey; and on the retirement of J. W. Salter he became palæontologist in 1863. Here his principal task was the naming of the invertebrate fossils collected during the progress of the geological survey and arranged in the Museum of Practical Geology at Jermyn Street; aid was also given at times to the officers in the field. Etheridge's results were embodied in memoirs published during 1858–81. He also assisted Professor Huxley by giving demonstrations in palæontology to students of the Royal School of Mines, and he and Huxley jointly prepared a catalogue of the fossils in the museum, which was published in 1865. At this date Etheridge began to make a list of all the known British fossils, with references to their geological formations and to published figures and descriptions. When completed up to 1888 it was reckoned that about 18,000 species had been catalogued. Only one volume of this great work, that dealing with the palæozoic fossils, was published ('Fossils of the British Islands, Stratigraphically and Zoologically arranged,' vol. i. Palæozoic Species, 1888). In 1881 Etheridge was appointed assistant keeper in geology at the British Museum natural history branch at Cromwell Road, where he laboured till his retirement from the public service in 1891.

Etheridge was elected F.R.S. in 1871, and afterwards served on the council and as vice-president of the Royal Society. He was awarded the Murchison medal by the council of the Geological Society in 1880, and was president from 1880 to 1882. He was also president of section C at the meeting of the British Association in 1882, and treasurer of the Palæontographical Society from 1880 to 1903. He was created an honorary fellow of King's College, London, in 1890, and received the first Bolitho medal from the Royal Geological Society of Cornwall in 1896. Etheridge was an assistant editor of the 'Geological Magazine' from 1865 until the close of his life. Always active and genial, he died at Chelsea, London, on 18 Dec. 1903, aged eighty-four, and was buried at Brompton cemetery. He was three times married, and by his first wife he had an only child, Robert Etheridge the younger, now curator of the Australian Museum at Sydney, New South Wales.

Among Etheridge's communications to scientific societies were papers on the palæontology of parts of Queensland, the Himalayas, Brazil, and the Arctic regions. In England he had given special attention to the Rhætic beds, and afterwards to the Devonian system. When the sequence of strata in North Devon was challenged by Joseph Beete Jukes [q. v.] in 1866, Etheridge was instructed by Murchison to investigate the evidence, and the results were published by the Geological Society in 1867 in an elaborate paper 'On the Physical Structure of West Somerset and North Devon, and on the Palæontological Value of the Devonian Fossils.' Later discoveries, by Dr. H. Hicks, of Lower Devonian (or possibly Silurian) fossils in the Morte slates, showed that the sequence of strata in North Devon was not so clear as Etheridge and others had maintained. To questions of water-supply Etheridge gave much practical attention, and in later years he acted as consulting geologist to the promoters of the Dover coal-boring.

Etheridge published 'Stratigraphical Geology and Palæontology' (1887). He also prepared the third edition of John Phillips's 'Illustrations of the Geology of Yorkshire' (part i. 1875), and he re-wrote the second edition of part ii. of Phillips's 'Manual of Geology' (1885).

[Obituary by Dr. Henry Woodward, Geol. Mag., Jan. 1904, p. 42 (with portrait and bibliography); memoirs by H. B. Woodward in Proc. Roy. Soc. lxxv. 1905, and in Proc. Bristol Nat. Soc. ser. 2, vol. x. 1904, p. 175 (with portrait).] H. B. W.

EUAN-SMITH, Sir CHARLES BEAN (1842–1910), soldier and diplomatist, one of several sons of Euan Maclauren Smith of George Town, British Guiana, by his wife Eliza Bean, was born at George Town on 21 Sept. 1842. He was educated at a preparatory school near Rugby, and subsequently by an English tutor at Bruges. Appointed ensign in the Madras infantry at the age of seventeen, he was promoted lieutenant in 1861, captain in 1870, major in 1879, lieutenant-colonel in 1881, and colonel in 1885, retiring in 1889. After serving in the expedition to Abyssinia in 1867 he was present at the capture of Magdala, was secretary in 1870–1 to Sir Frederick Goldsmid [q. v. Suppl. II] during the special mission of the latter to Persia, to settle various frontier questions, and accompanied Sir Bartle Frere [q. v.] in his special anti-slave trade mission to Zanzibar and Muscat in 1872 as military attaché. He was made C.S.I. in November of that year. Subsequently he was in charge of the consulate-general at Zanzibar from June to September 1875, was first assistant resident at Hyderabad in 1876, and received the appointment of consul at Muscat in July 1879. During the Afghan war of 1879–80 he was on special duty as chief political officer on the staff of Lieut.-general Sir Donald Stewart [q. v. Suppl. I], and subsequently took part in Lord Roberts's expedition for the relief of Kandahar, receiving the medal with two clasps and the bronze star for his share in the campaign. During the following years he held political appointments in Mewar, Banswara, Bhartpur and Karauli. In December 1887 he was appointed to succeed Sir John Kirk as British consul-general at Zanzibar. Here he was plunged into the various thorny discussions arising out of German annexations and claims advanced by France and other European countries to the immunities flowing from consular jurisdiction in the territories on the mainland, which had been acquired from the sultan by the British East Africa Company. He showed much skill in dealing with these questions, and in June 1890 he obtained the consent of the sultan to an agreement by which the latter placed himself under the protection of Great Britain, thus paving the way to the conclusion of agreements by the British government with France and Germany, and greatly facilitating an ultimate settlement. He had been made C.B. in 1889, and on this occasion was advanced to be K.C.B. in the civil division. In March 1891 he was appointed British envoy in Morocco, and was furnished by Lord Salisbury with special instructions, foremost among which was a direction to negotiate a new commercial treaty on a broad and liberal basis. In April 1892 he started from Tangier on a special mission to Fez, taking with him the draft of a commercial treaty, the terms of which had been settled in consultation with the Foreign Office, and provided also with instructions as to the language he should hold with regard to the questions of slavery and of the rights of protection exercised under treaty by the legations of foreign powers. A long and wearisome negotiation with the sultan and his ministers ensued. in which every device of intimidation, obstruction, and tergiversation was employed by the Moorish negotiators, and eventually, after the treaty had more than once been accepted by the sultan only to be again rejected or subjected to entirely inadmissible modifications, Euan-Smith left Fez with the staff of the mission. Fresh negotiations were opened by commissioners sent by the sultan, while the mission was on its way to the coast, but these proved equally delusive, and the British envoy returned to Tangier having effected little or nothing beyond the appointment of a British vice-consul at Fez, where France, Spain, and the United States already had consular agents. The objections of the sultan and his advisers to the proposals with which Euan-Smith had been charged were clearly too deep-rooted to be removed by arguments of persuasion, and Lord Salisbury decided on desisting from further efforts. But the effect of the negotiations and of episodes connected with them was seriously prejudicial to Euan-Smith's influence as British representative, and he ceased to hold the appointment in July 1893. In June of that year the University of Oxford conferred on him the honorary degree of D.C.L. and he was made hon. fellow of St. John's College, Oxford. He devoted his attention for the rest of his life to commercial business, taking an active part as chairman or director of several companies. In July 1898 he was offered by Lord Salisbury and accepted the appointment of minister resident at Bogota, in the republic of Colombia, but resigned it without proceeding to his post. He died in London on 30 Aug. 1910. He married in 1877 Edith, daughter of General Frederick Alexander, R.A., and had by her one daughter.

[The Times, 31 Aug. 1910; Foreign Office List, 1911, p. 417; India Office List; papers laid before Parliament.] S.

EVANS, DANIEL SILVAN (1818–1903), Welsh scholar and lexicographer, born at Fron Wilym Uchaf, Llanarth, Cardiganshire, on 11 Jan. 1818, was son of Silvanus Evans by his wife Sarah. Having commenced to preach as a member of Penycae congregational church, he entered the academy of Dr. Phillips of Neuaddlwyd with a view to the congregational ministry. In1843 he thought of emigrating to America, but later resolved to seek orders in the established church. In 1846 he entered St. David's College, Lampeter, where he was senior scholar, and was ordained deacon in 1848 and priest in 1849. His first curacy was at Llandegwining and Penllech, Carnarvonshire (1848–52), his second at Llangian in the same district (1852–62). In 1862 he became rector of Llanymawddwy near Machynlleth, and in 1876 exchanged to the neighbouring rectory of Llanwrin; the greater part of his life's work was done in these two retired parsonages. Evans made his first appearance before the Welsh public as a writer of verse; lyrical poems and hymns from his pen were published in 1843 and in 1846. But the study of the Welsh language soon absorbed all his attention. Already in 1847 he was planning the English-Welsh dictionary which was his first considerable work (*Archæologia Cambrensis*, first series, vol. ii. (1847), p. 282). Four years after his ordination the first volume of this appeared, and henceforward he was engaged without intermission in Welsh literary and philological studies. Through all his labours as editor and translator he kept steadily in view the more ambitious lexicographical work which was to be the coping-stone of his career, viz. the 'Dictionary of the Welsh Language,' planned on a great scale, of which the first part appeared in 1887. The heavy task, however, was carried no further than the letter E when he died. In later life Evans's eminence as a Welsh scholar received full recognition. In 1868 he received the honorary degree of B.D. from Lampeter; from 1875 to 1883 he was lecturer in Welsh in the University College of Wales, Aberystwyth; in 1897 he was elected to a research fellowship in Jesus College, Oxford, and in 1901 the newly established University of Wales gave him the honorary degree of D.Litt. He was made honorary canon of Bangor in 1888, prebendary of Llanfair in 1891, and chancellor of the cathedral in 1895. From January 1872 to August 1875 he was editor of 'Archæologia Cambrensis,' but archæology was not one of his special interests; his reputation rests on his encyclopædic knowledge of the whole range of Welsh literature and his skill in using this material as a lexicographer. He died on 12 April 1903, and was buried at Cemmes. He married Margaret, daughter of Walter Walters of Hendre, Cardiganshire, and left a son, John Henry Silvan Evans, who assisted his father in his great dictionary.

The 'Dictionary of the Welsh Language,' published by Spurrell of Carmarthen, appeared as follows: A, 1887; B, 1888; C, 1893; Ch, D, 1896; E–Enyd, 1906. The whole extends to 1923 pages, all words of importance being illustrated by examples of their use. Evans also published: 1. 'Blodau Ieuainc,' poems, Aberystwyth, 1843. 2. 'Telynegion,' lyrics, 1846 (2nd edit. 1881). 3. 'English and Welsh Dictionary' (Denbigh), vol. i. 1852; vol. ii. 1858. 4. 'Llythyraeth yr Iaith Gymraeg' (on Welsh orthography), Carmarthen, 1861. 5. 'Ystên Sioned' (jointly with John Jones), a collection of folk stories, Aberystwyth, 1882 (2nd edit., Wrexham, 1894). 6. 'Telyn Dyfi,' poems, Aberystwyth, 1898.

Evans edited, among other works, Ellis Wynne's 'Bardd Cwsg' (Carmarthen, 1853; 4th edit. 1891); the works of Gwallter Mechain (Rev. Walter Davies) (Carmarthen, 1868, 3 vols.); the Cambrian Bibliography of William Rowlands (Llanidloes, 1869); the works of Ieuan Brydydd Hir (Carnarvon, 1876); the second edition of Stephens's 'Literature of the Kymry' (1876); the 'Celtic Remains' of Lewis Morris (for the Cambrian Archæological Association, London, 1878). Evans was editor of the 'Brython,' a Welsh magazine issued at Tremadoc from 1858 to 1863, and contributed to Skene's 'Four Ancient Books of Wales' (Edinburgh, 1866) the translation into English of three of the four MSS. of ancient poetry therein edited.

[Who's Who, 1902; Y Geninen, 1905; T. R. Roberts, Dict. of Eminent Welshmen; Byegones (Oswestry), 22 April 1903.]

J. E. L.

EVANS, EDMUND (1826–1905), wood-engraver and colour-printer, born in Southwark on 23 Feb. 1826, was son of Henry Evans by his wife Mary. Educated at a school in Jamaica Row kept by Bart Robson, an old sailor, he in November 1839, at the age of thirteen, became 'reading boy' at Samuel Bentley's printing establishment at Bangor House, Shoe Lane. On the suggestion of an overseer, who found that the boy had a talent for drawing, his parents apprenticed him in 1840 to Ebenezer Landells [q. v.], the wood-engraver. Birket Foster, one year senior to Evans, was articled to Landells at the same time, and the two pupils often joined in sketching excursions. On the completion of his apprenticeship in May 1847, Evans started business as a wood-engraver on his own account, taking small premises at first in Wine Office Court, Fleet Street, and in 1851 moving to 4 Racquet Court. Orders soon came to him from the 'Illustrated London News' and from the allied firm of Ingram, Cooke & Co. In 1852 Birket Foster was preparing for Ingram, Cooke & Co. a set of illustrations to Madame Ida Pfeiffer's 'Travels in the Holy Land.'

These were handed over to Evans, who engraved them for three printings, a key-block giving the outlines in brown, and two other blocks adding tints in buff and blue. This experiment led to further work in colour, notably the preparation of an illustrated cover, then quite a novelty, for Mayhew's 'Letters Left at the Pastry-cook's' (1853). This was printed in blue and red on a white paper; but, finding that the white cover easily soiled, Evans substituted a yellow paper with an enamel surface, which had an immediate popularity and was greatly in request for railway novels, whence the term 'yellow-back.' During thirty years Evans produced a vast quantity of these and similar covers for various publishers.

Though he executed wood-engravings in black and white to illustrate Scott's poetical works (A. & C. Black, 1853–6), Cowper's 'Task' (Nisbet & Co., 1855–6), and other volumes, Evans became known from this time almost entirely as a colour engraver. His process of printing in oil colour from a series of wood blocks carried on the tradition which had descended from the early chiaroscuro engravers, and was almost identical with that of his immediate predecessor, George Baxter (1804–1867), except that he did not, like Baxter, use an engraved key plate of copper or steel.

Evans's first colour-printing of real importance as book illustration was for 'The Poems of Oliver Goldsmith' (1858), with pictures by Birket Foster. Foster made his drawings as usual on the block, and then coloured a proof pulled on drawing paper. This was followed most carefully by Evans, who bought the actual colours used by the artist, ground them by hand, and did the printing on a hand-press. Other successful publications between 1858 and 1860, with printing done in six to twelve colours on a hand-press, were 'Common Objects of the Sea Shore,' and 'Common Objects of the Country,' by the Rev. J. G. Wood, illustrated by W. S. Coleman [q. v. Suppl. II], and 'Common Wayside Flowers,' by T. Miller, containing drawings by Birket Foster. Another work, described by Evans as 'the most carefully executed book I have ever printed,' was 'A Chronicle of England' (1864), written and illustrated by James William E. Doyle [q. v. Suppl. I]. For that book, with its eighty-one illustrations, each produced by nine or ten colour-blocks, a hand press was employed for the last time. Evans also executed the first coloured plates presented by the 'Graphic' to its readers, a double-page picture of the Albert Memorial (1872) and 'The Old Soldier,' from a water-colour drawing by Basil Bradley (1873).

It was, however, by the colour-printing of children's books by Walter Crane, Randolph Caldecott, and Kate Greenaway, that Evans built his most enduring monument. From 1865 to 1869 he was occupied with the production of a series of sixpenny toy-books, published partly by Ward & Lock and partly by Routledge, with illustrations in colour by Walter Crane. In 1877 Evans arranged on his own account with Crane to illustrate a child's book entitled 'The Baby's Opera.' A first edition of ten thousand copies at five shillings apiece was sold, and a second edition was soon in demand. The volume was followed by many others in which artist and colour-printer worked in combination. At the end of 1879 Evans made another venture with 'Under the Window,' by Kate Greenaway [q. v. Suppl. II], a book that won immediate popularity, and was the forerunner of a fruitful partnership. Evans also printed the well-known 'Graphic' pictures by Randolph Caldecott [q. v.] and, by persuading him to embark on illustrations for children's books, inaugurated the famous series which began in 1878 with 'John Gilpin' and closed in 1885 with 'The Great Panjandrum Himself.' These three artists thoroughly grasped the possibilities and limitations of Evans's reproductive process, and worked in simple lines and flat washes of decorative colour, which the engraver could reproduce almost in facsimile. Shortly before his death Evans admitted that colour-printing from wood must yield to the three-colour process.

In 1864 Evans married Mary Spence Brown of North Shields, a niece of Birket Foster, and went to live at the Surrey village of Witley, which was the home of an interesting group of artists and authors. George Eliot, J. C. Hook, R.A., Birket Foster, Charles Keene, and Mrs. Allingham all belonged to his circle, and Kate Greenaway was a frequent visitor at his house.

Owing to ill-health, Evans retired from business in 1892, and settled at Ventnor, where he died on 21 Aug. 1905, being buried in Ventnor cemetery. His business is carried on by his two sons, Edmund Wilfred (*b.* 1869) and Herbert (*b.* 1871).

[Art Journal, Easter Art Annual, 1898; British and Colonial Printer, 31 March 1904, 7 Sept. 1905; Publishers' Circular, 14 Oct. 1905; Spielmann and Layard's Kate Greenaway, 1905; Hardie's English Coloured Books, 1906; Burch's Colour-Printing and Colour Printers, 1910; correspondence with Mr. Edmund Evans in 1904; private information.] M. H.

EVANS, GEORGE ESSEX (1863–1909), Australian poet, born at Cumberland Terrace, Regent's Park, London, on 18 June 1863, was youngest son of John Evans, Q.C., who was a bencher and treasurer of the Middle Temple and liberal M.P. for Haverford West (1847–52). After education at Haverford West grammar school and in the island of Guernsey, Evans emigrated to Australia in 1881. He attached himself to a survey party, and during a tour through the bush was first inspired to sing the praises of his adopted country. Subsequently he joined a brother, J. B. O. Evans, on a farm near Allora, Queensland; but cherishing literary ambitions he soon engaged in journalism. In 1882 he became a regular contributor to the 'Queenslander,' in which his earliest poems appeared under the pseudonym of Christophus, and after a struggling existence he established a connection with leading Australian papers like the 'Brisbane Courier' and the 'Sydney Bulletin.' In 1888 he settled at Toowoomba, where he was appointed district registrar by the Queensland government; he continued, however, to devote himself to literary pursuits. In 1892, 1893, and 1897 he edited a literary annual called 'The Antipodean'; but the venture, despite the collaboration of R. L. Stevenson, proved a failure owing to Evans's lack of business experience. His pen was also employed on less congenial tasks. In 1899 he compiled a guide to Darling Downs entitled 'The Garden of Queensland,' and later his services were enlisted by the government in preparing a report on the resources of Queensland, which was distributed in London at the Franco-British exhibition of 1908.

Evans's first volume of poetry, 'The Repentance of Magdaléne Despard, and other Verses' (London, 1891), containing some spirited patriotic utterances, attracted little attention. He was more successful with 'Loraine, and other Verses' (Melbourne, 1898), a long narrative poem, vividly descriptive of Australian life on a sheep farm, and in January 1901 he won the fifty-guinea prize offered by the New South Wales government for the best ode on the inauguration of the Australian commonwealth. He added to his reputation by the publication of 'The Sword of Pain' (Toowoomba, 1905) and 'The Secret Key, and other Verses' (Sydney, 1906), and both in England and America he was recognised as an Australian poet of power and individuality. With a view to fostering in Australia appreciation of art and literature, he founded the Toowoomba Austral Association in May 1903. In an enthusiastic ode entitled 'Queen of the North' (*The Times*, 7 Aug. 1909) he celebrated the fiftieth anniversary of the foundation of Queensland. He died at Toowoomba shortly afterwards, on 11 Nov. 1909. He married in 1899 Blanche, widow of E. B. Hopkins of Goodar station, Queensland, and daughter of the Rev. W. Eglinton, by whom he had one son. His admirers propose to commemorate him by a complete edition of his works.

Evans's poetic inspiration came from Australian life and country. He believed that Australian poetry should strike a new and distinctive note. Unlike some Australian poets, he was no pessimist. He encouraged his countrymen 'to face and subdue the resistance of nature,' and his verse breathes an intense appreciation of strenuous effort and robust courage. While his blank verse lacks technical finish, many of his stirring odes and lyrics reach a high level of poetic form.

[The Times, 14 Dec. 1909; Brisbane Courier, and Brisbane Daily Mail, 11 Nov. 1909; B. Stevens, Anthology of Australian verse, 1906; Sir J. Symon, Poetry and its claims, 1911.] G. S. W.

EVANS, Sir JOHN (1823–1908), archæologist and numismatist, born on 17 Nov. 1823 at Britwell Court, Burnham, Buckinghamshire, was second son of Arthur Benoni Evans, D.D. [q. v.], headmaster of the grammar school of Market Bosworth, Leicestershire, by his wife Anne, daughter of Thomas Dickinson, R.N. Anne Evans, [q. v.] was a sister, and Sebastian Evans [q. v. Suppl. II] a brother. John was educated at his father's school, and was entered in 1839 for matriculation at Brasenose College, Oxford, of which college he was towards the close of his life (1903) made an honorary fellow. He did not, however, proceed to the university, but after spending seven months in Germany entered in 1840, at the age of seventeen, the paper-manufacturing business of John Dickinson & Co., at Nash Mills, Hemel Hempsted, Hertfordshire, of which firm his uncle, John Dickinson, F.R.S., was founder and senior partner (*The Firm of John Dickinson*, 1896, p. 15). In 1850 Evans was admitted a partner. He proved a strenuous man of business, keenly alive to every scientific improvement and quick to grapple with complicated details.

Although he did not retire from the active duties of his firm till 1885, he always pursued many and diverse interests. When a boy of nine he had shown leanings towards natural science, and had hammered out for himself a collection of fossils from the Wenlock limestone quarries at Dudley. His later scientific studies were partly influenced by the practical requirements of his business. Water-supply being of primary importance to the paper-manufacturer, and his firm being engaged in an important law-suit, Dickinson *v.* The Grand Junction Canal Co., he made a special study of the subject, on which he became a recognised authority. He gave evidence before the royal commission on metropolitan water-supply, 1892. In his own district he explored the superficial deposits, as well as the deeper water-bearing strata, and investigated such matters as the relations between rainfall and evaporation, and the percolation of rain through soil. He kept in his own care the rain-gauges and percolation-gauges erected by his uncle at Nash Mills. In 1859 Evans accompanied Sir Joseph Prestwich [q. v. Suppl. I], the geologist, to France, as his assistant in an examination of flint-implements found in the old river-gravels of the valley of the Somme. Prestwich and Evans confirmed the opinion of the discoverer, Boucher de Perthes (*circ.* 1841–7), that these chipped flints were human handiwork and that they helped to prove the antiquity of man in western Europe. Evans wrote in 1860 in the 'Archæologia' on 'Flint Implements in the Drift, being an account of their discovery on the Continent and in England' (xxxviii. 280; cf. xxxix. 57). He now began to devote more continuous attention to the traces of early man in river-gravels and cavern-deposits, and formed a remarkable collection of stone and bronze implements, partly by the purchase of representative examples, partly by his own keenness in the discovery of specimens, even on ground already explored by other collectors. From time to time he published notices, in the 'Proceedings' of the Society of Antiquaries and of the Royal Society, of the discovery and distribution of new specimens. He was also interested in fossil remains of extinct animals and published an important paper, ('Nat. Hist. Rev.' 1865; cf. 'Geol. Mag.' 1884, pp. 418–24) on the 'Cranium and Jaw of an Archeopteryx.' Evans also formed various collections of mediæval and other antiquities, Anglo-Saxon, Lombardic jewellery, posy-rings, bronze weapons, and ornaments. In two books on primitive implements Evans gathered together all the evidence as to provenance, types, and distribution, and they were recognised as standard treatises. The first, 'The Ancient Stone Implements, Weapons and Ornaments of Great Britain,' was published in 1872 (French trans. 1878), a second and revised edition being issued in 1897. The other work, 'The Ancient Bronze Implements, Weapons, and Ornaments of Great Britain and Ireland,' was published in 1881 (French trans. 1882).

Evans had a special predilection for numismatics, and formed splendid collections of ancient British money, of gold coins of the Roman emperors, including some unique specimens, and of Anglo-Saxon and English coins, among which the gold series was especially noticeable. To the pages of the 'Numismatic Chronicle' he made more than a hundred contributions, many of them accounts of hoards and of unpublished coins from his own cabinets. His important paper ('Numismatic Chronicle,' 1865) on 'The "short-cross" Question,' was the outcome of an examination of more than 6000 specimens of the early silver pennies inscribed with the name Henricvs, and he was able to show that these coins belonged to several classes and that they were attributable to the respective reigns of Henry II. Richard, John, and Henry III. But his attention was chiefly concentrated on the coinage of the ancient Britons. His paper 'On the Date of British Coins,' published in the 'Numismatic Chronicle' for 1849–50 (xii. 127), was the first attempt to place the study of this coinage on a scientific basis. He showed, with pre-Darwinian instinct, that the appearance on these coins of horses, wheels, and ornaments, of which, previously, fanciful explanations had been given, was due to a slow process of evolution, and that the designs ('types') on the coins were the remote and degraded descendants of those on the gold *staters* of Philip of Macedon. Evans's conception of evolution as applied to the 'types' and 'fabric' of coins has since borne fruit in other branches of numismatics (cf. Keary, *Morphology of Coins,* and Evans's own paper, 'Coinage of the Ancient Britons and Natural Selection,' in the *Transactions of the Hertfordshire Natural History Society*, vol. iii. 1885). In 1864 he published the standard work, 'The Coins of the Ancient Britons,' for which he was awarded the Prix Allier de Hauteroche of the French Academy. A 'Supplement' was published in 1890, in which Evans described the discoveries subsequent to 1864, and inserted a map showing the find-spots of British coins.

Evans's varied knowledge, his grip of business, and habit of rapid decision made him a valuable officer of learned societies. He was elected F.R.S. in 1864, and for forty years took a conspicuous part in the society's business. He was a vice-president from 1876 and treasurer from 1878 to 1898. He joined the Geological Society in 1857, served as honorary secretary (1866–74), as president (1874–6), and acted as foreign secretary from 1895 till his death. In 1880 he received its Lyell medal for services to geology, especially post-tertiary geology, and his labours were eulogised as having bridged over the gulf that had once separated the researches of the archæologist from those of the geologist. He became a fellow of the Society of Antiquaries in 1852, and was its president from 1885 to 1892. The Numismatic Society of London (since 1904 the Royal Numismatic Society) was one of the earliest bodies that he joined. He became a member in 1849, was hon. secretary from 1854 to 1874, and president from 1874 till his death. From 1861 onwards he was a joint-editor of the society's journal, 'The Numismatic Chronicle.' In 1887 he received the society's medal (struck in gold) for distinguished services to numismatics.

He acted as president of the Anthropological Institute (1878–9), the Egypt Exploration Fund, the Society of Arts (chairman in 1900), the Paper-makers' Association, and the Society of Chemical Industry. He was president of the British Association in 1897–8 (Toronto meeting), when he gave an address on the Antiquity of Man, and was a trustee of the British Museum from 1885 till his death; he took an active part in the meetings of its standing committee. Evans was a member of numerous scientific and archæological bodies in foreign countries and had many academic honours. He was hon. D.C.L. of Oxford, LL.D. of Dublin and Toronto, Sc.D. of Cambridge, and a correspondent (elected in 1887) of the Institute of France (Academy of Inscriptions). In 1892 he was created K.C.B.

In spite of almost daily engagements in London, Evans lived nearly all his life at his home at Nash Mills, Hemel Hempsted, in an old-fashioned house, close to the mills. It was filled in every corner with books and antiquities (cf. *Herts County Homes*, 1892, p. 138). Here Evans was seen in his happiest mood, showing his treasures freely and with undisguised pleasure, and entertaining almost every European antiquary of note, not excluding many young scholars and collectors, from whom he never withheld encouragement. He was active too in county business. For some years he was chairman of quarter sessions, and vice-chairman and chairman of the county council, Hertfordshire. He served as high sheriff of the county in 1881. He was president and one of the founders (1865) of the Watford (afterwards the Herts) Natural History Society, and for more than twenty-three years chairman of Berkhamsted school.

In 1905 Sir John built a house, Britwell, on the edge of Berkhamsted Common, removing from Nash Mills in June 1906. He maintained his activities in old age, dying at Britwell on 31 May 1908, after an operation. He was buried in the parish church of Abbot's Langley, where there is a marble memorial of him, with a portrait-medallion by Sir William Richmond, R.A. A memorial window was placed by subscription in the chapel of Berkhamsted school.

Evans married in 1850 Harriet Ann, daughter of his uncle, John Dickinson, by whom he had three sons and two daughters. The eldest son, Sir Arthur John Evans, F.R.S., is the well-known archæologist and explorer of Crete. One daughter became the wife of Mr. Charles James Longman, the publisher. By his second marriage in 1859 to his cousin Frances, daughter of Joseph Phelps of Madeira, he had no children. He married, thirdly, in 1892, a lady of kindred archæological tastes, Maria Millington, daughter of Charles Crawford Lathbury of Wimbledon. Lady Evans and the one child of the marriage, a daughter Joan, survive him.

Evans left his principal collections of implements, coins, rings, and ornaments to his son, Sir Arthur Evans, who has presented certain portions of them to the Ashmolean Museum, Oxford. His collection of Lambeth pottery was sold at Christie's on 14 Feb. 1911. Many of the later varieties of his collection of Roman gold coins were sold by auction at the Hotel Drouot, Paris, on 26 and 27 May 1909.

An admirable portrait was painted by A. S. Cope, R.A., for the Royal Society (there are photogravure reproductions issued by the Fine Art Society, New Bond Street, London). A second portrait by the Hon.

John Collier was presented by subscription in 1905 in recognition of his public work in Hertfordshire (a replica is in the court house, St. Albans). A portrait-bust is on the obverse of the jubilee medal of the Numismatic Society of London (1887), engraved by Pinches from a drawing, and a large bronze cast medallion was executed by Frank Bowcher in 1899 for the Numismatic Society of London to celebrate Evans's fifty years' membership of the society (there is a reduced photograph of it in the 'Numismatic Chronicle,' 1899, pl. xi.). A good photograph is in the 'Geological Magazine,' 1908, plate i.

[Memoir by Sir Archibald Geikie in Proc. Roy. Soc. 1908, lxxx. B., p. l.; Geological Mag. 1908, pp. 1–10; Numismatic Chronicle, 1908, Proceedings, pp. 25–31 (B. V. Head); L. Forrer in Gazette numismatique française, 1909, with bibliography; Boule in L'Anthropologie, 1908; Proc. of Soc. of Antiquaries, 1909, p. 469 (C. H. Read); The Times, 1 June 1908; Athenæum, 6 June 1908; Men and Women of the Time, 1899; Burke's Landed Gentry, 1906; Who's Who, 1908; Rivista italiana di numismatica, pp. 459, 460; Cussans's Herts, iii. 93, 142; Pike's Herts in the Twentieth Century, 1908, pp. 19, 89; Victoria County Hist. Herts, geneal., 1907, p. 9; information kindly given by Lady Evans and Sir Arthur Evans; personal knowledge.] W. W.

EVANS, SEBASTIAN (1830–1909), journalist, born on 2 March 1830 at Market Bosworth, Leicestershire, was youngest son of Arthur Benoni Evans [q. v.] by his wife Anne, daughter of Captain Thomas Dickinson, R.N. Sir John Evans [q. v. Suppl. II] was his elder brother. Sebastian, after early education under his father at the free grammar school of Market Bosworth, won in 1849 a scholarship at Emmanuel College, Cambridge, graduating B.A. in 1853 and proceeding M.A. in 1856. In youth he showed promise as an artist and an aptitude for Latin and English verse. While an undergraduate he published a volume of sonnets on the death of the duke of Wellington (1852). On leaving the university he became a student at Lincoln's Inn on 29 Jan. 1855, but was shortly appointed secretary of the Indian Reform Association, and in that capacity was the first man in England to receive news of the outbreak of the mutiny. In 1857 he resigned the secretaryship and turned his talent for drawing to practical use by becoming manager of the art department of the glassworks of Messrs. Chance Bros. & Co., at Oldbury, near Birmingham. This position he occupied for ten years, and designed many windows, including one illustrating the Robin Hood legend for the International Exhibition in 1862.

Meanwhile he took a growing interest in politics as an ardent conservative. His work for the Indian Reform Association had brought him into touch with John Bright, and at Birmingham he made the acquaintance of Mr. Joseph Chamberlain, with whom, in spite of their political differences, he contracted a lasting friendship. In 1867 Evans left the glassworks to become editor of the 'Birmingham Daily Gazette,' a conservative organ. In 1868 he unsuccessfully contested Birmingham in the conservative interest and also helped to form the National Union of Conservative Associations. In the same year he took the degree of LL.D. at Cambridge. In 1870 he left the 'Gazette' to pursue an early design of a legal career. On 17 Nov. 1873 he was called to the bar at Lincoln's Inn, and joined the Oxford circuit. He quickly acquired a fair practice, but found time for both political and journalistic activity, writing leading articles for the 'Observer' and contributing articles and stories, chiefly of a mystical tenour, to 'Macmillan's' and 'Longman's' magazines. In 1878 he shared in the foundation of the 'People,' a weekly conservative newspaper, and edited it for the first three years of its career. When on the eve of the general election of 1886 the editor of the 'Birmingham Daily Gazette' died suddenly, Evans hurriedly resumed the editorship over the critical period.

Evans continued to cultivate art and poetry amid all competing interests. He exhibited at the Royal Academy and elsewhere pictures in oil, water-colour, and black and white, and practised wood-carving, engraving, and book-binding. As a poet, he combined a feeling for mediæval beauty with a humour which distinguishes him from the Pre-Raphaelites. He was an excellent translator in verse and prose from mediæval French, Latin, Greek, and Italian. In 1898 he published 'The High History of the Holy Graal' (new edit. 1910 in 'Everyman's Library'), a masterly version of the old French romance of 'Perceval le Gallois,' as well as an original study of the legend entitled 'In Quest of the Holy Graal.' Evans's versatility and social charm brought him a varied acquaintance. He knew Thackeray, Darwin, Huxley, Newman, Matthew Arnold, and Ruskin, and at a later period was the intimate friend of Burne-Jones, who shared his interests in mediæval legend and illustrated his history of the Graal. Towards the end of his life he retired to Abbot's Barton, Canterbury, where he died on 19 Dec. 1909.

In 1857 he married Elizabeth, youngest daughter of Francis Bennett Goldney, one of the founders of the London Joint Stock Bank. Of two sons, Sebastian and Francis, the latter assumed the name of Francis Bennett Goldney, and was returned to parliament as independent unionist member for Canterbury in December 1909, after serving several times as mayor of the town. He owns two portraits of Evans, one, a three-quarter length, in oils, painted by Roden about 1870; the other a silver point drawing by Delamotte about 1856.

Evans's published collections of poems, apart from those already mentioned, were: 1. 'Brother Fabian's Manuscripts and other Poems,' 1865. 2. 'Songs and Etchings,' 1871. 3. 'In the Studio, a Decade of Poems,' 1875. He also translated St. Francis of Assisi's 'Mirror of Perfection' (1898) and 'Geoffrey of Monmouth's History' (1904), and with his son, Mr. Goldney, 'Lady Chillingham's House Party,' adapted from Pailleron's 'Le Monde où l'on s'ennuie' (1901). In 1881 he re-edited his father's 'Leicestershire Words' for the English Dialect Society.

[The Times, 20 Dec. 1909; Miles's Poets and Poetry of the Century; Men and Women of the Time; Graduati Cantabrigienses; Foster's Men at the Bar; Lady Burne-Jones's Memorials of Edward Burne-Jones, 1904; Brit. Mus. Cat.] F. L. B.

EVERARD, HARRY STIRLING CRAWFURD (1848–1909), writer on golf, born at Claybrook House, Leicestershire, on 30 Jan. 1848, was only son of Henry Everard of Gosberton, Spalding, by his wife Helen Maitland, daughter by his second wife of Captain William Stirling of Milton and Castlemilk, Lanarkshire. After education at Eton (1862–6) he matriculated from Christ Church, Oxford, on 23 May 1866, graduating B.A. in 1871. He became a student at the Inner Temple in 1867, but was not called to the bar. He settled at St. Andrews, to which he was attracted by its renowned facilities for golf. He enjoyed the game keenly, and achieved success at it, winning in the competitions of the Royal and Ancient Golf Club the silver medal (second prize at the spring meeting) in 1889, the Calcutta cup in 1890, and the silver cross (the first prize) in 1891. Everard was also a good cricketer, tennis player, pedestrian and swimmer.

Everard became one of the best-known writers on golf, both from the practical and from the literary side, contributing to the 'Scots Observer' and to the 'National Observer' (under Henley's editorship), and to the 'Spectator,' 'Saturday Review,' and many golfing periodicals. He published 'Golf in Theory and Practice' (1897; 3rd edit. 1898); 'The History of the Royal and Ancient Club of St. Andrews' (1907), and he wrote chapter xiii. on 'Some Celebrated Golfers' for the Badminton Library manual (1890; 5th edit. 1895).

Everard died, after a short illness, on 15 May 1909 at St. Andrews. He married in 1880 Annie, eldest surviving daughter of Colonel Robert Tod Boothby of St. Andrews (*d.* 1907), and had issue two sons and two daughters.

[The Times, 17 and 20 May 1909; personal knowledge; private information.] W. W. T.

EVERETT, JOSEPH DAVID (1831–1904), professor of natural philosophy in Queen's College, Belfast, born at Rushmere, near Ipswich, Suffolk, on 11 Sept. 1831, was the eldest son of Joseph David Everett, a landowner and farmer of Rushmere, by his wife Elizabeth, eldest daughter of John Garwood, corn merchant of London. A younger brother, Robert Lacey Everett (*b.* 1833), was M.P. successively for the Woodbridge division (1885–6, 1892–5) and for south-east Suffolk (1906–10). Everett was educated at Mr. Buck's private school at Ipswich. On leaving he attended higher classes in mathematics at the Ipswich Mechanics' Institution under Stephen Jackson, proprietor of the 'Ipswich Journal,' who advised him to follow a scholastic life. After a short experience of teaching at a private school at Newmarket, where he had Charles Haddon Spurgeon [q. v.] as a colleague, he became, in 1850, mathematical master at Mr. Thorowgood's school at Totteridge, near Barnet. In 1854 he gained one of Dr. Williams's bursaries and became a student at Glasgow College (now University). After a most successful course he graduated B.A. in 1856 with honourable distinction in classics and mental philosophy, and M.A. in 1857 with highest distinction in physical science. He had thought of entering the ministry, but gave up the idea, and after acting for a short time as secretary of the Meteorological Society of Edinburgh, he became professor of mathematics in King's College, Windsor, Nova Scotia, in 1859. He returned to Glasgow in 1864 as assistant to Dr. Hugh Blackburn, professor of mathematics in the university (1849–79), and worked for a time in Lord Kelvin's laboratory. From 1867 till his retirement in 1897 he was professor of natural philosophy in

Queen's College, Belfast, serving on the council from 1875 to 1881.

Everett was elected F.R.S. Edinburgh in 1863; F.R.S. London in 1879; and was a vice-president of the Physical Society of London (1900–4). He acted as secretary and subsequently as chairman of the committee of the British Association for investigating the rate of increase of underground temperature downwards (1867–1904), and as secretary of the committee for the selection and nomenclature of dynamical units (1871–3). He was a fellow of the Royal University of Ireland.

Everett wrote many memoirs on dynamics, light, and sound (see *Royal Soc. Cat. of Scientific Papers*), which deal to a comparatively small extent with his own experimental work. He regarded it as his special mission to expound clearly the results of others. In his books and his lectures he spared no pains to make his statements precise and compact and to bring them up to date. His separate publications were: 1. 'Units and Physical Constants' (now 'The C.G.S. System of Units'), 1875; 3rd edit. 1886; Polish transl., Warsaw, 1885. 2. 'An Elementary Text Book of Physics,' 1877; 2nd edit. 1883. 3. 'Vibratory Motion and Sound,' 1882. 4. 'Outlines of Natural Philosophy,' 1887. He also translated Deschanel's 'Physics' (1870; 6th edit. 1882) and, in conjunction with his daughter Alice, Hovestadt's 'Jena Glass and its Scientific and Industrial Applications' (1902). The former work was largely rewritten by Everett.

He had many interests outside his professional work. He invented a system of shorthand which he published (1877 and 1883), was one of the pioneers of cycling, and invented a spring hub attachment for the spokes of bicycle wheels.

He moved from Belfast to London in 1898 and eventually settled at Ealing, regularly attending the meetings of scientific societies in London. He died from heart failure at Ealing on 9 Aug. 1904, and was interred at Ipswich. He married on 3 Sept. 1862 Jessie, daughter of Alexander Fraser, afterwards of Ewing Place Congregational Church, Glasgow (of the Frasers of Kirkhill, Inverness), and left three daughters and three sons, of whom the second, Wilfred, is professor of engineering in the Government Engineering College, Sibpur, Calcutta. A portrait by W. R. Symonds, presented in 1898, hangs in the great hall of Queen's College, Belfast.

[The Times, 12 Aug. 1904; Proc. Roy. Soc. London, lxxv. 377; Proc. Physical Soc. London, 1905, xix. 11; private information from Miss A. Everett, M.A., A. F. Everett, B.A., R. L. Everett, J.P., Prof. G. Carey Foster, Prof. W. B. Morton, and W. I. Addison, Registrar of the University of Glasgow.]

C. H. L.

EVERETT, Sir WILLIAM (1844–1908), colonel, born on 20 April 1844, was son of Thomas Ellis Everett, rector of Theddingworth, Leicestershire, by Gertrude Louisa, daughter of Joshua Walker, formerly M.P. for Aldborough. Spending a term in 1856 at Marlborough, he entered Sandhurst, and was commissioned as ensign in the 26th foot on 28 June 1864. On 23 August he was transferred to the 33rd foot, and was promoted lieutenant on 11 Jan. 1867. After the return of the regiment to England from the Abyssinian expedition, in which he took no part, he was made adjutant (25 Nov. 1868). He was an excellent draughtsman, and on 1 Feb. 1870 he was appointed instructor in military drawing at the Royal Military Academy, Woolwich. He remained there seven years, becoming captain in his regiment on 8 Sept. 1874. He passed through the Staff College in 1878.

In 1879 he was employed on the Turco-Bulgarian boundary commission under Sir Edward Bruce Hamley [q. v. Suppl. I], and on 12 July he was appointed vice-consul at Erzeroum, to see to the execution of the provisions of the Anglo-Turkish convention. In July 1880 he served on a commission to define the Turco-Persian frontier. During the famine of 1881 he was active at Erzeroum in the administration of Lady Strangford's relief fund. From 11 Sept. 1882 till the end of 1887 he was consul in Kurdistan. An attempt on his life was made on 13 April 1884 by a Roman catholic Armenian on account of his active vigilance, and he was severely injured in the hand and foot. He received 1000*l*. as compensation, and was made C.M.G. on 6 Aug. 1886.

From 11 Jan. 1888 till September 1892 Everett was professor of military topography at the Staff College. He left his regiment, in which he had become major on 1 July 1881, for an unattached lieut.-colonelcy. He was employed in the intelligence division of the war office as assistant adjutant-general, with the rank of colonel, from 7 June 1893 to 12 March 1901. He was technical adviser of the commission for the delimitation of the Sierra Leone frontier in 1895, and a commissioner for delimiting the Niger frontier in 1896–8, and the Togoland frontier in 1900. He was remarkable for tact, as well as for 'unfailing industry and a special skill in unravelling the complicated tangle of frontier questions.' Becoming K.C.M.G. on 27 June 1898, he was in charge of the intelligence division during 1899 (a time of exceptional stress), while Sir John Ardagh was absent at the Hague conference.

Placed on the retired list on 20 April 1901, Everett died at Interlaken of heart failure on 9 Aug. 1908, and was buried at Dunsfold, near Godalming. He had married in 1870 Marie Georgina, daughter of Pietro Quartano di Calogeras, doctor-at-law, Corfu. His wife survived him without issue.

[The Times, 12 August 1908; Lady Malmesbury, Life of Sir John Ardagh, 1909; private information.] E. M. L.

EWART, CHARLES BRISBANE (1827–1903), lieutenant-general and colonel commandant R.E., born at Coventry on 15 Feb. 1827, was fourth son of Lieutenant-general John Frederick Ewart. His elder brother, Sir John Alexander, is noticed below. After passing with credit through the Royal Military Academy at Woolwich Ewart received a commission as second-lieutenant in the royal engineers on 18 June 1845. Promoted lieutenant on 1 April 1846, he served at Woolwich, in Ireland, at Gibraltar, and at Chatham. In January 1854 he accompanied General Sir John Fox Burgoyne [q. v.] on a special mission to Turkey to examine the defences of the Dardanelles and the expediency of holding the straits as a base of operations in the event of a war with Russia. After surveying the ground at Gallipoli Ewart went to Varna, and acted as brigade major, while assisting in the preparations for the arrival of the allied army. He landed with it in the Crimea in September, was present at the affairs of Bulganak and McKenzie's Farm, and at the battles of the Alma, Balaklava, and Inkerman, was promoted captain on 13 December 1854, and was acting adjutant throughout the siege of Sevastopol until its fall in September 1855. Mentioned in despatches, he was promoted brevet-major on 2 Nov. 1855, and acted as major of brigade to the royal engineers, until the troops left the Crimea in June 1856. Returning from the Crimea, Ewart did duty at Shorncliffe and Dover, and from 1860 to 1865 was assistant quartermaster-general at the Horse Guards. In the early part of 1866 he was on special service in France and Algeria, and was commanding royal engineer of the London district for another five years. Created a C.B., military division, he was (1869–72) in the barrack branch of the inspector-general of fortifications' office, of which he was head as deputy director of works for barracks (1872–7). During these years his promotion had been steady: brevet lieut.-colonel on 3 March 1866; regimental lieut.-colonel on 4 March 1868; brevet colonel on 4 March 1873; and regimental colonel on 21 Oct. 1877.

As colonel on the staff and commanding royal engineer of the south-eastern district, he was at Dover (1877–9), and held a similar post at Gibraltar from 1879 to 1882. From Gibraltar he was sent in March 1881 to be commanding royal engineer of the Natal field force in the Boer war, but by the time of his arrival peace had been made. On returning from Gibraltar in Oct. 1882, he remained unemployed, living at Folkestone. In April 1883 he was appointed extra aide-de-camp to George, second duke of Cambridge [q. v. Suppl. II], and in April 1884 a member of the ordnance committee.

Promoted major-general on 27 Jan. 1885, Ewart was sent with the Soudan expedition under Sir Gerald Graham [q. v. Suppl. I] as a brigadier-general in command of the base and line of communications, including the general supervision of the railway construction from Suakin to Berber. For his services he was mentioned in despatches. After his return and two years' unemployment Ewart was lieutenant-governor of Jersey from Nov. 1887 until Nov. 1892. He was promoted lieutenant-general on 20 July 1888, retired from the service on 15 Feb. 1894, and was made a colonel-commandant of his corps on 30 March 1902. He died at Folkestone on 8 Aug. 1903, and was buried there.

Ewart married in 1860 his second cousin, Emily Jane, daughter of Peter Ewart, rector of Kirklington, Yorkshire, and sister of Major-general Sir Henry Peter Ewart, K.C.B., crown equerry; by her he had three sons and two daughters.

[War Office Records; Royal Engineers Records; Memoir in Royal Engineers Journal, 1903; Porter, History of the Corps of Royal Engineers, 1889, 2 vols.; The Times, 10 Aug. 1903.] R. H. V.

EWART, Sir JOHN ALEXANDER (1821–1904), general and colonel Gordon highlanders, born at Sholapore, Bombay, 11 June 1821, was third son in a family of four sons and a daughter of Lieutenant-general John Frederick Ewart, C.B., colonel of the 67th foot (*d.* 1854), by Lavinia, daughter of Sir Charles Brisbane [q. v.]. His younger brother, Charles Brisbane, is noticed above. Joseph Ewart [q. v.] was his grandfather. Educated at the Royal Military College, Sandhurst (1835–8), where he obtained special distinction, he entered the army on 27 July 1838 as ensign in the 35th (royal Sussex) regiment, and was promoted lieutenant on 15 April 1842. He was a good cricketer and captain of the regimental eleven. After doing garrison duty at Cape Town and Mauritius, Ewart exchanged into the 93rd Sutherland highlanders in 1846, and became captain on 12 May 1848, brevet-major on 12 May 1854, major on 29 Dec. 1854, and brevet lieutenant-colonel on 2 Nov. 1855.

Ewart served with his regiment throughout the Crimean war from the first landing at Gallipoli in April 1854 until the final evacuation of the Crimea in June 1856. He was present at the battle of the Alma (20 Sept.) and at the occupation of Balaklava (25 Sept.), being appointed a deputy - assistant - quartermaster - general next day. At the battle of Balaklava (25 Oct.) he commanded the sixth company of 'the thin red line.' On 5 Nov. at Inkerman he was the first to apprise Lord Raglan of the Russian advance (Kinglake, *Invasion of the Crimea*, vi. 36–38). He took part in the early siege operations before Sevastopol, but in May accompanied the expedition to the Sea of Azoff, and was at the capture of Kertch and Yenikale. He returned to the besieging force before Sevastopol and engaged in the assaults on 18 June and 5 Sept. He received the Piedmontese medal for valour, the British medal with five clasps, and French and Turkish decorations.

Ewart served with his regiment in India during the mutiny. He took part in an engagement near Bunnee, holding for a short time a command consisting of three squadrons of cavalry, five guns, and 500 infantry, and being specially named in despatches. On 16 Nov. 1857 Ewart commanded the leading party of stormers at the assault of the Secunderabagh; he personally captured a colour, and received two sabre wounds in an encounter with the two native officers who were defending it (G. B. Malleson, *History of the Indian Mutiny*, ii. 186). He was recommended for the Victoria Cross without result. When in action against the rebel Gwalior contingent at Cawnpore on 1 Dec. 1857 he was again very severely wounded by a cannon shot, his left arm being carried away. He received the mutiny medal with clasp, and was made C.B. on 24 March 1858. Promoted lieutenant-colonel on 16 April 1858, colonel on 26 April 1859, and aide-de-camp to Queen Victoria the same year, he commanded from 1859 to 1864 the 78th Ross-shire Buffs. Major-general on 6 March 1869, and lieutenant-general on 1 Oct. 1877, he commanded from 1877 to 1879 the Allahabad division of the Indian army. He was made a general on 13 Jan. 1884. In 1883–4 he was honorary colonel of 1st battalion duke of Edinburgh's regiment, from 1884 to 1895 of 92nd Gordon highlanders, and from 1895 to 1904 of the Argyll and Sutherland highlanders. In 1887 he was created K.C.B., and received the reward for distinguished service. He was promoted G.C.B. two days before his death, which took place on 18 June 1904 at his residence, Craigcleuch, Langholm, Dumfriesshire. He was buried in the cemetery of Stirling Castle. He was J.P. for Dumfriesshire and Staffordshire.

He married 16 Nov. 1858 Frances (*d.* 1873), daughter of Spencer Stone of Callingwood Hall, Stafford. He had issue four sons and a daughter. Three of his sons became officers in the army.

He published: 1. 'A Few Remarks about the British Army.' 2. 'The Story of a Soldier's Life,' 2 vols. 1881.

[Ewart's Story of a Soldier's Life, 2 vols. 1881; The Thin Red Line, regimental paper of the Sutherland Highlanders, June, July (portrait), 1904; P. Groves, History of the 93rd Sutherland Highlanders, 1895; Indian Mutiny, 1857–8, Selections from State Papers in the Military Department, ed. G. W. Forrest, 1902, ii. 340 seq.; Burke's Landed Gentry; Hart's and Official Army Lists.]

H. M. V.

EYRE, EDWARD JOHN (1815–1901), governor of Jamaica, born at Hornsea, Yorkshire, on 5 Aug. 1815, was third son of Anthony William Eyre (of the Eyres of Hope, Derbyshire), who was incumbent of Hornsea and Long Riston, East Riding of Yorkshire. His mother was Sarah Mapleton, daughter of the doctor of Bath to whom De Quincey makes friendly reference in his autobiography.

Edward was educated at the Louth and Sedbergh grammar schools. Intended for the army, he chafed against the delay in gaining a commission. At seventeen he took 150*l.*, which had been deposited as purchase money, and obtaining an additional 250*l.* emigrated to Australia. He arrived in 1833, and engaged in sheep farming, at first in New South Wales and then in South Australia on the Lower Murray river.

Becoming magistrate and protector of aborigines, he in 1836 began a series of adventurous journeys through the unknown sand deserts of the interior. He was the first of the 'overlanders,' that is he first found a way by which to drive live-stock overland from New South Wales to the new settlement at Adelaide. From this original and more practical purpose he was diverted by the absorbing attraction of exploring vast unknown regions. The most memorable of his journeys was that on which he, with white and native companions, started from Adelaide on 20 June 1840, and, all but one of his companions dropping off by the way, forced his own way, with a dogged tenacity of purpose and readiness of resource probably unsurpassed in history, round the head of the Great Australian Bight, through a region so utterly desolate and torrid as almost to preclude the passage of man, and with but a single companion, a native, reached King George's Sound on 13 July 1841. He proved himself a great explorer. In 1843 he received the founder's medal from the Royal Geographical Society. He described his journeys in 'Expeditions into Central Australia and Overland from Adelaide to King George's Sound, 1840–1' (2 vols. 1845), which were supplemented by papers on 'Expeditions Overland, Adelaide to Perth' in the 'Journal Roy. Geog. Soc.' (xiii. 161), 'Lower Course of the Darling' (xv. 327), and 'Considerations against an Interior Sea in Australia' (xvi. 200). Perhaps the most noticeable thing in Eyre's career in Australia was his exceptional kindliness, combined with firmness, toward the aborigines.

Eyre revisited England in 1845, and in 1846, chiefly because of his success in handling natives, was appointed lieutenant-governor of New Zealand, Sir George Grey being governor. He held the office till 1853. From 1854 to 1860 he was governor of St. Vincent, and in 1860–1 he acted temporarily as governor of the Leeward Islands. In 1861 he went to Jamaica to act as captain-general and commander-in-chief during the absence on other duty of Sir Charles Darling [q. v.]. In 1864 Darling definitely relinquished the appointment, and Eyre was confirmed as governor of Jamaica. There his experiences gave him a terrible notoriety.

The negro peasantry of Jamaica, which had not long been emancipated from slavery, outnumbered the white population by something like twenty-seven to one. The negroes were mostly quite uneducated and were seething with discontent, stirred by agitators, mostly of their own race, against the few European residents. The American war, moreover, had raised the price of the necessaries of life; and the example set by the neighbouring negroes in Haiti and St. Domingo, in setting up 'black republics' had made the situation with which Eyre had to deal very difficult.

On 7 Oct. 1865, in the planting district of Morant Bay in the county of Surrey, about five-and-twenty miles east of the capital, Kingston, some negroes successfully resisted the lawful capture of a negro criminal. On the 9th the police were forcibly prevented from arresting the chief rioters. On the 11th the 'Morant Bay rebellion' broke out, the court house of the district was burned, and at least twenty Europeans were killed and others wounded. The riot, which is believed to have been premeditated and organised, spread rapidly, and between 13 and 15 Oct. many atrocities were committed on the whites in outlying districts. Eyre, always prompt and self-reliant, called to his assistance all available naval and military officers, militia, European civilians, loyal negroes, and maroons. On 13 Oct., relying on a local statute, he held a council of war and proclaimed martial law throughout the county of Surrey except in Kingston. During the next eleven days he broke the back of the riot. Meanwhile George William Gordon, a coloured member of the legislature, who was long notorious for violence of speech and was believed to have instigated the rebellion, had been forcibly taken from Kingston (where martial law was not in force) into the zone of martial law at Morant Bay. There on 21 Oct. Gordon was tried by a court-martial presided over by Lieutenant Herbert Charles Alexander Brand, R.N. [q. v. Suppl. II], and being convicted he was sentenced to death. The next day being Sunday, the execution was deferred till Monday. Eyre, who was away at Kingston, was informed of the facts; and he—though not required to do so in the case of a sentence by court-martial—confirmed the sentence. Gordon was hanged on the morning of the 23rd. He had friends, and apart from the question of his guilt or innocence of a capital offence, these at once denounced the legality of Eyre's act in allowing the man to be taken within the zone of martial law for trial and punishment. Till the expiration of martial law, on 13 November, 608 persons were killed or executed, 34 were wounded, 600, including some women, were flogged, and a thousand dwellings, mostly flimsy leaf-built huts, were destroyed. Afterwards other culprits were tried and punished under the ordinary law of the colony—in some cases even by death.

The vast majority of the Europeans

resident in Jamaica were warm in their gratitude to Eyre. On 17 Jan. 1866 the legislative assembly voluntarily dissolved itself and abrogated the old popular constitution, leaving it to the home government to administer the island as a crown colony. Meanwhile the news of the riot and its manner of suppression reached England, and at first evoked approval of Eyre's prompt action; but presently passionate clamour arose from a large party, by which Eyre was held up to execration as a monster of cruelty. In turn another section of the public, with almost equal violence, made Eyre their idol. Lord Russell, the prime minister, surveyed the conflict with judicial impartiality. In December a royal commission of inquiry, consisting of Sir Henry Storks [q. v.], governor of Malta, Russell Gurney [q. v.], and John B. Maule, then recorder of Leeds, was sent to Jamaica, and Eyre was temporarily suspended from the governorship in favour of Storks. The commission arrived in Kingston on 6 Jan. 1866 and sat from 23 Jan. to 21 March. In February 1600*l.* was subscribed in Jamaica for Eyre's defence. On 9 April 1866 the commission reported that Eyre had acted with commendable promptitude and had stopped a riot which might have attained very serious dimensions, but that he had subsequently acted with unnecessary rigour, that Gordon's alleged offence of high treason was not proved, that there was no evidence of any organised conspiracy, and that many of the court-martials were improperly conducted. The House of Commons unanimously endorsed the findings of the commission. Lord Russell's government thanked Eyre for his promptitude, blamed him for excess in subsequent reprisal, and recalled him from his government. The accession of Lord Derby to power in June made no difference to Eyre. Sir J. P. Grant was gazetted in his place on 16 July.

Eyre arrived at Southampton on 12 Aug. 1866, and was publicly entertained there by his supporters, including Lord Cardigan and Charles Kingsley, on the 21st (cf. TREVELYAN'S *Ladies in Parliament*, 1869). But for the next three years his opponents, whom Carlyle styled a 'knot of nigger philanthropists,' maintained unceasing warfare upon him (cf. CARLYLE, *Shooting Niagara! and After*, *Crit. and Miscel. Essays*, London, 1899, v. 12). The 'Jamaica committee,' with John Stuart Mill as chairman, supported by Huxley, Thomas Hughes, Herbert Spencer, and Goldwin Smith, resolved on the prosecution for murder of Eyre and his chief associates in Jamaica (27 July 1866); and in September an equally influential committee, with Carlyle as chairman and Ruskin and Tennyson among its subscribers, undertook his defence. Eyre's effigy was burnt at a working-class meeting on Clerkenwell Green, and liberals and radicals lost no opportunity of denunciation. On 8 Feb. 1867 Brand, who had presided over the court-martial on Gordon, and Colonel (Sir) Alexander Abercromby Nelson [q. v.], who had confirmed the capital sentence, were committed for trial at Bow Street on a charge of murder. Eyre had retired to Adderley Hall, Shropshire, and was brought before the local bench, who dismissed the case on 27 March. He was defended by Hardinge Giffard, afterwards earl of Halsbury. In April Lord Chief Justice Cockburn elaborately went over the whole ground when charging the grand jury at the Old Bailey in regard to the defendants Nelson and Brand. He questioned Eyre's right to proclaim martial law and advised the grand jury to find a true bill. But this the jury declined to do and the prisoners were set free. Next year (2 June 1868) the proceedings against Eyre were revived. Under a mandamus of the queen's bench, which had jurisdiction under the Colonial Governors Act, he was charged at Bow Street with misdemeanour and was committed for trial. The grand jury at the Old Bailey were now charged by Mr. Justice Blackburn, who expressed dissent from Cockburn's view, and the bill against Eyre was thrown out. Finally, at the instigation of the Jamaica committee, a negro named Phillips brought a civil action for damages for false imprisonment against Eyre (29 Jan. 1869). Eyre pleaded the act of indemnity passed by the local legislature and obtained a verdict. Mill, in his 'Autobiography' (pp. 298–9), justified the part which he took in the attack on Eyre, but the hostile agitation was so conducted as to create an impression of vindictiveness. Carlyle's conclusion 'that Eyre was a just, humane, and valiant man, faithful to his trusts everywhere, and with no ordinary faculty for executing them' was finally accepted. On 8 July 1872, after discussion in the House of Commons, the government ordered payment of Eyre's legal expenses from the public funds. In his speech at Bow Street Eyre made a very dignified protest, and after the bill had been thrown out by the grand jury he published a defence in a letter to the newspapers. It is, however, impossible to understand the quiescent attitude of Eyre throughout the tragic crisis, unless his very remarkable habit of self-reliance, as shown in the story of his Australian journeys, is taken into account. Although he was not offered further public employment he received in 1874, from Disraeli's government, a pension as a retired colonial governor. From Adderley Hall, Shropshire, Eyre removed to Walreddon Manor, near Tavistock, where he continued to live in seclusion. There he died on 30 Nov. 1901, and there he was buried. He married in 1850 Adelaide Fanny Ormond, daughter of a captain R.N., and had four sons, all in the government service, and a daughter. His widow was awarded in 1903 a civil list pension of 100*l*. A characteristic portrait of Eyre is reproduced as a frontispiece to Hume's 'Life' (see below). Another, of much later date, hangs in the council room of the Royal Geographical Society.

[The Times, 1 Dec. 1901; Men and Women of the Time; Eyre's Expedition into Central Australia, 1845; Heaton's Australian Dictionary of Dates; Frank Cundall's Political and Social Disturbances in the West Indies, published for the 'Jamaica Institute,' 1896. For Eyre's part in the Jamaica riot and the subsequent controversy, see the Parliamentary Papers on Affairs of Jamaica, February 1866, Disturbances in Jamaica, 3 pts., February 1866, Report of the R. Commission, 2 pts., 1866, and Copy of Despatch from Rt. Hon. Edward Cardwell to Sir H. K. Storks, 1866. Among publications on behalf of the Jamaica committee (Eyre's opponents) the following are the most noteworthy: Facts and Documents relating to the Alleged Rebellion in Jamaica, and the Measures of Repression, including Notes of the Trial of Mr. Gordon, 1866; The Blue Books, n.d.; Statements of the Committee and other Documents, n.d.; A Quarter of a Century of Jamaica Legislation, n.d.; Martial Law, by Frederic Harrison, 1867; Illustrations of Martial Law in Jamaica, by John Gorrie, 1867; and Report of Proceedings at Bow Street Police Court, on the Committal of Col. Nelson and Lieut. Brand for the Murder of Mr. G. W. Gordon, 1867. More favourable to Eyre are Dr. Underhill's Testimony on the Wrongs of the Negro in Jamaica examined, in a Letter to the Editor of the Times, by A. L[indo], Falmouth, Jamaica, 1866; Case of George William Gordon, by Baptist Noel, 1866; Narrative of the Rebellious Outbreak in Jamaica, by Arthur Warmington, London, 1866; Addresses to H.E. Edward John Eyre, 1865, 1866 (Kingston, Jamaica, 1866); Charge of the Lord Chief Justice of England to the Grand Jury at the Central Criminal Court in the Case of the Queen against Nelson and Brand, revised and corrected by Sir Alexander Cockburn, edited by Frederick Cockburn, London, 1867; Treatise upon Martial Law . . . with illustrations . . . from . . . the Jamaica Case, by W[illiam] F[rancis] F[inlason], London, 1866; the same author's Commentaries on Martial Law, London, 1867, and his valuable History of the Jamaica Case, 2nd edit., London, 1869; and Life of Edward John Eyre, by Hamilton Hume, 1867. For useful summaries of the events, see Herbert Paul's Hist. of Modern England, vol. iii. passim; and an article by J. B. Atlay in Cornhill, Feb. 1902.] E. IM T.

THE

DICTIONARY
of
NATIONAL BIOGRAPHY

Founded in 1882

by

GEORGE SMITH

SUPPLEMENT

January 1901 – December 1911

Edited by Sir Sidney Lee

VOL. II. *FAED–MUYBRIDGE*

Now published by the

OXFORD UNIVERSITY PRESS

PREFATORY NOTE

578 memoirs appear in the present volume which is designed to furnish biographies of noteworthy persons dying between 22 Jan. 1901 and 31 Dec. 1911. The contributors number 180. The callings of those whose careers are recorded here may be broadly catalogued under ten general headings thus:

	NAMES
Administration of Government at home, in India, and the colonies	73
Army and navy	37
Art (including architecture, music, and the stage) . . .	80
Commerce and agriculture	16
Law	29
Literature (including journalism, philology, and philosophy) .	125
Religion	68
Science (including engineering, medicine, surgery, exploration, and economics)	90
Social Reform (including philanthropy and education) . .	39
Sport	21

The names of eighteen women are included on account of services rendered to art, literature, science, and social or educational reform.

Articles bear the initials of their writers save in a very few cases where material has been furnished to the Editor on an ampler scale than the purpose of the undertaking permitted him to use. In such instances the Editor and his staff are solely responsible for the shape which the article has taken, and no signature is appended.

*** In the lists of authors' publications only the date of issue is appended to the titles of works which were published in London in 8vo. In other cases the place of issue and size are specified in addition.

Cross references are given thus: to names in the substantive work [q.v.]; to names in the First Supplement[1] [q.v. Suppl. I]; and to names in the present Supplement[2] [q.v. Suppl. II].

[1] i.e. Vol. XXII (of the thin paper edition). [2] i.e. 1901–1911.

DICTIONARY
OF
NATIONAL BIOGRAPHY

1901–1911

FAED, JOHN (1819–1902), artist, born in 1819 at Barlay Mill, near Gatehouse-on-Fleet, in the Stewartry of Kirkcudbright, was eldest son of James Faed, a farmer, miller, and engineer there, whose cousin, Sir George Faed, K.C.B., fought at Waterloo. The family was notable for artistic talent. Thomas Faed, R.A. [q. v. Suppl. I], was the third son. Another brother was James Faed the engraver. John Faed's native taste for art was encouraged by his father. At the outset self-taught, he developed talent as a miniaturist. Leaving school in 1830, when only eleven, he visited next year many towns and villages of Galloway, painting miniatures for the gentry and middle-classes of the district, who regarded him as a prodigy. In 1839 he attended the art-classes at Edinburgh, and soon established a high reputation there as a miniaturist. For over forty years he practised in this department of art with eminent success. When he had obtained a secure position in Edinburgh, he brought thither his two brothers, Thomas and James, and supported them while they were studying art. From 1841 until near the close of his life Faed exhibited annually at the Royal Scottish Academy. He was chosen an associate of the Royal Scottish Academy in 1847, and an academician in 1851.

Gradually abandoning miniature-painting for figure-subjects, Faed found his themes in the Bible and the works of Shakespeare, Burns, Scott, and the ballad literature of Scotland. Among his characteristic pictures are the following:—'Boyhood' (1850); 'The Cruel Sister' (1851), and 'Burd Helen' (now in Kelvingrove Gallery, Glasgow); 'The Cottar's Saturday Night' (1854); 'Reason and Faith,' and 'The Philosopher' (1855); 'The Household Gods in Danger' (1856); 'Job and his Friends' (1858); and 'Boaz and Ruth' (1860). Other pictures were 'The Raid of Ruthven' (1856), 'Rosalind and Orlando,' 'Olivia and Viola,' and 'Shakespeare and his Friends at the Mermaid Tavern,' a companion picture to Thomas Faed's 'Scott and his Friends at Abbotsford.' Both of these last-named pictures were engraved by James Faed and were widely circulated.

'Annie's Tryst,' suggested by a Scottish ballad, his diploma picture for the Royal Scottish Academy, dated 1863, is in the National Gallery of Scotland, together with his notable picture 'The Poet's Dream' (1883), presented by him to the Royal Scottish Academy a few weeks before his death. 'The Wappinschaw,' an elaborate work, with numerous figures, was shown at the Royal Scottish Academy, and was purchased for 1200*l.* by James Baird of Cambusdoon.

From 1862 to 1880 Faed was in London, exhibiting regularly at the Royal Academy. Among the pictures shown there were 'Catherine Seyton,' 'Old Age,' 'The Stirrup Cup,' 'John Anderson my Jo,' 'Auld Mare Maggie,' 'After the Victory,' 'The Morning before Flodden,' 'Blenheim,' 'In Memoriam,' 'Goldsmith in his Study,' and 'The Old Basket-maker.'

Retiring to Ardmore, Gatehouse, near his birthplace, in 1880, Faed painted several landscapes in the neighbourhood, one being presented by him to Gatehouse town hall. He died at Ardmore on 22 Oct. 1902. Faed married in 1849 Jane, daughter of J. Macdonald, minister of Gigha in the Hebrides; she died in 1898. A painted portrait of Faed is in the possession of Mr. Donald Hall, Woodlyn, Gatehouse-on-Fleet.

Faed's practice as a miniaturist led to more elaboration of details in his pictures than contemporary taste approved. His art is typical of the best Scottish genre style of the late Victorian period.

[W. D. McKay's Scottish School of Painting; Bryan's Dict. of Painters and Engravers, revised ed.; Cat. of Nat. Gal. of Scotland, 42nd ed.; Scotsman, 23 Oct. 1902; Dundee Advertiser, 23 Oct. 1902.] A. H. M.

FAGAN, LOUIS ALEXANDER (1845–1903), etcher and writer on art, born at Naples on 7 Feb. 1845, was second son in a family of three sons and four daughters of George Fagan by his wife Maria, daughter of Louis Carbone, an officer in the Italian army. Robert Fagan [q. v.], diplomatist and artist, was his grandfather. The elder brother, Joseph George, a major-general in the Indian army, died in 1908; the younger, Charles Edward, is secretary of the Natural History Museum, South Kensington. His father, who joined the diplomatic service, was for many years from 1837 attaché to the British legation at Naples, then the capital of the kingdom of the Two Sicilies, and in his official capacity gave assistance to Sir Anthony Panizzi [q. v.] when on a political mission to Naples in 1851; he was made secretary of legation to the Argentine confederation in 1856, and after settling satisfactorily British claims in Buenos Aires in 1858 became consul-general successively to central America in 1860, to Ecuador (1861–5), and minister, chargé d'affaires, and consul-general to Venezuela (1865–9); he died of yellow fever at Caracas in 1869 (FAGAN, *Life of Panizzi*, ii. 101–2).

Fagan's boyhood was spent in Naples, where he early learned Italian and developed an interest in Italian life, literature, and art. In 1860 he was sent in charge of a queen's messenger to a private school at Leytonstone, Essex. In England, he was kindly received by his father's friend, Panizzi (*ibid.* ii. 213). While still a boy, on returning to Naples, he carried letters from Panizzi to the revolutionary leaders in the Two Sicilies, and he imbibed strong revolutionary sympathies. Accompanying his father to America, he served in the British legation at Caracas (1866–7). In 1868 he was secretary to the commission for the settlement of British claims in Venezuela. He returned from South America in June 1869, and in September stayed in Paris with Panizzi's friend, Prosper Mérimée, who wrote of him as 'conservant malgré toutes les nationalités par où il a passé l'air de *l'English boy*' (*ibid.* ii. 274–5).

The same month he obtained on Panizzi's recommendation a post of assistant in the department of prints and drawings in the British Museum, afterwards becoming chief assistant under George William Reid [q. v.] and (Sir) Sidney Colvin successively. He retired through ill-health in 1894. A somewhat hasty temper occasioned friction with his colleagues. Yet during the twenty-five years of official life he helped to increase the usefulness of his department alike for students and the general public.

He published a 'Handbook' to his department (1876) and a series of volumes of service to collectors and connoisseurs, viz. 'Collectors' Marks' (1883); 'One Hundred Examples of Engravings by F. Bartolozzi, with Descriptions and Biographical Notice' (4 pts. 1885); 'A Catalogue Raisonné of the Engraved Works of William Woollett' (1885); 'Descriptive Catalogue of the Engraved Works of W. Faithorne' (1888); and 'History of Engraving in England' (3 pts. fol. 1893). He also gave lantern lectures on the British Museum through the country and published in 1891 'An Easy Walk through the British Museum.'

His Italian training, which made the Italian language as familiar to him as English, focussed his main interests on Italian art and literature. His chief works on these subjects were 'The Works of Correggio at Parma, with Biographical and Descriptive Notes' (folio, 1873); 'Catalogo dei disegni, sculture, quadri e manoscritti di Michelangelo Buonarroti esistenti in Inghilterra' (in vol. ii. of Aurelio Gotti's 'Vita di M. Buonarroti') (1875); 'The Art of Michel' Angelo Buonarroti as illustrated by Various Collections in the British Museum' (1883), and 'Raffaello Sanzio: his Sonnet in the British Museum' (1884). He translated Marco Minghetti's 'The Masters of Raffaello' in 1882.

Fagan was also a practical artist, painting well in water-colours, drawing with refinement, and etching with much delicacy. He exhibited at the Royal Academy a series of etchings in 1872 depicting views and costumes of Naples; an etching of G. F. Watts's portrait of Sir Anthony Panizzi in 1878, and two etchings of Italian subjects in 1881. Some of these appeared in volume form in 'Twelve Etchings' (1873 fol.). He presented a collection of his etchings in various states of execution made between 1871 and 1877 to the British Museum in November 1879; they mainly depict Italian scenes and peasants.

Until Panizzi's death Fagan's relations with him remained close, and Panizzi appointed him his literary executor at his death in 1879. In 1880 Fagan published Panizzi's biography (2 vols.), which went through two editions and received Gladstone's commendation. In the same year Fagan edited and published at Florence 'Lettere ad Antonio Panizzi di uomini illustri e di Amici Italiani 1823–70,' and in 1881 he issued Mérimée's 'Lettres à M. Panizzi, 1850–1870,' of which English and Italian translations appeared the same year.

Fagan, who was a popular lecturer on art, travelled widely. He delivered the Lowell lectures at Boston in 1891, and in the course of long tours personally examined almost every art collection in Europe, America, and Australia. He advised on the arrangement of the art treasures at Victoria Museum, Melbourne.

A popular member of the Reform Club, Fagan published in 1886 'The Reform Club: its Founders and Architect.' After his retirement from the museum he lived for the most part in Italy, and built for himself a residence at Florence, where he died suddenly on 5 Jan. 1903. He married on 8 Nov. 1887 Caroline Frances, daughter of James Purves of Melbourne, Australia, who survived him. A portrait in oils (painted by J. S. Sargent, R.A., in 1894) was presented by his widow in 1911 to the Arts Club, Dover Street, London, W.

[The Times, 8 Jan. 1903; Mag. of Art, 1903, xxvii. 311; Bryan, Dict. of Painters and Engravers, 1903; Pratt, People of the Period, 1897; A. Graves, Royal Acad. Exhibitors, 1905; private information.]

W. B. O.

FALCKE, ISAAC (1819–1909), art collector and benefactor to the British Museum, born in 1819 at Yarmouth, was one of twenty children. His father removed to London soon after his son's birth and commenced business as an art dealer in Oxford Street, where in due course he was joined by his sons, David and Isaac. The business was eventually moved to New Bond Street (No. 92), and there before 1858 Isaac Falcke accumulated a comfortable fortune. Thenceforth he chiefly devoted himself to the study of art and to the collection of art treasures mainly for his own gratification. He soon formed a collection of majolica and lustre ware, which owing to some unfortunate investment he sold to a kinsman, Frederick Davis, a Bond Street dealer, who in his turn sold it to Sir Richard Wallace; it now forms part of the Wallace collection.

Falcke soon recovered his financial stability, and next bestowed his chief attention on bronzes of the fifteenth and sixteenth centuries, which were bought by Dr. Bode of Berlin, where they form the nucleus of the splendid collection in the Kaiser Friedrich Museum.

Falcke was through life deeply interested in Wedgwood china, and he ultimately made a collection of Wedgwood ware which was unique. It was exhibited at the opening of the Crystal Palace in 1856, at South Kensington in 1862, at Leeds in 1868, at Bethnal Green in 1875–6–7, and at Burslem in 1893. This collection Falcke presented to the British Museum on 17 June 1909. It comprises about 500 pieces, and includes one of the few original copies of the famous Barberini or Portland vase and a basalt bust of Mercury by John Flaxman (see *Guide to the English Pottery and Porcelain, British Museum*, 1910, pp. 74–76).

A fourth collection, a small one of Chinese and other porcelain, with some good bronzes, Falcke retained till his death. It was sold at Christie's on 19 April 1910, and fetched the large sum of 37,769*l.* 5*s.* 6*d.*

Falcke died in London on 23 Dec. 1909, and was buried in the Jewish cemetery at Willesden.

He married on 13 May 1847 Mary Ann, daughter of James Reid, of Edinburgh, but left no children.

[Jewish Chronicle, 2 July 1909, 29 Dec. 1909; The Times, 29 Dec. 1909, 20 April 1910; Frederick Litchfield, Pottery and Porcelain, 1905; private information.]

M. E.

FALCONER, LANOE (pseudonym). [See Hawker, Mary Elizabeth, novelist, 1848-1908.]

FALKINER, CÆSAR LITTON (1863–1908), Irish historian, born in Dublin on 20 Sept. 1863, was the second son of Sir Frederick Richard Falkiner [q. v. Suppl. II]. From the Royal School, Armagh, he went to the University of Dublin, graduating

B.A. in 1886 and proceeding M.A. in 1890. At college he wrote an essay on Macaulay as an historian, which showed that he then formed his conception of the study of history. In 1885 he was elected president of the college Philosophical Society. Much interested in politics, he entitled his presidential address 'A New Voyage to Utopia,' a kind of appeal from the new whigs to the old, which was suggested by the passing of the third reform bill. In 1887 he was called to the Irish bar, and in 1888 he began to work actively on behalf of the unionist cause. At the general election of 1892 Falkiner contested, unsuccessfully, South Armagh. He served on the recess committee whose labours resulted in the creation of the Irish department of agriculture. Devoting much thought to the Irish land problem, he mastered the intricacies of the many Irish Land Acts. In 1898 he was appointed temporary assistant land commissioner, and in 1905 this appointment became permanent. For the first half of his work his duty lay in the western counties, for the latter half in the southern counties.

Meanwhile Falkiner was spending much time and energy on the study of Irish history and literature. He diligently collected and sifted original material. His first book, 'Studies in Irish History and Biography, mainly in the Eighteenth Century' (1902), threw new and valuable light on the history of Ireland in the last quarter of the eighteenth century. But subsequently he mainly devoted himself to the seventeenth century. In 1896 he became a member of the Royal Irish Academy, and after serving on the council was elected secretary in 1907. Papers read before the academy formed the first part of his 'Illustrations of Irish History and Topography, mainly of the Seventeenth Century' (1904). His posthumous book, 'Essays relating to Ireland' (1909), dealt with the same century. In 1899 he was appointed, in the room of Sir John Thomas Gilbert [q.v. Suppl. I], inspector under the historical manuscripts commission, with the duty of editing the Ormonde papers. From 1902 to 1908 five volumes of these seventeenth-century papers appeared, containing over 3000 pages—a noble contribution to the raw material of history. The introductions show his power of handling vast masses of evidence.

Falkiner's interests extended to literature, and in this Dictionary and in Chambers's 'Cyclopædia of English Literature' he dealt with men of letters. In 1903 he edited the poems of Charles Wolfe and selections from the poems of Thomas Moore (in the 'Golden Treasury' series), and shortly before his death he designed editions of Moore's complete poetical works and of Dean Swift's letters.

Falkiner died on 5 August 1908, through an accident on the Alps while on a brief holiday at Chamonix. He was buried in the English churchyard in Chamonix.

On 4 Aug. 1892 he married Henrietta Mary, daughter of Sir Thomas Newenham Deane [q. v. Suppl. I], architect, of Dublin. She survived him with two daughters. A memorial tablet was placed by his friends in St. Patrick's Cathedral in 1910.

[Memoir by Prof. E. Dowden, prefixed to Falkiner's Essays relating to Ireland, 1909; Minutes, Royal Irish Acad. 1908–9.

R. H. M.

FALKINER, Sir FREDERICK RICHARD (1831–1908), recorder of Dublin, was third son of Richard Falkiner (1778–1833) of Mount Falcon, county Tipperary, who held a commission in the 4th royal Irish dragoons, by his wife Tempe Litton (1796–1888). Travers Hartley (*b.* 1829), an elder brother, was a well-known engineer; the fine railway line from Zurich to Chur was his design, and he supervised a large portion of the works in connection with the Forth Bridge. The family came to Ireland from Leeds in the time of the Protector, and was long engaged in the woollen manufacture.

Frederick, born at Mount Falcon on 19 Jan. 1831, was educated at Trinity College, Dublin, where he graduated B.A. in 1852. He was called to the Irish bar in the Michaelmas term of that year, and joined the north-east circuit. A man of great industry and natural eloquence, he soon won a foremost place in the ranks of the juniors and held briefs in many important cases. He took silk in 1867, and in 1875 he was appointed law adviser at Dublin Castle, an office since abolished, In the following year he was appointed recorder of Dublin, on the death of Sir Frederick Shaw [q. v.]. He threw himself with energy into the work of the court, and as the 'poor man's judge' he earned a reputation for humanity. During his early years as recorder he was called upon to decide many intricate points in the licensing laws. He took a keen interest in acts of parliament bearing on compensation to workmen for injuries received in the course of their employment, and when Mr. Chamberlain was engaged in drafting his bill on the subject in 1897 he adopted several of Falkiner's suggestions. In 1880 he was elected a bencher of the King's Inns, and in August 1896 he was knighted. He retired from his office on 22 Jan. 1905, when he was made a privy councillor.

Falkiner was one of the most prominent members of the general synod of the Church of Ireland, and in the debates of that body, especially on financial questions, he frequently intervened with much effect. He was chancellor to the bishops of Tuam, Clogher, Kilmore, and Derry and Raphoe. He was also chairman of the board of King's Hospital, better known as the Blue Coat School. Of this school he published in 1906 a history, which is in effect a history of Dublin from the Restoration to the Victorian era. Falkiner pursued literary interests; he wrote on Swift's portraits (SWIFT's *Prose Works*, 1908, vol. xii.), and a collection of his 'Literary Miscellanies' was published posthumously in 1909. He died at Funchal, Madeira, on 22 March 1908.

He married twice: (1) in 1861 Adelaide Matilda (*d.* 1877), third daughter of Thomas Sadleir of Ballinderry Park, county Tipperary; and (2) Robina Hall (*d.* 1895), third daughter of N. B. M'Intire of Cloverhill, county Dublin. By his first wife he had issue three sons, including Cæsar Litton Falkiner [q. v. Suppl. II], and four daughters.

A portrait by Walter Osborne is in the National Gallery, Dublin.

[A biography by Falkiner's daughter May, prefixed to his Literary Miscellanies; The Falkiners of Mount Falcon, by F. B. Falkiner, 1894; Burke's Landed Gentry of Ireland, 1904.]
R. H. M.

FANE, VIOLET (pseudonym). [See CURRIE, MARY MONTGOMERIE, LADY, 1843–1905, author.]

FANSHAWE, SIR EDWARD GENNYS (1814–1906), admiral, born at Stoke, Devonport, on 27 Nov. 1814, was eldest surviving son of General Sir Edward Fanshawe (1785–1858), R.E., and was grandson of Robert Fanshawe, who, after commanding with distinction the Monmouth in Byron's action off Grenada in 1779 and the Namur on 12 April 1782, was commissioner of the navy at Devonport, where he died in 1823. His mother was Frances, daughter of Sir Hew Whitefoord Dalrymple [q. v.], of whose services at Gibraltar and in Portugal in 1808 Fanshawe published (1895) a critical account. He entered the navy in 1828, and was promoted to be lieutenant in 1835. He was then in November appointed to the Hastings, in which, and afterwards in the Magicienne, he served on the home and Lisbon stations. During the greater part of 1838 he was flag lieutenant to Rear-admiral Bouverie, the superintendent of Portsmouth dockyard, and in November was appointed to the Daphne corvette, at first off Lisbon, whence he went out to the Mediterranean, where he took part in the reduction of Acre and the other operations on the coast of Syria in 1840. On 28 Aug. 1841 Fanshawe was promoted to the rank of commander, and in September 1844 went out to the East Indies in command of the Cruiser. His conduct in command of the boats at the reduction of a pirate stronghold in Borneo won for him his promotion to captain on 7 Sept. 1845. In the Russian war of 1854–6 he commanded the Cossack, and afterwards the Hastings in the Baltic and in the Channel; from May 1856 to March 1859 the Centurion in the Mediterranean; from June 1859 to April 1861 the Trafalgar in the Channel, and from 1 April 1861 he was superintendent of Chatham dockyard. In November 1863 he was promoted to be rear-admiral, and in 1865 was nominated a lord of the admiralty. From 1868 to 1870 he was superintendent at Malta dockyard, with his flag in the Hibernia. On 1 April he became vice-admiral, and in 1871 was nominated a C.B. From 1870 to 1873 he was commander-in-chief on the North American station; during 1875–8 was president of the Royal Naval College at Greenwich, in succession to Sir Cooper Key; and during 1878–9 was commander-in-chief at Portsmouth. On 27 Nov. 1879, his sixty-fifth birthday, he was placed on the retired list. In 1881 he was nominated a K.C.B., and at Queen Victoria's jubilee in 1887 was advanced to G.C.B. He continued to take an active interest in naval questions, serving as vice-president or member of council of the Navy Records Society till shortly before his death. He died on the anniversary of Trafalgar, 21 Oct. 1906. He married on 11 May 1843 Jane (*d.* 1900), sister of Edward, Viscount Cardwell [q. v.], and had issue four sons. Admiral of the Fleet Sir Arthur Dalrymple Fanshawe, G.C.B., is his third son.

[Royal Naval List; O'Byrne's Naval Biographical Dict.; Burke's Landed Gentry: The Times, 23 Oct. 1906; Clowes, Royal Navy, vi. and vii. 1901–3; information from Sir Arthur Fanshawe.]
J. K. L.

FARJEON, BENJAMIN LEOPOLD (1838–1903), novelist, second son of Jacob Farjeon (*d.* 1865), a Jewish merchant, by his wife Dinah Levy of Deal, was born in London on 12 May 1838. Educated at a private Jewish school until he was fourteen, he entered the office of the 'Nonconformist' newspaper. At the end of three years, unwillingness to conform to the Jewish faith caused a disagreement with his parents. At seventeen he embarked for Australia, travelling steerage; during the voyage he produced some numbers of a ship newspaper, 'The Ocean Record,' and was transferred by the captain to the saloon. From the goldfields of Victoria he went to New Zealand, on hearing of rich finds there. Soon abandoning the quest of gold, he settled at Dunedin as a journalist. He assisted (Sir) Julius Vogel [q. v. Suppl. I] in the management of the 'Otago Daily Times,' the first daily paper established in the colony, which Vogel founded in 1861. Farjeon became joint editor and part-proprietor; but journalism did not satisfy his ambition, and he wrote a novel, 'Christopher Cogleton,' for the weekly 'Otago Witness,' in which Vogel was also interested, a play 'A Life's Revenge,' and several burlesques in which the leading parts were taken by Julia Matthews, who subsequently won a reputation in London. In 1866 he published at Dunedin a successful tale of Australian life, 'Grif,' and a Christmas story, 'Shadows on the Snows,' which he dedicated to Charles Dickens.

Encouraged by an appreciative letter from Dickens, Farjeon in 1868 returned to England. He travelled by way of New York, where he declined the offer by Gordon Bennett of an engagement on the 'New York Herald'; and settled in chambers in the Adelphi. During the next thirty-five years he devoted himself to novel-writing with unceasing toil. The success of 'Grif,' which was republished in London (1870; new edit. 1885), was maintained in a series of sentimental Christmas stories, 'Blade o' Grass' (1874; new edit. 1899), 'Golden Grain' (1874), 'Bread and Cheese and Kisses' (1874; new edit. 1901), and in many conventional three-volume novels mainly treating of humble life—such as 'Joshua Marvel' (1871), 'London's Heart' (1873), and 'The Duchess of Rosemary Lane' (1876). As a disciple of Dickens, Farjeon won passing popularity, but he turned later to the sensational mystery in which Wilkie Collins excelled, and there his ingenuity was more effective. 'Great Porter Square' (1884) and 'The Mystery of M. Felix' (1890) are favourable examples of his work in this kind. His best novel is the melodramatic 'Devlin the Barber' (1888; new edit. 1901). A play by Farjeon, 'Home, Sweet Home,' was produced by Henry Neville at the Olympic Theatre in 1876, and in 1891 George Conquest put on at the Surrey Theatre Farjeon's dramatised version of his novel 'Grif,' which had already undergone unauthorised dramatisation. In 1873 he sat with Charles Reade and others on a committee formed by John Hollingshead [q. v. Suppl. II] to amend the law so as to prevent the dramatisation of novels without their writers' assent (Hollingshead, *My Lifetime*, ii. 54).

In October 1877 he gave readings in America from one of his early successes 'Blade o' Grass.'

Farjeon died at his house in Belsize Park, Hampstead, on 23 July 1903, and his remains were cremated and interred at Brookwood. He married on 6 June 1877 Margaret, daughter of the American actor, Joseph Jefferson; she survived him with four sons and one daughter. A head in pastels, by Farjeon's nephew, Emanuel Farjeon, a miniature-painter well known in the United States, belongs to the widow.

[The Times, 24 July 1903; Edmund Downey, Twenty Years Ago, 1905, p. 246; Tinsley, Random Recollections of an Old Publisher, 1900, ii. 309; private information.] L. M.

FARMER, EMILY (1826–1905), water-colour painter, was one of the three children of John Biker Farmer, of the East India Company's service, by his wife Frances Ann, daughter of William Churchill Frost. Alexander Farmer, a twin brother of her sister Frances, was an artist; he exhibited at the Royal Academy and elsewhere from 1855 to 1867, and is represented in the Victoria and Albert Museum by two small oil paintings of genre subjects; he died on 28 March 1869. Emily Farmer was born in London on 25 July 1826. She was educated entirely at home, and received instruction in art from her brother. In early life Miss Farmer painted miniatures, but she is best known for her refined and well-drawn groups of children and other genre subjects. She exhibited at the Royal Academy in 1847, and again in 1849 and 1850. In 1854 she was elected a member of the New Society (now the Royal Institute) of Painters in Water Colours, and she was a frequent contributor to its exhibitions until the year of her death. She resided for more than fifty years at Portchester House, Portchester, Hampshire, where she died on 8 May 1905. She is buried, with her mother, sister, and brother, in the churchyard of St. Mary's within the castle at Portchester. The Victoria and Albert Museum has two water-colour drawings by Miss Farmer, viz.

'In Doubt' and 'Kitty's Breakfast' (1883). Her best-known work is perhaps 'Deceiving Granny,' which was extensively reproduced. An oil portrait of Miss Farmer by her brother Alexander belongs to Miss M. A. Waller of Portchester.

[Information kindly supplied by Miss M. A. Waller; Catalogues of oils and water-colours, Victoria and Albert Museum; Graves, Dict. of Artists, Roy. Acad. Exhibitors, and British Institution Exhibitors; Cat. of the Roy. Acad. and Roy. Inst. of Painters in Water Colours; Art Journal, 1905, p. 224.]

B. S. L.

FARMER, JOHN (1835–1901), musician, born at Nottingham on 16 Aug. 1835, was eldest of a family of nine. His father, also John Farmer, was a lace manufacturer and a skilful violoncellist; his mother, whose maiden name was Mary Blackshaw, was markedly unmusical, but possessed of considerable mechanical inventiveness. An uncle, Henry Farmer, was a composer and the proprietor of a general music-warehouse in Nottingham. Farmer was apprenticed to him at a very early age after schooling at Hucknall Torkard and at Nottingham, and taught himself to play piano, violin, and harp. At the age of fourteen he was sent to the Conservatorium at Leipzig, where he studied under Moscheles, Plaidy, Hauptmann, and E. F. Richter, and sang in the Thomaskirche. After three years at Leipzig he moved to Coburg, studied under Spaeth, and rehearsed the choral work at the opera and elsewhere. In 1853 he returned to England, and took a position in the London branch of his father's lace business, where, though the work was very uncongenial, he stayed till the death, in 1857, of his mother, who had strongly opposed an artistic career. He then ran away to Zürich, to support himself by music-teaching, solely influenced by the residence of Wagner there at the time; he had helped in the production of 'Tannhäuser' at Coburg, and had experienced a strong reaction from the strict academicism of Leipzig.

In 1861 Farmer returned to England, and, after some fluctuations of fortune, was engaged to give daily piano performances at the International Exhibition of 1862. The association with Harrow school, which gave him his chief reputation, was a fruit of this engagement. Some old Harrovians who visited the exhibition and were struck with Farmer's playing invited him to take charge of a small musical society (unconnected officially with the school itself) in which they were interested. He took up his residence at Harrow at the end of 1862. In 1864, in spite of conservative scruples on the part of the authorities, he joined the staff of the school as music teacher. To words by Harrow masters [see BOWEN, EDWARD ERNEST, Suppl. II] he composed numerous songs which won great popularity and became an integral part of the permanent tradition of the school. In 1885, when Dr. Henry Montagu Butler, headmaster since 1859, who had given Farmer every encouragement, left Harrow, Farmer accepted an invitation (previously offered, but then declined) from Benjamin Jowett, Master of Balliol College, Oxford, to become organist there. At Balliol he remained till his death. Among numerous other college activities, he instituted, in the college hall, with the Master's full approval, classical secular concerts on Sunday evenings, which aroused for a short time considerable opposition.

There were many side outlets to Farmer's untiring energies. In 1872 a body of friends founded the Harrow Music School, an institution designed to systematise his method of instruction in classical piano music. Special stress was laid on the study of the work of Bach, the educational importance of which Farmer was one of the first in England to appreciate. He was also one of the earliest and firmest champions of Brahms. For the last twenty-five years of his life his method was adopted by the Girls' Public Day School Company, for which (as for many other schools) he acted as musical adviser and inspector. From 1895 onwards he was examiner to the Society of Arts, and he was also busily engaged in teaching and in lecturing in schools and in universities outside Oxford, taking up towards the end of his life a further interest—the music of soldiers and sailors. He died at Oxford on 17 July 1901, after a long paralytic illness.

Farmer married, at Zürich on 25 Oct. 1859, Marie Elisabeth Stahel, daughter of a Zürich schoolmaster; two of their seven children predeceased him.

Farmer's published compositions include numerous songs for Harrow, Balliol, St. Andrews, and elsewhere; oratorios, 'Christ and his Soldiers' (1878) and 'The coming of Christ' (1899); a fairy opera, 'Cinderella' (1882); a 'Requiem in memory of departed Harrow friends' (1884); and many works of smaller dimensions. Several extended pieces of chamber-music and other works remain in MS. He also edited many volumes of Bach and other standard composers; 'Gaudeamus, songs for colleges and schools' (1890); 'Hymns and chorales for schools and colleges' (1892); 'Dulce domum, rhymes and songs (old and new) for children' (1893); 'Scarlet and Blue, songs for soldiers and sailors' (1896). He had a remarkable gift for writing straightforward healthy tunes suitable for unison singing, and to these compositions he himself attached chief importance. A warmhearted enthusiast of magnetic personality, with a deep belief in the ethical influence of music, he did much to popularise the classical composers and to elevate musical taste in the circles in which he moved.

A portrait in oils is in the speech room at Harrow school.

[Personal knowledge; private information; Abbott and Campbell's Benjamin Jowett (1897); Harrow School, ed. E. W. Howson and E. Townsend Warner, 1898, passim; Musical Gazette, Dec. 1901.] E. W.

FARNINGHAM, MARIANNE (pseudonym). [See Hearn, Mary Anne, hymn-writer and author, 1834–1909.]

FARQUHARSON, DAVID (1840–1907), landscape painter, born at Lochend Cottage, Blairgowrie, on 8 Nov. 1840, was the younger son in the family of five children of Alexander Farquharson, dykebuilder there, and Susan Clark his wife. He served an apprenticeship in the shop of a painter and decorator in Blairgowrie in which was working about the same time another artist, William Geddes, who afterwards won a considerable reputation as a painter of fish. After following his trade in the south of Scotland, Farquharson returned to his native town, and with his brother started the business of A. and D. Farquharson, housepainters. On the dissolution of this partnership he devoted himself to the art of landscape painting, which, with little or no regular training, he had long practised in a desultory way. His first appearance at the Royal Scottish Academy, in 1868, was with a Solway landscape, and his sketching expeditions had already taken him as far as Ireland; but his main subjects throughout his career were found in his native glens and the Perthshire and western highlands.

About 1872–3 Farquharson removed to Edinburgh, and until 1882 had a studio there at 16 Picardy Place. His 'Last Furrow,' exhibited at the Scottish Academy in 1878, was purchased and engraved by the Royal Association for the Promotion of Fine Arts. It was followed by 'Noonday Rest' (R.S.A. 1879), 'Sheep plunging' (R.A. 1880), 'The Links of Forth' (R.S.A. 1883). In 1882 he was elected A.R.S.A., and in the same year he removed to London, settling at first in St. John's Wood, but spending many months each year in painting in the Scottish highlands and the west of England, with one or two visits to Holland. From 1886 onwards he was a regular exhibitor at the Royal Academy, where he first exhibited in 1877, and he contributed once or twice to the New Gallery, while his work was always on view at the galleries of Messrs. Tooth. In 1897 his picture at the Royal Academy, 'In a Fog,' was purchased for 420*l.* under the Chantrey Bequest.

By this time Farquharson had settled finally at Sennen Cove, Cornwall, which gave him the subject for a large landscape, 'Full Moon and Spring Tide,' hung in the place of honour in the large gallery in the Academy of 1904. This striking canvas, painted when the artist was sixty-four, first brought him into public notice, and it won him the associateship of the Royal Academy in the same year. With the exception of one or two of the foundation members, no artist became associated with the Academy at so advanced an age. 'Full Moon and Spring Tide' reappeared at the winter exhibition of the Academy in 1909, in the McCulloch collection, into which it had passed with several other of his large canvases, and again at the winter exhibition of 1911, with a selection of the painter's works, after his death. It was thus on view at Burlington House on three separate occasions in seven years —probably a unique record.

Farquharson's latest pictures included 'Birnam Wood' (R.A. 1906), also purchased by the Chantrey Trustees, and 'Dark Tintagel' (R.A. 1907). These, like all his large works, were painted with a broad and facile brush and a feeling for the large aspect of nature, but lacked the research and refinement of smaller landscapes painted earlier in the artist's life. The Manchester Art Gallery possesses one of Farquharson's oil-paintings; and there are two in the Glasgow Art Galleries.

Farquharson died at Balmore, Birnam, Perthshire, on 12 July 1907, and was buried in Little Dunkeld churchyard. Early in life he married Mary Irvine, whom he met in Ireland. She died in 1868. A son and daughter survived him.

[Private information; Scotsman, 13 July 1907; The Times, 13 July 1907; Graves, Royal Acad. Exhibitors, 1906; Cats. of Royal Acad. and Royal Scot. Acad.] D. S. M.

FARRAR, ADAM STOREY (1826–1905), professor of divinity and ecclesiastical history at Durham, born in London on 20 April 1826, was son of Abraham Eccles Farrar, president of the Wesleyan conference, by his second wife, Elizabeth, daughter of Adam Storey of Leeds. Educated at the Liverpool Institute, he matriculated in 1844 at St. Mary Hall, Oxford, obtaining a first class in the final classical school and a second in mathematics, and graduating B.A. in 1850. In 1851 he was the first winner of the prize founded in memory of Arnold of Rugby, with an essay on 'The Causes of the Greatness and Decay of the Town of Carthage,' and in the following year proceeded M.A. and was elected Michel fellow of Queen's College. In two successive years, 1853 and 1854, he won the Denyer prize for a theological essay, his themes being respectively 'The Doctrine of the Trinity' and 'Original Sin.' Ordained deacon in 1852 and priest in 1853, he became tutor at Wadham College in 1855, and acted both as mathematical moderator and examiner in classics in 1856. He was appointed preacher at the Chapel Royal, Whitehall, in 1858, and Bampton lecturer at Oxford in 1862, and became B.D. and D.D. in 1864.

While at Oxford Farrar published his chief literary work, 'Science in Theology, [nine] Sermons before the University of Oxford,' in 1859, and 'A Critical History of Free Thought,' the Bampton Lectures in 1862. In the former work he sought 'to bring some of the discoveries and methods of the physical and moral sciences to bear upon theoretic questions of theology.' The Bampton Lectures proved Farrar to be a learned and clear historian of ideas. In 1864 Farrar was appointed professor at Durham, and in 1878 he became canon of the cathedral. From this time onward, although he travelled widely in his vacation, not only through Europe but in Asia Minor, his life was identified with his work as teacher and preacher at Durham. His colleague, Dr. Sanday, who described him as 'a born professor,' doubted if 'any of the distinguished theologians of the last century . . . had at once the same commanding survey of his subject and an equal power of impressing the spoken word upon his hearers. . . . His knowledge was encyclopædic; and his method was also that of the encyclopædia. He was never more at home than in classifying, dividing, and subdividing. His experience in the study of natural science dominated his treatment of literature and the history of thought.' Of commanding height and appearance, and of stately manner, he by 'his physical presence heightened the effect of what he said.'

While at Durham, although he planned without executing an English church history, he only published a few sermons. He died at Durham on 11 June 1905, without issue, He married in 1864 Sarah Martha (1824–1905), daughter of Robert Wood, a Wesleyan minister.

[Guardian, 2 June 1905; Journal of Theological Studies, art. by Dr. Sanday, October 1905; Durham University Journal, 14 July 1905, with list of sermons.]

FARRAR, FREDERIC WILLIAM (1831–1903), dean of Canterbury, born on 7 Aug. 1831 in the fort at Bombay, was the second son of Charles Pinhorn Farrar, chaplain of the Church Missionary Society, by his wife Caroline Turner. At the age of three he was sent with his elder brother to England, and while under the care of two maiden aunts at Aylesbury attended the Latin school there. His parents came to England for a three years' furlough in 1839, and taking a house at Castleton Bay in the Isle of Man, sent their sons to the neighbouring King William's College, where they became boarders in the house of the headmaster, Dr. Dixon. The culture and comfort of the Aylesbury home and the comparative discomfort and roughness of the college are described by Farrar in his first story, 'Eric.' The religious teaching was strictly evangelical, but the standard of scholarship was inferior. In eight years Farrar rose to be head of the school, developing the strong self-reliance which distinguished him through life. Among his schoolfellows were Thomas Fowler [q. v. Suppl. II], Thomas Edward Brown [q. v. Suppl. I], and E. S. Beesly. In 1847, when his father left India and became curate-in-charge of St. James, Clerkenwell, Farrar lived with his parents, and attended King's College. Thenceforth, owing to his success in winning prizes and scholarships, his education cost his father nothing. He was first both in matriculation at London University and in the examination for honours, and graduated B.A. in 1852. His chief competitor was (Sir) Edwin Arnold [q. v. Suppl. II], and among the professors F. D. Maurice [q. v.] exercised a strong influence on him. From Maurice he learned a veneration for Coleridge's religious and philosophical writings. In October 1850 he went to Trinity College, Cambridge, with a sizarship and a King's College scholarship, and in 1852 he obtained a Trinity College scholarship. His novel 'Julian Home' draws freely on his Cambridge experiences. He was a member of the Apostles' Club. He took no part in games. In 1852 he won the chancellor's medal for English verse with a poem on the Arctic regions. In 1854 he was bracketed fourth in the classical tripos and was a junior optime in the mathematical tripos; he graduated B.A. in 1854, proceeded M.A. in 1857, and D.D. in 1874.

Before the result of the tripos was announced, Farrar accepted a mastership at Marlborough College, where his friends E. S. Beesly and E. A. Scott were already at work. The headmaster, G. E. L. Cotton [q. v.], afterwards bishop of Calcutta, was engaged in the task of revivifying the school. Farrar at once showed special gifts as a master, readiness to make friends of his pupils and power of stimulating their literary and intellectual energies. On Christmas Day 1854 he was ordained deacon, and priest in 1857. He left Marlborough after a year to take a mastership under Dr. Vaughan at Harrow (November 1855). In the same year he won the Le Bas prize at Cambridge for an English essay, and in 1856 he won the Norrisian prize for an essay on the Atonement, and was elected a fellow of Trinity College. Dr. Whewell is said to have been impressed by his familiarity with Coleridge's philosophy.

Farrar soon became a house-master at Harrow, where he remained fifteen years, serving for the last eleven years under Dr. H. M. Butler on Vaughan's retirement (see Dr. Butler's estimate of him as a schoolmaster in *Life*, p. 138). At Harrow, Farrar devoted all his leisure to literary work—a practice which he followed through life. Before he left Harrow he had won for himself a public reputation in three departments of literature —in fiction, in philology, and in theology. He began with fiction. In 1858 he published 'Eric, or Little by Little,' a tale of school-life, partly autobiographical, which long retained its popularity; thirty-six editions appeared in his lifetime. 'Eric' lacks the mellowness and the organic unity of 'Tom Brown's School Days,' which appeared a year earlier. But it influences boys through its vividness and sincerity, which reflect Farrar's ardent temperament and unselfish idealism. There followed in 1859 'Julian Home: a Tale of College Life' (18th edit. 1905). In 1862 'St. Winifred's, or the World of School' (26th edit. 1903), was printed anonymously. In 1873, under the pseudonym of F. T. L. Hope, 'The Three Homes: a Tale for Fathers and Sons,' was contributed to the 'Quiver.' It was not acknowledged till 1896; it reached its 18th edition in 1903.

Philology and grammar were Farrar's first serious studies, and he was a pioneer in the effort to introduce into ordinary education some of the results of modern philological research. In 1860 he published 'An Essay on the Origin of Language: based on Modern Researches and especially on the Works of M. Renan.' It was followed in 1865 by 'Chapters on Language,' of which three editions appeared, and in 1870 by 'Families of Speech,' from lectures delivered before the Royal Institution. The last two were re-issued together in 1878 under the general title of 'Language and Languages.' Farrar was an evolutionist in philology, and his first essay caught Darwin's attention and led to a friendship between the two. On Darwin's nomination Farrar in 1866 was elected a fellow of the Royal Society in recognition of his work as a philologist. In order to improve the teaching of Greek grammar he composed a card of 'Greek Grammar Rules,' which reached its 22nd edition, and published 'A Brief Greek Syntax' (1867; 11th edit. 1880). He explained his educational aims in two lectures at the Royal Institution, the first of which, 'On Some Defects in Public School Education,' urged the serious teaching of science and the defects in the current teaching of classics. His views elicited the sympathy of Darwin and Tyndall. In 1867 he edited, under the title of 'Essays on a Liberal Education,' a number of essays by distinguished university men advocating reforms. In theology Farrar first came before the public as contributor to Macmillan's 'Sunday Library for Household Reading' of a popular historical account of Seneca, Epictetus, and Marcus Aurelius, which he called 'Seekers after God' (1868; 17th edit. 1902). After the appearance of his first volume of sermons, 'The Fall of Man and other Sermons' (1868; 7th edit. 1893), he was appointed chaplain to Queen Victoria in 1869 (being made a chaplain-in-ordinary in 1873) and Hulsean lecturer at Cambridge in 1870. The Hulsean lectures were printed in 1871 as 'The Witness of History to Christ' (9th edit. 1892).

Farrar was a candidate in 1867 for the headmastership of Haileybury, but was defeated by Dr. Bradby, one of his colleagues at Harrow. In 1871 he was appointed headmaster of Marlborough

College in succession to George Granville Bradley [q. v. Suppl. II]. An outbreak of scarlet fever had just caused a panic among parents, but Farrar soon revived confidence and maintained the prestige of Bradley's rule, carried out sanitary improvements and the additional building which had been previously planned, and began the teaching of science in accordance with his principles of educational reform. While at Marlborough he made his popular reputation by writing the 'Life of Christ.' He sought to meet the requirements of the publishers, Messrs. Cassell, Petter & Galpin, who suggested that the sketch should enable readers to realise Christ's 'life more clearly, and to enter more thoroughly into the details and sequence of the gospel narratives.' In 1870 he visited Palestine with Walter Leaf, his pupil at Harrow, and his task was completed after much hard work in 1874. The success was surprising. Twelve editions were exhausted in a year, and thirty editions of all sorts and sizes in the author's lifetime. It has had a huge sale in America and has been translated into all the European languages. Despite its neglect of the critical problem of the composition of the gospels, and the floridity which was habitual to Farrar's style, his 'Life of Christ' combined honest and robust faith with wide and accurate scholarship. The value of the excursuses has been recognised by scholars. Farrar pursued his studies of Christian origins in the 'Life of St. Paul' (1879; 10th edit. 1904), an able and thorough survey of the Pauline epistles and the problems connected with them, and the most valuable of Farrar's writings; in 'The Early Days of Christianity' (1882, 5 edits.), in which the review of the writings of the New Testament was completed; and in his 'Lives of the Fathers: Church History in Biography' (1889), an attempt to bring his survey down to the end of the sixth century.

In 1875 Farrar declined the crown living of Halifax, but next year he accepted a canonry of Westminster with the rectory of St. Margaret's parish. His success as a preacher both at St. Margaret's church and in the Abbey was pronounced, and gave him the means of restoring the church. He thoroughly reorganised its interior, putting in many stained glass windows and spending 30,000*l.* on the building. At the same time he sought to restore to St. Margaret's its old position as the parish church of the House of Commons, and largely succeeded. In 1890 he was chosen chaplain to the House, and filled the position with distinction for five years. As a parish priest he earnestly faced his parochial responsibilities, and the drunkenness in Westminster slums made him a pledged abstainer and an eager advocate of temperance. In 1883 he was appointed archdeacon of Westminster.

In 1877 he roused a storm of criticism by a course of five sermons in the Abbey (Nov.–Dec.) on the soul and the future life, the subject of a current discussion in the 'Nineteenth Century.' He challenged the doctrine of eternal punishment. The sermons were published with a preface and other additions under the title 'Eternal Hope' in 1878 (18th edit. 1901), and the volumes called forth numerous replies, of which the most important was E. B. Pusey's 'What is of Faith as to Everlasting Punishment?' Pusey and Farrar corresponded, and in some measure Farrar modified his position in 'Mercy and Judgment: a Few Last Words on Christian Eschatology with reference to Dr. Pusey's "What is of Faith"' (1881; 3rd edit. 1900). Farrar's teaching largely repeated that of his master, F. D. Maurice, but he reached a far wider audience. At Farrar's suggestion the offer was made on Darwin's death in 1882 to inter his body in Westminster Abbey; Farrar was one of the pallbearers, and preached a notable funeral sermon on Darwin's work and character. In 1885 Farrar made a four months' preaching and lecturing tour through Canada and the United States. His lecture on Browning was reckoned the beginning of that poet's popularity in America. His preaching created a profound impression. His 'Sermons and Addresses in America' appeared in 1886. In the same year he served as Bampton lecturer at Oxford, his selection being an unusual compliment to a Cambridge divine. His theme was 'The History of Interpretation,' and was handled with scholarly effect.

His broad views long hindered his promotion, but in 1895 he became dean of Canterbury on the recommendation of Lord Rosebery. He threw himself with enthusiasm into his new duties. Repair and restoration of Canterbury Cathedral were urgent. In three years he raised 19,000*l.* by public subscription. The roofs were made watertight and the chapter house and crypt thoroughly restored. He improved the cathedral services and made the cathedral a centre of spiritual life for the town and diocese. In 1899 his right hand was affected by muscular atrophy which slowly attacked all his muscles. After a long illness he died on 22 March 1903. He was buried in the cloister-green of the cathedral, near Archbishop Temple. In 1860 he married Lucy Mary, third daughter of Frederic Cardew, of the East India Company's service, by whom he had five sons and five daughters.

His portrait by B. S. Marks was painted for Marlborough College in 1879, and a caricature by 'Spy' appeared in 'Vanity Fair' in 1891. Dean Farrar Street, a new street in Westminster, is named after him.

Farrar exerted a vast popular influence upon the religious feeling and culture of the middle classes for fully forty years by virtue of his enthusiasm, always sincere if not always discriminating, and of his boundless industry. In his religious views he occupied a position between the evangelical and broad church schools of thought.

In addition to those already mentioned, Farrar issued many other collections of sermons, which were widely read, and separate addresses or pamphlets; he also wrote much for 'The Speaker's Commentary,' 'The Expositor's Bible,' 'The Cambridge Bible for Schools,' and 'The Men of the Bible,' as well as for Smith's 'Dictionary of the Bible' and Kitto's 'Biblical Encyclopædia.' Among his independent publications were: 1. 'Lyrics of Life,' 1859. 2. 'General Aims of the Teacher and Form Management,' 1883. 3. 'My Object in Life,' 1883; 8th edit. 1894. 4. 'Darkness and Dawn: a Tale of the Days of Nero,' 1891; 8th edit. 1898. 5. 'Social and Present Day Questions,' 1891; 4th edit. 1903. 6. 'The Life of Christ as represented in Art,' 1894; 3rd edit. 1901. 7. 'Gathering Clouds: Days of St. Chrysostom,' 1895. 8. 'Men I have Known,' 1897. 9. 'The Herods,' 1897. 10. 'The Life of Lives: Further Studies in the Life of Christ,' 1900. Two selections from his works have been published under the titles 'Words of Truth and Wisdom' (1881) and 'Treasure Thoughts' (1886).

[Life by Farrar's son Reginald Farrar, 1905, with bibliography; The Times, 23 March 1903; Memoir by Dean Lefroy, prefixed to biographical edit. of the Life of Christ, 1903; 'Dean Farrar as Headmaster,' by J. D. R[ogers] in Cornhill Mag. May 1903; G. W. E. Russell's Sketches and Snapshots, 1910; Three Sermons preached in Canterbury Cathedral, 29 March 1903, by A. J. Mason, H. M. Spooner, and H. M. Butler; Farrar's Men I have Known, 1897, and other works, contain much autobiography.] R. B.

FARREN, ELLEN, known as Nellie Farren (1848–1904), actress, born at Liverpool on 16 April 1848, was daughter of Henry Farren [q. v.] by his wife Ellen Smithson, and was grand-daughter of William Farren (1786–1861) [q. v.]. Her first appearance is stated to have been made at the Theatre Royal, Exeter, on 12 Dec. 1853, when she appeared as the young duke of York in 'Richard III.' At nine she was at the old Victoria Theatre in Waterloo Road, London, singing a song which caught the popular ear, entitled 'I'm ninety-five.' At eleven she undertook juvenile parts in the provinces.

Her first regular appearance was made on the London stage at Sadler's Wells Theatre on 26 Dec. 1862, as the Fairy Star in 'The Rose of Blarney,' a Christmas extravaganza, in which she sang and acted very prettily. At the Victoria Theatre, Waterloo Road, then under the management of Frampton and Fenton, she played, 2 Nov. 1863, the Begum in 'Nana Sahib,' and on 26 Dec. Hymen in another Christmas piece, 'Giselle, or the Midnight Dancers,' as well as such parts as Lucy in 'The Flying Dutchman,' and Ducie in Boucicault's 'Colleen Bawn.'

From the Victoria she migrated to the Olympic Theatre, under the management of Horace Wigan, first appearing there, on 2 Nov. 1864, as Fanny in J. M. Morton's farce 'My Wife's Bonnet,' and as Gwynnedd Vaughan in Tom Taylor's 'The Hidden Hand.' She remained at this theatre until June 1868, playing leading parts in the burlesques which formed a prominent feature of the entertainment and laying the foundation of her fame as a burlesque actress. At the same time she secured genuine success in comedy characters like Charlotte in 'High Life below Stairs,' Sam Willoughby in 'The Ticket of Leave Man,' the Clown in Shakespeare's 'Twelfth Night,' Nerissa in 'The Merchant of Venice,' and Mary in 'Used Up' with Charles Mathews. Her renderings of Robert Nettles in Tom Taylor's 'To Parents and Guardians' and Nan in Buckstone's 'Good for Nothing' placed her for comic capacity beside Mrs. Keeley [q. v.]. She was next seen at the Queen's Theatre in Long Acre, under the management of Henry Labouchere, where Henry Irving was stage-manager and where the company included John L. Toole, Charles Wyndham, Lionel Brough, Alfred Wigan, John Clayton, and Nelly Moore. Here, on 20 June 1868, she appeared as Nancy Rouse in Burnand's burlesque of 'Fowl Play.'

On 21 Dec. 1868 she joined John Hollingshead's company for the opening of the Gaiety Theatre, appearing as Sprightley in 'On the Cards,' a comedy adapted from the French, and as Robert in W. S. Gilbert's burlesque 'Robert the Devil.' From that date until her retirement she was inseparably associated with the Gaiety Theatre, playing with success in every form of entertainment, from farce, burlesque, and comic opera to old English comedy and Shakespearean drama, under the management either of Hollingshead or of his successor, Mr. George Edwardes. As a boy 'Nellie Farren' proved at her brightest, and in that capacity became the idol of the Gaiety audiences. 'She could play anything,' wrote Hollingshead in 'My Lifetime,' 'dress in anything, say and do anything with any quantity of "go" and without a tinge of vulgarity. . . . She ought to go down to theatrical posterity as the best principal boy ever seen upon the stage since Sir William Davenant introduced ladies in the drama in the reign of Charles II. . . . She was essentially a boy-actress—the leading boy of her time—and for twenty years I tried to find her "double," and failed.'

She won immense popularity in rôles like Sam Weller in 'Bardell *v.* Pickwick' (24 Jan. 1871) and in comic singing parts like Leporello in Robert Reece's 'Don Giovanni' (17 Feb. 1873), Don Cæsar in H. J. Byron's 'Little Don Cæsar de Bazan' (26 Aug. 1876), Thaddeus in Byron's 'The Bohemian G'yurl' (31 Jan. 1877), Faust in his 'Little Dr. Faust' (13 Oct. 1877), Ganem in Reece's 'The Forty Thieves' (23 Dec. 1880), and Aladdin in Reece's burlesque of that name (24 Dec. 1881). Later, under Mr. George Edwardes's management, she played on 26 Dec. 1885 with enthusiastic acceptance Jack Sheppard in 'Little Jack Sheppard,' by Henry Pottinger Stephens and William Yardley, when she was first associated on the stage with Fred Leslie [q. v. Suppl. I]; she was Edmond Dantes in 'Monte Cristo, Jr.' by 'Richard Henry' (23 Dec. 1886), Frankenstein, by the same authors (24 Dec. 1887), and Ruy Blas in 'Ruy Blas, or the Blasé Roué,' by A. C. Torr (Fred Leslie) and F. Clarke (21 Sept. 1889).

In old comedy her best parts included Pert in 'London Assurance' (Drury Lane, 26 Feb. 1866), Miss Hoyden in 'The Man of Quality,' adapted from Vanbrugh's 'Relapse' (7 May 1870), Miss Prue in Congreve's 'Love for Love' (4 Nov. 1871), Charlotte in Bickerstaffe's 'Hypocrite,' with Phelps (15 Dec. 1873), Lydia Languish in 'The Rivals' (7 Feb. 1874), the chambermaid in 'The Clandestine Marriage,' with Phelps (6 Apr. 1874), Tilburina in Sheridan's 'The Critic' (13 May 1874), Lucy in 'The Rivals' (2 May 1877), and Betsy Baker (5 Dec. 1883). She well sustained her reputation by performances of Ursula in Shakespeare's 'Much Ado about Nothing' (Haymarket, 12 Dec. 1874) and Maria in 'Twelfth Night' (4 Mar. 1876). Pathos was combined with comic power in rôles like Clemency Newcome in Dickens's 'Battle of Life' (26 Dec. 1873), Smike in 'Nicholas Nickleby' (23 May 1886), Sam Willoughby in 'The Ticket of Leave Man,' as well as in Nan in 'Good for Nothing.'

In 1888–9 she visited America and Australia with Fred Leslie and the Gaiety company. She made her last regular appearance at the Gaiety as Nan on 6 April 1891, for the 'benefit' of the musical director and composer, Wilhelm Meyer Lütz [q. v. Suppl. II]. Sailing soon afterwards for Australia again, she opened at the Princess's Theatre, Melbourne, on 22 Aug. 1891, as Cinder-Ellen in Fred Leslie's burlesque 'Cinder-Ellen up too Late'; but before the end of the tour she was stricken with cardiac gout, which ultimately compelled her withdrawal from her profession. After returning to England a partial recovery allowed her in 1895 to undertake on her own account the management of the Opera Comique Theatre. The results were disastrous, and in three months all her savings vanished. A 'benefit' performance on 17 March 1899, at Drury Lane Theatre, on an unprecedented scale, brought her the substantial sum of 7200*l.*, which ensured her an adequate provision for life. By arrangement, she had the right to dispose of two-thirds of the capital sum by will, but 1000*l.* was reserved for the establishment at her death of a 'Nellie Farren' bed in a children's hospital, and 1000*l.* for division amongst theatrical charities.

Subsequently 'Nellie Farren' reappeared at other 'benefit' performances—for Lydia Thompson at the Lyceum Theatre, on 2 May 1899, as Justice Nell in a sketch of that name, specially written for her, and finally in the second scene of George Grossmith junior's *revue* 'The Linkman' on 8 April 1903, at the old Gaiety Theatre, which was then opened for the last time. She died from cardiac gout, at her residence in Sinclair Road, West Kensington, on 28 April 1904, and was buried in Brompton cemetery amid a concourse of admirers reckoned at 5000.

'Nellie Farren's' unbounded spirits and

good humour, her ready stores of drollery, and genuine sympathy with human weakness or distress gave her omnipotence over the average theatre-goer. She was neither tall nor beautiful, nor gifted with a wholly agreeable speaking or singing voice, but the charm of her individuality triumphed on the stage over all defects. An engraved portrait appears in John Hollingshead's 'Gaiety Chronicles.'

She married on 8 Dec. 1867 Robert Soutar (1827–1908), an actor and stage manager of the Gaiety Theatre, and left two sons, one of whom, Farren Soutar, has achieved success on the stage.

[Personal correspondence and recollections; Hollingshead's Gaiety Chronicles, 1898; The Times, 29 April 1904; Era, 5 May 1904; Farquharson's Short History of the Stage, 1909.]
J. P.

FARREN, WILLIAM (1825–1908), actor, born at 23 Brompton Square, London, on 28 Sept. 1825, was natural son of William Farren (1786–1861) [q. v.], 'old Farren.' Henry Farren [q. v.] was his elder brother. Their mother was wife of J. Saville Faucit; Helena Saville Faucit, Lady Martin [q. v. Suppl. I], was one of Mrs. Faucit's six legitimate children. Beginning life as a vocalist, 'young William Farren' sang at the Antient Concerts in 1848. Turning to the stage, he, after slight training in the country, made his London début in the name of Forrester at the Strand Theatre, under his father's management, on 6 Sept. 1849. On 5 March 1850 he was the original Moses in Sterling Coyne's version of 'The Vicar of Wakefield.' Later in the year he accompanied his father to the new Olympic, and acted under the name of William Farren, jun. In January 1852 he appeared as Cassio to his brother Henry's Othello, and was credited with promise.

On 28 March 1853 he made his first appearance at the Haymarket, under Buckstone, as Captain Absolute, and was identified with the fortunes of that house either in juvenile tragedy or light comedy until 1867. His more interesting rôles were Guibert in Browning's 'Colombe's Birthday' (25 April 1853), the leading part in Bayle Bernard's new play, 'A Life's Trial,' in March 1857 (cf. Henry Morley, *Journal*), Mercury in Burnand's farcical comedy, 'Venus and Adonis' (28 March 1864), and Romeo on 31 Aug. 1867. In October 1869 he was engaged by Mrs. John Wood for the St. James's, where he appeared as Brizard in Daly's version of 'Frou Frou' (25 May 1870), and Arthur Minton in 'Two Thorns' (4 March 1871), in which he struck the critic Dutton Cook as happily combining 'ease of manner with due impressiveness of delivery.' On 9 Sept. 1871 Farren migrated to the Vaudeville, with which he was long associated. There he was the original Sir Geoffrey Champneys in H. J. Byron's comedy 'Our Boys' on 16 Jan. 1875, and played the part, without intermission, until July 1878. Subsequently he was seen at the Royal Aquarium (afterwards Imperial Theatre) as Grandfather Whitehead (9 Nov. 1878), in which he was deemed inferior in pathos to his father; as young Marlow; as Archer in 'The Beaux' Stratagem' (Oct. 1879); as Sir Robert Bramble in 'The Poor Gentleman'; and as Adam in Miss Litton's revival of 'As You Like It'—a rôle which he repeated later at the opening of the Shaftesbury Theatre (20 Oct. 1888). Returning to the Vaudeville, he was Seth Pecksniff in 'Tom Pinch' (10 March 1881) and Sir Peter Teazle in the elaborate revival of 'The School for Scandal' (4 Feb. 1882). That part he resumed at the Criterion in April 1891 and at the Lyceum in June 1896. On 9 Dec. 1882 he challenged further comparison with his father by playing Sir Anthony Absolute. Subsequent parts included Colonel Damas at the Lyceum to the Pauline Deschappelles of Miss Mary Anderson (27 Oct. 1883).

In 1887, in conjunction with H. B. Conway, Farren started the Conway-Farren old comedy company at the Strand, appearing there as Lord Ogleby in 'The Clandestine Marriage,' old Dornton, and other characters. At the Criterion on 27 Nov. 1890 he played with great acceptance his father's original part of Sir Harcourt Courtly in 'London Assurance.' After 1896 his appearances on the stage were confined to occasional performances of Simon Ingot in 'David Garrick' with (Sir) Charles Wyndham. On his retirement in 1898 he settled at Rome. He died at Siena on 25 Sept. 1908, and was buried there.

Farren, like his father, ripened slowly. It was not until middle age, when juvenile rôles were abandoned, that he gradually established himself in public favour. One of the last of the traditional representatives of the Sir Anthony Absolutes and Mr. Hardcastles of classic English comedy, he achieved in Sir Peter Teazle, according to the critics of 1896, 'a masterpiece of sheer virtuosity,' but he lacked his father's powers, and his gifts of humorous expression were confined to the dry and caustic.

In 1846 Farren married Josephine

Elizabeth Davies, who was not connected with the stage, and by her had as surviving issue a daughter, who lived privately, and a son, Percy, an actor, known while his father was on the stage (from 1882) as William Farren, junior, and subsequently as William Farren.

[Pascoe's Dramatic List; W. Davenport Adams's Dict. of the Drama; Prof. Henry Morley's Journal of a London Playgoer; Mowbray Morris's Essays in Theatrical Criticism; Dutton Cook's Nights at the Play; Joseph Knight's Theatrical Notes; Dramatic Year Book, 1892; Tatler, 25 Sept. 1901; Green Room Book, 1908; Daily Telegraph, 28 Sept. 1908; private information; personal research.] W. J. L.

FAUSSET, ANDREW ROBERT (1821–1910), divine, born on 13 Oct. 1821 at Silverhill, co. Fermanagh, was the son of the Rev. William Fausset by his wife Elizabeth, daughter of Andrew Fausset, provost of Sligo. The family, of French origin, had been settled in co. Fermanagh for more than a century. Educated first at Dungannon Royal School, he obtained at Trinity College, Dublin, a Queen's scholarship in 1838, the first university scholarship and the vice-chancellor's prizes for Latin verse and Greek verse in 1841, the vice-chancellor's Greek verse prize and the Berkeley gold medal in 1842. He graduated B.A. in 1843 (senior moderator in classics), and won the vice-chancellor's Latin verse prize both in that year and in 1844. He obtained the divinity testimonium (second class) in 1845, and graduated M.A. in 1846, proceeding B.D. and D.D. in 1886.

On graduating, Fausset became a successful 'coach' at Trinity College, Dublin, but, drawn to parochial work, was ordained deacon in 1847 and priest in 1848 by the bishop of Durham, and served from 1847 to 1859 as curate of Bishop Middleham, a Durham colliery village. From 1859 until his death he was vicar of the poor parish of St. Cuthbert's, York. In 1885 he was made a prebendary of York. A good scholar and an eloquent preacher, he was an evangelical of strongly protestant sympathies, and wrote much in support of his convictions. He died at York on 8 Feb. 1910. Fausset was thrice married: (1) in 1859 to Elizabeth, daughter of William Knowlson, of York, by whom he had three sons and one daughter; (2) in 1874 to Agnes, daughter of Major Porter, of Hembury Fort, Honiton, by whom he had one son; and (3) in 1889 to Frances, daughter of the Rev. Dr. Strange, vicar of Bishop Middleham.

Fausset showed sound scholarship in critical editions of 'The Comedies of Terence' (omitting the 'Eunuch') (1844); of Homer's 'Iliad,' i.–viii. (1846), one of the first editions in English to take account of the criticism of Wolff, Niebuhr and Grote; and of 'Livy,' i.–iii., with prolegomena and notes (1849); and in translations of the 'Hecuba' (1850) and the 'Medea' (1851) of Euripides. His religious publications, most of which had wide circulation, were: 1. 'Scripture and the Prayer-Book in Harmony,' 1854; revised ed. 1894, an answer to objections against the liturgy. 2. Vols. ii. and iv. (Job, Ecclesiastes, Malachi, Corinthians I and Revelation) in the 'Critical and Explanatory Pocket Bible,' 1863–4. 3. Vols. iii., iv., and vi. (Psalms and Proverbs) in the 'Critical, Experimental and Practical Commentary,' 1864–70. 4. 'Studies in the CL. Psalms,' 1877; 2nd edit. 1885, an application of the argument from undesigned coincidences. 5. 'The Englishman's Critical and Expository Bible Cyclopædia,' originally issued in parts, in volume form, 1878. 6. 'Signs of the Times,' 1881. 7. 'Commentary on Judges,' 1885. 8. 'Guide to the Study of the Book of Common Prayer,' 1894, 3rd edit. 1903. Fausset also first translated into English J. A. Bengel's 'Gnomon of the New Testament' (1857), with notes and a life of Bengel.

[Record, 18 Feb. 1910; Gospel Magazine, April 1910; private information and personal knowledge.] A. R. B.

FAYRER, Sir JOSEPH (1824–1907), surgeon-general and author, born at Plymouth on 6 Dec. 1824, was second son of the six sons and two daughters of commander Robert John Fayrer, R.N. (1788–1849), by his wife Agnes (*d.* 1861), daughter of Richard Wilkinson.

His father, on retiring from active service in the navy, commanded steam-packets between Portpatrick and Donaghadee, and Liverpool and New York, and was thus a pioneer of ocean steam navigation; in 1843 he commanded H.M.S. Tenedos as a stationary convict-ship at Bermuda. In Joseph's youth the family lived successively at Haverbrack, Westmoreland, where Joseph made the acquaintance of Wordsworth, Hartley Coleridge, and John Wilson (Christopher North); at Dalrymple, where he was a pupil of the Rev. R. Wallace (1835–6), and at Liverpool, where he studied natural science at a day school. In 1840, after a brief study of engineering, he made a voyage to West Indies and South America as midshipman of the Thames in the new West Indian mail steam-packet service. In 1843 he accompanied his father to Bermuda, where an outbreak of yellow fever inclined him to the profession of medicine. Entering the Charing Cross Hospital in October 1844, where his fellow pupils included (Sir) William Guyer Hunter [q. v. Suppl. II] and Thomas Henry Huxley, he was appointed at the end of his second year house surgeon at the Westminster Ophthalmic Hospital. In July 1847 he was admitted M.R.C.S. England, becoming F.R.C.S. in 1878. On 4 Aug. 1847 he received a commission in the royal naval medical service, but soon resigned it to travel with Lord Mount-Edgcumbe through France, Germany, and Italy. While at Palermo the Sicilian revolution broke out, and Fayrer, with his friend Dr. Valentine Mott, son of the well-known American surgeon, obtained his first experience of gunshot wounds. At Rome, where he arrived in April 1848, he studied at the university, and in 1849 obtained there the degree of M.D.

On 29 June 1850 Fayrer left England for Calcutta, to become assistant surgeon in Bengal. His connection with the Indian medical service lasted for forty-five years. On the outward voyage Fayrer had medical charge of a batch of recruits who proved insubordinate; but when the commanding officer handed them over to Fayrer, he promptly put the ringleader in irons and restored quiet. Arriving at Fort William on 9 Oct. 1850, he spent two years at Chinsura, Cherrapunji in the Khasi Hills, and Dacca. His successful service as a field assistant-surgeon with the Burma field force in the Pegu war of 1852 led Lord Dalhousie to appoint him, in July 1853, residency surgeon at Lucknow.

At Lucknow he received on 8 Sept. 1854 the additional appointment of honorary assistant resident, involving political duties. On 20 March 1856 he was appointed civil surgeon of Lucknow and superintendent of charitable institutions. On the annexation of Oudh, Fayrer was placed in charge of the deposed king's stud of horses, elephants, camels, and wild animals.

During the Mutiny Fayrer's house was used both as hospital and fortress, and he himself played a prominent part through the siege from 30 June until the final relief on 17 Nov. 1857 (cf. his *Recollections*). In March 1858 he left for England on furlough, and studying in Edinburgh, was admitted M.D. in March 1859. On 29 April, on returning to India, he became professor of surgery at the Medical College, Calcutta. In January 1867 he was made president of the Asiatic Society of Bengal, which he had joined in January 1861, and in that capacity proposed a scheme for a Zoological society and gardens in Calcutta, which was finally carried out in 1875, when the gardens were opened by King Edward VII, then Prince of Wales.

In 1868 he was made C.S.I., and in 1869 surgeon in Calcutta to Lord Mayo, the new viceroy. On 1 Jan. 1870 he accompanied the Duke of Edinburgh on his travels through N.W. India. Owing to failing health he came home in March 1872. On his arrival he was elected F.R.C.P. London, and with (Sir) Lauder Brunton resumed his important researches on snake venoms which he had begun in India in 1867 and which he embodied in a great treatise, published in 1872. He joined the medical board of the India office in Feb. 1873 and was made president on 8 Dec., when he retired from the active list of the Indian army as a deputy surgeon-general. He continued president at the India office till January 1895, when he retired with the rank of surgeon-general and was awarded a good service pension in addition to his superannuation allowance.

Meanwhile, in 1875 Fayrer was selected to accompany Edward VII, when Prince of Wales, on his tour through India. The expedition left Brindisi on 16 October and returned to Portsmouth on 5 May 1876. On 7 March 1876, at Allahabad, Fayrer was made K.C.S.I. On his return he was gazetted honorary physician to the prince. With the prince he formed a cordial intimacy which lasted for life. He privately printed in 1876 'Notes' on the two royal visits to India.

On 19 April 1877 he was elected F.R.S., and joined the council in 1895. He was made honorary LL.D. of Edinburgh (July 1878) and of St. Andrews (1890). In 1879, as president of the Epidemiological Society, he gave an address on 'The Progress of Epidemiology in India' (1880). In 1881 he delivered the Lettsomian lecture before the Medical Society of London on 'Tropical Diseases' (published with papers on like subjects in that year), and in 1882 the Croonian lectures of the Royal College of Physicians on 'The Climate and some of the Fevers of India' (1882). He represented the government of India at the intercolonial congress at Amsterdam (with Dr. T. R. Lewis), and at the international sanitary congress at Rome (May-June 1885). He also represented both the Royal College of Physicians of London and the University of Edinburgh at the tercentenary of Galileo at Padua (Dec. 1892), when he made a speech in Italian and received the honorary degree of doctor of philosophy. On 11 January 1896 he was made a baronet. The remainder of his life was passed chiefly at Falmouth, where he died on 21 May 1907.

He married on 4 Oct. 1855, at Lucknow, Bethia Mary, eldest daughter of Brigadier-general Andrew Spens, who was in command of the troops there; by her he had six sons and two daughters. His eldest son, Robert Andrew, born on 27 June 1856, died on 28 Dec. 1904. He was succeeded as second baronet by his eldest surviving son, Joseph, who joined the Royal Army Medical Corps.

Despite official and professional calls upon his energies, Fayrer was a prolific writer on Indian climatology, the pathology of Indian diseases, sanitation, and above all on venomous snakes. His great work on 'The Thanatophidia of India,' the best book on the subject, published in folio in 1872 by government, was illustrated with admirable coloured plates from the life by native members of the Calcutta School of Art (2nd edit. 1874). The book embodies all Fayrer's experiments and researches, accounts of which were forwarded from India to Dr. F. C. Webb, who put them into literary shape. To Fayrer's inquiries is due the efficacious permanganate treatment of venomous snake-bites. But his main conclusions were that there is no absolute antidote, and that safety is only to be attained when the bite is in such a position as to make the application of a ligature between it and the heart possible, together with the use of the actual cautery. These opinions were somewhat modified after some later experiments by Fayrer, Brunton, and Rogers (*Proc. Roy. Soc.*, 1904, lxxiii. 323); it was there shown that recovery might be expected if a ligature were applied within half a minute or even a longer period after a bite, the site of the injury being then incised and solid permanganate of potassium rubbed in.

Of his other writings not already mentioned the following are the most important: 1. 'Clinical Observations in Surgery,' Calcutta, 1863. 2. 'Clinical Surgery in India,' 1866. 3. 'Osteomyelitis and Septicæmia and the Nature of Visceral Abscess,' 1867. 4. 'Fibrinous Coagula in the Heart and Pulmonary Artery as a Cause of Death after Surgical Operations,' 1867. 5. 'Clinical and Pathological Observations in India,' 1873. 6. 'On the Preservation of Health in India,' 1880 (new edit. 1894). 7. 'Epidemiology of Cholera,' 1888. 8. 'Sir James Ranald Martin,' 1897. 9. 'Recollections of My Life,' 1900. To 'Quain's Dictionary of Medicine' (1882) he contributed articles on 'Effects of Venom' and 'Venomous Animals,' and to 'Allbutt's System of Medicine' (1894) those on 'Sunstroke,' 'Climate,' and 'Fevers of India.'

Fayrer's portrait by Mr. Sydney P. Hall, in the Royal Medical College at Netley, was unveiled by Lord Wolseley.

[Lancet, 1 June 1907; Proc. Roy. Soc., B 80, 1908; Fayrer's Recollections of My Life, 1900.] H. P. C.

FENN, GEORGE MANVILLE (1831–1909), novelist, born in Pimlico on 3 Jan. 1831, was third child and the eldest of three sons of Charles and Ann Louisa Fenn. After a scanty education at private schools, Fenn studied at the Battersea Training College for Teachers under Samuel Clark [q. v.] from 1851 to 1854, and became on leaving master of the small national school at Alford, Lincolnshire. After some employment as a private tutor, he moved to London in quest of work, and became a printer. Purchasing a small press at Growle, Lincolnshire, he started 'Modern Metre,' a little magazine, entirely in verse, which was set up by himself, and ran from May to October 1862. In 1864 Fenn became part proprietor of the 'Herts. and Essex Observer,' published at Bishop's Stortford; but this venture proved no more successful. After endless disappointments, a short sketch entitled 'In Jeopardy' was accepted for 'All the Year Round' in 1864 by Dickens, and attracted the notice of other editors. Manuscripts were soon accepted by James Payn [q. v. Suppl. I] for 'Chambers's Journal' and by Edward Walford [q. v.] for 'Once a Week.' 'Readings by Starlight,' papers on working-class life, appeared in 1866 in the 'Star' newspaper under the editorship of Justin McCarthy, and were collected into four volumes in 1867. There soon followed 'Spots and Blots,' a similar series, in the 'Weekly Times' under Mr. (afterwards Sir John) Hutton.

'Hollowdell Grange,' Fenn's first boy's story, and 'Featherland,' a natural history tale for children, were both published by Messrs. Griffith & Farran in 1867; and from that date onwards he produced novel after novel, in magazine, newspaper, and volume form, with an industrious rapidity which few writers excelled. His separate books numbered more than 170. After 1881 his more successful works were books for boys, in which he often effectively embodied studies of natural history and geography. The boys' books met with some success in America, where several were reprinted under the general title of 'The Fenn Books.'

Meanwhile in 1870 he succeeded Hugh Reginald Haweis [q. v. Suppl. II] as editor of 'Cassell's Magazine'; and in 1873 he purchased from James Rice [q. v.] 'Once a Week,' which he carried on at a loss until the close of 1879. He never wholly abandoned journalism, and was for some years dramatic critic of the 'Echo' newspaper. In 1887 he produced at the Comedy Theatre a three-act farce, 'The Barrister,' and at Terry's Theatre next year he prepared a like piece, 'The Balloon,' in collaboration with Mr. John Henry Darnley. In 1903 he wrote for the family a privately printed memoir of B. F. Stevens, the American bookseller and man of letters. A lover of the country and of gardening, Fenn resided for some years on a remotely situated farm near Ewhurst, in Sussex; but from 1889 he lived at Syon Lodge, Isleworth, an old house with a large garden, where he amassed a library of some 25,000 volumes and amused his leisure in constructing astronomical telescopes of considerable size. On the day of the completion in 1907 of his last book, a memoir of his friend George Alfred Henty [q. v. Suppl. II], Fenn's health finally broke. He died after a long illness at Syon Lodge on 26 Aug. 1909, and was buried in Isleworth cemetery.

Fenn married in 1855 Susanna, daughter of John Leake, of Alford, Lincolnshire, who survived him. By her he had two sons and six daughters. The eldest son, Frederick, and the second son, Clive, engaged in literary pursuits.

[Personal knowledge; private information; Sketch, 6 Aug. 1902, an 'interview,' with excellent portraits; the Captain, Oct. 1909.] G. S. B.

FERGUSON, MARY CATHERINE, Lady (1823–1905), biographer, born at Stillorgan, co. Dublin, in 1823, was eldest daughter of Robert Rundell Guinness by his wife Mary Anne Seymour. She was educated partly at home and partly at Woodside, Cheshire. Keenly interested from an early age in Irish art and archæology, she made the acquaintance of (Sir) Samuel Ferguson [q. v.], and through him of George Petrie [q. v.], William Reeves [q. v.], and other workers in the same field. On 16 Aug. 1848 she married Ferguson, and thenceforth shared in his archæological and literary labours, and helped him to entertain in their house at 20 North Great George Street, Dublin, numerous native and foreign guests of like interests. In 1868 she published her popular book 'The Story of the Irish before the Conquest' (2nd edit. 1890), which is still in circulation. After her husband's death in 1886 she chiefly occupied herself in writing 'Sir Samuel Ferguson in the Ireland of his Day,' which appeared in 1896 (Edinburgh and London, 2 vols.), and pleasantly if discursively described the circle of which her husband was the centre. Her 'Life of William Reeves, D.D., Lord Bishop of Down, Connor and Dromore,' followed in 1893. Lady Ferguson also prepared for posthumous publication her husband's 'Ogham Inscriptions in Ireland, Wales and Scotland' (Edinburgh, 1887), 'The Hibernian Nights' Entertainments' (Dublin, 1887; three series), and popular editions of the 'Lays of the Western Gael' (Dublin, 1887; 3rd edit. 1897), 'Confession of St. Patrick' (1888), 'Congal' (Dublin, 1893), and 'Lays of the Red Branch' (1897). She died at her husband's house in Dublin on 5 March 1905, and was buried in her husband's grave at Donegore, co. Antrim. She had no children.

[Sir Samuel Ferguson in the Ireland of his Day, 1896; Life of William Reeves, D.D., 1893; Daily Express, Dublin, 7 March 1905; Who's Who, 1905; personal knowledge.] D. J. O'D.

FERGUSSON, Sir JAMES (1832–1907), sixth baronet of Kilkerran, governor of Bombay, born on 14 March 1832 in Edinburgh, was eldest of four sons of Sir Charles Dalrymple Fergusson (1800–1849), fifth baronet, of Kilkerran in Ayrshire, by his wife Helen, daughter of David Lord Boyle [q. v.], lord justice-general. Sir David Dalrymple, Lord Hailes [q. v.], was father of his father's mother. A younger brother, Charles Dalrymple, who substituted the surname Dalrymple for that of Fergusson, was created a baronet on 19 July 1887. James entered Rugby under Dr. Tait in August 1845, together with George Joachim (afterwards Lord) Goschen, Sir John Stewart, who served with him in the Crimea, and Sir Theodore Hope, afterwards a member of the supreme government in India. At school he gained some reputation in the debating club, and in 1850 he proceeded to University College, Oxford, having in the previous year succeeded his father in the baronetcy. His inclinations turned towards a military career, and leaving Oxford without a degree he entered the grenadier guards. With the 3rd battalion of that regiment he served in the Crimean war, 1854–5. He took part in the battle of Alma and was wounded at Inkerman on 5 Nov. 1854. On that day three of his brother officers were killed and five others wounded in the numerous encounters which the 1st division sustained, under George, duke of Cambridge. Close to him on the field of battle fell his friend and neighbour in Scotland, Colonel James Hunter Blair (KINGLAKE'S *Crimea*, vol. vi. chap. 6). At the dying man's suggestion, the electors chose Fergusson to take Blair's place in parliament as conservative member for Ayrshire, but he remained with the forces before Sevastopol until May 1855, when Lord Raglan advised him to enter upon his parliamentary duties. On his return home he received his medal from Queen Victoria, and retired from the army on 9 Aug. 1859. Although his active military career was thus brought to an early close, he remained an officer of the Royal Company of Archers, was colonel commanding the Ayr and Wigtown militia from 1858 to 1868, and also served in his county regiment of yeomanry.

In 1857 he lost his seat for Ayrshire, but recovered it in 1859, holding it until 1868. While attending to county business and the duties of a landlord, he devoted himself to his parliamentary work, and was appointed under-secretary of India under Lord Cranborne [see CECIL, LORD ROBERT, Suppl. II] in the Derby government of 1866. A year later he was transferred in a similar capacity to the home office, where there was need for efficient aid to Gathorne Hardy (afterwards Lord Cranbrook) [q. v. Suppl. II]. The public mind was agitated by trades union outrages, the Fenian movement, and the reform bill. After Disraeli succeeded Lord Derby as prime minister in February 1868 Fergusson was made a privy councillor and governor of South Australia, where he arrived on 16 Feb. 1869. Until 1885 (save for the period 1875–80) his career was identified with the oversea dominions.

In South Australia, which was prosperous and peaceful, the working of responsible government made small demands upon the governor. But Fergusson gave material assistance to his ministers in organising the telegraph system. In 1873 he left South Australia for New Zealand, but after Disraeli became premier (Feb. 1874) Fergusson resigned his post there in 1875, being made K.C.M.G. On his return to England he tried to resume his parliamentary career. His attempts to capture Frome in 1876 and Greenock in 1878 were unsuccessful. But he engaged actively in county affairs, and on 10 March 1880, on the eve of Lord Beaconsfield's fall from power, he accepted the post of governor of Bombay in succession to Sir Richard Temple [q. v. Suppl. II]. When the new governor was installed on 28 April 1880 Lord Lytton had tendered his resignation, Abdur Rahman was discussing terms with Sir Donald Stewart [q. v. Suppl. I] near Kabul, and Ayub Khan was meditating the attack upon Kandahar, which he successfully delivered at Maiwand on 27 July. Thus Fergusson's immediate duty was to push forward supplies and reinforcements through Sind. But his main duties were of an essentially civil character and connected with revenue administration. Before his arrival Sir Theodore Hope had carried through the supreme legislature the Dekhan Agriculturist Relief Act to enable the peasantry to shake off their indebtedness and meet the moneylender on more equal terms. The introduction of so novel an experiment met with opposition from the powerful lending classes and also from lawyers, who considered contracts sacred and the letter of bonds inviolable. New rules of registration were required, fresh courts instituted, and the system of conciliation organised. Fergusson, as a proprietor himself, threw his experience and heart into the work. The Act, which has been since amended, has abundantly vindicated its promoters. In another direction he sought the welfare of the Dekhan peasantry. Temple, while immensely increasing the area of forest reserves, had severely curtailed forest privileges long enjoyed by the cultivating classes in the uplands of the Ghat districts. Fergusson removed some part of the burden of forest conservancy which Temple had thrown on the people. He moreover inculcated moderation in assessing the land revenue and liberality in granting remissions in times of scarcity. To enable the state to deal more readily with famine, he gave attention to the alignment of the new Southern Maratha railway, mainly devised to carry food stuffs into districts liable to failure of the rains. In the same spirit he created the first agricultural department, and inaugurated experimental farms. In other departments he turned to account his experience at the home office. In the face of violent agitation he refused to exercise the clemency of the crown in favour of the high priest of the Vaishnava sect. This holy man had been convicted of complicity in postal robberies, and his religious followers regarded his punishment as an act of impiety. Fond of riding, Fergusson covered long distances in his tours through a province of 123,000 square miles. In earnestness of purpose and indefatigable energy he almost rivalled Sir Richard Temple. He did much to develop the port of Bombay, and took deep interes- in education, laying the foundation of tht native college at Poona which is called be his name. He was assisted in his governy ment by his colleague, Sir James Peile [q. v. Suppl. II], and at the close of it by (Sir) Maxwell Melvill (1834–1887), a man of rare distinction. With Peile's aid he was able to satisfy Lord Ripon by the steps taken in Bombay to develop rural and urban self-government. If the Bombay government was unable to go as far as that viceroy wished, it went further than any other province in India. Altogether Fergusson's administration in Bombay was successful, and he well merited the honour of G.C.S.I. which he received on 25 Feb. 1885.

Fergusson did not await the arrival of his successor, Lord Reay, but after making arrangements for the Suakin campaign relinquished the government on 27 March 1885, hurrying home to resume a political career. On 9 June 1885 Gladstone resigned, and on 27 Nov. Fergusson was returned as one of the members for Manchester (N.E. division). He held the seat until January 1906. On the return of Lord Salisbury to power on 3 Aug. 1886, Fergusson served from 1886 to 1891 as under-secretary in the foreign office, and was responsible for answering questions and otherwise representing that department in the House of Commons. He performed his duties with stolid discretion. In 1891 he was made postmaster-general, retaining the office until Gladstone's return to power in August 1892. He did not take office again, but at the opening of the new parliament in 1901 he proposed the re-election as speaker of William Court Gully, afterwards Viscount Selby [q. v. Suppl. II]. Meanwhile Fergusson's business capacity found scope as director of the Royal Mail Steam Packet Company, the National Telephone Company, and similar concerns. In the interests of the first-mentioned company he went to Jamaica in January 1907 to attend the conference of the British Cotton Growing Association. On the first day of the conference, 14 Jan., Kingston was overtaken by a terrible earthquake, followed by a destructive fire. Fergusson was walking in the street near his hotel, when he was killed by the fall of a wall. He was buried in the churchyard of Half Way Tree, near Kingston, and a memorial service was held on 21 Jan. in the Guards' Chapel, London.

Fergusson was thrice married: (1) at Dalhousie Castle on 9 Aug. 1859 to Lady Edith Christian, younger daughter of James Andrew Ramsay, first marquis of Dalhousie [q. v.]; she died at Adelaide on 28 Oct. 1871, leaving two sons and two daughters; (2) in New Zealand on 11 March 1873 to Olive, youngest daughter of John Henry Richman of Warnbunga, South Australia; she bore him one son, Alan Walter John (1878–1909), and died of cholera at Bombay on 8 Jan. 1882; (3) on 5 April 1893 to Isabella Elisabeth, widow of Charles Hugh Hoare, of Morden, Surrey, and daughter of Thomas Twysden, rector of Charlton, Devonshire. She survived him without issue. His elder son by his first wife, Major-general Sir Charles Fergusson, D.S.O., succeeded him in the title.

Fergusson's friends in Ayrshire, where he was much beloved for his charitable and kindly acts, erected to his memory a statue in bronze at the corner of Wellington Square in Ayr. It was executed by Sir Goscombe John, R.A., and unveiled by the earl of Eglinton in October 1910. In Jamaica, too, his memory is preserved in the restoration of the church of Half Way Tree and a mural tablet.

[The Times, 17 Jan. 1907; Kinglake's Crimea; Colonial and India Office Lists; Administration Reports of Bombay; Lucy's Salisbury and Balfourian Parliaments; and Parliamentary Reports.] W. L-W.

FERRERS, NORMAN MACLEOD (1829–1903), Master of Caius College, Cambridge, and mathematician, born on 11 Aug. 1829 at Prinknash Park, Gloucestershire, was only child of Thomas Bromfield Ferrers, stockbroker, of London (a descendant of the Taplow Court branch of the Ferrers family), by his wife Lavinia, daughter of Alexander Macleod of Harris. After spending three years, 1844–6, at Eton, he lived for about a year as a private pupil in the house of Harvey Goodwin [q. v. Suppl. I], the mathematician, then vicar of St. Edward's, Cambridge, afterwards bishop of Carlisle. Admitted a freshman of Caius College, Cambridge, on 6 March 1847, Ferrers graduated B.A. in 1851 as senior wrangler of his year, being also first 'Smith's prizeman.' Next year he was elected fellow of his college, and immediately afterwards went to London to study law. He was called to the bar, as a member of Lincoln's Inn, in 1855.

In 1856, owing to changes in the tutorial staff, there was an opening for a new mathematical lecturer in Caius College; and the Master, Dr. Edwin Guest [q. v.], invited Ferrers, who was by far the best mathematician amongst the fellows, to supply the place. His career was thus determined for the rest of his life. For many years head mathematical lecturer, he was one of the two tutors of the college from 1865. As lecturer he was extremely successful. Besides great natural powers in mathematics, he possessed an unusual capacity for vivid exposition. He was probably the best lecturer, in his subject, in the university of his day. He was ordained deacon in 1859 and priest in 1861.

On 27 Oct. 1880 he was elected Master of Gonville and Caius College, on Dr. Guest's resignation. He was admitted to the degree of D.D. on 7 June 1881. The honorary degree of LL.D. was conferred on him by the University of Glasgow in 1883.

For more than twenty years he was a member of the council of the senate at Cambridge: first in 1865, and continuously from 1878 to 1893, when increasing infirmity obliged him to decline re-election. In the mathematical tripos he acted as moderator or examiner more often, it is believed, than any one else on record. In 1876 Ferrers was appointed a governor of St. Paul's School, and in 1885 a governor of Eton College. He was elected F.R.S. in 1877.

In his early days Ferrers was a keen university reformer, within the limits in which reform was then contemplated. He heartily supported the abolition of religious tests, and the throwing open of all endowments to free competition; he introduced into his college a more systematic style of examination than was previously in vogue. But he held strongly the old view that a thorough training in mathematics was essential to a sound education. For new subjects, like natural science and mechanical engineering, he had scant sympathy. It was slowly, and probably with some reluctance, that he was induced to accept the principle that distinction in any subject which was recognised and taught in the university gave a valid claim to a scholarship or fellowship.

It was as a mathematician that Ferrers acquired fame outside the university. He made many contributions of importance to mathematical literature. His first book was 'Solutions of the Cambridge Senate House Problems, 1848–51.' In 1861 he published a treatise on 'Trilinear Co-ordinates,' of which subsequent editions appeared in 1866 and 1876. One of his early memoirs was on Sylvester's development of Poinsot's representation of the motion of a rigid body about a fixed point. The paper was read before the Royal Society in 1869, and published in their 'Transactions.' In 1871 he edited at the request of the college the 'Mathematical Writings of George Green' (1793–1841) [q. v.], a former fellow. Ferrers's treatise on 'Spherical Harmonics,' published in 1877, presented many original features.

His contributions to the 'Quarterly Journal of Mathematics,' of which he was an editor from 1855 to 1891, were numerous (see list in the *Roy. Soc. Cat. Scientific Papers*). They range over such subjects as quadriplanar co-ordinates, Lagrange's equations and hydrodynamics. In 1881 he applied himself to study Kelvin's investigation of the law of distribution of electricity in equilibrium on an uninfluenced spherical bowl. In this he made the important addition of finding the potential at any point of space in zonal harmonics. (*Quart. Journ. Mathematics*, 1881).

In 1879 Ferrers was troubled with the first symptoms of rheumatoid arthritis: this gradually increased until he was rendered a complete cripple. He died at the College Lodge on 31 Jan. 1903, at the age of seventy-three.

On 3 April 1866 he married Emily, daughter of John Lamb [q. v.], dean of Bristol and Master of Corpus Christi College, Cambridge. He had a family of four sons and one daughter.

There is a portrait of him, by the Hon. John Collier, in the college.

[Personal knowledge; College and University Records; Dr. Edward Routh's memoir in Royal Society's Proceedings; Ferrers Family History, by C. S. F. Ferrers.] J. V.

FESTING, JOHN WOGAN (1837–1902), bishop of St. Albans, born at Brook House, Stourton, Somerset, on 13 Aug. 1837, was eldest son of Richard Grindall Festing by his wife Eliza, daughter of Edward Mammatt, of Ashby-de-la-Zouch. A younger brother, Major-General Edward Robert Festing (*b.* 1839), R.E., C.B., F.R.S., was director of the science museum, South Kensington (1893–1904). The family, descended from Michael Christian Festing [q. v.], the musician, was of German origin.

Educated at King's school, Bruton, and King's College school, London, Festing graduated B.A. from Trinity College, Cambridge, in 1860 (D.D. *jure dig* 1890) as twenty-second senior optime, and in the same year was ordained deacon, becoming priest in 1861. From 1860 to 1873 he was curate of Christ Church, Westminster. In 1873 he was appointed to the vicarage of St. Luke, Berwick Street, a poor parish close to Seven Dials, which had recently been visited by cholera. Festing increased his reputation here for pastoral diligence, and on 19 May 1878 John Jackson, bishop of London, collated him to the important vicarage of Christ Church, Albany Street. There the church schools, in which he was always greatly interested, were a prominent feature of parish life, while the church itself was a recognised centre for the high church party, to which Festing adhered. He became rural dean of St. Pancras in 1887, and on 26 June 1888 prebendary of Brondesbury in St. Paul's Cathedral.

On 24 June 1890 Festing was consecrated bishop of St. Albans, succeeding Thomas Legh Claughton [q. v. Suppl. I], who had resigned but was retaining the use for life of the palace at Danbury. The choice of a parish priest of no fame for eloquence or erudition caused surprise. But Lord Salisbury, the prime minister, had asked both Henry Parry Liddon [q. v.], who had himself declined the see, and R. W. Church [q. v. Suppl. I], dean of St. Paul's, to suggest to him a man of parochial experience and zeal, and each independently suggested Festing. As bishop, Festing proved business-like, sympathetic towards hard work, and devout. While in private he urged obedience to the Prayer Book, his high church sympathies made him unwilling to hamper earnest clergy by coercive administration. His see embraced the counties of Essex and Hertfordshire; and he chose to reside at Endsleigh Street, London, W.C., near the chief railway termini. He afterwards secured a second house at St. Albans. His chief interest lay in the industrial and residential expansion of metropolitan Essex. Zealous in the cause of foreign missions, he mainly devoted himself to the Universities Mission to Central Africa, at the inauguration of which in the Cambridge senate-house he was present on 1 Nov. 1859. He was its assistant honorary secretary (1863–1882), treasurer (1882–1890), vice-president (1890–1892), and president and chairman (1892–1902), and advised on all the details of the mission's development.

Although no scholar, he was a studious reader, rising early each day for that purpose. He was fond of travel and skilful in water-colour drawing. He died unmarried at Endsleigh Street of angina pectoris on 28 Dec. 1902, and was buried at St. Albans. Choir-stalls were placed in his memory in St. Albans cathedral in 1903.

[The Times, 29 Dec. 1902; Guardian, 31 Dec. 1902; Record, 2 Jan. 1903; Central Africa (U.M.C.A. mag.), Feb. 1903.] E. H. P.

FIELD, WALTER (1837–1901), painter, youngest son of Edwin Wilkins Field [q. v.] by his second wife, Letitia Kinder, was born at Windmill Hill, Hampstead, on 1 Dec. 1837. He was a lineal descendant of Oliver Cromwell. After education at University College School, London, he was taught painting by John Rogers Herbert, R.A. [q. v.], and John Pye [q. v.] the engraver gave him lessons in chiaroscuro. Making art his profession, he painted outdoor figure subjects and landscapes, especially views of Thames scenery, which were often enlivened with well-drawn figures; he also produced a few portraits. At first he worked chiefly in oil, but subsequently executed many drawings in water-colour. His landscapes and coast scenes show skilful technique. Between 1856 and 1901 he exhibited at the Old Water Colour Society (Royal Society of Painters in Water Colours), at the Royal Academy (where he showed forty-two pictures), the British Institution (where he showed nine pictures), the Royal Society of British Artists, Dudley Gallery, and elsewhere. He was elected an associate of the Old Water Colour Society on 22 March 1880, but never attained full membership. He was also one of the earliest members of the Dudley Gallery, whose first exhibition was held in 1865. Field, who was devoted to his art, was a keen lover of nature; he was untiring in his efforts for the preservation of the natural beauties of Hampstead Heath, and was the chief founder of the Hampstead Heath Protection Society. A drinking fountain was erected on the Heath to his memory. He resided principally at Hampstead. He died at The Pryors, East Heath Road, on 23 Dec. 1901, and was buried in Hampstead cemetery.

The Victoria and Albert Museum has two water-colour drawings by Field, viz. 'Boy in a Cornfield' (1866) and 'Girl carrying a Pitcher' (1866); and three of his Thames views are in the Schwabe Collection in the Kunsthalle at Hamburg. Among his most popular works were 'The Milkmaid singing to Isaak Walton,' 'Henley Regatta,' which contains portraits from sittings of many famous oarsmen, and 'Come unto these Yellow Sands.' An exhibition of oil paintings by Field was held at the galleries of the Royal Society of Painters in Water Colours in September and October 1902; 216 works remaining in his studio after his death were sold at Christie's on 17 and 18 Nov. 1902.

By his wife, Mary Jane Cookson, whom he married on 14 May 1868, Walter Field had seven children.

[Information kindly supplied by Miss M. Field and Mr F. W. Hayward Butt; Müller und Singer, Allgemeines Künstler-Lexicon (date of death wrongly given in supplement: see death certificate at Somerset House); Graves, Dict. of Artists, Roy. Acad. and Brit. Inst. Exhibitors; Cats. of Old Water Colour Society (those of 1882–1901 contain reproductions of works by Field), Victoria and Albert Museum (water-colours), and the Hamburg Kunsthalle; The Year's Art, 1891, facing p. 86 (portrait); The Studio, Spring No., 1905, p. xlii; Illustrated London News, 27 Sept. 1902.] B. S. L.

FIELD, Sir WILLIAM VENTRIS, Baron Field of Bakeham (1813–1907), judge, born at Fielden, Bedfordshire, on 21 Aug. 1813, was second son of Thomas Flint Field of that place. After education at Burton grammar school he was articled to Messrs. Terrell, Barton & Smale, solicitors, of Exeter, his articles being subsequently transferred to Messrs. Picre & Bolton of Lincoln's Inn. In 1843 he became a member of the firm of Thompson, Debenham & Field, Salters' Hall Court, E.C. Having entered as a student at the Middle Temple on 15 Nov. 1843, and transferred himself on 17 Jan. 1846 to the Inner Temple, he practised as a special pleader from 1847 to 1850, and in the latter year was called to the bar. He first travelled the western circuit, where he enjoyed the friendship of John Duke (afterwards Lord) Coleridge [q. v. Suppl. I], but soon exchanged this for the Midland circuit. He was quickly recognised as a sound and painstaking lawyer, and obtained a large junior practice, chiefly of the kind known as commercial. Among his pupils at the bar was Sir James Fitzjames Stephen [q. v.], afterwards his colleague on the bench. In February 1864 he was appointed a queen's counsel, and in April of the same year was elected a bencher of his inn. He enjoyed for the next nine years a 'steady and lucrative' practice, and became the recognised leader of his circuit, though his name was not widely known to the general public.

In February 1875, upon the retirement from the bench of Mr. Justice Keating, and the transfer to the court of common pleas of Mr. Justice Archibald, Field was appointed by Lord Cairns to fill the consequent vacancy in the court of queen's bench. He was the last judge appointed to that ancient tribunal, which six months later became a division of the high court of justice, itself a part of the supreme court of judicature. He was also nearly the last person to be made a serjeant-at-law, and he was, like other judges in the same situation, re-admitted to the bench of his own inn when Serjeants' Inn was dissolved in 1876.

As a judge Field showed great learning, a keen and vigorous intellect, and a somewhat irascible temper, which was due to, or was stimulated by, a chronic disorder described by himself as a general irritation of the mucous membrane. But he never allowed physical inconvenience to interfere with the thoroughness of his work. In his later years he also suffered from increasing deafness, and as he insisted upon hearing everything that was said, proceedings before him usually lasted longer than his impetuous nature would have permitted in more favourable circumstances. His hastiness of manner occasionally involved him in warm controversy with counsel, but he showed no subsequent resentment.

Field had his share in the trial of important litigation. He decided in favour of the plaintiff in the first instance the remarkable case of Dobbs *v.* the Grand Junction Waterworks Co., and his judgment was ultimately confirmed by the House of Lords, which decided that houses were to be rated for water on the rated not the gross value; the successful litigant conducted his case personally against a great array of professional talent (Nov. 1883). The great licensing case of Sharpe *v.* Wakefield was also originally tried by Field. And in Dalton *v.* Angus, which decides the right of the owner of land to the 'lateral support' of his neighbour's land, the judgment of the House of Lords was in accordance with Field's answers to the questions which the peers had submitted to the judges.

In 1890 Field retired from the bench, taking leave of the profession in the chief justice's court. He was sworn of the privy council, and on 10 April was created a peer by the title of Baron Field of Bakeham near Staines, Middlesex. During the next two years he sat fairly often in the House of Lords, and with Lord Bramwell [q. v. Suppl. I] he differed in 1891 from the majority in the important case of the Bank of England *v.* Vagliano [see LIDDERDALE, WILLIAM, Suppl. II]. His closing years were passed principally at Bognor, and he died there on 22 Jan. 1907, and was buried in a family vault at Virginia Water. Field married in 1864 Louisa, daughter of John Smith, who died on 24 May 1880 without issue.

A caricature by 'Spy' appeared in 'Vanity Fair' in 1887.

[The Times, 24 Jan. 1907; Foster's Men at the Bar; Who's Who, 1901; personal recollections.] H. S.

FINCH-HATTON, HAROLD HENEAGE (1856–1904), imperialist politician, born at Eastwell Park, Kent, on 23 Aug. 1856, was fourth son of George William Finch-Hatton, tenth earl of Winchilsea [q. v.], by his third wife, Fanny Margaretta, daughter of Edward Royd Rice, of Dane Court, Kent. His brother, Murray Edward Gordon Finch-Hatton, twelfth earl of Winchilsea (1851–1898), M.P. for South Lincolnshire (1884–5) and the Spalding division (1885–7), was well known as a leading agriculturist. Finch-Hatton was educated at Eton, and matriculated at Balliol College, Oxford, on 20 Oct. 1874, but did not graduate. In 1876 he joined a brother in Queensland remaining in the colony till 1883. For some time he was engaged in cattle-farming at a settlement named Mt. Spencer, but subsequently went prospecting for gold in the Nebo goldfields, some forty miles further inland and about 100 from Mackay. Gold was found at Mount Britten and shares were bought in other claims; but the working expenses, chiefly owing to the defective communication with the coast, made the venture unremunerative, and after some eighteen months the Finch-Hatton brothers disposed of their rights to a Melbourne syndicate, retaining only a fourth share in the concern. Finch-Hatton always preserved his interest in Queensland, and as permanent delegate and chairman of the London committee of the North Queensland Separation League rendered energetic service to the colony. In 1885 he published a readable record of his Australian experiences in a book entitled 'Advance, Australia!' containing a sympathetic estimate of the 'Blacks' (aborigines) founded on individual intercourse, and thoughtful surveys of the sugar and mining industries. The final chapter on Imperial Federation condemned the action of Lord Derby as colonial secretary in dealing with the New Guinea question. (For a criticism of some views expressed in the book see A. PATCHETT MARTIN, *Australia and the Empire*, pp. 88–90.)

On his return to England Finch-Hatton occupied himself in financial work. But his chief interest was in imperial politics. He was one of the founders of the Imperial Federation League, and for some time acted as its secretary; he was also secretary to the Pacific Telegraph Company, formed for the promotion of cable communication between Vancouver and Australia. When, in the autumn of 1885, he contested East Nottingham as a conservative he strongly advocated imperial federation as a prelude to free trade within the empire. Finch-Hatton was defeated by a majority of 991. Twice afterwards, in July 1886 and July 1892, he was unsuccessful in the same constituency. His opponent at all three elections was Mr. Arnold Morley. At the general election of 1895 he was returned unopposed for the Newark division of Nottinghamshire. His political career, however, was brief. An able maiden speech (28 April 1896) on the second reading of the agricultural rating bill, in which he appealed to his twenty years' experience of Australian land legislation, was followed by bad health. Falling out of sympathy with his party, he resigned his seat rather suddenly in May 1898 (*The Times*, 13 May 1898). He regarded the conservative foreign policy as too timid, and disapproved of the Irish Land Act of 1896 and other domestic legislation. When not in London he henceforth lived at Harlech, and in 1903 was high sheriff of Merionethshire. Highly skilled in field sports, a good rifle shot and keen huntsman, he excelled at golf, often competing for the amateur championship. He could also throw the boomerang 'like a black.'

He died, unmarried, from heart-failure on his own doorstep at 110 Piccadilly, on 16 May 1904, 'after having completed the last of his morning runs round the park.' He was buried in Ewerby churchyard, near Sleaford, Lincolnshire.

[The Times, 18 May 1904; Burke's and G. E. C.'s Peerages; Foster's Alumni Oxon.; Finch-Hatton's 'Advance, Australia!' 1885; Hansard's Parl. Debates; Sleaford Gazette, 21 and 28 May 1904; Mennell's Dict. of Australasian Biogr.; R. Nevill and C. E. Jerningham's Piccadilly to Pall Mall, pp. 71–3.] G. LE G. N.

FINLAYSON, JAMES (1840–1906), Scottish physician, born in Glasgow on 22 Nov. 1840, was third son and fourth child of the seven children of Thomas

Finlayson, a manufacturer in that city, by his wife Georgina Campbell, the daughter of an army surgeon in India. His elder brother, Thomas Campbell Finlayson, was a distinguished congregational minister, first at Downing Place, Cambridge, and later at Rusholme, Manchester, and was hon. D.D. Glasgow (1891). James received his early education at the High School of Glasgow, and in 1856 entered the old college in High Street as an arts student. From 1857 to 1862 he was in his father's business; but in 1863 he began the study of medicine, and graduated M.B. at Glasgow University with honours on 16 May 1867, with a thesis on 'The value of quantitative methods of investigation in medicine and allied sciences'; he proceeded M.D. in 1869, and on 18 April 1899 was made hon. LL.D. He was admitted a fellow of the Royal Faculty of Physicians and Surgeons of Glasgow in 1871, and was successively honorary librarian (1877–1901), visitor (1899), and president (1900–3) of that body. After serving as house surgeon at the Children's Hospital, Manchester, he was assistant to Sir William Tennant Gairdner [q. v. Suppl. II] at the Glasgow Royal Infirmary, and in 1875 was elected physician to the Western Infirmary, Glasgow, where he was a recognised teacher until his death. He was also physician (1883–98) and later consulting physician to the Royal Hospital for Sick Children, Glasgow, and for many years was medical adviser to the Scottish Amicable Insurance Company. He set a high standard of professional conduct and learning, and had a large and important practice in and around Glasgow.

Finlayson was a prolific writer on all aspects of medicine, including diseases of children. He wrote 150 papers, 60 of which appeared in the 'Glasgow Medical Journal.' He was especially interested in the history of medicine, and gave a number of lectures at Glasgow under the title of 'Bibliographical Demonstrations on Hippocrates, Galen, Herophilus, and Erasistratus' (1893–5), the substance of which he contributed to 'Janus,' an international medical journal. His most important works were: 1. 'Clinical Manual for the Examination of Medical Cases,' 1878; 3rd edit. 1891. 2. 'Account of the Life and Works of Maister Peter Lowe, the Founder of the Faculty of Physicians and Surgeons of Glasgow,' 1889. 3. 'An Account of the Life and Works of Dr. Robert Watt, Author of the "Bibliotheca Britannica,"' 1897. To 'Keating's Cyclopædia of the Diseases of Children' (1889) he contributed an article on 'Diagnosis.'

Finlayson, who was unmarried, died suddenly from apoplexy on 9 Oct. 1906 at his residence, 2 Woodside Place, Glasgow; his remains were cremated at the Western Necropolis. A bust by McGillivray belongs to his sister. His friends endowed the Finlayson Memorial Lecture (on a subject connected with medicine, preferably its history) at the Royal Faculty of Physicians and Surgeons of Glasgow; the first lecture was delivered on 28 Feb. 1908 by Dr. Norman Moore on the 'Schola Salernitana.'

[Glasgow Med. Journ. 1906, lxvi. 360–7 (with portrait); Brit. Med. Journ. 1906, ii. 1067; information from Sir Hector Cameron, M.D.] H. D. R.

FINNIE, JOHN (1829–1907), landscape painter and engraver, son of John Finnie, brassfounder, by his wife Christian McIndoe, was born at Aberdeen, where he was baptised in the parish church on 4 May 1829. After serving apprenticeships to a house-painter at Edinburgh and a japanner at Wolverhampton he obtained employment with William Wales, a glass-painter at Newcastle, where he remained five years, attending the school of design under William Bell Scott [q. v.]. In 1853 he went to London, where he studied and taught in the Central School of Design at Marlborough House till, in 1855, he became master of the School of Art, then called the Mechanics' Institution, at Liverpool. In this position he continued forty-one years and six months, retiring at Christmas 1896. He is described as the dominating personality in the art life of Liverpool during that period. He began to send to the Liverpool Academy exhibitions in 1856, became an associate in 1861, a full member and trustee in 1865, and was president of the academy in 1887–8. He was also president of the Artists' Club and of the Liver Sketching Club. He joined the Royal Cambrian Academy in 1894 and became its treasurer in 1897. His earliest etching, the 'Head of Windermere,' dates from 1864. After some early experiments in etching and engraving Finnie adopted mezzotint as his favourite process in 1886. Though he exhibited pictures at the Royal Academy from 1861 onwards, and also at the British Institution and in Suffolk Street, he was best known in London by his original mezzotint engravings of landscape, exhibited at the Royal Academy and the Royal Society of Painters, Etchers, and Engravers, of which he became an associate on 24 Oct. 1887.

and a fellow on 6 April 1895. He sent forty-seven contributions in all to the society's gallery. His etchings and mezzotints, which are represented by specimens in the print-room of the British Museum, aim too much at a full pictorial effect, instead of observing the restrictions of graphic art. As a painter he is represented in the Walker Art Gallery at Liverpool. On retiring from the School of Art, in 1896, Finnie broke up his home in Huskisson Street and settled at Tywyn, near Llandudno, where he spent his life in painting, engraving, and music. He retained full vigour until an attack of influenza injured his heart in 1905. He returned to Liverpool, where he died on 27 Feb. 1907. He was buried at Smithdown Road cemetery beside his wife, Agnes James Ellison, who died on 8 July 1889. One son, Dr. Ellison Finnie, survived him. A memorial exhibition of his art, comprising 438 numbers, was held at the Walker Art Gallery, Liverpool, in 1907.

[Biographical Sketch by E. Rimbault Dibdin in Cat. of Finnie Memorial Exhibition, Liverpool, 1907; Graves, Royal Acad. Exhibitors, 1905; H. C. Marillier, The Liverpool School of Painters, 1904, p. 119.] C. D.

FISON, LORIMER (1832–1907), Wesleyan missionary and anthropologist, born on 9 Nov. 1832, was thirteenth child, in a family of twenty, of Thomas Fison of Barningham, Suffolk. His mother was a daughter of the Rev. John Reynolds, whose translations of Fénelon, Massillon, and Bourdaloue achieved some popularity. After education at Sheffield he matriculated as a pensioner from Caius College, Cambridge, on 27 June 1855. He studied mathematics under Robert Potts [q. v.], the editor of Euclid, whose second wife was Fison's sister, but left the university at the end of his second term after a boyish escapade, and sailed for Australia in search of gold. Coming under religious influence there, he joined at Melbourne the Wesleyan communion. In 1863 he was ordained a Wesleyan minister, and was almost immediately after sent to Fiji as a missionary. He served there for a first period of eight years, till 1871, winning the confidence of natives and Europeans.

While in Fiji Fison got into unusually close touch with the natives, and became much interested in the subject of family relationships. The publication of Lewis Morgan's 'Systems of Consanguinity' (1871) stimulated his interest and he met Alfred William Howitt [q. v. Suppl. II], who had been for very many years working at the same subject in Australia. Fison spent the years 1871–5 in New South Wales and Victoria, combining ministerial labour with anthropological research. Thenceforward the names of Fison and Howitt were associated as fellow-workers [see under Howitt, Alfred William, Suppl. II]. In 1875 he returned to Fiji, and remained there till 1884. During this period he was principal of the institution at Navuloa for the training of natives as teachers. Fison wrote a remarkable paper on the little understood subject of Fijian land tenure. Its substance was first published in the 'Journal of the Anthropological Institute' in 1881. It was reprinted in pamphlet form by the Fiji government press in 1903. Apart from this work and his collaboration with Howitt in 'Kamilaroi and Kurnai' (1880), he wrote in the 'Journal of the Royal Anthropological Institute' on Fijian antiquities (1881–95).

In 1884 Fison on returning to Australia engaged till 1888 in ministerial work at Hawthorn and at Flemmington in Victoria. In 1888 he settled at Melbourne and from that year to 1905 he edited the Melbourne 'Spectator,' a Wesleyan periodical. He also helped to found the (Wesleyan) Queen's College in Melbourne University and was active in its management.

In 1892 he was president of the anthropological section of the Australian Advancement of Science meeting at Hobart Town. In 1894 he attended the meeting of the British Association at Oxford, when the results of his scientific research into the organisation of Australian tribes received full recognition. Of brilliant gifts as a linguist Lorimer excelled in conversation and greatly impressed scholarly society in England. After his return to Australia his health soon compelled absolute repose. But in 1904 he published 'Tales from Old Fiji,' which—partly perhaps because of a natural hesitation to publish for general information all that he knew about Fijian mythology—is the least valuable of his contributions to scientific anthropology. In 1905 he was awarded a civil list pension of 150*l*. He died at a house which he had built at Essenden, Victoria, on 29 Dec. 1907. His widow survived him with two sons and four daughters.

[Fison's writings; Johns' Notable Australians, 1908; J. G. Frazer's Howitt and Fison, in Folklore, June 1909, p. 144 seq.; The Victorian Naturalist, vol. xxiv. April 1908; Australian Methodist Missionary Review, Sydney, 4 Feb. 1908 (by Dr. George Brown).] E. im T.

FITCH, Sir JOSHUA GIRLING (1824–1903), inspector of schools and educational writer, born in Southwark on 13 Feb. 1824, was second son in a family of six sons and two daughters of Thomas Fitch, a clerk in Somerset House, by his wife Sarah Tucker Hodges. Both parents were natives of Colchester. The eldest son, Thomas Hodges (1822–1907), became a Roman catholic and eventually was attached to the Marist Church, Notre Dame de France, in Leicester Square, London. The third son, William John (1826–1902), was headmaster of the Boys' British School, Hitchin, from 1854 till 1899. From a private school Joshua passed to the Borough Road school, Southwark, where he became a pupil teacher in 1838 and a full assistant in 1842. About two years later he was appointed headmaster of the Kingsland Road school, Dalston. Studying hard in his spare hours, he in 1850 graduated B.A. in the University of London, and in 1852 proceeded M.A. (in classics).

In 1852, after trial work there in the previous year, he joined the staff of the Borough Road Training College, soon after became vice-principal, and in 1856 succeeded to the principalship on the retirement of Dr. James Cornwell [q. v. Suppl. II]. He proved himself a brilliant teacher, especially stimulating his pupils by his lectures on 'Method' and by his enthusiasm for literature. Through life he laid stress on the importance to the teacher of literary training. After contributing to some of Cornwell's educational treatises, he entered in 1861 into the political arena with 'Public Education: Why is a New Code needed?' In 1862 he helped in the organisation of the education section of the International Exhibition, and in 1863 Lord Granville, lord president of the council, who on a visit to Borough Road was impressed by Fitch's power as a teacher, made him an inspector of schools.

The district assigned to Fitch was the county of York, with the exception of certain portions of the north and the west. His three reports on the Yorkshire district admirably describe its educational condition then. From 1865 to 1867 as assistant commissioner for the schools inquiry commission, he inspected the endowed and proprietary schools in the West Riding of Yorkshire and in the city and ainsty of York, as well as other endowed schools in the North and East Ridings of Yorkshire and in Durham, and his reports were most thorough and suggestive. In 1869 he acted as special commissioner on elementary education in the great towns (Manchester, Birmingham, Liverpool, and Leeds), and from 1870 to 1877 was an assistant commissioner of endowed schools.

From 1877 to 1883 Fitch performed ordinary official duties as inspector of East Lambeth. In 1883 he became chief inspector of schools for the eastern division, including all the eastern counties from Lincoln to Essex. From 1885 to 1889 he was inspector of elementary training colleges for women in England and Wales. He was continued in this post till 1894, five years beyond the normal age of retirement from government service.

Occasionally detached for special duties in the later period of his public service, he prepared in 1888, after a visit to America, a report on American education under the title 'Notes on American Schools and Training Colleges'; in 1891 a memorandum on the 'Free School System in the United States, Canada, France, and Belgium'; and in 1893 'Instructions to H.M. Inspectors, with Appendices on Thrift and Training of Pupil Teachers.'

Fitch's educational activities passed far beyond his official work. His association with the University of London was always close. From 1860 to 1865 and from 1869 to 1874 he was examiner in English language and history. In 1875 he was appointed to the senate, and on his retirement in 1900 was made a life fellow.

Much of his energy was always devoted to the improvement of the education of women. He was an original member of the North of England Council for the Higher Education of Women (founded in 1866) and one of those who helped to found in 1867 the College for Women at Hitchin, which in 1874 became Girton College, near Cambridge. He took an active part in the establishment of the Girls' Public Day School Company in 1874, and was foremost among those who secured, in 1878, the new charter for the University of London which placed women students on equal terms with men. In 1890 he with Anthony John Mundella [q. v. Suppl. I] and Anna Swanwick [q. v. Suppl. I] selected the women's colleges and schools among which was distributed the sum of 60,000*l.* left by Mrs. Emily Pfeiffer [q. v.] for the promotion of women's education. He was consulted by Thomas Holloway [q. v.] about the constitution of Holloway College, Egham, and by the founders of the Maria Grey Training College and the Cambridge Training College for the training of women teachers for secondary schools.

In both 1877 and 1878 Fitch lectured with great success on practical teaching at the College of Preceptors, where he was examiner in the theory and practice of education (1879–81) and moderator in the same subjects (1881–1903). In 1879–80 he lectured at Cambridge for the newly appointed teachers' training syndicates and he published his course in 1881 as 'Lectures on Teaching' (new edit. 1882). The book established Fitch's position in England and America as an expert on school management, organisation, and method. In 1897 he published 'Thomas and Matthew Arnold and their Influence on English Education' in the 'Great Educators' series, and in 1900 he collected his chief lectures and addresses in 'Educational Aims and Methods.' Written with unusual charm of style, these volumes emphasised Fitch's position as that of a pioneer, especially on the practical side of education, as an earnest advocate for the better training of the elementary teacher, and for the more systematic training of secondary teachers.

The National Home Reading Union established by Dr. John Brown Paton [q. v. Suppl. II] and Dr. Hill, Master of Downing College, owed much to Fitch's account of 'The Chautauqua Reading Circles,' which he contributed to the 'Nineteenth Century' after his return from America in 1888.

After his retirement from the board of education in 1894 he was still active in public work. In 1895 he was a member of departmental committees of the board of education on industrial and naval and dockyard schools. In 1898–9 he was chairman of the council of the Charity Organisation Society. In 1902 he helped in the organisation of a nature study exhibition in London.

Fitch, who was made hon. LL.D. of St. Andrews in 1888, and a chevalier of the legion of honour in 1889 by the French government in recognition of the services he rendered in England to French travelling scholars, was knighted in 1896. He died at his residence, 13 Leinster Square, Bayswater, London, on 14 July 1903, and was buried at Kensal Green. In 1856 he married Emma, daughter of Joseph Barber Wilks, of the East India Company. She survived him without issue, and in 1904 received a civil list pension of 100*l.*; she died on 1 April 1909.

A portrait of Sir Joshua by Miss Ethel King was presented to him in 1890 in recognition of his services to the cause of the higher education of women. It is now in the possession of Miss Pickton, niece of Lady Fitch and adopted daughter of Sir Joshua and Lady Fitch.

[The Rev. A. L. Lilley, Sir Joshua Fitch: an Account of his Life and Work (with a complete bibliography); Educational Record, Oct. 1903, pp. 422–3; private information.]

F. W.

FITZGERALD, GEORGE FRANCIS (1851–1901), professor of natural and experimental philosophy in the University of Dublin, born at 19 Lower Mount St., Dublin, on 3 Aug. 1851, was second of three sons of William FitzGerald [q. v.], rector of St. Ann's, Dublin, and afterwards successively bishop of Cork and of Killaloe. His mother, Anne Frances, was daughter of George Stoney of Oakley Park, Birr, King's County, and sister of George Johnstone Stoney [q. v. Suppl. II]. His younger brother, Maurice, was professor of engineering in Queen's College, Belfast, from 1884 to 1910. After education at home, under M. A. Boole, sister of George Boole [q. v.] the mathematician, he entered Trinity College, Dublin, at sixteen, and graduated B.A. in 1871 as first senior moderator in mathematics and experimental science, having won the university studentship in science. From boyhood he had shown an aptitude for mathematics, was athletic, and skilful with his fingers, but showed little ability for languages. For six years (1871–7), with a view to a fellowship, he studied the memoirs of mathematical physicists, and at the same time acquired a life-long reverence for the philosophy of Bishop Berkeley. He was awarded a fellowship in 1877 and became a tutor of the college. On the death of John R. Leslie in 1881 he became Erasmus Smith professor of natural and experimental philosophy, and held the post till his death.

Both as tutor and as professor FitzGerald exerted himself to bring the teaching of physical science at Trinity College up to the standard of the time, but he was hampered by lack of funds. He started, however, a physical laboratory, and gathered round him a small band of earnest workers whom he infected with his own enthusiasm. A large proportion of his teaching work was necessarily elementary, but his honours students fully appreciated his originality and suggestiveness.

FitzGerald showed a singular insight into difficult and obscure branches of physical science. His published work, 'not large in bulk but very choice and original,' deals mainly with the correction and development of the electromagnetic theory of radiation first put forward by Professor Clerk Maxwell [q. v.]. He suggested in 1882 the principle of the method of production of 'electric waves' which Hertz used in 1887, and he contributed much himself to our knowledge of their properties. He took a leading part in the discussion of electrolysis, and supported the view, since confirmed, that 'cathode rays' are streams of electrified particles. 'He possessed extraordinary versatility, and in the deepest subjects was more at home than in the trivial,' throwing out luminous suggestions 'with splendid prodigality and rejoicing if they were absorbed and utilised by others.' All his writings—chiefly contributions to the periodicals of scientific societies—have been collected by Sir Joseph Larmor and issued by the Dublin University Press as 'The Scientific Writings of the late George Francis FitzGerald' (1902).

FitzGerald was elected F.R.S. London in 1883, and in 1899 was awarded a royal medal by the society for his investigations in theoretical physics. In 1900 he was made an honorary fellow of the Royal Society of Edinburgh. He acted as honorary secretary of the Royal Dublin Society from 1881 to 1889, and as registrar of Dublin University School of Engineering from 1886. He was president of the mathematical and physical section of the British Association at Bath in 1888, president of the Physical Society of London in 1892–3, and chairman of the Dublin local section of the Institution of Electrical Engineers on its foundation in 1899. For many years he was examiner in physics in the University of London, and he took a prominent part in the educational affairs of Ireland, serving on the boards of national, of intermediate, and of technical education for Ireland. In educational matters 'self-satisfied unprogressiveness excited his indignation.'

FitzGerald died at 7 Ely Place, Dublin, on 22 Feb. 1901, and was buried at Mount Jerome. He married Harriette Mary, second daughter of John Hewitt Jellett, F.R.S. [q. v.], and had by her three sons and five daughters. His widow was awarded a civil list pension of 100*l.* in 1903. A charcoal portrait done about 1877 by John Butler Yeats belongs to his brother Maurice. An enlargement of the engraved portrait which forms the frontispiece of the 'Collected Works' hangs in the engineering school of Trinity College, Dublin.

[The Times, 25 Feb. 1901; Nature, 7 March 1901; Electrician, 1 March 1901; Proc. Roy. Soc. vol. 75, 1905; Journal Inst. Elect. Eng. 30, pp. 510. 1244; Physical Review, May 1901, reprinted in Collected Works; private information from Miss FitzGerald, Prof. F. T. Trouton, and Prof. W. E. Thrift.] C. H. L.

FITZGERALD, SIR THOMAS NAGHTEN (1838–1908), surgeon, born on 1 Aug. 1838 at Tullamore, Ireland, was son of John FitzGerald of the Indian civil service. After attending St. Mary's College, Kingston, he received his professional education at Mercers' Hospital in Dublin, became L.R.C.S. Ireland in 1857, and obtained a commission in the Army Medical Staff. A sudden attack of illness obliged him to abandon his course at Netley, and he made a voyage to Australia in search of health. Arriving at Melbourne in July 1858, he was immediately appointed house surgeon at the Melbourne Hospital, and held the post for two years, after which he began to practise privately as a surgeon in Lonsdale Street. In 1860 he was appointed full surgeon to the hospital, to which he was elected a consulting surgeon on his resignation in 1900. He was also consulting surgeon to the Queen Victoria, St. Vincent, and Austin hospitals. He excelled in the operative part of his profession, and wrote papers for medical journals on cleft palate, fractured patella, club foot, drilling in bone formations, and like surgical topics. When the medical school was started at Melbourne he proved himself as good a teacher as he was a surgeon. In 1884 he revisited Ireland, and after examination became F.R.C.S. Ireland. He was knighted in 1897 on the occasion of the diamond jubilee of Queen Victoria. He was president of the Medical Society of Victoria both in 1884 and in 1890, and of the Intercolonial Medical Congress in 1889. In 1900 he went to South Africa as consulting surgeon to the imperial forces then engaged in the Boer war, and for his services was made C.B. He published in the 'Intercolonial Medical Journal of Australasia' (1 Dec. 1900) an interesting account of his experiences in South Africa, in which the work of the Royal Army Medical Corps and the nursing staff was commended. He died on 8 July 1908 on board the s.s. Wyreema between Cairns and Townsville, while on a voyage for his health. He was buried in the Melbourne general cemetery. He married in 1870 Margaret, daughter of James Robertson, Launceston, Tasmania, and by her, who died in 1890, he had issue three daughters.

[Australian Med. Gaz. vol. 27, 1908, p. 428 (with portrait); Lancet, 1908, ii. 200.] D'A. P.

FITZGIBBON, GERALD (1837–1909), lord justice of appeal in Ireland, born in Dublin on 28 Aug. 1837, was eldest of the three children (two sons and a daughter) of Gerald FitzGibbon, K.C., master in chancery and a leading member of the Irish bar, by his wife Ellen, daughter of John Patterson of Belfast. His younger brother, Henry (*d.* 23 Feb. 1912), was at one time president of the Royal College of Surgeons in Ireland. Gerald became classical scholar in 1858 at Trinity College, Dublin, where he highly distinguished himself in classics, law, oratory, and English composition. He was made hon. LL.D. in 1895 (*Dublin Univ. Cal.* 1906–7, Suppl.). He was always deeply devoted to Trinity College, to which he said he owed everything and at whose service he constantly placed till death his eloquence and industry.

FitzGibbon was called to the Irish bar in Hilary Term, 1860, with Edward Gibson, afterwards Lord Ashbourne. The two were of the same age, and they subsequently took together on the same dates the various steps which brought them to the bench. FitzGibbon was soon the leading junior, both on his circuit (the Munster) and in Dublin. He refused silk in 1868, when offered it by Brewster, lord chancellor, but accepted the promotion from Lord Chancellor O'Hagan. He was called 'within the bar' in Trinity Term, 1872. FitzGibbon's senior practice was large, and he led the Munster circuit until his retirement from circuit on becoming a law officer. Even then he was taken 'special' in important cases throughout the country. Among the cases in which he proved his eminence as an advocate was that of O'Keeffe *v.* (Cardinal) Cullen (May 1873), in which he secured a verdict against the cardinal from a Dublin jury largely composed of catholics, though the verdict was afterwards set aside on technical grounds, and that of Bagot *v.* Bagot, a will case, lasting twenty-two days from 25 April 1878, in which his masterly statement for the plaintiff, Mrs. Bagot, secured her the verdict from a dubious jury, an adverse judge, and against the views of a host of medical experts (*Irish Times*, 26 April 1878 and following days; *Law Rep. Ireland*, vol. i.).

In 1876 FitzGibbon, who was a conservative in politics, became law adviser to Dublin Castle, an office since abolished. In 1877 he was made solicitor-general for Ireland in Lord Beaconsfield's government, and held the office until 13 Dec. 1878, when he was promoted lord justice of appeal. In the same year he was elected a bencher of the King's Inns, and next year was made a privy councillor of Ireland. FitzGibbon's career as a judge, which lasted for over thirty-one years, was highly distinguished. Many of his judgments were reviewed by the House of Lords, and in every case where he differed from the colleagues of his own court his opinion was upheld by the House of Lords. In Aaron's Reefs *v.* Twiss, where shares had been allotted on a fraudulent prospectus, FitzGibbon differed from the lord chancellor of Ireland, the master of the rolls, and in a minor degree from the other lord justice, and was upheld by the lords, Halsbury, Herschell, Watson, Macnaghten, Morris, and Davey (1896, *Appeal Cases*, p. 273; 1895, 2 *Irish Reports*, p. 207).

FitzGibbon was also a member of the English bar. Admitted to Lincoln's Inn on 12 Jan. 1857, he was called in Trinity Term, 1861, and was invited to the bench on 16 April 1901. He was made a privy councillor of England in 1900.

FitzGibbon was a man of many activities outside his profession. He did much for education in Ireland. He served with Lord Rosse and Lord Randolph Churchill on the commission appointed in 1878 to inquire into the condition and management of the endowed schools of Ireland (WINSTON S. CHURCHILL, *Lord R. Churchill*, pp. 78, 79; *Endowed Schools (Ireland), Report of the Royal Commissioners*, 1881). The Report led to the more important commission 'on educational endowments in Ireland,' of which FitzGibbon was chairman from 1885 to 1897. During its existence they framed schemes dealing with 1350 primary schools, eighty intermediate, and twenty-two collegiate schools and institutions, and the total annual income administered under these schemes was over 140,000*l.* Most of FitzGibbon's vacations were devoted to this commission. He was also a commissioner of national education in Ireland from 1884 to 1896, and in that capacity was specially successful in getting the rival denominations to agree.

In 1876 FitzGibbon joined the freemasons (Trinity College Lodge), and at once took a very active part in the charities. In 1879 he became a governor of the girls' school, and was devoted to its interest. In 1902 he defrayed the cost of the physical and chemical laboratory. After a visit to Canada in 1899 he became the representative in Ireland of the Grand Lodge of Canada. In 1908 he was elected president of the General Chapter of Prince Masons in Ireland, and published a volume of 'Addresses' delivered in that office. On his death the freemason brethren founded in his memory the 'FitzGibbon Memorial Gymnasium' in the girls' school, the 'FitzGibbon Memorial Burse' in the boys' school, and the 'FitzGibbon annuity.'

He was also active in the affairs of the Church of Ireland, serving for many years on the diocesan board of patronage for Dublin, and proving his skill in debate in the general synod. He was chancellor of many diocesan courts and lay diocesan nominator for the archdiocese of Dublin. He was one of the chief promoters of, and a generous contributor to, 'The Auxiliary Fund,' by which the great depreciation in the investments of the church and the poverty of the incumbents was supplemented.

At his country house at Howth, FitzGibbon long entertained at Christmas parties of men of all kinds of distinction. In later years his regular visitors included George Salmon [q. v. Suppl. II], provost of Trinity, Monsignor Molloy, John (Viscount) Morley, Mr. Arthur Balfour, Lords Roberts and Wolseley. But his most intimate friend among English politicians was Lord Randolph Churchill, whose acquaintance he first made at Dublin Castle in 1876, when Lord Randolph's father, the duke of Marlborough, was lord-lieutenant. Subsequently they constantly corresponded on frank and confidential terms. FitzGibbon wrote to Lord Randolph deprecating his acceptance of the chancellorship of the exchequer in 1886, and expressing a preference for Goschen.

FitzGibbon died at Howth on 14 Oct. 1909, and was buried in the graveyard attached to the old ruined church of St. Fintan at Howth. In the court of criminal appeal in England the lord chief justice expressed (15 Oct.) sympathy with the bench of Ireland on his death, describing him as 'a great judge, a profound lawyer, and a man of wide and varied learning' (*The Times*, 16 Oct. 1909). Such a reference to an Irish judge from the bench of England seems to have been unprecedented (*Law Times*, 23 Oct. 1909).

FitzGibbon married in 1864 Margaret Ann, second daughter of Francis Alexander Fitzgerald, baron of the exchequer in Ireland, and had issue three sons and four daughters. His eldest son, Gerald, is king's counsel in Ireland, being the third generation of the family to attain that honour.

Two portraits in oils by Walter Osborne, R.H.A., one in the Masonic girls' school, Dublin, the other at Howth, were presented by the Order to the school and to Mrs. FitzGibbon respectively. A full-length portrait was painted by Miss Harrison for the University Club, Dublin. A portrait in judicial robes for the banqueting hall of the King's Inns, by William Orpen, R.A., was subscribed for by the bench and bar of Ireland. A marble statue by A. Bruce Joy is to be placed in St. Patrick's Cathedral.

[Private information; Winston S. Churchill, Lord Randolph Churchill, 1906; Annual Report of the Masonic Female Orphan School of Ireland for 1909 (Dublin, 1910), and of the Grand Lodge of Free and Accepted Masons of Ireland for 1909; Thom's Directory, 1909; The Irish Reports, Common Law; The Irish Reports, Equity; The Irish Law Reports; Appeal Cases (both series) (England); Endowed Schools (Ireland) Report of the Royal Commission, 1881; Educational Endowments (Ireland), Reports of the Commission and Evidence, published in 1886; The Times, 16 Oct. 1909; The Law Times, 23 Oct. 1909.] D. F.

FLEAY, FREDERICK GARD (1831–1909), Shakespearean scholar, born at Deptford Broadway on 5 Sept. 1831, was son of John Goss Fleay, linen-draper, by his wife Jane. Both parents were of Somerset families. Of seven children, three—two sons and a daughter—alone lived to maturity.

Frederick, according to family tradition, was able to read at twenty months old. Entering, in 1843, King's College school, where Frederic Harrison was one of his companions, he rose to be captain, distinguishing himself alike in classics and mathematics. In Oct. 1849 he passed to Trinity College, Cambridge, his parents accompanying him in order to provide him with a home in the town. In his second year at Trinity he won an open mathematical scholarship, and after gaining several college prizes, graduated B.A. in 1853 as thirteenth wrangler, and sixth in the second class in the classical tripos. He was also placed third in the examination for Smith's prizes, and impressed the examiners with his aptitude for higher mathematics. Next year he obtained second place in the first class of the moral science tripos, and first place in the second class in the natural science tripos. Undergraduates dubbed him 'the industrious flea.' Despite the rare distinction of figuring in four tripos lists, Fleay just missed a fellowship at Trinity. He proceeded M.A. in 1856, and was ordained deacon in that year and priest in 1857.

Adopting a scholastic career, he was from 1856 to 1859 vice-principal of the Oxford

Diocesan Training College at Culham. From 1860 to 1866 he was second master and head of the scientific side at Leeds grammar school. After six months in 1867 as second master and head of the modern division at King Edward's School, Birmingham, he was headmaster of Hipperholme grammar school from 1868 to 1872, and filled a like post at Skipton grammar school from 1872 to 1876, when he abandoned the teaching profession. Although his teaching was mainly devoted to mathematics and science, he was an efficient instructor in both classics and English and interested himself in educational theory. Much practical value attaches to his 'Hints on Teaching,' which he published in 1874; and there is ingenuity in his 'Elements of English Grammar: Relations of Words to Sentences (Word Building)' (1859, 2 parts), and 'Logical English Grammar' (1884).

Fleay issued, while a schoolmaster, 'The Book of Revelation' (1864), a collection of orthodox sermons. But his independent and speculative habit of mind gradually alienated him from the Church of England, and on 7 February 1884 he relinquished his orders. He had studied sympathetically Comte's philosophy without accepting the Positivist religion. 'Three Lectures on Education' which show Comte's influence were read at Newton Hall in Nov. 1882, and published with a preface by Frederic Harrison in 1883. His love of more recondite speculation he illustrated in 1889 by privately circulating a highly complex mathematical study: 'Harmonics of Sound and Colour: their Law identical, their Use convertible.'

Meanwhile Fleay was devoting himself to literary work. From an early date he had interested himself in phonetics and in spelling reform. In 1858 he won the Trevelyan prize for an essay on phonetic spelling, which convinced one of the examiners, Max Müller, of his philological promise. There followed in 1878 his 'English Sounds and English Spelling.' In 1879 he joined the newly formed Spelling Reform Association and edited its journal, 'The Spelling Reformer' (1880–1). He devised two alphabets, the 'Victorian form' for educational purposes, and the 'Elizabethan form' for literary purposes. The former departed further than the latter from accepted orthography, but the method of both was sound.

In 1874 Fleay joined the New Shakspere Society on its foundation by Frederick James Furnivall [q. v. Suppl. II], and he applied much of his manifold industry for some twenty years to the elucidation of Shakespearean and Elizabethan drama. He contributed many papers to the 'Transactions of the New Shakspere Society.' His Shakespearean books began modestly with an 'Introduction to Shakespeare Study' (1877). There followed a useful 'Shakespeare Manual' (1878), with editions of Marlowe's 'Edward II' (1877), and of Shakespeare's 'King John,' and of the anonymous play on the theme (1878), as well as two pamphlets, 'Actor Lists, 1578–1642' (reprinted from 'Royal Hist. Soc. Trans.' 1881), and 'History of Theatres in London' (1882). All these efforts were preliminary to his three imposing compilations: 'A Chronicle History of the Life and Work of William Shakespeare' (1886), 'A Chronicle History of the London Stage,' 1559–1642' (1890), and 'A Biographical Chronicle of the English Drama, 1559–1642' (2 vols. 1891). The three works were handsomely printed in limited editions and quickly became scarce books.

Fleay's Shakespearean labours were severely practical, even statistical. Literary criticism lay outside his scope. He analysed with minuteness the changes in Shakespeare's metre and phraseology, and rigidly applied metrical and linguistic tests to a determination not only of the chronology of Shakespeare's and his fellow-dramatists' acknowledged work but of the authorship of anonymous plays of the era. His arbitrary identifications of the writers of the anonymous Elizabeth drama were often startling. He was no less dogmatic in his alleged detection of concealed topical or political allusions in text, plot, and character. At the same time the immense care with which he traced the history of the playing companies in the Shakespearean period threw much new light on English dramatic and theatrical history.

From Shakespearean and Elizabethan themes Fleay finally turned to Egyptology and Assyriology, chiefly in their bearing on biblical criticism. His main results were collected in 'Egyptian Chronology' (1899), dedicated to the memory of Edward White Benson [q. v. Suppl. I]. His latest inquiry concerned the Great Pyramid, on which he published a paper in 1905.

A self-denying and toilsome student who lived a secluded life. Fleay died at 27 Dafforne Road, Upper Tooting, London, on 10 March 1909, and was buried at Brookwood cemetery, Woking. He married on 14 Jan. 1869 Mary Ann Kite, who predeceased him in 1896. Their only child, John, survived him.

Besides the works cited Fleay published 'Almond Blossoms,' verse, in 1857; translations of 'Breton Ballads' (1870), and the 'Poetry of Catullus' and 'Vigil of Venus' (1874); 'A Guide to Chaucer and Spenser' (Glasgow, 1877, in 'Collins's School and College Classics'); and 'The Land of Shakespeare illustrated' (1889).

[Private information; Testimonials collected by Fleay, 1863–70 (privately printed); Athenæum, March 1909 (by Dr. A. W. Ward); Frederic Harrison's Autobiographical Memoirs, 1911.] S. L.

FLEMING, GEORGE (1833–1901), veterinary surgeon, born at Glasgow on 11 March 1833, was son of a working shoeing-smith there. Early in life he was taken by his father to Manchester, where both were employed in the farrier's shop of a veterinary surgeon. He subsequently entered the service of a well-known veterinary surgeon of Manchester, John Lawson, who sent him to Dick's College in Edinburgh. He took several medals and prizes, and in 1855 obtained the certificate of the Highland and Agricultural Society of Scotland, which was then recognised as a veterinary diploma. At the end of that year he entered the army veterinary service, and served in the Crimea until the termination of the war. In 1860 he volunteered for the expedition to North China, and was present at the capture of the Taku Forts and the surrender of Pekin, receiving for his services a medal with two clasps. Whilst in China he undertook an expedition beyond the Great Wall, which he described in 'Travels on Horseback in Manchu Tartary' (1865). In 1866 he obtained the diploma of the Royal College of Veterinary Surgeons, and in 1867 served with the army in Syria and Egypt. On his return he spent some years with the royal engineers at Chatham. In 1879 he was appointed inspecting veterinary surgeon at the war office, and in 1883 principal veterinary surgeon to the army. In 1887 he was made C.B. and in 1890 he retired from the army.

Fleming became a vice-president of the Royal College of Veterinary Surgeons in 1867, a year after his admission, and a member of council in 1868. He was elected president in 1880, when the agitation for an act of parliament to restrict the title of veterinary surgeon to the diploma-holders of the college had become acute, and by his energy and pertinacity he was mainly instrumental in securing the passage through parliament of the Veterinary Surgeons Act, 1881, which imposed a penalty upon unqualified persons who took or used the title of veterinary surgeon. The misuse of the title had become a public scandal. Fleming was in gratitude re-elected president for three years in succession (1881–4), and again in 1886–7. His portrait (full-length) was painted by B. Hudson, and presented to the college by subscription on 7 May 1883, 'as a token,' according to the inscription at the foot, 'of sincere esteem and gratitude.'

He received in 1883 the honorary degree of LL.D. from the University of Glasgow. He died on 13 April 1901 at Higher Leigh, Combe Martin, North Devon, his residence in later life. He was three times married: (1) to Alice, daughter of J. Peake of Atherstone in 1863; (2) to Susan, daughter of W. Solomon of Upchurch, Kent, in 1878; (3) to Anna, daughter of Colonel R. D. Pennefather of Kilbracken, co. Leitrim, who survived him and afterwards remarried.

Fleming was a voluminous writer, contributing largely to professional journals and to general reviews. He translated from the French Chauveau's 'Comparative Anatomy of the Domesticated Animals' (1873; 2nd edit. 1891), and from the German Neumann's 'Parasites and Parasitical Diseases of the Domesticated Animals' (1892; 2nd edit. 1905). His separately published works include: 1. 'Vivisection: Is it necessary or justifiable?' 1866. 2. 'Horse-Shoes and Horse-Shoeing—their Origin, History, etc.,' 1869. 3. 'Animal Plagues: their History, Nature, and Prevention,' vol. i. 1871; vol. ii. 1882. 4. 'Practical Horse-Shoeing,' 1872; 10th edit. 1900. 5. 'Rabies and Hydrophobia,' 1872. 6. 'A Manual of Veterinary Sanitary Science and Policy,' 2 vols. 1875. 7. 'A Text Book of Veterinary Obstetrics,' 1878; 2nd edit. 1896. 8. 'The Influence of Heredity and Contagion in the Propagation of Tuberculosis,' 1883. 9. 'Operative Veterinary Surgery,' vol. i. 1884. 10. 'The Practical Horse-Keeper,' 1886. His library of 900 volumes of books on professional subjects was given by him in 1900 to the Royal College of Veterinary Surgeons.

[The Times, 16 April 1901; Veterinary Record, vol. xiii. 27 April 1901; personal knowledge.] E. C.

FLEMING, JAMES (1830–1908), canon of York, born at Carlow on 26 July 1830, was youngest of five children of Patrick Fleming, M.D., of Strabane, who married in 1820 Mary, daughter of Captain Francis Kirkpatrick. Both families were of Scottish extraction. From 1833 to 1836 the boy was in Jamaica, his father having become paymaster to the 56th regiment; and on his father's death in 1838 his mother, who survived till September 1876, moved to Bath. His two brothers, William and Francis, were sent to Sandhurst, but ultimately took orders; William, an old-fashioned protestant, died vicar of Christ Church, Chislehurst, in May 1900. James went to King Edward VI's grammar school, Bath, in 1840, and to Shrewsbury in 1846, under Benjamin Hall Kennedy [q. v.]. He was in the school eleven, and won the Millington scholarship, matriculating on 15 Nov. 1849 at Magdalene College Cambridge, from which he graduated in 1853, proceeding M.A. in 1857 and B.D. in 1865. Ordained deacon in 1853 and priest in 1854, he was curate, first, of St. Stephen, Ipswich (1853–5), and then of St. Stephen, Lansdown, in the parish of Walcot, Bath (1855–9), with charge of the chapel of All Saints, where his plain evangelical preaching attracted good congregations. He started classes of instruction in elocution for working people in 1859, and was a strong advocate of total abstinence. In 1866 he was appointed by trustees to the incumbency of Camden church, Camberwell, formerly held by Henry Melvill [q. v.], and in 1873 was presented by the marquis (afterwards first duke) of Westminster to the vicarage of St. Michael, Chester Square. Admitted on 19 Feb. 1874, he retained this benefice till his death, becoming chaplain to the duke of Westminster in 1875. On 21 June 1899 the second duke of Westminster, on behalf of the congregation, presented him with an address and 2000*l.* on the completion of twenty-five years' incumbency. During the period parochial schools and local churches increased and a convalescent home, for which a parishioner gave Fleming 23,500*l.*, was built at Birchington. Outside his parish his chief interests were Dr. Barnardo's Homes [see Barnardo, Thomas John, Suppl. II]; the Religious Tract Society, of which he was an honorary secretary from 1880; and the Hospital Sunday Fund, to which he trained his congregation to make large annual contributions, amounting in twenty-eight years to nearly 35,000*l.*

Meanwhile on 30 May 1876 Lord Beaconsfield nominated Fleming to a residentiary canonry in York Minster (see *Debate in House of Lords*, 16 June 1879). William Thomson [q. v.], archbishop of York, made him succentor on 20 Aug. 1881, and precentor with a prebendal stall on 3 Jan. 1883. In 1880 Lord Beaconsfield was inclined to appoint him first bishop of Liverpool, but local pressure caused John Charles Ryle [q.v. Suppl. I] to be preferred. He afterwards declined the bishopric of Sydney with the primacy of Australia, Nov. 1884 [see Barry, Alfred, Suppl. II], and from reasons of income Lord Salisbury's successive offers of the deaneries of Chester (20 Dec. 1885) and of Norwich (6 May 1889). Honorary chaplain to Queen Victoria (1876) and chaplain in ordinary to her (1880) and to Edward VII (1901), Fleming from 1879 preached almost yearly before Queen Victoria, and before Edward VII, when Prince of Wales, at Sandringham. On 24 Jan. 1892 he preached at Sandringham the sermon in memory of the Duke of Clarence [see Albert Victor Christian Edward, Suppl. I], which was published as 'Recognition in Eternity,' and had a continuous sale, reaching in 1911 to about 67,000 copies. The author's profits, amounting by May 1911 to 1725*l.*, were distributed between two charities named by Queen Alexandra—the Gordon Boys' Home and the British Home and Hospital for Incurables. From 1880 Fleming was Whitehead professor of preaching and elocution at the London College of Divinity (St. John's Hall, Highbury). Three times—1901, 1903, and 1907—he was appointed William Jones lecturer (sometimes called the Golden lectureship) by the Haberdashers' Company. Fleming, who early in 1877 denounced the 'folly, obstinacy, and contumacy' of the ritualists in 'The Times' (25 Jan. 1877), ceased to wear the black gown in the pulpit after the judgment in Clifton *v.* Ridsdale (12 May 1877). But his suspicion of ritualism increased with his years (*cf.* Mrs. Creighton's *Life and Letters of Mandell Creighton*, ii. 308–309). In later life he supported the protestant agitation of John Kensit [q. v. Suppl. II]. His personal relations with C. H. Spurgeon [q. v.], William Morley Punshon [q. v.], and other nonconformist leaders were very cordial. Fleming died at St. Michael's Vicarage on 1 Sept. 1908, and was buried at Kensal Green cemetery. A reredos and choir stalls in memory of him were placed in St. Michael's (1911), and a statue of King Edwyn in York Minster. He married, on 21 June 1853, at Holy Trinity, Brompton, Grace, elder daughter of Admiral Purcell, who died on 25 May 1903. They had three sons and three daughters. A cartoon portrait of Fleming by 'Spy' appeared in 'Vanity Fair' in 1889.

Fleming's personal charm and grace of speech made him popular. but he was neither a student nor a thinker. 'The Stolen Sermon, or Canon Fleming's Theft,' a pamphlet issued in 1887 (embodying an article in the 'Weekly Churchman,' 6 May), showed that one of two sermons by Fleming, published as 'Science and the Bible' (1880), reproduced almost verbatim 'The Bible Right,' a sermon by Dr. Talmage ('Fifty Sermons,' 2nd series, 2nd edit. 1876, pp. 312–21). Fleming explained in a published letter that he had inadvertently transferred Dr. Talmage's sermon from his common-place book. Apart from some twenty separate sermons, chiefly for special occasions, Fleming published a useful manual on 'The Art of Reading and Speaking' (1896) and 'Our Gracious Queen Alexandra' (1901) for the Religious Tract Society.

[A. R. M. Finlayson, Life of Canon Fleming, 1909; The Times, 2 Sept. 1908; Record, 4 Sept. 1908; Guardian, 2 and 9 Sept. 1908; Crockford, Clerical Directory, 1908.]

E. H. P.

FLETCHER, JAMES (1852–1908), naturalist, born at Ashe, near Wrotham, Kent, England, on 28 March 1852, was second son of Joseph Flitcroft Fletcher by his wife Mary Ann Hayward. The eldest son, Flitcroft Fletcher, was an artist who exhibited five pictures at the Royal Academy (1882–6), dying at the age of thirty-six. Fletcher was educated at King's School, Rochester, and joined the Bank of British North America in London in 1871. In 1874 he was transferred to Canada and stationed at Montreal. In 1875 he entered the Ottawa office of the bank, and, resigning in May 1876, was employed in the library of parliament until 1 July 1887. Fletcher, whose leisure was devoted to the study of botany and entomology, was then appointed entomologist and botanist to the recently organised Dominion experimental farms. Since 1884 he had acted as Dominion entomologist in the department of agriculture. Elected a fellow of the Linnæan Society on 3 June 1886 and a member of the Entomological Society of America and other scientific societies, he was one of the founders of the Ottawa Field Naturalists' Club. At his death he was president of the Entomological Society of Ontario, and honorary secretary of the Royal Society of Canada. In 1896 he received the honorary degree of LL.D. from Queen's University.

Fletcher was a voluminous writer. To the 'Transactions' of the Ottawa Field Naturalists' Club he contributed a 'Flora Ottawaensis,' and with George H. Clark he published 'Farm Weeds of Canada' (1906). Valuable papers on injurious insects and on the diurnal *lepidoptera* appeared at intervals. Seventeen species of butterflies bear his name. He died at Montreal on 8 Nov. 1908, and is buried in Beechwood cemetery, Ottawa.

He married in 1879 Eleanor Gertrude, eldest daughter of Collingwood Schreiber, C.M.G., Ottawa, by whom he had two daughters.

The Ottawa Field Naturalists' Club erected in his memory a drinking-fountain with bronze medallion at the experimental farm, and had a portrait painted by Franklyn Brownell, R.C.A., which now hangs in the Ottawa public library.

[Information supplied by Fletcher's daughter, Mrs. R. S. Lake; memorial notices by the Ottawa Field Naturalists' Club in The Ottawa Naturalist, vol. xxii. No. 10, Jan. 1909.]

P. E.

FLINT, ROBERT (1838–1910), philosopher and theologian, born near Dumfries on 14 March 1838, was the son of Robert Flint, at that time a farm overseer, by his wife (born Johnston). His first school was at Moffat. In 1852 he entered Glasgow University, where he distinguished himself (without graduating) in arts and divinity. Having been employed as a lay missionary by the 'Elders' Association' of Glasgow, he was licensed to preach in 1858, and for a short time acted as assistant to Norman Macleod the younger [q. v.], at the Barony Church, Glasgow. He was minister of the East Church, Aberdeen (1859–62) and of Kilconquhar, Fife (1862–4), a country parish, which gave him leisure for study, improved by visits to Germany. On the death of James Frederick Ferrier [q. v.] in 1864 Flint was elected to succeed him in the moral philosophy chair at St. Andrews University, among the competing candidates being Thomas Hill Green [q. v.]. This chair he held till 1876, when he succeeded Thomas Jackson Crawford [q. v.] in the divinity chair of Edinburgh University. On this appointment he was made LL.D. of Glasgow and D.D. of Edinburgh. Thomas Chalmers [q. v.] had similarly migrated from the one chair to the other. Flint was appointed to a number of foundation lectureships. He was Baird lecturer (1876–7); in 1880 he crossed to America, and delivered a course as Stone lecturer at Princeton ; in 1887–8 he was Croall lecturer. He was elected on 21 May 1883 corresponding member of the Institute of France (Académie des sciences morales et politiques), and was a fellow of the Royal Society of Edinburgh. He resigned his chair to devote himself to literary work, a purpose hampered by failing health. For some time he lived at Musselburgh. He delivered the Gifford lectures in 1908–9. He died, unmarried, at his residence, 3 Royal Terrace, Edinburgh, on 25 Nov. 1910.

Flint was in person spare but well knit; his pale features wore an expression of self-command; his dark moustache gave distinction to his clerical garb. He had few intimates, and lived much of his life apart, devoted to his studies, always a hard reader, of extraordinary diligence in research and facile power of mastery. He had no taste for amusements, country walks being his one recreation. With his students he was popular, for he was patient and kind; yet it is said that of them all only two were ever privileged to accompany him in his walks. His methods were deliberate, his composition slow and sure in a small and neat handwriting, his speech measured and with some peculiarities of enunciation, e.g. 'awtoms,' 'know-ledge.' All his work was planned on a large scale; the cycle of his divinity lectures extended to seven sessions; his best-known books, complete in themselves, were parts of wider schemes; his sermons have been described as of 'magnificent length and toughness'; that his preaching was highly esteemed was due to his easy grasp of his subject, the elevation of his treatment, his straightforward style, and the convincing tones of his penetrating voice. As a thinker his characteristic was the confidence with which he brought all matters to the test of reason, trusting it as a guide to positive conclusions, and resting nothing on sentimental or prudential grounds. On lines of independent judgment he followed in the succession of Butler and Paley, welcoming every advance of physical science and speculative thought as enlarging the field for critical investigation and helping to clear the issue. His students were stimulated to the exercise of their own minds and to the attainment of a high intellectual standard. In church matters he kept aloof from many current controversies, but on occasion (1882) arguing strongly for the maintenance of the national church on a basis of 'mutual understanding, conciliation and peace.' In connection with the Edinburgh University tercentenary in 1884, in a series of professorial portraits by William Hole, Flint is etched in knightly armour as champion of the common faith. On his retirement in 1903 his portrait, painted by Sir George Reid, was presented to him by his students; it is now in his sister's possession, but is ultimately to belong to the Edinburgh University.

He wrote: 1. 'The Earth is the Lord's,' 1859 (sermon, Ps. xxiv. 1, 2). 2. 'Christ's Kingdom upon Earth,' 1865 (sermons). 3. 'The Philosophy of History in [Europe] France and Germany,' 1874; translated into French by Professor Ludovic Carrau of Besançon. 4. 'Theism,' 1877 (Baird Lecture); 7th edit., 1889. 5. 'Antitheistic Theories,' 1879 (Baird Lecture); 3rd edit. 1885. 6. 'A Sermon,' Edinburgh, 1881 (on Rev. i. 5). 7. 'The Covenant, 1660 to 1690,' Edin. 1881 (lecture). 8. 'Christianity in relation to other Religions,' Edin. 1882 (lecture). 9. 'The Duties of the People of Scotland to the Church of Scotland,' Edin. 1882 (lectures). 10. 'Vico,' 1884 (critical biography of Giovanni Battista Vico). 11. 'The Claims of Divine Wisdom,' Edin. 1885 (sermon to young). 12. 'The Church Question in Scotland,' 1891. 13. 'History of the Philosophy of History,' Edin. 1893 (first section, 'Historical Philosophy in France and French Belgium and Switzerland,' 1893). 14. 'Socialism,' 1894; 2nd edit. 1908. 15. 'Hindu Pantheism,' 1897. 16. 'Sermons and Addresses,' 1899. 17. 'Agnosticism,' 1903 (Croall Lecture). 18. 'Philosophy as Scientia Scientiarum,' 1904. 19. 'On Theological, Biblical and other Subjects,' 1905. Besides these, he wrote many articles, especially those on 'Theism' and 'Theology,' in the ninth edition of the 'Encyclopædia Britannica.'

[Scotsman, and The Times, 26 Nov. 1910; Hew Scott's Fasti Eccles. Scotic. 1869, ii. 458; 1871, iii. 516; W. Hole, Quasi Cursores, 1884, 145, sq. (with portrait); Vapereau, Dict. des Contemp. 1893; W. I. Addison, Roll of Graduates, Univ. Glasg. 1898, 198; information from Mr. Andrew Clark, S.S.C.; personal recollection.] A. G.

FLOYER, ERNEST AYSCOGHE (1852–1903), explorer, born on 4 July 1852 at Marshchapel, Lincs., was eldest surviving son of the Rev. Ayscoghe Floyer (*d.* 1872) by his wife Louisa Sara (1830-1909), daughter of the Hon. Frederic John Shore of the Bengal Civil Service. His mother, who was granddaughter of John Shore, first Baron Teignmouth [q. v.], and survived her son, was a pioneer in the movement for the systematic class teaching of plain needlework in English elementary schools, was inspector of needlework under the London school board, founder of the London Institution for Advancement of Plain Needlework, and author of several text-books upon the subject. After education at Charterhouse from 1865 until 1869, Floyer served for seven years in the Indian telegraph service, being stationed on the coast of the Persian Gulf. On receiving his long leave, in January 1876, he started for the unexplored interior of Baluchistan. His journeys there occupied him until May 1877, and his observations and surveys earned him a reputation as a bold and intelligent explorer. His results were published in 'Unexplored Baluchistan' (1882), with illustrations and map. The narrative describes a journey of exploration from Jask to Bampur; a tour in the Persian Gulf, visiting the island of Henjan and other places; and a journey of exploration from Jask to Kirman via Anguhran. There are appendices on dialects of Western Baluchistan and on plants collected. In January 1878 he was appointed inspector-general of Egyptian telegraphs, a post which he held until his death. He so administered the department as to convert an annual loss into a substantial annual surplus. He induced the government to devote a portion of this to experiments in the cultivation of trees and plants upon the soil of the desert. He took charge of these experiments in the capacity of director of plantations, state railways and telegraphs of Egypt. He cultivated successfully cactus for fibre, casuarina for telegraph poles, *Hyoscyamus muticus* yielding the alkaloid hyoscyamine, and other plants. Having discovered nitrate of soda in a clay in Upper Egypt, he was appointed by the government to superintend the process of its extraction. At the same time he engaged in exploration. In 1884 he made a journey from Halfa to Debba, and in 1887 surveyed two routes between the Nile and the Red Sea in about N. lat. 26°. In 1891 he was appointed by the Khedive to the command of an important expedition in a more southern part of the same desert (about N. lat. 24°). In this expedition he rediscovered the abandoned emerald mines of Sikait and Zabbara which had been worked at various epochs from early times. As the result of Floyer's report these mines were reopened. The outcome of this expedition, antiquarian, scientific, and economic, is fully described in his official publication, 'Étude sur la Nord-Etbai entre le Nil and la Mer Rouge' (Cairo, 1893, 4to, with maps and illustrations). For services to the military authorities Floyer received the British medal 'Egypt, 1882,' with clasp 'The Nile, 1884–5,' and the Khedive's bronze star. Floyer, who was popular with his native employés, had a mastery of Arabic and possessed an ear for minute differences of dialect.

Floyer died at Cairo on 1 Dec. 1903. He married in 1887 Mary Louisa, eldest daughter of the Rev. William Richards Watson, rector of Saltfleetby St. Peter's, Lincolnshire, by whom he left three sons.

Floyer described his Egyptian explorations in 'The Mines of the Northern Etbai' ('Trans. Roy. Asiatic Soc.' Oct. 1892); 'Notes on the Geology of the Northern Etbai' ('Trans. Geol. Soc.' 1892, vol. xlviii.); 'Further Routes in the Eastern Desert of Egypt' ('Geogr. Journ.' May 1893); and 'Journeys in the Eastern Desert of Egypt' ('Proc. Roy. Geogr. Soc.' 1884 and 1887). To the 'Journal' of the 'Institut Egyptien' for 1894–6 he contributed many papers on antiquarian, botanical, and agricultural matters.

[Personal knowledge; Journn. Roy. Asiatic Soc. April 1904.] V. C.

FORBES, JAMES STAATS (1823–1904), railway manager and connoisseur, born at Aberdeen on 7 March 1823, was eldest of the six children of James Staats Forbes, a member of a Scottish family long settled in England, by his wife Ann Walker. A brother, William, became manager of the Midland Great Western railway of Ireland, and was father of William, who is general manager of the London, Brighton and South Coast railway, and of Stanhope Alexander Forbes, R.A. Educated at Woolwich, James was brought up in London as an engineer, and showing skill as a draughtsman, he entered in 1840 the office of Isambard Kingdom Brunel [q. v.], who was then constructing the Great Western line. Joining the Great Western Company's service, he reached by successive steps the post of chief goods manager at Paddington. He next secured an appointment on the staff of the Dutch-Rhenish railway, then under English management, and soon rose to the highest post, bringing the line, then on the verge of bankruptcy, into a state of comparative success. On his retirement the directors retained his partial services as their permanent adviser. In 1861 the directors of the London, Chatham and Dover railway (which, formed by amalgamation in 1859, was then in the hands of a receiver) made him their general manager. He had previously been offered, and had twice refused, the post of general manager of the Great Western railway at a salary of 10,000*l*.

Debt, confusion, pressing creditors, and lack of money menaced the Chatham and Dover company, which was fighting for its very existence against two powerful neighbours, the South Eastern and the London and Brighton lines. Under Forbes's skilful and daring leadership the line held its own, and in 1871 he joined the board of directors, succeeding in 1873 to the post of chairman, which he held jointly with that of general manager until 1 Jan. 1899. On the amalgamation, at that date, of the Chatham line with the South Eastern, Forbes declined the chairmanship of the joint boards, but acted as their adviser. In his management of the finances of his own company, his tact in presiding at meetings of shareholders, and the exceptionally good terms which he secured for the Chatham railway in the amalgamation, Forbes proved himself a skilled diplomatist of great ability.

He also restored the fortunes of another bankrupt concern, the Metropolitan District railway; joined its board on 6 Oct. 1870, was chairman from 28 Nov. 1872 to 5 Sept. 1901, and from that date to 17 Feb. 1903 advisory director. For twenty-five years (1870–95) the rivalry between Forbes of the Chatham and the District and Sir Edward Watkin [q. v. Suppl. II] of the South Eastern and the Metropolitan was a source of anxiety to the shareholders and of much profit to lawyers. Forbes was at a great disadvantage, his opponent having control over two concerns which were solvent and successful and being himself a railway strategist of a high order. But for the suavity of temper and charm of manner of his rival, Watkin would probably have succeeded in crushing the two younger and poorer companies.

Forbes was connected with several other railways, most of them needing help to bring them out of difficulties. He was director and at one time deputy-chairman of the Hull and Barnsley line, and financial adviser to a still more unfortunate line, the Didcot, Newbury and Southampton; he was chairman of the Whitechapel and Bow railway, and of the Regent's Canal City and Docks railway. This last line was incorporated in 1882 for the construction of a line along the Regent's Canal from Paddington to the docks, but no progress has yet been made to carry out the scheme. His financial ability was widely in request. He was chairman of three important electric light companies, a director of the Lion Fire Insurance Company, and president of the National Telephone Company; from many of these boards he retired towards the end of his life.

Though a rigid economist, Forbes was always ready to introduce improvements when convinced that they were worth their cost. He adopted the block system, automatic brakes, and hydraulic stop blocks. To him were due the trials of the twin-ship system as represented by the Calais-Douvres, and he was largely responsible for the fine boats for the cross-Channel service belonging to the railway companies. Forbes excelled as an administrator on broad lines and in boldly taking an initiative, but had no taste for details. He was a frequent witness before Parliamentary Committees, and was a first-rate after-dinner speaker (cf. *Railway News*, 9 April 1904).

In September 1873, at a bye-election, he unsuccessfully contested Dover in the liberal interest, but did not again seek Parliamentary honours.

Forbes was much interested in art and, though his judgment was sometimes at fault, enjoyed a considerable reputation as a collector. His large collection of works of nineteenth-century artists included many examples of the Barbizon and modern Dutch schools. A selection (about one-twelfth) was exhibited at the Grafton Gallery in May 1905 (*Athenæum*, 27 May 1905, p. 664). A smaller exhibition, of which a printed catalogue appeared, was held in July 1908 at the Brighton Library and Art Gallery.

Forbes died on 5 April 1904 at his residence, Garden Corner, Chelsea Embankment, and was buried in the churchyard of West Wickham, Kent, the village where he formerly lived.

He married in 1851 Ann (*d.* 1901), daughter of John Bennett, by whom he had as surviving issue a son, Duncan, in the service of the Great Indian Peninsula railway, and two daughters, of whom Ann Bennett, the elder, married in 1897, as his second wife, Major-gen. Sir Charles Taylor Du Plat, K.C.B. (*d.* 1900).

There is a portrait of Forbes, executed in 1881, by Sir Hubert von Herkomer, and a marble bust (circ. 1893) by Trentenoir of Florence, both in the possession of his executors. A caricature by 'Spy' appeared in 'Vanity Fair' in 1900 (vol. xxxii. pl. 775).

[Authority above cited; Engineer, 8 April 1904; The Times, 6 April 1904; F. H. McCalmont, Parl. Poll Book, 7th edit. 1910, pt. 1, 87; Debrett; private information.]

C. W.

FORD, EDWARD ONSLOW (1852–1901), sculptor, born in Islington on 27 July 1852, was son of Edward Ford (*d.* 1864) by his wife Martha Lydia Gardner. His family moved to Blackheath while he was still a child. His father, who was in business in the City, died when he was barely twelve. After he had spent some time at Blackheath proprietary school, his mother determined that he should follow the strong bent towards art which he had already shown. She took him to Antwerp, where she sent him to the Academy as a student of painting. From Antwerp they moved after a time to Munich. There Ford studied under Wagmuller, who advised him to transfer his attention to modelling, which he did. Before leaving Munich Ford married, in 1873, Anne Gwendoline, the third daughter of Baron Frans von Kreuzer.

On returning to this country about 1874 Ford settled at Blackheath, whence he sent a bust of his wife to the Royal Academy of 1875. This at once attracted attention, and from that time onward the sculptor's career was watched with interest. Beginning with the statue of Rowland Hill at the Royal Exchange (1881), his more important works are: 'Irving as Hamlet' (1883), in the Guildhall Art Gallery; 'Gordon' (1890), the group of the famous general mounted on a camel, of which examples are at Chatham and Khartoum; the Shelley memorial in University College, Oxford (1892); the equestrian statue of Lord Strathnairn at Knightsbridge (1895); and the memorial to Queen Victoria at Manchester (1901). Besides these monumental works Ford executed many busts, invariably marked by taste in conception, delicate modelling, and verisimilitude. The best, perhaps, are the heads of Millais, Huxley, Herbert Spencer, Orchardson, Matthew Ridley Corbett, the duke of Norfolk, Mr. Briton Riviere, Sir Lawrence Alma-Tadema, Sir Walter Armstrong, Sir Hubert von Herkomer, and M. Dagnan-Bouveret. Ford also modelled a series of bronze statuettes. In each of these he endeavoured to embody some playful fancy which was, occasionally, less sculpturesque than literary. The most successful, perhaps, of these are 'Folly' (bought by the Chantrey trustees and now in the Tate Gallery), 'The Singer,' 'Applause,' 'Peace,' and 'Echo.' He was one of the first English sculptors to publish small replicas of his statues, which did much to extend his reputation.

Ford was elected A.R.A. in 1888 and R.A. in 1895, and became a corresponding member of the Institute of France. His example had much to do with that awakening of English sculpture in the last quarter of the nineteenth century which had its initial impulse in the teaching of Dalou at South Kensington and was helped by Ford's great personal popularity. Like most sculptors he was physically powerful, although of medium height, but, also like most sculptors, he overworked himself, and probably shortened his life by the energy with which he set about not only his own work but that of other people. On the death of Harry Bates [q. v. Suppl. I] he undertook to complete some of that artist's unfinished work, just at a time when commissions were coming in thick and fast to his own studio. About the middle of 1900 he was attacked by a dangerous form of heart disease, which left him, after a year of more or less precarious health, unable to resist the attack of pneumonia from which he died at 62 Acacia Road, N.W., on 23 Dec. 1901. He was buried at East Finchley. He was survived by his mother, his wife, four sons, and a daughter.

The best portrait of Onslow Ford is a head by John Macallan Swan [q. v. Suppl. II], which is the property of the painter's widow. He was also painted by Mr. Arthur Hacker, R.A., Sir Hubert von Herkomer, R.A., Mr. J. McLure Hamilton, and others. A memorial obelisk, including a medallion protrait in profile by A. C. Lucchesi and a replica of Ford's own figure of Poetry from the Shelley memorial, was set up at the junction of Grove End Road with Abbey Road, in St. John's Wood.

[The Times, 26 Dec. 1901; Men and Women of the Time; personal knowledge.]

W. A.

FORD, WILLIAM JUSTICE (1853–1904), cricketer and writer on cricket, the eldest of seven sons of William Augustus Ford, of Lincoln's Inn Fields, by his wife Katherine Mary Justice, was born in London on 7 Nov. 1853. Of his brothers, Augustus Frank Justice (*b.* 1858) and Francis Gilbertson Justice (*b.* 1866) distinguished themselves in Repton, Cambridge University, and Middlesex cricket, while a third, Lionel George Bridges Justice (*b.* 1865), became headmaster of Harrow in 1910. Educated at Eagle House, Wimbledon, and at Repton, where he played in the cricket eleven (1870–2). William entered

St. John's College, Cambridge, as minor scholar in 1872. became foundation scholar in 1874, and graduated B.A. with second-class classical honours in 1876, proceeding M.A. in 1878. He was a master at Marlborough College from 1877 to 1886, and from that year till 1889 was principal of Nelson College, New Zealand. On his return to England he became in April 1890 headmaster of Leamington college, from which he retired in 1893.

Of splendid physique (he was 6 ft. 3 in. in height and weighed in 1886 over 17 stone), Ford was as a cricketer one of the hardest hitters ever known, surpassed only by Mr. C. I. Thornton. His longest authenticated hit was 144 yards; in August 1885 at Maidstone he scored 44 runs in 17 minutes in the first innings, and 75 runs in 45 minutes in the second innings for Middlesex *v.* Kent. He was a slow round arm bowler and a good field at point. After retiring from his work as schoolmaster, he wrote much on cricket, publishing 'A Cricketer on Cricket' (1900); 'Middlesex County C.C. 1864–1899' (1900); and 'The Cambridge C.C. 1829–1901' (1902). He compiled the articles on 'Public School Cricket' for Wisden's 'Cricketers' Almanack' (1896–1904) and in Prince Ranjitsinhji's 'Jubilee Book of Cricket' (1897). He also contributed articles to the 'Cyclopædia of Sport' and to the 'Encyclopædia Britannica,' and the chapter on 'Pyramids and Pool' to the Badminton volume on 'Billiards.'

Ford died of pneumonia at Abingdon Mansions on 3 April 1904, and was buried at Kensal Green. He married in 1887 Miss K. M. Browning, of Nelson, New Zealand.

[The Times, 4 and 6 April 1904; Wisden's Cricketers' Almanack, 1905; Haygarth's Cricket Scores and Biographies, 1879, xii. 747; xiv. xcii; Cricket, 17 June 1886 (with portrait); J. Pycroft's Cricket Chat, 1886 (with portrait).] W. B. O.

FORESTIER-WALKER, Sir FREDERICK WILLIAM EDWARD FORESTIER (1844–1910), general, born at Bushey on 17 April 1844, was eldest of the four sons of General Sir Edward Walter Forestier-Walker, K.C.B. (1812–1881), of the Manor House, Bushey, Hertfordshire, by his first wife, Lady Jane, only daughter of Francis Grant, sixth earl of Seafield. His grand-uncle was Sir George Townshend Walker, first baronet [q. v.]. Educated at the Royal Military College, Sandhurst, he entered the Scots Guards as lieutenant on 5 Sept. 1862, and was promoted captain on 11 July 1865. In 1866–7 he served as A.D.C. to the major-general at Mauritius, and from 1869 to 1873 he was adjutant of his regiment. On 1 Feb. 1873 he became lieutenant-colonel, and afterwards he made his first acquaintance with South Africa, where he was thenceforth employed for the greater part of his active career. From 1873 to 1879 he was on the staff at the Cape of Good Hope acting as assistant military secretary to the general officer there. In that capacity, or on special service, he was engaged in much active warfare in South Africa. In 1875 he served in the expedition to Griqualand West. During 1877–8 he was with lieut.-general Sir Arthur Cunynghame [q. v.] through the sixth Kaffir war. He was mentioned in despatches, and was made colonel on 15 Oct. 1878 and C.B. on 11 Nov. following. In the course of 1878 he became military secretary to Sir Bartle Frere, the high commissioner. Throughout the Zulu war of 1879, of which Frederic Augustus Thesiger, second baron Chelmsford [q. v. Suppl. II] was in chief command, Forestier-Walker was employed on special service. In the early stages of the campaign he was principal staff officer to No. 1 column, being present at the action of Inyezane and during the occupation of Ekowe. Subsequently he was on the line of communications and in command of Fort Pearson and the Lower Tugela district. He received the medal with clasp, and was mentioned in despatches (*Lond. Gaz.* 5 March, 18 May 1879). Returning to England, he was from 1 August to 14 Nov. 1882 assistant adjutant and quartermaster-general of the home district; but from 12 Nov. 1884 till Dec. 1885 he was again in South Africa, serving with the Bechuanaland expedition under Sir Charles Warren as assistant adjutant and quartermaster-general. He was nominated C.M.G. on 27 Jan. 1886 and major-general on 31 Dec. 1887. From 1 April 1889 to Dec. 1890 he served as brigadier-general at Aldershot, and from 19 Dec. 1890 to 30 Sept. 1895 he was major-general commanding the troops in Egypt. On 26 May 1894 he was created K.C.B. for his services in Egypt. Subsequently he was lieut.-general commanding the western district of England from 1 Nov. 1895 to 18 Aug. 1899, with headquarters at Devonport. Shortly before the outbreak of the second Boer war it was decided to recall Sir William Butler [q. v. Suppl. II] from the command of the forces at the Cape, and the appointment was offered at very short notice to Forestier-Walker, who accepted it.

He arrived at Cape Town on 6 Sept. 1899, and was there during the chief stages of the Boer war. Placed in command of the lines of communication, he performed his exceedingly important duties with his usual thoroughness. At the outset he had to provide for the defence of a frontier 1000 miles long, and was active in support of Sir Redvers Buller's advance. He was twice mentioned in despatches. On 18 April 1901 he handed over his post to Major-general Wynne, and embarked for England. On 7 July 1902 he attained the rank of general, and on 1 Sept. 1905 he succeeded Sir George White (1835–1912) as governor and commander-in-chief of Gibraltar, having just before, on 31 July of the same year, been nominated colonel of the King's Own Scottish Borderers. He received the reward for distinguished service in 1893, and was nominated G.C.M.G. in 1900.

He died from heart failure at Tenby on 30 Aug. 1910, and was buried at Bushey, Hertfordshire. In 1887 he married Mabel Louisa, daughter of Lieut.-colonel A. E. Ross, late Northumberland fusiliers, and left one son.

A caricature portrait by 'Spy' appeared in 'Vanity Fair' in 1902.

[The Times, 1 Sept. 1910; T. Martineau, Life of Sir Bartle Frere, 1895, vol. ii.; Sir Frederick Maurice, History of the War in South Africa (1899–1902), 4 vols. 1906–1910; The Times History of the War in South Africa, ii. 114, iii. 207–8; Walford's County Families; Hart's and Official Army Lists; Burke's Peerage.] H. M. V.

FORSTER, HUGH OAKELEY ARNOLD- (1855-1909), secretary of state for war. [See Arnold-Forster.]

FORTESCUE, HUGH, third Earl Fortescue (1818–1905), eldest son of Hugh, second earl (1783–1861), by his first wife, Lady Susan (*d.* 1827), eldest daughter of Dudley Ryder, first earl of Harrowby, was born in London on 4 April 1818. A younger brother, Dudley Francis Fortescue (1820–1909), was M.P. for Andover (1857–1874) and a commissioner in lunacy (1867–1883). Known till his grandfather's death in 1841 as the Hon. Hugh Fortescue, and thenceforth till 1859 as Viscount Ebrington, he was educated at Harrow school and at Trinity College, Cambridge. He left the university in 1839 to become private secretary to his father, then lord-lieutenant of Ireland, and in 1840–1 he was private secretary to Lord Melbourne, the prime minister. Elected in 1841 M.P. for Plymouth in the whig interest, he held the seat for eleven years, having as his opponent in 1843 the chartist, Henry Vincent [q. v.]. Declining to stand again for Plymouth, he unsuccessfully contested Barnstaple in 1852, the constituency being disfranchised for bribery two years later. In 1854 he was returned for Marylebone, and he held the seat until 1859, when, owing to ill-health, he resigned, and on 5 December was raised to the peerage in his father's barony of Fortescue. On his father's death on 14 Sept. 1861, he succeeded to the earldom.

Ebrington, who had advocated the repeal of the corn laws, was appointed a lord-in-waiting in the Russell government of 1846, and from 1847 to 1851 was secretary to the poor law board. He was also appointed a member (unpaid) of the Metropolitan Consolidated Commission on Sewers in 1847, and was its chairman (unpaid) in 1849–51. He had no place in the Aberdeen goverment, but taking great interest in the health of the soldiers during the war with Russia, he visited in 1856 the barracks and military hospitals. Contracting ophthalmia, he lost an eye, and seriously injured his health. His speeches strenuously advocated sanitary improvements in the army, and he spoke frequently on the reform of local government in London. After his elevation to the peerage, Fortescue took little part in parliamentary life. Though a liberal by tradition, he differed from Gladstone on the Eastern crisis of 1878–9, and sat on the cross benches. He declared himself a liberal unionist on the home rule controversy in 1886.

A social reformer of much earnestness, Lord Fortescue was the author of numerous addresses and pamphlets on local government, health in towns, middle-class education, and other subjects. They included 'Unhealthiness of Towns,' a lecture delivered in the Mechanics' Institute at Plymouth (1846); 'Representative Self-Government for the Metropolis,' a letter to Lord Palmerston (1854); 'Public Schools for the Middle Classes' (1864); an address to the section of statistics and economic science, British Association, Plymouth (1877); and an address read at the Sanitary Congress, Exeter (1880). 'Our Next Leap in the Dark,' on the franchise bill, a reprint from the 'Nineteenth Century' (1884), showed the drift of his political ideas. He favoured the extension of the powers given to county authorities under the Local Government Act of 1888, and advocated the establishment of a local university in Devonshire. He supported Frederick Temple, then bishop of Exeter [q. v. Suppl. II], in establishing the diocesan conference, and spoke at its earlier meetings, besides subscribing liberally to schools and religious institutions. Fortescue, who was a good horseman, was the last man who habitually paid calls in London and made his way to the House of Lords on horseback. He encouraged stag-hunting, purchasing the reversion to the greater part of Exmoor on the death of Mr. F. W. Knight in 1897.

The earl died at Castle-hill, South Molton, on 10 Oct. 1905, having married on 11 March 1847 Georgiana Augusta Charlotte Caroline, eldest daughter of the Right Hon. George Lionel Dawson-Damer; she died on 8 Dec. 1866. Of his thirteen children, the eldest son, Hugh, is the fourth and present earl. Sir Seymour John, formerly captain R.N., served in Egypt in 1882 and at Suakin in 1885, and was an equerry-in-waiting to King Edward VII; Lionel Henry Dudley was killed in action near Pretoria on 11 June 1900, and John William is librarian at Windsor to King George V. A daughter, Lucy Eleanor, married Sir Michael Hicks-Beach, first Viscount St. Aldwyn.

A portrait in oils by Eden Upton Eddis (*c.* 1850) is in possession of the family at Castle-hill. A cartoon portrait of Earl Fortescue appeared in 'Vanity Fair' in 1881. A part of the chancel of Filleigh, the church of the parish in which Castle-hill stands, was adorned in his memory.

[The Times, 11 Oct. 1905; private information.] L. C. S.

FOSTER, Sir CLEMENT LE NEVE (1841–1904), inspector of mines and professor of mining at the Royal School of Mines, was second son of Peter Le Neve Foster [q. v.], secretary to the Society of Arts from 1853 to 1879. His mother was Georgiana Elizabeth, daughter of the Rev. Clement Chevallier. Born at Camberwell on 23 March 1841, he was educated first at the collegiate school in Camberwell, and afterwards at the Collège Communal of Boulogne. In 1857 he graduated Bachelier ès Sciences of the empire of France. In the same year he entered the School of Mines in London, where he took many prizes and left a brilliant record. Thence he went to the mining school of Freiberg. In 1860 he was appointed on the geological survey of England, and for five years he was engaged in field work in Kent, Sussex, Derbyshire, and Yorkshire. His first scientific publication was a memoir prepared with William Topley on the valley of the Medway and the denudation of the weald, and was published in the 'Quarterly Journal of the Geological Society' (vol. xxi). In 1865 he graduated D.Sc. at the University of London, and in the same year he resigned his post on the geological survey and became lecturer to the Miners' Association of Cornwall and Devon and secretary to the Royal Cornwall Polytechnic Society. In 1868 he was employed by the Khedive of Egypt on an exploring expedition to examine the mineral resources of the Sinaitic peninsula. He also reported in the same year on a Venezuelan goldfield, and from 1869 to 1872 he was engineer to a gold-mining company in Northern Italy. In 1872 he was nominated Inspector of Mines under the new Metalliferous Mines Regulation Act, being appointed to Cornwall. Eight years later—in 1880—he was transferred to North Wales, where he remained for twenty-one years. In 1890, on the death of Sir Warington Smyth [q. v.], he became professor of mining at the Royal School of Mines, an office which he held concurrently with his inspectorship. He proved an excellent teacher. In 1897, as inspector of mines, he investigated the cause of an underground fire in the lead mine of Snaefell in the Isle of Man. The cage in which he had descended with an exploring party was jammed in the shaft, and the party was subjected to a process of slow poisoning by the carbon monoxide generated by the fire. All the contemporary accounts of this accident attest the courage with which, in the face of apparently certain death, Foster noted his own sensations for the benefit of science. Foster never recovered from the cardiac injury sustained during the process of gradual suffocation. For nearly a year he was incapacitated.

Besides his official work, Foster produced numerous reports, and advised on many questions connected with mining and mining legislation. He served on various departmental committees and royal commissions, including those for the Chicago and the St. Louis Exhibitions. He was a juror at the Inventions Exhibition in 1885, at Paris in 1867, 1878, 1889, and 1900, also at Chicago in 1893. He received the legion of honour for services at Paris in 1889; became F.R.S. in 1892, and was knighted in 1903. In 1901 he resigned the inspectorship, but the professorship he retained until his death, which took place on 19 April 1904, at Coleherne Court, Earl's Court. He was serving on the royal commission on coal supplies at the time.

Foster translated from the Dutch of P. Van Diest a work on Banca and its tin stream works, learning the Dutch language for the purpose (Truro, 1867), and in 1876, with William Galloway, he published a translation from the French of Prof. Callon's treatise on mining. His principal work was a textbook on 'Ore and Stone Mining' (1894; 7th edit. revised by Prof. S. Herbert Cox, 1910), and he wrote the article on Mining in the 9th edition of the 'Encyclopædia Britannica.' He was also author of a textbook on 'Mining and Quarrying' (1903) and of numerous memoirs and papers in the 'Proceedings' of the Geological and other scientific societies and in various scientific periodicals. From 1894 he edited the mineral statistics issued by the home office, and the annual reports on mines and quarries. While he achieved considerable reputation as a geologist and metallurgist, it was as a miner and a mining expert that he was really eminent. Though at the beginning of his inspectorship his energy in imposing novel restrictions and in insisting on the reform and improvement of existing methods was little appreciated by the mining community, he ultimately won in both his districts the esteem alike of miners and mine-owners.

He married in 1872 his cousin, Sophia Chevallier, second daughter of Arthur F. Tompson of Belton, Suffolk, and had one son and two daughters. His widow received a civil list pension of 100*l*. in Aug. 1904.

[Proc. Roy. Soc. lxxv. 371 (by Prof. Judd); Nature, 28 April 1904 (by Hilary Bauerman); Journal of Soc. of Arts, 29 April 1904 (by the present writer); Trans. American Soc. of Mining Engineers, vol. 35 (1904), p. 662; Engineer, 22 April 1904.] H. T. W.

FOSTER, JOSEPH (1844–1905), genealogist, born at Sunniside, Sunderland, on 9 March 1844, was eldest of five sons and three daughters of Joseph Foster, a woollen draper of Bishop Wearmouth, by his wife Elizabeth, daughter of Emanuel Taylor. Myles Birket Foster, founder of the London bottling firm of M. B. Foster & Sons, was his grandfather, and Myles Birket Foster [q. v. Suppl. I], the water-colour painter, was his uncle. His ancestors were members of the Society of Friends from the earliest times until the resignation of his father a few years before his birth. Educated privately at North Shields, Sunderland and Newcastle, Foster began business in London as a printer, but soon abandoned it for genealogical research, to which he had devoted his leisure from an early age. To that pursuit he henceforth gave up all his time with self-denying enthusiasm and industry.

Foster's genealogical works began with pedigrees of the quaker families of Foster and Forster (1862; 2nd edit. 1871); of Wilson of High Wray and Kendal (1871); and of Fox of Falmouth with the Crokers of Lineham (1872), all of which were printed privately. There followed later pedigrees of the families of Pease, Harris, and Backhouse, as well as of Raikes.

In 1873 he projected his 'Pedigrees of the County Families of England.' The first volume, 'Lancashire Families,' appeared in that year, and it was followed by three volumes of 'Yorkshire Families' (1874). He printed 'Glover's Visitation of Yorkshire' in 1875; in 1877 there appeared his 'Stemmata Britannica,' part only of a collection of pedigrees of untitled gentry, and in 1878 the 'Pedigree of Sir John Pennington, Fifth Lord Muncaster.'

In 1879 he published, in collaboration with Mr. Edward Bellasis, Blue Mantle, his laborious 'Peerage, Baronetage and Knightage.' Foster pursued the main methods of Sir Bernard Burke's work; but aiming at greater accuracy, he exposed mythical ancestries, and placed in a section entitled 'Chaos' baronetcies of doubtful creation. Foster's undertaking was violently attacked by Stephen Tucker, Rouge Croix, in the 'Genealogist,' iv. 64, on account, principally, of its heraldry, and Foster and his colleague Bellasis defended themselves in a pamphlet, 'A Review of a Review of Joseph Foster's Peerage.' 'The Peerage,' which was re-isssued in 1881, 1882, and 1883, was ultimately amalgamated with Lodge's, which adopted much of its form.

In 1881 Foster established a periodical entitled 'Collectanea Genealogica et Heraldica,' which appeared at irregular intervals up to 1888. There he printed serially transcriptions of legal and other registers and genealogical researches, some of which (*i.e.* 'Members of Parliament. Scotland') (1882) were re-issued separately, and others were left uncompleted. In the periodical there also appeared much trenchant criticism and exposure of current genealogical myths, in which Foster had the assistance of Dr. J. Horace Round.

Meanwhile Foster, with heroic labour, transcribed the admission registers of the Inns of Court, and the institutions to livings since the Reformation. Some fruits of this labour were published in 'Men at the Bar: a Biographical Hand-List' (1888); 'Admissions to Gray's Inn, and Marriages in Gray's Inn Chapel' (1889); and 'Index Ecclesiasticus: or Alphabetical Lists of all Ecclesiastical

Dignitaries in England and Wales, 1800–1840' (1890).

In 1885 Foster undertook to edit for publication the transcripts by Joseph Lemuel Chester [q. v.] of the 'Oxford Matriculation Register,' and the 'Bishop of London's Register of Marriage Licences,' which had become the property of Mr. Bernard Quaritch. Foster copiously supplemented Chester's work from his own independent researches. The 'Oxford Matriculation Register,' alphabetically arranged, was published in eight volumes under the title 'Alumni Oxonienses'; four volumes, covering the period 1715–1886, appeared in 1887, and another four volumes, covering the period 1500–1714, in 1891. By way of recognition of this service the university gave him the honorary degree of M.A. in 1892. Next year he carried his work a stage further in 'Oxford Men and their Colleges.' 'London Marriage Licences' (1521–1869) was published from Chester's transcript in 1887.

In later life Foster wrote much on heraldry. There appeared in 1897 his 'Concerning the Beginnings of Heraldry as related to Untitled Persons'; in 1902 'Some Feudal Coats of Arms from Heraldic Rolls'. To a series of volumes, issued under the auspices of the eighth Lord Howard de Walden and called the 'De Walden Library,' Foster contributed 'A Tudor Book of Arms,' 'Some Feudal Lords and their Seals,' and 'Banners, Standards and Badges' (1904). Foster's heraldic work was severely censured by Mr. Oswald Barron, editor of the 'Ancestor,' to whose strictures he replied in two pamphlets, 'A Herald Extraordinary' and 'A Comedy of Errors from Ancestor III' (1902–3).

Foster's work met with very little support in his lifetime, though some of his compilations are of great and permanent value. He was not a scholarly archæologist, but his energy as a transcriber and collector of genealogical data has few parallels in recent times.

He died at his residence, 21 Boundary Road, St. John's Wood, on 29 July 1905, being buried at Kensal Green cemetery. His name is also inscribed on a memorial stone in Bishop Wearmouth cemetery. He married, on 12 Aug. 1869, Catherine Clark, eldest daughter of George Pocock of Burgess Hill, Sussex, and by her had two sons and three daughters.

Foster's library of books and manuscripts, many of them plentifully annotated, was privately dispersed at his death. Four volumes of grants of arms were secured for the British Museum, Add. MSS. 37147–37150.

Besides the works mentioned, Foster's publications include: 1. 'Our Noble and Gentle Families of Royal Descent,' 2 vols. 4to. 1883; large edit. 1885. 2. 'Noble and Gentle Families entitled to Quarter Royal Arms,' 1895. He also edited 'Visitation Pedigrees' for Durham (1887), for Middlesex (1889), for Northumberland (1891), and for Cumberland and Westmoreland (1891).

[Allibone's Dict. Suppl. 1891; Brit. Mus. Cat.; The Times, 1 Aug. 1905; private information.]

P. L.

FOSTER, SIR MICHAEL (1836–1907), professor of physiology in the University of Cambridge, born at Huntingdon on 8 March 1836, was eldest child in a family of three sons and seven daughters of Michael Foster, F.R.C.S., surgeon in Huntingdon, by his wife Mercy Cooper. Sir Michael's grandfather, John Foster, was a yeoman farmer of Holywell, Hertfordshire, with antiquarian tastes, who left to the British Museum a collection of coins found in his neighbourhood. The father was a baptist and his family lived in an atmosphere of fervent nonconformity. Foster was educated first at Huntingdon grammar school and later (1849–1852) at University College School, London. The religious tests demanded by the University of Cambridge stood in the way of his entering for a scholarship there. At the age of sixteen he matriculated at the University of London, and graduated B.A. in 1854 with the university scholarship in classics. Choosing his father's profession, Foster in 1854 began the study of science and medicine at University College. There in 1856 he obtained gold medals in anatomy and physiology, and in chemistry. In 1858 he proceeded M.B., and in 1859 M.D. of London University. The next two years were spent partly in medical study in Paris as well as at home, and partly in original investigation. Owing to threatenings of consumption he went on a sea voyage as surgeon on the steamship 'Union' without beneficial result. In 1861 he joined his father in practice in Huntingdon. His health improved, and in 1867 he accepted an invitation from Prof. Sharpey to become teacher in practical physiology in University College, London. There he rapidly showed his practical gifts as a teacher. Two years later he was appointed professor in the same subject, and he succeeded Huxley as Fullerian professor of physiology at the Royal Institution. In 1870 he left London for Cambridge, on his appointment, chiefly on Huxley's recommendation, to the new post of prælector of physiology in Trinity College. In 1883 he was appointed professor of physiology in the University. An honorary M.A. degree was conferred on him in 1873 and the complete degree in 1884. In 1872 he was elected F.R.S., and became one of the general secretaries of the British Association, a post which he resigned after four years, though he continued throughout his life to take an active part in the working of the association. In 1881 he succeeded Huxley as biological secretary of the Royal Society, an office which he held for twenty-two years. In 1899 he was president of the British Association, and in the same year was created K.C.B. In 1900 he was elected M.P. for the University of London, and this led him to apply for a deputy to perform the duties of his Cambridge professorship, and three years later to his resignation. In politics Foster was a liberal, but on the introduction of Gladstone's home rule bill he joined the liberal unionists and gave a general support to the conservative government. On entering the House of Commons he sat at first on the government side of the house. He found himself unable to support the government in several of its measures, notably the education bill of 1902, and finally crossed the floor of the house, thenceforth voting with the liberal opposition. At the general election of 1906 he stood for the university as a liberal, and was defeated by 24 votes. On 28 Jan. 1907 he died suddenly from pneumo-thorax in London, and was buried in the cemetery at Huntingdon, For more than thirty years he had lived at Great Shelford near Cambridge, where he engaged with ardour in gardening.

Foster was twice married: (1) in 1863 to Georgina (*d.* 1869), daughter of Cyrus Edmonds, by whom he had two children, a son, Michael George Foster, M.D. (Camb.), practising at San Remo and at Harrogate, and a daughter, Mercy, wife of J. Tetley Rowe, Archdeacon of Rochester; (2) in 1872 to Margaret, daughter of George Rust of Cromwell House, Huntingdon.

Foster left his mark on his generation chiefly as a teacher, a writer of scientific works, and an organiser. As a teacher he had a large share in the development of the present method of making practical work in the laboratory an essential part of the courses in biological science. In his student days, zoology, botany, physiology and histology—the latter two being generally regarded as insignificant parts of human anatomy—were taught by means of lectures and the exhibition of specimens, macroscopic or microscopic. Sharpey no doubt had somewhat extended this simple plan before he invited Foster to join him in London; but the first course of practical physiology given in England appears to have been that given by Foster. In 1870 Huxley instituted a course of practical biology, with Foster as one of his demonstrators. Foster's first care on coming to Cambridge was to introduce practical classes in physiology, physiological chemistry, histology, and biology, and these were soon followed by a class in embryology. In order to facilitate the conduct of these classes he co-operated with Burdon-Sanderson, Lauder Brunton, and Klein in writing a 'Text-Book for the Physiological Laboratory' (1873), with his pupil F. M. Balfour in writing 'The Elements of Embryology' (1874), and obtained the assistance of another of his pupils, John Newport Langley, in writing 'A Course of Elementary Practical Physiology' (1876), in which histology was included. His classes were the forerunners of those conducted in the laboratories of zoology and botany, subsequently established in Cambridge. The plan of teaching developed by Foster and by Huxley rapidly spread throughout Great Britain and America. Foster's belief in the value of direct observation of natural phenomena was accompanied by a belief in the virtue of research; and this he had a faculty of communicating to his pupils. It was through his influence that most of his early pupils devoted themselves to original inquiry. The earliest of these, H. N. Martin, became professor in Johns Hopkins University, U.S.A., and potently helped to develop biological research in America. Foster's many occupations prevented him taking a leading position as an original investigator (cf. *Journal of Physiology* xxxv. 233 for an account of his work). The experimental trend of his mind was shown in his main, and almost sole, relaxation—gardening. He hybridised several plants, but chiefly irises, and in these chiefly the oncocyclus section. Now and again he published a short article in one of the horticultural journals (cf. *The Garden*, 15 Nov. 1890, 18 Feb. 1893), but a good many of his hybrids he left undescribed.

Foster's 'Text-Book of Physiology,' published in 1876, gave a critical account of the state of physiology at the time;

the evidence for and against the current theories being dispassionately weighed. Its attractive style and its occasional passages of vivid literary merit placed it, amongst text-books, in a class by itself. Both at home and abroad it had an immediate success. Six editions were published and part of a seventh; the third edition was perhaps the best, since in the later remodelling it lost something of its original unity of purpose. He wrote also a 'Science Primer of Physiology' (1890), a life of Claude Bernard (1899), 'A History of Physiology during the Sixteenth, Seventeenth and Eighteenth Centuries' (1901), and 'Simple Lessons in Health for the Use of the Young' (1906). He was also joint-editor of the collected edition of Huxley's 'Scientific Memoirs' (1898–1902). Foster in 1878 founded the 'Journal of Physiology,' the first journal in the English language devoted solely to the subject, and remained its sole editor until 1894. Its pages were confined to accounts of original investigation, though for some years an appendix was issued giving a list of books and papers of physiological interest published elsewhere. In its early years most of the rising school of American physiologists used it as a means of publication.

Foster had great powers of organisation. It was chiefly through him that the Physiological Society was founded in 1875, and the International Congress of Physiologists established in 1889. During his long tenure of the office of secretary of the Royal Society he seized every opportunity of forwarding the cause of science, and took a prominent part in most of the plans for combined scientific action. He strengthened the connection between the Royal Society and the government, and the most varied forms of scientific expeditions and explorations found in him a strong supporter. His influence was perhaps more especially felt in the establishment of the International Association of Academies, and in the arrangements leading up to the publication of the 'International Catalogue of Scientific Papers.' He was a member of the committee appointed by the colonial office to advise as to the best means of combating disease; he served on the royal commissions on vaccination, disposal of sewage, and tuberculosis, and on the commission appointed to consider the reorganisation of the University of London.

Portraits of him were painted by Herkomer and by the Hon. John Collier; the former is in the possession of Trinity College, Cambridge; the latter belongs to his son, but a replica of the head and shoulders is in the possession of the Royal Society.

[Year Book of Roy. Soc. 1906, p. 13 (gives list of honours); Brit. Med. Journ. 9 Feb. 1907; Journ. of Physiol. xxxv. 233, March 1907; Rendiconti d. R. Accad. d. Lincei (Roma), xvi. Ap. 1907; Cambridge Rev. 30 May 1907; Proc. Linn. Soc. 1907, p. 42; Proc. Roy. Soc. B. lxxx. p. lxxi, 1908; Colorado Med. Journ. Oct. 1900; The Garden, 15 Nov. 1890, 18 Feb. 1893; Gardeners' Chron. 1883; Garden Life, 9 Feb. 1907.]

J. N. L.

FOULKES, ISAAC (1836–1904), Welsh author and editor, born in 1836 at the farm of Cwrt, Llanfwrog, Denbighshire, was son of Peter Foulkes by his wife Frances. At the age of fifteen he was apprenticed to Isaac Clarke, printer, Ruthin; in 1857 he entered the office of the 'Amserau' newspaper in Liverpool, and soon afterwards set up a printing business of his own in that city, which he conducted until his death. He issued in 1877–88 'Cyfres y Ceinion' (The Gem Series), a series of cheap reprints of Welsh classics which gave notable stimulus to the Welsh literary revival at the end of the nineteenth century. In May 1890 he began to issue the 'Cymro' (Welshman), a weekly Welsh newspaper intended primarily for Liverpool Welshmen, but soon read widely in Wales as well; Foulkes was both editor and publisher, and made the journal a literary medium of high value. He died at Rhewl, near Ruthin, on 2 Nov. 1904, and was buried in Llanbedr churchyard. He married (1) Hannah Foulkes, by whom he had two sons and three daughters; and (2) Sinah Owen.

Foulkes, who was known in bardic circles as 'Llyfrbryf' (Bookworm), was a keen student of Welsh literature, and as author, critic, editor and publisher, devoted to this cause literary judgment and unflagging energy. He wrote: 1. 'Cymru Fu' (a volume of folklore), pt. i. Llanidloes, 1862; pts. ii. and iii. Liverpool, 1863–4; 2nd edit. Wrexham, 1872. 2. 'Rheinallt ap Gruffydd' (a novel), Liverpool, 1874. 3. A memoir of the poet Ceiriog, Liverpool, 1887; 2nd edit. 1902; 3rd edit. 1911. 4. A memoir of the novelist, Daniel Owen, Liverpool, 1903. Among other works which he both edited and published are 'Enwogion Cymru,' a biographical dictionary of eminent Welshmen (Liverpool, 1870); the 'Mabinogion,' with a translation into modern Welsh (1880);

'The Poetry of Trebor Mai' (1883); 'Oriau Olaf,' by Ceiriog (1888). Editions of 'Dafydd ap Gwilym,' the 'Iolo MSS.,' and Yorke's 'Royal Tribes of Wales' were also issued from his press.

[Bygones (Oswestry), 9 Nov. 1904; 'Brython' (Liverpool), 25 May 1911; information from Mr. Lewis Jones, Ruthin.] J. E. L.

FOWLE, THOMAS WELBANK (1835–1903), theologian and writer on the poor law, born at Northallerton, Yorkshire, on 29 Aug. 1835, was son of Thomas Fowle, solicitor, and of Mary Welbank, both of Northallerton. After education at Durham school (1848–53) and at Charterhouse, he entered Exeter College, Oxford, in 1854; after a term's stay there he gained an open scholarship at Oriel College, graduating B.A. in 1858 (M.A. 1861). As an undergraduate he took an active part in the debates at the Union, and was president in 1858. His intimate associates included Thomas Hill Green [q. v.] and Prof. Albert Venn Dicey, and his sympathies, like theirs, were democratic. After rejecting thought of the bar, he took holy orders in 1859, becoming curate of Staines in Middlesex. In 1863 he was appointed vicar of Holy Trinity, Hoxton. Under his influence new schools were built, which, managed by a committee of churchmen and nonconformists, were the first to be governed under a conscience clause. Here in a poor and populous parish his advanced political ideas gathered strength, and he studied closely economic conditions. In 1868 he became vicar of St. Luke's, Nutford Place, and in the same year he reached a wider public through an essay on 'The Church and the Working Classes' in 'Essays on Church Politics,' to which Profs. Seeley and Westlake also contributed.

In 1875 he was presented to the rectory of Islip, and there he gave practical effect to his theories on social questions. He instituted and successfully managed an allotment system for agricultural labourers, and as a poor-law guardian helped to reduce out-door relief, to which he was strongly opposed.

Meanwhile Fowle's pen was actively devoted to both theology and social economy. An active-minded broad churchman, he endeavoured to reconcile new scientific discoveries with old religious beliefs in three articles on Evolution in the 'Nineteenth Century' (July 1878, March 1879, Sept. 1881), as well as in a pithy and suggestive volume called the 'New Analogy,' which he published in 1881 under the pseudonym of 'Cellarius.'

To social economy his most important contributions were an article in the 'Fortnightly Review' for June 1880 advocating the abolition of out-door relief and a concise manual on 'The Poor Law' in the 'English Citizen' series (1881; 2nd edit. 1890), a work which took standard rank at home and abroad.

Fowle actively supported the extension of the franchise to the agricultural labourer in 1884, but he declined to accept home rule in 1886 and for the next ten years was prominent among the liberal unionists. His authority on social questions was undiminished. To his advocacy was largely due the creation of parish and district councils under the local government act of 1894. In 1892 he urged the prudence of old-age pensions in a pamphlet called 'The Poor Law, the Friendly Societies, and Old Age Destitution—a Proposed Solution' (new edit. 1895).

The sudden death of Fowle's only son by his second wife in 1895 broke his health, and he was compelled by illness in 1901 to retire from Islip to Oxford, where he died on 14 Jan. 1903. He was buried at Islip by the side of his son.

Fowle was twice married: (1) in 1861, to Sarah Susannah (*d.* 1874), daughter of Richard Atkinson, medical practitioner at Richmond, Yorkshire, by whom he had seven daughters; (2) in 1876, to Mabel Jane, daughter of Jacob Isaacs, a West Indian merchant; she survived him with a daughter.

Fowle, by virtue of his liberal culture, his thorough knowledge of social conditions, especially in rural districts, and his persuasive eloquence, influenced public opinion alike among political leaders and the working classes. His published works, besides magazine articles, reviews, and books already mentioned, were: 1. 'Types of Christ in Nature: Sermons preached at Staines,' 1864. 2. 'The Reconciliation of Religion and Science,' 1873. 3. 'An Essay on the Right Translation of αἰὼν and αἰωνιος, regarded as exhibiting the Silence of the New Testament as to the Conditions of the Future Life,' 1877. 4. 'The Divine Legation of Christ,' 1879.

An enlarged photograph is in the debating hall of the Union Society, Oxford.

[Memoir by Prof. J. Cook Wilson, Oxford, 1903; Oxford Mag. 28 Jan. 1903; St. Luke's, Nutford Place, Parish Mag. Feb. 1903; Charity Organisation Rev. Sept. 1892; private information.] W. B. O.

FOWLER, THOMAS (1832–1904), president of Corpus Christi College, Oxford, born at Burton-Stather, Lincolnshire, on 1 Sept. 1832, was eldest son of William Henry Fowler, by his wife Mary Anne Welch. His intellectual development owed much in youth to his uncle by marriage, Joseph Fowler of Winterton (son of William Fowler of Winterton [q. v.]), who had married his father's sister. There was no known kinship between the two families of the same name.

After attending the Hull grammar school and the private school of R. Ousby, curate of Kirton-in-Lindsey, he entered as a day-boy, in January 1848, King William's College, Isle of Man, and was promoted to the head-form in August. Among his schoolfellows were Dean Farrar [q. v. Suppl. II], Professor Beesly, and the poet Thomas Edward Brown [q. v. Suppl. I], who, although a year and a half Fowler's senior, formed with him a life-long friendship (cf. *Letters of T. E. Brown*, with memoir by S. T. Irwin, i. 20). In half-holiday walks with Brown, Fowler began to cultivate that eye for beauty in nature which always stimulated his zest for travel. On 31 May 1850 he matriculated at Oxford, aged seventeen, as postmaster of Merton College. Brown was already at Christ Church. In 1852 Fowler obtained a first class in mathematical, and a second class in classical, moderations; and in the final examinations of 1854 a first in classics and a first in mathematics. In the same mathematical first classes was his friend Charles Lutwidge Dodgson (Lewis Carroll) [q. v. Suppl. I]; together the two read mathematics privately with Professor Bartholomew Price [q. v.].

As an undergraduate Fowler was in full sympathy with the 'Oxford movement'; but about 1854, when he graduated B.A., he gave up his tractarian opinions and connections, as well as the conservative political views in which he had been brought up, and adopted in permanence liberal, but moderate, opinions in theology and politics. In 1855 he was ordained, and became fellow and tutor, and in 1857 sub-rector of Lincoln College. In 1858 he won the Denyer theological prize for an essay on 'The Doctrine of Predestination according to the Church of England.'

It was during the twenty-six years of his residence in Lincoln College (1855–81) that he made his name as teacher, writer, and man of affairs. As proctor in 1862 he first came into close touch with university business. Thenceforth he took a leading part in it, either as member of Congregation and of the Hebdomadal Council, or as delegate of the Clarendon Press, the Museum, and the Common University Fund. His common sense, disinterestedness, bonhomie, and breadth and clearness of view account for his influence. His opinions on university reform received early direction from Mark Pattison [q. v.], fellow of his college. Fowler gave evidence before the University of Oxford commissioners on 26 Oct. 1877 (*Minutes of Evidence taken before the University of Oxford Commissioners*, part i. pp. 92–97) on lines which followed Pattison's 'Suggestions on Academical Organisation' (1868). 'I advocate,' he said, 'a transference of the more advanced teaching from the colleges to the university on the grounds that (1) it would tend to create a more learned class of teachers; (2) it would remedy certain gross defects in our present system of education [he refers here to the immaturity of teachers, and the subjection of teachers and taught to examinations]; and (3) it would establish a hierarchy of teachers [cf. his evidence before university commissioners 11 March 1873], the places in which could be determined by literary and educational merit.' In active co-operation with Dean Liddell, J. M. Wilson, Dean Stanley, Jowett, and others, Fowler played an effective part in promoting the important series of reforms which included the establishment of natural science as a subject of serious study in the university, the removal of tests, and the various provisions, financial and other, made by the commissioners of 1877, especially those by which a career at Oxford was opened to men willing to devote themselves to study and teaching.

As a teacher Fowler excelled in the small conversational lecture and especially in the 'private hour,' to which he devoted much time with individual pupils, trying to make them read and think for themselves. One of his earliest pupils at Lincoln was John (afterwards Viscount) Morley. Fowler was public examiner in the final classical school (1864–6, 1869–70, 1873 and 1878–9); and he was select preacher (1872–4). Fowler was professor of logic from 1873 to 1889. He had previously published 'The Elements of Deductive Logic' (1867; 10th edit. 1892) and 'The Elements of Inductive Logic' (1870; 6th edit. 1892), a manual which follows the lines of Mill's 'Logic' with independence and lucidity. While professor, Fowler made his chief contributions to literature. His edition of Bacon's 'Novum Organum,' which came out in 1878 (2nd edit. 1889), contains a valuable commentary on the text; the introduction clearly presents Bacon's place in the history of thought, and embodies much bibliographical research, for which Fowler had an aptitude. His monograph 'Locke' ('English Men of Letters' series, 1880) is notable for the historical setting of philosophical ideas, a feature already anticipated in his Denyer prize essay. An edition of 'Locke's Conduct of the Understanding, with Introduction,' followed (1881; new edit. 1901); monographs on 'Francis Bacon' (1881) and 'Shaftesbury and Hutcheson' (1882) appeared in the 'English Philosophers' series; the latter contains interesting new matter from the 'Shaftesbury Papers.'

'Progressive Morality' (1884; 2nd edit. 1895) is a short work remarkable for the insight with which moral experience is probed and analysed, always with the practical end in view of discovering principles which may be helpful for the education of character. Of 'The Principles of Morals,' part. i. was in print as early as 1875, but was first published in 1886 in the joint names of John Matthias Wilson [q. v.] and Fowler; part ii. (the larger part) came out in Fowler's name alone (see prefaces to the two volumes and art. Wilson, John Matthias). Like 'Progressive Morality,' 'The Principles of Morals' is of permanent value; it expresses, with a difference due to the altered circumstances of the nineteenth century, the philosophical temper and outlook of the great English moralists of the eighteenth century, and retains a flavour of their style. Exactness, and even elegance, of style, very noticeable in the sermons which he preached at St. Mary's, mark all Fowler's writings.

On 23 December 1881 Fowler was elected president of Corpus Christi College, in succession to his friend Wilson. Fowler entered thoroughly into the life of his new college, writing its history, making himself fully acquainted with its educational needs and its finance, piloting it skilfully through the difficulties of the period of transition which followed 1882, when the statutes made by the commissioners of 1877 came into operation, and winning the esteem and affection of seniors and juniors. His exhaustive 'History of Corpus,' published in 1893 (Oxford Historical Society), is of special interest as the history of a 'Renaissance Foundation.' In 1898 he issued a less elaborate account of the college in the 'Oxford College Histories' series, and between 1889 and 1900 he wrote a series of articles for this Dictionary on Corpus men of mark from Fox, the founder, to J. M. Wilson, his predecessor in the presidency. To this Dictionary he also contributed articles on the philosophical work of Bacon and Richard Price.

From 1899 till 1901 Fowler was vice-chancellor of the university. The work of the office was exceptionally heavy. The Boer war was in progress, and he as vice-chancellor, by arrangement with the war office, was charged with the duty of selecting for commissions in the army young university men ready to go to the front. From the strain of inquiry and correspondence involved his health never recovered. Largely through his influence the opposition in Oxford to conferring the honorary degree of D.C.L. at the encænia of 1899 upon Cecil Rhodes, whose munificent endowment the university a few years after began to enjoy, proved innocuous.

Fowler, who was made F.S.A. in 1873, and hon. LL.D. of Edinburgh in 1882, proceeded to the degree of D.D. in 1886; and was elected hon. fellow of Lincoln in 1900. He died unmarried in his house at Corpus on 20 Nov. 1904, and was buried in the cemetery at Winterton. In the church there a choir-screen, with inscription, was erected to his memory; and there is a tablet in the cloister of Corpus. By his will he was a benefactor of the three colleges, Merton, Lincoln, and Corpus, with which he had been connected. A cartoon portrait by E. T. D. appeared in 'Vanity Fair' in 1889 (xxxi. 763).

[Foster's Alumni Oxonienses; The Times, 21 Nov. 1904; Athenæum, 26 Nov. 1904; Oxford Magazine, 23 Nov. 1904; Letters of T. E. Brown, ed. with memoir by S. T. Irwin, 2 vols. 1900; Correspondence of William Fowler of Winterton in the county of Lincoln, ed. by his grandson Canon Fowler of Durham, 1907; Crockford, 1903; Who's Who, 1903; Minutes of Evidence taken before the University of Oxford Commissioners (of 1877), part i. pp. 92–97 (Fowler's evidence taken 11 March 1873 and 26 Oct. 1877); private information supplied by his cousin, Canon Fowler, and others; personal knowledge.] J. A. S.

FOWLER, Sir HENRY HARTLEY first Viscount Wolverhampton (1830–1911), statesman, born in Sunderland on 16 May 1830, was the second son of Joseph Fowler, a Wesleyan minister, who was secretary of the Wesleyan conference in 1848, by his third wife, Elizabeth McNeill, daughter of Alexander Laing of Glasgow, and step-daughter of John Hartley of Smethwick and Hunslet.

Educated at Woodhouse Grove school, a school for Methodist ministers' sons near Bradford, and at St. Saviour's grammar school, Southwark, he was intended for the university and the bar; but the premature death of his father made other plans necessary. Articled to Messrs. Hussey of London, he was admitted a solicitor in 1852. Meanwhile his mother on his father's death had settled in Wolverhampton, where her step-brother, John Hartley, was then living. There in 1855 Fowler joined her, and his long association with that city began. Next year he was taken into partnership there by Charles Corser, and remained a member of the firm until 1908. In 1876 he also entered into partnership with Sir Robert William Perks, becoming senior partner of the firm of Fowler, Perks & Co., London.

Fowler first showed his capacity for public life in municipal affairs. Owing to his vigour and grasp of business, he quickly made his mark in local administration, becoming mayor of Wolverhampton in 1863, and chairman of the first school board in 1870. Several important municipal schemes were carried largely owing to his zealous advocacy; he was also successful in opposing the introduction of politics into the municipal elections of the town. In 1892 his services to Wolverhampton were acknowledged by his being enrolled as the first freeman of the borough.

In addition to his municipal work Fowler took an active part in politics. A nonconformist liberal, he soon came to be recognised as a powerful representative of the party. At the great meeting which Gladstone addressed on the Eastern question at Birmingham on 31 May 1877 he was chosen to move one of the resolutions. His speech on that occasion deeply impressed Gladstone. It was not till 1880, however, that he entered parliament, when he was returned for Wolverhampton in the liberal interest as colleague of Charles Pelham Villiers [q. v.]. In 1885, when the borough was divided into three divisions, Fowler was re-elected for the eastern division, for which he sat until he was raised to the upper house in 1908.

In addition to his business capacity and masculine commonsense, he had a ready command of well-chosen language and the gift of lucidly presenting a complicated case. These qualities, combined with his straightforwardness and his moderation, gained for him with exceptional rapidity the ear of the house. It soon became clear that he was marked out for office. A strong party man, yet moderate and cautious in the expression of his views, a good Wesleyan, yet one who, after the custom of the early methodists, always remained in communion with the Church of England, he was respected and trusted by both sides of the house. On 25 July 1881 he seconded the liberal amendment to Sir Michael Hicks-Beach's vote of censure on the government's conduct after Majuba. In 1884 he became under-secretary for home affairs in Gladstone's second administration, and two years later financial secretary to the treasury. On assuming the latter office he was sworn a member of the privy council.

When, in 1886, Gladstone took up the cause of home rule, it was thought that Fowler would follow Lord Hartington and Mr. Chamberlain in their opposition to the measure. In the event, however, possibly with some searchings of heart, he remained faithful to his chief; and in the debates on the second reading (29 May 1886) he made 'an admirably warm and convinced defence of the policy of the bill.' Lord Morley described him at the time as 'one of the best speakers in the house' (*Life of Gladstone*, iii. 336).

During the six years of opposition which followed the rejection of the home rule bill (1886–92), Fowler, by his keen criticism of the financial policy of the unionist government, strengthened his position not only as an authority on finance but as an excellent debater.

When Gladstone returned to office in Aug. 1892, Fowler became president of the local government board with a seat in the cabinet for the first time. To him fell the duty of piloting the parish councils bill through the house. This was his greatest legislative achievement. From the first he determined to secure as far as possible the co-operation of both sides of the house in improving the bill. He knew his subject thoroughly, and was at the same time fair, courteous, and conciliatory; and in the end he carried a most complicated measure without once himself moving the closure.

On the reconstruction of the ministry in 1894 by Lord Rosebery, Fowler received promotion, becoming secretary of state for India. The appointment excited some cavil, but no previous secretary of state was in greater sympathy with her interests and the imperial questions involved. The chief events of his short tenure of the Indian secretaryship were the Chitral campaign in April 1895 and the revolt of the Lancashire members, led by Sir Henry James, against the reimposition of duties on cotton goods imported into India. In the debate on these duties Fowler made the speech of his life (5 Feb. 1895). He explained that the duties would not be protective because they would be accompanied by a countervailing excise, and he pleaded that parliament in adopting the duties would be acting for the people of India who could not act for themselves. The speech, which contained the memorable phrase 'Every member of this house is a member for India,' was one of those rare displays of argument and eloquence which affect votes. The cabinet was tottering when he rose to speak; when he sat down the situation was saved, and the government had a majority of 195. When asked subsequently whether he knew, while speaking, the effect he was producing, he replied 'The best part of that speech was never spoken; I saw that I had the house with me—and I sat down!' In June 1895 the government resigned after being defeated on the cordite vote, and Fowler received the G.C.S.I., in accordance, it is understood, with the wishes of Queen Victoria.

During the ten years of opposition which followed, Fowler was not a frequent speaker in the house. He devoted himself to his private affairs, and interested himself especially in the development of the telephone system. He was appointed director of the National Telephone Company in 1897, becoming president in 1901. Yet when Sir William Harcourt [q. v. Suppl. II] retired from the leadership of the liberal party in the House of Commons in Dec. 1898 Fowler's claims to the succession were seriously urged. The 'Spectator' (17 Dec. 1898) described him as 'a man thoroughly capable of directing the policy of his party, and, what is more, able, if need be, to govern the country with power and discretion.'

In the distracted councils of the liberal party which followed, Sir Henry was a strong supporter of Lord Rosebery, and was one of the vice-presidents of the Liberal League. He refused to join in the strictures of Sir Henry Campbell-Bannerman on the conduct of the Boer war, declaring that the war was 'just and inevitable.' While thus strengthening his position with moderate men on both sides, he incurred the hostility of the extreme radicals. But it was argued by many of the party that had he been ten years younger and 'inoculated with a dash of audacity' he would have been chosen to supersede Sir Henry Campbell-Bannerman (LUCY's *Balfourian Parliament*, 93). When Mr. Chamberlain startled the country with the tariff reform proposals in 1903, and thereby closed up the ranks of the liberal party, Fowler, as was natural in an old colleague of Villiers, joined heartily in the defence of free trade.

In the liberal administration which was formed in Dec. 1905, Sir Henry, feeling the burden of his seventy-five years, waived his claim to a secretaryship of state, and accepted the comparatively light office of chancellor of the duchy of Lancaster. His inclusion in the cabinet was welcomed by moderate men, who hoped that he would exercise a moderating influence on his younger and less cautious colleagues. But though, in Lord Rosebery's words, he probably gave the cabinet 'the soundest and most sagacious advice,' it is doubtful to what extent it was followed. He took little part in debate. The strain of constant attendance in the House of Commons told on him, but his business-like administration of the affairs of the duchy met with the warm approval of the sovereign. In March 1908, on Sir Henry Campbell-Bannerman's resignation, Mr. Asquith formed a ministry in which Fowler retained his former post. But he took the opportunity of leaving the lower house. On 13 April 1908 he was raised to the peerage as Viscount Wolverhampton, taking his seat in the upper house on the same day as his old friend, John Morley. Later in the same year (14 Oct.) he became lord president of the council. This was the culminating point of his political career, and was a remarkable position to have been won by a man who, aided by no adventitious circumstances, did not enter parliament until he was fifty, and owed everything there to intellect, resolution, and character.

Beyond taking charge of the old age pensions bill during 1908, Lord Wolverhampton took little part in debate in the House of Lords. In Oct. 1909 he received the honorary degree of LL.D. from the University of Birmingham, together with Mr. Balfour and other distinguished men, on the first occasion when the university conferred these degrees. Early in 1910 there were signs that his health was failing; both mind and memory were affected. With much in the advanced policy of the cabinet he was out of sympathy. But he retained his post until his medical advisers insisted on his taking a prolonged holiday. He resigned on 16 June 1910.

With complete rest his health greatly improved, but the death of his wife at Woodthorne, Wolverhampton, on 6 Jan. 1911 completely prostrated him. He died at Woodthorne on 25 Feb. 1911, and was buried in Tettenhall churchyard.

Fowler married on 6 Oct. 1857 Ellen, youngest daughter of George Benjamin Thorneycroft of Chapel House, Wolverhampton, and Hadley Park, Shropshire. To her devotion and wise counsel he owed much. She was made Lady of the Order of the Crown of India in 1895. Lord Wolverhampton left one son, Henry Ernest, who became second viscount, and two daughters. The elder daughter, Ellen Thorneycroft Fowler (Mrs. Alfred Felkin), has under her maiden name won fame as the author of 'Concerning Isabel Carnaby' and other novels; her sister, Edith Henrietta, wife of the Rev. William Robert Hamilton, is also a novelist of repute, and has written the biography of her father (1912).

There are portraits of Lord Wolverhampton, painted by A. S. Cope, R.A., in the Town Hall, Wolverhampton, and in the hall of the Law Society, London. A replica of the first is in the possession of his son. A cartoon portrait by 'Spy' appeared in 'Vanity Fair' in 1892.

[Private sources; Mrs. Hamilton's biography, 1912; The Times, 26 Feb. 1911; Burke's Peerage; Paul's History of Modern England.]

A. L. F.

FOX, SAMSON (1838–1903), inventor and benefactor, born at Bowling, near Bradford, Yorkshire, on 11 July 1838, was one of three sons of James Fox, a Leeds cloth-mill worker, by his wife Sarah Pearson. From the age of ten he worked with his father at the mill; but showing mechanical aptitude, was soon apprenticed to the Leeds firm of Smith, Beacock and Tannett, machine-tool makers, where he became foreman and later traveller. While there Fox designed and patented several tools for the machine cutting of bevelled gear and for the manufacture of trenails. Subsequently he started with his brother and another—Fox, Brother and Refitt—the Silver Cross engineering works for the manufacture of special machine tools. In 1874 he founded the Leeds Forge Company, and he acted as managing director until 1896 and was appointed chairman in May 1903. In 1877 he first patented the Fox corrugated boiler furnaces (by which the resisting power to external pressure was greatly increased), the plates being hammered by means of swage blocks under a steam hammer. This invention led to the practical application of triple expansion engines to marine boilers. The steamship Pretoria, built in 1878, was the first ocean-going steamer to be fitted with Fox's corrugated flues. Machinery for rolling in place of hammering was undertaken in 1882, and a Siemens steel plant was laid down. In 1886 Fox took out patents for the manufacture of pressed steel underframes for railway wagons instead of the old wrought-iron frames. The demand for the improved form of rolling stock led to great extension of the business in Leeds, and to the establishment of a factory at Joliet, near Chicago. There the first pressed steel cars used in America were made, as well as the 'Fox' pressed steel bogie trucks. The American business grew rapidly and new works were erected at Pittsburg, which were merged in 1889 in the Pressed Steel Car Company. Fox became a member of the Institution of Mechanical Engineers in 1875 and of the Institution of Civil Engineers in 1881. A member of the Society of Arts from 1879, he was awarded in 1885 the society's Howard gold medal for his invention of corrugated iron flues.

By way of facilitating and lessening the cost of his manufacturing processes, Fox first employed in England water-gas on a large scale for metallurgical and lighting purposes. The plant which he set up in September 1887 was capable in six months of producing 40,000 cubic feet per hour of water-gas, which was cheaper than ordinary coal gas, and had a far greater heating and lighting power (*The Times,* 2 Jan. 1889). Of the British Water-Gas Syndicate, formed in 1888, Fox became president, but it went into liquidation in 1893. In 1894 Fox produced the first carbide of calcium for making acetylene gas by the method discovered by T. L. Willson in America in 1888. He was the pioneer of the acetylene industry in Europe, for which works were set up at Foyers, N.B.

An enthusiastic lover of music, Fox gave in 1889 the sum of 45,000*l.* for the new buildings of the Royal College of Music, South Kensington, which were opened by King Edward VII (then Prince of Wales) on 2 July 1894 (*The Times,* 23 May 1889; 17 July 1894; *Strand Musical Mag.* Feb. 1895; GRAVES's *Life of Sir George Grove,* 1903). Fox's benefaction gave rise in 1897 to a prolonged libel action, in which Fox was plaintiff, against Mr.

Jerome K. Jerome and the publishers of 'To-day' for printing articles in the paper (May–Aug. 1894 and Jan. 1896) which reflected on Fox's conduct of his business and accused Fox of giving large sums to the college in order to give a wrong impression of his commercial prosperity. After sixteen days' trial, verdict was found for plaintiff without costs, the defendants undertaking not to republish the libel (see *The Times*, 1 April–11 May 1897).

Fox took a leading part in the political and municipal life of Leeds, and was thrice in succession (1889–91) mayor of Harrogate, which he represented on the West Riding county council. He was J.P. for Leeds and Harrogate, and was a member of the Legion of Honour of France. On his return from a tour in Canada and America, Fox died of blood poisoning at Walsall on 24 Oct. 1903, and was buried at Woodhouse cemetery, Leeds. There is a marble bust portrait at the Royal College of Music; painted portraits are at Grove House, Harrogate, where Fox resided, and at Leeds Forge, Leeds. Fox married on 18 May 1859 Marie Ann, daughter of Charles and Alice Slinger, and left issue one son and two daughters.

[The Times, 26 Oct. 1903; Proc. Inst. Civil Engineers, 1903–4, vol. clv.; Proc. Inst. Mechanical Engineers, Oct.–Dec. 1903; Journal, Soc. of Arts, 13 Nov. 1903; notes from the Leeds Forge Company; private information.] W. B. O.

FOX BOURNE. [See Bourne, Henry Richard Fox, 1837–1909, social reformer and author.]

FOXWELL, ARTHUR (1853–1909), physician, born at Shepton Mallet, Somerset, on 13 July 1853, was a younger son of Thomas Somerton Foxwell of Shepton Mallet and Weston-super-Mare by his second wife Jane, daughter of William Handcock of Jersey. His elder brother, Herbert Somerton Foxwell, is now professor of political economy in the University of London.

From Queen's College, Taunton, Arthur passed to St. John's College, Cambridge, graduating B.A. with honours in natural science in 1877, M.B. with first class in medicine in 1883, and proceeding M.A. and M.D. in 1891. Meanwhile in 1873 he graduated B.A. at London with honours in English and moral science, and pursued his medical education at St. Thomas's Hospital, London. In 1881 he became M.R.C.S. London. He became a licentiate of the Royal College of Physicians, London, in 1881, a member in 1885, and a fellow in 1892. At the college in 1889 he read the Bradshawe lecture, which he published in 1899 under the title 'The Causation of Functional Murmurs,' in which he deduced from clinical and pathological experience of cases and elaborate experiments the conclusion that functional murmurs are caused by dilatation of the pulmonary artery immediately beyond the valve and are not due to change in the viscosity of the blood. This view is now generally accepted. During the winter of 1887–8 he studied at Vienna, chiefly diseases of the throat and ear.

After holding the posts of house physician at St. Thomas's Hospital (1881), clinical assistant at the Brompton Hospital (1882), and junior resident medical officer at the Manchester Children's Hospital, Pendlebury (1882–3), he was elected as resident pathologist at the General Hospital, Birmingham (1884), and was honorary assistant physician there from 1885 to 1889. In 1889 he became honorary physician at the Queen's Hospital, Birmingham, where at his death he was senior honorary physician. At the hospital he was chiefly responsible for the construction of the roof ward, only partially covered in, and otherwise open to the air, in which considerable success was obtained in the treatment of various diseases apart from those of tuberculous nature. He was also for a time pathologist to the Birmingham Hospital for Women and demonstrator in medical pathology in the Queen's Faculty of Medicine (at Mason College), known as the Queen's College. From 1887 to 1901 he was honorary librarian at the Medical Institute, Birmingham, of which he was president at his death, and he edited for a time the 'Birmingham Medical Review' (1886–8). In 1906 he was appointed professor of therapeutics in the new Birmingham University and received the degree of M.Sc.

Of shy and reserved nature and weak health, Foxwell died, from the result of a bicycle accident, in the Warneford Hospital, Leamington, on 1 Aug. 1909, and was buried in the burial ground of the Franciscans at Olton. He married in 1889 Lisette, daughter of Charles Hollins of Torquay and widow of Robert Pollock of Birmingham. He left one daughter. A memorial tablet designed by his stepson, Mr. Courtenay Pollock, was placed in the Queen's Hospital, Birmingham, and an annual prize for a clinical essay, open to qualified residents in the Queen's, General, and Children's Hospitals, Birmingham, endowed in his memory.

Foxwell's chief publication, apart from the Bradshawe lecture, was 'Essays on Heart and Lung Disease' (1895), a collection of miscellaneous contributions to the 'Proceedings' of medical societies and similar pieces; papers on climate are included, as well as the Ingleby lectures on 'The Condition of the Vascular System in Anæmic Debility,' delivered at the Queen's College, Birmingham, 1892. He also published 'The Enlarged Cirrhotic Liver' (1896) and 'The Spas of Mid Wales' (1899).

[Brit. Med. Journal and Lancet, 14 Aug. 1909; Birmingham Med. Rev. Sept. 1909; information from Prof. H. S. Foxwell.]

E. M. B.

FRANKFORT DE MONTMORENCY, third VISCOUNT. [See DE MONTMORENCY, RAYMOND HARVEY, 1835-1902.]

FREAM, WILLIAM (1854-1906), writer on agriculture, born at Gloucester in 1854, was second son in the family of four sons and three daughters of John Fream, builder and contractor, by his wife Mary Grant. As a boy he was a chorister of Gloucester Cathedral, and was always devoted to music. After education in Sir Thomas Rich's Blue Coat Hospital, he entered the employment of a Gloucester corn and seed merchant; but gaining a royal exhibition at the Royal College of Science, Dublin, in May 1872, he studied there for three years, and took prizes in botany, practical chemistry, and geology, with special distinction in geology. While in Ireland he made long botanical walking tours to the wild district of Connemara and other distant parts of the country. He became an associate of the Royal College by diploma. He also matriculated in the University of London, and graduated in science with honours in chemistry at the first B.Sc. examination in 1877. From 1877 to 1879 he was professor of natural history at the Royal Agricultural College, Cirencester. In 1879 he filled a temporary vacancy as lecturer and demonstrator in botany at Guy's Hospital Medical School. The following winter he devoted to biological—more especially zoological—study at the Royal School of Mines in London and in writing for the agricultural press.

Early in 1880 he joined Professor John Wrightson in establishing and developing the College of Agriculture at Downton. He taught natural history there and instituted a series of field classes and laboratory demonstrations.

Fream paid visits to Canada in 1884, 1888 and 1891, to examine the agricultural conditions, which he described in a series of papers. These include a charming pamphlet 'The Gates of the West' (1892); 'Across Canada: a Report on Canada and its Agricultural Resources,' written for and published by the government of Canada (Ottawa, 1885); 'Canadian Agriculture' (parts i. and ii.), 'Journal of the Royal Agricultural Society' (1885); 'The Farms and Forests of Canada, as illustrated in the Colonial and Indian Exhibition of 1886' (Toronto, 1886); 'The Provincial Agriculture of Canada' (London, 1887). In 1888 he received from the M'Gill University of Montreal the hon. degree of LL.D.

In 1890 Eleanor Anne Ormerod [q. v. Suppl. II] chose Fream to be the first Steven lecturer in Edinburgh University on agricultural entomology; he had included the first course on the subject in Great Britain in his curriculum at Downton. He remained Steven lecturer till death. Fream, who was an unsuccessful candidate in March 1887 for the office of secretary and editor of the Royal Agricultural Society of England, was appointed in 1890 editor of the 'Journal' of the society, when it became a quarterly, relinquishing the office in 1900, when it was reduced to an annual publication.

For twelve years, from January 1894 till his death, Fream was agricultural correspondent of 'The Times,' writing very efficient weekly articles on agriculture and special annual reports on crop returns. His articles showed an intense love of country life and an intimate knowledge of wild flowers. He was a chief examiner in the principles of agriculture under the science and art department, South Kensington. In 1890 he was employed by the board of agriculture to report on agricultural education in Scotland.

Apart from his writings on Canada, and his journalistic work, Fream edited exhaustively the 13th and 14th editions of 'Youatt's Complete Grazier' (1893 and 1900). His most widely read book was 'The Elements of Agriculture' (British agriculture and live stock), published for the Royal Agricultural Society of England, in 1891 (7th edit. 1902); before his death some 36,000 copies were sold. 'The Rothamsted Experiments on the Growth of Wheat, Barley, and the Mixed Herbage of Grass-land' (1888) was a valuable textbook.

Fream resided chiefly at Downton, but he had working quarters in London, and was very popular in congenial society there. He died, unmarried, at Downton on 29 May

1906, and was buried in Gloucester cemetery.

A Fream memorial fund, subscribed by leading agriculturalists, was entrusted to the board of agriculture, the income to be awarded annually as prizes under special regulations.

[The Times, 31 May 1906.] R. W.

FRÉCHETTE, LOUIS HONORÉ (1839–1908), Canadian poet and journalist, born at Lévis, opposite Quebec, on 16 Nov. 1839, was eldest son of Louis Fréchette, a contractor, whose family was originally established in Ile de Ré, Saintonge. His mother was Marguerite Martineau de Lormière. After education at the Quebec Seminary and Nicolet College, young Fréchette passed to Laval University (Quebec), McGill University, and Queen's University. Becoming a law-student in Quebec in 1861 he published a first volume of (French) poetry 'Mes Loisirs' in 1863, and next year was called to the bar, but did not practise seriously, although he only retired from the profession in 1879. In 1865 he went to Chicago and there devoted himself for six years to journalism. He then edited 'L'Amérique,' and was for a time corresponding secretary of the Illinois Central railway in succession to Thomas Dickens, a brother of the novelist. His poetic reputation was enhanced by a second volume of verse 'La Voix d'un Exilé' (pt. i. 1866; pt. ii. 1868), in which he showed the strength both of his French patriotism and of his clerical antipathies. In 1871 he moved to New Orleans. There, while the siege of Paris was in progress, he showed his devotion to France by fighting a duel with a retired German officer, whom he had offended in a theatre by avowing his French sympathies; he had never used a sword before. In the same year he returned to Quebec.

Turning to politics, he unsuccessfully contested his native place, Lévis, at the general election of 1871 in the liberal interest; but in 1874, when Alexander Mackenzie [q. v.] came into power, he won the seat. He was a consistent supporter of the Mackenzie liberal government. He failed to retain the seat in 1878 and 1882, and thenceforward devoted to journalism all the energies that he spared from poetry. He edited his 'Journal de Québec,' contributed largely to 'L'Opinion Publique,' and during 1884–5 was editor of 'La Patrie.' He wrote frequently, too, for the American magazines the 'Forum,' 'Harper's,' and the 'Arena.' In 1889 the Mercier government appointed him clerk of the legislative council in Quebec, and he held the post till death.

Meanwhile Fréchette was publishing further volumes in verse: 'Pêle-Mêle' (Montreal, 1877), 'Les Oiseaux de Neige' (Quebec, 1880), 'Les Fleurs Boréales' (Dijon, 1881), 'Les Oubliés,' and 'Voix d'Outre Mer' (1886), 'La Légende d'un Peuple' (1887), and 'Les Feuilles Volantes' (1891). 'Les Fleurs Boréales' and 'Les Oiseaux de Neige' were crowned by the French Academy in 1880, and Fréchette was the recipient of the first Montyon prize for the year. He was also made an officier d'Académie lauréat of the Institute of France. The leading universities of Canada conferred honorary degrees upon him (LL.D. McGill University, Montreal, and Queen's University, Kingston, in 1881, and Toronto University in 1900; D.Lit. at Laval University in 1888), and in 1897, the year of the diamond jubilee, he was created C.M.G. He was furthermore president of the Royal Society of Canada. Besides poetry, Fréchette published prose works, including 'Lettres à Basile' (1872), 'Histoire Critique des Rois de France' (1881), and 'Originaux et Détraqués' (Montreal, 1892), the most lively and original of his prose compositions. A collection of tales, 'La Noël au Canada,' appeared in both English and French versions (1899–1900). Fréchette also attempted drama in 'Félix Poutré' (Montreal, 1871), 'Papineau,' and 'Véronica' (in five acts), but these, although vigorously written, lack dramatic instinct. At his death he had in preparation an authoritative edition of his poems. It appeared posthumously at Montreal in 1908 (three series), and it contains all the poems by which Fréchette desired to be remembered. Age softened his ardours against the church, and consequently the unclerical verses of 'La Voix d'un Exilé' find no place in this final edition. He died at Montreal on 31 May 1908.

As a poet Fréchette owes much to Victor Hugo, both in the mechanism of his lines and in the logical method of developing his themes. His poetry is held in high esteem by French-Canadians, who rank only Crémazie beside him. His friend Senator David said 'Fréchette n'avait pas le souffle, la puissance d'invention et de conception de Crémazie, mais il avait plus d'abondance, de souplesse, de forme, il était plus complet, plus émotif, plus chaud.' If Fréchette lack Hugo's vibrant lyrical quality, he is by no means his unsuccessful imitator in patriotic verse. The best measure of his talent will be found in 'La Légende d'un Peuple,' in which he commemorates with skill, vigour, and variety the history of the French race. In contrast to William Henry Drummond [q. v. Suppl. II], whose French types show no resentment against English rule, Fréchette presents the rarer French-Canadian sentiment which failed to reconcile itself to the events which brought 'perfide Albion' upon the scene in 1759. For purposes of poetry this attitude of mind may pass, but Drummond's is the truer picture.

Fréchette married in 1876 Emma, second daughter of Jean Baptiste Beaudry, banker, Montreal. She survived her husband with three daughters.

[The Times, 2 and 25 June 1908; Who's Who, 1908; Sir J. G. Bourinot, Story of Canada, 1896, p. 441 (portrait).] P. E.

FREEMAN, GAGE EARLE (1820–1903), writer on falconry, born on 3 June 1820 at Tamworth, Staffordshire, was son of Capt. Charles Earle Freeman of the 69th regiment by his wife Mary Parsons. After private education he was admitted a pensioner at St. John's College, Cambridge, on 8 July 1840, and graduated B.A. in 1845, proceeding M.A. in 1850. In later life he won at Cambridge four Seatonian prize poems on sacred subjects, 'The Transfiguration' (1882), 'Jericho' (1888), 'Damascus' (1893), and 'The Broad and the Narrow Way' (1894).

Ordained deacon in 1846 and priest in 1847, Freeman held a curacy at Geddington, Northants, from 1846 to 1854, and the perpetual cure of Emmanuel Church, Bolton-le-Moors, from 1854 to 1856. He was afterwards incumbent of Macclesfield Forest with Clough, Cheshire, till 1889, when he became vicar of Askham, near Penrith, and private chaplain to the earl of Lonsdale. This living he held until his death.

Through life he devoted his leisure to hawking, being introduced to the sport by William Brodrick of Belford, Northumberland, afterwards of Chudleigh, Devon [see SALVIN, FRANCIS HENRY, Suppl. II]. In Northamptonshire he enjoyed his first experience with a kestrel-hawk, equipped with a hood of home manufacture, and he afterwards flew sparrowhawks, merlins and peregrines at pigeons and larks. But he had his best sport later whilst in his lonely Cheshire parish, hawking grouse with peregrines on Buxton Moor and Swythamley, the property of his friend, Philip Brocklehurst of Swythamley Park, Staffordshire. Next to peregrines, Freeman preferred goshawks, with which he killed hares and rabbits, with or without ferrets. Lord Lilford affirmed that Freeman did more to keep English falconers in the right way than any man living (preface to *Lord Lilford on Birds*, 1903). To the 'Field' newspaper Freeman contributed articles on falconry for a quarter of a century over the signature 'Peregrine,' and on these articles he based two treatises of standard value. He had the chief share in 'Falconry; its Claims, History, and Practice' (1859), written in collaboration with Francis Henry Salvin [q. v. Suppl. II]. This is a handbook for beginners, with plates by Wolf, now long out of print. Freeman's 'Practical Falconry; and how I became a Falconer' (1869), is slightly more discursive and is now much sought after. Freeman's essay, 'On the Desirability of attempting to revive the Sport of Falconry by its Practice at Alexandra Park' (1871), won the second prize (the first being taken by Capt. C. Hawkins Fisher of Stroud) in a competition held by the Barnet committee for promoting the opening of Alexandra Park. Freeman contributed the section on Falcons and Falconry to 'Lord Lilford on Birds' (ed. A. Trevor-Battye, 1903). He also published 'Five Christmas Poems' (1860, reprinted from the 'Field,' with additions), and 'Mount Carmel, a Story of English Life' (1867).

He died at the vicarage, Askham, on 15 Dec. 1903, and was buried at Macclesfield Forest Chapel. Freeman was twice married: (1) on 5 Jan. 1848 to Christiana (*d.* 1886), daughter of John Slade of Little Lever, Bolton-le-Moors, by whom he had issue eight sons and two daughters; (2) in April 1891 to Mary, daughter of Francis William Ashton, cotton-spinner and calico printer, of Hyde, Cheshire, who survived him.

[Private information; Field, 19 Dec. 1903; The Times, 16 Dec. 1903 (copied in Guardian, 23 Dec.); Crockford's Clerical Directory; Eagle (St. John's Coll. Mag.), March 1904; J. E. Harting's Bibliotheca Accipitraria; E. B. Michell's Art and Practice of Hawking; Cox and Lascelles, Coursing and Falconry (Badminton Library); Penrith Observer, 22 Dec. 1903; Mid-Cumberland and North Westmorland Gazette, 19 Dec. 1903; Brit. Mus. Cat.; Allibone's Dict. Eng. Lit. (Suppl.); Freeman's Works. See also Major C. Hawkins Fisher's Reminiscences of a Falconer, pp. 55, 99–100, with a photographic portrait of Freeman.] G. LE G. N.

FRERE, MARY ELIZA ISABELLA (1845–1911), author, born at Bitton rectory, Gloucestershire, on 11 Aug. 1845, was eldest of the five children of Sir (Henry)

Bartle (Edward) Frere, first baronet [q. v.]. by his wife Catherine, second daughter of Lieut.-general Sir George Arthur [q. v.].

Privately educated at Wimbledon, she went out at the age of eighteen to Bombay, where her father was governor, and in the following year (1864), in her mother's absence in England, she was the hostess at government house. Profoundly interested in the Indian peoples, she accompanied her father on his tours, and gathered a large number of folk-lore tales from her ayah (Indian ladies' maid), to whom they had been handed down by a centenarian grandmother.

With an instructive introduction and notes by her father and illustrations by her sister Catherine, Miss Frere published twenty-four of these tales, in March 1868, under the title of 'Old Deccan Days.' The work was deservedly successful, and was four times reprinted (fifth impression 1898). Max Müller [q. v. Suppl. I] pointed out that Miss Frere's tales had been preserved by oral tradition so accurately that some of them were nearly word for word translations of the Sanskrit in which they were originally told. To Anglo-Indians the book 'opened up an entirely new field of scientific research . . . of inexhaustible wealth; and it gave a fresh impetus to the study of folk-lore in the United Kingdom, and throughout Europe and the Americas' (Sir G. Birdwood). 'Old Deccan Days' has been translated into German and Marathi, and recently selections have been included in Stead's 'Books for the Bairns' and in Sarah C. Bryant's 'Stories to tell the Children' (New York and London, 1911).

Miss Frere also wrote a pastoral play, 'Love's Triumph,' published anonymously in 1869, containing sonnets of poetic power and tenderness. One or two of her short poems subsequently appeared anonymously in the 'Spectator,' but most of her verse is unpublished.

Accompanying her father to South Africa when he was appointed high commissioner (March 1877), Miss Frere there, as in India, delighted in the country folk, and was a welcome guest at the old Dutch and English farmhouses. Here, too, she helped to dissipate racial prejudices. When she and a sister returned to England in 1880, shortly before the recall of their father by the Gladstone government, they were received with most gracious interest at Windsor by Queen Victoria.

In later years Miss Frere travelled extensively on the continent and in Egypt, and was in the Holy Land from the end of 1906 to August 1908. Living mainly at Cambridge, she studied Hebrew, and closely followed the results of biblical criticism. After some years of failing health, she died at St. Leonards-on-Sea on 26 March 1911, being buried at Brookwood cemetery.

[Miss Frere's books; Athenæum, 15 April 1911, memoir by Sir George Birdwood; Cambridge Daily News, 6 April 1911; South Africa, 8 April 1911; information kindly supplied by the family.] F. H. B.

FRITH, WILLIAM POWELL (1819–1909), painter, born on 9 Jan. 1819, at Aldfield, near Ripon, Yorkshire, was son of William Frith, by his wife Jane Powell, a member of the ancient but decayed family of Fitz, Shropshire. Both parents were in the domestic employment of Mrs. Lawrence of Studley Royal. When the boy was seven years old his family moved to Harrogate, where the father became the landlord of the Dragon Hotel. He sent his son to a school at Knaresborough which appears to have been a 'Dotheboys Hall.' The boy next passed to a large school at St. Margaret's, near Dover, his master being instructed to encourage a gift for art which Frith senior thought he could discern in his son. Young Frith was allowed to spend most of his time in various grotesque performances with pencil and chalk. On leaving school he had a narrow escape from becoming an auctioneer. He finally entered Sass's Academy in Charlotte Street, Bloomsbury. After two years under Sass he won admission to the schools of the Royal Academy. While still an academy student he commenced portrait painting. Through an uncle, Scaife, who kept an hotel in Brook Street, he obtained a practice chiefly among well-to-do farmers in Lincolnshire, who paid five, ten, and fifteen guineas for heads, kit-cats, and half-lengths respectively.

In 1837 Frith's father died, and his mother set up house with her son in London, at 11 Osnaburgh Street. In 1839 he exhibited a portrait of a child at the British Institution. In 1840 he painted his first subject pictures, exhibiting at the Academy that year 'Malvolio before the Countess Olivia' and 'Othello and Desdemona.' From that time for many years he was faithful to subjects from Scott, Sterne, Goldsmith, Molière, Cervantes, Shakespeare, Dickens, and the 'Spectator,' all of which gave him the opportunity of dressing up his models in picturesque clothes, and of incurring the odium of those young men who, as the Pre-Raphaelite

Brotherhood, were presently to vilify his ideals. In 1845 'The Village Pastor' secured his election as A.R.A. Among other well-known pictures which he contributed to the Academy during this middle period of his activity are: 'English Merry-making a Hundred Years Ago' (1847); 'Coming of Age in the Olden Time' (1849); 'Witchcraft'; 'Sir Roger de Coverley at the Saracen's Head' and a scene from 'The Good-Natured Man' (commissioned by John Sheepshanks [q. v.]), now in the Victoria and Albert Museum. In 1853 Frith was promoted to fill the vacancy left among the academicians by the death of Turner. Into his diploma picture, 'The Sleepy Model,' the artist introduced a good portrait of himself.

Frith visited Belgium, Holland, and the Rhine in 1850. A year later he spent the summer at Ramsgate, a visit which led to an abrupt change in his subjects. His diary for 30 Sept. 1851 contains the following entry (*Autobiography*): 'Began to make a sketch from Ramsgate sands which, if successful, will considerably alter my practice.' The result of this sketch was the large picture 'Ramsgate Sands,' sometimes called 'Life at the Seaside,' painted in 1853, exhibited in 1854, and now in the royal collection. It had a great popular success. There followed, in 1858, 'The Derby Day,' now in the national collection at the Tate Gallery, and, in 1862, 'The Railway Station,' now owned by Holloway College, both of which eclipsed even the 'Ramsgate Sands' in popularity. These three famous paintings enjoyed, like most of Frith's work, an immense circulation in engravings. Frith's success led to invitations from Queen Victoria to paint the marriage of the Princess Royal, and the marriage of Edward VII, as Prince of Wales. The first offer was declined; the second was accepted. The last pictures in which Frith showed his own peculiar talent in marshalling a crowd were 'Charles II's Last Whitehall Sunday' (1867) and 'The Salon d'Or, Homburg' (1871). Another crowd, painted twelve years later, 'The Private View of the Royal Academy' (1883), was far inferior to its predecessors. Frith made two ill-advised attempts to rival Hogarth. The first of these moralities, 'The Road to Ruin,' in five scenes, was at Burlington House in 1878; the second, 'The Race for Wealth,' in five pictures, was shown at a private gallery in King Street in 1880.

Besides those already named, Frith's better pictures include 'Dolly Varden' and the portrait of her creator, Charles Dickens (painted in 1859), in the Forster collection at South Kensington; 'Claude Duval' (1860); 'Uncle Toby and the Widow Wadman' (1866, now in the Tate Gallery); 'Pope and Lady Mary Wortley-Montagu'; and 'Swift and Vanessa.' 'The Dinner at Boswell's Rooms in Bond Street,' which was exhibited in 1869 at the Academy, was sold at Christie's in 1875 for 4567*l.*, the highest sum then reached for a work by a living painter. Frith also painted many anecdotic pictures during his later career; of these 'John Knox at Holyrood,' exhibited in 1886, is a familiar example. But here his gift for marshalling a crowd and for painting it with some vivacity had little or no scope.

Frith visited Italy in 1875, and made a second tour in the Low Countries in 1880. In 1890 he joined the ranks of the retired Royal Academicians, but he survived for nearly twenty years, painting to the end. He was a member of the Royal Belgian Academy and of those of Antwerp, Stockholm, and Vienna. He was a chevalier of the Legion of Honour, and personally received the badge of C.V.O. from Edward VII at Buckingham Palace on 9 Jan. 1908, his eighty-ninth birthday (cf. *Cornhill Mag.* 1909). He died at his residence in St. John's Wood, London, on 2 Nov. 1909, and was buried at Kensal Green after cremation at Golder's Green. A small collection of his better works was exhibited at Burlington House in the winter of 1911. It was then recognised that the 'Derby Day' and the 'Railway Station' possessed pictorial qualities, which it had become the fashion to deny.

Frith married on 22 June 1845 Isabelle, daughter of George Baker of York. She died on 28 Jan. 1880. Of twelve children, five daughters and five sons survived their father. His son, Mr. Walter Frith, is a dramatist and novelist.

Frith's friends included not only the chief artists of the day but many men of letters, including Dickens. He published: 'John Leech, his Life and Work' (1891), which is a description of Leech's work rather than a biography; 'My Autobiography and Reminiscences' (1887); and 'Further Reminiscences' (1888).

Portraits by himself at the ages respectively of eighteen and seventy belong to the family. A third portrait was painted in 1854 by Augustus Egg, R.A. Another good early portrait painted by an academy student friend, Cowper, who died young, was sold after Frith's death. His own head figures in the right-hand corner of 'Ramsgate Sands' (1853) and he introduced himself as paterfamilias with all his family into 'The Railway Station' (1861). A cartoon portrait by 'Spy' appeared in 'Vanity Fair' in 1873.

[The Times, 4 Nov. 1909; Academy Catalogues; A. Graves's Royal Academy Exhibitors; private information; Mrs. J. E. Panton, Leaves from a Life, 1911; Mrs. E. M. Ward, Reminiscences, 1911; Frith's Autobiography 1887, and Reminiscences, 1888.] W. A.

FRY, DANBY PALMER (1818–1903), legal writer, born in Great Ormond Street, London, on 1 Dec. 1818, was second son in the family of four sons and four daughters of Alfred Augustus Fry, a good scholar and linguist, who was accountant and for some years a partner in the firm of Thomas de la Rue & Co., wholesale stationers. His mother was Jane Sarah Susannah Westcott. He was named after his father's friend, Danby Palmer of Norwich [cf. PALMER, CHARLES JOHN]. The eldest son, Alfred Augustus Fry, was the first English barrister to practise in Constantinople.

Danby was educated at Hunter Street Academy, Brunswick Square, London, a well-known grammar school conducted by Jonathan Dawson, whose sons, George Dawson [q. v.] of Birmingham and Benjamin Dawson (subsequently proprietor of the school and long treasurer of the Philological Society), were Fry's schoolfellows. In 1836 he became a clerk in the poor law board, first at Somerset House and afterwards at Gwydyr House, Whitehall. On 1 April 1848, during the Chartist riots, he was officially deputed to report to headquarters the proceedings of the agitators on Kennington Common. Each hour he received messengers to whom he delivered his hastily written reports. Called to the bar at Lincoln's Inn on 30 Jan. 1851, he became in October 1871 inspector of audits, and on 15 Oct. 1873 assistant secretary to the local government board. From 1878 until his retirement in 1882 he was legal adviser to the board.

Fry made some reputation as author of legal handbooks. As early as 1846 he produced 'Local Taxes of the United Kingdom' (published officially). His 'Union Assessment Committee Act' (1862; 8th edit. 1897); his 'Lunacy Acts' (1864; 3rd edit. 1890); 'The Law Relating to Vaccination' (1869; 7th edit. 1890), and 'The Valuation [Metropolis] Act' (1869; 2nd edit. 1872) became standard works.

Through his father, whose circle of acquaintances included Lord Brougham, Leigh Hunt, and others interested in social and political reforms, Fry was friendly from an early age with Charles Knight and with Sir Rowland Hill's family. Economic and philanthropic problems occupied much of his attention, but his leisure was devoted to philology, and he became an expert student of both old English and old French. He helped his father in compiling in MS. an English dictionary with the words arranged according to roots. He was an original member of the Philological Society, founded in 1842, and its treasurer for many years, and was a contributor of well-informed papers on linguistic subjects to its 'Transactions.' He was one of the original committee of the Early English Text Society, founded by Dr. Furnivall [q. v. Suppl. II] in 1864. He was joint author with Benjamin Dawson of a small book 'On the Genders of French Substantives' (1876). His philological studies were pursued till his death. He died unmarried, on 16 Feb. 1903, at his house, 166 Haverstock Hill, and was buried at Highgate cemetery.

[Personal knowledge.] H. B. W–Y.

FULLER, SIR THOMAS EKINS (1831–1910), agent-general for Cape Colony, born at West Drayton on 24 Aug. 1831, was son of Andrew Gunton Fuller, baptist minister, who was a popular preacher and an amateur artist of some distinction. Andrew Fuller [q.v.], the baptist theologian, was his grandfather. His mother was Esther Hobson. Mr. Robert Fuller, author of 'South Africa at Home,' is his brother.

Educated at a private school, and then at the Bristol Baptist College, Fuller became baptist minister at Melksham, and afterwards served baptist chapels at Lewes and Luton. He subsequently turned his attention to literature and contributed freely to the press. In 1864 he went to South Africa to become editor of the 'Cape Argus.' He rapidly became a leader in the social and political life in Cape Colony. He won distinction for brilliant articles on social and educational work in the 'Argus,' and was one of the promoters of the Cape University. While editor of the 'Cape Argus' Fuller ardently advocated responsible government for the Cape Colony, which was granted by the imperial government in 1872. He was one of those chiefly instrumental in educating colonial opinion on the subject. In 1873 Fuller was appointed emigration agent to the Cape Colony in London, but in 1875 he returned to Cape Town to take up the post of general manager there of the Union Steamship Company. He held this office for twenty-three years.

Meanwhile he engaged actively in politics. In 1878 he was returned as one of the members for Cape Town in the House of Assembly, and retained the seat till his resignation in 1902. He was an eloquent and impressive speaker in parliament and advocated every progressive measure. He refused office, believing that he could serve the colony better as a private member. In his last years in parliament he was a steady and a prominent supporter of Cecil Rhodes's policy, and became his intimate friend. In 1898 he was made a director of De Beers Consolidated Mines Company, and thereupon he resigned his post with the Union Co. from a fear that the prominent part he took in party politics might react prejudicially on the welfare of the company. At the same time he found time for municipal work and was a member of the town council, a trustee of the public library, chairman of the harbour board, and a leading spirit in the chamber of commerce.

At the end of 1901 he returned to England, and on 1 Jan. 1902 assumed the office of agent-general to the Cape, resigning the De Beers directorship at the same time; he remained agent-general till 1907. In 1903 he was made C.M.G. and next year K.C.M.G. He died at Tunbridge Wells on 5 Sept. 1910. Fuller married (1) in 1855 Mary Playne, daughter of Isaac Hillier of Nailsworth, and by her had three sons and a daughter; (2) in 1875 Elizabeth, daughter of the Rev. Thomas Mann of Cowes. His eldest son, Mr. William Henry Fuller, commanded the East London town guard during the Boer war of 1899–1902.

Fuller was a man of high intellectual culture, and a profound student of philosophy. To the end of his life he reviewed literary works in the press and contributed a notable article to the 'Westminster Review' on 'Man's Relation to the Universe through Cosmic Emotion' (reprinted 1902). His last publication was 'Cecil Rhodes, a Monograph and Reminiscence' (1910), a valuable contribution to the biography of his friend.

[Anglo-African Who's Who, 1905; personal knowledge.] A. P. H.

FULLEYLOVE, JOHN (1845–1908), landscape painter, born at Leicester on 18 Aug. 1845, was son of John and Elizabeth Fulleylove. He was educated at day-schools in that town, and when about sixteen was articled as a clerk to Flint, Shenton and Baker, a local firm of architects. He developed a strong natural bent for the picturesque side of architecture by sketching from nature in his free hours, and received some instruction in painting from Harry Ward, a drawing-master of the school of Harding.

Fulleylove's earliest drawings were views of his native town and its neighbourhood. Taking up art professionally he began to exhibit English subjects in London in 1871. Subsequently he travelled widely at home and abroad in search of themes. In 1875 and again in 1880 he made tours in Italy. He spent the summer of 1878 in sketching at Tabley Old Hall, that of 1879 at Hampton Court, and that of 1882 at Versailles.

He was elected an associate of the Royal Institute of Painters in Water Colours in the spring of 1878, and became a member next year. Fulleylove moved from Leicester to London in 1883 and established himself at first in a house in Mecklenburgh Square, later moving (1893) to Great Russell Street, and ultimately (1894) to Church Row, Hampstead. Besides exhibiting an ever-widening range of subjects at the Institute, he held many exhibitions of his work at the Fine Art Society's galleries in Bond Street. Of these individual exhibitions, the first consisted of drawings of south-eastern France, 'Petrarch's Country' (1886); this was followed by views of Oxford (1888); views of Cambridge (1890); Parisian subjects and studies of Versailles (1894). In 1892 he exhibited a collection of local sketches at Leicester. In the summer of 1895 he visited Greece in company with his friends Alfred Higgins and Somers Clarke. Ninety drawings made during this tour, exhibited at the Fine Art Society's gallery in the following spring, mark the highest level of his achievement.

He occasionally practised painting in oil, was a member of the Institute of Painters in Oil, and contributed oil-paintings to the Academy and other exhibitions. In the summer of 1898 he executed a number of small panel pictures of Oxford which were exhibited at the Fine Art Society's Gallery in 1899. They were painted direct from nature, whereas the large oil pictures by which he was occasionally represented in later years at the Academy were worked up from water-colour sketches.

Fulleylove's next exhibition in Bond Street (1902) consisted of drawings of the

Holy Land, but Palestine did not inspire him so happily as Greece. In 1904 many excellent pencil sketches were exhibited at the Goupil Gallery in London, and at Edinburgh a series of local views, which like most of his latest work, such as the drawings of Westminster Abbey, the Tower of London, and some Middlesex subjects (1907), were executed for reproduction in colour as illustrations to books. Some of his Oxford oil sketches and of his drawings of Greece and Palestine were reproduced in similar form. He himself preferred the black-and-white reproductions of his earlier (1888) Oxford sketches by lithography, and of the Greek drawings in photogravure.

His health failed suddenly, and he died at Hampstead on 22 May 1908. He was buried in Highgate cemetery. Fulleylove married, in 1878, Elizabeth Sara, daughter of Samuel Elgood of Leicester; she with one son and two daughters survived him.

Fulleylove was an admirable architectural draughtsman. His early training had given him a thorough comprehension of construction and detail. His water-colour was always laid over a solid and carefully completed pencil sketch. In colour his earlier works are silvery, sometimes a little weak, but always harmonious. Greater breadth of tone and force of colour are noticeable in the Versailles drawings of 1893 and in the Greek series, which are not only his best productions but some of the most brilliant and accomplished water-colour work of his generation. A few of his drawings are in the Victoria and Albert Museum, and he is well represented in the Municipal Gallery at Leicester.

[Graves's Dictionary of Artists, 1760–1893; Catalogues of the Exhibitions of the Royal Institute of Painters in Water Colours and of the Fine Art Society; private information.]

FURNIVALL, FREDERICK JAMES (1825–1910), scholar and editor, born at Egham, Surrey, on 4 Feb. 1825, was second child and eldest son, in a family of five sons and four daughters, of George Frederick Furnivall by his wife Sophia Barwell. The father, a medical practitioner, who had been educated at St. Bartholomew's Hospital and was in 1805 assistant surgeon of the 14th foot, maintained a prosperous practice at Egham, and also kept a private lunatic asylum at his house, Great Fosters, out of which he made a fortune of 200,000*l.* He attended Shelley's wife, Mary, in her confinement at Marlow in 1817, and the son was fond of quoting his father's reminiscences of Shelley and his household. He died on 7 June 1865.

After attending private schools at Englefield Green, Turnham Green, and Hanwell, Furnivall in 1841 entered University College, London, and in July 1842 passed the London University matriculation in the first division. On 9 Oct. he matriculated from Trinity Hall, Cambridge. As a boy he hunted at Egham, and before entering the university he was a skilled oarsman. He quickly won a place in the college eight. During the long vacation of 1845 he built, with the aid of John Beesley, a Thames waterman, two sculling boats on a new plan. By narrowing the beam and extending the outriggers he gave an unprecedented leverage to the oar. A wager boat on Furnivall's lines was soon built for the champion sculler, Newell, who in it gave Henry Clasper, on the Tyne, one of his rare defeats (18 Jan. 1846). To sculling Furnivall remained faithful till death, and he always ardently advocated its superiority to rowing. Despite his lifelong devotion to the water he never learnt to swim. As an undergraduate he showed a characteristic impatience of convention and an undisciplined moral earnestness. He became a vegetarian, and remained one for a quarter of a century. To tobacco and alcohol he was a stranger through life. He read mathematics, and was admitted scholar of Trinity Hall on 1 June 1843. He graduated B.A. in 1847, taking a low place among the junior optimes in 1846. He proceeded M.A. in 1850.

On leaving Cambridge, Furnivall entered as a student at Lincoln's Inn (26 Jan. 1846). He read in the chambers of Charles Henry Bellenden Ker [q. v.], a friend of his father, a man of wide and enlightened interests. He was called to the bar at Gray's Inn (30 Jan. 1849), and set up as a conveyancer at 11 New Square. He rented various sets of rooms in Lincoln's Inn till 1873, but the law had small attraction for him, and his attention was soon diverted from it. Through Bellenden Ker he came to know many men and women who championed social reform and democratic principles. Of these John Malcolm Ludlow [q. v. Suppl. II] exerted a predominant influence on him. Through Ludlow he was drawn into the Christian Socialist movement, and accepted at first all its tenets. He heard Maurice preach at Lincoln's Inn, and attended his Bible readings. The doctrine of industrial co-operation appealed to him, and he joined the central co-operative committee. He supported trades unionism and identified himself with labour agitation, selling his books to give 100*l.* to the woodcutters who engaged in a strike in 1851. Meanwhile he wrote for the 'Christian Socialist,' and published in 1850 his first literary work, a pamphlet entitled 'Association a Necessary Part of Christianity.'

Philological study and music also engaged Furnivall's youthful attention. He joined the Philological Society in 1847, and heard Chopin play (26 July 1848) and Jenny Lind sing. The current literature which he chiefly admired was the early work of Ruskin, with whose outlook on life he avowed an eager sympathy. In 1849 a chance meeting with Mrs. Ruskin at a friend's house led to an invitation to Ruskin's London home. 'Thus began,' Furnivall wrote, 'a friendship (with Ruskin) which was for many years the chief joy of my life.' Of Ruskin, Furnivall was through life a wholehearted worshipper, and the habit of egotistic reflection which characterised his own writing is often a halting echo of Ruskin's style and temperament.

At the beginning of the intercourse Furnivall sought with youthful ardour to bring Ruskin into relation with Maurice. In 1851 he invited Maurice's opinion of Ruskin's theological argument in his 'Notes on the Construction of Sheepfolds.' Furnivall forwarded Maurice's criticisms to Ruskin, and an interesting correspondence passed through Furnivall between the two; but they had little in common. Furnivall, who inclined to Ruskin's rather than to Maurice's views, printed this correspondence for private circulation in 1890 (NICOLL AND WISE, *Anecdotes of the Nineteenth Century*, ii. 1–46).

In the spirit of Christian Socialism Furnivall at the same time devoted his best energies to endeavours to improve the social and educational opportunities of the working classes. With Ludlow and others he opened as early as 1849 a school for poor men and boys at Little Ormond Yard, Bloomsbury. In 1852 he joined the same friends in forming a working men's association for the purpose of giving lectures and holding classes at a house in Castle Street East, off Oxford Street. These efforts developed into the foundation on 26 Oct. 1854 of the Working Men's College in Red Lion Square, with Maurice as principal. Furnivall vigorously helped in the organisation of the new college. He spent there five nights a week, and actively identified himself with its social, athletic, and educational life. Furnivall taught English grammar and lectured on English poetry from Chaucer to Tennyson. He induced Ruskin to teach drawing to the students with profitable results. But it was in the development of the social side that he worked hardest. He accompanied the students in botanical walks and on rowing excursions. He arranged Sunday rambles, and organised concerts and dances. In 1858, on the advice of Ruskin, he took a party of working men on a tour abroad. It was Furnivall's only experience of foreign travel. He left London with his companions for Havre on 6 Sept., and spent three weeks walking in Normandy and visiting Paris. In 1859 he eagerly helped to organise a volunteer corps of college students, and became company commander, retaining the post for twelve years. Subsequently he inaugurated a college rowing club, which was named after Maurice. He induced the members to engage, under his leadership, in sculling four and eight races, which he introduced to the Thames in 1866; he was long the rowing club's guiding spirit.

Furnivall's devotion to the recreative aims of the college, and his emphatic advocacy of Sunday as a day of solely secular amusement, caused difficulties between him and Maurice and other members of the college council. His religious views had undergone a change. He had been brought up in conventional orthodoxy. This he abandoned in early manhood for an outspoken agnosticism and uncompromising hostility to the received faiths. Joining the Sunday League which combated Sabbatarianism, he described, during 1858, the Sunday amusements of the college in the League's organ, 'The People's Friend.' His somewhat insolent references to Maurice led the latter to tender his resignation of the principalship, and he was with difficulty persuaded to remain in office. Although a reconciliation was patched up, Maurice's relations with Furnivall lost all show of cordiality. Furnivall deemed Maurice and the college council to be not only unduly conservative in their religious views but undemocratic in refusing working men admission to the council. Furnivall's activity in the affairs of the college ceased only with his life. He never lost his early tone of impatience with those colleagues whose religious or political views differed from his own. But he retained to the last the ardent devotion of the students, and the social development of the institution stood deeply indebted to him.

Furnivall's zeal for literary study rapidly developed, and he tried to adapt to its pursuit the principles of association and co-operation which he advocated in other relations of life. Of the Philological Society he became one of two honorary secretaries in 1853, and was sole secretary from 1862 till his death. He supported with enthusiasm the society's proposals for spelling reform, which Alexander John Ellis [q. v. Suppl. I] devised, and always took an active part in promoting such reform, adopting in his own writings a modified phonetic scheme. In another direction his energetic participation in the Philological Society's work bore more valuable fruit. At the end of 1858 the society, at Archbishop Trench's suggestion, resolved to undertake a supplement to Johnson's and Richardson's Dictionaries. But Furnivall urged a wholly new dictionary, and his proposal was adopted. On the death in 1861 of the first editor of the suggested dictionary, Herbert Coleridge [q. v.], Furnivall took his place, and he worked at the scheme intermittently for many years. At the same time he planned a 'concise' dictionary which should be an abstract of the larger undertaking. Although he accumulated much material for the double scheme he made little headway owing to his varied engagements. In 1876 the Oxford University Press took over the enterprise, appointing Dr. (afterwards Sir) James A. H. Murray editor. The 'New English Dictionary' was the result. To that great work Furnivall continued to contribute to the end of his life.

Meanwhile Furnivall was concentrating his attention on early and middle English literature. He deemed it a patriotic duty to reprint from manuscript works which were either unprinted or imperfectly printed. He valued old literature both for its own sake and for the light it shed on social history. His literary endeavours at first centred in the literature of the Arthurian romances, and he inaugurated his editorial labours with an edition of Lonelich's fifteenth-century epic 'Seynt Graal,' which he prepared for the Roxburghe Club (1861, 2 vols.; re-edited for the Early English Text Society, 1874–8). Two prominent bibliophile members of the Roxburghe Club, Henry Huth [q. v. Suppl. II] and Henry Hucks Gibbs, afterwards Baron Aldenham [q. v. Suppl. II], enlisted his services. In 1862, for the Roxburghe club, he undertook one of his most valuable pieces of textual labour, the 'Handlyng Synne' of Robert of Brunne, to which he added the 'Manuel des Pechiez' of William of Waddington, unhappily from a MS. of inferior textual value. In 1862 he also printed a collection of early English poems from MSS. for the Philological Society, and in 1865 he published with Macmillan the more attractive 'Morte d'Arthur,' from an Harleian MS.

In 1864, with a view to more effectual pursuit of his literary aims, Furnivall founded the Early English Text Society. It began with 75 subscribers, Ruskin and Tennyson amongst them. Its first publication was Furnivall's edition of a short metrical 'Life of King Arthur.' The society flourished under Furnivall's energetic guidance, and he worked hard for it both as director and editor for more than forty years. He enlisted the co-operation of scholars all over the world, who edited texts for the society. At first the society's sole aim was to print mediæval MSS. But in 1867 a second or extra series was instituted to include reprints of the work of the earliest English printers. At his death the society had issued 140 volumes in the original series and 107 in the extra series. The vastness of the material with which Furnivall sought to deal led him to found other societies on similar lines for separate treatment of voluminous mediæval writers. Chaucer, Wiclif, and Lydgate each in his view needed a society exclusively devoted to his interests. It was chiefly at the suggestion of Henry Bradshaw [q. v. Suppl. I] that Furnivall started in 1868 the Chaucer Society. His hope was to form an accurate text of the poems by collation of all known manuscripts and to ascertain from both internal and external evidence the date at which each of Chaucer's known works was composed. His labour began in 1868 with the issue of his six-text edition of the 'Canterbury Tales,' which provides the best possible material for textual study. There followed parallel text editions of Chaucer's 'Minor Poems' (1871–9), and of his 'Troilus and Criseyde' (1881–2). Although he had collaborators, the most important of the Chaucer Society's publications are the fruit of Furnivall's own industry. He thus set Chaucerian study on a new and sure footing. Another enterprise diverted Furnivall's attention to English literature of a later period. In 1868 he and Prof. J. W. Hales edited and printed by subscription in three volumes the folio MS. of the 'Percy Ballads' [see Percy, Thomas]. With a view to continuing Percy's labours in rescuing old ballads from oblivion, Furnivall thereupon founded the Ballad Society, which was designed to make accessible the large store of ballad collections which was not accessible in modern reprints. The Roxburghe and Bagford collections of ballads in the British Museum were published (1868–99) by the society, together with illustrative pieces of popular literature of the sixteenth century.

Now that Furnivall's researches had reached the sixteenth century he proceeded to apply to Shakespeare's work the methods which had already served the study of Chaucer. In 1873 he founded the New Shakspere Society, with the object of determining 'the succession of his plays' and of illustrating his work and times. Many distinguished scholars became vice-presidents, and Robert Browning was induced to act as president. Furnivall organised reprints of early texts and of contemporary illustrative literature. To a translation of Gervinus's Commentaries on Shakespeare (1874) he prefixed an essay entitled 'The Succession of Shakspere's Work, and the Use of Metrical Tests in settling it.' There he laid a stress on the metrical tests, which became characteristic of the society's labours and evoked the ridicule of æsthetic critics (cf. [John Jeremiah] *Furnivallos Furioso,* 1874). Much controversy ensued. Swinburne, who at first treated Furnivall's learning with respect, was moved by the society's mechanical methods of criticism to satirise its proceedings in a skit called 'The Newest Shakespere Society' which appeared in 'The Examiner' in April 1876. Subsequently Swinburne denounced Furnivall and his friends as 'sham Shakespeareans.' Furnivall replied with heat (*Spectator*, 6 and 13 Sept. 1879). When Halliwell-Phillipps accepted in 1880 Swinburne's dedication of his 'Study of Shakespeare' Furnivall brought Halliwell-Phillipps as well as Swinburne within the range of his attack. In 'Forewords' to the facsimile of the second quarto of Hamlet, dedicated to Gladstone (1880), he dubbed Swinburne 'Pigsbrook,' and Halliwell-Phillipps 'H-ll-P.' In Jan. 1881 Halliwell complained to Browning of this 'coarse and impertinent language'; but Browning declined to intervene, and Halliwell-Phillipps privately printed the correspondence. Furnivall retorted in even worse taste in 'The "Co." of Pigsbrook & Co.' (1881). Furnivall's conduct had little to justify it. Many of the distinguished vice-presidents of the society resigned, and the society was thenceforth heavily handicapped. Nevertheless, it continued its work until 1890. Many of its publications were useful, notably its editions of Harrison's 'Description of England' (1877–8) and Stubbes's 'Anatomie of Abuses' (1879), which Furnivall himself prepared. By independent work outside the society, Furnivall also, despite his imprudences, stimulated Shakespearean study. In 1876 he wrote an elaborate preface to 'The Leopold Shakspere,' a reprint of Delius's text, which the publishers, Messrs. Cassell, dedicated to Prince Leopold, duke of Albany. The preface was re-issued separately in 1908 as 'Shakspere—Life and Work,' the preliminary volume of the 'Century' edition of Shakespeare. With a view to facilitating accurate textual criticism Furnivall supervised, too, the issue between 1880 and 1889 of photographic facsimiles, prepared by William Griggs [q. v. Suppl. II] and Charles Praetorius, of the Shakespeare quartos in 43 volumes, to eight of which he prefixed critical introductions by himself. One of the offshoots of the New Shakspere Society was the Sunday Shakspere Society, which was founded 18 Oct. 1874 as the outcome of an address given by Furnivall to members of the National Sunday League when on an excursion to Stratford-upon-Avon.

Three other literary societies were due to Furnivall's initiative. In 1881 he founded the Wiclif Society for the printing of the reformer's Latin MSS., and in the same year, at the suggestion of Miss E. H. Hickey, a devoted admirer of Browning, he inaugurated the Browning Society for the study and interpretation of Browning's poetry. Furnivall had read Browning's poetry with appreciation, and had come to know the poet, whose personality attracted him (cf. Furnivall, *How the Browning Society came into being*, 1884). The first meeting of the new society was held on 28 Oct. 1881, and excited much ridicule. But Furnivall and his fellow-members were undismayed, and their efforts greatly extended Browning's vogue. The poet was always grateful to Furnivall for his aid in popularising his work. Furnivall compiled an exhaustive 'Browning Bibliography' in 1881, and arranged for the production on the stage of several of Browning's plays, among them 'In a Balcony' (6 Dec. 1884), 'The Blot in the 'Scutcheon' (30 April and 2 May 1885), 'Return of the Druses' (26 Nov. 1891), and 'Colombe's Birthday' (19 Nov. 1893). In 1887 Furnivall became president of the society, which lasted till 1892. The final society which Furnivall founded was the Shelley Society, which lasted from 1886 to 1892. Besides reprinting many original editions of Shelley's poems, the society gave a private performance of the 'Cenci' at the Grand Theatre, Islington, on 7 May 1886.

Furnivall's work for his societies was unpaid, and though he found time for some external labour, including an edition of Robert de Brunne's 'Chronicle of England' for the Rolls Series in 1887, his literary activity was never really remunerative. His pecuniary resources were, during the last half of his life, very small. On his father's death on 7 June 1865 he received a substantial share of his large estate, but he invested all his fortune in Overend and Gurney's Bank, which stopped payment in 1867. Furnivall, left well-nigh penniless, was forced to dispose of his personal property, but this his rich friends, Henry Hucks Gibbs (afterwards Lord Aldenham) and Henry Huth, purchased and restored to him. In 1873 he was an unsuccessful candidate for the post of secretary to the Royal Academy. Among others who testified to his fitness were Tennyson, William Morris, Charles Kingsley, J. R. Seeley, M. Taine, and Delius. Thenceforth he lived on his occasional and small literary earnings and on an annual payment as trustee of a relative's property until 1884 when he was granted in addition a civil list pension of 150*l.*

In 1884 Furnivall, whose reputation as a scholar stood high in Germany, received the honorary degree of Ph.D. from Berlin University. In 1901, in honour of his 75th birthday, a volume entitled 'An English Miscellany,' to which scholars of all countries contributed, was printed at the Clarendon Press. At the same time the sum of 450*l.* was presented to the Early English Text Society, and an eight-sculling boat was given to Furnivall. His portrait was painted for Trinity Hall, of which he was made an hon. fellow on 21 April 1902. He received the hon. D.Litt. of Oxford University in 1901, and he was chosen an original fellow of the British Academy next year.

Till his death he advocated with characteristic warmth the value of sculling as a popular recreation. In 1891 he fiercely attacked the Amateur Rowing Association for excluding working men from the class of amateurs. By way of retaliation he founded on 15 Sept. 1891 the National Amateur Rowing Association on thoroughly democratic lines. In 1903 he became president in succession to the duke of Fife, the first president. In 1896 he formed, in accordance with his lifelong principles, the Hammersmith Sculling Club for girls and men, which was re-named the Furnivall Club in 1900. Until the year of his death he sculled each Sunday with members of the club from Hammersmith to Richmond and back, and took a foremost part in the social activities of the club.

Furnivall died at his London residence of cancer of the intestines on 2 July 1910, and his remains were cremated at Golder's Green. Until his fatal illness prostrated him, he carried on his varied work with little diminution of energy.

Furnivall's disinterested devotion to many good causes entitles him to honourable remembrance. The enthusiasm with which he organised societies for the purpose of printing inedited MSS. and of elucidating English literature of many periods stimulated the development of English literary study at home and abroad. His taste as a critic was, like his style, often crude and faulty. But he was indefatigable in research, and spared no pains in his efforts after completeness and accuracy. In his literary labour he was moved by a sincere patriotism. But there was no insularity about his sympathies. Powerful democratic sentiments and broad views dominated his life. He believed in the virtue of athletics no less than of learning, and he sought to give all classes of both sexes opportunities of becoming scholars as well as athletes.

Devoid of tact or discretion in almost every relation of life, he cherished throughout his career a boyish frankness of speech which offended many and led him into unedifying controversies. He cannot be absolved of a tendency to make mischief and stir up strife. His declarations of hostility to religion and to class distinctions were often unseasonable, and gave pain. But his defects of temper and manner were substantially atoned for not merely by his self-denying services to scholarship but by his practical sympathy with poverty and suffering, and by his readiness to encourage sound youthful endeavour in every sphere of work.

In 1862 Furnivall married at the registrar's office, Hampstead, Eleanor Nickel, daughter of George Alexander Dalziel. Separation followed in 1883. Of two children of the marriage, a daughter, Ena, died in infancy in 1866. The son, Percy, is a well-known surgeon.

Of portraits of Furnivall, one by Mr. William Rothenstein is at Trinity Hall, Cambridge; another by A. A. Wolmark was presented to the Working Men's College in 1908; a life-size head, drawn in crayons by C. H. Shannon in 1900, was offered after his death to the National Portrait Gallery; a fourth portrait, by Miss A. D. Staveley, is in the English Library at University College. In 1912 a small memorial fund was applied to the purposes of the Working Men's College.

[Frederick James Furnivall: a volume of personal record, with a biography by John Munro, Oxford University Press, 1911; The Working Men's College, 1854–1904, ed. J. Llewelyn Davies, 1904; Proc. Brit. Acad. (memoir by Prof. W. P. Ker), 1909–10, pp. 374–8; An English Miscellany, 1901, bibliography to date, by Henry Littlehales; personal knowledge.] S. L.

FURSE, CHARLES WELLINGTON (1868–1904), painter, born at Staines on 13 Jan. 1868, was fourth son of Charles Wellington Furse (1821–1900), vicar of Staines, principal of Cuddesdon (1873–83), rector of St. John the Evangelist, Westminster, and canon of Westminster (1883–94), and from 1894 to his death in 1900 canon and archdeacon of Westminster. The father was eldest son of Charles William Johnson (*d.* 1854) by his wife Theresa, daughter of the Rev. Peter Wellington Furse of Halsdon, Devonshire, and he assumed the surname of Furse in 1854 on succeeding to the Halsdon property. William Johnson, afterwards Cory [q. v. Suppl. I], was Archdeacon Furse's only brother. The artist's mother, Jane Diana, second daughter of John S. B. Monsell, vicar of Egham and granddaughter of Thomas Bewley Monsell of Dunbar, archdeacon of Derry, was his father's first wife, and died in 1877, when he was nine years old. Of her ten children, the eldest, John Henry Monsell Furse (*b.* 1860), became a well-known sculptor; and Michael Bolton Furse, fifth son, became bishop of Pretoria in 1909.

At an early age Charles showed a talent for drawing. During a long illness in childhood he read Scott's novels, and drew illustrations of the scenes which appealed to him. Later, he went to Haileybury, where he remained till he was sixteen. In the ordinary work of the school he displayed no special capacity, but continued to draw pictures of hunting scenes for his amusement. On leaving Haileybury he joined the Slade school, then under Alphonse Legros [q. v. Suppl. II], and speedily made his mark. He won the Slade scholarship within a year of entrance, and became a favourite pupil of his masters. Unfortunately, at this early stage, symptoms of consumption which was ultimately to prove fatal showed themselves, and he was forced to spend a winter at St. Moritz. His most intimate friend at this time was a fellow-pupil, now Sir Charles Holroyd, with whom he spent his holidays on the borders of the Lake district or near Maidstone, sketching and reading. From the Slade school he went to Paris, where he studied for some months in Julian's *atelier*, among not very congenial company. On returning from Paris he studied for a short time under Mr. (now Prof.) F. Brown at the Westminster School of Art; but at the age of twenty-one he set up for himself.

He had already exhibited at the Royal Academy (1888) a large figure entitled 'Cain'; but his first real success was a portrait of Canon Burrows (Royal Academy, 1889). This, and a head of his uncle, William Cory, shown at the Portrait Painters in 1891, secured his recognition as an artist of distinction. His father was now a canon of Westminster; and Furse lived at his house in Abbey Garden, renting a studio close by. Success appeared certain, but in the pursuit of his art he was hindered by frequent attacks of illness. He thought much about the principles of his art, and constantly discussed them, as well as literary questions, with his friends, among whom were prominent W. E. Henley [q. v. Suppl. II] and the group of men connected with the 'National Observer.' He read widely, but by predilection in the older literature, especially that of the sixteenth and seventeenth centuries. He occasionally wrote on artistic matters, gave lectures on great artists at Oxford University extension meetings in 1894 and subsequent years, and took part in debates at the Art Workers' Guild.

Although really independent and original, he was during early life unconsciously attracted by the merits of other painters. Thus he passed through several phases, at one time being influenced by Frank Holl, at another by Whistler, again by the Japanese artists, and above all by Mr. J. S. Sargent. The study of Tintoretto and Velasquez is also evident in many of his works. It is true that he assimilated rather than copied other styles; but it was not till near the end of his short life that he worked himself free of all these influences, and developed a noble and spontaneous manner of his own. Delighting in country life and in every variety of sport, he seldom painted landscape pure and simple, but introduced it habitually as a background or a setting for his figures.

Horses were his special study; and in his equestrian portraits the animal is, from the artistic point of view, as important as the man. A whole group of portraits of masters of hounds attests his peculiar skill in this direction. His excellence as a portrait-painter naturally led to his talent being employed chiefly in this line; but in the treatment of his subject he was always anxious to place it among suitable surroundings. In such pictures as the large portrait of Lord Roberts, that of 'Sir Charles Nairne,' and the 'Return from the Ride,' the accessories, studied with great care, form an essential part of the work.

In 1894 he became engaged to Eleanor, sister of Samuel Henry Butcher [q. v. Suppl. II], and her sudden death shortly afterwards was a blow from which it needed all his elasticity to recover. In the following year he was advised to winter in South Africa, and arrived at Johannesburg shortly after the Jameson Raid. He painted a picture of 'Doornkop,' choosing the moment when the British column was approaching the Boers in ambush. This picture was shown by the artist to President Kruger, but has since disappeared. He had some thoughts of volunteering for the Matabele war, but gave up the idea, and returned to England (1896). Two years later he accepted a commission, obtained for him by his friend, Prof. F. M. Simpson, to execute decorative paintings to fill four pendentives under the dome over the staircase in the Liverpool Town Hall. The remuneration was inadequate, but Furse undertook the task for the sake of the opportunity which it afforded of work on a grand scale and of a kind different from anything he had hitherto done. In making his designs he deliberately adopted the manner of Tintoretto, and, while eschewing the realistic reproduction of modern industrial and commercial conditions, adapted them to a treatment at once poetic and vigorous. These paintings, which were his chief occupation for nearly three years, are perhaps the most notable, though not the most popular, of all his works.

Meanwhile the state of his health had compelled him to pass a winter at Davos, where (in Feb. 1900) he became engaged to Katharine, the youngest daughter of John Addington Symonds. He married in October of the same year, and with his wife passed the following winter also at Davos. In 1901 they removed to a new house which he had had built for him on the high ground near Camberley. Here he took the greatest interest in laying out a small plot of land in formal eighteenth-century fashion, and speedily turned a sandy waste into a beautiful garden. Intensely happy in his marriage and a settled life in congenial surroundings, he worked harder than ever, and in these last three years produced some of his most successful pictures—the 'Return from the Ride,' 'Lord Charles Beresford,' 'Diana of the Uplands,' 'Cubbing with the York and Ainsty.' These works showed that he had at length found himself. But all the time the disease from which he suffered—tuberculosis—was making progress. He passed the winter of 1902–3 at Davos, spent the spring of 1903 in northern Italy and Spain, and took a studio, for the sake of his portrait-painting, in London. In the same year he was elected an associate of the Royal Academy. Never sparing himself, and still full of hope and enthusiasm, he gradually grew weaker, and died on 16 Oct. 1904. He was buried in Frimley churchyard. He left two sons, Peter and Paul, the second of whom was born three days before his death. In person Furse was tall and somewhat stout in later life, but muscular and vigorous. His features were rounded, the face oval, the eyes small but very keen, the complexion pale. He was a keen sportsman, a good shot and whip, and played most games well. His movements were quick, and he painted rapidly, with a fierce concentration, never hesitating to rub out his work over and over again if it did not satisfy him. His untiring energy, width of interest, and intellectual vitality showed themselves in his conversation. He liked nothing better than a good argument, but could listen as well as talk; and his criticism, though keen, was entirely free from jealousy and malice.

Many of his most notable pictures were exhibited in the gallery of the New English Art Club, of which he was an active member from 1891 to his death. He joined in the foundation of the International Society, and was a member of its council. He exhibited also at the Portrait Painters and the New Gallery. A collection of his works, 53 in number, was shown at the Burlington Fine Arts Club in 1906. The 'Return from the Ride' was bought after his death under the Chantrey Bequest; 'Diana of the Uplands' was purchased by the trustees of the National Gallery. Both these pictures are now at the Tate Gallery. The larger 'Lord Roberts (unfinished) has been lent by Mrs. Furse to the same institution. The best likeness of Furse extant is a photograph reproduced in the illustrated catalogue of the Burlington Fine Arts Club exhibition (1908). The same volume contains a selection from his writings (two articles were previously published in the 'Albemarle Magazine,' Aug. 1892, and the 'Studio,' i. 33), with a number of letters and the reports of some of his lectures.

[Memoir by Mr. D. S. MacColl, prefixed to the catalogue above mentioned (1908); private information.] G. W. P.

FUST, HERBERT JENNER- (1806–1904), cricketer. [See JENNER-FUST.]

G

GADSBY, HENRY ROBERT (1842–1907), musician, born at Hackney on 15 Dec. 1842, was son of William Gadsby. From 1849 to 1858 he was a chorister boy at St. Paul's at the same time as Sir John Stainer (*Mus. Times*, May 1901). He learnt rudimentary harmony under Mr. W. Bayley, the choirmaster, but was otherwise self-taught. In 1863 he became a teacher of the piano, the writer being one of his first pupils. Having also taught himself the organ, he became organist of St. Peter's, Brockley, holding this appointment till 1884. He succeeded John Hullah [q. v.] as professor of harmony at Queen's College, London, and Sir William Cusins [q. v. Suppl. I] as professor of pianoforte there. In 1880 he was appointed one of the original professors (of harmony) at the Guildhall School of Music, where he taught till his death. A member of the Philharmonic and other musical societies and fellow of the College of Organists, he was a well-known figure in the musical world. His published works include the following choral and orchestral cantatas: 'Psalm 130' (1862); 'Alice Brand' (1870); 'The Lord of the Isles' (Brighton Festival, 1879); 'Columbus' (male voices, 1881); 'The Cyclops' (male voices, 1883); music to 'Alcestis' (1876) and to Tasso's 'Aminta' (for Queen's College, 1898). Other instrumental works were a concert overture, 'Andromeda' (1873), an organ concerto in F, and a string quartet. Unpublished works include three other orchestral preludes, which have been performed: 'The Golden Legend,' 'The Witches' Frolic,' and 'The Forest of Arden.' Numerous part-songs, services, and anthems were printed, as well as 'A Treatise on Harmony' (1883) and 'A Technical Method of Sight-singing' (1897), which are useful text-books. Gadsby was a typical Victorian composer, whose works were always well received and never heard a second time. An earnest musician, whose mission in life was to teach others to be like himself, he died on 11 Nov. 1907 at 53 Clarendon Road, Putney, and was buried in Putney Vale cemetery. His widow died shortly after him, leaving two daughters.

[Grove's Dict. of Music; Brit. Mus. Cat.; Mus. Times, Dec. 1907 (a good obit. notice with portrait); Baker's Biog. Dict. Mus. 1900 (with portrait); personal knowledge.] F. C.

GAIRDNER, SIR WILLIAM TENNANT (1824–1907), professor of medicine at Glasgow, born in Edinburgh on 8 Nov. 1824, was eldest son of John Gairdner [q. v.], president of the Royal College of Surgeons, Edinburgh, by his wife Susanna, daughter of William Tennant. Educated at the Edinburgh Institution, Gairdner entered as a medical student in 1840 Edinburgh University, where he had a brilliant career. Immediately after graduation as M.D. in 1845, he went with Lord and Lady Beverley as their medical attendant to the Continent, spending the ensuing winter in Rome. On his return to Edinburgh in 1846 he acted for the customary two years' term as house physician and house surgeon to the Royal Infirmary, and then settled down to practice in Edinburgh in 1848. He was soon appointed pathologist to the Royal Infirmary, and immediately entered upon a career of great scientific energy, not only throwing himself into the teaching of his subject to large classes of undergraduates, but making numerous original observations. In 1853 he became physician to the Royal Infirmary. He at once lectured on the 'Principles and Practice of Medicine,' and continued his original observations, but restricted himself more and more to the clinical investigation of disease, at the same time paying close attention to the subject of public health, then in its infancy. In 1862 he brought out at Edinburgh both his classical work on 'Clinical Medicine' (12mo) and his notable volume, 'Public Health in relation to Air and Water.'

In the same year, 1862, Gairdner was appointed professor of medicine in the

University of Glasgow. From 1863 to 1872 he was also medical officer of health to the city, and during that period he remodelled the sanitary arrangements (cf. *Public Health Administration in Glasgow*, a memorial volume of the writings of Dr. J. B. Russell, Glasgow, 1905, with a preface by Gairdner; chaps. i. and ii. detail Gairdner's labours).

Gairdner was an exceptionally attractive lecturer, teaching the diagnosis of disease with singular thoroughness, and illuminating the subject in hand by means of a wide literary culture. Despite his activity as both teacher and consultant, he continued throughout his career his contributions to professional literature. In scarcely any department in medicine did he fail to add something new, in regard either to pathological changes or to clinical appearances. A series of early papers, 'Contributions to the Pathology of the Kidney' (Edinburgh, 1848), supplied an early description of waxy disease, and there was originality of view in 'The Pathological Anatomy of Bronchitis and the Diseases of the Lung connected with Bronchial Obstruction' (Edinburgh, 1850). Later he produced 'Insanity: Modern Views as to its Nature and Treatment' (Glasgow, 1885), and lectures upon 'Tabes Mesenterica' (Glasgow, 1888).

Among the matters on which he threw original light of great value were the intimate connection between arterial supply and myocardial changes; the reciprocal influence of the heart and lungs; hypertrophy and dilatation; the system of representing the sounds and murmurs of the heart by means of diagrams; the recognition of tricuspid obstruction, aneurism, and angina pectoris; and with Stokes, Balfour and Fagge he helped to make certain the diagnosis of mitral obstruction. His last contribution to circulatory disease was the article on aneurism in Clifford Allbutt's 'System of Medicine' (vol. vi. 1889).

Gairdner gave many public addresses on general topics. The chief of these were collected under the titles of 'The Physician as Naturalist' (Glasgow, 1889), and 'The Three Things that Abide' (1903).

Gairdner retired from the chair of medicine in Glasgow in 1890, when he returned to his native city. Many distinctions were granted him. He was made hon. LL.D. of Edinburgh in 1883, and hon. M.D. of Dublin in 1887; was F.R.S. in 1892; hon. F.R.C.P. Ireland in 1887; physician-in-ordinary to Queen Victoria in 1881; honorary physician to King Edward VII in 1901; member of the general council of medical education and registration, as representative of the University of Glasgow, 1894; president of the Royal College of Physicians of Edinburgh in 1893–4; and president of the British Medical Association when it met in Glasgow in 1888. He was created K.C.B. in 1898.

During the last seven years of his life, while his intellectual interests and energies were unimpaired, Gairdner suffered from an obscure affection of the heart, the symptoms of which he carefully recorded. He died suddenly at Edinburgh on 28 June 1907. In accordance with his wish, a complete account of the clinical and pathological conditions of his disease was published by the present writer, in association with Dr. W. T. Ritchie. His portrait, painted by Sir George Reid, is in the University of Glasgow.

Gairdner married, in 1870, Helen Bridget, daughter of Mr. Wright of Norwich; she survived him with four sons and three daughters.

[Proc. Roy. Soc. 80 B, 1908; Life, by G. A. Gibson, in preparation; Lancet and Brit. Med. Journal, 6 July 1907; Edinburgh Med. Journal, Scottish Med. and Surg. Journal, and Glasgow Med. Journal, Aug. 1907.] G.A.G.

GALE, FREDERICK (1823–1904), cricketer and writer on cricket under the pseudonym of 'The Old Buffer,' born at Woodborough, Pewseyvale, near Devizes, on 16 July 1823, was son of Thomas Hinxman Gale, rector of Woodborough and afterwards vicar of Godmersham, near Canterbury, by his wife Elizabeth, daughter of Dr. Poore of Andover. After attending Dr. Buckland's preparatory school at Laleham, Gale was from 1836 to 1841 at Winchester College, of which a great-uncle, Dr. W. S. Goddard [q. v.], was a former headmaster. While at Winchester he played in the cricket eleven against Eton and Harrow in 1841, and in 1845 he played once both for Kent and for the Gentlemen of Kent against the Gentlemen of England. He was a hard hitter and a good fieldsman, but after leaving Winchester gave little time to the practice of the game.

Articled to a member of the London firm of Messrs. Bircham & Co., solicitors, Gale long worked with them as parliamentary clerk, and afterwards as parliamentary agent on his own account. But, deeply interested in cricket and other games, he devoted much time to writing about them, and he gradually abandoned legal business for the work of an author and journalist. Usually employing the pseudonym of 'The Old Buffer,' he contributed to the 'Globe' and 'Punch,' to the 'Cornhill' and 'Baily's Magazine.' He lectured occasionally also and he wrote many books, the best known of which are 'Public School Matches and those we meet there' (1853), 'Ups and Downs of a Public School' (1859), 'Echoes from Old Cricket Fields' (1871); 'Memoir of the Hon. Robert Grimston' (1885); 'Modern English Sports: their use and abuse' (1885); 'The Game of Cricket' (with portrait of Gale) (1887); and 'Sports and Recreations' (1888). Through his brother-in-law, Arthur Severn, Gale became a close friend of Ruskin, to whom he dedicated his 'Modern English Sports.' Ruskin, who wrote a preface to the book, professed complete agreement with Gale's 'views of life, its duties and pleasures' (RUSKIN's Works, ed. Cook & Wedderburn, Index vol.). From 1865 till 1882 Gale resided at Mitcham. Interesting himself in Surrey cricket, he helped to discover and bring out four Surrey professional cricketers of distinction—H. Jupp, Thomas and Richard Humphrey, and G. G. Jones. In later life Gale, after some years spent with a son in Canada, became in 1899 a brother of the Charterhouse, London. He died in the Charterhouse on 24 April 1904, and was buried beside his wife at Mitcham. Gale married in 1852 Claudia Fitzroy (*d.* 1874), daughter of Joseph Severn [q. v.]; two sons and four daughters survived her.

[Personal knowledge; private information; Wisden's Cricketers' Almanack, 1905; Hist. of Kent County Cricket, 1907.] P. N.

GALLWEY, PETER (1820–1906), Jesuit preacher and writer, born on 13 Nov. 1820, at Killarney, was son of an agent to the Earl of Kenmare. At the age of six he was placed at school in Boulogne. Thence he passed to Stonyhurst, where he entered the Society of Jesus in 1836. Having completed his studies in literature and philosophy, he was appointed in 1843 to teach in the College of St. Francis Xavier, Liverpool, then at 36 Soho Street. In 1846 he returned to Stonyhurst to take charge of the higher forms. Three years later he began his theological studies at St. Beuno's College, near St. Asaph, and here he was ordained priest in 1852. By 1855 his course of training was completed, and in that year he was appointed prefect of studies at Stonyhurst. He was an excellent school organiser, with a rare power of exciting enthusiasm among his pupils, but his peculiar gifts fitted him still better for the spiritual ministry. In 1857 he was transferred to London, and placed in charge of the community which served the Farm Street church. Here he remained till 1869, when he was appointed master of novices at Manresa House, Roehampton. In 1873 he was appointed provincial of the Jesuit body in England. At the beginning of his term of office the question of opening a Jesuit school in Manchester involved him in a controversy with the bishop of Salford, Herbert (afterwards Cardinal) Vaughan [q.v. Suppl. II] (see SNEAD-COX's *Life of Cardinal Vaughan*, vol. i. chap. xii.). Despite episcopal opposition the Jesuits persisted in opening their school, and Vaughan then appealed to the Pope. The issue was decided in Rome in June 1875, when the Jesuit school in Manchester was closed by order of the Holy See. At the end of his period of office as provincial Gallwey was named rector of the College of St. Beuno, but he held the post for only a year. In 1877 he returned to the Farm Street church, and there continued his labours till his death on 23 Sept. 1906.

Gallwey was an effective preacher, but the effect was due not so much to any devices of oratory as to the note of intense personal sincerity and profound religious conviction which characterised his sermons. The same may be said of his longer published works. Possessed of a considerable fund of Irish humour, he made good use of it in controversy. 'The Committee on Convents' and other pamphlets issued in 1870 on the occasion of Mr. Newdegate's demand for the inspection of convents are noteworthy in this respect. Many of his funeral discourses on persons of note have been published. Of these may be mentioned that on Sir Charles Tempest (1865); on Hon. C. Langdale (1868); on Marcia Lady Herries (1883); on Lady Georgiana Fullerton (1885); on Mr. C. Weld (1885). Of his sermons on other subjects many have been issued in pamphlet form. The more important of his longer works are 'The Angelus Bell,' five lectures (1869); 'Lectures on Ritualism' (2 vols. 1879); 'Apostolic Succession' (1889); 'The Watches of the Sacred Passion' (3 vols. 1894).

[Father Gallwey, a Sketch, by Percy Fitzgerald, 1906; Discourse at the Requiem Mass for Fr. Gallwey, by Rev. M. Gavin, S.J., 1906; The Times, 25 Sept. 1906.] T. A. F.

GALTON, SIR FRANCIS (1822–1911), founder of the school of 'eugenics,' born at Birmingham on 16 Feb. 1822, was youngest of a family of four daughters and three sons born to Samuel Tertius Galton (1783–1844), banker, and his wife Frances Anne Violetta (1783–1874), daughter by a second marriage of Dr. Erasmus Darwin (1731–1802) [q. v.], the philosophical poet and man of science. The Galtons were members of the Society of Friends, and many of them were men of ability, amassing considerable fortunes as gunsmiths and bankers. Through his mother he was also related to men and women of mark.

After education at several small schools he was sent for two years (1836–8) to King Edward's School at Birmingham, but did not profit much from the classical curriculum in use there. Being intended for the medical profession, after preliminary apprenticeships to medical men at Birmingham, he studied for a year (1839–40) at the medical school of King's College, London. In 1840 he made a rapid tour to Vienna, Constantinople, and Smyrna; and at Michaelmas 1840 entered at Trinity College, Cambridge. He there made friendships with many notable men and read mathematics under William Hopkins (1793–1866) [q. v.], but illness prevented him from pursuing his course, and he took a 'poll' degree in 1844.

In 1844 his father died, and he found himself with means sufficiently ample to allow him to abandon the proposed medical career. He accordingly made a somewhat adventurous journey up the Nile to Khartum and afterwards in Syria. On his return he devoted himself from 1845 to 1850 to sport, but as this did not satisfy his ambition he determined to make a voyage of exploration at his own expense. Damaraland in south-west equatorial Africa (now German territory), then quite unknown to the civilised world, was fixed on as the scene of his exploration. Landing at Walfish Bay, he penetrated far into the interior amid many dangers and hardships, and on his return he published an interesting account of his journey entitled 'Tropical South Africa' (1853; 2nd edit. 1889).

This journey made him well known as an explorer, and from this time he played an important part on the council of the Royal Geographical Society, only retiring when deafness impeded his usefulness at their deliberations. In 1856 he was elected F.R.S., and frequently served on the council of the Royal Society.

As a result of his African journey he wrote a useful book, 'The Art of Travel' (1855; latest edit. 1872, and latest reprint 1893), describing artifices of use to travellers—a valuable *vade-mecum* for explorers. After his return from Africa, although he travelled extensively in Europe and became a member of the Alpine Club, he undertook no further exploration, because his health had suffered much from the hardships he had endured.

Galton took an active part in the administration of science. From 1863 to 1867 he was general secretary of the British Association; he was four times a sectional president, and twice declined the presidency. In 1863 he published 'Meteorographica, or Methods of Mapping the Weather.' In this work he pointed out the importance of 'anticyclones' (a word introduced by him), in which the air circulates clockwise (in the northern hemisphere) round a centre of high barometric pressure. This completed the basis of the system of weather forecasting now in operation throughout the civilised world. He also made other considerable contributions to meteorology. This work led to his membership from 1868 to 1900 of the meteorological committee and of the subsequent council, the governing body of the Meteorological Office. He had also previously been connected with Kew Observatory, an institution initiated by General Sir Edward Sabine (1788–1883) [q. v.] for magnetic and meteorological observations. He was a member of the Kew committee of the Royal Society from soon after its foundation, and was chairman from 1889 to 1901.

Meteorology did not nearly suffice to occupy Galton's active mind; already in 1865 he was occupied with those researches into the laws of heredity with which his name will always be associated. In the course of these investigations he was led to perceive the deficiency of tabulated data as to human attributes. He therefore initiated an anthropometric laboratory in connection with the International Health Exhibition of 1884–5, for the purpose of collecting statistics as to the acuteness of the senses, the strength, height, and dimensions of large numbers of people. He devised the apparatus and organised the laboratory himself. When the exhibition was closed the laboratory was moved elsewhere, and it was the forerunner of the biometric laboratory at University College, London.

Among the data collected in this way were impressions of fingers, and Galton thought they might be used for identification. Sir William Herschel had previously wished to use the method in India, and Dr. Faulds had made a similar suggestion in England.

Galton then confirmed earlier investigations which proved the permanence of finger-prints from youth to old age, and devised a dictionary of prints whereby an individual leaving a mark may surely be identified. The method is now in use in the criminal departments of every civilised country. An account of Galton's work is contained in his 'Finger Prints' (1893); 'Blurred Finger Prints' (1893); and 'Finger Print Directory' (1895).

It is due to Galton more than to any other man that many attributes generally regarded as only susceptible of qualitative estimate have been reduced to measurement. For example, he showed how to obtain a numerical measure of the degree of resemblance between two persons, and he made a map to show the geographical distribution of beauty in Great Britain. He devised the method of composite photographs in which each member of a group of persons makes an equal impress on the resulting portrait. Another attempt to annul the resemblance and to register only the individuality was not very successful.

To psychology Galton also made contributions which were important and very original. He showed that different minds work in different ways, and, for example, that visual images play a large part with some but not with others. He investigated visual memory as to illumination, definition, colouring, and the like, and the visions seen not very infrequently by the sane. Akin to this was an inquiry into the patterns or pictures associated in many minds with numbers. He also experimented on taste, on smell, on the muscular sense of weight, on the judgment of experts in guessing the weight of cattle, and on many cognate points. His investigations give him a high rank amongst experimental psychologists, and yet they were merely collateral to the main stream of his work.

On the publication in 1859 of the 'Origin of Species' by his cousin, Charles Robert Darwin (1809–1882) [q. v.], Galton at once became a convert to the views there enounced and began reflecting on the influence of heredity on the human race. He had been impressed by his own observation with the fact that distinction of any kind is apt to run in families. He therefore made a series of statistical inquiries whereby he proved the heritability of genius of all kinds. These investigations extended over forty years, and the results are set forth in his works: 'Hereditary Genius' (1869); 'English Men of Science' (1874); 'Human Faculty' (1883); 'Natural Inheritance' (1889); and 'Noteworthy Families' (1906).

Such investigations necessarily brought him to face the fundamental principles of statistics, and although his mathematical equipment was inadequate he obtained a remarkably clear insight into the subject. In the hands of Karl Pearson and of others his work led to the formulation of new statistical methods. The leading point is that he showed how the degree of relationship between any pair of attributes or any pair of individuals may be estimated by a numerical factor termed the correlation. He also gave a numerical estimate of the average contribution to each individual from his two parents and his remoter ancestry.

Collateral to these researches were experiments on Darwin's theory of pangenesis by transfusion of the blood of rabbits *inter se*; the results were however negative.

The study of heredity led Galton to the conviction that the human race might gain an indefinite improvement by breeding from the best and restricting the offspring of the worst. To this study he gave the name of 'eugenics,' and it is probably by this that he will be best known in the future. But he was under no illusion as to the rapidity with which favourable results may be attained, and he foresaw that it would need a prolonged education before an adequate knowledge of the power of heredity shall permeate the community. With the object of promoting this education he co-operated in the formation of 'eugenic societies,' and established in 1904 a eugenics laboratory to be worked in connection with the biometric laboratory mentioned above. He further founded in 1904 a research fellowship and in 1907 a scholarship in eugenic researches at University College. A quarterly journal entitled 'Biometrika' had already been initiated in 1901, and he was 'consulting editor.'

Galton received many honours, including medals from the English and French Geographical Societies in 1853 and 1854; a royal medal of the Royal Society in 1876; Huxley medal of the Anthropological Institute in 1901; Darwin medal of the Royal Society in 1902; Darwin-Wallace medal of the Linnæan Society in 1908; and the Copley medal of the Royal Society in 1910. He was made Officier de l'Instruction publique de France in 1891; hon. D.C.L. Oxford in 1894; hon. D.Sc. Cambridge in 1895; hon. fellow of Trinity College, Cambridge, in 1902; and was knighted by patent on 26 June 1909.

Galton lived chiefly in London, and for the latter part of his life at Rutland Gate, going much into society, principally in literary and scientific circles. He was universally popular and an excellent conversationalist, with a very keen sense of humour. During the last four or five years of his life he became very infirm in body, although his intellect remained as clear as ever. He died on 17 Jan. 1911 of acute bronchitis at Grayshott House, Haslemere, a house he had taken for the winter months. He was buried in the family vault at Claverdon near Warwick.

On 1 Aug. 1853 Galton married Louisa Jane, daughter of George Butler (1774–1853) [q. v.], dean of Peterborough and previously headmaster of Harrow School. Mrs. Galton died on 13 Aug. 1897 at Royat after a long period of ill health; she had no children.

He left by will his residual estate, amounting to about 45,000*l.*, for the foundation of a chair of eugenics in the University of London, and he wished Karl Pearson to be the first professor. The capital was to remain as far as possible untouched, and a laboratory was to be built from other sources. For the latter object a subscription has been started since his death.

Portraits of Galton by O. Oakley (ætat. 22, water-colour) and by Charles Wellington Furse in oils (1903) are in the possession of his nephew, Edward Galton Wheler, at Claverdon Leys, Warwick, and a copy of the latter by Francis William Carter hangs in the hall at Trinity College, Cambridge. There is a bronze bust of Galton by Sir George Frampton at University College, Gower Street, London. In 1908 he wrote an amusing work entitled 'Memories of my Life,' containing a complete list of his papers and books.

[Memories of my Life; personal knowledge and private information. A Life of Galton is being prepared by Professor Karl Pearson, F.R.S.] G. H. D.

GALVIN, GEORGE. [See Leno, Dan, 1860–1904.]

GAMGEE, ARTHUR (1841–1909), physiologist, born at Florence on 10 Oct. 1841, was youngest of the eight children of Joseph Gamgee (1801–1894) and Mary West. His father was a veterinary surgeon and pathologist whose researches, particularly on rinderpest, brought him recognition both in this country and abroad. Joseph Sampson Gamgee (1828–1886) [q. v.] was an elder brother.

Gamgee spent his early boyhood in Florence, and there imbibed a lifelong love of art and literature. When he was fourteen his family returned to England and he entered University College school, London. Afterwards he proceeded to the University of Edinburgh, where he studied physics under Peter Guthrie Tait [q. v. Suppl. II]. On taking his medical degree there he was appointed house-physician to the Royal Infirmary. Physiology, especially on its chemical side, early interested him; his inaugural thesis for the degree of M.D. was on the 'Contributions to the Chemistry and Physiology of Fœtal Nutrition'; it obtained the gold medal in 1862.

From 1863 to 1869 Gamgee was assistant to Dr. Douglas Maclagan, professor of medical jurisprudence at Edinburgh, and was at the same time lecturer on physiology at the Royal College of Surgeons and physician to the Edinburgh hospital for children. But his interests were centred in research, and then and later he published various papers elucidating problems of physiological chemistry and of the pharmacological action of chemical bodies. The most interesting of these were on 'The Action of the Nitrites on Blood' in 1868, and on 'The Constitution and Relations of Cystine,' issued jointly with Professor James Dewar in 1871.

In 1871 Gamgee worked with Kühne at Heidelberg and with Ludwig at Leipzig, and in the same year he was admitted M.R.C.P. Edinburgh, becoming F.R.C.P. in 1872. In the latter year he was also elected F.R.S. at the early age of thirty. In 1873 he was appointed the first Brackenbury professor of physiology in the Owens College, Manchester, now the Victoria University. He filled this post for twelve years, having Henry Roscoe, Balfour Stewart [q. v.], and Stanley Jevons [q. v.] among his colleagues, and he took his part with these men in making Owens College one of the most conspicuous scientific schools in the country. He worked with tireless enthusiasm as dean of the medical school, and sought with success to establish a working arrangement between the purely scientific and the applied aspects of medicine. A brilliant teacher, he left his impress on many men who have since distinguished themselves. In 1882 he was president of the biological section of the British Association which met at Southampton, and from 1882 to 1885 he was Fullerian professor of physiology at the Royal Institution, London. While in London he was admitted M.R.C.P. in 1885, and F.R.C.P. in 1896.

Gamgee resigned his chair in Manchester in 1885, and practised for a time as a consulting physician at St. Leonards. He was appointed assistant physician to St. George's Hospital, London, in 1887, where he was also lecturer on pharmacology and materia medica in the medical school. On resigning these appointments in 1889 he resumed his scientific work at Cambridge for a year, and then left England for Switzerland, residing first at Berne, then at Lausanne, and finally at Montreux, where he engaged in active practice as a consulting physician, devoting all his spare time to research in his own laboratory. In 1902 he visited the United States by invitation to inspect certain physiological laboratories where the work was chiefly directed towards the study of nutrition in health and disease. In the same year he delivered the Croonian lecture before the Royal Society on 'Certain Chemical and Physical Properties of Hæmoglobin.' He re-visited America in 1903, and at the celebration of Haller's bicentenary at Berne he represented the Royal Society.

He died of pneumonia while on a short visit to Paris on 29 March 1909, and was buried in the family vault in Arno's Vale cemetery, Bristol. He married in 1875 Mary Louisa, daughter of J. Proctor Clark. His widow was granted a civil list pension of 70*l.* in 1910. A son predeceased him and two daughters survived him.

Research was Gamgee's main interest through life. His intimate knowledge of physics and chemistry was linked with experience of German methods which he had gained more especially in the laboratories of his life-long friend, W. Kühne, the professor of physiology at Heidelberg. Whilst lecturing at Manchester Gamgee prepared a translation of Ludimar Hermann's 'Grundriss der Physiologie des Menschen' from the fifth German edition. This book, which appeared in 1875 (2nd edit. 1878), together with the publication of (Sir) Michael Foster's textbook of physiology in 1876, powerfully influenced the development of physiological research in England. In 1880 Gamgee published the first volume of 'A Textbook of the Physiological Chemistry of the Animal Body.' The second volume appeared in 1893. The publication of this book marked an epoch in the progress of English physiological study.

Certain parts of physiology possessed a peculiar fascination for Gamgee. Knowledge of the physical and chemical properties of hæmoglobin is largely due to him. He was engaged for many years on an elaborate research upon the diurnal variations of the temperature of the human body with specially devised apparatus for obtaining a continuous record throughout the twenty-four hours. The subject had always been in his mind since he had worked at Edinburgh under Tait. The paper recording his method and results appeared in the 'Philosophical Transactions of the Royal Society,' 1908, series B. vol. cc., but his death cut short the investigation. Gamgee believed that physiology stood in an intimate relation to the practice of medicine and that scientific training in a laboratory was essential to the advance of medicine. An excellent linguist, he could lecture fluently in French, German, and Italian. His conscientious modes of work relegated nothing of it to others; he did everything with his own hands.

Apart from the publications already mentioned, numerous contributions to the Proceedings of scientific societies and to scientific journals, Gamgee issued in 1884 'Physiology of Digestion and the Digestive Organs.'

[Lancet, 1909, i. 1144 (with portrait and bibliography); Brit. Med. Journal, 1909, i. 933; private information; personal knowledge.]

D'A. P.

GARCIA, MANUEL [PATRICIO RODRIGUEZ] (1805–1906), singer and teacher of singing, born at Zafra in Catalonia on 17 March 1805, belonged to a family of Spanish musicians. His father, Manuel del Popolo Vicente Garcia (1775–1832), made a reputation as singer, impresario, composer and teacher of singing. His mother, Joaquina Sitchès, was an accomplished actress. Manuel was the only son. Both his sisters, Maria Felicita (Madame Malibran) (1808–36) and Michelle Ferdinande Pauline (Madame Viardot-Garcia) (1821–1910), achieved the highest eminence as operatic singers. All three children were educated by their parents. At fifteen Manuel was studying harmony with Fétis in Paris and singing in opera with his father at Madrid. In 1825 the family migrated to America, and at New York the father founded an opera house. After eighteen months of brilliant success the company toured to Mexico, where they were robbed of their earnings—some 6000*l.*, it is said, in gold. They then returned to Paris, where the father pursued his career, but young Manuel, having no taste for the stage, became a teacher. In 1830 he temporarily interrupted his musical work to accept an appointment in the commissariat of the French army at Algiers, and on his return studied medicine in the military hospitals of Paris (art. in *Musical Times*, April 1905). In 1840 he presented to the French Institut his 'Mémoire sur la voix humaine,' which was accepted as the best authority on the subject. Appointed to a professorship at the Paris Conservatoire, he attracted many distinguished pupils, including Jenny Lind, whom he instructed in Paris from 26 Aug. 1841 to July 1842 (cf. Holland and Rockstro's *Jenny Lind Goldschmidt*, 1891, i. 109 seq.). In 1847 he published his world-famous 'Traité complet de l'art du chant,' of which a simplified abstract appeared as 'Hints on Singing' in 1894. In both the literary and artistic society of Paris Garcia filled a prominent place. Early in 1848 he resigned his position at the Conservatoire, and came to London in June. On 10 Nov. he was appointed a professor of singing at the Royal Academy of Music. He had long closely studied the physiology of the voice, and in 1854, for the purpose of examining his own larynx and that of some of his pupils, he invented the instrument since known as the laryngoscope. On 24 May 1855 he communicated to the Royal Society, through Dr. William Sharpey [q. v.], a paper called 'Observations on the Human Voice.' There he explained his invention, which proved of enormous value in the diagnosis of disease and in surgery (*Proc. Roy. Soc.* vol. 7, p. 399). After undergoing some improvement in 1857 by Johann Czermak of Pesth (1828–1873), the laryngoscope came into universal use as a medical and surgical appliance. Garcia held his professorship at the Royal Academy of Music for forty-seven years, only retiring in September 1895, at the age of ninety. But his bodily and mental activity seemed even then unimpaired, and he continued to teach privately and to maintain an interest in musical affairs until his death at Mon Abri, his house at Cricklewood, on 1 July 1906, at the age of 101 years and four months. He was buried in the private Roman catholic burying-ground of St. Edward's, Sutton Place, near Woking. On 17 March 1905, his hundredth birthday, he was received at Buckingham Palace by King Edward VII, who made him a C.V.O.; the German Emperor William II conferred on him the gold medal for science; the King of Spain admitted him to the order of Alphonso XII; the King of Sweden created him chevalier de l'ordre de mérite; a banquet which was attended by many distinguished persons was held in his honour; and his portrait, painted by John S. Sargent, R.A., was presented to him.

For more than half a century Garcia held, by general consent, the position of premier singing-teacher in the world. In person he was, from youth to old age, extremely handsome, with all his father's fiery and impetuous disposition. His chief recreation was chess. Mr. C. E. Hallé owns a sketch by Richard Doyle of Garcia and his friend, Sir Charles Hallé, at a game, which is reproduced in MacKinlay's 'Life,' p. 222. There is also a crayon sketch of Garcia, made by his sister Pauline soon after the invention of the laryngoscope. A portrait by Rudolf Lehmann was exhibited at the Royal Academy in 1869. Sargent's portrait Garcia left to the Laryngological Society.

Garcia married at Paris on 22 Nov. 1832 Cécile Eugenie Mayer (*b.* 8 April 1814; *d.* 18 Aug. 1880), by whom he had two sons—Manuel (1836–1885) and Gustav, a well-known singing teacher (*b.* 1837)—and two daughters—Maria (1842–1867) and Eugénie (*b.* 1844).

[M. Sterling MacKinlay, Garcia the Centenarian and his times, 1908; A. G. Tapia, Manuel García; su influencia en la laringología y en el arte del canto, Madrid, 1905; Grove's Dict. of Music; Mus. Times, April 1905 (with reproduction of Sargent's portrait); personal knowledge; private information.] F. C.

GARDINER, SAMUEL RAWSON (1829–1902), historian, born at Ropley, near Alresford, in Hampshire, on 4 March 1829, was eldest son of Rawson Boddam Gardiner by his wife Margaret, daughter of William Baring Gould. His grandfather, Samuel Gardiner of Coombe Lodge, Whitchurch, was high sheriff of Oxfordshire in 1794; his paternal grandmother, Mary Boddam, was descended from Bridget, eldest daughter of the Protector Cromwell, by her marriage with Henry Ireton. This pedigree, which has not been published, was carefully worked out by Colonel J. L. Chester. Gardiner was educated at Winchester College, which he entered about Michaelmas 1841, and matriculated at Christ Church, Oxford, in October 1847 (J. B. Wainewright, *Winchester College*, 1830–1906; Foster, *Alumni Oxonienses*). In 1850 he was given a studentship, and in 1851 he obtained a first class in the school of literæ humaniores. He graduated B.A. in 1851, but did not proceed M.A. till 1884, and was for theological reasons unable to retain his studentship. His parents were Irvingites; he married in 1856 the youngest daughter of Edward Irving, and was from 1851 to 1866 a deacon in the Irvingite church. His name was removed from the church register before 1872.

After his marriage Gardiner settled in London, and while maintaining himself largely by teaching began to study English history. He was admitted to read in the British Museum on 8 Nov. 1856, and to the Record Office on 1 July 1858. His desire from the first was to write the history of the Puritan revolution, but he thought it necessary to begin by studying the reign of James I. 'It seemed to me,' he afterwards wrote, 'that it was the duty of a serious inquirer to search into the original causes of great events rather than, for the sake of catching at an audience, to rush unprepared upon the great events themselves.' The first-fruits of these researches were some articles published in 'Notes and Queries' during 1860, which explained the causes of the quarrel between James and his parliament and threw fresh light on his policy towards the Roman catholics. Next, at the instigation of John Bruce (1802–1869) [q. v.], then director of the Camden Society, Gardiner edited for that body in 1862 a volume of reports and documents, entitled 'Parliamentary Debates in 1610.' In 1863 the first instalment of his history appeared, 'A History of England from the Accession of James I to the Disgrace of Chief Justice Coke, 1603–1616' (2 vols.). This was followed in 1869 by 'Prince Charles and the Spanish Marriage' (2 vols.). The reception of these books would have discouraged most men. About a hundred copies of the first work were sold, but most of the edition went for waste paper; the second had a circulation of about 500, but did not bring the author anything. Gardiner persevered, and his third instalment, published in 1875, 'A History of England under the Duke of Buckingham and Charles I, 1624–1628' (2 vols.), paid its expenses. The fourth instalment, 'The Personal Government of Charles I' (2 vols. 1877), and the fifth, 'The Fall of the Monarchy of Charles I' (2 vols. 1882), produced some small profit. This portion of his history was reissued under the title of 'History of England, 1603–1640' (10 vols. 1883–4). The next portion of his history consisted of three volumes issued separately in 1886, 1889, and 1891, under the title of 'The Great Civil War,' followed finally by three other volumes, called 'The History of the Commonwealth and Protectorate,' in 1895, 1897, and 1901.

The regular production of these sixteen volumes was made possible by Gardiner's methodical and strenuous industry. He examined systematically every source of information. He studied in the archives of different European capitals papers illustrating the diplomatic history of the Stuart period, and he presented to the British Museum two volumes of transcripts which he had made at Simancas, besides other documents copied elsewhere (*Add. MSS.* 31111–2). For many years he lived in Gordon Street, within easy reach of the British Museum and the Record Office; subsequently, while residing in succession at Bromley, Bedford, and Sevenoaks, he came up to London nearly every day to work in those two storehouses of historical materials. His chief recreation was cycling, and in his holidays he familiarised himself with the battle-fields of the English civil war and followed the campaigns of Montrose in Scotland and of Cromwell in Ireland. During the greater part of the period in which the history was produced Gardiner was actively engaged in teaching. From 1872 to 1877 he was a lecturer at King's College, London, and in 1877 he succeeded John Sherren Brewer [q. v.] there as professor of modern history. Between 1877 and 1894 he lectured regularly for the Society for the Extension of University Teaching in London. He also taught at Bedford College (1863–81) and in private schools near London, and lectured at Toynbee Hall.

Gardiner liked teaching and was an admirable popular lecturer. He used no notes and spoke in a simple, conversational manner, arranging his facts very clearly, and weaving the different threads of the subject into a connected whole with remarkable skill. His elevation of tone and his breadth of view made his verdicts on statesmen and his exposition of principles impressive as well as convincing. The six lectures on 'Cromwell's Place in History,' given at Oxford in 1896, are a good example of his style, though they are not printed exactly as they were delivered, because they were not written till he was asked by his audience to publish them.

Besides teaching, Gardiner found time to write a number of historical text-books. To the 'Epochs of English History,' published by Longmans, he contributed in 1874 'The Thirty Years' War,' and in 1876 'The Puritan Revolution' (15th impression 1902). He was the author of an 'Outline of English History for Children' (1881; new edit. 1901) and of a 'Student's History of England' for the higher classes in schools (3 vols. 1890). He also selected and edited, for use in the Modern History School at Oxford, a volume of 'Constitutional Documents of the Puritan Revolution' (1889; 3rd edit. 1906). These and other excellent text-books enjoyed a wide circulation. 'The Puritan Revolution' was translated into Russian, and portions of the 'Outline' were edited as a reading book for German schools.

In spite of the claims of his history and of his educational work, Gardiner contrived to take a leading part in all enterprises for the promotion of learning. From 1873 to 1878 he edited the historical department of the 'Academy.' To the 'Revue Historique' between 1876 and 1881 he supplied a series of 'bulletins' on the progress of historical literature in England. From the foundation of the 'English Historical Review' in 1886 he was one of its chief contributors, and from 1891 to 1901 its editor. He was director of the Camden Society from 1869 to 1897, editing for it no fewer than twelve volumes besides numerous contributions to its miscellanies. He edited two volumes of documents for the Navy Records Society and one for the Scottish History Society, and was a member of the council of each of these bodies. To this Dictionary he contributed twenty-one lives, and he wrote numerous articles for the ninth edition of the 'Encyclopædia Britannica.' Nor was it only by his writings that he forwarded scholarship. He could always find time to help other historians, and no one was more quick to recognise the merits of a beginner or so ready to give him advice and encouragement.

Recognition came slowly to Gardiner, who, in spite of his eminence as an historian, long maintained himself mainly by teaching and literary work, neither holding any post worthy of his powers nor receiving any aid from the endowments designed to promote learning. In 1878 Lord Acton unsuccessfully pressed Sir George Jessel, the master of the rolls, to appoint Gardiner deputy keeper in succession to Sir T. D. Hardy. In 1882, at Acton's instigation, Gladstone conferred upon Gardiner a civil list pension of 150*l*. a year (PAUL, *Letters of Lord Acton to Mary Gladstone*, 1904, pp. 129, 149). In 1884 All Souls College, Oxford, elected Gardiner to a research fellowship of the value of 200*l*. a year, in order to help him to continue his investigations. In 1892, when his tenure of that fellowship ended, he was elected by Merton College to a similar position, which he retained till his death. Many honorary distinctions were also conferred upon him at home and abroad. The academies or historical societies of various foreign countries elected him a member, as a recognition of the light his researches had thrown upon parts of their national history, viz. Bohemia (1870 ?), Massachusetts (1874), Copenhagen (1891), Upsala (1893), and Utrecht (1900). In 1887 the University of Göttingen gave him the degree of doctor of philosophy; Edinburgh that of LL.D. in 1881, Oxford that of D.C.L. in 1895, and Cambridge that of Litt.D. in 1899.

In 1894, on the death of Froude, Lord Rosebery offered Gardiner the regius professorship of modern history. He refused it, because he wished to reserve his time and strength for the completion of his book, and was reluctant to leave London, which was the most convenient place for his work. He consented, however, to fill in 1896 the newly created post of Ford lecturer at Oxford, and delivered the single course of lectures which was required, on 'Cromwell's Place in History' (3rd edit. 1897). During the later years of his life he published only two works of importance apart from the continuation of his history—a monograph on Cromwell for Goupil's series of illustrated biographies (1899; translated into German in 1903, with a preface by Professor Alfred Stern of Zurich) and a critical examination of the history of the gunpowder plot (1897) in answer to Father Gerard's endeavour to prove that the plot was devised by the government for its own ends.

By this time Gardiner's health was beginning to fail. He had intended to carry his history down to the restoration of Charles II, but he finally resolved to end it with the death of Cromwell. The third volume of the 'Commonwealth and Protectorate,' which brought the story down to the summer of 1656, was published in January 1901 (new edit. 4 vols. 1903). In March Gardiner was stricken by partial paralysis, and though he rallied for a time was never able to work again. A chapter of the history, which he left in manuscript, was published in 1903, and in accordance with his desires the book was completed by the present writer in his 'Last Years of the Protectorate' (2 vols. 1909).

Gardiner died at Sevenoaks on 23 Feb. 1902, a few days before the conclusion of his seventy-third year. He married (1) in 1856 Isabella, youngest daughter of Edward

Irving: she died in 1878; (2) in 1882 Bertha Meriton Cordery, who survived him and was granted a civil list pension of 75*l.* in 1903. He left six sons and two daughters.

Gardiner was buried at Sevenoaks, and tablets in memory of him were placed in Christ Church Cathedral and in Winchester Cathedral. His best memorial is his history. Its pages reveal the thoroughness of his workmanship and his single-minded devotion to truth. The book was based on a mass of materials hitherto unknown or imperfectly utilised, and those materials were weighed and sifted with scientific skill. Each new edition was corrected with conscientious care as fresh evidence came to light. In his narrative minute accuracy and wide research were combined with sound judgment, keen insight, and a certain power of imagination. Earlier historians of the period, and some of Gardiner's own contemporaries, had written as partisans. Gardiner succeeded in stating fairly and sympathetically the position and the aims of both parties. He did not confine himself to relating facts, but traced the growth of the religious and constitutional ideas which underlay the conflict. No side of the national life was neglected. He won the praise of experts by his accounts of military and naval operations, elucidated continually the economic and social history of the time, and was the first to show the interaction of English and continental politics. The result of his labours was to make the period he treated better known and better understood than any other portion of English history. A narrative which fills eighteen volumes and took forty years to write is necessarily somewhat unequal as a literary composition. Many critics complained that Gardiner's style lacked the picturesqueness and vivacity of Macaulay or Froude; others that his method was too chronological. There was truth in both criticisms; but the chronological method was chosen because it enabled the historian to show the development of events far better than a more artificial arrangement would have done. He sought to interest his readers by his lucid exposition of facts and the justice of his reflections rather than by giving history the charms of fiction, and was content with the distinction of being the most trustworthy of nineteenth-century historians.

[Personal knowledge; The Times, 25 Feb. 1902; Athenæum, 1 March 1902; English Hist. Rev., April 1902; Quarterly Rev., April 1902; Atlantic Monthly, May 1902; Proc. Brit. Acad. 1903–4; Revue Historique, lxxix. 232; Historische Zeitschrift, lxxxix. 190; Historisch-politische Blätter, cxxix. 7; J. F. Rhodes, Historical Essays, 1909; a bibliography of Gardiner's historical writings, compiled by Dr. W. A. Shaw, was published by the Royal Historical Society in 1903.]

C. H. F.

GARGAN, DENIS (1819–1903), president of Maynooth College, born at Duleek, co. Meath, in June 1819, was second son of Patrick Gargan and Jane Branagan.

Destined by his parents for the priesthood, he was sent at an early age to St. Finian's seminary, Navan. On 25 Aug. 1836 he entered St. Patrick's College, Maynooth, where he showed much promise, especially in physics and astronomy. He was ready for ordination before the canonical age. Ordained by Archbishop Daniel Murray on 10 June 1843, Gargan was sent to the Irish College, Paris, where he taught physics and astronomy till 1845. In that year he was appointed professor of humanity in Maynooth, and in 1859 he succeeded Matthew Kelly [q. v.] as professor of ecclesiastical history at the college. After many years of notable success in this position, he was in 1885 made vice-president of the college, and in 1894 became its president. Two historic events happened during his presidency, namely, the centenary celebration of the college foundation in 1895, and the visit of King Edward VII and Queen Alexandra in 1903. His management of both ceremonies was dignified and impressive. He died at Maynooth on 26 Aug. 1903, after sixty years' association with the college.

Though a man of wide and accurate scholarship, Gargan published only two books, 'The Charity of the Church a Proof of its Divinity,' a translation from the Italian of Cardinal Balluffi (1885), and 'The Ancient Church of Ireland, a Few Remarks on Dr. Todd's "Memoirs of the Life and Times of St. Patrick"' (Dublin, 1864).

[Irish Ecclesiastical Record, 1903, pp. 481–492; Freeman's Journal, 27 Aug. 1903; The Times, 28 Aug. 1903; Centenary History of Maynooth College, by Archbishop Healy.]

D. J. O'D.

GARNER, THOMAS (1839–1906), architect, son of Thomas Garner by his wife Louisa Savage, was born at Wasperton Hill, Warwickshire, on 12 Aug. 1839. Brought up in country surroundings, he acquired as a boy a love of riding and a knowledge of horsemanship which he retained through life. At the age of seventeen (1856) he entered as a pupil the office of (Sir) George Gilbert Scott [q. v.], where he was a fellow student with Mr. Thomas Graham Jackson, R.A., Mr. Somers Clarke, and John Thomas Micklethwaite [q. v. Suppl. II]. He had already made the acquaintance of George Frederick Bodley, R.A. [q. v. Suppl. II], who had served articles in the same office. After completion of his pupilage Garner returned to Warwickshire, and there began architectural practice, partly on his own account, partly as an assistant to Scott.

In 1868 Bodley sought his collaboration, and in 1869 they became partners, without any legal deed of association. A series of beautiful works in ecclesiastical, domestic and collegiate architecture was the result of this combination [see for description BODLEY, GEORGE FREDERICK, Suppl. II]. The fine churches of the Holy Angels, Hoar Cross, St. Augustine, Pendlebury, and St. German, Roath, are the chief buildings of definitely united authorship. During the partnership it was the practice of the two to give separate attention to separate works, and among the buildings which under this system fell mainly if not entirely to Garner's share the chief were St. Swithun's Quadrangle at Magdalen College, Oxford; the small tower in the S.E. angle of 'Tom' Quad, Christ Church; St. Michael's Church, Camden Town; Hewell Grange, a house for Lord Windsor; the reredos in St. Paul's Cathedral; the monuments of the bishops of Ely, Lincoln, and Chichester in their respective cathedrals, and that of Canon Liddon in St. Paul's. Other designs in which it appears that Garner's authorship was either sole or predominant were: churches at Bedworth, Peasdown, and Camerton; additions to Bosworth Hall, a house at Godden Green, Kent; the reconstruction of the chapel at St. Catharine's College, Cambridge; class-rooms, chapel, &c., at Marlborough College; the altar of King's College, Cambridge; and the restoration of Garner's own Jacobean home, Fritwell Manor House, Oxfordshire. After the perfectly friendly dissolution of partnership in 1897 Garner carried out as his own work exclusively Yarnton Manor, Oxfordshire; the Slipper Chapel, Houghton-le-dale; Moreton House, Hampstead; and the Empire Hotel, Buxton.

With his partner Bodley, Garner was regarded for many years as an authoritative ecclesiastical artist. Together they were responsible not only for many new buildings but also for the decoration, often the transformation, of buildings of earlier date. In 1902 Garner designed the cope worn by the dean of Westminster at the coronation of Edward VII. In his later years Garner joined the Church of Rome, and after the death of Edward Hansom he was appointed architect to Downside Priory, Bath, where he designed the choir in which his own interment was to take place. It is said that when John Francis Bentley [q. v. Suppl. II], the architect of the cathedral at Westminster, became aware of his own fatal illness, he suggested in answer to the question who should be his successor, 'Garner, for he is a man of genius.'

Garner died on 30 April 1906 at Fritwell Manor. He married in 1866 Rose Emily, daughter of the Rev. J. N. Smith of Milverton, Leamington Spa; she survived him without issue.

His residence was for a time at 20 Church Row, Hampstead, and his office was in Gray's Inn. His art collection was sold in January 1907.

'The Domestic Architecture of England during the Tudor Period,' a joint work by Garner and Mr. A. Stratton, was published in 1908, after Garner's death, under Mr. Stratton's editorship.

[Builder, xc. 523, 531 (1906); information from Mrs. Garner and from Mr. Edward Warren.] P. W.

GARNETT, RICHARD (1835–1906), man of letters and keeper of printed books at the British Museum, born in Beacon Street, Lichfield, on 27 Feb. 1835, was elder son of Richard Garnett [q. v.] by his wife Rayne, daughter of John Wreaks of Sheffield. His uncles Jeremiah Garnett and Thomas Garnett (1799–1878) are, like his father, noticed separately. Three years after his birth his father removed with his family to London on becoming assistant keeper of printed books at the British Museum. Richard was chiefly educated at home, but he spent some time at the Rev. C. M. Marcus's small private school in Caroline Street, Bedford Square, where his companions included Sir John Everett Millais [q. v. Suppl. I], Edward Hayes Plumptre [q. v.], and William Jackson Brodribb [q. v. Suppl. II]. He was also for a term at the end of 1850 at Whalley grammar school. Garnett showed exceptional intellectual precocity as a boy. He inherited his father's faculty for acquiring languages, and before he was fourteen he had read for his own amusement the whole of the 'Poetæ Scenici Græci,' Diodorus Siculus's History, the works of Boiardo, Ariosto, and Tasso, and the stories of Tieck and Hoffmann. All his life he studied not only the classics but the literature of France, Germany, Italy, and Spain. His interest in current affairs was at the same time singularly active in youth, and he assimilated with avidity details of home and foreign politics and records of sport.

After his father's death in Sept. 1850 he declined, from a confirmed if somewhat precocious distrust of the educational efficiency of both Oxford and Cambridge, his kinsfolks' proposal that he should prepare for one of the universities. In the autumn of 1851, through the good offices of Anthony Panizzi [q. v.], his father's colleague at the British Museum, he became an assistant in the library there. With the British Museum he was closely identified for the greater part of his career. His first employment was in copying titles for the catalogue, but he was soon engaged in the more responsible task of revising the titles. Panizzi quickly recognised his ability, and entrusted him with the duty of classifying fresh acquisitions and placing them on the shelves. Panizzi won his wholehearted admiration, and he set himself to carry on the traditions which Panizzi initiated at the museum. After devoting twenty years to subordinate labour at the museum, he was made in 1875 assistant keeper of printed books and superintendent of the reading-room. In spite of his shy and nervous manner he at once won golden opinions by the courteous readiness with which he placed his multifarious stores of knowledge at the disposal of readers. He was soon engaged on a heavy piece of work which added materially to the usefulness of the library to the public. In 1881 the printing of the general catalogue of books which had been suspended since 1841 was resumed. The superintendence of the enterprise fell to Garnett. He devoted immense energy to this great undertaking. In order to concentrate his energies upon it, he in 1884 retired from the reading-room, and was mainly occupied in editing the catalogue until 1890. In that year he was appointed keeper of printed books, and the catalogue was completed by other hands.

In 1882 Garnett was an unsuccessful candidate for the librarianship of the Bodleian library, Oxford, but his promotion to the headship of his department at the British Museum fully satisfied his ambitions. Many important additions were made to the library under his rule. 'A Description of Three Hundred Notable Books' (which he purchased for the museum during his term of office) was privately printed in 1899 in honour of his services on his retirement, and proves the catholicity and soundness of his judgment. He was keenly alive to the need of providing room for future accessions to the library, and in 1887 introduced 'the sliding press,' which greatly economised the space at his disposal. In 1899, a year before he attained the regulation age for retirement, he resigned his post, owing to his wife's failing health, after forty-eight years' service at the museum. Bishop Creighton called him 'the ideal librarian'—a title which was well justified by his width of literary knowledge and his zealous desire to adapt the national library to all reasonable public requirements. Although he was not a scientific bibliographer, he was interested in the purely professional side of his work, and won the regard of his fellow-librarians. In 1892–3 he was president of the Library Association of the United Kingdom, to whose 'Transactions' he frequently contributed. He edited a series of 'Library Manuals' and was president of the Bibliographical Society in 1895–7.

From early days Garnett devoted his leisure to literature, and during his career at the museum steadily won a general reputation as a man of letters. After his retirement from the museum his pen was exceptionally busy, and his literary work was in unceasing demand until his death.

In letters addressed between 1851 and 1864 to his younger brother, W. J. Garnett, who was then in Australia, he described his first literary endeavours as well as the varied experiences of his bachelor days in London. These letters, which have not been published, are now in the British Museum (*Add. MS.* 37489). Setting out with poetic ambitions which he never wholly abandoned, he published anonymously in 1858 his first volume, 'Primula; a Book of Lyrics.' This reappeared under his own name with additions next year as 'Io in Egypt, and other Poems,' and was thoroughly revised for a third issue in 1893. There followed 'Poems from the German' (1862); 'Idylls and Epigrams, chiefly from the Greek Anthology' (1869; republished as 'A Chaplet from the Greek Anthology,' 1892); 'Iphigenia in Delphi' (1891); 'One Hundred and Twenty-four Sonnets from Dante, Petrarch, and Camoens' (1896); 'The Queen and other Poems' (1901); a dramatic jeu d'esprit in blank verse called

'William Shakespeare, Pedagogue and Poacher' (1904); and finally 'De flagello myrteo' (1905; new edit. 1906), a collection (in prose form but of poetic temper) of three hundred and sixty rather subtle 'thoughts and fancies on love.' Garnett's verse displays a cultured, even fastidious, taste and much metrical facility, but much of it is a graceful and melodious echo of wide reading rather than original imaginative effort. The thought at times strikes a cynical note. Probably his most valuable poetic work was done in translation.

In prose Garnett's labours were extensive and unusually versatile. He was from early manhood a voluminous contributor to periodicals. At the outset he wrote for the 'Literary Gazette' when owned by Lovell Reeve, and for the 'Examiner.' Subsequently he regularly wrote on German literature for the 'Saturday Review.' Articles from his pen appeared from time to time in 'Macmillan's Magazine,' in 'Temple Bar,' and 'Fraser's Magazine.' At a later period he wrote critical introductions to innumerable popular reprints of standard books, and he diversified literary criticisms with many excursions into biography. In the 'Great Writers' series he published monographs on 'Milton' (1887), on 'Carlyle,' which was drastically reduced before publication (1887), and on 'Emerson' (1888). To this Dictionary and to the 'Encyclopædia Britannica' he supplied very many memoirs. He had no great powers of research and was prone to rely for his facts on his retentive memory, but his biographical work was invariably that of a tasteful, discriminating, and well-informed compiler. His range of biographical interest extended far beyond men of letters, and his biographies include those of Edward Gibbon Wakefield, the colonial pioneer (1898), and of William Johnson Fox, the social reformer (published posthumously and completed by Garnett's son Edward in 1910).

Garnett's most important publications were the volumes entitled 'Relics of Shelley' (1862) and 'The Twilight of the Gods' (1903). The former was a small collection of unpublished verse by the poet, which Garnett discovered among the poet's MSS. and notebooks, which had belonged to Shelley's widow, and passed on her death in 1851 to his son, Sir Percy Shelley. With Shelley he had many affinities. His good fortune in discovering the poet's unknown work gave great satisfaction to Sir Percy and to his wife, Lady Shelley. Garnett became their intimate friend, and they attested their regard for him by presenting him with Shelley's notebooks. These fetched 3000*l.* at the sale of Garnett's library after his death. Lady Shelley pressed on Garnett the task of preparing the full life of her father-in-law, but other engagements compelled him to yield the labour to Prof. Edward Dowden. Garnett's 'The Twilight of the Gods' is a series of semi-classical or oriental apologues of pleasantly cynical flavour in the vein of Lucian. The book came out in 1888, and attracted no attention, though the earl of Lytton, then English ambassador at Paris, promptly recognised in a long letter to the author the fascination of its imaginative power and dry humour. A reprint in 1903 was welcomed by a large audience and established Garnett's reputation as a resourceful worker in fiction and a shrewd observer of human nature.

Among Garnett's later works were a useful 'History of Italian Literature' (1897), and he joined Mr. Edmund Gosse in compiling an 'Illustrated Record of English Literature' (in 4 vols.); vols. i. and ii. were from Garnett's pen (1903).

Garnett cherished a genuine and somewhat mystical sense of religion which combined hostility to priestcraft and dogma with a modified belief in astrology. He explained his position in an article in the 'University Magazine' (1880), published under the pseudonym of A. G. Trent, which was re-issued independently in 1893 as 'The Soul and the Stars'; it was translated into German in 1894. Garnett maintained that astrology was 'a physical science just as much as geology,' but he gave no credit to its alleged potency as a fortune-telling agent.

In 1883 the University of Edinburgh conferred on Garnett the honorary degree of LL.D., and he was made C.B. in 1895. He died at his house, 27 Tanza Road, Hampstead, on 13 April 1906, and was buried in Highgate cemetery. The chief part of his library was sold at Sotheby's on 6 Dec. 1906.

Garnett married in 1863 Olivia Narney (*d.* 1903), daughter of Edward Singleton, co. Clare, and had issue three sons and three daughters. His second son, Edward (*b.* 1868), is well known as an author and dramatist.

On his retiring from the museum in 1899 Garnett's friends presented him with his portrait by the Hon. John Collier. The portrait belongs to Garnett's eldest son, Robert. A photogravure of it is prefixed to 'Three Hundred Notable Books' (1899). A better painting by Miss E. M. Heath is in the possession of Garnett's son Edward. A bust by (Sir) George Frampton, R.A., was exhibited at the Royal Academy in 1899. A caricature by 'Spy' appeared in 'Vanity Fair' in 1895.

Besides the works enumerated, Garnett was author of 'Shelley and Lord Beaconsfield' (privately printed, 1887); 'The Age of Dryden,' a literary handbook (1895); 'William Blake, Painter and Poet' ('Portfolio' monograph, 1895); 'Essays in Librarianship and Bibliography' (1899); 'Essays of an ex-Librarian' (1901). He also laboriously compiled from the voluminous MS. collections, chiefly dealing with Shropshire, of John Wood Warter [q. v.] 'An Old Shropshire Oak' (vols. i. and ii. 1886; vols. iii. and iv. 1891), and he lent his name as editor to 'The International Library of Famous Literature,' a popular anthology on a large scale, which an American publishing syndicate circulated in England in 1901.

[Notes kindly supplied by Garnett's brother, Mr. W. J. Garnett; H. Cordier, Le docteur Richard Garnett, 1906; The Times, 14 April 1906; Athenæum, 21 April 1906; personal knowledge.] S. L.

GARRAN (formerly Gamman), ANDREW (1825–1901), Australian journalist and politician, born at Bethnal Green, London, on 19 Nov. 1825, was third of the thirteen children of Robert Gamman, merchant, of London, by his wife Mary Ann, daughter of Henry Matthews, architect and engineer of the home department of the East India Company. Educated at Hackney grammar school, London, and at Spring Hill College, Birmingham, he matriculated in 1843 at London University, where he graduated B.A. in 1845 and M.A. in 1848. On the conclusion of his university career he visited Madeira for his health, and on the same ground finally emigrated to Australia.

On Garran's arrival at Adelaide in Jan. 1851 the controversy repecting state aid to religion was at its height, and of a paper called the 'Austral Examiner,' which was started to oppose the grant of state aid, Garran acted as editor for two years. The discovery of gold in Victoria, however, nearly depopulated Adelaide for the time, and brought the career of the paper to an abrupt conclusion. After serving as private tutor for a year in the family of Mr. C. E. Labillière on a station near Ballan, Victoria, he returned to Adelaide, and in 1854–5 edited the 'South Australian Register.'

In 1856 he became assistant editor under John West of the 'Sydney Morning Herald,' and his association with that newspaper lasted nearly thirty years. On West's death in 1873 he became editor-in-chief, and he held the post till the end of 1885, when his health compelled him to resign.

At the advanced age of sixty-two, Garran entered the political arena. In 1887 he was made a member of the legislative council of New South Wales by Sir Henry Parkes, and in that capacity his wide knowledge of affairs was always placed at the disposal of the house. In 1890 he suggested, and was made president of, a royal commission on strikes, and the report which he submitted resulted in the passing of the Trades Disputes Conciliation and Arbitration Act in 1892. Of the council of arbitration which this Act established Garran was made president (1 Oct. 1892), and he thereupon resigned his seat in the legislative council to avoid all suspicion of political bias. In his 'Fifty Years of Australian History' (ii. 294) Sir Henry Parkes bears testimony to Garran's 'care, patient labour and ability in conducting the inquiry.'

In December 1894 Garran withdrew from the arbitration council, and on 19 March 1895 was appointed vice-president of the executive council and representative of Mr. (now Sir George) Reid's government in the legislative council. Owing to failing health he resigned the vice-presidency in Nov. 1898, but remained a member until death. He was a member of the parliamentary standing committee on public works, a commissioner of the Sydney International Exhibition (1879), a member of the royal commission on noxious trades (1888), and of the Bay View lunatic inquiry commission (1894).

Garran took much interest in the University of Sydney, where in earlier years he attended the law lectures and took the degree of LL.D. in 1870. He was twice president of the Australian Economic Association. He edited in 1886 the 'Picturesque Atlas of Australasia,' the most comprehensive descriptive work on Australia hitherto published.

He died on 6 June 1901 at his residence, Elizabeth Bay, Sydney, and was buried in Rookwood cemetery. He married at Adelaide in 1854 Mary Isham, daughter of John Sabine, formerly of Bury St. Edmunds, and had one son and seven daughters. His son, Robert Randolph Garran, C.M.G. (*b.* 10 Feb. 1867), has made a reputation in the commonwealth as a constitutional lawyer.

A full-length panel portrait in oils, by Tom Roberts, an Australian artist, is in the possession of his widow.

[The Times, Melbourne Argus, and Sydney Morning Herald, 7 June 1901; Sydney Mail, 15 June 1901; Who's Who, 1901; University of London General Register, 1901; Johns's Notable Australians, 1908; Year Book of Australia, 1894–1902; Colonial Office Records.]

C. A.

GARRETT, FYDELL EDMUND (1865–1907), publicist, born on 20 July 1865, was fourth son of John Fisher Garrett, rector of Elton, Derbyshire, by his wife, Mary, daughter of Godfrey Gray. He was educated at Rossall school and Trinity College, Cambridge, where he graduated B.A. in the summer term of 1887 with a third class in classics. At the university he was more distinguished at the Union Debating Society, of which he was president in 1887, than in the schools. But though not taking a high degree, he gave in other ways early evidence of exceptional literary ability. Some of his translations from the classical poets, as well as his original pieces, contained in a small volume of undergraduate verse, 'Rhymes and Renderings,' published at Cambridge in 1887, are remarkable not only for their grace and ease of expression but for a real poetic feeling. On leaving the university Garrett joined the staff of the 'Pall Mall Gazette,' and rapidly made his mark as a journalist by the force of his convictions—he was at this time a very ardent radical—the freshness of his style, and a happy gift of humour. But he had always been delicate, and after two years of work in London his health broke down. The first symptoms of the disease to which he ultimately succumbed, phthisis, became apparent, and he was sent for cure to South Africa. The remedy was for the moment apparently successful, and in any case this visit to South Africa in the winter of 1889–90 led to other consequences most important to his career. South Africa was at that time entering the critical period of her history which terminated in the war of 1899–1902. Garrett, an ardent young man of exceptionally keen intelligence, not lacking in audacity, and of most winning manners and appearance, was quick to seize the salient points in an interesting situation and to make the acquaintance of the leading actors in the drama. He won the confidence of Sir Hercules Robinson [q. v. Suppl. I], then high commissioner for South Africa, and made great friends with Cecil Rhodes [q. v. Suppl. II], besides establishing more or less intimate relations with the leading Dutch politicians, including Jan Hofmeyr [q. v. Suppl. II] and President Kruger. The result was a series of articles in the 'Pall Mall Gazette,' subsequently published as a book, 'In Afrikanderland and the Land of Ophir' (1891, 2 edits.), which is still the best description of South Africa in that momentous phase of its development. The next four years were again devoted, as far as recurrent attacks of ill-health permitted, to journalistic work in London, first for the 'Pall Mall Gazette,' then, from 1893, for the 'Westminster Gazette,' in the opening years of its career, in either case under the editorship of Garrett's friend, (Sir) E. T. Cook. In 1894 he also produced a translation of Ibsen's 'Brand' into English verse in the original metres, which, if not perfect as a translation, for Garrett was not a great Norwegian scholar, is singularly successful in reproducing the spirit and poetry of the original.

In April 1895 Garrett returned to South Africa to become editor of the 'Cape Times,' the leading English newspaper in the sub-continent, and far the most important work of Garrett's life was done during his four and a half years' active tenure of that office (April 1895–August 1899). He was not only editor of the paper but the principal writer in it, and being a man of strong character and convictions, gifted moreover with extraordinary quickness of political insight, he on more than one occasion exercised by his trenchant pen a decisive influence on the course of affairs. In the rapid series of stirring events of these four years, the raid, the abortive rebellion in Johannesburg, the struggle between Rhodes and the Bond at the Cape, and between Kruger and the Uitlanders in the Transvaal, the Bloemfontein conference, and the growing tension between Great Britain and the South African republic, Garrett played a leading part. His position in South African politics became one of such importance that he was practically compelled to add to his arduous duties as editor of the 'Cape Times' those of a member of parliament. Returned at the Cape general election of 1898 as member for Victoria East, he immediately took a foremost place in the house of assembly, and in the two heated sessions preceding the war he was perhaps the most eloquent, and he was certainly the most persuasive, speaker on the 'progressive' (i.e. British) side, for, while warmly supporting Rhodes and the policy of Lord (then Sir Alfred) Milner, he showed great tact in dealing with the susceptibilities of his Dutch opponents. Indeed the policy which he always advocated, that of a United South Africa, absolutely autonomous in its own affairs, but remaining part of the British empire, is now an established fact, readily accepted by men of all parties. Garrett's important contribution to that result constitutes his chief title to remembrance. But the enormous physical strain was too much for his frail constitution. In the summer of 1899 his health broke down permanently. Obliged to leave South Africa, in an advanced stage of consumption, just before the outbreak of the war, he spent the next two or three years in sanatoria, first on the Continent and then in England, still hoping against hope that he might be able to return to an active political career. He had already in January 1900 resigned the editorship of the 'Cape Times,' and in 1902 he also gave up his seat in the house of assembly. He still from time to time, when his health permitted the exertion, wrote short articles and poems of exceptional merit, which are of permanent value, notably his brilliant 'Character Sketch' of Cecil Rhodes, published directly after Rhodes's death in the 'Contemporary Review' of June 1902, which is by far the most lifelike and best balanced picture of that great personality. Of much interest likewise are some of his memorial verses: 'The Last Trek,' written on the occasion of President Kruger's funeral progress from Cape Town to Pretoria (*Spectator*, 10 Dec. 1904), 'In Memoriam F. W. R.' (Frank Rhodes), (*Westminster Gazette*, 27 Oct. 1905), and 'A Millionaire's Epitaph' [Alfred Beit, q. v. Suppl. II], (*ibid.* 20 July 1906). In March 1903 Garrett, then a hopeless invalid, was married to Miss Ellen Marriage, whose acquaintance he had made, as a fellow patient, at the sanatorium at Nayland, Suffolk. Miss Marriage had been completely restored to health, and it was doubtless due to her care and devotion that Garrett's life was prolonged for another four years—years of great happiness, despite his complete physical prostration. In June 1904 Mr. and Mrs. Garrett settled in a cottage, Wiverton Acre, near Plympton, Devonshire. Garrett died there on 10 May 1907, and was buried at Brixton, Devonshire. To the last he occasionally wrote, chiefly on South Africa. Within a month of his death he contributed to the 'Standard' (12 April) an article on 'The Boer in the Saddle,' which showed no loss of his old brilliancy and force, although the effort involved in writing it was nearly fatal.

Besides the works mentioned Garrett published 'The Story of an African Crisis' (1897), and he contributed a chapter, 'Rhodes and Milner,' to 'The Empire and the Century' (1905). The Garrett Colonial Library, which was founded by colonial admirers in his memory, was opened at the Cambridge Union Society on 23 May 1911. A pencil portrait by Sir Edward Poynter is in the possession of his widow.

[An excellent Life by (Sir) E. T. Cook (1909) contains many extracts from his letters, a good photographic portrait, and, in the Appendix, some of his best fugitive pieces in prose and verse.] M.

GARROD, Sir ALFRED BARING (1819–1907), physician, born at Ipswich on 13 May 1819, was second child and only son of the five children of Robert Garrod of that town, by his wife, Sarah Enew Clamp. He was educated at the Ipswich grammar school, and after being apprenticed to Mr. Charles Hammond, surgeon to the East Suffolk Hospital, pursued his medical course at University College Hospital, where he graduated M.B. in 1842, and M.D. London in 1843, gaining the gold medal in medicine at both examinations. In 1847 Garrod was appointed assistant physician to University College Hospital, where he became physician and professor of materia medica and therapeutics and a professor of clinical medicine in 1849. He became a licentiate (corresponding to the present member), and in 1856 a fellow of the Royal College of Physicians, where he was Gulstonian lecturer in 1857, and lecturer on materia medica in 1864. He was elected F.R.S. in 1858. Having resigned his posts at University College Hospital he was in 1863 elected physician to King's College Hospital and professor of materia medica and therapeutics in King's College; on his retirement in 1874 he was elected consulting physician. At the Royal College of Physicians he was Lumleian lecturer in 1883, the first recipient of the Moxon medal in 1891, censor (1874–5, 1887), and vice-president in 1888. Knighted in 1887, he in 1890 became physician extraordinary to Queen Victoria, and was an honorary member of the Verein für innere Medicin in Berlin.

Garrod, a follower of Prout and Bence Jones, devoted himself to chemical investigation of the problems of disease. His name will always be known in connection with the discovery that in gout the blood contains an increased quantity of uric acid, and recent work has tended, in the main, to confirm his views. He announced this discovery in 1848 to the Royal Medical and Chirurgical Society (of which he was vice-president in 1880–1). He also separated rheumatoid arthritis from gout, with which it had previously been confused.

At the Medical Society of London, of which he was orator in 1858 and president in 1860, Garrod gave in 1857 the Lettsomian lectures 'On the Pathology and Treatment of Gout.' He long enjoyed an extensive practice, but when old age diminished his work as a consultant he returned with ardour to his chemical investigations.

Garrod died in London on 28 Dec. 1907, and was buried in the Great Northern cemetery, Southgate.

He married in 1845 Elizabeth Ann (*d.* 1891), daughter of Henry Colchester and Elizabeth Sparrow, of the Ancient or Sparrow House in Ipswich. Charles Keene of 'Punch' [q.v.] and Meredith Townsend [q. v. Suppl. II] of the 'Spectator' were Lady Garrod's first cousins. He had issue four sons and two daughters. The eldest son, Alfred Henry [q. v.], and the fourth son, Archibald Edward, were, like their father, elected fellows of the Royal Society. The third son, Herbert Baring, was general secretary of the Teachers' Guild of Great Britain and Ireland (1886–1909).

Garrod was author of: 1. 'Treatise on Gout and Rheumatic Gout,' 1859; 3rd edit. 1876, translated into French and German. 2. 'Essentials of Materia Medica and Therapeutics,' 1855; 13th edit. 1890, edited by Nestor Tirard, M.D. He also contributed articles on gout and rheumatism to Reynolds's 'System of Medicine,' 1866, vol. i.

[Brit. Med. Journ., 1908, i. 58; information from his son, A E. Garrod, M.D., F.R.S.]

H. D. R.

GARTH, Sir RICHARD (1820–1903), chief justice of Bengal, born at Morden, Surrey, on 11 March 1820, was eldest son of the six children of Richard Lowndes (afterwards Garth), rector of Farnham, Surrey, by his wife Mary, daughter of Robert Douglas, rector of Salwarpe, Worcestershire. His father was the second son of William Lowndes of Baldwin Brightwell, Oxfordshire, by his wife Elizabeth, daughter and heiress of Richard Garth of Morden, and assumed the name and arms of Garth on succeeding to his mother's property in 1837. In due course Richard became lord of the manor of Morden.

He was educated at Eton, where he played in the cricket elevens of 1837–8, and at Christ Church, Oxford, where he graduated B.A. in 1842 and M.A. in 1845. He was a member of the university cricket eleven from 1839 to 1842, and its captain in 1840 and 1841. Admitted a student of Lincoln's Inn on 9 July 1842, he was called to the bar there on 19 Nov. 1847. Joining the home circuit, he gained great popularity in the profession, and especial repute in commercial cases heard at the Guildhall. For many years he was counsel to the Incorporated Law Society. He took silk on 24 July 1866, and was two days later elected a bencher of his inn. In the 1866–8 parliament he represented Guildford in the conservative interest, but was defeated at the next general election.

In 1875 he was appointed chief justice of Bengal and was knighted (13 May). A bluff, genial, fresh-complexioned man, he looked more like a country squire or a naval officer than a judge. Popular with all classes of society in Calcutta, he did much to bring the European and Indian communities into closer social touch. His judicial decisions were marked by learning, patience, and practical good sense, and were rarely reversed by the judicial committee of the privy council.

Garth came into frequent conflict with the Bengal government. The views of the high court were then systematically sought on legislative proposals, and Garth framed confidential minutes. But at the same time he often gave subsequent public utterance to pronounced opinions about the proposed legislation. The most notable example of such practice was his vigorous propaganda against the Bengal tenancy bill, designed to give the cultivators in the permanently settled areas clearly defined and transferable occupancy rights, and passed into law after much controversy in 1885. In a published 'Minute' (Calcutta, 1882, 18 pp. folio) he declared the measure to be ruinous for the zamindars and to embody a policy of confiscation. His sincerity was unquestioned, but it was improper for the chief justice to engage in partisan controversy over legislation which he would probably have to interpret judicially. He showed sympathy with Indian aspirations. He promoted the Legal Practitioners Act of 1879, and he insisted that one of the three additional judges appointed to the Bengal high court in 1885 should be an Indian.

Ill-health led to his retirement in March 1886, shortly before he had qualified for full pension. He was named of the privy council in February 1888, but was not appointed to the judicial committee. A strong supporter of the Indian National Congress, he wrote 'A Few Plain Truths about India' (1888), largely in advocacy of its views. His vigorous reply (1895) to some criticisms of the movement by General Sir George T. Chesney [q. v. Suppl. I] has been constantly quoted by the congress authorities (see *Ind. Nat. Congress*, Madras, 1909, pt. ii. p. 24). Garth promoted in July 1899 a memorial to the India office from retired high court judges for the separation of executive and judicial functions in the administrative organisation of districts.

He died at his house in Cheniston Gardens, London, on 23 March 1903, and was buried at Morden. He married on 27 June 1847 Clara (*d.* 15 Jan. 1903), second daughter of William Loftus Lowndes, Q.C., by whom he had six sons and three daughters. A portrait of Garth by the Hon. John Collier is in the Calcutta high court.

[Foster's Men at the Bar, 1885; India List, 1903; Englishman Weekly Summary, 23 and 30 March 1886; Friend of India and Statesman Weekly, 26 March 1903; India, 27 March and 3 April 1903; Wisden's Cricketers' Almanack for 1904, lxxx; information kindly supplied by Lt.-col. Richard Garth, the eldest son; personal knowledge.] F. H. B.

GATACRE, Sir WILLIAM FORBES (1843–1906), major-general, born near Stirling on 3 Dec. 1843, was third son of Edward Lloyd Gatacre (1806–91) by his wife Jessie, second daughter of William Forbes of Callendar House, Falkirk, Stirlingshire. The second son is Major-general Sir John Gatacre, K.C.B. The father was squire of Gatacre in the parish of Claverley, Shropshire, a manor held by his ancestors from the time of Henry II or earlier, and was high sheriff of Shropshire in 1856. He taught his sons to be good horsemen, and it was to home life and parentage that Gatacre owed what was most characteristic of him—a mind and body which delighted in exercise and seemed incapable of fatigue.

Educated at Hopkirk's school, Eltham, and at Sandhurst, Gatacre was commissioned on 18 Feb. 1862 as ensign in the 77th foot, then stationed in Bengal. He was promoted lieutenant on 23 Dec. 1864. He went to Peshawur with the regiment in November 1866, and in 1867 he spent six months' leave alone in the upper valleys of the Indus, shooting and exploring. He was invalided home soon afterwards. The 77th returned to England in March 1870, and he was promoted captain on 7 Dec.

In February 1873 he entered the Staff College, and after spending two years there he was employed four years at Sandhurst as instructor in surveying. In August 1880, after a year's service on the staff at Aldershot, he went back to India with his regiment. He was promoted major on 23 March 1881, and lieutenant-colonel on 29 April 1882. He was then serving on the staff of Sir Harry Prendergast at Rangoon; but he returned to regimental duty in 1883, and succeeded to the command of the regiment at Secunderabad on 24 June 1884.

From 17 Dec. 1885 to 30 Sept. 1889 Gatacre was deputy quartermaster-general of the Bengal army. In the Hazara expedition of 1888 he gave striking proof of his activity and endurance. He was mentioned in despatches, and received the D.S.O. and the India medal with clasp. After being in temporary command of the Mandalay brigade for twelve months, and gaining a clasp for the Tonhon expedition, he was made adjutant-general of the Bombay army, with the substantive rank of colonel and temporary rank of brigadier-general (25 Nov. 1890). He had been made brevet-colonel on 29 April 1886. He was in command of the Bombay district from January 1894 to July 1897, but from March to September of 1895 he was engaged in the Chitral expedition. He commanded the 3rd brigade of the relief force under Sir Robert Low [q. v. Suppl. II], and on 20 April his brigade was sent forward as a flying column, as the Chitral garrison were in straits. It reached Chitral on 15 May, after a most arduous passage of the Lowari pass; but the garrison had already been relieved by Colonel Kelly's force from Gilgit. Gatacre received the medal and was made C.B.

On his return from Chitral Gatacre went to England for three months in the winter of 1895–6. During the summer of 1896 he was in temporary command at Quetta, and during the first half of 1897 he was fighting the plague at Bombay. The deaths there in January from this cause rose to more than 300 a day. Gatacre not only took care of his own troops but served as chairman of a committee to deal with the problem generally. Thanks to his energy and tact, the outbreak was well under control by July, when he left India to take command of a brigade at Aldershot. Five testimonials expressed the gratitude of the citizens of Bombay—Christian, Mussulman, and Hindu—for what he had done. In 1900 the gold medal of the Kaiser-i-Hind order was awarded him on this account.

In January 1898 he went to Egypt, with the local rank of major-general, to command the British brigade in the advance up the Nile for the recovery of Khartoum. He brought it into such condition that it was able to march 140 miles in a week. On 8 April the Anglo-Egyptian army under Sir Herbert Kitchener attacked the Mahdist forces under Mahmoud in their intrenched camp on the Atbara. The British brigade was on the left. Gatacre was one of the first men to reach the zariba, and would have been speared if his orderly had not bayoneted his assailant. Kitchener's despatch spoke of his untiring energy and devotion to duty, his gallant leading of his men, and his hearty co-operation throughout (*Lond. Gaz.* 24 May 1898). Some said that he drove his officers and men too hard, but he was unsparing of himself. 'In the ranks they call him "General Backacher" and love him' (Steevens, p. 61). He was promoted major-general on 25 June. In the further operations, which ended with the capture of Omdurman (2 Sept.), he commanded a division of two British brigades. He was again mentioned in despatches, received the thanks of parliament, and was made K.C.B. (15 Nov.). He received the British and Egyptian medals with two clasps and the Medjidie (2nd class). On 15 Dec. he was made a freeman of Shrewsbury, and in February 1899 he received a reward for distinguished service.

On 8 Dec. 1898 he took over command of the eastern district. On 21 Oct. 1899 he embarked for South Africa, to command the third division of the army corps sent out under Sir Redvers Buller [q. v. Suppl. II]. With one exception all the battalions of his division went to Natal to save Ladysmith, while Gatacre himself remained in Cape Colony, charged with the defence of the railway from East London to Bethulie and the country on each side of it. On 2 Dec. Buller asked Gatacre if he could not close with the enemy, or otherwise hinder their advance southward. On the night of 9 Dec. Gatacre made an attempt to seize the railway junction at Stormberg. He had by this time three battalions (Northumberland fusiliers, royal Irish rifles, and royal Scots), some mounted infantry, and two batteries of field artillery. Without good maps and led astray by the guides, his force, instead of surprising the enemy, was itself surprised on the march. A confused fight followed, in which some mischances occurred, and retreat became necessary. Many men were left behind, worn out with fatigue, and out of a total of 3035 there was a loss of 696. 'I think you were quite right to try the night attack, and hope better luck next time,' was Buller's reply to Gatacre's report of his failure. Lord Roberts on his arrival investigated the facts, and came to the conclusion that Gatacre had shown want of judgment and of ordinary precaution (*Lond. Gaz.* 16 March 1900).

By his orders Gatacre acted on the defensive for the next three months, barring reconnaissances on 23 Feb. and 5 March 1900. On 15 March he crossed the Orange river at Bethulie with his division, now numbering 5000 men, and came in touch with the main army, which was at Bloemfontein. He was placed in charge of the lines of communication. On the 19th he was told 'it is very desirable British troops should be seen all over the country,' and was asked if he could send a force to Smithfield, which he did. On the 28th Lord Roberts telegraphed, 'If you have enough troops at your disposal, I should like you to occupy Dewetsdorp,' and he sent there three companies of the Irish rifles and two of mounted infantry. On the 31st, in consequence of De Wet's successful stroke at Sannah's Post, there came orders to draw in outlying parties, especially the Dewetsdorp detachment. These were passed on without delay, and the detachment reached Reddersburg on 3 April. There it was surrounded, and surrendered after twenty-four hours' fighting, when Gatacre with a small relieving force was within a few miles of it. It is not easy to see where he was in fault; but he was held responsible for what had occurred, was relieved of his command on 10 April, and returned to England (Maurice, ii. 300–11 and 614). He was informed that there was no slur upon his honour, his personal courage, his energy and zeal, 'which are beyond all question.' He received the Queen's medal for South Africa with two clasps.

He resumed command of the eastern district at Colchester, and remained there till 8 Dec. 1903. He was placed on the retired list on 19 March 1904, but was employed for some months in connection with remounts and the registration of horses. Having joined the board of the Kordofan trading company, he went out to explore rubber forests in Abyssinia towards the end of 1905. He caught fever from camping in a swamp, died at Iddeni on 18 Jan. 1906, and was buried at Gambela. A tablet was put up to his memory in Claverley church, Shropshire.

Gatacre married (1) in 1876 Alice Susan Louisa, third daughter of Anthony La Touche Kerwen, D.D., dean of Limerick, by whom he had three sons, and whom he divorced in 1892; (2) on 10 Nov. 1895 Beatrix, daughter of Horace, Lord Davey [q. v. Suppl. II], who survived him without issue.

[An admirable life of him, by Lady Gatacre, 1910; The Times, 6 March 1906; Captains G. J. and F. E. Younghusband, The Relief of Chitral, 1895; G. W. Steevens, With Kitchener to Khartum, 1898; Sir F. Maurice, Official History of the War in South Africa; S.A. War Commission, Evidence, ii. 272–8.] E. M. L.

GATHORNE-HARDY, GATHORNE, first Earl of Cranbrook (1814–1906), statesman, born on 1 Oct. 1814 at the Manor House, Bradford, was third son of John Hardy (*d.* 1855), of Dunstall Hall, Staffordshire, the chief proprietor of Low Moor ironworks, judge of the duchy of Lancaster court at Pontefract and member of parliament for Bradford, by his wife Isabel, the eldest daughter of Richard Gathorne of Kirkby Lonsdale, Westmoreland. After attending preparatory schools at Bishopton near Studley, at Hammersmith, and at Haslewood near Birmingham, Gathorne was admitted in 1827 to Shrewsbury school, and in January 1833 he entered Oriel College, Oxford. He graduated B.A. in 1836 with a second class in classics, and proceeded M.A. in 1861 in order to vote against Gladstone. On 2 May 1840 Hardy was called to the bar at the Inner Temple, and joined the northern circuit. Shrewd business qualities combined with family interest and Yorkshire clannishness soon attracted clients. He rapidly attained prominence in his profession, and by 1855 he had acquired a complete lead on sessions and at the parliamentary bar. In the same year he applied for silk, but to his disappointment promotion was refused him. His father's death, however, in 1855 left him ample means, and allowed him to devote himself to politics.

Henceforth political interests became all-absorbing. In 1847 Hardy had unsuccessfully contested Bradford in the conservative interest, and in 1856 he entered the House of Commons as conservative member for Leominster, which he continued to represent till 1865. He rapidly won the esteem and confidence of Spencer Walpole [q. v.], and on his recommendation he was appointed under-secretary for the home department on 25 Feb. 1858, in Lord Derby's second administration. Like other members of the tory party, Hardy began by distrusting Benjamin Disraeli, then chancellor of the exchequer and leader of the House of Commons, as 'a shifty and unsafe tactician.' When a circular from the chief whip, Sir William Jolliffe [q. v.], requested closer attention to his parliamentary duties, Hardy impulsively tendered his resignation, which he withdrew on the interposition of Spencer Walpole. He remained in office till the fall of the Derby ministry on 14 June 1859.

In opposition Hardy found more scope for initiative and independence. His dashing attacks on John Bright and Lord John Russell contributed to the withdrawal of the abortive reform bill of 1860; and at the end of the session he declined an offer of the post of chief whip. Active in championing the rights and privileges of the Church of England, he helped in 1862 to reject a bill relieving nonconformists from the payment of church rates. Devotion to the established church recommended Hardy to the electors of the University of Oxford when they were bent, in 1865, on opposing Gladstone's re-election. Hardy somewhat reluctantly accepted the nomination of the conservatives. His victory by a majority of 180 on 18 July gave him a foremost place in the affairs of his party.

On the formation of Lord Derby's third administration Hardy was appointed on 2 July 1866 president of the poor law board, and was sworn of the privy council. After an exhaustive inquiry he introduced a poor law amendment bill on 8 Feb. 1867, and carried it through all its stages without any substantial alteration. This measure for the relief of the London poor established a metropolitan asylum for sick and insane paupers, provided separate accommodation for fever and smallpox patients, and gave some relief to poor parishes by a more equitable re-apportionment of the metropolitan poor rate and by charging the salaries of medical officers upon the common fund.

Hardy remained in the cabinet amid the dissensions over the reform bill of 1867, to which, despite misgivings, he gave a full support. Disraeli's personality told upon him and he had become an enthusiastic disciple.

In May 1867, on the resignation of Spencer Walpole after the Hyde Park riots, Hardy accepted the difficult post of home secretary. The liberal opposition compelled him to withdraw a bill declaring it to be illegal to use the parks for the purposes of political discussion. But he faced the Fenian conspiracy with courage. He refused to commute the capital sentence passed on the Fenian murderers at Manchester, although a disorderly mob forced its way into the home office. His life was repeatedly threatened, and warnings which he received compelled him to impose special restrictions on Queen Victoria's movements. The intimate relations which he established with Queen Victoria [q. v. Suppl. I] at this critical period were maintained throughout her reign.

After the resignation of the Disraeli ministry in 1868 Hardy rendered telling service to his party in debate, especially in conflict with Gladstone. His impassioned speech on the second reading of the Irish church disestablishment bill on 25 March 1869 proved a formidable, if 'an uncompromising, defence of laws and institutions as they are' (MORLEY, *Life of Gladstone*, 1903, ii. 265). As occasional leader of the opposition in Disraeli's absence he lost few opportunities of provoking collision with the prime minister. The appointment of Sir Robert Collier (afterwards Lord Monkswell) [q. v.] to the judicial committee of the privy council and the Ewelme rectory presentation in 1872 prompted him to scathing criticism, which damaged the government.

On the formation of Disraeli's second administration Hardy was appointed secretary of state for war on 21 Feb. 1874. Soon after assuming office he had a passing difference with his chief on church matters. A moderate although sincere churchman, he opposed on 9 July 1874 the public worship regulation bill, despite the protection given it by Disraeli, and he supported Gladstone in a speech which was listened to with some disapproval by his own side (LUCY, *Diary of the Disraeli Parliament*, 1885, p. 34). Hardy remained at the war office more than four years. The army reforms which Viscount Cardwell [q. v.] had inaugurated were still incomplete, and it fell to his successor to supplement and carry on his work. His regimental exchanges bill, which was passed in 1875, legalised the payment of money by officers to those desirous of exchanging regiments with them, and was denounced by the opposition as restoring the purchase system under another name. In the debates on the Eastern question (1876–8) Hardy took a prominent part, cordially supporting Disraeli's philo-Turkish policy, and busily occupying himself during 1878 in making preparations for the despatch of an expeditionary force to the Mediterranean in the event of war. In the debate on 4 Feb. 1878, when Gladstone urged the House of Commons to reject the vote of credit of 6,000,000*l.* which was demanded by the government, Hardy impressively denounced Gladstone's active agitation in the country (*ibid.* p. 385).

When Disraeli was forced by ill-health to leave the House of Commons in August 1876 Hardy expected to fill the place of leader, and he was disappointed by the selection of Sir Stafford Northcote [q. v.], but his strong instinct of party loyalty led him quickly to resign himself to the situation.

In the rearrangement of the cabinet which followed the resignation of the foreign minister, Edward Henry Stanley, fifteenth earl of Derby [q. v.], in March 1878, Hardy became secretary for India in succession to Lord Salisbury, who went to the foreign office. Reluctance to come into competition with Sir Stafford Northcote, the new leader of the House of Commons, mainly accounted for Hardy's retirement to the House of Lords on 11 May 1878, when he was raised to the peerage as Viscount Cranbrook of Hemsted. He took his title from his country seat in Kent, and at the desire of his family he assumed the additional surname of Gathorne.

Lord Cranbrook's first official duty at the India office was to sanction the Vernacular Press Act of 1878, which empowered the government to silence Indian newspapers that promoted disaffection, but he struck out the clause exempting from the act editors who submitted their articles to an official censor. He expressed doubt of the general principle of the act, declaring that the vernacular press was a valuable and one of the few available means of ascertaining facts of the Indian people's social condition and political sentiment (PAUL, *History of Modern England*, 1905, iv. 78). His relations with the viceroy, Lord Lytton, were invariably cordial. When Lytton exercised his prerogative of overruling his council on the question of reducing the cotton duties, Cranbrook in the council at home confirmed Lytton's action by his casting vote (*East India Cotton Duties, White Paper*, 1879). Lord Cranbrook fully shared the viceroy's apprehensions of Russian expansion in central Asia, and supported Lytton's forward policy on the north-west frontier, which aimed at restoring British influence in Afghanistan. When Ameer Shere Ali refused to receive the

British envoy, he was at one with Beaconsfield in regarding war as inevitable. In a powerful despatch dated 18 Nov. 1878 he justified the coercion of the Ameer, assigning the responsibility for Shere Ali's estrangement to the action of Gladstone's government in 1873 (H. B. HANNA, *The Second Afghan War,* 1899, ii. 135). On 5 Dec. 1878 he reaffirmed this conviction in the House of Lords, despite the attacks of Lord Northbrook [q. v. Suppl. II] and other liberals (*Hansard,* 3 S. ccxliii. 40). After the conclusion of the peace of Gandamak on 26 May 1879 Lord Cranbrook enthusiastically supported the appointment of a British resident to Cabul. But the murder of the resident, Sir Louis Cavagnari [q. v.], on 3 Sept. 1879 reopened the war. As soon as Lord Roberts' victories had once more restored Anglo-Indian supremacy he approved of Lytton's scheme for the separation of Kandahar from Kabul as the best means of counteracting Russian influence. But the practical difficulties of a partition proved stronger than he realised, for Abdurrahman, the new ameer, claimed the whole territory of his predecessor. The situation was still precarious when the ministers resigned on 22 April 1880.

After the fall of the Beaconsfield government Lord Cranbrook confined himself in opposition to occasional criticism of the government in the House of Lords. As an advocate of ecclesiastical reform on conservative lines he sat on the royal commission on cathedral churches from 1879 to 1885. His colleagues continued to place unbounded confidence in his integrity and shrewd judgment, but he played a less prominent part in public affairs. With Lord Salisbury he was in complete sympathy and on terms of close friendship. For Lord Randolph Churchill [q. v. Suppl. I] and the forward wing of the conservative party he had small regard. On 25 June 1885 he joined the conservative 'government of caretakers' as lord president of the council, a post which he again held in Lord Salisbury's second administration from 1886 to 1892. Owing to his inability to speak foreign languages he declined the foreign secretaryship in 1886, and likewise had the refusal of the Irish viceroyalty. As lord president of the council Cranbrook was mainly concerned with education. His churchmanship made him anxious to protect the voluntary schools. He cherished doubts of the prudence of the education bill of 1891, which established free education in elementary schools, but as a government measure he felt bound to give it official support.

Lord Cranbrook resigned with Lord Salisbury's ministry on 12 August 1892, and was created earl of Cranbrook on 22 August. After Gladstone was again in power Cranbrook denounced with unusual vigour and fluency the government's home rule bill in the second reading debate in the House of Lords on 7 Sept. 1893, when the government was heavily defeated; in 1886 and again in 1895 he refused the offer of the chairmanship of the house of laymen in convocation. After the general election of 1895 he retired from public life. He retained his clearness of mind to the end. He died at Hemsted Park on 30 Oct. 1906, and was buried at Benenden, Kent.

Lord Cranbrook, who was elected to the Literary Society in 1860, was the recipient of many honours. In 1865 Oxford conferred on him the hon. degree of D.C.L. In 1868 he was made a bencher of the Inner Temple; and in 1880, on his resignation of the India office, he became G.C.S.I. In 1892 he received the hon. degree of LL.D. from Cambridge, and in 1894 he was elected an hon. fellow of Oriel College, Oxford. A good portrait, painted by Frank Holl [q. v.], belongs to the family: a copy was presented to the Carlton Club by his eldest son. A drawing, made by George Richmond [q. v.] in 1857, hangs in the National Portrait Gallery. A caricature appeared in 'Vanity Fair' in 1872.

Cranbrook was a competent and strenuous administrator, an admirable 'House of Commons man,' a good debater and platform speaker. His speeches were straightforward, dashing party attacks; they excited the enthusiasm of his own side but reached no high intellectual level. Although combative by nature, he bore his political opponents no illwill. He had plenty of ambition, but was capable of suppressing it at the call of party and public interests. He was an ardent sportsman and a man of varied culture. Although he held strong views in church matters, he was free from prejudice. He disliked the opposition to the appointment of Frederick Temple [q. v. Suppl. II] to the bishopric of Exeter in 1869, and disapproved the attempt of the clerical party to oust Dean Stanley [q. v.] from the select preachership at Oxford in 1872. He regarded a broad and reasonable churchmanship as the foundation of conservatism.

Hardy married on 29 March 1838 Jane, third daughter of James Orr of Ballygowan and afterwards of Hollywood House, co. Down. She was made a Lady of the imperial order of the crown of India in 1878, and died on 13 Nov. 1897. By her he had issue four sons and five daughters, of whom one son and two daughters predeceased him. His eldest son, John Stewart, second earl (*b.* 1839), died on 13 July 1911, and was succeeded in the title by his eldest son, Gathorne, third earl of Cranbrook. The third son, Alfred Erskine (*b.* 1845), M.P. for Canterbury from 1878 to 1880 and for East Grinstead from 1886 to 1895, became a railway commissioner in 1905 and published a memoir of his father in 1910.

[A. E. Gathorne Hardy, Gathorne Hardy, 1st Earl of Cranbrook, a memoir, 1910; The Times, 31 Oct., 5 Nov. 1906, and Lit. Suppl. 24 March 1910; Athenæum and Spectator, 9 April 1910; Saturday Review, 19 March 1910; Paul, History of Modern England, 1905, vols. iii. and iv.; Clayden, England under Lord Beaconsfield, 1880; Lucy, Diary of the Home Rule Parliament, 1896; Lady Betty Balfour, Lord Lytton's Indian Administration, 1899; Sir John Mowbray, Seventy Years at Westminster, 1900; Annual Register, 1860–80; Grant Duff, Notes from a Diary.]
G. S. W.

GATTY, ALFRED (1813–1903), vicar of Ecclesfield and author, born in London on 18 April 1813, was second surviving son of Robert Gatty, solicitor, of Angel Court and Finsbury Square, London, by his wife Mary, daughter of Edward Jones of Arnold, Nottinghamshire. The family originally came from Cornwall, where it had been settled since the fifteenth century. Gatty entered Charterhouse in 1825, and was removed to Eton in 1829. For a time he prepared for the legal profession, but on 28 April 1831 he matriculated from Exeter College, Oxford, and graduated B.A. in 1836, proceeding M.A. in 1839 and D.D. in 1860. Gatty was ordained deacon in 1837 and priest in the following year. From 1837 to 1839 he was curate of Bellerby, Yorkshire. In the latter year he married, and was thereupon nominated by his wife's maternal grandfather, Thomas Ryder of Hendon, Middlesex, to the vicarage of Ecclesfield, near Sheffield, which he held for sixty-four years. Under his care the church was completely restored in 1861. In the same year he was appointed rural dean. He became sub-dean of York minster in 1862, and in the course of his career served under six archbishops of York. He died at Ecclesfield on 20 Jan. 1903. Gatty was twice married: (1) on 8 July 1839 to Margaret 1809–1873) [q. v.], youngest daughter of Alexander John Scott [q. v.], by whom he had six sons and four daughters; and (2) on 1 Oct. 1884 to Mary Helen, daughter of Edward Newman of Barnsley, Yorkshire, who survived him without issue. The third son of the first marriage, Sir Alfred Scott-Gatty, has been Garter King-of-arms since 1904, and the second daughter, Mrs. Juliana Horatia Ewing [q. v.], made a reputation as a writer for the young. A portrait of Gatty by Mrs. S. E. Waller, which was presented to him by his parishioners on the fiftieth anniversary of his incumbency, belongs to his second son, Reginald Gatty, rector of Hooton Roberts, Yorkshire.

Gatty's literary labours were prolonged and various. While still an undergraduate he published a slight volume of verse, 'The Fancies of a Rhymer' (1833). Later he collaborated with his wife, Margaret Gatty, in 'Recollections of the Life of the Rev. A. J. Scott, D.D., Lord Nelson's chaplain' (1842), in an edition of the 'Autobiography of Joseph Wolff' (1860), in a descriptive account of a tour in Ireland, entitled 'The old Folks from Home' (1861), and in the compilation of 'A Book of Sundials' (1872; 4th edit. 1900). Gatty repeatedly lectured before the Sheffield Literary and Philosophical Society, and published a useful 'Key to Tennyson's "In Memoriam"' (1881; 5th edit. 1894). But his name was best known as a writer on local topography and archæology. In 1847 appeared his learned essay on 'The Bell; its Origin, History, and Uses' (2nd edit. 1848). This was followed in 1869 by an enlarged folio edition of Joseph Hunter's 'Hallamshire' and in 1873 by a popular history of 'Sheffield, Past and Present.' Between 1846 and 1858 Gatty also issued four volumes of sermons.

[The Times, 21 Jan. 1903; A. Gatty, A Life at One Living, 1884; Men of the Time, 1899; private information from Sir Alfred Scott-Gatty.]
G. S. W.

GEE, SAMUEL JONES (1839–1911), physician, son of William Gee by his wife Lydia Sutton, was born in London on 13 Sept. 1839. His father had a position of trust in a business house and his mother was a person of remarkable ability. In 1847 he was sent to a private school at Enfield and then to University College school in London from 1852 till 1854. He matriculated at the University of London in May 1857, studied medicine at University College, graduated M.B. in 1861 and M.D. in 1865. He was elected a fellow of the Royal College of Physicians in 1870. He was appointed a resident house surgeon at the Hospital for Sick Children in Great Ormond Street, London, in 1865, and there became known to (Sir) Thomas Smith [q.v. Suppl. II], the surgeon, through whose influence he was elected assistant physician at St. Bartholomew's Hospital on 5 March 1868. On 24 Oct. 1878 he was elected physician and on 22 Sept. 1904 consulting physician, so continuing till his death. In the school of St. Bartholomew's he was demonstrator of morbid anatomy (1870–4), lecturer on pathological anatomy (1872–8), and lecturer on medicine (1878–93). He was also assistant physician and physician to the Hospital for Sick Children and became one of the chief authorities of his time on the diseases of children. At the Royal College of Physicians he delivered the Gulstonian lectures 'On the heat of the body' in 1871, the Bradshaw lecture 'On the signs of acute peritoneal diseases' in 1892, and the Lumleian lectures 'On the causes and forms of bronchitis and the nature of pulmonary emphysema and asthma' in 1899. He was a censor in the college in 1893–4 and senior censor in 1897. He attained a large practice and was consulted in all branches of medicine. He was appointed physician to George, Prince of Wales, in 1901. His observation was acute and systematic and his treatment always judicious. He deserved the reputation which he attained of being one of the first physicians of his time. He wrote many papers on medical subjects, nearly all of which have permanent value. The earliest were on chicken-pox, scarlet fever, and tubercular meningitis, and appeared in Reynolds's 'System of Medicine,' vols. i. and ii. (1866 and 1868), and forty-six others appeared in the 'St. Bartholomew's Hospital Reports.' He published in 1870 'Auscultation and Percussion, together with other Methods of Physical Examination of the Chest' (5th edit. 1906), which is at once the most exact and the most literary account of its subject in English. Robert Bridges in his 'Carmen Elegiacum' of 1877 has described Gee's appearance and methods of demonstration at the period of his work upon this book:

> 'Teque auscultantem palpantem et percutientem
> Pectora, sic morbi ducere signa vident.'

Gee's only other book was 'Medical Lectures and Aphorisms,' which appeared in 1902 and has had three editions. It contains fourteen lectures or essays and 272 aphorisms collected by Dr. T. J. Horder, once his house physician. The aphorisms represent very well the form of Gee's teaching at the bedside. Its dogmatic method he had learned from Sir William Jenner [q. v. Suppl. I], but his own reading of seventeenth-century literature coloured his expressions both in speaking and writing. His description of the child's head in hydrocephalus as distinguished from the enlarged skull of rickets and his observations on enlarged spleen in children are the passages of his writings which may most justly be considered as scientific discoveries. He wrote a short essay on Sydenham (*St. Bartholomew's Hospital Reports*, vol. xix.), one on Abraham Cowley (*St. Bartholomew's Hospital Journal*, 1903), and an article on the death of Andrew Marvell (*Athenæum*, 5 Sept. 1874).

He was librarian of the Royal Medical and Chirurgical Society from 1887 to 1899, and had a wide knowledge of books on medicine, his favourite English medical writers being Sydenham, Morton, and Heberden. He read Montaigne often, and had studied Milton, Phineas Fletcher, and Hobbes.

During the period of his active practice in London he lived first at 54 Harley Street, and then at 31 Upper Brook Street, Grosvenor Square. He died suddenly of heart disease at Keswick on 3 Aug. 1911. His remains were cremated, and his ashes deposited in the columbarium of Kensal Green cemetery, London. He married, on 7 Dec. 1875, Sarah, daughter of Emanuel Cooper, Mr. Robert Bridges, the poet, being his best man. His wife died before him, and they had two daughters, of whom one survived her father.

[Personal knowledge; St. Bart. Hosp. Reports, vol. xlvii.; St. Bart. Hosp. Journal, Oct. and Nov. 1911, obit. notices by Norman Moore, Howard Marsh, and T. J. Horder; works.] N. M.

GEIKIE, JOHN CUNNINGHAM (1824–1906), religious writer, born in Edinburgh on 26 Oct. 1824, was second son of Archibald Geikie, presbyterian minister in Toronto and subsequently at Canaan, Connecticut. Geikie received his early education in Edinburgh, and afterwards studied divinity for four years at Queen's College, Kingston, Ontario. Ordained a presbyterian minister in 1848, he first engaged in missionary work in Canada. From 1851 to 1854 he was presbyterian minister at Halifax, Nova Scotia. In 1860 he returned to Great Britain and held a presbyterian charge at Sunderland till 1867, and at Islington Chapel from 1867 to 1873. In 1876 he was ordained deacon in the Church of England and priest next year. He was curate of St. Peter's, Dulwich (1876–9), rector of Christ

Church, Neuilly, Paris (1879–81), vicar of St. Mary's, Barnstaple (1883–5), and vicar of St. Martin-at-Palace, Norwich (1885–90). In 1871 he was made hon. D.D. of Queen's College, Kingston, Ontario, and in 1891 hon. LL.D. of Edinburgh University. In 1890 he retired, owing to ill-health, to Bournemouth, where he died on 1 April 1906. He was buried at Barnstaple. He had been awarded a civil list pension of 50*l.* in 1898. He married in 1849 Margaret, daughter of David Taylor of Dublin. She survived him with two sons.

Geikie enjoyed a wide reputation as a writer of popular books on biblical and religious subjects. Spurgeon described him as 'one of the best religious writers of the age.' Scholarly, imaginative, and lucid, his chief writings dealt on orthodox lines with historical and practical rather than with theological themes. His most ambitious work was 'Hours with the Bible, or, the Scriptures in the Light of Modern Discovery and Knowledge' (10 vols. 1881–4; new edit. largely re-written, 12 vols. 1896–7). His 'Life and Words of Christ' (2 vols. 1877; new edit. 1 vol. 1891) reached a circulation of nearly 100,000 copies, and Delitzsch placed the book in 'the highest rank.' He was deeply interested in the exploration of Palestine under the direction of Claude Régnier Conder [q. v. Suppl. II], and several visits to the country supplied him with material for 'The Holy Land and the Bible: A Book of Scripture Illustrations gathered in Palestine' (2 vols. 1887; abridged edit. 1903). Among Geikie's other works were: 1. 'George Stanley, or Life in the Woods,' 1864; 2nd edit. 1874. 2. 'Entering on Life,' 1870. 3. 'Old Testament Portraits,' 1878; new edit. entitled 'Old Testament Characters,' 1880; enlarged edit. 1884. 4. 'The English Reformation,' 1879, a popular history from the ultra-Protestant standpoint which ran through numerous editions. 5. 'The Precious Promises, or Light from Beyond,' 1882. 6. 'Landmarks of Old Testament History,' 1894. 7. 'The Vicar and his Friends,' 1901. Geikie was also a voluminous contributor to religious magazines.

[Scotsman, 3 April 1906; Allibone's Dict.; Crockford's Clerical Directory.] W. F. G.

GELL, Sir JAMES (1823–1905), Manx lawyer and judge, born at Kennaa on 13 Jan. 1823, was second son of John Gell of Kennaa, Isle of Man. The family of Gell held land there for more than four centuries. After education at Castletown grammar school and King William's College, Gell at sixteen was articled to the clerk of the rolls, John McHutchin, in Castletown, and was admitted to the Manx bar on 16 Jan. 1845. He enjoyed a large and important practice, and became known as the chief authority on Manx law and custom. In 1854 he was appointed high bailiff of Castletown, and in May 1866, the year of the Manx Reform Act, became attorney-general. That office he filled with distinction for over thirty-two years. He drafted with much skill nearly all the Acts which came into operation during the period. From 1898 to 1900 he was first deemster, and from 1900 till death clerk of the rolls.

Gell temporarily filled the post of deputy governor in 1897, acting governor in July 1902, and deputy governor in November 1902. He was a member of the legislative council and of the Tynwald court for thirty-nine years. An intensely patriotic Manxman, he championed all the rights and privileges of the island. He took an active part in educational and religious work. He was chairman of the insular justices from 1879, a trustee of King William's College, and chairman of the council of education from 1872 to 1881. For many years he was chairman of the Manx Society for the Publication of National Documents, and he edited in 1867 vol. xii. of Parr's 'Abstract of Laws of the Isle of Man.' He was also editor for the insular government of the statute laws of the Isle from 1836 to 1848, and he supervised and annotated a revised edition of the statutes dating from 1417 to 1895.

An earnest churchman, he was for the greater part of his life a Sunday-school teacher, and was one of the church commissioners, the trustees of Manx church property. He was knighted in 1877. He was acting governor when King Edward VII and Queen Alexandra paid their surprise visit to the isle in 1902, and he received the honour of C.V.O. He died at Castletown on 12 March 1905. He married on 17 Dec. 1850 Amelia Marcia (*d.* 1899), daughter of William Gill, vicar of Malew, a well-known Manx scholar and representative of an ancient local family. Of four sons and three daughters, two sons, Mr. James Stowell Gell, high bailiff of Douglas and Castletown, and William Gell, vicar of Pontefract, Yorkshire, with one daughter, survive.

[The Times, 13 March 1905; Men of the Time, 1899; official Debates of the Legislature, vols. 1 to 22.] W. C.

GEORGE WILLIAM FREDERICK CHARLES, second Duke of Cambridge, Earl of Tipperary and Baron Culloden (1819–1904), field-marshal and commander-in-chief of the army, was only son of Adolphus Frederick, first duke [q. v.], the youngest son of George III. His mother was Augusta Wilhelmina Louisa, daughter of Frederick, landgrave of Hesse Cassel. He was born at Cambridge House, Hanover, on 26 March 1819, and being at that time the only grandchild of George III, his birth was formally attested by three witnesses —the duke of Clarence (later William IV), the earl of Mayo, and George Henry Rose, P.C. His father was governor-general of Hanover, and Prince George lived there till 1830, when he was sent to England to be under the care of William IV and Queen Adelaide. His tutor was John Ryle Wood, afterwards canon of Worcester, who had great influence over him and won his lasting attachment. At Wood's instance he began a diary, as a boy of fourteen, a singularly naive confession of his shortcomings, and he kept it up to within a few months of his death. In 1825 he was made G.C.H., and in Aug. 1835 K.G. In 1836 he rejoined his parents in Hanover, his tutor being replaced by a military governor, lieutenant-colonel William Henry Cornwall of the Coldstream guards. He had been colonel in the Jäger battalion of the Hanoverian guards since he was nine years old; he now began to learn regimental duty both as a private and an officer.

On the accession of his first cousin, Queen Victoria, in June 1837, Hanover passed to the duke of Cumberland, and the duke of Cambridge returned with his family to England. On 3 Nov. Prince George was made brevet colonel in the British army, and in Sept. 1838 he went to Gibraltar to learn garrison duties. He was attached to the 33rd foot for drill. After spending six months there and six months in travel in the south of Europe, he came home, and was attached to the 12th lancers, with which he served for two years in England and Ireland. On 15 April 1842 he was gazetted to the 8th light dragoons as lieutenant-colonel, but ten days afterwards he was transferred to the 17th lancers as colonel. He commanded this regiment at Leeds, and helped the magistrates to preserve the peace of the town during the industrial disturbances in August.

On 20 April 1843 he was appointed colonel on the staff, to command the troops in Corfu. He spent two years there, and on Lord Seaton's recommendation he received the G.C.M.G. He was promoted major-general on 7 May 1845. After commanding the troops at Limerick for six months, he was appointed to the Dublin district on 1 April 1847, and held that command five years. He had a large force under him, and worked hard at the training of the troops. In 1848 political disturbances made his post no sinecure. By the death of his father on 8 July 1850 Prince George became duke of Cambridge, and an income of 12,000*l.* a year was voted him by Parliament. He was made K.P. on 18 Nov. 1851. For nearly two years from 1 April 1852 he was inspecting general of cavalry at headquarters, and the memoranda on the state of the army which he then drew up (Verner, i. 39–59) show how much he concerned himself with questions of organisation. He was in command of the troops at the funeral of the duke of Wellington. On 28 Sept. 1852 he was transferred as colonel from the 17th lancers to the Scots fusilier guards.

In February 1854 the duke was chosen to command a division in the army to be sent to the Crimea. He accompanied lord Raglan to Paris on 10 April, and went thence to Vienna, bearing a letter from the Queen to the Emperor Francis Joseph. Leaving Vienna on 1 May, he reached Constantinople on the 10th. He was promoted lieutenant-general on 19 June, went with his division (guards and highlanders) to Varna, and thence to the Crimea. At the Alma (20 Sept.) he and his men were in second line, behind the light division; but when the latter fell back before the Russian counter attack, the guards and highlanders came to the front and won the battle. At Inkerman (5 Nov.) the duke with the brigade of guards (the highlanders were at Balaclava) came to the help of the 2nd division very early in the day, and retook the Sandbag battery. His horse was shot under him, and he found himself left with about 100 men, while the rest pushed on down the slope. Kinglake describes him 'with an immense energy of voice and gesture . . . commanding, entreating, adjuring' the men to keep on the high ground. By the advance of another Russian column he was nearly cut off from the main position, and he and his aide-de-camp 'had regularly to ride for it in order to get back' (Verner, i. 79). The guards lost 622 officers and men out of 1361 engaged.

The duke's courage was high, but he had not the imperturbability needed for war, and his health had suffered at Varna.

Of the Alma he notes, 'When all was over I could not help crying like a child' (VERNER, i. 73). Three days before Inkerman he had written to Queen Victoria gloomily about the situation of the army. He was 'dreadfully knocked up and quite worn out' by the battle, and was persuaded to go to Balaclava for rest. He was on board the frigate Retribution, when it narrowly escaped wreck in the great storm of 14 November. On the 25th he left the Crimea for Constantinople, and on 27 Dec. a medical board invalided him to England. He was mentioned in despatches (*Lond. Gaz.* 8 Oct., 12 and 22 Nov. 1854) and received the thanks of parliament, the medal with 4 clasps, the Turkish medal, and the G.C.B. (5 July 1855). He declined the governorship of Gibraltar, and was anxious to return to the Crimea. When general Sir James Simpson [q. v.] resigned command of the army there in November, the duke tried in vain to succeed him. In January 1856 he was sent to Paris, to take part in the conference on the further conduct of the war, but the conclusion of peace in March made its plans of no effect.

On 15 July Lord Hardinge [q. v.] resigned, and the duke succeeded him as general commanding in chief. He was promoted general, and on 28 July was sworn of the privy council. The breakdown in the Crimea had led to great changes in army administration. The secretary of state for war (separated in 1854 from the colonies) took over the powers of the secretary at war, and of the board of ordnance, which was abolished. He also took over the militia and yeomanry from the home office and the commissariat from the treasury. He became responsible to parliament for the whole military administration; but the general commanding in chief, as representing the crown, enjoyed some independence in matters of discipline and command, appointments and promotions. The abolition of the board of ordnance brought the artillery and engineers under his authority, and the duke was made colonel of these two corps on 10 May 1861. The amalgamation (of which he was a strong advocate) of the European troops of the East India Company with the army of the crown in 1862 gave him general control of troops serving in India.

The volunteer movement of 1859 brought a new force into existence. He was not unfriendly to it, but had no great faith in it, and was opposed to a capitation grant. He became colonel of the 1st City of London brigade on 24 Feb. 1860. He was president of the National Rifle Association, which was founded in 1859 and had till 1887 its ranges at Wimbledon, on land of which he was principal owner; then he found it necessary to call upon it to go elsewhere, and the ranges were transferred to Bisley. He took an active part in military education, and helped to found the Staff College. He had been appointed a commissioner for Sandhurst and for the Duke of York's school in 1850, and was made governor of the Military Academy at Woolwich in 1862. On the death of the Prince Consort he exchanged the colonelcy of the Scots fusilier guards for that of the Grenadier guards. On 9 Nov. 1862 he was made field-marshal.

During the first thirteen years of his command the duke was in accord with successive war ministers, though he was continually remonstrating against reductions or urging increase of the army. But in December 1868 Edward (afterwards Viscount) Cardwell [q. v.] became secretary of state, with Gladstone as premier, and they took in hand a series of reforms which were most distasteful to him. First of all, the so-called dual government of the army, which divided responsibility and was a hindrance to reform, was abolished. By the War Office Act of 1870 the commander-in-chief was definitely subordinated to the war minister, and became one of three departmental chiefs charged respectively with combatant personnel, supply, and finance. To mark the change, the duke was required in Sept. 1871 to remove from the Horse Guards to Pall Mall. He regarded this as a blow not only to his own dignity but to the rights of the crown, and the Queen intervened on his behalf; but he had to give way.

The reconstruction of the war office was followed by the adoption of short service, the formation of an army reserve, the linking of battalions, and their localisation. The purchase of commissions was abolished, and seniority tempered by selection became the principle of promotion. The duke was opposed to all these innovations. His watchwords were discipline, *esprit de corps*, and the regimental system, all of which seemed to him to be threatened. But holding it to be for the interest of the crown and the army that he should remain at his post, he accepted a system of which he disapproved. The system held its ground notwithstanding party changes, and in 1881 it was carried a stage further by H. C. E. Childers [q. v. Suppl. I], the linked battalions being welded into territorial regiments in spite of the duke's efforts to unlink them.

On 24 Nov. 1882 he was made personal aide-de-camp to Queen Victoria, to commemorate the campaign in Egypt; and on 26 Nov. 1887, when he had completed fifty years' service in the army, he was made commander-in-chief by patent. At the end of that year his functions were much enlarged, the whole business of supply being handed over to him. Cardwell had assigned it to a surveyor-general of the ordnance, who was meant to be an experienced soldier; but the office had become political, and the complaints about stores during the Nile campaign led to its abolition. Everything except finance now came under the control of the commander-in-chief, with the adjutant-general as his deputy. During the next few years much was done to fit the army for war: supply and transport were organised and barracks improved; but the secretary of state found that the military hierarchy hindered his personal consultation of experts.

In June 1888 a very strong commission was appointed, with Lord Hartington (afterwards duke of Devonshire) [q. v. Suppl. II] as chairman, to inquire into naval and military administration; and in May 1890 they recommended that the office of commander-in-chief should be abolished when the duke ceased to hold it, and that there should be a chief of the staff. Sir Henry Campbell-Bannerman [q. v. Suppl. II], who became war minister in 1892, dissented from this recommendation; but he thought the powers of the commander-in-chief ought to be diminished, and the duke's retirement was a necessary preliminary. The call for this step grew louder, and in the spring of 1895 the duke consulted the Queen. Though 76 years of age, he felt himself physically and mentally fit for his office. The Queen replied, reluctantly, that he had better resign (Verner, ii. 395), and on 31 October he issued his farewell order, handing over the command of the army to Lord Wolseley. To soften the blow, the Queen appointed him her chief personal aide-de-camp and colonel-in-chief to the forces, with the right of holding the parade on her birthday.

In announcing to the House of Commons the duke's approaching retirement, on the eve of his own fall (21 June) Campbell-Bannerman touched on his attractive personality, his industry and activity, his devotion to the interests of the army, and his familiarity with its traditions and requirements; but dwelt especially on his common sense and knowledge of the world, his respect for constitutional proprieties and for public opinion. The army was attached to him because of his fairness. He bore no ill-will to officers who differed from him, but could discuss points of difference with good temper (Verner, ii. 272, seq.). Though in the training of the troops, as in other things, he was conservative, his thorough knowledge of close-order drill, and his outspoken, not to say emphatic, comments made him a formidable inspecting officer and kept up a high standard.

Devoted as the duke was to the army, it by no means absorbed all his energies. He undertook with alacrity the duties that fell to him as a member of the royal family, which were especially heavy after the death of the Prince Consort. For instance, in 1862 he was called upon to open the international exhibition, to entertain the foreign commissioners, and distribute the prizes. He was connected with a large number of charitable institutions, and took real interest in them; but two were pre-eminent—the London Hospital and Christ's Hospital—over both of which he presided for fifty years. He was elected president of Christ's Hospital on 23 March 1854, and was the first president who was not an alderman of the City. From that time onward he worked unsparingly for it, though latterly his efforts were mainly in opposition to the removal of the school to Horsham, 'the most wanton thing that ever was undertaken' (Sheppard, ii. 322). He was in great request as a chairman at dinners and meetings for benevolent purposes, for though not eloquent he was fluent, and had the art of getting on good terms with his audience.

In private life he was the most affectionate of men. His mother lived long enough to send her blessing to 'the best son that ever lived,' while he was being entertained at the United Service Club to celebrate his military jubilee. She died on 6 April 1889, and within a year he had another heavy blow in the death of his wife. Disregarding the Royal Marriage Act, he had married morganatically on 8 Jan. 1840 Miss Louisa Fairbrother, an actress, then 24 years of age. She lived in Queen Street, Mayfair, as Mrs. Fitzgeorge till her death on 12 Jan. 1890. She was buried at Kensal Green, the duke being chief mourner.

The duke had rooms at St. James's Palace from 1840 to 1859, when he removed to Gloucester House, Park Lane, left to him by his aunt, the duchess of Gloucester. On the death of the duchess of Cambridge the Queen granted him Kew Cottage for his life. He had been made ranger of Hyde Park and St. James's Park in 1852, and of Richmond Park in 1857. In addition to the orders already mentioned, he was made K.T. on 17 Sept. 1881, grandmaster and principal grand cross of St. Michael and St. George on 23 May 1869, G.C.S.I. in 1877, G.C.I.E. in 1887, and G.C.V.O. in 1897. Of foreign orders he received the black eagle of Prussia in 1852, the grand cordon of the legion of honour in 1855, St. Andrew of Russia in 1874, and the order of merit of Savoy in 1895. He was made colonel-in-chief of the king's royal rifle corps on 6 March 1869, of the 17th lancers on 21 June 1876, and of the Middlesex regiment on 9 Aug. 1898. He was also colonel of two Indian regiments—the 10th Bengal lancers, and the 20th Punjabis; of the Malta artillery, the Middlesex yeomanry, and the 4th battalion Suffolk regiment; of the Cambridge dragoons in the Hanoverian army (1852–66), and of the 28th foot in the Prussian army (Aug. 1889). He received the honorary degree of D.C.L. Oxford on 1 June 1853; of LL.D. Cambridge on 3 June 1864; and of LL.D. Dublin on 21 April 1868; and became one of the elder brethren of the Trinity house on 11 March 1885. He received the freedom of the City of London, with a sword, on 4 Nov. 1857, and on 19 Oct. 1896 he was presented with an address from the corporation and his bust (by Francis Williamson) was unveiled at the Guildhall. He was made a freeman of York in 1897, of Bath and of Kingston in 1898.

A series of banquets at the military clubs and messes marked the duke's retirement, but he continued for several years to preside at regimental dinners and to keep in close touch with the army. He was very vigorous for his age, rode in Queen Victoria's diamond jubilee procession of 1897, and at her funeral in 1901. He paid his last visit to Germany in August 1903, but his strength was then giving way. He died at Gloucester House on 17 March 1904 of hæmorrhage of the stomach, having outlived by a few weeks the commandership-in-chief which he held so long. On the 22nd he was buried, in accordance with his wish, beside his wife at Kensal Green. The first part of the service was at Westminster Abbey with King Edward VII as chief mourner. Five field-marshals and thirteen generals were pall-bearers. Tributes were paid to his memory in both houses of parliament. He had three sons: Colonel George William Adolphus Fitzgeorge; Rear-admiral Sir Adolphus Augustus Frederick Fitzgeorge, K.C.V.O., who became equerry to his father in 1897; and Colonel Sir Augustus Charles Frederick Fitzgeorge, K.C.V.O., C.B., who was his father's private secretary and equerry from 1886 to 1895.

In June 1907 a bronze equestrian statue of him by Captain Adrian Jones was placed in front of the new war office in Whitehall, and there is also a statue at Christ's Hospital, Horsham. There is a memorial window in the chapel of St. Michael and St. George in St. Paul's Cathedral. Of the many portraits of him the chief are one, at the age of 18, by John Lucas (at Windsor), and three as a field-marshal, by Frank Holl (at Buckingham Palace), Arthur S. Cope (at the United Service Club), and Sir Hubert von Herkomer (at the R.E. mess, Chatham). A caricature portrait appeared in 'Vanity Fair' in 1870.

[Willoughby C. Verner, Military Life of the Duke of Cambridge, 1905; J. E. Sheppard, George, Duke of Cambridge, a memoir of his private life, 2 vols. 1906; The Times, 18 March 1904; Letters of Queen Victoria, 1907; Kinglake, Invasion of the Crimea, 1863, &c.; The Panmure Papers, 1908; Sir Robert Biddulph, Lord Cardwell at the War Office, 1904; E. S. C. Childers, Life of Hugh C. E. Childers, 1901; Pearce, Annals of Christ's Hospital, 1908; Third Report of Lord Northbrook's committee on army administration, 12 Feb. 1870 (c. 54); Report of Royal Commission (Penzance) on Army Promotion, 5 Aug. 1876 (c. 1569); Report of Royal Commission (Hartington) on Naval and Military Administration, 11 Feb. 1890 (c. 5979); Catalogues of the Duke's collection of plate, pictures, porcelain, books, &c., sold at Christie's in 1904.] E. M. L.

GEORGE, HEREFORD BROOKE (1838–1910), historical writer, born at Bath on 1 Jan. 1838, was eldest of the three children (two sons and a daughter) of Richard Francis George, surgeon, by his wife Elizabeth Brooke. He entered Winchester as a scholar in 1849, and succeeded in 1856 to a fellowship at New College, Oxford. He obtained first classes in both classical and mathematical moderations in 1858, a second class in the final classical school in 1859, and a second class in the final mathematical school in 1860. He graduated B.A. in 1860, proceeding M.A. in 1862.

George was called to the bar at the Inner Temple on 6 June 1864, and followed the western circuit till 1867, when he returned to New College as tutor in the combined school of law and history. He was ordained in 1868, but undertook no parochial work. After the separation of the law and history schools in 1872 he became history tutor of New College, and filled that office till 1891. He played a prominent part in the establishment of the inter-collegiate system of lecturing at Oxford. He remained a fellow of New College till his death. His historical writing and teaching were chiefly concerned with military history (in which he was a pioneer at Oxford) and with the correlation of history and geography. His chief publications, 'Battles of English History' (1895), 'Napoleon's Invasion of Russia' (1899), 'Relations of Geography and History' (1901; 4th edit. 1910), and 'Historical Evidence' (1909), all show critical acumen and fertility of illustration, if no recondite research. His 'Genealogical Tables illustrative of Modern History' (1874; 4th edit. 1904) and 'Historical Geography of the British Empire' (1904; 4th edit. 1909) are useful compilations.

George took a large part in the work of the university as well as in the re-organisation of his own college, which he described in his 'New College, 1856–1906' (1906). He was one of the first members of the Oxford University volunteer corps, and for many years he took an important share in the work of the local examinations delegacy. George's interests received a new direction from his first visit to Switzerland in 1860, when he met Leslie Stephen at Zermatt and accompanied him up to the Riffel by the Gorner glacier. In 1862 he accompanied Stephen on the first passage by the Jungfrau Joch (MAITLAND'S *Life of Stephen*, chap. vi.), and achieved a first ascent of the Gross Viescherhorn (*Alpine Journal*, i. 97). In 1863 he made a passage of the Col du Tour Noir with Christian Almer as guide, and 'finally settled the long-debated question about the relative positions of the heads of the Argentière, Tour, and Salène glaciers, which every successive map had professed to explain in a different way' (*ibid.* pp. 125, 286). Though he enjoyed the physical exercise, his interest in climbing was chiefly geographical and scientific. He was one of the first Alpine climbers to employ photography. He joined the Alpine Club in 1861, and the establishment of the 'Alpine Journal' was suggested at a meeting in his rooms at New College; he edited its first three volumes (1863–7). In 1866 he published 'The Oberland and its Glaciers,' written 'to popularise the glacier theory of Tyndall' (*Alpine Journal*, xxv.). George was the founder of the Oxford Alpine Club.

George, who inherited a moderate fortune from his father, was director of the West of England and South Wales Bank at Bristol, although he took no active part in the management of its affairs. The failure of the bank in 1880 not only injured George financially but involved him with his fellow-directors in an abortive trial for irregularities in keeping the accounts (*Annual Reg.* 3 May 1880, p. 38). George died at Holywell Lodge, Oxford, on 15 Dec. 1910. In 1870 he married Alice Bourdillon (*d.* 1893), youngest daughter of William Cole Cole of Exmouth, by whom he had two sons.

[Personal information; College and University Records; Alpine Journal, vol. xxv. May 1911.] R. S. R.

GERARD, [JANE] EMILY, MADAME DE LASZOWSKA (1849–1905), novelist, born on 7 May 1849 at Chesters, Jedburgh, near Airdrie, Roxburghshire, was eldest sister of General Sir Montagu Gilbert Gerard [q. v. Suppl. II for parentage]. Her great-grandfather was Gilbert Gerard [q. v.], formerly a Scottish Episcopalian. Her mother became a Roman catholic in 1848, and Emily belonged to that faith. Until the age of fifteen she was educated at home; for eighteen months of a long residence with her family in Venice (1863–6) she took lessons at the house of the Comte de Chambord with his niece, Princess Marguerite, afterwards wife of Don Carlos, and with her formed a life-long intimacy; the princess died in 1893. After three years at the convent of the Sacré Cœur at Riedenburg near Bregenz in Tyrol, Emily married on 14 Oct. 1869 Chevalier Miecislas de Laszowski, member of an old Polish noble family, and an officer in the Austrian army, whose acquaintance she made in Venice. She lived first at Brzezum, Galicia, and after the death of her mother in 1870 her sisters joined her there. From 1880 onwards she devoted much time to recording her foreign experience in the form of fiction. In 1883 her husband was appointed to the command of the cavalry brigade in Transylvania, and she spent two years in the province, at Hermannstadt and Kronstadt. She embodied her observations in 'The Land beyond the Forest: Facts, Figures and Fancies from Transylvania' (1888), an excellent description of the country and its inhabitants. In 1885 her husband retired from active service with the rank of lieutant-general, and they then made their permanent home in Vienna, where she died on 11 Jan. 1905. Her husband predeceased her by five weeks (December 1904). There were two sons of the marriage.

In 1880 Emily Gerard collaborated in a novel, 'Reata' (new edit. 1881), with her sister Dorothea, who in 1886 married Julius Longard de Longgarde, also an officer in the Austrian army. A like partnership produced 'Beggar my Neighbour' (1882), 'The Waters of Hercules' (1885), and 'A Sensitive Plant' (1891). She contributed without aid several short tales to Blackwood's and Longman's 'Magazines,' reprinted in the volumes 'Bis' (1890), and 'An Electric Shock and other Stories' (1897), and published six novels, of which the best is 'The Voice of a Flower' (1893). She wrote gracefully, and made the foreign setting effective, but lacked power of characterisation. She was a competent critic; for nearly two years she furnished monthly reviews of German literature to 'The Times,' and occasional articles on new German books to 'Blackwood's Magazine.'

Other works by Emily Gerard are: 1. 'A Secret Mission,' 1891. 2. 'A Foreigner,' 1896 (inspired by her own marriage). 3. 'The Tragedy of a Nose,' 1898. 4. 'The Extermination of Love, a Study in Erotics,' 1901. 5. 'The Heron's Tower,' 1904. 6. 'Honour's Glassy Bubble,' 1906; and a preface to S. Kneipp's 'My Water Cure,' 1893.

[Burke's Landed Gentry, 1906; The Times, 12–13 Jan. 1905; Athenæum, 21 Jan. 1905; Who's Who, 1904; Helen C. Black, Pen, Pencil, Baton and Mask: Biographical Sketches, 1896; William Blackwood and his Sons, vol. iii. (by Mrs. Gerald Potter), 1898, pp. 356–8.] E. L.

GERARD, Sir MONTAGU GILBERT (1842–1905), general, born at Edinburgh on 29 June 1842, was second son in a family of three sons and four daughters of Archibald Gerard (1812–1880) of Rochsoles, near Airdrie, Lanarkshire, by his wife Euphemia Erskine (*d.* 1870), eldest daughter of Sir John Robison [q. v.]. He was a great-grandson of Alexander Gerard [q. v.], philosophical writer, and of Archibald Alison [q. v.], father of the historian. The family was originally Scottish episcopalian, but the mother joined the church of Rome in 1848, the father a little later, and the children were brought up as Roman catholics. Montagu's eldest brother became Father John Gerard, S.J., and his eldest sister was Jane Emily, Madame de Laszowska [q. v. Suppl. II]. He was admitted to Stonyhurst in 1850, and subsequently passed four years at Ushaw (1855–9).

After spending some time on the Continent, Gerard went through the usual course at Woolwich. He was gazetted lieutenant in the royal artillery on 19 April 1864, and undertook garrison duty at Gibraltar. In 1866, on being transferred to the field artillery, he was stationed in the central provinces, India. In 1867–8 he was employed on the transport train during the Abyssinian expedition; he was mentioned in despatches and received the war medal. In 1870 he joined the Bengal staff corps, and was attached to the Central India horse. Promoted captain on 19 April 1876, he acted as brigade major throughout the second Afghan war (1878–80), and had his horse wounded at the action of Deh Sarak while escorting a convoy from Chara. He took part in the second Bazar valley expedition and in the defence of Jagdallak. He accompanied General (Sir) Charles Gough's brigade to Sherpur in December 1879, and Lord Roberts's march from Kabul to Kandahar, and was engaged at the battle of 1 Sept. 1880. He was twice mentioned in despatches, and received the medal with two clasps, the bronze star, and the brevets of major (22 Nov. 1879) and of lieut.-colonel (2 March 1881). Gerard served in the Egyptian campaign of 1882, and at Alexandria fought in all the actions that followed the bombardment. He was appointed deputy assistant adjutant and quartermaster general of the cavalry division, and was present at the reconnaissance of 5 Aug. 1882, the battles of Kassassin and Tel-el-Kebir, and the surrender of Arabi Pasha. In addition to being mentioned in despatches he was given the medal with clasp, the bronze star, the C.B., and the third class of the order of the Medjidie. He became major on 19 April 1884 and brevet-colonel on 2 March 1885.

Gerard had other qualities besides those of the successful soldier. In 1881 and again in 1885 he was despatched on secret missions to Persia. After serving as district staff officer of the first class in Bengal, he was selected to take charge of the tour which the Tsarevitch (afterwards Nicholas II) made in India (Dec. 1890–Feb. 1891), and the skill with which he discharged his duties resulted in his appointment in 1892 as British military attaché at St. Petersburg. In the negotiations concerning the Pamirs boundary dispute he played a conspicuous part, and when in March 1895 an agreement was signed between Great Britain and Russia for the delimitation of their spheres of influence in central Asia, Gerard was sent out to the Pamirs at the head of a British commission. He met the Russian mission under general Shveikovsky in June at Lake Victoria, and from that point eastwards to the Chinese frontier demarcated the line which henceforth divided Russian from British interests.

In 1896 he was nominated to the command of the Hyderabad contingent, and in 1899 was promoted to the command of a first-class district in Bengal. He was created C.S.I. in 1896, K.C.S.I. in 1897, and K.C.B. in 1902. He was promoted major-general on 1 April 1897, lieutenant-general on 12 Sept. 1900, and general on 29 Feb. 1904. On the outbreak of the Russo-Japanese war in 1904 he went out to Manchuria as chief British attaché in General Kuropatkin's army; but his health succumbed to the rigours of the campaign, and he died of pneumonia at Irkutsk on 26 July 1905 on his way home from Kharbin. A requiem mass was sung at the catholic church of St. Catherine's, St. Petersburg, at which both the Tsar and King Edward VII were represented. The body was subsequently conveyed to Scotland, and buried at Airdrie on 8 September. He married on 19 Sept. 1888 Helen Adelaide, third daughter of Edward Richard Meade, a grandson of John Meade, first earl of Clanwilliam; she survived him with one son. Gerard was devoted to all forms of sport, especially big-game shooting, and recorded his experiences in 'Leaves from the Diaries of a Soldier and a Sportsman, 1865–1885' (1903).

[The Times, 28 July, 22 Aug., 9 Sept. 1905; Tablet, 12 Aug. 1905; Army List, 1905; Stonyhurst Magazine, October 1905; H. B. Hanna, The Second Afghan War, 1910, iii. 257, 511; private information from Father John Gerard, S.J.] G. S. W.

GIBB, ELIAS JOHN WILKINSON (1857–1901), orientalist, born on 3 June 1857 at 25 Newton Place, Glasgow, was only son of Elias John Gibb, wine merchant, and Jane Gilman. Both parents survived their son. He was educated first at Park School, Glasgow, under Dr. Collier, author of the 'History of England,' and afterwards at Glasgow University, where he matriculated in 1873, and pursued his studies until 1875, but took no degree. Prompted on the one hand by a strong linguistic taste, and on the other by an early delight in the book of the 'Thousand and One Nights' (Alf Layla wa Layla), and other Eastern tales, Gibb, who was well provided for, devoted himself at an early period to the Arabic, Persian, and more especially Turkish languages and literatures. Gavin Gibb, D.D., a cousin of his grandfather, who was professor of oriental languages in the University of Glasgow from 1817 to 1831, seems to be the only connection in Gibb's family history with oriental scholarship. It was apparently without external help or suggestion that Gibb published in 1879, when only twenty-two, an English translation of the account of the capture of Constantinople by the Turks, given by Sa'du'd-Dín in the 'Tûju't-Teváríkh' or 'Crown of Histories.' In 1882 there followed his 'Ottoman Poems translated into English Verse in the Original Forms,' which was the forerunner of his detailed and ambitious 'History of Ottoman Poetry,' on which he gradually concentrated his energies. In 1884 he translated from the Turkish of Alī Azīz the 'Story of Jewad.'

Moving to London on his marriage in 1889, and collecting a fine oriental library, Gibb lived the life of a studious recluse, rarely going further from London than Glasgow to stay with his parents. He travelled in France and Italy in 1889, but never visited Turkey or any Eastern country, although he spoke and wrote the Turkish language correctly, and acquired through his reading a profound sympathy with Mohammedan thought. He joined the Royal Asiatic Society about 1881. The first volume of his work on Ottoman poetry, containing an introduction (pp. 1–136) to the whole subject, not less useful to students of Arabic and Persian than to those of Turkish literature, and an account of the earlier period of Ottoman poetry (A.D. 1300–1450), was published in 1900, but in November next year, while he was putting the final touches to the second volume, he was attacked by scarlet fever, of which he died on 5 Dec. 1901. He was buried at Kensal Green cemetery, his funeral being attended by the Turkish poet 'Abdu'l Ḥaqq Ḥámid Bey and other Mohammedan friends and admirers.

In 1889 Gibb married Ida W. E. Rodriguez (afterwards Mrs. Ogilvie Gregory). On his death his library was, with small reservations, divided among the libraries of the British Museum (which received his manuscripts), the Cambridge University (which received his Arabic, Persian and Turkish books), and the British Embassy at Constantinople (which received many valuable works on the East). A summary list of the Gibb MSS. is given in his 'History of Ottoman Poetry' (vol. ii. pp. xvi—xxxi, 1902). A list of the printed oriental books, 422 in number, in the Cambridge University Library was compiled by the present writer and published by the Cambridge University Press in 1906.

By desire of Gibb's widow and parents, the present writer edited, after Gibb's death, the remainder of his 'History of Ottoman Poetry,' which, though not complete, was in an advanced stage of preparation; vol. ii. was published in 1902; vol. iii. in 1904; vol. iv. in 1905; vol. v. (containing three chapters on the 'Rise of the New School' and indexes to the whole book) in 1907; and vol. vi. (containing the Turkish originals of the poems translated in the whole work) in 1909. A seventh supplementary volume, dealing with the most recent development of Turkish poetry, from Kemál Bey to the present time, has been written in French by Dr. Rizá Tevfíq Bey, deputy for Adrianople in the Turkish parliament (1911), and is being translated into English by the present writer.

[Personal knowledge and information supplied by Gibb's sister, Mrs. Watson; notices by present writer in Athenæum, 14 Dec. 1901, and Royal Asiatic Soc.'s Journal, 1902, p. 486.] E. G. B.

GIBBINS, HENRY DE BELTGENS (1865–1907), writer on economic history, born at Port Elizabeth, Cape Colony, on 23 May 1865, was eldest son of Joseph Henry Gibbins of Port Elizabeth, South Africa, by his wife Eleanor, daughter of the Hon. J. de Beltgens of Stanford, Dominica. Educated at Bradford grammar school, he won a scholarship at Wadham College, Oxford, in 1883, and obtained a second class in classical moderations in 1885, and a second class also in the final classical schools in 1887. He graduated B.A. in the following year. In 1890 he won the Cobden prize for an economic essay in the University of Oxford, and in 1896 received the degree of D.Litt. at Dublin.

From 1889 to 1895 he worked as assistant master at the Nottingham high school. In 1891 he was ordained deacon and in 1892 priest, serving the curacy of St. Matthew's, Nottingham, from 1891 to 1893. From 1895 to 1899 he was vice-principal of Liverpool College; from 1899 to 1906 headmaster of King Charles I school at Kidderminster; in 1906 he was made principal of Lennoxville University in Canada. Ill-health obliged him to leave Canada after a short stay. On 13 Aug. 1907 he was killed by a fall from the train in the Thackley tunnel between Leeds and Bradford. He married Emily, third daughter of Dr. J. H. Bell of Bradford, by whom he had one daughter.

Gibbins devoted himself to economic study from his Oxford days and published: 1. 'Industrial History of England,' 1890. 2. 'The History of Commerce in Europe,' 1891, 2nd edit. 1897. 3. 'English Social Reformers,' 1892, 2nd edit. 1902. 4. 'British Commerce and Colonies,' 1893, 4th edit. 1909. 5. 'Economics of Commerce,' 1894, Spanish trans. 1903. 6. 'Industry in England,' 1896. 7. 'The English People in the Nineteenth Century,' 1898; 2nd edit. 1900; Russian trans. 1901. 8. 'Economic and Industrial Progress of the Century,' 1901. He was a contributor to Palgrave's 'Dictionary of Political Economy' and edited for Messrs. Methuen their 'Social Questions of the Day' series (1891) and also their 'Commercial' series (1893). His economic work popularly illustrated the historical methods of economic study.

[The Times, 14 Aug. 1907; Foster's Alumni Oxon.; private information.] M. E.

GIBBS, HENRY HUCKS, first Baron Aldenham (1819–1907), merchant and scholar, born in Powis Place, Queen Square Bloomsbury, on 31 August 1819, was eldest son of George Henry Gibbs (1785–1842) of Aldenham, Hertfordshire, and Clifton Hampden, Oxfordshire, by his wife Caroline (*d.* 1850), daughter of Charles Crawley, rector of Stowe-nine-churches, Northamptonshire. His family came from Clyst St. George, and had been settled in Devonshire from the time of Richard II. Sir Vicary Gibbs [q. v.], the judge, was his great-uncle.

After education at Redland near Bristol and at Rugby, Gibbs entered Exeter College, Oxford, in 1838, and graduated B.A. with third-class classical honours in 1841, proceeding M.A. in 1844. On leaving the university he joined on 17 April 1843 the London house of Antony Gibbs & Sons, merchants and foreign bankers. His grandfather, Antony Gibbs (1756–1815), initiated the business in 1789 in Spain, and opened the London house in September 1808. In 1808 Gibbs's father, and in 1813 his uncle William (1790–1875), became partners. In 1821 a branch firm was opened in Peru. In 1875 Gibbs succeeded his uncle as head of the firm. In 1881 an older firm, Gibbs, Bright & Co., of Liverpool and Bristol, sometime under the headship of Gibbs's great-uncle George (1753–1818), elder brother of Antony Gibbs, was, with its Australian branches, taken over by Antony Gibbs & Sons.

Henry Hucks Gibbs took a leading part in London commercial affairs, serving as a director of the Bank of England (1853–1901) and governor (1875–7). He was specially interested in currency questions, was a strong advocate of bimetallism, and an active president of the Bimetallic League. In 1876 he published 'A Letter to the Marquess of Salisbury on the Depreciation of Silver'; in 1879 'Bimetallism in England and Abroad,' and in 1879 'Silver and Gold, a letter to M. Cazalet' (republished, with additions, in 1881 as 'The Double Standard'). In 1886 he issued, with Henry Riversdale Grenfell, 'The Bimetallic Controversy,' a collection of pamphlets, nine of which were from his pen; and in 1893 he wrote 'A Colloquy on Currency' (3rd edit. 1894).

Gibbs was a prominent member of the conservative party in the City of London, and was chairman of the Conservative Association there. He was returned to parliament as a member for the City at a bye-election on 18 April 1891, but retired at the general election in July 1892. In May 1880 Gibbs with other members of his family founded, in the conservative interest, the 'St. James's Gazette,' with Frederick Greenwood [q. v. Suppl. II] as editor, and the paper remained their property until 1888. He served in 1877–8 on the royal commission on the Stock Exchange, on the City parochial charities commission in 1880, and on the commission of 1885–6 upon the depression of trade. Gibbs, who was a J.P. for Hertfordshire and Middlesex, and high sheriff of Hertfordshire in 1884, was created Baron Aldenham, of Aldenham, on 31 Jan. 1896.

A strong churchman, Gibbs was a munificent benefactor to the church. With Lord John Manners, seventh duke of Rutland [q. v. Suppl. II], he liberally supported the Anglican sisterhood connected with Christ Church, Albany Street, one of the earliest established in London. He was a member of the council of Keble College, Oxford, which owes its chapel hall and library to his uncle William Gibbs and to the latter's sons, Antony and Martin. In conjunction with his mother he restored the church and endowed the living of Clifton Hampden on his Oxfordshire estate, and contributed to the support of St. Andrew's, Wells Street, and other churches. A member of the house of laymen of the province of Canterbury, and treasurer of the Church House, he joined the English Church Union in May 1862, became trustee in 1876, and was a member of its council until his death. One of his last public acts was to join in the appeal of prominent churchmen for the support of religious instruction in schools (*The Times*, 28 Jan. 1907).

Inheriting Aldenham House near Elstree in 1850 from his mother, he bought the rectory and advowson of Aldenham from Lord Rendlesham in 1877, and in 1882 thoroughly restored and reseated the church at a cost of 11,000*l.*, adding in 1902 an oak choir screen. He took an active part in the affairs of the diocese of St. Albans (founded in 1877), supporting the scheme for a new Essex bishopric and the Bishop of St. Albans Fund (of which he was a vice-president) for the extension of church work in East London. To the restoration of the Abbey of St. Albans as well as the support of the new diocese he devoted both time and money. A long and costly suit with Sir Edmund Beckett, Lord Grimthorpe [q. v. Suppl. II], deprived him of the honour of restoring the Lady chapel of the cathedral, but he obtained in spite of Grimthorpe's opposition two faculties (on 13 Jan. and 15 July 1890) to restore at his own cost the altar-screen, and to legalise the work which he had already carried out. He published in 1890 a full 'Account of the High Altar Screen in the Cathedral Church of St. Albans.' The reredos representing the Resurrection was executed in Carrara marble by Alfred Gilbert, R.A. The latest of his many benefactions to St. Albans Cathedral was the division and reconstruction of the great organ, by which a complete view of the building from east to west was obtained.

Aldenham, although staunch and outspoken both as tory and churchman, maintained the friendliest relations with those who differed from him. He cherished versatile interests outside commerce, politics, and ecclesiastical affairs. He was fond of shooting, and on 1 Sept. 1864 had the misfortune to lose his right hand in a gun accident, while he was shooting at Mannhead, Devonshire. Despite the disability, he continued to shoot, and also to play billiards. Endowed with a remarkable memory, he had a special gift for philology and lexicography. A prominent member of the Philological Society from 1859, he took great interest in the English Dictionary which was projected by the Philological Society in 1854, and he sub-edited letters C and K. When the project was taken up by the Oxford

University Press in 1880 with (Sir) James Murray as editor, Aldenham helped to settle the final form of the 'New English Dictionary,' and read and annotated every proof down to a few weeks before his death. He wrote many of the articles on words connected with banking, currency, and commerce, one of the last being 'pound.' For the Early English Text Society he edited in 1868 the 'Romance of the Chevelere Assigne.' For the Roxburghe Club, of which he was a member, he prepared in 1873 the 'Hystorie of the moste noble knight Plasidas,' and in 1884 the 'Life and Martyrdom of St. Katharine of Alexandria.' He was a good Spanish scholar, and wrote a booklet for private circulation (printed in 1874) on the game of cards called ombre. Aldenham was deeply versed in liturgical studies and a collector of old Bibles. An enthusiastic bibliophile, he described in 1888 the chief rarities in his library in 'A Catalogue of some Printed Books and Manuscripts at St. Dunstan's, Regent's Park, and Aldenham House, Herts.' His residence, St. Dunstan's, Regent's Park, he took on lease from the crown in 1856; it was formerly tenanted by the Marquis of Hertford, who bought and installed there the clock and automaton strikers of St. Dunstan's Church, Fleet Street, when the church was rebuilt in 1830.

Aldenham was appointed a trustee of the National Portrait Gallery on 18 Nov. 1890, was elected F.R.G.S. on 28 Nov. 1859, and F.S.A. on 4 June 1885, serving also on the council of the former society. He was president of Guy's Hospital from 1880 to 1896.

Aldenham died at Aldenham on 13 Sept. 1907; his youngest son, Henry Lloyd Gibbs, died on the following day, aged forty-six; both were buried at Aldenham. His will, dated 19 March (codicil 28 Aug.) 1906, was proved in December 1907; the gross estate was over 703,700*l.*, much of his property having been distributed during his lifetime. He married on 6 May 1845 at Thorpe, Surrey, Louisa Anne, third daughter of William Adams, LL.D., and Mary Anne Cokayne. His wife's brother, George Edward Cokayne [q. v. Suppl. II], married Lord Aldenham's sister, Mary Dorothea, on 2 Dec. 1856. Lady Aldenham died at St. Dunstan's, Regent's Park, on 17 April 1897, and was buried in Aldenham churchyard. Of their surviving children—four sons and a daughter—Alban George Henry succeeded to the peerage, having been previously M.P. for the City of London (1892–1906); Vicary, M.P. for St. Albans division, Hertfordshire (1892–1904), has re-edited the 'Complete Peerage' of his uncle, George Edward Cokayne; and Kenneth Francis is archdeacon of St. Albans and vicar of Aldenham.

A miniature portrait (æt. 20) by Sir William Ross, R.A.; a chalk drawing (with his eldest son) by E. U. Eddis (1859); a half-length portrait by Watts (1878), and a full-length by Ouless (1879), belong to the present Lord Aldenham. The Hon. Vicary Gibbs possesses a half-length by T. Gotch (1888) and a marble bas-relief of the head after death by J. Kerr Lawson. The Hon. Herbert Gibbs possesses a second portrait by Watts (1896).

[G. E. C. Complete Peerage, ed. Vicary Gibbs; The Times, 14 Sept. 1907; Kent's and Post Office London directories, 1808–26; Welch, Mod. Hist. of the City of London, 1896, pp. 375–6; Burke's Peerage; Herts Observer, 21 Sept. 1907; St. Albans Gazette, 18 Sept. 1907; Bankers' Mag. (sketch with portrait), xlviii. 267–9; Men of Note in Commerce and Finance, 1900–1, p. 20; Whitaker's Red Book of Commerce, 1910, p. 374; Proc. of Soc. of Antiquaries, xxii. 284–5; F. H. McCalmont, Parliamentary Poll Book, 1906, pt. 2, p. 159; Church Times, 20 Sept. 1907; Guardian, 18 Sept. 1907; Morning Post, 14 Sept. 1907; Daily Telegraph, 14 Sept. 1907; private information.] C. W.

GIFFEN, Sir ROBERT (1837–1910), economist and statistician, born at Strathaven, Lanarkshire, on 22 July 1837, was younger son of Robert Giffen, a small merchant and an elder of the presbyterian church, by his wife Janet Wiseman. Robert was educated at the village school and was put in charge of the Sunday-school library with an elder brother, John, who, destined for the ministry, died prematurely of consumption. The boys read all the books they could find, and wrote anonymously short articles and poems for a Hamilton newspaper. In 1850 Robert was apprenticed to a lawyer in Strathaven. Three years later he removed to a lawyer's office in Glasgow, and remained there seven years, attending lectures occasionally at the university. William Black [q. v. Suppl. I], the novelist, was one of his closest Glasgow friends (Reid, *William Black*, p. 18). In 1860 he definitely adopted journalism as a profession, becoming a reporter and sub-editor of the 'Stirling Journal.' In 1862 he came to London as sub-editor of the 'Globe' (1862–6). After serving for a time with Mr. John (afterwards Viscount) Morley on the 'Fortnightly Review' he joined the staff of the 'Economist,' under

Walter Bagehot [q. v.], as assistant-editor (1868–76), writing the City article from 1870 to 1876. He was also, from 1873 to 1876, City editor of the 'Daily News,' contributed to 'The Times' and the 'Spectator,' and was one of the founders of the 'Statist' in 1878. Goschen, in his classical 'Report on Local Taxation' (1871), acknowledged indebtedness to Giffen for assistance in the collection of historical material and in the compilation of the tables in the appendices. In 1876 Giffen was appointed to the board of trade as chief of the statistical department and controller of corn returns. In 1882 the commercial department of the board of trade, the main work of which had since 1876 been entrusted to the foreign office, was restored and united to the statistical department under Giffen, who became an assistant-secretary to the board. In 1892 a third department, the labour department, was added, and Giffen became controller of the commercial, labour, and statistical departments. He retired from the board in 1897 and removed to Chanctonbury, Haywards Heath. His varied services proved of great value to the board. Mr. Joseph Chamberlain, when president, in a minute written after the passing of the Bankruptcy Act of 1882, described Giffen as 'to a great extent the real author of the measure, to whose exhaustive memoranda on the subject I owe the best part of my own knowledge.' He served on various departmental committees, was a member of the royal commissions on the depression of agriculture in Great Britain (1893–7), and on the port of London (1900–2), and gave important statistical and economic evidence before numerous royal commissions, notably the depreciation of silver (1876), the London Stock Exchange (1878), gold and silver (1886–8), and local taxation (1898–9).

When accepting office in the civil service, Giffen obtained permission to continue to publish his views upon matters of economic interest. From 1876 to 1891 he edited the 'Journal of the Royal Statistical Society' (of which he was president, 1882–4), and wrote numerous articles and a regular contribution of City notes till his death for the 'Economic Journal,' the organ of the Royal Economic Society, of which he was one of the founders in 1890. Twice president of the section of economics and statistics of the British Association (1887 and 1901), he gave on the first occasion an address on 'The Recent Rate of Material Progress in England' and on the second an address on 'The Importance of General Statistical Ideas' (both afterwards published). Weighty and sagacious in debate, he was a pillar of the Political Economy Club from 1877 to 1910. Though he endeavoured to avoid political partisanship he presented on occasion the unusual spectacle of a civil servant criticising in public the policy of ministers of the crown. His examination of the finance of Gladstone's home rule proposals in 1893 was considered a 'most powerful and damaging indictment,' and led to the appointment of the royal commission on the financial relations between Great Britain and Ireland (1895–6) before which he was a witness. He regarded Ireland as overtaxed in comparison with Great Britain. Starting as a liberal, he became successively a liberal unionist in 1886, a unionist free-trader, abstaining from support of either of the great parties, in 1903, and finally 'on balance' a supporter of the unionist party owing to his dislike of the budget of 1909–10 as trenching too heavily upon capital and direct taxation, a view which he recorded in the 'Quarterly Review' for July 1909. Giffen was made an honorary LL.D. of Glasgow in 1884, and was created C.B. in 1891 and K.C.B. in 1895. He died of heart failure at Fort Augustus on 12 April 1910, while on a visit to Scotland, and is buried at Strathaven.

He married (1) in 1864, Isabella (*d.* 1896), daughter of D. McEwen of Stirling; (2) on 25 Nov. 1896, Margaret Anne, daughter of George Wood of Aberdeen. He had no children.

Giffen, a prolific writer on economic, financial, and statistical subjects, possessed a luminous and penetrating mind, great stores of information, an intimate acquaintance with business matters and methods, and shrewd judgment. His instructive handling of statistics and his keen eye for pitfalls contributed greatly to raise the reputation and encourage the study of statistics in this country, though he did not develop its technique by the higher mathematical treatment.

A sturdy individualist, Giffen viewed with suspicion any infraction of the maxim *laissez-faire*. He believed in the 'patience cure' for many social and financial evils. Though a strong free trader, he conceded that a slight customs' preference to colonial imports might be justified by political considerations. His frame of mind is reflected in his opinion that investors should inform themselves and judge for themselves, and not be guided by the advice of their bankers, brokers, or friends. He was in favour of 'free-banking,' under which a cheque might be drawn upon any person whether a banker or not. He advocated the reduction of the representation of Ireland in the imperial parliament, and the boring of a tunnel under the Irish Sea with a view to closer union.

His principal published writings, apart from separate addresses and pamphlets, are: 1. 'American Railways as Investments,' in Cracroft's Investment Tracts (1872; 2nd and 3rd edits. 1873), written at the suggestion of Mr. Bernard Cracroft of the Stock Exchange, who provided him with materials. This work served to dispel some of the indiscriminate mistrust of American railways by the British public. A French translation by E. de Laveleye was published at Liège, 1873. 2. 'The Production and Movement of Gold since 1848,' 1873. 3. 'Stock Exchange Securities; an Essay on the General Course of Fluctuations in their Prices,' 1877. 4. 'Essays in Finance' (contributions to periodicals), 1st series, 2 editions, 1880; 5th edit. 1890; 2nd series, 1886; 3rd edit. 1890. 5. The 'Statist' on Ireland; reprint of 'Economist's' [R. G.'s] letters to the 'Statist' on the Irish land and home rule questions, and of editorial comments thereon, 1886. 6. 'The Growth of Capital,' 1889. 7. 'The Case against Bimetallism,' 1892; 2nd edit. 1892. 8. 'Economic Enquiries and Studies' (contributions to periodicals), 2 vols. 1904. Giffen contributed 'Growth and Distribution of Wealth, 1837–1887,' to vol. ii. of T. H. Ward's 'Reign of Queen Victoria' (1887), and added a chapter to Lord Farrer's 'The State in its Relation to Trade' (1902). He left completed in manuscript a 'Handbook of Statistics,' not yet published.

[Personal knowledge; information from Lady Giffen; Statistical Soc. Journal, May 1909 (with excellent engraved portrait); Economic Journal, June 1909.] H. H.

GIFFORD, EDWIN HAMILTON (1820–1905), archdeacon of London and theologian, born at Bristol on 18 Dec. 1820, was sixth son of Richard Ireland Gifford by his wife Helen, daughter of William Davie of Stonehouse, Devonshire. After education at Elizabeth's Grammar School, Plymouth, he was admitted to Shrewsbury School in 1837, under Benjamin Hall Kennedy [q. v.], and in 1839 he proceeded to Cambridge, winning a scholarship at St. John's College. He had a distinguished university career. In 1842 he won the Pitt University scholarship. In 1843 he graduated B.A. both as senior classic and fifteenth wrangler in the mathematical tripos. In the same year he won the chancellor's medal, and was a fellow of his college from 4 April 1843 till 20 March 1844. He proceeded M.A. in 1846, and D.D. in 1861. In 1843 he returned to Shrewsbury as second master, and in 1848 he was appointed headmaster of King Edward's School, Birmingham. He proved a worthy successor of James Prince Lee [q. v.], and resigned in 1862 owing to ill-health. Gifford, who had been ordained in 1844, was honorary canon of Worcester (1853–77). In 1865 he became chaplain to Francis Jeune [q. v.], bishop of Peterborough, who presented him to the rectory of Walgrave, Northamptonshire. He subsequently held the post of examining chaplain to two successive bishops of London, Jackson and Temple. In 1875 he accepted the benefice of Much Hadham, Hertfordshire, and in 1877 was made an honorary canon of St. Albans. In 1883 he was nominated to the prebend of Islington in St. Paul's Cathedral, and the following year he succeeded Piers Calverley Claughton [q. v.] as archdeacon of London and canon of St. Paul's.

Though Gifford was select preacher at Cambridge (1864, 1869) and at Oxford (1879, 1890–1) he was not an effective preacher. He was better known as a scholar than as an ecclesiastic. On 24 April 1889 Gifford resigned his archdeaconry, and retired to Arlington House, Oxford, where he continued his studies to the last. In 1903 he was elected an honorary fellow of St. John's College, Cambridge. He died in London on 5 May 1905.

Gifford married (1) in 1844, Anne, daughter of John Yolland of Plymouth; (2) in 1873, Margaret Symons, daughter of Francis Jeune, bishop of Peterborough and sister of Francis Henry Jeune, baron St. Helier [q. v. Suppl. II]. He had issue one daughter.

Gifford's contributions to biblical and patristic learning, which were marked by insight and accuracy, included: 1. 'Voices of the Past' (1874), the Warburtonian lectures delivered at Lincoln's Inn 1870–4. 2. 'The Epistle to the Romans' (1881) in the 'Speaker's Commentary.' 3. 'Baruch and the Epistle of Jeremy' (1888) in the same series. 4. 'Authorship of Psalm cx.' (1892; 3rd edit. 1895). 5. 'The Catechetical Lectures of St. Cyril of Jerusalem' (1894), revised translation in vol. vii. of Nicene and Post-Nicene Library. 6. Eusebius's 'Præparatio Evangelica' (1903), 5 vols., text and translation.

[The Times, 6 May 1905; Guardian, 10 May 1905; Church Times, 12 May 1905; Shrewsbury School Register (1734–1908), 1909; Baker, History of St. John's College, Cambridge, 1869, i. 316; The Eagle, June 1905; Theologische Literaturzeitung, 24 Oct. 1903.] G. S. W.

GIGLIUCCI, Countess. [See Novello, Clara Anastasia, 1818–1908.]

GILBERT, Sir JOSEPH HENRY (1817–1901), agricultural chemist, born at Hull on 1 Aug. 1817, was one of four sons of Joseph Gilbert [q. v.], a congregational minister, by his wife Ann Taylor [see Gilbert, Mrs. Ann]. The family removed in 1825 to Nottingham, where Gilbert spent his boyhood. He was educated at a school at Mansfield, and in 1838 entered the University of Glasgow, specialising in analytical chemistry under Professor Thomas Thomson [q. v.]. A gun-shot accident in 1832, which caused the loss of one eye, impaired his general health for some time. He next worked at University College, London, in the laboratory of Professor Anthony Todd Thomson [q. v.], where he had as a fellow-student John Bennet Lawes [q. v. Suppl. I], with whom he was afterwards closely connected. In 1840 he went to Giessen, where he met Lyon Playfair [q. v. Suppl. I] and Augustus Voelcker [q. v.], worked in the laboratory of Liebig, and took the degree of doctor of philosophy. On his return from Giessen he acted in 1840–1 as assistant to Anthony Thomson at University College, and then devoted some time at Manchester to the chemistry of calico printing and dyeing.

On 1 June 1843 he joined as technical adviser John Bennet Lawes, who had shortly before started the first organised agricultural experiment station in the world at his ancestral home at Rothamsted; Gilbert lived at Harpenden close to the laboratory. From June 1843 to August 1900, when Lawes died, the two investigators lived in unbroken friendship and collaboration. 'What was Lawes' work was Gilbert's work; the two are indissolubly connected. . . . Lawes was essentially the practical agriculturist. . . . Gilbert on the other hand was possessed of indomitable perseverance, combined with extreme patience and careful watching of results. With the determination to carry out an experiment to the very close, he united scrupulous accuracy and attention to detail. Each of the partners had his own sphere, and the influence of the two minds, in themselves essentially different, materially contributed to the success which attended their joint efforts, and made the Rothamsted experiments a standard for reference, and an example wherever agricultural research is attempted' (Dr. J. A. Voelcker in *Journal Royal Agricult. Soc.* 1901, lxii. 348, 350).

Gilbert took an active part in the proceedings of various learned societies. He joined the Chemical Society in 1841, a few weeks after its formation, and became its president in 1882–3. He was admitted into the Royal Society in 1860, and received with Lawes its royal medal in 1867. He was elected in 1883 an honorary member of the Royal Agricultural Society, in the 'Journal' of which many of the results of the Rothamsted researches were published. In 1884 he was appointed Sibthorpian professor of rural economy at the University of Oxford, and held the professorship for six years, the full term allowed by the statute. In 1893 he went to the Chicago exhibition, and delivered in the United States seven lectures on the Rothamsted experiments. In 1894 Lawes and he were presented by the Prince of Wales at Marlborough House with the Albert gold medal of the Royal Society of Arts. He received honorary degrees from the universities of Glasgow (LL.D. 1883), Oxford (M.A. 1884), Edinburgh (LL.D. 1890), and Cambridge (Sc.D. 1894).

On the completion of fifty years of the joint labours of Lawes and Gilbert, a granite memorial of the event was dedicated at Rothamsted on 29 June 1893, and Gilbert was presented with an address and a piece of plate. On 11 Aug. 1893 he received the honour of knighthood. His activity of mind and body continued almost to the last, but the death of Lawes in 1900 was a great blow to him. He died at Harpenden on 23 Dec. 1901, in his eighty-fifth year, and was buried in the churchyard there close to the grave of Lawes.

Gilbert married twice: (1) in 1850, Eliza Laurie (*d.* 1853); (2) in 1855, Maria Smith, who survived him and was granted a civil list pension of 100*l.* in 1904. He had no family by either marriage. His portrait in oils, painted by Frank O. Salisbury in 1900, hangs in the directors' room at the laboratory at Rothamsted.

[Memoir (with portrait) by Dr. J. A. Voelcker in vol. 62 (1901) of the Journal Royal Agricult. Soc. of England; obit. notice by Robert Warington, F.R.S., in Proc. Roy. Soc. lxxv. 236–242; Trans. Chemical Soc., 1902, p. 625; Nature, 2 Jan. 1902; personal knowledge.] E. C.

GILBERT, Sir WILLIAM SCHWENCK (1836–1911), dramatist, born at 17 Southampton Street, Strand, the house of his mother's father, Dr. Thomas Morris, on 18 Nov. 1836, was only son in a family of four children of William Gilbert (1804–1890) [q. v. Suppl. I] by his wife Anne Morris. His second christian name was the surname of his godmother. As an infant he travelled in Germany and Italy with his parents. When two years old he was stolen by brigands at Naples and ransomed for 25*l*. In later days when visiting Naples he recognised in the Via Posilippo the scene of the occurrence. His pet name as a child was 'Bab,' which he afterwards used as a pseudonym. He is said to have been a child of great beauty, and Sir David Wilkie [q. v.] was so attracted by his face that he asked leave to paint his picture. At the age of seven he went to school at Boulogne. From ten to thirteen he was at the Western Grammar School, Brompton, and from thirteen to sixteen at the Great Ealing School, where he rose to be head boy. He spent much time in drawing, and wrote plays for performance by his schoolfellows, painting his own scenery and acting himself.

In Oct. 1855 he entered the department of general literature and science at King's College, London (*King's Coll. Calendar*, 1855–6, p. 89). Alfred Ainger [q. v. Suppl. II] and Walter Besant [q. v. Suppl. II] were fellow students. Some of his earliest literary efforts were verses contributed to the college magazine. He remained a student during 1856–7, intending to go to Oxford, but in 1855, when he was nineteen years old, the Crimean war was at its height, and commissions in the Royal Artillery were thrown open to competitive examination. Giving up all idea of Oxford, he read for the army examination announced for Christmas 1856 ('An Autobiography' in *The Theatre*, 2 April 1883, p. 217). But the war came to an abrupt end, and no more officers being required, the examination was indefinitely postponed. Gilbert then graduated B.A. at the London University in 1857, and obtained a commission in the militia in the 3rd battalion Gordon highlanders.

In 1857 he was a successful competitor in an examination for a clerkship in the education department of the privy council office, in which 'ill-organised and ill-governed office' he tells us he spent four uncomfortable years. Coming unexpectedly in 1861 into 300*l*., 'on the happiest day of my life I sent in my resignation.' He had already, on 11 October 1855, entered the Inner Temple as a student (Foster's *Men at the Bar*). With 100*l*. of his capital he paid for his call to the bar, which took place on 17 Nov. 1863 (cf. 'My Maiden Brief,' *Cornhill*, Dec. 1863). With another 100*l*. he obtained access to the chambers of (Sir) Charles James Watkin Williams [q. v.], then a well-known barrister in the home circuit, and with the third 100*l*. he furnished a set of rooms of his own in Clement's Inn, but he does not appear to have had any professional chambers or address in the 'Law List.' He joined the northern circuit on 15 March 1866, one of his sponsors being (Sir) John Holker [q. v.] (*MS. Circuit Records*). He attended the Westminster courts, the Old Bailey, the Manchester and Liverpool assizes, the Liverpool sessions and Passage Court, but 'only earned 75*l*. in two years.'

During the same period he was earning a 'decent income' by contributions to current literature. He appeared for the first time in print in 1858, when he prepared a translation of the laughing-song from Auber's 'Manon Lescaut' for the playbill of Alfred Mellon's promenade concerts; Mdlle. Parepa, afterwards Madame Parepa-Rosa [q. v.], whom he had known from babyhood, had made a singular success there with the song in its original French. In 1861 Gilbert commenced both as author and artist, contributing an article, three-quarters of a column long with a half-page drawing on wood, for 'Fun,' then under the editorship of Henry James Byron [q. v.]. A day or two later he was requested 'to contribute a column of "copy" and a half-page drawing every week' (*Theatre*, 1883, p. 218). He remained a regular contributor to 'Fun' during the editorship of Byron and that of Byron's successor, Tom Hood the younger [q. v.] (from 1865).

There is no evidence that he studied drawing in any school, but he was an illustrator of talent. In 1865 he made 84 illustrations for his father's novel, 'The Magic Mirror,' and in 1869 he illustrated another of his father's books, 'King George's Middy.' His illustrations of his own 'Bab Ballads' have much direct and quaint humour. In 1874 'The Piccadilly Annual' was described as 'profusely illustrated by W. S. Gilbert and other artists.' One of the 'other artists' was John Leech.

Having already both written and drawn occasionally for 'Punch,' Gilbert offered that periodical in 1866 his ballad called 'The Yarn of the Nancy Bell,' but it was refused by the editor, Mark Lemon [q. v.], on the ground that it was 'too cannibalistic for his readers' tastes' (*Fifty Bab Ballads*, pref., 1884). Gilbert's connection with 'Punch' thereupon ceased. 'The Nancy Bell' appeared, without illustrations, in 'Fun' on 3 March 1866. Gilbert's other work in 'Fun' may be traced by single figure drawings signed 'Bab.' A series of dramatic notices commencing 15 Sept. 1866 and 'Men we Meet, by the Comic Physiognomist' (2 Feb. to 18 May 1867) are thus illustrated. The first illustrated ballad was 'General John' (1 June 1867). From this date they became a regular feature of the paper. But not until 23 Jan. 1869, in connection with 'The Two Ogres,' was the title 'The Bab Ballads' used. They were first collected in volume form in the same year. Further 'Bab Ballads' continued to appear in 'Fun,' at varying intervals until 1871. A collected volume of 'More Bab Ballads' followed in 1873. The Bab Ballads established Gilbert's reputation as a whimsical humorist in verse.

At the same time Gilbert contributed articles or stories to the magazines—the 'Cornhill' (1863–4), 'London Society,' 'Tinsley's Magazine,' and 'Temple Bar'; he furnished the London correspondence to the 'Invalide Russe,' and, becoming dramatic critic to Vizetelly's 'Illustrated Times,' interested himself in the stage. In spite of these activities Gilbert found time to continue his military duties, and became captain of his militia regiment in 1867. He retired with the rank of major in 1883.

At the end of 1866 Gilbert commenced work as a playwright. To Thomas William Robertson [q. v.], the dramatist, he owed the needful introduction. Miss Herbert, the lessee of St. James's Theatre, wanted a Christmas piece in a fortnight, and Robertson recommended Gilbert for the work, which was written in ten days, rehearsed in a week, and produced at Christmas 1866. The piece was a burlesque on 'L'Elixir d'Amore,' called 'Dulcamara, or the Little Duck and the Great Quack.' Frank Matthews made a success in the title rôle, and it ran for several months and was twice revived. No terms had been arranged, and when Mr. Emden, the manager, paid Gilbert the 30*l.* that he asked, Emden advised him never again to sell so good a piece for so small a sum. Thenceforward Gilbert was a successful playwright, at first in the lighter branches of the drama. Another burlesque on 'La Figlia del Reggimento,' called 'La Vivandière, or True to the Corps,' was produced at the Queen's Theatre on 22 Jan. 1868, and in it John Lawrence Toole [q. v. Suppl. II] and Lionel Brough [q. v. Suppl. II] played. It ran for 120 nights. A third burlesque, on the 'Bohemian Girl,' entitled 'The Merry Zingara, or the Tipsy Gipsy and the Popsy Wopsy,' was produced at the Royal Theatre on 21 March 1868 by Miss Patty Oliver. On 21 Dec. 1868 the new Gaiety Theatre was opened by John Hollingshead [q. v. Suppl. II] with a new operatic extravaganza by Gilbert called 'Robert the Devil,' in which Nellie Farren [q.v. Suppl. II] played the leading part. Next year, at the opening of the Charing Cross (afterwards Toole's) Theatre, on 19 June 1869, the performance concluded with a musical extravaganza by Gilbert, 'The Pretty Druidess, or the Mother, the Maid, and the Mistletoe Bough, a travestie of Norma.' Gilbert was much attached to second titles. Between 1869 and 1872 he also wrote many dramatic sketches, usually with music, for the German Reeds' 'entertainment' at the Gallery of Illustration, 14 Regent Street. His musical collaborator was Frederick Clay [q. v. Suppl. I]. On 22 Nov. 1869 they produced together 'Ages Ago,' which was afterwards expanded into the opera 'Ruddigore'; on 30 Jan. 1871 'A Sensation Novel'; and on 28 Oct. 1872 'Happy Arcadia.' Arthur Cecil, Corney Grain, and Fanny Holland were the chief performers.

It was under the auspices of the German Reeds that Gilbert and (Sir) Arthur Sullivan [q. v. Suppl. I] first made each other's acquaintance. Sullivan was one of the composers of music for German Reed plays, and at the Gallery of Illustration in 1871 Clay introduced Sullivan to Gilbert (LAWRENCE'S *Life of Sullivan*, p. 84, and E. A. BROWNE'S *Gilbert*, p. 35). They soon were at work together on a burlesque, 'Thespis, or the Gods Grown Old,' which was produced at the Gaiety Theatre on 26 Dec. 1871 (JOHN HOLLINGSHEAD'S *Gaiety Chronicles*, 202–7). They often met at Tom Taylor's, and engaged together in amateur theatricals (ELLEN TERRY'S *Story of My Life*, 1908), but for the present no further dramatic collaboration followed.

Meanwhile Gilbert was assiduously seeking fame in more serious branches of the drama. On 8 Jan. 1870 'The Princess,' a respectful parody on Tennyson's poem, was produced at the Olympic with great success. This was afterwards the basis of the opera 'Princess Ida.' John Baldwin Buckstone [q. v.] now commissioned Gilbert to write a blank verse fairy comedy on

Madame de Genlis's story of 'Le Palais de la Vérité.' This was produced on 19 Nov. 1870 at the Haymarket under the title of 'The Palace of Truth,' with Buckstone, Madge Robertson (Mrs. Kendal), and W. H. Kendal in the cast. It ran for 230 nights. 'Pygmalion and Galatea,' a rather artificial classical romance, was produced also at the Haymarket on 9 Dec. 1871. It proved a remarkable success. The play was revived at the Lyceum with Miss Mary Anderson in 1884 and later in 1888, at the same theatre, with Miss Julia Neilson in the part. Gilbert is said to have made 40,000*l.* out of this play alone (*Daily Telegraph,* 30 May 1911). 'The Wicked World,' a fairy comedy, followed at the Haymarket on 4 Jan. 1873 and was not quite so successful as its forerunners.

In the meantime Gilbert wrote an extended series of comedies for Miss Marie Litton's management of the new Court Theatre in Sloane Square, London. This playhouse was opened by Miss Litton with Gilbert's 'Randall's Thumb' on 25 Jan. 1871; there followed during Miss Litton's tenancy 'Creatures of Impulse' (15 April 1871); 'Great Expectations' (28 May), an adaptation of Dickens's novel; 'On Guard' (28 Oct.); and 'The Wedding March' (under the pseudonym of F. Latour Tomline) (15 Nov. 1873). One of Gilbert's plays written for the Court Theatre, 'The Happy Land,' which Miss Litton produced on 17 March 1873, caused much public excitement. It was a burlesque version of Gilbert's 'Wicked World,' designed by himself, but mainly worked out by Gilbert Arthur à Beckett [q. v. Suppl. I]. Gilbert received 700*l.* for his share of the libretto (*W. S. Gilbert,* by Kate Field, *Scribner's Monthly,* xviii. (1879), 754). His name did not appear on the bill, where the piece was assigned to F. L. Tomline (i.e. Gilbert) and à Beckett. 'The Happy Land' was received with enthusiasm. But three of the actors, Walter Fisher, W. J. Hill, and Edward Righton (manager of the theatre), were made up to resemble respectively Gladstone, Robert Lowe (Lord Sherbrooke), and A. S. Ayrton, members of the liberal administration then in office. The lord chamberlain insisted on the removal of this feature of the performance.

Of more serious plays 'Charity,' produced on 3 Jan. 1874 at the Haymarket, was the story of a woman redeeming her one mistake in life by an after career of self-sacrifice. It was denounced as immoral by the general public, and was withdrawn after a run of eighty nights. There followed a series of successful comedies in which sentiment predominated over Gilbert's habitually cynical humour. 'Sweethearts' was produced at the Prince of Wales's on 7 Nov. 1874 under Mrs. Bancroft's management; 'Tom Cobb' at the St. James's, on 24 April 1875; 'Broken Hearts' on 17 Dec. 1875 at the Court Theatre under (Sir) John Hare's direction. 'Dan'l Druce,' a play of very serious tone, and 'Engaged' both came out at the Haymarket, on 11 Sept. 1876 and 3 Oct. 1877 respectively. 'Gretchen,' a four-act drama in verse on the Faust legend, was produced on 24 March 1879 at the Olympic. In 1884 Gilbert wrote an ambitious sketch, 'Comedy and Tragedy,' for Miss Mary Anderson to perform at the Lyceum Theatre (26 Jan. 1884).

Meanwhile Gilbert acquired a more conspicuous triumph in another dramatic field. The memorable series of operas in which he and Sullivan collaborated began with 'Trial by Jury,' which was produced at the Royalty Theatre by Madame Selina Dolaro on 25 March 1875. A sketch of an operetta under this title had appeared in 'Fun' on 11 April 1868. The words now took a new shape, Sullivan supplied the music, and the rehearsals were completed within three weeks. Gilbert's libretto betrayed the whimsical humour of his early 'Bab Ballads,' as well as the facility of his earlier extravaganzas and burlesques. Richard D'Oyly Carte [q. v. Suppl. II] was the manager of the Royalty. In view of the piece's success Carte formed a Comedy Opera Company, and gave Gilbert and Sullivan a commission to write a larger work together. The result was 'The Sorcerer,' which was first played at the Opera Comique on 17 Nov. 1877, and introduced George Grossmith and Rutland Barrington to the professional stage. This opera proved the forerunner of a long series of like successes. 'The Sorcerer' was followed by 'H.M.S. Pinafore, or the Lass that loved a Sailor,' under the same management on 25 May 1878. This ran for 700 nights and enjoyed an enormous popularity throughout the country. It was at once received in America with an 'enthusiasm bordering upon insanity' (Kate Field in *Scribner's Monthly,* xviii. 754), and after its first production in America Gilbert, with Sullivan, D'Oyly Carte, and Alfred Cellier, the musical conductor, went to New York (Nov. 1879) to give it the fresh advantage of Gilbert's personal stage management and Sullivan's own orchestral interpretation. While in New York they produced for the first time a new opera, 'The Pirates of Penzance, or the Slave of Duty,' which was brought out at the Fifth Avenue Theatre on New Year's Eve, 31 Dec. 1879. The party returned to England in time to produce 'The Pirates of Penzance' at the Opera Comique on 3 April 1880. This ran for a year. 'Patience, or Bunthorne's Bride' came out at the Opera Comique on 23 April 1881, and at the height of its triumph, on 10 Oct. 1881, it was transferred to the 'Savoy'—the new opera house built by D'Oyly Carte for the Gilbert and Sullivan operas. 'Patience' was a satire on the current 'æsthetic movement' and enjoyed great popularity.

The succeeding 'Savoy operas' were 'Iolanthe, or the Peer and the Peri' (25 Nov. 1882); 'Princess Ida, or Castle Adamant,' based on Gilbert's comedy 'The Princess' (5 Jan. 1884); and 'The Mikado, or the Town of Titipu' (14 March 1885). The last piece ran for two years, was played over 5000 times in America, and found favour on the Continent. It was the most popular of all Gilbert and Sullivan's joint works. It is said Gilbert, Sullivan, and Carte each made 30,000*l.* out of it. 'Ruddigore, or the Witch's Curse,' an elaboration of the German Reed piece 'Ages Ago,' followed on 22 Jan. 1887; 'The Yeoman of the Guard, or The Merryman and His Maid' on 3 Oct. 1888, and 'The Gondoliers, or The King of Barataria' on 7 Dec. 1889. The partnership was shortly afterwards interrupted. A disagreement on financial matters arose between Gilbert and Carte, and Gilbert thought that Sullivan sided with Carte. Separating for the time from both Sullivan and Carte, Gilbert wrote his next libretto, 'The Mountebanks,' for music by Alfred Cellier. It was produced at the Lyric Theatre on 4 Jan. 1892.

In writing these operas Gilbert first wrote out the plot as though it were an anecdote, and this he expanded to the length of a magazine article with summaries of conversations. This was overhauled and corrected and cut down to a skeleton, and then broken up into scenes with entrances and exits arranged. Not until the fifth MS. was the play illustrated by actual dialogue. Sometimes a piece would after a fortnight's rest be re-written entirely afresh without reference to the first draft. In arranging the scenes, too, no trouble was too great. In 'H.M.S. Pinafore' Gilbert went down to Portsmouth and was rowed round about the harbour and visited various ships, and finally pitched upon the quarter-deck of the Victory for his scene, which he obtained permission to sketch and model in every detail.

Gilbert's partnership with Sullivan and Carte was resumed in 1893, when he and Sullivan wrote 'Utopia Limited, or the Flowers of Progress.' It was produced at the Savoy on 7 Oct. 1893, but was not so popular as its predecessors, although it ran till 9 June 1894. Gilbert's next opera, 'His Excellency,' had music by Dr. Osmond Carr (Lyric, 27 Oct. 1894); it was followed by revivals of older pieces. In 'The Grand Duke,' which came out on 7 March 1896 at the Savoy, Gilbert and Sullivan worked together for the last time. Thenceforth Gilbert pursued his career as a playwright spasmodically and with declining success. A fanciful drama, 'Harlequin and the Fairy's Dilemma,' was produced without much acceptance by Mr. Arthur Bourchier at the Garrick Theatre (3 May–22 July 1904). On 11 Dec. 1909 his opera 'Fallen Fairies,' with music by Edward German, came out at the Savoy. His final production was 'The Hooligan,' a grim sketch of the last moments of a convicted murderer, played by Mr James Welch at the Coliseum in 1911.

Gilbert's successes as a dramatist brought him wealth, which he put to good purpose. He built and owned the Garrick Theatre in Charing Cross Road, which was opened in 1889. In 1890 he purchased of Frederick Goodall, R.A. [q. v. Suppl. II], the house and estate of Grims Dyke, Harrow Weald, Middlesex. The estate covered 100 acres and the house had been built for Goodall by Norman Shaw. Gilbert added an observatory and an open-air swimming lake. He was something of an astronomer as well as a dairy farmer, bee-keeper, and horticulturist. He was made J.P. in 1891 and D.L. for Middlesex, and devoted much time to his magisterial duties. In 1907 he was knighted. He was a well-known member of the Beefsteak, Junior Carlton, and Royal Automobile Clubs, and was elected by the committee to the Garrick Club on 22 Feb. 1906.

Gilbert died from heart failure brought on by over-exertion while saving a young lady from drowning in his swimming lake at Grims Dyke on 29 May 1911. The body was cremated at Golder's Green and the ashes buried at Great Stanmore church, Middlesex.

Gilbert was, perhaps, the most outstanding figure among Victorian playwrights. Few if any contemporary writers for the stage made so much money from that source alone, none acquired so wide a fame. In all his writing there is an effort after literary grace and finish which was in his early days absent from contemporary drama. His humour consists mainly in logical topsy-turveydom in a vein so peculiar to Gilbert as to justify the bestowal on it of the epithet 'Gilbertian.' He himself disclaimed any knowledge of Gilbertian humour, stating that 'all humour properly so called is based upon a grave and quasi-respectful treatment of the ludicrous.' His satire hits current foibles with unvarying urbanity and with no Aristophanic coarseness. The success of his operas was largely due to their freedom from vulgarity and to the excellence of the lyrics, which not only were musical and perfect in form but applied mastery of metre to the expression of the most whimsical and fanciful ideas. He had little or no ear for tune, but a wonderful ear for rhythm. Gilbert's words and metre underwent no change in the process of musical setting.

Gilbert believed that the playwright should dominate the theatre. He was a master of stage management. In a privately printed preface to 'Pygmalion and Galatea' he pointed out that 'the supreme importance of careful rehearsing is not sufficiently recognised in England.' His experience, for which he vouched by statistics, taught him that when his pieces were carefully rehearsed they succeeded, and when they were insufficiently rehearsed they failed. A sufficient rehearsal for a play he then considered to be three weeks or a month. His conduct at the rehearsals of his adaptation of 'Ought we to visit her' (a comedy in three acts by Messrs. Edwardes and Gilbert), produced at the Royalty on 17 Jan. 1874, led to a quarrel with Miss Henrietta Hodson [q. v. Suppl. II], which was renewed over the production of 'Pygmalion and Galatea' in January 1877. Miss Hodson published 'A Letter' in the same year complaining of Gilbert's dictatorial action, to which Gilbert replied in 'A Letter addressed to the Members of the Dramatic Profession.' Gilbert developed the practice of Tom Robertson, who was perhaps the first English playwright to impress his personal views at rehearsal on the actor. Gilbert rehearsed his pieces in his study by means of a model stage and figures, and every group and movement were settled in the author's mind before the stage rehearsals began. Until Gilbert took the matter in hand choruses were practically nothing more than a part of the stage setting. It was in 'Thespis' that Gilbert began to carry out his expressed determination to get the chorus to play its proper part in the performance.

Gilbert had in ordinary society a ready, subtle, and incisive wit. He was aggressive and combative and rarely let the discomfort of a victim deprive him and his companions of a brilliant epigram or a ready repartee. Nevertheless he had a kind heart, and was only a cynic after the manner of Thackeray. Many of the artists who worked under him bore testimony to his personal kindness. He was not interested in sport. He had a constitutional objection to taking life in any form. 'I don't think I ever wittingly killed a blackbeetle,' he said, and added 'The time will come when the sport of the present day will be regarded very much as we regard the Spanish bull-fight or the bear-baiting of our ancestors' (WILLIAM ARCHER, *Real Conversations*).

He married in 1867 Lucy Agnes, daughter of Captain Thomas Metcalf Blois Turner, Bombay engineers. His wife survived him without issue. A portrait painted by Frank Holl, R.A., in 1887 is destined for the National Portrait Gallery. He also owned a portrait of himself by Herman Gustave Herkomer and a bronze statuette by Andrea Lucchesi.

Besides the plays already mentioned, Gilbert wrote the following dramatic pieces: 'Harlequin Cock Robin and Jenny Wren, or Fortunatus, the Three Bears, the Three Wishes, and the Little Man who wooed the Little Maid,' pantomime (26 Dec. 1866) 'Allow Me to Explain,' farce, altered from the French (Prince of Wales's Theatre, 4 Nov. 1867); 'Highly Improbable,' farce (New Royalty, 5 Dec. 1867); 'No Cards' (German Reeds, 29 March 1869); 'An Old Score,' comedy-drama in three acts (Gaiety Theatre, 19 July 1869); 'The Gentleman in Black,' opera bouffe in two acts, music by Frederick Clay (Charing Cross Theatre, 26 May 1870); 'Our Island Home' (Gallery of Illustration, 20 June 1870); 'A Medical Man,' a comedietta (Drawing Room Plays, 1870); 'The Realms of Joy,' farce by F. Latour Tomline, i.e. Gilbert (Royalty Theatre, 18 Oct. 1873); 'Committed for Trial,' a piece of absurdity in two acts, founded on 'Le Réveillon' of H. Meilhac and L. Halévy (Globe Theatre, 24 Jan. 1874, revived at the Criterion, 12 Feb. 1877, as 'On Bail'); 'Topsy-turveydom,' extravaganza (Criterion Theatre, 21 Mar. 1873); 'King Candaules' (1875); 'Eyes and No Eyes, or the Art of Seeing,' a vaudeville, music by T. German Reed, founded on Hans Andersen's 'The Emperor's New Clothes' (St. George's Hall, 5 July 1875); 'Princess Toto,' comic opera in three acts, music by Frederick Clay (Strand Theatre, 2 Oct. 1876); 'The Ne'er-do-Weel,' drama (Olympic Theatre, 25 Feb. 1878); 'Foggerty's Fairy,' a fairy comedy (Criterion, 15 Dec. 1881); 'Brantinghame Hall,' drama (St. James's Theatre, 29 Nov. 1888); 'The Brigands,' opera bouffe in three acts, music by Offenbach, adapted from 'Les Brigands' of Meilhac and Halévy (Avenue Theatre, 16 Sept. 1889); 'Rosencrantz and Guildenstern,' a travesty on 'Hamlet,' in three tableaux (Vaudeville Theatre, 3 June 1891); 'Haste to the Wedding,' comic opera, music by George Grossmith (Criterion Theatre, 27 July 1892), a version of E. M. Labiche's 'Un Chapeau de Paille d'Italie,' played at the Court Theatre as 'The Wedding March' on 15 Nov. 1873; 'The Fortune Hunter,' drama (Theatre Royal, Birmingham, 27 Sept. 1897).

Collected editions of Gilbert's dramatic work appeared as 'Original Plays' (4 series, 1876–1911) and 'Original Comic Operas' (8 parts, containing 'Sorcerer,' 'H.M.S. Pinafore,' 'Pirates of Penzance,' 'Iolanthe,' 'Patience,' 'Princess Ida,' 'Mikado,' and 'Trial by Jury,' 1890). He also published 'Songs of a Savoyard,' a collection of songs from the Savoy operas, illustrated by Gilbert (1890), and 'Foggerty's Fairy and other Tales' (1890).

[William Schwenck Gilbert, an Autobiography in The Theatre, 2 April 1883, pp. 217 seq.; Edith A. Browne, W. S. Gilbert, 1907; Arthur Lawrence, Life of Sir Arthur Sullivan, 1899; William Archer, English Dramatists of To-day; William Archer, Real Conversations; Percy Fitzgerald, The Savoy Opera and the Savoyards; Daily Telegraph, 30 May 1911; The Times, 30 May–2 June, 18 Aug. (will), 1911; John Hollingshead's Gaiety Chronicles, 1898; Kate Field's W. S. Gilbert in Scribner's Monthly, 1879, xviii. 754; Smalley's London Letters, 2 vols., 1890; and his Anglo-American Memories, 1911; The English Aristophanes, art. by Walter Sichel, in Fortnightly Review, 1912; W. Davenport Adams, Dict. of the Drama.]

E. A. P.

GILLIES, DUNCAN (1834–1903), premier of Victoria, Australia, born in January 1834 at Over-Newton, a suburb of Glasgow, was second son of Duncan Gillies, a market gardener of that place, by Margaret his wife. After education at Glasgow High School he began a business career in a counting-house in his native city. He read much in his leisure, chiefly in history.

In 1852 he emigrated to Australia, and landing at Port Phillip, Victoria, proceeded to the Ballarat gold-fields, where for some time he worked as a digger. In 1853–4 he was one of the leaders of the miners in their resistance to the demands of the government, though from the outset he was strongly opposed to the use of violence and took no part in the affair of the Eureka stockade. Becoming known among his fellows as a ready speaker, he was elected a member of the local mining court, and in February 1858 he became a member of the Ballarat mining board, which then superseded that court.

Gillies, who had become a working partner in the Great Republic (mining) Company, was returned to the Legislative Assembly in 1859 as the miners' representative for Ballarat West, being re-elected in 1861, 1864, 1866, and 1868. He soon became one of the foremost debaters. On 11 May 1868 he took office as president of the board of land and works and commissioner of crown lands and surveys in the unpopular Sladen ministry, and was sworn a member of the executive council. Promptly rejected on seeking re-election, he sought a constituency where his growing antipathy to democracy might find favour. At the next general election, in March 1870, he was returned unopposed for Maryborough.

On 10 June 1872 he joined the Francis ministry as commissioner of railways and roads, and he retained the office when the cabinet was reconstructed under George Briscoe Kerferd in July 1874. He retired on 2 Aug. 1875, but was commissioner of lands and survey and president of the board of land and works and minister of agriculture in the last McCulloch government (25 Oct. 1875–21 May 1877). At the general election of May 1877 Gillies was returned for Rodney, but he was unseated on petition on the ground that undue influence had been exercised by the land department during the contest. He was exonerated from any personal knowledge of this abuse, and was re-elected for the same constituency on 2 Nov. 1877. He was prominent in the opposition to the party led by (Sir) Graham Berry [q. v. Suppl. II].

From 5 March to 3 Aug. 1880 he was commissioner of railways in the Service government, and although a strong conservative and free-trader he took office as commissioner of railways and minister of public instruction in the Service-Berry coalition which ruled the colony from 8 March 1883 to 18 Feb. 1886. When Service and Berry retired on the last date, and the ministry was reconstructed, again on a coalition basis, Gillies became premier and treasurer and Deakin chief secretary, each representing his own party in the cabinet and the Assembly.

The period of the Gillies-Deakin ministry was marked by great social and political activity. The revenue and expenditure of the colony increased to an unprecedented degree, whilst railways were extended in all directions. Useful legislation was promoted, of which the most important was the Irrigation Act of 1886 with its numerous off-shoots, but the government before its term of office ended had to contend with acute labour troubles, culminating in disastrous strikes. In 1887 Gillies declined the honour of K.C.M.G.

At the general election of March 1889 Gillies was returned for the Eastern Suburbs of Melbourne, and the government's power seemed unimpaired, though there were signs of coming difficulty. The first session passed without disaster, but in the second session a direct vote of want of confidence was carried on 30 Oct. 1890, by 55 votes to 35. Gillies resigned on 5 Nov. and led the opposition to the Munro and Shiels governments. Gillies was a consistent supporter of the cause of Australian federation. He represented Victoria at several intercolonial conferences as well as in the second and third sessions of the federal council of Australasia. He presided at the federal conference held in Melbourne in Feb. 1890, and was one of the representatives of Victoria at the national Australasian convention which met in Sydney in March and April 1891.

From 6 Jan. 1894 to 5 Jan. 1897 Gillies was agent-general for the colony in London. Returning to Melbourne, he again entered Parliament (14 Oct. 1897) as member for Toorak, and was re-elected in 1900. On 14 Oct. 1902 he was unanimously chosen as speaker of the House of Assembly. But failing health hampered the performance of his duties. He died of heart failure on 12 Sept. 1903 in the Speaker's apartments at the State Parliament House, and was buried in Melbourne general cemetery.

Gillies lacked many of the qualities of a popular leader. Even among his political supporters his general demeanour was somewhat cold and unsympathetic, but he gained respect by his conspicuous fairness and magnanimity. His speeches were models of clearness and force. He proved himself a powerful leader of the house, and in that capacity displayed tact and resource.

A portrait of Gillies in oils, three-quarter length, by Tennyson Cole, is in the National Gallery of Victoria at Melbourne.

[The Times, 14 Sept. 1903; Melbourne Age, 14, 15, 16 Sept. 1903; Melbourne Argus, 14 Sept. 1903; Australasian, 19 Sept. 1903; Johns's Notable Australians, 1908; Turner's History of the Colony of Victoria, vol. ii. 1904; Australian Year Book, 1904; Mennell's Dict. of Australas. Biog. 1902; Colonial Office Records.] C. A.

GIROUARD, DÉSIRÉ (1836–1911), Canadian judge, born at St. Timothy, co. Beauharnois, Province of Quebec, on 7 July 1836, was son of Jérémie Girouard by his wife Hippolite Piccard. He was descended on the father's side from Antoine Girouard, private secretary to De Ramezay, governor of Montreal in 1720. After attending the Montreal College he took the law course at McGill University, obtaining the first prize three years consecutively, and graduating B.C.L. in 1860, D.C.L. in 1874; he was also LL.D. of Ottawa University. He was called to the bar of Lower Canada in October 1860, and was appointed Q.C. in October 1880. He attained great distinction at the bar, especially in commercial cases, and was a well-known writer on legal and international questions. In 1860, before he was called, he published a useful treatise in French on bills of exchange. He also wrote on the civil laws of marriage and on the Insolvent Act. He was one of the chief collaborators in 'La Revue Critique,' which in 1873–4 gave expression to the dissatisfaction of the Montreal bar with the then existing Quebec court of appeals and led to the reconstitution of that court in 1874. He first stood for the Canadian Parliament in 1872, but was not successful till 1878, when he became conservative member for the constituency of Jacques Cartier, and held the seat for seventeen years, until the close of his political career. In Parliament, where he proved a good debater, he carried in 1882 a bill legalising marriage with a deceased wife's sister. Later, in 1885, with some other conservative French-Canadian members, he opposed the government on the subject of the execution of Louis Riel [q. v.]. He was chairman of the standing committee on privileges and elections, presiding in one well-known case—the Langevin-McGreevy case—over 104 sittings. He was offered a seat in the dominion cabinet, but preferred a judgeship, and was appointed in September 1895 to the bench of the supreme court of Canada. He was senior puisne judge when he died at Ottawa from a carriage accident on 22 March 1911.

Girouard was not only eminent as a lawyer and judge, but he was also an authority on the early history of the settlement of Montreal. In recognition of his historical researches he was presented by the governor-general with the Confederation medal in 1895. He began publishing the results of his studies in 1889, and in 1893 his papers, translated by his son, D. H. Girouard, were collected at Montreal under the title 'Lake St. Louis, Old and New, and Cavalier de la Salle.'

He was three times married: (1) in 1862 to Marie Mathilde, daughter of John Pratt of Montreal; she died in 1863; (2) in 1865 to Essie, daughter of Dr. Joseph Cranwill of Ballynamona, Ireland; she died in 1879; (3) on 6 Oct. 1881 to Edith Bertha, youngest daughter of Dr. John Beatty of Cobourg, Ontario. He left four daughters and six sons, one of his sons by his second wife being Sir Percy Girouard, at one time governor of the East Africa Protectorate.

[The Times, 23 March 1911; Montreal Daily Star, 22 March 1911; Canadian Parliamentary Guide; Canadian Who's Who, 1910; Morgan's Canadian Men and Women of the Time, 1898.]

C. P. L.

GISSING, GEORGE ROBERT (1857–1903), novelist, born in the Market Place, Wakefield, on 22 Nov. 1857, was eldest child in a family of three sons and two daughters of Thomas Waller Gissing (1829–1870), a Suffolk man of literary and scientific attainments, who settled at Wakefield as a pharmaceutical chemist, was author of a 'Wakefield Flora,' and corresponded on botanical subjects with Hooker, Bentham, and other botanists. The novelist's mother (still living) was Margaret, daughter of George Bedford of Dodderhill, a well-known solicitor in Droitwich. A younger brother, Algernon, enjoys some reputation as a novelist. George, who was profoundly influenced by his father, passed from private day schools in Wakefield to Lindow Grove, a Quaker boarding-school at Alderley Edge, where his unsociability and intellectual arrogance asserted itself at times unpleasantly, but where he shone on speech-days (see *Born in Exile*, chap. i.). In 1872 he came out first in the kingdom in the Oxford local examination, and obtained an exhibition at Owens College, Manchester. At the end of his first session he won Dr. Ward's English poem prize; he also gained a special prize for classics and the Shakespeare scholarship, and took a high place with honours in the London intermediate arts (see *Owens Coll. Union Mag.* Jan. 1904, p. 80). Unhappily, at this critical period, as at other times of his life, amorous propensities led him into serious trouble. His career at Owens broke off in disgrace, and his pride cut him adrift and made a temporary pariah of him; his health, too, was temporarily impaired by 'insane' overwork at college.

For eight or nine years after his disappearance from Manchester his resources were extremely precarious, and he was dogged by many hardships. After a brief period of clerkship at Liverpool he crossed as a steerage passenger to America, and was for a short time a classical tutor and then a gas-fitter at Boston. At Niagara he contemplated suicide; in Chicago he came near to absolute starvation. His experiences as a penniless rover in American cities are described with little deviation in 'New Grub Street' and elsewhere. Although he was neither morose nor eccentric in motive or bearing, he showed a curious inability to do the sane, secure thing in the ordinary affairs of life. An ill-considered marriage increased his embarrassment. He lacked social nerve, and the everyday conflicts of social intercourse bewildered and confounded him. Early attempts to obtain remunerative employment in the American press failed. In 1877, however, he managed to return to Europe, and then in the quiet atmosphere of Jena studied Goethe, Haeckel, and Schopenhauer, to be followed by Comte and Shelley. He became an adept in religious and metaphysical discussion, and boxed the compass of opinion like his own Godwin Peak (in *Born in Exile*). His correspondence at this time with a friend in Berlin, Herr Edward Bertz, author of 'Philosophie des Fahrrads' (1900) and other works, forms an autobiographical document of extraordinary impressiveness and candour.

On his return to England about the close of 1878 he illustrated his debt to Germany in a crude but powerful novel entitled 'Workers in the Dawn' (*Athenæum*, 12 June 1880), in which the Wertherian hero is, of course, the author, while Casti is his Teutonic confidante. Gissing, who risked the greater part of his ready money upon this book, confidently anticipated large profits. But the book was read by few save the critics, who denounced its 'dangerous' tendencies, and Gissing was once more faced by hunger and destitution. Copies, however, were sent to Mr. John Morley and to Mr. Frederic Harrison, both of whom recognised its power and interest. In 1882 the author became tutor to Mr. Harrison's sons; he obtained other pupils and an opening for occasional articles (such as a sketch 'On Battersea Bridge') in the 'Pall Mall Gazette.' His means were still small, but he was no longer destitute; yet his unpractical contempt for journalism, his idealism as an artist, no less than the necessity of providing an allowance, however small, for the wife from whom he was separated, involved him often in pecuniary difficulties. Devoted to classical literature, he read assiduously in the British Museum, neglecting the chance of obtaining further pupils and of contributing to the 'Fortnightly,' and cultivating the conception of himself as a social outlaw. His next books, 'The Unclassed' (1884; new edit. 1895), dedicated to his lifelong friend, Mr. Morley Roberts, 'Isabel Clarendon' (1886), 'Demos' (1886), and 'Thyrza' (1887), were all written from this point of view, and illustrated the degrading effects of poverty on character.

'Demos,' which was the first of his books to attract any popular attention, brought him 100*l.*, and with this sum he carried out a long cherished ambition of visiting the classic sites upon which he lived in imagination. He sailed on a collier to Naples, where he began 'The Emancipated' (published in 1890), described his first sight of Vesuvius as 'the proudest moment of his life,' and proceeded thence to Rome and Athens. On his return he put 'The Emancipated' for a time aside and wrote for serial publication in the 'Cornhill' 'A Life's Morning' (1888), the most vernal in atmosphere of any of his novels; but it was followed by the gloomy 'The Nether World' (1889), a full-length study of the animal conditions of semi-starvation, which goes far to justify Gissing's title as the 'spokesman of despair.' This and 'New Grub Street' (1891), a realistic study of the ruin by pecuniary care and overwork of an author's powers of imagination, for which he received 150*l.*, are the most closely observed and vigorously characterised of all his fuller developed novels.

Gissing's first wife was now dead, and in 1890 he married again, with unfortunate results. Comparative success enabled him to live away from London. At Exeter he wrote the disquieting and introspective 'Born in Exile' (1892) and began 'Denzil Quarrier' (1892; new edit. 1907), which he completed at Dorking, where he met George Meredith, one of his earliest appreciators. In 1892–3 he wrote at Clevedon 'The Odd Women' (new edit. 1907), an artistic study of three luckless and moneyless women. His novels henceforth, with the partial exception of 'In the Year of Jubilee' (1894), 'Eve's Ransom' (1895), and 'The Whirlpool' (1897), in which there is a recurrence of his old semi-autobiographical manner, show an inferior artistic sincerity. His critical study of 'Charles Dickens' (1898; illustr. edit. 1902) is a masterly vindication of Dickens, whom he had worshipped from youth.

During the last ten years of his life he re-visited Wakefield several times, and spent much time in southern England, at Budleigh, and at Epsom. His love of the countryside, of English living, and English manners he described in papers in the 'Fortnightly Review' under the title of 'An Author at Grass'; they were reprinted as 'Private Papers of Henry Ryecroft' in 1903. The autobiographical value with which they were credited is a testimony to their artistic success, but they faithfully reflect his lonely temper and his impatience of control. In the autumn of 1897 he revisited Italy with Mr. H. G. Wells, and his experiences in the Calabrian portion of his tour were recorded in the graphic pages of 'By the Ionian Sea' (1901). At Rome, too, fresh material was accumulated for 'Veranilda,' the most deliberate of his works, an historical romance of the city in the fifth century—the time of Theodoric the Goth. When in England again he contributed short stories to the weekly illustrated papers and wrote 'The Town Traveller' (1898) and 'Our Friend the Charlatan' (1901), inferior novels, refashioning some old material. The state of his lungs rendered it desirable for him to go south at the close of 1901. Moving from Paris to Arcachon, and thence to St. Jean Pied-du-Port, he there completed for bread and butter an easy-going romance of real life, 'Will Warburton' (1905), and in June began for fame his historical romance 'Veranilda.' He was not destined to finish the romance. In Nov. he moved to St. Jean de Luz, contracted a slight chill, and died of pneumonia on 28 Dec. 1903, at the age of forty-six. By his second wife, from whom he was long separated, he left issue two sons, Walter Leonard and Alfred Charles Gissing, to whom a joint pension of 74*l.* was in 1904 allotted during their minority from the civil list. The unfinished 'Veranilda' was published in 1904 (with a foreword by Mr. Frederic Harrison). Gissing carried his classical learning easily and lightly, but his classical romance will not rank with the novels of his early manhood.

The intellectual beauty and sincere friendliness of Gissing's nature were obscured by a peculiar pride or sensitiveness. His idiosyncrasies wore down as he grew older, but he lost also his extraordinary power of intensifying the misery of the world's finer spirits who are thrown among 'the herd that feed and breed' and are stupidly contented. His prose style is scholarly, suave, subtle, and plastic. Critics have deemed him a classicist who missed his vocation, but few classicists have written so much or so well. His imperfect understanding of the *joie de vivre* reduced his public while he lived; but there are signs that his work is obtaining a better co-ordinated appreciation since his death.

In addition to the works already enumerated Gissing wrote: 1. 'The Paying Guest,' 1895. 2. 'Sleeping Fires,' 1895. 3. 'Human Odds and Ends' (stories), 1898. 4. 'The Crown of Life' (early chapters semi-autobiog.), 1899. 5. 'The House of Cobwebs, and other Stories' (with an introductory survey of Gissing's books by the present writer), 1906.

A portrait appears in William Rothenstein's 'English Portraits' (1898), reduced in later (pocket) editions of the popular 'Ryecroft Papers.' A drawing by Mr. H. G. Wells is reproduced in the 'New York Critic.' The MSS. of Gissing's novels passed to his brother Algernon.

[The Times, 29 Dec. 1903; Guardian, 6 Jan. 1904; Outlook, 2 Jan. 1904; Sphere, 9 Jan. 1904 (portrait); Athenæum, 2 and 16 Jan. 1904, 7 July 1906; Academy, 9 and 16 Jan. 1904; New York Nation, 11 June 1903; Independent Rev., Feb. 1904; New York Critic, June 1902; Bookman, July 1906; Albany, Christmas No., 1904; Monthly Rev. vol. xvi.; Murray's Mag. iii. 506–18; National Rev., Oct. 1897, Nov. 1904, Nov. 1905; Saturday Rev., 19 Jan. 1895 and 13 April 1896; Gent. Mag., Feb. 1906; C. F. G. Masterman's In Peril of Change, 1905, pp. 68–73; Atlantic Monthly, xciii. 280; Upton Letters, 1905, p. 206; English Illustrated Rev., Nov. 1903; Nineteenth Cent., Sept. 1906; Fortnightly Rev., Feb. 1904; Manchester Guardian, 23 May 1906; Evening News, 18 June 1906; Manchester University Mag., May 1910; George Gissing, an Impression, by H. G. Wells, originally written as introduction to Veranilda; private information.] T. S.

GLADSTONE, JOHN HALL (1827–1902), chemist, born at 7 Chatham Place West, Hackney, London, on 7 March 1827, was the eldest son of John Gladstone by his wife Ali on Hall. The second son, George (1828–1909), a prominent educationalist, was for many years chairman of the School Board of Hove, Sussex. The father came from Kelso, where the family had been established since 1645, and after a successful career as a wholesale draper and warehouseman retired from business in 1842. John, after being privately educated, entered in 1844 University College, London, and attended the chemistry lectures of Professor Thomas Graham [q. v.], gaining a gold medal for original research, and publishing a paper on guncotton and xyloidine. In 1847 he went to Giessen University, where he was a pupil of Liebig, and after graduating Ph.D. there he returned to London in 1848. From 1850 to 1852 he was lecturer on chemistry at St. Thomas's Hospital, and in 1853 he was elected F.R.S. He sat on the royal commission which inquired into lighthouses, buoys and beacons from 1859 to 1862, and on the committee which the war office appointed in 1864 to investigate questions regarding guncotton. He succeeded Michael Faraday [q. v.] as Fullerian professor of chemistry at the Royal Institution in 1874, but resigned in 1877. Amongst the other important offices he held in scientific societies were president of the Physical Society (1874), of which he was a founder, and of the Chemical Society (1877–9); in 1892 he was made an honorary D.Sc. of Trinity College, Dublin, on the occasion of its tercentenary celebrations, and in 1897 he received the Davy medal from the Royal Society.

Gladstone was one of the founders of the new science of physical chemistry. A long series of papers—Professor Tilden estimates them at 140 by himself alone, and seventy-eight in collaboration—contributed to various learned societies through life contains the record of his researches. In his earlier years his chief discoveries concerned chemistry in relation to optics, and the refraction and the dispersion of liquids. He was one of the earliest students in spectroscopy, and published several papers, one written with Sir David Brewster, on the 'Solar Spectrum.' In 1872, with his assistant Alfred Tribe, he discovered that zinc covered with spongy copper would decompose water, and from that time the copper-zinc couple has become one of the most familiar pieces of chemico-electrical apparatus. The discovery was immediately followed by experiments as to the value of the copper-zinc union as a reducing agent for both organic and inorganic compounds. The results were published in the 'Journal of the Chemical Society' between 1872 and 1875. Papers on a similar subject, 'The Chemistry of the Secondary Batteries of Planté and Faure,' which were communicated to 'Nature' (1882–3), appeared in 1883 in volume form.

As reformer and promoter of education, Gladstone holds high rank. He was a pioneer of technical education and manual instruction, and one of the earliest advocates of the introduction of science into elementary schools. From 1873 to 1894 he sat on the London School Board, being vice-chairman from 1888 to 1891. In 1868 he contested the parliamentary representation of York as a liberal, but was unsuccessful, and though he was frequently asked to stand for other constituencies (cf. *Life of Lord Kelvin*, p. 761), his membership of the school board remained his only public office. To this he gave time and thought liberally, and as chairman of the school management and the books and apparatus committees he was responsible for many of the changes in the curriculum and improvements in the methods of education, which he described in the memorandum he contributed to the 'Life and Letters of Professor Huxley' (i. 350). He was an ardent advocate of spelling reform, and succeeded in 1876 in getting the school board to pass a resolution in its favour. The Spelling Reform Association was started in 1879 after a meeting in his house.

Gladstone was active in philanthropic and charitable work, and keenly interested in Christian endeavour, organising devotional meetings and bible classes among educated men and women. He was a vice-president of the Christian Evidence Society, and wrote and lectured frequently for it on Christian apologetics. He published 'The Antiquity of Man and the Word of God' (anonymously) (1864); 'Theology and Natural Science' (1867); 'Points of Supposed Collision between the Scriptures and Natural Science' (1880) (in Christian evidence lectures, 2nd ser.); and 'Miracles' (1880) (*ib.* 4th ser.). He was one of the earliest collaborators with Sir George Williams [q. v. Suppl. II] in the work of the Young Men's Christian Association, with which he was connected from 1850; he was specially active in its international relationships.

Gladstone died at 17 Pembridge Square, Notting Hill, London, on 6 Oct. 1902, and is buried in Kensal Green cemetery. He was twice married: (1) in 1852, to Jane May (*d.* 1864), only child of Charles Tilt, the publisher, by whom he had one son and six daughters; (2) in 1869, to Margaret, daughter of David King, LL.D. [q. v.]; she died in 1870, leaving a daughter. A cartoon portrait of Gladstone by 'Spy' appeared in 'Vanity Fair' in 1891.

Besides the works mentioned Gladstone was author of: 1. A memorial volume on his first wife (privately printed), 1865. 2. 'Michael Faraday,' 1872 (often reprinted), a work inspired by intimate personal knowledge and friendship. 3. 'Spelling Reform from an Educational Point of View,' 1878 (2nd edit. 1879). 4. 'Object Teaching,' 1882. He contributed to the 'Memoirs' issued by the Egypt Exploration Fund papers on the composition of the metals found in the course of the explorations (cf. the volume on 'Dendereh,' 1900). He also wrote a few hymns, which have been included in collections like 'Hymns for Christian Associations.'

[Proc. Roy. Soc., vol. 75, 1905; Trans. Chemical Soc., April 1905; Nature, 16 Oct. 1902; Phonetic Journal, 2 Jan. 1897; private information.] J. R. M.

GLAISHER, JAMES (1809–1903), astronomer and meteorologist, born at Rotherhithe on 7 April 1809, was son of James Glaisher, who soon removed with his family to Greenwich. There the boy, whose opportunities of education were slender, made the acquaintance of William Richardson, an assistant at the Royal Observatory, then under the direction of John Pond [q. v.], astronomer royal. Glaisher visited the observatory and was deeply impressed by Pond's delicate manipulation of the scientific instruments. A younger brother John became a computer in the observatory. From 1829 to 1830 James worked on the ordnance survey of Ireland under Lieut.-col. James. The occupation was thoroughly congenial, but serious illness brought on by exposure terminated the engagement. In 1833 Prof. (afterwards Sir George) Airy [q. v. Suppl. I], then director of the Cambridge University observatory, appointed Glaisher an assistant there, and with the equatorial he made a series of observations of the position of Halley's comet at its return in 1835. On 18 June 1835 Airy became astronomer-royal at Greenwich, and Glaisher followed him to the Royal Observatory on 4 Dec. He was succeeded at Cambridge by his brother John, who ten years later was assistant to Dr. John Lee (1783–1866) [q. v.] at Hartwell House, Aylesbury, and died in 1846.

In 1838 Airy put Glaisher in charge at Greenwich of the new magnetic and meteorological department, which was at first designed to last for a period of three years. But the term was afterwards extended to five, and the department was finally made permanent. As its chief till 1874 Glaisher organised the science of meteorology, and earned for himself the title 'Nestor of Meteorologists.'

Scientific meteorology was in its infancy when Glaisher began his work in it, and his first efforts were devoted to improving the instruments and organising observations. In February 1847 he communicated to the Royal Society his first important research—the result of three years' experiments—on 'The amount of the radiation of heat at night from the earth and from various bodies placed on or near the surface of the earth.' In 1847 he published his useful 'Hygrometrical Tables adapted to the Use of the Dry and Wet Bulb Thermometer,' which passed through very many editions. From 1848 to 1876 he regularly communicated to the Royal Society or the Meteorological Society tabulations and discussions of meteorological observations made at Greenwich. An error which Glaisher detected in 1847 in one of the registrar-general's quarterly meteorological reports led him to organise a system of precise meteorological observation which succeeded where all previous attempts had failed. He induced sixty volunteers (mostly medical men and clergymen) in different parts of the country to take daily weather notes with the accurate standard thermometer invented by Richard Sheepshanks [q. v.]. Filling up vacancies as they occurred among these volunteer observers, Glaisher succeeded in maintaining his voluntary service till his death. From 1847 to 1902 he prepared the meteorological reports for the registrar-general's returns of births, deaths and marriages. During 1849 he helped the 'Daily News,' by inspecting apparatus and offering various suggestions, to establish a daily weather report, which was first tried on 31 Aug. 1848, and being then soon abandoned, was revived in permanence with Glaisher's co-operation in the following year.

Glaisher joined the Royal Astronomical Society in 1841, and was elected F.R.S. in 1849. Other societies in whose affairs he was active were the Royal Microscopical, of which he was president in 1865–8, and the Photographic, of which he was president from 1869 to 1892. The British Meteorological Society, now the Royal Meteorological Society, was formed with Glaisher as secretary on 3 April 1850 at a meeting summoned by John Lee [q. v.] at Hartwell House. Glaisher remained secretary until 1872, but during 1867–8 retired from this office to serve as president. Through the Society's early years, Glaisher was its mainstay.

Glaisher endeavoured with energy to illustrate the practical value of meteorological research. He sought to define the relations between the weather and the cholera epidemics in London in 1832, 1849, and 1853–4 in a meteorological report for the general board of health in 1854. Glaisher often gave evidence before parliamentary committees on bills dealing with water supply, and in 1863 he prepared an official report on the meteorology of India. He studied the meteorological conditions affecting water supply and joined the board of directors of gas and water companies at Harrow and Barnet.

Glaisher was brought prominently into public notice by his active association with aeronautics. In 1861 the British Association reappointed a committee which had made some unsuccessful efforts in 1852 to pursue meteorological observation from balloons. A large balloon was constructed for the purpose by Henry Coxwell [q. v. Suppl. I], and in it he and Glaisher made with necessary instruments eight ascents in 1862. In four of these ascents from the Crystal Palace, and in one from Mill Hill, Hendon, Glaisher accompanied Coxwell as an ordinary passenger on ascents for public exhibition. The greatest height attained on these occasions was between six and seven thousand feet. Three ascents from Wolverhampton were arranged solely in the interest of the British Association's committee, and immense altitudes were scaled. On 17 July 1862, the first ascent from Wolverhampton, a height of 26,000 feet was reached, and on 18 August, 23,000 feet. The most remarkable feat was the third ascent from Wolverhampton on 5 September, when the height was reckoned at nearly seven miles (cf. *British Association Report*, 1862, pp. 384, 385). At an elevation of 29,000 feet Glaisher became unconscious. Coxwell temporarily lost the use of his limbs, but seized with his teeth the cord which opened the valve, and by this means caused the balloon to descend from an altitude of 37,000 feet. Neither Glaisher nor Coxwell suffered permanent injury. Glaisher made many later ascents: eight in 1863, eight in 1864, and four in

1865 and 1866. He published in full detail his meteorological observations in the 'British Association Reports' (1862-6). Subsequently he ascended in a captive balloon at Chelsea, at the invitation of its owner, Mr. Giffard, and made observations at low altitudes (cf. *British Association Report*, 1869). In 1869 Glaisher contributed an account of his ascents to 'Voyages Aériens,' in which C. Flammarion, W. D. Fonville, and G. Tissandier were his coadjutors. He afterwards superintended the production of the English edition of that book under the title 'Travels in the Air' (1871; new edit. 1880). The Aeronautical Society was founded in 1866, and Glaisher was its first treasurer. But his interest in aeronautics was always subsidiary to the scientific results to be obtained by their means.

In spite of his devotion to meteorology, Glaisher always maintained his interest in astronomy and mathematical science. In 1875 he joined the committee of the British Association on mathematical tables of which his son, Dr. J. W. L. Glaisher, was reporter. With help supplied by a grant from the association he completed for this committee the 'Factor Tables' begun by Burckhardt in 1814 and continued by Dase in 1862–5. Glaisher computed the smallest factor of every number not divisible by 2, 3, or 5 of the fourth, fifth, and sixth millions, those of the first, second, third, seventh, eighth, and ninth millions having been dealt with by his predecessors. Glaisher published his enumerations in 3 vols. 4to, 1879–83.

After retiring from the Royal Observatory at Greenwich, in 1874, Glaisher continued to supply his quarterly report to the registrar-general until the last year of his life. He took great interest in the Palestine Exploration Fund, being chairman of the executive committee from 1880; he contributed to the publications fifteen papers on meteorological observations made in Palestine.

Glaisher retained his vigour of mind and body until near his death at The Shola, Croydon, on 7 Feb. 1903, in the ninety-fourth year of his age. A bust presented by the fellows of the Royal Photographic Society in 1887 belongs to the Royal Meteorological Society.

Glaisher married in 1843 Cecilia Louisa, youngest daughter of Henry Belville, first assistant at the Royal Observatory. He had two sons and a daughter. Dr. James Whitbread Lee Glaisher, F.R.S., is his surviving son.

Besides the works cited and papers communicated to the Royal Society, the Royal Astronomical Society, the Meteorological Society, and the British Association, Glaisher translated Flammarion's 'Atmosphere' and Guillemin's 'World of Comets' (1876).

[Quarterly Journ. Roy. Meteorolog. Soc. (by Mr. Marriott), vols. xxix. and xxx.; Roy. Astron Soc. Monthly Notices (by W. Ellis) 1903; Observatory Mag., March 1903; private information.] H. P. H.

GLENESK, first Baron. [See Borthwick, Sir Algernon, 1830–1908.]

GLOAG, PATON JAMES (1823–1906), theological writer, born at Perth on 17 May 1823, was eldest son in the family of six children of William Gloag, banker, by his wife Jessie Burn. William Ellis Gloag, Lord Kincairney [q. v. Suppl. II], was a younger brother. His eldest sister, Jessie Burn Gloag, established in Perth one of the first ragged schools in Scotland. After finishing his school training at Perth Academy in 1839, Gloag studied at Edinburgh University (1840–3). Owing mainly to the disruption of 1843 he left Edinburgh and completed at St. Andrews (1843–6) the curriculum preparatory for the ministry of the Church of Scotland.

Licensed a preacher by Perth presbytery on 10 June 1846, Gloag, from 1848 to 1857, was first assistant, and then successor, to Dr. Russell at Dunning, Perthshire, and from 1860 to 1870 was parish minister of Blantyre, Lanarkshire, where he provided a new parish church, and established a savings bank. Meanwhile he published 'A Treatise on Assurance of Salvation' (1853), 'A Treatise on Justification' (1856), 'Primeval World, or Relation of Geology to Theology' (1859), 'The Resurrection' (1862), and 'Practical Christianity' (1866). In 1857, 1862, and 1867 he visited Germany, where he made friends with Tholuck and other divines, and familiarised himself with German theological literature.

In 1871 he became parish minister of Galashiels, and while there greatly extended his reputation as preacher and author. In 1879 he was Baird lecturer, taking for his subject 'The Messianic Prophecies.' A new church was completed in 1881 to meet the needs of his growing congregation. Although no ardent ecclesiastic, he moved in the general assembly of the Church of Scotland of 1887 for the relaxation of the eldership test. In 1889 he was moderator of the general assembly, and in his closing address he urged the importance of the highest possible culture for the Christian minister. In June 1892 he resigned his parochial charge, devoting himself in Edinburgh to theological research, and finding recreation in the study of numismatics. In 1896–9 he was interim professor of biblical criticism in Aberdeen University. In March 1867 Gloag had received the honorary degree of D.D. from St. Andrews, and he was made LL.D. of Aberdeen in April 1899. In 1897 his ministerial jubilee was celebrated by students and friends. After 1898 his health gradually failed. He died at Edinburgh on 9 Jan. 1906, and was interred in the family burying-ground in Dunning churchyard. The Galashiels parishioners placed a memorial window in St. Paul's Church, Galashiels. On 23 Jan. 1867 Gloag married Elizabeth S. Lang, third daughter of the Rev. Gavin Lang of Glasford. She survived him without issue. While Gloag was moderator the members of his congregation presented him with his portrait in oils, by Sir George Reid, P.R.S.A., which remains in Mrs. Gloag's possession.

Gloag's later theological publications show the influence of German scholarship of the liberal orthodox school. Chiefly valuable for their analytical criticism and exegesis of the New Testament, they give no support to the new higher criticism. The chief of them are: 1. 'Commentary on the Acts of the Apostles,' 2 vols. 1870. 2. 'Introduction to the Pauline Epistles,' 1874. 3. 'Commentary on the Epistle of St. James,' 1883. 4. 'Exegetical Studies,' 1884. 5. 'Introduction to the Catholic Epistles,' 1887. 6. 'Commentary on the Thessalonians,' 1887. 7. 'Introduction to the Johannine Writings,' 1891. 8. 'Introduction to the Synoptic Gospels,' 1895.

Gloag translated into English Lechler and Gerok's 'Apostelgeschichte' in 1865, Meyer's 'Apostelgeschichte' in 1887, Lünemann's 'Thessaloniker' in 1880, and Huther's 'St. James and St. Jude' in 1881. In 1880 he edited, with memoir, a volume of sermons by Dr. Veitch, Edinburgh. He issued as 'Bible Primers' a 'Life of St. Paul' (1881), and a 'Life of St. John' (1892). In 1891 he published 'Subjects and Mode of Baptism.'

[Mrs. Gloag's Paton J. Gloag, D.D., LL.D., 1908; information from Mrs. Gloag; Life and Work Magazine, July 1889 and February 1906; Scotsman and Glasgow Herald, 10 Jan. 1906; Border Standard, 6 July 1907.]

T. B.

GLOAG, WILLIAM ELLIS, Lord Kincairney (1828–1909), Scottish judge, born at Perth on 7 Feb. 1828, was son of William Gloag, banker in Perth, by his wife Jessie, daughter of John Burn, writer to the Signet, Edinburgh. Educated at Perth grammar school and Edinburgh University, he passed on 25 Dec. 1853 to the Scottish bar, where he enjoyed a fair practice. A conservative in politics, he was not offered promotion till 1874, when he was appointed advocate depute on the formation of Disraeli's second ministry. In 1877 he became sheriff of Stirling and Dumbarton, and in 1885 of Perthshire. In 1889 he was raised to the bench, when he took the title of Lord Kincairney. His career as a judge proved eminently successful. He died at Kincairney on 8 Oct. 1909, and was buried at Caputh. In 1864 Gloag married Helen, daughter of James Burn, writer to the Signet, Edinburgh, by whom he had one son, William Murray Gloag, professor of law at Glasgow University, and three daughters. There is a portrait of him, by Sir George Reid, at Kincairney.

[Scotsman, 9 Oct. 1909; Roll of the Faculty of Advocates; Records of the Juridical Society; History of the Speculative Society, pp. 32, 145, 201.]

G. W. T. O.

GODFREY, DANIEL (1831–1903), bandmaster and composer, eldest of four sons of Charles Godfrey, bandmaster of the Coldstream guards for fifty years, was born at Westminster on 4 Sept. 1831. His eldest brother, George William Godfrey, was well known as a playwright. Daniel was educated at the Royal Academy of Music, where he subsequently became professor of military music and was elected a fellow. In his early days he was a flute player in Jullien's orchestra and at the Royal Italian Opera. In 1856, on the recommendation of Sir Michael Costa, he was, through the influence of the Prince Consort, appointed bandmaster of the Grenadier guards, and one of his first duties was to play into London the brigade of guards returning from the Crimea. In 1863 he composed his famous 'Guards' waltz for the ball given by the officers of the guards to King Edward VII and Queen Alexandra, then Prince and Princess of Wales, on their marriage. This was followed by the 'Mabel' and 'Hilda' waltzes, which enjoyed universal popularity. During one of the visits of the guards band to Paris, Bizet, the composer of 'Carmen,' unconsciously caught the theme of one of them, and it figures in the finale to the first act of Bizet's 'Les Pêcheurs des Perles.' Godfrey made a tour with his band in the United States in 1876 in celebration of the centenary of American Independence. It was the first visit of an English military band since the creation of the republic, and a special Act of Parliament had to be passed to authorise it. At Queen Victoria's jubilee (1887) he was promoted second-lieutenant—the first bandmaster who received a commission in the army. He was also decorated with the jubilee medal and clasp. In 1891 he reached the age limit of sixty, but his period of service was extended for five years. He retired from the army on 4 Sept. 1896, with the reputation of England's leading bandmaster. Subsequently he formed a private military band which played at the chief exhibitions in England and with which he twice toured America and Canada. He rendered splendid service to the cause of military music, and was very successful as an 'arranger' of compositions for military bands. He died at Beeston, Nottinghamshire, on 30 June 1903. Godfrey married in 1856 Joyce Boyles, by whom he had two sons and three daughters. His eldest son, Dan Godfrey (*b.* 1868), a well-known conductor, is musical director to the corporation of Bournemouth. A cartoon of Godfrey by 'Spy' appeared in 'Vanity Fair' on 10 March 1888.

[Musical Times, Aug. 1903; British Musical Biogr.; Grove's Dict. of Music, 1906, ii. 192; Theatre, 1891, 1899 (portrait); private information.] J. C. H.

GODKIN, EDWIN LAWRENCE (1831–1902), editor and author, born on 2 Oct. 1831 at his maternal grandmother's house at Moyne, co. Wicklow, was eldest child of James Godkin [q. v.], presbyterian clergyman and journalist with strong nationalist sympathies. His mother, Sarah Lawrence, was of Cromwellian ancestry. Of delicate health, he spent his early childhood mainly in Wicklow, and when seven years old was sent to a preparatory school in Armagh, where his father was then living. For over four years, from 1841 to 1846, he was at Silcoates school for the children of congregational ministers, near Wakefield in Yorkshire. In 1846 he entered Queen's College, Belfast, Sir Robert Hart [q. v. Suppl. II] being a younger contemporary. He was first president of the Undergraduates' Literary and Scientific Society; at the time (he wrote later) 'John Stuart Mill was our prophet, but America was our Promised Land' (*Life and Letters*, i. p. 12). In 1851 he graduated B.A. and went to London to read for the bar at Lincoln's Inn, taking rooms in the Temple. He soon turned to authorship and journalism. Godkin undertook some literary work for Cassell's publishing house, with which his father was connected. In 1853 that firm published his first book, 'The History of Hungary and the Magyars from the Earliest Period to the Close of the Late War.' In October 1853 the 'Daily News' sent him out as special correspondent to Turkey on the eve of the Crimean war. He joined Omar Pasha's army, and was in the Crimea until the end of the war, returning home in September 1855. This experience gave him a lifelong hatred of war; he held that the most important result of the Crimean war was 'the creation and development of the special correspondents of newspapers' (*Life and Letters*, i. 100).

After writing for a short time for the 'Northern Whig' at Belfast, he went out in November 1856 to the United States, and almost immediately made a tour in the southern states, noting the effects of the slave system. He corresponded with the London 'Daily News,' and was admitted to the bar of the state of New York in Feb. 1858. In 1860 he made a tour in Europe for his health. While he was in Europe the American civil war broke out, and he strongly supported the North, writing to the 'Daily News' in condemnation of the British attitude with regard to the Trent incident. On returning to the United States in September 1862, while continuing his letters to the 'Daily News,' he wrote for the 'New York Times,' the 'North American Review,' and 'Atlantic Monthly.' He also took charge for a short time of the 'Sanitary Commission Bulletin.' In 1864 he wrote of himself 'I am by nature rather fitted for an outdoor than an indoor life. I have not got the literary temperament' (*Life and Letters*, i. 229). In July 1865 he established in New York a weekly journal 'The Nation,' to represent independent thought in the United States. The paper was started by subscription, but it did not pay in its early stages, and after the first year he took it over almost entirely as his private venture. He edited and wrote most of it till 1881, when he sold it to the 'Evening Post,' of which it became a kind of weekly edition. In 1883 he became editor in chief of both papers, retiring on account of ill-health in 1899. During most of this time his sub-editor was his friend, W. P. Garrison, son of William Lloyd Garrison.

The first prospectus of the 'Nation' stated

that it 'will not be the organ of any party, sect, or body' (*Life and Letters*, i. 238). It thus inaugurated a new departure in American journalism, and it influenced public opinion in the United States, not by the extent of its circulation, which was comparatively small, but by its literary power and transparent honesty. Its contributors included the most accomplished men of letters on both sides of the Atlantic. (Sir) Leslie Stephen [q. v. Suppl. II], who stayed with Godkin in New York in 1868 and formed a high opinion of his character and capacity, was English correspondent of the paper from that year till 1873 (Maitland's *Life*, i. 207–237). The 'Nation' 'was read by the two classes which in America have most to do with forming political and economic opinion, editors and university teachers' (Bryce, p. 378). Its superiority was 'due to one man, Mr. E. L. Godkin, with whom,' wrote J. R. Lowell, 'I do not always agree, but whose ability, information, and unflinching integrity have made the "Nation" what it is' (*Life and Letters*, i. 251). He was a determined opponent of corruption in political and municipal life in America. Though his political sympathies had lain with the republican as against the democratic party, yet on public grounds, as a civil service reformer and as a freetrader, in 1884, he supported Cleveland's candidature for the presidency as against Blaine. His paper was the recognised organ of the independents or 'Mugwumps' between 1884 and 1894. On the other hand he strongly opposed Cleveland when in 1895 he attacked England in his Venezuelan message. He was especially outspoken against Tammany Hall and its system, and was subjected in consequence to virulent attacks and constant libel actions by the leaders of Tammany. In December 1894, after the temporary defeat of Tammany, largely or mainly owing to his efforts, he was presented with a loving cup 'in grateful recognition of fearless and unfaltering service to the city of New York' (*Life and Letters*, ii. 181). He was opposed to the Spanish-American war, as well as to the South African war of Great Britain, and to the American annexation of Hawaii and the Philippines. He was also opposed, on economic grounds, to high tariffs, to the silver policy, and to bimetallism.

In 1870 he declined an offer of the professorship of history at Harvard University. In 1875 he removed to Cambridge, Massachusetts, but went back to New York in 1877. In 1875 he became a member of a commission appointed to devise a 'Plan for the government of cities in the State of New York,' which reported to the New York Legislature in 1877. In 1895 he was made an unpaid civil service commissioner. In 1889 he paid a visit to England, after an interval of twenty-seven years. Thereafter he kept in close touch with men and events in the United Kingdom, among the closest of his English friends being Mr. James Bryce and Professor A. V. Dicey. He was, like his father before him, a lifelong advocate of home rule for Ireland, and contributed two articles to the liberal 'Handbook of Home Rule' (1887) edited by Mr. Bryce. As home ruler, free trader, opponent of war and annexation, and advocate of honest and economical administration, he was in line with the advanced section of the liberal party in the United Kingdom, before socialism had come to the front, and he criticised with some bitterness the leaders on the tory side. His views are fully expounded in his 'Reflections and Comments' (New York, 1895); 'Problems of Modern Democracy' (New York, 1896); and 'Unforeseen Tendencies of Democracy' (Boston, 1898). In 1897 he was made, to his great pleasure, an hon. D.C.L. of Oxford. After serious illness in 1900 he sailed for England in May 1901, spent some time in the New Forest, died at Greenway on the Dart in Devonshire on 21 May 1902, and was buried in Hazelbeach churchyard in Northamptonshire. An inscription on his grave by Mr. Bryce describes him as 'Publicist, economist and moralist.' In his memory the 'Godkin Lectures,' on 'The Essentials of Free Government and the Duties of the Citizen,' were established at Harvard University.

Godkin was married twice: (1) in 1859, at Newhaven, Connecticut, to Frances Elizabeth (*d.* 1875), elder daughter of Samuel Edmund Foote, by whom he had three children, one of whom, a son, survived him; (2) in 1884 to Katherine, daughter of Abraham Sands. Both wives were of American birth.

Godkin was a man of marked talent. He combined with wide reading and knowledge of many countries a personal attraction which made him the 'faithful friend and charming companion' of the leaders of thought in both England and America. He gave his life's work to his adopted country, the United States, but he was never completely assimilated. Matthew Arnold considered him 'a typical specimen of the Irishman of culture' (*Life and Letters*, ii. 1). His Irish blood gave him singular frankness and buoyancy of spirits, especially in his earlier years, together with a trenchant style, powers of sarcasm and humour, and keen sympathies. His political views, which were deemed by many Englishmen the 'soundest' and 'sanest' in America, were those of a philosophic radical, though in later and more pessimistic years 'a disillusioned radical' (*Life and Letters*, ii. 238). He belonged to the school, without sharing the pedantry, of the early Benthamites, and he remained to the end of his life an advanced liberal in the sense which would have been given to that term between 1848 and 1870. He was not so much a man of original ideas as original in the strength and constancy with which he held by his principles and beliefs. By the mere force of his convictions and the ability with which he illustrated them he evoked a fervent enthusiasm for the commonplaces of good government and honest administration.

[Authorities cited; Life and Letters of Edwin Lawrence Godkin, edited by Rollo Ogden, 1907; James Bryce, Studies in Contemporary Biography, 1903; J. F. Rhodes, Historical Essays, 1909; Letters of Alexander Macmillan, p. 235; The Times, 23 May 1902; Annual Register, 1902; private information.]
C. P. L.

GODWIN, GEORGE NELSON (1846–1907), Hampshire antiquary, only surviving son of Edward Godwin, a draper of Winchester, and afterwards a farmer of Melksham, by his wife Mary Tugwell, was born at Winchester on 4 July 1846. With an only sister, Sarah Louisa, he was brought up at Winchester, and was educated there at a private school. After engaging in private tuition, and qualifying in 1868 at the London College of Divinity, he was ordained deacon in 1869 and priest in 1870. He subsequently proceeded to Trinity College, Dublin, where he gained the Cluff memorial prize in 1882, and graduated B.A. in 1884 and B.D. in 1887. After filling curacies at Heanor (1869–72), East Bergholt (1873–6), and Capel St. Mary (1876–7), he was appointed chaplain of the forces in 1877, and continued in the army until 1890, serving at Malta, Cairo, Dublin, the Curragh, and Netley Hospital. From 1890 to 1893 he was vicar of East Boldre, and after holding other parochial appointments, became curate in charge of Stokesby, Great Yarmouth, in 1904.

Godwin was best known as an antiquary and local historian. He was one of the founders of the Hampshire Field Club and Archæological Society, and was a leading authority on the history of Hampshire and neighbouring counties. His 'Civil War in Hampshire, 1642–45, and the Story of Basing House' (1882; new edit. 1904) embodies exhaustive researches into original authorities. He also wrote, amongst other topographical works, 'The Green Lanes of Hampshire, Surrey, and Sussex' (1882), and (with H. M. Gilbert) 'Bibliotheca Hantoniensis' (1891). He was editor of 'Hampshire Notes and Queries' 1896–9. His special knowledge was freely placed at the service of antiquarian and scientific societies. He died suddenly of heart failure while staying for the night at an inn in Little Walsingham on 10 Jan. 1907, and was buried in the churchyard of that village. Godwin was twice married: (1) on 13 Feb. 1870 to Mary Godwin (of a different family), by whom he had one daughter; (2) on 8 Aug. 1899 to Rose Elizabeth, daughter of George Jay of Camden Town, who survived him without issue.

In addition to the works mentioned, Godwin published: 1. 'A Guide to the Maltese Islands,' 1880. 2. 'Materials for English Church History, 1625–49,' 1895. He left unpublished 'French Prisoners of War at Rye and Winchester.'

[Hampshire Observer and Hampshire Chronicle, 19 Jan. 1907; Crockford's Clerical Directory; Brit. Mus. Cat.; private information.]
C. W.

GOLDSCHMIDT, OTTO (1829-1907), pianist and composer, was born of Jewish parents on 21 Aug. 1829 in the 'free city' of Hamburg, where Mendelssohn was born in 1809. His grandfather and father were Hamburg merchants, with an English connection, their firm having branches in Glasgow and Manchester. In early youth Otto was given pianoforte lessons by Jakob Schmitt (younger brother of Aloys), and harmony lessons by Fried. W. Grund. Mendelssohn opened the Leipzig Conservatorium on 3 April 1843, and Goldschmidt entered it in the following autumn. He studied there assiduously for three years, attending Mendelssohn's select class for pianoforte phrasing, and learning pianoforte technique from Plaidy and counterpoint from Hauptmann. He came to know Joachim, while W. S. Rockstro [q. v.] was a fellow-student. Jenny Lind [q. v.] appeared at the Gewandhaus at Leipzig on 4 Dec. 1845. From 1846 to 1848 Goldschmidt taught and played in Hamburg. In 1848 he was sent to Paris to study under Chopin, but the revolution drove him to England before he could fulfil his purpose. On 31 July 1848 he played in London at a concert given for charity by Jenny Lind (who was by this time abandoning the stage) in the concert-room of Her Majesty's Theatre; he also appeared in London on 27 March 1849 at Ella's Musical Union. In January 1850 he met Jenny Lind at Lübeck. In the same year she began a long American tour under Phineas T. Barnum. In May 1851, when her musical director, pianist, and accompanist, Benedict, was leaving for England, she sent for Goldschmidt to take his place. They were married at Boston according to the rites of the Episcopal Church on 5 Jan. 1852. Her age was then thirty-two, his twenty-three. From 1852 to 1855 they lived in Dresden, making frequent concert-tours. In 1856 they came to England, and shortly settled there. In 1859 Goldschmidt became naturalised in this country. In 1862 he began to edit with Sir William Sterndale Bennett [q. v.] the 'Chorale Book for England,' in which German stock-tunes were set to hymn-translations already made by Catherine Winkworth in her 'Lyra Germanica.' In 1863 and 1866 Goldschmidt conducted the choral portions of the festival when Jenny Lind appeared at Düsseldorf at the Whitsuntide Niederrheinisches Musikfest, where she had already sung in 1846 and 1855. In 1863 he joined the Royal Academy of Music as pianoforte professor, under Charles Lucas as principal. In 1866 Sterndale Bennett became principal, and Goldschmidt was from 1866 to 1868 vice-principal. From 1864 to 1869 he advised Dr. Temple about music at Rugby. In 1867 Jenny Lind sang at Hereford musical festival, and Goldschmidt produced there his 'Ruth, a Biblical Idyll'; this was heard again in 1869 at Exeter Hall, and in Düsseldorf on 20 Jan. 1870, when Jenny Lind made her last public appearance except for charity. In 1876 A. D. Coleridge, an enthusiastic amateur, got together an amateur choir for the first performance in England of Bach's B minor Mass (26 April 1876, St. James's Hall). The 'Bach Choir' thereupon came into being and Goldschmidt was appointed conductor. He held that office till 1885. His wife helped in the chorus. He edited many masterpieces for the collection called the 'Bach Choir Magazine.' In 1876 he was elected a member of the Athenæum Club under Rule II. His wife died on 2 Nov. 1887. In February 1891 he published a valuable collection of her cadenzas and fioriture. He died on 24 Feb. 1907 at his house, 1 Moreton Gardens, South Kensington, and was buried by his wife's side at Wynds Point on the Malvern Hills. He left two sons and a daughter.

Although Goldschmidt's opportunities came through his wife's celebrity, he used them wisely, and his German thoroughness, his sincerity of disposition, and his courtly manner made him a welcome factor in numberless musical activities. He was a knight of the Swedish order of the Vasa (1876), and was given the Swedish gold medal 'litteris et artibus,' with the commander ribbon of the polar star (1893). He was a chief officer or honorary member of the majority of London musical institutions. He owned the original autograph of Beethoven's 1802 letter to his brothers, called 'Beethoven's Will,' and presented this in 1888 to the Hamburg Stadtbibliothek. As a performer he was a surviving link with the Mendelssohn period, and his direct testimony to Mendelssohn's style as a pianist (clear and expressive, but almost pedalless) was important. He said that Mendelssohn stood always throughout his two-hour class. As a composer, Goldschmidt belonged to Mendelssohn's era; besides 'Ruth,' his published works were, 'Music, an Ode' (Leeds, 1898), a pianoforte concerto, a pianoforte trio, and various studies and pieces for the pianoforte. His publications are numbered down to op. 27.

[The Times, 26 Feb., 1 March, 13 May 1907 (will); Holland and Rockstro's Life of Jenny Lind; Musical Herald, May 1896; private information.] C. M–N.

GOLDSMID, Sir FREDERIC JOHN (1818–1908), major-general, born on 19 May 1818 at Milan, was only son of Lionel Prager Goldsmid, an officer of the 19th dragoon guards, and grandson of Benjamin Goldsmid [q. v.], Jewish financier. He early showed an aptitude for foreign languages, and after education at an English school in Paris he passed through King's College school to King's College, London. In January 1839 he received a commission in the East India Company's army, and in April joined the 37th Madras native infantry. In August 1840 his regiment was ordered to China, and there Goldsmid served as adjutant in the actions at Canton and along the coast, for which he received the Chinese war medal. In the course of the campaign he first turned his attention to the study of Oriental languages, for which he showed a marked faculty. Returning to India in 1845 he qualified as interpreter in Hindustani; he was appointed interpreter for Persian in 1849 and for Arabic in 1851. In the last year he obtained his company, and was promoted assistant-adjutant-general of the Nagpur subsidiary field force. Shortly after, thanks to the influence of General John Jacob [q. v.], Goldsmid entered the civil service, first as deputy collector and then as assistant-commissioner for the settlement of alienated lands in the newly acquired province of Sind.

On his return to England in 1855 he volunteered for active service in the Crimea, and was attached to the Turkish contingent at Kertch under General Sir Robert Vivian [q. v.]. Here he soon acquired a knowledge of Turkish. In recognition of his services he received the Turkish war medal, the order of the Medjidie (4th class), and a brevet majority in the army. He returned to India in 1856, and took up judicial work at Shikarpur. Subsequently he served on the staff of Sir Bartle Frere [q. v.], then chief commissioner of Sind, and during the Mutiny he distinguished himself in various dangerous missions.

In 1861 Goldsmid first became connected with the great scheme for linking up East and West by telegraph. In that year he arranged with the chiefs of Baluchistan and Makran for telegraph construction along the coast of Gwadar; his success in the negotiations was acknowledged by the Bombay government. In 1863 he was promoted brevet lieut.-colonel. In 1864 he was selected to superintend the gigantic task of carrying the wires from Europe across Persia and Baluchistan to India. He accompanied Col. Patrick Stewart when laying the Persian Gulf cable, and later proceeded by way of Bagdad and Mosul to Constantinople. There, after protracted negotiations, he carried through the Indo-Ottoman telegraph treaty. In 1865, on the death of Col. Patrick Stewart, he was appointed director-general of the Indo-European telegraph, and at once started for Teheran to assist in negotiating a telegraph treaty with the Persian government. For his services in securing the Anglo-Persian convention he was made a C.B. in 1866, and received the thanks of the government of India. From Teheran he travelled overland to India and back again to Europe to settle the terms of admission of the Indo-European telegraph to the European system. Subsequently Goldsmid personally superintended the construction of the telegraph line across the whole extent of Persia. Of that arduous work he gave an interesting and characteristically modest account in 'Travel and Telegraph' (1874).

After resigning the directorship of the Indo-European telegraph in 1870, Goldsmid was appointed in the following year a commissioner for the delimitation of the boundary between Persia and Baluchistan, and his award was eventually accepted by the Shah's government. In the same year Goldsmid was entrusted with the even more delicate task of investigating the claims of Persia and Afghanistan to the province of Seistan. A full account of the proceedings of the commission is contained in the voluminous collection of papers, entitled 'Eastern Persia' (1870–72), which was edited with an introduction by Goldsmid, and published under the authority of the India office in two volumes in 1876. It was a singular testimony to Goldsmid's tact and ability that despite the determined procrastination of the Persian commissioners a temporary settlement of this thorny question was reached, but not till the British commissioners had twice visited the disputed territory. The arbitral award was published at Teheran on 19 Aug. 1872; Persia was confirmed in the possession of Seistan, while a section of the Helmund was left in Afghan territory. The strict impartiality of the award satisfied neither party, but it had the desired effect of keeping the peace. For his services Goldsmid was created a K.C.S.I. in 1871, and received the thanks of the government of India. He retired from the army on 1 Jan. 1875 with a special pension and the rank of major-general.

Goldsmid's public career was not ended. In 1877 he was appointed British representative on the international commission to inquire into Indian immigration in Réunion. A joint report was issued in February 1878, and a separate report in the following April. In 1880 Goldsmid accepted the post of controller of crown lands (Daira Sanieh) in Egypt, and witnessed the outbreak there in September 1881. In June 1882 he was despatched by Lord Granville [q. v.] on a diplomatic mission to Constantinople; and on his return to Alexandria he rendered useful service in the campaign of 1882 by organising the intelligence department, for which he received the thanks of Viscount Wolseley and the war office. On his resigning the control of the crown lands on 1 May 1883 the Khedive bestowed on him the Osmanie decoration of the second class and the bronze star.

On leaving Egypt, Goldsmid accepted

from Leopold II, King of the Belgians, the post of 'administrateur déégué de l'association internationale' in the Congo, and he undertook the organisation of the administrative system in the new state. But soon after reaching the Congo Goldsmid's health broke down, and he returned to England on 31 Dec. 1883. Thenceforth he resided mainly in London, devoting himself to literary work connected with his Oriental studies, and taking an active interest in various religious and philanthropic institutions. He died at Brook Green, Hammersmith, on 12 Jan. 1908, and was buried at Hollingbourne, Kent. On 2 Jan. 1849 he married Mary (*d.* 1900), eldest daughter of Lieut.-general George Mackenzie Steuart, by whom he had issue two sons and four daughters.

In addition to the works already mentioned, and to many pamphlets and reviews, Goldsmid published 'Sáswi and Punhú,' a poem in the original Sindi, with a metrical translation (1863), and an authoritative life of 'Sir James Outram' (2 vols. 1880; 2nd edit. 1881). His knowledge of Eastern languages placed him in the forefront of Oriental critics. He joined the Royal Asiatic Society in 1864, and was an ordinary member of the council for brief periods between 1875 and 1889. He held the post of secretary from November 1885 to June 1887, and that of vice-president from 1890 to 1905. He was also a vice-president of the Royal Geographical Society, and presided over the geographical section of the British Association at the Birmingham meeting of 1886.

[The Times, 13 Jan. 1908; Journal, Royal Asiatic Soc., April 1908, art. by T. H. Thornton; Geographical Journal, Feb. 1908, art, by Sir T. H. Holdich; Sir Frederic Goldsmid, Travel and Telegraph, 1874; Sir Frederick Maurice, Campaign of 1882 in Egypt, 1908, p. 21; L. Fraser, India under Lord Curzon and After, 1911, p. 117.]

G. S. W.

GOODALL, FREDERICK (1822–1904), artist, born in St. John's Wood, London, on 17 Sept. 1822, was son of Edward Goodall [q. v.], the line engraver, by his wife Alice Le Petit, granddaughter of a Frenchman who was a printer of coloured engravings. Goodall's two brothers, Edward Goodall and Walter Goodall [q. v.], also made a reputation as artists.

Frederick, who as a child was fascinated by Turner's drawings, was educated at the Wellington Road Academy, a private school which Charles Dickens had attended. From thirteen to twenty-one he was a pupil of his father, who taught him oil painting; he also joined at sixteen a life class in St. Martin's Lane, where Etty had received instruction. In 1838 he went on a sketching tour through Normandy, and soon after extended his travels to Brittany and Ireland.

As early as 1836 Goodall exhibited water-colour paintings of Willesden Church and Lambeth Palace at the Society of Arts; the second picture was awarded the Isis medal of the society. At the same place he exhibited in 1838 an oil painting, 'Finding the Dead Body of a Miner in the Thames Tunnel,' which was awarded the large silver medal of the society. In 1839, when only seventeen, he showed at the Royal Academy his 'French Soldiers in a Cabaret.' Thenceforth he was a regular exhibitor at the Academy until 1902, only omitting the three years 1858, 1871, and 1874. Two of his early works, 'The Tired Soldier' (1842) and 'The Village Holiday' (1847), are now in the Vernon collection at the Tate Gallery and show the influence of Wilkie, a good copy of whose 'Penny Wedding' belonged to Goodall's father. A picture, 'Raising the Maypole,' at the Academy in 1851, proved very popular, and an engraving widely extended its vogue. In 1852 Goodall was elected A.R.A. His 'Cranmer at the Traitor's Gate' (1856) was engraved in line by his father. His promise attracted the notice of Samuel Rogers and Sir Robert Peel, and he early enjoyed the patronage of picture buyers. In 1857 Goodall visited Venice and Chioggia.

The winter of 1858 and the spring of 1859 were spent in Egypt, which Goodall revisited in 1870. From the date of his first Egyptian sojourn to the end of his career Goodall largely devoted himself to Eastern subjects, and thus vastly extended his popularity. The first of his Eastern paintings was 'Early Morning in the Wilderness of Shur' (Royal Academy in 1860). There followed 'The First Born' (1861) and 'The Return of a Pilgrim from Mecca' (1862). Elected R.A. in 1863, Goodall exhibited in 1864, as his diploma work, 'The Nubian Slave.' Among paintings of like theme which followed were: 'The Rising of the Nile' (1865), 'Hagar and Ishmael' (1866), 'Rebekah at the Well' (1867), 'Jochebed' (1870), 'Head of the House at Prayer' (1872), 'Subsiding of the Nile' (1873), 'Rachel and her Flock' (1875), 'The Return from Mecca' (1881), 'The Flight into Egypt' (1884), 'Gordon's Last Messenger' (1885), and 'By the Sea of Galilee' (1888), now at the People's Palace, Mile End. In 1889 he painted English landscapes such as 'A Distant View of Harrow on the Hill' (1889) and 'Beachy Head' (1896). Meanwhile he pursued his Eastern themes in 'Sheep-Shearing in Egypt' (1892) and 'Laban's Pasture' (1895). In 1897 'The Ploughman and the Shepherdess' was acquired for the Tate Gallery by public subscription. Goodall from time to time in later life painted portraits. Among his sitters were Sir Moses Montefiore (1890), William Beatty-Kingston, his wife (1890), his daughter, Rica (1894), and (Sir) Anderson Critchett (1898). Goodall's portrait by himself was exhibited at the Royal Academy in 1881.

In 1876 Goodall purchased the estate of Grims Dyke, Harrow, and on it his friend Norman Shaw built an imposing residence. But after some twelve years Goodall returned to London, and his Harrow house passed in 1890 to Sir William Schwenck Gilbert [q. v. Suppl. II]. At the end of his life he published a volume of gossiping 'Reminiscences' (1902). He died on 29 July 1904 at 62 Avenue Road, St. John's Wood, where he had resided since his removal from Harrow, and was buried in Highgate cemetery.

In 1872, then a widower, he married Alice Mary, daughter of T. W. G. Tarry, solicitor. Sons by his previous marriage were Frederick Trevelyan Goodall and Howard Goodall [qq. v.], both artists, who predeceased him.

Goodall fully satisfied the public taste, which liked a story told in paint clearly, correct in detail, and with a certain simple kind of sentiment. His painting throughout his career showed much technical ability but very little inspiration.

[Goodall's Reminiscences, 1902, with list of pictures and drawings; Graves's Royal Acad. Exhibitors, 1905–6; The Times, 1 August 1904.] F. W. G–N.

GOODMAN, Mrs. JULIA, whose maiden name was Salaman (1812–1906), portrait painter, born in London on 9 Nov. 1812, was eldest of the family of twelve sons and two daughters of Simeon Kensington Salaman by his wife Alice Cowen. Charles Kensington Salaman [q. v. Suppl. II] was her eldest brother After attending a private school in Islington, Julia developed a taste for art, receiving lessons from Robert Falkner, a pupil of Sir Joshua Reynolds. At first she successfully copied old masters but soon devoted herself to portrait painting, and obtained many commissions. In 1838 she exhibited for the first time at the Royal Academy, her last picture appearing there in 1901. Among her sitters were many persons prominent in society, including the Earl of Westmorland, Sir John Erichsen, Sir Francis Goldsmid, Sir G. A. Macfarren, Prof. David Marks [q. v. Suppl. II], and Gilbert Abbott à Beckett. Her portraits in oils or pastels numbered more than a thousand. She died at Brighton on 30 Dec. 1906, and was buried in the Golder's Green cemetery of the West London Synagogue of British Jews.

In 1836 she married Louis Goodman, a City merchant, who died in 1876. Among her seven children were Edward John Goodman, at one time sub-editor of the 'Daily Telegraph,' and Walter Goodman, a portrait painter, who painted a good portrait of his mother.

[Jewish Chronicle, 4 Jan. 1907.] M. E.

GORDON, JAMES FREDERICK SKINNER (1821–1904), Scottish antiquary, born at Keith, Banffshire, in 1821, claimed descent from the Gordons of Glenbucket, in Strathdon. Educated at Keith School and then at Madras College, St. Andrews, he gained, when fifteen years of age, the Grant bursary at St. Andrews University, and graduated there with distinction in 1840, proceeding M.A. in 1842. Appointed organising master in the (episcopal) national schools at Edinburgh, he was ordained deacon in the Scottish Episcopal Church in 1843 and priest the next year. After a first curacy to the bishop of Moray (Dr. Low) at Pittenweem, Fifeshire, he removed in 1843 to Forres as curate to Alexander Ewing, afterwards bishop of Argyll and the Isles at Forres (1843–4). His experiences at Pittenweem are narrated in his 'Scotichronicon.' In 1844 he was translated to the charge of St. Andrew's Episcopal Church, Glasgow, the oldest post-Reformation church in Scotland, and there he remained till 1890, when he retired owing to advancing years. At Glasgow he devoted much energy to the development of episcopacy, and raised funds wherewith to remodel and endow his church. He was a pioneer in effecting the removal of ruinous tenements and slums in the neighbourhood, thus initiating the movement which resulted in the Glasgow Improvement Act of 1866. His 'High Church' tendencies sometimes led to friction in his own denomination; but his earnest philanthropic work brought him general admiration.

Gordon led at the same time a strenuous literary life, closely studying the history of the catholic and the episcopal churches in Scotland, and the antiquities of Glasgow.

His chief publication was 'The Ecclesiastical Chronicle for Scotland' (4 vols. Glasgow, 1867), an elaborate and erudite work, which displayed much research; the first two volumes, entitled 'Scotichronicon,' contain a sketch of the pre-Reformation church, and an extended version of Keith's 'Catalogue of Scottish Bishops'; the third and fourth volumes, entitled 'Monasticon,' give the history of the Scottish monasteries, and biographies of the Roman catholic bishops of the post-Reformation mission. Gordon also published (all at Glasgow): 1. 'Glasghu Facies' (a history of Glasgow, written in a lively style), 1872. 2. 'The Book of the Chronicles of Keith, Grange, Ruthven, Cairney, and Botriphnie,' 1880. 3. New edition of Lachlan Shaw's 'History of the Province of Moray,' 1882. 4. 'Iona, a Description of the Island,' 1885. 5. 'Vade Mecum to and through the Cathedral of St. Kentigern of Glasgow,' 1894. Gordon also contributed an article on the 'Scottish Episcopal Church' to the 'Cyclopædia of Religious Denominations' (London, 1853), and wrote on 'Meteorology' to several encyclopædias and journals. In 1857 he received the degree of D.D. from Hobart College, U.S.A. He was an enthusiastic Freemason, having been initiated as a student at St. Andrews in 1841, and he was the oldest member of the craft at his death. After resigning the charge of St. Andrew's Church in 1890 he lived in retirement at Beith, Ayrshire, and died there on 23 Jan. 1904. He was interred with masonic honours in Beith cemetery.

[Glasgow Herald, 25 Jan. 1904; Scottish Guardian, 5 Feb. 1904; Clergy List, 1904; private information.] A. H. M.

GORDON, Sir JOHN JAMES HOOD (1832–1908), general, born on 12 Jan. 1832 at Aberdeen, was twin son of Captain William Gordon (1788–1834), 2nd Queen's royal regiment. The father served through the Peninsular war, and married at Santarem in 1818 Marianna Carlotta Loi, daughter of Luiz Conçalves de Mello, a government official in the province of Estremadura. His twin brother is General Sir Thomas Edward Gordon, K.C.B. The twins were the youngest children in a family of four sons and a daughter. John was educated at Dalmeny and at the Scottish Naval and Military Academy, Edinburgh, and with his twin brother entered the army, joining the 29th foot on 21 Aug. 1849, and becoming lieutenant on 9 Jan. 1854. He served in the Indian Mutiny campaign of 1857–8 with the Jaunpur field force, attached to 97th regiment. He was at the actions of Nasrutpur, Chanda (31 Oct.), Ameerpur, and Sultanpur, at the siege and capture of Lucknow, and storming of the Kaiser Bagh. The medal with clasp was awarded him. From September 1858 to April 1859 he acted as field-adjutant to Colonel (Sir) William Turner, commanding the troops on the Grand Trunk Road, near Benares, and the field force during operations in Shahabad. He was engaged in the final attack on Jugdespur, and in the action of Nowadi, and the subsequent pursuit. Mentioned in despatches, he was promoted captain on 2 Dec. 1859, and was made brevet-major on 30 Nov. 1860 (*Lond. Gaz.* 22 Feb. 1859). Gordon performed regimental duty in India for the next eighteen years; he was promoted major in 1860 and exchanged into the 46th regiment. Subsequently he was given the command of the 29th Punjab infantry, becoming lieut.-colonel on 21 Aug. 1875, and brevet colonel on 23 Feb. 1877. He served with the Jowaki Afridi expedition in 1877–8, and was thrice mentioned in despatches, receiving the medal and clasp.

In the Afghan war of 1878–9 he played a prominent part, commanding the 29th Punjab infantry, which was attached to the Kurram Valley column. He led a reconnaissance in force at Habib Kila on 28 Nov. 1878, and discovered that the Afghans, so far from abandoning their guns as had been reported, had taken up a strong position on the top of the pass. Gordon's report made Sir Frederick (afterwards Lord) Roberts abandon all idea of a frontal attack on the Peiwar Kotal (Lord Roberts, *Forty-one Years in India*, 1898, p. 354). Gordon's regiment formed the advance guard in the turning movement on the Spingawi Kotal on 2 Dec. During the night march some Pathans of the 29th Punjab infantry fired signal shots to warn the enemy of the British advance. The regiment was immediately displaced from its leading position. An inquiry instituted by Gordon resulted in the discovery of some of the culprits. Subsequently he was engaged in the Zaimukht expedition, including the assault of Zava, where he commanded the right column of General Tytler's force. For his services in the Afghan war he received the medal with clasp and was made C.B. in 1879. In expeditions to Karmana and against the Malikshahi Waziris in 1880 he was brigadier-general in command of the troops (*Lond. Gaz.* 4 Feb. and 7 Nov. 1879). He also served in the Mahsud Waziris expedition in 1881, when he commanded the second column; he was mentioned in despatches and was thanked by the government of India. From 1882 to 1887 he commanded a brigade of the Bengal army, and was made major-general on 20 Dec. 1886. In the Burmese expedition he commanded his brigade (1886–7), and he conducted the operations which succeeded in opening up the country between Manipur and Kendat. Once more he received the thanks of the government of India (*Lond. Gaz.* 2 Sept. 1887). Returning to England, he was made assistant military secretary at headquarters in 1890, and retained the office till 1896. He was promoted lieut.-general in 1891 and general in 1894. On 1 Jan. 1897 he was nominated member of the council of India, and held the post for ten years. He was advanced to K.C.B. in 1898, and to G.C.B. in 1908, and became colonel of 29th Punjab infantry in 1904. He resided in his last years at 35 Onslow Square, London, S.W. He died at Edinburgh on 2 Nov. 1908, and was buried in the Dean cemetery there. He married in 1871 Ella (*d.* 1903), daughter of Edward Strathearn, Lord Gordon of Drumearn [q v.], lord of appeal in ordinary, and had issue two surviving sons. both captains in the army.

In 1904 Gordon published a history of the Sikhs, illustrated by himself.

[The Times, 3 Nov. 1908; Lord Roberts, Forty-one Years in India, 30th edit. 1898; J. M. Bullock and C. O. Skelton, A Notable Military Family, The Gordons in Griamachary, 1907; Dod's Knightage; Official and Hart's Army Lists; Sir T. E. Gordon, A Varied Life: a record of military service in India, 1906, p. 236 seq.; H. B. Hanna, Second Afghan War, 1910, iii. 118; W. H. Paget, Records of Expeditions against the North-West Frontier Tribes, 1884; private information from Sir T. E. Gordon.] H. M. V.

GORDON-LENNOX, CHARLES HENRY, sixth DUKE OF RICHMOND AND first DUKE OF GORDON (1818–1903), lord president of the council, born on 27 Feb. 1818 at Richmond house, Whitehall (replaced by Richmond terrace after 1819; WHEATLEY and CUNNINGHAM'S *London*, iii. 162), was the eldest son of Charles Gordon-Lennox, fifth duke of Richmond [q. v.]. Known until his succession to the dukedom as the Earl of March, he was educated at Westminster School and Christ Church, Oxford, graduating B.A. in 1839. He entered as a cornet the royal regiment of horse guards, retiring as captain in 1844, but never saw active service. March was an aide-de-camp to the Duke of Wellington (1842–52), as was his father before him, and to Lord Hill, the duke's successor as commander-in-chief (1852–4). Meanwhile he was returned for West Sussex in the conservative interest at the general election of 1841, and held the seat until the death of his father on 21 Oct. 1860. He spoke with some frequency, and became a recognised authority on agricultural questions. In March 1859 he was appointed president of the poor law board in Lord Derby's second ministry, and was sworn of the privy council; but his tenure of office was brief, as the ministry fell in June. After the return of the conservatives to office in July 1866 Richmond was made knight of the garter on 15 Jan. 1867. He followed his leaders on parliamentary reform, and at the reconstruction of the government after the resignations of Lords Cranborne and Carnarvon and General Jonathan Peel [q. v.], he became president of the board of trade on 6 March 1867. In 1869, when the liberals had returned to office, he was 'sorely against opposing the second reading (of the Irish church bill), but went with his party' (GATHORNE HARDY'S *First Earl of Cranbrook*, i. 272). Next year he accepted the leadership of the conservative party in the House of Lords, which had been in abeyance since the retirement of Derby from public life in 1868 [see STANLEY, EDWARD GEORGE GEOFFREY SMITH]. The relations between Richmond and Disraeli were at first not altogether cordial. In parliament, though he never attempted high oratory, Richmond proved a vigorous upholder of conservative principles. In 1872, while permitting the ballot bill to pass its second reading without a division, he carried an amendment making secret voting optional by eighty-three votes to sixty-seven. On a subsequent amendment he retorted on Granville with so much warmth that the clerk had to read the standing order against 'sharp and taxing speeches' (FITZMAURICE'S *Granville*, ii. 108, 110; *Hansard*, ccxi., col. 1841). The commons having rejected his amendment, he pressed it to a division, and was defeated by 157 votes to 138.

On the formation of Disraeli's government in February 1874, Richmond became lord president of the council, though he would have preferred the secretaryship for war. He accepted his disappointment 'like a true man, professing himself ready to act for the best of the party' (*Gathorne-Hardy*, i. 335). On 18 May he introduced in a conciliatory speech the Scotch church patronage bill, substituting appointment by election for lay patronage in the Church of Scotland, and the measure became law. He also carried the Endowed Schools Act amendment bill, which had been hotly debated in the commons. Richmond's agricultural holdings bill of the following session, introduced on 12 March 1875, established presumption in favour of the tenant with compensation for various classes of improvements; it passed the lords without a division. During the debates he expressed himself strongly against any interference with liberty of contract between landlord and tenant (*Hansard*, ccxxii. col. 963). In 1876 he took charge of the elementary schools bill, a measure supplementary to the Act of 1870, and designed to enforce attendance; but his burials bill of 1877 was withdrawn after an amendment allowing nonconformist services in churchyards had been carried against him in the lords by 127 votes to 111. On 13 Jan. 1876 Richmond had been created Duke of Gordon and Earl of Kinrara in the peerage of the United Kingdom; the title of Duke of Gordon in the peerage of Scotland had expired in 1836 with his great-uncle, George, fifth Duke of Gordon [q. v.]. In August 1876, on Disraeli's promotion to the peerage, Richmond ceased to be leader in the lords. His efforts for the agricultural interest continued; in 1878, on the outbreak of cattle disease, he carried the contagious diseases (animals) bill, which dealt stringently with infection in the homesteads and made slaughter of imported beasts compulsory, except when the privy council was satisfied that the laws of the exporting country afforded reasonable security against disease. The measure did not go as far as Richmond wished, but he administered it drastically, reorganising the veterinary department of the privy council, which was afterwards replaced by the board of agriculture. The farming industry being grievously depressed, a royal commission on agriculture was appointed (4 Aug. 1879), and Richmond accepted the chairmanship. Admirably suited for the position, he conducted a wide inquiry lasting until July 1882, when his colleagues presented him with a token of esteem in silver. A preliminary report, dated 14 July 1881, dealt with Irish land tenure and cautiously admitted defects in the Ulster custom and 'Griffith's valuation.' The final report, signed unanimously, though with supplementary memoranda expressing dissidence on various points, recommended reforms connected with local administration, tithe rent-charge, the law of distress, and compulsory compensation for unexhausted improvements (*Preliminary Report, Parl. Papers*, 1881 [c. 2778], xv. 1; *Final Report, Parl. Papers*, 1882 [c. 3309], xiv. 1). Its chief outcomes were the Agricultural Holdings Act, passed by the liberal government in 1883, and the creation of the board of agriculture.

After the death of Lord Beaconsfield (19 April 1881), Richmond in a speech of 'excellent taste and judgment' proposed Salisbury for the leadership of the opposition in the lords, though privately 'giving indications that he would fain have kept it' (*Gathorne-Hardy*, ii. 163). The health of the duchess decided him not to advance his claims. He continued to take an active part in debate, while acting occasionally as a drag on the impetuosity of his new leader. He spoke incisively on the agricultural holdings bill of 1883, which went too far for his taste, and on the fall of Khartoum. Of his amendments, one making general the condition that in estimating compensation no account should be taken of the improved value which was due to the inherent qualities in the soil was accepted, after some demur, by the government. He declined, however, to do anything which, by risking the success of the bill, would be 'repugnant to the feelings of the whole of the tenant farmers of the country' (*Hansard*, cclxxxiii. col. 1828). During the crisis of 1884, produced by the refusal of the peers to pass a franchise bill unaccompanied by a redistribution of seats, Richmond's influence was on the side of peace. Summoned by Queen Victoria, who held him in high regard, he visited Balmoral on 13 Sept., and though Gladstone characterised what passed in the direction of compromise as 'waste of breath,' the ensuing correspondence with Sir Henry Ponsonby [q. v.] 'set up a salutary ferment' (Morley's *Gladstone*, iii. 130, 131). The duke opened communications with Lord Granville, making clear that the opposition was acting in good faith (*Gathorne-Hardy*, ii. 203). Northcote declared that the duke's action led 'to little more than a conference between the duke, Lord Salisbury, and Lord Cairns, and to a substantial agreement as to the course to be taken over the House of Lords' (A. Lang's *Stafford Northcote, First Earl of Iddesleigh*, ii. 205); it is clear that his mediation was of value. Richmond's part was nearly played. In the short-lived conservative ministry of 1885–6 he acted as secretary for Scotland, but when the second Salisbury government was formed in 1886 he 'went down to Scotland deliberately, and so put himself out of the way' (*Gathorne-Hardy*, ii. 254). Gradually ceasing to take part in public life, he died at Gordon castle after a short illness on 27 Sept. 1903, and was buried in the family vault in Chichester Cathedral.

Richmond, who was a conscientious and large-hearted man, by no means confined his public duties to politics. He was chancellor of the University of Aberdeen in 1861, receiving an hon. LL.D. in 1895; was appointed lord-lieutenant of the county of Banff in 1879, and ecclesiastical commissioner in 1885. In Sussex he succeeded his father as chairman of the county bench and was chairman of the West Sussex county council. He joined the Royal Agricultural Society in 1838, six months after its establishment, was member of the council from 1852 to 1857, and from 1866 to his death, was elected trustee in 1869, and was president both in 1868, when the show was held at Leicester, and in 1883, when it was held at York. At the general meeting of that year King Edward VII, then Prince of Wales, addressed him as 'the farmers' friend,' a title acknowledged by the duke to be the proudest he could bear. In 1894, when the show was held at Cambridge, he received the degree of hon. LL.D., having become hon. D.C.L. of Oxford in 1870. The duke was elected vice-president of the Smithfield Club in 1860, and was president in 1866 and 1875. He inherited and improved the famous flock of Southdown sheep at Goodwood and the herd of shorthorns at Gordon castle. He was a generous landlord; many of the crofters and small farmers on Speyside held on a merely nominal rent, and he built a concrete stone harbour for Port Gordon in 1878 at the cost of 15,000*l.*

Richmond was elected member of the Jockey Club in 1839, but took no active part in racing. Though the importance of the Goodwood meeting declined, owing to the rise of richer organisations elsewhere, he maintained its hospitality. The Tsar Alexander II and the Tsarina were his guests in 1873; the Crown Prince and Princess of Germany (afterwards the Emperor and Empress Frederick), King Edward VII, and Queen Alexandra visited him on many occasions. At his Scottish hunting seat, Glenfiddich Lodge, he shot grouse and stalked, and was a skilled salmon-fisher in the Gordon castle waters (*The Times*, 29 Sept. 1903, where a charge of undue exercise of proprietorial rights is refuted by Henry Ffennell). He revived the old hunt at Charlton, but eventually sold the hounds.

The duke married on 28 Nov. 1843 Frances Harriett, daughter of Algernon Frederick Greville, Bath king-at-arms and private secretary to the Duke of Wellington; she died on 8 March 1887. Of his four sons, the eldest, Charles Henry (*b.* 27 Dec. 1845), is the seventh and present duke. Of his two daughters, Caroline was his constant companion in later life; Florence died in 1895.

The duke's portrait, painted in 1886 by Sir George Reid, was presented to him by his Scotch tenantry, and is now at Gordon castle. Another portrait by Sir Francis Grant, P.R.A., presented by the Sussex tenantry, is at Goodwood. A cartoon portrait appeared in 'Vanity Fair' in 1870.

[Article by Sir Ernest Clarke in Journal Royal Agricultural Soc., vol. lxiv. 1903; The Times, 28 Sept. 1903; Paul, Modern England, 1905, iii. and iv.] L. C. S.

GORE, ALBERT AUGUSTUS (1840–1901), surgeon-general, born at Limerick in 1840, was eldest son of William Ringrose Gore, M.D., by his wife, Mary Jeners Wilson. He was educated in London, Paris, and Dublin, taking honours in science and medicine at Queen's College, Cork, in 1858, graduating M.D. at the Queen's University, Ireland, and being admited L.R.C.S., Ireland, in 1860. He joined the army medical staff in 1861, and was appointed assistant surgeon to the 16th lancers. When the regimental service was reduced he volunteered for service in West Africa, and took part in the bombardment and destruction of the Timni town of Massougha, on the Sierra Leone river, on 10 Dec. 1861, the attack on Madoukia on 27 Dec., and the storming and capture of the stockaded fetish town of Rohea on 28 Dec. He was mentioned in general orders for his services and for bravery in bringing in a wounded officer. In 1868 he was recommended for promotion on account of services rendered during an epidemic of yellow fever at Sierra Leone. He acted as sanitary officer to the quartermaster-general's staff during the Ashanti war in 1873, and was severely wounded in the action of 3 Nov. near Dunquah, and again at Quarman on 17 Nov. After six years' service at various base hospitals and as principal medical officer of the army of occupation in Egypt (1882) Gore was appointed principal medical officer north-west district, Mhow division, central India, and afterwards in a similar position to the forces in India. In this capacity he was responsible for the medical arrangements of the Chitral and

North-West Frontier campaigns of 1896 and 1897. He retired from the army in 1898, was made C.B. in 1899, and was granted a distinguished service pension.

He died at his residence, Dodington Lodge, Whitchurch, Shropshire, on 10 March 1901. He married in 1866 Rebecca, daughter of John White, by whom he had two sons and two daughters.

Gore was author of: 1. 'A Medical History of our West African Campaigns,' 1876. 2. 'The Story of our Service under the Crown,' 1879.

[Brit. Med. Journal, 1901, i. 679; information from Dr. W. R. Gore, his son.]

D'A. P.

GORE, GEORGE (1826–1908), electrochemist, born at Blackfriars, Bristol, on 22 Jan. 1826, was son of George Gore, a cooper in a small way of business in that city. He was educated at a small private school, from which he was removed at twelve to become an errand boy. At seventeen he was apprenticed to a cooper, following the trade for four years and supplementing his scanty education in his leisure hours. In 1851 he migrated to Birmingham, which was thenceforth his home.

He first found employment at Birmingham as timekeeper at the Soho works, next as a practitioner in medical galvanism; he subsequently became a chemist to a phosphorus factory, afterwards (1870–80) was lecturer in physics and chemistry in King Edward's School, and finally, from 1880 onwards, was head of the Institute of Scientific Research, Easy Row, Birmingham, which Gore conducted privately, and where he resided for the remainder of his life.

Gore possessed an intuition for research, and passed triumphantly from one field of physical inquiry to another. Between 1853 and 1865 he published in the 'Philosophical Magazine,' 'Pharmaceutical Journal,' 'Journal of the Chemical Society,' and elsewhere thirty papers embodying researches in chemistry and electro-metallurgy. Three dealing with the properties of electro-deposited antimony were published in the 'Philosophical Transactions of the Royal Society.' Other important researches related to the properties of liquid carbonic acid and hydrofluoric acid. In 1865 he was elected F.R.S. (with the support, among others, of Faraday, Tyndall, and Joule) on the ground of being the discoverer of amorphous antimony and electrolytic sounds, and for researches in electrochemistry.

Gore's discoveries in electro-metallurgy gave him a high reputation in Birmingham, where manufacturers eagerly availed themselves of new methods which he suggested for improving the art of electroplating. He was author of three valuable technical treatises: 'The Art of Electro-metallurgy' (1877; 5th edit. 1891); 'The Art of Scientific Discovery' (1878); 'The Electrolytic Separation and Refining of Metals' (1890). To wider fields of speculation Gore contributed 'The Scientific Basis of National Progress' (1882) and 'The Scientific Basis of Morality' (1899), where he gave expression to strong materialistic views. The University of Edinburgh made him hon. LL.D. in 1877, and in 1891 he was allotted a civil list pension of 150*l.* Of frugal habits, apparently denoting restricted means, he secretly amassed a moderate competence. He died at Birmingham on 20 Dec. 1908, and was buried there at Warstone Lane cemetery. He married in 1849 Hannah, daughter of Thomas Owen, baptist minister, and had issue one son and one daughter. His wife predeceased him in 1907. By his will he directed that his residuary estate (about 5000*l.*) should be divided equally between the Royal Society of London and the Royal Institution of Great Britain, to be applied in 'assisting original scientific discovery.' In view of the public disposal of his property, his daughter, Mrs. Alice Augusta Gore Fysh, was granted in 1911 a civil list pension of 50*l.*

[Roy. Soc. Proc. vol. lxxxiv. A.; Roy. Soc. Catal. Sci. Papers; Nature, vol. lxxix.; The Times, 24 Dec. 1908 (will); Birmingham Daily Post, 24 Dec. 1908; Men of the Time, 1899; private information. For list of Gore's electrical researches, see Electrician's Directory, 1892.]

GORE, JOHN ELLARD (1845–1910), astronomical writer, born at Athlone in Ireland on 1 June 1845, was son of John Ribton Gore, archdeacon of Achonry. After being educated privately he entered Trinity College, Dublin, where he obtained his engineering diploma with high distinction in 1865. Three years later, passing second in the open competition, he joined the Indian government works department and worked as assistant engineer on the construction of the Sirhind canal in the Punjab. There he began his observation of the stars, which had for first result the publication in 1877 of a small book entitled 'Southern Objects for Small Telescopes.' Gore retired from the Indian service in

1879 with a pension. Thenceforth he lived first at Ballisodare, co. Sligo, with his father until the latter's death, and afterwards in Dublin. He devoted himself to observations of the stars, principally with a binocular, for he never had a large telescope, and to writing on astronomy. Variable stars were chiefly the subject of his observations. In 1884 he presented to the Royal Irish Academy a 'Catalogue of Known Variable Stars' (enlarged and revised edit. 1888). A similar compilation by him, giving a list of the then computed orbits of binary stars, was published by the Irish Academy in 1890. At the same time Gore wrote much on astronomy for general reading. In some of his popular books he discussed with much judgment the theories of structure of the universe. 'Planetary and Stellar Studies' appeared in 1888; 'The Scenery of the Heavens' in 1890 (2nd edit. 1893); 'Astronomical Lessons' in 1890; 'Star Groups' in 1891; 'An Astronomical Glossary' in 1893; 'The Visible Universe' in 1893; 'The Worlds of Space' in 1894; and 'The Stellar Heavens' in 1903. In Studies in Astronomy' (1904) and in 'Astronomical Essays' (1907) he collected articles and essays that had appeared in magazines. His latest work, 'Astronomical Facts and Fallacies,' came out in 1909. Gore published many papers in the monthly notices of the Royal Astronomical Society. He was elected a fellow of the Royal Astronomical Society on 8 March 1878, was a member of council of the Royal Dublin Society, and a member of the Royal Irish Academy. He was at one time a leading member of the Liverpool Astronomical Society, and was chosen a vice-president of the British Astronomical Association on its foundation, and director of the variable star section. He died unmarried in Dublin from the effects of a street accident on 18 July 1910.

[Who's Who, 1910; Monthly Notices, Roy. Astr. Soc., Feb. 1911.] H. P. H.

GORST, Sir [JOHN] ELDON (1861–1911), consul-general in Egypt, born at Auckland, New Zealand, on 25 June 1861, was eldest son of the Right Hon. Sir John Eldon Gorst, who had gone out to New Zealand in 1860, by his wife Mary Elizabeth, daughter of the Rev. Lorenzo Moore of Christchurch. For a time he assumed the additional christian name of Lowndes to distinguish him from his father. Educated at Eton, he went to Trinity College, Cambridge, in 1880, graduating B.A. in 1883 as 21st wrangler, and proceeding M.A. in 1903. He was called to the bar at the Inner Temple in 1885, and in the same year was appointed, after a competitive examination, an attaché in the diplomatic service. In September 1886 he was sent as an attaché to the British agency at Cairo, and thus began his connection with Egypt. In May 1887 he was granted an allowance for knowledge of Arabic, and in October was promoted to be a third secretary in the diplomatic service; on 1 April 1892 he became a second secretary, and in May 1901 a secretary of legation. Meanwhile he had taken service under the Egyptian government, and had in November 1890 been appointed controller of direct revenues, serving in that capacity under Alfred (afterwards Viscount) Milner. In 1892 he succeeded Milner as under-secretary of state for finance, and in 1894 he was appointed to a newly created post, that of adviser to the ministry of the interior. This appointment was created with the object of decentralising the police, and combining an increase in the number of Egyptian as compared with European officers with efficient European control at headquarters, viz. at the ministry of the interior (Cromer, *Modern Egypt*, 1908, ii. 488). The selection of Gorst for the new appointment was evidence of the confidence which was felt in his ability and his tact, and was justified by the results (cf. Colvin, *The Making of Modern Egypt*, 1906, p. 339). In 1898 he succeeded Sir Elwin Palmer [q. v. Suppl. II] as financial adviser. The holder of the office is in effect 'the most important British official in Egypt' (Cromer, *Modern Egypt*, ii. 286; Milner, *England in Egypt*, 3rd edit., 1893, p. 105), and Gorst, who was made C.B. in 1900 and K.C.B. in 1902, filled it until 1904 with uniform success. After assisting at Paris in the negotiation of the Anglo-French agreement which settled outstanding questions with regard to Egypt, Gorst was transferred in May 1904 to the foreign office in London as an assistant under-secretary of state. Three years later, in 1907, he succeeded Lord Cromer as agent and consul-general in Egypt, ranking as minister plenipotentiary in the diplomatic service. He arrived at Cairo in April 1907, and Lord Cromer left on 4 May. In the House of Commons, on 11 April 1907, the foreign secretary, Sir Edward Grey, stated that the appointment had been made after consultation with Lord Cromer, who had full confidence in Gorst's ability to continue his work. Gorst was, in Lord Cromer's opinion, 'endowed with a singular degree of tact and intelligence' (*Modern Egypt*, ii. 292). He had proved himself a broad-minded administrator, hard-working, with great aptitude for finance and a good knowledge of the Arabic language. Gorst himself defined the aim of British policy in Egypt as 'not merely to give Egypt the blessings of good administration, but to train the Egyptians to take a gradually increasing share in their own government' (*Reports on Egypt and the Sudan in* 1910, Cd. 5633, May 1911, p. 1). The necessary qualifications were knowledge of the vernacular, sympathy with the feelings, the way, and the thought of the people, and even with their prejudices, and tact, power of effacement, and unlimited patience (*Reports for* 1909, Cd. 5121, April 1910, p. 50).

Gorst entered on his difficult duties at a very difficult time. The year 1907 was marked by financial depression due to overtrading and excessive credit, and by one of the worst Nile floods on record. Next year, 1908, he reported progress in satisfying the reasonable aspirations of the Egyptian people, but noted that Egyptian feeling had been affected by the unrest in other Mohammedan countries. The virulence of the extreme nationalist party made it necessary in 1909 to revive the press law and to pass a special 'Loi soumettant certains individus à la surveillance de la Police'; in February 1910 the Egyptian prime minister, Boutros Pasha, was murdered. In his report for 1910, the last which he wrote, Gorst recorded the comparative failure of representative institutions in Egypt in the form of the legislative council and general assembly, and he emphasised the necessity of caution in countenancing principles of self-government.

Like Lord Durham in his celebrated report on Canada; like Lord Dufferin in his report on Egypt; and like his own immediate predecessor, Lord Cromer, Gorst insisted on the wisdom of promoting municipal and local self-government, and one of the chief measures passed during his tenure of office was a law for enlarging the powers of the provincial councils, which came into force on 1 Jan. 1910. His administrative policy was subjected to criticism by politicians of both the advanced and the reactionary schools, but he was uniformly supported by the British government. He died prematurely, after a painful illness, on 12 July 1911, at his father's house, The Manor House, Castle Combe, Wiltshire, and was buried in the family vault at Castle Combe. He was succeeded as consul-general in Egypt by Lord Kitchener.

Gorst was made a G.C.M.G. in 1911 on the coronation of King George V, and held the first class of the Medjidie (1897) and the first class (grand cordon) of the order of Osmanie (1903). He was a keen sportsman. He married on 25 June 1903 Evelyn, daughter of Charles Rudd, of Ardnamurchan, Argyllshire, and had one daughter.

[The Times, 13 July 1911; Foreign Office List; Who's Who; Blue Books; Milner, England in Egypt, 3rd edit., 1893; Sir Auckland Colvin, The Making of Modern Egypt, 1906; Cromer, Modern Egypt, 1908.]

C. P. L.

GOSCHEN, GEORGE JOACHIM, first VISCOUNT GOSCHEN (1831–1907), statesman, born on 10 Aug. 1831 at his father's house in the parish of Stoke Newington, was eldest son and second child in the family of two sons and five daughters of William Henry Göschen, a leading merchant of the City of London, by his wife Henrietta, daughter of William Alexander Ohmann. His youngest brother, Sir William Edward Goschen, became British ambassador at Berlin in 1908. The father was son of Georg Joachim Göschen, an eminent publisher and man of letters at Leipzig, the intimate friend of Schiller, Goethe, Wieland and other 'heroes of the golden age of German literature' (see LORD GOSCHEN, *Life and Times of Georg Joachim Göschen*, 1903). In 1814 young William Henry Göschen came to London, where, with his friend Henry Frühling from Bremen, he founded the financial firm of Frühling & Göschen. A man of strong character, great industry, and deep religious convictions, he found time throughout an exceedingly busy life to indulge his love of literature and his taste for music.

From nine to eleven (1840–2) Goschen attended daily the 'Proprietary School' at Blackheath. Thence his father sent him for three years to Dr. Bernhard's school at Saxe Meiningen. During this period he only once visited England, usually spending his holidays with his German relations. His father, who intended his son for a business career, now thought he perceived in him qualities which would ensure success in public life in England. For this end it was desirable that young George should mix more than he had yet done with English boys; and it was with the view of making an Englishman of him that he was sent in August 1845 to Rugby entering the house of Bonamy Price [q. v.], afterwards professor of political economy at Oxford. After his first year, Goschen grew to like his surroundings and to be popular with his schoolfellows. He rose to be head of the school, and in that capacity he made his first reported speech, on the occasion of the resignation of the headmaster, A. C. Tait (afterwards archbishop of Canterbury). Amongst the boys he had been already recognised as the best debater in the school, especially in reply. Though his rise in the school had been rapid, it was not till June 1848 that he achieved positive distinction by winning the prize for the English essay; and shortly afterwards the English prize poem for the year. In 1849 he won the Queen's medal for the English historical essay; and in 1850, the prize for the Latin essay, 'Marcus Tullius Cicero.' In the autumn of 1850, after a couple of months of travel on the continent, Goschen entered Oxford as a commoner of Oriel. He failed to win scholarships at University and Trinity, but in 1852 his college awarded him an exhibition. Though in the technical Oxford sense his 'scholarship' was not considered preeminent, he obtained a double first in classical honours, with the general reputation in 1853 of having been 'the best first in.' At the Union he won great fame by his speeches on political and literary subjects; and in his last year was president of that society. In the previous year he had founded the 'Essay Club,' of which the original members were Arthur Butler, first headmaster of Haileybury, Charles Stuart Parker of University, H. N. Oxenham, the Hon. George Brodrick, W. H. Fremantle of Balliol, and Charles Henry Pearson (cf. *Memorials of Charles Henry Pearson*, 1900). Having graduated B.A. in 1853, Goschen entered actively into the business of his father's firm, by whom in October 1854 he was sent to superintend affairs in New Granada, now part of the United States of Colombia. After two years in South America he returned home, and on 22 Sept. 1857 married Lucy, daughter of John Dalley, a marriage which greatly conduced to the happiness of his future life. He now energetically devoted himself to business in London, rapidly making a reputation with commercial men, amongst whom he was known as the 'Fortunate Youth.' When only twenty-seven he was made a director of the Bank of England. In 1861 he achieved wider fame by publishing his 'Theory of the Foreign Exchanges' (5th edit. 1864), a treatise which won the attention of financial authorities and business men all over the world, and which has been translated into the principal languages of Europe. In 1863, a vacancy having occurred in the representation of the City of London, Goschen was returned unopposed as a supporter of Lord Palmerston's government. His views were those of a strong liberal, as liberalism was understood in those days; and he pledged himself to the ballot, abolition of church rates, and the removal of religious disabilities. On the latter subject, the abolition of tests in the universities, he took a leading position in the House of Commons, fiercely contending with Lord Robert Cecil (afterwards Lord Salisbury) [q. v. Suppl. II], who struggled hard to maintain the old close connection between the universities and the Church of England. At the opening of the session of 1864 Goschen achieved a marked success in seconding the address to the speech from the throne. But the pains which he took to distinguish his position in the liberal party, especially as regards foreign policy, from that taken up by Richard Cobden and John Bright, called forth, not unnaturally, vigorous remonstrance from the former (*Life*, i. 71). Before parliament was dissolved (July 1865), Goschen's knowledge of commercial matters, his brilliant speech on the address, and his ability in fighting the battle against tests, had given him a good standing in the House of Commons; and when the new parliament met, Lord Russell, who had succeeded Lord Palmerston as prime minister, invited him to join his ministry as vice-president of the board of trade (November 1865); and two months later to enter his cabinet as chancellor of the Duchy of Lancaster (January 1866). On the same day Lord Hartington (afterwards Duke of Devonshire) [q. v. Suppl. II], with whom in after years Goschen was to be closely associated, entered the cabinet for the first time.

Goschen now retired finally from business and from the firm of Frühling & Göschen, and henceforward devoted himself wholly to a political career. In the short-lived ministry of Lord Russell, and on the front bench of opposition during the Derby-Disraeli government which succeeded it, Goschen took an active part with Gladstone and other leading liberals in the reform struggles of the day. At the dissolution of 1868, standing as a strenuous advocate of Irish disestablishment, he was returned again for the City, this time at the head of the poll; and on Gladstone's forming his first administration, Goschen entered his cabinet as president of the poor law board. There he showed great zeal as a reformer of local government (see his remarkable *Report of the Select Committee of* 1870), and in substituting methodical administration for the chaotic system, or want of system, which had grown up. On the health of H. C. E. Childers breaking down, Goschen was appointed in March 1871 to succeed him as first lord of the admiralty, a department which at that time was subjected to much public censure. Here his administration proved extraordinarily successful in restoring the general confidence and in winning the enthusiastic admiration of the naval service. In 1874 the unwillingness of Goschen and Cardwell to reduce the estimates for 1874–5 below what they considered the needs of the country required was an important element in determining Gladstone's sudden dissolution (January 1874). This resulted in the advent to power for six years of Disraeli, and accordingly Goschen, who was again re-elected for the City, found himself for the first time in the House of Commons one of a minority, which on Gladstone's withdrawal was led by Lord Hartington. Until 1880 the interest of the public and parliament was mainly occupied with foreign affairs, and Goschen as a leading member of the liberal party was in continual consultation with Lord Hartington and Lord Granville on the serious condition of things in eastern Europe. His great position as a financier and a man of business, and his more than ordinary acquaintance with foreign politics, had led to his being chosen by the council of foreign bondholders, with the approval of the foreign office, and at the invitation of the viceroy of Egypt to proceed to that country, which was in a state bordering on bankruptcy, to investigate and report upon the financial position. With M. Joubert, representing the French bondholders, Goschen proceeded to Cairo, their joint efforts resulting in the promulgation of the Khedivial decree of 16 Nov. 1876, the Goschen decree, as it came to be called (Cromer, *Modern Egypt*, i. 13–15).

When Goschen returned to England, Gladstone's anti-Turkish agitation was at its height. In 1877, when Lord Hartington accepted on behalf of the liberal party the policy pressed upon parliament by Sir George Trevelyan, of equalising the county and borough franchise, Goschen's strong sense of duty compelled him to protest against what he believed must lead to the complete monopolising of political power by a single class of the community. This difference with his political friends as to a main 'plank' of the party 'platform' proved to be a turning-point in his career. At the general election in April 1880 Goschen, who had retired from the representation of the City of London, was returned for Ripon. The electorate repudiated Lord Beaconsfield, and Gladstone at the head of a large majority again became prime minister. Goschen felt it incumbent upon him to hold aloof from the new administration. Gladstone offered him the vice-royalty of India, which he declined. He consented, however, to go in May 1880 on a special and temporary mission to Constantinople as ambassador to the Sultan, without emolument; retaining, with the approval of his constituents, his seat in the House of Commons. The object of the British government was to compel the Turks, by means of the concert of Europe, to carry out the stipulations of the treaty of Berlin as regards Greece, Montenegro and Armenia, and to get established a strong defensive frontier between Turkey and Greece. Goschen has recounted at length the difficulties he encountered, and has described his interviews with Prince Bismarck at Berlin, and the negotiations at Constantinople with the representatives of the great powers (*Life of Lord Goschen*, vol. i. chap. vii.). His mission lasted for a year, and in June 1881 he was again back in London, receiving the congratulations of Gladstone and Granville upon the successful accomplishment of a most difficult task.

In the political situation at home he found much that he disliked. The fight over the Irish land bill was virtually at an end. A fierce struggle was raging between the government and the followers of Parnell, and Goschen felt it right at such a time to do what he could to strengthen the executive against the forces of disorder. In June 1882 he declined Gladstone's invitation to join his cabinet as secretary of state for war. In November 1883 Gladstone pressed him strongly to accept the speakership of the House of Commons, which he also declined, partly because he felt that his short sight would prove a disqualification for the successful performance of the duties of the chair. In truth Goschen was becoming more and more dissatisfied with the position of the liberal party, in which he feared the rapid growth of the influence of the advanced section led by Mr. Chamberlain and Sir Charles Dilke. He set himself to strengthen Gladstone against radical influences, and to secure for the present and future that due weight within the party should be given to moderate liberalism. But though disapproving much in Gladstone's conduct of affairs—foreign policy, Ireland, Egypt, South Africa—he was by no means disposed to place unlimited confidence in the conservative leader, Lord Salisbury. The ambition and influence of Lord Randolph Churchill in Goschen's eyes still further weakened the claims of party conservatism to the public confidence. He had, moreover, been disappointed that his own stand against a democratic franchise had found no conservative support. In January 1885 Goschen withdrew from the Reform and Devonshire Clubs; and his speeches to great meetings in the country gave further evidence of the independent standpoint he had now assumed. By moderate men of all parties those speeches were welcomed and admired.

The last session of the parliament elected in 1880 was momentous. In February 1885 came the news of the fall of Khartoum. A motion of censure on the Gladstone government was defeated only by fourteen votes, and Goschen voted in the minority. In June a combination between conservatives and Parnellites defeated the government on a clause of the budget. Goschen voted with the government. Lord Salisbury at once became prime minister, and Lord Randolph Churchill leader of the House of Commons.

The city of Ripon, which Goschen represented, was to lose its separate representation under the Reform Act of 1885, and an influential committee in Edinburgh invited Goschen to become a candidate for one of the divisions of that city at the coming general election. During the following autumn Goschen's speeches in Scotland and elsewhere made a great impression on the public (*Goschen's Political Speeches*, Edinburgh, 1886). Their high tone, their clear reasoning, the independent and disinterested character of the speaker, and the absence of claptrap or appeal to unworthy motives, were a refreshing contrast to much of the platform oratory of the day. At the same time the late ministers were freely disclosing their individual views to the public. Mr. Chamberlain was the spokesman of extreme radicalism, and found in Goschen his chief antagonist. Lord Hartington, whose allegiance to the liberal party had never wavered, spoke out as essentially a leader of moderate liberals, whilst Gladstone by studied indefiniteness endeavoured to keep all sections of liberals united under his 'umbrella.' Parnell threw the whole voting power of Irish nationalists on to the side of the conservatives. And though little was said about it at the general election, Goschen clearly saw that Parnell's policy of home rule, and Gladstone's line with reference to it, were the questions of the future. In vain he sought (July 1885) from Gladstone some explanation of his views (*Life of Lord Goschen*, vol. i. chap. ix.).

In November 1885 Goschen, supported by moderate liberals and conservatives, won an easy triumph in East Edinburgh over an advanced radical candidate. The effect, however, of the general election as a whole was to make it impossible for either of the great parties to hold power without the assistance of the Irish nationalists. Hence a remarkable development of the party position occurred. The majority of the liberal party coalesced with Parnell and his followers; and Gladstone was placed in power to carry out the policy of home rule. Goschen threw himself into the struggle for the union with conspicuous ability and zeal. With Lord Hartington he formed and inspired the liberal unionist party, and brought about that alliance with Lord Salisbury which was essential if the union was to be saved. At the great meeting at the Opera House on 14 April 1886, the first outward sign of this new alliance, Goschen's speech was the one that most deeply stirred the enthusiasm of his audience. In the House of Commons and all over the country he did battle for his cause with a fiery impetuosity which hitherto had hardly been recognised as part of his character. His hope that Lord Hartington should be the centre and leader of a strong body of moderate opinion was now realised. But the division in the liberal party was not so much between those who were known as whigs and radicals, as between unionists and home rulers; and thus many of the strongest radicals, such as Mr. Chamberlain and John Bright, were amongst Lord Hartington's most vigorous supporters. The union triumphed in the House of Commons, where Gladstone's home rule bill was defeated on 7 June 1886, and when the unionists secured a majority at the general election in July, Lord Salisbury formed a conservative administration. In East Edinburgh, however, Goschen was defeated by the home rule candidate, Dr. Wallace; but he did not relax his efforts outside the House of Commons in the unionist cause. On Lord Randolph Churchill's sudden resignation

(20 Dec. 1886) of the chancellorship of the exchequer in Lord Salisbury's government, and the lead of the House of Commons, Goschen, with the approval of Lord Hartington, accepted the offer made to him by Lord Salisbury to enter his cabinet as Lord Randolph's successor, W. H. Smith [q. v.] at the same time undertaking to lead the House of Commons.

Goschen's accession to the ministry at this crisis was of the greatest importance in keeping the unionist government on its feet. He met, nevertheless, one more personal reverse, in his failure to win back from the liberal home rulers the Exchange division of Liverpool (26 Jan. 1887). A fortnight later he was elected by a majority of 4000 for St. George's, Hanover Square, a seat which he retained till he went to the House of Lords. Henceforward, as a member of the Salisbury government, sharing the responsibility of his colleagues, Goschen necessarily played a less individual part than heretofore in the public eye, though he took a prominent share in the fierce conflicts inside and outside parliament against the powerful home rule alliance between liberals and Irish nationalists. For six years in succession he brought forward the budget, meeting with much skill the steadily growing expenditure of the country, whilst boasting with truth that at the same time he was gradually reducing its debt. His most memorable achievement whilst chancellor of the exchequer was his successful conversion of the national debt in March 1888 from a 3 per cent. to a $2\frac{3}{4}$, and ultimately a $2\frac{1}{2}$ per cent. stock. The great courage and ability required to carry through this operation received the recognition of political opponents, including Gladstone, not less than of his own friends. During the 'Baring crisis' in November 1890 his courage and firmness as finance minister were again demonstrated. The situation was saved; whilst he absolutely refused to yield to pressure to employ the funds or credit of the state to buttress up the solvency of a private institution (*Life*, vol. ii. chap. vii., and note in Appendix III. by Lord Welby). In the same year a good deal of unpopularity fell to Goschen's share, resulting from the 'licensing clauses' (ultimately abandoned) which it was proposed to introduce into the local taxation bill, for providing out of taxes on beer and spirits a compensation fund to facilitate the reduction in the number of public-houses.

At the end of 1891 Mr. Arthur Balfour succeeded to the leadership of the House of Commons (*Life*, ii. 186 seq.); but the days of the unionist ministry were already numbered, and the general election of the following June placed Gladstone once more in power. Over the home rule bill of 1893 the old controversy of 1886 was revived in all its bitterness, and Goschen was again in the front rank of the combatants. In opposition, he formally joined the conservative party, became a member of the Carlton Club, and repeated with undiminished power the efforts he had made nine years before to sustain the cause of the union. This time, however, Gladstone's policy was accepted by the House of Commons; but only to be rejected by the House of Lords, who were supported by the country at the general election of 1895.

Lord Salisbury's new administration was joined by Lord Hartington, Mr. Chamberlain, and other liberal unionists, whilst Goschen to his great satisfaction went to the admiralty (June 1895), where twenty years before he had won well-earned fame. His last period at the admiralty, which lasted till the autumn of 1900, was eventful; for though the country remained at peace with the great powers of the world, our foreign relations at times became severely strained. Difficulties connected with Venezuela, Crete, Nigeria, Port Arthur, Fashoda, and German sympathy with President Krüger, brought the possibility of rupture before the eyes of all men. Goschen felt that a very powerful British navy was the best security for the peace of the world, as well as for our own protection, and the vast increases of our naval establishments and the consequent growth of naval estimates were generally approved. The strain of these five years told upon his strength. The death of Mrs. Goschen in the spring of 1898 had been a heavy trial; and the weight of advancing years determined him to retire from office before the approaching general election. Accordingly on 12 Oct. 1900, to the regret of the public and the naval service, he resigned, and in December was raised to the House of Lords as Viscount Goschen of Hawkhurst, Kent.

The remainder of his life Lord Goschen hoped to spend mainly at Seacox Heath, his home in Kent, with more leisure than he had found in the past for seeing his family and friends, for indulging his strong taste for reading, and for attending to the interests of his estate. In 1903 he published the life and times of his grandfather, on which he had long been engaged; and in 1905 a volume of 'Essays and Addresses on Economic Questions.' This last consisted of contributions to the 'Edinburgh Review' and of addresses read to various bodies and institutions at different times, and of valuable comments by the author on the further light that the lapse of years had thrown upon the subjects treated. On the death of Lord Salisbury, Goschen was chosen chancellor of Oxford University (31 Oct. 1903), and devoted himself with energy to the interests of the university. He had been made hon. D.C.L. of Oxford in 1881, and hon. LL.D. of Aberdeen and Cambridge in 1888, and of Edinburgh in 1890.

Goschen's political life was by no means over. When in 1903 Mr. Chamberlain's fiscal policy was announced, causing rupture in the ministry and the unionist party, Goschen again came to the front as one of the foremost champions of free trade. He had, as he said, worked out these financial and commercial problems for himself; and accordingly he joined the Duke of Devonshire and other free-trade unionists in a vigorous effort to defeat a policy certain, in his opinion, to bring disaster on the nation. In the House of Lords and in the country, till the general election of January 1906 had made free trade safe, he threw himself into the conflict with much of his old energy and fire; and in the new parliament he once more solemnly warned conservative statesmen against the danger of identifying their party with the fiscal policy of Mr. Chamberlain. During the remainder of the session, he took part occasionally in the proceedings of the House of Lords, showing none of the infirmities of age excepting that his eyesight, never good, had deteriorated. On 7 Feb. 1907 he died suddenly in his home at Seacox, and was buried at Flimwell. Goschen left two sons and four daughters. His elder son, George Joachim, succeeded to the viscountcy.

Goschen showed throughout the whole of his career a remarkable consistency of character as a statesman, notwithstanding the fact that part of his official life was passed under Gladstone's, part under Lord Salisbury's leadership. Always moderate in his opinions, which were the outcome of honest and deep investigation, he disliked the exaggerations of party protagonists, and was as vehement in support of moderation as were the extremists on either side in fighting for victory. At the head of great departments, his industry, his grasp of principles, his mastery of details, and his determination to secure efficiency were conspicuous. But in the pressure of administrative work he remembered that his responsibilities as cabinet minister were not limited to his own department, and in all matters of general policy, especially as regards foreign affairs, of which he had exceptional knowledge, his counsels carried great weight. His courage and independence won him in a high degree the respect and confidence of his countrymen; and Queen Victoria placed much reliance on his judgment and his patriotism. Nature had not endowed him with the qualities that make an orator of the first rank. His voice was not good, nor his gestures and bearing graceful. Yet he proved again and again on public platforms that he possessed the power not only of interesting and leading men's minds but also of stirring their enthusiasm to a very high pitch. He never spoke down to his audience, or appealed to prejudice, but exerted himself to lead them to think and to feel as he himself thought and felt. His speeches very frequently contained some turn of expression or phrase which caught the public ear and for the time was in everyone's mouth. In 1885, 'He would not give a blank cheque to Lord Salisbury.' In his great fight against Irish nationalism, 'We would never surrender to crime or time.' In the fiscal controversy, 'He would be no party to a gamble with the food of the people.'

Goschen throughout his life did much useful public work outside the region of active politics. He had become an ecclesiastical commissioner in 1882. From its initiation in 1879 Goschen was a vigorous supporter of the movement for the extension of university teaching in London, and for many years he gave great assistance to the movement. With him the loss of office never meant the cessation of employment. In his private life his personal qualities and sympathetic nature won for him a large circle of real friends, whilst in society at large a strong sense of humour, his wide general knowledge of men and books, his power of conversation and of promoting good talk in others, made him highly valued. In his own house in the country and in London, where he delighted to gather round him friends and acquaintances, he carried the intenseness of interest characteristic of his working hours into the amusements of the day. It was not for the purposes of breadwinning alone that he set a high value on education. 'Livelihood is not a life,' he said to the Liverpool Institute (29 Nov. 1877, on *Imagination*). 'Education must deal with your lives as well as qualify you for your livelihoods.' He knew from his own experience how much education had done for his life outside those regions of business and politics where his chief energies had been spent.

A portrait in oils by Rudolf Lehmann (1880) is in the possession of the present viscount and is now at Seacox Heath; a second, by Mr. Hugh A. T. Glazebrook, is at Plaxtol, Kent, in the possession of his daughters. A cartoon portrait of Goschen by 'Ape' appeared in 'Vanity Fair' in 1869.

[Arthur D. Elliot, Life of Lord Goschen, 2 vols. 1911, compiled from private papers and correspondence; see also Bernard Holland, Life of the Eighth Duke of Devonshire, 2 vols. 1911, and Morley's Life of Gladstone, 1903; Hansard's Debates; Annual Register; Times reports of speeches.] A. R. D. E.

GOSSELIN, Sir MARTIN LE MARCHANT HADSLEY (1847–1905), diplomatist, born at Walfield, near Hertford, on 2 Nov. 1847, was grandson of Admiral Thomas Le Marchant Gosselin [q. v.] and eldest son of Martin Hadsley Gosselin of Ware Priory and Blakesware, Hertfordshire, by his wife Frances Orris, eldest daughter of Admiral Sir John Marshall of Gillingham House, Kent. Educated at Eton College and at Christ Church, Oxford, he entered the diplomatic service in 1868, and after working in the foreign office was appointed attaché at Lisbon in 1869. He was transferred to Berlin in 1872, where he remained till promoted to be second secretary at St. Petersburg in 1874. During the congress at Berlin in 1878 he was attached to the special mission of the British plenipotentiaries, Lord Beaconsfield and Lord Salisbury. He was transferred from St. Petersburg to Rome in 1879, returned to St. Petersburg in the following year, and to Berlin in 1882. In 1885 he was promoted to be secretary of legation, and was appointed to Brussels, where he served till 1892, taking charge of the legation at intervals during the absence of the minister, and being employed on occasions on special service. In November 1887 he was appointed secretary to the duke of Norfolk's special mission to Pope Leo XIII on the occasion of the pontiff's jubilee. In 1889 and 1890 he and Mr. (afterwards Sir Alfred) Bateman of the board of trade served as joint British delegates in the conferences held at Brussels to arrange for the mutual publication of customs tariffs, and in July of the latter year he signed the convention for the establishment of an international bureau for that purpose. He was also employed as one of the secretaries to the international conference for the suppression of the African slave trade, which sat at Brussels in 1889 and the following year and resulted in the General Act of 2 July 1890. In recognition of his services he was in 1890 made C.B. Later in that year he was one of the British delegates at the conference held by representatives of Great Britain, Germany, and Italy to discuss and fix the duties to be imposed on imports in the conventional basin of the Congo, and he signed the agreement which was arrived at in December 1890. In April 1892 he was promoted to be secretary of embassy at Madrid, was transferred to Berlin in the following year, and to Paris in 1896, receiving at the latter post the titular rank of minister plenipotentiary. In 1897 he was selected to discuss with French commissioners the question of coolie emigration from British India to Réunion, and in that and the following year he served as one of the British members of the Anglo-French commission for the delimitation of the possessions and spheres of influence of the two countries to the east and west of the Niger river. The arrangement arrived at by the commission was embodied in a convention signed at Paris on 14 June 1898, and provided a solution of questions which had gravely threatened the good relations between the two countries. At the close of these negotiations he was created K.C.M.G. From July 1898 to August 1902 he held the home appointment of assistant under-secretary of state for foreign affairs, and was then sent to Lisbon as British envoy, a post which he held till his death there on 26 Feb. 1905 from the effects of a motor-car accident. The relations of Great Britain with Portugal during Gosselin's residence were uneventful, but King Edward VII's sense of his services was marked by his preferment as K.C.V.O. in 1903 and as G.C.V.O. in 1904.

Gosselin possessed in a high degree fair judgment, good temper, and charm of manner. He was an accomplished musician, and possessed a delicacy of touch and a power of artistic interpretation on the pianoforte almost unrivalled even among professional artists.

Gosselin joined the communion of the Church of Rome in 1878. He married in 1880 Katherine Frances, daughter of the first Lord Gerard, and left one son, Alwyn Bertram Robert Raphael, captain in the Grenadier guards, and three daughters.

[The Times, 27 Feb. 1905; Oscar Browning's Memoirs, 1911; Foreign Office List, 1906, p. 397.] S.

GOTT, JOHN (1830–1906), bishop of Truro, born on 25 Dec. 1830, was third son of William Gott of Wyther Grange, Leeds, by Margaret, daughter of William Ewart of Mossley Hill, Liverpool. His grandfather was Benjamin Gott of Armley House, who introduced the factory system into the woollen trade of Leeds, and contributed greatly to the prosperity of the town. Educated first at Winchester, he matriculated at Brasenose College, Oxford, on 7 June 1849, and graduated B.A. in 1853, proceeding M.A. in 1854, B.D. and D.D. in 1873. After a year at Wells Theological College and some time spent in travel, he was ordained deacon in 1857 and priest in 1858. From 1857 to 1861 he was curate of Great Yarmouth, and from 1861 to1863 had charge of St. Andrew's Church. In 1863 the vicar of Leeds gave him the perpetual curacy of Bramley, Leeds; and in 1873, on the appointment of J. R. Woodford [q. v.] to the see of Ely, Gott was chosen by the crown his successor as vicar of Leeds. The appointment gave satisfaction from the intimate association of the Gott family with the commercial life of the city, and was amply justified by Gott's work. He started a church extension movement, with the result that, during his twelve years at Leeds, eight new churches were consecrated and the building of four others begun; he founded in 1875 Leeds clergy school; took a leading part in 1880 in the establishment of Victoria University, of the court of which the crown made him a member; promoted the university extension movement in the West Riding; and was the generous friend of all good works. In 1886 Gott was made dean of Worcester, a post which he filled till 1891. He extended the usefulness of the cathedral as a diocesan centre, and entered fully into the life of the diocese.

In 1891 Gott succeeded to the see of Truro on the resignation of George Howard Wilkinson [q. v. Suppl. II]. Consecrated at St. Paul's on 29 Sept. 1891, he saw in 1903 the completion of Truro Cathedral; founded a bishop's clergy fund for the aid of clergy in time of ill-health or other necessity; and diligently visited all parts of his diocese. A high churchman, but not a strong partisan, he signed in January 1901 the bishops' letter inviting clergy to accept the positions defined in the Lambeth 'Opinions.' He died suddenly at his residence, Trenython, near Par, on 21 July 1906 and was buried at Tywardreath.

Gott married in 1858 Harriet Mary, daughter of W. Whitaker Maitland of Loughton Hall, Essex; she died in London on 19 April 1906; by her he had one son and three daughters. A portrait by W. W. Ouless was exhibited at the Royal Academy in 1899. Another, painted in 1903, is in the dining-hall of Leeds clergy school.

Apart from his charge delivered in 1896 on 'Ideals of a Parish,' Gott wrote only one book, 'The Parish Priest of the Town' (1887), which had a wide circulation. He inherited a fine library, which was dispersed by sale at Messrs. Sotheby's in March 1908 and July 1910. It included a set of the four folio editions of Shakespeare, of which the first folio realised 1800*l.*, 22 July 1910.

[Yorkshire Post, 23 July 1906; Yorkshire Weekly Post, 6 May 1911; Guardian, 21 April and 28 July 1906; Record, 27 July 1906; The Times, 23 and 26 July 1910; and Foster, Alumni Oxonienses.] A. R. B.

GOUGH, Sir HUGH HENRY (1833–1909), general, born at Calcutta on 14 Nov. 1833, was third son in a family of four sons and four daughters of George Gough, Bengal civil service, of Rathronan House, Clonmel, co. Tipperary, by Charlotte Margaret, daughter of Charles Becher, Chancellor House, Tonbridge, Kent. His elder brother, Sir Charles John Stanley Gough, V.C. (*b.* 1832), still survives (1912). Field-marshal Viscount Gough [q. v.] was his grand-uncle. After education privately and at Haileybury College (1851–2) he joined the Bengal army on 4 Sept. 1853, becoming lieutenant on 9 Aug. 1855 and captain on 4 Jan. 1861.

On his arrival in India he perceived the likelihood of a sepoy revolt, but his warnings were disregarded by the authorities (Lord Roberts, *Forty-one Years in India*, 1898, p. 48). He was at Meerut on the outbreak of the Indian Mutiny, and served throughout the subsequent war. On 24 Aug. 1857 he was wounded in attempting to seize some mutineers at Khurkowdeh, and was rescued by his elder brother, Charles, who won in the campaign the Victoria cross. He served as adjutant of Hodson's horse throughout the siege of Delhi, and was at the action of Rohtuck (18 Aug.), where by a feigned retreat Hodson drew the enemy into the open and then completely routed them. Gough was wounded and his horse was shot under him. He accompanied the column under Colonel Greathed which was despatched to the relief of Cawnpore, and commanded a wing of the regiment in the actions at Bulandshahr (27 Sept.), Aligarh

(5 Oct.), and Agra (10 Oct. 1857), where he executed a dashing flank charge. On 12 Nov. 1857, when in command of a party of Hodson's horse near Alambagh, he charged across a swamp and captured two guns, which were defended by a vastly superior body of the enemy (LORD ROBERTS, *Forty-one Years in India*, p. 170). His horse was wounded in two places and his turban cut through by sword thrusts whilst he was in combat with three sepoys. He was mentioned in Sir Colin Campbell's despatches of 18 and 30 Nov. 1857 (*Selections from State Papers in Military Department*, 1857–8, ii. 339), and for his gallantry on this occasion he was awarded the Victoria cross, like his elder brother. Gough also distinguished himself in the operations round Lucknow on 25 Feb. 1858, when he set a brilliant example to his regiment on its being ordered to charge the enemy's guns. He engaged in a series of single combats, but was at length disabled by a musket ball through the leg while charging two sepoys with fixed bayonets. On this day Gough had two horses killed under him, a shot through his helmet and another through his scabbard. After the capture of Lucknow on 25 March 1858 he retired to the hills to recover from his wounds. Gough was mentioned in despatches on several occasions for 'distinguished bravery,' and was twice thanked by the governor-general of India, besides receiving the brevet of major and a medal with three clasps (*Lond. Gaz.* Dec. 1857, 16 and 29 Jan. 1858, and 15 Jan. 1859).

Gough subsequently took part in the Abyssinia campaign in 1868. He commanded the 12th Bengal cavalry, and was present at the capture of Magdala, being mentioned in despatches and receiving the medal and being made C.B. on 14 Aug. 1868 (*Lond. Gaz.* 16 and 30 June 1868). He was promoted lieut.-colonel in 1869, and received the brevet of colonel in 1877. Gough, who served throughout the Afghan war, was in command of the cavalry of the Kuram field force in 1878–9. At the forcing of the Peiwar Kotal on 2 Dec. 1878 he was the first to reach the crest, and pursued with his cavalry the flying enemy along the Alikhel road. At the action of Matun, by dismounted fire and several bold charges, he succeeded notwithstanding the difficult nature of the ground in driving the tribesmen to the highest ridges. from which they were dislodged by the artillery (7 Jan. 1879). In September 1879, on the renewal of the war after the massacre of the Cavagnari mission, he served with the Kabul field force as brigadier-general of communications, and was present at the engagement of Charasiab on 6 Oct. and in the various operations round Kabul in December 1879 (wounded). On Sir Frederick (afterwards Lord) Roberts's march to Kandahar Gough was in command of the cavalry brigade, and took part in the reconnaissance of 31 August at Pir Paintal (HANNA, *Second Afghan War*, iii. 498). He was in command of the troops engaged in the cavalry pursuit after the battle of Mazra on 1 Sept. 1880. For his services he was mentioned six times in despatches (*Lond. Gaz.* 4 Feb., 21 March, 7 Nov. 1879; 4 May, 3 and 31 Dec. 1880). He was awarded the medal with four clasps, the bronze decoration, and was created K.C.B. on 22 Feb. 1881.

Gough attained the rank of major-general in 1887 and of lieut.-general in 1891, and commanded the Lahore division of the Indian army (1887–92). He became general in 1894 and retired from the army in 1897. On 20 May 1896 he was nominated a G.C.B., and two years later was appointed keeper of the crown jewels at the Tower of London. There he died in St. Thomas's Tower on 12 May 1909, and was buried at Kensal Green cemetery. On 8 Sept. 1863 he married Annie Margaret, daughter of Edward Eustace Hill and his wife, Lady Georgiana Keppel; he had issue four sons and four daughters.

He published in 1897 his reminiscences of the Indian Mutiny, entitled 'Old Memories.'

[Sir Hugh Gough's Old Memories, 1897; G. W. Forrest, History of the Indian Mutiny, vol. ii. 1904; Burke's Peerage; L. J. Trotter, Hodson of Hodson's Horse, 1901; Men of the Time, 1899; Hart's and Official Army Lists; The Times, 14 and 19 May 1909; Indian Mutiny, selections from State Papers in Military Department, 1857–8, ed. G. W. Forrest, 3 vols. 1893; Lord Roberts, Forty-one Years in India, 30th ed. 1898; S. P. Oliver, The Second Afghan War, 1878–80, 1908; H. Septans, Les expéditions anglaises en Asie, Paris, 1897.]

H. M. V.

GOUGH-CALTHORPE, AUGUSTUS CHOLMONDELEY, sixth BARON CALTHORPE (1829–1910), agriculturist, born at Elvetham, Hampshire, on 8 Nov. 1829, was third son in the family of four sons and six daughters of Frederick Gough Calthorpe, fourth Baron Calthorpe (1790–1868), by his wife Lady Charlotte Sophia, eldest daughter of Henry Charles Somerset, sixth duke of Beaufort. The family descended from Sir Henry Gough (*d.* 1774), first baronet, of

Edgbaston, whose heir Henry, by his second wife, Barbara, heiress of Reynolds Calthorpe of Elvetham, succeeded in 1788 to the Elvetham estates, and taking the surname of Calthorpe, was created Baron Calthorpe on 15 June 1796 [see CALTHORPE, SIR HENRY]. Augustus was educated at Harrow from 1845 to 1847 and matriculated at Merton College, Oxford, on 23 Feb. 1848, graduating B.A. in 1851, and proceeding M.A. in 1855. In adult life he devoted himself to sport, agriculture, and the duties of a county magistrate. He lived on family property at Perry Hall, Staffordshire, serving as high sheriff of that county in 1881. At the general election of 1880 he stood with Major Fred Burnaby [q. v.] as conservative candidate for the undivided borough of Birmingham, near which a part of the family estates lay, but was defeated, P. H. Muntz, John Bright, and Mr. Joseph Chamberlain being returned. On the death on 26 June 1893 of his eldest brother, Frederick, fifth baron (1826–1893), who was unmarried (his second brother, George, had died unmarried in 1843), he succeeded to the peerage as sixth baron. On the family estates at Elvetham he started in 1900 what has become a noted herd of shorthorn cattle, and his Southdown sheep and Berkshire pigs were also famous. He showed generosity in devoting to public purposes much of his property about Birmingham. He made over to the corporation in 1894 the freehold of Calthorpe Park near that city, which his father had created in 1857, and took much interest in the development of the new Birmingham University. In 1900 he and his only son, Walter (1873–1906), presented 27½ acres of land, valued at 20,000*l.*, for the site of the university buildings, and in 1907 he gave another site, immediately adjacent, of nearly 20 acres, of the estimated value of 15,000*l.*, for a private recreation ground for the students. He died after a short illness at his London residence at Grosvenor Square on 22 July 1910, and was buried at Elvetham, after cremation at Golder's Green. He was succeeded in the title by his next brother, Lieut.-general Sir Somerset John Gough-Calthorpe (*b.* 23 Jan. 1831). He married on 22 July 1869 Maud Augusta Louisa, youngest daughter of the Hon. Octavius Duncombe, seventh son of Charles Duncombe, first Lord Feversham, by whom he had one son, Walter (who predeceased him), and four daughters.

[The Times, 23 and 28 July 1910; Harrow School Reg.; Foster's Alumni Oxon.; Burke's Peerage.] E. C.

GOULDING, FREDERICK (1842–1909), master printer of copper plates, was born at Holloway Road, Islington, on 7 Oct. 1842. His father, John Fry Goulding, foreman printer to Messrs. Day & Son, was married in 1833 to Elizabeth Rogers, who belonged to an old stock of Spitalfields weavers, and his grandfather, John Golding, also a copper-plate printer, was apprenticed in 1779 to a still earlier William Golding, a copper-plate printer of St. Botolph, Bishopsgate. In 1854 Frederick Goulding was sent to a day school conducted at the National Hall, Holborn, by William Lovett [q. v.], a well-known Chartist. On 24 Jan. 1857 he was apprenticed to Messrs. Day & Son, 6 Gate Street, Lincoln's Inn Fields, originally a firm of lithographic printers, but then concerned largely with the printing of engravings, to which branch of their business Goulding was attached. In his spare time through 1858 and 1859 he studied at the schools of art in Wilmington Square, Clerkenwell, and Castle Street, Long Acre, also attending lectures at the Royal Academy Schools. In 1859 he acted as 'devil' to James MacNeill Whistler [q. v. Suppl. II] in the printing of some of his etchings, and in the same year assisted his father in printing a series of etchings by Queen Victoria and the Prince Consort. At the Great Exhibition of 1862 he gave a daily demonstration of copper-plate printing for Messrs. Day & Son, from May till November, and began there the personal friendship with Sir Francis Seymour Haden [q. v. Suppl. II] which lasted till the end of his life.

By this time Goulding was a master of the 'art and mystery' of his craft, and began to use his spare time in the evenings and on Saturdays by working for private clients at his own residence, Kingston House, 53 Shepherd's Bush Road. Among those for whom he printed were Seymour Haden, Legros, Whistler, and Samuel Palmer. In 1881 he felt justified in embarking upon a printing business of his own, and built a studio, largely extended later, in the garden at the back of Kingston House. Among artists whose etchings he printed were Frank Short, Strang, Pennell, Rodin, Holroyd, Rajon and R. W. Macbeth; in fact few etchers or engravers did not claim Goulding's assistance. In 'About Etching' (1879) Haden described Goulding as 'the best printer of etchings in England just now.' From 1876 till 1882 he acted as assistant to Alphonse Legros [q. v. Suppl. II] in an etching class held weekly at the National Art Training School, now the

Royal College of Art, and from 1882 to 1891, when he was succeeded by Sir Frank Short, was entirely responsible for the conduct of the class. From 1876 to 1879 he also assisted Legros in an etching class held at the Slade School. On 7 Feb. 1890, at a full meeting of the council of the Royal Society of Painter-Etchers, he was unanimously elected the first master printer to the society.

In Goulding's case the craft of plate printing depended on something more than mere handicraft. He combined with remarkable dexterity of workmanship a singular understanding of each artist's aim, and so played no small part in the revival of etching in the nineteenth century. For his amusement and instruction he produced a few etchings of his own; their organic weakness of line is concealed by masterly printing.

He died, after five years' continuous ill-health, on 5 March 1909, and was buried in Kensal Green cemetery. On 16 Dec. 1865 he married Melanie Marie Alexandrine Piednue, and had three sons and a daughter (now Mrs. Pickford). A portrait in oils by Mr. Alfred Hartley, R.E., belongs to his daughter; there is also a dry-point etching by Mr. W. Strang, A.R.A., and a photo-engraving by Mr. Emery Walker from a photograph taken by Sir Frank Short.

[Frederick Goulding, Master Printer of Copper Plates, by the present writer, 1910, based on private information and on memoranda left by Goulding. The volume contains the full text of a lecture on the theory and practice of his craft delivered by Goulding to the Art Workers' Guild in 1904.] M. H.

GOWER, EDWARD FREDERICK LEVESON- (1819–1907). [See Leveson-Gower.]

GRACE, EDWARD MILLS (1841–1911), cricketer, born at Downend, near Bristol, on 28 Nov. 1841, was third of five sons of Henry Mills Grace (1808–1871) of Long Ashton, Somerset, medical practitioner and cricketing enthusiast, who had settled in 1831 at Downend. His mother was Martha, daughter of George Pocock, proprietor of a boarding school at St. Michael's Mill, Bristol. His brothers, Henry (1833–1895), Alfred (*b.* 1840), William Gilbert (*b.* 1848), and George Frederick (1850–1880), who all studied medicine, devoted themselves to cricket, the two youngest obtaining world-wide reputations for their all-round play. After education at Long Ashton, where he showed the family zeal for cricket, Grace studied medicine at the Bristol Medical School; he became M.R.C.S. England and L.R.C.P. Edinburgh in 1865, and L.S.A. in 1866. At first residing at Marshfield, he settled in 1869 at Thornbury, where he practised till his death, and took a prominent part in the life of the town. He was coroner for West Gloucestershire from 1875 till 1909, and held the office of district officer for the Thornbury board of guardians, was chairman of the Thornbury school board, and a member of the parish council. He died of cerebral hæmorrhage at his residence, Park House, Thornbury, on 20 May 1911. He was married four times, and left a widow, five sons and four daughters.

Grace, who was in youth a good athlete and fast runner, inherited from his father an aptitude for cricket, and was the first of the family to become famous at the game. On 7 August 1855, at the age of thirteen, he was chosen for his long-stopping to represent 22 of West Gloucestershire *v.* the All England eleven. William Clarke, the secretary and manager of the All England eleven, acknowledged his promise by presenting him with a bat (W. G. Grace's *Reminiscences*, pp. 5–6). He first appeared at Lord's in July 1861, playing for South Wales *v.* M.C.C., and next year he established his position as one of the finest batsmen in England. He first represented the Gentlemen *v.* Players in July 1862, and played on twelve occasions between 1863 and 1869, and after an interval of seventeen years played for the last time in 1886. He was the only amateur member of George Parr's team to Australia in 1863, but he met with small success. In August 1862, playing as a substitute for the M.C.C. *v.* the Gentlemen of Kent, at Canterbury, Grace carried his bat through the innings, scoring 192 not out, and captured all ten wickets in the second innings—a double feat only equalled by his brother William in 1886 and by Vyell Edward Walker [q. v. Suppl. II] in 1859. Grace's most notable seasons were those of 1863, of 1864, and of 1865. In 1863, when he made during the season 3000 runs, he, when playing for twenty of the Lansdown Club, Bath, scored 73 against a team which included Tinley, Jackson, and Tarrant, leading bowlers of England. In June 1865, when playing for eighteen of the Lansdown Club at Sydenham Field, Bath, he scored 121 against the United All England XI, 'an epoch-making event, as such achievements against the All England team were almost unheard of' (W. G. Grace's *Reminiscences*, p. 28). Although after 1865 Grace's fame was overshadowed by that of his younger brothers, William Gilbert and George Frederick, he long had a share in most of their triumphs in the matches between the Gentlemen and Players; from 1867 to 1874 the amateurs lost only a single match. The three Graces played for England against the Australians (6–8 Sept. 1880), an incident unparalleled in international cricket history. In August of the same year, at Clifton, Grace scored 65 and 43 (of 191 and 97 respectively) for Gloucestershire *v.* the Australians. The brilliant play of the Graces raised Gloucestershire to a first-class county in 1869, and champion county in 1876 and 1877. Grace was secretary of the Gloucestershire club from 1871 until 1909.

Quick of eye and limb, Grace was a rapid scorer and forcible hitter. Of unorthodox style, he was one of the first to employ the 'pull' stroke, hitting well-pitched off-balls to the on-boundary with consummate ease. His nerve, judgment, and speed made him '*the* best point' ever known, taking the ball almost off the bat (Daft, *Kings of Cricket*, p. 107). Grace ceased to play in county cricket in 1896, but played almost until his death for the Thornbury team, which he managed and captained for 35 years. In 1910, at the age of seventy, he played for them in some forty matches, meeting with much success as a lob bowler. During his cricketing career he scored over 76,000 runs and took over 12,000 wickets; he had an inexhaustible supply of cricketing recollections, which he would relate with much vivacity. He was a bold rider to hounds.

[W. G. Grace's Cricketing Reminiscences, 1899; Daft, Kings of Cricket, pp. 106–7 (with portrait, p. 13); K. S. Ranjitsinhji's Jubilee Book of Cricket, 1897, pp. 378–80; Haygarth's Scores and Biographies, vii. 114–5; Wisden's Cricketers' Almanack, 1911, p. 201 (for Thornbury performances); 1912 (for memoir); Lancet, 27 May 1911.] W. B. O.

GRAHAM, HENRY GREY (1842–1906), writer on Scottish history, born in the manse of North Berwick, on 3 Oct. 1842, was youngest of eleven children of Robert Balfour Graham, D.D., minister of the established church of North Berwick, by his wife Christina, daughter of Archibald Lawrie, D.D., minister of Loudon. At an early age he showed a great love of reading and spent most of his pocket-money on books. On the death of his father in 1855, his mother took him and her youngest daughter to Edinburgh, where, two years afterwards, he entered the university. Although showing no absorbing interest in the work of the classes and acquiring no university distinctions, he was a prominent and clever speaker in the debating societies. After being licensed as a probationer of the Church of Scotland in 1865, he was assistant at Bonhill, Dumbartonshire, until he was appointed in March 1868 to the charge of Nenthorn, Berwickshire. Here he made the acquaintance of Alexander Russel [q. v.], editor of the 'Scotsman,' who was accustomed to come to Nenthorn in summer; and he became a frequent contributor to the 'Scotsman' of reviews and leading articles. Of non-theological tendencies and widely tolerant in his opinions, he was, after the death of Dr. Robert Lee [q. v.], of Old Greyfriars church, Edinburgh, asked to become a candidate for the vacancy, but declined. In 1884 he was translated to Hyndland parish church, Glasgow, where he remained till his death on 7 May 1906. In 1878 he married Alice, daughter of Thomas Carlyle of Shawhill, advocate, and left a son, who died in Egypt, and a daughter.

Graham's principal work is 'Social Life of Scotland in the Eighteenth Century' (1899, 2 vols.; 3rd edit. 1906), graphically descriptive as well as learned. His 'Scottish Men of Letters of the Eighteenth Century' (1901; 2nd edit. 1908) is also very readable. For Blackwood's series of 'Foreign Classics' he wrote a monograph on 'Rousseau' (1882); and his 'Literary and Historical Essays' (published posthumously in 1908) include 'Society in France before the Revolution' (lectures at the Royal Institution, Feb. 1901) and a paper on 'Russel of the "Scotsman."'

[Scotsman, and Glasgow Herald, 8 May 1906; Graham's Essays, 1908, pref.] T. F. H.

GRAHAM, THOMAS ALEXANDER FERGUSON (1840–1906), artist, born at Kirkwall on 27 Oct. 1840, was only son of Alexander Spears Graham, writer to the signet and crown chamberlain of Orkney (like his father before him), by his wife Eliza Stirling. About 1850, some time after their father's death, Thomas and an only sister went to Edinburgh to live with their grandmother.

The boy's artistic instincts asserted themselves early. When little more than fourteen he was on the recommendation of the painter James Drummond [q. v.] enrolled (9 Jan. 1855) a student of the Trustees Academy. He proved an apt pupil in the talented group of McTaggart, Orchardson, Pettie, Chalmers, and the rest, who gathered round the recently appointed master, Robert Scott Lauder [q. v.]. Although he was the youngest of the coterie, Graham's talent and personal charm gave him a prominent place in it. He began to exhibit at the Royal Scottish Academy in 1859, but in 1863 he joined his friends Orchardson and Pettie in London. With Mr. C. E. Johnston, another Edinburgh-trained artist, the three shared a house in Fitzroy Square. Subsequently he occupied studios in Gloucester Road and Delancy Street, settling for good in 1886 at 96 Fellows Road, South Hampstead.

Save John MacWhirter, Graham spent more time abroad than any of his associates. As early as 1860 he went to Paris with McTaggart and Pettie, and two years later he paid, with Pettie and George Paul Chalmers, the first of several visits to Brittany, which supplied many pleasing and congenial subjects. In 1864 he was in Venice, where he did some charming sketches, and about 1885 he paid a prolonged visit to Morocco, then little exploited by artists, where he penetrated to Fez, and painted 'Kismet' (now in the Dundee Gallery) and other oriental subjects. But the picturesque Fifeshire fishing villages, the little seaports on the Moray Firth, and the wild west coast of Scotland were perhaps his favourite sketching grounds.

Graham's earlier pictures engagingly combine quaint naturalism and imaginative insight. 'A Young Bohemian' (1864), in the National Gallery of Scotland, is a delightful example of his work at that time. Later his handling broadened and his feeling for light and movement increased, and in pictures such as 'The Clang of the Wooden Schoon,' 'The Passing Salute,' or 'The Siren' he attained much rhythmic beauty of design, great charm of high-pitched and opalescent colour, and a fine sense of atmosphere. And, if lower in tone and more sombre in colour, 'The Last of the Boats' and a few other dramatic pictures of the sea are, in their different mood, equally successful. His art, however, was too sensitive and refined to command wide attention, and, owing to extreme fastidiousness, he was a somewhat uncertain executant. The only distinction conferred upon him was honorary membership of the Royal Scottish Academy, which he received in 1883. Latterly he gave much of his time to portraiture, in which his finest gifts had little scope. His most successful pictures rank with the best achievements of his school.

He died unmarried while on a visit to Edinburgh on 24 Dec. 1906. 'Tom' Graham, whose winning manners and brilliant conversational powers made him a great favourite with his friends, was exceptionally handsome. Excellent portraits of him by himself and by Orchardson and Pettie belong to his sister, and he served as model for these two artists on several occasions, notably in 'The First Cloud' by the former, and in 'The Jacobites' by the latter.

[Private information; personal knowledge; exhibition catalogues; Report of R.S.A. for 1907; Scotsman, 25 Dec. 1906; Sir W. Armstrong's Scottish Painters, 1887; J. L. Caw's Scottish Painting, 1908.] J. L. C.

GRAHAM, WILLIAM (1839–1911), philosopher and political economist, born at Saintfield, co. Down, in 1839, was a younger son of Alexander Graham, farmer and horse-dealer, by his wife Maria Crawford, a descendant of a Scottish presbyterian family which came to Ireland in Charles II's time to escape religious persecution. The father died poor while his son was very young, and it fell to the mother, a woman of spirit and intelligence, to bring up the children —four sons and a daughter—amid many hardships. William obtained a foundation scholarship at the Educational Institute, Dundalk, and being well grounded there in mathematics and English was soon engaged as a teacher in the royal school at Banagher, where he remained till he entered Trinity College, Dublin, in July 1860.

At Trinity College Graham won distinction in mathematics, philosophy, and English prose composition. During most of his college course he worked outside the university as headmaster successively of two important schools in or near Dublin. But a foundation scholarship in mathematics which he won in 1865 gave him an annual stipend together with free rooms and commons. He graduated B.A. in 1867, and thereupon engaged in coaching students in mathematics and especially philosophy. His success as private tutor enabled him to give up his school work. He devoted much time to the study of philosophy, and in 1872 he published his first book, 'Idealism, an Essay Metaphysical and Critical,' a vindication of Berkeley against Hamilton and the Scottish school.

Graham, who had proceeded M.A. in 1870, left Dublin in 1873 to become private secretary to Mitchell Henry, M.P. [q. v. Suppl. II], but resigned the post in 1874 and settled in London. In 1875 he was appointed lecturer on mathematics at St. Bartholomew's Hospital, and he engaged at the same time in literary and tutorial work; but the best part of his time for some years was given to the preparation of the most important of his books, 'The Creed of Science,' which appeared in 1881. This is a work of great freshness and power, discussing how far the new scientific doctrines of the conservation of energy, evolution, and natural selection necessitated a revision of the accepted theories in philosophy, theology, and ethics. It was well received, running to a second edition in 1884, and it evoked the admiration of Darwin, Gladstone, and Archbishop Trench. In bigoted circles Graham's argument was foolishly credited with atheistic tendencies. This wholly unfounded suspicion caused the Irish chief secretary, Sir Michael Hicks Beach, to withdraw an offer which he made to Graham of an assistant commissionership of intermediate education in Oct. 1886. In London Graham was soon a welcome figure in the best intellectual society. His many friends there included men of the eminence of Carlyle, Lecky, and Froude. Carlyle wrote of finding in him 'a force of insight and a loyalty to what is true, which greatly distinguish him from common, even from highly educated and what are called ingenious and clever men.' One of his strong points was his conversational gift. Professor Mahaffy wrote of him at the time of his death, 'His highest genius was undoubtedly for intellectual recreation. In this he had few equals' (*Athenæum*, 25 Nov. 1911).

Meanwhile his increasing reputation had led to his election in 1882 to the chair of jurisprudence and political economy in Queen's College, Belfast. This post he held till 1909, when ill-health compelled his retirement. At Belfast he enjoyed the enthusiastic regard of a long succession of pupils. He was professor of law for ten years before he joined the legal profession. In 1892 he was called to the bar at the Inner Temple without any intention of practising. His duties at Belfast allowed him still to reside most of the year in London, and in his leisure he produced a succession of works on political or economic subjects. 'Social Problems' came out in 1886, 'Socialism New and Old' in 1890, 'English Political Philosophy from Hobbes to Maine' in 1899, and 'Free Trade and the Empire' in 1904. He also read a paper on trusts to the British Association at Belfast in 1902, and was a frequent contributor to the 'Nineteenth Century,' 'Contemporary Review,' and 'Economic Journal.' He was for many years examiner in political economy and also in philosophy for the Indian civil service and the Royal University of Ireland, and in English for the Irish intermediate education department.

He received the honorary degree of Litt.D. from Trinity College, Dublin, in 1905. His health began to fail in 1907, and he died unmarried in a nursing home in Dublin on 19 Nov. 1911, being buried in Mount Jerome cemetery there.

[Graham's Autobiographical MS. notes; Irish Times, 20 Nov. 1911; personal knowledge.] J. R.

GRANT, GEORGE MONRO (1835–1902), principal of Queen's University, Kingston, Canada, born on 22 Dec. 1835 at Albion Mines, Pictou County, Nova Scotia, was third child of James Grant, who, springing from a long line of Scottish farmers, emigrated from Banffshire in 1826, and married five years later Mary Monro of Inverness.

Owing to the accident of losing his right hand at the age of seven, the boy was brought up to be a scholar. At Pictou Academy he gained in 1853 a bursary tenable at either Glasgow or Edinburgh University. He chose Glasgow, and seven years later, on the completion of a distinguished course, he received his testamur in theology, and was ordained (Dec. 1860) by the presbytery of Glasgow as a missionary for Nova Scotia. He declined an invitation from Norman Macleod [q. v.] to remain in Glasgow as his assistant.

After occupying various mission-fields in his native province and in Prince Edward Island, he accepted a call in 1863 to the pulpit of St. Matthew's Church, the leading Church of Scotland church in Halifax. Grant, who saw the need of a native trained ministry for the established presbyterian church in Nova Scotia, struggled without success to establish a theological hall at Halifax, by way of supplement to Dalhousie College, which largely through his efforts was reorganised as a non-sectarian institution in 1863. Meanwhile he directed his efforts to the union of the presbyterian church throughout Canada. The federation of the provinces in 1867, which Grant eagerly supported, gave an impulse to the spirit of union, and 15 June 1875 saw the first General Assembly of the united church.

In 1877 Grant, who had for some years identified himself with educational reform, became principal of Queen's University, Kingston, Ontario, a presbyterian foundation. He received the honorary degree of D.D. from Glasgow University in the same year. Queen's University was at the time in financial difficulties, and he undertook two strenuous campaigns in 1878 and 1887 to obtain increased endowment from private sources. The immediate financial situation saved, Grant concentrated his energies upon securing adequate recognition and aid from the provincial legislature; but he was faced by a prejudice against state-aided denominational colleges, which was encouraged by the claim of the University of Toronto to be the only properly constituted provincial university. In 1887 Queen's University rejected federation with Toronto. But Grant's political influence steadily grew, and he secured for his university in 1893 a state-endowed school of mines, which subsequently became the faculty of practical science in the university. In 1898 Grant sought to sever the tie between the presbyterian church and the arts faculty of Queen's. In 1900 he forced his views upon the church assembly, but he died two years later, and the assembly of 1903 reversed his policy, which was not enforced till June 1911. Grant's preponderating influence in education led to an invitation (which was refused) from Sir Oliver Mowat [q. v. Suppl. II] in 1883 to resign his principalship and accept the portfolio of education in his cabinet. Grant held that the education administration in the province should be wholly withdrawn from politics.

Grant acquired an intimate knowledge of the country, having twice traversed the continent. In 1872 he accompanied Mr. (afterwards Sir) Sandford Fleming on his preliminary survey of a route for the Canadian Pacific Railway, and in 1883, again with Mr. Fleming, he examined a route through the mountains. The first journey Grant recorded in 'Ocean to Ocean' (1873), and the impressions of both journeys are merged in four articles contributed to 'Scribner's Magazine' in 1880, and in 'Picturesque Canada,' a publication which he edited in 1884.

To the press and to periodicals Grant frequently communicated his views on public questions. His political comments in the 'Queen's University Quarterly' were widely read. He powerfully supported the new imperialism, and urged on Canada her imperial responsibilities. He became president of the Imperial Federation League, Ontario, in 1889. To religious literature Grant contributed one book of importance, 'Religions of the World' (Edinburgh 1894; 2nd edit., revised and enlarged, 1895). This has been translated into many European languages and into Japanese.

Grant showed his courage and independence at the close of his life in his trenchant criticism of the temperance party, which aimed at the total prohibition of the liquor traffic. To restore his health, which was impaired by his endowment campaign of 1887, Grant made a tour of the world in 1888. In 1889 he was elected moderator of the general assembly of the presbyterian church in Canada, and became LL.D. of Dalhousie University in 1892. In 1891 he was elected president of the Royal Society of Canada. He was president of the St. Andrew's Society, Kingston, from 1894 to 1896. In 1901 he was created C.M.G. He died at Kingston on 10 May 1902. He was buried in Cataraqui cemetery in the same town.

On 7 May 1867 Grant married Jessie, eldest daughter of William Lawson of Halifax, Nova Scotia. His only surviving child, William Lawson Grant, is professor of history in Queen's University, Kingston. A portrait of Grant by Robert Harris (1889) is in the Convocation Hall of Queen's University, Kingston; a bust by Hamilton McCarthy (1891) is in the library and senate room there.

[Life by W. L. Grant and Frederick Hamilton, Toronto, 1904, and Edinburgh and London 1905.] P. E.

GRANT, SIR ROBERT (1837–1904), lieutenant-general, royal engineers, born at Malabar Hill, Bombay, on 10 Aug. 1837, was younger son of Sir Robert Grant [q. v.], governor of Bombay, and was nephew of Lord Glenelg [q. v.]. His mother was Margaret (*d.* 1885), only daughter of Sir David Davidson of Cantray, Nairnshire, N.B., who married as her second husband Lord Josceline William Percy, M.P., second son of George fifth duke of Northumberland.

Robert was educated at Harrow with his elder brother Charles [see below]. When he was seventeen he passed first in a public competitive examination for vacancies in the royal artillery and the royal engineers caused by the Crimean war, and was gazetted second lieutenant in the royal engineers on 23 Oct. 1854, becoming first lieutenant on 13 Dec. of the same year.

After six months' training at Chatham Grant was sent to Scotland. In February

1857 he was transferred to the Jamaica command in the West Indies, and at the end of 1858 he served on the staff as fort adjutant at Belise in British Honduras. He passed first in the examination for the Staff College, just established; but after a few months there (Jan.–May 1859) he was aide-de-camp to Lieut.-general Sir William Fenwick Williams [q. v.], the commander of the forces in North America for six years. On 8 Aug. 1860 he was promoted second captain. He was at home for the final examination at the Staff College, in which he again easily passed first, despite his absence from the classes, and from January to June 1861 he was attached to the cavalry and artillery at Aldershot.

Finally returning from Canada in June 1865, Grant did duty at Chatham, Dover, and Portsmouth, and was promoted first captain on 10 July 1867 and major on 5 July 1872. From 1 Jan. 1871 to 1877 he was deputy assistant adjutant-general for royal engineers at the war office, and from 1877 was in command of the royal engineers troops, consisting of the pontoon, telegraph, equipment and depot units at Aldershot. He was promoted lieut.-colonel on 1 July 1878. In May 1880 he was appointed commanding royal engineer of the Plymouth subdistrict, and on 31 Dec. 1881 commanding royal engineer of the Woolwich district. He was promoted colonel in the army on 1 July 1882, and a year later was placed on half pay. He remained unemployed until 5 May 1884, when he was given the R.E. command in Scotland, with the rank of colonel on the staff.

On 20 March 1885 he left Edinburgh suddenly for Egypt to join Lord Wolseley, who had telegraphed for his services, as colonel on the staff and commanding royal engineer with the Nile expeditionary force. He served with the headquarters staff and afterwards in command of the Abu Fatmeh district during the evacuation, but he was taken seriously ill with fever and was invalided home in August. For his services he was mentioned in despatches of 13 June 1885 (*Lond. Gazette*, 25 Aug. 1885). Not anticipating so speedy a termination to the campaign, the authorities had filled up his appointment in Scotland and he had to wait nearly a year on half pay.

On 1 July 1886 Grant was appointed deputy adjutant-general for royal engineers at the war office. On 25 May 1889 he was created C.B., military division, and on 23 Oct. made a temporary major-general. Before he had quite completed his five years as deputy adjutant-general Grant was appointed to the important post of inspector-general of fortifications (18 April 1891), with the temporary rank of lieut.-general, dated 29 April 1891. He succeeded to the establishment of major-generals on 9 May 1891, and became lieut.-general on 4 June 1897. As inspector-general of fortifications Grant was an *ex-officio* member of the joint naval and military committee on defence, and president of the colonial defence committee. During his term of office important works of defence and of barrack construction were carried out, under the loan for defences and military works loan. His services were so highly valued that they were retained for two years beyond the usual term. He was promoted K.C.B. on 20 May 1896. On leaving the war office (17 April 1898) Grant's work was highly commended by the secretaries of state for war and the colonies, and he was awarded a distinguished service pension of 100*l.* a year. He was given the G.C.B. on 26 June 1902, and retired from the service on 28 March 1903. His health was failing, and he died on 8 Jan. 1904 at his residence, 14 Granville Place, Portman Square, London, and was buried in Kensal Green cemetery.

Always cool and self-contained, Grant was gifted with a sure judgment and a retentive memory. A portrait in oils by C. Lutyens, painted in 1897, hangs in the R.E. officers' mess at Aldershot, and a replica is in Lady Grant's possession. She has also a portrait in oils of Sir Robert Grant by Henty, painted in 1887. He married in London, on 24 Nov. 1875, Victoria Alexandrina, daughter of John Cotes of Woodcote Hall, Shropshire, and widow of T. Owen of Condover Hall in the same county. There were three children of the marriage, a daughter who died young, and twin sons, both in the army, of whom the younger, Robert Josceline, was killed at Spion Kop on 24 Jan. 1900.

Sir Charles Grant (1836–1903), elder brother of Sir Robert Grant, was born in 1836, and educated at Harrow, Trinity College, Cambridge, and at Haileybury. He entered the Bengal civil service in 1858, was appointed a commissioner of the central provinces in 1870, and acting chief commissioner in 1879, when he became an additional member of the governor-general's council. In 1880 he was acting secretary to the government of India for the home, revenue, and agricultural departments, and in 1881 was appointed foreign secretary to the government of India. He was created C.S.I. in 1881, and in 1885 K.C.S.I. on retirement. He died suddenly in London on 10 April 1903. He married: (1) in 1872 Ellen (*d.* 1885), daughter of the Rt. Hon. Henry Baillie of Redcastle, N.B.; and (2) in 1890 Lady Florence Lucia, daughter of Admiral Sir Edward Alfred John Harris, and sister of the fourth earl of Malmesbury. She was raised to the rank of an earl's daughter in 1890. Sir Charles Grant edited the 'Central Provinces Gazetteer' (2nd edit. 1870).

[War Office Records; Royal Engineers Records; The Times, 13 April 1903 and 9 and 10 Jan. 1904; Royal Engineers Journals, February 1904.] R. H. V.

GRANT DUFF, Sir MOUNTSTUART ELPHINSTONE (1829–1906), statesman and author, elder son of James Grant Duff [q. v.] by his wife Jane Catherine, daughter of Sir Whitelaw Ainslie [q. v.], was born at Eden, Aberdeenshire, on 21 Feb. 1829. He was educated at Edinburgh Academy, the Grange School, and at Balliol College, Oxford (1847–50). Among his contemporary friends at Oxford were Henry Smith, Henry Oxenham, Charles Pearson, Goldwin Smith, Charles Parker, and John Coleridge Patteson. He graduated B.A. in 1850 with a second class in the final classical school, and proceeded M.A. in 1853. On leaving Oxford he settled in London and read for the bar, and in 1854 passed with honours, second to James Fitzjames (afterwards Mr. Justice) Stephen, who later became one of his most intimate friends for life, in the LL.B. examination of London University. In the same year (17 Nov.) he was called to the bar by the Inner Temple, and while a pupil in the chambers of William Ventris (afterwards Lord) Field [q. v. Suppl. II] joined the Midland circuit, and obtained his first brief because he was the only person present who could speak German. He was one of the earliest contributors to the 'Saturday Review,' and lectured at the Working Men's College, of which Frederick Denison Maurice was first principal.

In December 1857 Grant Duff was returned as the liberal member for the Elgin Burghs, and held this seat without intermission until he was appointed governor of Madras in 1881. In 1860 and in each subsequent year he addressed to his constituents an elaborate speech, mainly on foreign policy, and he came to speak on this topic with recognised authority. His knowledge of the subject, largely derived from intimate conversation with foreigners of distinction in their own languages, was singularly wide and accurate, and his treatment of it entirely free from political acerbity. These speeches, which were from time to time re-published collectively, possess historical interest.

When Gladstone formed his first ministry in 1868, Grant Duff was appointed (8 Dec.) under-secretary of state for India, and he retained the office until the ministry finally resigned in 1874. In that year he paid a first visit to India. In 1880 he joined the second Gladstone ministry as under-secretary for the colonies, being sworn a member of the privy council on 8 May. It is probable that neither the domestic nor the colonial policy of the government during the next twelve months was supported by Grant Duff with unreserved enthusiasm, and on 26 June 1881 he accepted without hesitation the offer of the governorship of Madras, which brought to an end his twenty-four years' unbroken representation of his constituency in the House of Commons.

The presidency of Madras during the period of Grant Duff's government was free from critical events, but he devoted himself strenuously and successfully to his administrative duties, and the minutes in which from time to time he recorded and commented on the course of public affairs were models alike of assiduity and of style. Sir Louis Mallet [q. v.], under-secretary for India, commented upon the receipt of the last he wrote, 'I doubt whether any previous governor has left behind so able and complete a record.' Grant Duff left Madras in November 1886, and after making some stay in Syria returned to England in the spring of 1887. In March he was invested at Windsor with the G.C.S.I. He had been made C.I.E. in 1881.

On settling again in England Grant Duff made no effort to re-enter political life. The home rule controversy had embittered politics in his absence, and he had neither the requisite physical robustness nor any relish for violent conflict. A scholar, a calmly rational politician, and a man of almost dainty refinement both physically and morally, he devoted himself thenceforward to study, to authorship, and to the cultivation of the social amenities in which his experience was probably as wide and as remarkable as that of any one of his contemporaries. He was in the habit of meeting or corresponding with almost everyone of any eminence in social life in England, and with many similar persons abroad. He was a member of almost every small social club of the highest class. In February 1858, the month that he first took his seat in parliament, he was elected a member of the 'Cosmopolitan' and of the Athenæum. In 1889 he joined 'The Club,' and for some years before his death was its treasurer—'the only permanent official, and the guardian of its records.' He also belonged to the Literary Society (from 1872) and Grillion's (from 1889), and was in 1866 the founder of the Breakfast Club, and the most assiduous attendant at its meetings.

Grant Duff published numerous articles, essays, and memoirs, a volume of original verse (printed privately), and an anthology of the Victorian poets. All of them show learning, cultivation, and style; but the principal literary work he left behind him is his 'Notes from a Diary.' He began a diary in 1851, and from 1873 kept it with the intention that the bulk of it should be published. He published the first two volumes (1851–72) in 1897; further sets of two volumes each followed in 1898, 1899, 1900, 1901, 1904, and 1905. The fourteen volumes bring the record down to 23 Jan. 1901, when Grant Duff kissed hands as a privy councillor on the accession of King Edward VII. He declares in his preface to the first two volumes that his object has been to make it 'the lightest of light reading,' and the most 'good-natured' of books. The 'Notes' contain practically no politics, but are a purely personal record of the people he met, and the things they said. The result is a collection of excellent stories and memorable sayings, which form a valuable contribution to social history.

Grant Duff travelled much. He visited at different times Coburg, Dresden, Russia, Spain, Darmstadt (during the war of 1870), Athens, the Troad, India (seven years before his appointment to Madras), Syria (where he spent a winter at Haifa in a house lent to him by Laurence Oliphant), and Bucharest. In all these places he frequented the society of rulers, ambassadors, authors, and other remarkable people. He received from M. Ollivier a full and confidential account of the political events immediately preceding the Franco-Prussian war. He met Garibaldi in the height of his fame, and was for many years on terms of friendship with the Empress Frederick of Germany. From 1866 to 1872 he filled for two consecutive terms the office of lord rector of Aberdeen University. From 1889 to 1893 he was president of the Royal Geographical Society, and from 1892 to 1899 was president of the Royal Historical Society. He was elected F.R.S. in 1901, and was nominated a Crown trustee of the British Museum in 1903.

In person Grant Duff was slight, delicately made, and habitually gentle in speech and manner, though he would upon occasion express himself with great animation. He suffered through life from indifferent health, and in particular from astigmatic vision to such an extent that it was extremely difficult for him to read or write for himself.

He was the tenant for considerable periods of Hampden House, Berkshire, York House, Twickenham, and Knebworth House. Finally he bought Lexden Park, near Colchester, and in each of these houses he practised a wide hospitality. He died at his London house on Chelsea Embankment on 12 Jan. 1906, and was buried at Elgin cathedral.

Grant Duff married on 13 April 1859 Anna Julia, only daughter of Edward Webster of North Lodge, Ealing. By her he had four sons and four daughters. His elder sons, Arthur and Evelyn, are respectively minister at Dresden and consul-general, with the rank of minister, at Buda-Pest. Grant Duff's portrait in crayons by Henry T. Wells, drawn for reproduction for Grillion's Club, is in the possession of Lady Grant Duff at Earl Soham Grange, Framlingham.

Grant Duff published, besides 'Notes from a Diary': 1. 'Studies of European Politics,' 1866. 2. 'A Political Survey,' 1868. 3. 'Elgin Speeches,' Edinburgh, 1871. 4. 'Notes on an Indian Journey,' 1876. 5. 'Miscellanies, Political and Literary,' 1878. 6. 'Memoir of Sir Henry Maine,' 1892. 7. 'Ernest Renan,' 1893–8. 8. 'Memoir of Lord De Tabley,' 1899. 9. 'A Victorian Anthology,' 1902. 10 'Out of the Past: some Biographical Essays,' 2 vols. 1903. 11. 'Gems from a Victorian Anthology,' 1904.

[Notes from a Diary; Banffshire Herald, 16 Jan. 1906; The Times, 13 Jan. 1906; Burke's Landed Gentry; private information; personal knowledge.]
H. S.

GRANTHAM, Sir WILLIAM (1835–1911), judge, born at Lewes on 23 Oct. 1835, was second son of George Grantham of Barcombe Place, Sussex, by his wife Sarah, daughter of William Verrall of Southower Manor, Lewes. He was educated at King's College School, London, and was entered a student of the Inner Temple on 30 April 1860. A pupil in the chambers of James (afterwards Lord) Hannen [q. v. Suppl. I], he obtained in January 1863 the studentship given by the council of legal education, and was called to the bar on the 26th of the same month. Choosing the south-eastern circuit, a good local connection in Sussex aided him at the start, and his pleasant manner, combined with courage, pertinacity, and great industry, soon secured him a steady practice. He obtained the reputation of being 'a very useful junior in an action on a builder's account, in a running-down case, in a compensation case, and especially in disputes in which a combined knowledge of law and horseflesh was desirable.' He took silk on 13 Feb. 1877, and was made a bencher of his Inn on 30 April 1880, serving the office of treasurer in 1904.

As a leader Grantham achieved considerable success on circuit, but in London he failed to make any conspicuous mark. His real and absorbing interest was in politics; a conservative of the most orthodox school, gifted with an excellent platform manner and considerable rhetorical power, Grantham took a prominent part in the conversion to tory democracy of the working-men of London and the home counties. At the general election of February 1874 he was returned together with James Watney for East Surrey by a large majority, which he substantially increased in April 1880. After the redistribution of seats in 1885 he was selected to contest the borough of Croydon, carved out of his old constituency, and although the seat was regarded by the local conservatives as a forlorn hope, he defeated his liberal opponent, Mr. Jabez Balfour, by over 1000 votes. There was no more accomplished or successful electioneer in the south of England, and his services were widely in request as a platform speaker. By the death of his elder brother George in 1880 he had become squire of Barcombe and lord of the manor of Camois Court, a position which gave him additional prestige in 'the country party.' He became deputy chairman and eventually chairman of the East Sussex quarter sessions. In parliament he was a fairly frequent speaker, with a special mission to unmask and defeat the machinations of Gladstone; he was conspicuous among the militant spirits on the conservative benches. In January 1886, before he had the opportunity of taking his seat on his re-election for Croydon, he was made a judge of the Queen's Bench Division, in succession to Sir Henry Lopes [q. v. Suppl. I], and was knighted. It was Lord Halsbury's first judicial appointment, and there were many conflicting claims among conservative lawyers. In 'Whitaker's Almanack' for 1886 the name of Sir John Gorst, then solicitor-general, was printed among the judges instead of that of Grantham.

On the bench he showed himself indefatigable and painstaking, and he never failed to clear his list on circuit. He was shrewd in his judgment of character, had a varied assortment of general knowledge, and his manly, downright ways made a favourable impression on juries. He had a competent knowledge of law for the ordinary work of *nisi prius*, and his industry and energy made a strong contrast to the methods of some of his colleagues. But he lacked the breadth of mind and the grasp of intellect necessary for trying great and complicated issues, and he was a very unsatisfactory judge in commercial cases. Among his failings was an inability to refrain from perpetual comment; his 'obiter dicta' brought him into collision at one time or another with nearly every class of the community—deans, publicans, chairmen of quarter sessions, the council of the bar, the Durham pitmen, his brother judges. His love of talking was not conducive to the dignity of the bench, and towards the close of his career he was given strong hints in the press that the public interest would be best served by his retirement.

In the spring of 1906 Grantham found himself on the rota of judges appointed to try election petitions, a task for which his strong and somewhat intemperate political views rendered him peculiarly unfit. His decisions at Bodmin, at Maidstone, and at Great Yarmouth, all of which favoured the conservative claims to the seats, caused much dissatisfaction. On 6 July 1906 a motion to take into consideration his proceedings at Yarmouth was introduced into the House of Commons by Mr. Swift MacNeill, nationalist M.P. for South Donegal. Grantham was severely criticised and as strongly defended. At the suggestion of the prime minister, Sir Henry Campbell-Bannerman, the house declined 'to take the first step in a course which must lead to nothing less than the removal of the judge from the bench.' Grantham felt the stigma deeply, but was unwise enough to revive the memory of the debate, some five years later (7 Feb. 1911), by an indiscreet speech to the grand jury at Liverpool, which brought upon him in the House of Commons from Mr. Asquith, the prime minister, the severest rebuke which has ever been dealt to an English judge by a minister of the crown. Yet Grantham was perfectly sincere in his belief that in the discharge of his office he was uninfluenced by political partiality, nor was Mr. Arthur Balfour exceeding the truth when he declared in the course of the 1906 debate that 'a more transparently natural candid man than Mr. Justice Grantham never exercised judicial functions.'

A fine model of the English country gentleman, a liberal landlord, always ready to champion the cause of his poorer neighbours against local boards and the red tape of officialdom, Grantham was devoted to all out-of-door sports; he was a notable critic of horseflesh, was one of the founders of the Pegasus Club, and used to act as judge at the bar point to point races. An enthusiastic volunteer, he would sometimes appear at the 'Inns of Court' dinners in the scarlet coat, which had descended to him from an ancestor, of the old Bloomsbury Association or 'Devil's Own.' In the long vacation of 1910 he paid a visit to Canada, and won all hearts by his picturesque personality and outspoken opinions. Though he had sat on the bench for upwards of a quarter of a century, and had been for some years the senior puisne, his physical powers showed no sign of decay when he succumbed to a sharp attack of pneumonia, dying at his house in Eaton Square on 30 Nov. 1911. He was buried at Barcombe.

He married on 16 Feb. 1865 Emma, eldest daughter of Richard Wilson of Chiddingley, Sussex, who survived him; there was issue of the marriage two sons and five daughters. A portrait of Grantham by A. Stuart-Wortley is at Barcombe; an earlier oil painting by Bernard Lucas is in the possession of his younger son, Mr. F. W. Grantham.

[The Times, 1 Dec. 1911; Burke's Landed Gentry; Foster's Men at the Bar; Hansard, 4th series, clx. 370, 5th series, xxii. 366; personal knowledge.] J. B. A.

GRAY, BENJAMIN KIRKMAN (1862–1907), economist, son of Benjamin Gray, congregational minister, by his wife Emma Jane Kirkman, was born on 11 Aug. 1862 at Blandford, Dorset. He was educated privately by his father, and read omnivorously on his own account. In 1876 he entered a London warehouse, but found the work distasteful. His father vetoed, in 1882, a plan which he had formed of emigrating, and from 1883 to 1886 he taught in private schools, at the same time eagerly pursuing his own studies. Of sensitive and self-centred temperament, he interested himself early in social questions.

In September 1886 Gray entered New College, London, to prepare for the congregational ministry. He paid much attention to economics and won the Ricardo economic scholarship at University College. In 1892 he went to Leeds to work under the Rev. R. Westrope at Belgrave (congregational) Chapel. But congregational orthodoxy dissatisfied him, and in 1894 he joined the Unitarians. He served as unitarian minister at Warwick from that year till 1897. From 1898 to 1902 he was in London, engaged in social work at the Bell Street Mission, Edgware Road, and studying at first hand the economic problem of philanthropy. His views took a strong socialistic bent, and he joined the Independent Labour Party. But a breakdown in health soon compelled his retirement from active work. Removing to Hampstead he devoted himself to research into the history of philanthropic movements in England. In 1905 he lectured at the London School of Economics on the philanthropy of the eighteenth century. He died of angina pectoris on 23 June 1907, at Letchworth, whither he had been drawn by his interest in the social experiment of the newly established Garden City. His ashes were buried there after cremation. In 1898 Gray married Miss Eleanor Stone, who edited his literary remains.

'The History of English Philanthropy from the Dissolution of the Monasteries to the First Census' (1905) and 'Philanthropy and the State' (published posthumously, 1910) are substantial embodiments of much original research and thought. Gray traces through the social history of the nineteenth century a uniform tendency, whereby the effort of the individual is replaced by that of the State. In spite of his strong socialist convictions he writes with scholarly restraint and fairness, and throws light on tangled conditions of contemporary life.

[A Modern Humanist: miscellaneous papers by B. Kirkman Gray, with a memoir by H. B. Binns and Clementina Black, 1910.]

G. S. W.

GREEN, SAMUEL GOSNELL (1822–1905), baptist minister and bibliophile, born at Falmouth on 20 Dec. 1822, was eldest son of the family of five sons and four daughters of Samuel Green, baptist minister, of Falmouth and afterwards of Thrapston and London, by his wife Eliza, daughter of Benjamin Lepard, of cultured Huguenot descent. From 1824 to 1834 Green was with his family at Thrapston, and when they moved to Walworth in 1834 he was sent to a private school at Camberwell, where his literary tastes were encouraged. After leaving school, and until the age of nineteen, he worked in the printing-office of John Haddon in Finsbury, and then acted as tutor in private schools at Cambridge and Saffron Walden.

In 1840 he entered Stepney College (now Regent's Park College) to prepare for the baptist ministry, and graduated B.A. in the University of London in 1843. After ministerial posts at High Wycombe in 1844 and at Taunton in 1847, he became, in 1851, classical and mathematical tutor at Horton (now Rawdon) College, Bradford, and was from 1863 to 1876 president there. He impressed his students as a scholar of broad sympathies and a stimulating teacher (PROF. MEDLEY in *Centenary of Rawdon College*, 1904; REV. JAMES STUART in *Watford Observer*, Sept. 1905).

As a preacher Green proved a special favourite with children. Long connected with the Sunday School Union, where he succeeded his father as editor of the monthly 'Notes on Lessons,' he was elected in 1894 a vice-president of the union. His addresses and lectures to children on the Bible and his contributions to the 'Union Magazine' were afterwards separately published under various titles. He also wrote for children 'The Written Word' (12mo. 1871), a book of merit; 'The Apostle Peter' (1873; 3rd edit. 1883), and 'The Kingdoms of Israel and Judah' (2 vols. 1876–7). As the first Ridley lecturer at Regent's Park College in 1883, Green delivered the substance of his excellent 'Christian Ministry to the Young.'

In 1876 Green came to London to serve as editor, and in 1881 as editorial secretary, of the Religious Tract Society. Thenceforth his main energies were devoted to literary work, in which towards the end of his long life he was aided by his elder son, Prof. S. W. Green. His most important work was his 'Handbook to the Grammar of the Greek Testament,' published in 1870 (revised editions in 1880, 1885, 1892, and 1904), which was followed in 1894 by a primer which had also a wide circulation. A companion volume on the Hebrew of the Old Testament appeared in 1901. In 1898 he published his Angus lecture on 'The Christian Creed and the Creeds of Christendom'; in 1903 'A Handbook of Church History,' a compact and comprehensive manual; in 1904 a revised edition of Dr. Angus's 'Bible Handbook' (new and posthumous edition 1907), bringing that useful work up to date. In a revised edition of the English Bible (1877), designed by Joseph Gurney (1804–1879) [q. v.], Green, with Dr. George Andrew Jacob, headmaster of Christ's Hospital (1853–68), was responsible for the New Testament. For the Religious Tract Society's series of 'Pen and Pencil Sketches' he wrote wholly or in part 'Pictures from England' (1879 and 1889), 'France' (1878), 'Bible Lands' (1879), 'Germany' (1880), 'Scotland' (1883; new edit. 1886), and 'Italy' (1885).

Green was president of the Baptist Union at Portsmouth in 1895, and delivered from the chair two addresses, which were published. He also read a paper on 'Hymnody in our Churches,' a subject in which he was deeply interested. For John Rylands (1801–1888) [q. v.] of Manchester he printed for private circulation an admirable anthology, 'Hymns of the Church Universal' (1885), and was chairman of the editorial committee of the 'Baptist Hymnal.'

An appreciative and widely read critic of secular literature, he was the adviser of John Rylands's widow, of Stretford near Manchester, in various literary and benevolent schemes from the time of her husband's death in 1888. He and his third son, J. Arnold Green, assisted Mrs. Rylands in the collection of the John Rylands Library, Manchester, which was opened in 1899.

In 1900 Green received the honorary degree of D.D. from the University of St. Andrews. Retaining his vitality to the last, he died at Streatham on 15 Sept. 1905, and was buried in Norwood cemetery. He married in October 1848, at Abingdon, Berkshire, Elizabeth Leader, eldest daughter of James Collier; she died on 23 May 1905, having issue three sons and one daughter. His third son, J. Arnold Green, born on 23 Aug. 1860, died on 13 Sept. 1907.

A presentation portrait in oils by H. A. Olivier, subscribed for in 1900 by students of Rawdon and other friends, was handed by Green to the college at its annual meeting in June 1905.

Besides the works mentioned and other smaller religious and educational works, Green published: 1. 'Religious Hindrances to Religious Revival,' 1845. 2. 'The Working-Classes of Great Britain, their Present Condition, &c.,' 1850. 3. 'Clerical Subscription and National Morality' (Bicentenary Lectures), 1862. 4. 'What do I believe?' 12mo. 1880; Welsh translation, 1882. 5. 'The Psalms of David and Modern Criticism,' 1893. 6. 'The Story of the Religious Tract Society,' 1899.

[Memoir by Rev. James Stuart in the Watford Observer, Sept. 1905, reprinted and extended in the Baptist Handbook, 1906; Christian World, 21 Sept. 1905; Athenæum, 23 Sept. 1905, p. 403; personal information kindly supplied by Professor S. W. Green.] C. W.

GREENAWAY, CATHERINE or KATE (1846–1901), artist, was born at Cavendish Street, Hoxton, on 17 March 1846, being the second daughter of John Greenaway, a draughtsman and engraver on wood, long connected with the earlier days of the 'Illustrated London News' and 'Punch.' Her mother's maiden name was Elizabeth Jones. Early residence at a farmhouse at Rolleston, a Nottinghamshire village, served to nourish and confirm her inborn love of art; and she early developed that taste for childhood and cherry blossoms which became, as it were, her fitting pictorial environment. As a girl she studied drawing in various places, eventually joining the art school at South Kensington, where the headmaster, Richard Burchett [q. v.], thought highly of her abilities. One of her contemporaries was Elizabeth Thompson (afterwards Lady Butler); another was Helen Paterson, afterwards Mrs. William Allingham. She later 'took the life' at Heatherley's, and studied under Alphonse Legros [q. v. Suppl. II] in the Slade School at University College. In 1868, being then twenty-two, she exhibited at the Old Dudley Gallery a water-colour drawing entitled 'Kilmeny.' This was followed by other works, e.g. the 'Spring Idyll' ('Apple Blossom)' of 1870, in which year she also sent to Suffolk Street for the first time 'A Peeper' (children playing), which foreshadowed her later successes in the domain of little people. In 1877 she sent to the Royal Academy (and sold for twenty guineas) her first contribution, 'Musing'; and in 1889 she was elected a lady member of the Institute of Painters in Water Colours, to which she frequently contributed portraits, studies, and designs. But long ere this date she had achieved a wide and well-earned reputation as an inimitable exponent of child-life, and an inventor of children's books of a specific and very original kind. Her country experiences had stored her imagination with quaint costumes and unhackneyed accessories, and her quiet habit of mind and fondness for the subject enabled her to create a particularly engaging gallery of small folk. She was also fortunate enough to find in William John Loftie [q. v. Suppl. II] and Henry Stacy Marks, R.A. [q.v. Suppl. I], friends judicious enough to persuade her to cultivate her own bent of invention. After preluding for Messrs. Marcus Ward of Belfast and for others in valentines and Christmas cards, and drawing for minor magazines, she made a first success in 1879 with 'Under the Window,' the precursor of a long line of popular works, which brought her both fame and money, and a list of which is given hereafter. She was occasionally tempted from her predestined walk by demands for book illustrations (e.g. Bret Harte's 'Queen of the Pirate Isle'), or by efforts on a larger and more ambitious scale; but in the main she went her own way, and confined herself generally to the field in which, though she had many imitators, she had no formidable rivals. Now and then, as in 'Under the Window' and 'Marigold Garden,' she was her own rhymer; but although she possessed a true poetic impulse, her executive power was hardly on a level with it. As an artist she had, however, not only popularity but many genuine admirers, who fully appreciated the individuality of her charm. Ruskin, of whom she was long a favoured correspondent, wrote enthusiastically of her work in 'Præterita' and elsewhere; and both in Germany and France she was highly estimated. Three exhibitions of her works took place at the Fine Arts Society during her lifetime, namely, in 1880, 1891, and 1898; and these were followed in January 1902 by a fourth after her death. She died in her fifty-fifth year, on 6 Nov. 1901, at No. 39 Frognal, Hampstead, the house which had been built for her by Mr. Norman Shaw, and where she resided with her parents. She was cremated at Woking, and her remains were interred at Hampstead cemetery.

Much of Miss Greenaway's preliminary work was done for the old 'People's Magazine,' 'Little Folks,' 'Cassell's Magazine,' and the pictorial issues of Messrs. Marcus Ward and Co. She illustrated nine of Madame D'Aulnoy's 'Fairy Tales' (1871); Miss Kathleen Knox's 'Fairy Gifts' (1874); the 'Quiver of Love' (with Walter Crane), a collection of valentines (1876); Mrs. Bonavia Hunt's 'Poor Nelly' (1878); the 'Topo' of Lady Colin Campbell (1878), further described as 'A Tale about English Children in Italy'; and the 'Heir of Redclyffe' and 'Heartsease' (1879). Of her first real success, 'Under the Window, Pictures and Rhymes for Children' (1879), nearly 70,000 copies were sold in England, in addition to 30,000 French and German issues. Then came 'Kate Greenaway's

Birthday Book for Children' (1880), with verses by Mrs. Sale Barker; 'Mother Goose; or, the Old Nursery Rhymes' (1881); 'A Day in a Child's Life,' with music by Myles B. Foster, the organist of the Foundling Hospital (1881); and 'Little Ann and other Poems,' by Jane and Ann Taylor (1883). By the first three and the last of these five books she is said to have made a clear profit of 8000*l*. Next came a 'Painting Book of Kate Greenaway' (1884); the 'Language of Flowers' (1884); 'Mavor's English Spelling Book' (1884); 'Marigold Garden' (1885); 'Kate Greenaway's Alphabet' (1885); 'Kate Greenaway's Album' (1885); 'A Apple Pie' (1886); 'The Queen of the Pirate Isle,' by Bret Harte (1886); 'The Pied Piper of Hamelin,' by Robert Browning (1889); Kate Greenaway's 'Book of Games,' (1889); 'The Royal Progress of King Pepito,' by Beatrice F. Cresswell (1889); and the 'April Baby's Book of Tunes,' by the author of 'Elizabeth and her German Garden' (the Countess von Arnim) (1900). From 1883 (two issues) to 1895 she produced an annual 'Almanack.' In 1896 this was discontinued; but a final number appeared in 1897. She designed many very beautiful book-plates, that of Frederick Locker-Lampson [q. v. Suppl. I] being a fair example; and she also illustrated for Ruskin in 1885 (2nd edit. 1897) an old book of nursery rhymes for which he had a great admiration, 'Dame Wiggins of Lee and her Seven Wonderful Cats.'

[The chief authority for Kate Greenaway's life is the exhaustive volume published in 1905 by M. H. Spielmann and G. S. Layard. This, amply illustrated by reproductions of drawings and water-colours, and enriched by copious extracts from the artist's correspondence with Ruskin, is also written with much critical insight, and genuine sympathy for Miss Greenaway's aims and achievement. To a subsequent volume, Kate Greenaway: Sixteen Examples in Colour of the Artist's Work (Black's British Artists), 1910, Mr. Spielmann prefixed a short study. See also Ruskin's Fors Clavigera, and Præterita; Chesneau's La Peinture Anglaise, 1882; Alexandre's L'Art du Rire et de la Caricature, 1893; Recollections of Lady Dorothy Nevill, 1906; and the De Libris of the present writer, 1908, pp. 93–104. There is an attractive article in the Century Magazine, vol. 75, p. 183, by Mr. Oliver Locker-Lampson, M.P., with whose family Miss Greenaway was on terms of friendship.] A. D.

GREENIDGE, ABEL HENDY JONES (1865–1906), writer on ancient history and law, second son of Nathaniel Heath Greenidge by his wife Elizabeth Cragg Kellman, was born on 22 Dec. 1865 at Belle Farm Estate, Barbados, in which island his father's family had been settled since 1635. His father, for many years vicar of Boscobel parish, was afterwards headmaster of various schools, and enjoyed a high reputation as a teacher. The eldest son, Samuel Wilberforce, of St. John's College, Cambridge, was 25th wrangler in the Cambridge mathematical tripos of 1886, and died in 1890.

Greenidge was educated at Harrison College, Barbados, winning in 1884 the Barbados scholarship, and in the same year (15 Oct.) matriculating at Balliol College, Oxford. Elected to an exhibition in the following year, he was placed in the first class both in classical moderations in 1886 and in the final classical school in 1888. He graduated B.A. in the same year, and proceeded M.A. in 1891 and D.Litt. in 1904. On 5 Dec. 1889 he was elected, after examination, fellow of Hertford College. There he became lecturer in 1892 and tutor in 1902, and he retained these offices until his death. He was also lecturer in ancient history at Brasenose College from 1892 to 1905. He vacated his fellowship at Hertford on his marriage in 1895, and on 29 June 1905 was elected to an official fellowship at St. John's. He examined in the final classical school in 1895–6–7–8. He died suddenly at his residence in Oxford of an affection of the heart on 11 March 1906, and was buried in Holywell churchyard.

Greenidge married on 29 June 1895 Edith Elizabeth, youngest daughter of William Lucy of Oxford, and had issue by her two sons. On 28 March 1907 a civil list pension of 75*l*. was granted to his widow 'in consideration of his services to the study of Roman law and history,' but she died on 9 July 1907.

In spite of his early death, and constant employment in academic teaching, Greenidge's literary work is notable for its quality and quantity. Shortly after graduating he contributed numerous articles to a new edition of 'Smith's Dictionary of Antiquities' (1890–1). His first book, 'Infamia, its Place in Roman Public and Private Law,' was published at Oxford in 1894. There followed 'A Handbook of Greek Constitutional History' (1896); 'Roman Public Life' (1901), and 'The Legal Procedure of Cicero's Time' (Oxford, 1901), which was the most important of Greenidge's completed works. He also revised Sir William Smith's 'History of Rome' (1897), and the first part (down to the death of Justinian) of the 'Student's Gibbon' (1899). In 1903, in co-operation with Miss A. M. Clay, he produced 'Sources for Roman History, B.C. 133–70' (Oxford) designed to prepare the way for a new 'History of Rome.' In 1904 he contributed an historical introduction to the fourth edition of Poste's 'Gaius.' In the same year appeared the first volume of 'A History of Rome during the Later Republic and Early Principate,' covering the years 133 to 104 B.C. This work was designed to extend to the accession of Vespasian and to fill six volumes, but no second volume was issued. Much of Greenidge's most interesting work is to be found in scattered articles, more particularly in the 'Classical Review.' His merit as an historian lies in his accurate accumulation of detail, combined with critical insight and power of exposition, which were not unmixed with occasional paradox.

A portrait in oils, subscribed for by the boys of the school, hangs in the hall of Harrison College, Barbados.

[Oxford Magazine, vol. xxiv. nos. 16 and 17; Journal of Comp. Legislation, new series, vol. vii. pt. i. p. 282; private information.]

R. W. L.

GREENWOOD, FREDERICK (1830–1909), journalist, born in London on 25 March 1830, was eldest child in the family of eleven children of James Caer Greenwood, a coach-builder in Kensington, by his wife Mary Fish. His brother, James Greenwood, made a reputation as a voluminous story writer and journalist. Charles Greenwood (*d.* 1905), a popular sporting writer, best known as 'Hotspur' of the 'Daily Telegraph,' was no relation. Frederick, after being privately educated in Kensington, was apprenticed at about the age of fifteen to a firm of publishers and printers, but his indentures were voluntarily cancelled by the head of the firm in a year, and he was engaged as a reader. In 1851 Messrs. Clarke, Beeton & Co. consulted him as to the publication of the first English reprint of 'Uncle Tom's Cabin' (*Tatler*, 4 Dec. 1901). From the age of sixteen he supported himself, and at twenty he married (1850).

Greenwood was soon writing for papers and magazines. In 1853 he contributed a 'Life of Louis Napoleon Bonaparte' to a general account of 'The Napoleon Dynasty,' described as written 'by the Berkeley men and another.' It was republished under his own name with the title 'Life of Napoleon III, Emperor of the French,' in 1855; in a brief introduction Greenwood 'confesses to little knowledge of "politics" and less care.' The book shows a real comprehension of politics, and gives promise of the writer's mature style and method. For a time his chief ambition was to make a reputation as a novelist and story writer. In 1854 appeared 'The Loves of an Apothecary.' To 'Tait's Magazine' he contributed a story, 'The Path of Roses,' republished with numerous illustrations in 1859. A three-volume novel, 'Under a Cloud,' written in collaboration with his brother James, appeared first in 'The Welcome Guest' and then as a separate publication in 1860. He was a constant contributor to the 'Illustrated Times,' a paper started by Henry Vizetelly [q. v.] in 1855, just before the repeal of the Stamp Act (cf. VIZETELLY'S *Glances Back*, 1893).

In September 1861 Greenwood became first editor of the 'Queen,' at the outset a profusely illustrated paper, which gave a certain prominence to fashions but was largely literary and political. In July 1863 the 'Queen' was combined with the 'Lady's Newspaper,' and Greenwood's connection with it ceased. Meanwhile he had established close relations with George Smith, chief proprietor of the publishing firm of Smith, Elder & Co. He contributed (Feb. 1860) 'An Essay without an End' to the second number of the 'Cornhill Magazine,' which Smith inaugurated under Thackeray's editorship. Greenwood's strongest story, 'Margaret Denzil's History,' which contains powerful drawing of character, appeared in the magazine in 1863, and separately in November 1864 (2 vols.) When Thackeray resigned the editorship in 1862, Greenwood and George Henry Lewes [q. v.] directed the 'Cornhill' under George Smith's superintendence. Lewes withdrew in 1864, and Greenwood was sole editor till 1868. But his bent was to journalism of the highest kind. A scheme for an independent daily paper, to be largely modelled both in form and tone on Canning's 'Anti-Jacobin,' had been for some time in his mind, and he had proposed it to Mr. Parker, owner and publisher of 'Fraser's Magazine,' who declined immediate action. Greenwood did not contemplate acting as editor, and consulted Carlyle on the choice of one. Meanwhile George Smith was considering a like design, and when Greenwood brought his scheme to him in 1864, he at once resolved to give it effect. Greenwood, to his surprise, was appointed editor. Smith's partner, Henry Samuel King, declined responsibility, and the venture was Smith's personal concern. A brilliant band of contributors, most of whom were already in personal relations with Smith as a publisher, was collected. The paper was named the 'Pall Mall Gazette,' after the journal described in Thackeray's 'Pendennis.' The first number appeared on 7 Feb. 1865 [see SMITH, GEORGE, Suppl. I]. The 'Pall Mall' struggled with difficulty into financial success, but its triumph was secured early in 1866, by the publication in it of 'A Night in a Casual Ward, by an Amateur Casual,' three papers written by James Greenwood at the suggestion of his brother. In Greenwood's words they served 'to cut the rope of the balloon.' After 1868 Greenwood became entirely absorbed in the paper.

As editor he acquired an exceptional personal influence. Able writers covered under his guidance a wide field of interests, social, literary, and political. But the marked character of the 'Pall Mall' was given by Greenwood's individuality. (Sir) Leslie Stephen [q. v. Suppl. II], long a contributor, called the paper 'the incarnation of Greenwood.' His dominance was especially great on the political side. He had shared the liberal opinions of his generation, and he never became a conservative in the strict party sense. Thoroughly patriotic, he was no blind follower of any party leader. A vigilant observer of foreign affairs, and a profound admirer of Bismarck, he came to distrust Gladstone's domestic and foreign policy. The foreign policy of the conservative government of 1874–80 found in him an ardent champion. The keen watch he kept on events abroad enabled him in 1875 to acquire early information of the intention of the Khedive Ismail Pasha to sell his Suez Canal shares, and of the serious risk that they would pass into the possession of a French syndicate. He at once communicated first with the foreign secretary, Lord Derby, who was not inclined to move in the matter, and then with the prime minister, Lord Beaconsfield, who acted on his advice. There is no doubt that the purchase of the shares was first suggested by Greenwood, although his claim to that credit has been questioned (letters by Greenwood and others in *The Times*, 15 April, 11 May, 27 Dec. 1905; 13, 26 Jan., 10 Feb. 1906). Through the Russo-Turkish war of 1876–8 he vehemently attacked in the 'Pall Mall' Gladstone's sentimental crusade against Turkey, the maintenance of whose integrity was in his opinion a primary English interest.

In April 1880 the 'Pall Mall Gazette,' then (in Leslie Stephen's phrase) 'the most thorough-going of Jingo newspapers,' was presented by its proprietor, George Smith, to his son-in-law, Mr. Henry Yates Thompson, who avowed his intention to convert the paper into a radical political organ. Greenwood and all the members of the staff left. At the beginning of May the 'St. James's Gazette' was founded by some members of the firm of Antony Gibbs & Co., in order to give Greenwood the opportunity of continuing his advocacy of the old policy of the 'Pall Mall' [see GIBBS, HENRY HUCKS, LORD ALDENHAM, Suppl. II]. In the new paper Greenwood fought for the same cause with the same spirit and capacity as in the old. He powerfully advocated the occupation of Egypt in 1882, and was the wholehearted opponent of the Irish nationalists. No newspaper helped more effectively to destroy Gladstone's power and to prepare the way for the long predominance of the unionist party. But various causes, of which the strongest was the decline of a taste for serious journalism in the public, rendered it impossible for the 'St. James's' to attain to the prosperity of the 'Pall Mall.' After the death of one of the proprietors, George Gibbs, on 26 Nov. 1886 the financial control passed to his cousin Henry, who was not equally in harmony with Greenwood's views. In 1888 Greenwood persuaded Edward Steinkopff to buy the paper. But the new proprietor refused his editor the freedom he had so far enjoyed, and Greenwood retired suddenly and in anger within the year. In January 1891 he founded in pursuit of an early design the 'Anti-Jacobin,' at first as a threepenny and then as a sixpenny weekly paper. But the taste of the public was against him here also, and the 'Anti-Jacobin' was discontinued in January 1892.

Meanwhile Greenwood became a contributor to the 'Saturday Review' and other papers, and to 'Blackwood's' and the chief magazines, and he engaged anew in literature, publishing 'The Lover's Lexicon' in 1893 and 'Imagination in Dreams' in 1894. A series of papers which appeared in 'Blackwood's' under the general title of the 'Looker On' in 1898–9 ceased owing to the support given by the magazine to the war in South Africa. On that subject Greenwood shared the views of the pro-Boers. He always distrusted Mr. Chamberlain and the radical unionists, and had a scornful dislike of the South African financiers.

Greenwood, who was quick to detect

literary merit, was the private adviser of many literary men who achieved eminence. George Meredith was among his friends, and drew him as Richard Rockney in 'Celt and Saxon' (1910) (cf. W. T. STEAD in *Review of Reviews*, July 1910, p. 57). At a dinner given in his honour in London on 9 April 1905, Mr. J. M. Barrie spoke warmly of his debt to Greenwood's early encouragement. His editorial skill and instinct were only equalled by the perfect sincerity of his opinions, and his absolute disinterestedness. Greenwood died at his house in Sydenham on 14 Dec. 1909.

Greenwood's wife, Katherine Darby, whom he married in 1850, belonged to a landed family of Quaker connections in Hampshire. She died in 1900. Of Greenwood's five children, a son and two daughters survived him. His daughters were granted a civil list pension of 100*l*. in 1910.

[Information from the family; personal knowledge; Leslie Stephen's Life of Fitzjames Stephen, 1895; Herbert Paul's History of Modern England, 1905, vols. iii. and iv.; Tinsley, Random Recollections, i. 303. Maitland's Life of Leslie Stephen (1905) and Hyndman's Record of an Adventurous Career (1911) give estimates of Greenwood as editor from contributors' points of view.]

GREENWOOD, THOMAS (1851–1908), promoter of public libraries, son of William and Nanny Greenwood, was born at Woodley, near Stockport, Cheshire, on 9 May 1851, and educated at the village school. Benefiting by membership of a mutual improvement society conducted by William Urwick [q. v. Suppl. II.], then congregational minister of Hatherlow, Cheshire, he made excellent use of the Manchester public library and similar institutions. After serving as clerk in a local hat works he was for a short time a traveller with a Sheffield firm, and then for about three years assistant in a branch library at Sheffield. About 1871 he removed to London to join the staff of the 'Ironmonger.' In 1875 with W. Hoseason Smith he founded the firm of Smith, Greenwood & Co., afterwards Scott, Greenwood & Co., printers and publishers of trade journals and technical books. The firm at once founded the 'Hatters' Gazette,' and the 'Pottery Gazette,' an organ of the glass and china industries, and in 1879 the 'Oil and Colour Trades Journal.' Greenwood himself was the chief editor of these journals. He superintended all the publications of the firm, which included many important technical works.

His early acquaintance with public libraries and his personal gratitude to them convinced him of the need of increasing their number and improving their organisation. Thanks to his advocacy many rate-supported libraries were opened in London and elsewhere in commemoration of the jubilee of Queen Victoria. His manual on 'Public Libraries, their Organisation, Uses and Management,' appeared in 1886 and at once took standard rank. The work reached a fifth edition in 1894.

A warm admirer of Edward Edwards (1812–1886) [q. v.], a pioneer of municipal public libraries, Greenwood collected his personal relics and part of his library, and these he presented, with a handsome bookcase, to the Manchester public library, of which Edwards was the first librarian. In 1902 he wrote an interesting biography of Edwards, embodying the early history of the library movement, and he placed a granite monument over Edwards's grave at Niton, Isle of Wight.

Greenwood formed a large bibliographical library, illustrating all phases of bibliographical work and research, which he presented to the Manchester public library in 1906, making additions to it afterwards, and leaving at his death sufficient money for its maintenance. 'The Thomas Greenwood Library for Librarians' contains about 12,000 volumes. He also founded a small library at Hatherlow in honour of his old pastor William Urwick.

Formerly a fellow of the Royal Geographical Society, Greenwood travelled extensively, and in Japan in 1907 contracted an illness of which he died at Frith Knowl, Elstree, Hertfordshire, on 9 Nov. 1908. His remains after cremation at Golder's Green were interred at Hatherlow congregational church. He married Marianne, daughter of William Pettet, and had a son and two daughters.

In addition to the works named he wrote: 1. 'A Tour in the United States and Canada,' 1883. 2. 'Eminent Naturalists,' 1886. 3. 'Grace Montrose, an unfashionable novel,' 1886. 4. 'Museums and Art Galleries,' 1888. 5. 'Sunday School and Village Libraries,' 1892; 6. 'Greenwood's Library Year Book,' 1897, 1900, 1901.

[The Times, and Manchester Guardian, 11 Nov. 1908; Oil and Colour Trades Journal, 14 Nov. 1908 (with portrait); Who's Who, 1908; W. E. A. Axon in Library Association Record, June 1907 (description of the library for librarians); personal knowledge.] C. W. S.

GREGO, JOSEPH (1843–1908), writer on art, born on 23 Sept. 1843 at 23 Granville Square, Clerkenwell, was elder son of Joseph Grego (1817–1881), a looking-glass manufacturer, by his wife Louisa Emelia Dawley. His grandfather, Antonio Grego, a native of Como, settled in London before 1821 as a looking-glass manufacturer, the firm becoming Susan Grego & Sons in 1839, and Charles & Joseph Grego in 1845. After education at private schools Grego was for a time with Lloyds, the underwriters. Inheriting the spirit of collecting from his father, he drifted into that pursuit, combining it with dealing, art journalism, and authorship. He specialised as writer and collector in the work of Gillray, Rowlandson, Morland, and Cruikshank, and was an acknowledged authority on all of them. He was chiefly responsible for the edition of James Gillray's 'Works' in 1873, although the name of Thomas Wright (1810–77) [q. v.] alone appears in the title-page, and he edited 'Rowlandson the Caricaturist' (2 vols. 4to, 1880). Both books, which illustrate Grego's comprehensive and thorough method of work, became standard books of reference. He collected much material for a life of Morland, which he did not complete. In 1904 he published 'Cruikshank's Water Colours,' with an introduction and reproductions in colours. In 1874 he compiled a volume of 'Thackerayana' (dated 1875), based upon books with marginal and other sketches, from Thackeray's sale; owing to copyright difficulties the volume was immediately suppressed, but was reissued in 1898 (cf. *Athenæum*, 9 May 1908). A frequent writer on art in periodicals and the press, and editor of 'Pears' Pictorial,' 1893–6, he wrote 'History of Parliamentary Elections in the Old Days, from the Time of the Stuarts to Victoria' (1886; new edit. 1892), and edited R. H. Gronow's 'Reminiscences' with illustrations 'made up' from contemporary prints (1889); Vuillier's 'History of Dancing,' to which he contributed a sketch of dancing in England (1898); 'Pictorial Pickwickiana: Charles Dickens and his Illustrators' (2 vols. 1899); and Goldsmith's 'Vicar of Wakefield,' including Forster's essay on the story (1903).

Grego, who was always ready to lend prints and drawings for public exhibitions, occupied much of his time in organising exhibitions, chiefly of 'English Humorists in Art.' He was himself facile with his pencil, doing much work as a designer of theatrical costumes, and etching the designs of others. He invented a system of reproducing eighteenth-century colour prints in such exact facsimile that they have often been mistaken for originals. He was a director of Carl Hentschel, Ltd., photo-engravers, 1899–1908, and a substantial shareholder in the firm of Kegan Paul & Co. (of which company he was a director from Jan. 1903 till his death) and of the 'Graphic' Company.

He died unmarried on 24 Jan. 1908 at 23 Granville Square, where he was born and which he occupied all his life. His vast accumulations of prints, drawings, and books were dispersed on his death (at Christie's 28 April and 4 June 1908, and at Puttick and Simpson's April, June, and July 1908).

Jules Bastien-Lepage drew a small head of Grego in pen and ink on a visit to London, about 1880–1.

[The Times, 28 Jan. 1908; Athenæum, 2 Feb. 1908; Graphic, 1 Feb. 1908 (with portrait from a photo); information kindly supplied by his only sister, Mrs. Bruce-Johnston, by Mr. Thomas J. Barratt, and by Mr. H. Thornber.] W. R.

GREGORY, SIR AUGUSTUS CHARLES (1819–1905), Australian explorer and politician, born on 1 Aug. 1819 at Farnsfield, Nottinghamshire, was second son of Lieutenant Joshua Gregory, of an old Nottinghamshire family, by his wife Frances, sister of Charles Blissett Churchman of London. His father, a lieutenant in the 78th regiment (Ross-shire Buffs), was wounded at El Hamed in Egypt, and compelled to retire from the service, receiving in lieu of pension a grant of land in the new settlement on the Swan River (now Western Australia), whither he went with his wife and family in June 1829.

After being privately educated in England and in his new home, young Gregory in 1841 obtained employment in the survey department of Western Australia, and in August 1842 he was appointed assistant surveyor, holding the office till November 1854. In 1846, having obtained leave of absence, he began exploring work in the interior of the continent, starting on 7 August from Bolgart Spring, accompanied by his brothers Francis Thomas and Henry. He was soon stopped, however, in his progress eastward by an immense salt lake which compelled him to turn north-west, where he discovered some excellent seams of coal at the headwaters of the river Irwin. In September 1848 he led a party (sometimes known as the 'Settlers' Expedition') to the northward, and succeeded in reaching a point 350 miles north of Perth. The results of the expedition were to reveal the pastoral wealth of the Murchison and Champion Bay districts and the discovery of a lode of galena in the bed of the Murchison river. Later in the same year Gregory accompanied the governor, Capt. Charles Fitzgerald, R.N., on a visit to the mineral discovery, which proved to be of more importance than was at first supposed.

In 1855–6 Gregory undertook an expedition under the auspices of the Royal Geographical Society with the dual purpose of exploring the previously unknown interior of the northern territory of Australia and searching for traces of the lost explorer Friedrich Wilhelm Ludwig Leichhardt[q. v.]. Starting from the mouth of the Victoria river, the party ascended that river to its source, crossed the watershed to the southward-flowing Sturt creek, and then made its way to the gulf of Carpentaria and thence to the Dawson and across the northern peninsula to the east coast. The result was the shedding of much light on the rivers of this region, the discovery of the water parting formed by the Newcastle ranges, and the charting in sixteen months of 5000 miles of hitherto unknown wilds, but no certain traces of Leichhardt were found. For his achievements on this expedition Gregory was in 1857 awarded the founder's medal of the Royal Geographical Society.

In 1858 he undertook his last exploring expedition, when he was despatched by the New South Wales government to renew the search for Leichhardt. He started from Sydney on 12 Jan. and reached the Barcoo in April. In latitude 24° 25′ and longitude 145° S. he found a tree marked L and some stumps of others which had been felled with an axe. In May he reached the Thompson river, and followed it till it ran out in plains of baked clay. He then pushed down Cooper and Strzlecki Creek, and arrived at Adelaide after a seven months' exploration, which left the fate of Leichhardt as much in doubt as ever.

On his return from his last expedition he was employed in defining the southern boundary of Queensland, and became surveyor-general for the new colony, a post which he held from 23 Dec. 1859 to 11 March 1875. Thenceforward until 1 Sept. 1879 he was geological surveyor of the southern district of the colony. On 10 Nov. 1882 he was nominated a member of the legislative council, but did not take his seat till 26 June 1883. He played a prominent part in the debates, his intimate knowledge of the country and its resources and his fund of scientific and other information securing him an attentive hearing even from those who differed from him. It was his custom to sit always on the opposition benches, in order that he might be more free to criticise the various government measures.

Gregory took an active interest in municipal affairs. He was one of the first members of the Toowong shire council, and when the shire was gazetted a town in 1902 he was chosen first mayor. He was a trustee of the Queensland Museum from 1876 to 1899, and from 1876 to 1883 sat on the commission to inquire into the condition of the aborigines.

He took a keen interest in scientific work of all kinds, and in 1895 was president at Brisbane of the Australian Association for the Advancement of Science, devoting his opening address to a sketch of the geological and geographical history of Australia.

He was created C.M.G. on 27 Feb. 1875, and K.C.M.G. on 9 Nov. 1903. He died unmarried on 25 June 1905 at his residence, Rainworth, Brisbane, and was buried in Toowong cemetery.

Gregory, according to Sir Hugh Nelson, 'contributed more to the exact physical, geological, and geographical knowledge of Australia than any other man, for his explorations have extended to west, north, east, south, and central Australia.' He was joint author of 'Journals of Australian Exploration' (Brisbane, 1884) with his brother, Francis Thomas Gregory (1821–1888), who was in the survey office of Western Australia from 1842 to 1860; Francis accompanied his brother Augustus in his first exploring expedition in 1846, and led two expeditions himself in 1858 and 1861, being awarded the gold medal of the Royal Geographical Society in 1863; going to Queensland in 1862, he was nominated to the legislative council in 1874, and was for a short time postmaster-general in the first McIlwraith Ministry.

[The Times, and Brisbane Courier, 26 June 1905; West Australian, 27 June 1905; Geographical Journal, vol. 26, 1905; Western Australian Year Book for 1902–4; Mennell's Dict. of Australas. Biog., 1892; Burke's Colonial Gentry, 1891; Favence's History of Australian Exploration, 1888; Blain's Cyclopædia of Australasia, 1881; Heaton's Australian Dictionary of Dates, 1879; Howitt's History of Discovery in Australia, vol. ii. 1865; Tenison Woods's History of the Discovery and Exploration of Australia, vol. ii. 1865.]

C. A.

GREGORY, EDWARD JOHN (1850–1909), painter, born in Southampton on 19 April 1850, was grandson of John Gregory, engineer-in-chief of the auxiliary engines in Sir John Franklin's last Arctic expedition, and was eldest child (in a family of three sons and five daughters) of Edward Gregory, a ship's engineer, by his wife Mary Ann Taylor. On leaving Dr. Cruikshank's private school at fifteen he entered the drawing-office, in his native town, of the Peninsular and Oriental steamship company, in whose employ his father sailed; but though always keenly interested in all kinds of mechanism, he had set his mind upon being a painter. Making the acquaintance at Southampton of Hubert Herkomer (now Sir Hubert von Herkomer, R.A.), whose family had settled there, he started a life-class with him. In 1869 Gregory went to London, and with Herkomer joined the South Kensington Art School. Subsequently he studied for a short time at the Royal Academy. He was soon employed in the decorations of the Victoria and Albert Museum, and in 1871, with his friends Herkomer and Robert Walker Macbeth [q. v. Suppl. II], began working for the 'Graphic,' which had just been started by William Luson Thomas [q. v. Suppl. I]. Gregory at first contributed sketches from the theatres, but soon freely transcribed sketches sent home from the French army at the front by Mr. Sydney P. Hall. Gregory's illustrations, which were sometimes signed by both himself and Hall, discovered the variety and ingenuity of his draughtsmanship. He ceased to work regularly for the 'Graphic' about 1875.

Gregory was not a frequent exhibitor at Burlington House. His mark as a painter was first made by an oil-painting, 'Dawn' (now in the possession of Mr. John Sargent, R.A.), originally shown at Deschamps' gallery in 1879. Much of his best work appeared at the exhibitions of the Royal Institute of Painters in Water Colours, of which he was elected associate in 1871 and member in 1876. He succeeded Sir James Linton as president in 1898. From 1875 to 1882 his contributions to the Academy were mainly portraits, including that of Duncan McLaren, M.P., a replica of which is in the Scottish National Portrait Gallery. As early as 1883 he was elected with Macbeth to the associateship, and he became academician in 1898, after the completion and exhibition of his 'Boulter's Lock: Sunday Afternoon,' a work which hardly justified the years of elaboration spent upon it.

Gregory's art was honoured abroad, both his oils and his water-colours being awarded gold medals at the international exhibitions of Paris (1889 and 1900) and Brussels (1898), and at the Munich Jahresausstellung (1891). Probably his water-colours and some of his drawings on wood will have a more enduring fame than his oils. In all mediums he showed cleverness and resource as a draughtsman, and a technical skill that was especially remarkable in his water-colours. His art suffered in the end through a fastidious preoccupation with the technical problems of his craft. For many years his paintings, which were not numerous, were acquired as soon as they were finished by Charles J. Galloway of Manchester, at whose death they were dispersed with the rest of his collection at Christie's on 24 June 1905, Gregory's water-colours bringing large prices.

Besides 'Dawn' and 'Boulter's Lock,' Gregory's principal oil pictures were 'Piccadilly: Drawing-room Day' (R.A. 1883); 'Last Touches,' 'St. George' (which was etched by Paul Rajon), 'Miss Galloway,' 'The Intruders' (R.A. 1884); 'Marooning' (now in the Tate Gallery) (R.A. 1887); 'Fanny Bunter' and 'Après,' his diploma picture (R.A. 1890); and 'Spoils of Opportunity' (R.A. 1893). His chief contributions to the Royal Institute were: 'The Inception of a Song,' 'The Honeymoon,' 'Sir Galahad,' 'The Sanctum Invaded,' 'A Look at the Model,' 'Souvenir of the Institute,' 'The Fugitive,' 'Master Newall.'

Gregory, despite a bad stammer, showed unusual aptitude for affairs as president of the Institute and was a conscientious and popular visitor at the schools of the Academy, in the counsels of which he exerted much weight. He died at his residence, Brompton House, Great Marlow, on 22 June 1909, and was buried in Great Marlow churchyard. He married in 1876 Mary, daughter of Joseph Joyner, who survived him without issue.

'A Look at the Model' (the property of Mr. H. W. Henderson) and the 'Souvenir of the Institute' are self-portraits. Two other portraits of himself, painted by him in 1875 and 1883, are in the possession of Mrs. Alfred Henry, London. A portrait by John Parker, R.W.S., belongs to his widow. Early in his career Gregory was invited to contribute his portrait to the Uffizi Gallery at Florence, but never finished one to his satisfaction.

[Private information; Graves's Royal Academy Exhibitors, 1905–6.] D. S. M.

GREGORY, ROBERT (1819–1911), dean of St. Paul's, born at Nottingham on 9 Feb. 1819, was the eldest son of Robert Gregory, merchant, of Nottingham by his wife Anne Sophia, daughter of Alderman Oldknow, grocer, Nottingham. His parents were methodists; both died in 1824. Educated privately, Gregory entered a Liverpool shipping-office in 1835. At the age of twenty-one, influenced by the 'Tracts for the Times,' he resolved to be ordained. He was admitted a gentleman commoner of Corpus Christi College, Oxford, on 2 April 1840; graduated B.A. in 1843, proceeding M.A. in 1846, and D.D. in 1891; was Denyer theological prizeman in 1850; and was ordained deacon in 1843, priest in 1844, by the bishop of Gloucester and Bristol. After serving the curacies of Bisley, Gloucestershire (1843–7), Panton and Wragby, Lincolnshire (1847–51), and Lambeth parish church (1851–3), Gregory was from 1853 to 1873 vicar of St. Mary-the-Less, Lambeth. A zealous incumbent, he improved the church, built schools, founded a school of art, and closely identified himself with church work in elementary education. In 1867 he was select preacher at Oxford, and served on the royal commission on ritual.

In 1868 Gregory was appointed canon of St. Paul's, but for five years still held his Lambeth living. In 1870 H. P. Liddon [q. v.] became canon, and in 1871 R. W. Church [q. v. Suppl. I] was made dean. With them Gregory worked in fullest harmony for the attainment of Church's purpose, 'to set St. Paul's in order, as the great English cathedral, before the eyes of the country' (*Life and Letters of Dean Church*, p. 200). As treasurer of the cathedral he negotiated with the ecclesiastical commission the arrangement of the cathedral finances which helped to make reform possible. The changes made were not universally welcomed, but Gregory was unmoved by criticism. Church described him as 'of cast iron' (*Life and Letters*, p. 235). Four lectures contrasting the social conditions of England in 1688 and 1871, delivered by Gregory in St. Paul's in Nov. 1871, drew on him the charge of misusing the cathedral. The advance in the cathedral ritual and the decoration of the fabric led to hostility, which reached its height in the litigation of 1888–9 over the reredos, during which Gregory zealously supported the policy of Frederick Temple [q. v. Suppl. II], bishop of London.

For forty-three years Gregory was a member of the lower house of Canterbury convocation. He entered it as proctor for the archdeaconry of Surrey in 1868, and became proctor for the dean and chapter in 1874. His influence was immediately felt, more especially on educational questions and in defence of higher Anglican policy. W. C. Magee in 1881 wrote of him as 'the Cleon of the lower house' (*Life*, ii. 154); and J. W. Burgon, in a published letter of the same year, said 'In the lower house of convocation you . . . obtain very much your own way.' On the delivery of the Purchas judgment, Gregory joined Liddon in telling John Jackson [q. v.], bishop of London (2 March 1871), that the judgment would not be obeyed by them [see PURCHAS, JOHN]. In 1873 he was forward in defence of the Athanasian Creed; in 1874 he presented to convocation a petition in favour of retaining the impugned 'ornaments' of the church; in 1880, during the burials bill controversy, he favoured the abandonment by churchmen of the graveside service, if nonconformists could also be silenced. In 1881 he supported the memorial for the toleration of ritual, and in convocation presented a gravamen and reformandum to the same effect. An ardent supporter of church schools and long treasurer of the National Society, Gregory was elected a member of the London school board in 1873, but did not seek re-election when his three years' term ended. He was also a member of the education commission in 1886, and of the City parochial charities commission in 1888.

Appointed dean of St. Paul's on the death of Church in 1890, and installed on 5 Feb. 1891, Gregory continued his predecessor's policy, carried out in the face of some criticism the decoration of the cathedral with mosaics, and retained to advanced age the closest interest in the cathedral work. He resigned on 1 May, died at the deanery on 2 Aug. 1911, and was buried in the crypt of St. Paul's. He combined a simple faith and clear convictions, firmly held and boldly defended, with much administrative ability and singular devotion to the life and work of his cathedral. He was twice married: (1) in 1844 to Mary Frances, daughter of William Stewart of Dublin (*d.* 1851), by whom he had two sons who survived him; and (2) in 1861 to Charlotte Anne, daughter of Admiral the Hon. Sir Robert Stopford, by whom he had four daughters, of whom three survived him. A portrait by Sir William Richmond, exhibited at the Royal Academy in 1899, now hangs in the dining-room of the St. Paul's deanery.

In addition to some sermons, Gregory

published: 1. 'Are we better than our Fathers?' 1872. 2. 'The Position of the Priest ordered by the Rubrics in the Communion Service interpreted by themselves,' 1876. 3. 'Elementary Education: Some Account of its Rise and Progress in England,' 1895.

[The Times, 3 and 7 Aug. 1911; Guardian, 4 and 11 Aug. 1911; The Autobiography of Robert Gregory, ed. by Ven. W. H. Hutton, 1912; John Hannah, a Tribute of Affection, Two Sermons, with Memoirs of Robert and Anne Sophia Gregory (Nottingham, 1824); J. J. Hannah, The Lighter Side of a Great Churchman's Character, 1912; W. P. W. Phillimore, County Pedigrees, vol. i. Nottinghamshire; T. Fowler, History of Corpus Christi College, Oxford, pp. 318, 444; J. O. Johnston, Life of H. P. Liddon, 1904, pp. 145–8; Davidson and Benham, Life of A. C. Tait, 1891, vol. ii. chap. xxix.; M. C. Church, Life and Letters of Dean Church, 1895, pp. 200 seq.; J. W. Burgon, Canon Robert Gregory: a Letter of Friendly Remonstrance, 1881.] A. R. B.

GRENFELL, GEORGE (1849–1906), baptist missionary and explorer of the Congo, born at Ennis Cottage, Trannack Mill, Sancreed, near Penzance, on 21 Aug. 1849, was son of George Grenfell of Trannack Mill, afterwards of Birmingham, by his wife Joanna, daughter of Michael and Catherine Rowe of Botree, Sancreed. Grenfell shared with Francis Wallace Grenfell, first baron Grenfell, and William Henry Grenfell, first baron Desborough, a common ancestor in Paskow Greinfield (1658). Educated at a branch of King Edward's school, Birmingham, Grenfell was apprenticed to Messrs. Scholefield & Goodman, a hardware and machinery firm in Birmingham. The loss of an eye in early life in no way impaired his energy. Though his parents were anglicans he soon joined Heneage Street baptist chapel, where he was admitted to membership by baptism on 7 Nov. 1864. Influenced by the lives of David Livingstone [q. v.] and Alfred Saker (1814–1880), the 'Apostle of the Cameroons,' Grenfell, in September 1873, entered the Baptist College, Stokes Croft, Bristol, and on 10 Nov. 1874 the Baptist Missionary Society accepted him for work in the Cameroons under Alfred Saker. The two arrived there in January 1875. Grenfell's earliest work consisted in following the Yabiang river up to Abo and in discovering the lower course of the Sanaga river as far as Edea.

Grenfell, who moved to Victoria, Cameroons, in 1877, continued to explore the rivers inland, especially the Wuri, and in 1878 made an ascent of the Mongo ma Loba mountain. On 5 Jan. 1878 he was instructed to undertake pioneer work with the Rev. T. J. Comber up the Lower Congo. After the discoveries in 1877 of Sir Henry Morton Stanley [q. v. Suppl. II], Mr. Robert Arthington of Leeds had offered 1000*l.* to the Baptist Missionary Society for such work. A preliminary expedition, with the help of the (Dutch) Afrikaansche Handels-Vereeniging, preceded Grenfell and Comber's arrival at San Salvador on 8 Aug. 1878. Received there by the King of Kongo, Dom Pedro V or Ntolela, they pushed on to the Makuta country, but at Tungwa the chief forbade their proceeding towards the Upper Congo. Soon Grenfell co-operated with Comber and others in starting mission stations at Musuko, Vivi, Isangila, and Manyanga in July 1881, and so to Stanley Pool. On 28 Jan. 1884, in a small steel 'tender,' twenty-six feet long, Grenfell set out to survey the Congo up to the Equator at a point 18° long. E., passing the mouth of the Kwa river and visiting Bolobo, Lukolela, and Irebu, and inspecting the confluence of the Mubangi and the Congo. He now made his headquarters at Arthington, near Leopoldville, and on 13 June 1884 he successfully launched at Stanley Pool the Peace, a river steamer, with seven water-tight compartments of Bessemer steel, which was built by Messrs. Thornycroft, at Chiswick, at Mr. Arthington's cost, and under Grenfell's supervision, in 1882. It was constructed to draw only eighteen inches when carrying six tons of cargo, and to take to pieces at the cataracts.

On 7 July 1884 the Peace started on her first voyage of discovery, taking Grenfell and Comber along the Kwa, Kwango, and Kasai rivers. On the second Peace expedition (13 Oct. 1884) 'he was unquestionably the first to prove the independent status of the Mubangi'; discovered the Ruki or Black river; navigated the Ikelemba; found himself in contact with actual cannibals in the Bangala region; ascended the Itimbiri or Rubi river up to 2° 50′ N. lat.; visited Tippoo Tib (Tipu-Tipu) at Stanley Falls on 24 Dec. 1884; and followed the Mubangi for 200 miles up to what have since been called Grenfell Falls, 4° 40′ N. lat., 'by far the most northerly point yet reached in the exploration of the Congo basin' (Sir H. H. Johnston, *G. Grenfell and the Congo*, pp. 116, 127).

On the third voyage of the Peace (2 Aug. 1885) Grenfell was accompanied by his wife, his little daughter, von François, a German explorer, and eight native children from the mission schools. This time his object was to explore the affluents of the Congo from the east and the south—the Lulongo, the Maringa, and the Busira or Juapa, on which he found dwarf tribes (the Batwa).

His fourth journey (24 Feb. 1886), in company with Baron von Nimptsch, of the Congo Free State, and Wissmann, the German explorer, took him up the main stream of the Kasai, thence up the Sankuru, the Luebo, and the Lulua (careful notes being taken of the Bakuba and Bakete tribes), and so back to the Congo and on to Stanley Falls. On the fifth voyage (30 Sept. 1886) he passed up the Kwa and the Mfini to Lake Leopold II, and on the sixth (December 1886), with Holman Bentley, he explored the Kwango up to the Kingunji rapids. In all these journeys he made exact observations, which were published in 1886 by the Royal Geographical Society, and together with his chart of the Congo Basin gained for him the founder's medal of the society in 1887.

During his furlough he was received by King Leopold at Brussels in July 1887. Hearing (9 Aug.) of the death of Comber, he returned at once to the Congo and was busily occupied on the Peace in supplying the needs of the mission stations. But in September 1890 the Congo Free State, in spite of protest, impounded the vessel for operations against the Arabs. Grenfell came home and after long negotiations the Peace was restored, an indemnity being declined. A second steamer, the Goodwill, also made by Messrs. Thornycroft, was launched on the Upper Congo, December 1893.

On 13 Aug. 1891, Grenfell, who had received the Belgian order of Leopold (chevalier), was invited to be Belgian plenipotentiary for the settlement with Portugal of the frontier of the Lunda, and was allowed by the Baptist Missionary Society to accept the offer. On 17 Nov. 1892 Grenfell and his wife reached Mwene Puto Kasongo, the headquarters on the Kwango of the brutal Kiamvo, with whom they had a peaceful interview. Below the Tungila he met Senhor Sarmento, the Portuguese plenipotentiary, and after inspecting the rivers of the Lunda district the party reached St. Paul de Loanda (partly by railway) on 16 June 1893, the delimitation being agreed upon during July. He was made commander of the Belgian order of the Lion and received the order of Christ from the king of Portugal.

From 1893 to 1900 Grenfell remained chiefly at Bolobo on the Congo, where a strong mission station was established. After a visit to England in 1900, he started for a systematic exploration of the Aruwimi river, and by November 1902 had reached Mawambi, about eighty miles from the western extreme of the Uganda protectorate. Between 1903 and 1906 he was busy with a new station at Yalemba, fifteen miles east of the confluence of the Aruwimi with the Congo. Meanwhile he found difficulty in obtaining building sites from the Congo Free State, which accorded them freely to Roman catholics. He grew convinced of the evil character of Belgian administration, in which he had previously trusted. In 1903 King Leopold despatched at Grenfell's entreaty a commission of inquiry, before which he gave evidence, but its report gave him little satisfaction. Grenfell died after a bad attack of blackwater fever at Basoko on 1 July 1906. His salary never exceeded 180*l.* a year. Grenfell was twice married: (1) On 11 Feb. 1876, at Heneage Street baptist chapel, Birmingham, to Mary Hawkes, who died, after a premature confinement, at Akwa town on the Cameroon river on 10 Jan. 1877; (2) in 1878, at Victoria, Cameroons, to Rose Patience Edgerley, a West Indian. His eldest daughter, Patience, who, after being educated in England and at Brussels, returned to the Congo as a teacher, died of hæmaturic fever at Bolobo on 18 March 1899.

A memorial tablet was unveiled in Heneage Street baptist chapel, Birmingham, on 24 September 1907.

Grenfell was an observant explorer (cf. Bentley, *Pioneering on the Congo,* ii. 127–128) and an efficient student of native languages. He promoted industrial training, and gave every proof of missionary zeal.

[The Times, 1 Aug. 1906; Sir Harry Johnston, George Grenfell and the Congo, 1908, 2 vols.; George Hawker, Life of George Grenfell, 1909 (portraits); W. Holman Bentley, Life on the Congo (introduction by G. Grenfell), 1887; Shirley J. Dickins, Grenfell of the Congo, 1910; Lord Mountmorres, The Congo Independent State, 1906, pp. 110 ff.]

E. H. P.

GRENFELL, HUBERT HENRY (1845–1906), expert in naval gunnery, born at Rugby on 12 June 1845, was son of Algernon Grenfell, a clerk, by his wife Maria Guerin Price.

Joining the navy as a cadet on 13 Dec. 1859, when fourteen, Grenfell passed out first from the Britannia, and gained as sub-lieutenant the Beaumont Testimonial in

1865. He qualified as gunnery lieutenant in 1867, and was appointed first lieutenant on H.M.S. Excellent on 22 Sept. 1869. While holding this appointment he worked out with Naval Engineer Newman what are claimed to have been the first designs of hydraulic mountings for heavy naval ordnance. He also engaged in literary work of a technical character, contributing to 'Engineering' and service journals. On 31 Dec. 1876 he was made commander, and on 1 May 1877 was appointed, on account of his linguistic attainments, second naval attaché to the maritime courts of Europe. He also acted as naval adviser to the British representatives at the Berlin Congress of 1878. On 22 Sept. 1882 the sloop Phœnix, under his command, foundered off Prince Edward Island. No lives, however, were lost. Grenfell retired with the rank of captain on 2 Dec. 1887.

Grenfell was afterwards for many years associated with the experimental work of Armstrong, Whitworth & Co. He was the first to direct the Admiralty's attention to the night-sighting of guns; and about 1891, on the introduction of the incandescent electric lamp, he invented his 'self-illuminating night sights for naval ordnance.' The invention was for fifteen years attached to all heavy guns in the British navy, and was adopted by some foreign navies. Grenfell was also one of the first to suggest the use of sight-scales marked in large plain figures for naval guns, and advocated, though without success, the adoption of a telescopic light for day use. He also worked out the arrangement subsequently adopted for quick-firing field artillery, by which the changes of angle between the line of sight and the axis of the bore which are required when firing at a moving target can be effected without altering the line of sight.

In April 1877 Grenfell read before the Institution of Naval Architects an able paper advocating the trial of Grüson's chilled cast-iron armour in England, and in 1887 he published 'Grüson's Chilled Cast-Iron Armour' (translated from the German of Julius von Schutz). He helped to form the Navy League, and served at one time on its executive committee. He died at Alverstoke, Hampshire, on 13 Sept. 1906.

[The Times, 26 Sept. 1906; Engineering, 28 Sept. 1906; Capt. H. Garbett, Naval Gunnery, 1897; C. Orde Brown, Armour and its Attacks by Artillery, 1893; Clowes, History of the Royal Navy, vol. 7, 1903; the Navy List, Jan. 1888.] S. E. F.

GREY, Mrs. MARIA GEORGINA, whose maiden name was SHIRREFF (1816–1906), promoter of women's education, born on 7 March 1816, was younger daughter of Admiral William Henry Shirreff by his wife Elizabeth Anne, daughter of the Hon. David Murray; Emily Shirreff [q. v.] was her elder sister. In youth Maria was constantly abroad, and became an accomplished linguist. In later years, until she was prevented by ill-health, she went every winter to Rome. She early interested herself in the condition of women's education and position. On 7 Jan. 1841 she married her first cousin, William Thomas Grey (1807–1864), nephew of the second Earl Grey [q. v.] Her husband, who was a wine merchant in London, died on 13 March 1864. There were no children of the marriage.

Mrs. Grey collaborated with her sister, Miss Shirreff, in 'Passion and Principle' (1841), and in 'Thoughts on Self-Culture' (1850), but after her husband's death in 1864 concentrated her attention on women's education.

When the Report of the Schools Inquiry Commission of 1870 revealed the unsatisfactory condition of the education of girls in this country, Mrs. Grey read a paper at the Social Science Congress at Leeds, October 1871, advocating the establishment throughout England of large day schools for girls with boarding-houses in connection. For that purpose she formed in 1872 the 'National Union for the Higher Education of Women.' A mercantile company was created under the style of 'The Girls' Public Day School Company,' which provided the funds needed to give practical effect to the purposes of the union. Until 1879 Mrs. Grey was organising secretary of the union, which was dissolved in 1884. In 1906 the company was converted into a trust, which now (1912) has thirty-three schools and over 7000 pupils.

In order to ensure a supply of competent teachers for these new girls' schools, Mrs. Grey founded a training college for women teachers in secondary schools, of which again she acted as honorary organising secretary. The college was opened in 1878, with four students, in premises lent by William Rogers [q. v.], rector of Bishopsgate. After a removal in 1885, the college was installed in 1892 in its present quarters at Brondesbury, and became known as the Maria Grey Training College. Mrs. Grey throughout helped the college by donations of money and by unceasing effort to interest others in the work.

Mrs. Grey, who was an admirably persuasive speaker, was at the same time a strong advocate of the parliamentary enfranchisement of women, She was a member of the central society of the women's suffrage movement. In 1877 she wrote the pamphlet 'The Physical Force Objection to Woman's Suffrage.'

For the last fifteen years of her life Mrs. Grey was an invalid, but she maintained to the end her interest in women's education and progress. She died on 19 Sept. 1906 at 41 Stanhope Gardens, Kensington.

Many of her speeches were published as pamphlets. Besides the books in which she collaborated with Miss Shirreff, she published in 1858 a novel, 'Love's Sacrifice'; in 1887 a translation of Rosmini Serbati's 'The Ruling Principle of Method applied to Education'; and in 1889 'Last Words to Girls on Life in School and after School.'

[The Times, 21 and 24 Sept. 1906; Journal of Education, Oct. 1906; Burke's Peerage; cf. Hare's Story of My Life, vol. iv.; private information.] E. L.

GRIFFIN, Sir LEPEL HENRY (1838–1908), Anglo-Indian administrator, born at Watford, Hertfordshire, where his father was serving as locum tenens, on 20 July 1838, was only son of the three children of Henry Griffin, incumbent of Stoke-by-Clare, Suffolk, by his wife Frances Sophia, who had a family of four sons and six daughters by a first husband, Mr. Welsh.

Griffin was educated at Malden's preparatory school, Brighton, and then at Harrow, which he soon left, on account of illness. After tuition by Mr. Whitehead of Chatham House, Ramsgate, he passed the Indian civil service examination in 1859, and was posted to the Punjab as an assistant commissioner on 17 Nov. 1860. 'His conversational powers and ready wit made him popular in society; but he soon proved himself in addition an effective writer, a fluent speaker, and, despite a somewhat easy-going manner, a man of untiring industry' (*Journ. East India Assoc.* April 1908). He is the original of the brilliant civilian portrayed in Sir Henry Cunningham's novel 'Chronicles of Dustypore' (1875), and was credited with the authorship of Aberigh Mackey's 'Twenty-one Days in India' (1880), satiric sketches of Anglo-Indian life, which first appeared anonymously in 'Vanity Fair' (1878–9). Sir Robert Montgomery [q. v.], lieutenant-governor of the Punjab, turned Griffin's literary abilities to good purpose by selecting him to prepare historical accounts of the principal Punjab families and of the rulers of the native principalities. The work, which involved immense research, was based both on official documents and on records and information gathered from the chiefs and nobles themselves. His 'Punjab Chiefs,' historical and biographical notices of the principal families of the Punjab (Lahore, 1865); 'The Law of Inheritance to Sikh Chiefships previous to the Annexation' (Lahore, 1869); and 'The Rajas of the Punjab' (Lahore, 1870; 2nd edit. London, 1873), at once took rank as standard works.

Griffin served as under-secretary to the local government from April 1870; officiating secretary from March 1871; on special duty to frame track rules between the Punjab and Rajputana from February 1873; and as superintendent of the Kapurthala state from April 1875. He was on special duty at the Paris Exhibition of 1878, and was appointed permanent chief secretary of the Punjab in November of that year. His official minutes, rapidly dictated to shorthand writers, were models of style.

Griffin's great opportunity came in the later phases of the Afghan war. 'After lengthened consideration,' wrote Lord Lytton semi-officially in Feb. 1880, 'I have come to the conclusion that there is only one man in India who is in all respects completely qualified by personal ability, special official experience, intellectual quickness and tact, general commonsense and literary skill, to do for the government of India what I want done as quickly as possible at Kabul, and that man is Mr. Lepel Griffin.' Accordingly in March 1880 the viceroy furnished Griffin with an elaborate minute on the policy to be adopted in Afghanistan, and gave him superintendence of negotiations at Kabul, in subordination only to the military commander, Sir Frederick (now Earl) Roberts. Griffin reached Kabul on 20 March, and at once entered into communication with Abdur Rahman, who had returned to the country after ten years' exile in Russian territory, and was beginning to establish himself in Afghan Turkestan. Griffin by his masterly tact overcame Abdur Rahman's suspicions of English policy and finally, in circumstances which seemed most unpromising, helped to establish him on the Afghan throne and to inspire him permanently with a friendly feeling for England.

Before Griffin's labour was completed Lytton resigned; but the new viceroy, Lord Ripon [q. v. Suppl. II], offered Griffin sympathetic support. At a durbar at Kabul on 22 July the wishes and intentions of the government were explained to the Afghans by Griffin in a Persian speech, and Abdur Rahman was formally acknowledged as Ameer of Kabul, Griffin meeting him at Zimma, sixteen miles north of Kabul, a few days later, and discussing the conditions of British recognition and questions of future relationship. Griffin's official minute, dated 4 Aug., gave impressions of the new ruler which subsequent events proved singularly correct. 'The interview had the happiest results,' writes Lord Roberts in his 'Forty-one Years in India,' 'and must have been extremely gratifying to Mr. Griffin, whom we all heartily congratulated on the successful ending to the very delicate and difficult negotiations, which he had carried on with so much skill and patience.' The British defeat at the hands of Ayub Khan at Maiwand on 27 July slightly postponed the settlement, and Griffin remained at Kabul until the withdrawal of the British troops after the rout of Ayub Khan's army by General Roberts on 1 Sept. He was made C.S.I. in July 1879, and K.C.S.I. in May 1881. He also received the Afghan medal. The Ameer admired Griffin's skilful diplomacy, and wrote that 'he deserved the title of "Lord of Kabul" just as much as Roberts did that of "Lord of Kandahar"' (ABDUR RAHMAN'S *Life*, 1900, ii. 115).

After this triumph Griffin became agent to the governor-general in central India in February 1881. He was instrumental in effecting valuable reforms in Gwalior, Indore, Bhopal, and some smaller states, and he won the regard of the chiefs. His action in securing in 1884 the degradation of Sidik Hasan Khan, second consort of Shah Jehan, Begam of Bhopal from 1868 to 1901, for his usurpation of power and his covert disloyalty is warmly commended by her daughter, the present Begam Sultan Jahan, in 'An Account of My Life' (1912). When home on leave in 1886 Griffin was a royal commissioner for the Indian and Colonial Exhibition, and at the Queen Victoria jubilee in the following year he was on special duty with the Maharaja Shivaji Rao Holkar of Indore. Refusing Lord Dufferin's invitation to supervise the reorganisation of Burma, after the annexation of the upper province in 1886, Griffin remained in central India until his retirement from the service in January 1889. He had hoped for the lieutenant-governorship of his old province in 1887, when Sir Charles Aitchison [q. v. Suppl. I] retired, but his unconventional frankness seems to have made the government shy of giving adequate recognition to his exceptional abilities.

On educational policy in India Griffin held original views. His constant intercourse with the Indian aristocracy bred in him distrust of the system of making the English language the sole instrument of the higher native education. With Dr. G. W. Leitner (1840–1899), principal of the Government College, Lahore, he early in his career urged the employment in teaching of the Indian vernaculars, and the award of honours for proficiency in Eastern literature and learning, as well as for English. Ultimately at his instigation a university college was established in 1870 at Lahore to give effect to these principles, and when the Punjab University was created there in Oct. 1882, one of the five faculties was for Oriental learning. Yet the Oriental faculty which alone sought to employ in tuition other languages than English never flourished and is now practically defunct (*Quinquennial Report on Indian Education*, 1902–7). The Inayat Ali-Griffin prize is annually given in his memory for the highest marks in Mahommedan law in the first law examination. Griffin further helped Leitner to establish without much success the Oriental Institute at Woking, to enable Indian students in England to adhere to their caste and communal customs. Griffin also founded in 1885, with Leitner and Mr. Demetrius Boulger, the first editor, the 'Asiatic Quarterly Review,' which long enjoyed a prosperous career.

On settling in England Griffin interested himself in literature, finance, and politics. As chairman of the Imperial Bank of Persia he did much for British prestige in Persia, and in 1903 the Shah conferred upon him the imperial order of the lion and the sun. He was also chairman of the Burma ruby mines, and was on the boards of other companies. From 1894 to his death he was chairman of the East India Association, which disinterestedly advocated the interests of India. He took an active part in its proceedings, which were fully reported in the 'Asiatic Quarterly Review.'

He constantly wrote in the magazines and spoke in public on Indian questions, and while upholding the conservative view of Indian administration, showed a warm regard for the Indian people as well as for the native princes. He vigorously espoused the cause of Indians in the Transvaal and elsewhere in South Africa, heading deputations to the secretaries of state for India and the colonies on the subject in 1907. He was a supporter of the liberal unionist cause in home politics, and in 1900 he contested unsuccessfully West Nottingham in their interest.

Griffin died of pneumonia at his residence, Cadogan Gardens, London, on 9 March 1908. The body was cremated at Golder's Green and his ashes were deposited in the private chapel of Colonel Dudley Sampson, Buxshalls, Lindfield, Sussex.

He married on 9 Nov. 1889 Marie Elizabeth, elder daughter of Ludwig Leupold of La Coronata, Genoa, Italy, agent to the North German Lloyd S.N. Co. at Genoa; she survived him with two sons, born in 1898 and 1900 respectively. His widow afterwards married Mr. Charles Hoare. A drawing of Griffin by C. W. Walton is reproduced in the Begam's 'Account of My Life' (1912), p. 128.

In addition to the books already mentioned Griffin wrote: 1. 'The Great Republic,' a hostile criticism of the United States of America, 1884, reproducing articles in the 'Fortnightly Review.' 2. 'Famous Monuments of Central India,' fol. 1886. 3. 'Ranjit Singh' in 'Rulers of India' series, 1892.

[Record of Services, Bengal Estab., 1888; India Office List, 1907; Lord Lytton's Indian Administration, 1899; Roberts, Forty-one Years in India, 1898; Imp. Gaz. of India, vols. viii. and xx.; Sultan Jahan Begam's Life, 1912; Ameer Abdur Rahman's Life, 1900; Journ. East India Assoc., April 1908; The Times, and Standard, 11 March 1908; Indian Rev., June 1904; notes kindly supplied by Mr. F. L. Petre; personal knowledge.] F. H. B.

GRIFFITH, RALPH THOMAS HOTCHKIN (1826–1906), Sanskrit scholar, born at Corsley, Wiltshire, on 25 May 1826, was son of Robert Clavey Griffith (1792–1844), rector of Corsley (1815–44) and of Fifield Bavant, also in Wiltshire (1825–44), by his wife Mary Elizabeth Adderly, daughter of Ralph Hotchkin of Uppingham Hall. Educated first at Westminster school and then at Uppingham, Ralph proceeded with an exhibition from Uppingham to Queen's College, Oxford, which he entered as a commoner on 16 March 1843. Obtaining an honorary fourth class in classics, he graduated B.A. on 29 Oct. 1846, and proceeded M.A. on 22 June 1849. At Oxford he became a pupil of Professor Horace Hayman Wilson [q. v.], and gaining the Boden Sanskrit scholarship in 1849, continued the study of Sanskrit to the end of his life. From 1850 to 1853 he was assistant master of Marlborough College, of which he was also librarian. In 1853 he joined the Indian educational service, and on 17 December became professor of English literature at the Benares Government College. His promotion was rapid: on 1 June 1854 he became headmaster of the college. He encouraged sport, and showed thorough sympathy with Indian students. In the following year he was entrusted, in addition to his other duties, with the charge of the Anglo-Sanskrit department; and in 1856 he was appointed inspector of schools in the Benares circle.

During his first eight years in India (1853–61) Griffith devoted himself not only to the study of Sanskrit but to that of Hindī, the most widely spoken vernacular of northern India, under Pandit Rām Jason, the head Sanskrit teacher of the college, to whom he was much attached. Throughout the Mutiny Griffith worked quietly in his bungalow amid the surrounding disorder and tumult.

On the retirement of James Robert Ballantyne [q. v.] in 1861 Griffith succeeded to the principalship of the Benares College. He held the post for seventeen years, in the course of which he acted three times for short periods as director of public instruction. On 15 March 1878 he left the Benares College after a quarter of a century's service, and from that date till 1885 was director of public instruction in the North-west Provinces and Oudh. His success in official life, both as an administrator and a teacher, was uninterrupted. On his retirement he received a special pension, the honour of C.I.E., and the thanks of the government. Calcutta University made him a fellow.

Unmarried and without close family ties in England, Griffith, after reaching India in 1853, never saw his native country again. On his retirement he withdrew to Kotagiri, a beautiful hill station, some 7000 feet high, in the Nīlgiri district, Madras, residing with his brother Frank, an engineer in the public works department of the Bombay presidency, who had settled there in 1879. At Kotagiri he tranquilly engaged in the study and translation of the Vedas. He died (7 Nov. 1906) and was buried there.

An enthusiastic lover of flowers and of poetry, he was sensitive and reserved, but genial in sympathetic society. His pupils and admirers at Benares perpetuated his memory on his retirement in scholarships and prizes at the Sanskrit college. In the college library hangs a photograph of his portrait painted by F. M. Wood.

Griffith was attracted by the literary rather than by the linguistic side of Sanskrit. But he rendered a great service to the direct study of the language by founding in 1866 the 'Pandit,' a monthly journal of the Benares College, devoted to Sanskrit literature. This he edited for eight years. More than forty annual volumes have already appeared.

To the translation of Sanskrit poetry Griffith devoted himself for nearly half a century. He began at Marlborough College with his 'Specimens of Old Indian Poetry' (1852), containing selections tastefully translated in various rhyming metres from the two great epics, the 'Mahābhārata' and the 'Rāmāyaṇa,' and from the works of India's greatest poet, Kālidāsa. An extract from the drama 'Śakuntalā' is in blank verse. At Marlborough also he made a translation in heroic couplets of Kālidāsa's court epic, the 'Kumāra-sambhava,' under the title of 'The Birth of the War-god' (1853; 2nd edit. 1879). There followed 'Idylls from the Sanskrit' (1866), selections similar to those in his first book, and 'Scenes from the Rámáyan' (1868). His translation of the whole epic, the 'Rámáyan of Válmíki,' in rhyming octosyllabic couplets, occasionally varied by other metres, was completed in five volumes (1870–5). Having paid some attention to the study of Persian, he published in 1882 a version of 'Yuzuf and Zuleika,' which was his only excursion in translation outside Sanskrit.

After his retirement to the Nīlgiri Hills, Griffith turned from classical Sanskrit to the sacred scriptures of the Hindus, the Vedas. The 'Rigveda' or Veda of hymns, which represent the higher religion of the ancient Indo-Aryans, appeared in a verse translation entitled 'Hymns of the Rigveda, with a Popular Commentary,' in four volumes (Benares, 1889–92; 2nd edit. 2 vols. 1896–7). There followed the 'Hymns of the Sāmaveda,' or Veda of chants concerned with the Soma ritual (Benares, 1893); the 'Hymns of the Atharvaveda,' or Veda mainly consisting of magical spells (2 vols. Benares, 1895–6), and finally 'The Texts of the White Yajurveda,' or sacrificial Veda (Benares, 1899). In these translations Griffith abandoned rhyme and rendered each verse by one syllabically harmonising with the original and generally divided into corresponding hemistichs. Griffith's command of poetical diction enabled him to reproduce the form and spirit of the ancient hymns better than by means of prose or of rhyming verse. His method of interpretation is eclectic; it follows partly the mediæval commentators, partly the researches of Western scholars, supplemented by investigations of his own. His renderings cannot be reckoned authoritative, but they are the only versions that present the general spirit of the ancient hymns to the English reader in an attractive form. Thus Griffith was not only the most voluminous, but also the best translator of ancient Indian poetry that Great Britain has yet produced.

[Griffith's published works; Foster's Alumni Oxonienses; Who's Who, 1904; information furnished by the Provost of Queen's College, Oxford; letter from Mrs. H. L. Griffith (sister-in-law); note supplied by Pandit Rama Krishna (formerly professor of mathematics at Benares and at Agra, retired collector of Ghazipur).] A. A. M.

GRIFFITHS, ARTHUR GEORGE FREDERICK (1838–1908), inspector of prisons and author, born on 9 Dec. 1838, at Poona, India, was second son of Lieut.-colonel John Griffiths of the 6th Royal Warwickshire regiment. After education at King William's College, Isle of Man, he entered the army as ensign in the 63rd (now Manchester) regiment on 13 Feb. 1855. He was present at the siege and fall of Sevastopol, and took part in the expedition to Kinburn, for which he received the Crimean medal. He was promoted lieutenant on 27 July 1855. In 1856 his regiment was stationed at Halifax, Nova Scotia, but on being nominated aide-de-camp to Sir William Eyre [q. v.], commanding the troops in British North America, Griffiths was transferred to Toronto. The appointment, however, was not confirmed by the war office, and he returned home on leave. He pursued his military studies at the Hythe school of musketry, and in 1860 he passed fifth into the Staff College. In Nov. 1861, owing to the threatened war with the United States over the 'Trent' affair, Griffiths was ordered to rejoin his regiment at Halifax. He was promoted captain on 12 Feb. 1862.

From 1864 to 1870 he was brigade major at Gibraltar. His administrative capacity was recognised by his appointment to the temporary charge of the convict establishment at Gibraltar; and his success in enforcing discipline led him to enter the prisons service at home. Griffiths was deputy-governor of Chatham (1870–2), of Millbank (1872–4), and of Wormwood Scrubbs prisons (1874–81). From 1878 to 1896 he was inspector of prisons, and undertook the task of unifying the methods of administration throughout the country. He became an acknowledged authority on European prison systems and on the history of London gaols. His 'Memorials of Millbank' (1875; 2nd edit. 1884) and 'Chronicles of Newgate' (1884) were serious works of research; and he added to his reputation in 1890 by winning the Tsar's gold medal for a monograph on John

Howard [q. v.]. In 1896 he represented England at the international congress of criminal anthropologists at Geneva.

Griffiths retired from the army with the rank of major on 13 May 1875, and devoted his leisure to literature and journalism. He had already some experience as editor of the 'Gibraltar Chronicle' in 1864; and he became a frequent contributor to many journals. He edited papers and magazines so widely different as 'Home News' (1883–88), the 'Fortnightly Review' (1884), and the 'World' (1895). From 1901 to 1904 he was editor of the 'Army and Navy Gazette' in succession to Sir William Howard Russell [q. v. Suppl. II].

But it was as a writer of sensational tales of prison life that Griffiths was best known to the public, and in such stories as 'Secrets of the Prison House' (1893), 'A Prison Princess' (1893), 'Criminals I have known' (1895), 'Mysteries of Police and Crime' (1898; 3rd edit. 1904), 'The Brand of the Broad Arrow' (1900), and 'Tales of a Government Official' (1902), he revealed his extensive experience of the habits and characteristics of the criminal classes. His detective stories, like 'Fast and Loose' (1885), 'No. 99' (1885), 'The Rome Express' (1896), and 'A Passenger from Calais' (1905), were modelled on those of Gaboriau, and were inspired by his intimate acquaintance with French police methods. In his earlier novels, 'The Queen's Shilling' (1873), 'A Son of Mars' (1880; 2nd edit. 1902), and 'The Thin Red Line' (1886; 2nd edit. 1900), he drew mainly on his Crimean experiences, while 'Lola' (1878) was a faithful transcript of garrison life at Gibraltar. Altogether he published thirty novels.

He also contributed to the official 'History of the War in South Africa, 1889–1902' (1906–10; 4 vols.); and was author of several popular historical works.

Griffiths was a genial companion, a keen sportsman, and an amusing raconteur. He died at Victoria Hotel, Beaulieu, in the South of France, on 24 March 1908. He married on 18 Jan. 1881 Harriet, daughter of Richard Reily, who survived him.

[Fifty Years of Public Service, by Arthur Griffiths, 1904 (frontispiece portrait); The Times, 26 March 1908; Army and Navy Gazette, 28 March 1908; Brit. Mus. Cat.]

G. S. W.

GRIGGS, WILLIAM (1832–1911), inventor of photo-chromo-lithography, son of a lodge-keeper to the duke of Bedford at Woburn, Bedfordshire, was born there on 4 Oct. 1832. Losing his father in childhood, he was apprenticed at the age of twelve to the carpentering trade, and coming to London when eighteen, he was employed as an artisan in the Indian Court of the Great Exhibition of 1851. He improved his scanty education at night classes at King's College and elsewhere, and in 1855 was selected to be technical assistant to the reporter on Indian products and director of the Indian Museum, then in the India House, Leadenhall Street.

His artistic tastes and keen interest in photography were encouraged by Dr. John Forbes Watson [q. v.], who became his chief in 1858, and at his instance Griggs was installed at Fife House, Whitehall, pending completion of the India office, in a studio and workshops for photo-lithographic work. He had familiarised himself with the processes of photo-zincography discovered by the director-general of the Ordnance Survey, General Sir Henry James [q. v.]. By careful experiment he found that the use of cold, instead of hot, water in developing the transfer left the gelatine in the whites of the transfer, thus giving firmer adhesion to the stone and serving as a support to the fine lines. He also invented photo-chromo-lithography by first printing from a photo-lithographic transfer a faint impression on the paper to serve as a 'key,' separating the colours on duplicate negatives by varnishes, then photo-lithographing the dissected portions on stones, finally registering and printing each in its position and particular colour, with the texture, light and shade of the original.

He greatly cheapened the production of colour work by a simplified form of this discovery, viz. by a photo-lithographic transfer from a negative of the original to stone, printed as a 'key' in a suitable colour, superimposing thereon, in exact register, transparent tints in harmony with the original. Opaque colours, when necessary, were printed first. So far from keeping secret or patenting these improvements, Griggs described and gave practical demonstrations of them to the London Photographic Society (14 April 1868). He was thus a pioneer in the wide diffusion of colour work and half-tone block-making, and helped to bring about rapid cylindrical printing. But for his 'brilliant and painstaking work, chromo-lithography as a means of illustrating books would be almost a lost art, like that of coloured aquatint' (Martin Hardie's *English Coloured Books*, 1906, pp. 255–6).

Griggs established photo-lithographic works at his Peckham residence in 1868, soon after the publication of his first notable achievement—the beautiful plates illustrating Dr. Forbes Watson's 'Textile Manufactures and Customs of the People of India' (1866), which was followed by those illustrating 'Tree and Serpent Worship in India' (1868), by James Fergusson [q. v.]. He also reproduced some of the Prince Consort's drawings for Queen Victoria, and was thereafter chromo-lithographer to her Majesty and subsequently to King Edward VII. Though the contents of the India Museum were dispersed between South Kensington and elsewhere in 1878, he continued to serve the India office till Sept. 1885, thenceforth devoting himself exclusively to his own business.

In reproductions of old manuscripts and letterpress texts Griggs was as successful as in chromo-lithography. His production of fifty copies of the 'Mahābhāsya' (the standard authority on Sanskrit grammar), consisting of 4674 pages (1871), was carried out for 6000*l.* less than the estimate for a tracing of the original MS. by hand. More widely known, however, are his Shakespeare quartos, with critical introductions by Frederick James Furnivall [q. v. Suppl. II] and others, in 43 vols. (1881–91), which were sold at 6*s.* each, while the hand-traced facsimiles by E. W. Ashbee, superintended by James Orchard Halliwell-Phillipps [q. v.], had been sold at five guineas each.

On the initiative of Sir George Birdwood, who gave him constant encouragement, Griggs secured in 1881 the patronage of the committee of council on education for a series of shilling 'Portfolios of Industrial Art,' 200 of which have been issued, chiefly selected from the Chinese, Persian, Arabian, Sicilian, Italian, Russian, and Spanish specimens at South Kensington. Under an arrangement with the government of India, also negotiated at Sir George's instance, he issued from Jan. 1884 the quarterly 'Journal of Indian Art and Industry,' in imperial quarto (2*s.*), which is still carried on by his successors in business. A notable work in the same field, edited by Colonel T. H. Hendley, was his 'Asian Carpet Designs' (1905) of 150 coloured plates, sold at 18*l.* a copy. Nor was he less successful in illustrating such works as Dr. James Burgess's reports on the archæology of Western India through a long series of years, and his 'Ancient Monuments of India' (1897 to 1911); Colonel T. H. Hendley's many works on the art and history of Rajputana; facsimiles of illuminated MSS. at the British Museum (1889–1903), and other works for the trustees; Sir Richard Temple's 'Thirty-Seven Nats' in Burma (1906); and many scientific works, such as Dr. M. C. Cooke's 'Illustrations of British Fungi' (2nd edit. 6 vols. 1884–8) and his 'Handbook' thereof (2nd edit. 1887). The fullest, though by no means a complete, list of Griggs's works is given in the 'Journal of Indian Art,' Jan. 1912.

Griggs married in 1851 Elizabeth Jane Gill (*d.* 1903), and in his later years was assisted in business by his two sons. The firm of W. Griggs & Sons was formed into a public company on 20 Dec. 1906. He was for a time managing director, but owing to ill-health resigned all connection with the company in January 1910.

He died at Worthing on 7 Dec. 1911, being buried in the Forest Hill cemetery. His second son, Walter, carries on an independent business on his father's lines.

[Sir George Birdwood's introd. to Relics of Hon.E.I.Co., 1909; Martin Hardie's English Coloured Books, 1906; Journ. of Photographic Soc. of London, No. 192, 18 April 1868; Photo-Chromo-Lithography, pamphlet by Griggs, 1882; Journ. of Indian Art, Jan. 1912, obit. by Col. Hendley; The Times, 8 Dec. 1911; Printers' Register, 8 Jan. 1912; information supplied by Mr. Walter Griggs; personal knowledge.] F. H. B.

GRIMTHORPE, first Baron. [See Beckett, Sir Edmund, 1816–1905.]

GROOME, FRANCIS HINDES (1851–1902), Romany scholar and miscellaneous writer, second son of Robert Hindes Groome [q. v.], archdeacon of Suffolk, was born at his father's rectory of Monk Soham on 30 Aug. 1851. Through his father's mother there was a family connection with East Dereham, and, there is some ground for believing, blood-relationship with George Borrow [q. v.]. In 1861 he was at school at Wyke Regis, near Weymouth. From 1865 to 1869 he was at Ipswich grammar school under Dr. H. A. Holden [q. v. Suppl. I], where he distinguished himself both in Latin prose and in Latin verse. There too he won several cups for rowing, and helped to found and edit a school magazine. He read for a year with Francis de Winton at Boughrood on the Wye, and went up to Corpus Christi College, Oxford, matriculating in October 1870; in 1871 he was elected postmaster of Merton College. Even in early boyhood gypsy life seen in glimpses had exercised a singular fascination over him; an assistant master at Ipswich had given him some real knowledge of Romany and of gypsy lore; and at Oxford he came to know gypsies intimately, a fact which gave a new turn to his life. He left Oxford without taking a degree, spent some time at Göttingen, and for years lived much with gypsies at home and abroad; he travelled on the Puszta with Hungarian gypsies, and elsewhere with Roumanian and Roumelian companies, and he married in 1876 a wife of English gypsy blood, Esmeralda Locke, from whom he afterwards separated.

In 1876 Groome settled down to regular literary work in Edinburgh. He was soon one of the most valued workers on the staff of the 'Globe Encyclopædia' (6 vols. 1876–9). In 1877 he began to edit 'Suffolk Notes and Queries' in the 'Ipswich Journal.' He edited the 'Ordnance Gazetteer of Scotland' (6 vols. 1882–5; 2nd edit. 1893–5), which took rank as a standard work of reference. In 1885 he joined the literary staff of Messrs. W. & R. Chambers, and as sub-editor and copious contributor gave invaluable assistance in preparing the new edition of 'Chambers's Encyclopædia' (10 vols. 1888–92). He had a large share in a gazetteer (1 vol. 1895), and was joint-editor of a biographical dictionary, both published by the same house. Meanwhile he was an occasional contributor to 'Blackwood's Magazine,' the 'Bookman,' and other periodicals, wrote many articles for this Dictionary, and did much systematic reviewing for the 'Athenæum.' 'A Short Border History' was issued in 1887. The delightful sketches of his father and his father's friend, Edward FitzGerald, published as 'Two Suffolk Friends' in 1895, were expanded from two articles in 'Blackwood's Magazine' in 1889 and 1891.

At the same time Groome wrote much on gypsies. His article on 'Gipsies,' contributed to the ninth edition of the 'Encyclopædia Britannica,' made him known to the world as a gypsyologist. 'In Gipsy Tents' (1880; 2nd edit. 1881) recorded much of his own experience. He was joint-editor of the 'Journal of the Gypsy Lore Society' (1888–92; revived in 1907), and a paper by him on 'The Influence of the Gypsies on the Superstitions of the English Folk' was printed in 1891, in the 'Transactions of the International Folk-Lore Congress.' Mr. Watts-Dunton has said that in Groome's remarkable Romany novel with the oddly irrelevant name of 'Kriegspiel' (1896) 'there was more substance than in five ordinary stories,' the gypsy chapters, with autobiographical elements, being 'absolutely perfect.' 'Gypsy Folk Tales' (1899) contains over seventy tales with variants from many lands, and the elaborate introduction is a monument of erudition and ripe scholarship. He produced also an edition of Borrow's 'Lavengro' (1901), with notes and a valuable introduction. When his working powers failed him, Groome was assisting in the preparation of a new edition of 'Chambers's Cyclopædia of English Literature' (3 vols. 1901–1903); and for more than a year he was a confirmed invalid. He died in London on 24 January 1902, and was buried beside his father and mother in Monk Soham churchyard.

Nothing in Groome's life is more remarkable than that he should have passed so swiftly and cheerfully from a veritable Bohemia of romance into the bondage of systematic labour, and have worked in the new conditions with a rare efficiency. A singularly alert, swift, and eager intellect, he was unwearied in research, impatient of anything less than precision, a frank and fearless critic; thoroughly at home in wide fields of historical and philological research, and in some of them a master. A man of strong convictions and not a few prepossessions, he had a knowledge of the romantic side of Scottish history such as few Scotsmen possess, notably of Jacobite literature in all its ramifications native and foreign. His vivacious style showed a marked individuality. Men like Swinburne and Mr. Watts-Dunton cherished his friendship, and he maintained a correspondence with eminent scholars all over Europe (e.g. August Friedrich Pott and Franz von Miklosich); some of his many letters to C. G. Leland are quoted in Mrs. Pennell's 'Life of Leland' (1906).

[Who's Who, 1900; Scotsman, 25 Jan. 1902; Mr. Watts-Dunton's memoir in Athenæum, 22 Feb. 1902; information from brothers; personal knowledge.] D. P.

GROSE, THOMAS HODGE (1845–1906), registrar of Oxford University, born at Redruth in Cornwall on 9 Nov. 1845, was fourth son of James Grose. An elder brother, James, went to India in 1860 in the civil service, and died as member of council at Madras on 7 June 1898. Educated at Manchester grammar school, under the strenuous high-mastership of Frederick William Walker [q. v. Suppl. II], Grose was elected to a scholarship at Balliol College, Oxford, in 1864. He was one of the few to obtain four first classes, two in moderations and two again in the final schools (classics and mathematics).

He graduated B.A. in 1868, proceeding M.A. in 1871. He entered as a student at Lincoln's Inn, but his plans changed and he did not go to the bar. In 1870 he was elected to a fellowship at Queen's College, being appointed tutor in the following year, and there the rest of his life was spent. In 1872 he was ordained deacon, but his clerical work was confined to the duties of college chaplain and sermons in the chapel. In 1887 he was elected to the hebdomadal council, and in 1897 to the office of university registrar, which he held till his death. In 1871 he had been president of the Union; and in 1887, when the finances of the society were in low water, he was appointed to the new office of senior treasurer, which likewise he continued to hold till his death. Between 1876 and 1898 he served as examiner in the school of literæ humaniores no less than a dozen times. He was also president of the Association for the Education of Women and of the Women's Suffrage Society, and latterly a member of the education committee of the Nottinghamshire county council. His only contribution to literature was to assist Thomas Hill Green [q. v.] in editing 'The Philosophical Works of David Hume' (1874–5).

Grose's best work was done in his rooms at Queen's. Shy and reserved in manner, with gestures that were awkward and a voice that was gruff, he won the respect and affection of many generations of undergraduates. Himself unmarried, he devoted his time and his money to fatherly relations among an ever expanding circle of those who were to him in the place of sons. He followed closely every stage of his pupils' future life, however far removed they might be from Oxford. In his early years he had been a keen fives-player and an Alpine climber. He was a member of the Alpine Club from 1900 till death. Latterly his chief outdoor pursuit was field botany. Almost to the last he travelled much abroad, his interest being divided between natural scenery and art museums. In 1894 he paid a nine months' visit to India. His rooms ultimately became a storehouse of artistic objects and photographs brought back from foreign lands. He died in college, after a long and painful illness, on 11 Feb. 1906, and was buried at Holywell cemetery. The Union Society, who had two years before presented him with a service of silver plate inscribed 'Viro strenuo, suis carissimo, optime de societate merito,' adjourned their debate out of respect to his memory. His portrait by R. E. Morrison was presented by members of the college in 1903 and was hung in the college hall. After his death a memorial fund was formed for the assistance of undergraduates in need of aid.

[Personal knowledge; two pamphlets on the occasion of his death, printed at Oxford for private circulation, 1906.] J. S. C.

GUBBINS, JOHN (1838–1906), breeder and owner of race-horses, born on 16 Dec. 1838 at the family home, Kilfrush, co. Limerick, was fourth son of Joseph Gubbins by his wife Maria, daughter of Thomas Wise of Cork. Of three surviving brothers and five sisters, the third brother, Stamer, who was 6 feet 6 inches tall and of proportionate build, joined the army, and, attaining the rank of captain, distinguished himself in the Crimean war, where, discarding his sword, he carried a heavy blackthorn stick; subsequently he bred horses at Knockany, where he died on 7 Aug. 1879, aged forty-six, owing to the fall upon him of a horse which he had been 'schooling' over fences.

John Gubbins, after being educated privately, inherited the Knockany property from his brother Stamer, and purchased the estate of Bruree, co. Limerick. A fortune was also left him by an uncle, Francis Wise of Cork. Settling at Bruree in 1868, he spent about 40,000*l.* in building kennels and stables, and buying horses and hounds. He hunted the Limerick country with both stag and fox hounds, and was no mean angler, until forced to stop by the operations of the Land League in 1882.

From youth he took a keen interest in horse-racing. At first his attention was mainly confined to steeplechasers, and he rode many winners at Punchestown and elsewhere in Ireland. He was the owner of Seaman when that horse won the grand hurdle race at Auteuil, but had sold him to Lord Manners before he won the Grand National at Liverpool in 1882. Usna was another fine chaser in his possession. Buying the stallions Kendal and St. Florian, he bred, from the mare Morganette, Galtee More by the former and Ard Patrick by the latter. Galtee More won the Two Thousand Guineas and the St. Leger as well as the Derby in 1897, and was afterwards sold to the Russian government for 21,000*l.*, who later passed him on to the Prussian government for 14,000*l.* The latter government also bought Ard Patrick for 21,000*l.* a day or two before he won the Eclipse stakes of 10,000*l.* in 1903, when he defeated

Sceptre and Rock Sand after an exceptionally exciting contest. Other notable horses bred by John Gubbins were Blairfinde (winner of the Irish Derby) and Revenue. In 1897 he headed the list of winning owners with a total of 22,739*l*., and was third in the list in 1903. His horses were at various times trained by H. E. Linde (in Ireland), Joussiffe (at Lambourn), and S. Darling (at Beckhampton.) After 1903 John Gubbins was rarely seen on a racecourse owing to failing health, and in 1904 he sold his horses in training. In 1905, however, his health having apparently improved, he sent some yearlings to Cranborne, Dorset, to be trained by Sir Charles Nugent, but before these horses could run he died at Bruree on 20 March 1906, and was buried in the private burial ground at Kilfrush. He was high sheriff of co. Limerick in 1886, as well as J.P. and D.L. A warm-hearted, genial personality, he was a kind and indulgent landlord and employer, and a sportsman of the best type.

In 1889 he married Edith, daughter of Charles Legh, of Addington Hall, Cheshire; she predeceased him without issue. His estates passed to his nephew, John Norris Browning, a retired naval surgeon.

[Notes supplied by Mr. D. R. Browning, of Bruree, co. Limerick; Burke's Landed Gentry; Sportsman, 21 March 1906; Baily's Magazine, May 1906; Ruff's Guide to the Turf.] E. M.

GUINNESS, HENRY GRATTAN (1835–1910), divine and author, born on 11 Aug. 1835 at Montpelier House, near Kingstown, Ireland, was eldest son in the family of one daughter and three sons of John Grattan Guinness (1783–1850), captain in the army, who saw service in India. His mother was Jane Lucretia, daughter of William Cramer (an accomplished violinist and composer, who was son of Johann Baptist Cramer [q. v.], musical composer), and was widow of Captain J. N. D'Esterre, who was killed by Daniel O'Connell [q. v.] in a duel in Feb. 1815. His grandfather, Arthur Guinness of Beaumont, co. Dublin, established the first Sunday school in Ireland in Dublin in 1786. During their father's lifetime the family lived variously at Dublin, Liverpool, Clifton, and Cheltenham. After education at private schools at Clevedon and Exeter, Guinness at the age of seventeen went to sea, and travelled through Mexico and the West Indies. On his return to England in March 1853 he experienced religious 'conversion.' In Jan. 1856 he entered New College, St. John's Wood, London, was ordained as an undenominational evangelist in July 1857, and entered on evangelistic work, to which he thenceforth devoted his life at home and abroad. He met with great success as a preacher in London, rivalling Charles Haddon Spurgeon [q. v.] in popularity, and preaching often at the Moorfields Tabernacle, the charge of which he was offered but declined. There followed preaching tours on the Continent in Jan. 1858, in Ireland in Feb. 1858 and in 1859, and in America from Nov. 1859 to May 1860. After his first marriage on 2 Oct. 1860 he and his wife spent twelve years in incessant travelling. He visited Canada in 1861 and Egypt and Palestine in 1862. He then held a short pastorate at Liverpool, and afterwards worked in Ireland. Towards the close of 1865 Guinness took a house at 31 Bagot Street, Dublin, with a view to forming a training home for evangelists and missionaries. In 1866 he also conducted in Dublin the Merrion Hall Mission, and there he helped to bring Thomas John Barnardo [q. v. Suppl. II] under religious influence. In 1867 he left Dublin for Bath. Work in France occupied much of his time from 1868 to 1872. Next year he founded in London, and directed till his death, the East London Institute for Home and Foreign Missions, for the training of young men and women for home and foreign missionary work. The Institute was first located at 29 Stepney Green, and subsequently at Harley House, Bow. Barnardo was a co-director. During the first year the students numbered 32. At the end of three years branches were formed in London, and one was installed at Hulme Cliff College, Curbar, Derbyshire. Accommodation was provided for 100 men and women; over 1100 men and women have since been trained.

With the opening up of the Congo and the publication of H. M. Stanley's letters at the end of 1877, Guinness and his wife resolved to concentrate on foreign missions. A monthly magazine, 'The Regions Beyond,' was started in 1878. The Livingstone Inland Mission was formed in the Congo in 1878, and in 1880 became a branch of the institute, with Guinness as director and Mrs. Guinness as secretary. It was transferred to the control of the American Baptist Missionary Union in 1884 (see Mrs. Guinness's *The New World of Central Africa*, 1890). A new mission to the interior of Africa, the Congo Balolo Mission, was founded in 1889, and others followed in South America—in Peru in 1897, and the Argentine in 1899. The organisations were combined in 1899 to form 'The Regions Beyond Missionary Union,' an unsectarian body whose activities were further extended to India by the formation of the Behar mission in the Bengal presidency in 1901.

Although Guinness did not himself visit the interior of Africa, he went in the interest of his societies to Algeria in 1879, to America in 1889 (where he inspired the creation in Boston and Minneapolis of training institutions similar to his own), to India and Burma in November 1896, and to China and Japan in 1897. A second visit to Egypt in 1900 bore good fruit among the Sudanese. In 1903 Guinness went with his second wife on a five years' missionary tour round the world, visiting Switzerland (1903), America and Canada (1904), Japan and China (1905), Australia and New Zealand (1906), and South Africa (1907). He received the degree of D.D. from Brown University, Providence, U.S.A., in 1889.

Guinness died after four months' illness on 21 June 1910 at Bath, where he spent his last two years, and was buried in the Abbey cemetery there. He was twice married. His first wife, Fanny (1831–1898), daughter of Edward Marlborough Fitzgerald (*d.* 1839), and grand-daughter of Maurice Fitzgerald of Dublin, whom he married at Bath on 20 Oct. 1860, was one of the first women evangelists. She joined in all her husband's work, was secretary of the East London Institute and of the Livingstone Inland Mission, was editor of 'The Regions Beyond' from 1878, and, besides collaborating with her husband, independently published 'The Life of Mrs. Henry Denning' (Bristol, 1872) and 'The New World of Central Africa' (1890). She died at Cliff House, Curbar, Derbyshire, on 3 Nov. 1898, and was buried in Baslow churchyard. She had six daughters, of whom two only survived childhood, and two sons. All the children engaged in their parents' missionary efforts. The eldest son, Dr. Harry Grattan Guinness (*b.* 1861), is a director of the mission at Harley House. The younger daughter, Lucy Evangeline (Mrs. Karl Kumm, 1865–1906), edited 'The Regions Beyond' for some nine years after her mother's death, published books on South America and India, and was a writer of verse. Her father published a memoir of her in 1907. Guinness married secondly, on 7 July 1903, Grace, daughter of Russell Hurditch, by whom he had two sons.

In collaboration with his first wife Guinness published several works on prophecy. The most important, 'The Approaching End of the Age in the Light of History, Prophecy, and Science,' published in 1878 (8th edit. 1882), went through fourteen editions. Other joint publications were 'Light for the Last Days' (1886) and 'The Divine Programme of the World's History' (1888). Guinness published also in 1882 a translation of Brusciotto's grammar of the Congo language, and 'A Grammar of the Congo Language as spoken in the Cataract Region below Stanley Pool,' containing specimen translations from the Bible, which were printed separately as 'Mosaic History and Gospel Story.' His many other volumes included 'The City of the Seven Hills,' a poem (1891), and 'Creation centred in Christ' (2 vols. 1896).

[The Times, 22 June 1910; Men and Women of the Time, 1899; Thirteen Sermons, 1859 (with brief sketch of Guinness's life and portrait at age of 22); Harper's Weekly, 1860 (portrait); In Memoriam number of Regions Beyond, Jan.–Feb. 1911 (with portraits); Enter Thou, New Year's number of Regions Beyond, 1899, containing memoir of Mrs. Guinness with illustrations; J. S. Dennis, Christian Missions and Social Progress, 3 vols. 1906; Dwight, Tupper, and Bliss, Encyc. of Missions, 1904; James Marchant, Memoirs of Dr. Barnardo, 1907.] W. B. O.

GULLY, WILLIAM COURT, first Viscount Selby (1835–1909), Speaker of the House of Commons, born in London on 29 Aug. 1835, was second son of Dr. James Manby Gully [q. v.], the well-known physician of Great Malvern, by Frances, daughter of Thomas Court. He was educated privately, and at the early age of sixteen went to Trinity College, Cambridge. He was popular at the university and was chosen president of the Cambridge Union. In 1856 he graduated B.A. with a first class in the moral sciences tripos, then recently established, and proceeded M.A. in 1859. On 26 Jan. 1860 he was called to the bar at the Inner Temple, and joined the northern circuit. He shared the usual struggles of a junior barrister, and there is a well-authenticated story of a meeting between three members of the circuit who, despairing of their prospects at home, agreed to try their fortunes in India or the colonies. But they reconsidered their determination, and all of them rose to eminence in their own country. The three were Charles Russell [q. v. Suppl. I], afterwards lord chief justice of England, Farrer Herschell [q. v. Suppl. I], afterwards lord chancellor of Great Britain, and Gully, who gradually established a good practice at the bar, especially in commercial cases at Liverpool. He had a sound knowledge of law, and a fine presence and attractive personality.

According to a contemporary, who spoke with intimate knowledge, he 'was one of the straightest advocates a circuit ever saw.' He 'took silk' in 1877, was elected a bencher in 1879, and eventually became leader of the northern circuit.

In 1880 he felt that his position at the bar justified him in entering political life, and at the general election of that year he stood as a liberal candidate for Whitehaven, where the Lowther influence was strong against him. His opponent was George Cavendish Bentinck, and he was defeated by 182 votes. Nor was he more successful in 1885, when he tried again and was again defeated by the same opponent. It was not until 1892 that he obtained a seat in the House of Commons. Robert Ferguson, the liberal member for Carlisle, dissented from Gladstone's home rule policy, and at the general election of 1892 Gully was selected as a liberal candidate in his place. He was opposed by F. Cavendish Bentinck, but was returned by a majority of 143, and retained the seat until he left the House of Commons. In the same year he was appointed recorder of Wigan.

In the House of Commons Gully did not take a very active part in debates, but was known, and liked, as a quiet member, apparently more interested in his professional than in his political work. His opportunity came in 1895. In the April of that year Mr. Speaker Peel resigned his post. The liberal majority was small, dwindling and precarious, and the unionists resolved to nominate a member of their own party as his successor. The candidate whom they selected was Matthew White Ridley [q. v. Suppl. II], afterwards home secretary and first Viscount Ridley. On the liberal side Mr. Leonard Courtney (now Lord Courtney of Penwith), who had been chairman of ways and means, was suggested by the cabinet. But his attitude on the Irish question and his somewhat brusque individualism were certain to alienate liberal and nationalist votes. Sir Henry Campbell Bannerman [q. v. Suppl. II] avowed his willingness to take the post, and he would apparently have been accepted by the unionists. But Sir William Harcourt was unwilling to lose so valuable a colleague. Then Gully was suggested as a 'safe' man, whom all the sections of the liberal party would support. The suggestion is said to have come from Henry Labouchere. Gully was adopted as the liberal candidate, and on 10 April he was elected against Sir Matthew White Ridley by a majority of eleven votes. The opposition resented their defeat, and it was intimated that in the event of an early change of government the unionist party, if returned to power at a general election, would not feel bound to continue Gully as speaker in a new parliament. On 25 June, after Lord Rosebery's retirement, Lord Salisbury became prime minister, parliament was dissolved on 8 July, and at the general election the unionist party obtained a large majority. Gully's seat at Carlisle was contested, but he succeeded in retaining it by an increased majority. During the short interval which elapsed between Gully's election to the office of speaker and the dissolution of parliament he had firmly established his reputation as an excellent occupant of the chair, and when the new parliament met in August the notion of opposing his re-election was abandoned, the tradition of continuing in office an efficient speaker was maintained, and on the motion of Sir John Mowbray, the father of the house, he was unanimously re-elected. He retained his office, after another re-election in 1900, until his retirement in March 1905.

Gully had a difficult task to perform in succeeding the majestic and awe-inspiring Peel, but he proved himself equal to the task. Handsome, dignified, courteous, impartial, he sustained the judicial traditions of many parliamentary generations. His professional training enabled him to master quickly the rules and practice of the house, and his judicial temperament secured their impartial application. There were some who criticised his interpretation of them as too technical, to others it sometimes appeared that, as is natural to men of sensitive conscience, he inclined too much, in cases of doubt, to the side to which he was politically opposed; but no one ever questioned his fairness of mind. One re-regrettable incident lost him the confidence of the Irish nationalist party. On 5 March 1901, at a sitting of the committee of supply, the chairman, Mr. Lowther (afterwards speaker), had granted the closure, and a division was called; but when the order was given to clear the house, about a dozen Irish members refused to leave their seats. The speaker was sent for, and repeated the order; but the members refused to leave the house, and were forcibly removed by the police. The rule thus enforced was not embodied in any standing order and has since been expressly repealed. But there is no doubt that it represented the then existing practice of the House. Whether its enforcement could have been avoided is a question about which anyone acquainted with the difficulties of such situations would hesitate to express a confident opinion.

In March 1905, after nearly ten years' service, Gully found himself compelled, on the ground of health, to resign the office of speaker. The strain of his work was much increased by the serious illness of his wife, to whom he was devotedly attached. In accordance with custom, he received a peerage and a pension, and a vote of thanks from the House of Commons. He took as his title (Viscount Selby) the family name of his wife. Release from his official duties restored his health, and during the remaining years of his life he was a regular attendant at debates of the House of Lords, and served the public in many ways. He was chairman of the royal commission on motor cars, and also of the commission on vaccination; chairman of the board of trade arbitration committee in 1908, and a member of the permanent arbitration court at the Hague. He was also chairman of the executive committee of the Franco-British Exhibition of 1908. Gully was made an hon. LL.D. of Cambridge in 1900, and an hon. D.C.L. of Oxford in 1904, and received the freedom of the City of London on his resignation of the office of speaker. His health greatly suffered from his wife's death on 15 Nov. 1906. He was taken seriously ill whilst staying at Menaggio, on the lake of Como, in September 1909, and being brought home made a temporary recovery. He died on 6 November in that year at his country seat, Sutton Place, Seaford, and was buried at Brookwood. He married on 15 April 1865 Elizabeth Anne Walford (*d.* 1906), eldest daughter of Thomas Selby of Whitley and Wimbush in Essex. He had issue four daughters and two sons. His elder son, James William Herschell, succeeded to the peerage. His younger son, Edward Walford Karslake, was for many years private secretary both to his father and to his father's successor as speaker, and is now examiner of private bills for the two houses of parliament. The best portrait of Gully is that by Sir George Reid in the speaker's official house. Another portrait, painted by the Hon. John Collier in 1898, is in the hall of the Inner Temple. A cartoon portrait by 'Spy' appeared in 'Vanity Fair' in 1896.

[The Times, 8–11 Nov. 1909; Carlisle Express and Examiner, 13 Nov. 1909; A. I. Dasent, Lives of the Speakers, 1911; personal knowledge.] C. P. I.

GURNEY, HENRY PALIN (1847–1904), man of science, eldest son of Henry Gurney by his wife Eleanor Palin, was born in London on 7 Sept. 1847. He entered the City of London School in 1856, under the headmastership of Dr. Mortimer, and remained there until 1866; at the school he gained the Beaufoy mathematical medal, and was head of the school in science in 1865. In 1866 he proceeded to Clare College, Cambridge, where he specialised in science and mathematics. He rowed in his college boat, and ran for the university in the inter-university sports of 1868 and 1869. He graduated B.A. in 1870 as fourteenth wrangler, and was fourth in the first class of the natural science tripos. At the university Gurney studied mineralogy and crystallography under Professor William Hallowes Miller [q. v.], and acted for a while as Miller's deputy. Gurney was also the senior lecturer at Clare College in mathematics and natural sciences. Elected to a college fellowship in April 1870, he held it until 1883, when he was senior fellow of his college. In 1871 he took holy orders, and was appointed curate to Canon Beck, rector of the college living of Rotherhithe, and subsequently officiated for many years as curate at St. Peter's Church, Bayswater. Shortly after his marriage in 1872 he became lecturer for Walter Wren at Wren's tutorial establishment in Powis Square, Bayswater. Gurney's sound mathematical knowledge, clear method of teaching, and powers of organisation were found of such value that he became in 1877 managing partner of the firm of Wren & Gurney, which rapidly acquired celebrity as a preparatory establishment for young men wishing to enter the army, the Indian civil service, and other home or foreign office departments.

Meanwhile he had kept up his interest in mineralogy, and in 1875 he published his only book, a small but clear and useful work on crystallography, one of the manuals of elementary science issued by the Society for Promoting Christian Knowledge. In 1876 Gurney helped to found the Crystallogical Society, and was a member of its first council. In 1894 he was appointed to the post of principal of the Durham College of Science, Newcastle-upon-Tyne, in succession to Dr. William Garnett. At a critical period in the history of the College of Science Gurney showed tact, ability, and powers of conciliation and administration. Next year Gurney added the duties of professor of mathematics to the burden of the principalship, retaining the chair until 1904. In 1895 he took a prominent part in founding a department of mineralogy and crystallography at the college, and was himself the first lecturer, giving his services gratuitously. In 1896 the honorary degree of D.C.L. was conferred upon him by the University of Durham.

To meet the additional accommodation which the growth of the college made imperative, Gurney arranged an influential public meeting at Newcastle in 1899, where a strong committee was formed to collect subscriptions. In 1901, at Gurney's suggestion, the Armstrong Memorial Fund was devoted to the completion of the college, as a memorial of Lord Armstrong. The college thereupon took the name of Armstrong College. The new buildings were duly commenced in 1904.

Gurney died through a mountain accident in Switzerland on 13 Aug. 1904, having apparently lost his footing whilst out alone on La Roussette near Arolla. He was buried at Ganerew in Herefordshire. In 1872 he married at Whitchurch, Herefordshire, Louisa, daughter of the Rev. H. Selby Hele of Grays, Essex. He left a family of nine daughters; the eldest, Mary, is head mistress of the Newcastle high school for girls.

Gurney was essentially a teacher and an organiser of teaching, who combined great abilities as an administrator with a sound knowledge of scientific principles and marked powers of clear exposition. He acted as chaplain to the bishop of Newcastle, and warden and chaplain of the Newcastle diocesan house of mercy. For the first supplement of this Dictionary he wrote the memoir of Lord Armstrong. He also privately printed 'The Continuity of Life' (1876) and 'A Sermon on Words' (1882), and contributed notes on geology to the 'Transactions' of the Institute of Mining Engineers.

There is a bust of Gurney by Mr. C. Neuper in Armstrong College library, and an oil painting by A. H. Marsh in the hall.

[Mineralogical Mag., vol. xiv. Oct. 1904, No. 63, pp. 61–4; Newcastle Diocesan Gaz., Sept. 1904, p. 110; the Northerner, vol. v. No. 1, Nov. 1904, p. 2; Lady Clare Mag., vol iv. No. 1, Oct. term, 1904, p. 7; City of London School Mag., No. 169, March 1905, p. 3.] H. L.

GUTHRIE, WILLIAM (1835–1908), legal writer, born at Culhorn House, Stranraer, on 17 Aug. 1835, was son of George Guthrie of Appleby, chamberlain to the earl of Stair, by his wife Margaret, daughter of Robert McDonall. Educated at Stranraer Academy and at the Universities of Glasgow and Edinburgh, he passed to the Scottish bar in 1861, but never acquired much practice in the courts. Devoting himself to the study of law, he became editor of the 'Journal of Jurisprudence' (1867–74) and an official reporter of cases decided in the court of session (1871–4). In 1872 he was appointed registrar of friendly societies for Scotland, and in 1874 one of the sheriff-substitutes of Lanarkshire. In 1881 he received the honorary degree of LL.D. from Edinburgh University, and in 1891 represented the Faculty of Advocates at the International Law Association. In 1903 he was raised to the position of sheriff-principal at Glasgow, where he took a prominent and useful part in public affairs. He died in the house of his son, David Guthrie, C.A., Glasgow, on 31 Aug. 1908. He was buried in the Cathcart cemetery, Glasgow. He married Charlotte Carruthers, daughter of James Palmer of Edinburgh, by whom he had four sons and two daughters.

Guthrie was an industrious legal writer. His principal publications (all at Edinburgh) were: 1. The fourth edition of Robert Hunter's 'Treatise on the Law of Landlord and Tenant,' 1876. 2. 'Select Cases decided in the Sheriff Courts of Scotland,' 1878. 3. Translations of Savigny's 'Private International Law' (copiously annotated), 1869, 1880. 4. Editions of Erskine's 'Principles of the Law of Scotland,' 1870, 1874, and 1881. 5. Editions of Bell's 'Principles of the Law of Scotland,' 1872, 1885, 1889, and 1899. He also edited George Guthrie's 'Bank Monopoly the Cause of Commercial Crises' (1864 and 1866) and 'The Law of Trades Unions in England and Scotland under the Trade Union Act of 1871' (1873).

[The Times, Scotsman, and Glasgow Herald, 2 Sept. 1908.] G. W. T. O.

H

HADEN, Sir FRANCIS SEYMOUR (1818–1910), etcher and surgeon, the son of Charles Thomas Haden, M.D. (1786–1824), was born at 62 Sloane Street on 16 Sept. 1818. A biographical notice of his father by Dr. Thomas Alcock was prefixed to his work, 'Practical Observations on the Management and Diseases of Children,' published posthumously in 1827. His mother, Emma, was daughter of Samuel Harrison [q. v.], the vocalist, and was herself an excellent musician.

Haden received his general education at Derby School, Christ's Hospital, and University College, London, and continued his professional studies in the medical schools of the Sorbonne, Paris, and at Grenoble, where he acted as prosecteur in 1839, and, later, lecturer on surgical anatomy at the military hospital. In 1842 he became a member, and in 1857 a fellow, of the Royal College of Surgeons. From 1851 to 1867 he was honorary surgeon to the Department of Science and Art. He had settled in private practice at 62 Sloane Street in 1847, moving in 1878 to 38 Hertford Street, Mayfair. In addition to the labours of a large private practice, he found time for much public work in relation to surgical science, serving on the juries of the International Exhibitions of 1851 and 1862, and contributing in this capacity in 1862 an exhaustive report, remarkable for its championship of the operation of ovariotomy. He was consulting surgeon to the Chapel Royal, a vice-president of the obstetrical society of London, and one of the principal movers in the foundation of the Royal Hospital for Incurables in 1850. Throughout his life he maintained a vigorous campaign against cremation, as well as against certain abuses which had become more or less inseparable from the old-fashioned methods of burial, advocating a natural 'earth to earth' burial, which he effected by his invention of a *papier-mâché* coffin. He published on the subject several pamphlets, 'The Disposal of the Dead,' 'A Protest against Cremation,' 'Earth to Earth' (1875), and 'Cremation an Incentive to Crime' (2nd edit. 1892). Among his fellow practitioners he was noted for an instinctive power of diagnosis, due largely to a disciplined sense of vision. Much of his spare time in the evenings while a student in Paris was spent in the art schools, and quite apart from his purely artistic inclination he was always a staunch advocate of the use of drawing in training the hand and eye of the surgeon.

Haden sought relaxation from his professional work of surgeon, which he pursued till 1887, in the art and study of etching. His etched work, although technically that of an amateur, is the chief memorial of his life. Except for a few plates after Turner, and some family portraits after Wright of Derby, his work is entirely original. It includes a few portraits and figure studies, but is chiefly devoted to landscape. Here he was an artist of great truth and keenness of vision, and his best work shows a real sense of style, a true appreciation of the value of line, and a thorough command of an eminently virile technique. Most of his etchings, which number two hundred and fifty in all (Nos. 56 and 57 in Dr. Harrington's catalogue are in reality different states of a single plate), were done during the years of his greatest professional activity. He was not only assiduous in drawing and etching when in the country, but even on his professional rounds he was seldom without a plate in his pocket or in the carriage, ready to use the etching needle to record his impressions as another would a note-book.

Six of his plates, the records of an Italian journey, date as early as 1843–4, but there was an interval of fourteen years before he took up etching again in 1858. By that time Haden had come into close relations with James Abbott McNeill Whistler [q. v. Suppl. II], whose half-sister Dasha Delano Whistler, Haden married on 16 Oct. 1847. The etchings of Whistler and Haden bear traces of a mutual influence which is well exemplified in portraits by both (Harrington, No. 9; Wedmore, No. 25) of Lady Haden reading by lamplight. The two etchings were done on the same evening in 1858, the year in which Whistler published the thirteen prints of the 'French set.'

One half of Haden's etchings were produced in the decade succeeding 1859, sixty-eight being done in the two years 1864–5 alone. Then in 1877, when he was staying at Newton Manor with Sir John Charles Robinson, and afterwards travelling with Robinson in Spain, he completed his record number for one year, etching thirty-nine plates. Between 1859 and 1887 he was intermittently regular in his pastime, two years being the longest interval that he allowed to pass without etching a plate. After 1887 no plate is recorded until 1896, and in the next three years, 1896–8, he did eighteen plates, including a considerable number of mezzotints, a process which he chiefly practised at this late period of his activity. His last plate, a sketch of Woodcote Park, done on a pewter plate from the artist's bedroom window, is dated 1901.

Except for the twenty-five etchings which appeared in Paris under the title 'Études à l'eau-forte' in a portfolio with text by Philippe Burty (1865–6), nearly all Haden's etchings were put into commerce separately by the artist. Pieces of capital importance in the sale-room are the 'Thames Fishermen' (HARRINGTON, No. 11); 'By-road in Tipperary' (*ib.* No. 30); the larger 'Shere Mill Pond' (*ib.* No. 38); 'Sunset in Ireland' (*ib.* No. 51); 'La Belle Anglaise' (*ib.* No. 90); the 'River in Ireland' (*ib.* No. 91), and, most popular of all, the 'Breaking up of the Agamemnon' (*ib.* No. 145), a subject repeated in a later plate (*ib.* No. 229). But these *pièces capitales* are by no means the best of his work, which is as often found in the plates of less rarity and value. Special praise is due to the series of dry-points done in 1877 near Swanage, e.g. 'Windmill Hill,' No. 1 (H. No. 163); and for breadth and vigour of style in pure etching 'Sawley Abbey' (*ib.* No. 148); 'By Inveroran' (*ib.* No. 149); the 'Inn, Purfleet' (*ib.* No. 139); the 'Essex Farm' (*ib.* No. 155); and the 'Boat House' (*ib.* No. 156).

Haden's practical services to British etching include the foundation in 1880 of the Society (now the Royal Society) of Painter-Etchers, whose president he remained until his death. His public service was rewarded in 1894 by a knighthood, and his distinction recognised abroad by honorary membership of the Institut de France in 1905, the Académie des Beaux Arts, and the Société des Artistes Français. He was elected a member of the Athenæum in 1891 under Rule II. Among the medals awarded him at various times for etching were Grands Prix at the Expositions Universelles at Paris in 1889 and 1900. He exhibited etchings in the Royal Academy from 1860 to 1885, using the pseudonym of H. Dean in the exhibitions of 1860 to 1864. He also produced a large number of landscape drawings (now preserved in the collections of Mr. F. Seymour Haden, Dr. H. N. Harrington, the Victoria and Albert Museum, and elsewhere), some of the earliest being in water-colour, but the majority executed in black chalk, characterised by great breadth and vigour of handling; he received a medal for some exhibited at the International Exhibition, Chicago, 1893. Most of Haden's etchings were done direct on the copper without the aid of preliminary studies, but drawings which were used as studies for twenty-seven etchings are known.

The chief collections of his etchings are in the British Museum, the Avery collection in the New York Public Library, the Allbright Art Gallery, Buffalo, and the private collections of Dr. H. N. Harrington (who was one of Haden's executors) and Mr. Harris B. Dick of New York. Special exhibitions of his etchings were held by the Fine Art Society (1878–9), at the Corporation Art Gallery, Derby (1886), by the Royal Society of Painter-Etchers (1889), Wunderlich & Co., New York (1890), P. & D. Colnaghi (1901), F. Keppel & Co., New York (1901, 1903, 1904, 1906, 1908–9), Grolier Club, New York (1902), at the Salon d'Automne, Paris (1907), by Obach & Co., London (1907), T. & R. Annan & Co., Glasgow (1910), Ernest Brown & Phillips, Leicester Galleries (1911, Dr. H. N. Harrington's collection, with his valuable preface to the catalogue).

As a critic and writer on art, Haden will be chiefly remembered as a pioneer of the scientific criticism of Rembrandt's etchings (of which he had a considerable collection). He was largely responsible for the Rembrandt exhibition at the Burlington Fine Arts Club in 1879, and his introductory remarks to the catalogue gave the chief impetus to the criticism that has divided so much school work from the master's own etching. In addition to this introduction (published separately in 1879 as 'The Etched Work of Rembrandt'; French trans. 1880), his most valuable publications on art include 'About Etching' (1879; 3rd edit. 1881), 'The Relative Claims of Etching and Engraving to rank as Fine Arts and to be represented as such in the Royal Academy' (1883), 'The Art of the Painter-Etchers' (1890), 'The Royal Society of Painter-Etchers' (1891) (this and the preceding reprinted from the 'Nineteenth Century'), 'The Etched Work of Rembrandt, True and False' (a lecture, 1895), his 'Presidential Address to the Royal Society of Painter-Etchers, 1901' (1902).

On retiring from his London practice in 1887 Haden lived in the neighbourhood of Alresford, Hampshire. From 1888 he resided at Woodcote Manor, an old Elizabethan house, where he died on 1 June 1910. Lady Haden died in 1908. By her he had one daughter and three sons, his eldest son, Francis Seymour, C.M.G., being distinguished in the colonial service in South Africa.

There are two painted portraits of Haden, both done by Jacomb Hood in 1892, one being in the possession of his son, Mr. F. Seymour Haden, the other belonging to the Royal Society of Painter-Etchers. There is a portrait drawing by Alphonse Legros (done about 1883, and once in the possession of Messrs. Keppel of New York). His portrait was etched by himself (3 plates), L. Flameng (1875), L. Lacretelle (1878), W. Strang (1883), H. von Herkomer (2 plates, 1892), and Percy Thomas (1900); it was engraved by C. W. Sherborn (1880), and was mezzotinted by A. Legros (1881), G. Robinson (1887), and Sir Frank Short (1911, after the Painter-Etchers' portrait by Jacomb Hood).

[H. N. Harrington, Descriptive Catalogue, 1910 (including a complete series of reproductions of the etchings); The Times, 2 June 1910; information supplied by his son, Mr. Francis Seymour Haden.] A. M. H.

HAIG BROWN, WILLIAM (1823–1907), master of Charterhouse, born at Bromley by Bow, Middlesex, on 3 Dec. 1823, was third son of Thomas Brown of Edinburgh by his wife Amelia, daughter of John Haig, of the family of 'Haig of Bemersyde.' In his tenth year he received a presentation to Christ's Hospital, where he remained, first in the junior school at Hertford, and later on in London, until 1842. Throughout life he maintained a close connection with the Hospital, of which he became a 'donation governor' in 1864, and from that time took an active part in the work of the governing body, his experience being of especial service in connection with the removal of the school to Horsham in 1902. He was author, in 1899, both of 'The Christ's Hospital Carmen' in Latin, and of 'The School Song' in English, with an added version in Greek, French, and German. In 1842 he entered Pembroke College, Cambridge, graduating B.A. in 1846 as eighth junior optime in the mathematical and second in the first class in the classical tripos. Elected a fellow in October 1848 (M.A. 1849), and taking holy orders (deacon 1852 and priest 1853), he engaged in college work until 1857, when he was appointed headmaster of Kensington proprietary school.

In 1863, on the resignation of Dr. Richard Elwyn of the headmastership of Charterhouse, Haig Brown was appointed his successor on 12 Nov., in spite of the long established tradition that 'the Schoolmaster,' such was then his title, should have been educated at the school. On his first public appearance in Charterhouse at the Founder's Day dinner (12 Dec.), Haig Brown sat next to Thackeray, who died twelve days later. Next year Haig Brown proceeded LL.D. at Cambridge.

The position of Charterhouse was at this time critical. Placed in the heart of London, and with the new Smithfield Market at its doors, its existence as a boarding-school was rapidly becoming impossible, and the report of the Public Schools' Commission, issued early in 1864, definitely recommended its removal. Apart from the objections of politicians like A. S. Ayrton [q. v. Suppl. I], who denounced the removal as an injury 'to twenty, thirty, or even 50,000 families in the metropolis,' who had a claim to benefit by its endowments, a stubborn resistance was offered by the governors and their chairman, Archdeacon Hale, the master of the hospital, whose authority was then superior to that of 'the Schoolmaster.' Haig Brown thereupon issued a circular to old Carthusians, laying the whole case before them, the result being that they voted in the proportion of ten to one for removal, while he also won over Lord Derby, an influential governor, who became prime minister in June 1866, and he secured the support of Gladstone, who had recently been made a governor. In May 1866 the governors decided on the removal, and a private bill, giving the necessary powers, was introduced in the House of Lords, passed the House of Commons on 16 August, and became law four days later.

The new and admirable site at Godalming was accidentally discovered by Haig Brown, who, when on a visit to his wife's father at his rectory of Hambledon in the neighbourhood, heard that the 'Deanery Farm estate' was for sale, walked over the same day, and made up his mind. The governors, who had sold a large portion of their London estate to Merchant Taylors' school for a price far below its real value, refused, by what proved to be a very costly error, to purchase more than fifty-five acres, a large part of which was useless either for buildings or for playing-fields, and made provision for the accommodation of only about 180 boys. But the main point was carried; the first sod was turned on Founder's Day 1869, and on 18 June 1872 the new school was occupied by 117 old and 33 new boys. From that moment its progress was marvellous. 'The Schoolmaster' no longer occupied a position subordinate to the 'Master' of the hospital, but by the appointment of a 'new governing body of Charterhouse school' (distinct henceforth from the 'governors of Charterhouse'), in accordance with the Public Schools Act of 1868, he became a headmaster, with the very ample statutory powers which that act bestowed. Once Haig Brown held power he knew how to use it. Fearless himself, he inspired all around him with his own courage and confidence. Within a few years, in addition to the three houses originally built by the governors, eight others were erected by various masters entirely at their own risk, until by September 1876 the number of boys had grown to 500, the number to which it was then wisely limited, though it afterwards crept up to 560. In 1874 the school chapel was consecrated, and from then for more than thirty years frequent additions were made to the school in the shape of class-rooms, a hall, a museum, and new playing-fields. When Haig Brown retired in 1897 he had earned the title which he everywhere bore of 'our second Founder.'

In 1872 the future of Charterhouse was precarious; in 1897 it was secure; and the result was mainly due to the powerful, single-minded personality of the headmaster. He was not a great teacher, certainly no theorist about education, no lover of exact rules, and rather one who allowed both boys and masters the largest measure of independence. Like the other three great schoolmasters of the century, Arnold, Thring, and Kennedy, he neither sought nor received ecclesiastical preferment. Though bold to make changes, he was loyal to the past, so that he became the living embodiment of 'the spirit of the school,' both in its old and its new 'home.' A man 'of infinite jest,' though he could be very stern, he was always very human, so that 'Old Bill,' as he was called, was an object equally of awe and of affection.

On his retirement from the school in 1897 he was appointed master of Charterhouse (in London). He took an active part in the government of the hospital, and remained an energetic member of the governing body of the school. Among other distinctions bestowed on him were those of honorary canon of Winchester in 1891, and honorary fellow of Pembroke, his old college at Cambridge, in 1899. He was also made officier de l'Académie in 1882, and officier de l'Instruction publique in 1900. He died at the Master's lodge at the hospital on 11 Jan. 1907, and was buried in the chapel at Charterhouse School.

Haig Brown married, in 1857, Annie Marion, eldest daughter of the Rev. E. E. Rowsell. During the forty years of his school work she rendered him untiring assistance. By her he was father of five sons and seven daughters.

As a memorial of his work at the school a seated statue in bronze by Harry Bates, A.R.A. (who died before the work was wholly finished), was set up in front of the school chapel in 1899. His portrait by Frank Holl (etched by Hubert von Herkomer) was placed in the great hall in 1886.

Haig Brown's published works are the 'Sertum Carthusianum' (1870); 'Charterhouse Past and Present' (Godalming, 1879); and 'Carthusian Memories and other Verses of Leisure' (with portrait, 1905), a collection of various prologues, epilogues, epigrams, and other fugitive pieces. Three of his hymns, 'O God, whose Wisdom made the Sky,' 'O God, Thy Mercy's Fountains,' and 'Auctor omnium bonorum,' have a permanent place in the service for Founder's Day, and are worthy of any collection.

[William Haig Brown of Charterhouse, written by some of his pupils, edited by his son, H. E. Haig Brown, 1908; personal knowledge.] T. E. P.

HAIGH, ARTHUR ELAM (1855–1905), classical scholar, born at Leeds on 27 Feb. 1855, was third son, in a family of three sons and two daughters, of Joseph Haigh, chemist, by his wife Lydia, daughter of Charles James Duncan. He was educated at Leeds grammar school, where he gained nearly every school distinction. On 22 Oct. 1874 he matriculated from Corpus Christi College, Oxford, with a scholarship, and began his lifelong career of study and teaching at the university. As an undergraduate he was versatile and successful. He took a first class in classical moderations in 1875 and in literæ humaniores in 1878; he won the two Gaisford prizes for Greek verse (1876) and Greek prose (1877), the Craven scholarship (1879), and the Stanhope prize for an essay on the 'Political Theories of

Dante' (1878). He made pungent and witty speeches at the Union on the liberal side, and he rowed in the Corpus eight when it was near the head of the river. On graduating B.A. in 1878 (M.A. 1881) he was elected to a fellowship at Hertford, which he held till 1886. He became classical lecturer at Corpus also in 1878, and for the next twenty-seven years was constantly engaged in teaching at that and other colleges. In 1901 he was admitted fellow of Corpus, and was appointed senior tutor the following year. He was classical moderator in 1888–9, and again in 1897–8.

Haigh collaborated with T. L. Papillon in an edition of Virgil with a very careful text (1892); and he published 'The Attic Theatre' (1889) and 'The Tragic Drama of the Greeks' (1896). These works, which gave Haigh a general reputation, exhibit sound scholarship, independent judgment, the faculty of lucid exposition, and a wide range of classical and miscellaneous reading.

Haigh laid more stress than most Oxford tutors of his time on verbal accuracy and the need for close textual study. But the limitations of his method were consistent with broad and sympathetic literary interests. He studied English literature with the same fastidious diligence which he bestowed upon the classics, and was a cultivated and extremely well-informed critic of the English poets, and of some of the greater writers of Germany, France, and Italy.

Haigh took little part in university business or society, living a tranquil family life and cherishing a few intimate friendships. He died somewhat suddenly at his house in Norham Gardens, Oxford, on 20 Dec. 1905, and was buried in Holywell churchyard.

In Aug. 1886 he married Matilda Forth, daughter of Jeremiah Giles Pilcher, J.P., D.L. She predeceased him in July 1904, leaving four children.

[Personal knowledge; Foster's Alumni Oxonienses; article by A. G. (i.e. A. D. Godley, Fellow of Magdalen College, Oxford) in the Oxford Magazine, 24 Jan. 1906.] S. J. L.

HAINES, Sir FREDERICK PAUL (1819–1909), field-marshal, born on 10 Aug. 1819, at the Parsonage Farm, Kirdford, Sussex, was youngest child in the family of three sons and a daughter of Gregory Haines, C.B. (1778–1853), who was in Wellington's commissariat throughout the Peninsular war and at Waterloo, and ended his career as commissary-general in Ireland, by his wife Harriet, daughter of John Eldridge of Kirdford. The father was descended from prosperous Sussex yeomen, of whom the most remarkable was Richard Haines (1633–1685), author, among other works, of 'The Prevention of Poverty' (1674) and 'A Method of Government for Public Working Almshouses' (1679). Educated at Midhurst school and in Brussels and Dresden, Frederick, following the example of his two elder brothers, entered the army, being gazetted ensign in the 4th (the King's Own) regiment on 21 June 1839. He joined his regiment at Bangalore, where his eldest brother, Gregory, had just married a daughter of Sir Hugh (afterwards the first viscount) Gough [q. v.], who was in command of the Mysore division. This family connection led in 1844 to the appointment of Haines, who had been promoted lieutenant in 1840, as A.D.C. to Gough, then commander-in-chief in the East Indies. In the first Sikh war he was acting military secretary to the commander-in-chief, and fought at Moodkee and at Ferozeshah, where he was dangerously wounded. His services were rewarded by a captaincy, without payment, in the 10th foot (May 1846), whence he exchanged, in March 1847, into the 21st foot (the Scots fusiliers). From 23 May 1846 to 7 May 1849 he was military secretary to Lord Gough, and was present at the skirmish at Ramnuggur, the operations for the crossing of the Chenab, and the battles of Chillianwalla and Gujerat. For the services rendered in this capacity he was given a brevet majority in June 1849 and a brevet lieut.-colonelcy in August 1850.

In 1854 Haines accompanied the 21st foot to the Crimea, and was present at the actions of the Alma and Balaclava. His rank as a brevet lieut.-colonel placed him at the battle of Inkerman (5 Nov. 1854) in command of a small body of troops. The detachment held for six hours the barrier on the post road which guarded the approach to the second division camp, and the exploit in Kinglake's opinion 'augments the glory of the day as far as concerns the English, and gives much more simplicity, and consequently more grandeur, to the battle than would otherwise belong to it.' Haines was also responsible for sending troops to silence the Russian artillery on Shell Hill, and thus helped to bring the battle to its final crisis. After the battle of Inkerman he succeeded to a majority in the 21st foot, and he was promoted to a brevet colonelcy (28 Nov. 1854) in recognition of his conduct. In April 1855 he was gazetted lieut.-colonel, unattached, and from June 1855 to January 1856 he was assistant adjutant-general at Aldershot, where the camp was in course of construction. From June 1856 to June 1860 he was military secretary to the commander-in-chief at Madras, Sir Patrick Grant [q. v. Suppl. I], and accompanied him to Calcutta during the interval between the death of General Anson and the arrival of Sir Colin Campbell in the summer of 1857. In Oct. 1859 he was gazetted lieut.-colonel of the 8th foot, which he commanded from Sept. 1860 to Aug. 1861. After brief periods of service as an acting brigadier-general at Aldershot, as deputy adjutant-general at headquarters in Ireland, and as a brigadier-general in Ireland, he was promoted major-general (Nov. 1864) and held the command of the Mysore division from March 1865 to March 1870. On his return from India he became quartermaster-general at headquarters from Nov. 1870 to March 1871, and from May 1871 to Dec. 1875 was commander-in-chief at Madras, becoming a K.C.B. in 1871 and a lieutenant-general in 1873.

From April 1876 to April 1881 Haines was commander-in-chief in India. From the beginning of his term of office the attention of the Indian government was occupied by difficulties with Russia and with Afghanistan. When an Anglo-Russian war seemed imminent, in 1876, he strongly opposed a proposal of the viceroy, Lord Lytton [q.v.], for an invasion of central Asia by a small force (*Life*, pp. 216–24). He did not oppose Lytton's 'forward policy,' and he regarded the Afghan war as inevitable; but he differed entirely from the viceroy's estimate of the forces required for the purpose, and he disapproved of such measures as Cavagnari's suggestion of a surprise attack on Ali Musjid. He believed that the Kuram valley, to the strategic value of which Lytton and his confidential adviser, Sir George Colley [q. v.], attached great importance, was a *cul-de-sac* and useless as a military route to Kabul. The reinforcements on which Haines insisted at the outset of the campaign of 1878–9 proved to be required, and for his general supervision of the war he received the thanks of both houses of parliament and was given the grand cross of the Star of India in July 1879. He was made G.C.B. in 1877, and on the institution of the Order of the Indian Empire in 1878 he became, *ex officio*, C.I.E.

In the Afghan campaign of 1879–80 Haines had again serious differences with Lord Lytton about the Kuram route, the number of troops required, and the relation of the commander-in-chief to commanders in the field. His relations with Lytton's successsor, Lord Ripon [q. v. Suppl. II], were more cordial, but his warnings of the danger of an attack on Kandahar by Ayub Khan were disregarded by the viceroy. He acquiesced unwillingly in General Burrows' advance on the Helmund river, and ordered Bombay troops to move up in support. After the defeat of Burrows at Maiwand (27 July 1880) Haines suggested the relief of Kandahar by a force from Kabul commanded by General Roberts. For his services in the conduct of operations in the war of 1879–80 Haines received again the thanks of both houses of parliament, and was offered a baronetcy, which he declined. The close of his term of command was occupied with discussions about the recommendations of the Indian Army Commission of 1879, from which he dissented, urging the continuance of separate presidential armies.

From 1881 until his death Haines lived in London. He represented the British army at the Russian manœuvres of 1882 and at the German manœuvres of 1884. He had become a general in 1877 and was raised to the rank of field-marshal in 1890. He was colonel of the royal Munster fusiliers from 1874 to 1890, when he became colonel of his old regiment, the royal Scots fusiliers. In his closing years he was much interested in foreign policy, especially in central Asian questions, in art, the drama, and in cricket. He died in London on 11 June 1909, and was buried in Brompton cemetery.

Haines married in 1856 Charlotte (*d.* 1881), daughter of Col. E. Miller of the Madras army, and had three sons. A portrait by the Hon. John Collier (1891) is at the United Service Club, Pall Mall, London. A caricature by J. T. C. appeared in 'Vanity Fair' in 1876.

[Memoir of Richard Haines, 1633–85, by Charles Reginald Haines, privately printed, 1899; Army Lists; A. W. Kinglake, Invasion of the Crimea, vol. vi. 1877; G. B. Malleson, Ambushes and Surprises, 1885; Report and Evidence of the Indian Army Commission of 1879; R. S. Rait, Life of Hugh, First Viscount Gough, 1903, and Life of Sir Frederick Haines, 1911; Lady Betty Balfour's Lord Lytton's Indian Administration, 1899; H. B. Hanna, Second Afghan War, 3 vols. 1899–1910; The Times, 14 June 1909.] R. S. R.

HALIBURTON, ARTHUR LAWRENCE, first Baron Haliburton (1832–1907), civil servant, third son of Thomas Chandler Haliburton [q. v.] and Louisa, daughter of Capt. Lawrence Neville, was born at Windsor, Nova Scotia, on 26 Dec. 1832. He was educated at King's College in that town, the oldest university in the dominion, from which he received in 1899 an honorary D.C.L. degree. He was called to the Nova Scotian bar in 1855, but a few months later he received a commission in the commissariat department of the British army, and during the later stages of the Crimean war he served as a civil commissary at the base in Turkey. After the Peace of Paris he was posted to the forces in Canada. In November 1859 he was appointed deputy assistant commissary general, and transferred to the London headquarters; in 1869 he was made assistant director of supplies and transports, resigning his commission in the army and formally entering the civil service. In this capacity he consolidated and greatly simplified the chaotic arrangements which regulated the transport and travelling allowances of the army at home. In 1872 he was appointed deputy accountant general in the military department of the government of India, which post he held till 1875; on returning to the war office he acted as chairman of a committee which brought about a much-needed decentralisation and effected substantial economies in that office. In 1878 he was appointed director of supplies and transport, and it devolved upon him to supervise the victualling of the army during eight campaigns, which included the Nile expedition of 1884–5. On the testimony of Lord Wolseley no army that he had been associated with was so well fed as the British troops were on that occasion, in circumstances of unprecedented difficulty. In recognition of his services, Haliburton was made C.B. in 1880 and K.C.B. in 1885. On the abolition of the office of civilian director of supplies and transports in 1887 he was placed temporarily on the retired list; but after serving on several important public inquiries at home and abroad he became in May 1891 assistant under-secretary for war, and in 1895 permanent under-secretary, which office he held till his retirement by operation of the age-limit in 1897. He was made G.C.B. in that year, and in 1898 was raised to the peerage under the title of Baron Haliburton of Windsor in the province of Nova Scotia and dominion of Canada.

In 1891 he served as representative of the war office on the committee, of which Lord Wantage [q. v. Suppl. II] was the head, to investigate the terms and conditions of service in the army. His dissentient report contained a strong defence of the principle of the existing short service system, and effectually neutralised the recommendations in the direction of modifying it upon which the rest of the committee stood agreed. In December 1897, after his retirement from the war office, he conducted a vigorous newspaper campaign in 'The Times' against Arnold-Forster [q. v. Suppl. II] and others on the same topic of 'Short versus Long Service.' His letters were subsequently reprinted in pamphlet form; as were also another series contributed to the same newspaper in 1901 on 'Army Administration in Three Centuries.' It is no exaggeration to say that he was the first to explain to the public generally, and to not a few among military critics, the real nature of Lord Cardwell's reforms and of the army reserve created by them. During his later years he became a convert to the principle of universal service, and a few weeks before his death he formulated in the pages of the 'Nineteenth Century' a scheme for universal military training. He died at Bournemouth on 21 April 1907, and was buried at Brompton cemetery. Haliburton represented the finest type of civil servant, uniting indefatigable industry with great lucidity of expression and breadth of view. He worked, moreover, in complete harmony with the military officials in the war office, and his opinion was held in high regard by those soldiers on the active list who were best versed in the problems of military administration. On 3 Nov. 1877 he married Marian Emily, daughter of Leo Schuster and widow of Sir William Dickason Clay, second baronet; she survived him without issue.

[Lord Haliburton, a Memoir of his Public Services, by J. B. Atlay, 1909; private information.] J. B. A.

HALL, CHRISTOPHER NEWMAN (1816–1902), congregationalist divine, born at Maidstone on 22 May 1816, was son of John Vine Hall [q. v.], proprietor of the 'Maidstone Journal,' by Mary, daughter of James Teverill of Worcester. Educated at Rochester and at Totteridge, he entered his father's printing house at fourteen, working successively as compositor, reader, and reporter. In 1837 he went to Highbury College, in training for the congregational ministry, graduated B.A. at London University in 1841, and in 1842 was ordained pastor of Albion Church, Hull. There he gathered a large congregation, was in demand as a preacher, and in 1834 issued his first publication, a sermon on 'Christian Union.' His tract 'Come to Jesus,' issued in 1848, made his name widely known. Over 4,000,000 copies in some forty languages or dialects were circulated during the author's life.

In 1854 Hall became minister of Surrey Chapel, Blackfriars, the scene of Rowland Hill's labours. His success was pronounced. As a mental discipline, he read for the degree of LL.B. at London University, which with a law scholarship he obtained in 1856. During the American civil war he was conspicuous for his advocacy of the northern cause, and in 1866 he was appointed chairman of the Congregational Union. He was warmly welcomed on visiting Canada and the United States in 1867, was made D.D. of Amhurst University, and afterwards declined the offer of a pastorate in Chicago. During the controversy attending the education act of 1870 Hall sought to effect a reconciliation between W. E. Forster, the minister in charge of the measure, and nonconformist members of the Birmingham League, who distrusted Forster's policy. Hall was also the means of bringing Gladstone, with whom he became well acquainted, into conference with representative nonconformists. Throughout his career he sought to promote closer relations between church and dissent. In 1876 the congregation of Surrey Chapel moved to Christ Church, Westminster Bridge Road, built, mainly through Hall's exertions, at a cost of 64,000*l*. In 1892 he resigned his pastorate, and in the same year received the D.D. degree from Edinburgh University. He died in London on 18 Feb. 1902, and was buried at Abney Park cemetery.

Hall was an accomplished preacher, a man of wide sympathies, artistic feeling and evangelical fervour. For many years his work was done amid circumstances of great trial. He married, on 14 April 1846, Charlotte, daughter of Dr. Gordon of Hull. They separated in 1870. Litigation followed. Hall filed and withdrew a petition for divorce in 1873, but was successful in a second suit, which he initiated in 1879, when a counter-charge of adultery against him was withdrawn. A decree nisi was made absolute on 17 Feb. 1880. On 29 March 1880 he married Harriet Mary Margaret, eldest daughter of Edward Knipe, of Water Newton, Huntingdonshire, who survived him. There were no children of either marriage. Busts in terra cotta and bronze by Edward Onslow Ford [q. v. Suppl. II] were exhibited at the Royal Academy in 1878 and 1885 respectively.

Hall, in addition to many tracts, minor works, and several volumes of verse, containing seven hymns in 'common use' (JULIAN'S *Dictionary of Hymnology*), published: 1. 'The Author of "The Sinner's Friend,"' 1860, a brief memoir of his father, whose autobiography he edited in 1865. 2. 'Plain Truths Plainly Put,' 1861. 3. 'Sermons,' Boston and New York, 1868. 4. 'Homeward Bound and other Sermons,' 1869. 5. 'From Liverpool to St. Louis,' 1870. 6. 'Prayer: its Reasonableness and Efficacy,' 1875. 7. 'The Lord's Prayer: a Practical Meditation,' 1883. 8. 'Gethsemane: or Leaves of Healing from the Garden of Grief,' 1891. 9. 'Atonement, the Fundamental Fact of Christianity,' 1893. 10. 'Newman Hall: an Autobiography,' 1898.

[Hall's Autobiography, 1898; The Times, 9 Aug. 1879, 18 Feb. 1880, 19 Feb. 1902; T. W. Reid's Life of W. E. Forster, 1888, i. 539–42.] A. R. B.

HALL, FITZEDWARD (1825–1901), philologist, born at Troy, New York, on 21 March 1825, was eldest in the family of five sons and one daughter of Daniel Hall, lawyer, by his wife Anginetta Fitch. A younger brother, Benjamin Homer Hall, was a barrister and was city chamberlain of New York (1874–7 and 1884–5). After education at his native town, at Walpole, New Hampshire, and Poughkeepsie, Hall took the civil engineer's degree at Troy Rensselaer polytechnic in 1842. He early showed a passion for English words and phrases, which grew with his maturer years. He entered Harvard in 1846, but before his 'commencement' he was sent early in 1846 to Calcutta in pursuit of a runaway brother. Wrecked off the Ganges in September, and compelled for the moment to stay in India, Hall took lessons in Hindustani and Sanskrit, and finally resolved to remain in order to master the languages. After three years in Calcutta (where he studied Hindustani, Persian, Bengalee, and Sanskrit) and five months at Ghazipur, Hall removed to Benares in January 1850. At the government college there Hall was appointed tutor in Feb. 1850 and professor of Sanskrit and English in 1853. In July 1855 he became inspector of public instruction for Ajmere-Merwárá at Rajputana, and in Dec. 1856 for the central provinces at Saugor. There he served as a rifleman for nine months during the Sepoy mutiny. He then spent eighteen months in England, France, and America, and revisiting England in 1860 received the hon. degree of D.C.L. from Oxford University. He finally left India in 1862, and settled in London as professor of Sanskrit, Hindustani, and Indian jurisprudence in King's College, and librarian at the India office. From 1864 till his death he was examiner in Hindustani and Hindî for the civil service commissioners; he was also examiner in Sanskrit in 1880, and in English in 1887.

From his early years in India, Hall devoted himself with exceptional zeal and industry to the study of both Indian and English literature and philology. While at Benares he followed the example of the principal of the college, James Robert Ballantyne [q. v.], in discovering many unknown Sanskrit manuscripts, and in editing and translating several Sanskrit and Hindî works. He was the first American to edit a Sanskrit text, viz. 'The Âtmabodha, with its commentary, and the Tattvabodha,' two Vedanta treatises (Mirzapur, 1852). Subsequently he edited and published at Calcutta the 'Sankhyapravachana' (1856) and the 'Sankhyasâra' (1862), fourteenth- and sixteenth-century works respectively on the Sankhya materialist system of philosophy; the 'Sûryasiddhanta' (1859), the 'Vâsavadattâ' (1859), and the 'Daśarûpa, with its commentary and four chapters of Bharata's Nâṭyaśâstra' (1865). He also prepared in 1859 a valuable classified 'Index to the Bibliography of Indian Philosophical Systems.' Of works in Hindî, Hall published 'The Tarkasangraha, translated into Hindî from the Sanskrit and English' (Allahabad, 1850); 'The Râjanîti,' a collection of Hindu Apologues (Allahabad, 1854); and 'The Siddhântasangraha' (Agra, 1855). He also translated into Hindî Ballantyne's 'Synopsis of Science' (Agra, 1855) and edited his Hindî Grammar (London, 1868), and a Hindî Reader (Hertford, 1870). Other of Hall's works on India were 'Lectures on the Nyâya Philosophy,' in both Sanskrit and English (Benares, 1862); and 'A Rational Refutation of the Hindu Philosophical Systems, translated from the Hindî and Sanskrit' (Calcutta, 1862). He subsequently re-edited and annotated (Sir) Horace Hayman Wilson's translations of the 'Rigvedasaṁhitâ' (1866) and of the 'Vishnupurâna' (vols. 1–5 pt. 1, 1864–70; vol. 5 pt. 2 (index), 1877).

While librarian at the India office Hall directed much of his attention to English literature. He edited some books (1864–9) for the Early English Text Society, of which he was an original member of committee. In 1869 he retired from the India office and removed to The Hill House, Marlesford, Suffolk. There he divided his time between his edition of the 'Vishnupurâna' and research in English philology. 'Recent Exemplifications of False Philology' (New York, 1872) contained a pungent criticism of Richard Grant White's 'Words and their Uses' (New York, 1870). 'Modern English' (1873) and 'On English Adjectives in -able' (1877) contained much that was new and valuable. From 1878, when Dr. (afterwards Sir) James A. H. Murray became editor of the 'New English Dictionary,' Hall rendered the undertaking material aid. 'As a voluntary and gratituous service to the history of the English language, [he] devoted four hours daily to a critical examination of the proof sheets, and the filling up of deficiencies, whether in the vocabulary or the quotations' (Preface to *New Eng. Dict.*, Oxford, 1888). During the same period Hall contributed down to M some 2200 words and expressions in the Suffolk dialect, which he had heard and noted, to Prof. Wright's 'Dialect Dictionary.' He left at his death hundreds of long lists of quotations for Sir James Murray's use.

Hall died at his home at Marlesford, Suffolk, on 1 Feb. 1901. His ashes after cremation were interred in Oakwood cemetery, Troy, New York. He married at Delhi in 1854 Amelia Warde (*d.* 1910), daughter of Lieut.-colonel Arthur Shuldham of the East India Company's service. Of five children of the marriage, three died young; a son and daughter survived him. There is a brass tablet to Hall's memory in Marlesford church. He received in 1895 the hon. degree of LL.D. from Harvard, to which during his lifetime he gave some thousand Oriental manuscripts, many of them unique.

[New York Nation, 14 Feb. 1901 (memoir by Wendell Phillips Garrison); Modern Language Notes, Brooklyn, March 1901; Bookman, New York, xiii. 516, July 1901 (with portrait taken in 1893); Appleton's Cycl. of American Biogr. 1887; The Times, 15 Feb. 1901; information from Sir J. A. H. Murray, and from son, Mr. Richard D. Hall.]

W. O. B.

HALL, Sir JOHN (1824–1907), premier of New Zealand, born at Hull on 18 Dec. 1824, was third son of George Hall, shipowner, of Hull and of Elloughton, Yorkshire. In his eleventh year he went abroad to finish his education in Germany, Switzerland, and Paris. He spent the three years 1840–3 in a merchant's office at Hull. In 1843 he entered the secretary's department of the London General Post Office, and soon became private secretary to the secretary of the post office. He served as a volunteer in the hon. artillery company and as a special constable during the Chartist riots of 1848.

In 1852 he emigrated to Lyttelton, New Zealand, bought a neighbouring sheep run, and remained a prominent citizen of the province of Canterbury for the rest of his life. In 1853 the provincial councils were called into being by Sir George Grey [q. v. Suppl. I], and Hall became the member for Christchurch district of the Canterbury provincial council, on which he sat, except during his occasional absences from the colony, until the councils were abolished in 1876 by act of the central legislature. From 7 Feb. to May 1855 he was provincial secretary, and from May 1855 to 1859 was a member of the provincial executive. After a visit to England he became in 1862 member for the Mount Cook district; in 1864 he was re-elected to the provincial executive and was until 1869 secretary for public works.

Meanwhile he had been made resident magistrate for Lyttelton, sheriff, and commissioner of police on 27 Nov. 1856; a resident magistrate for the colony on 27 April 1857; and a justice of the peace in May 1857. From December 1858 to July 1863 he was a resident magistrate for Christchurch, and from January 1862 to 15 June 1863 first mayor of Christchurch. He was also the first chairman of Selwyn county council, and chairman (in 1869) of the Westland provincial council. In June 1863 he was commissioner of the Canterbury waste lands board. As a provincial politician he is best known as the originator of the road board system in Canterbury, and for his sheep ordinance.

In 1885 elections were held for the first responsible parliament that assembled in New Zealand, and Hall was one of the Christchurch members for the house of representatives until 1859. On 20 May 1856 he became colonial secretary under Sir William Fox [q. v. Suppl. I], but the ministry lasted only for a fortnight; during that period Hall spoke against voting by ballot. On his return from England in 1862 he was called to the legislative council (4 July). Resigning in February 1866, he was at once re-elected to the lower house by the Heathcote division as a supporter of Sir Frederick Aloysius Weld [q. v.] and an opponent of provincialism, holding the seat till 1872. He was a member of the executive council under the Stafford ministry (24 Aug. 1866–28 June 1869), postmaster-general (24 Aug. 1866–5 Feb. 1869), and electric telegraph commissioner (12 Oct. 1866–5 Feb. 1869). In 1867 he attended the intercolonial postal conference in Melbourne. During 1868 he acted as colonial treasurer during Sir William Fitzherbert's absence and drew up an able financial statement.

In 1872 he was called to the legislative council. He was a member of the executive council 20 July–10 November 1872, and colonial secretary in the Waterhouse cabinet from 11 Oct. 1872 till 3 March 1873. Ill-health then drove him to England till 1875. He became a member of the executive council under (Sir) Harry Atkinson [q. v. Suppl. I], without a portfolio, on 1 Sept. 1876. On 13 Sept. the government resigned, and he was not reappointed in the reconstituted ministry on account of his health.

As a prominent Anglican he strongly opposed the education act of 1877, which established secular education. Withdrawing from the upper house, he was chosen member for Selwyn in the general election of 1879. For some months he was leader of the opposition, and early in October he carried a hostile motion against Sir George Grey by a small majority. On the 8th he formed a ministry. He remained premier, supported by Sir Frederick Whitaker [q. v.] and Sir Harry Atkinson, until 21 April 1882; ill-health then compelled his retirement, but he continued to advise his colleagues. In the same year he visited England and was made a K.C.M.G. Premier during a period of great commercial depression, Hall was continually faced by a need for retrenchment and fresh taxation. The chief work of his government was the repeal of Sir George Grey's land-tax, the suppression of a Maori demonstration headed by the prophet Te Whiti, and the passing of the triennial parliaments bill and the universal suffrage bill, both measures which had been supported by the party he defeated.

Hall again sat in the house of representatives for Selwyn from 1883 until 1894, when he retired from political life. In 1890 he represented New Zealand at Melbourne, at the first conference on Australasian federation. In 1893 he introduced into the ministry's electoral bill an amendment conferring the vote upon women, a reform which he had always actively supported. It was passed into law on the eve of the general election. In 1905 he was chosen master of the Leathersellers' Company in London, but was unable to leave New Zealand to take the office. In 1906, the year of the New Zealand exhibition, he became first mayor of Greater Christchurch. On 25 Oct. he fell ill, and on 25 June 1907 he died at Park Terrace, Christchurch, and was buried in the family vault in Hororata cemetery.

He married in 1861 Rose Anne (*d.* 1900), daughter of William Dryden, of Hull. By her he had issue three sons and one daughter.

[Mennell's Dict. of Australasian Biog.; Gisborne's New Zealand Rulers and Statesmen, 1897 (with portrait); Rusden's Hist. of New Zealand; Reeves' The Long White Cloud; speeches and obituary notices in New Zealand Times, Auckland Star, Canterbury Times, 3 July 1907 (portrait).] A. B. W.

HALLÉ [formerly NORMAN-NERUDA], WILMA MARIA FRANCISCA, LADY HALLÉ (1839–1911), violinist, was third child and second daughter of Josef Neruda (1807–75), organist of the cathedral of Brünn, Moravia, where she was born on 21 March 1839. Almost in infancy Wilma began to play the violin. Her teacher was Leopold Jansa. At the age of seven she played one of Bach's sonatas at Vienna, and her fine rendering excited general astonishment. A tour through North Germany with her family followed. On 30 April 1849 she appeared at the Princess's Theatre, London, and on 11 June played a concerto of De Bériot at the Philharmonic concerts. Other tours through Europe spread her fame. In 1864 she made most successful appearances at Paris, and there she married in the same year Ludwig Norman, a Swedish musician, taking the surname of Norman-Neruda. She returned to London in 1869, appeared at the Philharmonic concerts, and remained till Christmas, leading the quartets at the Monday popular concerts. The favour accorded her brought her back to London every winter. She was specially distinguished as a quartet-leader. In 1876 Prince Alfred, afterwards duke of Saxe-Coburg and Gotha, joined with Earls Dudley and Hardwicke in presenting her with the celebrated Stradivarius violin that had belonged to Ernst. In 1885 she was left a widow. On 26 July 1888 she married her second husband, Sir Charles Hallé [q. v. Suppl. I], with whom she had long been professionally associated. After his death in 1895 King Edward VII, then Prince of Wales, became president of an influential committee which was formed to raise a fund for her benefit. As a result, the title-deeds of a palace at Asolo were presented to Lady Hallé. After the death on 11 Sept. 1898 of her only son (by her first husband) in a mountaineering accident in the Dolomites, Lady Hallé settled at Berlin as a teacher, re-visiting England every year and being formally appointed in 1901 violinist to Queen Alexandra. On 25 Jan. 1908 she played at the concert in London in memory of Joachim, who was one of her frequent associates. She died at Berlin from inflammation of the lungs on 15 April 1911. Effective technique, superb bowing, an indefinable touch of genius in her interpretations gave her a unique place among violinists; her tone scarcely yielded in fulness to the greatest male performers.

[The Times, 17 April 1911; Strad, May 1911; Musical Standard, 29 March 1902 (portrait); Grove's Dict. of Music, arts. Neruda, Stradivari, and Violin, and the Appendix; A. Ehrlich, Berühmter Geiger (Engl. edit. with portrait); personal reminiscences from 1872.] H. D.

HALLIDAY, SIR FREDERICK JAMES (1806–1901), first lieutenant-governor of Bengal, son of Thomas Halliday of Ewell, Surrey, was born there on Christmas Day 1806. A younger brother, General John Gustavus (*b.* 1822), long served on the Mysore commission. Halliday entered Rugby in 1814, and completed his education at the East India College, Haileybury, 1823–4. He was appointed to the Bengal civil service and arrived in Calcutta on 8 June 1825. Halliday first served as junior assistant to the company's agent in the Saugor division, and assistant registrar of the *Sadar* (supreme) court. He was joint magistrate and deputy collector in Bundelkhund and afterwards in Noakhali and Balu (1831–5); from Feb. 1835 magistrate and collector at Dacca, and next at Cuttack; and from April 1836 secretary to the board of revenue. In May 1838 he was appointed judicial and revenue secretary in Bengal, and, in addition, from March 1840 to 1843 he was junior secretary to the government of India both in the same and in the legislative departments. In 1849 he was made secretary in the home department by Lord Dalhousie, who held a high opinion of him and was distressed when, in July 1852, after twenty-seven years' uninterrupted service,

Halliday was compelled by ill-health to take long leave home. He was on sixteen occasions examined by the Parliamentary committees on the renewal of the East India Company's charter, granted in 1853.

Returning to India, he took his seat on the governor-general's council on 5 Oct. 1853, on the nomination of the court of directors. Bengal, hitherto directly administered by the governor-general, was constituted on 1 May 1854 a lieutenant-governorship, and Dalhousie appointed Halliday as 'the fittest man in the service . . . to hold this great and important office' of ruler of a territory comprising 253,000 square miles, with a population inadequately estimated at forty millions. Sir John Kaye credited him with natural ability, administrative sagacity, and a sufficiency in council which had won him general confidence (*Hist. of Sepoy War*, 9th edit. p. 58). Halliday sought with vigour to reform the administration of Bengal, the most backward of the great provinces of India (Sir JOHN STRACHEY'S *India*, chap. xxii.). In a valuable minute (30 April 1856) he submitted a scheme for the complete reorganisation of the police, and carried much of it into effect. Road communications were improved and extended, and Halliday supervised the up-country administration by prolonged and difficult tours in all directions. On several matters he came into conflict with members of the government of India, and in a private letter (6 Jan. 1856) Dalhousie was constrained to confess that 'he has so managed that I believe he has not in Bengal a single influential friend but myself' (DALHOUSIE'S *Private Letters*, 1901). In hearty sympathy with the policy of educational advance laid down in the despatch of Sir Charles Wood, first Viscount Halifax [q. v.], Halliday appointed a director of public instruction for Bengal in Jan. 1855, placed the presidency college on an improved footing, and in 1856 initiated the Calcutta University, the act of incorporation being passed in the following January.

A rebellion in June 1855 of the wild Santal tribes, who were suffering from the extortions of money-lending mahajans, was, in spite of preliminary protests from the supreme government, suppressed by martial law (Nov.–Dec.). The Santal country was placed under special officers and the five districts named the Santal Parganas. Halliday was also faced by agrarian difficulties. By the Act of 1859 —known as the 'Magna Charta of the ryots'—he restricted the landlord's powers of enhancement in specified cases, gave occupancy rights to tenants of twelve years standing, and improved the law relating to sales of land for revenue arrears.

Bengal was not the chief centre of the Sepoy mutiny, but Halliday was closely associated with its suppression. His influence over the governor-general Canning was great, and to facilitate constant communication he removed from his official residence, Belvedere, to rooms overlooking Government House, Calcutta. There was no member of the government whom Canning 'so frequently consulted or whose opinions he so much respected' (KAYE). It was under his strong persuasion that Canning allowed British troops to replace the Sepoy guard at Government House in August (Sir H. S. CUNNINGHAM'S *Earl Canning*, 1891, p. 126). In his final minute (2 July 1859) regarding the services of civil officers, Canning credited Halliday—the 'right hand of the government of India'—with effectually checking the spread of rebellion in Bengal. Halliday's 'Minute on the Bengal Mutinies' (30 Sept. 1858) gives full particulars of his activities (see BUCKLAND'S *Bengal under the Lieutenant-Governors*). He was included on 18 Mar. 1858 in the thanks which had been voted by both Houses of Parliament to the governor-general and others. He was also thanked by the East India Company (10 and 17 Feb. 1858), and the court of directors acknowledged his services in detail in a despatch dated 4 Aug. 1858. Retiring from the lieutenant-governorship on 1 May 1859, he was created (civil) K.C.B. a year later.

Halliday was inevitably exposed to the censure which Canning's clemency in restraining the spirit of revenge provoked. Halliday stoutly defended in an official minute his own educational policy, to which Sir George Russell Clerk [q. v. Suppl. I] and others attributed the revolt. But more persistent was a personal controversy in which Halliday was involved for some thirty years with a subordinate officer, William Tayler [q. v.], commissioner of Patna, Behar. With Tayler, Halliday's relations were strained before the Mutiny. Tayler had printed 'for private circulation' a violent 'Protest against the Proceedings of the Lieut.-Gov. of Bengal in the Matter of the Behar Industrial Institution' (Calcutta, 1857). Subsequently Halliday doubted the prudence of Tayler's procedure at the opening of the outbreak, and with the approval of the governor-general removed him from his commissionership (4 Aug.). Halliday appointed a Mahommedan to be deputy commissioner at Patna, and non-official Europeans resented so strongly Canning's sanction of the appointment that it was made one of the grounds in the Calcutta petition for Canning's recall. Anglo-Indian opinion rallied to the side of Tayler, whose published attacks on Halliday continued (see *The Patna Crisis*, 1858). Finally Tayler refused assurances of future good conduct, and, resigning the service on full pension on 29 March 1859, pursued his agitation for redress of alleged wrong till his death in 1892. The open controversy scarcely closed before 14 June 1888, when a motion by Sir Roper Lethbridge for a select committee on Tayler's case was opposed by the under-secretary for India (Sir John Gorst) and defeated by 164 to 20 (cf. *Parliamentary Papers: Halliday's Memorandum*, 1879, No. 238, and Tayler's reply, 1880, No. 143; vide also 1879, No. 308, and 1888, Nos. 226, 247, and 258). 'The Times' and the historians of the mutiny, Malleson and Mr. T. Rice Holmes, vehemently denounced Halliday's treatment of Tayler, while Sir John Kaye supported Tayler with reservations. The controversy is more judicially reviewed by Mr. G. W. Forrest in his 'History of the Indian Mutiny' (vol. iii. 1912), who shows Tayler to have been mistaken, theatrical, and nsubordinate.

Meanwhile on 29 Sept. 1868 Halliday was appointed to the council of India, and there being no statutory limit of tenure, remained a member until his resignation on 31 Dec. 1886. His salaried public service had then extended over sixty-one years.

Halliday was a musician of unusual capacity, performing on the contra basso. He gave and took part in concerts when lieut.-governor of Bengal, earning the sobriquet of 'Big Fiddle.' In later years his great stature and commanding figure made him conspicuous in many an orchestra at high-class concerts at the Crystal Palace and elsewhere. Retaining his faculties and memory unimpaired when a nonagenarian, he could vividly describe in the twentieth century as an eye-witness the last *suttee* (widow-burning) near Calcutta, just before the practice was prohibited by the regulation of 1829. He died on 22 Oct. 1901 at his residence, 21 Bolton Gardens, South Kensington, and was buried at Brompton cemetery.

He married in 1834 Eliza, daughter of General Paul Macgregor, of the East India Company's army. She died in 1886, and had a numerous family. The eldest son, Frederick Mytton, Bengal C.S., was sometime commissioner of Patna and member of the board of revenue; another son is Lieut.-general George Thomas, late of the Bengal cavalry; and a grandson, Sir Frederick Loch Halliday, is commissioner of police, Calcutta.

[C. E. Buckland's Bengal under the Lieut.-Governors, Calcutta, 1902, i. 1–162; Mutiny histories by Kaye, Malleson, Forrest, and Holmes; Sir W. Lee-Warner's Life of Dalhousie, 1904; Dalhousie's Private Letters, 1910; Parl. papers on Tayler's case, cited above, and Tayler's books and pamphlets; Parl. Debates, 1879, 1880, and 1888; India List, 1901; The Times, 24 Oct. 1901.]

F. H. B.

HAMBLIN SMITH. [See Smith, James Hamblin.]

HAMILTON, DAVID JAMES (1849–1909), pathologist, born on 6 March 1849 at Falkirk, was third child and second son of the nine children of George Hamilton, M.D., practitioner in that town, who wrote numerous articles in 'Chambers's Encyclopædia,' by his wife Mary Wyse, daughter of a naval surgeon. A sister Mary married on 9 Feb. 1891, as his second wife, Charles Saunders Dundas, sixth Viscount Melville. At the age of seventeen Hamilton became a medical student at Edinburgh, and was attracted to pathology by the influence of Professor William Rutherford Sanders [q. v.]. After qualifying in 1870 he was house surgeon at the old Edinburgh Infirmary, resident medical officer at Chalmers' Hospital, Edinburgh, and for two years at the Northern Hospital, Liverpool, where he wrote the essay on 'Diseases and injuries of the spinal cord' which in 1874 was awarded the triennial Astley Cooper prize of 300*l.* awarded by the medical staff of Guy's Hospital. This enabled him to spend two years in working at pathology in Vienna, Munich, Strassburg, and Paris. In 1876 he returned as demonstrator of pathology to Edinburgh, where his teaching came as a revelation to the students. He was also pathologist to the Royal Infirmary. During Professor Sanders's illness (1880–1) he delivered the lectures, but was disappointed in not being elected his successor. In 1882, when an extra-mural teacher in Edinburgh, he was appointed to the chair of pathology founded by Sir William James Erasmus Wilson [q. v.] at Aberdeen. There his life's work was done. He entirely organised the teaching, so that at his resignation through ill-health in 1908 the pathological department had a European reputation and pupils in all parts of the world, as was shown by the volume of 'Studies of Pathology' (edited by W. Bulloch) which they dedicated to him in 1906 at the quater-centenary of the University of Aberdeen. The book contains an article by Hamilton on 'The Alimentary Canal as a Source of Infection' and his portrait. An enthusiastic and inspiring teacher, with a strong personality and great powers of organisation, he was the first to introduce the practical teaching of bacteriology into general class work. He initiated the bacteriological diagnosis of diphtheria and typhoid fever in the north of Scotland, and did much to apply pathology to the uses of ordinary life. He investigated the diseases of sheep known as 'braxy' and 'louping ill,' and was chairman of the departmental committee on this question appointed by the board of agriculture in 1901, which presented its report in 1906. He confirmed the description of the 'braxy' microbe given in 1888 by Ivar Nielsen and discovered the bacillus of 'louping ill.' He wrote widely on all branches of pathology, especially on the nervous system, tuberculosis, and other diseases of the lungs, and on the healing of wounds. His textbook on pathology (2 vols. 1889–94) was recognised as a standard work.

He was F.R.S.Edin., and in 1908 was elected F.R.S.London. In 1907 the University of Edinburgh made him an honorary LL.D. He was a connoisseur in music and a facile draughtsman. He died on 19 Feb. 1909 at Aberdeen, and was buried there. Hamilton married: (1) in 1880, Elizabeth, daughter of Thomas Griffith, by whom he had two sons and one daughter; (2) in 1894, Catherine, daughter of John Wilson of South Bankaskine, Falkirk; she died without issue in June 1908.

[Information from his brother, G. G. Hamilton, and from W. Bulloch; Proc. Roy. Soc. 81 B.] H. D. R.

HAMILTON, Sir EDWARD WALTER (1847–1908), treasury official, born at Salisbury on 7 July 1847, was eldest son of Walter Kerr Hamilton [q. v.], bishop of Salisbury, whose friendship with Gladstone descended to his son. His mother was Isabel Elizabeth, daughter of Francis Lear, dean of Salisbury. Educated at Eton (1860–5) and Christ Church, Oxford (1866–8), he entered the treasury in 1870, before he could take his degree. He was private secretary to Robert Lowe, chancellor of the exchequer (1872–3), to his father's friend, Gladstone (1873–4), and again to Gladstone in his second administration (1880–5). With Gladstone his relations were always intimate. Gladstone wrote to him, on his ceasing to be his private secretary (30 June 1885): 'As to your services to me, they have been simply indescribable' (Morley's *Gladstone*, iii. 210–1). Hamilton published 'Mr. Gladstone,' a monograph, in 1898, in the preface to which he speaks of himself as 'one who was privileged to know Mr. Gladstone for nearly forty years and still more privileged to have been brought into the closest contact with him for a considerable time.'

In June 1885 Hamilton became a principal clerk in the finance branch of the treasury, in 1892 assistant financial secretary, in 1894 assistant secretary, and in 1902 permanent financial secretary and joint permanent secretary with Sir George Murray, until the autumn of 1907, when he was compelled by ill-health to retire from the service. He was made C.B. in 1885; K.C.B. in 1894; G.C.B. in 1906, and a privy councillor in 1908; he also held the honours of K.C.V.O. and I.S.O. He died, unmarried, at Brighton on 3 Sept. 1908, and was buried in Brighton cemetery.

As an official, Hamilton devoted himself to the financial rather than the administrative side of the treasury, and mastered the details of City business and banking. He was thus specially connected with Goschen's great financial measures, and published an account of them in 'Conversion and Redemption: an Account of the Operations under the National Debt Conversion Act, 1889' (1889).

Without striking brilliancy, Hamilton gained to a remarkable degree the confidence and affection of those whom he served. In nearly every case official relations led to private friendship. In personal life he found his chief interest in music, and he was the author of various musical compositions. His colleagues in the treasury presented him with his portrait by Mr. John da Costa in March 1908, after his retirement.

[Who's Who; The Times, 9 and 28 Oct. 1907, 4 Sept. 1908; private information.] C. P. L.

HAMILTON, EUGENE JACOB LEE (1845–1907), poet and novelist. [See Lee-Hamilton.]

HAMPDEN, Second Viscount. [See Brand, Henry Robert (1841–1906), governor of New South Wales.]

HANBURY, Mrs. ELIZABETH (1793–1901), centenarian and philanthropist, born in Castle Street, All Hallows, London Wall, on 9 June 1793, was younger daughter of John Sanderson of Arnthorpe, Yorkshire, and later of London. Her father, after coming to London, joined the Society of Friends; her mother died when she was under two years old. Intimacy with the Gurneys led to her assisting Elizabeth Fry [q. v.] in her work of visiting prisons; her elder sister, Mary, who became the wife of Sylvanus Fox, was already engaged in the like service. The sisters also took part in the anti-slavery movement. In 1826 Elizabeth married, as his second wife, Cornelius Hanbury, of Plough Court, Lombard Street, chemist, member of the old-established firm, now Allen & Hanburys Ltd. He was first cousin to the Gurneys of Earlham. His first wife was Mary, only child of William Allen [q. v.], his partner. By him she was mother of two children, a son, Cornelius, and a daughter, Charlotte.

Mrs. Hanbury was acknowledged a minister in the Society of Friends in 1833. With her husband she resided successively at Bonchurch, Stoke Newington, and on Blackdown Hills near Wellington, Somerset. Her husband died at The Firs, Blackdown, in 1869. Eighteen years later his widow moved with her daughter to the house of her son, Cornelius, at Richmond. She retained her clearness and activity of mind till the end of her long life, being keenly interested in the prison work of her daughter (see below) and in the missionary labours of two daughters of her son, Elizabeth and Charlotte Hanbury, in China and India. During May 1900, when in her 108th year, she sent a message to the Friends' yearly meeting in London, and afterwards through the Dowager Countess of Erroll forwarded a greeting to Queen Victoria from 'her oldest subject.' Mrs. Hanbury died at Dynevor House, Richmond, Surrey, on 31 Oct. 1901, aged 108 years 4 months and 3 weeks. She was buried at Wellington. Her portrait was painted in her 100th year by Percy Bigland, and now belongs to Lady Hanbury (widow of her husband's great-nephew) of La Mortola, Ventimiglia. A replica is in the possession of Mrs. Hanbury's son. Only four or five other British subjects have on authentic evidence died at the same advanced age. Since her death three persons have been certificated to die at a greater age.

The daughter, CHARLOTTE HANBURY (1830–1900), prison reformer, born at Stoke Newington on 10 April 1830, taught as a girl in ragged schools and visited the poor. On Blackdown she established several schools and mission rooms. She travelled largely in Europe and had friends in Germany, France, Spain, and Italy. In 1889 she commenced a series of visits to Morocco with a view to ameliorating the lot of Moorish prisoners. She established a Moorish refuge in Tangier and travelled in the interior of the country. At her death at Richmond, Surrey, on 22 Oct. 1900, she committed the care of the Tangier mission to her cousin, Henry Gurney. Her autobiography, a remarkable record, was edited by her niece, Mrs. Albert Head, in 1901.

[Annual Monitor, 1902, pp. 43–51; The Times, 1 Nov. 1901; Charlotte Hanbury: an Autobiography, 1901; Life of Mrs. Albert Head (Caroline Hanbury), by Charlotte Hanbury (the younger), 1905; information from Mrs. Hanbury's son, Mr. Cornelius Hanbury.]

C. F. S.

HANBURY, Sir JAMES ARTHUR (1832–1908), surgeon-general, born at Somerstoun House, parish of Laracor, near Trim, co. Meath, on 13 Jan. 1832, was one of the fourteen children of Samuel Hanbury, a large landowner, by his wife Louisa, daughter of Charles Ingham, rector of Kilmessan and Kilcool, co. Meath. A brother, William, also in the army medical service, was with the 24th regiment when it was annihilated at Chillianwallah in 1849, assisted Florence Nightingale [q. v. Suppl. II] in establishing the hospital at Scutari, and was in charge of Netley Hospital until his death. Another brother, Fleet-surgeon Ingham Hanbury, R.N., after distinguishing himself at Tel-el-Kebir (mentioned in despatches and the bronze decoration and C.B.), died on his way to India in 1884.

Hanbury graduated M.B. from Trinity College, Dublin, in 1853. He entered the army medical service as an assistant surgeon on 30 Sept. 1853; was promoted surgeon on 20 Feb. 1863; surgeon-major on 1 March 1873; brigade surgeon on 27 Nov. 1879; deputy surgeon-general on 5 May 1881; surgeon major-general on 14 June 1887, and retired from the service on 13 Jan. 1892. He was elected an honorary F.R.C.S. Ireland on 19 July 1883 and F.R.C.S. England, on 14 April 1887 (his diploma of membership being dated 23 Feb. 1859).

Hanbury was quartered for some years at Halifax, Nova Scotia, before he was sent to China and thence to India. He served with the Bazar valley expedition in the Afghan war of 1878–9, and was present during the march from Kabul to the relief of Kandahar. He was under fire in the battle of 1 Sept. in that campaign, was mentioned in despatches, received the medal and clasp, the bronze decoration, and the C.B. (1881). He was principal medical officer under Lord

Wolseley during the Egyptian campaign of 1882, when he was present at the battle of Tel-el-Kebir, and for the first time caused wounds to be dressed on the battlefield. Twice mentioned in despatches, he was made K.C.B. He served as principal medical officer at the Horse Guards and at Gibraltar (1887–8), and was surgeon-general of the forces in Madras (1888–92). In 1905 he received the reward for distinguished service. Tall (6 feet 1 inch in height), alert, and handsome, of great independence and energy, Hanbury was a popular master of hounds at Ootacamund. He died at Bournemouth on 2 June 1908.

He married in 1876 Hannah Emily, daughter of James Anderson of Coxlodge Hall, Northumberland, and widow of Colonel Carter, C.B.

[Brit. Med. Journal, 1908, i. 1463; Lancet, 1908, i. 1731; information from the Rev. S. Smartt, vicar of Newry.] D'A. P.

HANBURY, ROBERT WILLIAM (1845–1903), politician, born on 24 Feb. 1845 at Bodehall House, Tamworth, was only son of Robert Hanbury of Bodehall, a country gentleman of moderate landed estate but of ample means derived chiefly from collieries, by his wife Mary, daughter of Major T. B. Bamford of Wilnecote Hall, Warwickshire. Left an orphan in early childhood, Hanbury was educated at Rugby and at Corpus Christi College, Oxford, where he was well known as an 'oar.' He graduated B.A. in 1868 with a second class in literæ humaniores. At the age of twenty-seven he became in 1872 conservative member for Tamworth borough, and held that seat until 1878, when he was elected for North Staffordshire. He lost this seat at the general election of 1880, and for the next five years threw himself energetically into the work of conservative organisation. He contested Preston unsuccessfully in 1882, but won the seat in 1885, retaining it with increasing majorities until his death.

A vigilant and unsparing critic of the estimates even in the conservative parliament of 1886–92, he was regarded at first as something of a free-lance; but when the liberals returned to power in 1892, he and his allies, Mr. Thomas Gibson Bowles and (Sir) George Christopher Trout Bartley [q. v. Suppl. II], kept up a ceaseless warfare in committee of supply upon the policy of the government in every department. He was particularly energetic in attacking from the financial side Gladstone's home rule bill of 1893, and it was largely due to him that the question of the national store of cordite assumed the importance that inspired Mr. Brodrick's motion of June 1895, on which the Rosebery ministry was defeated.

When the Salisbury government came into power, Hanbury was made a privy councillor and financial secretary of the treasury. That post he held until 1900. The unionist ministry was then reconstructed after the general election of that year, and Hanbury succeeded Mr. Walter Long as president of the board of agriculture, with a seat in the cabinet. The change was regarded with some suspicion by the agricultural community; but Hanbury went amongst the farmers on all available occasions, delivered speeches at agricultural gatherings, and won general confidence.

A man of exceptionally fine physique, Hanbury died suddenly from pneumonia on 28 April 1903, at his London residence, Herbert House, Belgrave Square. Mr. Arthur Balfour, the prime minister, spoke in the House of Commons, with the approval of all parties, the same evening (28 April), of Hanbury's love for the House of Commons, of his accurate knowledge of its procedure, of his assiduous attendance; to the board of agriculture he had successfully brought an originality of method and desire to adapt a young office to the needs of the agricultural community. He was buried in the churchyard at his country residence, Ilam, near Ashbourne.

Hanbury was twice married (but left no issue): (1) in 1869 to Ismena Tindal (*d.* 1871), daughter of Thomas Morgan Gepp of Chelmsford; (2) in 1884 to Ellen, only child of Colonel Knox Hamilton; she survived him, marrying shortly after Victor Bowring, and taking the name of Bowring-Hanbury. Hanbury's eldest sister married Sir Archibald Milman, clerk assistant to the House of Commons, and there was a family lawsuit, carried up to the House of Lords, about the terms of his will. It was finally held on 7 Feb. 1905, by the earl of Halsbury and Lords Macnaghten, Davey, James, and Robertson (Lord Lindley dissenting) that upon the true construction of Hanbury's will there was an absolute gift of the testator's real and personal estate to his wife, subject to an executory gift of the same at her death to such of his nieces as should survive her (*The Times Law Reports*, xxi. 252).

A caricature by 'Spy' appeared in 'Vanity Fair' (1896).

[The Times, 29 April and 7 May 1903; Annual Register for 1903 [119], 130.] E. C.

HANKIN, ST. JOHN EMILE CLAVERING (1869–1909), playwright, born on 25 Sept. 1869 at Southampton, was third and youngest son of four children of Charles Wright Hankin, a descendant of the ancient Cornish family of Kestell, and at one time headmaster of King Edward VI's grammar school, Southampton. His mother was Mary Louisa (*d.* 1909), daughter of Edmund Thomas Wigley Perrot, who inherited estates at Craycombe, Worcestershire. In January 1883 Hankin entered Malvern College as house and foundation scholar, and at the age of seventeen he won an open postmastership at Merton College, Oxford, as well as a close Ackroyd scholarship, for which he was qualified hereditarily through his mother. He matriculated on 21 Oct. 1886, and took second classes in honour moderations (1888) and in the final classical school (1890). On leaving the university Hankin engaged in journalism in London. From 1890 he contributed to the 'Saturday Review.' In 1894 he joined the staff of the 'Indian Daily News' at Calcutta. After a year in India an attack of malaria drove him home. For a time Hankin worked on 'The Times,' and he contributed to other papers dramatic criticisms and miscellaneous articles. His keen wit and shrewd commonsense were seen to advantage in two series of papers which appeared in 'Punch' and were afterwards published independently, viz. 'Mr. Punch's Dramatic Sequels' (1901), which added supplementary acts to the great classics of the English drama, and 'Lost Masterpieces' (1904), a series of subtle parodies of eminent authors in both prose and verse.

Playwriting of a realistic frankness was Hankin's main ambition. The first of his plays to be acted was 'The Two Mr. Wetherbys,' which was privately performed in London by the Stage Society in Feb. 1903 and later by Mr. William Hawtrey in Australia and New Zealand. When in 1905 the strain of a journalist's life in London compelled him to retire to Campden in Gloucestershire, he mainly devoted himself to writing for the stage. His translation of Brieux's 'Les trois filles de Monsieur Dupont' was produced, again privately, by the Stage Society in 1905, and its boldness excited some censure. Hankin, who thoroughly believed in his own powers and principles, obtained genuine success in the witty and pungently ironical comedy called 'The Return of the Prodigal,' which was publicly produced on 26 Sept. 1905 by Messrs. Vedrenne and Barker at the Court Theatre, and was revived on 29 April 1907. 'The Charity that began at Home' and 'The Cassilis Engagement,' which was perhaps the most popular of his plays, proved less incisive; both were first performed privately by the Stage Society in London in 1906 and 1907 respectively, and were afterwards successfully repeated at repertory theatres in Manchester, Liverpool, and Glasgow. The three last-named plays were published in 1907 under the ironic title of 'Three Plays with Happy Endings,' with a preface in which he replied to adverse criticism in the press. In 'The Last of the De Mullins,' produced by the Stage Society in December 1908 and published in 1909, Hankin's merciless and outspoken realism went even further than before. He also wrote two one-act pieces, 'The Burglar who Failed,' which had a successful run at the Criterion Theatre in November 1908, and 'The Constant Lover,' which was produced at the Royalty Theatre in February 1912.

Hankin's dramatic work, in so far as it satirised middle-class conventional standards of morality, bore traces of Mr. Bernard Shaw's influence. But he showed originality in his absolute freedom from any semblance of romantic illusion and in his impatience of sentiment, which led him usually to end his comedies with the victory of the unscrupulous scamp. Although his plots were carefully elaborated, and his pieces technically well planned, he chiefly aimed at a coldly acute analysis of character. His finely pointed wit failed to reconcile the public at large or the critics in the press to his cynical attitude to life.

Never of robust health, Hankin suffered much since 1907 from neurasthenia, and he more than once derived benefit from the baths at Llandrindod Wells. Thither he went in the early summer of 1909, and in a fit of depression drowned himself in the river Ithon on 15 June 1909. His ashes were buried after cremation at Golder's Green. He married in 1901 Florence, daughter of George Routledge, J.P., the publisher. He left no children.

[The Times, 21 June 1909: Athenæum, 26 June 1909; Desmond MacCarthy's The Court Theatre, 1907; Malvern College Register, 1904; Foster's Alumni Oxon. 1888; Max Beerbohm, A Book of Caricatures, 1907, No. xix.; private information from Mrs. St. John Hankin.] G. S. W.

HANLAN (properly HANLON), EDWARD (1855–1908), Canadian oarsman, born of Irish parents at Toronto, Ontario, Canada, on 12 July 1855, was son in the family of two sons and two daughters of John Hanlon, hotel proprietor, and his wife Mary Gibbs. His nephew Edward Durnan was sculling champion of Canada. Educated at George Street public school, Hanlan developed an early taste for rowing, and he gained his first important success at the age of eighteen, when he became amateur champion of Toronto Bay. Turning professional, he beat all comers in 1876 at the centennial international exhibition at Philadelphia. In that year he took unsuccessful charge of an hotel in his native town. He became champion oarsman of Canada in 1877 and of America in 1878. Further successes in America led him in 1879 to test his powers in England; and on 15 June 1879 he defeated the English champion, W. Elliott of Blyth, rowing the course from Mansion House to Scotswood suspension bridge on the Tyne in the record time of 21 mins. 21 secs. On Hanlan's return to Toronto a public subscription of 4000*l*. was raised for his benefit. Hanlan revisited England in 1880, and on 15 Nov. beat Edward Trickett of Australia on the Thames for the world's championship. In four subsequent races (1881–4) Hanlan retained the title, but lost it on 16 Aug. 1884 to William Beach, a blacksmith of Illawana, in a race on the Paramatta river, and suffered further defeat from Beach on 28 March 1885 and 26 Nov. 1887. Two further efforts to regain the championship in 1888 were unsuccessful. With William O'Connor he beat Gaudaur and McKay for the double-scull championship of America on 8 Aug. 1898.

During his career Hanlan, who was 5 ft. 8¾ ins. in height and weighed 11 stone, won over 150 races, and as an oarsman was unsurpassed for finish and style. Unlike his English rivals, he used the slide simultaneously with the swing, kept his body well back, and held his arms straight long past the perpendicular before bending them to row the stroke, to which added strength was given by the skilful use of his great leg power.

Hanlan died on 4 Jan. 1908 at Toronto, where he was buried with civic honours. He married on 19 Dec. 1877 Margaret Gordon Sutherland of Picton, Nova Scotia, and had issue two sons and six daughters. A painted portrait of Hanlan, sitting in his boat, by H. H. Emmerson, which has been often engraved, belongs to his widow.

[Sportsman, and The Times, 6 Jan. 1908; Toronto Globe, 4, 6, and 7 Jan. 1908 (by H. J. P. Good); R. C. Lehmann, The Complete Oarsman, 1908, p. 49; Morgan, Canadian Men and Women of the Time; private information.]

W. S. J.

HARBEN, Sir HENRY (1823–1911), pioneer of industrial life assurance, born in Bloomsbury on 24 Aug. 1823, was eldest son of Henry Harben of Bloomsbury by his wife Sarah, daughter of Benjamin Andrade. He was first cousin to Mr. Joseph Chamberlain. The Harben family was originally engaged in banking at Lewes, but Henry's grandfather was a partner in the provision stores of Harben & Larkin of Whitechapel, London, and his father also carried on a wholesale business in the City. After a few years in his uncle's stores he was articled to a surveyor, but left that calling in March 1852, when he became accountant of the Prudential Mutual Assurance, Investment and Loan Association. The company was founded in a small way at Blackfriars in 1848 and had met with little success. Harben, who remained connected with the undertaking for sixty years, converted it into a colossal concern. In 1854 the company, mainly on Harben's advice, started a scheme of life assurance for the working classes; the new departure was at first hampered chiefly by the rivalry of the Safety Life Assurance Company, of which Cobden and Bright were directors, but which soon collapsed. Harben was appointed secretary of the Prudential on 26 June 1856, and soon proved that industrial life assurance was practicable. He also organised for the first time the valuation of industrial businesses on scientific principles.

On 24 Feb. 1870 Harben, who had become in 1864 a fellow of the Institute of Actuaries, was appointed actuary of the Prudential company in addition to the secretaryship. On 23 March 1873 he became resident director and secretary, resigning the latter office in the following year. He was made deputy-chairman on 19 Dec. 1878, chairman on 28 Dec. 1905, and president on 31 July 1907. In May 1879 the business was transferred to Holborn Bars, where the large block of buildings accommodates about 2000 clerks, whilst the company's annual income exceeds 14,500,000*l*. and its funds exceed 77,000,000*l*. Harben's services and advice were to the last available for the company. He presided at the weekly meeting of the board on 13 July 1911, five months before his death. He was knighted on Queen Victoria's diamond jubilee in June 1897.

Harben was a prominent member of the Carpenters' Company, joining the livery in 1878 and serving as master in 1893. Between 1889 and 1897 he gave large sums to assist the company in their various schemes of technical education and social philanthropy. These benefactions included an endowment for technical lectures and a gold medal in connection with the Institute of Public Health. The Convalescent Home for Working Men at Rustington, Littlehampton, the erection and partial endowment of which cost him over 50,000*l.*, was founded in 1895 and opened in 1897. It remained under his own management and that of his son during their lives, and then reverted to the Carpenters' Company, which now contributes liberally to its support.

Harben's London house for nearly half a century was at Hampstead, and he keenly interested himself in local affairs. For many years he was a leading member of the Hampstead vestry, and became its chairman. He represented Hampstead on the Metropolitan Board of Works from 1881 to 1889, and from 1889 to 1894 on the London county council. In 1900 he became the first mayor of Hampstead, and was elected for a second year, but resigned owing to failing health. A generous supporter of the local charities, he built a wing of the Hampstead General Hospital, liberally helped the Mount Vernon Hospital for Consumption and the School for the Blind, and gave 5000*l.* towards building the Central Public Library. He helped to secure Parliament-hill Fields and Golder's Green as open spaces for the public. For the London City Mission he built a hall at Hampstead, and was honorary colonel of the 1st cadet battalion of the royal fusiliers whose headquarters are at Hampstead.

His country seat was Warnham Lodge, near Horsham, where he built the Warnham village hall and club; he was a D.L. of Sussex, and served as high sheriff in 1898. An enthusiast for cricket, he constructed one of the best cricket grounds in Sussex, where important matches were played. A conservative in politics, he contested unsuccessfully Norwich in 1880 and Cardiff in 1885.

He died at his Sussex residence on 2 Dec. 1911, and was buried at Kensal Green cemetery. He married (1) on 1 Aug. 1846 Ann (*d.* 1883), daughter of James Such, by whom he had issue a son, Henry Andrade, his successor as chairman of the Prudential (1849–1910), whose death in August 1910 was a severe blow; and (2) on 8 Nov. 1890 Mary Jane, daughter of Thomas Bullman Cole. He was survived by a daughter and two grandsons, H. D. Harben and Guy P. Harben the artist.

Harben published: 1. 'The Weight Calculator,' 1849; 3rd edit. 1879. 2. 'Mortality Experience of the Prudential Assurance Company, 1867–70,' 1871. 3. 'The Discount Guide, Tables for the use of Merchants, Manufacturers . . .'; new edit. 1876.

A portrait by Mr. Norman Macbeth was painted in 1872 for the board-room of the Prudential Company. Another presentation portrait, by the Hon. John Collier (1889), is in the Hampstead Town Hall. A bust from life was modelled in 1902 by Mr. James Nesfield Forsyth.

[Insurance Record, 8 Dec. 1911, xlix. 579–80; Prudential Staff Gazette (portrait), May 1911, i. 120–1, and Dec. 1911, ii. 35; Post Mag. (portrait), 9 Dec. 1911, lxxii. 971–2, Ibis Mag. (portrait), Dec. 1911, xxxiv. 373–7; Burke's Peerage, 1911; Lodge's Peerage, 1912; The Times, 4 Dec. 1911; Hampstead and Highgate Express, 9 Dec. 1911; Hampstead and St. John's Wood Advertiser, 7 Dec. 1911; Brit. Mus. Cat.; notes kindly supplied by Sir Ernest Clarke.] C. W.

HARCOURT, LEVESON FRANCIS VERNON- (1839–1907), civil engineer. [See VERNON-HARCOURT.]

HARCOURT, SIR WILLIAM GEORGE GRANVILLE VENABLES VERNON (1827–1904), statesman, born on 14 Oct. 1827 in the Old Residence, York, was younger son in a family of two sons and five daughters of William Vernon Harcourt [q. v.] of Nuneham Park, Oxford, canon of York, by his wife Matilda Mary, daughter of Colonel William Gooch, whose father was Sir Thomas Gooch of Benacre, Suffolk, and whose grandfather was Sir Thomas Gooch [q. v.], bishop of Ely. Harcourt's grandfather, Edward Harcourt [q. v.], archbishop of York, son of George Vernon, Lord Vernon, took his mother's name of Harcourt on succeeding to the property of his first cousin, William Harcourt, third and last Earl Harcourt [q. v.], in 1830. Harcourt was proud of a descent which was traceable through many noble houses to the Plantagenet royal family. He had little in common with his elder brother, Edward William Harcourt (1825–1891), a staunch conservative, who succeeded to the Nuneham estates in 1871, and who, although he was M.P. for Oxfordshire from 1878 to 1886, mainly led the life of a country gentleman.

Harcourt's early days were spent in York and in the adjoining parish of Wheldrake, under a private tutor till the age of ten. For the next nine years (1837–46) he was a pupil with five other boys of Canon

Parr, until April 1840 at Durnford, near Salisbury, and from that time at Preston, where Parr was made vicar of St. John's. Chief of his friends and fellow-pupils at Durnford was Laurence Oliphant [q. v.]. At Preston he was an eye-witness of the bread riots of 1842, and the poverty and misery of the people made him a lifelong opponent of protection. From Preston he went to Cambridge University, entering Trinity College as a pensioner on 30 Sept. 1846. Already a good scholar and mathematician, he soon showed signs of brilliance. He matriculated in 1847 and became a scholar of Trinity in 1850. He took an active part in the debates of the Union and was admitted to the exclusive 'Society of Apostles.' There, as at the Union, his chief adversary in debate was (Sir) James Fitzjames Stephen [q. v.]. Harcourt championed the liberals and Stephen the conservatives. Their encounters were reckoned by contemporaries 'veritable battles of the gods,' though in 'adroitness' and 'chaff' Harcourt was Stephen's superior (L. STEPHEN, *J. F. Stephen*, 99 *seq.*). Although of magnificent physique he took no prominent part in sport. Whilst an undergraduate he was introduced by his tutor, (Sir) H. S. Maine, to John Douglas Cook [q.v.], then the editor of the 'Morning Chronicle,' a Peelite organ. He soon wrote regularly for that journal. In 1851 he graduated B.A. with a first-class in classics and a senior optime in the mathematical tripos. On 2 May 1851 he entered at Lincoln's Inn and settled down to the study of law in London. Three years later, on 1 May 1854, he was called to the bar of the Inner Temple, and he chose the home circuit. He soon acquired a large practice at the common law bar and, later, established a high reputation at the parliamentary bar, where his work yielded him a handsome income. Through the long struggle over the Thames Embankment scheme he acted as counsel for the Metropolitan Board of Works (see his letter to *The Times* of 7 July 1861, signed 'Observer'). During Nov. and Dec. 1863 public interest was centred in the court-martial trial of Lieut.-Colonel Thomas Crawley for alleged misconduct at Mhow in the previous year; Harcourt acted as Crawley's legal adviser, and his brilliant advocacy gained his acquittal.

He did not, however, confine his attention exclusively to his profession. He quickly made his mark in London society as an extremely clever young man who could both write and talk well. On the demise of the 'Morning Chronicle,' Beresford Hope inaugurated the 'Saturday Review,' in Nov. 1855, with Douglas Cook as editor. Cook at once enlisted Harcourt's services as one of the original contributors. Harcourt wrote continuously for the brilliant periodical from 1855 to 1859.

At the general election of May 1859 he contested the Kirkcaldy Burghs as an independent liberal against the official liberal candidate and old member, Robert Ferguson. The fight was fierce, and Harcourt was defeated by only eighteen votes. In the following January, at a great public demonstration at Kirkcaldy, he received a presentation 'as a tribute to his eminent talent, and in admiration of his eloquent advocacy of our cause.'

Meanwhile Harcourt was studying privately international law, which, in a letter to Lord John Russell, he described as 'my passion, not my profession.' He turned the study to advantage in the controversies over international law which occupied the cabinets of Europe after the first stages of the American civil war. To the 'London Review' of 30 Nov. 1861 he sent two letters, one on 'International Law and International Exasperation' and the other 'The case of the Nashville.' In 'The Times' of 5 Dec. 1861 appeared the first of a series of long and weighty letters, over the signature of 'Historicus,' dealing chiefly with questions of international law arising out of the American civil war. The letters were continued at intervals till 1876 and covered a wide field of political controversy. Throughout life he remained a constant correspondent of 'The Times' on all manner of political themes, in later years under his own name. The aim of the early 'Historicus' letters was to deny the Southern States the title to recognition as belligerents, and to define the obligation of neutrality on England's part. In 1863 Harcourt collected some of the letters under the title 'Letters by Historicus on Some Questions of International Law,' and in 1865 others appeared in a volume as 'American Neutrality.' The letters, which had a marked effect upon political opinion, established the writer's reputation. Lord John Russell wrote to Harcourt in 1868 thanking him for the help he had rendered to the maintenance of peace between England and the United States.

He was appointed a member of the Neutrality Laws Commission in the same year, and signed the report with a qualification deprecating any extension of the punishment to those engaged in shipbuilding for belligerents. He also served on the royal commissions on the laws of naturalisation and allegiance (1870) and on extradition (1878). In 1866 he was made a queen's counsel, according to Lord Selborne in recognition of his grasp of international law. But a more important recognition of the kind was his appointment in 1869 to the Whewell professorship of international law at Cambridge, which he held till 1887. Throughout that period he delivered lectures at increasingly irregular intervals and occupied rooms in Trinity College which he decorated with elaborate heraldic ornaments.

Meanwhile Harcourt was identifying himself with politics, though he was still reluctant to abandon his career at the parliamentary bar. He was generally reckoned to be independent of party ties, and Disraeli, whom he knew well socially, offered him in 1866 a safe conservative seat in Wales, which he declined. At the outset he chiefly confined his interposition in political discussion to the columns of 'The Times' above his old signature of 'Historicus.' There he urged the co-operation of both parties in passing a reform bill (12 March, 10 April, and 7 May 1866; cf. four letters on parliamentary reform, 4 Feb., 11 April, 2 and 9 May 1867, and on redistribution of parliamentary seats, 24 June). On 27 May 1867 he appealed, through 'The Times,' for the commutation of the death sentence passed on the Fenian convicts, and early in 1869 advocated in the same paper the disestablishment of the Irish Church.

On 29 June 1867 he delivered his first speech in London. The occasion was a public breakfast in St. James's Hall, held in honour of Lloyd Garrison, the American anti-slavery advocate. The chair was occupied by John Bright, and the list of speakers included Lord John Russell, the Duke of Argyll, John Stuart Mill, Lord Granville, and George Thompson (PASSMORE EDWARDS, *A Few Footprints*, 1906).

Next year he threw himself with growing energy into the party strife. He advocated the disendowment of the Church of Ireland at a great meeting held on 16 April 1868 in St. James's Hall, under the presidency of Earl Russell, and again on 22 June at a stormy meeting in the Guildhall. At a public breakfast, given to John Bright on 4 June by the Liberal Association, he eloquently acclaimed a new era of reform. On 18 Oct. he addressed a meeting of working men at Birmingham, and on 10 Nov. vigorously supported the liberal candidates for the City at Cannon Street Hotel during the general election. At the same time he agreed to stand for Oxford in the liberal interest in company with Edward Cardwell, the senior sitting member. His fine appearance and admirable platform manner greatly impressed the electors, and the two liberals were returned by a large majority (18 Nov.). On 3 Jan. 1870 and in many succeeding years Harcourt delivered to the Ancient Order of Druids at Oxford elaborate addresses on liberal policy which attracted vast public attention. By degrees he wholly abandoned his legal work for politics, and thereby sacrificed 10,000*l.* a year (GOSCHEN's *Life*, i. 149).

Harcourt's entry into parliament was looked forward to with interest. Gladstone on forming his first government in December 1868 offered him the post of judge advocate general, which carried with it a privy councillorship, but Harcourt declined the office because a privy councillorship was held at that time to debar the holder, when out of office, from legal practice. His maiden speech on 23 Feb. 1869, against a proposal to repeal the Act of Anne by which members accepting office under the crown vacate their seats, justified expectations. He was active in the discussion of the Irish Church bill during the session. Gladstone acknowledged his ability as a debater and anticipated for him a great parliamentary career. But Harcourt showed himself no docile party follower, and seated below the gangway, soon constituted himself a constant and candid critic of the liberal government. On 5 March he drew the attention of the house to the absence of any record of election petition judgments, and obtained a promise from the attorney-general to secure and lay them before the house. On the same day he carried a motion to appoint a select committee to inquire into the law affecting the registration of voters. He was appointed chairman of this committee, and its deliberations resulted in the registration of parliamentary voters bill of May 1871. During the session of 1870 he criticised many provisions of the government's Irish land bill, and of their elementary education bill. He opposed any sectarian religious education in the public schools apart from a reading of the Scriptures (cf. letters in *The Times*, 28 March and 10 June), with the result that a clause was inserted forbidding the use of formularism distinctive of any religious sect. He again championed religious equality during the debates on the university tests bill in June, and urged that 'every College incorporated with the universities should be open to persons of all religious opinions.'

Over the army regulation bill of 1871, which, among other reforms, sought to abolish the purchase of commissions in the army, Harcourt came into sharp collision with Gladstone. While denouncing the custom of 'purchase,' he protested against Gladstone using the Royal Warrant in procuring its abolition. The government's attitude was strongly defended by the attorney-general, Sir Robert Collier, afterwards Baron Monkswell, and the solicitor-general, Sir John Duke (afterwards Baron) Coleridge, on two different grounds of argument, and Harcourt delighted the house by asking 'in the language of Newmarket, whether the government was going to win with Attorney-General on Statute or with Solicitor-General on Prerogative.' Again in July he opposed that clause of the elections bill which sought to impose election expenses upon the constituencies on the ground that 'the people had long looked for the ballot as a boon; they were now going to give them the ballot as a tax.' With persistence he urged law reform on the notice of the country and the house (cf. address as president of the jurisprudence section of the Social Science Congress meeting at Leeds, Oct. 1871, and *The Times*, 8 Dec. 1871 and 3, 18, 21, and 28 Dec. 1872). On 26 July 1872 he moved 'that the administration of the law, under the existing system, is costly, dilatory, and inefficient. . . .' and, after a long debate, his motion was defeated only by a majority of fifteen. His activity both in and out of parliament helped to shape the Judicature Act of 1873, in the discussion of which he took a large part.

In discussions on the ballot bill in 1872 Harcourt carried against the government by 167 to 166 an amendment substituting 'with corrupt intent' for the word 'wilfully' in the clause making it punishable for a man 'wilfully' to disclose the name of the candidate for whom he voted. On 5 July he moved the second reading of the criminal law amendment bill, which provided that picketing should not be subject to a criminal charge. During November Harcourt attacked as an infringement of the right of public meeting A. S. Ayrton's bill for enabling the office of works to regulate public meetings in the London parks.

With equal independence and persistency Harcourt urged in parliament and the country the need of reducing the public expenditure, especially that on armaments (cf. *Hansard*, 1 April 1873). At his instance Gladstone appointed early in 1873 a select committee, with Harcourt as one of its members, to consider civil service expenditure. In debate on the Irish University bill, on 13 Feb., he denounced the clauses which prohibited the teaching of philosophy and modern history, declaring them to be 'the anathema of the Vatican against modern civilisation.' On the defeat of the second reading of this bill (March) Gladstone resigned, but he resumed office owing to Disraeli's refusal to form a ministry. Later in the year (Nov. 20) Sir John Duke Coleridge, then attorney-general, was promoted to the bench. His place was taken by Sir Henry James [q. v. Suppl. II], Harcourt's friend and companion in the House of Commons below the gangway, who had been made solicitor-general in the preceding September. Harcourt accepted Gladstone's offer of James's post of solicitor-general (20 Nov.). He deprecated receiving the customary honour of knighthood, but was overborne by Gladstone, and he was knighted at Windsor Castle on 17 Dec. He was returned unopposed for Oxford on 5 Dec.

Little opportunity was offered of testing his changed relations with a government of which he had been a somewhat rigorous critic and was now an official member. The dissolution of parliament, on 26 Jan. 1874, practically ended his first experience of office within three months. The liberals were heavily defeated in the country. The return of Disraeli to power on 21 Feb. placed Harcourt for the first time in opposition.

Re-elected for Oxford on 3 Feb. 1874, Harcourt proved a formidable enemy of the new conservative government. But his interest in the first session of the new parliament was concentrated on the public worship regulation bill, which, although not a government bill, was warmly supported by Disraeli. A staunch protestant throughout his career, Harcourt enthusiastically championed a measure which was designed to crush ritualism. Gladstone was no less vehement in opposition to the bill, and sarcastically twitted his follower with 'displays of erudition rapidly and cleverly acquired' (cf. HARCOURT in *The Times*, 11, 14, 20, 27, and 30 July 1874). But there was no permanent alienation. Through the sessions of 1875 and 1876 Harcourt was untiring in criticisms of conservative bills and policy, mainly on party lines. By his vigorous attack in 'The Times' of 4 and 5 Nov. (1875) on the Admiralty's 'Slave Circular' authorising the surrender of slaves taking refuge on British ships (13 July 1875) he hastened the withdrawal of the circular (5 Nov.). He ridiculed the royal titles bill of 1876, which made Queen Victoria Empress of India. He was foremost among the critics of the merchant shipping bill (May).

During the critical events in Eastern Europe (1876–8) Harcourt was in the forefront of the political battle at home, declaring the problem to be 'not how to maintain the Turkish government, but how safely to replace it' (speech at Oxford, 9 Jan. 1877). When Gladstone moved the vote of censure on the government for their support of Turkey on 7 May, Harcourt, speaking in support, declared that the knell of the Turkish empire had sounded. In Jan. 1878 he denounced the government's warlike preparations when a conference for the settlement of peace between Turkey and Russia was in process of formation, and later in the year ridiculed the new treaty of Berlin as already 'moribund' (*The Times*, 2 Nov. 1878). To the government's conduct of affairs in Afghan and South Africa during 1878 and 1879 Harcourt brought the same trenchant powers of attack. In a long speech on 31 March he put the blame of the Zulu war on Sir Bartle Frere for carrying on, under the British flag, those very injustices from which the Zulus had so long suffered under the Boers. Nor was his activity in the House of Commons confined to external policy. In April 1877 he urgently pleaded for a widening of the scope of education at Oxford and Cambridge and for increased endowment of research. During the session of 1879 he was indefatigable in seeking to amend in committee the army discipline and regulation bill.

It was not only in the House of Commons or in letters to 'The Times' that Harcourt made his influence felt during this period. His speeches at public meetings through the country proved the finest rhetorical efforts of his career. For the most part carefully prepared, yet delivered so skilfully as to appear extempore, they were masterpieces of dignified eloquence and brilliant epigram. At liberal demonstrations at Oxford, Scarborough, Sheffield, Southport, Liverpool, and Birmingham (20 Jan. 1880, with John Bright and Mr. Chamberlain) he ridiculed the government's policy of 'bluster and bravado,' and his rhetorical energy conspicuously supplemented that of Gladstone.

In March 1880 Parliament was dissolved, and a general election immediately followed. The contest in Oxford was very keen; the conservatives considerably reduced the liberal majorities, but Harcourt and his colleague (Sir) Joseph William Chitty [q. v. Suppl. I] were elected (3 April). The result of the general election was the return of 349 liberals, 243 conservatives, and 60 home rulers. Lord Beaconsfield resigned on 22 April. Despite their political differences, Harcourt's private relations with the conservative statesman remained friendly till Lord Beaconsfield's death on 19 April 1881, when Harcourt attended the funeral at Hughenden.

Delicate issues were involved in the choice in 1880 of a liberal prime minister. Gladstone had abandoned to Lord Hartington the leadership of the liberal party in 1875, and despite his active agitation in the country had not resumed his old post. Harcourt, while energetic in support and exposition of the liberal programme, inclined to whig doctrines. On 29 Dec. 1874 he had written to Goschen (*Life*, i. 152) 'I have been preaching whig doctrines *pur et simple*; they are my principles, and I mean to stick to them *coûte que coûte*.' He had urged on Hartington in Jan. 1875 the acceptance of the leadership, chiefly to save the party from radical predominance. Although he worked loyally with Gladstone, he was often puzzled by his apparent casuistry (*Life of Goschen*, i. 153). Now he urged Hartington to become prime minister in virtue of his formal place of leader. He believed, he wrote to him (18 April 1880), that his sobriety would have more effect on moderate public opinion than 'all the oratory in the world' (Holland, *Life of Duke of Devonshire*, i. 271). But events took another course. Gladstone declined to serve in any other situation save that of chief of the new government, and he again became prime minister. He at once formed a ministry. Harcourt was given the post of home secretary, and was sworn of the privy council (28 April). On seeking re-election as a minister Harcourt was again opposed at Oxford by his previous opponent, Alexander William Hall. The conservative organisation left no stone unturned to capture the seat, and Hall was returned by a majority of 54 (10 May). He was, however, shortly afterwards unseated on petition, and the borough was disfranchised for corruption for the whole of that parliament. Harcourt was not long absent from the House of Commons. Samuel Plimsoll [q. v. Suppl. I] generously resigned his seat at Derby in his favour, and he was elected without a contest on 26 May.

Harcourt's first legislative measure was the Ground Game Act, or the hares and rabbits bill, which he introduced on 27 May. The object of the bill was the better protection of the occupier of land against the ravages of hares and rabbits, and it provided that the occupier should have equal rights with the landlord to kill and take ground game. The bill aroused the bitterest opposition of a section of the tory party, and though the second reading was moved on 10 June, it was not finally passed until 27 August. The keen opposition brought out all Harcourt's adroitness in debate and retort. The effect of the bill was the extermination of the hare in many parts of England, but it went a long way towards conciliating the farmers and practically killed the agitation against the Game Laws.

Select committees to inquire into the state of British merchant shipping and the London water supply next occupied Harcourt's attention. As chairman of the last committee he drew up a report (3 Aug.) which recommended that a single body directly responsible to the people of London should take control of all the London water supply (cf. *Hansard*, 15 Feb. 1882). In the autumn he carefully considered the position of juvenile offenders, advocating the use of the birch instead of detention in prison. His recommendation led to a marked reduction in the number of juvenile criminal convictions (cf. speech at Cockermouth, 29 Oct. 1881). The revelations in Oct. 1881 of cruelty and abuses at St. Paul's Industrial School led him to propose a royal commission to inquire into the whole system of industrial and reformatory schools [see TAYLOR, HELEN, Suppl. II]. Harcourt firmly believed in capital punishment (cf. *Hansard*, 22 June 1881) and he administered the criminal law with merciful firmness.

But political disturbances in Ireland soon absorbed the attention of the government, and on Harcourt devolved the duty of carrying through the House of Commons, in the teeth of strenuous obstruction from the Irish members, the coercive measures which the government deemed necessary in the interests of order. After long and stormy debates (1–21 March 1881) he carried through the peace preservation (Ireland) bill, or the arms bill, which prohibited for five years, in certain districts proclaimed by the lord-lieutenant, the bearing of arms, and empowered the police to search for them. Next year, after the murder of Lord Frederick Cavendish and Mr. Burke in the Phœnix Park (6 May 1882), Harcourt introduced (11 May) the prevention of crimes (Ireland) bill, which empowered the lord-lieutenant, at discretion, to suspend trial by jury, and to substitute a commission of three judges of the Supreme Court, and granted an appeal to a court consisting of the whole of the judges. The bill, stringent though it was, met with the general approval of all parties in the house except the Irish members. The first reading was passed, after a short debate, by a majority of 305, although Mr. Dillon described Harcourt's speech as 'bloodthirsty.' The debate on the later stages of the bill proved a long struggle of endurance. The bill went into committee on 25 May, but it was not passed till 3 July, after a thirty-hours' continuous sitting of the house (30 June–1 July), in the course of which twenty-five Irish members were suspended for wilful obstruction. Throughout the proceedings Harcourt showed firmness, excellent temper and indifference to personal attack. The bill received the royal assent on 12 July. An autumn session, 24 Oct. to 2 Dec., was occupied in reforming the procedure of the House of Commons. Gladstone was absent owing to ill-health, and to Harcourt fell the task of defending the government's Irish policy against a spirited attack. The London campaign of the Irish dynamite conspirators in the spring of 1883 greatly increased Harcourt's responsibilities. In a circular to the police and local authorities, he urged the strictest supervision over the acquisition of explosives by the public. On 9 April he introduced into the house his explosive substance bill, which inflicted the severest penalties for the unlawful possession and illegal use of explosives. In the passing of the bill he achieved a record in parliamentary legislation. His introductory speech was concise and masterly, and so well suited to the temper of the house that, within two hours of his first rising, the bill was carried through all its stages. It was at once sent to the House of Lords, and its progress was marked by the same celerity there. Throughout the troublesome months that followed, Harcourt, who was never without police protection, succeeded in stamping out the dynamite conspiracy.

Meanwhile Harcourt continued in the recess to address great political gatherings throughout the country, defending with vigour the policy of the government and attacking the opposition. His reception was invariably enthusiastic. On 25 Aug. 1881 he was accorded the freedom of the city of Glasgow. At Burton-on-Trent

(22 Jan. 1882), and at the Drill Hall, Derby (25 April 1882), his audiences numbered many thousands. At Derby he pronounced a glowing eulogy on Gladstone, and when the prime minister at the end of the year contemplated resignation owing to illness, Harcourt urged him to hold on. On 16 Nov. many influential liberals met at the Westminster Palace Hotel to promote the foundation of the National Liberal Club, and Harcourt proposed the creation of a political and historical library to be called 'The Gladstone Library.'

The general legislation for which Harcourt was responsible during the rest of his tenure of office was small. In March he made a serious attempt to improve the conditions of labour in coal mines, and did much to extend the use of the Fleuss apparatus where the presence of injurious gases made conditions unhealthy. But the local government board (Scotland) bill, which he introduced on 29 June and which provided a board for Scotland, with full and independent jurisdiction over local Scottish affairs, passed the Commons on 17 Aug. 1883, only to be rejected by the House of Lords.

On 8 April 1884 Harcourt introduced his London government bill, which had been long in contemplation. It sought to consolidate the various governing bodies of the whole of London into a single corporation with full control of a large and defined area. The debate continued, with intervals, till 9 July, but the complexities of the bill and the ceaseless opposition which it aroused forced Harcourt reluctantly to abandon the measure. Meanwhile he was active both in parliament and the country in the struggle with the House of Lords over the franchise bill of 1884, and was as effective as the circumstances admitted in defence of the Egyptian policy of the government. He had supported Lord Hartington, the secretary for war, in despatching General Gordon in 1884 to the relief of Khartoum. On the fall of Khartoum and the death of Gordon (26 Jan. 1885) he resisted with rhetorical force the vote of censure on the government which was moved by Sir Stafford Northcote and brought the government majority down to fourteen. The government did not long survive. On 15 May 1885 Gladstone announced that a part of Harcourt's Crimes Act (Ireland) would be renewed, and on 8 June the Irish members and the tories combined on an amendment to the budget and the government was defeated by 264 to 252. Gladstone and his government at once resigned and Lord Salisbury became prime minister. Under the new government Harcourt succeeded in replacing a clause struck by the Lords out of the Registration Bill (July 23), which abolished the electoral disqualification of receipt of medical relief. During the month he censured the favourable reception by the government of Mr. Parnell's motion for an inquiry into the conduct of Lord Spencer's administration in regard to the Maamtrasna and other murder cases. At the same time he declared his unwillingness to support any future measure of coercion.

At the general election in November Harcourt's seat at Derby was contested, but he retained it without much difficulty. He devoted most of his time to an energetic campaign outside his constituency. While powerfully supporting his party, he dissociated himself at Blandford (24 Sept. 1885) from Mr. Chamberlain's extreme radicalism. The final result of the general election was that the conservatives and Parnellites exactly balanced the liberals, a difficult situation, which caused Harcourt disquietude. On 6 Dec. 1885 he wrote to Hartington that he looked 'forward to the tory government keeping up the Parnellite alliance, and so discrediting themselves' (*Life of Duke of Devonshire*, ii. 26). Speaking at Lowestoft next day he deprecated an early return of the liberals to office, preferring for his part that 'the tories should stew in the Parnellite juice, until they stank in the nostrils of the country' (*The Times*, 8 Dec. 1885). On 17 Dec. 1885 he declared himself in the depths of despair at party prospects, and divided the blame for the crisis between Mr. Chamberlain and Gladstone. Meanwhile rumours spread abroad that Gladstone was about to admit home rule into the party programme, but no word of that intention was communicated by Gladstone to his colleagues. On 28 Dec. Harcourt met Hartington, Mr. Chamberlain, and Sir Charles Dilke in London, and wrote jointly to Gladstone entreating him to give a straight answer respecting his intentions about home rule, and to consult his colleagues before committing himself to a new policy.

Parliament met on 12 Jan. 1886, and the current rumour of Gladstone's conversion to home rule was confirmed. The conservative government was defeated by a combination of liberals and home rulers, and Gladstone again became prime minister, 1 February. Lord Hartington, Sir Henry James, and Goschen at once declined to entertain a measure of home rule. Mr. Chamberlain and Sir George Trevelyan agreed to consider its details, without much hope of final assent. Harcourt had no hesitation in accepting Gladstone's guidance. Party loyalty was a paramount obligation. He would not desert the party ship and was sanguine of an early reunion with former colleagues who refused to join a home rule cabinet. He was very active in helping Gladstone to form the new ministry. He took the post of chancellor of the exchequer. He thus definitely became Gladstone's first lieutenant. He was acting leader of the house in the prime minister's absence, with the reversion, according to frequent precedent, to the headship of the government whenever a vacancy should arise.

Early in March Harcourt, while announcing the government's refusal to deal that session with disestablishment in Wales, treated the proposal with benevolence. On 8 April Gladstone introduced his home rule bill. Harcourt supported it in a powerful and impressive speech. All other methods of restoring tranquillity to Ireland had failed. The apparent suddenness of his conversion exposed him to bitter attack from the opposition and from dissentient liberals. He retorted that he had repudiated in the previous year the policy of coercion, and that home rule was the only alternative.

Harcourt's first budget, which he introduced on 15 April, was unexciting. A deficit of two and a half millions was to be supplied by existing taxes. The only innovation abolished, at a cost of 16,000*l.*, the tax upon beer brewed in cottages with a rental under 8*l.*

On the second reading debate of the home rule bill, which Gladstone moved on 10 May, Harcourt made one of the best speeches in defence, but the division, which was taken on 7 June, gave the government only 311 votes against 341.

At the general election which followed Harcourt retained his seat at Derby with difficulty, but outside his own constituency he prosecuted a vigorous campaign. With his aggressive temper there went a curious sensitiveness to attack by his former colleagues, and when Lord Hartington was announced (in June 1886) to speak against him at Derby, Harcourt wrote to protest, with the result that Lord Hartington cancelled his engagement. The conservatives, however, returned to power with a working majority of 113. Harcourt's term of office as chancellor of the exchequer ended on 20 July, having lasted less than six months. He was succeeded by Lord Randolph Churchill, and from the opposition benches mercilessly criticised the new government's Irish programme at the opening of the new parliament. But Harcourt still hoped to re-unite the liberal party, and at the end of 1886 he suggested a conference with that end. On 13 Jan. Lord Herschell, Harcourt, and Mr. (afterwards Viscount) Morley, representing the liberals, met Mr. Chamberlain and Sir George Trevelyan, representing the liberal-unionists, at Harcourt's London house. The deliberations continued at frequent intervals for two months, when the Round Table conference broke up without tangible results.

During the Salisbury parliament, 1886–1892, Harcourt, next to Gladstone himself, did more than any man by speeches in the House of Commons and the country to keep up the spirits of the liberal party. He was relentless in attack on the coercive policy of the conservative government in Ireland. Through 1887 he denounced the government's treatment of the attacks on Parnell and his colleagues by 'The Times' newspaper and strongly censured the constitution of the royal commission of inquiry into the charges. At the same time he fought hard for a reduction in national expenditure: he championed the social reforms of the party programme. Brilliant passages of arms with Mr. Chamberlain delighted the house. But Harcourt was no blind partisan. He helped to improve the government's Irish land bill, July, and the Allotments Act, Aug. 1887.

In the course of 1889 Harcourt delivered no less than nineteen set speeches at various liberal demonstrations in different parts of the country. His services to Gladstone proved invaluable and the relations between the two soon grew very close. During the Whitsuntide recess Gladstone stayed with him at Malwood, his country residence in the New Forest which he acquired in 1885, and Harcourt returned the visit to Hawarden in October. On the first night of the next session (12 Feb. 1890) Harcourt moved to condemn the publication of the Pigott letters in 'The Times' as a breach of privilege, but after a stormy debate, which lasted the whole evening, the motion was defeated by 260 to 212. During the session he opposed in his old 'Historicus' vein, by a long array of precedents and authorities, the cession of Heligoland to Germany. Towards the end of the summer the position of affairs was hopeful for the liberal party, but the condemnation of Parnell in the divorce court on 17 Nov. raised a new difficulty. On 21 Nov. Harcourt and Mr. John Morley attended the annual national liberal conference at Sheffield, and after the meeting they informed Gladstone of the delegates' opinion that the continuation of Parnell's leadership of the nationalists would be disastrous to home rule. Harcourt discussed the point with Gladstone, Mr. Arnold Morley, Mr. John Morley, and Lord Granville at Lord Rendel's house in London on 24 Nov. 1890. In the result Gladstone repudiated Parnell as leader of the Irish party. A split among the nationalists followed, and the liberal position in the House of Commons was weakened.

During the session of 1891 Gladstone's health often kept him away from the house, and Harcourt filled his place as leader of the opposition. Speaking in different parts of the country, he urged legislation in the interest of the agricultural labourer, the compulsory purchase of land for small holdings, local power to restrict the sale of liquor, declaring that home rule itself was insufficient to bring the liberals back to office. Home rule, disestablishment of the church in Wales, local control of liquor traffic, electoral reform, payment of members of parliament, the establishment of district councils, and the ending or mending of the House of Lords formed the Newcastle programme of the party which was formulated by the National Liberal Federation at Newcastle on 2 Oct. 1891, when Gladstone gave it his benediction. At Glasgow in October Harcourt championed with vigour the pronouncement which governed the policy of the party for the next four years. He was indefatigable in pressing the programme on the notice of the country, addressing upon it twenty-two public meetings next year. In the House of Commons he was not less active. In the session of 1892 he strenuously opposed Mr. Balfour's Irish local government bill, which passed its second reading on 24 May and was shortly afterwards withdrawn.

From the beginning of the year till after the dissolution of parliament on 29 June 1892, Harcourt sought to heal differences within the party and held several conferences at his private house with members of the extreme radical wing. At the end of June parliament dissolved, and at the ensuing general election 355 liberals and nationalists were returned, and 315 conservatives and liberal-unionists, thus giving a majority of 40 pledged to home rule. To Harcourt's efforts the result was largely due, but though returned at the head of the poll in his own constituency, it was by a considerably reduced majority. On 16 Aug Gladstone again became prime minister with Harcourt as chancellor of the exchequer.

Parliament met on 31 Jan. 1893, and the government's programme embraced not only home rule but bills for regulating a local veto, employers' liability, and local government. Gladstone's age and infirmities devolved on Harcourt, his lieutenant, a large share of the work of leading the house. Besides his budget, he took charge of the local veto bill, which provided that, on the demand of one-tenth of the municipal voters in any borough or ward, a vote might be taken which, by a majority of two-thirds of those actually voting, could extinguish every public-house licence in that area for a period of three years. The measure awoke bitter opposition, and was abandoned, to be reintroduced early in 1895. Harcourt's budget, which he introduced on 24 April, avoided surprises for lack of time. A deficit of 1,574,000*l.* was met by raising the income tax from 6*d.* to 7*d.* The session was mainly occupied by the home rule bill, which passed the third reading in the House of Commons on 1 Sept. by a majority of 34 and was rejected by the House of Lords on 8 Sept. by 419 against 41. The bill was thereupon for the time reluctantly dropped by the government. During the following autumn session Harcourt was prominent in the debates on the parish councils bill, which carried the session on to 10 Jan. 1894. At the beginning of Feb. the House of Lords amended the parish councils bill and greatly altered its powers. Harcourt, speaking at the annual conference of the National Liberal Federation at Portsmouth on 14 Feb., strongly denounced the action of the upper house, which he described as 'the champion of all abuses and the enemy of all reform.' On 1 March Gladstone made his last speech in the House of Commons, and on the same day attended his last cabinet council. Harcourt spoke a few words of 'acknowledgement and farewell,' of which Gladstone wrote to the Queen that they were 'undeservedly' kind. Two days later parliament was prorogued, and on the same day Gladstone resigned. The Queen on her own responsibility, and without consulting Gladstone, sent for Lord Rosebery, secretary for foreign affairs, and he consented to form a ministry.

The choice was a disappointment to Harcourt. He had well earned the reversion of the premiership. Entering public life when Lord Rosebery was at Eton, he had borne the brunt of a long stern fight and had acquired a wide experience of parliamentary ways. Since 1885 he had fought with untiring energy the battles of his party in and out of parliament. To the liberal cause he had been a pillar of strength. The majority of the liberal party regarded him as their champion. But Harcourt's loyalty to party and his conviction of its value were (in Lord Morley's phrase) 'indestructible instincts,' and he consented to serve under Lord Rosebery in his former office. When parliament met on 12 March 1894 he took his place as leader of the House of Commons.

The next sixteen months were the most strenuous period in Harcourt's political career. As leader in the House of Commons of a party with a small majority and a large and contentious programme, he exhibited unexpected skill, tact, and patience. His opinions did not always coincide with those of the prime minister, and, though for the most part they worked together in harmony, the cabinet councils were not free from friction. Both announced before the opening of parliament (12 March) adherence to the Newcastle programme, and Harcourt promised early legislation on the subject of temperance, to which he deemed himself personally pledged.

On the day after parliament re-assembled with Harcourt at the head of the House of Commons, the government suffered defeat. Henry Labouchere's amendment to the address, praying her Majesty to abolish the veto of the House of Lords, was carried against Harcourt's advice by 147 to 145. On 16 April Harcourt introduced his famous death duties budget. The estimated deficit for the year was 4,502,000*l.* The main principle of the bill was the abolition of the existing probate duty, the account duty, and Goschen's addition to the succession duty, and the imposition of a single graduated tax called the estate duty, chargeable on the principal value of all property, whether real or personal. The tax was graduated from one per cent. on estate of a value between 100*l.* and 500*l.* to a maximum of eight per cent. on estates over 1,000,000*l.* It proposed that the legacy and succession duties should be made identical in their application to realty and personalty. The income tax was raised from 7*d.* to 8*d.*, but the limit of exemption increased from 150*l.* to 160*l.* The abatement on incomes up to 400*l.* was raised from 120*l.* to 160*l.*, and a new abatement of 100*l.* created on incomes from 400*l.* to 500*l.* An increase of sixpence per barrel on beer and sixpence per gallon on spirits was imposed for one year only. A determined opposition was offered to the measure, and for three months it was subjected to every form of attack. But Harcourt had made himself familiar with every detail, and he met all criticisms with a firmness and conciliation which robbed the debate of much of its bitterness. Despite resistance, he carried his budget through the House of Commons on 17 July practically unimpaired, though by the narrow majority of 20, and without having once employed the closure. The bill was the most important legislative achievement of the year, and established Harcourt's reputation as a financier. Its results fully realised the expectations formed of them. Its main principles were not disturbed when the conservatives returned to power in the following year. During the rest of the session Harcourt helped to pass an evicted tenants (Ireland) bill and a local government bill for Scotland. The former bill was rejected by the House of Lords. The session closed on 25 Aug. During the recess, Harcourt abstained from platform speeches. He made a holiday tour in Italy. Consequent rumours of resignation were emphatically denied in a speech at Derby on 23 Jan. 1895, when amid scenes of great enthusiasm he denounced the House of Lords.

The session of 1895 opened on 5 Feb. under exceptional difficulties for the government, whose original majority of forty had fallen to less than twenty, mainly owing to the defection of the Parnellite group. The party programme included Welsh disestablishment, control of liquor traffic and plural voting. On 8 April Harcourt introduced his local liquor control bill, which mainly differed from that of 1893 by reducing the number of licences on the vote of a bare majority, at the same time as all licences were prohibited by a majority of two-thirds. The bill was read the first time before the Easter recess. On 2 May he introduced his fourth and last budget. He applied a realised surplus of 776,000*l.* to the reduction of debt and re-imposed the temporary tax of 1894 of sixpence per gallon of beer (yielding 500,000*l.*) in order to meet an estimated coming deficit of 319,000*l.* and provide a surplus of 181,000*l.* At the conclusion of his speech he declared that a continuation of the rise in national expenditure which had marked the last few years must inevitably lead to grave embarrassments. No serious opposition was offered to the measure, and it was finally passed on 10 May.

Most of May and June was devoted to the Welsh disestablishment bill. But the unexpected defeat of the government.

by a majority of seven, on 21 June, on a motion dealing with the supply of cordite, led to their immediate resignation. On 24 June, when Harcourt announced his retirement, he described the office of leader of the House of Commons as 'one of greater responsibility and higher obligation even than any office under the crown.' The highest of his ambitions was 'to stand well with the House of Commons.' It was his last speech as a minister of the crown.

The general election that followed was disastrous for the liberal party. Harcourt, while he appealed to his constituents for a mandate to deal with the House of Lords, and to pass the remainder of the Newcastle programme, emphasised the urgent need of temperance legislation. The plea was not popular. On 13 July the two liberal candidates at Derby, Harcourt and Sir Thomas Roe, were both defeated. The final result of the electoral conflict was to put the conservatives into power with the large majority of 152. For the second time Harcourt had to seek a new constituency, and West Monmouth was generously vacated in his favour by Cornelius Marshall Warmington, K.C., who was created a baronet in 1908. Although the liberal majority there was over 5000, the seat was contested, but Harcourt succeeded in slightly increasing the majority. Parliament met on 12 Aug. for the passing of supply, and was prorogued on 5 Sept. Harcourt spent the greater part of the next four months in retirement at Malwood.

Parliament met on 11 Feb. 1896, and Harcourt once more led the opposition with unabated vigour. Speaking at Bournemouth on 11 March 1896 he pledged the liberal party to the principle of self-government for Ireland, to a reform of registration and of the House of Lords, and to the cause of temperance. During the session he attacked the advance of the Anglo-Egyptian army into the Soudan, and asked for an inquiry into the circumstances of the Jameson Raid. After the trial of Dr. Jameson, Mr. Chamberlain moved for a select committee to inquire into recent events in Africa (30 July), and he accepted Harcourt's amendment to extend the inquiry to the raid itself. He was appointed a member of the committee, but only one meeting was held before Parliament was prorogued. From Feb. to July 1897 the committee continued its work at short intervals. Harcourt was prominent in examining witnesses, and his examination of Cecil Rhodes, though severe and searching, was universally admitted to be just. Finally in July Harcourt signed the majority report, which condemned the raid and censured Rhodes, but exonerated the colonial office and the high commissioner. Some members of his own party complained that the findings of the committee were inconclusive. Labouchere accused the two front benches of a conspiracy of silence, and declared that the committee had failed to probe the matter to the bottom. Harcourt defended the committee's decision, which was the only one that the evidence justified, but he failed to conciliate his critics. Some years later, on 20 Feb. 1900, when party feeling over South Africa was running high, he supported an abortive resolution to reopen the inquiry into the raid with a view to further investigation of the rumours that Rhodes's agents had endeavoured to implicate state officials in London and the Cape.

Meanwhile Harcourt offered uncompromising opposition to most of the domestic measures of the unionist government. The education bill, which was introduced on 31 March 1896 and withdrawn on 18 June, Harcourt denounced as extinguishing the school boards and reintroducing the religious difficulty. He treated with scarcely less vigour the agricultural rating bill, which was passed only after long and strenuous debates.

Internal differences hampered the influence of the party. Harcourt rarely referred in public to Lord Rosebery, his titular chief, whose followers showed small respect for Harcourt. The breach was widened by the Armenian massacres in Sept. 1896. Gladstone came forth from his retirement to urge on England a moral obligation to intervene between Turkey and her persecuted Armenian subjects. Harcourt expressed practical agreement with Gladstone in a speech to his constituents at Ebbw Vale on 5 Oct. Lord Rosebery promptly avowed his dissent from Gladstone's and Harcourt's views by resigning the liberal leadership. In a speech at Edinburgh (9 Oct.) he declared that the internal troubles of the party 'were not less than the external.' No immediate steps were taken definitely to elect a new leader. Mr. Morley asserted at Glasgow on 6 Nov. that it was at present enough for the party that Sir William Harcourt led them to admiration in the House of Commons. But Mr. Morley's applause was not universally shared within the liberal ranks, and the wounds left by Lord Rosebery's withdrawal failed to heal. Through the spring of 1897 Harcourt constantly commented in the house and in the country on the attitude of the government towards the war between Turkey and Greece. His sympathies lay with Greece, and he urged the annexation of Crete to that country. In the result Crete was liberated from Turkey, and a Christian administrator, Prince George of Greece, was made high commissioner. A political tour in East Scotland followed in November, in the course of which he addressed large audiences. Harcourt stayed with Sir Henry Campbell-Bannerman at Belmont Castle, receiving the freedom of Dundee (25 Nov.), and he revisited Kirkcaldy, the scene of his first parliamentary contest. During 1898 he constantly discussed the position of China. There at first he supported Lord Salisbury's policy of 'the open door' and the preservation of the integrity of China. But he opposed the lease by the British government of Wei-hai-wei (5 April) and attacked the government (29 April) for accepting the principle of spheres of influence in place of a recognition of commercial freedom and equal rights of all nations. In the House of Commons on 20 May, the day after Gladstone's death, he paid an eloquent and touching tribute to his old friend and leader, and at Gladstone's funeral in Westminster Abbey (28 May 1898) he acted as a pall-bearer.

Shortly afterwards he turned from current politics to ecclesiastical controversy. In stubbornly opposing the government's benefices bill through June, he resumed his early rôle of champion of protestantism and alleged a conspiracy in the Church of England to overthrow the principles of the Reformation. After the passing of the bill, until the end of the year he continued the controversy in letters to 'The Times' on 'Lawlessness in the Church,' which he collected in a volume called 'The Crisis in the Church.' He accused the clergy of violating the vows under which they were ordained. Harcourt's attack on ritualism excited a wide discussion and led to the prohibition by the bishops of some ritualistic practices which were current in advanced churches. The decision of the two archbishops against the ceremonial use of incense and processional lights (Aug. 1899) brought forth a triumphant letter from Harcourt in 'The Times.'

During the parliamentary recess of 1898 Harcourt's public appearances were rare, but at Aberystwith on 26 Oct., where he opened the new University College buildings, and at the City of London's banquet to Lord Kitchener on 4 Nov. he commended the handling by the government of the Fashoda difficulty. Meanwhile Harcourt's relations with the imperialistic section of his party who continued to regard Lord Rosebery as leader were growing increasingly strained. His authority was questioned through what he called the 'sectional disputes and personal interests' which divided the ranks.

On 8 Dec. he startled the public mind by announcing in a letter to Mr. Morley his resignation of the leadership of the liberal party in the House of Commons and his resolution to 'undertake no responsibility and to occupy no position the duties of which it is made impossible for me to fulfil.' His retirement was followed by that of Mr. Morley, who, in a speech to his constituents at Brechin on 17 Jan. 1899, announced his withdrawal from active participation in the policy of the front opposition bench. At a meeting of the liberal party in the Reform Club on 6 Feb. Sir Henry Campbell-Bannerman was elected Harcourt's successor in the leadership. Fine tributes were then paid to Harcourt, and, in addition to the formal resolution of regret, the meeting expressed 'its continued confidence in him.' But experience showed that there was small likelihood of his maintaining the unity of the party.

As a private member Harcourt showed from time to time activity in criticism of the government. He condemned the suspension of the sinking fund in April 1899 and scorned an imperial policy which failed to pay its way. At the beginning of May he supported the church discipline bill. At a dinner of the Welsh parliamentary party (6 May) he vehemently advocated, in opposition to advice which Lord Rosebery had lately tendered the party, the old programme of reform, and on 31 May, in a speech at Nantyglo, he urged England to develop her present possessions rather than increase her obligations by the addition of new ones.

Of the difficulties with the Transvaal Harcourt took a judicial view. He allowed the need of internal reform, but on the outbreak of war (Oct. 1899), while he condemned in the House of Commons the Boer ultimatum, he declared that he was not satisfied that the course pursued by the government had been 'in every respect most conducive to peace.' His prophecy that the war would cost 100,000,000*l.* was received with derision by the tories. On 30 Jan. 1900 he supported the vote of censure on the conduct of the war and blamed the government for basing their preparations on a contemptuous estimate of the character and resources of the Boers, but he expressed his confidence in the ultimate success of the British troops, whose valour he eulogised. Beyond some caustic criticisms of the government's financial proposals, he figured little in the House of Commons debates for the remainder of the first session of 1900, but during the general election in Sept. and Oct. he conducted a spirited campaign in his constituency of West Monmouthshire. He denounced the government's 'audacious' attempt to confine the election to the issue of the war, and discussed social problems, emphasising the need of comprehensive educational reform, with the elimination of all sectarian influence, and of legislation in the cause of temperance. He was in his seventy-third year, but his energy and eloquence were unabated. He retained his seat by a large majority. 'I wish I could join you in retiring' he wrote on 18 Oct. 1900 to Goschen who was resigning his place in the unionist government. 'Your party can, with regret, afford it. Mine is too short-handed to spare a single man at the ropes.'

In the new parliament Harcourt watched narrowly the course of events in South Africa. He declared that the cost of the war would have to be borne by the British tax-payer and that it was idle for the government to expect a contribution from the Transvaal (*Hansard*, 13 Dec. 1900). When on 14 June 1901 he and Campbell-Bannerman were entertained by the National Reform Union, Harcourt denounced the war as 'unjust and engineered' and 'recommended upon all sorts of false pretences,' but was less vehement in condemnation than his colleague. On 16 Jan. 1902 he elaborately denounced as an unconstitutional violation of the statute laws the action of the governor of Cape Colony in suspending, on the advice of the Cape ministers, the constitution of the colony. Throughout 1903, in both speeches and letters to 'The Times' (5 and 16 Feb. and 1 April), he vigorously protested against the introduction of forced labour into South Africa. In a letter to Lord Carrington, which was read (10 Feb. 1904) at a large protest meeting in Queen's Hall, he described the project as 'throwing back the moral sense of the nation a whole century since the final emancipation of the slave.' Other questions which engaged Harcourt's energies at this period were Sir Michael Hicks Beach's budget proposals of 1902, when he resisted the proposed tax on imported corn. On 12 May he moved an amendment (defeated by 296 to 188) to the finance bill asking the house to 'decline to impose customs duties on grain, flour, or other articles of first necessity for the food of the people.' During the same session he opposed Mr. Balfour's education bill, which he declared did nothing for the cause of elementary education but threatened an educational civil war; the bill not only destroyed the school boards but removed voluntary schools from popular control (cf. speeches to constituents, 8–9 Oct. 1902).

Mr. Chamberlain's advocacy of a reform in the fiscal system in 1903 roused Harcourt to fresh activity. Again both in speeches in the country and in letters to 'The Times' (13 July, 7 and 19 Aug., and 17 Nov. 1903) he reiterated his faith in free trade. Always loyal to the Crown, Harcourt was on friendly terms with the Prince of Wales, afterwards Edward VII. On 26 March 1901, at a public meeting at the Mansion House, he seconded the resolution, moved by Mr. Balfour, in favour of erecting a national monument to Queen Victoria in front of Buckingham Palace. At the coronation of Edward VII in 1902 he was offered a peerage, but this he respectfully but firmly declined. He was made honorary fellow of Trinity College, Cambridge, on 14 Nov. 1902. Early in 1904 his health showed signs of failing, and on 29 Feb. he announced to his constituents his intention of not seeking re-election, at the same time prophesying victory for the united party of progress. Even then his part in politics was not quite ended. In 'The Times' (14 March 1904), under the heading 'The Leader and the Led,' he wrote with his old incisiveness of the split in the tory ranks occasioned by the fiscal reform controversy.

On 17 May he spoke in the House of Commons for nearly an hour on the finance bill. His last speech was delivered at the annual reception of the National Liberal Club on 27 July, when he protested against the growing want of consideration exhibited towards the House of Commons by the employment of the closure and the 'guillotine' as the 'daily dram.' By the death, on 23 March 1904, of his nephew, Aubrey Vernon Harcourt, the only son of his elder brother, Edward William Harcourt, Sir William succeeded to the family estates at Nuneham, Oxfordshire. There his last days were spent in full possession of his faculties and of health. The evening before his death he appeared in his usual health. He retired to rest at his accustomed hour on Friday, 30 Sept., and quietly passed away in his sleep.

In a message of condolence from King Edward VII to Lady Harcourt the king described Harcourt as 'an old and valued friend.' He was buried in the old church within the grounds of Nuneham on 6 Oct. The funeral was attended only by the tenants and the immediate relatives. A memorial service was held at St. Margaret's, Westminster, on the same day.

Harcourt was twice married: first, on 5 Nov. 1859, to Maria Theresa, daughter of Thomas Henry Lister [q. v.] of Armitage Park, Yorkshire, and of Lady Theresa Lister, sister of Lord Clarendon. She died on 31 Jan. 1863, leaving two sons, of whom one died in infancy, and the other, Lewis, born on 31 Jan. 1863, after acting as private secretary to his father from 1882 to 1904, became first commissioner of works in Sir Henry Campbell-Bannerman's government in 1905 and colonial secretary in Mr. Asquith's administration in 1910. On 2 Dec. 1876 Harcourt married secondly Elizabeth, widow of Mr. J. P. Ives and a daughter of John Lothrop Motley, historian and sometime United States minister in London. Lady Harcourt survives with one son, Robert Vernon (*b.* 7 May 1878), liberal M.P. for Montrose burghs since 1908.

The figure of Justinian, in the fresco 'The School of Legislation' at Lincoln's Inn Hall, is a portrait of Harcourt at the age of thirty-three. It was painted from a sketch, now at Nuneham, which was taken by the artist, G. F. Watts, R.A., in 1860. The best portrait of Harcourt was painted by Mr. A. S. Cope, R.A., and was just finished at his death. It was intended as a gift to Harcourt himself; after his death it was presented to his son, Mr. Lewis Harcourt (in Feb. 1905), by a subscription of the liberal party, and it now hangs at Nuneham Park; a copy was at the same time subscribed for by the National Liberal Club. A bust by Mr. Waldo Story was modelled in Rome in 1899; the original plaster cast was presented by the sculptor to the National Portrait Gallery in 1907. A life-size statue of Harcourt, wearing the robes of a chancellor of the exchequer, stands in the members' lobby of the House of Commons. It is also by Mr. Waldo Story and was subscribed for by the members of the House of Commons; it was unveiled on 14 Jan. 1906 by Sir Henry Campbell-Bannerman. There were portraits in 'Vanity Fair' in 1870, 1892 (by 'Spy'), 1897, and 1899.

In his youth remarkably handsome, Harcourt assumed, later in life, robust proportions which were eminently suited to his vigorous and aggressive temperament. He sprang from a stock essentially conservative and inherited an immense respect for tradition; as soon, however, as he was convinced of the necessity for change, no man was more courageous or more earnest in his advocacy of radical measures of reform. Perhaps his greatest achievement was the passing of his death duties budget in 1894, a measure which almost revolutionised the existing system of taxation. Essentially a House of Commons man, he was a zealous guardian of its traditions, and he preserved to the twentieth century the grand manner of the whig orators of the eighteenth century. He was one of the last and one of the greatest of the old school of Parliamentarians.

Harcourt ranks with the few men who could talk as brilliantly as they could write. He was an indefatigable worker, and his speeches, which were monuments of closely reasoned arguments, teeming with facts and illuminated by witty epigrams, were generally most diligently prepared and delivered by the aid of copious notes. He was at his best, however, when suddenly called upon to debate, and was never so happy as when he was fighting a hopeless battle against overwhelming odds. Imbued with the spirit of the gladiator, he possessed the gift of the advocate and could quickly concentrate his powers of picturesque invective, sarcasm and paradox. Instinctively an aristocrat and living in an aristocratic atmosphere, he never hesitated to express his contempt for every form of meanness or pretension. Unable to suffer fools gladly, and impatient of mediocrity, he earned the reputation of irascibility and haughtiness. But beneath his aggressive manner he possessed a large-hearted tenderness which endeared him to those who knew him well, and he was one of the few who preserved his friendships intact through the home rule split in the liberal party. Valuing old associations, he delighted to treasure up souvenirs of his friends and colleagues. His wit and good-nature made him a favourite in society. Nothing delighted him more than to gather round him a few kindred spirits, irrespective of party or creed. In his home in the New Forest he was the happiest and merriest of men. There he pursued his favourite hobbies of gardening and dairy farming. A devoted husband and father, he found in the affection of his family a haven of rest amid a life of strenuous fighting.

[Herbert Paul's History of Modern England, 1904–6; Morley's Life of Gladstone, 1903; Earl of Selborne's Memorials Family and Personal; Holland's Life of the Duke of

Devonshire, 1911; Elliot's Life of Lord Goschen, 1911; Sir Robert Anderson's Lighter Side of Official Life, 1910; (Sir) Arthur Griffith Boscawen's Fourteen Years in Parliament, 1907; Justin McCarthy's History of Our Own Times; H. W. Lucy's The Disraeli Parliament, 1885, The Gladstone Parliament, 1886, The Salisbury Parliament, 1892, and The Balfourian Parliament, 1906; T. F. G. Coates's Lord Rosebery, 1900; T. P. O'Connor's Gladstone House of Commons, 1885; Hansard Parl. Reports, 1868–1904; Ann. Reg., 1868–1904; The Times 1 Oct., 1904, and passim; private papers in possession of Mr. Lewis Harcourt.] A. L. A.

HARDWICKE, sixth EARL OF. [See YORKE, ALBERT EDWARD PHILIP HENRY (1867–1904), under-secretary of state for war.]

HARDY, FREDERIC DANIEL (1827–1911), painter of domestic subjects, born at Windsor on 13 Feb. 1827, was son of George Hardy, a musician to George IV, Queen Adelaide, and Queen Victoria, who showed some taste for painting. The eldest brother also, George Hardy (1822–1909), was a painter of domestic subjects, especially cottage interiors. Brought up to the musical profession, Frederic soon abandoned music for painting, in which his eldest brother instructed him. In 1851 he began to exhibit at the Royal Academy and British Institution small but highly finished interiors with figures. Careful detail was combined with breadth and refinement. He excelled in depicting cottage interiors, reproducing the surfaces of walls and brick floors with notable effect. His work soon became popular. He exhibited ninety-three pictures at the Academy between 1851 and 1898, five at the British Institution, and a few at other galleries. High prices were paid for his pictures at sales. 'A Quartette Party' fetched 810 guineas at Christie's in 1873, and 'Reading the Will' 550 guineas in 1877. Other of his works were 'A Christmas Party' (1857), 'The Foreign Guest' (1859), 'Coal Heavers' (1865), 'The Late Arrival' (1873), 'Fatherless' (1876), 'A Music Party' (1879), and 'The Pet Lamb' (1888). He also painted a few portraits. 'Still Life' (1852) and 'Sunday Afternoon' (cottage interiors) are at the Victoria and Albert Museum; 'Children Playing at Doctors' (1863) at the Bethnal Green Museum; 'Try This Pair' and 'Little Helpers' at the Corporation Art Gallery, Guildhall, London; 'Interior of a Sussex Farmhouse' at the Leicester Corporation Art Gallery; 'Expectation' (interior of a cottage with mother and children, 1854) at the Royal Holloway College, Egham; eighteen pictures, of which two only 'Baby's Birthday' (1867) and 'A Misdeal' (1877) are dated, at the Municipal Art Gallery, Wolverhampton; and 'Tragedy' (four feet by six feet), lifesize figures in the box of a theatre (1880) at the City Art Gallery, Leeds.

On leaving Windsor, about 1852, Hardy after a short residence at Snell's Wood, near Amersham, Buckinghamshire, settled about 1854 at Cranbrook, Kent, where his brother George and his friends Thomas Webster, R.A. [q. v.], who was related to Hardy's mother, John Callcott Horsley, R.A. [q. v. Suppl. II], George Henry Boughton, A.R.A. [q. v. Suppl. II], and G. B. O'Neill also worked. Like Webster, he had a studio in the house known as the 'Old Studio' in the High Street. About 1875 he moved to Kensington but returned to Cranbrook about 1893. He died at 1 Waterloo Place, Cranbrook, on 1 April 1911, and was buried by the side of his wife in St. Dunstan's churchyard.

He married on 11 March 1852 Rebecca Sophia (*d.* 1906), daughter of William Dorrofield, of Chorley Wood, by whom he had five sons and one daughter.

[Private information; A. G. Temple, The Art of Painting, 302, 303; Ottley, Dict.; Graves, Dict. of Artists, Roy. Acad. and British Institution Exhibitors; Redford, Art Sales, ii. 49–50; J. C. Horsley, Recollections of a Royal Academician, p. 338.] B. S. L.

HARDY, GATHORNE GATHORNE-, first EARL OF CRANBROOK (1814–1906), statesman. [See GATHORNE-HARDY.]

HARE, AUGUSTUS JOHN CUTHBERT (1834–1903), author, born on 13 March 1834, at the Villa Strozzi, Rome, was youngest son in a large family of Francis George Hare of Hurstmonceaux, Sussex, by his wife Anne Frances, daughter of Sir John Dean Paul of Rodborough. Augustus Hare [q. v.] and Julius Hare [q. v.] were his uncles. In August 1835 he was adopted by his godmother, Maria, daughter of Oswald Leycester, rector of Stoke-upon-Tern, Shropshire, and widow of his uncle, Augustus Hare, his parents renouncing all further claim upon him. Educated first at Harnish Rectory (1843–6) he was sent in 1847 to Harrow, but ill-health compelled him to leave in the following year. He then studied under private tutors till 1853, when he matriculated at University College, Oxford, graduating B.A. in 1857. After residence abroad, mostly in Italy, from June 1857 till November 1858, he returned to England. In the following year he undertook for John Murray a handbook of

'Berks, Bucks and Oxfordshire' (1860). A 'Handbook to Durham,' in the same series, followed in 1863. His adoptive mother's failing health then made residence in a warm climate necessary, and, except for occasional visits to England, he remained abroad, mostly in Italy and the Riviera, from 1863 till June 1870. In November of that year his adoptive mother died, and he sought to perpetuate her memory in 'Memorials of a Quiet Life' (3 vols. 1872–6). The book subsequently ran into eighteen editions, and inaugurated a series of biographies written by him in the same mildly deferential key.

Hare mainly devoted his literary energy to the compilation of guide-books, material for which he gained in foreign tours. He sought to avoid the habitual conciseness and dryness of the ordinary guide-book, and mainly aimed at gathering up 'what had already been given to the world in a less portable form' (*Walks in Rome*, p. 3). The fruit of his own observation was combined with extracts from other books, often more copious than was justifiable. Freeman charged Hare with appropriating in 'Cities of Northern and Central Italy' (3 vols. 1876) articles of his in the 'Saturday Review.' He was accused, too, of copying 'Murray's Handbook to Northern Italy,' and was involved in consequence in legal proceedings. But despite these complaints Hare's practice remained unaltered.

Hare was also an artist of some power in water-colour, and he illustrated many of his own works. An exhibition of his water-colour sketches took place in London in the autumn of 1902.

In the latter part of his life Hare acquired a residence at Holmhurst, St. Leonards-on-Sea, where he collected books and pictures. He was a devotee of fashionable culture, and when in England much of his time was spent in visiting country-houses, where he was well known as a raconteur of ghost stories. His large circle of distinguished friends included Oscar II, King of Sweden, who decorated him with the order of St. Olaf in 1878. His 'The Story of My Life' (6 vols. 1896–1900), a long, tedious, and indiscreet autobiography, owed its vogue to its 'stories' of society. He died unmarried on 22 Jan. 1903 at Holmhurst, and was buried at Hurstmonceaux, Sussex.

Hare also published: 1. 'Epitaphs for Country Churchyards,' Oxford, 1856. 2. 'A Winter in Mentone,' 1862, 12mo. 3. 'Walks in Rome,' 2 vols. 1871; 17th edit. 1905. 4. 'Wanderings in Spain,' 1873. 5. 'Days near Rome,' 1875; 4th edit. 1905. 6. 'Walks in London,' 2 vols. 1878; 7th edit. 1901. 7. 'Life and Letters of Frances Baroness Bunsen,' 2 vols. 1878; 3rd edit. 1882. 8. 'Cities of Southern Italy and Sicily,' Edinburgh, 1883. 9. 'Florence,' 1884; 6th edit. 1904. 10. 'Venice,' 1884; 6th edit. 1904. 11. 'Cities of Central Italy,' 2 vols. 1884. 12. 'Cities of Northern Italy,' 2 vols. 1884. 13. 'Sketches in Holland and Scandinavia,' 1885. 14. 'Studies in Russia,' 1885. 15. 'Days near Paris,' 1887. 16. 'Paris,' 1887; 2nd edit., 2 vols., 1900. 17. 'North Eastern France,' 1890. 18. 'South Eastern France,' 1890. 19. 'South Western France,' 1890. 20. 'The Story of Two Noble Lives, Charlotte, Countess Canning, and Louisa, Marchioness of Waterford,' 3 vols. 1893. 21. 'Life and Letters of Maria Edgeworth,' 2 vols., 1894. 22. 'Sussex,' 1894. 23. 'North Western France,' 1895. 24. 'Biographical Sketches,' 1895. 25. 'The Gurneys of Earlham,' 2 vols. 1895. 26. 'The Rivieras,' 1896. 27. 'Shropshire,' 1898.

[The Athenæum, 31 Jan. 1903; The Times, 23, 27, and 28 Jan. 1903; The Story of My Life, 6 vols., 1896–1900; Who's Who, 1903.]

S. E. F.

HARLAND, HENRY (1861–1905), novelist, born at St. Petersburg on 1 March 1861, was only child of Thomas Harland, a lawyer of Norwich, Connecticut. He regarded himself as heir to the baronetcy of Harland of Sproughton, co. Suffolk, which was not claimed by his family on the death in 1848 of Sir Robert Harland, second baronet (G.E.C., *Complete Baronetage*, v. 155) because under the laws of Connecticut they would lose part of their property in that state. Brought up mainly in Rome, he studied in the University of Paris, acquiring a knowledge of the life of the Latin Quarter which he afterwards put to literary use. Subsequently he studied in Harvard University, though without graduating, and after returning for a year to Rome, where he wrote letters for the 'New York Tribune,' he entered the surrogate's office in New York.

Harland commenced his literary career with 'As it was Written: a Jewish Musician's Story,' which was published in London in 1885, under the name of 'Sidney Luska.' It was a sensational novel, dealing with Jewish-American life. Many stories of the same type followed under the same pseudonym, and although of no high literary merit they brought Harland both reputation and pecuniary profit in America. 'Grandison Mather' (1890), one of the last, was reviewed in the 'Athenæum' as 'a clever and lively novel by an author who deserves to be better known in England.' Soon after 1890 Harland resolved to abandon sensational fiction, and coming to England set himself deliberately to develop a literary style. Thenceforth he spent most of his time in London.

The first two books which appeared under his own name, 'Two Women or One?' (1890), an ingenious story of double personality, and 'Mea Culpa: a Woman's Last Word' (1891), show no marked breach of affinity with his earlier work. But in 1893, in 'Mademoiselle Miss and other Stories,' he gave the first, if imperfect, evidence of an independent style. This little book was followed by 'Grey Roses' in 1895 and 'Comedies and Errors' in 1898, delicate studies which proved the writer's mastery of the art of the short story. The influence of Mr. Henry James was visible in Harland's work. Discerning critics at once acknowledged his promise, and from its birth in 1894 until its demise in 1897 he was literary editor of the 'Yellow Book,' a quarterly literary and artistic magazine, which reckoned among its contributors authors and artists of an advanced æsthetic school. In 1900, through 'The Cardinal's Snuff Box,' a full-length novel of artistic charm, Harland first became known to the general public. Similar work followed until Harland's death at San Remo on 20 Dec. 1905. He married Aline Merriam, of French extraction. He had no children.

Besides the books already mentioned, Harland wrote, under the pseudonym 'Sidney Luska': 1. 'Mrs. Pexeida,' New York, 1886. 2. 'The Yoke of the Thorah,' New York, 1888. 3. 'My Uncle Florimond,' Boston, 1888. 4. 'A Latin Quarter Courtship, and other Stories,' 1890. Under his own name he also wrote: 5. 'The Lady Paramount,' 1902. 6. 'My Friend Prospero,' 1904. 7. 'The Royal End,' issued posthumously in 1909. He translated Matilde Serao's 'Fantasia' (1891), and wrote an introduction to a translation of Octave Feuillet's 'Roman d'un Jeune Homme Pauvre' (1902). Mrs. Harland translated Matilde Serao's 'Addio, Amore!' (1894).

A sketch portrait of Harland is reproduced in the 'Early Work of Aubrey Beardsley,' who also caricatured Harland in the frontispiece to John Davidson's 'Scaramouch in Naxos' (1889).

[The Times, 22 Dec. 1905; Athenæum, 30 Dec. 1905; New International Encyclopædia, 1910.] F. L. B.

HARLEY, ROBERT (1828–1910), congregational minister and mathematician, born in Liverpool on 23 Jan. 1828, was third son of Robert Harley by his wife Mary, daughter of William Stevenson, and niece of General Stevenson of Ayr, N.B. The father, after some success as a merchant, became a minister of the Wesleyan Methodist Association, and his frequent migrations on circuit gave his son Robert little opportunity of education. But his mathematical aptitude developed rapidly, and before he was seventeen he was appointed to a mathematical mastership at Seacombe, near Liverpool. He later served in the same capacity at Blackburn. In 1854 he entered the congregational ministry, and was stationed at Brighouse, Yorkshire, until 1868, filling in addition the chair of mathematics and logic at Airedale College during the latter portion of the time.

From 1868 to 1872 he was pastor of the oldest congregational church at Leicester, and from 1872 to 1881 was vice-principal of Mill Hill School, where he officiated in the chapel. At Mill Hill he was instrumental in erecting a public lecture hall where total abstinence was advocated, popular entertainments were held, and varied instruction given. From 1882 to 1885 he was principal of Huddersfield College, and from 1886 to 1890 minister of the congregational church at Oxford, where he was made hon. M.A. in 1886. Having fulfilled a ministerial appointment in Australia, he was pastor of Heath Church, Halifax, from 1892 until 1895, when he relinquished ministerial labours and settled at Forest Hill, near London. His energy and industry were unimpaired to the last; he fulfilled preaching engagements in London and the provinces, and was unceasing in the public advocacy of temperance.

Throughout his career mathematics remained Harley's chief study. He devoted much time to higher algebra, especially to the theory of the general equation of the fifth degree. His conclusions, which were published in 'Memoirs of the Manchester Lit. and Phil. Soc.' 1860, xv. 172–219, were independently reached at the same time by Sir James Cockle [q. v.]. Harley's two further papers on the 'Theory of Quintics' (in 'Quarterly Journal of Mathematics' 1860–2, iii. 343–59; v. 248–60), and an exposition of Cockle's method of symmetric products in 'Phil. Trans.' (1860) attracted the attention of Arthur Cayley [q. v. Suppl. I], who carried the research further. In 1863 Harley was admitted F.R.S. He acted as secretary of the A section of the British

Association at meetings at Norwich (1868) and Edinburgh (1871), and was a vice-president of the meetings at Bradford (1873), Bath (1888), and Cardiff (1891).

He failed to complete the treatise on quintics which he had begun, but continued to contribute papers of importance on pure mathematics to the transactions of various societies. A masterly sketch of the life and work of George Boole appeared in the 'British Quarterly Review' (July 1866), and a memoir of his friend, Sir James Cockle, is in the 'Proc. Roy. Soc.' vol. lix.

Harley died at Rosslyn, Westbourne Road, Forest Hill, on 26 July 1910, and was buried in Ladywell cemetery. In 1854 he married Sara, daughter of James Stroyan of Wigan; she died in 1905.

[Private information; Biograph, vi. 1881; The Times, 28 July 1910; Harley's Memoir of Sir James Cockle, Proc. Roy. Soc. lix. Men and Women of the Time, 1899; Memoir of Robert Harley by Prof. E. B. Elliott in Proc. London Math. Soc., ser. 2, vol. ix.] M. B.

HARRINGTON, TIMOTHY CHARLES (1851–1910), Irish politician, born in 1851 at Castletownbere, co. Cork, was son of Denis Harrington by his wife Eileen O'Sullivan. Educated at the local national school, he subsequently became an assistant teacher there. At twenty-six he joined the teaching staff of the Dominican School, Holy Cross, Tralee, co. Kerry, but withdrew almost immediately and engaged in journalism. With his brother Edward he founded the 'Kerry Sentinel' in 1877, and edited it during the land agitation in the south. He finally handed it over to his brother. He found time to enter the law school of Trinity College, Dublin, in 1884, but did not graduate. He was in full sympathy with the nationalist movement, and at the invitation of Mr. Parnell, who recognised his organising power, he accepted in 1882 the post of secretary of the Land League. The success of the organisation was largely due to Harrington's ability and endurance. He suffered two terms of imprisonment under Coercion Acts, once in 1881 for three months, again in 1883 for two months. When the Land League was dissolved and replaced by the National League in 1882 Harrington became secretary of the new organisation, and in 1886 was mainly responsible for devising the formidable 'Plan of Campaign' which greatly stimulated the land war (cf. DAVITT'S *Fall of Feudalism in Ireland*, pp. 514 sq.). In 1883, while in prison in Mullingar under the Coercion Acts, he was returned unopposed as nationalist M.P. for co. Westmeath. In 1885 he was elected M.P. for the Harbour division of Dublin, and retained the seat till his death. In 1887 he was called to the Irish bar, and during that and subsequent years he defended many of the political prisoners in the Irish courts. He had already made a strong stand in the press against what he believed was the unfair administration of justice in Ireland, and was specially prominent in asserting the innocence of Miles Joyce, executed for the Maamtrasna murders in 1885. He attended the trial and published in pamphlet form 'The Maamtrasna Massacres, Impeachment of the Trials' (1885; reprinted from the 'Freeman's Journal'). Much feeling was aroused by his denunciation. His most important brief was that of counsel for Parnell in the Parnell commission in 1888–9 at the law courts in Dublin. His knowledge of the country was of the greatest service to Parnell's leading counsel, Sir Charles Russell. While the commission was sitting he was fined 500*l.* for contempt of court for an article which appeared in the 'Kerry Sentinel.' When the split in the Irish party took place owing to Parnell's condemnation in the divorce suit, Harrington broke away from the majority and supported Parnell, with whom his relations were always personally close. On Parnell's death in 1891 he served under Mr. John Redmond, Parnell's successor. In 1901, being then a town councillor of Dublin, he was elected lord mayor of Dublin, and held the office for the exceptional period of three years. His conduct in the chair was eulogised by men of all parties. While lord mayor he took part in the land conference of 1902, which resulted in the Wyndham Land Act of 1903. It was largely due to his efforts that the disunited Irish party was reconstituted under Mr. Redmond in 1900. He filled many offices in Dublin with honour and dignity, and was appointed secretary of the Dublin committee under the Old Age Pensions Act of 1909. His health was at this time precarious, and he died on 12 March 1910 at his residence in Harcourt Street, Dublin, and was buried in Glasnevin cemetery near the grave of his famous leader.

Harrington never had full scope for his abilities. He showed first-rate capacity as a barrister, but his political sentiment was too strong to permit him to concentrate his powers on his profession. It is mainly on his record as secretary of the Land League that Harrington's reputation rests. His refusal of government positions when he was in sore financial straits proved his thorough disinterestedness. He was held in high esteem by his political opponents. He married in 1892 Elizabeth, second daughter of Dr. Edward O'Neill of Dublin, who, with five children, survived him.

Besides the pamphlet already cited, he published 'A Diary of Coercion' (1888).

[Davitt's Fall of Feudalism, pp. 514 &c.; O'Brien's Life of Parnell, passim; O'Connor's Parnell Movement, passim; D'Alton's History of Ireland, p. 348; Dod's Parl. Companion; Freeman's Journal and Irish Independent, 13 March 1910.] D. J. O'D.

HARRIS, THOMAS LAKE (1823–1906), mystic, was born of poor parents at Fenny Stratford, Buckinghamshire, on 15 May 1823. In 1828 his parents emigrated to Utica, New York state. He was an only child, and lost his mother in his ninth year. Before he was seventeen he began to write for the press, and his verses attracted notice. Brought up as a Calvinistic baptist, he joined the universalists about 1843, and became pastor of the 'fourth universalist church' of New York. In 1845 he married Mary Van Arnum (*d.* 1850), by whom he had two sons. A visit in 1847 to Andrew Jackson Davis, the Poughkeepsie 'seer,' confirmed him in 'spiritualism'; becoming a 'medium,' he retired, along with James D. Scott, another 'medium,' to Mountain Cove, Auburn, New York state; they edited the 'Mountain Cove Journal,' and gathered a small community. Harris broke with Scott, and in 1848 organised on Swedenborgian principles an 'independent Christian congregation' in New York (called later 'the Church of the Good Shepherd'). He was what is called an 'inspirational' preacher; the effect of his sermon (1850) on behalf of children was the founding of the New York Juvenile Asylum. With 1850 began his claim to be the 'medium' of lengthy poems. 'An Epic of the Starry Heaven,' the first of these, was 'suggested' in March 1850, 'dictated' between 24 Nov. and 8 Dec. 1853, and taken down by amanuenses, Harris being in a trance condition; other poems were alleged to be 'dictated' by Byron, Shelley, Keats, Coleridge, Pollok, or Poe; among the amanuenses were Charles Partridge and S. B. Brittan, his publishers. About 1855 he married Emily Isabella Waters (*d.* 1883). He wrote also in prose, and edited (May 1857–August 1861) the 'Herald of Light,' a spiritualist organ. He came to England in 1859, preaching in London, Manchester, Edinburgh, and Glasgow. Returning to America, with some English followers, in the autumn of 1861 he bought a small hill farm near the village of Wassaic, Duchess county, New York state, and here set up a community, styled 'the Use,' consisting of twelve persons in addition to his own family. By the end of 1863 he had acquired a mill, close to the village of Amenia. He further set up the 'first national bank' of Amenia, with himself as president, and began to engage in grape culture. His community, now numbering about sixty, was known as the 'brotherhood of the new life'; it included several persons of position, Japanese as well as American, some clergymen, and two Indian princes. Harris was in England in 1865–6, and in 1865 (March–September) Laurence Oliphant [q. v.] contributed anonymously to 'Blackwood' his 'Piccadilly,' in which there is a covert allusion (April, p. 504) to Harris as 'an apostle of a new church'; but it is not till the republication in 1870 that Harris is extolled (p. 84) as 'the greatest poet of the age,' and (p. 283) 'the greatest man in Piccadilly.' Oliphant in 1867 joined the 'brotherhood,' which in October migrated to Brocton, Chautauqua county, New York state, on the shore of Lake Erie; hence the settlement was known as Salem-on-Erie. Various farms here, purchased with the Oliphants' money and the proceeds of sale of previous holdings, were devoted to vine-growing and wine-making. Harris taught a new mode of breathing, 'open or divine respiration,' which was to secure immunity from death. In virtue of this mode of breathing Harris's wine had mystic qualities, freeing it from ill effects; hence he commended its use (and that of tobacco) to his followers, and opened a tavern for their benefit. Over Oliphant he established an autocratic sway, sending him back to Europe in 1870, and regulating his marriage relations. Obedient to command, Oliphant with his wife and mother left Paris in 1873 for Brocton and was completely enslaved by Harris. The 'brotherhood' removed in 1875 to Fountain Grove, near Santa Rosa, California, where Harris had 1200 acres under vine culture. He broached a theory of celestial marriages in 1876; his own 'counterpart' being the 'Lily Queen,' Jane Lee Waring, who became his third wife in 1892 in consequence of certain alleged 'revelations' by Miss Chevalier. The spell which bound the Oliphants to him was broken in 1881; legal measures compelled the restitution of Oliphant's property at Brocton; Oliphant's final estimate of Harris is given in 'Masollam' (1886). Though he published nothing between 1876 and 1891, he privately circulated many effusions in morbid verse. There was always the cunning of the charlatan about Harris's mysticism; latterly he abounded in ideas on sexual matters, sugar-coated for the modern taste. In 1891 he proclaimed that he had attained the secret of immortality; a partial rejuvenation of his powers was pleaded in confirmation. He came to England, making a long stay in Wales. To America he returned owing to his wine premises having been set on fire by a mob. He did not go to Santa Rosa, but remained in New York. In 1903 he was in Scotland. He died at New York on 23 March 1906; the fact (concealed by his followers, who professed to believe that he was asleep) was not made public till the following July. His remains were cremated. His widow—his third wife—still (1912) survives, in her eighty-fourth year.

A striking and not unkindly picture of Harris, drawn by Oliphant under the designation of David Masollam, portrays his 'leonine aspect,' his Semitic cast of features, his waving hair, overhanging and bushy brow, his eyes 'like revolving lights in two dark caverns,' his 'alternation of vivacity and deliberation,' with changes of voice and expression making him by turns 'much blacker and brighter than most people,' and 'looking very much older one hour than he did the next.' Oliphant holds that Harris was honest at the start, but gave way to greed, unrestraint, and love of power. His personal fascination was much akin to that exercised by John Wroe [q. v.]. His gift of language and power of dramatic utterance were remarkable; but he had nothing new to say, nor had his theology any distinctive mark, unless his doctrine of the fatherhood and motherhood of the divine being be so counted. To an unbeliever most of his verse appears to consist of echoes and high-pitched twaddle; he reminds the poet-laureate of Shelley (AUSTIN, *The Poetry of the Period*, 1870, p. 227, 'supernatural poetry'). He attracted a few like Oliphant, of more wit than wits, but most of his worshippers were of the class that mistakes conceit for culture, and is agape for novelty. Apart from numerous sermons, Harris's publications in verse and prose include: 1. 'Juvenile Depravity and Crime in our City. A sermon,' &c. [Mark x. 14], New York, 1850. 2. 'An Epic of the Starry Heaven,' New York, 1853; 4th edit. 1854. 3. 'A Lyric of the Morning Land,' New York, 1855; Glasgow, 1869. 4. 'A Lyric of the Golden Age,' New York, 1856 (dictated December–January 1854–5); Glasgow, 1870. 5. 'The Wisdom of Angels,' part i., New York, 1857. 6. 'Hymns of Spiritual Devotion,' New York, 1858, 12mo. 7. 'Arcana of Christianity,' part i., New York, 1858; Appendix, 1858; part iii., 1867. 8. 'Regina: a Song of Many Days,' New York, 1860. 9. 'The Breath of God with Man: an Essay. . . of Universal Religion,' 1867. 10. 'The Great Republic: a Poem of the Sun,' New York, 1867; 2nd edit. 1891. 11. 'A Celestial Utopia,' Frome, 1869 (account of the Brocton community, from the 'New York Sun'; authorised but apparently not written by Harris). 12. 'The Lord: the Two-in-One,' Salem-on-Erie, 1876 (by Harris and Lily C. Harris). 13. 'Hymns of the Two-in-One; for Bridal Worship in the Kingdom of the New Life,' Salem-on-Erie, 1876 (by the foregoing, under the pseudonyms of Chrysantheus and Chrysanthea). 14. 'A Wedding Guest,' 1877–8, 5 parts (privately printed at Fountain Grove), which was succeeded by many similar works from the same private press until 1887. 15. 'The Brotherhood of the New Life: its Fact, Law, Method,' Santa Rosa, 1891. 16. 'The New Republic,' Santa Rosa, 1891; London, 1891. 17. 'Lyra Triumphalis,' 1891 (dedicated to Swinburne). 18. 'God's Breath in Man and in Humane Society,' 1892 (photographic likeness prefixed). 19. 'Conversation in Heaven,' 1894. 20. 'The Dawnrise,' 1894. 21. 'The Marriage of Heaven and Earth,' 1903 (written 1866). 22. 'The Triumph of Life,' Glasgow, 1903. 23. 'The Song of Theos,' 1903. Posthumous was: 24. 'Veritas: a Word-Song,' Glasgow, 1910 (written 1898–9).

[Appleton's Cyclop. Amer. Biog., 1887; Oliphant, Life of L. Oliphant, 2nd edit. 1892; R. McCully on Harris, 1893, 1897; W. P. Swainson, T. L. Harris, Mad or Inspired, 1895; J. Cuming Walters, Athenæum, 28 July 1906; Annual Register, 1906; A. A. Cuthbert, Life and World-work of T. L. Harris, 1908; private information.] A. G.

HARRISON, REGINALD (1837–1908), surgeon, born at Stafford on 24 Aug. 1837, was eldest son of Thomas Harrison, vicar of Christ Church, Stafford, by Mary his wife. Harrison was educated at Rossall school, and after a short period of probation at the Stafford general hospital, he entered St. Bartholomew's Hospital, London. He was admitted M.R.C.S. England on 15 April 1859, and in the same year he obtained the licence of the society of apothecaries. He was then appointed house surgeon at the Northern Hospital, Liverpool, and shortly afterwards moved to the Royal Infirmary as senior house surgeon (1860–2), a post which carried with it the duty of attending the city lunatic asylum. He was surgeon to the Cyfarthfa iron works at Merthyr Tydfil (1862–4).

Returning to Liverpool in 1864 as assistant to Mr. E. R. Bickersteth, he practised as a surgeon first at 18 Maryland Street, in 1868 in Rodney Street. In 1864 he was appointed both surgeon to the Liverpool Bluecoat school and demonstrator of anatomy at the Royal Infirmary school of medicine, becoming in 1865 lecturer on descriptive and surgical anatomy in the school, and in 1872 lecturer on the principles and practice of surgery. On 13 Dec. 1866 he was admitted F.R.C.S. England; was surgeon to the Northern Hospital at Liverpool (1867–8); quarantine officer to the port of Liverpool; assistant surgeon to the Royal Infirmary (1867–74), and full surgeon from 1874 until he removed to London in 1889. In October 1889 he was elected surgeon to St. Peter's Hospital for stone and other urinary diseases on the resignation of Walter Coulson.

At the Royal College of Surgeons of England, Harrison was member of the council, 1886–1902, and vice-president, 1894–5. He was Hunterian professor of surgery and pathology 1890–1, when he delivered a course of lectures on stone in the bladder, enlarged prostate, and urethral stricture. In 1896 he was Bradshaw lecturer, taking as his subject vesical stone and prostatic disorders. In 1903 he visited Egypt officially, on behalf of the college, to inspect the school of medicine at Cairo. He was president of the Medical Society of London in 1890, having delivered there in 1888 the Lettsomian lectures, on the surgery of the urinary organs.

He ceased active professional work in April 1905, when he resigned his post at St. Peter's hospital; he died on 28 April 1908, and was buried at Highgate cemetery. He married in 1864 Jane, only daughter of James Baron of Liverpool, and left one son and two daughters.

Harrison was one of the small band of teachers who raised the Royal Infirmary school of medicine at Liverpool to the position of the well-equipped medical faculty of the University of Liverpool. In 1869 the private school of the infirmary became a joint-stock company, money was raised, and new laboratories were built. Harrison as secretary-manager sought to supply each lectureship as it fell vacant with a young and energetic man who was unhampered by the demands of private practice. The school, thus improved, became University College, which existed as a separate body from 1882 to 1903, when it was merged in the university.

Harrison also took part in establishing the system (on a plan already in vogue in America) of street ambulances which long made Liverpool remarkable amongst the towns of Great Britain. He was active in promoting the Street Ambulance Association for developing the system throughout England, and was president at his death.

Harrison's works include: 1. 'Clinical Lectures on Stricture of the Urethra and other Disorders of the Urinary Organs,' London and Liverpool, 1878. 2. 'Lectures on the Surgical Disorders of the Urinary Organs,' 2nd edit. 1880; 4th edit. 1893. 3. 'The Use of the Ambulance in Civil Practice,' Liverpool, 1881. 4. 'Selected Papers on Stone Prostate, and other Urinary Disorders, 1909.'

[Lancet, 1908, vol. i. p. 822 (with portrait); Brit. Med. Journal, 1908, vol. i. p. 601 (with portrait); Liverpool Medico-Chirurgical Journal, July 1908, p. 251; information kindly given by Mr. Reginald Harrison.]

D'A. P.

HART, Sir ROBERT, first baronet (1835–1911), inspector-general of customs in China, born on 20 Feb. 1835 at Portadown, co. Armagh, Ireland, was eldest of the twelve children of Henry Hart, a Wesleyan mill-owner and landed proprietor, by his wife Ann, second daughter of John Edgar of Ballybreagh. His ancestor on the father's side, Captain Van Hardt, came over from the Netherlands with King William III, distinguished himself at the battle of the Boyne, and was granted the township of Kilmoriarty. When Hart was twelve months old, his parents moved to Milltown on Lough Neagh, and about a year later to Hillsborough. Hart was sent to school at Hillsborough, then for a year to the Wesleyan school at Taunton, and afterwards to the Wesleyan Connexional school in Dublin. He reached the top of the last school at the age of fifteen, and won a scholarship at Queen's College, Belfast. There he was a younger contemporary of Edwin Lawrence Godkin [q. v. Suppl. II], and he graduated B.A. in 1853 with honours. He was always interested in the affairs of Queen's College, where he proceeded M.A. in 1871 and was made hon. LL.D. in 1882.

In the spring of 1854 a nomination for the consular service in China was given by the foreign office to each of the three Queen's Colleges in Ireland. Hart received without examination the nomination which fell to Queen's College, Belfast, and he left for China in May 1854, being then nineteen years old.

Starting as a supernumerary interpreter, Hart after three months at Hongkong was sent via Shanghai, which was then in the hands of the 'Triad Society,' to Ningpo. He was at first supernumerary and in 1855 assistant in the vice-consulate at Ningpo, and acted for some months as vice-consul. In March 1858 he was transferred to the consulate at Canton, and from April held the position of second assistant, acting also for some time as first assistant.

As the result of the Chinese war, which was temporarily concluded by the Treaty of Tientsin, Canton was in the earlier part of 1858 jointly occupied by an Anglo-French force. Hart was made secretary to the allied commissioners, serving in that capacity under Sir Harry Parkes [q. v.]. Subsequently his official chief at the consulate was Sir Rutherford Alcock [q. v. Suppl. I].

In May 1854, when the walled native city of Shanghai was occupied by Triad rebels against the Manchu government, the Chinese custom-house re-opened in the foreign settlement of Shanghai. It was resolved to collect there imperial revenue under the joint protectorate of Great Britain, the United States, and France. Each country was represented by its consul, the British consul being (Sir) Thomas Wade [q. v.]. It was thus that the imperial maritime customs of China were inaugurated. The American and French representatives soon resigned from the triumvirate, and were not replaced; and Wade was succeeded in the sole charge or superintendence of the imperial customs at Shanghai by H. N. Lay, vice-consul and interpreter in the Shanghai consulate.

The success of the new system at Shanghai led the viceroy of Canton to invite Hart to undertake the supervision of the customs at Canton. With the permission of the British government he resigned the consular service in 1859, and joined the new Chinese imperial maritime customs service as deputy-commissioner of customs at Canton. He remained in Canton till 1861. After the war of 1860 between Great Britain and France on the one side, and the Chinese government on the other, and the conclusion of the convention of Peking in Oct. 1860, the imperial collectorate of customs at the treaty ports was in 1861 formally recognised and invested with regular powers by the Chinese government.

During 1861–3 Lay, who had become inspector-general of the customs, was on two years' leave in Europe owing to injury in a riot. In Lay's absence Fitzroy, previously private secretary to Lord Elgin, and Hart acted for him as officiating inspectors-general. Fitzroy remained at Shanghai, while Hart organised the customs service at Foochow and other treaty ports. He also visited Peking at the invitation of the Tsungli Yamen, and stayed there with the British minister, Sir Frederick Bruce [q. v.]. The advice which Bruce gave him stood him in good stead in future dealings with the Chinese. On Lay's return in May 1863 Hart took up the duties of commissioner of customs at Shanghai with charge of the Yangtze ports. But Lay resigned a few months later, and Hart was appointed his successor. Thus at the age of twenty-eight Hart became inspector-general of the imperial maritime customs; and, although he tendered his resignation in 1906, he nominally held the post till his death.

When Hart became inspector-general the Taiping rebellion, which on his arrival in China was at the floodtide of success, was succumbing to the influence of Gordon and 'the ever-victorious army.' Hart met Gordon, with whom he formed a strong friendship, in the spring of 1864. He was largely responsible for reconciling Gordon and Li Hung Chang at Soochow in that year, and he was present at the taking of Chang Chow Fu. The rebellion ended in 1864, and Hart had much to do with the disbandment of the 'ever-victorious army.' In the same year he inspected the Chinese customs houses in the island of Formosa, and normal times having returned to China and its government, he was summoned to live at Peking, which thenceforward became his headquarters and permanent dwelling-place. There he exercised a genial hospitality, indulging a taste for music by maintaining a private band. He rarely moved from the capital during his long residence in China. A perfect master of the language, he wrote in Chinese, after his visit to Formosa in 1864, suggestions on Chinese affairs under the title of 'What a Bystander says.'

Until he finally left China—nominally on leave—in 1908, he only twice revisited Europe, the first time for six months in 1866, when he took with him some Chinese to see the world, and again in 1878, when he went as President of the Chinese commission to the Paris Exhibition.

Though not the first originator, Hart was the practical creator of the imperial maritime customs service of China, 'one of the most striking monuments ever produced by the genius and labour of any individual Englishman' (*The Times*, 10 Jan. 1899). The working of the system was largely dependent on his personal exertions. To his labours he brought great power of work and organisation, a strong memory and mastership of detail, thorough knowledge of Chinese methods and modes of thought, together with tact and Irish kindliness. As more ports were opened to foreign trade, the scope of Hart's duties extended, and owing to the efficiency of the service other than customs duties passed into its charge. The service included the lighting of the coast and inland waterways of China. The imperial post-office, which was formally established in 1896, became, too, one of its branches, and Hart's title was then changed to inspector-general of Chinese imperial customs and posts. Hart's department proved the one branch of Chinese administration which followed Western lines and was at once efficient and honest. It was worked scrupulously for the benefit of China. Hart's European officers were not drawn exclusively from British subjects, and he never subordinated Chinese to British interests.

Rarely absent from Peking, and taking, in the opinion of some, too exclusively a Chinese view of affairs, especially in later years, Hart long enjoyed the confidence of the Chinese government, and was entrusted by it with many negotiations affecting China's relations with other countries. In 1878 he, acting with Li Hung Chang, settled at Chefoo with the British minister at Peking, Sir Thomas Wade, the difficulty between China and Great Britain arising out of the murder in 1875 of Augustus Raymond Margary [q. v.], the result being the Chefoo convention of 1876. To Hart's co-operation was due the settlement of China's troubles in Formosa and on the Tongking frontier with France in 1885. France acknowledged his services by making him grand officer of the Legion of Honour. He was no less active in dealing with difficulties over the delimitation of the Burmese frontier and China's relations with Thibet. In May 1885 he was appointed by the English foreign secretary, Lord Granville, British minister at Peking in succession to Sir Harry Parkes, but he recognised that the Chinese wished to retain his services as inspector-general, and in August he resigned the position without taking up the duties. He had indeed identified himself too fully with Chinese interests and points of view to fit him for diplomatic work on behalf of another country.

Hart did not anticipate the collapse of China in the war with Japan of 1894–5; but after that war had been concluded by the Treaty of Shimonoseki, he used all his efforts to induce the Chinese government to introduce necessary reforms. He foresaw the Boxer outbreak in 1900, but he held that the movement was 'a purely patriotic volunteer movement, and its object is to strengthen China and for a Chinese programme' (*These from the Land of Sinim*, p. 52). The crisis came sooner than he had contemplated. He showed gallantry and endurance when the rebels occupied Peking, but his house and papers, including his diary of forty years, were burned (June), and he had to take refuge in the British legation. When the legation was besieged, false reports of his death were circulated in England (July), but he was unhurt. As soon as the rebellion was suppressed by an international force (14 Aug.) Hart resumed his office (21 Aug.), and became as before the friend and adviser of the Chinese government. He organised in 1901 a native customs service at the treaty ports, and he played a large part in the re-establishment of the Manchu dynasty with the empress dowager at its head. Although it was an 'alien government,' he insisted that it had been 'part and parcel of the nation for three hundred years' (*ib.* p. 96).

In 1901 he published, under the title 'These from the Land of Sinim,' essays on the Chinese question, part of which he had written during the Boxer rising. There, while dwelling eloquently on the populousness and fertility of the country, he explains the people's exclusiveness and distrust of foreign races. He optimistically looked for reform, he had written to a private friend in 1896, not from any individual action but from 'the healthy interaction of the forces now coming into play.'

Hart's unchallenged authority was rudely

and without warning terminated by the Chinese government in May 1906. The customs service was then subordinated to a board of Chinese officials under the title of Shui-Wu Ch'u. A remonstrance from the British government was disregarded. As a consequence Hart tendered his resignation in July 1906. It was never definitely accepted, but in Jan. 1908 he received formal leave of absence, and was accorded the title of president of the board of customs. He returned to England for good.

During his long sojourn in China the government had been profuse in acknowledgment of his services, and his Chinese honours excelled in number and distinction those bestowed on any other European. They included, brevet title of An Ch'a Ssu (civil rank of the third class), 1864; brevet title of Pu Cheng Ssu (civil rank of the second class), 1869; Red Button of the first class, 1881; Double Dragon, second division, first class, 1885; the Peacock's Feather, 1885; ancestral rank of the first class of the first order for three generations, with letters patent, 1889; brevet title of junior guardian of the heir apparent, 1901.

European governments, to whom he rendered a long succession of services, were also liberal in recognition. In 1870 he was made chevalier of the Swedish order of Vasa, and other high distinctions came from the governments of France, Belgium, Austria, Italy, Portugal, Holland, and Prussia, and from Pope Pius IX. The British government made him C.M.G. in 1879, K.C.M.G. in 1882, G.C.M.G. in 1889, and a baronet in 1893.

A north of Ireland man of retiring disposition, Hart, while he thoroughly assimilated Chinese influences, combined business capacity and courage with untiring patience and tolerance, habits of deliberation, and an Eastern equanimity under good or bad fortune. He had a fine memory and a stock of varied learning in oriental and other subjects. He was Förderer of the Museum für Völkerkunde, Leipzig, 1878; hon. member of the Royal Asiatic Society, Shanghai, 1879; of the Oriental Museum, Vienna, 1880; and of the Institut de Droit International, 1892. He was made an hon. fellow of the Royal Statistical Society in 1890. On his retirement from China he lived for the most part at Fingest Grove, near Great Marlow, where he died on 20 Sept. 1911. He was buried at Bisham on the Thames. On 23 Sept. 1911 an imperial edict was issued at Peking which, after reciting his services and enumerating the various Chinese honours already accorded him, added to these as a posthumous distinction the brevet rank of senior guardian of the heir apparent.

On 22 Aug. 1866 Hart married at the parish church of St. Thomas in the city of Dublin, Hester Jane, eldest daughter of Alexander Bredon, M.D., of Portadown. She survived him with one son, Edgar Bruce, his successor in the baronetcy, born in 1873, and two daughters.

A caricature appeared in 'Vanity Fair' in 1894.

[Sir Robert Hart—The Romance of a Great Career, told by his niece, Juliet Bredon, 1909 (with photogravure portrait as frontispiece); The Times, 10 Jan. 1899, 17 July 1900, 21 Sept. 1911; Foreign Office List; Who's Who, 1911.]

C. P. L.

HARTINGTON, MARQUIS OF. [See CAVENDISH, SPENCER COMPTON, eighth DUKE OF DEVONSHIRE (1833–1908).]

HARTSHORNE, ALBERT (1839–1910), archæologist, born at Cogenhoe, Northants, on 15 Nov. 1839, was the eldest survivor of the eight sons of Charles Henry Hartshorne [q. v.], rector of Holdenby, Northamptonshire, by his wife Frances Margaretta, youngest daughter of Thomas Kerrich [q. v.] of Denton, Norfolk. His education, which was begun at Westminster school (1854–7), was completed in France and at Heidelberg. Until 1865, when his father died, his home was Holdenby Rectory, and he soon developed the passion for archæology which he inherited from his father and grandfather.

Between 1876 and 1883 and from 1886 to 1894 he was secretary of the Archæological Institute of Great Britain and Ireland, and from 1878 to 1892 editor of the 'Archæological Journal.' He was elected F.S.A. on 8 June 1882, member of council on 4 May 1886, and local secretary for Derbyshire on 2 Dec. 1886.

His splendid monograph on 'Old English Glasses,' published in 1897 (4to), called attention to a neglected subject. Hartshorne was an authority also on monumental effigies, and published in 1876 'The Recumbent Monumental Effigies in Northamptonshire,' a folio volume of 128 photographic reproductions of scale drawings with historical descriptions. Valuable also was his 'Portraiture in Recumbent Effigies, and Ancient Schools of Monumental Sculpture in England, illustrated by Examples in Northamptonshire' (1899). An excellent draughtsman, Hartshorne illustrated his works with minute fidelity.

Hartshorne, who resided chiefly at Bradbourne Hall, Derbyshire, died at 7 Heene Terrace, Worthing, on 8 Dec. 1910, and was buried in Holdenby churchyard. He married in 1872 Constance Amelia (*d.* 1901), youngest daughter of the Rev. Francis MacCarthy of Ballyneadrig and Lyradane, but left no issue. A portrait-sketch, made in 1888 by Seymour Lucas, R.A., belongs to Mr. Hugh R. P. Wyatt at Cissbury, Worthing.

Besides the works above mentioned and contributions to the 'Archæological Journal' (xxxix. 376, on 'Collars of SS.,' 1882, and xlv. 238, on 'Monuments in St. Mary's Church, Warwick') and to other publications, Hartshorne published: 1. 'On Kirkstead Abbey, Lincolnshire, Kirkstead Chapel, and a Remarkable Monumental Effigy there preserved,' 1883. 2. 'Bradbourne Church, Derbyshire,' 1888. 3. 'Hanging in Chains,' 1891. 4. 'The Sword-belts of the Middle Ages,' 1891. 5. 'Oxford in the Time of William III and Anne, 1691–1712,' 1910. To 'Some Minor Arts as practised in England,' fol. 1894, by A. H. Church and others, Hartshorne contributed 'English Effigies in Wood.' He edited 'Memoirs of a Royal Chaplain, 1729–1763, the Correspondence of Edmund Pyle, D.D., with Samuel Kerrich, D.D.,' in 1905.

[Proc. Soc. Antiquaries, xxiii. 436; Who's Who, 1907; Athenæum, 3 Sept. and 17 Dec. 1910; The Times, 10 Dec. 1910; Cat. of Libr. of Soc. of Antiquaries; private information.] C. W.

HASTIE, WILLIAM, D.D. (1842–1903), professor of divinity at Glasgow, third son and fourth child in the family of four sons and three daughters of James Hastie by his wife Catherine Kell, was born on 7 July 1842 at Wanlockhead, Dumfriesshire, where his father was a manager of lead mines. After education in the local school he taught in the neighbourhood, and studied privately. Entering Edinburgh University in 1859, he distinguished himself in both his arts and divinity courses, graduating M.A. with first-class honours in philosophy in 1867 and B.D. in 1869. He supplemented his theological studies at Glasgow (1870–1), attending the class of Dr. John Caird [q. v. Suppl. I], professor of divinity. After becoming a licentiate of the Church of Scotland, he was for some years a wandering student among continental universities—in Germany, Holland, and Switzerland—mastering foreign languages and widening his theological knowledge. In the intervals passed at home he took occasional work as a university deputy, or as assistant to parish ministers, among them Paton James Gloag [q. v. Suppl. II], at Galashiels.

In 1878 Hastie was appointed principal of the Church of Scotland College at Calcutta. There he showed zeal and energy alike as academic organiser, as missionary, and as writer. In 1881 he published the first part of 'The Elements of Philosophy,' and in 1882 he issued an enlarged version of Dr. Th. Christlieb's 'Protestant Missions to the Heathen.' In 1883 his 'Hindu Idolatry and English Enlightenment' (a reprint of six letters from the Calcutta 'Statesman') gave educated natives some offence. Complaints, too, of the discipline of the college led the Foreign Missions Committee to relieve him of his post of principal in November 1883, and his able appeal to the general assembly at Edinburgh on 29 May 1884 was rejected by 193 to 90. A period of exclusion from ecclesiastical office followed, and Hastie occupied himself in translating from German, Italian, and French works on theology, philosophy, and law. He gave proof, too, of a poetic temperament in a sonnet sequence entitled 'La Vita Mia,' which he published in 1896 after contributing some of the poems to the 'Scotsman' and other newspapers. In 1892 Hastie was chosen to deliver in Edinburgh the Croall lecture. His course of philosophical lectures on 'The Theology of the Reformed Church in its Fundamental Principles' (published posthumously at Edinburgh in 1904) proved valuable. On 13 April 1894 Hastie received the honorary degree of D.D. from Edinburgh University, and in 1895 succeeded William Purdie Dickson [q. v. Suppl. II] as professor of divinity at Glasgow. There he was popular with his students, whom he impressed with his attainments and method. He died suddenly in Edinburgh on 31 Aug. 1903, and was interred in the family burying-ground at Wanlockhead. He was unmarried. A memorial 'Hastie Lecture' has been established in Glasgow University.

Besides his Croall lecture, Hastie contributed to learned dogmatic theology 'Theology as Science, and its Present Position and Prospects in the Reformed Church' (Glasgow, 1899), a compact and philosophic survey and argument. An intuitionist, he treated the divine immanence as a fundamental conception (*Theology as Science*, p. 98). In 1903 he gave a fresh illustration of poetical power and critical acumen in 'The Festival of Spring, from the Diván of Jeláleddin: Rendered in English Gazels after Rückert's Version, with an Introduction and Criticism of the Rubáiyât of Omar Khayyám.' The trenchant discussion of Omar is virile criticism. Other experiments in verse were a group of sonnets written at Oban, 'The Glory of Nature in the Land of Lorn' (Edinburgh, 1903) and 'The Vision of God: as represented in Rückert's Fragments' (Edinburgh, 1898).

Hastie's principal translations are: 'The Philosophy of Art,' by Hegel and C. L. Michelet (1886); Bernard Punjer's 'History of the Christian Philosophy of Religion from the Reformation to Kant,' with a preface by Prof. Flint (1887); 'History of German Theology in the Nineteenth Century,' by F. Lichtenberger (1889); 'History of Christian Ethics,' by Luthardt, with a useful introduction (1889); Kant's 'Principles of Politics, including his Essay on Perpetual Peace' (1891); Pfleiderer's Edinburgh Gifford Lectures on the 'Philosophy and Development of Religion,' 2 vols. (1894–1904); and Kant's 'Cosmogomy,' with an elaborate introduction (1900).

[The Aberdeen Doctors (introductory chapter), by the Rev. D. Macmillan, D.D.; The Curator of Glasgow University, by J. L. Galbraith; Scotsman, and Glasgow Herald, 1 Sept. 1903; private information; personal knowledge.] T. B.

HATTON, HAROLD HENEAGE FINCH- (1856–1904), imperial politician. [See Finch-Hatton.]

HATTON, JOSEPH (1841–1907), novelist and journalist, was son of Francis Augustus Hatton, a printer and bookseller at Chesterfield, who in 1854 founded the 'Derbyshire Times.' Hatton was born at Andover, Hampshire, on 3 Feb. 1841, and he was educated at Bowker's school, Chesterfield. Intended for the law, he entered the office of the town clerk at Chesterfield, William Waller, but marrying at the age of nineteen he engaged in journalism, publishing in 1861 'Provincial Papers,' being a collection of tales and sketches. In 1863 he was appointed editor of the 'Bristol Mirror.' He held that and other provincial posts until 1868, when he came to London. Pushing and energetic (Tinsley, *Random Recollections*, ii. 86), he was entrusted by Messrs. Grant & Co., newspaper and magazine proprietors, with the editorship of the 'Gentleman's Magazine,' the 'School Board Chronicle,' and the 'Illustrated Midland News.' Mark Lemon [q. v.], editor of 'Punch,' was among his early London acquaintances, and he published in 1871 a volume of reminiscences of Lemon under the title of 'With a Show in the North,' and subsequently in 'London Society' wrote a series of articles called 'The True Story of Punch' (cf. Spielmann's *Hist. of Punch, passim*). In 1874 Hatton retired from his editorship of Grant's periodicals and acted as London correspondent for the 'New York Times,' the 'Sydney Morning Herald,' and the Berlin 'Kreuz-Zeitung,' besides editing for a time the 'Sunday Times,' and making some reputation as a novelist. In 1881 the 'Standard' sent him to the United States to establish on its behalf an independent telegraph service (Hatton, *Journalistic London*, 144 n.), and he recorded his impressions of the country in a series of articles afterwards collected as 'To-day in America' (2 vols. 1881). It was during his visit that president Garfield was shot, and Hatton, who had early intelligence of the outrage, held the line for three hours and cabled the longest telegraphic message then recorded from America to the 'Standard.' That paper thus gave full details of the tragic event on 3 July 1881, a day before its London contemporaries (*People*, 4 Aug. 1907). A member of the Garrick Club, he was an intimate friend of (Sir) Henry Irving and of J. L. Toole, and accompanied the former on his first visit to America in 1883, which he described in 'Henry Irving's Impressions of America, narrated . . . by Joseph Hatton' (2 vols. 1884). In 1889 he 'chronicled' in like fashion Toole's reminiscences (2 vols.). In 1892 Hatton became editor of the 'People,' a conservative Sunday newspaper, and contributed to that paper (and also to a syndicate of provincial papers) his 'Cigarette Papers for After-dinner Smoking,' a weekly medley of reminiscences, stories, and interviews. He died in London on 31 July 1907, and was buried in Marylebone cemetery.

Hatton married in 1860 Louisa Howard (*d.* 1900), daughter of Robert Johnson, by whom he had an only son, Frank Hatton [q. v.], and two daughters, Ellen Howard, wife of William Henry Margetson, the artist, and Bessie, a novelist. His portrait, painted by his son-in-law, was exhibited at the Royal Academy in 1895. Hatton, who published in 1882 'The New Ceylon,' the first English book on North Borneo, issued in 1886 a biographical sketch of his son, who was killed in 1883 while exploring North Borneo.

Hatton's industry and fluency were great. Among his numerous novels, which suited popular taste, were 'Clytie' (1874); 'By Order of the Czar' (1890); and 'When Rogues Fall Out' (1899). He made several attempts at the drama. His dramatised version of his novel 'Clytie,' which was first produced at the Amphitheatre, Liverpool, on 29 Nov. 1875, and was transferred to the Olympic, London, on 10 Jan. 1876, proved highly successful. A dramatic version of his novel 'John Needham's Double' followed in 1885. His dramatic version of Hawthorn's 'Scarlet Letter' proved popular in America. Other works by him were: 1. 'Journalistic London,' 1882. 2. 'Old Lamps and New: an After-dinner Chat,' 1889. 3. 'Club-Land, London and Provincial,' 1890.

[The Times, and Standard, 1 Aug. 1907; People, 4 Aug. 1907; Who's Who, 1906; Hatton's Old Lamps and New and Journalistic London; private information.] L. M.

HAVELOCK, Sir ARTHUR ELIBANK (1844–1908), colonial governor, born at Bath on 7 May 1844, was fifth surviving son in a family of six sons and seven daughters of Lieut.-colonel William Havelock [q. v.] and Caroline Elizabeth (*d.* 1866), eldest daughter of Major Acton Chaplin of Aylesbury. He was a nephew of Sir Henry Havelock [q. v.]. In 1846 Arthur went to India with the rest of the family to join his father, who was then in command of the 14th light dragoons at Umballa. After the death of his father at the battle of Ramnuggur on 22 Nov. 1848, he and his family came back to England, but returning to India in August 1850 settled at Ootacamund in the Nilgiri hills. He attended Mr. Nash's school there, but completed his education in England at a private school at Lee, near Blackheath (1859–60).

In 1860 he passed into the Royal Military College, Sandhurst, and on 14 Jan, 1862 was gazetted ensign in the 32nd Cornwall light infantry. From 1862 to 1866 he performed garrison duty at Plymouth, the Curragh, Cork, and Colchester. Promoted lieutenant on 10 April 1866, he was stationed with his regiment at Gibraltar (1866–7), at Mauritius (1867–8), and at the Cape (1868–72). In August 1872 he returned to Mauritius, where he acted as paymaster; promoted captain on 1 Feb. 1873, he was successively aide-de-camp to Mr. Newton, the acting governor, and to Sir Arthur Gordon (afterwards Lord Stanmore), the governor. From February 1874 to 1875 he was chief civil commissioner in the Seychelles islands; from 1875 to 1876, on Sir Arthur Gordon's recommendation, colonial secretary and receiver-general in Fiji. On his return to England in 1876 he definitely joined the colonial civil service, and retired from the army with the rank of captain in March 1877. In the same year he went out to the West Indies as president of Nevis, and in August 1878 was transferred to St. Lucia, where he served for a year as administrator. In 1879 he returned to the Seychelles as chief civil commissioner, and in 1880 was made C.M.G.

In February 1881 Havelock became governor of the West African settlements in succession to Sir Samuel Rowe [q. v.]. Before assuming office he acted as British commissioner at a conference in Paris for the provisional demarcation of boundaries between Sierra Leone and French Guinea. During his administration he was actively engaged in a frontier dispute with the negro republic of Liberia. On 20 March 1882, by order of the colonial office, he proceeded to Monrovia with four gunboats. His demands for the immediate extension of the British protectorate to the river Mafa and for an indemnity of 8500*l.* for British merchants were reluctantly conceded by the Liberian government. A treaty was signed to this effect, stipulating that Havelock should intercede with the British government to fix the line of the river Mano as the frontier, and that Liberia should be repaid all the sums she had spent in acquiring territories west of the Mano. On the refusal of the Liberian senate to ratify the treaty Havelock returned to Monrovia with the gunboats on 7 Sept. 1882. A hostile collision was averted, thanks to Havelock's tact. But the senate persisted in its opposition to the treaty, and in March 1883 Havelock quietly occupied the territories between the rivers Sherbro and Mano, which were claimed by the British government (Sir Harry Johnston, *Liberia*, 1906, i. 277–9). The boundary between Sierra Leone and Liberia was eventually defined in 1903 by a mixed commission.

In 1884 Havelock was created K.C.M.G for his services, and the following year served as governor of Trinidad. In 1886 he assumed the responsible post of governor of Natal. The colony was passing through a period of financial depression, and the difficulties of administration were increased by the annexation of Zululand in May 1887 and Dinizulu's unsuccessful rebellion in 1888. Returning to England in 1889, Havelock served on the international anti-slavery commission at Brussels; and in 1890 was appointed governor of Ceylon. There he added to his reputation as an effective administrator. He carried out the railway extension to Kurunegala and Bandarawela, and acquired popularity with the natives by his abolition of the obnoxious 'paddy' tax, or levy on rice cultivation.

Nominated governor of Madras in 1895, he travelled all over the presidency, and proved himself a vigilant champion of its interests. In defiance of orders from the Calcutta government he firmly refused to allow the Mecca pilgrim ships to touch at Madras. His action was subsequently justified by the comparative immunity of the Madras presidency from the plague of 1899 and 1900. He was made G.C.M.G. in 1895, G.C.I.E. in 1896, and G.C.S.I. in 1901, when he left Madras. Long residence in the tropics had undermined his health, and in 1901 he refused the governorships of the Straits Settlements and of Victoria. Eventually he accepted the easier post of governor of Tasmania, but resigned in 1904, before completing his term of office. He retired to Torquay, and died at Bath on 25 June 1908. A competent and painstaking official, he showed practical sympathy with the people under his rule and anxiety to mitigate the rigours of the law. He married on 15 Aug. 1871 Anne Grace, daughter of Sir William Norris. She died on 6 Jan. 1908, leaving one daughter.

[The Times, 26 June 1908; Army List, 1874; J. Ferguson, Ceylon in 1903; addresses presented to and replies delivered by Sir A. E. Havelock on his fifteenth tour in the Madras presidency, 1900; Madras Weekly Mail, 2 July 1908; private information from Col. Acton Havelock.] G. S. W.

HAWEIS, HUGH REGINALD (1838–1901), author and preacher, born on 3 April 1838, at Egham, Surrey, was grandson of Thomas Haweis [q. v.], the friend and trustee of Lady Huntingdon, and was son of John Oliver Willyams Haweis by his wife Mary. His father (1809–1891) matriculated at Queen's College, Oxford, graduating B.A. in 1828, and proceeding M.A. in 1830. From 1846 he was morning preacher at the Magdalen Hospital in London, and from 1874 to 1886 rector of Slaugham in Sussex. In 1883 he was made Heathfield prebendary of Chichester Cathedral. He was the author in 1844 of 'Sketches of the Reformation,' a work of considerable learning.

Hugh Reginald, the eldest son in a family of four children, showed great musical sensibility and aptitude for violin playing from early years, but delicate health prevented systematic education. He suffered from hip-disease, and at the age of twelve Sir Benjamin Brodie pronounced his case hopeless. He was taken to his grandmother's house in Brunswick Square, Brighton, and recovered, although he remained almost a dwarf and had a permanent limp. At Brighton he practised the violin assiduously, receiving instruction from several masters and finally from Oury, a pupil of Paganini. He obtained orchestral practice as a member of the Symphony Society that met in the Brighton Pavilion. He also wrote much verse and prose for the Brighton papers. By the age of sixteen he had so much improved in strength that he was put under the care at Freshwater, Isle of Wight, of the Rev. John Bicknell, who prepared him for matriculation at Cambridge. In 1856 he matriculated at Trinity College, Cambridge, and quickly became a notoriety. He was the solo violinist of the Cambridge Musical Society, and formed a quartet society which met in his rooms. He read German poetry and philosophy with enthusiasm, and along with some friends of kindred tastes started a magazine called the 'Lion,' of which three numbers were issued. There was ability as well as originality in the magazine, but its extravagance laid it open to ridicule. (Sir) G. O. Trevelyan issued a rival sheet called the 'Bear,' which parodied all the eccentricities of the 'Lion.' Haweis says magnanimously that the greatest success of the 'Lion' 'was in calling forth the "Bear" which slew it.' He continued to contribute voluminously to any newspapers that would publish his writing, and he made the acquaintance of a French violinist, J. G. R. R. Venua, who interested him in the history and art of violin-making, a subject upon which he began researches. He graduated B.A. in 1859, and then travelled for his health. His father had wished him to avoid Italy, but falling in with Signor Li Calsi, a professional musician whom he knew at Brighton, he went with him to Genoa, whence Calsi was proceeding to join Garibaldi. Haweis followed him to the seat of war. He arrived when Garibaldi was besieging Capua. He incurred without injury many risks and privations from bad food, bad weather, and insanitary conditions. He made the acquaintance of King Victor Emmanuel, and was present at the peace celebrations in Milan. He described his experiences in the 'Argosy' in 1870.

Before leaving Italy Haweis read the newly issued 'Essays and Reviews,' and decided to seek orders in the English church. He had been for some years 'an irregular student of theology.' In 1861 he passed the Cambridge examination in theology and was ordained deacon, becoming priest in 1862 and curate of St. Peter, Bethnal Green. In East London he threw himself enthusiastically into parish work. He was much in the company of J. R. Green [q. v.], who was in sole charge of Holy Trinity, Hoxton, and Green greatly influenced his views on social questions. After two years in Bethnal Green he went as curate to St. James-the-Less, Westminster, and then to St. Peter, Stepney. In 1866 he was appointed incumbent of St. James, Westmoreland Street, Marylebone, being, according to his own account, the youngest incumbent in London. He found the church nearly empty and in need of immediate repair. By his energy, ability, and somewhat sensational methods he quickly filled his church, and kept it full and fashionable for the thirty-five years of his ministry. He remained at St. James's till death.

Haweis exercised great power in the pulpit. He always preached in a black gown. His theatrical manner and vanity frequently exposed him to charges of charlatanry and obscured his genuine spiritual gifts. But he was earnest and sagacious in his efforts. He organised in his church 'Sunday evenings for the people,' at which orchestral music, oratorio performances, and even exhibitions of sacred pictures were made 'to form portions of the ordinary church services.' His success encouraged him to use St. James's Hall, Regent Street, for Sunday morning services of a similarly unconventional character, and Dean Stanley invited him to preach at a course of 'services for the people' in Westminster Abbey. He was one of the first promoters of the Sunday opening of museums and picture galleries. He interested himself in the provision of open air spaces in London and in the laying out as gardens of disused churchyards. Haweis's literary activity was at the same time large. He wrote much for the magazines, for 'The Times' and the 'Pall Mall Gazette,' and was on the early staff of the 'Echo.' His first book, 'Music and Morals,' published in 1871 (16th edit. 1891), was a revision of magazine articles; it mingled pleasantly theories about music with biographical notices of musicians and criticisms of their music. There followed in 1884 'My Musical Life' (4th edit. 1891) and 'Old Violins' (1898, with a bibliography). As musical critic to 'Truth' Haweis helped to introduce Wagner's works to English notice. His soundest and most original literary work was on music, although his theological writings were bulkier. In 'Thoughts for the Times' (1872; 14th edit. 1891) he attempted to 'strike the keynotes of modern theology, religion, and life'; in 'Speech in Season' (1874) he 'applied these principles to present social needs and ecclesiastical institutions.' He continued his propaganda in 'Arrows in the Air' (1878); 'Winged Words' (1885); and 'The Broad Church; or, What is coming' (with a preface on Mrs. Humphry Ward's novel, 'Robert Elsmere,' 1891). He attempted a study of the origins of Christianity, which he published in 1886–7 in five volumes as 'Christ and Christianity.' The separate volumes were 'The Light of the Ages, 'The Story of the Four,' 'The Picture of Jesus,' 'The Picture of Paul,' and 'The Conquering Cross.' Throughout this work there was much that was acute and vivacious, but little that was original or new.

Haweis's chief success was achieved as a popular lecturer in England and the colonies, and in America, principally on musical themes. In 1885 he gave the Lowell lectures in Boston, U.S.A. During the Chicago Exposition in 1893 he lectured before the Parliament of Religions, and in the following year he visited the Pacific coast, preaching to crowded congregations in Trinity Church, San Francisco. Thence he toured through Canada, the South Sea Islands, Australia, and New Zealand, lecturing and preaching. He preached in nine colonial cathedrals. In 1897 he visited Rome for the third time, to lecture on Mazzini and Garibaldi. He described his American and colonial experiences in 'Travel and Talk' (2 vols. 1896).

For some years after D. G. Rossetti's death in 1882 Haweis occupied the poet's house in Cheyne Walk, Chelsea. He died suddenly of heart seizure at his residence in later years, 31 Devonshire Street, on 29 Jan. 1901, after preaching memorial sermons on Queen Victoria on the previous Sunday. His body was cremated at Woking, and the remains interred beside his wife. There is a tablet to his memory in Marylebone parish church. Two sons and a daughter survive him. His portrait in oils, painted by Felix Moscheles, belongs to his daughter. A cartoon portrait by 'Ape' appeared in 'Vanity Fair' in 1888.

Besides the works above mentioned and many sermons, Haweis, who was general editor (1886) of Routledge's 'World Library,' and for a year of 'Cassell's Magazine,' wrote: 1. 'Pet; or Pastimes and Penalties,' 1874. 2. 'Ashes to Ashes, a Cremation Prelude,' 1875. 3. 'Poets in the Pulpit,' 1880.

4. 'American Humorists,' 1883. 5. 'The Dead Pulpit,' 1896. 6. 'Ideals for Girls,' 1897. 7. 'The Child's Life of Jesus,' 1902. 8. 'Realities of Life: being thoughts gathered from the teachings of H. R. Haweis,' 1902. The family of Sir Morell Mackenzie [q. v.] entrusted Haweis with the delicate task of writing his life, which he published in 1893.

Haweis married in 1867 Mary, daughter of Thomas Musgrove Joy [q. v.] the artist. At the age of sixteen she exhibited in the Royal Academy, and contributed also to the Dudley Gallery. She illustrated her husband's books as well as her own. She was an enthusiastic student of Chaucer, and compiled in 1877 'Chaucer for Children, a golden key'; with coloured and plain illustrations (2nd edit. 1882). The book was educationally valuable. It led to 'Chaucer for Schools' (1880; 2nd edit. 1899), which was equally original in plan and execution, and to 'Chaucer's Beads, a Birthday Book' (1884), and 'Tales from Chaucer, adapted by Mrs. Haweis,' published in Routledge's 'World Library.' Mrs. Haweis was a copious writer of articles upon domestic art and dress for the magazines. Endeavouring to establish some sound canons of taste in the minor arts, she embodied her views with vivacity and piquancy in 'The Art of Beauty' (1878, with illustrations by the author). This was followed by 'The Art of Dress' (1879); 'The Art of Decoration' (1881); and finally by 'The Art of Housekeeping: a Bridal Garland' (1889). All were illustrated by the author. She published also 'Beautiful Houses: being a Description of certain well-known Artistic Houses' (2nd edit. 1882), and 'Rus in Urbe: or Flowers that thrive in London Gardens and Smoky Towns' (1886). She accompanied her husband in his tours on the Continent and to America, and interested herself in many philanthropic causes. She was a director of Lady Henry Somerset's Mercy League for Animals and a strong supporter of the women's franchise movement. Shortly before her death she published a novel, 'A Flame of Fire' (1897), 'to vindicate the helplessness of womankind.' She died on 24 Nov. 1898, and after cremation was buried at Boughton Monchelsea, Kent.

[There is much autobiography in My Musical Life and in Travel and Talk. See also The Times, 30 Jan. 1901; Men of the Time, 1899; Crockford; H. C. Marillier's University Magazines and their Makers (Opusculum xlvii. of Sette of Odd Volumes, 1899). For Mrs. Haweis, see The Times, 29 Nov. 1898; Men of the Time, 1899.] R. B.

HAWEIS, Mrs. MARY. [See under Haweis, Hugh Reginald.]

HAWKER, MARY ELIZABETH, writing under the pseudonym of Lanoe Falconer (1848–1908), novelist, born on 29 Jan. 1848 at Inverary, Aberdeenshire, was elder daughter of Major Peter William Lanoe Hawker (1812–1857), of the 74th highlanders, of Longparish House near Whitchurch, Hampshire, by his wife Elizabeth Fraser. Her grandfather was Lieutenant-colonel Peter Hawker [q. v.], author of 'Instructions to Young Sportsmen' (1841). Miss Hawker's education was desultory, but she read assiduously for herself. Her father died in 1857, and after her mother's second marriage in the autumn of 1862 to Herbert Fennell, the family lived for some years in France and Germany, and Miss Hawker became efficient in French and German. She was also an admirable pianist.

Miss Hawker early began to write, and a few stories and essays appeared in magazines and newspapers. Success did not come until 1890, when there appeared, as the initial volume of a series of novels issued by Mr. Fisher Unwin in the 'Pseudonym Library,' a story by Miss Hawker entitled 'Mademoiselle Ixe, by Lanoe Falconer.' The manuscript had been previously rejected by many publishers. The heroine was a governess in an English country house who was connected with Russian nihilists. The mystery was cleverly handled, and the artistic treatment showed a delicacy and refinement which were uncommon in English writers of short stories. The 'Saturday Review' declared it to be 'one of the finest short stories in England.' Success was great and immediate. Gladstone wrote and spoke the praises of the book, of which the circulation was forbidden in Russia; it was admired by Taine. Over 40,000 copies of the English editions were sold, and there were also continental and American editions. It was translated into French, German, Dutch, and Italian. Subsequently she published in 1891 'Cecilia de Noël,' an original and cleverly told ghost story, and 'The Hôtel d'Angleterre.' But failure of health interrupted her work, and her mother's death on 23 May 1901 proved a blow from which she never recovered.

She died from rapid consumption on 16 June 1908, at Broxwood Court, Herefordshire, and was buried at Lyonshall in that county.

Other works by Miss Hawker are 'Old Hampshire Vignettes' (1907) and two short tales, 'Shoulder to Shoulder' (1891) and 'The Wrong Prescription' (1893).

[The Times, 20 June 1908; Who's Who, 1907; Burke's Landed Gentry; Cornhill Magazine, Feb. 1912, article by Miss March Phillipps; private information.] E. L.

HAWKINS, Sir HENRY, Baron Brampton (1817–1907), judge, born at Hitchin on 14 Sept. 1817, was son of John Hawkins, a solicitor with a considerable 'family' practice, by his wife Susanna, daughter of Theed Pearse, clerk of the peace of Bedfordshire. After education at Bedford school, Hawkins was employed in his father's office long enough to take a dislike to legal work of that character, and with the reluctant consent of his parents on 16 April 1839 entered himself at the Middle Temple, and took out a special pleader's licence as soon as he was qualified. In 1841 he was the pupil of Frederick Thompson, a special pleader, and later of George Butt, who eventually became a Q.C. On 3 May 1843 Hawkins was called to the bar, and forthwith joined the home circuit and the Hertfordshire sessions. It appears that owing to his practice under the bar he was never quite without business, and although his earlier progress was not exceptionally rapid it was unbroken from the time of his call until he took silk in 1858. For the next eighteen years Hawkins occupied a place of increasing importance among the leaders of the bar. His lively intelligence, well-chosen language, and admirable manner made him exceedingly successful in winning the verdicts of juries, and he was the equal of his contemporaries, Serjeants Ballantine [q. v. Suppl. I] and Parry, in the forensic arts of which they were masters.

Hawkins was engaged in many cases of great ephemeral importance. In 1852 he was counsel for Simon Bernard, who was acquitted on a charge of complicity in the Orsini conspiracy against Napoleon III. As junior to Serjeant Byles [q. v.] he defended Sir John Dean Paul [q. v.], who was convicted in 1855 of fraud and sentenced to penal servitude. In 1862 he was junior to (Sir) William Bovill [q. v.] in Roupell *v.* Waite, in which Roupell confessed himself guilty of forgery and was subsequently sentenced to penal servitude for life. He also appeared for various defendants in the prosecutions instituted after the failure of Messrs. Overend and Gurney in 1866, all of them being acquitted. He was largely instrumental in securing the establishment by secondary evidence of the will and codicils of Lord St. Leonards, a case in which, with Frederick Andrew Inderwick [q. v. Suppl. II] and Dr. Henry Baker Tristram as his juniors, he appeared for Miss Sugden, and was able to hold his judgment on appeal (1875–6). He appeared in all but the earliest stages of the litigation of which Arthur Orton [q. v. Suppl. I], claiming to be Sir Roger Tichborne, was the principal figure (1871–2). When he was originally retained for the defence in the action of ejectment, it was no doubt intended that he should cross-examine the plaintiff, but before the case came on for trial John Duke Coleridge [q. v. Suppl. I], who had been instructed as one of the leaders of the western circuit, became solicitor-general, and as such the leader in the defence. In all the rhetorical art of cross-examination Hawkins was the greatest master, and he maintained his reputation in his cross-examination of several important witnesses, but the accident which deprived him of the right to cross-examine Orton was probably one of the bitterest disappointments of his life. When the trial at bar for perjury followed the collapse of the 'claimant's' action, Hawkins led for the crown (23 April 1872). His opening speech lasted six days and his reply nine days, while the prosecution lasted 188 days and Cockburn's summing-up eighteen days (Feb. 1874); in the action at nisi prius Coleridge had occupied twenty-three days in opening the case for the defence. There is no doubt that Hawkins's handling of the whole matter was worthy of the extraordinary occasion. From the time of his taking silk in 1858 to the end of the Tichborne case in 1874 he had no superior in the public estimation as a fighting advocate.

Besides his prolonged and lucrative practice in the courts, Hawkins was continually employed in compensation cases, before either juries or arbitrators. In particular he appeared for the royal commissioners engaged in the purchase of the site where the Royal Courts of Justice now stand. He had also a considerable practice in election petitions, being perhaps the most conspicuous counsel available for the purpose when, after the general election of 1868, those disputes were first tried before judges and decided independently of political considerations. Hawkins had stood as one of two liberal candidates for Barnstaple in 1865, but had not been returned; he made no other effort to enter the House of Commons.

In November 1876 Hawkins was appointed a judge of the queen's bench division, and being knighted was almost immediately transferred to the exchequer division. He was the first judge appointed to the exchequer division since the Judicature Acts had superseded the court of exchequer. Hawkins and Chief Baron Kelly deeply resented the provision of those acts by which every judge of the high court was to be styled 'Mr. Justice' and the old style of baron of the exchequer was dropped. Hawkins, who made vain efforts to secure the appellation of 'Baron Hawkins,' invariably called himself for private purposes 'Sir Henry Hawkins,' instead of 'Mr. Justice Hawkins.' The exchequer division was absorbed in the queen's bench division in 1880.

In Sept. 1877 Hawkins tried at the Central Criminal Court 'the Penge case,' when Louis and Patrick Staunton, the wife of Patrick, and a servant named Alice Rhodes were jointly indicted for the murder, by ill-treatment and intentional neglect, of the wife of Louis. The case was on the wide borderland between murder and manslaughter, and the sufficiency of the evidence of complicity against Alice Rhodes was open to question. All were convicted of murder and sentenced to death, Rhodes subsequently receiving a free pardon and the sentence on the others being commuted to penal servitude for life (cf. J. B. Atlay's *Trial of the Stauntons*, 1911). Hawkins tried at about the same time many other murder cases which attracted public attention, and this circumstance, together with the alliterative attractiveness of the phrase 'Hanging Hawkins,' gave rise to a loose popular impression that he was a judge of a peculiarly severe or even savage temper. For this idea there was no real foundation. Hawkins was an admirable criminal judge. Extremely patient and thorough, he took care that both the case for the crown and that for the accused person should be exhaustively stated and tested to the utmost. His summings-up—in which in his later years it was his invariable practice never to open his note-book unless for the purpose of reading to the jury some fragment of the evidence in which the actual words used were of great importance—were models of lucidity and completeness. His manner, while dignified, was considerate to the point of being almost gentle. He had a strong hatred of cruelty and of any serious and deliberate outrages against either person or property, and in the gravest cases he did not shrink from deserved severity. On the other hand the period of his judgeship practically covered the great change in the direction of leniency to criminals. In this movement Hawkins was one of the more progressive authorities. He greatly favoured the lightest punishment for first offences, even where the offences themselves were serious, but he never went to the lengths favoured by the more extreme reformers.

As a criminal judge Hawkins had very few equals during twenty-two years. As a civil judge he failed to convey the impression that to do justice between the parties was his single aim. Innumerable stories were told—some of them with substantial foundation—of the ingenious devices whereby he contrived that the case before him either should be referred by consent to arbitration or should not be tried out to a clear determination on the merits. These devices, usually extremely adroit, could hardly be described as otherwise than mischievous. Of the current explanations of this peculiarity that which was least wanting in plausibility was that the judge's principal motive was to avoid the reversal of his decisions on appeal. The author of 'The Life in the Law of Sir Henry Hawkins' states that Hawkins said to him 'I have a horror of adverse criticism, to which I am perhaps unduly sensitive.'

In another respect Hawkins's judicial character presented a strange contrast. When, while doing the work he liked, he was summing up important or complicated evidence in a criminal case, he had a command of excellent English, accurate, forcible, and dignified, which would have stood the test of absolutely literal reproduction in print. On the other hand, in delivering a considered judgment he was verbose and tautological; he failed to grasp the principles of the law and to deduce from them the true effect of the facts before him, and he involved himself in contradictions. Two of his judgments which establish these facts beyond question are those in Hicks *v.* Faulkner (8 Q.B.D. 167) on the law of malicious prosecution, and in R. *v.* Lillyman ([1896] 2 Q.B. 167) on a question of evidence in criminal cases. The latter judgment of the court for crown cases reserved was so unsatisfactory that for nine years, while it remained a leading authority, it was invariably construed as meaning the contrary of what it said, until in 1905, in the case of R. *v.* Osborne, in the same court, it was substantially overruled.

Hawkins resigned his judgeship in 1898 and was sworn of the privy council. He was created a peer on 27 Aug. 1899 by the title of Baron Brampton of Brampton in

Huntingdonshire. From that time till August 1902 he sat occasionally in the House of Lords or the judicial committee. His judgments in the House of Lords in Allen *v.* Flood, the famous Taff Vale railway case, and Quinn *v.* Leatham, exhibit to some extent the same sort of weakness as characterised his earlier performances in the same class of case. He died at his house in Tilney Street on 6 Oct. 1907, and was buried at Kensal Green cemetery.

Hawkins was a small man of slender build, but his features were handsome and imposing and his aspect eminently judicial. He was extremely fond of horse-racing. He never ran horses himself, but was elected an honorary member of the Jockey Club in 1878, and an ordinary member in 1889. He insisted to an unusual extent in enforcing his personal tastes upon those who did business before him. He shut off all access of the outer air to his court and maintained the atmosphere at the highest temperature. He not unfrequently sat while on circuit for exceedingly long hours, although in London he habitually rose quite punctually. Innumerable anecdotes were current illustrating these peculiarities. To the outside public he was probably the best known and also the most popular of the puisne judges.

Hawkins was twice married. His second wife, who survived him five weeks, was Jane Louisa, daughter of H. F. Reynolds of Hulme. He had no children by either marriage. Not long after his retirement from the bench he was received into the Roman catholic communion, and in 1903 with his wife presented the Chapel of SS. Augustine and Gregory to the Roman catholic cathedral at Westminster.

Several portraits exist. One in oils of Hawkins in judge's robes, by John Collier, was exhibited at the Royal Academy in 1878, and was left by Lady Brampton to the National Portrait Gallery; a second, 'Justice Hawkins sums up,' by Robert Barnes, A.R.S.A., was exhibited at the Royal Academy in 1891. Two portraits by J. A. Innes, one in crayons (1879) and the other in oils, belonged to the family, but were sold after Lady Brampton's death. There is also a bust—presented by Lady Brampton—at the Old Bailey. A caricature by 'Spy' appeared in 'Vanity Fair' (1873).

[The Times, 7–12 Oct. 1907; Law Reports; information from Messrs. Weatherby & Sons; personal knowledge. In 1904 Lord Brampton caused or permitted to be published a book in two volumes entitled 'The Reminiscences of Sir Henry Hawkins, Baron Brampton, edited by Richard Harris, K.C.' This book is written in the first person, but is undoubtedly the work of Richard Harris (1841–1906), who had practised for many years on the midland circuit, and was the author of 'Hints on Advocacy' and other legal and literary works. It has no pretence of arrangement and is a miscellaneous collection of anecdotes wholly lacking in literary skill and in verisimilitude, many of them being demonstrably inaccurate and none of them in any degree trustworthy. A pamphlet entitled 'The Life in the Law of Sir Henry Hawkins,' by 'E.' (London, 1907), published after Hawkins's death, is an account of his legal career compiled by the author for publication in a magazine substantially from Hawkins's dictation. It was not published during his life, because when it was completed he wrote to the anonymous author that he 'would not, after serious reflection, allow it to be published as it stood.' It cannot, therefore, be considered any more authoritative than Harris's book.] H. S.

HAYES, EDWIN (1819–1904), marine painter, born at Bristol on 7 June 1819, was son of Charles Hayes, an Irishman. After education at a private school in Dublin, he studied art at the Kildare Street School of Art, Dublin, where he was a fellow pupil of John Henry Foley [q. v.], the sculptor, and he subsequently served an apprenticeship to Telbin, the scene painter, in London. From the first, however, his ambition was to be a marine painter. He spent much time in a 10-ton yacht in the Irish Channel, drawing and sketching. A little later he improved his knowledge of the ocean by taking a trip as steward in a barque called the Mary Campbell across the Atlantic to Mobile. Returning to Dublin to pursue his art, he exhibited his first picture, 'A Scene at Ryde,' at the British Institution. The picture was well hung and quickly sold. In 1845 he showed his first painting at the Royal Academy, London; and he exhibited there every year until 1904, except 1864, 1867, 1882, and 1887. He was elected a member of the Royal Hibernian Academy in 1870, and was a member of the Royal Institute of Painters in Water Colours. His subjects were always maritime, the most noteworthy of his pictures being 'Off Dover,' 'Saved' (1891), and 'Crossing the Bar' (1895). He is represented in the Tate Gallery by 'Sunset at Sea,' from Harlyn Bay, Cornwall (1894), bought by the Chantrey Bequest Trustees in 1896, and in public galleries at Bristol, Liverpool, Melbourne, and Sydney.

The 'Sunset at Sea' in the Tate Gallery is Hayes's only picture in which the subject was simply sky and sea and nothing else. It was his habit to introduce shipping or boats. His work, which reflected elements in the style of Stanfield, was not strikingly original, nor was it fine in colour like that of Henry Moore, but Hayes painted with the vision of a sailor and possessed a sailor's knowledge and experience. He died on 7 Nov. 1904 at Bayswater, London, and was buried in the Kensal Green cemetery. He married in 1847 Ellen, youngest daughter of James Briscoe of Carrick-on-Suir. Of his eleven children, Mr. Claude Hayes, R.I., a well-known landscape painter, has exhibited at the Royal Academy since 1876. Hayes's portrait was painted by John Parker.

[Mag. of Art, May 1901; M.A.P., 19 Nov. 1904; The Times, 9 Nov. 1904; Graves's Royal Acad. Exhibitors, 1906; private information.] F. W. G–N.

HAYMAN, HENRY (1823–1904), honorary canon of Carlisle and headmaster of Rugby, born on 3 March 1823 in Surrey Street, Strand, London, was eldest son of Philip Bell Hayman, clerk in Somerset House (himself son of Henry Hayman, rector of Lewcombe and vicar of Halstock, Dorset), by his wife Jane, daughter of John Marshall. A brother was Marshall Hayman, barrister-at-law and a member of the staff of the 'Saturday Review,' who was lost on the Alps near Zermatt in 1876. In October 1832 Hayman entered Merchant Taylors' School, and becoming head monitor passed with a Sir Thomas White scholarship on 28 June 1841 to St. John's College, Oxford, where he graduated B.A. with a double second class in 1845, proceeding M.A. in 1849, B.D. in 1854, and D.D. in 1870. He was treasurer of the Union in Lord Dufferin's presidency, and was offered in 1845 a seat (number five) in the university eight, but family circumstances prevented him from accepting it. He was a fellow of his college from 1844 to 1855, and received the degree of M.A., *ad eundem*, at Cambridge in the latter year. He was ordained deacon in 1847 and priest in 1848. He was curate of St. Luke's, Old Street, London, from 1848 to 1849, and of St. James's, Westminster, from 1849 to 1851, and was assistant preacher at the Temple Church from 1854 to 1857.

In 1852 he adopted a scholastic career, and served till 1855 as an assistant master at Charterhouse under Dr. Saunders (afterwards dean of Peterborough) and Edward Elder [q.v.], and became master of the gown boys, a post only once before held by one who was not a Carthusian. In 1855 he was elected headmaster of St. Olave's grammar school, Southwark, and was headmaster of Cheltenham from 1859 to 1868, and of Bradfield from 1868 to 1869. He introduced science teaching at Bradfield and tried somewhat unsuccessfully to compel the boys to talk exclusively in Latin.

On 20 Nov. 1869 he was elected headmaster of Rugby in succession to Frederick Temple [q. v. Suppl. II]. The electors were the trustees of the Rugby charity, who at that date formed the governing body. All the assistant masters but one protested against the appointment. Hayman's conservative predilections were held to be in conflict with the liberal traditions of the school. The feeling of hostility grew when it became known that many of Hayman's testimonials were of old dates, and had been used without the consent of the writers. At first his disputed authority as headmaster was maintained by support of the trustees, but in December 1871 a new governing body, including Temple and G. G. Bradley [q. v. Suppl. II], was constituted under the Public Schools Act of 1868. Meanwhile the school discipline deteriorated, the numbers dwindled, and when a reduction of the assistant masters became necessary, the headmaster resolved on the dismissal of two of his most prominent opponents on the staff, Mr. Arthur Sidgwick and the Rev. C. J. E. Smith. Soon afterwards, on 19 Dec. 1873, the new governors passed a resolution removing Hayman from the headmastership. Hayman did not retire without a struggle. On 18 Feb. 1874 he instituted chancery proceedings to restrain the bishop of Exeter (Temple) and the governing body from enforcing his dismissal. The defendants replied by filing a demurrer. After a six days' hearing (13–19 March 1874), Vice-chancellor Sir Richard Malins [q. v.] decided against Hayman, but left each side to pay its own costs, and admitted that Hayman had suffered a 'grievous hardship.' Although feeling in the scholastic world ran high, his friends urged that he was treated with undue severity.

In 1874 he was nominated by Lord Beaconsfield to the crown living of Aldingham, Lancashire. He became honorary canon of Carlisle in 1884, was honorary secretary of the Tithe Owners Union in 1891, was secretary of King Alfred's League of Justice to Voluntary Schools in 1900, and served as proctor in convocation (1887–90).

On 21 March 1892 and 23 Jan. 1893 successful actions were brought against Hayman and other directors of the Canadian Pacific Colonisation Society, by two shareholders, claiming the repayment of their investments on grounds of misrepresentation. He died at Aldingham on 11 July 1904, and was buried in the churchyard there. He married on 19 July 1855, at St. George's, Hanover Square, Matilda Julia, second daughter of George Westby of Mowbreck Hall, Lancashire, and left a numerous family. There is an enlarged photograph of him at St. Olave's grammar school, and an oil painting belongs to the family.

Hayman was a cultured scholar and a fluent speaker and preacher. He contributed extensively to the 'Edinburgh,' 'Quarterly,' 'Nineteenth Century,' 'National Review,' and other leading periodicals, and was a voluminous writer for Smith's 'Dictionary of the Bible' between 1863 and 1893. His independent works include Greek and Latin verse translations, 1864, an edition of Homer's 'Odyssey' (3 vols. 1881–6), and the following: 1. 'Dialogues of the Early Church (1) Rome, (2) Smyrna, (3) Carthage,' 1851. 2. 'Retail Mammon, or the Pawnbroker's Daughter,' 1853. 3. 'Can we adapt the Public School System to the Middle Class?' 1858. 4. 'Sermons preached at Rugby School,' 1875. 5. 'Why we suffer, and other Essays,' 1890. 6. 'The Epistles of the New Testament,' an attempt to present them in current and popular idiom, 1900.

[The Times, 2 Jan. 1873, 13 July 1904; Rugby School, Remarks and Judgment of Vice-chancellor Sir Richard Malins on the Demurrer to the Bill filed by Rev. Dr. Hayman against the Governing Body of Rugby School, 1874; private information.]

HAYNE, CHARLES HAYNE SEALE-. [See Seale-Hayne, Charles Hayne (1833–1903), politician and benefactor.]

HAYWARD, ROBERT BALDWIN (1829–1903), mathematician, born on 7 March 1829, at Bocking, Essex, was son of Robert Hayward by his wife Ann Baldwin. The father, of an old Quaker family, withdrew from the Quaker community on his marriage. Educated at University College, London, Robert Baldwin entered St. John's College, Cambridge, in 1846, graduating as fourth wrangler in 1850. He was fellow from 30 March 1852 till 27 March 1860, and from 1852 till 1855 assistant tutor. From 1855 he was mathematical tutor and reader in natural philosophy at Durham University, leaving in 1859 to become a mathematical master at Harrow School. Hayward remained at Harrow till 1893, a period of thirty-four years. He improved the system of arithmetical teaching there, and ably advocated better methods. He was president (1878–89) of the Association for the Improvement of Geometrical Teaching (afterwards the Mathematical Association), and published in 1895 a pamphlet, 'Hints on teaching Arithmetic.' He was author of a text-book on 'Elementary Solid Geometry' (1890) and 'The Algebra of Coplanar Vectors and Trigonometry' (1899). In pure mathematics he made many researches, and published numerous papers in the 'Transactions' of the Cambridge Philosophical Society and the 'Quarterly Journal of Mathematics.' He was elected F.R.S. on 1 June 1876.

Hayward, whose interests were varied, was a capable mountain climber and an original member of the Alpine Club from its foundation in 1858, withdrawing in 1865. To the 'Nineteenth Century' (Feb. 1884) he contributed an article on 'Proportional Representation' which attracted notice. He died at Shanklin, Isle of Wight, on 2 Feb. 1903. He married in 1860 Marianne, daughter of Henry Rowe, of Cambridge; his wife's sister married Henry William Watson [q. v. Suppl. II]. He had issue two sons and four daughters.

[Proc. Roy. Soc. vol. lxxv.; Proc. Lond. Math. Soc. vol. xxxv.; Roy. Soc. Cat.]

T. E. J.

HEADLAM, WALTER GEORGE (1866–1908), scholar and poet, born in London on 15 Feb. 1866, was son of Edward Headlam, fellow of St. John's College, Cambridge, director of examinations in the Civil Service Commission (nephew of Thomas Emerson Headlam [q. v.]), and of Mary Anne Johnson Sowerby. He was educated at Elstree School, Hertfordshire, and at Harrow, in the house of the headmaster, Dr. H. M. Butler, subsequently Master of Trinity College, Cambridge.

In 1884 he entered King's College, Cambridge, as a scholar on the foundation. Both at Harrow and at Cambridge his career was distinguished. At Cambridge he gained many university prizes for verse composition (viz. seven Browne's medals and the Porson prize) in the years 1885–7. In 1887 he was placed in the first class (division 3) of the classical tripos, part i., graduating B.A. in 1887, and proceeded M.A. in 1891, and Litt.D. in 1903. In 1890 he became fellow of King's College, and shortly afterwards was appointed to a lectureship in classics. His best work as a teacher was done with small classes, where his striking personality had free play. In Jan. 1906 he was a candidate for the regius professorship of Greek vacated by the death of Sir R. C. Jebb [q. v. Suppl. II]. His prelection on this occasion made a profound impression. On 20 June 1908 he died suddenly at an hotel in London. He was buried in the churchyard of Wycliffe, Yorkshire. During the last years of his short life his work had gained recognition from a rapidly growing circle, and he was deservedly looked upon as one of the leading Greek scholars of his time; but at the moment of his death the greater part of what he had published consisted of contributions to classical periodicals. For many years the plays of Æschylus formed the central subject of his studies, and he contemplated a full critical edition of them, towards which he had made large collections. One of his most important contributions to learning was a paper on 'Greek Lyric Metres' which appeared in the 'Journal of Hellenic Studies' in 1902. Headlam's writings possess distinction throughout, and give evidence of his fastidious taste and keen sensibility to all forms of beauty. Of his Greek versions of English and other poetry it was said that they are not surpassed, if indeed they are equalled, by any existing productions of the same kind. His English verse also is of high quality. His numerous emendations of Greek texts were founded upon a close study of the causes of textual corruption, coupled with an almost unrivalled sense of the genius of the Greek language.

During his lifetime he published: 1. 'Fifty Poems by Meleager, with a translation,' 1890. 2. 'On Editing Æschylus: a Criticism,' 1891. 3. 'The Plays of Æschylus translated from a Revised Text,' 1900–8; republished in a collected form in 1909 (in this volume the translations of the 'Persæ' and 'Septem contra Thebas' are the work of his brother, C. E. S. Headlam). 4. 'A Book of Greek Verse,' 1907. 5. 'Restoration of Menander,' 1908. Posthumous publications: 1. 'The Agamemnon of Æschylus,' revised text and English translation, with some notes, 1910, edited by A. C. Pearson. 2. 'Letters and Poems,' with Memoir by his brother, Cecil Headlam, and a full bibliography by L. Haward, 1910.

[Personal knowledge; memoir and bibliography cited; Academy, 8 Oct. 1910, memoir (by Shaen Leslie).] M. R. J.

HEARN, MARY ANNE, 'Marianne Farningham' (1834–1909), hymn-writer, daughter of Joseph Hearn, village postmaster, was born at Farningham, Kent, on 17 Dec. 1834. Her kinsfolk were baptists of the rigid Calvinistic type. A teacher at Bristol (1852–7), at Gravesend (1857–9), and at Northampton (1859–66), she gave up school work in 1866 to devote herself entirely to literature. In 1857 she had joined the outside staff of the newly founded 'Christian World,' for which she wrote regularly till her death. To the 'Sunday School Times' she was first a contributor, and from 1885 editor. In later life she retired to Barmouth. A keen supporter of educational movements, and in request as a speaker at free church meetings, and as a lecturer, she died at Barmouth on 16 March 1909.

Adopting the pseudonym of 'Marianne Farningham,' a combination of her Christian names with the name of her birthplace, she published nearly forty volumes, most of them poems or papers collected from the 'Christian World' or from publications associated with it. The chief are: 1. 'Lays and Lyrics of the Blessed Life,' 1861. 2. 'Poems,' 1865. 3. 'Morning and Evening Hymns for the Week,' 1870. 4. 'Songs of Sunshine,' 1878. 5. 'A Working Woman's Life,' an autobiography, 1907. Three or four of her hymns passed into occasional use. The most popular, 'Watching and waiting for me,' is in Sankey's 'Songs and Solos.' Some of her dramatic poems, notably 'The Last Hymn,' 'A Goodbye at the Door,' 'A Blind Man's Story,' 'Jairus,' and 'Rebekah,' achieved a vogue as recitations.

[Autobiography, 1907; Christian World, 18 March 1909; Julian's Dict. of Hymnology.] J. C. H.

HEATH, CHRISTOPHER (1835–1905), surgeon, born in London on 13 March 1835, was son, by Eliza Barclay his wife, of Christopher Heath [q. v.], minister of the Catholic Apostolic church in Gordon Square, London. Heath entered King's College School in May 1845, and after apprenticeship to Nathaniel Davidson of Charles Street, Manchester Square, began his medical studies at King's College, London, in October 1851. Here he gained the Leathes and Warneford prizes for general proficiency in medical subjects and divinity, and was admitted an associate in 1855. From 11 March to 25 Sept. 1855 he served as hospital dresser on board H.M. steam frigate Impérieuse in the Baltic fleet during the Crimean war, and for this service he was awarded a medal. He became M.R.C.S. England in 1856, and F.R.C.S. in 1860. He was appointed assistant demonstrator of anatomy at King's College, and served as house surgeon at King's College Hospital to Sir William Fergusson [q. v.] from May to November 1857. In 1856 he was appointed demonstrator of anatomy at the Westminster Hospital, where he was made lecturer on anatomy and assistant surgeon in 1862.

In 1858 he was consulting surgeon to the St. George and St. James Dispensary; in 1860 he was appointed surgeon to the West London Hospital at Hammersmith, and in 1870 he was surgeon to the Hospital for Women in Soho. Meanwhile in 1866 he was appointed assistant surgeon and teacher of operative surgery at University College Hospital, becoming full surgeon in 1871 on the retirement of Sir John Eric Erichsen [q. v.] and Holme professor of clinical surgery in 1875. He resigned his hospital appointments in 1900, when he was elected consulting surgeon and emeritus professor of clinical surgery.

At the Royal College of Surgeons of England Heath was awarded the Jacksonian prize in 1867 for his essay upon the 'Injuries and Diseases of the Jaws, including those of the Antrum, with the treatment by operation or otherwise.' He was a member of the board of examiners in anatomy and physiology (1875–80), an examiner in surgery (1883–92), and in dental surgery (1888–92), and was member of the council (1881–97). He was Hunterian professor of surgery and pathology (1886–7), Bradshaw lecturer in 1892, and Hunterian orator in 1897, when he chose as his subject 'John Hunter considered as a great Surgeon.' He succeeded John Whitaker Hulke [q. v. Suppl. I] as president of the college on 4 April 1895, and was re-elected for a second term.

In 1897 Heath visited America to deliver the second course of 'Lane Medical Lectures' recently founded at the Cooper Medical College in San Francisco. During this visit the McGill University of Montreal made him hon. LL.D. He was president of the Clinical Society of London in 1890–1, a fellow of King's College, London, and an associate fellow of the College of Physicians, Philadelphia.

He lived for many years at 36 Cavendish Square, a house which is now rebuilt, and died there on 8 Aug. 1905. He married (1) Sarah, daughter of the Rev. Jasper Peck; and (2) Gabrielle Nora, daughter of Captain Joseph Maynard, R.N., and left a widow, five sons, and one daughter.

Heath was a brilliant surgeon and a great teacher both of anatomy and surgery. It was his ill-fortune as a surgeon to be in his prime when the older surgery based on anatomy with all its rapidity of execution was giving way before the advances of modern pathology, with the slower methods bred of a secure anæsthesia and a more cumbrous technique. His intimate knowledge of anatomy made him a dexterous surgeon, but his comparative inability to appreciate the new truths of bacteriology cut him off from the scientific side. As a teacher he combined the older methods of the 'coaches' or 'grinders' with the practical knowledge of hospital work from which they were debarred. He was a born controversialist, hitting hard, and with a confident belief in his own opinion.

Heath's works, all published in London, were: 1. 'A Manual of Minor Surgery and Bandaging,' 1861; 12th edit. 1901. 2. 'Practical Anatomy, a Manual of Dissections,' 1864; 9th edit. 1902; translated into Japanese, Osaka, 1880. 3. 'Injuries and Diseases of the Jaws,' 1868; 4th edit. 1894; translated into French, 1884. 4. 'Essay on the Treatment of Intrathoracic Aneurism by the Distal Ligature,' 1871; re-issue 1898. 5. 'A Course of Operative Surgery,' 1877; 2nd edit. 1884; translated into Japanese Osaka, 1882. 6. 'The Student's Guide to Surgical Diagnosis,' 1879; 2nd edit. 1883. Philadelphia, 1879; New York, 1881. 7. 'Clinical Lectures on Surgical Subjects,' 1891; 2nd edit. 1895; second series 1902. He edited the 'Dictionary of Practical Surgery,' in 2 vols. 1886.

A marble bas-relief portrait by Mr. Hope Pinker commemorates Heath in the hall of the medical school buildings of University College Hospital.

[Lancet, 1905, vol. ii. p. 490 (with portrait); Brit. Med. Journal, 1905, vol. ii. p. 359; additional particulars kindly given by Mr. P. Maynard Heath, M.S., F.R.C.S.Eng., his fourth son; personal knowledge.] D'A. P.

HEATH, Sir LEOPOLD GEORGE (1817–1907), admiral, a younger son of George Heath (*d.* 1852), serjeant-at-law, by his wife Anne Raymond Dunbar, was born in London on 18 Nov. 1817. Douglas Denon Heath [q. v. Suppl. I] was his eldest brother. He entered the R.N. College, Portsmouth, in Sept. 1830. He gained the first medal on passing out in 1831, and in Dec. 1840 received a prize commission as lieutenant on passing his final examination. In that rank he served on the Mediterranean and East Indies stations. He was promoted to commander on 3 Aug. 1847, and in July 1850 was appointed to command the steam sloop Niger, and sent to the west coast of Africa. There he had his first war service, being present in the small squadron under Commodore Henry Bruce at the attack on and destruction of Lagos, in which affair the British loss was 15 killed and 75 wounded. At the end of 1852 the Niger was transferred to the Mediterranean, and Heath, remaining in her, was employed at the outbreak of the Russian war in blockade work along the Black Sea coasts. He accompanied the expedition to the Crimea, and from 14 Sept. 1854 was beach-master at Eupatoria during the landing of troops and stores. At the bombardment of Sevastopol on 17 Oct. 1854 the Niger was lashed alongside the line-of-battle ship London, and towed her into action. On 18 Nov. following, Heath was appointed acting captain of the Sans Pareil, flagship of Sir Edmund (afterwards Lord) Lyons [q. v.], and this appointment was afterwards confirmed by the admiralty. A few days afterwards he was made captain of the port of Balaclava, and it is clear that the adverse criticisms of the state of that port while under his management which were published by some London newspapers were both ill-informed and prejudiced. Sir Edmund Lyons was perfectly satisfied with Heath's work, and in January 1855 recommended him to the admiralty for the important post of principal agent of transports. Heath was appointed, and held the post until the war was practically over. In November 1855 he left for England, and in December was appointed to command the screw-mortar ship Seahorse, which was intended for the bombardment of Kronstadt. This ship was rendered useless by the peace, and Heath returned to the Black Sea to help in bringing back the troops. Though almost the junior captain in the Black Sea fleet, he was among the first to receive the C.B., which was awarded to him on 25 July 1855. He also received the Legion of Honour, the 4th class of the Medjidie, and the Crimean and Turkish medals.

Following the peace Heath for some years commanded the coast-guard ship in Southampton Water, and in April 1862 became captain of the Cambridge, gunnery school ship at Devonport. A year later he was transferred for special service to the Portsmouth gunnery school, where he remained till appointed, in July 1867, to the Octavia as commodore in command in the East Indies. He arrived on the station in time to help on the preparations for the expedition from Bombay under Sir Robert Napier [q. v.] against King Theodore of Abyssinia, and afterwards assisted to land the troops, though for this duty Captain (afterwards Sir George) Tryon [q. v.] was sent out from England as transport officer. For his services during his command Heath was awarded the K.C.B. and received the thanks of parliament. On his return to England in 1870 he was appointed vice-president of the ordnance select committee, and held that post until promoted to be rear-admiral on 20 Dec. 1871. Heath was not actively employed as a flag officer, and retired on 12 Feb. 1873. He rose on the retired list to be vice-admiral on 16 Sept. 1877, and admiral on 8 July 1884. He died on 7 May 1907 at his home, Anstie Grange, Holmwood, near Dorking.

Heath married in 1853 Mary Emma, (*d.* 1902), daughter of Cuthbert Marsh, of Eastbury, Hertfordshire, and had issue five sons and two daughters. The eldest son, Arthur Raymond Heath, was from 1886 to 1892 M.P. for the Louth division of Lincolnshire. Brigadier-general Gerard Moore Heath, D.S.O., R.E., is the youngest son.

Heath published, in 1897, his 'Letters from the Black Sea,' written during the Crimean war.

[The Times, 9 May 1907; Heath's Letters from the Black Sea (portrait), 1897.]

L. G. C. L.

HECTOR, Mrs. ANNIE FRENCH, writing as Mrs. Alexander (1825–1902), novelist, born in Dublin on 23 June 1825, was only daughter of Robert French, a younger member of the family of French of Frenchpark, Roscommon, a Dublin solicitor, by his wife Anne, daughter of Edmund Malone of Cartrons. A son died in infancy. On her father's side Miss French was a direct descendant of Jeremy Taylor, and was connected with the poet Charles Wolfe (1791–1823) [q. v.]. On her mother's side she was related to Edmund Malone (1741–1812) [q. v.]. Educated under governesses at home, she read much for herself. In 1844 her parents, owing to pecuniary losses, left Dublin for Liverpool, and after sojourning at Chester, Jersey, and other places, settled in London. Miss French only once again visited Ireland. In London she made many literary acquaintances, including Mrs. Basil Montagu and Mrs. S. C. Hall. In 1856 she began lifelong friendships with Eliza Lynn (afterwards Mrs. Lynn Linton) [q. v. Suppl. I], and W. H. Wills [q. v.], editor of 'Household Words,' and his wife. She first attracted public attention by a little paper in 'Household Words' called 'Billeted in Boulogne,' in 1856. Her novels, 'Agnes Waring' and 'Kate Vernon,' published in 1854 and 1855, were entirely neglected.

On 15 April 1858 she married, in London, Alexander Hector (1810–1875), a man of enterprise and ability. Beginning life in the East India Company's navy, he joined Richard Lemon Lander [q. v.] in his exploration of the Niger, in 1832, and General Francis Rawdon Chesney [q. v.] in the exploration of the Euphrates and Tigris (1835–7). When Chesney's expedition broke up Hector settled at Bagdad, and was the first merchant in recent times to open up trade between Great Britain and the Persian Gulf. He assisted Sir Henry Layard [q. v.] in his Assyrian excavations, and excavated on his own account, the British Museum purchasing some of his finds. He returned to England with a large fortune in 1857, but after his marriage his health broke, and he died, having long been partially paralysed, in 1875.

During her husband's lifetime Mrs. Hector wrote little, owing to his dislike of the vocation for a woman. Nevertheless 'Which shall it be?' came out in 1866, and before Hector's death she published her best known novel, the 'The Wooing o't.' It appeared as a serial in 'Temple Bar' during 1873, being re-issued in three volumes at the end of that year. She adopted as a pseudonym her husband's Christian name.

After Hector's death his widow, left with one son and three daughters, and with smaller means than she had anticipated, began to write in good earnest. Spending six years with her family in Germany and France and then three years at St. Andrews, she settled in London in 1885, and thenceforth rarely left it, busily occupied with novel-writing till her death.

In 1875 came out 'Ralph Wilton's Ward,' and 'Her Dearest Foe' in 1876. There followed forty-one novels, which enjoyed popularity among habitual readers of fiction both here and in America. Eleven passed into a second edition; 'The Freres' (1882) was translated into Spanish, 'By Woman's Wit' (1886) into Danish, and 'Mona's Choice' (1887) into Polish. The fresh and vivacious style reflects the Irish temperament, and the tone is always wholesome. 'Kitty Costello' (1904), a novel which presents an Irish girl's introduction to English life, and has autobiographic touches, was written when Mrs. Hector was seventy-seven and was barely completed at her death. A witty, clever talker, of quick sympathies and social instincts, Mrs. Hector was in many ways abler and broader-minded than her writings show. She died in London, after ten years' suffering from neuritis, on 10 July 1902, and was buried in Kensal Green cemetery.

A portrait painted at the time of her marriage by an artist named Fitzgerald, living at Versailles, and another painted just before her death by her youngest daughter, Miss May Hector (reproduced in 'To-day,' 23 July 1902), belong to her daughters.

[Who's Who, 1901; Brit. Mus. Cat.; Helen C. Black, Notable Women Authors of the Day, 1893; private information.] E. L.

HECTOR, Sir JAMES (1834–1907), Canadian geologist, born in Edinburgh on 16 March 1834, was son of Alexander Hector, writer to the signet, by his wife Margaret Macrostie. Educated at the Edinburgh Academy, he matriculated at the university in 1852, and qualified M.D. in 1856. During the short period in 1854 when Edward Forbes [q. v.] filled the chair of natural history in the university, his lectures deeply interested Hector, who became his assistant and worked zealously at geology and other branches of natural science. Medical studies were likewise pursued with ardour, and Hector acted as assistant to Dr. (afterwards Sir James Young) Simpson [q. v.].

Through the influence of Sir Roderick Impey Murchison [q. v.], Hector was chosen as surgeon and geologist to accompany the government exploring expedition to the western parts of British North America, under the command of Captain John Palliser [q. v.], during 1857–60. An immense tract of country from Lakes Superior and Winnipeg to Vancouver Island was traversed with a view to colonisation. Hector then discovered the pass, now known as Hector's Pass, by which the Canadian Pacific railway crosses the Rocky Mountains. Many other important geographical as well as ethnological and geological observations were made and communicated, some to the British Association (1858–60), others to the Geological Society of London (1861). Hector drew attention to the erratic blocks and the evidence of extensive glaciation; he noted the general structure of the Rocky Mountains, and described beds of tertiary and cretaceous lignite and coal in the country east of the mountains and at Nanaimo in Vancouver Island.

In 1861, on Murchison's recommendation, Hector was appointed geologist to the provincial government of Otago, New Zealand. Four years later he became director of the geological survey of the colony (now dominion), and from 1866 director of the meteorological and weather department of the New Zealand Institute, and of the colonial museum and the botanical gardens at Wellington. He resided in Wellington until his retirement in 1903.

During this service of forty-two years Hector gained a world-wide reputation as a naturalist and geologist. His numerous official reports included several on the coal-deposits of New Zealand and on the geological structure and other economic deposits of various districts. His first sketch map of the geology of the islands was published in 1869, and later editions, embodying the work of F. von Hochstetter, Julius von Haast, and others, in 1873 and 1885. A table of the fossiliferous formations of New Zealand accompanied his reports for 1879–1880 (1881). He edited the 'Transactions and Proceedings of the New Zealand Institute' for 1869–76. To scientific societies and journals in England as well as in New Zealand he communicated many and important observations on such subjects as the volcanic and earthquake phenomena; the thermal and mineral springs; the eruption of Tarawera in 1886; the rock-basins; the glacial phenomena; the meteorology; recent and fossil fauna and flora, notably fishes, reptiles, birds and cetacea; and the Moas. He also obtained from tertiary strata in Nelson the remains of a gigantic penguin described by Huxley under the name of Palæeudyptes antarcticus.

He was appointed C.M.G. in 1875 and K.C.M.G. in 1887, and received the order of the Golden Cross from the German emperor in 1874.

He was elected F.R.S.Edinburgh in 1861, and F.R.S.London in 1866, and also a corresponding member of the Zoological Society of London. The Lyell medal was awarded to him in 1876 by the Geological Society, and the founder's gold medal in 1891 by the Royal Geographical Society. He was president of the Wellington Philosophical Society in 1873–74, and president of the Australasian Association for the advancement of science in 1891. In his later years he was chancellor of the New Zealand University. He died at Wellington, N.Z., on 5 Nov. 1907.

Hector married in 1868 Maria Georgiana, daughter of Sir David Monro [q. v.], speaker of the house of representatives in New Zealand.

His published works include: 1. 'Handbook of New Zealand,' 1879; 4th edit. 1886. 2. 'Outlines of New Zealand Geology,' 1886 (with geological map, 1885).

[The Times, 7 Nov. 1907; obituary by Prof. J. W. Gregory in Nature, 14 Nov. 1907; see also Geology of New Zealand, by Prof. James Park, 1910 (bibliography).]

H. B. W.

HELLMUTH, ISAAC (1817–1901), bishop of Huron, born of Hebrew parents near Warsaw, Poland, on 14 Dec. 1817, attended Rabbinical schools, and at the age of sixteen passed to the University of Breslau, where he convinced himself of the truths of Christianity. Coming to England in 1841, he was received into the Church of England at Liverpool. Trained for holy orders by Hugh McNeile [q. v.] and James Haldane Stewart, Liverpool clergymen of strong evangelical views, Hellmuth emigrated to Canada in 1844, bearing letters to George Jehoshaphat Mountain [q. v.], bishop of Quebec, from Archbishop Sumner of Canterbury, and other eminent men. Bishop Mountain ordained him deacon and priest in 1846 and appointed him to be professor of Hebrew and Rabbinical literature at Bishop's College, Lennoxville, of which he soon became also vice-principal. At the same time he was made rector of St. Peter's church, in the neighbouring town of Sherbrooke, then the chief centre of English settlement in the province of Lower Canada. His learning and zeal were widely recognised. He received the degree of D.D. from Lambeth in 1853 and from Lennoxville University in 1854, as well as the degree of D.C.L. from Trinity College, Toronto, in the latter year. He afterwards resigned his posts in the province of Quebec to become superintendent of the Colonial and Continental Church Society in British North America. In this capacity he was very successful. He joined Dr. Cronyn, bishop of Huron, in an endeavour to set up in the diocese an evangelical theological college by way of opposition to Trinity College, Toronto. During a visit to England in 1861 Hellmuth collected a sum sufficient to endow the new Huron college in the diocese. It was established in London, Ontario, and when it was opened in 1863 Hellmuth became first principal and professor of divinity. He was also appointed archdeacon of Huron, dean of Huron, and rector of St. Paul's cathedral. His continued interest in education led him to institute at London, Ontario, in 1865 the Hellmuth Boys' College and in 1869 Hellmuth Ladies' College.

On 19 July 1871 Hellmuth was made coadjutor bishop of Huron to Dr. Cronyn, with the title of bishop of Norfolk. and on Cronyn's death in September following Hellmuth succeeded him as the second bishop of Huron. In his first charge to the diocesan synod, the bishop showed his strong evangelical views by recommending the canons of the Church of Ireland for use in his diocese, by way of preventing ritualism. In 1872 he opened a chapter-house, which was intended to form part of a new cathedral. In 1878 he attended the Lambeth conference. The crowning achievement of his episcopate was the foundation of the Western University in connection with Huron College. The university was incorporated by an act of the Ontario legislature in 1878, and was inaugurated by Hellmuth at the chapter-house on 6 Oct. 1881. He contributed of his own means $10,000 (over 2000*l.* sterling) to its endowment, and had visited England in 1880 to collect subscriptions. On 29 March 1883 Hellmuth resigned the see of Huron owing to a misunderstanding. His friend Robert Bickersteth [q. v.], bishop of Ripon, asked him to leave Canada to become his bishop-suffragan as bishop of Hull, an appointment to which Bickersteth publicly announced that the royal assent had been given. But as an ordained bishop, Hellmuth was declared by the law officers of the crown ineligible for the post of suffragan. Thereupon Bickersteth installed him in the less satisfactory position of coadjutor-bishop, which lapsed with Bickersteth's death in 1884. Hellmuth became successively rector and rural dean of Bridlington (1885–91), chaplain of Trinity Church, Pau (1891–7), and rector of Compton Paunce-foot, Somerset (1897–9). He died at Weston-super-Mare on 28 May 1901, and was buried there.

Hellmuth married (1) in 1847 Catherine (*d.*1884), daughter of General Thomas Evans, C.B., by whom he had two sons and one surviving daughter; (2) in 1886 Mary, daughter of Admiral the Hon. Arthur Duncombe and widow of the Hon. Ashley Carr-Glynn, by whom he had no issue.

Besides numerous controversial and other pamphlets, he published 'The Divine Dispensations and their Gradual Development,' a critical commentary on the Hebrew Scriptures (Edinburgh 1866); 'The Genuineness and Authenticity of the Pentateuch' (1867), and 'A Biblical Thesaurus (Polyglot Bible), with an Analysis of every Word in the Original Languages of the Old Testament' (1884).

Two paintings of Hellmuth in the possession of his elder son were destroyed by fire in Toronto.

[Morgan, Canadian Men and Women of the Time, 1898; Mockridge, Bishops of the Church of England in Canada, 1896 (with engraved portrait); Canadian Biog. Dict. 1880; Hist. of the County of Middlesex, 1889; Annual Register, 1901; F. J. Lowndes, Bishops of the Day, 1897.] D. R. K.

HEMMING, GEORGE WIRGMAN (1821–1905), mathematician and law reporter, born on 19 Aug. 1821, was second son of Henry Keene Hemming of Grays, Essex, by his wife Sophia, daughter of Gabriel Wirgman of London. Educated at Clapham grammar school, he proceeded to St. John's College, Cambridge, where in 1844 he was senior wrangler, and first Smith's prizeman, and was elected to a fellowship. He entered as a member of Lincoln's Inn in the same year, but was not called to the bar until 3 May 1850, meanwhile continuing his mathematical studies. His work as a reporter in the chancery courts began in 1859, and continued without a break until 1894. From 1871 to 1875, when he took silk, he was junior counsel to the treasury —generally a stepping-stone to the bench. From 1875 to 1879 he was standing counsel to his university, and was appointed a commissioner under the Universities Act, 1877. As a Q.C. he practised before Vice-chancellor Bacon, and in 1887 was appointed an official referee. Elected a bencher in 1876, he in 1897 served as treasurer of Lincoln's Inn. He died at 2 Earl's Court Square, South Kensington, on 6 Jan. 1905, and was buried in old Hampstead church.

Hemming married in 1855 his second cousin Louisa Annie, daughter of Samuel Hemming of Merrywood Hall, Bristol, and had four sons and four daughters. Of these the eldest son, Harry Baird (*b.* 1856), is law reporter to the House of Lords; a daughter, Fanny Henrietta (1863–1886), exhibited at the Royal Academy.

A water-colour sketch of Hemming when a young man, in fancy dress, by his lifelong friend, Sir John Tenniel, and a miniature exhibited at the Royal Academy by his niece, Edith Hemming, belong to the family.

Hemming wrote 'An Elementary Treatise on the Differential and Integral Calculus' (Cambridge, 1848; 2nd edit. 1852); 'First Book on Plane Trigonometry' (1851); and 'Billiards Mathematically Treated' (1899; 2nd edit. 1904). He published 'Reports of Cases adjudged in the High Court of Chancery, before Sir William Page Wood' for 1859–62 (2 vols. 1861–3, with Henry Robert Vaughan Johnson); and for 1862–65

(2 vols. 1864–5, with Alexander Edward Miller). On the establishment of the council of law reporting, Hemming acted as an editor of the 'Equity Cases' and 'Chancery Appeals,' subsequently merged in the chancery division series of the 'Law Reports.'

He was a regular contributor to the 'Saturday Review,' from which a pamphlet on the 'Fusion of Law and Equity' was reprinted in 1873.

[The Times, 7 Jan. 1905; Foster, Men at the Bar; Neale, Honours Reg. of University of Cambridge; Law Journal, 14 Jan. 1905; private information.] C. E. A. B.

HEMPHILL, CHARLES HARE, first Baron Hemphill (1822–1908), lawyer and politician, born in August 1822 at his father's residence in Cashel, was youngest of the five children—two sons and three daughters—of John Hemphill (1777–1833) of Cashel and Rathkenny, co. Tipperary, whose grandfather was Samuel Hemphill [q. v.], the Presbyterian divine and controversialist, and whose mother, Elisabeth Bacon of Rathkenny, was a niece of Matthew Bacon, author of 'Bacon's New Abridgment of the Law,' and a descendant of Sir Nicholas Bacon [q. v.]. Charles's mother, Barbara Hemphill [q. v.], was youngest daughter of Patrick Hare, D.D. His elder brother served as lieutenant in the 69th regiment, and died unmarried in Oct. 1840. Hemphill after his father's death in 1833 was placed at Dr. Walls's school, Dublin. In 1839 he matriculated at Trinity College, Dublin, of which his maternal uncle and godfather, Charles Hare, D.D., was a distinguished fellow and tutor. Hemphill's academic career was brilliant: he obtained a classical scholarship in 1842 and first classical moderatorship and the large gold medal for classics in 1843, when he graduated B.A. He was moreover auditor of the Trinity College Historical Society, in whose debates he took a prominent part. Amongst his friends and contemporaries in the society were William Magee, archbishop of York [q. v.], and Sir Edward Sullivan, Lord chancellor of Ireland [q. v.]. After serving his terms at the Middle Temple, London, and the King's Inns, Dublin, he was called to the Irish bar in midsummer term 1845, along with (Sir) Charles Gavan Duffy [q. v. Suppl. II] and Lord Justice Barry. Hemphill went the Leinster circuit, and rapidly acquired a large practice.

Hemphill's ambition from the first was for a political rather than a forensic career. In 1857 and again in 1859, while a stuff gownsman, he unsuccessfully contested Cashel, his birthplace, in the liberal interest and was defeated, polling on the first occasion thirty-nine votes against fifty-four for Sir Timothy O'Brien. His high standard of electoral morality explains his defeat. He took silk in 1860, and next year declined an offer of a judgeship in the high court of Bengal. In 1863 he was appointed chairman of a county, the title at the time of a county court judge in Ireland. The office did not preclude him from practising at the bar, but rendered him ineligible for election to the House of Commons. He was successively chairman of the counties of Louth, Leitrim, and Kerry. The administration of the Irish Land Act of 1870 was entrusted to county court judges, and Hemphill strenuously endeavoured to carry out the intention of the legislature by securing for tenants capriciously evicted from their holdings compensation for improvements made by themselves. On the coming into operation of the County Courts (Ireland) Act of 1877, whereby county court judges were no longer permitted to practise at the bar, he elected to vacate his county court judgeship on a pension and to pursue his profession. In January 1882 he was appointed a bencher of the King's Inns, and in the same year was made one of three serjeants-at-law, in Ireland, who take precedence at the bar immediately after the law officers of the crown.

In 1886, on the split in the liberal party on the Home Rule question, Hemphill threw in his lot with the Gladstonian liberals. At the general election of that year, after nearly a generation, he was once more a parliamentary candidate, contesting unsuccessfully the West Derby division of Liverpool in the Gladstonian interest, and at the general election of 1892 he was defeated in a contest for the representation of Hastings. On the fall of Lord Salisbury's administration in August 1892 Hemphill, although he had completed his seventieth year, became Irish solicitor-general in Gladstone's fourth administration. He held the post till the fall of Lord Rosebery's administration in 1895, when he was sworn of the Irish privy council, an honour not previously accorded to an outgoing solicitor-general. At the general elections of 1895 and 1900 Hemphill was returned in the liberal interest by majorities of ninety-nine and forty-four respectively as member for North Tyrone, and was the only member of the Gladstonian party in the House of Commons representing an Irish constituency. Although he entered the House of Commons at an advanced age, his intellectual alertness, legal knowledge, powerful memory, and physical vigour made him a power in debate; while his geniality and old-world courtesy rendered him personally popular. On the formation of Sir Henry Campbell-Bannerman's administration in December 1905 Hemphill's years precluded his appointment to the Irish lord chancellorship. A peerage which he did not seek was conferred on him. He was created Baron Hemphill of Rathkenny and of Cashel on 12 Jan. 1906. He died on 4 March 1908 at his residence, 65 Merrion Square, Dublin, and was buried at Deansgrange cemetery, near Dublin.

Of distinguished presence, above the medium height, and of erect carriage even in old age, Hemphill was entertaining in conversation owing to his wide reading and varied experience.

A portrait by Morant is in the possession of his son, the second Lord Hemphill.

Hemphill married on 11 April 1849 Augusta Mary, younger daughter of the Hon. Sir Francis Stanhope, K.H., and grand-daughter of Charles Stanhope, third earl of Harrington. She died on 12 April 1899. Two sons and a daughter of the marriage survive; the elder son, Stanhope Charles John, succeeded his father as second Baron Hemphill.

[Freeman's Journal, 5, 6, 7 March 1908; Law Times, 7, 14, 21 March 1908; information derived from the first Lord Hemphill and his family.] J. G. S. M.

HENDERSON, GEORGE FRANCIS ROBERT (1854–1903), colonel and military writer, born on 2 June 1854 at St. Helier, Jersey, was eldest son of William George Henderson, afterwards dean of Carlisle [q. v. Suppl. II], by Jane Melville, daughter of John Dalyell of Lingo, Fife. Henderson was educated at Leeds grammar school while his father was headmaster, became head of the school, was captain of the cricket eleven and a good amateur actor. In 1873 he gained a history scholarship at St. John's College, Oxford, and an exhibition from his school, but did not graduate. In November 1876 he entered Sandhurst, being fourth in the list, and was also captain of the cricket eleven there.

On 1 May 1878 he was commissioned as second-lieutenant in the York and Lancaster regiment, and joined the first battalion (65th) at Dinapore. On promotion to lieutenant on 24 June 1879, he passed to the second battalion (84th); and after serving at Dover and in Ireland, he went with it to Egypt, where it formed part of Graham's brigade. In 1882 he was engaged at Magfar and Tel-el-Maskhuta, and commanded a company at Kassassin and Tel-el-Kebir. He received the medal with clasp, the bronze star and Medjidie (5th class), and on General Graham's recommendation he obtained a brevet majority on his promotion to captain on 2 June 1886. In 1883 he went with his battalion to Bermuda, and thence to Halifax, Nova Scotia, visiting Virginia to examine the battlefields of the American civil war.

In January 1885 he joined the ordnance store department, and served in it five years, being stationed at Woolwich, Edinburgh, Fort George, and Gibraltar. During this time he was at work on the history of the American civil war and the Franco-Prussian war. In 1886 he published anonymously 'The Campaign of Fredericksburg' (3rd edit. 1891), which attracted the notice of Lord Wolseley, and led to Henderson's appointment in January 1890 as instructor at Sandhurst, at first in military topography, but afterwards in tactics and administration. In 1891 he published 'The Battle of Spicheren,' a masterly study in its breadth and minuteness. From 17 Dec. 1892 to 22 Dec. 1899 he was professor of military art and history at the Staff College, where 'he exercised by his lectures and his personality an influence upon the younger generation of the officers of the British army for which it would be difficult to find a parallel nearer home than that of Moltke in Prussia' (*The Times*, 7 March 1903). The publication in 1898 of 'Stonewall Jackson and the American Civil War' (2 vols. 3rd edit. 1902) placed him in the first rank of military historians. Lord Wolseley wrote a preface for the second edition. Lord Roberts stated that it helped to shape his plans for the campaign in South Africa.

He embarked for the Cape with Lord Roberts on 23 Dec. 1899. He left the York and Lancaster regiment, in which he had become major on 10 Nov. 1897, and was made substantive lieutenant-colonel. On 10 Jan. 1900 he was appointed director of military intelligence with the local rank of colonel. Maps were much needed: in the post office at Capetown he discovered some hundreds of maps of the Transvaal, intended for the Boer government, and he prepared maps of the Free State. He accompanied Roberts to the Modder camp, and witnessed the beginning of the turning movement against Cronje; then his health failed, and he went home. He was mentioned in the despatch of 31 March, and was made C.B. on 29 Nov.

He was placed on the staff of the war office on 29 Aug. 1900 as an assistant adjutant-general, to write the history of the war; but he was employed first on revision of the infantry drill-book. In the autumn of 1901 he went to South Africa to examine the battlefields, but he worked too hard and broke down again. He returned to England in February 1902, and at the end of that year he was sent to Egypt for the winter. He died at Assouan on 5 March 1903, and was buried in the Roman catholic cemetery at Cairo, where there is a memorial to him. In 1883 he married Mary, daughter of Pierce Joyce of Galway, who survived him. She received a civil list pension of 100*l.* in 1904. They had no children.

Henderson had rare gifts as a military historian. He meant the history of the South African war to be a great picture, not a cold catalogue of facts. He had completed the first volume, on the antecedents of the war; but after his death it was decided that the history should be confined to the military contest, and what he wrote was not published.

The following articles in the 'Edinburgh Review' were Henderson's: 1. 'The American Civil War,' April 1891. 2. 'Clarke's Fortification,' October 1891. 3. 'Von Moltke's Campaign in Bohemia,' April 1894. 4. 'Lord Wolseley's "Marlborough,"' October 1894. 5. 'Army Organisation,' January 1896. 6. 'National Defence,' April 1897. 6. 'The War in South Africa,' January 1900. He published a translation of Verdy du Vernois' study of the battle of Custozza in 1894, and an original study of the battle of Wörth in 1899. He wrote a preface to Count Sternberg's 'Experiences of the Boer War' (1901) in which he dealt with foreign criticism; and he contributed articles on war, strategy and tactics to the 'Encyclopædia Britannica' (10th edit.). He also wrote in 'The Times' on manœuvres. He was a frequent lecturer at the United Service Institution and before the military societies of Aldershot and Ireland. Some of these lectures have been reprinted with other of his papers in 'The Science of War,' 1905, with a prefatory memoir by Lord Roberts, who writes of Henderson's 'most fascinating personality,' his gifts as a lecturer and a writer, and his value as a staff officer.

[In addition to the above memoir, The Times, 7 March 1903; Spectator, 14 March 1903; the Leodiensian (school journal), April 1903; private information.] E. M. L.

HENDERSON, JOSEPH (1832–1908), portrait and marine painter, born on 10 June 1832 at Stanley, Perthshire, was the third son—he had a younger twin brother—of a stone-carver, Joseph Henderson, by his wife, Marjory Slater. The family removing to Edinburgh, the father died there about 1840 in poor circumstances, and the four boys were sent to business at a very early age. Joseph was apprenticed to a firm of drapers in George Street, but he was allowed time to attend the classes of the Trustees' Academy in the mornings and evenings. On the recommendation of Alexander Handyside Ritchie [q. v.], sculptor, he was enrolled a student on 2 Feb. 1849. William Quiller Orchardson [q. v. Suppl. II] and Robert Herdman [q. v.] were fellow students. He left the academy on 10 May 1853, about a year after Robert Scott Lauder [q. v.] was appointed headmaster, and settled in Glasgow. From 1852 onward, Henderson supported himself entirely by his art. His early work bears the impress of the earlier Scottish tradition, as modified by Duncan and Thomas Faed [q. v. Suppl. I], rather than that of Lauder and his pupils, although evidences of Lauder's suggestion appear in Henderson's genre pictures such as 'The Ballad' (1858) and 'The Sick Child' (1860). After spending some twenty years chiefly on pictures of that kind, Henderson, during a holiday on the Ayrshire coast about 1871, discovered that his real bent was sea-painting. Although he continued to paint portraits, he paid chief attention to the sea. At first figure incidents of considerable importance were usually introduced, and his colour inclined to be black and his handling hard; but gradually the figures became accessory to the effect, his colour gained in freshness and his brushwork in freedom. His best work was done during the last fifteen years of his life. While his principal pictures were in oils, he painted in watercolour also, and was a member of the Royal Scottish Water-Colour Society. In celebration of his jubilee as a professional artist the Glasgow Art Club, besides entertaining him to dinner and presenting him with a souvenir, organised a special exhibition of his work (1901), and after his death the Royal Glasgow Institute of the Fine Arts, of which he was a vice-president, arranged a memorial exhibition. Between 1871 and 1886 he exhibited twenty pictures at the Royal Academy, but his chief pictures were usually shown at the

Glasgow Institute. His art is represented in the Glasgow Gallery by an admirable sea-piece, 'The Flowing Tide,' and by full-length portraits of two lord provosts, and the collection of the Scottish Modern Arts Association contains his 'Storm.'

He died at Ballantrae, Ayrshire, where for many years he had spent the summer, on 17 July 1908, and was buried in Sighthill cemetery, Glasgow.

Henderson married thrice: (1) in 1855, Helen, daughter of James Cosh, Buchanan, and by her (*d.* 1866) had four children, a daughter Marjory, who became second wife of William McTaggart, R.S.A. [q. v. Suppl. II], and three sons, all of whom became artists; (2) in 1869, Helen Young of Strathaven (*d.* 1871), by whom he had one daughter; and (3) in 1872, Eliza Thomson, who survived him with two daughters.

There are admirable portraits of him by his son John (in the artist's possession) and by William McTaggart (in his widow's possession). John Mossman executed a double medallion of him and his third wife.

[Private information; Scots Pictorial, 15 Jan. 1901; International Studio, 1902, xvi. 207; Glasgow Herald, 18 July 1908; exhibition catalogues; Percy Bate, The Art of Joseph Henderson, 1908; J. L. Caw, Scottish Painting, 1908.] J. L. C.

HENDERSON, WILLIAM GEORGE (1819–1905), dean of Carlisle, born at Harbridge, Hampshire, on 25 June 1819, was eldest son of Vice-admiral George Henderson of Harbridge, by his wife Frances Elizabeth, daughter of Edward Walcott-Sympson. Educated first at Laleham, and then at Bruton school, Somerset, he matriculated from Wadham College, Oxford, on 30 June 1836, was elected to a demyship at Magdalen College in July, won the Chancellor's prize for Latin verse in 1839, and graduated B.A. with a first class in classics and a second class in mathematics in 1840, proceeding M.A. in 1843, D.C.L. in 1853, and D.D. in 1882. He won the prize for Latin essay in 1842 and the Ellerton theological prize next year. In 1844 he was ordained deacon but from some doctrinal hesitation did not take priest's orders until 1859. In 1845 he was appointed headmaster of Magdalen College school, but left it in the following year to become tutor in the University of Durham. In 1847 he was elected to a fellowship at Magdalen, holding it till 1853. In 1851 he was appointed principal of Hatfield Hall, Durham, and in 1852 became headmaster of Victoria College, Jersey. Henderson's success here was pronounced, and in 1862 he obtained the headmastership of Leeds grammar school. A born teacher and good organiser, devoted to his school, and winning the lasting affection of his pupils, he remained at Leeds until 1884. He took little part in public affairs, but was an active member and editor of the Surtees Society.

In 1884 Henderson was appointed to the deanery of Carlisle. He sought to popularise the cathedral services, and interested himself in philanthropic work, but owing to weak health his later years were spent in comparative retirement. He died suddenly at Rose Castle, Carlisle, on 24 Sept. 1905. A decided high churchman, Henderson took no active part in controversy, but he signed the memorial in 1881 for the toleration of ritual. He married Jane (*d.* 1901), daughter of J. Dalyell of Lingo, Fifeshire, by whom he had eight sons (one of whom was Lieut.-colonel G. F. R. Henderson [q. v. Suppl. II]) and six daughters. Twelve of his children survived him. His portrait by Mr. W. W. Ouless R.A. (1887) is at Victoria College, Jersey.

Henderson edited for the Surtees Society: 1. 'Missale ad usum Insignis Ecclesiæ Eboracensis,' vols. 59 and 60, 1874, for which he collated the extant MSS. and the five printed editions. 2. 'Manuale et Processionale ad usum Insignis Ecclesiæ Eboracensis,' vol. 63, 1875, to which he added in an appendix an abbreviated reprint of the Sarum manual and of such manual offices as occur in the Hereford missal or manual. 3. 'Liber Pontificalis Christophori Bainbridge Archiepiscopi Eboracensis,' vol. 61, 1875, the last surviving pontifical of the old English use. He also published 'Missale ad usum Percelebris Ecclesiæ Herfordensis' (1874), a reproduction of the printed edition of 1502 collated with a fourteenth-century MS.

[Yorkshire Post, 25 Sept. 1905; Guardian, 27 Sept. 1905; Foster, Alumni Oxon.; Honours Register of the University of Oxford; private information; J. R. Bloxam, Fellows, &c., of Magdalen College, Oxford, vii. 342; R. B. Gardiner, Wadham College Register, 1895, p. 375.] A. R. B.

HENLEY, WILLIAM ERNEST (1849–1903), poet, critic, and dramatist, born at Gloucester on 23 Aug. 1849, was eldest of five children, all sons, of William Henley, a bookseller in Gloucester, by his wife Emma Morgan. His father came of an old yeoman stock and his mother was descended from Joseph Warton, the critic [q. v.]. Of his brothers, Edward John was a well-known London actor, and later toured in America, where he died in 1898; and

Anthony Warton is a landscape painter. William Ernest was educated at the Crypt grammar school, Gloucester, of which, in 1861, Thomas Edward Brown [q. v. Suppl. I], the poet, became head master. That he had Brown for a teacher, Henley was accustomed to deem a rare piece of good fortune. His presence, he says, was 'like a call from the world outside, the great, quick, living world. . . . What he did for me, practically, was to suggest such possibilities in life and character as I had never dreamed' (*Works*, iv. 207–8). Brown's influence was all the greater in that Henley was partly severed from 'the great, quick, living world,' during the late period of his youth and his early manhood, by a tuberculous disease which from his twelfth year made him a cripple and long threatened his life. His consolation was reading and study, and in 1867 he passed the Oxford local examination as a senior candidate. The progress of the disease soon necessitated the amputation of one foot, and having been told by the doctors that his life could be saved only by the amputation of the other leg he, in 1873, went to Edinburgh to place himself under the care of Prof. Joseph (afterwards Lord) Lister in the infirmary. There he was a patient for twenty months. By Lister's skilful attention the leg was saved, and although his health always remained precarious, he was able, with occasional intervals of severe illness, to apply himself to literary labour until the close of his life. The character of his nights and days in the infirmary is vividly disclosed in the 'Hospital Verses,' a portion of which appeared in the 'Cornhill Magazine' for July 1875. His mood of mind is depicted in 'Out of the night that covers me.'

Some verses previously sent from the infirmary to the 'Cornhill Magazine' led the editor (Sir) Leslie Stephen, when in Edinburgh in 1875, to visit him on his sick-bed and to introduce him to R. L. Stevenson, who describes him as sitting 'up in his bed with his hair all tangled,' and talking 'as cheerfully as if he had been in a king's palace' (letter of Stevenson, 13 Feb. 1875). Henley portrayed Stevenson to the life in the hospital sonnet 'Apparition.' Henceforth their relations became intimate. Their temperaments had strong affinities; both were unconventional; both were devoted to the art of literature, and their sympathy, as Stevenson states, was 'nourished by mutual assistance.' 'As I look back in memory,' he wrote in his dedication to Henley of 'Virginibus Puerisque' (1881), 'there is hardly a stage of that distance but I see you present with advice, reproof or praise.' Subsequently their personal relations grew less intimate owing to a private disagreement, and on the appearance of Stevenson's biography by Mr. Graham Balfour in 1901, Henley contributed to the 'Pall Mall Magazine' (Dec. 1901) a disparaging article called 'R. L. S.' Yet in an essay on Hazlitt (1902, *Works*, ii. 158) he referred to Stevenson as an artist in letters, 'who lived to conquer the English-speaking world.'

On leaving the infirmary in 1875, Henley remained in Edinburgh for a few months to work on the staff of the 'Encyclopædia Britannica.' His contributions, mainly in French biography, included Chénier and Chastelard; but he felt hampered by the conditions of the work. Already he had begun to contribute to the London journals, and in 1877–8 he settled in London to become editor of a weekly paper, 'London,' founded by George Glasgow Brown, a friend of Stevenson and himself, in which appeared many of his early poems, several of the essays included in 'Views and Reviews,' and Stevenson's unique 'New Arabian Nights.' On the discontinuance of the paper he did critical work for the 'Athenæum,' the 'St. James's Gazette,' the 'Saturday Review,' and 'Vanity Fair.' From 1882 to 1886 he was editor of the 'Magazine of Art,' where he made known to England the sculptural genius of Rodin, championed the pictorial art of Whistler, and found for Robert Alan Mowbray Stevenson [q. v. Suppl. I] opportunity to begin his work as art critic. In 1889 he returned to Edinburgh to become editor of a weekly paper, the 'Scots Observer,' the headquarters of which were in 1891 removed to London, the title having been changed to the 'National Observer.' Patriotic imperialism, or anti-Gladstonianism, was the dominating note of the paper's politics; but Henley's main purpose was the promotion of what he deemed the higher interests of literature and art. While iconoclasm, sometimes extreme and one-sided, was a conspicuous feature of its criticism, its appreciation of excellence only partially recognised or not recognised at all was as common as its disparagement of what was supposed to have obtained an undeserved repute. Its 'middles' included contributions from several writers who had won fame, and from more who were on the way to win it. Among the many contributors were J. M. Barrie, T. E. Brown.

Thomas Hardy, Rudyard Kipling, Andrew Lang, Arthur Morrison, (Sir) Gilbert Parker, G. S. Street, G. W. Steevens, R. L. Stevenson, H. G. Wells, and W. B. Yeats. Exacting as an editor, Henley was yet a benevolent autocrat, and stimulated his contributors by his strong literary enthusiasm and blend of friendly correction with generous praise. After retiring from the editorship of the 'National Observer' in 1894 he was until 1898 editor of a monthly magazine, the 'New Review,' which, notwithstanding notable contributions in fiction and essays, was a financial failure. From 1899 till his death he contributed occasionally a literary article to the 'Pall Mall Magazine.'

Meanwhile, he had, in 1888, obtained reputation as a poet, though more instantly and widely in America than in England, by a 'Book of Verses,' which embraced the whole graphic hospital series, of which the more poignant, in the unrhymed form, had been refused admission to the 'Cornhill Magazine'; the 'Bric-à-Brac Poems,' some in the sonnet form and the majority in the modish forms of old French verse, but often wrought with such deft command of phrase, and so alive with poetic fancy, or emotion, that all sense of artificiality disappears; and various other verses entitled 'Echoes,' the majority of which accord with his own definition of a lyric, 'a single emotion temperamentally expressed in terms of poetry' (Preface to *English Lyrics*, p. 1). In 1892 he published the 'Song of the Sword and other Verses,' including the 'London Voluntaries'; and in 1893 a second edition, with additions, appeared under the title 'London Voluntaries and other Verses.' In the 'Voluntaries,' 'a rich and lovely verbal magic,' wrote Francis Thompson, 'is mated with metre that comes and goes like the heaving of the Muse's bosom' (*Academy*, 18 July 1903). The technical accomplishment attains here its most difficult triumphs. In 1898 the two collections of verse were reprinted in a definitive edition, with omissions, additions and changes under the title 'Poems,' with a photogravure of the author's bust by Rodin. A series of drawings of London types by William Nicholson with picturesque quatorzains by Henley appeared in the same year; and in 1900 he published a small volume of verse entitled 'For England's sake: Verses and Songs in Time of War,' voicing his patriotic fervour during the Boer struggle. The two most notable poems are 'Pro Rege Nostro,' which has been set to music as a song by Miss Frances Allitsen, and for choral purposes by Mr. Ernest Dicks, and 'Last Post,' set to music for chorus and orchestra by Sir Charles Villiers Stanford. The lyric sequence, 'Hawthorn and Lavender' (1901, first printed in the 'North American Review'), a kind of parable of the spring, summer, autumn, and winter of manhood, contains a more intimate revelation of himself than the earlier poems. This volume also includes among other pieces the 'Threnody for Queen Victoria' which, first appearing in the 'Morning Post,' was printed for private circulation as a broadside. 'Hawthorn and Lavender' he intended to be his last poetic utterance; but his first experience of the delights of motoring inspired him to write 'A Song of Speed,' which appeared in the 'World's Work' in April 1903, and shortly afterwards was published separately.

Henley's verse was the occasional recreation of a life mainly occupied with editing and the criticism of literature and art. In 1890 he published 'Views and Reviews,' described by himself as 'a mosaic of scraps and shreds from the shot rubbish of some fourteen years of journalism,' and consisting mainly of vignette impressions of the great English and French writers. A companion volume on art appeared in 1902, selected from the memorial catalogue (1887) of the loan collection of French and Dutch pictures in the Edinburgh International Exhibition (1886), from the 'Century of Artists' (1889), prepared as a memorial of the art portion of the Glasgow Exhibition of 1888, and from the catalogue (1889) of the loan collection of pictures of the great French and Dutch romanticists of the nineteenth century, prepared for the art publishers, Messrs. Dowdeswell. For the last catalogue he wrote an elaborate note on 'Romanticism.' The volume also includes a study of Sir Henry Raeburn, which prefaced a sumptuous book, published in 1890, by the Association for the Promotion of the Fine Arts in Scotland, as well as a study of two modern artists (Charles Keene and Rodin) contributed to the 'National Observer' in 1890; and a tribute to R. A. M. Stevenson from the 'Pall Mall Magazine' in July 1900.

'As critic,' wrote Meredith of Henley, 'he had the rare combination of enthusiasm and wakeful judgment. Pretentiousness felt his whip smartly, the accepted imbecile had to bear the weight of his epigrams. But merit under a cloud, or just emerging, he sparkled on or lifted to the public view. He was one of the main supports of good literature in our time' (*The Henley*

Memorial, p. 7). Impressionist and emotional, Henley's criticism represents artistic sensibilities that are exceptionally keen. In painting he proposed to ignore any qualities except those strictly pictorial, and sculpture he pronounced to be 'wholly a matter of form, surface and line.' His literary sympathies were restricted by peculiarities of temperament, but realist and humorist as well as poet, he was an expert critic of those forms of literature that deal primarily with concrete human nature. His prose style, elaborately polished and occasionally mannered, is notable for elasticity, and vivid appositeness of phrase.

Henley collaborated with R. L. Stevenson in four plays, 'Deacon Brodie' (privately printed in 1880, and in a finished version in 1888), 'Beau Austin' and 'Admiral Guinea' (both printed in 1884), and 'Macaire' (in 1885). A collected edition of the first three plays was published in 1892, and 'Macaire' was added in 1894. 'Deacon Brodie' was produced at Pullan's Theatre of Varieties, Bradford, on 28 Dec. 1882, and was performed at the Prince's Theatre, London, on 2 July 1884, and in the same year at Edinburgh. With the finished version, which has not been performed in this country, Henley's brother, Edward John, made a successful tour in America in 1888. 'Beau Austin' was produced by Mr. (now Sir) Beerbohm Tree at the Haymarket Theatre, London, on 3 Nov. 1890. 'Admiral Guinea,' first produced on 29 Nov. 1897, was revived at the Royalty Theatre, Glasgow (the Repertory Theatre) on 19 April 1909 and at His Majesty's Theatre, London, on 4 June of the same year. 'Macaire' was played twice by the Stage Society, London (on 4 Nov. 1900 at the Strand Theatre, and on 8 Nov. at the Great Queen Street Theatre). 'Beau Austin' and 'Macaire' were performed at a matinee in Her Majesty's Theatre on 3 May 1901 on behalf of the Prince of Wales's Hospital Fund, all the parts being filled by leading actors and actresses. 'Deacon Brodie' is dramatically the most effective of the four pieces, none of which attained popular success, though all helped to promote a higher ideal of playwriting in Great Britain.

Henley was also the author of 'A new and original travestie by Byron M'Guiness,' entitled 'Mephisto,' new music by Mr. D. Caldicott and Mr. Ernest Bucalossi, which, produced on Whit Monday, 14 June 1887, was played for some weeks as an after piece at the Royalty Theatre, London; his brother taking the part of Mephisto, and Miss Constance Gilchrist that of Marguerite.

A warm admirer of Elizabethan prose, Henley projected the republication of a series of Tudor translations which, edited and prefaced by special scholars and begun in 1892 with Florio's translation of Montaigne's 'Essays,' was completed by the issue of the Tudor Bible, the preface for which he did not live to finish. With Mr. J. S. Farmer he was engaged for many years in compiling a 'Dictionary of Slang and its Analogues,' issued in parts only to subscribers (1894–1904), which was almost finished at the time of his death. With Mr. T. F. Henderson he prepared the centenary edition of the poetry of Robert Burns, in four vols. (1896–7), contributing to the last volume an elaborate essay, which was also published separately, on the poet's 'life, genius and achievement.' An edition of 'Byron's Letters and Verse,' volume i., with vivid biographical sketches of Byron's friends and other persons mentioned in the letters, appeared in 1897; but, owing to copyright difficulties, the project was abandoned. In 1901 he edited the Edinburgh folio Shakespeare. He contributed a preface to the poetry of Wilfrid Blunt (1895), and to the collected edition of the poems of T. E. Brown (1900); introductory essays to editions of Smollett (1899), Hazlitt (1902–4), and Fielding (1903); and prefaces to various novels in the American edition de luxe of the works of Charles Dickens. Amongst his latest essays was that on 'Othello,' for the Caxton Shakespeare (1910), edited by Sir Sidney Lee. In 1891, under the title of 'Lyra Heroica,' he published a selection of English verse 'commemorative of heroic action or illustrative of heroic sentiment,' of which a school edition with notes by L. Cope-Cornford and W. W. Greg was printed in 1892; in 1894 with Mr. Charles Whibley, a 'Book of English Prose'; in 1895 a 'London Garland from Four Centuries of Verse,' and in 1897 'English Lyrics: Chaucer to Pope.'

In 1893 Henley received the degree of LL.D. from the University of St. Andrews; in 1898 he was granted a civil list pension of 225*l.* a year. Considerations of health induced him, after experimenting with various suburban residences about London, to remove in 1899 to Worthing, though he retained a flat in London, which he occupied at intervals. In 1901 he removed to Woking. A nervous shock, due to an accident while leaving a moving railway carriage, seriously affected his health.

and he died at Woking on 11 June 1903. His body was cremated at Woking and the ashes were brought to Cockayne Hatley, Bedfordshire.

Henley married at Edinburgh, in Jan. 1878, Anna, daughter of Edward Boyle, engineer, of Edinburgh, and Marianne Mackie. She survived him and in 1904 was granted a civil list pension of 125*l.* The only child, Margaret, died at the age of five years in 1894. She is the 'Reddy' of Mr. J. M. Barrie's 'Sentimental Tommy'; there is a painting in oil of her by Charles Wellington Furse, A.R.A. [q. v. Suppl. II], and a crayon sketch by the Marchioness of Granby (Duchess of Rutland). She was buried in the churchyard of Cockayne Hatley, where a tombstone, designed by Onslow Ford, with beautiful bronze work by the artist, is erected to her.

Henley was over the average height, broad-shouldered, and, notwithstanding his illnesses, physically vigorous and energetic. His powerful head was crowned by strong, bushy yellow hair, which had a tendency towards the perpendicular; latterly it became white. He possessed pleasant and expressive blue eyes, but was extremely short-sighted. Physically he contrasted strikingly with the shadowy R. L. Stevenson. Debarred by his lameness and uncertain health from various pastimes and diversions, he obtained much enjoyment from conversation, and was an admirable listener and inquirer as well as talker. In Stevenson's essay, 'Talk and Talkers,' he is cleverly portrayed under the pseudonym 'Burly'; but the description applies chiefly to his earlier years and largely to special bouts of discussion with the Stevensons; in his later years his manner was less 'boisterous and piratical.' Although capable under excitement of much picturesque denunciation, he was in conversation, for the most part, quietly humorous, frank, robust, and genial.

Henley's collective works appeared in 1908 in a limited edition in six volumes; vols. i. and ii. poems, including, in an appendix, some published in earlier volumes or in anthologies but not reprinted by him in his definitive edition; vols. iii. and iv. essays not previously collected; and vols. v. and vi. 'Views and Reviews.' The essays include those on Fielding, Smollett, Hazlitt and Burns; 'Byron's World'; and an unrevised selection from contributions to the 'Pall Mall Magazine.'

A bust of Henley by Rodin (1886) was presented by Mrs. Henley to the National Portrait Gallery in April 1913. A drawing was made by William Rothenstein in 1897, and an oil painting by William Nicholson in 1901. A sketch by 'Spy' (Leslie Ward), which, though touched with caricature, is an admirable likeness, was made for 'Vanity Fair' in 1897. On 11 July 1907 a memorial of Henley, subscribed for by friends and admirers, was unveiled by the Earl of Plymouth in the crypt of St. Paul's Cathedral, London; it consists of a replica of Rodin's bust in bronze (the sculptor's gift) set in white marble.

[Obituary notices; Stevenson's Life and Letters; the Henley Memorial, 1907; A Blurred Memory of Childhood, by Roden Shields (a fellow patient as a boy with Henley in the Infirmary), in Cornhill Mag., Aug. 1905; William Ernest Henley, by Sidney Low, ib., Sept. 1903; Mrs. W. Y. Sellar's Recollections, ib., Dec. 1910; Portraits of the Henleys by Francis Watt in Art Journal, Feb. 1906; information from Mrs. Henley and Mr. Alfred Wareing; personal knowledge. A list of Henley's signed contributions to magazines and reviews is in English Illustrated Mag., vol. xxix.] T. F. H.

HENNELL, SARA. [See under Bray, Mrs. Caroline (1814–1905), friend of George Eliot and author.]

HENNESSEY, JOHN BOBANAU NICKERLIEU (1829–1910), deputy surveyor-general of India, born at Fatehpur, Northern India, on 1 Aug. 1829, was son of Michael Henry Hennessey by a native mother. After being educated locally, he was admitted to the junior branch of the great trigonometrical survey on 14 April 1844. For some years he worked in the marshy jungle tracts of Bengal and the north-west provinces bordering the Nepal Terai. Of the party of 140 officers and assistants which he joined, forty were carried off by fever in a few days, and he was often incapacitated by illness. But his zeal and thoroughness attracted notice, and, transferred to the Punjab in 1850, he fixed the longitudinal position of Lahore, Amritsar, Wazirabad, and other places.

Attached to the superintendent's field office in 1851, he helped the astronomical assistant to collate the various computations of latitude observations and in other work. In Oct. 1853 he was placed in charge of the branch computing office, and in the following year assisted the surveyor-general at the Chach base line. Promoted to the senior branch on 25 April 1854, he was employed at headquarters (Dehra Dun) in reducing the measurements of the Chach base line, and preparing (in triplicate manuscript) a general report on the north-east longitudinal series. During the Mutiny he was at Mussoorie, a hill station ten miles beyond Dehra Dun. For nearly five months he was under arms and on harassing duty.

After service with the base line at Vizagapatam, in the south, he took two years' leave to England in March 1863. Entering Jesus College, Cambridge, on 31 Oct. as a fellow commoner, he pursued mathematical studies with great aptitude under professors Adams, Challis, and Walton. With the sanction of the secretary of state he learned the new process of photo-zincography at the ordnance survey offices, Southampton, and returning to duty in India (April 1865) took out an extensive apparatus with which he established the process at survey headquarters. By this means the rapid reproduction of maps and survey sheets became possible, and the great cost and delay of sending orders to England were avoided.

Hennessey, appointed to the charge of the amalgamated computing office and calculating branch, made (1866) the comparisons of standards and determined the 10 feet standard bar of the trigonometrical survey. He also took in hand the vast accumulations of material provided by the labours of William Lambton [q. v.], Sir George Everest [q. v.], and Sir Andrew Scott Waugh [q. v.], and with the help of a large staff reduced them to order.

Hennessey assisted his chief, General James Thomas Walker [q. v.], in the editorship of the monumental 'Account of the Operations of the Great Trigonometrical Survey of India,' of which the first volume was issued in 1870. He was a large contributor to some of the volumes, fourteen of which were issued during his tenure of office. He also wrote the report on 'Explorations in Great Tibet and Mongolia, made by A——k in 1879–82' (Dehra Dun, 1884). He was designated deputy superintendent of the trigonometrical survey in Sept. 1869, officiated as its superintendent in 1874, and after the three branches of survey operations had been amalgamated under the title of the Survey of India, he was appointed (Feb. 1883) deputy surveyor-general.

On 9 Dec. 1874, with the equatorial of the Royal Society, he observed from Mussoorie (6765 ft.) the transit of Venus (see *Trans. Roy. Soc.* Nos. 159 and 161, 1875). This won him the fellowship of the society (1875), to the 'Transactions' of which he had contributed in 1867, 1870, 1871, and twice in 1873. Cambridge conferred upon him the honorary M.A. degree in 1876, and after his retirement on 1 Oct. 1884 on a special pension granted by government, he was made a C.I.E. (6 June 1885).

At Mussoorie, where he at first lived after retirement, he was an active member of the municipality, captain of the local volunteer corps, and discoverer of the spring from which the water-supply is obtained. Coming to London, he resided in Alleyn park, West Dulwich, where he died on 23 May 1910, being interred at Elmer's End cemetery.

He married at Calcutta in March 1868 Elizabeth Golden, only daughter of R. Malcolm Ashman; by her he had a son and daughter. The son, Lieut. J. A. C. Hennessey, 45th (Rattray) Sikhs, was killed in action at Jandola, Waziristan, in Oct. 1900; memorial prizes for moral worth were founded at his old school, Dulwich.

[Memoir on Indian Surveys, by Sir C. Markham, 1878, and cont. by C. E. D. Black, 1891; List of Officers in Survey Dept. to Jan. 1884, Calcutta; Indian Survey Report for 1888–5, Calcutta; The Times, 26 May 1910; personal knowledge.] F. H. B.

HENNESSY, HENRY (1826–1901), physicist, born at Cork on 19 March 1826, was the second son of John Hennessy of Ballyhennessy, co. Kerry, by his wife Elizabeth, daughter of Henry Casey of Cork. Sir John Pope-Hennessy [q. v.] was a younger brother. Educated at Cork under Michael Healy, he received an excellent training in classics, modern languages, and mathematics. Deprived as a Roman catholic of a university education, he adopted the profession of an engineer. His leisure was from early youth devoted to mathematical research, in which he engaged quite spontaneously. From an early period he made original and valuable contributions to British and foreign scientific journals, which he continued through life. In 1849 he was made librarian of Queen's College, Cork, and in 1855, on the invitation of Cardinal Newman, he became professor of physics at the Roman catholic University, Dublin. In 1874 he transferred his services to the Royal College of Science, Dublin, where he was appointed professor of applied mathematics. His work there was of exceptional merit, and he was dean of the college in 1880 and again in 1888. Hennessy was made a member of the Royal Irish Academy in 1851, and was its vice-president from 1870 to 1873. He was also elected F.R.S. in 1858.

In 1890 he resigned his chair under the recent compulsory rules for superannuation in the civil service at the age of 65. A memorial to the government protesting against his retirement was influentially signed but was without effect. Owing to the inadequacy of his pension he resided much abroad, but returning to Ireland under medical advice, he died on 8 March 1901, at Bray, co. Wicklow. He married Rosa, youngest daughter of Hayden Corri, and had issue.

Hennessy was remarkable for his versatile interests and scientific ingenuity. In his earliest paper, which was published in 1845, when he was only nineteen, in the 'Philosophical Magazine,' he proposed to use photography for the registration of barometric and thermometric readings. In 'Researches in Terrestrial Physics' (*Phil. Trans.* 1851) he argued from the figure and structure of the earth and planets, that they were of fluid origin, and that a fluid nucleus at a high temperature was enclosed within their crust. He also wrote on meteorology and on climatology (*British Assoc. Rep.* 1857), deducing laws which regulate the distribution of temperature in islands. The excellence of a paper 'On the Influence of the Gulf Stream' (*Proc. Roy. Soc.* 1857–9) led to a request to report on the temperature of the seas surrounding the British Isles for the Committee on Irish Fisheries in 1870. Among his other proposals was one for a decimal system of weights and measures founded on the length of the polar axis of the earth, a quantity capable of more accurate determination than the earth's quadrant, on which the metric system is based. Standards such as the polar foot and the polar pound, and a complete set of weights and measures on the polar system, constructed under Hennessy's supervision, are in the Museum of the Royal College of Science, Dublin. In the same museum are many models of his mechanical inventions, one of them illustrating the structure of sewers best adapted to obtain the greatest scour with due provision for a great influx of storm water (cf. 'Hydraulic Problems on the Cross-sections of Pipes and Channels,' *Proc. Roy. Soc.* 1888).

Hennessy, besides his papers in scientific periodicals, published separately: 1. 'On the Study of Science in its Relation to Individuals and Society,' Dublin, 1858; 2nd edit. 1859. 2. 'On the Freedom of Education' (a paper at the Social Science Congress, Liverpool, in 1858), 1859. 3. 'The Relation of Science to Modern Civilisation,' 1862.

[Men of the Time, 1899; Proc. Roy. Soc. vol. 75 (1905) p. 140; Who's Who, 1901; Pratt, People of the Period, 1897.]

HENRY, MITCHELL (1826–1910), Irish politician, born at Ardwick Green, Manchester, in 1826, was younger son of Alexander Henry, M.P. for South Lancashire in the liberal interest (1847–52), who died 4 Oct. 1862, by his wife Elizabeth, daughter of George Brush, of Dromore, co. Down. Having been educated privately and at University College School, Henry joined the Pine Street school of medicine in Manchester, afterwards incorporated in the medical department of the Owens College. He graduated M.R.C.S. in 1847 and having established himself in practice as a consulting surgeon at No. 5 Harley Street, Cavendish Square, he was next year appointed surgeon to the Middlesex Hospital, and in 1854 was elected a fellow of the Royal College of Surgeons. In 1862, however, he abandoned his profession and became a partner in the family firm of A. & S. Henry, merchants and general warehousemen, of Manchester and Huddersfield. In 1865 he unsuccessfully contested Woodstock in the liberal interest, and was defeated at Manchester both at a bye-election in 1867 and at the general election in 1868. During his second Manchester candidature he founded the 'Evening News' as an electioneering sheet, and after his defeat he disposed of the paper to the printer, William Evans.

Henry was an enthusiastic angler, and his interest in the sport brought him frequently to the west of Ireland. As a consequence he successfully contested county Galway in 1871. He warmly supported the political principles of Isaac Butt [q. v.] and was a member of the council of the Home Rule League; his election was therefore regarded as a great victory for the national party (O'CONNOR, *The Parnell Movement*, p. 226). His first important speech in parliament was in support of Butt's motion for an inquiry into the judgment of Mr. Justice Keogh (see KEOGH, WILLIAM NICHOLAS) in the matter of the Galway election petition in 1872. He opposed Gladstone's Irish university bill, chiefly on the ground that it did not concede the principle of sectarian education demanded by public opinion in Ireland, and on 2 July 1874, in seconding Butt's motion to consider the parliamentary relations between Great Britain and Ireland, he dealt effectively with the financial side of the question, arguing strongly that Ireland had for years been paying more than her due share of the taxation of the empire, as fixed by the Act of Union. In July 1877 he returned to the subject of the over-taxation of Ireland, and at the opening of parliament in January next year, being called on, owing to Butt's illness, to act as leader of the Irish party, he urged that the most pressing needs of Ireland were the assimilation of the Irish franchise to that of England, a reasonable university bill, and the acknowledgment of Ireland's right to manage her own domestic affairs.

Meanwhile he had purchased from the Blakes a large estate of some 14,000 acres in county Galway between Letterfrack and Lenane. It consisted mostly of bog land, which he reclaimed, and at Kylemore Lough he erected a stately mansion, known as Kylemore Castle, now the property of the duke of Manchester. These operations and the fact of his residing there brought money into the district, and his relations with the peasantry were on the whole very friendly till the days of the Land League. His position as an Irish landlord seems, however, to have modified his political views; anyhow he came to view with apprehension the development of the home rule agitation under Parnell's leadership. Independent of his rents for his income, he suffered less than his neighbours from the Land League movement, but he disapproved its operations. The home rule which he advocated was, he declared, intended to draw Ireland closer to England, whereas the object of the Parnellites was to sever Ireland from England (HANSARD, *Debates*, cclv. 1884–90). His warm support of Forster's efforts to suppress the league brought about an open breach with his former colleagues. While supporting the land bill of 1881 he deprecated the working of it by the county court judges (12 May 1881, *ibid.* cclxii. 342–51), and described the Land League as a 'dishonest, demoralising and un-Christian agitation.' Henry was unseated at the general election in 1885 by what he called Parnellite 'intimidation.' He was, however, elected for the Blackfriars division of Glasgow, and returning to parliament he reopened the campaign against his former colleagues and their Gladstonian allies (*ib.* ccciv. 1275), and voted against the second reading of Gladstone's home rule bill on 7 June 1886. He failed to obtain re-election at the general election that year and retired from parliament. In 1889 the firm of A. & S. Henry was turned into a limited liability company, of which Henry was chairman till 1893. His interest in Ireland declined and his pecuniary position was not maintained. Disposing of his Galway estate, he established himself at Leamington, where he died on 22 Nov. 1910. Henry married in 1850 Margaret, daughter of George Vaughan of Quilly House, Dromore, county Down, by whom he had three sons and three daughters. His wife predeceased him in 1874 and was buried in a mausoleum erected by him near Kylemore Castle.

A cartoon by 'Spy' appeared in 'Vanity Fair' (1879).

[Manchester Guardian, 24 Nov. 1910; The Times, 23 Nov. 1910; Annual Register, 1910, p. 144; Burke's Landed Gentry; Hansard's Parliamentary Debates; Lucy's Diary of Two Parliaments; Locker-Lampson's Consideration of the State of Ireland; O'Donnell's Hist. of Irish Parliamentary Party; information kindly supplied by Mr. Percy Robinson and Mr. C. W. Sutton.]

R. D.

HENTY, GEORGE ALFRED (1832–1902), writer for boys, born at Trumping ton, near Cambridge, on 8 Dec. 1832, was the eldest son of three children of James Henty, stockbroker, and Mary Bovill, daughter of Dr. Edwards, physician, of Wandsworth. In September 1847 he was admitted to Westminster School, and in 1852 he proceeded to Gonville and Caius College, Cambridge, but left the university prematurely without taking a degree. On the outbreak of the Crimean war Henty and his younger brother, Frederick, volunteered for active service. Both entered the hospital commissariat, and in the spring of 1855 went out to the Crimea. Later in the year the brother died of cholera at Scutari. Henty's Crimean experience gave him a taste both for soldiering and for journalism. His letters describing the siege of Sevastopol were accepted by the 'Morning Advertiser,' and he continued his contributions until he was incapacitated by fever. On being invalided home, he was promoted purveyor of the forces, and received the Turkish order of the Medjidie. His administrative capacity was recognised, and in 1859 he was chosen to organise the Italian hospitals during the war with Austria. On his return he held various posts in the commissariat department at Belfast and Portsmouth, but he soon wearied of routine and resigned his commission. For a time Henty helped his father in the management of a colliery in Wales, an experience he afterwards turned to account in his story

'Facing Death' (1883; 3rd edit. 1907), and subsequently he went out to Sardinia as manager of a mine, but this occupation proved equally uncongenial.

In 1865 Henty adopted the calling of a journalist and wrote miscellaneous articles, mainly for the 'Standard.' Roving instincts, however, would not let him settle down. His chance came in 1866, when he was commissioned to serve as correspondent of the 'Standard' during the Austro-Italian war. While following Garibaldi's Tyrolese campaign he became acquainted with George Meredith [q. v. Suppl. II], who was then a correspondent of the 'Morning Post'; and he witnessed from an Italian man-of-war the disastrous naval battle of Lissa (20 July 1866). In the course of the next ten years Henty, in the service of the 'Standard,' accompanied Lord Napier's expedition to Abyssinia in 1867–8, his articles being reprinted as 'The March to Magdala' (1868); attended the inauguration of the Suez Canal in 1869; saw something of the winter campaign of 1870–1 during the Franco-German war, afterwards starving in Paris during the Commune; witnessed the Russian conquest of Khiva in 1873; followed Lord Wolseley's victorious expedition to Ashanti (1873–4), his letters being reissued as 'The March to Coomassie' (1874); watched guerilla warfare in Spain during the Carlist insurrection in 1874; was with the Prince of Wales (afterwards King Edward VII) during his tour through India in 1875, and saw some desperate hand-to-hand fighting while with the Turkish army in the Turco-Servian war (1876). Hard work and rough experiences told on Henty's health, and except for a visit to the mining camps of California he did no more correspondent's work abroad.

Meanwhile Henty made occasional excursions into fiction. His first boys' book, 'Out in the Pampas' (1868; 4th edit. 1910), was followed by 'The Young Franc-Tireurs,' a tale of the Franco-Prussian war (1872; 6th edit. 1910). After 1876 he settled down to writing stories largely based on his own experiences. He issued about a dozen orthodox novels, including 'Colonel Thorndyke's Secret,' published as late as 1898, but none of them achieved much success. His real strength lay in writing tales of adventure for boys, which came out at the rate of three or four volumes a year. Military history was his favourite theme, but he took all history for his province, from that of ancient Egypt in 'The Cat of Bubastes' (1889; 3rd edit. 1908) to that of current affairs in 'With Roberts to Pretoria' (1902). He prided himself upon his historical fidelity and manly sentiment. From 1880 to 1883 he was editor of the 'Union-Jack,' in succession to W. H. G. Kingston [q. v.]; from 1888 to 1890 he was the mainstay of Beeton's 'Boys' Own Magazine,' and in 1889 he collaborated with Archibald Forbes [q. v. Suppl. I] in a boys' annual, 'Camps and Quarters.' These magazines all died young.

Of tall, burly, athletic figure, bluff face, and patriarchal beard, Henty devoted his leisure to sailing. In 1887 he purchased a yacht, and more than once he was an unsuccessful competitor in the race from Dover to Heligoland for the Kaiser's cup. He died on board his yacht Egret in Weymouth harbour on 16 Nov. 1902 and was buried in Brompton cemetery.

Henty was twice married: (1) in 1858 to Elizabeth Finucane, by whom he had two sons and two daughters, his elder son, Captain Charles Gerald Henty, alone surviving him; (2) late in life to Elizabeth Keylock, who survived him.

In addition to those works already mentioned, Henty's chief volumes include: 1. 'The Young Buglers: a Tale of the Peninsular War,' 1880; 4th edit. 1910. 2. 'In Times of Peril: a Tale of India,' 1881; 4th edit. 1911. 3. 'Friends though Divided: a Tale of the Civil Wars,' 1883; 3rd edit. 1910. 4. 'Under Drake's Flag,' 1883; 2nd edit. 1896. 5. 'With Clive in India,' 1884; 2nd edit. 1896. 6. 'St. George for England: a Tale of Cressy and Poitiers,' 1885; 2nd edit. 1896. 7. 'In Freedom's Cause: a Story of Wallace and Bruce,' 1885; 3rd edit. 1906. 8. 'For Name and Fame: or, Through the Afghan Passes,' 1886; 3rd edit. 1900. 9. 'The Dragon and the Raven: or, the Days of King Alfred,' 1886; 3rd edit. 1908. 10. 'The Lion of the North: a Tale of the Times of Gustavus Adolphus,' 1886; 3rd edit. 1906. 11. 'The Young Carthaginian,' 1887; 3rd edit. 1906. 12. 'The Bravest of the Brave; or, With Peterborough in Spain,' 1887; 2nd edit. 1896. 13. 'Queen Victoria, Scenes from her Life and Reign,' 1887; 3rd edit. 1901. 14. 'For the Temple: a Tale of the Fall of Jerusalem,' 1888; 2nd edit. 1896. 15. 'Orange and Green: a Tale of Boyne and Limerick,' 1888; 3rd edit. 1910. 16. 'One of the 28th: a Tale of Waterloo,' 1889; 3rd edit. 1908. 17. 'The Lion of St. Mark: a Tale of Venice,' 1889; 2nd edit. 1897.

18. 'By Pike and Dyke: a Tale of the Rise of the Dutch Republic,' 1890; 3rd edit. 1905. 19. 'By Right of Conquest; or, With Cortez in Mexico,' 1891; 3rd edit. 1910. 20. 'Redskin and Cowboy,' 1892. 21. 'A Jacobite Exile,' 1894; 2nd edit. 1909. 22. 'In the Reign of Terror,' 1896. 23. 'Through the Russian Snows: a Story of Napoleon's Retreat from Moscow,' 1896. 24. 'With Frederick the Great,' 1898; 2nd edit. 1909. 25. 'With Moore at Corunna,' 1898; 2nd edit. 1909. 26. 'Torpedo-Boat 240: a Tale of the Naval Manœuvres,' 1900. 27. 'With Buller in Natal,' 1901. 28. 'John Hawke's Fortune: a Story of Monmouth's Rebellion,' 1901; 2nd edit. 1906. 29. 'With Kitchener in the Soudan,' 1903. 30. 'With the Allies to Pekin,' 1904.

[G. Manville Fenn's George Alfred Henty, 1907 (photographs); The Times, and Standard, 17 Nov. 1902; Athenæum, 22 Nov. 1902; Life and Adventures of George Augustus Sala, 1896; Edmund Downey, Twenty Years Ago, 1905; private information from Capt. C. G. Henty.] G. S. W.

HERBERT, AUBERON EDWARD WILLIAM MOLYNEUX (1838–1906), political philosopher and author, born at Highclere on 18 June 1838, was the third son of Henry John George Herbert, third earl of Carnarvon [q. v.], by his wife Henrietta Anne, eldest daughter of Lord Henry Molyneux Howard, a brother of Bernard Edward Howard, twelfth duke of Norfolk. Henry Howard Molyneux Herbert, fourth earl of Carnarvon [q. v.], was his eldest brother. Herbert was educated at Eton, entering the school in Sept. 1850. He had a high reputation for scholarship and general ability, but left early, having been elected to a founder's kin fellowship at St John's College, Oxford, at Easter 1855. He took a second in classical moderations in the Michaelmas term 1857, but did not seek final honours. In May 1858 he joined the 7th hussars at their depot at Canterbury as cornet by purchase, and in June 1859 became a lieutenant, also by purchase. In the autumn of 1860 he joined the service troops at Umballa. In 1861 he returned to England, and in Feb. 1862 sold his commission. He then returned to Oxford, where he was president of the Union in Hilary Term 1862; he graduated B.C.L. in 1862 and D.C.L. in 1865. He lectured in history and jurisprudence at St. John's College, and resigned his fellowship in 1869.

During these years Herbert displayed his father's love of adventure. In March 1864 he visited the scene of the Prusso-Danish war, and distinguished himself at Dybböl, near Sonderburg, by sallies from the Danish redoubts for the purpose of rescuing the wounded. As a recognition of his bravery he was made a knight of the Order of the Dannebrog (*The Times*, 4 April 1864; *Nationaltidende*, Copenhagen, 13 Nov. 1906). His impressions of the campaign are recorded in his letters to his mother published under the title 'The Danes in Camp' (1864).

The American civil war drew him to the United States, and he witnessed the siege of Richmond. An intention to witness the war of 1866 between Prussia and Austria was frustrated owing to its short duration. During the Franco-German war he went to France, and was present at Sedan. He was outside Paris during the siege, and was one of the very first to enter the city after the capitulation, being nearly shot as a spy on his way in. He remained there during the Commune in the company of his second brother, Alan Herbert, who practised medicine in Paris. In later life he received the Austrian Order of the Iron Crown, third class, for helping to rescue the crew of the Parc, an Austrian vessel wrecked off Westward Ho!

Herbert had early been attracted by politics, and while at Oxford he founded the Chatham and Canning Clubs, conservative debating societies. In July 1865 he was defeated as a conservative candidate in an election in the Isle of Wight. In the summer of 1866 Sir Stafford Northcote, who had just been made president of the board of trade, chose him as his private secretary, a post he held till the autumn of 1868, when he resigned, surprising his chief with the news that he was about to contest Berkshire as a liberal. This election he lost, but in Feb. 1870 he was returned at a bye-election for Nottingham with the support of Mundella. A fortnight after entering the house he made his first speech in the second reading debate on the education bill of 1870; he supported the principle that all provided schools should be secular or strictly unsectarian. In July 1871, when the House of Lords had rejected the bill for the abolition of the purchase system, he criticised Gladstone's solution of the difficulty by royal warrant, and urged the House of Commons to take effective action against the veto of the House of Lords, 'a body which was wholly irresponsible' (Hansard, third series, vol. 208). On 19 March 1872 he seconded Sir Charles Dilke's motion for an inquiry into the expenses of the civil list, and followed Sir

Charles's example by declaring himself a republican. This led to a scene of great disorder, and the latter part of his speech was inaudible (HANSARD, third series, vol. 210). He took a leading part in the passing of the Wild Birds' Protection Act, 1872 (HANSARD, third series, vol. 211). At all points an advanced radical, he was an ardent supporter of Joseph Arch and spoke at the mass meeting at Leamington on Good Friday 1872, when the Warwickshire Agricultural Labourers' Union was formed (JOSEPH ARCH, *The Story of his Life, told by himself*, 1898). At the dissolution of 1874 he retired from parliamentary life, but he took an active part in the agitation caused by the Bulgarian atrocities, organised in 1878 the great 'anti-Jingo' demonstration in Hyde Park against the expected war with Russia, and in 1880 championed the cause of Charles Bradlaugh [q. v.], speaking at some of the stormy Hyde Park meetings.

Meanwhile Herbert had become an ardent but independent disciple of Herbert Spencer's philosophy. His creed developed a variant of Spencerian individualism which he described as voluntaryism. But his devotion to Spencer's great doctrine was life-long, and Spencer made him, at his death in 1903, one of his three trustees (SPENCER'S *Autob.* 1904, *preliminary note*). In 1884 Herbert published his best-known book, 'A Politician in Trouble about his Soul,' a reprint with alterations and additions from the 'Fortnightly Review.' In the first chapters the objections to the party system are discussed, and in the last chapter Spencerian principles are expounded and the doctrine of *Laissez-faire* is pushed to the extreme point of advocating 'voluntary taxation.'

In 1890 Herbert started a small weekly paper, 'Free Life,' which first appeared under the same cover as his friend St. George Lane Fox's 'Political World,' but 'Free Life,' later called 'The Free Life,' soon became a small separate monthly paper, the 'Organ of Voluntary Taxation and the Voluntary State.' The last number was printed on 13 August 1901. In 1906 he summarised his views in the Herbert Spencer lecture which he delivered at Oxford. In 1889 he edited 'The sacrifice of education to examination. Letters from all sorts and conditions of men,' a result of the influentially signed 'Protest' against examinations in the 'Nineteenth Century,' Nov. 1888. He explained his view of the capital and labour problem in 'The True Line of Deliverance,' a criticism of trade unionism, which appeared in a volume of essays called 'A Plea for Liberty' (1891). In an article 'Assuming the Foundations' (*Nineteenth Century and After*,' Aug., Sept. 1901), he expounded his agnostic position towards religion.

On leaving parliament he took to farming, purchasing Ashley Arnewood farm near Lymington, where he lived till his wife's death in 1886. He then moved to the neighbourhood of Burley in the New Forest, and built, after a pre-existing building, 'The Old House,' which was his home till death. At the same time he travelled much, re-visited America in 1902–3, and often wintered abroad. At first at Ashley Arnewood Farm on a small scale, and subsequently at 'The Old House' on a large scale, Herbert once every summer entertained at tea all comers, without distinction of class, to the ultimate number of several thousands, the gypsies clearing off the remains.

Herbert, a man of singular charm, always scrupulously anxious to distinguish the system he attacked from the men who upheld or lived under it, was penetrated by the belief that the law of equal freedom is the supreme moral law. A keen sportsman and a fine rider in his youth, he gave up sport in later life on account of his objection to taking life, and for the same reason became a vegetarian. But his interests outside his philosophic propagandism were varied. He was one of the first to take to bicycling, and was very fond of adventurous sailing in a small boat. An ardent climber he was a member of the Alpine Club from 1863 to 1872. He was interested in prehistoric remains and made a fine collection of flint implements. He followed with sympathy the investigations of psychic research and made vigorous efforts to preserve the historic character of the New Forest (cf. art. 'The Last Bit of Natural Woodland' in *Nineteenth Century*, Sept. 1891). He has been compared to Tolstoi, but he always repudiated the gospel of non-resistance, meeting it with his favourite formula 'Use force only to restrain force and fraud.'

He died at 'The Old House' on 5 Nov. 1906, and was buried at his desire in a grave in the grounds.

Herbert, who was a voluminous writer of letters to 'The Times' and other journals, published, besides the books cited already: 1. 'The Right and Wrong of Compulsion by the State,' 1885. 2. 'Bad Air and Bad Health,' 1894. 3. 'Windfall and Water-drift,' a small volume of verses, 1894. 4. 'The Voluntaryist Creed,' 1908, posthumously issued, consisting of the Herbert Spencer lecture of 1906, and 'A Plea for Voluntaryism,' an essay completed just before his death.

Herbert married in 1871 Lady Florence Amabel, daughter of George Augustus Frederick Cowper, sixth earl Cowper. She died in 1886. They had four children: two sons, of whom the elder died in boyhood, while the younger, Auberon Thomas, born in 1876, succeeded his uncle, Francis Thomas de Grey Cowper, seventh earl Cowper [q. v. Suppl. II], as Lord Lucas and Dingwall in 1905, and two daughters, of whom the elder died in 1893.

[The Times, Daily Telegraph, Tribune, 6 Nov. 1906; Westminster Gazette, 7 Nov. 1906; Ringwood Almanac, 1907; family and private information. For his conversion to Spencer's political principles see his Spencer lecture, 1906, p. 6; for letters to him from J. S. Mill and Spencer see Letters of John Stuart Mill, 1910, and Life and Letters of Herbert Spencer, 1908, by Dr. Duncan; for his connection with the Dominicans, a Sunday dining club founded by J. S. Mill in 1865, see Frederic Harrison's Autobiographic Memoirs, 1911, ii. 83.]

A. H–s.

HERBERT, Sir ROBERT GEORGE WYNDHAM (1831–1905), colonial official, born on 12 June 1831 at his father's house at Brighton, was only son (in a family of three children) of Algernon (1792–1855), youngest son of Henry Herbert, first earl of Carnarvon, by his wife Marianne, daughter of Thomas Lempriere, seigneur de Dielamont and cadet of the old house of Rozel of Jersey. Robert's third name of Wyndham was derived from his grandmother on his father's side, Elizabeth Alicia Maria, daughter of Charles Wyndham, second earl of Egremont [q. v.]. In 1834 his parents removed to Ickleton in Cambridgeshire, to an old house and spacious garden which came to Robert's father on the death of his uncle, Percy Wyndham. Algernon Herbert, a cultivated man and a keen botanist, at once began improvements which were continued throughout his own life and those of his children to whom the property descended.

From his seventh to his ninth year Robert attended the Rev. Mr. Daniel's school at Sawston, four miles from Ickleton. After further preparation under private tutors Herbert was sent to Edward Coleridge's house at Eton in 1844. Though apparently lacking in assiduity, he soon proved himself a brilliant scholar. At Eton he won the Newcastle scholarship in 1850, and in the same year a scholarship at Balliol College, Oxford. At Oxford he gained the Hertford scholarship in 1851, and the Ireland scholarship and the Latin verse prize in 1852. He took a first class in classical moderations in Easter term 1852, but only a second class in the final classical schools in Michaelmas 1853, when G. C. Brodrick, G. J. Goschen, and Lewis Campbell were among those in the first class. In 1854 he was elected Eldon law scholar and a fellow at All Souls. The All Souls fellowship he held for life. He graduated B.A. in 1854 and proceeded D.C.L. in 1862.

Coming in 1855 to London, where he shared rooms with his lifelong friend (Sir) John Bramston, like himself of Balliol and a fellow of All Souls, Herbert acted for a short time as private secretary to Gladstone, and his friendly relations with his chief were never interrupted. Called to the bar at the Inner Temple on 30 April 1858, he next year went out with Bramston to Queensland, he as colonial secretary and Bramston as private secretary to the governor, Sir George F. Bowen [q.v. Suppl. I]. Queensland had just been separated from New South Wales and made into an independent colony. Herbert and Bramston built for themselves a bungalow in what were then the outskirts of Brisbane, calling it 'Herston,' a combination of their respective names. From 1860 to 1865 Herbert was member of the legislative council and first premier of the colony, discharging his duties with distinction.

Herbert acquired an interest in considerable tracts of land in Queensland, and greatly developed his own taste for natural history, especially for birds and horses. At the same time many young men from the neighbourhood of Ickleton were drawn by his example to settle in the colony, and he looked after these settlers' interests with characteristic kindliness. He visited England in 1865, and came home for good in 1867, bringing back to Ickleton many Australian birds.

In 1868 he became assistant secretary at the board of trade, and in February 1870 went to the colonial office, first as assistant under secretary, and then, in 1871, as permanent under secretary of state for the colonies. The last office he retained for over twenty-one years, giving constant and conspicuous proof of his tact, business acumen, geniality, and courteous bearing. He retired from the service in 1892, but he returned to the colonial office, by request, for a few months in 1900. Meanwhile he acted as agent-general for Tasmania (1893–

1896), was high sheriff of London (1899), and was for a time adviser to the Sultan of Johore. He was made C.B. and K.C.B. in 1882, G.C.B. in 1902; he was chancellor of the order of St. Michael and St. George from 1892 to his death; and was made hon. LL.D. of Cambridge in 1886. A member of several clubs, including 'The Club' and Grillion's, Herbert passed much time in his last years in London, but he made his real home at Ickleton. He died there, unmarried, on 6 May 1905, and was buried there. A memorial bust by Sir George Frampton is in a corridor at the colonial office (cf. for unveiling by Lord Crewe, colonial secretary, *The Times*, 10 July 1908).

[Family papers and information; Colonial Office Records; The Times, 8 May 1905.]

E. IM T.

HERFORD, BROOKE (1830–1903), unitarian divine, born at Altrincham, Cheshire, on 21 Feb. 1830, was eighth child of John Herford, and younger brother of William Henry Herford [q. v. Suppl. II for account of parents]. From the school of John Relly Beard [q. v.] he entered in his fourteenth year the Manchester counting-house of his father, a wine merchant and insurance agent. Six months in Paris at the age of sixteen gave him a command of French. He engaged in Sunday school work, and the influence of Philip Pearsall Carpenter [q. v.] made him a teetotaler. He began to prepare for the Unitarian ministry, this purpose being strengthened by the influence of Travers Madge, whose life he afterwards wrote. In Sept. 1848 he entered Manchester New College (then at Manchester, now at Oxford); there his proficiency was conspicuous; but preaching was even more to him than scholastic attainment: he did missionary work in vacations, and as the college authorities refused to sanction his combining with his studies a regular engagement as preacher at Todmorden, he withdrew to become (February 1851) the settled minister there, and married soon after. From Todmorden he removed in January 1856 to Upper Chapel, Sheffield, including with his pastorate much missionary work in both Sheffield (leading to the formation of the Upperthorpe congregation) and Rotherham, and in Yorkshire and Derbyshire villages. Hence, in 1859, he was appointed missionary tutor to the Unitarian Home Missionary Board (now College) in Manchester, and added this engagement to his Sheffield work. In 1861 he was one of the founders and editors of the 'Unitarian Herald,' and in 1862 he began the publication of 'Home Pages,' a popular series of religious tracts. Economy of time combined with sagacious method enabled him to get through an enormous amount of strenuous labour. The success of his Sheffield ministry was largely based upon his intelligent sympathy with the working classes; his lecture to them on 'Trade Outrages' (1861) was a striking example of plain and wise speaking. His sermons were not rhetorical, but clear and devout, and 'packed with good sense' (CUCKSON). In November 1864 he succeeded Beard in the ministry of New Bridge Street chapel, Strangeways, Manchester, accepting the call on condition that seat rents and subscriptions should be abolished, and the minister's stipend be dependent on an offertory; the experiment so long as Herford remained was successful. On the death of John Harland [q. v.] in 1868, Herford undertook the completion of the new edition of Baines' 'Lancashire,' travelling up and down the county in search of particulars, to the detriment of his health. The second and last volume, which appeared in 1870 (4to), is by Herford; the edition is superseded by the improved edition by James Croston (1886–93, 5 vols. 4to).

Herford visited the United States in 1875, and removed thither later in the same year on a call to the Church of the Messiah, Chicago, where he ministered from January 1876 to July 1882. He had declined in 1881 a call to Cambridge, Massachusetts, but now accepted one to Arlington Street church, Boston (the scene of Channing's labours); here he remained till January 1892. In America his powerful and genial personality found scope for abundant activities. He was chairman of the council of the American unitarian conference (1889–91), became preacher in 1891 to Harvard University, and received its degree of D.D. in June 1891. Herford returned to England in February 1892 in order to succeed Thomas Sadler [q. v.] in the ministry of Rosslyn Hill chapel, Hampstead. This, his last ministry, was full of vigour. He put new life into the British and Foreign Unitarian Association, doubling its income, and acting as its president (1898–9). In June 1901 he retired from active duty, and was presented with a testimonial of over 3000*l*. Herford's position in his denomination was that of an open-minded and warm-hearted conservative, especially in Biblical matters; his relations with members of other churches and of no church were extremely cordial. He died at Hampstead on 20 Dec. 1903.

He married on 22 June 1852 Hannah (*d.* April 1901), daughter of William Hankinson, of Hale, Cheshire, and had issue three sons and six daughters. His third son, Oliver (Brooke) Herford, is well known in America as author of ironical prose and poetry, illustrated by himself.

In addition to a multitude of sermons, tracts, and a few good hymns, Herford published: 1. 'Travers Madge: a Memoir,' 1867, 12mo; 3rd edit. 1868. 2. 'The Story of Religion in England: a Book for Young Folk,' 1878. 3. 'The Forward Movement in Religious Thought as interpreted by Unitarians,' 1895. 4. 'Brief Account of Unitarianism,' 1903. Posthumously published were: 5. 'Anchors of the Soul,' 1904 (sermons, with biographical sketch by Philip Henry Wicksteed, and portrait). 6. 'Eutychus and his Relations,' 1905 (sketches reprinted from the 'Unitarian Herald').

[Memoir by John Cuckson, 1904 (three portraits); biographical sketch by P. H. Wicksteed, 1904 (portrait); Roll of Students, Manchester New College, 1868; C. S. Grundy, Reminiscences of Strangeways U.F. Church, 1888; G. E. Evans, Record of Provincial Assembly, Lanc. and Chesh., 1896; J. E. Manning, Hist. of Upper Chapel, Sheffield, 1900; Julian, Dict. of Hymnology, 1907, p. 1718.] A. G.

HERFORD, WILLIAM HENRY (1820–1908), writer on education, born at Coventry, 20 Oct. 1820, was fourth son in a family of six sons and three daughters of John Herford by his first wife, Sarah, daughter of Edward Smith of Birmingham, uncle of Joshua Toulmin Smith [q. v.]. Brooke Herford [q. v. Suppl. II] was a younger brother. The father, who was through life a strong liberal and convinced unitarian, became a wine merchant in Manchester in 1822, residing at Altrincham, where his wife, a woman of cultivation and an accomplished artist, conducted a successful girls' school. After attending a school kept by Charles Wallace, unitarian minister at Hale Barns, William was from 1831 to 1834 a day boy at Shrewsbury under Samuel Butler [q.v.]. From 1834 to 1836 he was at the Manchester grammar school. Then, being destined for the unitarian ministry, he was prepared for entry at the ministerial college at York by John Relly Beard [q. v.], from whom 'I first learned by experience that lessons might be made interesting to scholars.' From 1837 to 1840 he studied at Manchester College in York, and there came into contact with German philosophy and theology. He removed with the college from York to Manchester in the summer of 1840, and thus came under the influence of three new professors, Francis Newman [q. v. Suppl. I], James Martineau [q. v. Suppl. I], and John James Tayler [q. v.], the last of whom he regarded as his spiritual father. Graduating B.A. of London University in the autumn of 1840, he began to preach in unitarian pulpits, but declined a permanent engagement as minister at Lancaster in order to accept a scholarship for three years' study in Germany. In 1842 he went to Bonn, where he attended the courses of Arndt, A. W. Schlegel, and F. C. Dahlmann, and formed an intimate friendship with his contemporary, Wilhelm Ihne. After two years at Bonn he spent eight months in Berlin, where he was admitted to the family circles of the Church historian Neander and the microscopist Ehrenberg. In the summer of 1845 he accepted an invitation from a unitarian congregation at Lancaster, where he remained a year. In 1846 Lady Byron, widow of the poet, invited him, on James Martineau's recommendation, to undertake the tuition of Ralph King, younger son of her daughter, Ada, Countess of Lovelace. Herford, early in 1847, accompanied the boy to Wilhelm von Fellenberg's Pestalozzian school at Hofwyl, near Bern. Herford grew intimate with Wilhelm von Fellenberg, became a temporary teacher on the staff, and accepted with enthusiasm Pestalozzi's and Froebel's educational ideas.

In Feb. 1848 he resumed his pastorate at Lancaster, and soon resolved to work out in a systematic way the ideas which he had developed at Hofwyl. In Jan. 1850 Herford, while retaining his ministerial duties, opened at Lancaster a school for boys on Pestalozzian principles. Prosperous on the whole, but never large, the school continued with some distinction for eleven years, when a decline in its numbers caused him to transfer it to other hands. Resigning his pastorate at the same time, he with his family went for eighteen months to Zurich in charge of a pupil. On his return in September 1863 he filled the pulpit of the Free Church in Manchester until 1869, acquiring increasing reputation as a teacher and lecturer, especially to women and girls. He was an ardent advocate of the opening of universities to women. Some of his teaching was given at Brooke House School, Knutsford, whose headmistress, Miss Louisa Carbutt (afterwards Herford's second wife), was educating girls upon principles closely akin to his own. Herford formed a plan of a co-educational school for younger children. In 1873 he opened his co-educational school at Fallowfield, Manchester, and afterwards moved it to Ladybarn House, Withington. For twelve years he directed it with an individuality of method which diffused through the neighbourhood a new educational ideal. Resigning the school to his second daughter in 1886, he thenceforth devoted his leisure to authorship and to travel, publishing in 1889 his chief work, 'The School: an Essay towards Humane Education,' a masterpiece of English educational writing, which he described as 'the fruits of more than forty years of teaching; various in the sex, age, class and nation of its objects.' In 1893 he published 'The Student's Froebel,' adapted from 'Die Menschenerziehung' of F. Froebel (1893; revised edit., posthumous, with memoir by C. H. Herford, 1911). This is the best English presentment of the educational doctrine which it summarises and expounds. In 1890 he settled at Paignton in South Devon. In 1902 he published 'Passages from the Life of an Educational Free Lance,' a translation of the 'Aus dem Leben eines freien Pädagogen' of Dr. Ewald Haufe. He died at Paignton on 27 April 1908, and was buried there. Herford married (1) in Sept. 1848 Elizabeth Anne (*d.* 1880), daughter of Timothy Davis, minister of the Presbyterian chapel, Evesham, by whom he had three sons and four daughters; (2) in 1884 Louisa, daughter of Francis Carbutt of Leeds, and from 1860 to 1870 headmistress of Brooke House, Knutsford, who died in 1907 without issue. A medallion of Herford by Helen Reed, made in Florence in 1887, hangs in Ladybarn House School, Manchester.

Herford spoke of himself as having been for the first quarter of a century of his teaching an unconscious follower of F. Froebel, and for the following fifteen years his professed disciple. With Pestalozzi he urged the teacher never to deprive the child of 'the sacred right of discovery,' and to seek to bring things, both abstract and concrete, into actual contact with the pupil's senses and mind, putting words and names, 'those importunate pretenders,' into a subordinate place. Moral training, 'practised not by preaching and as little as possible by punishment, but mainly by example and by atmosphere,' he held to be of supreme importance, and its primary purpose to be 'an intellectual clearing and purifying of the moral sense.' To physical training (including play, gymnastics, singing, and handwork) he attached importance only less than that which was assigned to moral culture. Himself a teacher of genius, he disdained any compromise with educational principles or conventions of which he disapproved.

[Memoir of W. H. Herford by Prof. C. H. Herford, prefixed to revised edit. of Herford's Student's Froebel (1911); autobiographical statements in preface to The School; family information and personal knowledge.]

M. E. S.

HERRING, GEORGE (1832–1906), philanthropist, born in 1832 of obscure parentage, is said to have begun working life as a carver in a boiled beef shop on Ludgate Hill (*The Times*, 3 Nov. 1906), but this statement has been denied. By judicious betting on horse-races he soon added to his income. He then became, in a small way at first, and in a very large way later, a turf commission agent. In 1855, during his early days on the turf, he was an important witness against William Palmer [q. v.], a betting man, who was convicted of poisoning another betting man, John Parsons Cook. At Tattersall's and at the Victoria Club Herring became known as a man of strict integrity, and was entrusted with the business of many leading speculators, who included the twelfth earl of Westmorland, Sir Joseph Hawley, and the duke of Beaufort. For a short time Herring owned racehorses. In 1874 Shallow, his best horse, was a winner of the Surrey Stakes, Goodwood Corinthian Plate, Brighton Club Stakes, and Lewes Autumn Handicap, four races out of ten for which he ran. Although remaining a lover of the turf and interesting himself in athletics, Herring soon left the business of a commission agent for large financial operations in the City of London, where in association with Henry Louis Bischoffsheim he made a fortune. He was chairman of the City of London Electric Lighting Company, and was connected with many similar undertakings. His powers of calculation were exceptionally rapid and accurate.

Of somewhat rough exterior and simple habits, Herring devoted his riches in his last years to varied philanthropic purposes. From 1899 till his death he guaranteed to contribute to the London Sunday Hospital Fund either 10,000*l.* in each year or 25*l.* per cent. of the amount collected in the churches In 1899, 1900, and 1901 the fund, exercising its option, took 10,000*l.* annually; in 1902, 11,575*l.*; in 1903, 12,302*l.*; in 1904, 11,926*l.*; in 1905, 12,400*l.*; in 1906, 11,275*l.* The form of the benefaction spurred subscribers' generosity. He supported a 'Haven of Rest,' almshouses for aged people at Maidenhead, where he had a house; he started with Mr. Howard Morley the Twentieth Century Club at Notting Hill for ladies earning their own livelihood, and was a generous benefactor to the North-west London Hospital at Camden Town, of which he was treasurer. In 1887 he first discussed with 'General' Booth the 'Back to the Land Scheme,' an original plan of the Salvation Army for relieving the unemployed. In 1905 he proposed to place 100,000*l.* in the hands of the Salvation Army for the purpose of settling poor people on neglected land in the United Kingdom, in establishing them as petty cultivators, and supporting them and their families until the land should become productive; the advance to be paid back by the settlers, and then to be given by the Salvation Army to King Edward's Hospital Fund in twenty-five annual instalments. Herring defended the scheme with eagerness when it was criticised as impracticable (*The Times*, 13 Feb. 1906), and it was put into operation. The sum actually received from Herring was 40,000*l.* under a codicil to his will. With this an estate was purchased at Boxted, Essex, comprising about fifty holdings, which was visited and approved by Herring not long before his death. The entire control of the scheme was, in accordance with a decision of the court of chancery, vested in the Salvation Army, with 'General' Booth as sole trustee (*The Times*, 19-20 Dec. 1907).

Herring, who lived in much retirement, and deprecated public recognition of his generosity, died on 2 Nov. 1906 at his Bedfordshire residence, Putteridge Park, Luton, after an operation for appendicitis. He also had residences at 1 Hamilton Place, Piccadilly, and Bridge House, Maidenhead. The urn containing his remains, which were cremated at Woking, was buried under the sundial at the Haven of Rest Almshouses at Maidenhead. His estate was sworn for probate at 1,371,152*l.* 18*s.* 8*d.* gross. After legacies to his brother William, to other relatives, friends, and charities, the residue was left to the Hospital Sunday Fund, which benefited to the extent of about 750,000*l.* The bequests to charities under the will reached a total of about 900,000*l.* (*The Times*, 10 May 1907).

On 15 June 1908 a marble bust of Herring, by Mr. George Wade, presented by the Metropolitan Sunday Hospital Fund as residuary legatees under his will, was placed in the Mansion House. On a brass plate beneath the bust is inscribed a letter received in 1905 by Herring from King Edward VII, who warmly commended Herring's disinterested philanthropy.

[The Times, 3 Nov. 1906, 16 June 1908; Sporting Life, 3 Nov. 1906; Who's Who, 1907.] C. W.

HERSCHEL, ALEXANDER STEWART (1836–1907), university professor and astronomer, second son of Sir John Frederick William Herschel, first baronet [q. v.], and grandson of Sir William Herschel [q. v.], was born on 5 Feb. 1836 at Feldhausen, South Africa, where his father was temporarily engaged in astronomical work. The family returned to England in 1838, and after some private education Alexander was sent to the Clapham grammar school in 1851, of which Charles Pritchard [q. v.], afterwards Savilian professor of astronomy, was headmaster. In 1855 he proceeded to Trinity College, Cambridge, where he graduated B.A. as twentieth wrangler in 1859, proceeding M.A. in 1877. While an undergraduate he helped Prof. Clerk Maxwell [q.v.] with his illustrations of the mechanics of rotation by means of the apparatus known as 'the devil on two sticks.' From Cambridge Herschel passed in 1861 to the Royal School of Mines, London, and began the observation of meteors which he continued to the end of his life. He early wrote, chiefly on meteorological subjects, papers for the British Meteorological Society, and he contributed, between 1863 and 1867, many articles to the 'Intellectual Observer,' a scientific periodical.

From 1866 to 1871 Herschel was lecturer on natural philosophy, and professor of mechanical and experimental physics in the University of Glasgow. From 1871 to 1886 he was the first professor of physics and experimental philosophy in the University of Durham College of Science, Newcastle-on-Tyne. At the Durham College Herschel provided, chiefly by his personal exertions, apparatus for the newly installed laboratory, some being made by his own hands. When the college migrated as Armstrong College to new buildings, the new Herschel Physical Laboratory was named after him.

Herschel made some accurate records of his observations of shooting stars in a long series of manuscript notebooks. He also accomplished important work in the summation, reduction, and discussion of the results of other observers with whom he corresponded in all parts of the world. With R. P. Greg he formed extensive catalogues of the radiant points of meteor streams, the more important of these being published in the 'Reports' of the British Association for 1868, 1872, and 1874. A table of the radiant points of comets computed by Herschel alone is in the 'Report' for 1875. He was reporter to the committee of the British Association on the 'observations of luminous meteors,' and from 1862 to 1881 drew up annually complete reports of the large meteors observed, and of the progress of meteoric science. For the British Association (1874–81) he prepared reports of a committee, consisting of himself, his colleague at Newcastle, Prof. A. G. Lebour, and Mr. J. T. Dunn, which was formed to determine the thermal conductivities of certain rocks. For the 'Monthly Notices' of the Royal Astronomical Society he prepared the annual reports on meteoric astronomy each February from 1872 to 1880 and contributed many other important papers to the 'Notices.' In one of these (June 1872), on meteor showers connected with Biela's comet, he predicted the shower which recurred at the end of November of that year. Herschel acquired great precision in noting the paths of meteors among the stars. From his determination of the radiant point of the November Leonids, Professor Schiaparelli deduced the identity of their orbit with that of Tempel's comet of 1866.

Besides meteoric astronomy, Herschel was interested in many branches of physical science, and became a member of the Physical Society of London in 1889 and of the Society of Arts in 1892. He contributed frequently to 'Nature,' an article on 'The Matter of Space' in 1883 being specially noteworthy. He worked much at photography, and in 1893 the Amateur Photographic Association presented an enlarged carbon print portrait of Alexander Herschel to the South Kensington Museum for the British Museum Portrait Gallery.

Herschel became fellow of the Royal Astronomical Society in 1867, and in 1884 was elected F.R.S., an honour already conferred on his grandfather, his father, and his younger brother John. In 1886 he gave up his professorship, and was made D.C.L. of Durham University. In 1888, with other members of his family, he reoccupied the house, now called Observatory House, Slough, where his grandfather, Sir William Herschel, had lived. Here he resided till his death, absorbed in study, but late in life he made a journey to Spain to observe the solar eclipse of 1905.

He died unmarried at Slough on 18 June 1907, and was buried in St. Lawrence's church, Upton, in the chancel of which his grandfather lies.

[Obituary notices in the Observatory Mag., July 1907, and Monthly Notices of the Royal Astronom. Soc., Feb. 1908; Annual Reports of the British Assoc.] H. P. H.

HERTSLET, Sir EDWARD (1824–1902), librarian of the foreign office, born at 16 College Street, Westminster, on 3 Feb. 1824, was youngest son of Lewis Hertslet [q.v.], of Swiss descent, by his first wife, Hannah Harriet Jemima Cooke. Educated privately near Hounslow, he was on 23 March 1840 temporarily attached to the library of the foreign office under his father, who was then librarian. On 8 Jan. 1842 he received a permanent appointment, on 28 Aug. 1844 became second clerk, and a little later the senior clerk. On 1 April 1855 he became sub-librarian, and on 19 Nov. 1857 librarian.

Hertslet carried on his father's tradition. He was long a main pivot of the foreign office work. Preliminary memoranda by him (now in the foreign office archives) focussed the history, geography, or international law incident to the chief public questions which came before the government while he held office. With the post of librarian he combined up to 1870 the agency for members of the diplomatic and consular services, and received an annual compensation on its abolition in that year.

He was attached to the special mission of Lord Beaconsfield to the Berlin congress in 1878, and was knighted for his services. He was one of the delegates for the examination of the question of boundary between British and Dutch territory in Borneo in June 1889.

Hertslet was retained at the foreign office long after the normal retiring age of sixty-five, discharging his duties up to 2 Feb. 1896. He was made C.B. on 21 Feb. 1874, and K.C.B. on 20 Aug. 1892. He died at his residence, Bellevue, Richmond, after an operation, on 4 Aug. 1902. He had resided at Richmond since 1852 and was active in local affairs.

Hertslet married Eden (*d.* 1899), daughter of John Bull, clerk of the journals of the House of Commons. Of his nine sons and three daughters, six sons and a daughter survived him. His third son, Mr. Godfrey L. P. Hertslet, in the library of the foreign office, succeeded him as editor of the 'Foreign Office List' and is also assistant editor of 'Hertslet's Commercial Treaties.'

Hertslet continued many publications which his father began; the principal were: 1. The 'Foreign Office List,' of which he was joint-editor from its third year (1855), and sole editor and proprietor from 1864 to his death. 2. Vols. xii.–xvi. with the index to the whole series and with the help of his eldest son, Sir Cecil Hertslet, vols. xvii.–xix. of the collection of treaties and conventions, known as 'Hertslet's Commercial Treaties' (1871–1895). 3. 'British and Foreign State Papers,' of which he was responsible for vols. 27–82, though his name appears only on the later volumes. These state papers are now government publications. Hertslet also compiled 'The Map of Europe by Treaty,' vols. i.–iii. 1875; vol. iv. 1896, as well as 'The Map of Africa by Treaty,' 2 vols. 1894. He was author of 'Recollections of the Old Foreign Office' (1901).

[The Times, 5 Aug. 1902; Who's Who, 1902; Foreign Office List, 1902; notes from a private biography given by Mr. Godfrey Hertslet; personal knowledge.] C. A. H.

HIBBERT, Sir JOHN TOMLINSON (1824–1908), politician, born on 5 Jan. 1824 at Lyon House, Oldham, was eldest son of Elijah Hibbert, one of the founders of the firm of Hibbert, Platt & Sons, machinists, by his wife Betty, daughter of Abraham Hilton of Cross Bank, near Oldham. At thirteen he was sent to a private school, Green Brow, Silloth, Cumberland. Entered at Shrewsbury school in June 1837, under Benjamin Hall Kennedy [q. v.], he there distinguished himself as an athlete. In later life he was chairman of the governors of the school. He was admitted at St. John's College, Cambridge, on 15 May 1843, and graduated B.A. as next above the 'wooden spoon' in the mathematical tripos in 1847, proceeding M.A. in 1851.

Called to the bar at the Inner Temple in the Easter term 1849, Hibbert at once developed a keen interest in politics. In 1857 he unsuccessfully contested his native town in the liberal interest, but was returned unopposed at a bye-election on 6 May 1862. Being re-elected after contests on 13 July 1865 and 18 Nov, 1868, he lost the seat in February 1874, but regained it on 1 March 1877, having in the interval unsuccessfully contested Blackburn. He was re-elected for Oldham on 31 March 1880 and on 25 Nov. 1885, was defeated in 1886, regained the seat on 6 July 1892, and lost it finally on 15 July 1895. In all he was candidate for Oldham eleven times.

An enthusiastic supporter of Gladstone he held subordinate office in Gladstone's four administrations, being parliamentary secretary of the local government board from 1871 to 1874, and again from 1880 to 1883; under secretary of the home department (1883–4); financial secretary to the treasury (1884–5 and 1892–5); and secretary to the admiralty (1886). He was a business-like administrator. He also served on three Royal commissions: the sanitary commission (1868); the boundary commission (1877); the Welsh Sunday closing commission (1890); as well as on the parliamentary committee on secondary education (1893). He materially helped the passing of the Execution within Gaols Act (1868), the Married Women's Property Act (1870), the Clergy Disabilities Act (1870), and the Municipal Elections Act (1884). Always keenly interested in poor law reform, he was long president of the north-western poor law conference.

To his native county, where he became J.P. in 1855 and D.L. in 1870, Hibbert's services were manifold. On the passing of the Local Government Act, 1888, he was elected a county councillor for Cartmel, was chosen an alderman on 24 Jan. 1889, was first chairman of the Lancashire county council on 14 Feb. following, and was first chairman of the County Councils Association. Other local offices included that of governor of Owens College and of the courts of the Victoria University (where he was made D.C.L. in 1902) and of Liverpool University. Hibbert was sworn a privy councillor in 1886, and made K.C.B. in 1893. He was appointed constable of Lancaster Castle in May 1907. He died at Hampsfield Hall, Grange-over-Sands, on 7 Nov. 1908, and was buried at Lindall-in-Cartmel. He married (1) in 1847 Eliza Anne (*d.* 1877), eldest daughter of Andrew Scholfield of Woodfield, Oldham; and (2) in January 1878 Charlotte Henrietta, fourth daughter of Admiral Charles Warde, of Squerryes Court, Westerham, Kent. He left one son and one daughter.

Portraits are at Oldham art gallery (by J. J. Shannon, R.A.), and at the county offices at Preston and the Royal Albert Asylum, Lancaster (both by Robert E. Morrison).

[The Times, 9 Nov. 1908; Manchester Faces and Places, vol. x.; Memories, by Lady Hibbert, 1911; private information.]

T. C. H.

HILES, HENRY (1828–1904), musical composer, born at Shrewsbury on 31 Dec. 1828, was youngest of six sons of James Hiles, a tradesman there. After studying as a boy under his brother John Hiles (1810–82), a musician of some repute and the author of several useful catechisms on musical subjects, Hiles left home to become in 1845 organist of the parish church, Bury, whence he removed to Bishop Wearmouth in 1847. But close study injured his health, and from 1852 to 1859 he travelled in Australia and elsewhere. On his return to London in 1859 he was organist of St. Michael's, Wood Street, for a few months and was then appointed organist and teacher of music to the Blind Asylum, and organist of St. Thomas, Old Trafford, Manchester. From Manchester he went to the parish church, Bowden, in 1861, and was at St. Paul's, Hulme, from 1863 to 1867. He graduated Mus.Bac. at Oxford in 1862 and Mus.Doc. in 1867.

In 1876 Hiles was appointed lecturer on harmony and composition at Owens College, Manchester, and in 1879 he was reappointed to Victoria University. Under the new charter of the Victoria University of 1891 he drew up a scheme for the establishment of a faculty of music, and was appointed permanent senior examiner and lecturer. He was also professor of harmony and counterpoint at the Royal Manchester College of Music, and took an active part in founding the Incorporated Society of Musicians. As a choral conductor he was much in request among societies at Manchester and neighbouring towns.

Hiles also made some reputation as a composer and writer of educational works. He gained the first prize for an organ composition at the College of Organists in 1864, and four others consecutively for anthems and organ music; he also won the prize for a serious glee, 'Hushed in Death,' 1878, offered by the Manchester Gentlemen's Glee Club, and in 1882 won the Meadowcroft prize. His musical compositions comprise: oratorio, 'The Patriarchs,' 1872; cantatas, 'The Ten Virgins,' 'The Crusaders,' 'Fayre Pastorel'; operetta, 'War in the Household,' 1885; concert overtures, 'Youth' and 'Harold,' 1893; fourteen anthems; services in G and F; sonata in G minor; two sets of six impromptus and other works for organ and pianoforte. His educational works are: 1. 'Harmony of Sounds,' three editions, 1871–2–9. 2. 'Grammar of Music,' 2 vols. 1879. 3. 'First Lessons in Singing.' 4. 'Part Writing or Modern Counterpoint,' 1884. 5. 'Harmony or Counterpoint?' 1889. 6. 'Harmony, Choral or Contrapuntal,' 1894. Hiles acted as editor of the 'Wesley Tune Book' and the 'Quarterly Musical Review,' 1885–8.

He died at Worthing on 20 Oct. 1904. He was twice married: (1) to Fanny Lockyer, and (2) to Isabel Higham. Two sons and one daughter by the latter survived him.

A self-educated musician, who was never a cathedral chorister nor studied in any particular school, Hiles showed as a teacher and writer remarkable modern tendencies. He had little respect for the old contrapuntists or the mere philosophic 'theory' of harmony. His modern sympathies failed, however, to influence his own musical compositions, which as a rule contain clear-cut and beautiful melody, orthodox though rich harmony, and regular form. He essayed no work on a large scale, and was too old to be much influenced as a composer by modern orchestration.

[Musical Times, 1 July 1900; Grove's Dict. of Music; Brown and Stratton's Brit. Musical Biogr.; private information.] J. C. B.

HILL, ALEXANDER STAVELEY (1825–1905), barrister and politician, was only son of Henry Hill of Dunstall Hall, Staffordshire, where he was born on 21 May 1825, by his wife Anne, daughter of Luke Staveley of Hunmanby, Yorkshire. Educated at King Edward School, Birmingham, in the house of James Prince Lee [q. v.], he was in the first form with Joseph Barber Lightfoot [q. v.] and Brooke Foss Westcott [q. v. Suppl. II]. Matriculating at Exeter College, Oxford, in 1844, he graduated B.A. in 1852, B.C.L. in 1854, and D.C.L. in 1855. From 1854 to 1864 he held a Staffordshire fellowship at St. John's College. The volunteer movement found in him an enthusiastic supporter, and he was one of the first to join the Victoria rifles in 1859. Admitted to the Inner Temple on 6 Nov. 1848, he was called to the bar on 21 Nov. 1851, joined the Oxford circuit, and took silk in 1868. He was elected a bencher of his inn the same year, and served the office of treasurer in 1886. He was recorder of Banbury from 1866 to 1903 and deputy high steward of Oxford University from 1874 until his death. Meanwhile he acquired a large practice at the parliamentary bar. This he was obliged to relinquish on entering the House of Commons in 1868. But until 1887 he enjoyed a good common law practice, besides holding a leading position in the probate, divorce, and admiralty division and frequently acting as arbitrator in important rating cases. He was leader of the Oxford circuit from 1886 to 1892. He was counsel to the admiralty and judge advocate of the fleet from 1875 till his retirement through failing health in 1904.

A staunch conservative in politics, Hill, after two unsuccessful attempts, at Wolverhampton in 1861 and at Coventry in March 1868, was elected for Coventry in December 1868. He sat in the house for thirty-two years—representing Coventry (1868–74), West Staffordshire (1874–85), and the Kingswinford division of Staffordshire (1885–1900). He was created a privy councillor in 1892. One of the earliest supporters of the policy afterwards known as tariff reform, he pressed in 1869 for an inquiry on behalf of the silk weavers of Coventry into the effect of the commercial treaty with France, and in speeches delivered in 1869 and 1870 showed the weakness of Great Britain's position in endeavouring to maintain a free trade policy against the operation of foreign tariffs.

In 1881 Staveley Hill went to Canada to study its suitability as a centre for emigration. He formed a large cattle ranch seventy miles south of Calgary, then in the North-West Territory, and since included in the province of Alberta. To this ranch, which was called New Oxley, he often returned, and he published a volume descriptive of the life among the foothills of the Rocky Mountains entitled 'From Home to Home: Autumn Wanderings in the North West, 1881–1884' (1885), illustrated by his wife. Toronto University made him an hon. LL.D. in 1892. He died at his residence, Oxley Manor, Wolverhampton, 28 June 1905. Staveley Hill married (1) on 6 Aug. 1864 Katherine Crumpston Florence (*d.* 14 May 1868), eldest daughter of Miles Ponsonby of Hale Hall, Cumberland; and (2) in 1876 Mary Frances (*d.* 1897), daughter of Francis Baird of St. Petersburg. A portrait of him by Desanges belongs to his only child, Henry Staveley Staveley-Hill (*b.* 22 May 1865), who succeeded him as recorder of Banbury and became in 1905 M.P. for the Kingswinford division.

Besides the volume mentioned above Staveley Hill wrote a treatise on the 'Practice of the Court of Probate' (1859).

[The Times, 30 June 1905; Foster, Alumni Oxonienses; Foster, Men at the Bar; Men and Women of the Time, 15th ed. 1899; Dod's Parliamentary Companion, 1900; private information.] C. E. A. B.

HILL, ALSAGER HAY (1839–1906), social reformer, born on 1 Oct. 1839 at Gressonhall Hall, Norfolk, was second son in a family of five sons and six daughters of John David Hay Hill, lord of the manor of Gressonhall, by his wife Margaret, second daughter of Ebenezer John Collett, of Hemel Hempsted, M.P. from 1814 to 1830.

He was educated at Brighton College (1850–4) and at Cheltenham College (1854–7), and while a schoolboy published at Cheltenham a small volume of poems, 'Footprints of Life,' in 1857. Two years later he competed unsuccessfully for the prize for the Burns centenary poem. In 1857 he obtained an exhibition at Caius College, Cambridge, migrating as scholar to Trinity Hall, where he graduated LL.B. in 1862. At Cambridge he started the 'Chit Chat' debating club, which still exists, and was treasurer of the Union. Becoming a student of the Inner Temple on 3 Oct. 1860, he was called to the bar on 26 Jan. 1864. He joined the south-eastern circuit, but soon devoted his energies to journalism and to literature, interesting himself especially in poor law and labour questions, and doing active work as almoner to the Society for the Relief of Distress in the East of London.

In letters to the press during 1868 Hill called attention to weaknesses in the poor law, and urged a more scientific classification of paupers (*The Times*, 9 Jan. 1868). His pamphlet on 'Our Unemployed,' prepared as a competition essay for the National Association for the Promotion of Social Science, and published in 1867, was one of the first to call public attention to the problem of unemployment, and to suggest a national system of labour registration. Other pamphlets followed: 'Lancashire Labour and the London Poor' in 1871; 'Impediments to the Circulation of Labour, with a Few Suggestions for their Removal,' in 1873; 'The Unemployed in Great Cities, with Suggestions for the Better Organisation of Labourers,' in 1877, and 'Vagrancy' in 1881. Hill was a pioneer of the system of labour exchanges in England, and in 1871 established in Greek Street, Soho, 'The Employment Inquiry Office and Labour Registry,' which was subsequently transferred to 15 Russell Street, Covent Garden, as the 'Central Labour Exchange, Employment, Emigration, and Industrial Intelligence Office.' There as director Hill gave advice to applicants for assistance. In connection with the exchange and at the same offices he founded and edited in 1871 the 'Labour News,' which became an organ of communication between masters and men seeking work in all parts of the kingdom. Hill had agents and correspondents in the chief industrial centres, who sent notes on the condition of the local labour markets. Hill's venture, which was not profitable, diminished his strength and resources; on his retirement a committee of working men managed the paper, and contributed from the profits to Hill's maintenance. From 1877 onwards he also edited 'The Industrial Handbook' and superintended the publication in 1881 of 'The Industrial Index to London,' by H. Llewelyn Williams, as well as 'Business Aspects of Ladies' Work.' These pamphlets were handy guides to employment, for both men and women. He also edited in 1870–1 a series of penny 'Statutes for the People,' which aimed at giving the labouring class cheap legal advice. Hill likewise took a prominent part, from its foundation in 1869, in the work of the Charity Organisation Society, acting as honorary secretary of the council until July 1870, and as an active member of the council until 1880 (see *Charity Organisation Review*, 1892).

Through life Hill continued to write verse, collecting his poems in 'Rhymes with Good Reason' (1870–1), in 'A Scholar's Day Dream' (1870; 2nd edit. 1881), and in 'A Household Queen' (1881). His lyrics are somewhat rough in style, but show earnest sympathy with the labouring classes, with whose interest he identified himself. One of his poems, 'Mrs. Grundy's Sunday,' was widely circulated to further the aims of the National Sunday League for rational Sunday recreation. He was a vice-president of the league from 1876 to 1890, and lectured at its Sunday Evenings for the People. The Working Men's Club and Institute Union also found in Hill a zealous supporter. Hill fell in his last years into ill-health and poverty, living in retirement at Boston, Lincolnshire. He died there unmarried on 2 August 1906, and was buried at Gressonhall. He was elected a member of the Athenæum Club in 1877, and was president of the Cheltonian [Old Boys'] Society (1877–8).

[Burke's Landed Gentry; Foster's Men at the Bar; The Times, 4 Feb. 1910 (letter from Lionel G. Robinson on Hill's work in regard to Labour Exchanges); Cheltenham Coll. Reg. 1911, p, 171; notes from Hill's brother, the Rev. Reginald Hay Hill, Wethersfield Vicarage, Braintree.] W. B. O.

HILL, FRANK HARRISON (1830–1910), journalist, baptised on 4 March 1830 at Boston, Lincolnshire, was younger son of George Hill, merchant of that city, by his wife Betsy, daughter of Pishey Thompson [q. v.]. Educated at the Boston grammar school, Hill in September 1846 entered as a divinity student the Unitarian New College, Manchester, where he studied under Dr. James Martineau [q.v. Suppl. I]. In June 1851 he completed the five years' 'course of study for the Christian ministry prescribed by that institution.' There is no evidence that he availed himself of his right to preach. Meanwhile in 1848 he had matriculated at the University of London, and having graduated B.A. in the first class in 1851 acted from 1853 to 1855 as private tutor in the family of Dukinfield Darbishire of Manchester; the elder of his pupils, S. D. Darbishire, was subsequently the famous 'stroke' of the Oxford University boat (1868–70), and afterwards practised as a doctor at Oxford. Somewhat later Hill became tutor in the family of Mrs. Salis Schwabe, also of Manchester.

Hill seems to have owed his introduction to journalism to Henry Dunckley [q. v.], 'Verax' of the 'Manchester Times and Examiner,' and to Richard Holt Hutton [q. v. Suppl. I], editor of the 'Spectator.' He was sufficiently well known in 1861 to become, on the death of James Simms, editor of the 'Northern Whig,' the chief organ of the Ulster liberals. He took up his work at Belfast at the time when the Fenian movement in the south of Ireland was becoming dangerous, and when the civil war in the United States was influencing party politics at Westminster. Alone of Irish journalists he supported the north in the American struggle, and he risked temporary unpopularity in the cause (cf. address presented on resigning editorship, Jan. 1866).

After leaving New College, Manchester, Hill kept up friendly relations with his teacher, Dr. James Martineau, who had officiated at Hill's marriage at Little Portland Chapel, London, in 1862. Through Martineau he made the acquaintance of Harriet Martineau, then on the staff of the 'Daily News' and like himself a staunch supporter of the northern states. He also came to know Crabb Robinson, Robert Browning, and W. J. Fox. At the suggestion of Mr. Frank Finlay, proprietor of the 'Northern Whig' (his wife's brother), Hill was hastily summoned at the end of 1865 to London to become assistant editor of the 'Daily News.' It was a critical moment in parliamentary politics. After the death in 1865 of Lord Palmerston, the liberal prime minister, and the succession of Earl Russell to his office, the party demanded stronger measures and methods than the whig tradition countenanced.

Hill energetically championed a forward liberal policy. Whilst the conservative reform bill of 1866 was passing through parliament he contributed to a volume of essays, 'Questions for a Reformed Parliament' (1867), an enlightened article on the political claims of Ireland. At the same time he wrote for the 'Saturday Review,' and a high place among London journalists was soon won. On the retirement of Thomas Walker [q. v.] from the editorship of the 'Daily News' in 1869, Edward Dicey [q. v. Suppl. II] filled the post for a few months; but Hill soon succeeded Dicey, and he held the editorship for seventeen years. The price had been reduced from threepence to one penny a year before he assumed office. Hill continued to give steady support to Gladstone's administration, and the journal became an influential party organ. Under his editorship and the management of (Sir) John Richard Robinson [q. v. Suppl. II] the 'Daily News' attained an influence and a popularity which it had not previously enjoyed. Hill collected a notable body of leader-writers. Amongst these, in addition to Peter William Clayden [q. v. Suppl. II], the assistant editor, were Justin McCarthy, (Professor) William Minto [q. v.], (Sir) John Macdonell, Prof. George Saintsbury, Andrew Lang, and later Mr. Herbert Paul—whilst William Black the novelist, Sir Henry Lucy, and Frances Power Cobbe [q. v. Suppl. II] were occasional writers or auxiliary members of the staff. Hill himself wrote constantly, notably a series of 'Political Portraits,' which was published separately in 1873 and went through several editions. His intimate relations with the political leaders of the day enabled him to gauge accurately their aims and ambitions, and his keen insight had at its service a caustic pen.

Hill declined to accept Gladstone's home rule policy in 1886. The proprietors were unwilling to sanction Hill's claim to independence of the party leaders' programme, and early in 1886 his services were somewhat abruptly dispensed with. He returned the cheque for a year's salary sent by the proprietors on his retirement. Thereupon Hill's political friends wished to show, by means of a pecuniary testimonial, their appreciation of his services to the party, but the proposal was abandoned in deference to his wish. Before the close of the year he became the regular political leader-writer of the 'World,' and held that post for twenty years.

Hill contributed to the 'Fortnightly Review' (1877–8) a bitter and trenchant article on 'The Political Journeyings of Lord Beaconsfield,' and to the 'Edinburgh Review' (July 1887) an appreciative article on 'Mr. Gladstone and the Liberal Party.' After leaving the 'Daily News' he was a frequent contributor to the 'Nineteenth Century.' A life of George Canning which he wrote for the 'English Worthies' series (1881) contained few new facts, but showed a clearer appreciation of Canning's political aims and difficulties than previous biographers had presented.

Hill was called to the bar at Lincoln's Inn in 1872, but never practised. He died suddenly at 13 Morpeth Terrace, Westminster, on 28 June 1910, and by his will bequeathed 1000*l.* to the Boston grammar school to found an exhibition from the school to any English university.

In June 1862 he married Jane Dalzell Finlay, daughter of the proprietor of the 'Northern Whig,' and a contributor to the literary section of that paper. After her marriage Mrs. Hill continued to write literary articles and reviews, chiefly in the 'Saturday Review.' She died in 1904.

[Private information; F. Moy Thomas's Recollections of Sir John R. Robinson, 1904; Justin McCarthy's Reminiscences; Notes and Queries, 15 Oct. 1910.] L. R.

HILL, GEORGE BIRKBECK NORMAN (1835–1903), editor of Boswell's 'Life of Johnson,' born at Bruce Castle, Tottenham, Middlesex, on 7 June 1835, was second son of Arthur Hill and grandson of Thomas Wright Hill [q. v.], whose sons, Sir Rowland and Matthew Davenport, are separately noticed (for his paternal ancestry see his *Life of Sir Rowland Hill* and *History of the Penny Postage*). His mother, Ellen Tilt, daughter of Joseph Maurice, was of Welsh, and, through her mother, Theodosia Bache, of Huguenot origin. Educated at his father's school, he imbibed in youth strictly liberal principles. On 1 March 1855 he entered Pembroke College, Oxford, and there came under other influences. William Fulford, editor of the 'Oxford and Cambridge Magazine,' introduced him to the circle of Burne Jones, William Morris, and Rossetti, and he joined the Old Mortality Club, of which Swinburne, Professor Dicey, Professor Nichol, and Mr. Bryce were members. Ill-health condemned him to an 'honorary' fourth class in literæ humaniores. He graduated B.A. in 1858, and proceeded B.C.L. in 1866 and D.C.L. in 1871.

Eager to marry, he adopted the family

vocation of private schoolmaster. In 1858 he became an assistant in his father's school, and ten years later succeeded to the headship on his father's retirement. The contemporary development of the public schools, the deterioration of Tottenham as a suburb, and Hill's over-anxious and valetudinarian temperament militated against his success. He and his wife continued the work under a sense of increasing strain until his health broke down seriously in 1875. Prematurely aged, he was henceforth a chronic invalid.

From 1869 onwards Hill was a frequent writer for the press, mainly of pungent criticisms in the 'Saturday Review.' After two winters in the south Hill found the rest and quiet he needed at Burghfield in the Reading district. There he devoted himself to the elucidation of the literary anecdote and literary history of the later eighteenth century, concentrating his main attention on the life of Dr. Johnson. In 1878 he published, with a dedication to his uncle, Sir Rowland Hill, 'Dr. Johnson: his Friends and his Critics,' wherein he reviewed the judgments passed on Dr. Johnson by Macaulay, Carlyle, Goldsmith, Boswell, and others, and depicted the Oxford of 1750. Next year he edited Boswell's correspondence with Andrew Erskine and the 'Tour in Corsica.' Hill interrupted his Johnsonian studies in order to write a life of Sir Rowland Hill (1880, 2 vols.). The account of the Hill family and ancestry is excellent, but the historical portions from the pen of the postal reformer are heavy. In 1880 also he wrote 'Gordon in Central Africa, 1874–1879,' from original letters and documents belonging to Gordon's sister (2nd edit. 1899). The loss of his favourite son, Walter, caused further delay in the resumption of his Johnsonian work. In 1881 the Clarendon Press consented through Jowett's influence to his proposal for a new edition of 'Boswell's Life' upon a classical scale. It was eventually published in six volumes (with a dedication to Jowett as 'Johnsonianissimus') in 1887, after nearly twelve years intermittent work, much of it done on the Riviera or Lac Leman. The edition was accepted as a masterpiece of spacious editing. The index, forming the sixth volume, is a monument of industry and completeness. Mr. Percy Fitzgerald, a preceding editor of Boswell, alleged inaccuracy and inadequacy, but Hill's work was valiantly defended by Sir Leslie Stephen. Hill pursued his Johnsonian exegesis in seven further volumes: 'Johnson's Letters' (1892, 2 vols.); 'Johnsonian Miscellanies' (Lives subsidiary to Boswell) (1897, 2 vols.), and 'Johnson's Lives of the English Poets' (1905, 3 vols.), specially valuable from the wealth of annotation, which was revised for the press after his death by Hill's nephew, Mr. Harold Spencer Scott. In 1887 he edited for the first time nearly ninety interesting 'Letters of David Hume to William Strahan.' This book he dedicated to Lord Rosebery, who had purchased the manuscript letters at Jowett's suggestion.

In the autumn of 1887 Hill settled in Oxford at 3 Park Crescent, and his pen remained active on his favourite theme. He was made an honorary fellow of his old college (and Dr. Johnson's) and greatly enjoyed the social amenities of university life. He became the 'prior' (1891–2) and oracle of the Johnson Club in London.

In 1889 he made a tour in the footsteps of Boswell and Johnson in Scotland, which he described in 'Footsteps of Samuel Johnson (Scotland), with Illustrations by Lancelot Speed.' In 1890 he published a miscellaneous volume, 'Talks about Autographs.' In 1892 Hill left his Oxford house and divided his time thenceforth between his favourite winter residences, Clarens and Alassio, his daughter's house, The Wilderness, Hampstead, and a cottage at Aspley Guise, Bedfordshire. In 1893 he and his wife visited a daughter settled at Cambridge, near Boston, Massachusetts, and he wrote an instructive volume on Harvard College, which was warmly acclaimed in New England for its friendly tone of comparison. Williams College conferred a doctorate upon him on 10 Oct. 1893. In 1897 his 'Letters of Dante Gabriel Rossetti to William Allingham' renewed memories of the Old Mortality Club at Oxford and of the old house in Red Lion Square where Burne Jones and William Morris had their rooms.

He died at Hampstead on 27 Feb. 1903, and was buried at Aspley Guise by the side of his wife, who predeceased him barely four months. He had married Annie, daughter of Edward Scott of Wigan, in the parish church there on 29 Dec. 1858, and by her he had five sons and two daughters. His eldest son, Maurice (*b.* 1859), is K.C., and his third son, Leonard Erskine, M.B., F.R.S., is professor of physiology at London Hospital.

A crayon drawing by W. R. Symonds, of 1896, reproduced as frontispiece in 'Talks about Autographs,' is in the common room of Pembroke College, Oxford, to which he bequeathed his Johnsonian library; a portrait by Ellen G. Hill, dated 1876, is reproduced as frontispiece to the 'Letters' of 1906.

Hill was the benevolent interpreter of Johnson's era to his own generation, and brought to his work a zeal and abundant knowledge which gave charm to his discursiveness. In addition to the works already cited he edited Johnson's 'Rasselas' (Oxford, 1887); Goldsmith's 'Traveller' (Oxford, 1888); 'Wit and Wisdom of Samuel Johnson' (Oxford, 1888); Lord Chesterfield's 'Worldly Wisdom: Selection of Letters and Characters' (Oxford, 1891); 'Eighteenth Century Letters, Johnson, Lord Chesterfield' (1898) and Gibbon's 'Memoirs' in the standard text (1900). He also issued in 1899 'Unpublished Letters of Dean Swift' (the dean's correspondence with Knightly Chetwood of Woodbrook, 1714–31, from the Forster Collection, since embodied in Ball's new 'Swift Correspondence'). There appeared posthumously his 'Letters written by a Grandfather' (selected by Hill's younger daughter, Mrs. Lucy Crump, 1903) and 'Letters of George Birkbeck Hill' (arranged by Mrs. Crump, 1906).

[Brief Memoir of Dr. Birkbeck Hill, by Harold Spencer Scott, prefixed to Lives of the English Poets, vol. i. 1905; Hill's published Letters, 1903, 1906; The Times, 28 Feb. 1903, 9 Nov. 1906; Percy Fitzgerald's hostile Editing à la mode—an examination of Dr. Birkbeck Hill's new edition of Boswell's Life of Johnson (1891), his A Critical Examination of Dr. B. Hill's Johnsonian Editions (1898), and his James Boswell, an autobiography (1912); personal knowledge and private information.]

T. S.

HILL, ROSAMOND DAVENPORT- (1825–1902), educational administrator, born at Chelsea on 4 Aug. 1825, was eldest of the three daughters of Matthew Davenport Hill [q. v. for family history]. In 1826 the family moved to the father's chambers in Chancery Lane, and thence, in 1831, to Hampstead Heath. Here they became intimate with Joanna [q. v.] and Agnes Baillie. At the age of eight Rosamond went to a day school, where she was taught practical botany, a subject which affected her future attitude towards practical education. Most of her education was acquired at home, where her mother's failing health threw much of the household management on her. During girlhood, on 1 March 1840, she had an interview in London with Maria Edgeworth [q. v.], of which she has left a long account (*Memoir*, p. 11). After a move to Haverstock Hill, where Thackeray and other distinguished men visited them, the family travelled abroad, in 1841 in France, in 1844 in Belgium, and later in Switzerland and Italy. In 1851 the father's appointment as a commissioner in bankruptcy took the family to Bristol, where Mary Carpenter [q. v.] enlisted Rosamond's services in her 'St. James's Back Ragged School.' Rosamund took the arithmetic classes and taught the children practical household work. Rosamond was soon acting as private secretary to her father, and eagerly identified herself with his efforts at educational and criminal law reform. In 1856 she visited Ireland and wrote 'A Lady's Visit to the Irish Convict Prisons.' In 1858 she and her father visited prisons and reformatories in Spain, France, and Germany. The temperance question and the treatment of prisoners occupied her pen. In 1860 Davenport Hill and his daughters published 'Our Exemplars, Rich and Poor.' Meanwhile in 1855 Rosamond and her father had inspected together the reformatory at Mettray, founded on the family system by M. Frédéric Auguste Demetz, of whom Rosamond became a lifelong friend. After the ruin of the Mettray school during the war of 1870, she helped to raise nearly 2500*l*. in England for its restoration. In 1866 Miss Carpenter and Rosamond started at Bristol on the Mettray principles an industrial school for girls, which is still at work.

On the death of her father in 1872 Rosamond and her sister Florence went to Adelaide on a visit to relatives named Clark, of whom Emily Clark was a notable worker on behalf of children. In Australia the sisters inspected schools, prisons, and reformatories with the aid of (Sir) Henry Parkes [q. v.]. Miss Hill gave evidence in Sydney before a commission on reformatory treatment, and the report issued in 1874 quoted her evidence and included an important paper by her, 'A Summary of the Principles of Reformatory Treatment, with a Special Reference to Girls' (printed in the *Memoir*). She argued that the treatment should aim at fitting the girls to govern themselves.

In 1875, after returning home by way of Egypt and Italy (in 1874), the sisters published 'What we saw in Australia,' and they completed in 1878 a biography of their father. In 1879 the two sisters settled in Belsize Avenue, Hampstead, and now added to their surname their father's second name, Davenport, in order to avoid confusion between Miss Rosamond Hill and Miss Octavia Hill (1838–1912), the active social reformer, who was no relation

Miss Hill at the same time left the Church of England for the unitarians.

On 5 Dec. 1879 she was elected as a progressive member to the London school board for the City of London, being second on the poll. She retained her seat till 1897, fighting successfully six triennial elections. As a member of the board, she showed an administrative capacity which was acknowledged by all parties to be of the first rank. At the outset she joined the industrial school committee and school management committee. She also acted as chairman of the managers of the Greystoke Place school in Fetter Lane, when it was the only board-school in the City of London, and there social or domestic economy was first made a school subject. In 1882 she became with admirable results chairman of the cookery committee, contributing a valuable article, 'Cookery Teaching under the London School Board,' to 'Macmillan's Magazine' (June 1884; reprinted in 'Lessons on Cookery,' 1885).

In 1886 she opposed the board's pension scheme for teachers, which in 1895 was abolished as actuarially unsound. She visited, in 1888, at Naas, Herr Abrahamson, the inventor of the Slöyd system of hand and eye training by means of woodwork, and described the system in the 'Contemporary Review' (May 1888). In the autumn of the same year she visited schools in the United States and Canada, and as a result she secured, in the face of much hostility, the introduction of pianos (for the purpose of marching and drill) into the London schools. With characteristic independence she resisted the provision by the board of meals for children, and in 1893 she opposed the denominational tendency of the board, though she was an ardent advocate of daily religious teaching. In 1896 she gave evidence before the departmental committee on reformatory and industrial schools and wrote a paper on 'How to deal with Children pronounced by the Authorities to be unfitted for Industrial Training' (*Memoir*, p. 132).

On her retirement from the board, owing to failing health, in 1897, she settled with her sister at a house near Oxford named Hillstow by Professor Skeat. The Brentwood industrial school was on her retirement re-named 'The Davenport-Hill Home for Boys.' She died at Hillstow after a long illness on 5 Aug. 1902.

To the end she was interested in the prevention of crime by education as well as in reformatories and industrial schools, which had first excited her philanthropic instincts, and she contributed two letters on these subjects to 'The Times' in her last days (24 Dec. 1900 and 16 April 1901). She was long a member of the Froebel Society, and was in 1894 made a governor of University College, London. She wrote in 1893 'Elementary Education in England,' at the request of the women's education sub-committee at the Chicago exhibition.

[Memoir of Rosamond Davenport-Hill, by Ethel E. Metcalfe (with three photographic portraits and a reproduction from miniature as a child); The Times, 7 Aug. 1902.]

J. E. G. de M.

HILLS, Sir JOHN (1834–1902), major-general, royal (Bombay) engineers, born at Neechindipore, Bengal, on 19 August 1834, was the third son in a family of six sons and four daughters of James Hills of Neechindipore, one of the largest land-owners and indigo planters in Bengal. His mother was Charlotte Mary, daughter of John Angelo Savi of Elba, and grand-daughter of General Corderan, commanding the French forces at Pondicherry. The second son is Lieutenant-general Sir James Hills-Johnes.

Educated at the Edinburgh Academy and at the Edinburgh University, where he won the Straton gold medal, Hills entered the East India Company's College at Addiscombe on 6 Aug. 1852, and was made second lieutenant in the Bombay engineers on 8 June 1854. After instruction at Chatham, Hills arrived at Bombay in August 1856, was posted to the Bombay sappers and miners, and having passed in Hindustani was appointed, on 14 Jan. 1857, assistant field engineer with the 2nd division of the Persian expeditionary force under major-general Sir James Outram [q. v.]. He was present at the capture of Mohumra, and for his services with the expedition received the medal with clasp. He was promoted lieutenant on 5 Nov. 1857. While at home on furlough he was elected a fellow of the Royal Society of Edinburgh, on 21 March 1859.

Returning to India, Hills was for a time garrison engineer at Fort William, Calcutta, and in January 1862 became assistant to the chief engineer in Oude in the public works department at Lucknow. Promoted captain on 1 Sept. 1863, he was appointed executive engineer in Rajputana in 1865. In 1867 he joined the Abyssinian expedition under major-general Sir Robert Napier (afterwards Lord Napier of Magdala) [q. v.]. He was at first employed as field engineer at Kumeyli camp, at the foot of the hills, to which the railway was made from the base at Zula, ten miles away, on the Red Sea. There he was mainly occupied in sinking wells for water supply. Later he helped to construct the road from rail head at Kumeyli to Senafeh, a distance of over 50 miles, with elevations rising to over 7000 feet, a most difficult undertaking. He was mentioned in despatches and received the medal.

After the campaign Hills resumed work at Lucknow. From 1871 to 1883 he was commandant of the Bombay sappers and miners at Kirkee, bringing this native corps into a high state of efficiency. Meanwhile he was promoted major on 5 July 1872, lieutenant-colonel on 1 Oct. 1877, and brevet colonel on 1 Oct. 1881.

During the Afghan war of 1879–80, and while still commandant of the Bombay sappers and miners, Hills was commanding royal engineer of a division of the Kandahar field force as well as of the South Afghanistan field force in 1881. He took part in the defence of Kandahar and distinguished himself on several occasions; was mentioned in despatches for his services, was created C.B. on 22 Feb. 1881, and received the medal.

After a furlough Hills served as commanding royal engineer of the expeditionary force to Burma in 1886–7. He retired on 31 Dec. 1887 with the honorary rank of major-general. He was created K.C.B. in May 1900. He died unmarried at 50 Weymouth Street, London, on 18 June 1902, and was buried in the family vault at Kensal Green.

Hills was an all-round sportsman, a first-rate cricketer, a powerful swimmer, a fine swordsman, and an excellent shot; many tigers fell to his gun. He published 'The Bombay Field Force, 1880' (with plans, 1900), and 'Points of a Racehorse' (1903, 4to), which embodied the results of thirty years' close study.

[India Office Records; Royal Engineers Records; The Times, 20 June 1902; Carmarthen Journal, June 1902; Aberystwyth Observer, 23 May 1900; private information.] R. H. V.

HIND. [See Archer-Hind, Richard Dacre (1849–1910), classical scholar.]

HIND, HENRY YOULE (1823–1908), geologist and explorer, born at Nottingham on 1 June 1823, was third of five sons of Thomas Hind, by his wife Sarah Youle.

Educated till fourteen with his cousin John Russell Hind [q. v. Suppl. I], the astronomer, as a private pupil of the Rev. W. Butler, headmaster of the Nottingham grammar school, he spent two years (1837–9) at the Handels-Schule at Leipzig. In 1843 he studied at Queens' College, Cambridge, but left without graduating. He then travelled and studied in France, returning to England in 1846 and leaving for Canada the same year. In 1848 he was made lecturer in chemistry and mathematical master in the provincial normal school, Toronto. From 1853 till his resignation in 1864 he was professor of chemistry and geology in Trinity University, Toronto. Attached as geologist by the government of Canada to the first expedition to the Red River district (now the province of Manitoba) in 1857, he was in command of the explorations in the Assiniboine and Saskatchewan districts of the North West Territory in 1858, and was employed in the exploration of Labrador and its river system in 1861, when his brother, William George Richardson Hind, accompanied the expedition as artist. He also conducted, in 1864, a geological survey of New Brunswick for the government of the province. In 1869–71 he examined officially the goldfields of Nova Scotia. During an exploration of the mineral fields in north-east Newfoundland and the Labrador coast in 1876, he discovered the extensive cod banks that extend north-west for several hundred miles off the shore above the straits of Belle Isle. The Newfoundland government desired him to investigate further and report on this important discovery the following year, but the Canadian government required his services in preparing scientific evidence on behalf of the Canadian plea in the controversy over the fisheries with the United States, which was discussed before the commission then sitting at Halifax, N.S. At the close of the proceedings in 1877 the records and evidence were entrusted to his care for arrangement and indexing at the suggestion of the commissioners for the United States.

Hind received the degrees of M.A. from Trinity University, Toronto, in 1853, and D.C.L. from King's College, Windsor, Nova Scotia, in 1890. In the latter year he was made president of the newly formed church school at Edgehill. In 1878 he was awarded a gold medal and diploma from the Paris exposition for charts showing the movements of seal and other fish on the coast of North America during the different seasons

Hind died on 9 Aug. 1908 at Windsor, Nova Scotia, and was buried in the Maplewood cemetery. He married, on 7 Feb. 1850, Katherine, second daughter of Lieutenant-colonel Duncan Cameron, C.B., of the 79th Highlanders, who was wounded at Quatre Bras. By her he had issue two surviving sons, Duncan Henry, rector of Sandwich, Ontario, and Kenneth Cameron, canon of All Saints' cathedral, Halifax, Nova Scotia, and two daughters.

Hind was the editor of the 'Canadian Journal' (3 vols. 4to, 1852–55); of the 'Journal of the Board of Arts and Manufactures for Upper Canada' (1861–63); and of the 'British American Magazine' (1863). All were published at Toronto. He contributed to the journals of the Royal Geographical Society, of which he was elected a fellow in 1860, and other learned societies. His chief independent publications are: 1. 'The Narrative of the Canadian Red River Exploring Expedition of 1857 and of the Assiniboine and Saskatchewan Exploring Expedition of 1858,' Toronto, 1859, and London, 1860, 2 vols. with maps; containing the first detailed account and map of the now famous fertile belt. 2. 'Explorations in the Interior of the Labrador Peninsula, 1863,' 2 vols., with illustrations by Hind's brother, William George Richardson Hind. 3. 'Notes on the Northern Labrador Fishing Ground,' Newfoundland, 1876, which contains an account of the newly discovered cod banks. 4. 'The Effect of the Fishery Clauses of the Treaty of Washington on the Fisheries and Fishermen of British North America,' 1877, which attracted wide-spread attention.

[Art. in Frank Leslie's Illustrated, 26 Feb. 1881; Evening Mail, Halifax, N.S., 10 Aug. 1908, and Hants Journal, Windsor, N.S., 12 Aug. 1908; Morgan, Canadian Men and Women of the Time; information supplied by Miss Margaret Hind (daughter), Sunny Side, Nova Scotia.] W. S. J.

HINGESTON-RANDOLPH [formerly HINGSTON], FRANCIS CHARLES (1833–1910), antiquary, born at Truro on 31 March 1833, was son of Francis Hingston (1796–1841), controller of customs at Truro, who belonged to a family long settled at St. Ives, had literary tastes, and wrote poems (edited by the son in 1857). His mother was Jane Matilda, daughter of Captain William Kirkness.

From Truro grammar school Francis passed in 1851 to Exeter College, Oxford, as Elliott exhibitioner. He graduated B.A. in 1855 with an honorary fourth class in the final pass school, and proceeded M.A. in 1859. Ordained in 1856, he served as curate of Holywell, Oxford, until 1858, when he moved to Hampton Gay, in the same county, succeeding to the incumbency of the parish next year. In 1860 he became rector of Ringmore, near Kingsbridge, Devonshire, the patronage to which living afterwards became vested in his family. He remained at Ringmore for the rest of his life. On his marriage in 1860 to Martha, only daughter of Herbert Randolph, incumbent of Melrose, Roxburghshire, he added, at the wish of his father-in-law, the name of Randolph to his own and adopted Hingeston, the earlier form of the spelling of his family surname.

Hingeston-Randolph developed antiquarian tastes early. At seventeen he published 'Specimens of Ancient Cornish Crosses and Fonts' (London and Truro, 4to, 1850). Much historical work followed, but his scholarship was called in question. In the 'Rolls' series he edited Capgrave's 'Chronicle' (1858); Capgrave's 'Liber de Illustribus Henricis' (1859), and 'Royal and Historical Letters during the Reign of Henry the Fourth,' vol. i. 1399–1404 (1860). The last volume was especially censured, and when Hingeston-Randolph had completed a second volume in 1864 collation of it by an expert with the original documents led to the cancelling and reprinting of sixty-two pages and the adding of sixteen pages of errata. Two copies of the volume are in the British Museum, one in the revised form and the other in the original state. Of each version eight copies were preserved, but none was issued to the public.

In 1885 Frederick Temple, then bishop of Exeter, made Hingeston-Randolph a prebendary of Exeter Cathedral, and at the bishop's suggestion he began editing the 'Episcopal Registers' of the diocese. Between 1886 and 1909 he completed those of eight bishops of the thirteenth, fourteenth, and fifteenth centuries (11 pts.). He mainly restricted himself to indexing the contents of the registers, a method which limited the historical utility of his scheme.

Hingeston-Randolph specially interested himself in church architecture, and was often consulted about the restoration of west country churches. He wrote 'Architectural History of St. Germans Church, Cornwall' (1903), and contributed many architectural articles to the 'Building News' and the 'Ecclesiologist.' For ten years (1879–90) he was rural dean of Woodleigh, and brought the work of the district to a high state of efficiency. In his articles 'Up and down the Deanery,' which he contributed to the 'Salcombe Parish Magazine,' he gave an interesting historical account of every parish under his charge. He died at Ringmore on 27 Aug. 1910, and was buried in the churchyard there. His wife predeceased him in 1904. He left four sons and six daughters.

Besides the works cited, Hingeston-Randolph published 'Records of a Rocky Shore, by a Country Parson . . .' (1876) and 'The Constitution of the Cathedral Body of Exeter' (1887). He was also a contributor to 'Devon Notes and Queries' (iv. 73, 180, 1906–7), 'Notes and Gleanings' (1882–92), and 'Western Antiquary' (vi. 1886–7, xi. 1891–2, and xii. 1893).

[Devon and Cornwall Notes and Queries; Boase and Courtney, Bibliotheca Cornubiensis; Boase, Collectanea Cornubiensia; private information.] H. T-S.

HINGLEY, Sir BENJAMIN, first baronet (1830–1905), ironmaster, born at Cradley in Worcestershire on 11 September 1830, was youngest son of Noah Hingley (1796–1877) of Cradley Park, at one time mayor of Dudley, by his first wife, Sarah, daughter of Noah Willett of Coalbournbrook, Kingswinford. Noah Hingley, like his father before him, began life as a chainmaker in a small factory on the banks of the Stour, and ultimately founded the chain making and cable firms of Noah Hingley & Sons, and Hingley & Smith of Netherton. Benjamin, after private education, worked with his father and his elder brothers, Hezekiah (1825–1865) and George (1829–1901), in the manufacture of anchors. The introduction of the Nasmyth hammer enabled the firm to make a specialty of forgings of a large size, and the father, instead of purchasing the iron for the purpose, erected large ironworks at Netherton for the manufacture. Additional ironworks were subsequently acquired at Old Hill and Harts Hill, and the business grew until it became one of the largest and most important in the Midlands. In 1865, on the death of his brother Hezekiah, Benjamin became head of the firm, which was converted into a limited company in 1890. But Benjamin retained a controlling interest and continued in command until his death. For nearly thirty years he was chairman of the South Staffordshire and East Worcestershire Ironmasters' Association, and president of the Midland iron and steel wages board. He was also for many years a prominent member of the South Staffordshire coal trade wages board. His sense of fairness, good judgment, and scrupulous integrity rendered him an important factor in the preservation of industrial peace in the Black Country. He was also for thirty years chairman of Lloyd's British Testing Company, Limited, Netherton, chairman of the Cradley Gas Company, and a director and for some time chairman of the South Staffordshire Mond Gas Company. In 1903 he was elected president of the Mining Association of Great Britain. In 1883 he joined the Iron and Steel Institute, became a member of council in 1891 and a vice-president in 1903. In 1890 he was mayor of Dudley, and in 1900 was High Sheriff of Worcestershire.

In 1885 Hingley began a parliamentary career, being elected liberal member of parliament for North Worcestershire. He represented the constituency for ten years, but in 1886 he joined the unionist wing of his party during the home rule controversy. In 1892 he rejoined the liberal ranks, While in the House of Commons he served on numerous committees dealing with trade and commercial questions, and was specially thanked for his services on the admiralty committee on dockyard management appointed in July 1886. He retired owing to ill-health in 1895. On 8 August 1893 he was created a baronet, with special remainder, in default of issue, to his elder brother and his male issue. He died, unmarried, at his residence, Hatherton Lodge, near Cradley, on 13 May 1905, and was buried at Halesowen. The baronetcy descended to his nephew, George Benjamin Hingley, son of his brother Hezekiah. A presentation portrait in oils, by A. S. Cope, R.A., was exhibited at the Royal Academy in 1901.

[Journal of the Iron and Steel Institute, vol. lxvii.; Burke's Baronetage; The Times, 15 May 1905.] L. P. S.

HINGSTON, Sir WILLIAM HALES (1829–1907), Canadian surgeon, born at Hinchbrook, Huntingdon, province of Quebec, on 29 June 1829, was eldest son in a family of two sons and two daughters of Lieut.-colonel Samuel James Hingston by his second wife, Eleanor McGrath of Montreal. His father, an Irish Roman catholic, was lieutenant-colonel in the Canadian militia. After the disbanding of the troops at the conclusion of the war of 1812 he settled upon a grant of land at Hinchbrook. As a pioneer he was unsuccessful, and died deep in debt in 1831. Hingston was educated at a grammar school in Huntingdon, kept by John (afterwards Sir John) Rose, and then at the Montreal College of St. Sulpice (1842–3). In 1844 he became apprentice to R. W. Rexford, chemist, at Montreal, and managed to save sufficient from his small earnings as a clerk to obtain a medical training without other assistance. In 1847 he entered McGill University in the medical faculty; he graduated in pharmacy at the College of Physicians and Surgeons of Lower Canada in 1849, and took a degree at the university in 1851. The same year he went to Edinburgh and studied under (Sir) James Young Simpson [q. v.] and James Syme [q. v.]. Simpson showed Hingston the rare mark of confidence of taking his pupil with him on his visits to private patients. He was made L.R.C.S.Edin. in 1852. From Edinburgh Hingston passed to St. Bartholomew's Hospital, London, and thence for a few months to Dublin, where he worked under Stokes, Corrigan, and Graves. Having acquired a fair knowledge of German he next proceeded for two years to the Continent, where he engaged in medical study in Paris, Berlin, Heidelberg, and Vienna. Although Simpson urged him to remain at Edinburgh as his personal assistant, Hingston began practice in Montreal in 1854.

During the second year of his practice he faced a cholera epidemic with heroic self-sacrifice, and won the devotion of poor Irish emigrants. In 1860 he was nominated to the staff of the Hôtel Dieu. On his first patient there he successfully performed for the first time in Canada the new operation of resection of a diseased joint. In 1865 he, with a few others, was instrumental in reviving the Montreal Medico-Chirurgical Society, of which he became president, and he founded the Women's Hospital. He remained on the active staff of the Women's Hospital till its amalgamation with the new Western Hospital, of which he was a charter member and consulting surgeon and chairman of the medical board. In 1867 he revisited Edinburgh, and Sir James Simpson gave him an opportunity of proving his operative skill. In 1873 he was made dean of the medical faculty at Bishop's College, and in 1878 professor of clinical surgery at Laval University. He was president of the College of Physicians and Surgeons of Quebec in 1886. Hingston, who worked hard to make vaccination compulsory in Montreal, and to improve the public health, won a high reputation as a surgeon possessing courage, decision, and rapidity in operation. In 1872 he removed in one opeıation, for the first time on record, the tongue and lower jaw. In ovariotomy for cystic and other tumours he was not at first successful, but in 1885 he had a remarkable series of thirteen cases without a death. Hingston failed to master the meticulous routine of modern asepsis. He kept to the last his faith in the old system. His surgical ability was, however, widely acknowledged. In 1892, when the British Medical Association held its annual meeting in Nottingham, he delivered the address on surgery. In 1900 he received the honorary fellowship of the Royal College of Surgeons of England.

Hingston was prominent in the public life of Montreal. He was mayor of the city in 1875, and was re-elected in 1876 by acclamation, but declined a third term. He was chairman of the board of health of the city and also of the board for the province of Quebec in 1885. He interested himself locally in financial matters, was president in 1875 of the City Passenger Railway Company, which has since become the Montreal Street Railway System, and of the Montreal City and District Savings Bank from 1895, besides being a director of the Montreal Trust and Deposit Company. He was made hon. D.C.L. of Bishop's College, Lennoxville, and hon. LL.D. of Victoria University, Toronto. He was appointed commander of the Roman order of St. Gregory in 1875, and on 24 May 1895 he was knighted. In the same year he was defeated as conservative candidate in Montreal Centre for the House of Commons, but he was appointed to the Senate in 1896.

Hingston, whose catholicism was uncompromising but not aggressive, died in Montreal on 19 Feb. 1907, and was buried in Mount Royal cemetery. He married on 16 Sept. 1875 Margaret Josephine, daughter of David Alexander Macdonald, lieut.-governor of Ontario. She survived him. They had four sons and one daughter. The eldest son is a Jesuit priest; the second, Dr. Donald Hingston, is on the surgical staff of the Hôtel Dieu. A portrait by J. Colin Forbes is in the possession of the family, and another by Delfosse is at the City and District Savings Bank, Montreal.

Hingston published in 1885 'Climate of Canada and its Relation to Life and Health,' and pamphlets on vaccination and other subjects. He was a frequent contributor to professional periodicals.

[The Times, 20 Feb. 1907; Montreal Medical Journal, xxxvi. 194–202; Morgan, Canadian Men and Women of the Time, 1898; private information.] A. M.

HIPKINS, ALFRED JAMES (1826–1903), musical antiquary, born at 22 Medway Street, Westminster, on 17 June 1826, was only son of James Hipkins (1800–1882), a cabinet and pianoforte maker, who also wrote verse, by his wife Jane Mary Grant (1802–1865). He had an only sister, Ellen (1838–1911). As a boy he desired to become a painter, but in 1840 he was placed by his father in Messrs. Broadwood's pianoforte factory, where he remained all his life. A music-seller in the Strand, named Fenton, gave him a few pianoforte lessons in 1841, and Marcellus Higgs taught him the organ in 1844; in spite of such limited tuition be became a charming performer on the piano, having the unique reputation of rendering the music of Chopin according to the composer's intention. His chief energies were devoted to a study of the science of music and of the history and quality of keyboard instruments. On the latter subject he became an unrivalled authority. He reintroduced equal temperament in tuning into this country in 1846, and wrote profusely on musical history, contributing largely to 'Grove's Dictionary,' as well as to the ninth edition of the 'Encyclopædia Britannica.' In 1881 he made a journey through Germany to examine historic pianofortes in the royal palaces. His chief publication was 'Musical Instruments, Historic, Rare, and Unique' (1881), a standard work illustrated in colour by William Gibbs. Between 1885 and 1896 he lectured on his special theme at the principal musical institutions as well as at the Royal Institution, and superintended the arrangement of many exhibitions of musical instruments.

He was elected F.S.A. on 14 Jan. 1886, and was a member of the council and honorary curator of the Royal College of Music. A familiar and genial figure in musical circles, he died at Kensington on 3 June 1903, and was buried at Kensington cemetery, Hanwell. A memorial brass, designed by Sir Lawrence Alma-Tadema (see *Musical Times*, Oct. 1908), was placed in St. Margaret's church, Westminster, where he was christened and where his kinsfolk lie. He left an interesting collection of tuning-forks to the Royal Institution and a fine collection of musical instruments to the Royal College of Music.

Hipkins married on 2 Oct. 1850 Jane Souter Black, of Scotch family, at Orange Street chapel, Leicester Square. Of their two children a son, who was deaf and dumb, was a distinguished wood engraver (*b.* 1851), while the daughter, Edith (*b.* 1854), a portrait painter, has frequently exhibited at the Royal Academy.

[Musical Times, Sept. 1898 and July 1903; private information.] F. C.

HOARE, JOSEPH CHARLES (1851–1906), bishop of Victoria, Hong-kong, born at Ramsgate on 15 Nov. 1851, was fourth son of Edward Hoare, vicar of Holy Trinity, Tunbridge Wells, and hon. canon of Canterbury. His mother was Maria Eliza (*d.* 1863), daughter of Sir Benjamin Collins Brodie [q. v.], surgeon. Educated first at Brighton, then (1863–1870) at Tonbridge school, he passed with a scholarship to Trinity College, Cambridge, graduating B.A. in 1874 with a second class in the classical tripos, and proceeding M.A. in 1878 and D.D. in 1898. In December 1874 he was ordained deacon by the Bishop of London for missionary work, and, after acting for some months as his father's curate, sailed in October 1875 to join the Church Missionary Society's Mid-China mission at Ningpo. He was ordained priest by the Bishop of North China in 1876. His chief work at Ningpo was the founding and successful conduct of a training college for Chinese evangelists. Hoare rapidly acquired a knowledge of the Ningpo colloquial language, and in it produced versions of 'Pearson on the Creed,' 'Trench on the Parables,' and 'Ryle on St. Matthew.' By 1891 he had sent out 164 students, of whom 61 were then either evangelists or school teachers.

In 1898 Frederick Temple, Archbishop of Canterbury, invited Hoare to succeed John Shaw Burdon [q. v. Suppl. II] as Bishop of Victoria, Hong-kong, and he was consecrated at St. Paul's cathedral on 11 June 1898. The change from mid-China to south China entailed the learning of two new dialects, and, as a bishop, Hoare had the oversight of a colony, as well as of missionary work in several provinces. He won the respect of all classes in the colony, worked amongst the sailors of the port, and continued his policy of fostering a spirit of self-reliance amongst the Chinese Christians. Unswervingly loyal to the Church Missionary Society, he was not always at one with the home authorities. On 14 Sept. 1906 he set out from Hong-kong in his house-boat on a preaching tour along the coast. Caught in the typhoon of 16 Sept., he headed back to Hong-kong, but the boat capsized in Castle Peak bay, 12 miles from Hong-kong, and two Chinese sailors alone escaped. Hoare's body was not recovered.

Both at Ningpo and at Hong-kong Hoare left a permanent mark on the work of his mission by the influence of a fine personality and by his contributions to vernacular literature. Hoare was twice married: (1) in 1882 to Alice Juliana (*d.* 1883), daughter of Canon John Patteson, of Norwich; and (2) to Ellen, daughter of the Rev. F. F. Gough, who survived him, and by whom he had two sons and three daughters. In addition to the works already noticed, there were issued after his death two volumes of comments on books of the Bible, edited by Walter Moule.

[Record, 28 Sept. 1906; Church Missionary Intelligencer, November and December 1906; private information and personal knowledge.]

A. R. B.

HOBBES, JOHN OLIVER, pseudonym. [See Craigie, Mrs. Pearl Mary Teresa (1867–1906), novelist.]

HOBHOUSE, ARTHUR, first Baron Hobhouse of Hadspen (1819–1904), judge, born at Hadspen House, Somerset, on 10 Nov. 1819, was fourth and youngest son of Henry Hobhouse [q. v.] by his wife Harriet, sixth daughter of John Turton of Sugnall Hall, Stafford. Edmund Hobhouse [q. v. Suppl. II], bishop of Nelson, and Reginald Hobhouse (1818–95), archdeacon of Bodmin, were elder brothers. Passing at eleven from a private school to Eton, he remained there seven years (1830–7). In 1837 he went to Balliol College, Oxford, graduated B.A. in 1840 with a first class in classics, and proceeded M.A. in 1844. Entering at Lincoln's Inn on 22 April 1841, he was called to the bar on 6 May 1845, and soon acquired a large chancery practice. In 1862 he became a Q.C. and a bencher of his inn, serving the office of treasurer in 1880–1. A severe illness in 1866 led him to retire from practice and accept the appointment of charity commissioner. Hobhouse threw himself into the work with energy. He was not only active in administration but advocated a reform of the law governing charitable endowments. The Endowed Schools Act, 1869, was a first step in that direction, and under that act George fourth baron Lyttelton [q.v.], Hobhouse, and Canon H. G. Robinson were appointed commissioners with large powers of reorganising endowed schools. Much was accomplished in regard to endowed schools, but the efforts of Hobhouse and his fellow commissioners received a check in 1871, when the House of Lords rejected their scheme for remodelling the Emanuel Hospital, Westminster. There followed a controversy which was distasteful to Hobhouse, and with little regret he retired in 1872 in order to succeed Sir James Fitzjames Stephen [q. v.] as law member of the council of the governor-general of India. Hobhouse had meanwhile served on the royal commission on the operation of the Land Transfer Act in 1869.

Hobhouse 'on his departure for India received strong hints that it would be desirable for him to slacken the pace of the legislative machine,' which had been quickened by the consolidating and codifying activities of Fitzjames Stephen and of Stephen's immediate predecessor, Sir Henry Sumner Maine [q. v.] (Ilbert, *Legislative Methods and Forms,* p. 138). That suggestion he approved. Whitley Stokes [q. v. Suppl. II], secretary in the legislative department, was mainly responsible for the measures passed during Hobhouse's term of office, with the important exception of the Specific Relief Act, 1877, in which Hobhouse as an equity lawyer took an especial interest, and a revision of the law relating to the transfer of property, which became a statute after he left India. Of strong liberal sentiment, Hobhouse had small sympathy with the general policy of the government of India during the opening of Lord Lytton's viceroyalty. The attitude to Afghanistan was especially repugnant. On the conclusion of his term of office in 1877 he was made a K.C.S.I., and returning to England soon engaged in party politics as a thoroughgoing opponent of the Afghan policy of the conservative government. In 1880 he and John (afterwards Viscount) Morley unsuccessfully contested Westminster in the liberal interest against Sir Charles Russell, third baronet, of Swallowfield, and W. H. Smith [q. v.]. Hobhouse was at the bottom of the poll.

In 1878 he was made arbitrator under the Epping Forest Act (41 & 42 Vict. c. ccxiii.) and in 1881 he succeeded Sir Joseph Napier [q. v.] on the judicial committee of the privy council. There without salary he did useful judicial work for twenty years. He delivered the decision of the committee in 200 appeals, of which 120 were from India. Several cases were of grave moment. In Merriman *v.* Williams (7 Appeal Cases 484), an action between the bishop and dean of Grahamstown, Hobhouse set forth fully the history of the relationship of the Church of South Africa with the Church of England, and decided that the South African Church is independent of it. In the consolidated appeals in 1887 by several Canadian banks (12 Appeal Cases, 575) against the decisions of the court of queen's bench for Quebec, which involved the respective limits of the power of the dominion and provincial legislatures to regulate banks, Hobhouse's judgment upheld the right of the province to tax banks and insurance companies constituted by Act of the dominion legislature. In a case from India in 1899 (26 Indian Appeals, Law Reports 113) which necessitated the review of a number of conflicting decisions of the Indian courts, Hobhouse settled a long disputed point in Hindu law and decided, contrary to much tradition, that when an individual person was adopted as an only son, the fact of adoption should be legally recognised and the parents' plenary powers admitted.

In 1885 Hobhouse accepted a peerage with a view to assisting in the judicial work of the House of Lords, but a statutory qualification by which only judges of the high courts of the United Kingdom could sit to hear appeals had been overlooked. In 1887 the disqualification was removed by Act of Parliament in regard to members of the judicial committee; but Hobhouse did not take up the work of a judge in the House of Lords. He only sat there to try three cases, in two of which, Russell *v.* Countess of Russell (1897 Appeal Cases 395) and the Kempton Park case (1899 Appeal Cases 143), he was in a dissenting minority. As a judge Hobhouse, who was always careful and painstaking, invariably stated the various arguments fully and fairly, but he was tenacious of his deliberately formed opinion.

While engaged on the judicial committee, Hobhouse devoted much energy to local government of London. From 1877 to 1899 he was a vestryman of St. George's, Hanover Square. In 1880 he assisted to form and long worked for the London Municipal Reform League, which aimed at securing a single government for the metropolis. From 1882 to 1884 he was a member of the London School Board. Upon the creation of the London County Council in 1888 Hobhouse was one of the first aldermen. Advancing years and increasing deafness led him to retire from the judicial committee in 1901. He died at his London residence, 15 Bruton Street, on 6 Dec. 1904, and was cremated at Golder's Green.

To the last an advanced liberal and constructive legal reformer, Hobhouse, all of whose judicial work was done gratuitously, urged many legal changes, which won adoption very slowly. Much influence is assignable to an address by him before the Social Science Congress at Birmingham in 1868 on the law relating to the property of married women (1869; new edit. 1870), and to 'The Dead Hand' (1880), a collection of addresses on endowments and settlements of property (reprinted from the 'Transactions of the Social Science Association').

Hobhouse married, on 10 Aug. 1848, Mary (*d.* 1905), daughter of Thomas Farrer, solicitor, and sister of Thomas, first Baron Farrer [q. v.], Sir William Farrer (*d.* 1911), and Cecilia Frances (*d.* 1910), wife of Stafford Henry Northcote, first earl of Iddesleigh. He left no issue, and the peerage became extinct on his death. Two portraits, a drawing by George Richmond and an oil painting by Frank Holl (1882), are in the possession of his nephew, the Rt. Hon. Henry Hobhouse.

[Lord Hobhouse, a Memoir, by L. T. Hobhouse and J. L. Hammond, 1905; Burke's Peerage, 1899; Foster, Alumni Oxonienses; Foster, Men at the Bar; The Times, 7 and 10 Dec. 1904; private information.]

C. E. A. B.

HOBHOUSE, EDMUND (1817–1904), bishop of Nelson, New Zealand, antiquary, born in London on 17 April 1817, was elder brother of Arthur, first Baron Hobhouse of Hadspen [q. v. Suppl. II], and was second son of Henry Hobhouse [q. v.], under-secretary of state for the home department. He entered Eton in 1824, but left it in 1830 from ill-health and read with tutors. He matriculated at Balliol College, Oxford, on 16 Dec. 1834, and graduated B.A. in 1838, proceeding M.A. in 1842, B.D. in 1851, and D.D. in 1858. He rowed in the Balliol boat for four years (1835–8), and was stroke in 1836–7. Oxford giving no facilities for theological study, Hobhouse went to Durham University, where he graduated L.Th. in 1840. At his father's wish, he entered for a fellowship at Merton, and was elected at his third trial in 1841. He was ordained deacon in the same year and priest in 1842. In 1843 he became vicar of the college living of St. Peter in the East, Oxford, which he held with his fellowship till 1858.

Hobhouse worked his parish with zeal and declined offers of better preferment. Bishop Samuel Wilberforce [q. v.] made him rural dean, and as secretary of the diocesan board of education he did much for the church schools, and helped to found the Culham training college for schoolmasters. On his father's death in 1854 he devoted part of his patrimony to providing at St. Edmund Hall and St. Alban Hall, Oxford, help for necessitous students. On the subdivision of the diocese of New Zealand, Bishop G. A. Selwyn [q. v.] obtained the appointment of Hobhouse to the new see of Nelson, for which he was consecrated in 1858. The diocese, extending over 20,000 square miles, had a sparse and scattered population, with few roads. Its difficulties were increased by the outbreak of the Maori war, and by the discovery of gold. Hobhouse was diligent in ministering to his scattered flock, was generous in hospitality, provided a residence for the holder of the see, and founded the Bishop's School. But the work broke down his health; he resigned the see in 1865 and returned home in 1866. In 1867 he became incumbent of Beech Hill, near Reading. On Bishop Selwyn's translation to Lichfield he made Hobhouse, in 1869, his assistant bishop, and in 1871 gave him the rectory of Edlaston, Derbyshire. During 1874–5 he was chancellor of the diocese, though he had no legal training (*Life and Episcopate of G. A. Selwyn*, ii. 350). On the death of Selwyn in 1878, the new bishop, W. D. Maclagan [q. v. Suppl. II], retained him as assistant; but ill-health led him to resign in 1881. He retired to Wells, lending aid to clergy around him but refusing office. The Somerset Archæological Society gained in him an active member, and he helped to found the Somerset Record Society. He died at Wells on 20 April 1904.

Hobhouse was twice married: (1) in 1858 to Mary Elizabeth, daughter of General the Hon. John Brodrick (*d.* 1864), by whom he had two sons; and (2) in 1868 to Anna Maria, daughter of David Williams, warden of New College, Oxford, who survived him.

Hobhouse, who was from his Oxford days a zealous student of English mediæval history, more especially on its ecclesiastical side, published 'A Sketch of the Life of Walter de Merton' (1859), and edited the 'Register of Robert de Norbury, Bishop of Lichfield and Coventry' (in 'Collections for a History of Staffordshire,' vol. i. 1880). For the Somerset Record Society he edited 'Calendar of the Register of John de Drokensford, 1309–1329' (1887); 'Churchwardens' Accounts of Croscombe, &c.' (1890); 'Rentalia et Custumaria Michaelis de Ambresbury' (1891); and (with other members of the council) 'Two Cartularies of the Augustinian Priory of Bruton and the Cluniac Priory of Montacute' (1894). A volume of sermons and addresses was printed in 1905.

[Memoir by his son, Walter Hobhouse, prefixed to Sermons and Addresses, 1905; The Times, 22 April 1904; Guardian, 27 April 1904; Athenæum, 30 April 1904.] A. R. B.

HODGETTS, JAMES FREDERICK (1828–1906), commander and archæologist, son of James Hodgetts (*d.* 1830) by his wife Judith, daughter of Richard May, portrait painter, was born in London on 18 Jan. 1828. After his father's death his mother married Edward William Brayley [q. v.]. Hodgetts did not get on with his stepfather, who educated him for a scientific career. As a boy he assisted Sir Samuel Rush Meyrick [q. v.] in the arrangement of the Tower armoury. At an early age he went to sea, was in the East India Company's service in the Burmese war of 1851, became commander in the Indian navy, was wrecked, and had a narrow escape from drowning off the coast of Australia. He volunteered for service in the Crimean war; not being accepted, he became professor of seamanship at the Prussian naval cadets' school in Berlin till 1866, when the school was abolished. Having studied Russian in India, he transferred his services at the suggestion of Sir Roderick Impey Murchison [q. v.] to St. Petersburg and Moscow, where he lectured as professor in the Imperial College of Practical Science till his retirement in 1881. Coming to London, he patented a design for ships' hulls, which was not carried out; wrote stories for boys in the 'Boys' Own Paper' ('Harold the Boy Earl' being the first), afterwards published separately; and wrote and lectured on archæological subjects, contributing to the 'Journal of the British Archæological Association' and to the 'Antiquary.' He was engaged on an unfinished life of Alfred the Great. He died at his residence, 24 Cheniston Gardens, Kensington, on 24 April 1906. He married (1) in 1858 Isabella Gough (*d.* 1862), by whom he had a son, Edward Arthur Brayley Hodgetts; and (2) in 1867 Augusta Louisa von Dreger, by whom he had one daughter.

Among his publications were: 1. 'Ivan Dobroff: a Russian Story,' Philadelphia, 1866. 2. 'Anglo-Saxon Dress and Food,' &c., 1884 (lectures at the International Health Exhibition). 3. 'Anglo-Saxon Dwellings,' &c., 1884 (ditto). 4. 'Older England,' &c., 1884 (six lectures at the

British Museum). 5. 'Older England,' &c., second series, 1884 (ditto). 6. 'The Champion of Odin; or, Viking Life,' &c., 1885. 7. 'The English in the Middle Ages,' 1885. 8. 'Greater England,' &c., 1887 (on the consolidation of the colonial empire). 9. 'Edwin, the Boy Outlaw,' 1887.

[The Times, 26 April 1906; Athenæum, 5 May 1906; Annual Register, 1906; private information.] A. G.

HODSON, HENRIETTA (afterwards Mrs. Henry Labouchere) (1841–1910), actress, born at Upper Marsh, in St. Mary's parish, Westminster, on 26 March 1841, was eldest daughter of George Alfred Hodson, Irish comedian and singer (1822–1869), by his wife Henrietta Elizabeth Noel. Her father kept the Duke's Arms inn at Westminster (*Reg. Births*, Somerset House). Her two sisters, Kate (afterwards Mrs. Charles Fenton) and Sylvia, were also on the stage. As a girl Henrietta Hodson was entrusted by her parents for instruction in acting to Edmund Glover of the Theatre Royal, Glasgow, where she made her first appearance as a mute 'super' in 1858. At the end of nine months she was promoted to small parts. Early in 1860 she was acting at Greenock, and there first met Henry Irving. With the view of bettering their positions the two journeyed on speculation to Manchester, where they were engaged by Knowles for his Theatre Royal stock company, both making their first appearance in the city on 29 Sept. in 'The Spy; or a Government Appointment.' In the autumn of 1861 Henrietta Hodson became a member of Mr. J. H. Chute's Bath and Bristol companies, and in both cities soon acquired popularity as a soubrette and burlesque actress. On 4 March 1863, at the opening of the Theatre Royal, Bath (newly built after destruction by fire), she played Oberon in 'A Midsummer Night's Dream'; the cast included Ellen Terry and Madge Robertson. Shortly afterwards she married Walter Richard Pigeon, a Bristol solicitor, and retired from the profession; but on the early death of her husband she returned to the stage in her maiden name, which she used professionally to the last.

On 26 Dec. 1866 Henrietta Hodson made an auspicious first appearance in London at the Prince of Wales's Theatre, during the second season of H. J. Byron and Marie Wilton's management, as Prometheus in Byron's new extravaganza, 'Pandora's Box; or The Young Spark and the Old Flame.' In 1867 the Queen's Theatre, Long Acre, was built by Samuel Lamon, and opened by a syndicate which included Henry Labouchere, then M.P. for Windsor. The responsible manager was Alfred Wigan. Miss Hodson joined the original company, which included (Sir) Charles Wyndham, (Sir) Henry Irving, J. L. Toole, Lionel Brough, and Ellen Terry. The new theatre opened on 24 Oct. 1867 with Charles Reade's 'The Double Marriage,' in which Miss Hodson appeared as Jacintha. On 8 Jan. 1868 she gave a pathetic rendering of Lucy Garner in Byron's 'Dearer than Life,' and in the following April played Oliver Twist to Irving's Bill Sikes and Toole's Artful Dodger in Oxenford's dramatisation of Dickens's novel.

During 1868 she married Henry Labouchere, one of the proprietors of the Queen's Theatre, but she continued on the stage, where she fully maintained her reputation. Terminating her engagement at the Queen's in August 1870, she opened the Royalty on 3 Sept. for a season under her own management, appearing with acceptance in Reece's 'Whittington and his Sensation Cat' and other pieces, chiefly burlesques. In November she returned to the Queen's to play Ariel in a spectacular revival of 'The Tempest.' Henry Labouchere had then bought out the other lessees and the proprietor, and had assumed control of the theatre. Miss Hodson's technical knowledge and experience proved invaluable to her husband. Her sister Kate (acting as Miss Kate Gordon) joined the company as the principal soubrette. In April 1871 Miss Hodson made a new departure by appearing as Imogen in 'Cymbeline,' and, although somewhat lacking in dignity and passion in the earlier scenes, showed discretion and grace in the boy's disguise.

In the following October Henrietta Hodson entered upon a second period of management at the Royalty by reviving 'The Honeymoon,' with herself as Juliana. Here she inaugurated the system (frequently adopted since) of the unseen orchestra. In Dec. 1871 came a popular revival of 'Wild Oats,' compressed into three acts, with (Sir) Charles Wyndham as Rover and the manageress as Lady Amaranth. Miss Hodson won lavish praise in January 1874 for the naturalness of her acting as Jane Theobald in the new comedy 'Ought we to visit her?' although the conduct of one of the authors, (Sir) William Schwenck Gilbert [q. v. Suppl. II], at the rehearsals was highly distasteful to her.

In July 1874 she concluded her management by appearing as Peg Woffington to the Triplet of the veteran Benjamin Webster. On 29 Nov. 1875, at the Amphitheatre, Liverpool, she was the first Clytie in Joseph Hatton's dramatisation of his novel of that title, and played the part at the Olympic in London on 10 Jan. 1876.

After other engagements she played, in January 1877, Cynisca in a revival of Gilbert's 'Pygmalion and Galatea' at the Haymarket, and during the rehearsal had a fresh dispute with the author, whose dictatorial control she attacked in a pamphlet-letter addressed to the profession [see under GILBERT, SIR WILLIAM SCHWENCK, Suppl. II]. On 3 Jan. 1878 Miss Hodson appeared to signal advantage at the Queen's as Dolores, Countess Rysoor, in 'Fatherland,' her husband's adaptation of Sardou's 'Patrie.' Shortly afterwards she retired from the stage.

Thenceforth she was chiefly known as the tactful hostess at her husband's successive residences, Pope's Villa, Twickenham, and in Old Palace Yard, Westminster. In 1881 she was instrumental in introducing Mrs. Langtry to the stage, and in 1882 accompanied her to America, but made a quick return owing to a violent dispute with her protégée. In 1903 Labouchere acquired Villa Christina, near Florence, and thither Mrs. Labouchere retired. She died there suddenly of apoplexy on 30 Oct. 1910. She left a daughter, Dora, married, in 1903, to the Marquis Carlo di Rudini. Henry Labouchere died at the Villa Christina on 16 Jan. 1912.

An actress of individuality and high technical accomplishment, Henrietta Hodson was seen at her best in characters where she could mingle demureness with an underlying sense of fun and mischief. When pathos or sentimentality was demanded she was found wanting. Her art was somewhat too delicate and refined for burlesque, in which she showed a lack of animal spirits.

[Pascoe's Dramatic List; The Stage Door (Routledge's Christmas Annual, 1880); Ellen Terry's Story of My Life (with portrait of Miss Hodson); Belville St. Penley's The Bath Stage, 1892; The Bancrofts, 1909; Mrs. T. P. O'Connor, I myself, 1911; Michael Williams's Some London Theatres, 1883; The Stage of 1871, by Hawk's Eye; Strand Mag., May 1894, p. 517; Dutton Cook's Nights at the Play, 1883; Joseph Knight's Theatrical Notes, 1893; Daily Telegraph, 1 Nov. 1910; private information and personal research.]

W. J. L.

HOEY, MRS. FRANCES SARAH, 'MRS. CASHEL HOEY' (1830–1908), novelist, born at Bushy Park, co. Dublin, on 14 Feb. 1830, was one of the eight children of Charles Bolton Johnston, secretary and registrar of the Mount Jerome cemetery, Dublin, by his wife Charlotte Jane Shaw. Frances was educated at home, chiefly by her own efforts. On her sixteenth birthday, 14 Feb. 1846, she married Adam Murray Stewart. There were two daughters of the marriage. In 1853 she began to contribute reviews and articles on art to the 'Freeman's Journal' and the 'Nation' and other Dublin papers and periodicals. Thenceforth until her death she was continuously occupied in journalism, novel-writing or translation.

Her husband Stewart died on 6 Nov. 1855, and his widow then came to London with an introduction to Thackeray. She soon wrote reviews for the 'Morning Post,' to whose editor William Carleton introduced her, and for the 'Spectator.' On 6 February 1858 she married John Cashel Hoey (1828–1893), C.M.G., a knight of Malta and a well-known Dublin journalist. He was a member of the Young Ireland party, and assisted Sir Charles Gavan Duffy [q. v. Suppl. II] when he revived the 'Nation' in 1849, and was editor during 1856–7 after Duffy's departure for Australia (cf. C. G. DUFFY, *My Life in Two Hemispheres*, 1898). He was a devout Roman catholic, and after her marriage his wife adopted his faith. Later Hoey was called to the bar of the Middle Temple (18 Nov. 1861), and was secretary to the agent-general of Victoria in London (1872–3 and 1879–92) and of New Zealand (1874–9) (see FOSTER's *Men at the Bar*).

In 1865 Mrs. Hoey began with a story entitled 'Buried in the Deep' a long connection with 'Chambers's Journal,' then under the editorship of James Payn [q. v.]. Until 1894 she was a constant contributor, writing articles, short stories, and two serial novels, 'A Golden Sorrow' (1892) and 'The Blossoming of an Aloe' (1894).

Mrs. Hoey wrote in all eleven novels, dealing for the most part with fashionable society. Her first novel, 'A House of Cards' (3 vols. 1868; 2nd edit. 1871), two later novels, 'Falsely True' (1870) and 'The Question of Cain' (1882), and her last novel, 'A Stern Chase' (1886), each passed into a second edition, and some enjoyed a vogue in Canada and the United States. Mrs. Hoey was also largely responsible for 'Land at Last' (1866), 'Black Sheep' (1867), 'Forlorn Hope' (1867),

'Rock Ahead' (1868), and 'A Righted Wrong' (1870), five novels which were published under the name of Edmund Yates [q. v.]; of the last work Mrs. Hoey was sole author, and the secret of her authorship was divulged. Mrs. Hoey, too, helped Yates in 1874 to plan the 'World,' for which she wrote much.

Mrs. Hoey was a frequent visitor to Paris, and was well known to English residents there. On Easter Day 1871 she was the only passenger from London to Paris, whence she returned next day with the news of the Commune. An article by her, entitled 'Red Paris,' appeared in the 'Spectator.' Mrs. Hoey was 'reader' for publishers at various periods, and was the first to send a 'Lady's Letter' to an Australian paper, a piece of work which she performed fortnightly for more than twenty years. She also translated twenty-seven works from the French and Italian, seven in collaboration with John Lillie. They include memoirs, travels, and novels.

Mrs. Hoey, who was a humorous talker and generous to literary beginners, was granted a civil list pension of 50*l.* in 1892. She was left a widow next year, and died on 8 July 1908 at Beccles, Suffolk; she was buried in the churchyard of the Benedictine church at Little Malvern, Worcestershire.

[Who's Who, 1908; The Times, 15 July 1908; Allibone, Suppl. ii.; Tinsley, Random Recollections of an Old Publisher, 1900, i. 138–143; Brit. Mus. Cat.; private information.]

E. L.

HOFMEYR, JAN HENDRIK (1845–1909), South African politician, born at Capetown on 4 July 1845, was eldest of the five children of Jan Hendrik Hofmeyr, a farmer in the Cape Peninsula. The family came from the Netherlands to South Africa in the eighteenth century. Educated at the South African College at Capetown, he left school at the age of sixteen, meaning to enter the government service; but having no interest and no money he became a journalist in the colony. He started on the staff of the 'Volksvriend,' which he bought. In 1871 he amalgamated it with the 'Zuid Afrikaan,' and gave the combined journal the title 'Ons Land.' At one time he also edited the 'Zuid Afrikaansche Tijdschrift.'

In 1878 he formed the Boeren Vereeniging or Farmers' Association, with headquarters at Capetown. The original aims of this association were purely agricultural, but, the Afrikander Bond having been started in 1882 with less loyal and more political objects, Hofmeyr in 1883 amalgamated the Farmers' Association with it, modified its programme, and secured control of its working. He acted as chairman of the Bond till 1895, when he resigned, but resumed the office after 1902, when the South African war was over. Meanwhile he had in 1879 entered the Cape parliament as member for Stellenbosch. He remained in parliament for sixteen years, till 1895, and filled the position of leader and spokesman of the Dutch party in the colony. He was a member without portfolio of Sir Thomas Scanlen's ministry for six months in 1882, and was offered the premiership in 1884, but he held aloof alike from office and from distinction of any kind. At the same time he was a member of the executive council of the Cape Colony, and represented the colony on important occasions. He was one of the Cape delegates to the first colonial conference held in London in 1887, and moved a memorable motion: 'To discuss the feasibility of promoting a closer union between the various parts of the British empire by means of an imperial tariff of customs, to be levied independently of the duties payable under existing tariffs, on goods entering the empire from abroad, the revenue derived from such tariff to be devoted to the general defence of the empire.' He contended 'that the British empire should have some other consolidating force in addition to mere sentiment, that it should have the force of self-interest.' His scheme 'would produce revenue for imperial purposes and at the same time would leave the various fiscal tariffs of the different parts of the empire, of the colonies as well as England, untouched.' His proposal implied the creation of some kind of fiscal parliament for the empire, and was put forward at once as a unifying and as a revenue measure. It is noteworthy not only on its merits but also as the suggestion of the leader of the Dutch-speaking population of South Africa (*Proc. Colonial Conference of* 1887, C. 5091, 2 vols., July 1887, i. 463–8).

In 1889 Hofmeyr was a member of the South African customs conference. In 1890, when Sir Henry (afterwards Lord) Loch [q. v. Suppl. I] was governor of the Cape and high commissioner for South Africa, he negotiated with President Kruger the Swaziland convention between the British and the Transvaal governments. Neither to the more extreme section of the Afrikander party in South Africa nor to President Kruger was Hofmeyr's part in the negotiation quite congenial. Between Hofmeyr, who became 'the leader of constitutional Afrikanderdom,' and Kruger, who was 'the leader of militant Afrikanderdom,' difference of view was inevitable (*The Times Hist. of War in South Africa*, i. 291). In 1894 Hofmeyr again represented the Cape Colony at the colonial conference held at Ottawa to consider the question of trade and communication among the different colonies and between the colonies and the mother country.

Until the Jameson Raid of 1895 Hofmeyr was a close friend and supporter of Cecil Rhodes [q. v. Suppl. II]. 'People have disputed,' Rhodes is reported to have said, 'whether I led Mr. Hofmeyr or Mr. Hofmeyr led me' (EDMUND GARRETT, *The Story of a South African Crisis*, 1897, pp. 158–9). Mr. Schreiner, in his evidence before the select committee on British South Africa, stated that Hofmeyr 'has been during the six years of Mr. Rhodes's tenure of office as prime minister his constant confidant on every matter of public importance' (*Second Report from the Select Committee on British South Africa*, H. of C. paper 311, 13 July 1897, 'Minutes of Evidence,' p. 177). From the date of the raid Hofmeyr's relations with Rhodes were permanently broken off. At the time of the raid Hofmeyr urgently advised the high commissioner, Sir Hercules Robinson (afterwards Lord Rosmead) [q. v. Suppl. I], to issue the proclamation of 31 Dec. 1895, which disowned and condemned the movement (*The Times History*, i. 169). Hofmeyr, who had been the adviser and friend of British governors and ministers in the Cape Colony, and was at the same time the powerful and trusted leader of the Dutch party, was placed in a difficult position by the bitterness which thenceforth divided the British and the Dutch. In May 1899 he was largely responsible for initiating the Bloemfontein conference between Lord Milner and President Kruger (C. 9345, June 1899, p. 239), and at the beginning of July in that year, on the eve of the Boer war, he went to Bloemfontein and Pretoria in the hope of promoting a peaceful settlement. During the earlier part of the war he was in South Africa, and acted as chairman of the committee of the fund for the relief of Boer widows and orphans and of wounded Boers. During its later stages he was absent from South Africa on the ground of health, but was in South Africa again at the time of Mr. Chamberlain's visit, and at a deputation to Mr. Chamberlain at Capetown in February 1903 he made a speech in favour of conciliation. He took no very prominent part in advocating the South African Union. He was more in favour of federation than of unification, for he was essentially a citizen of Cape Colony and much concerned to maintain the position of the colony in a united South Africa. He was, however, one of the delegates who came to England in 1909 to effect the final settlement. After seeking medical treatment at Nauheim he died of angina pectoris in London on 16 Oct. 1909. Hofmeyr married twice: (1) in 1880, Aleda Hendrikz (*d.* 1883) of Somerset West; (2) on 1 Sept. 1900, her sister, Johanna Hendrikz. He left no children. He was buried among his wife's people in the Dutch reformed churchyard at Somerset West.

Hofmeyr had no gift of eloquence, but was on occasion an effective speaker. He wrote English well, had an excellent memory for both books and men, encouraged games, and was wide in his sympathies in normal times. He is credited with having helped through the Cape parliament an Act desired by the leaders of the Anglican church of South Africa, which was not his own communion (WIRGMAN'S *History of the English Church and People in South Africa*, 1895, p. 273). He was not rich, and coveted neither money nor distinction. Disinterested, and seeking no personal aggrandisement, he exerted very great personal influence on behalf of his people as a diplomatist and organiser behind the scenes. 'Mr. Hofmeyr,' said Mr. Schreiner in July 1897, 'is practically the leader of something very like half the popular house, although he is not now in the house' (*Second Report from the Select Committee on British South Africa*, as above). By means of the Afrikander Bond, which he moulded and controlled, he educated the Dutch of South Africa, and more especially of the Cape Colony, gave them political cohesion, and made them a political force. His Dutch fellow-countrymen felt unbounded confidence in his leadership and cherished strong personal affection for 'Onze Jan.' Despite the racial rancours which the Boer war aggravated and which for the time coloured his political views, Hofmeyr was a conspicuous advocate of the doctrine that nationalism within the empire is compatible with and not antagonistic to cohesion of the whole.

A bronze bust of him stands in the Parliament Buildings at Capetown, and when he retired from the legislature he was presented by his fellow members with a life-size portrait. A fund for a memorial to him is now being raised in South Africa.

[Blue Books; Anglo-African Who's Who, 1907; The Times History of the War in South Africa, 7 vols. 1900–9; The Times, 18 Oct. 1909; South Africa, 23 Oct. 1909.]

C. P. L.

HOGG, QUINTIN (1845–1903), philanthropist, fourteenth child and seventh son of Sir James Weir Hogg [q. v.] and Mary Claudine, daughter of Samuel Swinton, of the Indian civil service, was born on 14 Feb. 1845 in Grosvenor Street, London. Sir James MacNaghten McGarel Hogg, first Baron Magheramorne [q. v.], was his eldest brother; four other brothers were in the service of the Indian government. After attending preparatory schools, Quintin entered Mr. Joynes' house at Eton in 1858, and there took a prominent part in athletics, especially in association football, which was then a recent development. He long maintained an active interest in the game, playing in some early international matches. While at Eton, too, he showed strong religious leanings, which coloured his whole life (*Story of Peter*, p. 44). In 1863 he left Eton for the office of Messrs. Thompson, tea merchants, in the City of London; eighteen months later, by the influence of Charles McGarel, who had married a sister, he entered the firm of Bosanquet, Curtis and Co., sugar merchants. He soon became a senior partner of the house, which was renamed Hogg, Curtis and Campbell, and under his active direction greatly prospered. The firm's factories were concentrated in Demerara, which Hogg frequently visited. After 1882 the continental bounties for the protection of lime-grown sugar injured the East India trade, and Hogg's income suffered. He retired from the firm in 1898, but pursued other commercial interests till death.

Philanthropy was the main concern of Hogg's life. In the winter of 1864–5, with the help of Arthur (afterwards 11th Baron) Kinnaird, he started in 'Of Alley' (now York Place, Charing Cross) a ragged school for boys. Larger premises were taken in Castle Street, off Hanover Street. In a portion of the building Hogg soon started for thirty-five boys of a better class a 'Youths' Christian Institute.' In 1878 the institute was transferred to Long Acre, and the Ragged School, which was soon superseded by the board schools, was dissociated from it. In the new premises, which accommodated 500 members, Hogg offered courses of technical education, which proved almost as attractive as the schemes of recreation, for which in 1880 he provided a ground at Mortlake.

In 1881 the Royal Polytechnic Institution in Regent Street came into the market. The building, which was erected in 1838, had been at first devoted to scientific exhibitions, and since 1860 to technical classes in addition. The concern was wound up in 1881. Next year, to meet the growing needs of his institute, Hogg purchased the lease for 15,000*l.* and spent larger sums on alterations. Hogg retained the name Polytechnic, but gave it the new significance of an institution under public management which should provide young men and women of the lower middle classes with instruction, recreation, and social intercourse. Its comprehensive aims were thus described by Hogg: 'What we wanted to develop our institute into was a place which should recognise that God had given man more than one side to his character, and where we could gratify any reasonable taste, whether athletic, intellectual, spiritual, or social.' The new Polytechnic was opened on 25 Sept. 1882, with 2000 members. During the first winter the numbers rose, under Hogg's energetic direction, to 6800. Hogg greatly increased and improved the technical classes. New developments included a debating society, a savings bank, a Christian workers' union, and a volunteer corps. In 1886 Hogg opened a day school with professional, commercial, and industrial sections, and organised holiday tours and holiday accommodation for members. Almost all parts of the world were ultimately included in the Polytechnic itineraries, the cost of which remained low, and travellers' circular excursion tickets were sold to the general public. A further development in 1891 embraced a labour bureau for members and non-members, and on Hogg's suggestion, after a conference at the Polytechnic in 1902, an Act of Parliament was passed authorising metropolitan borough councils to establish labour bureaus at the public expense.

Hogg continued to be as generous with his purse as with his energies and counsel. He bought a new athletic ground at Merton. In 1888 he paid off a deficit in working expenses of 6000*l.*, and his aggregate contributions rose to a total of 100,000*l.* But financial help was now forthcoming from outside sources. In 1889 the commissioners for the redistribution of London parochial charities made a grant of 11,500*l.*, with a yearly endowment of 3500*l.*, and by 1891 an endowment of 35,000*l.* was subscribed by the public. Hogg, who regarded religious instruction as essential to his scheme, agreed that the official subvention should be applied exclusively to secular work. In 1896 Hogg's friends celebrated his silver wedding by raising nearly 14,000*l.* whereby to reduce outstanding liabilities.

By his successful inauguration and administration of the Regent Street Institute Hogg initiated the Polytechnic movement in London. In January 1889 he was elected an alderman of the first London County Council, and holding the office till 1894, encouraged the formation by the Council of other London polytechnics.

Hogg's activities told on his health, and he often sought recuperation in foreign travel or in yachting. He died of heart failure at the Polytechnic on 17 Jan. 1903. The evening before was spent as usual in directing and advising the members. After cremation his ashes were buried in the Marylebone cemetery at Finchley. On 16 May 1871 Hogg married Alice, eldest daughter of William Graham, M.P. He had three sons and two daughters.

In 1880 Hogg started and edited 'Home Tidings of the Young Men's Christian Institute,' which was continued in 1887 as the 'Polytechnic Magazine.' Later he appointed a paid editor, but remained till his death a frequent contributor. In 1900 he published 'The Story of Peter,' a series of religious addresses delivered at a Sunday afternoon class at the Polytechnic, 1896–97.

In memory of Hogg a new Quintin Hogg recreation ground and boathouse at Grove Park, Chiswick, were provided in 1904 at the cost of 25,000*l.*, and a bronze group statue, by Sir George Frampton, R.A., was erected in 1906 in Langham Place, opposite the Polytechnic. There is a portrait by Lowes Dickinson, and another by E. W. Appleby hangs in the hall of the institute. A sum of 90,000*l.* was also raised in 1910 by Hogg's friends and admirers for the purpose of rebuilding the old premises. In 1911 the daily attendance at the Polytechnic averaged 3000, and 600 classes were held weekly.

[Quintin Hogg, by his daughter, Ethel M. Hogg, with photograph as frontispiece, 1904; The Times, 19 Jan. 1903; information from the secretary of the Polytechnic; Encyclopædia Britannica, vol. xxii., Polytechnics; Century Magazine, June 1890; Sidney Webb, the London Polytechnic Institutes, 1898.]

G. S. W.

HOLDEN, LUTHER (1815–1905), surgeon, born on 11 Dec. 1815, in his grandfather's house at Birmingham, was second son of the Rev. Henry Augustus Holden (1785-1870), who married his cousin Mary Willetts' daughter of Hyla Holden of Wednesbury in Staffordshire. His father, on retiring from the army with the rank of lieutenant, matriculated at Worcester College, Oxford, in 1814 (B.A. 1817), and held the curacies of Wolstanton in Shropshire and of Warmington near Banbury, where he took pupils, but on being left a small fortune gave up his curacy and lived at Brighton and afterwards in London. His eldest son was Henry Holden (1814–1909) [see under HOLDEN, HUBERT ASHTON, Suppl. I]. His fourth son, Philip Melanchthon Holden (1823–1904), was for forty-two years rector of Upminster in Essex.

Luther, after successive education at home with his father's pupils, at a private school in Birmingham, and at Havre in 1827, where he made rapid progress in French, entered St. Bartholomew's Hospital in 1831. Apprenticed for five years to Edward Stanley [q. v.], he was admitted M.R.C.S.England in 1838, and then studied for one year in Berlin and another in Paris, where an Italian student taught him to speak and to read Italian. He was surgeon to the Metropolitan Dispensary, Fore Street, from 1843, living in the Old Jewry and teaching anatomy to private pupils, among whom was William Palmer, the poisoner [q. v.]. Holden was one of the twenty-four successful candidates at the first examination for the newly established order of fellows of the College of Surgeons (24 Dec. 1844).

Appointed in 1846 with A. M. McWhinnie superintendent of dissections (or demonstrator) at St. Bartholomew's Hospital, he was elected in 1859 jointly with Frederick Skey [q. v.] to lecture upon descriptive and surgical anatomy. This office he resigned in June 1871. Elected assistant surgeon to the hospital in July 1860, and full surgeon in August 1865, he became consulting surgeon in 1881. He then resigned his hospital appointments on attaining the age of sixty-five, and retiring from his house in Gower Street to Pinetoft, Rushmere, near Ipswich, he thenceforth spent much time in travel, visiting Egypt, Australia, India and Japan. In 1898 he was entertained by the medical profession at Johannesburg. He remained surgeon to the Foundling Hospital from 1864 until his death. At the Royal College of Surgeons Holden was a member of the council (1868–84); an examiner in surgery (1873–83); in anatomy (1875–6), and a member of the board of dental examiners (1879–82). He was vice-president (1877–8), president in 1879, and Hunterian orator in 1881.

Holden died at Putney on 5 Feb. 1905, and was buried in the cemetery of the parish church at Upminster. By his will he bequeathed 3000*l.* to the medical school of St. Bartholomew's Hospital to endow a scholarship in surgery. He also made handsome bequests to St. Bartholomew's Hospital and to the Foundling Hospital.

He was twice married (both wives bore the same name and were of the same family): (1) in July 1851 to Frances, daughter of Benjamin Wasey Sterry of Upminster, Essex; and (2) in 1868 to Frances, daughter of Wasey Sterry, who survived him. He had no children.

A fluent linguist and a good classic, as well as a keen sportsman, he was a conspicuously handsome member of a handsome family, and was seen at his best in the hunting field. A three-quarter length portrait—an admirable likeness—in oils, by Sir J. E. Millais, R.A., presented on Holden's retirement, hangs in the great hall at St. Bartholomew's Hospital. It has been engraved.

Holden, one of the last members of the anatomical school of surgery of the mid-nineteenth century, was primarily interested in anatomical, and only in a subordinate degree in surgical, study, and then in its clinical rather than in its operative aspect. He held that anatomy could be learnt only by personal dissection and examination of the dissected subject, and not by lectures, books, or pictures. An unpublished paper by him, 'On the Mechanism of the Hip Joint,' read at the Abernethian Society at St. Bartholomew's Hospital (24 Nov. 1850), exerted much influence. It dealt with the effect of atmospheric pressure in retaining the ball-shaped head of the femur within the socket of the acetabulum, and with the importance of keeping the anterior part of the capsular ligament in the erect attitude.

Holden published: 1. 'Manual of the Dissection of the Human Body,' a book enjoying a large circulation, 1850, 4 pts. without illustrations; 1851, 1 vol. copiously illustrated; 5th edit. 1885; Philadelphia, 7th edit. 1901, 2 vols. 2. 'Human Osteology,' 1855, 2 vols.; later editions 1 vol.; 8th edit. 1899; this work marked a distinct advance in the study of the human skeleton; the illustrations by Holden and etched on stone by Thomas Godart, librarian of the medical school of St. Bartholomew's Hospital, are of the highest order; they formed at the time a new feature in the teaching of anatomy, for the origins and insertions of the muscles were shown upon the figures of the bones in red and blue lines. 3. 'Landmarks Medical and Surgical,' first published in the 'St. Bartholomew's Hospital Reports,' vol. 2 (1866), and vol. 6 (1870), separately issued in an enlarged and revised form in 1876; 4th edit. 1888; translated into Spanish by D. Servendo Talón y Calva (Madrid, 1894): a study of the application of anatomy to surgery, proving how much anatomy can be learnt on the surface of the living body whilst the skin is yet unbroken.

[Brit. Med. Journal, 1905, i. 337; Lancet, 1905, i. 450 (each with a portrait); p. 1297 (an interesting note upon Holden's Osteology); St. Bartholomew's Hospital Reports, vol. xli. 1905, p. xxxi (with portrait); Medico-Chirurgical Trans., vol. lxxxviii. 1905, p. cxxiii; Bagnall's History of Wednesbury, Wolverhampton, 1854, p. 173, and Baker's Hist. of Northampton, i. 317, containing a genealogy of the family; private information; personal knowledge.] D'A. P.

HOLDER, Sir FREDERICK WILLIAM (1850–1909), first speaker of the house of representatives in the Australian commonwealth, born at Happy Valley, South Australia, on 12 May 1850, was son of James Morecott Holder of Adelaide by Martha Breakspear Robey, his wife. After education at St. Peter's College, Adelaide, he was for a time a state schoolmaster, and subsequently editor and proprietor of the 'Burra Record.' From 1886 to 1890 he was mayor of Burra.

He entered the legislative assembly of South Australia as member for the Burra district in April 1887, and was returned for the same constituency at the elections of 1890, 1893, 1896 and 1899. He was a member of several committees and royal commissions, including the land laws commission in 1887, Barrier trade select committee in 1888, intercolonial free trade commission in 1890, mails commission in 1890, pastoral lands commission in 1891, and the Orroroo railway commission in 1892. He took a prominent part in the movement for Australian federal union and was a member of the convention which framed the Commonwealth constitution in 1897–8.

From 27 June 1889 to 19 Aug. 1890 he was treasurer of the colony in Dr. Cockburn's ministry. After having been for some time virtually leader of the opposition, he was sent for in June 1892 on the defeat of the Playford ministry, and succeeded in forming a government, in which he again took the position of treasurer in addition to that of premier. His administration lasted only till 15 Oct. of the same year, when it was defeated by four votes on a want of confidence motion. On 16 June 1893 he returned to office as commissioner of public works in Mr. Kingston's ministry, and on 17 April 1894 became treasurer. On 1 Dec. 1899 the government was defeated by one vote and resigned; but within a few days Holder was again sent for and formed his second administration, in which he was premier, treasurer, and minister of industry.

In May 1901 Holder was returned as one of the representatives of South Australia to the federal parliament of the Commonwealth, and was unanimously elected speaker of the lower house. He was re-elected in 1904 and 1907. He died in office in tragic circumstances. He was about to prorogue the House after a turbulent all-night sitting, when he was seized with a fit, and expired within a few hours in the parliament house on 23 July 1909. He was accorded a state funeral at Adelaide on 26 July. Mr. Deakin, prime minister of the Commonwealth, in moving the resolution of regret in the house of representatives, said: 'No speaker more gentle, patient, or equitable has presided over any deliberative assembly with which I am acquainted' (*Commonwealth of Australia, Parliamentary Debates*, 1909, i. 1629–30).

Holder was a member of the South Australian School of Mines and Industries, and served in the military forces of his state from 1858 to 1899. He actively helped to found a national library, and he was a prominent office-bearer and preacher in the methodist church. He was created a K.C.M.G. on 26 June 1902.

Holder married on 29 March 1877 Julia Maria, daughter of John Ricardo Stephens, M.D., and left issue. Lady Holder has been president of the Women's Christian Temperance Union in South Australia, and is a vice-president of the National Council of Women.

[The Times, 27 July 1909; Johns's Notable Australians, 1906; Year Book of Australia, 1901; Mennell's Dict. of Australasian Biog. 1892; Colonial Office Records.] C. A.

HOLE, SAMUEL REYNOLDS (1819–1904), dean of Rochester and author, born at Ardwick, near Manchester (where his father was then in business), on 5 Dec. 1819, was only son of Samuel Hole, of Caunton Manor, Nottinghamshire, by his wife Mary, daughter of Charles Cooke of Macclesfield. After attending Mrs. Gilbey's preparatory school at Newark, he went to Newark grammar school. Of literary tastes, he edited at sixteen a periodical called 'The Newark Bee.'

Foreign travel preceded Hole's matriculation from Brasenose College, Oxford, on 26 March 1840. Fox-hunting, to which he was devoted for fifty years, occupied much of his time at the university. He was, too, secretary of the Phœnix (the oldest social club in Oxford) in 1842, and presided at its centenary dinner on 29 June 1886. In 1847 he published a sprightly *jeu d'esprit* illustrative of Oxford life and recreation, entitled 'Hints to Freshmen.' He graduated B.A. on 25 May 1844 and proceeded M.A. on 23 May 1878.

Hole was ordained deacon in 1844 and priest in 1845. He became curate of Caunton in the former year, and was vicar from 1850 to 1887. In 1865 he was appointed rural dean of Southwell, and in 1875 prebendary of Lincoln. He was chaplain to Archbishop Benson from 1883, and in 1884 was elected proctor to convocation.

At Caunton he instituted daily services and never omitted a daily visit to the village school; but his clerical duties were varied by hunting, shooting, and other rural sports, and he was an enthusiastic gardener. After the death of his father in 1868 he was squire of Caunton as well as vicar, and his genial humour made him popular with all ranks.

In 1858 Hole came to know John Leech [q. v.], and a close friendship followed. In the summer of 1858 the two, who often hunted together, made a tour in Ireland, of which one fruit was Leech's illustrated volume, 'A Little Tour in Ireland' (1859), with well-informed and witty letterpress by 'Oxonian' (i.e. Hole). A reprint of 1892 gives Hole's name as author. Hole made many suggestions for Leech's pictures in 'Punch,' and much correspondence passed between them (cf. JOHN BROWN'S *Horæ Subsecivæ*, 3rd ser., 1882, which contains Hole's biographic notes on Leech). Hole's friendship with Leech also led to his election to the 'Punch' table in 1862, but he was never a regular contributor to 'Punch,' only writing occasionally while Mark Lemon was editor. At Leech's house in Kensington Hole met Thackeray, who was, he wrote, of his own height (6ft. 3in.). The novelist proposed him for the Garrick Club. At Thackeray's invitation, too, Hole contributed to the 'Cornhill'; Dean Church quoted in the pulpit some verses by Hole there in the belief that they were by Hood.

Hole was long a rose-grower, and he came into general notice as promoter and honorary secretary of the first national rose show, which was held in the old St. James's Hall on 3 July 1858. Thenceforth he was an enthusiastic organiser of flower-shows. At Caunton he grew upwards of 400 varieties of roses, and afterwards at Rochester had 135 in his deanery garden. He edited 'The Gardener's Annual' for 1863, and came to know the leading horticulturists in France and Italy as well as at home. The establishment of the National Rose Society in December 1876 was largely due to his efforts; and his 'Book about Roses, how to grow and show them' (1869; 15th edition 1896), though of no great scientific value, did much to popularise horticulture. The work was translated into German and circulated widely in America. Hole presided at the National Rose Conference at Chiswick in 1889, and Tennyson, in writing to him, hailed him as 'the Rose King.' Hole's more general work on gardening, 'The Six of Spades' (i.e. the name of an imaginary club of six gardeners), appeared in 1872, and was reprinted, with additions, in 1892, as 'A Book about the Garden and the Gardener.'

A moderate high churchman, Hole proved popular as a preacher, especially to parochial home missions and as a platform orator. He spoke without notes. A rather raucous voice was atoned for by a fine presence, earnestness, plain language, and common sense. While he denounced drunkenness, gambling, and horse-racing, he frankly defended moderate drinking, at the Church Congress of 1892 (cf. *The Dean and the Drink*, by W. KEMPSTER, 1892), and publicly justified the playing of whist for small stakes. For several years he was a mid-day preacher at St. Paul's cathedral during Lent, and he was a select preacher at Oxford in 1885–6.

In 1887 Hole was made dean of Rochester. There his activity was undiminished. Besides popularising the cathedral services and continuing for a time his home mission work, he made in 1894 a four months' lecture tour in the United States, by which he raised 500*l.* for the restoration of his cathedral. He described his experiences in 'A Little Tour in America' (1895). The crypt and west front of Rochester cathedral were restored under Hole's supervision, the screen decorated, and vestries built. The new tower, which formed part of his plans, was erected after his death. Hole received the Lambeth degree of D.D. in 1887, was appointed almoner of the chapter of St. John of Jerusalem in 1895, and grand chaplain of Freemasons in 1897. In 1899 his brother masons placed a stained glass window in the clerestory at Rochester. His last sermon in the cathedral was preached on Christmas Day 1903; and he died at the deanery on 27 Aug. 1904. He was buried at Caunton.

Hole married, on 23 May 1861, Caroline, eldest daughter of John Francklin of Gonalston, Nottinghamshire, and Great Barford, Bedfordshire, by whom he had an only son, Samuel Hugh Francklin Hole (*b.* 1862), barrister-at-law, Inner Temple. A large portrait, painted by Charles Wellington Furse [q. v. Suppl. II], is at Caunton; and in Rochester cathedral there is a sculptured recumbent figure by F. W. Pomeroy, A.R.A. A cartoon appeared in 'Vanity Fair' (1895).

Hole was a humorous and charming letter-writer, sometimes embellishing his paper with clever sketches. His correspondents were of all classes, but they included Leech, Millais, Thackeray, Dr. John Brown, Dean Bradley, Sir George Grove, J. H. Shorthouse, and Archbishop Benson. A selection was edited by Mr G. A. B. Dewar in 1907. Hole's 'Memories' (1892) are prolific in good stories and wise observation; frequently reprinted, they were included in 1908 in Nelson's Shilling Library. 'More Memories,' which followed in 1894, contains Hole's addresses in America, as well as early contributions to periodicals. Another rather more reflective volume of reminiscence, 'Then and Now,' 1901, was the author's favourite work. Hole wrote several hymns which were set to music by his friend Sir John Stainer. One of them, 'Father, forgive,' had a sale of more than 28,000, and realised nearly 100*l.* for the Transvaal war fund. 'Sons of Labour' is included in 'Hymns Ancient and Modern.'

Besides the works above cited, and separate addresses and sermons, Hole published: 1. 'Hints to Preachers; with Sermons and Addresses,' 1880. 2. 'Nice and her Neighbours,' 1881 (an account of the Carnival). 3. 'Addresses spoken to Working Men from Pulpit and Platform,' 1894. 4. 'Our Gardens' (Haddon Hall Library), 1899.

[Memoir by G. A. B. Dewar prefixed to Letters of Dean Hole, 1907; Hole's autobiographical works; Burke's Landed Gentry; Men of the Time, 1899; The Times, 29, 31 Aug., 1, 2 Sept. 1904; Guardian, 31 Aug.; Church Times, 2 Sept.; Gardeners' Chronicle, 3 Sept. (with two portraits); Newark Advertiser

31 Aug.; Nottingham Daily Express (portrait), 29, 30 Aug.; Foster's Alumni Oxonienses, 1888; F. Madan's A Century of the Phœnix Common Room; Brasenose Quatercentenary Monographs, 1910; A. C. Benson, Life of Archbishop Benson, 1899, i. 506–7; Overton and Wordsworth, Life of Bishop Christopher Wordsworth, 1888, pp. 260–3; Frith, John Leech, 1891, vol. ii. ch. 8; Spielmann, Hist. of Punch, 1895, pp. 362, 434; Brit. Mus. Cat.; Dean Pigou, Phases of My Life, pp. 355–6; private information.] G. Le G. N.

HOLLAMS, Sir JOHN (1820–1910), solicitor, born at Loose, Kent, on 23 Sept. 1820, was son of John Hollams, curate in charge of Loose, by his wife Mary Pettit. His grandfather, Sir John Hollams (knighted in 1831), was five times mayor of Deal. After being educated privately Hollams was articled to a firm of solicitors in Maidstone, and in 1840 came to London. There he served his articles with the firm of Brown, Marten and Thomas. He was admitted a solicitor in 1844, and next year his firm took him into partnership. By hard work and integrity of character he obtained a foremost place in his profession. While still under forty he declined the offer of appointment as solicitor to the Admiralty, and on more than one occasion refused the office of chief clerk in chancery. In 1866 he was elected to the council of the Law Society, and in 1867 became a member of the Judicature Commission, upon which he did valuable work, but refused the knighthood offered in recognition of his services. He was president of the Law Society in 1878–9, and his portrait by the Hon. John Collier was placed in the society's hall. He was a generous supporter of the Solicitors' Benevolent Society. In 1902 he found his name included among the knights in the birthday list of honours. The crowning event in his career was the unique honour paid to him by the bench and bar in entertaining him at a dinner in the hall of the Inner Temple on 6 March 1903. He was made a deputy-lieutenant for the county of London in 1882, and was a J.P. for the county of Kent. He died at his country residence, Dene Park near Tonbridge, on 3 May 1910.

Hollams married in 1845 Rice (*d.* 1891), daughter of Edward Allfree, rector of Strood, Kent, by whom he left three sons. Under the title of 'Jottings of an Old Solicitor' (1906), he published a collection of reminiscences, useful for a description of the procedure of the courts before the passing of the Judicature Act.

[Jottings of an Old Solicitor, 1906; The Times, 4 May 1910; Dod's Peerage, 1909; private information.] C. E. A. B.

HOLLINGSHEAD, JOHN (1827–1904), journalist and theatrical manager, born in Union Street, Hoxton, London, on 9 Sept. 1827, was son (by his wife Elizabeth) of Henry Randall Hollingshead. The father failed in business, and was confined in the debtors' prison of Whitecross Street, but became in 1847 clerk to the secretary of the Irish society for administering the Irish estates of the London corporation, retiring on a pension in 1872 and dying next year. Miss Sarah Jones, great-aunt of John's mother, was long nurse to Charles Lamb's sister Mary, who lived for the last six years of her life (1841–7) under the care of Miss Jones's sister, Mrs. Parsons, at her house in Alpha Road, St. John's Wood (Lucas, *Life of Lamb*, ii. 285–6). Hollingshead as a child saw something of Lamb, and as a young man saw much of Mary Lamb and her literary circle. Educated at a Pestalozzian academy at Homerton, Hollingshead at an early age took a nondescript situation in a soft goods warehouse in Lawrence Lane, Cheapside. A taste for literature early manifested itself, and he read in his spare time at Dr. Williams's Library (then in Cripplegate), and at the London Institution. He quickly developed an ambition to write for the press; at nineteen he contributed to 'Lloyd's Entertaining Journal' an article called 'Saturday Night in London,' and soon sent miscellaneous verse to the 'Press,' a conservative newspaper inspired by Benjamin Disraeli. After some experience as a commercial traveller, he entered into partnership as a cloth merchant in Warwick Street, Golden Square; but the venture failed, and he turned to journalism for a livelihood. In 1856 he became a contributor to the 'Train,' a shilling magazine founded and edited by Edmund Yates [q. v.], and then joined his friend, William Moy Thomas [q. v. Suppl. II], as part proprietor and joint editor of the 'Weekly Mail.' In 1857 he sent to 'Household Words,' then edited by Charles Dickens, a sketch of city life, called 'Poor Tom, a City Weed.' The article pleased the editor, whose sentiment and style Hollingshead emulated, and he joined the staff. He was a voluminous contributor of graphic articles, chiefly descriptive of current incident and of out-of-the-way scenes of London life. 'On the Canal' was the title of several articles describing a journey in a canal boat from London to

Birmingham, and he reported the classic Sayers-Heenan fight. Many of his contributions to 'Household Words' and other periodicals he collected in volumes entitled 'Bow Bells' (1859); 'Odd Journeys in and out of London' (1860); 'Rubbing the Gilt off' (1860); 'Underground London' (1862), and 'Rough Diamonds' (1862). He was one of the first contributors to the 'Cornhill Magazine,' which was founded in 1859. When Thackeray, the editor, asked him where he learnt his 'pure style,' he replied 'In the streets, from costermongers and skittle-sharps.'

In 1861, when London suffered from famine, he wrote for the 'Morning Post' 'London Horrors' (republished as 'Ragged London' the same year). He also wrote much in the 'Leader' for his friend, F. J. Tomlin, for the 'London Review,' edited by Charles Mackay, and for 'Good Words,' edited by Norman Macleod. Sir Charles Wentworth Dilke [q. v.], a commissioner of the Great Exhibition of 1862, entrusted him with the 'Historical Introduction to the Catalogue.' From 1863 to 1868 he acted in succession to Yates as dramatic critic to the 'Daily News.' He wrote once or twice for 'Punch' when Shirley Brooks was editor, and in 1880, under Sir F. C. Burnand's editorship, became an occasional contributor. There he pleaded with effective satire for improvements in the government of London, especially attacking the Duke of Bedford, whom he christened the Duke of Mudford, for his mismanagement of his Bloomsbury property. His articles entitled 'Mud Salad (i.e. Covent Garden) Market' and 'The Gates of Gloomsbury' attracted wide attention. Many of his contributions to 'Punch,' in verse and prose, reappeared in his volumes 'Footlights' (1883), 'Plain English' (1888), and 'Niagara Spray' (1890).

Meanwhile he took a spirited part in other public movements. In 1858 he became a member of the committee for the abolition of the paper duty, which was effected in 1861. With Dion Boucicault he agitated in favour of 'Free Trade for Theatres,' and against the licensing regulations. In 1866 and again in 1892 a special committee of the House of Commons reported favourably on his general view, but no action was taken. To his efforts was largely due the Public Entertainments Act in 1875, sanctioning performances before 5 o'clock, which the Act 25 Geo. II c. 36 previously made illegal. In 1873 he led another agitation for the reform of copyright law so as to prevent the dramatisation of novels without the author's sanction. A royal commission reported in 1878 in favour of the novelist. From 1860 onwards he fought the closing of the theatres on Ash Wednesday, and in 1885 the restriction was removed by Lord Lathom, then lord chamberlain.

Hollingshead helped to found the Arundel Club and the New Club, Covent Garden (*My Lifetime*, ii. 209), and joined with zest in Bohemian society. He first turned theatrical manager in 1865. Although he did not abandon journalism, his main interest lay for nearly a quarter of a century in theatrical enterprise. From 1865 to 1868 he was stage director of the Alhambra, where he thoroughly reformed the performances. For acting a pantomimic sketch in contravention of the theatrical licensing law he was fined 240*l*. or 20*l*. a performance.

On 21 Dec. 1868 Hollingshead opened as manager the Gaiety Theatre in the Strand, which had been newly built by Charles John Phipps [q. v. Suppl. I] for Lionel Lawson. It was erected on the site once partly occupied by the Strand music-hall. A theatre and restaurant were now first combined in London in one building. At the Gaiety, Hollingshead made many innovations, including the system of 'No fees,' and inaugurated continual Wednesday and Saturday matinees. In August 1878, outside the theatre, he first introduced the electric light into London, and later, he was the first to make use of it upon the stage. He mainly devoted himself to burlesque, which he first produced in three acts. In his own phrase, he kept 'the sacred lamp of burlesque' burning at the Gaiety for eighteen years. His chief successes in burlesque were Reece's 'Forty Thieves,' Hervé's and Alfred Thompson's 'Aladdin,' H. J. Byron's 'Little Dr. Faust' and 'Little Don César de Bazan,' and 'Blue Beard,' 'Ariel,' and other pieces by Sir F. C. Burnand. His actors and actresses included Toole, Edward Terry, Nellie Farren, Fred Leslie, and Kate Vaughan. His scene painters were Grieve, Telbin and Son, Gordon, John O'Connor, and W. Hann, and his musical conductor was Meyer Lütz [q. v. Suppl. II]. Hollingshead did not confine himself to burlesque. He produced serious new plays by T. W. Robertson, W. S. Gilbert, H. J. Byron, Charles Reade, and Dion Boucicault; operas and operettes (in which Charles Santley, Cummings and Emmeline Cole sang) by Hérold, Hervé, Offenbach, Lecocq, and Suppé; while Shakespeare and old and modern English comedy were interpreted by, among others, Phelps, Charles Mathews, and Toole

Compton, Hermann Vezin, Forbes Robertson, Ada Cavendish, Mrs. John Wood, and Rose Leclercq. He produced 'Thespis' on 26 Dec. 1871, the first work in which Gilbert and Sullivan collaborated, and was the first English manager to stage a play by Ibsen ('Quicksands or Pillars of Society,' 15 Dec. 1880). Some of the work which he produced was from his own pen. He himself wrote the farce 'The Birthplace of Podgers,' first represented at the Lyceum on 10 March 1858, in which Toole acted the part of Tom Cranky for thirty-six years; the plot was suggested by Hollingshead's investigations in early life into the identity of the house in which the poet Chatterton died in Brook Street, Holborn (HATTON'S *Reminiscences of Toole*, i. 96); in 1877 he adapted 'The Grasshopper' from 'La Cigale' of Meilhac and Halévy. In 1879 he arranged through M. Mayer for the complete company of the Comédie Française, including Sarah Bernhardt, Got, Delaunay, the two Coquelins, Febvre, and Mounet Sully, to give six weeks' performances (42 representations) from 2 June to 12 July. He paid 9600*l.* in advance, and the total receipts were 19,805*l.* 4*s.* 6*d.*, an average of 473*l.* for each representation.

With characteristic public spirit, benevolence, and success, he organised many benefits for old actors or public objects.

At Christmas 1874, in addition to the 'Gaiety,' he took and managed for a short time the Amphitheatre in Holborn and the Opéra Comique in the Strand. In 1888 he resigned the management of the Gaiety to Mr. George Edwardes. The receipts from the theatre, which contained 2000 seats, were, for fifteen years of his control, 1869–1883, 608,201*l.* The house was closed for only eighteen weeks in seventeen years. Hollingshead was responsible for 959 matinées in the period. In eighteen years Hollingshead made 120,000*l.* profit, after paying away about 1¼ million sterling. His salaries were on a high scale. He paid Phelps, Toole, and Charles Mathews 100*l.* a week each for appearing in a revival of Colman's 'John Bull' in 1873.

On 12 March 1888 Hollingshead started, at a hall near Queen Anne's Gate, Westminster, a spectacular panorama of Niagara, which he carried on till 29 Nov. 1890. In his later years he contributed a weekly letter to the 'Umpire,' a Manchester sporting paper, and lost the fortune which he had derived from the Gaiety in speculation in theatres and music-halls. He died of heart failure at his house in the Fulham Road on 10 Oct. 1904, and was buried in Brompton cemetery near Sir Augustus Harris and Nellie Farren. He was married on 4 April 1854, and had issue two sons and one daughter. Edward Linley Sambourne [q. v. Suppl. II] did an excellent drawing of Hollingshead for 'Punch.'

In addition to the works already mentioned, Hollingshead published: 1. 'Ways of Life,' 1861. 2. 'To-day: Essays and Miscellanies,' 1865, 2 vols. 3. Miscellanies,' 1874, 3 vols. (selections from earlier collections). 4. 'The Story of Leicester Square,' 1892. 5. 'My Lifetime,' 1895, 2 vols. with photogravure portraits. 6. 'Gaiety Chronicles,' 1898 (with caricature portraits). 7. 'According to my Lights: Miscellanies in Prose and Verse,' 1900. 8. 'Charles Dickens as a Reader,' 1907.

[Hollingshead's My Lifetime, 2 vols. 1895, and his Gaiety Chronicles, 1898; William Tinsley's Random Recollections of an Old Publisher, ii. 1–3; G. A. Sala's Life and Adventures, i. 41, ii. 179–181; Edmund Yates's Recollections and Experiences, i. 286–7, 335–6; Sir F. Burnand's Records and Reminiscences; The Times, 11 and 15 Oct. 1904.] A. F. S.

HOLLOWELL, JAMES HIRST (1851–1909), advocate of unsectarian education, born in St. Giles's Street, Northampton, on 25 Feb. 1851, was son of William Hollowell, shoemaker and a local preacher in the reformed Wesleyan denomination. His mother's maiden name was Mary Anne Swinfield. He left school early to earn a living, but read widely by himself, and also attended a class which met three times a week from five to six in the morning.

In early youth he showed a gift for public speaking, and at eighteen became a temperance agent and lecturer. Joining the congregationalists at Dumfries, he decided to study for the congregational ministry. He was already married when in 1871 he entered Nottingham (congregational) institute. He went on to Cheshunt College in the following year, and there won a scholarship. From 1875 to 1882 he was pastor at Bedford chapel, Camden Town, London, and from 1882 to 1889 was minister of Park Hill congregational church, Nottingham. At Nottingham he was for a time chairman of the school board. Subsequently he was pastor of Milton church, Rochdale, from October 1889 till December 1896. This charge he relinquished in order to devote himself to the work of organising secretary of the Northern Counties Education League for promoting unsectarian state education. He was practically the founder of this league. His faith in unsectarian education was strong and uncompromising. In 1903 he took a leading part in organising with the Rev. John Clifford 'the passive resistance movement' against the payment of rates and taxes, on the ground that the Education Act of 1902 gave an inequitable support at state expense to church schools which taught church doctrine. Learned in educational legislation, he was a forcible speaker and an untiring pamphleteer. He also wrote a novel entitled 'Ritualism Abandoned or a Priest Redeemed' (1899), under the pseudonym of K. Ireton, and 'What Nonconformists stand for' (1901; 2nd edit. 1904).

In 1904 Hollowell unsuccessfully contested the South Birmingham division against Viscount Morpeth. In 1908 he was elected chairman of the Lancashire Congregational Union.

His exertions broke down his health, and he died of cerebral apoplexy at Rochdale on 24 Dec. 1909. He was buried at Rochdale cemetery. A memorial bust, by John Cassidy, was unveiled at the Congregational Church House, Manchester, on 3 April 1911.

He married at Dumfries, in 1870, Sarah, daughter of James Lacey of Crewkerne, Somerset, and had one son and five daughters.

[W. Evans and W. Claridge, James Hirst Hollowell and the Movement for Civic Control in Education, 1911 (with portraits); Congregational Year Book, 1911, p. 176; Manchester Guardian, 27 Dec. 1909.] C. W. S.

HOLMAN HUNT, WILLIAM. [See Hunt, William Holman (1827–1910), painter.]

HOLMES, AUGUSTA, properly Augusta Mary Anne (1847–1903), composer, born in Rue de Berri, Paris, on 16 Dec. 1847, was granddaughter of Captain John Holmes of New Park, co. Tipperary, and daughter of Captain Dalkeith Holmes, who settled in Paris in 1820, and married Augusta Macgregor in 1828. As a child Augusta Holmes became passionately devoted to music, though her parents—neither of them musically inclined—gave her no encouragement. Her mother died at Versailles in 1857, and next year her father allowed the child to take up music seriously. From 1859 to 1865 she attracted attention as a piano prodigy and singer of French songs of her own composition. As early as 1862 she published some pieces under the pseudonym of 'Hermann Zenta.' After a course of instruction from H. Lambert, Klosé, and Saint-Saëns, she became a pupil of César Franck in 1875, having previously acquired no little fame by her setting of 'In Exitu Israel,' in 1873, and an opera 'Héro et Léandre,' produced at the Opéra Populaire in 1874. Her studies with Franck bore fruit in her 'Orlando Furioso' Symphony in 1877, and in her prize symphony 'Lutèce,' which was awarded second place, after Dubois and Godard (who tied for the first place), in the competition offered by the city of Paris in 1878. In 1879 she became a French citizen, and thenceforth wrote her name as Holmès. Her orchestral piece 'Les Argonautes' was performed under Pasdeloup's direction at the Concerts Populaires (24 April 1881) and was followed by the symphonic poem 'Irlande' (2 March 1882), which betrayed innate Irish sympathy, was described by Jullien as 'a creation of great worth, evincing by turns a charming tenderness, ardent passion, and masculine spirit,' and firmly established Miss Holmes's reputation. Another patriotic symphony, 'Pologne,' was given at the Concerts Populaires (9 Dec. 1883), and in 1884 she published a volume of songs, 'Les Sept Ivresses.' Her symphonic ode 'Ludus pro patria' was well received at the concerts of the Conservatoire on 4 March 1888. Its reception was, however, surpassed by her 'Ode Triomphale,' performed by a very large chorus and orchestra at the Paris Exhibition in 1889. She wrote a 'Hymn à la Paix' for the Florence Exhibition in 1890, and a symphonic suite, 'Au pays bleu,' in 1891.

Turning her attention to the lyric stage, Miss Holmes composed a four-act opera, 'La Montagne noire,' which was successfully given at the Grand Opera, Paris, on 8 Feb. 1895. Two other operas, 'Astarte' and 'Lancelot du Lac,' were from her prolific pen. Her interest in Ireland grew, and after reading much about the country she revised her symphonic poem 'Irlande,' for production at the first Feis Ceoil, in Dublin, on 18 May 1897, and she planned an Irish opera in the following year. For a time a theosophist and afterwards a spiritualist, Miss Holmes finally became a Roman catholic, and was baptised in the Dominican friary church, in the Faubourg St. Honoré, in 1902. She died at Versailles on 28 Jan. 1903. A splendid monument was unveiled to her memory in the St. Louis cemetery, Versailles, on 13 July 1904. A weeping muse is represented holding a lyre, and on the monument is inscribed a quotation from her choral symphony 'Lutèce.'

[Flood's Hist. of Irish Music, 1905; Grove's Dict. of Music, new edit. 1906; Musical Times and Musical Herald, March 1903.]

W. H. G. F.

HOLMES, Sir RICHARD RIVINGTON (1835–1911), librarian of Windsor Castle, born in London on 16 Nov. 1835, was second of five children of John Holmes [q. v.], assistant keeper of manuscripts at the British Museum, by his wife Mary Anne, eldest daughter of Charles Rivington, bookseller, and sister of Francis Rivington [q. v.]. An elder brother, the Rev. Charles Rivington Holmes (*d.* 1873), was father of Mr. Charles John Holmes, director of the National Portrait Gallery since 1909. Richard was educated at Highgate school (1843–53), where he obtained a foundation scholarship, and after spending a short time in a merchant's office he assisted his father unofficially at the British Museum until the latter's death in April 1854, when he was appointed an assistant in the manuscript department. Here he rapidly acquired a fair knowledge of palæography, and thanks to these attainments and his skill as a draughtsman he was selected for the post of archæologist to the Abyssinian expedition of 1868. On the capture of Magdala, Holmes purchased from Abyssinian owners for the British Museum about 400 manuscripts, which had been taken by King Theodore from Christian churches, as well as the gold crown of the sovereigns of Abyssinia and a sixteenth-century chalice, which are now in the Victoria and Albert Museum, South Kensington. The transactions, which were held to condone sacrilegious treatment of objects connected with religious worship, were severely criticised by Gladstone, but Holmes's conduct won the approval of the authorities, and he was awarded the war medal.

In 1870 Queen Victoria appointed Holmes librarian at Windsor Castle in succession to Bernard Bolingbroke Woodward [q. v.]. Though more of an antiquary than a bibliographer, Holmes showed a collector's zeal for the acquisition of books connected with the history of the castle and of the royal family, and he took a special interest in the drawings, miniatures, and etchings at Windsor. Under his supervision the rearrangement of drawings by Holbein, Leonardo da Vinci, and other old masters was completed, and on his advice the collection of royal and historical miniatures was enriched by important purchases. He further took advantage of his personal friendship with Whistler to secure an almost complete set of that artist's etchings, but the collection was sold after Whistler's death. Nominated serjeant-at-arms to Queen Victoria in 1898, he was continued in that office by King Edward VII as well as in that of royal librarian. He was made M.V.O. in 1897, C.V.O. in 1901, and promoted K.C.V.O. in 1905. He retired from the Windsor library in the following year.

Holmes shared with his brothers a natural aptitude for drawing, but received no regular training. While an assistant at the British Museum he executed two series of 'Outlines for Illumination' (xv. century), and in 1860 he assisted Henry Le Strange [q.v.] and Thomas Gambier Parry [q. v.] in the decoration of Ely cathedral. The influence of Rossetti may be traced in some exceedingly delicate pen drawings, dating from about the same time; the majority of these are now in the possession of Mrs. Robert Barclay. Holmes's artistic talents developed in other directions. He executed five stained glass windows in 1867 and three more in 1889 for Highgate school chapel. At Windsor he devoted his leisure to designing bookbindings for the royal library and to landscape painting in water-colour. He was a frequent exhibitor at the Royal Academy, the Grosvenor and New Galleries, and drew a series of illustrations for Mrs. Oliphant's 'Makers of Venice' (1887).

Holmes, who was a zealous volunteer, attained the rank of lieut.-colonel in the first volunteer battalion of the Berkshire regiment, and received the volunteer decoration. Elected fellow of the Society of Antiquaries on 22 March 1860, he became vice-president in 1907. In his last years he was a treasurer of the Royal Literary Fund. He died in London on 22 March 1911, and was buried at Upton, Buckinghamshire. He married on 27 Oct. 1880 Evelyn, eldest daughter of Richard Gee, canon of Windsor, and had issue two daughters, of whom the elder predeceased her father in 1904.

A drawing of Holmes made by Heinrich von Angeli in 1877 is in the possession of the widow; an oil portrait by William Gibb (*c.* 1895) belongs to Mrs. Johnstone of Anne Foord's House, Windsor; a silver-point drawing was executed by Alphonse Legros about 1902, and a chalk drawing by William Strang, A.R.A. (1907), is in the royal collection at Windsor.

Holmes, who was always a favourite with the royal family, compiled popular and slight biographies of Queen Victoria (4to, 1897; new edit. 1901) and of 'Edward VII; his life and times' (fol. 1910). Other published works included:

1. 'Specimens of Bookbinding in the Royal Library, Windsor Castle,' fol. 1893. 2. 'Naval and Military Trophies,' fol. 9 parts, 1896–7. 3. 'The Queen's Pictures,' 1897. 4. 'Windsor,' illustrated by M. Henton, 1908.

[The Times, 23 March 1911; Athenæum, 25 March 1911; the Cholmeleian, May 1911; private information from Mr. C. J. Holmes.]

G. S. W.

HOLMES, TIMOTHY (1825–1907), surgeon, born on 9 May 1825, was son of John Holmes, warehouseman, living in Colebrooke Row, Islington, by his wife Elizabeth. He entered Merchant Taylors' School in November 1836, and gained a Stuart's exhibition to Pembroke College, Cambridge, in 1843. In 1845 he was admitted a scholar of the college, graduating B.A. in 1847 as forty-second wrangler and twelfth classic. He proceeded M.A. in 1853; in 1900 the further degree of Master in Surgery was conferred upon him, and in the same year he was made an honorary fellow of Pembroke College.

Holmes returned to London on the completion of his Cambridge course, and became a student at St. George's Hospital; he was admitted F.R.C.S.England on 12 May 1853 without previously taking the usual diploma of membership. He then served as house surgeon and surgical registrar at St. George's Hospital. He acted for a time as curator of the museum and demonstrator of anatomy until in June 1861 he was elected assistant surgeon and lecturer on anatomy. Holmes became full surgeon to the hospital in December 1867 upon the resignation of Thomas Tatum (1802–1879). This post Holmes held until 1887, when he retired on a time limit of service and was appointed consulting surgeon. In 1894 he accepted the onerous position of honorary treasurer, and was appointed a vice-president on his retirement from active work in 1904. Elected assistant surgeon to the Hospital for Sick Children in Great Ormond Street in May 1859, he was full surgeon (Sept. 1861–8). For twenty years he was chief surgeon to the metropolitan police.

In 1872 Holmes was elected Hunterian professor of surgery and pathology at the Royal College of Surgeons of England. A member of the court of examiners (1873–1883), he joined the newly appointed board of examiners in anatomy and physiology, and in 1880 he was a surgical examiner on on the board of examiners in dental surgery. In 1877 Holmes was elected a member of the council of the college, but did not seek re-election at the end of his first term of office in 1885.

Holmes took an active interest in the Royal Medical and Chirurgical Society of London (now merged in the Royal Society of Medicine). He was chairman of the building committee which arranged the removal of the society from its old quarters in Berners Street to its house in Hanover Square in 1899, and in 1900 he was elected president of the society, after filling all the subordinate offices. He joined the Pathological Society of London in 1854, and while honorary secretary (1864–7) prepared a general index to the volumes of its transactions. He was an original member of the Clinical Society, and was a vice-president from 1873 to 1875. After a long residence at 18 Great Cumberland Place he removed to 6 Sussex Place, Hyde Park, where he died on 8 Sept. 1907. He was buried at Hendon. He married Sarah Brooksbank, but left no issue. His portrait, painted by Sir W. B. Richmond, R.A., in 1889, is now at St. George's Hospital.

Holmes was a scientific surgeon possessed of an unusually clear and logical mind. Gifted with the power of incisive speech, he was fearless in expressing his conclusions, and exposed the fallacy in an argument mercilessly. The loss of an eye owing to an accident during his hospital work, a harsh and somewhat monotonous voice, and a manner carefully cultivated to hide any interest he might feel in those whom he examined, made him a terror to students, although his lack of sympathy was superficial, and he was the friend and trusted adviser of all who sought his help. He was a surgeon of the older school before the advent of bacteriological methods, and he made anatomy the foundation of his surgery. He was a skilled writer, always lucid, pure in style, and well read in Greek and Latin as well as in the best English literature.

Holmes edited several editions of Henry Gray's 'Anatomy,' which has remained a standard text-book and he designed and edited 'A System of Surgery, Theoretical and Practical' (4 vols. 1860–4; 2nd edit. 5 vols. 1869–71; 3rd edit. 3 vols. 1883), under the joint editorship of himself and J. W. Hulke [q. v.]. Holmes also published: 1. 'A Treatise on the Principles and Practice of Surgery,' 1875, which long formed a text-book for medical students; 4th edit. 1884; 5th edit. 1888, rewritten by T. Pickering Pick. 2. 'A Treatise on the Surgical Treatment of the Diseases of Infancy and Childhood' (the results of his ten years' experience as surgeon to the Children's Hospital in Great Ormond Street), 1868; 2nd edit. 1869; translated into French and German. 3. A life of Sir Benjamin Collins Brodie [q. v.] for the 'Masters of Medicine' series in 1898.

Holmes translated C. E. A. Wagner's 'On the Process of Repair after Resection and Extirpation of Bones,' with an appendix of cases (Sydenham Society, London, 1859). With Dr. John Syer Bristowe [q. v. Suppl. I] he also prepared a valuable report upon hospitals and their administration, which was published as an appendix to the sixth annual report of the public health department of the Privy Council.

[St. George's Hosp. Gazette, vol. xv. 1907, p. 127; Lancet (with portrait), 1907, ii. 803; Brit. Med. Journal, 1907, ii. 704; personal knowledge.] D'A. P.

HOLROYD, HENRY NORTH, third Earl of Sheffield (1832–1909), patron of cricket, born at 58 Portland Place, St. Marylebone, on 18 Jan. 1832, was elder surviving son of George Augustus Frederick Charles Holroyd, second earl of Sheffield, by Harriet, eldest daughter of Henry Lascelles, second earl of Harewood. His grandfather, John Baker Holroyd, first earl of Sheffield [q. v.], was the patron and friend of Edward Gibbon, the historian [q. v.]. Until he succeeded to the earldom in 1876 he bore the courtesy title of Viscount Pevensey. Educated at Eton, he entered the diplomatic service and was attached successively to the embassies at Constantinople (1852), Copenhagen (1852–3), and again at Constantinople (1853–6). From 1857 to 1865 he sat in the House of Commons as conservative M.P. for East Sussex.

Sheffield, although he never gained distinction as a player, deeply interested himself in cricket. From 1855 he was a member of the M.C.C., the presidency of which he several times declined. From 1879 to 1897 and from 1904 till death he was president of the Sussex County Club, which owed its secure financial position to his active interest and generosity. Many Sussex players, notably Mr. George Brann, owed their first appearance for the county to Lord Sheffield's discerning interest. In 1887, at his own expense, he engaged Alfred Shaw [q. v. Suppl. II], then lately retired from the Nottinghamshire XI, and William Mycroft to coach the young players of Sussex. At Sheffield Park, Fletching, his Sussex seat, Sheffield kept up one of the finest private cricket grounds in the kingdom. On this ground the visiting Australian teams of 1884, 1886, 1890, 1893, and 1896 all opened their tours with matches against more or less representative English XI's raised by Lord Sheffield. King Edward VII (then Prince of Wales) was present in 1896. The ground was freely placed at the service of local cricket, Lord Sheffield discouraging the use of boundaries in club matches. In 1891–2 Lord Sheffield, at his sole expense, took to Australia a team including Dr. W. G. Grace, under the management of Alfred Shaw. This enterprise greatly stimulated Australian cricket; the earl presented the Sheffield Shield, a trophy to be competed for annually by cricketers of Victoria, New South Wales, and South Australia. Sheffield was actively interested in the volunteer and, later, in the territorial movements. He gave a recreation ground to Newhaven in 1889 at a cost of 4000*l*.

In 1894 Sheffield served as president of the Gibbon Commemoration Committee of the Royal Historical Society, and lent the Gibbon MSS. and relics in his possession to the centenary exhibition in the British Museum, November 1894. The MSS. he sold to the Museum in the following year (Add. MSS. 34874–87), having previously allowed the publication of variant readings and passages omitted from his grandfather's edition of Gibbon's 'Autobiography,' justifying himself by the passage of time for acting contrary to the first earl's injunction that no further publication be made from Gibbon's MSS. To this volume 'The Autobiographies of Edward Gibbon,' edited by Mr. John Murray (1896), and to 'Private Letters of Edward Gibbon,' edited by Mr. Rowland E. Prothero (2 vols. 1896), Lord Sheffield contributed introductions. Other Gibbon papers of lesser interest were sold by auction after the earl's death, together with the Sheffield Park library and pictures.

Lord Sheffield, who was unmarried, died at Beaulieu in the south of France on 21 April 1909, and was buried in the family vault in Fletching churchyard. His younger brother, the Hon. Douglas Edward Holroyd (*b.* 20 June 1834), had predeceased him on 9 Feb. 1882. His sister, Lady Susan Holroyd, married in 1849 Edward William Harcourt (*d.* 1891) of Nuneham, and was mother of Aubrey Harcourt (1852–1904), who died unmarried, and of Edith, wife of the twelfth earl of Winchilsea. On Sheffield's death the Irish earldom became extinct. The English barony of Sheffield passed by special remainder to Edward Lyulph Stanley, fourth Baron Stanley of Alderley, heir male of the elder daughter of the first Lord

Sheffield; Lord Stanley was thenceforth known as Lord Sheffield.

[The Field, 24 April 1909; Cricket, 29 April 1909; Sussex Daily News, 22 April 1909; Haygarth's Scores and Biographies, xiv. 1007; A. W. Pullen, Alfred Shaw, Cricketer, 1902; Burke's Peerage.] P. L.

HOLYOAKE, GEORGE JACOB (1817–1906), co-operator and secularist, born at 1 Inge Street, Birmingham, on 13 April 1817, was eldest son and second of thirteen children of George Holyoake, engineer, by his wife Catherine Groves. His mother carried on independently a business for making horn buttons, and George practised when still a child some of the processes of the manufacture. He was apprenticed to a tinsmith, and afterwards worked with his father at the Eagle Foundry as a whitesmith. Later, the father bought some machinery then newly invented for making bone buttons and placed his son in charge of it.

The boy's inclinations lay, however, towards intellectual pursuits, and at the age of seventeen he became a student at the Old Mechanics' Institute, where he showed aptitude for mathematics and the making of mechanical instruments. He began to teach mathematics in Sunday schools when he was twenty, and about the same time to assist with classes at the Mechanics' Institute. In 1839, on the occasion of a machinery and art exhibition at Birmingham, he was selected to explain to the public the working of some of the machines.

Deeply moved in youth by the aspirations which produced the Owenite and Chartist movements, Holyoake joined the Birmingham reform league at the age of fourteen (1831), and became a Chartist a year later. In 1837 he attended meetings addressed by Robert Owen [q.v.]. In 1838 he delivered his first lecture on socialism and co-operation and enrolled himself a member of the Owenite 'Association of all Classes of all Nations.' He was present at the great Chartist riots, known as the Bull Ring riots, at Birmingham on 15 July 1839.

Holyoake had been brought up in the strictest evangelical tenets, which his mother firmly held, but his association with liberal movements broadened his beliefs. Abandoning the life of a workman, he accepted in 1840 an invitation from the Owenites of Worcester to minister for them at their hall of science. These halls, which were springing up in many towns, were centres of educational and propagandist work. Under such influences Holyoake's beliefs rapidly grew rationalistic. Next year, on the invitation of the congress of the Universal Community Society of Rational Religionists, he went to Sheffield to lecture and conduct a school. In 1841 he was one of the editors of 'The Oracle of Reason' (published at Bristol), and when a colleague, Charles Southwell, was imprisoned next year for blasphemy, Holyoake continued the paper, and, being compelled to examine the evidences of Christianity with some thoroughness, finally rejected them altogether. On 24 May 1842, in the course of a walk from Birmingham to Bristol, where Southwell was in prison, he lectured at the Mechanics' Institution, Cheltenham, and in reply to a question by an auditor made flippant reference to the deity. Arrested on a charge of blasphemy on 1 June, he was committed by the magistrates for trial at the Gloucester Assizes, and on declining to swear to his own recognisances, was refused bail. He was tried at the Gloucester Assizes on 15 Aug. 1842, before Justice Thomas Erskine [q. v.], on a charge of blasphemy at common law, and after defending himself in a nine hours' speech, was convicted and sentenced to six months' imprisonment. A report of the trial was published in the same year, and in 1851 Holyoake, in 'The History of the Last Trial by Jury for Atheism in England,' appealed to the attorney-general and the clergy for some change in the law. But no alteration was made, and several trials on the like charge have taken place since (cf. J. F. Stephen, *Hist. of Criminal Law*, ii. 473–6).

On his release from prison Holyoake came to London, and, opening a shop for the sale of advanced literature, continued his varied propaganda. He was secretary of the anti-persecution union, which demanded freedom of theological thought and speech. He was editor of 'The Movement' (1843), a republican and radical journal. But practical social reform also occupied his mind. Supporting the principle of co-operative production and distribution, he presided at the opening of the Toad Lane store at Rochdale in 1845. To his enthusiasm the spread of the co-operative idea owed much. During 1845 he was in Glasgow as lecturer again to a body of Owenites. But he soon returned to London, and started the 'Reasoner' on 3 June 1846. This was the most sustained of the many journals which he conducted. It was followed in 1850 by the 'Leader.'

Drifting away both from Owenism and

from the anti-Christian propaganda of his early years, he defined his developing religious views by the word 'secularism,' which he invented and first used in the 'Reasoner' (10 Dec. 1846). He fully explained his position in 'Secularism, the Practical Philosophy of the People,' a pamphlet published in 1854. His religious development led to differences with Charles Bradlaugh and other associates who remained avowed atheists, and Holyoake defended his opinions in public debates with them and their supporters. Meanwhile he was steadfast in his advocacy of the freedom of the press, of abolition of the Christian oath, and of republican radicalism, the political creed which he adopted on the death of Chartism. A presentation of 250*l.* from sympathisers in 1853 enabled him to start in business as a bookseller and publisher at 147 Fleet Street, and his shop became the headquarters of his agitation. There he with especial boldness defied the law for taxing newspapers. For publishing without stamps in 1854 the 'War Chronicle' and 'War Fly Sheets,' journals denouncing the Crimean war, he was summoned before the court of the exchequer (31 Jan. 1855). The fines he had incurred amounted to 600,000*l.* But the prosecution was abandoned, for the Newspaper Stamp Act was repealed during the year. Holyoake continued the agitation for the abolition of the remaining duties on paper, which were removed in 1861. He strenuously advocated extension of the franchise, and defended the ballot in a pamphlet against John Stuart Mill (1868). In July 1866 he played a prominent part in the demand for electoral reform which led to the Hyde Park riot, and in later life he was active in the effort to pass the affirmation bill which finally became law in 1888.

Holyoake did not confine his energies to home questions. He was acting secretary to the British legion sent out to Garibaldi in 1863, and he twice travelled in the United States and Canada with a view to studying problems of colonisation. The second visit was paid in 1882. Meanwhile failing health and eyesight reduced Holyoake's activities. In 1874 he received an annuity by public subscription. He still wrote copiously for the press, starting in 1876 a new periodical, 'The Secular Review.' To the end he was persistent in his support of the co-operative movement, and he sympathised with the co-partnership development which deprecated the mere pursuit of dividends. He recognised that distributing stores was not the fulfilment of the Rochdale purpose, and advocated co-operative production through the self-governing workshop. In his last years he removed to Brighton and was president of the Liberal Association there. He thrice tried to enter parliament—in 1857, when he issued an address to the electors of Tower Hamlets; in 1868, when he offered himself as candidate for Birmingham; and in 1884, when he addressed the Liberal Association of Leicester on the death of Peter Alfred Taylor [q. v.]. But on no occasion did he go to the poll, and after the Leicester failure he published a pamphlet setting out how handicapped a poor man was in public life. It was at his suggestion, made in 1866 to Lord John Manners, first commissioner of works, that the limelight was placed over the clock tower at Westminster at night to denote that parliament was sitting.

Holyoake died at Brighton on 22 Jan. 1906, and after cremation at Golder's Green his ashes were buried in Highgate cemetery. He was twice married: (1) on 10 March 1839 to Eleanor Williams, daughter of a soldier, by whom he had four sons and three daughters (she died at Brighton in January 1884); (2) in 1886 to Mrs. Jane Pearson.

His chief works were: 'A History of Cooperation in England' (1875–7; revised edit. 1906); 'Self-Help by the People,' a history of the Rochdale Pioneers (1855; 10th edit. 1893), and biographies of Richard Carlile (1848), Tom Paine (1851), Robert Owen (1859; 3rd edit. 1866), John Stuart Mill (1873), and Joseph Rayner Stephens (1881). Among other of his numerous writings, which included many controversial pamphlets and educational manuals, are: 1. 'Handbook of Grammar,' 12mo, 1846. 2. 'Paley refuted in his own Words,' 1847. 3. 'Mathematics no Mystery,' 1848. 4. 'Rudiments of Public Speaking and Debate,' 1849 (repeatedly revised and republished). 5. 'The Logic of Death,' 1851; 101st edit. 1902; German translation 1865. 6. 'History of Fleet Street House,' 1856. 7. 'The Trial of Theism,' 1858; new edit. 1877. 8. 'Principles of Secularism,' 1859. 9. 'Outlaws of Free Thought,' 1861. 10. 'Travels in Search of a Settlers' Guide Book of America and Canada,' 1884. 11. 'The Co-operative Movement To-day,' 1891. 12. 'Sixty Years of an Agitator's Life,' 2 vols. 1892; 3rd edit. 1893. 13. 'Origin and Nature of Secularism,' 1896. 14. 'Bygones Worth Remembering,' 1905. He wrote in this Dictionary on Richard Carlile and Henry Hetherington, with whose careers he was associated.

A portrait by a nephew, Rowland Holyoake, is in possession of the Rationalist Press Association, and a replica is in the National Liberal Club. A pen portrait by Mr. Walter Sickert belongs to Mr. Fisher Unwin.

[Holyoake's autobiographical works, cited above; MacCabe's Life and Letters of Holyoake, 2 vols. 1908; George Jacob Holyoake: a bibliography by C. W. F. Goss, 1908; Life of Charles Bradlaugh, by his daughter, Mrs. Bonner (1894); Holyoake's 'Warpath of Opinion' [1896] correcting misstatements regarding his career in Mrs. Bonner's Life of Bradlaugh and in W. J. Linton's Memories (1895).] J. R. M.

HOOD, ARTHUR WILLIAM ACLAND, first Baron Hood of Avalon (1824–1901), admiral, born at Bath on 14 July 1824, was second son of Sir Alexander Hood, second baronet (1793–1851), by his wife Amelia Annie, youngest daughter and co-heiress of Sir Hugh Bateman, baronet. Alexander Hood (1758–98) [q. v.] was his grandfather. Entering the navy in 1836, he saw early service on the north coast of Spain, and afterwards on the coast of Syria and at the reduction of Acre. In January 1846 he was promoted to be lieutenant of the President, on the Cape station, from which he was paid off in 1849. In 1850 he was appointed to the Arethusa, with captain (afterwards Sir Thomas M. C.) Symonds [q. v.], and in the Channel, Mediterranean, Black Sea, and in the Crimea in front of Sevastopol, remained attached to her for nearly five years. On 27 Nov. 1854 he was promoted to be commander, especially for service with the naval brigade, and in 1856 went out to China in command of the Acorn brig. In her or her boats he was engaged at Fatshan on 1 June 1857, and at the capture of Canton on 27–28 Dec. 1857, for which he received his promotion to the rank of captain, 26 Feb. 1858. After nearly five years on shore he was appointed in December 1862 to the Pylades, for the North American station, from which in the autumn of 1866 he was ordered home to take command of the Excellent and the Royal Naval College at Portsmouth. This may be described as to a great extent the turning-point in his service, leading him to settle down almost entirely as an administrator. The Excellent was, and is, the school of scientific gunnery, and after three years in her Hood was appointed director of naval ordnance. Here he remained for five years; a careful, painstaking officer, though without the genius that was much needed in a period of great change, and clinging by temperament to the ideas of the past, when they had ceased to be suitable. In May 1871 he was nominated a C.B.; and in 1874, as he still wanted some sea time to qualify him for his flag, he was appointed to the Monarch in the Channel fleet. In March 1876 he became rear-admiral, and from January 1877 to December 1879 was a lord commissioner of the admiralty. He was then appointed to the command of the Channel fleet, which he held till April 1882, becoming vice-admiral in July 1880. In June 1885 he was named as first sea lord of the admiralty in succession to Sir Astley Cooper Key [q. v.], being promoted to the rank of admiral on 1 July 1885, and nominated K.C.B. in the December following. The four years which followed were years of great change and great advance, but it was commonly supposed that Hood's efforts were mainly devoted to preventing the advance from becoming too rapid. Like his predecessor, he scarcely understood the essential needs of England as a great naval power; and several of his public declarations might be thought equivalent to an expression of belief that, useful as the navy was, the country could get on very well without it. On 11 July 1889, having attained the age limit of sixty-five, he was placed on the retired list, and at the same time resigned his seat at the admiralty. He continued, however, to take an active interest in naval affairs, and showed, in occasional letters in 'The Times' and elsewhere, a more correct appreciation of the problems of naval supremacy than he was supposed to have done during his official life.

In September 1889 he was nominated G.C.B., and in February 1892 was raised to the peerage as Lord Hood of Avalon. He died at Wooten House, Glastonbury, the residence of his nephew, Sir Alexander Hood, fourth baronet, on 16 Nov. 1901. He married in October 1855 Fanny Henrietta, third daughter of Sir Charles Fitzroy Maclean; she survived him with two daughters.

[Royal Navy Lists; The Times, 18 Nov. 1901; Burke's Peerage; Clowes, Royal Navy, vol. vii. 1903.] J. K. L.

HOOK, JAMES CLARKE (1819–1907), painter, born in Northampton Square, Clerkenwell, on 21 Nov. 1819, was eldest son of James Hook, who was at first a draper in London, and after a failure in business became judge of the mixed commission court of Sierra Leone; his mother was Eliza, the second daughter of Dr. Adam Clarke [q. v.], the Bible commentator. After a general education at the North London grammar school in Islington he studied art in London, first at the British Museum, then in the schools of the Royal Academy, to which he was admitted a student in 1836. As a boy he received some advice from Constable and John Jackson. In 1839 he went to Dublin to paint a few portraits. In 1842 he won medals both in the life and in the painting school at the Academy; in 1845 he received the gold medal for historical painting, and in the following year the travelling studentship. He first exhibited at the Academy in 1839, sending 'The Hard Task.' This work was hung at the British Institute from 1844. In the latter year his 'Pamphilus relating his Story' from Boccaccio also appeared at the Academy. From Florence he sent 'Bassanio commenting on the Caskets' to the same exhibition in 1847, and 'Otho IV at Florence' in 1848. The revolution of 1848 drove him from Venice back to England before the end of the year. First settling at Brampton, he afterwards built a house, Tor Villa, on Campden Hill. He continued his devotion to the old-fashioned genre of historical anecdote, scenes from Scott and from romantic literature generally. Among his best-known pictures of this period were: 'The Rescue of the Brides of Venice' (R.A. 1851), 'Othello's description of Desdemona' (R.A. 1852), and 'Isabella of Castile and the Idle Nuns' (R.A. 1853). In 1850 he was elected A.R.A. and in 1860 R.A.

Meanwhile in 1853 Hook had moved to Abinger, in Surrey, and in 1854 he first visited Clovelly. A complete change of subject followed and he began to modify his style, at first betraying some Pre-Raphaelite influences. In his 'A Few Minutes to Wait before Twelve o'clock' (1853) he first turned his attention to English landscape, but he thenceforth confined himself chiefly to the scenery and life on the English coast and in the narrow seas. Such subjects he treated with a vigorous sense of movement and of briny atmosphere which was as far removed as possible from studies like 'Bassanio and the Caskets.' He was, in short, converted to the faith of Constable, and devoted the rest of his life to the honest painting of the sea and of nature as he saw it. His development roused the enthusiasm of Ruskin, who deemed his feeling superior to his execution, however. His general reputation was made in 1859 by his 'Luff, Boy!' Among other well-known works of his later period are: 'The Fisherman's Goodnight' (1856); 'A Signal on the Horizon' (1857); 'The Coast Boy gathering Eggs' (1858); 'The Trawlers' (1862); 'Fish from the Dogger Bank' (1870); 'The Samphire Gatherer' (1875); 'The Broken Oar' (1886); 'Breadwinners of the North' (1896); and 'The Stream' (1885, bought by the Chantrey bequest and now in the Tate Gallery). Hook is also represented there by 'Home with the Tide' (1880), 'Young Dreams' (1887), 'The Seaweed Raker' (1889), and 'Wreckage from the Fruiter' (presented in 1908). He painted a few portraits, the best known, perhaps, being one of his son, Allan (1897).

He was through life a strong radical and nonconformist, frequently attending primitive methodist chapels. He died at his house, Silverbeck, Churt, Surrey, which he had built for himself and occupied for forty years, on 14 April 1907, and was buried in Farnham cemetery. His portrait, painted in 1882, in which he resembles a weather-beaten salt, is one of the best works of Sir John Millais, Bart., P.R.A. A portrait by Opie belongs to his son Bryan. A small pencil sketch made by Charles Lear in 1845–6 is in the National Portrait Gallery. In 1891 he painted a portrait of himself for the Uffizi gallery at Florence.

In 1846 he married the third daughter of James Burton, solicitor, and by her had two sons, Allan and Bryan, both artists. His wife predeceased him in 1897. He left gross personalty 112,108*l.* and 96,901*l.* net.

Hook's art during his first period was in no way distinguished above that of other practitioners of a genre now obsolete, but his maritime pictures have a force and character of their own which will never fail to exercise a certain charm. Many of his works were exhibited at the winter exhibition of the Royal Academy in 1908.

[Men of the Time; The Times, 16 and 19 April, 6 and 21 May 1907; Graves, Royal Acad. and Brit. Inst. Exhibitors; Ruskin, Academy Notes, ed. Wedderburn and Cook, 1904; D. G. Rossetti, Letters to W. Allingham, 285–7; private information.] W. A.

HOOKER, Sir JOSEPH DALTON (1817–1911), botanist and traveller, younger son of Sir William Jackson Hooker [q. v.] and his wife Maria, eldest daughter of Dawson Turner, F.R.S. [q. v.], was born at Halesworth, Suffolk, on 30 June 1817. At Glasgow he received in the high school the old-fashioned Scottish liberal education which enabled him afterwards to write Latin with facility. In the university, where his father was regius professor of botany, Lord Kelvin [q. v. Suppl. II] and Lord Sandford [q. v.] were fellow-students and remained lifelong friends; he studied moral philosophy, which he thought in after life had been of little service to him. Devoting himself mainly to medicine, he graduated M.D. in 1839.

Hooker imbibed from his father a passion for botanical research, and from his youth was inspired with a keen desire to indulge it by foreign travel. This was first gratified when Sir James Clark Ross [q. v.], a friend of his father, offered to take him, if he qualified in time, nominally as assistant surgeon, but actually as naturalist, on his own ship, the Erebus, on the Antarctic expedition. Thus Hooker, like Darwin and Huxley, 'began his scientific career on board one of Her Majesty's ships.' The filiation of Hooker's life-work to that of Darwin had an accidental origin. Charles Lyell of Kinnordy, father of Sir Charles Lyell [q. v.], had lent Hooker the proof-sheets of Darwin's 'Journal.' He was hurrying on with his studies and slept with them under his pillow to read at daybreak. They impressed him 'despairingly with the variety of acquirements, mental and physical, required in a naturalist who should follow in Darwin's footsteps.' He was casually introduced to Darwin in Trafalgar Square, and Lyell sent him a published copy of the 'Journal' on the eve of his departure.

The Erebus sailed from Chatham on 29 Sept. 1839. Besides magnetic survey the collection of 'various objects of natural history' was 'enjoined to the officers.' There were three breaks in the voyage during southern winters, in Tasmania, New Zealand, and the Falklands, and these afforded Hooker ample opportunity for collecting.

On the return of the expedition in 1843 Hooker at once commenced the publication of the botanical results. They fill six quarto volumes (1844–60), with 2214 pages and 528 plates; two are devoted to the flora of the Antarctic Islands ('Flora Antarctica,' 1844–7), two to that of New Zealand (1852–4), and two of Tasmania (1855–60). The treasury made a grant of 1000*l.* to be expended on the plates. But beyond an honorarium of 350*l.* from each of the two colonies he received no remuneration.

Darwin had through the elder Lyell read the letters sent home by Hooker, and began a lifelong correspondence by warmly congratulating him on his return in December 1843. The intercourse of the two for the next fifteen years is a memorable page in scientific history. The permanence of species was substantially the belief with which Darwin, Hooker, and Huxley started on their expeditions. Fossil remains in South America convinced Darwin that the present inhabitants of a given area though similar were not identical with their predecessors in the past; there had been an evolution in time. The animals and plants (worked out by Hooker in 1845–6) of the Galapagos, though related, differed in each island; the inevitable conclusion was that there had been an evolution in space. Species were clearly not permanent; and an explanation was needed. Hooker found that identical species occurred in islands 'separated by 3000 miles of ocean'; was it to be concluded, as Agassiz thought, that species had multiple origins?

On 14 Jan. 1844 Darwin wrote to Hooker, 'I think I have found out the simple way by which species become exquisitely adapted to various ends.' This was natural selection; Hooker was the first to whom the theory was confided, and he read at the same time the first sketch of the 'Origin' (printed in 1909 by Mr. Francis Darwin). The confidence proved afterwards of no small importance. During the next fourteen years in which Darwin was occupied in elaborating his theory, he was almost in continuous correspondence with Hooker with regard to its details. 'The intimacy,' which began in 1843, 'ripened [on Hooker's side] into feelings as near to those of reverence for [Darwin's] life, work and character as is reasonable and proper' (*L. L.* ii. 20). Darwin for his part could write to him in 1862: 'For years I have looked to you as the man whose opinion I have valued more on any scientific subject than anyone else in the world' (*M. L.* ii. 284). Writing to Lyell in 1866, Darwin said: 'his [Hooker's] mind is so acute and critical that I always expect to hear a torrent of objections to anything proposed; but he is so candid that he often comes round in a year or two' (*M. L.* ii. 138).

Darwin and Hooker were both ultimately inspired by Lyell. Darwin's problem was how species originate; Hooker's how they are distributed over the surface of the earth. If they worked on parallel lines, they mutually re-acted on one another, and Darwin saw clearly that the distribution problem was an essential feature in any evolutionary theory. Writing to Hooker in 1845, he said, 'I know I shall live to see you the first authority in Europe on that grand subject, that almost keystone of the laws of creation, geographical distribution' (*L. L.* i. 336).

In his 'Flora Antarctica' Hooker rejected emphatically the theory of 'multiple origins,' the supposition that the same species may have originated in more than one area. Darwin thought their occurrence in widely separated islands was explained by physical means of transport, and the present trend of opinion is on his side. Hooker told him that following Edward Forbes [q. v.] he was driven to 'the necessity of assuming the destruction of considerable areas of land to account for it' (*L. L.* ii. 20). This was the view adopted in the 'New Zealand Flora' in 1854.

In 1845 Hooker was a candidate, with the support of Humboldt and Robert Brown [q. v.], for the chair of botany at Edinburgh, but was unsuccessful. Immediately afterwards he was appointed botanist to the Geological Survey. His work in a new field was brilliant; in papers published in 1845 he threw light on the structure of *Stigmaria* and *Lepidostrobus*, and in 1852 explained *Trigonocarpon*. He did no further work in fossil botany after 1855.

Hooker wrote to Darwin in 1854, 'from my earliest childhood I nourished and cherished the desire to make a creditable journey in a new country' (*M. L.* i. 70). This was gratified in 1847 (in which year he was elected F.R.S.), when Lord Carlisle, then chief commissioner of woods and forests, obtained for him a grant of 400*l.* wherewith to explore for two years the central and eastern Himalaya. The earl of Auckland wished this to be followed by a visit to Labuan, for which he received a commission in the navy. But this part of the scheme fell through with Lord Auckland's death in 1849. The admiralty sent him out to Egypt in H.M.S. Sidon with Lord Dalhousie, who attached him to his suite. Part of 1848 and 1849 was spent in exploring Sikkim, where he was the guest of Brian Hodgson [q. v.]. In the latter year he was joined by Dr. Campbell, the government agent, and owing to some intrigue in the Sikkim court they were both temporarily imprisoned. He was able to explore part of Eastern Nepal, in which no traveller has since succeeded in following him. He surveyed single-handed the passes into Tibet, and the Lhasa expedition in 1903 sent him a telegram from Khambajong congratulating him on the usefulness of his survey. His observations on the geology and meteorology of Sikkim are still fundamental, and he explained the terracing of mountain valleys by the formation of glacial lakes. He succeeded in introducing into cultivation through Kew the splendid rhododendrons of Sikkim, which were worthily illustrated from his drawings in a work edited by his father (1849–51) and published during his absence. Hooker spent 1850 in travelling with Thomas Thomson (1817–1878) [q. v.] in Eastern Bengal and the Khasia Hills. They returned to England together in 1851. The result of the expedition was a collection of plants representing 6000 to 7000 species. The treasury gave him a grant of 400*l.* per annum for three years to name these and distribute the duplicates (sixty herbaria were recipients), and to write the 'Himalayan Journals' (1854; 2nd edit. 1855), which have become a classic. In 1855 he published 'Illustrations of Sikkim-Himalayan Plants,' including *Hodgsonia*, the gigantic cucurbit dedicated to his friend Hodgson.

In 1855 Hooker was appointed assistant director at Kew, and with Thomson published his first volume of a 'Flora Indica,' which, planned on too large a scale, did not proceed further. It was prefaced by an introductory essay on the geographical relations of the flora which has never been superseded. The authors regard species as 'definite creations' (p. 20). But both Darwin and Hooker were always in agreement that species for purposes of classification must be accepted as facts, whatever view be taken as to their origin. Huxley, however, thought Hooker in the following year '*capable de tout* in the way of advocating evolution' (*L. L.* ii. 196).

In 1858 an event happened which Darwin's friends had long anticipated. On 15 June Darwin received from Dr. Alfred Russel Wallace, who was then in the Celebes Islands, an essay which substantially embodied his own theory. The position became tragic, for on 29 June Darwin was prostrate with illness; scarlet fever was raging in his family and an infant son had died of it the day before. Lyell and Hooker acted for him; an extract from an abstract of the theory shown by Darwin to Hooker and read by the latter in 1844 was communicated with Wallace's essay to a meeting of the Linnean Society on 1 July 1858. Darwin's 'Origin' itself appeared in Nov. 1859. Four months earlier Hooker published his 'Introductory Essay on the Flora of Tasmania,' by far the most noteworthy of his speculative writings. In this he frankly adopts, in view of the Darwin-Wallace theory, the hypothesis 'that species are derivative and mutable.' The essay is in other respects remarkable for the first sketch of a rational theory of the geographical distribution of plants, besides giving a masterly analysis of the Australian flora.

In the autumn of 1860 John Washington [q. v.], hydrographer of the navy, invited Hooker to take part in a scientific expedition to Syria. The cedar grove on Lebanon was examined and found to be on an old moraine 4000 feet below the summit, which is no longer covered with perpetual snow. The climate must formerly, therefore, have been colder. Under such conditions he speculated as to the possibility of the Lebanon, Algerian, and Deodar cedars having been parts of continuous forest at a lower level.

In the same year Hooker began with his friend George Bentham [q. v.] the 'Genera Plantarum,' a vast undertaking, the first part of which was issued in 1862, the concluding in 1883. It is written in Latin; it aims at establishing a standard of uniformity in classification; it is based throughout on first-hand study of material; and it is a mine of information for the study of distribution. Reichenbach found in Hooker's work that 'touch of genius which resolves difficult questions of affinity where laborious research has often yielded an uncertain sound.'

In 1862 he contributed to the Linnean Society his classical memoir 'Outlines of the Distribution of Arctic Plants,' in which he worked out in detail 'the continuous current of vegetation which extends from Scandinavia to Tasmania, the greatest continuity of land of the terrestrial sphere.'

In 1865 Hooker's father died. At the time Hooker was himself prostrated with rheumatic fever. He succeeded his father in the directorship at Kew, and for the next twenty years administrative duties of the most varied kind limited seriously the time available for scientific work. At the British Association at Nottingham in 1866 he delivered a lecture on 'Insular Floras.' He described the problem as the *bête noire* of botanists. He frankly abandoned 'sinking imaginary continents,' and found a rational explanation in trans-oceanic migration. In 1867 was completed a 'Handbook of the New Zealand Flora' for the colonial government, and he edited the fourth volume of the 'Illustrations of the Genus Carex' left unfinished on the death of his friend Francis Boott [q. v.].

Hooker in 1868 presided over the British Association at Norwich. After the lapse of ten years he found 'natural selection an accepted doctrine with almost every philosophical naturalist.' He discussed Darwin's later theory of pangenesis which, at the time received with little favour, is now thought, as Hooker considered possible, 'to contain the rationale of all the phenomena of reproduction and inheritance.' In 1869 he attended at the instance of the government the International Botanical Congress at St. Petersburg.

In 1870 he produced his 'Student's Flora of the British Islands' (3rd edit. 1884). He had pointed out in 1853 that he knew of no 'Flora' 'which attempts to give a general view of the variation and distribution of the species described in it.' He now showed how this should be done.

An expedition to Morocco occupied April to June of 1871 in company with John Ball (1818–1889) [q. v.] and George Maw as geologist. The main object was to explore the Great Atlas. The highest point reached was the Tagherot Pass (11,843 feet), the first time by any European; descent into the Sous Valley was forbidden. An important result was the discovery that the Arctic-Alpine flora did not reach the Atlas. The interesting fact was observed that the practice of sacrificing animals as a propitiatory rite survived amongst the Berbers, and the travellers were themselves on one occasion the object of it. Hooker was unable to write more than a portion of the published 'Journal,' which was completed by Ball in 1878.

In 1850 Kew had passed from the generous control of the woods and forests to the less sympathetic of the office of works. In 1872 Hooker had what have been euphemistically described as 'protracted differences' with Acton Smee Ayrton [q. v. Suppl. I], the first commissioner. The scientific world saw clearly that the underlying question was the degradation of Kew to a mere pleasure garden. The differences were not settled without debates in both houses of parliament. Public opinion declared itself on Hooker's side. Gladstone transferred Ayrton in August 1873 to another office, and the electorate dismissed him in 1874 from political life.

In 1873 the Royal Society elected Hooker president, with Huxley as joint secretary. Hooker's policy was to bring the society more into touch with the social life of the community. The ladies' soirée was instituted. On the other hand the privilege of election without selection was taken away from peers and restricted to privy councillors. In 1876 the Challenger returned from the voyage round the world 'originated' by the Royal Society and 'crowned with complete success.' In 1872 Hooker had drawn up for Henry Nottidge Moseley [q. v.] suggestions as to what could be done in the way of botanical collecting. Hooker was chairman of the committee of publication of the Reports (1876–95);

fifty volumes were produced, the work of seventy-five authors, at an expenditure from public funds of some 50,000*l*. In 1878 Hooker laid down his office in a valedictory address. He was able to make one announcement which gave him peculiar pleasure. The Royal Society has little endowment, and the fees 'occasionally prevented men of great merit from having their names brought forward as candidates.' To allow of their reduction Hooker almost single-handed raised amongst his personal friends a sum of 10,000*l*.

This was in other ways a period of intense activity. In 1874 Hooker presided over the department of zoology and botany of the British Association at Belfast. He chose as the subject of his address 'The carnivorous habits of some of our brother organisms—plants.' In such cases he showed that vegetable protoplasm is capable of availing itself of food such as that by which the protoplasm of animals is nourished. In 1877, at the close of the session of the Royal Society, Hooker obtained an extended leave of absence to accept an invitation from Dr. Hayden, geologist in charge of the United States Geological and Geographical Survey of the Territories, 'to visit under his conduct the rocky mountains of Colorado and Utah, with the object of contributing to the records of the survey a report on the botany of those states.' Professor Asa Gray and Sir Richard Strachey [q.v. Suppl. II] were also members of the party. Hooker's report was published by the American government in 1881. His general conclusion was that the miocene flora had been exterminated in western North America by glaciation, but had been able to persist on the eastern side and in eastern Asia. In 1879 he returned to Antarctic botany, and rediscussed the flora of Kerguelen's Land as the result of the transit of Venus expedition in 1874. Its Fuegian affinities were confirmed though 4000 miles distant. He was more disposed to admit transoceanic migration, though still inclined to a former land-connection. In 1881 Hooker made geographical distribution the subject of his address as president of the geographical section at the jubilee meeting of the British Association at York.

With the completion of the 'Genera Plantarum' in 1883 Hooker was able to make a determined attack on his 'Flora of British India,' commenced with the collaboration of other botanists in 1855. This was completed in seven volumes in 1897; the number of species actually described approaching 17,000. The last four volumes were almost wholly from his own hand; the *Orchideæ* alone occupied him for two years.

His health began to fail, and under medical advice he retired from the directorship of Kew in 1885 to a house which he had built for himself at Sunningdale. While relieved of official cares he was able to continue his scientific work at Kew with renewed strength.

Shortly before his death Darwin had expressed a wish to aid 'in some way the scientific work carried on at Kew.' This took the shape of the 'Index Kewensis,' a catalogue of all published names of plants with bibliographical references and their native countries. The preparation entrusted to Mr. Daydon Jackson in 1882 occupied him for ten years; the printing took from 1892 to 1895, during which time Hooker imposed on himself the laborious task of revising the whole.

In 1896 Hooker edited the 'Journal' of Sir Joseph Banks during Cook's first voyage from a transcript in the British Museum made by his aunts, Dawson Turner's daughters; the original manuscript is now in the Mitchell Library at Sydney. Hooker next occupied himself (1898–1900) with the completion of Trimen's 'Handbook of the Flora of Ceylon.' In the 'Imperial Gazetteer of India' (1907) he gave his final conclusions on the Indian flora, published in advance in 1904. His last literary effort was 'a sketch of the life and labours' of his father (*Ann. of Bot.* 1902).

Hooker's position in the history of botanical science will rest in the main on his work in geographical distribution. His reputation has amply fulfilled Darwin's early prophecy. It is difficult to say whether it is more remarkable for his contributions to its theory or to its data. De Candolle's classical work, 'Géographie Botanique raisonnée,' published in 1855, raised problems which he left unanswered; Hooker solved them. As Asa Gray has justly said: 'De Candolle's great work closed one epoch in the history of the subject, and Hooker's name is the first that appears in the ensuing one.' As a systematist, his works exhibit a keen appreciation of affinity and a consistent aim at a uniform standard of generic and specific definition. As with his predecessor Robert Brown [q. v.], this was accompanied by great morphological insight. It was exhibited in his early palæontological work and in numerous studies of remarkable plants throughout life. His explanation of the origin of the pitcher in *Nepenthes* is substantially accepted. In 1863 he produced his great paper on the South African *Welwitschia,* which Darwin thought 'a vegetable ornithorhynchus' and Asa Gray 'the most wonderful discovery, in a botanical point of view,' of the century. In his last years he found recreation in studying the copious material which the exploration of Eastern Asia supplied in the genus *Impatiens* (balsams). They were the subject of thirteen papers, the last only appearing shortly after his death. Beginning with 135 species in 1862, he finally was able to recognise some 500.

The eminence of his work received general recognition. He received honorary degrees from Oxford, Cambridge, Dublin, Edinburgh and Glasgow. He was created C.B. in 1869; K.C.S.I. in 1877; G.C.S.I. in 1897; in 1907 the Order of Merit was personally presented to him at Sunningdale on behalf of King Edward VII on his ninetieth birthday, and he had the Prussian *pour le mérite*. From the Royal Society he received a royal medal in 1854, the Copley in 1887, and the Darwin in 1892; from the Society of Arts the Albert medal in 1883; from the Geographical their Founder's medal in 1884, and from the Manchester Philosophical its medal in 1898; from the Linnean in 1888, one specially struck on the completion of the 'Flora of British India' in 1898, and that struck on the occasion of the Darwin celebration in 1908; in 1907 he was the sole recipient from the Royal Swedish Academy of the medal to commemorate the bicentenary of the birth of Linnæus. He was one of the eight *associés étrangers* of the French Académie des Sciences, and member of other scientific societies throughout the world.

Hooker was five feet eleven inches in height and spare and wiry in figure. There are portraits by George Richmond (1855) in the possession of his son C. P. Hooker, by the Hon. John Collier at the Royal Society, and by Sir Hubert von Herkomer at the Linnean, and a bronze medallion modelled from life by Frank Bowcher for the same society. He possessed great powers of physical endurance, and could work continuously with a small amount of sleep. In temperament he was nervous and high-strung; he disliked public speaking, though when put to it he could speak with a natural dignity and some eloquence. He completely outlived some heart trouble in middle life (doubtless of rheumatic origin). His mental powers retained unabated vigour and activity until the end. The summer of 1911 enfeebled him. What seemed a temporary illness compelled him at last to remain in bed. He passed away unexpectedly in his sleep at midnight at his house at Sunningdale on 10 Dec. 1911.

The dean and chapter of Westminster offered with public approval the honour of burial in the Abbey, where it would have been fitting that his ashes should be placed near Darwin. But at his own expressed wish he was interred at Kew, the scene of his labours.

Hooker was twice married: (1) in 1851 to Frances Harriet (*d.* 1874), eldest daughter of John Stevens Henslow [q. v.], by whom he left four sons and two surviving daughters; (2) in 1876 to Hyacinth, only daughter of William Samuel Symonds [q. v.], and widow of Sir William Jardine, seventh baronet [q. v.], by whom he left two sons.

[Personal knowledge; Gardeners' Chronicle, 16 Dec. 1911 to 30 Jan. 1912; Kew Bulletin, 1912, pp. 1–34 (with bibliography); Life and Letters of Charles Darwin, 3 vols. 1887 (cited as L.L.), and More Letters of Charles Darwin, 2 vols. 1903 (M.L.).] W. T. T-D.

HOPE, JOHN ADRIAN LOUIS, seventh Earl of Hopetoun and first Marquis of Linlithgow (1860–1908), first governor-general of the commonwealth of Australia, born at Hopetoun on 25 Sept. 1860, was eldest son of John Alexander Hope, sixth earl of Hopetoun, by his wife Ethelred Ann, daughter of Charles Thomas Samuel Birch-Reynardson of Holywell-hall, Lincolnshire. He succeeded to the earldom in 1873 and was educated at Eton. After leaving school he travelled in the East and in America Hopetoun, who identified himself with the conservative party, was a lord-in-waiting to Queen Victoria in Lord Salisbury's first and second administrations (1885–6 and 1886–9). At the same time he took a strong interest in Scottish affairs. He became deputy-lieutenant of the counties of Linlithgow, Lanark, Haddington and Dumfries. From 1887 to 1889 he acted as high commissioner to the general assembly of the Church of Scotland, and discharged his duties with ease and hospitality.

In spite of physical weakness and strong attachment to domestic life and sport, Hopetoun's public career was mainly spent in appointments overseas. In September 1889 he became governor of Victoria, Australia, receiving at the same time the honour of G.C.M.G. He was in office during the financial crisis, due to excessive speculation in lands, which began in 1891, attained formidable proportions in 1892, when the government sanctioned a *moratorium* of five days to enable the banks to collect their resources, and reached its height in the following year. Hopetoun handled with discretion the ministerial reconstructions which were necessitated by popular discontent. He also generously acquiesced in the reduction of his salary from 10,000*l.* to 7000*l.* A further proposal for its reduction to 5000*l.* was rescinded by the government after it had been carried in the assembly. Hopetoun's accessibility and keen interest in horse-racing and other forms of sport admirably fitted him for his post. In March 1895 his term of office came to an end.

On his return home he was paymaster-general in Lord Salisbury's third administration from 1895 to 1898, when he succeeded the earl of Lathom as lord chamberlain. In 1895, too, he stood as unionist candidate for the lord rectorship of Glasgow University, but was defeated by Mr. Asquith. In the same year Hopetoun, who had always shown a keen interest in all that concerned ships and sailors, was elected president of the Institution of Naval Architects in succession to Lord Brassey, who had taken his place in Victoria, and in 1896 he accompanied the members on a visit to Germany. He discharged his arduous duties with tact and success for five years, presiding over the International Congress of Naval Architects, opened in London by King Edward VII (when Prince of Wales) in 1897.

On the creation of the commonwealth of Australia Hopetoun seemed indicated by colonial opinion as the first governor-general, and the office was conferred on him in August 1900. He was made Knight of the Thistle and G.C.V.O. On his way out he visited India, where he had a severe attack of typhoid fever. Landing at Sydney, where he was received with great enthusiasm, on 16 Dec. 1900, he invited Sir William Lyne, the premier of New South Wales, to form the first federal ministry, and on his failure he had recourse to (Sir) Edmund Barton, also of New South Wales. On 1 Jan. 1901 he represented the queen-empress at the inauguration of the Australian commonwealth, and at the opening of the federal parliament by King George V (when Duke of Cornwall and York) on 7 May, he delivered an address, declaring that a common tariff, which 'must operate protectively as well as for the production of revenue,' would be the first work of the new parliament. His hospitality and felicity of speech largely contributed to the success of the royal tour (Sir Donald Mackenzie Wallace, *The Web of Empire*, 1902). The governor-general travelled freely from state to state, placing himself in touch with the various interests. His relations with his ministers were harmonious, though he hesitated long over the alien immigration restriction bill, passed to carry into effect the 'white Australia' feeling, and did not give it his consent until December 1901.

Hopetoun had pointed out from the first that his salary of 10,000*l.* was insufficient for his position. But an attempt to supplement it by contributions from the states failed and a bill for its increase was rejected on 1 May 1902. Consequently Hopetoun asked for his recall by the imperial government, and his resignation was announced in the senate on 14 May 1902 to the general surprise and regret. On 17 July he left Australia amid demonstrations of popular sympathy. On his return home Hopetoun was created marquis of Linlithgow on 27 Oct. 1902.

For some time after his recall Linlithgow took little part in public life, but on 3 Feb. 1905 he became secretary of state for Scotland in Mr. Balfour's administration, and held office until the resignation of the government in the following December. Two years before, the price (122,500*l.*) at which he had sold Rosyth to the government, for the purpose of constructing a naval base, received unfavourable criticism; but the ministerial defence was that the amount was little above the valuation, and that the difference would have gone in costs if recourse had been had to compulsory purchase after arbitration (*Hansard*, 4th series, vol. cxxiv. cols. 1266–1282, and vol. cxxv. col. 695).

Linlithgow died at Pau, after a year's illness, on 29 Feb. 1908. As became an ardent Scotsman, Linlithgow was brigadier-general of the Royal Company of Archers and served in the Lanarkshire yeomanry. He rode vigorously but unluckily to hounds, and kept both harriers and beagles.

He married in 1886 Hersey Alice, third daughter of Dayrolles Blakeney Eveleigh-de-Moleyns, fourth Lord Ventry, by whom he had issue two sons and one daughter. He was succeeded by his elder son, Victor Alexander John, eighth earl of Hopetoun, born in 1887.

His portrait, by Robert Brough, was presented to him in 1904, after his return from Australia, by Linlithgowshire and the adjoining counties, Lord Rosebery, always a close friend, making the presentation;

it is now at Hopetoun House. Lord Rosebery also, on 5 Oct. 1911, unveiled at Linlithgow a statue of the marquis by Sir George Frampton, R.A. Lord Linlithgow, said Lord Rosebery on that occasion, regarded himself as unequal to high office, but proved himself 'more than adequate' (*The Times*, 6 Oct. 1911). A second statue, by Bernie Rhind, R.S.A., erected in Melbourne, was unveiled by Sir John Fuller, governor of Victoria, on 15 June 1911. A cartoon by 'Spy' appeared in 'Vanity Fair' in 1900.

[The Times, and the Scotsman, 2 March 1908; Transactions of Institution of Naval Architects, 1908.] L. C. S.

HOPE, LAURENCE, pseudonym. [See NICOLSON, MRS. ADELA FLORENCE (1865–1904), poetess.]

HOPETOUN, seventh EARL OF. [See HOPE, JOHN ADRIAN LOUIS (1860–1908), first governor-general of Australia.]

HOPKINS, EDWARD JOHN (1818–1901), organist, born at Westminster on 30 June 1818, was son of George Hopkins (1789–1869), a clarinet player. John Hopkins (1822–1900), organist of Rochester cathedral, and Thomas Hopkins (*d.* 1893), organ builder, were his brothers. Edward Hopkins (1818–1842), organist of Armagh cathedral, and John Larkin Hopkins, Mus.Doc. [q. v.], organist successively of Rochester cathedral (1841–56), and of Cambridge University (1856–73), were his cousins. After serving as a chorister at the Chapel Royal, St. James's, from 1826 to 1834, Hopkins was organist in turn of Mitcham church, Surrey, from 1834, of St. Peter's, Islington, from 1838, and of St. Luke's, Berwick Street, from 1841.

In October 1843 he was elected organist at the Temple church, London, and remained there for fifty-five years. On completing his jubilee in 1893 he received a valuable testimonial from the benchers, and on his retirement in 1898 was made hon. organist. He sang at Westminster Abbey in the choir at the coronation of William IV in 1831 and at Queen Victoria's diamond jubilee celebration in 1897.

He received the honorary degree of Mus.Doc. from the archbishop of Canterbury in 1882, and from the University of Toronto in 1886.

Hopkins was an excellent organist and a fine extemporaneous player. His compositions, though neither numerous nor of large calibre, are always melodious and pleasing. His anthems 'Out of the Deep' and 'God is gone up' won the Gresham prize medals in 1838 and 1840 respectively. His two services in A and F, and many of his chants and hymn tunes, which number 160, have obtained world-wide celebrity.

Hopkins was one of the first to issue a series of elaborate arrangements for the organ. For the services at the Temple church he arranged and edited a 'Book of Responses,' and a collection of chants, all of which were incorporated in the 'Temple Church Choral Service Book' (1867; 2nd edit. 1880) and the 'Temple Psalter' (1883). He also issued a collection of '165 single chants of the 16th, 17th, 18th, and 19th centuries' and 'single chants with additional harmonies for unison use.' His historical prefaces to the Temple service books exhibit much scholarly research. He also edited Purcell's organ music and several volumes for the Musical Antiquarian Society, and contributed many musical articles to the press. As an authority on organ construction Hopkins was without an equal, and standard rank has long been accorded his book, 'The Organ, its History and Construction' (1855; third edit. with Dr. Rimbault, 1877).

Hopkins died on 4 Feb. 1901, and was interred in Hampstead cemetery. He married in 1845 Sarah Lovett, by whom he had four sons and five daughters.

[The Life and Works of Edward John Hopkins, by Dr. C. W. Pearce, 1910; Grove's Dict. of Music; private information.] J. C. B.

HOPKINS, JANE ELLICE (1836–1904), social reformer, born at Cambridge on 30 Oct. 1836, was younger daughter of William Hopkins [q. v.], mathematician and geologist, by his second wife, Caroline Boys.

Educated by her father, she developed a faculty for scientific thinking, combined with poetic insight, humour, and religious fervour. Devoting herself to social reform, she held, when about twenty, large meetings of navvies who were employed in a suburb of Cambridge. A club and institute were built through her efforts. Elihu Burritt, the American writer, attested the power of her addresses in his 'Seed Lives' (1863). In 1865 she published 'English Idylls and other Poems,' dedicated to her father, 'to whom I owe all I am.' After his death in 1866, an incurable illness caused her at intervals acute suffering but failed to affect her spirit. Removing with her mother to Brighton, she wrote 'Active Service' (1872–4) and other pamphlets in aid of Sarah Robinson's

Soldiers' Institute, Portsmouth. After a year abroad, she made, at Freshwater, the acquaintance of Julia Margaret Cameron [q. v.], George Frederick Watts [q.v. Suppl. II], and Charles Tennyson Turner [q.v.]. During 1872 she met James Hinton [q. v.], under whose medical training and at whose request she embarked on her lifework—the endeavour to raise the moral standard of the community, and to secure the legal protection of the young from ill-usage.

At Hinton's death in 1875 she edited his 'Life and Letters,' and for ten years she arduously wrote and lectured through the three kingdoms on the theme of pure living. Engaged on what George Macdonald [q. v. Suppl. II] called her 'great sad work,' she addressed huge meetings of men in Edinburgh, Newcastle, Gateshead, Sunderland, Carlisle, Swansea, Cardiff, Hull, Liverpool, Manchester, and Dublin, and of mill-girls in Halifax. Although personally frail and insignificant, she exerted over her audiences an instantaneous influence by virtue of her beautiful voice, spiritual intensity, and absence of self-consciousness or sentimentality. Among those who aided her work were Bishop Lightfoot, who said she did the work of ten men in the time, and Bishops Wilkinson, Maclagan, and Fraser. Of 'True Manliness,' one of her many pamphlets which appeared anonymously, 300,000 copies were sold in a year. Her efforts led to an amendment in 1880 of the Industrial Schools Act, which rendered the protection of children under sixteen legally possible, and they helped to pass the Criminal Law Amendment Act of 1886.

The aim of her work was preventive while that of Mrs. Josephine Butler [q. v. Suppl. II] was remedial. With Bishop Lightfoot's help she founded the White Cross League in 1886, and saw England and the Colonies dotted over with branches.

In 1888 failure of health compelled her active work to cease. During illness she wrote 'The Power of Womanhood; or Mothers and Sons' (1899), and in 1902 'The Story of Life' (2nd edit. 1903), a book of instruction for the young based on natural history and physiology, of which 7000 copies were sold in a year. She died on 21 August 1904 at Brighton, and was buried there.

Among her other writings are: 1. 'An Englishwoman's Work among Workingmen,' 1875; 4th edit. 1882. 2. 'Rose Turquand,' a novel, 1876. 3. 'Notes on Penitentiary Work,' 1879. 4. 'Christ the Consoler, Comfort for the Sick,' with introduction by the Bishop of Carlisle, 1879; 7th edit. 1904. 5. 'Preventive Work, or the Care of our Girls,' 1881. 6. 'Village Morality,' 1882. 7. 'Legal Protection for the Young,' 1882. 8. 'Grave Moral Questions addressed to the Men and Women of England,' 1882. 9. 'Autumn Swallows, a book of lyrics,' 1883. 10. 'The Present Moral Crisis, 1886. 11. 'Girls' Clubs and Recreative Evening Homes,' 1887.

[Life by Rosa M. Barrett, 1907; The Times, 24 Aug. 1904; Guardian, 31 Aug. 1904.]

C. F. S.

HOPWOOD, CHARLES HENRY (1829–1904), recorder of Liverpool, born at 47 Chancery Lane, London, on 20 July 1829, was fifth son, in a family of eight sons and four daughters, of John Stephen Spindler Hopwood (1795–1868), solicitor, of Chancery Lane, by his wife Mary Ann (1799–1843), daughter of John Toole of Dublin. After education successively at a private school, at King's College School, and at King's College, London, he became a student at the Middle Temple on 2 Nov. 1850, and was called to the bar on 6 June 1853. He joined the northern circuit and obtained a good practice. He took silk in 1874, and was elected a bencher of his Inn in 1876, becoming 'reader' in 1885, and treasurer in 1895. He edited two series of reports of 'Registration Cases'; the first series (1863–7), in which he collaborated with F. A. Philbrick, appeared in 1868, and the second series (1868–72), in which he collaborated with F. J. Coltman, appeared in 1872–9 (2 vols.).

In 1874, and again in 1880, Hopwood was elected member of parliament for Stockport in the liberal interest. He was defeated in the same constituency at the general election in 1885. In 1892 he was elected for the Middleton division of Lancashire and sat till 1895. During Gladstone's short ministry of 1886 Hopwood was appointed recorder of Liverpool.

Throughout his public life Hopwood supported energetically and with singular tenacity and consistency the principle of personal liberty. He was a loyal supporter of radical measures, but at the time of his death he was justly described as 'the last of those liberals who were all for freedom—freedom from being made good or better as well as freedom from worse oppression; freedom from state control; freedom from the tyranny of the multitude, as well as from fussy, meddlesome legislation.' In parliament he opposed unrelentingly the Contagious Diseases Acts and the Vaccination Acts, denying that it was justifiable to curtail the personal liberty of such persons as chose to expose themselves and others to risks of infection. As recorder he discouraged prosecutions for such offences as keeping disorderly houses. Towards the end of his life he spoke with indignation of an Act forbidding —on the ground of public safety—the carrying of pistols without a licence. He was also a constant advocate in the House of Commons of trade unions, and of the reform of the laws then regulating the relation of master and servant. While at the bar he constantly defended trades unionists who were prosecuted for offences against the Conspiracy Acts, and sought to protect the funds of the union from legal distraint. As recorder of Liverpool he made himself the protagonist of the current reaction from greater to less severity in awarding punishment for crime. In his own court he carried the remission of severity to a pitch which his friends could not justify. He claimed that by his substitution of sentences of about three months' imprisonment for sentences of about seven years' penal servitude he greatly diminished crime within his jurisdiction; but in quoting statistics in support of this contention he made no allowance for the facts that the magistrates, disapproving of his intemperance in reform, committed to the assizes many persons who would naturally have been sent for trial to his sessions, and themselves dealt summarily with very many more. He proposed legislation in favour of short sentences, and in 1897 he founded the Romilly Society to reform the criminal law and prison administration. He sought to establish a court of appeal in criminal cases. He was a warm advocate of an extension of the suffrage to all adults, including women.

Hopwood was a man of handsome features and good presence, wore a full black beard, and preserved an almost juvenile complexion to the end of his life. He had the power of attracting the warm personal regard of many of his friends who considered his exaggerated insistence upon his own opinions to be mischievous. He died unmarried at Northwick Lodge, St. John's Wood Road, N.W., on 14 Oct. 1904, and his remains, after cremation at Golder's Green, were buried in a family grave at Kensal Green. A portrait in oils by Jamyn Brooks belongs to Hopwood's younger brother, Canon Hopwood, Louth, Lincolnshire.

Hopwood edited: 1. 'Observations on the Constitution of the Middle Temple,' 1896. 2. 'A Calendar of the Middle Temple Records,' 1903. 3. 'Middle Temple Records,' 1904.

[The Times, 17 and 19 Oct. 1904; Men of the Time, 1898; Foster's Men at the Bar; personal knowledge.]

HORNBY, JAMES JOHN (1826–1909), provost of Eton, born at Winwick, Lancashire, on 18 Dec. 1826, was younger son of Admiral Sir Phipps Hornby [q. v.] by his wife Sophia Maria, daughter of Lieutenant-general John Burgoyne (1722–1792) [q. v.]. Hornby was entered as an oppidan at Eton in 1838, and after a successful career as a scholar and as a cricketer went to Balliol College, Oxford, in 1845, where he enjoyed similar success in the schools and as an athlete. He gained a first class in the final classical school in 1849, and rowed in the Oxford Eight in 1849 and 1851. Graduating B.A. in 1849, in which year he was elected a founder's fellow of Brasenose College, and proceeding M.A. in 1851, he was principal of Bishop Cosin's Hall at Durham University from 1853 to 1864, when he returned to Oxford and took up work at Brasenose as junior bursar. In 1867 he was appointed second master at Winchester, but shortly after was selected for the important post of headmaster of Eton on the resignation of Archdeacon Balston. For several generations the headmaster had been an Eton colleger and scholar of King's College, Cambridge, and at Eton was the subordinate officer of the provost. Since 1861 a royal commission had been engaged in an inquiry into the administration of the great public schools of England with special reference to Eton College. As a result of this commission the whole administration of Eton College was changed, and placed in the hands of a new governing body under new statutes. The old connection between Eton and King's College, Cambridge, was made less binding, and the powers of the provost of Eton were very considerably curtailed. The headmaster's position became one of increased independent authority. In these altered circumstances Hornby entered on his duties as headmaster of Eton early in 1868. The appointment of an oppidan, an Oxonian, and a gentleman of high breeding and aristocratic birth, who had not served his apprenticeship as an Eton master, marked the new era in the history of the school. In accordance with the spirit of the age and the new statutes many reforms were introduced by Hornby into the school curriculum. He was, however, a progressive rather than a radical reformer, with a tendency to become more conservative as years went on. In matters of strict discipline, both with assistant-masters and boys, he did not escape criticism, occasionally hostile in tone, but his innate good-breeding and tact, his courtesy and sympathetic manner, together with a strong sense of genuine humour, enabled him to maintain a personal popularity. In July 1884 Hornby ceased to be head-master on being appointed provost in succession to Charles Old Goodford [q. v.]. He held the dignified and less arduous post of provost until his death at Eton on 2 Nov. 1909. He was buried in the Eton cemetery. He married in 1869 Augusta Eliza, daughter of the Rev. J. C. Evans of Stoke Poges. She died in 1891, leaving three sons and two daughters.

Hornby was of handsome appearance, and retained his bodily vigour throughout life. From 1854 to 1867 he distinguished himself as one of the pioneers of Alpine climbing, and was a member of the Alpine Club from December 1864 until his death. He made many new ascents, which called for the highest physical and mental qualities in a mountaineer. After his appointment to Eton, his athletic feats were chiefly confined to skating, in which he was an accomplished proficient up to the date of his death. Although he did not pretend to any literary gifts, he was an accomplished scholar and an admirable public speaker. Hornby, who proceeded D.D. at Oxford in 1869 and was made hon. D.C.L. of Durham in 1882, was appointed honorary chaplain to Queen Victoria in 1882, and in 1901 to King Edward VII, who made him C.V.O. in 1904. A portrait by the Hon. John Collier is in the provost's lodge at Eton College. A monumental brass to his memory is in the ante-chapel.

[The Times, 3 Nov. 1909; Lyte's History of Eton College; Brasenose College Register, Oxford Hist. Soc., 1909; Eton under Hornby, by O.E. [i.e. H. S. Salt]; Alpine Journal, xxv., No. 187; personal knowledge.]
L. C.

HORNIMAN, FREDERICK JOHN (1835–1906), founder of the Horniman Museum, born at Bridgwater on 8 Oct. 1835, was second son of John Horniman of Bridgwater by his wife Ann, daughter of Thomas Smith of Witney, Oxfordshire. His parents belonged to the Society of Friends and he was educated at the Friends' School, Croydon (founded in 1702). After joining the large tea-packing business founded at Newport, I.W., by his father and moved to Wormwood St., London, 1852 (now W. H. and F. J. Horniman & Co., Limited), he travelled extensively in the east and west, during a period of forty years, collecting objects illustrative of the natural history, arts, and manufactures of the world. These he placed in his private residence, Surrey House, Forest Hill, and first opened the exhibition to the public on 24 Dec. 1890. About 1879 he removed to Surrey Mount adjoining, where he made additions in 1893. On 1 June 1895 the enlarged building, with surrounding grounds of five acres, was freely opened to the public. Horniman compiled a guide for visitors, and employed a curator and librarian as well as a naturalist. The collection and the visitors increased rapidly, and in 1897 Horniman erected at a cost of 40,000*l.* a new and handsome edifice near at hand from the designs of C. Harrison Townsend, F.R.I.B.A., having on the exterior wall a mosaic panel, thirty-two feet by ten feet, designed by R. Anning Bell to represent the course of human life, and a memorial tablet by F. W. Pomeroy, A.R.A.; a bronze fountain by J. W. Rollins was given by Horniman's son. Finally in 1901 Horniman presented his museum and surrounding estate to the London county council. The museum is now a lecture centre, and an annual report is issued. A new lecture hall and reading room, erected at the museum by his son, was opened on 28 Jan. 1912.

Horniman was liberal M.P. for the Falmouth and Penryn boroughs (1895–1904). He died in London on 5 March 1906. He married (1) on 3 June 1859 Rebekah, daughter of John Emslie of Dalston; (2) on 30 Jan. 1897 Minnie Louisa, daughter of G. W. Bennett of Charlton, Kent. His son by the first marriage, Emslie John Horniman, was liberal M.P. for Chelsea (1906–10), and his only daughter, Annie Elizabeth Frederica Horniman, is the founder of the Irish Theatre, Dublin, and of the Repertory Theatre, Manchester. His portrait by William Henry Margetson was exhibited at the Royal Academy in 1897.

[The Times, 6 March 1906; Who's Who, 1906; An Account of the Horniman Free Museum and Recreation Grounds, Forest Hill (illustrated), 1901.] C. F. S.

HORSLEY, JOHN CALLCOTT (1817–1903), painter, born in London on 29 Jan. 1817, was elder son of William Horsley [q. v.], the well-known composer of glees, by his wife Elizabeth Hutchins, daughter of John Wall Callcott [q. v.], musical composer, brother of Sir Augustus Wall Callcott [q. v.], the painter. Horsley had one brother and three sisters, one of whom married Isambard Kingdom Brunel [q. v.]. He showed a bent towards pictorial art while still very young. His general education was obtained at a school on a site now filled by the Carmelite convent and church, Kensington, and his early training as an artist at Sass's academy in Bloomsbury. In due time he became a student at the Royal Academy, where he won the gold medal in 'the antique.' Before he was twenty he earned the praise of Sir David Wilkie for an ambitious picture called 'Rent Day at Haddon Hall in the Sixteenth Century.' The first picture he exhibited was 'Rival Musicians,' but the first sent to the Royal Academy was 'The Pride of the Village' (1839), now in the Tate Gallery. While yet very young he was appointed headmaster to the figure class in the National School of Design in Somerset House. In 1843, in 1844, and again in 1847, he was successful in winning prizes in the competitions for employment in the decoration of the new houses of parliament, the result of which was the painting of two large wall-pictures, 'The Spirit of Religion' and 'Satan surprised at the Ear of Eve,' in the new palace. At Somerleyton he also painted two wall-pictures dealing with incidents in the youth of Alfred the Great. But large historical pictures were not to his taste, and his power of treating them was affected for the worse by his reluctance to go to the root of all knowledge of structure and movement, the study of the naked model. Against that study he headed an abortive agitation in 1885, when the spirit of the Paris Salon was, he thought, invading English art too boldly. A letter by him (signed H.) in 'The Times' (2 May 1885), following one from 'A British Matron' a day earlier, led to a long and animated newspaper controversy. Horsley's real preference was for domestic scenes, conceived somewhat in the style of Terborch and De Hooghe. Among the best of these are 'Malvolio practising Deportment to his own Shadow,' 'Attack and Defence,' 'Holy Communion,' 'The Lost Found,' 'The Gaoler's Daughter,' 'Negotiating a Loan,' 'Le Jour des Morts,' and two pictures commissioned by the Prince Consort, 'L'Allegro' and 'Il Pensieroso.' His 'Healing Mercies of Christ' forms the altarpiece in the chapel of St. Thomas's Hospital, London. He also painted a few portraits, the best known and most accessible being that of Martin Colnaghi, in the National Gallery. Although painted when both artist and sitter were very old men, this in some degree compensates by its vivacity and fidelity for its shortcomings as a work of art. Another of his portraits is that of the Princess Beatrice (Princess Henry of Battenberg) at the age of thirteen months.

Horsley was elected A.R.A. in 1855 and R.A. in 1856. He will be chiefly remembered at the Academy for the part he took in organising the epoch-making series of 'Old Masters' at Burlington House. From 1875 to 1890 he was the moving spirit of these exhibitions. He was indefatigable in searching for desirable pictures, and in persuading their owners to lend. For such duties he was remarkably well fitted, being at once extremely popular and yet quite ready with his 'no' when inadmissible claims were made on behalf of this or that 'masterpiece.' Horsley was treasurer of the Academy from 1882 to 1897, when he retired from the active list of academicians.

In 1858 Horsley bought a house at Cranbrook, Kent, commissioning the then unknown Mr. Norman Shaw to repair and add to it. There several of his more rustic pictures were painted.

Horsley inherited a lively interest in music and its professors. With many of the latter he was intimate, especially with Mendelssohn, who, when in London, was his frequent visitor. In early life he had suggested to his intimate friend, John Leech, many themes for his drawings in 'Punch.' He died on 18 Oct. 1903, in his eighty-seventh year, at the house in High Row, Kensington, which had been the property of his family for nearly a century, and was buried at Kensal Green. He was twice married: (1) in 1847 to Elvira Walter; (2) in 1854 to Rosamund, daughter of Charles Haden, surgeon, of Derby and London, who survived him with three sons and two daughters. His sons are Walter Charles Horsley, painter, Sir Victor Horsley, the surgeon, and Gerald Horsley, architect. Of two portraits by his eldest son, Walter Charles Horsley, one painted in 1891 is in the possession of Horsley's widow; the other (*c.* 1898) is at the Royal Academy, Burlington House. Before his death in 1903 there was published Horsley's 'Recollections of a Royal Academician' (edited by Mrs. Edmund Helps).

[Horsley's Recollections, 1903; The Times, 20 and 23 Oct. 1903; Cat. Nat. Gallery of British Art (Tate Gallery); Spielmann's Hist. of Punch; Graves' Roy. Ac. and Brit. Inst. Exhibitors; personal knowledge.] W. A.

HOSKINS, Sir ANTHONY HILEY (1828–1901), admiral, born at North Perrott near Crewkerne, Somerset, on 1 Sept. 1828, was fourth son of Henry Hoskins (1790–1876), rector of North Perrott, by his wife Mary, daughter of the Rev. William Phelips of Montacute. The Somerset branch of the Hoskins family settled in that county in the seventeenth century. Mary, daughter of Richard Hoskins, of a related branch of the family (of Beaminster, Dorset), married Samuel Hood and was mother of the two admirals, Samuel Hood, first Lord Hood [q. v.], and Alexander Hood, first Lord Bridport [q. v.]. From school at Winchester Hoskins entered the navy in April 1842, taking with him a proficiency in classical learning unusual at his early age. In his first ship, the Conway, he is said, probably with some exaggeration, to have acted as Greek coach to one of the lieutenants, Montagu Burrows [q. v. Suppl. II]. In the Conway Hoskins remained for some years, participating in several fights with Arab slavers in the Mozambique and in the attack on Tamatave (Clowes, vi. 345–6). Afterwards, in the President, he continued on the same station, employed on similar service. On 26 May 1849 he was made lieutenant, and while in the Castor on the Cape station was lent to Sir Henry Smith as A.D.C. during the Kaffir war of 1851–2. In 1857 he took the Slaney gunboat out to China, and in her took part in the capture of Canton on 28 Dec. This won for him his promotion to commander's rank on 26 Feb. 1858; but remaining in the Slaney, he was in her in May in the gulf of Pe-che-li, and was present at the reduction of the Taku forts and in the operations in the Pei-ho leading to the occupation of Tien-tsin. On 12 Dec. 1863 he was promoted to be captain. In 1869–72 he commanded the Eclipse on the North American station; in 1873–4 the Sultan, in the Channel fleet; and in 1875–8 was commodore in Australian waters. In 1877 he was nominated a C.B., became a rear-admiral on 15 June 1879, and from 1880 was a lord commissioner of the admiralty, from which post he was sent out to the Mediterranean, where the Egyptian troubles after the bombardment of Alexandria were urgently calling for reinforcements. On his return in the winter he was nominated K.C.B., and to June 1885, when he became vice-admiral, he was superintendent of naval reserves, and was then for nearly four years again a lord commissioner of the admiralty. From March 1889 he was commander-in-chief in the Mediterranean till 20 June 1891, when he was promoted admiral, and was appointed senior naval lord of the admiralty. He retired on reaching the age limit, 1 Sept. 1893. He was nominated G.C.B. on 17 Nov. 1893. In his retirement he lived mostly in London, taking much interest in naval and geographical societies till his death, which took place at Capel, near Dorking, on 21 June 1901. He was buried at North Perrott, when the king and the admiralty were officially represented. His portrait was executed by Henry Tanworth Wells, R.A., in 1901 for Grillion's Club. A caricature by 'Spy' appeared in 'Vanity Fair' (1883). Stern, strict, and even severe in his service relations, he was in his private and personal character one of the most genial of men.

He married, on 27 Oct. 1865, Dorothea Ann Eliza, second daughter of the Rev. Sir George Stamp Robinson, seventh baronet. She died on 7 Oct. 1901, without issue.

[Royal Navy Lists; The Times, 22, 27 June 1901; Clowes, Royal Navy, vols. vi. and vii., 1901–3.] J. K. L.

HOWARD, GEORGE JAMES, ninth Earl of Carlisle (1843–1911), amateur artist, was the only son of Charles Wentworth George Howard, fifth son of George Howard, sixth earl [q. v.] and M.P. for East Cumberland, 1840–79, by his wife Mary, second daughter of Sir James Parke, Baron Wensleydale [q. v.]. George William Frederick Howard, seventh earl of Carlisle [q. v.], the statesman, was his father's eldest brother. Born in London on 13 Aug. 1843, Howard was educated at Eton and Trinity College, Cambridge, where in 1861 he was one of a few undergraduates selected to join King Edward VII when Prince of Wales in attendance at a private course of lectures on history by Charles Kingsley. He graduated B.A. in 1865. On the death of his father in 1879 he was elected liberal M.P. for East Cumberland, lost the seat in 1880, but regained it in 1881 and held it till 1885. At the disruption of the party over Irish home rule he joined the liberal unionists, but did not sit in the 1886 parliament. He succeeded his uncle, William George Howard (1808–1889), the invalid and bachelor eighth earl of Carlisle, in 1889. In the House of Lords he continued to vote with the liberal unionists, while his wife had become an ardent public worker on the radical side. On one question of social reform, the temperance question, they were wholly agreed. On his accession to the earldom the public-houses both on the Yorkshire and on the Cumberland estates were closed, and one of his very rare speeches in the House of Lords was in favour of the licensing bill of the liberal government in 1908. Politics, however, were but a secondary interest to him; and though fond of country life and sports, especially shooting, he had from the beginning left the administration of his great estates in Cumberland, Northumberland, and Yorkshire in the hands of his wife. His real devotion was to art. Having shown as a boy a remarkable gift for likeness and caricature, he took up the practice of painting in earnest after leaving Cambridge, and was the pupil successively of Alphonse Legros and Giovanni Costa. Of his many friendships the most intimate were with artists, especially with the two above named and with Burne-Jones, Leighton, Watts, Thomas Armstrong, Pepys Cockerell, and latterly Sir Charles Holroyd. He had an intense sympathy for Italy and the Italians, and in early life cherished a close and reverential friendship for Mazzini. He became a skilled and industrious painter of landscape, principally in water-colour. His work was conceived in a topographical spirit, and he was at his best in studies made direct from nature rather than in work carried out afterwards in his studio. In later life he suffered much from gastric trouble, and partly for the sake of health made frequent winter journeys abroad, to Egypt, India, and East Africa, painting wherever he went; but the scenery which best inspired him was that of his beautiful north country homes, Naworth and Castle Howard. In the last year of his life he published 'A Picture Song-Book' (1910), a set of coloured reproductions from drawings in illustration of old English songs done to amuse his grandchildren. He was an influential trustee of the National Gallery for more than thirty years. He died at his daughter's residence, Brackland, Hindhead, Surrey, on 16 April 1911, and was buried at Lanercost Priory, Naworth.

Just before his fatal illness Carlisle had taken an active part in the movement for stopping the alterations of the bridge and paths in St. James's Park proposed by the office of works. He had at the same time agreed to offer to the National Gallery for a price much below its market value the masterpiece of Mabuse, the 'Adoration of the Magi,' which had been bought by the fifth earl and been for a century the chief glory of the Castle Howard collection. His wish in this respect was carried out by his widow after his death, and the picture is now the property of the nation. His private tastes and distastes in art were very decided, but he knew on occasion how to suppress them and support reasonable views which were not his own. He was a man of remarkable social charm, though not free from moods of cynicism and irony. A portrait of him in early life by Watts is in the gallery at Limnerslease. A sketch of him was executed for Grillion's Club by Henry Tanworth Wells in 1894. In 1864 he married Rosalind, youngest daughter of the second Lord Stanley of Alderley, by whom he had six sons, three of whom predeceased him, and five daughters, of whom one died in infancy. The eldest daughter, Lady Mary, is the wife of Professor Gilbert Murray; another daughter, Lady Cecilia, is wife of Mr. Charles Henry Roberts, liberal M.P. for Lincoln since 1906.

Carlisle was succeeded by his son, Charles James Stanley Howard, tenth earl (1867–1912), who was born on 8 March 1867, educated at Rugby and Balliol College, Oxford, and married in 1894 Rhoda Ankaret, daughter of Colonel Paget W. L'Estrange, by whom he had one son and three daughters. He was captain in the third battalion Border regiment of militia, with which he served in South Africa in 1902; was an active member of the London school board (1894–1902); contested without success in the unionist interest Chester-le-Street, the Hexham division of Northumberland, and Gateshead; was unionist M.P. for South Birmingham (1904–11), and latterly one of the parliamentary whips for his party. His health was already failing when he succeeded to the title, and he died at 105 Eaton Place, London, on 21 Jan. 1912; he was buried at Lanercost.

[Private information; The Times, 18 and 21 April 1911; International Studio, 1903, xxi. 121.]

HOWELL, DAVID (1831–1903), dean of St. David's, son of John Howell, farmer and calvinistic methodist deacon, of Treos, in the parish of Llangan, Glamorganshire, was born on 16 Aug. 1831. His mother being of weak health, he was brought up for the most part by his grandmother, Mary Griffiths of Tynycaeau, a churchwoman. At the age of fifteen he returned to his father's home, which was now at Bryn Cwtyn, near Pencoed. Farming, however, was not to his mind, and, having shown a decided bent for letters, he was persuaded by his mother and the rector of St. Mary Hill (afterwards well known as Archdeacon Griffiths of Neath) to prepare for orders in the Church of England. After passing through the Eagle School, Cowbridge, the Preparatory School, Merthyr, and the Llandaff Diocesan Institute at Abergavenny, he was ordained deacon in 1855 and priest in 1856. A curacy of two years at Neath under Griffiths was followed by his appointment in 1857 as secretary for Wales to the Church Pastoral Aid Society; he then became vicar of Pwllheli in 1861. In 1864 he was transferred to the important vicarage of St. John's, Cardiff, where his abilities found a congenial field; he endeavoured to adapt the machinery of the church to the needs of a rapidly growing community, and raised no less than 30,000*l.* for the purpose. In 1875 he was elected a member of the first Cardiff school board. In this year he became vicar of Wrexham, where he remained until 1891, when he removed to the neighbouring vicarage of Gresford. At Wrexham, as at Cardiff, he greatly extended the activities of the church. He received the degree of B.D. from the archbishop of Canterbury in 1878, was appointed prebendary of Meliden and honorary canon of St. Asaph in 1885, and became archdeacon of Wrexham in 1889. Popular opinion marked him out for yet greater responsibilities, and the bestowal upon him in 1897 of the deanery of St. David's was regarded as a kind of retirement. The restoration of the Lady chapel showed that he had not lost his zest for work. He died on 15 Jan. 1903 at St. David's, and was buried in the chapel of St. Nicholas in the cathedral. An altar tomb and a bronze tablet commemorate him there.

His gifts and his temperament, no less than his family connections (his brother William became a calvinistic methodist deacon and his sister married Dr. David Saunders of the same body), fitted him to become a mediating influence between the church and Welsh nonconformity. He was well versed in Welsh literature, particularly its hymnology, and in warm sympathy with every Welsh patriotic movement. Party politics did not interest him, and after 1875 he held aloof from political strife. He was a highly gifted orator, powerful not only in the pulpit but also in a remarkable degree on the eisteddfod platform, where he was known by the bardic name of 'Llawdden.' He brought the evangelical temper and the methodist fervour into all his church work. Yet his 'churchmanship though always broad was never really vague' (*The Times*, 16 Jan. 1903). His parochial work was thorough, and he was a believer in the voluntary school system. He married Anne Powell of Pencoed, and left four sons, of whom the youngest, William Tudor Howell, was conservative M.P. for the Denbigh boroughs from 1895 to 1900.

[Article in Geninen, April 1903, by W. Howell; Byegones (Oswestry), 28 Jan. 1903; The Times, 16 Jan. 1903; Welsh Religious Leaders in the Victorian Era, ed. J. V. Morgan, 1905.] J. E. L.

HOWELL, GEORGE (1833–1910), labour leader and writer, born at Wrington, Somerset, on 5 Oct. 1833, was son of a mason, who fell into financial difficulties. Howell was sent to farm service when he was eight. Two years later he became a mortar boy, assisting masons. In 1847 he became a member of a Chartist society; he was then an eager reader of books which he borrowed from the village library. At the age of twenty he went to Bristol, where he worked as a bricklayer; he continued to spend his spare time in reading and was one of the first members of the Young Men's Christian Association. In 1854 he journeyed to London, where he came to know William Rogers (1819–96) [q v.], who helped him with his studies. In London he increased his political activities, making the acquaintance of Mazzini, Kossuth, Ernest Jones, and other prominent democratic leaders, and he developed an interest in trade unionism. He was prominent in the historical nine hours' struggle (1859) in the building trade, and gradually took his place with men like William Newton and William Allan as a trade union leader. While still working at his trade he was threatened by an employer with imprisonment under the Master and Servants Act, and that threat he never forgot. In 1864 he ceased to work as a bricklayer.

Meanwhile trade unionism was entering politics, goaded by the civil disabilities under which labour combinations suffered (1860–75). Howell joined the body of unusually able men, including Alexander MacDonald, George Odger [q. v.], and Robert Applegarth, which, known as 'the Junta,' directed trade union affairs at the time. He became secretary to the London trades council (1861–2), and was secretary to the Reform League (1864–7), in which capacity he was one of the marshals of the procession that broke down Hyde Park railings in 1866. He was secretary to the parliamentary committee of the Trade Union Congress (1871–5) and to the Plimsoll and Seamen's Fund committee (1873). A leading spirit in the Garibaldi and Polish agitations amongst the London workmen, he served as a member of the council of the International Working-men's Association (1865).

The best service which Howell did to the trade union movement was as a parliamentary lobbyist. He became known as 'the champion bill passer.' Year after year from 1870 he buttonholed, interviewed and pulled wires in parliamentary lobbies. He saw the old Master and Servants Act drastically amended in 1867 and repealed in 1889, and the Trade Union Acts of 1871 and 1876 were passed largely owing to his efforts. In his 'Labour Legislation, Labour Movements, and Labour Leaders' (1902) he gave a lively account of those years. His first attempt to enter parliament was in 1868, when he contested Aylesbury as a liberal trades-unionist and polled 942 votes, but was defeated. A similar result attended another contest in the same constituency in 1874, when he polled 1144 votes. In 1875 he addressed election meetings at Norwich but did not persist in his candidature. In 1881 he contested Stafford but was rejected with 1185 votes. He was successful, however, in 1885 at Bethnal Green. In 1886 he urged the issue of a cheap official edition of the statutes of the realm. His suggestion was adopted, and his part in initiating the useful enterprise was acknowledged in the preface of the first volume. He represented Bethnal Green until 1895, when he was defeated. He did not seek to enter parliament again. He remained a liberal, and opposed the movement among trade unionists (the controversy lasted from 1890 to 1900, when the labour party was formed) for the creation of a political party which would be independent of the existing parties.

In 1897 a public subscription was raised for him, and in 1906 he received a pension from the civil list of 50*l.* per annum. In 1906 his library, largely consisting of works on economic and social questions, was purchased for 1000*l.*, also raised by public subscription, and was presented to the Bishopsgate Institute, London.

He died at 35 Findon Road, Shepherd's Bush, on 17 Sept. 1910, and was buried at Nunhead cemetery.

Howell's works, to whose value for students of trades union history Mr Sidney Webb bears witness, are: 1. 'Handy Book of the Labour Laws,' 1876; 3rd edit. 1895. 2. 'Conflicts of Capital and Labour Historically Considered,' 1878; 2nd revised edit. 1890. 3. 'National Industrial Insurance and Employers' Liability,' 1880. 4. 'Trade Unionism New and Old,' 1891. 5. 'Trade Union Law and Cases' (with H. Cohen, K.C.), 1901. 6. 'Labour Legislation, Labour Movements, and Labour Leaders,' 1902.

Howell also edited the 'Operative Bricklayers' Society's Trade Circular' (1861); wrote 'Life of Ernest Jones' for the 'Newcastle Chronicle,' Jan. to Oct. 1898 (not published separately); compiled quarterly abstracts of parliamentary bills, reports, and transactions (1886–7); prepared (with A. J. Mundella) the chapter on 'Industrial Associations' in vol. ii. of T. H. Ward's 'Reign of Queen Victoria' (1887), and that on 'Liberty for Labour' in Thomas Mackay's 'A Plea for Liberty' (1891); and contributed a preface to Lord Brassey's 'Work and Wages' (1894).

Two portraits hang in the Bishopsgate Institute, one by Mr. George A. Holmes and the other by Mrs. Howard White.

[Works cited; Beehive, 10 May 1873 and 19 June 1875; Millgate Monthly, August 1908; Webb's History of Trade Unionism; Howell Library, Bishopsgate Institute.]

J. R. M.

HOWES, THOMAS GEORGE BOND (1853–1905), zoologist, born at Kennington on 7 Sept. 1853, of Huguenot descent, was eldest son of Thomas Johnson Howes by his wife Augusta Mary, daughter of George Augustus Bond, captain in the East India Company's service. After private education, he was introduced to Professor Huxley in 1874 as a good draughtsman and keen naturalist. For five years he assisted in the development of Huxley's practical instruction in biology at the Normal School of Science and Royal School of Mines (now Royal College of Science), and in 1880 succeeded T. J. Parker as demonstrator of biology at the Royal School of Mines. In 1885 Howes was made an assistant professor of zoology at the Normal School of Science, and on the retirement of Huxley in 1895 was appointed first professor of zoology at the Royal College of Science, South Kensington. He held this appointment at the time of his death on 4 Feb. 1905. In 1881 Howes married Annie, daughter of James Watkins, and had one daughter. His widow was awarded a civil list pension of 50*l.* in 1905.

Howes excelled as a teacher and colleague. The thoroughness of the training in biology at South Kensington was largely due to his knowledge and zeal. His reading in zoological literature was very wide and was freely dispensed to all who sought his advice. He devoted much time and energy to founding or extending the work of societies that promote natural knowledge, and he occupied a responsible position on most of the London societies. At the Belfast meeting of the British Association in 1902 Howes was president of section D (zoology). His skill as a draughtsman was great, and the work by which he is best known to students, 'Atlas of Elementary Biology' (1885), was entirely illustrated from his own drawings; the zoological part was revised as 'Atlas of Elementary Zootomy' (1902); another well-known text-book, Huxley and Martin's 'Elementary Biology' (1875), was issued in a revised form by Howes in conjunction with Dr. Dukinfield Scott in 1888.

As an investigator, Howes dealt chiefly with the comparative anatomy of the vertebrata, to the knowledge of which he made many contributions, his chief memoir being an account, written in collaboration with Dr. H. H. Swinnerton, of the development of the skeleton of the rare Norfolk Island reptile, 'Sphenodon' (*Trans. Zool. Soc.* 1901). He was elected F.R.S. in 1897, LL.D. St. Andrews in 1898, and D.Sc. Manchester, 1899.

[Proc. Roy. Soc. 79, B. 1907; Nature, vol. 71, 1905, p. 419; Proc. Linn. Soc., Oct. 1905, p. 34; private sources.] F. W. G.

HOWITT, ALFRED WILLIAM (1830–1908), Australian anthropologist, born on 17 April 1830 at Nottingham, was eldest son in a family of four sons and three daughters of William Howitt [q. v.] and his wife Mary Howitt [q. v.], the well-known writers. After home instruction at Nottingham and Esher, his parents in 1840 took him and their other children to Heidelberg to continue their education. They returned in 1843, living successively at Clapham (1843–8) and St. John's Wood (1848–52), while Alfred studied at University College, Gower Street. In 1852 William Howitt with two of his sons, Alfred and Herbert Charlton, went to Australia, partly to visit his own brother Godfrey, who had been for some time settled at Melbourne in medical practice. After two years' wandering in Australia William Howitt returned to England, leaving his two sons in Australia. Herbert Charlton was subsequently drowned while bridge-making in New Zealand.

Alfred first farmed land belonging to his uncle at Coalfield near Melbourne, and then took to cattle droving. He soon acquired the reputation of an able, careful, and fearless bushman. In Sept. 1859 a committee at Melbourne commissioned him to explore Central Australia from Adelaide. He reported adversely on the character of the country. After serving as manager of the Mount Napier cattle station near Hamilton he was sent by the Victoria government in 1860 to prospect for gold in the unknown region of Gippsland. He made a scientific and practical study of gold mining and of the local geology, and by his advice the goldfields on the Crooked, Dargo, and Wentworth rivers were opened. On 18 June 1861 he was appointed leader of the expedition in search of the explorers Robert O'Hara Burke [q. v.], and William John Wills [q. v.], who had disappeared the year before in the then unknown region toward the Gulf of Carpentaria. He was absent from Melbourne from 14 July to 28 Nov. 1861, advancing rapidly despite the difficulties of travel, and found the one survivor of the last expedition (John King) on Cooper's Creek, far in the north, and brought him back to Melbourne. At the end of the same year Howitt again visited Cooper's Creek, and succeeded, after a leisurely journey, in bringing back the remains of Burke and Wills to Melbourne on 28 Dec. 1862. For these services Howitt was made in 1863 police magistrate and warden of the goldfields in Gippsland. He held these posts till 1889.

From his early days in Australia he had devoted himself to scientific observation. With especial eagerness he studied the aboriginal population. During the expedition of 1862 he thoroughly familiarised himself with the social organisation of the Dieri tribe about Cooper's Creek. At Gippsland he came into close touch with the Kurnai tribe, who adopted him by formal initiation as a member and admitted him to their secret ceremonies. He thus went beyond any other European in his study of the Australian aboriginal. Moreover, he spared himself no pains in corresponding with others who were to any extent in a position to observe any facts in connection with his own favourite subject, and he sifted and arranged the information thus gained with extraordinary care and aptitude. To Brough Smith's 'Aborigines of Victoria' (Melbourne, 1878) Howitt contributed 'Notes on Aborigines of Cooper's Creek' and 'Notes on the System of Consanguinity and Kinship of the Brabrolong Tribe, North Gippsland.' Lorimer Fison [q. v. Suppl. II], whom he had casually met in the bush some years before, joined him in 1871 in his investigations, and helped him to interpret his facts. Together the two friends published 'Kamilaroi and

Kurnai' (Melbourne, 1880), which embodied the results of their inquiries and reflections on group marriage and relationship and marriage by elopement, drawn chiefly from the usages of the Australian aborigines. In 1880 Howitt and Fison also published 'The Kurnai Tribe, their Customs in Peace and War,' with an introduction by Lewis H. Morgan (Melbourne, 1880). Again in 1885 Howitt contributed an important paper on Kurnai rites to the 'Journal of the Royal Anthropological Institute.' Other important memoirs on the tribal systems by Howitt, writing either separately or jointly with Fison, followed in the same periodical until 1907.

In 1889 Howitt left Gippsland to become secretary of mines in Victoria, and in 1896 was appointed commissioner of audit and a member of the public service board; these two appointments he held until his retirement from public service in 1901. Until his death he pursued his studies in ethnology and other branches of science. An important treatise, 'The Eucalypti of Gippsland,' was issued together with a valuable paper on the 'Organisation of the Australian Tribes' in the 'Transactions of the Royal Society of Victoria' in 1889. Finally in 1904 Howitt published his chief book, 'The Native Tribes of South East Australia.'

Fison and Howitt may fairly claim to be pioneers of the new anthropology, and by their researches into the organisation of the human family to have given the study the character of an exact science. The American investigator, Lewis Morgan, in his great book on the 'Systems of Consanguinity and Affinity of the Human Family' (1869), led the way, but they went on their own lines further than he, notably in regard to systems of marriage and relationship among aboriginal Australians.

After retirement from the public service in 1901, Howitt lived chiefly at Melbourne in the enjoyment of widespread recognition as an ethnologist. In 1904 he received the Clarke memorial medal from the Royal Society of New South Wales. In 1905–6 he was chairman of the Royal Commission on coal mining in Victoria. On 27 June 1906 he was made C.M.G. In 1907 he was president of the meeting at Adelaide of the Australasian Association for the Advancement of Science; and in the same year he was the first recipient from the same association of the newly instituted Mueller medal. He died at Melbourne on 7 March 1908 (barely three months after the death of his associate Fison). He married on 18 Aug. 1864, at Adelaide, Maria, daughter of Benjamin Boothby, judge of the supreme court at Adelaide; she died in 1902, leaving two sons and three daughters. A portrait of Howitt in bas relief is on the monument to Burke and Wills at Melbourne, Victoria.

[The Victorian Naturalist, vol. xxiv. April 1908, by Howitt's friend, Prof. W. Baldwin Spencer; (Melbourne) Argus, 9 March 1908; Man, viii. 1908; Johns's Notable Australians, 1908; J. G. Frazer's Howitt and Fison, art. in Folk Lore, June 1909, pp. 144 *seq.*; unpublished despatches; public records; information supplied by G. Harry Wallis of the City Museum, Nottingham.]

E. IM T.

HOWLAND, Sir WILLIAM PEARCE (1811–1907), Canadian statesman, born at Paulings, New York, on 29 May 1811, was son of Jonathan Howland, a descendant of John Howland, who migrated from England in 1620. His mother's maiden name was Lydia Pearce. After education at the common school of his native place and at Kinderhook Academy, Howland went to Canada in 1830 and found employment in a general store at Cooksville, Ontario. His business interests rapidly grew, and in association with his brother Peleg he soon owned a number of country stores, and made large profits in lumbering and rafting ventures. For some years he was in business near Brampton, Ontario, and later went into the milling and grain business with his brothers Peleg and Frederick. He bought the Lambton mills, near Toronto, in 1840.

In 1857 Howland was elected to parliament, representing West York as a follower of the advanced liberal leader, George Brown [q. v. Suppl. I]. In 1862 he alienated himself from that leader by accepting the portfolio of finance in the (John Sandfield) Macdonald-Sicotte liberal administration. Brown and Mowat refused to join on the ground that the cabinet was hostile to the principle of representation by population. Howland and McDougall, the only Ontario liberals in the ministry, defended themselves from the charge of party disloyalty by asserting that they were acting solely in the interests of confederation. Howland remained in cabinet office for six years.

In 1862 he was sent to England with Sicotte on militia matters. At the same time he pursued negotiations with reference to the Intercolonial railway and to the proposed cession of Rupert's Land by the Hudson's Bay Company. He had an acute prevision of the rich possibilities of the Canadian north-west. Subsequently he founded the Rescue Company for the purpose of capturing the growing traffic between the British settlers in the Red River country and the Americans at St. Paul, Minnesota, and with a view to establishing communications linking the trade of Toronto with the north-west and ultimately with the Pacific coast. Finally in 1880 Howland headed a syndicate for the building of the Canadian Pacific Railway.

Meanwhile in 1863 Howland had exchanged his financial portfolio for that of receiver-general. This he retained till the following year, when he became postmaster-general (1864–6). In 1865 he and (Sir) Alexander Galt [q. v. Suppl. I] visited Washington as commisioners for Canada to consider reciprocal trade with the United States. Next year he succeeded Galt as finance minister. In Dec. 1866 he took part in the London conference which resulted in the confederation of the Canadian provinces, and he became minister of inland revenue in 1867 in the first confederation cabinet under Sir John Alexander Macdonald [q. v.]. He resigned his portfolio in July 1868 to become lieutenant-governor of Ontario, and he filled that post until 1873. Thenceforth he confined his attention to business. For his services at the time of confederation he was appointed C.B., and in 1879 he was created K.C.M.G. He died at Toronto on 1 Jan. 1907, and was buried there.

He married thrice: (1) in 1843 Marianne Blythe (*d.* 1849), by whom he had a daughter and two sons, both subsequently mayors of Toronto, and both dying before their father; (2) in 1866 Susanna Julia (*d.* 1886), widow of Captain Hunt; and (3) Elizabeth Mary Rattray, widow of James Bethune, Q.C.; she survived him.

Of two portraits in oil, one is in Government House and the other in the National Club, Toronto; there is a bust by Miss Mildred Peel, R.C.A. (Lady Ross), in the normal school.

[The Times, 3 Jan. 1907; Toronto Globe; Canadian Men and Women of the Time; Dent, Canadian Portrait Gallery, 1881, iii. 124; private information.] P. E.

HUBBARD, LOUISA MARIA (1836–1906), social reformer, born in St. Petersburg on 8 March 1836, was eldest in the family of four sons and three daughters of William Egerton Hubbard, Russian merchant, younger brother of John Gellibrand Hubbard, first Baron Addington [q. v.]. Her mother, Louisa Ellen (*d.* 1883), was daughter of Captain William Baldock. In 1843 her family left Russia for England, and settled at Leonardslee near Horsham. She was educated privately. Her father interested himself in philanthropic work, especially that of the Church Missionary Society; he died in 1882, and his widow survived him for a year. From that time till 1893 Miss Hubbard resided at Beedinglee in Sussex.

Miss Hubbard devoted her life and means to improving the condition of women of her own class who had to work for their living. She brought to her task much business capacity, a strong religious sense, and abundant culture. In 1864 she began her labours by interesting herself in the order of deaconesses, which had been formed in 1861, and she sought to train and organise them for teaching and nursing. In 1871 (under the initials 'L. M. H.') she issued 'Anglican Deaconesses: or, Is there no Place for Women in the Parochial System?' But her main aim was to open to women new fields of work in all directions. From 1869 to 1878 she compiled annually 'A Guide to all Institutions for the Benefit of Women.' The number of such institutions rose, she points out, from five in 1854 to over a thousand in 1898. On 19 Aug. 1871 Miss Hubbard began in the church and tory newspaper 'John Bull' a series of letters on work for ladies, which were published collectively in 1872, with an introduction by Sir James Kay-Shuttleworth [q. v.], as 'Work for Ladies in Elementary Schools, with an Introduction by an Old Educator.' Her proposals, supported by her father's influence, led to the transformation in February 1873 of the college founded by Bishop Otter [q. v.] at Chichester into a college for training as elementary teachers girls from secondary schools. In 1878 she further proved her interest in education in 'Why Should I send my Child to School?' and in 1880, 'A Few Words to the Mothers of Little Children.' In 1875 she published a 'Handbook for Women's Work,' which in 1880 became 'The Englishwoman's Year Book.' This Miss Hubbard edited until 1898. In 1875 she started the 'Woman's Gazette' (afterwards named 'Work and Leisure'), and edited it till 1893. There she advocated nursing as a profession, a proposal which won the active sympathy of Florence Nightingale [q. v. Suppl. II]. Miss Hubbard was also one of the earliest advocates of massage and of typewriting as women's occupations and also suggested gardening fifteen years before the foundation of the woman's department of the Swanley Horticultural College. Miss Hubbard helped Lady Mary Feilding to form in 1876 the Working Ladies' Guild, and an article (1881) by Miss A. Wallace in Miss Hubbard's 'Woman's Gazette' on the 'Co-operation of Governesses' led to the formation of the Teachers' Guild in 1884. In 1889 Miss Hubbard founded a friendly society for gentlewomen. The British Women's Emigration Society, formed in 1880 (now at the British Institute), the Matrons' Aid Society (now the Midwives' Institute), and the Church of England Women's Help Society, an offshoot of the Girls' Friendly Society, all owed much to Miss Hubbard's activity. In 1889 she provided considerable funds for the Gentlewomen's Employment Club, in Lower Belgrave Street, London, which was a result of her endeavour to solve the problem of providing homes for gentlewomen.

Apart from her philanthropic interest, Miss Hubbard was an adept at landscape painting and an enthusiastic horsewoman. In 1885 she published an allegory, 'The Beautiful House and Enchanted Garden,' and in 1887 'Where to Spend a Holiday.' In 1893 her health showed signs of failure, and she gave up most of her work. In 1899 a paralytic stroke completely disabled her while she was in Tyrol. She remained there until her death at Gries bei Bozen on 25 Nov. 1906.

[Information supplied by Miss Hubbard's brother, Mr. William Egerton Hubbard, J.P.; The Times, 1 Dec. 1906; A Woman's Work for Women, being the Aims, Efforts, and Aspirations of L. M. H. (Miss Louisa M. Hubbard), (with portrait), 1898, by Edwin A. Pratt.]

J. E. G. DE M.

HUDDART, JAMES (1847–1901), Australian shipowner, born at Whitehaven on 22 Feb. 1847, was the son of William Huddart, ship-builder, of Whitehaven, Cumberland, by his wife Frances Lindow. He was educated at St. Bees College. He left school at the age of sixteen, and went to Australia, where he joined the shipping firm of his uncle, Captain Peter Huddart of Geelong, Victoria. In 1866 his uncle left Australia, and James Huddart took charge of the firm, then engaged in bay traffic between Geelong and Newcastle (New South Wales) In 1870 he founded Huddart, Parker & Co., an intercolonial steamship line. In 1887 he came to England, where he organised a new and improved passenger service between Australia and New Zealand. He was chairman of the Employers' Union during the Australian maritime strike in 1890.

Huddart's main object in life was to establish the 'All Red Route'—a series of fast steamship lines which, with the help of the Canadian Pacific railway, should link New Zealand, Australia, and Canada to Great Britain, and keep within the empire a large amount of trade which is now carried across foreign countries. He began work to this end in 1893 by starting a fast line of steamers, the Canadian-Australian Royal Mail Steamship line, which ran between Sydney and Vancouver. The next step was a fast line between Canada and this country. At Huddart's instigation a conference among all the colonies concerned was held at Ottawa in 1894. The Canadian government subsequently voted a subsidy of 150,000*l.* a year for the first ten years, and 100,000*l.* for the years following, and the co-operation of the Canadian Pacific railway was secured. It was determined that Great Britain should be asked to contribute 75,000*l.* for the Canadian service, for which Huddart completed his preparations. Mr. Chamberlain, the colonial secretary, welcomed the scheme, but called for tenders, which were sent in 1896 by Huddart and by the Allan line. Nothing was done with them. Meanwhile some of the subsidies for which Huddart had hoped were not forthcoming to help the Sydney-Vancouver line, and in 1897 he was forced to give up the project after sinking his private fortune in order to maintain it. On 27 Feb. 1901 he died at his house in Chatsworth Gardens, Eastbourne. He was buried in Ocklynge cemetery, Eastbourne. On 1 Sept. 1869 he married Lois, daughter of James Ingham of Ballarat, consulting engineer. He had issue three sons and a daughter. The youngest, Midshipman Cymbeline A. E. Huddart of H.M.S. Doris, was killed in the battle of Graspan in the South African war (25 Nov. 1899), and after death was awarded the conspicuous service cross.

[The Times, 1 and 4 March 1901, 8 Jan 1910; Sydney Morning Herald, 1 March 1901; Australian, and Sydney Mail, 2 March 1901; information supplied by Mrs. James Huddart.]

A. B. W.

HUDLESTON (formerly SIMPSON), WILFRED HUDLESTON (1828–1909), geologist, born at York on 2 June 1828, was eldest son of Dr. John Simpson of Knaresborough (the third in succession to practise medicine) by his wife Elizabeth, daughter of Thomas Ward of Dore House, near Handsworth. His mother was heiress through her mother, Eleanor Hudleston (*d.* 1856), of the family of Hudleston of Hutton John, Cumberland. Wilfred, who with the rest of his family assumed the surname of Hudleston by royal licence in 1867, was educated first at St. Peter's school, York, and afterwards at Uppingham, proceeding to St. John's College, Cambridge, where he graduated B.A. in 1850 and M.A. in 1853.

At Cambridge he was interested chiefly in ornithology, which he had begun to study at school. In 1855 he spent a summer in Lapland, collecting with Alfred Newton [q. v. Suppl. II] and John Woolley. After visiting Algeria and the Eastern Atlas with Henry Baker Tristram [q. v. Suppl. II] and Osbert Salvin [q. v.], he spent more than a year in Greece and Turkey adding to his collections. From 1862 to 1867 he systematically studied natural history and chemistry, attending courses of lectures at the University of Edinburgh, and afterwards at the Royal College of Chemistry in London. Undecided at first whether to make chemistry or geology his chief subject, he was drawn to the latter by the influence of Professor John Morris [q. v.].

Settling in London, although he lived part of the year on property at West Holme, Dorset, and at Knaresborough, he began his career as a geologist. Engaging actively in the work of the Geologists' Association, he served as secretary from 1874 to 1877, and supplied many careful reports of their excursions. He was president of the association (1881–3). He became a fellow of the Geological Society in 1867, was secretary (1886–90), and president (1892–4). He contributed to the society's 'Journal,' among others, an important paper (with the Rev. J. F. Blake) on the corallian rocks of England. Other papers on the jurassic system appeared in the 'Geological Magazine,' and in 1887 he began to publish in the Palæontographical Society's volumes a monograph on the inferior oolite gasteropods, which, when completed in 1896, comprised 514 pages of letterpress and 44 plates. It was largely founded on his own fine collection of these fossils, which he bequeathed to the Sedgwick Museum, Cambridge.

In 1884 Hudleston was elected F.R.S. In 1886 and the following year he undertook some dredging in the English Channel, for he was hardly less interested in recent mollusca than in fossils, and greatly aided the foundation of a marine laboratory at Cullercoats, Northumberland. Early in 1895 he made a journey in India, travelling from Bombay as far as Srinagar. Hudleston, who received the Geological Society's Wollaston medal in 1897, presided over the geological section of the British Association in 1898. He received, with the other three original members, a gold medal at the jubilee of the British Ornithologists' Union in Dec. 1908. He was also a president of the Devonshire Association and other local societies.

His memoirs and papers, about sixty in number, cover an unusually wide field and are characterised by thoroughness. They discuss, besides British subjects, questions of Indian, Syrian, and African geology, two of the most important being on the eastern margin of the North Atlantic basin and the supposed marine origin of the fauna of Lake Tanganyika. His presidential addresses to societies are conspicuous for painstaking research and breadth of view. Tall, spare, and strongly built, a keen sportsman with both rod and gun, he enjoyed good health till the last few years of his life. He was J.P. for both Dorset and the West Riding. He died suddenly at West Holme, Dorset, on 29 January 1909. In 1890 he married Rose, second daughter of William Heywood Benson of Littlethorpe, near Ripon, who survived him without issue. A portrait in oils is in the possession of Mrs. Hudleston.

[Burke's Landed Gentry, s.v. Hudleston of Knaresborough; Geol. Mag. (with portrait), 1904 and in 1909; Quarterly Journal of Geol. Soc., 1909; Proc. Roy. Soc. 81 B. (with portrait), 1909; Ibis Jubilee Supplement, 1909; private information; personal knowledge.] T. G. B.

HUDSON, CHARLES THOMAS (1828–1903), naturalist, third of five sons of John Corrie Hudson, chief clerk of the legacy duty office (1795–1879), and Emily (1794–1868), daughter of James Hebard, of Ewell, Surrey, was born at Brompton, London, on 11 March 1828. The father in youth was an advanced radical and friend of William Godwin [q. v.], of the Shelleys, Charles Lamb, and William Hazlitt; in later life his opinions changed (*Athenæum*, 1879, i. 506). He was author of 'A letter on the cruelty of employing children in sweeping chimneys' (*Pamphleteer*, xxii. 407–30, for 1823); and also of: (1) 'The Executor's Guide,' 2nd edit. 1838 (many edits.); (2) 'Plain Directions for making Wills,' 2nd edit. 1838 (many edits.); (3) 'Tables for valuing Annuities,'

2nd edit. 1842; (4) 'The Parent's Handbook, or Guide to the Choice of Professions,' 1842. Of other sons, Franklin Hudson (1819–1853), a surgeon, compiled 'Monumental Brasses of Northamptonshire' (1853), and Corrie Hudson (1822–1880), also in the legacy duty office, published two official handbooks.

Charles Thomas Hudson was educated at Kensington grammar school and The Grange, Sunderland. Family circumstances compelled him to earn his living by teaching at an early age, first at Glasgow and afterwards at the Royal Institution, Liverpool. It was largely through his own exertions that he was able in 1848 to go to St. John's College, Cambridge. He graduated as fifteenth wrangler in 1852, proceeding M.A. in 1855 and LL.D. in 1866. After leaving Cambridge he became on 25 July 1852 second master of the Bristol grammar school, and on 30 March 1855 was appointed headmaster. He resigned this post at midsummer 1860, and in 1861 opened a private school at Manilla Hall, Clifton, formerly the residence of Sir William Draper [q. v.], which he conducted till 1881. His varied interests and sympathies explain his school's success. Afterwards he lived at 6 Royal York Crescent, Clifton, whence he moved in 1891 to Dawlish, Devon, and in 1899 to Shanklin, Isle of Wight. During his later years he often gave lectures, chiefly at public schools, on natural history, which he illustrated with ingenious coloured transparencies of his own construction.

Hudson, a born naturalist, devoted his leisure to microscopical research, and in particular to the study of the Rotifera. His first printed paper was on 'Rhinops Vitrea' in the 'Annals and Magazine of Natural History' for 1869. Afterwards he published numerous papers in the 'Microscopical Journal' and the 'Quarterly Journal of Microscopical Science,' describing new genera and species of Rotifera, of which 'Pedalion mirum' was a noteworthy discovery. A list of these papers is given in the 'Journal of the Royal Microscopical Society' for 1904, p. 49. He was elected fellow of the Royal Microscopical Society in 1872, was president from 1888 to 1890, and an honorary fellow from 1901 till his death. With the assistance of Philip Henry Gosse [q. v.] he published in 1886–7 'The Rotifera: or Wheel-Animalculæ.' In recognition of this, the standard monograph on the subject, he was elected F.R.S. in 1889. Lord Avebury (*Pleasures of Life*, ch. 9) quotes the charming introduction of this work as showing that the true naturalist was no mere dry collector.

Hudson's natural gift for drawing found expression in the beautiful illustrations of 'The Rotifera.' He was also musical, and as a young man wrote and composed songs.

Hudson died at Shanklin on 23 Oct. 1903, and was buried there. He married (1) on 19 June 1855 Mary Ann, daughter of William Bullock Tibbits of Long Ashton, near Bristol, by whom he had one daughter, Florence; and (2) on 24 June 1858, at Clifton, Louisa Maria Fiott, daughter of Freelove Hammond of the Inner Temple; by his second wife he had four sons and five daughters.

[Personal knowledge; private information; Men of the Time, 15th edition, 1899; Journal of Royal Micr. Soc., 1904, pp. 48, 49; Brit. Mus. Cat.] C. L. K.

HUGGINS, Sir WILLIAM (1824–1910), astronomer, born at Stoke Newington, London, on 7 Feb. 1824, was son of William Thomas Huggins, silkmercer and linendraper of Gracechurch Street, by his wife Lucy Miller of Peterborough (*d.* 1868). Entering the City of London School in February 1837 on its foundation, he left at Easter 1839 to pursue his education under private tutors. He worked at classics, mathematics, and modern languages, but his inclination lay towards science. Early in life he spent much time in microscopical research, especially in connection with physiology. He joined the Royal Microscopical Society in 1852 and also occupied himself with chemistry and physics. After a few years of business life Huggins came into the possession of a moderate competence and decided to devote himself to observational astronomy. He joined the Royal Astronomical Society on 12 April 1854, and in 1856 built for himself an observatory attached to his house at Tulse Hill, which is briefly described in the society's 'Monthly Notices,' 9 May 1856. That house he occupied for life. The observatory there, on its foundation, contained a 5-inch equatorial by Dollond, a transit-circle by Jones of 3¼ inches aperture, with a circle 18 inches in diameter, and a clock by Arnold. Huggins's earliest observations were of ordinary geometrical or visual astronomy, and his first communications to the 'Monthly Notices' are records of his observations of occultations of stars by the moon (vol. xxii.). In 1858 he purchased from the Rev. W. R. Dawes for

200*l*. an object-glass of 8 inches diameter made by the American firm of Alvan Clark, which was mounted equatorially and provided with a clock motion by Messrs. Cooke of York. With this instrument he observed between 1858 and 1860 the changes in the forms of the belts and spots on Jupiter, and the periodic disappearance of Saturn's rings in 1862 (cf. *R. Astr. Soc. Notices*). The publication in 1862 of Kirchhoff's interpretation of the Fraunhofer lines in the spectrum as showing the chemical constitution of the sun turned Huggins's attention in a new and more fruitful direction. To his neighbour at Fulse Hill, William Allen Miller [q. v.], professor of chemistry at King's College, who had worked much on chemical spectroscopy, Huggins confided a scheme for applying Kirchhoff's methods to the stars, and asked Miller to join him in the research. Huggins and Miller devised a new instrument, a star spectroscope, which enabled them to determine the chemical constitution of stars. They described their star spectroscope in the 'Philosophical Transactions of the Royal Society' for 1864, pp. 415–17. The light-dispersing portion of the apparatus consisted of two prisms of very dense and homogeneous flint glass made by Ross, which were attached to the 8-inch refractor. Mr. Rutherford in America had already devised similar apparatus quite independently. Miller and Huggins owed nothing to his invention. As a preliminary to work on the stars with this instrument it was necessary to have convenient maps of the spectra of terrestrial elements, and Huggins devoted a large part of 1863 to making twenty-four such maps with a train of six prisms. These were published in a paper read before the Royal Society in December of that year (*Phil. Trans.* 1864, cliv. 139). Earlier in 1863 Miller and Huggins had presented to the Royal Society the results of their first investigations with their star spectroscope in a paper on the 'Lines of the Spectra of some of the Fixed Stars' (*Proc. Roy. Soc.* 1863, xii. 444); this was followed by a more complete paper on the 'Spectra of some of the Fixed Stars' (*Phil. Trans.* 1864, cliv. 413–35). The conclusion was that 'in plan of structure the stars, or at least the brightest of them, resemble the sun. Their light, like that of the sun, emanates from intensely white-hot matter, and passes through an atmosphere of absorbent vapours. With this unity of general plan of structure there exists a great diversity amongst the individual stars. Star differs from star in chemical constitution' (cf. his addresses, *Brit. Assoc.* 4 Aug. 1866). On 29 Aug. 1864 Huggins made an important observation. Examination with the spectrum apparatus showed that the light from a certain planetary nebula in Draco was such as would emanate from a luminous gas, and hence it was to be concluded that so-called nebulæ were not in all cases aggregations of stars too far distant to be resolved into their constituent units, as had hitherto been supposed. In a paper 'On the Spectra of some of the Nebulæ' (*Phil. Trans.* 1864, cliv. 437) Huggins showed that eight nebulæ he had examined exhibited gaseity. This paper, by Huggins alone, was published as a supplement to the joint paper on the 'Spectra of the Fixed Stars,' and like the former papers was communicated by Dr. Miller, Huggins not being then a fellow of the Royal Society. He was elected a fellow in June 1865.

In May 1866 Huggins first subjected to spectroscopic examination a Nova, or new star, one having appeared in the constellation Corona Borealis. He suggested that, owing to some great convulsion, the star had been suddenly enveloped in flames of burning hydrogen (*Proc. Roy. Soc.* 1866, xv. 146). By 1866 ten papers in all had been published. In that year the Royal Society awarded a royal medal to Huggins for his researches. Miller, as a member of the council, was excluded from this honour, and his other engagements soon prevented him from working with Huggins by night, but in 1867 the gold medal of the Royal Astronomical Society was given to Huggins and Miller jointly for their work in astronomical physics. From 1867 to 1870 Huggins was one of the hon. secretaries of the Royal Astronomical Society, vice-president from 1870 to 1873, and from 1873 to his death, except for two years (1876–8) when he was president, was foreign secretary.

In the years following 1864 Huggins extended his series of observations of nebulæ, examining amongst others the great nebula in Orion (cf. *Phil. Trans.* clvi. 381, clviii. 540; *Phil. Mag.* xxxi. 475; *Proc. Roy. Soc.* 1865, xiv. 39; *Monthly Notices R.A.S.* xxv. 155). From 1866 onwards he observed the spectrum of several comets as they appeared, and found the spectrum of Brorsen's comet of 1868 to indicate a chemical constitution different from that of the nebulæ (cf. *Proc. Roy. Soc.* 1868, xvi. 386), whilst spectroscopic examination of the second comet of 1868 (Winnecke's) revealed volatilised carbon, which has since proved to be typical of many cometary spectra.

In Feb. 1868 Huggins in the annual report of his observatory to the Royal Astronomical Society referred to experiments he had made in following up suggestions made by (Sir) Norman Lockyer for observing the red flames on prominences in the sun's chromosphere, which had previously been only observed at times of the sun's eclipse. He was not successful in this attempt until the end of the same year, and meanwhile he had been anticipated by Lockyer and Janssen, who saw these prominences immediately after the eclipse in Aug. 1868. Huggins, however, made an essential advance in the method by widening the slit of the spectroscope. About 1862–3 Huggins thought to apply to spectroscopic astronomy the principle enunciated by Doppler in 1841 that the positions of spectrum lines change as the object moves to or from the spectator. After consultation in 1867 with James Clerk Maxwell [q. v.], but wholly independently of him, Huggins presented to the Royal Society early in 1868 some observations on the spectrum of Sirius (*Phil. Trans.* 1868, clviii. 529), from which a motion of the star from the earth could be deduced of about 25 miles per second. In 1870 the Royal Society came into possession of the Oliveira bequest. This was placed at Huggin's disposal for the construction of a large telescope to enable him to pursue more effectively his researches into the motions of stars. The dome of his observatory was enlarged to a diameter of 18 feet instead of 12, and a new instrument procured from Sir Howard Grubb consisting of a 15-inch refractor and an 18-inch Cassegram reflector, with mirrors of speculum metal which could be used on one mounting. From 1870 to 1875 Huggins used the refracting telescope for determining the velocity of stars in the line of sight by visual observation; the results appeared in the 'Proceedings of the Royal Society' in papers 'On the Spectrum of the Great Nebula in Orion, and on the Motion of Stars towards and from the Earth' (1872, xx. 379), and 'On the Motions of some of the Nebulæ towards or from the Earth' (1874, xxii. 251). Later observers, Vogel, Belopolsky, Frost, Adams, Newall, and Campbell, have greatly developed Huggins's method of this kind of observation with immense advantage to astronomical knowledge. Meanwhile Huggins soon turned his attention with important consequences to the application of photography to stellar spectroscopy. As early as 27 Feb. 1863 he had attempted to photograph the spectrum of Sirius; but the result was unsatisfactory and the effort was not pursued (*Phil. Trans.* 1864). In 1872 Dr. Draper in America photographed with greater success a spectrum of Vega. In 1876 Huggins secured improved apparatus, and using the gelatine dry-plate, which dates from 1871, he obtained a still better photograph of the spectrum of Vega (cf. *Proc. Roy. Soc.* 1876, xxv. 445). There followed photographs of great precision of the spectra of the larger stars, of the moon and the planets (cf. 'On the Photographic Spectra of Stars,' *Phil. Trans.* 1880, part ii. p. 669; 1890, xlviii. 216). Applying photography to solar research, he announced to the Royal Society on 21 Dec. 1882, that he had obtained photographs of the solar disc showing also the characteristic rays and structure of the corona round the sun, hitherto seen only during a total solar eclipse. But the promise implied in this communication has not since been realised. 'The Corona of the Sun' formed the subject of the Bakerian lecture delivered by Huggins before the Royal Institution on 20 Feb. 1885. In 1882 the photographic method of spectroscopy was applied to the Great Nebula in Orion, and this object was observed again both visually and photographically some years later, mainly to determine the origin of the chief nebular line (cf. *Proc. Royal Soc.* 1882, xxxiii. 425; 1889, xlvi. 40, with Mrs. Huggins; and 1890, xlviii. 213). On this subject Huggins's conclusions differed from those which (Sir) Norman Lockyer had reached, but finally the observations of Prof. Keeler at the Lick Observatory corroborated Huggins's view that the nebular line is not a remnant of the magnesium fluting and that its origin is still unknown.

Huggins's reputation as an astronomer of the first rank was early recognised. In 1870 he received the degree of hon. LL.D. from Cambridge, and of hon. D.C.L. from Oxford in 1871 (at Lord Salisbury's installation as chancellor). The Universities of Edinburgh, Dublin and St. Andrews all conferred on him the honorary degree of LL.D. From the Royal Society he received the royal medal in 1866, the Rumford in 1880, and the Copley in 1898. The Royal Astronomical Society awarded to him the gold medal for his researches on velocity in the line of sight in 1885. The Paris Academy of Sciences bestowed on him the Lalande prize in 1882, and in 1888 he received the Prix Janssen of the Institute of France, and from the National Academy of Sciences of Washington he obtained the Draper gold medal in 1901. His private means were not large, and in 1890 a civil list pension of 150*l.* a year was granted him. In 1891 he was president of the British Association meeting at Cardiff. His address was an eloquent statement of recent progress in astronomy, chiefly of the discoveries which had been made since 1860, owing to the introduction into the observatory of the spectroscope and the dry plate, and he spoke of the quite recent application of photography to star-charting. In 1897, at the diamond jubilee of Queen Victoria, Huggins was created a K.C.B., and in 1902 he was one of the original members of the Order of Merit. In 1900 he was chosen president of the Royal Society, and held the office till 1906. In that capacity he delivered four annual addresses, two on the 'Importance of Science as a Part of General Education,' and two on the 'Duty of the Royal Society to the Specialised Scientific Societies, and secondly on its Duty as Adviser to the State.' The four addresses were collected with some notes on the history of the Royal Society in 'The Royal Society, or Science in the State and in the Schools' (1906).

Huggins continued his spectroscopic researches almost to his death. He made especially important observations of the new star in the constellation of Auriga in 1892 (*Proc. Roy. Soc.* 1892, l. 465; 1892, li. 487; 1893, liv. 30). His final conclusion was that the cause of the Nova was the casual near approach of two bodies previously possessing considerable velocities in space; that enormous forces of a tidal nature were set at work, and caused an outburst of hot matter, and that the phenomenon had some analogy to the periodic outbursts on the sun, but on a grander scale (cf. lecture at Royal Institution on 13 May 1892, and *Fortnightly Review* for June). In 1895 he examined the helium line in the spectrum of the sun, which after a first unsuccessful attempt (*Chemical News*, No. 1855) he found to be double, and so procured additional evidence that helium is a terrestrial element. In 1897 he did much to settle the vexed question in solar physics regarding the extent and the presence of calcium in the sun (cf. *Proc.* 1897, lxi. 433). The discovery of radium by Professor and Madame Curie in 1903 again led to laboratory experiments by Huggins with the spectroscope (*Proceedings of the Royal Society*, 1903, lxxii. 196; 1903, lxxii. 409; 1905, lxxvii. 130).

Through life Huggins occasionally pursued scientific inquiries outside the range of astronomy. In a paper on 'Prismatic Examination of Microscopic Objects' he described the application for the first time of the spectroscope to the microscope (*Quarterly Journal Microsc. Soc.* 1865). In 1883 he wrote 'On the Function of the Sound Post, and on the Proportional Thickness of the Strings of the Violin' (*Proc. Roy. Soc.* 1883, xxxv. 241). In his later years Huggins with the co-operation of Lady Huggins collected into two volumes the results of his work. Volume i. entitled 'An Atlas of Representative stellar Spectra from λ 4870 to λ 3300,' comprises a discussion of the evolutional order of the stars and the interpretation of the spectra, preceded by a short history of the observatory and its work (1900). The second volume, 'The Scientific Papers of Sir William Huggins' (1909), contains the complete set of his contributions to scientific literature, in most cases verbatim, and with some additions.

At the end of 1908 Huggins found it necessary, owing to advancing years, to give up astronomical work, and the instruments provided in 1870 by the Royal Society reverted to that body, who gave them to the syndicate of the Cambridge University Observatory. On a brass tablet fixed in 'the Huggins dome' of that observatory the following words were inscribed: '1870–1908. *These telescopes were used by Sir William Huggins and Lady Huggins in their observatory at Tulse Hill in researches which formed the foundation of the Science of Astrophysics.*' He died in London on 12 May 1910 rather suddenly, following a surgical operation, and, according to his wish, his body was cremated at Golder's Green, where his ashes remain.

In 1875 Huggins married Margaret Lindsay, daughter of John M. Murray of Dublin, who survived him. He had no children. In his wife Huggins found a devoted and helpful coadjutor, and her services to astronomy were recognised by the Royal Astronomical Society in 1901, when she and Agnes Mary Clerke [q. v. Suppl. II] were chosen honorary members of that society.

Huggins was a representative of the Royal Society on the Board of Visitors of the Royal Observatory, Greenwich, from 1898 until his death, and served in a like capacity at the University Observatory at

Oxford. When the organisation of astronomical amateurs known as the British Astronomical Association was founded in 1896 it had the warm approval of Dr. Huggins, who was present at the initiatory meeting and was a vice-president for many years.

A portrait by the Hon. John Collier hangs in the rooms of the Royal Society; it is reproduced in the volume of Huggins's scientific papers.

[The Scientific Papers of Sir William Huggins, edited by Sir Wm. Huggins, K.C.B., O.M., and Lady Huggins, Hon.M.R.A.S.; Proc. Roy. Soc., series A, vol. 86, 20 Feb. 1912; Monthly Notices of the Royal Astronomical Soc., Feb. 1911.] H. P. H.

HUGHES, EDWARD (1832–1908), portrait-painter, born on 14 Sept. 1832, at Myddelton Square, Pentonville, was son of George Hughes, painter and exhibitor at the Royal Academy, by his wife Mary Lucas. From his father and John Pye [q. v.], the engraver, Hughes received his earliest training in art. In December 1846 he was admitted to the Royal Academy school, and in 1847, when still only fourteen, was awarded the silver medal of the Royal Society of Arts for a chalk drawing. His precocious ability rapidly developed, and in the same year Hughes's earliest painting, 'The First Primer,' won distinction on the line at Burlington House. A more ambitious subject, 'Nourmahal's dream; Light of the Harem,' from 'Lalla Rookh,' was hung the following year. From 1855 to 1876 Hughes was regularly represented at the Academy by subject-pictures, which he afterwards abandoned for the more remunerative work of portraiture. From 1878 to 1884, when his contributions ceased, he exclusively exhibited portraits at the Royal Academy, the most noteworthy being those of Miss Louisa Parnell (Hon. Mrs. Francis Errington) and Dr. Lightfoot, bishop of Durham. 'Very many artists,' Millais is reported to have said, 'can paint the portrait of a man, but very few can paint the portrait of a lady, and Edward Hughes is one of those few.' Hughes's popularity steadily increased, and in 1886 his whole-length painting of Miss Jeannie Chamberlain (Lady Naylor Leyland), exhibited at Messrs. Agnew's Galleries, brought him important commissions.

In 1895 Hughes received his first royal commission. He painted a whole-length seated portrait of Queen Mary, when Duchess of York (now at Buckingham Palace). Of Queen Alexandra Hughes painted three whole-length portraits. The first of these, standing in a landscape, as Princess of Wales, and now at Sandringham, was exhibited at the Guildhall in 1897. The second portrait, in the mourning robes worn at the opening of parliament in 1902, is now at Marlborough House, and was reproduced in photogravure by J. B. Pratt; the third portrait (at Buckingham Palace), which shows Queen Alexandra in coronation robes, was engraved by E. L. Haynes, while replicas were executed for the King of Denmark and the Durbar Hall, Patiala, India. Hughes also painted the Princess Royal, the Princess Victoria, the Queen of Norway (these portraits are at Sandringham), the Duchess of Teck, the Prince of Wales, his brother Prince Albert, and his sister Princess Mary (these are at Buckingham Palace).

Hughes's later work was confined entirely to portraits of ladies and children; among his sitters being Louise, Duchess of Devonshire, and her daughters, Lady Mary and Lady Alice Montagu. The Countess of Leven and Melville, Mrs. William James, and Mrs. Miller Mundy were painted at whole length with their children. The group of the Earl and Countess of Minto's three daughters, painted in 1905, was Hughes's largest picture. Hughes's many American sitters included Miss Jean Reid (afterwards the Hon. Mrs. John Ward), daughter of Mr. Whitelaw Reid, American Ambassador in London from 1904.

Hughes died on 14 May 1908 at his residence, 52 Gower Street, W.C., and was buried at Highgate cemetery. His unfinished portrait of himself is in the possession of his daughter. He married first Mary Pewtner, and secondly Kate Margetts, and was survived by two sons and a daughter, Alice Hughes, who resided with her father for many years at Gower Street, and earned a wide reputation as a professional photographer.

Hughes, who studied the masters of portraiture from Reynolds onwards to the modern workers of the French school, devoted his technical skill chiefly to an idealistic treatment of his sitters.

His earliest portrait of Queen Alexandra, those of Queen Mary, Lady Naylor Leyland, and seven others were reproduced in photogravure in 'The Book of Beauty,' 1896. No specimen of his work is in any public collection.

[The Times, 16 May 1908, and other press notices; The Book of Beauty, 1896, edit. by Mrs. F. Harcourt Williamson; Art Journal, 1902; Royal Academy Exhibitors, 1905–6.

by Algernon Graves; Lists of the Printsellers' Association; information from the Hon. Charlotte Knollys, Miss Alice Hughes, and Sir H. T. Wood, Royal Society of Arts.]

J. D. M.

HUGHES, HUGH PRICE (1847–1902), methodist divine, born at Carmarthen, on 8 Feb. 1847, was grandson of Hugh Hughes, a well-known Welsh preacher, and son of John Hughes, surgeon, of Carmarthen, by his wife, Anne Phillips, of Jewish descent on her father's side. Educated first at Carmarthen grammar school, then at the Mumbles, near Swansea, he was, as a schoolboy, placed on the 'plan' as a Wesleyan local preacher. In 1865 he entered Richmond College in preparation for the Wesleyan methodist ministry. There his independence of character brought him into conflict with the authorities. In 1869 he graduated B.A. at London University, proceeding M.A. in 1881. Placed by the Wesleyan conference on the itinerating 'plan,' he began work at Dover; was moved in 1872 to Brighton, in 1875 to Tottenham, in 1878 to Dulwich, and in 1881 to Oxford. At each station marked success attended his work.

In 1884 Hughes was brought to London as superintendent minister at Brixton Hill, and speedily became the leader of a 'forward' party in methodism. He advocated new methods and especially new energy, inspired others with his own enthusiasm, and, despite much opposition, won a majority of the connection to his side. The Wesleyan methodist 'forward movement' took formal shape in 1885, and in 1886 Hughes was chosen to start a West London mission, with a social as well as a religious side. He began its services in St. James's Hall in October 1887, and remained until his death the leader of the work. Meanwhile the 'Methodist Times' was started in 1885, with Hughes as its editor, to support the policy of the forward party. Hughes's characteristic ardour made the journal a powerful influence, politically and ecclesiastically, in methodism. In 1886 he raised in it the question of methodist reunion, and saw his suggestion bear fruit. The publication of articles by 'A Friend of Missions' (Dr. (afterwards Sir) H. S. Lunn) attacking methodist missionary methods in India led to a commission of inquiry, which reported in 1890 against the charges. Hughes supported his contributor through a long and bitter controversy. In 1892 he was a conspicuous figure at a 'reunion of the churches' conference at Grindelwald, and suggested terms of reunion. Desiring to consolidate the influence of nonconformity, he was a chief promoter of the Free Church Congress, which met in 1892, and of the national council of the Evangelical Free Churches, of which he was, in 1896, the first president. In 1898 he was elected president of the Wesleyan methodist conference, and threw himself into the task of raising the Million Guineas Fund. Throughout his career he was a keen advocate of social reform, and in such work joined hands with representatives of other churches. Worn out with many labours he broke down in 1902, and died in London of apoplexy on 17 Nov.

Hughes was one of the most distinct personalities in the religious life of his day. An evangelical in faith, a preacher and speaker of magnetic power, with the capacity for communicating enthusiasm to others, he carried his influence far beyond his own denomination. In politics a radical, he helped to make the phrase 'the nonconformist conscience,' by challenging the title to take part in political life of Sir Charles Wentworth Dilke after the divorce case of Crawford *v.* Crawford in 1886, and of Parnell after his exposure in O'Shea *v.* O'Shea in 1890. During the Boer war he defended the imperialist side. His ministerial life was a struggle against conservatism; but he lived to be denounced as 'steeped in ecclesiasticism.' In the Education Acts controversy he supported the Free Church policy, but expressed his own willingness to accept the Apostles' Creed as a basis of teaching. He had no sympathy with laxity in doctrine, and successfully opposed the admission of unitarians to the Free Church council.

Hughes married, on 20 Aug. 1873, Mary Katherine Howard, daughter of the Rev. Alfred Barrett, governor of Richmond College, who survived him with two sons and two daughters.

His chief publications were: 1. 'The Atheist Shoemaker: a Page in the History of the West London Mission,' 1889, for which he was attacked by G. W. Foote. 2. 'The Philanthropy of God,' 1890. 3. 'Social Christianity,' 1890. 4. 'Ethical Christianity,' 1891. 5. 'Essential Christianity,' 1894. 6. 'The Morning Lands of History: a Visit to Greece, Palestine and Egypt,' 1901.

[The Life of Hugh Price Hughes, by his daughter, Dorothea P. Hughes, 1904; Life, by J. Gregory Mantle, 1903; Hugh Price

Hughes as we knew him, by J. Armitage Robinson and others, 1902; The Times, 18 Nov. 1902; Christian World, 20 Nov. 1902; Guardian, 19 Nov. 1902; Review of Reviews, 1890; personal knowledge and private information.] A. R. B.

HUGHES, JOHN (1842-1902), Wesleyan methodist divine and editor, son of John Hughes and Jane his wife, was born on 15 April 1842, at Cwm Magwr Isaf, in the parish of Llanfihangel y Creuddyn, Cardiganshire. Left an orphan at an early age, he had little schooling, and found employment first as a farm lad and afterwards as a lead miner. In 1863 he became a slate quarryman at Blaenau Festiniog; here his interest in literary and theological questions made him a leader among his fellow-workers, and he was designated a Wesleyan lay preacher. Resolving to enter the ministry, he passed a brief period of preparation at Jasper House, Aberystwyth, and was accepted by his connexion in 1867. He travelled until 1878 in the South Wales district; he was then transferred to the North Wales district, a sphere of labour in which he took a more and more important place, until in 1897 he was appointed Welsh connexional editor and superintendent of the bookroom at Bangor. He took an active part in the affairs of his connexion, and to his advocacy was largely due the establishment of an annual general assembly for North and South Wales. In 1901 he received the degree of D.D. from the South Western University, Georgetown, Texas. He died at Bangor on 24 Feb. 1902. In March 1873 he married Emily, daughter of Rev. Henry Wilcox, by whom he had four sons and two daughters. One of the sons, Henry Maldwyn Hughes, B.A., D.D., is a Wesleyan methodist minister.

Hughes, best known by his bardic name of 'Glanystwyth,' was of versatile gifts, holding a high place as a preacher and as a writer of Welsh prose and verse. He edited the 'Winllan' from 1874 to 1876, the 'Gwyliedydd' newspaper in 1890, and the 'Eurgrawn Wesleyaidd' from 1897 to 1902. He published: 1. 'John Penri,' a poem, Machynlleth, 1888. 2. A Welsh Life of Christ, Holywell, 1891. 3. 'Oesau Bore y Byd' (The World's Infancy), Holywell, 1892. 4. A Life of Rev. Isaac Jones, Liverpool, 1898. 5. 'Delw y Nefol,' a volume of sermons, Holywell, 1900. 6. A Commentary on Colossians, Bangor, 1901.

[Memoir by D. Gwynfryn Jones and H. Maldwyn Hughes, Bangor, 1904.] J. E. L.

HULME, FREDERICK EDWARD (1841-1909), botanist, only son of Frederick William Hulme, landscape painter, was born at Hanley, Staffordshire, on 29 March 1841. Brought to London as a child, and sent first to the Western grammar school, he studied art at South Kensington from his seventeenth year and became art-master of Marlborough College, in 1870 professor of geometrical drawing at King's College, London, in 1885 lecturer to the Architectural Association, and examiner to the Science and Art Department and the London Chamber of Commerce. A lover of nature rather than a student of natural science, he interested himself in the folklore of plants and sketched with skill plants and flowers. He was a voluminous writer on various themes, and his chief works were illustrated by coloured plates from his own drawings. In 1875 he began the issue of 'Familiar Wild Flowers,' his best-known work, with numerous plates. Eight volumes appeared in his lifetime, and a ninth was just ready at his death. The whole work has been repeatedly reissued serially.

Hulme also furnished plates for books by other writers, notably 'Familiar Garden Flowers,' by Shirley Hibberd, the companion series to his own 'Familiar Wild Flowers' (1879); and 'Sylvan Spring' (1880), by Mr. Francis George Heath.

Hulme was elected a fellow of the Linnean Society in 1869, and fellow of the Society of Antiquaries in 1872. For several years he was also a vice-president of the Selborne Society, with whose principles he was in thorough sympathy. He died at Kew on 11 April 1909, and was buried at Brookwood. He married in 1866 Emily, daughter of John Napper of Herfield Place, Sussex. His wife, two sons, and two daughters survived him, the elder son, Frank Howell Hulme, being dean of Bloemfontein.

Hulme's chief works were: 1. 'The Principles of Ornamental Art,' 1875. 2. 'The Town, College and Neighbourhood of Marlborough,' 1881. 3. 'The History, Principles and Practice of Heraldry,' 1891; 2nd edit. 1897. 4. 'The History of Symbolism in Christian Art,' 1891; revised 1899. 5. 'The Birth and Development of Ornament,' 1893; reissued in 1894. Minor works which chiefly consisted of art students' text-books include: 1. 'Sketches from Nature of Plant Form,' 1867. 2. 'The Garland of the Year with twelve chromographs of flowers,' issued anonymously, 1873. 3. 'Plants, their Natural Growth and Ornamental Treatment,' 1874. 4. 'Art Instruction in

England,' 1882. 5. 'Myth Land,' 1886. 6. 'Wayside Sketches,' 1889. 7. 'Natural History Lore and Legend,' 1895. 8. 'Wild Fruits of the Countryside,' with 36 coloured plates, 1902. 9. 'Butterflies and Moths of the Countryside,' with 35 coloured plates, 1903. 10. 'Wild Flowers in their Seasons,' with 80 coloured plates, 1907. 11. 'Familiar Swiss Flowers,' with 100 coloured plates, 1908. 12. 'That Rock-garden of Ours,' with 50 illustrations, 1909.

[The Times, 14 April 1909; Journal of Botany, 1909, p. 235; Journal of Horticulture, 1909, lviii. 360; Proc. Linnean Soc., 1908–9, pp. 41–2; Selborne Mag., 1909, xx. 77; information from the family.] G. S. B.

HUME, MARTIN ANDREW SHARP (1843–1910), author, born in London on 8 Dec. 1843, was second son of William Lacy Sharp, of the East India Company's service, who married Louisa Charlotte Hume in 1840. Educated at a private school at Forest Gate, he had some practical training in business, and began early to learn Spanish. A branch of his mother's family had settled at Madrid towards the end of the eighteenth century. In 1860 he paid his Spanish kinsfolk a first visit, which had a decisive influence on his career. His relatives received him with affectionate cordiality. Though he declined their invitation to make his home with them, he visited them annually for long periods, perfected his knowledge of Spanish, witnessed the revolution of 1868, and became acquainted with the chief organisers of the movement. The last of the Spanish Humes, a lady advanced in years, died in 1876, bequeathing her property to Martin Sharp, and in August 1877, in compliance with her wish, he assumed the name of Hume. He was now independent. A keen volunteer officer, he was attached to the Turkish forces during the campaign on the Lom in 1878–9; he then spent some time in exploration on the west coast of Africa, and travelled extensively in Central and South America.

Till 1882 Hume's sympathies had been vaguely conservative. Then his views changed, and during the next eleven years he actively engaged in English political conflict. He stood unsuccessfully as a liberal candidate at Maidstone in 1885, at Central Hackney in 1886, and at Stockport in 1892 and 1893. After some practice in journalism, he meanwhile produced his first book, a 'Chronicle of King Henry VIII of England' (1889), a translation from the Spanish. Though this attracted little attention, Hume persevered, and 'The Courtships of Queen Elizabeth; a History of the Various Negotiations for her Marriage,' and 'The Year after the Armada, and other Historical Studies,' both issued in 1896, were received with a degree of popular favour which led him to adopt authorship as a profession. In 1897 he published 'Sir Walter Ralegh' and 'Philip II of Spain,' the latter monograph showing insight and independence of view.

Next year Hume succeeded Pascual de Gayangos at the Public Record Office as editor of the 'Spanish State Papers,' and did sound work in this capacity. But his official duties did not absorb all his energies. In 1898 he published 'The Great Lord Burghley,' a readable study, and 'Spain, its Greatness and Decay, 1479–1789,' a useful historical outline, which he completed in the following year by the publication of 'Modern Spain, 1788–1898' (1899; new edit. 1906). The substance of the two latter volumes was recast in a more popular form under the title of 'The Spanish People: their Origin, Growth and Influence,' in 1901, and in the same year Hume issued 'Treason and Plot. Struggles for Catholic Supremacy in the Last Years of Queen Elizabeth.' His unflagging industry and gift of picturesque narrative were again displayed in 'The Love Affairs of Mary Queen of Scots,' which appeared in 1903, as did also 'Españoles é Ingleses en el siglo XVI' (Madrid), a work for which Hume had an unaccountable preference. In 1904 and 1906 respectively he contributed to the third and fourth volumes of 'The Cambridge Modern History.' By that time the pressure of work was beginning to tell upon him, and the result is visible in the hastily improvised lectures, delivered early in 1904, on 'Spanish Influence on English Literature' (1905). Henceforward he devoted himself to the production of works whose titles are enough to show that they were meant to appeal rather to general readers than to scholars: 'The Wives of Henry the Eighth, and the Parts they played in History' (1905); 'Queens of Old Spain' (1907); 'The Court of Philip IV; Spain in Decadence' (1907); 'Two English Queens and Philip' (1908), and 'Queen Elizabeth and her England' (1910). In addition to executing these publishers' commissions, Hume was busily engaged in reviewing books in the 'Daily Chronicle' and the 'Morning Post,' in lecturing on Spanish history at Pembroke College, Cambridge, and in examining at the universities of Birmingham and London. Deafness, which had long troubled him, increased during his last year. He died unmarried, on 1 July 1910, at his sister's house at Forest Gate of inflammation of the brain. A posthumous volume, entitled 'True Stories of the Past' (1910), bears witness to his untiring diligence and dexterous treatment of romantic episodes.

In addition to the works mentioned above, Hume edited a reprint of 'A History of Spain' (1900) by U. R. Burke [q. v.], translated a novel, 'Face to Face and Dolorosa,' from the Spanish of F. Acebal (1906), wrote a study on 'Fashion in Femininity' for Mary Craven's 'Famous Beauties of two Reigns' (London, 1906), and published 'Through Portugal,' an account of a short tour in that country, in 1907. In 1907 he also, amid much similar work, collaborated with F. B. Harbottle in a 'Dictionary of Quotations (Spanish),' supervised 'The South American Series' of historical manuals, and edited another series entitled 'Romantic History.'

Hume's interest in Spanish history and politics was genuine and well-informed, and he did good service in popularising these subjects. But his work at the Record Office shows that he was capable of better things. He took little pains to conceal his dislike for the academic type of mind, and professional critics were sometimes blind to the real merits which lay behind his emphatic style and journalistic methods. He was sensitive to criticism and was much chagrined at his failure to obtain chairs in history and Spanish for which he applied at the universities of Glasgow and Liverpool respectively. His merits were recognised in other ways; he was made hon. M.A. of Cambridge in 1908; he was a corresponding member of the Royal Spanish Academy, of the Royal Spanish Academy of History, and of the Royal Galician Academy, and a knight grand cross of the order of Isabel the Catholic. As a retired officer of the 3rd battalion of the Essex regiment he was known to the public as Major Hume; to his intimates and friends as 'Don Martin.'

[Private information; The Times, 4 July 1910. A memoir by R. B. Cunninghame Graham is in preparation.] J. F-K.

HUNT, GEORGE WILLIAM. [See under MACDERMOTT, GILBERT HASTINGS (1845–1901), music-hall singer.]

HUNT, WILLIAM HOLMAN (1827–1910), painter, born in Wood Street, Cheapside, London, on 2 April 1827, was eldest son in a family of two sons and five daughters of William Hunt, warehouseman there, by his wife, Sarah, daughter of William Holman. He was baptised in the famous church of St. Giles, Cripplegate. His father, William Hunt, who had some taste for art and books, took his son, while a child, to call on John Varley, the water-colour painter, but young William's early artistic ambitions were not encouraged by his father. After education at private schools the boy, in his thirteenth year, had his first touch of commercial life, engaging himself as assistant to a surveyor or estate agent, and afterwards to the London agent of Richard Cobden [q. v.], calico printer and politician. Finding these employments uncongenial, he obtained the reluctant permission of his family to spend his evenings in learning something of the practice of art. In this he was assisted by one Henry Rogers, a portrait painter living in the City of London, in whom lingered some of the traditions of Reynolds. Holman Hunt's own early efforts in portraiture attracted the attention of his master. In 1843 he left his mercantile employment and began work as a student at the British Museum. He spent three days a week there, and soon devoted another two days to copying at the National Gallery. In 1844 he was received into the Academy schools as a probationer after failing in a first attempt, and was promoted to studentship the following year. Millais, two years younger than himself, was already known among Holman Hunt's fellow-students at the Museum as a precocious genius. At the Academy the two youths made each other's acquaintance, and became friends for life. With another Academy student, Dante Gabriel Rossetti [q. v.], Holman Hunt was soon on 'nodding terms,' but he did not form a close acquaintance with him till they had left the school. In 1846 Holman Hunt began to exhibit at the Academy, sending from a studio at Hackney a picture entitled 'Hark!' a little girl holding a watch to her ear. In 1847, when he had removed to 108 High Holborn, he sent to the Academy 'Dr. Rochecliffe performing Divine Service in the Cottage of Joceline Joliffe at Woodstock,' a scene from Scott's novel. At the British Institution he exhibited in the same year 'Little Nell and her Grandfather.' These paintings were followed in 1848 by the 'Flight of Madeline and Porphyro,' from Keats's 'Eve of St. Agnes' (now the property of Walton Wilson). Like Holman Hunt's former Academy picture, this performance fired the enthusiasm of Rossetti, then a pupil of Ford Madox Brown. Rossetti told the artist that the illustration of Keats was 'the best picture of the year,' and asked permission to call on him. In August Holman Hunt acceded to Rossetti's request to work under him in his studio in Cleveland Street, Fitzroy Square. For the following nine years the two artists remained on intimate terms. To Holman Hunt Rossetti owed his introduction to Millais.

In the autumn of 1848 the three young men laid the foundation of the Pre-Raphaelite Brotherhood, a movement of wide significance which sought a new veracity in art. Ford Madox Brown [q. v. Suppl. I] was already working independently in the same direction. But Brown never joined the Brotherhood, of which Holman Hunt was at the outset the moving spirit, being ardently seconded by Millais. Rossetti was soon recruited, and suggested developments. Subsequently Thomas Woolner, W. M. Rossetti, James Collinson, and F. G. Stephens were admitted to the band. The title of the Brotherhood, and its initial-mark, P.R.B., were formally adopted in 1849. These seven men alone formed the genuine Brotherhood, although various other artists have from time to time been erroneously credited with membership. After the death of Dante Gabriel Rossetti in 1882, much controversy took place as to the relative responsibilities of Holman Hunt and others in initiating the movement. Rossetti, whose intimacy with Holman Hunt declined after 1857, was then represented to be its creator, while Ford Madox Brown was also put forward as the source of inspiration. Many influences were doubtless at work, but Millais alone can share with Holman Hunt the honours of parentage of the P.R.B., and Dante Rossetti's place was no more than that of first and chief disciple of these two. As Holman Hunt was the original conceiver, so was he the most faithful member of the little school, carrying on its principles without relaxation to the end of his long life.

The first thoroughly Pre-Raphaelite picture which Holman Hunt completed was 'Rienzi,' which was hung in the Academy of 1849 as a pendant to Millais's 'Isabella.' It was not sold at the exhibition, but on its return to Holman Hunt's studio Augustus Leopold Egg, R.A. [q. v.], found a customer for it at 105*l.* in a collector named Gibbons, through whom it passed to F. W. Cosens. It is now the property of Thomas Clarke. Holman Hunt was at the time threatened with distraint by his landlord, and the 105*l.* proved of great service.

At the end of 1849 Holman Hunt went abroad for the first time. He and Rossetti together visited Paris and afterwards Antwerp, Ghent, and Bruges. Holman Hunt's admiration was chiefly stirred in France by Delaroche, Flandrin, and Ingres. On returning to England he moved into new lodgings near old Chelsea church. While there he took his share in starting the Pre-Raphaelite organ 'The Germ,' the first number of which, issued on 1 Jan. 1850, opened with an etching by Holman Hunt—two subjects on a single plate, in illustration of a poem by Woolner; a copy of the etching is at the Tate Gallery. Meanwhile Holman Hunt was working on his picture of 'Christians escaping from Druid Persecution,' which was exhibited at the Academy in 1850. For the first time the Brotherhood roused a storm of censure among the critics, including Dickens (in 'Household Words'), and Holman Hunt's contribution shared the general denunciation. No buyer was found for it at the Academy, but Millais later in the year met casually at Oxford Thomas Combe [q. v.] of the Clarendon Press, who, on Millais's suggestion, bought it for 100 guineas. Combe, who left this and other pictures by Holman Hunt to the Ashmolean Museum at Oxford, thenceforth proved an invaluable friend to the painter, who was frequently entertained by Combe and his wife at Oxford.

At this period Holman Hunt was greatly depressed by want of substantial recognition, and fell into debt. He contemplated giving up art for farming. An offer to (Sir) Austen Henry Layard [q. v. Suppl. I] to accompany him as draughtsman on his archæological exploration of Nineveh arrived too late. He accepted employment, however, from William Dyce [q. v.] in copying and restoring old masters, and took Robert Braithwaite Martineau [q. v.] as a pupil. In the meantime, in 1851, he improved his position by exhibiting at the Royal Academy 'Valentine rescuing Sylvia from Proteus,' a scene from Shakespeare's 'Two Gentlemen of Verona.' The first design for the picture had been made in the previous October, when Holman Hunt, Rossetti, and F. G. Stephens were staying together at Sevenoaks painting sylvan backgrounds in Knole Park. The Sylvia was studied from Eleanor Siddal (afterwards Rossetti's wife), and the Valentine from James Lennox Hannay, subsequently a London magistrate. This notable picture was attacked by 'The Times,' but happily and unexpectedly it found a powerful defender in John Ruskin [q. v. Suppl. I], who in a letter to the newspaper compared Holman Hunt's art to that of Dürer. Thenceforth Ruskin was the chief public champion of Holman Hunt and his school (cf. his *Præraphaelitism*, 1851). Holman Hunt soon included Ruskin among his closest friends, and their affection for each other lasted till death. Holman Hunt's 'Valentine' was exhibited a second time in 1851 at the Liverpool Exhibition, where it won the premium of 50*l.* offered for the 'most approved painting.' It was bought in 1854 by (Sir) Thomas Fairbairn, who became another sympathetic patron and whose portrait Holman Hunt painted in 1874. The 'Valentine' was resold in 1887.

In the course of 1851 Holman Hunt and Millais spent some time at Ewell, near Epsom, afterwards removing to Worcester Park Farm. Each painted backgrounds for important pictures. Holman Hunt was beginning his 'Hireling Shepherd' and 'The Light of the World,' both of which were completed slowly at his Chelsea studio. 'The Hireling Shepherd' was finished in time for exhibition at the Royal Academy in 1852. Carlyle, Hunt's neighbour at Chelsea, had seen 'The Hireling Shepherd' in the studio, and had declared it to be 'the greatest picture he had seen painted by any modern man.' It was hung on the line, and ultimately passed to Manchester Art Gallery, while a replica became the property of Sir William Agnew [q. v. Suppl. II]. During that year he worked hard on three very different subjects. 'Claudio and Isabella' illustrated a scene from Shakespeare's 'Measure for Measure,' which after exhibition at the Academy in 1853 won a Liverpool prize of 50*l.* (it is now in the possession of Mrs. Ashton). 'Our English Coasts, 1852,' a study of the Downs near Hastings, was also exhibited at the Royal Academy in 1853; it was subsequently renamed 'Strayed Sheep,' and became the property of George Lillie Craik. Yet a third picture, 'New College Cloisters, 1852,' was shown at the Academy of 1853; it is at Jesus College, Oxford.

In 1854 Holman Hunt still further increased his reputation by sending to the Academy two of his best pictures, 'The Awakened Conscience' and 'The Light of the World.' The former was bought by (Sir) Thomas Fairbairn. 'The Light of the World' was acquired for 400 guineas by Thomas Combe, and in 1872 was presented by his widow to Keble College, Oxford. Ruskin in letters to 'The Times' wrote admiringly of the ethical and spiritual significance of both the paintings of 1854. He attributed to Holman Hunt a religious passion new to English art. In later years Holman Hunt was grieved by injury done to 'The Light of the World' owing to what he regarded as want of care at Keble College. He therefore painted the subject again on a life-size scale in 1904. The second version was purchased by Mr. Charles Booth, who arranged for its exhibition in the chief colonial cities and finally presented it to St. Paul's Cathedral, where it now hangs. Engravings and reproductions have made the original version one of the most familiar of modern pictures.

Holman Hunt's growing success enabled him in the meantime to carry out a project which had been slowly forming itself in his mind, to visit Palestine and treat sacred subjects among their actual surroundings. He resolved, he said, to find out with his own eyes what Christ was like.

Leaving England in January 1854 for two years, he travelled to Palestine by way of Paris, Malta, Egypt and Jaffa. At Cairo Thomas Seddon [q. v.] joined him. Settling down in Jerusalem, he soon began the well-known painting 'The Finding of the Saviour in the Temple,' which he finished six years later. Then, encamping on the western shore of the Dead Sea, he started on 'The Scapegoat.' Much other work was designed, and he made numberless studies of Jewish types and of the natural scenery. He explored the Holy Land with thoroughness, and formed useful friendships with English and other European tourists. At the close of 1855 he travelled from Beyrout to the Crimea, by way of Constantinople. In February 1856 he was again in London. The P.R.B. was then practically in a state of dissolution as a brotherhood but remained an ever-increasing force as a body of principles.

Holman Hunt settled for a time in Pimlico (49 Claverton Street). There he worked on designs for the illustrated edition of Tennyson's Poems for which Moxon the publisher had already enlisted the services of Millais, Rossetti, Maclise, Mulready, Stanfield, and others. Hunt undertook six drawings, including 'The Lady of Shalott,' 'Haroun al Raschid,' and 'Oriana.' Long afterwards, in 1886 he happily repeated his design for 'The Lady of Shalott' in oil. The edition of Tennyson was published in May 1857. Tennyson criticised Holman Hunt's interpretation of his 'Lady of Shalott,' but the artist who met the poet at Mrs. Prinsep's residence, Little Holland House, was soon on good terms with him, visiting him at Farringford, in the Isle of Wight, in

1858, and accompanying him with Palgrave, Woolner, and Val Prinsep, on a walking tour in Devonshire and Cornwall in 1860.

Holman Hunt's 'Scapegoat' was sent to the Academy of 1856. It arrested attention but puzzled the critics. Sir Robert Peel [q. v.] offered 250*l.* for it; he wished to hang it as a pendant to a Landseer! It was ultimately sold to Mr. Windus of Tottenham, a well-known collector, for 450*l.* It subsequently passed to Thomas Fairbairn, and in 1887 into the collection of Sir Cuthbert Quilter. At the exhibition of 1856 Holman Hunt also showed three Oriental landscapes.

At the suggestion of Combe, Holman Hunt offered himself as a candidate for the associateship of the Academy in the same year, but he was rejected, receiving only a single vote. His relations with the Academy were thenceforth strained. He sent nothing to the Academy again till 1860, and only eight pictures in the succeeding fourteen years, altogether ceasing to contribute after 1874. He took part in 1858 in the formation of the Hogarth Club, originally formed of artists who had failed to win official recognition (it lasted till 1897). In 1863 he gave evidence before a royal commission on the Academy, in which he adversely criticised its management. Millais and many artist friends soon, however, became influential members of the Academy, and they subsequently assured Hunt that he would be welcomed by that body, would he consent to join it. But he resolved to remain outside, and from that resolution he never swerved.

Late in 1856 Holman Hunt moved from Pimlico to Campden Hill, where he took a house, Tor Villa, which had just been vacated by James Clarke Hook [q. v. Suppl. II]. He occupied it for some ten years. There he busied himself for a time with the designing of furniture, helping to set a fashion which, under the subsequent influence of William Morris and others, developed into a movement scarcely less important than that of the P.R.B. His 'Finding of the Saviour in the Temple,' which he had begun in Jerusalem in 1854, was finished at Campden Hill in 1860. It fetched a price far in excess of any in Holman Hunt's previous experience. It was sold for 5500 guineas to the picture-dealer Gambart, who exhibited it at his gallery in Bond Street with great success. It passed in 1891 from the collection of C. P. Matthews into that of Mr. John T. Middlemore, M.P. for Birmingham, who presented it to the Birmingham Art Gallery in 1896. It was engraved by Lizars and Greatbach.

For the nine following years Holman Hunt's position was well maintained. 'A Street Scene in Cairo: the Lantern-maker's Courtship,' exhibited at the Academy in 1861, became the property of William Kenrick of Birmingham. In 1863 two pictures were shown at the Academy, 'The King of Hearts,' portrait of a boy, now the property of the earl of Carnarvon, and a portrait of Stephen Lushington [q. v.], painted for his son Vernon.

In 1866 Holman Hunt exhibited on his own account at a gallery in Hanover Street some new pictures, including 'London Bridge on the Night of the Prince of Wales's Wedding, March 10, 1863,' into which he introduced a portrait of Combe (now in the Combe bequest, Ashmolean Museum, Oxford), and 'The After-glow.' Next year he showed at the Academy 'Il dolce far niente' and 'The Festival of St. Swithin,' a lifelike study of pigeons (also now at the Ashmolean Museum).

In August 1866 Holman Hunt had resolved on a second visit to the East. But quarantine regulations, owing to an outbreak of cholera, prevented him from going farther than Florence, where he took a studio. He had married (for the first time) before leaving England in 1865, and his wife, who accompanied him to Florence, died there in 1866. Holman Hunt was soon at work in his Florentine studio on his 'Isabella and the Pot of Basil.' This picture, which was rendered popular by Blanchard's engraving, was purchased by Gambart, and in 1867 exhibited by itself. It ultimately became the property of Mrs. Hall of Newcastle. Hunt stayed in Italy, with an occasional visit to England, for some two years. He visited Naples, Salerno, and Ravello, and saw Venice for the first time under Ruskin's guidance. He was elected member of the Athenæum Club under Rule II in 1868.

After fourteen years' absence from Palestine, Holman Hunt landed at Jaffa in the autumn of 1869. He remained in the Holy Land for another two years. In Dec. 1869 he was staying at Bethlehem, but soon took a house at Jerusalem, and slowly painted one of his most characteristic works, 'The Shadow of Death,' also called 'The Shadow of the Cross.' He returned with it to England in 1871. Sir Thomas Fairbairn negotiated its sale to Messrs. Agnew and Son, who exhibited it separately in London and through the country; 5500*l.* down was paid for it and the original study, an equal sum being promised later. Sir William Agnew finally presented the painting to the

Manchester Art Gallery. The head of Christ in this picture was copied by command of Queen Victoria under the title of 'The Beloved,' and is now in the Chapel Royal.

Holman Hunt now remained in London, painting a few portraits, till 1875. He then left for Neuchâtel, where he was married for the second time. Thence he passed once again to Jerusalem by his old route of Alexandria and Jaffa. He arrived in the course of 1875, and stayed in Jerusalem or the neighbourhood for two and a half years. On the voyage out through the Mediterranean he painted 'The Ship,' which remained the property of the painter till 1906, when in honour of his eighty-first birthday it was purchased by a number of admirers and presented to the Tate Gallery. 'Nazareth, overlooking Esdraelon,' and a first design for the most elaborate labour of his life, 'The Triumph of the Innocents,' were executed during this third sojourn in Jerusalem. Difficulties over 'The Triumph' caused by a bad canvas bought in Jerusalem proved a source of grave anxiety.

While Holman Hunt was still in Palestine the Grosvenor Gallery was built and opened by Sir Coutts Lindsay in 1877. Hunt encouraged the enterprise, and to the first exhibition sent his completed 'Nazareth' (now in the Ashmolean at Oxford). He subsequently sent 'The Ship' (1878), portraits of his sons Cyril (1880) and Hilary 'The Tracer' (1886), Sir Richard Owen (1881), and Dante Rossetti (1884, worked from an earlier pastel), as well as 'The Bride of Bethlehem' (1885) and 'Amaryllis' (1885).

On returning in 1878 from the Holy Land, Holman Hunt, who still kept on his house at Jerusalem, worked anew on his 'Triumph of the Innocents' at a Chelsea studio. The first picture he temporarily abandoned, and began a new version, which was finished in 1885. After exhibition in the Fine Art Society's Galleries, this was acquired by Mr. J. T. Middlemore of Birmingham. Meanwhile Holman Hunt had repaired and repainted the earlier version, which was acquired by the Liverpool Art Gallery for 3500 guineas. The original design of the picture, which varies considerably from both the large versions, is in the collection of Sidney Morse.

A water-colour, 'Christ among the Doctors,' which now belongs to Mr. Middlemore, was executed in 1886, in which year as complete a collection of Holman Hunt's works as could be brought together was shown by the Fine Art Society in London. Holman Hunt's next important picture was 'May Morning on Magdalen Tower, Oxford,' which he began in 1888 on a small canvas, and finished in 1891, when it was shown in a private gallery in Old Bond Street. This original version was presented by Mr. and Mrs. Barrow Cadbury to the Birmingham Art Gallery in 1907.

In 1892, accompanied by his wife, Holman Hunt travelled through Italy and Greece to Egypt, and thence paid a last visit to Palestine. There he prepared designs for Sir Edwin Arnold's 'Light of the World,' and painted 'The Miracle of Sacred Fire, Church of the Sepulchre,' which he exhibited at the New Gallery in 1899 and afterwards lent to Liverpool, but kept in his own possession.

Holman Hunt occasionally practised modelling, and some of his designs, especially 'The Triumph of the Innocents,' show that if he had taken up that branch of art, he might have succeeded better than he did in painting. He was a ready writer. In 1888 he contributed three articles on the Pre-Raphaelite movement to the 'Contemporary Review.' In 1891 he contributed to 'Chambers's Encyclopædia' an able article on the same subject. In 1905 he published a work in two volumes entitled 'Pre-Raphaelitism and the Pre-Raphaelite Brotherhood,' which forms a history of his own life and throws much light on the lives of his friends.

In 1905, on the death of George Frederick Watts [q. v. Suppl. II], Holman Hunt was admitted to the Order of Merit, and at the encænia of the same year he received the honorary degree of D.C.L. from the University of Oxford. Another collection of his works was exhibited at the Leicester Galleries in 1906, when the catalogue had a preface by Sir William B. Richmond, K.C.B., R.A. Holman Hunt died at his residence, 18 Melbury Road, Kensington, on 7 Sept. 1910, and his remains, after cremation at Golder's Green, were interred in the crypt of St. Paul's Cathedral near the graves of Sir Christopher Wren, Sir Joshua Reynolds, J. M. W. Turner, Lord Leighton, and Sir J. E. Millais.

He was twice married: (1) in 1865 to Fanny, daughter of George Waugh, and granddaughter of Alexander Waugh [q. v.], who died at Florence in the following year leaving a son Cyril Benoni; and (2) in 1875 to Marion Edith Waugh, his deceased wife's sister, by whom he had a son, Hilary Lushington, and a daughter, Gladys Mulock.

Holman Hunt painted his own portrait three times, at the age of fourteen, seventeen, and forty-one; the last portrait is in the Uffizi Gallery, Florence. He was twice painted by Sir William Richmond; for the first time in 1878, and for the second in 1900. The earlier picture belongs to Sir William Richmond; the latter was presented to Holman Hunt by his friends, with an address written by (Sir) Leslie Stephen. Both portraits are reproduced in photogravure in Hunt's 'Pre-Raphaelitism' (1905).

Holman Hunt's lifelong adherence to Pre-Raphaelite principles and his strong religious convictions give him a unique place in the history of English art. The determined realism with which he treats the scenes of New Testament history has recalled to many critics the genius of Bunyan. In Ruskin's view, the New Testament 'became' to Holman Hunt, after he quitted worldly subjects, 'what it was to an old Puritan or an old Catholic of true blood'—'the only Reality.' Holman Hunt's minute search after what he believed to be truth did not permit him to paint many pictures. But all show the same conscientious fidelity to fact, and bright, if not always harmonious, colouring. Æsthetic unity is too often sacrificed to excess of detail, producing occasionally the crudest effects. His genius was essentially Germanic, finding expression not in the intrinsic powers of the material in which he worked, but in the forceful detail of his representations. He ignored the virtues of concentration and subordination, and endeavoured to say as much as he could on every subject he treated. Yet few artists can claim a more distinctive individuality or have made a bolder stand against the artistic conventions of their own day than Holman Hunt; whether those conventions were always for the worse is a different question.

[Holman Hunt's Pre-Raphaelitism and the Pre-Raphaelite Brotherhood, 2 vols. 1905; William Holman Hunt and his Works (published anonymously, but by F. G. Stephens), 1860; Pre-Raphaelite Diaries and Letters, ed. W. M. Rossetti, 1900; Dante Gabriel Rossetti, his Family Letters, with a Memoir by W. M. Rossetti, 2 vols. 1895; Ruskin's Art of England (Lecture I, on Rossetti and Hunt) in his collected works, ed. Wedderburn and Cook (see the admirable index vol. for numerous references to Hunt); Millais's Life of Sir J. E. Millais; W. Bell Scott's Autobiography; Rowley, Fifty Years of Work without Wages, 1911; Graves, Royal Academy Exhibitors, 1905; Catalogues of Tate Gallery and Birmingham, Manchester, and Liverpool Art Galleries; Cat. of Exhibition at Leicester Galleries, 1906, with preface by Sir W. B. Richmond; private information.]

W. A.

HUNTER, COLIN (1841–1904), sea-painter, born at Glasgow on 16 July 1841, was youngest child in the family of three sons and two daughters of John Hunter and his wife, Anne MacArthur. Owing to failing health the father gave up business in Glasgow about 1844, and removing to Helensburgh, opened a library and book-shop there, and became post-master. Colin Hunter was thus brought up on the coast. On leaving school he spent four years in a shipping-office in Glasgow, and soon made the acquaintance of William Black, the novelist, who became a lifelong friend. From early youth his bias towards art was strong. He devoted all his leisure to sketching from nature, and after a little study at the local school of art he at twenty abandoned business to become a landscape-painter. He practically taught himself to paint by working out of doors, frequently in the company of J. Milne Donald, the best-known painter in the west of Scotland, who encouraged him and gave him hints. From the first his work was vigorous, and, for its period, strong and rich in tone. A few months spent in Paris in the studio of M. Léon Bonnat at a later date left no obvious traces on his style.

Many of Hunter's earlier pictures appeared in the Royal Scottish Academy and the Glasgow Institute. For the most part they were closely studied and carefully painted scenes in the neighbourhood of Helensburgh, near the Trossachs or in Glenfalloch. Rustic figures were occasionally introduced. But towards 1870 he took seriously to painting the sea, and thenceforth, although frequently producing admirable inland landscapes, his finest, and certainly his most characteristic, work was inspired by the Firth of Clyde and Arran, or by the sea-fringed and fretted highlands and islands of the west.

Until 1870 he lived principally at Helensburgh, although from 1868 to 1872 he had a studio in Edinburgh. Meanwhile his work commenced to attract attention at the Royal Academy. He had first exhibited there in 1868. Four years later he went to London. After occupying studios in Langham Place and Carlton Hill, he removed in 1877 to Melbury Road, Kensington, where he built a fine house and studio. In 1873 the power and originality of 'Trawlers waiting for Darkness' had evoked general admiration. His career was thenceforth one of almost unbroken success. His pictures formed for many years one of the features of the Academy exhibitions, where he showed ninety-seven pictures in all. Many were acquired for public collections. The 'Salmon Stake Nets' (1874) went to Sydney and 'Waiting for the Homeward Bound' (1882) to Adelaide. 'Their Only Harvest' (1878), one of the best purchases of the Chantrey trustees, is in the Tate Gallery, London; 'The Herring Market at Sea' (1884) at Manchester, and 'The Pool in the Woods' (1897), a charming landscape, at Liverpool. The Glasgow Gallery contains 'Goodnight to Skye' (1895) and 'Niagara Rapids' (1901), the latter a reminiscence of a visit to America. Preston possesses 'Signs of Herring' (1899), one of his finest works. In 1884 he was elected A.R.A.

Hunter's handling of oil-paint was heavy and lacked flow and flexibility, and his drawing was effective and robust rather than constructive and elegant; but he had an instinctive feeling for ensemble and chiaroscuro, was a powerful, if restricted, colourist, and possessed a poetic apprehension of certain effects of light and atmosphere. He was at his best perhaps in pictures in which some incident of fisher-life or sea-faring was associated with the pathetic sentiment of sunset or dusky after-glow, and his most characteristic pieces are low in tone and somewhat sad in feeling. Occasionally painting in water-colour with vigour and freshness, he was a member of the Royal Scottish Water-Colour Society. As an etcher he also attained some distinction, his plates being effective in arrangement, sparkling in effect, and drawn with vigour and decisiveness.

Some time before his death Colin Hunter's health failed and his right hand was paralysed. He died at Lugar, Melbury Road, on 24 Sept. 1904, and was buried at Helensburgh. He married on 20 Nov. 1873, in Glasgow, Isabella, daughter of John H. Young, surgeon-dentist. His wife, with two sons (the elder of whom, Mr. J. Young Hunter, is an artist) and two daughters, survived him. Mrs. Hunter possesses a portrait of her husband, exhibited at the Royal Academy in 1878, by John Pettie, R.A.

[Information from the family; exhibition catalogues; Sir W. Armstrong's Scottish Painters, 1887; Art Journal, 1891, vol. 43, p. 187; J. L. Caw, Scottish Painting, 1908; Wemyss Reid's Life of William Black, passim; Scotsman, 26 and 29 Sept. 1904.] J. L. C.

HUNTER, Sir WILLIAM GUYER (1827–1902), surgeon-general, born at Calcutta in 1827, was eldest son of Thomas Hunter of Catterick near Richmond in Yorkshire. Educated at King's College school, he began his professional training at Charing Cross Hospital in 1844; became M.R.C.S. England in 1849; F.R.C.S.Edinburgh in 1858; M.D. Aberdeen, and M.R.C.P. London in 1867, and F.R.C.P. in 1875.

Nominated an assistant surgeon in the Bengal medical service in May 1850, he served through the second Burmese war of 1852–3 which led to the annexation of Pegu. For this campaign, during which his life was endangered by cholera, he received a medal and clasp. In 1854 he received high commendation from the Bombay Medical Board for successfully establishing dispensaries in Raligaum, Alighur, and Shikapur, and in 1857 the thanks of the government for zeal and skill during a fever epidemic in Shikapur, and for repressing a revolt of eight hundred prisoners in the jail of that station. During the Mutiny he acted as civil surgeon in Upper Scinde and obtained brevet rank of surgeon. He again received the thanks of government and was granted a medal. His health being shattered by the experiences of the year he came home on furlough, but was recalled to Bombay to take up the appointment of physician to the Jamsetji Jijibhoy hospital and professor of medicine in the Grant Medical College, of which he was made principal in 1876. The institution prospered under his administration; he found it with sixteen students, he left it with two hundred. He was made deputy surgeon-general in 1876, and was specially promoted to the rank of surgeon-general in 1877, when he received the thanks of government for organising the medical and hospital equipment for active service when troops were sent to Malta from India. His scheme was ultimately adopted throughout India.

In 1880 he was appointed by Sir Richard Temple [q.v. Suppl. II] vice-chancellor of the University of Bombay, a distinction usually reserved for members of the legislative council and judges of the high court in India. On his retirement from the service in 1880 he received much honourable recognition. He was appointed honorary surgeon to Queen Victoria; the inhabitants of Bombay presented him with a public address, gave his portrait to the Grant Medical College, and founded a scholarship. On his return to England he was elected a consulting physician to the Charing Cross Hospital, London.

In 1883, on the occasion of a severe outbreak of epidemic cholera in Egypt, Hunter at the request of the Indian Medical Board, was sent on a special mission to investigate it. He wrote an able report showing the urgent need of efficient sanitation in Egypt and emphasising the superior value of sanitary measures to quarantine regulations. The report was adversely criticised, but its main conclusions seem justified. In 1885 he pressed his views on the sanitary conference at Rome, which he attended as the official representative of Great Britain. He was made K.C.M.G. in 1884 and hon. LL.D. of Aberdeen in 1894.

In his last years he was prominent in English public life. From 1886 to 1887 he was a member of the London school board for the Westminster division, and from 1885 to 1892 he was conservative M.P. for Central Hackney. While in parliament he was chairman of the Water Inquiry Committee of the City of London, and a member of the departmental committee to 'enquire into the best mode of dealing with habitual drunkards.' He also did admirable service in connection with the vaccination commission, the shop hours bill, and the midwives' registration bill.

During 1884–5 he was especially interested in the formation of the volunteer medical staff corps (now the royal army medical corps, territorial), of which he was the first honorary commandant.

He died at his residence, Anerley Hill, Upper Norwood, on 4 March 1902, and was buried at Paddington cemetery.

Hunter married (1) in 1856 a daughter of Christopher Packe, vicar of Ruislip, Middlesex; (2) in 1871 the second daughter of Joseph Stainburn.

[Medico-Chirurgical Transactions, 1903, vol. lxxxvi. p. cvii; Lancet, 1902, vol. ii. p. 856; Brit. Med. Journal, 1902, vol. i. p. 749.]

D'A. P.

HUNTINGTON, GEORGE (1825–1905), rector of Tenby, born at Elloughton near Hull, on 25 Aug. 1825, was youngest of the family of four sons and three daughters of Charles William Huntington of Elloughton by his wife Harriet, daughter of William Mantle, curate in charge of Siderston, Norfolk. After education at home he studied from 1846 to 1848 at St. Bees theological college (closed in 1896). Ordained deacon in 1848 and priest in 1849 by the bishop of Manchester, he first served as curate at St. Stephen's, Salford. In 1850 he removed to Wigan, where his work among the Lancashire colliers came to the notice of the earl of Crawford and Balcarres, who made him his domestic chaplain.

After acting as clerk in orders of Manchester cathedral from 1855 to 1863, and receiving the Lambeth degree of M.A. in 1855, he became rector of St. Stephen's, Salford, in 1863. Huntington was active in Manchester during the cotton famine, and his 'Church's Work in our Large Towns' (1863) gave him a high reputation. On 6 Jan. 1867 he was inducted into the crown rectory of Tenby, in Pembrokeshire, where he remained until his death at Bath on 8 April 1905. He was buried at Tenby.

Huntington was an earnest high churchman, and at first came into conflict with evangelical sentiment in Tenby. A mission conducted there in 1877 by ritualist clergy under Huntington's auspices led to controversy in which William Basil Jones, bishop of St. David's, took part (cf. *Three Letters on the Subject of the Late Tenby Mission*, 1877). But the hostility gradually disappeared, and Huntington was able to restore and beautify his church, with the active support of his parishioners. He was an impressive preacher, at once practical and somewhat mystical. He was also a governor of the county school, chairman of the managers of the parish schools, and an energetic freemason.

Besides the work mentioned, Huntington published sermons, addresses, articles in magazines, and three volumes exhibiting some power in describing character, viz. 'Autobiography of John Brown, Cordwainer' (1867), of which he represented himself as editor and which went into five editions; the 'Autobiography of an Alms-Bag' (1885) which depicts some local figures, and his 'Random Recollections' (1895) which contains attractive sketches of friends and neighbours.

Huntington married on 26 April 1849 Charlotte Elizabeth, daughter of John Henry Garton of Hull, who survived him. He had issue five daughters and two sons.

[The Times, 14 April 1905; Church Times, 14 April 1905; obituary by J. Leach in Tenby and County News, 12 April 1905; Crockford's Clerical Directory; St. Bees College Calendar, 1848; Brit. Mus. Cat.; private information.]

E. S. H-R.

HURLSTONE, WILLIAM YEATES (1876–1906), musical composer and pianist, born at 12 Richmond Gardens, Fulham, on 7 Jan. 1876, was grandson of Frederick Yeates Hurlstone [q. v.], president of the Royal Society of British Artists, and only son of the four children of Martin de

Galway Hurlstone, a surgeon, by his wife Maria Bessy Styche.

Without receiving any regular training, he at the age of nine was allowed to publish a set of five waltzes for piano, and in 1894 he gained a scholarship at the Royal College of Music. There he studied composition under (Sir) Villiers Stanford and piano under Algernon Ashton and Edward Dannreuther, leaving the college in December 1898 an excellent pianist and performer of chamber-music and a composer of decided promise. He thereupon published some trifling songs and pieces, but public attention was soon drawn to the fine series of orchestral variations on a Swedish air which he produced at the first concert of the Patrons' Fund on 20 May 1904. At the second (chamber) concert his pianoforte quartet was played and warmly received. In 1906 he won a prize of 50*l.* offered by the Worshipful Company of Musicians for the best 'Fantasy-Quartet' for strings. Always of a delicate constitution, he died of consumption on 30 May 1906, and was buried at Mitcham, Croydon. He was unmarried. After his death many of his MS. compositions were published at the expense partly of private friends and partly of the Society of British Composers, of which he was a valued member.

Besides the works mentioned his chief pieces were his pianoforte concerto in D, his suite 'The Magic Mirror,' and a cantata 'Alfred the Great.' There is an engaging sincerity and simple charm in his music that seemed to promise a brilliant future.

[Grove's Dict. of Music; Mus. Times, July 1906; Society of British Composers' Year-book for 1907, giving full list of works.] F. C.

HUTH, ALFRED HENRY (1850–1910), bibliophile, born in London on 14 Jan. 1850, was second son of Henry Huth [q. v.] and of Augusta, third daughter of Frederick Westenholz of Waldenstein Castle, Austria. When not quite twelve years old, Huth was taken, with an elder brother, from a private school at Carshalton, to travel in the East under the care of Henry Thomas Buckle [q. v.], the historian. The tour, which began on 20 Oct. 1861, was broken by the death of Buckle at Damascus on 29 May 1862, and Huth's education was continued less adventurously at Rugby in 1864, and afterwards at the University of Berlin. On 16 Jan. 1872 he married his first cousin, Octavia, fourth and youngest daughter of Charles Frederick Huth, his father's eldest brother. Possessed of an ample fortune, and devoting himself to study and collecting he published in 1875 his first book, a study of 'The Marriage of Near Kin' (2nd edit. 1887), following it in 1880 by an account in two volumes of 'The Life and Writings of Henry Thomas Buckle,' written with considerable vivacity and containing an attack on Buckle's fellow traveller, John Stuart Stuart Glennie, which the latter answered in the 'Athenæum' and in the third edition (1880) of his 'Pilgrim-Memories.' After the death of his father in 1878 the fine library which he had formed passed into the possession of Alfred Huth, who saw to its completion in 1880 the catalogue which his father had begun to print. The care and augmentation of the collection formed one of his chief interests to the end of his life. He became a member (subsequently treasurer and vice-president) of the Roxburghe Club, and in 1888 contributed to its publications an edition of a manuscript in his own possession, 'The Miroure of Mans Saluacionne,' an English fifteenth-century verse translation of the 'Speculum Humanæ Saluationis.' The next year he published a verse translation of the first part of Goethe's 'Faust' in language 'partly Jacobean, partly modern' and closely literal. Of this a second edition, much revised, was published in 1911. In 1892 he took part in founding the Bibliographical Society, acting as its first treasurer and subsequently as president. During these years he lived at Bolney House, Ennismore Gardens, but subsequently removed to Fosbury Manor, near Hungerford. In 1894 he published anonymously 'A True Relation of the Travels and Perilous Adventures of Mathew Dudgeon, Gentleman: wherein is truly set down the Manner of his Taking, the Long Time of his Slavery in Algiers, and Means of his Delivery. Written by Himself, and now for the first time printed.' This Jacobean romance was presented with some attempt to reproduce the typographical characteristics of its period. In the same year he read before the Bibliographical Society a paper urging the compilation of 'a general catalogue of British works,' but the project proved too large to be carried out. Huth himself continued to work at his own collection, and at the time of his death on 14 Oct. 1910, from heart failure, while out shooting with a neighbour in Hampshire, he was engaged on a 'Catalogue of the Woodcuts and Engravings in the Huth Library,' which appeared posthumously. He was buried at Fosbury, Wiltshire. His wife survived him without issue.

By his will he directed that on the sale

of his collection the trustees of the British Museum should have the right of selecting fifty volumes from it, a bequest acknowledged as of greater value to the Museum library than any received since that of Thomas Grenville [q. v.] in 1846. A sumptuous catalogue of the books thus chosen was published early in 1912. The Huth autographs and engravings were sold in June and July 1911, the former realising 13,081*l.*, the latter 14,840*l.* The first portion of the library (A–B, and the Shakespeariana), sold in November 1911, fetched 50,821*l.*, exclusive of the price paid for the Shakespeares, bought privately by Mr. W. A. Cochrane for presentation to Yale University, Newhaven, U.S.A. The sale of the second portion followed on 5–7 June 1912 and realised 30,169*l.* 15*s.* 6*d.*

In addition to the books named above, Huth wrote an article on 'The Fertilisation of Plants' in the 'Westminster Review' (October 1877), a pamphlet on the 'Employment of Women' (1882), and a memoir of his father for this Dictionary. He contributed also letters to 'The Times' on land legislation and on the death-duties, especially as to their inequitable incidence on collectors of rare books and works of art.

[Cat. of Huth Books in Brit. Mus. 1912; The Times, 18 and 19 Oct., 19 and 24 Dec. (Will) 1910; 17 Jan. 1911; private knowledge.]

A. W. P.

HUTTON, ALFRED (1839–1910), swordsman, born at Beverley on 10 March 1839, was eleventh and youngest child and seventh son of Henry William Hutton (1787–1848) of Walker Gate, Beverley, captain in the 4th (Royal Irish) dragoon guards (retired 1811). His mother was Marianne (*d.* 1879), only child of John Fleming of Beverley. A brother, Edward Thomas, was father of Lieut.-general Sir Edward Hutton, K.C.M.G. (*b.* 1848). Educated at Blackheath, Alfred matriculated at University College, Oxford, on 25 Nov. 1857, but left without graduating to join the 79th (Cameron) highlanders (31 May 1859). At the age of twelve he had taken his first fencing lessons at the school in St. James's Street from Henry Angelo the younger (*d.* 1852), his father having been a pupil of Henry Angelo the elder [see Tremamondo, Henry]. On arrival at the depot of his regiment at Perth he soon proved himself an expert fencer. Upon joining the headquarters of his regiment in India, at the request of his commanding officer, Colonel Hodgson, he organised in the regiment the Cameron Fencing Club, for which he prepared his first book, 'Swordsmanship' (1862). In 1864 he exchanged into the 7th hussars, and in 1866 into the 1st (king's) dragoon guards, popularising fencing in both regiments. He was gazetted captain on 30 Sept. 1868, and retired from the service in 1873.

Invalided home in 1865, he had become the pupil and friend of McTurk, Angelo's successor, at the school of arms in St. James's Street. On leaving the army he devoted himself to the practice of modern fencing with foil, sabre, and bayonet, but chiefly to the study and revival of older systems and schools. His chief work, 'Cold Steel' (a title sometimes transferred from the book to the writer by his friends), was published in 1889. This was a practical treatise on the sabre, based on the old English backsword play of the eighteenth century, combined with the method of the then modern Italian school. Hutton successfully advocated the use by cavalry of a straight pointed sword for thrusting rather than a cutting sword. In 1890 he published 'Fixed Bayonets,' but his views of bayonet fighting were regarded in the army as too theoretical for modern practical instruction.

Under Hutton's instruction the school of arms of the London rifle brigade reached a high level of all-round swordsmanship. For its benefit 'The Swordsman' was written in 1891 (enlarged edit. 1898). In 1892 he published 'Old Sword Play,' a summary history of fencing as practised in the fifteenth, sixteenth, and seventeenth centuries. In 1894 he was elected F.S.A., and an honorary member of the Cercle d'Escrime de Bruxelles, on whose invitation he took the chief part with several English pupils in a historical display of 'L'Escrime à travers les Ages,' held at the opera-house on 22 May. From 1867 he was a member of the London Fencing Club, and from 1895 till death he was first president of the Amateur Fencing Association, originally the fencing branch of the Amateur Gymnastic Association, the earliest attempt at organising English fencing. His last published work was 'The Sword and the Centuries' (1901), a popular illustrated epitome of his deeper researches.

Hutton was one of the founders of the Central London Throat and Ear Hospital in 1874, and for thirty years its first chairman. Of tall and picturesque figure, handsome face, and chivalrous bearing, traits suggestive to friends of Don Quixote, he was wholehearted in his devotion to the science of arms, which he did much to rescue from neglect. He died unmarried at his chambers in 76 Jermyn Street, London, on

18 Dec. 1910, and was buried in Astbury churchyard, Cheshire. A memorial tablet was unveiled at Astbury Church by Lieut.-general Sir Edward Hutton on 8 Oct. 1911.

Besides the works mentioned and articles in periodicals, he published: 1. 'Swordsmanship for the Use of Soldiers,' 1866. 2. 'Swordsmanship and Bayonet Fencing,' 1867. 3. 'The Cavalry Swordsman,' 1867. 4. 'Bayonet Fencing and Sword Practice,' 1882. 5. 'A Criticism of the Infantry Sword Exercise,' 1895. 6. 'Sword Fighting and Sword Play,' 1897. 7. 'Examples of Ju-Jitsu for Schoolboys.'

Hutton's fine collection, of fencing and duelling literature, with some admirable specimens of Oriental sword-cutlery, he bequeathed to the Victoria and Albert Museum.

Hutton was often painted, usually in ancient or modern fencing costume. A portrait by John Ernest Breun, entitled 'Cold Steel,' won the gold medal at the Paris Salon in 1892, and is reproduced in Hutton's book so named (1889). Another portrait by W. Howard Robinson, foil in hand and mask under arm, was reproduced in 'The Field,' 25 June 1910; a caricature by 'Jest,' rapier in hand, was in 'Vanity Fair,' 13 Aug. 1903.

[Arthur W. Hutton, Some Account of the Family of Hutton of Gate Burton, Lincolnshire, 1898 (privately printed); private information supplied by Colonel Cyril G. R. Matthey, F.S.A., one of Hutton's executors; Thimm, Fencing Bibliography; Saturday Review, 6 July 1889 (Cold Steel), 14 June 1890 (Fixed Bayonets); The Times, 19 Dec. 1910; personal knowledge.] A. F. S.

HUTTON, FREDERICK WOLLASTON (1836–1905), geologist, born on 16 Nov. 1836 at Gate Burton, Lincolnshire, was second of the seven sons (and ten children) of Henry Frederick Hutton, rector of Gate Burton, and afterwards of Spridlington, near Lincoln (where he inherited an estate from a godfather). His mother was Louisa, daughter of Henry John Wollaston, rector of Scotter, a relation of William Hyde Wollaston [q. v.]. Wealth came to the father's family through his great-grandfather, Thomas Hutton, a lawyer at Gainsborough, whose son purchased Gate Burton Hall for the family seat, with the advowson of the rectory. Frederick's eldest brother, Henry Wollaston (*b.* 1835), is prebendary of Lincoln; his youngest brother, Arthur Wollaston (1848–1912), was rector of St. Mary-le-Bow, Cheapside.

Frederick, educated at Southwell and the Naval Academy, Gosport, served for three years in the Indian mercantile marine. Afterwards he entered King's College, London, and in 1855 obtained a commission in the 23rd royal Welsh fusiliers, becoming lieutenant in 1857 and captain in 1862. He saw service in the Crimea 1855–6; and in the Indian Mutiny he shared in the capture of Lucknow and in the defeat of the Gwalior mutineers by Sir Colin Campbell, afterwards Lord Clyde [q. v.], receiving medals for both campaigns. In 1860–1 he passed with distinction through the Staff College, Sandhurst, and thenceforth his interest in scientific studies rapidly developed.

In 1865 Hutton sold out of the army, and the following January emigrated with his family to New Zealand. As a colonist on the Waikato he was hardly successful, but in 1871 he was appointed assistant-geologist to the New Zealand geological survey and removed to Wellington. In 1873 he left that town for Dunedin on being appointed provincial geologist of Otago and curator of the museum. In 1877 he became professor of natural science in the Otago University. In 1890 he went to Christchurch as professor of biology and geology in the university of New Zealand, but resigned that post in 1893 for the curatorship of the museum. In March 1905 he revisited England, after an absence of thirty-nine years. On the return voyage, near Cape Town, he died at sea (where he was buried) on 27 Oct. 1905.

Besides geology, Hutton had a good knowledge of ornithology and ethnology; and many of the skeletons of the extinct moa (*Dinornis*) now in Europe were obtained by him. In addition to thirteen official catalogues and reports, he wrote more than a hundred scientific papers, the majority contributed to the 'Transactions of the New Zealand Institute.' Eight appear in the 'Quarterly Journal' of the Geological Society (London), among them being a valuable description of the Tarawera district, shortly after the great eruption in 1886. He was also the author of a 'Class-book of Elementary Geology' (1875); of 'Darwinism and Lamarckism, Old and New' (1899); and 'Index Faunæ Novæ Zealandiæ' (1904); and was joint author of 'Nature in New Zealand' (1902) and 'Animals of New Zealand' (1904). In 1902 he published 'The Lesson of Evolution,' a series of essays, which at the time of his death he had enlarged and almost rewritten. This was printed for private circulation in 1907, but deserves to be more widely read. His last article, written while in England on

'What is Life?' appeared in the 'Hibbert Journal' (1905). Hutton maintained life to be something immaterial and independent of matter, which, however, it required in order to display itself. He was an original thinker and was often involved in controversy, where he fought strenuously but fairly.

He was elected F.G.S. in 1861, a corresponding member of the Zoological Society of London in 1872, and F.R.S. in 1892. He was also a corresponding member of other European, colonial and American societies, was president of the Australasian Association for the Advancement of Science in 1901 at the Hobart Town meeting, and was first president of the board of governors of the New Zealand Institute, by which a memorial medal and prize was founded.

In 1863 Hutton married Annie Gouger, daughter of Dr. William Montgomerie of the Bengal military service, who introduced gutta-percha into practical use in Europe. His wife, three sons (one an officer in the royal engineers) and three daughters survived him.

[Geol. Mag. 1905; Quarterly Journal Geol. Soc. 1906; Proc. Roy. Soc. 79 B; memoir prefixed to The Lesson of Evolution, 1907; information from Prebendary H. W. Hutton.]

T. G. B.

HUTTON, GEORGE CLARK (1825–1908), presbyterian divine and advocate of disestablishment, born in Perth on 16 May 1825, was eldest of twelve children, of whom only three outlived childhood. George's surviving brother, James Scott Hutton (*d.* 1891), was principal of the Deaf and Dumb Institution, Halifax, Nova Scotia. His father, George Hutton, was a staunch supporter of secession principles. He taught a private school in Perth, took an active interest in the deaf and dumb, and invented a sign language. His mother, Ann Scott, came of a Cromarty family. Hutton, who received his early education from his father, was for a time a teacher, and at the age of fifteen had sole charge of a school near Perth. In Oct. 1843 he entered Edinburgh University, where he won prizes for Latin and Greek, the gold medal for moral philosophy under John Wilson ('Christopher North') [q. v.], and three prizes for rhetoric, one for a poem, 'Wallace in the Tower,' which his professor, William Edmondstoune Aytoun [q. v.], caused to be printed.

He entered the divinity hall of the Secession Church in July 1846, was licensed to preach by the presbytery of Edinburgh on 5 Jan. 1851, and on 9 Sept. of the same year was ordained and inducted minister of Canal Street United Presbyterian church, Paisley. There he remained for the rest of his life, celebrating his ministerial jubilee on 21 Oct. 1901.

Hutton was an able evangelical preacher and a capable exponent of traditional theology, but he was mainly known through life as the active advocate of the 'voluntary' movement in Scotland which condemned civil establishments of religion as unscriptural, unjust, and injurious. In 1858 he joined the Liberation Society, and from 1868 until death was a member of its executive. He was the chief spokesman of a branch of the society formed in Scotland in 1871, and in 1886 helped to form the disestablishment council for Scotland. From 1872 to 1890 he was the convener of a disestablishment committee of the synod of the United Presbyterian church. He spoke in support of disestablishment in tours through Scotland, and not merely urged his views in pamphlets and in the press, but from 1880, when Gladstone formed his second administration, he in letters and interviews entreated the prime minister, without avail, to give practical effect to his opinions. On his representations on behalf of his cause the Teinds (Scotland) bill in 1880 was dropped by the government. In 1883 Hutton mainly drafted an abortive bill for the disestablishment and disendowment of the Church of Scotland, which John Dick Peddie, M.P. for Kilmarnock burghs, introduced into the House of Commons. To Hutton's pertinacity may be partly attributed Gladstone's support of a motion for Scottish disestablishment in the House of Commons in 1890. When in January 1893 Gladstone's government announced a measure to prevent the creation of vested interests in the established churches of Wales and Scotland, Hutton wrote urging the substitution of a final measure for the suspensory bill. On 25 Aug. Gladstone gave a somewhat evasive reply to a deputation from the disestablishment council, who pressed the government to accept Sir Charles Cameron's Scottish disestablishment bill. With Gladstone's resignation in March 1894 legislative action was arrested. Gladstone's hesitating attitude to the Scottish disestablishment question disappointed Hutton, but friendly relations continued between them, and in May 1895 he was invited to Hawarden, and was cordially received.

Hutton also promoted temperance and educational legislation. In regard to education, he held strongly that a state system must be entirely secular. He strenuously opposed the provision in the education bill of 1872 for the continuance of 'use and wont' in regard to religious teaching. In 1873 he was elected a member of Paisley school board; he lost his seat in 1876, but served again from 1879 to 1882.

Hutton exerted a dominant influence on the affairs of the United Presbyterian church in the years preceding its union in 1900 with the Free church. He represented his church at the pan-presbyterian council at Philadelphia in 1880 and at Toronto in 1892. In 1884 he was moderator of synod, became convener of the synod's business committee in 1890, and principal of the theological hall of his church in 1892, succeeding Dr. John Cairns [q. v. Suppl. I]. He was a qualified supporter of the first negotiations for the amalgamation of the Free and United Presbyterian churches (1863–1873), nor when the negotiations were resumed in 1896 and were brought to a successful issue in 1900, did he favour an early union. Union seemed to him to endanger the cause of disestablishment, but he finally accepted the assurance that in the united church there would be no attempt to limit the expression of his 'voluntary' opinions. Once the union was accomplished he became one of its most enthusiastic champions and was co-principal with George Cunninghame Monteath Douglas [q. v. Suppl. II] of the United Free Church College, Glasgow, until 1902. In 1906 he was elected moderator of the general assembly of the United Free church in succession to Dr. Robert Rainy [q. v. Suppl. II]. True to the last to his 'voluntary' principles, he unflinchingly opposed the movement for a reunion of the established and United Free churches, and his final words in the general assembly of his church, on 27 May 1908, resisted a proposal of conference on the subject from the established church. He died two days later, 29 May 1908, in his hotel at Edinburgh and was buried in Woodside cemetery, Paisley. Hutton married on 16 May 1853 Margaret Hill (*d.* 1893), by whom he had five children.

Hutton was a born controversialist—trenchant and argumentative, with an intense belief in the spiritual mission of the church and the need of freeing it of civil ties. His opinions made him unpopular with a large and influential section of his countrymen. In his later years there was little enthusiasm for his cause, even in his own church. Hutton was made hon. D.D. of William's College, Massachusetts, U.S.A., in 1875, and of Edinburgh in 1906. His portrait, painted on his ministerial jubilee in 1901 by Sir George Reid, P.R.S.A., hangs in the United Free Church Assembly Hall in Edinburgh.

Hutton's chief published writings are: 1. 'The Nature of Divine Truth and the Fact of its Self-Evidence,' Paisley, 1853. 2. 'The Rationale of Prayer,' Paisley, 1853. 3. 'Law and Gospel: Discourses on Primary Themes,' Edinburgh, 1860. 4. 'The Word and the Book,' Paisley, 1891.

[Life, by Alexander Oliver, 1910; Life and Letters of John Cairns, by Alexander R. MacEwen, 1895 (4th edit. 1898); Life of Principal Rainy by Patrick Carnegie Simpson, 2 vols. 1909; personal knowledge.]

W. F. G.

I

IBBETSON, Sir DENZIL CHARLES JELF (1847–1908), lieutenant-governor of the Punjab, was born on 30 Aug. 1847 at Gainsborough in Lincolnshire. He sprang from a branch of the Yorkshire family, to which Henry John Selwin-Ibbetson, first baron Rookwood [q. v. Suppl. II], belonged. His grandfather was commissary general at St. Helena during the captivity of Napoleon, and used his humour and talents of vivid portraiture in drawing caricatures of the great exile and his staff. His father, Denzil John Hart Ibbetson, married Clarissa, daughter of the Rev. Lansdowne Guilding, and at the time of his son's birth was employed as an engineer in the construction of the Manchester, Sheffield, and Lincolnshire railway. Having subsequently taken holy orders, he became vicar of St. John's, in Adelaide, South Australia. Denzil was educated first at St. Peter's College, Adelaide, and then at St. John's College, Cambridge. In 1868 he passed third in the open competition for the civil service of India, and next year graduated B.A. at Cambridge as a senior optime in the mathematical tripos.

Ibbetson proceeded to India, joining the Punjab commission at the end of 1870. His future distinction rested upon a thorough grounding in revenue administration and settlement work, which brought him into close touch with the realities of district life and agrarian questions. In December 1871 he was appointed assistant settlement officer at Karnal, and he was placed in independent charge of the settlement operations in 1875. Ibbetson's report, owing to its accuracy, variety of interest, and lucidity of style, at once brought the writer's name to the front. Published in 1883, it dealt with one portion of the Karnal district, 892 square miles, lying between the Jumna on the east and the high-lying lands of Jind on the west. Its scholarly investigation of tribal organisation and the social life of the villagers, of their agricultural partnerships and systems of cultivation, riveted attention. He received the thanks of government for the 'ability, patience, and skill' with which he had discharged his duty, and the student of India's agrarian problems still turns to Ibbetson's work for information and suggestion. His treatment of the Punjab census of 1881 displayed the same qualities. His report was a mine of facts in regard to castes, customs, and religions, as well as of high anthropological value. From its pages he afterwards quarried his 'Outlines of Punjab Ethnography' (1883). He entered on a fresh field of labour in the compilation of the 'Punjab Gazetteer' in 1883. In the following year his career took a new direction for some twenty months, as head of the department of public instruction. The comprehensive report of the commission appointed by Lord Ripon to inquire into the state of education had pointed out defects in the administration of the Punjab. Under the direction of Sir Charles Aitchison, Ibbetson introduced the needed reforms. At length in 1887, having completed sixteen strenuous years, Ibbetson took furlough and went to England.

On his return to India at the end of 1888, government lost no time in turning his experience to account. Hitherto he had not worked in the political field, and he was now entrusted with the conduct of British relations with the Kapurthala state. Other special duties entrusted to him were conferences on census operations and jail administration in 1890, followed by an inquiry regarding cantonment administration. But the most fruitful of all his labours was an investigation, commenced in 1891, into the working of the Deccan Agriculturists' Relief Act of 1879. The result was amending legislation of the highest importance, which was calculated to relieve more efficiently the Deccan peasantry of their indebtedness and to prevent the gradual transfer of their incumbered holdings to the trading and money-lending classes. The report of Ibbetson and his colleagues led not merely to an amendment of the Deccan Act itself in 1895, but to a more general alteration throughout the empire of the Indian laws of contract and evidence. Another resultant reform was the introduction into Bombay of a proper record of proprietary rights. In 1896, as secretary to the government of India in the revenue department, he became Lord Elgin's right hand in dealing with agricultural problems, and prepared the ground for the Punjab Land Alienation Act. That Act, ably piloted in 1900 by Sir Charles Rivaz, did not go as far as Ibbetson wished, but it restricted the alienation of land so as to keep its occupation in the hands of the agricultural tribes to the exclusion of the commercial castes. For his services he was made C.S.I. in 1896.

Passing from the secretariat to the more congenial task of administration, Ibbetson was in 1898 sent to take charge of the Central Provinces as chief commissioner. The province, then comprising 87,000 square miles, was still staggering under the blow of the famine of 1897 when, in October 1899, another failure of the monsoon occurred in a season of epidemics of fatal diseases. By July 1900 subsistence was required for 2,250,000 of the famished population. A vacancy for a few months on the executive council of the governor-general brought him a change of work without relaxation, and he was compelled to seek rest in furlough.

After his return from England he joined in 1902 the council of Lord Curzon. As a member of that vigorous administration Ibbetson gathered up the fruits of the reports of the famine commissioners of 1898 and 1901, translating their recommendations into rules and regulations for the conduct of future campaigns. Other gigantic schemes of reform resulting from the labours of the irrigation commission of 1902 and the reorganisation of the police department fell upon his shoulders. In addition to these exceptional labours and ordinary duties, he took a leading part in legislative business. Amongst other measures he carried the Co-operative Credit Act of 1904, a Poison Act, the Transfer of Property Amendment, the Punjab Village Sanitation, and the Central Provinces Municipal Acts. In 1903 he was promoted K.C.S.I.

In 1905 he temporarily filled the highest position in his service, that of lieutenant-governor of the Punjab, and on the retirement of Sir Charles Rivaz, on 6 March 1907, he was confirmed in that office. The seditious acts of revolutionists had then brought matters to a serious crisis. Famine and devastating plague had laid heavy hands on the peasantry. The vernacular press, used for the purpose by the leaders of revolution, had disseminated false news, which agitated their simple minds. Even the latest triumph of British enterprise in bringing three million acres under canal irrigation was turned against the government. The new irrigation colonies had over-taxed the administrative resources of their rulers, and mistakes had been made. The yeomen peasants were led to believe that these were the result of deliberate policy, and the first-fruits of breach of faith. Foremost among the instigators of the extreme agitation were Lala Lajpat Rai and Ajit Singh. Serious riots broke out in Lahore and Rawalpindi. With prompt vigour, Ibbetson repressed the disorders. He secured the authority of the supreme government for the deportation of the two ringleaders without trial under the regulation of 1818. He applied an ordinance hastily promulgated by the governor-general to the suppression of seditious meetings, and enforced the law against rioters. Troops were kept in readiness, and he employed his police with alert discrimination.

Meanwhile Ibbetson was under the shadow of a fatal malady, but he allowed no bodily infirmity to relax his activity. When at length an operation could not be avoided, he quietly proceeded to London in June 1907, and returned at the earliest moment to his post to disprove false rumours of enforced retirement and allegations of a want of confidence in his policy on the part of superior authority. But the progress of his malady was not to be stayed. He resigned his office on 21 Jan. 1908, and his departure from Lahore called forth public manifestations of sympathy and respect. He died in London on 21 Feb. following, and his body was cremated at Golder's Green. When the news of his death reached the Punjab a public subscription was raised, part of which was applied to a portrait executed by Mr. H. Olivier, which now hangs in the Lawrence Hall at Lahore; a memorial tablet bearing an inscription of just eulogy was also erected to his memory in Christ Church, Simla, at the expense of Lord Curzon.

He married on 2 Aug. 1870 Louisa Clarissa, daughter of Samuel Coulden of the Heralds' College. His widow survived him with two daughters, Ruth Laura and Margaret Lucy; the latter in 1899 married Mr. Evan Maconochie of the Indian civil service.

[Times, 22 Feb. 1908; Pioneer, 23 Feb. 1908; Statesman, Calcutta, 23 Feb. 1908; Administration Reports of the Punjab; Report on the Settlement of the Karnal District, 1883; Census Report of the Punjab, 1881; Outlines of Punjab Ethnography; Gazetteer of the Districts of the Punjab; Reports of Famine Commissions and on the Working of the Deccan Agriculturists Relief Act.] W. L-W.

IBBETSON, HENRY JOHN SELWIN-. [See SELWIN-IBBETSON, HENRY JOHN, first BARON ROOKWOOD (1826–1902), politician.]

IGNATIUS, FATHER. [See LYNE, JOSEPH LEYCESTER (1837–1908), preacher.]

INCE, WILLIAM (1825–1910), regius professor of divinity at Oxford, born in St. James's parish, Clerkenwell, London, on 7 June 1825, was son of William Ince, sometime president of the Pharmaceutical Society of London, by his wife, Hannah Goodwin Dakin. Educated at King's College School, London, where he began a lifelong friendship with William Henry Smith, afterwards leader of the House of Commons, he was elected to a Hutchins' scholarship at Lincoln College, Oxford, on 10 Dec. 1842. He graduated B.A. with first-class honours in classics in Michaelmas term 1846; he proceeded M.A. on 26 April 1849; and D.D. on 7 May 1878. He was ordained deacon in 1850 and priest in 1852.

Early in 1847 he was elected to a Petrean fellowship in Exeter College, became tutor of the college in 1850, and sub-rector in 1857. He held all three posts till 1878. He was at once recognised as 'one of the ablest and most popular tutors of his day' (W. K. STRIDE's *Exeter College*, 1900, p. 181), his lectures on Aristotle's 'Ethics' and on logic being especially helpful. As sub-rector he earned the reputation of a tactful but firm disciplinarian. He was a constant preacher in the college chapel.

He served the university offices of junior proctor in 1856–7; of select preacher before the university, 1859, 1870, and 1875; of Oxford preacher at the Chapel Royal, Whitehall, 1860–2; and of classical examiner, 1866–8. From 1871 till 1889 he was examining chaplain to J. F. Mackarness, bishop of Oxford, who was fellow of Exeter (1844–6).

On 6 April 1878 Ince was appointed

regius professor of divinity at Oxford and canon of Christ Church. Keenly alive to the intellectual side of his official duties, he read widely and gave his pupils the benefit of his studies. His duties included that of presenting candidates for honorary degrees in divinity, and his happily expressed and enunciated Latin speeches on such occasions recalled the days when Latin was still a spoken language. He took an active share in the administration of Christ Church, both as a cathedral body and as a college, and he showed a well-informed and even-minded judgment in such university offices as curator of the Bodleian library, chairman of the board of theological studies, and member of the hebdomadal council. He preached frequently both as professor in the university church and as canon in the cathedral, and although lacking magnetic qualities he attracted his congregations by the manliness of his delivery and the directness of style. His theological position was that of a moderate Anglican, loyal to the formularies and to what he considered to be the spirit of the Church of England, but inclining, especially in his later days, to evangelical interpretations, and rejecting ritualism alike in form and doctrine.

He died, after some years of failing health, in his official house at Christ Church on 13 Nov. 1910, in his 86th year, and was buried on 16 Nov. in the cemetery at the east end of Christ Church cathedral. He was elected honorary fellow of King's College, London, in 1861, and of Exeter College in 1882.

He married at Alvechurch, Worcestershire, on 11 Sept. 1879, Mary Anne, younger daughter of John Rusher Eaton of Lambeth, and sister of John Richard Turner Eaton, fellow of Merton (1847–65) and rector of Alvechurch (1879–86). She died at Fairford, Gloucestershire, on 21 March 1911, and was buried in Christ Church cemetery in the same grave with her husband.

Ince published many occasional sermons, addresses, and pamphlets dealing with controversial topics in university administration or church doctrine. The following are of chief interest: 'The Past History and Present Duties of the Faculty of Theology in Oxford,' two inaugural lectures read in the Divinity School, Oxford, in Michaelmas term, 1878 (these led to a published correspondence with Rev. H. R. Bramley, fellow of Magdalen College, afterwards precentor of Lincoln, as to the patristic and liturgical interpretation of Τοῦτο ποιεῖτε, 1879). 2. 'The Education of the Clergy at the Universities,' 1882. 3. 'The Luther Commemoration and the Church of England,' 1883. 4. 'The Life and Times of St. Athanasius,' 1896 (lectures delivered in Norwich Cathedral). 5. 'The Doctrine of the Real Presence: a Letter about the Recent Declaration of the English Church Union, and its Appended Notes,' 1900. 6. 'The Three Creeds, specially the so-called Athanasian Creed: a Sermon preached before the University of Oxford, 7 Feb. 1904' (advocating the excision of the Athanasian creed from the public services of the church).

[Boase, Registrum Collegii Exoniensis (1894), p. 186; The Times, 14 Nov. 1910; Oxford Times, 19 Nov. 1910; appreciation by Dr. W. Walrond Jackson, rector of Exeter College, in the Stapledon Magazine, iii. 6.] A. C.

INDERWICK, FREDERICK ANDREW (1836–1904), lawyer, fourth son of Andrew Inderwick, R.N., and Jane, daughter of J. Hudson, was born in London on 23 April 1836. He was educated privately and at Trinity College, Cambridge, where he matriculated in Michaelmas term 1853, but did not graduate. He was admitted a student of the Inner Temple on 16 April 1855, and was called to the bar on 26 Jan. 1858. In the preceding year the jurisdiction of Doctors' Commons over matrimonial and testamentary causes was abolished, and the courts of probate and divorce were created by 20 & 21 Victoria, c. 77 and c. 85. Inderwick attached himself to this branch of the profession which speedily developed a special bar of its own. He had learnt from Dr. Spinks, in whose chambers he had been a pupil, the working of the old 'Commons' practice, and he soon made his reputation as a very capable and effective advocate. He took silk on 19 March 1874, and was made a bencher of his inn on 5 June 1877. He rapidly obtained a complete lead in what became from 1876 the Probate Divorce, and Admiralty Division of the High Court of Justice, while still occasionally accepting briefs on the south-eastern circuit, which he had joined immediately after his call. Inderwick enjoyed the advantage of a most pleasing voice and presence, and to a thorough knowledge of his own branch of law and practice he brought the gifts of clear statement and forcible exposition; but his style in cross-examination was not always as virile as divorce court witnesses require, and in the more important or sensational cases he was generally reinforced by some conspicuous figure from the common law bar. His elevation to the bench was confidently predicted; but promotion never came, and in August 1903, in the full enjoyment of a highly lucrative practice, he accepted the post of commissioner in lunacy. He was then suffering from a painful malady, of which he died just a twelvemonth later.

After two unsuccessful attempts to enter parliament in the liberal interest—for Cirencester in 1868 and Dover in 1874—he was returned for Rye in April 1880, but was defeated at the general election in December 1885, when he stood for the Rye division of the county of Sussex.

His interests were closely bound up with the Cinque Ports, and he twice (1892–3) served as mayor of Winchelsea, near which he had a residence. Inderwick was a prolific writer on historical and antiquarian subjects, and his work on the records of the Inner Temple holds high rank in legal and topographical literature. He was elected F.S.A. in 1894. He died at Edinburgh on 18 August 1904, and was buried at Winchelsea. He married on 4 Aug. 1857 Frances Maria, daughter of John Wilkinson of the exchequer and audit department. A fine bust of Inderwick by Sir George Frampton, R.A., stands in one of the corridors of the Royal Courts of Justice outside the bar library, in the formation and management of which he displayed much judgment and activity. A cartoon by 'Spy' appeared in 'Vanity Fair' (1896).

Besides early legal works, 'The Divorce and Matrimonial Causes Acts' (1862), 'The Law of Wills' (1866), and his 'Calendar of the Inner Temple Records, 1505–1714,' vols. 1–3 (1896–1901), he published, amongst other works: 1. 'Side-lights on the Stuarts,' 1888. 2. 'The Interregnum, 1648–1660,' 1891. 3. 'The Story of King Edward and New Winchelsea,' 1892. 4. 'The King's Peace,' an historical sketch of the English Law Courts, 1895.

[The Times, 19 Aug. 1904; The Book of Cambridge Matriculations and Degrees; private information.] J. B. A.

INGRAM, JOHN KELLS (1823–1907), scholar, economist, and poet, born at the rectory of Temple Carne, co. Donegal, on 7 July 1823, was eldest son of William Ingram, then curate of the parish, by his wife, Elizabeth Cooke. Thomas Dunbar Ingram [q. v. Suppl. II] was his younger brother. The family was descended from Scottish Presbyterians, who settled in co. Down in the seventeenth century. John Ingram, the paternal grandfather, was a prosperous linen-bleacher at Lisdrumhure (now Glenanne), co. Armagh; he conformed to the Established Church of Ireland and raised at his own expense in 1782 the Lisdrumhure volunteers. Ingram's father, who was elected in 1790 a scholar of Trinity College, Dublin, died in 1829, and his five children were brought up by his widow, who survived till 22 Feb. 1884. Mother and children removed to Newry, and John and his brothers were educated at Dr. Lyons' school there. At the early age of fourteen (13 Oct. 1837) John matriculated at Trinity College, Dublin, winning a sizarship next year, a scholarship in 1840, and a senior moderatorship in 1842. He graduated B.A. early in 1843.

In his undergraduate days Ingram showed precocious promise alike as a mathematician and as a classical scholar. In December 1842 he helped to found the Dublin Philosophical Society, acting as its first secretary, and contributing to its early 'Transactions' eleven abstruse papers in geometry. He always said that the highest intellectual delight which he experienced in life was in pure geometry, and his geometrical papers won the praise of his teacher, James MacCullagh [q. v.], the eminent mathematical professor of Trinity. But from youth upwards Ingram showed that intellectual versatility which made him well-nigh the most perfectly educated man of his age. After contributing verse and prose in boyhood to Newry newspapers, he published two well-turned sonnets in the 'Dublin University Magazine' for Feb. 1840, and three years later sprang into unlooked-for fame as a popular poet. On a sudden impulse he composed one evening in Trinity in March 1843 the poem entitled 'The Memory of the Dead,' beginning 'Who fears to speak of Ninety-eight?' It was printed in the 'Nation' newspaper on 1 April anonymously, but Ingram's responsibility was at once an open secret. Though his view of Irish politics quickly underwent modification, the verses became and have remained the anthem of Irish nationalism. They were reprinted in 'The Spirit of the Nation' in 1843 (with music in 1845); and were translated into admirable Latin alcaics by Professor R. Y. Tyrrell in 'Kottabos' (1870), and thrice subsequently into Irish. Ingram did not publicly claim the authorship till 1900, when he reprinted the poem in his collected verse.

In 1844 Ingram failed in competition for a fellowship at Trinity College, but was consoled as *proxime accessit* with the Madden prize. He was elected a fellow two years later, obtaining a dispensation from the obligation of taking holy orders. He had thought of the law as a profession, in case he failed to obtain the dispensation. At a later period, in 1852, he was admitted a student of the King's Inns, Dublin, and in 1854 of Lincoln's Inn. But after taking his fellowship he was actively associated with Trinity College in various capacities for fifty-three years.

Elected a member of the Royal Irish Academy on 11 Jan. 1847, Ingram gave further results of geometrical inquiry in papers which he read in the spring on 'curves and surfaces of the second degree.' At the same time he was extending his knowledge in many other directions, in classics, metaphysics, and economics. Although Carlyle met him as a young member of Trinity during his tour in Ireland in 1849, he only recognised him as author of the 'Repeal' song, and described him as a 'clever indignant kind of little fellow' who had become 'wholly English, that is to say, Irish rational in sentiment' (CARLYLE'S *Irish Journey*, 1849 (1882), pp. 52, 56). In 1850 Ingram visited London for the first time, and also made a first tour up the Rhine to Switzerland. In London he then made the acquaintance of his lifelong friend, George Johnston Allman [q. v. Suppl. II]. Other continental tours followed later.

In 1852 Ingram received his first professorial appointment at Trinity, becoming Erasmus Smith professor of oratory. Three years later the duty of giving instruction in English literature was first attached to the chair. Thus Ingram was the first to give formal instruction in English literature in Dublin University, although no independent chair in that subject was instituted till 1867. A public lecture which he delivered in Dublin on Shakespeare in 1863 showed an original appreciation of the chronological study of the plays, and of the evidence of development in their versification (see *The Afternoon Lectures on English Literature*, Dublin, 1863, pp. 93–131; also *ibid.* 4th ser., 1867, pp. 47–94). A notable paper on the weak endings of Shakespeare, which, first read before a short-lived Dublin University Shakespeare Society, was revised for the New Shakspere Society's 'Transactions' (1874, pt. 2), defined his views of Shakespearean prosody.

In 1866 Ingram became regius professor of Greek at Dublin, a post which he held for eleven years. Although he made no large contribution to classical literature, he proved his fine scholarship, both Greek and Latin, in contributions—chiefly on etymology—to 'Hermathena,' a scholarly periodical which was started at Trinity College in 1874 under his editorship. A sound textual critic, he had little sympathy with the art of emendation.

In 1879 Ingram became librarian of Trinity College, and displayed an alert interest in the books and especially in the MSS. under his charge. He had already described to the Royal Irish Academy in 1858 a manuscript in the library of Roger Bacon's 'Opus Majus' which supplied a seventh and hitherto overlooked part of the treatise (on moral philosophy). He also printed 'Two Collections of Medieval Moralised Tales' (Dublin, 1882) from medieval Latin manuscripts in the Diocesan Library, Derry, as well as 'The Earliest English [fifteenth century] Translations of the "De Imitatione Christi"' from a MS. in Trinity College library (1882) which he fully edited for the Early English Text Society in 1893. Ingram was also well versed in library management. Two years before becoming university librarian he had been elected a trustee of the National Library of Ireland, being re-elected annually until his death, and he played an active part in the organisation and development of that institution. When the Library Association met in Dublin in 1884, he was chosen president, and delivered an impressive address on the library of Trinity College.

In 1881, on the death of the provost, Humphrey Lloyd [q. v.], Ingram narrowly missed succeeding him. Dr. George Salmon [q. v. Suppl. II] was appointed. He became senior fellow in 1884, and in 1887 he ceased to be librarian on his appointment as senior lecturer. The degree of D.Litt. was conferred on him in 1891. In 1893 he received the honorary degree of LL.D. from Glasgow University. In 1898 he became vice-provost, and on resigning that position next year he severed his long connection with Dublin university.

Throughout his academic career Ingram was active outside as well as inside the university. He always took a prominent part in the affairs of the Royal Irish Academy, serving as secretary of the council from 1860 to 1878, and while a vice-president in 1886 he presided, owing to the absence through illness of the president (Sir Samuel Ferguson), at the celebration of the centenary of the academy. He was president from 1892 to 1896. In 1886 Ingram became an additional commissioner for the publication of the Brehon Laws. In 1893 he was made a visitor of the Dublin Museum of Science and Art, and he aided in the foundation of Alexandra College for Women in 1866.

Meanwhile economic science divided with religious speculation a large part of his intellectual energy. In economic science he made his widest fame. In 1847 he had helped to found the Dublin Statistical Society, which was largely suggested by the grave problems created by the great Irish famine; Archbishop Whately was the first president. Ingram took a foremost part in the society's discussions of economic questions. He was a member of the council till 1857, when he became vice-president, and was the secretary for the three years 1854–6; he was president from 1878 to 1880. In an important paper which he prepared for the society in 1863—'Considerations on the State of Ireland'—Ingram took an optimistic view of the growing rate of emigration from Ireland, but argued at the same time for reform of the land laws, and an amendment of the poor law on uniform lines throughout the United Kingdom. Wise and sympathetic study of poor law problems further appears in two papers, 'The Organisation of Charity' (1875), and 'The Boarding out of Pauper Children' (1876). In 1878, when the British Association met in Dublin, Ingram was elected president of the section of economic science and statistics, and delivered an introductory address on 'The present position and prospects of political economy.' Here he vindicated the true functions of economic science as an integral branch of sociology. His address was published in 1879 in both German and Danish translations. In 1880 he delivered to the Trades Union Congress at Dublin another address on 'Work and the Workman,' in which he urged the need for workmen of increased material comfort and security, and of higher intellectual and moral attainments. This address was published next year in a French translation. From 1882 to 1898 he was a member of the Loan Fund Board of Ireland.

Ingram's economic writings covered a wide range. To the ninth edition of the 'Encyclopædia Britannica' he contributed sixteen articles on economists or economic topics. His most important contributions —on political economy (1885) and slavery (1887)—were each reprinted in a separate volume. The 'History of Political Economy' (1888) traced the 'development of economic thought in its relation with general philosophic ideas rather than an exhaustive account of economic literature.' The book quickly obtained worldwide repute. Translations were published in German and Spanish (1890; 2nd German edit. 1905), in Polish and Russian (1896; 2nd edit. 1897), in Italian and Swedish (1892), in French (1893), (partly) in Czech (1895), in Japanese (1896), in Servian (1901), and again in French (1908). Ingram's 'History of Slavery and Serfdom' (1895) was an amplification of the encyclopædia article. It was translated into German in 1905. He was also a contributor to Palgrave's 'Dictionary of Political Economy' (1892–9).

Ingram's economic position was coloured by his early adoption of Comte's creed of positivism. His attention was first directed to Comte's views when he read the reference to them in John Stuart Mill's 'Logic' soon after its publication in 1843. It was not till 1851 that he studied Comte's own exposition of his religion of humanity; he thereupon became a devoted adherent. In September 1855 he visited Comte in Paris (*Comte's Correspondence*, i. 335; ii. 186). To Comte's influence is attributable Ingram's treatment of economics as a part of sociology, and his conception of society as an organism and of the consensus of the functions of the social system. Though Ingram never concealed his religious opinions, he did not consider himself at liberty publicly to avow and defend them, so long as he retained his position in Trinity College. In 1900, the year after his retirement, when he was already seventy-seven, he published his 'Outlines of the History of Religion,' in which he declared his positivist beliefs. In the same year there appeared his collected verse, 'Sonnets and other Poems,' which was largely inspired by Comte's principles. Several other positivist works followed: 'Human Nature and Morals according to Auguste Comte' (1901); 'Passages [translated] from the Letters of Auguste Comte' (1901); 'Practical Morals, a Treatise on Universal Education' (1904), and 'The Final Transition, a Sociological Study' (1905). Between 1904 and 1906 he contributed to the 'Positivist Review,' and on its formation in 1903 he accepted a seat on the Comité Positiviste Occidental. Ingram sided with Richard Congreve [q. v.] in the internal differences of 1879 as to organisation within the positivist ranks.

Despite his sympathy with the Celtic people of Ireland and their history, Ingram distrusted the Irish political leaders of his time. He attended the great unionist demonstration at Dublin in November 1887. In theory he judged separation to be the real solution of the Irish problem, but deemed the country unripe for any heroic change (cf. *Sonnets,* 1900). To all military aggression he was hostile. He strenuously opposed the South African war (1899–1902). One of his finest sonnets commemorated the death of Sir George Pomeroy Colley [q. v.] at the battle of Majuba Hill on 27 Feb. 1881. It formed a reply (in the *Academy,* 2 April 1881) to an elegiac sonnet by Archbishop Trench in 'Macmillan's Magazine' of the same month. Ingram, while honouring Colley's valour, denounced as 'foul oppression' the cause for which he fought.

Ingram died at his residence, 38 Upper Mount Street, Dublin, on 1 May 1907, and was buried in Mount Jerome cemetery.

His portrait, painted by Miss Sarah Purser, R.H.A., was presented by friends to the Royal Irish Academy on 22 Feb. 1897.

Ingram married on 23 July 1862 Madeline, daughter of James Johnston Clarke, D.L., of Largantogher Maghera, co. Londonderry. She died on 7 Oct. 1889, leaving four sons and two daughters. Many of Ingram's published sonnets are addressed to his wife; one of them, entitled 'Winged Thoughts,' commemorates the death in South Africa, in 1895, of his third son, Thomas Dunbar Ingram, two of whose own sonnets appear in the volume.

[Memoir in Royal Irish Academy Abstract of Minutes, Session 1907–8, pp. [16]–[24]; Bibliography of Ingram's writings with a brief chronology by Thomas W. Lyster in an leabarlann, vol. iii. No. 1, June 1909 (Dublin), with photograph of Miss Purser's portrait; Memoir by C. Litton Falkiner (an account chiefly of Ingram's work for the Dublin Statistical Society, and of his economic writings), Dublin, 1907; Memoir in Palgrave's Dictionary of Political Economy, App. 1908; Positivist Review, ed. S. H. Swinny, June 1907—Ingram's Religious Position, by E. S. Beesly and Personal Reminiscences by the Editor; A Treasury of Irish Poetry in the English Tongue, ed. Stopford A. Brooke and T. W. Rolleston, 1905, pp. 142, 513; notes from Prof. R. Y. Tyrrell and Mr. S. H. Swinny.]

INGRAM, THOMAS DUNBAR (1826–1901), Irish historical writer and lawyer, born in Newry on 28 July 1826, was second son of William Ingram by his wife Elizabeth Cooke. John Kells Ingram [q. v. Suppl. II] was his elder brother. After a preliminary education in Newry, he was sent to Queen's College, Belfast, where he matriculated in 1849 and graduated B.A. and LL.B. in 1853. Proceeding to London in 1854, he entered London University and graduated LL.B. there in 1857. He entered Lincoln's Inn as a student on 24 Jan. 1854, obtained a law studentship in January 1855, and was called to the bar on 17 Nov. 1856. In 1864 he published 'Compensation to Land and House Owners, being a Treatise on the Law of Compensation for Interests in Lands, payable by Public Companies' (new edit. 1869). In 1866 he obtained the post of professor of jurisprudence in Hindu and Mohammedan law in Presidency College, Calcutta, and filled the chair till 1877. At the same time he practised in the high court of judicature. In 1871 he published 'Two Letters on some Recent Proceedings of the Indian Government.'

Leaving India in 1877, he settled in Dublin and devoted himself to historical research, chiefly on Irish themes, which he treated from a pronouncedly unionist point of view. The fruits of his Irish studies appeared in the volumes: 'A Critical Examination of Irish History' (2 vols. 1904); 'A History of the Legislative Union of Great Britain and Ireland' (1887) and 'Two Chapters of Irish History' (1888). There followed 'England and Rome, a History of the Relations between the Papacy and the English State Church from the Norman Conquest to the Revolution of 1688' (1892). Ingram's works on Irish history contain valuable material and are written with great earnestness and sincerity, but they fail in their purpose of controverting Lecky's conclusions respecting the corrupt means whereby the union of 1800 was brought about.

He died unmarried in Dublin on 30 Dec. 1901, and was buried in Mount Jerome cemetery.

[Daily Express, Dublin, 31 Dec. 1901; Brit. Mus. Cat.; University Calendars; information from Mr. J. K. Ingram.]

D. J. O'D.

INNES, JAMES JOHN McLEOD (1830–1907), lieutenant-general royal (Bengal) engineers, born at Bhagalpur, Bengal, India, on 5 Feb. 1830, was only son of surgeon James Innes of the Bengal army, of the family of Innes of Thrumster in Caithness, by his wife Jane Alicia McLeod, daughter of Lieut.-general Duncan McLeod (1780–1856) and sister of Sir Donald Friell McLeod (1810–1872) [q. v.].

Educated at a private school and at

Edinburgh University, where he won the mathematical medal for his year, he entered the East India Company's military college at Addiscombe in February 1847. He passed out at the head of his term, was awarded the Pollock medal (presented to the most distinguished cadet of the outgoing term), and was commissioned as 2nd lieutenant in the Bengal engineers on 8 Dec. 1848.

After passing through the usual course at Chatham, Innes arrived in India in November 1850. He was at first employed in the Public Works Department on the construction of the Bari Doab canal in the Punjab. On 1 Aug. 1854 he was promoted lieutenant, and in 1857, shortly after the annexation of Oude, he was transferred to that province as assistant to the chief engineer.

When the Mutiny began in May 1857 Innes was at Lucknow. He was given charge of the old fort the Machi Bhowan, with orders to strengthen it, so that it would both overawe the city and serve as a place of refuge. After the siege began in June the disastrous action of Chinhut made it necessary to concentrate the whole of the garrison at the Residency. Orders were given for the evacuation of the Machi Bhowan and Innes, one of the most fearless and energetic of the subalterns, assisted to blow it up. On the morning of 20 July the rebels assembled in large masses and exploded a mine in the direction of the Redan battery, leaving an enormous crater. They advanced boldly to the assault, but Lieutenant Loughman in command, with Innes and others, drove them back after four hours' fighting.

Innes was especially employed in mining. On 21 Aug. after sixty-four hours' hard work and no sleep he blew up Johannes's house, from which the rebel sharpshooters had fired with deadly effect and had practically silenced a British battery. During the relief by General Havelock Innes took part in all the sorties, and after the general had entered the city on 25 Sept. 1857, he was placed in charge of the mining operations in the new position occupied by Havelock's force in the palaces on the bank of the river. The defence was then chiefly confined to mining and countermining until the final relief by Sir Colin Campbell on 22 Nov. Innes's book, entitled 'Lucknow and Oude in the Mutiny' (1895), stands almost alone for sobriety and balance among accounts of the defence of Lucknow and the operations in Oude.

After the evacuation of Lucknow, Innes was posted to Brigadier-general Franks's division, and during its march through Oude he was present at the affairs of Miratpur, Chandi and Amirpur. He greatly distinguished himself at the battle and capture of Sultanpur on 23 Feb. 1858. For a splendid act of gallantry during the advance in putting out of action by his single-handed boldness a dangerous gun of the enemy General Franks recommended him for the Victoria Cross, observing that his courage was 'surpassed by none within his experience.' Subsequently on 4 March, the day on which Franks effected his junction with Sir Colin Campbell to besiege Lucknow, Innes was severely wounded at the attack on the fort at Dhowrara, eight miles from Lucknow. He was promoted 2nd captain on 27 Aug. 1858.

For his services in the Indian Mutiny Captain Innes was three times mentioned in despatches; he received the brevet rank of major on 28 Aug. 1858, the Victoria Cross, the medal with two clasps, and a year's service for the defence of Lucknow. When the military college at Addiscombe was closed in June 1861, the secretary of state for India, in addressing the last batch of cadets, read out Lord Canning's speech on presenting Innes with the Victoria Cross. After the Mutiny campaign Innes was appointed garrison engineer at Fort William, Calcutta; he then served in various grades of the public works department in the central provinces and in the Punjab until 1867. In the following year he was appointed a member of the commission to investigate the failure of the bank of Bombay. In 1869 he started the upper section of the Indus valley railway, and in the following year he was appointed accountant-general of the public works department, and held that important post for seven years. In the meantime his military promotion had run on. He was promoted 1st captain in his corps on 29 Feb. 1864; brevet lieut.-colonel on 14 June 1869; regimental major on 5 July 1872; regimental lieut.-colonel on 1 April 1874; and brevet colonel on 1 Oct. 1877.

In 1882 Innes was appointed inspector-general of military works. He was a member of the Indian defence committee, and many new defences were carried out under his orders. He was promoted major-general on 28 Nov. 1885, and retired from the service with the honorary rank of lieut.-general on 16 March 1886. On the jubilee celebration of the defence of the Residency at Lucknow in June

1907 he was created C.B., military division.

After his retirement Innes devoted himself to literary pursuits. His principal works besides that already mentioned were: 1. 'The Sepoy Revolt of 1857,' 1897. 2. 'Sir Henry Lawrence' ('Rulers of India' series), 1898. 3. 'Life of Sir James Browne, K.C.S.I., R.E.,' 1905.

Innes died, after a long illness, at his residence, Pemberton Terrace, Cambridge, on 13 Dec. 1907. He married at Jalander, India, on 30 Oct. 1855, Lucy Jane Macpherson, youngest daughter of Dr. Hugh Macpherson, professor and sub-principal at King's College, Aberdeen. By her he had three sons, of whom two survived him, and a daughter.

[India Office Records; Royal Engineers' Records; Vibart, Addiscombe; histories of the Indian Mutiny; The Times, 16 December 1907; Royal Engineers Journal, 1908; private information.] R. H. V.

IRBY, LEONARD HOWARD LOYD (1836–1905), lieutenant-colonel and ornithologist, born at Boyland Hall, Morningthorpe, Norfolk, on 13 April 1836, was son of Rear-admiral Frederick Paul Irby [q. v.] of Boyland Hall by his second wife, Frances (*d.* 1852), second daughter of Ichabod Wright of Mapperley Hall, Nottinghamshire. The father was second son of Frederick Irby, second baron Boston. Charles Leonard Irby [q. v.], captain R.N., was his uncle. After education at Rugby and at the Royal Military College, Sandhurst, he entered the army in 1854, and served with the 90th light infantry in the Crimea from 5 Dec. 1854 to 20 March 1855. He was present at the siege of Sevastopol, and received the medal with clasp and Turkish medal. In 1857 he was wrecked in the ship Transit with Captain (afterwards Lord) Wolseley and his regiment in the straits of Banca, Sumatra, on his way to China. The arrival of the news of the Indian Mutiny caused the destination of the regiment to be changed, and it at once proceeded to Calcutta. He served throughout the Mutiny from 12 August 1857 until the close of the campaign. He was engaged in the defence of Brigadier-general Sir Henry Havelock's baggage at the Alambagh; advanced to the relief of Lucknow with Lord Clyde, and after the relief and withdrawal of the garrison of Lucknow he remained with Sir James Outram to defend the Alambagh till the final advance of Lord Clyde to the siege and capture of Lucknow. He was present throughout those operations, and was awarded the medal with two clasps and a year's extra service. In October 1864 he exchanged into the 74th highlanders, and was with that regiment at Gibraltar till 1872. He retired as a lieut.-colonel on 1 April 1874.

While stationed at Gibraltar Irby devoted himself to ornithological study, and continuing the labours begun by Thomas Littleton Powys, fourth Lord Lilford [q. v. Suppl. I], proved a pioneer in investigations into Spanish ornithology. He embodied his research and observations in his 'Ornithology of the Straits of Gibraltar' (1875; enlarged 2nd edit. 1894), including south-west Andalucia and northern Morocco. The book enjoys a standard repute. Irby pursued his studies with ardour at home on his retirement. He prepared a useful 'Key List of British Birds' (1888), and contributed several papers to the 'Ibis.' As an ornithologist he denounced the wanton destruction of bird life and the needless multiplication of species by scientists. Latterly he took up lepidopterology, and with the help of his sons formed a very good collection of European butterflies and British moths. The former belongs to his son, Major Frederick Irby of Boyland Hall, Norfolk, and the latter is in the Norwich Museum. Irby was a member of the council of the Zoological Society of London from 1892 to 1900. He assisted in the formation of the life groups in the Natural History Museum, South Kensington, where some of the most remarkable cases of British birds bear his name.

He died on 14 May 1905 at 14 Cornwall Terrace, Regent's Park, and was buried at Kensal Green. He married (1) on 31 Aug. 1864 Geraldine Alicia Mary (*d.* 1882), daughter of J. B. Magenis, rector of Great Horkesley, by whom he had two sons; (2) on 22 Jan. 1884 Mary, daughter of Col. John James Brandling, C.B., of Low Gosforth, co. Northumberland, by whom he had a daughter.

[The Times, 16 May 1905; Ibis, July 1905, obit. notice by Willoughby C. Verner; Nature, 18 May 1905; Burke's Peerage, s.v. Boston; Hart's Army List; Lord Wolseley's Story of a Soldier's Life, 2 vols. 1903; private information from his son, Major J. Irby.] H. M. V.

IRELAND, WILLIAM WOTHERSPOON (1832–1909), physician, born at Edinburgh on 27 Oct. 1832, was son of Thomas Ireland, a publisher of Edinburgh. Through his father's grandmother he was a lineal descendant of John Knox through Mrs. Welsh, daughter of the reformer. His mother was Mary, daughter of William Wotherspoon, writer to the signet, and first manager and secretary of the Scottish Widows' Life Assurance Society. Ireland was educated at the Edinburgh high school, and afterwards at the university, where he graduated M.D. in 1855. He then studied for a short time at Paris and became resident surgeon at the Dumfries Infirmary. He was appointed an assistant surgeon in the East India Company's service on 4 Aug. 1856, was attached to the Bengal horse artillery, and was present at the siege of Delhi, where he treated the wounds of Lieutenant (now Lord) Roberts. He took part in the battles of Bedli-Ka-Serai and Najafgarh. He was himself wounded by a bullet which destroyed one of his eyes and passed round the base of the skull towards the opposite ear. He also had a second wound though of a less serious character; a ball entered the shoulder and lodged in his back. In the list of casualties in the East India Register and Army List for 1858 he is shown as 'killed before Delhi 26 August 1857.' He received the medal and clasp and was granted three years' furlough counting as service; but after two years' convalescence he was retired from the service with a special pension. After ten years' work, partly spent at Madeira and partly on the continent of Europe, he was from 1869 to 1879 medical superintendent of the Scottish National Institution for Imbecile Children at Larbert. In 1880 he opened a private home for the treatment of cases of arrested mental development, first at Stirling, afterwards at Prestonpans and Polton. In 1905 he was the recipient from his friends of a jubilee gift and an illuminated address presented to him by Dr. T. S. Clouston. He retired to Musselburgh after the death of his wife and died there on 17 May 1909.

He married Margaret Paterson in 1861, and left one son and a daughter.

Ireland, a man of striking individuality, became an authority upon idiocy and imbecility. He had a wide knowledge of literature and history and was well acquainted with the French, German, Italian, Spanish, Norse, and Hindustani languages. His most original and interesting work was the application of his medico-psychological knowledge to explain the lives and actions of many celebrated men. These sketches are contained in 'The Blot upon the Brain, Studies in History and Psychology' (Edinburgh, 1885; 2nd edit. 1893; New York, 1886; translated into German, Stuttgart, 1887), where he considers the hallucinations of Mohammed, Luther, and Joan of Arc; the history of the hereditary neurosis of the royal family of Spain, and kindred subjects. A companion volume 'Through the Ivory Gate, Studies in Psychology and History,' Edinburgh, 1889, deals with Emanuel Swedenborg, William Blake, Louis II of Bavaria, Louis Riel, and others. His 'Life of Sir Harry Vane the Younger, with a History of the Events of his Time,' 1905, is a careful study from original documents.

Besides the works mentioned, Ireland published: 1. 'A History of the Siege of Delhi by an Officer who served there,' Edinburgh, 1861. 2. 'Randolph Methyl, a Story of Anglo-Indian Life,' 1863, 2 vols. 3. 'What Food to eat,' 1865. 4. 'Studies of a Wandering Observer,' 1867. 5. 'Idiocy and Imbecility,' 1877, 2nd edit. renamed 'The Mental Affections of Children: Idiocy, Imbecility, and Insanity,' London and Edinburgh, 1898; Philadelphia, 1900. 6. 'Golden Bullets, a Story of the Days of Akber and Elizabeth,' Edinburgh, 1891. To the 'Journal of Mental Science' he contributed literary and psychological studies of Torquato Tasso, Auguste Comte and Friedrich Nietzsche.

[Journal of Mental Science, 1909, lv. p. 582; Edinburgh Med. Journal, June 1909, p. 563; Lancet, 1909, i. 1643; Brit. Med. Journal, 1909, i. 1334; additional information kindly given by Lieut.-col. D. G. Crawford, I.M.S., and Miss Ireland.] D'A. P.

IRVINE, WILLIAM (1840–1911), Mogul historian, born at Aberdeen on 4 July 1840, was only son of William Irvine, an Aberdeen advocate, by his wife Margaret Garden. On the death of his father when he was a child, his mother, of Aberdeen family but a Londoner by birth, brought him to London. He owed most of his education to his mother and grandmother. Leaving a private school before he was fifteen, he served a short apprenticeship to business, and after spending some years as a clerk in the admiralty passed for the Indian Civil Service. He landed in Calcutta late in 1863, and being posted to the North-Western Provinces (now the United Provinces of Agra and Oudh) served there as a magistrate and collector until he retired in 1889. In India Irvine was chiefly known as an authority on the provincial laws of rent and revenue. In 1868, while yet an assistant, he published his 'Rent Digest,' a digest of the rent law of the province, and he was employed for eight years in revising the rent and revenue settlement records of the Ghazipur district, an arduous undertaking. He left India in 1889 with the reputation of an excellent officer, hard working, judicious, and accurate.

While in India Irvine devoted his leisure to Indian history. In 1879 he produced a history of the Afghan Nawabs of Fatehgarh or Farukhabad (*Journ. Asiatic Soc. of Bengal*, 1879). On retiring to England he began a history of the decline of the Mogul empire from the death of Aurangzeb in 1707 to the capture of Delhi by Lord Lake in 1803. The work was based on a wide study of the authorities, chiefly native, and was planned on a very large scale. Various chapters appeared in the 'Journal of the Asiatic Society of Bengal' between 1896 and 1908, and Irvine accumulated materials down to 1761; but the history itself was not carried later than the accession of Mahomed Shah in 1719. Numerous papers on cognate subjects appeared in the 'Journals' of the Royal Asiatic Society of London and the Asiatic Society of Bengal, the 'Asiatic Quarterly Review,' and the 'Indian Antiquary'; and in 1903 Irvine published a large work on the Mogul army, entitled 'The Army of the Indian Moghuls: its organisation and administration.' He also contributed in 1908 the chapter on Mogul history to the new 'Gazetteer of India.' His last publication of importance was a life of Aurangzeb in the 'Indian Antiquary' for 1911; a résumé appeared the same year in the 'Encyclopédie d'Islam.'

Meanwhile in 1893 Irvine's attention was drawn to the Venetian traveller, Niccolao Manucci, who spent fifty years in India, and was, after Bernier, the chief contemporary European authority for the history of India during the reign of Aurangzeb (1658–1707). Manucci's work was only known in a garbled French version. After a search of eight years Irvine discovered not only a Berlin codex which gives a part of the text but a Venice MS. which supplied the whole. Manucci had dictated his work in Latin, French, Italian, or Portuguese according as the nationality or knowledge of his chance amanuenses might requre. Irvine not only translated but edited it with such a fulness of knowledge and illustration that on its publication by the government of India in 1907 as 'Storia di Mogor' (3 vols.) it at once took rank as a classic. Irvine's fame rests mainly on this work.

Irvine was unrivalled in his intimate knowledge of the whole course of Mogul history, and was much consulted by other scholars. In 1908 the Asiatic Society of Bengal made him an honorary member. He was a vice-president and member of the council of the Royal Asiatic Society; he served also on the council of the Central Asian and various other learned societies. He died at his house in Castelnau, Barnes, after a long illness on 3 Nov. 1911, and is buried in the Old Barnes cemetery. In 1872 he married Teresa Anne, youngest daughter of Major Evans, and grandniece of Sir George de Lacy Evans [q. v.]. She died in 1901, and is buried in the same grave with her husband. Irvine left one son, Henry, an electrical engineer in the West Indies, and a daughter.

[Buckland, Dict. of Indian Biog.; The Times, 7 Nov. 1911; Calcutta Englishman, and Journal Roy. Asiat. Soc., Jan. 1912, with list of Irvine's minor writings; personal knowledge.] J. K.

IRVING, Sir HENRY (1838–1905), actor, whose original name was John Henry Brodribb, was born at Keinton Mandeville, Somerset, on 6 Feb. 1838. His father, Samuel Brodribb, came of yeoman stock, and was a small and not prosperous shopkeeper; his mother, Mary Behenna, was a Cornishwoman. When their only child was four years old, the parents moved to Bristol; later, on their leaving Bristol for London, the boy was sent to live at Halsetown, near St. Ives in Cornwall, with his mother's sister, Sarah, who had married Isaac Penberthy, a Cornish miner, and had three children. The household was methodist and religious, and Mrs. Penberthy a woman of stern but affectionate nature. The life was wholesome and open-air. In 1849, at the age of eleven, the boy joined his parents, who were living at 65 Old Broad Street (on the site of the present Dresdner Bank), and attended school at Dr. Pinches' City Commercial School in George Yard, Lombard Street. Here he acted with success in the school entertainments. In 1851 he left school, and entered the office of Paterson and Longman, solicitors, Milk Street, Cheapside, whence, at the age of fourteen, he went to be clerk in the firm of W. Thacker & Co., East India merchants, Newgate Street. A year later he joined the City Elocution Class, conducted by Henry Thomas. Here he won a reputation among his fellows as a reciter, and was always 'word-perfect' in the parts he acted. His first visit to a theatre had been to Sadler's Wells, to see Samuel Phelps play Hamlet; and he took every opportunity of seeing Phelps act, studying each play for himself before going to the theatre. At sixteen he made the acquaintance of a member of Phelps's company, William Hoskins, who gave him tuition in acting, and later introduced him to Phelps, who offered him an engagement. Brodribb had, however, determined to begin his career in the provinces: he continued to read, to study plays, to learn fencing and dancing, and to carry on his office work until, in 1856, Hoskins introduced him to E. D. Davis, who engaged him for the stock company at the Lyceum Theatre, Sunderland.

At this theatre, under the name of Henry Irving, Brodribb made his first public appearance on the stage on 18 Sept. 1856, he being between eighteen and nineteen years old. His part was Gaston, Duke of Orleans, in Lytton's 'Richelieu.' On one occasion he broke down in the part of Cleomenes in 'The Winter's Tale,' because the religious notions imbibed at Halsetown prevented him from learning the part on a Sunday. This was said to be the only time in his career in which he failed for lack of previous study. He received no salary for the first month, and 25*s.* a week during the remainder of his engagement, and out of this he contributed to the support of his parents. In Feb. 1857, when just nineteen, he left Sunderland for Edinburgh, where he remained two and a half years under the management of R. H. Wyndham. Among the parts he played there were Horatio, Banquo, Macduff, Catesby, Pisanio (to the Imogen of Helen Faucit) and Claudius in 'Hamlet'; while he appeared with success also in pantomime and burlesque. His reception by the Edinburgh public and press was by no means altogether favourable. From the outset he was praised for his 'gentlemanly' air, his earnestness, and the care he took over his costume and 'make-up'; but he was often taken to task for the mannerisms of which much was to be heard later.

From Edinburgh Irving passed to his first engagement in London. On 24 Sept. 1859 he appeared in a small part in Oxenford's 'Ivy Hall,' produced by Augustus Harris, the elder, at the Princess's Theatre, Oxford Street. The parts allotted him being beneath his ambition, he obtained a release from his contract. Readings of 'The Lady of Lyons' and 'Virginius' at Crosby Hall in the following winter and spring led to a four weeks' engagement at the Queen's Theatre, Dublin, which began in March 1860. Replacing a popular actor who had just been dismissed, Irving was received by a section of the audience with three weeks of active hostility. When the nightly disturbances had at last been stopped. his Laertes, Florizel, and other performances won him general favour. From Dublin he went to Glasgow and Greenock, and in Sept. 1860 obtained an engagement at the Theatre Royal, Manchester, under Charles Calvert.

In Manchester Irving spent nearly five years. His progress was slow and disheartening. Calvert, however, was a staunch friend and adviser, and in time the good qualities of Irving's acting—his earnestness, his intelligence, and the effort to be natural—made themselves felt. It was at the Theatre Royal, Manchester, that he first appeared as Hamlet. In April 1864 he had impersonated Hamlet (or rather J. P. Kemble as Hamlet) in one of a series of tableaux illustrating a reading by Calvert. On 20 June following he chose the part for his benefit. For his 'make-up' on this occasion he copied that of Fechter and wore a fair wig. Lack of physical and vocal power were the chief faults urged by the critics. The periods during which the theatre was closed Irving spent in giving readings in various places, and the vacation of 1864 was spent at Oxford, where he acted Hamlet and other parts. In October 1864 Calvert moved from the Theatre Royal to the new Prince's Theatre. Irving remained at the Theatre Royal, playing unimportant parts, till the early part of 1865. In February of that year he and two others gave in public halls in Manchester an entertainment burlesquing the spiritualistic *séances* of the Davenport Brothers; and his refusal to demean (as he considered) the leading theatre by repeating this entertainment on its stage was the ostensible reason for the termination of his engagement. For a few weeks he played under Calvert at the Prince's, and then returned to Edinburgh. Between April and Dec. 1865 he acted at Edinburgh, Bury, Oxford, and Birmingham. Having received and refused an offer to join Fechter's company at the Lyceum Theatre, London, he began in Dec. 1865 an engagement at Liverpool. In the summer of 1866 he went touring with his lifelong friend, John Lawrence Toole [q. v. Suppl. II], whom he had first met at Edinburgh in 1857, and in July 1866 he created at Prince's Theatre, Manchester, the part of Rawdon Scudamore, the villain in Boucicault's drama 'The Two Lives of Mary Leigh,' afterwards called 'Hunted Down.' His arrangement with Boucicault was that, should he succeed in the part, he should be engaged to play it in London; and the arrangement was duly carried out.

When he joined Miss Herbert's company at the St. James's Theatre in Oct. 1866 Irving was twenty-eight and a half years old, had been on the stage ten years, and had played nearly 600 parts (BRERETON, ii. 345). His first part at the St. James's was not Rawdon Scudamore, but Doricourt in 'The Belle's Stratagem.' Boucicault's play 'Hunted Down' was produced in November, and Irving's performance made a favourable impression. In Feb. 1867 there followed Holcroft's 'The Road to Ruin,' in which he played Young Dornton. A brief engagement with Sothern to play Abel Murcott in 'Our American Cousin' at the Théâtre des Italiens, Paris, was followed by a tour with Miss Herbert in England, and in Oct. 1867 Irving returned to the St. James's, now under the management of J. S. Clarke, only to leave it very soon for the new Queen's Theatre in Long Acre. Here, under Alfred Wigan, he appeared in Dec. 1867 as Petruchio in 'Katherine and Petruchio,' the Katherine being Miss Ellen Terry, whom he then met for the first time. His Petruchio was not liked, but during his engagement at the Queen's, which lasted till March 1869, he played with success three villains, two in plays by H. J. Byron, the third being Bill Sikes in Oxenford's 'Oliver Twist.' Like Macready, he was almost confined for a time to villains, for after a brief and unsuccessful engagement at the Haymarket in July, in August 1869 he was playing yet another villain at Drury Lane. In April 1870 he joined the company at the Vaudeville, and here, on 4 June, he made his first notable success in London, in the part of Digby Grant in Albery's 'Two Roses.' The run was a long one, and on his benefit night in March 1871 Irving added to his fame by reciting 'The Dream of Eugene Aram.'

In this year, 1871, the Lyceum Theatre was taken by an American, H. L. Bateman, whose daughters, Kate and Isabel, were actresses. Irving, rather against his will, left the Vaudeville to join the newly formed company, of which Miss Isabel Bateman was the leading lady. On the opening night, 11 Sept. 1871, he played Landry Barbeau in 'Fanchette,' an adaptation from the German by Mrs. Bateman, the manager's wife. On 23 Oct. this play gave place to Albery's 'Pickwick,' in which Irving took what proved to be the leading character, Alfred Jingle. Bateman's resources were now almost exhausted; and as a measure of despair he accepted Irving's urgent entreaty to put on 'The Bells,' a version by Leopold Lewis [q. v.] of Erckmann-Chatrian's 'Le Juif Polonais.' 'The Bells,' produced at the Lyceum on 25 Nov. 1871, was a complete success. Irving, now between thirty-three and thirty-four, 'woke to find himself famous.' In place of the easy-going, comfortable Burgomaster represented in the original and other versions of the play he created a conscience-haunted wretch, and made horror the chief emotion of the play. 'The Bells' ran till the middle of May 1872 and during its run Irving acted nightly, in addition to Mathias, first Jingle and later Jeremy Diddler. On 28 Sept. 1872 Bateman put up 'Charles I.' by W. G. Wills [q. v.]. Despite much protest against the dramatist's treatment of Cromwell, the play was successful, and the pathos and dignity of Irving's performance of the King increased his fame. On 19 April 1873 Bateman put on Wills's 'Eugene Aram,' in which Irving took the title-part; and on 27 Sept. he appeared as the Cardinal in Lytton's 'Richelieu.' Here, for the first time, he came into comparison with Macready and Phelps. In spite of his nervousness, the originality of his conception, and the inadequacy of his support, his success was almost complete, only one critic of importance accusing him of monotony and feebleness of voice. On 7 Feb. 1874 'Richelieu' gave place to Hamilton Aïdé's 'Philip,' where Irving snatched a personal success from a poor play.

Meanwhile, somewhat against Bateman's wishes, Irving was preparing a bolder stroke; and on 31 Oct. 1874 he appeared as Hamlet. The excitement among playgoers was great; and though the play was cheaply mounted and the audience failed during the first two acts to see the drift of a very quiet and original performance, in the end the rendering was a triumph. The play ran for 200 nights. Tennyson and others liked the new Hamlet better than Macready's, and Irving had now attained the supreme position among living actors. Criticism and even scurrilous attack were not wanting, and they broke into greater activity when in September 1875 he appeared as Macbeth. His Macbeth was not the robust butcher to whom the public were accustomed, and in bringing out the imagination in Macbeth, Irving doubtless, in this his first rendering, brought out too strongly his disordered nerves. The play ran for eighty nights. In February 1876 'Othello' was produced. Salvini had appeared as Othello in London only the year before, and Irving's very different reading of the character was even more hotly attacked than his Macbeth, while with this play his mannerisms of voice and movement probably reached their worst. In Tennyson's 'Queen Mary,' which followed in April 1876, they were less obvious; but the part of Philip of Spain was, by comparison, a small one, and the play, as staged, uninteresting, and in June 'The Bells' was revived, together with 'The Belle's Stratagem,' in which Irving played Doricourt. The autumn was spent in a tour, during which the graduates and undergraduates of Trinity College, Dublin, presented him in the dining-hall of the university with an address. On 29 January 1877 Irving appeared at the Lyceum as Richard III in Shakespeare's play, which then for the first time ousted Colley Cibber's version from the stage. In the following May came 'The Lyons Mail,' Irving taking the two parts of Lesurques and Dubosc; and this play, which ran till the end of July, remained in his repertory till the end of his career. His next appearance in a new part was in May 1878, when he played the King in Boucicault's 'Louis XI,' and enthralled his audiences in the death scene. In June came the unsuccessful production of 'Vanderdecken,' by Wills and Percy Fitzgerald, to be followed in July by 'The Bells' and 'Jingle,' the latter being a new version by Albery of his 'Pickwick.' Bateman had died in June 1875; and the theatre had since been managed, not illiberally, by his widow, who naturally desired that her daughters should have good opportunities, and retained Miss Isabel Bateman as leading lady. The time had now come when Irving felt the necessity of choosing his own company and conducting his own management. On his proposing to leave the Lyceum, Mrs. Bateman resigned in August 1878, and the theatre passed into Irving's hands. He was then a few months over forty years old.

During his autumn tour in 1878 the theatre was altered and improved. For his leading lady he engaged Miss Ellen Terry, who began a famous association of twenty-four years when she appeared as Ophelia to his Hamlet on the opening night of his management, 30 Dec. 1878. Joseph Knight summed up in the 'Athenæum' (4 Jan. 1879) the aims of the new manager: 'Scenic accessories are explanatory without being cumbersome, the costumes are picturesque and striking and show no needless affectation of archæological accuracy, and the interpretation has an *ensemble* rarely found in any performance, and never during recent years in a representation of tragedy.' Irving's second production was 'The Lady of Lyons' (27 April 1879), of which only forty performances were given, and which he never afterwards played. His summer holiday he spent cruising with the Baroness Burdett-Coutts in the Mediterranean, where he gathered some ideas for a production of 'The Merchant of Venice.' In the season of 1879–80 a short run of 'The Iron Chest,' by George Colman the younger, was followed by a hurried (STOKER, chap. 9) but brilliant production of that play, in which Irving showed a new Shylock, the grandest and most sympathetic figure in the play. The season of 1880–1 was opened with 'The Corsican Brothers'; and on 3 Jan. 1881 came Tennyson's 'The Cup,' one of the most beautiful stage productions that Irving achieved. In May began a series of twenty-two performances of 'Othello,' in which Irving and the American actor, Edwin Booth (who had just before been playing with ill-success at the Princess's Theatre, and who came to the Lyceum on Irving's invitation), alternated weekly the parts of Othello and Iago. During Irving's autumn tour the theatre was once more altered and improved; and in March 1882 came the production of 'Romeo and Juliet,' to which Irving restored the love of Romeo for Rosaline. This play was even more finely mounted than 'The Merchant of Venice'; it was Irving's first really elaborate production, and here for the first time he showed his ability in handling a stage crowd, having possibly taken some hints from the visit to London in the previous year of the Meiningen company. Though Romeo was not a part in which Irving excelled, the play ran till the end of the season and opened the season of 1882–3. In Oct. 1882 he produced 'Much Ado about Nothing,' playing Benedick to the Beatrice of Miss Terry, and the comedy was at the height of its success when it was withdrawn in June 1883.

In Oct. 1883 Irving and his company set sail for the first of his eight tours in America. The tour lasted till March 1884, and included New York and fifteen other towns, the repertory containing eight plays. Everywhere he was received with enthusiasm by press and public. At the end of May 1884 he was back at the Lyceum, where in July he produced 'Twelfth Night.' His Malvolio was not generally liked, and the run of the play was brief. In September he sailed for his second American tour (which at the time he intended should be his last), during which he played in the chief towns of Canada, as well as in those of America. His return to the Lyceum in May 1885 was marked by a mild disturbance owing to his attempt to introduce the practice of 'booking' seats in the hitherto unreserved pit and gallery, an attempt which he surrendered in deference to the objections raised. After a few revivals he put on, towards the end of the month, a slightly altered version of Wills's 'Olivia,' in which Miss Terry had appeared with great success elsewhere. Irving took the part of Dr. Primrose, and the play ran till the end of the season. Once more the theatre was redecorated and altered. On 19 Dec. came one of the greatest financial successes of Irving's management, Wills's 'Faust.' In this production Irving for the first time indulged in scenic effects for their own sake, and used them rather as an amplification of the author's ideas than as a setting for the drama. His Mephistopheles was one of his weirdest and most striking impersonations, and the play ran continuously for sixteen months, that is, till April 1887, new scenes of the students' cellar and the witches' kitchen being introduced in the autumn of 1886. In June 1887 Irving gave two special performances: one of Byron's 'Werner' (as altered by F. A. Marshall), in which he played Werner, and one of A. C. Calmour's 'The Amber Heart,' in which he did not appear. From Nov. 1887 to March 1888 he and his company made their third tour in America, 'Faust' being the principal thing in the repertory. In the week before he sailed for home, Irving gave at the Military Academy, West Point, a performance of 'The Merchant of Venice' without scenery. 'Faust,' 'The Amber Heart,' and 'Robert Macaire,' in which Irving played the title part, filled the short summer season of 1888 at the Lyceum, and the winter season opened with a revival of 'Macbeth.' The production was sumptuous, and Irving was now capable of expressing his idea of Macbeth more fully and with less extravagance than in 1875. In April 1889 a command performance at Sandringham enabled Queen Victoria, who was a guest there, to see Irving and Miss Terry for the first time. The programme consisted of 'The Bells' and the trial scene from 'The Merchant of Venice.' For his first production in the autumn of 1889 Irving chose Watts Phillips's drama, 'The Dead Heart,' as re-modelled by Mr. W. H. Pollock. He played Landry, and induced Sir Squire (then Mr.) Bancroft, who had retired in 1881, to play the Abbé Latour. On 20 Sept. 1890 he opened his winter season with 'Ravenswood,' a new version by Herman Merivale of 'The Bride of Lammermoor.' The play was too gloomy to be popular. After this there was no new production at the Lyceum till 5 Jan. 1892, when 'King Henry VIII' with music by Edward German was mounted with more splendour than Irving had allowed even to 'Faust.' The cost of production, which exceeded 11,000*l.*, was too great to be profitable, though the piece remained in the bill for six months. In November 'King Lear' was put on; and in Feb. 1893 came the performance of Tennyson's 'Becket.' This play had been sent to Irving by Tennyson in 1879 (*The Theatre*, Oct. 1879, p. 175); and Irving, though he refused it at first (*Alfred, Lord Tennyson*, ii. 196), had frequently thought it over. Not till 1892 (Stoker, i. 221–2; but see *Alfred, Lord Tennyson, loc. cit.*) did Irving decide to produce it; he then obtained Tennyson's approval of his large excisions, and persuaded him to write a new speech for Becket for the end of act i. sc. iii. Produced on 6 Feb. 1893, four months after the poet's death, 'Becket' proved to be one of Irving's greatest personal and financial triumphs; its first run lasted till 22 July, and it was frequently revived. Soon after its first production it was acted by command before Queen Victoria at Windsor.

Irving's fourth American tour lasted from Sept. 1893 till March 1894, 'Becket' being the piece most often played. This was Irving's most successful tour, the total receipts being over 123,000*l.* In the provincial tour which occupied the autumn of 1894 Irving appeared for the first time as Corporal Gregory Brewster in A. Conan Doyle's 'A Story of Waterloo,' or 'Waterloo,' as it was afterwards called. On 12 Jan. 1895 he produced at the Lyceum Comyns Carr's 'King Arthur,' which was followed in May by a bill consisting of Pinero's 'Byegones,' 'Waterloo,' and 'A Chapter from the Life of Don Quixote,' a condensed version of a play written to Irving's order by Wills in 1878. The fifth American tour occupied the months from Sept. 1895 to May 1896, and included towns in the south which Irving had not before visited, 'King Arthur' being the principal piece in the repertory. The following September saw him back at the Lyceum, where he produced 'Cymbeline,' himself playing Iachimo. On 19 Dec.

1896 he revived 'King Richard III.' On his return to his rooms after the play he fell and injured his knee, and it was not till the end of Feb. 1897 that he was able to return to work and resume the interrupted run of that play. In April 1897 he played Napoleon in Comyns Carr's adaptation of Sardou and Moreau's 'Madame Sans-Gêne.' The year 1897 had not been a successful one; the year 1898 was disastrous. 'Peter the Great,' a tragedy by Irving's son Laurence, and 'The Medicine Man,' by H. D. Traill and Robert Hichens, both failed outright; and in February Irving's immense stock of scenery, comprising the scenes of all his productions except 'The Bells' and 'The Merchant of Venice,' was destroyed by fire. During his autumn tour he was taken with pleurisy and lay dangerously ill at Glasgow. The result of these heavy losses was the sale of his library by auction in Feb. 1899, and the transference, early in the same year, of his interest in the Lyceum Theatre to a company. Not till April was Irving well enough to reappear on the stage; he then produced Laurence Irving's translation of 'Robespierre,' a play written for him by Sardou. After a brief autumn tour he sailed for his sixth tour in America, which lasted from October 1899 to May 1900, the company visiting more than thirty towns, and playing five plays in addition to 'Robespierre.' In April 1901 he produced at the Lyceum 'Coriolanus'—his last new Shakespearean production. In October began his seventh American tour, which lasted till March 1902. It was at the conclusion of this tour that Miss Ellen Terry left Irving's company, though she appeared once or twice at the Lyceum in the next London season, and took part in the autumn provincial tour of 1902. In April 1902 Irving revived 'Faust' at the Lyceum, and closed the season on 19 July with a performance of 'The Merchant of Venice.' This was his last performance in that theatre. The company which had taken over the Lyceum Theatre had lost so much money over their ventures during his tours that they were unable to carry out certain structural alterations demanded by the London County Council. The contract was annulled; the Lyceum Theatre remained empty till it was converted into a music-hall, and Irving had to find a house elsewhere.

It was at Drury Lane that he produced on 30 April 1903 'Dante,' written for him by Sardou, and translated by Laurence Irving. The expenses of production and running were enormous, and the play failed to attract either in England or in America, where Irving made his eighth and last tour from Oct. 1903 to March 1904. In April he began a provincial tour which ended in June, and in September another, which he intended to be his last. 'Becket' was the play chiefly performed. Broken by a brief holiday at Christmas, the tour went on till Feb. 1905, when ill-health compelled Irving to rest. In April he revived 'Becket' at Drury Lane, and played it, with other pieces, with success till June. This was his last London season, and the last performances of it were, as if prophetically, scenes of enthusiasm as wild as any that had attended him in his early popularity. On 2 Oct. he resumed at Sheffield his provincial tour. In the following week he was at Bradford. On the evening of 13 Oct. 1905 he played 'Becket,' and on returning to his hotel collapsed and died almost immediately. His age was sixty-seven years and eight months. His body was taken to the London house of the Baroness Burdett-Coutts, where it was visited by crowds of mourners; and after cremation the ashes were buried in Westminster Abbey on 20 Oct. 1905.

Irving occasionally gave recitations and readings. His recitation of Lytton's poem, 'The Dream of Eugene Aram,' was his most famous *tour-de-force*. His earlier readings have been mentioned; of those given later and for public objects the most important were his reading of 'Hamlet' in the Birkbeck Institute in Feb. 1887, of scenes from 'Becket' in the chapter-house at Canterbury in May 1897, and at Winchester during the celebration of the tercentenary of Alfred in Sept. 1901. Among the many addresses he delivered were the following: 'Acting: an Art,' before the Royal Institution in February 1895; 'The Theatre in its Relation to the State,' the Rede Lecture for 1898 to the University of Cambridge; and 'English Actors,' delivered before the University of Oxford in June 1886. The last was published in 1886, and, together with three other addresses, was reprinted, under the title of 'Four Great Actors,' in 'The Drama, by Henry Irving' (1893). 'The Stage,' an address delivered before the Perry Bar Institute in March 1878, was published in the same year. To the 'Nineteenth Century' he contributed short articles, under the collective heading of 'An Actor's Notes,' in April and May 1877, Feb. 1879, and June 1887, a note on 'Actor Managers' in June 1890, and 'Some Misconceptions about the Stage' in Oct. 1892.

Irving also published acting editions of many of his productions, including 'Becket,' and himself prepared with the assistance of Francis Albert Marshall [q. v.] and many other coadjutors the text, with suggestions for excisions in performance, of the 'Henry Irving Shakespeare,' to which he contributed an essay on 'Shakespeare as a Playwright' (1888).

Irving opened many memorials, among them the Shakespeare fountain presented to Stratford-upon-Avon by G. W. Childs in Oct. 1887, the memorial of Marlowe at Canterbury in Sept. 1891, and the statue of Mrs. Siddons on Paddington Green in June 1897.

His degrees and honours included the LL.D. of Dublin (1892), the Litt.D. of Cambridge (1898), the LL.D. of Glasgow (1899), and the Komthur Cross of the Ernestine Order of the second class, conferred upon him by the Dukes of Saxe-Coburg-Gotha and Saxe-Meiningen. In 1883 he was approached on the subject of a knighthood, and declined the honour (*The Times*, 24 Oct. 1905, p. 12); in 1895 he accepted it, and thus, being the first actor to be knighted for his services to the stage, obtained for his profession the 'official recognition' which he had declared to be its due. He was the first actor to speak at the annual banquet of the Royal Academy, and the inclusion of the toast of 'The Drama' dates from that occasion.

Irving married on 15 July 1869 Florence, daughter of Daniel James O'Callaghan, surgeon-general in the East India Company, and niece of John Cornelius O'Callaghan [q. v.], author of 'The Green Book, or Gleanings from the Desk of a Literary Agitator.' There were two children of the marriage: Henry Brodribb, born on 5 Aug. 1870, and Laurence Sidney Brodribb, born on 21 Dec. 1871. Early in 1872 the husband and wife ceased to live together, and a deed of separation was executed in 1879. During the greater part of his London career Irving lived in rooms at 15A Grafton Street, Bond Street; in 1899 he moved to a flat at 17 Stratton Street, Piccadilly.

In figure Irving was tall and very thin, in constitution wiry and capable of great and prolonged exertion. The beauty and nobility of his face and head increased with years (on his appearance in youth see Ellen Terry, *The Story of my Life*, pp. 147–8, and *The Bancrofts*, p. 324); and he had expressive features and beautiful hands. In character he was ambitious, proud, lonely, and self-centred ('an egotist of the great type' is Miss Terry's phrase for him), but gentle, courteous, and lavishly generous. His personal magnetism was very strong; he inspired devotion in those who worked with him and adulation in his admirers. His resentment of parody and caricature may probably be ascribed to his jealousy for the dignity of his art as much as to sensitiveness in himself; of direct attack (and perhaps few actors have been so virulently attacked as Irving was in his earlier years at the Lyceum) he took little notice. Though open to suggestion, he relied almost entirely upon his own mind, and had sufficient power of genius and will to force acceptance of his always sincere and original views. As an actor, he had many disabilities, natural and contracted, a voice monotonous and not powerful, a peculiar pronunciation, a stamping gait, and a tendency to drag his leg behind him, angular and excessive gesture, and a slowness of speech which became more marked when powerful emotion choked his utterance. These mannerisms, which were at their height between 1873 and 1880, were less pronounced after his second American tour in 1884; and through most of his career he may be said to have either kept them in check or made good use of them. It has been said that in all his parts he was 'always Irving'; this is true inasmuch as his physical characteristics and commanding personality could not be disguised, but his assumptions of character were nearly always complete 'from the mind outwards.' He has been called an intellectual actor. If the phrase is meant to state that he could not express great passion, it is unjust: unsurpassed in the portrayal of fear, horror, scorn or malignity, he could draw tears as freely as any 'emotional' actor. His intellectuality lay in the thought which he brought to bear on any part or play he undertook. The dregs of the old school in tragedy still lingered on the stage when he forced his audiences to think out Shakespeare's characters anew, and helped forward the revolution begun by Fechter, a revolution which aimed, no less than did that of Garrick, at restoring nature and truth. Irving's bent led him towards the bizarre and fantastic, and touches of these appeared in all his work. He kept it, however, in check, and his distinction of appearance and manner, with a power of donning a noble simplicity, enabled the impersonator of Mathias and of Mephistopheles to be admirable also as Charles I, Dr. Primrose, or Becket. Of his Shakespearean characters, his finest was probably his Hamlet in which his thought, his princely air, his fantasy, his tenderness, and his power of suggesting coming doom, all had play. His much debated Macbeth, his Iago, and his Shylock were also very fine; as Othello and Romeo he was less successful. A sardonic humour and a raffish air were the best things in such comic parts as Jingle and Robert Macaire.

For the modern drama of his own country Irving did little or nothing. It did not appeal to him, nor did it suit his large theatre or his love of beautiful production. His excursions into it were few and ill-judged; but he has the honour of having staged Tennyson's 'The Cup,' 'Queen Mary,' and 'Becket.' The other dramatists whom he employed gave him nothing of permanent value.

The sumptuousness and elaboration of his mountings have been exaggerated. In the early days of his management they were very modest. As time went on they grew more complete and splendid; but, if they left little to the imagination, and if his example has led to subsequent extravagance and vulgarity, Irving himself never mangled Shakespeare in order merely to make room for more scenery (though he altered him in order to secure the kind of dramatic effects demanded by the modern stage). Not himself a man of wide culture or trained taste, he took advantage of the contemporary revival in art, and knew where to go to find beauty; and among those who designed scenes or costumes for him were Burne-Jones, Alma-Tadema, and Seymour Lucas, while his music was supplied by the leading composers of the time. In rehearsing he was even more fixed than Macready (though more courteously so) in his own opinion on the smallest details; and the result was a perfection in the *ensemble*, a single artistic impression, which in tragedy had not been known before, even in the accurate archæology of the Shakespeare productions of Charles Kean. By these means and by his own acting, he drew back to the theatre the intelligent and distinguished people who had deserted it. He numbered among his personal friends the leading men in the country, was invited to meet royalty at country houses, and entertained magnificently (indeed, almost officially as head of the English stage) in his own theatre. The effect was to fulfil one of his dearest wishes, that the drama might be raised to an acknowledged place of honour among the arts and influences of civilisation. Its maintenance there he believed to be impossible without an endowed national theatre.

The portraits of Irving in oil, statuary, and other media are very many. The principal oil-portraits are (1) full-length as Philip II by Whistler (about 1875), now in the Metropolitan Museum, New York; an etching after this picture was made by the painter; (2, 3, and 4) as Richard Duke of Gloucester (1878), as Hamlet (1880), and as Vanderdecken (1880), all by Edwin Long, and in the collection of Mr. Burdett-Coutts; (5) three-quarter length, seated, in modern dress, by J. Bastien-Lepage (1880), in the National Portrait Gallery; (6) half-length, seated, in modern dress, by the Hon. John Collier (1886); (7) three-quarter length, standing, in modern dress, by Millais (1884), in the Garrick Club (engraved by T. O. Barlow, 1885); a copy of this picture, presented by the Garrick Club to the National Portrait Gallery, is on loan to the Shakespeare Memorial Gallery, Stratford-upon-Avon. Oil-portraits of Irving as Mathias and as Charles I, by James Archer, R.S.A., were exhibited in the Royal Academy in 1872 and 1873 respectively. An oil portrait by J. S. Sargent, R.A., which was exhibited in the Royal Academy in 1889, was afterwards destroyed by Irving (*The Bancrofts*, p. 337). In statuary the following portraits are known: (1) a marble statue by R. Jackson, exhibited in the Royal Academy in 1874; (2) a marble bust, by W. Brodie (1878), in the possession of Mr. Burdett-Coutts; (3) a marble statue of Irving as Hamlet, by E. Onslow Ford, R.A. (1883–5), in the Guildhall Art Gallery; (4) a bronze bust by Courtenay Pollock, R.B.A. (1905), in the Garrick Club; (5) a small figure as Tamerlaine, by E. Onslow Ford, forming part of the Marlowe Memorial at Canterbury; (6) a colossal statue in academic robes, by Thomas Brock, R.A., erected by subscription of actors and actresses in front of the north side of the National Portrait Gallery and unveiled by Sir John Hare on 5 Dec. 1910. Many sketches and studies of Irving were made by Bernard Partridge; among these, one, a pen-and-ink sketch of Irving as Richard III, is in the possession of Mr. Burdett-Coutts, who also owns sketches and drawings of Irving by F. W. Lawson and James Pryde, and miniatures of Irving at twenty-five and at thirty-seven by an artist unknown. Drawings by Fred Barnard are frequent. A pastel of Irving as Dubosc, by Martin Harvey, is in the possession of Mr. Charles Hughes of Kersal, Manchester, and a drawing by Martin Harvey is in the possession of Sir George Alexander. Mr. Gordon Craig owns a pencil head of Irving by Paul Renouard; and drawings by Val Bromley and Gordon Craig, a lithograph by W. Rothenstein, and wood engravings by James Pryde and W. Nicholson are also known. A cartoon by 'Ape' appeared in 'Vanity Fair' in 1874.

[The authoritative biography of Irving is that by Mr. Austin Brereton, 2 vols. 1908 (with bibliography). In 1906 Mr. Bram Stoker, many years his manager, published 2 vols. of Personal Reminiscences of Henry Irving. The most vivid portrait of the man and the actor is to be found in Miss Ellen Terry's The Story of my Life, 1908. Mr. Percy Fitzgerald published a life of Irving in 1906, and presented to the Garrick Club a very large collection of press-cuttings and other papers concerning him. See also William Archer, Henry Irving, Actor and Manager: a critical study, 1883; F. A. Marshall (pseud. Irvingite), Henry Irving, Actor and Manager, 1883; John Hollingshead, My Life, 2 vols. 1895; Clement Scott, Some Notable Hamlets of the Present Time, 1905; Bernard Shaw, Dramatic Opinions and Essays, 1907; W. H. Pollock, Impressions of Henry Irving, 1908; The Bancrofts, by Sir Squire and Lady Bancroft, 1909. On his knighthood, see Neue Freie Presse, 20 Oct. 1905, and The Times, 24–27 Oct. 1905.] H. H. C.

IWAN-MÜLLER, ERNEST BRUCE (1853–1910), journalist, born at 8 Hereford Square, South Kensington, on 26 March 1853, was only son of Sévère Félicité Iwan-Müller by his marriage with Anne, daughter of John Moule of Elmsley Lovett, Worcestershire. His mother and an only sister, Elizabeth, survived him. His paternal grandfather, a Russian by birth, named Troubetskoy, was exiled from his native country for political reasons and led for some years a wandering life under the assumed name of Iwan-Müller. He finally settled in England and married the daughter of Charles Wilkin, artist and engraver.

After four years (1863–7) spent at a preparatory school at Thurmanston in Leicestershire, young Iwan-Müller was sent to King's College School, London, where he remained till the end of the summer term of 1871. In October 1873 he entered New College, Oxford, as a commoner, and graduated B.A. (with a first class in literæ humaniores) in December 1876. He proceeded M.A. in 1880. As an undergraduate he was a prominent speaker at the Union and also a frequent contributor to the 'Shotover Paper,' a humorous journal, modelled on the Cambridge 'Light Green,' which enjoyed great popularity in the university.

After graduating, Iwan-Müller was senior classical master at Brackenbury's school, Wimbledon, and in 1879 he returned to Oxford, remaining there till 1884, as a private tutor and 'coach.' Both as an undergraduate and as 'coach' he was a well-known figure in Oxford, and very popular among the young men of literary and political proclivities. He always declared himself an 'out and out Tory' and scouted the more modern title of conservative; but despite the outspokenness of his political opinions, his geniality and humour won him friends among men of all parties. In May 1884 he left Oxford to become editor of the 'Manchester Courier,' a post which he held till June 1893, and in which he did much to promote a great revival of conservatism in Lancashire. In June 1893 he came to London as assistant editor of the 'Pall Mall Gazette' under Mr. Harry Cust. In February 1896 he left the 'Pall Mall' for the 'Daily Telegraph,' on which he remained till his death. Besides his regular work as a leader-writer, he undertook several special missions for that journal, including a long visit to South Africa during the Boer war, a visit to Ireland in 1907 and another to Paris during the crisis caused by the Austrian annexation of Bosnia and Herzegovina in the autumn of 1908. While living in London he also contributed many articles on political subjects to the 'Quarterly Review,' the 'Fortnightly Review,' and other leading magazines. His published works are 'Lord Milner in South Africa' (1902), which is a mine of information on events leading up to the Boer war, and 'Ireland To-day and To-morrow' (1907). At the time of his death he was busily at work on a book dealing with the 'Life and Times of Sir Robert Morier,' for which he had collected much valuable material, which was subsequently embodied in the 'Life' (2 vols. 1911) written by Sir Robert's daughter, Mrs. Wemyss.

Iwan-Müller was conspicuous among the journalists of his time by the range of his knowledge, especially in the field of foreign politics. He enjoyed the confidence of some of the leading statesmen of his time, notably Mr. Arthur Balfour and Lord Salisbury, and perhaps no journalist was ever better acquainted with the inner history of important public events. His discretion was unfailing, and he was trusted and consulted by the leaders of his party to an extent as exceptional as it was, owing to his own modesty and reticence, unsuspected by the outside world. A 'genial giant' of exuberant vitality, he was welcome in every society, while his generosity, especially to the less successful members of his own profession, was unbounded.

Iwan-Müller died in London, unmarried, on 14 May 1910, and was buried at Brookwood. An excellent oil portrait by Hugh de T. Glazebrook belongs to the artist.

[Personal knowledge; Musings without Method, in Blackwood's Mag., July 1910, pp. 143–146, a brilliant and appreciative sketch. See also The Times, 16 May 1910, and Daily Telegraph, 16 May 1910.] M.

J

JACKS, WILLIAM (1841–1907), ironmaster and author, born at Cornhill, Berwickshire, on 18 March 1841, was son in a family of six children of Richard Jacks, shepherd, by his wife, Margaret Lamb. After attending the village school of Swinton, Berwickshire, he became an apprentice in Hartlepool shipyard. Presently he was advanced to the counting-house, where his growing knowledge of continental languages and his business tact led to more responsible occupation. Having managed the Seaham engine works at Sunderland for a time, he was appointed in 1869 manager for Messrs. Robinow and Marjoribanks, ironmasters of Glasgow. On 6 Dec. 1880 he established on his own account at Glasgow a concern which speedily developed into the well-known firm of William Jacks and Co., iron and steel merchants, of Glasgow, Middlesbrough, Sheffield, and Grangemouth. In 1893 he was president of the British Iron Trade Association.

Jacks was elected in the liberal interest M.P. for Leith Burghs in 1885. Unwillingness to accept Gladstone's Irish policy cost him his seat at the general election of 1886, but he represented the county of Stirling as a liberal from 1892 to 1895. Thenceforth he gave his leisure to literary work. He had shown scholarship and taste in a translation of Lessing's 'Nathan the Wise,' which appeared in 1894 with an introduction by Dean Farrar. 'Robert Burns in other Tongues' (1896) presented and discussed versions of the Scottish poet in sixteen foreign languages. 'The Life of Prince Bismarck' (1899) and 'James Watt' (1901) are compact biographies. 'Singles from Life's Gathering' (1902; 2nd edit. 1903), with an introduction by Dean Farrar, who suggested the book, is largely autobiographical. 'The Life of his Majesty William II, German Emperor' (1904), brought a hearty acknowledgment from the Kaiser, with a signed portrait.

Jacks was a D.L. for Stirlingshire, and in 1899 he was created LL.D. of Glasgow University. He died on 9 Aug. 1907 at The Gart, Callander, and was interred in Callander cemetery. He bequeathed 20,000*l.* to Glasgow University, for the endowment of a chair of modern languages to be named after him. To the Glasgow Athenæum Commercial College and the Glasgow Chamber of Commerce respectively he left 1000*l.*, and he bequeathed 1000*l.* each to the Edinburgh Border Counties Association and the Glasgow Border Counties Association to establish scholarships to be called by his name. Jacks married on 23 Oct. 1878 Matilda Ferguson, daughter of John and Emily Stiven, Glasgow. His wife survived her husband, but there was no family.

[Information from Mr. H. Arnold Wilson, of Messrs. William Jacks and Co.; Who's Who, 1906; Glasgow Herald, 10 Aug. 1907; Chambers's Journal, April 1902; Scottish Field, Dec. 1906; personal knowledge.] T. B.

JACKSON, JOHN (1833–1901), professional cricketer, born at Bungay, Suffolk, on 21 May 1833, was taken to Nottinghamshire in infancy and was brought up near Newark, where in the hunting season he was wont to run barefoot after the hounds. He learned his early cricket at Southwell, and after engagements as a professional at Newark, Edinburgh, and Ipswich, he joined the Notts XI, whom he served for ten years. He first appeared at Lord's for the North *v.* South in 1856, and in 1857, when he captured 8 wickets for 20 runs in the same match, was the most prominent bowler in England. In 1858, when helping Kent *v.* England, he took 9 wickets for 27 runs at Lord's, and 13 wickets for 90 runs at Canterbury. His highest batting score in first-class cricket, when scores were rarely very high, was 100 for Notts *v.* Kent in 1863. From 1859 to 1864 he played in twelve matches for the Players *v.* Gentlemen, and in the match at Lord's in 1861 he and Edgar Willsher bowled unchanged through both innings of the Gentlemen. In 1859 he went with the first English team to America, meeting with great success against local teams. He was a member of George Parr's All England XI and visited Australia with Parr's team in the winter of 1863. In 1866 his career was cut short by an accident to his leg while playing for Notts *v.* Yorkshire. From 1870 till his death he lived mainly at Liverpool, where from 1870 to 1872 he was professional at Princes Park, and in 1871 caterer, groundman, and bowler to the Liverpool club. In 1875 he was employed in a Liverpool warehouse, but in later years he fell into poverty, and died in Liverpool workhouse infirmary on 4 Nov. 1901.

Fully six feet in height, and weighing over 15 stone, Jackson was a first-class round arm bowler, with an easy action, combining variety and accuracy with tremendous pace, which gained for him the title of the 'demon bowler.' Jackson figures in many of Leech's famous 'Punch' cricket sketches, where the village cricketer is seen bandaged after bruises inflicted by Jackson's lightning deliveries, but showing pride in his sufferings (see *Punch*, 29 Aug. 1863).

[The Times, 9 Nov. 1901; Wisden's Cricketers' Almanack, 1902, lxvi.; Read's Annals of Cricket, 1895; Haygarth's Cricket Scores and Biographies, v. 199–200; W. Caffyn's Seventy-one not out, 1899; pp. 72–4, passim; notes kindly supplied by Mr. P. M. Thornton.] W. B. O.

JACKSON, JOHN HUGHLINGS (1835–1911), physician, born at Providence Green, Green Hammerton, Yorkshire, on 4 April 1835, was the youngest son in the family of four sons and one daughter of Samuel Jackson, a yeoman owning his own land at Providence Green, and at one time also a brewer. His mother, whose maiden surname was Hughlings, was of Welsh extraction. His three brothers settled in New Zealand, where one of them, Major William Jackson, greatly distinguished himself in the Maori war, and was afterwards accidentally drowned. From the village school of Green Hammerton, Jackson passed successively to schools at Tadcaster, Yorkshire, and at Nailsworth, Gloucestershire, but owed, in his own opinion, little to his instruction there. Apprenticed at York to William C. Anderson, M.R.C.S. (father of Dr. Tempest Anderson), he began his medical education at the York Medical and Surgical School, and continued it at St. Bartholomew's Hospital, where Sir James Paget was one of his teachers. After matriculating at London University and qualifying M.R.C.S. and L.S.A. in 1856, he was until 1859 house surgeon to the dispensary at York, and was there intimately associated with Thomas Laycock [q. v.], then physician to the dispensary. Returning to London in 1859, he thought of giving up medicine in order to devote himself to philosophy, but was dissuaded by (Sir) Jonathan Hutchinson, to whom he had an introduction, and was, through Hutchinson's influence, appointed to the staff of the Metropolitan Free Hospital. He also became in 1859 lecturer on pathology at the London Hospital, and in the summer session he lectured on histology and the microscope. In 1860 he graduated M.D. at St. Andrews. In 1863 he was appointed assistant physician to the London Hospital and lecturer on physiology in the medical school. He became physician in 1874, and remained on the active staff till 1894. He was for a time one of the physicians to the Islington Dispensary, and a clinical assistant to Mr. Poland at the Moorfields Eye Hospital.

Meanwhile in May 1862 Jackson was made assistant physician to the National Hospital for the Paralysed and Epileptic in Queen Square. This institution was established in 1859. When Dr. Jackson joined the staff, Dr. Charles Edward Brown-Séquard [q. v. Suppl. I] was one of the physicians there, and he was succeeded in 1863 by Dr. Charles Bland Radcliffe [q. v.]. Brown Sequard led Jackson to devote his attention chiefly to diseases of the nervous system. Jackson remained on the active staff of the hospital until 1906, when he became consulting physician.

In 1868 Jackson, who had become M.R.C.P. London in 1860, was elected F.R.C.P., and in 1869 he delivered the Gulstonian lectures at the College of Physicians—an honour usually conferred on the most distinguished newly elected fellow. His subject was 'Certain Points in the Study and Classification of Diseases of the Nervous System.' He was also Croonian lecturer at the college in 1884, his subject being 'Evolution and Dissolution of the Nervous System,' and he became Lumleian lecturer in 1890, choosing the subject of 'Convulsive Seizures.' Thus he had the unusual distinction of being chosen to deliver three courses of lectures before the college. He was a member of the council of the college in 1888 and 1889. He was elected F.R.S. in 1878.

Jackson's main work was done in neurology. His investigations fall roughly into three series. His earliest interest was apparently in speech defect in brain disease, and by careful and detailed study of numerous cases he was able to associate such defect in most cases with disease in the left cerebral hemisphere. His papers with these detailed facts and conclusions were published chiefly in the 'London Hospital Reports' in and about 1864. Two years previously Broca had definitely associated loss of speech with disease of the posterior part of the third left frontal convolution. These investigations were unknown to Jackson at the date of his early research, and on learning of them he generously acknowledged that his independent conclusions had 'on every point of importance been anticipated by M. Broca.' The exceptions noted by Jackson were subsequently found to be explained in most instances by the observation that in left-handed persons the speech centre was as a rule situated in the right hemisphere.

The second series of Dr. Jackson's investigations was concerned with the occurrence of local epileptic discharges. These are now known as instances of Jacksonian epilepsy, although Jackson did not himself use that term. He always acknowledged Bravais's earlier recognition of this form of convulsion (1824), and the observation of 'epileptic hemiplegia'—the temporary paralysis following such convulsions—by Dr Robert Bentley Todd [q. v.]. But it was by the observation of a large number of such cases of convulsions starting locally, by careful examination of the subsequent paralysis or weakness, and the correlation of these with the actual position of the lesion in the brain giving rise to the phenomena, that Jackson was able, in 1870, to indicate certain regions of the brain as definitely related to certain limb movements, as well as to confirm incidentally the earlier work by Broca on the speech centre. Fritsch and Hitzig in Germany, and Ferrier in England, soon supplied experimental corroboration.

Jackson's third series of investigations had reference to the hierarchy of the nervous system, and although it may seem more theoretical and suggestive than practical, yet his hypotheses were constantly fortified and illustrated from clinical observation and the study of actual disease. He conceived the nervous system to consist of a series of levels—a lower, a middle, and a higher. In the lowest level, movements are represented in their simplest and least complex form; these centres are situated in the medullary and spinal structures. The middle level consists of the so-called motor area of the cortex, and the highest motor levels are found in the præfrontal area. Jackson did not attempt to formulate definitely the application of this theory of levels to sensory structures. His conception of the nervous system, as an evolution of the complex out of the simple, renders intelligible the theory of nervous disease as a process of dissolution—a term borrowed from Herbert Spencer. The highest and most lately developed functions are those to go first in the process of disease. The removal of the inhibition of the highest centres results in the uncontrolled action of the lower, and we thus have the explanation of such widely different conditions as post-hemiplegic rigidity and the illusions of the insane. Negative or destructive lesions do not produce positive symptoms; these are the outcome of the action of normal structures acting without the control or restraint of the more highly developed structures or structures of the higher level. The last subject at which he worked was the form of epilepsy which has been designated 'uncinate,' from the fact, which he was the first to point out, that its symptoms were associated with a lesion in the uncinate gyrus of the temporo-sphenoidal lobe. His first case of this disorder was published in 1866, and he returned to the subject in several later contributions to medical literature.

Jackson's researches depended on an immense amount of detailed observation. Thousands of cases were carefully diagnosed, and their symptoms and signs noted in the greatest detail. His work combines attention to the minutest details with a power of the widest generalisation. As a clinical assistant at Moorfields Eye Hospital Jackson was one of the first physicians to use the ophthalmoscope in this country, and he employed it habitually and diligently in his observations on disease. He was the first to point out that well-marked optic neuritis may co-exist with perfect vision.

Jackson, whose personal character was notable for its simplicity and consideration for others, died at 3 Manchester Square on 7 Oct. 1911, and was buried at Highgate. He married in 1865 his cousin, Elizabeth Dade Jackson; she died in 1876, leaving no issue.

Jackson's writings have not been collected. They are scattered through various periodicals. The 'London Hospital Reports,' 1864–1869, contain some of his earliest and most important work. He contributed many articles to 'Brain,' the 'West Riding Hospital Reports,' the 'Lancet,' 'British Medical Journal,' 'Medical Times and Gazette,' 'Medical Press and Circular,' the 'Proceedings of the International Medical Congress in London,' the 'Moorfields Hospital Reports,' and the 'Proceedings' of the Ophthalmological and Medical Societies.

[The Times, 9 Oct. 1911; British Med. Journ. and Lancet, 14 Oct. 1911; London Hosp. Gaz., Oct. and Dec. 1895; Sir Jonathan Hutchinson in Brit. Med. Journal, 9 Nov. 1911; information from Mr. Charles Jackson (cousin); personal knowledge.] J. T.

JACKSON, MASON (1819–1903), wood-engraver, was born of humble parentage at Ovingham, Northumberland, on 25 May 1819. He came to London at the age of eleven to reside with his elder brother, John Jackson [q. v.], joint author with William Andrew Chatto of the 'Treatise on Wood Engraving' (1839). Mason received from his brother his first lessons in wood-engraving. By 1836 he was sufficiently advanced to take part in the engraving of Richard Seymour's design for the green wrapper of the monthly parts of 'Pickwick Papers. Between 1850 and 1860 Jackson made himself a name by his wood-engravings for the Art Union of London; by his engraved illustrations to Knight's Shakespeare (1851–2), Walton's 'Compleat Angler' (1856), and the 'Arabian Nights' (1859); and by his work in the 'Illustrated London News.' On the death of Herbert Ingram [q. v.] in 1860 Jackson joined the staff of the 'Illustrated London News' as art editor, a position which he filled with great ability till his retirement some thirty years later. Like his brother, Mason Jackson took a literary and historical as well as a practical interest in his profession. His book 'The Pictorial Press: its Origin and Progress' (1885) is a valuable work, tracing the rise and progress of illustrated journalism from its crudest beginnings to its modern development. He died in London on 28 Dec. 1903, and was buried in Brompton cemetery.

Jackson married Lucy Tippetts on 16 July 1864, and had two sons and a daughter. His daughter married Professor Sir Walter Raleigh in July 1890.

His elder son, ARTHUR MASON JACKSON (1866–1909), was educated at Westminster School and Brasenose College, Oxford, and entered the Indian Civil Service in 1887. After being collector at Nasik for two years he was murdered there by a young Brahmin on 21 Dec. 1909, on the eve of his departure to take over the duties of collector at Bombay. During his service in India he devoted his great talents especially to the study of Sanskrit and the vernaculars, and was recognised as one of the best Oriental scholars of his day.

[The Times, 2 Jan. 1904 and 23 Dec. 1909; Illustrated London News, 2 Jan. 1904; private information.] M. H.

JACKSON, SAMUEL PHILLIPS (1830–1904), water-colour artist, born at Bristol on 4 Sept. 1830, was only son of four children of Samuel Jackson [q. v.], landscape-painter, by his wife Jane Phillips. One sister married Mr. Roeckel, musical composer; another is Mrs. Ada Villiers, a musician. He received early instruction in art from his father at Bristol, and studied figure drawing at the life school of the academy there. Among his early Bristol friends were James Francis Danby [q. v.] and Charles Branwhite [q. v.]. He soon directed his attention mainly to land- and sea-scape, and first exhibited in London at the age of twenty. In 1851 his 'Dismasted Ship off the Welsh Coast' was shown at the British Institution, where between that year and 1857 he exhibited nine pictures. He first exhibited at the Royal Academy in 1852, and from that year to 1881 sent eight paintings and eight drawings. On 14 Feb. 1853 he was made associate of the Royal Water Colour Society, and henceforth confined himself to water colours, sending the maximum number of pictures—eight a year—to each summer exhibition of the society until 1876, when he was elected full member. By 1881 he had sent some 500 works to the winter and summer exhibitions. His earlier works, mainly in oils, showed a preference for Devon and Cornish coast scenes, and many of them won the praise of Ruskin. His 'Coast of North Devon' (Brit. Instit.) was bought by Mr. Bicknell. The more important were 'A Roadstead after a Gale, Twilight' (R.A. 1852), 'Towing a Disabled Vessel' (R.A. 1852), 'Hazy Morning on the Coast of Devon' (1853), (the two latter now in Vict. and Alb. Museum, South Kensington), 'A Summer Day on the Coast' (1855), 'The Breakwater and Chapel Rock, Bude,' and 'The Sands at Bude' (1856), 'Dartmouth Harbour' (1858), 'On the Hamoaze, Plymouth' (1858, now at South Kensington), 'Styhead Tarn, Cumberland' (1858), and 'A Dead Calm far at sea' (1858). A tour in Switzerland in 1858 with his father produced his 'Lake of Thun—Evening,' exhibited in 1859. Other sea-scapes followed, viz. 'Bamborough' in 1859, 'Whitby Pier in a Gale' in 1863, and 'St. Ives' Pier' in 1864. From 1856 he passed some time at Streatley-on-Thames, Reading, and subsequently at Henley-on-Thames. Thenceforward he chiefly devoted himself to views of the Thames. 'The Thames at Wargrave, Mid-day' (now at South Kensington) is dated 1866, and 'The Thames from Streatley Bridge' 1868. Jackson's strength lay in firm and careful execution, and in restrained harmonies of tone and colour. In such early work as his 'Hazy Morning on the Coast of Devon' he favoured restful sunlight effects. His handling of grey mist and clouds always skilfully interpreted the placid west country atmosphere. Jackson had other than artistic interests. He was interested in photography, and invented an instantaneous shutter for which he gained a medal from the Royal Photographic Society. Most of his life was spent at Bristol and he died unmarried at his residence there, 62 Clifton Park Road, on 27 Jan. 1904.

[The Times, 2 Feb. 1904; Western Daily Press, Bristol, 2 Feb. 1904; Athenæum, 6 Feb. 1904; J. L. Roget, Old Water Colour Society, 1891, ii. 379–81; Victoria and Albert Mus. Cat. of Water Colour Paintings, 1908; Graves's Exhibitors Royal Acad. and British Institution; The 'Old' Water Colour Society in Studio, Spring number 1905; Ruskin Acad. Notes, ed. Cook and Wedderburn, 1904, pp. 80, 198, 249.] W. B. O.

JAMES, Sir HENRY, first Lord James of Hereford (1828–1911), lawyer and statesman, born at Hereford on 30 Oct. 1828, was third and youngest son of Philip Turner James, surgeon, of Hereford, by his wife Frances Gertrude, daughter of John Bodenham of The Grove, Presteign, Radnorshire. One of his brothers, Gwynne James, became a leading solicitor at Hereford, and a nephew is Judge Gwynne James. He was educated at Cheltenham College, which was opened in 1841, and was the first boy on the roll. In after years he was president of the council of governors of the school, and founded the James of Hereford entrance scholarships, primarily for Herefordshire boys. At school he played in the cricket elevens of 1844 and 1845, and never lost his interest in the game, playing occasionally for the old boys, and becoming president of the M.C.C. in 1889. He gained no special distinction in school studies, and on leaving began training as an engineer, but soon joined the Middle Temple as a student (12 Jan. 1849). He was lecturer's prizeman in 1850 and 1851, and was one of the earliest and foremost members of the Hardwicke Debating Society, where he developed a power of lucid speaking. Called to the bar in 1852, he joined the Oxford circuit, among his contemporaries being Mr. (afterwards Baron) Huddleston [q. v.] and Henry Matthews, now Lord Llandaff. His rise at the bar was not rapid. He practised at first mainly in the mayor's court, of which he became leader. Comparatively early in his career he became known to (Sir) John Hollams [q. v. Suppl. II], and through him obtained much commercial work at the Guildhall. In 1867, after fifteen years at the bar, he was appointed 'postman' of the Court of Exchequer—an office now extinct—and became a Q.C. in 1869. Next year he was elected bencher of his Inn, and in 1888 served as treasurer. In 1870 he joined (Sir) Henry Drummond Wolff [q. v. Suppl. II] in an expedition to the seat of the Franco-German war, and came under the fire of French artillery at Strassburg.

In 1869 James entered the House of Commons as liberal member for Taunton. There he came to the front more quickly than at the bar. In company with (Sir) William Harcourt [q. v. Suppl. II] he was soon a prominent figure on the ministerial side below the gangway, occasionally criticising his leaders with effect. As a parliamentary speaker he was rarely brief, but he held the ear of the house. A speech which he made in 1871 against a bill introduced by Jacob Bright for giving the parliamentary franchise to unmarried female householders attracted attention as 'a bold and incisive speech . . . the speech of a man who was weary of talking around a subject and went straight to the root of the matter' (*Ann. Reg.* 1871, p. 92). During the same session he took an active part as a private member in the debates on the elections (parliamentary and municipal) bill, which was thrown out by the Lords. In 1872 he increased his reputation by a speech supporting Mr. Justice Keogh's judgment in the Galway election petition, a 'powerful and conclusive argument' (*ib.* 1872, p. 85), upon which he was complimented by Disraeli among many others. In 1873 he was prominent in the debates on Lord Selborne's Judicature Act. In Sept. 1873 he became solicitor-general in Gladstone's government in succession to Sir George Jessel [q. v.], and was knighted. Two months later, when the attorney-general (Sir) John Duke Coleridge [q. v. Suppl. I] became lord chief justice, James succeeded him as attorney-general, Sir William Harcourt becoming solicitor-general in his place. Parliament was dissolved immediately afterwards, and James was re-elected for Taunton, but the defeat of his party deprived him of office. While in opposition, he was active in debate, and when Gladstone returned to office after the general election of 1880 James, who retained his seat for Taunton, again became attorney-general. He held the post until the liberal government went out in 1885, the solicitor-general being Farrer Herschell (afterwards Lord Herschell) [q. v. Suppl. I]. James performed both his political and professional work, which was exceptionally heavy, with unsparing energy. In parliament his chief exploit was the drafting and carrying through its various stages the corrupt practices bill of 1883. He had already championed the cause of electoral purity, and his skill and temper in the conduct of his bill evoked Gladstone's admiration. In all relations James won the prime minister's 'peculiarly warm regard,' which James fully reciprocated (*Life of Gladstone*, iii. 110). On 24 June 1885 he was made a privy councillor.

At the general election of 1885, after the new reform bill had become law, he was returned as member for Bury in Lancashire, and he represented that constituency for the rest of his time in the House of Commons. When Gladstone declared for home rule early in 1886, James declared unhesitatingly against the change of Irish policy. Gladstone offered him first the lord chancellorship and then the home secretaryship in his new ministry, but James, with rare self-denial, declined both. He was already a warm intimate friend of Lord Hartington (afterwards duke of Devonshire), and with him he thenceforward acted in close personal sympathy, becoming a leader of the newly formed liberal-unionist party. Returned for Bury at the elections of 1886 and 1892, James, now a private member of parliament, continued his private practice at the bar. He appeared for 'The Times' with Sir Richard Webster, the attorney-general, before the Parnell commission of 1888–9, and summed up his clients' case, in reply to Sir Charles Russell's final speech for Parnell, in a twelve days' speech, 'perhaps the most notable of all his forensic achievements' (31 Oct. to 22 Nov. 1889) (*Law Journal*). From 1892 to 1895 he acted as attorney-general of the Duchy of Cornwall to King Edward VII, then Prince of Wales, with whom he had formed a close intimacy. In 1892 he was made hon. LL.D. of Cambridge.

On 22 April 1893 James spoke at great length against Gladstone's home rule bill, and in Feb. 1895 he, on behalf of the Lancashire cotton spinners, led the opposition to the liberal government's proposal to reimpose duties on cotton imported into India. On the return of the unionists to power in August 1895 James was raised to the peerage as Lord James of Hereford, and for the first time became a cabinet minister (5 Aug.), holding the office of chancellor of the Duchy of Lancaster in the unionist administration. In 1896 he joined the judicial committee of the privy council, and took part in the judicial work of that body as well as of the House of Lords. He made no great mark as a lord of appeal, possibly owing to his advanced age and distraction by other work. He resigned his position on the judicial committee before his death. He had, however, eminently a judicial mind. As arbitrator in industrial disputes, and notably as chairman of the coal conciliation board from 1898 to 1909, he gave a series of important decisions, which were accepted by all parties without demur. Between 1895 and 1902 he sat, too, on a committee of the privy council appointed to deal with university education in the north of England.

James resigned office in July 1902, when Mr. Balfour succeeded Lord Salisbury as prime minister. Trained in old whig principles, he was not in sympathy with the education policy of the unionist government. In the same year he was made G.C.V.O. Next year, when Mr. Chamberlain formulated his policy of tariff reform, James declared his resolute adherence to the principle of free trade. As in the home rule crisis, he acted with the duke of Devonshire, and stiffened the latter in his opposition to the new policy. In Nov. 1909 he opposed, as unconstitutional, the rejection of the budget by the House of Lords. During his later years he took much interest in the Imperial Institute, and was for a long time chairman of the advisory committee.

Although no eloquent speaker nor profound lawyer, James was an admirable advocate, especially in the conduct of criminal cases. He had in a high degree the good judgment of a strong, clear, and business-like mind. He was not too legal for the House of Commons, where his tact and clearness of exposition rendered him one of the most successful of all law officers of the crown. His political views were of the whig type, cautious and moderate, but unhesitating.

A good sportsman, especially with the gun, he maintained through life a large circle of friends. King Edward VII was constantly a guest at his shooting parties. He was an intimate friend of Millais; he knew Dickens, Charles Reade, Tom Taylor, and other men eminent in literature or art, although he had few intellectual interests outside his profession. His chief associates were engaged in the law, and he was generous in encouragement to young barristers. To the bar, as he told his constituents at Bury, he was more indebted than most men. 'I worked my way into its ranks . . . there my friendships have been formed.' He was munificent in private charity. He died on 18 Aug. 1911 at Kingswood Warren near Epsom. Previously he had made his country home at Breamore near Salisbury, and there he was buried in the parish churchyard. He was unmarried, and the peerage became extinct at his death. A portrait by Mr. J. St. H. Lander is in the Benchers' Rooms at the Middle Temple, and there are other portraits at the Devonshire Club and at Cheltenham College. A cartoon by 'Ape' appeared in 'Vanity Fair' in 1874.

A fund in his memory for the endowment of Cheltenham College was inaugurated in July 1912.

[Authorities cited; The Times, 19 Aug. 1911; Law Journal, 26 Aug. 1911; Holland's Life of the Duke of Devonshire, 1911; Sir Algernon West in Cornhill Mag., Jan. 1912; Men of the Time, 1899; Burke's Peerage; private sources.] C. P. L.

JAMES, JAMES (1832–1902), composer of 'Land of my Fathers,' the Welsh national anthem, born on 4 Nov. 1832 at the 'Ancient Druid' inn, Argoed, in the parish of Bedwellty, Monmouthshire, was son of Evan James (1809–1878) by his wife Elizabeth Stradling of Caerphilly. The father, a Welsh versifier under the penname of Ieuan ab Iago, removed with his family about 1844 to Pontypridd, where he carried on the business of weaver and wool merchant. His son James assisted him in the business. On a Sunday evening in January 1856 the father wrote a Welsh song of three verses, to which the son, a good singer and harpist, shortly afterwards composed original music, giving it the name of 'Glan Rhondda' (original score reproduced in 'Graphic' for 5 Aug. 1893). The words and the simple and tuneful melody, which owed nothing to any folksong of England or Scotland, caught the public taste when sung locally by the son at an eisteddfod at Pontypridd in 1857 and on other occasions. Thomas Llewelyn, a harpist of Aberdare, to whom James communicated the song. included it, without disclosing its authorship, in a collection of unpublished Welsh airs, now in the possession of Mrs. Mary Davies, which he submitted for competition at the Llangollen eisteddfod of 1858, in the course of which it seems to have been also sung (*Eisteddfod Programme*). The air so impressed the adjudicator, John Owen (Owain Alaw) (1821–1883), that he included it, with symphonies and accompaniments of his own (and an English translation of the words by Eben Fardd), in his 'Gems of Welsh Melody' (Ruthin, 1860, No. 1). He gave it the name of 'Hen Wlad fy Nhadau,' or 'Land of my Fathers,' from the opening words of the first verse.

The song gradually grew in popularity, and was sung at the national eisteddfod at Bangor in August 1874. During the following decade it became recognised by Welshmen in all parts of the world (*Cymru Fu*, 30 Nov. 1889) as the national anthem of Wales, being generally sung at the close of meetings, all persons present meanwhile standing uncovered or at the salute, and joining in the chorus. The son composed music for several other songs of his father, but none was published. Leaving Pontypridd in 1873, James lived at Mountain Ash (1873–91) and at Aberdare, where he died at Hawthorn Terrace on 11 June 1902, being buried at Aberdare cemetery. He married in 1850 Cecilia, daughter of Morgan and Joan Miles of Pontypridd, by whom he had two sons and three daughters, his eldest and only surviving son, Taliesin, being a teacher of the harp. A fund has been raised for providing a memorial for the joint authors of the song, but its form has not yet been decided.

[Information from James's son Mr. Taliesin James, Cardiff, and Mrs. Mary Davies; T. R. Roberts, Dict. of Eminent Welshmen (1908), p. 202; T. Mardy Rees, Notable Welshmen (1908), p. 381; Morien, Hist. of Pontypridd (1903), pp. 68–71 (with portraits of father and son); Graphic, 5 Aug. 1893 (with illustrations); Grove's Dict. of Music and Musicians (1907), v. 499; Mr. D. Emlyn Evans's notes on the song in 'Gem Selection —Songs of Wales,' published by Valentine; circular issued by Pontypridd Memorial Committee (1909). A long correspondence as to the alleged similarity of the song to 'Rosin the Beau' appeared in the South Wales Daily News for March 1884 (see especially James James's letter 17 March) and in Western Mail (Cardiff) for 4, 7, 8, and 9 April 1884.] D. Ll. T.

JAMESON, ANDREW, Lord Ardwall (1845–1911), Scottish judge, born at Ayr on 5 July 1845, was eldest son of Andrew

Jameson, sheriff of Aberdeen and Kincardine, by his wife Alexander, daughter of Alexander Colquhoun Campbell of Barnhill, Dumbartonshire. Educated at Edinburgh Academy, he graduated M.A. from the University of St. Andrews in 1865. He afterwards attended Edinburgh University, and on 19 May 1870 he passed at the Scottish bar, where he gradually acquired a considerable practice. In 1882 he was appointed junior counsel to the department of woods and forests. On 27 April 1886 he was made sheriff of Roxburghshire, Berwickshire, and Selkirkshire. Having taken a prominent part in politics as a liberal unionist, he received from Lord Salisbury's government the office of sheriff of the counties of Ross, Cromarty, and Sutherland on 28 Nov. 1890, and became sheriff of Perthshire on 27 Oct. 1891. On the resignation of Henry James Moncreiff, second Baron Moncreiff [q. v. Suppl. II], he was raised to the bench, on 6 Jan. 1905, with the title of Lord Ardwall. In the same year he was made hon. LL.D. of St. Andrews. After an illness of about six months he died, at 14 Moray Place, Edinburgh, on 21 Nov. 1911, and was buried at Anwoth in Kirkcudbrightshire.

In addition to legal and political work Jameson was active in other spheres of public life. He conducted several important inquiries on behalf of the government, frequently acted as an arbiter in industrial disputes, and was for some years, in succession to Lord James of Hereford, chairman of the board of conciliation, between the coalowners and Scottish Miners' Federation. He was keenly interested in Scottish religious affairs, as a member of the Free church, and he supported Dr. Robert Rainy [q.v. Suppl. II] in promoting the union of that body with the United Presbyterians (1900), though he had strongly opposed him during the agitation for disestablishing the Church of Scotland. He was also devoted to country life, and during the later part of his career paid much attention to agriculture. Of frank and boisterous speech, he shared the tastes and pursuits of the Scottish judges of the old school, of which George Fergusson, Lord Hermand [q. v.], was the last survivor (*Scotsman*, 22 Nov. 1911).

In 1875 Jameson married Christian, daughter of John Gordon Brown of Lochanhead and niece of Walter McCulloch of Ardwall in Kirkcudbrightshire, from whom she inherited the estate after which the judge took his title. There were born of this marriage one daughter and three sons, the eldest and youngest of whom entered the army. The second, John Gordon Jameson, advocate, unsuccessfully contested East Edinburgh, as a unionist, at a by-election in January 1912. There are three paintings of Lord Ardwall by Sir George Reid, two of which are (1912) at 14 Moray Place, Edinburgh, and the third at Ardwall.

[Roll of the Faculty of Advocates; Scotsman, and Perthshire Constitutional Journal, 22 Nov. 1911; personal knowledge.]

G. W. T. O.

JAPP, ALEXANDER HAY (1837–1905), author and publisher, born at Dun, near Montrose, on 26 Dec. 1837, was youngest son of Alexander Japp, a carpenter, by his wife Agnes Hay. After the father's early death, the mother and her family moved to Montrose, where Alexander was educated at Milne's school. At seventeen Japp became a book-keeper with Messrs. Christie and Sons, tailors, at Edinburgh. Three years later he removed to London, and for two years was employed in the East India department of Smith, Elder and Co. Smith Williams, the firm's literary adviser, once took him to see Leigh Hunt. Returning to Scotland owing to illness, he worked for Messrs. Grieve and Oliver, Edinburgh hatters, and in his leisure in 1860–1 attended classes at the university in metaphysics, logic, and moral philosophy. He became a double prizeman in rhetoric, and received from Professor W. E. Aytoun a special certificate of distinction, but he did not graduate. At Edinburgh he was much in the society of young artists, including John Pettie [q. v.] and his friends. Turning to journalism, he edited the 'Inverness Courier' and the 'Montrose Review.' Having settled in London in 1864, he joined for a short time the 'Daily Telegraph.' While writing for other papers, he acted as general literary adviser to the publishing firm of Alexander Strahan, afterwards William Isbister and Co., and aided in editing their periodicals, 'Good Words,' 'Sunday Magazine' (from 1869 to 1879), as well as the 'Contemporary Review' from 1866 to 1872, while Dean Alford was editor. He also assisted Robert Carruthers [q. v.] in the third edition of Chambers's 'Cyclopædia of English Literature,' and his services were acknowledged by his being made LL.D. of Glasgow in 1879. In 1880 he was elected F.R.S. of Edinburgh.

In October of 1880 Japp started as a publisher, under the style Marshall Japp and Co., at 17 Holborn Viaduct; but bad health and insufficient capital led him to make the venture over to Mr. T. Fisher Unwin in 1882. From that year to 1888 he was literary adviser to the firm of Hurst and Blackett.

Japp was soon a versatile and prolific writer, often writing under pseudonyms as well as in his own name. In his own name he issued in 1865 'Three Great Teachers of our own Time: Carlyle, Tennyson, and Ruskin,' of which Ruskin wrote to Smith Williams: 'It is the only time that any English or Scotch body has really seen what I am driving at—seen clearly and decisively.' As 'H. A. Page' he published 'The Memoir of Nathaniel Hawthorne' (1872; with several uncollected contributions to American periodicals); an analytical 'Study of Thoreau' (1878); and his chief book, 'De Quincey: his Life and Writings, with Unpublished Correspondence' (supplied by De Quincey's daughters) (2 vols. 1877; 2nd edit. 1879, revised edit. in one vol. 1890). In his own name Japp issued a selection of De Quincey's 'Posthumous Works' (vol. i. 1891; vol. ii. 1893) and 'De Quincey Memorials: being Letters and other Records here first published' (1891).

Japp's interest in Thoreau brought him the acquaintance of Robert Louis Stevenson. The two men met at Braemar in August 1881, and Japp's conversation attracted Stevenson and his father. Stevenson read to Japp the early chapters of 'Treasure Island,' then called 'The Sea Cook,' and Japp negotiated its publication in 'Young Folks.' Subsequently Stevenson and Japp corresponded on intimate terms; and Japp's last work, 'Robert Louis Stevenson: a Record, an Estimate, and a Memorial' (1905), was the result of the intercourse.

Japp essayed many forms of literature. Under a double pseudonym he issued in 1878 'Lights on the Way' (by the late J. H. Alexander, B.A., with explanatory note by H. A. Page), a semi-autobiographical fiction. There followed 'German Life and Literature' (1880; studies of Lessing, Goethe, Moses Mendelssohn, Herder, Novalis, and other writers), and three volumes of verse: 'The Circle of the Year: a Sonnet Sequence with Proem and Envoi' (privately printed, 1893); 'Dramatic Pictures, English Rispetti, Sonnets and other Verses' (1894); and 'Adam and Lilith: a Poem in Four Parts' (1899; by 'A. F. Scot'). Scientific speculation and observation are themes of his 'Animal Anecdotes arranged on a New Principle' (by 'H. A. Page') (1887), an attempt to show that the faculties of certain animals differ in degree rather than in kind from those of men; 'Offering and Sacrifice: an Essay in Comparative Customs and Religious Development' by 'A. F. Scot' (1899); 'Some Heresies in Ethnology and Anthropology' dealt with under his own name (1899); 'Our Common Cuckoo and other Cuckoos and Parasitical Birds' (1899), a criticism of the Darwinian view of parasitism; and 'Darwin considered mainly as Ethical Thinker' (1901), a criticism of the hypothesis of natural selection.

From 1884 till 1900 he lived at Elmstead, near Colchester, where he cultivated his taste for natural history. After three years in London he finally settled at Coulsdon, Surrey, in September 1903. There, busy to the last, he died on 29 Sept. 1905, and was buried in Abney Park cemetery. His temperament was almost morbidly sensitive, but he was generous to young authors. When past fifty he taught himself Hebrew. He left in manuscript a work on Hebrew rites and customs, as well as a study of social life in the middle ages.

Japp married (1) in 1863 Elizabeth Paul (*d.* 1888), daughter of John Falconer of Laurencekirk, Kincardineshire; (2) Eliza Love, of Scottish descent (*d.* Sept. 1912). By his first wife he had seven children; a son and two daughters survived him.

In addition to 'H. A. Page' and 'A. F. Scot,' he wrote under the pseudonyms 'E. Conder Gray' and 'A. N. Mount Rose.' In 1857 William McTaggart [q. v. Suppl. II] painted his portrait, which is in the possession of the family.

[Private information, based chiefly on an unpublished autobiographical fragment; obituary notices in Scottish Patriot, by R. W. J[ohnstone] (with portrait), and in Weekly Budget; Mr. Sidney Whitman in Westminster Gaz. 12 Oct. 1905; The Times, 2 Oct. 1905 (gives wrong date of birth); Nature, 1905, vol. 72; Athenæum, 7 Oct.; Montrose Review and Montrose Standard, 6 Oct.; Roll of Glasgow Graduates, ed. W. J. Addison; Graham Balfour's Stevenson, i. 191, 192 n.; Stevenson's Letters (ed. Colvin), ii. 45–6, 51–2–3, 74–5, and Preface to 'Familiar Studies; R. F. Sharp's Dict. of English Authors (appendix); Japp's works; Allibone's Dict. Eng. Lit. (suppl. vol. ii.). Cf. also Miss Betham-Edwards's Friendly Faces of Three Nations (1911) and Mrs. Isabella Fyvie Mayo's Recollections of Fifty Years (1911).] G. Le G. N.

JARDINE, Sir **ROBERT**, first baronet (1825–1905), East India merchant and racehorse owner, born on 24 May 1825, was the seventh son of David Jardine of Muir househead, Applegarth, Dumfriesshire, and Rachel, daughter of William Johnstone of Linns, Dumfriesshire. After education at Merchiston College, Edinburgh, he went to China with his uncle, Dr. William Jardine, a pioneer in the East India trade and then head of Jardine, Matheson and Co. He did much to extend the business of the firm. Returning in 1859, he took up a partnership in the London branch, Matheson and Co., Lombard Street, and on the death of his brother Andrew in 1881 became head of the firm, inheriting also the Lanrick Castle estate, Perthshire, as well as much property in Dumfriesshire. He had already acquired Castlemilk, Lockerbie, where in 1865 he erected a modern mansion. In the same year he entered parliament as liberal M.P. for Ashburton. In 1868 he was elected by a small majority for Dumfries burghs, being opposed by a radical. He unsuccessfully contested Dumfriesshire against Mr. Hope Johnstone (conservative) in 1874, but carried the seat in 1880 and continued to hold it till his retirement from public life in 1892, though he had broken with his party on the home rule question. He was created a baronet on 20 July 1885.

Active in county business, Jardine was for twenty-four years captain of the Lockerbie company of the king's own Scottish Borderers. He was prominent also as an agriculturist and a breeder of stock, his Galloway cattle winning many prizes at shows.

Jardine was best known as a devotee of sport. He began to run horses when in China. In 1862 his colours were registered, and in 1877 he was elected to the Jockey Club, but for fifteen years his horses ran in the name of his cousin, John Johnstone of Hallheaths, his racing partner. Their horses were mostly trained on Middleham Moor by Thomas, brother of Matthew Dawson [q. v.], and Fred Bates. Their first successes were with Rococo in the Northumberland Plate in 1866 and with Mandrake in the Great Ebor Handicap in 1867. Their chestnut colt Pretender won the 2000 guineas in 1869, and beat Pero Gomez by a head in the Derby the same year, when he was ridden by John Osborne, but failed in the St. Leger. Two years later Bothwell won the Two Thousand. In 1877 Jardine's three-year-old Hilarious won the Cesarewitch. The Manchester Cup was taken by him three times, and the Lincolnshire Handicap won in 1889. But he was most successful at Ascot, winning the Queen's Vase in 1869 and 1871, the Royal Hunt Cup in 1884, the Wokingham twice, and the Stakes seven times (twice each with Teviotdale and Lord Lorne). When the Sheffield Lane joint stud was broken up, Jardine for many years bred his own horses. His last year as an owner was 1896.

Jardine was even more interested in coursing than in horse-racing, and the continuance of the sport under the disadvantages entailed by the Ground Game Act owed much to his influence. An active member of the Altcar, Ridgway and Scottish National Clubs, he was elected to the National Coursing Club in 1884. He established the Corrie and Mid-Annandale Meetings, and held Waterloo Cup nominations for thirty-nine years. The Castlemilk kennel first made its mark after 1860 and reached its zenith in 1873, when Muriel won the Waterloo Cup. The Purse and Plate were also taken several times in subsequent years. Jardine was much attached to his dogs and is said to have made selections for the Waterloo meeting in his bedroom in the last year of his life. At one time also Jardine hunted and was a founder of the Dumfriesshire foxhounds pack and a member of the Caledonian hunt. A fine specimen of the country gentleman and sportsman of the old school, he collected at Castlemilk pictures as well as turf trophies. He died there after a year's illness on 17 Feb. 1905, and was buried in St. Mungo's churchyard. Jardine's portrait by Henry Tanworth Wells was exhibited at the Royal Academy in 1876. A cartoon by 'Spy' appeared in 'Vanity Fair' (1890).

Jardine married on 4 April 1867 Margaret Seton, daughter of John Buchanan Hamilton of Leny, Perthshire. She died on 7 March 1868, leaving an only son, Robert William Buchanan Jardine, who succeeded to the baronetcy.

[Burke's Peerage and Baronetage; The Times, 18 and 22 Feb. 1905; Field, 25 Feb.; Sportsman, Dumfries and Galloway Standard, Glasgow Herald, and Scotsman, 18 Feb.; Who's Who, 1905.] G. Le G. N.

JEAFFRESON, JOHN CORDY (1831–1901), author, born at Framlingham, Suffolk, on 14 Jan. 1831, was second son and ninth child of William Jeaffreson (1789–1865), surgeon of that place, who revived in England, after long disuse, the operation of ovariotomy in 1836. His mother was Caroline (*d.* 1863), youngest child of George Edwards, tradesman, also of Framlingham. He was named after his mother's uncle by marriage, John Cordy

(1781–1828), a prosperous tradesman of Worlingworth and Woodbridge. After education at the grammar schools of Woodbridge and Botesdale, he was apprenticed to his father in August 1845, but, disliking surgical work, he matriculated from Pembroke College, Oxford, on 22 June 1848. Among his undergraduate friends were Henry Kingsley [q. v.] and Arthur Locker [q. v. Suppl. I]. After graduating B.A. in May 1852 he settled in London, and was for some six years a private tutor and lecturer at private schools.

In his leisure he tried his hand at novel writing, publishing 'Crewe Rise' in 1854 and next year 'Hinchbrook,' which ran serially through 'Fraser's Magazine.' During the next thirty years a long series of novels in the orthodox three-volume form followed; some like 'Live it down' (1863) and 'Not dead yet' (1864) were well received on publication, but none won a permanent repute. In 1856 he abandoned teaching for journalism and for literature of a journalistic quality. From 1858 to his death he was a regular contributor to the 'Athenæum,' and on the recommendation of the editor of that paper, Hepworth Dixon, he collaborated with Prof. William Pole [q. v.] in the authorised biography of Robert Stephenson, engineer (1864 2 vols.). A volume, 'Novels and Novelists from Elizabeth to Victoria' (1858), which he compiled at the British Museum, evinced facility in popularising literary research, which became Jeaffreson's main work in life. Five works, each in two volumes, which he designed to illustrate anecdotally social history, appealed to a wide audience. The first, 'A Book about Doctors,' came out in 1860. Like ventures were 'A Book about Lawyers' (1866); 'A Book about the Clergy' (1870); 'Brides and Bridals' (1872); and 'A Book about the Table' (1874).

Jeaffreson became a student at Lincoln's Inn on 18 June 1856 and was called to the bar on 30 April 1859. He did not practise law, but he joined the Inns of Court volunteers, and was a familiar figure in legal as well as in literary society. In 1860 he joined 'Our Club,' then a dining club, meeting weekly at Clunn's Hotel, Covent Garden. There he often met Thackeray and leading members of most of the professions. In 1872 Sir Thomas Duffus Hardy, a literary friend, who was deputy keeper of the Public Records, invited Jeaffreson to become an inspector of documents for the Historical MSS. Commission. Jeaffreson protested that he had no qualifications for such a post. But Hardy was persistent, and after a two years' discursive palæographical training at the Public Record Office Jeaffreson began work as an inspector of MSS. in 1874. Although he did not abandon his literary pursuits, he chiefly devoted the next fourteen years to reporting on and calendaring manuscript records. Between 1876 and 1887 he published reports of twenty-nine MS. collections in various parts of the country. Apart from private collections, he dealt with the archives of the boroughs of Chester, Leicester, Pontefract, Barnstaple, Plymouth, Ipswich, Wisbech, Great Yarmouth, Eye, Southampton, and King's Lynn, as well as of the West Riding and North Riding of Yorkshire and the county of Essex. His most laborious work was done at Leicester, where, besides preparing a general report, he also compiled an index to the muniments (1881). For the Middlesex County Record Society he edited four volumes of Middlesex county records (1886–92). Jeaffreson's work as an archivist proved his industry, but it exhibited many traces of his lack of historical training.

In his official capacity Jeaffreson inspected the valuable collection of MSS. formed by Alfred Morrison [q. v. Suppl. I], and he obtained the owner's permission to work up into connected narratives, independently of his official report, unpublished correspondence of Byron and Nelson. In 'The Real Lord Byron: New Views of the Poet's Life' (2 vols. 1883) Jeaffreson wrote with candour, but not always with full knowledge, of both Byron and Shelley. Abraham Hayward [q. v.] denounced the book in the 'Quarterly Review,' and J. A. Froude sought to expose its defects in the 'Nineteenth Century' (Aug. 1883). Jeaffreson defended himself at length in the 'Athenæum,' and then proceeded in 'The Real Shelley: New Views of the Poet's Life' (2 vols. 1885) to expand in detail his frank censure of that poet's career and character. Prof. Dowden condemned Jeaffreson's methods and conclusion both in the 'Academy' and in his authorised 'Life of Shelley' next year. Jeaffreson in a like spirit digested the Nelson papers in the Alfred Morrison collection. 'Lady Hamilton and Lord Nelson' appeared in 1888 (2 vols.), and 'The Queen of Naples and Lord Nelson' in 1889 (2 vols.; new edit. 1897). In all these volumes Jeaffreson described himself as a 'realistic' biographer, but his work was done too perfunctorily to be exhaustive, and although he gave new and important information from unpublished sources he failed to cover adequately the field of research.

After many years of failing health, which brought his work to an end, Jeaffreson died on 2 Feb. 1901 at his house in Maida Vale, and was buried in Paddington cemetery, Willesden Lane. He married on 2 Oct. 1860, at St. Sepulchre's Church, Holborn, Arabella Ellen, only surviving daughter of William Eccles, F.R.C.S.; she survived him with a daughter who died 28 Sept. 1909. A portrait in oils belonging to Mrs. Jeaffreson was painted after his death by Mary Hector (Mrs. Robb), youngest daughter of 'Mrs. Alexander,' the novelist [see HECTOR, MRS. ANNIE FRENCH, Suppl. II].

Jeaffreson's chief works, besides those cited, were: 1. 'The Annals of Oxford,' 1870 (a popular compilation which was severely criticised). 2. 'A Young Squire of the Seventeenth Century, from the Papers of [an ancestor] Christopher Jeaffreson of Dullingham House, Cambridgeshire,' 2 vols. 1878. 3. 'A Book of Recollections,' 2 vols. 1894.

[Jeaffreson's Recollections, as above; The Times, 5 Feb. 1901; Athenæum, 9 Feb. 1901; Men of the Time, 1899; Allibone's Dict. Engl. Lit.; W. M. Rossetti's Some Recollections, 1911; private information.] S. L.

JEBB, SIR RICHARD CLAVERHOUSE (1841–1905), Greek scholar, eldest of the four children of Robert Jebb, an Irish barrister, by his wife Emily Harriet, third daughter of Heneage Horsley, dean of Brechin, was born on 27 Aug. 1841 at Dundee, where his parents were visiting his maternal grandfather, the dean of Brechin; to the place of his birth he owed his second name. His father's grandfather, Richard Jebb, came from Mansfield, Nottinghamshire, to settle at Drogheda in Ireland early in the eighteenth century. Richard Jebb, an Irish judge, was his grandfather; John Jebb [q. v.], bishop of Limerick, was his great-uncle.

Jebb's early life was spent in or near Dublin. In 1850 his father retired from the bar, and the family removed from Dublin to Killiney, nine miles off. After receiving early education from his father, Jebb was sent to St. Columba's College, Rathfarnham, in 1853, and two years later to Charterhouse School, still in the City of London, where he remained till 1858. When little more than seventeen he entered at Trinity College, Cambridge, in October of the same year. Though few worked harder than Jebb in manhood, his undergraduate years were not devoted exclusively to study; but he had learnt much at school, and his natural gifts—his memory and mastery of language—were altogether exceptional. Without any apparent effort he gained all the highest prizes that Cambridge offered for classical learning: he was Porson scholar in 1859, Craven scholar in 1860, and senior classic and first Chancellor's medallist in 1862. In 1863 he was elected fellow of Trinity College.

For the next twelve years Jebb was a classical lecturer of his college; in 1869 he was elected public orator of the university. Jebb found time and energy for much beyond the duties of these offices. He took part in a re-organisation of classical lectures in the university on the inter-collegiate plan; together with Edward Byles Cowell [q. v. Suppl. II] he founded the Cambridge Philological Society in 1868, and was the first secretary; he acted as examiner in London University in 1872; he served for some time on the staff of 'The Times' as leader-writer and reviewer. Besides all this he published four books during this period. To the series called 'Catena Classicorum' he contributed editions of Sophocles' 'Electra' (1867) and of 'Ajax' (1868). An edition of 'The Characters of Theophrastus' followed in 1870, and a collection of translations into Greek and Latin verse in 1873. The editions of Sophocles showed for the first time that schoolbooks may be works of literature; the Theophrastus was so popular that it was soon impossible to procure a copy; the 'Translations,' which included a version of Browning's 'Abt Vogler' into Pindaric metres, a brilliant tour-de-force, were pronounced by experts to be masterpieces of their kind. In 1888 he composed another Pindaric ode addressed to the University of Bologna, which was celebrating the 800th year of its existence; to this effort Tennyson referred when next year he dedicated his 'Demeter and Persephone' to Jebb:

> Bear witness you, that yesterday
> From out the Ghost of Pindar in you
> Roll'd an Olympian.

In 1875 Jebb left Cambridge on being elected professor of Greek at Glasgow in succession to Edmund Law Lushington [q. v.]. He remained at Glasgow for fourteen years, admirably performing the duties of his chair. Much of the work was elementary, but his teaching was thoroughly business-like and practical: he kept his large classes in excellent order and drilled them methodically in the rudiments. To his advanced students he gave of his best.

There was one remarkable novelty in his teaching: on one day in each week he lectured upon modern Greek, which he knew well and spoke with ease. He visited Greece in 1878 and explored its archæology, receiving from the King of Greece the gold cross of the order of the Saviour. For the six winter months of each year at Glasgow his teaching work was heavy, but the long summer vacations, which he spent at Cambridge, gave him the opportunity to write; and books came at short intervals from his pen. The first of these was an important work on the 'Attic Orators from Antiphon to Isæus.' Published in two volumes in 1876, this book was well received in general, but Prof. J. P. Mahaffy, reviewing the book in the 'Academy' (1 April 1876), brought against Jebb a charge of excessive obligation to the work of F. Blass in the same field. Jebb thought it necessary to reply to his critic in 'Some Remarks' (1876), Mahaffy's reply to which elicited a 'Rejoinder' from Jebb (1877). It might have been better if Jebb had relied for his defence upon the evidence of his later books. In 1877 he published a 'Primer of Greek Literature'; in 1878 a further book of 'Translations in and from Greek and Latin Verse and Prose,' in collaboration with Henry Jackson and W. E. Currey; in 1879 a volume of selections from the 'Attic Orators' with an excellent commentary, which he seems to have completed in a single month; in 1880 'Modern Greece,' two lectures with papers on 'The Progress of Greece' and 'Byron in Greece,' and in 1882 a monograph on Bentley in the 'English Men of Letters' series, a model of its kind. 'Homer: an Introduction to the Iliad and Odyssey,' appeared at Glasgow in 1887 (3rd edit. 1888); it was a masterly and concise statement of most complicated questions.

In 1884 Jebb paid a first visit to America, and received the degree of LL.D. from Harvard University. In 1889 he was recalled from Glasgow to Cambridge to take the place of Benjamin Hall Kennedy [q. v.] as regius professor of Greek. He was re-elected at the same time to a fellowship at his old college. These posts he held for the rest of his life. He at once took an active part in instruction and administration of the university. His carefully prepared lectures, which remain unpublished, dealt mainly with the history of Greek literature, and were attended by large audiences of undergraduates. Yet Jebb probably taught more successfully through his books than by means of lectures; his hearers, while admitting the excellence of his matter, were apt to complain of his manner as deficient in life and vigour.

Soon after his return to Cambridge he began to address an audience of a different kind. In the summer of 1891 Henry Cecil Raikes [q. v.], M.P. for the University of Cambridge, died, and Jebb was chosen to succeed him in the conservative interest. He was re-elected in 1892, 1895, and 1900. It may be questioned whether he did wisely in trying to combine the life of politics with the life of study; he carried the double burden with distinction, but not for long. He was not content to follow the example of his most famous predecessor, Sir Isaac Newton, and merely to sit and vote with his party. In discussions concerning education and the Church he spoke fairly often and was favourably heard. For debate he was not well equipped, but few men could be more impressive in a set speech upon a formal occasion. He gave a fine proof of his eloquence in the speech which he delivered at Charterhouse in July 1903, when a cloister was dedicated in commemoration of those Carthusians who had fallen in the recent war. Jebb, besides serving on parliamentary committees, sat on the royal commission on secondary education in 1894, on the London University commission of 1898, and the commission on Irish University education in 1901. He was also a member of the consultative committee of the board of education from 1900. He spoke from the platform at many meetings, political and educational, in different parts of the country. Jebb contrived to carry on his literary work together with this public activity. He delivered the Rede lecture at Cambridge in 1890 and the Romanes lecture at Oxford in 1899; the subject of the first was 'Erasmus' and of the second 'Humanism in education.' In 1892 he revisited the United States and delivered at Johns Hopkins University lectures on 'The Growth and Influence of Greek Poetry,' which he published next year. He published an elaborate commentary on the newly discovered poems of Bacchylides in the last year of his life (1905).

Meanwhile Jebb had begun and completed the great work of his life, his edition of Sophocles. He had started on the enterprise in 1880; the first volume, containing the 'Œdipus Tyrannus,' appeared in 1883. He published a volume upon each of the remaining extant plays—'Œdipus Coloneus' (1885), 'Antigone' (1888), 'Philoctetes' (1890), 'Trachiniæ' (1892), 'Electra' (1894), and 'Ajax' (1896); he intended to publish an eighth volume containing the fragments. To the Greek text are added a translation into English prose, critical notes upon the text, and a commentary. In the first two plays the critical notes were written in Latin; it was in deference to an appeal from Matthew Arnold that English was used for this purpose in the later volumes.

A man of affairs as well as a scholar, Jebb helped to shape and to start upon its career the Society for the Promotion of Hellenic Studies in 1879. He was one of the originators of the society and one of its most active members; he made important contributions to the Journal issued by the society. Similarly, to Jebb more than to any other man the British School of Archæology at Athens owes its existence. Since his visit to Greece in 1878 he kept urging upon the British public the duty of doing what had already been done by France and Germany. In 1887 his ideal was realised, and the British School at Athens entered on its career of excavation and discovery. Lastly, he took a leading part in the meetings and discussions which ultimately led to the formation of the British Academy. When the Academy received its charter of incorporation in 1902, Jebb was one of the original fellows.

Although he was very shy in manner, Jebb's friends and admirers included the leading men of letters of his time, and with Tennyson, whom he had gratified by a review of 'Harold' in 'The Times' (18 Oct. 1876), he formed a close intimacy. He stayed with the poet at Aldworth, and wrote admiringly of Tennyson's work in T. H. Ward's 'English Poets' (vol. iv. 1894). His own literary eminence and public services were fittingly recognised. In 1888 he was elected an honorary fellow of Trinity College, Cambridge. He was made hon. LL.D. of Edinburgh in 1879; hon. Litt.D. of Cambridge in 1885; hon. LL.D. of Dublin and hon. Ph.D. of Bologna in 1888; and hon. D.C.L. of Oxford in 1891. He was a fellow of London University, appointed by the crown in 1897, and a corresponding member of the German Institute of Archæology. In 1898 the Royal Academy elected him to fill Gladstone's place as their professor of ancient history; in 1903 he was elected a trustee of the British Museum in succession to Lord Acton. In 1900 he accepted the honour of knighthood, which he had declined three years earlier. Lastly, in 1905 he received the distinction of the Order of Merit.

When the British Association met at Cambridge in 1904 Jebb became a member, and was elected a vice-president of the section of education. He was chosen president of the section for the following year, when the association met in South Africa. He reached Capetown on 15 Aug. 1905. His address on education, delivered in Capetown, was so successful that he had to repeat it at Johannesburg. The travelling, sightseeing, and general business of the next month was arduous and overtaxed his strength. Soon after reaching England on 19 Oct. his health failed, and he died at Springfield, his house in Cambridge, on 9 December 1905. On 13 Dec. he was buried in St. Giles's cemetery at Cambridge after a funeral service in the chapel of Trinity College. He left no family.

A portrait of Jebb, painted by Sir George Reid in 1903, hangs in the Hall of Trinity College. It is a faithful likeness; but the sitter was suffering at the time from hay-fever, and the expression is consequently harassed.

Jebb was married on 18 Aug. 1874, at Ellesmere in Shropshire, to Caroline Lane, daughter of the Rev. John Reynolds, D.D., of Philadelphia and widow of General Slemmer of the United States army. Lady Jebb survived her husband. To her the edition of Sophocles was dedicated: Jebb wrote that his work had owed more to her sympathy than to any other aid.

Sir John Sandys re-edited Jebb's 'Characters of Theophrastus' in 1909, and prepared for the press in the same year the translation of Aristotle's 'Rhetoric' which was left unpublished at Jebb's death. Lady Jebb issued in 1907 a selection from his 'Essays and Addresses,' as well as his 'Life and Letters.' Jebb was a leading contributor to the 9th edition of the 'Encyclopædia Britannica.' He wrote for this Dictionary the articles on Bentley and Porson, and for the 'Cambridge Modern History' (vol. i. 1902) a brilliant chapter on 'The Classical Renaissance.'

Never idle, Jebb worked faster than other men, and few accomplished more. He took little exercise, although in later life he rode a tricycle, and he occasionally fished. He wrote a beautiful hand, clear and large; in working for the press he preferred pencil to pen and ink. While he did many things well he was far more distinguished as a scholar and man of letters than as a politician and public speaker; and his reputation will depend chiefly upon his edition of 'Sophocles,' which is the most completely satisfactory commentary on a classical author that has been written in the English language. Though each volume is of moderate compass, nothing is omitted that can throw light on the matter in hand. The compression is marvellous; yet the statement is everywhere perfectly lucid. Every part of the edition is good, but best of all is the commentary. Jebb had an exquisite apprehension of every shade of meaning in the most delicate and precise of languages; and there was a natural harmony between the poet and his expositor, by virtue of which Jebb seems to wind his way into the very mind of Sophocles. In a hundred places where the text had been suspected and alteration suggested, Jebb's subtle analysis proved the text to be sound and showed why Sophocles used precisely those words and no others. Few men of Jebb's time had received as great gifts from nature as he, and few worked as hard to exercise and improve them.

[Life and Letters, by Caroline Jebb, 1907, with an estimate by A. W. Verrall, pp. 429–487; The Times, 11 Dec. 1905; Athenæum, 16 Dec. 1905; Proc. Brit. Acad., 1905–1906, notice by Prof. R. Y. Tyrrell, p. 445; Tennyson's Life of Tennyson, 1897; Grant Duff, Notes from a Diary, 1889–1901 (1901–5); J. E. Sandys' Hist. of Classical Scholarship, vol. iii.; private information; personal knowledge.] J. D. D.

JELF, GEORGE EDWARD (1834–1908), Master of Charterhouse, eldest son of seven children of Richard William Jelf [q. v.] and Emmy, Countess of Schlippenbach, lady-in-waiting to Frederica, Duchess of Cumberland (afterwards Queen of Hanover), was born on 19 Jan. 1834 at Berlin, where his father was tutor to Prince George of Cumberland. His uncle was the scholar, William Edward Jelf [q. v.]; his younger brothers are Hon. Sir Arthur Richard Jelf, judge of the high court, who retired from the bench in 1910, and Colonel Richard Henry Jelf, formerly governor of the Royal Military Academy, Woolwich. Educated at preparatory schools at Hammersmith and Brighton, Jelf was admitted to Charterhouse under Dr. Saunders in 1847, and matriculated at Christ Church, Oxford, on 2 June 1852. He held a studentship at Christ Church from 1852 to 1861, and won a first class in classical moderations in 1854. He graduated B.A. with a third class in lit. hum. in 1856, and he proceeded M.A. in 1859 and D.D. in 1907. In 1857 he entered Wells Theological College, and the following year he was ordained deacon, becoming priest in 1859. He held curacies at St. Michael's, Highgate (1858–60), St. James's, Clapton (1860–6), and at Aylesbury (1866–8). On the presentation of Roundell Palmer, first Earl of Selborne [q. v.], he became vicar of Blackmoor, Hampshire, in 1868, and in 1874 he accepted from Lord Braybrooke the living of Saffron Walden. In 1878 he was made an honorary canon of St. Albans.

Jelf's long connection with Rochester began with his appointment in 1880 to a residentiary canonry, a position he held for twenty-seven years. He continued his parish work at Saffron Walden till 1882, and from 1883 to 1889 he had the onerous charge of St. Mary's, Chatham; subsequently he devoted himself to mission work in the diocese. Straitened means compelled him to undertake extra clerical duties. His tenure of the rectory of Wiggonholt near Pulborough (1896–7), in addition to his canonry, involved too great a division of interests, and in the latter year Jelf accepted the incumbency of St. German's, Blackheath, where he enjoyed comparative freedom from parochial responsibilities. In 1904 he resigned this benefice and definitely retired to Rochester. But in 1907 he was appointed to the dignified position of Master of Charterhouse in succession to William Haig Brown [q. v. Suppl. II]. His health, however, failed soon after moving to London, and he died on 19 Nov. 1908 at the Master's lodge, Charterhouse. He was buried in Highgate cemetery, and on the same day a memorial service was held in Rochester cathedral.

Jelf married (1) in 1861 Fanny (*d.* 1865), daughter of G. A. Crawley of Highgate, by whom he had one surviving son, and three daughters, who all died of scarlet-fever in 1871; (2) in 1876 Katherine Frances, younger daughter of prebendary C. B. Dalton, vicar of St. Michael's, Highgate, who survived him; by her he had three sons and four daughters.

A moderate high churchman, Jelf was a trusted friend and godson of Edward Bouverie Pusey [q. v.], whose 'Christus Consolator' (1883) he edited. From 1895 he acted as proctor in convocation for the dean and chapter of Rochester; but he took little part in current controversy. The bent of his mind was devotional rather than critical, and he exercised considerable influence through his numerous popular homiletic publications, of which the most important are: 1. 'The Secret Trials of the Christian Life,' 1873. 2. 'The Rule of God's Commandments,' 1878. 3. 'The Consolations of the Christian Seasons,' 1880. 4. 'Work and Worship,' 1888, sermons preached in English cathedrals. 5. 'Mother,

Home and Heaven,' 1891. 6. 'Sound Words, their Form and Spirit,' 1907, addresses on the English Prayer-Book.

[The Times, 20 Nov. 1908; Guardian, 25 Nov. 1908; Chatham and Rochester News, 21 Nov. 1908; Katherine Frances Jelf, Memoir of George Edward Jelf, 1909; Roundell Palmer, Earl of Selborne, Memorials Personal and Political (1865–95), 1898, 2 vols.] G. S. W.

JENKINS, EBENEZER EVANS (1820–1905), Wesleyan minister and missionary, born at Exeter on 10 May 1820, was second son of John Jenkins, cabinet maker, by his wife Mary Evans, a Welshwoman. His parents were earnest methodists. Educated at Exeter grammar school, he showed as a boy literary leanings and soon became assistant master in the school of William Pengelly [q. v.]. Resolving on the methodist ministry, he was ordained at Great Queen Street Wesleyan chapel, London, on 31 Oct. 1845, and was sent out to Madras. Stationed at first at Mannargudi, he was able by September 1846 to prepare a Tamil sermon. After a move to Negapatam, he settled, about 1848, at Black Town chapel, Madras, and soon started the Royapettah school (now college) there, the oldest Wesleyan educational institution. He was absent (1855–7) from India on account of health during the Mutiny, but in 1857 he returned as chairman of the Madras district, continuing to minister in his old chapel, which he enlarged. A volume of sermons preached there was issued at Madras in 1863 (2nd edit. 1866); but his health again failed, and returning home by way of Australia, where he gave many lectures, he was appointed in 1865 superintendent of the Hackney circuit. He at once gained a high reputation as a preacher and speaker through the country, and made several foreign tours in an official capacity, speaking at the Evangelical Alliance convention at New York in 1873, and in 1875–6 and again in 1884–5 visiting missions in China, Japan, and India. From 1877 to 1888 he was a general secretary of the Mission House, remaining an honorary secretary until his death. In 1880 he was president of the Wesleyan conference.

His last years were spent in Southport, where he died on 19 July 1905. He was buried at Norwood cemetery. Jenkins published many addresses and sermons, chiefly on missionary aims and work.

He married twice: (1) in 1850, at Madras, Eliza Drewett (*d.* 27 April 1869); (2) in October 1871, Margaret Heald, daughter of Dr. Wood of Southport; she died on 7 March 1875 at the birth of her second son.

[Memoir by son, J. H. Jenkins, M.A., 1906; The Times, 20 July 1905.] C. F. S.

JENKINS, JOHN EDWARD (1838–1910), politician and satirist, born at Bangalore, Mysore, Southern India, on 28 July 1838, was the eldest son of John Jenkins, D.D., Wesleyan missionary, by his wife Harriette, daughter of James Shepstone of Clifton. His father removed to Canada, where he became minister of St. Paul's Presbyterian church, Montreal, and moderator of the general assembly. The son, after having been educated at the High School, Montreal, and McGill University, and later at the University of Pennsylvania, came to London, and was called to the bar at Lincoln's Inn on 17 Nov. 1864. He secured some practice, and in 1870 he was retained by the Aborigines Protection and Anti-Slavery Society to watch the proceedings of the British Guiana coolie commission. He visited the colony and became the champion of the Indian indentured labourers there, publishing in 1871 'The Coolie: his Rights and Wrongs.' His zeal for social reform, however, turned him aside from his profession, and in 1870 he suddenly became famous as the anonymous author of 'Ginx's Baby, his Birth and other Misfortunes,' a pathetic satire on the struggles of rival sectarians for the religious education of a derelict child, which attracted universal notice and had its influence on the religious compromise in the Education Act of 1870. An edition, the 36th, of 'Ginx's Baby' (1876) was illustrated by Frederick Barnard [q.v. Suppl. I].

Jenkins was a strong imperialist and in 1871 he organised the 'Conference on Colonial Questions' which met at Westminster under his chairmanship. His inaugural address was entitled 'The Colonies and Imperial Unity: or the Barrel without the Hoops.' This originated the Imperial Federation movement as opposed to the policy of imperial disintegration advocated by Prof. Goldwin Smith [q. v. Suppl. II] and others, and led in 1874 to Jenkins's appointment as first agent-general in London for the dominion of Canada, an office which he held only two years. His imperialism did not, however, hinder him from protesting against the Act by which Queen Victoria became in 1876 empress of India, when he published anonymously 'The Blot on the Queen's Head' (1876). Notwithstanding his imperialism Jenkins was an ardent radical with political ambition. After unsuccessfully contesting in the radical interest Stafford and Truro, he was during his absence in Canada returned at the general election of 1874 as member of parliament for Dundee, and retained the seat until the dissolution of 1880. He then at a by-election in January 1881 contested Edinburgh as an independent liberal, but was defeated by Lord McLaren, then lord advocate [q. v. Suppl. II]. Subsequently, his dislike for Gladstone's views in imperial politics overcame his radicalism in home politics, and in 1885 he attempted to recover his seat for Dundee as a conservative, but he failed both then and in 1896. He was a fluent and popular speaker. He served on the royal commission on copyright in 1876–7.

Jenkins, who wrote articles on 'Imperial Federation' in the 'Contemporary Review' for 1871, made some unsuccessful attempts to repeat the popular success of 'Ginx's Baby,' publishing 'Lord Bantam,' a satire on a young aristocrat in democratic politics (2 vols. 1871); 'Barney Geoghegan, M.P., and Home Rule at St. Stephen's,' reprinted with additions from 'Saint Paul's Magazine' (1872); 'Little Hodge,' supporting the agitation led by Joseph Arch on behalf of the agricultural labourer (1872); 'Glances at Inner England,' a lecture (1874); 'The Devil's Chain,' a tale (1876); 'Lutchmee and Dilloo,' a tale (3 vols. 1877); 'The Captain's Cabin, a Christmas Yarn' (1877); 'A Paladin of Finance,' a novel (1882); 'A Week of Passion: or, The Dilemma of Mr. George Barton the Younger,' a novel (3 vols. 1884); 'A Secret of Two Lives,' a novel (1886), and 'Pantalas and what they did with him,' a tale (1897). He was from 1886 editor of the 'Overland Mail' and the 'Homeward Mail,' newspapers of which his brother-in-law, Sir Henry Seymour King, is the proprietor. From the beginning of Sir Henry King's political career he acted as his parliamentary secretary.

Jenkins died in London on 4 June 1910, after some years' suffering from paralysis. He married in 1867 Hannah Matilda, daughter of Philip Johnstone of Belfast, and left a family of five sons and two daughters.

[The Times, and Morning Post, 6 June 1910; Overland Mail, 10 June 1910; Dod's Parliamentary Companion; Brit. Mus. Cat.; Sir Leslie Stephen, Life of Sir James Fitzjames Stephen.] R. E. G.

JENNER-FUST, HERBERT (1806–1904), cricketer, born on 23 Feb. 1806 at 38 Sackville Street, Piccadilly, was eldest son and one of fourteen children of Sir Herbert Jenner, afterwards Jenner-Fust [q. v.], dean of arches, by his wife Elizabeth, daughter of Major-general Francis Lascelles. Two brothers, both in holy orders, played in the Cambridge University cricket eleven —Charles Herbert, the second son, and the eighth son, Henry Lascelles Jenner, first bishop of Dunedin, from 1866 to 1871. Jenner after education at Eton from 1818 to 1823 spent a year at a private tutor's. Like his father before him, he matriculated in 1824 at Trinity Hall, Cambridge, where he gained a scholarship and afterwards a fellowship. In 1826 he was first in college examinations, and next year was third in the law honour list, graduating LL.B. in 1829 and proceeding LL.D. in 1835. Called to the bar at Lincoln's Inn in 1831 and admitted an advocate in the ecclesiastical court of Doctors' Commons in 1835, he practised there with success until 1857–8, when that court was abolished and its business transferred to Westminster. After residing successively at Beckenham, at Carshalton, and at Sidcup, he finally settled on the family property at Hill Court, Gloucestershire, in 1864, when he adopted the additional surname of Fust.

Jenner was best known as a cricketer. He was a member of the Eton eleven in 1822–3, and at Cambridge distinguished himself in more than one branch of the game. On 4 June 1827 he played as the captain of the Cambridge eleven in the first match between Oxford and Cambridge Universities, scoring forty-five runs in the single innings out of a total of ninety-two, and taking five wickets, among them that of Charles Wordsworth [q. v.], the Oxford captain, afterwards bishop of St. Andrews. A few weeks later he was one of the seventeen Gentlemen who defeated eleven Players. Thenceforth, until his retirement in 1836, he was prominent in almost all first-class cricket, appearing for the Gentlemen, for England, for Kent, and two or three times, in a friendly way without county qualifications, for Norfolk. He was an excellent batsman, and a successful underhand bowler, roundhand bowling from 1816 to 1828 being expressly forbidden. But Jenner chiefly shone as a wicket-keeper. In 1833 he was elected the annual president of the Marylebone cricket club at the early age of twenty-seven, and was from 1882 till death president of the West Kent cricket club.

After 1836 Jenner often took part in local matches, proving himself an admirable captain. In 1877 he was a prominent guest at the dinner in London which celebrated the jubilee of the Oxford and Cambridge match.

In 1880, at the age of seventy-four, he played for his parish of Hill in a match against Rockhampton, scoring eleven (run out), and as bowler and wicket-keeper getting ten wickets, besides running out two. Outliving by nearly twelve years all players in the university match of 1827, he died at Hill Court on 30 July 1904, in his ninety-ninth year.

An oil portrait hangs in the pavilion at Lord's cricket ground.

In 1833 he married Maria Eleanora (*d.* 1891), third daughter of George Norman and sister of George Warde Norman [q. v.], and had issue Herbert, general inspector under the Local Government Board (1884–1906), and two daughters.

[Personal knowledge; Lillywhite's Cricket Scores and Biographies, i. 462; Hist. Kent County Cricket, 1907; Scores and Annals of the West Kent Cricket Club, 1897; Wisden's Cricketers' Almanack 1905.] P. N.

JEPHSON, ARTHUR JERMY MOUNTENEY (1858–1908), African traveller, born at Hutton Rectory, Brentwood, Essex, on 8 Oct. 1858, was fifth and youngest son of John Mounteney Jephson, vicar of Childerditch, Essex, and Ellen, daughter of Isaac Jermy, of Stanfield Hill, Norfolk [q. v.]. He was educated at Tonbridge School (1869–74) and on H.M.S. Worcester (1874–76). In 1880 he joined the Antrim regiment of the royal Irish rifles, but resigned his commission in 1884. At the desire of his friend, Helena Comtesse de Noailles, he joined [Sir] Henry Morton Stanley's [q. v. Suppl. II] expedition for the relief of Emin Pasha. Leaving Europe in 1887, Stanley and he travelled up the Congo, and left the ill-fated rear-guard at Yambuya on the Aruwimi on 28 June. Jephson accompanied Stanley on the difficult journey through the forests to Lake Albert, and in April 1888 he was despatched over the lake to find Emin. He brought Emin to Stanley at the end of the month. With Emin, at Stanley's and the Pasha's request, he travelled through Emin's equatorial province, and in accordance with instructions, offered to guide all inhabitants who wished to follow Emin and himself out of the province by way of Zanzibar to Egypt. The proposal for the evacuation of the province met with opposition from the people, and Jephson was engaged for nine months with Emin in resisting their rebellion. Both were imprisoned at Dufile in August 1888. In October the Mahdists came down upon the province, and at the beginning of December, on the news of their successes in the north, the native soldiers at Dufile besought Emin to lead them in retreat. Emin's own unwillingness to quit the province, the affairs of which were in great confusion, added to Jephson's difficulties. The council of native rebel officers at Wadelai condemned both Emin and Jephson to death, but early in February 1889 he succeeded in rejoining Stanley at Kavali, and subsequently they managed to rescue Emin. Returning to England in 1890, Jephson became a queen's messenger in 1895 and held a similar post under King Edward VII (1901).

He was awarded a medal by the Royal Geographical Society of London in 1890 and a diploma by that at Brussels in the same year.

He died on 22 Oct. 1908 at Sunninghill, Ascot, and was buried there. He married in 1904 Anna, daughter of Addison Head of San Francisco, and left one son.

Jephson told the story of his part in the relief expedition in 'Emin Pasha and the Rebellion at the Equator' (1890; German tr. Leipzig, 1890; French tr. Paris, 1891). He collected a number of native folk-tales, and admirably presented them in 'Stories told in an African Forest by Grown-up Children of Africa' (1893). He also wrote 'The Story of a Billiard Ball' (1897).

[Geogr. Journ. xxxii. 630; The Times, 23 Oct. 1908; Jephson's Emin Pasha, 1890; Sir H. M. Stanley's Autobiography, 1909, and In Darkest Africa, 1890; private information.] O. J. R. H.

JEUNE, FRANCIS HENRY, Baron St. Helier (1843–1905), judge, was eldest son of Francis Jeune, bishop of Peterborough [q. v.], by his wife Margaret Dyne, only child of Henry Symons of Axbridge, Somerset. Born on 17 March 1843 at St. Helier, where his father was then rector and dean of Jersey, Jeune was sent as a boy to the school kept at Exmouth by Penrose, a teacher of great ability, though freely addicted to the use of corporal punishment. Thence he went to Harrow (1856–61), where he obtained a scholarship at the same time as the first Viscount Ridley and won many prizes, his English essays in particular showing an unusual amount of information, an original thoughtfulness, and a command of forcible English. When Lord Brougham visited the school on a speech day he pronounced Jeune's performance 'perfect oratory.' In 1861 he obtained a Balliol scholarship, and was placed in the first class in moderations in 1863 and in the final classical school in 1865. In 1863 he obtained the Stanhope prize for an essay on 'The Influence of the Feudal System on Character,' and in 1867 the Arnold prize for one upon 'The Mohammedan Power in India.' He was called to the bar by the Inner Temple on 17 Nov. 1868. In 1874, upon the establishment in its present form of Hertford College, he was made one of the original fellows.

Before his call to the bar Jeune worked for some time in the office of Messrs. Baxter, Rose, and Norton, the well-known firm of solicitors, and in 1869 he proceeded, upon their instructions, to Australia, to inquire into and report upon the evidence proposed to be adduced in support of the claim of Arthur Orton to be 'Sir' Roger Tichborne. After his return he was counsel for the plaintiff in the famous action of ejectment, Tichborne *v.* Lushington, which was tried for 103 days before chief justice Bovill, from June 1871 to March 1872, when the jury stopped the case, and the claimant was committed for trial for perjury. Jeune's leaders were Serjeant William Ballantine [q. v. Suppl. I], Mr. Giffard, Q.C. (now Earl of Halsbury), and Mr. Pollard. He held no brief in the criminal trial which followed.

Jeune won a great reputation as a junior of exceptional learning and industry, and a large proportion of his practice was in ecclesiastical courts, or before the judicial committee of the privy council. In ecclesiastical litigation he was engaged usually but not always on the evangelical side—that being the party to which his father, the bishop, had belonged. He was on that side in the Mackonochie case, in the litigation of Green *v.* Lord Penzance, in the cases of Dale, and Enraght, and that of Julius *v.* the Bishop of Oxford, and in Cox [Mr. Bell-Cox] *v.* Hake. Another case in which he appeared before the judicial committee was an application for leave to appeal by Louis Riel [q. v.], a Canadian who was hanged for armed rebellion in 1885. He served on the royal commission on ecclesiastical patronage in 1874, and on that on ecclesiastical courts in 1881, and before his appointment to the bench was chancellor of the dioceses of St. Albans, Durham, Peterborough, Gloucester and Bristol, St. Asaph, Bangor, and St. David's.

In 1880 he stood as conservative candidate for Colchester, and was defeated by two votes by William (afterwards Judge) Willis, Q.C. [q. v. Suppl. II]. After this election he sat with Messrs. Holl, Q.C., and Turner as a commissioner to inquire into the corruption reported after the trial of an election petition to have prevailed at Sandwich, then a parliamentary borough. The commission reported the existence of the most flagrant corruption. The borough was consequently disfranchised, until by the Redistribution Act of 1885 it became part of one of the divisions of Kent.

In 1888 Jeune was appointed a queen's counsel, and in June 1891 was elected a bencher of the Inner Temple. The last case of great importance in which he appeared at the bar was the prosecution before the archbishop of Canterbury (Benson), with assessors, of Edward King [q. v. Suppl. II], bishop of Lincoln, for alleged unlawful ritual. Jeune was counsel for the accused bishop, and the result of the trial was that some of the practices impugned were held to be lawful and others unlawful.

In 1890 the suggestion was authoritatively made to Jeune that he should again stand for parliament, with a view to his appointment as solicitor-general upon the occurrence of an expected vacancy in that office, but he declined the proposal on the ground that his health would be unequal to the strain of parliamentary and official work. In 1891 Sir James Hannen [q. v. Suppl. I] was created a lord of appeal, and Jeune accepted the office of judge of the probate, divorce and admiralty division in place of Hannen's junior colleague, Sir Charles Parker Butt [q. v. Suppl. I], who succeeded Hannen as president. Jeune was knighted in the usual course. The work of the division fell principally upon his shoulders for the following year and a half, owing to Butt's illness, which terminated fatally in May 1892. It was then determined to cure by legislation an ambiguity in the Judicature Acts as to the precise conditions in which a judge succeeded to the office of president of the probate division. An Act was passed creating a definite office of president of the probate, etc., division, with the judicial rank of one of the lords justices of appeal. The new arrangement practically involved that the president should always be a privy councillor. Of this office Jeune was the first holder.

Jeune's tenure of this office, which lasted thirteen years, was distinguished and successful. A sound lawyer and a strong man, he gave a conspicuous example of the patience and personal courtesy which towards the end of the nineteenth century became, more conspicuously than at some previous periods of legal history, characteristic of the judges of the high court. With the assistance of his colleague, Mr. Justice Gorell Barnes, now Lord Gorell, he made his small division a model of efficiency and despatch. The lists in probate, divorce, and admiralty were increasingly full at the beginning of each year, and arrears were practically unknown. In each of the three classes of work Jeune was an efficient and capable judge. Of admiralty work he had little or no special knowledge at the time of his appointment as a judge, but fortifying himself with much reading he speedily became sufficiently master of the necessary technical knowledge. He was naturally best known to the general public as the judge in divorce cases. In these delicate and sometimes difficult litigations he did much to restore to his court the decorum and gravity which had been most marked in the time of Hannen, and had somewhat declined during the presidency of Sir Charles Butt. In all three branches Jeune secured the confidence of those who practised before him.

When the liberal government came into office in 1892 a difficulty arose as to the payment of the judge-advocate-general, and Gladstone, acting on the precedent of the appointment to that office of Sir Robert Joseph Phillimore, first baronet [q. v.], when judge of the court of admiralty, eventually requested Jeune to add these duties to his own. Jeune accordingly held the office until 1904. He received no salary, but his services in this respect were recognised by his creation as K.C.B. in 1897 and as G.C.B. at the close of the South African war in 1902. During these ten years, as previously, the daily work of the office was performed by two deputies, one legal and the other military, but the finding of every 'general court-martial' had to be confirmed or quashed by the judge-advocate-general himself, who was also required to advise the sovereign personally in many cases, for which reason it was necessary that the office should be held by a privy councillor. Jeune was the last holder, as the post was practically abolished by statute in 1904, the title and some of the duties being transferred to a legal official of the war office. Jeune found that his tenure of the office occupied him for several hours weekly in time of peace, and during the South African war the addition to his public duties which it involved was considerable.

In 1898 and 1902 Jeune was chairman of board of committees respectively on the load line regulations as to winter North Atlantic freeboard, and on the effect of employment of lascars and other foreigners upon the reserve of British seamen available for naval purposes. In 1904 he was a member of Sir Michael Hicks Beach's commission on ecclesiastical discipline.

In January 1905, upon medical advice, he resigned the presidency of the probate, etc., division, and was created a peer by the title of Baron St. Helier. His failing health, which had been gravely affected by grief for the death of his only son in 1904, did not permit of his taking his seat in the House of Lords, and he died at his house in Harley Street on 9 April 1905. He was buried in the churchyard at Chieveley, Bucks.

Jeune married in 1881 Susan Mary Elizabeth, elder daughter of the Hon. Keith William Stewart-Mackenzie, and widow of Lieut.-colonel the Hon. John Constantine Stanley, second son of the second Lord Stanley of Alderley. His domestic happiness was complete and unbroken. His manifold activities and hospitable disposition brought him a large circle of friends, whom he entertained both in London and at his country house, Arlington Manor, Newbury, Berkshire. His only son, Christian Francis Seaforth (*b.* 1882), of the Grenadier guards, A.D.C. to Lord Lamington, the governor of Bombay, died in 1904, of enteric fever, at Poona.

In person Jeune was tall and of distinguished appearance. He was one of the first of the judges to wear a full beard and moustache, his forensic wig notwithstanding. An oil painting by Sir Hubert von Herkomer, representing him seated, without a wig, but otherwise in the state dress of a lord justice of appeal, belongs to Lady St. Helier, and is an admirable likeness. A cartoon by 'Stuff' appeared in 'Vanity Fair' in 1891.

[Private documents and personal recollection; The Times, 11 April 1905; Lady St. Helier's Memories of Fifty Years, 1909.]

H. S.

JOHNSON, LIONEL PIGOT (1867–1902), critic and poet, born at Broadstairs, Kent, on 15 March 1867, was third son of Captain William Victor Johnson of the 90th regiment light infantry (1822–91) by his wife Catherine Delicia Walters. The father was second son of Sir Henry Allen Johnson, second baronet (1785–1860), and grandson of General Sir Henry

Johnson, first baronet [q. v.]. During Lionel's boyhood his family resided at Mold, Flintshire, and afterwards settled at Kingsmead, Windsor Forest. He was educated at Durdham Down, Clifton, and at Winchester College, where he gained a scholarship in 1880 and remained six years. He rose rapidly in the school, and won the prize for English literature in 1883, the prize for an English essay in 1885, and the medal for English verse in 1885 and 1886, the subjects being 'Sir Walter Raleigh in the Tower' and 'Julian at Eleusis.' He edited the school paper, 'The Wykehamist,' from 1884 to 1886, and converted it, so far as he dared, into a literary review, with articles on Wykehamical poets and discussions of the technique of verse. From early boyhood he was a writer of verse, mainly imitative, and an omnivorous reader, with a retentive memory and an inveterate habit of quotation. At Winchester he wrote his first critical essay of any importance, on the 'Fools of Shakespeare,' which was published in 'Noctes Shakesperianæ' (1887). Small in stature and of frail physique, he took no exercise save walking, making vacation tours in Wales, the Lake country, and Cornwall.

In December 1885 Johnson won a Winchester scholarship at New College, Oxford, and in July 1886 he gained the Goddard scholarship for proficiency in classics. He went up to New College in October 1886, taking a second class in classical moderations in 1888 and a first in literæ humaniores in 1890. At Oxford, as at Winchester, he was something of a literary dictator. There he formed his prose style by the study chiefly of his namesake, Samuel Johnson, and was profoundly influenced by Walter Pater.

On leaving Oxford in 1890 he entered on a literary career in London, at first living at 20 Fitzroy Street with a little group of artists and men of letters. The publisher Charles Kegan Paul [q. v. Suppl. II] helped to start him in journalism, and he was soon hard at work reviewing for the 'Academy,' 'Anti-Jacobin,' 'National Observer,' 'Daily Chronicle,' and 'Pall Mall Gazette.' His ambition to become known as a poet was delayed by the necessity of earning money to free himself of debts contracted at Oxford by lavish expenditure on books and prints. This he had accomplished by the end of 1891; but his first eagerness for publication had passed off, and he continued to write and revise. While preparing his first prose book, on Thomas Hardy, he walked for a month (June 1892) in Dorset. Some of the best of his early poems made their first appearance in the 'Century Guild Hobby-Horse' and the first and second 'Book of the Rhymers' Club' (1892–4). Even before he went to Oxford Johnson had grown sceptical about the validity of Anglican claims, and, though he still conformed outwardly to the Church of England, he read deeply in Roman catholic theology and cultivated the acquaintance of priests as well as poets. On 22 June 1891 he was received into the Church of Rome, and talked for a time of taking orders. Asceticism, reverence for catholic tradition, sympathy with catholic mysticism, and a love of the niceties, rather than the splendours, of ritual—catholic puritanism, as he called it—became henceforth prominent in the subject-matter of his poems, of which a first collection came out in 1895. Another leading factor of his poetry, his love for Ireland, was of later growth, and tells especially in his second volume, 'Ireland and other Poems' (1897). His interest in nationalist politics and in the Irish literary revival was fostered by a visit to Ireland in September 1893, which he often repeated, but his own alleged Irish origin was a literary pose, and Celtic influences had reached him first through Wales.

In October 1895 Johnson removed to 7 Gray's Inn Square, Gray's Inn, a few years later to New Square, Lincoln's Inn, and again to Clifford's Inn, where the close of his life was spent in illness and absolute seclusion. His health had been undermined by intemperance and the habit, formed in boyhood, of working late at night. On 22 Sept. 1902 he sent his last poem, on Pater, to the editor of the 'Academy.' A week later he fell in Fleet Street, fractured his skull, and died in St. Bartholomew's Hospital, without recovering consciousness, on 4 October. He was buried at Kensal Green. A tablet to his memory was placed in the cloisters of Winchester College in 1904. He was unmarried.

Johnson published: 1. 'The Gordon Riots' (No. 12 of Historical Papers, edited by John Morris, S.J.), 1893. 2. 'Bits of Old Chelsea' (letterpress written by Johnson jointly with Richard Le Gallienne), 1894 fol. 3. 'The Art of Thomas Hardy,' 1894. 4. 'Poems,' 1895. 5. 'Ireland, with other Poems,' 1897. His scattered critical essays, among which an essay on Walter Pater in the 'Fortnightly Review,' September 1894, is especially worthy of mention, were collected as 'Post

Liminium; Essays and Critical Papers,' with an introduction by Thomas Whittemore, in 1911. Selections of Johnson's poems appeared at the Dun Emer Press, Dundrum, 1904, and in the 'Vigo Cabinet' series, 1908.

Johnson's best work, both in prose and verse, was done in the decade of 1886–95. The brilliant promise of his youth was hardly fulfilled. But his criticism was acute and based on profound learning, even if the omniscience that he was apt to affect sometimes provoked distrust. As a poet he had a genuine though limited inspiration. Often ornate, almost always felicitous in language, he knew how to be simple, but was rarely passionate. There are lyrics, however, like 'The Dark Angel,' that spring from profound inward experience and are faultless in expression.

[Academy, 11 Oct. 1902; Athenæum, 18 Oct. 1902; Wykehamist, Oct. 1902; Atlantic Monthly, Dec. 1902; Rolleston's Treasury of Irish Poetry; Memoir by Clement K. Shorter in Vigo Cabinet series, No. 34 (Elkin Mathews), 1908; private information.] C. D.

JOHNSTON, WILLIAM (1829–1902), of Ballykilbeg, Orangeman, born at Downpatrick, co. Down, on 22 Feb. 1829, was the eldest child in a family of four sons and three daughters of John Brett Johnston (*d.* 8 March 1853) of Ballykilbeg, near Downpatrick (a descendant of Archbishop Francis Marsh [q. v.]), by his wife Thomasina Anne Brunette (*d.* 1852), daughter of Thomas Scott, a local surgeon. From the diocesan school at Downpatrick he went in 1848 to Trinity College, Dublin, graduating B.A. in 1852, proceeding M.A. in 1856. Originally intended for the medical profession, on his father's death in 1853 he turned to the law, and was eventually called to the Irish bar in Hilary term, 1872. On 8 May 1848 he entered the Orange order, in which he ultimately rose to be deputy grand master of Ireland, and sovereign grand master of the Black institution; the triennial council of Orangemen, instituted 1866, was due to his proposal (Dec. 1865). Conceiving that the Party Processions Act (12 March 1850; since repealed) was being enforced in the north of Ireland and not in the south, Johnston organised a demonstration against it at Ballykilbeg (12 July 1866) and led an Orange procession to Bangor, co. Down (12 July 1867). Brought before the magistrates in September, he was committed for trial, which took place at Downpatrick in March 1868 before Justice Morris [see MORRIS, SIR MICHAEL, LORD MORRIS and KILLANIN, Suppl. II], who sentenced him to two months' imprisonment, reducible to one month if Johnston would give securities for good behaviour (himself 500*l.*, and two sureties of 250*l.*); this Johnston indignantly declined. His cell at Downpatrick was afterwards visited as the shrine of a protestant confessor. He was released four days before the expiry of the two months by medical order, the object being to frustrate an apprehended demonstration; but his friends were on the alert, and he made a triumphal progress to Ballykilbeg, his carriage being drawn by his Orange followers.

On 15 Nov. 1868 he was elected for Belfast as an independent conservative, defeating in conjunction with Sir Thomas McClure (liberal) the official conservatives, Sir Charles Lanyon and John Mulholland (afterwards Lord Dunleath). A petition against the return of Johnston and McClure failed, after a month's trial before Baron Fitzgerald. Re-elected in 1874, Johnston resigned his seat in March 1878, on his appointment by Lord Beaconsfield as inspector of Irish fisheries. After several warnings, called forth by his political speeches against the Land League and home rule, he was dismissed from office by Earl Spencer, the lord-lieutenant, on account of a vehement oration in the General Synod of the Church of Ireland at Dublin in 1885. He had impoverished his estate in order to serve his cause, having lost considerably by financing an Orange newspaper, the 'Downshire Protestant' (7 July 1855–12 Sept. 1862); his necessities were relieved by a public subscription. In 1885 he was returned for South Belfast, and held the seat till his death, speaking frequently against the project of a Roman catholic university, the policy of home rule, and the toleration of 'ritualism.' As representative of the Orange order he thrice crossed the Atlantic, the only year in which he missed attendance at a 12 July celebration in Belfast being 1891, when he was on his way to Canada. In Irish economics he was a firm advocate of 'the three F's' (fair rent, free sale, fixity of tenure); he supported Gladstone's land bill of 1890, and the leasehold tenant right bill. As a member of the Irish Temperance League he supported the Sunday Closing Act. His personal adhesion to the temperance cause was extreme: urged to take stimulant in his last illness, his answer was 'I would die first.' On 9 July 1902 he left London to open an Orange bazaar at Lurgan on the 10th, and to speak at a demonstration on the 12th at Ballynahinch;

this was his last effort; he was seized with faintness and a chill, and died at Ballykilbeg on 17 July 1902. He was buried in Rathmullan churchyard on 21 July; a monument over his grave was erected by public subscription. He was thrice married: (1) on 22 Feb. 1853 to Harriet, daughter of Robert Allen of Kilkenny, by whom he had issue two sons and two daughters; (2) on 10 Oct. 1861 to Arminella Frances, daughter of Thomas Drew, D.D.; (3) in 1863 to Georgiana Barbara (*d.* 1900), youngest daughter of Sir John Hay of Park, seventh baronet, by whom he had issue three sons and four daughters. His portrait adorns many Orange banners.

Although a man with a mission, Johnston was a gentleman in grain, 'transparently upright and honest,' and simply and devoutly religious. He never lost the esteem of his opponents. The Belfast nationalist organ, in recording his death, spoke of his 'courage and consistency,' adding that he was 'loved by his catholic tenants and neighbours.' One of his daughters joined the Roman catholic church, and it was characteristic of his sense of duty and his goodness of heart that he drove her to mass on the way to his own parish church. He contributed from time to time to various journals but he was not distinguished as a writer; his separate literary efforts were early, and of no great moment. He published: 1. 'Nightshade: a Novel,' 1857; 2nd edit. 1858. 2. 'Ribbonism and its Remedy: a Letter,' Dublin, 1858. 3. 'Freshfield,' 1859 (a novel). 4. 'Under which King?' 1872 (a story).

[Belfast News-Letter, 18 and 22 July 1902; Northern Whig, 18 and 22 July 1902; Irish News and Belfast Morning News, 18 July 1902; Burke's Landed Gentry of Ireland, 1904; information from Mr. John McBride, Holywood, co. Down; personal recollections.] A. G.

JOLY, CHARLES JASPER (1864–1906), royal astronomer of Ireland, born at St. Catherine's rectory, Tullamore, on 27 June 1864, was eldest son in the family of three sons and two daughters of John Swift Joly, successively rector of St. Catherine's, Tullamore, and of Athlone, by his wife Elizabeth, daughter of the Rev. Nathaniel Slator. His father's family, of French origin, settled in Ireland in the eighteenth century. After a short attendance at school at Portarlington, and nearly four years at Galway grammar school, Joly in October 1882 entered Trinity College, Dublin, where he won a mathematical scholarship. He graduated in 1886 with the first mathematical honour of his year—the 'studentship,' candidates for which were required to offer a second subject in addition to mathematics. Joly chose physics, the experimental side of which so much interested him that he went to Berlin in order to work in Helmholtz's laboratory. The death of his father in 1887 rendered it needful for him to seek a competency without delay, and abandoning a design of devoting himself wholly to experimental science, he returned to Ireland to read for a fellowship in Trinity College. The conditions of the examination discouraged strict specialism in mathematics or science, and Joly failed to win election till 1894. He then engaged in tuition at the college, and was junior proctor in 1896.

Joly's career as a productive mathematician began almost as soon as he was admitted to a fellowship. In his first paper, on 'The theory of linear vector functions,' which was read to the Royal Irish Academy on 10 Dec. 1894, he proved his discipleship to Sir William Rowan Hamilton [q. v.], the discoverer of quaternions, and first applied the quaternionic analysis to difficult and complex problems of geometry, using it as an engine for the discovery of new geometrical properties. The properties of linear vector functions were further studied in 'Scalar invariants of two linear vector functions' (*Trans. R.I.A.* 1896, xxx. 709) and 'Quaternion invariants of linear vector functions' (*Proc. R.I.A.* 1896, iv. 1), while the extension of the quaternion calculus to space of more than three dimensions was discussed in 'The associative algebra applicable to hyperspace' (*Proc. R.I.A.* 1897, v. 75); the algebras considered are those that are associative and distributive, and whose units satisfy equations of the same type as the units of quaternions. Other more purely geometrical investigations were published about this time under the titles 'Vector expressions for curves' (*Proc. R.I.A.* 1896, iv. 374) and 'Homographic divisions of planes, spheres, and space' (*Proc. R.I.A.* 1897, iv. 515).

In 1897 Joly resigned his work at Trinity College on his appointment as royal astronomer of Ireland at Dunsink observatory, where the rest of his life was spent. In this quiet retreat Joly devoted himself to advanced study and research. From 1898 to 1900 he was engaged in editing Hamilton's 'Elements of Quaternions,' originally published shortly after its author's death in 1865, and now out of print. Joly made considerable additions, including an appendix of 114 pages; the first volume of the new edition was published in 1899, and the second in 1901. While occupied with this work, Joly communicated several memoirs to the Royal Irish Academy: 'Astatics and quaternion functions,' 'Properties of the general congruency of curves,' and 'Some applications of Hamilton's operator in the calculus of variations' were all read in 1899; in the first, quaternions are applied to the geometry of forces, in the second to pure geometry, and in the third to some of the equations of mathematical physics. Early in the following year he presented a paper 'On the place of the Ausdehnungslehre in the general associative algebra of the quaternion type,' in which he showed that Grassmann's analysis for *n* dimensions, which is distributive but only partially associative, may be regarded as a limited form of the associative algebra of $n+1$ dimensions. In the course of the following five years Joly continued his labours in such memoirs (in the publications of the Royal Irish Academy or the Royal Society) as 'Integrals depending on a single quaternion variable'; 'The multilinear quaternion function'; 'The interpretation of a quaternion as a point symbol'; 'Quaternion arrays'; 'Representation of screws by weighted points'; 'Quaternions and projective geometry'; 'The quadratic screw-system'; 'The geometry of a three-system of screws,' and 'Some new relations in the theory of screws.' Finally in 1905, the centenary year of Hamilton's birth, he brought out 'A Manual of Quaternions,' which at once superseded all other introductory works on the subject.

During Joly's tenure of the office of royal astronomer he directed much observational work, the fruits of which appeared in the 'Dunsink Observations and Researches.' In 1900 he accompanied an eclipse expedition to Spain, and obtained some excellent photographs of totality; an account of the results was published in 'Trans. R.I.A.' xxxii. p. 271. He also edited Preston's 'Theory of Light' (3rd edit. 1901).

He was elected F.R.S. in 1904, and was a trustee of the National Library of Ireland and president of the International Association for Promoting the Study of Quaternions. Of outdoor sports he was fondest of climbing, being a member of the Alpine Club from 1895 to death. In literature he was well versed in Dante's work. Joly died at the observatory of pleurisy following typhoid fever on 4 Jan. 1906; he was buried at Mount Jerome cemetery, Dublin. On 20 March 1897 Joly was married to Jessie, youngest daughter of Robert Warren Meade of Dublin. His wife and three daughters survived him.

[Personal knowledge; private information from the surviving relatives of Dr. Joly; Proc. Roy. Soc. 78A; Monthly Notices Roy. Astronom. Soc. lxvi. 177; Alpine Journal, 1906.] E. T. W.

JOLY DE LOTBINIÈRE, Sir HENRY GUSTAVE (1829–1908), Canadian politician, born on 5 Dec. 1829 at Épernay, France, was son of Gaspard Joly, the owner of famous vineyards at Épernay, who became seigneur of Lotbinière, Canada, on his marriage with Julie Christine, daughter of Chartier de Lotbinière, speaker of the Quebec Assembly (1794–7). His mother's grandfather, Gaspard Michel Chartier de Lotbinière, marquis de Lotbinière, served as one of Montcalm's engineers at Quebec. In 1888 Henry assumed his mother's surname of de Lotbinière with the sanction of the Quebec legislature. He received his education at the Sorbonne in Paris, and joining his father at Lotbinière, was called to the bar of Lower Canada in 1855.

In Canada Joly early espoused the liberal cause in politics, and represented Lotbinière in the Canadian House of Assembly in 1861. In 1864 he effectively attacked the Taché-Macdonald government for remitting the canal dues, and subsequently supported Sir Antoine Aimé Dorion [q. v. Suppl. I] in his opposition to the federation movement. On the passing of the British North America Act he sat for his old constituency both in the first federal House of Commons at Ottawa and in the Quebec Legislative Assembly from 1867 to 1874. In the latter year a law was passed enacting that no one should hold a seat in both legislatures. Joly accordingly resigned his seat in the federal house and devoted his energies to the leadership of the liberal opposition in the Quebec Assembly. In 1872 he obtained the appointment of a parliamentary committee to inquire into corrupt practices. In 1874 and again in 1877 he declined the offer of a seat in the senate. In 1878 on the dismissal of the Boucherville ministry Luc Letellier St. Just, lieut.-governor of Quebec, called on Joly to form an administration. His government had only a bare majority, and his proposal to abolish the upper house led to its defeat after eighteen months of office. During that brief period he adopted a policy of retrenchment, and strove hard to purify the administration. Meanwhile he continued his legal duties at the bar, and was made Q.C. in 1878. In 1883 he was elected vice-chairman of the Liberal Dominion Federation. In the same year he retired from the leadership of the liberal opposition in Quebec, and in 1885 on his refusal to countenance the nationalist agitation led by Honoré Mercier [q. v. Suppl. I] against the execution of Louis Riel [q. v.] for high treason, he withdrew altogether from public life.

In 1895, when he was made K.C.M.G., he was induced to emerge from his retirement and to take an active part in the party campaign. On the return of the liberals to power in the following year Joly, who re-entered the federal House of Commons as member for Portneuf, was appointed controller of inland revenue. In 1897 he accepted the portfolio of minister of inland revenue in Sir Wilfrid Laurier's dominion cabinet, and was nominated a privy councillor. From 1900 to 1906 he held the post of lieut.-governor of British Columbia, and in that capacity he entertained at Victoria, the capital, the Prince and Princess of Wales (afterwards King George V and Queen Mary) when they visited Canada in 1901. Through life Joly actively promoted the interests of agriculture, forestry, and horticulture. At Quebec he brought about important reforms in the administration of timber lands and he warmly advocated the systematic preservation of the Canadian forests. He was vice-president of the American Forestry Congress in 1885, and helped to found the Canadian Forestry Association. Joly's disinterestedness was fully recognised among Canadian politicians. The last of the grand seigneurs, an aristocrat and yet a liberal, Joly sympathised intensely with the ideals of self-government held by the Rouge party. He died at Quebec on 16 Nov. 1908. He married on 6 May 1856 Margaretta Josepha (*d.* 1904), daughter of Hammond Gowen of Quebec, by whom he had issue three sons and three daughters. His two younger sons, Alain Chartier, C.I.E., and Gustave Henri, D.S.O., are both majors in the royal engineers.

[The Times, and Toronto Globe, 17 Nov. 1908; Castell Hopkins, Canadian Annual Review of Public Affairs, 1909; J. C. Dent, Canada since the Union of 1841, 2 vols. 1881; L. P. Turcotte, Canada sous l'Union, 1871; M. Bibaud, Le Panthéon Canadien, 1891; E. Collins, Life of Sir J. A. Macdonald, 1883; J. Pope, The Royal Tour in Canada, 1901.]

G. S. W.

JONES, Sir ALFRED LEWIS (1845–1909), man of business, born at Carmarthen on 24 February 1845, was son of Daniel Jones of Carmarthen by his wife Mary, eldest daughter of Henry Williams, rector of lanedi, South Wales. He was one of nin children, most of whom died young, and came to Liverpool with his parents when two years old. Here after being educated at different schools he began to earn his living in 1860, when he became first a ship's apprentice and then a clerk to the firm of Fletcher and Parr of Liverpool, which did business in a small way with the West Coast of Africa as agents of the African Steamship Co. Of an evening he attended classes at the Liverpool College. His energy was rewarded by his becoming manager of the firm; but owing to some changes in the business Jones on 1 Jan. 1878 started on his own account as a shipping and insurance broker, gradually making for himself a good position. Messrs. Elder, Dempster had absorbed much of his old firm's business, and in 1876 he boldly offered to take control of their concern or buy them out. Quickly raising substantial capital, he became in 1879 junior partner and was soon the master spirit of Messrs. Elder, Dempster's business. His first aim was to monopolise the whole shipping trade of the West African ports, and with this object he absorbed competing lines, British or foreign, including the British and African Steam Navigation Company, for which he paid nearly 1,000,000*l*. From shipping he passed to promotion of the general trade of the West Coast ports, including banking arrangements and hotels. In 1894 he started oilmills in Liverpool for the manufacture of the West African produce, and purchased mines in South Wales from which to draw steam coal. In 1897 he founded the Bank of British West Africa.

Jones's chief success was in revivifying the Canaries, which about 1880 were on the verge of bankruptcy. Visiting them in 1884 on coaling business, he urged their people to grow bananas; then he brought their fruit, especially bananas, to England, inaugurated a tourist traffic, employed the islands as sanatoriums (cf. Taylor's *Canary Islands*, London, 1893, p. 57) for invalided officers from the West Coast colonies, and established a coaling station and works at Las Palmas.

In 1900 Mr. Chamberlain, secretary of state for the colonies, invited Jones's co-operation in developing the trade of the West Indies. Although by no means satisfied with the government subsidy, Jones energetically carried out the contract which he undertook in 1901 to inaugurate a new steamship service with Jamaica. He built a new class of steamer, and gave liberal terms to tourists, for whom he bought new hotels at Constant Spring and Myrtle Grove. His new line he worked from the docks at Avonmouth, near Bristol, thus restoring to Bristol its ancient West Indian trade. He established a branch house at Bristol and formed a branch firm named Elders and Fyffes, which popularised the Jamaica banana in the West of England. He many times revisited the Canary Islands, and twice he was in Jamaica, the second time during the serious earthquake in Kingston in January 1907.

In the interest of the colonial territories with which he was in contact, Jones, readily following the lead of the colonial office, helped to found in 1899 the Liverpool School of Tropical Medicine, to which he gave generous support. The London School of Tropical Medicine had been established the year before. Again, in June 1902 he founded and acted as first president of the British Cotton Growing Association. In June 1903 he became chairman of the Liverpool Institute of Tropical Research. He was also president of the Liverpool Chamber of Commerce, and a member of Mr. Chamberlain's tariff commission formed in 1904. He was consul in Liverpool for the Congo Free State.

Jones was made a K.C.M.G. in 1901, and was elected an honorary fellow of Jesus College, Oxford, in 1905, by way of acknowledgment more especially of the services he rendered to tropical medicine. He also received foreign decorations from Belgium, Spain, Russia, Portugal, and the Liberian republic. He died on 13 Dec. 1909 from heart failure at his residence, Oaklands, Aigburth, Liverpool, and was buried at Anfield cemetery, Liverpool. He was unmarried; his sister, Mrs. Pinnock, lived with him from her early widowhood.

Jones's organising capacity was very great, and his energy tireless. With cheery and vigorous self-assertiveness he combined genuine benevolence and public spirit.

The Alfred Jones professorship in tropical medicine at Liverpool University was largely endowed by Jones, who bequeathed his fortune of some 500,000*l.* for educational and scientific purposes tending to benefit Liverpool or the West Coast of Africa.

A portrait in oils, presented by the merchants of Liverpool, hangs in the Walker art gallery of that city. A memorial to include a statue is proposed at Liverpool.

[Liverpool Courier, 14 Dec. 1909 (which has autobiographical notes); Times, 14 Dec. 1909; Who's Who, 1909; a sketch in Pitman's Commercial Reader, p. 118; private information from Mrs. Pinnock; personal knowledge.] C. A. H.

JONES, HENRY CADMAN (1818–1902), law reporter, born on 28 June 1818 at New Church in Winwick, Lancashire, was eldest son of Joseph Jones, at the time vicar of Winwick and afterwards of Repton, Derbyshire, by his wife Elizabeth Joanna Cooper of Derby. Educated privately he entered Trinity College, Cambridge, in 1837, and graduated B.A. in 1841 as second wrangler and second Smith's prizeman, being elected a fellow in the same year. The senior wrangler and first Smith's prizeman of his tripos was (Sir) George Gabriel Stokes [q. v. Suppl. II]. Admitted to Lincoln's Inn on 7 June 1841, and called to the bar on 24 Nov. 1845, he became a pupil of Sir John Rolt [q. v.]. From 1857 until 1865, when the official law reports were founded, Jones was associated with Sir John Peter De Gex [q. v.] in three successive series of chancery reports. He continued to report chancery appeals for the law reports until within three years of his death. In 1860 he drafted with J. W. Smith the consolidated orders of the court of chancery and later with Sir Arthur Wilson the rules under the Judicature Acts of 1873 and 1875. Of retiring disposition and of deep religious convictions he actively engaged in the work of the Religious Tract Society and took part, with his university competitor, Sir George Stokes, in the proceedings of the Victoria Institute, founded for the discussion of Christian evidences. Much leisure was spent on an unpublished concordance to the Greek Testament.

He died at St. Matthew's Gardens, St. Leonards-on-Sea, on 18 Jan. 1902, and was buried in Repton churchyard.

He married (1) on 4 Sept. 1851 Anna Maria (*d.* 10 May 1873), daughter of Robert Steevens Harrison of Bourn Abbey, Lincolnshire; (2) on 4 Sept. 1879 Eliza (*d.* 26 Oct. 1909), third daughter of the Rev. Frederick Money of Offham, Kent. By his first wife he had eight children, of whom a son and four daughters survived him. A portrait by Eden Upton Eddis [q. v. Suppl. II] belongs to the family.

[The Times, 21 Jan. 1902; Law Journal, 25 Jan. 1902; Foster, Men at the Bar; private information.] C. E. A. B.

JONES, JOHN VIRIAMU (1856–1901), physicist, born at Pentrepoeth near Swansea on 2 Jan. 1856, was second son of Thomas Jones (1819–1882) [q. v.]. His elder brother, Sir David Brynmor Jones, K.C., has been M.P. for Swansea district since 1895. John was named after John Williams, missionary of Erromango [q. v.], 'Viriamu' being the pronunciation of 'Williams' by South Sea natives. He was educated successively at a private school at Reading, at University College School, London, at the Normal College, Swansea, at University College, London, and finally at Balliol College, Oxford (1876–81). He had a distinguished university career. At London he was first in honours at matriculation, graduated B.Sc. with honours, and became university scholar in geology, being elected fellow of University College. At Balliol, where he matriculated on 24 Jan. 1876 and was the centre of a circle of singularly able undergraduates, he was elected Brackenbury scholar in natural science in 1876, and won a first class in mathematical moderations in 1877, and a first class in the final schools of mathematics in 1879 and of natural science in 1880. He graduated B.A. in 1879, and proceeded M.A. in 1883. In May 1881 he was appointed principal of Firth College (now University College), Sheffield, acting as professor of physics and mathematics. In June 1883 he was selected as the first principal of the University College of South Wales at Cardiff, and in a few years collected the sum of 70,000*l.* for building, obtaining a grant of the site from the corporation. From that time much of his energy was devoted to the movement for creating a national university of Wales, and when the charter was granted in 1893 he became the first vice-chancellor of the new Welsh University. In this capacity he had a preponderating influence in determining the course of studies in the arts and sciences, and in giving the new university's degrees a standard value.

His position in the scientific world was one of high promise and of substantial achievement. His researches were mainly directed towards the precise determination of electrical and physical standards, and to the construction of measuring instruments which should satisfy the utmost demands of engineering theory. His first paper appeared in the 'Proceedings of the Physical Society' in 1888 and treated of the mutual induction of a circle and of a coaxial helix; in 1890 he published in the 'Electrician' a determination of the ohm by the use of a Lorenz apparatus. From this time forward a series of more and more accurate determinations of this constant occupied his leisure. He was elected F.R.S. in 1894, and in 1897 he laid before the Royal Society a simplification and more general solution of the problem attacked in his first paper. In 1898 a description was given of a new ampere balance, which he did not live to see constructed. Jones's sympathies were wide and his personality attractive. He was an expert mountaineer and was a member of the Alpine Club from 1887 till death. He died at Geneva on 2 June 1901 and was buried at Swansea. A statue by Sir William Goscombe John, R.A., stands in front of the college at Cardiff. The Physical Research Laboratory at the new college buildings in Cathays Park, Cardiff, was erected in his memory. He married in 1882 Sarah Katherine, eldest daughter of W. Wills of Wylde Green, near Birmingham. She survived him without issue, and was granted in 1902 a civil list pension of 75*l.* a year.

[John Viriamu Jones and other Memories, by Prof. E. B. Poulton (with portrait), 1910; The Times, 4 June 1901; Nature, 13 June 1901; Alpine Journal, Feb. 1902.] R. S.

JONES, THOMAS RUPERT (1819–1911), geologist and palæontologist, born in Wood Street, Cheapside, London, on 1 Oct. 1819, was the son of John Jones, silk merchant and throwster (a descendant of the old Powys family of North Wales), by his wife Rhoda Burberry of Coventry. Jones was educated at private schools, first at Taunton, where his father conducted a part of his business, and afterwards at Ilminster, where he began to take interest in geology, collecting ammonites and other fossils from the stone-beds of the Upper and Middle Lias, then largely quarried in the neighbourhood. In 1835 he was apprenticed to Hugh Norris, surgeon, at Taunton, but owing to Norris's death his apprenticeship was completed with Dr. Joseph Bunny at Newbury, Berkshire, in 1842. There he carried on geological researches, results of which were published in papers on the geological history of Newbury (1854), and the geology of the Kennet Valley (1871). During the years 1842–50 he was engaged as a medical assistant, chiefly in London, and continuing his natural history studies, he gave special attention with the aid of the microscope to the foraminifera and entomostraca, both recent and fossil. As a result of these early researches his 'Monograph on the Cretaceous Entomostraca of England' was published in 1849, and in course of time he became the leading authority in Britain on the entomostracan orders of phyllopoda and ostracoda, as well as on the foraminifera.

In 1851 Jones was appointed assistant secretary of the Geological Society, then at Somerset House, where his most important duty was the editing of the society's 'Quarterly Journal,' work which he carried out with the utmost zeal and precision. As an editor, and in the knowledge he acquired of geological bibliography, he excelled. After the death of Gideon Algernon Mantell [q. v.] he edited the 3rd edition of that author's 'Geological Excursions round the Isle of Wight' (1854), the 2nd edition of the 'Medals of Creation' (1854), and the 7th edition of the 'Wonders of Geology' (2 vols. 1857–8).

In 1858 he became lecturer on geology, and in 1862 professor, at the Royal Military College, and afterwards at the Staff College, Sandhurst, resigning his post at the Geological Society in 1862, when he took up residence at Farnborough. He retired in 1880 on the abandonment by the military authorities of the teaching of geology.

During his residence in Hampshire, and, after his retirement, in London he continued his researches on microzoa, contributing many papers, some in conjunction with H. B. Brady, H. B. Holl, J. W. Kirkby, and W. K. Parker, to the 'Quarterly Journal of the Geological Society,' the 'Annals and Magazine of Natural History,' the 'Reports of the British Association,' and the 'Geological Magazine.' He edited the 'Reliquiæ Aquitanicæ' of E. Lartet and H. Christy (1875), and, with much addition and revision, the 2nd edition of F. Dixon's 'Geology of Sussex' (1878). He utilised his extensive knowledge by publishing useful summaries of information with original observations on quartz, flint, &c. (1876), on the antiquity of man (1877), on peat and peat bogs (1880), on chalk and flint (1885), on the history of the sarsens (1886, 1901), on the plateau implements of Kent (1894); articles contributed to the 'Proceedings of the Geological Association' and to local scientific societies and field clubs. In South African geology he was keenly interested; he mastered the literature, wrote many articles and reviews on the subject, and rendered much help to A. G. Bain and other pioneers in that country. Ever ready to give assistance to others, he counted as recreations the editing of friends' papers and correcting proofs.

Jones was elected F.R.S. in 1872, and in 1890 the Lyell medal was awarded to him by the council of the Geological Society. He was president of the Geologists' Association 1879–81, and president of the geological section of the British Association at Cardiff in 1891, when he gave an address on coal.

Sturdy in build, but below the average height, he was cheery in disposition and full of humour, and as a lecturer clear and fluent. During the later years of his life he resided at Chesham Bois, where he died on 13 April 1911, and was buried.

He married twice: (1) Mary, daughter of William Harris of Charing, Kent, who had a fine collection of chalk fossils; they had issue, two sons and three daughters; the eldest son, William Rupert, became assistant librarian to the Geological Society; (2) Charlotte Ashburnham, daughter of Archibald Archer (an instructor in portrait-painting in the Royal Academy schools), by whom he had two sons and three daughters. His widow was granted a civil list pension of 50*l.* in 1912.

His published works include the following monographs issued by the Palæontographical Society: on 'Cretaceous Entomostraca' (1849; supp. with Dr. G. J. Hinde, 1890); 'Tertiary Entomostraca' (1856; supp. with C. D. Sherborn, 1889); 'Fossil Estheriæ' (1862); 'Foraminifera of the Crag' (1866 and 1895–7); 'Carboniferous Bivalved Entomostraca,' with Dr. G. S. Brady (1874); and 'Palæozoic Phyllopoda,' with Dr. Henry Woodward (1888).

[Biography (with portrait) in Geol. Mag., Jan. 1893; Supp. notice, with portrait, on 90th birthday, ibid. Nov. 1909; Men and Women of the Time, 1899; obit. by H. B. W., Nature, 27 April 1911. The best published portrait is in Life and Letters of Sir Joseph Prestwich, 1899, p. 376.] H. B. W.

JONES, WILLIAM WEST (1838–1908), archbishop of Capetown, born at South Hackney on 11 May 1838, was the sixth and youngest son of Edward Henry Jones, wine merchant, of Mark Lane, by his wife Mary Emma Collier. From Merchant Taylors' School, which he entered in April 1845, he passed in 1856 as a foundation scholar to St. John's College, Oxford. He took a second class in classical moderations in

1858, but owing to ill-health from overwork was unable to take honours in the final schools, and was given an honorary fourth both in the final classical school and in mathematics. From 1859 until his marriage in 1879 he was fellow of St. John's, and was made an honorary fellow of the college in 1893. He graduated B.A. in 1860, proceeded M.A. in 1863, B.D. in 1869, and was made an hon. D.D. on being consecrated a bishop in 1874. Ordained deacon in 1861 and priest in 1862, he was licensed to the curacy of St. Matthew's in the City Road, and from 1864 to 1874 held the living (in the gift of his college) of Summertown on the outskirts of Oxford.

He was preacher at the old Whitehall Chapel (1870–2), and rural dean of Oxford (1871–4). On 17 May 1874 Jones was consecrated in Westminster Abbey, bishop of Capetown, in succession to Robert Gray [q. v.], first bishop of Capetown and metropolitan of South Africa. Jones accepted the difficult post only on the urgent advice of Samuel Wilberforce, bishop of Oxford, with whom he was in cordial relations (*Guardian*, 27 May 1908). The protracted conflict between Gray and Bishop Colenso [q. v.] as to the South African church's independence of the Church of England was still a living issue on Jones's appointment. But when at his consecration he took the oath of allegiance to A. C. Tait, archbishop of Canterbury, he and the archbishop signed a document which safeguarded the independent rights and privileges of the South African church. The thirty-four years of Jones's episcopate were years of constant war of races in South Africa. But he steadily sought to encourage peace in both church and state without sacrificing principles or concealing his own views. In 1897 the see of Capetown was elevated to the dignity of an archbishopric. A strong high churchman and a member of the English Church Union, by virtue of his simplicity of character, courtesy, bonhomie, business aptitude, and dignified presence, Jones won the respect and friendship of English and Dutch, high church and low church.

At the close of the Boer war in 1902 he took part in the great peace thanksgiving service at Pretoria, and was busy at his death in raising funds for the completion of the Anglican cathedral at Capetown, in memory of those who had fallen in the war. Early in 1908 he came to England to attend the Lambeth conference, and died at the Lizard on 21 May 1908; he was buried in Holywell cemetery, Oxford, the third archbishop to be buried at Oxford, the other two being Laud and Juxon, all three members of St. John's College. He married in 1879 Emily, daughter of John Allen of Altrincham, Cheshire, and had two sons.

A portrait by Charles Wellington Furse, A.R.A., is in the possession of his widow, and another by William Orpen, A.R.A., is in the hall of St. John's College, Oxford. A third by Mr. C. H. Thompson is in the Diocesan College, Capetown; and a fourth by Mr. Tennyson Cole in the Diocesan Library, Capetown. A recumbent statue by Mr. Hartwell is in the memorial chapel of the cathedral at Capetown.

[Anglo-African Who's Who, 1907; The Times, 22 May 1908; Guardian, 27 May 1908; Cape Church Monthly, June and July 1908; Wirgman's History of the English Church and People in South Africa 1895; private information.] C. P. L.

K

KANE, ROBERT ROMNEY (1842–1902), writer on Irish land law, born at Gracefield, Blackrock, county Dublin, on 28 Oct. 1842, was eldest son of Sir Robert Kane [q. v.], first president of the Queen's College, Cork. His mother, Katherine, daughter of Henry Baily, of Berkshire, and niece of Francis Baily [q. v.], president of the Royal Astronomical Society, wrote (before her marriage) a well-known 'Irish Flora.' After attending Dr. Quinn's private school in Harcourt Street Kane passed to Queen's College, Cork, whence he graduated M.A. in 1862, and received in 1882 the honorary degree of LL.D. Becoming a member of Lincoln's Inn, he studied law in London in the chambers of an eminent conveyancing lawyer, W. H. G. Bagshawe, and in 1865 he graduated LL.B. with honours in London University. Being called to the Irish bar the same year he went the Munster circuit and soon enjoyed a good practice. In 1873 he was appointed professor of equity, jurisprudence, and international law at the King's Inns, and, acquiring the reputation of an authority on Irish land legislation, he was in 1881 appointed a legal assistant commissioner under the Land Law Act of that year. He retained that post till 1892, when he was made county court judge for the united counties of Kildare, Carlow, Wexford and Wicklow.

Kane collaborated with Francis Nolan, Q.C., in an admirable treatise on the 'Statute Law of Landlord and Tenant in Ireland' (1892). But the whole subject of Irish history, literature, and antiquities appealed to him. He was a member of the Royal Irish Academy, a fellow of the Royal Society of Antiquaries of Ireland, for many years one of the two honorary secretaries of the Royal Dublin Society, and a trustee of the National Library of Ireland. His edition of 'Lectures on Irish History,' by his friend A. G. Richey [q. v.], published in 1887 under the slightly misleading title of 'A Short History of the Irish People,' displayed wide reading, ripe judgment, and independence. After some years of feeble health he died at his residence, 4 Fitzwilliam Place, Dublin, on 26 March 1902.

Kane married on 29 Dec. 1875 Ellinor Louisa, second daughter of David Coffey, taxing master in chancery, by whom he had two sons and three daughters. The elder son, Harold, lieutenant in the 1st battalion of the South Lancashire regiment, fell in the Boer war while fighting against great odds on the summit of Mount Itala on 26 Sept. 1901 (*Irish Times*, 4 Oct. 1901).

[Information from Kane's lifelong friend and brother-in-law, Mr. Valentine J. Coppinger, Dublin; The Times, 28 March 1902; Ann. Reg. 1902.] R. D.

KEAY, JOHN SEYMOUR (1839–1909), Anglo-Indian politician, born at Bathgate, Linlithgowshire, on 30 March 1839, was younger of the two sons of John Keay (*d.* 15 July 1841), minister of the Church of Scotland, of Bathgate, by his wife Agnes Straiton (*d.* 3 June 1864). Educated at Madras College, St. Andrews, Keay was apprenticed in 1856 to the Commercial Bank of Scotland, and in 1862 went to India to manage branches of the Government Bank of Bengal, which was recently started to develop the cotton trade between India and England. He next entered the service of Sir Salar Jung, minister of Hyderabad. After a successful public career he opened a private banking and mercantile business at Hyderabad, and founded the cotton spinning and weaving mills now known as the Hyderabad (Deccan) Spinning and Weaving Co. Ltd.; he remained a director of the company until his death.

After twenty years in India Keay returned to England in 1882, and busily engaged in both home and Indian politics. In an exhaustive treatise entitled 'Spoiling the Egyptians, a Tale of Shame told from the Blue Books' (1882, three editions) he warmly protested against the claim of the Indian government to the province of Berar in Hyderabad, and his voluminous protest was loudly upheld by the radical party in England (cf. H. M. HYNDMAN's *Record of an Adventurous Life*, 1911, p. 170). He sympathised with the native Indian cry for a larger share in the government, and was a member of the British committee of the Indian National Congress. In 'The Great Imperial Danger: an Impossible War in the near Future' (1887) he deprecated the fear of war with Russia, and discussed with first-hand knowledge the Afghan frontier question. As an advanced liberal, he unsuccessfully contested West Newington at the general election in Feb. 1886, but he won a seat at the bye-election for Elgin and Nairn on 8 Oct. 1889. Keay constantly intervened in the debates on the land purchase bill of 1890, concerning which he published an elaborate 'Exposure,' and won the reputation of a bore (cf. LUCY, *Diary of Salisbury Parliament*, 1892, p. 371 seq., with sketch portrait by Harry Furniss). He was re-elected at the general election of 1892, but was defeated after a close contest in that of July 1895, and was again unsuccessful in the Tamworth division of Warwickshire in January 1906, when he attacked tariff reformers in 'The Fraud of the Protection Cry.' He had a country residence at Minchinhampton, Gloucestershire, and was president of the Stroud (Gloucestershire) liberal club. He died on 27 June 1909 at his London residence, 44 Bassett Road, North Kensington, and his remains were cremated at Golder's Green.

He married on 22 Oct. 1878 Nina, second daughter of William Carne Vivian of Penzance. She died on 16 Jan. 1885, leaving two daughters. A caricature by 'Spy' appeared in 'Vanity Fair' (1892).

[The Times, 29 June and 24 Aug. 1909; India, 2 July 1909, p. 3; Thacker's Indian Directory, 1910; Gloucester Journal, 28 Aug. 1909; Linlithgowshire Gazette, 2 July 1909; Hansard's Parl. Debates, 1889–95; Dod's Parl. Companion, 1890; Debrett's House of Commons; F. H. McCalmont, Parl. Poll Book, 1910, pt. 2, 81; Who's Who, 1909; Brit. Mus. Cat.; private information.] C. W.

KEETLEY, CHARLES ROBERT BELL (1848–1909), surgeon, born on 13 Sept. 1848 at Grimsby, was son of Robert

Keetley by his wife (born Waterland). Both his father and mother came of a seafaring stock. His father, a shipbuilder and a mayor of Grimsby, fell into financial straits. The son, who was mainly brought up by his grandparents and by his uncle, T. B. Keetley, a medical practitioner of Grimsby, was educated at Browne's school there, and acted as 'surgery help' or unarticled apprentice to his uncle during the last years of his school life. He then attended the lectures on botany and anatomy at the Hull school of medicine. He entered St. Bartholomew's Hospital in 1871, matriculated at the London University, and in 1874 obtained the two gold medals at the intermediate examination in medicine, one for anatomy, the other for organic chemistry, materia medica, and pharmaceutical chemistry. He took no degree. He was admitted M.R.C.S.England, and F.R.C.S. in 1876. He became L.R.C.P. in 1873. After serving in 1875 as house-surgeon to the Queen's Hospital, Birmingham, and taking general practice at Bungay in Suffolk, he was from 1876 to 1878 an assistant demonstrator of anatomy in the medical school of St. Bartholomew's Hospital.

In 1878 he was elected assistant surgeon at the West London Hospital, and with this hospital he was associated until his death. During his thirty years' service, and mainly by his advice, the hospital grew from a small suburban venture into a great charity, to which was attached a post-graduate medical school of the first importance. At the outset Keetley introduced into the wards and operating theatre the antiseptic methods of modern surgery before they had been adopted to any great extent by the other hospitals in London. He advocated the operation of appendicotomy and wrote a valuable handbook on orthopædic surgery (London, 1900). In 1882 he was foremost in founding, and was the first president of, the West London Medico-Chirurgical Society. He also originated and organised with Mr. Herbert Chambers an army medical civilian reserve, which was afterwards merged into the territorial force as the Third London General Hospital corps.

A slight but incurable deafness and want of business aptitude hampered Keetley's professional success. A keen athlete in early life, he was well known as a football player, boxer, and oarsman; he was a skilful artist and caricaturist with pen and pencil, and had a gift for impromptu rhymes. He died on 4 Dec. 1909 at Brighton, and was buried in Kensal Green cemetery.

He married Anna, daughter of Henry Holmes Long of the East India Company, but had no children.

Keetley, who was co-editor of the 'Annals of Surgery,' vols. i.–xiv. (London and New York, 1885–91), published: 1. 'The Student's Guide to the Medical Profession,' 1878; 2nd edit. 1885. 2. 'An Index of Surgery,' 1881; 4th edit. 1887. 3. 'Orthopædic Surgery; a Handbook,' 1900. 4. 'Kallos. A Treatise on the Scientific Culture of Personal Beauty and the Cure of Ugliness,' 1883; this work deals with the influence of Hellenic culture on the world's ideal of beauty, and in it Keetley anticipated some of the ideals of the later eugenics school.

[Lancet, 1909, vol. 2, p. 1788 (with portrait); Brit. Med. Journal, 1909, vol. 2, p. 1721 (with portrait); West London Medical Journal, January 1910; 'In Memoriam C. B. Keetley,' by Herbert W. Chambers (with portrait); additional information kindly given by Dr. G. S. Stephenson of Great Grimsby; personal knowledge.] D'A. P.

KEKEWICH, Sir ARTHUR (1832–1907), judge, born on 26 July 1832 at Peamore, Exeter, was second son of Samuel Trehawke Kekewich of Peamore, the head of an old Devonshire family, and M.P. for Exeter in 1826 and for South Devon in 1858, by his first wife Agatha Maria Sophia, daughter of John Langston of Sarsden, Oxfordshire. His elder brother Trehawke Kekewich (1823–1909) took a prominent part in Devonshire affairs. Sir George William Kekewich, formerly permanent secretary of the board of education and M.P. for Exeter (1906–10), was his half-brother and Major-general Sir Robert Kekewich, K.C.B., the defender of Kimberley, was his nephew. Educated at Eton and at Balliol College, Oxford, where he matriculated on 11 March 1850, Arthur Kekewich was placed in the second class by the mathematical moderators in 1852, and graduated B.A. in 1854 with a first class in literæ humaniores and a second in the final school of mathematics. In the same year he was elected to a fellowship at Exeter College, which he held until his marriage on 23 Sept. 1858, with Marianne, daughter of James William Freshfield. He proceeded M.A. in 1856. Having entered as a student at Lincoln's Inn on 8 Nov. 1854, he was called to the bar on 7 June 1858. His connection through his wife with the great firm of Freshfield & Son, solicitors, gave him an excellent start, and brought him at an early period in his professional career the post of junior standing counsel to the Bank of England; for many years he was in the enjoyment of one of the largest junior practices at the chancery bar. He was made Q.C. on 4 May 1877, and a bencher of his inn on 4 July 1881. Though he possessed a sound knowledge of law and practice, he proved deficient in the qualities of a leader. He never obtained a firm footing in any one of the chancery courts, and his business dwindled to very modest proportions. He unsuccessfully contested, in the conservative interest, Coventry in 1880 and Barnstaple in 1885. There was some surprise in Lincoln's Inn when on the retirement of Vice-Chancellor Bacon [q. v.], in November 1886, Kekewich was appointed by Lord Halsbury to fill the vacancy, and he received the honour of knighthood early in the following year. On the bench Kekewich showed an expedition and despatch not usually associated with proceedings in Chancery; he had a thorough knowledge of the minutiæ of equity practice, and was especially conversant with the details arising out of the administration of estates in chancery. But his quickness of perception and his celerity in decision were apt to impair the accuracy of his judgments, and he failed to keep sufficiently in control a natural tendency to exuberance of speech. Most kindly and courteous in private life, he was apt to be irritable on the bench. His judgments were appealed against with uncomplimentary frequency, and though he was occasionally avenged by the House of Lords, it was his lot to be reversed in the court of appeal to an extent which would have been disconcerting to a judge of less sanguine temperament. Several of his juniors on the bench were promoted over his head to the court of appeal; but by the legal profession his shrewdness, sense of duty, and determination to administer justice with the minimum of delay were fully recognised. He died after a very short illness on 22 Nov. 1907 at his house in Devonshire Place; there were no arrears in his court, and he had sent, a day or two before his death, his only two reserved judgments to be read by one of his colleagues. He was buried at Exminster near Exeter. Kekewich was a strong churchman and conservative. A man of fine physique and active habits, a keen shot and fisherman, he became in his later years an enthusiastic golf-player. His wife with two sons and five daughters survived him. A caricature by 'Spy' appeared in 'Vanity Fair' in 1895.

[The Times, 23 Nov. 1907; personal knowledge.] J. B. A.

KELLY, MARY ANNE, 'EVA' (1826–1910), Irish poetess. [See under O'DOHERTY, KEVIN IZOD.]

KELLY, WILLIAM (1821–1906), Plymouth brother and biblical critic, only son of an Ulster squire, was born at Millisle, co. Down, in May 1821. His only sister married a Canadian clergyman. He was educated at Downpatrick and at Trinity College, Dublin, where he graduated B.A. with the highest honours in classics. Left fatherless at an early age, he became tutor in the family of the then Seigneur of Sark. Though he was brought up as a protestant churchman he had leanings to Puseyism, but became a Plymouth brother in 1841, and shortly after left Sark for Guernsey. At the age of twenty-four he met John Nelson Darby [q. v.], the founder of the Darbyites (a seceding sect of the Plymouth brethren), became Darby's chief lieutenant, and edited his collected writings (34 vols. 1867–83). In 1879 Kelly supported Dr. Edward Cronin, who was excommunicated, in his dispute with Darby on a question of church discipline. Kelly and his party maintained the superiority of individual conscience over church control in matters not fundamental, but they remained true to all of Darby's narrow doctrinal views except as to the baptism of infants. Charles Haddon Spurgeon said of Kelly that he was 'born for the universe,' but 'narrowed his mind by Darbyism.'

After nearly thirty years (1844–71) in Guernsey, Kelly spent his last thirty-five years at Blackheath. He died at The Firs, Denmark Road, Exeter, on 27 March 1906, and was buried near his second wife in Charlton cemetery. He married (1) Miss Montgomery, of Guernsey; (2) Elizabeth Emily (*d.* 1884), daughter of H. Gipps, rector of St. Peter's, Hereford.

Shortly before his death Kelly presented his library of 15,000 volumes to the town of Middlesbrough.

Kelly was a prolific writer and lecturer on scriptural subjects. From 1848 to 1850 he edited the 'Prospect' and from 1857 to his death the 'Bible Treasury' (still in progress), periodicals devoted to the discussion of scriptural topics from the ultra-protestant point of view. From 1854–6 he contributed to the 'Christian Annotator,' for which Samuel Prideaux Tregelles [q. v.] and Philip

Henry Gosse [q. v.] also wrote. As editor he came into contact with theologians of every school of thought, with Dean Alford [q. v.], Principal Thomas Charles Edwards [q. v. Suppl. I], and others. His writings displayed much logical faculty. A keen critic and controversialist, and an uncompromising opponent of all forms of higher biblical criticism, he obtained a wide reputation as a scholar. His critical Greek text of the 'Revelation of St. John,' 1860 (the first Greek work printed in Guernsey), met with the warm approval of Heinrich von Ewald, the German theologian.

His published works, whose titles fill four pages of the British Museum catalogue, include: 1. 'The Book of Revelation, translated from the Greek,' 1849. 2. 'Lectures on the Book of Revelation,' 1861. 3. 'Lectures on the Second Coming and Kingdom of Jesus Christ,' 1865. 4. 'Lectures on the New Testament Doctrine of the Holy Spirit,' 1867; new edit. 1906. 5. 'On the Gospel of Matthew,' 1868. 6. 'Lectures introductory to the Study of the Pentateuch . . .,' 1871. 7. 'Isaiah expounded,' 1871; new edit. 1897. 8. 'Lectures on the Earlier Historical Books of the Old Testament,' 1874. 9. 'Elements of Prophecy,' 1876. 10. 'In the Beginning, and the Adamic Earth,' 1894; revised edit. 1907. 11. 'The Gospel of John expounded,' 1898. 12. 'The Revelation expounded,' 1901; 3rd edit. 1904. 13. 'God's Inspiration of the Scriptures,' 1903.

[The Times, 31 March 1906; Memories of the Life and Last Days of William Kelly, by Heyman Wreford, 1906 (with portrait); E. E. Whitfield on Plymouth Brethren and William Kelly, in Schaff-Herzog's Religious Encyclopædia, new edit. 1908–11; W. Blair Neatby's History of the Plymouth Brethren, 2nd edit. 1902; William Kelly as a Theologian in Expositor, 7th ser. No. 17; Brit. Mus. Cat.; information supplied by Mr. F. E. Race, of Paternoster Row.] W. B. O.

KELVIN, first Baron. [See Thomson, Sir William (1824–1907), man of science.]

KEMBALL, Sir ARNOLD BURROWES (1820–1908), general, colonel commandant royal artillery, born in Bombay on 18 Nov. 1820, was one of five sons of Surgeon-general Vero Shaw Kemball, of the Bombay medical staff, by his wife Marianne, daughter of Major-general Shaw, formerly of the Black Watch. Kemball's brothers did good service in the Bombay presidency: George and Alick in the Bombay cavalry, Vero Seymour in the Bombay artillery, Charles Gordon in the civil service, rising to be a judge of the supreme court, and John in the 26th Bombay infantry. Passing through the Military College at Addiscombe, Arnold received his commission as a second-lieutenant in the Bombay artillery on 11 Dec. 1837. He served in the first Afghan war with a troop of Bombay horse artillery, and was present at the storming and capture of Ghazni on 28 July 1839 and at the subsequent occupation of Kabul. On the march back to Bombay he took part in the capture of the fortress of Khelat. For this campaign he received the medal. After his return to the Bombay presidency he passed in the native languages, and was appointed assistant political agent in the Persian Gulf, in the neighbourhood of which he remained from 1842 until the close of his military career in 1878. Kemball, who was promoted captain in 1851, took part in the Persian war of 1856–7, and was specially mentioned in the despatches of Sir James Outram [q. v.], who had applied for his services. Lord Canning, the governor-general of India, in general orders of 18 June 1857 especially commended his share in the brilliant expedition against Ahwaz. For the Persian campaign Kemball received a brevet majority, the C.B., and the Indian general service medal, with clasp for Persia. At the close of the war Kemball resumed his political duties in the Persian Gulf, and two years later was appointed consul-general at Baghdad. In 1860 he became lieut.-colonel, and in 1863 attained the rank of colonel in the royal artillery. In 1866, on the extension of the order of the Star of India, he became one of the first knights commander, and in 1873 he was attached to the suite of the Shah of Persia during that monarch's visit to England.

In 1875 Kemball was nominated British delegate on the international commission for delimiting the Turco-Persian frontier, and on the outbreak of the war between Turkey and Servia he was appointed military commissioner with the Turkish army in the field. He was present at all the operations in the vicinity of Nisch and Alexinatz, and at the close of the campaign was nominated president of the international commission to delimit the frontiers between Turkey and Servia. His intimate knowledge of the Turkish language, added to his imperturbable calmness under fire, endeared him to the Turkish soldiery. In the spring of the following year, on the outbreak of the war with Russia, he was transferred in his former capacity to the Turkish army in Asia. The Turkish troops continued to show the fullest confidence in his judgment and gallantry, and fully appreciated his kindness to the wounded. Wherever the fight was hottest he was on observation (*The Times*, 20 July 1878). The Russians were well aware of the veneration in which Kemball was held by the Turks, and like the Servians in the preceding campaign were under the mistaken impression that he was in command of the Turkish forces. After the battle of Zewin Duz on 16 June 1877 a determined effort was made to capture him. Cossack pursuers were only thrown off after an exciting chase of more than twenty miles, and Kemball by a daring swim across the Araxes river found shelter in a Turkish camp. He firmly protested against Kurdish atrocities, and at his insistence the Ottoman commander-in-chief took steps to suppress them.

At the close of the Russo-Turkish war Kemball was made K.C.B. and was promoted lieut.-general. The Sultan also bestowed on him the medal for the campaign. Recalled to England, Kemball was designated to be military adviser to Lord Beaconsfield's special mission to the Berlin congress, but his uncompromising objection to the cession of Batum to Russia led to the withdrawal of this offer, and he was not afterwards employed. At the close of the Russo-Turkish war he was entertained by the officers of the royal artillery at Woolwich.

Kemball took a keen interest in the construction of the then projected railway from Constantinople to the Persian Gulf, and was more or less intimately bound up with the Euphrates Valley railway scheme (see *Journal of the Royal United Service Institution*, June 1878). After his retirement from active service he was prominently associated with Sir William Mackinnon [q. v. Suppl. I] and others in the development of East Africa, and was one of the founders in 1888 and first chairman of the Imperial East African Company. To his prescience is mainly due the construction of the Uganda railway and the sovereignty of Great Britain over the East African Protectorate (see *The Times*, 20 Sept. 1892).

Kemball, who attained the rank of full general in Feb. 1880, died at his London residence, 62 Lowndes Square, Knightsbridge, on 21 Sept. 1908, and was buried in Kensal Green cemetery. He married in 1868 his cousin, Anna Frances, third daughter of Alexander Nesbitt Shaw of the Bombay civil service. His only daughter, Wynford Rose, married in 1902 Bentley Lyonel, third Baron Tollemache. A tablet to his memory has been erected in St. George's garrison church, Woolwich, by his widow. A cartoon by 'Ape' was reproduced in 'Vanity Fair' in 1878.

[The Times, 10 Jan. and 21 June 1878, 20 Sept. 1892, and 22 Sept. 1908; Illustrated London News, 21 July and 29 Sept. 1877; Journal Royal United Service Institution, June 1878; Sir F. Goldsmid, Life of Sir James Outram, 1880; G. W. Hunt's History of the Persian War; C. B. Norman's Armenia and the Campaign of 1877, 1878; C. Williams, The Armenian Campaign, 1878; Royal Artillery Institution Leaflets, Oct. 1908 and Feb. 1909; Amoris memoria, privately printed by Lady Kemball.] C. B. N.

KEMBLE, HENRY (1848–1907), actor, born in London on 1 June 1848, was son of Henry Kemble, captain of the 37th foot. Charles Kemble [q. v.] was his grandfather. He was educated by his aunt, Fanny Kemble [q. v. Suppl. I], at Bury St. Edmunds and King's College school, London. In 1865 he entered the privy council office, but devoted most of his time to amateur theatricals. Yielding to the hereditary bias, he made his professional debut on the stage at the Theatre Royal, Dublin, on 7 Oct. 1867, and for a year and a half remained a minor member of Harris's stock company there. Subsequently he acted old men and character parts at Edinburgh, Glasgow, Scarborough, and Newcastle-on-Tyne. On 29 Aug. 1874 he made his first appearance in London at Drury Lane, under Chatterton's management, as Tony Foster in a revival of 'Amy Robsart.' On 26 Sept. he was the original Philip of France in Halliday's 'Richard Cœur de Lion,' and later was favourably received as Dr. Caius in 'The Merry Wives of Windsor.' In 1875 he joined John Hare's company at the Court Theatre, and was seen to advantage as Dr. Penguin in 'A Scrap of Paper.' On 30 Sept. 1876 he appeared at the Prince of Wales's as Crossley Beck in 'Peril,' then beginning his long association and friendship with the Bancrofts. Among his later characters here were Dolly Spanker in 'London Assurance,' Sir Oliver Surface in 'The School for Scandal,' and Algie Fairfax in 'Diplomacy.' On 27 Sept. 1879 he was the original Mr Trelawney Smith in 'Duty,' an adaptation by Albery from Sardou.

Following the Bancrofts to the Haymarket, Kemble appeared there on the opening night of their management (31 January 1880) as Mr. Stout in 'Money,' and subsequently played Dr. Sutcliffe in a revival of 'School.' During the recess he toured the provinces with Miss Ellen Terry, returning to the Haymarket on 20 Sept. to play Captain Mouser in a revival of Buckstone's 'Leap Year.' A few weeks later he played Sir Lucius O'Trigger to the Bob Acres of John S. Clarke. On 26 Oct. 1881 he was the original Cranmer in W. S. Raleigh's 'Queen and Cardinal,' but the play proved a failure, and Kemble went for a time with Mrs. Scott-Siddons (the Anne Boleyn of the cast) into the provinces. On 15 Feb. 1882 he reappeared at the Court in two new characterisations—as the Rev. Mr. Jones in D. G. Boucicault's adaptation 'My Little Girl' and Mr. Justice Bunby in Burnand's farcical comedy 'The Manager.' Other original characters followed. On 20 July 1885 he played his old part of Mr. Snarl in 'Masks and Faces' at the Bancroft farewell.

A variety of engagements of small importance occupied him for the next fifteen years, during which he was the original Mr. Parr on 5 Jan. 1888 in Robert Buchanan's 'Partners' at the Haymarket, where he remained for some time, and he made an acceptable Polonius at the Theatre Royal, Manchester. on 9 Sept. 1891, the occasion of (Sir) Herbert Beerbohm Tree's first performance of 'Hamlet.' Subsequently joining Sir Herbert Beerbohm Tree at Her Majesty's, he was, on 1 Feb. 1902, the original Ctesippus in Stephen Phillips's 'Ulysses.' On 4 Nov. following he was seen to advantage at the Duke of York's as the Earl of Loam in Mr. J. M. Barrie's 'The Admirable Crichton.' His last appearance on the stage was made at the Criterion in April 1907 as Archibald Coke in a revival of Mr. Henry Arthur Jones's 'The Liars.' On 17 Nov. following he died, unmarried, at Jersey.

Kemble was an excellent comedian, and revelled in strongly marked character parts. His stout figure and somewhat short stature enhanced the comicality of his mien. Much beloved by his associates, he was affectionately known at the Garrick Club as 'The Beetle,' due to his early habit of wearing a long brown cloak with a large collar, which he pulled over his head in cold weather.

[Pascoe's Dramatic List; Bancroft Memoirs; Ellen Terry's Story of My Life; Dramatic Notes for 1881–6; William Archer's Theatrical World of 1896; Charles Brookfield's Random Reminiscences, 1902; Green Room Book, 1908.] W. J. L.

KENSIT, JOHN (1853–1902), protestant agitator, born in the City of London on 12 Feb. 1853, was only son of John Kensit by his wife Elizabeth Anne. Educated at Bishopsgate ward schools, he became, in 1868, a choir-boy at the church of St. Lawrence Jewry, under Benjamin Morgan Cowie [q. v.], afterwards dean of Exeter. He subsequently entered the warehouse of Messrs. J. and R. Morley as draper's assistant, but found the work uncongenial. About 1871 he opened a small stationer's shop in East Road, Hoxton, and soon extended his business by becoming a sub-postmaster. From an early age he was interested in the cause of militant protestantism, and actively engaged in agitation against what he deemed romanising tendencies in the Anglican church. In 1885 he started the City protestant book depot in Paternoster Row. The bookshop rapidly expanded into a publishing house. Profits were derived not only from evangelical sermons and ultra-protestant pamphlets but from strongly anti-sacerdotal publications which exposed regardless of decorum alleged procedure of the confessional, and paraded isolated instances of monastic asceticism as practices generally prevalent in the Church of England. To advance his views he instituted and edited 'The Churchman's Magazine.' In 1890 the Protestant Truth Society was founded, of which Kensit became secretary. Subscriptions flowed in, and the credit of the society was not shaken by the attacks in the press on the failure of the secretary to issue a balance sheet (*Truth*, 14 Feb. 1895). In 1894 and again in 1897 Kensit was an unsuccessful candidate for the London school board.

The ecclesiastical agitation of 1898, 1899, and 1900, caused by the growth of ritualism, gave Kensit his opportunity. He now organised a band of itinerant young preachers, named 'Wicliffites,' who created disturbances in ritualistic churches throughout the country. In January 1897 he first attained general notoriety by publicly objecting in the church of St. Mary-le-Bow to the confirmation of Mandell Creighton [q. v. Suppl. I] as bishop of London. Early in 1898 he began an organised anti-ritualist campaign in London. Selecting St. Ethelburga's, Bishopsgate, as the object of an attack, he qualified himself by residence as a parishioner, and frequently interrupted the services. On Good Friday 1898 he protested against the adoration of the cross at St. Cuthbert's, Philbeach Gardens. He was fined 3*l.* for brawling in church, but was acquitted on appeal to the Clerkenwell quarter sessions. Bishop Creighton forbade the extreme practices to which Kensit objected, but disregarded his threats of further interference. In the same year at the Bradford church congress Kensit denounced the bishop's weakness.

At the general election of 1900 Kensit unsuccessfully contested Brighton as an independent conservative, and made the district the scene of frequent anti-ritualist disturbances. In 1901 he again achieved prominence in London by his public protests in the church of St. Mary-le-Bow against the elections of bishop Winnington-Ingram to the see of London, and of Charles Gore to that of Worcester. In the autumn of 1902 he and his followers transferred their activities to Liverpool, where their propaganda excited violent outbreaks. After addressing a meeting at Claughton Hall, Birkenhead, Kensit was returning to Liverpool, when a chisel was flung at him and severely wounded him in the left eye-lid. Kensit was removed to the Liverpool Royal Infirmary, and died on 18 Oct. 1902 of double pneumonia, unconnected with the wound. He was buried in Hampstead cemetery. John Mackeever, who was charged with flinging the chisel, was tried for manslaughter and acquitted at the Liverpool assizes on 11 Dec. 1902. A sincere but narrow-minded fanatic, Kensit was unfitted by education and judgment to lead the protestant cause. On 14 Sept. 1878 he married Edith Mary, daughter of Alfred Eves of the Corn Exchange, Mark Lane, who survived him with two daughters and a son, Mr. J. A. Kensit, who carried on his father's propaganda.

[J. C. Wilcox, John Kensit, 1903 (portrait frontispiece); J. Britten, A Prominent Protestant, 1899; The Times, and Liverpool Post, 9 Oct. 1902; Churchman's Magazine, 1892 and 1902; Louise Creighton, Life of Mandell Creighton, 1904, ii. 288 seq.]

G. S. W.

KENT, CHARLES, whose full Christian names were William Charles Mark (1823–1902), author and journalist, born in London on 3 Nov. 1823, was eldest son in a family of five sons and two daughters of William Kent, R.N., and grandson of William Kent, captain R.N. [q. v.]. His mother was Ellen, only daughter of Charles Baggs, judge of the vice-admiralty court, Demerara, and sister of Charles Michael Baggs, Roman catholic bishop [q. v.]. Both parents were Roman catholics, and Kent was educated first at Prior Park, Bath, and then at St. Mary's College, Oscott (13 Feb. till Christmas 1838). At an early age he adopted the profession of letters and began writing prose and verse. At Christmas 1845, when only twenty-two years of age, he succeeded William Frederick Deacon [q. v.] as editor of the 'Sun,' an evening newspaper, which, founded in 1792 by William Pitt, had sunk into a struggling condition. Its politics had long been liberal, and it advocated free trade. Since 1833 it was the sole property of Murdo Young, whose daughter Kent married in 1853. In 1850 Kent purchased the paper of his future father-in-law for 2024*l.* Kent remained both editor and proprietor, but he failed, despite his zeal and industry, to restore the fortunes of the paper, which expired on 28 Feb. 1871.

The 'Sun' was one of the first journals to publish reviews of books, and Kent was a voluminous contributor of these as well as of leading articles. Some of his political sketches were published separately under pseudonyms. 'The Derby Ministry, by Mark Rochester,' appeared in 1858 and was reissued as 'Conservative Statesmen'; 'The Gladstone Government, by A Templar,' followed in 1869. After his connection with the 'Sun' ceased, Kent edited, from 1874 to 1881, the 'Weekly Register,' a Roman catholic periodical.

Meanwhile Kent was called to the bar at the Middle Temple (10 June 1859), but he did not practise. He was busy seeking a literary reputation in fields outside journalism. 'Catholicity in the Dark Ages, by an Oscotian' (1847) gave promise of enlightened learning. 'The Vision of Cagliostro, a Tale of the Five Senses,' which appeared in 'Blackwood's' in 1847, was reissued in the first series of 'Tales from Blackwood.' His earliest independent volume under his own name, 'Aletheia, or the Doom of Mythology; with other Poems' (1850), showed poetic thought and feeling. One of the poems, 'Lamartine in February [1848]' accidentally came to the notice of the French poet and statesman three years after its publication and drew from him an enthusiastic letter of gratitude. At the same time Kent wrote largely for 'Household Words' and 'All the Year Round,' and came into intimate relations with Dickens, the editor and proprietor. To the 'New Monthly Magazine' he contributed 'Stereoscopic Glimpses,' twenty poems descriptive of as many English poets' home life, beginning with Shakespeare at Shottery and ending with Wordsworth at Rydal. These he collected in 1862 as

'Dreamland; or Poets in their Haunts.' He welcomed Longfellow to England in a poem which appeared in 'The Times,' 3 July 1868. A collected edition of Kent's 'Poems' was published in 1870.

Kent's literary acquaintance was large. It early included, besides Charles Dickens, Leigh Hunt, both the first and the second Lord Lytton, Charles Reade, Robert Browning, George Meredith, and Matthew Arnold. He caused Leigh Hunt's line, 'Write me as one that loves his fellow-men,' to be placed on Hunt's tomb at Kensal Green. Dickens wrote a letter to Kent within an hour of the novelist's death (8 June 1870), and Kent presented it to the British Museum in 1879. The first letter which he received from the second Lord Lytton (4 July 1866) he also presented to the Museum in 1887.

His later years were largely devoted to preparing popular complete editions of the works of great writers. The collected works of Burns appeared in 1874. In 1875 he brought out a centenary edition of Lamb's works with a memoir which contained among other new facts an authentic record of Lamb's relations with Frances Maria Kelly, the actress, the information coming from Miss Kelly herself. There succeeded editions of Thomas Moore (1879), Father Prout (1881), besides 'Leigh Hunt as an Essayist' (1888), the miscellaneous works of the first Lord Lytton (12 vols. Knebworth edition), 'The Wit and Wisdom of Lord Lytton' (1883), and 'The Humour and Pathos of Charles Dickens,' 1884. A literary curiosity called 'Corona Catholica. De Leonis XIII assumptione, epigramma in 50 linguis' (sm. 4to, 1880), supplied translations of an English epigram into fifty languages; among the many eminent scholars who supplied the translations were Max Müller, who turned the epigram into Sanskrit, Prof. Sayce, who turned it into Assyrian, and Prince Lucien Bonaparte who rendered it in Basque. The MS. of this compilation is now in the British Museum.

Kent received a civil list pension of 100*l.* on 14 Jan. 1887. In his last years he was a frequenter of the Athenæum Club, which he joined in 1881. He was a contributor to this Dictionary, writing among other articles those on Chatterton and Charles Reade. He died on 23 Feb. 1902 at his house at Campden Hill, and was buried at St. Mary's catholic cemetery, Kensal Green.

He married in 1853 Ann (1824–1911), eldest daughter of Murdo Young of Ross, N.B. She wrote in youth several novels: 'Evelyn Stuart' (3 vols. 1846); 'Maud Hamilton'; 'The Gilberts of Ashton,' and was a contributor to the press until 1906. She died in London on 16 Aug. 1911. She was received into the Roman catholic church in 1851. She had issue five sons and two daughters.

[The Times, 24 Feb. 1902; Biograph, Feb. 1879; Grant's Newspaper Press, i. 330 seq.; Allibone, Dict. Eng. Lit. Suppl.; J. Collins Francis, Notes by the Way, 1909; private information]. S. L.

KENYON, GEORGE THOMAS (1840–1908), politician, second son of Lloyd Kenyon, third baron Kenyon, by his wife Georgina, daughter of Thomas de Grey, fourth baron Walsingham, was born in London on 28 Dec. 1840. He was educated at Harrow (1854–60), entered Christ Church, Oxford, in 1860, graduated B.A. with second class honours in law and history in 1864, and proceeded M.A. in 1870. In 1869 he became a barrister of the Middle Temple. He contested the Denbigh boroughs unsuccessfully as a conservative in 1874 and 1880, but won the seat in 1885 and held it until 1895, and again from 1900 to 1905. In 1897 he stood unsuccessfully for East Denbighshire at a bye-election. He promoted the Wrexham and Ellesmere railway and was its first chairman (1891–1908). In 1873 he published a life of his ancestor, the first baron Kenyon (1732–1802). His chief interest was the promotion of secondary and higher education in Wales, and to his enlightened zeal was largely due the passing of the Welsh Intermediate Education Act of 1889, which established the present comprehensive system of secondary schools in Wales. The bill was introduced by Stuart (afterwards Lord) Rendel, the leader of the Welsh liberal members. But the conservatives were in power, and it was Kenyon's influence which secured its passage, with some slight changes. Kenyon took an active part in the establishment of the University of Wales and was its junior deputy-chancellor from 1898 to 1900. He died on 26 Jan. 1908, at his seat of Llannerch Panna, near Ellesmere. On 21 Oct. 1875 he married Florence Anna, daughter of J. H. Leche, of Carden Park, Chester. He left no issue. There is a portrait by E. Miller at Llannerch Panna.

[Who's Who, 1907; Alumni Oxonienses; The Times, 28 Jan. 1908; information supplied by Lord Kenyon.] J. E. L.

KENYON-SLANEY, WILLIAM SLANEY (1847–1908), colonel and politician, born on 24 Aug. 1847 at Rajcot in India, where his father was serving in the

East India Company's army, was eldest son of William Kenyon, a captain in the second regiment of the Bombay light cavalry. Lloyd, first Lord Kenyon [q. v.], was his great-grandfather. His mother was Frances Catharine, daughter and coheiress of Robert Aglionby Slaney [q. v.] of Hatton Grange, Shropshire, on whose death in 1862 the family assumed by royal licence the additional surname of Slaney.

Kenyon-Slaney entered Eton in Sept. 1860, and becoming an inmate of William Evans's house he proved himself a fair scholar and an enthusiastic footballer and cricketer; he played in the school eleven at football in 1864 and 1865. Through life he was a good all-round sportsman; he did much to popularise Association football, playing for England in the International Association match against Scotland on 8 March 1873, and for the Old Etonians in the final for the Association Cup in 1876.

Kenyon-Slaney left Eton in Dec. 1865, having already (13 Oct. 1865) matriculated at Christ Church, Oxford, where he only resided a year (1866–7). Destined for the army, he was gazetted on 20 Nov. 1867, and joined the 3rd battalion of the Grenadier guards at Dublin, becoming on 10 July 1870 lieutenant (and captain) without purchase, on 8 Sept. 1878 captain (and lieutenant-colonel), on 21 July 1883 major, and on 21 July 1887 colonel of the regiment. In 1882 his battalion formed part of a brigade of guards in the Egyptian war, and he was present at the action of Mahuta and at the battle of Tel-el-Kebir (13 Sept. 1882), for which he received the medal with clasp and the Khedive's bronze star. On 23 Nov. 1887 he was placed on half-pay, retiring from the army in 1892.

A conservative in politics, Kenyon-Slaney failed in his first candidature for parliament at the general election in 1885, when he contested the Wellington division of Shropshire, but he was returned at the general election in 1886 for the Newport division, and sat for that constituency till his death, being re-elected after a contest in 1892 and 1906 and without a contest in 1895 and 1900. In his maiden speech in committee of supply on 8 Sept. 1886 he urged the war office to provide a recreation ground for the garrison of the metropolis. In Nov. 1890 he moved the address in reply to the Queen's speech, confining himself for the first time to a single sentence of thanks. He spoke frequently in the house on agriculture, the army, Ireland, the death duties, and pure beer, on which topic he introduced a bill. As a platform orator through the country he stood in the first rank. He was an ardent tariff reformer.

Although Kenyon-Slaney took no keen interest in education, he is chiefly remembered as the author of 'the Kenyon-Slaney clause' in Mr. Balfour's Education Act of 1902. This clause provides that the religious instruction given in non-provided schools shall be under the control of the whole body of managers and not of the foundation managers or of any individual clergyman. It was carried in committee, on 7 Aug. 1902, by 211 to 41, and although it raised a storm in ecclesiastical circles, it worked well. In Nov. 1902 he declined the offer of a baronetcy, but in 1904 became a privy councillor.

A model landlord, who saw that every cottage on his estate had at least three bedrooms, proper drainage, and a good water supply, Kenyon-Slaney was involved in 1904 in an acute controversy with one of his tenant-farmers, Mr. Frederic Horne, whose activities as a radical politician seemed to Kenyon-Slaney to be incompatible with personal superintendence of his farm and with their mutual good relations. Mr. Horne gave up his farm, and his political friends represented him through Shropshire as a martyr to Kenyon-Slaney's political zeal. In 1895 Kenyon-Slaney was prominent in Shropshire, the first county to take the matter up, in inaugurating the movement for relief of naval and military veterans which was merged in 1902 in the Imperial Service Fund. Kenyon-Slaney died at Hatton Grange on 24 April 1908, and was buried in the churchyard of Ryton near Shifnal. He married at Weston, on 22 Feb. 1887, Lady Mabel Selina Bridgeman, elder daughter of the third earl of Bradford, by whom he had a son and a daughter.

Portraits of himself and his wife, painted by Mr. Mark Milbanke, were at his death ready for presentation to him by his constituents in celebration of his twenty-one years' service in the House of Commons.

[Memoir of Colonel William Kenyon-Slaney, M.P., edited by Walter Durnford, 1909; The Times, 25 and 30 April 1908; Shrewsbury Chronicle, 1 May 1908; Newport Advertiser, 26 April 1908; Eton School Lists; Foster's Alumni Oxonienses; Army Lists; Burke's Peerage and Landed Gentry; private information.]

W. G. D. F.

KEPPEL, Sir HENRY (1809–1904), admiral of the fleet, born in Kensington on 14 June 1809, was sixth surviving son of William Charles, fourth earl of Albemarle, by his wife Elizabeth Southwell, daughter of Edward, 20th Lord de Clifford. His grand-uncle was Augustus, Viscount Keppel [q. v.], and his elder brothers, Augustus Frederick and George Thomas, became successively fifth and sixth earls of Albemarle. Henry entered the navy on 7 Feb. 1822. After leaving the Royal Naval College at Greenwich he was appointed to the Tweed, of twenty-eight guns, and went out to the Cape. He passed his examination in 1828, and was promoted to lieutenant on 29 Jan. 1829. Early in 1830 he was appointed to the Galatea, Capt. Charles Napier [q. v.], which, after a spell of home service, went to the West Indies. At Barbadoes Keppel jeopardised his career by breaking an arrest in order to attend a dignity ball. He was next appointed to the Magicienne, Capt. James H. Plumridge [q. v.], going out to the East Indies, where he saw active service during the war between the East India Company and the Rajah of Nanning. His promotion to commander, dated 20 Jan. 1833, recalled him, and in 1834 he was appointed to command the Childers, brig, in which he served first on the south coast of Spain, co-operating with the forces of the Queen Regent against the Carlists, and afterwards on the west coast of Africa. On 5 Dec. 1837 he was promoted to be captain. In August 1841 he commissioned the Dido, corvette, for the China station, where he served with distinction during the latter part of the war under Sir William Parker. When peace was made in August 1842 Keppel was sent to Singapore as senior officer on that part of the station. There he made friends with Sir James Brooke [q. v.], with whom he returned to Sarawak. For eighteen months he co-operated with Brooke for the suppression of Borneo piracy, and, after many boat actions, the Dido, together with the East India Co.'s steamship Phlegethon, destroyed the chief stronghold of the pirates, together with some 300 prahus. After two years on half-pay Keppel was appointed in 1847 to the Mæander, frigate, and returned to the same station, where his intercourse with Brooke was resumed. Towards the end of the commission he visited Australia, and in 1851 returned to England by the Straits of Magellan (*The Times*, 22, 25, and 26 Jan. 1904).

In 1853 Keppel was appointed to the St. Jean d'Acre, then considered the finest line-of-battle ship in the navy, and served with distinction in her during the Baltic campaign of 1854, following which the ship was sent to the Black Sea. In July 1855 Keppel was moved into the Rodney, and took command of the naval brigade ashore before Sevastopol, continuing with it till the fall of the fortress. In addition to the Baltic and Crimean medals, he received the cross of the Legion of Honour, the third class of the Medjidie, and, on 4 Feb. 1856, was made a companion of the Bath.

When in the autumn of 1856 Keppel commissioned the Raleigh, frigate, as commodore and second in command on the China station, his reputation for courage and conduct combined with his family interest to give the ship a certain aristocratic character somewhat uncommon in the service; among the lieutenants were James G. Goodenough [q. v.], Lord Gillford [see Meade, Richard James, fourth earl of Clanwilliam, Suppl. II], and Prince Victor of Hohenlohe [q. v.], while Lord Charles Scott [q.v. Suppl. II], Henry F. Stephenson, Arthur Knyvet Wilson, and Hon. Victor Montagu were midshipmen on board. During the Raleigh's passage war broke out in China, and every effort was made to hurry the ship to Hong Kong, shortly before reaching which she struck upon an uncharted pinnacle rock. The ship was totally lost, but there was no loss of life, and Keppel was acquitted by the subsequent court-martial. He next hoisted his broad pennant in the chartered river steamer Hong Kong, and took part in the operations in the Canton River. The attack delivered on the grand fleet of war junks in the upper reaches of Fatshan Creek on 1 June 1857 was entrusted to Keppel, under whose personal command practically the whole of the junks, to the number of about seventy, were burnt. The Chinese had obstructed the stream, measured the distances, and made other careful preparations for the defence of their position, and they fought stoutly. Keppel's galley was sunk, and five of her crew were killed or wounded. He was warmly complimented by the commander in chief [see Seymour, Sir Michael], on whose recommendation he was awarded the K.C.B. On 22 August following he was promoted to his flag, and returned home.

In Sept. 1858 Sir Henry was appointed groom-in-waiting to Queen Victoria, a post which he resigned in May 1860 to hoist his flag on board the frigate Forte as commander-in-chief on the Cape station. There was some friction between Keppel and the governor at the Cape [see GREY, Sir GEORGE], and he was shortly transferred to the Brazilian command. He became a vice-admiral on 11 Jan. 1864, and in December 1866 was chosen to be commander-in-chief on the China station, where he had his flag in the Rodney. On 3 July 1869 he was promoted to admiral, and returned home. In April 1870 he was awarded an admiral's good service pension, and in May 1871 was advanced to the Grand Cross of the Bath. From November 1872 to 1875 he was commander-in-chief at Devonport; on 5 Aug. 1877 he received his promotion to be admiral of the fleet; and in March 1878 he was appointed first and principal naval aide-de-camp to the queen. By a special order in council his name was retained on the active list of the navy until his death, which took place in London on 17 Jan. 1904. He was buried at Winkfield with naval honours, a memorial service being held in the Chapel Royal, St. James's.

Keppel's social reputation stood as high as his service character. He was no less remarkable for the charm of his personality than for his love of sport and exuberant vitality. With King Edward VII, especially while Prince of Wales, he was on terms of intimate friendship; and with Queen Alexandra and the whole royal family his relations were such as are rarely permitted to a subject.

A bust by Count Gleichen was presented to the United Service Club by King Edward VII in 1905. Cartoon portraits appeared in 'Vanity Fair' in 1876 and 1903.

Keppel was twice married: (1) in 1839 to Katherine Louisa (*d.* 5 June 1859), daughter of Gen. Sir John Crosbie, G.C.H.; (2) on 31 Oct. 1861 to Jane Elizabeth, daughter of Martin J. West and sister of Sir Algernon West. By his second wife, who died on 21 April 1895, he left issue Colin Richard, *b.* 3 Dec. 1862, now a rear-admiral, and Maria Walpole, who married Capt. (now Vice-admiral) Frederick Tower Hamilton, R.N.

Keppel published his memoirs in 1899 with the title 'A Sailor's Life under Four Sovereigns,' 3 vols.

[Keppel's Sailor's Life, 1899; Memoir by Keppel's brother-in-law, Sir Algernon West, G.C.B., 1905; The Times, 18 Jan. 1904, based chiefly on Keppel's book.]

L. G. C. L.

KERR, JOHN (1824–1907), physicist, born on 17 Dec. 1824 at Ardrossan, Ayrshire, was second son of Thomas Kerr, a fish-dealer. He was educated at a village school in Skye, and proceeded to the University of Glasgow, attending classes from 1841 to 1849. From 1846 he studied under William Thomson, afterwards Lord Kelvin [q. v. Suppl. II], and on graduation in 1849 he obtained Lord Eglinton's prize as the most distinguished student in mathematics and natural philosophy. Although a divinity student, he was one of the earliest to engage in research work in the 'coal-hole' in which Thomson had set up the first physical laboratory in Great Britain. After some time spent in teaching, Kerr was ordained a minister of the Free church, but did not take clerical duty. In 1857 he was appointed lecturer in mathematics to the Glasgow Free Church Training College for Teachers. This post he held for forty-four years, until his retirement in 1901. Here he set up a small laboratory, spending all his spare time in research.

His name is associated with two great discoveries affecting the nature of light—the bi-refringence caused in glass and other insulators when placed in an intense electric field, and the change produced in polarised light by reflection from the polished pole of an electromagnet. The series of papers describing the first of these phenomena appeared in the 'Philosophical Magazine' from 1875 onwards; the second discovery was communicated to the British Association at its Glasgow meeting in 1876, and caused intense excitement among the physicists there. The mathematical theory of this 'Kerr effect' was first worked out by George Francis FitzGerald [q. v. Suppl. II], and more recently by Sir Joseph Larmor. Kerr's only independently published works are 'The Metric System' (1863) and 'An Elementary Treatise on Rational Mechanics' (1867). The latter of these procured him the honorary degree of LL.D. from his university. He was elected F.R.S. in 1890, and received the royal medal in 1898. He continued to publish the results of his researches in the 'Philosophical Transactions' till near his death. He was awarded in 1902 a civil list pension of 100*l.* a year. He died at Glasgow on 18 Aug. 1907. He married Marion, daughter of Col. Balfour of Orkney, and had three sons and four daughters.

[Proc. Roy. Soc., 82a, 1909, p. 1; The Times, 19 Aug. 1907; Nature, 3 Oct. 1907; Who's Who, 1907.]

R. S.

KERR, ROBERT (1823–1904), architect, born at Aberdeen on 17 Jan. 1823, was son of Robert Kerr by his wife Elizabeth, daughter of Thomas McGowan, yeoman, of Peterhead, and cousin of Joseph Hume [q. v.]. Kerr's only brother, Thomas, who settled at Rockford, Illinois, was a doctor both of medicine and divinity. After education in Aberdeen, Kerr was articled in that town to John Smith, the city architect. Early in his professional career he attempted practice in New York, but returned to England, where he acquired a practice.

In 1852 Kerr put forward a scheme for architectural training, and soon ranked as a pioneer in the educational movement among architects. He was appointed examiner in the voluntary examination established by the Royal Institute of British Architects, and in 1857 was elected a fellow of that body, on whose council he served in 1861–2 and again in 1870–2, and in whose development and organisation he played an important part. For forty years he was a constant contributor to the literature and the debates of the Institute.

From 1861 to 1890 he was professor of the arts of construction (and a fellow) at King's College, London. From 1892 to 1896 he was lecturer on 'Materials, their nature and application,' to the Architectural Association, a body of which he was one of the founders and was the first president in 1847. From 1860 to 1902 he was district surveyor (under the metropolitan board of works and the London county council) for St. James's, Westminster.

Kerr's chief works as a designer were the National Provident Institution, Gracechurch Street (corner of Eastcheap); Ascot Heath House, Berkshire; Ford House, Lingfield, Surrey; Bearwood, Berkshire, a large country house for John Walter [q. v.], proprietor of the 'Times'; Dunsdale, Westerham, Kent, for Joseph Kitchin; and two important competition designs, one (in 1857) for the Home and Foreign Offices, the other for the Natural History Museum at South Kensington, which was awarded the second premium.

Kerr's forcible personality was better displayed in his writings, lectures and trenchant speeches than in his architecture. He died on 21 Oct. 1904 at his residence, 31 Cathcart Road, West Brompton, and was buried at the Church of the Annunciation, Chislehurst.

Kerr's chief publications, apart from technical articles in periodicals, were: 1. 'Newleafe Discourses on the Fine Art Architecture,' 1846. 2. 'The English Gentleman's House,' 1865. 3. 'Ancient Lights,' 1865. 4 'The Consulting Architect,' 1886. 5. 'Chapters on Plan and Thoroughfare in the Principles and Practice of Modern House Construction,' edited by Lister Sutcliffe, 1900. He edited (with introduction and enlargement) the third edition of Fergusson's 'History of Modern Architecture' in 1891. For many years Kerr wrote the leading article in the 'Architect.'

Kerr married in 1848 Charlotte Mary Anne Fox, and was survived by eight of his nine children. Of four sons three became architects.

[Journ. Royal Inst. Brit. Architects, vol. xii. 3rd series, p. 14; Builder, 12 Nov. 1904; information from Henry N. Kerr.] P. W.

KILLEN, WILLIAM DOOL (1806–1902), ecclesiastical historian, born at Church Street, Ballymena, co. Antrim, on 5 April 1806, was third of four sons and nine children of John Killen (1768–1828), grocer and seedsman in Ballymena, by his wife Martha, daughter of Jesse Dool, a farmer in Duneane, co. Antrim. His paternal grandfather, a farmer at Carnmoney, co. Antrim, married Blanche Brice, a descendant of Edward Brice [q. v.], first of the Scottish founders of the Irish presbyterian church. A brother, James Miller Killen (1815-1879), D.D., minister in Comber, co. Down, was author of 'Our Friends in Heaven' (Edinburgh, 1854), which ran through many editions, and 'Our Companions in Glory' (Edinburgh, 1862). Thomas Young Killen [q. v.] was his father's grand-nephew.

After attending local primary schools, Killen went about 1816 to the Ballymena Academy, and in November 1821 entered the collegiate department of the Royal Academical Institution, Belfast, where Professor James Thomson [q. v.], father of Lord Kelvin, took a special interest in him. Passing here through the usual curriculum for the ministry of the Synod of Ulster, he was in 1827 licensed to preach by the Presbytery of Ballymena, and on 11 Nov. 1829 ordained minister at Raphoe, co. Donegal. While diligently performing his pastoral duties, he read extensively in church history and allied subjects. Killen was active in a bitter north of Ireland controversy concerning the relative merits of prelacy and presbyterianism, which was provoked by four sermons preached in 1837 in St. Columb's cathedral, Londonderry, by Archibald Boyd [q. v.]. Killen and three other Presbyterian ministers replied in four sermons preached in Londonderry and published in 1839 with the title: 'Presbyterianism Defended . . . .' A reply from Boyd and counter-replies from the four ministers ensued. One of these, 'The Plea of Presbytery' (1840), which reached a third edition, earned for its authors a vote of thanks from the Synod of Ulster.

In July 1841 Killen was unanimously appointed by the general assembly of the presbyterian church in Ireland professor of church history, ecclesiastical government, and pastoral theology in their college, Belfast, in succession to James Seaton Reid [q. v.]. Henceforth he resided in Belfast, proving himself an able professor and devoting his increased leisure to the special study of ecclesiastical history. In 1869 he was appointed president of the college in succession to Dr. Henry Cooke [q. v.], and in this capacity helped to raise large sums of money for professorial endowments and new buildings. In 1889 he resigned his chair, owing to advanced years, but continued in the office of president. He died on 10 Jan. 1902, and was buried in Balmoral cemetery, Belfast, where a fitting monument marks his resting-place. He married in 1830 Anne (*d.* 1886), third daughter of Thomas Young, Ballymena, by whom he had three sons and five daughters.

Killen received the degrees of D.D. (1845) and of LL.D. (1901) from the University of Glasgow. His portrait, painted by Richard Hooke, hangs in the Gamble library, Assembly's College, Belfast.

Killen's historical writing was voluminous. He was painstaking in research, and threw much new light on the history of the Irish presbyterian church and other subjects.

His chief works, some of which circulated widely in the United Kingdom and in America, were: 1. Continuation of Reid's 'History of the Presbyterian Church in Ireland to 1841,' Belfast, 1853. 2. 'The Ancient Church. Its History, Doctrine, Worship, and Constitution traced for the First Three Hundred Years,' 1859. 3. 'Memoir of John Edgar, D.D., LL.D.,' Belfast, 1867. 4. 'The Old Catholic Church. The History, Doctrine, Worship, and Polity of the Christians traced from the Apostolic Age to the Establishment of the Pope as a Temporal Sovereign, A.D. 755,' Edinburgh, 1871. 5. 'The Ecclesiastical History of Ireland from the Earliest Period to the Present Times,' 2 vols. 1875. 6. 'The Ignatian Epistles entirely Spurious. A Reply to Bishop Lightfoot,' Edinburgh, 1886. 7. 'The Framework of the Church. A Treatise on Church Government,' Edinburgh, 1890. 8. 'Reminiscences of a Long Life,' 1901. He edited, with introductions and notes: 1. 'The Siege of Derry,' by John Mackenzie [q. v.], Belfast, 1861. 2. 'The Rise and Progress of the Presbyterian Government in the North of Ireland,' by Patrick Adair [q. v.]. 3. 'History of the Church of Ireland,' by Andrew Stewart [q. v.], Belfast, 1866. 4. 'History of Congregations of the Presbyterian Church in Ireland,' chiefly by Seaton Reid, Belfast, 1886.

[Personal knowledge; Killen, Reminiscences of a Long Life, 1901; Belfast News-letter, 11 Jan. 1902; private information.]

T. H.

KIMBERLEY, first EARL OF. [See WODEHOUSE, JOHN (1826–1902), statesman.]

KINAHAN, GEORGE HENRY (1829–1908), geologist, born in Dublin on 19 Dec. 1829, was one of the fifteen children of Daniel Kinahan, barrister-at-law, by his wife Louisa Stuart Millar. Passing out from Trinity College, Dublin, with an engineering diploma in 1853, he was employed as an assistant on the construction of the railway viaduct over the Boyne at Drogheda. In 1854 he entered the Irish branch of the geological survey, under J. Beete Jukes [q. v.], and gained an intimate acquaintance with the geology of Ireland during thirty-six years of energetic work. He became district surveyor in 1869, and a large part of the geological map on the scale of one inch to one mile is due to his personal investigation. At his death no one had so wide a knowledge of local facts of Irish geological structure, or of the history of mining and kindred enterprises in the country. Kinahan was interested also in Irish archæology. He was a member of the Royal Irish Academy, and served long upon its council.

Kinahan was eminent in geology as a field-worker rather than as a writer; but his books and his contributions to the 'Memoirs of the Geological Survey of Ireland' and to scientific periodicals in Ireland and England are mines of information. His style, especially in controversy, was often more vigorous than precise. His 'Manual of the Geology of Ireland' (1878) contains the results of much original observation. The classification adopted for the palæozoic strata was modelled on certain suggestions of Jukes, and has ceased to meet with acceptance. An important compilation, largely from his own notes, entitled 'Economic Geology of Ireland,' which appeared as a series of papers in the Journal of the Royal

Geological Society of Ireland, was issued separately in 1889.

Kinahan was of strong and massive build; he died at his residence, Woodlands, Clontarf, Dublin, on 5 Dec. 1908, being buried in the Protestant churchyard at Ovoca, co. Wicklow. He married Harriet Ann, daughter of Capt. Samuel Gerrard, 3rd King's own dragoon guards, and had by her three sons and five daughters.

Kinahan's smaller works are: 1. (With Maxwell Henry Close [q. v. Suppl. II]) 'The General Glaciation of Iar-Connaught,' 1872. 2. 'Handy-book of Rock-names,' 1873. 3. 'Valleys and their Relation to Fissures, Fractures, and Faults,' 1875. 4. (With A. McHenry) 'Reclamation of Waste Lands in Ireland,' 1882. 5. 'Superficial and Agricultural Geology, Ireland,' 2 pts. 1908.

[Abstract of Minutes, Royal Irish Acad., 16 Mar. 1909; Geol. Mag. 1909, p. 142 (with portrait); Irish Naturalist, 1909, p. 29 (with portrait); personal knowledge.]

G. A. J. C.

KINCAIRNEY, LORD. [See GLOAG, WILLIAM ELLIS (1828-1909), judge of court of session.]

KING, EDWARD (1829-1910), bishop of Lincoln, born on 29 Dec. 1829 at 8 St. James's Place, Westminster, was third child and second son in a family of five boys and five girls of Walker King (1798-1859), rector of Stone, Kent, and canon and archdeacon of Rochester, who married in 1823 Anne (*d.* 1883), daughter of William Heberden the younger [q. v.]. Edward King's grandfather, Walker King (1751-1827), was bishop of Rochester.

After some teaching from his father at Stone, King became a daily pupil of the curate there, John Day; and when Day became incumbent of Ellesmere, Edward went with him. He showed as a boy a strong feeling for religion, but at the same time was fond of dancing, fishing, and swimming, and was an excellent horseman. Through life his chief recreation was foreign travel, chiefly in Switzerland and Italy.

In February 1848 King matriculated at Oriel College, Oxford. Edward Hawkins [q. v.] was provost. At 'collections'—the formal review of work and conduct—at the end of King's first term, Hawkins made the characteristic comment on King's habits of life 'that even too regular attendance at chapel may degenerate into formalism.' King had been brought up in a school of old-fashioned churchmanship, but the influences of the Tractarian movement had already reached him; and at Oxford they were deepened by his intercourse with Charles Marriott [q. v.], fellow and tutor of Oriel. As an undergraduate he observed the extreme and methodical strictness in daily life and devotion, including fasting and abstinence, which Tractarianism inculcated. His punctilious rule of attending afternoon chapel at 4.30 'made boating difficult and cricket quite impossible,' but he managed to spend some time on the river.

King did not read for honours; but under the able tuition of his college he was well grounded in Plato and Aristotle. He was more an Aristotelian than a Platonist, and to the end of his life he used 'The Ethics' as a text-book on which he grounded his social and moral teaching. In early life he completely mastered Italian by reading it with an invalid sister, and Dante was the author from whom he most frequently quoted. He graduated B.A. in 1851, and in the interval between his degree and his ordination he acted as private tutor to Lord Lothian's brothers, and made a journey to Palestine.

King, who always looked forward to holy orders as his appointed sphere in life, received in 1854 the offer of a curacy from Edward Elton, vicar of Wheatley, near Cuddesdon, in Oxfordshire. He was ordained both deacon (11 June 1854) and priest (3 June 1855) by Samuel Wilberforce, bishop of Oxford. Wheatley was at that time a rough and lawless village, and King's zeal in pastoral work powerfully reinforced Elton's efforts at moral reformation. In dealing with the boys and youths of the parish he first manifested that remarkable power of influencing young men which was the special characteristic of his later ministry.

In 1858 Bishop Wilberforce, alarmed by the outcry against alleged romanising tendencies in the theological college at Cuddesdon, which he had founded in 1853, changed the staff, and bestowed the chaplaincy on King. It was by no means a welcome change. Next spring the bishop forced the vice-principal, Henry Parry Liddon [q. v.], to resign, and begged King to succeed him. King, however, declined, and remained chaplain till, at the beginning of 1863, on the death of the Rev. H. H. Swinny, the bishop made him principal of the college and vicar of Cuddesdon. As vicar of the parish he had fuller scope for pastoral work, and as principal of the college he developed an unique power of winning the confidence and moulding the character of the students, They were attracted by his profound piety, his cheerfulness, his persuasiveness, and his companionable habits. His rule, though gentle, was firm. He taught a theology which, while fundamentally catholic, was free from exotic peculiarities. He aimed at turning out men saturated with the spirit of the Prayer Book. Among his students at Cuddesdon was Stephen Edward Gladstone, son of W. E. Gladstone, whose attention was thus called to King's gifts as a trainer of young clergymen. In February 1873, on the death of Charles Atmore Ogilvie [q. v.], the first professor of pastoral theology at Oxford, Gladstone offered the chair to King. He was installed in the canonry of Christ Church (annexed to the professorship) on 24 April 1873, and took up residence at Oxford. His mother lived with him till her death ten years later.

King treated pastoral theology as the systematic inculcation, not of abstract theories, however venerable, but of lessons practically learnt in pastoral intercourse with the poor, the tempted, and the perplexed. In addition to his statutory lectures, he held every week during the term a voluntary gathering of undergraduates, who assembled in the evening in a kind of adapted wash-house in his garden, which he called his 'Bethel.' There he gave addresses of a more directly spiritual kind, and their influence was profound and permanent. He took a full though not a very conspicuous part in the social and academic life of the university; he preached in the university pulpit, and in the parish churches of Oxford; and, aided by his mother, exercised a genial hospitality. As Dr. Pusey (1800–1882) grew old and feeble, and Dr. Liddon (1829–1890) resided less and less in Oxford, King became the most powerful element in the religious life of the university.

In February 1885, on the resignation of Christopher Wordsworth [q. v.], bishop of Lincoln, Gladstone appointed King to the vacant see. He was consecrated in St. Paul's Cathedral on St. Mark's Day, 25 April 1885, the sermon—a highly polemical discourse on the claims of the episcopal office—being preached by his friend Liddon. As soon as King became bishop of Lincoln he arranged to get rid of Riseholme, a huge and straggling house which had been since 1841 the episcopal residence; and he restored the Old Palace at Lincoln, close to the cathedral, where he spent the rest of his life. He entered with much interest into the public life of the city. In February 1887 he prepared for death and attended on the scaffold a young murderer in Lincoln gaol; a circumstance which was felt to mark a new type of episcopal life and ministration. From that time on, the bishop always ministered to similar cases in Lincoln gaol. The form of episcopal work in which he took the keenest interest was confirming. A round of confirmations was to him a renewal of the best and happiest activities of his earlier manhood; and, whether he was addressing the schoolboys and apprentices of Lincoln, or the fisher-lads of Grimsby, or the ploughboys of the rural districts, he was equally at his ease and equally effective.

King earnestly adhered to the higher form of the Anglican tradition. He held and taught the real objective Presence and the eucharistic sacrifice, and he practised and received confession. His doctrine with regard to the cultus of the Blessed Virgin and the invocation of saints was strictly moderate; and he discouraged all romanising forms in worship, and all unauthorised additions to the appointed services of the Prayer Book. He had no personal taste for ritualism, but he wore the cope and mitre, and also the eucharistic vestments when celebrating in his private chapel, or in churches where they were used. Some of the more fiery protestants in his diocese began to murmur against these concessions to what they abhorred, and before long the Church Association resolved to prosecute the bishop for illegal practices in divine worship. The only possible method of trying the bishop was to cite him before the archbishop of Canterbury; but the precedents were doubtful, and the archiepiscopal court had only a nebulous authority. After much preliminary discussion, it was decided that the trial before the archbishop should go forward. It began on 12 Feb. 1889 in the library of Lambeth Palace, the archbishop having as assessors the bishops of London (Temple), Oxford (Stubbs), Rochester (Thorold), Salisbury (Wordsworth), and Hereford (Atlay). Sir Walter Phillimore was counsel for King. The charge was that, when celebrating the Holy Communion in Lincoln Cathedral on 4 Dec. 1887, and in the parish church of St. Peter-at-Gowts, Lincoln, on 18 Dec. 1887, the bishop had transgressed the law in the following points: 1. Mixing water with the sacramental wine during the service, and subsequently consecrating the 'mixed cup.' 2. Standing in the 'eastward position' during the first part of the communion service. 3. Standing during the prayer of consecration on the west side of the holy table, in such manner that the congregation could not see the manual acts performed. 4. Causing the hymn 'Agnus Dei' to be sung after the prayer of consecration. 5. Pouring water and wine into the paten and chalice after the service, and afterwards drinking such water and wine before the congregation. 6. The use of lighted candles on the holy table, or on the re-table behind, during the communion service, when not needed for the purposes of light. 7. During the Absolution and Blessing making the sign of the cross with upraised hand, facing the congregation. These facts were not disputed, and all the archbishop had to do was to decide whether they were or were not conformable to the laws of the church.

The trial was delayed by various protests made on behalf of the bishop, and the actual hearing of the case did not begin till 4 Feb. 1890. The archbishop's judgment, delivered on 21 Nov. 1890 after due deliberation, was substantially in the bishop's favour, although each party was ordered to pay its own costs. The archbishop decided (1) that the mixture of the cup must not be performed during the service; (2) and (3) that the eastward position was lawful if so managed as not to make the manual acts invisible; (4) that the 'Agnus Dei' might be sung; (5) that the ablutions after the service were permitted; (6) that lighted candles on the holy table, if not lighted during the service, were permitted; (7) that the sign of the cross at the absolution and the blessing was an innovation which must be discontinued. Much dissatisfied by this result, the Church Association appealed to the judicial committee of the privy council; but on 2 Aug. 1892 the appeal was dismissed, and the archbishop's judgment upheld. It had no widespread effect, but was scrupulously obeyed by the bishop of Lincoln, even when celebrating in his private chapel.

The duration of these proceedings and the anxieties and distresses inseparable from them told heavily on the bishop's health and spirits. But great sympathy was evoked, and his hold on the affections of his diocese was sensibly strengthened. Henceforward he was beyond question 'the most popular man in Lincolnshire.' In January 1900, at a representative gathering of the county, his portrait, painted by public subscription, was presented to him by the lord-lieutenant, Lord Brownlow; and on his seventy-ninth birthday he received a cheque from the clergy and laity of the diocese amounting to nearly 2000*l*. This he devoted to the Grimsby Church Extension Fund.

After, as before, the trial, he was unremitting in the discharge of his episcopal duties. He played an active part in opposition to the education bills of the liberal government, and he continued to take his annual holiday abroad, but went less and less to London, though he always attended convocation and the bishops' meetings at Lambeth. On 1 June 1909 he presided, as visitor of the college, at the opening of the new buildings at Brasenose, and on 30 Nov. following he was present in the House of Lords to vote for Lord Lansdowne's amendment to the budget.

In January 1910 his health began to fail; but he took three confirmations in February. On 2 March he dictated a farewell letter to the diocese, and on the 8th he died at the Old Palace. He was buried in the Cloister Garth of Lincoln Cathedral. He was unmarried. He did not in the least condemn the marriage of the clergy, but he did not feel himself called to it.

Late in life King separated himself from the high church party as a whole by sanctioning the remarriage of the innocent party in a divorce suit. In politics he was a staunch tory: 'I have been voting against Gladstone all my life,' he said, 'and now he makes me a bishop.' Yet he favoured the franchise bill of 1884, on the ground that the agricultural labourers must be taught to be citizens of the kingdom of God by being citizens of the kingdom of England. King's character and career manifested with peculiar clearness the power of purely moral qualities. He had no commanding gifts of intellect, no great learning, and no eloquence; but his faculty of sympathy amounted to genius, and gave him an intuitive knowledge of other people's characters, and a power of entering into their difficulties, which drew them to him with no effort on his part. To this must be added the most perfect refinement of thought and bearing, a sanctified commonsense, and a delicate humour.

King published, besides sermons and charges and pamphlets on the 'Lincoln Case': 1. 'The Communicant's Manual' (edited), 1869, &c. 2. 'A Letter to the Rev. C. J. Elliott . . . being a reply to Some Strictures, &c.' by E. King, &c. 1879. 3. 'Ezra and Nehemiah,' 1874. 4. 'Meditations on the Last Seven Words of our Lord

Jesus Christ,' 1874; translated into Kafir, S.P.C.K., 1887.

After his death there appeared: 1. 'The Love and Wisdom of God: a Collection of Sermons,' 1910. 2. 'Spiritual Letters,' 1910. 3. 'Counsels to Nurses,' 1911. 4. 'Duty and Conscience—being Retreat Addresses,' 1911. 5. 'Sermons and Addresses,' 1911.

A portrait in oils by George Richmond, R.A., now at Cuddesdon College, was engraved by Thomas Lewis Atkinson in 1877. The presentation portrait by W. W. Ouless, R.A. (1899), is at the Old Palace, Lincoln.

The bishop is commemorated by a church at Great Grimsby, which was built with money presented to him in 1908. Another church at Grimsby has been built with money subscribed to a memorial fund. A statue by Sir William Richmond, R.A., has been placed in Lincoln Minster, and a bursary has been endowed at St. Chad's Hall, Durham.

[The present author's Life of King, 1911; Cuddesdon Coll. Jubilee Record; information from the bishop's family.] G. W. E. R.

KING, Sir GEORGE (1840–1909), Indian botanist, son of Robert King and Cecilia Anderson, was born at Peterhead, where his father was a bookseller, on 12 April 1840. King's father soon moved to Aberdeen, and with an older brother, George, who was the boy's godfather, founded the publishing firm of G. and R. King. Both brothers possessed literary aptitudes, the elder writing much on social and religious subjects and the younger compiling a meritorious history of 'The Covenanters in the North.' King's father died, aged thirty-six, in 1845 and his mother five years later. Thereupon King became his uncle's ward, and, after passing through the grammar school, where Mr. (subsequently Sir) W. D. Geddes was his form master, in 1854 joined his uncle's business. At school King showed a marked predilection for natural science; and on coming of age in 1861 left his uncle's service for the University of Aberdeen in order to study medicine as an avenue to a scientific career. There King came under the influence of the botanist George Dickie [q. v.], and, becoming his assistant, devoted all his spare time to botanical work. Graduating as M.B. with highest academical honours in 1865, King on 2 Oct. entered the Indian medical service, and reached India on 11 April 1866. In 1868 he was temporarily appointed to the Saharanpur Botanic Garden, and next year joined the Indian forest service. His efficiency in these positions led the duke of Argyll, secretary of state for India, to promote him in March 1871 to the post of superintendent of the Royal Botanic Garden, Calcutta, and of cinchona cultivation in Bengal. The Calcutta garden had been seriously damaged by two great cyclones in 1864 and 1867, but King completely renovated it, formed an adequate herbarium collection to replace that dispersed by the East India Company in 1828, and organised a botanical survey of India, of which in 1891 he became the first director. As manager of the cinchona department King substituted quinine-yielding cinchonas for the poorer kinds previously grown, inaugurated in 1887 an economic method of separating quinine, and established in 1893 a method of distributing the drug on self-supporting lines at a low price. Both the governments of Bengal and of India recognised King's administrative capacity. On their behalf he acted as a visitor of the Bengal Engineering College, as a manager of the Calcutta Zoological Gardens, and as a trustee of the Indian Museum. He was created C.I.E. in 1890 and K.C.I.E. in 1898. The humane services which he rendered in connection with quinine were acknowledged by the grade of Officier d'Instruction Publique and by the gift of a ring of honour from the Czar Alexander III.

King's early writings, mainly official reports and contributions to the journals of learned societies, although scanty, were sufficiently valuable to lead his university to confer on him the degree of LL.D. in 1884. He was elected F.R.S. in 1887. In the same year he founded the 'Annals of the Royal Botanic Garden, Calcutta, to which, during the next eleven years, he contributed a series of monographs of Ficus, Quercus, Castanopsis, Artocarpus, Myristica, Anonaceæ, and Orchidaceæ, marked by a lucidity and completeness which placed him among the foremost systematic writers of his time. In 1889 he further undertook a sustained study of the flora of the Malayan Peninsula; ten parts of his 'Materials' for a Flora of the region were issued before 1898.

King retired from India on 28 Feb. 1898. Failing health thenceforth reduced his public activity, although in 1899 he was president of the botanical section of the British Association at Dover. Under medical advice he mainly resided at San Remo, where he prosecuted his Malayan studies, but each summer he worked at Kew. With the co-operation of various botanists he carried his Malayan research to the end of the twenty-first part, the revision of which had just been completed when he died of an apoplectic seizure at San Remo on 12 Feb. 1909. A memorial tablet marks his burial place there and records his philanthropic labours. King's services to botanical science were recognised by the award of medals by the University of Upsala, the Linnean Society, and the Royal Horticultural Society.

King married, in 1868, Jane Anne, daughter of Dr. G. J. Nicol, Aberdeen; she died in 1898. Of their two sons the elder, Robert, became an officer in the royal engineers.

A bronze medallion portrait, by F. Bowcher, was presented by Indian friends in 1899 to the Zoological Garden, Calcutta, a replica being placed in the Calcutta Botanic Garden. A copy, formerly in King's possession, is now in the Scottish National Portrait Gallery, Edinburgh.

[Obituary notice by the present writer in Proc. Roy. Soc. vol. 81, p. xi, based on official notifications, original papers, and the memoranda and letters of King's relatives and friends; Kew Bulletin, 1909, pp. 193–7, for bibliography.] D. P–N.

KING, HAYNES (1831–1904), genre painter, born at Barbados in Dec. 1831, was son of Robert M. King by his wife Maria. Coming to London in 1854, he became a student at Leigh's (afterwards Heatherley's) Academy in Newman Street, London. He first exhibited in 1857 at the Society of British Artists, of which he was elected a member in 1864; many of his works appeared at its exhibitions, and forty-eight were shown at the Royal Academy between 1860 and 1904. He worked at one period with Thomas Faed, R.A. [q. v.], whose influence is shown in his work. He painted efficiently, if without original power, genre subjects, interiors, landscapes, and coast scenes with figures. Among his works were 'Looking Out' (1860), 'The Lace Maker' (1866), 'A Water-Carrier, Rome' (1869), 'Homeless' (1872), 'News from the Cape' (1879), 'Approaching Footsteps' (1883), 'Getting Granny's Advice' (1890), 'The New Gown' (1892), and 'Latest Intelligence,' which appeared at the Royal Academy in 1904. His 'Jealousy and Flirtation' (a cottage interior dated 1874) is at the Bethnal Green Museum, and 'An Interesting Paragraph' is at the City Art Gallery, Leeds.

King resided latterly at 103 Finchley Road, N.W. After some months of ill-health he committed suicide on 17 May 1904 at the Swiss Cottage station of the Metropolitan railway, London. He married in 1866 Annie Elizabeth Wilson, a widow, and left no family.

[Information kindly supplied by Mr. Yeend King, V.P.R.I.; The Times, 18 and 21 May 1904; Art Journal, 1904, p. 272; H. Blackburn, English Art in 1884, p. 228 (reproduction); Graves, Dict. of Artists and Roy. Acad. Exhibitors; Cats. of R.B.A. (some containing reproductions), Victoria and Albert Museum (oil paintings), and City Art Gallery, Leeds.] B. S. L.

KINGSCOTE, Sir ROBERT NIGEL FITZHARDINGE (1830–1908), agriculturist, born at Kingscote, Gloucestershire, on 28 Feb. 1830, was only son of Thomas Henry Kingscote, squire of Kingscote (1799–1861), by his first wife, Lady Isabella (1809–1831), sixth daughter of Henry Somerset, sixth duke of Beaufort. Educated privately at a school at Weymouth, he afterwards went abroad with a tutor until at the age of sixteen he obtained a commission in the Scots fusilier guards through the influence of his maternal great-uncle Lord Fitzroy Somerset (afterwards Lord Raglan) [q. v.]. On the outbreak of hostilities with Russia he went out to the Crimea as aide-de-camp to his kinsman, Lord Raglan, and was in close attendance on the commander-in-chief, whose remains he escorted back to England. For his war services he was made brevet major on 12 Dec. 1854, and subsequently lieutenant-colonel and C.B. He sold out of the guards in 1856, and lived the ordinary life of a country gentleman. He had been elected in 1852 as a liberal to represent the western division of Gloucestershire; he retained that seat for thirty-three years. On the death of his father on 19 Dec. 1861 he came into possession of the estate at Kingscote, and kept up the family traditions as a squire, breeder of pedigree live stock, and follower of the hounds. From 1859 to 1866 he was parliamentary groom-in-waiting to Queen Victoria, and thus began a lifelong intimacy with the royal family, especially with the Prince of Wales (afterwards King Edward VII). In May 1864 he was appointed, in succession to Colonel Thomas, superintendent of the Prince of Wales's stables, a post which he held until 1885. In 1867 he was appointed extra equerry to the prince, and on the accession of the prince to the throne was made extra equerry to the king. In March 1885 Colonel Kingscote accepted from Gladstone a commissionership of woods and forests, from which he retired in 1895, on reaching the age of sixty-five. He became paymaster-general of the royal household on King Edward VII's accession. He was made K.C.B. (civil) on 2 July 1889 and G.C.V.O. on 9 Nov. 1902. He was also a member of council of the Prince of Wales (from 1886), and receiver-general of the Duchy of Cornwall (from 1888).

Kingscote died at Worth Park, Sussex, on 22 Sept. 1908; he married (1) on 15 March 1851 Caroline, daughter of Colonel George Wyndham, first Lord Leconfield (she died in 1852, leaving no issue); (2) on 5 Feb. 1856 Lady Emily Marie Curzon, third daughter of Richard William Penn, first Earl Howe (1836–1910), by whom he had one son and two daughters. A portrait in oils, done by A. de Brie in 1908, belongs to the son. A cartoon by 'Spy' appeared in 'Vanity Fair' (1880).

Kingscote was a recognised authority on agriculture. He joined the Royal Agricultural Society in 1854, and was elected a member of the council in 1863, only finally retiring in November 1906. He was chairman of the finance committee for thirty-one years (1875–1906), and was president of the society at Bristol in 1878. When the Royal Agricultural Society met at Cambridge in 1894, Kingscote was made an hon. LL.D. He was chairman of the governors of the Royal Veterinary College, and an active member of the council of the Royal Agricultural College at Cirencester, of the Smithfield Club, Shorthorn Society, Hunters' Improvement Society, and numerous other agricultural organisations. He was also a member of the two royal commissions on agriculture of 1879 and 1893. In personal appearance he was tall, slim, and upright, with an aristocratic face and the aquiline nose of the Somersets, which he inherited from his mother. His courteous bearing and his kindly and tactful manners were of the old school.

[Memoir by the present writer in the Journal of the Royal Agricultural Society for 1908, vol. 69 (with photogravure reproduction of his portrait in oils).] E. C.

KINGSTON, CHARLES CAMERON (1850–1908), Australian statesman, born at Adelaide, South Australia, on 22 Oct. 1850, was the younger son of Sir George Strickland Kingston, who accompanied Colonel Light, the first surveyor-general of the colony, to South Australia in 1836, and was elected in April 1857 first speaker of the House of Assembly, holding the office in all for eighteen years; he was knighted by patent on 30 April 1870, and died on 26 Nov. 1881. Kingston's mother, his father's second wife, Ludovina Rosa Catherine da Silva Cameron, was of Portuguese descent on her mother's side; her father, Lieut.-colonel Charles Cameron of the 3rd regiment (the Buffs), served with distinction in the American and Peninsular wars.

After education at the Adelaide Educational Institution, Kingston was early in 1868 articled to the law in the office of Mr. (now Chief Justice Sir Samuel James) Way, and was admitted to the colonial bar in 1873, remaining with Mr. Way till the latter was appointed chief justice in 1876. Kingston then commenced practice as a barrister and solicitor on his own account. He quickly acquired a leading practice, and was very successful in the criminal courts. In 1889 he was made Q.C.

He was first returned to the house of representatives of South Australia on 8 April 1881, as member for West Adelaide, which he continued to represent until 7 Feb. 1900. Entering parliament as a liberal, he soon developed into an advanced radical, identifying himself closely with social reform in the interest of the working classes, and helping to secure the franchise for women, factory legislation, and the establishment of a state bank.

He first held office as attorney-general in the second ministry (16 June 1884–16 June 1885) of (Sir) John Colton [q. v. Suppl. II] and he held the same office in Mr. Thomas Playford's first ministry (11 June 1887–27 June 1889). On the fall of Playford's government he became a prominent member in opposition to the Cockburn ministry. On 16 Jan. 1892 he joined the second Playford administration as chief secretary, and acted as premier during Playford's absence in India from January to May 1892. On 16 June 1893, on the appointment of Playford as agent-general in London, he became premier and attorney-general, and his government remained in power until 1 Dec. 1899, a notable fact in the history of the colony; no former ministry had held office for more than three years.

Kingston had few equals in Australia as a parliamentary draftsman. While a member of the Colton government he drafted the bill for the imposition of land and income taxes. He also prepared and carried the employers' liability bill and a measure to amend the laws of inheritance. Whilst a member of the Playford government he rendered valuable assistance in securing the adoption of a protective tariff and the payment of members. He was a strong opponent of Chinese immigration, and was one of the representatives of his colony in June 1888 at the Australasian conference held in Sydney on the subject. The measure which he framed for regulating the immigration was adopted by all the colonies represented at the conference with the exception of Tasmania.

His name is intimately associated with the federation of Australia. In 1888, as attorney-general in the Playford government, he took charge of the bill for securing the entry of South Australia into the federal council, and after a severe struggle succeeded in passing it. He was one of the representatives of the colony at the session of the council held at Hobart in February 1889. He was a member of the federal convention held at Sydney in 1891, and assisted Sir Samuel Griffith in preparing the original Commonwealth bill. Acting with Sir George Turner, he also drafted the federal enabling bill, which was adopted at the conference of Australian premiers at Hobart in 1895, and when the second federal convention assembled at Adelaide in March 1897, Kingston was elected président and presided also over the adjourned meetings at Sydney and Melbourne in 1897–8. He was a member of the premiers' conference at Melbourne in 1899, which finally settled the federal constitution bill which was ultimately approved by the referendum.

In 1897 he represented South Australia at Queen Victoria's diamond jubilee celebrations in London, and as president of the federal convention he presented a loyal address. He was made an honorary D.C.L. of Oxford on 30 June and was sworn a member of the privy council on 7 July 1897. He visited England again in May 1900, when he resigned his seat in the House of Representatives. He then accompanied (Sir) Edmund Barton and Mr. Deakin to London to assist in the passing of the commonwealth constitution bill through the imperial parliament.

On his return to Australia he was elected (22 Sept. 1900) to the legislative council of South Australia. He resigned on 31 Dec., and at the first federal elections in March 1901 South Australia returned him at the head of the poll to the commonwealth House of Representatives.

When the first commonwealth administration was formed by Sir Edmund Barton on 1 Jan. 1901 Kingston became minister of trade and customs, and introduced a customs tariff bill, imposing high duties which aroused vehement discussion. He fought it successfully through parliament, and when it became law administered it with unprecedented severity. He resigned his position in the ministry on 7 July 1903 owing to differences of opinion with his colleagues over the conciliation and arbitration bill, in which he was more in harmony with the labour party than with other members of the cabinet.

Re-elected without a contest to the commonwealth parliament for the district of Adelaide at the general elections of 1903 and 1906, he took little further part in public affairs. He died at Adelaide on 11 May 1908, and was buried in West Terrace cemetery in that city.

Kingston married in 1873 Lucy May, daughter of Lawrence McCarthy of Adelaide, but there was no issue. He had adopted a son who pre-deceased him.

[Turner's First Decade of the Australian Commonwealth, 1911; The Times, 12 May 1908; Adelaide Chronicle and Adelaide Observer, 16 May 1908; Johns's Notable Australians, 1908; Year Book of Australia, 1908; Dod's Peerage, 1908; Hodder's History of South Australia, 2 vols. 1893; Mennell's Dict. of Australas. Biog. 1892; Colonial Office Records.] C. A.

KINNS, SAMUEL (1826–1903), writer on the Bible, born in 1826, was educated at Colchester grammar school and privately. He received the degree of Ph.D. from the University of Jena in 1859. For twenty-five years he was principal and proprietor of a prosperous private school, The College, Highbury New Park. Ordained deacon in 1885 and priest in 1889, he held a curacy at All Souls, Langham Place (1885–9), and was rector of Holy Trinity, Minories, from 29 March 1889 until the closing of the church on 1 Jan. 1899, under the Union of Benefices Act. In 'Moses and Geology,' which he published in 1882 (14th edit. 1895), he endeavoured to show that the account of the creation in the first chapter of Genesis harmonises with the latest scientific discoveries. His next work, 'Graven in the Rock,' published in 1891 (4th edit. 1897), deals with the confirmation of Biblical history afforded by the Egyptian and Assyrian monuments. Kinns was a popular lecturer on the subjects of his books at the British Museum and in London churches, but his pious zeal was greater than his scholarship. He died at Haverstock Hill on 14 July 1903.

He also published: 1. 'Holy Trinity, Minories, its Past and Present History,' 1890. 2. 'Six Hundred Years, or Historical Sketches of Eminent Men and Women of Holy Trinity, Minories,' 1898; two editions.

[Pratt's People of the Period; Edw. Murray Tomlinson, Holy Trinity Minories, 1907; Brit. Mus. Cat.; Crockford's Clerical Directory.]

C. W.

KINROSS OF GLASCLUNE, first Baron. [See Balfour, John Blair (1837–1905), president of the court of session.]

KITSON, JAMES, first Baron Airedale (1835–1911), iron and steel manufacturer, second of the four sons of James Kitson of Elmete Hall, Yorkshire (1807–1885), by his wife Ann, daughter of John Newton of Leeds, was born at Leeds on 22 Sept. 1835. His father, who started life in humble circumstances and was a friend of George Stephenson, established engineering works at Airedale and proved a pioneer of engineering industry in the north of England; the first locomotive seen in the West Riding came from his workshop; he was mayor of Leeds in 1860–2.

Educated first at Wakefield proprietary school and afterwards at University College, London, young Kitson was placed, with his elder brother Frederick William, in charge of the Monkbridge ironworks, which had been purchased by his father in 1854 to supply his Airedale foundry at Hunslet and other engineering works with sound Yorkshire iron. On the death of his brother in 1877 James assumed the sole direction of the ironworks, and assisted his father also at the Hunslet works. These now (1912) cover twelve acres and give employment to 2000 workmen. Although builders of stationary engines and other machinery, the firm is best known as constructors of locomotives especially suited to the various requirements of mountain ranges, deserts, or swamps. The business was converted into a limited liability company in 1886, but Kitson retained an active supervision of its affairs, assisted by his eldest son and his nephew, F. J. Kitson.

A successful ironmaster, he soon attained eminence in the industrial world. He was an original member of the Iron and Steel Institute, was its president in 1889–91, and was awarded the Bessemer gold medal in May 1903. He became a member of the Institution of Mechanical Engineers in 1859, and a member of the Institution of Civil Engineers in December 1876, serving on its council from 1899 to 1901. He was also president of the Iron Trade Association.

Kitson was a devoted citizen of Leeds. He was its first lord mayor in 1896–7, and was president of the Leeds Chamber of Commerce in 1880–1, taking a lifelong interest in social and educational movements. In 1862 he had instituted a model-dwelling scheme for Leeds workers, was a generous supporter of the Leeds General Infirmary, and president of the Hospitals for Poor Consumptives organised by the Leeds Tuberculosis Association. To the Leeds Art Gallery he gave Lord Leighton's picture 'The Return of Persephone.' In October 1904 the Leeds University conferred on him the honorary degree of D.Sc. He also received on 23 May 1906 the honorary freedom of the city, and at the beginning of 1908 was elected president of the Leeds Institute.

In his early business career he became honorary secretary of the Yorkshire Union of Mechanics' Institutes, one of the earliest institutions of its kind in the country, and helped to establish the Holbeck Institute, of which he became trustee. He was also connected with the National Education League, and acted as secretary of the Leeds branch. A warm supporter of the liberal party, he first became prominent as a politician at the time of the Education Act of 1870. He was chosen in 1880 president of the Leeds Liberal Association, and in the same year took a conspicuous part in securing the return of Gladstone for the borough. He was from 1883 to 1890 president of the National Liberal Federation. After unsuccessfully contesting central Leeds in 1886, he represented the Colne Valley division of the West Riding from 1892 to 1907. He was active in promoting old age pensions, and was elected president of the National Old Age Pensions League at its inauguration on 24 October 1894. Kitson, who was created a baronet on 28 Aug. 1886, was made a privy councillor on 30 June 1906, and was created Baron Airedale of Gledhow on 17 July 1907. An ardent free trader, he had charge in 1906 of the motion by which the liberal government contested the question of tariff reform.

Amongst other activities, he was honorary colonel of the 3rd volunteer battalion of the West Yorkshire regiment; chairman of the London and Northern Steamship Co., the Yorkshire Banking Co., and the Baku Russian Petroleum Co.; and director of the London City and Midland Bank and of the North Eastern Railway Company. A member of the Unitarian body, he devoted much of his time and means to religious and philanthropic objects.

Airedale died in Paris from a cardiac affection on 16 March 1911, and was buried in St. John's churchyard, Roundhay, Leeds.

He was twice married: (1) on 20 Sept. 1860 to Emily Christiana (*d.* 1873), second daughter of Joseph Cliff of Wortley, Yorkshire, by whom he had three sons, Albert Ernest, who succeeded to the peerage, James Clifford, and Edward Christian, and two daughters; (2) on 1 June 1881 to Mary Laura, only daughter of Edward Fisher Smith of the Priory, Dudley, by whom he had one son, Roland Dudley, and a daughter. He left an estate provisionally sworn at 1,000,000*l.*

A portrait painted by Mr. J. S. Sargent in 1905 is in possession of the family at Gledhow Hall, Leeds. A bust by Mr. Spruce, a local sculptor, is to be placed in Leeds Town Hall, by gift of Mr. Middlebrook, M.P. A memorial sundial at the Springfield Convalescent Home, Horsforth, was subscribed for by the firm's workmen in October 1911.

[The Times, 17, 23, and 29 March 1911; Lodge's Peerage, 1912; Proc. Inst. Civ. Engineers, v. 186, pp. 446–7; McCalmont's Parliamentary Poll Book, 1910, pp. 145, 267–8; Yorkshire Post, 17 Mar. 1911; Pall Mall Mag. (portrait) 1907, v. 40, pp. 417–24; the Rev. C. Hargrove's In memory of James Kitson, first Baron Airedale (reprint from Yorkshire Post, with additions and portrait), 1911; Leeds Hospital Mag., Nov. 1911, pp. 221–3; Morley's Life of Gladstone; private information.] C. W.

KITTON, FREDERICK GEORGE (1856–1904), writer on Dickens, born at Golding Street, Heigham, Norwich, on 5 May 1856, was son of Frederick Kitton, tobacconist, who made some reputation as a microscopist. His mother's maiden name was Mary Spence. Coming to London at seventeen to follow the occupation of an artist and wood-engraver, he served as apprentice on the staff of the 'Graphic.' He attained much skill as an etcher, and contributed to artistic journals. Inheriting from his father a capacity for research, he soon turned to literary pursuits. With the exception of a few minor efforts, including memoirs of Hablot K. Browne (1882), of John Leech (1883), and of his father (1895), he mainly devoted himself with immense zeal to illustrating the life and works of Charles Dickens, in a long series of books, the chief of which were: 'Dickensiana, a bibliography of the literature relating to Charles Dickens and his writings' (1886); 'Charles Dickens by Pen and Pencil' (1890); 'Dickens and his Illustrators' (1899); 'Charles Dickens, his Life, Writings, and Personality' (1901), in which he supplemented Forster's biography; and 'The Dickens Country,' published posthumously (1905; 2nd edit. 1911). He also annotated the 'Rochester' edition of Dickens's works (1900), and at the time of his death he was working for a New York publisher upon the costly 'Autograph,' or 'Millionaire's,' edition, and with Mr. M. H. Spielmann on a like edition of Thackeray.

Kitton was one of the founders, and an active member of, the Dickens Fellowship, and compiled the catalogue of the Dickens Exhibition (1903).

From 1888 Kitton lived at St. Albans, where he helped to procure the purchase for the Hertfordshire County Museum of the Sir John Evans collection of books, manuscripts, drawings, etc., relating to the county; these he catalogued and arranged. Besides writing much on St. Albans and its neighbourhood, he helped to save from destruction many old buildings. Kitton died at St. Albans on 10 Sept. 1904, and was buried there. In 1889 he married Emily Clara, second daughter of H. A. Lawford, C.E., but had no children.

His large Dickens library was purchased from his widow by a subscription organised by the Dickens Fellowship, as a nucleus for a national Dickens library, and was formally presented to the Guildhall Library by Lord James of Hereford on 7 Feb. 1908.

[Memoir by Arthur Waugh in The Dickensian, 1895, prefixed to Kitton's posthumous The Dickens Country, 1905; Athenæum, 17 Sept. 1904; Academy, lxvii. 192, 225 (article by Walter Jerrold); Hertfordshire Standard, 16 Sept. 1904; Brit. Mus. Cat.; Cat. of Guildhall Lib.] C. W.

KNIGHT, JOSEPH (1837–1909), landscape painter and engraver, son of Joseph and Eliza Knight, was born in London on 27 Jan. 1837. At the age of seven he met with an accident which necessitated the amputation of his right arm at St. Bartholomew's Hospital. In 1845 the family removed to Manchester, where Knight spent the earlier part of his career as an artist, visiting France, Holland, and Italy. In 1871 he removed to London and in 1875 to North Wales, where he thenceforth chiefly resided. He made some reputation alike as a painter in oil and in water-colour, and as an engraver and etcher. Welsh scenery furnished the subjects of many of his pictures and engravings, and he was a member of the Royal Cambrian Academy. Knight exhibited from 1861 onward at various London galleries, contributing to the Royal Academy for the first time in 1869. He was elected in 1882 a member of the Royal Institute of Painters in Water Colours and an associate of the Society of Painter Etchers, of which he became a fellow on 13 April 1883. From 1883 to 1908 he sent 104 original mezzotint engravings, varied occasionally by etchings, to the exhibitions of the Painter Etchers; his work was rather monotonous and lacking in expression. He is represented as a painter in the Tate Gallery (Chantrey bequest), Victoria and Albert Museum, the City Art Gallery and Peel Park Gallery, Manchester, the Walker Art Gallery, Liverpool, and at Oldham; some engravings are in the British Museum. He died at Bryn Glas, near Conway, on 2 Jan. 1909. In 1859 he married Elizabeth Radford of Manchester, who survived him.

[Graves, Dict. of Artists and Royal Acad. Exhibitors, iv. 346; The Times, 6 and 11 Jan. 1909; private information.] C. D.

KNIGHT, JOSEPH (1829–1907), dramatic critic, born at Leeds on 24 May 1829, was elder son of Joseph Knight, cloth merchant, who was a native of Carlisle. His mother, Marianne daughter of Joseph Wheelwright, became blind in middle life but lived to the age of seventy-three. Educated at a private boarding school, Bramham College, near Tadcaster, Knight early showed a taste for poetry and rose to be head of the school. In 1848 a promising poem by him, 'The Sea by Moonlight,' was printed at Sheffield by the headmaster for circulation among his pupils' parents.

Joining his father in business at nineteen, he devoted his leisure to literature, collecting and reading books, and taking a prominent part in the literary activities of Leeds. Elizabethan and early French poetry especially moved his youthful enthusiasm, and he never lost his admiration for the work of Drayton, Wither, and Ronsard. With his fellow-townsman, Mr. Alfred Austin, afterwards poet laureate (his junior by six years), he helped to found a Mechanics' Institute at Leeds, at which he lectured on literary subjects. On 7 April 1854 he lectured on 'The Fairies of English Poetry' before the Leeds Philosophical and Literary Society. At Leeds, too, he made the acquaintance of William Edward Forster [q. v.], who stayed at Knight's house while he was parliamentary candidate for the constituency in 1859. Knight seconded Forster's nomination.

In 1860 Knight adventurously abandoned a business career in Leeds for journalistic life in London. He found early employment as dramatic critic for the 'Literary Gazette,' through a chance meeting with the editor, Mr. John (afterwards Viscount) Morley. Thenceforth he largely occupied himself in writing of the contemporary stage. In 1869 he succeeded John Abraham Heraud [q. v.] as dramatic critic of the 'Athenæum,' and he retained that post till his death. In 1871, during the siege of Paris, he used his influence to secure the invitation to the Comedie Française to act at the Gaiety Theatre in London. He also acted as dramatic critic for the 'Sunday Times,' the 'Globe,' and for the 'Daily Graphic' from 1894 to 1906. But Knight's dramatic interests always ranged far beyond the contemporary theatre. He was thoroughly well versed in dramatic history, and from 1883 to the close of the first supplement in 1901 Knight was the chief contributor of the lives of actors and actresses to this Dictionary. His articles numbered over 500. On the notice of Garrick in these pages he based an independent memoir which appeared in 1894.

Knight's social charm, handsome presence, courteous bearing, and fine literary taste made him welcome in literary and dramatic circles from his first arrival in London. His early associates there included John Westland Marston [q. v.] and Sebastian Evans [q. v. Suppl. II], to both of whom he owed counsel and encouragement. At Marston's house he met leading authors and playwrights. Thomas Purnell [q. v.], a Bohemian journalist, introduced him to Swinburne, and with that poet and with Swinburne's friend, Dante Gabriel Rossetti, he was long on terms of intimacy. Rossetti valued Knight's discernment in poetical and other matters and liked his manly geniality (cf. W. M. Rossetti's *Life of D. G. Rossetti*). One of Dante Rossetti's last letters was addressed to Knight (5 March 1882), and in 1887 Knight published a sympathetic and discriminating 'Life of Rossetti' in the 'Great Writers' series.

Knight found varied opportunities of proving his literary knowledge. He contributed the causerie signed 'Sylvanus Urban' to the 'Gentleman's Magazine' from 1887 till near his death, and he was a reviewer of general literature for the 'Athenæum.' In July 1883, on the death of Henry Frederick Turle [q. v.], he became editor of 'Notes and Queries,' and retained that office for life. In that capacity he indulged his versatile antiquarian and literary tastes and formed many new acquaintances. On 4 May 1893 he was elected F.S.A.

With strong affinities for Bohemian life, Knight was long a leading member of the Arundel Club. But after 1883, when he was elected to the Garrick Club (3 March), his leisure was mainly spent there. He was an ideal club companion, convivial, chivalric, and cultured. With actors and actresses he maintained cordial relations without prejudicing his critical independence. On 4 July 1905 the dramatic profession entertained him, as the oldest living dramatic critic, to dinner at the Savoy Hotel. Sir Henry Irving took the chair, and M. Coquelin and Madame Réjane were among the guests.

Knight was an ardent book collector through life, but twice he was under the necessity of parting with his collection—on the second occasion in 1905. He died at his house, 27 Camden Square, on 23 June 1907, and was buried in Highgate cemetery.

He married at the parish church, Leeds, on 3 June 1856, Rachel (*d.* 1911), youngest daughter of John Wilkinson of Gledhall Mount near Leeds. He had issue a son Philip Sidney, *b.* 2 Feb. 1857, now in Australia, and two daughters, Mrs. Ian Forbes Robertson and Mrs. Mansel Sympson of Lincoln. A posthumous portrait in oils by Miss Margaret Grose was presented to the Garrick Club in 1912 by Knight's friend Mr. H. B. Wheatley. A coloured chalk drawing by Leslie Ward is dated June 1905. William Bell Scott designed a book plate for Knight, embodying his likeness, in 1881.

Besides the books mentioned Knight published in 1893 'Theatrical Notes 1874–1879,' a collection of articles on the drama from the 'Athenæum,' and he edited in 1883 Downes's 'Roscius Anglicanus.'

[The Times, 24 June 1907; Athenæum, June 1907; Notes and Queries, 29 June 1907; J. Collins Francis, Notes by the Way, 1909, pp. i–xliii (pp. xl–xliii contain a full list of Knight's contributions to this Dictionary); V. Rendall, Some Reminiscences of Joseph Knight (Nineteenth Cent., Dec. 1911); personal knowledge.] S. L.

KNOWLES, Sir JAMES THOMAS (1831–1908), founder and editor of the 'Nineteenth Century' and architect, born at Reigate, Surrey, on 13 Oct. 1831, was eldest child in the family of two sons and three daughters of James Thomas Knowles, architect, by his wife Susanna, daughter of Dr. Brown. About 1839 his father built for himself a large house in Clapham Park, and there or in the near neighbourhood Knowles lived till 1884.

After education at University College, London, Knowles entered his father's office and spent some time in studying architecture in Italy. He published a prize essay on 'Architectural Education' in 1852, became an associate of the Royal Institute of British Architects in 1853, and a fellow in 1870. Knowles practised his profession with success for some thirty years. He built, according to his own account, 'many hundreds of houses, besides several churches, hospitals, clubs, warehouses, stores, roads, and bridges.' His chief commissions were three churches in Clapham (St. Stephen's, St. Saviour's, and St. Philip's), Albert Mansions, Victoria Street, The Thatched House Club in St. James's Street in 1865, and Sir Erasmus Wilson's enlargement of the Sea Bathing Hospital at Margate in 1882. Baron Albert Grant [q. v. Suppl. I] was at one time a client. In 1873 Knowles designed a palatial residence for Baron Grant which was erected in Kensington High Street on the site of demolished slums, but the house was never occupied and was pulled down in 1883, when its place was taken by Kensington Court. In 1874, too, when Baron Grant purchased Leicester Square with a view to converting it into a public open space, he entrusted Knowles with the task of laying out the ground, and of adorning it architecturally.

But Knowles's activity and alertness of mind always ranged beyond the limits of his professional work. A little volume, compiled from the 'Morte d'Arthur' of Sir Thomas Malory, 'The Story of King Arthur and his Knights of the Round Table,' which he published in 1862, reached an eighth edition in 1895, and met with Tennyson's approval. In contributions to the magazines and periodicals he showed a varied interest in literary and philosophic questions, and he grew ambitious of the acquaintance of leaders of public opinion. In 1866 he called on Tennyson at Freshwater and became an intimate for life. He designed for the poet without charge his new house at Aldworth in 1869.

Early in the same year, when Knowles was entertaining Tennyson and a neighbour, Charles Pritchard [q. v.], at his house at Clapham, the possibility was canvassed of forming a representative 'theological society' for determining in discussion the bases of morality. With characteristic energy Knowles communicated with champions of all schools of thought, and obtained their assent to join such a society. A first meeting was held at Willis's Rooms on 21 April 1869 and the Metaphysical Society was then constituted. The original members included Dean Stanley, Manning, W. G. Ward, R. H. Hutton, James Martineau, Bishop Ellicott, Bagehot, Huxley, Tyndall, Gladstone, and Froude. Knowles acted as general secretary. Early anticipations of failure were belied, and under Knowles's direction the society flourished for twelve years. The members dined together month by month at an hotel, and the discussion followed. Important recruits were Ruskin, who joined in 1870, and Fitzjames Stephen. A chairman was elected annually, and he was occasionally re-elected. The chairmen were Sir John Lubbock, Manning, Huxley, Gladstone, W. G. Ward, James Martineau, Lord Selborne, and Lord Arthur Russell. The society dissolved in 1881 because, said Tennyson, the members failed to define what metaphysics meant. According to Knowles, all possible subjects had then been exhausted, while pressure of other work compelled his withdrawal from the direction.

Knowles's management of the Metaphysical Society brought him into personal touch with the chief intellectual men of the day. With Gladstone his relations were soon as close as with Tennyson. He turned such relationships to much public advantage. In 1870 he became editor of the 'Contemporary Review' in succession to Dean Alford, and he induced many members of the Metaphysical Society to contribute to the pages of the magazine either papers which they had read at the society's meetings or original articles. Such contributions gave the magazine a high repute. In 1877 the 'Contemporary' changed hands, and a disagreement with the new proprietors led Knowles to sever his connection with it. Thereupon he founded under his sole proprietorship and editorship a new periodical which he called the 'Nineteenth Century.' The first number appeared in March and was introduced by a sonnet of Tennyson. Members of the Metaphysical Society continued to support Knowles, and Gladstone, Manning, Sir John Lubbock, Bishop Ellicott, and Fitzjames Stephen were early contributors to the new venture, whose professed aim was to provide a platform from which men of all parties and persuasions might address the public in their own names. 'Signed writing' was the essential principle of the 'Nineteenth Century.' No anonymous articles were admissible. Every topic of current interest was to be discussed openly by the highest authority. With diplomatic skill Knowles induced writers of renown to engage in controversy with one another in his magazine on matters of moment, at times in symposia, but commonly in independent articles. Gladstone, who was persuaded frequently to meet in religious debate Fitzjames Stephen and Huxley, deservedly complimented Knowles on his success in keeping 'the "Nineteenth Century" pot boiling' (13 May 1888, MORLEY'S *Life*, iii. 360). The result was a triumph for periodical literature, and the profits were substantial. Few contemporaries of distinction in any walk of life failed to contribute to the magazine, over which Knowles exercised an active and rigorous control till his death. When the nineteenth century ended, he renamed the magazine 'The Nineteenth Century and After' (Jan. 1901).

Knowles, who gave up architectural practice in 1883, moved next year from Clapham to Queen Anne's Lodge by St. James's Park, where he constantly entertained a distinguished circle of friends and collected pictures and works of art. He caused to be painted for his collection Tennyson's portrait by Millais in 1881, and Gladstone's portrait by Troubetzkoi in 1893. Although his interests were mainly absorbed by the 'Nineteenth Century,' he found time to engage in a few other public movements. In 1871 he organised the Paris Food Fund for the relief of the besieged population in Paris, and induced Manning, Huxley, Lubbock, and Ruskin to act with him on the committee. In 1882 he energetically opposed the Channel Tunnel scheme; he not merely condemned it in an article from his own pen in the 'Nineteenth Century,' but brought together in the magazine a vast number of adverse opinions from eminent persons. When the proposal was revived in 1890, Knowles repeated his denunciation in the 'Nineteenth Century,' and in Gladstone's view crushed the design. 'The aborted channel tunnel,' wrote Gladstone, 'cries out against you from the bottom of the sea.' In philanthropic enterprise Knowles was also active. He joined Lord Shaftesbury, the Baroness Burdett Coutts, and Miss Octavia Hill in starting the Sanitary Laws Enforcement Society, and he originated the first fund for giving toys to children in hospitals and workhouses.

Knowles was well known to Queen Alexandra and other members of the Royal

Family. When on a visit to her and King Edward VII at Sandringham in 1903 he was made K.C.V.O. In his last years he had a house at Brighton as well as in London. He died at Brighton of heart failure on 13 Feb. 1908, and was buried in the extramural cemetery there.

Knowles was twice married: (1) in 1861 to Jane Emma, daughter of the Rev. Abraham Borradaile; (2) in 1865 to Isabel Mary, daughter of Henry William Hewlett. His second wife survived him with one son and two daughters. His pictures and works of art were dispersed by sale at Christie's 26–29 May 1908.

[A short autobiographical MS. kindly lent by Lady Knowles; The Times, 14 Feb. 1908; Journal Roy. Institute Brit. Architects, 22 Feb. 1908; Tennyson and his Friends, ed. Lord Tennyson, 1911; Lord Ronald Gower's Old Diaries, 1902. For the Metaphysical Society see Knowles's prefatory note to R. H. Hutton's paper, The Metaphysical Society, a Reminiscence (Nineteenth Century, Aug. 1885); Ruskin's Works, ed. E. T. Cook and Wedderburn, xxxiv. pp. xxviii–xxix; Macdonald's Life of W. C. Magee, i. 284; Tennyson's Life, 2 vols. 1897; Leslie Stephen's Life of Sir J. Fitzjames Stephen, 1895.] S. L.

KNOX, Mrs. ISA, born Craig (1831–1903), poetical writer, only child of John Craig, hosier and glover, was born in Edinburgh, 17 Oct. 1831. In childhood she lost both parents, and was reared by her grandmother, leaving school in her tenth year. A close study of standard English authors developed literary tastes; and, after contributing verses to the 'Scotsman' with the signature 'Isa,' she was regularly employed on the paper in 1853. Coming to London in 1857 she was appointed secretary to the National Association for the Promotion of Social Science, and held the position till she married, in May 1866, her cousin, John Knox, an iron merchant of London. In 1858 she won with a resonant ode a prize of 50*l.* offered at the Crystal Palace for a centenary poem on Burns. There were 621 candidates, among them being Frederic William Henry Myers [q. v. Suppl. I], Gerald Massey [q. v. Suppl. II], and Arthur Joseph Munby [q. v. Suppl. II]. After her marriage she contributed occasionally to 'Fraser,' 'Good Words,' and the 'Quiver,' edited the 'Argosy' for a short time, and published some volumes of poems and juvenile histories. She died at Brockley, Suffolk, on 23 Dec. 1903.

In verse Mrs. Knox produced nothing that surpassed the Burns ode. Her first volume, 'Poems by Isa' (1856), showed some promise, and some lyric quality appeared in 'Poems: an Offering to Lancashire' (1863); 'Duchess Agnes, a Drama, and other Poems' (1864); and 'Songs of Consolation' (1874). Dr. A. H. Japp edited a 'Selection from Mrs. Knox's Poems' in 1892. Of Mrs. Knox's prose work 'The Essence of Slavery' (1863) summarised F. A. Kemble's 'Journal of a Residence on a Georgian Plantation,' and 'Esther West' (1870; 6th edit. 1884) was a well-constructed story. Mrs. Knox's 'Little Folk's History of England' (1872) reached its 30th thousand in 1899, and the author adapted from it a successful 'Easy History for Upper Standards' (1884). 'Tales on the Parables,' two series, appeared in 1872–7.

[Rogers's Modern Scottish Minstrel; Grant Wilson's Poets and Poetry of Scotland; Edwards's Modern Scottish Poets, 2nd series, Brechin, 1881; Burns Centenary Poems, 1859; Miles's Poets and Poetry of the Nineteenth Century, vol. ix.; information from Dr. A. H. Millar, Dundee; Brit. Mus. Cat.] T. B.

KYNASTON (formerly Snow), HERBERT (1835–1910), canon of Durham and classical scholar, born in London on 29 June 1835, was second son of Robert Snow by his wife Georgina, daughter of Roger Kynaston and sister of Herbert Kynaston [q. v.], high-master of St. Paul's school. His maternal grandmother was Georgina, daughter of Sir Charles Oakeley [q. v.], governor of Madras. From 1844 to 1847 Herbert Snow was at a private school at Beaconsfield, and from 1847 to 1853 was an oppidan at Eton, where he was among the selected candidates for the Newcastle scholarship, and made his mark on the football field and the river, rowing in both the Britannia and Monarch. In 1853 he gained a scholarship at St. John's College, Cambridge. His university career was brilliant and exceptionally versatile. In 1855 he won the Porson scholarship, which was then awarded for the first time, together with Camden's gold medal for Latin hexameters and Browne's gold medal for Latin alcaic ode, and in 1857 he was bracketed senior classic with (Sir) John Robert Seeley [q. v.] and two others. He became fellow of St. John's college on 22 March 1858, graduating B.A. in 1857 and proceeding M.A. in 1860 when he vacated the fellowship on his marriage. Nor was it only in scholarship that Snow excelled as an undergraduate. He rowed seven in the university boat in the Oxford and Cambridge race of 1856, and was stroke in 1857. He was a member of the Alpine Club from 1862 to 1875. He was one of the earliest members of the Amateur Dramatic Club, and became a freemason. Throughout his life he was devoted to the craft, passing the chair in Foundation Lodge, Cheltenham, and afterwards being grand chaplain of England and one of the founders of Universities Lodge, Durham.

In 1858 Snow returned to Eton as assistant master and was ordained deacon in 1859 and priest in 1860. After sixteen years at Eton, he was elected principal of Cheltenham College in 1874. In 1875 he assumed his mother's family surname of Kynaston. In 1881 he proceeded B.D. and the next year D.D. at Cambridge; for the former degree he wrote a Latin thesis on the use of the expression 'The Kingdom of God' in the New Testament, and for the latter an English essay on 'The Influence of the Holy Spirit on the Life of Man.'

Resigning Cheltenham in 1888, Kynaston was for nearly a year vicar of St. Luke's, Kentish Town. In 1889 Bishop Lightfoot appointed him canon of Durham and professor of Greek in the university, in succession to the distinguished scholar and teacher, Thomas Saunders Evans. He remained at Durham till his death there on 1 Aug. 1910.

He married (1) in 1860 Mary Louisa Anne, daughter of Thomas Bros, barrister; and (2) in 1865 Charlotte, daughter of Rev. John Cordeaux of Hooton Roberts. He had four sons and three daughters.

Kynaston's academic distinctions fail to exhibit the range of his powers. Always devoted to music, of which he had a practical as well as a theoretical knowledge, he had a good tenor voice. As a linguist he was at home in five or six languages, and could improvise effective poetical translations. Once, in less than two hours, he rendered an Italian song into English verse which fitted the music.

An admirable composer in Greek and Latin, Kynaston was too fastidious a writer to make any contribution to scholarly literature commensurate with his capacities. His best-known book is an edition of Theocritus with English notes (Oxford, 1869; 5th edit. 1910). His other works are: 1. 'Nucipruna: exercises in Latin Elegiac Verse,' 12mo, 1873. 2. 'Sermons preached in the College Chapel, Cheltenham,' 1876. 3. 'Poetæ Græci,' extracts with English notes, 1879. 4. 'Exercises in Greek Iambic Verse' and Key, 12mo, 1879–80. 5. 'Exemplaria Cheltoniensia,' 1880. 6. 'Selections from the Greek Elegiac Poets,' 18mo, 1880. He also published translations of Euripides's 'Alcestis' into English verse (1906) and of the prayers from 'Vita Jesu Christi' of Ludolphus of Saxony (1909).

[The Times, 2 and 8 Aug. 1910; Eagle, Dec. 1911; Life of Kynaston, by E. D. Stone, 1912; Classical Review, Nov. 1910; personal knowledge; private information.] H. E.

L

LABOUCHERE, Mrs. **HENRY**. [See Hodson, Henrietta (1841–1910), actress.]

LAFONT, EUGÈNE (1837–1908), science teacher in India, born at Mons, Belgium, on 26 March 1837, was eldest son of Pierre Lafont by his wife Marie Soudar. Educated at St. Barbara's College, Ghent, and at the Jesuits' seminary, he was admitted to the order in 1854, and did educational work in Belgium until 1865. He was then sent to Calcutta to inaugurate science teaching at St. Xavier's College, which had been founded by the Jesuit fathers in 1860 for the 'domiciled' European and Eurasian communities. He was rector of the college from 1873 to 1904, when failing health caused his retirement. After leaving Europe he only revisited it twice, in 1878 to recruit after severe illness, and in 1900 to visit the Paris exhibition for scientific purposes.

Indian education on Lafont's arrival in India was almost exclusively literary, and Lafont was the pioneer of scientific teaching in Bengal. He combined a thorough knowledge of experimental physics with great skill as a teacher and lecturer. He equipped St. Xavier's with a fine meteorological and solar observatory, and with a physical laboratory second to none in India. He was one of the founders of the Indian Association for the Cultivation of Science, and for nineteen years gave weekly honorary lectures under its auspices, and was its senior vice-president. A popular and eloquent preacher, he also frequently lectured on Christian evidences, claiming that true science was the handmaid of faith.

Lafont was a member of the Institutes of Mechanical and Electrical Engineers, and was chairman of the Calcutta section of the latter from 1889. Appointed a fellow of Calcutta University in 1877, he took an active part in the work of the senate, filling at various times the offices of syndic (thrice), dean of the arts faculty (1904–7), and president of the board of studies in physics (1904–6). At the jubilee celebrations of the university in March 1908 he received the honorary degree of D.Sc. He had been created C.I.E. on 1 Jan. 1880, and was made an officer of the French Academy, while in 1898 the king of the Belgians made him a knight of the order of Leopold. His devotion to science, his constant labour for the welfare of the 'domiciled' white community, his gentleness, and his charm of manner won him general esteem. He died at Darjeeling on 10 May 1908, and was buried there.

[Journ. Inst. of Elect. Eng. vol. xxxxi. no. 192, 1908; The Times, 11 May 1908; Englishman (Calcutta), weekly edit., 14 and 21 May 1908.] F. H. B.

LAIDLAW, ANNA ROBENA, afterwards Mrs. Thomson (1819–1901), pianist, daughter of Alexander Laidlaw, a merchant, by his wife Ann Keddy, was born at Bretton, Yorkshire, on 30 April 1819. Her family, who were intimate with Sir Walter Scott, claimed connection with the Laidlaws of Chapelhope and Glenrath; Scott's Willie Laidlaw and James Hogg's wife, Margaret Laidlaw, were kinsfolk (cf. Patterson's *Schumann*, 1903). In 1827 Robena Laidlaw went to Edinburgh, where she studied music with Robert Müller. Her family removed to Königsberg in 1830, and there she continued her musical studies under Georg Tag, subsequently taking lessons from Henri Herz, in London, in 1834. In that year she played at William IV's court and at Paganini's farewell concert. Returning to Germany, she gave pianoforte recitals in Berlin with much applause, and visited Warsaw, St. Petersburg, Dresden, and Vienna. She made the acquaintance of Schumann, who dedicated to her his 'Fantasiestücke,' Op. 12, and wrote of her playing at the Gewandhaus Hall, Leipzig, in July 1837, as 'thoroughly good and individual.' 'This artiste,' he added, 'in whose culture are united English solidity and natural amiability, will remain a treasured memory to all who have made her closer acquaintance' (*Neue Zeitschrift für Musik*, 11 July 1837). Several letters were addressed to her by Schumann, one of which is given in facsimile in Dr. Patterson's biography of the composer (pp. 106, 107). At Schumann's suggestion she transposed, as being more 'musical,' the original order of her Christian names, from Robena Anna to Anna Robena. She was appointed pianist to the Queen of Hanover, and remained in Germany until 1840, when she settled in London. After her marriage to George Thomson in 1852 she retired from public life. She died in London on 29 May 1901, and was buried at Woking after cremation. She had four daughters.

[Mendel's Musikalisches Conversations Lexikon, 1875; Dr. Annie W. Patterson's Schumann, 1903; Zeitschrift Int. Mus. Ges. iii. 188 ff.; Rellstab's Life of Ludwig Berger, 1846; Grove's Dict. of Music, 1906, ii. 622; information from her daughter, Miss Robena Thomson.] J. C. H.

LAIDLAW, JOHN (1832–1906), presbyterian divine and theologian, born in Edinburgh on 7 April 1832, was only child of Walter Laidlaw by his wife Margaret Brydon. His ancestors for generations were sheep farmers. He studied at the Normal School of Edinburgh, with a view to the teaching profession, but ultimately decided to prepare for the ministry. At Edinburgh University, where he matriculated in October 1851, he distinguished himself in classics, mathematics, and philosophy, winning four gold medals, and carried off (1853) Sir William Hamilton's [q. v.] prize in philosophy and the Bulwer-Lytton [q. v.] prize for an essay on the relations of mind and matter. In 1854 he was made M.A. *honoris causa*.

After spending three sessions in the divinity hall of the Reformed Presbyterian church, Laidlaw in 1856 joined the Free church of Scotland and studied for two sessions (1856–8) at New College, Edinburgh. During the summer of 1858 he attended classes at Heidelberg and other German universities, and in the following year began his ministry at Bannockburn. On 6 August 1863 he was inducted to the Free West church, Perth, where the membership greatly increased under his charge. A handsome church was built, and he made his mark as an evangelical preacher. In 1868 he declined an invitation to become colleague to Dr. Robert Smith Candlish [q. v.]. From 1872 to 1881 he was minister of the Free West church, Aberdeen. On 25 May 1881 he was appointed to the chair of systematic theology in New College, Edinburgh; he held the post until 1904.

Laidlaw was a conservative theologian, basing his lectures on the teaching of the Reformation divines. 'In his best work, there was a fine combination of the biblical, the experimental, and the historical' (*Memoir* by H. R. Mackintosh, D.D., p. 37). While unsympathetic towards the views of William Robertson Smith [q. v.], he spoke in the general assembly of 1880 in support of a rejected resolution which confined the assembly's censure of Smith to a general admonition of caution in his public utterances on the theological questions in dispute.

In 1878 Laidlaw delivered the Cunningham lectures at New College, his subject being 'The Biblical Doctrine of Man.' The lectures were published in 1879 (Edinburgh; new edit. entirely recast, 1895; reprint, 1905). His most popular book, 'The Miracles of Our Lord,' in which scholarship was combined with orthodoxy (1890; 4th edit. 1902), also originated in a course of lectures. He further published 'Foundation Truths of Scripture as to Sin and Salvation' (Edinburgh, 1897, Bible Class Handbooks). His 'Studies in the Parables, and other Sermons' appeared posthumously in 1907.

An ardent advocate of the reunion of Scottish presbyterianism, it was largely owing to Laidlaw's influence that the union of the Reformed Presbyterian church with the Free church of Scotland was brought about in 1876. Nine years later, in 1885, he was active in inducing representatives of the three large presbyterian churches to debate the possibility of union. The conference, though abortive at the time, bore fruit later.

In 1880 Laidlaw became hon. D.D. of Edinburgh University. He died after some years of ill-health in Edinburgh on 21 Sept. 1906, and was buried in the Grange cemetery, Edinburgh.

In December 1869 he married Elizabeth, daughter of Samuel Hamilton, who survived him with one daughter.

[Memoir by H. R. Mackintosh, D.D., prefixed to Laidlaw's posthumously published 'Studies in the Parables, and other Sermons' (1907); Scotsman, 22 Sept. 1906; private information.] W. F. G.

LAMBERT, BROOKE (1834–1901), vicar of Greenwich, born at Chertsey, Surrey, on 17 Sept. 1834, was fourth son and fifth of the eight children of Francis John Lambert (1798–1876), younger son of Sir Henry Lambert (1760–1803), fourth baronet. Sir John Lambert (*d.* 1723), the first baronet, belonging to a Huguenot family of the Ile de Rhé, settled as a merchant in London soon after 1685. Brooke's mother, Catherine (*d.* 1851), only daughter of Major-general Wheatley, a Peninsular officer, was of Welsh descent. The family during Brooke's boyhood removed to Kensington.

After education at home and at a small school kept by James Chase, a clergyman of strong evangelical views, Lambert went in 1849 to Brighton College. Deciding to seek holy orders, he became a student at King's College, London. The excitement caused by the ejection of F. D. Maurice in 1853 from his professorship there stirred in him a regard for Maurice which influenced his churchmanship for life. In 1854 he matriculated at Brasenose College, Oxford, as a commoner, and graduated B.A. in 1858; he proceeded M.A. in 1861 and B.C.L. in 1863. He deliberately chose a pass degree in order that he might pursue his own wide course of reading without interference. He attended Stanley's lectures on ecclesiastical history and formed a friendship with him. At Whitsuntide 1858 he was ordained deacon, and was successively curate of Christ Church, Preston (1858–60), and of St. John's, Worcester (1860–3). After some months at Hillingdon, near Uxbridge, he offered himself as curate to the Rev. R. E. Bartlett, vicar of St. Mark's, Whitechapel. On the promotion of Bartlett, Lambert succeeded to the vicarage early in 1866.

As vicar of St. Mark's, Whitechapel, Lambert performed many duties which lay outside the ecclesiastical range. He joined the Whitechapel board of trustees and the vestry and became a member of the board of works and a guardian. His force of character and business capacities admirably fitted him for such offices. He began a thorough study of poor law administration and local government, on which while he was in Whitechapel his views matured very quickly. They found expression in a small volume called 'Pauperism: seven sermons preached at St. Mark's, Whitechapel, and one preached before the University, Oxford, with a Preface on the work and position of clergy in poor districts' (1871). Lambert here put on record the results of a census that he made of a portion of his parish and of careful inquiries into the earnings of the district, with calculations of the cost of living. He thus anticipated the scientific statistical methods of Mr. Charles Booth, as well as the teaching of the Charity Organisation Society on the uselessness of indiscriminate charity. The book is a permanent contribution to economic science and contemporary history. In the year of Lambert's appointment cholera visited the parish. He circulated papers of directions, organised the distribution of medicine and visited the sick assiduously; he notes that on one day he buried forty-four corpses. He founded a penny bank, a soup kitchen, a working-man's club, and a mutual improvement society; he renovated the church. At the general election of 1868 he arranged a course of sermons in his church on the duties of electors. Among the preachers were H. R. Haweis, Stopford Brooke, F. D. Maurice, and J. R. Green. Under the constant strain of work Lambert's health broke down and he resigned the living in the autumn of 1870. He spent the winter abroad with J. R. Green, then vicar of St. Philip's, Stepney, and a visit to the West Indies, where his family had property, subsequently restored his health. In June 1872 he was instituted to the living of Tamworth, Staffordshire, where he remained for six years. There he made a careful and thorough restoration of the fine old parish church, nearly completed two district churches, and was instrumental in establishing a school board. But he found a provincial town more impervious to new ideas and methods than East London. A serious falling off in his private income owing to the decline of the West Indian sugar trade led to his resignation at the end of 1878.

On leaving Tamworth Lambert engaged in London in voluntary work for the London school board, and educational problems absorbed his attention. He helped to establish the London University Extension Society, and in June 1879 became organising secretary. He was chairman of the Local Centres Association from 1894 to 1900 and vice-chairman of the society in 1898 and 1899. In the autumn of 1879 he became curate-in-charge of St. Jude's, Whitechapel, while the vicar, Canon Barnett, was out of England. In August 1880 he was appointed by Mr. Gladstone vicar of Greenwich, where he remained till his death twenty years later. The position afforded an almost unlimited field for honest and wise public work. The income of the charities of the ancient royal borough amounted to nearly 20,000*l.* per annum, and into the work of wise administration Lambert threw himself with energy. Boreman's Educational Foundation, and the Roan Trust, which maintains two large secondary schools, absorbed much of his attention, and he was also chairman of all the Greenwich groups of elementary schools. He was a member of the Greenwich board of works and a guardian, being the chairman of the infirmary committee and interesting himself minutely in the management of the poor law schools. By his discharge of these public duties he earned for himself a unique position of influence and respect. In his parish work he was equally successful. The parish church was renovated with sound æsthetic judgment. He entrusted his parish council with control of finance and consulted it with regard to changes in worship and ritual. When this council became aware in 1888 of the smallness of the vicar's stipend it established a vicar's fund which contributed 400*l.* per annum to Lambert's income till his death. A university extension centre and a committee of the Charity Organisation Society were successfully established in Greenwich, and in 1885 the Greenwich Provident Dispensary was founded, which quickly reached a membership of 3000. Lambert joined the Mansion House committee appointed to inquire into distress (1888), the departmental committee appointed by the local government board to inquire into the management of poor law schools (1894), and the departmental committee appointed to consider reformatory and industrial schools (1895). From 1880 till his death he was first chairman of the Metropolitan Association for Befriending Young Servants. In the kindred Association for Befriending Boys, founded in 1898, he was also active. As early as 1883 he helped to found the Art for Schools Association, and remained its chairman till 1899.

Lambert, who was a prominent freemason and past grand chaplain of England, combined in his manifold endeavours high ideals with great business aptitudes. He travelled widely in his vacations. His health failed in 1900, and a long journey to South Africa and then up the Nile to Khartoum failed to restore it. He died unmarried at Greenwich vicarage on 25 Jan. 1901, and after cremation was buried at Old Shoeburyness parish church.

A marble bust, executed towards the end of his life by Joy, a sculptor of Tamworth, was presented after his death to the Roan Schools at Greenwich.

Lambert wrote frequently in the 'Contemporary Review' and other magazines, and published many single sermons. He was author of 'The Lord's Prayer: Ten Sermons'

(1883). After his death was published 'Sermons and Lectures by the late Rev. Brooke Lambert, edited by Rev. Ronald Bayne; with a Memoir by J. E. G. de Montmorency.'

[Mr. de Montmorency's Memoir cited above; The Times, 26 Jan. 1901; Spectator, 2 March 1901; Guardian, 30 Jan. and 6 Feb. 1901; A Thanksgiving for Brooke Lambert, a Sermon preached in Tamworth Parish Church on St. Lambert's Day, 1903, by C. W. Stubbs, D.D., Dean of Ely, afterwards bishop of Truro, 1903.] R. B.

LANG, JOHN MARSHALL (1834–1909), principal of the University of Aberdeen, born on 14 May 1834 at the manse of Glassford, Lanarkshire, was second son in a family of eleven children of Gavin Lang, minister of the parish, a 'small living' of 150*l*. a year. His mother, Agnes Roberton Marshall of Nielsland, granddaughter of a wealthy Lanarkshire laird, traced her descent to John Row [q. v.]; she proved an admirable housewife and exercised great influence on her children. Sir Robert Hamilton Lang, K.C.M.G., is Marshall Lang's surviving brother.

After a somewhat superficial education under private tutors at the manse, Lang spent a year at the High School of Glasgow, and then studied at Glasgow University under Professors William Ramsay [q. v.], Edmund Lushington [q. v. Suppl. I.] and Lord Kelvin [q. v. Suppl. II]. He was chiefly influenced by the professors of philosophy, William Fleming and Robert Buchanan [q. v.], but he did not graduate. Proceeding to the divinity hall, he was stimulated by some senior fellow-students, including John Caird [q. v. Suppl. I], A. K. H. Boyd [q. v. Suppl. I], and George Washington Sprott [q. v. Suppl. II], but it was only when he received licence that his capabilities became apparent. A brief assistantship at Dunoon sufficed to make him widely known as a preacher. At twenty-two he was called to the important charge of the East Parish of St. Nicholas, Aberdeen, where he was ordained on 26 June 1856. His ministry in Aberdeen, although it lasted only two years, formed an epoch in the religious life not only of the city but of the district. In the reform of church worship he took a forward step. He remarked, in a sermon, that if there was reason for the choir standing at praise, that reason was valid for the congregation also standing. The congregation stood for the next act of praise. He printed his sermon and it ran through three editions. The presbytery interfered, and notice was given for its next meeting of a motion censuring him and inhibiting the innovation. Dr. Robert Lee [q. v.] wrote from Edinburgh begging him to stand firm; but he feared obduracy might hurt the cause, and he cautiously obeyed the presbytery's direction to return to use and wont. If he could not be a protagonist in the movement, he proved again and again that he was a pioneer.

In 1858, owing to ill-health, Lang left Aberdeen for the country parish of Fyvie, Aberdeenshire, where he learned much of rural Scottish life and its needs. In Jan. 1865 he removed to Glasgow to a newly built church in the Anderston (or west end) district of the great parish of the Barony. There he formed a large congregation, and introduced with due caution the ritual improvements which he desired. In Anderston church the first organ actually used in the worship of the Church of Scotland was set up, and psalms were chanted in the prose version. When Glasgow was threatened with a visitation of cholera, Lang, aided by Alexander Neil Somerville [q. v.], of the Free church, and (Sir) William Tennant Gairdner [q. v. Suppl. II], pressed on the town council the adoption of sanitary measures which averted the plague. In 1868 he was transferred to the Edinburgh suburban parish of Morningside. In 1872 he, with Professor William Milligan [q. v. Suppl. I], was deputy from the Church of Scotland to the general assembly of the Presbyterian Church of America.

Next year Lang succeeded Norman Macleod [q. v.] at the Barony of Glasgow, where his incumbency lasted twenty-seven and a half years. He took from the outset a full share in the public life of Glasgow; for nine years he served on the school board; for twenty-seven years he was chaplain to the 1st Lanark volunteers; he acted on the commission for the housing of the poor, and was for many years chairman of the Glasgow Home Mission Union, an effort to unite all the churches in charitable work. His ministerial labours were unceasing. He began, what was then rare in Glasgow, services on Sunday evenings, which were crowded. He raised the hitherto unexampled sum of 28,000*l*. for the purpose of rebuilding his church. The new church was dedicated in 1889; it contained a chapel provided by his sister, Mrs. Cunliffe, in memory of her husband, which was adorned with the first fresco painting of our Lord that had been seen in the Church of

Scotland (*Aberdeen Ecclesiol. Soc. Trans.*). There he instituted daily service, mostly taken by himself, and, in the church, services every day in Holy Week, and at Christmas.

At the same time he was prominent in the general assembly, where he became convener of its committee on correspondence with the foreign reformed churches. In that capacity he attended the assembly of the Moravian church at Klobuck in Hungary, and of the Danish church at Copenhagen. In 1887 he went to Australia to take the services in the Scots church, Melbourne, for four months, returning by way of San Francisco, Buffalo, and New York. He was made convener in 1890 of the Assembly's commission to 'inquire into the religious condition of the people of Scotland.' The work occupied six years, and meant a personal visitation of almost all the parishes of Scotland. Lang's annual speech, as he gave in his reports, was the great event of successive general assemblies. In 1893 he was moderator of the general assembly.

Anxious to heal division in the church he actively promoted the Pan-Presbyterian Alliance; he attended and spoke at all its quadrennial conferences, from the first at Edinburgh in 1876 to that of which he was president at Washington in 1899. For the Philadelphia Conference (1881) he wrote a 'Letter of Greeting,' which was translated into many languages. He joined in the conferences for Christian unity in Scotland initiated by Bishop George Wilkinson [q. v. Suppl. II] and in his company he addressed the general assembly of the United Free church.

In 1900, on the death of Sir William Geddes [q. v.], principal of Aberdeen University, Lang offered himself for the vacant office and was chosen by the Crown. He rapidly vindicated the appointment by tact and business capacity. The chief events of his principalship took place in Sept. 1906, when the (belated) quatercentenary of the university was celebrated, and King Edward VII and Queen Alexandra opened the new buildings which his energy largely helped to complete, at Marischal College. Lang was made C.V.O. in celebration of the occasion. He had received from Glasgow the degree of D.D. after his appointment to the Barony, and that of LL.D. in 1901. He was also an honorary member of the Imperial University of St. Petersburg, of the Imperial Academy of St. Petersburg, and of the Egyptian Institute (1906). He was Baird lecturer at Glasgow in 1901.

In Dec. 1908 his health began to fail. He died at Aberdeen on 2 May 1909. He was buried beside Bishop Patrick Forbes [q. v.] within the ruined transept of Aberdeen Cathedral.

Lang married at Fyvie in 1859 Hannah Agnes, daughter of P. Hay Keith, D.D., minister of Hamilton. By her he had seven sons and a daughter. His third son, Cosmo Gordon Lang (*b.* 1864, and named after Lang's patron at Fyvie) became Archbishop of York in 1909.

Lang was author of several devotional volumes, including: 1. 'Heaven and Home, a Book for the Fireside,' 1880. 2. 'The Last Supper of Our Lord,' Edinburgh, 1881. 3. 'Ancient Religions of Central America,' Edinburgh, 1882. 4. 'Life: is it worth living?' London, 1883. 5. 'The Anglican Church,' Edinburgh, 1884. 6. 'Homiletics on St. Luke's Gospel,' 1889. 7. 'Gideon, a Study Practical and Historical,' 1890. 8. 'The Expansion of the Christian Life' (Duff Lectures), Edinburgh, 1897. 9. 'The Church and its Social Mission' (Baird Lectures), Edinburgh, 1902.

A portrait by his friend and elder, Mr. E. R. Calterns, hangs in the session-house of the Barony church. A bronze memorial medallion was unveiled on 9 Dec. 1911 in the same church.

[Memories of John Marshall Lang, by his widow, privately printed, Edinburgh, 1910; information from members of his family; The Renascence of Worship, by the Rev. John Kerr, Edinburgh, 1909; Reports of the Schemes of the Church of Scotland; personal knowledge.] J. C.

LANGEVIN, Sir HECTOR LOUIS (1826–1906), Canadian statesman, born at Quebec on 25 August 1826, was son of Lieut.-colonel Jean Langevin, a Quebec merchant, of Anjou stock, who had served as assistant and secretary to Lord Gosford, governor-general of Canada, and had been for a time corresponding clerk of crown lands. His mother was Sophie Scholastique, daughter of Major La Force, who had distinguished himself in the defence of Canada in 1812–14. Langevin received his education at the Seminary of Quebec (1836–46) and studied law at Montreal. Entering the office there of (Sir) George Etienne Cartier [q. v.], he identified himself with Cartier's conservative political principles and was very intimately associated with him in public life. He found time for journalism in the early course of his legal career and edited successively at Montreal 'Mélanges Religieux' (from 1847) and the 'Journal of Agriculture.' Langevin was called to the bar of Lower Canada in 1850. Settling in Quebec, he became editor in 1857 of the 'Courrier du Canada.' He was elected to the Quebec city council in the same year and was mayor of Quebec from 1858 to 1860. He entered political life in 1857, when he was elected member for Dorchester in the legislative assembly of Canada. He held the seat till 1867. In 1864, when he was made Q.C., he was admitted to the Taché-Macdonald conservative ministry as solicitor-general for Lower Canada. In 1866 he was promoted to be postmaster-general and remained in office till the Confederation Act was passed. Langevin played an active part in the negotiations which led to the formation of the Dominion of Canada. On the passing of the Act of Confederation in 1867, when he was sworn a privy councillor of Canada, he became a member of the Dominion House of Commons, and sat there till 1896. He represented his old constituency of Dorchester until 1874, and Three Rivers from 1878 to 1896. In Sir John Macdonald's first Dominion administration he filled the office of secretary of state (1867–9), and was minister of public works (1869–73). He was postmaster-general on Macdonald's return to power in 1878, and from 1879 to 1891 resumed the ministry of public works. His resignation of that post in 1891 followed charges of corruption against his department. He was exonerated from blame save as to negligence. In 1873 he had succeeded Sir George Etienne Cartier [q. v.] as leader of the French-Canadian conservative party. He owed his political influence to his consistent support of the ultramontane forces in the church. In 1870 Pope Pius IX created him Knight Commander of the Order of St. Gregory. He was appointed C.B. in 1868 and K.C.M.G. in 1881. He was made LL.D. of Laval University in 1882.

Langevin died in Quebec on 11 June 1906, and was buried in the church of the Hôtel Dieu du Précieux Sang.

He married on 10 Jan. 1854 Marie Justine (*d.* 1882), eldest daughter of Lieut.-colonel Charles H. Têtu of Quebec; of nine children only two daughters survive (1912).

[The Times, 12–13 June 1906; Debrett's Peerage; Rose, Cycl. of Canadian Biography, 1888.]
P. E.

LANGFORD, JOHN ALFRED (1823–1903), Birmingham antiquary and journalist, born in Crawley's Court, Bradford Street, Birmingham, on 12 Sept. 1823, was second surviving son of John Langford, who, coming to Birmingham from Wales in 1815, started business in 1828, as a chair-maker, in Bradford Street, Cheapside (PIGOT'S *National Commercial Directory*, 1835, col. 41).

Langford owed his early education to his mother, Harriet Eaton, a paralysed invalid. After attending a private school in Brixhall Street, Deritend (1829–33), he entered his father's chair-making business at ten, and was duly apprenticed when thirteen in 1836. In his scanty leisure he read widely for himself. At nineteen, while still an apprentice, he married his first wife, and at twenty-one was a journeyman earning a guinea a week. In 1846 he became hon. secretary of the newly established Birmingham Co-operative Society.

Langford soon contributed to various periodicals, including 'Howitt's Journal.' William Howitt described a visit to him in June 1847 under the title of 'A Visit to a Working-man' (*Howitt's Journal*, ii. 242–4). In August 1847 he joined the new unitarian 'Church of the Saviour,' which George Dawson [q. v.] started. In a widely circulated pamphlet he defended Dawson against an attack by George Gilfillan in 'Tait's Edinburgh Magazine' (1848, pp. 279–285). In the winter of 1850–1 he taught evening classes in the schools of Dawson's church, gave up chair-making, and opened a small newsvendor's and bookseller's shop. From 1852 to 1855 he carried on a printing business (45 Ann Street), and then became sub-editor of the newly founded 'Birmingham Daily Press' (7 May 1855). From 1862 to 1868 he was closely associated with the 'Birmingham Daily Gazette' (a liberal-conservative daily paper), from which he withdrew on account of his radical convictions. Always an ardent liberal, he was honorary secretary of a Birmingham branch of the 'Friends of Italy,' formed in 1851, aided in the organisation of the liberal party when its headquarters were at Birmingham under the control of Francis Schnadhorst, and joined Dawson in conducting the 'Birmingham Morning News,' an advanced liberal paper, (2 Jan. 1871 to 27 May 1876); after the split in the liberal party in 1886 he allied himself with the Gladstonian section, but gradually abandoned political work.

Langford helped in the acquisition for the public of Aston Hall and Park in 1858, and served as manager with a residence at the Hall until the purchase of the property by the corporation in 1864. He was teacher of English literature in the

Birmingham and Midland Institute (1868–1874); member of the Birmingham School Board (1874–85 and 1886–91); and did much for the public libraries of the city, publishing an account of them and of the art gallery in 1871. In 1875–6 Langford made a tour round the world with his friend (Sir) Richard Tangye (cf. his poem *On Sea and Shore*, 1887).

He died on 24 Jan. 1903 in his 80th year at 85 Fernley Road, Sparkhill, Birmingham. He was buried at the Key Hill cemetery, Hockley. By his first wife, Anne Swinton (*d.* 1847), one of his father's workwomen, he had four children, of whom only a daughter, wife of Dr. George Craig, survived. By his second wife, Mary Anne, eldest daughter of F. Pine, a printer, whom he married 7 April 1849, he had six children.

Langford's best known publications are 'Century of Birmingham Life, 1741–1841' (2 vols. Birmingham, 1868), and 'Modern Birmingham and its Institutions' (2 vols. 1873–7). Both works were largely derived from the files of 'Aris's Birmingham Gazette,' of which the 'Birmingham Daily Gazette' was an offshoot.

Among Langford's other publications (in prose) were: 1. 'Religious Scepticism and Infidelity; their History, Cause, Cure, and Mission,' 1850. 2. 'English Democracy; its History and Principles,' 1853; 2nd edit. 1855. 3. 'Staffordshire and Warwickshire Past and Present' (with C. S. Mackintosh and J. C. Tildesley), 1884, 4 vols.

He wrote much poetry of pure and tender sentiment, but not great in sustained inspiration. His poetical publications include commemorative poems on Shakespeare in 1859 and 1864; 'The Drama of a Life' (in 5 scenes) and 'Aspiranda' (1852); 'The King and the Commoner,' an historical play (Birmingham, 1870); and 'A Life for Love, and other Poems' (Birmingham, 1900).

[A full account of his early career will be found in the British Controversialist, 1871, xxv. 54–62, 221–30, 303–12, 383–91. See also Birmingham Faces and Places, 1888, i. 102–4; Men and Women of the Time, 1899; Birmingham Daily Post, 27 and 29 Jan. 1903; The Times, 26 Jan. 1903; Dr. Stuart Reid's Sir Richard Tangye, 1907; Brit. Mus. Cat.]

C. W.

LASZOWSKA, MADAME DE. [See Gerard, Emily (1846–1905), novelist.]

LATEY, JOHN (1842–1902), journalist, born in Wenlock Road, City Road, London, on 30 Oct. 1842, was only son of John Lash Latey (1808–1891) of Tiverton, Devonshire, contributor from 1842 and editor from 1858 to 1890 of the 'Illustrated London News,' by his wife Eliza Bentley, of South Molton, Devonshire, daughter of a coal merchant. John Lash Latey was a trenchant advocate of liberal principles from the time of the Reform Bill of 1832, and an early contributor under the pseudonym of 'Lash' to 'Lloyd's News' (cf. T. Catling's *My Life's Pilgrimage*, 1911).

Educated at Barnstaple and at the Working Men's College, London, from 1860 to 1864, Latey joined in 1861 the staff of the 'Penny Illustrated Paper,' then newly founded by (Sir) William Ingram of the 'Illustrated London News,' and from that year till 1901 was both art and literary editor. Under his guidance the paper, which was staunchly liberal, filled an important place in popular journalism. Mr. Harry Furniss and Phil May [q. v. Suppl. II] were among his artists. With the latter he contributed in 1878 a series of 'Bird's-eye Views,' and from 1878 to 1889 he wrote a weekly article by 'The Showman,' genially criticising society and affairs.

Under the pseudonym of 'The Silent Member,' Latey was for fifteen years parliamentary reporter to the 'Illustrated London News,' of which he was also for a time dramatic critic, as well as literary editor and editor of the Christmas annual in 1899. With Mayne Reid [q. v.] he was co-editor (1881–2) of 'The Boys' Illustrated News,' the first illustrated newspaper for the young, and from June 1899 to 1902 he was editor of the 'Sketch.' Latey was a founder of the London Press Club and a fellow of the Journalists' Institute. He was a fine chess player, excelled in his youth in running and swimming, and was one of the earliest volunteers as a private in the Working Men's College company of the 19th Middlesex regiment. He died at 11 North Villas, Camden Square, on 26 Sept. 1902 after a long illness, and was buried at Highgate cemetery. He married in August 1872 Constance, daughter of Louis Lachenal, who improved the English concertina; she survived him with three sons and a daughter, who became wife of Mr. W. Heath Robinson, black and white artist. A portrait painted by John Edgar Williams in 1873 is in the widow's possession.

Latey's separately published works included: 1. 'The Showman's Panorama,' by Codlin (*i.e.* J. Latey) and illustrated by Short (*i.e.* Wallis Mackay), 1880. 2. 'The River of Life: A London Story,' 1886; new edit. 1894. 3. 'Love Clouds: a Story of Love and Revenge,' 1887; new edit. 1894.

He also wrote a short history of the Franco-German War (1872) and a 'Life of General Gordon' (1885).

[The Times, 27 Sept. 1902; Sketch, Oct. 1902 (with portrait); Penny Illustr. Paper and Illustr. London News, 4 Oct. 1902 (with portraits); Who's Who, 1902; Men and Women of the Time, 1899; information from son, Mr. William Latey.] W. B. O.

LATHAM, HENRY (1821–1902), master of Trinity Hall, Cambridge, born at Dover on 4 June 1821, was second son of John Henry Latham, a paymaster of exchequer bills, by his first wife, Harriet, only child of Edward Broderib, M.D., of Bath. His paternal grandfather, Samuel Latham, was a banker at Dover and consul for several foreign countries. His father settled at Eltham soon after his son's birth, but Henry was considered delicate and was sent to Dover to the house of his mother's father, who had retired thither from Bath. Here he went to a private school and enjoyed the run of his grandfather's large library. In 1836 he returned home. He read with two curates at Eltham, attended lectures, and travelled on the Continent. He entered Trinity College, Cambridge, in 1841, was elected a scholar in 1844, and graduated B.A. as eighteenth wrangler in 1845. He continued to reside at Trinity till he was called to his life's work at Trinity Hall in 1847. Trinity Hall was then a small and almost exclusively a law college. The master, Sir Herbert Jenner-Fust [q. v.], was dean of arches. The fellows were advocates of Doctors' Commons or barristers, with the exception of two clerical fellows, who were almost always brought from other colleges and acted as tutors. There were thirty-nine undergraduates. The men rarely took degrees except in civil law.

On the recommendation of Trinity friends, Latham was admitted to a vacant clerical fellowship, to which a tutorship was attached, 29 Dec. 1847, and was ordained deacon by the bishop of Ely in 1848 and priest in 1850. He proceeded M.A. in 1848. In 1855, on the retirement of his colleague, he became senior tutor. Latham set himself not only to make such general reforms as were then needed everywhere, but to broaden the aims of the college by destroying its exclusively legal associations, and thus raise it to the front rank among the smaller colleges. The abolition in 1857 of the independent profession of civil lawyers made a change on the legal side imperative. He attracted promising men from other colleges, like Henry Fawcett from Peterhouse, by the prospect of foundation scholarships and lay fellowships to follow, and he originated the system of open scholarships to be awarded before admission. Of this innovation Sir Robert Romer (afterwards lord justice), senior wrangler in 1863, was one of the first to take advantage. As a conservative reformer he helped to recast the college statutes in 1857. An innovator from another college, Latham provoked criticism from some of his colleagues, but his personal influence as a college tutor on pupils of all capacities, his sound judgment, and breezy commonsense steadily overcame all obstacles. His interest was always rather in men than in books, and his conversational and anecdotal powers were remarkable.

In 1877, when the master, Dr. Thomas Charles Geldart, died, Latham was disappointed in not succeeding him. Fawcett was a rival candidate. Sir Henry Sumner Maine [q. v.] was elected. Latham built himself a house near Cambridge in 1880, and in 1885 resigned the tutorship. The undergraduates then numbered 178 in place of thirty-nine at the date of his appointment. His old pupils presented him with his portrait by Frank Holl, and with the surplus money collected for that purpose founded a college prize for English literature. In 1888, on Maine's death, he became master.

As master Latham continued to take lectures and pupils in order to keep in touch with the undergraduates. But a practical rebuilding of the college remains the visible monument of his mastership. He suggested and largely paid for a new block of rooms, the Latham Buildings. He had the Lodge reconstructed, the hall enlarged, and at his own expense built a new combination room, the old being converted into a reference library. His health failed in 1901, and he died, unmarried, at the Lodge, on 5 June 1902. He was buried in Little Shelford churchyard.

In 1877 he brought out 'The Action of Examinations,' and late in life surprised his friends by publishing studies on the life of Christ which still command wide interest. In 1890 appeared his 'Pastor Pastorum,' in 1894 'A Service of Angels,' and in 1901 'The Risen Master.' The copyright of these books Latham left to Trinity Hall.

Of three portraits, one as a young man by Lowes Dickinson belongs to his nephew's widow; another by Frank Holl, painted in 1884–5, is in Trinity Hall Lodge; and the third, as master, painted by the same artist, hangs in the college hall.

[College Books of Trinity College and Trinity Hall; private information; personal knowledge.] H. E. M.

LAURIE, JAMES STUART (1832–1904), inspector of schools, born in Edinburgh in 1832, was younger brother of Simon Somerville Laurie [q. v. Suppl. II]. Educated in the Universities of Edinburgh, Berlin, and Bonn, he became a private tutor in the family of Lord John Russell. Becoming attracted to the study of educational theory and practice, he was chosen in 1854 inspector of schools, and was appointed by the government from time to time to make special educational investigations. In 1863 he resigned as a protest against the revised code of Robert Lowe (Lord Sherbrooke) [q. v.]. He was subsequently special commissioner to the African settlements, assistant commissioner under the royal commission of inquiry into primary education (Ireland), 1870, and director of public instruction in Ceylon. He entered the Inner Temple as a student on 2 Nov. 1867, and after leaving Ceylon was called to the bar on 6 June 1871. Thenceforth he mainly devoted himself to literary work, which consisted of educational handbooks and science manuals, together with the following: 'Christmas Tales' (1863); 'Religion and Bigotry' (1894); 'The Story of Australasia' (1896); 'Gospel Christianity *versus* Dogma and Ritual' (1900). He died at Bournemouth on 13 July 1904. He married on 7 Oct. 1875 Emily Serafina, eldest daughter of Frederick G. Mylrea of London.

[The Times, 19 July 1904.] F. W.

LAURIE, SIMON SOMERVILLE (1829–1909), educational reformer, born in Edinburgh on 13 Nov. 1829, was eldest of five sons of James Laurie, chaplain to the Edinburgh Royal Infirmary, by his wife Jean, daughter of Simon Somerville, united presbyterian minister at Elgin. Thomas, a publisher in London, and James Stuart [q. v. Suppl. II] were younger brothers. Owing to the family's narrow means Simon at eleven was earning money by teaching. Educated at the High School, Edinburgh, between 1839 and 1844, he entered the University of Edinburgh in 1844, and soon acted as class assistant to Professor James Pillans [q. v.]. He graduated M.A. in May 1849. After five years spent in travel with private pupils on the Continent, in London, and in Ireland, he was from 1855 till 1905 secretary and visitor of schools to the education committee of the Church of Scotland at Edinburgh. The committee, until the Act of 1872, controlled the parish schools of Scotland and administered till 1907 the Church of Scotland training colleges for teachers in Edinburgh, Glasgow, and Aberdeen. During his fifty years' secretaryship Laurie directed all his great influence towards improving the schools by raising the education and status of the teachers. He insisted that the students preparing in training colleges to become teachers should receive their general education in the classes of the universities, in association with the students preparing for other professions, and should obtain only their strictly professional training in the training college. Not till 1873 was the cause won; then Scottish training college committees were granted permission by the board of education to send their best students to university classes. The movement for establishing university (day) training colleges in England had his hearty support, and in 1890 he delivered the inaugural address to the Liverpool day training department of the University College, one of the first established in England.

In 1856 Laurie was appointed visitor and examiner for the Dick Bequest Trust, and he remained in office till 1907. The trust was formed by James Dick in 1828 to distribute substantial grants of money, formerly averaging 5000*l.* yearly, among the best equipped and most efficient parochial schoolmasters in the counties of Aberdeen, Banff, and Moray. The funds were apportioned in agreement with Laurie's reports, which, published in 1865 and 1890, form masterly expositions of educational principles and practice.

In 1868, at the request of the Merchant Company of Edinburgh, Laurie inspected and reported on the Edinburgh schools known as Daniel Stewart's Hospital, George Watson's Hospital, the Merchant Maiden Hospital and James Gillespie's Free School, while the governors of the Heriot Trust asked him to include in his inquiry the George Heriot's Hospital. Laurie pointed out that these schools lacked 'moral and intellectual ventilation,' self-dependence, and family life, and financially the sum spent on them annually in Edinburgh was larger than the total assessment for the maintenance of the parochial schools of Scotland, and more than half the expenditure of the privy council on schools of all kinds in the northern part of the kingdom. Laurie reported against distinctive dress, and advised that the boys should be sent for education to the Edinburgh High School, and the opening of a high school as a day-school for the girls. Laurie's suggestions, submitted in 1868, were embodied in the Act of Parliament (1869) which enabled the Merchant Company of Edinburgh to remove the monastic and to a great extent the eleemosynary aspects of the 'hospitals.' In 1872 Laurie became secretary to the royal commission on endowed schools in Scotland. On the recommendations of the third and final report of this commission (1875), the organisation of secondary education proceeded under the executive commissions of Lord Moncrieff in 1878 and of Lord Balfour in 1882–9.

Laurie also took active part in the voluntary educational movements. He was one of those who co-operated with Mrs. Crudelius in founding in 1867 the Edinburgh Ladies' Educational Association, to provide lectures for women on university subjects with a view to women becoming students within the university. This movement issued in the admission of women to the University of Edinburgh in 1892 on the same terms as men for arts subjects. In 1876 he suggested, and as honorary secretary organised, in conjunction with Sir Edward Colebrook, the Association for promoting Secondary Education in Scotland, which held meetings and issued reports until in 1880 the Endowed Institutions Act was passed.

In 1876 the Bell Trustees (who controlled the fund commemorating Dr. Andrew Bell [q. v.], the reformer of elementary education), instituted the Bell chairs of the theory, history, and art of education, one in St. Andrews University, and the other in the University of Edinburgh. John Miller Dow Meiklejohn [q. v. Suppl. II] was made professor at St. Andrews. Laurie was appointed to the Edinburgh chair, and occupied it till 1903. The number of his students rose from twelve in his first year to 120 in his last. During his tenure of the professorship no man in Great Britain did more to set pedagogy upon a scientific and philosophical basis, and to secure for teachers a position similar to that of members of other professions. As a member of the professorial body he was one of the leaders of the reforming party by whose efforts the Universities (Scotland) Act, 1889, was passed and the universities remodelled by subsequent ordinances. In 1891, when he was president of the Teachers' Guild of Great Britain and Ireland, he gave evidence before a select parliamentary committee in favour of the registration and organisation of teachers for public schools of all grades. He was in fact a leader in every educational advance of his time. He fought persistently against bureaucratic dictation in education, and stoutly championed the freedom of local educational authorities from the central control of the board of education.

Throughout a strenuous life of administration, teaching, and writing, the study of metaphysics and philosophy was his constant pre-occupation. In 1866 he published the 'Philosophy of Ethics: an Analytical Essay,' and in 1868 'Notes, Explanatory and Critical, on Certain British Theories of Morals.' In 1884 there appeared his important philosophical work 'Metaphysica Nova et Vetusta' (under the pseudonym of Scotus Novanticus) and in 1885 followed, under the same pseudonym, 'Ethica, or the Ethics of Reason.' These were republished, the former in 1889, the latter in 1891, and in these editions Laurie acknowledged the authorship. Both were translated into French, the former in 1901, the latter in 1902, by Georges Remacle, professeur à l'Athénée royal de Hasselt.

After resigning the chair of education at Edinburgh in 1903 Laurie delivered the Gifford lectures in natural theology there for 1905–6. The first course was on 'Knowledge' and the second on 'God and Man.' These lectures were embodied in 1906 in his last book 'Synthetica: being Meditations, Epistemological and Ontological,' a work which gave Laurie high rank among speculative writers. The book was the basis of the exposition in French by Georges Remacle, 'La Philosophie de S. S. Laurie.' He died on 2 March 1909 at 22 George Square, Edinburgh, and was buried in the Grange cemetery there. Laurie married twice: (1) in 1860 Catherine Ann (*d.* 1895), daughter of William Hibburd of Berkshire, by whom he had two sons and two daughters; (2) in 1901 Lucy, daughter of Professor Sir John Struthers [q. v. Suppl. I]. A portrait of Laurie in oils, painted by Fiddes Watt, was presented to Laurie from many admirers on 11 Jan. 1907, and is in the possession of Mrs. Laurie. Laurie received the honorary degree of LL.D. from the universities of St. Andrews in 1887, of Edinburgh in 1903, and of Aberdeen in 1906.

Besides the work already cited, Laurie's published works include: *On the theory of education:* 1. 'On Primary Instruction in Relation to Education,' 1867; 6th edit. 1898. 2. 'Training of Teachers and other

Educational Papers,' 1882. 3. 'Occasional Addresses on Educational Subjects,' 1888. 4. 'Language and Linguistic Method in the School,' 1892; based on lectures at the College of Preceptors in 1890. 5. 'Institutes of Education, comprising an Introduction to Rational Psychology,' 1892. 6. 'Teachers' Guild Addresses,' 1892, a masterly compendium of educational doctrine on a philosophical basis. 7. 'The Training of Teachers and Methods of Instruction,' 1901 (chiefly reprints from earlier essays). *On the history of education:* 1. 'The Life and Writings of John Amos Comenius,' 1881. 2. 'The Rise and Early Constitution of Universities, with a Survey of Mediæval Education,' 1886. 3. 'A Historical Survey of Pre-Christian Education,' 1895. 4. 'Studies in the History of Educational Opinion from the Renaissance,' 1903.

[Private information; biography prefixed to M. Remacle's Philosophie de S. S. Laurie, which gives an impression of the breadth and attractiveness of Laurie's character (Paris and Brussels, 1909); Sir Ludovic Grant's address on presenting Professor Laurie for the LL.D. degree in University of Edinburgh; excerpts from minutes of the Senatus Academicus of the University of Edinburgh (5 June 1903) and of the Dick Bequest Trustees (11 July 1907); Address from Dick Bequest Schoolmasters (May 1908) and from Students of the Edinburgh University Class in Education (March 1903).] F. W.

LAW, DAVID (1831–1901), etcher and water-colour painter, son of John Law, was born in Edinburgh on 25 April 1831. Apprenticed at an early age to George Aikman, steel-engraver, he was in 1845, on his master's recommendation, admitted to the Trustees' academy, where he studied under Alexander Christie [q. v.] and Elmslie Dallas [q. v.] until 1850. On the termination of his apprenticeship he obtained an appointment as 'hill' engraver in the ordnance survey office, Southampton, and it was not until twenty years later that he realised his ambition, and, resigning his situation, became a water-colour painter. In this venture he had considerable success, but his early training as an engraver had prepared him to be a pioneer in the revival of etching, and he was one of the founders of the Royal Society of Painter-Etchers in 1881. He was perhaps rather an interpreter by etching of other men's work than an original etcher, and his style, while delicate in drawing and sensitive to effects of light, was somewhat mechanical, and more reminiscent of the labours of the steel-engraver than of the spontaneity or incisiveness of the real etcher. But his plates after Turner and Corot and some modern landscape painters had many admirers, and during the time (1875–90) that reproductive etching was in high fashion they were in great demand. Probably, however, his best and most vital etched work was done from water-colours by himself. This was the case with the 'Thames,' the 'Castle,' and the 'Trossachs' sets, all of which were popular. Law, who settled in London in 1876, died at Worthing on 28 Dec. 1901, after some years of declining health. A portrait by Mr. Seymour Lucas, R.A., was reproduced in the 'Art Journal' (1902), for which magazine Law had occasionally etched a plate.

[Register of Trustees' academy; The Times, 30 Dec. 1901; Art Journal, March 1902; Bryan's Dict. of Engravers.] J. L. C.

LAW, Sir EDWARD FITZGERALD (1846–1908), expert in state finance, born at Rostrevor House, co. Down, on 2 Nov. 1846, was third son of the nine children of Michael Law, senior partner of Law and Finlay's bank, Dublin, and afterwards director of the Bank of Ireland, by his wife Sarah Anne, daughter of Crofton FitzGerald. His eldest brother, Robert, lived on his Irish estates. His second brother, Michael, was an early member of the international courts in Egypt. Law went to schools at Brighton and St. Andrews, and thence to the Military Academy at Woolwich. He was gazetted to the royal artillery in July 1868, and served in India. There he became known as a sportsman and a fine steeple-chaser, while his instinct for topography and linguistic aptitude in French, German, and Russian promised well for a military career. But, invalided home, he retired from the army for private reasons in October 1872, keeping his name on the reserve of Officers. Going to Russia, he next started business there as an agent for agricultural machinery, and, after mastering many difficulties, prospered until he was ruined by the conduct of his partners, against whom he brought legal proceedings. Thereupon he joined Messrs. Hubbard, the English firm of Russian merchants, and in their behalf visited every part of the Russian empire. His intimate knowledge of the country and the people was turned to account in a long series of magazine articles on Russian ambitions in Central Asia.

From December 1880 to March 1881, and

from August to September 1881, Law acted as consul at St. Petersburg. In 1883 he declined the offer of a post which the war office was asked by King Leopold II to fill in the Belgian service in Central Africa [see STANLEY, SIR HENRY MORTON, Suppl. II.] and he accepted the managership of the Globe Telephone Company in London. That company was then fighting the United Telephone Company. Law pushed through a scheme of amalgamation in the interests of the shareholders in 1884, and thereby abolished his own post. Volunteering for duty in the Sudan in 1885, he served with the commissariat and transport staff of the guards' brigade. He received the medal and clasp and the Khedive's bronze star, was mentioned in despatches, and promoted to the rank of major (June 1886). He was meanwhile recalled to England for work in the army intelligence department in connection with troubles with Russia over the Penjdeh incident on the Afghan frontier.

After visiting Manchuria to develop the services of the Amur River Navigation Company, he was associated with Colonel E. J. Saunderson [q. v. Suppl. II] in the anti-home rule campaign of the Irish Loyal and Political Union. Of inventive mind, he patented a machine for setting up type at a distance by the transmission of electric impulses, and a flying machine, the precursor of the aeroplane.

In January 1888 Law was posted to St. Petersburg as commercial and financial attaché for Russia, Persia, and the Asiatic provinces of Turkey. He rendered valuable service to the English ambassador, Sir R. Morier [q. v.]. After visiting Persia in the course of 1888, he was attached next summer to Nasiruddin, Shah of Persia, on his visit to England. In 1890 he acted as British delegate for negotiation of a commercial treaty with Turkey. In 1892 he went to Greece to make an exhaustive inquiry into the financial situation there, his report appearing early in 1893. In March 1894 he was promoted to a commercial secretaryship in the diplomatic service. After a riding tour all through Asiatic Turkey he reported on railway development there in October 1895, and was the first to suggest British association with Germany in the Baghdad railway and British control of the section from Baghdad to the Persian Gulf; that policy he advocated to the end of his life.

In December 1896 Law was transferred as commercial secretary to Vienna with supervision of Austria-Hungary, Russia, Italy, Greece, and the Balkan States. In that capacity he, with Mr. (now Sir Francis) Elliot, British minister at Sofia, negotiated a commercial treaty with Bulgaria in the winter of 1896–7. He represented Great Britain at Constantinople on the international committee for determining the indemnity payable by Greece after her war with Turkey in 1897. His influence helped to keep the amount within reasonable limits, and in the autumn he served at Athens on the international commission for the due payment of the indemnity and the regulation of Greek finance.

When the international financial commission of Greek finance was founded in 1898, Law was unanimously elected president. He devised an ingenious system of consolidation of revenues, which rendered the international commission acceptable and useful to Greece, and he won a high place in the affections of the people throughout the country. While engaged on the business he was created a K.C.M.G. in May 1898, and given the rank of resident minister in the diplomatic service. He declined the Grand Cross of the Grecian Order of the Saviour and other foreign decorations. At the close of 1898 he went to Constantinople to represent British, Belgian, and Dutch bondholders on the council of the Ottoman debt.

In March 1900 Law went out to India as finance member of the government and took wide views of his responsibilities. He lost no time in completing the currency reform begun in 1893, setting aside the large profits from rupee coinage to form a gold standard reserve fund as a guarantee for stability of exchange. A great famine was afflicting the country when he took office, but a period of prosperity followed, and notwithstanding the cost of the many administrative improvements which Lord Curzon effected, Law was able to write off heavy arrears of land revenue and to make the first serious reduction of taxation for twenty years. The limit of income-tax exemption was raised from Rs. 500 to Rs. 1000 per annum, and the salt tax—the burden of which upon the masses had been a subject of perennial criticism of government—was reduced from Rs. 2.8 as. (equivalent to 3*s.* 4*d.*) to Rs. 2 per maund. In the budget of 1905–6, promulgated after Law left office, but for the framing of which he was mainly responsible, the salt tax underwent a further reduction of 8 as., and the district boards (roughly corresponding to the English county councils) received a material annual subvention. One of Law's useful reforms was to give the local governments a larger interest in the revenue and expenditure under their control—a principle which was permanently adopted and extended later. As Lord Curzon testified, Law came into closer touch with the commercial community than any predecessor. To projects like the Tata iron and steel works at Sakchi, Bengal [see TATA, JAMSETJI NASARWANJI, Suppl. II], he gave earnest encouragement, and he eagerly advocated the new system of co-operative rural credit under government supervision initiated in 1904.

Law, who was made C.S.I. on 1 Jan. 1903, and K.C.S.I. in 1906, resigned his membership of the council on 9 Jan. 1905, some three months before the completion of his term. He dissented from the views of the viceroy in his controversy with Lord Kitchener over army administration, and on coming home served on the committee appointed by the secretary of state in May 1905 to make recommendations on the subject. This report advised changes, which led to Lord Curzon's resignation (*East India Army Administration*, 1905, Cd. 2718).

To a despatch (22 Oct. 1903) of Lord Curzon's government deprecating participation in the imperial preference policy, which Mr. Chamberlain had begun to advocate, Law appended a dissenting minute. Law's minute was utilised in party discussions in Great Britain and the colonies, and was cited with approval by Mr. Deakin, prime minister of Australia at the imperial conference of 1907 (*Official Report of Conf.* 1907). On return home, Law became a vice-president of the Tariff Reform League, and actively championed its policy.

Law represented Great Britain on the Cretan reform commission in January 1906, and on the committee which sat in Paris under the provisions of the Act of Algeciras (April 1906) to found the bank of Morocco. Appointed English censor of the bank, he paid thenceforth a fortnightly visit to Paris. Law, who was also connected with many financial enterprises in the City of London, died in Paris on 2 Nov. 1908, his sixty-second birthday. He was buried at Athens on 21 Nov. with the public and military honours due to a Grand Cross of the Order of the Saviour. A central street of Athens is named after him, and tablets to his memory are to be unveiled in the British chapel at Athens, and in St. Patrick's Cathedral, Dublin. In a chapter contributed to his 'Life,' Mr. J. L. Garvin describes him as 'fearing no responsibility, yet able to show himself . . . a safe and dexterous tactician, audacious in instinct, prudent in method, and yet full of emotional strength, of passionate possibilities, and all manner of great-heartedness.' He married on 18 Oct. 1893 Catherine only daughter of Nicholas Hatsopoulo, a prominent member of an old Byzantine family, who had long owned property in Attica, and had established themselves in Athens on the erection of the Greek kingdom. There were no children of the union.

[Life by Sir Theodore Morison and G. P. Hutchinson, 1911; Gen. Sir H. Brackenbury's Memories, 1909; Sir T. Raleigh's Lord Curzon in India, 1906; E. India: Finan. Statements and Discussions thereon, 1901–2 to 1905–6 and 1911–2; Greece, No. II; Cor. relating to Greek Finances, 1898; Papers on Preferential Tariff for India, 1904, Cd. 1931; For. Office List, 1908; The Times, 4 Nov. 1908; Pioneer Mail of various dates; information kindly supplied by Lady Law.]

F. H. B.

LAW, THOMAS GRAVES (1836–1904), historian and bibliographer, was great-grandson of Edmund Law, bishop of Carlisle [q.v.], and grandson of Edward Law, first earl of Ellenborough [q. v.]. Born on 4 Dec. 1836 at Yeovilton in Somersetshire, Law was third son and fourth of eight surviving children of William Towry Law (1809–1886), Lord Ellenborough's youngest son, by his first wife, Augusta Champagné (*d.* 1844), fourth daughter of Thomas North Graves, second Baron Graves. The eldest son, Augustus Henry [q. v.], was a jesuit missionary, and the second son, General Francis Towry Adeane Law, C.B. (1835–1901), saw much military service. The father originally served in the Grenadier guards, but in 1831 had taken orders in the Church of England, and at the time of his son's birth was rector of Yeovilton and chancellor of the diocese of Bath and Wells, of which his kinsman, George Henry Law [q. v.], was bishop.

On the death of his mother in 1844, Law was sent to school at Somerton, but in the following year, on his father's removal to the living of Harborne in Staffordshire, he was successively sent to St. Edmund's School, Birmingham, and (as founder's kin) to Winchester School, then under the charge of Dr. Moberly. In 1851 his father joined the Roman catholic church, a step which necessitated his son's leaving Winchester. In 1852 he studied at University College, London, where he had De Morgan and Francis Newman among his teachers, and in 1853 he entered the

Roman catholic college at Stonyhurst. For a time he hesitated between the church and the army as a profession, and his father actually obtained for him a cadetship in the military service of the East India Company. In 1855, however, under the influence of his father's friend, Father Faber, he entered the Brompton Oratory, London, where he was ordained priest in 1860. He remained in the Oratory till 1878, when, owing to the loss of his faith in the teaching of the church, he definitively left its communion.

In 1879 Law, who had long devoted himself to historical and literary study, was appointed keeper of the Signet library in Edinburgh, and there he passed the remainder of his life. In this capacity he did valuable service in promoting the study of Scottish history. He was one of the founders, in 1886, of the Scottish History Society, and acted as its honorary secretary. In 1898 the University of Edinburgh made him hon. LL.D. 'in recognition of his learned labours and indefatigable industry'; and in the last year of his life the Scottish History Society presented him with a valuable gift in recognition of his disinterested zeal. After a long and painful illness he died at his home at Duddingston, near Edinburgh, on 12 March 1904. Law was married on 15 April 1880 to Wilhelmina Frederica, daughter of Captain Allen of Errol, Perthshire, by his wife Lady Henrietta Dundas, and left one son, Duncan, and five daughters.

Law's main historical interests lay in the sixteenth century, and specially in its religious and ecclesiastical aspects. In his treatment of contending religious forces he shows remarkable freedom from partisanship, and everything that he wrote was based on all the accessible sources relative to his subject.

His most important historical work is 'The Conflicts between Jesuits and Seculars in the reign of Queen Elizabeth' (1889); but he also wrote many reviews and articles, the most important of which will be found in 'Collected Essays and Reviews of Thomas Graves Law, LL.D.' (Edinburgh, 1904). To this Dictionary he contributed sixteen memoirs, including those of David Laing, Edmund Law, bishop of Carlisle, Robert Parsons, and Nicholas Sanders. For the Camden Society he edited 'The Archpriest Controversy,' 2 vols. (1896–8); and for the Scottish Text Society, 'Catholik Tractates of the Sixteenth Century,' 1901, and 'The New Testament in Scots,' 3 vols. (1901–3). Of special note among Law's contributions to Scottish history are his edition of 'Archbishop Hamilton's Catechism,' with preface by Gladstone (Oxford, 1884), and a chapter on Mary Stuart in the 'Cambridge Modern History' vol. iii.

[Memoir by the present writer, prefixed to Law's Collected Essays, Edinburgh, 1904, with photographic portrait and bibliography.]

P. H. B.

LAWES (afterwards LAWES-WITTEWRONGE), Sir CHARLES BENNET, second baronet (1843–1911), sculptor and athlete, born at Teignmouth on 3 Oct. 1843, was only son of Sir John Bennet Lawes, first baronet [q.v. Suppl. I], of Rothamsted, Hertfordshire, by his wife Caroline, daughter of Andrew Fountaine of Narford Hall, Norfolk. Educated at Eton and Trinity College, Cambridge, Lawes was placed in the third class of the natural sciences tripos in 1865, and graduated B.A. next year. Of splendid physique, he excelled in athletics both at school and college. At Eton he won the first prize for the 100 yards, hurdle race, quarter-mile, mile, steeplechase, sculls, and pair oars. At Cambridge he was the chief amateur athlete of his period. He won the half-mile race, the mile (1864), and the two miles (1865) at the university sports; the mile (1864 and 1865) at the inter-university athletic meeting, and the one mile amateur championship at the meeting of the Amateur Athletic Club in 1865. He won the Cambridge sculls in 1862, the diamond sculls at Henley in 1863, and the Wingfield sculls, also at Henley, in 1865. In the last year he was also amateur champion oarsman, and stroked the losing Cambridge eight in the university boatrace. In 1898, at the age of fifty-five, he took up speed cycling, and at one time kept a pacing team at the Crystal Palace, where in 1899 he scored a twenty-five miles amateur record of fifty-one minutes, fifteen and four-fifths seconds.

After leaving Cambridge he made sculpture his profession, and long rented a studio at Chelsea. He began his training in London under J. H. Foley, R.A., and in 1869 he studied under Professor Hagen at Berlin. Between 1872 and 1908 he exhibited twelve works at the Royal Academy, including 'Girl at the Stream,' 'Daphne,' and 'The Panther.' A few other examples of his art appeared at the Royal Society of British Artists and elsewhere. His figures and portraits showed real ability, though his success was not quite equal to his ambition. In later life he expended much labour upon a colossal group of 'The Punishment of Dirce'; it was exhibited in 1911 at the International Fine Arts Exhibition at Rome, where Lawes assisted in arranging the British sculpture. It was set up in 1912 in the grounds at Rothamsted. A smaller bronze replica is in the Tate Gallery. He was the first president of the Incorporated Society of British Sculptors, which was founded in 1904.

In 1882 Richard Claude Belt, a sculptor of some repute, brought an action against Lawes for alleged libels in 'Vanity Fair' for 20 August 1881, and elsewhere. Lawes accused Belt of the fraudulent imposture of putting forward under his name sculpture executed by other persons. The case (Belt *v.* Lawes), which excited immense attention, was opened before Baron Huddleston on 21 June 1882, and occupied the court for forty-three sittings. Leading artists were called as witnesses on each side. Finally on 28 Dec. 1882 the jury decided in Belt's favour, and awarded him 5000*l.* damages. The case was the last heard at the old law courts at Westminster. After an appeal the verdict was upheld in March 1884.

On 31 Aug. 1900 Lawes, on the death of his father, succeeded to the baronetcy and the Rothamsted property. He became chairman of the Lawes Agricultural Trust and vice-chairman of the incorporated society for extending the Rothamsted experiments in agricultural science, in which he was keenly interested. On 18 April 1902 he assumed by royal licence the additional surname of Wittewronge, after a kinsman, Thomas Wittewronge (*d.* 1763), from whom his family had derived the estate of Rothamsted. He died at Rothamsted on 6 Oct. 1911 after an operation for appendicitis, and was cremated at Golder's Green. He married on 8 April 1869 Marie Amelie Rose, daughter of Charles George Fountaine, and had an only son, John Bennet Fountaine, who succeeded to the baronetcy.

At Rothamsted there is a life-size marble statue of Lawes-Wittewronge, executed by J. H. Foley, R.A., in 1870, as well as a portrait in oils painted by Frank Salisbury in 1905. A memorial portrait was placed in the pavilion at Fenner's, Cambridge, in July 1912. A cartoon appeared in 'Vanity Fair' for 12 May 1883.

[The Times, June, Nov., and Dec. (esp. 29 Dec., leading art.) 1882, 22 Dec. 1883, 18 March 1884, 4 April and 7 Oct. 1911, 23 Jan. 1912; Burke's Peerage, 1912; Graves, Dict. of Artists and Royal Acad. Exhibitors; Cats. of Royal Acad. and British section of Rome Exhibition; private information.] B. S. L.

LAWES, WILLIAM GEORGE (1839–1907), missionary, son of Richard Lawes by his wife Mary, daughter of Joseph Pecover of Reading, was born at Aldermaston, Berkshire, on 1 July 1839. After education at the village school, he entered at fourteen a Reading house of business. In 1858 his thoughts turned towards missionary work. He was accepted by the London Missionary Society, and after training at Bedford was ordained to the congregational ministry on 8 Nov. 1860. A few months' voyage brought him to Niué (Savage Island) in the South Seas in August 1861, and he worked on the island until 1872. Besides general work in the mission and the industrial training of the people, he engaged in linguistic study, and in 1886 completed the task begun by others of rendering the New Testament into Niué. In 1872 he came home on furlough, taking with him corrected versions of Exodus, the Psalms, and the New Testament in the vernacular. Whilst at home he was appointed to the New Guinea mission, for which he sailed in April 1874. He settled first at Port Moresby, and again devoted himself to labours of translation. He reduced the Motu language to writing, prepared simple books in the language, set himself to the translation of the New Testament, and founded a training institution for New Guinea natives. When the British protectorate over New Guinea was proclaimed in 1884, Lawes, with James Chalmers [q. v. Suppl. II], gave much help to the British authorities. For twenty years his home was at Port Moresby, but on the training institution being moved to Vatorata, Lawes made that his centre His position among both the settlers and the natives enabled him to give much help to the British administration—help gratefully acknowledged by Sir William Macgregor, 'first ruler of British New Guinea' (*Life*, p. 289). By the influence of Sir William, Lawes received the degree of D.D. from Glasgow University in April 1895. In the following year he visited Australia, and during his stay in Sydney saw through the press several works in Motu—selections from Old Testament history, a collection of 204 hymns, a catechism, forms of service, a Motu grammar and dictionary, and a manual of geography and arithmetic. In 1901 he took to England a revised Motu version of the New Testament.

In 1898 Lawes explored the mountainous region at the back of Vatorata. In 1905 he marked on a map ninety-six villages with the inhabitants of which he had been friendly. On his leaving New Guinea in March 1906, an address signed by the acting lieutenant-governor and the chief commercial men in the island noted his services to geographical and philological science, as well as to the missionary cause.

Lawes settled at Sydney, and died there from pneumonia on 6 Aug. 1907. He married, in November 1869, Fanny Wickham, who proved a zealous co-worker both in Niué and New Guinea, and survived him. They had four sons and one daughter.

Lawes, though to some extent obscured by the more striking achievements of his colleague Chalmers, efficiently helped to set the New Guinea work on firm foundations and to secure for it the general respect of the official and commercial communities.

[King's W. G. Lawes of Savage Island and New Guinea; Lovett's James Chalmers: his Autobiography and Letters; Lindt's Picturesque New Guinea, 1887 (portrait); Lovett's Hist. of the London Missionary Soc., vol. i.; Canton's Hist. of the Brit. and Foreign Bible Soc., vol. v.; private information.] A. R. B.

LAWLEY, FRANCIS CHARLES (1825–1901), sportsman and journalist, born on 24 May 1825, was fourth and youngest son of Sir Paul Beilby Lawley-Thompson, first Baron Wenlock, by his wife Catherine, daughter of Richard Neville, second Lord Braybrooke. After attending a school at Hatfield, he entered Rugby on 24 May 1837, and matriculated from Balliol College, Oxford, on 21 March 1844. In 1848 he won a second class in literæ humaniores, graduated B.A., and was elected a fellow of All Souls. In 1847 he entered the Inner Temple as a student, but was not called to the bar. He proceeded B.C.L. in 1851. Resolving on a political career, he was elected M.P. for Beverley as an advanced liberal in July 1852. Gladstone, when he became chancellor of the exchequer in December, made him a private secretary, and he performed his duties to the satisfaction of his chief, who remained his friend for life. Lawley gave up his Oxford fellowship in 1853. In May 1854 the duke of Newcastle, the colonial secretary, sounded Lawley as to his willingness to accept the governorship of South Australia. After the duke of Newcastle's retirement on 8 June 1854, his successor at the colonial office, Sir George Grey, made the offer in formal terms, and Lawley accepted it—with disastrous result to his career.

From an early age Lawley had interested himself in horse-racing—although while a fellow of All Souls' he could not (he said) run horses in his own name—and he soon involved himself disastrously in gambling and speculation. The colt Clincher, which he bought in 1849 jointly with the earl of Airlie, started favourite for the Derby of 1850, but ran third only to Voltigeur and Pitsford, with the result that Lawley lost many thousands. In 1851 he was to some extent interested in the fortunes of Teddington, who won the Derby. Subsequently he was owner of the well-known horse Gemma di Vergy, who won thirteen races as a two-year-old. Meanwhile dealings on the stock exchange exposed him to serious imputations. He was freely charged with turning to profitable personal use private information acquired as Gladstone's secretary, and he made admissions on being challenged by Sir George Grey which led to the cancelling of his colonial appointment. On 3 August Lawley's position was fully explained in the House of Commons by Sir George Grey, and in the discussion which followed Disraeli, Bright, Gladstone, and many others took part. Apart from questions of conduct, the bestowal of the governorship was censured on the ground of Lawley's youth; Gladstone defended his secretary on this and every count (*Hansard*, 3rd series, cxxxv. 1226–59).

Amid these embarrassments Lawley quitted England for the United States, and remained there for nine years, with little interruption. In America he acted as special correspondent of 'The Times' with the confederate army during the civil war. His despatches were admirable, both as to style and matter, and his valuable 'Account of the Battle of Fredericksburg' was published separately. He was in close touch with the Generals Stonewall Jackson, Longstreet, and Stuart. Returning to England in May 1865, he settled in London as a sporting writer and journalist, and quickly acquired a literary reputation. He was a frequent contributor to the 'Daily Telegraph,' with which he was connected until his death. He also published much in 'Baily's Magazine.' An accurate and polished style, a retentive memory, and a vast fund of first-hand knowledge and anecdote, gave value to his work. His range of topic in newspaper and magazine was wide, extending over 'Trainers, New and Old,' 'Sport in the Southern States,' 'Napoleon's Chargers,' 'Decline of Irish Humour,' 'A Word for Pugilism,' and 'Mr. Gladstone's Coaching Days.' To this Dictionary he contributed a memoir of

Admiral Rous. In 1889 he intervened in the bitter controversy respecting the conduct of Charles Wood, the jockey, with a pamphlet in Wood's defence, entitled 'The Bench and the Jockey Club.'

As a writer of books Lawley's most successful effort was 'The Life and Times of "The Druid"' [i. e. Henry Hall Dixon, q. v. Suppl. I] (1895). In conjunction with John Kent he published in 1892 'The Racing of Lord George Bentinck.' Of handsome presence and courtly demeanour, Lawley proved a fascinating companion. He died on 18 Sept. 1901, in King's College Hospital, London, from an illness which had seized him that day in the street. In 1860 he married Henrietta, daughter of Frederick Zaiser, chaplain to the King of Saxony. He left no issue.

[The Times, 21 Sept. 1901; Daily Telegraph, 21 Sept. 1901; Sportsman, 20 Sept. 1901; Baily's Mag., Feb. 1902 (portrait); Lawley's The Bench and the Jockey Club, 1889.] E. M.

LAWSON, GEORGE (1831–1903), ophthalmic surgeon, born in London on 23 Aug. 1831, was second son of William Lawson of the firm of Trower, Trower and Lawson, wine merchants, of the City of London, by his wife Anne Norton. After education at the Blackheath proprietary school, he entered King's College Hospital in 1848. Admitted M.R.C.S. in 1852, he served for a year as house surgeon to Sir William Fergusson [q. v.]. In 1852 he became a licentiate in midwifery of the College of Surgeons and licentiate of the Society of Apothecaries. Early in 1854 Lawson entered the army as an assistant surgeon, and in March of that year he left England with the first draft of troops for Malta. On the outbreak of the Crimean war he was detailed for duty at Varna with the third division under General Sir Richard England; from Varna he went to the Crimea and saw the first shot fired at Bulganak. He was present at the battles of Alma and Inkerman and was sent to Balaclava about the middle of January 1855. He had a severe attack of typhus fever in May 1855, followed by complete paraplegia. Although he had been gazetted assistant surgeon to the third battalion of the rifle brigade he was invalided home and at the end of the war he resigned his commission.

Lawson then decided to practise in London. Elected F.R.C.S. in 1857, he settled at 63 Park Street, Grosvenor Square, and turned his attention more especially to ophthalmic surgery, probably at the suggestion of Sir William Bowman [q. v. Suppl. I], who had been assistant surgeon at King's College Hospital whilst Lawson acted as house surgeon. Becoming clinical assistant to Bowman at the Royal London Ophthalmic Hospital, Moorfields, he was in 1862 elected surgeon to the hospital on the retirement of Alfred Poland (1822–1872), was appointed full surgeon in 1867 and consulting surgeon in 1891. He held the post of surgeon to the Great Northern Hospital for a short time. To the Middlesex Hospital he was elected assistant surgeon in 1863, surgeon in 1871, lecturer on surgery in 1878, and consulting surgeon in 1896. He served as a member of the council of the College of Surgeons from 1884 to 1892, and in 1886 was appointed surgeon-oculist to Queen Victoria. He died in London on 12 Oct. 1903, and was buried at Hildenborough, Kent. He married, on 5 March 1863, Mary, daughter of William Thomson, of the Indian medical service, by whom he had seven sons.

Lawson practised ophthalmic surgery as a part of general surgery and was little affected by the tendency towards specialism which completely divorced the two subjects before his death.

His works are: 1. 'Injuries of the Eye, Orbit and Eyelids; their immediate and remote effects,' 1867. 2. 'Diseases and Injuries of the Eye; their medical and surgical treatment,' 1869; 6th edit. 1903.

[Lancet, 1903, ii. 1184 (with portrait); Brit. Med. Journal, 1903, ii. 1019 (with portrait); private information.] D'A. P.

LAWSON, GEORGE ANDERSON (1832–1904), sculptor, born at Edinburgh in 1832, was son of David Lawson by his wife Anne Campbell. After early education at George Heriot's Hospital and training under Alexander Handyside Ritchie [q. v.] and in the schools of the Royal Scottish Academy, Lawson went to Rome, where he was a critical admirer of John Gibson [q. v.]. Returning to England, he made his home for some years at Liverpool, gaining a considerable local reputation for imaginative groups and figures in terra-cotta. In 1862 he exhibited at the Royal Academy a marble statuette of 'Jeannie Deans,' and in 1866 he went to London. In 1868 his 'Dominie Sampson,' a humorous representation, free from all exaggeration, of the old pedant in Scott's 'Guy Mannering,' was exhibited at the Royal Academy and gained wide popularity. Lawson continued to exhibit regularly, gradually abandoning, however, the picturesque and romantic style of his earlier works for a greater classical severity. He produced some charming studies of adolescence, among them 'Callicles' (R.A. 1879; now in the possession of Lady Pease), suggested by Matthew Arnold's 'Empedocles on Etna,' and 'Daphne' (R.A. 1880). More ambitious, though not more successful, works were 'In the Arena' (R.A. 1878) and 'Cleopatra' (R.A. 1881), the former a spirited representation of a struggle between athlete and panther, while the latter shows the Egyptian queen dying of the asp's sting. 'The Danaid' (R.A. 1882), a listless figure full of weariness and dejection carrying an urn to the fountain, and 'Old Marjorie' (R.A. 1890), a fine study of an old Scottish woman's head, also had admirers.

In portraiture the Burns memorial at Ayr (R.A. 1893), a replica of which was erected in Melbourne in 1903, was his best-known work. He also executed the Wellington monument in Liverpool, and statues of Joseph Pease for Darlington and James Arthur for Glasgow, and he exhibited at the Royal Academy busts of George Macdonald (1871) and others. All his work showed intellectual effort, but at times it lacked spontaneity and freshness.

Lawson died at Richmond, Surrey, on 23 Sept. 1904. He married on 28 Aug. 1862 Jane, daughter of Matthew Frier of Edinburgh; they had no issue. A portrait in oils of Lawson, by John Pettie, R.A., is in the possession of his nephew, Mr. Matthew F. Lawson, at Seaforth, Bridge of Allan.

[The Times, 24 Sept. 1904; Spielmann's British Sculpture, 1901; art. on Sculpture in Encyc. Brit. 11th edit.; art. by Edmund Gosse in Century Mag., July 1883; Graves's Roy. Acad. Exhibitors.] S. E. F.

LAWSON, Sir WILFRID, second baronet (1829–1906), politician and temperance advocate, born on 4 Sept. 1829 at his father's house, Brayton, near Carlisle, was eldest son in a family of four sons and four daughters of Sir Wilfrid Lawson (1795–1867), by his wife Caroline, daughter of Sir James Graham, first baronet, of Netherby, and sister to Sir James Robert George Graham [q. v.], the Peelite statesman. The family surname was originally Wybergh. The politician's father was younger son of Thomas Wybergh of Clifton Hall, Westmoreland, whose family was settled there since the fourteenth century. Thomas Wybergh's wife Elizabeth was daughter of John Hartley of Whitehaven, and sister of Anne, wife of Sir Wilfrid Lawson, tenth and last baronet, of Isel Hall, Cockermouth, who died without issue on 14 June 1806; this Sir Wilfrid's property passed by his will to the eldest son of his wife's sister, another Thomas Wybergh, who assumed the surname of Lawson, and dying unmarried on 2 May 1812 was succeeded in his estates by his next brother, Wilfrid Wybergh, who also took the name of Lawson and was made a baronet on 30 Sept. 1831.

Young Lawson was brought up at home. His father, an advanced liberal, was devoted to the causes of temperance, peace, and free trade. He held dissenting opinions, and he chose as tutor for his boys a young man, J. Oswald Jackson, who had just left the dissenting college at Homerton, and was in after years a congregationalist minister. The instruction was desultory, and Lawson declared in after life that he 'had never had any education,' and that Adam Smith's 'Wealth of Nations' was the book which taught him all he knew. He was, however, early initiated into the sports of hunting, shooting, and fishing, and was a capital shot and a hard rider. In 1854 he bought the hounds which had belonged to John Peel [q. v.] of the hunting song, amalgamated them with a small pack which he already possessed, and became master of the Cumberland foxhounds. He took a keen interest in agriculture, woodcraft, and all rural pursuits. He was early made J.P., and was active in the social and public life of the county.

His father, whose political convictions he shared, wished him to enter parliament at the earliest opportunity. On 21 March 1857 Lawson contested in the liberal interest West Cumberland, which had always been represented by two tory members. During the contest Lawson first gave proof of his faculty for public speaking, in which humour and sarcasm played a chief part. But he was at the bottom of the poll, with 1554 votes against 1825 recorded for the second tory. The new parliament was dissolved in 1859, and on 31 May Lawson, standing for Carlisle with his uncle, Sir James Graham, was returned to the House of Commons, in which he sat with few intervals till his death, forty-seven years later. His maiden speech was made with unusual self-possession in 1860, and Lawson early made a reputation as, in his own words, 'a fanatic, a faddist, and an extreme man.' Joining the radical section of his party, which was out of sympathy with the liberal prime minister, Lord Palmerston, he doggedly voted for the old principles of 'peace, retrenchment, and reform,' for abstention from interference in foreign affairs, and for the promotion of religious equality.

To the furtherance of temperance reform, which the majority of liberals scouted as a crotchet, Lawson was already committed, although he was not yet a professed abstainer, and with this cause he chiefly identified himself in the House of Commons and the country. In the session of 1863 he supported a motion in favour of Sunday closing, and the home secretary, Sir George Grey, who opposed it, said that Lawson's argument was equally good for total prohibition. 'That' (wrote Lawson) 'was just where I wanted my argument to tend.' Thus encouraged, he produced on 8 June 1864 his 'permissive bill,' which provided that drink-shops should be suppressed in any locality where a two-thirds majority of the inhabitants voted against their continuance. The bill was rejected by 294 to 37.

On the dissolution of parliament in July 1865 Lawson stood again for Carlisle, and was defeated by fifteen votes. His radicalism had offended moderate liberals; and the 'permissive bill' had aroused the fury of the liquor-trade. Excluded from parliament, Lawson bestirred himself on the platform, speaking in favour of extension of the suffrage, abolition of church rates, Irish disestablishment, and, above all, liquor-law reform. He became closely associated with the United Kingdom Alliance (founded in 1853 for the total suppression of the liquor traffic), and he was elected president in 1879. He sought every opportunity of pleading for legislation on the lines of his 'permissive bill' of 1864, but the policy acquired the new name of 'local option,' or 'local control,' and later it was known as 'local veto.' Lawson's lifelong principle was: 'No forcing of liquor-shops into unwilling areas.'

In 1867 Lawson's father died, and he succeeded to the baronetcy and estates. After the dissolution of 1868 Lawson, who was an enthusiastic champion of Gladstone's policy of Irish disestablishment, and indeed upheld disestablishment everywhere, was returned for Carlisle at the top of the poll. In the new parliament he was active in support of the government measures, but also identified himself with many unpopular causes. He advocated women's rights; in 1870 he moved a resolution condemning the opium-traffic, which was heavily defeated. At the end of the session of 1870 he voted, with five supporters, against some addition to the army which had been judged expedient in view of the Franco-German war. In 1872 he moved a resolution to the effect that we should, as soon as possible, extricate ourselves from all treaties with foreign powers, by which we bound ourselves to fight for them and their dominions. He was opposed by Gladstone, and beaten by 126 to 21. To the end of his life he maintained that his proposal was sound and struck at the root-danger of our foreign policy.

On his permissive bill he still concentrated his main energies. He reintroduced it on 12 May 1869, 17 May 1871, 8 May 1872, 7 May 1873, and 17 June 1874. The adverse majorities fluctuated from 257 in 1864 to 72 in 1871, but Lawson's enthusiasm never slackened. During the recess of 1871–2 he was busy through the country speaking in favour of his measure. Accompanied by (Sir) George Trevelyan, he met in some large towns a furiously hostile reception. From the republican agitation of Sir Charles Dilke [q. v. Suppl. II] and others Lawson held aloof, but on 19 March 1872 he voted in the minority of two for Dilke's motion of inquiry into Queen Victoria's expenditure, which Auberon Herbert seconded.

In the next parliament (1874–80), for which Lawson was again returned for Carlisle, but in the second place, he continued his fight for temperance, introducing his proposals in each of four sessions, and incurring heavy defeats, but abstaining in debate from controversial questions on which he had no special knowledge. In 1875 the bill was rejected by a majority of 285. He advocated in 1875–6 Sunday closing in Ireland, a measure which was carried in 1879. In 1877 he supported with some misgivings Mr. Joseph Chamberlain's 'Gothenburg system' for municipal control of liquor traffic, which eliminates the element of private profit. In 1879 he changed his permissive bill for a local option resolution, which was rejected by a majority of 88.

Despite Lawson's love of sport and horses, his development of puritan energy led him to oppose in 1874 the traditional 'adjournment for the Derby.' For many years he annually waged war on the proposal to make the day a holiday, and in 1892 he carried his point, with the result that the motion for adjournment was not renewed. On this and all other topics he seasoned his speech with welcome humour and apt quotation.

To the parliament of 1880–5 Lawson was again returned for Carlisle in the second place. He argued for religious freedom when Charles Bradlaugh, an avowed atheist, was excluded from the house [q. v. Suppl. I]. He voted against Forster's Irish coercion bill in 1881, and with the Irish nationalists. He persistently resisted the liberal government's policy in Egypt in 1882–3. To his proposed reform of the liquor traffic a majority of the new house was favourable, and in June 1880 he for the first time carried by twenty-six votes his resolution in favour of local option. In the following year he carried it by forty-two, and in 1883, when Gladstone voted with him, by eighty-seven.

At the general election of November 1885, which followed the extension of the suffrage to the agricultural labourers, Lawson was defeated in the Cockermouth division of Cumberland by ten votes. Five hundred Irish constituents voted against him. There was a paradox in his defeat by the labourers and the Irish, in both of whose interests he had consistently worked hard during the last parliament. He watched from the Riviera the subsequent struggle in parliament over Gladstone's home rule bill, with which he was in complete sympathy. In June 1886 he stood as home rule candidate for the Cockermouth division, and won by 1004 votes. In the new parliament he zealously supported the Irish cause, and resisted Mr. Balfour's policy of coercion in all its phases. In 1888 he successfully opposed the clauses in the local government bill which would have provided compensation for publicans whose licences were not renewed.

Lawson was re-elected for the Cockermouth division in 1892 and 1895, but took a less conspicuous part in the parliament, although he was steadfast to all the causes which he had earlier espoused. A reduction in his majority at Cockermouth in 1895 he attributed to the unpopularity of the local veto bill, on which Sir William Harcourt (though not the prime minister, Lord Rosebery) had appealed to the country. To the South African war, which broke out in October 1899, he was absolutely opposed, and as a pro-Boer he was defeated at Cockermouth by 209 votes. He found comfort in polling upwards of 4000 votes. During the autumn and winter of 1901 he engaged anew, after a holiday on the Riviera, in political agitation outside parliament. In April 1903 he was returned at a bye-election for the Camborne division of Cornwall, on the understanding that, at the expiration of the parliament, he should be at liberty to contest his old constituency. He now rarely missed a day's attendance at the house, or failed to take part in a division. The fiscal controversy which opened in 1903 gave him the opportunity of avowing his passionate attachment to the cause of free trade. At the general election of January 1906 he was again returned for the Cockermouth division. After the election the liberal prime minister, Sir Henry Campbell-Bannerman, offered him a privy councillorship; and it is characteristic of Lawson that no one heard of the offer till it had been declined. Lawson was elated by the liberal triumph of 1906, but his health showed signs of failure. He had long given up hunting, and latterly did not ride; but he went on shooting to the end. On 29 June 1906 he voted in the house for the last time in a division on clause iv. of Mr. Birrell's education bill. He died at his London house, 18 Ovington Square, S.W., on 1 July 1906, and was buried in the churchyard of Aspatria, in which parish Brayton is situated. On 12 November 1860 Lawson married Mary, daughter of Joseph Pocklington-Senhouse of Netherhall, Cumberland, by whom he had four sons and four daughters. There is an oil painting (by C. L. Burns) at Brayton. A statue of Lawson by Mr. David M'Gill is on the Victoria Embankment, and a drinking-fountain, with a medallion portrait by Roselieb, at Aspatria. A cartoon portrait appeared in 'Vanity Fair' in 1880.

Lawson, despite his strong and unchanging convictions, was absolutely just to friend and foe alike, and his justice was tempered by a tenderness which had its root in a singularly humane disposition. He always claimed for others the same freedom of opinion and expression which he claimed for himself. His power of speech was well adapted to great popular audiences. His humour was spontaneous and unforced; his jokes, like those of Sydney Smith, were rich and various, and always served the purposes of his serious argument. He had a vein of sarcasm which, though never personal, was extremely keen, wrote light verse with quickness and ease, and often combined in it humour and sarcasm with great pungency. His main political aim was as simple and sincere as his character. He saw in the liquor traffic the great moral and material curse of England; and he devoted all his energies to the attempt to destroy it. From first to last, he was the most disinterested of politicians.

Selections from Lawson's speeches were published under the titles: 'Gay Wisdom,' first series (reprinted from the Liverpool 'Argus'), 1877; 'Wit and Wisdom,' 1886; and 'Wisdom, grave and gay,' chiefly on temperance and prohibition, selected and edited by R. A. Jameson (1889). His verses on political themes were collected with illustrations by Sir F. Carruthers Gould in 'Cartoons in Rhyme and Line' in 1905, 4to. He also issued in 1903 verses entitled 'The Conquest of Camborne, 9 April 1903.'

[Sir W. Lawson's manuscript diary; Sir Wilfrid Lawson, a Memoir, edited by G. W. E. Russell, 1909; private information; Lucy's Diary of Parliaments, 1874–1905.]

G. W. E. R.

LEADER, JOHN TEMPLE (1810–1903), politician and connoisseur, born at his father's country house, Putney Hill Villa, sometimes called Lower House, on 7 May 1810, was younger son (in a family of two sons and four daughters) of William Leader, a wealthy merchant of London (*d.* 1828), by his wife Mary (1762–1838).

The father, son of a coachmaker of the same names, was engaged in business as coachbuilder, distiller, and glass manufacturer; he sat in the House of Commons from 1812 to 1818 as whig member for Camelford, a pocket borough which he bought of Lord Holland for 8000*l.* From 1820 to 1826 he represented Winchelsea, a pocket borough of Lord Darlington, afterwards duke of Cleveland, and there he had as colleague Henry, afterwards Lord Brougham, with whom he grew intimate. A patron of art, he commissioned George Henry Harlow [q. v.] to paint several portrait groups of his children, in one of which (now at Holmwood, Putney Heath) John figures as a boy.

After education at private schools, John entered Charterhouse in 1823, and won a gold medal there, but soon left to study under a private tutor, the Rev. Patrick Smyth of Menzies, with whom he visited Ireland, Norway, and France. The accidental death at Oxford of his elder brother William in February 1826 made him heir to the main part of his father's large fortune, which he inherited on his father's death on 13 Jan. 1828. On 12 Feb. following he matriculated as a gentleman commoner from Christ Church, Oxford. Although he was an idle and spendthrift undergraduate, he formed the acquaintance of some serious contemporaries, including James Robert Hope Scott, W. E. Gladstone, and Sir Stephen Glynne. With the last he made archæological excursions which stimulated a lifelong taste. His favourite recreation in youth was swimming, which he practised to extreme old age. In his Oxford vacations he continued his foreign travels. He was in Paris during the revolution of 1830, and there, through the introduction of his father's friend, Brougham, came to know many liberal politicians like Arago, Cuvier, and Armand Carrel. He took no degree at the university, and after leaving Oxford actively engaged in politics. He attached himself to the advanced wing of the liberal party, and in that interest was elected M.P. for Bridgwater in January 1835. He at once made a mark in political circles. In the house he generally acted with Grote, Molesworth, and the philosophical radicals, and was among the most thoroughgoing champions of 'The People's Charter.' In his first session he seconded Grote's resolution in favour of the ballot. John Arthur Roebuck [q. v.] regarded him as a useful politician, but feared his addiction to social amusements. Some of his party friends complained that his political speeches were too violent and bitter. In 1836 he joined the Reform Club, of which he remained a member till his death. In February 1837, as a disciple of Brougham and Grote, he was admitted to the first council of the new London University and in the same month he presided at a dinner to Thomas Wakley, which was attended by Daniel O'Connell, Joseph Hume, and most of the forward radicals.

In May 1837 Leader adventurously accepted the Chiltern hundreds in order to contest Westminster at a bye-election against Sir Francis Burdett. Having abandoned his radical principles, Burdett had resigned the seat, and was challenging his constituents to return him anew as a conservative (cf. Grego's *Parliamentary Elections* and H. B., *Key to Political Sketches*, 1841, pp. 332 seq.). Leader was defeated, polling 3052 votes against 3567, but he renewed his candidature at the general election in August, when his opponent was Sir George Murray, and he was elected by 3793 against 2620. He was re-elected in July 1841, and remained the representative of Westminster till the dissolution in 1847. He continued to advocate chartism and radicalism with unabated energy. On 2 May 1842 he seconded Thomas Duncombe's motion 'that the petitioners for the national charter be heard at the bar of the house.' In the same session (18 Feb.) he supported C. P. Villiers's motion for the total repeal of the corn laws. On 13 Feb. 1844 he spoke in behalf of the liberties of Canada, which he joined Roebuck in championing. He was not heard in the house again (HANSARD, *Debates*, 1836–44).

While in the house Leader was prominent in all phases of London society, and extended his large acquaintance on holiday tours in Italy and France. His intimacy with Brougham grew and he was his only companion, on 21 Oct. 1839, in the carriage accident near Brougham Hall, Cumberland, which led to the sensational report of Brougham's death (LORD BROUGHTON'S *Reminiscences*, v. 229). He entertained largely at his residence at Putney and at a house which he rented in Stratton Street. His friend Edward John Trelawny [q. v.] long lived with him at Putney. Other of his guests there included Richard Monckton Milnes, Charles Austin, and French, Italian, and American visitors to the country (see for list R. E. LEADER'S *Autob. of J. A. Roebuck*, 1897, pp. 106–7). He saw much in London of Louis Napoleon, afterwards Napoleon III, who, when projecting his descent on Boulogne in 1840, solicited Leader's influence with his French friends. He cultivated intercourse with men of letters and artists, and showed an interest in Gabriele Rossetti, the father of Dante Gabriel Rossetti (W. M. ROSSETTI'S *Reminiscences*, 1906, pp. 366–7).

In 1844 Leader's career underwent, without explanation, a sudden change. Abandoning his promising political prospects and his manifold interests at home, he left England for the Continent, and although his life was prolonged for nearly half a century he thenceforth paid his native country only rare and brief visits. At first he spent much time at Cannes with his friend Brougham, and here Cobden met them both in 1846. Like Brougham, Leader acquired property at Cannes, and exerted himself to improve the place. He built a residence there, which was known as the 'Château Leader,' and the municipality named a thoroughfare 'Boulevard Leader.' But he parted with his possessions at Cannes some time before his death.

It was with Florence that Leader's exile was mainly identified. In that city and its near neighbourhood he purchased many old buildings of historic interest, elaborately restoring them at munificent cost and filling them with works of art and antiquities. On 16 Feb. 1850 he bought the ancient Villa Pazzi, in the village of Majano near Florence. On 5 March 1855 he purchased the ruined medieval castle of Vincigliata, in 1857 a house in the Piazza dei Pitti in Florence itself, and on 8 April 1862, the Villa Catanzaro, also at Majano. All these edifices were practically rebuilt under his supervision. The two houses at Majano were each renamed Villa Temple Leader (*La parocchia di S. Martino e Majano: Cenni storici*. Florence, 1875. G. MARCOTTI, *Simpatie di Majano, Lettere dalla Villa Temple Leader*, Florence, 1883). In the restoration of the gigantic castle of Vincigliata Leader took immense interest. The exhaustive reconstruction was the work of Giuseppi Fancelli, son of the fattore or steward of Leader's Florentine estates, whom he had had trained as an architect. As at his villas at Majano, Leader provided at Vincigliata a spacious swimming-bath in the grounds, where he indulged his favourite pastime winter and summer till near his death. Although he lived part of each year in the restored castle, he freely opened it to the public. His pride in it increased with his years, and he delighted in conducting through it distinguished visitors. His visitors' book at Vincigliata abounded in autographs of persons of eminence in royal, artistic, and literary circles throughout Europe; Queen Victoria signed the book on 15 April 1888. He commemorated many of these visits by inscriptions on marble slabs which he affixed to the castle walls. Some of his Florentine guests renewed old associations. In January 1888 he acted as cicerone to Gladstone and his family, and he opened an intimate correspondence with the statesman which continued till the end of Gladstone's life. He surprised Gladstone by his vitality, and interested him in a collection which he formed of English words derived from the Italian (cf. *Philological Pastimes of an Englishman in Tuscany, with some Letters of Gladstone to J. T. Leader*, 1898).

Leader's practical interest in Florentine archæology, which extended beyond his own possessions, was rewarded by the bestowal on him of the knight commandership of the crown of Italy by King Victor Emmanuel. Under his auspices many archæological treatises concerning Vincigliata and Majano were compiled and published, and several Italian manuscripts of literary, historical, or genealogical interest were printed at his expense. Zealously studying the careers of historical personages who were associated with his Italian properties, Leader with the aid of competent scholars made especially exhaustive researches into the biographies of Sir John Hawkwood [q. v.] and Robert Dudley, titular duke of Northumberland [q. v.]. His life of Hawkwood, 'Giovanni Acuto,' which came out at Florence in 1889 in the joint names of himself and Giuseppe Marcotti, is a standard work; it was translated into English by 'Leader Scott' in 1889 [see Baxter, Lucy, Suppl. II]. Hardly less elaborate is Leader's 'Life of Sir Robert Dudley, Duke of Northumberland' (Florence, 1895), in the preface to which he acknowledges 'Leader Scott's' assistance. An Italian translation appeared at Florence in 1896.

Leader died, active to the last, at 14 Piazza dei Pitti, Florence, on 1 March 1903. Late in life he adopted the Roman catholic faith, and in accordance with a codicil to his will he was buried with Roman catholic rites.

On 19 Aug. 1867 Leader married, on one of his few visits to London, by special licence, Maria Louisa di Leoni, widow of Count Antonio di Leoni and daughter of Constantine Raimondi. She died at Florence on 5 Feb. 1906, without issue.

A fine medallion portrait of Leader in bronze, dated 1895 (presented by himself), is in the audience room of the Reform Club, Pall Mall. Portraits of him and his wife by Italian artists are at the Piazza dei Pitti at Florence and the Villa Temple Leader, Maiano.

Leader's fortune amounted to 250,000*l.* He made several bequests to educational and charitable institutions in Florence, including the sum of 7000*l.* for the restoration of the central bronze door of the Duomo. The rest of his property in England and Italy, including Vincigliata, was bequeathed to his grandnephew, Richard Luttrell Pilkington Bethell, third Lord Westbury, whose maternal grandfather, the Rev. Alexander Fownes-Luttrell, had married Leader's sister, Anne Jane. Leader still owned at his death the family residence on Putney Hill. He proved his lifelong interest in the district by giving 2000*l.* in 1887 for the restoration of St. John's Church there.

[Authorities cited; information from the third Lord Westbury; The Times, 3 March 1903, 11 May (will); Tablet, 16 May 1903; Leader's Rough and Rambling Notes, chiefly of my Early Life, Florence 1899 (with reprint of a contemporary memoir of Leader in Saunders's Portraits and Memoirs of the Most Eminent Political Reformers, 1838); R. E. Leader's Autob. of Roebuck, 1897, passim; J. C. Francis's Notes by the Way, 1909, p. 188. Accounts of Leader's chief Italian residences appeared under his auspices in 'Il Castello di Vincigliata e i suoi contorni,' Florence, 1871; Giuseppe Marcotti's 'Vincigliata,' Florence, 1870; and 'Majano Vincigliata Settignano,' by Alessandro Papini (Leader's maestro di casa), Florence, 1876. Largely working on Marcotti's book, Leader Scott (Mrs. Lucy Baxter) prepared for Leader her 'Vincigliata and Maiano,' Florence, 4to, 1891, and her 'Guide to Vincigliata,' Florence, 1897.]

S. L.

LEAKE, GEORGE (1856–1902), premier of Western Australia, born at Perth, Western Australia, in 1856, was eldest son of George Walpole Leake, Q.C. His family had long taken a prominent part in the parliamentary and official life of Western Australia. His father (after filling many public offices in the colony between 1870 and 1890) was a member of the first legislative council under responsible government from 1890 until July 1894, when the council under the Constitution Act of 1889 became elective. His uncle, Sir Luke Samuel Leake, was speaker of the legislative council from 19 Oct. 1870 till his death on 1 May 1886.

After education at Bishop's Boys' School (now Perth High School) and St. Peter's Collegiate School, Adelaide, George Leake, having been articled to his father, was admitted to the bar of the supreme court in May 1880 and was taken into partnership by his father. From 1878 to 1880 he was clerk to the registrar of the supreme court and assistant clerk of the legislative council, and after acting for a time as crown solicitor, he held the office permanently, except for a brief interval, from May 1883 to July 1894. In 1886 he acted temporarily as attorney-general and member of the executive council.

Leake, who attained a prominent position in his profession, was returned to the first legislative assembly as member for Roebourne in 1890, when the colony was granted responsible government. He declined the offer of a post in the ministry of Mr. (afterwards Sir John) Forrest. In June 1894 he was elected member for Albany in opposition to the Forrest ministry, was re-elected in May 1897, and resigned in August 1900 on visiting England. In April 1901 he returned to parliament as member for West Perth. He was made a Q.C. in 1898 on the recommendation of Sir John Forrest. Leake, a strong advocate of federation, was president of the Federation League of Western Australia, and a delegate to the

Australian Federal Convention at Adelaide in 1897.

On the resignation of Mr. Throssel in May 1901 Leake formed a ministry in which he was both attorney-general and premier. His government had no working majority and was defeated in October, Leake resigning on 21 Nov. 1901. An attempt to form a coalition ministry failed, but Mr. Morgans, his successor, proved unable to carry on the government, and Leake formed on 23 Dec. 1901 his second administration, which lasted till his death six months later at Perth on 24 June 1902. Accorded a public funeral, he was buried in the East Perth cemetery. The London Gazette of 26 June 1902 stated that it was King Edward VII's intention to confer the C.M.G. on him at the coronation. He was a keen lover of sport and a prominent cricketer in his younger days. In later life he took a strong interest in racing, and was chairman of the Western Australia Turf Club. Leake married in 1881 Louisa, eldest daughter of Sir Archibald Paull Burt, sometime chief justice of Western Australia, and had issue.

[Colonial Office List, 1902; Who's Who, 1902; The Times, 26 June 1902; West Australian, 25 June 1902; Year Book of Australia, 1897–1902; Mennell's Dict. of Australasian Biog., 1892; Colonial Office Records.] C. A.

LECKY, SQUIRE THORNTON STRATFORD (1838–1902), writer on navigation, born at Down, co. Down, Ireland, in 1838, was son of Holland Lecky of Bally Holland House, Bangor, co. Down, and Castle Lecky, co. Derry.

Lecky was sent to school at Gracehill, co. Antrim. At fourteen, without permission of his parents, he began his career at sea as midshipman on board the Alfred (1291 tons), a sailing merchantman, bound for Calcutta. But on his return home he showed an ambition for wider experience by apprenticing himself to James Beazley, a Liverpool shipowner. After serving his time on sailing ships voyaging to India, he became in 1857 second mate of Beazley's Star of the East, 'a magnificent China clipper.' He was subsequently second mate of an American ship, and then for two years first-class second master in the Indian navy, serving in the ships Indus, Frere, and Napier until the Indian fleet was disbanded. Thereupon he rejoined the merchant service, and made voyages to North and South America, in one of which he sought in vain to run the blockade of Charleston harbour during the American civil war. In 1864 he obtained his master's certificate, and was for some years second officer in the Inman Company's service. He was afterwards employed successively by Messrs. Lamport Holt of Liverpool (for four and a half years) and by the Pacific Steam Navigation Company (for six years).

In these employments he became an expert in the navigation of the Pacific, and made a great reputation in shipping circles for his nautical surveys. He was frequently of service in detecting 'danger-spots' not marked on existing charts. In 1865 he detected off Rio de Janeiro what has since been called 'Lecky Rock,' a steep and but slightly submerged rock, surrounded on all sides by seven fathoms of water. Shortly afterwards he located a similar danger-spot near Rat Island, and the 'Lecky Bank' to the north-east of the River Plate entrance. In 1869 he published, as the result of his first trip to Ceará in Brazil, a plan showing wide errors in earlier charts, both as to the shape of the land and depth of the water. In 1874 plans of his were published by the Admiralty showing similar errors in existing charts of Port Tongoy, Chile. For many years his running surveys for the Strait of Magellan and for a large part of Smyth's Channel (off Chile) and the water between Punta Arenas and Cape Pillar were the only trustworthy guides to safe navigation. His nautical surveying work, which was highly appreciated by the Admiralty, covered the greater part of the coast of South America.

In 1876 he sailed as a guest on Lord Brassey's yacht, the Sunbeam, when she started on her voyage round the world. But he left her at Buenos Aires, and then, for lack of a better engagement, sailed for Calcutta as boatswain on the City of Mecca. In the evening he gave classes in navigation to the officers from the captain downwards, and in the morning wielded the hose as boatswain. In 1878 he became commodore captain of the British steamers of the American line from Liverpool to Philadelphia, and thoroughly enjoyed the responsibility. He commanded the British Prince transport in the Egyptian war of 1882, and going to the front won the medal and the Khedive's bronze star, and received a complimentary letter from the lords commissioners of the admiralty on his zealous and able conduct. Lecky had previously received a commission as a royal naval reserve officer, and eventually retired with the rank of commander.

In his spare time Lecky wrote on navigation. He had acquired by his own diligent study at sea a knowledge of mathematics and astronomy, which betrayed exceptional strength of intellect and character. His healthy and vigorous style, and avoidance, where possible, of technical language, gained for his books a world-wide popularity among seamen. His 'Wrinkles in Practical Navigation' (1881; 15th edit. 1908, with photogravure portrait) is the best work of its kind. In 1882 he published 'The Danger Angle and Off-Shore Distance,' and in 1892 'Lecky's A, B, C and D Tables.' The latter were labour-saving tables for solving problems in navigation and nautical astronomy, which he recast from varied material. He was an extra master, and passed the board of trade examination in steam machinery, a knowledge of which frequently stood him in good stead.

In 1884 Lecky was appointed marine superintendent of the Great Western Railway Company, being selected from some 600 applicants. With great energy and efficiency he supervised the Irish steamship service from Milford Haven, the fast Weymouth and Channel Island steamers, and those running between Weymouth and Cherbourg, besides looking after the company's docks. He practically designed their ships and supervised their building, drawing up the specifications in his own hand. He also kept for eight years an automatic tide-gauge, which demonstrated that the Admiralty tide-tables for Pembroke Dock were in error. In 1898 Lecky's health failed and he retired on a pension, but the company retained him as their consultant adviser in all marine matters. He was a younger brother of the Trinity House, and an enthusiastic fellow of both the Royal Astronomical and the Royal Geographical societies. He was for many years a member of the Mercantile Marine Association, and served on its council. Till within a few weeks of his death he was busy on a 'Star Atlas.' He died at Las Palmas on 23 Nov. 1902, and was buried in the English cemetery at that place. Lecky married twice, and a son by his first wife and a son and daughter by his second wife survived him.

[The Nautical Mag. 1902; The Times, 5 Dec. 1902; F. T. Bullen's A Great Merchant Seaman, in Cornhill Mag., Feb. 1903; information from Lecky's son, Lieut. H. S. Lecky, R.N.]

LECKY, WILLIAM EDWARD HARTPOLE (1838–1903), historian and essayist, was born at Newtown Park, co. Dublin, on 26 March 1838. He was only son of John Hartpole Lecky and of his first wife, Mary Anne Tallents; she was married in 1837, and died in 1839. The Leckys were of Scottish origin, connected by tradition with Stirlingshire, and had apparently migrated to Ireland early in the seventeenth century. Lecky's grandfather was of the Carlow branch of the family, and married Maria Hartpole, who, with her sister, was the last representative of the Hartpoles of Shrule Castle, near Carlow. The historian's mother was descended from a family long connected with Newark; her father, W. E. Tallents, was a solicitor of high reputation in that town. Lecky thus had English, Scotch, and Irish blood in his veins. Lecky's father had been called to the bar, but, having private means, did not practise. He lived near Dublin, owned property in Queen's County, and was a magistrate there. In 1841 he married again. His second wife was Isabella Eliza, daughter of Colonel Eardley Wilmot, who acted as a mother to the boy, and throughout her life remained on the best of terms with him. A son, George Eardley, and a daughter, were the issue of this marriage. In 1847 Lecky's parents spent some months in England, and he went to school with a Dr. Stanley, first at Walmer, then at Lewes. In 1848 he returned to his parents in Ireland, and went to a day-school at Kingstown, then to Armagh school, and in the autumn of 1852 to Cheltenham. A few weeks after this event his father died; but his stepmother continued to live in Ireland, at Monkstown near Dublin, till she became second wife, on 2 May 1855, of Thomas Henry Dalzell, eighth earl of Carnwath (she died on 16 Oct. 1902).

Lecky remained for three years at Cheltenham, but did not find school life at all congenial. In 1855 he left school, and, after a short time with a private tutor, entered Trinity College, Dublin, as a fellow commoner, in February 1856. There he was free to study as he pleased, and made good use of his opportunities, if in a somewhat desultory way. He has himself traced, in an interesting essay, the 'formative influences' he underwent at college. Probably the companionship of chosen friends, such as David Plunket (now Lord Rathmore), Edward Gibson (now Lord Ashbourne), Gerald FitzGibbon [q. v. Suppl. II], Edward, son of Smith O'Brien, and his cousin Aubrey, and Thomas (afterwards Canon) Teignmouth Shore, was the most stimulating of these influences; but he himself attributes much to his reading Bishop Butler, Whately, Bossuet, Hobbes, and particularly Buckle. With his friends he discussed history and philosophy, took part in debates in the College Historical Society, and won the gold medal for oratory in 1859. In the same year he graduated B.A.

His first publication was a small volume entitled 'Friendship, and other Poems,' issued under the name 'Hibernicus' (1859), which attracted little attention. This he followed up by a volume of essays called 'The Religious Tendencies of the Age,' published anonymously in 1860. He had long had a leaning towards theological studies, and even contemplated taking orders. But the book was remarkable for its wide outlook and spirit of tolerance, and foreshadowed no adhesion to any particular church. Meanwhile his family had gone abroad; and his holidays were chiefly spent on the Continent, in Belgium, Switzerland, and elsewhere. He thus imbibed that love of travelling which distinguished him through life. Spain and Italy were afterwards his predilection, and few Englishmen can have known those countries better than he. He was in Rome early in 1861, and was enthusiastic for the cause of Italian unity. In July 1861 he published, also anonymously, his 'Leaders of Public Opinion in Ireland.' The volume fell still-born from the press; and the later issues (1871 and 1903) were so radically altered as to form practically a new book. His first literary ventures had not been successful, and he passed through a period of uncertainty and discouragement. He gave up the idea of entering the church, but could not fix on any other profession. He hesitated between standing for parliament and adopting a literary career; but, though he believed he had failed as an author, literature eventually carried the day over politics. His next publication was to show the justice of this decision. He read widely in the history of the early Middle Ages, studied the lives of the saints and the development of the early church, and carried cargoes of books with him during his travels in Spain, the Pyrenees and Italy. In 1863 he proceeded M.A., and published an essay on 'The Declining Sense of the Miraculous,' which subsequently formed the first two chapters of his 'History of Rationalism,' published in two volumes in January 1865.

The book achieved great and immediate success, and at once raised Lecky, then only twenty-seven years old, into the front rank of contemporary authors. It is a striking combination of history and philosophy, of the essay and the narrative. It displays wide and often abstruse reading, with a great power of thought and generalisation; and it derives unity from the dominance of a central idea—the development of reason, and the decay of superstition as a power in human society. It traces this evolution from the days of the early church, through the 'Dark Ages,' down to the Reformation. After discussing the belief in magic and witchcraft and in miracles, the author examines the æsthetic, scientific, and moral developments of rationalism, pointing out the connection between artistic changes and the progress of physical science on the one hand, and the evolution of moral ideas on the other. This prepares the way for a long chapter on the history of religious persecution, which is traced to the doctrine of exclusive salvation, and on its gradual elimination by the spirit of tolerance, arising from the growth of reason and the decay of dogmatic religion. Finally, a similar evolution is traced in politics and industry, and illustrated by the coincidence between the growth of protestantism and that of political liberty, the abolition of slavery, and the like. The survey is very wide; the facts and illustrations cited are occasionally somewhat overwhelming; and there is some tendency to discursiveness. The book would probably have been the better for a more rigid compression and a clearer and more logical sequence of its parts. Nevertheless, it remains a remarkable contribution to the history of the human mind and of human society. It is written throughout in a polished and dignified style, which, though seldom brilliant, is always lucid, and occasionally rises into impassioned eloquence.

The defects and virtues of this work are characteristic of Lecky throughout, and are clearly to be seen in his next book. With one stride Lecky had become famous; his society was sought in the highest literary and political circles; he was elected to the Athenæum in 1867, and became intimate with Lord Russell, Sir Charles Lyell, Dean Milman, Carlyle, Henry Reeve, and other distinguished men. He now established himself in London (6 Albemarle St.), lectured at the Royal Institution on 'The Influence of the Imagination on History,' and paid much attention to politics. His letters show him a strong liberal, though not a radical (as he said himself) 'like Mr. Bright or Mr. Disraeli.' He condemned the tories for bringing in the reform bill of 1867, and supported the disestablishment of the Irish church, and (with some reservations) the Irish Land Act of 1870. Meanwhile he was working hard at his 'History of European Morals,' which appeared, in two volumes, in the spring of 1869. The book was attacked by both the utilitarians and the orthodox, but achieved a success no less great than its predecessor, with which it was so closely connected as to be in some sense a sequel or an expansion in a particular direction. Lecky himself, in a letter, indicates this connection by saying that both books 'are an attempt to examine the merits of certain theological opinions according to the historical method. . . . The "Morals" is a history of the imposition of those opinions upon the world, and attempts to show how far their success may be accounted for by natural causes. . . . The "Rationalism" is a history of the decay of those opinions.' The author was always an 'intuitional' moralist, but held strongly to the belief that moral intuitions are susceptible of development, and that history shows a continuous advance in moral concepts. This is the main thesis of the book. 'The path of truth (he says) is over the corpses of the enthusiasms of our past.' The treatment, however, is not entirely historical. The author begins with a long discussion, not altogether in place, of the dispute between the intuitionists and the utilitarians, and decides in favour of the former. He then proceeds to show the progressive character of moral intuitions, and the gradual changes in the standard and mode of action of human morality. These he traces through the later periods of the Pagan empire and the *Völkerwanderung*, down to the re-establishment of the empire of the west. He covers no little of the same ground which he covered in his previous book; and there is some repetition, notably in the treatment of religious persecution. He concludes with an examination of the position of women under the Roman empire and in the later Middle Ages.

In the following year (1870) Lecky first met, at Dean Stanley's, Queen Sophia of the Netherlands and her maid-of-honour, Elizabeth, eldest daughter of General Baron van Dedem and his first wife, Baroness Sloet van Hagensdorp. He subsequently visited Queen Sophia at the House in the Wood, and became engaged to her lady-in-waiting, Elizabeth van Dedem. Meanwhile the Franco-German war had broken out. Lecky inclined at the outset to favour Germany, believing that the conflict had arisen from unprovoked aggression on the part of France; but as the war proceeded his opinion changed, and he strongly condemned the terms of peace. In June 1871 he married, and shortly afterwards settled down at 38 Onslow Gardens, which was thenceforward his home. The Leckys had a wide circle of distinguished friends, among whom may be mentioned, in addition to those named above, Sir Henry and Lady Taylor, Froude, Sir Henry Holland, Sir Leslie Stephen, Browning, Tennyson, Lord and Lady Derby, Lady Stanley of Alderley, Kinglake, Huxley, Tyndall, and Herbert Spencer—in fact all that was best in the literary and scientific society of the day. In 1873 he was elected a member of the 'Literary Society,' and in 1874 of 'The Club,' which Dr. Johnson had founded—an event which gave him much gratification.

But social claims did not abate his ardour for work. In December 1871 he brought out a revised edition of his 'Leaders of Public Opinion in Ireland,' but was disappointed at its reception. Meanwhile he was collecting materials for his *magnum opus*, the 'History of England in the Eighteenth Century.' For this purpose he paid several visits to Ireland, and made extensive researches in Dublin. These visits resulted in many discoveries and rectifications, which give his chapters on Ireland a special value. The first two volumes of the book appeared in January 1878, and achieved immediate success. His aim, as he himself explains in his preface, was not to write a detailed or personal history, but 'to disengage from the great mass of facts those which relate to the permanent forces of the nation, or which indicate some of the more enduring features of national life.' But an immediate object, very near his heart, was (as he also says in a letter) to refute what he held to be the calumnies of Froude against the Irish people. This explains the otherwise disproportionate amount of space allotted to Ireland in the book. In the subsequent (cabinet) edition Irish history occupies five volumes, as compared with seven devoted to that of England. The work occupied Lecky for nineteen years. The third and fourth volumes were published in 1882, the fifth and sixth in 1887, the seventh and eighth in 1890. Each successive instalment heightened and confirmed the author's fame. Lord Acton, writing of vols. iii. and iv., said that they were 'fuller of political instruction than anything that had appeared for a long time.' American critics recognised the impartiality of the author in dealing with the American revolution, and the thoroughness of his investigations. By this great work Lecky's name will chiefly live. The style is sound, lucid, and elevated throughout, never rhetorical or declamatory, and never sinking below itself. The narrative moves steadily forward, with due regard to chronological sequence; but the events and episodes are so grouped and connected as to make the whole intelligible. The limitations of the subject and the necessities of historical narrative help to correct that tendency to diffuseness, recurrence, and defective arrangement which are noticeable in the earlier works. Attention is mainly concentrated on political movements and ideas, but society, commerce, industry, art, and literature, and especially ecclesiastical affairs and religious thought, receive their share. But perhaps the most valuable qualities in Lecky's historical work are the philosophical character of his summaries and deductions, the soundness of his judgments of men and of events, and the scrupulous impartiality with which he treats all parties and all creeds. There is doubtless some want of colour; but as a truthful picture of eighteenth-century Britain in its most important aspects the book excelled all previous efforts, and will be hard to supersede.

In Irish affairs Lecky always took a keen interest. He saw the dangers of Gladstone's land legislation. Although he never became a tory, he was, from the date of Gladstone's adoption of the policy of home rule in 1886, a liberal unionist. He intervened actively in the struggle over Gladstone's policy by writing several weighty letters to 'The Times' (1886) and by an article in the 'Nineteenth Century' (April 1886). When, in 1892, the home rule project was revived, he again denounced it in letters to the Irish Unionist Convention and to the 'Scotsman,' and in articles published in the 'National Observer,' the 'Pall Mall Gazette,' and the 'Contemporary Review' (May 1893). Meanwhile he was occupied in rearranging his 'History' for the cabinet edition, which appeared in 1892, and in working up the materials for 'Democracy and Liberty.' In 1891 he published a volume of poems, which, though not reaching the higher flights of poetic imagination or expression, were marked by elevated feeling, a tender melancholy, and a sincerity and self-restraint, truly representing the author's temperament. In 1892, on the death of Professor Freeman, Lecky was offered the regius professorship of modern history at Oxford, but declined it. He had been made hon. D.C.L. of Oxford in 1888 and hon. Litt.D. of Cambridge in 1891. In 1895 he was elected hon. secretary for foreign correspondence to the Royal Academy, and received the honorary degree of LL.D. at Glasgow. In October of the same year he accepted an invitation to stand for the seat in parliament, as representative of Dublin University, vacated by the elevation of Mr. Plunket to the peerage; some of the clerical electors demurred to his religious opinions, but after a contest he was elected by a considerable majority. It is noteworthy that his first speech (February 1896) was made on behalf of the Irish prisoners condemned under the Treason Felony Act thirteen years before. He speedily made a mark in parliament, and was listened to with attention when he rose to speak. He discharged his parliamentary duties with exemplary regularity; and his tall, thin, somewhat stooping, but impressive figure was well known in the house. But he never acquired the parliamentary manner; his speaking was so fluent, even, and rapid as to become monotonous; and he excelled rather in set speeches than in debate. Although he had a distinct turn for politics, and his sincerity, ability, and wide knowledge always carried weight, he must be ranked among those whom training and character fitted better for other fields, and whom distinction won elsewhere carried too late into the rough-and-tumble of parliamentary life.

In 1896 he published his 'Democracy and Liberty' in two volumes. This book, though full, like all his works, of learning, and marked by profound thought, impartiality, and sobriety of judgment, hardly met with the success which, in many respects, it deserved. Like his 'Rationalism' and his 'Morals,' it to some extent falls between the two stools of essay and narrative, of history and philosophical discussion. The book is very discursive. The great question—the effect of democracy upon liberty—is obscured by the importation of many matters, such as marriage and divorce, whose connection with the main subject is not obvious, or of others, like nationality, the bearing of which upon it is insufficiently brought out. The weight of the illustrative matter and the very fairness of the tone have also hindered its popularity. In these respects it may profitably be compared with Sir James Stephen's 'Liberty, Equality, Fraternity,' and Sir Henry Maine's essay on 'Popular Government'—far shorter books, and, from this and their very one-sidedness, far more effective. 'Democracy and Liberty' is largely a treatise on contemporary politics. It provides a storehouse of admirable, if somewhat disjointed, reflections, made, on the whole, from a distinctly conservative point of view, and without much hope for the future of democracy. It is largely a doubt, a protest, and a regret.

In regard to Irish university education, Lecky recognised the necessity of doing something for the Roman catholics, and favoured the establishment of a Roman catholic university, in which candidates for the priesthood should be educated along with laymen. On the financial question he held that Ireland was entitled to separate treatment; but found a remedy not in abated taxation, but an equivalent grant. He had doubts about the Irish local government bill, and sought to amend it in several details. He opposed the grant of compulsory powers of purchase to the congested districts board, as well as the proposal to make that body more representative, but warmly supported the agricultural policy of Sir Horace Plunkett. He also opposed the introduction of old age pensions, preferring a reform of the poor law. He favoured international arbitration, but believed more in a great and gradual revolution in public sentiment. In these and many other questions he displayed his characteristic independence of thought and mental balance, and a genuine interest in the public welfare without a tinge of fanaticism.

In 1899 he issued a revised edition of 'Democracy and Liberty,' with a new introduction, containing what is probably the best summary and estimate of Gladstone's work and character which has yet appeared. In the autumn of the same year he brought out, under the title of 'The Map of Life,' a volume of reflections on life, character, and conduct, which achieved and still enjoys considerable popularity. It cannot be said that the reflections are very profound, nor are they epigrammatically expressed; but there is a mellow wisdom, a good sense, a hopeful trust in the force of resolution, a mingled gentleness and firmness, which give the book a certain charm. It would be profitable reading for the young, but has probably found more readers among the old. In the spring of 1903 a finally revised edition (the third) of his 'Leaders' appeared. The life of Swift was now omitted, being included (in an enlarged form) in Messrs. Bell's edition of Swift's works. Beginning with an introductory chapter on the Irish parliament in the eighteenth century, the author narrates the lives of Flood, Grattan, and Daniel O'Connell, the last of which occupies the whole of the second volume, while that of Grattan occupies two-thirds of the first. The book had gradually won its way to public acceptance, and taken its place as a highly important contribution to Irish history. A volume of 'Historical and Political Essays' was posthumously published by his widow in 1908. In making this collection Mrs. Lecky was fulfilling an intention of the author which he had not lived to carry out. The essays are partly biographical sketches of Carlyle, Madame de Staël, Sir Robert Peel, Lord Derby, Henry Reeve, Dean Milman, Queen Victoria, and his solitary chapter of autobiography 'Formative Influences'—partly discussions on historical and political topics. An address on 'The Empire, its Value and Growth,' displays his genuine warmth of patriotic feeling and a tempered imperialism. But perhaps the most interesting are two essays entitled 'Thoughts on History' and 'The Political Value of History.' The latter, while holding that history cannot predict, proves the value of historical study to the statesman, but concludes that 'its most precious lessons are moral ones.'

Many honours were conferred on Lecky. He was hon. LL.D. of Dublin (1879) and of St. Andrews (1885). In 1897, at Queen Victoria's diamond jubilee, he was made a privy councillor. When the British Academy was founded in 1902, he became one of its original members. In the same year he received the high distinction of the Order of Merit, being one of the first twelve recipients of that honour. He also now became a full member of the French Institute, of which he had been a corresponding member since 1893. Meanwhile his health, which during the greater part of his life had been good, began to fail. In the spring of 1901 an attack of influenza led to dilatation of the heart, from which he never entirely recovered. Ill-health compelled him in December 1902 to resign his seat in parliament. He gradually grew weaker, and on 22 Oct. 1903 he died quietly and suddenly in his own study, among his books. His body was cremated, and the remains, after a service at St. Patrick's, were buried in Mount Jerome cemetery, Dublin. His wife Elizabeth, eldest daughter of General Baron van Dedem, by whom he had no issue, survived till 23 May 1912; she was buried beside her husband in Mount Jerome cemetery. The Lecky chair of history at Trinity College, Dublin, was endowed by Mrs. Lecky from the proceeds of her husband's landed property in Queen's County and co. Carlow. All Lecky's MSS., published and unpublished, were left by his widow to Trinity College, as well as a bronze bust of him by Boehm (*The Times*, 23 June 1912).

In person Lecky was very tall and slim. His head was dome-shaped, the hair (which he wore rather long) was fair, the brow lofty, the eyes thoughtful and with a gentle expression, the nose long and nearly straight, the mouth somewhat large, the lips full and drawn down at the corners, the chin rounded. The front of the face was shaved, but he wore side-whiskers, the hair being allowed to meet under the chin. Lecky indulged in no sport, and played no games, but he was a good walker, and in his younger days habitually made long excursions on foot, preferably in beautiful scenery. Pictures of him by Watts and Henry Tanworth Wells are in the National Portrait Gallery, and several good photographs are given in the 'Memoir.' A drawing, by H. T. Wells, is in the Royal Library at Windsor. A cartoon portrait by 'Spy' appeared in 'Vanity Fair' in 1882.

Lecky's most important works, all of which were published in London, are: 1. 'Leaders of Public Opinion in Ireland,' 1861; revised edits. in 1871 and (2 vols.) 1903. 2. 'History of the Rise and Influence of the Spirit of Rationalism in Europe,' 2 vols. 1865; cabinet edit. 1869. 3. 'History of European Morals from Augustus to Charlemagne,' 2 vols. 1869; cabinet edit. 1877. 4. 'History of England in the Eighteenth Century,' 8 vols. 1878–1890; cabinet edit. separating the English and Irish histories, 1892. 5. 'Democracy and Liberty,' 2 vols. 1896; cabinet edit. 1899. 6. 'The Map of Life: Conduct and Character,' 1899; cabinet edit. 1901. 7. 'Historical and Political Essays,' 1908; cabinet edit. 1908.

[Memoir of W. E. H. Lecky, by Mrs. Lecky, 1909; Notice sur la vie et les travaux du très-honorable W. E. H. Lecky, par le Comte de Franqueville, Paris, 1910; J. F. Rhodes, Historical Essays, 1909; The Times, 23 Oct. 1903; Acton's Letters to Mary Gladstone, 1904, pp. 131–2; Letters to William Allingham, 1911, p. 197; Tollemache, Old and Odd Memories; and note in Spectator, 13 Nov. 1909; Proc. Brit. Acad. 1903–4, p. 307; private information.] G. W. P.

LEE, FREDERICK GEORGE (1832–1902), theological writer, born at Thame, Oxfordshire, on 6 Jan. 1832, was eldest son of Frederick Lee of Thame, sometime rector of Easington, Oxfordshire, and vicar of Stantonbury, Berkshire, by his wife Mary, only daughter and sole heir of George Ellys of Aylesbury. Educated at Thame grammar school, he matriculated at St. Edmund Hall, Oxford, on 23 Oct. 1851, but did not graduate (FOSTER'S *Alumni Oxonienses*, p. 830). Whilst an undergraduate he won the Newdigate prize in 1854, for an English poem on 'The Martyrs of Vienne and Lyons,' which passed through five editions. He was admitted S.C.L. (student of civil law) the same year, and, after spending some time at Cuddesdon Theological College, was ordained deacon by the bishop of Oxford in 1854 on a title to Sunningwell, Berkshire, and priest in 1856. He then became assistant-minister of Berkeley Chapel in London, and in 1858–9, at the time of the ritualist riots at St. George's in the East, he showed his sympathy with Charles Fuge Lowder [q. v.], Alexander Heriot Mackonochie [q. v.], and the other clergy there by preaching and taking part in the services of that church. Lee next became incumbent of St. John's, Aberdeen, but introduced non-communicating attendance, then almost unknown in the Anglican church, which caused a schism in the congregation, and his adherents built St. Mary's church for him; this however soon came to an end, as the bishop of Aberdeen refused to consecrate it, or in any way sanction it. Returning to London, he was in 1867 appointed vicar of All Saints', Lambeth. An eloquent preacher, with a musical and melodious voice, he ministered zealously to this poor parish for thirty-two years.

From the time of his taking holy orders, Lee's views were of the most advanced high church type. In conjunction with Mr. Ambrose Lisle March Phillipps de Lisle [q. v.], a prominent Roman catholic, he founded in 1857 the Association for Promoting the Union of Christendom, a society whose object was to reunite the churches of Rome and England with that of Russia. From 1863 to 1869, when the association was dissolved, Lee edited 'The Union Review.' In 1868, when de Lisle was high sheriff of Leicestershire, he appointed Lee his chaplain, but Canon David James Vaughan [q. v. Suppl. II], then vicar of St. Martin's,

Leicester, refused to allow him to preach the assize sermon before the judges. In 1870 Lee issued 'The Validity of the Holy Orders of the Church of England maintained and vindicated,' perhaps the best book written on this subject. Lee's investigations ultimately led him to doubt the validity of Anglican orders, and in conjunction with some other clergymen who shared his distrust of the validity of their ordination he founded the Order of Corporate Reunion. The object of the society was to restore to the Church of England valid orders which were supposed to have been lost at the Reformation. Accordingly Lee was consecrated a bishop by some catholic prelates, whose names were kept—even from members of the 'Order'—a profound secret, at or near Venice in the summer of 1877; he took the title of 'Bishop of Dorchester.' On his return to England he consecrated two other Anglicans in the little chapel at All Saints' vicarage, Lambeth, as bishops—the Rev. Thomas Wimberley Mossman, rector of East and West Torrington, Lincolnshire, as 'Bishop of Selby,' and Dr. J. T. Seccombe, an Anglican layman, as 'Bishop of Caerleon.' In this chapel, too, Lee and his coadjutors re-ordained some few clergy who felt doubtful about their orders, and administered confirmation to laity who felt the like scruples. The 'Reunion Magazine' (1877–9) was founded by Lee, in order to spread the tenets of the order. Every one connected with the Order of Corporate Reunion was bound to secrecy, and some six or seven years before his death Lee destroyed every paper relating to it.

In 1879 Lee was created honorary D.D. of the Washington and Lee University, Virginia. He was elected F.S.A. on 30 April 1857, but resigned in 1892.

Lee was throughout life a voluminous writer of history, archæology, theology, and poetry, besides being actively engaged in journalism. At one time Lee edited the 'Church News' and 'Church Herald,' both newspapers of the tory and high church school, and the 'Penny Post,' and he was for many years a leader writer for 'John Bull,' a weekly paper of moderate high church tendencies. He also founded and edited the shortlived periodicals 'The Pilot,' 'The Anchor,' and 'Lambeth Review.' His best antiquarian work is his 'History and Antiquities of the Prebendal Church of the Blessed Virgin Mary of Thame' (1886). As an historian Lee was a thorough-going and blind partisan, and his historical works are untrustworthy. The best known of these are 'Historical Sketches of the Reformation' (1879), 'Edward the Sixth, Supreme Head' (1886; 2nd edit. 1889), 'Cardinal Reginald Pole, Archbishop of Canterbury' (1888), and 'The Church under Queen Elizabeth' (3rd edit. 1897), where he impugns the validity of Anglican orders.

His poetical works, besides the Newdigate prize poem, include 'Poems' (1855), 'The King's Highway and other Poems' (1872), 'The Bells of Botteville Tower' (1874), and 'Petronilla and other Poems' (1889). Most of these reached more than one edition. His 'Directorium Anglicanum,' a manual for the right celebration of Holy Communion, passed into a fourth edition in 1878, and was much used by the Anglican clergy. He also brought out an 'Altar Service Book of the Church of England' (1867, 3 vols. 4to).

In 1881, in a novel, 'Reginald Barentyne, or Liberty without Limit: a Tale of the Times,' Lee caricatured a ritualistic priest, and gave offence to high church Anglicans. His position during his closing years grew ambiguous. He retired from All Saints', Lambeth, on 1 Nov. 1899, when the church was acquired by the South Western Railway Company and demolished. On 11 Dec. 1901 he was received into the Roman catholic church, at his own request, by his old friend Father Best of the Oratory. After a short illness he died at his residence in Earl's Court Gardens on 22 Jan. 1902; his body was interred at Brookwood cemetery in the same grave with his wife. Lee had married, on 9 June 1859, Elvira Louisa, daughter of Joseph Duncan Ostrehan, vicar of Creech St. Michael, Somerset, by whom he had three sons and one daughter. His wife predeceased him in 1890, having previously joined the Roman catholic church. His second son, Gordon Ambrose de Lisle Lee, fills the post of York herald.

Other works include: 1. 'The Words from the Cross,' 1861; 3rd edit. 1880. 2. 'Parochial and Occasional Sermons,' 1873. 3. 'The Christian Doctrine of Prayer for the Departed,' 1875. 4. 'Memorials of the Rev. R. S. Hawker,' 1876. 5. 'Glossary of Liturgical and Ecclesiastical Terms,' 1877. 6. 'Glimpses of the Supernatural,' 2 vols. 1877. 7. 'More Glimpses of the World Unseen,' 1880. 8. 'The Sinless Conception of the Mother of God,' 1881. 9. 'Order out of Chaos,' 1881. 10. 'Glimpses of the Twilight,' 1885. 11. 'A Manual of Politics,' 1889. 12. 'Lights and Shadows, being Examples of the Supernatural,' 1894.

[The Times, 25 Jan. 1902; The Tablet, 1, 8, and 22 Feb. 1902; Men and Women of the Time, 1899; Alumni Oxonienses; Pedigree of Lee in his History and Antiquities of Thame Church, pp. 635–42; Brit. Mus. Cat., where the list of his publications fills twenty-one pages; private information.] W. G. D. F.

LEE, RAWDON BRIGGS (1845–1908), writer on dogs, born on 9 July 1845, was son of George Lee, unitarian minister at Kendal, and proprietor and editor of the 'Kendal Mercury.' His mother was Jane Agnes, daughter of Joseph Whitaker of Kendal, who was intimate there with the painter Romney.

After education at the Friends' school, Kendal, Lee learned journalism under his father, whom he ultimately succeeded in the editorship of the 'Mercury,' retaining it till 1883. But he gave much time to field sports, especially fishing, otter-hunting, and cricket, becoming also an authority upon wrestling, and in spite of defective eyesight one of the finest fly-fishers in England, with an unrivalled knowledge of angling in the Lake district. He made his chief reputation, however, as a breeder of dogs. In 1869 he first formed a kennel, and his pack of Fellside terriers became well known to otter-hunters. But fox-terriers were his especial fancy. In 1871 he won the cup at the national show at Birmingham with a dog (Mac II) of this breed; and other prize-winners, such as Nimrod and Gripper, were exceptionally fine specimens. He was also successful with Dandie Dinmonts, pointers, collies, bull-terriers, Skye-terriers, and Clumber spaniels. His English setter, Richmond, after winning the highest honours at home, went to Australia to improve the breed. Lee acted as judge at dog-shows held at Bath, Darlington, and Lancaster, but declined to adjudicate abroad. He finally retired from the show-ring in 1892. A powerful advocate of field-trials for sporting dogs, he did much to extend the movement which began in 1865.

Meanwhile, Lee, who had for several years written in the 'Field' on angling and dog-breeding, came to London in 1883, and joined its staff, succeeding John Henry Walsh [q. v.] as kennel-editor, and holding that post until June 1907. He also contributed occasionally to 'Land and Water,' the 'Fishing Gazette,' the 'Stock-keeper,' and other papers. His health failed owing to injury in a carriage accident at Kendal. He died from paralysis in a nursing home at Putney on 29 Feb. 1908. His body was cremated at Golder's Green, the ashes being afterwards buried in the family vault at Kendal.

He had married in Feb. 1907 Emily, daughter of Lieut. Charles Dyer, and widow of Edward King, of Wavington, Bedfordshire.

Lee, who, whilst living in London, formed an excellent collection of books and pictures on sporting subjects, published the following works, which are standard authorities: 1. 'History and Description of the Fox-terrier,' 1889; 4th edit., enlarged, 1902. 2. 'History and Description of the Collie or Sheep Dog in his British Varieties,' illustrated by Arthur Wardle, 1890. 3. 'History and Description of the Modern Dogs of Great Britain and Ireland—Non-sporting Division,' illustrated by A. Wardle and R. H. Moore, 1894; new edit. 1899. 4. 'History and Description of the Terriers,' illustrated by the same artists, 1894; 3rd edit. 1903. 5. 'History and Description of the Modern Dogs of Great Britain and Ireland—Sporting Division,' illustrated by A. Wardle, 2 vols. 1897; 3rd edit. 1906.

He also wrote, with Fred Gresham, the article on the Dog in the 'Encyclopædia of Sport.'

[Private information; The Times, 2 March 1908; Field, Sporting and Dramatic News, and Westmorland Gazette, 7 March 1908; Kendal Mercury, 6 March; Lee's works.] G. Le G. N.

LEE-HAMILTON, EUGENE JACOB (1845–1907), poet and novelist, born in London on 6 Jan. 1845, was son of James Lee-Hamilton, who died soon after his son's birth, by his wife Matilda Abadam. Eugene as a child lived with his widowed mother and her brother, William Abadam, at the Château de Biranos, near Pau, until Abadam's death about 1854, when his mother took him to Paris. There she married her second husband, Henry Ferguson Paget, an engineer, whose active sympathy with the Polish insurrection had compelled him to leave his employment in Poland.

Eugene was educated in France and Germany, partly at school and partly under tutors at home. In 1864 he entered Oriel College, Oxford, gaining a Taylorian scholarship for 'French with German' in that year, and leaving the university without a degree. In July 1869 he was nominated an attaché, and was employed for some months in the foreign office. He was appointed to the embassy at Paris under Lord Lyons on 21 Feb. 1870. He was with the embassy at Tours, Bordeaux, and Versailles during the Franco-German war. In 1871 he acted as secretary to Sir Alexander Cockburn at Geneva in the Alabama arbitration, and suffered in health from the pressure of work.

In January 1873 he was promoted to be third secretary, and transferred to the legation at Lisbon under Sir Charles Murray on 10 Feb. He was unemployed from 1 Jan. to 8 Sept. 1875, when he resigned on account of illness. He had been an accomplished skater and dancer, but nervous disease developed, with the result that for twenty years he was incapacitated from all physical exertion and had to lie on his back. He lived at Florence with his mother and his half-sister, Miss Violet Paget ('Vernon Lee'), spending the summers at Siena or the Bagni di Lucca. His intellectual vitality was uninjured by his physical disablement. His health was soon sufficiently restored to enable him to indulge his gifts as a talker, and his room became one of the centres of intellectual cosmopolitan society in Florence. His visitors included Mr. Henry James and M. Paul Bourget.

In time, too, he was able to compose and to dictate fragments of verse. Most of 'The Sonnets of the Wingless Hours' (published in 1894), his most characteristic production, were written between 1880 and 1888. By 1896 his recovery was completed. From a visit to Canada and the United States in 1897 he returned a 'new man,' and he married on 21 July 1898, at Boldre, Hampshire, Annie E. Holdsworth, the novelist. They settled in a villa between Florence and Fiesole. A volume of verse, entitled 'Forest Notes,' in which both husband and wife collaborated, appeared in 1899. In 1900 they moved to the Villa Benedettini, San Gervasio, where in 1903 a daughter, Persis Margaret, was born. The child died in 1904, and the father's grief is recorded in 'Mimma Bella' (published in 1909), a volume of elegiac sonnets. The depression culminated in a paralytic stroke, from which Lee-Hamilton died on 7 Sept. 1907, at the Villa Pierotti, Bagni di Lucca; he was buried in the new protestant cemetery outside the Porta Romana, Florence.

A portrait painted during his last illness by Stephen Haweis and a beautiful death mask are in the possession of his widow.

Poetry was Lee-Hamilton's consolation throughout his long illness. His earliest volume, 'Poems and Transcripts,' appeared in 1878; then followed 'Gods, Saints, and Men' (1880), 'The New Medusa and other Poems' (1882), 'Apollo and Marsyas and other Poems' (1884). He excelled in the poetic form of the sonnet, of the technique of which he had a perfect mastery, and the dramatic impersonal 'Imaginary Sonnets' (1888) and the autobiographic 'Sonnets of the Wingless Hours' (1894) rank with the best of their kind.

Lee-Hamilton wrote also 'The Fountain of Youth,' a fantastic tragedy in verse (1891); two novels, 'The Lord of the Dark Red Star, being the Story of the Supernatural Influences in the Life of an Italian Despot of the 13th Century' (1903), and 'The Romance of the Fountain' (1905); and a metrical translation of Dante's 'Inferno' (1898). In 1903 he made a selection from his poems for the 'Canterbury Poets' series, for which William Sharp wrote a preface.

[Preface by Annie Lee-Hamilton to Mimma Bella, 1909; The Times, 11 Sept. 1907; Foreign Office List, 1876; private information.]

E. L.

LEFROY, WILLIAM (1836–1909), dean of Norwich, born in Dublin on 6 Nov. 1836, was eldest of the four children of Isaac and Isabella Lefroy, whose circumstances were humble. Educated at St. Michael-le-Pole Latin school, Dublin, he entered a printing office in youth, afterwards working as a journalist on the 'Irish Times.' With the help of an ex-scholar, John Galvan, he prepared himself for Trinity College, Dublin, where he graduated B.A. in 1863, proceeding B.D. in 1867 and D.D. in 1889. Ordained deacon in 1864, and priest in 1865 by the bishop of Cork, John Gregg [q. v.], he was licensed to the curacy of Christ Church, Cork. The fame of his preaching power quickly spread, and in 1866, when he was thirty, he was appointed incumbent of St. Andrew's chapel, Renshaw Street, Liverpool, in succession to Robert William Forrest, afterwards Dean of Worcester. Originally a broad churchman, he was influenced by the evangelical preaching of D. L. Moody, of Northfield, U.S.A. The first bishop of Liverpool, J. C. Ryle [q. v. Suppl. I], made him honorary canon in 1880, rural dean of South Liverpool in 1884, and archdeacon of Warrington in 1887. He was elected a proctor in convocation in 1886, and was appointed Donnellan lecturer at Dublin in 1887. He exerted much influence over the young men of his congregation, many of whom took holy orders. He was a prominent member of the Liverpool school board in the 'voluntary' interest from 1876.

At Easter 1889 he succeeded Edward Meyrick Goulburn [q. v. Suppl. I] in the deanery of Norwich, after the post had been declined by James Fleming [q. v. Suppl. II]. He soon effected some reforms in the management of the cathedral, especially as to 'appropriated' seats, and he instituted a simple evening service. He paid attention to the fabric under the advice of John Loughborough Pearson, R.A. [q. v. Suppl. I]. The choir, the walls of which were unflaked and the pillars strengthened, was re-opened by Archbishop Benson [q. v. Suppl. I] on 1 May 1894; then the exterior, the cloisters, and the stonework of the nave were repaired with the help of Sir Samuel Hoare, M.P. Lefroy collected 6623*l.* for a new organ, which was dedicated on 12 Dec. 1899. His financial efforts on behalf of Norwich grammar school were equally successful.

Lefroy, who closely studied the problem of clergy sustentation, put forward at the church congress, Norwich, 1895, a scheme to which the Queen Victoria clergy fund of 1897 owes much. He sat for twenty-three years in convocation, where he, as elsewhere, preferred vigorous argument to gentle persuasion. He was a strong advocate of the reform both of convocation and of cathedral establishments.

Lefroy was devoted to Switzerland, and he was one of the summer chaplains of the Colonial and Continental Church Society annually from 1867 to the year of his death. From 1875 to 1878 he was a member of the Alpine Club, but although fond of mountain climbing made no great expeditions. He helped to build the English churches at Zermatt, Riffel Alp, Gletsch, and Adelboden. He preached in the church at Riffel Alp on 1 Aug. 1909, twenty-five years after he had opened it on 27 July 1884. Seized with illness just afterwards, he died at the Riffel hotel on 11 Aug. 1909, and was buried in the churchyard of Holy Trinity, Riffel Alp. The dean was twice married. By his second wife, Mary Ann, daughter of Charles MacIver, of Calderstone, Liverpool, whom he married at Malta on 11 Feb. 1878, he left two daughters, of whom Mary Ann is the wife of Sir Percy Bates, fourth baronet.

An oil painting by Blackden is at the Deanery, Norwich. Lefroy's published works include: 1. 'The Christian Ministry: its Origin, Constitution, Nature, and Work' (the Donnellan lectures, 1887–8), 1890. 2. 'Agoniæ Christi' ('Preachers of the Age' series), 1893. 3. 'The Immortality of Memory and other Sermons,' 1898. 4. 'Christian Science contrasted with the Christian Faith and with itself,' 1903.

[The Times, 12 Aug. 1909; Record, 13, 20, and 27 Aug., 3 Sept. 1909; Guardian, 18 Aug. 1909; Lefroy's introduction to Echoes from the Choir of Norwich Cathedral, 1894; Greater Britain Messenger, Oct. 1909; H. Leeds, Life of Dean Lefroy, Norwich, 1909; private information.] E. H. P.

LEGROS, ALPHONSE (1837–1911), painter, sculptor, and etcher, born at Dijon on 8 May 1837, was the second son in a family of seven brothers and sisters of Lucien Auguste Legros, an accountant who came from the neighbouring village of Véronnes. His mother was Anne Victoire, daughter of Jean Baptiste Louis Barrié, mechanic, of Dijon. Legros spoke French all his life. Sent to the Ecole des Beaux-Arts at Dijon at an early age, he was intended to qualify for an artistic trade. To the end of his career early wanderings to the farms of his relatives around Dijon supplied him with subjects for his works. Leaving the Dijon school in 1850, he was apprenticed to one Maître Nicolardo, house decorator and painter of images. In 1851 he travelled towards Paris to take up another situation, but passing through Lyons he worked for six months as journeyman wall-painter with the decorator Beuchot, who was at work in the chapel of Cardinal Bonald in the cathedral. Legros was employed on the ornamental work in fresco. One day an Italian engaged in laying the mosaic pavement was in difficulties over the design, and asked Legros to draw it out for him. The boy designed it afresh, to the Italian's admiration. 'Ce fut,' Legros said, 'mon premier orgueil d'artiste et ma première sensation d'art.'

Arrived in Paris, Legros worked with Cambon, scene-painter and decorator of theatres, an experience which developed breadth of handling and decorative quality in his work and incidentally a gift for histrionic mimicry. At the same time he attended the drawing school of M. Lecoq de Boisbaudran in the rue de l'Ecole de Médecine, a master who developed in his pupils a power of drawing from memory both scenes of nature and pictures in the Louvre. Legros, like his fellow-pupils Bonvin, Fantin-Latour, and Régamey, spent whole days in the Louvre, and the excellence of Legros's drawing from memory of Holbein's portrait of Erasmus excited Lecoq's especial interest in his pupil, who thenceforth worked in his master's studio. Legros's drawing of the Erasmus is reproduced in Lecoq's 'Training of the Memory of Art,' translated by L. D. Luard (1911). The profile portrait by Holbein had a lasting influence on Legros; it may be seen even in his later works, such as 'Prière de

Noël,' perhaps the best picture he painted. In 1855 Legros attended the evening classes at the Ecole des Beaux-Arts, and acquired there a lifelong love of drawing from the antique; some of these studies, done at various periods in chalk and in gold-point, are in the British Museum print room.

Legros sent to the Salon of 1857 two portraits; one was rejected and was sent to the exhibition of protest organised by Bonvin in his studio; the other, which was accepted, was a profile portrait of his father, a beardless head recalling the Erasmus, now in the museum at Tours, presented by the artist when his friend Cazin was conservateur. Champfleury, who noticed the work in the Salon, sought out the artist and enlisted him in the group of so-called 'Realists,' a school of protest against the academical trifles of the degenerate Romantics. Legros was already associated with men like Bonvin, Bracquemond, Fantin-Latour, Manet, and Ribot, and was dubbed 'Realist' more because it was the war-cry for the time than for any other reason. Legros thus won the support of Baudelaire, Champfleury, and Durantez, who hoped for a revival of art through the young 'realists.' He appears in Fantin-Latour's well-known group of portraits called 'Hommage à Delacroix.'

In 1859 Legros's 'Angelus' was in the Salon, the first of those quiet church interiors with kneeling figures of patient women by which he is best known in England. It was in the collection of Sir Francis Seymour Haden [q. v. Suppl. II]. Baudelaire, in an article devoted to this little masterpiece, called Legros a religious painter gifted with the sincerity of the old masters. 'Ex Voto,' a work of great power, painted in 1861, and now in the Museum of Dijon, was received by his friends with enthusiasm, but only got a mention at the Salon. During this period Legros made his living by the occasional sale of his etchings and lithographs, and by private teaching. A pupil, son of M. de Laborde, Directeur des Archives, took him for a fortnight's tour through Catalonia in Spain. He saw nothing of the Galleries, but in the Louvre he had come under the influence of the Spanish school, and the Spanish places and people now excited his imagination and sympathy. 'Le Lutrin,' exhibited in 1863, had no better success than 'Ex Voto'; it was very badly hung, but the same picture with one figure painted out obtained a medal in 1868. Legros's reputation was confined to a narrow circle, and at the time that 'Le Lutrin' was painted he, according to Dalou, was in a state of great poverty, disheartened, ill, living in dread of creditors, although not 'devoid of that saving quality of humour, which never left him.'

Encouraged by James Abbott McNeill Whistler [q. v. Suppl. II], who heartened him with the hope of finding work in London, Legros left France for England in 1863. Not wholly unknown, he was welcomed with great kindness by Dante Gabriel Rossetti [q. v.] and George Frederick Watts [q. v. Suppl. II]. At first he lived by his etching and by teaching. On the recommendation of (Sir) Edward Poynter he was appointed teacher of etching at the South Kensington School of Art, and his success in that post led to his election in 1875 to the Slade professorship of fine art at University College, London. Leighton, Burton, Poynter, and Watts supported his candidature. In due course Legros became a naturalised British subject. He remained professor till 1892, and among the many young artists who came under his care were Mr. Henry Tuke, Mr. Thomas Gotch, Charles Furse, William Strang, who was his most faithful disciple, Countess Féodora Gleichen, Miss Hallé, (Sir) Charles Holroyd, and Miss Swainson. Legros encouraged truth of character and severity in the work of his pupils, with a simple technique and a respect for the traditions of the old masters after the manner of the schools of Raphael and the Carracci. He painted before the students, and would draw before them from the life and from the antique. All varieties of art work were practised: sculpture, modelling, decoration, etching, medal-making and even gem-engraving. As Legros had casually picked up the art of etching by watching a comrade in Paris working at a commercial engraving, so he began making medals after studying Pisanello in the British Museum and the Cabinet des Médailles.

Much of Legros's work outside his classroom continued to bear trace of the rebellious romantic spirit of his youth. Such is the characteristic of his etchings from Edgar Allan Poe, the 'Bonhomme Misère,' and 'La Mort du Vagabond.' In his last years, after he had resigned the professorship, he etched in the early spirit 'Le Triomphe de la Mort,' and beautiful idyls of fishermen by willow-lined streams, labourers in the fields, farms in Burgundy, and castles in Spain. In 1897, at the instance of S. Arthur Strong [q. v. Suppl. II], he was commissioned by the Duke of Portland to design fountains for the gardens at Welbeck. These were carried out with the help of Professor Lanteri. In the same year he undertook the decoration for the top of the Bank of England at the diamond jubilee of Queen Victoria.

Legros first exhibited at the Royal Academy in 1864, and sent paintings or etchings each year till 1874. Subsequently he only exhibited at the Academy in 1881 and 1882, in the last year sending six bronze medals. He was elected fellow of the Society of Painter-Etchers in July 1880, but resigned in 1885. He was re-elected a fellow in April 1895, and made an honorary fellow in Dec. 1910. He was elected an honorary fellow of the Royal Scottish Academy in March 1911. He was also a member of the International Society and of the Society of Twelve.

For many years Legros had been devoted to the work of Alfred Stevens [q. v.], and his last labour was to serve as the president of the committee of the Stevens Memorial, now at the Tate Gallery. He was present at the opening of the exhibition of Stevens's work held at the Tate Gallery to commemorate the presentation of that memorial on 15 Nov. 1911. He died at his home in Watford on 7 Dec. following, and was buried in Hammersmith cemetery; almost his last words were those of gratitude at the recognition of Stevens, saying 'Il a été reconnu.'

He married in 1864, the year after he came to England, Frances Rosetta, third daughter of Samuel Hodgson of Kendal. Of their four sons and five daughters two sons and three daughters survived him. He made several portraits of himself at various periods of his life, both etchings and drawings; one, in gold-point, he did by invitation for the Uffizi Gallery in Florence. In addition to the portrait by Fantin-Latour in 'Hommage à Delacroix,' there is an early head of Legros by the same artist, which was in the collection of Mr. Van Wisselingh. The present writer has a profile study in oils and two etchings. A bronze head of Legros by Rodin is in the Manchester City Art Gallery and a terracotta head by Dalou in the museum at Dijon.

Many pictures and drawings by Legros besides those mentioned are in public galleries and in important private collections. At the Luxembourg, Paris, are the painting 'L'Amende Honorable,' 'Dead Christ,' and portrait of Gambetta, with bronzes, medals, and some twenty-two drawings. At Dijon is the 'Ex Voto,' his masterpiece. At the Victoria and Albert Museum, South Kensington, are landscapes, 'The Tinker,' the study of a head, and the portraits (among others) of Browning, Burne-Jones, and Huxley. At the National Gallery of British Art are 'Femmes en prière' and a portrait. In the collection of Rosalind, Countess of Carlisle, are 'A Christening,' 'Barricade,' 'Psyche,' 'The Poor at Meat,' two portraits and several drawings and etchings. Thirty-five drawings and etchings are in the print room British Museum. 'Jacob's Dream' and twelve drawings after the antique are at the Fitzwilliam Museum, Cambridge. His work is also represented at Manchester, Liverpool, and Peel Park Museum, Salford. Of Legros's etchings the principal collections are those of the late Mr. T. G. Arthur of Carrick House, Ayr, and Mr. Guy Knowles of 17 Kensington Gore, London; these two collections would form almost a complete set. Mr. F. E. Bliss of 21 Holland Park, W., has some 900 proofs in his possession. Mr. Guy Knowles also possesses the best collection of Legros's sculpture and medals, including the mask of Miss Swainson, two masks for a fountain, and the highly finished little torso, a cast of which is in the Victoria and Albert Museum, South Kensington. An exhibition of sixty of his paintings and a number of etchings, lithographs, drawings, and bronzes was held, shortly after his death, in the National Gallery of British Art, Millbank.

[Catalogue raisonné de l'œuvre, gravé et lithographié, de M. Alphonse Legros, Slade Professor of Art au Collège de l' Université de Londres, Professeur de gravure à l'eau-forte à l'Ecole de South Kensington, par MM. A. P. Malassis et A. W. Thibaudeau, 1855–1877, Paris, édit. 1877; Baudelaire, Curiosités esthétiques, Salon, 1859, et l'Art romantique, peintres et aquafortistes; Castagnary, Salons (1857–1870), 2 vols. Paris, 1892; Alphonse Legros, aquafortiste, in Gazette des Beaux-Arts, 1 April 1867, by Ch. Gueullette; Exposition d'œuvres d'art exécutées en noir et blanc, by Louis Décamps, and an unsigned letter by Dalou in L'Art, 27 Aug. 1876; M. Alphonse Legros, au salon du 1875, by A. P. Malassis; Contemporary Portraits, No. xxvi., by W. E. Henley in University Mag., Feb. 1880; Four Masters of Etching, by F. Wedmore, Fine Art Society, 1883. See also the Critiques of Paul Mantz, Lagrange, Burty, Duranty, Gonse (with Legros's Study of the prints of Rembrandt, 1 Dec. 1885), in the Gazette des Beaux-Arts; Rapport à l'Académie de Dijon, par Henri Chabeuf, 1888; Les Graveurs du xix siècle, Legros, by Henri Béraldi, Paris, 1889; Exhibition of Pictures, Water-colours, Drawings, and Etchings by M. Alphonse Legros (late Slade Professor) at The Dutch Gallery, by R. A. M. Stevenson, 1897; Alphonse Legros, Exposition de son œuvre à L'Art Nouveau: Mot d'hommage à Legros, par Arsène Alexandre, 1898; Alphonse Legros, by Dr. Hans W. Singer in Die Graphischen Künste, 1898; Alphonse Legros, art. in L'Estampe et l'Affiche, 15 March and 18 April 1899; Alphonse Legros, by Léonce Bénédite, art. in Revue de l'Art Ancien et Moderne, 10 May 1900; Sir F. Wedmore in The Times, 11 Dec. 1911 and 17 Feb. 1912; Exhibition of Legros's Works, Fine Art Society, by D. S. MacColl, 7 Jan. 1912; Exhibition of the Etchings of Legros, by Sir F. Wedmore, 7 Jan. 1912; arts. by Thomas Okey and Sir Charles Holroyd in Burlington Mag., 7 Feb. 1912; Graves's Royal Academy Exhibitors.] C. H.

LEHMANN, RUDOLF (1819–1905), painter, born on 19 Aug. 1819, at Ottensen, near Hamburg, was a younger son of Leo Lehmann, a miniature-painter practising in the town, by his wife Friederike Dellevie. Educated at the Johanneum, Hamburg, he left in 1837 for Paris, where his eldest brother, Henry, then a student under Ingres and later professor at the Ecole des Beaux-Arts, undertook his art-training. At an aunt's salon in Paris Lehmann met many celebrated persons and inaugurated a cosmopolitan friendship with men of letters, artists, and musicians. From Paris he went to Munich, studying there under Kaulbach and Cornelius, and in 1838 joined his brother at Rome, where he spent six years copying, studying, and painting genre pictures of the peasantry, and greatly extending his acquaintance. Lehmann's first noteworthy compositions were paintings of a girl in the Abruzzi costume and a Capri grape-gatherer, 'Grazia.' The latter was awarded a gold medal at the Paris Salon in 1843, and both subjects were engraved by Julien. The French government commissioned a 'Madonna and Child,' for which Adelaide Ristori sat as the Madonna, and a 'St. Sebastian' for provincial churches, and also purchased for the museum at Lille his large painting 'Pope Sixtus V blessing the Pontine Marshes,' exhibited at the Salon of 1847. Returning to Paris, Lehmann witnessed the revolutions of 1847 and 1848, and, after a year at Hamburg, paid his first visit to London in April 1850. His first contribution to the Royal Academy, 1851, was a portrait of Earl Granville (engraved by W. Walker); 'Graziella,' taken from Lamartine's 'Confidences,' was exhibited in 1856.

Ten years' further residence in Italy (1856–66), mostly at Rome, where his studio was much frequented by foreign visitors, were marked by his large painting 'Spurgo di Canale,' and broken by a visit to London and marriage there in 1861 to Amelia, the accomplished daughter of Robert Chambers [q. v.], the Scottish publisher. Lehmann returned with his family to London in 1866 and became a regular contributor of subject-pictures and portraits to the Royal Academy. Among his best-known works of this period were portraits of Sir Henry Bessemer (1867) and Baron Reuter, both engraved by T. O. Barlow, R.A., of Sir William Fergusson (Royal College of Surgeons), and of Helen Faucit (Shakespeare memorial gallery, Stratford), both engraved by Toubert, and of Lady Enfield (1874). Of Robert Browning, who became an intimate family friend, Lehmann drew four portraits, two drawings and two paintings. The painting of 1875 was exhibited with 'La Lavandaja' and other of his works at Paris in 1878, and the modified replica of 1884 was presented by the artist to the National Portrait Gallery in 1890.

Portraiture occupied Lehmann's later years, but occasionally he produced such paintings as 'Undine' (1890) and 'Cromwell at Ripley Castle' (1892). Among his later sitters were Lord Revelstoke (engraved by Barlow), Earl Beauchamp (1877; replicas at Oxford and Worcester), Sir W. Siemens, George Joachim Goschen [q. v. Suppl. II], Sir T. Spencer Wells (Royal College of Surgeons), Sir Andrew Clark (Royal College of Physicians), and Miss Emily Davies (Girton College), one of his most successful portraits.

Lehmann's portraits, usually signed with his monogram and the date, though smooth and painstaking in effect, possess a quiet dignity and are accurate likenesses. He contributed 111 subjects to Burlington House, and many others to the Grosvenor Gallery and New Gallery. He was awarded three gold medals and made a knight of the falcon of Saxe-Weimar. His portrait by himself is in the Uffizi Gallery, Florence, and another by Sir H. von Herkomer, R.A., belongs to his daughter, Mrs. Barry Pain. Lehmann, who was a naturalised British subject, died on 27 Oct. 1905 at Bournemede, Bushey, and his cremated remains were buried in Highgate cemetery. He was survived by three married daughters, Mrs. Bedford (Madame Liza Lehmann), Mrs. Charles Goetz, and Mrs. Barry Pain.

Lehmann's well-written 'Reminiscences' (1894) contain interesting biographical notes and information concerning social life in Rome. 'Men and Women of the Century' (1896, 4to) gives reproductions of twelve oil-portraits and seventy-two portrait-sketches from his 'Album of Celebrities,' now in the department of prints and drawings at the British Museum. This valuable series of crayon drawings from life, begun at Rome with portraits of Pius IX, Chopin, and Liszt, was continued during the artist's long career in England and abroad.

[The Times, 28 Oct. 1905; Athenæum, 4 Nov. 1905; An Artist's Reminiscences, by R. Lehmann, 1894; Memories of Half a Century, by R. C. Lehmann, 1908; Men and Women of the Century, ed. by H. C. Marillier, 1896; Royal Academy Exhibitors, by A. Graves, 1905; various exhibition catalogues; Royal Academy Pictures, by Cassell & Co.; Vapereau's Dictionnaire universel des Contemporains, 1880; Men and Women of the Time, 1899; information from his daughter, Mrs. Barry Pain, and nephew, Mr. R. C. Lehmann.] J. D. M.

LEICESTER, second Earl of. [See Coke, Thomas William (1822–1909), agriculturist.]

LEIGHTON, STANLEY (1837–1901), politician and antiquary, was second son of Sir Baldwin Leighton (1805–1871), of Loton Park, Shropshire, seventh baronet, and an authority on economic policy, by his wife Mary, daughter and eventual heiress of Thomas Netherton Parker of Sweeney Hall, Oswestry, the author of several pamphlets on rural economy. The Leighton family, which traces its pedigree from Richard de Leighton, knight of the shire for Shropshire in 1313, had held Loton in the male line since the reign of Henry VII, and the baronetcy dates from 1693. Sir Baldwin (1747–1828), sixth baronet, married Margaret Louisa Anne, daughter of Sir John Thomas Stanley of Alderley (1735–1807) and sister of John Thomas Stanley, first baron Stanley of Alderley.

Stanley, born at Loton on 13 Oct. 1837, was educated at Harrow and at Balliol College, Oxford (B.A. and M.A., 1864). In 1861 he was called to the bar from the Inner Temple, but relinquished the law on succeeding in 1871 to his mother's property at Sweeney Hall, where he devoted himself to local affairs. At the general election in 1874 he was a candidate in the conservative interest for Bewdley, but was beaten by 99 votes. In 1876, when a vacancy occurred in the representation of North Shropshire, Leighton promptly offered himself as a candidate. Although a conservative, his candidature was not acceptable to the majority of the county gentry, who adopted S. K. Mainwaring; but Leighton was returned by a majority of 37, due to liberal support given to him as the opponent of the nominee of the county gentry. Yet his principles were uncompromisingly conservative, and, though preserving a considerable independence of judgment, he quickly won the confidence of those who originally opposed him, and continued to represent North Shropshire and (after the division of the county in 1885) the Oswestry division until his death. His style of speaking was not well suited to the House of Commons, and his influence there was mainly due to his recognised position as a convinced supporter of church and state. He was a devoted churchman, and took a leading part in the establishment of the Clergy Pensions Institution. In the House of Laymen he represented the diocese of Lichfield. He also took a prominent part in all public matters in North Shropshire, and commanded the Oswestry volunteer corps from 1871 to 1880.

Apart from public life, antiquarian study was Leighton's strongest taste. He became F.S.A. in 1880 and was a vice-president of the Shropshire Archæological Society from its foundation. Papers by him on the 'Records of the Corporation of Oswestry' and the 'Papers and Letters of Gen. Mytton during the Civil Wars' appear among its 'Transactions.' He was president of the Cambrian Archæological Association in 1893, and in 1897 he founded the Shropshire Parish Register Society. He was an accomplished amateur artist, and made large collections for an illustrated history of the fine ancient houses with which Shropshire abounds. One volume, 'Shropshire Houses Past and Present' (1901), containing drawings and descriptions of 50 houses, was in the press at the time of his death. Materials remain for at least eight more volumes.

Deeply interested in religious education, he helped to re-organise the school for Welsh children of both sexes which had existed in London under the auspices of the Society of Antient Britons since 1715. The Act of 1870 rendered superfluous its original purpose of giving elementary education, and mainly through Leighton's initiative it was converted in 1882 into the flourishing school for the secondary education of girls of Welsh parentage at Ashford in Middlesex.

Leighton died somewhat suddenly in

London on 4 May 1901, and was buried at Oswestry. In 1873 he married Jessie Marie, daughter and co-heiress of Henry Bertie Watkin Williams Wynn, of Nantymeiched, Montgomeryshire. He left a son, Bertie Edward Parker, now (1912) captain in the 1st dragoons, and a daughter, Rachel. His portrait, the last work of Sir J. E. Millais, was presented to him by his constituents in 1896, and is now at Sweeney Hall.

[Oswestry Advertiser, 8 May 1901; memoir by W. P. W. P[hillimore] in Shropshire Parish Registers, Hereford Diocese, vol. vi. 1902; personal knowledge.] F. G. K.

LEININGEN, Prince ERNEST LEOPOLD VICTOR CHARLES AUGUSTE JOSEPH EMICH (1830–1904), admiral, reigning prince of Leiningen, was born at Amorbach, Bavaria, on 9 Nov. 1830. He was elder son of Charles, reigning prince of Leiningen (1804–1856), by his wife Marie, countess of Klebelsberg. His father was only son of Princess Victoria Maria Louisa of Saalfeld, by her first husband, Emich Charles, reigning prince of Leiningen; the princess's second husband was the duke of Kent, and by him she was mother of Queen Victoria, who was thus half-sister of Prince Charles of Leiningen, the admiral's father. The Duchess of Kent took much interest in her grandson Prince Ernest as a boy, and through the influence of his step-aunt, Queen Victoria, he entered the British navy on 14 March 1849. As a midshipman of the Hastings, flagship of Rear-admiral Austen, commander-in-chief in the East Indies, and afterwards in the paddle sloop Sphinx, he served during the second Burmese war of 1851–2, being present at the capture of Prome. At the end of 1853 he was appointed to the Britannia, flagship of Vice-admiral Sir James Whitley Deans Dundas [q. v.] in the Mediterranean, and at the end of June 1854 was sent up the Danube, with a small party from the Britannia under Lieut. Glyn, to man some river gunboats at Rustchuk, then the headquarters of Omar Pasha, the Turkish commander-in-chief. Travelling overland, the party reached Rustchuk on 10 July. Three days before a small Turkish force had seized Giurgevo on the north bank of the Danube. Prince Gortschakoff with 70,000 men was moving on this Turkish force to drive it south across the Danube, and Omar, immediately turning the gunboats over to Glyn, directed him at any cost to hold a creek which separated the Turkish position from the Russian advance. The Russians were checked, and the English and Turks meanwhile succeeded in throwing a bridge of boats across the river. Gortschakoff saw that this meant his having to face the whole Turkish army, and drew off accordingly to Bukarest, leaving the Turks masters of the lower Danube. Prince Leiningen received from the Turkish government a gold medal for distinguished service in the field, and on passing his examination was promoted to lieutenant on 2 April 1855. He was at once appointed to the Duke of Wellington, the flagship of Vice-admiral Dundas in the Baltic, and in her and in the Cossack took part in the Baltic campaign, being present at the bombardment of Sveaborg. His remaining service as lieutenant was in the paddle frigate Magicienne, on the Mediterranean station, and in the royal yacht, from which he was promoted to commander on 1 Feb. 1858. From this time onwards he was employed almost continuously in the yacht, first as commander, then as captain, his only foreign service being in 1862–3, when he commanded the Magicienne in the Mediterranean. His promotion to captain was dated 25 Oct. 1860, and he was still serving in the yacht when he reached flag rank on 31 Dec. 1876. On 18 Aug. 1875 the Alberta, with Queen Victoria on board, was crossing from Cowes to Portsmouth when, in Stokes Bay, she ran down the schooner yacht Mistletoe, which sank with a loss of four lives. The accident caused much excitement, especially locally, the tendency being to lay the blame on the royal yacht and her captain. It is important, therefore, to notice that at the time of the accident the prince, the commander, and the navigating officer of the Alberta were all on the bridge; also that it was a common thing for pleasure craft to go as near to the royal yacht as possible when a chance of seeing the queen offered itself. The coroner's jury at Portsmouth brought in a verdict of manslaughter against the prince and the navigating officer, Staff-captain Welch; but when the case went to the assizes the grand jury threw out the bill. Meanwhile a court of inquiry was held at Portsmouth, and completely exonerated the prince and his officers; but this decision was, in the popular opinion, rendered somewhat obscure by the action of the admiralty, which voluntarily paid compensation for the loss of the yacht.

Early in 1880 the prince was selected for the post of second-in-command of the Channel squadron; but in April, after the appointment had been gazetted, the Gladstonian government came into office, and at once set the appointment aside. During the continuation of that ministry he was not employed, either as rear-admiral or after his promotion to vice-admiral on 1 Dec. 1881; but when Lord Salisbury's government was formed in 1885 he was, on 1 July, appointed commander-in-chief at the Nore, a post which he held until his promotion to admiral on 7 July 1887. This was his last service, and on 9 Nov. 1895 he reached the age for retirement. He was made G.C.B. in 1866 and G.C.V.O. in 1898. After hauling down his flag he resided chiefly at Amorbach, where he died on 5 April 1904. He married at Carlsruhe, on 11 Sept. 1858, Princess Marie Amalie of Baden, daughter of Leopold, grand duke of Baden; she died on 21 Nov. 1899. His only son, Prince Emich Edward Carl, succeeded him as reigning prince; his only daughter, Princess Albertine, died in 1901.

A marble bust by the prince's cousin, Prince Victor of Hohenlohe [q. v. Suppl. I], is at Wald Leiningen. A small head, painted by D'Albert Durade at Geneva in 1847, together with a painting by J. R. Say (1857) of the prince with his cousin, Prince Victor, both in naval uniform, are at Buckingham Palace.

[The Times, 6 April 1904.] L. G. C. L.

LEISHMAN, THOMAS (1825–1904), Scottish divine and liturgiologist, born at his father's manse on 7 May 1825, was the eldest son, in a family of thirteen children, of Matthew Leishman, D.D., minister of Govan, who was leader of the middle party in the secession controversy of 1843, and whose portrait was painted by John Graham-Gilbert [q. v.]. His mother was Jane Elizabeth Boog. A brother, William, was professor of midwifery in the university of Glasgow from 1868 to 1894. Ancestors on both sides led distinguished clerical careers, and family tradition claims collateral connection with Principal William Leishman of Glasgow University. After education at Govan, Thomas passed to Glasgow High School and Glasgow University, where graduating M.A. in 1843, he distinguished himself in classics, and acquired a love of books and sense of style. After the usual course at the Divinity Hall, he was licensed as a probationer by the presbytery of Glasgow on 7 Feb. 1847, and became assistant at Greenock. From 1852 to 1855 he served the parish of Collace, near Perth, and from 1855 till 1895 that of Linton, Teviotdale, in the presbytery of Kelso. Leishman, while effectively ministering to a rural district, soon became a leader in presbytery and synod. With a view to reviving the old order of public worship which had deteriorated (he thought) through borrowings from English dissent, he was among the first to join the Church Service Society (formed in 1865), and in 1866 he became a member of its editorial committee, where he worked hard, chiefly in collaboration with George Washington Sprott [q. v. Suppl. II]. In 1868 Sprott and Leishman published an annotated edition of 'The Book of Common Order,' commonly called Knox's Liturgy, and the 'Directory for the Public Worship of God agreed upon by the Assembly of Divines at Westminster,' which became a standard authority.

He proceeded D.D. from Glasgow University with a thesis on 'A Critical Account of the Various Theories of the Sacrament of Baptism' (Edinburgh, 1871). In 1875 he published a plea for the observance by the Church of Scotland of the five great Christian festivals, entitled: 'May the Kirk keep Pasche and Yule?' 'Why not,' he answered, in the words of Knox, 'where superstition is removed.' Owing to broken health, the winter of 1876–7 was spent in Spain and in Egypt, and Leishman added to earlier studies in the continental reformed liturgies an investigation of the Mozarabic and Coptic service-books. A warm defender of the validity of presbyterian ordination he joined Sprott and others in a formal protest against the admission by the general assembly of 1882 of two congregational ministers to the status of ordained ministers. The precedent of 1882 was not acted on again. In 1892 Leishman helped William Milligan [q. v. Suppl. I] to found the Scottish Church Society in the interest of catholic doctrine as set forth in the ancient creeds and embodied in the standards of the Church of Scotland. He took an active part in the work of this society, contributing papers to its conferences, and three times (1895–6, 1902–3, and 1905–6) acting as its president. To a work in four volumes, 'The Church of Scotland Past and Present,' edited by Robert Herbert, and primarily intended as a contribution to church defence (1891), he contributed a valuable section on 'The Ritual of the Church of Scotland.' Leishman defined his ecclesiastical position in 'The Moulding of the Scottish Reformation' (Lee lecture for 1897);

'The Church of Scotland as she was, and as she is' (John Macleod Memorial lecture for 1903); in an address on 'The Vocation of the Church' at the Church of Scotland Congress, 1899, and in devout and practical lectures on pastoral theology which were delivered by appointment of the general assembly at the four Scottish universities, 1895–7, and are not yet published. He was moderator of the general assembly of 1898, where the archbishop of Canterbury, Dr. Temple, pleaded the cause of temperance. The speeches of both Temple and Leishman on the occasion were published in a pamphlet.

Leishman's third son, James Fleming, was ordained to succeed him at Linton (7 March 1895), and thereupon Leishman removed to Edinburgh. There he died on 13 July 1904, and was buried at Linton. At Hoselaw, in a remote corner of the parish where Leishman used to conduct cottage services, a chapel was erected by public subscription to his memory in 1906 (*Scot. Ecclesiological Soc. Trans.* iii. 90). Leishman married, on Lady Day 1857, his cousin, Christina Balmanno Fleming, who died on 15 June 1868. Five sons and two daughters survived him.

Leishman, whose manners abounded in gentle dignity, was described by A. K. H. Boyd [q. v. Suppl. I] as 'the ideal country parson, learned, devout, peace-loving, pretty close to the first meridian of clergyman and gentleman.' A fine photograph hangs in the moderators' portrait gallery in the Assembly Hall, High Street, Edinburgh.

Besides the works mentioned, Leishman contributed to the Church Service Society's series of Scottish liturgies and orders of divine service, an edition with introduction and notes of the Westminster Directory (Edinburgh, 1901).

[Diaries and correspondence in possession of his son; personal knowledge; Border Mag. iii. 28; publications of the Scottish Church Society; Blackwood's Mag., Nov. 1897; New Liturgies of the Scottish Kirk; Funeral Sermon by Rev. Dr. Sprott.] J. C.

LE JEUNE, HENRY (1819–1904), historical and genre painter, born in London on 12 Dec. 1819, was of Flemish extraction, being the third of the five children of Anthony Le Jeune. His grandfather, his father, and his brothers were professional musicians. His brothers occupied posts as organists at Farm Street, and Sardinian and Moorfields chapels. His sister gave up music for photography, at which she worked nearly all her life at Naples; Garibaldi was among her sitters. Le Jeune himself showed pronounced musical tastes, but at an early age he evinced a desire to become an artist, and was sent to study at the British Museum. In 1834 he was admitted as a student at the Royal Academy schools; there, after obtaining four silver medals in succession, he was awarded the gold medal in 1841 for his painting of 'Samson bursting his Bonds,' which was shown at the British Institution in the following year. He first exhibited at the Royal Academy in 1840, sending a picture of 'Joseph interpreting the Dream of Pharaoh's Chief Butler.' In 1847 the Prince Consort purchased his 'Liberation of the Slaves.'

From 1845 to 1848 he was headmaster of the morning class at the government school of design at Somerset House, and from 1848 until 1864 curator of the painting school of the Royal Academy, an office which included the duty of giving instruction in painting. In 1863 he was elected an A.R.A., but he never attained the rank of academician. In 1886 he became an honorary retired associate.

Le Jeune painted both in oil and water-colour. He exhibited eighty-four pictures at the Royal Academy between 1840 and 1894, twenty-one at the British Institution between 1842 and 1863, and a few at other galleries. The subjects of his earlier paintings were principally derived from the Bible, Shakespeare, or Spenser, and included 'The Infancy of Moses,' 'Una and the Lion' (1842), 'Prospero and Miranda' (1844), 'Ruth and Boaz' (1845), and 'The Sermon on the Mount' (1851). Subsequently he devoted himself to child subjects, and it was as a painter of children that he was mainly known. His figures are well grouped, gracefully drawn, and carefully finished. To the later phase of his work belong 'Little Red Riding Hood' (1863), 'The Wounded Robin' (1864), 'Little Bo-Peep' (1873 and 1881), and 'My Little Model' (1875). One of his best works was 'Much Ado about Nothing' (1873), a fishing party of three children seated catching minnows on an old river sluice. One of his early paintings of scriptural subjects, 'Ye Daughters of Israel, weep over Saul' (1846), is at the Royal Museum and Art Galleries, Peel Park, Salford. The Royal Holloway College, Egham, has one of his genre pictures, 'Early Sorrow' (1869); and another, his 'Children with Toy Boat,' is in the Manchester City Art Gallery. He painted a few portraits.

Le Jeune always lived in London, and resided for over forty years at Hampstead. In his last years deafness largely withdrew him from society. He was keenly interested in chess problems. He died at 155 Goldhurst Terrace, Hampstead, N.W., on 5 Oct. 1904, and was buried at Kensal Green cemetery.

He married on 21 June 1844 Dorothy Lewis, daughter of James Dalton Lewis, by whom he had five sons and three daughters.

[Information kindly supplied by Miss F. Le Jeune; Art Journal (engravings, &c.), 1858, pp. 265–267, 1860, p. 36, 1867, p. 60, 1871, p. 236, 1874, p. 40; Illust. London News, 25 July 1863, pp. 80 (portrait), 94; Ottley, Dict. of Recent and Living Painters and Engravers; Men of the Time, 1865, p. 509; Clement and Hutton, Artists of the Nineteenth Century, ii. 55; G. H. Shepherd, Short Hist. of the British School of Painting, 96–7; Hodgson and Eaton, The Roy. Acad. and its Members, 362, 363, 385; A. G. Temple, Art of Painting in the Queen's Reign, 303; Müller und Singer, Allg. Künstler-Lexicon; Cats. of Art Galleries of Manchester City, Salford, and Royal Holloway College; Champlin and Perkins, Cyclopedia of Painters and Paintings, iii. 55 (portrait); Graves, Dict. of Artists, Roy. Acad. and British Institution; Athenæum, 15 Oct. 1904; Who's Who, 1905.] B. S. L.

LEMMENS-SHERRINGTON, Madame HELEN (1834–1906), soprano vocalist, born on 4 Oct. 1834 at Preston, Lancashire, was daughter of John Sherrington (of a Roman catholic family long settled in the town), who managed a mill owned by his father. Her mother, whose maiden surname was Johnson, a beautiful and promising young singer, retired from the profession on her marriage. A sister José enjoyed some success as a soprano singer.

At the time of Helen's birth the family were ruined by a bank failure. In 1838 her father obtained an appointment at Rotterdam, where good music was available both publicly and privately. Amid Dutch surroundings Helen was taught music by her mother, and quickly showed the possession of a rich and pure soprano voice. At an early age she sang in the Roman catholic church at Rotterdam and fascinated the congregation. Her serious studies were begun in 1852 at the Brussels Conservatoire under Cornelis; in 1855 she was awarded the first prize for singing and elocution. Already in great request as a concert-singer abroad, she became betrotned to Nicolas Jacques Lemmens (1823–1881), an organist, who induced her to return to England in 1856. A stranger in her own country, she at first experienced difficulty in securing engagements, but at a concert of the Amateur Musical Society in the Hanover-square Rooms on 7 April, conducted by Henry Leslie, she 'produced quite an impression,' singing a florid bolero by Victor Massé and Schubert's 'Ave Maria.' In the same week she sang with Sims Reeves in a miscellaneous programme at Hullah's concerts, and again with brilliant success. She appeared at Charlotte Dolby's concert, in two performances of Mendelssohn's 'Hymn of Praise,' and gave a concert of her own on 19 June (see *Musical Gazette*). Critics agreed as to her high promise (*Athenæum*, 19 April). After some study of English oratorio, by which her style was greatly improved, she appeared in Mendelssohn's 'Elijah' and Macfarren's 'May-day' at the Bradford festival (1 Aug.), at the inauguration of the Free Trade Hall, Manchester, in October, and at Liverpool in December. On 3 Jan. 1857 she married Lemmens; they settled permanently at 53 Finchley Road, London. On 23 Jan. she made her first appearance with the Sacred Harmonic Society, Exeter Hall, in Mendelssohn's 'Athalie.'

Madame Lemmens-Sherrington had now taken her place as one of the first English sopranos; and after the retirement of Clara Novello [q. v. Suppl. II] in 1860 had hardly a rival. From 1860 to 1865 she sang in English opera, and in 1866 in Italian opera at Covent Garden. But she was mainly a concert-singer, and with Janet Patey, Sims Reeves, and Charles Santley she completed the quartet of great vocalists which from 1870 stood for all that was best in English art. Her husband had small success as a pianist, though in some demand for performances on the harmonium, and the task of providing for their seven children fell mainly on her. She worked too hard, travelling great distances to keep engagements; two concerts a day, followed by a performance at an evening party, were not uncommon. Oratorio music displayed her powers to greatest advantage, and she was peculiarly successful in Haydn's 'Creation,' where the elaborate air 'On mighty pens' precisely suited her. In the autumn of 1875 Lemmens arranged a provincial tour, at which she sang in scenes from Wagner's 'Lohengrin,' then new in England and much discussed. In 1876 she took part at St. James's Hall in the first performance in England of Bach's 'High Mass.'

Lemmens in 1879 opened a school for

catholic church musicians at Malines, and in January 1881 she accepted the offer of a post as teacher of singing at the Brussels conservatoire. But just before she took up the office her husband died (30 Jan. 1881). She completed her engagements in England, making no formal farewell; her last or almost her last appearance was in Mendelssohn's 'Elijah,' at Mr. Kuhe's musical festival in the Dome, Brighton, on 19 Feb. Proceeding to Brussels, she retained her post there till 1891. She occasionally revisited England, re-appearing during 1883–4, and showing little abatement of her earlier powers. Subsequently she sang at a performance of Benoît's 'Lucifer' in 1889, in the Albert Hall, and for a time engaged in teaching in London at the Royal Academy of Music, and at the Royal College of Music, Manchester. On 1 Nov. 1894 she appeared for the last time in public, singing at Manchester in Haydn's 'Creation'; she stipulated that she should receive no fee. Her last years were spent in retirement at 7 Rue Capouillet, Brussels, where she lived with two sisters.

Madame Lemmens-Sherrington died at Brussels on 9 May 1906. Her daughters May and Ella sang at Louvain in Nov. 1881 and subsequently in England; they afterwards took the veil. The sons followed engineering.

[Interview, with portrait, in Musical Herald, July 1899, revised by her; Clayton's Queens of Song (with portrait); British Musical Biography; information from Miss Padwick; biographical sketch in Le Guide Musical, translated with additions in Musical World, 19 Feb. 1881; obituaries in the musical press, May and June 1906; personal reminiscences.]
H. D.

LEMPRIERE, CHARLES (1818–1901), writer and politician, born at Exeter on 21 Sept. 1818, was second son of John Lempriere, D.D. [q. v.], compiler of the 'Classical Dictionary,' by his second wife Elizabeth, daughter of John Deane of Salisbury. Entering at Merchant Taylors' School in Feb. 1825, he matriculated at St. John's College, Oxford, in 1837, with a scholar-fellowship of the old type. He graduated B.C.L. in 1842 and D.C.L. in 1847, and remained a law fellow of the college until his death.

He was called to the bar from the Inner Temple on 22 Jan. 1844, and for a time did work for (Sir) Alexander James Edmund Cockburn [q. v.], who always remained his friend. Joining the western circuit, he made good progress; but he early fell into the hands of unscrupulous financiers, whose schemes involved him in difficulties which lasted almost till his death. In pursuance of these schemes he travelled for some time in Egypt and the Levant. Meanwhile he interested himself in politics on the conservative side. He had been one of the earlier members of the Conservative Club (1841). From 1850 onwards he was a trusted agent of the conservative party, and engaged actively in political work. When it was resolved in 1859 to oppose Gladstone's election for Oxford University, Lempriere was deputed to approach the marquis of Chandos, afterwards duke of Buckingham, to induce him to stand. Premature revelation of the position of things by the conservative leaders at Oxford brought grave discredit upon Lempriere, who was really not in fault. The marquis ultimately stood (1 July 1859), and was defeated by 859 to 1050 votes. Two years after, Lempriere was despatched by Sir Moses Montefiore [q. v.] on a private mission to Mexico, then in the midst of civil and financial disturbance, to defend, as far as was possible, the threatened British interests in the country. Travelling by way of the United States, Lempriere recorded his impressions of the position there in the best of his literary productions, 'The American Crisis considered' (1861). Believing as most Englishmen did in the claims of the South to independence, he saw and exposed most vividly the danger to be apprehended from the emancipation of the negro population. There followed his 'Notes on Mexico' (1862). The confused condition of the country is reflected in the traveller's impressions. Vera Cruz had been occupied by the Spaniards, and there were fears that the French might establish permanent control of the country. Brigandage was rampant, and disorder universal. The book was attacked for inaccuracy in statistics and faultiness of style. Yet it is probably the best extant account of Mexican affairs in those days of turmoil.

In 1865 Lempriere was back in England and taking an active part in elections. When in June 1866 John Bonham Carter, liberal member for Winchester, accepted the office of junior lord of the treasury in Lord John Russell's administration, and offered himself for re-election, Lempriere contested the seat to prevent an unopposed return. He only polled 46 votes. In 1867, under Lord Derby's administration, his services were rewarded by the colonial secretaryship of the Bahamas. Political feeling at that time ran high in the islands, and it was not long before Lempriere's strong tory opinions brought him into difficulties. He was accused of interfering in elections, and had to resign. Scenes of great disorder followed; Lempriere's house was plundered and his papers destroyed. Instead of returning to England he proceeded to the United States, where he had previously made the acquaintance of Horace Greeley, who now employed him as a writer for the 'Tribune.' After Greeley's death in 1872 Lempriere entered on the most singular stage of his career. He organised a colony of young Englishmen at Buckhorn in Western Virginia, on the lines of that afterwards attempted at Rugby, Tennessee, by Thomas Hughes, who is vaguely said to have suggested the idea to Lempriere. The 'colony' failed, the colonists were half starved, and in 1879 Lempriere was back in England and again engaged in financial projects. In the pursuit of these he travelled in most countries of Europe. His last undertaking was in connection with the valuation of the great Partagas tobacco estates in Cuba, in which he was employed by a syndicate (1887–9). From that time onwards he remained in England, occasionally residing for some months at a time in Belgium and Luxemburg, where he had many friends. He died at West Kensington on 30 Oct. 1901.

Lempriere's powers were not displayed to best advantage in his literary work. His reputation was that of a persuasive speaker and a brilliant conversationalist. There are oil paintings of him in the Common Room of St. John's College and at the Seigneurie of Rozet in Jersey, with which his family was connected.

[J. Bertram Payne, Monograph of the House of Lempriere, 1862; Robinson, Register of Merchant Taylors' School, ii. 223; Foster, Alumni Oxonienses, and Men at the Bar; Register of St. John's College, Oxford.]

A. T. G.

LENG, Sir JOHN (1828–1906), newspaper proprietor, born at Hull on 10 April 1828, was younger brother of Sir William Christopher Leng [q. v. Supp. II]. Educated at Hull grammar school, he acted there as joint-editor with Charles Cooper (afterwards editor of the 'Scotsman') of a manuscript school magazine. Becoming assistant teacher at a private school, he sent letters to the 'Hull Advertiser' which attracted the notice of Edward Francis Collins, then editor, and led to his appointment in 1847, at nineteen, as sub-editor and reporter. This post, which embraced dramatic and musical criticism, he held for four years. In July 1851 Leng was selected from among seventy candidates as editor of the then bi-weekly 'Dundee Advertiser.' The paper was founded in 1801, but had fallen into a backward state. Leng soon raised the 'Advertiser' to high rank, both in local and imperial affairs. His wide practical knowledge of newspaper work enabled him to reorganise both the literary staff and machinery. The old premises were quickly found too small; and in 1859 he built the first portion of new premises in Bank Street, which, before his death, attained gigantic proportions. As early as 1852 Leng was made a partner by the proprietors of the 'Advertiser,' and the imprint thenceforth bore the name of John Leng & Co.

After the abolition of the 'taxes on knowledge' in 1861, the 'Advertiser' was issued daily. In June 1870 Leng was one of the first Scottish newspaper proprietors to establish an office in Fleet Street, London, with direct telegraphic communication with Dundee. When stereotyping was adopted, after printing from rolls of paper instead of sheets was introduced, he caused a stereotype-foundry to be erected as a portion of the plant. In 1851 the single machine in use could only produce 350 copies per hour; fifty years afterwards Leng had four elaborate machines in operation, each capable of throwing off 20,000 copies per hour. He was the first to attempt illustrations in a daily paper; and when the primitive pantographic method was superseded by zincography, he founded a zincographic and photographic studio as part of the office equipment. The difficulty of obtaining an adequate paper supply was overcome in 1893, when the Donside paper-mills were acquired by a private limited liability company, of which Leng was chairman.

Leng proved to be a notable pioneer in other departments of journalistic enterprise. In May 1859 he founded the first halfpenny daily newspaper in Scotland, under the title of the 'Daily Advertiser,' but the limited machinery then available compelled him to suspend this venture. In January 1858 he established the 'People's Journal,' a weekly newspaper which soon reached the largest circulation of any similar paper in Scotland. A literary weekly paper, the 'People's Friend,' was founded by him in 1869; and he lived to see it reach a circulation which rivalled that of London periodicals of its kind. The 'Evening Telegraph,' a halfpenny daily newspaper, was started in 1877, and had a successful career, being amalgamated in 1900 with the 'Evening

Post,' another local paper. In 1869 he suggested the introduction of sixpenny telegrams, printing specimen forms similar to those afterwards adopted.

In September 1889, on the death of J. B. Firth, one of two members of parliament for Dundee, Leng was returned without opposition in the liberal interest. He was re-elected by large majorities in 1892, 1895, and 1900, retiring from the House of Commons at the dissolution in 1905. An advanced radical and a supporter of home rule all round, he made his maiden speech, on 26 March 1890, in support of the parliamentary elections (Scotland) bill, which proposed that the expenses of returning officers at such elections should be paid out of the rates. Among the topics which he brought before the House of Commons were the excessive hours of railway guards, engine-drivers, and firemen; appointment of female inspectors of factories and workshops; boarding-out of pauper children by parochial boards. He was prominent in 1893 in support of the home rule bill of Mr. Gladstone, and of the employers' liability bill. In the same year he was knighted and was made deputy-lieutenant for the county of the city of Dundee. He was made an honorary burgess of Dundee in 1902; and in 1904 hon. LL.D. of St. Andrews.

Despite his journalistic and parliamentary activity he found time for extensive travel. He visited the United States and Canada in 1876, and frequently toured in France, Germany, and Holland. His first Western journey was recorded in a volume entitled 'America in 1876' (Dundee, 1877); and a visit to India in 1896 was detailed in his book 'Letters from India and Ceylon' (1897), a work translated and widely circulated in Germany. Two journeys in the Near East produced 'Some European Rivers and Cities' (1897) and 'Glimpses of Egypt and Sicily' (1902). A second American tour in 1905 was commemorated in 'Letters from the United States and Canada' (1905). In October 1906 he set out on a third tour in America, but fell ill at Delmonte, California, and died there on 12 Dec. 1906. His body was cremated and the ashes brought home and interred at Vicarsford cemetery, near Newport, Fife.

Leng married twice: (1) in 1851, Emily, elder daughter of Alderman Cook of Beverley; she died at Kinbrae, Newport, Fifeshire, in 1894, leaving two sons and four daughters; (2) in 1897, Mary, daughter of William Low, of Kirriemuir, who survived him.

A portrait by James Archer, R.S.A., was presented to him in 1889 by the staff of the 'Dundee Advertiser' when he entered parliament. In 1901 a portrait by Sir William Quiller Orchardson, R.A., presented to him by the people of Dundee, was given by him to Dundee Permanent Art Gallery. The unspent balance of the subscriptions was increased by Leng so as to form the Leng Trust, designed to encourage the study of Scottish literature and music.

Besides the volumes mentioned, Leng published numerous pamphlets on socialism, free trade, and economic subjects. A posthumous work, edited by Lady Leng, is entitled 'Through Canada to California' (1911).

[Dundee Year Book, 1901 and 1906; Dundee Advertiser, 1851–1906; Centenary of Dundee Advertiser, 1901; private information.] A. H. M.

LENG, Sir WILLIAM CHRISTOPHER (1825–1902), journalist, born at Hull on 25 Jan. 1825, was elder son of Adam Leng of Hull by Mary, daughter of Christopher Luccock, of Malton, architect. Sir John Leng [q. v. Suppl. II] was a younger brother. His father had served in the navy during the Napoleonic wars on board the Termagant; but from 1815 he engaged in commerce at Hull. After education at a private school, where he showed a taste for literature, William was apprenticed in 1839 to a wholesale chemist in Hull, and afterwards acted as town-traveller. In 1847 he began business on his own account. Meanwhile in anonymous contributions to the 'Hull Free Press,' including sketches of notable citizens (issued in book form in 1852), he championed with vigour a variety of reforms. Denouncing the overloading and mismodelling of cargo steamships, he first suggested to Samuel Plimsoll [q. v. Suppl. I] the crusade which led to the introduction of the Plimsoll 'load-line.' Proposals for municipal reforms in Hull like the demolition of slum-property were defeated in his opinion by the self-interest of prominent liberals, whose party he hitherto supported. Thereupon he declared himself a conservative, and remained through life a devoted adherent of the conservative cause. Brought up as a Wesleyan, he joined the evangelical party in the Church of England.

In spite of divergent political opinions, William was a regular contributor of articles on municipal and national affairs to the 'Dundee Advertiser,' after his brother John became editor in 1851. In 1859 William gave up his chemist's business in Hull and resided in Dundee till 1864, writing in the 'Advertiser.' During the civil war in America he was almost the only journalist in Scotland to support the cause of the North.

In 1864 Leng joined Frederick Clifford [q. v. Suppl. II] in acquiring on easy terms the 'Sheffield Daily Telegraph.' He became managing editor, and at Sheffield the remainder of his life was passed. On 1 Jan. 1864 the 'Sheffield Daily Telegraph' became his property and first bore the imprint of 'Leng & Co.' In 1872 more extensive premises were purchased in Aldine Court, and there linotype machines were first employed in England to set up a newspaper entirely. The paper, which was almost moribund when he undertook its direction, quickly became in Leng's vigorous hands a great conservative power in the north of England.

Leng was fearless in advocacy of what he deemed the public interest. At personal risk he denounced in 1867 the terrorism practised by Sheffield trade-unionists upon non-union workmen under the leadership of William Broadhead [q. v. Suppl. I]. Leng induced the government to appoint a royal commission of inquiry which fully established his allegations (September 1867). He is the original of Mr. Holdfast in Charles Reade's 'Put Yourself in his Place' (1870), a novel dealing with Broadhead's crimes. In recognition of his services he was presented (28 April 1868) with his portrait by H. F. Crighton and a purse of 600 guineas, subscribed by men of all political opinions. The picture now hangs in Sheffield town hall.

Leng established at Sheffield as supplementary to the 'Telegraph,' the 'Weekly Telegraph,' the 'Evening Telegraph and Star,' the 'Weekly News,' and the 'Sunday Telegraph,' all of which became flourishing concerns. At different times he visited the Continent, writing for the 'Telegraph' descriptive articles, some of which he republished in book form. For many years vice-chairman of the Sheffield Conservative and Constitutional Association, he was afterwards chairman. In 1895-6 he was elected chairman of the Sheffield Chamber of Commerce. He was knighted in 1887 on the occasion of Queen Victoria's jubilee. Dying at Sheffield on 20 Feb. 1902, he was buried in Ecclesall churchyard. He married in 1860 Anne (*d.* 1893), daughter of David Stark of Ruthven, Forfarshire, and widow of Harry Cook of Sandhurst, Australia. Her sister was first wife of his brother John. His two sons, C. D. Leng and W. St. Quentin Leng, became partners in the 'Sheffield Telegraph.' A cartoon portrait by 'Spy' appeared in 'Vanity Fair' in 1890.

[In Memoriam, Sir William Christopher Leng, Kt. (1902); Sheffield Daily Telegraph, 20 Feb. 1902; Dundee Advertiser, 20 Feb. 1902; Dundee Year Book, 1902; private information.] A. H. M.

LENNOX, CHARLES HENRY GORDON-. [See GORDON-LENNOX, CHARLES HENRY, sixth DUKE OF RICHMOND AND first DUKE OF GORDON (1818–1903), lord president of the council.]

LENO, DAN, whose true name was GEORGE GALVIN (1860–1904), music-hall singer and dancer, was born on 20 Dec. 1860 at 4 Eve Court, Somers Town, afterwards demolished to make room for St. Pancras terminus. His father and mother, who were known professionally as Mr. and Mrs. Johnny Wilde, were itinerant music-hall performers who trained the child as a tumbler and contortionist. The father at any rate was Irish, and to that circumstance and the boy's occasional sojourns in Ireland may be attributed his marked Irish voice, which was no small part of his attraction in later years. He made his first appearance as early as 1864 as 'Little George, the Infant Wonder, Contortionist and Posturer' in the Cosmotheca off the Edgware Road, since destroyed. His father dying about this time, his mother married another member of the same profession, named Grant, whose stage name was Leno. The boy with his mother, stepfather, and a brother, also an acrobat, began to tour the United Kingdom and to some extent the continent. Described as 'The Great Little Lenos,' the brothers were performing in various places in 1867. The brother soon disappeared, and in 1869 Dan, who had been forced through an accident to substitute clog-dancing for tumbling, was known as 'The Great Little Leno, the Quintessence of Irish Comedians,' and had presumably added singing and patter to his agility. In 1869 he was in Belfast, among the audience being Charles Dickens, then lecturing in Ireland, who is said to have spoken to the boy and prophesied success for him (JAY HICKORY WOOD, *Dan Leno*, 1905).

The boy's name was changed from George to Dan owing to a misapprehension on the part of either the printer or deviser of a playbill. The boy's stepfather appreciated the accidental change and saw the value of it, and as Dan Leno the stage name was crystallised. For many years the touring life continued, with moderate success, and then in 1880 Dan Leno, now nearly twenty, entered for a clog-dancing competition and the championship of the world silver belt at the Princess's Music Hall, Leeds, and won it. He subsequently lost it, but recaptured it in 1883, at the People's Music Hall, Oldham, and emerged from the contest into the successful period of his life. In 1883, in St. George's Church, Hulme, Manchester, he married Miss Lydia Reynolds, a music-hall singer, and not long afterwards made his first appearance as Dan Leno in London, at the Foresters' Music Hall, where at a salary of *5l.* a week he sang and danced. His first song, 'Going to Buy the Milk for the Twins,' a mixture of singing and monologue such as he practised to the end, was so successful that he obtained an engagement at the Oxford Music Hall and there attracted the attention of George Conquest [q. v. Suppl. II], of the Surrey Theatre, who engaged Leno and his wife at a joint salary of *20l.* a week to play in the 1886–7 pantomime of 'Jack and the Beanstalk.' Dan accepted, and played Jack's mother. From this point his career was a triumph.

In 1887 he made his appearance at the Empire theatre, Leicester Square, on the occasion of its being converted into a music hall, and sang one of his earliest successes, a parody of 'Queen of My Heart' in 'Dorothy.' Next year Sir Augustus Harris [q. v. Suppl. I] engaged him for the Drury Lane pantomime of 1888–9 — 'Babes in the Wood'—for which he worked so acceptably as the Wicked Aunt that it ran from 26 Dec. until 27 April, and his engagement was renewed for a term of years which ended only with his death. Every winter he was the particular star of Drury Lane; while during the rest of the year he made a tour of the principal music halls in the United Kingdom. No other comedian of his time had drawing power to compare with him. On 26 November 1901 the culminating point of his success was reached when he was commanded to Sandringham to sing before King Edward VII, Queen Alexandra, and their guests—the first music-hall performer to be thus honoured.

In September 1902 Dan Leno's health broke down. His continuous and excitable activity exhausted his strength. He was able to return to the stage during the early months of 1903 and for the Drury Lane pantomime of 1903-4; but he died at Balham from general paralysis of the brain on 31 Oct. 1904 at the early age of forty-three. His funeral on 8 Nov. at Lambeth cemetery, Tooting, was attended by an immense crowd of admirers.

Dan Leno throughout the best years of his career, which covered his connection with Drury Lane, signally excelled all other music-hall comedians in intelligence, humour, drollery, and creativeness. He used the words provided for him only as a basis, often suggested by himself, on which to build a character. Although essentially a caricaturist, with a broad and rollicking sense of fun which added myriad touches of extravagance beyond experience, the groundwork of his creations was true, and truth continually broke through the exuberance of the artist. His most memorable songs in his best period were a mixture of monologue and song, in male or female character, but the song came gradually to count for less and less. 'The Shopwalker' perhaps first convinced the great public of his genius. Leno's long series of largely irresponsible but always human pantomime figures at Drury Lane differed from all pantomime figures by their strange blend of fun and wistfulness. It was his special gift to endear himself to an audience, and compel its sympathies as well as applause.

The recipient of large salaries, he was correspondingly lavish. He was President of the Music Hall Benevolent Fund, and himself the distributor of much private charity. He carried his fun into private life and was much addicted to practical jokes. His hobbies were farming live stock in the meadow attached to his house at Balham and painting or modelling in the wooden studio in his garden. For one evening in 1902 he edited the 'Sun,' a short-lived newspaper then under Mr. Horatio Bottomley's ownership. He also wrote a burlesque autobiography entitled 'Dan Leno: his Book' (1901), which is not wholly without nonsensical merit.

He left a widow and several children, among them a married daughter, Georgiana, who had appeared on the stage. A bust of the comedian is in the entrance hall of Drury Lane Theatre.

[The Times, 1 Nov. 1904; Daily Telegraph, 1 Nov. 1904; Era, 5 Nov. 1904. Dan Leno, by Jay Hickory Wood, 1905; James Glover, Jimmy Glover his book, 1911; pp. 74 seq. (with portrait of Leno from bust by himself).]

E. V. L.

LEVESON-GOWER, [EDWARD] FREDERICK (1819–1907), politician and autobiographer, second son of Granville Leveson-Gower, first Earl Granville [q. v.], by his wife Lady Henrietta, or Harriet, Cavendish, daughter of the fifth duke of Devonshire, was born on 3 May 1819. He was always called by his second Christian name. His early years were partly spent with his parents at the British embassy, Paris. As a boy he was a frequent visitor at Holland House (cf. his autobiography, *Bygone Years*, 1905, ch. iii.; LADY GRANVILLE'S *Letters*, ii. 3). Educated at Eton and Christ Church, Oxford, he graduated B.A. in 1840; he was judge's marshal to Lord Denman and Baron Parke, and was called to the bar at the Inner Temple in 1845. In 1846 he was returned as liberal member for Derby at a by-election, and was re-elected at the general election next year, but was unseated, his agent having illegally engaged voters as messengers. Returned for Stoke-on-Trent in 1852, he was at the bottom of the poll at the election five years later, the Chinese war having divided the liberals in the constituency. In 1859 he was returned for Bodmin, and held the seat until 1885, when he retired from political life.

Leveson-Gower's speeches in the House of Commons were not numerous, though he seconded the address on the meeting of parliament in the autumn of 1854. Gladstone offered him the posts of chief whip and postmaster-general, but he refused both, thinking that there were others more deserving of promotion (*Bygone Years*, p. 258). He was for several years chairman of railway committees, a tribunal of which he formed no high opinion (*ibid.* p. 259).

In 1874 he became first chairman of the National School of Cookery, and held the position until 1903, when he became vice-chairman. He acted for some twenty years as a director of Sir W. G. Armstrong & Co., Ltd.

Leveson-Gower took much pleasure in foreign travel. In 1850–1 he visited India. In 1856 he went to Russia as attaché to his brother, Lord Granville, the special envoy on the coronation of the Czar Alexander II (*Bygone Years*, ch. viii.; FITZMAURICE'S *Granville*, ch. viii.). But it was as a social figure that he was most conspicuous. Gifted with agreeable manners, conversational tact, and a good memory, he excelled as a diner-out and giver of dinners. These qualities are reflected in his 'Bygone Years' (1905), a pleasant volume of reminiscences, which contains many well-told anecdotes. His editing of his mother's 'Letters' (1894) also shows an intimate knowledge of several generations of society. In August 1899 he published an article with the object of showing that the author of 'Werner' was not Byron, but Georgiana, duchess of Devonshire (*Nineteenth Century*, vol. xlvi. pp. 243–250). The theory is discredited by Mr. Hartley Coleridge (*The Works of Lord Byron*, 1901, v. 329–333; see also *Bygone Years*, pp. 325–6, and the correspondence in *Literature*, 12, 19, and 26 August 1899). He was a member of Grillion's Club, and also of the Political Economy Club, of which science he made a serious study. He was J.P. for the county of Surrey and D.L. for Derbyshire.

Leveson-Gower married on 1 June 1853 Lady Margaret Mary Frances Elizabeth, second daughter of Spencer Joshua Alwyne Compton, second marquis of Northampton; she died on 22 May 1858. After her death he lived with his mother at Chiswick House, Chiswick, until she died in 1862, when he took No. 14 South Audley Street. In 1870 he also purchased Holmbury, near Dorking. There Gladstone visited him at least once a year, and other frequent guests were his brother, Lord Granville, to whom he was much attached, Mrs. Grote, Bishop Wilberforce, Tennyson, and Russell Lowell. Leveson-Gower died in London on 30 May 1907, and was buried at Castle Ashby, Northamptonshire. His only child, George Granville Leveson-Gower, who has been a commissioner of woods and forests since 1908, owns at 12 Norfolk-crescent, London, W., three portraits, including a half-length chalk portrait by H. T. Wells, R.A., done in 1871 for Grillion's Club. In the apartments of the Dowager Lady Granville, Leveson-Gower's sister-in-law, at Kensington Palace are two portraits of him: one in water-colours taken at the age of seventeen by the Vicomtesse de Caraman, and the other in oils believed to be by Manana.

[Bygone Years, by the Hon. Frederick Leveson-Gower, 1905; Letters of Harriet, Countess Granville, edited by the Hon. Frederick Leveson-Gower, 1894; G. W. E. Russell, Sketches and Snapshots, 1910; The Times, 31 May 1907.] L. C. S.

LEWIS, BUNNELL (1824–1908), classical archæologist, born in London on 26 July 1824, was the eldest of the twelve children of William Jones Lewis of London by his first wife Mary Bunnell, a descendant of Philip Henry, the nonconformist divine. Samuel Savage Lewis [q. v.] was his half-brother. Educated under Dr. Jackson, afterwards bishop of London, at Islington proprietary school and at University College, London, Lewis, after reading with Charles Rann Kennedy [q. v.], graduated B.A. in 1843 in the University of London, obtaining the university scholarship in classics. He became fellow of University College in 1847, and proceeded M.A. in classics in 1849, taking the gold medal, then first awarded. He was appointed the same year professor of Latin at Queen's College, Cork, an appointment which he held until 1905. He laboured to make archæology an integral part of university education, and with that end in view collected objects of art and antiquity for the museum of his college. At the foundation of the Queen's University in Ireland he took an active part in its administration, and held the office of examiner in Latin for four years.

Lewis early devoted his attention to archæology, being elected F.S.A. on 2 Feb. 1865, and was in 1883 appointed foreign corresponding associate of the National Society of Antiquaries of France. In 1873–1874 he delivered courses of lectures on classical archæology at University College in connection with the Slade School of Art. The inaugural lecture was published. His special study was the survival of Roman antiquities in various parts of Europe, and his inquiries took him during the summer recesses to Norway, Sweden, Denmark, Germany, France, Switzerland, Italy, Sicily, and Turkey. His discoveries of Roman antiquities, which shed much new light on the interpretation of Latin literature, were embodied in papers contributed between 1875 and 1907 to the 'Archæological Journal.'

Lewis died at his residence, 49 Sunday's Well Road, Cork, on 2 July 1908, and was buried at Cork. He was twice married: (1) on 2 Oct. 1855 to Jane (*d.* 31 Dec. 1867), second daughter of the Rev. John Whitley, D.D., chancellor of Killaloe; and (2) on 4 Oct. 1871 to Louise Emily (*d.* Nov. 1882), daughter of Admiral Bowes-Watson of Cambridge. He left no issue. He bequeathed to University College, London, his classical and archæological library and 1000*l.* for a 'Bunnell Lewis prize' for proficiency in original Latin verse and in translations from Latin and Greek.

Besides his archæological papers and contributions to the second (revised) edition of Dr. William Smith's Latin Dictionary, he published a 'Letter to J. Robson, Esq., on the Slade Professorships of Fine Art' (1869) and 'Remarks on Ivory Cabinets in the Possession of Wickham Flower, Esq., (1871).

[Summary of the Life of the Rev. George Lewis, D.D., and Genealogy, 1873; Q.C.C., conducted by the Students of Queen's College, Cork (portrait), 1906, ii. 25–6; Cork Constitution, 3 July 1908; Irish Times, 3 July 1908; The Times, 17 Aug. 1908 (will); Men and Women of the Time, 1899; information kindly supplied by Miss Mary Bunnell Burton.]

C. W.

LEWIS, EVAN (1818–1901), dean of Bangor, born at Llanilar, Cardiganshire, on 16 Nov. 1818, was second (and posthumous) son of Evan Lewis of that place (who was descended from the Lewis family of Dinas Cerdyn and Blaen Cerdyn in that county) by his wife Mary, daughter of John Richards, also of Llanilar. His mother married, for her second husband, John Hughes of Tyn-y-beili, Llanrhystyd.

His elder brother, David Lewis (1814–1895), fellow of Jesus College, Oxford (1839–1846) and vice-principal (1845–6), served as curate of St. Mary's, Oxford, under John Henry Newman, and joined the Roman catholic communion in 1846. In 1860 he settled for life at Arundel. Devoting himself to a study of the canon law and the lives of the saints, he translated from the Latin 'The Rise and Growth of the Anglican Schism,' by Nicholas Sanders, with an elaborate introduction and notes (1877); and among other works from the Spanish, the writings of St. John of the Cross (1864; 2nd edit., with numerous changes, 1889; new edit. 3 vols., with an introduction by Father Benedict Zimmermann, 1909).

Evan Lewis, after education at Ystrad Meurig and Aberystwyth, went to a school at Twickenham kept by his father's brother, David Lewis, D.D. (1778–1859) (FOSTER, *Al. Oxon.*; G. JONES, *Enwogion Sir Aberteifi*, 98). Following his elder brother David to Jesus College, Oxford, Lewis matriculated on 7 April 1838, and graduated B.A. in 1841, proceeding M.A. in 1863. Of powerful physique, he rowed 'stroke' in the college boat when it was head of the river, and in after life was a great walker. Ordained deacon and priest in 1842 by Christopher Bethell, Bishop of Bangor [q. v.], he was successively curate of Llanddeusant (1842), Llanfaes with Penmon (1843–5), Llanfihangel Ysceifiog (1845–6), all in Anglesey, and Llanllechid, Carnarvonshire (1847–59). He was vicar of Aberdare, Glamorganshire (1859–66), rector of Dolgelly, Merionethshire, and rural dean of Estimaner (1866–84), proctor in convocation for the diocese of Bangor (1868–80), chancellor of

Bangor (1872–6), canon residentiary (1877–1884), and dean from 1884 till his death at the deanery on 24 Nov. 1901. He was buried at Llandegai churchyard.

He married (1) in October 1859 Anne, youngest daughter by his first wife of John Henry Cotton, dean of Bangor, at one time his vicar; she died on 24 Dec. 1860 at Aberdare, leaving no issue; (2) in 1865 Adelaide Owen, third daughter of the Rev. Cyrus Morrall of Plas Iolyn, Shropshire (Burke's *Landed Gentry, s. v.*); she survived him with three sons and three daughters.

While at Oxford, Lewis, like his brother David, came under the influence of the tractarians, and on returning to Wales he inculcated their doctrines by speech and pen. At Llanllechid he introduced choral services for the first time in the Bangor diocese, and gradually adopted a dignified ritual. This he supplemented by direct 'catholic' teaching as to the sacraments, being the first Anglican in the nineteenth century to preach in Wales the doctrines of apostolic succession and baptismal regeneration (Archdeacon David Evans' *Adgofion*, i.e. *Reminiscences*, 1904, pp. 35–6). Some of the younger clergy followed Lewis's lead, and the movement resulted in a latter-day Bangor controversy (*Dadl Bangor*). The Rev. John Phillips attacked the ritualist position in two famous lectures delivered at Bangor in November 1850 and January 1852 respectively and shortly afterwards published. Lewis replied to the first lecture in a series of Welsh letters in 'Y Cymro,' signed 'Aelod o'n Eglwys' (a member of the church), reprinted in 1852 in book form. His best work was an elaborate Welsh treatise on the apostolic succession, described as by a Welsh clergyman (*Yr Olyniaeth Apostolaidd gan Offeiriad Cymreig:* Bangor, 1851, London, 1869). He also wrote, besides occasional papers on Welsh church questions, and on the Wesleyan succession (*Yr Olyniaeth Wesleyaidd*), under the pseudonym of 'Amddiffynydd' (i.e. Defender) in 1858. He was much interested in church music, co-operated in the production of the 'Bangor Diocese Hymn Book,' and himself translated into Welsh Faber's 'Good Friday Hymns' and 'Adeste Fideles.'

[For Dean Lewis see Western Mail (Cardiff), 25 Nov. 1901; North Wales Chronicle (Bangor), 30 Nov.; Church Times, 29 Nov. 1901; T. R. Roberts, Eminent Welshmen (1908), p. 306. See also Welsh articles in Y Geninen for March 1902, p. 37, and March 1903, p. 23, and (with portrait) in Yr Haul, 1902, p. 3; private information.] D. Ll. T.

LEWIS, Sir GEORGE HENRY, first baronet (1833–1911), solicitor, second son in a family of four sons and four daughters of James Graham Lewis, solicitor (1804–73), by his wife Harriet, daughter of Henry Davis of London, was born on 21 April 1833 at 10 Ely Place, Holborn, where, after the fashion of the day, his father resided over the offices of his firm. Educated at a private Jewish school at Edmonton and at University College, London, Lewis was articled to his father in 1851 and was admitted a solicitor in the spring of 1856, joining the firm of Lewis & Lewis, which his father had founded and in which the only other partner was his uncle, George Lewis. Their business, which strongly resembled in many ways that of Mr. Jaggers as described by Dickens in 'Great Expectations,' dealt largely with criminal matters, with insolvency, and with civil litigation arising out of fraud, barratry, and the like, and the firm was largely employed by members of the theatrical profession. Besides the general work of the office the younger George Lewis gained experience in advocacy by constant practice in the police courts. He showed remarkable ability and acuteness at the Mansion House in Jan. 1869 on behalf of the prosecutor, Dr. Thorn of the Canadian bar, who brought charges of fraud against the directors of the bankrupt firm Overend, Gurney & Co.; but his popular reputation was first established in July 1876 in connection with the so-called Balham mystery [see under Gully, James Manby], where at the coroner's inquest he represented the relatives of Mr. Charles Bravo, whose death was the subject of the inquiry. His searching and relentless cross-examination, which for the first time made clear the relationship of the various parties in the drama, though it failed to fix the guilt on any of the persons involved, brought him much notoriety and was the cause of a substantial increase in the business of the firm.

Gradually he obtained what was for more than a quarter of a century the practical monopoly of those cases where the seamy side of society is unveiled, and where the sins and follies of the wealthy classes threaten exposure and disaster. He was the refuge, with fine impartiality, of the guilty and the innocent, of the wrongdoer and of the oppressed. But though he was employed on one side or the other in almost every *cause célèbre* which was tried in London for five-and-thirty years, the bulk of his practice lay in the cases which by adroit handling he kept out of court, largely to the benefit of all concerned. He possessed an unrivalled knowledge of the past records of the criminals and adventurers of both sexes, not only in England and on the continent of Europe, but in the United States, which was peculiarly serviceable to him and to his clients in resisting attempts at conspiracy and blackmail. It has been said of him that 'he was not so much a lawyer as a shrewd private inquiry agent; audacious, playing the game often in defiance of the rules, and relying on his audacity to carry him through.' 'For a trial,' wrote Mr. Smalley, who knew him well, 'he prepared with a thoroughness which left no opening for surprise. He had methods of investigation which were his own, and intuitions beside which the rather mechanical processes of Sherlock Holmes seemed the efforts of a beginner.' These qualities were never more conspicuously exhibited than in the proceedings before the Parnell commission in 1888–9, where he represented the majority of the incriminated nationalists, and where he laid the train which resulted in the exposure of the forgeries of Richard Pigott [q. v.].

Lewis's extraordinary memory for detail enabled him to reduce written notes to a minimum, and some time before his death he declared that he had destroyed all record of his strange experiences. It was impossible to lead such a life without incurring much fierce resentment, and the causes he championed were not always those of right and justice; but he was the author of many acts of great kindness and generosity, and he was a staunch and loyal friend. Wealthy and hospitable, he was a familiar figure in the artistic and theatrical world, and there was no phase of society with which his professional experience had not, at one time or another, brought him into touch. Though a Jew by birth, a fact of which he was conspicuously proud, and having enjoyed few advantages as a young man, George Lewis became a familiar figure in very exalted circles and was one of those admitted to the intimacy of King Edward VII, by whom he was made a Companion of the Victorian Order in 1905. In 1892 he was knighted, in recognition, it was supposed, of his services in connection with the Parnell commission. On the coronation of King Edward VII in 1902 he obtained a baronetcy.

In the later years of his life Lewis was active in promoting certain much-needed reforms in the criminal law. He was a strong advocate of the Prisoners' Evidence Act of 1898, by which prisoners and their wives were made competent witnesses in criminal as well as in civil cases, as well as of the court of criminal appeal created in 1908. His practice had made him acquainted with every phase of conjugal unhappiness, and he proved a highly illuminating witness before the royal commission appointed in 1909 to inquire into the working of the divorce laws. He argued in favour of equal rights for both sexes, of the cheapening of procedure, and of the establishment of local divorce courts. He contributed also to the movement which led to the Moneylenders Act of 1900, intended to put a curb upon usurious extortion.

Lewis died, after a prolonged illness, at his house in Portland Place, on 7 Dec. 1911, and was buried at the Jewish cemetery, Willesden; he had done very little professional work for some years before his death. He was married twice: (1) in 1863 to Victorine, daughter of Philip Kann of Frankfort-on-Maine; she died in 1865, leaving a daughter; (2) in 1867 to Elizabeth, daughter of Ferdinand Eberstadt of Mannheim, by whom he had two daughters and one son, George James Graham, who succeeded him in the baronetcy and as head of the firm of Lewis & Lewis. A portrait in oils by John S. Sargent, R.A., was exhibited at the Royal Academy in 1896. A cartoon portrait by 'Spy' appeared in 'Vanity Fair' in 1896.

[The Times, 8 Dec. 1911; the New York Daily Tribune, 31 Dec. 1911 (article by George W. Smalley); Burke's Baronetage; private information.] J. B. A.

LEWIS, JOHN TRAVERS (1825–1901), archbishop of Ontario, born on 20 June 1825, at Garrycloyne Castle, Cork, the seat of his great-uncle on the mother's side, John Travers, was son of John Lewis, M.A., curate of St. Ann's, Shandon, Cork, of Welsh descent, by his wife Rebecca Olivia, daughter of John Lawless of Kilcrone, Cloyne. Educated at Hambin and Porter's School, Cork, he entered Trinity College, Dublin, winning the first Hebrew prize, and graduating B.A. in 1848 as senior moderator and gold medallist in ethics and logic. Ordained deacon in 1848, and priest in 1849, he visited Canada in the latter year and settled there for life. He first received charge of the mission at West Hawkesbury in the Ottawa Valley. In 1854 he was appointed to the rectory of St. Peter's,

Brockville; and on 13 June 1861 was elected first bishop of the new diocese of Ontario. He was at the time the youngest bishop in the whole Anglican church, and the last in Canada to be created by royal letters patent. In 1893 he was elected by the house of bishops to the office of metropolitan of the ecclesiastical province of Canada, and in 1894 to the dignity of archbishop of Ontario.

In 1861, in his first address as bishop of Ontario, he advocated the incorporation of a synod board to manage the funds and direct the mission work of the diocese, a system since adopted throughout the Dominion. In his address of 1864 he spoke in favour of a national council of representatives for the whole Anglican church, to affirm the catholic doctrines. At the meeting of the provincial synod in 1865 he moved an address to the archbishop of Canterbury in behalf of the proposed council. He then visited England and urged acceptance of the scheme, and the result was the first Lambeth conference of 1867. At the same time his steady interest in scientific questions led him to be the original promoter of the first meeting of the British Association in Canada, held at Montreal 1884. He was author of some published sermons and contributor to religious periodicals in Canada and England.

Lewis was made hon. D.D. of Oxford (1897), hon. LL.D. of Dublin, and hon. D.C.L. by Trinity University, Toronto, and by Bishop's College University, Lennoxville. In 1885 the governor-general of Canada presented him with the memorial medal of the confederation of the provinces in acknowledgment of his 'important services in the cause of literature and science.' He died at sea in the Atlantic on his way from Canada to England on 6 May 1901, and was buried at Hawkhurst, Kent. An altar was erected to his memory in the cathedral, Kingston, Ontario. A painted portrait of Lewis is in possession of his widow; two pastels in colours are owned by his eldest son.

Lewis twice married: (1) on 22 July 1851, Annie Henrietta Margaret, daughter of the hon. Henry Sherwood, Q.C., successively solicitor-general and attorney-general for Upper Canada; she died on 28 July 1886, leaving six children, the eldest of whom, John Travers Lewis, K.C., is chancellor of the diocese of Ottawa; (2) on 20 Feb. 1889, Ada Maria, daughter of Evan Leigh, C.E., of Manchester. Lewis's second wife, by whom he had no issue, was well known before her marriage for her pious works in France, where she founded the British and American homes for young women and children in Paris and built Christ Church at Neuilly-sur-Marne.

[Private information; Kingston Daily Whig, 7 May 1901; Morgan's Canadian Men and Women of the Time, 1898.] W. S. J.

LEWIS, RICHARD (1821–1905), bishop of Llandaff, second son of John Lewis (*d.* 1834), barrister-at-law, of Henllan in the parish of Llanddewi Velfrey, Pembrokeshire, by his first wife, Eliza, daughter of Charles Poyer Callen of Grove, Narberth, in the same county, was born at Henllan on 27 March 1821. His father was a prominent supporter of the reform bill of 1832 (cf. Nicholas, *Annals of County Families*, 904). An ancestor had married into the family of Col. John Poyer [q. v.], whose estate of Grove, with that of Henllan and Molleston amounting together to 3500 acres, passed to the bishop on the death of his only brother, John Lennox Griffith Poyer Lewis (1819–1886), a barrister of Lincoln's Inn and high sheriff of Carmarthenshire for 1867.

Educated at the grammar school of Haverfordwest and at Bromsgrove school (Feb. 1835 to 1839), he matriculated at Worcester College, Oxford, 18 June 1839, being Cookes scholar 1839–43. Owing to ill-health, he graduated B.A. in 1843 in the 'pass' examination with an honorary fourth class. He then travelled for two years with his brother through central and south-eastern Europe, Egypt, as far as the second cataract, and, crossing the desert, through Palestine, Asia Minor, and Greece. He was ordained deacon in 1844 and priest in 1846 by the bishop of Oxford. After serving a curacy at Denchworth near Wantage he was on 17 Sept. 1847 presented by his grandfather to the vicarage of Amroth, Pembrokeshire, a Poyer living of which he afterwards became patron. This he relinquished for a curacy at Flaxley, Gloucestershire, and in 1851 he was preferred by the lord chancellor to the rectory of Lampeter Velfry, a purely agricultural parish, with a Welsh-speaking population of about 1000, adjoining his native place and comprising a part of the family estate. Bishop Thirlwall refused to institute him, on the ground of his inadequate knowledge of Welsh, but an appeal to the archbishop was decided in his favour (23 June 1852) (Dean Roberts of Bangor in *Y Geninen*, January 1906). He became rural dean of Lower Carmarthen in the same year.

He catechised the scholars in the Sunday school every Sunday, and the number of communicants rose from fifteen in 1851 to one hundred and ten in 1883 (see his 7th Visitation Charge, 1903). He was prebendary of Caerfarchell in St. David's Cathedral from 1867 to 1875, archdeacon of St. David's, prebendary of Mydrim, and chaplain to the bishop (Basil Jones) from 1875 to 1883, the archdeaconry, which was *pro hac vice* in the gift of the crown, being conferred on him by the prime minister, Disraeli. He was exceptionally active throughout his archdeaconry, but he was scarcely known outside before the Church Congress held at Swansea in 1879, when as chairman of the subjects committee and of one of the public meetings he gave an impression of tact and judgment (DEAN ROBERTS, *loc. cit.*). On the advice of Dean Vaughan and Dean Allen (of St. David's) he accepted in Jan. 1883, with some hesitation, when sixty-two years old, and with little experience of urban or industrial conditions, Gladstone's offer of the see of Llandaff, which had not been held by a Welshman since 1675. He was consecrated on 25 April 1883 at St. Paul's Cathedral by Archbishop Benson—it being his first consecration—was enthroned on 1 May, and soon afterwards received the degree of D.D. from Oxford by diploma.

The Church Extension Society founded by Lewis's predecessor, Alfred Ollivant [q. v.], in 1850 had practically exhausted all its funded capital before the end of 1883. After visiting every parish in the diocese and after realising the deficient provision in the industrial districts, Lewis inaugurated the Bishop of Llandaff's Fund for the erection of inexpensive churches in populous districts, and for the support of additional curates. Starting the fund with a personal contribution of 1000*l*. (to which later he added 1000 guineas), he asked for 50,000*l*., of which 20,000*l*. was raised within a year, and the total reached before his death was 60,155*l*. 18*s*. 3*d*., of which 27,061*l*. had been expended in building grants and 23,232*l*. in grants for the stipends of curates. In 1897 he started a Poor Benefice Fund, which has since been affiliated to the Queen Victoria Clergy Pension Fund. In 1898 he established a diocesan Sunday, on which collections should be made throughout the diocese for the four chief diocesan funds, namely, the two already mentioned and those of the Church Building Society (established by Ollivant in 1845) and the Church Schools Association. A million shilling thank-offering fund, opened by the bishop in 1901 (to commemorate the nineteenth century) proved disappointing; only some tenth of that sum was realised. During his episcopate he confirmed 83,844 candidates, some 30 new parishes were formed, 100 new churches built or rebuilt, and 130 restored.

One of the earliest acts of the bishop was to establish an annual Diocesan Conference, which first met in October 1884. His addresses at these conferences and even his visitation charges were mainly devoted either to administrative matters or to a spirited defence of the church and its property, including exposure of what he regarded as unfair treatment of its schools. A broad churchman, he pursued a policy of toleration in matters of ritual, and secured the obedience of clergy who inclined to ritualist excesses.

After the death of William Basil Jones [q. v. Suppl. I] in 1897, he, as senior Welsh bishop, was frequently consulted by the primate on questions relating to Wales, especially as to education. He refused to countenance any compromise on the question of church schools (*South Western Daily News*, 28 Feb. and 29 April 1903); with much reluctance he met the teachers' representatives in an abortive conference at Llandaff on 23 Nov. (*ibid.*). He was unable, from stress of work or disinclination, to take any part in the administration of the South Wales University College. To him was largely due in 1892 the establishment, within his diocese, of a theological college (St. Michael's) for the post-graduate training of candidates for orders.

Lewis was president of the Church Congress at Cardiff in 1889, spoke at the Rhyl Congress of 1891 on the church revival in Wales, and presided at a meeting on the church in Wales at the London Congress in 1899. He also presided over a committee of the Lambeth Conference of 1887 which considered the care of emigrants. He took his seat in the House of Lords on 14 April 1885. He attended rarely, but uniformly voted on the conservative side.

Somewhat lacking in sympathy with modern Welsh nationalism, he took little part in any Welsh movement unconnected with the church, but was keenly alive to the necessity of utilising the Welsh language in the services of the church and also for church defence. He insisted on Welsh-speaking clergy serving parishes where Welsh was spoken, and declined to institute patrons' nominees who could not speak

Welsh. The exercise of such discretion on his part was upheld in the law courts (*Law Reports*, 20 Q.B.D. 460; 58 *Law Times*, 812).

The bishop died at Llandaff on 24 Jan. 1905, and was buried at Llanddewi Velfrey. He preserved his physical vigour till near the end. A life-size gilt-bronze statue, in ecclesiastical robes, by (Sir) W. Goscombe John, R.A., was erected in the cathedral, being unveiled on behalf of the subscribers by Viscount Tredegar on 17 Dec. 1908. A portrait in the Palace, Llandaff, by Mr. A. S. Cope, R.A., was presented on the twenty-first anniversary of his accession to the see (3 Nov. 1904).

In April 1847, while a curate at Denchworth, Lewis married Georgiana King, daughter of Major John Lewis of the Hon. East India Company. She died at Llandaff on 24 Feb. 1895. Their only child, Arthur Griffith Poyer Lewis (1848–1909), educated at Eton and University College, Oxford, where he rowed in the university boatrace of 1870, was called to the bar at Lincoln's Inn on 17 Nov. 1873, and joined the South Wales circuit. He was registrar to the diocese of Llandaff from January 1885 to April 1898, secretary to the bishop from 1897 to 1908, and chancellor of the dioceses of Llandaff and St. David's (1908–9). He was also recorder of Carmarthen (1890–1905), stipendiary magistrate for Pontypridd from July 1905, and chairman of the quarter sessions of Haverfordwest from 1907 and of Carmarthenshire from 1908 (FOSTER'S *Men at the Bar*; *Who's Who*, 1909; *Western Mail*, 6 May 1909).

[South Wales Daily News and Western Mail (Cardiff) of 25 Jan. 1905 and a Welsh article in Y Geninen (Carnarvon) for January 1906 by the Dean of Bangor give the fullest and most reliable account of Bishop Lewis. See also articles by Mr. J. E. Ollivant in the Llandaff diocesan magazine for March 1905 and in Guardian 1 Feb. 1905; Foster's Alumni Oxon.; Distinguished Churchmen (1902), by Charles H. Dant. The primary authorities for the bishop's episcopal work are the reports of the Llandaff Diocesan Conference from 1884 on (notably that for 1904, containing his own review of the progress made), and his visitation charges (both published at Cardiff), and also, from March 1899 on, the Llandaff diocesan magazine, each number of which gives *inter alia* a list of the public engagements fulfilled by the bishop in the preceding quarter. A summarised account of Dr. Lewis's episcopacy was given by his successor (Dr. Hughes) to the Welsh Church Commission on 11 June 1908 (Minutes of Evidence, book iii. pp. 511 et seq.] D. LL. T.

LIDDERDALE, WILLIAM (1832–1902), governor of the Bank of England, born at St. Petersburg on 16 July 1832, was second of the six sons of John Lidderdale, a Russia merchant, by his wife Ann Morgan. When ten years old he was brought to England, and after education at a private school at Birkenhead he began his commercial career in 1847 in the office of Heath and Co., Russia merchants of Liverpool. He next became cashier to Rathbone Bros. and Co. of Liverpool, representing that firm in New York from 1857 to 1863. Becoming a partner in 1864, he started the Rathbones' London house, and his business ability quickly brought him to the front rank of London merchants. He became a director of the Bank of England in 1870, deputy-governor in 1887, and governor in 1889.

During Lidderdale's deputy-governorship effect was given by the bank to the reduction of the interest on the national debt, in accordance with the National Debt Conversion Act passed in 1888, by George Joachim Goschen [q. v. Suppl. II], the chancellor of the exchequer. During his second year of office as governor Lidderdale was faced by the gravest responsibility. The money market had been for some months in an unsettled state owing to the large drain of gold to foreign parts, especially to South America. On Friday, 7 Nov. 1890, the bank rate was suddenly raised to 6 per cent. On the following day Lidderdale was informed that the great accepting house of Baring Bros. was in need of assistance being called upon to meet certain commitments in respect of the Buenos Ayres harbour and water works. Their liabilities were 22,000,000*l.*, against which were liquid assets immediately available of 15,000,000*l.*, whilst the personal estates of the partners were valued at about 11,000,000*l.* Lidderdale immediately consulted not only his fellow directors but the leading bankers and merchants. By the following Wednesday afternoon he had purchased 1,500,000*l.* of gold from Russia and borrowed 3,000,000*l.* from France. On Thursday, 14 Nov., Messrs. Baring laid a statement of their affairs before the directors; on Friday Lidderdale placed the British government in full possession of the facts of the coming emergency and of the steps taken and proposed to be taken to meet it. On the same afternoon a guarantee fund was opened at the bank, and by noon the next day a subscription of 16,000,000*l.* had been secured, and he was able to announce to the public that the situation was saved.

The bank, supported by the chief joint-stock banks, discount houses, and a few leading firms, undertook the liquidation of Messrs. Baring's affairs by means of a committee to last for three (eventually extended to four) years, during which it was hoped that the whole of the firm's assets would be satisfactorily realised. In his dealing with the inevitable difficulties of the liquidation, Lidderdale, by his firm action, still further increased the confidence of the City in his financial leadership.

At the close of this alarming crisis, which the country had hardly time to realise before it disappeared, the services of Lidderdale and his fellow directors received marked public recognition. On 30 Dec. 1890 a committee from the Stock Exchange presented the governor and directors with an appreciative address. On 27 Feb. 1891 Lidderdale was presented with the honorary freedom of the Grocers' Company. On 6 May he was admitted to the honorary freedom of the City of London; at the banquet in his honour which followed at the Mansion House, Lidderdale insisted that the maintenance of a sufficient reserve for national wants was the concern not only of the Bank of England, but of all the banks of the country. He was made a privy councillor on 30 May 1891.

Lidderdale was continued in office as governor for a year beyond the usual term, so that he might bring to a conclusion negotiations with the government for changes in the management of the bank, which eventually took shape in the Bank Act of 27 June 1892. To his personal investigation of the details was largely due the judgment of the House of Lords on 5 March 1891 (reversing the decision of the lower courts), in the intricate case, Vagliano Bros. *versus* the Bank of England. Thereby the bank was finally relieved, after three years' litigation, of a claim to pay the plaintiffs a sum of 71,500*l.* which a clerk of theirs had fraudulently drawn from the firm's account at the Bank of England in 1888. The result was warmly welcomed by the banking interest.

Lidderdale, who became a commissioner of the Patriotic Fund in 1893, and held (among other financial offices) the presidency of the council of the Corporation of Foreign Bondholders, died on 26 June 1902 at 55 Montagu Square, London, W., and was buried at Winkfield, near Windsor. He married in 1868 Mary Martha, elder daughter of Wadsworth Dawson Busk of Winkfield, Berkshire (formerly of St. Petersburg), by his wife Elizabeth Thielcke; of his eight children four sons and three daughters survived him.

[Journ. Inst. of Bankers, xxiii. 400–3; Joseph Burn, Stock Exchange Investments in Theory and Practice, 1909, pp. 54–7; Arthur D. Elliot, Life of Viscount Goschen, 1911, ii. 169–75, 283–4; Men and Women of the Time, 1899; Men of Note in Finance and Commerce, 1900–1, p. 139; The Times, 27 June and 23 July 1902; City Press, 6 and 9 May 1891; private information.] C. W.

LINDSAY, JAMES GAVIN (1835–1903), colonel R.E., born on 21 Oct. 1835, was younger son of Colonel Martin Lindsay, C.B. of Dowhill, co. Londonderry, who commanded the 78th highlanders.

Educated at Addiscombe from 1852 to 1854, he obtained a commission in the Madras engineers, becoming second lieutenant on 9 Dec. 1854 and lieutenant on 27 April 1858. He served in the Indian Mutiny campaign in 1858 under Sir George Whitlock, and was present at the affairs of Jheejung and Kabrai, the battle of Banda, and the relief of Kirwi. He was in the reserve at the storming of the heights of Punwarree and received the medal and clasp. He was made second captain on 29 June 1863. Subsequently he entered the railway department as deputy consulting engineer, and in April 1870 he was appointed executive engineer of the first grade for the railway survey of Mysore. In 1872 he undertook as engineer-in-chief the construction of the Northern Bengal railway. His administrative capacity was seen to advantage during the Bengal famine of 1873–4, when he employed on public works large numbers who were out of work owing to the failure of the crops. He was promoted captain on 30 July 1871; major on 5 July 1872; lieut.-colonel on 31 Dec. 1878; and colonel on 31 Dec. 1882.

During the second Afghan war in 1879–1880 he showed his organising power by building for military purposes the Sukkur-Sibi railway, of which he was engineer-in-chief. It was constructed in three months and opened for traffic on 27 Jan. 1880. He also started the Harnai and Gulistan-Karez sections of the Kandahar railway. Afterwards he took part in the march from Quetta to the relief of Kandahar with the force under Major-general Sir Robert Phayre [q. v. Suppl. I] and in the destruction of the towers of Abu Saiad Khan's fort (cf. *Lond. Gaz.* 25 Jan. 1881). He again received the medal.

Returning from the frontier at the close

of the war, he became chief engineer of the Southern Mahratta railway in 1881, and by exercise of his great organising powers and by his gift of obtaining the devoted services of his staff he finished the railway in 1891. The line proved of great service in ameliorating distress during the subsequent famines. Meanwhile in 1885, when Russian intrigues had caused unrest on the north-west frontier, he as engineer-in-chief made arrangements for carrying out the railroad from Sibi up the Bolan towards Quetta. Incapacitated by breaking his arm, he retired from the service in 1891 before the completion of this line. On returning home he became deputy chairman of the Southern Mahratta railway and in 1896 chairman.

Lindsay, an able and trusted officer, was a leader of railway work in India, his name being identified with the establishment of the North Bengal State railway, the Southern Mahratta, the Ruk-Sibi and Bolan railways. His influence over those who worked with him enabled him to carry out fine work rapidly. He died on board the P. & O. steamship Caledonia near Aden on 19 Dec. 1903 on his way to Bombay, where he had intended to visit railway works with which he was associated. He was twice married, but left no issue. Both his wives predeceased him.

[Royal Engineers Journal, Feb. 1904; Engineer, 1 Jan. 1904; The Times, 23 Dec. 1903; Official and Hart's Army Lists; H. B. Hanna's Second Afghan War, vol. iii. 1910.] H. M. V.

LINDSAY, afterwards **LOYD-LINDSAY, ROBERT JAMES**, Baron Wantage (1832–1901), soldier and politician, was younger son of General James Lindsay of the Grenadier guards, a cadet of the family of which the earls of Crawford are the head. His mother was Anne, eldest child of Sir Coutts Trotter, banker and first baronet. His elder brother, Sir Coutts Lindsay (*b.* 1824), inherited in 1837 the baronetcy of his maternal grandfather, Sir Coutts Trotter. Of two sisters, the elder, Margaret, married her cousin, Alexander William Crawford Lindsay, 25th earl of Crawford [q. v.]; the younger, Mary Anne, married Robert Stayner-Holford, of Westonbirt, Gloucestershire.

Born on 16 April 1832, Robert James Lindsay was educated at Eton, and in 1850 received a commission in the Scots guards, then the Scots fusilier guards. Ordered to the Crimea with his regiment in Feb. 1854, he carried the queen's colour at the battle of the Alma as senior subaltern, and distinguished himself by helping to rally the regiment, which had been thrown into momentary confusion by a mistaken order; for this service he was thanked next morning on parade by the Duke of Cambridge. He played a conspicuous part at Inkerman in command of his company, and in the early spring of 1855 he was appointed A.D.C. to General Sir James Simpson [q. v.], which position he vacated in August of the same year to take up the adjutancy of his regiment. On the return of the British troops from the Crimea in July 1856 he received a brevet majority and was made musketry instructor in the recently created school at Hythe. On 24 Feb. 1857 he was gazetted to the Victoria Cross, with a double recommendation for his services at Alma and Inkerman, and he received this decoration from Queen Victoria on 27 June. Early in 1858 he was appointed equerry in the household of Edward VII, then Prince of Wales, which was then constituted for the first time. On 17 Nov. 1858 he was married to Harriet Sarah, only surviving child and heiress of Samuel Jones Loyd, Baron Overstone [q. v.], and he assumed the name of Loyd-Lindsay.

In 1859 he retired from the army with the rank of lieutenant-colonel, and devoted himself to the management and embellishment of the estate of Lockinge near Wantage in Berkshire, which had been settled on him and his wife by Lord Overstone. Loyd-Lindsay was one of the pioneers of the volunteer movement, and took a main part in the raising of the Berkshire corps, of which he was made colonel commandant in 1860, and on the reorganisation of the force in 1888 he became brigadier-general of the home counties brigade. He also held the command, by special request of the Prince of Wales, from 1866 to 1881, of the Honourable Artillery Company. From the first he was a strong advocate of the institution of bodies of mounted infantry among the volunteers, and his enthusiasm for rifle shooting is commemorated by the Loyd-Lindsay prize, which he founded, and which is annually competed for at Bisley. In 1865 he entered the House of Commons as conservative member for Berkshire, and he retained his seat until his elevation to the peerage in 1885; he held the office of financial secretary to the war office from August 1877 to the fall of Lord Beaconsfield's government in April 1880. On the outbreak of the Franco-Prussian war a letter from Loyd-Lindsay in 'The Times' of 22 July 1870 led to the formation of the National Society for Aid to the Sick and Wounded, which developed into the Red Cross Aid Society. Of that body he was chairman from the first, and he visited in this capacity the scene of the war in France, being received at the Prussian headquarters at Versailles, and penetrating into besieged Paris. In July 1876, as commissioner of the society, he was present during the campaign between Turkey and Servia, and his private letters from the front to his father-in-law attracted the attention of Lord Beaconsfield. In the spring of 1900 he was with difficulty prevented, though the hand of death was visibly upon him, from sailing for South Africa to direct the operations of the Red Cross Aid Society during the Boer war. In 1881 he was made K.C.B. on the occasion of the 'coming of age' of the volunteer force, and he was raised to the peerage in July 1885 under the title of Baron Wantage of Lockinge, becoming lord-lieutenant of Berkshire in the same year. In 1891 he was chosen by the secretary for war, Edward Stanhope [q. v.], to preside over a committee appointed to inquire into the length and conditions of service in the army, the recommendations of which were the source of some much-needed ameliorations in the lot of the private soldier. In 1892 Lord Wantage succeeded the duke of Clarence as provincial grand master of the freemasons of Berkshire.

The death of Lord Overstone in 1883 placed a princely fortune at the disposal of Lord Wantage and his wife. The owner of large estates in Berkshire and Northamptonshire, he became one of the leading agriculturists in the country, devoting special attention to the breeding of shire horses and pedigree cattle. A man of lofty personal character, he cherished a strong sense of the duties and responsibilities attendant upon wealth and high station. He was a generous and discriminating patron of art, and assisted by his wife's judgment added largely to the fine collection of pictures formed by Lord Overstone. He was one of the founders and chief supporters of the Reading University College, which since his death has benefited largely by the munificence of Lady Wantage. He died at Lockinge Park, Wantage, and was buried at Ardington, after a long illness, on 10 June 1901; there was no issue of the marriage, and the title became extinct.

Wantage was of singularly fine presence, and his massive head and refined features served more than one artist as models for King Arthur and the ideal 'Happy Warrior'; he was frequently painted, the best portraits being respectively by Mr. W. W. Ouless, R.A., now at Lockinge, and by Sir William Richmond, R.A., painted in 1899, now at Carlton Gardens. A cartoon portrait by 'Spy' appeared in 'Vanity Fair' in 1876.

[Memoir of Lord Wantage by Harriet Lady Wantage, 1907; Edinburgh Review, Jan. 1902; Spectator, 4 Jan. 1908; private information.]

J. B. A.

LINGEN, Sir RALPH ROBERT WHEELER, Baron Lingen (1819–1905), civil servant, born in Birmingham on 19 Feb. 1819, was only son of Thomas Lingen of the old Herefordshire family [see Lingen, Sir Henry] by his wife Ann, eldest daughter of Robert Wheeler of Birmingham. Lingen was sent to Bridgenorth grammar school at the beginning of 1831, the head boy of the school at the time being Osborne Gordon [q. v.]. In May 1837 he won a scholarship at Trinity College, Oxford, and went into residence in the same year. His contemporaries included James Fraser [q. v.], afterwards bishop of Manchester, an old schoolfellow, Frederick (afterwards Archbishop) Temple [q. v. Suppl. II], with whom he was brought much into contact in later years on educational matters, Sir Stafford Northcote, and Froude. One of his closest friends through life was Benjamin Jowett, who, writing to him in 1890, spoke of 'a friendship of more than fifty years' standing.' From school Lingen brought a high reputation for scholarship, which was fully sustained at the university. In 1838 he gained the Ireland scholarship, in 1839 the Hertford. In 1840 he took a first class in the final classical school, and next year became a fellow of Balliol. In 1843 he won the Latin essay, and in 1846 the Eldon scholarship. In 1881 he received the hon. degree of D.C.L., and in 1886 he was made hon. fellow of his old college, Trinity.

Lingen, who became a student at Lincoln's Inn on 4 May 1844, read in chambers until 6 May 1847, when he was called to the bar. Shortly afterwards he entered the education office, then under a committee of the privy council, and in 1849, when he was only 30 years old, became secretary in succession to Sir James Kay-Shuttleworth [q. v.], the first holder of the office. 'This post he filled for twenty years, and during the creation of our elementary education system he was the controlling executive force, if not also the virtual creator of successive codes' (*Ann. Reg.* 1905). While Lingen was serving under Kay-Shuttleworth, the latter remarked to him, in respect of some change, 'Get it done, let the objectors howl' (ABBOTT and CAMPBELL'S *Jowett*, i. 185). As secretary, Lingen acted on this maxim, though his strength lay perhaps not so much in his capacity to make changes as in his ability to negative claims upon the public purse. The growth of educational expenditure led to the appointment in 1858 of a commission on the subject; the Duke of Newcastle served as president and the enquiry lasted nearly three years. At this time Lord Granville was president of the council, and the vice-president, in charge of education, was Robert Lowe, afterwards Lord Sherbrooke [q. v.]. With Lord Granville and more especially with Lowe, whom at a later date he joined at the treasury, Lingen worked with loyalty and in entire harmony (FITZMAURICE'S *Lord Granville*, i. 426; PATCHETT MARTIN'S *Robert Lowe, Viscount Sherbrooke*, ii. 478). The staunch adherence to 'sound principles,' with which Lingen credited Lowe, was equally characteristic of himself, and he proved fearless and tenacious in the face of public criticism.

The Newcastle commission, which reported in March 1861, gave a lead in the direction of payment by results, but the revised code which was first issued at the end of July in that year, though it did not come before parliament until the following February, went far beyond the committee's recommendations. All assistance from state funds to the schools of the country was merged in a capitation grant depending upon the children passing an examination in the three R's. Examination was, according to the opponents of the scheme, substituted for inspection. Financial considerations were paramount in Lowe's and Lingen's minds in drawing up the revised code. 'As I understand the case, you and I [wrote Lowe later] viewed the three R's not only or primarily as the exact amount of instruction which ought to be given, but as an amount of knowledge which could be ascertained thoroughly by examination, and upon which we could safely base the parliamentary grant. It was more a financial than a literary preference . . . One great merit of the scheme, as it seems to me, was that it fixed a clear and definite limit' (*Life of Lord Sherbrooke*, ii. 217). Matthew Arnold reckoned Lingen, while in charge of the education office, as 'one of the best and most faithful of public servants, who saw with apprehension the growth of school grants with the complication attending them, and was inclined to doubt whether government had not sufficiently done its work and the schools might now be trusted to go alone' (HUMPHRY WARD, *Reign of Queen Victoria*, ii. 258).

The publication of the code aroused a storm of criticism, among its opponents being the late secretary, Sir James Kay-Shuttleworth; a compromise was arrived at, but the authors of the scheme were not forgiven, and on 12 April 1864 Lord Robert Cecil, afterwards Lord Salisbury [q. v. Suppl. II], moved a vote of censure in the House of Commons on the education department for alleged mutilation of the inspectors' reports in favour of the views which the revised code had embodied. He was supported among others by W. E. Forster [q. v.], the motion was carried, and Lowe resigned, demanding a committee of inquiry, whose report exonerated the education office and showed the allegations to be groundless. The attack was clearly directed as much against Lingen as against Lowe himself, and it is testimony to Lingen's power and strength of character that he attracted the animosity which is usually reserved for the parliamentary chiefs of a government department. 'If rumour does not much belie him,' wrote the 'Saturday Review' (16 April 1864), 'Mr. Lingen is quite as powerful (as Mr. Lowe) and a good deal more offensive. It is from Mr. Lingen that all the sharp snubbing replies proceed' (PATCHETT MARTIN, ii. 223). It was alleged by his opponents 'that the whole department over which Mr. Lowe and Mr. Lingen presided was in a state of revolt' (p. 221), which no doubt meant that Lingen upheld discipline and kept a strong hand on the public purse strings. The result of the committee of inquiry was necessarily to strengthen his position, which he continued to hold till towards the end of 1869, when he was given the C.B. and promoted to be permanent secretary of the treasury, the highest post in the home civil service.

Gladstone was then prime minister and Lowe chancellor of the exchequer. Lingen was well qualified to preside over the treasury under a government which carried almost aggressively into practice the old liberal doctrine of economy. He was head of the treasury under the first Gladstone government, then under Disraeli's government from 1874 to 1880, and again under Gladstone's government from 1880 to 1885. On the fall of that government he retired. During the conservative tenure of office he had as chancellor of the exchequer his old Oxford contemporary, Sir Stafford

Northcote [q. v.], and that his services were appreciated by both parties in the state is shown by his being given the K.C.B. in 1878. On his retirement in 1885 he was raised to the peerage as Baron Lingen.

At the treasury Lingen, although he was concerned with administrative control rather than with purely financial questions, proved himself an enemy of growing expenditure and a vigilant guardian of the public purse, who neither cared for nor sought popularity. Like Gladstone, with whom he was largely brought into contact, he combined scholarship with business capacity, and brought principle and character to bear upon details in a high degree. After his retirement he was an alderman of the first London County Council (1889–92), and chairman of the finance committee, a most important post in the early days of the council; but he gradually withdrew from public life in consequence of growing deafness. He died at his London house on 22 July 1905, and was buried at Brompton cemetery. In 1852 he married Emma, second daughter of Robert Hutton, at one time M.P. for Dublin. She died on 27 Jan. 1908. There was no issue of the marriage, and the peerage became extinct on Lingen's death.

[Authorities cited; The Times 24 July 1905; Osborne Gordon, a memoir with a selection of his writings, edited by Geo. Marshall, M.A., with sketch of Gordon's school and college life by Lingen, Oxford, 1885; Evelyn Abbott and Lewis Campbell, Life and Letters of Benjamin Jowett, 1897; Patchett Martin's Life and Letters of Robert Lowe, Viscount Sherbrooke, 2 vols 1893; Letters of Matthew Arnold, 1848–88, by G. W. E. Russell, 1901; G. W. Smalley's London Letters, 1890, ii. 192; private information.] C. P. L.

LINLITHGOW, first MARQUIS OF. [See HOPE, JOHN ADRIAN LOUIS (1860–1908), first governor-general of Australia.]

LISTER, ARTHUR (1830–1908), botanist, born at Upton House, Upton, Essex, on 17 April 1830, was youngest son in a family of four sons and three daughters of Joseph Jackson Lister [q. v.]. Joseph, afterwards Lord, Lister (1827–1912) was his elder brother. A member through life of the Society of Friends, Lister was educated at Hitchin. Leaving school at sixteen to engage in business, he soon joined as partner the firm of Messrs. Lister and Beck, wine merchants, in the City of London. He retired from the concern in 1888.

Lister's name is specially identified with painstaking researches on the Mycetozoa. From 1888 onwards he published many valuable memoirs in the 'Annals of Botany,' the 'Journal' of the Linnean Society, and the 'Proceedings' of the Essex Field Club, in reference to the species and life-history of these organisms. His principal work, 'A Monograph of the Mycetozoa' (with 78 plates), issued by the trustees of the British Museum in 1894, is an exhaustive catalogue of the species in the national herbarium. He was also the compiler of the museum's 'Guide to the British Mycetozoa' (1895).

Elected F.L.S. on 3 April 1873, he served on the council (1891–6), and was vice-president (1895–6). He became F.R.S. on 9 June 1898, and was president of the Mycological Society 1906–7. He was a J.P. for Essex. Lister died at Highcliff, Lyme Regis, on 19 July 1908, and was buried at Leytonstone. He married on 2 May 1855 Susanna, daughter of William Tindall of East Dulwich, by whom he had issue three sons and four daughters. The eldest son, Joseph Jackson Lister, was elected F.R.S. in 1900.

[Proc. Linn. Soc. 1909; Bradford Scientific Journal, vol. ii. 1909; Stratford Express, 25 July 1908 (with portrait); Nature, 6 Aug. 1908; The Times, 22 July 1908, 1 Sept. (will).] T. E. J.

LISTER, SAMUEL CUNLIFFE, first BARON MASHAM (1815–1906), inventor, born at Calverly Hall, near Bradford, on 1 Jan. 1815, was the fourth son in a large family of Ellis Cunliffe Lister-Kay (*d.* 1854) of Manningham and Farfield, D.L. and J.P., by the second of three wives, Mary, the daughter of William Kay of Cottingham. The original family name was Cunliffe; the father, Ellis Cunliffe, a wealthy manufacturer and the first M.P. for Bradford after the Reform Bill of 1832, assumed the name of Lister by the will of a cousin, Samuel Lister of Manningham, and the name Kay on the death of William Kay, father of his second wife.

Samuel's paternal grandmother, Mary, daughter of William Thompson, had bequeathed him in 1834 Addingham rectory on condition that he took orders; but, after education at a private school at Balham Hill, Clapham Common, he was placed, at his own request, in the employ of Sands, Turner and Co., merchants, of Liverpool, for whom while still young he made repeated visits to America, gaining an insight into American business methods. In 1837 his father built for him and his elder brother, John, a worsted mill at Manningham, opened in 1838 under the style J. and S. C. Lister. The partnership lasted till 1845, when John retired, becoming his father's heir by the death of the eldest brother, William. From 1845 to 1864 Samuel was successively in partnership with J. Ambler and J. Warburton. He carried on the business alone from 1864 till 1889, when the Manningham Mills became a limited company, of which he remained the chief shareholder and chairman.

Lister devoted great part of his long career to invention, taking out over 150 patents, apart from early inventions not patented. His first invention, in 1841, was a swivel shuttle for inserting a silk figure on a plain ground; his earliest patent, in 1844, a method for fringing shawls. In 1841 also he first turned his attention to mechanical wool-combing, the object of which is to separate the long hairs from the short, the long making better cloth, the short being used for blankets and rough material. Previously such work was done by hand in conditions harmful to the workers. Lister in 1842 bought from George Edmund Donnisthorpe a wool-combing machine, which, like earlier machines patented by Edmund Cartwright [q. v.] in 1790, a French inventor named Heilmann, and others, proved unsatisfactory. Unable to resell it, he determined to improve it, and evolved by 1845 the Lister-Cartwright machine, with which he combed the first pound of Australian wool combed in England. Improvements in the machine itself and subsidiary processes led in 1846 to the 'square-motion' machine, a type to the invention of which Sir Isaac Holden [q. v. Suppl. I] had rival claims, and in 1850 to the 'square-nip' machine. The demand for this type was so great that machines built for 200*l.* were sold for 1200*l.*, and the profit was great. Involved in legal proceedings with the French inventor, Heilmann, who claimed that his patent rights had been infringed, Lister assured his position by purchasing the Heilmann machine, though he made little use of it, and in 1853 he acquired the Noble machine, an improved type invented by one of his own mechanics. For some years he commanded the wool-combing industry. His inventions in this connection made clothing permanently cheaper, brought prosperity to Bradford, and helped to create the Australian wool trade. Ultimately Sir Isaac Holden took Lister's place as chief controller of the industry.

About 1853 Lister devoted himself to further inventions with what seemed to be reckless zeal. In that year he took out nine patents, in 1855 twelve, all for textile processes. In 1855 also he first thought of utilising silk-waste. The stuff, which is produced when the fibre is reeled off the cocoon, was then purchasable at ½*d.* a pound. In 1859 Lister, though ignorant of the silk industry, invented a machine which answered his purpose, yet for years, despite continual improvements, spinners would not look at it. Bad business followed, and costly experiments brought him face to face with ruin. In 1864 his partner, Warburton, fearing bankruptcy, left him, and his loss on the machine reached a total of 250,000*l.* At last, in the latter half of that year, his machine established confidence, and he regained his financial standing. Silk waste, shipped from China, India, Italy, and Japan, and bought at 6*d.* a pound, was converted into silk velvets, carpets, imitation seal-skin, poplins, and other silk products. A second fortune was made. This was increased in 1878, when a velvet loom, bought in Spain in 1867, and developed through eleven years by experiments costing 29,000*l.*, at last began to pay. The old Manningham Mills, burnt down in 1871, had been replaced by new mills on a far larger scale, and by 1889 Lister's annual profit was 250,000*l.* He also invented in 1848, though he made no commercial use of it, a compressed-air brake for railways, anticipating by twenty-one years the Westinghouse patent (1869) in America. His last invention was a process of compressing corn for storing it by way of provision for time of war. In after years decreased profits, due to high American tariffs, made Lister an early advocate of tariff retaliation.

In later life Lister bought for nearly 1,000,000*l.* three adjoining estates in the north, Swinton Park, Jervaulx, and Middleham Castle. He also purchased Ackton Colliery at Featherstone, Yorkshire. Here during the coal strike of 1893 some of the colliery works were destroyed and the military fired on the rioters, causing loss of life. Under Lister's ownership the mine's coal-output multiplied twelve times.

Though a hard man of business, Lister was a generous benefactor to Bradford, presenting the city with, among other gifts, Lister Park. He also readily acknowledged the claims of all who in any way anticipated or helped in his inventions, contributing 47,500*l.* to the Cartwright Memorial Hall and the statue of Cartwright erected in Lister Park, and also commissioning the sculptor, Matthew Noble [q. v.], in 1875, to make two busts of Donnisthorpe, one for his widow, the other to be placed at the entrance to Manningham Mills.

Lister owned pictures by Reynolds, Romney, Gainsborough, and other great painters. He was fond of every kind of sport, a good shot, and devoted to coursing, being a member of the Altcar Club from 1857. Though an ambition to win the Waterloo Cup was never gratified, he owned, among other successful greyhounds, 'Liverpool,' which in 1863 divided the Croxteth Stakes with N. B. Jones's 'Julia Mainwaring,' and 'Chameleon,' which out of seventy-nine courses in public lost only twelve, winning the Altcar Cup in its fourth season, and beating J. Lawton's 'Liberty' for the Waterloo purse in 1872.

Lister's great gifts received public recognition during his lifetime. In 1886 he was awarded the Albert medal of the Society of Arts. In 1887 he was offered, but refused, a baronetcy; and on 15 July 1891 he was made first Baron Masham. He was an hon. LL.D. of Leeds University, deputy-lieutenant and justice of the peace in North and West Ridings, high sheriff of Yorkshire in 1887, and at one time colonel of the West Riding volunteers.

In old age Lister retained all his activity, and in 1905 he published 'Lord Masham's Inventions,' an account of his main labours. He died at Swinton Park on 2 Feb. 1906.

There is a statue (1875) of Lister by Matthew Noble in Lister Park, Bradford, a marble bust by Alfred Drury in the Cartwright Memorial Hall, Bradford, and portraits by Frank Holl [q. v.] and Hugh Carter [q. v. Suppl. II] in the possession of the family.

Lister married on 6 Sept. 1854 Annie (*d.* 1875), eldest daughter of John Dearden of Hollin's Hall, Halifax. He had two sons and five daughters.

[The Engineer (with portrait), and Engineering, 9 Feb. 1906; The Times, 3 Feb. 1906; Burke's Peerage, 1911; Lord Masham's Inventions, 1905; Encyc. Brit. 11th edit.] S. E. F.

LITTLER, Sir RALPH DANIEL MAKINSON (1835–1908), barrister, second son of Robert Littler, minister of the Lady Huntingdon Chapel at Matlock Bath, where he was born on 2 Oct. 1835. His father was cousin of Sir John Hunter Littler [q. v.], and his mother was Sarah, daughter of Daniel Makinson, cotton spinner and borough reeve of Bolton-le-Moors, Lancashire. He was educated at University College School and University College, London, where he graduated B.A. in 1854. Admitted to the Inner Temple on 14 Nov. 1854, he was called to the bar on 6 June 1857. He went the northern and afterwards the north-eastern circuit, but acquiring no large practice, he was appointed a revising barrister for Northumberland in 1868. In 1866 he contributed to a treatise by (Sir) John Henry Fawcett on 'The Court of Referees in Parliament' a chapter on engineering and a digest of the reports made by the referees. Turning his attention to the parliamentary bar, he obtained a position there. His interest in engineering proved useful as counsel for the railway companies, and he became an associate of the Institution of Civil Engineers in 1877. He took silk in 1873. He was made a bencher of the Middle Temple (to which he had been admitted *ad eundem* on 28 April 1870) on 24 Nov. 1882, and was treasurer 1900–1. He was created C.B. in 1890 and was knighted in 1902. From 1889 till death Littler was chairman of the Middlesex sessions. While anxious to assist the young offender to reform, he gave long sentences even for small offences to the habitual criminal, and his judicial action was often adversely criticised in the press. At the time of his death he was taking proceedings for libel against two newspapers, 'Reynolds's Newspaper' and 'Vanity Fair.' He was also chairman of the Middlesex county council from 1889, and in recognition of his long service in the two capacities he was presented in July 1908 with a testimonial amounting to 1300*l.* (*The Times*, 8 July 1908). As a freemason he attained the rank of past deputy grand registrar and past provincial grand senior warden for Middlesex. He died on 23 Nov. 1908 at his residence, 89 Oakwood Court, Kensington, and was buried at Hampstead.

Two portraits commissioned by Littler's fellow justices—one painted by Sir Hubert von Herkomer and the other by Miss B. O. Offer—are in the Guildhall, Westminster.

In addition to various pamphlets and the book already mentioned Littler wrote (with Richard Thomas Tidswell) a volume on 'Practice and Evidence in Cases of Divorce and other Matrimonial Causes' (1860), and (with Mr. Arthur Hutton) 'The Rights and Duties of Justices' (1899).

[The Times, 24 Nov. 1908; Law Journal, 28 Nov. 1908; Foster, Men at the Bar; Brit. Mus. Cat.; private information.]
C. E. A. B.

LIVESEY, Sir GEORGE THOMAS (1834–1908), promoter of labour co-partnership, born at Islington on 8 April 1834, was the eldest of three children of Thomas Livesey (1806-1871) by his wife Ellen Hewes (1806–1886). His father, at first in the employ of the Gas Light and Coke Company, in Brick Lane, Shoreditch, was from 1839 till his death chief clerk and secretary of the South Metropolitan Gas Company, and inaugurated many reforms in the status of the workmen, starting a sick fund in 1842 and a superannuation fund in 1855. A younger brother, Frank (1844–1899), was chief engineer of the same company from 1882 to 1899.

George at the age of fourteen entered the South Metropolitan Gas Company, and gradually became expert in all branches of gas technics and soon devised many improvements in its manufacture and purification. He was made assistant manager in 1857, engineer in 1862, and on his father's death in October 1871 was appointed to the dual post of engineer and secretary. In that position he continued the beneficent policy inaugurated by his father towards the company's workmen, who thenceforth received, for example, an annual week's holiday with double pay. He became in 1882 a director and in 1885 chairman of the board. Under Livesey's long and energetic control the company prospered greatly. From 1862, when he became engineer, to his death in 1908 the annual gas output of the company rose from 350 million to 12,520 million cubic feet. Gradually the company absorbed almost all the London gas companies south of the Thames.

An engineer of great ability and originality, Livesey soon enjoyed a world-wide reputation on matters connected with the gas-industry; the modern design of gas-holders is based upon his models. But it was in the economic organisation of industry that Livesey's chief work was done. After adopting in 1876 the principle of the sliding scale, whereby a decrease or increase in the price of gas to consumers regulated inversely the shareholders' dividends, Livesey proved his growing faith in the community of all industrial interests by admitting in 1886 officers and foremen to a share in the profits along with consumers and shareholders. In 1889, a year of much labour unrest, of which the dockers' strike was the first outcome, Livesey felt that the time was ripe to inaugurate a system which he had long had in his mind of profit-sharing among his workmen. The national union of gas-workers with other trade unions opposed Livesey's policy, to which he resolutely adhered. In the result the unions ordered a strike in December, but after two months Livesey won a costly victory (5 Feb. 1890). Livesey's workmen were ultimately unanimous in favour of his plan, and in spite of opposition from trade unions outside, his system was permanently adopted, with very satisfactory results. In 1894 mere profit-sharing was replaced by the capitalising of the workmen's bonus; the workmen became shareholders, and entered into a well-considered scheme of labour co-partnership. Livesey's proposal for the betterment of industrial conditions culminated, after some struggle with the shareholders, in the election by the employees of two workmen shareholders to seats on the board of directors on 28 Oct. 1898. Two years later the salaried staff elected one of their number to the board. The innovation was fully justified by its success. In 1906 a record bonus of $9\frac{3}{4}$ per cent. was paid on wages and salaries; in 1910 nearly 5500 employees had more than 340,000*l.* invested in the company, and three of the number had seats on the board of ten directors. Subsequently all the London gas companies and a number of provincial gas companies accepted Livesey's industrial system. Thus Livesey by his strong personality, excellent judgment, and organising capacity, did much to promote industrial stability.

Livesey sat on the Labour Commission of 1891–4. He was also a member in 1906 of the war office committee for the employment of ex-soldiers. He was a member of the Institution of Civil Engineers (councillor 1906), of the Institute of Mechanical Engineers, of the Institution of Gas Engineers, and many kindred societies. He was knighted in June 1902, on the coronation of King Edward VII. Livesey was a keen churchman, and contributed generously to religious and philanthropic movements. He erected in 1890, at his own cost, the 'Livesey' library, Old Kent Road, the first public library in Camberwell.

Livesey died at his residence, Shagbrook, Reigate, on 4 Oct. 1908; 7000 working men attended his burial in Nunhead cemetery. He married in 1859 Harriet, daughter of George and Harriet Howard; she died in 1909 without issue.

A portrait of Livesey (in oils) by W. M. Palin, presented in 1890 by the shareholders, is in the board room of the South Metropolitan Gas Co., Old Kent Road; a bronze statue by F. W. Pomeroy, A.R.A., subscribed for by shareholders and employees, was erected in 1910 in front of the company's offices, and was unveiled by Lord Grey on 8 Dec. 1911. The Livesey Memorial Hall, erected in his memory on the premises of the South Suburban Gas Company at Lower Sydenham, was opened on 18 Aug. 1911. In May 1910 the 'Livesey professorship of coal gas and fuel industries' was founded at Leeds University, the endowment fund of 10,700*l.* being raised by subscriptions of gas engineers and manufacturers.

[Engineering, 9 Oct. 1908; Journal of Gas Lighting, 6 Oct. 1908; Gas World, 10 Oct. 1908; The Times, 2 Jan. 1897, 17 Feb. 1898, 5 Oct. 1908; Proc. Inst. Civil Engineers, 1907–8, vol. clxxiv. pt. iv.; Proc. Inst. Mech. Engineers, 1908; Trans. Inst. Gas Engineers, 1908; Edinburgh Review, April 1909; H. D. Lloyd, Labour Co-partnership, New York, 1898, ch. x. pp. 191–213 (summarised in N. P. Gilman's A Dividend to Labour, Boston, 1899, pp. 317–323); David F. Schloss, Methods of Industrial Remuneration, 3rd edit. 1898, pp. 358–9; R. H. I. Palgrave, Dict. of Political Economy, vol. iii., Appendix, 1908, arts. Co-partnership and Profit-sharing; Report on Gain Sharing, Bd. of Trade (Labour Department), c. 7848, 1895; numerous arts. by Livesey in Co-partnership Journal publ. by South Metropolitan Gas Company, vols. i.–v. (1904–8); papers by Livesey in Proc. Brit. Assoc. of Gas Managers, Trans. Gas Institute, and Trans. Inst. Gas Engineers; private information.] W. B. O.

LOATES, THOMAS (1867–1910), jockey, born at Derby on 6 Oct. 1867, was a younger son in the family of eight children of Archibald Loates, an hotel keeper there. Two of his brothers, Charles (generally known as 'Ben') and Samuel (who, after he gave up riding, became a trainer of horses at Newmarket), were also professional jockeys. Tom Loates was apprenticed to Joseph Cannon (training at that time for Lord Rosebery at Primrose House, Newmarket) and was fifteen years of age when, in 1883, he rode his first winner, a filly belonging to Lord Rosebery, at Newmarket. During that season he had five mounts. Next year, when he rode in twenty-two races, he was again successful once only. In 1885 he rode four winners, in 1886 twelve, and in 1887 twenty-one. In 1888 he came into prominence by riding fifty-eight winners out of 288 mounts, and thenceforward held a foremost place. In 1889 he was victorious for the first time in a classic race, winning the Derby on the duke of Portland's Donovan, and in the same year headed the list of jockeys by riding 167 winners out of 674 mounts, a percentage of winners to mounts of 24·77. He again occupied the first place in 1890, and, after a two years' retirement, for a third time in 1893, his most successful season, when, with 222 winning mounts out of 857, he had the fine percentage of 25·90. He was attached to Jewitt's stable at the time, and in that year rode Isinglass for Harry McCalmont when he won the 'Triple Crown' (the Two Thousand Guineas, Derby, and St. Leger), the Ascot cup, and other valuable races. In 1893 he also won the One Thousand Guineas on Sir Blundell Maple's Siffleuse, and rode Red Eyes in the dead-heat with Cypria for the Cesarewitch. Having accepted a retainer from Mr. Leopold de Rothschild, he rode St. Frusquin in 1896, when that horse won the Two Thousand Guineas, and again when it was beaten in the Derby by a neck by the Prince of Wales's (afterwards Edward VII) Persimmon. He rode sixteen seasons, had 7140 mounts, was placed first 1425 times, second 1145 times, and third 920 times. In all, Loates rode eight times in the Two Thousand Guineas. He twice won in that race as well as the One Thousand Guineas and the Derby; he won the St. Leger once. He rode nine times in the Oaks, without winning. For several seasons his chief rival was Mornington Cannon. If not to be classed among the great English jockeys, Loates showed many excellent qualities. A very resourceful rider, he was quick to take advantage of openings that presented themselves during a race.

In 1900 Loates had trouble with his eyes, and relinquishing his licence at the end of that season, retired into private life. For some years he lived at Newmarket, nearly always in bad health. In 1909 he went to live at York Cottage, Aldbourne, near Brighton, where he died in a convulsive fit, on 28 Sept. 1910. He was buried at Brighton. His will was proved for 74,342*l.*, one of the largest fortunes ever accumulated by a jockey. He married in 1909 Isabella Dale, daughter of Charles Simpson Watt of Perth. He left no issue. A cartoon portrait by 'Spy' appeared in 'Vanity Fair' in 1890.

[Sporting Life, 29 Sept. 1910 and 14 Feb. 1911; Sportsman, 29 Sept. 1910; H. Sydenham Dixon, From Gladiateur to Persimmon, p. 186; Ruff's Guide to the Turf, vols. 1883–1900.] E. M.

LOCKEY, CHARLES (1820–1901), tenor vocalist, son of Angel Lockey of Oxford, was born at Thatcham, near Newbury, on 20 March 1820. After being a choir-boy at Magdalen College, Oxford, from 1828 to 1836, he studied singing with Edward Harris at Bath, and afterwards became (in 1842) a pupil of (Sir) George Smart, then the fashionable 'coach' for singers. Lockey sang in the choirs of St. George's chapel, Windsor, and Eton College chapel. In 1843 he became a vicar-choral of St. Paul's Cathedral. His first public appearance in oratorio was in October 1842, when he sang in Rossini's 'Stabat Mater' for the Melophonic Society with excellent success. In 1848 he was appointed a gentleman of the Chapel Royal, and for the next ten years was much in demand at provincial festivals. The most noteworthy incident of his career was his being chosen to create the tenor part at the first production of Mendelssohn's 'Elijah' at Birmingham on 26 Aug. 1846, when he elicited the warmest praises of the composer. On the same occasion he sang at first sight a recitative which Mendelssohn had to vamp up hastily for an anthem of Handel (cf. *Musical Times*, 1846). Lockey retired from public life about 1862 on account of a throat affection, and entered into business at Gravesend and Dover. He nominally held his position at St. Paul's till his death, but for forty-three years Fred Walker, Joseph Barnby, and Edward Lloyd were his deputies. He died on 3 Dec. 1901 at Hastings. On 24 May 1853 he married Martha Williams, an excellent contralto singer, who predeceased him in 1897, leaving one son, John.

[Notice, by son, in Grove's Dictionary; private information.] F. C.

LOFTIE, WILLIAM JOHN (1839–1911), antiquary, born at Tandraghee, co. Armagh, Ireland, on 25 July 1839, was eldest son of John Henry Loftie of Tandraghee by his wife Jane, daughter of William Crozier. After private education he entered Trinity College, Dublin, where he graduated B.A. in 1862. Taking holy orders in 1865, he served curacies at Corsham, Wiltshire (1865–7), St. Mary's, Peckham (1867–8), and St. James's, Westmoreland Street, London (1869–71). He was assistant chaplain at the Chapel Royal, Savoy, from 1871 to 1895, when he retired from clerical work. He was elected F.S.A. in 1872.

Loftie early devoted himself in London to literary and antiquarian study, and wrote voluminously in periodicals. At the outset he contributed frequently to the 'People's Magazine,' of which he became editor in 1872. He also wrote in the 'Guardian' from 1870 to 1876, joined the staff of the 'Saturday Review' in 1874, and of the 'National Observer' in 1894, and occasionally contributed to the 'Quarterly' and other reviews.

During many winter vacations in Egypt he visited out of the way parts of the country, and described one tour in 'A Ride in Egypt from Sioot to Luxor in 1879, with Notes on the Present State and Ancient History of the Nile Valley' (1879). He sent papers on Egyptology to the 'Archæological Journal,' and described a fine collection which he formed of scarabs in an 'Essay of Scarabs: with illustrations by W. Flinders Petrie' (1884).

Loftie at the same time issued many volumes on British art and architecture, editing from 1876 the 'Art at Home' series (twelve volumes). 'Inigo Jones and Wren: or the Rise and Decline of Modern Architecture in England' (4to, 1893) is a volume of merit. He found his chief recreation in exploring unrestored churches, and was one of the founders of the Society for the Protection of Ancient Buildings. It was on his advice that Kate Greenaway [q. v. Suppl. II] devoted her energies solely to the illustration of children's books.

The history of London was, however, Loftie's longest sustained interest. His books on the topic combine much research with an attractive style. The chief of them are his 'Memorials of the Savoy: the Palace, the Hospital, the Chapel' (1878) and 'A History of London' (2 vols. 1883–4; 2nd edit. enlarged, 1884). The latter work was a first attempt to give an accurate yet popular account of recent research in London history; the later periods are treated hurriedly, but the early chapters remain an indispensable authority.

Loftie died on 16 June 1911 at his residence, 3A Sheffield Terrace, Kensington, and was buried in Smeeth churchyard, Kent. He married on 9 March 1865, at St. George's, Hanover Square, Martha Jane, daughter of John Anderson and widow of John Joseph Burnett of Gadgirth, Ayrshire, and had issue one daughter. Mrs. Loftie was the author of 'Forty-six Social Twitters' (16mo, 1878), 'The Dining Room' in 'Art at Home' series (1878), and 'Comfort in the Home' (1895).

Besides the cited works on London, Loftie published: 1. 'In and Out of London: or the Half-Holidays of a Town Clerk,' 1875. 2. 'Round about London,' 12mo, 1877; 6th edit. 1893. 3. 'The Tourists' Guide through London,' 1881. 4. 'London' (in the 'Historic Towns' series), 1886. 5. 'Authorised Guide to the Tower,' 1886; revised edit. 1910. 6. 'Kensington

Picturesque and Historical,' 1888. 7. 'Westminster Abbey,' 1890; abridged edit. 1894. 8. 'London City,' 1891. 9. 'The Inns of Court and Chancery,' 1893; new edit. 1895. 10. 'Whitehall' ('Portfolio' Monographs, No. 16), 1895. 11. 'London Afternoons,' 1901. 12. 'The Colour of London,' illustrated by Yoshio Markino, 1907.

Loftie's books on art include: 13. 'A Plea for Art in the House' 12mo, 1876. 14. 'Catalogue of the Prints and Etchings of Hans Sebald Beham,' 16mo, 1877. 15. 'Lessons in the Art of Illuminating: Examples from Works in the British Museum,' 4to, 1885. 16. 'Landseer and Animal Painting in England,' 1891. 17. 'Reynolds and Children's Portraiture in England,' 1891. 18. 'The Cathedral Churches of England and Wales,' 1892.

Other publications were: 19. 'A Century of Bibles, or the Authorised Version from 1611 to 1711,' 1872. 20. 'Windsor: a Description of the Castle, Park, Town, and Neighbourhood,' folio, 1886.

[The Times, 17 June 1911; Men of the Time, 1899; Allibone's Dict. of Eng. Lit. Suppl.; Crockford's Clerical Directory; private information.] W. B. O.

LOFTUS, Lord AUGUSTUS WILLIAM FREDERICK SPENCER (1817–1904), diplomatist, born at Clifton, Bristol, on 4 Oct. 1817, was fourth son of John Loftus, second marquis of Ely in the peerage of Ireland (1770–1845), by his wife Anna Maria, daughter of Sir Henry Watkin Dashwood, baronet, of Kirtlington Hall, Oxfordshire. His mother was lady of the bedchamber to Queen Adelaide, and his sister-in-law, Jane (daughter of James Joseph Hope-Vere), wife of his brother, John Henry Loftus, third marquis, held the same post in the household of Queen Victoria from 1857 till 1889. Having been privately educated by Thomas Legh Claughton [q. v. Suppl. I], afterwards bishop of St. Albans, Lord Augustus spent several months in 1836–7 abroad with his father, and saw King Louis-Philippe, Talleyrand, and other notabilities. He was early introduced at the court of King William IV, who undertook to 'look after him' in the diplomatic service. His first appointment, which he received from Lord Palmerston, was dated 20 June 1837, the day of the king's death, in the name of his successor, Queen Victoria.

Until 1844 he was unpaid attaché to the British legation at Berlin, at first under Lord William Russell, and from 1841 under John Fane, Lord Burghersh, afterwards eleventh earl of Westmorland [q. v.]. The intimate relations into which Loftus came with the Prussian court lasted, with a few interruptions, till 1871. In 1844 he was appointed paid attaché at Stuttgart. Russia was represented there by Prince Gortchakoff, with whom Loftus formed an enduring intimacy. The British legation was also accredited to Baden; and in the summer months Loftus accompanied his chief to Baden-Baden, where he maintained a summer residence till 1871.

Just before the outbreak of the Revolution of 1848, Loftus, at the request of Sir Stratford Canning (afterwards Viscount Stratford de Redcliffe) [q. v.], joined his special mission to several European courts, when on his way to Constantinople. He thus witnessed many episodes in the revolutionary movement at Berlin, Munich, and Trieste. He persuaded Canning to desist from attempting mediation at Venice between the insurgents and the government. During the Baden revolution of 1849 Loftus remained in Carlsruhe or Baden-Baden. In personal meetings with insurgents he showed himself cool and outspoken; and he witnessed amid personal peril the surrender of Rastatt to the Prince of Prussia, which ended the rebellion.

An appointment in 1852 as secretary of legation at Stuttgart, to reside at Carlsruhe, was quickly followed in February 1853 by promotion to the like post at Berlin. In September 1853 Loftus acted there as chargé d'affaires in the absence of the British minister, Lord Bloomfield [q. v.]. The moment was one of critical importance in European affairs. The Crimean war was threatening, and the direction of the foreign policy of Prussia was passing at the time into the hands of Bismarck, whom Loftus 'always considered to be hostile to England, however much he may have occasionally admired her' (*Reminiscences*, 1st ser. i. 207). With the diplomatic history of the Crimean war Berlin was little concerned. Loftus warmly repudiated the charge brought against him in the memoirs of Count Vitzthum of having obtained by surreptitious means the Russian plan of proposed operations at Inkerman; the plan was supposed to have been communicated by the Tsar to Count Münster, and by him to the King of Prussia (*ibid.* 1st ser. i. 251; Count Vitzthum, *St. Petersburg and London*, 1852–64, i. 90). At the close of the war, Loftus reported as to the British consulates on the German shores of the Baltic, several of which had been denounced for slackness in reporting intelligence, especially as to the entrance into Russia of contraband of war. An appendix descriptive of the state of trade in the districts led to the subsequent foreign office regulation requiring all secretaries of embassies and legations to furnish annual reports on the trade and finance of the countries in which they resided.

In March 1858 Loftus left Berlin to become envoy extraordinary to the Emperor of Austria (MALMESBURY, *Memoirs of an Ex-Minister*, 1885, p. 428). He did all that he could to avert the coming war between Austria and France, but owing to a shy and reserved manner he did not exercise much influence at Vienna. Acting under the successive instructions of the foreign secretaries, Lord Malmesbury [q. v.] and Lord John Russell [q. v.], he made clear to Count Buol, the head of the Austrian government, the sympathy felt in England for the cause of the national liberation of Italy (*Reminiscences*, 1st ser. i. 377). On the outbreak of the war with Italy in April 1859 Loftus continued to keep Austrian statesmen informed of the strength of the English feeling against Austria.

Towards the end of 1860 the legation at Vienna was converted into an embassy, and Loftus was transferred to the legation at Berlin, where the 'Macdonald' affair was causing friction. Loftus was instructed to restore friendly relations, but he was soon immersed in the Schleswig-Holstein crisis, in which at first he frankly expressed personal views which were favourable to Denmark (*ibid.* 1st ser. i. 298 seq.). In September 1862 he met Lord John Russell, his chief, at Gotha during Queen Victoria's visit to Rosenau, and was informed of the intention of the government to raise the legation at Berlin to the rank of an embassy. He was disappointed in the well-grounded expectation that he would himself be immediately named ambassador. The office was conferred on Sir Andrew Buchanan [q. v.], and in January 1863 Loftus began a three years' residence at Munich, where Lord Russell considerately made the mission first class. At Munich he formed the acquaintance of Baron Liebig, the chemist, of whose beneficent inventions he made useful notes.

In February 1866 he returned to Berlin as ambassador. He at once perceived the determination of Prussia to solve her difficulties with Austria by 'blood and iron' (*Reminiscences*, 2nd ser. i. 43). The crisis soon declared itself. Loftus records a midnight talk with Bismarck on 15 June 1866, in the course of which the latter, drawing out his watch, observed that at the present hour 'our troops have entered' the territories of 'Hanover, Saxony and Hesse-Cassel,' and announced his intention, if beaten, to 'fall in the last charge.' On the British declaration of neutrality, which immediately followed the outbreak of the Austro-Prussian war Loftus commented: 'We are, I think, too apt to declare hastily our neutrality, without conditions for future contingencies' (*ibid.* i. 78). In July 1866 Loftus was created a G.C.B. under a special statute of the Order. During his residence at Berlin he was offered, subject to the Queen's permission to accept it, the Order of the Black Eagle, but steadily declined the honour. In March 1868 he was accredited to the North German Confederation; and in November of the same year he was made a privy councillor. Loftus anxiously watched the complications which issued in the Franco-Prussian war of 1870–1, and when the conflict began he was faced by many difficulties. Bismarck took offence at the ready acceptance by the British government of the request that French subjects in Germany should be placed under its protection during the war; averring that 'there is already a feeling that Her Majesty's government have a partial leaning towards France, and this incident will tend to confirm it' (*ibid.* ii. 288). Loftus and his secretary, Henry Dering, managed the complicated system of *solde de captivité* for the 300,000 French prisoners of war in Germany to the satisfaction of those concerned.

Already in 1861 Loftus had sagaciously urged in a communication to Lord Clarendon that England and France should take the initiative in ridding Russia of the obnoxious article in the Treaty of Paris which excluded ships of war from the Black Sea (*ibid.* 1st ser. i. 213). Russia's endeavour to abrogate the article by her sole authority in 1870 produced critical tension with England, which would have been averted had Loftus's advice been taken.

After the creation of the German Empire fresh credentials had to be presented to its sovereign ruler at Berlin. Loftus, who was desirous of a change, was at his own suggestion removed to St. Petersburg in February 1871, where he remained eight years. The moderation and humane disposition of Alexander II, and the marriage of his daughter Marie to the Duke of Edinburgh in January 1874 seemed to favour peace between England and Russia; but the period proved to be one of diplomatic difficulty. Loftus attended the Tsar on his visit to England in 1874; but subsequently disturbances in the Balkan provinces of the Turkish empire brought the Russian and British governments to the verge of war. In October 1876 Loftus was sent to the Crimea to confer with Prince Gortchakoff, the chief Russian minister, then in attendance upon Alexander II at Livadia, as to the basis of a conference for the preservation of peace to be held at Constantinople. But the proposal of a conference was rejected by the Porte; and war between Turkey and Russia broke out in June 1877.

During the progress of the war Loftus was often an object of suspicion to the Russian government (*Reminiscences*, 2nd ser. ii. 230–8). Before the Congress of Berlin met in July 1878, he wisely suggested a preliminary Anglo-Russian understanding; and this, notwithstanding some doubts on the part of de Giers, Russian assistant minister for foreign affairs, was brought about by means of a discussion of the San Stefano Treaty between Count Schouvaloff, Russian ambassador in London, and Lord Salisbury [q. v. Suppl. II], then British foreign secretary. In the course of a leave of absence at Marienbad during 1878 he met, at Baden-Baden, Gortchakoff, now released from the regular conduct of foreign affairs, and they discussed the Russian mission to Kabul, which de Giers had denied at St. Petersburg. The mission was subsequently withdrawn after the Treaty of Berlin.

Early in 1879 Loftus expressed to Lord Salisbury his desire for a more genial climate and less arduous duties. Accordingly Lord Dufferin [q. v. Suppl. II] succeeded him at St. Petersburg, and he was appointed governor of New South Wales and Norfolk island. He held office in Australia from 1879 to 1885. During his first year there he opened the first international exhibition held at Sydney. In 1881 he entertained Princes Albert Edward and George (afterwards King George V) of Wales, while on their tour round the world in the Bacchante. To Loftus's suggestion was due the sending of a New South Wales contingent of troops to the Sudan expedition in 1884.

After his return home he wrote at Linden House, Leatherhead, his 'Diplomatic Reminiscences' (1837-62, 2 vols. 1892; second series, 1862-99, 2 vols. 1894). The personal element in these is small, and the chronological order is not always precise. Without literary pretensions, the reminiscences have few rivals among later English records as a continuous narrative of diplomatic life and letters extending over more than forty years. He died at Englemere Wood Cottage, near Ascot, the house of his sister-in-law, Lady Eden, on 7 March 1904. He was buried at Frimley. Loftus married at Fulham, London, on 9 Aug. 1845, Emma Maria (*d.* 1902), eldest daughter of Admiral Henry Francis Greville, C.B. He had issue three sons and two daughters. His elder daughter, Evelyn Ann Francis, died at Berlin on 28 Sept. 1861, and in her memory her parents began the building of the English church at Baden-Baden, which was completed with the aid of the Empress Augusta and Mrs. Henry Villebois. The eldest son, Henry John, joined the diplomatic service, and the third, Montagu Egerton, M.V.O., is British consul at Cherbourg.

[The Times, 10 March 1904; Loftus's Diplomatic Reminiscences (with portrait); H. Kohl, Anhang zu den Gedanken u. Erinnerungen von Fürst Bismarck, i. 126; Lord Fitzmaurice, Life of Lord Granville, 2 vols. 1905; Memoirs and Letters of Sir Robert Morier, 2 vols. 1911; Count Vitzthum von Eckstädt, London, Gastein und Sadowa, Stuttgart, 1899, 2 series, 1892–4; Burke's Peerage; private information.]

A. W. W.

LOHMANN, GEORGE ALFRED (1865–1901), Surrey cricketer, second of five children of Stewart Lohmann, member of the London Stock Exchange, by his wife Frances Watling, of a Gloucestershire family, was born at Kensington on 2 June 1865. After education at Louvain school, Wandsworth, he was for a time employed in the settlement department of the Stock Exchange. He showed early promise as a cricketer with the Church Institute Club at Wandsworth Common (1876–8); in 1883 he attracted the notice of Walter William Read [q. v. Suppl. II], and turning professional, first appeared for Surrey at the Oval in 1884. As a medium pace bowler he met with great success in 1885, when he took 150 wickets with an average of 14½ runs a wicket. His most brilliant seasons were from 1888 to 1890, when in first-class cricket he took 209, 202, and 220 wickets respectively. Lohmann played in the Gentlemen *v.* Players matches from 1886 to 1896. He visited Australia thrice: in 1886–7 and 1887–8, both times with Shaw and Shrewsbury's teams, and in 1891–2 with Lord Sheffield's team. His best bowling performances were against the Australians at Sydney, where in February 1887 he took

8 wickets for 35 runs, in Jan. 1892, 8 for 58, and in Feb. 1888, with John Briggs [q. v. Suppl. II], he bowled unchanged through both innings. As a bowler he took the Australian cricketer Spofforth as his model, and cultivated great variety of pace; he had a high delivery and a swinging run, and was largely responsible for the cultivation of the off theory. He had no equal as a 'head' bowler, with his command of subtle devices for getting batsmen out, and a unique capacity for fielding his own bowling. As a batsman he was a good hitter, and in May 1889 at the Oval he scored 105 for Surrey *v.* Essex, adding with Sharpe 149 for the last wicket. As a fieldsman his catches at coverslip were marvellous, and gave that position a new importance in first-class cricket. His fine all-round play was largely the means of restoring Surrey to her leading position among the cricketing counties.

Lung trouble in 1892 compelled him to go to South Africa, where he remained in 1893–4. On his return he played for Surrey in 1895 and 1896. In 1896 he finally appeared at Lord's for England *v.* Australians. Differences with the Surrey club in that year led to his retirement from first-class cricket. He subsequently returned to South Africa, and died unmarried of consumption at Matjesfontein on 1 Dec. 1901. There in 1902 the Surrey Cricket Club erected a marble tombstone to his memory.

[The Times, 2 Dec. 1901; Daft's Kings of Cricket (with portrait, p. 233); Wisden's Cricketers' Almanack, 1902, p. liii; W. G. Grace's Cricketing Reminiscences, 1899; Giants of the Game, ed. R. H. Lyttelton, pp. 58–61; Pycroft's Cricket Chat, 1886, pp. 32–5; private information; notes from Mr. P. M. Thornton.] W. B. O.

LONGHURST, WILLIAM HENRY (1819–1904), organist and composer, son of James Longhurst, organ-builder, was born at Lambeth on 6 Oct. 1819. In 1821 his father started business in Canterbury, and Longhurst began his seventy years' service for the cathedral there when he was admitted a chorister in January 1828. He had lessons from the cathedral organist, Highmore Skeats, and afterwards from Skeats's successor, Thomas Evance Jones. In 1836 he was appointed under-master of the choristers, assistant-organist, and lay clerk. He was the thirteenth successful candidate for the fellowship diploma of the College of Organists, founded in 1864. In 1873 he succeeded Jones as organist of Canterbury Cathedral, and held the post until 1898. His services were recognised by the dean and chapter in granting him, on his retirement, his full stipend, together with the use of his house in the Precincts. The degree of Mus.Doc. was conferred on him by the archbishop of Canterbury in 1875. He died at Harbledown, Canterbury, on 17 June 1904.

As a composer Longhurst devoted himself chiefly to church music. His published works include twenty-eight short anthems in three books, and many separate anthems; a morning and evening service in E; a cantata for female voices, 'The Village Fair'; an 'Andante and Tarantella' for violin and piano; many hymn tunes, chants, songs, and short services. An oratorio, 'David and Absalom,' and other works remain in MS.

[Musical Age, Aug. 1904 (with portrait); Grove's Dict. of Music; Brit. Musical Biog.; Musical Times, June 1906.] J. C. H.

LOPES, SIR LOPES MASSEY, third baronet (1818–1908), politician and agriculturist, born at Maristow, Devonshire, on 14 June 1818, was eldest son of Sir Ralph Lopes, second baronet, by his wife Susan Gibbs, eldest daughter of Abraham Ludlow of Heywood House, Wiltshire. [For his descent see LOPES, SIR MANASSEH MASSEH, first baronet.] Henry Charles Lopes, first Baron Ludlow [q. v. Suppl. I], was a younger brother. Educated at Winchester College and at Oriel College, Oxford, where he graduated B.A. in 1842 and proceeded M.A. in 1845, he adopted a political career, and in 1853 unsuccessfully contested in the conservative interest the borough of Westbury, which his father had represented at intervals for twenty years. Elected for that constituency in 1857, he held it until 1868, when he was invited to contest South Devon against Lord Amberley [see RUSSELL, JOHN, VISCOUNT AMBERLEY]. Winning the seat, he kept it until 1885, when owing to ill-health he retired from parliament.

Lopes joined a group of members, including Mr. Henry Chaplin, Albert Pell [q. v. Suppl. II], and Clare Sewell Read [q. v. Suppl. II], who supported farming interests, and was chairman of the agricultural business committee. In several successive sessions he urged the grievance of the increasing burden of local taxation; and on 16 April 1872 he carried against Gladstone's government, by a majority of 100 (259 votes to 159), a resolution declaring that it was unjust to impose taxation for national objects on real property only, and demanding the transfer to the exchequer in whole or in part of the cost of administering justice, police, and lunatics (*Hansard*, ccx. cols. 1131–1403; *The Reminiscences of Albert Pell*, edited by Thomas Mackay, p. 259). Lopes's speech showed mastery of his subject. Relief came to landowners and farmers in the Agricultural Ratings Act, passed by the conservative government in 1879. Lopes was also the author of an amendment to the public health bill of 1873, transferring to the national exchequer the payment of half the salaries of medical officers and inspectors of nuisances. He advocated, but vainly, the division of local rates between owner and occupier.

When Disraeli came into power in 1874 Lopes was appointed civil lord of the admiralty, and retained that office until 1880. He was chairman of a committee which reorganised the admiralty office, and added to the efficiency of the Naval College, Greenwich, by causing the property of the foundation to give a better return. Ill-health compelled him in 1877 to refuse the secretaryship to the treasury in succession to William Henry Smith [q. v.]. On his retirement from parliamentary life in 1885 he was sworn of the privy council, but declined a peerage.

Lopes, who had been high sheriff of Devonshire in 1857, continued to make his influence felt in local politics, though his public appearances were not numerous. From 1888 to 1904 he was an alderman of the Devonshire county council, and in the last year he resigned a directorship of the Great Western railway, which he had held for forty years. A liberal supporter of the charitable institutions of Plymouth, he endowed the South Devon and East Cornwall Hospital to the amount of 14,000*l.*, besides other donations. He was also a large subscriber to Church of England extension and endowment. A scientific farmer of much sagacity, he greatly increased the value of his estates at Maristow. On his accession to the property he had to rebuild throughout, owing to the system of long leases which prevailed; he computed that in forty years he spent 150,000*l.* on improvements. By prize-giving he encouraged the raising of sound stock, and he instituted a pension system for the aged poor.

Lopes died at Maristow on 20 Jan. 1908 after a few days' illness. His portrait by Mr. A. S. Cope, R.A., painted in 1900, is in the committee-room of the South Devon and East Cornwall Hospital, Plymouth. A cartoon portrait by 'Ape' appeared in 'Vanity Fair' in 1875. He married twice: (1) Bertha (*d.* 1872), daughter of John Yarde-Buller, first Lord Churston; (2) Louisa (*d.* 27 April 1908), daughter of Sir Robert W. Newman, first baronet, of Mamhead, Devonshire. He had three children by his first wife, Henry Yarde Buller Lopes, fourth and present baronet, and two daughters.

[The Times and Western Morning News, 21 Jan. 1908; Royal Agricultural Society Journal, 1887, xxiii. 23; Albert Pell's Reminiscences, p. 267.] L. C. S.

LORD, THOMAS (1808–1908), congregational minister, born of poor parents at Olney, Buckinghamshire, on 22 April 1808, was son of John Lord by his wife Hannah Austin. Mainly self-taught, he was apprenticed to a shoemaker. After his family removed to Northampton in 1816 he became a Sunday school scholar and teacher. Having preached in the villages for some years he was ordained for the congregational ministry on 14 Oct. 1834. He filled successively the pastorates of Wollaston, Northamptonshire (1834–45), Brigstock (1845–63), Horncastle (1863–66), Deddington, Oxfordshire (1866–73). In 1873 he accepted a call to Great Bridge, Staffordshire, and resigning that pastorate in 1879 continued to live there, and frequently delivered occasional sermons. In 1899 he returned to Horncastle, where his only daughter, Mrs. Hodgett, resided, and still pursued his career as preacher. His hundredth birthday was celebrated at Horncastle in 1908, when he received a congratulatory telegram from King Edward VII. In his 101st year he occupied the pulpits at Horncastle, Peterborough, Lincoln, Alford, Louth, Wainfleet, Skegness, Boston, Kirkstead, and Tuddenham near Ipswich. When unable to read he recited the scriptures.

He was one of the founders of the Congregational total abstinence association, and a member of the Peace Society from its foundation and of the Liberation Society. He is said to have preached over 10,000 sermons. He died at Horncastle after a few hours' illness on 21 Aug. 1908, aged 100 years and 121 days. He married in 1830 Elizabeth Whimple (*d.* 1889) and left two sons and a daughter.

Lord published in 1859 a memorial sermon on Sir Arthur de Capell Broke of Great Oakley Manor, Northamptonshire, who maintained an open-air mission at Stanion, a neighbouring village. Lord also printed 'Heavenly Light, The Christian's

Desire' (1861), and 'Precept and Practice' (1864).

[Congregational Year Book, 1909, p. 179, with engraving of portrait taken on his 100th birthday; The Times, 22 Aug. 1908; private information.] C. F. S.

LOTBINIÈRE. [See JOLY DE LOTBINIÈRE, SIR HENRY GUSTAVE (1829–1908), lieut.-governor of British Columbia.]

LOVELACE, second EARL OF. [See MILBANKE, RALPH GORDON NOEL KING (1839–1906), author.]

LOVETT, RICHARD (1851–1904), author, son of Richard Deacon Lovett and Annie Godart his wife, was born at Croydon on 5 Jan. 1851. Nine years of boyhood (1858–67) were spent with his parents at Brooklyn in the United States. Leaving school there at an early age, he was employed by a New York publisher. In 1867 he returned to England, and in 1869 entered Cheshunt College, the president of which, Dr. Henry Robert Reynolds [q. v. Suppl. I], powerfully influenced him. He graduated B.A. with honours in philosophy at London University in 1873, and proceeded M.A. in 1874, when he left Cheshunt and was ordained to the ministry of the Countess of Huntingdon's connexion. He began ministerial work at Bishop's Stortford, also acting as assistant master at the school there.

In 1876 he accepted an independent charge as minister of the Countess of Huntingdon church at Rochdale. Lovett was a thoughtful, able preacher, and he made many friends in Lancashire. But his leaning was towards authorship rather than pastoral work, and in 1882 he was appointed book editor of the Religious Tract Society in London. In his new office Lovett's interest in foreign missions grew. He became a director of the London Missionary Society, and wrote the society's history for its centenary, a task which he completed in 1899 after three years of strenuous labour. Interest in missionary work brought him into close touch with James Chalmers of New Guinea [q. v. Suppl. II] and James Gilmour of Mongolia, both of whose lives he wrote. He revisited the United States as a delegate to the œcumenical missionary conference of 1900.

A close student of all that concerned the English printed Bible, and more particularly the works of William Tindale, Lovett, on the foundation of the Rylands library at Manchester, gave advice in regard to the biblical section, and compiled its bibliographical catalogue of Bibles. He formed for himself a good collection of early English Bibles and kindred works, which was dispersed after his death. In 1899, on the retirement of Samuel Gosnell Green [q. v. Suppl. II], Lovett became one of the secretaries of the Religious Tract Society, being specially charged with the Society's continental interests, while retaining much of his former work as book editor. Towards the end of his life the affairs of Cheshunt College, of which he acted as honorary secretary, occasioned him anxiety, and he was among the early workers for the reconstitution of the Congregational Union. Incessant labour impaired his health, and he died suddenly of heart failure at Clapham, London, on 29 Dec. 1904.

He married on 29 April 1879 Annie Hancock, daughter of William Reynolds of Torquay, who, with one son and two daughters, survived him.

Lovett, although warmly attached to his own communion, was far from sectarian in sympathies and outlook. He was a prolific author, contributing freely to periodical literature. His chief books were: 'Norwegian Pictures' (1885); 'Pictures from Holland' (1887); 'Irish Pictures' (1888); 'London Pictures' (1890); 'United States Pictures' (1891); 'James Gilmour of Mongolia' (1892); 'The Printed English Bible' (1895); 'The History of the London Missionary Society' (1899); 'The English Bible in the John Rylands Library' (1899); 'James Chalmers' (1902); and 'Tamate: the Life of James Chalmers for Boys' (1903).

[Christian World, 5 Jan. 1905; private information and personal knowledge.] A. R. B.

LOW, ALEXANDER, LORD LOW (1845–1910), Scottish judge, born on 23 Oct. 1845, was son of James Low of The Laws, Berwickshire, by his wife Jessy, daughter of George Turnbull of Abbey St. Bathans, Berwickshire. After education at Cheltenham College and at St. Andrews University, he proceeded to St. John's College, Cambridge, where he graduated B.A. with a first class in the moral science tripos in 1867. He studied law at Edinburgh University and passed to the Scottish bar on 22 Dec. 1870, joining the Juridical Society on 18 Jan. 1871. For some time he edited the 'Scottish Law Reporter,' and, becoming known as a sound lawyer and judicious pleader, rose steadily. He was a conservative, but never active in politics. In 1889 he was appointed sheriff of the counties of Ross, Cromarty, and Sutherland, and in 1890 was raised to the bench. As a judge he was even more successful than as an advocate. One most important lawsuit which came before him, when sitting as a judge of first instance, was that in which the property of the 'Free Church' was claimed by members of that body who objected to its union with the 'United Presbyterians' (1900). Low decided against this claim, and his judgment was adhered to by the inner house of the court of session, whose decision was, however, reversed on appeal to the House of Lords (1904). He resigned, owing to bad health, in the autumn of 1910, died at The Laws on 14 October of that year, and was buried at Whitsome, Berwickshire. Low, who married (1875) Annie, daughter of the Hon. Lord MacKenzie (Scottish judge), left one son, Mr. James A. Low, C.A., Edinburgh, and two daughters. A portrait of him by Fiddes Watt is at The Laws.

[Scotsman and The Times, 15 Oct. 1910; Roll of the Faculty of Advocates; Records of the Juridical Society.] G. W. T. O.

LOW, Sir ROBERT CUNLIFFE (1838–1911), general, born at Kemback, Fifeshire, on 28 Jan. 1838, was second in a family of four sons and two daughters of Sir John Low [q. v.], general in the Indian army, by his wife Augusta, second daughter of John Talbot Shakespeare, of the East India Company's civil service. His eldest brother is Mr. William Malcolm Low, formerly of the Bengal civil service, who was M.P. for Grantham from 1886 to 1892.

After education at a private school Low received a commission as cornet in the Indian army on 26 Aug. 1854, and was posted to the 4th Bengal cavalry. His first service was in the expedition against the Santals, and won him promotion to lieutenant on 29 Sept. 1855. On the outbreak of the Indian Mutiny his regiment joined the rebels, and Low was subsequently attached to the Delhi field force. He took part in the action at Badli-ke-Serai on 8 June 1857 and in the brilliant victory of John Nicholson [q. v.] at Najafghar (25 Aug.). During the siege and fall of Delhi (20 Sept.) he served as A.D.C. to General (Sir) Archdale Wilson [q. v.], and was mentioned in despatches (*Lond. Gaz.* 15 Dec. 1857). After accompanying Sir Colin Campbell (afterwards Lord Clyde) [q. v.] on his march to the second relief of Lucknow (19 March 1858), Low was appointed brigade-major to the Agra field force, and rendered useful service in the pursuit and capture of rebels in Central India. At the end of the campaign he received the medal with two clasps and the thanks of the governor-general of India.

Promoted captain on 1 Jan. 1862, he commanded a company in the second Yusafzai expedition under Sir Neville Chamberlain [q. v. Suppl. II], and was awarded the medal with clasp. He attained the rank of brevet-major on 15 Feb. 1872 and of lieut.-colonel on 8 Feb. 1878. The following year he commanded the 13th Bengal lancers in the campaign against the Zakha Khel Afridis of the Bazar valley. On the renewal of the Afghan war Low shared in the punitive expedition against the Zaimukhts in Dec. 1879, and was present at the assault of the Zava heights. In June 1880 Sir Frederick (afterwards Lord) Roberts secured his appointment as director of the transport service. Under Low's energetic and intelligent management the transport organisation worked smoothly and efficiently (Lord Roberts, *Forty-one Years in India*, 30th edit. 1898, p. 465); and his services on the march from Kabul to Kandahar were generously acknowledged by the commander-in-chief (*Lond. Gaz.* 7 Nov. 1879, 3 Dec. 1880). He was rewarded with the C.B., the medal with clasp, and the bronze star.

Low became colonel on 8 Feb. 1882, and was nominated brigadier-general in May 1886 to command the second-class district of Bareilly. In the following July he was detached for service in Upper Burma, where a desultory armed resistance was prolonged for two years after the annexation of the country. He was given the command of a brigade at Minbu, and during the period of pacification he was incessantly engaged in arduous guerrilla warfare. He was mentioned in despatches (*Lond. Gaz.* 2 Sept. 1887), received the thanks of the governor-general of India, and was created K.C.B. In 1888 he resumed charge of the Bareilly district, and held the command of the first-class district of Lucknow from 1892 to 1895. Meanwhile he was promoted major-general on 5 Oct. 1893.

His proved capacity for organisation led to his nomination as commander-in-chief of the Chitral relief expedition. Advancing from Nowshera in the spring of 1895 Low concentrated his whole force on the Malakand pass, and on 3 April stormed the heights, which were held by 5000 Pathans. The enemy were again defeated at the Panjkora, and a flying column, despatched by Low under Sir William Gatacre [q. v. Suppl. II], reached Chitral on 15 May after a most arduous passage of the Lowari pass. But meanwhile the garrison had already been relieved by Colonel Kelly's force from Gilgit. It was generally recognised that the favourable issue of the campaign was mainly due to the soundness of Low's dispositions and the rapidity of his movements. For his services he received the thanks of the governor-general of India (*Lond. Gaz.* 15 Nov. 1895). Next year he was promoted lieut.-general and advanced to G.C.B. From 1898 to 1903 he commanded the Bombay army, and after attaining the rank of general in 1900 he retired from the service in 1905. In 1909 he succeeded Sir Hugh Henry Gough [q. v. Suppl. II] as keeper of the crown jewels at the Tower of London. He died there on 6 Aug. 1911, and was buried at Dorchester. He married in 1862 Mary Constance (*d.* 1900), daughter of Captain Taylor of the East India Company's service, and left issue two sons and three daughters. A portrait by Miss E. Taylor, painted in 1907, is in the possession of his eldest son, Lieut.-colonel Robert Balmain Low, D.S.O., of the 9th Bengal lancers. A brass tablet has been erected in the church of St. Peter-ad-Vincula in the Tower of London.

[The Times, 7 Aug. 1911; Sir W. Lee-Warner, Memoirs of Sir Henry Norman, 1908; W. H. Paget, Record of Expeditions against the North-West Frontier Tribes, 1884; H. B. Hanna, The Second Afghan War, vol. iii. 1910; G. J. and F. E. Younghusband, The Relief of Chitral, 1895; Sir George Robertson, Chitral, 1898; private information from Mr. W. M. Low.] G. S. W.

LOWE, Sir DRURY CURZON DRURY-. [See Drury-Lowe, Sir Drury Curzon (1830–1908), lieut.-general.]

LOWRY, HENRY DAWSON (1869–1906), journalist, novelist and poet, eldest son of Thomas Shaw Lowry, bank clerk at Truro, afterwards bank manager at Camborne, by his wife Winifred Dawson of Redhill, was born at Truro on 22 Feb. 1869. He was educated at Queen's College, Taunton, and at Oxford University (unattached), where he graduated in the honour school of chemistry in 1891. His original purpose was to devote himself to chemistry, but his literary predilections gradually conquered his scientific inclinations. After contributing to the 'Cornish Magazine,' he was encouraged by the acceptance, in 1891, of his Cornish stories by W. E. Henley [q. v. Suppl. II] for the 'National Observer.' He continued to write for the 'National Observer' so long as Henley remained editor; and coming to London in 1893, he obtained a connection with the 'Pall Mall Gazette,' joining the staff in 1895. Subsequently he went to 'Black and White.' Early in 1897 he became editor of the 'Ludgate Magazine,' and the same year he joined the staff of the 'Morning Post.' Latterly he also wrote as 'Independent' in the 'Daily Express,' and he was an occasional contributor to other papers. He died, unmarried, at Herne Hill on 21 Oct. 1906. Warm-hearted, impulsive, and sociable, he was popular with his colleagues and friends.

It is in his short stories, dealing with Cornish life, which he thoroughly knew, that Lowry is at his best. Refined, sympathetic, and emotional, he was also a facile writer of tasteful verse. His works are: 1. 'Wreckers and Methodists,' 1893. 2. 'Women's Tragedies,' 1895. 3. 'A Man of Moods,' 1896. 4. 'Make Believe,' 1896. 5. 'The Happy Exile,' 1897. 6. A book of poems, 'The Hundred Windows,' 1904.

[Men and Women of the Time; Morning Post, 23 Oct. 1906; information from Mr. James Greig of the Morning Post and Mr. John Lane, publisher.] T. F. H.

LOWTHER, JAMES (1840–1904), politician and sportsman, born at Swillington House, Leeds, on 1 Dec. 1840, was younger son in a family of two sons and a daughter of Sir Charles Lowther, third baronet (1803–1894), of Swillington House, Leeds, and Wilton Castle, Redcar, by his wife Isabella (*d.* 1887), daughter of Robert Morehead, rector of Easington. His grandfather, Sir John (created a baronet in 1824), was second son of Sir William Lowther [q. v.], who succeeded his cousin as Baron and Viscount Lowther in 1802, and was created Earl of Lonsdale in 1807. James Lowther was educated at Westminster School and at Trinity College, Cambridge, graduating B.A. in 1863 and proceeding M.A. in 1866. He entered at the Inner Temple on 1 Nov. 1861, and was called to the bar on 17 Oct. 1864, but never practised.

His interests were divided between public affairs and sport. Through life he championed the uncompromising principles of conservatism in which he was bred. In 1865 he stood for York city in the conservative interest, and was returned at the head of the poll. His maiden speech was delivered in opposition to the abortive reform bill brought in by Lord Russell's government in 1866. In the following year Lord Derby's government produced their reform bill. This also Lowther opposed, denouncing it as an extremely bad measure and speaking disrespectfully of Disraeli, its framer. But his independent action did not prevent him from being offered nor from accepting the post of parliamentary secretary to the poor law board in Disraeli's first administration (1867–8). At the general election of 1868 he was again returned at the head of the poll at York, and in the following years he took a vigorous part in opposition to Gladstone's government in Parliament. He was never afraid of controversy with the prime minister, and was one of the minority of eleven against 442 in the division on the second reading of the Irish land bill (1870). At the general election of 1874 he was for a third time returned for York, but on this occasion second at the poll. When Disraeli formed his second administration in 1874 he appointed Lowther under-secretary for the colonies. In 1878 Disraeli, now Lord Beaconsfield, gave further proof of his confidence in Lowther by nominating him chief secretary to the lord-lieutenant of Ireland in succession to Sir Michael Hicks Beach. He was sworn of the privy council at the same time. This was Lowther's highest official appointment, and his last. It caused surprise at the time. His character and temperament always appeared to greater advantage in the freedom of opposition than under the restraint of office, and it was remembered to his detriment in Ireland that he had voted against the land bill of 1870. He showed no lack of ability in conducting the business of his department, nor any vacillation in dealing with the spirit of disorder which was becoming manifest in the country. But the duke of Marlborough was lord-lieutenant; Lowther was not in the cabinet, and consequently was not charged with full responsibility. He held the appointment till the general election of 1880, which was fatal alike to the government and himself. He lost his seat at York after a fifteen years' tenure of it. For eight years his efforts to re-enter the House of Commons proved unsuccessful. In Feb. 1881 he stood and was beaten in East Cumberland, and in September in North Lincolnshire. At the general elections of 1885 and 1886 he was defeated in the Louth division of Lincolnshire and the Eskdale division of Cumberland. In 1888 he was returned at a bye-election for the Isle of Thanet, and that constituency he represented until his death. On his return to the house he made a reputation as a rare survival of old toryism. He deplored Ritchie's bill for the establishment of county councils (1888), which he was not in the house in time to resist. He was always an unwavering advocate of protection, and welcomed the prospect, which was realised in his last year in parliament, of tariff reform becoming an accepted principle of his party. He had great knowledge of parliamentary procedure and paid constant attention to forms and precedent. He was popular among all parties in the house. It was his annual habit during his last years in parliament to oppose the sessional order of the house prohibiting lords-lieutenant and peers from taking part in elections, on the ground that it was an anomaly and that it was not rigidly enforced. It continued to be passed until 1910, when it was finally dropped.

Outside politics Lowther had many public interests. He served as alderman of the county council for the North Riding of Yorkshire and on the Tees Fishery Board, and he was one of the founders and sometime president of the Darlington Chamber of Agriculture. On his father's death in 1894 he inherited Wilton Castle, Redcar, and took personal interest in his estate. In 1873 he began to breed horses at Wilton Castle, and registered his colours—blue and yellow hoops, red cap. He trained at Newmarket with Joseph Enoch, who was Lord Zetland's private trainer. Enoch died in 1902, and thenceforth Lowther trained with John Watts and, after Watts's death, with Golding. During these years Lowther won many races, but none of first-rate importance. His first success was in 1877, when he won the Gimcrack Stakes with King Olaf, ridden by Archer. His most successful horse was King Monmouth, who began by winning the Great Yorkshire Handicap in 1885, and ended with a record in 1889 of twenty-three races and upwards of 11,000*l.* in stakes. Lowther's best year was in 1889, when he won fourteen races and over 7000*l.* in stakes. He ran his horses regularly in the north of England, and was a constant attendant at meetings at York, Stockton, and Redcar. Lowther's reputation did not, however, depend only or mainly on his achievements as an owner. He did not bet, and was known to be a good judge of racing and to demand as high a standard of honesty in its conduct as was required in any other occupation. He became a member of the Jockey Club in 1877; he first served as a steward in 1880. When senior steward in 1889 he was appointed a member of a special commission with Prince Soltykoff and Lord March (duke of

Richmond) to inquire into the charge of slander brought by Sir George Chetwynd against Lord Durham in consequence of words uttered in a speech at the Gimcrack Club dinner. Sir George claimed 20,000*l.* damages. The trial was held under unusual circumstances at the Law Courts in London, and attracted much attention. The verdict, which exonerated the plaintiff of the graver charges, laid the damages at one farthing (29 June 1889). In 1903 Lowther's health was obviously failing. He sold his horses and was obliged to forgo active work in parliament. There was no appreciable recovery, and on 12 Sept. 1904 he died at Wilton Castle. His body was cremated at Darlington, and his ashes were deposited in Wilton churchyard.

He was unmarried. At his death Wilton Castle passed to his nephew, Mr. John George Lowther.

His portrait, painted by Mr. E. Miller after his death, is at Wilton Castle. Caricature portraits by 'Spy' appeared in 'Vanity Fair' in 1877 and 1900.

[The Times, Yorkshire Post, Yorkshire Herald, Yorkshire Daily Observer, Sportsman, all of 13 Sept. 1904; Field, 17 Sept. 1904; private sources.] R. L.

LÖWY, ALBERT or ABRAHAM (1816–1908), Hebrew scholar, born on 8 Dec. 1816, at Aussee in Moravia, was the eldest son of thirteen children (seven sons and six daughters) of Leopold Löwy by his wife Katty. His father's family had been settled for several generations at Aussee, and had produced many learned men, after one of whom, Rabbi Abraham Leipnik, author of a MS. account (in Hebrew) of the destruction of the synagogue in Aussee in 1720, Löwy was called. In 1822 his father left Aussee for Friedland, on the border of Silesia, where he owned a brewery. In 1829 Albert left home for schools in Leipzig, Jägendorf, and Olmütz, and eventually attended the University of Vienna. Among his friends and fellow students there were Moritz Steinschneider, the German Hebraist, and Abraham Benisch [q. v.].

Löwy intended, on the completion of his studies, to migrate to Italy, where Jews enjoyed much liberty. But in 1838, with his two friends, Steinschneider and Benisch, he founded 'Die Einheit,' a society of some two hundred students of the Vienna University, most of them Jews, who were endeavouring to promote the welfare of the Jews, one of their aims being to establish colonies in Palestine. In 1840 Löwy visited England to seek support for the scheme, and there he settled for life. A section of the Jewish community in London was at the time seeking to reform both ritual and practice. The reformers seceded from the main body of their co-religionists, opening on 27 Jan. 1842 the West London Synagogue of British Jews, in Burton Street. Löwy became one of the first two ministers; David Woolf Marks [q. v. Suppl. II] was the other. With his colleague he edited the prayer-book of the new congregation, which he served until 1892.

In 1870, under the guidance of Löwy and Benisch, the Anglo-Jewish Association was formed in London to champion the cause of persecuted Jews and to maintain Jewish schools in the Orient. In 1874 Löwy, after attending a Jewish conference at Königsberg on the Russo-Jewish question, was sent by the Anglo-Jewish Association on a secret mission to Russia. His report on the position of the Russian Jews was published as an appendix to the 'Annual Statement of the Anglo-Jewish Association' for 1874. Löwy was secretary of the Anglo-Jewish Association from 1875 until his resignation in 1889. On 31 Oct. 1892 he resigned his ministry at the West London Synagogue, but he took part in public affairs until his death in London on 21 May 1908; he was buried at the Ball's Pond cemetery of the West London Synagogue of British Jews.

Löwy was an accurate and erudite Hebrew scholar. In 1872 Lord Crawford entrusted him with the preparation of a catalogue of his unique collection of Samaritan literature, and in 1891 he completed his chief task as a scholar, the 'Catalogue of Hebraica and Judaica in the Library of the Corporation of the City of London.' He engaged in the controversy over the Moabite stone at the Louvre, the genuineness of which he warmly contested. In 1903 he printed for private circulation 'A Critical Examination of the so-called Moabite Inscription in the Louvre.' Löwy also won repute as a teacher of Hebrew, and among his pupils were Archbishop Tait, the Marquess of Bute, and Thomas Chenery, editor of 'The Times.' He was a member of the council of the Society of Biblical Archæology, and founded in 1870 the Society of Hebrew Literature (continued until 1877), and edited its publications. In 1893 he was made honorary LL.D. of St. Andrews.

In January 1851 Löwy married Gertrude (died January 1879), eldest daughter of Israel Levy Lindenthal, minister of the

New Synagogue, Great St. Helen's, by whom he had nine children. His daughter, Bella Löwy, edited the English translation of Graetz's 'History of the Jews' (5 vols. 1891).

A tablet in the hall of the West London Synagogue, Upper Berkeley Street, W., commemorates Löwy's fifty years' ministry. An oil painting by Solomon J. Solomon, R.A., belongs to his son Ernest.

[Jewish Chronicle, 15 Feb. 1907 and 22 May 1908; private information.] M. E.

LOYD-LINDSAY. [See LINDSAY, ROBERT JAMES, BARON WANTAGE (1832–1901), soldier and politician.]

LUARD, SIR WILLIAM GARNHAM (1820–1910), admiral, born on 7 April 1820 at Witham, Essex, was eldest son in a family of five sons and six daughters of William Wright Luard (1786–1857) of Witham, by his wife Charlotte (*d.* 1875), daughter of Thomas Garnham. The family was of Huguenot origin and had migrated to England on the revocation of the Edict of Nantes, the chief branch settling at Blyborough, Lincolnshire, in 1747. To the elder line belonged Henry Richards Luard [q. v.], John Luard [q. v.], John Dalbiac Luard [q. v.], and Charles Edward Luard (1839–1908) of Ightham, Kent, who served in the royal engineers, becoming colonel in 1886 and major-general in 1887.

William was educated at the Royal Naval College, Portsmouth, and in 1835 was rated midshipman and appointed to the Actæon frigate. By his service as mate during the first China war he earned his commission as lieutenant, dated 4 May 1841. He was present in the squadron under Sir Gordon Bremer at the storming of Fort Taecocktow on 7 Jan. 1841, and at the capture of the Bogue Forts on 25 Feb., when the ships silenced the batteries of Anunghoy and on North Wantong, which the Chinese believed to be impregnable. As a lieutenant he served in the Isis, of 44 guns, on the Cape station, in the Grecian, sloop, on the south-east coast of America, and in April 1848 was appointed first lieutenant of the Hastings, of 72 guns, flagship of Sir Francis Collier [q. v.] in the East Indies. On 29 Sept. 1850 he was promoted to commander, and was appointed on the same day to command the Serpent, of 12 guns, in which he continued during the second Burmese war, taking part in the capture of Rangoon in April 1852, of Pegu in the following June, and other operations. He was mentioned in despatches and received the medal with the clasp for Pegu. He subsequently commanded the Star, sloop, on the south-east coast of America, and from her was in August 1855 moved into the flagship as executive officer. On 11 March 1857 he was promoted to captain. In July 1860 he was appointed flag captain to the commander-in-chief at the Nore, and in November to the screw line-of-battleship Conqueror for the China station. In her he took part in the operations in Japan, superintending the landing of storming parties at the destruction of the Nagato batteries in the Straits of Shimonoseki in Sept. 1864, for which service he received the C.B. and 4th class of the legion of honour. In Jan. 1869 he became flag-captain to the admiral superintendent of naval reserves, and was captain-superintendent of Sheerness dockyard from May 1870 until he was promoted to flag rank on 1 Jan. 1875.

Luard had no employment afloat as a flag-officer, but was superintendent of Malta dockyard from March 1878 until promoted to vice-admiral on 15 June 1879. He afterwards served as chairman of several departmental committees, including that which inquired into the bursting of the Thunderer's gun in Jan. 1879, and in Nov. 1882 succeeded Sir Geoffrey Hornby [q. v. Suppl. I] as president of the Royal Naval College, Greenwich. He reached the rank of admiral on 31 March 1885, and a week later was placed on the retired list under the age clause; but he held his appointment at Greenwich for six months after retirement. He was a deputy-lieutenant and J.P. for Essex, and in 1897 received the K.C.B.

Luard died at Witham on 19 May 1910 as the result of a carriage accident, and was buried at All Saints' Church there.

He married in 1858 Charlotte, third daughter of the Rev. Henry du Cane of Witham, Essex, by whom he had three sons and eight daughters. Commander Herbert du Cane Luard, R.N., is the second surviving son. A portrait painted by Sidney Luard in 1905 is at 'Ivy Chimneys,' Witham.

[The Times, 20 and 25 May 1910; Burke's Landed Gentry.] L. G. C. L.

LUBY, THOMAS CLARKE (1821–1901), Fenian, born in Dublin in 1821 (RUTHERFORD, *Fenian Conspiracy*, i. 46, says 1828), was the son of James Luby, a clergyman of the established Church of Ireland. He attended Mr. Murphy's school, and with a view to entering the church he matriculated at Trinity College, Dublin, as a pensioner and a protestant on 2 July 1839, Thomas Luby [q. v.] being his college tutor. He graduated B.A. in 1845 (*Cat. of Graduates in the University of Dublin*), but falling under the influence of the Young Ireland propaganda he abandoned his theological studies and became an occasional contributor to the 'Nation' newspaper. In 1848 he was involved in the revolutionary movement headed by William Smith O'Brien [q. v.]. With his friend Eugene O'Reilly he planned a rising on the borders of Dublin and Meath, and after the failure of what was known as the Blanchardstown affair (Duffy, *Four Years of Irish Hist.*, pp. 671–5) he went south to join O'Brien in Tipperary. Undismayed by O'Brien's defeat at Ballingarry, he and several others of the party conceived a plan for a fresh rising in 1849. The rising proved a fiasco, but Luby was captured at Cashel and suffered a short imprisonment. After his release he is said (Rutherford) to have gone to Australia, whence he returned to Europe about 1853 to assist James Stephens [q. v. Suppl. II], who was at that time in Paris, in starting a new conspiracy, known subsequently as the Fenian movement. The next two years were spent by Luby in Stephens's company, travelling about Ireland and collecting information as to the state of public opinion. Finding that beneath the apparent tranquillity the embers of the rebellion were still aglow, he was detached to assist Charles Joseph Kickham [q. v.] in the editorship at Dublin of the short-lived revolutionary 'Tribune' newspaper. In 1858 the Irish Republican Brotherhood, a secret society, of which the members were bound together by an oath formulated by Luby (O'Leary, *Fenians and Fenianism*, i. 120), was founded for the purpose of forcibly separating Ireland from England. During Stephens's absence in America in 1858–9 the work of extending the society in Ireland was energetically carried on by Luby. Numerous 'circles' were established by him at this time and the following years in Leinster and Munster. The funeral of Terence Bellew MacManus [q. v.] in 1861, followed closely by the 'Trent' affair, gave a great impetus to the movement, and Luby was despatched by Stephens as special envoy to America in 1863 for the purpose of procuring the necessary funds. He landed at New York on 25 Feb. During the next four months he covered, in his own words, '6000 miles of space,' generally in the company of John O'Mahony [q. v.], the 'head centre' of the Fenian brotherhood, addressing public meetings at Philadelphia, Crawfordsville, Chicago, and other places.

His mission from a pecuniary point of view was not a success, and, returning to Ireland at the end of July, he found the movement languishing there. Luby's energy restored confidence, and the 'Irish People' newspaper was successfully launched at Dublin as the organ of the party. He accepted the post of co-editor along with John O'Leary [q. v. Suppl. II] and Kickham. The paper was rationalistic as well as revolutionary and was therefore boycotted by the catholic clergy. Nevertheless it had a large sale in the east and south of Ireland and was both a pecuniary and literary success. Luby's contributions can generally be distinguished by their inordinate length and sanguine tone (O'Leary, i. 257). The first number of the paper appeared on 28 Nov. 1863, the last was dated 16 Sept. 1865. On the evening of the previous day the offices of the 'Irish People,' in Parliament Street, were raided by the police. Luby, O'Leary, and the principal members of the conspiracy, with the exception of Stephens and Kickham, were arrested nearly at the same time and removed to Richmond prison. The trials commenced at Green Street police court on 27 Nov. before a special commission presided over by Justices Keogh and Fitzgerald. Luby was the first to be called up, and after a three days' trial he was condemned to twenty years' penal servitude for treason-felony. In 1869, by way of protest against the continued misgovernment of Ireland, it was proposed to nominate him a candidate for the representation of county Longford (O'Connor, *Parnell Movement*, p. 219), but John Martin (1812–1875) [q. v.] was substituted and was defeated. By the exertions of the Amnesty Association, presided over by Isaac Butt [q. v.], Luby, with other political prisoners, was restored to liberty in 1871, but not being allowed to return to Ireland he settled with his wife and family in New York, where he devoted himself to journalism. He continued to take a lively interest in Irish affairs and, according to Le Caron (*Secret Service*, pp. 104, 120, 137–8), was one of the founders of the Irish Confederation and a trustee of the so-called skirmishing fund. But he ceased to play an active part in Irish-American politics. Like O'Leary and the Fenians generally, he regarded the home rule movement under Butt and Parnell with distrust, and he was open in his condemnation of the Land League agitation. Apart from his journalistic work he wrote 'The Lives and Times of Illustrious and Representative Irishmen' (New York, 1878; vol. i. only), and in 1882 he contributed a series of articles on the Fenian movement to the New York 'Irish Nation.' O'Leary dedicated his 'Recollections of Fenians and Fenianism' to him in acknowledgment of the assistance rendered by him in its composition; a portrait in vol. i. confirms the description of him in the Dublin papers in 1865 as 'a quiet-faced, pale and somewhat sad-looking man.' He died in New York on 1 Dec. 1901.

[The chief authorities for Luby's Life are his own reminiscences incorporated in O'Leary's Recollections of Fenians and Fenianism. See in addition to the authorities mentioned Report of Proceedings at the Special Commission, Dublin, for trial of Thomas Clarke Luby and others for Treason Felony, Dublin, 1866; The Times, 3 Dec. 1901.] R. D.

LUCKOCK, HERBERT MORTIMER (1833–1909), dean of Lichfield, born on 11 July 1833, at Great Barr, Staffordshire, was second son of the Rev. Thomas George Mortimer Luckock by his wife Harriet, daughter of George Chune of Madeley, Shropshire. Educated at Marlborough College (1848–50) and Shrewsbury School (1850–3), he was elected to a scholarship at Jesus College, Cambridge, and graduated B.A. with a second class in the classical tripos in 1858, proceeding M.A. in 1862 and D.D. in 1879. In 1859, 1861, and 1862 he won the members' prize for an essay. In 1860 he was placed in the first class of the theological examination (middle bachelors), and won the Carus and Scholefield prizes for proficiency in the Greek Testament and the Septuagint. In 1861 he was awarded the Crosse scholarship; in 1862 the Tyrwhitt Hebrew scholarship. Ordained deacon in 1860 by the bishop of Oxford, he worked for a time at Clewer with T. T. Carter [q. v. Suppl. II], and as a private tutor at Eton. He was elected to a fellowship at Jesus College, took priest's orders in 1862, and was appointed to the college living of All Saints, Cambridge. From 1863 to 1865 he was rector of Gayhurst with Stoke-Goldington, Buckinghamshire, but returned to the vicarage of All Saints in 1865, held it for ten years, and completed a new church for the parish. He was select preacher at Cambridge in 1865, 1874, 1875, 1883, 1884, 1892, and 1901.

In 1873 Bishop Woodford of Ely (three volumes of whose sermons he afterwards edited) appointed Luckock one of his examining chaplains, made him hon. canon of Ely in 1874, and entrusted him with the organisation of Ely Theological College. He was principal of the college from 1876 to 1887, exercising a marked influence on the men under his care. He was residentiary canon of Ely from 1875 to 1892, and warden of the society of mission preachers in the diocese. In 1892 he was appointed dean of Lichfield, where he advanced the character of the cathedral services, and promoted the restoration of the fabric, rebuilding at his own cost St. Chad's Chapel. He died at Lichfield on 24 March 1909, and was buried there in the cathedral close.

He married in 1866 Margaret Emma (*d.* 1890), second daughter of Samuel Henry Thompson of Thingwall, Liverpool; of eight children six survived him.

A decided high churchman, though standing aloof from party organisations, a born teacher, unemotional and precise, Luckock exercised a wide influence, largely through his books. The more important were: 1. 'After Death,' an examination of the testimony of primitive times respecting the state of the faithful dead and their relation to the living, 1879; 5th edit. 1886. 2. 'Studies in the History of the Book of Common Prayer,' 1881. 3. 'Footprints of the Son of Man as traced by St. Mark,' 1885; 3rd edit. 1890. 4. 'The Divine Liturgy,' 1889. 5. 'The Intermediate State,' a sequel to 'After Death,' 1890; 2nd edit. 1891. 6. 'The Church in Scotland,' 'National Churches' series, 1892. 7. 'The History of Marriage, Jewish and Christian, in relation to Divorce and certain Forbidden Degrees,' 1894; 2nd edit. 1895. 8. 'Footprints of the Apostles as traced by St. Luke in the Acts,' 1897; 2nd edit. 1905. 9. 'Special Characteristics of the Four Gospels,' 1900. 10. 'Spiritual Difficulties in the Bible and Prayer Book, with Helps to their Solution,' 1905. 11. 'Eucharistic Sacrifice and Intercession for the Departed both consistent with the Teaching of the Book of Common Prayer,' 1907.

[Guardian, 31 March 1909; Church Times, 26 March 1909; Brit. Mus. Cat.; Cambridge University Calendar; private information.]
A. R. B.

LUDLOW, JOHN MALCOLM FORBES (1821–1911), social reformer, second son of Colonel John Ludlow, C.B., of the East India Company's service, by his wife Maria Jane Brown, daughter of Murdoch Brown of Tellicherry, Madras, was born at Nimach in India on 8 March 1821. His father was a younger brother of Edmund Ludlow, head of the

Hill Deverell branch of the Wiltshire family, to which Edmund Ludlow [q. v.] the regicide belonged. Major-general John Ludlow (1801–1882), to whom the suppression of widow-burning in Rajputana was chiefly due, was his first cousin. Ludlow's mother was in Boulogne when war broke out after the peace of Amiens, and was detained with her governess, but allowed to reside in Paris for purposes of education. The intimacy with France thus formed led to her living there after her husband's death, and thus her son witnessed the revolution of 1830. He was sent in 1832 to the Collège Bourbon in Paris, where he obtained many prizes, and graduated bachelier ès lettres of the University of France on 10 July 1837. His education inclined him to wish to become a French subject, but his father's wish that he should be an Englishman determined him to leave France. He paid a visit to Martinique, where he acquired a horror of slavery, and thence returned to England, read law in the chambers of Bellenden Ker, and was called to the bar at Lincoln's Inn on 21 Nov. 1843. He practised as a conveyancer from 1843 to 1874, but had many interests outside the law. One of the first of these was the British India Society, an association for promoting reforms in India. At its inaugural meeting he heard and admired Daniel O'Connell. He attended a conference on the abolition of slavery, where Thomas Clarkson [q. v.] presided, and elsewhere became familiar with the speaking of Lyndhurst and Brougham, and heard Carlyle lecture. In 1841 he visited Manchester, where he became acquainted with John Bright [q. v.], Richard Cobden [q. v.], and R. R. R. Moore [q. v.], and a little later he became a member of the anti-corn law league. In the same year he paid a second visit to the West Indies, and in 1844, after an attack of hæmoptysis, spent a winter in Madeira. When the revolution of 1848 broke out he went to Paris to look after his two surviving sisters, who lived there. He mixed with the populace, was struck by the general good-humour, and made one or two speeches from a chair in the streets. From 1847 onwards he sought in London to interest young men in looking after the poor. He had called upon F. D. Maurice, then chaplain of Lincoln's Inn, in relation to work in his district. On 10 April 1848 Charles Kingsley called upon him on the suggestion of Maurice, and Ludlow went with Kingsley to see the Chartists on their way from Kennington Common. They walked back to the house of Maurice to give him the news that Feargus O'Connor [q. v.] had advised the people to disperse quietly. In May 1848 'Politics for the People' was issued, and this was the starting-point of the Christian Socialist movement. The paper only lasted till July, but the founders, with Charles Mansfield, Archibald Campbell, Frank Penrose, and others, continued to meet, generally in Ludlow's chambers, and a result of their discussions was the foundation of a night school in Little Ormond Yard. Thomas Hughes [q. v. Suppl. I] joined in the work soon after it started, and always continued to be a friend of Ludlow. In the last week of Dec. 1849 these associates, with W. J. Evelyn of Wotton and two working men, met together with the object of encouraging work for mutual profit, and co-operative production in certain trades. Ludlow afterwards presented the Labour Co-partnership Association with a table bearing an inscription on a brass plate recording that it was 'the one used by the Christian Socialists when drawing up the first code of rules for a workmen's co-operative productive society,' in 1848. The table is now at 6 Bloomsbury Square, London. He founded and edited in 1850 a penny weekly paper called the 'Christian Socialist.' Lectures and classes were held in 1853 for working men and women in Castle Street East (by Oxford Street), and Ludlow conducted there a successful French class. From these, and partly in consequence of a resolution of a conference of delegates from co-operative bodies, the Working Men's College in Great Ormond Street arose in November 1854. Ludlow was the chief practical worker in its foundation. He lectured there on law, on English, and on the history of India. These last lectures were published in two volumes in 1858. He wrote a pamphlet in the same year on the war in Oude, and in 1859 'Thoughts on the Policy of the Crown towards India'; several parts of 'Tracts for Priests and People' (1861–2); 'A Sketch of the History of the United States' (1862); 'Woman's Work in the Church' (1865); 'Popular Epics of the Middle Ages' (2 vols. 1865); 'President Lincoln self-portrayed' (1866); 'A Quarter Century of Jamaica Legislation' (1866); 'Progress of the Working Classes' (1867); 'The War of American Independence' (1876), besides articles in 'Good Words' (1863–4), on slavery, in the 'Edinburgh Review,' 'Fraser's' and 'Macmillan's Magazine,' the 'Fortnightly' and the 'Contemporary Review,' and other periodical publications. He contributed biographies to the 'Dictionary of Christian Biography' and to the 'Biographical Dictionary' of the Society for the Diffusion of Useful Knowledge. In 1869 he was active in originating the first co-operative congress in London. He was secretary of the royal commission on friendly and benefit societies from 1870 to 1874. On the death of John Tidd Pratt [q.v.] he was made registrar of friendly societies in England on 27 Feb. 1875, and was appointed to the newly created office of chief registrar of friendly societies on 13 Aug. 1875, an office which he held till 1891 and in which he rendered laborious services to the friendly societies of the United Kingdom, the value of which they several times publicly acknowledged. He was created C.B. on 20 June 1887. After his retirement he still continued to take interest in the causes which he had begun to serve in his youth, and a few days before his death signed a manifesto with Lord Courtney and others in favour of the adoption of co-partnership as a remedy for existing disturbed conditions of labour. He died at 35 Upper Addison Gardens, Kensington, of a pneumonic attack, on 17 Oct. 1911. He married on 20 March 1869 Maria Sarah, youngest daughter of Gordon Forbes of Ham Common. She died without issue in 1910.

Ludlow was a small, slightly built man of gentle manners. He had a finely shaped head and brown eyes of peculiar brightness. He was active in mind and body to the end. The 'constans et perpetua voluntas' of Justinian animated his whole life. He was always ready to sacrifice everything in support of his principles. His reputation for knowledge of the part of the law which interested him was high. He was learned in both men and books, and knew more than a dozen languages. His political creed was based on faith in the people. He was firmly attached to Christianity, and his deep religious feelings were apparent in his speeches, writings, and conduct, and are illustrated in a short account which exists in manuscript of seven great crises in his spiritual and moral life.

[The manuscript notes of Ludlow's reminiscences have been kindly lent for the purpose of this life by his executor, Mr. Urquhart A. Forbes; see also The Times, 19 Oct. 1911; Working Men's College Journal, Nov. 1911 and Feb. and March 1912; Co-Partnership, Sept. and Nov. 1911; Commonwealth, Nov. 1911; Co-operative News, 21 and 28 Oct. 1911; Scottish Co-operator, Oct. 1911; F. Maurice, Life of F. D. Maurice, 2 vols., 4th edit. 1885; Charles Kingsley, Letters and Life, by his wife, 1908; The Working Men's College (1854–1904), 1904 (with portrait, p. 13); Sir Henry Cotton, Indian and Home Memories, 1911; personal knowledge.] N. M.

LUKE, Mrs. JEMIMA (1813–1906), hymn-writer, daughter of Thomas Thompson, was born at Islington, London, on 19 Aug. 1813. Her father was one of the pioneers of the Bible Society, assisted in the formation of the Sunday School Union, and helped to support the first floating chapel for sailors. In 1843 she married Samuel Luke, a congregational minister, who died in 1873. After his death she resided at Newport, Isle of Wight, where she died on 2 Feb. 1906. An ardent nonconformist, she was an active opponent of the Education Act of 1902, and was summoned among the Isle of Wight 'passive resisters' in September 1904—the oldest 'passive resister' in the country.

Mrs. Luke, who edited 'The Missionary Repository,' published among other books: 'The Female Jesuit' (1851), 'A Memoir of Eliza Ann Harris of Clifton' (1859), and 'Early Years of my Life' (1900), an autobiography. She is best known by her children's hymn, 'I think when I read that sweet story of old,' which became classical. It was written in 1841 while Mrs. Luke was travelling in a stage-coach between Wellington and Taunton, prompted by a previous hearing at the Normal Infant School in Gray's Inn Road, London, of the tune associated with it. The hymn was printed first in the 'Sunday School Teachers' Magazine' (1841); in 1853 it appeared, anonymously, in 'The Leeds Hymn Book,' and has since been admitted to all hymn-books of repute.

[Private information; Julian's Dictionary of Hymnology; British Weekly, 8 Feb. 1906; Musical Times, February 1905.] J. C. H.

LUPTON, JOSEPH HIRST (1836–1905), scholar and schoolmaster, born at Wakefield on 15 Jan. 1836, was second son of Joseph Lupton, headmaster of the Greencoat School at Wakefield, Yorkshire, by his wife Mary Hirst, a writer of verse, some of which is included in 'Poems of Three Generations' (privately printed, Chiswick Press, 1910). In the cathedral at Wakefield Lupton placed a stained glass window, by Kempe, in memory of his parents. Educated first at Queen Elizabeth grammar school, Wakefield, and then at Giggleswick school, where he became captain, he was admitted on 3 July 1854 to a sizarship at St. John's College, Cambridge. In 1858 he graduated B.A., being bracketed fifth in the first class in the classical tripos. In June of the same year he was awarded one of the members' prizes for a Latin essay.

After assisting the headmaster of Wakefield grammar school Lupton was appointed, in 1859, second classical master in the City of London school, then in Milk Street, Cheapside. Among his pupils there were Henry Palin Gurney [q. v. Suppl. II] and James Smith Reid, now professor of ancient history at Cambridge. Ordained deacon in 1859 and priest in 1860, he served as curate at St. Paul's church, Avenue Road, N.W., and afterwards to W. Sparrow Simpson, rector of St. Matthew's church, Friday Street, E.C. Proceeding M.A. in 1861, he succeeded to the fellowship at St. John's College, Cambridge, vacated by (Sir) John Eldon Gorst on 19 March 1861. In 1864 he was appointed sur-master and second mathematical master in St. Paul's school, London, then in St. Paul's churchyard, and from 1884 at Hammersmith. He remained sur-master for thirty-five years, the high masters being successively Herbert Kynaston [q. v.] and Frederick William Walker [q. v. Suppl. II]. In 1897 Lupton became Latin master of the upper eighth and honorary librarian. After his retirement in 1899 the Lupton prize (for a knowledge of the Bible and Book of Common Prayer) was founded to commemorate his long service at the school.

Lupton, who had published in 1864 'Wakefield Worthies,' an account of the town and its chief inhabitants, subsequently devoted his leisure to researches into the life and works of Dean Colet, the founder of St. Paul's school. He published for the first time the following works of Colet: 'De Sacramentis Ecclesiæ' (1867) from the MS. in the library of St. Paul's; 'On the Hierarchies of Dionysius' (1869); 'Exposition of St. Paul's Epistle to the Romans' (1873); 'Exposition of St. Paul's First Epistle to the Corinthians' (1874); and 'Letters to Radulphus on the Mosaic Account of the Creation, together with other Treatises' (1876). Each of these volumes (save the first) included a translation and an erudite introduction. There followed, in 1883, a translation of the letters of Erasmus to Jodocus Jonas (1519), containing the lives of Jehan Vitrier, warden of the Franciscan convent at St. Omer, and of Colet. In 1887 Lupton's chief original work, 'The Life of Dean Colet' (new edit. 1909), gave a scholarly presentment of Colet's aims and career.

Lupton was Hulsean lecturer at Cambridge in 1887, became preacher to Gray's Inn in 1890, won the Seatonian prize for a sacred poem at Cambridge in 1897, and proceeded B.D. in 1893 with a thesis on 'The Influence of Dean Colet upon the Reformation of the English Church,' and D.D. in 1896 with a dissertation on Archbishop Wake's 'Project of Union between the Gallican and Anglican Churches (1717–1720).' He died at Earl's Terrace, Kensington, on 15 Dec. 1905, and was buried in Hammersmith cemetery.

Lupton married twice: (1) on 30 Aug. 1864 Mary Ann (*d.* Oct. 1879), daughter of Thomas St. Clair MacDougal, a colleague at the City of London school (by her he had three sons and two daughters); (2) in 1884 Alice (*d.* 1902), daughter of Thomas Lea of Highgate.

In memory of his first wife Lupton erected a drinking fountain at Brook Green and founded the 'Mary Lupton' prizes for French and German at St. Paul's School for Girls. In memory of his second wife he founded the 'Alice Lupton' prizes for music at St. Paul's School for Girls, and for scripture and church history at the North London Collegiate School for Girls.

Lupton, whose speech and writing were both characterised by a graceful dignity, published, besides the works already mentioned: 1. 'St. John of Damascus' in the 'Lives of the Fathers for English Readers' series, 1882. 2. 'An Introduction to Latin Elegiac Verse Composition,' 1885; with key, 1886; reprinted, 1888; with vocabulary, 1893. 3. 'An Introduction to Latin Lyric Verse Composition,' 1888; with a key, 1888. 4. 'Commentary on the First and Second Books of Esdras in the Apocrypha.' He also edited More's 'Utopia' in Latin from the edition of March 1518, and in English from the first edition of 1551; with introduction, notes and facsimiles (1895); and 'Erasmi Concio de Puero Jesu,' a sermon on the Child Jesus by Desiderius Erasmus, in an old English version of unknown authorship, with Introduction and Notes (1901). He was a contributor to this Dictionary, to Smith and Wace's 'Dictionary of Christian Biography,' to Hastings's 'Dictionary of the Bible,' and to 'Notes and Queries.'

[Private information; the Eagle (St. John's College, Cambridge), vol. xxvii. No. 139, March 1906; Pauline (St. Paul's School magazine, published at the school, West Kensington), July 1899, pp. 95–97, and April 1906, pp. 12–19; Res Paulinæ (the eighth half-century of St. Paul's School, 1859–1909), pp. 28, 104, 112, 221, and 223; the Paulina (St. Paul's (Girls) School magazine, Hammersmith), March 1906.]

F. W.

LUSK, Sir ANDREW, first baronet (1810–1909), lord mayor of London, born on 18 Sept. 1810 at Pinmore, in the parish of Barr, Ayrshire, was son of John Lusk, a small farmer and a strict presbyterian, by his wife Margaret, daughter of John Earl, of Knockdolian. Brought up at home in strong religious principles, Lusk was educated at the parish school. At twenty-five he left home with his brother Robert to start a small wholesale grocery business in Greenock, where he gained some experience in journalism. The business, helped by the rapidly expanding sugar trade of Greenock, greatly prospered, and Andrew, leaving it in charge of his brother, came to London. In 1840 he opened premises at 63 Fenchurch Street as a dealer, first in groceries for export (*P.O. London Directory*, 1846) and afterwards in ships' stores. A wide connection was soon built up, and the firm still exists under the style of Andrew Lusk & Co. Lusk was chairman of the Imperial Bank in Lothbury from its establishment in 1862 until its incorporation with the London Joint Stock Bank in 1893, when he joined the board of the last-named bank. He was for many years chairman of the General Life Insurance Company, which under his supervision became prosperous.

In 1857 Lusk was elected common councilman for Aldgate ward, and on 8 Oct. 1863 alderman of that ward; he removed to Bridge Without on 12 Feb. 1892. In 1860–1 he served as sheriff, with alderman Abbiss as his colleague, and on Michaelmas Day 1873 was chosen lord mayor. During his mayoralty he raised a fund of 150,000*l.* for the relief of the Bengal famine; entertained Sir Garnet Wolseley at the Mansion House on his return from the Ashanti campaign; presided at the banquet given by the corporation at Guildhall on 18 May 1874 to the Tsar Alexander II, after his daughter's marriage with the Duke of Edinburgh; and on 4 Aug. 1874 received a baronetcy. As a City magistrate he was shrewd and genial. He was a prominent member of the Fishmongers' Company, then a stronghold of City liberalism, and served as prime warden in 1887. He was twice master of the Company of Spectacle Makers, in 1869–70 and 1870–1. He was also J.P. for Middlesex.

On 13 July 1865 Lusk was elected liberal M.P. for Finsbury, then one of the largest constituencies in London, as a colleague of William McCullagh Torrens [q. v.]. He retained the seat until the division of the constituency in November 1885, when he retired. Lusk was a useful member of committees and a critic of the estimates, but took little part in the debates. After the liberal split on the home rule question in 1886 he became a liberal unionist.

Lusk, who resigned his alderman's gown on 24 Sept. 1895, died in his ninety-ninth year at his residence, 15 Sussex Square, Hyde Park, on 21 June 1909, and was buried in Kensal Green. He had no issue, and the baronetcy became extinct. Of his estate (96,659*l.* 13*s.* 1*d.* in gross value) he left over 15,000*l.* to charitable institutions. He married on 24 Oct. 1848 Elizabeth, daughter of James Potter of Grahamstown, Falkirk, by Jane his wife, daughter of John Wilson of Falkirk. Lady Lusk died on 28 Jan. 1910.

In 1888 a marble bust of Lusk by H. McCarthy was placed at the expense of the corporation in the corridor of the Guildhall council chamber. A portrait by T. MacKinley, painted in 1868, belongs to Sir Andrew's nephew, Mr. Andrew Lusk. A cartoon portrait by 'Spy' appeared in 'Vanity Fair' in 1871.

[J. Ewing Ritchie, Famous City Men, 1884, 75–82; A. B. Beaven's Aldermen of the City of London, 1908; Corporation Pocket Book; Welch, Modern Hist. of the City of London; F. H. McCalmont, Parl. Poll Book; Burke's Peerage; Dod's Parl. Companion, 1884; Men of Note in Finance and Commerce, 1900; Bankers' Mag. 1887, xlvii. 1111–14 (with portrait); The Times, 22 and 25 June, and 5 Aug. 1909; J. R. Dicksee, Cat. of Works of Art belonging to the Corporation, 1893, p. 52; information from Mr. Andrew Lusk.] C. W.

LUTZ, WILHELM MEYER, commonly known as Meyer Lutz (1829–1903), musical composer, was born probably in 1829, though other dates have been given, at Münnerstadt, near Kissingen, Bavaria, where his father was organist and harmony professor at the Schullehrer Anstalt. Meyer Lutz, growing up in a musical atmosphere, became a good pianist in childhood, and at twelve years old played in public with orchestral accompaniment. He afterwards studied at the Gymnasium, Würzburg, passing in due course to the university, and pursued his musical studies under Eisenhofer and Keller. In 1848 he was in England, where he remained for life. He was organist of St. Chad's, Birmingham, and then of St. Ann's, Leeds. He conducted at the Surrey Theatre, London, 1851–5, and went on tours through the provinces with Italian operatic artists and the Pyne-Harrison company. He finally settled in London as conductor at the newly opened Gaiety

Theatre. He held the office from March 1869 till 1896. He was also organist and choirmaster at St. George's Roman catholic cathedral, Southwark. For the church he composed several grand masses, five Magnificats (published), a Tantum Ergo, and much other music. He edited a complete collection of motets for the ecclesiastical year, including some of his own, which were rather trivial. He was far better known by the very many settings of the lightest kind of musical entertainments which he composed for the Gaiety Theatre (cf. for details, the *Sketch*, 18 April 1894). His most successful tune was the 'Pas de Quatre' in 'Faust Up to Date' (1888). In a rather larger style he produced the operettas 'Faust and Marguerite' (1855), 'Blonde and Brunette' (1862), 'Zaida' (1868), 'Miller of Milburg' (1872), 'Legend of the Lys' (1893), and a concert-cantata 'Herne the Hunter' (1863). He left also unpublished works in the more ambitious forms of instrumental music. Lutz died in West Kensington, London, on 31 Jan. 1903. He married in succession two sisters, whose maiden name was Cooke.

[Meyer Lutz's works in Brit. Mus. Library; Grove's Dict. of Music; John Hollingshead's Gaiety Chronicles, 1898 (with portrait); Musical Times, and Musical Herald, March 1903; information from Dr. Hornsey Casson and Mr. Leopold Stern.] H. D.

LYALL, Sir ALFRED COMYN (1835–1911), Anglo-Indian administrator and writer, born on 4 Jan. 1835 at Coulsdon in Surrey, was second son in the family of seven sons and four daughters of the Rev. Alfred Lyall. His father and two uncles, William Rowe Lyall, dean of Canterbury [q. v.], and George Lyall [q. v.], chairman of the East India Company, are already noticed in this Dictionary. Lyall's mother was Mary, daughter of James Broadwood of Lyne, Sussex. His younger brother, Sir James Broadwood Lyall, was at one time lieutenant-governor of the Punjab. The families of both father and mother had originally lived on the Scottish Border; but, on the mother's side, there was also a Swiss derivation from the Tschudis of Glarus, and a Highland from the Stewarts of Appin.

Lyall passed his childhood and early youth with his family first at Godmersham and then at Harbledown in East Kent. He was at Eton as a foundation scholar from 1845 to 1852. In 1853 he obtained a nomination for the Indian civil service at Haileybury College. Arriving in India on 2 Jan. 1856, he held his first appointment at Bulandshahr in the Doab. This district borders on the Meerut and Delhi districts, so that when the Mutiny broke out at Meerut on 10 May 1857 Lyall found himself near the heart of the troubles, and one of his early Indian experiences was that of riding away from his own bungalow, fired at by the rebels. Lyall then joined at Meerut a corps of volunteer cavalry, and fought in several minor actions, in one of which his horse was killed under him. On the day after the storming of Delhi (20 Sept. 1857) he rode into that city with Sir George Campbell [q. v. Suppl. I]. Later in the month he joined Greathed's column, which was charged with clearing the road to Agra, and took part, together with Frederick (afterwards Lord) Roberts and (Sir) Henry Norman [q. v. Suppl. II], in an action near Bulandshahr, where he remained in his civil capacity in a district still seething with disaffection when the column marched on. In 1858 he volunteered for the campaign in Rohilcund and on the borders of Oudh. He was noticed for these services in Lord Canning's Minute of July 1859, and received the Mutiny medal.

Subsequently Lyall rose rapidly in the Indian civil service. He was sent to the Central Provinces in 1864. In 1865 he was appointed to act as commissioner of Nagpur, and in 1867 he was made commissioner of West Berar. His 'Statistical Account or Gazetteer of Berar' was considered to be an excellent piece of work, and was one of the earliest, if not the first, of its kind. In 1873 Lyall was appointed by Lord Northbrook [q. v. Suppl. II] to be home secretary to the government of India, but in 1874 was made the governor-general's agent in Rajputana. Here, amid other work, he carried out important negotiations with native states relative to the salt treaties, and again distinguished himself with his pen by drawing up the 'Statistical Account or Gazetteer of Rajputana.'

In 1878 Lyall was appointed by Lord Lytton [q. v.] to the very important post of foreign secretary to the government of India, and held this office during the critical period of the Afghan war and the subsequent settlement, serving under Lord Lytton until the resignation of that viceroy in April 1880, and then under the Marquis of Ripon [q. v. Suppl. II]. Both viceroys testified to the value of his services. Lyall visited Kabul early in 1880, when the negotiations which led to the accession of Abdurrahman to the Afghan throne were in progress, and was sent by Lord Ripon to Kandahar in the autumn of the same year, when it was a question whether the plan of Lord Lytton to make the province of Kandahar a separate state under the Wali Sher Ali should be maintained or abandoned. On Lyall's report of the Wali's weakness and desire to leave Kandahar, and in view of other considerations of policy, that scheme was abandoned. Lyall was a strong advocate of the retention of Quetta and the Sibi and Pishin districts, a step which, after some delay, was sanctioned by the imperial government. On retiring from the foreign secretaryship in 1881 Lyall wrote a note strongly advocating the policy of a definite treaty with Russia with regard to the position of Afghanistan, a policy which eventually prevailed, and led up to the convention of 1907 between England and Russia, with results beneficial to both Asia and Europe. In recognition of his services he was made C.B. in 1879 and K.C.B. in 1881.

In 1881 Lyall was appointed lieutenant-governor of the North-West Provinces and Oudh, now called the United Provinces, and entered upon that office in April 1882. 'During nearly six years' (in the words of Sir William Hunter) 'he laboured with unflagging devotion for the welfare of the people. It fell to him to introduce Lord Ripon's scheme of local self-government in towns and districts. He carried out, by means of the supreme legislative council, a reform of the land laws in Oudh, for the protection of tenants. . . . Through his influence a separate legislative council was created for what are now the United Provinces, and a new university was founded at Allahabad' (*The Times*, April 1911). These institutions were intended, Lyall wrote 'to be important steps towards a kind of provincial autonomy, which I hold to be one of the cardinal points of our constitutional policy in India.' His administration was also marked by an extension of railways and other public works.

Lyall retired from the Indian civil service in Dec. 1887, and immediately on his return to England was appointed to be a member of the India Council in London. This post he held for the unusually long period of fifteen years, being re-appointed in 1897 by the secretary of state at the close of the ten years which then formed the usual term. In the India Council he adhered consistently to his views both as to Indian foreign policy and as to the extension of local self-government, or devolution of powers, in India. Lord Knutsford, then colonial secretary, offered him in 1888 the governorship of Cape Colony, but this he declined. In Feb. 1887 he had been made a K.C.I.E., and in 1896 he was promoted to be a G.C.I.E. On his retirement from the India office in 1902 he was made a privy councillor by King Edward VII.

During the twenty-three years between his return from India and his death Lyall was one of the best-known and most distinguished men in English society. His many-sided character brought him into relation with statesmen, soldiers, officials, philosophers, historians, and poets, and he was also the friend of many cultivated women; he belonged to such dining clubs as The Club, the Literary Society (1888), Grillion's, as well as to Grant Duff's Breakfast Club (1890), and was also a member of the Athenæum Club. He was one of the earliest members of the Synthetic Society formed in June 1896, with a view to the discussion of religious and philosophic questions. The members included E. S. Talbot, then bishop of Rochester, Mr. Arthur Balfour, Frederic Myers, Lord Rayleigh, R. H. Hutton, Canon Scott Holland, and others. His social position was due to his original genius, his singular personal charm, and to the wide range of his interests. In a rare way he united the faculty for, and experience of, the active life with a philosophic mind tinged by melancholy, a poetic imagination, and the power of vivid and realistic expression. Lyall's cousin, the Countess Martinengo di Cesaresco, in her 'Outdoor Life in Greek and Roman Poets' (1912), recognised in Lyall a counterpart of the Roman public servant, who could both think and do 'He was the only man I have ever known,' the countess writes, 'who gave me the idea that he would have been at home in the Roman world.'

From an early period in his Indian career Lyall had made himself known by occasional poems and by essays upon Indian subjects contributed to the London reviews. Both the poems and the essays revealed an imaginative genius by which he was able to enter into the minds and feelings of men of remote races. The poems after a period of private circulation were published in 1889 in a volume called 'Verses written in India,' and, with some later additions, have gone through several editions. The sixth edition was published in 1905. The best-known and most popular of these poems are, perhaps, those entitled 'The Old Pindaree,' 'Theology in Extremis,' 'The Rajput Chief,' and the 'Meditations of a Hindu Prince.'

Lyall's chief prose essays were collected in 1882 under the title of 'Asiatic Studies,' of which the first essay had appeared in the 'Fortnightly Review' under John (afterwards Viscount) Morley's editorship in Feb. 1872. Hindu religion and custom were here treated by an administrator who had seen how these things actually worked out in real life. 'He drew attention,' it has been said, 'to the necessity of examining Hinduism not only from the evidence in the Sacred Books, but as a popular religion actually existing and undergoing transformation before our eyes.' A second series of the 'Asiatic Studies' was published in 1899. This series included the Rede lecture, 'Natural Religion in India,' which Lyall delivered at Cambridge in 1891, and also three 'letters' originally published under the pseudonym of Vamadeo Shastri. Lyall represented the author to be 'an orthodox Brahmin, versed in the religion and philosophy of his own people, who is chiefly interested in the religious situation, and who surveys from that standpoint the moral and material changes that the English rule is producing in India.' This series also includes an interesting chapter on the relations between history and fable.

'Asiatic Studies' is mainly a masterly contribution to the comparative study of religions. History came next to that study in Lyall's intellectual interests. His 'Rise and Expansion of the British Dominion in India' (1893), which was developed in successive editions, is, like Seeley's 'Expansion of England,' a luminous essay upon determining causes and their results rather than mere narration. Other books were the short life of Warren Hastings (1889) in the 'English Men of Action' series; a critical appreciation in the 'Men of Letters' series (1902) of Tennyson, of whom he had been a friend from 1881 until the poet's death; and the 'Life of the Marquis of Dufferin' (2 vols. 1905). In 1908 he delivered the Ford lectures on Indian history at Oxford, and he gave an address at Oxford in the same year to the 'Congress of Religions' over which he presided. He was a frequent contributor to the 'Edinburgh Review' upon subjects connected with Indian history and philosophy, and with general literature. In recognition of his position as both a distinguished public servant and a man of letters and of philosophic intellect he received the D.C.L. degree from Oxford in 1889 and the LL.D. degree from Cambridge University in 1891; and he became an honorary fellow of King's College, Cambridge in 1893, a fellow of the British Academy in 1902, and a member of the Academic Committee of the Royal Society of Literature in 1910. He was a governor of Dulwich College from 1891, and became chairman of that board in April 1907. He was appointed a trustee of the British Museum in 1911.

In home politics Lyall was a liberal unionist, a strong free trader, and an active opponent of the movement for extending the suffrage to women. In his last years he took an active part in the central administration of the Charity Organisation Society.

Lyall died suddenly from heart disease on 10 April 1911 at Farringford in the Isle of Wight, where he was on a visit to Lord Tennyson, the son of his friend the poet-laureate. He was buried at Harbledown near Canterbury, the home of his boyhood, after a funeral service in the cathedral. He married in 1863 Cora, daughter of P. Cloete of Cape Colony, and left two sons and two daughters.

Of four portraits in oils, one, by J. J. Shannon, R.A. (1890), is at Allahabad University; a second, by Mr. Christopher Williams (1908), is at Dulwich College; and two, respectively by Lady Stanley (1889) and by Lady Walpole (1896), are in Lady Lyall's possession. A memorial tablet is to be affixed in the nave of Canterbury Cathedral.

[The Times, 11 April 1911; Sir C. P. Ilbert in Proc. of British Academy, vol. v. 1911; Dr. G. W. Prothero in Proc. of Academic Committee of Royal Soc. of Lit. 1912; Grant Duff, Notes from a Diary, 1886–1901; private information. A Life by Sir Mortimer Durand is in preparation.] B. H. H.

LYALL, EDNA, pseudonym. [See Bayly, Ada Ellen (1857–1903), novelist.]

LYNE, JOSEPH LEYCESTER, 'Father Ignatius' (1837–1908), preacher, born in Trinity Square in the parish of All Hallows Barking, on 23 Nov. 1837, was the second son of seven children of Francis Lyne, merchant of the City of London, by his wife Louisa Genevieve (*d.* 1877), daughter of George Hanmer Leycester, of White Place, near Maidenhead, Berkshire, who came of the well-known Cheshire family, the Leycesters of Tabley. In October 1847 Lyne entered St. Paul's school under Herbert Kynaston [q. v.]. In 1852, after suffering corporal punishment for a breach of discipline, he was removed, and his education was completed at private schools at Spalding and Worcester. He early developed advanced views of sacramental doctrine. An acquaintance with Bishop Robert Eden [q. v.] procured his admission to Trinity College, Glenalmond. There he studied theology from 1856 to 1858 under William Bright [q. v. Suppl. II], and impressed the warden, John Hannah [q. v.], by his earnest piety. After a year's lay work as catechist at Inverness, where his eccentricity and impatience of discipline brought him into collision with Bishop Eden, Lyne was ordained in 1860, on the express condition that he should remain a deacon, and abstain from preaching for three years. He became curate to George Rundle Prynne [q. v. Suppl. II], vicar of St. Mary's, Plymouth, and soon started a guild for men and boys with himself as superior. Encouraged by Priscilla Lydia Sellon [q. v.], and largely influenced by Edward Bouverie Pusey [q. v.], who presented him with his first monastic habit, he projected a community house on a monastic pattern, when illness interrupted his activities. At Bruges, where he went to recruit, he studied the rule of the Benedictine order. On his return in 1861 he replaced Alexander Heriot Mackonochie [q. v.] as curate of St. George's-in-the-East, London, and took charge of St. Saviour's mission church. Now convinced of his monastic vocation, he assumed the Benedictine habit. The innovation was challenged by Charles Fuge Lowder [q. v.], his ritualist vicar, and after nine months Lyne resigned rather than abandon his monastic dress.

In 1862 Lyne, who henceforth called himself 'Father Ignatius,' issued a pamphlet in favour of the revival of monasticism in the Church of England. This publication excited vehement controversy. Together with one or two kindred spirits Lyne formed at Claydon, near Ipswich, a community, which was frequently menaced by protestant violence. The bishop of Norwich, John Thomas Pelham [q. v.], refused him a licence to preach and subsequently inhibited him. In 1863 Lyne acquired premises at Elm Hill, near Norwich, in face of local opposition. Special masses celebrated for the community by the sympathising vicar in the church of St. Lawrence, Norwich, at Lyne's instigation, produced further conflicts between him and the bishop. Lyne's appeal for support to Bishop Samuel Wilberforce [q. v.] only elicited a recommendation of submission. Forcing himself upon public notice by addressing the Bristol Church Congress of 1863, he could only secure a hearing through the interposition of Bishop Charles John Ellicott [q. v. Suppl. II]. His life at Norwich was varied by a mission in London and by quarrels within the community. In 1866, owing to a flaw in the title-deeds, Lyne found himself dispossessed of his Elm Hill property, and he retired to a house at Chale lent him by Dr. Pusey, who remained his friend. In 1867 he removed to Laleham, and at Feltham near by he started a Benedictine community of Anglican sisters, who subsequently seceded to Rome. From 1866 to 1868 he preached regularly at St. Bartholomew's, Moor Lane, and other City churches. But his conduct was so extravagant that he was suspended by Archibald Campbell Tait [q. v.], bishop of London.

In 1869 Lyne purchased land in the Black mountains, South Wales, and built Llanthony Abbey. The cost of the buildings, which remained incomplete, was defrayed by friends and the pecuniary returns of Lyne's mission preaching. Accounts of miracles and supernatural visitations enhanced the local prestige of the monastery, of which 'Father Ignatius' constituted himself abbot. But the life of the community never ran smoothly. Few joined the order; in many cases those who joined soon fell away. In 1873 Lyne was summoned before Vice-chancellor Sir Richard Malins [q. v.] for detaining Richard Alfred Todd, a ward in chancery, as a novice at Llanthony, and was ordered to release the young man (*The Times*, 26 July 1873). His difficulties were increased by family quarrels. His father, who had persistently opposed his son's extreme Anglican practices, repudiated him altogether after his mother's death in 1877, and publicly denounced his conduct and doctrines.

'Father Ignatius' combined the profession of a cloistered monk with the activities of a wandering friar. When the churches were closed to him, he preached in lecture halls and theatres, and impressed the public everywhere by his eloquence. On 12 Dec. 1872 he appeared as the champion of Christianity in an interesting public encounter with Charles Bradlaugh [q. v.] at the Hall of Science in Old Street, London.

In 1890–1 he made a missionary tour through Canada and the United States. He was cordially invited to preach in the churches of all denominations; but his zeal for heresy-hunting was not appreciated by the episcopal church of America. On his return he initiated a petition to the archbishops and convocation for coercive measures against the higher critics of the scriptures; and at the Birmingham Church Congress of 1893 he denounced Dr. Gore for his essay on inspiration in 'Lux Mundi' (1889). In 1898 he was irregularly admitted to the priesthood by the Syrian Archbishop and Metropolitan for the Old Catholics of America, Mar Timotheus (Joseph Villatte). He died unmarried at Camberley on 16 Oct. 1908, and was buried at Llanthony Abbey. The abbey was left to the few remaining monks, subject to the right of an adopted son, William Leycester Lyne; in 1911 it passed into the hands of the Anglo-Benedictine community of Caldey. A caricature by 'Ape' appeared in 'Vanity Fair' in 1887.

'Father Ignatius's' effort to revive monasticism in England bore little fruit. His persuasive oratory and his courage in the face of persecution were combined with extravagance of conduct and an impatience of authority which rendered him unable to work even with sympathisers. Of versatile talent, Lyne composed sacred music, and wrote a volume of verse, 'The Holy Isle: a legend of Bardsey' (1870); and two monastic tales, 'Brother Placidus, and why he became a Monk' (1870) and 'Leonard Morris, or the Benedictine Novice' (1871). Two volumes of addresses, 'Mission Sermons' (1886; 2nd ed. 1890) and 'Jesus only' (1889), were edited by J. V. Smedley.

[Baroness de Bertouche, Memoir of Father Ignatius, 1904; Father Michael, O.S.B., Father Ignatius in America, 1893; The Times, 17 Oct. 1908; Guardian, 21 Oct.; Church Times, 23 Oct.; Life of Samuel Wilberforce, 1883, iii. 165; Life of Archibald Campbell Tait, 1891, i. 502–5; Charles Bradlaugh, his Life and Work, 1894, i. 342; Edmund Yates, Celebrities at Home, 2nd ser., 1878, p. 207 seq.; The other side, being the award of Augustus A. Leycester in the matter of arbitration between Francis Lyne and Rev. J. L. Lyne (i.e. father and son), 1886.] G. S. W.

LYONS, Sir ALGERNON McLENNAN (1833–1908), admiral of the fleet, born at Bombay on 30 August 1833, was second son of Lieut.-general Humphrey Lyons, Indian army, by his first wife, Eliza Bennett. Admiral Sir Edmund (Lord) Lyons [q. v.] was his uncle. After education at a private school at Twickenham, he entered the navy in 1847. His first service was in the Cambrian, frigate, bearing the broad pennant of Commodore (Sir) James Hanway Plumridge [q. v.] on the East Indies and China station, and on the return of the ship to England in Nov. 1850 Lyons joined the Albion, of 90 guns, in the Mediterranean. In Oct. 1853 he was promoted to mate, and on 28 June 1854 was transferred, as acting lieutenant, to the Firebrand, paddle-frigate, Captain Hyde Parker [q. v.]. The Crimean war was in progress, and Parker, with the Vesuvius and a gunboat, had for some weeks been blockading the mouths of the Danube; on 27 June he had destroyed the Sulineh batteries. He now decided to try to destroy the guard houses and signal stations higher up the river, through which communication was maintained with all the Russian forts, and on 8 July entered the river with the ship's boats, one division of which was commanded by Lyons. The first station reached was defended by a stockade and battery, and the banks were lined by Cossacks, who maintained a heavy fire. Parker fell, shot dead, and the command of the Firebrand's boats devolved on Lyons. The attack was successful, five signal stations being destroyed and the Cossacks dispersed. Lyons was mentioned in despatches for his gallant conduct on this occasion, and, his promotion to lieutenant having already been confirmed, he was noted for future consideration. On 17 Oct. the Firebrand took an important part in the bombardment of Sevastopol, towing into action the Albion, flagship of his uncle, Sir Edmund Lyons. The Albion being set on fire by the batteries was for some time in a dangerous position, and the Firebrand had a difficult task to tow her off. In Dec. 1854 Sir Edmund Lyons became commander-in-chief, and chose his nephew to be his flag-lieutenant. Lyons shared in the further operations in the Black Sea, especially at Kertch and at Kinburn, and was promoted to commander on 9 Aug. 1858 in his uncle's hauling down vacancy.

In 1861–2 Lyons commanded the Racer on the North America station during the civil war, a duty which called for the exercise of tact in the protection of British interests. On 1 Dec. 1862 he was promoted to captain, and, after waiting, as was then customary, for employment, was appointed in Jan. 1867 to command the Charybdis in the Pacific, where he remained till 1871. In Oct. 1872 he was appointed to the Immortalité, frigate, and acted as second in command of the detached squadron. From 1875 he was for three years commodore in charge at Jamaica, and in April 1878 took command of the Monarch on the Mediterranean station, where he served till promoted to rear-admiral on 26 Sept. of that year. In Dec. 1881 Lyons was appointed commander-in-chief in the Pacific, on 27 Oct. 1884 he became vice-admiral, and in Sept. 1886 assumed command of the North America and West Indies station, whence he was recalled home by promotion to admiral on 15 Dec. 1888. For three years from June 1893 he was commander-in-chief at Plymouth; he rose to be admiral of the fleet on 23 Aug. 1897, and reached the age for retirement on 30 Aug. 1903. Lyons was made K.C.B. in 1889, and G.C.B. in June 1897. In Feb. 1895 he was appointed first and principal naval aide-de-camp to Queen Victoria. He died on 9 Feb. 1908 at Kilvrough, Parkmill, Glamorganshire, of which county he was a deputy lieutenant and a J.P.

Lyons married in 1879 Louisa Jane, daughter and heiress of Thomas Penrice of Kilvrough Park, Glamorganshire. She survived him with two sons and two daughters.

[The Times, 10 Feb. 1908.] L. G. C. L.

LYTTELTON, ARTHUR TEMPLE (1852–1903), suffragan bishop of Southampton, born in London on 7 Jan. 1852, was fifth son of George William Lyttelton, fourth Baron Lyttelton [q. v.], by his first wife Mary, daughter of Sir Stephen Richard Glynne (eighth baronet). Educated at Eton and at Trinity College, Cambridge, he was placed in the first class of the moral science tripos in 1873, graduated B.A. in 1874, proceeding M.A. in 1877 and D.D. in 1898. After a year at Cuddesdon Theological College he was ordained deacon in 1876 and priest in 1877. From 1876 to 1879 he served the curacy of St. Mary's, Reading; and from 1879 to 1882 was tutor of Keble College, Oxford, receiving the Oxford M.A. degree in 1879. His work at Keble was designed to prepare him for becoming the first Master of Selwyn College, a similar foundation at Cambridge. In 1882 he was appointed Master of Selwyn at the age of thirty, but its rapid growth was largely due to the confidence he inspired. A pronounced liberal in politics, he helped to draw up in December 1885 a declaration on disestablishment signed by liberal members of the Cambridge senate. He acted as examining chaplain to the bishop of Ripon, Dr. Boyd Carpenter (1884–8), and to Bishop Creighton both at Peterborough (1891–6) and at London (1896–8). In 1891 he was Hulsean lecturer at Cambridge.

Desiring pastoral work, Lyttelton in 1893 left Selwyn College to become vicar of Eccles, Lancashire; he was made rural dean, was elected in 1895 proctor for the clergy in York convocation, and in 1898 was appointed to an honorary canonry of Manchester. He put into practice in his parish some of his liberal views on Church reform. In his youth Lyttelton had been a page at the court of Queen Victoria. In 1895 she made him an hon. chaplain, and in 1896 a chaplain in ordinary. In 1898 the bishop of Winchester, Dr. Randall Davidson, invited him to become his suffragan, and he was consecrated bishop of Southampton in St. Paul's Cathedral on 30 Nov. 1898. In the same year he was made provost of St. Nicholas's College, Lancing, which gave him authority over the southern group of the Woodard schools, and in 1900 he was appointed archdeacon of Winchester. Lyttelton seemed marked out for the highest office in the church, but in 1902 he fell ill of cancer, died at Castle House, Petersfield, on 19 Feb. 1903, and was buried at Hagley, Worcestershire. He married in 1880 Mary Kathleen, daughter of George Clive of Perrystone Court, Herefordshire; she died on 13 Jan. 1907, leaving two sons and a daughter.

Lyttelton gave everywhere the impression of a noble character, strong in a faith held rigidly though without intolerance. In politics a liberal, ecclesiastically a high churchman, he was distinguished by broad general culture but attempted no specialised study. For many years a contributor to periodical literature, and the author of an essay on the Atonement in 'Lux Mundi' (1889), he also published: 'College and University Sermons' (1894) and 'The Place of Miracles in Religion' (1899), being the Hulsean lectures for 1891. After his death there appeared 'Modern Poets of Faith, Doubt and Unbelief, and other Essays' (1904), with portrait.

[Memoir by E. S. Talbot, bishop of Winchester, prefixed to 'Modern Poets of Faith,' &c., 1904; The Times, 21 Feb. 1903; Guardian, 25 Feb. 1903; Church Times, 27 Feb. 1903; Louise Creighton, Life and Letters of Mandell Creighton, 1904, i. 349; Debrett's Peerage, Baronetage and Knightage, ed. 1911.]

A. R. B.

M

MACAN, Sir ARTHUR VERNON (1843-1908), gynæcologist and obstetrician, born at 9 Mountjoy Square, Dublin, on 30 Jan. 1843, was eldest of three sons in a family of five children of John Macan, of a co. Sligo family, who was formerly a scholar of Trinity College, Dublin (1809), and became a leading Q.C. on the Connaught circuit, and first commissioner in bankruptcy in the High Court in Ireland. His mother, Maria Perrin, was daughter of a Liverpool merchant of Huguenot extraction. Of his brothers Jameson John Macan (*d.* 1910) for several years assisted in editing the 'British Gynæcological Journal'; and Reginald Walter Macan became Master of University College, Oxford, in 1906.

Arthur Macan was educated at St. Columba's College (1858–9), co. Dublin, entered Trinity College, Dublin, in 1859, and graduated B.A. in December 1864. He studied medicine in the School of Physic, Trinity College, and at the House of Industry Hospital. He proceeded M.B. and M.Ch. in 1868, and took the degree of M.A.O. in 1877. Having joined a class in London with a view to entering the army medical service, he changed his mind, and early in 1869 he went to Berlin. The next three years were spent in intermittent study abroad, working under Langenbeck, Hebra, Braun, Rokitansky, and others. He varied his work by prolonged walking tours, in one of which he walked from Berlin to Milan and thence to Vienna. A tour through Sicily and Greece brought him to Constantinople. In 1870 he served as volunteer with the Prussian army, and was at Versailles when the royal palace was used as a German military hospital. Returning to Dublin in 1872, he was appointed assistant physician at the Rotunda Lying-in Hospital, and after three years' tenure of this post was elected gynæcologist to the City of Dublin Hospital.

In 1877 he was elected fellow of the King and Queen's College of Physicians, Ireland, and in 1878 was appointed lecturer in midwifery in the Carmichael school of medicine. His chief opportunity came in 1882, when he succeeded Lombe Atthill [q. v. Suppl. II] as master of the Rotunda Hospital, a post which is the prize of the obstetric profession in the United Kingdom.

Macan, who throughout life was a radical and a reformer, found, on his return from abroad, obstetric practice in the United Kingdom far behind that on the Continent. He set himself to introduce the newer methods, in face of the opposition of the profession. He and other progressives were dubbed the 'German band,' and treated with scant courtesy at medical meetings. But their teachings have become the commonplaces of obstetric practice. Macan was one of the earliest in the kingdom to apply Listerian principles in midwifery, and later substituted, as far as possible, aseptic for antiseptic methods. He became master of the Rotunda Hospital at a time when there was serious debate whether the very existence of maternity hospitals was justified, on account of the terrible mortality from puerperal sepsis. Macan vigorously developed the reforms which had been instituted by his predecessor, Atthill. He improved the system of nursing. In the last eighteen months of his term of office there was no death from septic causes. Just before the usual term of seven years at the Rotunda Hospital expired, Macan was elected king's professor of midwifery in the School of Physic, Trinity College, a post which carried with it the duties of obstetric physician and gynæcologist to Sir Patrick Dun's Hospital. From 1902 to 1904 he was president of the Royal College of Physicians of Ireland, and in 1903 he was knighted. He was also president of the British Gynæcological Society (1890), of the section of obstetrics of the Royal Academy of Medicine in Ireland (1886–7; 1899–1901), and of the obstetric section of the British Medical Association in 1887. He was honorary president of the obstetric section of the International Congress of Medicine in Berlin in 1890, and of the Congress of Gynæcology and Obstetrics in Geneva in 1896, and in Amsterdam in 1899. It was by Macan's personal force of character that he mainly influenced the development of obstetrics in the United Kingdom. Although he wrote no book, he published between 1872 and 1908 no fewer than seventy reports and communications from his pen in the 'Dublin Journal of Medical Science' alone. Many others appeared elsewhere.

He died on 26 Sept. 1908 of heart failure at his residence, 53 Merrion Square, Dublin. He was buried in Mount Jerome cemetery, Dublin. Of robust physique, he was fond of outdoor sports. A portrait in oils by Miss Sara Purser, R.H.A., is in the possession of his son, Mr. A. V. Macan.

Macan married, on 30 Jan. 1877, Mary Agnes, daughter of John Bradshaw Wanklyn, of Cheam, Surrey. She died in 1886 of puerperal sepsis, the disease which few had done more to combat than Macan. There were three sons and four daughters of the marriage.

[Journal of Obstetrics and Gynæcology of the British Empire, Nov. 1908; Dublin Journal of Medical Science (by Sir J. W. Moore), Nov. 1908; Todd's Cat. of Graduates in Dublin Univ.; MS. Entrance Book, Trin. Coll., Dublin; private information; personal knowledge.] R. J. R.

McARTHUR, CHARLES (1844–1910), politician and writer on marine insurance, born at Kingsdown, Bristol, in May 1844, was son of Charles McArthur of Port Glasgow by his wife Harriet. Educated at Bristol grammar school, McArthur entered the office of North, Ewing & Co., underwriters and marine insurance brokers, Liverpool, in 1860. He made his mark in his profession by the publication in 1871 of 'The Policy of Marine Insurance popularly explained, with a Chapter on Occasional Clauses' (2nd edit. 1875). In 1874 he went into business on his own account as an average adjuster, with Mr. Court as partner, and established the firm of Court & McArthur of Exchange Buildings, Liverpool, and Cornhill, London. In 1885 he published 'The Contract of Marine Insurance' (2nd edit. revised, 1890). McArthur became chairman of the Association of Average Adjusters of Great Britain, and was made chairman of the commercial law committee of the Liverpool Chamber of Commerce in 1887, vice-president of the chamber in 1888, and president from 1892 to 1896. In 1892 he read an important paper on bills of lading reform at the international conference at Genoa on the codification and reform of the law of nations. In 1895 he advised the government in regard to the marine insurance bill and the Companies Amendment Act. His services were acknowledged by the presentation at Liverpool on 8 Sept. 1896 of a service of plate.

McArthur entered parliament in Nov. 1897 as liberal-unionist member for the Exchange division of Liverpool, after a close contest with Mr. Russell Rea. He was re-elected by an increased majority in 1900, but lost the seat in 1906, when he stood as a conservative free-trader. He was returned for another division of Liverpool (Kirkdale) in September 1907, was re-elected in January 1910, and retained the seat till his death. In the House of Commons he was an active champion of shipping and commercial interests. Though a convinced free trader, he advocated subsidies to British shipping companies to enable them to meet foreign state-aided competition, and the meeting of bounties by bounties. He also urged the improvement of the status of the merchant service by the establishment of training-ships on the coasts and a pension scheme for sailors, and the transference of the cost of lighthouses and beacons to the board of trade. He was on the committee of 1904–5 which reported in favour of the application of British statutory regulations to foreign ships in British ports. As a strong evangelical, McArthur played in parliament a persistent, if not very effective, part in church questions. In May 1899 he moved unsuccessfully the second reading of a bill 'to secure a prompt and inexpensive means' for settling ritual disputes. He proposed to overrule the episcopal veto on prosecutions by a lay court and to substitute inhibition for imprisonment in case of contumacy. He resisted the appointment of the royal commission on ecclesiastical discipline in 1904, but in 1908 he introduced the ecclesiastical disorders bill, in which he claimed to give effect to the commission's report. To the bill for amending the royal accession declaration (carried in 1909) he offered a stout resistance.

McArthur died rather suddenly at his London residence on 3 July 1910, and was buried at Wallasey cemetery, Liverpool. His wife Jessie, youngest daughter of John Makin, survived him without issue.

Besides his works on marine insurance, McArthur published 'The Evidences of Natural Religion and the Truths established thereby' (1880).

[The Times, 4, 7 July 1910; Liverpool Daily Post, 4 July (with portrait); Hansard's Parliamentary Debates; Who's Who, 1910; Brit. Mus. Cat.] G. Le G. N.

MACARTNEY, Sir SAMUEL HALLIDAY (1833–1906), official in the Chinese service, born near Castle Douglas on 24 May 1833, was youngest son of Robert Macartney of Dundrennan House, Kirkcudbrightshire, and Elizabeth, daughter of Ebenezer Halliday of Slagnaw. He belonged to the Macartneys of Auchinleck in Kirkcudbrightshire, to which Earl Macartney [q. v.], ambassador to China in 1792–93, also belonged. Educated at the Castle Douglas Academy, Halliday, at the age of fifteen, went as a clerk into a merchant's office in Liverpool, and in 1852 entered Edinburgh University in order to study medicine. In 1855, while still a medical student, he joined the medical staff of the Anglo-Turkish contingent in the Crimean war, and was with them at the occupation of Kertch. He graduated M.D. at Edinburgh in 1858, and, joining the army medical department, was in Sept. of that year gazetted to the 99th regiment as third assistant surgeon. The regiment was under orders for India, in consequence of the Mutiny, and he went with it to Calcutta, where it remained through 1859. Early in 1860 it was ordered to China, and he served in the Chinese war of that year, taking part in the advance on Pekin. Thus began his connection with China which lasted through life. From Dec. 1860 he was stationed for fifteen months with part of the regiment in Canton, and at the end of February 1862 he went with two companies to Shanghai, which was then threatened by the Taipings. He served under General (Sir) Charles William Dunbar Staveley [q. v.], but seeking a wider career than that of an army doctor, in October 1862 he resigned the army medical service (being gazetted out in January 1863), in order to join the Chinese service. In Nov. 1862 he became military secretary to Burgevine, when the latter succeeded Ward in command of the 'Ever Victorious Army.' On Burgevine's dismissal in Jan. 1863, Macartney was spoken of as a possible successor, and at a later date, when 'Chinese' Gordon contemplated resigning the command, he offered the reversion of it to Macartney, who was prepared to take it. Macartney, however, desired not so much to take up a temporary appointment as permanently to enter the Chinese government service in the capacity of interpreter and adviser, for which he had qualified himself by learning the language.

He became closely attached to Li Hung Chang, and was by him appointed, with the grade of colonel in the Chinese service, to command a separate contingent of Chinese troops which co-operated with Gordon. In the late summer of 1863 he took Fung Ching and Seedong. At this time also he turned to account his knowledge of chemistry acquired at Edinburgh 'by instructing experts in the manufacture of gunpowder, percussion caps, and munitions of war' (Mossman, pp. 200–1). With Li Hung Chang's support, he made at Sungkiang the beginning of an arsenal, which was developed at Soochow, when that place had been recaptured from the Taipings; finally, after the close of the rebellion it was permanently established in 1865 at Nankin.

Macartney's diplomatic tact and knowledge of Chinese language and character were brought into play when he was called upon to act as intermediary between Gordon and the Chinese generals, especially Li Hung Chang, with whom Gordon was incensed for the treacherous murder of the Taiping leaders at Soochow after the surrender of that city. Macartney's intervention aroused Gordon's resentment. Gordon denounced Macartney in a letter which was published in a blue book in 1864, but subsequently made full apology; intimate friendship between the two men was renewed, and Gordon by his Woolwich connection helped the starting of the Chinese arsenal. Gordon said of Macartney that he 'drilled troops, supervised the manufacture of shells, gave advice, brightened the Futai's intellect about foreigners, and made peace, in which last accomplishment his forte lay' (Boulger, *Life of Gordon*, i. 90; *Life of Macartney*, 75).

Macartney was in charge of the arsenal at Nankin for ten years, 1865–75, during which he paid a short visit to Europe in 1873–4. In 1875 his appointment was terminated owing to disagreement with the Chinese authorities, but the murder at Manwein of Augustus Raymond Margary [q. v.] in the same year led to the sending next year of a Chinese mission to London and the permanent appointment of a Chinese representative at the Court of St. James. Macartney was appointed secretary to the embassy, with which he reached England in Jan. 1877. He never returned to China, but remained in Europe, helping to organise the diplomatic relations of the Chinese government, visiting Paris and St. Petersburg, and for nearly thirty years, from 1877 to 1906, holding the position first of secretary and then of councillor and English secretary to the Chinese legation in London. In that capacity he advised the Chinese government in all negotiations and entirely identified himself with Chinese interests. He was made a mandarin of the second degree, with the distinction of the peacock's feather, and was given the first class of the Chinese order of the Paton Sing. He was made a C.M.G. in 1881, and K.C.M.G. in 1885. He retired at the beginning of 1906. He died at his home at Kenbank, Dalry, Kirkcudbrightshire, on 8 June in that year, and was buried in the family burying ground at Dundrennan.

In appearance he was tall and fair, with a calm expression and deliberate manner, possibly the result of long contact with the East. He married (1) at Soochow in 1864 a Chinese lady who died in 1878, leaving one daughter and three sons; the eldest son is Mr. George Macartney, C.I.E., British consul-general at Kashgar; and (2) in 1884 a French lady, Jeanne, daughter of M. Léon du Sautoy of Fontainebleau, who died in 1904, leaving one daughter and three sons.

[Life by Demetrius Charles Boulger, 1908; The Times, 9 June 1906; London and China Telegraph, 11 June 1906; Annual Register, 1906; A. J. Sargent's Anglo-Chinese Commerce and Diplomacy, 1907; Life of Gordon by D. C. Boulger, 1896; General Gordon's private diary of his exploits in China amplified by S. Mossman, 1885; authorities cited]. C. P. L.

MACAULAY, JAMES (1817–1902), author, born in Edinburgh on 22 May 1817, was eldest son of Alexander Macaulay (1783–1868), M.D. and F.R.C.S. Edinburgh, who in his later years removed from Edinburgh to practise in London, and was author of a 'Dictionary of Medicine designed for Popular Use' (Edinburgh, 1828; 14th edit. 1858). James was educated at the Edinburgh Academy; A. C. Tait [q. v.], the future archbishop, was among his schoolfellows. He then proceeded to Edinburgh University, were after taking the arts course, he devoted himself to medicine. With his fellow-student and lifelong friend, Edward Forbes [q. v.], he went to Paris in 1837–8, and witnessed François Majendie's experiments on animals. Both, according to Macaulay, left the room 'disgusted less by the cruelty of the professor than by the heartlessness of the spectators.' He was thenceforth a strenuous opponent of vivisection. Macaulay graduated both M.A. and M.D. at Edinburgh in 1838, and next year published 'An Essay on Cruelty to Animals,' which he followed up in later life with 'A Plea for Mercy to Animals' (1875; new edit. 1889) and 'Vivisection: is it scientifically useful or morally justifiable?' (1881); both questions were answered in the negative.

On leaving the university, Macaulay travelled as a tutor in Italy and Spain, and spent some months in Madeira, contributing careful 'Notes on the Physical Geography, Geology and Climate' of the island to the 'Edinburgh New Philosophical Journal' for Oct. 1840. He supplied the letterpress to 'Madeira, illustrated by A. Picken,' and edited 'The Stranger' (Funchal), both published in the same year. Macaulay was elected F.R.C.S. Edinburgh on 7 July 1862; but meanwhile he had abandoned medicine for literature and journalism. Settling in London, he joined the staff of the 'Literary Gazette' in 1850. From 1858 to 1885 he was editor of two weekly periodicals, the 'Leisure Hour' (founded in 1852) and 'Sunday at Home' (founded in 1854); he shared the editorship with Mr. William Stevens from 1885 to 1894. Both papers had moral and religious aims, and long enjoyed a wide circulation among young readers. Macaulay's contributors to the 'Leisure Hour,' who were usually anonymous, included at the outset Archbishop Whately [q. v.], and afterwards Frank Buckland [q. v.], Canon Rawlinson [q. v. Suppl. II], and Arminius Vambéry. Macaulay was also for many years general editor of the Religious Tract Society's periodicals. The 'Boy's Own Paper' and the 'Girl's Own Paper' were founded in 1879 and edited under his direction.

In 1871 Macaulay travelled through the United States of America, and wrote a series of roseate articles in the 'Leisure Hour,' called 'First Impressions of America,' which were collected as 'Across the Ferry' (1871; 3rd edit. 1884). A visit to Ireland next year produced 'Ireland in 1872: a Tour of Observation' (1873; new edit. 1876). The author advocated a restricted home rule.

Macaulay's independent publications were thenceforth chiefly narratives of adventure for boys and girls; a series of anecdotes of great men, Gordon, Luther, Livingstone, Whitefield, and Cromwell, proved popular. He died at 41 Wynnstay Gardens, Kensington, on 18 June 1902. He married in 1860 a daughter of G. Stokes, vicar of Hope, Hanley.

Besides the works mentioned and many other collections of tales of adventure, Macaulay published: 1. 'What Great Englishmen have said concerning the Papacy,' 1878 (reissued as 'Witness of Great Englishmen,' 1900). 2. 'All True: Records of Peril and Adventure by Sea,' 1879 (new edit. 1880). 3. 'Sea Pictures drawn with Pen and Pencil,' 1882 (new edit. 1884), a work praised highly by Ruskin. 4. 'Gray Hawk: Life and Adventures among the Red Indians,' 1883 (reissued

1909), a story founded on fact. 5. 'Stirring Stories of Peace and War by Land and Sea,' 1885 (new edit. illustrated in colour by George Soper, 1910). 6. 'Victoria, R.I.: Her Life and Reign,' 1887 (5 portraits). 7. 'From Middy to Admiral of the Fleet: the Story of Commodore Anson retold,' 1891. He also edited 'Speeches and Addresses of the Prince of Wales [Edward VII]' (1889).

[Men of the Time, 1899; Lists of Edinburgh medical graduates and fellows of Roy. Coll. Surg. Edinb.; Daily News, 20 June 1902; British Weekly, 25 June; The Times, 19 Feb. 1868; Literary World (Boston, Mass.), 1885, p. 348; Seed Time and Harvest (R.T.S.), Aug. 1902; Introd. to Index vol. of Leisure Hour, 1852–76; Allibone's Dict. Eng. Lit. vol. ii. and Suppl.; Brit. Mus. Cat.] G. Le G. N.

MACBAIN, ALEXANDER (1855–1907) Celtic scholar, born at Glenfeshie, Badenoch, Inverness-shire, on 22 July 1855, was son of John Macbain, crofter, of Glenfeshie. Educated at the schools of Insch and Alvie, he became a pupil-teacher; subsequently for a short time he was engaged on the Ordnance Survey in Wales. In 1874 he entered the grammar school of Old Aberdeen, and in 1876 matriculated as a bursar at King's College, Aberdeen. He won distinction in both classics and philosophy, and graduated in 1880 with honours. For a brief period he acted as assistant at his Aberdeen school, and in 1881 was appointed rector of Raining's School, Inverness, under the government of the Highland Trust. In 1894 the school was transferred to the Inverness school board to form a higher grade school, and was incorporated with the high public school, where Macbain taught till his death. His leisure was devoted to Celtic studies. In 1901 Aberdeen University conferred upon him the hon. degree of LL.D., and he received on 1 April 1905, on the recommendation of Mr. A. J. Balfour, then prime minister, a civil list pension of 90*l.* He died of apoplexy in an hotel at Stirling on 6 April 1907. He was buried in Rothiemurchus churchyard, Badenoch. A study for a picture-portrait of him was made in 1885 by Colin J. Mackenzie, and was in possession of F. Maciver, Inverness. He was unmarried.

Macbain was recognised as one of the most learned Celtic scholars of his time. His first book, 'Celtic Mythology and Religion,' was published at Inverness in 1885. His useful book, 'Personal Names and Surnames of the Town of Inverness,' was issued at the same place in 1895, as was also 'An Etymological Dictionary of the Gaelic Language' in 1896. Macbain's 'Dictionary,' which occupied him from 1882 till 1896, contains 6900 words, traced etymologically with great erudition. The first edition was exhausted in a year; and Macbain was arranging for a new edition at his death. In 1892 he edited Dr. Cameron's 'Reliquiæ Celticæ,' and in 1900 he edited and recast Alexander Mackenzie's 'History of the Mathesons,' which had come out in 1882. Macbain also edited Skene's 'Highlanders,' 'The Book of Deer,' and MacEachen's 'Gaelic Dictionary,' all of which were published at Stirling. He edited the 'Celtic Magazine' (Inverness) from 1886 till 1888, and was joint editor of 'The Highland Monthly' (Inverness) from 1889 till 1902. He was a frequent contributor to these magazines and to the 'Proceedings' of various societies, notably the Inverness Gaelic Society and the Inverness Scientific Society and Field Club. He wrote on the Picts in 'Chambers's Encyclopædia.'

[Inverness Courier, 9 April 1907; Northern Chronicle, 10 April 1907; Celtic Monthly, April 1907; private information.] A. H. M.

MACBETH, ROBERT WALKER (1848–1910), painter and etcher, born at Glasgow on 30 Sept. 1848, was second son of Norman Macbeth [q. v.], R.S.A. He received his general education partly in Edinburgh, partly at Friedrichsdorf in Germany. Returning home, he studied art in the schools of the Royal Scottish Academy. In 1871 he came to London, where with his friend Edward John Gregory [q. v. Suppl. II] and (Sir) Hubert (von) Herkomer he joined the staff of the newly founded 'Graphic' newspaper and entered the Royal Academy schools. His early practice was chiefly in water-colour, and in 1874 he was elected a member of the Royal Water Colour Society. He was also a constant exhibitor at the Royal Academy, where his work showed something of the influence of Frederick Walker [q. v.]. At the Academy he exhibited, among other oil paintings which attracted attention, 'A Lincolnshire Gang' (1876), 'Potato Harvest in the Fens' (1877), and 'A Fen Flood' (1883). His 'Cast Shoe' was purchased by the Chantrey bequest in 1890 for 630*l.* It was however as an etcher that Macbeth was most widely known. During the vogue enjoyed by reproductive etching from 1880 onwards, he etched a series of large plates after pictures by Velazquez and Titian, in the Prado Gallery, Madrid.

They are remarkable for the vigour and richness with which they suggest the colour and handling of their originals. He also etched the 'Le Chant d'Amour' of Burne-Jones (R.A. 1896).

Macbeth was elected an associate of the Royal Academy in 1883, at the same time as Gregory, and a full academician in 1903, and became an original member of the Society of Painter-Etchers.

During his latter years he lived chiefly at Washford, near Dunster, and hunted with the Exmoor staghounds. His London studio was in Tite Street, Chelsea. He died at Golder's Green on 1 Nov. 1910, and was buried there.

Macbeth married in 1887 Lydia, eldest daughter of General Bates of the Bombay native cavalry. His widow survived him with a daughter, Mrs. Reginald Owen. A portrait in oils was painted by Carlo Pellegrini [q. v.].

Some of his work was shown at the winter exhibition of the Royal Academy in January 1911.

[Men and Women of the Time; Hodgson and Eaton, Royal Academy and its Members, 1905, p. 359; Graves, Royal Academy Exhibitors; The Times, 3, 4, and 8 Nov. 1910; private information.] W. A.

MACCALLUM, ANDREW (1821–1902), landscape painter, born at Nottingham in 1821, of Highland descent, was son of an employé at Messrs. William Gibson & Sons' hosiery manufactory in that town. Living in boyhood near Sherwood Forest, he early developed a love of landscape art, of which his family disapproved. Being apprenticed against his will to his father's business, he devoted his leisure to drawing, and was encouraged by Thomas Bailey [q. v.], father of Philip James Bailey [q. v. Suppl. II] the poet, who allowed him to copy pictures in his collection.

On his twenty-first birthday young MacCallum left his uncongenial home, it is said, without a shilling. He maintained himself by teaching, and is stated to have sold his first picture to W. Enfield, then town clerk of Nottingham. At the age of twenty-two he became a student in the recently founded Government School of Art at Nottingham. He exhibited a view of Flint Castle at the British Institution in London in 1849, and probably in the same year became a student at the Government School of Design at Somerset House, where J. R. Herbert [q. v.], R. Redgrave [q. v.], and J. C. Horsley [q. v. Suppl. II] were among his instructors. In 1850 he first exhibited at the Royal Academy. From that year till 1852 he was assistant master at the Manchester School of Art, and from 1852 to 1854 he was headmaster of the School of Art at Stourbridge, where he resided at the Old Parsonage, New Street. In 1854 he went to Italy with a travelling studentship awarded by the Science and Art Department. Part of his time was devoted to procuring facsimiles of mural decorations for use in schools of art. His manuscript 'Report of a Sojourn in Italy from the year 1854 to 1857' is in the library of the Victoria and Albert Museum.

Returning to England in 1857, he decorated the western exterior of the Sheepshanks Gallery at the South Kensington Museum with panels of sgraffito. Thenceforth he devoted himself to landscape, which he had practised in Italy, and he found congenial subjects at Burnham Beeches and in Windsor Forest. Among purchasers of his pictures were John Phillip, R.A. [q. v.], and James Nasmyth [q. v.], and he was awarded a silver medal by the Society for the Encouragement of the Fine Arts. Towards the end of 1861 he painted at Fontainebleau; in 1864 he worked in Switzerland and on the Rhine; in 1866 he was in Italy; in the winter of 1866–7 he was in the neighbourhood of Paris. Between 1870 and 1875 he paid several visits to Egypt. About 1875 he was commissioned by Queen Victoria to paint five views near Balmoral.

MacCallum sent fifty-three pictures to the Royal Academy (1850–1886) and a few to the British Institution, Society of British Artists, and International Exhibitions (1870–1). Special exhibitions of his paintings were held at the Dudley Gallery in 1866 (6 water-colours and 29 oils, including his large 'Charlemagne Oak, Forest of Fontainebleau,' and 'A Glade in Sherwood Forest') and at Nottingham in 1873. His 'Sultry Eve' was shown at the Centennial Exhibition at Philadelphia in 1876. His reputation rests mainly upon his woodland subjects, but he also produced imaginative compositions such as 'The Eve of Liberty' (1876). He endeavoured to exemplify in his paintings the compatibility of breadth and detail. His presentation of trees betrayed a laborious fidelity which is hardly known elsewhere, but his meticulous attention to intricate branching and other details exposed him to the criticism that he lacked spiritual power and imagination. He not infrequently used water-colour, and he drew in pastel and in gold, silver, and copper point. He sometimes lectured on art subjects.

He died on 22 Jan. 1902 at 5 The Studios, Holland Park Road, Kensington. He had lived in the neighbourhood since 1858, when he leased from Thomas Webster, R.A. [q. v.], his house in The Mall, Kensington. He was twice married: (1) to Miss Tetlow (*d. c.* 1875) of Altrincham, a cultured lady of independent means; and (2) to Miss Salway of Ludlow, by whom he had two sons, who both served in the South African war. His portrait was painted by J. H. Sylvester in 1888.

The Tate Gallery has his 'Silvery Moments, Burnham Beeches' (1885), and 'The Monarch of the Glen'; to the Victoria and Albert Museum belong 'In Sherwood Forest—Winter Evening after Rain' (1881), 'S. Maria delle Grazie, Milan' (1854), 'Rome from the Porta San Pancrazio' (1855–6), 'The Burning of Rome by Nero, and the Massacre of the Christians' (1878–9), a 'Head of Christ' after Daniele Crespi, two pencil and two water-colour studies of trees, and numerous drawings of ornament; and at the City of Nottingham Art Gallery are 'The Major Oak, Sherwood Forest' (1882), which measures about 9 ft. by 12 ft., and 'The Opening Scene in Bailey's "Festus."'

[Private information; Illustr. London News, 23 June 1866; Art Journ. 1866, p. 218, and 1877, pp. 321–324 (illustr. art. by J. Dafforne); Fine Arts Quarterly Review, 1866, i. 373; Clement and Hutton, Artists of the Nineteenth Century; Sir H. Cole, Fifty Years of Public Work, 1884, i. 329; P. G. Hamerton, in English Painters of the Present Day (1871), pp. 60, 61; G. H. Shepherd, Minor Masters of the old British School, 39; Müller and Singer, Allg. Künstler-Lexicon; Graves, Dict. of Artists, Roy. Acad. Exhibitors, and British Institution; Cat. Tate Gallery, Victoria and Albert Museum (oils and water-colours), Nottingham Art Gall., and Dudley Gall. (1866); The Times, 31 Jan. 1902.] B. S. L.

McCALMONT, HARRY LESLIE BLUNDELL (1861–1902), sportsman, born on 30 May 1861, was only son (in a family of three children) of Hugh Barklie Blundell McCalmont (1836–1888), barrister, of Lincoln's Inn, living at Hampton Court, by his wife Edith Florence, daughter of Martin Blackmore of Bonchurch, Isle of Wight. From Eton, Harry passed in 1881 into the 6th foot, and in 1885 was gazetted to the Scots guards, from which he retired in 1889. Meanwhile he became heir of an immense fortune left him by his great-uncle, Hugh McCalmont, of Abbeylands, co. Antrim, who died unmarried on 20 October 1887, leaving an estate valued at 3,121,931*l.* The residuary estate, amounting to about 3,000,000*l.*, was left in trust to pay 2000*l.* a year to his grand-nephew for seven years after the testator's death, and then the capital and interest were to be transferred to the heir. In 1894 McCalmont thus came into possession of some 4,000,000*l.* A keen sportsman, he engaged largely in racing, yachting, and shooting. He purchased from John James Robert Manners, seventh duke of Rutland [q. v. Suppl. II], the Cheveley estate at Newmarket, where game was very plentiful, and he delighted in hospitality and benevolence.

On the turf McCalmont placed himself under the guidance of Captain Machell [q. v. Suppl. II]. One of the first horses he owned was Timothy, who in 1888 carried his colours (light blue and scarlet, quartered; white cap) to victory in the contests for the Gold Cup and Alexandra Plate at Ascot. From Machell he purchased for 500*l.* the Wenlock mare Deadlock, who, bred to Isonomy, produced in 1890 the colt Isinglass. During the four seasons this horse was in training he won the huge sum of 57,455*l.*—as a two-year-old 4577*l.*, at three years old 18,860*l.*, at four 31,498*l.*, and at five 2520*l.* This is the largest amount won by any one horse on the English turf. In 1893 Isinglass was successful in the Two Thousand Guineas, Derby. and St. Leger; the following year he won the Princess of Wales's Stakes of 10,911*l.*, the Eclipse Stakes of 9285*l.*, and the Jockey Club Stakes of 11,302*l.*, and in 1895 he carried off the Ascot Cup. At the stud Isinglass became the sire of two 'classic' winners—Cherry Lass, who won the One Thousand Guineas and Oaks in 1905, and Glass Doll, who won the Oaks in 1907. One of his sons, Rising Glass, ran second in the Derby and St. Leger, and won the Jockey Club Stakes as his sire had done. Among many other good horses that carried the colours of McCalmont were Suspender (winner of the Royal Hunt Cup), Amphora (winner of the Stewards' Cup at Goodwood), and St. Maclou, who won the Lincolnshire Handicap, beating Sceptre, finished second in the Cambridgeshire, and won the Manchester November Handicap in 1902.

McCalmont, who was elected a member of the Jockey Club in 1893, was returned as conservative M.P. for the Newmarket division of Cambridgeshire in 1895 and was re-elected in 1900. At the time of the latter election he, as colonel of the 6th battalion of the Royal Warwickshire regiment, was serving in Cape Colony and the Orange Free State during the South African war; for his South African services he was made C.B.

On 16 Jan. 1902 he moved in the House of Commons the address in reply to the King's speech. On 8 Dec. 1902 he died suddenly from heart failure at his house, 11 St. James's Square, and was buried in the churchyard at Cheveley.

He was twice married: (1) to Amy, daughter of Major John Miller, who died in 1889; and (2) in 1897 to Winifred, daughter of Sir Henry de Bathe. He left no issue, and the bulk of his fortune passed to his second cousin, Dermot McCalmont, son of his father's first cousin, Colonel Sir Hugh McCalmont, K.C.B. Cartoon portraits by 'Spy' appeared in 'Vanity Fair' in 1889 and 1896.

[Burke's Landed Gentry; The Times, and Sportsman, 9 Dec. 1902; Ruff's Guide to the Turf; Baily's Mag. 1895 (portrait); H. Sydenham Dixon, From Gladiateur to Persimmon; Badminton Mag., Feb. 1903.]

E. M.

McCLEAN, FRANK (1837–1904), civil engineer and amateur astronomer, born at Glasgow on 13 Nov. 1837, was only son of John Robinson McClean, M.P., F.R.S., a civil engineer of repute, who besides receiving many commissions from the British government, carried out works in Paris for Emperor Napoleon III, and was one of the engineers invited by the Viceroy of Egypt to report upon the Suez Canal. His mother was Anna, daughter of William Newsam. On 18 Jan. 1850 Frank was admitted to Westminster school as a 'home-boarder,' his family living in the neighbourhood. From Westminster he passed in 1853 to the university of Glasgow, and thence in 1855 to Trinity College, Cambridge, where he gained a scholarship and graduated as twenty-seventh wrangler in 1859. In the same year he was articled to Sir John Hawkshaw [q. v. Suppl. I], the engineer, and in 1862 was made a partner in his father's engineering firm of McClean and Stileman. For four years he was resident engineer of the Barrow docks and of the Furness and Midland Railway, and other work of the firm fell to his control, but in 1870 he withdrew from his profession in the enjoyment of a large income. Thenceforth he divided his time between a town residence in South Kensington and a country house near Tunbridge Wells.

On his retirement McClean occupied himself with natural science and with the collection of illuminated manuscripts, early printed books, ancient coins, enamels, and ivories. In order to perfect his collections he studied foreign languages and visited the museums and galleries of the Continent.

His scientific interest at first inclined to electrical work, but he soon turned to astronomy, and in 1875 he completed an observatory at his country house at Ferncliffe, near Tunbridge Wells, where he devoted himself to astronomical spectroscopy. A star spectroscope designed by him and named after him still figures in instrument makers' catalogues. In 1884, when he built a new country residence at Rusthall, he arranged a laboratory there, and an ingenious apparatus comprising a heliostat for spectroscopic observation of the sun. He described his first results in papers contributed to the Royal Astronomical Society (1887–91).

In 1895 McClean began astronomical spectroscopic work of another kind, and with a telescope of 13 inches aperture made by Sir Howard Grubb, with a prism placed in front of the object-glass, he began a systematic survey of the spectra of all the stars brighter than magnitude 3½ in the northern heavens. This was completed in 1896, and in 1897 McClean at the invitation of Sir David Gill took the prism to the Cape of Good Hope Observatory, and having mounted it on a similar telescope belonging to that observatory, extended his survey to the whole sky. The account of the northern survey is published in the 'Philosophical Transactions of the Royal Society' (vol. cxci.) and of the southern in a quarto volume, 'Spectra of Southern Stars' (1898). For this work he received the gold medal of the Royal Astronomical Society in 1899. It was characteristic of McClean that he did with his own hand the routine photography which his astronomical work entailed, instead of leaving it to an assistant.

McClean generously employed his ample fortune in the advancement of astronomy. In 1894 he presented to the Royal Observatory at the Cape of Good Hope a photographic telescope of 24 inches aperture, with a twin visual telescope of 18 inches aperture having a slit spectroscope and an object-glass prism attached. This instrument, called the Victoria telescope, is housed at McClean's expense in an excellent dome with a rising floor. A still more munificent gift was the foundation, at a cost of 12,500*l.* of the Isaac Newton studentships in the university of Cambridge for the encouragement of study and research in astronomy and physical optics. This foundation has proved eminently successful. In 1911 five important government positions in astronomy were filled by former Isaac Newton students.

McClean joined the Royal Astronomical Society in 1877, and served on the council from 1891 until his death. He received the honorary degree of LL.D. from the university of Glasgow in 1894. He was elected F.R.S. in 1895. He died at Brussels, from pneumonia, on 8 Nov. 1904, and was buried at Kensal Green cemetery. He bequeathed his collection of illuminated manuscripts and early printed books and a large part of his art treasures to the FitzWilliam Museum at Cambridge, and made large money bequests to that university, to the university of Birmingham, to the Royal Institution, and to the Royal Astronomical Society for furthering astronomical and physical science. In 1865 he married Ellen, daughter of John Greg of Escowbeck, Lancaster, and by her had two daughters and three sons. The youngest, Frank Kennedy McClean, is an observing astronomer and an aviator.

[Proc. Roy. Soc. vol. lxxviii.; Roy. Astron. Soc. Monthly Notices, Feb. 1905, vol. lxv.]
H. P. H.

McCLINTOCK, Sir FRANCIS LEOPOLD (1819-1907), admiral, born at Dundalk on 8 July 1819, was the eldest son of Henry McClintock, formerly of the 3rd dragoon guards, by his wife Elizabeth Melesina, daughter of the Ven. George Fleury, D.D., archdeacon of Waterford. He entered the navy in 1831 and passed his examination in Oct. 1838; but promotion at that date was slow and uncertain, and McClintock remained a mate for nearly seven years. He was made lieutenant on 29 July 1845, when serving in the Gorgon on the South American station, and a few days later was moved into the Frolic, sloop, on board which he served for two years in the Pacific. On 7 Feb. 1848 he was appointed to the Enterprise, Captain Sir James Clark Ross [q. v.], for a voyage to the Arctic; and in Feb. 1850 he was chosen to be first lieutenant of the Assistance [see Ommanney, Sir Erasmus, Suppl. II], proceeding on a similar voyage of discovery. In these expeditions he established his reputation as an Arctic traveller, more especially by making an unprecedented sledge journey of 760 miles in 80 days in the winter and spring of 1851, when the Assistance was frozen up at Griffith Island. On his return home he received his promotion to commander, dated 11 Oct. 1851. In Feb. 1852 a larger Arctic expedition of five ships was fitted out and placed under the command of Captain Sir Edward Belcher [q. v.]. Two of the ships had auxiliary steam power, and McClintock was given the command of one of these, the Intrepid, which was officially described as tender to the Resolute, Capt. Kellett, under whose immediate orders he was. The Intrepid wintered on the south side of Melville Island, whence many sledge expeditions were sent out. McClintock himself made a journey of 1210 geographical miles in 105 days, during which he examined and charted the west coast of Prince Patrick Island and Ireland's Eye. The comparative perfection to which Arctic sledge travelling attained was in great measure due to improvements introduced by McClintock. In the summer of 1854 Belcher decided to abandon the Intrepid and three other ships, and the party returned home in the North Star and two relief ships. On 22 Oct. 1854, a day after McClintock received his promotion to captain, Dr. Rae arrived with the first certain intelligence of the fate of Franklin's expedition [see Franklin, Sir John]. The Admiralty was satisfied of the truth of the news and took no action to confirm it, but Lady Franklin determined on a search expedition. For this purpose she bought the Fox yacht and had her fitted out, principally at her own cost, giving the command to McClintock who, like the other officers of the expedition, offered his services gratuitously. McClintock published in 1859 an account of this service, entitled 'The Voyage of the Fox in the Arctic Seas: a Narrative of the Fate of Sir John Franklin and his companions,' a work which has gone through many editions. The expedition returned to England in 1859, bringing with it the written memorandum of Franklin's death, of the abandonment of the ships, and of the fate of the whole party. In recognition of his success McClintock was allowed by the Admiralty to count the period of his command of the Fox as sea-time, and in 1860 he was knighted.

From Feb. 1861 to Dec. 1862 McClintock commanded the Doris, frigate, in the Mediterranean, and in Nov. 1863 commissioned the Aurora for service with the Channel squadron. In her he cruised in the North Sea during the Danish war of 1864, and on 9 May of that year, by his presence at Heligoland, prevented the development of what might have been a serious problem in international law. From 1865 he was for three years commodore in charge at Jamaica, and on 1 Oct. 1871 he reached flag rank. From April 1872 to May 1877 he served as admiral superintendent of Portsmouth Dockyard, and on 5 Aug. 1877 was promoted to vice-admiral. In Nov. 1879 McClintock was appointed commander-in-chief on the North America and West Indies station, where, with his flag in the Northampton, he remained for the customary three years. This was his last active service. In Feb. 1884 he was elected an elder brother of the Trinity House, and on 7 July of the same year reached the rank of admiral, one day before being overtaken by the age for retirement. He was created a K.C.B. in the birthday honours of 1891.

McClintock offered himself as candidate for Drogheda at the general election of 1868, but withdrew in consequence of dangerous rioting. He died in London on 17 Nov. 1907, and was buried at Kensington cemetery, Hanwell. He married in 1870 Annette Elizabeth, second daughter of Robert Foster Dunlop of Monasterboice, co. Louth. One son, John William Leopold, entered the navy and was promoted commander in 1905.

Two portraits of McClintock, painted by Stephen Pearce, are in the collection of Arctic explorers at the National Portrait Gallery; one was painted in 1856. A third portrait by Frederick Yates (1901) belongs to Lady McClintock.

[A Life, with portrait from photograph, was published by Sir Clements R. Markham in 1909; see The Times, 18 and 23 Nov. 1907; and Journal of Roy. Geograph. Soc., Jan. 1908.] L. G. C. L.

McCOAN, JAMES CARLILE (1829–1904), author and journalist, born at Dunlow, co. Tyrone, Ireland, on 14 July 1829, was only son of Clement McCoan of Charlemont, Armagh, by Sarah, daughter of James Carlile of Culresoch, Moy.

After education at Dungannon school and Homerton College, London, he matriculated at London University in 1848. Having entered at the Middle Temple on 15 November 1851, he was called to the bar on 17 November 1856, and joined the south-eastern circuit. But he did not seek practice in England. Engaging in journalism, he acted as war correspondent for the 'Daily News' during the Crimean war. At the close of the war McCoan travelled in Georgia and Circassia, and afterwards settled at Constantinople, where he practised in the supreme consular court until 1864, and founded and edited the first English newspaper in Turkey, the 'Levant Herald,' which was for a time subsidised by the English government. In 1870 McCoan disposed of the paper, and, returning to England, embodied full information which he had collected during visits to Egypt in his exhaustive and readable 'Egypt as it is' (1877). 'Egypt under Ismail: a Romance of History,' with appendix of official documents (1889), carried on the story. Some articles which McCoan contributed to 'Fraser's Magazine,' after the conclusion of the Anglo-Turkish convention of 1878, he expanded into 'Our New Protectorate: Turkey in Asia, its Geography, Races, Resources, and Government, with Map showing existing and projected Public Works' (2 vols. 1879).

McCoan represented Wicklow county as a protestant home-ruler in the parliament of 1880–5. In 1881 he volubly attacked the government's coercive legislation (cf. LUCY, *Diary of the Gladstone Parliament*, pp. 117, 118). On 3 February McCoan was among the home-rulers suspended for defying the authority of the Speaker. Subsequently he disavowed sympathy with the illegal action and unconstitutional methods of the Land League, and supported Gladstone's land bill, while endeavouring to amend it. Denounced for disloyalty to his party by Patrick Egan, treasurer of the Land League (cf. HANSARD, 20 May 1881), McCoan thenceforth gave an independent support to the liberal government. He frequently spoke at length on the politics of the Near East, championing the Turks from personal knowledge.

McCoan was an unsuccessful liberal candidate for the Lancaster division in 1885, for Southampton in 1886, and for the Macclesfield division in 1892. He died at his residence, 42 Campden Hill Square, Kensington, on 13 January 1904, and was buried at Kensal Green.

He married on 2 June 1857 Augusta Janet, the youngest daughter of William Jenkyns of Elgin, and left one son, and a daughter who married the Rev. J. C. Bellew. Besides the works mentioned he was author of 'Protestant Endurance under Popish Cruelty: a Narrative of the Reformation in Spain' (1853), and 'Consular Jurisdiction in Turkey and Egypt' (1873).

[Private information; Foster's Men at the Bar; The Times, 15 Jan. 1904; Daily News, 16 Jan. 1904; Levant Herald, 25 Jan.; Hansard's Parl. Debates; Brit. Mus. Cat.;

Allibone's Dict. Eng. Lit. (Suppl.); Lucy's Memories of Eight Parliaments, pp. 303-4; Northern Whig (weekly), 23 Jan. 1904.]

G. LE G. N.

MACCOLL, MALCOLM (1831-1907), divine and author, born at Glenfinnan, Inverness-shire, on 27 March 1831, was the son of John MacColl of Glenfinnan by his wife Martha, daughter of Malcolm Macrae of Letterfearn in Kintail. His childhood passed mainly at Kintail and Ballachulish. At about fifteen he was at school at Dalkeith, and on 14 Sept. 1854 he entered the theological department of Trinity College, Glenalmond. Ordained deacon in 1856 and priest in 1857 by the bishop of Glasgow, he was in 1856-7 in charge of Castle Douglas. He was curate of St. Mary's, Soho, London (1858-9); in 1860 curate of St. Barnabas, Pimlico; in 1861 of St. Paul's, Knightsbridge; in 1862-3 chaplain at St. Petersburg; in 1864-7 again at St. Paul's, Knightsbridge; in 1867-9 chaplain in Southern Italy; and in 1869 curate of Addington, Buckinghamshire. While at Glenalmond he attracted the notice of Gladstone, with whose political and religious views he identified himself through life. In 1865 he published (as 'Scrutator') a pamphlet in Gladstone's support, 'Mr. Gladstone and Oxford.' A book, 'Science and Prayer,' which reached a fourth edition in 1866, also aided his progress. In 1868 he published 'Is there not a Cause?' (2nd edit. 1869), a defence of Gladstone's Irish church policy. In 1870 he was chaplain to Lord Napier and curate of St. Giles's, Camberwell. In 1871 he was presented by Gladstone to the City living of St. George's, Botolph Lane. The church was closed in 1891, but MacColl continued to receive the stipend. In 1875, during the controversy over the Public Worship Regulation Act, he issued a clever attack on the judicial committee of the privy council, entitled 'Lawlessness, Sacerdotalism and Ritualism.' In the same year he was present at the second Bonn conference on reunion. In 1876 he visited eastern Europe with Henry Parry Liddon [q. v.], and joined Liddon in denouncing Bulgarian atrocities which they believed they had seen (JOHNSTON'S *Life and Letters of H. P. Liddon*, pp. 210-11). He gave evidence before the Ecclesiastical Courts Commission of 1881. In 1884 he was presented by Gladstone to a residentiary canonry at Ripon. He defended that statesman's Irish policy in 'Reasons for Home Rule' (1886, nine edits.). Few political or ecclesiastical controversies escaped his pen. In 1899 he received the hon. D.D. degree from Edinburgh University, and published 'The Reformation Settlement' (10th edit. 1901). He gave evidence (with parts of which he was afterwards dissatisfied) before the royal commission appointed in 1904 to inquire into ritual excess. In 1903 he formally left the liberal party over its education policy. He died suddenly in London on 5 April 1907. He married in 1904 Consuelo Albinia, youngest daughter of Major-general W. H. Crompton-Stansfield, of Esholt Hall, Yorkshire, who survived him without issue.

MacColl was largely self-educated, and raised himself by industry, resolution, and literary aptitude. Controversy was the breath of his nostrils. Gladstone called him 'the best pamphleteer in England,' but apparently distrusted his learning (A. C. BENSON, *Life of E. W. Benson*, ii. 657). In addition to many contributions to periodicals, various pamphlets, and works referred to, MacColl published: 1. 'Life Here and Hereafter,' sermons, 1894. 2. 'Christianity in Relation to Science and Morals,' 1889, 4th edit. 1890. 3. 'England's Responsibility towards Armenia,' 1895. 4. 'The Sultan and the Powers,' 1896. 5. 'The Royal Commission and the Ornaments Rubric,' 1906.

[The Times, 6 April 1907; Guardian, 10 April 1907; A. Macrae, History of the Clan Macrae (in proof), p. 471; Men of the Time, 1887; D. C. Lathbury, Correspondence on Church and Religion of W. E. Gladstone, 1910, ii. 62, 318; Clergy List, 1857 and following years, and Crockford's Clerical Directory, 1886 and following years, where the dates of MacColl's ordination and early preferments are variously given; private information.]

A. R. B.

MACCOLL, NORMAN (1843-1904), editor of the 'Athenæum' and Spanish scholar, born on 31 August 1843 at 28 Ann Street, Edinburgh, was only child of Alexander Stewart MacColl by his wife Eliza Fulford of Crediton. His grandfather, Donald MacColl, clergyman of the Scottish episcopal church, became, later, factor to the duke of Gordon on his Lochaber estates. MacColl's father, a good classical scholar, kept a private school of repute in Edinburgh, and his mother was an accomplished woman. Norman was brought up at home together with his first cousin, Alice Caunter, now widow of James R. Jackson. He entered at Christ's College, Cambridge, in 1862, but migrated next year to Downing, and was elected a scholar there in 1865. He took a high second class in the classical tripos of 1866, a disappointing position, due partly to ill-health, partly, as his coach,

Richard Shilleto [q. v.], recognised, to reading outside examination subjects. He was in 1869 elected a fellow of Downing, having won the Hare prize in 1868 with an essay on 'Greek Sceptics from Pyrrho to Sextus,' which was published and indicated the bent of his mind. He graduated B.A. in 1866 and proceeded M.A. in 1869. He became a student of Lincoln's Inn on 21 Jan. 1872, and was called to the bar on 17 Nov. 1875.

At Cambridge MacColl began an acquaintance with Sir Charles Dilke [q. v. Suppl. II] proprietor of the 'Athenæum,' and in 1871 Dilke appointed him editor of that paper. He held the office to the end of 1900, working without any regular assistance till 1896.

As editor of the 'Athenæum' MacColl, whose general knowledge was great and whose interests were wide, was faithful to sound ideals of criticism, thorough, independent, and well-informed. An artist in language, he kept a keen eye on the style of his contributors. He was cautious in his policy, but, once having settled it, was not easily moved. He claimed to be something of a tactician, when new ideas, as in the case of Darwin, made changes of view imperative, and he allowed his reviewers when they were wrong to be corrected in published correspondence.

His temperament encouraged independence and a certain measure of isolation, partly from reserve and shyness, partly from his unwillingness to associate himself with any clique, and partly from a horror of self-advertisement; he went comparatively little into society, although he visited occasionally Westland Marston's Sunday parties, went regularly in later life to the Athenæum Club, was one of Leslie Stephen's Sunday tramps, and played a steady game of golf. His private generosity was notable, and much kindness lay underneath a somewhat sardonic humour.

MacColl travelled much on the Continent in his vacations, making one Spanish tour. He devoted himself seriously to the study of Spanish from 1874. He published in 1888 'Select Plays of Calderon,' with introduction and notes; in 1902 a translation of Cervantes' 'Exemplary Novels' (Glasgow, 2 vols.), and at the time of his death he was engaged on an edition of the 'Miscellaneous Poems of Cervantes' which was published posthumously (1912). His Spanish publications reflect his scrupulous methods of scholarship. He died suddenly at his residence, 4 Campden Hill Square, Kensington, on 16 Dec. 1904, from heart failure, and was buried at Charlton cemetery, Blackheath, in the same grave with his parents. He was unmarried.

A portrait by Clegg Wilkinson, painted shortly before his death, belongs to his cousin, Mrs. Jackson, who presented a replica to Downing College, now in the Combination Room. A small but vivid sketch occupies the centre of Harry Furniss's view of literary characters at the reading-room of the British Museum (*Punch*, 28 March 1885). He endowed by will a lectureship at Cambridge in Spanish and Portuguese which bears his name, and left to the university library his Spanish books.

[Information from Mrs. Jackson and college authorities; personal knowledge; Athenæum, 24 Dec. 1904; Morning Leader, 17 Dec. 1904; Publishers' Circular, 10 Feb. 1905; Cambridge University Reporter, 8 June 1905; J. C. Jeaffreson, Book of Recollections; memoir by Fitzmaurice Kelly, before Miscellaneous Poems of Cervantes, 1912.] V. R.

MACCORMAC, Sir WILLIAM, first baronet (1836–1901), surgeon, the elder son of Henry MacCormac [q. v.], a physician of Belfast, and Mary Newsham his wife, was born at Belfast on 17 Jan. 1836. The younger son, John, became a director of the Northern Linen Company at Belfast.

William, after education at the Belfast Royal Academical Institution, studied at Dublin and Paris. In October 1851 he entered Queen's College, Belfast, as a student of engineering and gained engineering scholarships there in his first and second years. He then turned aside to the arts course, graduating B.A. in the old Queen's University in 1855 and proceeding M.A. in 1858. He won the senior scholarship in natural philosophy in 1856, and next year was admitted M.D., subsequently receiving the hon. degrees of M.Ch. in 1879 and of D.Sc. in 1882, with the gold medal of the university. The hon. degrees of M.D. and M.Ch. were also bestowed upon him in later life by the University of Dublin in June 1900.

After graduation MacCormac studied surgery in Berlin, where he made lasting friendships with von Langenbeck, Billroth, and von Esmarch. Becoming M.R.C.S. England in 1857, he was elected in 1864 F.R.C.S. Ireland. MacCormac practised as a surgeon in Belfast from 1864 to 1870, becoming successively surgeon, lecturer on clinical surgery, and consulting surgeon to the Royal Hospital. He then moved to 13 Harley Street, London, where he resided until death.

At the outbreak of the Franco-German

war in 1870 MacCormac volunteered for service. Appointed to hospital duties at Metz, he was treated on his arrival as a spy and returned to Paris. Here he joined the Anglo-American association for the care of the wounded, and with others arrived at Sedan on the night of 30 Aug. 1870. Bivouacked in the waiting-room of the deserted railway station, MacCormac, unable to sleep, wandered up and down the platform, and at 2 A.M. witnessed the arrival of Napoleon III and two attendants in a solitary cattle truck attached to an engine, and following the party at a distance was sole spectator of the Emperor's hardly-gained entrance to the town which he soon left again as a prisoner. The battle of Sedan began at 4 A.M. on 1 Sept., and during the first day more than a thousand soldiers were brought for treatment to the Caserne d'Asfeld, a deserted infantry barracks on the ramparts, which MacCormac and his companions had hastily converted into a hospital of 384 beds.

Returning to London at the end of the Franco-German war, he was admitted in 1871 at the Royal College of Surgeons of England to the rare distinction of an *ad eundem* fellowship. In the same year he became, after a severe struggle, assistant surgeon at St. Thomas's Hospital, which had just moved to the Albert Embankment. He was made full surgeon in 1873 upon the resignation of Frederick le Gros Clark (1811–1892), and he was for twenty years lecturer on surgery in the medical school. He was elected consulting surgeon to the hospital and emeritus lecturer on clinical surgery in the medical school on retiring from active work in 1893.

Meanwhile MacCormac saw more war service. In 1876, as chief surgeon to 'the National Aid Society for the Sick and Wounded' during the Turco-Servian campaign, he was present at the battle of Alexinatz. As honorary general secretary, he contributed largely to the success of the seventh International Medical Congress in London in 1881, the 'Transactions' of which he edited; he was knighted on 7 Dec. for these services. He was president of the Medical Society of London in 1880 and of the metropolitan counties branch of the British Medical Association in 1890. MacCormac was also surgeon to the French, the Italian, Queen Charlotte's, and the British lying-in hospitals. He was an examiner in surgery at the University of London and for her majesty's naval, army, and Indian medical services. In 1897 he was created a baronet and was appointed surgeon in ordinary to the Prince of Wales, afterwards King Edward VII; on 27 Sept. 1898 he was made K.C.V.O. in recognition of professional services rendered to the Prince when he injured his knee.

At the Royal College of Surgeons of England, MacCormac was elected a member of the council in 1883, and in 1887 of the court of examiners. He delivered the Bradshaw lecture in 1893, taking as the subject 'Sir Astley Cooper and his Surgical Work,' and he was Hunterian orator in 1899. He was elected president in 1896, and enjoyed the unique honour of re-election on four subsequent occasions, during the last of which he presided over the centenary meeting held on 26 July 1900. His war service was still further extended, and his great practical knowledge was utilised in the South African campaign of 1899–1900, when he was appointed 'government consulting surgeon to the field force.' In this capacity he visited all the hospitals in Natal and Cape Colony, and went to the front on four occasions. In 1901 he became K.C.B. for his work in South Africa, and an honorary serjeant-surgeon to King Edward.

He died at Bath on 4 Dec. 1901, and was buried at Kensal Green. He married in 1861 Katharine Maria, daughter of John Charters of Belfast, but left no issue.

MacCormac was six feet two inches high, and well built in proportion. His industry, mastery of detail, rapidity of work, and Irish bonhomie made him a first-rate organiser. At home in the medical circles of Europe, he broke down the insularity which still militates against the progress of English surgery, and he learned and taught what was done at home and abroad.

Of four portraits in oils, one, by Mr. H. Harris Brown, was presented to Queen's College, Belfast, on 9 March 1897; two by Prince Troubetskoi belong to Lady MacCormac, and the fourth is in the medical committee room at St. Thomas's Hospital. A marble bust by A. Drury, A.R.A., is in the central hall at St. Thomas's Hospital. A cartoon portrait by 'Spy' appeared in 'Vanity Fair' in 1906.

MacCormac published: 1. 'Notes and Recollections of an Ambulance Surgeon, being an Account of Work done under the Red Cross during the Campaign of 1870,' 1871; translated into German by Professor Louis Stromeyer, Hanover, 1871, and into Italian by Dr. Eugenio Bellina, Firenze, 1872. 2. 'Surgical Operations,' part 1, 1885, 2nd edit. 1891; part 2, 1889. 3. 'On Abdominal Section for the Treatment of Intraperitoneal Injury,' 1887; translated into

German, Leipzig, 1888. 4. 'An Address of Welcome on the Occasion of the Centenary Festival of the Royal College of Surgeons of England,' 1900; with biographical accounts, often with portraits, of the sixty-one masters or presidents.

[Belfast News Letter, 5 Dec. 1901; Northern Whig, 5 Dec. 1901; St. Thomas's Hosp. Reports, vol. xxx. 1901, p. 322; private information; personal knowledge.] D'A. P.

MACDERMOT, HUGH HYACINTH O'RORKE, THE MACDERMOT (1834–1904), attorney-general for Ireland, born on 1 July 1834 at Coolavin, co. Sligo, was eldest of the twelve children of Charles Joseph MacDermot, titular 'Prince of Coolavin,' by his wife Arabella O'Rorke, the last lineal descendant of the Breffny family. The family, which was Roman catholic, lost most of their lands in the civil wars in Ireland in the seventeenth century, and they lived for generations in great retirement at Coolavin, where the head, despite his narrow means, maintained much personal state (cf. ARTHUR YOUNG'S *Tour in Ireland*, i. 219).

A brother, John MacDermot (known locally from his swarthy complexion as 'The Black Prince'), became a canon of Achonry and was a notable rider to hounds.

Educated at home by his father until 27 Aug. 1852, at eighteen he entered the Royal College of St. Patrick, Maynooth, as a candidate for the priesthood. He was 'head of his year' there in every subject. He remained at Maynooth until 1856, when he abandoned the ecclesiastical career, and obtaining a burse on the nomination of the bishops, entered in November the catholic university in St. Stephen's Green, Dublin, of which Newman was rector. There during 1857 and 1858 he gained various distinctions in classics and English (*Calendars*, 1856–9).

On leaving the university in 1859 MacDermot read law in Dublin and London, and won a studentship of 50*l.* a year given by the Council of Legal Education in London. Admitted a student of the King's Inns, Dublin, in Michaelmas term 1857, he was called in Michaelmas term 1862, and was summoned to the inner bar in Feb. 1877. He was elected a bencher on 11 Jan. 1884.

MacDermot went the Connaught circuit, on which he became the chief junior. He later acquired leading Dublin business. Though no great orator, he was a first-rate lawyer, and understood the management of witnesses and juries.

At the celebrated Galway election petition in 1872 before Judge Keogh, MacDermot held the junior brief for Colonel Nolan, the sitting member. He was a senior counsel in the action for libel brought against Lord Clanricarde by Frank Joyce, his former agent, in 1883; and appeared for A. M. Sullivan [q. v.] in the prosecution for sedition in 1880, and for Mr. Wilfrid Scawen Blunt in an attempt to quash on *certiorari* Blunt's conviction by a crimes court in 1887. After taking silk MacDermot held a leading brief in nearly every important case from the West of Ireland, especially in those of a political complexion.

On the death of his father on 5 Dec. 1873 MacDermot became 'The MacDermot' and titular 'Prince of Coolavin.' A strong liberal in politics, he was made in May 1885 solicitor-general for Ireland in Gladstone's second administration. He retired with the ministry in the following July, but held the office again from February to August 1886 in Gladstone's third administration. When Gladstone became prime minister for the fourth time in 1892 MacDermot was made attorney-general and was sworn of the privy council in Ireland. He remained attorney-general till 1895. MacDermot never sat in the House of Commons. He failed in his only attempt to obtain a seat in 1892, when he contested West Derbyshire against Mr. Victor Cavendish, afterwards ninth duke of Devonshire. He said laughingly that the voters mistook him for 'the Great Macdermott,' the music-hall singer [see MACDERMOTT, GILBERT HASTINGS, Suppl. II].

MacDermot died on 6 February 1904 at 10 FitzWilliam Place, Dublin, and was buried in the catholic church, Monasteraden, co. Sligo. He married twice: (1) on 1 Dec. 1861, Mary (*d.* 1871), daughter of Edward Howley, D.L., of Belleek Castle, by whom he had three sons; (2) in 1872, Henrietta Maria, daughter of Henry Blake, J.P., by whom he had five sons.

[Burke's Landed Gentry of Ireland, 1904, p. 368; Thom's Directory for 1904; Irish Times and Independent, 8 Feb. 1904; The College Register of the Royal College of St. Patrick, Maynooth (27 Aug. 1852 and 7 Feb. 1853).] D. F.

MACDERMOTT, GILBERT HASTINGS, whose real surname was FARRELL (1845–1901), music-hall singer, born on 27 Feb. 1845, served in youth in the royal navy. As 'Gilbert Hastings' he made his first appearance on the stage in 1869, as 'utility' actor at Dover. A few months later he came to London, making his first appearance as 'G. H. Macdermott' at the Oriental Theatre, Poplar. Later he played at the Grecian (1870–1), Britannia (1871–2), Sanger's (1873), and the Gaiety (1873). A fair actor in parts like Myles-Na-Coppaleen in 'The Colleen Bawn,' Richard Varney in 'Amy Robsart,' he was also a versatile playwright in melodrama, and among plays of his which were produced in London were 'The Headsman's Axe' at the Grecian (1870), 'Driven from Home,' at the Grecian (1871), 'The Mystery of Edwin Drood,' 'Brought to Book' (with Henry Pettitt, [q.v.], 1876), both produced at the Britannia, and 'Racing' (1887), at the Grand Theatre, Islington.

Meanwhile, in 1873 Macdermott made his first appearance at the London Pavilion music-hall, singing 'The Scamp,' the first of a highly successful series of comic songs. In 1874 he accompanied the *opera-bouffe* artiste, Julia Matthews, to America as both stage manager and actor. He appeared with her at the Eagle theatre, New York, in such pieces as 'The Irish Heiress' (1 Nov. 1875) and 'Giroflé-Girofla,' and played Bob Brierley in 'The Ticket of Leave Man' (February 1876). On his return to England in April 1876 he acted at the Britannia Theatre in 'Brought to Book,' and then returned to the London Pavilion, where he sang such popular songs as 'I'll strike you with a Feather' and 'The Two Obadiahs.'

Early in 1878, when political excitement in England over the Russo-Turkish war ran high, and Lord Beaconsfield, the prime minister, sent a British fleet into Turkish waters to resist the advance of Russia, Macdermott leapt into universal fame by his singing of a song written and composed by George William Hunt (1829 ?–1904), a most fertile composer of music-hall songs, who was author of some ballet music and of the incidental music to the burlesque 'Monte Christo, Jr.,' and was also a painter of some merit (he died in Essex County Asylum of softening of the brain on 3 March 1904; cf. *Musical Herald,* April 1904; *Referee,* 22 Oct. 1911). Hunt's patriotic song of 1878, with a swinging tune and a refrain beginning:

We don't want to fight,
But *by Jingo,* if we do,
We've got the ships, we've got the men,
We've got the money too,

became at Macdermott's instigation the watchword of the popular supporters of England's bellicose policy. The 'Daily News' on 11 March 1878 first dubbed the latter 'Jingoes' in derision, and George Jacob Holyoake [q. v. Suppl. II] wrote to the paper on 13 March 1878 of 'The Jingoes—the new type of music-hall patriots who sing the Jingo song.' Macdermott continued singing the 'Jingo' song for two years, and at his call the words 'jingo' and 'jingoism' passed permanently into the English language in the sense of 'aggressive patriot' and 'aggressive patriotism' (cf. *New English Dict.* s.v. 'Jingo').

Later songs which owed their popularity to Macdermott were 'On the Strict Q.T.' and 'Jubilation Day,' which, set to the Boulangist tune 'Le Père de Victoire,' was popular during Queen Victoria's jubilee year, 1887.

'The Great Macdermott' was of fine stature and commanding presence, and possessed a powerful if unmelodious voice. He was practically the last of the 'lion comiques' of the English music-hall, resplendent in evening dress with a vast expanse of shirt-front. In his later years Macdermott performed in dramatic sketches at music-halls, making a hit in 'Our Lads in Red.' His last appearances were at the London Pavilion and Tivoli music-hall in 1894. Subsequently he was proprietor and managing director of several music-halls.

He died of cancer at his residence in Clapham on 8 May 1901, and was buried at West Norwood cemetery. He was twice married, his second wife being well known on the music-hall stage as Annie Milburn. An engraved portrait appeared in the 'Era,' 11 May 1901.

[Personal recollections; Daily Telegraph, 9 May 1901; The Times, 10 May 1901; Era, 11 May 1901; Notes and Queries, 20 July 1901; information from Mr. Henry Davey.] J. P.

MACDERMOTT, MARTIN (1823–1905), Irish poet and architect, was born of catholic parents at 8 Ormond Quay, Dublin, on 8 April 1823. His father, John MacDermott (1785–1842), was a merchant; his mother, Amelie Therese Boshell, was of French descent. He was educated as a catholic in Dublin and Boulogne-sur-Mer, but became a protestant in early life. He was articled to Patrick Byrne, R.H.A., a well-known Dublin architect, but his studies were interrupted by participation in the Young Ireland movement. He occasionally wrote, chiefly in verse, for the 'Nation' from 1840 onwards. When, in 1848, the Young Irelanders desired to enlist the sympathy of the French government in their struggle for Irish independence, MacDermott was one of the delegates sent to Paris to interview Lamartine, then foreign minister in the new republican government. Lamartine made MacDermott and his friends a glowing speech of welcome but published so disappointingly colourless a report of the interview in the official 'Moniteur' as to convince them of the impossibility of practical help. Lamartine appears to have understood the Irishmen to ask for armed aid, whereas they only looked for moral support (cf. GAVAN DUFFY, *Four Years of Irish History*, pp. 567, 568). MacDermott remained in Paris as the representative of the 'Nation,' but soon after its suppression in 1848 went to Birkenhead, where he completed his training in a local architect's office. Coming to London after 1850, he entered the office of (Sir) Charles Liddell, and was employed chiefly on the stations of the Metropolitan railway extension. He obtained the post of chief architect to the Egyptian government, and spent some years in Alexandria from 1866 onwards. Some twelve years later he retired and settled in London. His subsequent years were devoted to literary work. In 1879 he translated Viollet-le-Duc's 'Essay on the Military Architecture of the Middle Ages.' A constant correspondent of Sir Charles Gavan Duffy [q. v. Suppl. II], he was intimately associated with him in 1892–5 in his scheme of the 'New Irish Library,' a series of books designed to continue the successful national library inaugurated in 1843. For the series, which was not well supported, MacDermott prepared an anthology of Irish poetry called 'The New Spirit of the Nation,' 1894. He died at his residence at Cotham, Bristol, on 25 April 1905.

MacDermott's poems are few and of homely quality. Two of them, 'The Coulin' and 'Exiles Far Away,' have achieved great popularity. He is represented in 'Brooke and Rolleston's Treasury of Irish Poetry' (1905) by 'Girl of the Red Mouth.' Besides the publications already cited, MacDermott edited 'Irish Poetry' for the 'Penny Poets' series; 'Poems and Ballads of Young Ireland' (1896); and, with additions, Thomas Moore's 'Life of Lord Edward Fitzgerald' (1897).

He married about 1860 Miss Martha Melladew of Liverpool, and by her had nine children, of whom three sons and three daughters survived him.

[Freeman's Journal, 27 April 1905; correspondence with present writer; information kindly supplied by Miss Maud MacDermott of Taunton; the Architect and Contract Reporter, May 1905; personal knowledge; Duffy's Young Ireland.] D. J. O'D.

MACDONALD, GEORGE (1824–1905), poet and novelist, born on 10 Dec. 1824 at Huntly, West Aberdeenshire, was descended from one of the 120 MacDonalds who made good their escape from the massacre of Glencoe in Feb. 1692. His Jacobite great-grandfather was born on 16 April 1746, the day of the battle of Culloden, in which his great-great-grandfather, a red-haired piper, lost his sight. From Portsoy in Banffshire the family ultimately moved to Huntly, where George MacDonald's grandfather, who spoke Gaelic, was farmer and banker. The author's father, also George MacDonald, grew up on the farm, marrying as his first wife Helen, daughter of Captain MacKay, of Celtic lineage, and sister of the Gaelic scholar, Mackintosh MacKay [q. v.]. His parents were congregationalists. Of five sons, George was the youngest. His mother dying soon after his birth, his father married as his second wife, in 1839 Margaret MacColl, who proved a kind stepmother to George and his brothers. George began his education on his father's farm and then at a small school at Huntly. In the autumn of 1840 he won at King's College, Aberdeen, a Fullerton bursary of 14*l.* as 12th bursar, and he attended college for four years from 1840–1 to 1844–5, omitting 1842–3. He studied hard to the injury of his health, eking out his narrow means by teaching. Sir William Duguid Geddes [q. v. Suppl. I] was among his contemporaries. George took the third prize in chemistry and was fourth prizeman in natural philosophy.

Already a poet who saw symbolic meanings in what others found commonplace, he was regarded by the students as something of a visionary. Of his university life he gave a graphic picture in his poem 'Hidden Life' (in *Poems*, 1857). He graduated M.A. in March 1845, and on 28 February 1868 his university made him hon. LL.D.

Seeking a livelihood in tutorial work, MacDonald removed to London soon after graduating, and in Sept. 1848 he entered the theological college at Highbury to prepare for the congregational ministry.

Finding the ways of Highbury College uncongenial, he did not finish his course there, but he was duly ordained to his first and only charge, the Trinity congregational chapel at Arundel, in 1850. His spiritual and intellectual independence dissatisfied his congregation. Proposals to reduce his small stipend on the ground of lack of doctrine in his sermons led to his resignation at the close of 1853. Resolving to devote himself to literature, he moved to Manchester. There he grew intimate with Alexander John Scott [q. v.], principal of Owens College, and with Henry Septimus Sutton [q. v. Suppl. II], a religious poet who was a friend of Coventry Patmore. Both men deeply influenced MacDonald. Although ill-health and poverty made his position difficult, his work at Manchester brought him his earliest recognition. In 1855 he published his first book, a poem 'Within and Without,' of which the first draft had been written at Arundel in the winter of 1850. It is a poetic tragedy of married love and misunderstanding. In the ardour of their religious aspiration, many lines recall Browning's earlier poems, especially 'Pauline,' though without Browning's obscurity. The book won the appreciation of Tennyson and the intense admiration of Lady Byron, who became at once one of MacDonald's close friends. A volume of poems published in 1857 strengthened MacDonald's reputation, and in 1858 there appeared in prose 'Phantastes,' a faerie allegorical romance equally attractive as allegory and fairy-tale. It quickly took rank with 'Undine' and other classics of the kind. Its lyrics are among MacDonald's most fascinating and impressive verse.

MacDonald's energy was thenceforth largely absorbed by prose fiction of two kinds, one of which dealt with the mystical and psychic and the other described humble life in Scotland. 'David Elginbrod' (1863; new edit. 1871), dedicated to Lady Byron's memory, 'Adela Cathcart' (1864), and 'The Portent,' a story of second sight (1864), were early studies in the first category, and effectively challenged the materialism of the day. 'Alec Forbes' (1865) and 'Robert Falconer' (1868) will rank among the classics of Scottish literature in their powerful delineation of Scottish character, their sense of the nobility of country work, and their appreciation of ideal beauty. A quaint humour tinged MacDonald's stern opposition to the rigid theology of Scottish orthodoxy, and these books did much to weaken the force of Calvinism and to broaden spiritual ideals. The same aim was pursued with growing effect in the succeeding novels, chiefly in Scottish settings, 'Malcolm' (1875), 'St. George and St. Michael' (1876), 'The Marquis of Lossie' (1877), a sequel to 'Malcolm,' 'Paul Faber, Surgeon' (1879), in which philosophic reflection both in prose and verse predominates, 'Sir Gibbie' (1879), and 'Castle Warlock, a homely romance' (1882)

After he gave up his formal ministry at Arundel, MacDonald long continued to preach as a layman. From his first settling in Manchester he delivered sermons to a company of working men who rented a room for the purpose, and when a serious illness compelled him in 1856 to winter in Algiers, his hearers subscribed the cost of the expedition. From Algiers he returned to Hastings, and there three years (1857–1860) were spent before he finally settled in London. His first house was in Queen Square, Bloomsbury, and thence he moved to Tudor Lodge in Albert Street, Regent's Park. In London his social circle quickly extended. His friendship with Frederick Denison Maurice led him to become a lay member of the Church of England. Maurice was godfather to his fourth son. But his relations with nonconformists remained close, and he continued to accept invitations to preach in their pulpits as a layman.

Like Robert Browning, who became a friend, he often heard the Welsh poet preacher, Thomas Jones [q. v.]. Ruskin was another admiring associate and visitor at MacDonald's London house, and he cited MacDonald's poem, 'Diary of an Old Soul' (1880), with Longfellow's 'Hiawatha' and Keble's hymns as evidence 'that the generation . . . might fairly claim to be an age not destitute of religious poetry' (*Pleasures of England*). MacDonald formed intimate friendships with such widely differing people as the Carlyles, William Morris, Burne Jones, Lord Tennyson, Octavia Hill, Dean Stanley, Matthew Arnold, the eighth duke of Argyll, John Stuart Blackie, Lord Houghton, Lord and Lady Mount-Temple, Arthur Hughes, and his publisher, Alexander Strahan, to whose generosity he owed much.

Besides writing and preaching without intermission, MacDonald was sole editor of 'Good Words for the Young' (1872–3), and he also lectured on Shakespeare and other literary themes in London with great success. His lectures were at once scholarly and imaginative; they were delivered extempore. For a short time he held an evening lectureship in literature at King's College, London, and in 1872 he went on a lecturing tour in America, where he found enthusiastic audiences. There he met Whittier, Longfellow, Oliver Wendell Holmes, C. D. Warner, R. W. Gilder, and Emerson.

Despite his activity, MacDonald's income was still small. In 1877 he was granted by the special desire of Queen Victoria a civil list pension of 100*l*. In the interests of health from 1881 to 1902 he spent the greater part of each year at Casa Coraggio at Bordighera. The house was built by himself largely out of contributions by friends. At Bordighera as in London, where his charities were unceasing, he proved a friend to all the neighbouring poor. In 1902 he returned to England to a house built for him at Haslemere by his eldest son. He died after a long illness at Ashtead, the home of his youngest daughter, now Lady Troup, on 18 Sept. 1905. His ashes after cremation at Woking were buried in the English cemetery at Bordighera.

Of two portraits in oil by Sir George Reid, one is in the library of King's College, Aberdeen, and the other belongs to Dr. Greville MacDonald, of 85 Harley Street, who also owns a portrait in red chalk by E. R. Hughes, dating about 1880. A bust by George Anderson Lawson [q. v. Suppl. II] was shown at the Royal Academy in 1871.

MacDonald married in 1851 Louisa, daughter of James Powell, who was in complete sympathy with his ideals. She adapted for stage representation a series of scenes from the 'Pilgrim's Progress,' in which her husband and her children took part, and the experiment led the way for later revival by others of old miracle plays. She died and was buried at Bordighera in 1902 soon after the celebration of her golden wedding. Of a family of six sons and five daughters, five sons and two daughters survived their father. The eldest son is Dr. Greville MacDonald, and the youngest daughter, Winifred Louisa, is wife of Sir Charles Edward Troup, K.C.B., LL.D.

MacDonald was above all else a poet. 'The Diary of an Old Soul' must rank with the best work of Crashaw and Vaughan. Both his verse and his stories for children have a dainty humour and an unobtrusive symbolism which place them in much the same category as Hans Andersen's tales. In the beautiful simplicity of his character and in his courtly charm of manner MacDonald has been likened to Count Tolstoy, but to an extent unknown to Tolstoy's later life he mingled with the world. Besides the books already named, MacDonald's works include: 1. 'Unspoken Sermons' (3 vols. 1867, 1885, and 1889). 2. 'The Disciple, and other Poems,' 1868. 3. 'England's Antiphon,' 1868; new edit. 1874. 4. 'At the Back of the North Wind,' 1871. 5. 'The Princess and the Goblin,' 1872. 6. 'Ranald Bannerman's Boyhood,' 1871. 7. 'Gutta Percha Willie,' 1873. 8. 'Thomas Wingfold, Curate' (in 'The Day of Rest'), 1876, new edit. 1880. 9. 'Letters from Hell,' with preface by George MacDonald, 1884. 10. Shakespeare's 'Hamlet,' study with the text of the folio of 1623 (1885). 11. 'Miracles of our Lord,' 1886. 12. 'Home Again,' 1887. 13. 'There and Back,' 1891. 14. 'The Hope of the Gospel,' 1892. 15. 'Heather and Snow,' 1893. 16. 'A Dish of Orts,' a volume of essays, 1893. 'Works of Fancy and Imagination,' a collective edition (excluding the novels), appeared in 1886 (10 vols.). MacDonald's 'Poetical Works' (2 vols.) appeared in 1893 (new edit. 1911). In 1904 a new collected edition of 'The Fairy Tales' followed, and in 1905 a new edition of 'Phantastes' illustrated by Arthur Hughes.

[The Times, 19 Sept. 1905; Contemporary Review, Dec. 1871, art. signed Henry Holbeach; Bookman, Nov. 1905; Blackwood's Magazine, Mar. 1891, a generous appreciation by Sir William Geddes; George MacDonald, a biographical and critical appreciation, by Joseph Johnson, 1906; private information.

A. M–n.

MACDONALD, Sir HECTOR ARCHIBALD (1853–1903), major-general, youngest of five sons of William Macdonald, a crofter-mason, by his wife Ann, daughter of John Boyd, was born at Rootfield, Urquhart, on 13 April 1853. After employment in a draper's shop at Dingwall, he enlisted as a private in the 92nd Gordon highlanders in August 1870, when eighteen, and served about nine and a half years in the ranks and as colour-sergeant. He first saw active service in the second Afghan war. On 27 Sept. 1879 he showed skill and energy in driving the enemy from the Hazardarakt pass near Karatiga and thereby enabling Lord Roberts to continue his march to Kushi. He again distinguished himself at the action of Charasiab on 6 October following by dislodging a picquet, which was causing much annoyance by its fire. He was mentioned in despatches on both occasions. He took part in the Maidan expedition, in the operations round Kabul in December 1879, including the defence of the Sherpur cantonments, the attack upon Takt-i-Shah, the engagement of Childukhtan, and the second action at Charasiab. He accompanied Lord Roberts on his march from Kabul to Kandahar in August 1880, and was engaged at the reconnaissance of 31 August and at the battle of 1 September, distinguishing himself at the capture of Ayub Khan's camp at Baba Wali. His dash and prowess in the field, which won him the sobriquet of 'Fighting Mac,' led General Roberts to promote him at Kabul to the rank of second lieutenant in the Gordon highlanders; his commission was ratified on 7 Jan. 1880, when his claymore was presented to him by his brother officers. He was awarded the Afghan medal with three clasps and the bronze decoration (Despatches, *Lond. Gaz.* 16 Jan. 1880). On the way home from India Macdonald and two companies of the 92nd Highlanders were landed in Natal to join Sir George Colley [q. v.] in his attempt to relieve the British garrisons in the Transvaal. At the battle of Majuba 'Fighting Mac' displayed heroic courage (*Lond. Gaz.* 3 May 1881). He was taken prisoner, but General Joubert was so impressed with the bravery of his defence that on his release his sword was returned to him. He became full lieutenant on 1 July 1881.

In 1883 Macdonald's appointment to a post in the Egyptian constabulary under Valentine Baker [q. v. Suppl. I] opened a new phase in his career. Incidentally he shared in the Nile expedition of 1885, serving as garrison adjutant at Assiout from 22 Jan. to 5 June 1885. After the failure of that expedition Macdonald played an important part in reorganising the Egyptian army, and was mainly associated with the training of the 11th Sudanese regiment, which he modelled on the Highlanders. He became captain in 1888, and was transferred to the Egyptian army. The Sudan campaign of 1888–91 gave Macdonald the opportunity of testing the steadiness of the Sudanese troops under his command. Their conduct at Toski (3 Aug. 1889) and the capture of Tokar (19 Feb. 1891) reflected great credit on Macdonald's training and example (*Lond. Gaz.* 11 Jan. 1889 and 6 Sept. 1889). He received the medal with two clasps, bronze star with clasp, third-class of the Medjidie, and the distinguished service order (25 Feb. 1890), as well as the third-class of the Osmanie. He was promoted major on 7 July 1891 and was attached to the 7th royal fusiliers, while remaining in Egypt. In 1896, when Sir Herbert (afterwards Viscount) Kitchener began the reconquest of the Sudan, Macdonald was appointed to the command of a brigade of Egyptian infantry in the expedition to Dongola. Both at Ferkeh on 7 June and Hafir on 19 September he showed a rare gift for handling troops, and for his services received the brevet of lieut.-colonel on 18 Nov. 1896 and the Egyptian medal with two clasps. He served also in the Nile expedition of 1897–8, and commanded an Egyptian brigade at the action of Abu Hamed (*Lond. Gaz.* 25 Jan. 1898, two clasps to Egyptian medal), and at the battle of Atbara (8 April 1898). The adroitness he displayed at Omdurman (2 Sept. 1898) in wheeling round his brigade through a complete half circle, half battalion by half battalion, to meet an unexpected flank attack of the Dervishes, turned what might have proved disaster into victory (*Lond. Gaz.* 24 May and 20 Sept. 1898). 'Fighting Mac' became a popular hero on his return, and the enthusiasm was enhanced by the fact that he had risen from the ranks. He had been nominated C.B. on 22 June 1897, and was appointed A.D.C. to Queen Victoria, with brevet of colonel, on 16 Nov. 1898. He was thanked by both Houses of Parliament and received the Egyptian medal with two clasps.

From 24 Oct. 1899 till 3 Jan. 1900 he was a brigadier-general in India, commanding the Sirhind district in the Punjab with headquarters at Umballa; he attained the rank of major-general on relinquishing the command. On the death of Major-general Wauchope [q. v. Suppl. I] at the battle of Magersfontein (10 Dec. 1899) Macdonald succeeded him in the command of the Highland brigade, and at once proceeded to South Africa. There he maintained his high reputation. He prepared the way for Lord Roberts's march to the relief of Kimberley by seizing Koodoesberg (5–8 Feb. 1900), and by this demonstration the attention of the Boers was distracted from the main advance. He was present at the operations which resulted in the surrender of General Cronje's army at Paardeberg (16–27 Feb. 1900). In the attack on the Boer laager on 18 Feb. he was slightly wounded while leading the Highland brigade. During the reduction of the Free State he was attached to the ninth division under Sir Henry Colvile [q. v. Suppl. II]. On the march from Lindley to Heilbron he took part in several stubbornly contested actions (27–31 May 1900), and was engaged in the operations that led to the surrender of General Prinsloo at Brandwater. During the subsequent guerilla warfare he directed bodies of troops in the south-east of the Orange River Colony, being from the beginning of 1901 stationed at Aliwal North. For his services in South Africa he was created a K.C.B. in 1900, and given the command of the Belgaum district in southern India in 1901. In May 1902 he was transferred to the command of the troops in Ceylon.

There disaster befel him. Early in 1903 an opprobrious accusation against him was reported to the governor of Ceylon (Sir West Ridgeway), who at once granted Macdonald's request for leave to return to

London and discuss the matter with the war office authorities. The latter directed a court of inquiry to be held in Ceylon. Macdonald left London on his way thither on 24 March, and shot himself next day at the Hôtel Regina in Paris. He was buried in the Dean cemetery, Edinburgh. In 1884 he married Christina McDonald, daughter of Alexander MacLouchlan Duncan of Leith; she died at Edinburgh on 11 March 1911, leaving one son.

Macdonald holds an exceptional place in the history of the British army as a private who rose wholly by virtue of his soldierly capacity and physical courage to all but the highest military rank. As a dauntless fighter and a resourceful leader of men in battle he acquired well-merited fame. A rough tongue always showed traces of his origin. Among the Highlanders his memory was idolised. A memorial in the form of a tower 100 feet high was completed at Dingwall, overlooking his birthplace, on 23 May 1907.

[The Times, 26 March 1903; T. F. G. Coates, Hector Macdonald, 1900; D. Campbell, Major-General Hector A. Macdonald, 1900; D. L. Cromb, Hector Macdonald, 1903; Hart's and Official Army Lists; S. P. Oliver, The Second Afghan War, 1878–80, 1908; Lord Roberts, Forty-One Years in India, 30th edit. 1898; G. W. Steevens, With Kitchener to Khartum, 1898, pp. 57, 278 seq.; Winston Churchill, The River War, 1899; Maurice, History of the War in South Africa, 4 vols. 1906–10.] H. M. V.

McDONALD, JOHN BLAKE (1829–1901), Scottish artist, son of James McDonald, wood merchant, was born at Boharm, Morayshire, on 24 May 1829. He was educated there, but, going to Edinburgh with a taste for art, he entered the academy of the Board of Trustees in Edinburgh in 1853. He proved a good student both then and later in the life school of the Royal Scottish Academy, where in 1862 he won the first prize for painting from the life. But retaining much of the chiaroscuro of the earlier school, and being, in spite of a certain dexterity and force of execution, heavy in handling and dull in colour, his pictures lacked the charm and fine quality which mark those of Lauder's best pupils. They were effective, however, and popular, for most of the more important dealt with dramatic or picturesque episodes in highland history or Jacobite romance, and in 1862 he was elected an associate of the Royal Scottish Academy and academician in 1877. In 1874 he was in Venice, where he painted a number of pictures, and after 1878 he practically abandoned figure for landscape, in which he did some vigorous work of the transcript kind in both oil and water-colour. One of his best pictures, 'Prince Charlie leaving Scotland,' is in the Albert Institute, Dundee, and his diploma work, 'Glencoe, 1692,' is also a characteristic example. Dying in Edinburgh on 20 Dec. 1901, he was survived by his second wife and a grown-up family.

[Scotsman, 21 Dec. 1901; R.S.A. Report, 1902; Nat. Gall. of Scotland Cat.] J. L. C.

MACDONALD, Sir JOHN DENIS (1826–1908), inspector-general of hospitals and fleets, born at Cork on 26 Oct. 1826, was youngest son of James Macdonald, artist, by his wife Catherine, daughter of Denis McCarthy of Kilcoleman, co. Cork. His father was the representative of the Castleton branch of the Macdonald family, and claimant of the Annandale peerage through his great-grandfather, the Hon. John Johnston of Stapleton. He was privately educated, and after attending the Cork school of medicine went to King's College medical school to finish his course. Having qualified, he entered the navy as assistant surgeon in 1849 and was appointed to the Royal Hospital, Plymouth. In 1852 he was appointed to the Herald, and continued in her on surveying service in the South Pacific until 1859. In the same year he was elected a fellow of the Royal Society for his unremitting microscopic studies with the aid of the sounding-lead, dredge, and towing-net, and was promoted to surgeon. In 1862 he was awarded the Makdougall-Brisbane medal by the Royal Society of Edinburgh for his deep-sea investigations. In 1864 he was appointed to Haslar Hospital, and in June 1870 as staff surgeon to the Lord Warden, flagship in the Mediterranean. In 1871 he was awarded the Gilbert Blane medal. In March 1872 he was appointed to the flagship at Portsmouth for service as professor of naval hygiene at Netley; this post he continued to hold after his promotion to deputy inspector-general in Feb. 1875. In July 1880 he was promoted inspector-general, and in that rank was in charge of the Royal Naval Hospital at Plymouth from 1883 to 1886. He retired on 24 May 1886. He was made K.C.B. in 1902. His chief publications were 'The Analogy of Sound and Colour' (1869); 'Outlines of Naval Hygiene' (1881); and a 'Guide to the Microscopical Examination of Drinking Water' (1883). He died at Southall on 7 Feb. 1908.

Macdonald was twice married: (1) in 1863 to Sarah Phœbe (*d.* 1875), daughter of Ely Walker of Stainland, Yorkshire, by whom he had two sons and two daughters; (2) to Erina, daughter of William Archer, prebendary of Limerick. She died in 1893, without issue.

[The Times, 11 Feb. 1908; information from the family.] L. G. C. L.

MACDONELL, Sir HUGH GUION (1832–1904), soldier and diplomatist, was second son of Hugh MacDonell, who as British consul-general at Algiers rendered important services, and with his second wife, daughter of Admiral Ulrich, the Danish consul-general, went through a period of great personal suffering and danger during Lord Exmouth's mission and the bombardment of the town in 1816. Owing to subsequent protests of the Dey against the elder MacDonell's continuance in the office of consul-general, he was pensioned off, and retired to Florence, where his son, Hugh Guion, was born on 5 March 1832, being one of a family of two sons and six daughters. His elder brother, General Sir Alexander F. MacDonell, died in 1891. His eldest sister, married to the Marquis de la Marismas, was Dame du Palais to the Empress Eugénie and died in 1908.

Hugh was educated for the army at the Royal Military College, Sandhurst. He joined the rifle brigade in 1849, and served for three years in British Kaffraria. He retired from the army on 11 March 1853, and entered the diplomatic service in the following year, becoming attaché at Florence. He was promoted to be paid attaché at Constantinople in December 1858, and served there till 1866, when he was transferred to Copenhagen. In 1869 he was appointed secretary of legation at Buenos Ayres, was transferred to Madrid in 1872, and after three years of service there was promoted to be secretary of embassy at Berlin (1875–8) and subsequently at Rome (1878–82). After serving as chargé d'affaires at Munich from 1882 to 1885, he held in succession the appointments of British envoy at Rio (1885–8), at Copenhagen (1888–93), and at Lisbon (1893–1902). The outbreak of war between Great Britain and the two South African republics in October 1899 raised some very difficult and delicate questions between this country and Portugal, whose port at Lourenço Marques was directly connected with the Transvaal by rail and afforded the principal, if not the only, channel for supplies and external communications when access through the British colonies had been closed. MacDonell's management of the discussions which he had to conduct on these subjects was perfectly tactful and conciliatory, and contributed in no small degree to the maintenance of cordial relations.

His services were recognised by the distinction of C.M.G. in 1889; C.B. in 1890; K.C.M.G. in 1892; and G.C.M.G. in 1899. On his retirement in 1902 he was made a privy councillor, and died in London on 25 Jan. 1904. MacDonell married in July 1870, while at Buenos Aires, Anne, daughter of Edward Lumb, of Wallington Lodge, Surrey, by whom he had four sons and one daughter.

[The Times, 26 Jan. 1904; Foreign Office List, 1905, p. 268; The Scourge of Christendom, by Lieut.-col. Playfair, pp. 249–305.] S.

MACE, JAMES, 'Jem Mace' (1831–1910), pugilist, born on 8 April 1831 at Beeston, near Swaffham, Norfolk, was son of a tenant on the Windham Estates there. Early in life he was associated with a travelling booth, where he played the violin and gave boxing exhibitions. While thus engaged he attracted the notice of Nat Langham, a showman and former boxing champion, the only vanquisher of Tom Sayers [q.v.], who invited Mace to join his show. Mace made great strides in boxing; his first important fight took place on 2 Oct. 1855 at Mildenhall, Suffolk, when he defeated a local boxer named Slack. His fame soon reached London, and on 17 Feb. 1857 he met and easily beat Bill Thorpe at Canvey Island. Mace was thenceforth acknowledged to be one of the best boxers of his generation. With boxing matches Mace long combined the avocations of publican and circus performer. In 1858 he kept the Swan Inn, Swan Lane, Norwich, and in 1861 the 'Old King John,' Holywell Lane, Shoreditch. He toured with Pablo Fanque's circus during 1861, and with Ginnett's circus in 1862. At one time he was proprietor of the Strawberry recreation grounds, Liverpool.

Meanwhile his fame as a boxer grew, and his matches were numerous. He defeated Bob Brettle, a former victor, on the Essex coast, on 19 and 20 Jan. 1860, thus becoming middle-weight champion. Mace's victory on 18 June 1861 over Sam Hurst (a Lancashire giant, 6 ft. 2½ ins. in height and weighing 15 stone) greatly increased his reputation, and he was challenged for the championship by Thomas King [q.v.] for 200*l.* a side. The meeting took place on 28 Jan. 1862, and after forty-three rounds of very even fighting Mace won by scientific methods; but he was in turn beaten at

Aldershot by King on 26 Nov. following. On King's retirement Mace resumed the title of champion, was challenged by and beat Joe Goss after a severe battle at Plumstead Marshes, Purfleet, on 1 Sept. 1863, and again defeated him decisively on 6 Aug. 1866. A championship match with an Irish giant, O'Baldwin (afterwards Ned Baldwin), 6 ft. 4½ ins. in height, was arranged for 15 Oct. 1867; but the laws against prize-fighting were at length rigidly enforced, and Mace was arrested, having been chased by the police from Woodford, Essex, and bound over to keep the peace. Mace then went to America, where at New Orleans he outfought Tom Allen of Birmingham on 10 May 1870, and drew with Joe Coburn on 30 Nov. 1871. A visit to Canada preceded his return to London. Subsequently he continued his boxing career in Australia, and carried on a publican's business at Melbourne. He again returned to England, and in 1901 was in charge of the 'Black Bull,' Colville Street, Birmingham, but later, falling into poverty, toured the country with travelling shows and gave sparring exhibitions till his death at Jarrow on 30 Nov. 1910.

Mace married twice late in life and had issue. A black and tint portrait appeared in the 'Licensed Victuallers' Gazette,' 14 April 1899.

The last of the representatives of the old prize ring, Mace, who had a fine constitution and was of great strength and agility, had few if any superiors in his art. He had a graceful and effective style, combined with accurate and scientific judgment and straight hitting, especially with the left. In his matches with Joe Goss he maintained the old traditions of the ring, and remained incorruptible at a time when boxing was on its decline. He never met his contemporary, Tom Sayers [q. v.], whose superior some judges considered him to be.

[The Times, 1 Dec. 1910; Licensed Victuallers' Gazette, 2 Dec. 1910; Manchester Guardian, 2 April 1910 (interview); H. D. Miles, Pugilistica, 1906, iii. 444–488; Fistiana, 1868; F. W. J. Henning, Some Recollections of the Prize Ring, 1888, and Fights for the Championship, 1902, ii. 440 seq. (with portrait).] W. B. O.

MACFADYEN, ALLAN (1860–1907), bacteriologist, born on 26 May 1860 at Glasgow, was youngest of the four sons of Archibald Macfadyen, brass founder in Glasgow, by his wife Margaret, daughter of D. McKinlay of Stornaway. He was educated at Dr. Bryce's collegiate school at Edinburgh from 1871, and became a student in the university of Edinburgh in 1878, graduating M.B., C.M. (1883), M.D. with gold medal (1886), and B.Sc. in hygiene (1888). He studied chemistry and bacteriology in Berne, Göttingen, and Munich, and returning to England became a research scholar of the Grocers' Company (1889–1892), and lecturer on bacteriology at the College of State Medicine in London, which was subsequently amalgamated with the Jenner Institute of Preventive Medicine (afterwards called the Lister Institute), of which Macfadyen was made director in 1891. In 1903 Macfadyen was appointed secretary of the governing body as well as head of the bacteriological department. To him fell a very large share in planning and organising the present building of the Lister Institute on the Chelsea Embankment. He contracted typhoid fever in 1902 while engaged in investigating its bacillus. From 1901–4 he was Fullerian professor of physiology at the Royal Institution, where he delivered lectures on 'The Cell as the Unit of Life,' posthumously published in 1908. In 1905 he resigned his official position at the institute, and devoted himself entirely to original work, in the pursuit of which he accidentally infected himself with Malta fever and typhoid fever. He died at Hampstead a martyr to science on 1 March 1907 and was buried there.

Macfadyen's main bacteriological work was on the intracellular juices or endotoxins of certain bacteria. While some germs such as those which produce diphtheria and tetanus give off poisons as they grow, others, such as those responsible for cholera and typhoid fever, retain their poisons, which are therefore known as endotoxins. In order to obtain these endotoxins Macfadyen froze bacteria by means of Sir James Dewar's liquid air to a temperature of – 190° C., and then ground up the bacteria thus rendered brittle. He showed that by injecting small doses of these endotoxins into animals immunity from the disease could be established. In much of this work he was assisted by Mr. S. Rowland. Proofs of immunity had just been reached at the date of Macfadyen's death. He investigated, too, thermophilic bacteria, namely those which can live at a temperature of 140° C.; and with Sir James Dewar proved that the vital processes of some bacteria are not destroyed by a temperature of – 250° C. or only 23 above that of absolute zero. His early work dealt largely with the fermentative action of bacteria.

Besides the work mentioned, Macfadyen published many memoirs in medical and scientific periodicals, including the 'Journal of Anatomy and Physiology,' vols. xxi., xxv.–xxvi.; 'Proceedings of the Royal Society,' 1889; 'Transactions of the International Congress of Hygiene,' vol. ii.; 'Journal of Pathology and Bacteriology,' 1894.

He married on 7 Jan. 1890 Marie, daughter of Professor Cartling, director of the botanical gardens at Dettingen, but left no issue.

[Memoir by Prof. R. Tanner Hewlett, M.D., appended to The Cell as the Unit of Life, 1908 (with photograph and list of published papers); Brit. Med. Journ. 1907, i. 601; information from his brother, Archibald Macfadyen.] H. D. R.

MACFARREN, WALTER CECIL (1826–1905), pianist and composer, born in Villiers Street, Strand, London, on 28 Aug. 1826, was youngest son of George Macfarren [q. v.], dramatist, and brother of Sir George Alexander Macfarren [q. v.]. Having from his fourth year shown gifts for music, he was a choir-boy at Westminster Abbey under James Turle (1836–41), and sang at Queen Victoria's coronation. When his voice broke, he had thoughts of becoming an artist, and took some lessons in painting, and then served as salesman in a Brighton pianoforte warehouse. At the persuasion of his brother, he entered the Royal Academy of Music in October 1842, learning the pianoforte under W. H. Holmes and composition under his own brother and Cipriani Potter. In January 1846 he became a sub-professor of the pianoforte, and remained on the staff of the Royal Academy fifty-seven years, for many years lecturing there six times annually as well as teaching the piano. He always remained a sound performer of the older school. He also composed many small but solid pianoforte pieces, natural, pleasing, and always highly finished in style, recalling Mendelssohn and Sterndale Bennett. His vocal works included two church services and many short secular pieces; the part-song 'You stole my Love' proved very successful. He produced an overture to 'The Winter's Tale' (1844); an overture to 'The Taming of the Shrew' (1845); 'Beppo,' a concert overture (1847). He suffered from weak eyesight, but did not share his brother's fate of total blindness. From 1873 to 1880 he conducted the concerts at the Royal Academy, and from 1877 to 1880 was treasurer of the Philharmonic Society. Resuming the composition of large works, he produced with success at Kuhe's Brighton Festivals his 'Pastoral Overture' (1878), 'Hero and Leander' (1897), and a complete symphony in B flat (1880); none was sufficiently original to retain a place in the concert repertory. In 1881 there followed a concert-piece for pianoforte and orchestra, written for his pupil, Miss Kuhe, and the only large composition of his to be printed, and he produced an overture to 'Henry V' at the Norwich Festival.

Macfarren was appointed musical critic to the 'Queen' newspaper in 1862, and contributed articles, moderately conservative in tone, till his death. For the music publishers Ashdown and Parry (afterwards Edwin Ashdown) he edited 'Popular Classics,' which reached 240 numbers; he also edited Mozart's complete pianoforte works and Beethoven's sonatas. His complete 'Scale and Arpeggio Manual' (1882) took standard rank.

On the occasion of his jubilee in 1896 he founded two prizes, gold medals for pianoforte-playing, at the Royal Academy. In 1904 he retired from all active work, save that of contributor to the 'Queen'; on this occasion an illuminated address, signed by several hundreds of his friends, was publicly presented to him. He lived in Osnaburgh Terrace, usually spending his vacations at Brighton. He published in the summer of 1905 'Memories,' an autobiography which was insufficiently revised. He died in London on 2 Sept. 1905, and was buried in St. Pancras cemetery, East Finchley.

He married in 1852 Julia Fanner, daughter of an artist; her mind gave way in 1878. She died in 1902 without issue.

[Macfarren's Memories; interviews, with portraits, in Musical Herald, April 1893, and Musical Times, Jan. 1898; Musical Herald, Dec. 1901, Sept. 1903, Nov. 1905, p. 363 (will); personal reminiscences.] H. D.

MACGREGOR, JAMES (1832–1910), moderator of the general assembly of the Church of Scotland, born at Brownhill, Scone, Perthshire, on 11 July 1832, was son of James MacGregor, farmer, by his wife Margaret MacDougall. After receiving elementary education at his parish school and at Perth academy, MacGregor studied for the ministry of the Church of Scotland at St. Andrews University, 1848–55. Licensed as a preacher by Perth presbytery on 18 May 1855, he was minister of the High Church, Paisley, from 8 Nov. following till May 1862, when he was appointed to the parish of Monimail, Fifeshire. Translated to Tron Church, Glasgow (10 March 1864), as colleague and successor to Dr. James Boyd, father of A. K. H. Boyd [q. v. Suppl. I], he won great popularity as preacher and pastor. After four years in Glasgow he succeeded Dr. Maxwell Nicholson on 9 Jan. 1868, in the Tron Church, Edinburgh. There he fully maintained his reputation for pulpit oratory. A well-organised parochial visitation committee, which he initiated, was at length amalgamated with the Association for Improving the Condition of the Poor. On 30 Nov. 1873 MacGregor became first minister of St. Cuthbert's parish, Edinburgh, which has the largest of Scottish congregations. With various colleagues he completed there a distinguished record during the remaining thirty-seven years of his life. Mainly through his exertions the old parish church was superseded in 1894 by a new edifice, which, with its equipment, cost about 50,000*l.*

From 1885 MacGregor effectively defended on the platform the existing relations between church and state. As moderator of the general assembly in 1891, he guided the proceedings with notable success. 'I heard his closing address,' wrote A. K. H. Boyd, 'and all the old indescribable fire and charm were there. . . . MacGregor is a born orator. You have to listen with rapt attention to every word he says. He is equally great, too, as Guthrie was, in pulpit and on platform.' Although a staunch churchman he was considerate and tolerant when his cherished principles were not assailed, and was not without hope that divided presbyterians might ultimately recognise one inclusive Church of Scotland.

MacGregor proved the most popular Scottish preacher of his day. In 1870 St. Andrews conferred on him the honorary degree of D.D. In 1877 he was elected chaplain to the Royal Scottish Academy and to the Midlothian volunteer artillery, earning in his latter capacity the long service medal. In 1886 he became chaplain-in-ordinary to Queen Victoria (who gave him frequent tokens of her esteem), and the appointment was renewed by Edward VII in 1901 and by George V in 1910. MacGregor was also a fellow of the Royal Society of Edinburgh.

Although apparently of fragile physique MacGregor travelled much. In 1861 he was in the countries adjoining the Levant. When the marquis of Lorne was governor-general of Canada, he accompanied him in 1881 into the north-west provinces and witnessed the progress of the Canadian Pacific railway. One of the railway stations, named 'MacGregor' in his honour, is now a flourishing township, with a church that contains his portrait and is appropriately named St. Cuthbert's. In 1889 he was one of the Scottish presbyterian representatives at the jubilee celebration of the Australian presbyterian church. He described some of his travels in the 'Scotsman,' but published nothing else. He died at his manse on 25 Nov. 1910, and was interred in the Grange cemetery, Edinburgh.

MacGregor married twice: (1) in 1864 Helen, daughter of David Robertson, publisher, Glasgow; she died in 1875 and her two children both died young; (2) in 1892 Helen Murray, who survived him.

About 1875 a portrait of MacGregor was painted by Otto Leyde, and in 1898 another by Sir George Reid, P.R.S.A., was presented to him by his congregation and friends. These are family possessions. A third, a study by John Bowie, A.R.S.A., for a group of 'Queen's Chaplains,' is in the session house of St. Cuthbert's parish church.

[Information from Mrs. MacGregor and Miss Story, Glasgow; Memoir of Principal Story, by his daughters; Dr. A. K. H. Boyd's Twenty-five Years of St. Andrews; Scotsman and Glasgow Herald, 26 Nov. 1910.] T. B.

MACHELL, JAMES OCTAVIUS (1837–1902), owner and manager of racehorses, born at Etton rectory, near Beverley, on 5 Dec. 1837, was son of Robert Machell, vicar of Marton-in-Cleveland, who descended from an old Westmorland family, by his wife Eliza Mary, daughter of James Zealy and heiress to the Sterne and Waines property at Little Weighton and Beverley.

After education at Rossall school, where he distinguished himself in athletics, James joined, when seventeen years old, the 14th foot (afterwards the West Yorkshire regiment) as ensign. In 1858 he was gazetted lieutenant, and in 1862 captain. For some time he was quartered in Ireland, where he had ample opportunities for indulging his love of sport. He won many a bet by jumping over the mess-room table or from the floor to the mantel-shelf. He exchanged into the 59th in 1863, but retired from the service the same year, owing (it is said) to the commanding officer's refusal to permit him to go to Doncaster for the St. Leger.

Thereupon Machell settled at Newmarket, taking with him a three-year-old horse called Bacchus, which he had bought for a very small sum. With this animal he at once won a big handicap. The race was worth 1000*l.*, and he was said to have won a bet of 10,000*l.* to 400*l.* Thus he quickly obtained a firm footing on the turf, and was very soon one of its conspicuous figures. In 1865 he became associated with Mr. Henry Chaplin, who, at his instigation, bought that season the yearling Hermit for 1000 guineas. Two years later Hermit won the Derby and incidentally put some 70,000*l.* into Machell's pocket. From time to time Machell gave his guidance to newcomers to the turf, among them Sir Charles Legard, Lord Aylesford, the earl of Lonsdale, Lord Calthorpe, Sir John Willoughby, Lord Rodney, and Harry McCalmont [q. v. Suppl. II]. McCalmont was indebted to Machell's insight for his ownership of Isinglass. The horse's dam, Deadlock, which belonged originally to Lord Alington, was purchased by Machell for a small sum, and he bred from her a useful animal called Gervas. But before the merits of Gervas were ascertained Deadlock was sold, and all trace of her lost, until one day Machell recognised her in a farmer's cart and, obtaining her for a trifling consideration, sold her for 500*l.* to McCalmont, who in 1890 bred from her Isinglass to Isonomy. Machell superintended the training of Isinglass, who won stakes to the value of 57,455*l.*, and carried off in 1893 the Two Thousand Guineas, Derby, and St. Leger.

Machell was also mainly responsible for the victories (for various owners) of Knight of the Thistle for the Royal Hunt Cup at Ascot, Petronel in the Two Thousand Guineas (1880), Pilgrimage in the Two Thousand Guineas and One Thousand Guineas (1878), Harvester, who dead-heated with St. Gatien in the Derby (1884), Seabreeze, winner of the Oaks and St. Leger (1888), and Rockdove in the Cesarewitch (1895). Three of his own horses won the Grand National Steeplechase—Disturbance in 1873; Reugny in 1874; and Regal in 1876. He was also interested in Lord Manners's Seaman, who won in 1882. Between 1864 and 1902 Machell's own horses won 540 races, worth 110,010*l.* Apart from his sound knowledge of horses, Machell's success was largely attributable to his judgment of human character, to his business-like methods, and to his patience. Machell, who in his early days proved himself a swift short-distance runner, died at St. Leonards, Sussex, on 11 May 1902, and was buried in Newmarket cemetery. A portrait in oils of Machell, mounted on a grey Arab horse, watching a training gallop on Newmarket Heath, is at Crackanthorpe Hall, Appleby. It was painted by H. Hopkins and E. Havell. A cartoon portrait by 'Spy' appeared in 'Vanity Fair' in 1887.

[Notes supplied by Mr. P. W. Machell, C.M.G. (nephew); Sportsman, and Pall Mall Gaz., 12 May 1902; Ruff's Guide to the Turf; Baily's Mag. 1889 (portrait); W. C. A. Blew, Hist. of Steeplechasing, 1901; Badminton Library, Racing, 1900.] E. M.

MACHRAY, ROBERT (1831–1904), archbishop of Rupert's Land, born in Aberdeen, Scotland, on 17 May 1831, of Highland ancestry, was son of Robert Machray, advocate of Aberdeen, by his wife Christian Macallum. His parents were presbyterians. After early education at Nairn Academy and at Coull parish school, he graduated M.A. from King's College, Aberdeen, in 1851, being head of his year, and winning the highest prizes. Proceeding to Sidney Sussex College, Cambridge, he graduated there in 1855 as 34th wrangler, and was elected to a fellowship. He proceeded M.A. in 1858. He was dean of his college in 1858. Meanwhile he had joined the Church of England, and was ordained deacon in 1855 and priest in the following year. He became vicar of Madingley, near Cambridge, in 1862. In 1865 Machray was Ramsden preacher at Cambridge, and in the same year he accepted the bishopric of Rupert's Land, as successor to David Anderson, the first bishop, being consecrated at Lambeth on 24 June 1865. He proceeded D.D. of Cambridge, and was made hon. LL.D. of Aberdeen in the same year.

Machray's diocese covered 2,000,000 square miles of territory, with headquarters at Winnipeg, then a hamlet with a population of 150. To assist him in the administration of the diocese he had only eighteen clergymen. In 1866 he made a difficult tour of inspection of the Indian missions and held a first conference of the diocese on 30 May 1866. A first diocesan synod met on 29 May 1867. Machray was active in introducing new methods of education. He renewed and reorganised the disused St. John's College, Winnipeg, securing John Maclean [q. v.], later first bishop of Saskatchewan, as warden and theological tutor; he himself lectured in ecclesiastical history and liturgiology as well as in mathematics. He also formed a college school for boys, of which he took charge. In 1878 he founded

Machray exhibitions at the college for sons of clergymen and contributed to the foundation of St. John's Ladies' College. When the University of Manitoba was constituted in 1877, Machray became chancellor, holding the office until his death. St. John's College was made a constituent college of the university. He was also chairman successively of the provincial board of education and the advisory board; and exerted in that capacity constant influence upon the educational development of the province.

Meanwhile Machray was faced by great difficulties in organising his diocese. Frequent destruction of the crops by locusts and the rebellion of Riel in 1870 arrested his progress. At the same time the population was growing, and Machray did all in his power to organise the diocese on lines likely to serve the future. In course of time the bishopric was subdivided into eight sees (Moosonee, 1872; Mackenzie River, 1874; Saskatchewan, 1874; Athabasca, 1884; Qu'Appelle, 1884; Calgary, 1888; Selkirk, 1891; Keewatin, 1901). One hundred and ninety clergy and numerous lay readers were enlisted in church work. In 1875 Machray became metropolitan of Canada under the primacy of the Archbishop of Canterbury, and at the union of the Canadian Anglican churches in 1893 he was created archbishop of Rupert's Land and primate of all Canada. He aided in the formation of the general synod of the Dominion which met in that year, when he was also created prelate of the Order of St. Michael and St. George. Machray attended the Lambeth Conferences in 1878 and 1888, and in the latter year preached before Cambridge University. He received the honorary degree of D.D. from Manitoba University in 1883; from Durham in 1888, and that of D.C.L. from Trinity College, Toronto, in 1893. He died unmarried at Winnipeg on 9 March 1904. A state funeral was decreed, and he was buried in the cemetery of St. John's Cathedral.

A portrait by Colin Forbes was presented to Machray in 1882.

[Robert Machray, Life of Archbishop Machray, 1909; Morgan, Canadian Men and Women of the Time; Dent, Canadian Portraits; Mockridge, Bishops of the Church of England in Canada and Newfoundland; Lowndes's Bishops of the Day, 1897.] P. E.

MACINTYRE, DONALD (1831–1903), major-general Bengal staff corps, born at Kincraig House, Ross-shire, on 12 Sept. 1831, was second son of Donald Macintyre of Calcutta by his wife Margaret, daughter of John Mackenzie of Kincraig House, Ross-shire. Educated at private schools in England and abroad, he was at the East India Company's Military College, Addiscombe, from 1848 to 1850, obtained his first commission in the Bengal army on 14 June 1850.

With the 66th Gurkhas he served under Sir Colin Campbell, afterwards Lord Clyde [q. v.], in the two expeditions of 1852 against the hill tribes on the Peshawar frontier, including the destruction of the fortified village of Pranghur and the action at Ishkakot. He also joined the expeditionary force against the Boree Afridis in Nov. 1853. In 1856 he took part with the 66th Gurkhas in the expedition under Sir Neville Chamberlain [q. v. Suppl. II] to Kuram Valley, Afghanistan, and with the Doaba field force in Peshawar Valley in 1864, receiving the medal with clasp. He was made lieutenant on 23 Nov. 1856. During 1857 and 1858, when engaged in raising an extra Gurkha regiment (now the 4th Gurkhas), he took part in protecting the hill passes on the Kale Kumaon frontier from the Rohilkund rebels and in keeping the district in order. For these services he was awarded a medal. He was promoted captain in June 1862 and major on 14 June 1870. He served with the Lushai expedition in 1871–2, being several times mentioned in despatches, and being made brevet lieut.-colonel on 11 Sept. 1872. For an act of gallantry in this campaign, at the storming of the stockaded village of Lalgnoora on 4 Jan. 1872, he received the Victoria Cross. Macintyre, who was serving as second in command to Colonel (Sir) Herbert Macpherson, C.B., V.C., commanding the 2nd Gurkhas, while leading the assault, was the first to reach the stockade, which was from 8 to 9 feet high. To climb over it and disappear among the flames and smoke of the burning village was the work of a very short time. The stockade was successfully stormed by Macintyre under the heaviest fire which the Lushai delivered that day.

Macintyre, who became lieut.-colonel on 14 Jan. 1876 and colonel on 1 Oct. 1887, commanded the 2nd Prince of Wales's Own Gurkhas with Sir Garnet Wolseley's force at the occupation of Cyprus and also with the Khyber column, directed against the Zakha Khel Afridis, in the Afghan war of 1878–9. He was also in both expeditions to the Bazar Valley under Lieut.-general Sir Francis Maude, V.C. (medal). He retired with the rank of major-general on 24 Dec. 1880, and thenceforth lived at Mackenzie Lodge, Fortrose, Ross-shire.

Macintyre, who was a traveller and sportsman, published an account of his experiences in 'Hindu Koh, Wanderings and Wild Sports on and beyond the Himalayas' (1889; new edit. 1891). He was a J.P. for Ross-shire and an F.R.G.S. He died at Fortrose on 15 April 1903 and was buried in Rosemarkie churchyard. He married Angelica, daughter of the Rev. T. J. Patteson, Kirmetties, Forfar.

[The Times, 17 April 1903; Hart's and Official Army Lists; W. H. Paget, Record of Expeditions against the North-West Frontier Tribes, 1884, p. 296; Who's Who, 1902.]

H. M. V.

MACKAY, ÆNEAS JAMES GEORGE (1839–1911), Scottish legal and historical writer, born at Edinburgh on 3 Nov. 1839, was grandson of Captain Mackay of Scotstoun, Peeblesshire, a distinguished soldier in India, and was son of Thomas George Mackay, W.S., by his wife Mary, daughter of John Kirkcaldy of Baldovie, Forfarshire. He was educated at Edinburgh Academy, proceeding thence to King's College, London, where he gained distinction in divinity and history. He continued his course of study at University College, Oxford, where he graduated B.A. in 1862, proceeding M.A. in 1865, and then at Heidelberg, completing his legal curriculum at Edinburgh University, where he was one of the first to obtain the degree of LL.B. He was admitted advocate at the Scottish bar in 1864, and attained considerable repute in consultation rather than as a pleader. He devoted much time to studies in law and history, and in 1874 he succeeded Cosmo Innes [q. v.] as professor of constitutional law and history in Edinburgh University. While he occupied this chair he brought out his greatest work, 'The Practice of the Court of Session' (2 vols. 1877–9), which is still a standard authority. In 1881 he was appointed advocate-depute and resigned the professorship. In 1886 he was made sheriff-principal of Fife and Kinross, retaining that office till 1901, when failing health compelled him to resign. During the last ten years of his life illness condemned him to inactivity. His latest labours were connected with the statute law revision (Scotland), for which he prepared an elaborate and exhaustive account of pre-union legislation, issued as a Blue Book. During his term as sheriff he busily engaged in literary work, writing many articles on Scottish subjects for this Dictionary and for the 'Encyclopædia Britannica.' He was made LL.D. of Edinburgh in 1882, and was a fellow of King's College, London. He died at Edinburgh on 10 June 1911. He married in 1891 Lilian Alina, daughter of Colonel Charles W. St. John, 94th regt., who survived him without issue.

Besides his legal works Mackay took much interest in Scottish literature, and made several notable contributions to it. He was one of the founders of the Scottish History Society in 1885, and was an active member of the Scottish Text Society. For the former society he wrote a prefatory life of John Major for Archibald Constable's translation of Major's 'History of Great Britain' (1892), and for the latter he supplied in 1884 an introduction and appendix for an edition of the 'Poems of William Dunbar,' and also edited Lindsay of Pitscottie's 'Chronicles of Scotland' in 1899. Other works of interest were: 1. 'Memoir of Sir James Dalrymple of Stair,' 1873. 2. 'William Dunbar: a Study in the Poetry and History of Scotland,' 1889. 3. 'A Sketch of the History of Fife and Kinross,' Cupar Fife, 1890. 4. 'A Century of Scottish Proverbs and Sayings, in Prose and Rhyme, current in Fife,' Cupar Fife, 1891. 5. 'Manual of Practice in the Court of Session,' Edinburgh, 1893. 6. 'A History of Fife and Kinross' ('County Histories' series), Edinburgh, 1896.

[Book of Mackay; Scotsman, and Glasgow Herald, 12 June 1911; Scots Law Times, 17 June 1911; private information.]

A. H. M.

MACKAY, ALEXANDER (1833–1902), promoter of education in Scotland, born at Bonar Bridge, Sutherland, on 22 Feb. 1833, was son of William Mackay, tailor and clothier, of Bonar Bridge, by his wife Elizabeth Macgregor. Educated at Bonar Bridge parochial school, he passed to St. Andrews University, where he was a prizeman, graduated M.A., and subsequently in 1891 was admitted to the honorary degree of LL.D. After a short engagement as a teacher at Cameron in Fifeshire he removed to Torryburn, where he was parish schoolmaster for twenty-six years. There he carried on the best Scottish teaching traditions and made a special effort to train boys for the colonies. From 1862 till his death he was an elder of the established church. On the passing in 1861 of the Parochial and Burgh Schoolmasters Act, which refashioned the old system of Scottish education, Mackay devoted himself to the development of educational methods and administration and in the organisation of the teaching profession. A further step in advance was made in 1872 by the great Compulsory Education (Scotland) Act. To a weekly paper, 'Educational News,' established at Edinburgh on 1 Jan. 1876 by William Ballantyne Hodgson [q. v.] and other enlightened educational leaders as the official organ of Scottish teachers, Mackay became a chief contributor, and on 1 July 1878 undertook its editorship, at first without salary. He improved the financial position of the paper, and received a salary from 1881. Under his control the paper, in which he wrote on a wide range of themes, did much to increase the efficiency of the statutory system of education and to improve the position of the teaching profession. From 1876 till death he was treasurer of the Educational Institute of Scotland, was president in 1881, and greatly extended the influence of the body. In 1897 he was elected a member of the school board of Edinburgh and was re-elected in 1900. He was convener of the evening school committee. A conservative in politics, he possessed much force of character, independence of mind, and clarity of judgment. He died at 13 Warriston Crescent, Edinburgh, on 4 Dec. 1902. In 1863 he married Jane Watt, who survived him with a son, Major Mackay, and four daughters.

Mackay published several works of value in the teaching profession. They include: 1. 'Foreign Systems of Education.' 2. 'Æsthetics in Schools.' 3. 'A History of Scotland.' 4. 'A Plea for our Parish Schools.' 5. 'Free Trade in Teaching.'

[The Times, 8 Dec. 1902; Scotsman, 5 Dec. 1902; Educational News, 13 Dec. 1902 (with portrait); information from the family; Scottish Educational Statu tes.]

J. E. G. de M.

MACKENNAL, ALEXANDER (1835–1904), congregational divine, born at Truro on 14 Jan. 1835, was the third of seven children of Patrick Mackennal, a Scotsman from Galloway. His mother was Cornish. In 1848 the family removed to London, and Mackennal entered the school of William Pinches, Ball Alley, George Yard, Lombard Street; among his schoolfellows was John Henry Brodribb (afterwards Sir Henry Irving [q. v. Suppl. II]). After passing through another school, at Hackney, he entered Glasgow University in October 1851, learning much from John Nichol [q. v. Suppl. I] and leaving in 1854 without graduation, but recognised as a leader among his fellow-students in liberal thought and politics. His first bent was towards medicine, but in 1852, when acting as tutor in a highland family of Scottish baptists, he resolved upon the congregational ministry, and entered Hackney College (1854); while there he graduated B.A. (October 1857) at London University. As a student he was influenced by Thomas Toke Lynch [q. v.] and deeply by Frederick Denison Maurice. His first settlement was at Burton-on-Trent (May 1858); a strongly Calvinistic section of his flock was not in sympathy with his breadth of view, and, after his removal, seceded to form a presbyterian congregation, but in the village chapel at Branstone, connected with Burton, he found lifelong friends. In 1862 he removed to Surbiton, Surrey, where John Carvell Williams [q. v. Suppl. II] was one of his deacons. Here he transferred his congregation from a hall to a church building largely planned by himself, and co-operated with Dean Stanley, Robert William Dale [q. v. Suppl. I], and others in a volume of addresses to working people. In 1870 he succeeded James Allanson Picton as minister of Gallowtree-gate Church, Leicester. He established a local mission, and became secretary of the Leicester and Rutland County Union of his denomination. He declined to stand as a candidate for the Leicester school board, being equally opposed to the Cowper Temple compromise and to the secular system, maintaining throughout life that the true solution of the educational difficulty was to be found in 'the frank recognition of schools of different types.' He did much for the Leicester Literary and Philosophical Society, of which he became president in 1876. In 1877 he moved to Bowdon, Cheshire, where he remained till death, declining calls to London and elsewhere. In 1887 he filled the chair of the Congregational Union of England and Wales, and in the same year received the degree of D.D. from Glasgow University.

Two years later he made the first of several visits to America in 1889, representing the Congregational Union at the triennial council of American congregational churches. This visit formed a turning point in Mackennal's career. It led to the holding of an international congregational council in London (July 1891), of which Mackennal as secretary was the efficient organiser. He took part in the reunion conferences begun at

Grindelwald in 1891, but his ideal was a co-operative rather than a corporate union. The 'historic episcopate' stood in the way of amalgamation. Subsequently he worked for a federation of the evangelical free churches initiated at a congress in Manchester in Nov. 1892. The constitution of the National Free Church Council, adopted at Nottingham in March 1896, was drawn up by him; for six years (1892–8) he acted as secretary, and was president in 1899. Meanwhile he had become in 1891 chairman of the council of Mansfield College, Oxford, in succession to Dale, and on two occasions delivered courses of lectures in the college ('ministerial jurisprudence' and 'pastoral theology').

Despite his varied energy, Mackennal remained through life a close student, a finished preacher, and an assiduous pastor. His thoughts on critical and theological questions were at once broad and deep; exaggeration and excitement he abhorred, and he had no liking for 'reckless evangelising' of the Moody type. In his limitation of the Divine omniscience he falls unconsciously into a Socinian position (*Life*, p. 137). In politics he was no prominent figure, but a consistent advocate of an anti-war policy. He died at Highgate on 23 June 1904, and was buried at Bowdon. He married in 1867 Fanny (*d.* 12 Jan. 1903), daughter of Dr. Hoile of Montrose, and widow of Colin Wilson, by whom he had three sons and two daughters.

In addition to single sermons and addresses, he published: 1. 'Christ's Healing Touch, and other Sermons,' 1871 (sermons at Surbiton). 2. 'The Life of Christian Consecration,' 1877 (sermons at Leicester). 3. 'Sermons from a Sick Room,' Manchester, 1880. 4. 'Memoir,' prefixed to 'Sermons by George James Proctor,' 1881. 5. 'The Christian Testimony: Four Pastoral Lectures,' Manchester, 1883. 6. 'The Biblical Scheme of Nature and Man,' Manchester, 1886 (four lectures). 7. 'Life of John Allison Macfadyen,' D.D., 1891 (father of his own biographer; an excellent piece of work). 8. 'The Story of the English Separatists,' 1893, 4to. 9. 'The Seven Churches in Asia: Types of the Religious Life,' 1895; 1898. 10. 'Homes and Haunts of the Pilgrim Fathers,' 1899, 4to (illustrations by C. Whymper). 11. 'The Kingdom of the Lord Jesus,' 1900. 12. 'Sketches in the Evolution of English Congregationalism,' 1901 (Carew lecture at Hartford, Conn.). 13. 'The Eternal Son of God and the Human Sonship,' 1903.

[D. Macfadyen, Alexander Mackennal, Life and Letters, 1905 (two portraits); Congregational Year Book, 1905; Dale, Hist. Eng. Congregationalism, 1907, pp. 745–7; Addison's Graduates Univ. Glasgow, 1898; The Times, 14 Jan. 1903; 25 and 27 June 1904; Proceedings, First Nat. Council of Free Churches, 1896; Free Church Federation Movement, Historical Sketch, 1900 (portrait).]

A. G.

MACKENZIE, Sir ALEXANDER (1842–1902), lieutenant-governor of Bengal, born at Dumfries on 28 June 1842, was eldest son of the eleven children of John Robertson Mackenzie, D.D. (1811–1877), minister of the established church at Dumfries till the disruption, then minister of Free St. Mary's church there, minister at Birmingham (1847–74), and sometime moderator of the English presbyterian synod. His mother was Alexandrina, fourth daughter of James Christie, M.D., of Huntly. At King Edward VI's school, Birmingham, he passed through all the classes and became head boy on the classical side. Entering Trinity Hall, Cambridge, with a founder's exhibition in 1859, he did well in the college examinations, but declined to compete in the classical tripos, owing to his inability to subscribe to the Anglican test for a fellowship. In the Indian civil service examination of July 1861 he came out second to (Sir) James Westland [q. v. Suppl. II].

Arriving in India on 11 Dec. 1862, he served in Bengal as assistant magistrate and collector, and from February 1866 as under secretary and junior secretary to the local government. Here he had charge of the political correspondence of the province, which then included Assam, and at the request of Sir William Grey [q. v.] he wrote a 'Memorandum on the North-East Frontier of Bengal' (Calcutta, 1869), which he subsequently brought up to date in his 'History of the Relations of Government with the Hill Tribes of the North-East Frontier of Bengal' (Calcutta, 1884). A standard authority, the work is singularly candid, and drew some protest from the government of India (*Foreign Depart. Letter*, Simla, 23 May 1884).

Placed on special duty in December 1873 in connection with the Bengal-Behar famine, he injured his eyesight by his application, and took long furlough home (May 1874 to November 1875). On return he served as secretary to the board of revenue; magistrate and collector of Murshidabad from April 1876; again secretary to the board from March 1877; financial secretary to the Bengal government from October 1877; and, concurrently, from January 1879, member of the lieut.-governor's legislature. Appointed home secretary to the government of India in April 1882, he earnestly identified himself with the plans of Lord Ripon [q. v. Suppl. II] for the extension of local self-government and for the encouragement of capital and private enterprise in the country. He had a large share in shaping the Bengal Tenancy Act and Rent Law of 1885.

Made a C.S.I. in May 1886, he went to the Central Provinces as chief commissioner in March 1887, but his programme of reform was hampered by disagreement with the military members of the provincial commission. In December 1890 he was transferred to Burma as chief commissioner, and was created a K.C.S.I. in January. Mackenzie suppressed the predatory raids of the hill tribes who were still disturbing the peace by sending out some seventeen or eighteen compact expeditions of military police. By 1892 he reported complete tranquillity and proposed substantial reductions in the number of military police. He was home on leave for two years from May 1892, and his actual service in Burma was short. In April 1895 he joined the government of India as temporary member, and in December he became lieutenant-governor of Bengal in succession to Sir Charles Elliott [q. v. Suppl. II].

His connection with Lord Ripon assured him a welcome from the native press; but the Bengalis disliked a sanitary survey of Calcutta which he ordered and questioned his view of the need for amending the Calcutta Municipal Act (cf. Speech, 26 Nov. 1896) by substantially qualifying the authority of the existing elected and nominated commissioners of the municipality. His amending bill provided for three coordinate municipal authorities, for the adequate representation of the European commercial community, and for reform of the building regulations. The bill finally passed in 1899, after Mackenzie's retirement; it reduced the number of elected representatives, and, though the Bombay model was largely followed, it was held to infringe just principles of local self-government. Mackenzie's object, however, was to remedy the insanitary condition of the then Indian capital. Meanwhile he sought to protect Bengal from the financial encroachments of the government of India, likening the province to a lamb thrown on its back and close sheared for the benefit of the central administration. By an Act passed in 1896 he enlarged the powers of municipalities outside the capital. He co-operated with the Assam administration in the successful completion of the south Lushai expedition in 1895–6; and he hastened the progress of the important land settlement operations which his predecessor had inaugurated in Behar and Orissa [cf. Elliott, Sir Charles Alfred, Suppl. II]. Other of his agrarian measures were the amendment of the Bengal Tenancy, 1885, and the Partition of Estates, 1876, Acts.

In dealing efficiently with the severe famine of 1896–7 Mackenzie, owing to ill-health, exercised little personal supervision in the field, but he directed the policy, and the economical results were due to him. The invasion of plague was a greater difficulty. The guidance of experience was wanting, and frequent changes of plan were ordered from headquarters; but his arrangements kept the disease out of Bengal until April 1898, nearly two years after its appearance in Bombay (cf. Buckland's *Bengal under the Lieutenant-Governors*). At the same time the severe earthquake of 12 June 1897 did serious damage in Calcutta and in many parts of the province. Mackenzie's health broke down under the varied strains, and on 23 June 1897 he left for six months' leave. He returned at the end of the year, but resigned in April 1898. In none of the three provinces which he ruled was Mackenzie's work completed, and his high promise was not fulfilled. He was 'stronger in office work and on paper than in active administration' (*Pioneer Mail*, 26 April 1912). But he was unquestionably 'one of the ablest men of his time in India' (Sir Charles Crosthwaite's *Pacification of Burma*, 1912). A rapid worker, candid in speech, he was a strict and none too sympathetic chief, but no one in real trouble or want went to him in vain.

Returning to England, he became a director of several companies; spoke on missionary platforms, and took an active part in the work of the Marylebone presbyterian church. Towards the close of 1901 he was adopted as one of the liberal candidates for Plymouth, but in October 1902 ill-health compelled his withdrawal. He died at his residence, Radnor, Holmbury St. Mary, Surrey, on 10 Nov. 1902, and was buried at Ewhurst church, where a marble tomb has been erected.

He married (1) in 1863 Georgina Louisa (*d.* 1892), youngest daughter of Colonel W. Bremner of the Madras army, niece of Patrick Robertson [q. v.], lord of session;

(2) in August 1893 Mabel Elizabeth, third and youngest daughter of Ralph Elliot, eldest son of Sir George Elliot, first baronet, M.P., by whom he had a son (*d.* while at Eton College, June 1910) and a daughter; she survived him and married secondly the Hon. Noel Farrer, second son of the first Baron Farrer [q. v.].

[Mackenzie's N.E. Frontier of Bengal; C. E. Buckland's Bengal under the Lieut.-Governors, 1902; L. G. Fraser's India under Curzon and After, 1911; J. Nisbet's Burma under Brit. Rule and Before, 1901; Birmingham Daily Post, 5 March 1877 and 11 Nov. 1902; The Times, 11 Nov. 1902; Western Mercury, Calcutta Statesman, 12 Nov. 1902; Indian Daily News, Hindu Patriot, 13 Nov. 1902; Indian Mirror, 14 Nov. 1902; Presbyterian, 20 Nov. 1902; Pioneer Mail, 21 Nov. 1902 and 26 April 1912; information kindly given by the Hon. Mrs. Farrer.] F. H. B.

MACKENZIE, Sir GEORGE SUTHERLAND (1844–1910), explorer and administrator, born at Bolarum, India, on 5 May 1844, was third son of Sir William Mackenzie, K.C.B., M.D., inspector-general of Madras medical service, by his wife Margaret, daughter of Edmund Prendergast, of Ardfinan Castle, co. Tipperary. Educated at Clapham under Dr. Charles Pritchard [q. v.], he went into commercial life, joining the firm of Gray, Dawes & Co., East India merchants, in London, and agents for the British India Steam Navigation Co., and, ultimately becoming a partner in the firm, was closely connected with the British India Steam Navigation Co., of which he was made a director. In 1866, at twenty-two years of age, he went to the Persian Gulf as the representative of his firm, and after some time at Bushire was sent into the interior, to establish agencies at Shiraz and Ispahan. With a view to meeting the need of improved communication between the coast of the Persian Gulf and the interior, in 1875 he travelled from Ispahan through the Bakhtiari country by way of Shuster to the head of the Gulf. Though unarmed and with three attendants only, he travelled in safety, and by his courage and tact made friends with the chiefs of the tribes. In 1878 he made the reverse journey, starting from Mahommerah, steaming up the Karun river, and then proceeding by way of Shuster. He thus tried to open up a trade route by the Karun river, a scheme which was more successfully negotiated with the Persian government at a later date by Sir Henry Drummond Wolff [q. v. Suppl. II]. At his death Mackenzie was 'the doyen of Persian explorers' (*Geographical Journal*, July–Dec. 1910, p. 738).

After the Anglo-German agreement of 1886, the British East African Association, of which Mackenzie was a member, obtained from the Sultan of Zanzibar in May 1887 a concession of the coastline of East Africa between the Umba River and Kipini near the mouth of the Tana. A founders' agreement dated 18 April 1888, in which Mackenzie figures as a contributor and a director, was followed by a royal charter which, on 3 Sept. 1888, incorporated Mackenzie and the other members of the association under the name of the Imperial British East African Co. Mackenzie gave the name of Ibea to the company's territories. In the autumn of 1888 he arrived at Zanzibar to take over, as managing director, the coast leased to the company, and then went on to Mombasa. The time was critical. The coast tribes in the German sphere were in revolt against the German East Africa Co. A joint blockade of the whole East African coast by Great Britain and Germany was found necessary; and in the British sphere the Arabs were on the eve of an armed rising owing to runaway slaves being harboured at the mission stations. Mackenzie averted this last imminent danger, and conciliated the Arab slave-owners by paying them compensation for the fugitive slaves at the mission stations at the rate of $25 a head, the gross sum amounting to 3500*l.* Sir Charles Euan-Smith [q. v. Suppl. II], British consul-general at Zanzibar, described this act as one of 'unparalleled generosity and philanthropy,' and bore the strongest testimony to Mackenzie's 'tact and good judgment.' His experience with a cognate people in Persia stood him in good stead (Keltie, *Partition of Africa*, p. 329). The admiral on the station, Fremantle, commented on his 'tact, care and discretion,' and reported that 'he has literally won golden opinions, the Arabs spontaneously giving him a feast' (*Parl. Pap. Africa*, No. 1 (1889), August 1889, pp. 13, 17, 21, 36, &c.).

Mackenzie paid a visit to England in 1889, but returned to Mombasa again in December of that year accompanied by Captain (now Sir Frederick) Lugard, who wrote of 'the personal affection which Mackenzie inspired in all who served under him.' By way of developing East Africa he introduced Persian agriculturists, improved Mombasa town and harbour, sent caravans into the interior as far as Uganda, and with a well-selected staff organised the territory (*C.O. List* for 1890). He was also of much assistance to the Italians in negotiating treaties for them with the Somali tribe, and received the grand cross of the crown of Italy. He ceased to be administrator in May 1890, when he returned to England, and in 1895 the company surrendered their charter to the government. He was made C.B. in 1897 and K.C.M.G. in 1902. He also held the grand cross of the brilliant star of Zanzibar. He was a member of the council of the Royal Geographical Society 1893–1909 and vice-president 1901–5. He died suddenly in London on 1 Nov. 1910, and was buried at Brookwood cemetery. He married (1) in 1883 Elma (*d.* 1904), daughter of Major William Cairns Armstrong, 15th East Yorkshire regiment; (2) in 1905 May Matilda, widow of Archibald Bovill, and daughter of Hugh Darby Owen. He left no family. A portrait is in the possession of his sister, Mrs. Mackinnon, 10 Hyde Park Gardens; a photograph of this picture is at the Royal Colonial Institute, of which he was a prominent member.

[Authorities cited; The Times, 3 Nov. 1910; Geographical Journal, July–December 1910; Scott Keltie's Partition of Africa, 1893; P. L. McDermott, British East Africa or Ibea, 1893; Lugard's Rise of an East African Empire, 1893; Colonial Office List, 1890; Blue Book, 1889.] C. P. L.

M'KENZIE, Sir JOHN (1836–1901), minister of lands in New Zealand, born at Ardross, Ross-shire, Scotland, in 1836, was son of a farmer. After education at the parish school he worked on his father's farm. In 1860 he emigrated to Otago, New Zealand, and became working manager of the Pakitapu station near Palmerston. Then he farmed on his own account in the Shag valley. In 1865 he became clerk and treasurer to the local road board, and secretary to the local school committee. In 1868 he was an unsuccessful candidate for the provincial council of Otago, but in 1871 he won the seat for Waihemo, which he retained until the abolition of the provinces in 1875. In 1881 he became a member of the House of Representatives for Moeraki, and in 1884 he was promoted to be junior whip under the Stout-Vogel combination. When John Ballance [q. v. Suppl. I] became premier in 1881 M'Kenzie received the portfolio of lands and immigration, which he held until his retirement in 1900. He was identified with the liberal policy of purchasing large estates, cutting them up, and settling small farmers upon them. His efforts were strongly oppossed at the time, but his scheme proved substantially successful. In the years following the death of Ballance in 1893, when Richard John Seddon [q. v. Suppl. II] began his long tenure of the premiership, M'Kenzie was the most respected member of the cabinet. He introduced his first repurchase bill in 1891. It was passed by the legislative council in 1892 shorn of its compulsory clauses. A certain amount of land was bought under this Act, notably the Cheviot estate in 1893. In 1894 M'Kenzie induced both houses to pass his Lands for Settlement Act, which gave him power to compel unwilling owners to sell. He made many voluntary alterations in this Act during his term of office, and introduced a consolidating and amending Act in 1900. In 1894 he devised a scheme for helping the unemployed to get on to the land by setting them to clear forest land and prepare it for cultivation. While thus engaged the men gained both capital and experience, and when the land was cleared they were allowed to lease it on favourable terms. M'Kenzie also instituted a successful system of advancing loans to settlers on the security of their farms. The question of land tenure was keenly debated at this time, and in order to maintain the custom of not selling Crown lands he compromised with the opposition in 1892 and introduced the 'lease in perpetuity' (lease for 999 years), under which the tenant escaped periodical revaluations. In 1896, his health having given way, he went to London for a serious operation. He came back in 1899, and returned to his parliamentary duties, but his illness continued, and he retired from office on 15 June 1900. In 1901 he was appointed a member of the legislative council, and in June of that year the duke of York (afterwards King George V), then visiting New Zealand with the duchess, made him K.C.M.G. On 6 August 1901 he died at his home at Heathfield, Bushey, New Zealand. A memorial cairn was erected to his memory at Bushey. He left a widow, two sons, and three daughters.

[Mennell, Dict. of Australas. Biog.; W. Pember Reeves, State Experiments in Australia and New Zealand, 2 vols. 1902; Gisborne, New Zealand Rulers, 1897 (portrait); Otago Daily Times, 7, 8, and 10 Aug. 1901; Lyttelton Times, 7 and 8 Aug. 1901; private information.] A. B. W.

MACKENZIE, Sir STEPHEN (1844–1909), physician, born on 14 Oct. 1844 at Leytonstone, was seventh child of four sons and five daughters of Stephen Mackenzie, who in addition to his medical practice had a large establishment for the treatment of hysterical patients. His mother, Margaret Frances, was the daughter of Adam Harvey, a wine merchant of Lewes and Brighton. Sir Morell Mackenzie [q. v.], the laryngologist, was the eldest child. An uncle, Charles Mackenzie, known as Henry Compton [q. v.], was a Shakespearean actor. Mackenzie's father was killed in a carriage accident in 1851, and he left his family in somewhat straitened circumstances. Stephen, after education at Christ's Hospital (1853–9), began his medical career as apprentice to Dr. Benjamin Dulley of Wellingborough, whose daughter he afterwards married. He entered the medical college of the London Hospital in 1866, and became M.R.C.S.England in 1869. After holding a number of resident appointments at the London Hospital, he lived for a year at Aberdeen, and there graduated M.B. with highest honours in 1873 and M.D. in 1875. He became M.R.C.P. of London in 1874 and F.R.C.P. in 1879. After working at the Charité Hospital, Berlin, in 1873, he returned to the London Hospital, and was appointed in succession medical registrar (9 Dec. 1873), assistant physician (17 March 1874), physician to the skin department (7 Dec. 1875 to 19 Oct. 1903), physician (14 Sept. 1886), and consulting physician (6 Dec. 1905). In 1877 he was appointed lecturer on pathology jointly with H. G. Sutton, and in 1886 lecturer on medicine in the medical college.

Mackenzie was distinguished not only as a general physician but for special knowledge of skin diseases, to which he made many original contributions, and of ophthalmology, which by his teaching he did much to introduce into general medicine. He was physician (1884–1905) and consulting physician to the London Ophthalmic (Moorfields) Hospital, and wrote on changes in the retina in diseases of the kidneys. In 1891 he delivered the Lettsomian lectures before the Medical Society of London on anæmia. He also made some original observations on the distribution of the filarial parasites in the blood of man in relation to sleep and rest. He employed glycerinated calf lymph for vaccination, thus reviving the practice instituted by Dr. Cheyne in 1853. He was knighted in 1903, and soon afterwards resigned his hospital appointments owing to increasing asthma.

Mackenzie died on 3 Sept. 1909, and was buried at Dorking. He married in 1879 Helen, daughter of Dr. Benjamin Dulley of Wellingborough, and had one daughter and three sons. Mackenzie's portrait in oils, painted by Henry Gibbs in 1882, is in the possession of his widow at The Croft, Dorking.

Mackenzie wrote numerous articles in Quain's 'Dictionary of Medicine,' Allbutt's 'System of Medicine,' and other medical publications, but published no independent treatise.

[London Hosp. Gaz. 1909–10, xvi. 6; Brit. Med. Journal, 1909, ii. 732; private information.] H. D. R.

MACKINLAY, Mrs. JOHN. [See Sterling, Antoinette (1843–1904), singer.]

MACKINTOSH, JOHN (1833–1907), Scottish historian, son of William Mackintosh, a private soldier, was born at Aberdeen on 9 Nov. 1833. He was educated at Botriphinie parish school, Banffshire, and at an early period settled in Aberdeen as stationer and newsagent. An eager student of Scottish history, by strenuous application he taught himself the art of composition, and devoted every spare minute to study and research. In 1878 he brought out the first volume of a 'History of Civilisation in Scotland,' which was in 1888 completed in four volumes, a new edition appearing 1892–6. While showing indications of imperfect culture, it is characterised by independent judgment, shrewd thoughtfulness, and clear and well-balanced exposition. He also wrote 'The Story of Scotland' (1890), a 'History of the Valley of the Dee' (1895), and 'Historical Earls and Earldoms' (1898). In 1880 he received the degree of LL.D. from the University of Aberdeen, and in 1900 a civil list pension of 50*l*. He died at Aberdeen on 4 May 1907.

[Who's Who; Scotsman and Glasgow Herald, 6 May 1907.] T. F. H.

McLACHLAN, ROBERT (1837–1904), entomologist, born at 17 Upper East Smithfield, London, on 10 April 1837, was one of five children of Hugh McLachlan, ship-chandler (*d.* 1855), a native of Greenock, who settled in London in early life, living at the close of his life near Hainault Forest.

Possessed of private means, McLachlan, in 1855, when eighteen years old, made a voyage to Australia and China, where he collected much botanical material, which Robert Brown, keeper of the botanical department of the British Museum, subsequently examined. His interests soon centred on entomology, and, prompted by the writings of Hagen, he commenced the work of elucidating the families of British and foreign Neuroptera, his first paper on the order appearing in the 'Entomologist's Annual' (1861). This was followed by various important monographs. His 'Catalogue of British Neuroptera' was published by the Entomological Society in 1870. Meanwhile, as a zealous collector, he had brought together an unequalled series of specimens and maintained a voluminous correspondence at home and abroad relating to the study. His chief independent publication was 'A Monographic Revision and Synopsis of the Trichoptera [caddis-flies] of the European Fauna' (1874–84), a great work which was illustrated by his own detailed drawings, made under the camera lucida. For the 'Encyclopædia Britannica,' 9th edition, he wrote the article 'Insects.'

McLachlan was a member of many English and foreign scientific societies. He was elected F.R.S. on 7 June 1877 (being supported by Charles Darwin and George Bentham), and gave valued honorary assistance for several years in the editing of the society's 'Catalogue of Scientific Papers.' He successively filled the offices of secretary of the Entomological Society (1868–72) and treasurer (1873–5, 1891–4), serving as president (1885–6.) On the establishment of the 'Entomological Monthly Magazine' (1864) he acted as an editor, eventually (1902) becoming proprietor, without relinquishing editorial work. He was elected a fellow of the Linnean Society in 1862, and served on the council (1879–83).

McLachlan, who was unmarried, died on 23 May 1904, at his home at Lewisham, and was buried in Tower Hamlets cemetery, London.

[Proc. Roy. Soc., vol. lxxv., and Catal. Sci. Papers; Trans. Entomol. Soc., 1904, Presidential Address; Proc. Entomol. Soc., 1886, Presidential Address; Entomol. Month. Mag. July 1904; Entomological News, Sept. 1904; Proc. Linn. Soc., 1905; Proc. Roy. Hort. Soc., vol. xxix.; Nature, 2 June 1904.]

T. E. J.

MACLAGAN, CHRISTIAN (1811–1901), Scottish archæologist, born at Underwood, near Denny, Stirlingshire, in 1811, was daughter of George Maclagan (*d.* 1818), distiller and chemist of good education, by his wife Christian, daughter of Thomas Colville, printer, of Dundee. Her great-great-grandfather, Alexander Maclagan (1653–1722), was parish minister of Little Dunkeld, Perthshire, and was succeeded in that charge by his only son, Alexander Maclagan (1694–1768), a strong Hanoverian in a Jacobite parish. Her grandfather, Frederick (1738–1818), who just outlived her father, was ordained parish minister of Melrose in 1768, and she was engaged on a life of him at her death.

Christian was brought up by her mother at Underwood, and at Braehead Farm, Stirlingshire. After the disruption in 1843 she joined the Free church, and built a mission church in St. Mary's Wynd, Stirling; but having quarrelled with Dr. Beith, the Free church minister, she joined the established church, and transferred the building to that denomination; it is now a *quoad sacra* parish church.

In later life she resided at Ravenscroft, near Denny, and devoted much time and money to the removal of slums in Stirling, providing houses for the working-classes outside the burgh. Her father and grandfather had both been interested in Roman forts in Scotland, and this subject engrossed the greater part of her long life. Her researches in prehistoric remains in Scotland are valuable, though her conclusions and theories have not been generally accepted. She was made a lady associate of the Society of Antiquaries of Scotland in 1871, and her name remained on the roll till her death, although she wished to withdraw because the society refused her the rights of a fellow. Miss Maclagan was an artist of ability, although her right hand was rendered useless by a bone-disease and she could only employ her left hand. She devised a special method for taking rubbings from sculptured stones, and exhibited the results of her work at the Glasgow Exhibitions of 1888 and 1901, but she never disclosed the secret of her plan. In consequence of her dispute with the Society of Antiquaries of Scotland, she sent all her rubbings from stones to the British Museum.

Her published writings, all relating to prehistoric studies, were: 1. 'The Hill Forts, Stone Circles, and other Structural Remains of Ancient Scotland,' Edinburgh, 1875. 2. 'Chips from Old Stones,' published privately, 1881. 3. 'What mean these Stones? with Plates of Druidic Stones in Scotland,' Edinburgh, 1894. 4. 'A Catalogue Raisonné of the British Museum Collection of Rubbings from Ancient Sculptured Stones,' Edinburgh, 1895. She contributed papers to the Stirling Natural History and Archæological Society in 1882 and 1893, showing rubbings of sculptured stones at Islay and Ardchattan priory, prepared by her method. She died at Ravenscroft,

Stirling, on 10 May 1901, and was buried in Stirling cemetery.

[Scotsman, 13 May 1901; Sentinel (Stirling), 14 May 1901; Athenæum, 18 May 1901; Scots Magazine, 1818; Hew Scott's Fasti Eccles. Scot.; notes from Miss Maclagan's MS. autobiography, supplied by J. W. Barty, LL.D.; notes from W. B. Cook, Stirling; private information.] A. H. M.

MACLAGAN, WILLIAM DALRYMPLE (1826–1910), successively bishop of Lichfield and archbishop of York, born in Edinburgh on 18 June 1826, was fifth son of Dr. David Maclagan, 'physician to the forces,' who served with distinction as a medical officer in the Penisular war, and was president of both the Royal Colleges of Physicians and Surgeons at Edinburgh. His mother was Jane, daughter of another physician, Dr. Philip Whiteside, and granddaughter of Dr. William Dalrymple of Ayr ('D'rymple mild') [q. v.]. His eldest brother, Sir Douglas Maclagan (1812–1900), who was knighted in 1880, distinguished himself at Edinburgh in his father's profession, being president, like his father, of the two Scottish royal colleges and serving as professor of medical jurisprudence and public health at Edinburgh University from 1869 to 1896.

William, after education at the Edinburgh High School, attended law classes in the university, and in 1846 became a pupil in the office of Messrs. Douglas & Co. As early as 1843 he had joined the episcopal church. Changing his plans, he sailed for India in Feb. 1847, and in April landed at Madras. where he joined the 51st regiment of Madras native infantry. He retired in Oct. 1849, when, having attained the rank of lieutenant, in obedience to medical advice he came home invalided. He drew his modest military pension to the last. In later periods of his life there were signs of his training as a soldier and of the habit which it had engendered of expecting as well as yielding obedience to orders.

In 1852 he went into residence at Peterhouse, Cambridge, graduating B.A. in 1857 as a junior optime in the mathematical tripos of the previous year. Among his college contemporaries was his lifelong friend George Palmer (afterwards canon and a successor of his at Newington); out of college he was intimate with Montagu Butler (the present Master of Trinity). To his college Maclagan remained warmly attached through the rest of his life. On Trinity Sunday 1856 he was ordained and was licensed to the curacy of St. Saviour's, Paddington. From 1858 he served as curate at St. Stephen's (Avenue Road), Marylebone, until 1 Jan. 1860, when he became organising secretary of the London Diocesan Church Building Society, in which capacity his power of organisation first found scope. Shortly before this he had issued a popular tract, 'Will you be confirmed? a Word to the Young. By a London Curate' (1859). From 1865 to 1869 he was curate in charge at Enfield, where some of the first parochial missions were held during his tenure of office. In Sept. 1869 he was appointed by the lord chancellor, Lord Hatherley, to the rectory of the large south London parish of Newington, where he remained till 1875. His labours there are commemorated by an east window in the little mission church of St. Gabriel, the building of which had at first exposed him to many attacks. Always a moderate high churchman, Maclagan in 1870 and 1872 edited with Dr. Weir, vicar of Forty Hill, Enfield, two series of essays entitled 'The Church and the Age,' treating of the 'principles and position' of the Church of England. To the earlier series Maclagan contributed an essay, 'The Church and the People,' which is distinguished by its candid and cheerful tone, but still more by a characteristic determination to apply direct and practical remedies to the alienation of the working classes from the church and her services. In 1873 he visited Rome and Naples with Dr. Weir in the interests of his health. In 1875 he was transferred to the living of St. Mary Abbots, Kensington, where his renown as a parish clergyman and as the organiser of parochial religious agencies rapidly rose. In 1876 he declined Lord Beaconsfield's offer of the bishopric of Calcutta; but in 1878, after being named prebendary of Reculverland in St. Paul's Cathedral and chaplain-in-ordinary to Queen Victoria, he accepted the bishopric of Lichfield, vacant by the death of George Augustus Selwyn [q. v.].

He was enthroned at Lichfield Cathedral on 11 July 1878. Practical work and efficient discharge of pastoral duties distinguished his episcopate. He brought his clergy together in synods and retreats, and directed the aid of the laity into various concurrent channels. He issued many letters to the diocese in the 'Lichfield Diocesan Magazine,' the most important of them being a series addressed 'Ad Clerum.' A volume of 'Pastoral Letters and Synodal Charges,' published by him later, in 1892, notably illustrates his spirit of moderation and gentle sympathy. In October 1887, at the request of Archbishop Benson and in company with John Wordsworth, bishop of Salisbury [q.v. Suppl. II], he attended a conference of Old Catholics at Bonn, where he had an interview with Döllinger. In 1890 he testified in a different way to his desire for unity among Christians by welcoming a body of nonconformists to his palace and to the cathedral service, a proceeding which in 1895 he repeated at Bishopthorpe. So late as 1904, in an address on Christian Brotherhood, he advocated the admission of nonconformists to Holy Communion.

In 1891 Archbishop Magee died after but two months' tenure of the see of York, and Lord Salisbury offered the archbishopric to Maclagan. He was confirmed at St. George's, Hanover Square, and was enthroned in the Minster on 15 Sept. 1891. At York he worked on the same lines which he had followed at Lichfield. He introduced the same regulations restricting the preaching of deacons which he had promulgated there; on the other hand, he established guilds of youths inclined to pastoral life. In 1892 he established at York a training college for clergy under the name of 'Scholæ Episcopi.' From the same year onwards he spent much time in visiting his clergy, and within three years became personally acquainted with the 650 parishes of his diocese. He was generous in diocesan gifts, more especially to the Poor Benefices Fund, which he started; and on two occasions—in 1897 and in 1906—he offered to surrender 2000*l.* of his annual income in order to facilitate the subdivision of his diocese. He discouraged the more advanced usages, from the practisers of which his chief troubles as a bishop proceeded. In 1889 and 1890 he took part in the hearing at Lambeth of the charges against Edward King, bishop of Lincoln [q. v. Suppl. II], and was in full accordance with both Archbishop Benson and his successor, Archbishop Temple. A protracted struggle with Sir Edmund Beckett, Lord Grimthorpe [q. v. Suppl. II], vicar-general of his province and chancellor of his archdiocese, who insisted on the issue of licences to guilty divorcees, ended only in 1900 when Lord Grimthorpe was succeeded in these offices by Sir Alfred Cripps.

Maclagan was responsible, with Archbishop Temple, for the substance if not for the form of the 'Responsio' made in 1896 to the bull 'Apostolicæ Curæ,' in which Pope Leo XIII had denied the validity of Anglican orders (see Lord Halifax's account in F. D. How's *Archbishop Maclagan*, ch. xxxiii.). In the following year, accompanied by W. J. Birkbeck, he paid a private visit to Russia, where he was cordially received by the authorities of the Russian Church as well as by the Tsar Nicholas II and the Tsaritsa. At the coronation of Edward VII in 1902 he crowned Queen Alexandra, although it was decided that this function appertained to the Archbishop of York by grace rather than by right. In 1906 Maclagan celebrated the eightieth year of his life, and the fiftieth of his ministry, by a special offering of 2000*l.* for charitable purposes. But his physical powers — especially those of memory — were then declining, and in the autumn of 1908, after taking a passive part in the Lambeth Conference and many meetings incidental to the Pan-Anglican Congress, he resigned his archbishopric (thereby setting a precedent). At the beginning of 1909 he took up his abode at Queen's Gate Place, London, where, after a short illness, he died on 19 Sept. 1910. He was buried in Bishopthorpe churchyard, in the grave next to that of his lifelong friend Canon Keble. At Lichfield a large stone cross, erected by himself, marks the spot which he had chosen for his grave.

Maclagan's pastoral activity has been rarely surpassed. Although his literary style was pure and clear he never attained great renown as a preacher. Late in life he prefixed a brief monograph to an edition of 'The Grace of Sacraments' (1905) by Alexander Knox [q. v.], a forerunner of the Tractarians. In 1855 he published for private circulation a small volume of sonnets and other short poems. But those of his writings which will live longest are his hymns. Among them is the beautiful hymn for All Saints' Day ('The Saints of God'), two Good Friday hymns, and one for St. Luke's Day (for list see JULIAN'S *Dictionary of Hymnology* (1892), p. 709). He also composed the tunes of a number of hymns, among them those of the Communion hymn 'Bread of Heaven,' of Wesley's 'O Thou before the world began,' and of the hymn 'Palms of Glory' (for festivals of martyrs). He wrote some other 'Ancient and Modern' hymn tunes; others have been published in the 'Church Monthly,' a magazine begun in 1888.

Maclagan was twice married: (1) in April 1860 to Sarah Kate (*d.* July 1862), daughter of George Clapham, by whom he had two sons; and (2) in Nov. 1878 to Augusta Anne, youngest daughter of

William Keppel Barrington, sixth Viscount Barrington, a lady whose powers of organisation well matched his own. She survived him with a son and daughter.

A portrait was painted by Sir William Richmond; another, by the Hon. John Collier, is in the hall of Peterhouse, Cambridge; a third is to be placed in the Maclagan Memorial Hall, under which name the ancient St. William's College, York (the church and convocation house of the province), was restored in 1909, after the archbishop's resignation.

[F. D. How's Life, 1911; The Times, 20 Sept. 1910; The Guardian, 23 Sept. 1910; private information from Mr. F. D. How and others.] A. W. W.

MACLAREN, ALEXANDER (1826–1910), baptist divine, born in Glasgow on 11 Feb. 1826, was youngest son of David McLaren (1785–1850) by his wife Mary (Wingate). The son always signed his name McLaren, though the spelling Maclaren is that of all his published works. His father, a business man and lay pastor (1823–36) of a congregation of Scottish baptists, was the pioneer manager (1836–40) of the South Australian Company, his family remaining in Glasgow; his name survives in the Maclaren wharf at Adelaide, and Maclaren Vale. While at the Glasgow High School, where Robert Rainy [q. v. Suppl. II] was his schoolfellow, Maclaren was baptised on 17 May 1840 (McLaren) by James Paterson, minister of Hope Street baptist chapel. He studied at Glasgow University 1838–9 (junior Latin) and 1839–40 (Greek). In 1842, the family having removed to London on the return of the father (1840), he entered Stepney College to study for the baptist ministry under William Harris Murch, D.D. (1784–1859), followed (1844) by Benjamin Davies, LL.D. [q. v.], who put Maclaren on the way to be a good Hebraist. At the London University, to which Stepney was affiliated, he graduated B.A. (Oct. 1845), and took a prize (1845) in the 'first scripture' examination. While at college he was much influenced by Thomas Binney [q. v.], who taught him to preach, and by Edward Miall [q. v.]. He left college (1846) for the ministry at Portland Chapel, Southampton, with a guaranteed stipend of 60*l.*, room for three hundred hearers, and a membership of twenty. His dress was unclerical and his ways unconventional; Spurgeon thought him a 'dangerous man.' His preaching, always brief, had genius and fire, with great self-command. His chapel filled. Never given to pastoral visitation, he devoted much time to Sunday-school work and the preparation of teachers. At the Southampton Athenæum he became a popular lecturer, both on literary and on ecclesiastical topics. His Southampton ministry closed on 20 June 1858, in consequence of a call to Manchester.

On 27 June 1858 he began his ministry at Union Chapel (building now owned by United Free Methodists) in Oxford Road, Manchester. The trust-deed requires the pastor to be a baptist and recognises only 'believers' baptism' by submersion, but opens membership to others; though a convinced baptist, Maclaren's views about all 'ritual' approximated to those of Friends. The building soon proved to be inadequate, and the present Union Chapel (opened 16 Nov. 1869), and the adjoining lecture hall, were erected farther down Oxford Road at a cost of 22,000*l.*; school premises were added in 1880. From this church proceeded (1872) the People's Institute in Rusholme, and, by way of denominational extension, two churches in Gorton and three missions in poor districts, for Maclaren believed in 'denominational walls' but not in 'the broken bottles on the top.'

Apart from his personal magnetism, Maclaren's pulpit power, which throughout his Manchester life placed him above all rivalry, is ascribed by his friend Alexander Mackennal, D.D. [q. v. Suppl. II], to his 'rare exegetical skill, the power of illuminating his subject by side-lights, and focussing all side-lights on his central theme' (*Life of J. A. Macfadyen, D.D.*, 1891, p. 115). The present Master of Peterhouse, when principal of Owens College, spoke of Maclaren's preaching as 'one of the chief literary influences in the city of Manchester' (Carlile). His 'exegetical skill' was based on a minute and accurate philology, to which his valuable version of the Psalms bears witness; he maintained the habit of reading every day, in the originals, a chapter of each Testament. He was a good German scholar, acquainted with the 'higher' criticism, but he deemed the 'most precious elements in the Psalms' to be 'very slightly affected' by 'questions of date and authorship' (preface to *Psalms*, 1893). While declining numerous invitations to leave Manchester, he preached for the Baptist Missionary Society at Surrey chapel (1864), for the London Missionary Society (same place, 1870), was president of the Baptist Union (1875, and again 1901), and was president of the

Baptist World Congress (1905) in London. In 1877 he was made D.D.Edinburgh; in 1902, Litt.D.Manchester; on 23 April 1907, D.D.Glasgow.

In 1865 he made a tour in Italy, and although his strictures on the Roman church were severe, he believed that 'true and devout souls' dwelt in that communion. With Cardinal Vaughan [q. v. Suppl. II], when bishop of Salford, Maclaren was on excellent terms, as he was with James Fraser [q. v.], bishop of Manchester, and the Anglican clergy generally. In 1881 reasons of health led to his resting for nearly a year. In 1883 he visited the baptist churches of Australia. He revisited Italy early in 1903.

On 28 June 1903 he retired from active duty, but was made pastor emeritus and occasionally preached; an annuity of 200*l.* he declined. He left Manchester for Edinburgh in June 1909, presenting his library to the Baptist College, Manchester. At 4 Whitehouse Terrace, Edinburgh, he died on 5 May 1910; a funeral service was held at Union Chapel on 9 May; the remains, after cremation, were buried in Brooklands cemetery near Manchester. His portrait, painted in 1896 by Sir George Reid, is in the Manchester Art Gallery; a replica by Sir George is in the deacons' vestry at Union Chapel. He married on 27 March 1856 his cousin Marion Ann (*b.* 18 Aug. 1828; *d.* 21 Dec. 1884), daughter of James Maclaren of Edinburgh; of their five children, a son, Alister Maclaren, and two daughters survived him.

In addition to single sermons and addresses he published: 1. 'The Student: his Work and . . . Preparation,' 1864, 12mo. 2. 'Sermons preached in Manchester,' series 1–3, 1865. 3. 'A Spring Holiday in Italy,' 1865. 4. 'Sermons preached in Union Chapel' [1872], three series. 5. 'Week-day Evening Addresses . . . in Manchester,' 1877. 6. 'The Union Psalter . . . selected' [1878]. 7. 'The Life of David as reflected in his Psalms,' 1880. 8. 'The Secret of Power, and other Sermons,' 1882. 9. 'A Year's Ministry,' 1884; 2nd series, 1885 (reprinted from the 'Christian Commonwealth'). 10. 'Christ in the Heart,' 1886. 11. 'The Epistles . . . to . . . Colossians and Philemon,' 1887 (in 'Expositor's Bible'). 12. 'The Unchanging Christ, and other Sermons,' 2nd edition, 1890. 13. 'The Holy of Holies,' 1890 (sermons on John xiv.–xvi.). 14. 'The God of the Amen, and other Sermons,' 1891. 15. 'After the Resurrection,' 1892 (sermons). 16. 'The Conquering Christ, and other Sermons,' 1892. 17. 'Bible Class Expositions,' 1892–4, six vols. (covers Gospels and Acts). 18. 'The Wearied Christ, and other Sermons,' 1893; 19. 'Paul's Prayers, and other Sermons,' 1893 (revised). 20. 'The Psalms,' vols. 1 and 2, 1893; vol. 3, 1894 (in 'Expositor's Bible,' with original translation). 21. 'Christ's "Musts," and other Sermons,' 1894. 22. 'The Victor's Crowns,' 1895. 23. 'The Beatitudes,' 1895. 24. 'Triumphant Certainties, and other Sermons' [1897]. 25. 'Leaves from the Tree of Life,' 1899; 1906. 26. 'Last Sheaves, Sermons,' 1903. 27. 'Expositions of Holy Scripture,' three series, 6 vols. in each, 1904–10. 28. 'Pulpit Prayers,' 1907 (taken in shorthand).

Selections from his sermons were made by J. H. Martyn in 'Pictures and Emblems' [1885]; by George Coates in 'Creed and Conduct,' 1897; in 'Music for the Soul,' 1897; and by F. A. Aitkins in 'A Rosary of Christian Graces,' 1899.

[University of London, General Register, 1860; brief sketch from the Freeman, 1875; J. C. Carlile, A. Maclaren, the Man and his Message, 1901 (portrait); D. Williamson, Life of A. Maclaren, 1910 (5 portraits); E. T. McLaren, Dr. McLaren, of Manchester, 1911 (six portraits); Baptist Handbook, 1911 (memoir by J. E. R[oberts]; portrait); information from Mr. W. Innes Addison, assistant clerk of senate, Glasgow.]

A. G.

MACLAREN, IAN (pseudonym). [See Watson, John (1850–1907), preacher and author.]

McLAREN, JOHN, Lord McLaren (1831–1910), Scottish judge, born at Edinburgh on 17 April 1831, was son of Duncan McLaren [q. v.], M.P. for Edinburgh, by his first wife, Grant, daughter of William Aitken, merchant in Dunbar. Owing to delicate health John was unable to attend school, and was privately educated. He went to Edinburgh University, and joined the Scots Law Society (20 Nov. 1854). On 6 Dec. 1856 he passed to the Scottish bar, and next year became a member (18 March 1857) of the Juridical Society, of which he was librarian (1859–1860). His progress at the bar was hindered by the state of his health, which forced him to spend at least one winter abroad. In 1869, however, he was made sheriff of chancery, and thereafter gradually acquired a considerable practice.

Like his father, who was the active leader of Scottish radicals and senior M.P.

for Edinburgh since 1865, McLaren was an advanced liberal, and, though personally very popular with the bar, incurred the hostility of the whig influence which was at that time strong in the Parliament House.

After the Gladstone government retired in 1874 McLaren played an active part in re-organising the Scottish liberals, and in arranging the 'Midlothian campaign' of 1879–80. He moved the vote of thanks to Gladstone after his first speech (24 Nov. 1879), and helped William Patrick Adam [q. v.], the liberal whip, in preparing for the general election of 1880, when he was himself returned for the Wigton district. On the formation of the Gladstone government (April 1880) he was appointed lord advocate, by way of recognition of his services to the party, but was defeated on seeking re-election by Mark John Stewart (afterwards Sir M. J. Mactaggart Stewart). The like ill-fortune pursued him when he stood for Berwick-on-Tweed in July 1880. He remained without a seat till January 1881, when his father retired in his favour, and he was elected for Edinburgh, after a contest. McLaren's parliamentary career was cut short against his wish. Sir William Harcourt, then home secretary, and he were on bad terms, and their differences came to a head in August 1881. The resignation of Adam Gifford, Lord Gifford [q. v.], then created a vacancy on the Scottish bench. The lord advocate, in accordance with the usual practice, recommended to the prime minister an advocate for the appointment. Gladstone requested McLaren to take the post himself. McLaren declined. He had just fought three costly elections within the last eighteen months, and wished to remain in parliament. But Gladstone under pressure from Harcourt was insistent. John Bright, then chancellor of the Duchy of Lancaster, whose sister (Priscilla) was third wife of McLaren's father, exerted his influence with Gladstone on McLaren's behalf, but without avail; and McLaren was forced out of the House of Commons into the vacant judgeship. He was succeeded as lord advocate by John Blair Balfour, Lord Kinross, [q. v. Suppl. II]. On the bench, where his judgments were noted as models of clear reasoning and concise statement, McLaren was eminently successful during a judicial career of nearly thirty years. He died at Brighton on 6 April 1910, and was buried in the Grange cemetery at Edinburgh.

While at the bar McLaren was editor and author of several legal works: 1. 'Collection of Public General Statutes and Acts of Sederunt relating to Procedure in the Supreme Courts of Scotland,' 1861. 2. 'Treatise on the Law of Trusts and Trust Settlements,' 1863. 3. Edition of Professor More's 'Lectures on the Law of Scotland,' 1864. 4. 'Law of Scotland relating to Wills,' 1868; new edit. 1894, still a leading authority. 5. Edition of Professor Bell's 'Commentaries on the Law of Scotland,' 1870. He also studied astronomy and mathematics, and various mathematical papers by him were published by the Royal Society of Edinburgh, of which he was several time a vice-president. He was for some years president of the Scottish Meteorological Society, and a director of the Ben Nevis Observatory. He received the honorary degree of LL.D. from the universities of Edinburgh (1882), Glasgow (1883, along with John Bright, who was then installed as rector), and Aberdeen (1906, at the fourth-centenary celebration of that university), and was an intimate friend of Sir William Thomson (Lord Kelvin) [q. v. Suppl. II], Professor Peter Guthrie Tait [q. v. Suppl. II], and other men of science.

McLaren married in 1868 Ottilie, daughter of H. L. Schabe of Glasgow, by whom he had three sons and three daughters. He was survived by one son, Duncan, now (1912) residing in British Columbia. Of his daughters, the eldest, Katharine, married F. S. Oliver of Checkendon Court, Oxfordshire, author of 'The Life of Alexander Hamilton,' and the youngest, Ottilie, wife of William Wallace, musical composer, has shown much ability as a sculptor.

There are three oil portraits of McLaren; two, by Otto Leyde and John Lavery respectively, are in the possession of his widow. The third, by Meg Wright, belongs to his half-brother, Sir Charles Benjamin Bright McLaren, Lord Aberconway. Two busts in bronze, by John Hutchinson, R.S.A., and by his daughter, Mrs. Wallace, belong to his widow.

[Scotsman and The Times, 7 April 1910; Roll of the Faculty of Advocates; Roll of the Scots Law Society; Records of the Juridical Society; Proc. Roy. Soc. Edin., vol. xxxi. part 5, p. 694; personal knowledge.]

G. W. T. O.

MACLEAN, JAMES MACKENZIE (1835–1906), journalist and politician, was born on 13 Aug. 1835 at Liberton, near Edinburgh. His father, a native of Uist, an island in the Hebrides, spent some years in Jamaica before settling at Liberton, where he died in 1839. His mother belonged to the Biagrie family and was of French extraction. James was educated first at Circus Place school, Edinburgh, then at Dr. Bruce's grammar school, Newcastle-on-Tyne, whither his mother removed with her two boys on her husband's death. In 1845, after a year at the preparatory school at Hertford, he entered Christ's Hospital as a foundationer and became a 'Grecian.' The necessity of earning his living compelled him to forgo his intention of proceeding to Cambridge. He was for a short time mathematical tutor at his old school at Newcastle. In 1854 he joined the editorial staff of the local 'Newcastle Chronicle,' then a weekly paper, and edited it from 1855 to the spring of 1858. On the recommendation of Alexander Russel [q. v.] of the 'Scotsman' he subsequently became a leader-writer for the 'Manchester Guardian,' and at the close of 1859 Russel's influence procured for him the editorship of the 'Bombay Gazette.' He held the office for more than a year when differences with the proprietor led him to resign early in 1861. Persuaded by friends to remain in Bombay, he thereupon started the 'Bombay Saturday Review,' which, while modelled on its London prototype, gave more prominence to commercial affairs. He gathered round him many eminent contributors, including Sir Alexander Grant [q. v.], Sir George Birdwood, Thomas Chisholm Anstey [q. v.], and occasionally even the governor, Sir Bartle Frere [q. v.]. The advertisement revenue was greatly benefited by the share mania (1861–5) arising from the American civil war and the consequent expansion of the Bombay cotton trade.

Early in 1864 Maclean purchased the principal share in the 'Bombay Gazette,' of which he resumed the editorship, and before long became the sole proprietor. To the 'Gazette' he mainly devoted himself, writing largely for it, and discontinuing the 'Bombay Saturday Review.' His candour and independence imported new vigour into the discussion of public affairs in Western India, and while severely criticising native political aspirations, he was at times equally uncompromising in attack on the policy of government. His vituperative style, which extended the circulation of his paper, especially appealed to young Indians, and he set the model of licence which the native press in Western India subsequently adopted (*Times of India Proclamation Supplement*, 4 Nov. 1908). At the same time Maclean organised public opinion in Bombay to many beneficent ends. Sir George Birdwood pronounced him to be 'the ablest publicist we ever had in India' (*Roy. Soc. of Arts Journal*, 14 June 1901).

Appointed in 1865 to the bench of justices, which had a general supervision of municipal affairs, Maclean initiated the agitation which resulted in the creation of a semi-elective municipal corporation (1872). A member of this body for many years, he read as its chairman in 1875 the address of welcome to the Prince of Wales (afterwards King Edward VII). On the occasion of this royal visit he compiled an historical and descriptive 'Guide to Bombay' (1875), which ranks among the best works of its kind and was re-issued annually till 1902. He was a fellow of Bombay University.

At the close of 1879 Maclean sold the 'Gazette' in order to take part in politics at home. An upholder of Lord Beaconsfield's motto, 'Imperium et Libertas,' he was an unsuccessful conservative candidate for the Elgin burghs at the general election of 1880. For a time he associated himself with Lord Randolph Churchill, and helped to secure his election to the chairmanship of the National Union of Conservative Associations (Feb. 1884). But an estrangement followed when it seemed to Maclean that Lord Randolph was seeking to supplant Lord Salisbury as party leader. A motion which Maclean submitted to the council (2 May 1884) with a view to restoring harmony in the party was carried and led Lord Randolph to resign the chairmanship and to withdraw for the time from the political arena (WINSTON CHURCHILL'S *Life*, i. chap vii.).

At the general election of 1885 Maclean won for his party the second seat at Oldham, and at the election of 1886 he headed the poll. Lord Randolph, now leader of the house, became reconciled to him, and he seconded the address in October 1886. He soon won a reputation as an effective speaker; he also displayed antagonisms to his leaders on various questions. He notably offended trade unionists and bi-metallists, and at the election of 1892 lost his seat at Oldham, being at the bottom of the poll.

In 1882 Maclean had acquired a large interest in the 'Western Mail,' Cardiff, to which he contributed for many years a weekly political letter. He stood for the borough at the general election of 1895, and, defeating Sir Edward James Reed [q. v. Suppl. II], became the first conservative member for Cardiff after forty years. While maintaining his reputation as a parliamentary debater, he developed a distrust and dislike of Mr. Chamberlain, which ruined his parliamentary career. He opposed the conservative government on many critical questions, of which the chief were the retention of Chitral, the negotiations leading up to the South African war, and the imposition in 1899 of countervailing sugar duties in India. In the matter of the sugar duties he seconded on 15 June 1899 a motion of want of confidence moved by the opposition, and owing to the angry interruptions on his own side he crossed the floor of the house to finish his speech. The Cardiff conservatives withdrew their support. He disposed of his interest in the 'Western Mail,' and retired from parliament at the dissolution of 1900.

An ardent free trader, Maclean spoke and wrote against tariff reform after its promulgation by Mr. Chamberlain. In a paper read before the Royal Society of Arts (10 Dec. 1903), he emphasised the objections from the Indian point of view (cf. his *India's Place in an Imperial Federation*, 1904). He now wrote for liberal journals, such as the 'Manchester Guardian' and the 'South Wales Daily News.' Some of these contributions were revised and collected as 'Recollections of Westminster and India' (Manchester, 1902).

An original member of the Institute of Journalists, he was president of the conference at Cardiff in 1899, when he deprecated 'a growing spirit [in the press] of obsequiousness to personages in high social or political positions' (*Proc. Inst. Journalists*, No. 21, Sept. 1897). He revisited India at the end of 1898, and was received with enthusiasm in Bombay. He died at Southborne, Bournemouth, on 23 April 1906, and was buried at Chiswick.

He married (1) in 1867 Anna Maria (*d.* 1897), daughter of Philip Whitehead, of the 'Bombay Gazette'; and (2) on 23 July 1900 Mrs. Sarah Kennedy, third daughter of Dr. D. Hayle of Harrogate, who survives; there were no children. A pastel portrait was executed by his widow.

[Maclean's Recollections, Guide to Bombay, and other writings; Churchill, Life of Lord Randolph Churchill, 1906; The Times, and Manchester Guardian, 24 April 1906; Times of India, 25 April 1906; Cardiff Times, Stalybridge Standard, and Bombay Gazette Weekly Summary, 28 April 1906; Oldham Chronicle, 30 April 1906; Lucy's Diary of Salisbury Parliament, 1886–92, and of the Unionist Parliament, 1895–1900; personal knowledge; private papers, &c., kindly lent by Mrs. Maclean.] F. H. B.

MACLEAR, GEORGE FREDERICK (1833–1902), theological writer, born at Bedford on 3 Feb. 1833, was the eldest son of the Rev. George Maclear, M.A., chaplain of Bedford county prison (1832–69), by his wife Isabella Ingle. Educated at Bedford grammar school, he obtained a scholarship at Trinity College, Cambridge, in 1852 and had a distinguished academic career. He won the Carus Greek Testament prize in 1854 and 1855, and after graduating B.A. with a second class in the classical tripos of 1855, he was placed in the first class in the theological tripos of 1856 (its first year). He gained the Burney prize in 1855, the Hulsean in 1857, the Maitland in 1858 and 1861, and the Norrisian in 1863. All five prize essays were published. His Maitland essay of 1858, 'The Christian Statesman and our Indian Empire; or the legitimate sphere of government countenance and aid in promoting Christianity in India,' reached a second edition. That of 1861, on 'Christian Missions during the Middle Ages,' was recast as 'Apostles of Mediæval Europe' (1869), and was the first of a series of important volumes on missionary history. Maclear proceeded M.A. in 1860, B.D. in 1867, and D.D. in 1872. Ordained deacon in 1856 and priest in 1857, he held curacies at Clopton, Bedfordshire (1856–8), and St. Barnabas, Kennington (1858–60); was assistant-preacher at Curzon Chapel, Mayfair (1860–5); and reader at the Temple (1865–70); select preacher at Cambridge in 1868, 1880, and 1886, and at Oxford in 1881–2; and Ramsden preacher at Cambridge in 1890. He delivered the Boyle lectures at Whitehall in 1879–80 'On the Evidential Value of the Holy Eucharist' (1883; 4th edit. 1898).

Meanwhile Maclear was an assistant master at King's College School, London (1860–6), and headmaster (1867–80). He showed great ability as teacher and organiser, doubled the numbers and greatly raised the standing of the school. While headmaster he declined an offer of the see of Colombo in 1875. Eventually he accepted the post of warden of St. Augustine's Missionary College, Canterbury, in 1880, and held it till his death. In this capacity he worked untiringly as preacher, lecturer, and adviser on foreign mission work. In 1885 he was made an hon. canon of Canterbury Cathedral. He died at St. Augustine's College, after a long illness, on 19 Oct. 1902, and was buried in St. Martin's churchyard, Canterbury.

Maclear was twice married: (1) on 10 June 1857 to Christiana Susan, daughter of J. Campbell, rector of Eye, Suffolk (she died on 31 May 1874, being predeceased by an only daughter); and (2) on 27 Dec. 1878 to Eva, eldest daughter of William Henry D'Olier Purcell, vicar of Exmouth; she died on 1 March 1890, leaving three sons and a daughter. A portrait by Mr. Sydney P. Hall, unveiled on 5 Dec. 1902, hangs in the hall of the new King's College School at Wimbledon.

Maclear enjoyed a wide reputation as a theological writer. His lucid and well-arranged text-books, which were long in general use, include the 'Class Books of Old and New Testament History' (1862), the 'Class Book of the Catechism' (1868), 'An Introduction to the Articles' (written with the Rev. Watkin Wynn Williams) (1895; new edit. 1909). To missionary history he contributed, besides the work mentioned, 'The Conversion of the West' (4 vols. 1878) and 'St. Augustine's, Canterbury: its Rise, Ruin, and Restoration' (1888); and he wrote on missions in the 'Encyclopædia Britannica' (9th edit.). Maclear also published, with several devotional books, 'An Elementary Introduction to the Book of Common Prayer' (1868) and 'The Baptismal Office and the Order of Confirmation' (1902), in both of which he collaborated with Francis Procter [q. v. Suppl. II]; he edited portions of the Cambridge Bible for Schools; and contributed to Smith's Dictionaries of 'Christian Antiquities' and 'Christian Biography,' and to Cassell's 'Bible Educator.' 'Lectures on Pastoral Theology,' a selection from his unpublished manuscripts, was edited by the Rev. R. J. E. Boggis, D.D., in 1904.

[Private information; Lectures on Pastoral Theology, with portrait and Dedication by Dr. Boggis, 1904; King's College School Magazine, Dec. 1902, by Prof. Hales, Rev. H. Belcher, and others; Crockford's Clerical Directory; Guardian, 22 Oct. 1902, and Church Times, 24 Oct. 1902; Kentish Observer, 23 Oct.; The Times, 20, 23 Oct.; Brit. Mus. Cat.] G. Le G. N.

MACLEAR, JOHN FIOT LEE PEARSE (1838–1907), admiral, son of Sir Thomas Maclear [q. v.], astronomer royal at the Cape of Good Hope, was born at Cape Town on 27 June 1838. He entered the navy in Sept. 1851 as a cadet on board the Castor, frigate, then bearing the broad pennant of Christopher Wyvill, commodore in command on the Cape station. In her he saw service during the Kaffir war of 1851, and afterwards, as a midshipman of the Algiers, served in the Baltic and in the Black Sea from 1854 to 1856, receiving the Baltic, Turkish, and Crimean medals, with the clasp for Sevastopol. He passed his examination in July 1857, and served on board the Cyclops in the Red Sea as mate during the outbreak at Jeddah in 1858. On 19 May 1859 he was promoted to lieutenant, and shortly afterwards appointed to the Sphinx, in which he served on the China station until 1862, being present at several engagements during the second Chinese war, and especially at Taku Forts, for which he received the clasp. In 1863 he went to the Excellent to qualify as a gunnery lieutenant, and in Feb. 1864 was appointed to the Princess Royal, flagship on the China station. He returned home in her, and in Oct. 1867 was chosen to be first lieutenant of the Octavia, frigate, flagship of Commodore Heath [see Heath, Sir Leopold George, Suppl. II] in the East Indies. In her he took part in the Abyssinian campaign of 1868, earning the medal and his promotion to commander, which was dated 14 Aug. 1868.

In 1872 the Challenger was commissioned by Sir George Nares, with Maclear as his commander, for the voyage of scientific discovery in which the ship went round the world. Returning home in her in 1876, Maclear was on 14 August promoted to captain. In 1879 he succeeded Sir George Nares in command of the Alert, sloop, and remained in her until 1882, completing the survey of the Straits of Magellan. From 1883 to 1887 he commanded the Flying Fish on surveying service, carrying out other valuable scientific work during the same time. On 20 June 1891 he reached flag rank, and two months later retired. He was promoted to vice-admiral on the retired list in 1897, and to admiral in 1903. After leaving the sea, Maclear assisted in the compilation of several volumes of the official sailing directions, especially those for the Eastern Archipelago (1890 and 1893) for the West Coasts of Central America and the United States (1896), for Bering Sea and Alaska (1898), and the 'Arctic Pilot' (vol. ii. 1901 and vol. iii. 1905). He was a fellow of the Royal Geographical and Royal Meteorological societies.

He died from heart failure in an hotel at Niagara on 17 July 1907, and his body was brought to England for burial. He married on 4 June 1878 Julia, sixth daughter of Sir John Frederick William Herschel [q. v.].

[The Times, 19 July 1907; Journal of Roy. Geogr. Soc. 1907; Proc. Meteorol. Soc. 1907; Sir Charles Wyville Thomson, The Voyage of the Challenger, 2 vols. 1877; W. J. J. Spry, Cruise of H.M.S. Challenger, 1876.] L. G. C. L.

MACLEOD, FIONA (pseudonym). [See SHARP, WILLIAM (1855–1905), man of letters.]

MACLEOD, HENRY DUNNING (1821–1902), economist, born at Moray Place, Edinburgh, on 31 March 1821, was the second son and youngest child of Roderick Macleod (1786–1853) of Cadboll and Invergordon Castle, lord-lieutenant of Cromarty, and for several years M.P. successively for the county of Cromarty, the county of Sutherland, and the Inverness burghs. His mother was Isabella, daughter of William Cunninghame of Laimshaw, Ayrshire. He was called Dunning after his great-uncle, John Dunning, the first Lord Ashburton [q. v.]. He had one brother, Robert Bruce Æneas, fifth of Cadboll, and three sisters.

Macleod was educated first at Edinburgh Academy, then at Eton. He matriculated at Trinity College, Cambridge, in 1839, graduated B.A. as senior optime in 1843, and proceeded M.A. in 1863. On 5 May 1843 he was admitted a student of the Inner Temple. He was abroad for the greater part of the next two years, and then read as a pupil in the chambers of Edward Bullen, special pleader (1846–8), being called to the bar on 26 Jan. 1849. His subsequent legal career was intermittent. He established a certain reputation as a mercantile lawyer, joined the midland circuit in 1863, and was employed by the government from June 1868 till March 1870 in preparing a digest of the law of bills of exchange.

Macleod's life was mainly devoted to the study of political economy. In 1847, while still a law student, he acted as chairman of a committee formed in Easter Ross, a district in which his father was the largest landowner, to devise an improved system of poor law relief. A plan drawn up by Macleod was adopted with success in Easter Ross, and was described in the report issued by the Board of Supervision for the Relief of the Poor in 1852. It was subsequently imitated extensively throughout Scotland. Macleod remained for six years in Easter Ross supervising its working, and during that time he was also active in advocating free trade at the elections of 1847 and 1852.

In 1853 Macleod went to London, residing at Kensington for the rest of his life. He had suffered severely from bank-failures and was often thenceforth in straitened circumstances. Soon after settling in London he was engaged in a law case in which he successfully contested the claim of the board of trade to prohibit a joint-stock bank, founded under Sir Robert Peel's Act of 1845, from increasing its capital. Macleod expounded the general conclusions to which the litigation brought him in his first work, 'The Theory and Practice of Banking' (1856; 5th edit. 1892–3; Italian translation). It was highly commended for its independence in Tooke's 'History of Prices.' Other works in which Macleod combated the views of orthodox economists were now published at frequent intervals. From 1860 till 1868 he acted as coach in political economy to selected candidates for the Indian civil service. He also lectured on banking at Cambridge in 1877, at King's College, London, in 1878, at Edinburgh and Aberdeen in 1882, and he read many papers on the subject before learned societies.

Macleod, who agreed in the main with Archbishop Whately's views, regarded value as consisting in exchangeability, not as dependent on utility or cost of production. He made valuable contributions to the historical side of economic science (*Econ. Journal*, Dec. 1902), and was the first writer to give due prominence to the phenomenon of credit and to the exchanges in which it plays part (*Quarterly Review*, Oct. 1901). In his 'Elements of Political Economy' (1858; re-issued in 1872–5 as 'The Principles of Economical Philosophy,' and again in 1881–6 as 'The Elements of Economics') he enriched the economic vocabulary with the name 'Gresham's Law.' This term he first applied to the well-known principle of currency that 'bad money drives out good,' or that 'where two media come into circulation at the same time, the more valuable will tend to disappear.' Macleod did not assume that this conclusion was first reached by Sir Thomas Gresham [q.v.] when seeking to restore the debased coinage of Queen Elizabeth's reign, for it was well understood before the sixteenth century. Macleod's term is universally adopted by writers on currency. The 'Dictionary of Political Economy' (1858), of which only one volume appeared, was the attempt of one man to do what was afterwards accomplished by Mr. R. H. I. Palgrave with collaborators.

Macleod's views and attainments were not much regarded by orthodox economists (cf. CLIFFE LESLIE in *Academy* vii. 363). He was an unsuccessful candidate for the chairs of political economy at Cambridge in 1863, at Edinburgh in 1871, and at Oxford in 1888. A somewhat over-confident style of controversy told against him. On the

Continent and in America he was treated with more respect than at home. He was elected a fellow of the Cambridge Philosophical Society on 25 February 1850, and was corresponding member of the Société d'Economie Politique of Paris and of the Royal Academy of Jurisprudence and Legislation, Madrid.

In 1887 he drew up, at the request of the gold and silver commission, a memorandum on the relation of money to prices. He died at Norwood on 16 July 1902, and was buried at West Norwood cemetery. He had been in receipt of a civil list pension of 100*l.* since 20 June 1892.

Macleod married on 18 Aug. 1853 Elizabeth Mackenzie, eldest daughter of Hugh J. Cameron, sometime provost of Dingwall. He had three sons and four daughters. Of the sons two, Roderick Henry and Keith William Bruce, have won distinction in the Indian and Ceylon civil services respectively. One daughter, Mary, is a successful writer of books for children.

Besides the works cited, Macleod published: 1. 'Elements of Banking,' 1876. 2. 'Economics for Beginners,' 1883. 3. 'The Theory of Credit,' 1889–91, 2 vols.; 2nd edit. 1893–7; re-issued in one volume, 1898. 4. 'Bimetalism,' 1894. 5. 'History of Banking in Great Britain,' being vol. ii. of 'The History of Banking of All Nations,' 1896. 6. 'The History of Economics,' 1896. 7. 'Indian Currency,' 1898. 8. 'Draft Tentative Scheme for Restoring a Gold Currency to India,' privately printed, fol. 1898.

[The Times, 18 July 1902; Men at the Bar, 1885; Allibone's Dict. of Eng. Lit., 1891; Statement and Testimonials of Henry Dunning Macleod, Candidate for the Chair of Commercial and Pol. Econ. and Mercantile Law in Univ. of Edinburgh, 1871; An address to the Board of Electors to the Professorship of Pol. Econ. in the Univ. of Oxford, 1888; Burke's Landed Gentry; Quarterly Review, Oct. 1901; Economic Journal, Dec. 1902; Law Lists, 1890; Encyc. Brit. 11th edit. vols. 12 and 17; private information.]

S. E. F.

MACLURE, EDWARD CRAIG (1833–1906), dean of Manchester, born in Upper Brook Street, Manchester, on 10 June 1833, was eldest son of John Maclure, merchant, by his marriage with Elizabeth, daughter of William Kearsley, also a merchant. Educated at Manchester grammar school (1844–50), he won a Hulmeian scholarship at Brasenose College, Oxford, and matriculated there on 28 Jan. 1852. He graduated B.A. in 1856 and proceeded M.A. in 1858, being created B.D. and D.D. in 1890. Taking holy orders, he was curate of St. John's, Ladywood, Birmingham (1857–61), of St. Pancras, London (1861–3), and vicar of Habergham Eaves, Burnley (1863–77). In the public life of Burnley he took a prominent part, becoming chairman of the school board. Dr. Fraser, bishop of Manchester, appointed him in 1877 to the important vicarage of Rochdale, in 1878 to an honorary canonry of Manchester, and in 1881 to the rural deanery of Rochdale. He carried out great improvements at Rochdale parish church, for which he raised 10,000*l.*, as well as on the vicarage estate. In 1887 he acted as honorary secretary of the church congress at Manchester.

Designated archdeacon of Manchester in 1890, he was before his induction appointed dean of Manchester on the death of John Oakley [q. v.], being installed on 28 October. As dean Maclure won the goodwill of all classes by his broad sympathies, humour and love of fair play. Through his incessant care the daily service in the cathedral increased in dignity and beauty, and the Sunday evening services grew to be an important element in the religious life of the city. To his energy was due the rearrangement of the boundaries of the old churchyard and the building of the western annexe and the new vestries and library at the north-east corner of the cathedral.

Maclure largely devoted his abundant energy to promoting popular education of a religious kind. He was elected a member of the Manchester school board in 1891, and was unanimously appointed chairman. That position he held until the board was abolished in 1903 by the Education Act of the previous year. He was afterwards deputy-chairman of the education committee of the city council until his death, and was also a member of the Salford education committee. His practical knowledge of the details of the administration of education was recognised by government by his appointment in 1894 as a member of the royal commission on secondary education and in 1899 by his being placed on the consultative committee of the board of education. From 1895 to 1902 he was chairman of the School Board Association of England and Wales. He was also principal of the Scholæ Episcopi at Manchester and a governor of Owens College, Manchester University, of Manchester grammar school, of Chetham Hospital, and of Hulme's Trust. He was made hon. LL.D. at the Victoria University, Manchester, in 1902.

Maclure died at Manchester on 8 May 1906, and was buried at Kersal church, near that city. A monumental brass is in the chancel of the cathedral, and another memorial is in the grammar school.

He married on 7 May 1863 Mary Anne (*d.* 17 Oct. 1905), daughter of Johnson Gedge of Bury St. Edmunds, and had three sons, of whom William Kenneth took holy orders, and three daughters.

His brother, SIR JOHN WILLIAM MACLURE (1835–1901), born at Manchester on 22 April 1835, and educated at Manchester grammar school, engaged with success in commerce and financial enterprise. He came into prominence as honorary secretary to the committee of the Lancashire cotton relief fund, instituted in 1862 for the relief of the operatives thrown out of work through the stoppage of supplies of cotton during the American civil war. Over 1,750,000*l.* was raised for this object, and Maclure received a public testimonial. He was an enthusiastic volunteer, becoming major of the 40th Lancashire rifles. As churchwarden of Manchester (1881–96) he was instrumental in collecting large sums of money for a thorough restoration of the cathedral. A strong churchman, he was in politics a conservative, and was elected in 1886 M.P. for the Stretford division of Lancashire, which seat he retained until his death on 28 Jan. 1901. His cheery temperament made him popular in the House of Commons. On 7 April 1892 he and three other directors of the Cambrian railways were admonished by the speaker by direction of the house for a breach of privilege in dismissing a stationmaster on account of his evidence before the committee on the hours of railway servants. He was created a baronet on 1 Jan. 1898. There is a tablet to his memory in Manchester cathedral. He married on 13 Dec. 1859 Eleanor, second daughter of Thomas Nettleship of East Sheen, Surrey, by whom he had three sons and four daughters.

[Manchester Guardian, 9 May 1906 (with portrait); The Times, 9 May 1906; Manchester Courier, 14 May 1906; Guardian (London), 30 May 1906; C. H. Drant, Distinguished Churchmen (with portrait), 1902; Crockford's Directory, 1906; Ulula, the Manchester grammar school magazine, 1906, p. 69; Dod's Parliamentary Companion, 1900; Burke's Peerage, 1901; Axon's Annals of Manchester.] C. W. S.

McMAHON, CHARLES ALEXANDER (1830–1904), general and geologist, born at Highgate on 23 March 1830, was son of Captain Alexander McMahon of Irish descent, formerly in the Indian service, by his wife Ann, daughter of Major Patrick Mansell (British army). After education at a private school, he obtained a commission in the 39th Madras native infantry on 4 Feb. 1847, but after eight years' service in that regiment became a member of the Madras staff corps, and was transferred in 1856 to the Punjab commission, on which he served for thirty years, holding the rank of commissioner for the last fourteen. At the outbreak of the Mutiny, McMahon, then a lieutenant and assistant commissioner of the Sialkot district, in which was a cantonment, was in full charge owing to his superior's illness. On 9 July 1857 the native troops rose, and after murdering some Europeans, including four of their officers, decamped to join the rebels. But McMahon contrived to send a note to General John Nicholson [q.v.], who restored order at Sialkot so completely that McMahon was able to force the surrender of some 140 refugee rebels. In 1865 his ability as a judge was proved in a civil suit against the government of India which came before him as a Punjab commissioner. An intricate question, involving about 1,500,000*l.*, had been remitted by the privy council for trial on its merits. McMahon's decision (against the plaintiff) was upheld on appeal by the superior courts of the Punjab and the privy council in England.

While commissioner of Hissar in 1871 McMahon began to work seriously at geology, and six years later published his first important paper in the 'Records of the Geological Survey of India' (vol. x.). This and its successors dealt with a group of crystalline rocks, some of which, after examination with the microscope, he maintained to be eruptive. Subsequently, in 1879, while on a furlough in England, with the rank of lieutenant-colonel, he entered himself as a student at the Royal School of Mines. On returning to India he investigated its rocks with increased vigour, contributing in all twenty-one papers to the 'Records.'

He retired in 1885 with the rank of colonel, becoming major-general in 1888 and lieutenant-general in 1892. Settling in London, he devoted himself to petrological studies, taking part in the proceedings of kindred societies and publishing papers in their journals, the total number of his contributions to geology being nearly fifty. As an investigator he was scrupulously careful and accurate. In petrology he merits a high place among the pioneers, for in 1881 he had independently arrived at the conclusion, which then found only a very few supporters in England, that, as a general rule, the extent of metamorphism affords an indication of the relative age of ancient rocks, and in 1884 he maintained, as is now generally admitted, that foliation, in certain crystalline rocks, was due to a flowing of the mass while it was still viscid or partly crystallised. His valuable collection of rock slices was presented by his widow to Manchester University.

He became a fellow of the Geological Society in 1878, and was awarded its Lyell medal in 1899. He was president of the Geologists' Association in 1894–5 and of the geological section at the meeting of the British Association in 1902. In 1898 he was elected F.R.S., and a contribution to the 'Geological Magazine' was published in November 1903. He died at his London house on 21 Feb. 1904.

He was twice married: (1) in 1857 to Elizabeth (*d.* 1866), daughter of Lieutenant-Colonel Charles Franklin Head, late 93rd highlanders; of his family by her, two sons, the elder being Colonel Sir Arthur Henry McMahon, K.C.I.E., C.S.I., a distinguished officer in the Indian army, who is also a geologist, and one daughter, are still living; (2) in 1868 to Charlotte Emily, daughter of Henry Dorling of Stroud Green House, Croydon, who, with a son and daughter, survived him.

[Proc. Roy. Soc., vol. lxxv.; Geol. Mag. 1904; Quart. Journ. Geol. Soc., 1905; private information; personal knowledge.] T. G. B.

MACMILLAN, HUGH (1833–1903), presbyterian divine and religious writer, born at Aberfeldy on 17 Sept. 1833, was eldest son in the family of six sons and three daughters of Alexander Macmillan, merchant of Aberfeldy, by his wife Margaret Macfarlane. After attending a school in his native place and Hill Street Academy, Edinburgh, he entered the university of Edinburgh, where he went through the arts course and also studied medicine. Deciding to enter the ministry of the Free church, he studied at New College, Edinburgh, and being licensed by the presbytery of Breadalbane in January 1857, became minister of the Free church at Kirkmichael, Perthshire, in 1859. The fine scenery of this parish stimulated his love of nature, to which he gave expression in his preaching and writings. In 1861 he published 'Footnotes from the Page of Nature, or First Forms of Vegetation' (2nd edit. 1874, entitled 'First Forms of Vegetation'), the first of many popular volumes in which he brought study of scientific research to illustrate moral and spiritual truths. He was especially well versed in botany. In 1864 he accepted the pastorate of Free St. Peter's church, Glasgow. There, while faithfully discharging his pastoral duties, he continued his studies in natural history, which he supplemented by foreign travel. In 1867 there appeared his best-known work, 'Bible Teachings in Nature' (15th edit. 1889), in which he enforced the harmony subsisting between the natural and the spiritual world. The work was translated into French, German, Italian, Norwegian, and Danish, and at the author's death upwards of 30,000 copies had been printed in this country, besides many thousands in America. His next book, 'Holidays on High Lands, or Rambles and Incidents in Search of Alpine Plants' (1869; 2nd edit. 1873), was a detailed account of the Alpine plants found in this country. There followed 'The Ministry of Nature' (1871; 8th edit. 1888)

On 19 Sept. 1878 he became minister of the Free west church, Greenock. There he remained until 1901, when he retired from the active ministry. His labours received wide recognition. He was made in 1871 both hon. LL.D. of St. Andrews University and a fellow of the Royal Society of Edinburgh, and he became hon. D.D. of the universities of Edinburgh (1879) and Glasgow. In 1883 he was elected a fellow of the Scottish Society of Antiquaries.

During his later years he filled practically every post of honour and influence in the Free church. He delivered the Thomson lectures at the Free Church College, Aberdeen, in 1886; the Cunningham lectures at New College, Edinburgh, in 1894, his subject being the archæology of the Bible in the light of recent researches; and the Gunning lectures at Edinburgh University in 1897, when he dealt with the relations of science and revelation. In the last year he was moderator of the general assembly of the Free church, and in that capacity was present at the celebration in London of the diamond jubilee of Queen Victoria, who was a warm admirer of his books.

Devoted to the Highlands and its people, Macmillan was the first chief of the Clan Macmillan Society (1892–9). He was a diligent student of art, and one of his last literary undertakings was a monograph on George Frederick Watts, R.A. ('Temple Biographies' series), posthumously published in 1903.

He died at his residence in Edinburgh on 24 May 1903, and was buried in the Dean cemetery. He married on 14 June 1859 Jane, second daughter of William Patison of Williamfield, near Edinburgh. She survived him with one son and five daughters.

Besides the works cited, Macmillan published the following, chiefly dealing with the relations of religion and science, and characterised by beauty of thought and diction, and by devotional feeling: 1. 'The True Vine, or the Analogies of our Lord's Allegory,' 1871; 5th edit. 1883. 2. 'The Garden and the City, with other Contrasts and Parallels of Scripture,' 1872; 2nd edit. 1873. 3. 'Sun Glints in the Wilderness,' 1872. 4. 'The Sabbath of the Fields, being a Sequel to Bible Teachings in Nature,' 1876; 6th edit. 1889. 5. 'Our Lord's Three Raisings from the Dead,' 1876. 6. 'Two Worlds are Ours,' 1880; 4th edit. 1889. 7. 'The Marriage in Cana of Galilee,' 1882. 8. 'The Riviera' (one of the best books on the subject), 1885; 3rd edit. 1902. 9. 'The Olive Leaf,' 1886. 10. 'Roman Mosaics, or Studies in Rome and its Neighbourhood,' 1888; 2nd edit, 1892. 11. 'The Gate Beautiful and Other Bible Teachings for the Young,' 1891. 12. 'My Comfort in Sorrow,' 1891. 13. 'The Mystery of Grace and Other Sermons,' 1893. 14. 'The Daisies of Nazareth,' 1894; 2nd edit. 1901. 15. 'The Clock of Nature,' 1896. 16. 'The Spring of the Day,' 1898. 17. 'Gleanings in Holy Fields' (the outcome of a visit to Palestine), 1899. 18. 'The Corn of Heaven,' 1901. 19. 'The Christmas Rose, and Other Thoughts in Verse,' 1901. 20. 'The Highland Tay from Tyndrum to Dunkeld,' 1901. 21. 'The Poetry of Plants,' 1902. The following were posthumously published: 'The Touch of God and Other Sermons' ('World's Pulpit' series 1903); 'Rothiemurchus,' a fascinating account of a picturesque Highland neighbourhood (1907); and 'The Isles and the Gospel and other Bible Studies' (1907). Macmillan was also a voluminous contributor to scientific and religious periodicals.

[Memoir by George A. Macmillan, prefixed to The Isles and the Gospel and other Bible Studies, 1907; Sunday Magazine, 1897, p. 374; In Memoriam: Hugh Macmillan, (printed for use of members of West United Free church, Greenock); Scotsman, and Glasgow Herald, 25 May 1903; private information.] W. F. G.

McNAIR, JOHN FREDERICK ADOLPHUS (1828–1910), Indian and colonial official, born at Bath on 23 Oct. 1828, was eldest son of Major Robert McNair, staff officer, London. After education at King's College, London, and at the School of Mines, he entered the Madras (royal) artillery in 1845, was promoted captain in 1858 and major (retired) in 1870. He was employed with his battery in India until 1850. In 1853 he proceeded to the Straits Settlements and served at Malacca and in Labuan. After qualifying in the Hindustani and Malay languages he was appointed in 1856 staff officer and subsequently adjutant of artillery for the Straits district. After serving during 1857 as A.D.C. and private secretary to the governor, E. A. Blundell, he became executive engineer and superintendent of convicts at Singapore. He received the approval of the governor-general of India, Sir John (afterwards Lord) Lawrence, in council on the completion of the military works at the latter place, and the government of Netherlands India thanked him for services in connection with the introduction into Java of the Straits system of prison discipline.

From 1865 to 1867 McNair was in England as deputy governor and in charge of public works at Woking prison. In 1867, when the administration of the Straits Settlements was transferred from the Indian to the colonial department, he returned to Singapore as colonial engineer and controller of convicts and member of the legislative council of the colony (14 Feb.). He was colonial secretary during 1868, a member of the executive council from 1869, and colonial engineer and surveyor-general from 1873. In Feb. 1881 he was transferred to Penang as acting lieutenant-governor and resident councillor of that province. He retired on a pension on 10 Aug. 1884. McNair meanwhile was officially employed on important missions to Siam in 1868, 1874, 1875, and 1878. In 1875–6 he was officiating chief commissioner in Pêrak during the disturbances in that state, and took part in the affair of Kotah Lamah on the Pêrak river, for which he received the medal and clasp. He was special commissioner to Selangor to inquire into piracy, and to Pêrak in connection with the Pangkor treaty in 1874. McNair was made C.M.G. on 24 May 1878.

After his retirement McNair occupied his time principally in writing. He had already issued in 1878 'Pêrak and the Malays,' a descriptive account of the

Malayan peninsula, and in 1899, in collaboration with W. D. Bayless, he published 'Prisoners their own Warders,' an interesting account of the old Singapore convict prison. He also issued (for private circulation) 'Oral Traditions from the Indus,' and wrote many articles for the 'Asiatic Quarterly' on Eastern topics.

McNair died at Brighton on 17 May 1910, and was buried in the town cemetery. He was twice married: (1) in 1849 to Sarah des Granges, daughter of the Rev. J. Paine, M.A. (she died in 1903); and (2) to Madalena, daughter of E. Vallence of Brighton, and widow of surgeon-major G. Williamson, R.A.M.C. He had two sons and three daughters.

A portrait in oils, three-quarter length, belongs to his second son, Arthur Wyndham, of the Indian civil service.

[The Times, 20 May 1910; Colonial Office List, 1910; Straits Settlements Civil Service List, 1884; Colonial Office Records; information supplied by relatives.] C. A.

McNEILL, Sir JOHN CARSTAIRS (1831–1904), major-general, born at Colonsay House on 29 March 1831, was eldest son in a family of four sons of Capt. Alexander McNeill (1791–1850) of the islands of Colonsay and Oronsay in the Hebrides, by his wife Anne Elizabeth, daughter of John Carstairs of Stratford Green, Essex, and Warboys, Huntingdonshire. Duncan McNeill, Lord Colonsay [q. v.], the Scottish judge, and Sir John McNeill [q. v.], the diplomatist, were his uncles. After education at the university of St. Andrews and at Addiscombe, he entered the army on 9 Dec. 1850 as ensign in the 12th Bengal native infantry. He was promoted lieutenant on 30 Aug. 1855. During the Indian Mutiny, 1857–8, McNeill won distinction as aide-de-camp to Sir Edward Lugard during the siege and capture of Lucknow. He took part in the engagement at Jaunpur, in the relief of Azimghur, and in various operations at Jugdespur, and received the medal with clasp and brevet of major. He became captain on 31 Aug. 1860 and major on 8 Oct. 1861, and in the latter year, being transferred to the 107th foot, he proceeded to New Zealand as aide-de-camp to General Sir Duncan Alexander Cameron [q. v. Suppl. I]. He served there till 1865, engaging in the Maori war of 1864. He was present at the engagements on the Katikara river, the Kalroa, Rangiriri, the Gate Pah, and various other encounters with the Maoris. During the war he won the Victoria Cross for an act of gallantry on 30 March 1864, when he was threatened, while engaged in carrying despatches, by a force of the enemy, and managed to effect the escape of both himself and a private, who was in imminent peril of his life (*Lond. Gaz.* 21 Aug. and 23 Oct. 1863; 19 Feb. and 14 May 1864, and 12 April 1865). McNeill also received the medal and the brevet of lieut.-colonel.

From 1869 to 1872 McNeill was military secretary to Sir John Young, Lord Lisgar [q. v.], governor-general of Canada, and was on the staff of the Red River expedition in Canada under Sir Garnet (afterwards Viscount) Wolseley in 1870. He became colonel on 25 April 1872, and for his services on this expedition he was nominated C.M.G. on 2 Dec. 1876. As chief of the staff in the Ashanti war of 1873–4 he showed daring, determination, and a first-rate capacity for organisation, and was so severely wounded in the wrist at the destruction of Essaman that he had eventually to be sent home. (*Lond. Gaz.* 18 Nov. 1873 and 7 and 31 March 1874). He was awarded the medal and was made C.B. on 31 March 1874. By Queen Victoria's command he accompanied Prince Leopold (afterwards duke of Albany) to Canada, and on his return was appointed K.C.M.G. on 17 Aug. 1880. In 1882 he was promoted major-general, and served in the Egyptian campaign on the staff of the duke of Connaught (*Lond. Gaz.* 2 Nov. 1882). He received the medal, bronze star, and the 2nd class Medjidie, and was nominated K.C.B. on 24 Nov. 1882.

In the Soudan campaign of 1885 he commanded the second infantry brigade. On 20 March he took part in the action at Hashin, where his troops stormed Dihilibat hill. On 22 March a force under McNeill started from Suakin for Tamai to escort a convoy of camels with supplies. A halt was made half-way at Tofrik, and while a zeriba was being formed, the enemy attacked in force. After severe fighting the Arabs were repulsed with loss. Sir Gerald Graham [q. v. Suppl. I], who had started out to McNeill's assistance, soon returned on hearing that reinforcements were not required. Graham deprecated the sharp criticism to which McNeill's conduct was subjected on the ground of lack of caution (*Lond. Gaz.* 25 Aug. 1885). For his services in the campaign he received two clasps. He retired from the service in 1890. Inheriting the family estates in the Hebrides, McNeill was made J.P. and D.L. for Argyllshire in 1874.

He became an equerry to Queen Victoria and A.D.C. to George, duke of Cambridge. In 1898 he was appointed king at arms to the Order of the Bath, and, on the accession of Edward VII, G.C.V.O. on 2 Feb. 1901. Of foreign orders he held the first class of the Red Eagle and of the order of the Crown of Prussia. His love of sport made him a favourite with the royal family.

He died unmarried, on 25 May 1904, at St. James's Palace, London, and was buried at Oronsay Priory, Argyllshire.

[The Times, 27 and 28 May 1904; Burke's Landed Gentry; Hart's and Official Army Lists; Indian Mutiny: Selections from State Papers in Military Department, 1857–8, iii. 558; Lord Wolseley, Story of a Soldier's Life, 1903, ii. 279; R. H. Vetch, Life, Letters, and Diaries of Lieut.-general Sir Gerald Graham, 1901, p. 293; H. E. Colvile, History of the Sudan Campaign, 2 parts, 1889.]

H. M. V.

McQUEEN, Sir JOHN WITHERS (1836–1909), major-general, born in Calcutta on 24 Aug. 1836, was the eldest of the three sons of John McQueen, chaplain of the Kidderpur Orphan Asylum in that city. McQueen was sent home at an early age and educated at Glenalmond College, Perthshire, under Bishop Charles Wordsworth [q. v.]. Before he had completed his seventeenth year he received a direct cadetship in the East India Company's military service, and returning to India he was appointed ensign in the 27th Bengal native infantry on 4 August 1854 On the outbreak of the Mutiny of the Bengal army in May 1857 the 27th proved unfaithful, and McQueen, who had been promoted lieutenant on 3 June in that year, was attached to the 4th Punjab rifles, one of the newly raised frontier regiments, which had been ordered by Sir John Lawrence to proceed to Delhi to assist in the siege of that fortress. On its way down country the 4th turned aside to take part in an attack on the Hindustani fanatics at Narinji on 21 July 1857, and reached Delhi on 6 Sept., after a march of 1035 miles, in time to engage in the assault on the city on the 14th, and the six days' continuous street fighting which ensued. Here McQueen soon earned a name for conspicuous bravery. On 19 Sept., accompanied by one sepoy, he reconnoitred up to the very gates of the King's Palace, thus enabling that important post to be captured with trifling loss (Lord Roberts, *Forty-One Years in India*, i. 247). Subsequently McQueen took part in the relief of Lucknow by Sir Colin Campbell [q. v.], and on 17 Nov. 1857 at the capture of the Secundarabagh, he was severely wounded; for his gallantry on this occasion he was recommended (without result) for the Victoria Cross. On 15 May 1858, after eleven months' continuous fighting, the 4th Punjab rifles marched back to the frontier, having lost thirteen out of fifteen British officers and upwards of 370 non-commissioned officers and men. For his services in the Mutiny McQueen was twice mentioned in despatches (*Lond. Gaz.* 28 July 1858 and 4 Feb. 1859), and received the medal with two clasps, besides being made adjutant of the regiment. In this capacity he took part in the expedition against the Kabul Khel Waziris on the Trans-Indus frontier in 1859 under Sir Neville Chamberlain [q. v. Suppl. II], and in April 1860 he was promoted second in command of his regiment. On 4 Aug. 1866 he was promoted captain, and on 10 June 1870 was appointed commandant of the 5th (now 58th) Punjab rifles. This corps he commanded in the Jowaki expedition under Sir Charles Keyes in 1877–8, being repeatedly mentioned in despatches, acquiring a reputation for personal gallantry, and for marked skill in mountain warfare. On the outbreak of the Afghan war in 1878 the 5th rifles was attached to the Kuram Valley column under the command of Sir Frederick (afterwards Earl) Roberts. Here McQueen's long service on the frontier, his knowledge of the various frontier tribes and of their languages, coupled with his wide experience of mountain warfare, proved most valuable to the commander-in-chief. At the forcing of the Peiwar Kotal on 2 Dec. 1878 and again in the operations round Kabul in December 1880 General Roberts bore testimony to McQueen's value as a soldier. For his services in the Afghan war McQueen received the medal with two clasps, the C.B., and a brevet lieutenant-colonelcy (*Lond. Gaz.* 4 Feb. 1879). In 1881 he commanded the 5th Punjab rifles in the Mahsud Waziri expedition under Brigadier-general T. G. Kennedy, C.B., and in December following he was made A.D.C. to Queen Victoria with the rank of colonel in the army. In Sept. 1885 he was promoted brigadier-general and given the command of the Hyderabad contingent, and on 15 Oct. 1886 he was transferred to the command of the Punjab frontier force. Two years later he commanded the expedition against the Black Mountain tribes on the Hazara border with the rank of major-general, and at the close of the campaign was given the K.C.B. Promoted major-general in 1891, McQueen vacated the command of the Punjab frontier force and returned to England, settling at Bath. He was advanced to G.C.B. on 22 June 1907, and died on 15 August 1909 at Richmond, Surrey, being buried at Wimbledon. In addition to his other honours McQueen wore Queen Victoria's jubilee and King Edward's coronation medals.

He married in 1872 Charlotte Helen, daughter of Major-general Charles Pollard of the royal (Bengal) engineers; his eldest son, Malcolm Stewart, was killed in the South African war in 1900; his surviving son, Lieutenant J. A. McQueen, is in the royal engineers; he also left two daughters.

[W. H. Paget, Record of Expeditions against the North West Frontier Tribes, 1884; Lord Roberts, Forty-One Years in India, 30th edit. 1898; The Official History of the Second Afghan War, 1908; H. B. Hanna, The Second Afghan War, 3 vols. 1899–1910; Sir J. L. Vaughan, My Service in the Indian Army; The Times, 16 Aug. 1909.] C. B. N.

MACRORIE, WILLIAM KENNETH (1831–1905), bishop of Maritzburg, born at Liverpool on 8 Feb. 1831, was eldest son of David Macrorie, a Liverpool physician, by his wife Sarah, daughter of John Barber. Admitted to Winchester in 1844, he matriculated at Brasenose College, Oxford, on 2 Feb. 1849. He graduated B.A. in 1852, and was elected to a senior Hulme exhibition at his college in 1854. On proceeding M.A. in 1855 he became a fellow or assistant-master at St. Peter's College, Radley. Ordained deacon in the same year and priest in 1857, he was successively curate of Deane (1858–60), and of Wingates, Lancashire (1860–1). In 1861 A. C. Tait, bishop of London, presented him to the rectory of Wapping, and in 1865 Hulme's trustees nominated him to the perpetual curacy of Accrington.

In January 1868 Robert Gray [q. v.], bishop of Cape Town, offered Macrorie the bishopric of the church in Natal. J. W. Colenso [q. v.] was still in Natal, having declined to recognise his canonical deposition from the see, which had been pronounced in 1863. Since that date Bishop Gray had made unsuccessful efforts to establish, in the colony, a new rival episcopate. After some hesitation Macrorie accepted the post, being the first colonial bishop not appointed by the crown. Since Colenso enjoyed a legal right to the title of bishop of Natal, Macrorie was designated bishop of Maritzburg. The government of Lord Derby disapproved the appointment, and refused to grant the Queen's mandate for Macrorie's consecration in any place where the Act of Uniformity was in force. Archbishop Longley vetoed the ceremony in the province of Canterbury, and the Scottish bishops declined to take any part in the rite. Eventually Bishop Gray himself consecrated Macrorie at Cape Town on 25 Jan. 1869, regardless of a protest signed by 129 adherents of Colenso.

Macrorie's uncompromising high churchmanship tended to prolong the schism in the Natal church. He showed zeal and energy in the performance of his duties, and owed much influence to the financial support of the S.P.G. and the S.P.C.K., which had been withdrawn from Colenso. But his want of tact alienated moderate opinion, and his fierce denunciations of Colenso's supporters widened the prevailing breach. Archbishop Benson sought in vain to reconcile the contending parties. At length in June 1883, on the death of Colenso, Benson suggested to Macrorie the propriety either of resigning or of accepting the see of Bloemfontein. But Macrorie declined to entertain the 'cowardly thought.' Macrorie's difficulties diminished on the refusal of the archbishop to consecrate either George William Cox [q. v. Suppl. II] or William Ayerst [q. v. Suppl. II], whom the Colenso party, on their leader's death, elected to the bishopric of Natal. At length Macrorie resigned his see in 1891, and being appointed next year to a canonry in Ely Cathedral, served the diocese as assistant-bishop. He died at the College, Ely, on 24 Sept. 1905, and was buried in the cathedral close. In 1863 he married Agnes, youngest daughter of William Watson of South Hill, Liverpool. In 1876 he was created hon. D.D. of Oxford and D.C.L. of the university of South Africa.

[The Times, 25 and 29 Sept. 1905; H. Paul, History of Modern England, 1905, iii. 185; Farrer, Life of Bishop Robert Gray, 1876; G. W. Cox, Life of J. W. Colenso, 1888, vol. ii.; A. T. Wirgman, Hist. of English Church and People in South Africa, 1895; Life of James Green, Dean of Maritzburg, 2 vols. 1909; Men and Women of the Time, 1899.] G. S. W.

McTAGGART, WILLIAM (1835–1910), artist, born on 25 Oct. 1835 at Aros, a croft on the edge of Durry Moss in the Laggan of Kintyre, Argyllshire, was third son in the family of five brothers and three sisters of Dugald McTaggart, a crofter, by his wife Barbara Brolochan. When the father's croft was absorbed in a larger farm, he moved into Campbeltown. There William attended the school founded by the Society for the Promotion of Christian Knowledge in Scotland. After receiving a sound elementary education, he became apprentice when thirteen in the drug dispensary of Dr. Buchanan, who proved a wise counsellor and a kind friend. Juvenile attempts in modelling and surreptitious sketches of local characters or portrait drawings of friends early displayed an artistic impulse, but so removed was he from all art influences and effort that at first he thought he had discovered portraiture for himself. Dr. Buchanan lent him books, encouraged his efforts to paint, and showed him portraits by Scottish artists in the houses of well-to-do patients. At sixteen McTaggart, despite the discouragement of parents and friends, went to Glasgow, to devote himself to painting, with an introduction from Buchanan to Daniel Macnee [q. v.], the portrait painter. After a short stay in Glasgow he proceeded to Edinburgh, where, on Macnee's recommendation, he was admitted (19 April 1852) a pupil at the Trustees' Academy. Robert Scott Lauder [q. v.] had just been appointed headmaster, and McTaggart joined the talented group of students which included W. Q. Orchardson [q. v. Suppl. II], John Pettie [q. v.], G. P. Chalmers [q. v.], Tom Graham [q. v. Suppl. II], and John MacWhirter [q. v. Suppl. II]. In this coterie McTaggart soon took a conspicuous place, and the ardent friendships which he then formed were lifelong. Supporting himself in Edinburgh by portrait-sketching, often in chalk, he spent the summer vacations from 1853 to 1856 on similar work in Dublin. In 1857 he went home to Campbeltown, where he painted genre pictures which attracted attention when shown at the Royal Scottish Academy, where he first exhibited in 1855. Those of the following year were even more successful, and led to his election as associate on 9 Nov. 1859. He was only twenty-four years of age, and was still enrolled as one of Lauder's pupils.

At this time and for some years afterwards his subjects were chiefly drawn from the everyday life and scenery of the parish, half-landward and half-seaboard, in which he had been reared. These were varied occasionally by motives derived from Scottish song or modern poetry. McTaggart went to Paris in 1860 with Pettie and Tom Graham, spent a few weeks' holiday on the Riviera in 1876, and in 1882 made a fortnight's trip to the capitals of central Europe with his friend J. G. Orchar of Dundee. Otherwise he was never abroad. Chosen academician of the Royal Scottish Academy in 1870, he took for a time a lively interest in its affairs, exhibiting regularly there until 1895. At the Royal Academy in London he exhibited eleven pictures between 1866 and 1875. In 1878, the year of its foundation, he became vice-president of the Royal Scottish Water Colour Society.

From about 1870, when McTaggart spent several summers at Tarbert on Loch Fyne, incidents of sea-faring figured more frequently in his work, although landscape and rural life were not abandoned. Later he began to paint the open sea. At Machrihanish, Carnoustie, Carradale and Southend he produced many splendid pictures of the sea, sometimes in its utter loneliness, but more often associated with episodes in child-play or in the fisher's perilous calling. Up till 1889 McTaggart continued to paint portraits of men and women, and in the case of a child or a family group it became his practice to unify the group or to give significance to the action of a single figure by fixing upon some simple incident—fishing in a highland burn, gathering flowers, playing on the shore, or idling on the sea-braes—thus investing the portrait with the spontaneity and charm of a picture. In 1889 McTaggart retired from Edinburgh to Broomieknowe, a beautifully situated village about six miles away, where he built a large studio in the garden. There he lived in comparative isolation, devoting himself to the expression of his original views of nature. His later work was divided between landscape and the sea. Figure incident became less prominent and was more closely knit with its setting.

In later years he rarely left Broomieknowe except for an annual summer visit to Kintyre. His liberty-loving temperament ultimately alienated him from the Scottish Academy, of which he was latterly a member in little more than name, but he maintained his connection with the Royal Scottish Water Colour Society, and, always interested in younger contemporaries, he became a vice-president of the Society of Scottish Artists in 1898. Save with these two societies, he rarely exhibited in his later years. In 1901 an exhibition of thirty-two of his more recent pictures was organised by Messrs. Aitken, Dott & Son in Glasgow, Edinburgh, and Dundee, and widened his reputation, although it did not spread beyond Scotland.

He died at his house, Dean Park, Broomieknowe, on 2 April 1910, and was buried in Newington cemetery, Edinburgh, three days later. He was married twice: (1) on 9 June 1863 to Mary Brolochan (*d.* 1884), daughter of Hugh Holmes, builder, Campbeltown; and (2) on 6 April 1886 to Marjory, eldest daughter of Joseph Henderson [q.v. Suppl. II]. Of the first marriage two sons and two daughters survived him, and of the second two sons and four daughters. Of several good portraits of him probably the best are by G. P. Chalmers (about 1870) and by himself (1892), both in the possession of Mrs. McTaggart, and by Henry W. Kerr, R.S.A. (1908), in the possession of his eldest son.

McTaggart's painting gradually gained in expressiveness and power. In his later work he subordinated the minor facts to the broader effects of reality, and expressed the inner spirit of nature rather than its merely visual appearances. This tendency revealed itself first in water-colour. Soon his oil pictures also expressed that sensitiveness to the sparkle and flicker of light and the brilliance and purity of colour, and that apprehension of the rhythmical movement and the emotional significance of nature, which were the essential qualities of his gift. Quite independently McTaggart anticipated the discoveries regarding light and movement commonly associated with the French impressionists, but, while he shared their intense interest in the appearances of reality, he combined with that an imaginative passion and a refined pictorial intention which transformed his work and made it art of a high creative order.

[Private information and personal knowledge; exhibition catalogues; R.S.A. Reports; Art Journal, April 1894; Good Words, November 1899; Studio, July 1909; introduction to catalogue of McTaggart exhibition, 1901; notes to Catalogue of Thirty-six Paintings by William McTaggart, R.S.A., 1907; J. L. Caw, Scottish Painting, Past and Present, pt. ii. chap. iv. 1908; E. Pinnington, G. P. Chalmers and the Art of his Time, 1896; Martin Hardie, John Pettie, R.A., 1908; Manchester Guardian, 4 April 1910.]

J. L. C.

MACWHIRTER, JOHN (1839-1911), landscape painter, was born at Slateford, near Edinburgh, on 27 March 1839. His father, George MacWhirter, a descendant of an old Ayrshire family, was a paper manufacturer at Colinton, but had achieved some distinction as a draughtsman, geologist and botanist. His mother, Agnes Laing, was George MacWhirter's second wife, and sister of Major Alexander Gordon Laing [q. v.], the African explorer. John was the fourth of six children (two daughters and four sons). His sister, Agnes MacWhirter (1833–1882), was a still-life painter of considerable repute. He was sent to school at Colinton, but his father dying when the boy was eleven, he was apprenticed at the age of thirteen to Oliver & Boyd, booksellers at Edinburgh. He left his employment after five months and entered the Trustees' Academy, then conducted by Robert Scott Lauder [q. v.]. Of his fellow students William McTaggart [q. v. Suppl. II], John Pettie [q. v. Suppl. I], William Quiller Orchardson [q. v. Suppl. II], and Tom Graham [q. v. Suppl. II] became lifelong friends. Apart from the excellent training of his masters, MacWhirter devoted himself from the first to outdoor sketching and direct study of nature, and made such rapid progress that as early as 1854 one of his pictures, 'Old Cottage at Braid,' was exhibited at the Royal Scottish Academy.

In the next year he undertook the first of what proved to be annual journeys to the Continent, visiting on this occasion some of the old cities of Germany, Tyrol, and the Salzkammergut. A picture of Lake Gosan, which was a fruit of this journey, was bought by the Royal Association for the Promotion of the Fine Arts in Scotland. In the course of his many travels MacWhirter visited Italy, Sicily, Switzerland, Austria, Turkey, Norway, and the United States, ever in search of material for his busy brush. In 1867 he exhibited at Edinburgh six pictures of Rome and the Campagna and was elected associate of the Royal Scottish Academy. Two years earlier he had made his first appearance at the Royal Academy of London, with 'The Temple of Vesta.' This was followed in 1868 by 'Old Edinburgh: Night.' In 1869 the artist moved to London, and remained there for the rest of his life. In 1879 he was elected A.R.A.; in 1882 he became hon. R.S.A.; and in 1893 he was made R.A. In 1901 he published a book on 'Landscape Painting in Water-Colours.' He died at 1 Abbey Road, St. John's Wood, on 28 Jan. 1911, and was buried at Golder's Green. MacWhirter married in 1872 Katherine, daughter of Prof. Menzies of Edinburgh University. He had two sons and two daughters, one of whom married Charles Sims, A.R.A.

MacWhirter owed his popularity largely to the tinge of sentiment which invested his otherwise naturalistic landscapes with a certain literary significance, and which is reflected in the fanciful titles he gave to his landscapes and studies of trees: 'The Lady of the Woods' (1876), 'The Three Graces' (1878), 'The Lord of the Glen' (1880), 'The Three Witches' (1886), 'Crabbed Age and Youth' (1899), 'A Fallen Giant' (1901). MacWhirter is represented at the National Gallery of British Art by 'June in the Austrian Tyrol.' In the Royal Academy diploma gallery is his 'Nature's Archway.' 'A Fallen Giant' is at the municipal art gallery, Pietermaritzburg, Natal; 'Spindrift' at the Royal Holloway College; and 'Constantinople and the Golden Horn' at the Manchester municipal gallery. MacWhirter is also represented at the Walker art gallery, Liverpool, the Derby corporation art gallery, and the municipal galleries of Dundee, Aberdeen, and Hull.

A portrait of the artist as a young man (1871), by John Pettie, R.A., and a later one in water-colours by Sir Hubert von Herkomer, R.A., are in the possession of his family. MacWhirter was also painted by Mr. Wolfram Onslow Ford and by Mr. J. Bowie.

(Fifty Years of Art, part 7 (Virtue & Co.); The Art of J. MacWhirter, by M. H. Spielmann (F. Hanfstaengl); John MacWhirter, R.A., by W. Macdonald Sinclair, D.D. (Art Journal Christmas Annual, 1903); Martin Hardie's Life of Pettie; J. L. Caw's Scottish Painting, 1908; private information.] P. G. K.

MADDEN, FREDERIC WILLIAM (1839–1904), numismatist, eldest son of Sir Frederic Madden [q. v.], keeper of the manuscripts in the British Museum, by Emily Sarah, his wife, was born at his father's official residence in the museum on 9 April 1839. Entering Merchant Taylors' School in April 1846, he passed to St. Paul's in March 1848, and being presented in 1851 by Prince Albert to Charterhouse School, remained there till 1856. In 1859 he became an assistant in the department of antiquities and coins in the British Museum. He resigned this post in 1868, and in 1874 became secretary and librarian to Brighton College. In 1888 he was appointed chief librarian of the public library of Brighton, resigning the post in 1902, when his health began to fail. He died at Brighton on 20 June 1904.

Madden was a member of the Numismatic Society of London from December 1858, its joint-secretary 1860–8, and joint-editor of its journal, the 'Numismatic Chronicle,' from 1861 to 1868. In 1896 he was awarded its silver medal for distinguished services to numismatics (*Num. Chron.* 1896, proceedings, p. 18). He was a member of the Royal Asiatic Society from 1877.

Madden contributed nearly forty papers to the 'Numismatic Chronicle,' mainly on Jewish and Roman numismatics. Of chief value were his papers (1865 and 1867–8) on the Roman gold coins acquired by the British Museum from the famous Wigan and Blacas collections and the series of articles on the Christian symbols occurring on coins of the Constantinian period. His chief work, 'A History of Jewish Coinage' (1864) was republished as 'The Coins of the Jews' in an enlarged and revised edition (1881, 4to). This exhaustive and fully illustrated treatise remains a standard book; it includes, besides the Jewish coinage proper, a discussion of all the various notices of money in the Bible.

Madden also published a 'Handbook of Roman Numismatics' (1861, 12mo), a sound but somewhat arid manual. He completed and published in 1889 Seth William Stevenson's 'Dictionary of Roman Coins,' and contributed articles on Biblical coins to Kitto's 'Cyclopædia.'

[Numismatic Chronicle, 1905; Proc. Numismatic Soc. pp. 27–28; Athenæum, 2 July 1904; information from Mr. H. A. Grueber, F.S.A.] W. W.

MADDEN, KATHERINE. [See Thurston, Mrs. Katherine Cecil (1875–1911), novelist.]

MADDEN, THOMAS MORE (1844–1902), Irish gynæcologist, son of Richard Robert Madden [q. v.] by his wife Harriet, daughter of John Elmslie, a West Indian planter, was born in 1844 at Havana, Cuba, where his father was the British representative in the international commission for the abolition of the slave trade. His West Indian origin was clearly discernible in his features. When his father returned to his practice in Dublin, the son was apprenticed to James William Cusack, a well-known surgeon there, but threats of consumption led to a long sojourn abroad. He completed his medical education at Malaga and in the University of Montpellier. In 1862 he qualified as M.R.C.S. (London)

He then travelled in Africa and Australia. At length in 1865 he returned to Dublin to practise, specialising in obstetrics. In 1868 he became assistant-master of the Rotunda Lying-in Hospital, and in 1872 physician to the Hospital for Children. He was subsequently appointed master of the National Lying-in Hospital and obstetric physician and gynæcologist to the Mater Misericordiæ Hospital in 1878. In 1872 he was decorated by the French government for his share in raising the Irish Ambulance corps which served in the Franco-Prussian war, and was soon recognised in the United Kingdom and elsewhere as one of the foremost gynæcologists. He became F.R.C.S. (Edinburgh) in 1882. He served as vice-president of the British Gynæcological Society (1878), as vice-president of Dublin Obstetrical Society (1878), as president of obstetric section of Royal Academy of Medicine of Ireland (1886), as honorary president of the first International Congress of Obstetrics and Gynæcology, held at Brussels in 1892, and as president of the obstetric section of the British Medical Association.

He died at his country house at Tinode, co. Wicklow, on 14 April 1902. In 1865 he married Mary Josephine, daughter of Thomas McDonnell Caffrey, by whom he had three sons and two daughters.

Madden was a voluminous writer, chiefly on medical subjects. Besides articles in medical journals and contributions to Quain's 'Dictionary of Medicine,' he published the following books, several of which ran through three editions, and were reckoned standard works: 1. 'Change of Climate in Chronic Disease,' 1864; 3rd edit. 1873. 2. 'The Spas of Belgium, Germany, France, and Italy,' 1867; 3rd edit. 1874. 3. 'Contributional Treatment of Chronic Uterine Disorders,' 1878. 4. 'Mental and Nervous Disorders Peculiar to Women,' 1883; 2nd edit. 1884. 5. 'On Uterine Tumours,' 1887. 6. 'Lectures on Child Culture, Moral, Mental and Physical,' 3rd edit. 1890. 7. 'Clinical Gynæcology,' 1893. He edited 'The Dublin Practice of Midwifery' and 'A Manual of Obstetric and Gynæcological Nursing,' 1893.

Madden wrote accounts of his father and family in 'Memorials of R. R. Madden' (1886); 'The Memoirs (chiefly autobiographical) of R. R. Madden' (1891); 'Genealogical, Historical, and Family Records of the O'Maddens of Galway and their Descendants' (1894).

[Madden's O'Maddens of Galway, 1894, and his Memoirs of R. R. Madden, 1891; Brit. Mus. Cat.; Men of the Time, 1899; Medical Register; Dublin Directories; Freeman's Journal, April 1902.] D. J. O'D.

MAITLAND, AGNES CATHERINE (1850–1906), principal of Somerville College, Oxford, born on 12 April 1850 at 12 Gloucester Terrace, Hyde Park, was second daughter of David John Maitland of Chipperkyle, Galloway, by his wife Matilda Leathes Mortlock. Her father settled as a merchant in Liverpool when Agnes was five years old, and she was educated at home there in a presbyterian atmosphere.

Between 1880 and 1885 she studied cookery at the Domestic science training school in Liverpool, and from 1885 to 1889 acted as an examiner in cookery in elementary schools, and of teachers trained by the 'Northern Union of Schools of Cookery.' She was soon recognised as an authority on domestic economy. She wrote several cookery books, of which the most important are 'The Rudiments of Cookery: a Manual for Use in Schools and Homes' (35th thousand, 1910); the 'Afternoon Tea Book' (1887; 3rd edit. 1905); 'What shall we have for Breakfast?' (1889; 2nd edit. 1901). She also published between 1875 and 1889 some educative novels and tales suited to young girls.

Miss Maitland, who was keenly interested in the higher education of women, left Liverpool in 1889 to succeed Miss Shaw Lefevre as principal of Somerville Hall, Oxford. Her experience of public work and talent for administration and organisation proved of value to Somerville, which, founded in 1879 and incorporated as a college in 1881, retained the style of 'Hall' until 1894. During Miss Maitland's tenure of the principalship the number of students rose from thirty-five to eighty-six, and the buildings were proportionately extended. She developed the tutorial system with a view to making Somerville a genuine college and no mere hall of residence, and she urged the students to take the full degree course so as to prove their title to the degrees.

Although she was something of an autocrat, she worked in full harmony with her staff, won the complete confidence of the students, and showed faith in democratic principles. On her initiative a proportion of the council of the college was elected by duly qualified old students; while the latter were quite unfettered in their choice, Miss Maitland was always anxious that some of themselves should be on the council. A strong liberal in politics, and a broad-minded churchwoman (in spite of her presbyterian training), she preserved the undenominational atmosphere of the college.

To Miss Maitland the college owes the erection of its library, which contains 15,000 volumes and was opened in 1894 by Mr. John (afterwards Viscount) Morley. At Lord Morley's suggestion Helen Taylor [q. v. Suppl. II] presented to Somerville the library of John Stuart Mill, free of conditions.

She died after some two years' illness, on 19 Aug. 1906, at 12 Norham Road, Oxford, and was buried in Holywell cemetery, Oxford.

A portrait, a chalk drawing in three colours, made by William Strang, A.R.A., in 1905, is in the library at Somerville College. A memorial dining-hall, to be called after her, and panelled and furnished by the Maitland Memorial Fund, is in course of erection.

Besides the works cited, Miss Maitland published: 1. 'Elsie, a Lowland Sketch,' 1875. 2. 'Madge Hilton, or left to themselves,' 1884; 2nd edit. 1890. 3. 'Rhoda,' a novel, 2 vols. 1886. 4. 'Cookery Primer for School and Home Use,' 1888. 5. 'Cottage Lectures,' 1889. 6. 'Nellie O'Neil,' 1889; 2nd edit. 1910.

[The Times, 20, 23 Aug. 1906, not accurate in all details; Who's Who, 1906; private information.] E. L.

MAITLAND, FREDERIC WILLIAM (1850–1906), Downing professor of the laws of England, Cambridge, born on 28 May 1850 at 53 Guilford Street, London, was only son in a family of three children of John Gorham Maitland [q. v.] by his wife Emma, daughter of John Frederic Daniell, F.R.S. [q. v.]. From his grandfather, Samuel Roffey Maitland [q. v.], he received not only a small manorial estate at Brookthorpe in Gloucestershire, but also a love of historical research. His mother died in 1851, and his father, a scholar and a linguist, in 1863. Frederic's youth was mainly passed in charge of his aunt, Charlotte Louisa Daniell. After education at home, where German governesses gave him early command of that language, and at a preparatory school at Brighton, he passed in 1863 to Eton, where E. D. Stone was his private tutor. In 1869 he entered Trinity College, Cambridge, as a commoner. Abandoning, in 1870, mathematics for moral and mental science, he came under the influence of Henry Sidgwick [q. v. Suppl. I]. In 1872 he was elected a scholar and was bracketed senior in moral sciences tripos. He became Whewell international law scholar in 1873. A fluent, caustic, and persuasive speaker, he was successively secretary and president of the Cambridge Union Society; he was also a good runner, and represented the university in the three-mile race. He graduated B.A. in 1873, and proceeded M.A. in 1876, being made hon. LL.D. in 1891.

Maitland joined Lincoln's Inn as a student on 6 June 1872, and was called to the bar on 17 Nov. 1876, and for the next eight years practised as conveyancer and equity draftsman, mainly as 'devil' for Mr. Benjamin Bickley Rogers, a scholar as well as a lawyer of repute. Although Maitland received at Lincoln's Inn a thorough training in practical law, his bent was for scientific, theoretical, historical law. His knowledge of German introduced him early to Savigny's 'Geschichte des Römischen Rechts' (of which he began a translation never completed or published) and to the works of Brunner on Anglo-Norman law. Through Stubbs's 'Constitutional History' he was led to study the publications of the Record Commission, and the vast materials for the original study of English law. He soon formed the aim of doing for English law what Savigny had done for Roman law, that is, to produce, after due investigation and collation of the undigested and scattered materials, a scientific and philosophical history of English law from the earliest times in all its bearings upon the economic, political, constitutional, social and religious life of the English people. He rapidly trained himself by his unaided endeavours in palæography and diplomatic. Both training and character, in which quick wit and wide sympathies were combined with singular independence of mind, fitted him admirably for his task.

In 1884 Maitland was elected to the newly established readership in English law in the university of Cambridge, and there he mainly resided till his death. In 1888 he was elected Downing professor of English law, and moved to West Lodge, his official residence in Downing College. His inaugural lecture as professor, 'Why the History of English Law is not Written,' was a popular exposition of his aims and an appeal for fellow workers. As professor, while he lectured regularly to the students, he corresponded with or entertained the leading lawyers, jurists, and historians of England, Europe, and America. By lecture, review, and essay he was always pressing upon English readers, and acknowledging his own debt to, the labour of foreign writers, and was always generous in help and encouragement to fellow-workers.

Soon after settling at Cambridge, Maitland perceived that his vast design of interpreting English law stood in need of co-operative effort. He consequently succeeded in 1887 in founding the Selden Society, 'to encourage the study and advance the knowledge of the history of English law' by publishing needful material, with headquarters in the Inns of Court in London, and under the direction of the legal authorities. In the twenty years intervening between its foundation and Maitland's death the society issued twenty-one volumes on the history of different branches of the law, edited either by himself or by editors selected and supervised by himself. In 1887, too, the year of the Society's foundation, he published his first important work, 'Bracton's Note-book' (3 vols.). It was an edition of a British Museum MS. which he put forward as the actual materials collected by Bracton [q.v.] for his great treatise 'De Legibus et consuetudinibus Angliæ,' temp. Henry III, one of the best sources of English history and law in the period immediately preceding Edward I. In 1887–8 he delivered a course of lectures at Cambridge on 'The constitutional history of England' from the death of Edward I to his own time (published after his death). In 1889 he published two most important contributions to periodicals: 'The Materials for English Legal History' in the 'Political Science Quarterly,' being a thorough analysis and classification of all known available materials for each period from Ethelbert to Henry VIII, and 'The History of the Register of Original Writs' in the 'Harvard Law Review,' an admirable illustration of the proper method of dealing with one of the most abstruse branches of his materials—the development of the forms of action at common law. Meanwhile Maitland was actively engaged on his 'History of English Law before the Time of Edward I,' a *magnum opus* which he planned in consultation and co-operation with Sir Frederick Pollock. The work, published in 1895 (2 vols.), bears the names both of Sir Frederick Pollock and Maitland on the title-page, but it was substantially carried out by Maitland. It was at once universally adopted as an authoritative textbook on this period and a model for other periods. In the same year (1895) he was made literary director of the Selden Society.

Maitland next turned his attention to a different theme, the action and reaction of Roman civil law, whether ancient or mediæval, upon English law. In 1895 he traced the sources of the influences of Roman law upon English law in the thirteenth century, in a volume, 'Bracton and Azo,' issued by the Selden Society (viii.).

Carrying his study of the topic down to the sixteenth century, he confuted, to the annoyance of Anglican apologists, the partisan theory that there was in England before the Reformation a system of Anglican canon law independent of the Roman canon law. After several essays in periodicals through 1896–7 (see *Collected Papers*) he published in 1898 his 'Roman Canon Law in the Church of England,' finally proving that the pre-Reformation canon law enforced in England was purely Roman. His judgment was accepted, even by Stubbs, who was in part responsible for the other theory. Free from all theological bias, Maitland regarded the Reformation as a national movement of statesmen, using royal necessities and reformers' enthusiasm to deliver England from the actual oppression of Papal canon law and the prospective infliction of the mediæval civil law. Further researches into the legal effect of the Reformation led to dissertations on 'The Corporation Sole, the Crown as Corporation,' 'The General Law of Corporations,' and 'Trust and Corporation'—a study of the growth of 'trusts' as an elusive but effective substitute for the strict legal corporation. Maitland's scholarly impartiality received conspicuous recognition. On Lord Acton's invitation he wrote on the 'Anglican Settlement and Scottish Reformation' in the 'Cambridge Modern History' (1903).

Convinced of the inadequacy of the printed texts of the Year Books in old legal Anglo-French, Maitland persuaded the Selden Society to undertake a new edition, selecting the period of Edward II, with a careful collation of all MSS., translation, illustrations from the plea rolls, and introductory essays. With the assistance of Mr. G. J. Turner, Maitland produced the first three volumes in 1903–4–5. The fourth volume was completed after Maitland's death by Mr. Turner in 1907. For his own use Maitland compiled a grammar of the old law-French, and published it in the introduction to the first volume.

At the same time Maitland, apart from his historical studies, advocated many plans of legal reform, such as the simplification of English law by the abolition of the separate law of real property 'founded on worn-out theories and obsolescent ideas' ('The Law of Real Property,' 1879; 'Survey of a Century,' 1901, in *Coll. Papers*), and a prompt codification of the English law so simplified ('The Making of the German Civil Code,' 1906, in *Coll. Papers*). 'Strenuous endeavours to improve the law,' he wrote, 'are not hindered but forwarded by a zealous study of legal history.'

Maitland found relief from his literary researches in varied recreation. He was devoted to music. He rowed and walked and was an Alpine mountaineer. In 1881 he became secretary of the 'Sunday Tramps,' a body of pedestrians organised by (Sir) Leslie Stephen [q. v. Suppl. II], with whom he formed a close friendship.

In 1897 he delivered the Ford lectures at Oxford on 'Township and Borough.' Next year his health, which had always been delicate, was weakened by pleurisy. Thenceforward he wintered abroad, passing the colder months with his family in the Grand Canary, where with the help of MSS. or photographs of MSS. he steadily pursued literary work. His reputation grew rapidly in his last years at home and abroad. He was made hon. D.C.L. of Oxford in 1899, as well as LL.D. of Glasgow, Cracow, and Moscow Universities. He was a corresponding member of Royal Prussian Academy and Royal Bavarian Academy. In 1901 he delivered the Rede lecture at Cambridge. In 1902 he was chosen an original fellow of the British Academy, a bencher of Lincoln's Inn, and also an honorary fellow of Trinity College, Cambridge. On his last voyage to the Grand Canary in Nov. 1906 he was attacked by pneumonia, and died at Quiney's Hotel, Las Palmas, on 19 Dec. 1906. He is buried in the English cemetery there.

At Cambridge there was founded in 1907 'The F. W. Maitland Memorial Fund,' for the promotion of research and instruction in the history of law and legal language and institutions. At Oxford, 'the Maitland Library' of legal and social history acquired his own copy of Domesday Book and other favourite volumes. A portrait painted by Miss Beatrice Lock (now Mrs. Leopold Fripp) in August 1906 is in the possession of the present writer; it was reproduced in photogravure in vol. 22 of the Selden Society's publications; a replica painted after Maitland's death hangs in the hall of Downing College. A posthumous bust, executed in bronze by Mr. S. Nicholson Babb for the Maitland Memorial fund, was presented to the university of Cambridge, and is placed in the Squire law library.

Maitland married on 20 July 1886 Florence Henrietta, eldest daughter of Herbert Fisher, the last judge of the Court of Stannaries for the Duchy of Cornwall, and niece of Julia Prinsep, second wife of (Sir) Leslie Stephen [q. v.]; he had issue two daughters, born in 1887 and 1889. His widow and daughters survive him.

Maitland published: 1. 'Pleas of the Crown for the County of Gloucester, 1221,' 1884. 2. 'Justice and Police,' 'English Citizens' series, 1885. 3. 'Bracton's Notebook,' 3 vols. 1887. 4. 'Select Pleas of the Crown, 1200–1225,' Selden Society, vol. i. 1888. 5. 'Select Pleas in Manorial and other Seignorial Courts, Henry III and Edward I,' Selden Society, vol. 2, 1889. 6. 'Three Rolls of the King's Court, 1194–5,' Pipe Roll Society, vol. 4, 1891. 7. 'The Court Baron' (jointly with W. P. Baildon), Selden Society, vol. 4, 1891. 8. 'Records of the Parliament holden at Westminster, 28 Feb. 1305,' Rolls series, 98, 1893. 9. 'The History of English Law before the Time of Edward I' (jointly with F. Pollock), 2 vols. 1895; 2nd edit. 1898. 10. 'The Mirror of Justices' (jointly with W. J. Whittaker), Selden Society, vol. 7, 1895. 11. 'Bracton and Azo,' Selden Society, vol. 8, 1895. 12. 'Domesday Book and Beyond, Three Essays,' 1897. 13. 'Township and Borough, the Ford Lectures of 1897,' 1898. 14. 'Roman Canon Law in the Church of England, Six Essays,' 1898. 15. 'Political Theories of the Middle Ages, by Dr. Otto Gierke,' translation and introduction, 1900. 16. 'The Charters of the Borough of Cambridge' (jointly with Mary Bateson), 1901. 17. 'English Law and the Renaissance,' Rede lecture, 1901. 18. 'Year Books of Edward II, vol. i. 1307–9,' Selden Society, vol. 17, 1903. 19. 'Year Books of Edward II, vol. ii. 1308–9–10,' Selden Society, vol. 19, 1904. 20. 'Year Books of Edward II, vol. iii. 1309–10,' Selden Society, vol. 20, 1905. 24. 'Life and Letters of Leslie Stephen,' 1906.

Many essays, articles, and reviews from 1872 to 1906 were collected by his brother-in-law, H. A. L. Fisher, and reprinted as 'The Collected Works of Frederic William Maitland' (1911). Other works posthumously published are 'Year Books of Edward II, vol. iv. 1309–11,' Selden Society, vol. 22, 1907 (completed by G. J. Turner, and containing a memoir and photogravure); 'The Constitutional History of England' (being lectures delivered at Cambridge, 1887–8, edited by H. A. L. Fisher), 1908; and 'Equity and the Forms of Action at Common Law' (lectures delivered at Cambridge, edited by A. H. Chaytor and W. J. Whittaker), 1909. Maitland also contributed to 'Social England,' 'Dictionary of Political Economy,' 'Encyclopædia Britannica,' 'Encyclopædia of the Laws of England,' and this 'Dictionary of National Biography,' and he wrote a preface to Smith's 'De Republica Anglorum,' edited by L. Alston, 1906.

[MS. memoir by his eldest sister, Mrs. Reynell (not published); Frederic William Maitland, two lectures and a bibliography, by A. L. Smith, Oxford, 1908 (the best appreciation of his work and fullest bibliography); Frederic William Maitland: a biographical sketch, with portrait, by H. A. L. Fisher, Cambridge, 1910. Proceedings of the British Academy, Dec. 1906, pp. 455–60, by Sir Frederick Pollock; Athenæum, 5 Jan. 1907, pp. 15–16, and Solicitors Journal, Jan. 1897; Quarterly Review (Sir F. Pollock), April 1907; English Historical Review (P. Vinogradoff); Law Quarterly Review (notices by foreign jurists); Juridical Review (by D. P. Heatley); Political Science Quarterly (American impression), June 1907; Cambridge University Reporter (Report of Memorial Meeting), 22 July 1907; Preface to vol. 22 of Selden Society's publications, Nov. 1907; see also J. H. Round's Peerage and Pedigree, i. 146, 1910; Prof. Maitland: biographical notice and portrait, Journal of Soc. of Comp. Legislation, No. 13, 1904; and Maitland's Life and Letters of Leslie Stephen, 1906.] B. F. L.

MALET, Sir EDWARD BALDWIN, fourth baronet (1837–1908), diplomatist, born in the British legation at the Hague on 10 Oct. 1837, was second son of Sir Alexander Malet, second baronet [q. v.], by his wife Marianne, daughter of John Spalding of the Holme, and step-daughter of Henry, first Lord Brougham. Educated at Eton from 1850 to 1853, he entered the diplomatic service in 1854 at the exceptionally early age of seventeen, being appointed attaché to his father at Frankfort. On 14 April 1856 he matriculated from Corpus Christi College, Oxford. But a brief stay at the university scarcely interrupted his progress in diplomacy. Transferred from Frankfort to Brussels in 1858, he was appointed paid attaché at Paraná, Argentina, in August 1860, after passing the necessary examination. He was transferred to Rio de Janeiro in 1861, and thence to Washington in 1862, where he served three years under Richard Bickerton Pemell, Lord Lyons [q. v.]. During the various difficult discussions which followed the American civil war Malet was one of the most trusted members of Lord Lyons's staff. After four months in Lisbon in 1865 Malet rejoined Lord Lyons on the latter's appointment to Constantinople, and followed him to Paris in 1867. In September 1870, after the battle of Sedan, he was despatched by Lord Lyons on an adventurous journey to the German headquarters at Meaux with a letter to Count Bismarck, inquiring whether he would entertain negotiations with Jules Favre for an armistice. Bismarck, who had known him as a boy and as Prussian representative in the Diet had been on terms of friendship with his father and mother at Frankfort, received Malet cordially, but merely gave him a verbal promise to receive a member of the government of national defence. Jules Favre's first interview with the German chancellor at Ferrières was the result. On the investment of Paris by the German forces, Malet accompanied Lord Lyons, who followed the provisional government to Tours and afterwards to Bordeaux. On the conclusion of peace in March 1871 the embassy returned to Paris, but during the outbreak of the Commune, when Lord Lyons went to Versailles with the French government, Malet was left in charge at Paris from 19 March to 6 June 1871. For his zealous services during this trying period he was made C.B. Lyons and Malet remained close friends and constant correspondents till the former's death, but they separated, to their great mutual regret, in August 1871, when Malet became secretary of legation at Peking. After a year in China he was transferred to Athens, and thence to Rome in August 1875, where he remained three years, becoming secretary of embassy when the mission was raised to that rank in 1876. He took an active part in the negotiations for the renewal of the treaty of commerce of 1863 between Great Britain and Italy and acted in November 1875 as joint commissioner with (Sir) Charles Malcolm Kennedy in conferences at Rome.

In April 1878 he was transferred to Constantinople. The situation there was critical. The treaty of San Stefano had been signed on 3 March 1878. Russia had agreed to submit the treaty to a European congress, reserving the right of accepting or refusing discussion on any question. The British government demanded that all the provisions of the treaty should be unreservedly open to consideration. The Russian army was encamped outside Constantinople, while the British fleet was in the Sea of Marmora. Owing to the bad health of Sir Austen Henry Layard [q. v. Suppl. I], the British ambassador, Malet received the provisional rank of minister plenipotentiary in case of the absence of the ambassador. Malet rendered Layard substantial assistance until February 1879, when the ambassador was compelled to take leave of absence, and Malet, who assumed charge, was largely instrumental in procuring the acceptance by the Turkish government of various arrangements necessitated by the provisions of the treaty of Berlin—among others those for the occupation of Bosnia by Austria-Hungary and the policing of Eastern Roumelia after the withdrawal of the Russian troops. His straightforward but considerate demeanour gained the confidence of the sultan, Abdul Hamid II, who, several years later, on the occurrence of a vacancy in the embassy, expressed a hope that Malet would leave the embassy at Berlin for Constantinople.

In October 1879 he was appointed British agent and consul-general in Egypt. Three months before Tewfik Pasha had succeeded as Khedive on the abdication of his father Ismail. Malet was at once occupied with negotiation for financial and administrative reform which Ismail's reckless extravagance and mismanagement made imperative. There followed in 1881 the native unrest and revolt of the Egyptian army under Arabi, Toulba, and Ali Fehmi. Malet, who was made K.C.B. in October 1881, was in sympathy with the movement for constitutional government, and sought means of reconciling it with due observance of financial obligations. But as the disturbances grew more acute he deemed intervention necessary, and recommended Turkish intervention under European control, or, failing that, intervention by Great Britain and France jointly, or by one of them alone. On the outbreak of the rebellion and the native attacks on Europeans, Malet, under instructions from his government, followed the representatives of the other European powers to Alexandria, but, declining the offer of accommodation on board the British admiral's flagship, took up his residence in an hotel in the centre of the town, and endeavoured to restore confidence among the European community and promoted measures of protection. In the midst of this work he was struck down by sudden illness—whether due to natural causes or to poison seems doubtful—and after remaining on board H.M.S. Helicon for some days in a critical condition returned to England. Meanwhile the British government undertook to subdue the rebellion single-handed. Malet resumed his place in Egypt on 10 August, as soon as his health permitted, and after the defeat of Arabi's forces by Sir Garnet Wolseley's army at the battle of Tel-el-Kebir (13 Sept. 1882) he accompanied the Khedive on his reentry into his capital. In the angry controversy over the fate of Arabi and his leading associates Malet deprecated capital punishment, and after the exercise of considerable pressure on the Egyptian government, the sentence of death which was pronounced on the ringleaders was commuted to one of perpetual banishment to Ceylon. These discussions and the task of reconstituting the complicated machinery of government in Egypt were over-taxing Malet's weakened health, and Lord Dufferin [q. v. Suppl. II], then ambassador at Constantinople, was sent to Egypt (November 1882) on a special mission. Lord Granville, referring to this appointment in the House of Lords (15 Feb. 1883), said: 'If any man ever deserved the confidence of his country, Sir E. Malet deserves it in consideration of the way in which he conducted the affairs of Egypt in times of extraordinary difficulty. But we thought it would not be fair to centre in one man constructive as well as diplomatic duties.' Malet aided Lord Dufferin in drawing up a scheme of reorganisation, and after Lord Dufferin's departure superintended the development of the scheme, helped actively and courageously to cope with an epidemic of cholera in July 1883, and left amidst general expressions of affection and regret on promotion to be British envoy at Brussels in September following. In a speech delivered at a farewell luncheon given to him by the British community at Cairo, he strongly emphasised his feeling that the great need for Egypt was a well-ordered system of justice. After a year in Belgium he became British ambassador at Berlin on the death of Lord Ampthill [q. v.] in August 1884. There he served eleven years. Among various thorny questions with which he had to deal were those of the rival British and German claims in East and West Africa, the settlement of the international agreements affecting the navigation of the Niger and Congo rivers, the recognition of the Congo Free State, and the complications which had arisen in the Samoa Archipelago. He took part as British plenipotentiary in conferences held at Berlin on these questions in 1884 and 1885. He had been sworn a privy councillor in 1885, and became G.C.M.G. in the same year and G.C.B. in 1886. He resigned on grounds of ill-health in 1895, when the German court and government expressed regrets which amounted almost to reproaches and testified to his great popularity. Subsequently Lord Salisbury appointed him one of the British members of the international court of arbitration, established at the Hague under the convention of 29 July 1899. He succeeded to the baronetcy on the death of his elder brother, Henry Charles Eden, without male issue, on 12 Jan. 1904. During his remaining years he suffered from constant attacks of asthma, and he died at Chorley Wood, Hertfordshire, on 29 June 1908. He married in March 1885 Lady Ermyntrude Sackville Russell, daughter of Francis Charles Hastings, ninth duke of Bedford, but had no children. A portrait in oils, painted by Sir William Richmond at the embassy at Berlin, is in the possession of Lady Ermyntrude Malet. A cartoon portrait by 'Spy' appeared in 'Vanity Fair' in 1884.

Malet published in 1901 a book entitled 'Shifting Scenes,' in which he gave an interesting but somewhat disjointed account of various episodes in his diplomatic career. He left an unfinished memoir of his service in Egypt, which was supplemented by extracts from his correspondence and printed in 1909 for private circulation.

[Malet's own accounts of his experiences; The Times, 30 June 1908; Foreign Office List, 1909, p. 403; Papers laid before Parliament; Cambridge Modern History, xii. 435; Lord Cromer, Modern Egypt, 2 vols. 1908.] S.

MALONE, SYLVESTER (1822–1906), Irish ecclesiastical historian, born in the parish of Kilmally, co. Clare, in 1822, was son of Jeremiah Malone by his wife Mary Slattery. Having discovered his vocation, he was educated for the priesthood and was ordained in 1854. His first curacy was at Cooraclare in his native county, but after a year and a half he was successively transferred to Kilkee, where he remained fourteen years, and to Newmarket-on-Fergus. In 1875 he became parish priest of Sixmilebridge, and in 1889 of Clare Castle. Finally, in 1892 he was appointed to Kilrush as vicar-general, and there he remained for the rest of his life. He was raised soon after to the dignities of canon and archdeacon.

Malone, who cherished strong nationalist sympathies, was always devoted to study and was well versed in the Irish language. He made valuable researches into the history of the catholic church in Ireland, and among Irish critics his 'Church History of Ireland from the Invasion of the English in 1169 to the Beginning of the Reformation in 1532' (1867; 2nd edit. 2 vols. Dublin, 1880) takes standard rank.

He was keenly interested in the movement for the preservation of the Irish language, and was a member of the various societies started to achieve that object. To the Society for the Preservation of the Irish Language he bequeathed 100*l.* for the best essays in Irish on 'Irish Prose' and 'Irish Poetry.' Dr. Douglas Hyde and the Rev. P. S. Dinneen, both well known in the Gaelic movement, were the successful candidates. Malone died at Kilrush on 21 May 1906.

Besides the work named, Malone published: 1. 'Tenant Wrong illustrated in a Nutshell; or a History of Kilkee in Relation to Landlordism during the last Seven Years, in a Letter addressed to the Rt. Hon. W. E. Gladstone,' Dublin, 1867. 2. 'Chapters towards a Life of St. Patrick,' Dublin, 1892, 12mo. 3. 'Adrian IV and Ireland,' Dublin, 1899, 16mo. 4. 'The Life of St. Flannan of Killaloe,' Dublin, 1902. 5. 'Irish Schools and their Managers,' 1904.

[Freeman's Journal, 22 May 1906; information kindly supplied by the Very Rev. J. F. Hogan, D.D.; Irish Catholic Directories; Brit. Mus. Cat.] D. J. O'D.

MANLEY, WILLIAM GEORGE NICHOLAS (1831–1901), surgeon-general, born at Dublin in 1831, was second son of the Rev. William Nicholas Manley, his mother being a daughter of Dr. Brown, a surgeon in the army. He was educated at the Blackheath proprietary school and was admitted M.R.C.S.England in 1851. He joined the army medical staff in March 1855 and was attached to the royal artillery, with which he served in the Crimea from 11 June 1855. He was present at the siege and fall of Sebastopol, and was granted the medal with clasp and the Turkish medal. He remained attached to the royal artillery throughout the New Zealand war, 1863–6, in the course of which he won the Victoria Cross. Having volunteered to accompany the storming party in the assault on the Pah near Tauranga, on 29 April 1864, he attended Commander Hay, R.N., when that officer was carried away mortally wounded, and then volunteered to return in order to see if he could find any more wounded. Manley was also present under the command of Sir Trevor Chute at the assault and capture of the Okotukou, Putahi, Otapawa, and Waikohou Pahs, and for his services he was again mentioned in despatches and promoted to the rank of staff surgeon. For rescuing from drowning a gunner of the royal artillery who had fallen overboard in the Waitotara river, he received the bronze medal of the Royal Humane Society.

When the Franco-Prussian war broke out in 1870, Manley was placed in charge of the B division of the British ambulance corps, which was attached to the 22nd division of the Prussian army. He was present at several engagements, and afterwards received the German steel war medal and the Bavarian order of merit. William I, the German Emperor, at the request of the Crown Prince, decorated him with the second class of the iron cross for his conduct in seeking for the wounded of the 22nd division in the actions of Châteauneuf and Bretoncelle on 18 and 21 Nov. and the battles of Orleans and Cravant on 10 Dec. 1870. He was also present at the siege of Paris, and for his attention to wounded Frenchmen he received the cross of the Société de Secours aux Blessés. Manley served with the Quetta field force in the Afghan war of 1878–9, and was present at the occupation of Kandahar, receiving the thanks of the viceroy and the medal. He was principal medical officer under Sir Edward Hamley during the war in Egypt of 1882, and he was present at the battle of Tel-el-Kebir. He was promoted to the rank of deputy surgeon-general, and retired from the army in 1884 with the honorary rank of surgeon-general, being made C.B. in 1894. In 1896 he was granted a distinguished service pension.

Manley, who was noted for his physical and moral courage, was a trustworthy and pleasant comrade. He spared no pains to keep himself abreast of scientific progress in his profession both as it affected military surgery and hospital administration. He died at Lansdown Terrace, Cheltenham, on 16 Nov. 1901.

He married in 1869 Maria Elizabeth, eldest daughter of Thomas Harwood Darton of Temple Dinsley, Hertfordshire, and left five sons and one daughter.

[Lancet, 1901, ii. 1459; Brit. Med. Journal, 1901, ii. 1554; The Times, 19 Nov. 1901.]

D'A. P.

MANNERS, Lord JOHN JAMES ROBERT, seventh Duke of Rutland (1818–1906), politician, born at Belvoir Castle on 13 Dec. 1818, was second son in the family of three sons and four daughters of John Henry Manners, fifth duke of Rutland, by Lady Elizabeth, daughter of Frederick Howard, fifth earl of Carlisle [q. v.]. His elder brother was Charles Cecil John Manners, sixth duke of Rutland [q. v.]. After education at Eton, he entered Trinity College, Cambridge, as a fellow-commoner on 17 Oct. 1836 and graduated M.A. in 1839. Neither at school nor at college did he show much promise, but at Cambridge he was an active member of the Camden Society, which had for its object the 'restoring of English churches on Gothic principles,' and inclined to advanced Anglicanism. On leaving the university he travelled with his elder brother in France, Switzerland, Italy, and in Spain. In the last country he visited Don Carlos, with whose cause he was in sympathy. The impressions made on him by this journey he set forth in verse under the title of 'Memorials of other Lands.' These 'Memorials' appeared in 1841 as part of a volume called 'England's Trust and other Poems,' which was dedicated to Lord John's friend, George Augustus Smythe, afterwards seventh Viscount Strangford [q. v.]. A couplet in the chief poem:

Let wealth and commerce, laws and learning die,
But leave us still our old nobility,

obtained permanent currency, and exposed its author to much ridicule. The ingenuous lines did an injustice to Lord John's real beliefs and aspiration. In spite of conservative temperament and firm faith in aristocracy, he entertained no selfish claims to privilege of caste, and was ambitious, before all things, of helping to improve the condition of the poor. He continued his endeavours in patriotic poetry in a second volume, 'English Ballads and other Poems' (1850), and also published in early life 'Notes of an Irish Tour' (1849) and 'A Cruise in Scotch Waters on board the Duke of Rutland's yacht "Resolution" in 1848' (folio, 1850), illustrated by John Christian Schetky [q. v.]. Although he thenceforth only published occasional political speeches and lectures, he cultivated literary tastes till the end of his life.

Meanwhile, in 1841, in his twenty-third year, Manners entered parliament as conservative member for Newark. Gladstone, still a tory, was his colleague, and he described Manners as an excellent candidate, a popular and effective speaker, and a good canvasser by virtue of his kindly disposition (Morley's *Gladstone*, i. 238). With Gladstone Manners's personal relations, despite the divergence of their political views, were always close, and he was one of the pall-bearers at Gladstone's funeral in Westminster Abbey in 1898. In parliament Lord John at once associated himself with George Smythe, Alexander Cochrane-Baillie (afterwards first Baron Lamington), and Benjamin Disraeli, and was prominent in the literary and artistic society which Lady Blessington gathered about her. As in the case of his friends, a love of history and literature was combined with zeal for the regeneration of the labouring classes. Disraeli exerted a powerful influence on him, and largely under Disraeli's guidance Manners and his political friends gradually formed themselves into the 'Young England party.' The party sought to supplant whig and middle-class predominance in politics and society by setting the aristocracy at the head of a movement for raising the condition of the proletariat intellectually and materially. The church too and the government of Ireland were to be recovered from Whig influences. During 1843 and 1844 the party played an active part within and without the House of Commons, and was free in its criticism of Peel's administration. Manners mainly identified himself with the Young England party's advocacy of social reform. In 1843 he supported Viscount Howick's motion for an inquiry into the condition of England and the disaffection of the working classes. He sought to establish public holidays by Act of Parliament, publishing 'A Plea for National Holidays' in 1843. In 1844 he associated himself with Lord Ashley, who was devoting himself to factory reform, in endeavouring to secure a ten hours' day for labour (*Hansard*, 22 March 1844). The measure, which the Manchester school stoutly opposed, became law in May 1847. Manners urgently advocated the allocation of waste lands for the use of the agricultural population, and of a general system of allotments such as already existed on the Belvoir property. In the autumn of 1844 he accompanied Disraeli and Smythe on a tour through Lancashire and other manufacturing districts with a view to promulgate the principles of the party, and to ascertain the facts of current industrial depression. At Birmingham on 26 Aug. 1844 he declared that his friends and himself were seeking to 'minister to the wants, direct the wishes, listen to the prayers, increase the comfort, diminish the toil, and elevate the character, of the long-suffering, industrious, and gallant people of England.' On 3 Oct. he was on the platform with Disraeli at the Manchester Athenæum when that statesman gave a famous lecture on the acquirement of knowledge, and both he and Disraeli spoke at Bingley in Yorkshire on 11 October.

The chivalrous and romantic mould in which Manners's political views were cast led George Smythe when dedicating to him his 'Historic Fancies' in 1844 to describe him as 'the Philip Sidney of our generation.' Disraeli authoritatively defined the principles of the 'Young England party' in 'Coningsby,' also in 1844. In that novel Manners figured as Lord Henry Sydney, who was shocked at the substitution of the word 'labourers' for 'peasantry' and who was charged by his critics with thinking to make people prosperous by setting up village maypoles. In Disraeli's 'Sybil' (1845) and in 'Endymion' (1880) many of Lord John's views are placed on the lips of Egremont and Waldershare respectively.

The 'Young England party' was not destined to live long. Religious and political differences led to its dissolution. Manners, like many of his colleagues, while strong in his attachment to the Church of England, was disposed to sympathise with Newman and the 'Tractarians.' Frederick William Faber [q. v.] became his intimate friend, and strongly influenced his views. He gave no sign of joining the Church of Rome, but he advocated a generous treatment of the Roman priesthood in Ireland, the maintenance of friendly relations with the Vatican, and the disestablishment of the Irish Church. In 1845 he supported the proposed grant to Maynooth College; Smythe voted with him, but Disraeli and other of his friends opposed the grant. The 'Young England party' was thereby divided. In the same year Faber with James Hope, afterwards Hope-Scott [q. v.] of Deepdene, and others followed Newman into the communion of Rome, and Manners's friendships and sympathies were further shaken.

A larger disturbance of social and political ties attended Peel's change of attitude towards the Corn Laws. Manners was no thick and thin supporter of protection. Although his first considerable speech in parliament was delivered against a motion by C. P. Villiers for the total repeal of the Corn Laws (18 Feb. 1842), he made no emphatic profession of opinion. He 'did not say that the Corn Laws might not be improved . . . but he felt that hon. members were wrong in attributing distress entirely to the Corn Laws' (*Hansard*, lx. 711). On Peel's sudden adoption of the principle of free trade he maintained that since Sir Robert had come into office professing contrary principles, there ought to be a special appeal to the constituencies upon the issue. He told the electors of Newark that he would in that event seek their suffrage as a free trader. When it became evident that no such reference was to be made, Manners by way of protest joined the protectionist party. George Smythe accepted free trade: Disraeli allied himself with Lord George Bentinck in opposition to free trade, and the 'Young England party' was thereupon dispersed.

Manners, at the general election in Aug. 1847, retired from Newark, where as a protectionist he had no chance of re-election, and stood for Liverpool without success. In 1849 he was again defeated in the City of London by Baron Lionel de Rothschild; but in 1850 he was returned for Colchester in the protectionist interest. This seat he exchanged for North Leicestershire in 1857, and he represented that constituency until 1885; after the Redistribution Act, he sat for the Melton Division of the county until he succeeded his brother in the dukedom in 1888. Manners quickly filled a prominent place in the conservative party and in the House of Commons. His parliamentary gifts were not those of an orator but of a dexterous and resourceful debater. His wisdom in council was of greater value than his capacity for action.

In February 1852, when Lord Derby formed his first administration, Manners became first commissioner of works, with a seat in the cabinet, and was made a privy councillor. The government only lasted till 16 Dec. During the administrations of Lord Aberdeen (1852–5) and Lord Palmerston (1855–8) he took his share in the opposition's criticism of the conduct of the Crimean war and the Indian Mutiny campaign, but he refrained from seeking party advantage in national troubles, although he fell under that suspicion through a question which he put with a view to fixing upon government the responsibility for Lord Dalhousie's annexation of Oude (Feb. 1856; *Hansard*, cxl. 1855).

In Feb. 1858, on the formation of the second Derby ministry, Manners resumed his former office. He thus superintended the unveiling in St. Paul's Cathedral of Stevens's monument to the duke of Wellington, for which preparations had been begun under his authority in 1852. The government survived little more than a year, and Lord John was again in opposition until July 1866, when he returned for the third time to the office of works under Lord Derby, and retained the post under Disraeli (Feb.–Dec. 1868). In spite of his tory principles, he accepted Disraeli's reform bill of 1867, when General Peel, Lord Carnarvon, and Lord Cranborne (Lord Salisbury) retired rather than support the measure. The government resigned after their defeat at the general election of 1868 (Dec. 2), and Lord John was in opposition with his party until Feb. 1874.

Throughout Disraeli's second government (1874–80) Manners held the office of postmaster-general, again with a seat in the cabinet. It was the most important political post that fell to him. He returned to it during Lord Salisbury's short first administration (June 1885 to Feb. 1886). No important reforms distinguished his career at the post office, but under his régime the minimum telegram charge was reduced from a shilling to sixpence (Oct. 1885). During his first tenure of the postmastership he was chairman of the copyright commission (1876–8).

Meanwhile Manners, while staunch to the essentials of the conservative faith, showed no unreadiness to consider impartially the practical application of some democratic principles. In 1875, while he opposed Sir George Trevelyan's abortive household franchise (counties) bill, he based his opposition on the argument that an extension of the electorate would diminish the opportunity for the entry into the House of Commons of men of small or moderate means, and would render it more accessible to men of wealth and influential local position (*Hansard*, ccxxv. 1119). During the controversy over the liberal government's proposals for an extension of the franchise, 1884–5, Manners only resisted the proposals as originally set forth on the ground that no extension of the franchise was equitable in the absence of a scheme for the redistribution of seats (*Hansard*, ccxciii. 1468).

Lord John's last period of office was from 1886 to 1892, when he joined the cabinet as chancellor of the duchy of Lancaster during Lord Salisbury's second administration. In March 1888 he succeeded to the dukedom on the death of his brother, and he was made K.G. in 1891. When Lord Salisbury's government left office in the summer of 1892, Lord John's official career came to an end. But he never ceased to take an interest in public affairs. In 1903 he welcomed Mr. Chamberlain's new policy of tariff reform, and declared his allegiance anew to his early principles.

The duke was not deeply interested in sport, but he held for a time the hereditary mastership of the Belvoir hounds, the private pack of the dukes of Rutland which was instituted in 1720, and has since been in their ownership. For a short period Lord Edward Manners (*d.* 1900) was field master under his father; since 1896 Sir Gilbert Greenall has hunted the hounds with a subscription.

The ducal property lay principally in Leicestershire and Derbyshire, and the duke had a London house in Cambridge Gate, Hyde Park. In 1892 he sold his Cheveley estate, near Cambridge, to Harry Leslie Blundell McCalmont [q. v. Suppl. II], giving as his reason the injurious consequences of a system of free trade. On 17 June 1896 he was granted the additional title of Baron Roos of Belvoir.

The duke was made LL.D. of Cambridge in 1862; D.C.L. of Oxford in 1876; and G.C.B. in 1880. He was master of the Shipwrights' Company; chairman of the Tithes Redemption Trust; high steward of the borough of Cambridge; and hon. colonel of the 3rd battalion of the Leicestershire regiment.

He died at Belvoir on 4 Aug. 1906, and was buried there. He married twice: (1) on 10 June 1851 Catherine Louisa Georgiana (*d.* 1854), only daughter of Colonel George Marlay, C.B., of Belvedere, co. Westmeath; and (2) in 1862 Janetta (*d.* 1899), eldest daughter of Thomas Hughan of Airds, Galloway. By the first marriage he had one son, Henry John Brinsley, who succeeded him as eighth duke. By his second wife the duke had five sons and three daughters.

A kit-cat portrait by J. R. Herbert and a full-length by Sir Hubert von Herkomer are at Belvoir, together with two other paintings. Cartoon portraits appeared in 'Vanity Fair' in 1869 (by 'Ape') and in 1881.

[The Times, Standard, Manchester Guardian, and Leicester Post, 5 Aug. 1906; W. F. Monypenny's Life of Lord Beaconsfield; Gathorne Hardy's First Earl of Cranbrook, 2 vols. 1910; Croker Papers, 1884, vol. iii.; Sir W. Fraser, Disraeli and his Day, 1891; private sources. A life by Mr. Charles Whibley is in preparation.] R. L.

MANNING, JOHN EDMONDSON (1848–1910), unitarian divine, son of John Manning, schoolmaster in Liverpool, was born there on 22 March 1848. His preparation for the ministry was largely due to his brother-in-law, George Beaumont, unitarian minister at Gateacre. He studied at Queen's College, Liverpool (1866–8), Manchester New College, London (1868–73), and at Leipzig (1875–6); he graduated B.A. at London University in 1872; was Hibbert scholar in 1873, and proceeded M.A. in 1876. His settlements in the ministry were Swansea (1876–89) and Upper Chapel, Sheffield (1889–1902). While at Swansea he was (1878–88) visitor and examiner in Hebrew and Greek to the Presbyterian College, Carmarthen. Of the Unitarian Home Missionary College, Manchester, he was visitor (1892–4), and from 1894 till his death tutor in Old Testament, Hebrew, and philosophy. His ministries had been greatly successful, and his sound learning gave distinction to his academic career.

He died (of the effects of pleurisy, contracted on a holiday in Italy) on 30 April 1910, at his residence, Harper Hill, Sale, Manchester. He was buried in the Dan-y-Graig cemetery, Swansea. He married in 1879 Emma, youngest daughter of George Browne Brock, J.P. (formerly minister at Swansea), who survived him with three daughters.

He published, besides separate sermons and tracts: 1. 'A History of Upper Chapel, Sheffield,' Sheffield, 1900 (one of the best congregational histories). 2. 'Addresses at the Unitarian Home Missionary College,' Manchester, 1903 (six addresses biennially from 1895, on topics of his chair, also separately issued). 3. 'Thomas a Kempis, and the "De Imitatione Christi,"' Manchester, 1907 (a valuable excursus).

[Christian Life, 7 May 1910 (memoir by present writer); Manning's Hist. Upper Chapel, 1900.] A. G.

MANNS, Sir AUGUST (1825–1907), conductor of the Crystal Palace concerts, born at Stolzenburg, near Stettin, Pomerania, on 12 March 1825, was fifth child of the foreman in a glass factory. He learnt music from a musician at Torgelow, and was then apprenticed to Urban of Elbing. Having mastered the violin and several wind instruments, he entered the band of a Danzig regiment as clarinettist. In 1849 he led Gung'l's orchestra at Berlin; at Christmas he obtained his first conductor's post, at Kroll's Garten. Theoretical instruction he received from Professor Geyer. After Kroll's Garten was burnt down in 1851 Manns became bandmaster in Von Roon's regiment at Koenigsberg;

then at Cologne, where he also conducted the Polyhymnia Society. In 1854 he came to England as sub-conductor under Henry Schallehn at the Crystal Palace, then just opened. Manns soon disagreed with Schallehn (letter in the *Musical World*, 8 Nov. 1854) and took posts successively at Leamington and at Edinburgh, in the summer conducting at Amsterdam. On 14 Oct. 1855 he returned to the Crystal Palace as full conductor.

There had been only a wind band, which played in the centre transept. At once Manns began to improve both material and locality. The wind-band became a complete orchestra, which played in a suitable court, and afterwards a concert room was built and enclosed. Daily concerts were given, and on Saturdays a large body of extra strings soon came to assist in special programmes. These Saturday concerts were continued for forty years, and became a most important element in London musical life. Manns played a violin concerto of his own composition on 8 Dec. 1855, and there were some other performances of his works; but he soon relinquished all work except conducting. The music at the Crystal Palace induced leisured people to settle at Sydenham and attend daily. Already in the first season Manns introduced Schumann's symphony in D minor (15 March 1856) and Schubert's in C major (5 and 12 April), novelties to England. The concerts acquired a repute for programmes then considered 'advanced.' Brahms's name appeared in 1863. Schubert, partly owing to the enthusiasm of Sir George Grove [q. v. Suppl. I], then secretary to the Crystal Palace company, was specially cultivated. A choral society was started, to assist in the performances. The most distinguishing and useful feature of the concerts was introduced on 13 April 1861, when the programme was devoted to living English composers, who till then had practically no opportunity of hearing their works. Afterwards all new compositions were welcomed; every young musician could reckon on his attempts being given a hearing. Manns allowed no one but himself to conduct. The influence on the development of English music was of the first importance.

Outside these concerts Manns did little. He conducted promenade concerts at Drury Lane in 1859, and the Glasgow concerts in 1879 and later. On Costa's retirement the Handel triennial festivals were entrusted to Manns (1883–1900), as well as the Sheffield festivals of 1896 and 1899. He was much less successful with the chorus than the orchestra; his beat was eccentric and very puzzling to the uninitiated.

After 1890 the Crystal Palace concerts declined. Orchestral music could be heard elsewhere in London, and the old popularity of the palace had died out. The band was lessened, and the season of Saturday concerts shortened. A testimonial was subscribed for, and presented to him on 30 April 1895, by Sir George Grove, the duke of Saxe-Coburg also speaking on Manns's services to English music. Manns conducted till the season of 1900–1, concluding on 24 April, and at a choral concert on 22 June 1901, after which he retired. He was knighted on 9 Nov. 1903. His last appearance as a conductor was at the jubilee of the Crystal Palace on 11 June 1904. He died on 1 March 1907 at Norwood, and was buried at West Norwood cemetery.

He was married three times—twice in early life and thirdly in 1897 to Wilhelmina Thellusson. By the second marriage he had a daughter. His portrait in oils was painted by John Pettie, R.A., in 1892. A cartoon portrait by 'Spy' appeared in 'Vanity Fair' in 1895.

[Musical Herald, July 1900 and April 1907 (obit. with opinions from several leading composers, reminiscences from 1854, portrait, and list of decorations and presentations); Musical Times, February 1897 and April 1907 (obit.); Graves's Life of Sir George Grove; Saxe-Wyndham's August Manns and the Saturday Concerts, 1909; personal reminiscences.] H. D.

MANSEL-PLEYDELL, JOHN CLAVELL (1817–1902), Dorset antiquary, born at Smedmore, Dorset, on 4 Dec. 1817, was eldest son of Colonel John Mansel (1776–1863) of Smedmore by his wife Louisa, fourth daughter of Edmund Morton Pleydell of Whatcombe, Dorset.

Educated privately, he entered St. John's College, Cambridge, in 1836, and graduated B.A. in 1839. He was admitted a student of Lincoln's Inn on 2 May 1840, but was not called to the bar. For thirty years he was an officer in the Queen's Own yeomanry cavalry. He was one of the promoters of the Somerset and Dorset railway, and suffered considerable financial loss in consequence. In 1856 he built at his own expense the Milborne Reformatory, which was converted in 1882 into an industrial school. In 1857 he was made a fellow of the Geological Society, and was later a fellow of the Linnean Society. He succeeded on his mother's death to the family estate of Whatcombe, Dorset, and to landed property in the Isle of Purbeck in 1863. In 1872 he assumed the additional name of Pleydell, his mother's maiden name. He founded the Dorset Natural History and Antiquarian Field Club in 1875, and was its president till his death. In 1876 he was high sheriff of Dorset, and he was a member of the county council from its establishment in 1887 till his death. He was an evangelical churchman. A liberal in politics till 1886, he changed his party in consequence of the home rule bill. He died at his Dorset residence on 3 May 1902.

Mansel-Pleydell married twice: (1) on 6 June 1844, Emily (*d.* 4 Nov. 1845), daughter of Captain A. Bingham; and (2) on 21 June 1849, Isabel, the daughter of F. C. Acton Colville (sometime captain in the Scots guards and A.D.C. to Lord Lynedoch in the Peninsular war). He celebrated his golden wedding on 21 June 1899. Of three sons, two survived him.

Mansel-Pleydell was a keen student of geology, botany, and ornithology. To the County Museum of Dorset he presented many valuable geological finds made by himself, including a perfect fore paddle of the Pleiosaurus macromerus and the tusks and molars of the rare Elephas meridionalis. He was the author of: 1. 'The Flora of Dorsetshire,' 1874; 2nd edit. 1895. 2. 'The Birds of Dorsetshire,' 1888. 3. 'The Mollusca of Dorsetshire,' 1898. He also contributed many papers on natural science and archæology to the journals of learned societies.

[The Times, 5 and 20 May 1902; Who's Who; The Eagle (Mag. of St. John's Coll. Cambridge), June 1902; Quart. Journ. of the Geol. Soc. 1903.] S. E. F.

MANSERGH, JAMES (1834–1905), civil engineer, born on 29 April 1834 at Lancaster, was second son of John Burkit Mansergh of that town. After being educated locally and at Preston, he was sent in 1847 to Queenwood College, Hampshire ('Harmony Hall'), which he entered on the same day as Henry Fawcett [q. v.], afterwards postmaster-general. Mansergh and Fawcett edited together the 'Queenwood Chronicle,' and among their teachers were John Tyndall [q. v.] and (Sir) Edward Frankland [q. v. Suppl. I].

In 1849 Mansergh was apprenticed to Messrs. H. U. McKie and J. Lawson, engineers, of Lancaster. In 1855–9 he was engaged in Brazil as engineer to Mr. E. Price, the contractor for the Dom Pedro II railway; and on his return to England he became a partner of his former master, McKie, in Carlisle. The firm laid out the first sewage-farm in England at Carlisle. The partnership was dissolved in 1860, and from 1862 to 1865 Mansergh was engaged on the construction of the Mid-Wales and the Llandilo and Carmarthen railways. In 1866 he entered into partnership with his brother-in-law, John Lawson, in Westminster. Lawson died in 1873, and thenceforward Mansergh practised alone until he took his two sons into partnership towards the end of his life.

Mansergh specialised chiefly in waterworks, and in sewerage and sewage-disposal works. In accordance with advice which he had given the corporation of Birmingham in 1871 and repeated in 1890, the corporation obtained powers to construct impounding-reservoirs in the valleys of the Elan and Claerwen rivers, and an aqueduct 73½ miles in length to convey the water to Birmingham. The work was commenced in 1894, and the supply was inaugurated by King Edward VII and Queen Alexandra on 21 July 1904. The complete scheme will provide 75,000,000 gallons per day for the use of Birmingham and district, after giving 27,000,000 gallons of compensation-water per day to the River Wye. The total cost of the works up to the present has been about five and three-quarter millions sterling. They have been described recently by Mansergh's sons (*Minutes of Proc. Inst. Civ. Eng.* cxc.).

Mansergh also carried out sewerage and sewage-disposal for Southport, Burton-on-Trent, Coventry, Derby, and Plymouth, and water-supply works for Lancaster, Stockton, Middlesbrough, and many other places. His consulting practice and parliamentary work reached large dimensions. He appeared more than six hundred times before parliamentary committees, acted for three hundred and sixty municipalities or local authorities, wrote more than two hundred and fifty reports on sewerage and waterworks alone, and gave evidence at about three hundred public inquiries. In 1889 he reported to the Victorian government on the sewerage of Melbourne and its environs; in 1895 on a scheme for a supply of water from Lake Simcoe for the city of Toronto; and in the same year on the sewerage of Colombo, Ceylon. He prepared two schemes for the sewerage of the Lower Thames valley; to the first, in 1878, was awarded one of three premiums, while the second (prepared in conjunction with Mr. J. C. Melliss) was defeated in Parliament. He was a member of the royal commission on metropolitan water-supply in 1892–3, and supported the local government board in the London water transfer bill, 1902.

Mansergh was high sheriff of Radnorshire in 1901–2, was J.P. for that county from December 1902, and was presented with the freedom of his native city of Lancaster in March 1903. He was elected F.R.S. in 1901. An associate of the Institution of Civil Engineers in 1859, a member in 1873, and a member of council in 1885, he was elected president for 1900–1. His presidential address (*Proc.* cxliii. 2) was a history of waterworks engineering. He received in 1882 a Telford medal and premium from the Institution for a paper on 'The Lancaster Waterworks Extension' (*Proc.* lxviii. 253). He lectured on water-supply at the School of Military Engineering, Chatham, in 1882. He was president of the engineering congress held in connection with the Glasgow exhibition of 1901. He was also a member of the Institution of Mechanical Engineers, and served on its council from 1902. He was chairman of the engineering standards committee from its inception in 1901 until his death.

Mansergh died at his residence, 51 Fitzjohn's Avenue, Hampstead, on 15 June 1905, and was buried in Hampstead cemetery. His portrait in oils, by W. M. Palin, a son-in-law, is in the possession of the Institution of Civil Engineers.

He married (1) in 1859, a daughter of Robert Lawson of Skirton, Lancs., by whom he had two sons and two daughters; and (2) in September 1898, the widow of Nelson Elvey Irons of Tunbridge Wells.

[Minutes of Proceedings of the Inst. Civil Eng. clxi. 350; Engineering, 16 June 1905; The Times, 16 June 1905.] W. F. S.

MANSFIELD, ROBERT BLACHFORD (1824–1908), author and oarsman, born at Rowner, Hampshire, on 1 Feb. 1824, was second son of John Mansfield, rector of Rowner, and younger brother of Charles Blachford Mansfield [q. v.]. His mother was Winifred, eldest daughter of Robert Pope Blachford, of Osborne House, Isle of Wight. After attending preparatory schools at Romsey and Guildford, he was admitted to the foundation of Winchester College in 1835, the first year of Dr. Moberly's headmastership. There he spent five years, of which he wrote later a lively account, but he never rose above the status of a fag. Two private tutors, one of whom was William Henry Havergal [q. v.], prepared him for Oxford, where he matriculated as a commoner at University College in 1842, graduating B.A. in 1846. Admitted student of Lincoln's Inn in 1845, he was called to the bar at the Inner Temple in 1849, and joined the western circuit, but never practised seriously.

Mansfield long lived a roving life, in Scotland and on the Continent. An excellent shot, he visited the moors of Scotland almost every year from 1843 to 1859, and was one of the first Englishmen to take up golf, which he first learned at Pau in 1857, and afterwards introduced at Southampton, Malvern, Winchester, and Brighton. But his fame rests on his prowess with the oar. Coached by a more famous oarsman, F. N. Menzies, in his freshman's year (1842–3), he helped to raise his college boat to the head of the river. He also rowed in 1843, as a temporary substitute, in the Oxford crew that afterwards with seven oars beat Cambridge at Henley. In the following year (1844) he broke down when in training for the university race. The pioneer of English rowing on the rivers of Germany, he recorded his achievements in two books, which, first published anonymously, passed through many editions: 'The Log of the Water-Lily (four-oared Thames gig), during a Rowing Excursion on the Rhine and other Streams of Germany. By an Oxford Man and a Wykehamist' (1851; 2nd ed. 1854); and 'The Water-Lily on the Danube, being a Brief Account of the Perils of a Pair Oar, during a voyage from Lambeth to Pesth. Illustrated by one of the Crew' (1852). A third trip down the Saône and Rhone in France was less successful. He described his companions on these expeditions in 'New and Old Chips from an Old Block' (1896), a little volume of good autobiographical gossip. The record of another portion of his life is contained in 'School Life at Winchester College, or the Reminiscences of a Winchester Junior, with a Glossary of Words, &c., peculiar to the College' (1866), of which a third edition appeared on the occasion of the quingentenary celebration (1893). He also edited a posthumous work by his brother Charles on 'Aerial Navigation' (1877), and 'Letters from the Camp before Sebastopol' by Col. C. F. Campbell (1894), a dearly loved cousin, whom he visited in the Crimea at the close of the war. Late in life he finally settled down in London, becoming a member of the vestry and guardian for St. George's, Hanover Square.

Mansfield died at Linden House,

Headington, on 29 April 1908. He married on 29 July 1858, at the British embassy, Brussels, Sophie, daughter of Lieut.-colonel L'Estrange of Moystown, King's Co., Ireland, by whom he had two daughters.

[The Times, 19 May 1908.] J. S. C.

MAPLE, Sir JOHN BLUNDELL, first baronet (1845–1903), merchant and sportsman, born on 1 March 1845, at 145 Tottenham Court Road, was elder son of John Maple (*d.* 1900) by his wife Emily Blundell. The father, after some years as an assistant with Messrs. Atkinson in Westminster Bridge Road, started in 1840 in Tottenham Court Road, under the name Maple & Cook, a furnishing and drapery business, which, after ten years of steady progress, grew to great dimensions. John, who was educated at Crawford College and King's College school, joined his father in 1862 and greatly aided in the development of the concern. Although the father took part in the business till near his death in 1900, the son from 1880 was practically head of the firm. In 1891 it was converted into a limited liability company (with a capital of 2,000,000*l.*) of which Maple was chairman.

Maple's abundant energies were not absorbed by his business. He contested unsuccessfully the parliamentary division of South St. Pancras as a conservative in 1885, but in 1887, at a bye-election, became member for the Dulwich division, and represented that constituency until his death. In parliament he safeguarded the interests of the shop assistants, and for twelve years was the president of the Voluntary Early Closing Association. He was also a member of the London County Council. He was knighted on Lord Salisbury's resignation of office in 1892, and at Queen Victoria's diamond jubilee in 1897 received a baronetcy.

Maple's association with the turf was marked by characteristic boldness and thoroughness. In 1883 he registered the racing colours of 'sky blue, black sleeves, gold cap,' which were eventually changed to 'white and gold stripes, claret cap.' For several years he raced under the pseudonym of 'Mr. Childwick,' from the name of his country seat, Childwickbury, near St. Albans, where he established an extensive breeding stud. Previously he had run a few horses in hunter races under the *nom de course* of 'Mr. Hodges,' the name of one of his friends. Although during the later years of his life the farm was overstocked, he bred many useful racehorses. During the twenty-one years that he had horses in training they won 544 races of the value of 186,169*l.* In each of eight seasons his winnings ran into five figures. His most successful year was 1901, when twenty-four of his horses won fifty-eight races worth 21,364*l.*, a total which placed him at the head of the winning owners.

In addition to breeding thoroughbreds, he was a bold buyer of blood stock. He gave 4000 guineas for the yearling filly Priestess, and 6000 guineas for the yearling colt Childwick, with which he won the Cesarewitch in 1894. Childwick long ranked as the highest-priced yearling bought by auction, but the record is now held by Sceptre, who made 10,000 guineas. Maple purchased Common from Lord Alington and Sir Frederic Johnstone for 15,000 guineas the day after that horse won the St. Leger in 1891.

Among Maple's horses bred at Childwickbury were Siffleuse (1893) and Nun Nicer (1898), each of which won the One Thousand Guineas, and Mackintosh, a very useful horse that was unbeaten as a three-year-old. With the colt Kirkconnel, which he had bought, Maple won the Two Thousand Guineas in 1895. In 1885 Maple's Royal Hampton ran third to Melton and Paradox in the Derby, and Kirkconnel was third to Sir Visto and Curzon in 1895. In 1888, after Fred Archer's death, Maple purchased Falmouth House, Newmarket. Percy Peck was then his private trainer. In 1895 Peck was succeeded by J. Day, who the following year gave way to William Waugh. In September 1903 Maple was elected a member of the Jockey Club.

Maple died at Childwickbury, St. Albans, on 24 Nov. 1903, and was interred in the churchyard there. His estate was valued for probate at 2,153,000*l.* During his life he had bestowed large sums on charitable institutions. He had undertaken in 1897 the rebuilding of University College Hospital, which immediately adjoined his business premises. The work was nearly completed at the time of his death, and he empowered his executors to carry the scheme through, with the proviso that the total cost was not to exceed 200,000*l.* The new building was opened by the duke of Connaught on 6 Nov. 1906. He married in 1874 Emily Harriet, daughter of Moses Merryweather of Clapham, but left no heir. His only daughter married first Baron von Eckardstein, from whom she obtained a divorce, and secondly Captain Archibald Weigall, M.P. for the Horncastle division of Lincolnshire.

A painted portrait by Sir Luke Fildes is in the possession of his widow, who married Mr. Montague Ballard in 1906. A cartoon portrait by 'Spy' appeared in 'Vanity Fair' in 1891.

[Notes supplied by Mr. Charles Hodges; The Sportsman, 25 Nov. 1903; Kingsclere, by John Porter; Ruff's Guide to the Turf; The Times, 25 Nov. 1903; Burke's Peerage, Baronetage, and Knightage.] E. M.

MAPLESON, JAMES HENRY (1830–1901), operatic manager, born in 1830, was brought on the stage at Drury Lane Theatre as the infant in the christening scene of Shakespeare's 'Henry VIII,' acted on 21 May of that year (*Musical Times*, 9 Dec. 1901). He was educated at the Royal Academy of Music, which he entered on 5 Sept. 1844. Cipriani Potter, the principal, recorded that Mapleson showed 'some disposition' for violin and pianoforte. After two years at the academy, where he chiefly studied the violin, he played in 1848–9 in the orchestra of the Royal Italian Opera at the same desk with Remenyi, then a refugee in England. Balfe the conductor took interest in Mapleson, gave him singing lessons, and urged him to adopt the career of a tenor vocalist; Gardoni and Belletti gave him like encouragement. In 1849 he organised an autumn concert tour. On the advice of Sims Reeves, he went to Milan and studied for three years under Mazzucato, and sang in opera at Lodi. He returned to England in 1854, but immediately afterwards underwent a surgical operation which destroyed his voice. He opened a concert and dramatic agency, and in 1858 was engaged by E. T. Smith, lessee of Drury Lane Theatre, to manage a season of Italian opera there. Three years later Mapleson took the Lyceum Theatre for a season of his own, engaging Mlle. Titiens, Alboni, and Giuglini, with Arditi as conductor. He became a volunteer officer, and was soon known as Colonel Mapleson. In 1862 he secured a lease of Her Majesty's Theatre for 21 years. The most remarkable event of his tenancy was the production of Gounod's 'Faust,' on 11 June 1863. The engagement of Christine Nilsson in 1867 was a brilliant success. On 6 Dec. 1867 Her Majesty's Theatre was burnt down; the next morning Mapleson secured Drury Lane Theatre. In 1869–70 he was in partnership with Gye at Covent Garden; then he returned to Drury Lane, although Her Majesty's Theatre had been rebuilt. He projected a grand National Opera-house on the Thames Embankment; the first brick of the substructure was laid by Mlle. Titiens on 7 Sept. 1875, and the first stone of the building by Prince Alfred (the duke of Edinburgh) on 16 Dec. But money was wanting, and the unfinished building was finally demolished in 1888. Mapleson returned to Her Majesty's Theatre in 1877; but his first season was seriously marred by the fatal illness of Titiens, who had been his mainstay not only in London, but also in his autumn provincial tours, and especially in Ireland. In 1878 he had a stroke of good fortune in the discovery of Bizet's 'Carmen,' which had not succeeded in Paris, but at its first London performance, on 22 June, at once obtained its enduring success. Mapleson then took his company to the United States, and during the rest of his career divided his life between England and America. He managed a London season in the summer, and toured in America during the winter. In 1881–2 he engaged Adelina Patti, who was then at New York; and she was a member of his company till July 1885. Always in low water, yet never crushed by adversity, Mapleson carried on a losing struggle for several years, till in April 1886 he was entirely at the end of his resources in San Francisco, without means and with the theatre shut against him. His company camped out among their luggage, which they dared not touch, and many of the versatile Italians prepared to start as small street-traders. A benefit concert enabled Mapleson to begin his journey eastward; at each successive stage he arranged a performance which paid for the next stage, and thus after some time he reached New York. In the autumn of 1887 he resumed tours in the English provinces, but found himself out of touch with the public. The old-fashioned Italian operas on his repertory had lost their vogue, and his singers no longer attracted. Italian opera in London seemed for the time on the verge of extinction; but in 1888 Augustus Harris took Covent Garden with a very strong financial backing, against which Mapleson could not contend. New enterprises on Mapleson's part were often reported later; he succeeded in opening the Academy of Music at New York in 1896, but the rivalry of the Metropolitan Opera-house soon compelled him to close his season. He died in London of Bright's disease on 14 Nov. 1901, and was buried in Highgate cemetery.

In 1888 he published two volumes of memoirs, frank and egotistic, but amusing in their revelations of operatic management. He married the soprano singer Marie Roze, who made a first appearance on the English operatic stage under his auspices in London on 18 May 1872, but a separation took place.

[Mapleson's Memoirs, 1888 (the main but rather vague source of his biography); Arditi's Reminiscences; Entry-book of the Royal Academy of Music, kindly examined by Prof. Corder; The Times, 15 Nov. 1901.]
H. D.

MAPOTHER, EDWARD DILLON (1835–1908), surgeon, born at Fairview, near Dublin, on 14 Oct. 1835, was son of Henry Mapother, an official of the Bank of Ireland, and of Mary Lyons, both of co. Roscommon. Richard Mapother (son of Sir Thomas Mapother of Mappowder, Dorsetshire) came to Ireland during Queen Elizabeth's reign, and was granted land in co. Roscommon. Mapother was apprenticed to John Hatch Power (1806–1863), professor of surgery at the Royal College of Surgeons of Ireland in Dublin. He received his professional education in the college, at the Carmichael school of medicine, at the Jervis Street, the Richmond, and allied hospitals. He obtained letters testimonial of the Royal College of Surgeons of Ireland on 21 April 1854, and passed as a fellow on 30 Aug. 1862. In 1857 he graduated M.D. with first honours and gold medal at the Queen's University, Dublin. Before he was nineteen he began to teach anatomy, and with John Morgan (1829–1876) conducted large classes with great success at the Royal College of Surgeons of Ireland. On 30 May 1864 he was elected to the chair of 'Hygiene or political medicine' in the college, which had been vacant since the resignation of Henry Maunsell (1806-1879) in 1846. On 21 February 1867 he succeeded Arthur Jacob [q. v.] as professor of anatomy and physiology. In 1879 he was elected president of the college, and it was largely due to his exertions during his year of office that the dental diploma was instituted, whilst later he took a leading part in the movement which ended in the amalgamation of the Carmichael and Ledwich schools of medicine with that of the college.

Mapother was elected surgeon to St. Vincent's Hospital, Dublin, in 1859, and he was also surgeon to St. Joseph's Hospital for Children. He was the first medical officer of health for Dublin, was surgeon in ordinary to the lord-lieutenant of Ireland from 1880 to 1886, and was also president of the statistical society of Ireland.

Mapother left Dublin in 1886, and after spending some time in studying syphilis and diseases of the skin at various schools in Europe, he settled in London in 1888 as a specialist, at first in the house, 32 Cavendish Square, which had been occupied by the surgeon Richard Quain [q. v.]. He died at 16 Welbeck Street on 3 March 1908.

He married in 1870 Ellen, daughter of the Hon. John Tobin, M.P., of Halifax, Nova Scotia, and by her had one son and six daughters.

Mapother was author of: 1. Physiology and its Aids to the Study and Treatment of Disease,' Dublin, 12mo, 1862; 2nd edit. 1864; 3rd edit., edited by John Knott, M.D., 1882. 2. 'Lectures on Public Health delivered at the Royal College of Surgeons,' Dublin, 1864; 2nd edit. 1867. 3. 'The Medical Profession and its Educational and Licensing Bodies,' Dublin, 1868. (This essay won the first Carmichael prize of 200*l.* for 1868, the bequest coming from Richard Carmichael (1776–1849), who left 3000*l.* in trust to the College of Surgeons for the purpose of a first prize of 200*l.* and a second of 100*l.* every fourth year for two essays on medical education.) 4. 'Animal Physiology' (Gleig's school series), 1871; 2nd edit. 1891. 5. 'The Dublin Hospitals, their Grants and Governing Bodies,' Dublin, 1869. 6. 'The Body and its Health, a Book for Primary Schools,' Dublin, 16mo, 1870; 4th edit., Dublin, 8vo, 1870; the work had a wide circulation and was designed for children in the Irish national schools. 7. 'Lisdoonvarna Spa and Seaside Places of Clare,' Dublin, 1871, 16mo; 3rd edit., London, 8vo, 1878. 8. 'Treatment of Chronic Skin Diseases,' three lectures delivered at St. Vincent's Hospital, London and Dublin, 1872; 2nd edit. 1875. 9. 'Papers on Dermatology and Allied Subjects,' 1889; 2nd edit. 1899.

[History of the Royal College of Surgeons in Ireland, by Sir C. A. Cameron, Dublin, 1886, p. 435; Lancet, 1908, i. 823; British Med. Journal, 1908, i. 661; Men and Women of the Time, 1899; information from Sir Lambert H. Ormesby and Dr. John Knott.] D'A. P.

MAPPIN, SIR FREDERICK THORPE, first baronet (1821–1910), benefactor to Sheffield, born at Sheffield on 16 May 1821, was eldest son of Joseph Mappin, cutler, of Broomgrove, Sheffield, by his wife Mary Ann (*d.* 25 Aug. 1841), daughter of Thomas Thorpe of Haynes, Bedfordshire. Receiving his early education at Sheffield, young Mappin at the age of fourteen entered his father's cutlery business, and was only twenty when his father's death threw upon him the sole burden of its management. He afterwards took his younger brothers into partnership, but in 1859 retired himself from the firm, which continued to flourish, in order to become the senior partner in the works of Thomas Turton & Sons, steel manufacturers. He showed his interest in the progress of mechanical science by joining as a member the Institution of Mechanical Engineers in 1862, and the Institution of Civil Engineers as an associate on 7 Feb. 1865. He was president of the File Manufacturers' Association in 1870. He retired from active business in 1885, but became a director when the Turton firm was converted into a limited liability company, and held the office until almost the close of his life.

Largely released from business responsibilities in middle life, Mappin threw himself with much energy into public and local work. He was a member of the Sheffield town council in 1854, chairman of the town trustees (a wealthy and important Sheffield body dating from the thirteenth century), and mayor of Sheffield in 1877–8. Mappin was a prominent member of the Cutlers' Company (of Hallamshire), serving as assistant (1846–9 and 1857–60), searcher (1850–1853), senior warden (1854–5), and master cutler (1855–6).

Greatly interested in education, he was chief founder of the Sheffield Technical School and its munificent supporter. He also liberally contributed to Firth College and university College, which with the technical school was incorporated into the new university of Sheffield in 1905. To the funds of the university, of which he became the first senior pro-chancellor, he contributed 15,000*l.*, besides founding various scholarships and exhibitions. From 1873 to 1903 he was chairman of the Sheffield United Gas Company; he was a director of the Bridgwater navigation, was a working director of the Midland railway (1869–1900), and as juror at the Paris Exhibition of 1878 was made an officer of the legion of honour. Mappin, who was an early supporter of the volunteer movement, joined the 4th (Hallamshire) York and Lancaster regiment in March 1861, and retired as captain in March 1872.

An influential leader of local liberalism, he was president of the Hallamshire Liberal Association, and of the Sheffield United Liberal Association. He entered parliament in 1880 as member for East Retford, and in 1885 was elected for the Hallamshire division of the West Riding, which he represented until 1906. Although he was an advocate of home rule and free trade, his liberalism was of a pronounced whiggish type. On 27 Aug. 1886 he was created a baronet. His lifelong devotion to the interests of his native city was recognised in 1900 by the bestowal on him of the first presentation of its honorary freedom. He retired from public life in 1905, having been for many years familiarly known as the 'grand old man' of Sheffield. Mappin was brought up as a congregationalist, but became later a member of the Church of England, and was a generous supporter of church work.

A lover of art, he added (in two gifts) eighty pictures to the Mappin Art Gallery at Western Park, Sheffield, founded under the will of his uncle, John Newton Mappin of Birchlands in 1887. His own collection of pictures consisted almost exclusively of works by artists of the mid-Victorian period. They were dispersed at two public sales which began respectively on 5 May 1906 and 17 June 1910; the prices realised at the former sale were much below those originally paid for the pictures, owing to change in public taste.

He died at his residence, Thornbury, Sheffield, on 19 March 1910, and was buried at the Ecclesall burial-ground. He left an estate valued for probate at 931,086*l.* Besides his Sheffield residence, he had a town house, 32 Prince's Gate.

Mappin married on 25 Sept. 1845 Mary Crossley (*d.* 10 April 1908), daughter of John Wilson of Oakholme, Sheffield, by whom he had three sons, Frank, who succeeded to the baronetcy, Wilson, and Samuel Wilson.

His portrait was frequently painted for presentation by public bodies. In October 1892 his portrait by Ouless was placed in the Mappin Art Gallery, and a portrait of Lady Mappin by Mr. J. J. Shannon was presented to him, both being paid for by public subscription. His bust in bronze was placed in the Botanic Gardens, Sheffield, in November 1903 as a public recognition of the part he took in securing the transfer of the gardens to the town trustees. In October 1905 his portrait by Mr. Ernest Moore, presented by the town trustees, was placed in their rooms at the court house; a replica was subscribed for in 1906 by the directors and chief officials of the gas company, to be placed in their board-room. There are portraits also at the Sheffield Reform Club and in the council-room of the Sheffield University.

[Burke's Peerage and Baronetage, 1910; Sheffield and District Who's Who, 1905, p. 14; Thomas Asline Ward's Peeps into the Past, 1909, pp. 326, 328; Robert E. Leader's History of the Cutlers' Company of Hallamshire, ii. 41; Sheffield University Calendar, 1911–12, p. 598; Debrett's House of Commons, 1905; Pike's Contemporary Biographies, no. 4, Sheffield, 1901; Mappin Art Gall. Cat., 1887, 1892; Athenæum, 25 June 1910; The Times, 21 and 24 Mar. 1910, 16 May 1910; Sheffield Daily Telegraph, and Sheffield Daily Independent, 19 Mar. 1910.]

C. W.

MARJORIBANKS, EDWARD, second Baron Tweedmouth (1849–1909), politician, born in London on 8 July 1849, was eldest son in a family of four sons and two daughters of Sir Dudley Coutts Marjoribanks, first baronet, a very capable man of business and a collector of works of art, who sat in parliament as liberal member for Berwick-on-Tweed from 1853 to 1868 and subsequently from 1874 to 1881; having been created a baronet on 25 July 1866, he was raised to the peerage as Baron Tweedmouth (12 Oct. 1881). Among his ancestors was Thomas Marjoribanks of Ratho, who was member for Edinburgh in the Scottish parliament and was in 1532 one of the founders of the Court of Session, becoming afterwards lord clerk register and a lord of session. His mother was Isabella, daughter of Sir James Weir Hogg, first baronet [q. v.] and sister of Sir James Macnaghten McGarel Hogg, first Lord Magheramorne [q. v.], and of Quintin Hogg [q. v. Suppl. II], founder of the Regent Street Polytechnic. Of his sisters the elder, Mary Georgiana, married Matthew Ridley, first Viscount Ridley [q. v. Suppl. II], and the younger, Ishbel Maria, married John Campbell, seventh earl of Aberdeen. Educated at Harrow, Marjoribanks matriculated at Christ Church, Oxford, on 9 March 1868. At the university he devoted himself chiefly to sport and took no degree. He was through life a fine horseman and devoted to hunting, a splendid shot alike with gun and with rifle, a keen fisherman, and an enthusiastic deer-stalker. After leaving Oxford in 1872 he went for a tour round the world, and on his return he studied law, being called to the bar at the Inner Temple on 17 Nov. 1874. He worked for a time in the chambers of Sir John Duke Coleridge [q.v. Suppl. I], afterwards lord chief justice, and was employed by him to collect and arrange material for the Tichborne trial. Coleridge formed a high opinion of his abilities, but he made little further progress at the bar, and deserted law for politics. His political and family connections were strong in Berwickshire, where his father had purchased considerable estates. An invitation to stand in June 1873 as a liberal candidate there on the sudden occasion of a vacancy failed to reach him in time. After failing in 1874 in a contest in Mid-Kent he became prospective liberal candidate for North Berwickshire in 1875. At the general election of 1880 he was elected by a majority of 268. He held the seat until the death of his father in 1894 removed him to the House of Lords.

During his earlier years in parliament, although Marjoribanks spoke little, he was active in promoting many public objects and measures in which his constituents were interested, and he was a leading supporter of the movement for legalising marriage with a deceased wife's sister, being destined in due course to conduct the bill to its final victory in the House of Lords in 1907. In 1882 he moved the address in reply to the speech from the throne. He was soon in frequent requisition at political gatherings in many parts of the kingdom but especially in Scotland. When the home rule ministry of Gladstone was formed in 1886 Marjoribanks received his first official appointment as comptroller of Queen Victoria's household and second whip to the party, and was sworn a member of the privy council. For the next eight years he was indefatigable in promoting the interests of his party alike in parliament and in the constituencies. After the rejection of the home rule bill in June 1886 and the downfall of Gladstone's ministry, Marjoribanks, with Mr. Arnold Morley as his chief, served as second whip to the opposition until 1892. On Gladstone's return to office in 1892 Marjoribanks became parliamentary secretary to the Treasury, or chief liberal whip, Mr. Arnold Morley having accepted office in the cabinet. His engaging manners, assiduity, imperturbable good humour, and devotion to all manly sports made him an almost ideal whip, with few equals and no superiors among his contemporaries.

On the death of his father on 4 March 1894 he succeeded to the peerage as Lord Tweedmouth, and was invited by Lord Rosebery, who, on Gladstone's resignation, had just become prime minister, to join the cabinet as lord privy seal and chancellor of the Duchy of Lancaster. Tweedmouth's sure grasp of the internal mechanism and sentiment of the party gave him due weight in the inner counsels of the ministry. When the government of Lord Rosebery fell in 1895 and a general election converted the liberal party into a divided, distracted, and enfeebled opposition, Tweedmouth earnestly devoted himself to the up-hill task of restoring its fallen fortunes. He was prominent in society, and entertained largely both in London at Brook House and at his beautiful home in Scotland, Guisachan in Inverness-shire. He had married on 9 June 1873 Lady Fanny Octavia Louisa, third daughter of John Winston Spencer-Churchill, seventh duke of Marlborough, and sister of Lord Randolph Churchill. Lady Tweedmouth was endowed with a native gift for society, and shared her husband's labour in bringing together liberal politicians of all shades of opinion. She initiated the Liberal Social Council and did as much as social agencies can to restore courage, confidence, and concord to the party. Her death on 5 Aug. 1904 dealt her husband a blow from which he never completely recovered. At the same time financial losses, due to a crisis in the affairs of Meux's brewery, which he bore with cheery fortitude, compelled Tweedmouth to part with Brook House and Guisachan and to sell many of the art treasures which his father had collected.

When a liberal government was formed in Dec. 1905 with Sir Henry Campbell-Bannerman [q. v. Suppl. II] as prime minister, Tweedmouth became first lord of the admiralty. He took office at a critical moment, for the expansion of the German navy was then in full swing and yet there was a section of the liberal party which was disposed to insist on a large reduction of naval expenditure. Some slight and temporary reductions were made at the outset, but on the whole Tweedmouth stood firm to the policy of maintaining England's naval supremacy, and he gave a cordial support to the many and drastic measures of reform initiated by Lord Selborne and steadfastly pursued by Lord Cawdor [q. v. Suppl. II], his two immediate predecessors, both acting on the vigorous inspiration of the first sea lord, Sir John (now Lord) Fisher. He represented the admiralty in the House of Lords with becoming dignity and discretion, and he displayed a firm grasp of the business of his department. His term of office was not eventful until March 1908, when it was bruited abroad that the German Emperor had written to Tweedmouth on matters connected with naval policy and that in the course of a reply Tweedmouth had communicated to the Kaiser many details of the forthcoming navy estimates before these had been presented to the House of Commons. Tweedmouth was on these grounds popularly credited with something like an act of treason. A private and unpublished correspondence with the German Emperor had taken place, and the public knowledge of that fact may have been due to a conversational indiscretion on Tweedmouth's part. In other respects the circumstances were misrepresented and Tweedmouth was unjustly censured by public opinion. No one can blame a minister for receiving a private letter from a foreign sovereign. Nor can he in common courtesy refrain from answering the letter. All that is required of him is to frame his answer with the full knowledge and sanction of his colleagues. This condition was scrupulously fulfilled by Tweedmouth, though the fact was not fully disclosed at the time. There was no premature disclosure of the estimates to the Kaiser. Tweedmouth sent in his reply no information except what was also given to Parliament at the same time. An indispensable act of courtesy was controlled throughout by ministerial authority higher than Tweedmouth's own. The first insidious assaults of cerebral malady may account for Tweedmouth's sole fault in talking too unreservedly about the correspondence.

Sir Henry Campbell-Bannerman's resignation followed soon after this misunderstanding (5 April 1908), one of his last official acts being to nominate Tweedmouth for a knighthood of the Thistle. On Mr. Asquith's succession as prime minister and some reconstruction of the government, Tweedmouth relinquished the admiralty and became lord president of the council. But his ministerial career was practically at an end. Within a few weeks he was stricken down by a cerebral attack from when he never recovered sufficiently to resume any kind of public work. He finally resigned his office in Sept. 1908. During the last few months of his life he resided at the chief secretary's lodge in the Phœnix Park at Dublin, which had been lent by his colleague Mr. Birrell in order that he might be under the care of his sister, the Countess of Aberdeen, the wife of the viceroy. There he died on 15 Sept. 1909. He was buried in the family burying-ground in Chirnside churchyard, Berwickshire, where his wife had previously been buried. In her memory he had restored and greatly beautified this church, which was not far from Hutton Castle, a residence which his father had purchased, restored, and enlarged. He was succeeded in the title by his only child, Dudley Churchill.

A cartoon portrait by 'Spy' appeared in 'Vanity Fair' in 1894.

[Private information; The Times, 16 Sept. 1909; a volume entitled Edward Marjoribanks, Lord Tweedmouth, Notes and Recollections, was edited in 1909 by Tweedmouth's sister, the Countess of Aberdeen, and besides biographical notes, apparently from the pen of the editor, it contains a series of recollections by many of his friends and colleagues. To these are appended brief appreciations of Fanny, Lady Tweedmouth, his wife, and of Isabella, Lady Tweedmouth, his mother.] J. R. T.

MARKS, DAVID WOOLF (1811–1909), professor of Hebrew at University College, London, born in London on 22 Nov. 1811, was eldest son of Woolf Marks, merchant, by his wife Mary. From the Jews' free school, in Bell Lane, Spitalfields, he went for five years as pupil-teacher to Mr. H. N. Solomon's boarding school for Jews at Hammersmith. After acting as assistant reader at the Western Synagogue, St. Alban's Place, Haymarket, he became in 1833 assistant reader and secretary to the Hebrew congregation at Liverpool. There he taught Hebrew to John (afterwards Sir John) Simon [q. v.], and the two became close friends. Simon, who was an early advocate of reform in Jewish ritual and practices in England, enlisted Marks's aid in the movement, and in 1841 Marks was chosen senior minister of the newly-established reformed West London congregation of British Jews, retaining the post until the end of 1895, first at the synagogue in Burton Street, which was opened on 27 January 1842, then at Margaret Street, whither the congregation removed in 1849, and lastly at the existing building in Upper Berkeley Street which was opened in 1870 (J. Picciotto, *Sketches of Anglo-Jewish History*, 1875, pp. 374 seq.). With his colleague, Albert Löwy [q. v. Suppl. II], he prepared the reformed prayer-book, and mainly owing to his persistent efforts his synagogue was legalised for marriages. Sir Moses Montefiore, the orthodox president of the Board of Deputies of British Jews, a body which alone enjoyed the right of registering or certifying places of worship for Jewish marriages, long refused to certify the reformed synagogue. A clause covering Marks's synagogue was removed in 1857 by Montefiore's influence during the committee stage in the House of Commons from a bill for legalising dissenters' marriages in their own places of worship. Bishop Wilberforce and the earl of Harrowby, however, at Marks's persuasion, reintroduced the clause in the House of Lords, and it became law.

Marks was Goldsmid professor of Hebrew at University College, London, from 1844 to 1898, and was dean of the college during the sessions 1875–7. He was also for a time professor of Hebrew at Regent's Park Baptist College, and was one of the Hibbert trustees, a trustee of Dr. Williams's library, and for thirty-five years member of the Marylebone vestry. The Hebrew Union College in Cincinnati conferred the honorary degree of D.D. upon him. He died at Maidenhead on 2 May 1909, and was buried at the Ball's Pond cemetery of the West London Synagogue.

Marks published four volumes of sermons (1851–85); a biography of Sir Francis Goldsmid (1879, part i., part ii. being by his colleague Löwy); and 'The Law is Light,' a course of lectures on the Mosaic law (1854). He was a contributor to Smith's 'Dictionary of the Bible.'

In 1842 Marks married Cecilia (*d.* 1882), daughter of Moseley Woolf of Birmingham; by her he had two daughters and four sons, of whom Harry Hananel Marks, J.P., was at one time M.P. for the Isle of Thanet, and is proprietor and editor of the 'Financial News,' and Major Claude Laurie Marks, D.S.O. (1863–1910), served with distinction in the South African war.

A tablet in commemoration of his long ministry was placed in the hall of the West London Synagogue, Upper Berkeley Street, and in the committee room there hangs a portrait in oils, executed and presented by Julia Goodman [q. v. Suppl. II] in Nov. 1877. An oval crayon drawing by Abraham Solomon [q. v.] in 1853 (belonging to Mr. Israel Solomon) was engraved by S. Marks (see *Cat. Anglo-Jewish Hist. Exhibition*, 1887).

[Jewish Chronicle, 7 May 1909; private information.] M. E.

MARRIOTT, Sir WILLIAM THACKERAY (1834–1903), judge-advocate-general, born in 1834, was third son of Christopher Marriott of Crumpsall, near Manchester, by his wife Jane Dorothea, daughter of John Poole of Cornbrook Hall, near Manchester.

He was admitted to St. John's College, Cambridge, in 1854 and became prominent in the debates of the Union society. He graduated B.A. in 1858. In the same year he was ordained deacon, and appointed curate of St. George's, Hulme, a parish mainly inhabited by the working classes. In 1859 he started the 'Hulme Athenæum,' one of the first working-men's clubs established in England. All the members were working men. In 1860 Marriott issued a pamphlet, 'Some Real Wants and Some Legitimate Claims of the Working Classes,' in which he advocated the formation of parks, gymnasiums and clubs for the people. A year later, when the time came for him to take priest's orders, he declined on conscientious grounds, giving his reasons in the preface to his farewell sermon, 'What is Christianity ?' (1862).

Renouncing his orders, Marriott became a student of Lincoln's Inn on 4 May 1861 and began writing for the press. He was called to the bar on 26 Jan. 1864, and the following year published a pamphlet on the law relating to 'Clerical Disabilities.' Endowed with considerable rhetorical powers, he soon acquired a lucrative practice in railway and compensation cases. He was made a Q.C. on 13 Feb. 1877, and was elected a bencher of Lincoln's Inn on 26 Nov. 1879. Like many rising lawyers he cherished political ambitions, and was returned as liberal member for Brighton on 5 April 1880. In his election address he described himself as a follower of Lord Hartington [q. v. Suppl. II], then the official head of the liberal party; but when Gladstone became prime minister, he showed signs of dissatisfaction. He vehemently opposed the government's proposal to remedy obstruction by means of the closure, and on 30 March 1882 he moved an amendment to the closure resolution, which was defeated by 39 (Lucy, *The Gladstone Parliament*, 1886, p. 228). In 1884 he published a pamphlet entitled 'The Liberal Party and Mr. Chamberlain,' a violent attack on what he regarded as the revolutionary radicalism of Mr. Joseph Chamberlain, and there ensued an acrimonious personal controversy, which Marriott afterwards regretted. Meanwhile his alienation from the liberal party became complete. Repeated visits to Egypt confirmed his opinion of the disastrous consequences of Gladstone's Egyptian policy, which he denounced in an open letter to Lord Salisbury, entitled 'Two Years of British Intervention in Egypt' (1884). He vacated his seat early in 1884, offered himself for re-election as a conservative, and was elected (3 March 1884). On the accession of the conservatives to office Marriott was made a privy councillor (9 July 1885), and was appointed judge-advocate-general in Lord Salisbury's first administration (15 July). He was again gazetted judge-advocate-general on 9 Aug. 1886 in Lord Salisbury's second administration, and retained the office till 1892. He was knighted in 1888. He supported the conservative cause with ardour. He joined the grand council of the Primrose League, and in May 1892 he succeeded Sir Algernon Borthwick, Lord Glenesk [q. v. Suppl. II], as chancellor of the league, and was mainly instrumental in organising the monster petition against the home rule bill of 1893. In the same year he retired from parliament to resume practice at the parliamentary bar. He had been re-elected as a conservative for Brighton at the general elections of 1885, 1886, and 1892.

In 1887 and 1888 Marriott had acted as counsel for the ex-Khedive Ismail Pasha in settling claims for the arrears of his civil list against the Egyptian government. He persuaded the ex-Khedive to moderate his demands, with the result that he secured for him the handsome compensation of 1,200,000*l.* He was less successful in prosecuting similar claims of Zobehr Pasha, the Sudanese slave trader. After his retirement from parliament he embarked in unfortunate financial speculation. On 3 May 1899 he obtained a judgment of 5000*l.* and costs against Mr. Hooley. Later he transferred his attentions to South Africa and migrated thither. Residing at Johannesburg, he carried on legal business there, and acted as political adviser of the Dale Lace party in opposition to Lord Milner's policy. He died at Aix-la-Chapelle on 27 July 1903. On 17 December 1872 he married Charlotte Louisa, eldest daughter of Capt. Tennant, R.N., of Needwood House, Hampshire.

Marriott's literary work showed some critical power. His change of profession and his political conversion exposed him to constant attack, and detraction confirmed a characteristic cynicism.

A caricature appeared in 'Vanity Fair' in 1883.

[The Times and Morning Post, 30 July 1903; The Eagle, Dec. 1903; Men of the Time, 1899; Leslie Stephen, Life of Henry Fawcett, 1885, p. 29; Annual Register, 1888, p. 382.]

G. S. W.

MARSDEN, ALEXANDER EDWIN (1832–1902), surgeon, born on 22 Sept. 1832, was son by his first wife of William Marsden [q. v.], surgeon. He was educated at Wimbledon school and King's College, London, and was admitted a licentiate of the Society of Apothecaries in 1853 and M.R.C.S.England in 1854; he graduated M.D. at St. Andrews in 1862 and became F.R.C.S.Edinburgh in 1868.

Entering the army in 1854 as staff assistant surgeon, he served in the Crimean war. For three months he was in the general hospital at Scutari; early in 1855 he was sent to Sevastopol with the 38th regiment, and he acted afterwards as a surgeon to the ambulance corps until the end of the war, when he received the Crimean and Turkish medals. On his return to England he was appointed surgeon to the Royal Free Hospital, London (founded by his father), where he was also curator of the museum and general superintendent. At the cancer hospital at Brompton (also founded by his father) he was surgeon from 1853 to 1884; consulting surgeon from 1884 until his death; trustee from 1865; member of the house committee from 1870, and chairman of the general committee from 1901.

In 1898 he was master of the City company of cordwainers, and on his retirement he presented to the company the service of plate given to his father in 1840 in recognition of his philanthropic work in opening the first free hospitals in London. Marsden died at 92 Nightingale Lane, Wandsworth Common, S.W., on 2 July 1902.

In 1856 he married Catherine, only daughter of David Marsden, banker.

Marsden published: 1. 'A New and Certain Successful Mode of treating Certain Forms of Cancer,' 1869; reissued 1874 (a collection of extracts, 1870). 2. 'The Treatment of Cancers and Tumours by Chian Turpentine,' 1880. 3. 'Our Present Means of successfully treating or alleviating Cancer,' 1889. He also edited in 1871 the fourth edition of his father's treatise on 'Malignant Diarrhœa, better known by the Name of Asiatic or Malignant Cholera.'

[Men and Women of the Time, 1899; Lancet, 1902, ii. 118; Brit. Med. Journal, 1902, ii. 157; private information.] D'A. P.

MARSHALL, GEORGE WILLIAM (1839–1905), genealogist, born at Ward End House, near Birmingham, on 19 April 1839, and descended from a family settled for several generations at Perlethorpe, Nottinghamshire, was only child of George Marshall, a Birmingham banker, by his second wife, Eliza Henshaw Comberbach. Educated privately and at St. Peter's College, Radley, he entered Magdalene College, Cambridge, in 1857, but soon removed to Peterhouse, whence he graduated with the degree of LL.B. in 1861, and proceeded LL.M. in 1864, and LL.D. in 1874. In 1861 he entered the Middle Temple, was called to the bar on 9 June 1865, and for some time practised on the Oxford circuit.

Genealogy was Marshall's lifelong study from his Cambridge days. He collected manuscript material and published much. His earliest publication was 'Collections for a Genealogical Account of the Family of Comberbach' (his mother's family) in 1866. In 1877 he founded 'The Genealogist,' and edited the first seven volumes. For the Harleian Society he edited in 1871 'The Visitations of Nottinghamshire in 1569 and 1614,' and in 1873 'Le Neve's Pedigrees of Knights.' He also printed privately in 1878 'The Visitation of Northumberland in 1615,' and in 1882 'The Visitation of Wiltshire in 1623.' His chief work was 'The Genealogist's Guide,' an alphabetical list of all known printed pedigrees (1879; 2nd edit. 1885; subsequent editions came out at Guildford in 1893 and 1903). Another valuable work is his 'Handbook to the Ancient Courts of Probate' (1889; 2nd edit. 1895). On the various families bearing the surname of Marshall he printed two volumes entitled 'Miscellanea Marescalliana' (1883–1888). He issued a list of printed parish registers in 1891 and 1893, and a revised list in 1900, with an appendix in 1904. Six Nottinghamshire registers were issued by him between 1887 and 1896, namely those of Perlethorpe, Carburton, Edwinstow, Worksop, Wellow, and Ollerton. Other of his works were: 'A Pedigree of the Descendants of Isaac Marshall' (1868); 'Notes on the Surname of Hall' (Exeter, 1887); and 'Collections relating to the Surname of Feather' (Worksop, 1887).

On 30 May 1872 Marshall was elected a fellow of the Society of Antiquaries; and he was one of the founders in 1896 of the Parish Register Society, to the publications of which he contributed. In 1887 he was appointed Rouge Croix Pursuivant of Arms and in 1904 was promoted to be York Herald. Several valuable and novel suggestions by him in regard to the entering of pedigrees and additions thereto in the books of the College of Arms were adopted by the chapter. For the college he collected a unique collection of manuscript and printed parish registers. He also presented, either in his lifetime or by bequest on his death, many volumes of manuscripts, abstracts of wills, marriage licences, and pedigrees. As a herald he had a great liking for allusive or canting coats-of-arms and crests. A keen and truth-seeking antiquary, with an intuitive power of research, he had a lawyer's love of conciseness and accuracy.

In 1891 Marshall purchased the Sarnesfield Court estate in Herefordshire, formerly the seat of the Monington family, and was made J.P. In 1902 he served the office of high sheriff, and was appointed D.L. He was also a freemason. At Sarnesfield Court he formed a rich library of genealogical and heraldic works and an extensive collection of armorial china.

He died at his London residence, Holmbush, Barnes, on 12 Sept. 1905, and was buried at Sarnesfield, his tabard as York herald, with the collar of SS, sword, and cap, being placed on his coffin. Marshall was twice married: (1) at Walton-on-the-Hill, Surrey, on 26 Sept. 1867, to Alice Ruth, younger daughter of Ambrose William Hall, sometime rector of Debden, Essex; (2) to Caroline Emily, elder sister of his first wife. He left issue six sons and two daughters. There are two portraits of him at Sarnesfield, one as a boy by Poole of Birmingham, and the other by Levine in 1884.

[Memoir by J. P. R. (John Paul Rylands) in Genealogist, new ser. xxii. 198–202, with a good portrait of Marshall in his tabard; The Times, 15 and 18 Sept. 1905; Miscellanea Genealogica et Heraldica, original series, ii. 62–69; Men and Women of the Time, 1899; private information.] W. G. D. F.

MARSHALL, JULIAN (1836–1903), art collector and author, born at Headingley House, near Leeds, on 24 June 1836, was third son and youngest of the five children of John Marshall, jun. (1797–1836), of Headingley, Leeds, M.P. for Leeds (1832–5), by his wife Mary, eldest daughter of Joseph Ballantyne Dykes of Dovenby Hall, Cockermouth. His grandfather, John Marshall of Headingley (1765–1845), M.P. for Yorkshire (1826–30), greatly improved modes of flax-spinning and inaugurated successful factories at Leeds and Shrewsbury. Educated first at the private school of the Rev. John Gilderdale at Walthamstow, Julian was at Harrow from 1852 to 1854. From 1855 he was employed in the family flax-spinning business at Leeds, but, having no taste for a business life, he left in 1861.

Before he was twenty he began to form a collection of prints, and from 1861 to 1869 he devoted himself exclusively to perfecting it. He became a noted connoisseur of the art of engraving, and brought together choice examples of the leading works of the ancient and modern schools. His collection was dispersed at a twelve days' sale at Sotheby's on 30 June to 11 July 1864, and realised 8352*l.* 1*s.* 6*d.* Marshall was also a capable musical amateur, singing in the Leeds parish church choir under Samuel Sebastian Wesley [q. v.], and actively promoting the first Leeds Musical Festival in 1858. In later years he formed a valuable collection of musical autographs and portraits, wrote much on musical subjects, and contributed to Grove's 'Dictionary of Music and Musicians.' He was for many years honorary secretary to the Mendelssohn Scholarship Fund, founded by Madame Jenny Lind in memory of the composer.

As a boy Marshall won the champion racket at Harrow. He was through life keenly interested in the practice and literature of games, and above all of tennis. He is chiefly known by his 'Annals of Tennis' (1878), a work of minute and exhaustive research. Towards the end of his life he formed a notable collection of book plates.

Marshall died on 21 Nov. 1903 at his residence, 13 Belsize Avenue, N.W., and was buried in Hampstead churchyard. He married on 7 Oct. 1864 Florence Ashton, eldest daughter of Canon Thomas, vicar of Allhallows Barking, and granddaughter of Archbishop Sumner. Three daughters survived him. Mrs. Marshall, who is a composer and conductor, besides contributing to Grove's Dictionary, published in 1883 a 'Life of Handel' in Hueffer's 'Great Musicians' series, and in 1889 the 'Life and Letters of Mary Wollstonecraft Shelley.'

Besides the works above mentioned Marshall published: 1. 'Lawn-tennis, with the Laws adopted by the M.C.C. and A.A.C. and L.T.C. and Badminton,' 1878. 2. 'Tennis Cuts and Quips, in prose and verse, with rules and wrinkles,' 1884. 3. 'Tennis, Rackets, Fives' (with Major James Spens and Rev. J. A. Arnan Tait), in the 'All-England' series, 1890. 4. 'A Catalogue of Engraved National Portraits in the National Art Library, with a Prefatory Note,' South Kensington Museum, 1895.

[M. G. Dauglish, Harrow School Register, 1801–1900, p. 217; Rev. R. V. Taylor, Biographia Leodiensis, 1865, pp. 364–6, 411–415; Ann. Register, 1903, p. 165; Athenæum, 26 Dec. 1903; G. W. Reid, Cat. of the Coll. of Engravings, the property of J. Marshall, 1864; information kindly supplied by Mrs. Julian Marshall.] C. W.

MARTIN, Sir THEODORE (1816–1909), man of letters, born at Edinburgh on 16 Sept. 1816, was only son in a family of ten children of a well-to-do Edinburgh solicitor, James Martin, who was for some years private secretary to Andrew, Lord Rutherfurd [q. v.]. His grandfather, also Theodore Martin, was ground officer on the estate of Cairnbulg, near Fraserburgh. His mother was Mary, daughter of James Reid, shipowner of Fraserburgh. From Edinburgh high school under Dr. Adam he passed to Edinburgh University (1830–3), of which he was created hon. LL.D. in 1875. At the university a love of literature was awakened in him by the lectures of James Pillans [q. v.], professor of humanity, and there he first caught sight of William Edmonstoune Aytoun [q. v.], a student three years his senior, with whom he was to form ten years later a close friendship and a literary partnership. As a young man he studied German and interested himself in music and the stage.

Martin was bred to the law, and practised as a solicitor in Edinburgh until June 1846. In that year he migrated to London in order to pursue the career of a parliamentary solicitor or agent. In 1847 he joined in that capacity, at Westminster, Hugh Innes Cameron, and his business was carried on under the style of Cameron & Martin until 1854. Then Cameron left the firm, and Martin conducted it single-handed for eight years. In 1862 Martin took a partner, William Leslie of the Edinburgh firm of Inglis & Leslie, for whom he had acted as London agent. Leslie died in 1897, when Martin was joined by two other partners, but the firm was known as Martin & Leslie until 1907, when the style was changed to Martin & Co. Martin's parliamentary business in London was extensive, profitable, and important. Among the earliest private bills which he prepared and piloted through parliamentary committees were those dealing with the Shrewsbury and Chester railway and the river Dee navigation. He was thus brought into close relations with North Wales, which he subsequently made a chief place of residence. He also carried the bill for the extension to London of the Manchester, Sheffield, and Lincolnshire (now the Great Central) railway. During 1879 he was closely engaged in negotiating, for Lord Beaconsfield's government, the purchase of the undertakings of all the London water companies, and in preparing a bill for vesting them in a public trust; but the measure was dropped during the last days of Lord Beaconsfield's ministry, and was not revived on Gladstone's return to office in 1880. Martin's parliamentary work was his main occupation through life, and he conducted it with unsparing energy and much ability.

Before leaving Edinburgh he contributed to 'Tait's' and 'Fraser's' magazines and to other periodicals humorous pieces in prose and verse. The poems he ascribed to Bon Gaultier, a 'bon compagnon' whose name had caught his fancy in Rabelais (*Prol.* livre i.). In 1841 Aytoun was attracted by one of these papers, 'Flowers of Hemp; or The Newgate Garland. By One of the Family,' a satire on the fashionable novel in the style of Harrison Ainsworth's 'Dick Turpin' and 'Jack Sheppard.' At Aytoun's request the naturalist Edward Forbes [q. v.] brought the young men together, and 'a kind of Beaumont and Fletcher partnership,' as Martin called it, was the result. From 1842 to 1844 they wrote together a series of humorous pieces for 'Tait's' and 'Fraser's' magazines. Besides comic poems there were parodies in prose, including a set of prize novels, prior in date to Thackeray's, and a series of humorous colloquies in the fashion of 'Noctes Ambrosianæ,' called 'Bon Gaultier and his Friends.' Most of the verse was collected in 1845 in 'Bon Gaultier's Ballads,' a volume which achieved immediate popularity and reached a sixteenth edition in 1903. The attractions of the volume were enhanced by the illustrations—in the first edition by 'Alfred Crowquill' (A. H. Forrester [q. v.]), to whose drawings Richard Doyle and John Leech added others in later editions.

The Bon Gaultier verse mainly parodied the leading poetry of the day, especially the 'new poetry' of Tennyson. A few of the mock poems pretended to be competition exercises for the poet-laureateship vacated by Southey's death. 'The Lay of the Lovelorn,' a parody of 'Locksley Hall,' which was elaborated by Martin out of ten or a dozen lines by Aytoun, was perhaps the most popular piece. Lockhart (in *Spanish Ballads*), Macaulay, Mrs. Browning, Moore, Leigh Hunt, Uhland, and even Aytoun himself were all among the victims of Martin or his partner's ridicule, together with the German student and the American patriot. Martin was the larger contributor, but Aytoun's work is the better. If the 'Ballads' are more on the surface than the 'Rejected Addresses' with which they invite comparison, they are hardly less amusing. The fun, whatever shape it takes, is always healthy, and the reaction against the extravagance of transitory fashions in literature is generally sound in spirit.

Before the Bon Gaultier partnership ended in 1844, Martin and Aytoun also worked together in a series of translations which appeared in 'Blackwood's Magazine' in 1843–4, and were published collectively in 1858 as 'Poems and Ballads of Goethe.' Martin's friendship with Aytoun continued till Aytoun's death in 1865, when Martin paid him the tribute of a sympathetic, if discursive, 'Memoir' (1867), which he subsequently summarised for this Dictionary.

Martin's early affection for the drama developed steadily. Edmund Kean was one of his first theatrical heroes. On a visit to London in 1840 he first saw Helen Faucit [q. v. Suppl. I] act, and after witnessing her performance of Rosalind at Glasgow in Dec. 1843 he wrote some 'prophetic lines,' in which he fancied himself Orlando. In July 1846 he extolled her powers in an article, 'Acting as one of the Fine Arts,' in the 'Dublin University Magazine.' In the same year he translated for her the little Danish romantic drama of Henrik Hertz, 'King René's Daughter,' which she produced in 1849. (It was first published in 1850.) The extreme refinement of the piece, and the fictitiousness of a situation impossible in real life, convey an impression of artificiality, but Helen Faucit rendered to perfection its tenderness of touch, to which Martin's verse—some of his best—rendered full justice. The blind Iolanthe was long one of her most popular parts.

Miss Faucit's fascination grew on Martin, who is said to have followed her from place to place until he made her his wife (Mrs. Sellar's *Recollections*, p. 37). They were married on 25 Aug. 1851 at the old Church of St. Nicholas in Brighton, and spent their wedding tour in Italy. After their return in November she resumed her connection with the stage, which continued practically till 1871. In April 1852 she appeared at Manchester in Martin's adaptation of 'Adrienne Lecouvreur.' In the same year they bought a house, 31 Onslow Square, where Thackeray was their near neighbour, and where they formed the centre of a large and cultivated social circle. This remained Martin's London residence till the end of his life, although he was almost driven out of it at the last by the noise of passing motor omnibuses, a nuisance which, in 1906, he denounced in 'The Times.' The summer and autumn of 1861 were spent at Bryntysilio on the banks of the Dee, about two miles above Llangollen, to which Martin's parliamentary work on Dee navigation had introduced him. Martin was charmed with the place, and in 1865 he bought the house and adjoining grounds, both of which were considerably enlarged as the years went on. Bryntysilio remained the favourite country residence of Martin and his wife. He associated himself effectively with the industrial activities of the locality and took a great interest in Welsh music.

Martin's literary activity increased after his marriage and his reputation widened. In 1859 he was one of the umpires for the prize offered by the Crystal Palace Company at the Burns centenary festival. His literary energies were chiefly divided between essays on the stage for the magazines, and translations from Latin, German, and Italian, with occasional adaptations for the theatre. In 'Fraser's Magazine' (Feb. 1858, Dec. 1863, and Jan. 1865) he lamented the decay of the English drama, subsequently arguing in 'The Drama in England,' a paper on the 'Kembles' (*Quarterly Review*, Jan. 1872), that a cardinal necessity for the recovery of the English stage was the presence of a governing mind in control of a national theatre. To the 'Quarterly Review' he also contributed excellent biographical essays on David Garrick (July 1868) and Macready (Nov. 1872). Most of his writings on the drama Martin collected for private circulation as 'Essays on the Drama' (1874). At later dates he wrote on 'Rachel' in 'Blackwood's Magazine' (Sept. 1882), while in a paper, 'Shakespeare or Bacon?' reprinted in 1888 from 'Blackwood's Magazine,' he sought to dispel the 'Baconian' delusion. The essays on Garrick, Macready, the Kembles, and Rachel, with a vindication of Baron Stockmar (*Quarterly Rev.* Oct. 1882), reappeared in a volume of 'Monographs' (1906).

Martin's labours as translator were singularly versatile. In 1854 and 1857 he published, from the original Danish or from the German, English versions of Oehlenschläger's romantic dramas 'Aladdin' and 'Correggio.' In 1860 he printed his translation of the 'Odes' of Horace, which, like all Martin's versions of Latin poetry, is more fluent than scholarly. This was subsequently incorporated in his 'Works of Horace' (2 vols. 1882) with the tasteful rather than learned monograph on the Roman poet which Martin contributed in 1870 to Collins's 'Ancient Classics for English Readers,' and the substance of two lectures on 'Horace and his Friends,' delivered at the Edinburgh Philosophical Institution in Oct. 1881. His 'Catullus, with Life and Notes,' followed 'Horace's Odes' in 1861, and books i.–vi. of the 'Æneid' as late as 1896. In 1862 he published his translation of Dante's 'Vita Nuova,' which he dedicated in a charming sonnet to his 'own true wife.'

German poetry occupied Martin's energies with more marked success. In Nov. 1850 he had printed in the 'Dublin University Magazine' a translation of Goethe's 'Prometheus,' and in 1865 he published a version of the 'First Part of Faust.' The 'Second Part' followed in 1886. The 'First Part' was constantly reprinted, and reached a ninth edition in 1910. A second revised edition of the 'Second Part' came out in the same year. Of the beautifully illustrated edition of the 'First Part' (1876) Queen Victoria made a Christmas present to Lord Beaconsfield. Martin's English version—one of many—of Schiller's 'Camp of Wallenstein' (*Blackwood's Mag.* Feb. 1892), although full of spirit and gaiety, wants the dignified atmosphere of the original. In 1878 appeared a translation of 'Poems and Ballads of Heinrich Heine,' and in 1889 'The Song of the Bell, and other Translations from Schiller, Goethe, Uhland and Others,' an anthology of modern German lyric poetry. No metrical or other difficulty is shirked by the translator, but there is a lack of precision and finish in the execution. A spirited translation of Friedrich Halm's (Baron von Münch-Bellighausen) 'Gladiator of Ravenna' (1854), an essentially theatrical type of German romantic drama, was printed for private circulation. It was reprinted in 1894 with 'Madonna Pia' (founded on the Marquis du Belloy's 'La Malaria' of 1853), 'King René's Daughter,' and 'The Camp.' Martin also translated the poems of Giacomo Leopardi in 1904.

Meanwhile, Martin engaged in literary labour of a different kind. In 1866, while he was occupied with his memoir of Aytoun, his friend (Sir) Arthur Helps [q.v.] recommended him to Queen Victoria to write the biography of the Prince Consort. The life had originally been entrusted to General Charles Grey, the Queen's private secretary, and Grey had published in 1868 'The Early Years of the Prince Consort,' only bringing the memoir as far as the Prince's marriage. Grey's other occupations prevented him from carrying the work further, and Helps's health unfitted him for the task. Martin's knowledge of German and his literary facility were his main recommendations. He was not personally known to the Queen, nor had he been acquainted with the Prince. He frankly stated his doubts and difficulties in a letter for the Queen's eye, but in an interview with her on 14 Nov. he accepted the task on his own condition—viz. that he should have a free hand as to both the time and the manner in which the work was carried out (*Queen Victoria as I knew her*, p. 19). The Queen, who undertook that the sifting of the documents to be placed at his disposal should be the business of herself, Grey, and Helps, placed in Martin the fullest trust. When on 10 Jan. 1868 Martin, while staying at Osborne, was confined to his room through a serious accident on the ice, his wife was invited to the palace and remained there for three weeks. Thenceforth the Queen showed Martin's wife as well as himself unceasing kindness. With him the Queen maintained until her death a very confidential intercourse and correspondence.

The first volume of the Prince's biography was published in 1875, and carried the narrative to 1848. The second volume, which appeared in 1876, largely dealt with the attacks on the Prince in the press, and his vindication in both houses of parliament. The third volume, which covered the period of the Crimean war, came out in Dec. 1877, when English relations with Russia were again strained. Martin's description of the influence which the Prince had exerted against that power and Prussia provoked a controversy as to the authority of the Crown in the constitution; Henry Dunckley [q.v. Suppl. I], writing under the pseudonym of 'Verax' in the 'Manchester Examiner and Times' and the 'Manchester Guardian,' vigorously questioned the right of the Crown to intervene in matters of policy (cf. his 'The Crown and the Cabinet,' 1878). Of Martin's fourth volume (1879) the Indian Mutiny formed the political background; and vol. v. brought to a close in 1880 the biographer's devoted labour of thirteen years (see his letter in *Queen Victoria as I knew her*, p. 8). The biography abounds in letters and papers previously unpublished and is an especially valuable contribution to current diplomatic history. Though the view taken of the Prince is highly favourable, Martin's tone is essentially candid and free from courtly adulation. Martin's services were recognised by the Queen's bestowal on him of the honours of C.B. in 1878 and of K.C.B. in 1880. A cheap edition of the biography (six parts at 6*d.* each) came out in 1881–2.

Martin followed up his 'Life of the Prince Consort' with a second effort in political biography, 'A Life of Lord Lyndhurst. From Letters and Papers in possession of his Family' (1883). It is an attempt to correct the unpleasing impression given of Lyndhurst by Lord Campbell in 'Lives of the Chancellors' (1869, vol. viii.), and although Martin's refutation wearies by its length he paints a successful portrait.

In 1881 Martin was elected lord rector of St. Andrews University, and in Oct. he delivered his inaugural address on education. During that and the next year some time was spent in Italy. In 1887 Martin and his wife made a final journey abroad to the Riviera. Until that period, when Lady Martin's health began to fail, Martin and she continued their social activities in London and Wales. In their London home between 1882 and 1887 they and their friends, including Henry Irving and Canon Ainger, took part in readings of Shakespeare, whose excellence attracted attention. The summer and autumn were still spent at Bryntysilio, where Robert Browning and other literary friends frequently sought them out. In 1896 Queen Victoria sent Martin, on his 80th birthday, the insignia of K.C.V.O. Lady Martin died at Bryntysilio on 31 Oct. 1898, and Sir Theodore devoted himself to her biography, which appeared in 1900. In 1901 he issued for private circulation 'Queen Victoria as I knew her,' which was published in 1908. His pen continued active till near the end. His last contribution to 'Blackwood' was an article on Dante's 'Paolo and Francesca,' published in 1907. For many years he was an active worker on the Royal Literary Fund, becoming a member of the fund in 1855, an auditor in 1862, a member of the general committee in 1868, and registrar in 1871. He resigned the office of registrar and his seat on the committee in 1907, but was re-elected to the committee next month. In succession to James Orchard Halliwell-Phillipps [q. v.] he became a trustee of Shakespeare's birthplace on 6 May 1889, and retained the office till his death. He was a frequent visitor to Stratford-on-Avon, and placed in the church there in 1900, in memory of his wife, a marble pulpit, designed by G. F. Bodley, R.A. In 1906 he celebrated his 90th birthday at Bryntysilio. He died there on 18 Aug. 1909, and was buried, by the side of his wife, in Brompton cemetery. He left no issue.

Martin's industry—literary as well as professional—was exceptional. In all his work he wrote everything to the last in his own hand, never employing an amanuensis. His literary versatility—both in prose and verse—has within its limits been rarely surpassed. His varied translations show unusual receptivity of mind. As a biographer he accomplished, in the 'Life of the Prince Consort,' an important piece of work which needed doing, and he did it well. A staunch conservative, he grew impatient of innovation in his old age. Although a rigorous man of business, he was generous in private charity, especially to unsuccessful authors. His romantic devotion to his wife and his faith in her genius are the most distinctive features of his career.

A portrait by Thomas Duncan of Martin at the age of ten is in the National Portrait Gallery at Edinburgh. A second portrait, painted in 1878 by James Archer, R.S.A., was presented by Sir Theodore to Mr. William Blackwood, and hangs in the 'Old Saloon' in Blackwood & Sons' publishing house at Edinburgh, among those of many other early contributors to 'Maga.' A third portrait, by Robert Herdman, R.S.A., also belongs to Mr. Blackwood. A fourth painting, by F. Dixon, was presented by Martin in 1905 to his partner, Mr. Bernard Hicks, and a fifth painting, by J. Mordecai, was given by him in 1907 to his partner Mr. W. F. Wakeford. Lord Ronald Gower, one of Martin's many friends, presented to the National Portrait Gallery a sixth painting, by F. M. Bennett, which is a bad likeness; it hangs in the east wing. In 1873 a crayon portrait was drawn by Rudolf Lehmann, and a caricature by 'Spy' appeared in 'Vanity Fair' in 1877.

[The Times, the Scotsman, and Western Morning News, 19 Aug. 1909; private information; personal knowledge.] A. W. W.

MARTIN, Sir THOMAS ACQUIN (1850–1906), industrial pioneer in India and agent-general for Afghanistan, born at Four-oaks, Sutton Coldfield, Birmingham, on 6 March 1850, was son of Patrick William Martin, leather manufacturer, of Birmingham, by his wife, Mary Anne Bridges. After education at the Oratory, Edgbaston, he entered the engineering firm of Walsh, Lovett in Birmingham, and in 1874 went out to Calcutta to start a branch for them. Possessed of exceptional business capacity, he soon founded the firm which bears his name, of Clive-street, Calcutta, and Laurence Pountney-hill, E.C. As the head of this firm he notably fostered the material development of India. The firm took over in 1889 the management of the

Bengal Iron and Steel Company, which inaugurated at Burrakur Indian production and manufacture on a capitalised basis permitting of competition with imported steel and iron. The out-turn of pig iron was then 9000 tons per annum; but the works have been modernised, rich deposits at Manharpur are being worked, and the present productive capacity is 75,000 tons yearly. The firm also pioneered the construction of light railways along district roads in India, to serve as feeders of the main lines. It built and has the management of the Howrah-Amta, Howrah-Sheakhalla, Bukhtiarpur-Behar, Baraset-Basirhat, Shahdara (Delhi)-Saharanpur, and the Arrah-Sasaram light railways, which aggregate a length of 300 miles. Many jute mills in Bengal were constructed by the firm, and up to Martin's death it had the management of the Arathoon jute mills, Calcutta. Three large collieries in Bengal, and the Hooghly Docking and Engineering Company are under its control. The Tansa duct works, providing Bombay with a constant water-supply from a lake forty miles distant, were engineered by the firm, which has carried out the water-supplies of the suburbs of Calcutta, and of a large number of Indian mofussil towns, including Allahabad, Benares, Cawnpore, Lucknow, Agra, and Srinagar (Kashmir). With Mr. Edward Thornton, F.R.I.B.A., as principal architect, it erected chiefs' palaces and important public buildings in various parts of India, and particularly in Calcutta, where they are contractors for the All-India Victoria memorial hall.

Early in 1887 Martin was appointed agent by Abdur Rahman Khan, Ameer of Afghanistan, and he sent to Kabul (Sir) Salter Pyne, the first European to reside there since the war of 1879–80 (with the exception of a French engineer who was there for a very brief period and afterwards disappeared). Pyne, on behalf of Martin's firm, built for the Ameer an arsenal, a mint, and various factories and workshops, subsequently introducing, as state monopolies, a number of modern industries.

Martin was constantly consulted by the Ameer on questions of policy, and he and his agents were able to render frequent political service to Great Britain. Abdur Rahman selected him to be chief of the staff of Prince Nasrullah Khan, his second son, on his mission to England in 1895. The stay here lasted from 24 May to 3 Sept., and in August Martin was knighted. Though the Ameer's main object in arranging the visit—the opening of direct diplomatic relations with Great Britain—was not achieved, Abdur Rahman still retained the fullest confidence in him. On his return to Kabul, Nasrullah Khan was accompanied by Martin's younger brother Frank, who succeeded Pyne as engineer-in-chief (cf. F. MARTIN, *Under the Absolute Amir*, 1907).

A man of genial manner and generous disposition, Martin was a close student of human nature. He proved his commonsense and catholicity of temper by admitting into partnership, in 1889, an able Bengali, (Sir) R. N. Mukherji, K.C.I.E., who shares with Martin's sons, Ernest and Harold, and Mr. C. W. Walsh the proprietorship of the firm. Martin, who was broken in health by severe toil in a tropical climate, spent much of his later life in Europe. He died at Binstead House, Isle of Wight, on 29 April 1906, and was buried in Ryde cemetery. A painting from a miniature is in the Calcutta office. He married on 2 April 1869, at Birmingham, Sarah Ann, daughter of John Humphrey Harrby, of Hoarwithy, Herefordshire, who survives with a daughter and five sons, four in the firm, and Captain Cuthbert Thomas, Highland light infantry.

[Ameer Abdur Rahman's autobiography, 2 vols. 1900; Gray's At the Court of the Ameer, 1905; Cyclopædia of India, Cal., 1905; V. Chirol's Indian Unrest, 1910; Admn. Rept. Ind. Rlys. for 1910; The Times, 1 and 14 May 1906; Englishman (Calcutta), 17 Feb. 1912; Birmingham Post, 2 May 1906; private information.] F. H. B.

MARWICK, SIR JAMES DAVID (1826–1908), legal and historical writer, born at Leith on 15 July 1826, was eldest son of William Marwick, merchant of Kirkwall, and Margaret, daughter of James Garioch, also a merchant there. Educated at Kirkwall grammar school, he removed in 1842 to Edinburgh, where he was apprenticed as clerk to James B. Watt, solicitor before the supreme courts (whose daughter he married later). He also attended the law classes at Edinburgh University. Subsequently he became a lawyer's clerk at Dundee and, qualifying as a procurator, he, in partnership with William Barry, son of the town clerk, carried on legal business in Dundee till 1855. In that year Marwick returned to Edinburgh to found with the son of his first employer, J. B. Watt, then lately dead, the firm of Watt and Marwick, which soon gained a high position. In 1857 he entered the Edinburgh town council. Before his three years' term was complete the office of town clerk fell vacant. Town councillors were prohibited from accepting any paid appointment under the council till they had been a year out of office. But the post was kept vacant till Marwick was eligible, and in December 1860 he was chosen to fill it.

Marwick remained town clerk of Edinburgh until 1873, and became during that period a chief authority on Scottish municipal law and practice. On 11 March 1873 he was appointed town clerk of Glasgow at a salary of 2500*l.* (raised afterwards to 3500*l.*), with a retiring allowance of 1500*l.* after fifteen years' service. At Glasgow Marwick carried out the extension of the city by the annexation of fourteen suburban burghs. This labour, begun in 1881, was completed in 1891; and in 1893 he drafted the enactment whereby Glasgow was made a county. He resigned the office of town clerk of Glasgow in 1903.

Marwick was the recipient of many honours. In 1878 he was made an LL.D. of Glasgow University; he was knighted in 1888; in 1893 he was presented with the freedom of the burgh of Kirkwall. In 1864 he was elected F.R.S.Edinburgh.

He died at Glasgow on 24 March 1908, and was buried at Warriston cemetery, Edinburgh. He married in 1855 Jane, third daughter of James B. Watt; she survived him with two sons and five daughters. Before leaving Edinburgh in 1873 Marwick's wife was presented with a portrait of her husband, painted by Robert Herdman, R.S.A. Of two busts by George S. Templeton, R.A., publicly subscribed for in 1905, one in marble was given to Glasgow Art Galleries and the other in bronze was retained by Lady Marwick.

Marwick was a voluminous writer, chiefly upon Scottish municipal history. He was one of the founders of the Scottish Burgh Record Society, Edinburgh, and edited the publications (many of which were compiled by himself) from 1868 till 1897. His principal works are: 1. 'Extracts from the Burgh Records of Edinburgh, 1403–1589,' Scottish Burgh Record Society, 4 vols., and index vol. 1869–92. 2. 'Observations on the Law and Practice of Municipal Corporations in Scotland,' 1879. 3. 'Charters and Documents relating to the City of Edinburgh, 1143–1540,' Scot. Burgh Rec. Soc. 1871. 4. 'Extracts from the Records of the Burgh of Glasgow, 1573–1662,' 2 vols., Scot. Burgh Rec. Soc. 1876–81. 5. 'Miscellany of the Scottish Burgh Record Society,' edited 1881. 6. 'Report on Markets and Fairs in Scotland, prepared for the Commission,' 1890. 7. 'Charters and Documents relating to the Collegiate Church of the Holy Trinity and the Trinity Hospital, Edinburgh, 1460–1661,' Scot. Burgh Rec. Soc. 1891. 8. 'Charters and Documents relating to the City of Glasgow, 1175–1649,' 3 vols., Scot. Burgh Rec. Soc. 1894–99, 1906. 9. 'The River Clyde and the Harbour of Glasgow,' 1898. 10. 'The Water Supply of the City of Glasgow,' 1901. 11. 'Extracts from the Records of the Burgh of Glasgow, 1691–1717,' jointly with Robert Renwick, Scot. Burgh Rec. Soc. 1908. Posthumously published were: 12. 'The River Clyde and the Clyde Burghs,' Scot. Burgh Rec. Soc., with portrait, and memoir by John Gray M'Kendrick, 4to, 1909. 13. 'Edinburgh Guilds and Crafts,' Scot. Burgh Rec. Soc. 1909. 14. 'History of the Collegiate Church and Hospital of the Holy Trinity and the Trinity Hospital, Edinburgh, 1460–1661' (founded on No 7, supra), Scot. Burgh Rec. Soc. 1911. 15. 'Early Glasgow,' ed. by Robert Renwick, 1911. Marwick was editor of the 'Records of the Convention of Royal Burghs of Scotland' from 1866 till 1890.

[A Retrospect, autobiography, privately printed, 1874; Glasgow Herald, and Scotsman, 25 March 1908; Memoir by John Gray M'Kendrick, in above posthumous volume; private information.] A. H. M.

MASHAM, first Baron. [See Lister, Samuel Cunliffe (1815–1906), inventor.]

MASKELYNE, MERVYN HERBERT NEVIL STORY- (1823–1911), metallurgist. [See Story-Maskelyne.]

MASSEY, GERALD (1828–1907), poet, born in a hut at Gamble Wharf, on the canal near Tring, on 29 May 1828, was son of William Massey, a canal boatman, by his wife Mary. His father brought up a large family on a weekly wage of some ten shillings. Massey said of himself that he 'had no childhood.' After a scanty education at the national school at Tring, Massey was when eight years of age put to work at a silk mill there. His hours were from 5 A.M. to 6 P.M., and he earned from ninepence to one shilling and threepence a week. He then tried straw-plaiting. But the marshy districts of Buckinghamshire induced ague, and at fifteen he found employment as an errand-boy in London. Reading was an absorbing passion with him from childhood, and as a lad he developed poetical ambitions. He devoted his leisure in London to a study of Cobbett's 'French without a Master,' and of books by Tom Paine, Volney, and Howitt. As early as 1848 he published with a bookseller at Tring a first volume, 'Poems and Chansons,' and sold some 250 copies at a shilling each to his fellow-townsfolk. The revolutionary spirit of the times caught his enthusiasm, and joining the Chartists he applied his pen to the support of their cause. With one John Bedford Leno, a Chartist printer of Uxbridge, he edited in 1849, at twenty-one, a paper written by working-men called 'The Spirit of Freedom.' Next year he contributed some forcible verse to 'Cooper's Journal,' a venture of the Chartist, Thomas Cooper [q. v.] (cf. COOPER'S *Life*, 4th edit. 1873, p. 320). But Massey's sympathies veered to the religious side of the reforming movement, and in the same year he associated himself with the Christian Socialists under the leadership of Frederick Denison Maurice, who wrote of him at the time to Charles Kingsley as 'not quite an Alton Locke,' but with 'some real stuff in him' (MAURICE, *Life of F. D. Maurice*, ii. 36). Massey acted as secretary of the Christian Socialist Board and contributed verse to its periodical 'The Christian Socialist.' During the same year (1850) he brought out a second volume of verse, 'Voices of Freedom and Lyrics of Love,' which showed genuine poetic feeling, although the style was rough and undisciplined. Next year he welcomed Kossuth to England in a poem, and he enthusiastically championed the cause of Italian unity.

Massey fully established his position as a poet of liberty, labour, and the people with a third volume, 'The Ballad of Babe Christabel and other Poems,' which appeared in Feb. 1854. The book, which dealt with conjugal and parental affection as well as with democratic aspirations, passed through five editions within a year, and was reprinted in New York, where Massey's position was soon better assured than in London. Despite obvious signs of defective education and taste, Massey's poetry deserved its welcome. Hepworth Dixon in the 'Athenæum' (4 Feb. 1854) called him 'a genuine songster.' The best-known poets of the day acknowledged his 'lyrical impulse and rich imagination.' Alexander Smith likened him to Burns, while Walter Savage Landor in the 'Morning Advertiser' compared him with Keats, Hafiz, and Shakespeare as a sonneteer. Tennyson was hardly less impressed, although he thought that the new poet made 'our good old English crack and sweat for it occasionally' (TENNYSON'S *Life*, i. 405). Ruskin regarded Massey's work 'as a helpful and precious gift to the working classes.' Sydney Dobell, a warm admirer, became a close personal friend, and Massey named his first-born son after him.

To 'Babe Christabel' there succeeded five further volumes of verse, viz. 'War Waits' (1855, two editions), poems on the Crimean War; 'Craigcrook Castle' (1856); 'Robert Burns, a Song, and other Lyrics' (1859); 'Havelock's March,' poems on the Indian Mutiny (1860); and 'A Tale of Eternity and other Poems' (1869). The poem on Burns was sent in for the Crystal Palace competition at the Burns centenary in 1859, and although it failed to win the prize, was placed in the first six of the competing works. [See KNOX, Mrs. ISA.] Other of the volumes include ballads breathing an admirable martial and patriotic ardour. Massey's ballad 'Sir Richard Grenville's Last Fight' is for its fine spirit worthy of a place beside Tennyson's 'Revenge,' which was written much later, and his tribute to England's command of the sea in 'Sea Kings' clearly adumbrates Rudyard Kipling's 'Song of the Dead' in 'The Seven Seas' (1896). Massey's narrative verse embodies mystical speculation and was less successful; his range and copiousness suffered from laxity of technique; but both in England and America he long enjoyed general esteem. In 1857 Ticknor & Field of Boston published his 'Complete Poetical Works,' with a biographical sketch, and in 1861 a similar collection came out in London with illustrations and a memoir by Samuel Smiles. In his lectures on 'Self-help' in 1859 Smiles set Massey high among his working-class heroes. After 1860 Massey gradually abandoned poetry for other interests which he came to deem more important, and his vogue as a poet decayed. In 1899 Massey's eldest daughter, Christabel, collected for her father his chief poems in two volumes under the title of 'My Lyrical Life.' This anthology goes far to justify the admiration of an earlier generation.

Meanwhile Massey sought a livelihood from journalism. For a time he worked with John Chapman [q. v. Suppl. I], the radical publisher in the Strand. 'George Eliot' who was also in Chapman's employ (1851–3) afterwards based on Massey's career some features of her 'Felix Holt—

the Radical' (1866). From 1854, on the invitation of the editor, Hepworth Dixon, Massey wrote occasionally for the 'Athenæum.' He was also a contributor to the 'Leader,' which Thornton Leigh Hunt edited. Charles Dickens accepted verse from him for 'All the Year Round.' To the first number of 'Good Words' in 1860 he sent a poem on Garibaldi, and Alexander Strahan, the publisher of that periodical, gave him valuable encouragement.

Yet despite his popularity and his industry, Massey, who was now married, found it no easy task to bring up a family on the proceeds of his pen. With a view to improving his position, he had in 1854 left London for Edinburgh, where he wrote for 'Chambers's Journal' and Hugh Miller's 'Witness.' There, too, he took to lecturing at literary institutes on poetry, Pre-Raphaelite art, and Christian socialism. His earnestness drew large audiences. In 1857 he moved from Edinburgh to Monk's Green, Hertfordshire, and then to Brantwood, Coniston, which was at the time the property of a friend, William James Linton [q. v. Suppl. I]; it was acquired by Ruskin in 1871. During four years' subsequent residence at Rickmansworth, Massey found a helpful admirer in Lady Marian Alford [q. v. Suppl. I], who resided with her son the second Earl Brownlow at Ashridge Park, Berkhamsted. Lord Brownlow provided him in 1862 with a house on his estate, called Ward's Hurst, near Little Gaddesden. There Massey remained till 1877. In 1867 the second Earl Brownlow died, and his brother and successor married next year. Both episodes were celebrated by Massey in privately printed volumes of verse. While at Ward's Hurst, Massey closely studied Shakespeare's sonnets, on which he contributed an article to the 'Quarterly Review' in April 1864. He argued that Shakespeare wrote most of his sonnets for his patron Southampton. He amplified his view in a volume called 'Shakespeare's Sonnets never before interpreted' in 1866. This he rewrote in 1888 under the title of 'The Secret Drama of Shakespeare's Sonnets.' Despite his diffuseness, self-confidence, and mystical theorising, Massey brings together much valuable Shakespearean research.

At Ward's Hurst, too, Massey developed an absorbing interest in psychic phenomena. In 1871 he issued a somewhat credulous book on spiritualism which he afterwards withdrew. Subsequently he made three lecturing tours through America. The first tour lasted from Sept. 1873 to May 1874, and extended to California and Canada. The second tour, which began in Oct. 1883 and ended in Nov. 1885, included Australia and New Zealand, as well as America. A third American tour opened in Sept. 1888, but the fatal illness of a daughter brought it to an early close. His lectures dealt with many branches of poetry and art, but they were chiefly concerned with mesmerism, spiritualism, and mystical interpretation of the Bible. He printed privately many of his discourses. His faith in spiritualistic phenomena was lasting, and monopolised most of his later thought.

Massey's resources, which were always small, were augmented in 1863, on Lord Palmerston's recommendation, by a civil list pension of 70*l.*, to which an addition of 30*l.* was made by Lord Salisbury in 1887. On leaving Ward's Hurst he lived successively at New Southgate (1877–90), at Dulwich (1890–3), and from 1893 at South Norwood. His closing years were devoted to a study of old Egyptian civilisation, in which he thought to trace psychic and spiritualistic problems to their source and to find their true solution. 'A Book of the Beginnings,' in two massive quarto volumes, appeared in 1881, and a sequel of the same dimensions, 'The Natural Genesis,' appeared in 1883. Finally he published 'Ancient Egypt the Light of the World, in twelve books' (1907). Massey believed that these copious, rambling, and valueless compilations deserved better of posterity than his poetry.

Massey died on 29 Oct. 1907 at Redcot, South Norwood hill, and was buried in Old Southgate cemetery. He was twice married: (1) on 8 July 1850 to Rosina Jane Knowles (buried in Little Gaddesden churchyard on 23 March 1866), by whom he had three daughters and a son; (2) in Jan. 1868 to Eva Byron, by whom he had four daughters and a son. Two daughters of each marriage survived their father.

[Massey's Poetical Works, with memoir by Samuel Smiles, 1861; J. Churton Collins's Studies in Poetry and Criticism, 1905, pp. 142–67; A. H. Miles, Poets and Poetry of the Century, v. 347 seq.; Allibone's Dict. Engl. Lit.; The Times, 30 Oct. 1907; Athenæum, 9 Nov. 1907; Review of Reviews, Dec. 1907 (with portrait); Book Monthly (by James Milne), July 1905 and Sept. 1907 (with portrait); private information from Miss Christabel Massey, the eldest surviving daughter.] S. L.

MASSON, DAVID (1822–1907), biographer and editor, born at Aberdeen on 2 Dec. 1822, was son of William Masson, stonecutter in that city, and Sarah Mather, his wife. After education at the grammar school of Aberdeen (1831–5) under James Melvin [q. v.], he matriculated in October 1835 at Marischal College and Aberdeen University, and at the close of his course, in April 1839, took the first place among the Masters of Arts of his year. With the intention of qualifying for the ministry of the Church of Scotland, he proceeded to Edinburgh and spent three years (1839–42) in the divinity hall of the university, where Dr. Thomas Chalmers [q. v.] was one of his teachers; but towards the close of his curriculum, during the stir of the Disruption, he resolved not to enter the church. He returned to Aberdeen and undertook (1842–4) the editorship of a weekly journal, 'The Banner.' In the summer of 1843 he visited London for the first time as the guest of his fellow-townsman Alexander Bain [q. v. Suppl. II], and made the acquaintance of Mrs. Carlyle. In the following year, during his second visit to London, he met Thomas Carlyle [q. v.], who introduced him to the editor of 'Fraser's Magazine,' in which his first article appeared in that year. From 1844 to 1847 he was engaged in Edinburgh on the staff of W. and R. Chambers, publishers, in the preparation of their Miscellanies and Educational Series. A little book on the history of Rome, written in 1847, was published in 1848; and in the same year he brought out, anonymously, another on ancient history. Other text-books on mediæval history (1855) and modern history (1856) followed after his direct association with the firm of Chambers had come to an end.

In 1847 Masson removed to London and began to contribute to the magazines and reviews, including 'Fraser's,' the 'Quarterly,' the 'Westminster,' the 'Leader,' and the 'North British,' and to the 'Encyclopædia Britannica.' He enjoyed the friendship of the Carlyles, and enlarged his circle of literary acquaintances through his membership of 'Our Club,' where his companions included Thackeray, Douglas Jerrold, Charles Knight, Mark Lemon, Dr. Doran, Peter Cunningham, and others. In these early years of hard work he found relaxation with the corps of the London Scottish volunteers; and in 1851–2 he acted as secretary of the London Society of the Friends of Italy.

In 1853, the year of his marriage, he was appointed professor of English literature in University College, London, in succession to Arthur Clough [q. v.]; and in 1856 he published a volume of 'Essays, Biographical and Critical: Chiefly on English Poets.' This was followed in 1859 by his 'British Novelists and their Styles,' and by the first volume of an extensive 'Life of Milton, narrated in connection with the Political, Ecclesiastical, and Literary History of his Time.' On the latter work (1859–80, 6 vols.) his reputation as a biographer and historian chiefly rests, and there must be few rivals in this *genre* in any literature so painstaking and thorough in the recovery of the setting of a great career. The book was received with general approbation, and such criticism as has suggested that the reader cannot see the poet in the crowd of contemporary interests has misjudged the author's deliberate purpose. The book remains the standard authority. To the labours of this undertaking Masson added, towards the close of 1858, the task of starting and editing a new magazine for Alexander Macmillan, the first number of which appeared on 1 Nov. 1859, two months before Thackeray inaugurated the rival 'Cornhill.' Its title, 'Macmillan's Magazine,' was 'Editor David's' suggestion, and was accepted by the publisher after a long friendly battle for the name 'The Round Table.' Shortly before the issue of the first number, Masson and Macmillan spent three days in September 1859 with Tennyson in the Isle of Wight, and on the return journey they visited Kingsley at Eversley. Masson continued to edit the 'Magazine' with success till 1867, when his place was taken by Sir George Grove [q. v. Suppl. I]. In the autumn of 1863 he undertook, in addition, the editorship of the short-lived 'Reader.' Two years later he published a volume of essays entitled 'Recent British Philosophy.'

On the death of William Edmonstoune Aytoun [q. v.] in 1865, Masson was appointed professor of rhetoric and English literature in the university of Edinburgh; and from that date to the close he resided in Edinburgh. There he completed his 'Life of Milton'; edited the works of 'Goldsmith' (1869), 'Milton' (1874), and 'De Quincey' (1889–90); wrote an exhaustive biography of 'Drummond of Hawthornden' (1873); and recast and reissued the matter of the essays of 1856, with additions, in three separate volumes entitled 'Wordsworth, Shelley, and Keats,' 'The Three Devils,' and 'Chatterton' (1874). To the same period belong, among other works, his volume on De Quincey for the 'English Men of Letters' series (1878), and 'Edinburgh Sketches and Memories' (1892), a reprint of magazine articles. During the thirty years of academic life in Edinburgh (1865–95), where more than 5000 students passed through his class-room, he achieved a popularity which remains a pleasant tradition in Scottish university life. From 1867 he interested himself in the movements for the 'higher education' and the medical education of women, and gave annually, under the auspices of the 'Association for the University Education of Women' (1868), a course of lectures on English literature until the admission of women to the Scottish universities. The Masson Hall, a residence for women undergraduates, erected by the committee of this association, and opened on 24 November 1897, bears his name, in recognition of his labours. From 1880 to 1899 he acted as editor of the 'Privy Council Register of Scotland,' in succession to John Hill Burton [q. v.], and contributed historical introductions or digests to each of the thirteen volumes which he supervised; and in 1886 he delivered the Rhind lectures before the Society of Antiquaries of Scotland. In 1893, on the death of William Forbes Skene [q. v.], he was appointed historiographer-royal for Scotland; and on 12 Feb. 1896 the Royal Scottish Academy elected him an honorary member and professor of ancient literature. He was an honorary graduate of the universities of Aberdeen (LL.D.), Dublin (Litt.D.), and Moscow. From 1869 to 1878 he resided at 10 Regent Terrace, Edinburgh (where he was visited by John Stuart Mill and Carlyle); and from 1882 at 58 Great King Street. His closing years were spent at Lockharton Gardens, Edinburgh. He died on the night of Sunday, 6 Oct. 1907, and was buried in the Grange cemetery, Edinburgh.

Masson's long association with Carlyle and his admiration of his friend's genius have to some extent obscured the individuality of his own work; and an alleged physical likeness, more imagined than true to fact, has encouraged the popular notion of discipleship. He was too independent in character to owe much to another, and the trait by which his authority was won—sincerity in workmanship, that 'indisputable air of truth' which is felt in everything he wrote and did—was not derived from, and hardly confirmed by, the intercourse at Chelsea. In his literary work he sometimes sacrificed the claims of art to the importunities of research; yet no sound judgment could deny the accuracy, the sanity of judgment, and the geniality of critical temper, which distinguish his work as historian and essayist. On his large circle of friends and pupils he left a lasting impression of vigorous personality and high purpose. From his prime, but especially in his later years, he was, if not the dictator, the confidant in every important literary and public enterprise, and by his broad-minded patriotism, untainted by the parochialism which he heartily condemned, was accepted by his contemporaries as the representative of what counts for best in Scottish character.

He married, on 27 Aug. 1853, Emily Rosaline, eldest daughter of Charles and Eliza Orme, at whose house in Avenue Road, Regent's Park, he had been one of a group of writers and painters (including Coventry Patmore, Dante Gabriel Rossetti, Thomas Woolner, and Holman Hunt), in sympathy with the Pre-Raphaelite Brotherhood. They had one son, Orme, professor of chemistry in the university of Melbourne and F.R.S., and three daughters, Flora, editor of two posthumous works by her father, Helen (Mrs. Lovell Gulland), and Rosaline, author of several books.

Sir George Reid painted three portraits of Masson: (*a*) a three-quarter length in oil, presented to him by Lord Rosebery in the name of the subscribers on 23 Nov. 1897, on the occasion of his retirement (now in the possession of Professor Orme Masson); (*b*) a smaller canvas, in oil, commissioned by Mr. Irvine Smith for his private collection, and now in the possession of Mr. Charles Green, publisher, Edinburgh; (*c*) a canvas, in oil, presented by the artist to the National Portrait Gallery, Edinburgh, and there preserved. An etching ($12\frac{1}{2}'' \times 16''$) was made by F. Huth in 1898 from the Irvine Smith canvas; and an etched portrait-sketch by William Hole appears in 'Quasi Cursores,' published in 1884, on the occasion of the tercentenary of the university of Edinburgh. Two portraits (from photographs of Masson in later life) were published in 1911: (*a*) in the Scottish History Society's edition of Craig's 'De Unione,' and (*b*) in the posthumous volume of 'Memories of Two Cities.' A marble bust by J. P. Macgillivray, R.S.A., presented by subscription to the university of Edinburgh in 1897, is less successful than the portraits by Reid and Huth.

Masson's published writings comprise:

1. 'History of Rome' (Chambers's Educational Course), 1848. 2. 'Ancient History' (the same), 1848. 3. 'The British Museum, Historical and Descriptive' (Chambers's Instructive and Entertaining Library), 1848. 4. 'College Education and Self Education. A Lecture,' 1854. 5. 'Mediæval History' (Chambers's Educational Course), 1855. 6. 'Modern History' (the same), 1856. 7. 'Essays, Biographical and Critical: chiefly on English Poets,' 1856 (see Nos. 16, 17 and 18). 8. 'British Novelists and their Styles,' 1859. 9. 'Life of Milton, narrated in connection with the Political, Ecclesiastical, and Literary History of his Time,' vol. i. 1859; vol. ii. appeared in 1871; the sixth and last in 1880; and a new edition of the first in 1881. 10. 'Recent British Philosophy,' 1865; 3rd edit. 1877. 11. 'The State of Learning in Scotland. A Lecture,' 1866. 12. 'University Teaching for Women,' introductory lectures to the second series of lectures in Shandwick Place, 1868. 13. 'The Works of Goldsmith' (Globe edit.), 1869. 14. 'Drummond of Hawthornden,' 1873. 15. 'The Poetical Works of John Milton,' 3 vols. 1874, re-issued in 1877, 1878, 1882, 1890, and in 3 vols. in the 'Golden Treasury' series, in a separate edition in 1882, and later in the 'Eversley' series. 16. 'Wordsworth, Shelley, and Keats, and other Essays,' 1874. 17. 'The Three Devils: Luther's, Milton's, and Goethe's. With other Essays,' 1874 (new edit. 1875). 18. 'Chatterton: a story of the year 1770,' 1874; new edit. 1899; Nos. 16, 17 and 18 are reprints, with additions, of No. 7. 19. 'The Quarrel between the Earl of Manchester and Oliver Cromwell' (Camden Society), 1875. 20. Introduction to 'Three Centuries of English Poetry' (an anthology by his wife), 1876. 21. 'The Poetical Works of John Milton' (Globe edit.), 1877. 22. 'De Quincey' ('English Men of Letters' series), 1878; revised 1885. 23. 'Register of the Privy Council of Scotland,' 1st series, vols. iii.-xiv., 2nd series, vol. i. (13 vols. covering the years 1578–1627), 1880–1899. 24. 'The Vicar of Wakefield' (Globe readings), 1883. 25. 'Carlyle personally and in his Writings. Two Lectures,' 1885. 26. 'Select Essays of De Quincey,' 1888. 27. 'The Collected Writings of Thomas De Quincey, a New and Enlarged Edition,' (14 vols.), 1889–90. 28. 'Edinburgh Sketches and Memories' (reprints of articles), 1892. 29. 'James Melvin, Rector of the Grammar School of Aberdeen,' Aberdeen, 1895 (reprinted from 'Macmillan's Magazine,' 1864). 30. 'Memories of London in the Forties,' published posthumously and edited by his daughter, Flora Masson, 1908, containing reprints from 'Blackwood's' and 'Macmillan's' magazines. 31. 'Memories of Two Cities,' posthumously edited by Flora Masson, 1911. Masson also contributed the first article (on Milton) in a volume entitled 'In the Footsteps of the Poets,' published by Messrs. Isbister & Co. (n.d.).

[Autobiographic references in works, especially Nos. 25, 28, 29, and 30; Scotsman, 24 Nov. 1897 (which contains Lord Rosebery's eulogy on the occasion of the presentation of the portrait) and 8 Oct. 1907; The Times, 8 Oct. 1907; Who's Who, 1903; Carlyle's Letters, 1889; Letters of Alexander Macmillan, 1908; J. M. Barrie, An Edinburgh Eleven, 1889; Quasi Cursores, 1884; Strand Magazine, Feb. 1896 (with reproduction of a series of early photographs); arts. by Miss Flora Masson in Cornhill, Nov. 1910 and June 1911; information supplied by Miss Rosaline Masson from family papers; personal recollections.] G. G. S.

MASSY, WILLIAM GODFREY DUNHAM (1838–1906), lieutenant-general, born at Grantstown, co. Tipperary, Ireland, on 24 Nov. 1838, was eldest of four sons of Major Henry William Massy (1816–1895) of Grantstown and Clonmaine, co. Tipperary, by his wife Maria, daughter of Patrick Cahill. Educated at Trinity College, Dublin, he graduated B.A. in 1859, and was made LL.D. in 1873.

Meanwhile he had entered the army as ensign on 27 October 1854, and was promoted lieutenant on 9 February 1855. Going out to the Crimea, he served at the latter part of the siege of Sevastopol, was under fire at the battle of Tchernaya, and commanded the grenadiers of the 19th regiment at the assault of the Redan on 8 Sept. During the last engagement he showed great gallantry. Returning to the trenches for reinforcements, he was dangerously wounded by a ball which passed through his left thigh, shattering the bone. Being left on the ground, he fell during the ensuing night into the hands of the enemy, who abandoned him, believing him to be mortally wounded. He was finally rescued, and recovered after a confinement to his camp stretcher of nearly six months. His courage was commended in a special despatch by Sir James Simpson [q. v.], and he became popularly known as 'Redan' Massy. Promoted captain on 20 Feb. 1860, he was awarded the 5th class of the Legion of Honour and Turkish medal.

In 1863 he obtained his majority, and served as assistant adjutant-general in India. On his promotion as lieutenant-colonel he commanded in India the 5th royal Irish lancers from 1871 to 1879. On 4 Sept. 1879 Massy was proceeding with a small escort to Kabul, when the news of the massacre of Sir Louis Cavagnari [q. v.] reached him at Shutargarden; and he at once telegraphed the news to Sir Frederick (afterwards Lord) Roberts. During the Afghan war of 1879–80 he commanded a cavalry brigade and took a prominent part in the battle of Charasiab on 6 Oct. 1879, capturing 75 pieces of Afghan artillery. During the subsequent operations in the Charde Valley, Massy was despatched in pursuit of the enemy (7 Oct.), but he failed to cut off the Afghan line of retreat. Next taking part in the actions round Kabul, he was ordered (11 Dec. 1879) to start from Sherpur with the cavalry under his command and effect a junction with General Macpherson's brigade. Advancing too far, Massy was cut off by 10,000 Afghans at Killa Kazi, and after an unsuccessful charge and the abandonment of guns he was extricated from a difficult position by the timely arrival of the main body. General Roberts in his report laid the responsibility for the disaster on Massy, who was severely censured and removed from his command. General Roberts's strictures were regarded as unduly harsh, and Massy was soon reappointed to a brigade by George, duke of Cambridge, the commander-in-chief (*Despatches, Lond. Gaz.* 16 Jan. and 4 May 1880). He received the Afghan medal with two clasps.

He became major-general on 23 Aug. 1886 and was nominated C.B. on 21 June 1887. He held the command of the troops in Ceylon from 1888 to 1893, when he attained the rank of lieutenant-general. On 4 Oct. 1896 he obtained the colonelcy of the 5th royal Irish lancers, and on 1 April 1898 was placed on the retired list. He received the reward for distinguished service. He was a J.P. and D.L. for co. Tipperary, and high sheriff in 1899. He died on 20 Sept. 1906 at the family residence, Grantstown Hall, Tipperary. He married in 1869 Elizabeth Jane, eldest daughter of Major-general Sir Thomas Seaton, K.C.B., of Ackworth, Suffolk, and widow of George Arnold, by whom he left issue one daughter, Gertrude Annette Seaton, who married in 1893 Colonel James George Cockburn (*d.* 1900).

[The Times, 21 and 22 Sept. 1906; Lord Roberts, Forty-one Years in India, 30th edit. 1898; H. B. Hanna, The Second Afghan War, iii. 1910; S. P. Oliver, The Second Afghan War, 1908; J. Duke, Recollections of the Kabul Campaign, 1883; Septans, Les expéditions anglaises en Asie, Paris, 1897, p. 213 *seq.*; Burke's Landed Gentry of Ireland, 1904; Hart's and Official Army Lists.]

H. M. V.

MASTERS, MAXWELL TYLDEN (1833–1907), botanist, born at Canterbury on 15 April 1833, was youngest son of William Masters (1796–1874), a nurseryman of scientific ability, known as the raiser of elm and other seedlings, as a hybridiser of passion flowers, aloes and cacti, and as the compiler of a valuable catalogue, 'Hortus Duroverni' (1831); he corresponded with Sir William Hooker [q. v.] from 1846 to 1862, became alderman and mayor of Canterbury, and was founder of the museum there in 1823.

Masters, after education at King's College, London, of which he became an associate, qualified L.S.A. in 1854 and M.R.C.S. in 1856. He graduated M.D. *in absentia* at St. Andrews in 1862.

While at King's College he attended the lectures of Edward Forbes [q. v.] and those of Lindley at the Chelsea physic garden. On the acquisition of the Fielding herbarium by the university of Oxford, Masters was appointed sub-curator under Dr. Daubeny, the professor of botany, and his first paper, one on air-cells in aquatic plants, was communicated to the Ashmolean Society in 1853. He delivered courses of lectures on botany at the London and Royal Institutions, and was an unsuccessful candidate in 1854 for the botanical chair which Edward Forbes vacated at King's College on his appointment to Edinburgh; Robert Bentley [q. v. Suppl. I] was elected. From 1855 to 1868 Masters was lecturer on botany at St. George's Hospital medical school. In 1856 he began to practise as a general practitioner at Peckham.

It was at this period that his attention was first drawn to the study of malformations, especially those of the flower, and their connection with the theory of the foliar nature of its parts. His first teratological paper, one on a monstrosity in Saponaria, was published in 1857 in the 'Journal of the Linnean Society,' of which he became a fellow in 1860. After other preliminary papers, his volume on 'Vegetable Teratology,' to which he was prompted by his friend Samuel James Salter, F.R.S. (1825–97), and whick was on the whole his most original contribution to science, was issued by the

Ray Society in 1869. Although the author never had leisure to prepare a second edition, he furnished many additions to the German version published in 1886, and in 1893 he prepared a descriptive catalogue of the specimens of vegetable teratology in the museum of the Royal College of Surgeons. On the death of Lindley, its founder, in November 1865, Masters, whose elder brother William was associated with the 'Gardeners' Chronicle' at its establishment in 1841, was appointed principal editor of that journal, and henceforth the horticultural side of botany was his dominant interest for life. Under his direction the paper maintained a high standard. Botanists of eminence were among the writers, and he encouraged beginners. Masters acted as secretary to the International Horticultural Congress of 1866, and edited its 'Proceedings.' Out of the large surplus, Lindley's library was purchased for the nation and vested in trustees, of whom Masters was chairman, whilst 1000*l*. was given to the Gardeners' Royal Benevolent Institution, in which Masters always took keen interest. He was an assiduously active supporter of the Royal Horticultural Society, and succeeded Sir Joseph Dalton Hooker [q. v. Suppl. II] as chairman of the scientific committee. He kept in close touch with the progress of horticulture on the Continent.

Masters continued to work at pure botany, studying in the Kew herbarium from 1865. He was a large contributor to Lindley and Moore's 'Treasury of Botany' (1866; revised edit. 1873), elaborated the Malvaceæ and allied orders and the passion-flowers for Oliver's 'Flora of Tropical Africa' (vol. i. 1868; vol. ii. 1871), and the passion-flowers for the 'Flora Brasiliensis' (1872); and after much study, prepared a monograph on the same family Restiaceæ for De Candolle's supplement to the 'Prodromus' (1878). On the conifers, which divided his chief attention with the passion-flowers, he wrote in the 'Journals' of the Linnean and Horticultural Societies, the 'Journal of Botany,' and in the 'Gardeners' Chronicle,' and in 1892 he presided over the Conifer Conference of the Horticultural Society. He also contributed to Hooker's 'Flora of British India' and to his edition of Harvey's 'South African Plants,' and to Sir William Thiselton-Dyer's 'Flora Capensis.'

As lecturer and examiner, Masters knew the requirements of students, and met them successfully in thorough revisions of Henfrey's 'Elementary Course of Botany,' which he brought abreast of the time (2nd edit. 1870; 3rd edit. 1878, with the section on fungi re-written by George Milne Murray [q. v. Suppl. II]; 4th edit. in 1884, with the sections relating to the cryptogamia re-written by Alfred William Bennett [q. v. Suppl. II]). Masters also published two primers, 'Botany for Beginners' (1872) and 'Plant Life' (1883), both of which were translated into French, German, and Russian, and he contributed articles on horticulture and other subjects to 'Encyclopædia Britannica' (9th edit.).

Masters was elected a fellow of the Royal Society in 1870, and a correspondent of the Institute of France in 1888; and was also a chevalier of the order of Leopold. He died at the Mount, Ealing, on 30 May 1907. His body was cremated at Woking. In 1858 he married Ellen, daughter of William Tress, by whom he had four children. His wife and two daughters survived him.

His services have been commemorated by the endowment of an annual series of Masters lectures in connection with the Royal Horticultural Society.

[Gardeners' Chronicle, xli. (1907), pp. 368, 377, 398, 418, by William Botting Hemsley (with two portraits); Kew Bulletin, 1907, pp. 325–334, with bibliography.] G. S. B.

MATHESON, GEORGE (1842–1906), theologian and hymn writer, known as 'the blind preacher,' born at 39 Abbotsford Place, Glasgow, on 27 March 1842, was the eldest son in the family of five sons and three daughters of George Matheson, a prosperous Glasgow merchant. His mother, Jane Matheson, his father's second cousin, was the eldest daughter of John Matheson of the Fereneze Print Works, Barrhead. As a child he suffered much from defective eyesight, and while a boy he became blind. This calamity did not deter him from an early resolve to enter the ministry.

After attending two private schools, he proceeded in 1853 to Glasgow Academy, where, notwithstanding his disability, he gained a competent knowledge of the classics, French, and German, and carried off many prizes. At Glasgow University, which he entered in 1857, he had a distinguished career, graduating B.A. in 1861, the last occasion on which the degree was granted, with 'honourable distinction in philosophy,' and proceeding M.A. in 1862. In the latter year he passed to the divinity hall, where he was much influenced by John Caird [q. v. Suppl. I].

In January 1867, after being licensed by the presbytery of Glasgow, he was appointed assistant to the Rev. Dr. MacDuff of Sandyford church, Glasgow, and on 8 April 1868 became minister of Innellan church on the shores of the Firth of Clyde, then a chapel of ease in the parish of Dunoon, but through Matheson's efforts soon erected into a parish church. There Matheson was minister for eighteen years, and his preaching gifts rapidly matured. For a time he grew dissatisfied with the calvinistic theology in which he was brought up, and according to his own account was inclined to reject all religion (cf. *Life of Matheson*, pp. 121–2). But a study of the Hegelian philosophy saved him from agnosticism. Innellan afforded Matheson leisure and tranquillity for study and writing. In 1874 he published anonymously 'Aids to the Study of German Theology,' in which he sought to show that German theology was positive and constructive. The work passed into a third edition within three years. In 1877 appeared 'The Growth of the Spirit of Christianity' (Edinburgh, 2 vols.), a philosophic presentment of the history of the church to the Reformation. In 'Natural Elements of Revealed Theology' (Baird lecture, 1881) 'he endeavoured to employ the results of the science of comparative religion in the defence of Christianity as a revealed religion' (A. B. BRUCE, *Brit. and For. Evangel. Rev.* 1881). In his 'Can the Old Faith live with the New? or, the Problem of Evolution and Revelation' (Edinburgh, 1885; 2nd edit.), he argued that the acceptance of evolution was calculated to strengthen belief in the Christian faith.

While at Innellan Matheson also began a long series of devotional books which made a wide appeal, and wrote much sacred poetry. A selection of his verses appeared as 'Sacred Songs' in 1890. The third edition (1904) included the hymn 'O Love that wilt not let me go,' which has found a place in almost every modern hymnal. At the Sunday-school convention held in Jerusalem in 1904 representatives of fifty-five different Christian communions, gathered from twenty-six different nations, sang it on the slopes of Calvary.

In October 1885 Matheson preached with success at Balmoral before Queen Victoria, by whose direction the sermon was printed for private circulation. Meanwhile in 1879 he declined an invitation to succeed Dr. John Cumming [q. v.] of Crown Court church, London, but in 1886 he became minister of St. Bernard's parish church, Edinburgh. His lack of sight proved no bar to the capable discharge of onerous parochial duties. His influence was specially strong among the educated classes, who were attracted by his intellectual force, as well as by his eloquence and dramatic power. In 1897 indifferent health led him to relinquish a portion of pastoral responsibility to a colleague, and the joint pastorate lasted until July 1899, when he finally retired. The later years of his life were devoted almost entirely to study and authorship. He was made D.D. of Edinburgh in 1879, and LL.D. of Aberdeen in 1902, but declined the Gifford lectureship at Aberdeen. In 1890 he was elected a fellow of the Royal Society of Edinburgh.

Matheson, whose learning was varied rather than profound, was a conspicuous representative of liberal theology. Despite his blindness, he was invariably radiant and cheerful. He died at Avenell House, North Berwick, after a brief illness, on 28 Aug. 1906, and was buried in the family vault in Glasgow Necropolis on 1 Sept. He was unmarried. He shared his home with his eldest sister, Jane Gray Matheson, to whom he attributed much of his happiness and success.

His portrait, painted by Otto Leyde, hangs in the vestry of St. Bernard's parish church, Edinburgh.

Matheson's many devotional works included: 'My Aspirations' (Cassell's 'Heart Chords' series, 1883); and 'Words by the Wayside' (1896); both of which were translated into German. His contributions to theology other than those cited were: 1. 'The Psalmist and the Scientist, or, the Modern Value of the Religious Sentiment,' Edinburgh, 1887, which popularised the views set forth in 'Can the Old Faith live with the New?' 2. 'Landmarks of New Testament Morality' (Nisbet's Theological Library), 1888. 3. 'The Spiritual Development of St. Paul,' Edinburgh, 1891; translated into Chinese. 4. 'The Distinctive Messages of the Old Religions,' Edinburgh, 1892. 5. 'The Lady Ecclesia,' 1896, an allegorical treatment of the development of the Spirit of Christ in the Church and in the individual. 6. 'Sidelights from Patmos,' 1897. 7. 'The Bible Definition of Religion,' 1898. 8. 'Studies of the Portrait of Christ' (vol. i. 1899; vol. ii. 1900), a characteristic work, of which 11,000 copies were sold within one year. 9. 'The Representative Men of the Bible,' first series, 1902; second series, 1903. 10. 'Representative Men of the New Testament,' 1905. 11. 'The

Representative Women of the Bible,' posthumously, 1907.

[Life of George Matheson, by D. Macmillan, 1907; Matheson's Times of Retirement, with brief memoir also by Dr. Macmillan; Julian's Dict. of Hymnology; personal knowledge.]

W. F. G.

MATHEW, Sir JAMES CHARLES (1830–1908), judge, born at Lehenagh House, Cork, on 10 July 1830, was eldest son of Charles Mathew of Lehenagh House by his wife Mary, daughter of James Hackett of Cork. Father Theobald Mathew [q. v.], the apostle of temperance, was his uncle, and it was largely due to his representations that the nephew, after receiving his early education at a private school at Cork, was sent at the age of fifteen to Trinity College, Dublin, a most unusual step at that period for a member of a Roman catholic family. Here he graduated as senior moderator and gold medallist in 1850. He entered as a student at Lincoln's Inn on 1 June 1851, and read in the chamber of Thomas Chitty [q. v.], the special pleader; he was called to the bar in Hilary term 1851, having obtained in the previous November an open studentship. He was made a bencher in Easter term 1881. For some ten years his progress was very slow. In the meantime he found scope for his debating and argumentative powers at the Hardwicke Society, of which he was one of the founders; and the humour and sarcasm which never forsook him brought him into prominence at the social gatherings of the Home Circuit mess. When business at last came to him, it found him thoroughly versed in the intricacies of pleading and practice and ready to seize every opportunity. He had a strong natural aptitude for the practical side of law, and from the outset of his career at the bar he showed impatience of technicalities and determination to get at the real points at issue. His services were in especial demand at the now defunct Guildhall sittings, where the heavy City special jury cases were tried, and after the way was cleared by Mr. (now the Right Hon.) Arthur Cohen being made a Q.C. in 1874, Mathew and Charles (afterwards Lord) Bowen [q. v. Suppl. I] were invariably retained by one side or the other; but in spite of his vast practice as a junior, Mathew steadily refrained from applying for a silk gown: a weak and rather harsh voice may have rendered him distrustful of his powers as a leader. In 1873 he was among the treasury counsel on the prosecution of the Tichborne claimant, Arthur Orton [q. v. Suppl. I], and he was the only one of his opponents with whom Dr. Kenealy [q. v.] did not quarrel (cf. Sir H. S. Cunningham's *Life of Lord Bowen*).

In March 1881, though still a stuff gownsman, he was appointed a judge in the Queen's Bench Division and he was knighted. At first he was hardly the success on the bench that his friends had predicted. He was often over hasty in speech, and he showed himself too impatient of slowness and dulness. These defects, however, wore away, and he became eventually the best nisi prius judge of his time. On the criminal side, though his previous experience in that branch of the profession was small, he showed acuteness and broad common sense, with occasionally, as was observed, a slight leaning to the prisoner. But it is by the institution of the commercial court that he will be best remembered. He had always held strong views on the question of costs and of legal procedure, and shortly before his elevation to the bench he had served on a royal commission appointed to inquire into the former subject. In 1895 he persuaded the other judges of the Queen's Bench, in which Lord Russell of Killowen [q. v. Suppl. I] had just been appointed chief justice, to assent to the formation of a special list for commercial cases to be heard in a particular court, presided over by the same judge sitting continuously and with a free hand as to his own procedure. Of this office Mathew was the first and by far the most successful occupant. He swept away written pleadings, narrowed the issues to the smallest possible dimensions, and allowed no dilatory excuses to interfere with the speedy trial of the action. His own judgments, 'concise and terse, free from irrelevancies and digression,' won the approval of all who practised in the court, and the confidence of the mercantile community. To a man of Mathew's alert, energetic, and radical mind the procedure in Chancery, especially in chambers, seemed a cumbersome survival of medievalism; and when sitting occasionally as a chancery judge he tried to introduce some of the reforms he had found efficacious in the commercial court. But the soil was not congenial, and some of his criticisms caused a good deal of umbrage to the members of the chancery bar.

Shortly after the return of the liberal party to office in August 1892, Mathew was made chairman of a royal commission appointed to inquire into the case of the evicted tenants in Ireland, with especial reference to their reinstatement and resettlement. The selection was not very fortunate. As a convinced home ruler, later the father-in-law of Mr. John Dillon, a leading Nationalist M.P., he was regarded with distrust by the landlords and the unionists generally. The opening day, 7 Nov., was marked by a disagreeable altercation between the chairman and Mr. (now the Right Hon. Sir) Edward Carson. Following the example of Sir John Day [q. v. Suppl. II] at Belfast, Mathew refused to allow cross-examination by counsel. Carson thereupon stigmatised the inquiry as 'a sham and a farce,' and Mathew pronounced this observation to be 'impertinent and disgraceful to the Irish bar.' Counsel were ordered to withdraw, two of the chairman's colleagues took speedy opportunity of resigning, and the landlords as a body refused to take any further part in the proceedings. The commission, however, continued to take evidence, and reported in due course; some of its recommendations bore fruit in the clauses of Mr. Wyndham's Land Purchase Act of 1903. It should be said that the lines of procedure laid down by Mathew have been consistently followed in subsequent royal commissions.

Not improbably owing to this episode Mathew was not raised to the court of appeal until 1901. In his new capacity he displayed all his old qualities of accuracy, common sense, and vigour, but he deprecated elaborate arguments and voluminous citation of authorities, the 'old umbrellas of the law,' as he used to call them. On 6 Dec. 1905 he was seized with a paralytic stroke at the Athenæum Club, and his resignation was announced shortly afterwards. He died in London on 9 Nov. 1908, and was buried in St. Joseph's cemetery at Cork.

In many respects Mathew was a typical representative of the south of Ireland. Ready and facile of speech, he was gifted with a delightful flow of humour and a strong appreciation of the lighter side of life. An ardent radical and a devout Roman catholic, he maintained the happiest relations with many who were vehemently opposed to him in religion and politics; on circuit he was always a welcome visitor at the houses of the dignitaries of the Church of England. A man of wide reading and culture, he was a warm-hearted and faithful friend.

He married on 26 Dec. 1861 Elizabeth, daughter of Edwin Biron, vicar of Lympne near Hythe; she survived him. There were two sons and three daughters of the marriage. Of these latter the eldest, Elizabeth, married in 1895 Mr. John Dillon, M.P.; she died in 1907.

An oil painting of Mathew by Frank Holl, R.A., is in the possession of his widow. A cartoon portrait by 'Spy' appeared in 'Vanity Fair' in 1896.

[The Times, 10 Nov. 1908; Men and Women of the Time; Annual Register, 1892; Reports of Commercial Cases, by T. Mathew and M. Macnaghten, vol. i. introduction, 1895; personal knowledge.] J. B. A.

MATHEWS, CHARLES EDWARD (1834–1905), Alpine climber and writer, born at Kidderminster on 4 Jan. 1834, was third of six sons of Jeremiah Mathews, a Worcestershire land agent, by his wife Mary Guest. Of his five brothers, the eldest, William (1828–1901; educated at St. John's College, Cambridge, 20th wrangler 1852), was one of the leading pioneers of Alpine exploration and the largest contributor to 'Peaks, Passes, and Glaciers' (1859 and 1862); he was president of the Alpine Club 1869–71. The fourth brother, George Spencer Mathews (1836–1904, 7th wrangler in 1859 and fellow of Caius College, Cambridge), was also a noted mountaineer. Both brothers were prominent figures in municipal and social life at Birmingham.

Charles Edward was educated at King Charles I's school, Kidderminster, served his articles in Birmingham and London from 1851, and was admitted solicitor in 1856. He practised with great success in Birmingham, acted as solicitor to the Birmingham school board throughout its existence, and as clerk of the peace from 1891 till his death. He was a member of the town council from 1875 to 1881 and for nearly fifty years exerted much influence on the public and social affairs of Birmingham. One of the founders and subsequently chairman of the parliamentary committee of the Education League, he founded in 1864 the Children's Hospital, in conjunction with Dr. Thomas Pretious Heslop [q. v.], and took part for many years in its management; he set on foot the agitation which led to the reorganisation of King Edward's school, and served as a governor of the school from its reconstitution in 1878 till his death; a lifelong friend of Mr. Joseph Chamberlain, he was from 1886 one of the local leaders of the liberal unionist party.

Outside professional and civic interests, Mathews's abounding energy found its main outlet in mountaineering. He was introduced to the Alps in 1856 (*Peaks, Passes and Glaciers*, 1st series, ch. iv) by his brother

William, with whom the idea of forming the Alpine Club originated; and the foundation of the club was definitely decided upon in November 1857 by the two brothers, a cousin, Benjamin Attwood Mathews, and Edward Shirley Kennedy; the last, aided by Thomas Woodbine Hinchliff [q. v. Suppl. I], taking the leading share in its actual formation (Dec. 1857–Jan. 1858). Charles Edward Mathews played his part in the conquest of the Alps which followed during the succeeding decade, and he continued to climb vigorously for more than forty years, long after all the other original members of the Alpine Club had retired from serious mountaineering. He was president of the club from 1878 to 1880, and took a prominent part in its affairs till the last year of his life: 'no one has on the whole done so much [for mountaineering and for the Alpine Club] because no one has continued his Alpine activity over so long a period.' He was also one of the founders (1898) and the first president of the Climbers' Club, an association formed with the object of encouraging mountaineering in England and Ireland.

Besides numerous papers in the 'Alpine Journal' (vols. i.–xxii.) he contributed articles on the guides Melchior and Jakob Anderegg to 'Pioneers of the Alps' (1887), and a retrospective chapter to C. T. Dent's 'Mountaineering' in the Badminton Library (1892); but his most important work in Alpine literature is 'The Annals of Mont Blanc' (1898), an exhaustive monograph, containing a critical analysis of the original narratives of the early ascents of the mountain, and a history and description of all the later routes by which its summit has been reached. Mathews himself climbed it at least twelve times.

He died at Edgbaston on 20 October 1905, and was buried at Sutton Coldfield. There is a monument to his memory in the garden of Couttet's hotel at Chamonix. Mathews married in 1860 Elizabeth Agnes Blyth, and had two sons and two daughters.

[The Times, 21 Oct. 1905; Birmingham Daily Post, 21, 23, 24, and 25 Oct. 1905; 24 Aug. 1907; Alpine Journal, xxii. 592, xxiii. 427; personal knowledge; private information.] A. L. M.

MATHEWS, Sir LLOYD WILLIAM (1850–1901), general and prime minister of Zanzibar, born in 1850, was son of Captain William Mathews, one of the pioneers of the volunteer movement. Entering the royal navy in 1863 as a naval cadet, he became a midshipman on 23 Sept. 1866, and in 1868 was stationed in the Mediterranean.

He first saw active service in the Ashanti campaign of 1873–4. He received the war medal and won promotion to the rank of lieutenant. On 27 Aug. 1875 Mathews was appointed lieutenant on board H.M.S. London, which was engaged in suppressing the slave trade on the east coast of Africa. He proved himself a capable and enterprising officer, capturing many Arab dhows and receiving the thanks of the admiralty. He retired from the navy with the rank of lieutenant in 1881.

Meanwhile in 1877 he was selected to command the army of Bargash, the Sultan of Zanzibar, who wished his troops to be drilled on the European model. Mathews trained and equipped a military force of 1000 regulars and 5000 irregulars, and henceforth devoted his services entirely to the Zanzibar government. He was given the rank of brigadier-general in the Zanzibar army, and in 1881 he was successful in capturing the Arab slave dealers who had murdered Captain Brownrigg, R.N. Mathews retained the confidence of Bargash's successors, and devoted his main energies to urging the suppression of slavery. In 1889 a decree was issued purchasing the freedom of all slaves who had taken refuge in the sultan's dominions; and in 1890 the sale or purchase of slaves was prohibited in Zanzibar. In November following, in accordance with the Anglo-German convention, Zanzibar was formally declared a British protectorate. In 1891 Mathews was appointed British consul-general for East Africa, but he never took up the duties of the post. He preferred to remain in the sultan's immediate service, and in October following he became prime minister and treasurer of the reconstituted Zanzibar government. Under his enlightened rule the machinery of administration was reorganised with a minimum of friction, and the old order of things was rapidly transformed. Mathews's strong personality impressed itself on successive sultans. In 1896, on the death of Sultan Hamed bin Thwain, he opposed the attempt of Khalid to seize the throne. The palace was bombarded by British warships, and Khalid was compelled to submit. Mathews then secured the installation of Sultan Hamed bin Mahommed, who was entirely favourable to British interests (27 Aug. 1896). Thanks to the prime minister's reforming energies, the legal status of slavery was abolished in 1897, compensation being given to the slave owners. Farms were established for the cultivation of new products, and modern methods of agriculture were introduced. The value of his work was officially recognised by the British government. He was created C.M.G. in 1880, and raised to K.C.M.G. in 1894. In addition to these honours he held the first class of the Zanzibar order of the Hammudie, and the order of the crown of Prussia. Mathews's prestige remained unshaken till the end. His name became a household word throughout East Africa for strict justice and honest administration. He died at Zanzibar on 11 Oct. 1901, and was buried in the English cemetery outside the town.

[The Times, 12 Oct 1901; Navy Lists; R. N. Lyne, Zanzibar in Contemporary Times (portrait, p. 100), 1905; Sir Gerald Portal, The British Mission to Uganda in 1893, 1894; H. S. Newman, Banani: the Transition from Slavery to Freedom in Zanzibar, 1898; E. Younghusband, Glimpses of East Africa and Zanzibar, 1910.]

MAWDSLEY, JAMES (1848–1902), trade union leader, born at Preston on 9 Feb. 1848, was son of Thomas Mawdsley, an operative cotton spinner, by his wife Jane Fawcett. At the age of nine he went to the mill as a half-timer. He soon became interested in trade unionism, and was elected in 1875 assistant secretary to the Preston Spinners' Association. He took an active part in the historic Preston lockout of 1878, and in September of that year became secretary to the Amalgamated Association of Cotton Spinners. He belonged to what is somewhat inaccurately called 'the old school of trade union leader.' Mr. Sidney Webb entitles him 'the cautious leader of the Lancashire cotton spinners,' but his policy was steadily directed to resist reductions in wages and secure a minimum scale agreement. His opposition to the reductions forced upon the operatives in 1879 and 1885 became an essential link in the development of trade union policy in Lancashire. But it was not till 1892–3 that he fought his great battle. The employers then sought to enforce a further reduction in wages of five per cent.; the operatives refused to accept it, and for twenty weeks the mills of south-east Lancashire were idle. The industrial result of this dispute was a reduction of under three per cent. and the famous conciliation scheme known as the Brooklands agreement, by which the men and the masters agreed to fix wages for periods of years by consent and refer disputes to an arbitrator. But a farther reaching effect was that as the operatives were very dissatisfied with the result it threw them into political agitation and so opened the door for the political labour party.

From 1882 to 1897 he was a member of the parliamentary committee of the trade union congress, and joined in the constant endeavours of the committee to widen its field of activity in home and foreign politics. Although he did not welcome the growing power of the independent labour political movement, he was forced along on its currents. He visited America in 1895 as a trade union delegate, and repeatedly went to the Continent on the same errand. He was made a J.P. for the city of Manchester in 1888 and for the county of Lancaster in 1894. He was a member of the royal commission which inquired into labour questions in 1891–4, opposed a general scheme of arbitration, and was one of the signatories of the minority report which advocated 'public for capitalist enterprise.' He was also a member of several local authorities. In 1900 he unsuccessfully contested Oldham as a trade unionist candidate for parliament.

He married in January 1871 Ann Wright, by whom he had five sons and four daughters. He died at Taunton, Ashton-under-Lyne, on 4 Feb. 1902, and was buried at Christ Church cemetery there.

[Factory Times, 7 Feb. 1902; The Times, 5 Feb. 1902; Sidney Webb's Industrial Democracy, 1897; family information.]

J. R. M.

MAY, PHILIP WILLIAM, called PHIL MAY (1864–1903), humorous draughtsman, born at 66 Wallace Street, New Wortley, Leeds, on 22 April 1864, was seventh child of Philip William May, an engineer. His father's father was Charles May, squire of Whittington, near Chesterfield, a sportsman and amateur caricaturist. His mother's father was Eugene Macarthy (1788–1866), an Irish actor and for a while manager of Drury Lane Theatre. An elder sister of his mother, Maria (1812–1870), was an actress of repute, and married Robert William Honner [q.v.], manager of the Sadler's Wells and Surrey Theatres. Charles May being a friend of George Stephenson, his son Philip (the artist's father) was admitted as a pupil to Stephenson's locomotive works at Newcastle-on-Tyne, but failed to succeed in business on his own account, with the result that his family were in very needy circumstances. Phil May was sent to St. George's School, Leeds, but left very early. His own wish was to be a jockey; but when still quite a child he was employed as timekeeper in a foundry, and at twelve years of age had begun to help the scene painter and make himself generally useful at the Leeds theatre. Subsequently he joined a touring company as an actor, his first appearance being at the Spa Theatre, Scarborough. He played among other parts François in 'Richelieu' and the cat in 'Dick Whittington.' In his fifteenth year he set out for London to earn his fortune, suffering there great hardships. Part of the return journey he performed on foot. In Leeds again, he took to drawing in earnest, contributed to a paper called 'Yorkshire Gossip,' and designed pantomime costumes. At the age of nineteen he married Sarah Elizabeth Emerson.

In 1883, after more London poverty, May drew a caricature of Irving, Bancroft, and Toole leaving a Garrick Club supper, which was published by a print-seller in the Charing Cross Road. The print caught the eye of Lionel Brough, the actor, who bought the original (cf. *The Bancrofts: Recollections of Sixty Years*, 1909, p. 330, with reproduction). Replicas were subsequently acquired by King Edward VII, Sir Arthur Pinero, and Sir Squire Bancroft. Brough recommended May to the editor of 'Society.' For 'Society' he did some work, and then passed to 'St. Stephen's Review,' of which paper he was the artistic mainstay until a break down of health made it advisable to go to Australia, where he had an offer of 20*l.* a week from the 'Sydney Bulletin.' He left London in 1885 and remained in Australia until 1888, completing altogether some 900 drawings for the 'Bulletin.' For a while after leaving that paper he remained in Melbourne practising painting, and then settled in Paris to study art as seriously as he was able. Returning to live in London in 1892, he resumed his labours on 'St. Stephen's Review,' to which from Paris he had contributed his first widely successful work, the illustrations to 'The Parson and the Painter,' published as a book in 1891. In 1892 appeared the first 'Phil May's Winter Annual,' destined to be continued until 1903, containing some thirty to fifty drawings by himself, with miscellaneous literary matter. There were fifteen issues in all (three being called 'Summer Annual'), and these shilling books probably did as much to make the artist's reputation as a humorist as any of his journalistic drawings. His first important newspaper connection was with the 'Daily Graphic,' for which paper he started on a tour of the world, which however came to an abrupt close in Chicago, and he returned to London in 1893, never to leave it again. There followed a very busy period, during which he contributed not only to the 'Daily Graphic' and 'Graphic' but, among other illustrated papers, to the 'Sketch' and 'Pick-me-up,' and steadily acquired a name for comic delineations of low life such as none could challenge. In 1895 there appeared 'Phil May's Sketch Book: Fifty Cartoons,' and in 1896 his 'Guttersnipes: Fifty Original Sketches,' containing some of his most vivid and characteristic work, on the strength of which he was elected to the Royal Institute of Painters in Water Colours. In the same year he succeeded to a chair at the 'Punch' Table. Although he retained it until his death the traditions of the paper were a little cramping to one so essentially Bohemian as he, while some of his contributions to it, such as the illustrations to the 'Essence of Parliament' (reissued in Lucy's 'Balfourian Parliament,' 1906), must be considered a misapplication of his genius. Portraits were not his forte, and any time which he spent on drawing from photographs was lost. In 1897 appeared 'Phil May's Graphic Pictures' and also 'The ZZG., or Zig-Zag Guide. Round and about the beautiful and bold Kentish coast. Described by F. C. Burnand and illustrated by Phil May,' to which the artist contributed 139 illustrations; in 1899 followed both 'Fifty hitherto unpublished Pen and Ink Sketches' and the 'Phil May Album, collected by Augustus M. Moore,' with a biographical preface.

Phil May once stated that all he knew about drawing had come from Edward Linley Sambourne [q. v. Suppl. II]. Although the initial line work of the two men is very similar, the difference in the completed drawings is wide. Sambourne progressed by multiplying strokes; May by the process of omitting them. Phil May struck out line after line until only the essentials remained. His usual method for his 'Punch' contributions was to draw more or less fully in pencil and then work over this with pen and ink, with the utmost economy of stroke, and finally rub out the pencil. But latterly he often omitted the pencil foundation. Those who attended his lectures, which he illustrated as he talked, or were present at Savage Club entertainments at which he acted as 'lightning cartoonist,' say that the rapidity and sureness of his hand were miraculous. May's line at its best may be said to be alive.

It is certain that no English draughtsman has ever attained greater vigour or vivacity in black and white. In this frugal and decisive medium he drew thousands of droll and cynical scenes of Bohemian and street life, becoming thereby as pre-eminently the people's illustrator of the end of the Victorian period as Keene had been during its middle years and Leech during its earlier ones. None could set down London street types, whether of Seven Dials or the Strand, with greater fidelity and brilliance. Critics and artists alike united to praise him. Whistler once remarked that modern black and white could be summed up in two words—Phil May.

In private life May was a man of much humour and a curious amiability and gentleness, qualities which unhappily carried with them a defect of weakness that made him the victim both of sociability and of impecunious friends. He earned large sums but was too easily relieved of them. His 'Punch' editor, Sir Francis Burnand, tells a story illustrative at once both of his generosity and of his inherent sweetness, to the effect that on being asked at a club for a loan of 50*l.*, May produced all he had—namely half that amount—and then abstained from the club for some time for fear of meeting the borrower, because he felt that 'he still owed him 25*l.*'

Before his health finally broke May had been a sedulous horseman. He was greatly interested in boxing, although rather as a spectator than a participator, and another of his hobbies was the composition of lyrics, usually of a sentimental order, some of which were set to music. Not long before his death he made a serious arrangement to return to the stage, as Pistol, in a revival of 'Henry V'; but his appearance did not extend beyond one or two rehearsals taken with impossible levity. A full-length portrait of May in hunting costume by J. J. Shannon was exhibited at the Academy of 1901, so realistic in character as to distress many who saw it and were unaware of May's besetting weakness. A cartoon portrait by 'Spy' appeared in 'Vanity Fair' in 1895. He also introduced himself in his pictures probably more frequently than any other artist, often with a whimsical and half-pathetic sidelong glance at his foibles. He died on 5 Aug. 1903 at his home in Medina Place, St. John's Wood, and was buried at Kensal Green. His widow, who received a civil list pension of 100*l.* a year, married again and died in 1910. He left no family.

After his death there were published further collections of published and unpublished sketches in 'Phil May's Sketches from Punch,' 1903, his 'Picture Book,' 1903, with a biographical and critical preface by G. R. Halkett; his 'Medley,' 1904, his 'Folio of Caricature Drawings and Sketches,' 1904, with a biography, and in the same year 'Phil May in Australia,' with both an excellent biography and iconography. On 25 June 1910 a mural tablet subscribed for by the public was unveiled on the house in Leeds where he was born, recording the circumstance and calling him 'the great black and white artist' and 'a fellow of infinite jest.'

[The Times, 6 August 1903; biographical prefaces to Phil May in Australia, Bulletin Office, Sydney, 1904, and The Phil May Folio, London, 1904; James Glover, Jimmy Glover: his book, 1911 (with portrait of May by himself, Leeds, 1880); private information.]

E. V. L.

MAYOR, JOHN EYTON BICKERSTETH (1825–1910), classical scholar and divine, third son of the Rev. Robert Mayor (*d.* 1846), was born on 28 Jan. 1825 at Baddegama in Ceylon, where his father was a missionary of the Church Missionary Society from 1818 to 1828. His mother was Charlotte (1792–1870), daughter of Henry Bickersteth, surgeon, of Kirkby Lonsdale, and sister of Henry Bickersteth, Baron Langdale [q. v.], and Edward Bickersteth, rector of Watton [q. v.]. He was named John Eyton in memory of his father's friend, the Rev. John Eyton (*d.* 1823), rector of Eyton in Shropshire, who had prompted the elder Mayor to abandon the medical profession and to become a missionary (*The Eagle*, xxv. 333).

From his early boyhood Mayor delighted in books. At the age of six he 'revelled in Rollin (in default of Plutarch)' and in English prose versions of Homer and Virgil (*First Greek Reader*, p. xxi, n. 2). After attending the grammar school of Newcastle-under-Lyme as a day boy, he was from 1833 to 1836 at Christ's Hospital, whence he was removed owing to an attack of scarlet fever. For several years he was at home, learning Greek, as well as Latin, from his mother. In 1838, with the aid of his uncle, Robert Bickersteth, a successful surgeon in Liverpool, he was sent to Shrewsbury, the school which won his lifelong devotion. He read much out of school, for his own improvement. He bought for himself and 'perused carefully' the works of Joseph Butler and Richard Hooker (*The Latin Heptateuch*, p. lxvii f.), and was familiar with the writings of 'Leighton and Burnet and Chalmers—from very early days' (*The Eagle*, xxiii. 106). He 'thumbed the "Corpus Poëtarum" from Lucretius to Ausonius.' Milton's verse, English and Latin, he 'nearly knew by heart' (*First Greek Reader*, p. xxxvi).

In Oct. 1844 he began residence at St. John's College, Cambridge (on his interests as an undergraduate, see *ib.* pp. xli seq. and *The Eagle*, xxiii. 308). His college tutor was the Rev. Dr. Hymers, his private tutor William Henry Bateson [q. v.], ultimately Master of St. John's. He also read classics with Richard Shilleto [q.v.]. In the classical tripos of 1848 he was third in the first class. An elder brother, Robert Bickersteth, was third wrangler in 1842; his younger brother, Joseph Bickersteth, was second classic in 1851; all the three brothers were elected fellows of the college, the date of John's admission as fellow being 27 March 1849.

From 1849 to 1853 Mayor was master of the lower sixth at Marlborough College, and there he prepared his erudite edition of 'Thirteen Satires of Juvenal.' This was first published in a single volume with the notes at the foot of the page (1853). A second edition was published in two volumes (1869–78) with the notes at the end of each, and a third edition (1881) with the text of the 'Thirteen Satires' and the notes on Satires i., iii.–v., vii. in the first volume, and the notes on Satires viii., x.–xvi. in the second. A fourth edition of the first volume appeared in 1886.

In 1853 Mayor returned for life to St. John's, at first as an assistant tutor or lecturer in classics, but the vastness of his learning prevented him from being a good lecturer. He was ordained deacon in 1855 and priest in 1857. He subsequently kept the act for the B.D. degree (taking the subject of vernacular services *versus* Latin), preached a Latin and an English sermon, but never took the degree (*The Eagle*, xxiii. 107). To the 'Journal of Classical and Sacred Philology,' founded by Hort, Lightfoot, and Mayor in 1854, he contributed two learned and comprehensive articles on Latin lexicography (Nov. 1855 and March 1857).

Throughout life Mayor applied himself with exceptional ardour to various forms of literary and antiquarian research, and he proved indefatigable in amassing information. He brought together an immense library, which he stored until 1881 in his college rooms over the gateway of the second court. In that year he acquired a small house in Jordan's Yard to make room for the overflow of books and papers. An accomplished linguist, he was familiar not only with Latin and Greek but with French, Italian, and Spanish, and notably with German and Dutch. To the collecting of biographical material he devoted immense energy, and in later life he placed his biographical notes at the disposal of contributors to this Dictionary.

His early publications include biographies of Nicholas Ferrar (1855), of Matthew Robinson (1856), of Ambrose Bonwicke (1870), and William Bedell (1871), as well as an edition of Roger Ascham's 'Scholemaster' (1863; new edit. 1883). But the history of his own university was one of his most absorbing interests, and he emulated the antiquarian zeal of Thomas Baker [q. v.], the ejected fellow of the 18th century. He printed the four earliest codes of the college statutes (1859). He transcribed the admissions to the college from 1630, and his transcript was edited as far as 1715 by himself (1882–93), and as far as 1767 by Mr. R. F. Scott (1903). He calendared Baker's voluminous MSS. in the university library. He supplied material to Prof. Willis and John Willis Clark [q. v. Suppl. II] for their 'Architectural History of Cambridge,' and he gave every aid and encouragement to Charles Henry Cooper [q. v.] in his labours on Cambridge history and biography, and accumulated manuscript notes for a continuation of Cooper's 'Athenæ Cantabrigienses.' Mayor foretold that his own biographical collections would survive with the manuscripts of Baker and Cole. In 1869 Mayor published for the first time Baker's 'History of St. John's College,' a solid work in two large volumes; he continued Baker's text, and added abundant notes to the lives of all the Masters of the college and of the bishops trained within its walls.

In 1864 Mayor was elected without a contest university librarian. He held the post for three years, and was never absent from his duties for more than eight days together. During his tenure of office the catalogue of MSS. was completed, and he substituted for the various series of class-marks a single series of Arabic numerals (a reform which was subsequently abandoned). Although his energy increased the life and vigour of the library, all his literary and antiquarian projects were in his own words put 'out of gear' by his duties, and in 1867 he withdrew to resume his private work. The revision of his 'Juvenal' chiefly occupied him between 1869 and 1872, and in the last year (1872) he was elected professor of Latin in succession to Hugh Andrew Johnstone Munro [q. v.]. He remained professor till his death. His favourite subjects for lectures were Martial and the Letters of Seneca and the younger Pliny, with Minucius Felix and Tertullian. But, like his college lectures, those delivered before the university were too closely packed with references to parallel passages to be appreciated by the ordinary student. His lectures on Bede bore fruit in 1878 in a joint edition (with Dr. J. R. Lumby) of the 'Ecclesiastical History' (bks. iii. and iv.), in which the learned and multifarious commentary fills a little more space than the text.

Mayor pursued his studies unremittingly, 'taking no exercise for its own sake' and rarely going abroad except on academic or learned business. In 1875 he represented Cambridge University at the tercentenary of Leyden, where he met Madvig and Cobet. In the same year he paid his only visit to Rome, where, apart from its ancient associations, he was mainly interested in the modern schools, where the boys learnt by heart whole books of Virgil and Tasso. A keen interest in the Old Catholics led him to attend the Congress convened at Constance in 1873, when he delivered a German as well as an English discourse (Mayor's *Report of Congress,* 1873; also his edit. of *Bishop Reinkens' Second Pastoral Letter and Speeches, and Prof. Messmer's Speech,* 1874).

His physical constitution was remarkably strong. He attributed the vigour of his old age to his strict adherence to vegetarian diet, which he adopted in middle life and thenceforth championed with enthusiasm. He set forth his views on diet first in 'Modicus Cibi Medicus Sibi, or Nature her Own Physician' (1880); and subsequently in the selected addresses published in 'Plain Living and High Thinking' (1897). In 1884 he became president of the Vegetarian Society, and held office till death. Throughout that period he was a frequent contributor to the 'Dietetic Reformer and Vegetarian Messenger'; and the Vegetarian Society in 1901 printed selections by him from the Bible and from English poets under the title of 'Sound Mind in Body Sound: a Cloud of Witnesses to the Golden Rule of not too much.' He was also keenly interested in missionary work at home and abroad, and especially in the college mission in Walworth.

Mayor became president of his college in Oct. 1902, and at the fellows' table he charmed visitors of the most varied tastes by his old-fashioned courtesy, and by his learned and lively talk. His interests within their own lines remained alert to the last. When the National Library of Turin was partly destroyed by fire on 26 Jan. 1904, he promptly sent the library no fewer than 710 volumes (*The Eagle,* xxvi. 264 f.). In 1907 he easily mastered Esperanto.

Mayor's wide learning received many marks of respect in his later years. He received the honorary degree of D.C.L. from Oxford in 1895, that of LL.D. from Aberdeen in 1892 and from St. Andrews in 1906, and that of D.D. from Glasgow in 1901. He was one of the original fellows of the British Academy (1902). In 1905, on his 80th birthday, a Latin address of congratulation written by Prof. J. S. Reid and numerously signed, was presented to him at a meeting held in the Combination Room of St. John's, under the presidency of Sir Richard Jebb. Until 1908 he preached in the college chapel and occasionally in the university church. He printed his sermons immediately after delivery, without his name, but with the date and place, and with an appendix of interesting notes. His style in the pulpit reflected the best seventeenth and eighteenth century examples, and his sermons dealt exhaustively with subjects of importance. 'The Spanish Reformed Church' was the theme of two sermons in 1892 and 1895, the first of which was partly delivered in the university church and was published in 'Spain, Portugal, the Bible' (1895). His last sermon, that on 'The Church of Scotland' (1908), was in praise of Scottish learning and Scottish missionary enterprise. A selection of his sermons was edited for the Cambridge University Press by the Rev. H. F. Stewart in 1911, after his death. Mayor, who was unmarried, died suddenly of heart failure within two months of completing the 86th year of his age, on 1 Dec. 1910, while he was preparing to leave his Cambridge residence, with a view to reading prayers in the college chapel. He was buried in St. Giles's cemetery, on the Huntingdon road, Cambridge.

Mayor possessed an unusual power of accumulating knowledge. He had small faculty of construction, and much of the work that he designed was not attempted, or if attempted was uncompleted. A projected commentary on Seneca never appeared. A Latin dictionary, which might have been his *magnum opus,* was never seriously begun. Contemplated editions of Milton and of Boswell's 'Life of Johnson,' and an ecclesiastical history of the first three centuries came to nothing. Yet his publications are very numerous and cover a wide range. Some of these have been already mentioned. His scholarly reputation mainly rests on his edition of Juvenal. Apart from this, his chief contributions to classical learning are an edition of Cicero's 'Second Philippic,' founded on that of Halm (1861); a bibliography of Latin literature, founded on that of Hübner (1875); and an independent edition of the 'Third Book of Pliny's Letters' (1880). In 1868 he published an excellent 'First Greek Reader,' with a vigorous preface on classical education, interspersed with interesting touches of autobiography. Of proposed editions of 'The Narrative of Odysseus' ('Odyssey,' books ix.–xii.), and of the 'Tenth Book of Quintilian,' only a small portion was published (1872). His annotated editions of Burman's and Uffenbach's visits to Cambridge, printed in 1871, were posthumously published, as part of 'Cambridge under Queen Anne,' in 1911. In 1889 he published a critical review of the 'Latin Heptateuch' of Cyprian, the sixth-century poet and bishop of Toulon. Among miscellaneous works may be reckoned Mayor's edition of Richard of Cirencester's 'Speculum Historiale de gestis Regum Angliæ' for the Rolls series (2 vols. 1863–9), devoting many pages of the preface to indicating the exact sources of all the borrowed erudition of the forger of the treatise 'De Situ Britanniæ,' which its first editor (and, indeed, author), Charles Bertram [q. v.] of Copenhagen, had falsely attributed to Richard of Cirencester. In 1874 he edited Cooper's 'Memoir of Margaret Countess of Richmond and Derby,' and in 1876 published, for the Early English Text Society, 'The English Works of Bishop Fisher.' His latest work was a 'First German Reader, with Translation and Notes,' which he had printed for himself and published at the Cambridge University Press in Jan. 1910 with the title 'Jacula Prudentium, Verse and Prose from the German.'

His annotated copies of Juvenal and Seneca are among the books presented by his executors to the library of his college, and his interleaved Latin dictionaries are among those presented to the university library, which he named as the ultimate destination of his biographical collections. Of the rest of his library more than 18,000 volumes were sold in Cambridge after his death (Catling's catalogue of sale on 14–18 March 1911).

A presentation portrait painted by (Sir) Hubert (von) Herkomer in 1891 is in the hall of St. John's College. An etching by the same artist formed the frontispiece of 'Minerva' (1903–4), and is reproduced in 'The Eagle' (xxv. 129).

[Autobiographical passages in prefaces to First Greek Reader, Juvenal (ed. 1886), The Latin Heptateuch, and in Spain, Portugal, the Bible; also in Commemoration Sermon, 1902, in The Eagle, xxiii. 307f. and 106f.; Report of Meeting of Subscribers to Portrait of Prof. Mayor, ib. xvi. 268–76, xvii. 81; Presentation of Address, ib. xxvi. 241–7, with reprint of articles on Prof. Mayor in National Observer, 26 Dec. 1891, and Daily Mail, 25 Aug. 1904; obituary notices by the present writer in The Times, 2 Dec. 1910; Guardian, 9 Dec. p. 1717; Cambridge Review, 8 Dec.; Classical Review, Feb. 1911; Proceedings of the British Academy, April; and The Eagle, xxxii. pp. 189–98, followed on pp. 199–232 by notices by Rev. C. E. Graves, Rev. H. F. Stewart, J. B. Mullinger, and others, and reprint of articles in The Athenæum, 10 Dec. 1910, and Blackwood's Magazine, Jan. 1911, with bibliography of contributions to Notes and Queries; writings on Vegetarianism, ib. pp. 232, 316f., and articles in classical periodicals, ib. xxxiii. pp. 58–62; university tributes to his memory in Cambridge University Reporter, xli. pp. 608, 1270, and xlii. 37; lastly, Memoir in Select Sermons, edit. by the Rev. H. F. Stewart (with portrait), Cambridge, 1911.] J. E. S.

MEADE, RICHARD JAMES, fourth Earl of Clanwilliam in the Irish peerage, and second Baron Clanwilliam in the peerage of the United Kingdom (1832–1907), admiral of the fleet, born on 3 Oct. 1832, was eldest son in the family of four sons and a daughter of Richard Charles Francis Meade [q. v.], third earl of Clanwilliam and Baron Gillford in the Irish peerage and Baron Clanwilliam in the peerage of the United Kingdom, by his wife Lady Elizabeth, eldest daughter of George Augustus Herbert, eleventh earl of Pembroke. He had his early education at Eton, and entered the navy on 17 Nov. 1845; he passed his examination in Nov. 1851 and was promoted to lieutenant on 15 Sept. 1852. In Dec. of the same year he was appointed to the Imperieuse, frigate, in which he served during the whole of the Russian war. The Imperieuse was senior officer's ship of the advanced squadron and followed up the ice and established the blockade of the Gulf of Finland as early in the spring as possible, and before the navigation was thought safe for heavy ships. In Sept. 1856 Lord Gillford was appointed to the Raleigh, Captain Keppel [see Keppel, Sir Henry, Suppl. II], for the China station, and when the Raleigh was wrecked near Hong Kong on the passage out, he followed Keppel and with him took part in the boat actions of Escape Creek on 25 May 1857 and of Fatshan Creek on 1 June. In August he was appointed to the Calcutta, flagship of Sir Michael Seymour [q. v.], and in Dec. he landed with the naval brigade before Canton. At the storming of Canton on 29 Dec. Gillford was severely wounded in the left arm by a gingal bullet; he was mentioned in despatches, received the medal with clasps for Fatshan and Canton, and on 26 Feb. 1858 was promoted to commander and appointed to the Hornet, which he took to England. On 22 July 1859 he was promoted to captain. From 1862 to 1866 he commanded the Tribune in the Pacific, and from Oct. 1868 to 1871 the battleship Hercules in the Channel. In 1872 he became an aide-de-camp to Queen Victoria, and was given the command of the steam reserve at Portsmouth. On the formation of Disraeli's ministry in 1874 he joined the Board of Admiralty as junior sea lord, and continued at Whitehall until the change of government brought in a new board in May 1880. He was promoted to flag rank on 31 Dec. 1876, received the C.B. in June 1877, and succeeded to the earldom on 7 Oct. 1879. From 1880 to 1882 he had command of the flying squadron, reaching the rank of vice-admiral on 26 July 1881, and being awarded the K.C.M.G. in March 1882; from Aug. 1885 to Sept. 1886 he flew his flag as commander-in-chief on the North American and West Indies station, laying down the command in consequence of his promotion to admiral on 22 June 1886. In June 1887 he was raised to the K.C.B., and in 1888 became a commissioner of the patriotic fund. He was commander-in-chief at Portsmouth from June 1891 to June 1894, was promoted to admiral of the fleet on 20 Feb. 1895, received the G.C.B. in May following, and reached the age for retirement on 3 Oct. 1902.

In the words of one of his messmates, Clanwilliam 'throughout his life was before everything a sailor, studious of the interests of the service and of those under his command, and probably valued his rank as an admiral much more than his title as an Irish earl or English baron.' He died on 4 Aug. 1907 at Badgemore, Henley on Thames, and was buried in the family vault at Wilton, near Salisbury.

He married on 17 June 1867 Elizabeth Henrietta, eldest daughter of Sir Arthur Edward Kennedy [q. v.], G.C.M.G., governor of Queensland, and had four sons and four daughters. The eldest son, Richard Charles, Lord Gillford, born in 1868, entered the navy, was made lieutenant in 1891, was flag lieutenant to Sir George Tryon [q. v.] in the Victoria in 1893, and leaving the navy shortly afterwards, died in 1905. The second son, Arthur Vesey Meade, Lord Dromore, born in 1873, succeeded to the earldom; the third, Herbert, entered the navy and reached the rank of commander in 1908; and the youngest, Edward Brabazon, was a captain in the 10th hussars.

A portrait by Rudolf Lehmann was exhibited at the Royal Academy in 1899; a 'Vanity Fair' cartoon by 'Spy' was published in 1903; and an engraved portrait was published by Messrs. Walton of Shaftesbury Avenue.

[The Times, 5 and 9 Aug. 1907; Burke's Peerage.] L. G. C. L.

MEAKIN, JAMES EDWARD BUDGETT (1866–1906), historian of the Moors, born at the house of his mother's brother at Ealing Park, London, on 8 Aug. 1866, was the eldest son in a family of three sons and two daughters of Edward Ebenezer Meakin, then a tea-planter in Almora, India, by his wife Sarah, only daughter of Samuel Budgett of Bristol. He was educated first at Mr. Hill's preparatory school, Redhill, and then at Reigate grammar school.

His father, who was keenly interested in oriental peoples and religion, visited Morocco, and founded there on 15 July 1884 the first English newspaper, the 'Times of Morocco,' which urged sympathetic consideration of native interests. James joined his father in Morocco for reasons of health. He acted first as assistant editor of the paper and then as editor. He at once studied the Moorish people and their language. Adopting native dress and the native name Tahar bil Mikki, he mixed freely with all classes, soon mastered the Moorish dialect of Arabic, of which he published in 1891 a word-book with English explanations ('An Introduction to the Arabic of Morocco'), and closely observed Moorish life. In 1890 he returned to England, to consider means of preparing a work on Morocco, which should be as authoritative as Lane's 'Modern Egyptians' on Egypt. But no publisher would encourage the scheme, which was abandoned. Nor would the Royal Geographical or the Scottish Geographical Society accept Meakin's proposal to explore under their auspices the mountainous district of the Central Atlas behind Morocco. After another year in Morocco (1892), he in 1893 began a journey round the world by way of Turkey and Persia, visiting all the important Mohammedan settlements in Asia and Africa. He returned to Morocco for some months in 1897, and afterwards fixed his permanent home in England, where he devoted himself to literature, journalism, and public lecturing.

Besides Morocco, Meakin now made questions of social reform a special subject of study. In 1901, with a view to raising the standard of health and comfort among the working classes and to exposing the evil conditions of city slums, Meakin organised a scheme for the delivery through the country of lectures on such themes, known as the 'Shaftesbury Lectures.' He often lectured himself, and in 1905 he took a leading part with Dr. John Brown Paton [q. v. Suppl. II] in forming the British Institute of Social Service, under whose auspices the 'Shaftesbury Lectures' were continued. In 1906 he acted as special correspondent of the 'Tribune,' a short-lived London daily newspaper, at the conference of Algeciras. In 1902 he received the Turkish order of the Medjidie in recognition of his studies of Islam. He died in Hampstead Hospital, after a brief illness, on 26 June 1906, and was buried at Highgate cemetery.

Meakin married in 1900 Kate Alberta, daughter of C. J. Helliwell, sometime of Liverpool and afterwards of Vancouver. He had one son.

As a writer on Morocco, Meakin, though without any particular gift of style, was thorough and trustworthy. His chief publications 'The Moorish Empire' (1899, an historical epitome); 'The Land of the Moors' (1901, a general description); 'The Moors' (1902, a minute account of manners and customs), are standard works. Other books of his are: 'Life in Morocco and Glimpses beyond' (1905); 'Model Factories and Villages' (1905); 'Sons of Ishmael.' With his wife, who helped him in many of his books, he wrote the article on Morocco in the 'Encyclopædia Britannica' (11th edit.).

[The Times, 30 June 1906; Who's Who, 1906; Progress, October 1906; introduction to The Moors, 1902; Athenæum, June 1906; private information.] S. E. F.

MEDD, PETER GOLDSMITH (1829–1908), theologian, born on 18 July 1829, was eldest son of John Medd, F.R.C.S., of Leyburn, Yorkshire. who practised at Stockport, by his wife Sarah, daughter of William Goldsmith. After education at King's College, London, where he was associate in theology in 1849 and subsequently honorary fellow, Medd matriculated at St. John's College, Oxford, on 1 March 1848, whence he migrated as scholar to University College, graduating B.A. there in 1852, and proceeding M.A. in 1855. He was fellow of University College from 1852 to 1877, bursar in 1856, tutor from 1861 to 1870, dean and librarian (1861). Taking holy orders in 1853, he served the curacy of St. John the Baptist, Oxford (1858–67), and leaving Oxford in 1870 was rector of Barnes until 1876. He declined in 1875 an offer of the bishopric of Brechin; from 1876 till his death he was rector of North Cerney, Cirencester. In 1877 Medd was made honorary canon of St. Albans. He took a leading part in the establishment of Keble College, Oxford, of the council of which he was senior member in 1871. He was select preacher at Oxford in 1881 and Bampton lecturer in 1882. His Bampton lectures, 'The One Mediator,' published in 1884, although condensed and harsh in style, show great learning. In 1883 he was proctor in convocation for the diocese of Gloucester and Bristol.

Medd took a keen interest in the higher education of women, and represented his university on the council of Cheltenham Ladies' College. He died, after a long illness, at North Cerney on 25 July 1908, and was buried there. He married on 19 Jan. 1876 Louisa, daughter of Alexander Nesbitt of Byfield House, Barnes, who with six sons and two daughters survived him.

A learned authority on the liturgy, Medd edited with William Bright [q. v. Suppl. II] in 1865 the 'Liber precum publicarum ecclesiæ Anglicanæ,' the Latin version of the Prayer Book. He contributed in 1869 an historical introduction to Henry Baskerville Walton's edition of the first Prayer Book of Edward VI and the ordinal of 1549, and in 1892 he edited Andrewes's 'Greek Devotions' from a manuscript annotated by Andrewes himself, which was discovered by Robert George Livingstone, tutor of Pembroke College. This manuscript was an earlier and more authentic transcript than that made in 1648 for Richard Drake, on which all previous editions had been based. Besides the works mentioned, Medd published several sermons and devotional volumes, including: 1. 'The Christian Meaning of the Psalms and the Supernatural Character of Christian Truth,' 1862. 2. 'The Church and Wesleyanism,' 1868. 3. 'Home Reunion,' 1871. 4. 'Catholic Unity,' 1875. 5. 'The Country Clergyman's Ideal,' 1887. He also contributed the introductory memoir to 'Selected Letters of William Bright,' 1903.

[The Times, 28 July 1908; Brit. Mus. Cat.; private information.] W. B. O.

MEDLICOTT, HENRY BENEDICT (1829–1905), geologist, born at Loughrea, co. Galway, on 3 Aug. 1829, was second of three sons of Samuel Medlicott, rector of Loughrea, by his wife Charlotte, daughter of Colonel H. B. Dolphin, C.B. The eldest son, Joseph G. Medlicott (*d.* 1866), of the geological survey of India, afterwards in the Indian educational service, was author of a 'Cotton Hand-book for Bengal' (1862). The youngest son, Samuel, became rector of Bowness in Cumberland in 1877.

Medlicott received his early education partly in France, partly in Guernsey, and then entered Trinity College, Dublin, where he graduated B.A. in 1850, with diploma and honours in the school of civil engineering, proceeding M.A. in 1870. In 1851 he joined the geological survey of Ireland, and worked for two years under Joseph Beete Jukes [q. v.], when he was transferred to the English staff and was engaged during 1853 in field-work in Wiltshire. On 24 March 1854 he joined the geological survey of India, and from August till 1862 was professor of geology at the Thomason College of Civil Engineering at Rurki. During his vacations he carried on geological field-work for the survey under Dr. Thomas Oldham [q. v.]. In 1857, as a volunteer, he joined the garrison of Rurki against the mutineers, and for his services was awarded the Indian Mutiny medal. In 1862 he rejoined the geological survey as deputy superintendent for Bengal.

During his early years in India, Medlicott, with his brother Joseph, investigated the stratigraphical position of the Vindhyan series, and sought to separate these ancient unfossiliferous and possibly pre-Cambrian strata from the Gondwana series which ranges from upper palæozoic into mesozoic. In a memoir published by the Indian survey in 1864 Medlicott dealt with the structure of the southern portion of the Himalayan ranges, and expressed the view that the elevation of the mountains did not commence before tertiary times. He instituted some comparisons between the structure of the Alps and the Himalayas in a paper published by the Geological Society in 1868. In his opinion too little attention had been given to the effects of shrinkage and subsidence, and he questioned whether the sea-level has permanently maintained the same radial distance from the centre of the earth. In the words of William Thomas Blanford [q. v. Suppl. II], 'Some of the views expressed by him required and have since received revision, but as an original description of mountain-building, from a uniformitarian as opposed to a catastrophic point of view, it deserves far more attention than it has received.'

In 1876 Medlicott succeeded Oldham as superintendent of the geological survey of India, the title being altered to director in 1885. His duties kept him mainly in Calcutta, where he gave the most painstaking attention to editing the survey publications.

He retired on 27 April 1887, and died at Clifton, Bristol, on 6 April 1905. He was elected F.R.S. in 1877, and in 1888 the Wollaston medal was awarded to him by the Geological Society. He was president of the Asiatic Society of Bengal 1879–81, and was a fellow of Calcutta University.

On 27 Oct. 1857 he married at Landour (Landhaur) Louisa, second daughter of the Rev. D. H. Maunsell, by whom he had three sons and three daughters. His wife, with one son and one daughter, survived him.

His published works include: 1. 'Sketch of the Geology of the Punjab,' 1874; revised 1888. 2. 'Manual of the Geology of India,' two vols. (with W. T. Blanford), 1879; new edit., revised by R. D. Oldham, 1893. 3. 'Agnosticism and Faith,' 1888. 4. 'The Evolution of Mind in Man,' 1892.

[Obituaries by W. T. Blanford, Proc. Roy. Soc. lxxix. B. 1906, p. xix, and Nature, lxxi. 1905, p. 612.] H. B. W.

MEIKLEJOHN, JOHN MILLER DOW (1836–1902), writer of school books, born in Edinburgh on 11 July 1836, was son of John Meiklejohn, an Edinburgh schoolmaster. Educated at his father's private school (7 St. Anthony Place, Port Hopetoun), he graduated M.A. at Edinburgh University on 21 April 1858, when he was the gold medallist in Latin. At an early age he devoted himself to German philosophy, and when still under twenty produced for Bohn's Philosophical Library a translation of Immanuel Kant's 'Critique of Pure Reason.' Meiklejohn became a private schoolmaster, first in the Lake district and then in Orme Square and York Place, London. He also lectured and engaged in journalism. His linguistic powers and general interest in affairs induced him in 1864 to act as a war correspondent in the Danish-German war, when he was arrested as a spy. But he was already busy with useful compilations for the schoolroom. Between 1862 and 1866 he issued 'An Easy English Grammar for Beginners, being a Plain Doctrine of Words and Sentences' (Manchester, 4 parts). For some years he published his schoolbooks for himself in Paternoster Square. In 1869 he issued (jointly with Adolf Sonnenschein) 'The English Method of Teaching to Read,' and this was followed in 1870 by 'The Fundamental Error in the Revised Code, with Special Reference to the Problem of Teaching to Read.' In 1874 Meiklejohn's educational energy was rewarded by his appointment as assistant commissioner to the endowed schools commission for Scotland. To the report of that commission he contributed valuable educational suggestions. In 1876 Dr. Bell's trustees instituted a chair of the theory, history, and practice of education in St. Andrews University, and Meiklejohn was appointed as the first professor. In his new capacity Meiklejohn from the outset exerted much influence on educational ideas at a time when the national system of education was undergoing complete reconstruction. He was a frequent contributor to the 'Journal of Education' and was a fair and humorous controversialist. Meanwhile Meiklejohn steadily continued to compile and edit school textbooks on history, geography, and literature. His works, apart from numerous school texts and reading books for Blackwood's educational series (1883–7) and the like, included 'The Book of the English Language' (1877), 'The English Language: its Grammar, History, and Literature' (1886), and 'The British Empire: its Geography, Resources, Commerce, Land-ways, and Water-ways' (1891). His numerous geographical manuals adapted to modern use the work of James Cornwell [q.v. Suppl. II]. Meiklejohn's series of school books, which was inaugurated in 1894, included a book on Australasia (1897) and 'The Art of Writing English' (1899; 4th edit. 1902). There followed 'English Literature: a New History and Survey from Saxon Times to the Death of Tennyson' (posthumous, 1904). Meiklejohn did much to raise the standard of school books in use throughout the country. A keen politician, he unsuccessfully contested the Tradeston division of Glasgow as a Gladstonian liberal in 1886.

He died at Ashford, Kent, on 5 April 1902, and was buried there. He married Jane Cussans or de Cusance. Of his sons and daughters, Lieutenant H. B. Meiklejohn, R.N., died on 18 May 1902.

Besides the works mentioned Meiklejohn was author of 'An Old Educational Reformer, Dr. Andrew Bell' (Edinburgh, 12mo, 1881), and he edited the 'Life and Letters of William Ballantyne Hodgson' (Edinburgh, 1883).

[The Times, 7 April 1902; The Journal of Education, May 1903; Post Office Edinburgh and Leith Directory, 1846–7; Meiklejohn's works; Brit. Mus. Cat.] J. E. G. DE M.

MELDRUM, CHARLES (1821–1901), meteorologist, born at Kirkmichael, Banffshire, in 1821, was son of William Meldrum, farmer, of Tomintoul, Banffshire. Educated at Marischal College, Aberdeen, he was lord rector's prizeman, and graduated M.A. in 1844. In 1846 he was appointed to the education department, Bombay, and two years later was transferred to the Royal College of Mauritius as professor of mathematics. There later (Sir) Walter Besant [q. v. Suppl. II] was a colleague and intimate friend. In 1851 Meldrum founded the Mauritius Meteorological Society, which he served for many years as secretary.

In 1862 he was appointed government observer in charge of the small meteorological observatory then maintained at Port Louis. Here he devoted himself to the examination of ships' logs, and worked out the laws of cyclones in the Indian Ocean, work of great practical benefit to navigators, which brought considerable credit to the Mauritius observatory. The site at Port Louis was unsuitable for a meteorological observatory, and with the support of Sir E. Sabine he was able to obtain the erection of a new station at Pamplemousses—a site unhappily marshy and fever-stricken. Here the foundation stone of the Royal Alfred Observatory was laid in 1870 by the Duke of Edinburgh. The principal work of the observatory was as before the study of the movement of storms, but from 1880 photographs of the solar surface have been taken daily to supplement the series made at Greenwich and Dehra Dun for a continuous record of the number of spots on the sun.

In 1876 Meldrum was elected a fellow of the Royal Society, and in the same year the degree of LL.D. was conferred on him by the university of Aberdeen. He was made C.M.G. in 1886, and was a member of the governor's council from 1886 until his retirement from service in 1896, when he returned to England, settling at Southsea.

He died at Edinburgh on 28 August 1901. He married in 1870 Charlotte, daughter of Percy Fitzpatrick.

[Monthly Notices, Royal Astron. Soc. lxii. 243, 1902; P. J. Anderson, Records of Marischal College, ii. 510; Proc. Roy. Soc. 1905; Who's Who, 1901.] A. R. H.

MELLON, Mrs. SARAH JANE, formerly Sarah Jane Woolgar (1824–1909), actress, born at Gosport, Hampshire, on 8 July 1824, was daughter of a tailor named Woolgar, who went on the stage in 1829 and proved an indifferent tragedian. He gave his child an excellent professional training. Making her first appearance at Plymouth in May 1836, as Leolyn in 'The Wood Demon,' she quickly acquired a reputation as a 'young phenomenon,' performing at Halifax, York, Nottingham, and on the Worcester circuit. Subsequently she studied music, and at Birmingham in 1841, during the visit of Mr. and Mrs. Wood, the operatic vocalists [see Paton, Mary Ann], sang for five nights as Adalgisa in 'Norma.' In November 1842 she fulfilled a successful engagement at the Theatre Royal, Manchester, where she appeared as Ophelia.

On 9 Oct. 1843 Miss Woolgar made her London début at the Adelphi as Cleopatra in Selby's burletta 'Antony and Cleopatra.' With the Adelphi she was long associated. Her first original character there was in T. Egerton Wilks's romantic drama 'The Roll of the Drum' on 16 October. On 8 April 1844 she joined the Keeleys at the Lyceum, and after appearing in several light pieces she rendered to great advantage the part of Mercy in Stirling's version of 'Martin Chuzzlewit.'

In the autumn of 1844 the Adelphi reopened under the management of Benjamin Webster and Madame Celeste, and the golden period of Miss Woolgar's career at that theatre began. On 14 October she showed dramatic feeling as Lazarillo in Boucicault's 'Don Cesar de Bazan.' At the Haymarket on 18 Nov. (owing to the sudden illness of Madame Vestris) she played Lady Alice Hawthorn, on half a day's notice, in the same author's new comedy 'Old Heads and Young Hearts.' She returned to the Adelphi at Easter 1845, and afterwards fulfilled some provincial engagements with her father. At the Adelphi on 11 March 1847 she was the original Lemuel in Buckstone's melodrama 'The Flowers of the Forest.' Dickens spoke of this performance as the most remarkable and complete piece of melodrama he had seen. Appearances in a variety of unimportant dramas, farces, and burlesques followed. After a severe illness she reappeared at the Adelphi on 1 March 1852 as Phœbe to Wright's Paul Pry, acting 'with her usual correct perception of character and vivacity.' In April 1853 she was Mrs. Vane in 'Masks and Faces,' and among her original characterisations in 1854 was Anne Musgrave in Tom Taylor and Charles Reade's 'Two Loves and a Life' (20 May).

In 1856 Miss Woolgar joined the Lyceum company under Charles Dillon, appearing there on 15 Sept. as Florizel in the burlesque of 'Perdita,' to the Perdita of Miss Marie Wilton (Lady Bancroft), who then made her metropolitan début. On 16 Oct. she was the original Constance in 'The Three Musketeers.' In March 1857 she gave a notable rendering of Ophelia, and in the following Christmas sustained a leading character in the Oriental pantomime of 'Lalla Rookh.' On 20 Jan. 1858 she was the original Countess de Montelons in Leigh Hunt's comedy 'Lovers' Amazements.' At this period she was married to Alfred Mellon [q. v.], the musician, and thenceforth acted under her married name.

On the opening of the new Adelphi Theatre on 27 Dec. 1858, Mrs. Mellon played Memory in the apropos sketch 'Mr. Webster's company is requested at a Photographic Soirée,' afterwards delivering Shirley Brooks's inaugural address in the same character. Her finest original rôle at this period was Catherine Duval in Watts Phillips's 'The Dead Heart' (10 Nov. 1859). In January 1860 her Mrs. Cratchit in 'The Christmas Carol' was highly praised by Prof. Henry Morley. On 29 March 1860, at Covent Garden, in aid of the funds of the ill-fated Dramatic College, she played Black-Eyed Susan in Douglas Jerrold's drama to T. P. Cooke's William, notable as Cooke's last appearance on the stage. At the Adelphi on 10 Sept. 1860, when 'The Colleen Bawn' was performed for the first time in England, Mrs. Mellon played Anne Chute, 'winning, perhaps, the foremost honours of the night' (Morley). Her acting with J. L. Toole at the Adelphi in Oct. 1864 in 'The Area Belle' Dickens described in a letter as quite admirable. In September 1865 her Nan in 'Good for Nothing' was said by a competent critic to be as excellent in its way as Jefferson's Rip Van Winkle, which it then preceded. On 5 Oct. 1867 the Adelphi was reopened under her own supervision (but not responsible management). She then demonstrated her versatility by playing Peg Woffington in 'Masks and Faces' and Tom Croft in 'The School for Tigers.' On 26 Dec. 1867 she was the original Sally Goldstraw in Charles Dickens and Wilkie Collins's drama 'No Thoroughfare.' In March 1875 she played Mrs. Squeers in a revival of Halliday's version of 'Nicholas Nickleby,' and in the following October Gretchen to Joe Jefferson's Rip Van Winkle. But, failing to keep step with the steady march towards naturalness, she came to be considered stilted and over pronounced, and she gradually lost caste. On 15 May 1878 a testimonial performance of 'The Green Bushes' was given on her behalf at Drury Lane, when Madame Celeste made her last appearance on the stage. On 14 May 1879 she reappeared at the Adelphi as Mrs. Candour in a revival of 'The School for Scandal,' and there on 24 April 1880 she played Mrs. O'Kelly in the first performance given in England of 'The Shaughraun.' On 2 August following, at the Haymarket, she was the original Miss Sniffe in Boucicault's comedy 'A Bridal Tour.' She remained on the stage till 1883.

Mrs. Mellon died at her residence, Vardens Road, Wandsworth Common, after a very brief illness, on 8 Sept. 1909, and was buried in Brompton cemetery beside her husband, whom she survived forty-two years. She left two daughters, of whom the younger, Miss Mary Woolgar Mellon, became an actress.

'In her prime,' writes John Coleman, 'Miss Woolgar was one of the most accomplished all-round actresses of her day; tragedy, comedy, melodrama, farce, or burlesque—nothing came amiss to her. . . . In high comedy she lacked distinction and hauteur; but a plenitude of sprightliness, piquancy, and even elegance, atoned for this drawback.' At the Victorian Era Exhibition in Earl's Court in 1897 was shown a water-colour drawing, by T. Harrington Wilson, of Mrs. Mellon as Laura in 'Sweethearts and Wives' (1849), lent by the artist. At the Toole sale at Sotheby's in November 1906 were sold an oil-painting by R. Clothier of Toole and Miss Woolgar in the milkmaid scene from 'The Willow Copse' (1869) and a water-colour sketch by Alfred Edward Chalon of Miss Woolgar as the Countess in 'Taming a Tartar.'

[Thomas Marshall's Lives of the Most Celebrated Actors and Actresses (1847); Theatrical Journal, vol. xi. 1854; Era Almanacks for 1875 and 1877; Gentleman's Magazine, Oct. 1888; T. Edgar Pemberton's Dickens and the Stage; Prof. Henry Morley's Journal of a London Playgoer; John Coleman's The Truth about 'The Dead Heart,' 1890; The Bancroft Memoirs, 1909; Daily Telegraph, 10 Sept. 1909; Athenæum, 18 Sept. 1909; personal research.] W. J. L.

MELVILLE, ARTHUR (1855–1904), artist, born at Loanhead of Guthrie, Forfarshire, on 10 April 1855 (*Parish Register*), was fourth son (in the family of seven sons and two daughters) of Arthur Melville, a coachman, by his wife Margaret Wann. When Arthur was quite young the family removed to East Linton, a picturesque village on the Haddingtonshire Esk. There he went to school, and at an early age was apprenticed to a grocer. Devoted to drawing from childhood, he gave up a situation at Dalkeith, when about twenty, and went to Edinburgh, determined to become an artist. He worked with energy and enthusiasm in the school of art, and later in the life school of the Royal Scottish Academy, receiving encouragement from J. Campbell Noble, R.S.A., of whom he was a personal pupil.

In 1875 he exhibited for the first time at the Scottish Academy, and during the next few years painted some oil pictures of homely incident, which secured the interest of one or two local connoisseurs and led to his going to Paris in 1878. There he studied at Julien's Passage Panorama atelier and sketched on the quays. He also painted at Grez and Granville, and it was in the work then done in water-colour, though his oil pictures possessed distinctive qualities also, that he began to reveal the special qualities which developed rapidly and distinguished his art to the end. Three years later, in 1881, he went to Egypt, where he found material and effects eminently suited to stimulate his artistic development. From Egypt he went by Suez and Aden to Kurrachi, whence he found his way up the Persian Gulf to Bagdad, rode across Asia Minor to the Black Sea, and took steamer to Constantinople. During these two years he made many striking drawings and stored up a wealth of impressions, which bore fruit in future years.

When Melville returned to Scotland, the artistic movement, which issued in what came to be known as the Glasgow school, had already begun. There was a certain affinity between his work and that of the young Glasgow painters. Meeting Mr. (now Sir James) Guthrie and E. A. Walton at Cockburnspath in 1883,

Melville associated himself with them. He had already achieved a more individual style than they, and his strong personality helped to accelerate and mould the Glasgow movement, but he on his part was influenced by the Glasgow artists' enthusiasm and audacity in experiment. During the following years, besides completing many Eastern sketches, he painted in water-colours in the Orkneys; but the most important pictures which he produced before leaving Edinburgh for London in 1888 were several oil portraits, amongst them 'The Flower Girl' (1883), 'Miss Ethel Croall' (1886), and the 'Portrait of a Lady' shown at the Royal Scottish Academy in 1889, each in its way a *tour de force.* A visit to Spain and Tangier in 1889–90 was followed in 1892 by an expedition to northern Spain with Mr. Frank Brangwyn. These journeys supplied Melville with motives for a series of important drawings executed on a larger scale and more subtle and masterly in style and finer in colour than their predecessors. Venice in 1894 was his next fruitful venture. After 1897 he devoted more attention to oil painting. There, however, his work, although always interesting and powerful, was more experimental and less satisfying, and, in portraiture at least, tended to extravagance. In 1904 he was again in Spain, at San Sebastian, Granada, and Barcelona, but he contracted typhoid fever while there, and on 29 Aug. he died from its after-effects, at his residence, Redlands, Witley, Surrey. His body was cremated and his ashes lie in Brookwood cemetery.

On 18 Dec. 1899 he married in London Ethel, daughter of David Croall of Southfield, Liberton, Midlothian, who, with a daughter, survived him. Mrs. Melville has a charcoal drawing of him by Sir James Guthrie; Mr. Graham Robertson, an intimate friend, made two sketches of him, which remain in his own possession.

Melville was elected an associate of the Royal Scottish Academy in 1886, and was for some years a member of the Royal Scottish Water-Colour Society. In London he became an associate of the Royal Water Colour Society in 1889 and full member in 1900. The National Gallery of Scotland possesses 'A Moorish Procession,' one of the finest of his Tangier drawings, and 'Christmas Eve,' one of four large oil pictures illustrating Christmas carols, upon which he was engaged at his death; the Glasgow Gallery has an important water-colour, 'The Capture of a Spy,' and in the water-colour collection at the Victoria and Albert Museum, London, is 'The Little Bull Fight—Bravo Toro!' There are also notable drawings by him in the Luxembourg, Paris, and the Metropolitan Museum, New York.

[Information from Mrs. Melville and Mr. J. C. Noble; exhibition catalogues; R.S.A. Report, 1904; Baldwin Brown, The Glasgow School of Painters, 1908 (with photographic portrait); J. L. Caw, Scottish Painting, 1908.]

J. L. C.

MEREDITH, GEORGE (1828–1909), novelist and poet, was born at 73 High Street, Portsmouth (the Lymport of 'Evan Harrington'), on 12 Feb. 1828. His great-grandfather, John Meredith, was living at Portsea in the middle of the eighteenth century, and there in the parish church his son Melchizedek or Melchisedec was baptised in June 1763. 'Mel' early in life became a tailor and naval outfitter in the chief street of Portsmouth, and his business soon became the leading one of its kind in the port (there is a reference to it in chap. vi. of the second vol. of Marryat's *Peter Simple*, 1834). His ambitions ranged beyond the counter; he was on friendly terms with many distinguished customers, was welcomed as a diner-out, and talked like Sydney Smith. He kept horses and hunted, was a member of a local Freemasons' Lodge, and joined the Portsmouth yeomanry as an officer on Napoleon's threat of invasion. In 1801 and 1803–4 he was a churchwarden in the parish church of St. Thomas, to which he presented two offertory plates. He died on 10 July 1804, leaving a large family by his wife Anne, like himself, tall, handsome, and (it is said) the daughter of a solicitor in good practice. 'Mel's' son, Gustave Urmston (1797–1876), whose name was changed subsequently to Augustus Armstrong, succeeded to the business. Though not without commercial ability, he was wild and extravagant, being, possibly, hampered by his father's grand ideas. He married in 1824 Jane Eliza (1802–1833), daughter of Michael Macnamara of the Point, Portsmouth, 'an old inhabitant' of the town. The only child of this marriage was George Meredith, born above the ancestral shop and baptised on 9 April 1828 in the church of St. Thomas, just seven months before the death of Mrs. 'Mel,' his grandmother. In July 1833 his mother died, the business fell into a rapid decline, and the father migrated first to London and subsequently to Cape Town. He retired after 1860 to 2 Oxford Villas (now 50 Elm Grove), Southsea, where his son visited him occasionally, and he died there on 18 June 1876. His second wife (his cook), Matilda (Buckett), died in 1885, aged sixty-seven, and they are interred together in the Highland Road cemetery, Southsea. The four 'daughters of the shears,' as Meredith called the great Mel's daughters in 'Evan Harrington,' were all exceedingly beautiful, and they married men somewhat above their own social station. The eldest, Anne Eliza, married in April 1809 Thomas Burbey, banker, of 46 High Street, Portsmouth, who became mayor of the town in 1833. The second, Louisa, married in March 1811 John Read, consul-general for the Azores. The third, Harriet, married John Hellyer, a brewer; and the youngest, Catherine Matilda, married, also in St. Thomas's church, on 28 Oct. 1819, (Sir) Samuel Burdon Ellis [q. v.]. Three of these aunts can be identified without difficulty, mutatis mutandis, for Meredith never mimicked environment too closely, in 'Evan Harrington.'

Meredith's first ten or twelve years were spent at Portsmouth, where he enjoyed the hospitality of his aunts, their friends and relatives. He went as a day boy to St. Paul's church school, Southsea; afterwards the trustees of his mother's small estate put him to a boarding school in the town, his chief recollections of which centred round the dreariness of the Sunday services and the reading of the 'Arabian Nights.' Early in 1843 he was sent to the Moravian School at Neuwied on the Rhine, ten miles north-west of Coblentz, where Professor Henry Morley had preceded him about five years. He remained there until the close of 1844, when he returned home to be articled to a solicitor in London. He began to learn in earnest, though never very systematically, at Neuwied, and his ideas were much enlarged, but he was mainly self-educated. He studied Goethe and Richter. His sympathy with the German point of view in 'Farina,' 'Harry Richmond,' 'The Tragic Comedians,' 'One of our Conquerors,' and elsewhere is sometimes attributed to his sojourn upon the Rhine when he was fifteen; but his stay at Neuwied was brief and his allusions to it in later life were very limited and inconclusive. He read German with perfect ease, but spoke it indifferently, with less ease, indeed, than he spoke French, which he wrote with facility.

In 1845 he was articled to Richard Stephen Charnock of 10 Godliman Street, lawyer and antiquary, who is thought to have combined certain of the traits of the two uncles in 'Richard Feverel.' Charnock was a Bohemian and a 'character' who, in 1847–8, when he became accessible to Meredith, was one of the 'old boys' of the Arundel Club. George's income during this period was very small and irregular, and he frequently lived on a single bowl of porridge a day. His recreation was walking out into Surrey. His patrimony had dwindled, and seeing no definite prospect in the law he turned instinctively to journalism. At or through the Arundel Club he obtained introductions to R. H. Horne, Lord John Manners, and Charles Dickens, through whom he hoped to obtain work on the 'Standard,' 'Household Words,' and other papers. Twenty-four of his earliest poems were contributed to 'Household Words,' while he acted as 'writing master' to a small circle of amateurs who sent other poems to the same periodical. In 1849 he began sending contributions, including a piece on Kossuth, to 'Chambers's Journal,' and on 7 July a poem by him on 'Chillianwallah' was printed there. He had already made the acquaintance of 'Ned' [Edward] Gryffydh, son of Thomas Love Peacock [q. v.]; had walked with him to Brighton, and afterwards met, at his rooms near the British Museum, his attractive if flighty sister, Mary Ellen, who had married, in Jan. 1844, Lieutenant Edward Nicolls (commander of H.M.S. Dwarf) and was left a widow within four months of the marriage. Extraordinarily gifted, young, poor, ambitious, Meredith was admitted into the intimacy of the Peacock circle. He played cricket with Mrs. Nicolls's little daughter, Edith, and took his place among Mrs. Nicolls's many admirers. In successive months he, young Peacock, Mrs. Nicolls, Charnock, and other friends, edited the manuscript periodical 'The Monthly Observer,' which ran from March 1848 to July 1849 (cf. *Athenæum*, 24 Aug. 1912). Mrs. Nicolls was at least seven years older than Meredith, but they were married at St. George's, Hanover Square, on 9 Aug. 1849. They paid visits to Felixstowe and elsewhere, and then, depending chiefly upon a small Portsmouth legacy, spent a year or more abroad before taking up their residence at Weybridge. There they boarded at The Limes, the house of Mrs. Macirone, a highly cultured woman, where Meredith met, among others, Sir Alexander Duff Gordon, his accomplished wife (Lucy), Eyre Crowe, Tom Taylor, and Samuel Lucas of 'The Times,' whose 'Mornings of the Recess' formed the literary causerie most valued by men of letters. Two miles across the ferry stood Peacock's house at Lower Halliford. Meredith's youthful admiration for Peacock bore fruit in a genuine though not very close influence. While still at Weybridge Meredith dedicated his 'Poems' of 1851 to 'Thomas Love Peacock, Esq. . . . with the profound admiration and affectionate respect of his son-in-law, Weybridge, May 1851.' In all probability Peacock had assisted in the publication of the volume, which was issued by Peacock's friends, J. W. Parker & Son of West Strand, and which cost the poor author about 60*l.* (a single copy has since fetched as much as 30*l.*). Parker & Son also published 'Fraser's Magazine,' to the pages of which Peacock's daughter and son-in-law were early contributors. An 'Essay on Gastronomy and Civilisation' (Dec. 1851) is signed M[ary] M[eredith]; it was subsequently expanded into a little book. Two among George Meredith's earliest identified single poems, 'Invitation to the Country' and 'Sweet of the Year,' also appeared in 'Fraser' (Aug. 1851, June 1852). While still at Weybridge, with 'duns knocking at the door,' Meredith began working at 'The Shaving of Shagpat,' much of it being read aloud to his little step-daughter, and many passages declaimed to Janet Duff Gordon, his literary Egeria of a few years later. In 1853 Peacock invited Meredith and his wife, whose struggle with poverty threatened to overwhelm them, to live in his house. There Arthur Gryffydh (1853–90), the only child of the union, was born on 11 June 1853. Soon after Peacock installed the young family in a cottage (still standing) at Lower Halliford.

'No sun warmed my roof-tree,' Meredith was said to have exclaimed in later years; 'the marriage was a blunder.' The course of estrangement, though not its cause, is traced implicitly in 'Modern Love.' Outwardly relations were amicable, and visits were paid to the FitzGeralds (nephews of the author of 'Omar') at Seaford, and were returned. In 1858 Mrs. Meredith went off to Capri with the artist Henry Wallis, eventually returning to Weybridge, where she died at Grotto Cottage in 1861. Meredith claimed his son, and for a time they lived together in London, no one knows where, or upon what resources. Ned Peacock and his son, however, were still occasional visitors, as they continued to be for at least another ten years.

In Meredith's first volume, 'Poems' of 1851, there is nothing, perhaps, altogether first rate, for the 'Love in the Valley,' as we know it, was rewritten in 1878. But the general level of accomplishment and beauty is high; there is daring in the young poet's rhythmical experiments without rhyme. Although Meredith often complained later of the lack of encouragement extended to his early efforts, his first volume won much praise. W. M. Rossetti, then twenty-two years old, described it as Keatsian in the 'Critic' (15 Nov.), and Charles Kingsley in 'Fraser' (Dec. 1851) put the 'Love Poems' above Herrick's. Tennyson also wrote that he found the verse of 'Love in the Valley' very sweet upon his lips. The quinine, so distinctive of Meredith's later verse, was imported later. Meredith's second venture, 'The Shaving of Shagpat: An Arabian Entertainment,' followed in 1855. It is a fantasia on the subject-matter of 'The Arabian Nights,' easily outstripping its forerunner, Beckford's 'Vathek,' in the skill with which it catches the oriental spirit. Arabic students have indeed sought a lost original. The author expressly repudiated any elaborate allegorical intention. George Eliot in 'The Leader' (5 Jan. 1856) described it as a work of genius—poetical genius, and as 'an apple tree among the trees of the wood.' 'Farina: a Legend of Cologne,' which followed the Arab tale in 1857, is a rather slighter burlesque or ironical sketch, something in the vein of Peacock, aimed at the mediæval and romantic tale. George Eliot praised it, though without very much emphasis, in the 'Westminster Review' October 1857.

All three volumes had been easel-pieces from which the author could hardly with reason expect pecuniary return, and from 1856, when Meredith severed his connection with Halliford, down to the close of 1858, we can only conjecture his means of support. Extremely poor, he almost despaired of literature while doing a certain amount of hackwork and supplementing his slender income by occasional journalism. He may possibly have received some assistance from his father's sisters. His home was temporarily fixed in London. There at 8 Hobury Street, Chelsea, 'The Ordeal of Richard Feverel,' commenced at The Limes, was concluded with comparative rapidity, during 1858–9. Published in 1859, it was reviewed with enthusiasm in 'Cope's Tobacco Plant' by James Thomson [q. v.] in May, and favourably by the 'Athenæum' on 9 July 1859; on 14 October 'The Times' devoted three columns to it. Mudie, it seems, took three hundred copies, but then lost nerve owing to suspicion of 'low ethical tone' formulated by the 'Spectator'

The main idea of the book, the victimisation of the Fairy Prince hero by a fond paternal system of education, was suggested by Herbert Spencer's famous article in the 'British Quarterly Review' (April 1858), with occasional hints from 'Tristram Shandy,' 'Émile,' and the more recent 'The Caxtons.' In this book Meredith first and successfully assumes the airily Olympian and omniscient manner which is the inspiration of his genius and is not explained by anything in his personal experience or training. But his power was little recognised. Nineteen years elapsed before a second edition was called for, and Meredith realised that he could not look to books for a living. He thereupon definitely accepted regular work for the 'Ipswich Journal,' a Conservative newspaper since dead. The offer was due to connections formed in his early London days through Charnock with Foakes, proprietor of the 'Ipswich Journal,' and other newspaper men, among whom was Algernon Borthwick. Every Thursday or Friday he posted a leading article (occasionally two, for the second of which he was expressly paid) and two columns of news-notes, for which he received approximately 200*l.* per annum. He spoke with feeling later of the Egyptian bondage of (tory) journalism; but the leaders and notes were admirably done (DOLMAN, *New Review*, March 1893). Indirectly 'Richard Feverel' did Meredith service, for it brought him into nearer contact with Swinburne, Monckton Milnes, and the Pre-Raphaelite group. At a meeting with Swinburne during the summer of 1859 in the Isle of Wight, Swinburne at one sitting 'composed before our eyes his poem "Laus Veneris"' (M. PHOTIADÈS), and in a letter to the 'Spectator' of 7 June 1862 Swinburne protested with chivalrous eloquence against the freezing reception accorded to 'Modern Love' in the 'Spectator.' In 1859–60 Meredith had returned to the sand and pines and river that he loved, and it was while he was lodging in High Street, Esher, that Janet Duff Gordon stumbled accidentally upon him and his son Arthur. The Duff Gordons' proximity, between Esher and Oxshott, determined his settlement at Copsham in a fit dwelling for a poet, on a breezy common, close to the humming pine woods, behind Claremont and the Black Pool—a small lake surrounded by tall dark trees and frequented by a stately heron (JANET ROSS, *Early Days Recalled*, 1891). At the Duff Gordons, he was introduced to notable people, such as Mrs. Norton, Kinglake, Millais, Sir F. B. Head, G. F. Watts, and at Copsham he continued to live for six years. An epicure of aristocratic type in his zest for choice living and varied society, he was afflicted with a weak stomach and tormented by a constitutional flatulence which he sought to exorcise by many-sided activity; thence came conference with and observation of all sorts and conditions of men. He scoured the countryside by night and day with a hawk's eye for uncommon types; of sportsmen, cricketers, prize-fighters, boxers, race meetings, and alehouse assemblies he was ever, as his books attest, a connoisseur. During the second half of 1859 he contributed six poems to successive numbers of 'Once a Week,' including 'The Last Words of Juggling Jerry' (3 Sept.), and on 11 Feb. 1860, besides submitting one or two short stories, traces of which have since disappeared, he began in the same periodical the serial publication of 'Evan Harrington, or He would be a Gentleman,' which was illustrated by Charles Keene. Keene, Sandys, Millais, and Rossetti were among the illustrators of 'Once a Week,' and with these Meredith became familiar. 'Evan Harrington' is the most real, and perhaps the most generally entertaining, of all Meredith's novels. It describes in a sardonic vein the frantic attempts of Evan's sisters (and sidelights here are assumed to have been drawn from a whimsical observation of his own paternal aunts) to escape from the Demogorgon of Tailordom. The spirit of 'Great Mel,' who dies before the action begins, pervades the book. In so far as he ever drew his characters direct from life Janet Duff Gordon (Mrs. Janet Ross from 1860), who begins now to be a regular correspondent, was his model for Rose Jocelyn (see MRS. ROSS, *The Fourth Generation*, 1912). 'Evan Harrington' was much more remunerative than its predecessor, and was pirated in America before the year was out. But again it proved a disappointment. The 'Saturday Review,' which had condemned 'Richard Feverel' for its affectations, wearisome word-painting, and immorality, described 'Evan Harrington' as a surprisingly good novel; the other papers either ignored or damned it with vapid mouthings.

The next three years (1861–4) were among the busiest in Meredith's life, although his novel-writing was temporarily interrupted. He wrote much poetry, publishing in 1862 an autobiographical commentary (now in the mood of Hamlet, now in that of Leontes) upon his first love and his disillusion in 'Modern Love (perhaps 'the most intensely modern poem ever written') and Poems of the English Roadside.' The book included 'Juggling Jerry,' 'The Old Chartist,' and other poems reprinted from 'Once a Week,' besides twelve new poems. He became a contributor to the 'Morning Post,' and in 1862 began reading for the publishers Messrs. Chapman & Hall, in addition to his editorial contributions to the 'Ipswich Journal.' His connection with Chapman & Hall was soon close. Batches of manuscripts were forwarded periodically, and on blank enclosed slips headed by the titles, Meredith inscribed crisp, sharp, and epigrammatic criticism. Once a week or thereabouts he interviewed authors in the firm's old office, 193 Piccadilly. By rejecting 'East Lynne' it has been estimated that he lost the firm a round sum of money. He also declined works by Hugh Conway, Mrs. Lynn Linton, Mr. Baring Gould, Herman Merivale, Cuthbert Bede, Stepniak's 'Underground Russia,' 'The Heavenly Twins,' and 'Some Emotions and a Moral.' Samuel Butler's 'Erewhon' he dismissed with a 'Will not do,' and Shaw's 'Immaturity' with a 'No.' On the other hand he encouraged William Black, Sir Edwin Arnold, Thomas Hardy, Olive Schreiner, and George Gissing. Meredith was deeply interested in the work of his younger contemporaries; Gissing and Thomas Hardy confessed no small obligation to his encouragement. But he often vacillated in his opinions of both current and past literature.

Meredith was now earning probably over 500*l.* a year; the death of his wife in 1861 and of her mother-in-law, Lady Nicolls, within two years, meant the ultimate as well as the actual pecuniary responsibility for his son Arthur, to whom he had become perilously devoted. He was in Tirol and Italy with his son during the summer of 1861. Arthur was first sent in October 1862 to Norwich grammar school under Dr. Jessopp, who had become a close friend, and then to a Pestalozzi school near Berne (recommended by G. H. Lewes, suggestive in some ways of Weyburn's school in 'Lord Ormont'), and eventually to Stuttgart. A post was afterwards obtained for him in the De Koninck's firm at Havre and later (through Benecke) in a linseed warehouse at Lille. He was provided for subsequently by a legacy from a great-aunt, and resided at Bergamo and Salò on Lake Garda; he wrote some agreeable travel sketches (one of a raft journey from Bale to Rotterdam in 'Macmillan's Magazine'). Meredith sent him many stimulating, sympathetic, and profoundly touching letters, rarely of reproof, more often of reconciliation and bracing exhortation. Spoiled in childhood, of a jealous, self-conscious temperament, suspicious, not without just cause, of a certain lack of consideration on the part of his father, Arthur became, in spite of welcome offered, an incompatible figure at his father's home; his health was ever declining, and he died at Woking at the house of his half-sister, Mrs. Clarke (Edith Nicolls).

Meredith was still in the early 'sixties living economically at Copsham, but his friendships were extending and his visitors were numerous. His intimate circle included William Hardman (later of the 'Morning Post'), Mr. H. M. Hyndman, Frederick Jameson, Frederic Chapman the publisher, J. A. Cotter Morison, Rossetti, Swinburne (who interchanged satires and squibs with him), William Tinsley, Mr. Lionel Robinson, and Frederic Maxse. He was known among them as 'Robin,' Hardman as 'Friar Tuck,' and Mr. Robinson as 'Poco.' To Frederick Augustus Maxse [q. v. Suppl. I.], a very close associate, he dedicated 'By the Rosanna' (Oct. 1861), as well as 'Modern Love' (1862); with him he sailed on a stormy voyage to Cherbourg in The Grebe, a cutter yacht, in 1858, and he took a brief walking tour round Godalming in July 1861. In May 1862 Meredith and Hardman tramped round Mickleham and Dorking. Entertainment was drawn from the associations of Burford Bridge (Keats), The Rookery (Malthus), and Albury (Tupper), and many aphorisms were read by 'Robin' from his note-books. Soon after this Meredith paid a visit to his friend Hyndman at Trinity College, Cambridge, and made acquaintance with university life for the first time. He spent Christmas 1862 with the Hardmans. In the early summer of 1863 he was at Seaford with Burnand, Hyndman, and the FitzGeralds, and Hyndman relates how, after much fine open talk, a good deal of it monologue, upon the beach, Burnand exclaimed 'Damn you, George, why don't you write as you talk?' In August, Meredith and Hyndman were at Paris together, reading Renan's 'Vie de Jésus,' and visiting Véfour's, Versailles, Sèvres, and admiring the ædileship of Napoleon III. On 23 August Meredith left to join his friend Mr. Lionel Robinson at Grenoble, trudging thence like a packman through Dauphiné and the Graian Alps. He went abroad upon several occasions with Mr. Robinson, and began to store up material for his marvellous Alpine effects, making a study of passes and visiting more than once the villa of friends on Lake Como. In January and again in October 1863 he went on a cruise in Cotter Morison's yacht, Irene, on the second occasion to the Channel Islands. The acquaintance with Morison was begun some three years earlier, when Morison was fresh from Oxford, where he had formed an intimacy with Mr. John Morley. In 1862 Morison sought Meredith's counsel in correcting the proofs of his 'Life of St. Bernard' (Meredith always called him 'St. Bernard' afterwards). Meredith denounced him for writing in Carlylese, 'a wind-in-the-orchard style,' and Morison was eventually induced to re-write and simplify much of it. Through Morison, Meredith grew rapidly more intimate with Mr. John Morley, and this friendship proved of material importance to him. He meanwhile resisted pressing invitations to leave Copsham to settle in London with Rossetti and Swinburne at their 'phalanstery,' the Queen's House (Tudor House), Cheyne Walk, Chelsea. Meredith went so far as to take a room in their house in 1861–2. But Rossetti's Bohemianisms were distasteful to him; he seldom went to the house, and after three months paid no more rent. About this time he joined the Garrick Club (elected 23 April 1864, resigned 1899), where he was soon to meet Frederick Greenwood and others, who admired and helped him much.

Of his personal appearance at this period Meredith's friends have recorded ample impressions. Sir F. Burnand, who first saw him at Esher talking to his publisher, 'Pater' Evans (of Bradbury & Evans), and was introduced by Maurice FitzGerald, nephew of Edward FitzGerald [q. v.], wrote: 'George strode towards us . . . he never merely walked, never lounged; he strode, he took giant strides. He had on a soft, shapeless wide-awake, a sad-coloured flannel shirt, with low open collar turned over a brilliant scarlet neckerchief tied in a loose sailor's knot; no waistcoat; knickerbockers, grey stockings, and the most serviceable laced boots which evidently meant business in pedestrianism; crisp curly brownish hair, ignorant of parting; a fine brow, quick observant eyes, greyish, if I remember; beard and moustache a trifle lighter than the hair. A splendid head, a memorable personality. Then his sense of humour, his cynicism, and his absolutely boyish enjoyment of mere fun, of any pure and simple absurdity. His laugh was something to hear; it was of short duration, but it was a roar.' A portrait of the same date exists in the pen-drawing of 'Mary Magdalen at the Gate of Simon the Pharisee' by D. G. Rossetti, in which the figure of Christ was George Meredith drawn from the life. According to another friend, H. M. Hyndman, Meredith's physical strength in early manhood was great. 'He was all wire and whipcord. . . . I shall never forget a playful struggle I had with him in the Dolphin Hotel at Chichester, where we were staying with a party for Goodwood races. I was then strong and active and thought I was pretty good at a rough and tumble, but he wore me down by sheer endurance' (*Justice*, May 1910). He was addicted to throwing up and catching a heavy iron weight at the end of a wooden shaft—which he called his 'beetle exercise.' Over-indulgence in this, it is thought, sowed the seeds of future spinal trouble. His robustness, never so great in reality as in appearance, was also impaired for a time about 1862 and (later) by a fanatical but generally short-lived ardour for vegetarianism, with which his friend Maxse infected him. From Hardman he imbibed a faith in homœopathy. He was habitually fastidious and often difficult (to the utmost acerbity) about the quality and dressing of his food.

In 1863, while still at Copsham, Meredith reconcentrated upon fiction, and submitted to the gradual intensification of labour which the completion of a novel always involved. In April 1864 he brought out 'Emilia in England' (afterwards re-christened 'Sandra Belloni'), the only story which he furnished with a sequel (in 'Vittoria,' 1866). Emilia's passion for Italy forms the central theme of the whole. Her figure, the most beautiful and elaborate he had yet portrayed, dominates the two novels. Nowhere are the gems of his insight more lavishly scattered. There are admirable woodland scenes. At the same time he first formulates his anti-sentimental philosophy and his growing belief in the purifying flame of the Comic Spirit. The reception of the book was, however, meagre.

In September 1864 Meredith married Marie, fourth daughter of Justin Vulliamy (*d.* 1870), of the Old House, Mickleham; her mother Elizabeth Bull came of an old Cheshire family. Meredith got to know the Vulliamys through his friend N. E. S. A. Hamilton of the British Museum, and first met his future wife in Norfolk. The

Vulliamys were of Swiss Huguenot origin [see VULLIAMY, BENJAMIN LEWIS]. After a few weeks at Pear Tree Cottage, Bursledon, Meredith and his wife took lodgings and then a lease of Kingston Lodge, Norbiton, almost opposite the gates of Norbiton Hall, where Hardman resided. Meredith was at the moment full of schemes, 'laying traps for money.' He had hopes of conducting a review, writing rambling remarks, an autobiography. He settled down in a chastened frame of mind to complete 'Rhoda Fleming,' but in the meantime he had improved his position with Chapman & Hall. His enthusiasm for Norbiton, where his son, William Maxse, was born on 26 July 1865, cooled down as buildings began to close in his horizon, and at the end of 1867 he moved to Flint Cottage, facing Box Hill, near Burford Bridge, in Mickleham. There, the scene of Miss Austen's 'Emma,' his opportunities of seeing and knowing people who were useful to him as types were ever enlarging. He became attached to the literary associations of the place, its connections with Keats, with the French exiles of Juniper Hall, and with the Burneys. He knew mid-Surrey extraordinarily well, and, devoted to outdoor life, he acquired a detailed and intimate knowledge of the natural history of the countryside (cf. GRANT ALLEN, in *Pall Mall Gazette*, May 1904). He is probably the closest observer of nature among English novelists. At the top of the sloping garden, about four minutes' remove from Flint Cottage, he put up in 1875–6 a Norwegian chalet where, in one of the two rooms, he slung his 'hammock-cot,' and could live alone with his characters for days together. On the terrace in front of the chalet, whence he descended to meals, he was often to be heard carrying on dialogues with his characters and singing with unrestrained voice. Whimsical and sometimes Rabelaisian fabrications accompanied the process of quickening the blood by a spin (a favourite word with him) over Surrey hills. There he wrote his master-works, 'Beauchamp's Career' and 'The Egoist,' and welcomed his friends, often reading aloud to them in magnificent recitative unpublished prose or verse.

After his second marriage Meredith mainly devoted himself to 'Vittoria,' the sequel of 'Emilia,' Marie, his 'capital wife' and 'help-meet,' copying the chapters. G. H. Lewes, editor of the 'Fortnightly,' eventually offered 250*l.* for the serial rights, and 'Vittoria' in an abbreviated form ran through that Review (January–December 1865). Meanwhile he completed a new novel, 'Rhoda Fleming.' He had promised upon his marriage to 'write now in a different manner,' and 'Rhoda' (originally 'The Dyke Farm'), expanded and much altered in process of construction, yet written consistently against the grain, was the fruit of this conformity. It was adequately reviewed on 18 Oct. 1865 in the 'Morning Post,' with whose proprietor Borthwick his relations were cordial, and hardly anywhere else. 'Rhoda Fleming' is, comparatively speaking, a plain tale, mostly about love, and concerned primarily with persons in humble life. He attempts the delicate task of describing the innate purity of a woman after a moral lapse.

In May 1866 Meredith was sent out by the 'Morning Post' as special correspondent with the Italian forces then in the last phase of the war with Austria. He stayed at the Hotel Cavour in Milan, and afterwards at the Hotel Vittoria in Venice, awaiting events and forgathering with the other special correspondents at the Café Florian. Hyndman was there, and Charles Brackenbury, and G. A. Sala, an antipathetic figure, with whom Meredith was nearly drawn into a serious quarrel. He saw something of the inconclusive operations in Italy and addressed thirteen interesting and vivid letters in plain prose to the paper, the first dated Ferrara, 22 June 1866, and the last Marseilles, 24 July 1866 (reprinted in memorial edition, vol. xxiii. and privately printed as 'Correspondence from the Seat of War in Italy'). For a time Meredith had some hopes of becoming 'The Times' correspondent in Italy, Paris, or elsewhere. As he went home over the Stelvio pass and then by way of Vienna, where he met Leslie Stephen for the first time, he collected fresh material for the revision and expansion of his 'Fortnightly' novel, 'Vittoria' (or 'Emilia in Italy'), which was published on his return to England in 1866. This novel of the revolution of 1848–9 has a complex plot in which Charles Albert, Mazzini, and other historic persons figure; the opening scene on the summit of Monte Motterone, walked over in company with 'Poco,' ranks with that of 'Harry Richmond' or 'The Amazing Marriage.' On its publication the style of the book was complained of as that of prose trying to be poetry, and the author in essaying the novel of history was warned against handicapping himself by extra weight. Swinburne, however, overflowed with generous praise. In 1867 Mr. John

Morley became editor of the 'Fortnightly Review,' and Meredith's contributions to it, which included some reviews of new books, grew frequent. During part of 1867–8 Mr. Morley was absent in America and Meredith was left in charge of the magazine. In 1868 Meredith made his single incursion into active politics by assisting his friend Maxse, who was standing as radical candidate for Southampton. His powers were now at their ripest, and during 1869 and 1870 he was engaged on the great first-person romance of 'The Adventures of Harry Richmond.' Serial publication in the 'Cornhill' was arranged on liberal terms (500*l.* for copyright and 100*l.* on sale of 500 copies), and the first part appeared in Sept. 1870. There were fifteen illustrations by Du Maurier. The father and son theme of 'Feverel' is reanimated in an atmosphere at times dazzlingly operatic; Richmond Roy, on whose character Meredith lavished all his powers, stalks larger than life alongside of Wilkins Micawber and My Uncle Toby. Not one of the author's books rivals this one in invention.

Meanwhile Meredith, whose sympathy with France was increasing in strength, though he admitted now that the war was chargeable on France and its emperor, wrote for the 'Fortnightly' (Jan. 1871) a rather cryptic defensive poem—'France, 1870,' which formed the nucleus of his 'Odes in Contribution to the Song of French History.' French history and memoir (especially Napoleonic) and the fruitage of European travel remained his favourite pastime to the end. In 1872 his friend Leslie Stephen welcomed to the 'Cornhill' his 'Song of Theodolinda.' Meredith spent short holiday seasons more than once in the early seventies in the neighbourhood of Dreux at Nonancourt on the Avre, where his wife's brothers owned wool-spinning mills. His succeeding book, 'Beauchamp's Career,' is enriched by local colour derived from observations made during this Norman sojourn as well as at the Café Florian in 1866. The next two novels, 'Beauchamp's Career' and 'The Egoist,' mark the summit of Meredith's power of concentration. The first, 'Beauchamp's Career' (refused by 'Cornhill'), began to appear in a painfully condensed form in the 'Fortnightly' in August 1874. The book protests through the brains of Beauchamp, the young naval officer (a reflection of Maxse), on the one hand against lolling aristocrats who refuse to lead and against the false idols of Manchester on the other; the complex hero is hampered by apple-fever (as Meredith styles his prepossession for some of the fairest daughters of Eve) and at times by a species of megalomania. The construction keeps the interest intensely alive, and the book ends with the sting of the hero's death by drowning.

Meredith was at this time acquiring new friends, among whom were Moncure Conway, R. L. Stevenson, Russell Lowell, and W. E. Henley; his books were becoming known among the younger generation at Oxford; he was seen in London, though never a familiar figure there, at picture exhibitions or concerts, or dining at Krehl's in Hanover Square. He was preparing to drop his work for the Ipswich paper, done as he said with his toes to leave room for serener operations above, but was still dependent pecuniarily to a considerable extent upon journalism and reading for Chapman & Hall. He managed to combine with his weekly expedition to London a reading engagement to Mrs. Benjamin Wood, 'the great lady of Eltham,' a great-aunt of Sir Evelyn Wood, a woman of marked intelligence, with whom he often discussed contemporary topics. This brought in an appreciable addition to his income. After the reading he returned to the Garrick to dine and then by the 8.40 train from London Bridge to Box Hill. The cool reception accorded to his 'favourite child,' 'Beauchamp's Career' (despite a highly favourable notice by Traill in the 'Pall Mall'), chilled him. Mark Pattison spoke of his name on a book as a label to novel-readers, warning them not to touch. Two short stories in the 'New Quarterly Magazine'—'The House on the Beach' (Jan. 1877) and 'The Case of General Ople and Lady Camper,' a little masterpiece (July 1877)—added range to his repute. In a lecture on 'The Idea of Comedy and the Uses of the Comic Spirit,' which he delivered at the London Institution on 1 Feb. 1877, he defined one of his dominant conceptions of life—the destined triumph of comedy in its tireless conflict with sentimentalism. The lecture was printed with amendments in the 'New Quarterly Magazine' and not separately until 1897. Meredith continued to harp upon the function of the Comic Spirit, notably in the prelude to 'The Egoist,' in the 'Ode to the Comic Spirit,' and in 'The Two Masks.'

After the lecture a new period in Meredith's career as a novelist opens. For a quarter of a century he had been producing novels of the first rank. Yet his best work was still addressed to empty benches.

Henceforth he abandoned any idea of a compromise with his readers. He determined to write in his own way, upon his own themes uninterruptedly. In 'The Egoist' (3 vols. 1879) or 'Sir Willoughby Patterne, The Egoist,' as it was first called when it began to run through the 'Glasgow Weekly Herald' in June 1879, he develops a new novel-formula consisting of a kind of fugue —innumerable variations upon one central theme, that of the fatuity of a pontifical egoism, mercilessly exposed by the searchlights of the Comic Spirit. 'I had no idea of the matter,' wrote Stevenson when rereading the novel, 'human red matter he has contrived to plug and pack into this strange and admirable book. Willoughby is of course a fine discovery, a complete set of nerves not heretofore examined, and yet running all over the human body—a suit of nerves . . . I see more and more that Meredith is built for immortality.' The noble but 'coltish' Vernon Whitford is sketched after the author's friend Leslie Stephen. The book was hastily written in five months, by night as well as by day, to the injury of health. It was the first among Meredith's novels to provoke a crossfire of criticism. Henley reviewed it three (or four) times, frankly as regarded the ingrained peculiarities of the style, but with an almost reverential admiration for its analytic power. Mr. William Watson attacked (in *National Review,* October 1889) the plethoric mentality of the writer, his fantastic foppery of expression, oracular air of superiority, and sham profundity. The controversy did the author no harm. The three volumes of 1879 were followed by a second one-volume edition in 1880. This fact, the reprints of 'Shagpat' and 'Feverel' and 'Love in the Valley,' the appearance of 'Feverel' and 'Beauchamp's Career' in Tauchnitz editions, and the reproduction of several of the novels in America, all began to point to a rediscovery on the part of the public of the Meredith revealed by 'The Times' in 1859 and then obscured for twenty years.

Meredith next published 'The Tale of Chloe,' a short story of a singular and grievous pathos, in the 'New Quarterly Magazine' (July 1879), and then began sketching in the first instance from newspaper reports, and from 'Meine Beziehungen zu Ferdinand Lassalle' by Hélène von Racowitza (Breslau, 1879), a contemporary romance, the love story and death in a duel of Ferdinand Lassalle, the German socialist. Meredith called his dramatic recital 'The Tragic Comedians,' and enriched it with some of his most brilliant and original epigrams. It first appeared in the 'Fortnightly' (Oct. 1880–Feb. 1881), and was enlarged for separate publication (by Kegan Paul) in December 1880. In spite of his imperfect materials, Meredith accurately assessed the values of his hero and heroine, Alvan (Lassalle) a Titan, a sun-god, inured to success, of Jewish race, a revolutionary and a free-liver, and Clotilde (Hélène von Dönniges) a Christian girl from a noble and exclusive, demagogue-hating family of the Philistines. The book attracted attention, was taken over by Chapman & Hall in 1881, and was reprinted in America and in the Tauchnitz collection.

In 1879 he had by hard exertion carved out a good holiday, spent partly in Patterdale with Mr. John Morley, and partly in Dauphiné and Normandy. But premonitions of advancing ill-health, a growing sense of neglect, and the necessities of unremitting labour saddened him. For a time he was estranged from his son Arthur, but news of Arthur's spitting blood in June 1881 awoke the old tenderness, and next year he made a Mediterranean excursion with him. Meanwhile the enthusiastic devotion of literary friends was increasing. In 1882 he joined Leslie Stephen's society of Sunday Tramps, which more than once made Box Hill a base for the ascent of Leith Hill. In 1882 the Stevensons visited him. In 1883 he met Sir Charles Dilke and Prof. R. C. Jebb for the first time. He was cheered by Browning's appreciation of his verse.

In May 1883 he brought out his most notable poetic volume, 'Poems and Lyrics of the Joy of Earth,' no testimony to his wisdom, he describes it. Here we have, with a few personal poems, such as the verses to J[ohn] M[orley] and 'To a Friend Lost' (Tom Taylor, whose 'Lady Clancarty' he had applauded), the finished version of 'Love in the Valley,' and lyrics such as 'The Lark Ascending,' 'Earth and Man,' 'Melampus,' and 'The Woods of Westermain,' which satisfactorily answer the complaint that Meredith's 'Philosophical Lyrics' contain too much brain and too little music or magnetism. He urges the need of the mutual working of blood (the flesh, senses, bodily vigour) and brain, and the steering of a course between ascetic rocks and sensual whirlpools, in quest of spiritual exaltation.

In 1884–5 there ran through the 'Fortnightly Review' chapters i.–xxvi. of 'Diana of the Crossways' (so named after a beautiful old Surrey farm house, pictured in the memorial edition). The book (with a dedication to one of his

Sunday Tramp friends, Sir Frederick Pollock) appeared in 1885, and three editions were exhausted during the year. At length the general public was captured. Diana was clearly modelled upon the brilliant Caroline Sheridan, the Hon. Mrs. Norton [q. v.], whom he had met at the Duff Gordons before 1860, and who was long a favourite theme of society gossip. The legend of her having betrayed to 'The Times' the secret confided to her by Sidney Herbert that Peel had resolved on the repeal of the Corn Laws was of later growth, and Meredith was subsequently persuaded by the Dufferins to repudiate the popular identification of Mrs. Norton's career with that of his heroine. The book was blessed by Henley in the 'Athenæum' and the heroine celebrated as of the breed of Shakespeare and of Molière. A parody appeared among 'Mr. Punch's Prize Novels,' and society grew alive to the peculiar flash of the Meredithian epigram. Invitations from society and societies inundated him, and Box Hill became a place of pilgrimage. Collective editions of his works were arranged and proposals were made to dramatise 'Evan Harrington' and 'The Egoist.' The belated success coincided tragically with the insidious development of a spinal complaint and with the serious and soon hopeless malady of his wife. Two operations proved ineffectual, and she died on 17 Sept. 1885. Despite ebullitions of temper, which appeared at times almost uncontrollable, Meredith was devotedly attached to one who protected him not only from himself but also from adroit strangers, concerning whose claims upon his attention he was often far too sanguine. It was to the poetic mood that his mind reverted during this period of privation and suffering. The years 1887–8 yielded two of his most characteristic volumes of verse, 'Ballads and Poems of Tragic Life' and 'A Reading of Earth'—the last containing 'The South-Wester,' 'The Thrush in February,' 'Nature and Life,' 'Dirge in Woods,' and above all the 'Hymn to Colour,' with the touching epitaph 'M. M.' The 'Nature Poems' were collected with beautiful drawings by W. Hyde, 1898 (sm. fol.).

His temper mellowed greatly during his last twenty years, and he became in a sense far more approachable. In 1887 he spent a month at St. Ives in Cornwall to be near his friends the Leslie Stephens. In July 1888 he dined at the Blue Posts tavern in Bond Street with (Lord) Haldane and Mr. Asquith, sitting between Mr. A. J. Balfour and Mr. John Morley. In August 1888 he paid a visit to his younger son William, who was interested in an electrical engineering firm with business in South Wales, and was at Tenby, Llandilo, Towyn, and Brecon (see *Cardiff Western Mail,* 12 Feb. 1908). In 1889 he was at Browning's funeral. 'The Ring and the Book' and Tennyson's 'Lucretius' were among his favourite poems. Similarity of temperament with his elder son Arthur precluded equable relations, but he was distressed and made despondent by the news of Arthur's death at Woking in March 1890, when he himself was shaken and ill. In 1892 he underwent the first of three operations for stone in the bladder.

Meanwhile in 1889 Meredith returned to fiction. The most individual of the later novels, a new study of modern femininity, 'One of our Conquerors,' ran simultaneously through the 'Fortnightly,' 'Australasian,' and 'New York Sun' (Oct.–May 1890–1). 'When I was sixty,' Meredith wrote, 'and a small legacy had assured my pecuniary independence, I took it into my head to serve these gentlemen (the critics) a strong dose of my most indigestible production. Nothing drove them so crazy as "One of our Conquerors."' In the prologue Meredith's mania for analogy, epigram, and metaphors runs riot. 'Lord Ormont and his Aminta,' in which a similar motive—that of people rendered strangers to themselves by a false position—is reinvoked, first appeared in the 'Pall Mall Magazine' (Dec. 1893–Aug. 1894). Issued separately in three volumes by Chapman & Hall in 1894 (and by Scribners in America), it was gratefully inscribed to the surgeon who had operated on him, George Buckston Browne. The basis of the story is to be found in the secret marriage of the famous Charles Mordaunt, earl of Peterborough [q. v.], in 1735 with Anastasia Robinson. The novel, which reverts to an easier style of writing than 'One of our Conquerors,' contains many of the writer's adroitest sayings. Meredith still had several novels in solution in his mind, the names of which have partially survived, such as 'Sir Harry Firebrand of the Beacon,' 'A Woman's Battle,' and a novel dealing with the career of Lady Sarah Lennox, in addition to the half-finished 'Celt and Saxon' (sketch on a great scale in 1890), the torso of which appeared in the 'Fortnightly' in 1910 and subsequently in the memorial edition (vol. xx.); but the last completed novel at which he travailed hard in 1894 was 'The Amazing Marriage,' in which the character of Woodseer, the virtuoso of nature and style, was a long-promised sketch of one of his friends, in this case R. L. Stevenson. The story had been begun and laid aside in 1879; it was resumed in 1894 at the urgent instance of his friend Frederick Jameson, to whom the work was dedicated. 'The Amazing Marriage' shows no declension of power—the style is less mannered than that of its three predecessors, but the subject-matter is almost extravagantly varied and complex. The arrangement affords the reader two peeps at English society of an almost Disraelian luxuriance, respectively in 1814 and 1839. The work appeared serially in 'Scribner's Magazine' (Jan.–Dec. 1895), and was published in two volumes in the same year by Constable & Co. His son William had recently joined this firm, which now assembled (under the author's direction) the copyrights of all his works and in 1896 commenced a collective edition de luxe in thirty-six volumes (completed 1910–11).

Meredith's life-work in prose fiction, which taxed his brain and health far more severely than his verse, was now completed. Henceforth he was regarded by the enlightened public as literary and political arbitrator and court of appeal, and in that capacity wrote during his later years various poems, platform letters, introductions, and the like, his opinions being cited in the newspapers in every form and context. His mental activity though still formidable was evidently more upon the surface than it had been during the harassing turmoil of the creative period. For the last sixteen years, owing to paraplegia, he had to abandon the physical activities which had been such an important element in his life and thought.

In 1892, upon the death of Tennyson, Meredith was elected president of the Society of Authors. In 1894 he relinquished his long established relation as reader with Chapman & Hall. In 1895 his quiet routine was broken by visits from the Daudets and Mr. Henry James and in July by a visit of ceremony of the Omar Khayyam Club, upon which occasion Mr. Edward Clodd ('Sir Reynard') 'discovered his brush' by eliciting a speech in answer to laudatory apostrophes by Thomas Hardy and George Gissing. Five years later he welcomed a similar visitation from the Whitefriars Club. In 1898 Leslie Stephen forwarded him a parchment bearing the felicitations of the authors of the day upon the attainment of his seventieth birthday. A similar tribute was paid him ten years later on his eightieth birthday. Among other honours were the vice-presidency of the London Library in 1902 and the Order of Merit in 1905, together with the rarely bestowed gold medal of the Royal Society of Literature.

In 1905 Meredith had the misfortune to break his leg, but he made an excellent recovery. Keenly alert and abreast of modern movements and interested in the work of the younger men, he envied only the power to be one of the active workers. On 13 April 1909 he wrote his last letter—an expression of condolence—to Mr. Watts-Dunton, on Swinburne's death. He insisted on being taken out in his bath-chair in all weathers. On 14 May 1909 he caught a slight chill; on the 16th he was taken ill. He died quietly on 18 May at Flint Cottage in the presence of his son, William Maxse, his daughter, Marie Eveleen ('Dearie'), wife of Henry Parkman Sturges, and his faithful nurse, Bessie Nicholls. A request from leading men of the day (and the expressed wish of Edward VII) for Meredith's burial in Westminster Abbey was refused by the dean. After cremation his ashes were laid beside his wife in Dorking cemetery (23 May), as he had himself arranged that they should be. On the day of his funeral some verses in terza rima by Mr. Thomas Hardy appeared in 'The Times,' and a memorial service was held in the Abbey. At Browning's funeral he had expressed the sentiment 'better the green grass turf than Abbey pavements.' On the headstone of his simple grave reclines an open book with the lines from 'Vittoria,' 'Life is but a little holding, Lent to do a mighty labour.' His will, dated Aug. 1892, was proved by his son, Lord Morley, and Mr. J. C. Deverell of Pixham Firs, Dorking (see *The Times*, 26 June 1909), his property being divided between son and daughter, with remainder to their children.

Meredith inherited a fine figure, and (strikingly good looking as a young man, when his abundant hair was chestnut red) his face grew handsomer as he grew older. He was in his heyday vividly and victoriously alive and had the optimism of high vitality. 'When I ceased to walk briskly part of my life was ended.' He was devoted to English fare; a connoisseur of cigars, he glowed over a generous wine and was proud of his small cellar; his hospitality was exquisite. He had a delicate, untrained ear for good music, and could play well by ear. He talked rotundly and resonantly (and several good phonographic records of his reading voice are preserved) on every topic discussed in Burton's 'Anatomy.'

Many thought him greater in conversation than in any other art.

Meredith's novels are more like Platonic dialogues than works of fiction. His characters have as a rule singularly little volition or speech of their own. The voice of their creator can be heard perpetually prompting them from behind a screen. The poems fill the interstices of thought in the novels. Oscar Wilde said with some point that Meredith had mastered everything but language: as a novelist he could do anything except tell a story, as an artist he was everything except articulate. To this it might be replied that he sought commonly to adumbrate conceptions not susceptible to lucid or exact statement, that he did not wish to narrate a story but to exemplify projections of his individual imagination. He was articulate enough when he desired to be so. He never pretended to make or take things easy; and the 'pap and treacle' style in fiction or poetry was his special abhorrence. But the novel was more or less accidental to him. It was his object in the capacity of virtuoso to express a code of connoisseurship in life and conduct. He delineates character by a strange shorthand process of his own; his men, and especially his women, transcend ordinary human nature, yet his heroines, and chief among them his 'English roses,' can hardly be matched outside Shakespeare. His descriptive power and insight into the secret chambers of the brain were indeed superb. But description, character, plot were in the novels wholly subservient to the ideals of his imagination. Thoroughly tonic in quality, his writings are (as Lamb said of Shakespeare) essentially manly.

Of posthumous works by Meredith the chief were the unfinished story of 'Celt and Saxon' ('Fortnightly Review,' Jan.–Aug. 1910), containing an interesting résumé of some of his frequent race speculations; 'The Sentimentalists,' a conversation comedy (of two distinct periods) begun at the period of his conception of the Pole family in his most laboured work, 'Emilia in England.' It was produced at the Duke of York's Theatre on 1 March 1910, and subsequently achieved a succès d'estime (see *Eye-Witness,* 2 Nov. 1911); and 'Last Poems by George Meredith,' including 'Milton,' 'Trafalgar Day,' 'The Call,' 'The Crisis,' 'The Warning,' and other poems emphasising England's need of a general defensive service. In the same year the definitive memorial edition was begun, and has been completed in twenty-seven volumes (1909–11); it includes all his writings (letters only excluded), together with various readings and a bibliography. A collection of Meredith's letters edited by his son appeared in 1912. The most notable portraits are the painting by G. F. Watts in 1893 in the National Portrait Gallery (not a good likeness), the dry-point etching of Mortimer Menpes (1900), drawings by Mr. J. S. Sargent of 1901, and William Strang's portrait commissioned by King Edward VII for the royal collection at Windsor. Two caricatures appeared in 'Punch,' by E. J. Wheeler, 19 Dec. 1891, and by E. T. Reed, 28 July 1894. A caricature by Max Beerbohm appeared in 'Vanity Fair,' 24 Sept. 1896. Of the later portraits the photograph by his friend Mrs. Seymour Trower (*Mem. Ed.* xxii.) is inferior to that at the age of eighty given in the second volume of the Letters. But Meredith was a refractory subject, and though he had a fine portrait of his wife by his friend Frederick Sandys in his sitting-room he would never consent to give Sandys an adequate sitting. An early photograph is given in memorial edition, vol. vii., and two others first appear in the Letters (Oct. 1912). A bronze medallion by Theodore Spicer-Simpson was placed in the miniature room, National Portrait Gallery, in 1910.

Of Meredith's manuscripts, which attest throughout the intense and laborious character of the author's workmanship, the original autographs of 'Celt and Saxon,' 'The Egoist,' and 'One of our Conquerors' were deposited on loan in the British Museum by the novelist's son and daughter in 1910. Other MS. works were given by Meredith as a means of provision to his faithful attendant, Frank Cole, and his trained nurse, Bessie Nicholls, his seven years attendant. Of these 'The Tragic Comedians' fetched 220*l.*, 'A Conqueror of our Time' (an early version of 'One of our Conquerors,' with no fewer than four versions of chapter xiv.) 260*l.*, 'Diana of the Crossways,' in the early serial form, 168*l.*, 'A Reading of Earth,' 205*l.*; 'The Amazing Marriage' and 'The Tale of Chloe' were also offered for sale (see *The Times,* 2, 4, 26 Nov., 1 and 2 Dec. 1910).

[The article is based primarily upon the numerous accounts and reminiscences which appeared in the London press in May 1909 (see The Times 20 and 27 May); on two well-packed articles by Mr. Edward Clodd in the Fortnightly (July 1909) and by Mr. Stewart M. Ellis in the same review, April 1912 (invaluable for ancestral details); on personal information kindly given by several of Meredith's friends, among them Mr. Clodd, Mr. Lionel Robinson, Mr. F. Jameson, Dr. Plimmer, and Mr. Kyllmann; and on Meredith's Collected Letters (1912, 2 vols.), kindly put at the writer's disposal before publication by Mr. W. M. Meredith. Of the many books about Meredith J. A. Hammerton's George Meredith in Anecdote and Criticism, 1909, and C. Photiadès's George Meredith, Paris, 1910, will probably be found most useful for biographical purposes. In 1890 appeared the rhapsodical medley on G. Meredith: Some Characteristics, by R. Le Gallienne, which has gone through five editions, and this was rapidly followed by Hannah Lynch's George Meredith, 1891; Walter Jerrold's George Meredith: an Essay towards Appreciation, 1902; Richard Curle's Aspects of George Meredith, 1908; Thomson's George Meredith, Prose Poet, 1909; Sydney Short's On Some of the Characteristics of Meredith's Prose Writing, Birmingham, 1907; A. Henderson's Interpreters of Life and the Modern Spirit: Meredith, 1911; J. W. Beach's The Comic Spirit in George Meredith, an Appreciation, 1911; Von Eugen Frey's Die Dichtungen George Meredith, Zurich, 1910; Ernst Dick's George Meredith, Drei Versuche, 1910. Among the critical interpretations the first place is held by George Meredith, Some Early Appreciations, 1909 (a most useful collection); George Meredith, by Mrs. Sturge Henderson, 1907; The Poetry and Philosophy of George Meredith, by G. M. Trevelyan, 1906; and George Meredith, a Primer to the Novels, by James Moffatt, 1909. The bibliography by John Lane appended to Le Gallienne's book and revised in the fifth edition of 1900, though incomplete after 1892, is still most useful (it includes personalia, portraits, articles, dedications, appreciations, translations and parodies) and is supplemented now by the Bibliography of the Writings in Prose and Verse by Mr. Arundel Esdaile, 1907, and the bibliog. (or chronology) of works in full appended to the Memorial Edition, vol. xxvii. (1911) by the same compiler. Other books of service are Van Doren's Life of Peacock, 1911; The Pilgrim's Scrip, or Wit and Wisdom of George Meredith, with Selections from his Poetry and an Introduction (by Mrs. Gilman), Boston, 1888; Hyndman's Reminiscences, 1911, 46–92; Tinsley's Random Recollections, 1–137; Maitland's Life of Leslie Stephen; Gleeson White's English Illustration: 'The Sixties,' 25, 42–3; Grant Duff's Notes from a Diary; Janet Ross's The Fourth Generation, 1912, and Three Generations of Englishwomen, 1888; Marcel Schwob's Spicilège, 1894; Firmin Roz's Le Roman Anglais Contemporain, 1912; Mme. Daudet's Notes sur la Vie; Daily News, 12 Feb. 1908; New Princeton Rev., March, April 1887 (Flora Shaw); Bookbuyer, Jan. 1889 (home life); Bookman, Jan. 1905; Rev. des Deux Mondes, 15 June 1867, Feb. 1908; Westminster Rev., July 1864; Fortnightly Rev., Nov. 1883, June 1890, Feb. 1891 (Wilde), June 1886, March 1892, Nov. 1897; Contemp. Rev., Oct. 1888 (J. M. Barrie); Henley's Views and Reviews, 1890; New Review, March 1893; Edin. Rev., Jan. 1895; Free Rev., Sept. 1896; Sat. Rev., 27 Mar. 1897 (G. B. Shaw); Nineteenth Century, Oct. 1895 (Traill); Longman's Mag., Nov. 1882 (R. L. S.); Independ. Rev., 1904–5, and Dec. 1906 (important articles on the Poems); Canadian Mag., July 1905 (MacFall); Atlantic Mo., June 1902; Rev. Germanique, March–April 1906; Athen., 29 May 1909; Quarterly Rev., July 1897, July 1901; Tribune, 7 Jan. 1906 (Elton); Engl. Illustr., Feb.–March 1904; Pall Mall Mag., May 1904; Acad., Jan. 1891 (Arthur Symons); The Times, 24 Oct. 1909, 13 Feb. 1908.] T. S.

MERIVALE, HERMAN CHARLES (1839–1906), playwright and novelist, born in London on 27 Jan. 1839, was only son of Herman Merivale, permanent under-secretary of the India office [q.v.]. Herman was educated first at a preparatory school and then at Harrow, where C. J. Vaughan, the headmaster, became much attached to him. He gives a full account of his schooldays in 'Bar, Stage, and Platform' (1902; cf. pp. 168–214). On leaving school in 1857 Merivale entered Balliol College, Oxford, where Swinburne and Charles Bowen were his contemporaries. He graduated B.A. in 1861, with a first class in classical moderations and a second in the final classical school. From early youth Merivale had been devoted to the drama, and was a good amateur actor, but his endeavour to found a dramatic club at Oxford, as Sir F. C. Burnand did at Cambridge, was foiled by the opposition of the dons. He was called to the bar of the Inner Temple on 26 Jan. 1864; he went the western circuit, and also the Norfolk circuit, where Matthew Arnold was his companion. Later he was through his father's influence junior counsel for the government on Indian appeals, and in 1867 boundary commissioner for North Wales under the Reform Act. From 1870 to 1880 he edited the 'Annual Register.' At his father's house he met many distinguished men, including Lord Robert Cecil, afterwards Lord Salisbury, who was a lifelong friend.

After his father's death in 1874 Merivale gave up the law, and, following his real tastes, devoted himself to literature and the drama. As early as 1867 he had written, under the pseudonym of Felix Dale, a farce, 'He's a Lunatic,' in which John Clayton [q. v.] played the chief part, and in 1872 Hermann Vezin produced at the Court Theatre 'A Son of the Soil,' which Merivale adapted from Ponsard's 'Le Lion Amoureux.'

His first dramatic success was 'All for her,' founded on Dickens's 'Tale of Two Cities,' written in collaboration with J. Palgrave Simpson, and produced by John Clayton at the Mirror Theatre (formerly the Holborn) on 18 Oct. 1875. In the autumn of 1879 Miss Genevieve Ward produced 'Forget-me-not,' by Herman Merivale and F. C. Grove (cf. BRAM STOKER, *Personal Reminiscences of Sir Henry Irving*, 1907, p. 350), and she played the part of the heroine, Stéphanie de Mohrivart, for ten years (over 2000 times) in all parts of the world (cf. HELEN C. BLACK, *Pen, Pencil, Baton and Mask*, p. 180). In 1882, at Bancroft's invitation, Merivale adapted with admirable skill Sardou's 'Fédora.' Merivale's 'The White Pilgrim,' produced by Hermann Vezin in 1883, is poetic drama of the highest quality. Merivale published the piece in a volume with other poems in the same year.

Merivale wrote many excellent farces and burlesques. At John Hollingshead's invitation he produced 'The Lady of Lyons Married and Settled' (Gaiety Theatre, 5 Oct. 1878), and 'Called There and Back' (Gaiety, 15 Oct. 1884). 'The Butler' (1886) and 'The Don' (1888) were both written for Toole, who took great pleasure in playing them, especially 'The Don' (cf. J. HATTON, *Reminiscences of J. L. Toole*, 1892, pp. 264–5). In 1882 Merivale sold the acting rights of 'Edgar and Lucy,' a play adapted from Scott's 'Bride of Lammermoor,' to Irving, who produced it on 20 Sept. 1890, under the title of 'Ravenswood' (cf. BRAM STOKER, *Sir Henry Irving*, 1907, pp. 120–2).

Meanwhile Merivale won a reputation as a novelist with 'Faucit of Balliol' (3 vols. 1882), the earlier chapters of which give an admirable picture of Oxford life. He proved his literary facility in a fairy tale for children, 'Binko's Blues' (1884), and 'Florien,' a five-act tragedy in verse (1884), and in frequent contributions to 'Blackwood,' the 'Cornhill,' the 'Spectator,' 'Punch,' 'Saturday Review,' the 'World,' and 'Truth.' But it was in poetic drama that Merivale's ability, which combined fancy and wit with a poetic imagination, showed to best advantage.

Merivale's health required him to live at Eastbourne. There he interested himself in politics as an ardent liberal, working hard for his party between 1880 and 1890. A brilliant speaker, he refused many invitations to stand for parliament, including the offer of an Irish seat from Parnell.

In 1891 Merivale's health broke down while he was engaged on a memoir of Thackeray, for the 'Great Writers' series of Messrs. Walter Scott, which Sir Frank Marzials completed. Ordered a long sea-voyage to Australia, he and his wife were shipwrecked when six degrees north of the line, and on being rescued were taken to Pernambuco, where Merivale's increasing illness compelled a hasty return to England. Recovery followed, and Merivale was again at work. On leaving for Australia he had been induced to give his solicitor and trustee, Cartmell Harrison, a 'power of attorney,' and in 1900, through Harrison's default, he lost the whole of his fortune of 2000*l.* a year. A civil list pension of 125*l.* was awarded him on 25 May 1900. In June a matinée was given for his benefit at Her Majesty's Theatre. He died suddenly of heart failure on 14 Jan. 1906, at 72 Woodstock Road, Bedford Park, W. A few years before, he became a Roman catholic. He was buried in his father's grave in Brompton cemetery.

Merivale married in London, on 13 May 1878, an Irish lady, Elizabeth, daughter of John Pitman, who often assisted him in his work, notably in 'The Don.' They had no children. His widow was granted a civil list pension of 50*l.* in 1906.

Two portraits, one by Claude Calthrop, M.A., belong to Mrs. Merivale.

Besides the plays cited, Merivale was author of : 1. 'A Husband in Clover' (Lyceum Theatre, 26 Dec. 1873). 2. 'Peacock's Holiday' (Court Theatre, 16 April 1874). 3. 'The Lord of the Manor,' founded on 'Wilhelm Meister' (Imperial Theatre, 3 April 1880). 4. 'The Cynic' (Globe Theatre, 14 Jan. 1882). 5. 'The Whip Hand,' with Mrs. Merivale (Cambridge Theatre Royal, 21 Jan. 1885). 6. 'Our Joan' (Grand Theatre, 3 Oct. 1887).

[The Times, 17 Jan. 1906; Who's Who, 1905; Pratt, People of the Period, 1897; H. C. Merivale, Bar, Stage and Platform, 1902, informative reminiscences, lacking in dates; Hollingshead, Gaiety Chronicles, 1898; The Bancrofts, Recollections of Sixty Years, 1909; private information.] E. L.

MERRIMAN, HENRY SETON (pseudonym). [See SCOTT, HUGH STOWELL (1862–1903), novelist.]

MEYRICK, FREDERICK (1827–1906), divine, born at Ramsbury vicarage, Wiltshire, on 28 Jan. 1827, was the youngest son of Edward Graves Meyrick, vicar of

Ramsbury, by his wife Myra Howard. He claimed descent from the ancient family of Meyricks of Bodorgan, Anglesey, through Rowland Merrick or Meyrick, bishop of Bangor, 1559–66 [q. v.]. Educated first at Ramsbury school, he won a scholarship at Trinity College, Oxford, and matriculated on 12 June 1843. He graduated B.A., with a second class in final classical school, in 1847, and proceeded M.A. in 1850. Elected fellow of Trinity in 1847, he travelled on the Continent with pupils, closely observing ecclesiastical affairs. One result was the establishment in 1853 of the Anglo-Continental Society, of which Meyrick for forty-six years acted as secretary. The results of his observations in Spain he published as 'The Practical Working of the Church of Spain (1851).'

Returning to Oxford, Meyrick was ordained deacon in 1850 and priest in 1852; became tutor of Trinity; took an active part in the discussion of university reform; crossed swords with H. E. Manning [q. v.] over Roman catholic ethics as represented by Liguori's works; was select preacher at Oxford (1855–6 and 1875–6), and Whitehall preacher (1856–7). In 1859 he was appointed an inspector of schools, and resigned his fellowship in the following year. In 1868 Meyrick was instituted to the rectory of Blickling with Erpingham, Norfolk, where he spent the remainder of his life. From 1868 to 1885 he served the bishop of Lincoln, Christopher Wordsworth [q. v.], as examining chaplain, and in 1869 became a non-residentiary canon of Lincoln.

The Vatican Council of 1870 gave new life to Meyrick's interest in continental affairs. He visited Döllinger at the time of his excommunication, and attended the Bonn conferences on reunion (1874 and 1875), which he helped to organise. During 1886 he was principal of Codrington College, Barbadoes, a theological training institution. In 1892 he accompanied the archbishop of Dublin, Lord Plunket [q. v. Suppl. I], on a journey in Spain for the aid of the reformed church; and on the archbishop's consecration in 1894 of Bishop Cabrera he drew up an address, largely signed, in support of Lord Plunket's action. In 1898 he resigned the secretaryship of the Anglo-Continental Church Society, and in 1899 ended the publication of the 'Foreign Church Chronicle,' which he had edited for twenty years. In 1904 he took part in the ritual controversy, identifying himself more intimately with the moderate evangelicals. He died at Blickling on 3 Jan. 1906, and is commemorated in the church by a window. A wide traveller, an accomplished linguist, and a clever disputant, he hindered his ecclesiastical advancement by his controversial zeal. He married in 1859 Marion E. Danvers, who with two sons and five daughters survived him.

Meyrick contributed to periodical literature; to Smith's 'Dictionary of the Bible' (1860, 1863), to the 'Dictionary of Ecclesiastical Antiquities' (1875), and to 'A Protestant Dictionary' (1904); to the 'Speaker's Commentary' (Joel and Obadiah, 1876; Ephesians, 1880); to the 'Pulpit Commentary' (Leviticus, 1882); and to the 'One Volume Commentary' (1905). His 'Memories' (1905) is especially useful for its account of his contemporaries at Oxford and for its view of Anglican interest in the Old Catholic and other reform movements on the Continent. In connection with these movements he translated into Latin and other languages standard works of English divines, and was the author of several anti-Roman pamphlets. He also published: 1. 'Moral Theology of the Church of Rome,' 1856. 2. 'The Outcast and the Poor of London,' 1858. 3. 'University and Whitehall Sermons,' 1859. 4. 'Is Dogma a Necessity?' 1883. 5. 'The Doctrine of the Church of England on the Holy Communion restated,' 1885; 4th edit. 1899. 6. 'The Church in Spain,' 1892. 7. 'Scriptural and Catholic Truth and Worship,' 1901; 2nd edit. 1908.

[F. Meyrick, Memories of Life at Oxford, &c., 1905; The Times, 4 and 17 Jan. 1906; Guardian, 10 Jan. 1906; J. H. Overton and E. Wordsworth, Christopher Wordsworth, Bishop of Lincoln, 1888, p. 379; G. W. Kitchin, Edward Harold Browne, D.D., 1895, pp. 229–231; D. C. Lathbury, Correspondence on Church and Religion of W. E. Gladstone, 1910, i. 135, 215; A. F. Hort, Life and Letters of F. J. A. Hort, 1896, i. 348; private information.] A. R. B.

MICHIE, ALEXANDER (1833–1902), writer on China, born at Earlsferry, Fifeshire, on 1 March 1833, was only son of Alexander Michie, a weaver, by his wife Ann Laing. On his father's death his mother married again, and Robert Thin, M.D.Edinburgh (*d.* at Shanghai in 1867), and George Thin, M.D.Edinburgh, of London, were Michie's stepbrothers. Educated for commercial life at Kilconquhar school, Michie was for some time a bank assistant at Colinsburgh; but in 1853 he left England to join Lindsay and Co., merchants, at Hong-Kong. Encouraged to depend largely on his own judgment in his work for the firm, he was allowed by tradition to trade independently and for his own profit. Michie made rapid progress, and in 1857 became a partner of his firm and its representative at Shanghai. Subsequently he transferred his services successively to Chapman, King and Co., to Dyce, Nichol and Co., in which he obtained a partnership, and finally to the leading Chinese firm, Jardine, Matheson and Co. He was meanwhile a prominent member of the Chamber of Commerce, Shanghai, and was for some years chairman.

Michie was active in acquiring information likely to be serviceable to British commerce. After the drafting of the treaty of Tientsin, ratified in 1860, which proposed to open new ports in the north, Michie in the spring of 1859 engaged in a secret trading expedition to the Gulf of Pechili, and was one of the first European traders to gain direct knowledge of Wei-hai-Wei, Chefoo, Newchang, and other places on that then unknown coast. In 1861 he helped Sir James Hope [q. v.] in his negotiations with the Taiping rebels. He went up the River Yangtze with the expedition which was to protect British trade, and at Nanking, Michie, with Lieutenant-colonel (afterwards Lord) Wolseley and J. P. Hughes, vice-consul designate of Kiu-Kiang, was allowed to land, and the three remained for some weeks as the voluntary guests of the rebels, as to whose strength and intentions they acquired useful information.

In 1863 Michie returned temporarily to England by the unusual route of Siberia. He described in the 'Journal of the Geographical Society' his journey between Tientsin and Mukden, and in 1864 published 'The Siberian Overland Route,' a description of the whole journey from Peking to St. Petersburg.

In 1869 Michie, on behalf of the Shanghai Chamber of Commerce, accompanied Mr. Swinhoe, consul of Taiwan, on an expedition into the interior. A revision of the Treaty of Tientsin was contemplated, and Michie and his companion undertook to study the conditions of trade in the districts likely to be affected. After passing through the canal district of the Yangtze valley, he explored Szechuan and made a report of permanent value.

In 1883 Michie settled at Tientsin, where he not only carried on his private business but acted as correspondent of 'The Times.' For some years too he edited the 'Chinese Times,' published at Tientsin, and wrote occasionally for 'Blackwood,' 'Leitner,' and other magazines. In 1895 he was 'The Times' special correspondent during the Chino-Japanese war. Subsequently he left China for England, only returning in 1901 in order to visit his daughter, who with her husband had been shut up in the legations at Peking. He died on 8 Aug. 1902 at the Hotel Cecil, London, and was buried at Highgate cemetery.

In 'The Englishman in China' (2 vols. 1900) Michie supplied a clear and comprehensive account of European relations with China through the Victorian era. The central figure of the narrative is Sir Rutherford Alcock [q. v.]. Michie's criticisms of English diplomacy and English officials are the fruit of personal observation and first-hand knowledge. He also published 'Missionaries in China' (1891) and 'China and Christianity' (1900).

Michie married on 16 Dec. 1866 Ann, daughter of Charles Morley Robinson of Forest House, Leytonstone, Essex. He had issue one daughter and one son, Alexander, an official in the Chinese customs service.

[The Times, 12 Aug. 1902; Geog. Journ. x. xvii. and xx.; Stanley Lane Poole, Life of Sir Harry Parkes, 1894; Sir Henry Keppel, A Sailor's Life under Four Sovereigns, 1899; private information.] S. E. F.

MICKLETHWAITE, JOHN THOMAS (1843–1906), architect, born at Riskworth House, Wakefield, Yorkshire, on 3 May 1843, was son of James Micklethwaite of Hopton, Mirfield, worsted spinner and colliery owner, by his wife Sarah Eliza Stanway of Manchester.

After education at Tadcaster and Wakefield, and subsequently at King's College, London, which afterwards granted him an hon. fellowship, he became a pupil in 1862 of (Sir) George Gilbert Scott [q. v.], and formed a lifelong friendship with a fellow pupil, Mr. Somers Clarke. He began independent practice in 1869 and was in constant collaboration with Mr. Somers Clarke, who definitely became his partner in 1876 and remained in that capacity till his retirement from active work in 1892.

An earnest churchman and a master of historic ritual, Micklethwaite brought sympathy and knowledge to bear on his work as a designer. His productions, though not strikingly original, were invariably scholarly and correct. The individual responsibilities of Micklethwaite and his partner are not always easy to distinguish. Of their joint works the church of St. John, Gainsborough, the churches of All Saints, Brixham, and St. Paul's, Wimbledon Park, as well as the enlargement of the parish church at Brighton, were all designed and begun by Mr. Somers Clarke, and were completed by Micklethwaite after 1892. At Brighton church Micklethwaite modified his colleague's design, and at All Saints' church, Haydon Lane, Wimbledon, Micklethwaite, besides completing Mr. Somers Clarke's plans, designed the screens and furniture. The church at Stretton was designed by Mr. Clarke but was carried out by Micklethwaite after 1892.

Among the works which were distinctly or exclusively Micklethwaite's are: St. Hilda's church, Leeds; St. Bartholomew's, Barking Road, East Ham (1902); St. Peter's, Bocking; Widford church vestry; the rebuilding (tower excepted) of All Saints', Morton, near Gainsborough (1891–3); the House of Mercy, Horbury; St. Saviour's, Luton, and the restoration of Madingley church. Micklethwaite's ecclesiological skill was often in demand for the completion or furnishing of chancels and the like, for example at St. John's, Wakefield. The screens and rood of St. Mary Magdalene's, Munster Square, London, are of his design. He was often engaged in restoration, as at Kirkstall Abbey, the churches of Oundle, Thornhaugh, Inglesham, Orford, Winchelsea, West Malling, Lydney North, and All Saints, Great Sturton. The York county council appointed him, with Mr. W. H. Brierley, to restore Clifford's Tower at York, and in 1900 he was made architect to St. George's Chapel, Windsor. At Ranworth, Norfolk, he repaired the celebrated screen, and at St. Andrew's, Cherry Hinton, he restored the chancel.

Of his less frequent domestic and secular work there are examples in the addition to Stapleford Park, and the Technical Schools at Wimbledon.

Micklethwaite's critical knowledge of Westminster Abbey and his affection for the fabric were rewarded in 1898 by his appointment as surveyor to the dean and chapter, on the death of John Loughborough Pearson [q. v.]. The works of renewal on the south transept and west front were carried out during his period of office in collaboration with Mr. W. D. Caröe, F.S.A. As custodian of the Abbey he aimed primarily and essentially at conservation. With the possible exception of the decoration on the west side of the Confessor's shrine carried out at the time of the coronation of King Edward VII (when he also designed some of the vestments for the ceremonial), he made few if any attempts at conjectural renovation.

Throughout his career Micklethwaite devoted himself to archæological inquiry and writing as well as to architectural work. In 1870, when he wrote a paper on the Chapel of St. Erasmus in Westminster Abbey, he was elected F.S.A. He served for many years on the executive committee of the Antiquaries' Society, was several times a member of council, and became a vice-president in 1902. A series of articles begun in 'The Sacristy' as early as 1870 were collected in 1874 as 'Modern Parish Churches, their Plan, Design and Furniture.' Among his more important monographs were two essays on Saxon churches and two on Westminster Abbey, all in the 'Archæological Journal,' one on the sculptures of Henry VII's Chapel in 'Archæologia,' and a treatise on the Cistercian plan in the 'Yorkshire Archæological Journal.' He was one of the founders of the Alcuin Club, the Henry Bradshaw Society, and the St. Paul's Ecclesiological Society. His tract on the 'Ornaments of the Rubric' was the first publication of the Alcuin Club in 1897, and reached a third edition. He was a member, and in 1893 master, of the Art Workers' Guild, and took a leading part in the affairs of the Archæological Institute. In 1874 he issued, in conjunction with Mr. Somers Clarke, a pamphlet, 'What shall be done with St. Paul's?' in reference to the internal alterations then in progress.

After some years of failing health, he died, unmarried, on 28 Oct. 1906, at his residence, 27 St. George's Square, London, S.W., and was accorded the honour of burial in the west cloister, Westminster Abbey.

[Athenæum, 10 Nov. 1906, p. 589, article by Prof. Lethaby; Builder, vol. xci. 1906, p. 516; obituary notice by the president, Soc. Antiq. Proceedings, 23 April 1907; Index Proc. Soc. Antiq., second ser., i.–xx. 267 (list of Micklethwaite's contributions); information from Mr. Somers Clarke.] P. W.

MIDLANE, ALBERT (1825–1909), hymn writer, born at Newport, Isle of Wight, on 23 Jan. 1825, was the posthumous child and youngest of the large family of James Midlane (*d.* Oct. 1824) by his wife Frances Lawes, a member of the congregational church then under Thomas Binney [q. v.]. Midlane, after an ordinary education, was employed for some three years in a local printing office, then became an ironmonger's assistant, and ultimately was in business for himself as tinsmith and ironmonger. His religious training was in the congregational church and its Sunday school, in which he became a teacher; he states that instead of listening to sermons he studied the hymn-book; subsequently he joined the Plymouth brethren. Prompted by his Sunday-school teacher, he began to write verse as a child, contributing to magazines as 'Little Albert.' His first printed hymn, written in September 1842, appeared in the 'Youth's Magazine,' Nov. 1842. The hymn which came first into use ('God bless our Sunday Schools,' to the tune of the National Anthem) was written in 1844. The hymn on which his fame rests ('There's a Friend for little children') was composed on 7 Feb. 1859; it has been translated into a dozen languages, including Chinese and Japanese; it was included in the supplement to 'Hymns Ancient and Modern' (1868), when Sir John Stainer wrote the tune 'In Memoriam' for it. Midlane's output of hymns was amazing; in one year he wrote about 400, chiefly for American newspapers; Julian (July 1907) credits him with having produced over 800 hymns, of which 83 had been introduced into widely used hymnals. Many were published in magazines and in very numerous tiny collections; for the year 1908 he wrote that he counted 'just upon 200 published compositions, which is about the annual average.' This, however, included verses on national and local topics in the 'Isle of Wight County Press' and other periodicals, and historical prose. For some time he edited a local magazine, 'Island Greetings.' He made nothing by his pen, and having become guarantor for a friend he was reduced to bankruptcy. His friends throughout the country, in conjunction with the Sunday School Union, raised a sum which enabled the bankruptcy to be annulled and provided an annuity for Midlane and his wife. He was a man of wide sympathies; his hymns, with little claim to genius, are marked by a winsome religious emotion, and a passionate love of children. He died at Forest Villa, South Mall, Newport, I.W., on 27 Feb. 1909, as the result of an apoplectic seizure, and was buried in Carisbrooke cemetery. He married Miriam Granger, who survived him with two sons and one daughter.

The following works are believed to contain most of his hymns: 1. 'Poetry addressed to Sabbath School Teachers,' 1844, 12mo. 2. 'Vecta Garland,' 1850, 12mo. 3. 'Leaves from Olivet,' 1864, 12mo. 4. 'Gospel Echoes,' 1865, 16mo. 5. 'Above the Bright Blue Sky,' 1867, 16mo; 1889, 24mo. 6. 'Early Lispings,' 1880, 16mo. 7. 'God's Treasures,' 1890, 16mo. 8. 'The Bright Blue Sky Hymn Book,' 1904, 12mo (315 hymns); 1909, 12mo (323 hymns; portrait). 9. 'The Gospel Hall Hymn Book,' 1904, 12mo (218 hymns additional to those in No. 8, 1904). 10. 'A Colloquy between the Gallows and the Hangman,' 1851 (verse). 11. 'Chronological Table of Events . . . Carisbrooke Castle,' Newport, I.W., 1877, 12mo.

[The Times, 1 March 1909; Isle of Wight County Press, 6 March 1909; Miller's Singers and Songs, 1869, p. 572; Julian's Dictionary of Hymnology, 1907, pp. 733 sq., 1672; private information.] A. G.

MILBANKE, RALPH GORDON NOEL KING, second Earl of Lovelace (1839–1906), author of 'Astarte,' born at 10 St. James's Square, London, on 2 July 1839, was second son of William King, afterwards King-Noel, first earl of Lovelace (1805–1893), by his first wife, Ada Augusta, daughter of Lord Byron the poet [q. v.]. The father, who succeeded as eighth Baron King in 1833, was created earl of Lovelace on 30 June 1838. He was lord-lieutenant of Surrey from 1840 to his death in 1893, and interested himself in agricultural and mechanical engineering.

During 1847–8 Ralph was a pupil at Wilhelm von Fellenberg's Pestalozzian school at Hofwyl, near Berne [see under Herford, William Henry, Suppl. II]. Subsequently educated privately, he matriculated at University College, Oxford, in 1859, but did not graduate. On the death on 1 Sept. 1862 of his elder brother, Byron Noel, Viscount Ockham, who had succeeded his grandmother, Lady Byron, as twelfth Baron Wentworth, Ralph himself became thirteenth Baron Wentworth. He had assumed the surname of Milbanke, Lady Byron's maiden surname, by royal licence on 6 Nov. 1861. Taking little part in public life, he read widely and showed independent if rather erratic judgment. At the age of twenty-two he spent a year in Iceland, and was a zealous student of Norse literature. In early life a bold Alpine climber, he spent much time in the Alps, while a peak of the Dolomites bears his name. An accomplished linguist, he was especially conversant with Swiss and Tyrolese dialects. His intimate acquaintance with French, German, and English literature was combined with a fine taste in music and painting. He enjoyed the intimacy of W. E. H. Lecky and other men of letters. In 1893 he succeeded his father as second earl of Lovelace. In 1905 he privately printed 'Astarte: A Fragment of Truth concerning

George Gordon Byron, first Lord Byron,' dedicated to M. C. L. (his second wife). This vigorous if somewhat uncritical polemic purported to be a vindication of Lovelace's grandmother, Lady Byron, from the aspersions made upon her after the 'revelations' of Mrs. Beecher Stowe in 1869–70. Lovelace alleged, on evidence of hitherto undivulged papers left by Lady Byron, and now at his disposal, that Byron's relations with his half-sister, Mrs. Augusta Leigh, were criminal, and that she was the 'Astarte' of the poet's 'Manfred.' Lovelace printed a statement signed in 1816 by Dr. Lushington, Sir Robert Willmot, and Sir Francis Doyle, and various extracts from correspondence. He also cited a letter in support of his conclusion from Sir Leslie Stephen, who had examined the papers. 'Astarte' provoked replies from Mr. John Murray (*Lord Byron and his Detractors*, 1906) and from Mr. Richard Edgcumbe (*Byron: the Last Phase*, 1909).

Lovelace died very suddenly at Ockham Park, Ripley, Surrey, on 28 Aug. 1906. After cremation at Woking his ashes were buried in the King chapel over the family vault in Ockham church. He was twice married: (1) on 25 Aug. 1869, to Fanny (*d.* 1878), third daughter of George Heriot, vicar of St. Anne's, Newcastle; (2) on 10 Dec. 1880, to Mary Caroline, eldest daughter of the Rt. Hon. James Stuart Wortley; she survived him. There was no male issue. Lovelace's daughter, Ada Mary, by his first wife, succeeded to her father's barony of Wentworth. The earldom of Lovelace devolved on his half-brother Lionel Fortescue King, son of the first earl by his second wife.

[G. E. C.'s and Burke's Peerages; The Times, 30 Aug., 3 and 10 Sept. 1906; Spectator, 15 Sept. 1906 (letter by 'O.' (Mrs. Ady); Brit. Mus. Cat.; Lovelace's Astarte and works cited.] G. Le G. N.

MILLER, Sir JAMES PERCY, second baronet (1864–1906), sportsman, born at Manderston on 22 Oct. 1864, was eldest surviving son of Sir William Miller, first baronet (1809–1887), of Manderston, Berwick, a Leith merchant, who was M.P. for Leith (1859–64) and Berwickshire (1893–4). James, after education at Eton and Sandhurst, joined the army, becoming captain in the 14th hussars on 8 Sept. 1888. On 10 Oct. 1887 he succeeded to the baronetcy on his father's death. He was afterwards major of the Lothians and Berwickshire imperial yeomanry, and served in South Africa (1900–1) with the 6th battalion imperial yeomanry, being mentioned in despatches, and receiving the D.S.O. He was a J.P. and D.L. for Berwickshire.

In 1889 Miller, who had previously owned a few steeplechasers, appeared upon the turf as an owner of racehorses, run under Jockey Club rules. In that year he purchased with rare judgment, of Sir Robert Jardine and John Porter, Sainfoin, which had won the Esher Stakes at Sandown Park very easily. The price was 6000*l.* and half the value of the Derby, if the horse won that prize. Sainfoin won the Derby of 1890 from Le Noir, Orwell, and Surefoot.

Miller's next stroke of luck was the purchase in 1894 for 4100 guineas, as a yearling, of the mare Roquebrune (foaled in 1893), by St. Simon, who had been bred by the Duchess of Montrose. With Roquebrune he won the New Stakes at Ascot and the Zetland Stakes at Doncaster. Mated in 1899 with Sainfoin, Roquebrune produced Rock Sand, her first foal. With this colt Sir James won in 1902 the Woodcote Stakes at Epsom, the Coventry Stakes at Ascot, the Champagne Stakes at Doncaster, and the Dewhurst Plate at Newmarket. In the following year Rock Sand won the Two Thousand Guineas, Derby, and St. Leger. During the three seasons he was in training, this horse won stakes to the value of 45,618*l.*, and was chiefly instrumental in placing Sir James at the head of the list of winning owners in 1903 and 1904, with totals of 24,768*l.* and 27,928*l.* Meanwhile Miller had in 1895 won the Oaks with La Sagesse, a daughter of Wisdom, and in 1901 his filly Aïda, by Galopin, won the One Thousand Guineas. The most important of his successes in handicaps was that gained in the Cesarewitch of 1898 with Chaleureux, destined to become the sire of the filly Signorinetta, who in 1908 won the Derby and Oaks for the Chevalier Ginistrelli. During the seventeen years he had horses in training Miller won 161 races, worth 114,005*l.*

Miller established a high-class breeding farm at Hamilton Stud, Newmarket, where Rock Sand was foaled. He was elected a member of the Jockey Club in 1903, and was a steward of that body when he died in 1906. In December 1905 he sold by auction most of his mares, and Roquebrune was purchased by a Belgian breeder for 4500 guineas. Six weeks later, on 22 Jan. 1906, Sir James died at Manderston, his Scottish home, from a chill caught in the hunting-field. His remains were interred at Christ Church, Duns. Rock Sand was shortly afterwards sold to Mr. August

Belmont of New York for 25,000*l*. Married in 1893 to the Hon. Eveline Mary Curzon, third daughter of the fourth Baron Scarsdale, Miller left no issue, and was succeeded in the baronetcy by his brother, John Alexander. A cartoon portrait appeared in 'Vanity Fair' in 1890.

[The Times, 23 Jan. 1906; Kingsclere (by John Porter), pp. 124–5; Ruff's Guide to the Turf; Debrett's Peerage; Burke's Peerage.]
E. M.

MITCHELL, Sir ARTHUR (1826–1909), Scottish commissioner in lunacy and antiquary, born at Elgin on 19 Jan. 1826, was son of George Mitchell, C.E., by his wife Elizabeth Cant. He was educated at Elgin Academy, and graduated M.A. at Aberdeen University in 1845, prosecuting his studies for the medical profession at Paris, Berlin, and Vienna, and proceeding M.D. at Aberdeen in 1850. Devoting himself to lunacy, he quickly showed an aptitude for this branch of practice. When the Lunacy Act of 1857 was passed, he was chosen one of the deputy commissioners for Scotland, and was commissioner from May 1870 to September 1895. Improved methods for treating the insane, which he helped to bring into use in Scotland, he developed effectively in his book 'The Insane in Private Dwellings' (Edinburgh 1864). Presenting his views persuasively rather than argumentatively, he won for them wide support. In 1880 he was appointed a member of the English commission on criminal lunacy, and his experience largely influenced the report upon which the Act of 1880 was founded. In 1885 he served on the departmental committee on criminal lunatics in Ireland. From May 1869 till March 1872 he acted as Morison lecturer on insanity to the Royal College of Physicians of Edinburgh. In his lectures, many of which were published in book form, and in other works, he dealt authoritatively with various aspects of lunacy—individual, social, and medical.

Mitchell combined with his professional work much antiquarian study. In 1861 he was appointed a corresponding member, and in 1867 he was elected a fellow, of the Society of Antiquaries of Scotland, and continued an active member till his death, serving from time to time as secretary and vice-president. His researches largely dealt with existing superstitions in the Scottish Highlands, especially in their bearing on problems of insanity. He contributed many papers to the 'Proceedings,' the latest being a series on Scottish topographers (1901–9). In 1876 Mitchell was the first Rhind lecturer in archæology, and delivered three courses of six lectures each, which were published under the title 'The Past in the Present: What is Civilisation?' (Edinburgh 1880); the book took standard rank. Mitchell was one of the founders of the Scottish History Society, and was a member of council and vice-president. He edited for the society 'Macfarlane's Topographical Collections' (3 vols. 1906–8). He was also president of the Scottish Text Society and professor of ancient history to the Royal Scottish Academy from 1878. He was a member of the royal commission on Scottish universities in 1889, and served till 1900.

In 1886 Mitchell was made C.B., and in 1887 K.C.B. He received the hon. degree of LL.D. from Aberdeen in 1875; and became hon. fellow of the Royal College of Physicians of Ireland in 1891. He died at 34 Drummond Place, Edinburgh, on 12 Oct. 1909, and was buried in Rosebank cemetery, Edinburgh. He married in 1855 Margaret, daughter of James Houston, Tullochgriban, Strathspey; she died on 4 Nov. 1904, leaving one son, Sydney Mitchell.

Besides the works mentioned and editions of Andrew Combe's 'Observations on Mental Derangement' (1887) and 'Management of Infancy' (1896), Mitchell published in 1905 'About Dreaming, Laughing, and Blushing.'

There are two portraits of Mitchell, one painted in 1880 by Norman Macbeth, R.S.A., and the other by Sir George Reid, P.R.S.A., in 1896. Both are in possession of the family.

[Scotsman, and Dundee Advertiser, 13 Oct. 1909; Lancet, 23 Oct. 1909; private information.]
A. H. M.

MITCHELL, JOHN MURRAY (1815–1904), presbyterian missionary and orientalist, born in Aberdeen on 19 Aug. 1815, was fourth son in the family of five sons and three daughters of James Mitchell, burgess of Aberdeen, by his wife Margaret Gordon. Both parents were related to Patrick Copland [q. v.]. Three brothers, James (1808–1884), Gordon (1809–1893), and Alexander (1822–1901), became ministers of the Church of Scotland. After attending the parish school of Kinneff, Kincardineshire, Mitchell in 1828 entered the grammar school of Aberdeen, where he was strongly influenced by the rector James Melvin [q.v.]. With the second highest bursary, gained by his Latin prose, he entered Marischal College, Aberdeen, at fourteen, and graduated M.A.

with distinction in 1833. Deciding to enter the ministry of the Church of Scotland, he began his divinity course in that year, studying first at Aberdeen, where he won the lord rector's prize for an essay on 'The Septuagint and other Greek Versions of the Old Testament.' In 1837 the fame of Thomas Chalmers [q. v.] drew him to Edinburgh University, where he won a gold medal offered by Professor David Welsh [q. v.] for an essay on 'Eusebius as an Ecclesiastical Historian.' During the session 1837–8 he took charge of a class at Aberdeen grammar school, and among his scholars was James Augustus Grant [q. v. Suppl. I], the African traveller.

Mitchell was from youth interested in foreign missions and was deeply impressed by the labours of Alexander Duff [q. v.]. Ordained in 1838 and appointed by the foreign mission committee of the Church of Scotland to be a missionary to Bombay, he readily mastered the Marathi language and literature and became proficient in Sanskrit and the Parsi Zend. Among the Marathis he made many converts and gave an impulse to missionary work by originating the Bombay missionary conference. While at Bombay he made missionary tours annually throughout Central India. At the disruption of the Church of Scotland in 1843, Mitchell, with his colleagues in India, joined the Free church and bore a leading part in organising the Free church mission. He succeeded in inaugurating a flourishing mission in the British cantonment at Poona, where Scottish missionaries had previously been forbidden, and began work among the Mangs and Mahars of Jalna and North Haidarabad. After a four years' visit to Scotland (1863–7), where he ministered at Broughty Ferry, he proceeded in 1867, at Dr. Duff's request, to Calcutta, and remained in Bengal for the next six years. Mainly through his efforts the 'Union Church,' an important European congregation, was formed at Simla, and he helped to found a mission to the Santals.

On returning home in 1873 he acted as secretary to the foreign mission committee of the Free church. In 1880, after attending the pan-presbyterian council at Philadelphia, he went by way of Japan and China to India, where he spent two years in lecturing and preaching. From 1888, when he retired from the mission field, until 1898 he was minister of the Scottish church at Nice. Here his friends included the Dutch novelist, Maarten Maartens, who wrote admiringly of Mitchell's 'pure and child-like heart' and of his 'noble aspirations and beliefs.'

Mitchell's closing years were devoted to literary work in Edinburgh. He had published 'Hinduism, Past and Present' (1885; 2nd edit. 1897), a capable introduction to the study of Indian religion. As Duff missionary lecturer in 1903 he gave an exhaustive course on 'The Great Religions of India,' which was posthumously published in 1905 with a prefatory note by his nephew, Dr. James Mitchell.

In December 1858 Mitchell was made hon. LL.D. of Marischal College and the university of Aberdeen. He died at his house in Edinburgh on 14 Nov. 1904, and was buried on 18 Nov. in the Dean cemetery, Edinburgh. On the sixtieth anniversary of his ordination as a missionary to India, his portrait, painted by W. E. Lockhart, R.S.A., was presented (May 1898) to the Free church, and now hangs in the general assembly hall of the United Free church in Edinburgh.

Besides several lectures, contributions to periodicals, and admirable metrical translations from classical and Indian poets, he published: 1. 'Letters to Indian Youth regarding the Evidences of the Christian Religion, with a Brief Examination of the Evidences of Hinduism, Parseeism and Mohammedanism' (Bombay 1850; 11th edit. 1894; trans. into several Indian languages). 2. 'The Conflict of Ancient Paganism and Christianity' (n.d.). 3. 'Memoir of Rev. Robert Nesbit, Missionary,' London 1858. 4. 'In Western India: Recollections of my Early Missionary Life,' Edinburgh 1899.

On 22 Dec. 1842 he married Maria Hay, daughter of the Rev. Alexander Flyter, minister of Alness, Ross-shire. There were no children. Mitchell's wife, who died on 31 March 1907, was distinguished for her missionary zeal and literary ability. Many books by her had a large circulation; the chief of them were: 1. 'A Missionary's Wife among the Wild Tribes of South Bengal,' 1871. 2. 'In Southern India,' 1885. 3. 'Sixty Years Ago,' 1905.

[Scotsman, 16 Nov. 1904; Mitchell's writings private information.] W. F. G.

MOBERLY, ROBERT CAMPBELL (1845–1903), theologian, born at Winchester on 26 July 1845, was third son of George Moberly [q. v.], headmaster of Winchester and afterwards bishop of Salisbury. His mother Mary Ann was daughter of Thomas Crokat, a Scottish merchant at Leghorn. The family of seven sons and eight daughters was brought up in close personal friendship with their near neighbours at Winchester, Rev. John Keble and Miss Charlotte M. Yonge. (Miss C. A. E. Moberly, *Dulce Domum: George Moberly, his Family and Friends*, 1911.)

After two years at a preparatory school at Twyford near Winchester, Moberly became a commoner of Winchester in 1856, and obtained a scholarship there in 1857. Thence he passed in 1863 to New College, Oxford, with a Winchester scholarship. In Easter term 1865 he obtained first-class honours in classical moderations, but in the final classical schools, in 1867, he was placed in the second class. He was awarded the Newdigate prize in June 1867 for a poem on Marie Antoinette. He graduated B.A. in 1867, proceeding M.A. in 1870, and D.D. in 1892. He was ordained deacon in 1869 and priest in 1870. In December 1867 he was elected senior student of Christ Church, and held his studentship till his marriage in 1880. He was engaged in lecturing and teaching in classical subjects at the college, 1868–75. From 1871 to 1885, he was domestic chaplain to his father, the bishop of Salisbury.

In January 1876 he accompanied his friend Reginald Stephen Copleston (*Dulce Domum*, p. 254) to Colombo, where Copleston had been appointed bishop. The visit lasted six months, and on his return to Oxford Moberly published a pamphlet, 'An Account of the Question between the Bishop and the C.M.S. in the Diocese of Colombo.' In 1876 he became principal of St. Stephen's House, Oxford, then founded for the training of Anglican clergy for foreign mission work. In 1878, at his father's urgent request, he undertook the principalship of the Diocesan Theological College at Salisbury. In 1880, on the nomination of the dean and chapter of Christ Church, he became vicar of Great Budworth, Cheshire. As a parish clergyman, he proved himself an earnest and fair-minded champion of Anglican opinions, on such questions as the jurisdiction of church courts, the laws as to marriage, and the educational problem. He had an exceptional clearness of perception of the principles that lay behind practical questions. In 1884 his diocesan, William Stubbs [q. v. Suppl. II], bishop of Chester, brought him out of this retirement to act as his examining chaplain, and to address clerical meetings in the diocese. Stubbs's successor, Francis John Jayne, retained Moberly as examining chaplain (1889–92); and nominated him honorary canon of Chester in 1890.

Moberly established a reputation as an exponent of philosophical theology by the paper, entitled 'The Incarnation as the Basis of Dogma,' which he contributed to 'Lux Mundi' in 1889, and his position was strengthened by his paper, 'Belief in a Personal God,' read before the Church Congress at Rhyl in 1891. In 1892 he was appointed regius professor of pastoral theology at Oxford, and canon of Christ Church. His professorial lectures were thoughtful, and he preached with ability in the university pulpit and in the cathedral. In 1900 he became proctor for the dean and chapter of Christ Church in the Lower House of Convocation, and showed brilliant powers of advocacy. From 1893 he was examining chaplain to William Stubbs, bishop of Oxford, and he was honorary chaplain to Queen Victoria, 1898–1901, and chaplain in ordinary to Edward VII, 1901. Moberly died on 8 June 1903, and was buried in the burial-place at the east end of Christ Church Cathedral. In 1880 he married Alice Sidney, second daughter of Walter Kerr Hamilton [q. v.], bishop of Salisbury. His son, Walter Hamilton Moberly, is now fellow of Lincoln College, Oxford.

Moberly judged his true sphere of activity to be that of a writer. His chief work was 'Atonement and Personality' (1901), a treatise dealing with the highest problems of dogmatic theology in an unusually systematic and original manner. Prof. William Sanday, reviewing it in the 'Expositor,' said that, to find its equal in importance, one must go back to Butler and Hooker. Other works are: 1. 'Is the Independence of Church Courts really impossible?' 1886; republished 1899. 2. 'Sorrow, Sin, and Beauty,' 1889 (three devotional addresses); republished posthumously, 1903. 3. 'Considerations upon Disestablishment and Disendowment,' 1894. 4. 'Reason and Religion: Some Aspects of their Mutual Interdependence,' 1896. 5. 'Ministerial Priesthood, with an Appendix upon Romanist Criticism of Anglican Orders,' 1897; republished 1899. 6. 'Doctrinal Standards': No. 1 of 'Pusey House Occasional Papers,' 1898. 7. 'Christ our Life: Sermons chiefly preached in Oxford,' 1902. 8. 'Undenominationalism as a Principle of Primary Education,' 1902. 9. Published after his death, 'Problems and Principles' (a selection of his papers and pamphlets on theological subjects and church problems), 1904.

[Foster, Alumni Oxon.; Crockford, Clerical Directory; The Times, 9 June 1903; Oxford

Times, 12 June 1903; Guardian, 1903, pp. 817, 822. Appreciations by Dr. William Sanday in the Journal of Theological Studies, 1903, p. 499, and by Dr. Henry Scott Holland in Personal Studies, 1905, p. 272. A. C.

MOCATTA, FREDERIC DAVID (1828–1905), Jewish philanthropist, born in London on 16 Jan. 1828, was elder son in a family of two sons and two daughters of Abraham Mocatta (1797–1880). His father was an active member of the movement in England in 1840 for reform of Jewish worship and practice. His mother was Miriam, daughter of Israel Brandon. The Mocatta family, originally named Lumbrozo, was driven from Spain in 1492, when one branch migrated to Italy and the other, after a settlement in Holland, moved to England about 1670. Frederick David represented the seventh generation of the English settlers. In 1790 Abraham Lumbrozo de Mattos, his great-grandfather, who founded the firm of Mocatta & Goldsmid, bullion brokers to the Bank of England, was permitted by George III to change the family name to Mocatta, after a maternal ancestor. Rachel, a daughter of this Abraham, was mother of Sir Moses Montefiore [q. v.].

Educated at home by private tutors, among them Albert Löwy [q. v. Suppl. II], he was taught Hebrew and Latin by his father, and came to speak five or six languages. About 1843 he entered his father's business, from which he retired in 1874. His chief recreations through life were the study of history and antiquities, and foreign travel which extended over Europe, Asia Minor, Palestine and Egypt.

Enjoying a large income, Mocatta was best known as a broad-minded philanthropist. Among the first questions that engaged his attention were the better housing of the working classes and the administration of charity in such a way as not to demoralise the poor. He was an active promoter and vice-president from its formation in 1869 of the Charity Organisation Society, and was chairman from 1901 of the Charity Voting Reform Association, with whose efforts to abolish electioneering in charity administration he was in fullest sympathy. He was specially interested in hospital and nursing work, and he liberally supported almost every hospital in London.

To Jewish charities he devoted the greater part of his wealth and leisure. He was active in organising the Board of Guardians of the Jewish Poor (founded in 1859), and was chairman of a Jewish workhouse started in 1871, and reorganised in 1897 as the Home for Aged Jews, with himself as president; he also helped to form the Jews' Deaf and Dumb Home in 1865. The situation of the Jews in eastern Europe engaged his constant attention. He was vice-president of the Anglo-Jewish Association, was member of the Alliance Israélite in Paris, and member of the Roumanian committee which was founded in London in 1872 to watch over the affairs of the Roumanian Jews. In 1882 he took active part in administering the Mansion House Committee Fund for assisting Jews to leave Russia.

Mocatta did all he could to promote education, especially that of the Jewish poor, and he encouraged Jewish literature and research. In whole or part he defrayed the expenses of many important publications, including Zunz's two books, 'Zur Geschichte und Literatur' (Berlin, 1850) and 'Literaturgeschichte der Synagogalen Poesie' (Berlin, 1855), Berliner's 'Juden in Rom' (Frankfort, 1893), and the English translation of Graetz's 'History of the Jews' (London and Philadelphia, 1891). In 1887 he was president of the Anglo-Jewish Historical Exhibition at the Albert Hall, which led to the establishment of the Jewish Historical Society of England. He was president of the society in 1900. He bequeathed to public uses his valuable collection of books, principally on Jewish history; it now forms the Mocatta Library at University College, Gower Street, the room being the headquarters of the Jewish Historical Society. He was elected F.S.A. in 1889. He was chairman of the council of founders of the West London Synagogue (1896–1904). On 16 Jan. 1898, his seventieth birthday, he was presented with a book containing signatures of the Empress Frederick and of 8000 other representatives of 250 public bodies to which Mocatta had given his support; the book now belongs to his nephew, Mr. B. Elkin Mocatta.

Mocatta died in London on 16 Jan. 1905, and was buried at the Ball's Pond cemetery of the West London Synagogue of British Jews. There is a drinking fountain to his memory outside St. Botolph's Church, Aldgate. An enlarged photograph is in the committee room of the West London Synagogue.

Mocatta published 'The Jews and the Inquisition' (1877), which has been translated into German, Italian, and Hebrew, and 'The Jews at the Present Time in their Various Habitations,' a lecture (1888).

He married in 1856 Mary Ada, second daughter of Frederick David Goldsmid,

M.P. for Honiton, and sister of Sir Julian Goldsmid; he had no issue.

[F. D. Mocatta: a memoir, lectures, and extracts from letters, 1912; Jewish Chron. 20 Jan. 1905, 17 Feb. (will); Charity Organisation Rev., Feb. 1905; private information.]
M. E.

MÖENS, WILLIAM JOHN CHARLES (1833–1904), Huguenot antiquary, born at Upper Clapton on 12 Aug. 1833, was second son of Jacob Bernelot Möens, a Dutch merchant who, born in Rotterdam on 18 Jan. 1796, settled in youth in London, and died at Tunbridge Wells on 19 July 1856. His mother was Susan Baker, daughter of William Wright of the City of London, solicitor. The family, of old standing in Flanders, derived its name from Mons in Hainault. A great uncle, Adrian Möens (1757–1829), became a naturalised British subject in 1809, and was from 1800 consul for the Netherlands in Bristol, where he died 18 May 1829.

Möens, who was privately educated, began his career on the Stock Exchange, but soon retired to a house which he had bought at Boldre in Hampshire, devoting himself to yachting, and later to antiquarian researches. In January 1865 he proceeded with his wife to Sicily and Naples, and on 15 May, while returning from Pæstum with a party, including, besides his wife, the Rev. John Cruger Murray Aynsley and Mrs. Aynsley, the two men were suddenly captured by a band of about thirty brigands near Battipaglia. Möens, a pioneer of amateur photography, had been photographing the temples. The two ladies took refuge in the village, and Aynsley was released next morning to negotiate a ransom fixed at 8000*l.* Möens remained in the brigands' custody for four months, being dragged over the mountains, insufficiently clad and often starving. Italian soldiers hotly pursued the band, without capturing them, and Möens, being very tall, was often a mark for the soldiers' bullets. Strenuous efforts for his release were made by his friends. On 26 Aug. the brigands gave him up after receiving from him the sum of 5100*l.* In January 1866 Möens published a lively account of the episode in 'English Travellers and Italian Brigands.' A new edition was called for in May, and the book was translated into several languages. The proceeds of sale Möens devoted to building a school near his residence at Boldre, Hampshire. In 1867 he bought the estate of Tweed in the same county. In 1869 he sailed his steam yacht Cicada from Lymington up the Rhine to Strassburg, and by French canals to Paris and Havre. A similar trip followed in 1875, and next year he published 'Through France and Belgium by River and Canal in the Steam Yacht Ytene.' Möens deeply interested himself in the New Forest. He made a special study of forest law, and fought several battles for the commoners' rights. By his support of the New Forest Pony Association he did much to improve the breed. He was a member of the Hampshire county council from its formation. He published pamphlets on the working of the Allotment Acts in 1890 and Parish Councils Act in 1894.

Möens closely studied genealogy, especially that of Flemish families settled in England. In 1884 he edited 'The Baptismal, Marriage, and Burial Registers of the Dutch Church, Austin Friars.' In 1885 he was one of twelve persons who founded the Huguenot Society of London. He read the first paper on 13 May, on 'The Sources of Huguenot History,' and edited the earliest publications. He was elected a vice-president in 1888, and was president from 1899 to 1902. His work for the society was untiring and of great value. Elected F.S.A. in 1886, he was appointed a local secretary, and was a member of the Hampshire Field Club and Archæological Society.

He died suddenly at Tweed on 6 Jan. 1904, and was buried at Boldre church. He married on 3 Aug. 1863 Anne, sixth daughter of Thomas Warlters, of Heathfield Park, Addington, but left no issue. By his will he divided his library between the Hampshire county council and the French Hospital, Victoria Park, London.

Besides the works cited, Möens edited: 1. 'The Walloons and their Church at Norwich: their History and Registers, 1565–1832,' Lymington, 1887–8, with an historical introduction (which was reprinted separately with a new preface, 1888; 150 copies). 2. 'Chronic Hist. der Nederland, Oorlogen, Troublen,' &c., 1888, an account of an anonymous work by Philip de St. Aldegonde, printed at Norwich in 1579 by Antony de Solemne, a Brabant who came there in 1567 (reprinted from *Archæologia*, li. 205). 3. 'Hampshire Allegations for Marriage Licences granted by the Bishop of Winchester, 1689 to 1837' (Harleian Soc. Publications, vol. 34), 1893. 4. 'Registers of the French Church, Threadneedle St.' (Huguenot Soc.), 1896. 5. 'Register of Baptisms in the Dutch Church at Colchester from 1645 to 1728' (Huguenot Soc.), 1905.

[Burke's Landed Gentry; Athenæum, 16 Jan. 1904; Huguenot Soc. Proc., vol. vii. 1901–4, p. 324 (with portrait); Möens's works.]
C. F. S.

MOIR, FRANK LEWIS (1852–1904), song composer, was born at Market Harborough on 22 April 1852. Early in life he showed musical and other artistic talents, and while still a boy composed a song. After acting as tuner in London and Nottingham, he became an art student at South Kensington. Though he had no musical training, he won a scholarship at the National Training School for Music, where he studied under Prout, Stainer, and Bridge; and while there Boosey & Co. engaged him to compose ballads for four years. He won the Madrigal Society's prize in 1881. Possessing a good baritone voice, he gave recitals and taught singing at a studio in Oxford Street, London. He composed sentimental drawing-room ballads with extraordinary facility; many had very great popularity, especially 'Only once more' (1883) and 'Down the Vale' (1885). He wrote both music and words in many cases, including a comic opera, 'The Royal Watchman.' He tried a higher style in a harvest cantata, a communion service in D, and some elaborate songs, which met with little success. He published a work on 'Natural Voice Production' (1889), and contributed organ solos, of little value, to the collections 'Abbey Voluntaries,' 'Chancel Echoes,' 'Cathedral Voluntaries,' and 'Stark's Select Series.'

The music-pirates, who surreptitiously printed popular songs and sold them in the streets at a penny, ruined Moir. Publishers refused his compositions; he fell into despondency and penury, and after a painful illness died at Deal on 14 July 1904. He had married Eleanor Farnol, a vocalist from Birmingham, and left three children.

[Goodworth's Musicians of All Times; Musical Herald and Musical Times, August 1904 (obit.); Moir's works in Brit. Museum.]
H. D.

MOLLOY, GERALD (1834–1906), rector of the Catholic University of Dublin, born at Mount Tallant, near Dublin, on 10 Sept. 1834, was second son of Thomas Molloy by his wife Catharine, daughter of Patrick Whelan. He received his early education at Castleknock College, and thence passed to Maynooth College, the theological seminary of the Irish catholic priesthood. The capacity for sustained work which distinguished him through life carried him with such success through his college course that at its close in 1857, when only twenty-three years old, he was appointed professor of theology at Maynooth. But his bent was not for theology. With his professorial duties he combined a study of the natural sciences, for which he had special aptitudes. In 1870 he published, under the title 'Geology and Revelation,' a work which testified to his scientific gifts as well as to his acquirements as a theologian. In 1874 he resigned his chair in Maynooth (where he received the degree of D.D.) for the professorship of natural philosophy in the Catholic University, Dublin.

In 1878 he was appointed one of the two assistant commissioners for regulating intermediate education in Ireland according to the new Act of Parliament passed in that year. But after a few months he retired, and resumed his professorship at the Catholic University. Of this institution he became rector in 1883, but the title was then little more than honorary. The Royal University of Ireland had been established in 1879, and on its foundation the buildings of the Catholic University became merely a college in which the Dublin fellows of the new university lectured, and students were prepared for its degrees. Molloy was among the first senators of the Royal University, and was made D.Sc.; in 1882 he resigned the position of senator for a fellowship in the department of physical science, which he held till 1887. In 1885 the government named a commission to inquire into educational endowments in Ireland and to formulate improved schemes for their application. Of two paid commissioners Molloy was one. This appointment he held till the commission concluded its work in 1894. In 1890 he was reappointed a senator of the Royal University, and in 1903 became its vice-chancellor. As vice-chancellor he represented the Royal University at Aberdeen when in 1906 the university there celebrated the four hundredth anniversary of its foundation. During the festivities he died suddenly of heart failure on 1 Oct. 1906. He was buried in Glasnevin cemetery, Dublin. A man of broad sympathies and genial manners, he was a favourite with every rank and section of Irish society.

Molloy's gifts did not lie in the direction of original research, but he had a singular power of lucid exposition, and a faculty to translate scientific knowledge into language comprehensible to the lay mind. His lectures in his own classroom, in the theatre of the Royal Dublin Society, and elsewhere, always attracted large audiences. His more notable works are, besides 'Geology and Revelation' (1870), 'Outlines of a Course of Natural Philosophy' (1880), 'Gleanings in Science' (1888), and 'The Irish Difficulty—Shall and Will' (1897).

[Freeman's Journal, and Irish Times, 2 Oct. 1906; Irish Ecclesiastical Record, Nov. 1906.]
T. A. F.

MOLLOY, JAMES LYNAM (1837–1909), composer, born at Cornalaur, King's Co., Ireland, on 19 Aug. 1837, was eldest son of Dr. Kedo J. Molloy by his wife Maria Theresa. His brother, Bernard Charles Molloy, born in 1842, was nationalist M.P. for King's Co. 1880–5, and for Birr division 1885–1900. James was educated at St. Edmund's College, Ware, and at the catholic university, Dublin, where he won a junior classical scholarship in 1855, under the rectorship of Cardinal Newman, and graduated in arts in 1858. Among his class fellows were the Roman catholic archbishop of Dublin (Dr. Walsh), and Hugh Hyacinth O'Rorke the MacDermot [q. v. Suppl. II]. He showed much musical ability during his college course, and his singing of the services during Holy Week in 1857 and 1858 attracted attention. The degree of M.A. from the catholic university not being legally recognised, he continued his studies at London University, Paris, and Bonn, and was called to the English bar from the Middle Temple on 6 June 1863. He joined the south-eastern circuit and became a member of Brighton sessions, but did not practise. For a time he acted as secretary to Sir John Holker [q. v.], attorney-general, and resided for many years in London. In 1889 he was made private chamberlain to Pope Leo XIII.

As early as 1865 Molloy issued a number of songs, some of them with words by himself, but he became more ambitious and ventured on an operetta, 'The Students' Frolic,' to a libretto by Arthur Sketchley [see Rose, George, 1817–1882]. Though the piece was not very successful, yet the melody of one of the songs, 'Beer, beer, beautiful beer,' was subsequently utilised and became extremely popular as 'The Vagabond,' words by Charles Lamb Kenney [q. v.]. In 1873 he brought out an edition of Irish tunes entitled 'Songs of Ireland,' of which an enlarged edition appeared in 1882. Between 1865 and 1900 Molloy was responsible for nearly one hundred songs, many of which had a wide vogue, e.g. 'Songs from Hans Andersen,' 'Darby and Joan,' 'The Kerry Dance,' 'Love's Old Sweet Song,' 'Thady O'Flynn,' 'The Clang of the Wooden Shoon,' and 'By the River.' A keen sportsman and in early life an athlete, he showed his versatility in a charmingly written prose work, 'Our Autumn Holiday on French Rivers' (1874; 2nd edit. 1879), illustrated by Linley Sambourne [q. v. Suppl. II]. This book describes a voyage up the Seine and down the Loire in a four-oared outrigger, and suggested to Robert Louis Stevenson the similar expedition described in 'An Inland Voyage' (1878) (Balfour's *Life of Stevenson*, 1910, p. 143). Molloy also furnished music for one of Sir Francis Burnand's early comic operas, 'My Aunt's Secret.'

He spent the remainder of his life at Woolleys, Hambleden, Henley-on-Thames. He died there on 4 Feb. 1909. In 1874 Molloy married Florence Emma, youngest daughter of Henry Baskerville, of Crowsley Park, Henley-on-Thames. He left issue two sons and one daughter.

[Brown and Stratton's Brit. Musical Bio. 1897; O'Donoghue's Poets of Ireland, 1892–3; J. A. O'Shea, Roundabout Recollections, 1892, ii. 98–100; Flood's Hist. of Irish Music, 1905; private information.] W. H. G. F.

MOLLOY, JOSEPH FITZGERALD (1858–1908), miscellaneous writer, born in New Ross, co. Wexford, on 19 March 1858, was son of Pierce Molloy and his wife Catherine Byrne, and received his early education at St. Kieran's College, Kilkenny. Originally intended for the ministry of the Roman catholic church, he devoted himself to literature and music, and acted for a time as organist of the Augustinian friary church, New Ross. When twenty years old he decided on a literary career, and, armed with letters of introduction to Mr. and Mrs. S. C. Hall, he went to London in the winter of 1878. Both Mr. and Mrs. Hall proved staunch friends, and he was at once employed on the 'Art Journal,' which Hall edited. Sir Charles Gavan Duffy [q. v. Suppl. II], who had been M.P. for New Ross in 1853, also proved a friend, and engaged him as his private secretary, subsequently obtaining for him a clerkship in the London office of the agent-general for New Zealand.

Molloy was a fertile writer, and won popularity as a biographical and historical compiler. His first work was 'Songs of Passion and Pain' (under the pseudonym of 'Ernest Wilding') (1881). There followed 'Court Life below Stairs, or London under the First Georges' (2 vols. 1882), which was well received and reached a second edition in 1885. A sequel, 'London under the Last Georges' (2 vols.), appeared in 1883. 'Life and Adventures of Peg Woffington' (2 vols. 1884); 'Royalty Restored, or London under Charles II' (2 vols. 1885); 'Famous Plays' (1886), and 'The Life and Adventures of Edmund Kean' (2 vols. 1888), were works of like calibre. His 'Romance of the Irish Stage' (2 vols. 1897) had a very large sale. Molloy also published serially many novels in leading London and Liverpool papers, as well as in 'Temple Bar,' 'English Illustrated Magazine,' 'Graphic,' and 'Illustrated London News.' Among his separately published novels were: 'Merely Players' (3 vols. 1881); 'It is no Wonder' (2 vols. 1881); 'What hast thou done?' (1883); 'That Villain Romeo' (1886); 'A Modern Magician' (3 vols. 1887); 'An Excellent Knave' (1893); 'His Wife's Soul' (1893; 2nd edit. with the title, 'Sweet is Revenge,' 1895), and 'A Justified Sinner' (1897).

Molloy travelled much on the continent of Europe in search of health, which was never robust, journeying through France, Spain, Belgium, Italy, and Algiers. Despite failing strength he was engaged shortly before his death on 'Victoria Regina,' published posthumously in two volumes. He died unmarried at his residence, 20 Norland Square, Notting Hill, W., on 19 March 1908, and was buried at St. Mary's cemetery, Kensal Green.

Besides the works mentioned above, Molloy wrote: 1. 'The Faiths of the Peoples,' 2 vols. 1892. 2. 'The Most Gorgeous Lady Blessington,' 2 vols. 1896. 3. 'Historical and Biographical Studies,' 1897. 4. 'The Queen's Comrade: the Life and Times of Sarah, Duchess of Marlborough,' 2 vols. 1901. 5. 'The Sailor King: William IV, his Court and his Subjects,' 2 vols. 1903. 6. 'Romance of Royalty,' 2 vols. 1904. 7. 'The Russian Court in the Eighteenth Century,' 1905. 8. 'Sir Joshua and his Circle,' 2 vols. 1906. Molloy also edited, with introduction and notes, the 'Memoirs of Mary Robinson' in 1895.

[Private information from his sister, Miss K. Molloy; Freeman's Journal and Irish Times, 20 March 1908; personal knowledge.]

W. H. G. F.

MOLYNEUX. [See More-Molyneux, Sir Robert Henry, G.C.B. (1838–1904), admiral.]

MONCREIFF, HENRY JAMES, second Baron Moncreiff of Tullibole (1840–1909), Scottish judge, born at Edinburgh on 24 April 1840, eldest son of James Moncreiff, first Baron Moncreiff [q. v.], by his wife Isabella, daughter of Robert Bell, procurator of the Church of Scotland. After education at Edinburgh Academy and at Harrow School, he went in 1857 to Trinity College, Cambridge, where he graduated B.A. and LL.B. in 1861 (with a first class in the law tripos). Having attended law lectures at Edinburgh University, and becoming a member of the Speculative Society, he passed on 14 July 1863 to the Scottish bar, where he acquired a fair practice. A whig in politics according to the tradition of his family, he was appointed advocate-depute in 1865 by his father, who was then lord advocate, but lost that office when the Russell ministry went out in June 1866. He was re-appointed under Gladstone's administrations of 1868 and 1880. In 1881 he became sheriff of Renfrew and Bute. On Gladstone's adoption of his home rule policy Moncreiff joined the liberal unionists. In 1888 he was raised to the bench, with the title of Lord Wellwood. In 1895, on the death of his father, he succeeded to the peerage, and in 1901 was appointed lord-lieutenant of Kincardineshire. He resigned his judgeship owing to failing health in 1905, died at Bournemouth on 3 March 1909, and was buried in the Grange cemetery at Edinburgh.

Moncreiff, who was a versatile writer, with a keen sense of humour, contributed many articles and short stories to 'Blackwood's Magazine,' the 'Cornhill Magazine,' the 'World,' 'Fraser's Magazine,' the 'Badminton Magazine,' and other periodicals, and wrote 'General Remarks on the Game of Golf' for the volume on golf in the 'Badminton Library.' A collection of his articles and stories was printed for private circulation in 1898 and 1907. He was also author of a useful treatise on 'Review in Criminal Cases' (1877).

Moncreiff married (1) in 1866 Susan (*d.* 1869), daughter of Sir William Dick Cunyngham of Prestonfield, Midlothian; (2) in 1873 Millicent (*d.* 1881), daughter of Colonel Fryer of Moulton Paddocks, Newmarket. He had no family, and was succeeded in the peerage by his brother, the Hon. and Rev. Robert Chichester Moncreiff (*b.* 1843). A portrait was painted by Fiddes Watt shortly before Moncreiff's death.

[Scotsman, 4 March 1909; Harrow School Register; Roll of the Faculty of Advocates; History of the Speculative Society, p. 151; personal knowledge.]

G. W. T. O.

MONCRIEFF, Sir ALEXANDER (1829–1906), colonel and engineer, born at 27 George Square, Edinburgh, on 17 April 1829, was eldest son of Captain Matthew Moncrieff, of the Madras army, by Isabella, daughter of Alexander Campbell. His father was a descendant of Alexander Moncrieff [q. v.]. He retained the 'superiority' and designation of Culfargie, but the estate had passed to Lord Wemyss, and he lived at Barnhill near Perth.

Moncrieff was educated at Edinburgh and Aberdeen universities, and spent some time in a civil engineer's office, but did not settle down to a profession. He was commissioned as lieutenant in the Forfarshire artillery (militia) on 16 April 1855, and obtained leave to go to the Crimea during the siege of Sevastopol. He was promoted captain on 16 Sept. 1857, was transferred to the city of Edinburgh artillery (militia) on 9 Nov. 1863, became major on 26 March 1872, and was made colonel of the 3rd brigade, Scottish division, R.A., on 20 Feb. 1878.

As he watched the bombardment of 6 June 1855, and the silencing of the Russian guns in the Mamelon by shots through the embrasures, his mind turned to the problem of raising and lowering guns, so that they might fire over the parapet and then descend under cover for loading. He conceived the idea of mounting guns on curved elevators, which would allow them to recoil backwards and downwards, the energy of recoil being used to raise a counterweight which would bring the gun up again to the firing position. This method had the further advantage, that it lessened the strain on the platform by interposing a moving fulcrum between it and the gun. He carried out experiments at his own expense for several years. and a 7-ton gun mounted on his system was tried at Shoeburyness and favourably reported on in 1868.

From 1867 to 1875 Moncrieff was attached to the royal arsenal, to work out the details of his disappearing carriage, adapt it to heavier and lighter guns, and devise means of laying and sighting guns so mounted. He received 10,000*l.* for his invention and for any improvements on it. In 1869 he submitted designs for a hydro-pneumatic carriage, in which air was compressed by the recoil of the gun and formed a spring to raise it again. This was intended for naval use in the first instance, but it was adapted to siege and fortress guns, and eventually superseded the counterweight system. It met with opposition at first, being thought too complicated; and Moncrieff complained bitterly of the obstacles placed in his way. He had controversy also with officers of the royal engineers, who held that he claimed too much for his system, and was not entitled to dictate how and where it should be used. There was substantial agreement, however, as to the great merit of his inventions. He published in 1873 a pamphlet on the Moncrieff system, which he explained or defended in lectures at the Royal Institution (7 May 1869) and the United Service Institution (*Journal*, vols. x. xi. xiv. xvii. xix. xxviii.), in the 'Proceedings of the Royal Artillery Institution' for 1868, and the R.E. professional papers of 1870. He was a member of the Institution of Civil Engineers, was elected F.R.S. in 1871, was made C.B. in 1880, and K.C.B. in 1890.

A man of many interests, genial and sociable, he went to South Africa and Canada in search of sport, and exhibited at the Scottish Academy as an amateur artist. He was captain of the Wimbledon Golf Club in 1894. In later life he was a director of two banks, acquired wealth, and bought the estate of Bandirran in Perthshire. He claimed to be head of his family as the heir male of William Moncrieff, who died in 1570; but this claim affected the title to the baronetcy created in 1626, and was opposed by Lord Moncreiff of Tullibole, the holder of the baronetcy. The case came into court in June 1905, and the evidence produced led to the withdrawal of his petition. He died at Bandirran on 3 Aug. 1906, and was buried at Abernethy, Perthshire. In 1875 he had married Harriet Mary, only daughter of James Rimington Wilson of Broomhead Hall, Yorkshire. They had five sons and two daughters. The eldest son, Malcolm Matthew (in the carabiniers), and a younger son, Alaric Rimington (in the Scots Greys), served throughout the South African war, the former being severely wounded.

[The Times, 6 Aug. 1906; Seton, The House of Moncrieff, 1890; information from Mr. A. R. Hope Moncrieff.] E. M. L.

MOND, LUDWIG (1839–1909), chemical technologist, manufacturer, and collector of works of art, born at Cassel on 7 March 1839, was of Jewish parentage. His father, Moritz B. Mond, was a well-to-do merchant. His mother's maiden name was Henriette Levinsohn. After studying at the Realschule and the polytechnic school at Cassel, Mond worked in 1855 under

Hermann Kolbe at Marburg and went in 1856 to Heidelberg to work under Robert Wilhelm Bunsen. In 1859 he began his industrial career in a miniature soda-works at Ringkuhl near Cassel, where he began the researches that led to his sulphur recovery process; he next became manager of a factory at Mainz for the production of acetic acid by wood distillation. Thence proceeding to Cologne, he worked there at the production of ammonia from waste leather. Subsequently he spent some time at other factories in Germany and Holland. He came to England in 1862 and took out an English patent for the recovery of sulphur from the Leblanc alkali-waste, by a method of partial oxidation and treatment with acid, and in 1863 he went to John Hutchinson & Co. at Widnes to perfect the process. In 1864 he took over the construction and management of a Leblanc soda-works at Utrecht, but returned to Widnes in 1867, entering into partnership with J. Hutchinson of Hutchinson & Earle in order to push his sulphur recovery process. From this time forward he was domiciled in England; he became a naturalised British subject in 1880. M. Schaffner had invented a process somewhat similar to that of Mond almost simultaneously, and manufacturers in Widnes, Newcastle, and Glasgow for a number of years used a combination of Mond's and Schaffner's processes by which about 30 per cent. of the total sulphur was recovered from the alkali-waste. The process was also used in France; but by 1894 the Mond and Schaffner processes were entirely replaced by the Claus-Chance process (G. Lunge, *Sulphuric Acid and Alkali*, 2nd edit. ii. 827–51).

In 1872 Mond made the acquaintance of Ernest Solvay, a Belgian chemist, who had effected great improvements in a rival process to that of Leblanc, the ammonia-soda process which had been invented by Harrison Gray Dyer and John Hemming in 1838. Solvay had started a small factory at Couillet near Charleroi for working his process. Mond, with much searching of heart, invested his small capital derived from the sulphur recovery process, in purchasing the option to work Solvay's patents in England. He entered into partnership with Mr. (now the Rt. Hon. Sir) John Tomlinson Brunner, his friend since 1862, who had been in the commercial department of Hutchinson's works. Not without difficulty, the two men raised the capital necessary to start works at Winnington, near Northwich. The Solvay process was imperfect; during the first year of the working at Winnington 'everything that could explode, exploded, and everything that would break, broke'; but by ceaseless labour Mond by 1880 had succeeded in perfecting the process so that it became a financial success. In 1881 the concern was turned into a limited liability company, of which Mond remained a managing director till his death; and the firm of Brunner, Mond & Co. are now the largest alkali makers in the world, employing about 4000 workmen. The firm was one of the first to adopt an eight hours' day and to provide model dwellings and playing-fields for their workpeople. Mond left 20,000*l.* in trust for the benefit of disabled and aged workpeople belonging to the firm.

In 1879 Mond returned to the problem of the production of ammonia, which was important for the use of its compounds as artificial manure. A series of investigations carried out with his assistant, Dr. Joseph Hawliczek, based on the use of cyanides, was not followed up industrially; a further series carried out with Mr. G. H. Beckett, Dr. Carl Markel, and Dr. Adolf Staub led to the invention of the Mond producer-gas plant, which Mond patented in 1883, and continued to improve till the end of his life. By carefully regulating the temperature of a furnace in which air and steam are led over heated coal or coke, Mond succeeded in converting all the nitrogen of the fuel into ammonia, which could easily be recovered, and generating at the same time a very cheap and useful form of producer-gas. Over three million tons of bituminous fuel, lignites, and peats are now used annually at Dudley Port, Staffordshire, and in other places in various parts of the world in the production of 'Mond-gas.' Mond's next step in 1885 was to try, with the help of Dr. Carl Langer, to convert the heat energy of fuel, and in particular of producer-gas directly into electrical energy by improving the gas battery invented by Sir William Robert Grove [q. v. Suppl. I]. The use of porous plates moistened with sulphuric acid and faced on either side with platinum and platinum black, to separate the hydrogen from the oxygen, led to interesting results; but the inventors were unable to overcome the defects of the cells (of which they published an account in 1889). Mond, in connection with this work, carried out a series of researches with Sir William Ramsay and Dr. John Shields on the occlusion of hydrogen and oxygen by platinum and palladium (*Phil. Trans.*

clxxxvi. 657 (1895); cxc. 129 (1897); cxci. 124 (1898).

The work on the gas battery was interrupted by investigations of more urgent importance. Mond from 1886 directed his efforts to recover the chlorine wasted in the ammonia-soda process as calcium chloride. By using first nickel oxide, and later magnesia, instead of lime to decompose the ammonium chloride formed, he obtained easily decomposable chlorides, from which chlorine could be recovered by treatment with air or steam, either in the elementary form or in that of hydrochloric acid. Between 1886 and 1889 he took out a number of patents bearing on this point, some independently, some with G. Eschellmann, and his processes were used industrially for some time. The use of nickel compounds, and of nickel valves in the chlorine process, and the use of finely divided nickel to purify producer-gas for use in the gas battery led Mond, in collaboration with Langer and Quincke, to discover nickel carbonyl, a gaseous compound of nickel and carbon monoxide. Mond, after two years' work, based on this discovery a remarkable method for the extraction of metallic nickel from its ores, unlike any metallurgical process previously known (see paper 'On the extraction of nickel from its ores by the Mond process,' by W. C. ROBERTS-AUSTEN, F.R.S., *Proc. Inst. Civil Engineers*, cxxxv. 29, 1899). Mond formed the 'Mond Nickel Company' to work the process, with mines in Canada and a model works at Clydach, near Swansea, with a considerable output of nickel yearly. Mond pursued the scientific investigation of the carbonyls, and with Quincke and Langer obtained iron carbonyls; he suggested to Sir James Dewar an investigation on the production of nickel carbonyl under high pressure, for which Dewar took out a patent in 1902; and a posthumous paper, with a note by Mr. R. L. Mond, gives an account of investigations with Dr. Heinrich Hirtz and Mr. M. Dalton Cowap on carbonyls of cobalt, molybdenum, and ruthenium (*Trans. Chem. Soc.* 1910, p. 798). This was Mond's last research.

In the work of scientific societies Mond was extremely active. In January 1880 he took a leading part in the foundation of a Lancashire Chemical Society, and in the following April urged that it should become a national society; as a result of the movement, which was largely helped by Sir Henry Roscoe, the Society of Chemical Industry was founded in 1881, and became later one of the largest scientific societies in the world. In August 1881 Mond undertook the arrangements for the foundation of the Society's 'Journal,' drew up a plan for it, and guaranteed the cost till it should become self-supporting. He acted as foreign secretary of the society till his election as president in 1888. In 1906 he was awarded the society's medal for conspicuous services to applied chemistry.

Mond was elected F.R.S. in 1891, honorary member of the German Chemical Society and member of the Società Reale of Naples in 1908, and corresponding member of the Prussian Akademie der Wissenschaften in 1909. He received honorary doctorates from the universities of Padua (1892), Heidelberg (1896), Manchester (1904), and Oxford (1907). He was awarded the grand cordon of the Crown of Italy in 1909.

Mond lived at Winnington from 1867 till 1884, when he removed to London; he spent most of his winters in Rome, where he acquired the Palazzo Zuccari. For some years he had suffered from heart disease, from which he died at his house, The Poplars, Avenue Road, Regent's Park, on 11 Dec. 1909. He was buried with Jewish rites in a family mausoleum at the St. Pancras cemetery, Finchley.

Mond married in 1866 his cousin Frida Loewenthal, who survives him. He left two sons, Robert Ludwig Mond, and Sir Alfred Moritz Mond, liberal M.P. for Swansea, who was created a baronet in 1910.

Mond was a man of great scientific attainments, of indomitable resource and energy, and with a genius for divining the industrial possibilities of discoveries in pure science. Apart from inventions of detail, he will be remembered, as an industrial chemist, for having placed the ammonia-soda process on a practical basis, for his nitrogen recovery process and producer-gas, and for his nickel process. He left a fortune of over 1,000,000*l*. But his commercial success was 'the result and not the object of his work.'

The obituary of Mond by Carl Langer (*Berichte der deutschen chem. Gesellschaft* for 1911, p. 3665) gives a list of his English patents, forty-nine in number, and a list (incomplete) of the papers published by Mond whether independently, with the collaborators previously mentioned, or with R. Nasini (on the physical properties of certain nickel compounds).

Apart from his daily occupations Mond's interests were mainly in pure science, music, and art, and the improvement of the condition of his workpeople. In his address to students at the opening of the Schorlemmer laboratory at Owens College, Manchester, on 3 May 1895 (*Journ. Soc. Chem. Ind.* xiv. 552), he insisted on the importance to industrial chemists of a training in pure science. None of his great benefactions were devoted to the teaching of applied science. He was inclined to deny that such teaching was of any value in the training of a chemist (NASINI, see bibliography below). In 1896 he gave 100,000*l.* under a special trust to found and equip the Davy-Faraday Laboratory, in a house next to the Royal Institution, for research in chemistry and physics; and by his will he left two sums of 50,000*l.* to the Royal Society and to the University of Heidelberg respectively, for the encouragement of research and other purposes. Between 1892 and his death he gave to the Royal Society sums amounting to 16,000*l.* for the continuance and improvement of the society's catalogue of scientific papers. In 1908 he founded a biennial prize of 400*l.* for chemistry at the Accademia dei Lincei (of which he had been elected an honorary member in 1899) in memory of his friend, the chemist, Stanislao Cannizzaro. He left to the town of Cassel a sum of 20,000*l.*, together with 5000*l.* for a Jewish charitable foundation. In his lifetime he made large gifts for charitable purposes, but as a rule these remained anonymous.

From 1892 onwards Mond formed a remarkable collection of pictures, mainly early Italian, of which a detailed description was published by Dr. J. P. Richter, who acted as Mond's adviser (*The Mond Collection, an Appreciation*, 2 vols. London, 1910). Mond bequeathed, subject to the life-interest of his wife, the greater portion of his pictures to the National Gallery, with a sum to provide for their housing. He also left 20,000*l.* to the Munich Akademie der bildenden Künste for the training of art students.

Though not above the middle height, Mond was a man of impressive presence, with a massive head, full beard, dark piercing eyes, and strongly marked features of an Oriental type. A marble bust (1896) by Joseph von Kopf; a bronze bust by Henrik Glicenstein; a bronze full figure (1906) by Ferdinand Seeboeck; a monumental bronze bas relief (1909) by C. Fontana, presented to Mond by a committee of Italian chemists; a portrait medallion by E. Lantéri (1911), and an oil painting by Solomon J. Solomon, R.A. (at Sir Alfred Mond's house), belong to Mrs. Mond.

[Obituaries in The Times, 13 Dec. 1909; Nature, lxxxii. 222 (1909), by Sir Edward Thorpe, F.R.S.; Rendiconti della R. Accademia dei Lincei, ser. 5, **xix.** p. 409 (1910), by Raffaele Nasini; Rendiconti della Società chimica Italiana, ii. (1910), by Luigi Gabba; Journ. Soc. Chem. Industry, xxviii. 1304 (1910); The Recovery of Sulphur from Alkali-waste, by L. Mond, Liverpool, 1868; On the Origin of the Ammonia-Soda Process, by L. M., Journ. Chem. Soc. Ind. iv. 527 (1885); presidential address on the production of ammonia, Journ. Soc. Chem. Industry, viii. 505 (1889); presidential address on Chlorine to the chemical section of the British Association; Brit. Assoc. Report for 1896, p. 734; History of my Process of Nickel Extraction, by L. M., Journ. Soc. Chem. Ind. xiv. 945 (1895); personal knowledge; private information from Mrs. Mond, Mr. R. L. Mond, Sir William Ramsay, Sir Henry Roscoe, and Sir Edward Thorpe.] P. J. H.

MONKHOUSE, WILLIAM COSMO (1840–1901), poet and critic, born in London on 18 March 1840, was son of Cyril John Monkhouse, a solicitor, by his wife Amelia Maria Delafosse, of a Huguenot family which came to England after the revocation of the edict of Nantes. Monkhouse entered St. Paul's School on 3 Oct. 1848, and left in 1856 to take up a nomination to a supplementary clerkship in the board of trade, then under the presidency of Lord Stanley of Alderley. Rising through various grades, he was assistant secretary to the finance department at his death. In 1870–1 he was sent by the board to South America in connection with Seamen's Hospitals; in 1894–6 he acted as a member of the committee on the Mercantile Marine Fund.

Monkhouse's literary career began betimes. He wrote much verse while at school, and he was an early contributor to 'Temple Bar,' the 'Argosy,' the 'Englishwoman's' and other magazines. It was not until 1865 that Moxon put forth his first volume, 'A Dream of Idleness, and other Poems.' The volume was of promise, and some of its pieces, e.g. 'The Chief Ringer's Burial' and 'The Night Express,' found their place in anthologies. But it had no great success, pecuniary or otherwise. The moment was perhaps unfavourable to one who was a disciple of Wordsworth and Tennyson. After an essay in the three-volume novel, 'A Question of Honour' (1868), Monkhouse for some years practically abandoned poetry for literary and art criticism. He became a frequent contributor to the 'Academy,' to the 'Magazine of Art' (then under the editorship of W. E. Henley), and eventually to the 'Saturday Review.'

In 1869 he published 'Masterpieces of English Art'; in 1872 he edited and prefaced a photographic edition of Hogarth's works; in 1877 came a 'Handbook of Précis Writing'; in 1879 an excellent short life of Turner for Cundall's 'Great Artists,' and in 1887 a little guide-book on the 'Italian Pre-Raphaelites' in the National Gallery. In 1890 followed a valuable volume on the 'Earlier English Water Colour Painters' (2nd edit. 1897).

In 1890 Monkhouse returned to poetry with 'Corn and Poppies,' some portions of which had appeared in the 'Magazine of Art.' This volume contained many of his best pieces, and notably his highest effort, the stately 'Dead March.' Of a fine ballad entitled 'The Christ upon the Hill,' a limited edition was issued with etchings by William Strang in 1895; and after his death appeared a slender volume entitled 'Pasiteles the Elder and other Poems,' in which this ballad was included. Other prose works were: 'A Memoir of Leigh Hunt' in the 'Great Writers' series, 1893; 'In the National Gallery,' 1895; 'British Contemporary Artists,' chiefly contributed to 'Scribner's Magazine,' 1899; 'A History of Chinese Porcelain,' 1901; and 'Life of Sir John Tenniel' (for the 'Art Journal'), 1901. To this Dictionary Monkhouse was a diligent contributor of lives of artists, including Reynolds and Turner. As a critic he had the happy faculty of conveying a well-considered and weighty opinion without suggesting superiority or patronage; as a poet, though he lacked the leisure to realise his full ambition, he left much which no true lover of finished and thoughtful work can wisely afford to neglect.

Monkhouse died at Skegness on 2 July 1901. He was twice married: (1) in 1865 to Laura, daughter of John Keymer of Dartford in Kent; (2) in 1873 to Leonora Eliza, the daughter of Commander Blount, R.N., by whom he had two sons and six daughters. There are painted portraits of him by C. E. Johnson, R.I., and J. M'Lure Hamilton, and an etching by William Strang, A.R.A.

[Monkhouse's works; personal knowledge. See also art. in Art Journal for March 1902, by Edmund Gosse, on Cosmo Monkhouse as an Art Critic.] A. D.

MONRO, CHARLES HENRY (1835–1908), author, born in London on 17 March 1835, was second of three sons of Cecil Monro, chief registrar of the court of chancery, by his wife Elizabeth, daughter of Colonel Henry Howe Knight-Erskine of Pittodrie. Alexander Monro [q. v.], principal of Edinburgh University in 1685, was an ancestor, six of whose descendants are already commemorated in this Dictionary. His elder brother, Cecil James, a man of extraordinary powers, was incapacitated by phthisis soon after his election to a fellowship at Trinity in 1855. His younger brother, Kenneth, a brilliant artillery officer, died in early manhood of phthisis in Nova Scotia. Charles Henry entered Harrow in 1847, proceeded to Gonville and Caius College, Cambridge, as Sayer scholar in 1853, graduated B.A. in 1857 with a first class in classics, and in the same year was elected to a fellowship, of which he resigned the emoluments in 1897. Called to the bar at Lincoln's Inn in 1863, he did not practise, but continued his study of law, though his work was hampered by ill-health, necessitating much residence abroad. From 1872 to 1896 he was law lecturer at his college. In 1900 he represented Cambridge University at the 500th anniversary of the second foundation of the University of Cracow.

In 1891 he published an annotated text and translation of the title 'Locati Conducti' in Justinian's 'Digest'; in 1893 'De Furtis'; in 1896 'Ad legem Aquiliam'; in 1900 'De Adquirendo Dominio'; and in 1902 'Pro Socio.' Meanwhile he had begun the heavy task of translating the whole 'Digest.' One volume of this work appeared in 1904 and another in 1909, after his death, covering, altogether, about one-fourth of the book. His work was marked by great acuteness and independence of judgment and accuracy of scholarship. He had a peculiar gift for translation, and his rendering of the 'Digest,' so far as it proceeded, was much superior to any earlier attempt.

Monro, who was an accomplished linguist, and was specially interested in Celtic, died, unmarried, at Eastbourne on 23 Feb. 1908, and was buried there. By his will he left a large sum to his college, which has perpetuated his memory by a Monro fellowship, a Monro lectureship in Celtic, a Monro endowment to the Squire law library in Cambridge, and a Monro extension to the college library.

[Venn, Biogr. Hist. of Gonv. and Caius Coll., ii. 310; memorial notices in The Caian, xvii. 161; Burke's Landed Gentry, s.v. Knight-Erskine; Cass, Hist. of Monken Hadley, p. 181; notices of members of the family in this Dictionary; school and college records; communications from friends; personal knowledge.] W. W. B.

MONRO, DAVID BINNING (1836–1905), classical scholar, born at Edinburgh on 16 Nov. 1836, was eldest child of the four sons and two daughters of Alexander Monro Binning, writer to the signet (1805–1891), of Auchinbowie, Stirlingshire, and Softlow, Roxburghshire, by his wife and cousin Harriet, daughter of Alexander Monro, M.D. [q. v.], of Craiglockhart. On his marriage his father assumed his wife's surname, which his own ancestors had borne, and on his death in 1891 his Scottish estates passed to his eldest son. Monro was as a boy educated privately. He entered Glasgow University in 1851, and there distinguished himself in logic and mathematics, but the influence of Edmund Lushington [q. v. Suppl. I], professor of Greek, determined the direction of his studies for life. He matriculated at Oxford as scholar of Brasenose College on 16 June 1854, and in November of the same year was elected to a scholarship at Balliol College, where he afterwards held a Snell exhibition. He was placed in the first class in moderations, both in classics and mathematics, in 1856, in the first class in the final classical school, and the second class in the final mathematical schools in 1858. He won the Ireland scholarship (1858) and the prize for a Latin essay (1859), and was elected fellow of Oriel in the same year. He entered at Lincoln's Inn as a student, but was not called to the bar, returning to Oxford in 1862 as lecturer of Oriel College. He became tutor in 1863, and was elected vice-provost in 1874, on the retirement of Dr. Edward Hawkins [q. v.] from Oxford. On Hawkins's death in 1882 Monro was chosen provost.

As tutor at Oriel, Monro raised the standard of the teaching, and won the enthusiastic regard of his pupils by his devotion to their best interests. He lectured, as the manner then was, on a great variety of subjects, comparative philology, early Greek history and philosophy, Homer, Thucydides, Herodotus, early Roman history, Roman constitutional history, and Roman public law, and though his delivery was weak and he lacked fluency, his lectures were valued. Here, as with his pupils in his rooms, his strength lay not merely in the abundance and accuracy of his knowledge, but even more in his method of interpreting an author and of marshalling his facts. As provost he ruled his college in a wise and liberal spirit; a sound judgment and a rare grasp of principle were linked to fine courtesy and warmth of heart. In the life and work of the university he played a leading part. He was more than once public examiner; he served on the delegacy of the press, was a curator of the museum, and a member of the hebdomadal council, and he filled the office of vice-chancellor (1901–4).

Meanwhile Monro devoted his literary interests and energies to the elucidation of the 'Homeric Poems,' and to questions arising out of them. In October 1868 he wrote in the 'Quarterly Review' an article on the 'Homeric Question,' which he recast for the 'Encyclopædia Britannica' (edit. 1880). He collated the 'Venetian MSS. of Scholia' to the 'Iliad' for Dindorf's edition (1875–7); published a school edition of 'Iliad I' (1878), a 'Grammar of the Homeric Language' (1882; 2nd edit. 1891), and a school edition of the 'Iliad' (i.–xii. 1884, 3rd edit. 1899; xiii.–xxiv. 1889, 3rd edit. 1901). A complete text of 'Homeri Opera et Reliquiæ' appeared in 1896, and in 1902 there followed, in collaboration with T. W. Allen, a text of the 'Iliad' with an apparatus criticus. The later years of his life were given to an edition of the last twelve books of the 'Odyssey' (1901), with notes and introductions embodying the results of his work. He contributed papers on Homeric questions to the 'Academy,' the 'Journal of Philology,' the 'Journal of Hellenic Studies,' and other periodicals. If the quantity of his published work is small, this is due to his powers of compression, to his self-criticism, and his reluctance to put out anything for which he could not vouch. His school edition of 'Iliad I,' which served the purpose of a 'ballon d'essai,' embodied the results of years of work, and gives concisely the writer's views on disputed points of interpretation and the principles underlying them, whilst the publication of the 'Homeric Grammar' put Monro at once among the first authorities on the subject.

Monro held that the solution of all Homeric questions must be found in philology. He was thoroughly familiar with the work of archæologists and the contribution made by them to our knowledge, but he did not hold it to be of equal value or certainty. Unwearying industry, a sound judgment, and a true sense of literary form combined to make him a model interpreter of his author; his dislike of anything premature or superfluous, his wide range of knowledge of comparative philology, and his clearness of statement gained for his writings exceptional authority. Monro spoke French, German, and Italian with accuracy of idiom and accent, having a very sensitive ear, whilst his 'Modes of Greek Music' (1894) attests his fondness for music and his knowledge of it.

Monro founded the Oxford Philological Society in 1870, and was for many years its president; he took part in founding the Hellenic Society and the Classical Association, and was vice-president of both; he was a member of the council of the British School at Athens, officier de l'instruction publique in France, and an original fellow of the British Academy. He was created hon. D.C.L. of Oxford in 1904, LL.D. of Glasgow in 1883, and Doc.Litt. of Dublin in 1892. He died suddenly of heart disease at Heiden, Switzerland, on 22 Aug. 1905, and was buried in Holywell cemetery, Oxford. His portrait by Sir William Quiller Orchardson, R.A., is in the Oriel common room. He was unmarried.

[Personal knowledge; David Binning Monro, a short Memoir, translated with slight alterations from a notice by J. Cook Wilson in the Jahresbericht über die Fortschritte der Klassischen Alterthumswissenschaft, Oxford, Clarendon Press, 1907.]

L. R. P.

MONSON, Sir EDMUND JOHN, first baronet (1834–1909), diplomatist, born at Chart Lodge, Seal, near Sevenoaks, on 6 Oct. 1834, was third son of William John Monson, sixth Baron Monson, by his wife Eliza, youngest daughter of Edmund Larken. Educated first at a private school in the Isle of Wight, and then at Eton, he entered Balliol College, Oxford, where he graduated B.A. with a first-class degree in law and modern history in 1855. Elected a fellow of All Souls College in 1858, and proceeding M.A. in the same year, he acted as examiner in modern languages for the Taylorian scholarship in 1868. He entered the diplomatic service in 1856, and on passing an examination was appointed attaché at Paris in July of that year. After a few months in Florence in 1858 he was retransferred to Paris, and thence to Washington, where for nearly five years he acted as private secretary to Lord Lyons [q. v.]. During that period Lyons was occupied with the critical questions which resulted from the outbreak of the American civil war. In 1863 Monson was removed to Hanover, and thence after a few months to Brussels. In 1865 he quitted the diplomatic service and sought election to parliament as member for Reigate in the liberal interest, but was unsuccessful, and remained unemployed till May 1869, when he became consul in the Azores. This appointment was intended as a stepping-stone to renewed diplomatic employment, for which he was eminently fitted both by disposition and training. In 1871, when the independent position conceded to Hungary by the dual constitution was found to render the presence of a British agent at the Hungarian capital desirable, Monson was selected for the newly created post of consul-general at Buda-Pesth, the diplomatic nature of the appointment being subsequently emphasised by the additional rank of second secretary to the embassy at Vienna. In February 1876, when it grew evident that Servia and Montenegro were in danger of being driven into active hostilities against Turkey in aid of the insurgents in Bosnia and Herzegovina, it was deemed prudent to have a British representative at the Montenegrin capital, and Monson was sent on a special mission to Cettigne. He remained there, though suffering severely in health, during the war of the Servians and Montenegrins with the Turks which broke out in June following, through the subsequent mediation by Great Britain for the purpose of procuring an armistice, and the deliberations of the conference at Constantinople. The declaration of war by Russia against Turkey, in April 1877, rendered his presence at Cettigne no longer necessary, and he returned to Buda-Pesth, being made C.B. in January 1878. In June 1879 he was appointed minister resident in Uruguay, and five years later was promoted to the rank of envoy at Buenos Ayres. At the close of 1884 he was transferred to Copenhagen, and in February 1888 to Athens, becoming in 1886 K.C.M.G. Before he left Denmark, the Danish and United States governments bore testimony to their 'entire confidence' in his learning, ability, and impartiality by selecting him as arbitrator on the claims of the American firm of Butterfield & Co. against the Danish government on account of the treatment of two of their vessels by the Danish authorities of the island of St. Thomas in 1854 and 1855. This case had been a subject of diplomatic controversy for over thirty years. It was settled in the Danish government's favour by Monson's award, delivered in January 1900. In 1892 he was transferred to Brussels and was made G.C.M.G. Next year he was promoted to be ambassador at Vienna and was sworn a privy councillor. After three years' residence at the Austrian capital he was transferred to Paris in October 1896, having a few months previously been made G.C.B. In his new post he was called upon to deal with numerous embarrassing disputes arising out of conflicting colonial claims and interests. The themes included the rights of fishery enjoyed by the French in the waters and on the coast of Newfoundland, the exercise of jurisdiction in the New Hebrides, and questions of boundary and spheres of influence in East and West Africa. Monson, calm and judicial by temperament, and grave and courteous in manner, avoided unnecessary irritation, and was personally much liked by the French ministers and officials with whom he was brought in contact. In June 1898 he signed a convention for the delimitation of the possessions and spheres of influence of the two countries in the region of the Niger. Later in the same year Lord Kitchener in his progress up the Nile, after the final defeat of the Dervishes at Omdurman, discovered that a French exploring party from the Congo under Captain Marchand had established themselves on the bank of the river at Fashoda and there hoisted the tricolor, which Captain Marchand refused to lower except on instructions from home. An acute controversy ensued, which at one time seemed likely to lead to very serious results. More moderate counsels, however, prevailed, Captain Marchand's party was withdrawn, and in March 1899 a declaration was signed in London defining the respective spheres of influence of the two countries in central Africa, which disposed of this subject of dispute. Monson's management of his share in the discussions was unexceptionable. But in December 1898, while the question was still awaiting final solution, he caused no little commotion by a speech delivered at the annual meeting of the British chamber of commerce in Paris, in which, after some frank comments on the novel methods recently practised in diplomacy, he expressed his conviction that neither in France nor in Great Britain was there any deep-rooted feeling of animosity against the other country, and made an earnest appeal to those in France who 'were directly or indirectly responsible for the national policy to abstain from the continuance of a policy of pin-pricks which, while it could only procure some ephemeral gratification to a short-lived ministry, must inevitably perpetuate across the Channel an irritation which a high-spirited nation must eventually feel to be intolerable.' It was naturally supposed by many that this utterance was the result of some instructions from home, but it may safely be asserted that to the British cabinet it came as unexpectedly as to the public at large. It had, however, no evil effects. The allusion to the brief duration of French ministries was made the subject of interpellation and attack in the French chamber of deputies, and it was a striking tribute to Monson's popularity that his defence was warmly and successfully undertaken by the French government, and that the incident in no degree affected his position. He remained at Paris till the end of 1904, and had the satisfaction of seeing a general settlement of the principal questions at issue between the two countries affected by the agreements signed in London in the spring of that year (8 April 1904). He had received the honorary degree of D.C.L. of Oxford University in 1898 and that of LL.D. of Cambridge in 1905, acted in 1900 as one of the British commissioners for the Paris exhibition of 1900, was made G.C.V.O. in 1903, and was created a baronet on his retirement (23 Feb. 1905), being granted also by King Edward VII as a personal favour the use of the 'Thatched House Lodge' in Richmond Park. He also received from the French government the grand cross of the legion of honour. After much ill-health he died in London on 28 Oct. 1909, and was buried in the family mausoleum adjoining South Carlton church near Lincoln.

Monson married in 1881 Eleanor Catherine Mary, daughter of Major Munro, who had held the office of British consul-general at Monte Video, and had by her three sons.

A portrait by the Hungarian artist, Beremy, was subscribed for by Monson's colleagues at Paris, but the painter became bankrupt and the picture disappeared.

[The Times, 30 Oct. 1909; Foreign Office List, 1910, p. 417; papers laid before Parliament.] S.

MONTAGU, Lord ROBERT (1825–1902), politician and controversialist, born at Melchbourne, Bedfordshire, on 24 Jan. 1825, was second son of George Montagu, sixth duke of Manchester, by his first wife, Millicent, daughter and heir of Brigadier-general Bernard Sparrow of Brampton Park, Huntingdonshire. Educated privately, he graduated M.A. from Trinity College, Cambridge, in 1849.

In April 1859 he was returned as a conservative M.P. for Huntingdonshire, and held the seat in successive parliaments till February 1874. He early made his mark as a speaker, championing church rates and winning the congratulations of Sir Stafford

Northcote for his substantial success in persistently urging the need of revival of parliamentary control over the estimates and government expenditure. Montagu, who published in 1852 a treatise on shipbuilding, suggesting a new method of laying down vessels, on 19 May 1862 pleaded with practical effect for expert advice in shipbuilding, for plated ships of war in the place of wooden vessels, and for the establishment of a naval school of architecture and engineering on the model of the Woolwich military academy. In foreign affairs Montagu was no less active and sensible. He opposed Roebuck's resolution (30 June 1863) for recognition of the confederation of the southern states of America, and he spoke strongly in favour of non-intervention between Denmark and the German powers (5 July 1864). In later years he gave much attention to the Eastern question. On the reform question Montagu showed individuality. He feared the policy of multiplying the ignorant voter, and advocated plurality voters, with additional franchises to property and the professions. On social questions Montagu's attitude was more liberal. So early as 1860 he supported a measure for a council of conciliation in labour disputes; and in 1875, in a debate on the employers and workmen bill, he declared trades unions to be 'not only a natural right but a preservative of order.' On Montagu's motion (April 1864) a select committee on which he sat inquired into the disposal of sewage in large towns; and subsequent legislation on the subject owed much to his labours. On 19 March 1867 Montagu was made, on the reconstruction of Lord Derby's third ministry, vice-president of the committee of council on education, and was appointed first charity commissioner, being sworn of the privy council. He held office till Disraeli's resignation in December 1868. As education minister Montagu sought vigorously to enforce the conscience clause in all schools which received grants from public funds, and advocated the extension of technical education. He carried a bill assimilating the vaccination procedure of England to that of Scotland and Ireland, and took effective measures to deal with a serious cattle plague which had spread from the Continent to England. While in opposition Montagu, as an adherent of the old system, actively criticised the education bill of 1870 and its successors. His views on the Irish question came to differ from those of his party, and during the parliament of 1874–80 he sat for Westmeath as a conservative home ruler. He left the home rule organisation in 1877, but remained out of harmony with Disraeli's government. To its vacillation he mainly assigned the Bulgarian agitation, and he condemned the Afghan policy of Lords Salisbury and Lytton.

On his retirement from parliament in 1880 Montagu devoted himself to religious controversy. In 1864 he had defended church establishments and upheld Anglicanism in 'The Four Experiments in Church and State and the Conflicts of Churches'; but in 1870 he became a Roman catholic, and in 1874, in 'Expostulation in extremis,' attacked Gladstone's 'Political Expostulation on the Vatican Decrees.' In the same year, too, he published, as the first volume of St. Joseph's theological library (a Jesuit series), a treatise 'On Some Popular Errors in Politics and Religion,' an adaptation of P. Secondo Franco's 'Risposte popolari alle obiezioni più diffuse contro la religione.' In 1882 Montagu rejoined the English church on ethical and political rather than on theological grounds (see his *Reasons for leaving the Church of Rome*, 1886). Thereupon he pursued a vigorous campaign against Romanist doctrine and practice, professing to expose a conspiracy in which the leaders of both political parties were involved, to bring England under the dominion of the papacy (cf. his *Recent Events, and a Clue to their Solution*, 1886, 3rd edit. 1888; *Scylla or Charybdis, which? Gladstone or Salisbury?* 1887). 'The Sower and the Virgin' (1887) was an exhaustive confutation of the doctrines of the immaculate conception and papal infallibility. 'The Lambeth Judgment, or the Marks of Sacerdotalism' (1891) minutely analysed Bishop King's case.

Montagu, whose independence and sincerity unfitted him for success in political life, was widely read and spoke with fluency. He died at 91 Queen's Gate, Kensington, on 6 May 1902, and was buried at Kensal Green. He married (1) on 12 Feb. 1850 Mary (*d.* 1857), only child and heiress of John Cromie, of Cromore, co. Antrim, by whom he had two sons and two daughters; (2) on 18 Oct. 1862 Catherine (*d.* 1897), daughter of William Wade; by her he had three sons and two daughters.

In addition to the works cited and other tracts, theological and political, Montagu published: 1. 'A Few Words on Garibaldi,' three edits. 1861. 2. 'A Mirror in America,' 1861 (a polemic against party spirit). 3. 'Foreign Policy: England and the

Eastern Question,' 1877 (a vigorous exposure of the inconsistencies of English foreign policy).

A spirited cartoon by 'Ape' of Montagu as 'A Working Conservative' appeared in 'Vanity Fair,' on 1 Oct. 1870.

[Burke's Peerage; Men of the Time, 1899; Luard's Grad. Cant.; The Times, 7 and 12 May 1902; Who's Who, 1902; Hansard's Parl. Debates; Brit. Mus. Cat.] G. Le G. N.

MONTAGU, Sir SAMUEL, first Baron Swaythling (1832–1911), foreign exchange-banker and Jewish philanthropist, born at Liverpool on 21 Dec. 1832, was second son and youngest child of Louis Samuel (1794–1859), watchmaker and silversmith, of Liverpool, by his wife Henrietta, daughter of Israel Israel of Bury Street, St. Mary Axe. His parents were orthodox Jews, and he was through life a strict adherent of orthodox Judaism. Whilst still a lad his parents reversed his original name of Montagu Samuel to Samuel Montagu, and he obtained a royal licence for the change in 1894. By a second licence in 1904 he assumed the surname of Samuel-Montagu.

After education at the Mechanics' Institution, Liverpool, now the Liverpool Institute, he came to London when his father retired from business in 1845. He obtained his earliest employment at thirteen with his brother-in-law, Adam Spielmann, a foreign banker in Lombard Street. Soon dissatisfied with his salary and prospects he became manager of the London branch of a Paris banker named Monteaux, opened at 21 Cornhill. Quickly cancelling this engagement he acted as a bullion-broker on his own account, but in Feb. 1853 he resolved on founding a new foreign exchange and banking business. He was still under age, and a small capital, stated to be 3000*l.*, was advanced by his father in his behalf to his elder brother Edwin, a small banker in Liverpool, who became Montagu's partner without an active rôle in the concern. The firm was first known as Samuel & Montagu and had an office in Leadenhall Street. Two years later Montagu took over Monteaux's London branch which was in difficulties, and he moved to its premises in Cornhill. From the start Ellis Abraham Franklin, who afterwards married Montagu's sister, was in the effectual position of Montagu's partner, and he was made a full partner in 1862, when the firm's style was changed to Samuel Montagu & Co. New premises were taken in 1863 at 60 Old Broad Street. The house at Cornhill then became a branch, and later, with capital of Samuel Montagu & Co.'s provision, the independent concern of A. Keyser & Co. By subsequent agreement two sons of each of the three partners of Samuel Montagu & Co. were taken into that firm's partnership. Five survivors of the six younger partners carry on the business at 60 Old Broad Street.

At the outset Montagu and his colleagues took up with energy the foreign exchange operations from which great firms like those of Rothschild and Baring were withdrawing in view of other occupation. Montagu's house quickly secured a large proportion of the exchange business, and, while establishing its own fortune, helped to make London the chief home of the clearing-house of the international money market. Montagu's knowledge of intricate exchanges was, even among Jewish exchange dealers, remarkable. He calculated profit in the most complicated transactions, involving the conversion and re-conversion of foreign currencies, with a miraculous rapidity. In the silver market his firm's transactions were on an exceptionally large scale. He owed much in later life to his partners' sagacity and to his choice of able assistants.

Self-confident, and of a masterful personality, Montagu soon exerted much influence alike in general financial and public affairs, as well as in the Anglo-Jewish community. The demonetisation of the French copper coinage in England was largely due to his agitation. Mainly owing to his representations the Royal Exchange was roofed in by the City authorities, and the merchants assembling there were protected from the inclemency of the weather. In 1897 he gave one of the picture panels in the Exchange, painted by Solomon J. Solomon, R.A., depicting Charles I's visit to the Guildhall in 1641–2 to demand the surrender of the Five Members.

Montagu, who in politics was a staunch liberal, was elected in the liberal interest M.P. for the Whitechapel division of the Tower Hamlets in 1885 and held the seat for fifteen years. He grew intimate with the party leaders but took little part in the business of the House of Commons save on financial matters and on those touching the Jews. He was chief author of the Weights and Measures Act (1897), which legalised the use of metric weights and measures, and he procured the insertion of a clause in the Finance Act of 1894 (sec. 15) exempting from the death duties bequests to public libraries, museums, and art galleries. An ardent supporter of bimetallism, he was a member of the gold and silver commission (1887–90), and he was president of the

Decimal Association, of the principles of which he was an ardent advocate. In 1888 he was a member of the select committee of the House of Commons on alien immigration, which in the interest of persecuted foreign Jews he was averse from restricting unduly.

With the public work of the Anglo-Jewish community Montagu from an early period intimately identified himself, but he had many differences with leading fellow-workers. He was a life member of the council of the United Synagogue, but disagreement with Lord Rothschild led him to forgo active association. For some years he was a prominent member of the Jewish board of deputies, of the Jewish board of guardians, and of the Religious Education Board, but from the two latter bodies he withdrew before his death. In 1870 he founded in Aldgate, and became president of, the Jewish Working-men's Club. He was until 1909 president of the Shechita board (for supervising the slaughtering of animals according to Jewish ritual), and was chairman of the building committee of the New West End Synagogue in Bayswater (his own place of worship), of which he was first warden. One of his greatest services to the Jewish community was his successful effort to form in 1887 the federation of the smaller East End synagogues. By insisting on English being the official language at meetings of the members of these synagogues he helped to anglicise the foreign Jewish population.

His efforts on behalf of the East London poor, both Jewish and Christian, were unremitting. He was treasurer of the Jews' Temporary Shelter. To facilitate the distribution of working Jews among the less populated provincial districts he founded without much success the Congregational Union and Dispersion Committee. In 1887 he established the East London Apprenticeship Fund, of which he was president. He was also a trustee of the People's Palace at Mile End, a member of the house committee of the London Hospital, and a director of the Four per Cent. Industrial Dwellings Company. On 28 July 1903 he gave 10,000*l.* to the London County Council for its housing scheme for the poor of Tottenham.

He frequently travelled abroad in the interests of his oppressed co-religionists. In 1875 he visited the Holy Land and subsequently founded with Lord Rothschild the first secular and industrial school in Jerusalem. On the outbreak, in 1882, of the violent Jewish persecution in Russia he went to the Continent, at the request of the Mansion House Committee for the relief of Russian Jews, to control and direct the ensuing stream of emigration. Two years later he visited the United States to assist in the establishment of Jewish agricultural colonies in the Far West. In 1886 he visited all the chief towns of Russia, investigating the condition of the Jews there and discouraging emigration. He was well received, until on his arrival at Moscow the Russian government's suspicions were aroused and 'the Jew Montagu' was ordered to leave the country in 48 hours (*Hansard*, 1886, cccviii. 263–4). The Mansion House Fund developed into the Russo-Jewish Committee, of which Montagu was president from 1896 until 1909. The fund rendered inestimable services to persecuted Russian Jews.

Montagu, who was a collector of works of art, was a member of the Burlington Fine Arts Club, and was elected F.S.A. on 14 Jan. 1897. He was a frequent exhibitor at the Old Masters' Exhibitions of the Royal Academy, the Burlington Fine Arts Club, Guildhall, Whitechapel, and elsewhere. Besides possessing many choice pictures, he was a discriminating purchaser of old English silver. His notable collection included the earliest known 'font-shaped' cup, two mazer bowls, early silver-mounted stoneware flagons, Tudor and Jacobean tankards, salts, steeple cups, and Lamerie plate.

Montagu, who was made a baronet on 23 June 1894, retired from the representation of Whitechapel in the House of Commons in 1900, and was succeeded there by his nephew and partner, Mr. Stuart Montagu Samuel, who was created a baronet in 1912. Montagu, however, unsuccessfully contested the central division of Leeds against Mr. Gerald Balfour at the general election of 1900. On 18 July 1907, on Campbell-Bannerman's recommendation, he was raised to the peerage as Baron Swaythling, taking his title from Swaythling near Southampton, where he had a country residence.

A man of great tenacity of purpose and opinion, Swaythling was long a pillar of conservative Judaism and warmly deprecated any breach of Jewish custom on the part of his family or of the Jewish community. At the same time he was a vigorous opponent of the Zionist movement for the formation of a Jewish state in Palestine. He retired from active business life in September 1909, and died on 12 Jan. 1911 at his London residence, 12 Kensington Palace Gardens. He was buried with full Jewish ritual at the cemetery of the Federation of Synagogues, Edmonton.

He married on 5 March 1862 Ellen, youngest daughter of Louis Cohen of Gloucester Place, Portman Square, and the Stock Exchange, sister of Sir Benjamin Louis Cohen, first baronet; her grand-aunt Judith was wife of Sir Moses Montefiore. She survived him with four sons and six daughters. Louis Samuel Montagu, the eldest son, succeeded to the peerage, and Edwin Samuel Montagu, the second son, has been M.P. for the Chesterton division of Cambridgeshire since 1906, and became under-secretary for India in 1910. By a provision of his will Swaythling debarred his children and those claiming through them from participation in his estate (beyond a life annuity of 100*l.*) should they at his death not themselves be professing, or be married to a person not professing, the Jewish religion.

The congregation of the New West End Synagogue presented him in 1902 with his portrait by Sir W. Q. Orchardson [q.v. Suppl. II]; it belongs to the family, and was reproduced in the 'Magazine of Art' (new series, ii. 361). A cartoon appeared in 'Vanity Fair' in November 1886 (No. 505).

Besides contributions to 'Palgrave's Dictionary of Political Economy' and to the 'Encyclopædia Britannica,' and articles to periodicals on finance and decimal currency, Swaythling published 'A Plea for a British Dollar' (reprinted from 'Murray's Magazine'), 1888.

[The Times, 11, 13, 16, 17 and 22 Jan., 6 March 1911; Jewish Chronicle, 13 and 20 Jan. 1911 (with portrait); Bankers' Magazine, 1888, xlviii. 963–5 (with early portrait), Nov. 1909, lxxxviii. 667–70 (with later portrait), Feb. 1911, xci. 282–6; Who's Who, 1911; Lodge's Peerage; Pike's London in the 20th century, p. 113; Character Sketch by Lily Montague, 1913; private information.] C. W.

MONTAGU-DOUGLAS-SCOTT, LORD CHARLES THOMAS (1839–1911), admiral. [See SCOTT.]

MONTGOMERIE, ROBERT ARCHIBALD JAMES (1855–1908), rear admiral, born at Rothesay, Isle of Bute, on 11 Sept. 1855, was son of James Montgomerie, M.D., of Edinburgh, by his wife Mary Campbell of Lochnell, and entered the navy on board the Britannia in Aug. 1869. He became sub-lieutenant in September 1875, and while serving in that rank on board the Immortalité in the detached squadron, jumped overboard to save life on 6 April 1877. It was a dark night, the sea was rough, the ship before the wind, and the latitude was infested with sharks; Montgomerie therefore, in addition to the Albert medal and the silver medal of the Royal Humane Society, was awarded the Stanhope gold medal for the act of greatest gallantry during the year, and shortly afterwards was appointed to the royal yacht. From her he was promoted to lieutenant on 13 Sept. 1878. He was serving in the Carysfort, Captain H. F. Stephenson, during the Egyptian war of 1882, and, being landed with the naval brigade, was present at the battle of Tel-el-Kebir on 13 Sept. He received the medal with clasp for Tel-el-Kebir, and the Khedive's bronze star. In Jan. 1885 the naval brigade under Lord Charles Beresford was organised to attempt the relief of Gordon, and Montgomerie, then a lieutenant of the Inflexible, joined it at Gubat and served in the gunboat Safieh in some of the operations above Metemneh. From March to July 1885 he was naval transport officer at Dongola, and was specially mentioned in Lord Wolseley's despatches; from Aug. 1885 to June 1886 he served on the staff of Gen. Sir Frederick Stephenson [q. v. Suppl. II], and was placed in command of all the armed steamers on the Nile, and appointed to superintend the river transport. He received the Nile clasp, and was appointed to the royal yacht, an appointment almost invariably awarded for services which otherwise would go unrequited. From the yacht he was promoted to commander on 24 Aug. 1887. In that rank he served on the East Indies station in the Boadicea, flagship of Sir E. R. Fremantle, and in Oct. 1890 took part in the Vitu expedition, being placed in command of the field battery, which was actively engaged (FREMANTLE, *The Navy as I have known it*, 381 et seq.). He received the medal with Vitu clasp, was mentioned in despatches, and in May 1892 was nominated a C.B. In Sept. 1891 he was appointed to command the Lion, training ship, and on 1 Jan. 1894 was promoted to captain. After commanding the Bonaventure, cruiser, on the China station, and the Prince George, battleship, in the Channel, he was appointed to the Charybdis in Nov. 1901 for the North American station, and was commodore in Newfoundland waters during the fishery season. He served as commodore under Sir Archibald Douglas during the Venezuelan operations of Dec. 1902, and conducted the blockade of the coast and the bombardment of Puerto Cabello (*Blue Book: Venezuela*, No. 1 (1903), Cd. 1399). In April 1904 he was appointed a naval aide-de-camp to King Edward VII, and in May became inspecting captain of boys' training ships. In the birthday honours of 1904 he was awarded the C.M.G., and on 5 July 1905 was promoted to rear-admiral. He hoisted his flag on 1 Jan. 1907 in command of the destroyers and submarines in commission with nucleus crews, and held the appointment for a year. On the occasion of the review of the home fleet in the Solent in Aug. 1907 he received the C.V.O. He died in London on 1 Sept. 1908, and was buried at Hunsdon.

Montgomerie was a distinguished athlete, and at one time was heavy-weight champion boxer of the navy; a keen sportsman, he hunted big game in many parts of the world. He married in 1886 Alethe Marian, eldest daughter of Spencer Charrington of Hunsdon House, Hertfordshire, and for many years M.P. for the Tower Hamlets. He had issue one son. A portrait, painted in 1908 by Mr. J. Kay Robertson, belongs to his widow.

[The Times, 3 Sept. 1908]. L. G. C. L.

MONTMORENCY, RAYMOND HARVEY DE, third VISCOUNT FRANKFORT DE MONTMORENCY (1835–1902), major-general. [See DE MONTMORENCY.]

MOOR, SIR RALPH DENHAM RAYMENT (1860–1909), first high commissioner of Southern Nigeria, born on 31 July 1860 at The Lodge, Furneux Pelham, Buntingford, Hertfordshire, was son of William Henry Moor, surgeon, by his wife Sarah Pears. Educated privately, and destined for business, he engaged in 1880–1 as a learner in the tea trade. On 26 Oct. 1882 he entered the royal Irish constabulary as a cadet, and becoming in due course a district inspector resigned on private grounds on 9 Feb. 1891.

In March 1891 Moor took service under Sir Claude Macdonald, the consul-general of the Oil Rivers Protectorate, as commandant of constabulary in the protectorate. Of a striking personality, he soon made his mark. In July 1892 he was appointed by the foreign office vice-consul for the Oil Rivers district, and from 6 Sept. 1892 to 15 Feb. 1893 acted as commissioner. During January 1896 he served the office of consul, and on 1 Feb. 1896, when the district was formed into the Niger Coast Protectorate, he was made commissioner and consul-general for the territory, and consul for the Cameroons and Fernando Po.

When in 1900 the protectorate passed from the foreign office to the colonial office, Moor became high commissioner of Southern Nigeria and laid the foundations of the new administration, which developed into the present flourishing colony; his health failing, he retired on pension on 1 Oct. 1903. He then allied himself with Sir Alfred Jones [q. v. Suppl. II]; he gave valuable advice on West African affairs, and aided in the development of the British Cotton Growing Association. He also served on certain committees at the nomination of the secretary of state.

He was found dead in bed at his residence, the Homestead, Barnes, on 14 Sept. 1909; the inquest pointed to suicide during temporary insanity. He was buried at the new Barnes cemetery.

Moor became C.M.G. in 1895 and K.C.M.G. in 1897. He married in 1898 Adrienne, widow of J. Burns.

[The Times, 15, 16, 17 Sept. 1909; Foreign Office List, 1908; official information; personal knowledge.] C. A. H.

MOORE, ARTHUR WILLIAM (1853–1909), Manx antiquary, born on 6 Feb. 1853 at Cronkbourne, Douglas, Isle of Man, was one of ten children (five sons and five daughters) of William Fine Moore, J.P., owner and controller of the Tromode Sail-cloth Mills and a member of the self-elected House of Keys. His mother was Hannah, daughter of Henry Curwen Christian Curwen, of a Cumberland family. William Christian, 'Illiam Dhône' [q. v.], was an ancestor. Entering Rugby under Dr. Temple on 6 Feb. 1867, he passed to Trinity College, Cambridge, where he was bracketed second in the historical tripos of 1875 with Mr. Gordon Duff and graduated B.A. in 1876, proceeding M.A. in 1879. He distinguished himself in athletics at Cambridge and won his blue for Rugby football.

Moore devoted his adult activities to the welfare of his native island in all its phases. Succeeding his father as head of the sail-cloth firm, he managed it with success until steamship competition destroyed the business. He was also director of the Isle of Man Steam Packet Co., of which he published an historical account, and of the Isle of Man Banking Co. Placed on the commission of the peace in 1877, he became member of the House of Keys in 1881, and being elected speaker in 1898, held the office till death. He ably championed the rights and privileges of the house, when the house came into conflict with the governor and council. He took part in drawing up the petition for a reform of the Manx Constitution in 1907. He was also a member of the council of education for the island (1888), of the harbour board (1899), and of the Manx Diocesan Church Commissioners, and became deputy receiver-general in 1905. He interested himself in meteorology, publishing a pamphlet on the climate of the island in 1899 and a record of 'Earth Temperatures at Cronkbourne, 1880–9,' in the 'Royal Meteorological Soc. Quarterly Journal' (xx., Oct. 1894). He was president of the Isle of Man Agricultural Society in 1883. In 1902 he received King Edward VII on his visit to the island, and was created C.V.O. in the same year.

On Manx antiquities Moore was the chief authority in the island, and was one of the museum and ancient monuments trustees from the formation of that body in 1886. Moore's chief title to fame is as the promoter of the study of the Manx language and of Manx history. He only learned the language in early manhood, at a time when it and its literature were despised by his educated fellow countrymen and threatened with extinction. He sketched the history of the language and the sources of knowledge respecting it in a paper printed by the Natural History and Antiquarian Society of the isle in 1887. In 1899 he founded the Manx Language Society and became its first president. Assisted by (Sir) John Rhys, he in 1893 edited for the Manx Society for the Publication of National Documents 'The Book of Common Prayer in Manx Gaelic,' the earliest and longest MS. in the language. He sought to conserve not only the language but the music, lore, and tradition of the island, and published the results of his labours in such volumes as 'The Surnames and Place Names of the Isle of Man' (1890); 'Folk-Lore of the Isle of Man' (1891); 'Manx Carols' (1891); 'Further Notes on Manx Folk-Lore' in 'The Antiquary' (1895); and 'Manx Ballads and Music' (1896). Moore's 'History of the Isle of Man' (1900) is the one authoritative book on the subject. He also published 'The Diocese of Sodor and Man' (1893); 'Manx Worthies' (1901); 'Bishop Hildesley's Letters' (1904); 'Douglas 100 Years Ago' (1904); and 'Extracts from the Records of the Isle of Man' (1905). He edited the periodical 'The Manx Note Book' (1885–7), and contributed many articles to that and other learned magazines.

Moore, who was appointed official translator of the Acts of Tynwald into Manx, was a vice-president of the Celtic Association, and at the eisteddfod held at Cardiff in 1899 the degree of Druid was conferred upon him in recognition of his services to Manx literature. He collected materials for a book on Anglo-Manx dialect, which was not completed at his death. He died at Woodbourne House, Douglas, on 12 Nov. 1909, and was buried at Kirk Braddan cemetery.

On 24 Feb. 1887 he married Louisa Elizabeth Wynn, daughter of Dr. Hughes-Games, then Archdeacon of Man and subsequently vicar of Hull. He left one son and two daughters. A bust executed by Mr. Taubman, a Manx sculptor resident in London, and unveiled at Douglas by Lord Raglan on 10 Oct. 1911, stands in the chamber of the House of Keys; and a portrait by the Liverpool artist, R. E. Morrison, President of the Liverpool Manx Society, was presented by the artist to the House of Keys.

[Celtic Review, 15 Jan. 1910; Isle of Man Weekly Times, 13 Nov. 1909; Isle of Man Examiner, 20 Nov. 1909; information from the Misses Moore.] S. M.

MOORE, STUART ARCHIBALD (1842–1907), legal antiquary, born in Sept. 1842, was fourth son of Barlow Brass Moore of The Lawn, South Lambeth, Surrey, by his wife Harriet Adcock. Educated at the Philological School, Marylebone Road, he became secretary to Sir Thomas Duffus Hardy [q. v.], deputy keeper of the public records, and afterwards practised as a record agent. Elected F.S.A. on 2 May 1869, he contributed to 'Archæologia' in 1886 a paper on the 'Death and Burial of King Edward II.' Moore quickly obtained distinction as an antiquarian lawyer and an authority on questions relating to foreshore, fishery, and cognate matters. On 24 Jan. 1880, somewhat late in life, he became a student of the Inner Temple, and being called to the bar on 25 June 1884, at once obtained a lucrative practice. He fought with great pertinacity and success the claims of the crown to foreshore, arguing that the crown parted long ago with its foreshore rights to the lords of manors bounded by the sea. His 'History of the Foreshore and the Law relating thereto' (1888) is full of interesting extracts from ancient records, and constitutes the subject's brief against the crown.

Moore loved yachting, and was one of the finest amateur seamen of his time; he commanded his own 80-ton fishing ketch, in which he carried the vice-commodore's flag of the Royal Cruising Club all round Great Britain and the greater part of Ireland, with little regard for weather. He was a frequent correspondent of 'The Times,' chiefly on yachting and other seafaring matters. About two years before his death he was seized with paralysis of the lower limbs and retired to his vessel, in which he continued to live, bearing his affliction with courage and cheerfulness. Shortly before his death he wrote two letters to 'The Times' on secret commissions (8 Jan.) and on the Channel tunnel (8 Feb.). He died somewhat suddenly on 29 June 1907, on board his yacht at Southwick, and was buried there. He married Isabel Kate, daughter of John Knight Higgins of Southampton, and had issue two sons.

Besides the work mentioned, he published: 1. 'The Thames Estuary: its Tides, Channels, &c., a Practical Guide for Yachts,' 1894. 2. 'History and Law of Fisheries' (with his son Hubert Stuart Moore), 1903. He also edited 'Letters and Papers of J. Shillingford, 1447–50,' for the Camden Society (1871), and 'Cartularium Monasterii Sancti Johannis Baptiste in Colecestria,' for the Roxburghe Club (1897), as well as 'Domesday Book for Northamptonshire, extended and translated,' 1863.

[The Times, 6 July 1907; Foster, Men at the Bar; Law Times, 13 July 1907, p. 264; personal information.] C. W.

MORAN, PATRICK FRANCIS (1830–1911), cardinal archbishop of Sydney, born at Leighlinbridge, co. Carlow, Ireland, on 16 Sept. 1830, was the son of Patrick Moran by his wife Alicia, sister of Cardinal Cullen [q. v.], whom at the age of twelve he accompanied to Rome. There educated at the Irish College of St. Agatha, he gave early proof of capacity, was ordained priest by special dispensation as to age on 19 March 1853, and was from 1856 to 1866 vice-principal under Monsignor Kirby of the College of St. Agatha, and professor of Hebrew at the College of Propaganda. Enjoying a right of access to the Vatican archives, he made a special study of Celtic ecclesiastical history, and published at Dublin 'An Historical Sketch of the Persecution suffered by the Catholics of Ireland under Cromwell and the Puritans' (1862; new edit. 1884), 'Essays on the Origin, Doctrines, and Discipline of the Early Irish Church' (1864), and other scholarly works.

Returning to Ireland in 1866, Moran became private secretary to his uncle, Cardinal Cullen, then archbishop of Dublin. He held the post till 1872. He became coadjutor to the bishop of Ossory in 1872, and bishop of Ossory in 1873. In 1884 he succeeded Roger William Bede Vaughan [q.v.] as archbishop of Sydney. Early in 1885 he was summoned by Leo XIII, a college comrade and lifelong friend, on a secret mission to Rome, 'The Times' announcing that he was to be made archbishop of Dublin, an office he was known to covet. The rival claims of Dr. Walsh, the popular favourite, would appear to have occasioned a papal dilemma, which was finally surmounted by making Walsh archbishop of Dublin and Moran a cardinal. He was consecrated at Rome in Aug. 1885, returning to Sydney immediately afterwards. Subsequently, as primate of Australia, Moran presided at the plenary councils in 1885, 1895, and 1905. He visited Rome in 1888, 1893, 1898, 1902, and again in 1903 to attend the papal conclave which resulted in the election of Pope Pius X. He celebrated his silver jubilee as archbishop of Sydney in 1909. He died suddenly on 16 Aug. 1911 at Manby Palace, Sydney, and was buried in St. Mary's cathedral.

Moran was most exact in the performance of his episcopal duties, a strict disciplinarian, and a most militant churchman, holding apathy to be the worst enemy to his faith. He appeared to love religious strife, and opposed with vigour the strong and aggressive Orange element in Eastern Australia. He advocated undenominational education by the state, protested unceasingly against any possible Roman catholic disabilities, and by brusque declarations in the press and on the platform provoked hostility and religious controversy. He was, however, a wise educational reformer, and on his arrival in Australia a severe critic of existing Roman catholic schools and seminaries. His zeal in building new schools, churches, and hospitals was remarkable, at least 1,500,000*l.* being spent on these objects during his primacy. Among other buildings in New South Wales which owe their origin to him are St. Ignatius' college, Riverview, St. Columba's Seminary, Springwood, St. Vincent's Hospital, Darlinghurst, St. Joseph's College, Hunter's Hill, the Franciscan Friary, Waverley, Rose Bay Convent, St. Vincent's Girls' College, Waitura Foundling Hospital, and the Mater Misericordiæ Hospital in North Sydney. His ambition to complete St. Mary's Cathedral, which had been begun by Archbishop John Bede Polding [q. v.] and continued by

Archbishop Vaughan, remained unfulfilled, though enough was done to render it a lasting memorial to Moran's activity.

In Australian politics Moran was a prominent and at times disturbing figure, who shared with ministers the attentions of parliamentary cartoonists. Although a strenuous advocate of home rule, he had as bishop of Ossory in 1880 spoken boldly in opposition to the Land League agitation. In Australia he received, and gave every assistance to, delegates from the Irish Nationalist party. Possessed of democratic sympathies, he was on friendly terms with the Australian labour leaders, and received during the maritime strike in 1890 deputations of workmen at St. Mary's presbytery. He enthusiastically supported Australian federation, took part, by invitation, in a preliminary discussion of the project at an informal assembly of Australian statesmen at Bathurst, and was an unsuccessful candidate, though by a small number of votes only, for the National convention elected in 1907 to draft the commonwealth constitution. He was in favour of sending an Australian contingent to take part in the Soudan campaign of 1898.

Moran was deeply read in history, particularly Irish ecclesiastical history, hagiology, and archæology. His best-known works were his 'History of the Catholic Archbishops of Dublin' (Dublin, 1864) and 'Spicilegium Ossoriense' (3 series, Dublin, 1874–84), a collection of documents illustrating Irish church history from the Reformation till 1800. An article in 1880 in the 'Dublin Review' identifying Old Kilpatrick in Scotland as the 'Birthplace of St. Patrick, Apostle of Ireland,' excited wide comment at the time. He also published, mostly at Dublin: 1. 'Memoirs of the Most Rev. Oliver Plunkett,' 1861. 2. 'Acta Sancti Brendani,' 1872. 3. 'Monasticon Hibernicum,' 1873. 4. 'The Bull of Adrian IV,' 1873. 5. 'Irish Saints in Great Britain,' 1879. 6. 'Occasional Papers,' 1890. 7. 'Letters on the Anglican Reformation,' 1890. 8. 'History of the Catholic Church in Australasia,' 1896; 2nd edit. 1897. 9. 'Reunion of Christendom and its Critics,' 1896. 10. 'The Mission Field of the Nineteenth Century,' 1896. 11. 'The Catholics of Ireland under the Penal Laws in the Eighteenth Century,' 1899. Moran also edited 'Pastoral Letters of Cardinal Cullen' (1882); 'The Catholic Prayer Book and Manual of Meditations' (16mo, 1883); David Roth's 'Analecta . . . de rebus Catholicorum in Hibernia (1616)' (1884).

[Who's Who, 1911; Catholic Who's Who, 1911; Tablet, 19 Aug. 1911; The Times, and Manchester Guardian 17 Aug. 1911; Sydney Daily Telegraph, 17 and 18 Aug. 1911; History of Catholic Church in Australasia, 1896; Men and Women of the Time, 15th edit.; Johns's Notable Australians; O'Brien's Life of Parnell, i. 246; ii. 27.] S. E. F.

MORE-MOLYNEUX, Sir ROBERT HENRY (1838–1904), admiral, born on 7 Aug. 1838, was third and youngest son of James More-Molyneux of Loseley Park, Guildford, by his wife Caroline Isabella, eldest daughter of William F. Lowndes-Stone of Brightwell Park, Oxfordshire. After being privately educated he entered the navy in 1852. As a cadet and midshipman of the Sans Pareil he served in the Black Sea during the campaign of 1854, and was present at the bombardment of Odessa and the attack on Sevastopol on 17 Oct. 1854; and as a midshipman of the Russell took part in the Baltic expedition of 1855. He received the Crimean medal with clasp for Sevastopol, the Turkish and the Baltic medals. In 1859 he was a mate of the Vesuvius, employed on the west coast of Africa in the suppression of the slave trade, and was mentioned in despatches for services in a colonial gun-boat up the Great Scarcies river; in the same year, with two boats, he captured an armed slaver brig off the Congo, and for this service received his promotion to lieutenant, dated 28 June 1859. In that rank he served from Jan. 1860 to 1865 on the Mediterranean station, first in the St. Jean d'Acre, afterwards in the flagship Edgar, and on 18 Dec. 1865 was promoted to commander. In June 1866 he was appointed executive officer of the Doris, frigate, on the North America and West Indies station, and while serving in her received the thanks of the admiralty and of the French government for valuable services rendered to the Gironde, transport, wrecked in a dangerous position off Jamaica; also the thanks of the admiralty for other services rendered after the great hurricane at St. Thomas in 1867. In July 1869 he was appointed to command the St. Vincent, training ship for boys, and on 6 Feb. 1872 was promoted to be captain. In May 1877 he was appointed to command the Ruby, in which he served in the Levant during the Russian war of 1877–8, and afterwards in Burma. He was captain of the Invincible at the bombardment of Alexandria, and afterwards during the war, and received the Egyptian medal with clasp for Alexandria, the Khedive's bronze star, the 3rd class of the Osmanie, and was also awarded the C.B. In May 1884 he was appointed commodore commanding the ships in the Red Sea, and protected Suakin till the arrival of Sir Gerald Graham's expedition in 1885. Special reference was made to this service by the secretary to the admiralty in parliament, and More-Molyneux was mentioned in despatches by the commander-in-chief and by Lord Wolseley, received the clasps for Suakin and the Nile, and was advanced to the K.C.B. He next served as captain-superintendent of Sheerness dockyard till promoted to his flag on 1 May 1888. He was an aide-de-camp to Queen Victoria from 1885 to 1888.

His further service was administrative and advisory. In 1889 he was one of the British representatives at the International Marine Conference held at Washington; from Aug. 1891 to Aug. 1894 he was admiral-superintendent at Devonport; on 28 May 1894 he became vice-admiral, and on 13 July 1899 reached the rank of admiral. From Oct. 1900 he was president of the Royal Naval College at Greenwich, until his retirement in Aug. 1903. He was promoted G.C.B. in Nov. 1902, and died at Cairo on 29 Feb. 1904. His body was embalmed, sent home, and buried at St. Nicholas's church, Guildford.

More-Molyneux married in 1874 Annie Mary Carew, daughter of Captain Matthew Charles Forster, R.N.; she died in 1898, leaving a daughter, Gwendolen.

[The Times, 5 and 28 March 1904; Burke's Landed Gentry; portraits from photographs were published in the Illustrated London News in 1886, 1900, 1902, and 1904; and an engraving was issued by Messrs. Walton of Shaftesbury Avenue.] L. G. C. L.

MORFILL, WILLIAM RICHARD (1834–1909), Slavonic scholar, born at Maidstone, Kent, on 17 Nov. 1834, was eldest son of William Morfill, professional musician, of Huguenot origin. Educated first at the grammar school of his native town, he was sent in 1848 to Tonbridge school, where he rose to be head boy in 1853, winning a Judd exhibition to the university. In the same year he was elected to a scholarship at Oriel College, Oxford. He was placed in the first class in classical moderations, but a break-down in health compelled him to take a pass degree (B.A. 1857; M.A. 1860). During the remainder of his life he stayed at Oxford, first as a 'coach' or private tutor. For some time he lectured on English literature at Wren's in London, and was always busy reading, writing, and reviewing. His long vacations were spent in travelling on the Continent, especially in Slavonic countries, where he made many friends. In very early life he acquired an interest in the literature, languages, and history of the Slav and his neighbours in the Near East, which became the main study of his life; he owed almost everything to self-teaching. His knowledge of Russian is said to date from his school days, when one of the masters presented him with a Russian grammar. In 1870, and again on two subsequent occasions, he was nominated by the curators of the Taylorian Institution to deliver the lectures on the Ilchester foundation upon Slavonic literature. In 1889 he was appointed, on the recommendation of the same body, to be university reader in Russian, a position which was raised in 1900 to that of professor of Russian and of the Slavonic languages. He was a corresponding member of many learned societies on the Continent, and Ph.D. of the Czech university of Prague. In 1903 he was elected fellow of the British Academy, in the philological section.

Morfill was a voluminous author in the subjects that he had made his own. He wrote grammars of Polish (1884), Serbian (1887), and Bulgarian (1897) for Trübner's series of 'Simplified Grammars'; of Russian (1889) and Czech (1889) for the Clarendon press; for 'The Story of the Nations' histories of Russia (1885; 6th edit. 1904) and Poland (1893); for 'Religious Systems of the World' a sketch of Slavonic religion; besides many articles in the 'Encyclopædia Britannica.' He also published 'Slavonic Literature' (1883) and 'A History of Russia from Peter the Great to Alexander II' (1902). In conjunction with Dr. R. H. Charles he translated the Slavonic version of the 'Book of the Secrets of Enoch' (1896) and other Apocryphal literature. At the time of his death he was engaged on a translation of the ancient 'Novgorod Chronicle.' His interests, however, were by no means confined to Slavonic. From a boy he had read widely in English literature, and he possessed a most retentive memory. His first publication was an edition of ballads from MSS. of the reign of Elizabeth for the Ballad Society (1873). He kept up his classics to the last, and found time to make himself acquainted with Welsh and Old Irish, and also with Georgian and Turkish. This fortunate gift of tongues was valued by him, not so much for linguistic purposes, as affording a key to the knowledge of national character and history. He was an old-fashioned humanist, rather than a philologer of the modern type. So too in social intercourse he was no scholastic recluse but a genial man of the world. His house at Oxford was the meeting place of a small but brilliant circle, who may not have been prominent in academical business, but who there sharpened one another's wits for the distinction they gained in the outer world.

Morfill married, about 1862, Charlotte Maria Lee, of a Northamptonshire family, who died in 1881, leaving no children. After he had passed his seventieth year, his health gradually failed, though he retained his vivacity and his devotion to work almost to the end. He died peacefully in his chair at his house in Oxford on 9 Nov. 1909. He bequeathed his valuable collection of Slavonic books to Queen's College, which elected him in 1885 an honorary member of its common room.

[Personal knowledge; memoir by Sir J. A. H. Murray in Proc. Brit. Acad., vol. iv.; Oxford Mag., Nov. 1909.] J. S. C.

MORGAN, EDWARD DELMAR (1840–1909), linguist and traveller, born at Stratford, Essex, on 19 April 1840, was only son of Edward John Morgan, an officer in the Madras artillery and later a member of the English factory or merchants' company in St. Petersburg, by his wife Mary Anne Parland. Educated at Eton, he early became a brilliant linguist. After leaving school he resided with his parents in St. Petersburg, and completely mastered the Russian language.

In 1872 he travelled first in Asia, making a journey in Persia with Sir John Underwood Bateman-Champain [q. v.], a director of the Indo-European telegraph. Morgan subsequently visited Kulja and the neighbouring parts of Central Asia. In 1876 he translated from the Russian the Central Asian explorer Przhevalsky's 'Mongolia, the Tangut Country and the Solitudes of Northern Tibet' (1876, 2 vols., with an introduction and notes by Colonel Henry Yule, C.B.). He also joined Sir Thomas Douglas Forsyth [q. v.] in translating the same author's 'From Kulja across the Tian-Shan to Lobnor' (1879). Morgan made later expeditions to Little Russia, in the language and literature of which he was learned, to the lower part of the Congo (1883), which gave him an intimate interest in the affairs of the Free State, to East Africa, and to the Baku oil region of Caucasia. Morgan, who was a fellow of the Royal Geographical Society for forty years, and served on its council, contributed much to its 'Journal.' He was also honorary secretary of the Hakluyt Society (1886–92), and collaborated with C. H. Coote in editing for it (1886) the 'Early Voyages and Travels to Russia and Persia, by Anthony Jenkinson and other Englishmen.' He was honorary treasurer for the Ninth International Congress of Orientalists (1892), in London, under Max Müller's presidency, and edited its transactions (1893). He died in London on 18 May 1909, and was buried at Copthorne, Sussex, where he chiefly resided in his later years. He married on 25 Sept. 1873 Bertha, daughter of Richard Thomas, by his wife Louisa de Visme, who died on 18 Feb. 1911 aged 101. Morgan had issue four sons and three daughters; the eldest son, Edward Louis Delmar Morgan, lieutenant R.N., died in 1900.

Besides the works mentioned, Morgan contributed a chapter on Askja to J. Cole's 'Summer Travelling in Iceland' (1882), and wrote a critical survey of the state of knowledge in 1894 of the Central Asian mountain systems, in the 'Scottish Geographical Magazine,' x. 337.

[Geographical Journal, xxxiv. 94; private information.] O. J. R. H.

MORIARTY, HENRY AUGUSTUS (1815–1906), captain in the navy, the second son of Commander James Moriarty, R.N., by his wife Catherine Webb, was born on 19 May 1815 in the signal tower on Dursey Island, co. Cork. He was educated at Portsmouth, and entered the navy on 18 Dec. 1829 on board the North Star, frigate. In 1837 he was promoted to second master and appointed to the Caledonia, flagship, in the Mediterranean, and during the war on the coast of Syria in 1840 served on board the Ganges, of 84 guns, receiving the English and Turkish medals. He was promoted to master in June 1844, and in 1848, while master of the Penelope, flagship on the west coast of Africa, had command of a paddle-box boat in an expedition to destroy the slave barracoons on the river Gallinas. In the Russian war he was master of the Duke of Wellington, flagship of Sir Charles Napier [q. v.], in the Baltic; he was mentioned in despatches for surveying work done under fire, and was employed under Captain Sulivan [see SULIVAN, SIR BARTHOLOMEW J.] in placing the mortar vessels preparatory to the bombardment of Sveaborg on 9 Aug. 1855. In 1857 and in 1858 Moriarty was appointed to navigate the line-of-battle ship Agamemnon, lent by the admiralty to lay the first Atlantic telegraph cable. In June 1863 he was promoted to staff commander, and in August was appointed to the Marlborough, of 121 guns, flagship in the Mediterranean. He navigated the Great Eastern in 1865 and 1866 when she was employed in laying the second and third Transatlantic cables; and, when the cable broke in mid ocean in 1865, he fixed the position so accurately as to ensure the subsequent recovery of the broken end. When the Great Eastern had hooked the lost cable and was heaving it up to her bows, the mark-buoy placed by Moriarty was bumping against the ship's side. He was in 1866 awarded the C.B. for this success, and received a valuable testimonial from his brother officers. In Dec. 1867 he reached the rank of staff-captain, and was appointed to Portsmouth dockyard as assistant master attendant, becoming master attendant and Queen's harbour-master in Nov. 1869. Moriarty held this post until 3 Dec. 1874, when he was placed on the retired list with the rank of captain. After his retirement he was occasionally employed as nautical assessor to the judicial committee of the privy council, and frequently as nautical expert before parliamentary committees, among which those on Barry Docks, the Tay Bridge, the Forth Bridge, and the Tower Bridge may be mentioned. His chief publications were four volumes of sailing directions (1887–93), compiled for the admiralty, and the articles on 'Log,' 'Navigation,' and 'Seamanship' in the 'Encyclopædia Britannica' (9th edit.)

Moriarty died at Lee, Kent, on 18 Aug. 1906, and was buried in the cemetery there. Moriarty married (1) on 30 July 1852 Lavinia Charlotte (*d.* Sept. 1874), daughter of William Page Foster, by whom he had two sons and two daughters; (2) in 1875 Harriet Elizabeth, daughter of Robert Avent of St. Budeaux, Devonshire; she died without issue in March 1892.

[The Times, 20 Aug. 1906; information from the family.] L. G. C. L.

MORLEY, third EARL OF. [See PARKER, ALBERT EDMUND (1843–1905), politician.]

MORRIS AND KILLANIN, LORD. [See MORRIS, Sir MICHAEL (1826–1901), lord chief justice of Ireland.]

MORRIS, SIR LEWIS (1833–1907), poet and Welsh educationist, eldest surviving son of Lewis (Edward Williams) Morris, solicitor of Carmarthen, by Sophia, daughter of John Hughes, shipowner and merchant of the same town, was born in Spilman Street, Carmarthen, on 23 Jan. 1833. His father, who was grandson of Lewis Morris (1703–1765) [q. v.], Welsh poet, originally of Anglesey and later of Penbryn, near Aberystwyth, was first registrar of the Glamorgan circuit of county courts, and from the subdivision of the office till his death on 30 June 1872 registrar of the Swansea court. He possessed 'great political influence (on the liberal side) in the town and county of Carmarthen' (J. LLOYD MORGAN, *Life of Prof. Morgan,* p. 39). Besides an elder brother and a sister who died in infancy, Morris had three brothers, William Hughes (*d.* 1903) and Charles Edward, both solicitors, and John, rector of Narberth since 1885.

Morris was educated at Queen Elizabeth's grammar school, Carmarthen (1841–7), and at Cowbridge (1847–50) under Hugo D. Harper, whom he followed, with a number of other Welsh boys, to Sherborne, where he remained one year (1850–1). With Harper he formed a lifelong friendship. At Cowbridge he wrote a prize poem on Pompeii; at Sherborne he won the Leweston prize for classics and a prize for an English poem, 'A Legend of Thermopylæ.' He proceeded to Jesus College, Oxford, matriculating on 26 June 1851, and took first class in both classical moderations in 1853 and literæ humaniores in 1855 (HARRIET THOMAS, *Father and Son*, p. 51). He graduated B.A. in 1856, proceeding M.A. in 1858, and was awarded the chancellor's prize for the English essay on 'The Greatness and Decline of Venice' in 1858. 'Nothing but the possession of more than the statutable amount of property prevented his election to a fellowship' (HARDY, *Jesus College*, p. 201). For the same reason he had been ineligible for an entrance scholarship, but had been granted the rank of an honorary scholar. A college literary club, including among its members John Richard Green (who entered as a scholar in 1855), jointly produced a poem entitled 'The Gentiad,' satirising the more exclusive and wealthier set to which Morris belonged (*Letters of J. R. Green*, p. 15). One of its most caustic lines, attributed by Morris to Green, though it is authoritatively stated it was not written by him, gave great offence to Morris owing to a subtle imputation on his father's professional conduct. The breach between Morris and Green was never healed, not even in 1877, when both were simultaneously elected fellows of the college, shortly after the appointment, as principal, of Morris's old master (Dr. Harper).

Morris was admitted a student of Lincoln's Inn on 21 Nov. 1856, was awarded a certificate of honour on 7 Jan. 1861, was called to the bar on 18 Nov. 1861, and practised, chiefly as a conveyancer, till 1880. Two poems, 'At Chambers' and 'A Separation Deed,' are based on incidents in his professional life.

In 1871 there appeared anonymously the first series of his 'Songs of Two Worlds, by a new writer.' It consisted chiefly of lyrical poems contributed from 1865 downwards to a small literary and artistic society, 'The Pen and Pencil Club,' meeting at the house of Peter Taylor [q. v.] (*The New Rambler*, p. 112). The sonorous verse and placid optimism won for these 'Songs' great popularity, and a second series which followed in 1874, and a third issued in 1875, proved equally attractive. Though published anonymously, the last poem in the third series, 'To My Motherland,' indicated the writer's identity (cf. *Athenæum*, 23 Sept. 1876). A new edition of the three series in one volume was issued in 1878.

Meanwhile Tennyson's 'Tithonus' had suggested to Morris (*New Rambler*, p. 121) a series of blank verse monologues put into the mouths of the chief characters of Greek mythology. His three earliest poems on this plan—'Marsyas,' 'Eurydice,' and 'Endymion'—were rejected by various magazines (*ibid.* 112). Other poems expressed in a like spirit the preconceptions and moral ideals of his own age. The pieces were linked together by the device of a pilgrimage to the Shades. Finally all were collected under the general title of 'The Epic of Hades' in three sections named Hades, Tartarus, and Olympus. The Hades section appeared as book ii. of the 'Epic' early in 1876; this was followed by books i. and iii. in the subsequent year, when a complete edition in one volume was also issued. The work, which was mostly written 'amid the not inappropriate sounds and gloom of the (London) Underground Railway' (*ibid.* p. 117), was described as 'by the author of "Songs of Two Worlds."' The success of the volume was surprising: it ran through three editions of 1000 copies each in its first year, and some forty-five editions (exceeding fifty thousand copies) during the author's lifetime A quarto edition with illustrations by George R. Chapman appeared in 1879. The lucidity of expression, the many idyllic pictures, the passages of spiritual exaltation, coupled with a strongly didactic character, made the work specially popular with the middle class, whose appreciation was voiced by John Bright when in his speech on Cobden at Bradford, 25 July 1877, he described it as 'another gem added to the wealth of the poetry of our language.'

Morris owed his vogue as a poet, which lasted throughout his lifetime, to his enforcement of simple truths in simple language and metre. He earnestly taught in verse a cheerful optimism, and if he often excited critical scorn for his lack of subtlety, he exerted a wide moral influence. Much of his work betokens discipleship to Tennyson. After 'The Epic of Hades' came in 1879 'Gwen: a Drama in Monologue, in Six Acts.' The theme was the tragedy of a secret marriage. Its form may have been suggested by Tennyson's 'Maud.' There is an interesting picture of Llangunnor church, where the author was himself buried. 'The Ode of Life' (1880), consisting of a series of poems descriptive of various stages and phases of life, maintained the 'Epic's' note of high moral purpose.

'Songs Unsung' (1883) was the first volume issued under the author's name. It was described on the title-page as 'by Lewis Morris of Penbryn.' He had used the same designation in 1876, when he first published a poem under his own name, namely, an elegiac poem in memory of his great-grandfather's poet-friend Goronwy Owen [q. v.], in 'Y Cymmrodor,' vol. i., and in the 'Poetical Works of G. Owen,' ed. by R. Jones (1876), ii. 309–312, but this was never included in any edition of Morris's works. Penbryn was the name of the house near Aberystwyth where his great-grandfather had spent his later years, and Morris bestowed it on a house on the outskirts of Carmarthen bought by his father about 1840. This 'territorial' description of the author was the main theme of a savage attack on him in the 'Saturday Review' for 24 Nov. 1883. Lewis Morris was contrasted with 'William Morris of Parnassus.' Yet the 'Saturday Review' had already hailed 'The Epic of Hades' as 'one of the most considerable and original feats of recent English poetry' (*ibid.* 31 March 1877).

'Gycia: a Tragedy, in Five Acts' (1886), written 'with a view to stage representation,' and based on a story (*circa* 970 A.D.) recorded by Constantine Porphyrogenitus in his 'De Administratione Imperii,' displays more of a Greek spirit than any other of Morris's works. 'Songs of Britain' (1887) contains some patriotic odes like that on Queen Victoria's Jubilee (1887); three long poems based on Welsh legends are inferior in treatment to his verse on classical subjects.

Collected editions of Morris's works were issued in three volumes in 1882, and in one volume in 1890. 'A Vision of Saints' (1890) was Morris's last poem of first-rate importance, and was intended to be the Christian counterpart of his pagan 'Epic of Hades,' consisting of a series of monologues of nineteen saintly characters, concluding with Elizabeth Fry and Father Damien. His remaining volumes were three collections of lyrics—'Songs without Notes' (1894); 'Idylls and Lyrics' (1896); and 'Harvest Tide' (1901)—and 'The Life and Death of Leo the Armenian (Emperor of Rome): a Tragedy, in Five Acts' (1904). When in 1907 Morris carefully revised his collected works for a sixteenth edition, he announced in the preface that he 'brought to a definite close his long career as a writer of verse.' An authorised selection of his poems was issued in 1904, and after his death a volume of selections, 'reprinted under the author's supervision' from the fourteenth edition of the collected works, appeared in 'The Muses' Library.'

In 1905 Morris issued a volume of essays, appreciations, and addresses under the title 'The New Rambler: from Desk to Platform' (Longmans, Green & Co.). The work, in which he discusses his ideals as a poet, and answers some of his severest critics, is largely autobiographical. Most of the addresses deal with problems of Welsh education, which was the second great interest of his life. Until 1876, Morris, who then lived chiefly in London, took no active interest in Welsh affairs. He had not mastered the Welsh language (cf. his poem, *The Eisteddfod:* 'Hardly the fair tongue I know'), nor did he know much of the history and literature of Wales, while Welsh archæology did not appeal to him. Hugh Owen [q. v.] first interested him in Welsh education (*New Rambler*, 262). In Oct. 1878 he became one of the joint honorary secretaries to the University College of Wales, Aberystwyth, which from its opening in 1872 depended entirely on voluntary contributions. Thenceforth he was concerned with all its varying fortunes, drafting various appeals on its behalf and (with another) its amended constitution in 1885 (after its receipt of a government grant). He was joint treasurer of the college from March 1889 to March 1896, and from the latter date till his death one of its two vice-presidents.

He was one of the five members of a departmental committee appointed in Aug. 1880, with Lord Aberdare as chairman, to inquire into the state of intermediate and higher education in Wales. The committee's report (C. 3047), issued in August 1881, resulted in the establishment of two new colleges and eventually of the University of Wales, and the passing of the Intermediate Education (Wales) Act of 1888, 'the educational charter of modern Wales.' During the inquiry Morris specially interested himself in the higher education of women, to which he was 'early a convert' (*New Rambler*, 280, 301). He threw himself with vigour into the propaganda and constructive effort which followed the issue of the report.

After the establishment of the university in 1893 he became its junior deputy chancellor for 1901–3, and received from it the honorary degree of D.Litt. in 1906. He was a member of the council of the Cymmrodorion Society from 1877 to Dec. 1892, and thenceforth one of its vice-presidents. He served as a member of the Carmarthenshire intermediate education committee, and was a justice of the peace for Carmarthen. When Sir Hugh Owen's proposals for the reform of the eisteddfod by the formation of a National Eisteddfod Association were adopted, Morris was in Sept. 1880 appointed chairman of the council of the executive committee of the new body. That office he held till his death.

During Tennyson's later years Morris was a frequent guest of his (*Lord Tennyson, by his Son*, ii. 389), and on Tennyson's death in 1892 he was disappointed of the poet-laureateship (cf. *New Rambler*, p. 180). In 1893 he wrote the odes on the marriage of the Duke of York (now George V) and on the opening of the Imperial Institute, and in 1895, during Lord Rosebery's premiership, he was knighted.

Next to the laureateship his main ambition was a seat in parliament, which he also failed to win. An advanced liberal in politics, and from 1887 till his death a member of the political committee of the Reform Club, he was in favour of home rule and Welsh disestablishment. But his chief interest lay in social reform (see his odes for the first co-operative festival in 1888, for the trade union congress at Swansea in 1901, and on the opening of the West Wales Sanatorium in 1905). In 1868, and again in 1881 and 1883, he was invited to contest the Carmarthen Boroughs, but withdrew in favour of another liberal. In July 1886 he unsuccessfully contested the Pembroke Boroughs (cf. his idyll, *In*

Pembrokeshire, 1886). In 1892 Morris and another liberal submitted to arbitration their respective claims to be the official liberal candidate for Carmarthen Boroughs, but the award went against Morris (*Western Mail*, 14 April 1892). He was not a popular speaker, and suffered from a shyness often mistaken for hauteur.

He died at Penbryn on 12 Nov. 1907, and was buried at Llangunnor. By his will he left to the Aberystwyth College, for the Welsh national library (in the promotion of which he had been interested), the autograph letters of the Morris brothers, 1728–65 (edited by J. H. Davies, 2 vols. Oxford, 1906–9), and certain books. He married in 1868 Florence Julia, widow of Franklin C. Pollard, and by her, who survived him, he had two daughters and one son, Arthur Lewis, a naval constructor at Elswick. He did not announce his marriage till 1902. His portrait, painted in 1906 by Mr. Carey Morris (of Llandilo), is at Penbryn. A bust by Sir William Goscombe John, R.A., was exhibited at the Royal Academy in 1899.

[Private information and personal knowledge; The New Rambler, passim; The Times, 13 Nov. and 24 Dec. 1907; Western Mail, and South Wales Daily News (Cardiff), 13 Nov. 1907; Athenæum, 16 Nov. 1907; Carmarthenshire Antiquarian Society's Reprint (1906–7), ii. 190–2; Men and Women of the Time, 1899; Allibone's Dict. Eng. Lit., Suppl.; A. H. Miles, Poets and Poetry of the Century (1892), v. 591–620. As to Morris's work in connection with Welsh movements, especially education, see Sir Hugh Owen, his Life and Life Work (1885), by W. E. Davies (for which Morris wrote a preface); Report of the Hon. Society of Cymmrodorion for 1906–7 in Transactions for that year, p. v; Annual Reports of the National Eisteddfod Association from 1881 on; The University of Wales (in College Histories series), by W. C. Davies and W. L. Jones (1905), 111–118, 129, 221; The Welsh People, by Rhŷs and Brynmor Jones, 492, 495; Students' Handbook (Univ. Coll. of Wales, Aberystwyth), 1909, pp. 22–3.] D. Ll. T.

MORRIS, Sir MICHAEL, Lord Morris and Killanin (1826–1901), lord chief justice of Ireland and member of the judicial committee of the privy council in England, belonged to an ancient Roman catholic family which formed one of 'the fourteen tribes of Galway' and acquired the estate of Spiddal, co. Galway, by marriage in 1684. Michael Morris was elder son of Martin Morris, J.P. (1784–1862), who was high sheriff of co. Galway in 1841, being the first Roman catholic to hold that office since 1690. His mother, Julia, daughter of Dr. Charles Blake, of Galway, died of cholera in 1837. His younger brother, George (1833–1912), high sheriff of co. Galway (1860–1) and M.P. for Galway city (1867–8 and 1874–80), was an official of the Irish local government board (1880–98), being made a K.C.B. on his retirement.

Born at Spiddal on 14 Nov. 1826, Michael Morris, after education at Erasmus Smith School, in Galway, entered Trinity College, Dublin, as an exhibitioner in 1842. His religion disqualified him from competing for a scholarship. In 1846 he graduated brilliantly as first senior moderator in ethics and logic and won a gold medal. At Trinity his chief recreation was racquet-playing, and he acquired a skill which he retained to an advanced age. After a year's foreign travel he was called to the Irish Bar in Trinity term 1849, joining the Connaught circuit. His rise in his profession was rapid, his abounding commonsense, his wit, and strong Galway brogue, which never diminished, attracted clients. Following his father's example, he was high sheriff of his county for 1849–50. From 1857 to 1865 he held the post of recorder of Galway. In February 1863 he took silk.

In July 1865 Morris was returned to parliament as member for Galway. He issued no address and identified himself with no party, yet 90 per cent. of the electors voted for him owing to the local popularity of himself and his family. He at once made his mark in the House of Commons, where he sat with the conservative party. Although of independent temperament and impatient of party ties he was distrustful of democracy, was devoted to the union and hostile to the cry of home rule. In July 1866 he was appointed solicitor-general for Ireland by Lord Derby, and was the first Roman catholic to hold that office in a conservative government. He was re-elected unopposed by his constituents. In November he was promoted to the attorney-generalship. In 1866 he was sworn of the Irish privy council; and his intimate knowledge of local affairs enabled him to do useful work on the judicial committee.

In 1867 Morris was raised to the Irish bench as puisne judge of the court of common pleas. He was succeeded in the representation of Galway by his brother George. He became chief of his court in 1876, and lord chief justice of Ireland in 1887. On the bench his good-humour and shrewd wisdom stood him in good stead. He managed juries with admirable bonhomie, and even at the height of the land league agitation (1880–3) rarely failed to secure a right verdict. He was created a baronet in 1885, and on 25 Nov. 1889 was promoted to the judicial committee of the English privy council, receiving a life peerage by the title of Lord Morris. Although his new duties compelled his removal to London, his permanent residence and substantial interests, as he said on taking leave of the Irish bar, remained in his native country.

As appellate judge of the privy council Morris distinguished himself by his good-humoured contempt for legal subtleties, and his witty shrewdness. He not infrequently dissented from the majority of the committee, but well held his own in argument with his colleagues. In the suit McLeod *v.* St. Aubyn, which raised in 1899 a question of contempt on account of scandalous reflections on a court of justice, he delivered a characteristically robust judgment in pronouncing committals for such contempt obsolete, because 'courts are satisfied to leave to public opinion attacks or comment derogatory or scandalous to them' (*Law Reports*, Appeal Cases, 1899, p. 561). Morris was a popular figure in English society. He became a member of Grillion's Club, and in 1890 he received the unprecedented honour of being elected a bencher of Lincoln's Inn, though he had never been called to the English bar.

Morris always took a keen interest in Irish education. From 1868 to 1870 he was a member of the Powis commission on primary education in Ireland; in 1868 he became a commissioner of national education and, later, chairman of the board. On the foundation of the Royal University in 1880 he was appointed a senator, and in 1899 was elected vice-chancellor. He was a visitor of Trinity College, Dublin, and in 1887 received the honorary degree of LL.D. from his old university.

Morris retired from the privy council and from public life in 1900, when he accepted the hereditary barony of Killanin in the peerage of the United Kingdom. He was thenceforth known as Lord Morris and Killanin. He died at Spiddal on 8 Sept. 1901.

On 18 Sept. 1860 Morris married Anna, daughter of Henry George Hughes [q. v.], baron of the court of exchequer in Ireland. His wife died on 17 Oct. 1906. Of a family of four sons and six daughters, two sons and a daughter predeceased their father. He was succeeded in the barony of Killanin by his eldest son, Martin Henry Fitzpatrick, in whose triumphant election, in defiance of the home rule organisation, as conservative member for Galway in 1900, Morris played a conspicuous part.

Morris's judicial decisions were vigorously phrased and were marked by greater regard for the spirit than for the letter of the law. He made no pretence to legal erudition and boldly scorned precedent. Yet his insight into human nature compensated for most of his defects of legal learning. His popularity with his fellow-countrymen, and especially with his Galway tenantry, never waned. He ridiculed the political views of the nationalists; but he could jest in the Irish language, and his strong Celtic sympathies reduced political differences to a minimum. During his whole career, which covered the Fenian outbreak and the land league movement, he never received a threatening letter. He rather cynically assigned Ireland's distresses to natural causes—to a wet climate and the absence of coal. Local developments or improvements, which laid fresh expenses on poor localities, he deprecated. He was at one with the nationalists in regarding the existing financial relations between England and Ireland as unfair to Ireland, and spoke to that effect in the House of Lords on 23 March 1894 (*Hansard* [38], 1582). Though he always treated home rule as a wild and impracticable dream, he was impatient of much of the routine which England practised in its government of Ireland. His epigram on the Irish political problem—'a quick-witted nation was being governed against its will by a stupid people'—was quoted by his friend Lord Randolph Churchill in the home rule debate on 17 April 1893, and is characteristic of his caustic sagacity (Lucy, *Diary of the Home Rule Parliament*, p. 108). His witticisms, if at times coarse and extravagant, usually hit the mark.

There is no good portrait of Lord Morris. A drawing by Henry Tanworth Wells [q. v. Suppl. II] was made for Grillion's Club, and a large photograph hangs in the reception room of the King's Inns at Dublin. A caricature portrait by 'Spy' appeared in 'Vanity Fair' in 1893. An engraving from photographs was made after Morris's death by Messrs. Walton & Co., of Shaftesbury Avenue.

[The Law Mag. and Rev., Nov. 1901 (art. by Richard J. Kelly); The Times, 9 Sept. 1901; Annual Register, 1901.] G. S. W.

MORRIS, PHILIP RICHARD (1836–1902), painter, born at Devonport, Devonshire, on 4 Dec. 1836, was the youngest of the five children of John Simmons Morris, an iron founder, by his wife Anne Saunders. He was taken to London at the age of fourteen, with a view to being trained for his father's profession. But his mind was set upon an artist's career, and, largely owing to Holman Hunt's advice, his father overcame a rooted objection to his pursuit of art. Philip was soon allowed to work at the British Museum, where he applied himself particularly to drawing from the Elgin marbles. Having entered the Royal Academy Schools, Morris made striking progress, gaining three silver medals for drawing, painting, and portrait. In 1858 he won the gold medal and a travelling studentship which enabled him to visit Italy. He exhibited at the Royal Academy for the first time in the same year, and, save for five years, was represented there annually till 1901. He exhibited at the British Institution from 1857 to 1865. The beginning of his professional career was brilliantly successful and raised hopes in his brother artists and in the public that were destined to be disappointed by the achievement of his maturity. After Morris's election as A.R.A. in 1877 his powers began to wane, and in 1900 he retired voluntarily from the associateship. He died in London on 22 April 1902, and was buried at Kensal Green. He was married to a widow, Mrs. Sargeantson, daughter of J. Evans of Llangollen, and had two sons and three daughters.

For his earliest work Phil Morris chose his subjects from the drama of the sea and the sailor's life. It was his instinct for dramatic effectiveness and sentiment that made his art popular, both on the walls of exhibitions and in the form of engraved plates, and atoned to a certain extent for his shortcomings as a colourist. His landscape backgrounds were almost invariably the feeblest part of his pictures. Among his early sea pictures were: 'Voices from the Sea' (R.A. 1860); 'Drift-wreck from the Armada' (1867); and 'Cradled in his Calling' (B.I. 1864). Then came a period during which he was almost exclusively attracted by religious subjects, such as 'The Shadow of the Cross' (acquired by the Baroness Burdett-Coutts and never exhibited); 'Where they Crucified Him' (B.I. 1864); 'Jesus Salvator' (1865); 'The Summit of Calvary' (1871); 'The Shepherd of Jerusalem.' None of his pictures, however, attained to more popularity than 'Sons of the Brave' (1880), depicting the orphan boys of soldiers, Royal Military Asylum, Chelsea. Among other well-known works by him are 'The Knightly Mirror,' 'Good-bye, God Bless You' (1873), 'The Mowers' (1875), 'The Sailor's Wedding' (1876), 'The First Communion,' and 'The Reaper and the Flowers.'

[Mag. of Art, 1902; Victoria Mag., 1880; Graves's Royal Acad. Exhibitors; British Institution Exhibitors; private information.]

P. G. K.

MORRIS, TOM (1821–1908), golfer, second son of John Morris, a letter carrier in St. Andrews, and Jean Bruce, a native of Anstruther, was born in North Street, St. Andrews, on 16 June 1821. An elder brother, George, was also an accomplished golfer and was said to have had 'a prettier style than Tom,' though not such a reliable player. Tom received a good elementary education at the Madras College, St. Andrews. He began to play golf, he was accustomed to say, when he was 'six or seven, maybe younger'; and immediately on leaving school he was apprenticed to a golf ball maker, Allan Robertson, perhaps the most finished golfer St. Andrews has produced and then in the height of his fame. Serving under Robertson for four years as an apprentice and five as a journeyman, Morris had many opportunities of practising the game with him, until he was able to meet him on almost equal terms; and the two as partners were more than able to hold their own against any golfers of their time. Shortly after his marriage to Nancy Bayne, the daughter of a coachman, he went in 1851 to Prestwick, Ayrshire, where, besides being keeper of the golf links, he set up as a golf club and ball maker. Having in 1853 beaten his old master, Robertson, in a single round for a small stake, he challenged him to play him for 100*l.*, but Robertson did not respond. Morris, however, found a worthy rival in Willie Park of Musselburgh, who was some years his junior. Park was the more brilliant and stylish player, a longer driver, and also a better putter than Morris; but Morris was the more careful and imperturbable, excelled in approaching, and but for an occasional tendency to be short with his putts would always have had the advantage. Of six matches played in 1854 each won three. Of matches played, each over four different greens, that of 1856 was won by Park by 8 and 6 to play; that of 1862 was won by Morris by 17 holes; that of 1870 was unfinished, the referee, on account of the behaviour of the crowd on the last green (Musselburgh), postponing the playing of the last six holes until next day, and Park, who was leading by one hole, refusing to abide by the decision; and that of 1882 was won by Morris, then in his sixty-first year, by 5 up and 3 to play. In the first year of its institution, in 1860, the open championship was won by Park, in the next two years by Morris, then by Park, and again by Morris, who also won it in 1866, Park winning it as late as 1875.

From 1863 to 1903 Morris was green keeper to the Royal and Ancient Club, St. Andrews, and during the forty years his sturdy, blackbearded figure—in his later years gradually whitening—might be seen regulating the starting of the players in all the principal tournaments. From the time that the modern furore for golf began he was also largely employed in the planning of golfing greens in all parts of the kingdom, and latterly he occupied a unique position as a kind of golf patriarch. He had, amongst his contemporaries, no superior when in his prime, nor until he was outplayed by his son Tom. So long did he retain his exceptional powers that in 1893, in his 72nd year, he won the first prize and medal in the annual competition of St. Andrews club makers; and, although allowed 5, his score of 83 was the lowest by three. In his eightieth year he went round the links in 86. He was in fairly good health when his death was brought about, on 24 May 1908, by accidentally falling down a stair. He attributed his good health to the fact that he always slept with his bedroom window open, and to his morning swim in the sea, summer and winter. He was a ruling elder in the parish church, St. Andrews, and on one occasion was chosen a representative elder to the general assembly. He had two sons—both in the business with him as club makers—and a daughter.

The elder son, Tom, known as 'Young Tom,' achieved the unique feat of winning the open championship in 1868 when only in his seventeenth year, and of winning it during three successive years, and this with record scores. He died suddenly on 25 Sept. 1875. A monumental tombstone, with his figure three quarter size, was erected, by subscriptions obtained through the different golf clubs of the kingdom, over his grave in the cathedral burying ground, St. Andrews. The second son 'J. O. F.,' a fairly good golfer, died in 1906.

In 1903 the portrait of Morris was painted for the Royal and Ancient Golf Club, St. Andrews, by Sir George Reid.

[Life by W. W. Tulloch, D.D., 1906; the Badminton Book of Golf; Scotsman, and Glasgow Herald, 25 May 1908; personal recollections.] T. F. H.

MORRIS, WILLIAM O'CONNOR (1824–1904), Irish county court judge and historian, born in the city of Kilkenny on 26 Nov. 1824, was son of Benjamin Morris, sometime rector of Rincurran in the diocese of Cork and Cloyne, and Elizabeth, youngest daughter and co-heiress of Maurice Nugent O'Connor of Gartnamona, near Tullamore, King's County. A delicate boy, he was placed when ten years of age under the care of a physician at Bromley in Kent. From 1837 to 1841 he was at a private school at Epsom, and from 1841 at a school in South Wales, where, under the tuition of the rector of Laugharne, in Carmarthenshire, he studied classics and history, and enjoyed ample opportunity for outdoor sports—shooting, fishing, and hunting. In Michaelmas term 1843 he entered Oriel College, Oxford, and in the summer of 1844 he was elected a scholar. Straitened circumstances, due to the great famine in Ireland, compelled a year and a half's absence (1846–7) from the university, but returning in the autumn of 1847 he obtained a second class in literæ humaniores in 1848. His father had died in 1846, and Morris, having abandoned an early predilection for a military career, raised three years after leaving Oxford the necessary fees of 100*l.* wherewith to enter the King's Inns, Dublin, as a law student. In Michaelmas term 1852 he was admitted a member of Lincoln's Inn and he was called to the Irish bar in 1854. Choosing the home circuit, he gradually worked his way upwards, and in 1862 he was elected a professor of common and criminal law in the King's Inns. Next year he was appointed a commissioner to investigate the rights of owners of fixed nets for salmon in Ireland, but owing to a difference of opinion between him and Sir Robert Peel, the third baronet, then chief secretary, he was compelled to resign. The county court judgeship given him later he regarded as reparation for this injustice.

Meanwhile he married, established himself at Blackrock, and became owner, through his wife, of Gartnamona. He began to contribute articles on historical, legal, social, and political subjects to the 'Edinburgh Review,' whose editor, Henry Reeve [q. v.], he had come to know. For 'The Times' he reviewed books, chiefly on military history—a favourite subject of study. As a landlord he paid close attention to the conditions of land tenure in Ireland, and when Gladstone, after the disestablishment of the Irish Church, announced his intention of dealing with the Irish land question, Morris, at the request of John Thadeus Delane [q. v.], contributed a series of special articles on the subject to 'The Times.' Travelling through the country he collected his information at first hand. His letters in 'The Times' (reprinted in 1870 with a map), advising the legal recognition of Ulster tenant-right wherever it existed, attracted attention, and the Land Act of 1870, though not entirely to his satisfaction, embodied many of his ideas. In 1869–70 Morris served on a commission to inquire into the corrupt practices attending the election of freemen of the city of Dublin, and his report throws light on municipal government in Ireland. In 1872 he was appointed county court judge for the county of Louth, and after six years was transferred to county Kerry. The change did not prove agreeable. He had no sympathy with the home rule movement and detested the accompanying agrarian agitation, which was violent in Kerry. Of the Land Act of 1881, which he administered, he disapproved, and he never lost an opportunity of denouncing it. He reduced rents from 15 to 20 per cent. on well-managed estates, and from 30 to 40 per cent. on badly managed ones; but his refusal to submit to local opinion led to many stormy scenes between him and the bar. In 1880 he removed with his family from Dublin to Gartnamona, and was, at his own request, transferred in 1886 to the county judgeship of the united counties of Sligo and Roscommon. His position there was easier, but his attitude towards the de Freyne tenants in 1901, and his pungent remarks on men and measures in connection with recent Irish legislation, drew down on him hostile criticism.

Thenceforth Morris devoted himself largely to literary work, and published in quick succession 'Hannibal . . . and the Crisis of the Struggle between Carthage and Rome,' and 'Napoleon . . . and the Military Supremacy of Revolutionary France,' both in the 'Heroes of the Nations' series (1890); 'Great Commanders of Modern Times,' reprinted from the 'Illustrated Naval and Military Magazine' (1891); 'Moltke: a Biographical and Critical Study' (1893); 'Ireland from 1494 to 1868,' in the 'Cambridge Historical' series (1894); 'Memories and Thoughts of a Life,' being his autobiography (1895); 'The Great Campaign of Nelson' (1898); 'Ireland from '98 to '98' (1898); 'The Campaign of 1815' (1900); 'Present Irish Questions' (1901); 'Wellington . . . and the Revival of the Military Power of England,' in the 'Heroes of the Nations' series (1904); besides numerous articles in the 'Edinburgh' and several in the 'English Historical Review' on Turenne, Sedan, Waterloo, and Ireland from 1793 to 1800. He wrote too much and too superficially to become an authority of first rank on either military or Irish history. He had no personal experience of military affairs, and except in the case of Ireland of his own day his knowledge of Irish history was largely second-hand. His style was that of an accomplished journalist, content for the most part to build on other men's foundations; but such writings as his 'Napoleon' and 'Ireland from '98 to '98' possess permanent interest from their strongly personal character and independent judgment. But he often failed to take the trouble to collect all the facts on which a sound or impartial judgment could be passed. He admired Napoleon and O'Connell, but unduly depreciated their contemporaries, and formed low estimates of Moltke and Parnell. A liberal unionist of the type of W. E. H. Lecky, he united the best characteristics of the English and Irish races. Morris was in private life honest, courageous, imaginative, fond of outdoor sports, an admirable raconteur, and a just landlord.

Morris died on 3 Aug. 1904 at Gartnamona. He married in 1858 Georgiana, eldest daughter of 'handsome' George Lindsay, by whom he had five daughters and a son, Maurice Lindsay O'Connor Morris.

[Morris's autobiography and writings; Burke's Landed Gentry; The Times, 4 Aug. 1904.] R. D.

MOUNTFORD, EDWARD WILLIAM (1855–1908), architect, born on 22 Sept. 1855 at Shipston-on-Stour, Worcestershire, was son of Edward Mountford by his wife Eliza Devonshire, daughter of William and Mary Richards of Northampton. After private education at Clevedon, Somersetshire, he was articled in 1872 to Habershon & Pite, architects, Bloomsbury Square, London. Starting independent practice in 1881, he achieved distinction by winning in 1890 the open competition for the Sheffield town hall. Throughout his career Mountford was exceptionally successful in competitions. The Museum and Technical School at Liverpool, an important group of buildings near St. George's Hall, followed shortly after the Sheffield work.

In Battersea he erected the town hall and the Polytechnic, and among other London buildings he designed St. Olave's grammar school, Southwark (1893); the Northampton Institute, Clerkenwell (1898); and finally his chief work, the Central Criminal Court at Old Bailey, occupying the site of Newgate Prison (1907) [see DANCE, GEORGE, the younger].

Mountford believed in the association of first-rate sculpture and painting with architecture, and the Central Criminal Court affords a good example of such a union of the arts. His style developed from a free Renaissance method as exhibited at Sheffield to the more normal classic of the Old Bailey. He became an associate of the Royal Institute of British Architects in 1881 and a fellow in 1890. He was for fourteen years a member of the council. In 1893–5 he was president of the Architectural Association. Though failing in health he was in January 1908 one of the eight specially selected competitors for the designing of the London County Council Hall. He died at his residence, 11 Craven Hill, London, W., on 7 Feb. 1908.

Mountford was twice married: (1) on 28 June 1888 to Jessie Elizabeth, daughter of John Saunders Smith of Northampton; (2) on 11 July 1903 to Dorothy, daughter of A. G. Hounsham of Hampstead Heath. He had a son by his first marriage, and a daughter by his second.

[R.I.B.A. Journal, vol. xv. 3rd ser. 1908, p. 274; Builder, 15 Feb. 1908; Architectural Rev., March 1908, xxiii. 136; information from Mr. F. Dare Clapham.] P. W.

MOWAT, SIR OLIVER (1820–1903), Canadian statesman, born at Kingston, Upper Canada (now Ontario), on 22 July 1820, was eldest son in a family of three sons and two daughters of John Mowat of Canisbay, Caithness-shire, who had come out to Canada as sergeant with the 3rd Buffs in 1814, had taken his discharge to occupy a grant of land near Kingston, and had married Helen Levack of Caithness in 1819. A younger brother, John B. Mowat, D.D., was professor of Hebrew in Queen's University, Kingston, from 1857 until his death in 1900.

After education at private schools in Kingston, Mowat, who was brought up and remained a presbyterian, was articled in 1836 to (Sir) John Alexander Macdonald [q. v.] as a student-at-law. In Nov. 1840 he left Mr. Macdonald's office for Toronto. When, in May 1841, the governor, Lord Sydenham, temporarily moved the seat of government from Toronto to Kingston, Mowat followed the court of chancery to that place, and being there called to the bar of Upper Canada in Nov. 1841, was at once admitted into partnership with his principal, Robert Easton Burns. In Nov. 1842 the firm moved back to Toronto with the court of chancery, and from that time until his death Mowat lived almost continuously in Toronto. He rapidly gained distinction in equity practice, and was for many years the acknowledged leader of the chancery bar. He was a bencher of the Law Society of Canada from 1853 until his death, save from 1864 to 1872, and was made Q.C. in 1856. In January 1856, on the motion of Macdonald, he was appointed by the Taché-Macdonald government one of the commissioners to revise and consolidate the statutes of Upper Canada, and such of the other statutes as affected the upper province. At a later date he was also a commissioner for the consolidation of the statutes of Ontario.

Mowat's first incursion into public life was in Dec. 1856, when he was elected an alderman for the city of Toronto; his first entry into the political field was at the general election of 1857, when he was elected to the legislative assembly by the riding of South Ontario. Mowat supported the radical party, which was led by George Brown [q. v. Suppl. I], and advocated a reform of parliamentary representation by population and the secularisation of state schools.

In July 1858 the Macdonald-Cartier ministry resigned on a vote censuring the selection of Ottawa as the proposed capital, and Mowat became provincial secretary in the George Brown cabinet, which lived only forty-eight hours. The new ministers had resigned their seats to seek re-election, and the opposition snatched the opportunity to carry a vote of want of confidence. Within a few hours the old Macdonald-Cartier administration was installed in office as the Cartier-Macdonald government, and carried on the government until their defeat in the house shortly after the general elections of 1862. It was meanwhile becoming increasingly evident that some method must be devised to simplify the machinery of government of Canada, which the division between the two provinces hampered. At a great convention of reformers held at Toronto in 1859, which discussed the situation, Mowat forcibly presented what appeared to him to be the only possible alternatives, viz. a dissolution of the union between the two provinces, which he would deprecate, or the federation of the two provinces with a local legislature established in each, whereby alone, he held, could representation by population be attained, and the wealthy and more populous province be relieved from the domination of the French minority. He declined office in the John Sandfield Macdonald-Sicotte ministry of 1862, which refused to countenance the principle of representation by population. When the seventh parliament of Canada assembled in 1863, the J. S. Macdonald-Dorion ministry in control left representation by population an open question, and Mowat accepted the office of postmaster-general in the administration. His chief reforms were acts of retrenchment. He cancelled the existing Allan contract for ocean mails, renewing it on much more favourable terms, and he fixed the Grand Trunk railway postal subsidy at $60 a mile in lieu of the $300 to $800 a mile which the company claimed. In 1864, after the accession to office and early defeat of the Taché-John A. Macdonald government, George Brown's proposal of a coalition government for the purpose of 'settling for ever the constitutional difficulties between Upper and Lower Canada' was adopted. Mowat joined the coalition and took part in the conference on federation which met at Quebec (10 to 28 October 1864). Mowat advocated a senate elected for a fixed term, instead of an appointed senate which might prove a mere mechanical device for registering the acts of the party in power.

Mowat's labours on confederation were cut short by his appointment, on 14 Nov. 1864, as one of the vice-chancellors of Ontario. He held that office until Oct. 1872. In 1872, when Edward Blake and Alexander Mackenzie [q. v.], leaders of the Ontario legislature, abandoned, in accordance with the new constitution, local for federal politics, Mowat at their request resigned his judgeship and, rejoining the local legislature as member for North Oxford, became premier of Ontario on 29 Nov. 1872. He remained at the head of the province until 1896, when he entered Dominion politics as a supporter of Sir Wilfrid Laurier.

The enactments for which Mowat was responsible during his twenty-four years' premiership of Ontario aimed, as in the Ballot Act of 1874 and the Manhood Suffrage Act of 1888, at democratising Ontario institutions. At the same time he sought to simplify and cheapen the operation of justice. By the Administration of Justice Acts (1873 and 1874) and the Judicature Acts of 1880 and 1881 he effectively assimilated the practice and procedure of the common law and equity courts. Finally Mowat was responsible for an important series of measures which, checked by the federal veto and sanctioned in six instances on appeal to the privy council, served to define the proper limits of provincial rights under the constitution and rendered Mowat the victorious champion of provincial rights. In the first year of his premiership Mowat claimed the right of the lieutenant-governor-in-council to appoint queen's counsel with precedence in Ontario courts. In 1876 the province secured the right to regulate by legislation companies incorporated whether under a Dominion, British, or foreign charter. Again in 1883 the privy council pronounced, after much litigation, in favour of Mowat's claims on behalf of the province to enact liquor legislation in spite of the general control of trade and commerce vested in the Dominion parliament, and the judgment at the same time declared the power of the provincial legislature to be within prescribed limits 'as plenary and as ample as the imperial parliament in the plenitude of its power possessed and could bestow.' Among other of Mowat's victories was the final delimitation by a decision of the privy council in 1884 of the boundaries of Upper Canada (in Ontario) after a long and heated struggle with the Dominion parliament and with the neighbouring province of Manitoba. The ownership and control of 144,000 square miles of territory were thereby secured to Ontario. Mowat was made K.C.M.G. in 1892 and G.C.M.G. in 1893.

In 1896 Mr. Laurier, the liberal leader of the Dominion, induced Mowat to resign the premiership of Ontario and assist the liberal party in the general elections of that year. The dominant issue was the Manitoba school question, touching the claims of Roman catholics to separate state education, which the Manitoba legislature declined to admit. Mowat was in accord with his leader in advocating a compromise between the catholics and the Manitoba legislature which should not prejudice liberal and unsectarian principles. The result was a victory for Mr. Laurier and his party, and Mowat accepted a seat in the senate, and the office of minister of justice in the Laurier cabinet. In 1897 he retired to accept the office of lieutenant-governor of Ontario. In 1898 his health began to fail, but in spite of a partial paralysis he continued his official duties. He died at Government House, Toronto, on 19 April 1903, and was accorded a public funeral in Mount Pleasant cemetery.

Mowat's consistent success as a party leader was due to his tact, political sagacity, and integrity. The province recognised that to him its affairs were safely entrusted. The conservative opposition was powerless in the presence of the popularity and prestige which Mowat gained by his successful championship of provincial rights. In Dominion politics Mowat advocated the policy of unrestricted reciprocity with the United States, while he was an ardent supporter of the British connection. He denounced as 'veiled annexation' Goldwin Smith's proposal that Canada and the United States should maintain a uniform tariff against the world, and free trade between themselves. He was a member of the senate of the university of Toronto (1852–72), president of the Canadian Institute (1864–6), president of the Evangelical Alliance (1867–87), vice-president of the Upper Canada Bible Society (1859–1903), and hon. president of the Canadian Bar Association (1897). He held honorary degrees from Queen's university, Trinity university, and the university of Toronto.

On 19 May 1846 Mowat married Jane, daughter of John and Helen Ewart of Toronto. There were two sons and three daughters from this marriage. The eldest son, Frederick Mowat, is sheriff of the city of Toronto.

There are portraits in the Ontario Legislative Buildings by Robert Harris, C.B.; in Government House, Toronto, by Dixon Patterson; in the National Club, Toronto, and in the board room of the Imperial Life Assurance Company by E. Wyly Grier; and in Sheriff Mowat's house by J. Colin Forbes.

[Sir Oliver Mowat, a biographical sketch by C. R. W. Biggar, K.C., Toronto, 1905; private information.] P. E.

MUIR, SIR WILLIAM (1819–1905), Indian administrator and principal of Edinburgh University, born in Glasgow on 27 April 1819, was youngest of four sons of William Muir, merchant in Glasgow, by his wife Helen Macfie, of an Ayrshire family. John Muir [q.v.], the Sanskrit scholar, was his eldest brother. The eldest sister, Margaret, married the painter, Sir George Harvey [q.v.]. Left a widow two years after William's birth, his mother took her four sons and four daughters to Kilmarnock, where William attended the grammar school. On the removal of the family to Manor Place, Edinburgh, he entered the university there, and subsequently the university of Glasgow. Before he had the opportunity of graduating, his grand-uncle, Sir James Shaw [q. v.], chamberlain of the City of London, previously lord mayor, gave Mrs. Muir four writerships for the East India Company's civil service, and all her four sons went successively to Haileybury College and to the North-West Provinces of India. The second and third sons, James and Mungo, died there after short service.

On 16 Dec. 1837 William Muir landed in Bombay. There he at once entered on the work of settling the periodical assessments of land revenue, and with that work his service of thirty-nine years was mainly identified. He was stationed successively in the districts of Cawnpore, Bundelkhund, and Fatehpur. Following in the footsteps of Robert Merttins Bird [q.v.] and of James Thomason [q. v.], the creators of the land revenue system, he passed into the board of revenue, and then became secretary to Thomason's government of the North-West Provinces at Agra in 1847.

The sepoy Mutiny broke out at Meerut on 10 May 1857 and spread rapidly. Muir, at Agra, where the situation was soon critical, advised vigorous action from the first. Akbar's great fort of Agra became the refuge of the Christians, and John Russell Colvin [q. v.], the lieutenant-governor, just before his death there on 9 Sept. 1857, nominated Muir and two others to keep the wheels of government in motion. Muir vividly told the story of his experience for his children in his 'Agra in the Mutiny' (1896). Soon there was neither government nor revenue; but as head of the intelligence department Muir held the dangerous position of centre of communication between the viceroy, Lord Canning, and the civil and military authorities right across India to Delhi, Lahore, and Peshawar, to Gwalior, Indore, and Bombay. The invaluable correspondence which he controlled, after being partially utilised by Kaye in his history, was published in Edinburgh in two volumes in 1902, edited by W. Coldstream.

On the virtual suppression (save in Oudh) of the rebellion at the end of 1857 Lord Canning personally undertook the lieutenant-governorship of the North-West Provinces, and removed the headquarters from Agra to Allahabad. At the end of

January 1858 he summoned Muir to join him there as secretary to his government. Muir's experience and influence became all-important in the reorganisation of the provinces through 1858. To form after the Mutiny a permanent settlement of the North-West Provinces which should at once content the people and satisfy the revenue was the problem which Muir solved in his masterly minute of 5 Dec. 1861, when he was senior member of the board of revenue. He showed how the desired result could be reached gradually, on the basis of corn rents. That great state paper convinced the government of India. Political changes at the India office in London first delayed sanction and then indefinitely postponed the decision. To that delay was largely due the loss of life, property, and revenue since caused by famines in northern and central India.

After acting as provisional member of the governor-general's legislative council from 1864 Muir became foreign secretary under John first Lord Lawrence in 1867, when he was created K.C.S.I. Next year he became lieutenant-governor of the North-West Provinces, and held office till 1874. The sympathy and the efficiency which he brought to his administration obliterated the last traces of the rebellion. He mitigated the severity of the land assessment, and passed two acts which consolidated and amended the land laws of the North-West Provinces. He checked, and finally abolished, Hindu female infanticide, without creating political discontent. He promoted the spread of both primary and university education. The Muir college, which bears his name, at Allahabad, and the university which he instituted there, perpetuate his memory, and he devoted his leisure to the welfare of the Christian natives. From 20 Nov. 1874 to Sept. 1876 he held the high office of financial member of Lord Northbrook's council.

When Queen Victoria became Empress of India she adopted, as the translation of that title, the phrase, which Muir suggested, of Kaisar-i-Hind. At a later period, when a guest at Balmoral, he assisted Queen Victoria in her Hindustani studies.

On his retirement from India in 1876 he accepted the invitation of Lord Salisbury, secretary of state for India, to join the council of India in London. But he resigned his seat there on 15 Dec. 1885 on being appointed principal of Edinburgh University. That office he held till his death. Finding the official residence insufficient, he acquired Dean Park House, which became the centre of a gracious hospitality, that soon obliterated the memory of old academic feuds. In the words of Sir Ludovic Grant, son of Sir Alexander Grant [q. v.], his immediate predecessor, he 'cemented cordial relations between the university and all sections of the community.' He proved a generous benefactor to the university, and was generally known as 'the students' principal.'

Meanwhile Muir amid his official labours made a universal reputation as an Arabic scholar and an historian of Islam. To the 'Calcutta Review,' while it was edited by the present writer from 1857 onwards, Muir contributed fifteen articles, and on these he based his standard 'Life of Mahomet—History of Islam to the Era of the Hegira' (4 vols. 1858–61). He acquired the MSS. of the first authorities, Wâkidi, Hishâmi, and Tabari, and subsequently presented his valuable MS. of Wâkidi to the India office, after giving a transcript to the Edinburgh University library. A third edition of Muir's 'Life,' in one volume, omitting the introductory chapters and most of the notes, appeared in 1894 and was out of print at his death. In 1881 Muir delivered the Rede lecture at Cambridge on 'The Early Caliphate and Rise of Islam.' In 1883 his 'Annals of the Early Caliphate' and in 1896 his 'Mameluke or Slave Dynasty of Egypt' completed his great history down to the assumption of the title of Caliph by the Osmanli Sultanate. To the last volume Muir prefixed a lecture which he delivered to the Edinburgh students in 1894 on the Crusades, 'that great armament of misguided Christianity.' Meanwhile he also published 'The Corân: its Composition and Teaching, and the Testimony it bears to the Holy Scriptures' (1878); 'Extracts from the Corân, in the Original, with English rendering' (1880); 'The Apology of al-Kindy' (1881 and 1887); 'The Old and New Testaments, Tourat, Zubûr and Gospel; Moslems invited to see and read them' (1899), and other small treatises. 'Ancient Arabic Poetry: its Genuineness and Authenticity,' in Royal Asiatic Society's 'Journal' in 1879, is of high value.

He was elected president of the Royal Asiatic Society of Great Britain and Ireland in 1884, and in 1903, in recognition of 'the great value, importance, and volume' of his work on Islamic history and literature, was awarded the triennial jubilee gold medal, previous holders being E. B. Cowell [q. v. Suppl. II] and E. W. West [q. v. Suppl. II]. He was made hon. D.C.L. of Oxford in 1882, LL.D. of Edinburgh and Glasgow.

and in 1888 Doctor of Philosophy of Bologna University, at the eighth centenary of the foundation of which he represented Edinburgh.

Muir died at Edinburgh on 11 July 1905, and was buried in Dean cemetery. He married in 1840 Elizabeth Huntly (*d.* Oct. 1897), daughter of James Wemyss, collector of Cawnpore and a cadet of the family of Wemyss Castle in Fifeshire. She was identified with her husband in all his undertakings. Of the fifteen children of the marriage, the eldest son is Colonel William James Wemyss Muir, Bengal artillery and political department.

In 1862 Muir joined his brother John in endowing the Shaw professorship of Sanskrit and comparative literature at Edinburgh in memory of their grand-uncle, Sir James Shaw. Busts of Muir are in the Muir College, Allahabad, and in Edinburgh University. A crayon portrait belongs to the eldest son.

[The Friend of India, 1873–1874; The Times, 12 July 1905; the Royal Asiastic Society's Journal, 1905, by Sir Charles J. Lyall (a good estimate of Muir's Arabic scholarship and general character); the Student, Edinburgh University Magazine, Sir William Muir Number, 1905; Sir William Muir Memorial Service, an address by Rev. John Kelman, M.A., D.D., in the M'Ewan Hall, Sunday, 16 July 1905.] G. S.

MÜLLER. [See Iwan-Müller, Ernest Bruce (1853–1910), journalist.]

MULLINS, EDWIN ROSCOE (1848–1907), sculptor, born in London on 22 Aug. 1848, was a younger son and sixth child in a family of five sons and three daughters of Edward Mullins of Box, Wiltshire, solicitor, by his wife Elizabeth Baker. After being educated at Louth grammar school and Marlborough College (1863–5), Mullins was trained in the art schools of Lambeth and the Royal Academy, and subsequently under John Birnie Philip [q. v.]. In 1866 he went to Munich, where he studied under Professor Wagmüller, and in 1872 gained a silver medal at Munich and a bronze medal at Vienna for a group entitled 'Sympathy.' In 1874 he returned to London and became a constant exhibitor at the Royal Academy and other galleries. He devoted himself preferably to ideal work, which was marked by simplicity and restraint. The best of his works of this kind was probably 'Cain: My punishment is greater than I can bear' (New Gallery, 1896). The bronze statue of a 'Boy with a top' (R.A. 1895) was shown at the International Exhibition at Brussels in 1897; while other works possessing both charm and simplicity were the marble figure of a girl personifying 'Innocence' (R.A. 1876), 'Rest' (Grosvenor Gallery, 1881; acquired by Miss Hoole), 'Morn waked by the Circling Hours' (Grosvenor Gallery, 1884), 'Autolycus' (R.A. 1885), a bronze group entitled 'The Conquerors' (R.A. 1887), 'Love's Token' (R.A. 1891), and 'The Sisters' (1905).

Mullins also possessed considerable powers of portraiture. He exhibited at the Royal Academy busts of, among others, Dr. Martineau (1878), Mr. W. G. Grace (1887), Rt. Hon. C. T. Ritchie (1889), and Sir Evelyn Wood (1896). He also executed statuettes of Gladstone (1878), Val Prinsep, A.R.A. (R.A. 1880), Sir Rowland Hill, and Edmund Yates (1878), a marble effigy of Queen Victoria for Port Elizabeth (1900), a bronze equestrian statue of the Thakore Saheb of Morvi (1899), and statues of General Barrow (marble, 1882) for the Senate House of Lucknow, of Henry VII (stone, 1883), for King's College, Cambridge, and William Barnes, the Dorsetshire poet (1887), for Dorchester. His most curious work was the circus-horse in Brighton cemetery, executed in 1893 as a memorial to Mr. Ginnett, a well-known circus-owner.

Mullins embellished many prominent London buildings by carvings, panels, and other effective decorative work. He executed the carvings for the buildings of the Fine Arts Society, Bond Street (1881), a pediment for the Harris Free Library, Preston, representing 'The Age of Pericles' (1886), and the frieze, representing the entry of Charles II into London, for the drawing-room of the Grocers' Hall (1892).

In 1889 Mullins published 'A Primer of Sculpture.' He died at Walberswick, Suffolk, on 9 Jan. 1907. His remains after cremation at Golder's Green were buried at Hendon Park. He married on 4 June 1884 Alice, daughter of John Pelton, J.P., of Croydon, and had issue three sons and one daughter.

[The Times, 14 Jan. 1907; Spielmann's British Sculpture, 1901; Encyc. Brit. 11th edit. art. on Sculpture; Century Mag., July 1883; Portfolio, Aug. 1889 (art. by Sir Walter Armstrong); Builder, 21 Jan. 1888; Art Journ. 1907; private information from Mr. W. E. Mullins.] S. E. F.

MUNBY, ARTHUR JOSEPH (1828–1910), poet and civil servant, born in 1828, was eldest of six sons and one daughter of Joseph Munby of Clifton Holme, Yorkshire, solicitor, a member of an old Yorkshire family, by his wife Caroline Eleanor Forth (see *Memorial of Joseph Munby*, by A. J. MUNBY, 1876). He was educated at St. Peter's School, York, and Trinity College, Cambridge, where he graduated B.A. in 1851, proceeding M.A. in 1856. He entered Lincoln's Inn on 11 June 1851, and was called to the bar on 17 Nov. 1855. From 1858 to 1888 he held a post in the ecclesiastical commissioners' office, retiring at the age of sixty. A competent and conscientious official, he was known to his friends as an accomplished poet and man of letters. His first volume, entitled 'Benoni,' was issued in 1852. Seven years later he was a competitor for the fifty-guinea prize offered by the Crystal Palace Company for a poem on the Burns centenary of 1859, when he was one of six competitors whose excellence was held to be not far short of that of the winner, Miss Isa Craig, afterwards Mrs. Craig-Knox [q. v. Suppl. II]. Others of the six were Gerald Massey [q. v. Suppl. II] and Frederic William Henry Myers [q. v. Suppl. I]. To 'Benoni' succeeded, in 1865, 'Verses New and Old,' a collection of contributions to 'Fraser,' 'Macmillan,' 'Temple Bar,' 'Once a Week,' and other magazines. In 1880 came 'Dorothy,' a 'country story,' in the elegiac verse which its writer had employed for his Burns poem. Published anonymously, and dedicated to a lifelong friend, the novelist, Richard Doddridge Blackmore [q. v. Suppl. I], its idyllic grace and vivid pictures of country scenes and life obtained for it a recognition which had not been accorded to its acknowledged predecessors. Robert Browning, to whom a copy had been forwarded through the publisher, received it with the warmest admiration, praising especially its signal 'exquisitenesses of observation' and consummate craftsmanship; and it was speedily reprinted in America, going into three editions in 1882. 'Vestigia Retrorsum' (Rosslyn series of poets) followed in 1891. This included a sonnet which in the previous year had received the diploma of the committee of the Beatrice Exposition at Florence. 'Vulgar Verses' (that is, 'verses of common life') 'in dialect and out of it,' written under the pseudonym of 'Jones Brown' (1891); 'Susan, a Poem of Degrees' (1893); 'Ann Morgan's Love, a Pedestrian Poem' (1896); 'Poems, chiefly Lyric and Elegiac' (1901); and a final volume, 'Relicta' (1909), make up the sum of Munby's metrical output. To this last collection he prefixed the following Landor-like quatrain:

'There was a morning when I follow'd Fame:
There was a noonday when I caught her eye:
There is an evening when I hold my name
Calmly aloof from all her hue and cry.'

He also produced a few magazine articles and a compilation entitled 'Faithful Servants: Epitaphs and Obituaries' (based on an earlier anthology of 1826), which included 'A Historical Preface and a Prefatory Sonnet.

Munby's poetry is characterised by its absolute sincerity, its scholarship, its technical skill, its descriptive power, and its keen feeling for and close observation of nature and rural life. Outside this, his dominant note may be said to have been what has been called 'the glorification of the working woman,' with especial insistence on the dignity of manual labour.

Munby travelled widely, was a clever raconteur, and an F.S.A. with a genuine love of antiquity. For many years he was a regular contributor to 'Notes and Queries'; and he was a warm supporter of the Working Men's College, then in Great Ormond Street, where, between 1860 and 1870, he taught a Latin class. He was a member of the Pen and Pencil Club which assembled, *circa* 1864–74, at Aubrey House, Notting Hill, under the auspices of Mrs. Peter Taylor. A selection from its proceedings, entitled 'Auld Lang Syne,' was printed privately in 1877, and includes verses by Munby.

Munby died at his little cottage at Pyrford, near Ripley in Surrey, on 29 Jan. 1910, and was buried at Pyrford. The publication of his will in the following July disclosed the fact that on 14 January 1873 he had married his servant, Hannah Cullwick, who had died in July 1909. Owing to the refusal of his wife to quit her station, the marriage (ran the will), though known to her relations and to three of her husband's friends, had never been made known to his own family. The circumstances supply an explanation of many passages in Munby's poems which must otherwise remain obscure to his readers; and several of the pieces contained in his last volume, 'Relicta,' issued after his wife's death, read in this light, have great beauty and pathos. He left no issue.

He bequeathed many of his books to Trinity College, Cambridge; and to the British Museum two deed-boxes containing photographs, MSS., diaries, &c., on condition that they were not to be opened or examined before 1 Jan. 1950.

[Personal knowledge; The Times, 5 Feb. 1910; Daily Telegraph, and Daily Mail, 4 July 1910; art. in Gent. Mag. ccxcvii. 503–514, by Thomas Bayne; Working Men's College Journal, March 1910, and works.]

A. D.

MUNRO, JAMES (1832–1908), premier of Victoria, Australia, born on 7 Jan. 1832 at Glen Dubh in the parish of Eddrachillis, Sutherlandshire, was second son of Donald Munro of Glen Dubh, by his wife Georgina Scobie Mackay. Educated at the village school of Armadale, Sutherlandshire, he began life as a printer, serving his apprenticeship in Messrs. Constable's printing-works at Edinburgh. He emigrated to Victoria in 1858 and worked as a printer until 1865, when he founded the Victorian Permanent Property Investment and Building Society, of which for seventeen years he acted as secretary. He was also instrumental in starting the Melbourne woollen mills and the Victorian Permanent Fire Insurance Co. Taking advantage of the steady appreciation in land values, Munro founded in 1882 the Federal Banking Company and for three years conducted its operations as managing director. In 1887 he established the Real Estate Bank.

In 1863 he turned his attention to politics. After an unsuccessful attempt to enter the legislative assembly for Dundas, he was elected in 1874 for North Melbourne as a supporter of James Goodall Francis [q. v.], and in 1877 for Carlton. He was defeated in 1880, but re-entered parliament for North Melbourne in April 1881. In March 1886 and March 1889 he was returned for Geelong.

Always a staunch liberal, Munro was minister of public instruction in the first Berry ministry from 10 Aug. to 20 Oct. 1875. He declined office in the second Berry administration in 1877, and joined with J. J. Casey in forming a 'corner party' on the liberal side. He led the opposition to the Gillies-Deakin government, and in 1890, on his return from a visit to England, he attacked the financial policy of that cabinet and carried a vote of want of confidence. As a result he took office as treasurer and premier on 5 Nov. 1890. At the meeting of the federal convention in Sydney in 1891, Munro was one of the representatives of Victoria. Financial pressure due to the depreciation of land values led Munro to resign the premiership in February 1902 and become agent-general of the colony in London. Returning to Melbourne in November following, amid financial difficulties and failing health, he resigned that office and retired from public life.

Apart from politics Munro's chief interest lay in temperance work. For many years he was the leader of the temperance party in the Victorian parliament, and was at one time president of the Victorian Alliance and the Melbourne Total Abstinence Society and chief officer of the Order of Rechabites.

He was an executive commissioner at the Melbourne exhibitions of 1880–1 and 1888–9, and at the Philadelphia, the Sydney, and Paris exhibitions.

Munro died at his daughter's residence at Malvern, a suburb of Melbourne, on 25 Feb. 1908. He married, on 31 Dec. 1853, Jane, only daughter of Donald Macdonald of Edinburgh, and had four sons and three daughters.

[Victorian Men of the Time, 1878; Burke's Colonial Gentry, ii. 638; Mennell's Dict. of Australasian Biog. 1892; The Times, 27 Feb. 1908; Melbourne Argus, 26 Feb. 1908; Turner's Hist. of the Colony of Victoria, vol. ii.; Colonial Office Records.]

C. A.

MURDOCH, WILLIAM LLOYD (1855–1911), Australian cricketer, born at Sandhurst, Victoria, Australia, on 18 Oct. 1855, fourteen days after his father's death, was son of Gilbert William Lloyd Murdoch, at one time an officer in the American army, by his wife Edith Susan Hogg.

Educated at Dr. Bromley's school in Ballarat, he removed in youth to New South Wales. Having been articled at Sydney to G. Davis, a solicitor, he practised at Cootamundra. Showing early aptitude for cricket, he was a member of the Albert cricket club at Sydney, and at the age of twenty he began to play for New South Wales, and from 1875 to 1884, in eleven inter-colonial matches, he had the fine average of 47 runs for 20 innings. The score by which his name is chiefly remembered was that of 321 (out of a total of 775) made for New South Wales *v.* Victoria at Sydney in Feb. 1882. He also scored 279 not out for the Fourth Australian team *v.* Rest of Australia at Melbourne in 1883. In the colonies he was known as the 'W. G. Grace of Australia,' and was the earliest of a long series of great Australian batsmen. Originally his fame was partly due, however, to his merits as a wicket-keeper. He claimed to be the first to dispense with the longstop, a course which Blackham, the best of all wicket-keepers, subsequently popularised in Australia and

England. But he soon gave up wicket-keeping to his colleague Blackham, and thenceforth generally fielded at point.

Murdoch first came to England as a member of the first Australian eleven (captained by D. W. Gregory) which visited England in 1878. He owed his selection to his capacity as a wicket-keeper. During this tour he learned much in the art of batting, and became one of the leading batsmen of the world. He captained the Australian teams which visited England in 1880, 1882, 1884, and 1890, heading the Australian batting averages on each of these tours. At Kennington Oval in Sept. 1880, in the match in which Australia met for the first time the full strength of England, Murdoch showed his calibre by carrying his bat in an uphill game through the second innings for 153 (Dr. W. G. Grace scored 152 for England in the first innings). The teams of 1882 and 1884 were the strongest ever sent to England, and as a batsman Murdoch was at that period surpassed only by Dr. Grace. His outstanding innings of 1882 was that of 286 not out *v.* Sussex at Brighton, a score which was until 1899 unbeaten by an Australian in England. In the match *v.* England at the Oval in Aug. 1884 he scored 211 out of a total of 551, still the highest score made by an Australian in England in a representative match. He also scored 132 *v.* Cambridge University in June of that year. After an absence from the game for six years he returned to England in 1890 as captain of a weak Australian team, which met with little success. He also visited America in 1878, and went with W. W. Read's team to South Africa in 1891–2.

Settling in England in 1891, he qualified for Sussex, and captained that county between 1893 and 1899. For Sussex his best scores during this period were 172 *v.* Hampshire at Southampton (1894), 144 *v.* Somersetshire at Brighton (1896), 130 *v.* Gloucestershire at Bristol (1897), and 121 not out *v.* Notts at Nottingham (1898); but with increasing years and weight his batting deteriorated. He subsequently played (1901–4) for the London County Cricket Club founded by Dr. W. G. Grace at the Crystal Palace, Sydenham, making many good scores against first-class counties. His last memorable score was 140 at the Oval in 1904, when he played as substitute for the Gentlemen *v.* Players. Of fine physique, Murdoch was an orthodox and consistent batsman, playing with a straight bat and a perfect defence; a master of the off drive and the cut, he was quick to jump out to slow bowling and hit hard and clean. As a batsman he was excelled by Dr. W. G. Grace only on hard true pitches, and by few in defence on soft treacherous wickets. As a captain he was a master of tactics, full of pluck and resource, and showed great nerve in uphill games.

Murdoch, who visited Australia on business in 1910, died of apoplexy at Melbourne cricket ground on 18 Feb. 1911, while a spectator of the test match there between South Africa and Australia. His remains were embalmed and brought to England, and were interred at Kensal Green. He married in 1884, at Melbourne, Jemima, daughter of John Boyd Watson, a wealthy goldminer of Bendigo, and had issue two sons and three daughters.

Murdoch published in 1893 a little handbook on cricket. There is a small steel engraving portrait of Murdoch on the title-page of vol. 42 of 'Baily's Magazine' (1884).

[The Times, 20 Feb. 1911; Mennell's Dict. of Australasian Biog. 1892; W. G. Grace, Cricketing Reminiscences, 1899; Wisden's Cricketers' Almanack, 1912; private information.] W. B. O.

MURRAY, ALEXANDER STUART (1841–1904), keeper of Greek and Roman antiquities in the British Museum, born at Arbirlot, near Arbroath in Forfarshire, on 8 Jan. 1841, was eldest son in a family of four brothers and four sisters of George Murray, a tradesman, and of his wife Helen Margaret Sayles. His younger brother, George Robert Milne Murray [q. v. Suppl. II], was keeper of the department of botany at the British Museum (1895–1905), this being the only instance in the history of the British Museum of two brothers being keepers at the same time.

After being educated at the Royal High School, Edinburgh, Murray attended Edinburgh University during 1863–4, and graduated M.A. He also studied at Berlin University in 1865, where he worked at philological and archæological subjects under Böckh, Hübner, and Zumpt, and had Henry Nettleship for a fellow student.

Murray was appointed assistant in the department of Greek and Roman antiquities at the British Museum on 14 Feb. 1867. (Sir) Charles Newton [q. v. Suppl. I] was then keeper. The Blacas and Castellani collections had just been purchased, and Wood's excavations were in progress at Ephesus. Between 1867 and 1886 Murray worked actively under Newton's direction, and acquired minute familiarity with the whole collection of Greek and Roman antiquities. On 13 Feb. 1886 he succeeded Newton as keeper of the department of Greek and Roman antiquities. The recent removal of the natural history collections to the new buildings in Cromwell Road, Kensington, the completion of the new building known as the 'White Wing' at Bloomsbury, and other alterations, had greatly increased the available space for the exhibition of the collections. Hence a thorough reorganisation of the galleries devoted to Greek and Roman antiquities was rendered at once practicable, and this was for many years Murray's chief preoccupation. The specimens were set out with greater consideration than before for general effect and space, and at the same time all the fittings and labels were improved. He was always helpful to visitors to his department, and patiently answered inquiries of correspondents from a distance. Although he carried through the press no departmental catalogue of his own, he was a careful reader and critic of all that was published by assistants in his department, and contributed introductions to several volumes by them. He wrote the letterpress to the 'Terracotta Sarcophagi, Greek and Etruscan, in the British Museum' (1898), and most of the Enkomi section of the 'Excavations in Cyprus' (Brit. Mus.).

For many years he made it a practice to visit the Continent, especially Greece, Italy, Sicily, or Spain, and so was familiar with the chief classical sites and foreign collections, and with foreign archæologists. The only occasions on which he took part in work in the field were in 1870, when he visited the site of Priene with Newton, and in 1896, when he was temporarily in charge of the excavations at Enkomi (Salamis) in Cyprus.

He died of pneumonia, supervening on influenza, at his house in the museum precincts, on 5 March 1904, and was buried at Kensal Green.

He was twice married: (1) to Jenny Hancock (who died on 3 Nov. 1874, and is buried at Weybridge); (2) on 5 April 1881, to Anne Murray, youngest daughter of David Welsh, of Tillytoghills, Kincardineshire, who survived. There was no family by either marriage.

Murray was made LL.D. of Glasgow in 1891. He was a corresponding member of the Royal Prussian Academy and of the Académie des Inscriptions of the French Institute; a member of the German Archæological Institute, a fellow of the Society of Antiquaries (1889), of the British Academy (1903), and a vice-president of the Society for the Promotion of Hellenic Studies.

He was through life an adherent of the Scottish presbyterian church. Although somewhat quick-tempered, he was courteous and warm-hearted.

Murray wrote much on classical archæology independently of his official work. His writings showed the width of his knowledge, and were full of curious observations on points of detail; but his power of broad elementary exposition was limited, and though he was always interesting and suggestive, it was by no means easy to follow the general drift of his thought. From 1879 onwards all his writings dealing with early Greece were coloured by his reluctance to accept the early date, which was gradually being established beyond controversy, for Mycenæan culture.

His chief independent works were: 1. 'A Manual of Mythology,' 1873. 2. 'A History of Greek Sculpture,' vol. i. 'From the Earliest Times down to the Age of Pheidias,' 1880; vol. ii. 'Under Pheidias and his Successors,' 1883; 2nd edit. of both volumes, 1890. 3. 'Handbook of Archæology: Vases, Bronzes, Gems, Sculpture, Terracottas, Mural Paintings, Architecture, &c.,' 1892. 4. 'Greek Bronzes,' 1898. 5. 'The Sculptures of the Parthenon,' 1903.

Murray was also a frequent writer in the leading archæological organs and in the ninth edition of the 'Encyclopædia Britannica,' as well as in the 'Contemporary' and 'Quarterly' reviews (cf. *Bursiane-Kroll*, p. 102).

[Proc. Brit. Acad. 1903–4, p. 321 (by Sir E. Maunde Thompson); Bursiane-Kroll, Biograph. Jahrb. für die Altertumswiss. 1907, p. 100 (A. H. Smith); personal knowledge and private information.] A. H. S.

MURRAY, CHARLES ADOLPHUS, seventh Earl of Dunmore (1841–1907), born in Grafton Street, London, on 24 March 1841, was only son of Alexander Edward Murray, sixth earl of Dunmore, by his wife Catherine, fourth daughter of George Augustus Herbert, eleventh earl of Pembroke [q. v.]. He succeeded his father as seventh earl on 15 July 1845.

Educated at Eton, he entered the Scots fusilier guards on 18 May 1860, and remained with the regiment till 1864. A conservative in politics, he was lord-in-waiting to Queen Victoria throughout Disraeli's second government from 1874 till 1880. He was also lord-lieutenant of

Stirlingshire from 1874 till 1885, and hon. colonel of the 1st volunteer battalion of the Cameron Highlanders from 1896 till 1907.

A man of powerful physique, Dunmore travelled in many parts of the world, including Africa and the Arctic regions; but his chief fame as an explorer rests on a year's journey made in 1892 in company with Major Roche of the third dragoon guards through Kashmir, Western Thibet, Chinese Tartary and Russian Central Asia. They started from Rawal Pindi on 9 April 1892, and remained together till 12 Dec., when they parted at Kashgar in Chinese Turkestan. Major Roche, having no passport for the Central Asian frontier, then returned to India, while Dunmore continued his route westward through Ferghana and Transcaspia, reaching Samarcand towards the end of January 1893. He had ridden and walked 2500 miles, traversing forty-one mountain passes and sixty-nine rivers. On 3 July 1893 he read a paper on his experiences before the Royal Geographical Society (*Geog. Journ.* ii. 385), and in the same year published an account of his exploration in 'The Pamirs.' Though interesting and written in a simple and manly style, the book had small geographical value. Dunmore's scientific outfit was meagre. Indications for altitude were based on the readings of ordinary aneroids, and were not trustworthy. The ground had been covered by previous explorers and, according to experts, Dunmore lacked the necessary training for making fresh observations of value (*Geog. Journal*, iii. 115). Dunmore was also the author of 'Ormisdale,' a novel, published in 1893.

A few years before his death he, together with other members of his family, joined the Christian Scientists' Association. He attended the dedication of the mother church of the community at Boston, U.S.A., in June 1906. In 1907, at a Christian science meeting at Aldershot, he declared that his daughter had cured him of rupture by methods of Christian science. He died suddenly on 27 Aug. 1907 at Manor House, Frimley, near Camberley, and was buried at Dunmore, near Larbert, Stirlingshire. At an inquest, on 28 Aug. 1907, death was pronounced to be due to syncope caused by heart failure.

Lord Dunmore married on 5 April 1866 Lady Gertrude, third daughter of Thomas William Coke, second earl of Leicester, K.G. An only son, Alexander Edward, succeeded as eighth earl of Dunmore.

[The Times, 28 Aug. 1907; Who's Who; Burke's Peerage; Geog. Journ., Oct. 1907.]

S. E. F.

MURRAY, DAVID CHRISTIE (1847–1907), novelist and journalist, born on 13 April 1847 in High Street, West Bromwich, was one of a family of six sons and five daughters of William Murray, printer and stationer of that town, by his wife Mary Withers. David attended private schools at West Bromwich and Spon Lane, Staffordshire, but at the age of twelve was set to work in his father's printing office. He early entered on a journalistic career by writing leaders for the 'Wednesbury Advertiser.' He was soon on the staff of the 'Birmingham Morning News' under George Dawson, reporting police court cases at twenty-five shillings a week, and rapidly winning the approval of his employer as an admirable descriptive writer. In Jan. 1865 Murray went to London without friends, funds, or prospects, and found casual employment at Messrs. Unwin Brothers' printing works. In May he enlisted as a private in the fourth royal Irish dragoon guards, and accompanied his regiment to Ireland, but after a year a great-aunt purchased his discharge. Thenceforth journalism or foreign correspondence was his profession, varied by novel-writing. When in London, he passed his time in Bohemian society. In 1871 he became parliamentary reporter for the 'Daily News.' In 1892 he was editor of the 'Morning,' a short-lived conservative daily London paper. A few years later he contributed to the 'Referee' ethical, literary and political articles, which were collected as 'Guesses at Truth' (1908).

Murray travelled much, and was constantly absent from London for long periods. He represented 'The Times' and the 'Scotsman' in the Russo-Turkish war of 1877–8. On his return he described in a series of articles for 'Mayfair' a tour through England in the disguise of a tramp. From 1881 to 1886 he lived mainly in Belgium and France, and from 1889 to 1891 Nice was his headquarters. Subsequently he resided for a time in North Wales. He made some success as a popular lecturer, touring through Australia and New Zealand in that capacity in 1889–91, and through the United States and Canada in 1894–5. He described Australia in articles in the 'Contemporary Review' (1891). In 'The Cockney Columbus' (1898) he collected letters on America from the 'New York Herald.' From 1898 onwards he devoted much energy to the support by writing and lecturing of Emile Zola's plea in behalf of Captain Dreyfus, a French officer, who had been wrongfully condemned for espionage.

Meanwhile Murray used his literary power to best effect in fiction. In 1879 he contributed his first novel, 'A Life's Atonement,' periodically to 'Chambers's Journal.' From that date until his death scarcely a year passed without the publication of one and at times two novels. Between 1887 and 1907 he occasionally collaborated with Henry Herman [q. v. Suppl. I] or Mr. Alfred Egmont Hake. Murray's novels 'Joseph's Coat' (1881) and 'Val Strange' (1882) achieved a notable success. 'By the Gate of the Sea' (1883) and 'Rainbow Gold' (1885), which first appeared in serial form in the 'Cornhill Magazine' under the editorship of James Payn [q. v. Suppl. I], fully maintained Murray's repute. 'Aunt Rachel' (1886) was equally attractive. Murray's fiction abounded in vigour. His plots are loosely constructed and he drew his incidents freely from his journalistic experiences. His style shows the hand of the journalist, but he is effective in describing the neighbourhood and inhabitants of Cannock Chase.

Murray died on 1 Aug. 1907 in London after a long illness, during which he endured much privation. He was buried at Hampstead. A memorial tablet in copper with pewter medallion was unveiled at West Bromwich public library in December 1908. He was twice married. By his first wife, Sophie Harris of Rowley Regis, whom he married in 1871, he had a daughter, who died young; by his second wife, Alice, whom he married about 1879, he had one son, Archibald. Two sons and two daughters were born out of wedlock.

Besides his novels, Murray was author of several rambling volumes of autobiography. Such were: 'A Novelist's Notebook' (1887); 'The Making of a Novelist, an Experiment in Autobiography' (1894); and 'Recollections' (1908).

[Who's Who, 1907; The Times, 2 Aug. 1907; Allibone, Suppl. II., 1891; Henry Murray, A Stepson of Fortune, 1909, p. 445 (autobiographic recollections by D. C. Murray's brother); Murray's Recollections, 1908 (with photogravure portrait), and other autobiographic works, which are deficient in dates; private information.] E. L.

MURRAY, GEORGE ROBERT MILNE (1858–1911), botanist, younger brother of Alexander Stuart Murray [q. v. Suppl. II], was born at Arbroath, Forfarshire, on 11 Nov. 1858. He was educated at Arbroath High School, and in 1875 studied under Anton de Bary at Strasburg. In 1876 he became an assistant in the botanical department of the British Museum, having charge of the cryptogamic collections, and in 1895, on the retirement of Dr. William Carruthers, he became keeper of the department, a post which he was compelled by ill-health to resign in 1905. He was lecturer on botany at St. George's Hospital medical school from 1882 to 1886, and to the Royal Veterinary College from 1890 to 1895. In 1886 Murray acted as naturalist to the solar eclipse expedition to the West Indies; and again visited the same area on a dredging expedition in 1897; in 1898 he chartered a tug for a dredging expedition in the Atlantic, 300 miles west of Ireland, on which he was accompanied by a party of naturalists; and in 1901 he became director of the civilian scientific staff of the national Antarctic expedition in H.M.S. Discovery, under Captain R. F. Scott. He was, however, only able to accompany the expedition as far as Cape Town. For some years he devoted much of his vacation to the collection of diatoms and algæ in the Scottish lochs from the fishery board's yacht Garland. Murray was elected a fellow of the Linnean Society in 1878, apparently in contravention of the bye-laws, as he was then under age. He became a vice-president in 1899, and was elected a fellow of the Royal Society in 1897. He died at Stonehaven on 16 Dec. 1911.

He married in 1884 Helen, daughter of William Welsh of Walker's Barns and Boggieshallow, Brechin, and left one son and one daughter. His wife died in 1902.

Murray's contributions to botany refer mainly to marine algæ, but he wrote the section on fungi in Henfrey's 'Elementary Course of Botany' (3rd edit. 1878); he contributed the articles on Fungi and Vegetable Parasitism to the ninth edition of the 'Encyclopædia Britannica' (1879 and 1885); and between 1882 and 1885 he published three reports upon his investigations of the salmon disease, undertaken at the instance of Professor Huxley. In 1889 he published a 'Handbook of Cryptogamic Botany,' together with Alfred William Bennett [q. v. Suppl. II]; from 1892 to 1895 he edited 'Phycological Memoirs, being Researches made in the Botanical Department of the British Museum,' of which three parts appeared, each containing papers by him; and in 1895 he published an 'Introduction to the Study of Seaweeds.' He also edited 'The Antarctic Manual' for the expedition of 1901, arranging the contents and securing contributors, but only writing some four pages of instructions on plant-collecting.

[The Times, 19 and 21 Dec. 1911; Gardeners' Chronicle, i. (1911) 466; Journal of Botany (1912), 73 (with photographic portrait).]

G. S. B.

MUSGRAVE, Sir JAMES, first baronet (1826–1904), benefactor of Belfast, born at Lisburn, co. Antrim, on 30 Dec. 1826, was seventh of nine sons (and one of the twelve children) of Dr. Samuel Musgrave (1770–1836), a leading physician of Lisburn, by his wife Mary (*d.* 1862), daughter of William Riddel, Comber, co. Down. The Ulster branch of the Musgraves came thither from Cumberland in the seventeenth century. Musgrave's father, who sympathised with the United Irishmen, was arrested on 16 Sept. 1796 on a charge of high treason and imprisoned in 'The New Gaol,' Dublin (*Belfast News-Letter*, 19 Sept. 1796). Released in 1798, he resumed professional work in Lisburn; but in 1803 he was again arrested and imprisoned for a time on a similar charge.

After attending local schools and receiving private tuition, James began early a business career in Belfast, and ultimately, with two of his brothers, John Riddel and Robert, he established the important firm of Musgrave Brothers, iron founders and engineers. Soon, taking part in the public life of Belfast, he was in 1876 elected at the head of the poll one of the Belfast harbour commissioners, and was thenceforth regularly re-elected. From 1887 to 1903 he was chairman, in succession to Sir Edward J. Harland, M.P.; under his direction the harbour was greatly improved, and new docks, quays, and deep water channels constructed for the increasing trade, one of these being named the 'Musgrave Channel' in his honour. He resigned the chairmanship in 1903. In 1877 he was elected president of the Belfast chamber of commerce. He was the moving spirit in the establishment of the Belfast technical school, helped greatly in the erection of the Royal Victoria Hospital in Belfast, in commemoration of the jubilee of Queen Victoria, and founded in 1901 the Musgrave chair of pathology in Queen's College, Belfast. Musgrave worked hard as a member of the 'Recess Committee' which was formed in 1895 by Sir Horace Plunkett to devise means for the amelioration of the agricultural and economic condition of Ireland, and whose proposals were embodied in 1899 in an act of parliament. In 1866 he and his brother John had purchased an estate of some 60,000 acres in co. Donegal. During part of every year he resided on the estate at Carrick Lodge, Glencolumbkille, taking a deep interest in the welfare of the tenantry. He was appointed J.P. and D.L. of co. Donegal, and served as high sheriff 1885–6. He was chairman of the Donegal railway company, in the establishment of which he had a large share. In 1897 he was created a baronet of the United Kingdom. Musgrave died unmarried at Drumglass House, his Belfast residence, on 22 Feb. 1904, and was buried in the cathedral churchyard, Lisburn. A stained-glass window to his memory, and to that of other members of the family, is in the First Lisburn presbyterian church, to which his ancestors belonged. A marble bust by A. M'F. Shannan, A.R.S.A., and an oil painting by Walter Frederic Osborne [q. v. Suppl. II], were placed in the Belfast Harbour Office in memory of his services.

[Personal knowledge; information kindly supplied by Mr. Henry Musgrave, D.L.; Belfast News-Letter, 23 Feb. 1904.] T. H.

MUYBRIDGE, EADWEARD (1830–1904), investigator of animal locomotion, born at Kingston-on-Thames on 9 April 1830, was the son of John Muggeridge, corn-chandler, of Kingston, by his wife Susannah. His original names of Edward James Muggeridge he soon converted into Eadweard Muybridge. Migrating to America in early life, he at first adopted a commercial career, and then, turning his attention to photography, he became director of the photographic surveys of the United States government. In 1872, whilst engaged in his official duties on the Pacific coast, he was consulted as to an old controversy in regard to animal locomotion, viz. whether a trotting horse at any portion of its stride has all its feet entirely off the ground. On the race-course at Sacramento, California, in May 1872, he made several negatives of Occident, a celebrated horse, while trotting laterally in front of his camera at speeds varying from 2 mins. 25 secs. to 2 mins. 18 secs. per mile. These experiments showed that the horse's four feet were at times all off the ground. He continued his experiments with a view to determining the actual visual appearance of various kinds of animal locomotion and their proper representation.

The photographs for his earliest experiments were made with a single camera, and required a separate trotting for each exposure. His next experiments were made in 1877 on the stud-farm of Mr. Leland Stanford at Palo Alto, San Francisco, where he employed a number of cameras placed in a line, thus obtaining a succession of exposures at regulated intervals of time or distance. The cameras were arranged to obtain photographs of the subject from three different points of view; each movement was taken by a different camera on extremely rapid wet plates, the exposure at times being only one six-thousandth part of a second. The shutters of the cameras were operated by means of thin thread stretched across the path of the animal the record of whose movements was to be taken. Some of the results of these early experiments illustrating the action of horses whilst walking, trotting, or galloping were published in 1878 under the title of 'The Horse in Motion.' In his analysis of the quadrupedal walk, Muybridge arrived at the conclusion that the successive foot-fallings are invariable and are probably common to all quadrupeds. His investigations led to much modification of the treatment of animal movements in the works of painters and sculptors.

In order to project the pictures upon a screen so that they would appear to move, Muybridge invented, in 1881, a machine which he called the 'zoopraxiscope,' and which he claimed to be the first instrument devised for demonstrating, by synthetical reconstruction, movements originally photographed from life. The 'zoetrope,' or 'wheel of life,' which was invented about 1833 and had long been in popular use as a toy, had no like scientific pretension. Muybridge's 'zoopraxiscope' was widely employed. By its means horse-races were reproduced on a screen with such fidelity as to show the individual characteristics of the motion of each animal, flocks of birds flew with every movement of their wings clearly perceptible, two gladiators contended for victory, athletes turned somersaults, and the like. At the electrical congress in Paris in September 1881 Muybridge lectured before the assembled men of science with his newly animated illustrations for the first time in Europe at the laboratory of Dr. E. J. Marey (who was independently experimenting on Muybridge's lines). He also lectured in London, before the Royal Institution, in March 1882 and in March 1889 and at a conversazione given by the Royal Society.

A wider investigation of animal movements was undertaken by Muybridge in 1884–5 under the auspices and at the charge of the university of Pennsylvania. More than 100,000 photographic plates were obtained and embodied in a work published at Philadelphia in 1887 as 'Animal Locomotion, an Electro-photographic Investigation of Consecutive Phases of Animal Movement, 1872–1885.' The work contains over 2000 figures of moving men, women, children, beasts, and birds, in 781 photo-engravings, bound in eleven folio volumes. The great cost of preparing and printing this work restricted its sale to a very few complete sets, and a selection of the most important plates on a reduced scale was published in London in 1899 as 'Animals in Motion.'

Muybridge's efforts led the way to the invention of the cinematograph, which was the immediate result of Dr. Marey's invention of the celluloid roll film in 1890.

When in England Muybridge resided at his birthplace, Kingston-on-Thames. He was there in 1895, but returned more than once to the United States before finally settling at Kingston in 1900. There he lived at 2 Liverpool Road with Mr. George Lawrence, whom he appointed his executor. In the grounds there he dug out a miniature reproduction to scale of the Great Lakes of America.

Muybridge died on 8 May 1904, and his remains were cremated at Woking. He bequeathed to the Kingston public library 3000*l.*, in reversion after the death of a lady relative, the income to be applied to the purchase of works of reference, together with his lantern slides, zoopraxiscope, and a selection from the plates of his 'Animal Locomotion.'

Besides the works above mentioned, Muybridge published: 1. 'Descriptive Zoopraxography, or the Science of Animal Locomotion made Popular,' 1893 (abridged edition same year). 2. 'The Human Figure in Motion' (abridged from 'Animal Locomotion'), 1901. 3. 'The Science of Animal Locomotion (Zoopraxography),' n.d.

[The Bioscope, 1 Sept. 1910, pp. 3–5; H. V. Hopwood's Living Pictures, 1899 (with bibliography and list of patents); Haydn's Dict. of Dates, s.v. Zoopraxiscope; Illustrated Lond. News, 18 March 1882 and 25 May 1889 (portrait, p. 645); Proc. of the Royal Institution, 1882, x. 44–56, 1889, xii. 444–5; information kindly supplied by Mr. B. Carter, librarian of the Kingston Public Library.] C. W.

THE DICTIONARY of NATIONAL BIOGRAPHY

Founded in 1882

by

GEORGE SMITH

SUPPLEMENT

January 1901 — December 1911

Edited by Sir Sidney Lee

VOL. III. *NEIL—YOUNG*

Now published by the

OXFORD UNIVERSITY PRESS

PREFATORY NOTE

In the present volume which is designed to furnish biographies of noteworthy persons dying between 22 Jan. 1901 and 31 Dec. 1911, the memoirs reach a total of 557. The contributors number 177. The callings of those whose careers are recorded may be broadly catalogued under ten general headings thus:

	NAMES
Administration of Government at home, in India, and the colonies	68
Army and navy	39
Art (including architecture, music, and the stage) . . .	75
Commerce and agriculture	17
Law	26
Literature (including journalism, philology, and philosophy) .	132
Religion	51
Science (including engineering, medicine, surgery, exploration, and economics)	115
Social Reform (including philanthropy and education)	24
Sport	10

The names of twenty-eight women appear in this volume on account of services rendered in art, literature, science, and social or educational reform.

Articles bear the initials of their writers save in a very few cases where material has been furnished to the Editor on an ampler scale than the purpose of the undertaking permitted him to use. In such instances the Editor and his staff are solely responsible for the shape which the article has taken, and no signature is appended.

⁂ In the lists of authors' publications only the date of issue is appended to the titles of works which were published in London in 8vo. In other cases the place of issue and size are specified in addition.

Cross references are given thus: to names in the substantive work [q.v.]; to names in the First Supplement[1] [q.v. Suppl. I]; and to names in the present Supplement[2] [q.v. Suppl. II].

[1] i.e. Vol. XXII (of the thin paper edition). [2] i.e. 1901 – 1911.

DICTIONARY

OF

NATIONAL BIOGRAPHY

1901–1911

NEIL, ROBERT ALEXANDER (1852–1901), classical and Oriental scholar, the second son of Robert Neil, minister of the *quoad sacra* parish of Glengairn near Ballater, Aberdeenshire, by his wife Mary Reid, was born at Glengairn Manse on 26 Dec. 1852. Both parents were sprung from Aberdeenshire families which had produced many clergymen and medical men. Robert, who was always interested in books, was educated under Mr. Coutts, the master of the local school, but was taught classics by his father. In 1866, while still under fourteen, he entered Aberdeen University, having obtained a small scholarship at the annual bursary competition. At the end of the session he was first prizeman in the class of Prof. (Sir) William Geddes [q. v. Suppl. I]. In 1870 he graduated at Aberdeen with first-class honours in classics, the Greek prize being divided between him and Mr. A. Shewan, now well known as an Homeric scholar. The following winter Neil acted as an assistant in the university library and next year studied anatomy and chemistry with the intention of graduating in the medical faculty. He soon changed his mind and was elected a classical scholar of Peterhouse, Cambridge. Meantime he had been reading omnivorously; but his early training, in which classical composition had played but a small part, handicapped him for the Cambridge course. Under the tuition, however, of Dr. J. S. Reid, of Dr. Verrall for a short time, and later of Richard Shilleto [q. v.], he made such rapid progress that in 1875 against strong competition he won the Craven scholarship and in 1876 graduated as second classic. Soon after he was elected a fellow of Pembroke College, where till his death twenty-five years later he was a classical lecturer, though his public lectures were given for many years at his old college, Peterhouse. Soon after taking his degree he published 'Notes on Liddell and Scott' in the 'Journal of Philology' (viii. 200 seq.); but his teaching work left him little leisure for writing, which his caution and fastidious taste made a somewhat laborious task, while his wide range of literary interests rendered reading more congenial. Almost immediately after his degree Neil began to read Sanskrit with Prof. Edward Byles Cowell [q. v. Suppl. II]. For the rest of his life Neil spent one or two afternoons a week in term time working with Cowell. In the earlier years they read parts of the 'Rig Veda,' of Indian drama, grammar, and philosophy, but gradually turned their attention more and more to Buddhist literature. In 1886, under their joint names, appeared an edition of the 'Divyāvadāna,' a Buddhist work in Sanskrit. The edition was founded on the collation of a number of MSS. which were supplied to the editors from various libraries, including those of Paris and St. Petersburg. After the publication of this work Neil, though still reading the 'Veda' with Cowell, took up seriously the study of Pāli, and formed one of the little band of scholars who under Cowell's superintendence translated the 'Jātaka,' or Birth Stories, into English (6 volumes, Cambridge University Press,

1895–1907). Neil's own contribution forms part of vol. iii. During these years Neil was also busy with much classical work. For many years he had in the press an edition of Aristophanes' 'Knights,' which but for the introduction was completed at his death and was issued soon afterwards by the Cambridge University Press. Here in brief space is concentrated a great amount of sound scholarship and delicate observation of Aristophanic Greek. The history of Greek comedy, Pindar, and Plato were subjects on which Neil frequently lectured and on which he accumulated great stores of knowledge. He was also thoroughly familiar with all work done in the comparative philology of the classical languages, Sanskrit, and Celtic. His emendation of a corrupt word, ἀσαγεύοντα, in Bacchylides into ἀωτεύοντα was at once accepted by Prof. (Sir) Richard Jebb [q. v. Suppl. II]. Besides his professional work as a classical lecturer and as university lecturer on Sanskrit—a post to which he was appointed in 1883—Neil took much interest in architecture both ancient and mediæval, and had a wide and intimate knowledge of the cathedrals of the western countries of Europe. He was interested in women's education, and before his college work became very heavy lectured at both Girton and Newnham. But his greatest influence was manifested in work with individual students, where his kindliness, care, and quiet humour attracted even the less scholarly. He was popular in Cambridge society, and amid his multifarious duties could always spare time to solve difficulties for his friends. He was for long a syndic of the University Press, where he helped many young scholars with advice and oversight of their work as it passed through the press. He served for four years upon the council of the senate, but the work was not congenial to him, and he refused to be nominated a second time.

In 1891 Aberdeen University conferred upon him the honorary degree of LL.D. Neil took a keen interest in Scottish history and literature, and was for long a member of the Franco-Scottish Society. In 1900, on the death of Mr. C. H. Prior, he took with some hesitation the work of senior tutor of Pembroke. He died after a brief illness on 19 June 1901, and was buried in the churchyard at Bridge of Gairn, not far from his birthplace. He was unmarried. In appearance Neil was a little over the average height and strongly built, with brown hair and large expressive eyes. There are several good photographs of him.

[Obituary notices by personal friends in Cambridge Review (Dr. Adam, October 1901); British Weekly, 27 June 1901 (Sir W. Robertson Nicoll, a class mate at Aberdeen); Alma Mater, the Aberdeen University Mag., 20 Nov. 1901 (Dr. J. F. White); information from the family, and personal knowledge for nineteen years.] P. G.

NEIL, SAMUEL (1825–1901), author, born at Edinburgh on 4 August 1825, was second of three sons of James Neil, an Edinburgh bookseller, by his wife Sarah Lindsay, a connection of the Lindsays, earls of Crawford. On the death of the father from cholera in 1832, the family went to live at Glasgow. After education at the old grammar school at Glasgow, Neil entered the university; while an undergraduate he assisted the English master in the high school and worked for the 'Glasgow Argus' (of which Charles Mackay [q. v.] the poet was editor) and other newspapers. For a time he was a private tutor and then master successively of Falkirk charity school in 1850, of Southern Collegiate School, Glasgow, in 1852, and of St. Andrew's school, Glasgow, in 1853. Finally he was rector of Moffat Academy from 1855 to 1873.

With his school work Neil combined much literary activity. He promoted in 1857, and edited during its existence, the 'Moffat Register and Annandale Observer,' the first newspaper published in Moffat, and wrote regularly for other Scottish periodicals and educational journals.

In 1850 Neil planned, and from that date until 1873 edited, the 'British Controversialist' (40 vols. in all), a monthly magazine published in London for the discussion of literary, social, and philosophic questions. He himself contributed numerous philosophical articles, many of which he subsequently collected in separate volumes. Of these his 'Art of Reasoning' (1853) was praised for its clarity and conciseness by John Stuart Mill, George Henry Lewes, Archbishop Whately, and Alexander Bain. Other of his contributions to the 'British Controversialist' were published independently, under the titles of 'Elements of Rhetoric' (1856), 'Composition and Elocution' (1857; 2nd edit. 1857, 12mo), 'Public Meetings and how to conduct them' (1867, 12mo).

On resigning his rectorship of Moffat Academy in 1873 Neil settled in Edinburgh, devoting himself to English literature, and especially to Shakespeare. He founded and was president of the Edinburgh Shakespeare Society, and gave the annual lecture from 1874 till his death. To the 'British Controversialist' in 1860 he had contributed a series of papers which he reissued in 1861 as 'Shakespeare: a Critical Biography.' The work enjoyed a vogue as a useful epitome of the facts, although Neil accepted without demur the forgeries of John Payne Collier. It was translated into French and German. Neil, who was a frequent visitor to Warwickshire, issued a guide to Shakespeare's birthplace at Stratford-on-Avon as 'Home of Shakspere described' (Warwick, 1871, 12mo), and he edited the 'Library Shakespeare' (3 vols.) in 1875, besides several separate plays for school use.

Neil took a leading part in educational and philanthropic affairs in Edinburgh, where he was on intimate terms with Professors John Stuart Blackie, Henry Calderwood, John Veitch, and David Masson. He helped to found the Educational Institute of Scotland for granting fellowships to teachers. For the Craigmillar School for the Blind there, which he managed for some years, he compiled a book of poems on the blind and by the blind, entitled 'Dark Days brightened.'

In 1900 his health failed. He died on 28 Aug. 1901, while on a visit at Sullom Manse, Shetland, and was buried in Sullom churchyard. He married on 7 April 1848 Christina, youngest daughter of Archibald Gibson, who served in the navy and was with Nelson on the Victory at the battle of Trafalgar. She predeceased him on 26 Jan. 1901. He had issue three sons and five daughters, of whom one son and three daughters, all married, survive.

A painted portrait by George Barclay is in possession of his daughter at 53 Craiglea Drive, Edinburgh. His head was done in white alabaster by a sculptor of Glasgow in 1853.

Other of Neil's works include: 1. 'Cyclopædia of Universal History,' 1855; 2nd edit. 1857 (with I. McBurney). 2. 'Synopsis of British History,' 1856, 12mo. 3. 'Student's Handbook of Modern History,' 1857. 4. 'The Young Debater,' 1863. 5. 'Culture and Self-culture,' 1863. 6. 'Martin Luther,' 1863, 12mo. 7. 'Epoch Men and the Results of their Lives,' 1865, 12mo. 8. 'The Art of Public Speaking,' 1867, 12mo. 9. 'The Debater's Handbook and Controversialist Manual,' 1874, 12mo; new edit. 1880. Neil edited and compiled the larger part of 'The Home Teacher, a Cyclopædia of Self-instruction' (1886, 6 vols. 4to).

[James Love's Schools and Schoolmasters of Falkirk, 1898, pp. 232–8; Ardrossan and Saltcoats Herald, 20 Sept. 1901 (memoir by Neil's son-in-law, Rev. Charles Davidson); Moffat Express, 5 Sept. 1901; Educational News, 7 Sept. 1901; private information; notes from Mr. James Downie.] W. B. O.

NELSON, ELIZA (1827–1908), actress. [See under Craven, Henry Thornton.]

NELSON, Sir HUGH MUIR (1835–1906), premier of Queensland, born at Kilmarnock on 31 Dec. 1835, was son of the Rev. William Lambie Nelson, LL.D. Educated first at Edinburgh High School, and then at the university, where he came under the influence of Prof. John Wilson (Christopher North), he did not graduate, his father having decided in 1853 to go to Queensland, which was then attracting a number of enterprising Scotsmen.

The father settled in the colony at Ipswich, and Nelson entered a merchant's office; but, of fine physique, he soon sought open-air work on a farm at Nelson's Ridges, some six miles from Ipswich; thence he went to manage the Eton Vale station at Darling Downs. When he married in 1870, he settled with good results on the London estate in the Dalby district.

In 1880 Nelson entered the local public life as a member of the Wambo district under a new scheme of divisional boards. In 1883, while absent on a visit to Scotland, he was elected member of the house of assembly for Northern Downs. When in 1887 this electoral district was split up, he became member for the portion known as Murilla, which he represented continuously for the rest of his public life.

On 13 March 1888 Nelson for the first time took office, as minister for railways, under Sir Thomas McIlwraith [q. v. Suppl. I], continuing when the ministry was reconstituted under Boyd Dunlop Morehead till 7 August 1890. Throughout 1891, he was leader of the opposition. Although he seems to have been a supporter of Sir Samuel Griffith, it was not till Griffith's resignation on 27 March 1893 that he took office, joining McIlwraith as colonial treasurer. On 27 October 1893 he became premier and vice-president of the executive council, combining in his own hands the offices of chief secretary and treasurer. The colony was in the throes of the anxiety and depression which followed the bank crisis of

1893; in no part of Australia was that crisis worse than in Queensland. Thus the task before the new premier was no light one; but his broad grasp of finance, coupled with extensive knowledge of the circumstances and requirements of the people, enabled him to render excellent service to Queensland during a most critical period of its history (*Queensland Hansard*, 1906, vol. xcvi. pp. 1–16).

In 1896 Nelson was created K.C.M.G., and in 1897 came to England to represent his colony at the Diamond Jubilee of Queen Victoria. On this occasion he was made a privy councillor and received the honorary degree of D.C.L. at Oxford. After his return he continued his dual office till 13 April 1898, when he sought a less arduous position as president of the legislative council. On 4 Jan. 1904 he received a dormant commission as lieutenant-governor of Queensland.

In 1905 he visited New Guinea, in which he was much interested: there he contracted fever, from which he never really recovered (see *Queensland Parly. Deb.*, 1906, xcvi. 15), and he died at his residence, Gabbinbar, near Toowoomba, on 1 Jan. 1906. His death was the signal for general mourning, and he was accorded a public funeral. He was buried at Toowoomba cemetery.

Nelson was a strong man, and the greatest authority on constitutional questions that the colony had had up to that time, although he was opposed to the federation of the Australian states (*Daily Record, Rockhampton*, 1 Jan. 1906). He founded the Royal Agricultural Society of Toowoomba and the Austral Association. He was president of the Royal Geographical Society of Queensland.

Nelson married in 1870 Janet, daughter of Duncan McIntyre, who survived him. They had issue two sons and three daughters.

[Brisbane Courier, 2 Jan. 1906; Mennell's Dict. of Australas. Biog.; John's Notable Australians; Who's Who, 1905.] C. A. H.

NERUDA, WILMA. [See Hallé, Lady (1839–1911), violinist.]

NETTLESHIP, JOHN TRIVETT (1841–1902), animal painter and author, born at Kettering, Northamptonshire, on 11 Feb. 1841, was second son of Henry John Nettleship, solicitor there, and brother of Henry [q. v.], of Richard Lewis [q. v.], and of Edward, the ophthalmic surgeon. His mother was Isabella Ann, daughter of James Hogg, vicar of Geddington and master of Kettering grammar school. Music was hereditary in the family, and Nettleship was for some time a chorister at New College, Oxford. Afterwards he was sent to the cathedral school at Durham, where his brother Henry had preceded him. Having won the English verse prize on 'Venice' in 1856, he was taken away comparatively young, in order to enter his father's office. There he remained for two or three years, finishing his articles in London. Though admitted a solicitor and in practice for a brief period, he now resolved to devote himself to art, in which he had shown proficiency from childhood. Accordingly he entered himself as a student at Heatherley's and at the Slade School in London, but to the last he was largely independent and self-taught. His first work was in black and white, not for publication, but to satisfy his natural temperament, which always led him to the imaginative and the grandiose. It is to be regretted that none of the designs conceived during this early period was ever properly finished. They include biblical scenes, such as 'Jacob wrestling with the Angel' and 'A Sower went forth to sow,' which have been deservedly compared with the work of William Blake. Nothing was published under his own name, except a poor reproduction of a 'Head of Minos,' in the 'Yellow Book' (April 1904). But the illustrations to 'An Epic of Women' (1870), by his friend, Arthur William Edgar O'Shaughnessy [q. v.], are his; and his handiwork may likewise be traced in a little volume of 'Emblems' by Mrs. A. Cholmondeley (1875), where his name erroneously appears on the title-page as 'J. J. Nettleship.'

These designs reveal one aspect of his character, a delight in the manifestations of physical vigour. He was himself in his youth a model of virility. As a boy he was a bold rider in the hunting field. When he came to London he took lessons in boxing from a famous prize-fighter, and more than once walked to Brighton in a day. He accompanied a friend, (Sir) Henry Cotton, on a mountaineering expedition to the Alps, for which they trained together bare-footed in the early morning round Regent's Park. It was this delight in physical prowess and in wild life that now induced him to become a painter of animals. His studies were made almost daily in the Zoological Gardens; and for twenty-seven years (1874–1901) he exhibited spacious oil pictures of lions, tigers, etc., at the Royal Academy and for most of the period at the Grosvenor Gallery. Though always noble in conception and often effective in grouping and in colour, these pictures failed somewhat in technique and were not simple enough for the popular taste. At one time more than a dozen of them were exhibited together in the Corn Exchange at Gloucester; but a scheme for purchasing the collection fell through, and they are now dispersed. In 1880 Nettleship was invited to India by the Gaekwar of Baroda, for whom he painted a cheetah hunt as well as an equestrian portrait, and was thus enabled to see something of wild animals in their native haunts. In his later years he took to the medium of pastel, and, painting his old subjects on a smaller scale, acquired a wider measure of popularity.

Nettleship was far more than a painter. His intellectual sympathies were unusually wide. In 1868, when only twenty-seven, he published a volume of 'Essays on Robert Browning's Poetry,' which was probably the first serious study of the poet, and has passed through three editions with considerable enlargements, of which the latest is entitled 'Robert Browning: Essays and Thoughts' (1895). The book brought about an intimate friendship between the poet and his critic. Another book that shows both his mature power of literary expression and his opinions about his own art is 'George Morland and the Evolution from him of some Later Painters' (1898). Here there are touches of self-portraiture. Among the books illustrated by him may be mentioned 'Natural History Sketches among the Carnivora,' by A. Nicols (1885), and 'Icebound on Kolguev,' by A. B. R. Trevor Battye (1895).

After a long and painful illness, Nettleship died in London on 31 Aug. 1902, and was buried at Kensal Green cemetery. He married in 1876 Ada, daughter of James Hinton [q. v.], the aural surgeon; she survived him with three daughters, the eldest of whom was married to Augustus E. John, and died in Paris in 1909.

A memorial tablet in bronze, designed by Sir George Frampton, with the aid of two brother artists, who were born in the same town, Sir Alfred East and Thomas Cooper Gotch, has been placed in the parish church at Kettering.

[Personal knowledge; Sir Henry Cotton, Indian and Home Memories, 1911; Graves's Royal Academy Contributors.] J. S. C.

NEUBAUER, ADOLF (1832–1907), orientalist, was born at Kottesó, in the county of Trentsen, in the north of Hungary, on 7 March 1832. His father, Jacob Neubauer, a Jewish merchant, who was a good Talmudic scholar, belonged to a family which had received the right of residence in the same neighbourhood in 1610; his mother was Amalie Langfelder.

Designed by his father for the rabbinate, Neubauer received his first education from his cousin, Moses Neubauer, also a good Talmudist. About 1850 he became a teacher in the Jewish School at Kottesó. Soon afterwards he went to Prague, where he attended the lectures of the critical rabbinical scholar, S. J. L. Rapoport, learnt French, Italian, and Arabic, studied mathematics, and finally (15 Dec. 1853) matriculated in the university. Between 1854 and 1856 he studied oriental languages at the University of Munich. In 1857 he went to Paris, where he resided till 1868, except for visits to libraries to examine manuscripts, and a somewhat long sojourn in Jerusalem, where he held a post at the Austrian consulate. At Paris he was attracted by the rich MS. treasures of the imperial library, and made the acquaintance of Salomon Munk, who was engaged in the study of the Judæo-Arabic literature of the middle ages, of Joseph Derenbourg, of Ernest Renan, and other orientalists. The influence of his Paris surroundings led Neubauer to adopt as his life's work the study, description, and, where circumstances permitted, the publication, of mediæval Jewish manuscripts. Thus in 1861–2 he published in the 'Journal Asiatique' (vols. 18–20) numerous extracts and translations from a lexical work of David ben Abraham of Fez (10th century), the MS. of which he had discovered in a Karaite synagogue in Jerusalem; and in 1866, after a visit to St. Petersburg, he published a volume 'Aus der Petersburger Bibliothek,' consisting of excerpts from MSS. preserved there, relating to the history and literature of the Karaites. He did not altogether lay aside other studies, and in 1863 won the prize offered by the Académie des Inscriptions et Belles-Lettres for a critical exposition of the geography of Palestine, as set forth in the two Talmuds and other post-Biblical Jewish writings. His work 'La Géographie du Talmud: Mémoire couronné par l'Académie' appeared in 1868. Though not free from errors, it displayed a remarkable thoroughness and mastery of facts; and at once placed its author in the first rank of Rabbinical scholars.

Already in 1866 Neubauer had visited Oxford, for the purpose of examining the large collection of Hebrew MSS. in the

Bodleian Library. The printed Hebrew books in the library had been catalogued shortly before (1852–60) by Moritz Steinschneider; and in 1868 the curators entrusted to Neubauer the task of cataloguing the Hebrew MSS. in the library. Oxford became henceforth Neubauer's home till 1901. The work of cataloguing and properly describing the MSS. was long and arduous. In the end the catalogue appeared in 1886—a large quarto volume of 1168 columns, containing descriptions of 2602 MSS. (many consisting of from 20 to 50 distinct works), and accompanied by an atlas of forty facsimile plates, illustrating the Hebrew palæography of different countries and periods. In spite of his engrossing labours on the catalogue, Neubauer found time for much important literary work besides. In 1873 he was appointed sub-librarian of the Bodleian Library. His knowledge, not merely of Hebrew, but of foreign literature generally, was extensive; and while he was sub-librarian both the foreign and the Oriental departments of the library were maintained with great efficiency. The first to recognise, in 1890, the value for Jewish literature of the 'Genizah,' or depository attached to a synagogue, in which MSS. no longer in use were put away, he obtained for the library, in course of time, from the 'Genizah' at Old Cairo, as many as 2675 items, consisting frequently of several leaves, and including many of considerable interest and value. The catalogue of these fragments, with very detailed descriptions, was begun by Neubauer (vol. i. 1886); but it was completed and published by (Dr.) A. E. Cowley, his successor in the library, in 1906.

Neubauer also, during 1875, edited from a Bodleian and a Rouen MS. the Arabic text of the Hebrew dictionary (the 'Book of Hebrew Roots') of Abu-'l-Walid (11th century), a work of extreme importance in the history of Hebrew lexicography, which was known before only from excerpts and quotations. In 1876 he published, at the instance of Dr. Pusey, an interesting catena of more than fifty Jewish expositions of Isaiah liii., which was followed in 1877 by a volume of translations, the joint work of himself and the present writer. In the same year (1877) there appeared, in vol. xxvii. of 'L'Histoire littéraire de la France,' a long section (pp. 431–753) entitled 'Les Rabbins Français du commencement du XIVe siècle,' which, though its literary form was due to Renan, was based throughout upon materials collected by Neubauer. A continuation of this work, called 'Les Ecrivains Juifs français du XIVe siècle' (vol. 31 of 'L'Histoire littéraire,' pp. 351–802) based similarly on materials supplied by Neubauer, appeared in 1893. These two volumes on the French rabbis, stored as they are with abundant and minute information, drawn from the most varied and recondite sources, including not only Hebrew and German journals, but unpublished MSS. in the libraries of Oxford, Paris, the south of France, Spain, Italy, and other countries, form perhaps the most remarkable monument of Neubauer's industry and learning. In 1884 he was appointed reader in Rabbinic Hebrew in the University of Oxford. In 1887 he published (in the series called 'Anecdota Oxoniensia') a volume (in Hebrew) of 'Mediæval Jewish Chronicles and Chronological Notes,' which was followed in 1895 by a second volume bearing the same title. He also issued, in 1878, a previously unknown Aramaic text of the Book of Tobit, from a MS. acquired in Constantinople for the Bodleian Library; and in 1897 edited, with much valuable illustrative matter, the original Hebrew of ten chapters of Ecclesiasticus from some manuscript leaves, which had been discovered in a box of fragments from the Cairo Genizah. A constant contributor to learned periodicals both at home and abroad, he published in the 'Jewish Quarterly Review' (1888–9, vol. i.) four able articles entitled 'Where are the Ten Tribes?' and valuable essays in the Oxford 'Studia Biblica' in 1885, 1890, and 1891.

Neubauer's unremitting labours told upon his health. About 1890 his eyesight began to fail him. In 1899 he resigned his librarianship, and in 1900 his readership. He resided in Oxford, in broken health, till 1901, when he went to live under the care of his nephew, Dr. Adolf Büchler, a distinguished Rabbinical scholar, at Vienna. When Büchler was appointed vice-president of Jews' College, London, in 1906, Neubauer returned with him to England, and died unmarried at his nephew's house on 6 April 1907.

Neubauer was created M.A. of Oxford by diploma in 1873, and he was elected an hon. fellow of Exeter College in 1890. He was an hon. Ph.D. of Heidelberg, an hon. member of the Real Academia de la Historia at Madrid, and a corresponding member of the Académie des Inscriptions et Belles-Lettres in Paris. A portrait, painted by L. Campbell Taylor in 1900, is in the Bodleian Library.

Neubauer was nowhere more at home

than among the manuscripts of a library. He quickly discovered what manuscripts of value a library contained, and habitually excerpted passages of interest. As a Hebrew bibliographer, he was second only to Steinschneider (1816–1907). At Oxford he stimulated and encouraged the studies of younger scholars. By example and precept he taught the importance of independent research. He retained his racial shrewdness and his quaint humour almost to the last. Though he did not practise Jewish observances, he was strongly Jewish in sympathy. He wrote an excellent Hebrew style.

[Personal knowledge; Jewish Chronicle, 8 March 1901, 12 April 1907; Jewish World, 19 April 1907; Allgemeine Zeitung des Judentums, 3 and 10 Jan. 1908.]

S. R. D.

NEVILLE, HENRY (1837–1910), actor, whose full name was THOMAS HENRY GARTSIDE NEVILLE, born at Manchester on 20 June 1837, was son of John Neville (1787–1874), manager of the Queen's Theatre, Spring Gardens, and of his second wife, Marianne, daughter of Capt. Gartside of Woodbrow, Saddleworth, Lancashire. He was the twentieth child of a twentieth child, both being the issue of a second marriage. A brother George was also an actor.

At three he was brought on the stage in his father's arms as the child in 'Pizarro'; but he forfeited all help from his father by refusing to join the army like other members of the family. In 1857, at Preston, he took to the stage as a profession. When John Vandenhoff bade leave to the stage on 29 Oct. 1858, at the Theatre Royal, Liverpool, Neville played Cromwell to the tragedian's Cardinal Wolsey in 'King Henry VIII,' act iii. After a stern novitiate in the north of England and in Scotland, he first appeared in London at the Lyceum Theatre, under Madame Celeste, on 8 Oct. 1860, as Percy Ardent in a revival of Boucicault's 'The Irish Heiress.' Prof. Henry Morley hailed him as 'a new actor of real mark.' After other provincial engagements he spent four years at the Olympic under Robson and Emden (1862–6), and the experience proved the turning-point in his career. On 2 May 1863 he was the original Bob Brierley in Tom Taylor's 'The Ticket of Leave Man,' a character in which he made the success of his life. He played it in all some 2000 times. In May 1864, while Tom Taylor's play was still running, Neville also appeared as Petruchio in the afterpiece of 'Catherine and Petruchio,' and was highly praised for his speaking of blank verse. On 27 Oct. 1866 he was the first professional exponent of Richard Wardour in Wilkie Collins's 'The Frozen Deep,' a character originally performed by Charles Dickens.

Neville's impassioned and romantic style of acting, which gave a character to the Olympic productions, contrasted with the over-charged, highly coloured style then current at the Adelphi. But early in 1867 he migrated to the Adelphi, where, on 16 March, he was the original Job Armroyd in Watts Phillips's 'Lost in London,' and on 1 June the original Farmer Allen in Charles Reade's version of Tennyson's 'Dora.' On 31 Aug., on Miss Kate Terry's farewell, he played Romeo to her Juliet, and on 26 Dec. he was the original George Vendale in Dickens and Collins's 'No Thoroughfare.' On 7 Nov. 1868 'The Yellow Passport,' Neville's own version of Victor Hugo's 'Les Misérables,' was produced at the Olympic with himself as Jean Valjean. At the Gaiety on 19 July 1869 he played an important rôle in Gilbert's first comedy, 'An Old Score,' and at the Adelphi in June 1870 he originated the leading character of the industrious Sheffield mechanic in Charles Reade's 'Put Yourself in his Place.'

From 1873 to 1879 Neville was lessee and manager of the Olympic Theatre. After experiencing failure with Byron's comedy 'Sour Grapes' (4 Nov. 1873) and Mortimer's 'The School for Intrigue' (1 Dec.) he scored success through his acting of Lord Clancarty in Tom Taylor's 'Lady Clancarty' (March 1874), and with Oxenford's 'The Two Orphans' (14 Sept.), which enjoyed a great vogue and was revived at the end of his tenancy. Other of his original parts which were popular were the badly drawn title-part in Wills's 'Buckingham' (4 Dec. 1875), the hunchback in his own version of Coppée's 'The Violin-maker of Cremona' (2 July 1877), Franklin Blake in Wilkie Collins's 'The Moonstone' (22 Sept.), and Jeffrey Rollestone in Gilbert's 'The Ne'er-do-Weel' (2 March 1878). Subsequently he played at the Adelphi for two years, opening there on 27 Feb. 1879 as Perrinet Leclerc in Clement Scott and E. Mavriel's 'The Crimson Cross,' and acting to advantage on 7 Feb. 1880 St. Cyr in Wills's new drama, 'Ninon.' In a successful revival of 'The School for Scandal' at the Vaudeville, on 4 Feb. 1882, he proved a popular, if somewhat heavy, Charles Surface. A little later he was supporting Madame Modjeska in the provinces as the Earl of Leicester in Wingfield's 'Mary Stuart' and as Jaques in 'As You Like It.' On 25 Oct. 1884 he was the original George Kingsmill in Mr. Henry Arthur Jones's 'Saints and Sinners' at the Vaudeville.

Thenceforth Neville chiefly confined himself to romantic heroes in melodrama. On 12 Sept. 1885 he was the original Captain Temple in Pettitt and Harris's 'Human Nature' at Drury Lane, and after playing in many like pieces he went to America in 1890 with Sir Augustus Harris's company to sustain that character. He opened at the Boston Theatre, Boston, and appeared as Captain Temple for 200 nights, the play then being re-named 'The Soudan.' On his return to London he appeared at the Princess's on 11 Feb. 1892 as Jack Holt in 'The Great Metropolis,' a nautical melodrama, of which he was part author. During the succeeding fourteen years he continued with occasional interruptions to originate prominent characters in the autumn melodramas at Drury Lane. His last appearance on the stage was at His Majesty's at a matinee on 29 April 1910, when he played Sir Oliver in a scene from 'The School for Scandal.'

Neville's art reflected his buoyant, breezy nature and his generous mind. A romantic actor of the old flamboyant school, he succeeded in prolonging his popularity by an adroit compromise with latter-day conditions. He believed that the principles of acting could be taught, and in 1878 established a dramatic studio in Oxford Street, in whose fortunes he continued for many years to take a vivid interest. In 1875 he published a pamphlet giving the substance of a lecture on 'The Stage, its Past and Present in Relation to Fine Art.'

Although he lived for the theatre, Neville was a man of varied accomplishments. He painted, carved, and modelled with taste, took a keen interest in sport, was a volunteer and crack rifle shot, and once placed the St. George's Vase to the credit of his corps. He was also a man of sound business capacity, and long conducted the George Hotel at Reading.

Neville died at the Esplanade, Seaford, Sussex, on 19 June 1910, from heart failure as the result of an accident, and was buried at Denshaw, Saddleworth, Lancashire. By his marriage with Henrietta Waddell, a non-professional, he left four sons, none of them on the stage. The gross value of his estate was estimated at 18,671*l.* (see his will in *Evening Standard* of 23 Nov. 1910). A full-length portrait in oils of him as Count Almaviva in Mortimer's 'The School for Intrigue' (1874), by J. Walton, is in the Garrick Club.

[Pascoe's Dramatic List; Prof. Henry Morley's Journal of a London Playgoer; R. J. Broadbent's Annals of the Liverpool Stage; The Era Almanack, 1887, p. 36; Dutton Cook's Nights at the Play; Mowbray Morris's Essays in Theatrical Criticism; Joseph Knight's Theatrical Notes; The Green Room Book, 1909; Daily Telegraph, 20 June 1910; private information and personal research.] W. J. L.

NEWMARCH, CHARLES HENRY (1824–1903), divine and author, born at Burford, Oxfordshire, on 30 March 1824, was second son of George Newmarch, solicitor, of Cirencester, by Mary his wife. He traced his descent as far back as the Norman Conquest. After education from March 1837 at Rugby, whither his elder brother, George Frederick, had gone in 1830, he spent some time in the merchant shipping service and in Eastern travel. Of his Eastern experience he gave an account in 'Five Years in the East,' published in 1847 under the pseudonym of R. N. Hutton, which attracted favourable attention. In 1848 appeared anonymously his interesting 'Recollections of Rugby, by an old Rugbeian' (12mo), and in the same year a novel, 'Jealousy' (3 vols.). Settling in Cirencester, Newmarch showed keen interest in the antiquities of the neighbourhood, and in 1850 wrote with Professor James Buckman [q. v.] 'Illustrations of the Remains of Roman Art in Cirencester' (4to; 2nd edit. 1851). He was chiefly instrumental in founding in 1851 the 'Cirencester and Swindon Express,' which was soon amalgamated with the 'Wilts and Gloucester Standard.' He was joint editor of the paper, and till the end of his life was a regular contributor under the name of 'Rambler.' He issued with his brother in 1868 a brief account of the 'Newmarch pedigree.'

Newmarch matriculated at Corpus Christi College, Cambridge, in 1851, graduating B.A. in 1855. Taking holy orders in 1854, he was from 1856 to 1893 rector of Wardley-cum-Belton, Rutland, and rural dean of the district from 1857 to 1867. He was greatly interested in agricultural matters, contributing much to 'Bell's Life' on the subject; he championed the cause of the village labourers, who stoutly defended him against the attacks of Joseph Arch, when Arch visited Belton in his tour of the village districts in 1872. He took an active part in church building in Rutland, and restored the chancel of his parish church. Increasing deafness led to his retirement in 1893 to 37 Upper Grosvenor Road, Tunbridge Wells, where he died on 14 June 1903.

Newmarch married on 6 Feb. 1855, at Leckhampton, Anne Straford of Cheltenham and Charlton Kings, and had issue two sons and three daughters. One daughter survived him. A tablet to his memory was erected in Belton church in 1912.

[The Times, 20 June 1903; Guardian, 1 July 1903; Rugby School Register, 1901, ii. 293; information from son-in-law, the Rev. J. B. Booth.] W. B. O.

NEWNES, Sir GEORGE, first baronet (1851–1910), newspaper and magazine projector, born at Glenorchy House, Matlock, on 13 March 1851, was youngest son of three sons and three daughters of Thomas Mold Newnes (*d.* 1883), a congregational minister at Matlock, by his wife Sarah (*d.* 1885), daughter of Daniel Urquhart of Dundee. Educated at Silcoates, Yorkshire, and at the City of London School, he was apprenticed when sixteen to a wholesale firm in the City of London. Three years after completing his apprenticeship he was placed by another London firm of dealers in fancy goods in charge of a branch business in Manchester, and there suddenly conceived the idea of a journal which should consist wholly of popularly entertaining and interesting anecdotes, or, as he termed, them 'tit-bits,' extracted from all available sources. This idea proved the foundation of his fortune. Within twelve months he made plans for producing such a periodical. Negotiations in Manchester for financial help to the extent of 500*l.* failed. Scraping together all the money he could, Newnes accordingly produced with his own resources on 2 Oct. 1881 the first number of the weekly paper which he christened 'Tit-Bits.' He engaged the Newsboys' Brigade to sell it in the streets. Within two hours 5000 copies were sold.

The paper grew in popularity, and after producing it in Manchester for three years with increasing success, Newnes transferred the publication to London, where he opened offices first in Farringdon Street, and later in Burleigh Street and Southampton Street. Other bold innovations upon a publisher's business followed. By instituting the 'Tit-Bits' prize competitions, including the offer (on 17 Nov. 1883) of a house, 'Tit-Bits Villa,' at Dulwich, of the value of 800*l.* as one of the first prizes, he appealed in a new fashion to a widespread popular instinct which has since been developed to immense profit and in endless ways by the proprietors of other publications. Equally original and successful was his insurance plan, which constituted each copy of 'Tit-Bits' a railway accident policy for the purchaser. These expensive schemes, which were launched by Newnes only after most careful consideration, and in spite of general predictions of failure, gave excellent returns. One of his prizes, a situation in the office of 'Tit-Bits,' was won in Sept. 1884 by Mr. Cyril Arthur Pearson, who rose to be manager of the paper, and left in July 1890 to start 'Pearson's Weekly.' A frequent contributor to the page 'Answers to Correspondents' was Mr. Alfred Harmsworth (now Lord Northcliffe), who as a result founded in 1888 'Answers,' a rival paper to Tit-Bits. The popularity of the competitions became so great that in one day no less than two hundred sacks of letters were received. The paper meanwhile improved. It ceased to be a collection of extracts only and included in increasing proportion contributions by authors of note.

In 1890 Newnes, at the suggestion of his schoolfellow, William Thomas Stead, brought out the first number of the 'Review of Reviews,' with Stead as editor; but after a few months Stead and Newnes separated, Stead taking sole charge of the 'Review,' while Newnes in 1891 started the 'Strand Magazine,' combining on a large scale popular illustration with popular literary matter at the price of sixpence. In January 1893 he made a still bolder venture. At the close of 1892 the 'Pall Mall Gazette,' an evening daily newspaper, which was then a liberal journal, edited by (Sir) E. T. Cook, suddenly changed hands and politics. Newnes promptly engaged the services of the whole superseded literary staff of the 'Pall Mall Gazette' and started on 31 Jan. 1893 the 'Westminster Gazette' as a new organ of the liberal party. Newnes's friends in the party were nervous about investing their money, but Newnes had full confidence in himself, and succeeded in giving the paper financial stability. His publishing firm was incorporated in 1891 as a limited company with a capital of 400,000*l.* and reconstructed in 1897, when the capital was increased to 1,000,000*l.* Among the new ventures which followed from the house of George Newnes, Ltd., were: 'Country Life' (1897), the 'Ladies' Field,' the 'Wide World Magazine' (both in 1898), and 'C. B. Fry's Magazine' (1904).

Newnes entered Parliament in 1885 as member for the Newmarket division of Cambridgeshire, which he represented in the liberal interest until 1895, when he lost his seat, and was rewarded for his services to his party by a baronetcy. The prime minister, Lord Rosebery, stated that the honour was conferred on him as a pioneer of clean popular literature. Newnes was returned for Swansea Town in 1900, and represented that constituency until the general election of 1910.

Newnes applied much of his wealth to public purposes. His London residence was on Putney Heath, and he took great interest in the welfare of Putney. In 1897, the year of the diamond jubilee, he presented a new and spacious library at a cost of 16,000*l.*, the building being opened by Lord Russell of Killowen, the lord chief justice, in May 1899. In 1898 he fitted out at his own expense the South Polar Expedition, under the guidance of the Norwegian explorer C. E. Borchgrevinck. His sympathy with suffering was always strong. The painful sight of horses toiling up the steep ascent from Lynmouth to Lynton in Devon, where he acquired a country residence, led him to build a cliff railway there. Similarly he met the difficulty which was felt by invalids in mounting to the heights at his birthplace, Matlock, by building a cable railway for their use, which he presented to the town on 28 March 1893. He died at his residence in Lynton on 9 June 1910, and was buried at Lynton.

Newnes married in 1875 Priscilla Jenney, daughter of the Rev. James Hillyard of Leicester, by whom he had two sons, of whom the younger, Arthur, died in childhood. The elder son, Frank Hillyard Newnes, his successor in the baronetcy, has been since 1906 M.P. for Bassetlaw, Nottinghamshire.

A memorial tablet in the corridor near the entrance to the Putney library was unveiled on 23 May 1911; it consists of a bronze bust of Newnes in relief against a white marble background, designed by Mr. Oliver Wheatley. A cartoon portrait by 'Spy' appeared in 'Vanity Fair' in 1894.

[Life of Sir George Newnes, by Hulda Friederichs (with portrait), 1911; T. H. S. Escott, Masters of English Journalism, 1911; Mitchell's Newspaper Directory, 1911, p. 16; Putney News-letter, 12 June 1910; Tit-Bits, 25 June 1910; The Times, 10 June 1910; Whitaker's Red Book of Commerce; private information.] C. W.

NEWTON, ALFRED (1829–1907), zoologist, born at Geneva on 11 June 1829, was fifth son of William Newton of Elveden, Suffolk, sometime M.P. for Ipswich, and Elizabeth, daughter of Richard Slater Milnes of Fryston, Yorkshire, and aunt of Richard Monckton Milnes first Baron Houghton [q. v.]. In 1848 Newton left home for Magdalene College, Cambridge. He obtained the English essay prize there in two successive years and graduated B.A. in 1853. From 1854 until 1863 he held the Drury travelling fellowship, making use of the endowment in the study of ornithology, a subject to which he had been attached from boyhood. He visited Lapland with John Wolley, the ornithologist, in the summer of 1855, and in 1858 they went together to Iceland and sought out the last nesting-place of the great auk. Newton stayed in the West Indies in 1857 and went thence to North America. In 1864 he paid a visit to Spitzbergen on the yacht of Sir Edmund Birkbeck, and he made several summer voyages round the British Isles with the ornithologist Henry Evans of Derby, so that he was acquainted with almost all the breeding-places of their sea-birds. All these travels he accomplished in spite of lameness due to hip-joint disease in childhood, which later in life was aggravated by an injury to the other leg. Newton made no complaint, though he had to use two sticks instead of one, and went about his work with undiminished assiduity. He wrote the 'Zoology of Ancient Europe' in 1862 and the 'Ornithology of Iceland' in 1863. A chair of zoology and comparative anatomy was founded at Cambridge, and Newton was appointed the first professor in March 1866; he held office till his death. His lectures were the least important part of his work as professor. The subject was almost unknown in the university, whether among the undergraduates or the ruling authorities, and the professor had to create a general interest in it and to improve the museum and other apparatus for its study. Newton did his best to make the acquaintance of every undergraduate who had any taste for natural history and to encourage him. Every Sunday evening at his rooms in the old lodge of Magdalene such undergraduates found a cheery welcome and pleasant talk, and many of them became lifelong friends of the professor and of one another. Charles Kingsley was sometimes there and talked on the land tortoise and the red deer or on the natural history of the New Forest. George Robert Crotch, the first coleopterist of his time, was generally present, and started fresh paradoxes on every possible subject every evening. Newton's own talk, which was most often on birds or on the countries to which he had travelled, was always full, exact, and interesting, and exhibited a pleasant sense of humour. The rooms in which this circle met contained a fine ornithological library, and where the walls were vacant a few pictures of birds, of which the finest was a drawing of gerfalcons by Wolff, the celebrated artist of birds. The accuracy which Newton encouraged in others he required from himself, and for this reason his works often took long to complete. His large book 'Ootheca Wolleyana,' an account of the collection of birds' eggs made by his friend John Wolley, appeared from 1864 to 1902, and contains an interesting biography of the collector. The collection of eggs was given to Newton by Wolley's father, and Newton presented it, with his own large collection, to the University of Cambridge. The 'Dictionary of Birds,' which appeared 1893–6, is probably his greatest work. He had prepared himself for such a book by his 'Ornithology of Iceland,' published in Baring Gould's 'Iceland' in 1863; his 'Aves' in the 'Record of Zoological Literature,' vols. i.-vi.; his 'Birds of Greenland,' printed in the 'Arctic Manual'; and by many papers in the 'Ibis' and other scientific journals. He wrote the article on ornithology in the ninth edition of the 'Encyclopædia Britannica,' and that on Gilbert White in this Dictionary; he edited the 'Ibis' from 1865 to 1870, the 'Zoological Record' from 1870 to 1872, and the first two volumes of the fourth edition of Yarrell's 'British Birds,' 1871–82. He was elected F.R.S. in 1870, and received the royal medal of the society in 1900, and the gold medal of the Linnæan Society in the same year. He used to attend the meetings of the British Association, and it was due to its action, stimulated by him, that the first three acts of parliament for the protection of birds were passed. He was for several years chairman of the committee for studying the migration of birds appointed by that association, and he was constantly referred to by the public and by individual students as the chief authority of his time on ornithology, and always promptly endeavoured to answer the questions put to him. He was one of the founders of the British Ornithologists' Union and was a frequent contributor to its journal, the 'Ibis.' The dodo and the great auk were birds in which he took particular interest, and when his brother, Edward Newton, brought him from Mauritius a fine series of dodo bones Newton generously sent some as a gift to Professor Schlegel of Leyden, who had been one of his chief opponents as regards the columbine affinities of the bird. Towards the end of his life he appointed Mr. William Bateson to lecture for him, but continued to show active interest in all the other work of his professorship, and was always a constant resident during term-time at Cambridge. Throughout his career he took a large part in university affairs, and conducted with his own hand a very heavy public and private correspondence. In his last years some of the fellows of Magdalene thought him too arbitrary in his attachment to simple food and old usages, but outside their microcosm the Johnsonian force with which he expressed his convictions only added to the charm of his society. His final illness was a cardiac failure, and when the Master of Magdalene paid a last visit to him Newton said 'God bless all my friends, God bless the college, and may the study of zoology continue to flourish in this university!' He died unmarried on 7 June 1907. He was buried in the Huntingdon Road cemetery at Cambridge.

His portrait, by Lowes Dickinson, is at Magdalene College, Cambridge.

[Proc. Roy. Soc., 80 B., 1908; Trans. Norfolk Nat. Soc. viii. 1908; W. H. Hudleston's account in the Ibis, 1907; Newton's Memoir of John Wolley, 1902; C. B. Moffat, Life and Letters of A. G. More, 1898; F. Darwin, Life and Letters of Charles Darwin, 1887; H. E. Litchfield, Emma Darwin: a Century of Family Letters, Cambridge, 1904 (privately printed); A. C. Benson, Leaves of the Tree, 1911, pp. 132 seq.; Field, 15 June 1907; Newton's works; personal knowledge.] N. M.

NICHOLSON, Sir CHARLES, first baronet (1808–1903), chancellor of the University of Sydney, New South Wales, born at Bedale, Yorkshire, on 23 Nov. 1808, was only surviving child of Charles Nicholson of London, by Barbara, youngest daughter of John Ascough of Bedale. Graduating M.D. at Edinburgh University in 1833, he emigrated to Australia, and settled on some property belonging to his uncle near Sydney in May 1834. Here for some time he practised as a physician with success. A good classical scholar, well read in history and science, an able writer and lucid speaker, he soon prominently identified himself with the social and political interests of the colony. In June 1843 he was returned to the first legislative council of New South Wales as one of the five members for the Port Phillip district (now the state of Victoria). In July 1848, and again in Sept. 1851, he was elected member for the county of Argyle. From 2 May 1844 to 19 May 1846 he was chairman of committees of the legislative council, and on 20 May 1847, in May 1849, and October 1851, he was chosen speaker, retaining the office until the grant to the colony of responsible government in 1855–6, when he became for a short time a member of the executive council.

When in 1859 the district of Moreton Bay was separated from New South Wales and formed into the colony of Queensland, Nicholson was nominated on 1 May 1860 a member of the legislative council of the new colony, and was president during the first session, resigning the office on 28 Aug. 1860.

Nicholson was from the first a powerful advocate of popular education in New South Wales. He was a member of the select committee to inquire into the state of education in the colony moved for by Robert Lowe (afterwards Lord Sherbrooke), on whose report the educational systems of the Australian colonies have in the main been based. But his name is more intimately associated with the foundation of the University of Sydney. He watched over its early fortunes with unremitting care, was a generous donor to its funds, and endowed it with many valuable gifts, including the museum of Egyptian, Etruscan, Greek, and Roman antiquities which he collected with much personal exertion and at considerable cost. He was instrumental in obtaining a grant of arms from the Heralds' College in 1857, and the royal charter from Queen Victoria in 1858. On 3 March 1851 he was unanimously elected vice-provost, and delivered an inaugural address at the opening of the university on 11 Oct. 1852. He was chancellor from 13 March 1854 till 1862, when he left Australia permanently for England. There he chiefly resided in the country near London, actively occupied as a magistrate, as chairman of the Liverpool and London and Globe Insurance Co., and as director of other undertakings, at the same time interesting himself in Egyptian and classical and Hebrew scholarship. Gardening was his chief source of recreation. Preserving his vigour till the end, he died on 8 Nov. 1903 at his residence, The Grange, Totteridge, Hertfordshire, and was buried in Totteridge churchyard.

Nicholson was knighted by patent on 1 March 1852, and was the first Australian to be created a baronet (of Luddenham, N.S.W.) (8 April 1859). He was made hon. D.C.L. of Oxford in 1857, hon. LL.D. of Cambridge in 1868, and hon. LL.D. of Edinburgh in 1886.

Nicholson married on 8 Aug. 1865 Sarah Elizabeth, eldest daughter of Archibald Keightley, registrar of the Charterhouse, London, and had three sons, of whom the eldest, Charles, succeeded to the baronetcy. A portrait by H. W. Phillips hangs in the hall of the university at Sydney; another by H. A. Olivier belongs to his widow.

[Burke's Colonial Gentry, i. 289; The Times, 10 Nov. 1903; Mennell's Dictionary of Australasian Biography, 1892; Martin's Life and Letters of Robert Lowe, Viscount Sherbrooke, 1893; Sir G. Bowen's Thirty Years of Colonial Government, 1889; Barff's Short Historical Account of Sydney University, 1902; Lancet, 21 Nov. 1903; Colonial Office Records; information from relatives.] C. A.

NICHOLSON, GEORGE (1847–1908), botanist, born at Ripon, Yorkshire, on 4 Dec. 1847, was son of a nurseryman, and was brought up to his father's calling. After spending some time in the gardens of Messrs. Fisher Holmes at Sheffield, he went for two years to the municipal nurseries of La Muette, Paris, and then to those of Messrs. Low at Clapton. In 1873 he was appointed, after competitive examination, clerk to John Smith, the curator at Kew; in 1886 he succeeded Smith as curator. He retired owing to ill-health in 1901, but continued his botanical researches at Kew as far as his strength allowed.

A fluent speaker in French and German, Nicholson paid holiday visits to France and Switzerland, and travelled in Germany, Northern Italy, and Spain. Impressed with the value of a knowledge of foreign languages to young gardeners, he devoted much of his leisure to teaching some of them French. In 1893 he went officially to the Chicago Exhibition, as one of the judges in the horticultural section; and he took the opportunity to study the forest trees of the United States. In 1902, the year after his retirement, he visited New York as delegate of the Royal Horticultural Society to the Plant-Breeding Conference.

Until 1886 Nicholson devoted much attention to the critical study of British flowering plants. His first published work, 'Wild Flora of Kew Gardens,' appeared in the 'Journal of Botany' for 1875. In the same year he joined the Botanical Exchange Club, and to its 'Reports' and to the 'Journal of Botany' he contributed notes on such segregates as those of *Rosa* and of *Cardamine pratensis*. The 'Wild Fauna and Flora of Kew Gardens,' issued in the 'Kew Bulletin' in 1906, which expanded his paper of 1875, was largely his work. Out of 2000 fungi enumerated, 500 were found by Nicholson. His herbarium of British plants was presented, towards the close of his life, to the University of Aberdeen, through his friend James Trail, professor of botany there.

When Sir Joseph Hooker [q. v. Suppl. II] was reorganising and extending the arboretum at Kew, he found an able coadjutor in Nicholson, who wrote monographs on the genera *Acer* and *Quercus* and twenty articles on the Kew Arboretum in the 'Gardeners' Chronicle,' during 1881-3. A valuable herbarium which he formed of trees and shrubs was purchased by the trustees of the Bentham fund in 1889 and presented to Kew. His 'Hand-list of Trees and Shrubs grown at Kew' (anon. 2 pts. 1894–6) attested the fulness of his knowledge of this class of plants. Nicholson's *magnum opus* was 'The Dictionary of Gardening' (4 vols. 1885–9; enlarged edit. in French, by his friend M. Mottet, 1892–9; two supplementary vols. to the English edition, 1900–1). This standard work of reference, most of which was not only edited but written by Nicholson, did for the extended horticulture of the nineteenth century what Philip Miller's Dictionary did for that of the eighteenth.

Of gentle, unselfish character, he was chosen first president on the foundation of the Kew Guild in 1894. Elected an associate of the Linnean Society in 1886, Nicholson became a fellow in 1898, and he was awarded the Veitchian medal of the Royal Horticultural Society in 1894, and the Victoria medal in 1897. To him was dedicated in 1895 the 48th volume of the 'Garden,' a paper to which he was a large contributor. Dr. Udo Dammer in 1901 named a Central American palm *Neonicholsonia Georgei*. Fond of athletic exercises, he brought on, by his devotion to mountaineering, heart trouble, of which he died at Richmond, on 20 Sept. 1908. His remains were cremated. He married in 1875 Elizabeth Naylor Bell; but she died soon after, leaving a son, James Bell Nicholson, now a lieutenant in the navy.

[Gardeners' Chron. 1908, ii. 239 (with portrait); Journal of Botany, 1908, p. 337 (with the same portrait); Proc. Linnean Soc. 1908–9, pp. 48–9; Journal of the Kew Guild.]

G. S. B.

NICOL, ERSKINE (1825–1904), painter, born in Leith on 3 July 1825, was eldest son (in a family of five sons and one daughter) of James Main Nicol of that city by his wife Margaret Alexander. After a brief commercial education he became a house-painter, but quickly turned to art. He was an unusually youthful student at the Trustees' Academy, Edinburgh, where he came under the joint instruction of Sir William Allan [q. v.] and Thomas Duncan [q. v.]. At fifteen he exhibited a landscape at the Royal Scottish Academy, and two years later two (one painted in England) and a chalk portrait. For a time he filled the post of drawing-master in Leith Academy.

After a hard struggle at Leith to earn a living by his pencil, he went to Dublin in 1846, and for the next four or five years taught privately there, and not, as is frequently said, under the Science and Art Department. At Dublin he discovered the humours of Irish peasant life, the unvarying subject for his brush for a quarter of a century. From Ireland, where he had a patron in his friend Mr. Armstrong of Rathmines, he sent two examples of this kind to the Scottish Academy exhibitions of 1849–50. In 1850 he settled in Edinburgh, where his reputation was already established. Most of the work he exhibited at the R.S.A. was purchased by well-known collectors like Mr. John Miller of Liverpool and Mr. John Tennant of Glasgow. He was elected an associate of the Scottish Academy in 1851 and a full member in 1859. His diploma work for the Scottish Academy, 'The Day after the Fair,' is in the National Gallery, Edinburgh.

In 1862 Nicol left Edinburgh for London, at first renting a studio in St. John's Wood, and from 1864 till the end of his painting career residing at 24 Dawson Place, Pembridge Square, W. Though he finished his canvases in Edinburgh or London, Nicol for several months of each year studied his Irish subjects at first hand in co. Westmeath, where he built himself a studio at Clonave, Deravaragh. When his health no longer permitted the journey to Ireland, he abandoned Irish humble life for that of Scotland, which he studied at Pitlochry, where he fitted up a disused church as a studio.

Nicol contributed to the Royal Academy first in 1851, and then in 1857–8; from 1861 to 1879, there was only a break in 1870. Elected an associate in 1866, he joined the retired list after an acute illness in 1885. His portrait of Dr. George Skene Keith, which was exhibited at the R.A.

in 1893, is dated the previous year, but he practically ceased to paint in oils in 1885. He excelled also in water-colours, and occasionally painted in that medium at a later date. One of his water-colours, 'Clout the auld' (1886), is in the Ashbee collection in the Victoria and Albert Museum.

Although Nicol's humour was broader in his earlier than in his later canvases, he was always successful as a comic story-teller whose first-rate craftsmanship was never sacrificed to the pursuit of popularity. His mature drawing was generally sound and quick, and his colour was pleasing and sometimes rich and even subtle. After 1885 he lived in retirement, dividing his time between Crieff, Torduff House, Colinton, Midlothian, and The Dell, Feltham, where he died on 8 March 1904. He was buried in the burial-ground of his second wife's family at Rottingdean.

The jovial element in Nicol's canvases had no place in his life. His disposition was grave, shy, and reserved. Nicol was twice married: (1) in 1851 to Janet Watson, who died in 1863, leaving a son (Mr. John Watson Nicol, a painter) and a daughter; (2) in 1865 to Margaret Mary Wood, who survived him, and by whom he had two sons (the elder, Mr. Erskine Edwin Nicol, a painter) and a daughter.

Nicol's principal works, many of which were engraved, were: 'Irish Merry Making' (R.S.A. 1856); 'Donnybrook Fair' (1859); 'Renewal of the Lease Refused' (R.A. 1863), 'Waiting for the Train' (R.A. 1864); 'A Deputation' (R.A. 1865); 'Paying the Rent,' 'Missed it,' and 'Both Puzzled' (R.A. 1866, the last engraved by W. H. Simmons); 'A Country Booking-office' (R.A. 1867); 'A China Merchant' and 'The Cross-roads' (R.A. 1868); 'A Disputed Boundary' (R.A. 1869); 'The Fisher's Knot' (R.A. 1871); 'Steady, Johnnie, Steady' (R.A. 1873, engraved by Simmons); 'The New Vintage' (R.A. 1875); 'The Sabbath Day' (R.A. 1875, engraved by Simmons); 'Looking out for a Safe Investment' (engraved by Simmons) and 'A Storm at Sea' (R.A. 1876); 'Unwillingly to School' (R.A. 1877); 'The Missing Boat' (R.A. 1878); 'Interviewing their Member' (R.A. 1879, engraved by C. E. Deblois).

For the first volume of 'Good Words,' 1860–1, Nicol did three drawings. He is represented in the Glasgow Corporation Galleries by an oil painting, 'Beggar my Neighbour,' and in the Aberdeen Gallery by a water-colour. His oil paintings 'Wayside Prayers' (1852) and 'The Emigrants' (1864) in the Tate Gallery are poor examples.

Nicol's portrait, by Sir William Fettes Douglas, exhibited at the R.S.A. in 1862, belongs to the Scottish Academy.

[Private information; Graves's Royal Academy Exhibitors; James Caw's Scottish Painting, Past and Present.] D. S. M.

NICOLSON, Mrs. ADELA FLORENCE, 'Laurence Hope' (1865–1904), poetess, born at Stoke House, Stoke Bishop, Gloucestershire, on 9 April 1865, was daughter of Arthur Cory, colonel in the Indian army, by his wife Fanny Elizabeth Griffin. She was educated at a private school in Richmond, and afterwards went to reside with her parents in India. In 1889 she married Colonel Malcolm Hassels Nicolson of the Bengal army [see below] and settled at Madras. The name Violet, by which her husband called her, was not baptismal. Mrs. Nicolson devoted her leisure to poetry. Her first volume, in which she first adopted the pseudonym of 'Laurence Hope,' 'The Garden of Kama and other Love Lyrics from India, arranged in Verse by Laurence Hope,' was published in 1901. Generally reviewed as the work of a man, it attracted considerable attention and was reissued as 'Songs from the Garden of Kama' in 1908. How far the substance of the poems was drawn from Indian originals was a matter of doubt. They are marked by an oriental luxuriance of passion, but the influence of Swinburne and other modern English poets is evident in diction and versification. Two other volumes under the same pseudonym, 'Stars of the Desert' (1903) and 'Indian Love,' published posthumously in 1905, display similar characteristics and confirmed without enhancing their author's reputation. Some of her shorter poems have become popular in musical settings. Mrs. Nicolson died by her own hand, of poisoning by perchloride of mercury, on 4 Oct. 1904, at Dunmore House, Madras. She had suffered acute depression since her husband's death two months before. She was buried, like General Nicolson, in St. Mary's cemetery, Madras. She left one son, Malcolm Josceline Nicolson.

Malcolm Hassels Nicolson (1843–1904), general, son of Major Malcolm Nicolson of the Bengal army, was born on 11 June 1843. He entered the army in 1859 as ensign in the Bombay infantry, and was promoted lieutenant in 1862. Serving in the Abyssinian campaign of 1867–8, he was present at the action at Azogel and at the capture of Magdala, and received the Abyssinian medal. He attained the rank of captain in 1869. During the Afghan war of 1878–80 he saw much active service. He took part in the occupation of Kandahar and fought at Ahmed Khel and Urzoo. He was mentioned in despatches, and in 1879, while the war was in progress, he was promoted major. After the war he received the Afghan medal with one clasp, and in March 1881 the brevet rank of lieutenant-colonel. He became army colonel in 1885 and substantive colonel in 1894. For his services in the Zhob Valley campaign of 1890 he was again mentioned in despatches, and he was made C.B. in 1891. From 1891 to 1894 he was aide-de-camp to Queen Victoria, being promoted major-general in the latter year and lieutenant-general in 1899. A good service pension was conferred on him in 1893. He died on 7 Aug. 1904 at Mackay's Gardens nursing home, Madras, and was buried in St. Mary's cemetery. General Nicolson was an expert linguist, having passed the interpreter's test in Baluchi, Brahui, and Persian, and the higher standard in Pushtu.

[Madras Mail, 5 Oct. 1904; Athenæum, 29 Oct. 1904; Gent. Mag., N.S. viii. 634; The Times, 11 Aug. 1904; Army Lists; information supplied by friends.] F. L. B.

NIGHTINGALE, FLORENCE (1820–1910), reformer of hospital nursing, born at the Villa La Columbaia, Florence, on 12 May 1820, was named after the city of her birth. Her father, William Edward Nightingale (1794–1874), was son of William Shore, long a banker at Sheffield; he was a highly cultured country gentleman of ample means, and a great lover of travel. When he came of age on 21 Feb. 1815 he assumed by royal sign-manual the surname of Nightingale on inheriting the Derbyshire estates of Lea Hurst and Woodend of his mother's uncle, Peter Nightingale (*d.* unmarried 1803). On 1 June 1818 he married Frances, daughter of William Smith (1756–1835) [q. v.], a strong supporter of the abolition of slavery. The issue was two daughters, of whom Florence was the younger. Her elder sister, Frances Parthenope (*d.* 1890), so called from the classical name of Naples, her birthplace, married in 1858, as his second wife, Sir Harry Verney [q. v.], second baronet, of Claydon, Buckinghamshire.

Florence Nightingale's first home was at her father's house, Lea Hall, in Derbyshire. About 1825 the family moved to Lea Hurst, which Nightingale had just built. In 1826 he also bought Embley Park, in Hampshire, serving the office of high sheriff of that county in 1828. It became the custom of the family to spend the summer at Lea Hurst and the winter at Embley Park, with an occasional visit to London. Miss Nightingale enjoyed under her father's roof a liberal education, but she chafed at the narrow opportunities of activity offered to girls of her station in life. She engaged in cottage visiting, and developed a love of animals. But her chief interest lay in tending the sick. Anxious to undertake more important responsibilities than home offered her she visited hospitals in London and the country with a view to finding what scope for activity offered there. Nursing was then reckoned in England a menial employment needing neither study nor intelligence; nor was it viewed as a work of mercy or philanthropy. Sidney Herbert, afterwards Lord Herbert of Lea [q. v.], and his wife were Miss Nightingale's neighbours at Wilton House, not far from Embley Park. A close friendship with them stimulated her philanthropic and intellectual instincts. Her horizon was widened, too, by intercourse with enlightened members of her mother's family, by acquaintance with Madame Mohl and her husband, and possibly by a chance meeting in girlhood with Mrs. Elizabeth Fry.

Miss Nightingale's hospital visits seem to have begun in 1844, and were continued at home and abroad for eleven years. She spent the winter and spring of 1849–50 with friends of her family, Mr. and Mrs. Bracebridge, in a long tour through Egypt. On the journey from Paris she met two sisters of St. Vincent de Paul, who gave her an introduction to the house of their order at Alexandria, where she carefully inspected their schools and 'Miséricorde.' She recognised that the Roman Catholic sisterhoods in France, with their discipline and their organisation, made better nurses than she found in her own country (cf. MISS NIGHTINGALE, *Letters from Egypt*, privately printed). On her way back to England she paid a first visit (31 July to 13 Aug. 1850) to the Institute of Protestant Deaconesses at Kaiserswerth on the Rhine near Düsseldorf. The institute had been founded on a very humble scale in 1833 for the care of the destitute by Theodor Fliedner, protestant pastor of Kaiserswerth, and had since grown into a training school for women teachers and for nurses of the sick. The institution was run on the lines of poverty, simplicity, and common sense. A very brief experience of the Kaiserswerth

Institute convinced Miss Nightingale of the possibilities of making nursing a 'calling' for ladies and no mere desultory occupation. Next year she spent some four months at Kaiserswerth (July to October), and went through a regular course of training as a sick nurse. On her return to her home at Embley Park she published a short account of Kaiserswerth, in which she spoke frankly of the dulness of the ordinary home life of English girls. Late in life she wrote of her visits to Kaiserswerth, 'Never have I met with a higher love, a purer devotion, than there. There was no neglect. It was the more remarkable, because many of the deaconesses had been only peasants: none were gentlewomen when I was there.' There followed further visits to London hospitals, and in the autumn of 1852 she inspected those of Edinburgh and Dublin. Great part of 1853 was devoted to various types of hospitals at Paris. Late in the same year she accepted her first administrative post. On 12 Aug. 1853 she became superintendent of the Hospital for Invalid Gentlewomen, which was established in 1850 in Chandos Street by Lady Canning. Miss Nightingale moved the institution to No. 1 Upper (now 90) Harley Street. In 1910 it was resettled at 19 Lisson Grove, N.W., and was then renamed after Miss Nightingale.

In March 1854 the Crimean war broke out, and the reports of the sufferings of the sick and wounded in the English camps stirred English feeling to its depths. In letters to 'The Times' (Sir) William Howard Russell [q. v. Suppl. II], the correspondent, described the terrible neglect of the wounded, and the 'disgraceful antithesis' between the neglect of our men and the careful nursing of the French wounded. 'Are there no devoted women among us,' he wrote, 'able and willing to go forth to minister to the sick and suffering soldiers of the East in the hospitals of Scutari? Are none of the daughters of England, at this extreme hour of need, ready for such a work of mercy? Must we fall so far below the French in self-sacrifice and devotedness?' (cf. *The Times*, 15 and 22 Sept. 1854). On 14 Oct. Miss Nightingale offered her services to the War Office; but before her offer reached her friend, Sidney Herbert, then secretary of state for war, he himself had written to her on the same day, and proposed that she should go out to the Crimea: 'I receive numbers of offers from ladies to go out' (he told Miss Nightingale), 'but they are ladies who have no conception of what a hospital is, nor of the nature of its duties. . . . My question simply is, Would you listen to the request to go out and supervise the whole thing? You would, of course, have plenary authority over all the nurses, and I think I could secure you the fullest assistance and co-operation from the medical staff, and you would also have an unlimited power of drawing on the government for whatever you think requisite for the success of your mission.' Miss Nightingale made her plans with extraordinary speed. On 17 Oct. Lady Canning, who helped her in the choice of nurses, wrote of her, 'She has such nerve and skill, and is so gentle and wise and quiet; even now she is in no bustle or hurry, though so much is on her hands, and such numbers of people volunteer their services' (HARE'S *Story of two Noble Lives*). On 21 Oct., within a week of receiving Herbert's letter, Miss Nightingale embarked for the Crimea, with thirty-eight nurses (ten Roman Catholic sisters, eight sisters of mercy of the Church of England, six nurses from St. John's Institute, and fourteen from various hospitals); her friends, Mr. and Mrs. Bracebridge, also went with her. Scutari was reached on 4 Nov., the eve of the battle of Inkerman. Miss Nightingale's official title was 'Superintendent of the Female Nurses in the Hospitals in the East'; but she came to be known generally as 'The Lady-in-Chief.'

Her headquarters were in the barrack hospital at Scutari, a huge dismal place, reeking with dirt and infection. Stores, urgently needed, had not got beyond Varna, or were lost at sea. 'There were no vessels for water or utensils of any kind; no soap, towels, or clothes, no hospital clothes; the men lying in their uniforms, stiff with gore and covered with filth to a degree and of a kind no one could write about; their persons covered with vermin.' One of the nurses, a week after arrival, wrote home, 'We have not seen a drop of milk, and the bread is extremely sour. The butter is most filthy; it is Irish butter in a state of decomposition; and the meat is more like moist leather than food. Potatoes we are waiting for, until they arrive from France.' Sidney Godolphin Osborne went out to visit Scutari soon after Miss Nightingale's arrival, and in a report on the hospital accommodation described the complete absence of 'the commonest provision for the exigencies' of the hour (cf. OSBORNE'S *Scutari and its Hospitals*, 1855). Miss Nightingale's difficulties are incapable of exaggeration. The military and medical authorities already on the spot viewed her intervention as a reflection on themselves. Many of her own volunteers were inexperienced, and the roughness of the orderlies was offensive to women of refinement. But Miss Nightingale's quiet resolution and dignity, her powers of organisation and discipline rapidly worked a revolution.

Before the end of the year Miss Nightingale and her companions had put the Scutari barrack hospital in fairly good order. The relief fund organised by 'The Times' newspaper sent out stores, and other voluntary associations at home were helpful. In December Mary Stanley, daughter of the bishop of Norwich, and sister of Dean Stanley, came out with a reinforcement of forty-six nurses. Miss Nightingale quickly established a vast kitchen and a laundry; she made time to look after the soldiers' wives and children, and to provide ordinary decencies for them. She ruled, but at the same time she slaved: it is said that she was on her feet for twenty hours daily. Although her nurses were also overworked, she allowed no woman but herself to be in the wards after eight at night, when the other nurses' places were taken by orderlies. She alone bore the weight of responsibility. Among the wounded men she naturally moved an ardent devotion. They christened her 'The Lady of the Lamp.' Longfellow in his poem, 'Santa Filomena,' tried to express the veneration which her endurance and courage excited.

But the battle for the reform of the war hospitals was not rapidly won. Early in 1855, owing to defects of sanitation, there was a great increase in the number of cases of cholera and of typhus fever among Miss Nightingale's patients. Seven of the army doctors died, and three of the nurses. Frost-bite and dysentery from exposure in the trenches before Sevastopol made the wards fuller than before. The sick and wounded in the barrack hospital numbered 2000. The death-rate rose in February 1855 to 42 per cent. At Miss Nightingale's persistent entreaties the war office at home ordered the sanitary commissioners at Scutari to carry out at once sanitary reforms. Then the death-rate rapidly declined until in June it had dropped to 2 per cent. The improved conditions at Scutari allowed Miss Nightingale in May to visit the hospitals at and near Balaclava. Her companions on the journey included Mr. Bracebridge and the French cook, Alexis Benoît Soyer [q. v.], who had lately done good service at Scutari. The fatigues attending this visit of inspection brought on an attack of Crimean fever, and for twelve days she lay dangerously ill in the Balaclava sanatorium. Early in June she was able to return to Scutari, and resumed her work there. To her nursing work she added efforts to provide reading and recreation rooms for the men and their families. In March 1856, when peace was concluded, she returned to Balaclava, and she remained there till July, when the hospitals were closed. She then went back for the last time to Scutari. It was not till August 1856 that she came home.

A ship of war was offered Miss Nightingale for her passage, but she returned privately in a French vessel and, crossing to England unnoticed, made her way quietly to Lea Hurst, her home in Derbyshire, although the whole nation was waiting to demonstrate their admiration of her. Queen Victoria, who abounded in expressions of devotion, had in Jan. 1856 sent her an autograph letter of thanks with an enamelled and jewelled brooch designed by the Prince Consort (*Queen Victoria's Letters*, iii. 215), and the Sultan of Turkey had given her a diamond bracelet. In Sept. 1856 she visited Queen Victoria at Balmoral. 'She put before us,' wrote the Prince Consort, 'all that affects our present military hospital system and the reforms that are needed: we are much pleased with her. She is extremely modest' (SIR THEODORE MARTIN, *Prince Consort*, iii. 503). In Nov. 1855, at a meeting in London, a Nightingale fund had been inaugurated for the purpose of founding a training school for nurses, the only recognition of her services which Miss Nightingale would sanction. By 1860 50,000*l.* was collected, and the Nightingale School and Home for Nurses was established at St. Thomas's Hospital. Although Miss Nightingale's health and other occupations did not allow her to accept the post of superintendent, she watched the progress of the new institution with practical interest and was indefatigable in counsel. Her annual addresses to the nurses, which embody her wisest views, were printed for private circulation. The example thus set was followed by other great hospitals, to the great advantage both of hospital nurses and of hospital patients.

In spite of the strain of work and anxiety in the Crimea, which seriously affected her health, Miss Nightingale thenceforth pursued her labours unceasingly, and sought to turn to permanent advantage for the world at large the authoritative position and experience which she had attained in matters of nursing and sanitation. She settled in

London, and, although she lived the retired life of an invalid, she was always busy with her pen or was offering verbally encouragement and direction. In 1857, after publishing a full report of the voluntary contributions which had passed through her hands in the Crimea, she issued an exhaustive and confidential report on the workings of the army medical departments in the Crimea. Next year she printed 'Notes on Matters affecting the Health, Efficiency and Hospital Administration of the British Army.' The commission appointed in 1857 to inquire into the sanitary condition of the army set a high value on her interesting evidence. With her approval an army medical college was opened in 1859 at Chatham; a first military hospital was established in Woolwich in 1861; and an army sanitary commission was established in permanence in 1862. Everywhere her expert reputation was paramount. During the American civil war of 1862–4 and the Franco-German war of 1870–1 her advice was sought by the foreign governments concerned.

In regard to civil hospitals, home nursing, care of poor women in childbirth, and sanitation, Miss Nightingale's authority stood equally high. In 1862, in Liverpool Infirmary, a nursing home was founded with special reference to district nursing, and was placed under the care of Agnes Elizabeth Jones (1832–1868), who had been trained at Kaiserswerth. In 1867, at the request of the poor law board, she wrote a paper of 'Suggestions for the improvement of the nursing service in hospitals and on the methods of training nurses for the sick poor.' Miss Nightingale had a hand in establishing in 1868 the East London Nursing Society, in 1874 the Workhouse Nursing Association and the National Society for providing Trained Nurses for the Poor, and in 1890 the Queen's Jubilee Nursing Institute.

In 1857, on the outbreak of the Indian Mutiny, Miss Nightingale had written from Malvern to her friend Lady Canning, wife of the governor-general, offering in spite of her bad health 'to come out at twenty-four hours' notice, if there were anything for her to do in her line of business' (HARE, *op. cit.*). She never went to India. But the sanitary condition of the army and people there became one of the chief interests of her later life. The government submitted to her the report of the royal commission on the sanitary state of the army in India in 1863, and she embodied her comments in a paper entitled 'How People may live and not die in India,' in which she urged the initiation of sanitary reform. She corresponded actively with Sir Bartle Frere, governor of Bombay, and in August 1867 was in constant communication with Sir Stafford Northcote, then secretary of state for India, as to the establishment of a sanitary department of the Indian government. With every side of Indian social life she made herself thoroughly familiar, exchanging views personally or by correspondence with natives, viceroys, and secretaries of state, and constantly writing on native education and village sanitation. She wrote to the 'Poona Sarvajanik Sabha' in 1889: 'There must be as it were missionaries and preachers of health and cleansing, if any real progress is to be made.' In other published papers and pamphlets she discussed the causes of famine, the need of irrigation, the poverty of the peasantry, and the domination of the money-lender. She urged native Indians to take part in the seventh international congress of hygiene and demography held in London in 1887, and to the eighth congress at Buda-Pesth in 1890 she contributed a paper on village sanitation in India, a subject which, as she wrote in a memorandum addressed to Lord Cross, secretary of state for India, in 1892, she regarded as especially her own.

Miss Nightingale wrote well, in a direct and intimate way, and her papers and pamphlets, which covered all the subjects of her activity, greatly extended her influence. Her most famous book, 'Notes on Nursing,' which first appeared in 1860, went through many editions in her lifetime.

Miss Nightingale, in spite of her withdrawal from society, was honoured until her death. Among the latest distinctions which she received was the Order of Merit in 1907, which was then for the first time bestowed on a woman, and in 1908 she was awarded the freedom of the City of London, which had hitherto only been bestowed on one woman, the Baroness Burdett-Coutts [q. v. Suppl. II]. She had already received, among many similar honours, the German order of the Cross of Merit and the French gold medal of Secours aux blessés militaires. On 10 May 1910 she was presented with the badge of honour of the Norwegian Red Cross Society.

She died at her house in South Street, Park Lane, London, on 13 Aug. 1910, at the age of ninety. An offer of burial in Westminster Abbey was in accordance with her wishes refused by her relatives. She was buried in the burial place of her family at

East Wellow, Hampshire, on 20 August. Memorial services took place in St. Paul's Cathedral, where the government was officially represented, at Liverpool Cathedral, and many other places of worship.

Miss Nightingale raised the art of nursing in this country from a menial employment to an honoured vocation; she taught nurses to be ladies, and she brought ladies out of the bondage of idleness to be nurses. This, which was the aim of her life, was no fruit of her Crimean experience, although that experience enabled her to give effect to her purpose more readily than were otherwise possible. Long before she went to the Crimea she felt deeply the 'disgraceful antithesis' between Mrs. Gamp and a sister of mercy. The picture of her at Scutari is of a strong-willed, strong-nerved energetic woman, gentle and pitiful to the wounded, but always masterful among those with whom she worked. After the war she worked with no less zeal or resolution, and realised many of her early dreams. She was not only the reformer of nursing but a leader of women.

After her death a memorial fund was instituted for the purpose of providing pensions for disabled or aged nurses and for erecting a statue in Waterloo Place. Memorial tablets have been fixed on her birthplace at Florence as well as in the cloisters of Santa Croce there.

A marble bust executed by Sir John Steell in 1862 and presented to Miss Nightingale by the non-commissioned officers and men of the British army was bequeathed by her to the Royal United Service Museum, together with her various presentation jewels and orders. A plaster statuette by Miss J. H. Bonham-Carter (*c.* 1856) (standing figure with lamp in right hand) is at Lea Hurst; of five replicas, one is at St. Thomas's Hospital, another is at the Johns Hopkins Hospital School for Nurses, Baltimore, and the others belong to members of the family. Of two portraits in oils, one by Augustus Leopold Egg, R.A., executed about 1836, is in the National Portrait Gallery; another, by Sir William B. Richmond, R.A., dated about 1886, is at Claydon House. A chalk drawing by Countess Feodora Gleichen, made in 1908, is at Windsor Castle among portraits of members of the Order of Merit. Several water-colour and chalk drawings are either at Lea Hurst or at Claydon House: one (with Miss Nightingale's mother and sister) by A. E. Chalon is dated about 1835; another is by Lady Eastlake; a third, dated about 1850, by her sister, Lady Verney, was lithographed. Others were executed by Miss F. A. de B. Footner in 1907. A picture of Miss Nightingale receiving the wounded at Scutari hospital in 1856 is by Jerry Barrett.

[M. A. Nutting and L. L. Dock's History of Nursing (with bibliography of Miss Nightingale's writings), New York, 1907, vol. ii., chaps. 3–6; The Times, 14–23 Aug. 1910; Burke's Landed Gentry; Soyer's Culinary Campaign, 1857; Lord Stanmore's Lord Herbert of Lea, 1906; J. B. Atkins, Sir William Howard Russell, 1911; Martineau's Sir Bartle Frere; Bosworth Smith's Lord Lawrence; Trans. Seventh Internat. Congress on Hygiene and Demography, 1887; Journal of the Poona Sarvajanik Sabha, 1889; private information.] S. P.

NODAL, JOHN HOWARD (1831–1909), journalist and writer on dialect, was son of Aaron Nodal (1798–1855), of the Society of Friends, a grocer and member of the Manchester town council. Born in Downing Street, Ardwick, Manchester, on 19 Sept. 1831, he was educated at the Quaker school at Ackworth, Yorkshire (1841–5). At seventeen he became a clerk of the old Electric Telegraph Company, and rose to be manager of the news department in Manchester. From the age of nineteen he also acted as secretary of the Manchester Working Men's College, which, formed on the lines of the similar institution in London, was subsequently absorbed in Owens College.

Nodal began early to contribute to the local press. During the volunteer movement of 1860–2 he edited the 'Volunteer Journal,' and in January 1864 he gave himself up to journalism on being appointed sub-editor of the 'Manchester Courier' on its first appearance as a daily paper. From 1867 to 1870 he was engaged on the 'Manchester Examiner and Times.' Meanwhile he edited the 'Free Lance,' an able literary and humorous weekly (1866–8), and a similar paper called the 'Sphinx' (1868–71). For thirty-three years (1871–1904) he was editor of the 'Manchester City News.' Under his control the 'City News' besides chronicling all local topics was the recognised organ of the literary and scientific societies of Lancashire. Many notable series of articles were reprinted from it in volume form. Two of these, 'Manchester Notes and Queries' (1878–89, 8 vols.) and 'Country Notes: a Journal of Natural History and Out-Door Observation' (1882–3, 2 vols.), developed into independent periodicals. Nodal was also a frequent contributor to 'Notes and Queries,' and from 1875 to 1885 was on the staff of the 'Saturday Review.'

Two prominent Manchester institutions owed much to Nodal's energies: the Manchester Literary Club, of which he was president (1873–9) and whose annual volumes of 'Papers' he started and edited for those years, and the Manchester Arts Club, which he was mainly instrumental in founding in 1878. For the glossary committee of the Literary Club he wrote in 1873 a paper on the 'Dialect and Archaisms of Lancashire,' and, in conjunction with George Milner, compiled a 'Glossary of the Lancashire Dialect' (2 parts, 1875–82). When the headquarters of the English Dialect Society were removed in 1874 from Cambridge to Manchester, Nodal became honorary secretary and director. He continued in office to the dissolution of the society in 1896. With Prof. W. W. Skeat (1835-1912) he compiled a 'Bibliographical List of Works illustrative of the various English Dialects,' 1877. His other works include: 1. 'Special Collections of Books in Lancashire and Cheshire,' prepared for the Library Association, 1880. 2. 'Art in Lancashire and Cheshire: a List of Deceased Artists,' 1884. 3. 'A Pictorial Record of the Royal Jubilee Exhibition, Manchester,' 1887. 4. 'Bibliography of Ackworth School,' 1889.

He died at the Grange, Heaton Moor, near Manchester, on 13 Nov. 1909, and was interred at the Friends' burial-ground, Ashton-on-Mersey. He married (1) Helen, daughter of Lawrence Wilkinson, by whom he had two sons and three daughters; (2) Edith, daughter of Edmund and Anne Robinson of Warrington.

[Momus, 10 April 1879; Journalist, 12 July 1889; Manchester City News, 19 Dec. 1896, 20 Nov. 1909, and 9 July 1910; Papers of Manchester Literary Club, 1910; Nodal's Bibliography of Ackworth School; personal knowledge.] C. W. S.

NORMAN, CONOLLY (1853–1908), alienist, born at All Saints' Glebe, Newtown Cunningham, on 12 March 1853, was fifth of six sons of Hugh Norman, rector of All Saints', Newtown Cunningham, and afterwards of Barnhill, both in co. Donegal, by his wife Anne, daughter of Captain William Ball of Buncrana, co. Donegal. Between 1672 and 1733 several members of the Norman family served as mayors of Derry, and two represented the city in parliament. Educated at home owing to delicate health, Norman began at seventeen the study of medicine in Dublin, working at Trinity College, the Carmichael Medical School, and the House of Industry Hospitals. In 1874 he received the licences of the King's and Queen's College of Physicians and the Royal College of Surgeons of Ireland, becoming a fellow of the latter college in 1878, and of the former in 1890.

Norman's professional life was spent in the care of the insane. In 1874, on receiving his qualifications, he was appointed assistant medical officer in the Monaghan Asylum, and he remained there till 1881. After study at the Royal Bethlem Hospital, London, under (Sir) George Savage (1881–2) he was successively medical superintendent of Castlebar Asylum, co. Mayo (1882–5), and of Monaghan asylum (1885–6). From 1886 till his death he was medical superintendent of the most important asylum in Ireland, the Richmond Asylum, Dublin, where he proved his capacity for management and reform. When he took charge of the Richmond Asylum it was insanitary and overcrowded, and more like a prison than a hospital. He introduced a humane régime, made the wards bright and comfortable, and found regular occupation for some 75 per cent. of the patients. By his advice a large branch asylum was built a few miles away in the country. In 1894, and again in 1896, 1897, and 1898, the asylum was visited by beriberi, the outbreak in 1894 being specially severe. He wrote a very complete article on the clinical features of the disease in 1899 (*Trans. Royal Acad. of Medicine in Ireland*, vol. xvii.). In later years he was interested in the problem of the care of the insane outside asylums. He studied the methods adopted in Gheel in Flanders and elsewhere, and advocated in many papers the inauguration in the United Kingdom of a system of boarding out.

Norman was president of the Medico-Psychological Association of Great Britain and Ireland in 1894, when the annual meeting was held in Dublin. In 1907 he was president of a section of the Medico-Psychological Congress at Amsterdam. At the time of his death he was vice-president of the Royal College of Physicians of Ireland. In 1907 the honorary degree of M.D. was conferred on him by the University of Dublin. He was long an editor of the 'Journal of Medical Science,' contributed many papers on insanity to medical periodicals, and was an occasional contributor to this Dictionary.

Norman had many interests outside his speciality. He read widely, and collected books, engravings, and pewter. He was an indefatigable letter-writer, and a humorous and whimsical conversationalist.

Norman died suddenly on 23 Feb. 1908, while out walking in Dublin. He was buried in Mount Jerome cemetery, Dublin. He married, on 6 June 1882, Mary Emily, daughter of Randal Young Kenny, M.D., of Killeshandra, co. Cavan. There were no children of the marriage. On St. Luke's Day, 18 Oct. 1910, a memorial with medallion portrait by Mr. J. M. S. Carré, erected by public subscription in the north aisle of St. Patrick's Cathedral, was unveiled by the lord-lieutenant, the earl of Aberdeen. On the same day the subscribers presented to the Royal College of Physicians of Ireland a portrait in oils by Miss Harrison. Neither artist knew Norman, and both portraits are faulty.

[Journal of Mental Science, April 1908; Medical Press and Circular, 4 March 1908; Burke's Landed Gentry of Ireland; private sources and personal knowledge.] R. J. R.

NORMAN, Sir FRANCIS BOOTH (1830–1901), lieutenant-general, younger brother of Sir Henry Wylie Norman [q. v. Suppl. II], was born on 25 April 1830 in London. He entered Addiscombe, and obtained his commission in the Bengal army 8 Dec. 1848. On the mutiny of his regiment he was attached to the 14th (the Ferozepore Sikh) regiment of the Bengal infantry, and remained at Ferozepore during subsequent operations. In 1863 he took part in the second expedition against the Yusafzais at Ambela, and was present at the storming of the Conical hill and at the destruction of Laloo. He was mentioned in despatches, and added the frontier medal with clasp to the Mutiny medal. In the three following years he was engaged during the Bhutan campaign in the capture of Dewangiri and of the stockades in the Gurugaon Pass, serving as assistant quartermaster-general and receiving the clasp and brevet majority. In 1868 he took part in the Hazara campaign as second in command of the 24th (Punjab) regiment, again receiving the clasp. After an interval of ten years the Afghan war (1878–80) brought him fresh opportunities of distinction. He commanded the 24th regiment in the Bazar valley and the defence of Jagdallak, marching with Roberts's force from Kabul to Kandahar and taking part in the battle of Kandahar. Mentioned in several despatches, he received the medal with clasp, the bronze star, a C.B., and brevet colonelcy. During the war with Burma in 1885–6, he commanded the Bengal brigade of the Upper Burma field force, assisting in the occupation of Mandalay and Bhamo. He was thanked by the government of India and promoted to be K.C.B. He attained the rank of major-general on 1 Sept. 1889, and left India in 1891.

He died on 25 June 1901 at Dulwich, and was buried in West Norwood cemetery. He was twice married: (1) in 1852 to Eliza Ellen, daughter of lieutenant Nisbett, Bengal army, who died at Rawal Pindi in 1870; and (2) in March 1892 to Caroline Matilda, daughter of the Rev. W. W. Cazalet and widow of Major E. F. J. Rennick, Bengal staff corps, who survived him. He left three sons and three daughters, one of the latter, Edith, being the wife of Sir Louis W. Dane, G.C.I.E., C.S.I., lieutenant-governor of the Punjab.

[The Times, 27 June 1901; Indian army lists, and official reports.] W. L-W.

NORMAN, Sir HENRY WYLIE (1826–1904), field-marshal and administrator, was born in London on 2 Dec. 1826. His father, James Norman, exchanged an adventurous life at sea for business at Havana in Cuba, and then married Charlotte Wylie of Dumfries. He subsequently moved to Calcutta, carrying on his business there until his death in March 1853. His widow died at an advanced age at Sandgate on 13 Sept. 1902. Henry Norman did not enter Addiscombe College (as stated in *The Times*, 27 Oct. 1904), but after a very imperfect education joined his father in Calcutta in 1842 with a strong desire to go to sea, meanwhile taking such clerical work as offered itself. Even at this age, however, he impressed others with the qualities which Earl Roberts regarded as his special gifts, 'extraordinary memory' and 'a natural liking and aptitude for work.' The 'soldierly instincts' within him were kindled by news of Sir Charles Napier's campaign in Sind in 1843, and of Sir Hugh Gough's victories at Maharajpur and Gwalior, and fortune favoured him by bringing him a direct appointment as cadet in the infantry of the Company's Bengal army (1 March 1844). In April he joined the 1st Bengal native infantry as ensign, devoting his whole heart to his regimental duties; and in March 1845 he was transferred to the 31st native infantry (afterwards 2nd Queen's own Rajput light infantry), which remained loyal in 1857. He thus escaped the cruel fate of his brother officers in the 1st native infantry. Throughout his active service he seemed to possess a charmed life, and was constantly unhurt when men were struck down by his side.

His regiment was stationed at Lahore after the first Sikh war in 1846, as part of the force under Colin Campbell (afterwards Lord Clyde) [q. v.]. He became lieutenant on 25 Dec. 1847, and was soon made adjutant. When Vans Agnew and Anderson were murdered at Multan on 20 April 1848, Norman was on sick leave at Simla, but was at once recalled to his regiment, then stationed at Ferozepore. In the 'war with a vengeance' that followed Norman shared in every incident and battle. He witnessed the opening scene at Ramnagar, took part in Thackwell's inconclusive operations at Sadulapur on 3 Dec. 1848, joined in the confused and bloody mêlée at Chilianwala on 13 Jan. 1849, and shared the conspicuous honour won by his regiment in the decisive attack on Kalra at the crowning victory of Gujarat on 21 Feb. 1849. He was present at the grand surrender of the Sikh army at Rawalpindi, and helped to chase the Afghans back to their hills, finally receiving the Sikh war medal and two clasps. In December 1849 he was brigade-major at Peshawar to Sir Colin Campbell. In 1850 he accompanied Sir Charles Napier on the Kohat pass expedition, and afterwards took part in expeditions against the Afridis, the Mohmands, and the Utman Kheyls. While he was at Panjpao on 15 April 1852 he was specially mentioned in despatches. Becoming deputy assistant adjutant-general and A.D.C. to General Sir Abraham Roberts [q. v.], he was credited in divisional orders (15 Dec. 1853) with 'all the qualifications for a good soldier and first-rate staff officer.'

A brief interlude in Norman's service on the staff occurred when the Santals in 1855 rose against the extortionate money-lenders. He at once joined his regiment, taking part in the suppression of disturbances. In May 1856 he was at headquarters in Calcutta as assistant adjutant-general, and in the following year he reached Simla with the commander-in-chief, General George Anson [q. v.], a few days before news of the outbreak at Meerut and of the arrival of the mutineers at Delhi simultaneously reached headquarters. General Sir Henry Barnard [q. v.] took command of the relief force on the death of Anson (27 May 1857), united his forces at Alipur with those of Sir Archdale Wilson [q. v.] on 7 June, and next day defeated the rebels at Badli-ki-Serai, establishing himself on the Ridge of Delhi in sight of the walled city filled with some 10,000 mutineers and soon receiving 20,000 more trained sepoys. Chester, the adjutant-general, lay dead amongst the 183 killed and wounded, and upon Norman devolved his duties. From 8 June to 8 Sept., when the arrival and establishment in position of the siege guns enabled the assault to be delivered, Norman was invaluable to the several commanders of the Delhi field force: first to Barnard until he died of cholera on 5 July, then to (Sir) Thomas Reed [q. v.] until he left with the sick and wounded on 17 July, and then to Archdale Wilson until he established his headquarters in the palace of captured Delhi on 21 Sept. Neville Chamberlain [q. v. Suppl. II] arrived on 24 June to assume the duties of adjutant-general, but on 14 July he was severely wounded. Notwithstanding the strain and sufferings of the siege, Norman without any hesitation left Delhi with Greathead's column, and took part in the fighting at Bulandshahr, Aligarh, and Agra. He was able early in November to report his arrival to Sir Colin Campbell, commander-in-chief, and proceed with him as deputy adjutant-general to the relief of Lucknow. In the attack on the Shah Nujeef on 16 Nov. his horse was shot under him, but he rallied and led some soldiers on the point of retreating; and when the relief was accomplished he was present at the battle of Cawnpore and took part in the defeat of the Gwalior troops (6 Dec. 1857). Then followed the final capture of Lucknow in March 1858, the Rohilkhand campaign (April to May), and the battle of Bareilly (5 May), at which he received his only wound. The cold season campaign in Oudh, 1858–9, found him present at the engagements of Buxar Ghat, Burgudia, Majudia, and on the Rapti, and at the close of these operations the commander-in-chief brought his merits to the notice of the viceroy. Up to this time, indeed, he had been mentioned twenty-three times in despatches or in general orders. But his rewards lagged, because his years were fewer than his services. Even so late as 2 Dec. 1860 he was gazetted as a captain in the new staff corps, on the heels of which followed a brevet majority, 3 Dec., and then a brevet lieutenant-colonelcy on 4 Dec. He became C.B. on 16 August 1859, and A.D.C. to Queen Victoria on 8 Sept. 1863, an honour which he held until 22 March 1869, when he was promoted major-general. Worn out by all he had endured, he proceeded home in December 1859, and was at once welcomed by the press and invited to

Windsor Castle. On 1 Oct. 1860 he was made assistant military secretary to the Duke of Cambridge, who always entertained a high regard for him. In the following year he was ordered back to India to take part in the great scheme of army reorganisation.

From this time his career, which promised so much success in the military service, was gradually diverted to civil administration. As first secretary to the government of India in the military department (12 Jan. 1862–31 May 1870), he had to endure the criticism and attacks of many vested interests affected by the financial stress and the reorganisation schemes of the period following the Mutiny. Stricken with fever, he was sent home in December 1865. Returning to India in 1867, he resumed his secretarial duties and became a major-general on 23 March 1869. From 1 June 1870 to 18 March 1877 he was member of the council of the governor-general of India, and took a prominent part in the discussion of Afghan affairs and the scientific frontier. He advocated on every occasion friendly relations with Russia, forbearance towards the Amir, and scrupulous avoidance of any advance beyond existing frontiers. He never forgot 'the dangers of our position in India,' and urged measures of economy and internal administration in order to keep our forces concentrated and our subjects contented. These views were not in harmony with Lord Lytton's forward policy, and he resigned his office in March 1877. He had been made K.C.B. on 24 May 1873, and was promoted lieutenant-general on 1 Oct. 1877. On 25 Feb. 1878 he was appointed member of the council of India, and when Lord Hartington [q. v. Suppl. II] became secretary of state for India on 28 April 1880 his strenuous opposition to the retention of Kandahar was rewarded with success. On 1 April 1882 he became general, and he was deputed to Egypt to settle various financial questions as to the liability of Indian and British revenues for the Indian contingent. On 30 Nov. 1883 he resigned his post at the India office to take up a colonial appointment as governor of Jamaica, where Lord Derby warned him that 'there will be a great deal to do' (*Letter*, 27 Sept. 1883).

Norman was received coldly on arrival. He bore unknown instructions on the constitutional crisis which had succeeded the resignation of the non-official members of the legislative council owing to the obligation imposed on the island for paying damages arising out of the seizure of the Florida. Queen Victoria's order in council of 19 May 1884 at least terminated uncertainty if it failed to satisfy hopes. But the introduction of the new representative scheme of legislation was so firmly and tactfully effected that 'the people were satisfied with even the little they had received' (speeches of the chairman of the standing committee for raising funds and others March 1886). For his services he received in May 1887 the G.C.M.G., and the military distinction of G.C.B. in the following month. In 1889 he disinterestedly accepted the governorship of Queensland in order to relieve the home government of a difficulty caused by their unpopular appointment of Sir Henry Blake. In Queensland quiet times succeeded to angry constitutional controversies. The colony was, however, soon involved in financial troubles, and Norman showed his public spirit in offering to share the reduction of salary to which the members of the legislative assembly had to submit. The responsible ministers freely sought his advice, and when he retired after the close of 1895 Mr. Chamberlain expressed his high appreciation of the governor's long and valuable services.

During Norman's term of office in Queensland Lord Kimberley, secretary of state for India, offered him, through Lord Ripon, secretary of state for the colonies, on 1 Sept. 1893, the post of governor-general of India on the resignation of that office by Lord Lansdowne. On 3 Sept. Norman accepted the office, but in the course of the next few days he found that the excitement and anxieties so upset him at the age of nearly sixty-seven years, that he could not expect to endure the strain of so arduous an office for five years. On 19 Sept. he withdrew his acceptance. After his return to England he was employed on various duties and commissions of a less onerous but important character. In December 1896 he was appointed president of a royal commission to inquire into the conditions of the sugar-growing colonies in West India. This involved a cruise round the islands and gratified his taste for the sea, cruising and voyaging having been Norman's chief recreation during his life. His views in favour of countervailing duties on bounty-fed sugar imported into the United Kingdom were not shared by his colleagues. In 1901 he was made governor of Chelsea Hospital, being raised to the rank of field-marshal on 26 June 1902. In the following year, despite his failing health, he took part in the South African war commission. On 26 Oct. 1904 he died at Chelsea Hospital, and was buried with full military honours at Brompton cemetery.

Norman was thrice married: (1) in 1853 to Selina Eliza, daughter of Dr. A. Davidson, inspector-general of hospitals; she died on 3 Oct. 1862 at Calcutta, having had issue four daughters, and one son, Henry Alexander, who died at sea in March 1858; (2) in September 1864 to Jemima Anne (*d.* 1865), daughter of Capt. Knowles and widow of Capt. A. B. Temple; and (3) in March 1870 to Alice Claudine, daughter of Teignmouth Sandys of the Bengal civil service. By her he had two sons, Walter and Claude, who both entered the army, and one daughter. Mural memorial tablets were erected by public subscription in Chelsea Hospital, at Delhi, and in the crypt of St. Paul's cathedral. This last, unveiled on 3 June 1907 by Lord Roberts, bore the simple legend 'Soldier and administrator in India, governor of Jamaica and Queensland, through life a loyal and devoted servant to the state.'

A portrait in oils, painted by Lowes Dickinson for the city of Calcutta, was exhibited at the Royal Academy in 1879. A cartoon portrait of Norman by 'Spy' appeared in 'Vanity Fair' in 1903.

[W. Lee-Warner, Memoirs of Field-Marshal Sir Henry Norman, 1908; Narrative of the Campaign in 1857 at Delhi, by Lieut. H. W. Norman, 2nd Asst. Adjutant-General; Selections from state papers preserved in the Mil. Dept. of the Govt. of India, 1857–8, ed. G. W. Forrest, 3 vols. 1893–1902; Kaye and Malleson's History of the Sepoy War in India; Parliamentary papers, including Mutiny of Native Regiments, 1857–8, Organisation of the Indian Army, 1859, Afghan campaign, 1878–79; G. W. Forrest, Field-Marshal Sir Neville Chamberlain, 1909]. W. L-W.

NORMAN-NERUDA, Wilma Maria Francisca (1839–1911), violinist. [See Hallé, Lady.]

NORTHBROOK, first Earl of. [See Baring, Thomas George (1826–1904), viceroy of India.]

NORTHCOTE, HENRY STAFFORD, Baron Northcote of Exeter (1846–1911), governor-general of the Australian commonwealth, born on 18 Nov. 1846 at 13 Devonshire St., Portland Place, London, was second son of Sir Stafford Henry Northcote, first earl of Iddesleigh [q.v.]; his mother was Cecilia Frances, daughter of Thomas Farrer, and sister of Thomas Farrer, first Lord Farrer. He went to Eton in 1858 and Merton College, Oxford, in 1865, graduating B.A. in 1869 and proceeding M.A. in 1873. On leaving Oxford he was appointed to a clerkship in the foreign office on 18 March 1868. In Feb. 1871 he was attached to the joint high commission, of which his father was one of the members and which sat at Washington from Feb. to May 1871, to consider the Alabama claims and other outstanding questions between Great Britain and the United States. The negotiation having resulted in the Treaty of Washington of 8 May 1871, he became secretary to the British member of the claims commission which was constituted under the 12th article of that treaty, and assistant to the British claims agent in the general business of the commission. The commission sat at Washington from Sept. 1871 to Sept. 1873. In Nov. 1876 Northcote became an acting third secretary in the diplomatic service. When Lord Salisbury went as British plenipotentiary to the Constantinople conference at the end of 1876, Northcote accompanied him as private secretary. In Feb. 1877 he was made assistant private secretary to his father, who was then chancellor of the exchequer, and he was private secretary from October 1877 to 15 Mar. 1880. On that date he resigned the public service to stand in the conservative interest for Exeter, the city near which the home of his family lay. He was duly elected and represented Exeter in the House of Commons from 1880 till 1899. From June 1885 till Feb. 1886, in Lord Salisbury's short first government, he was financial secretary to the war office. In Lord Salisbury's second government he held the post of surveyor-general of ordnance from August 1886 to Dec. 1887, resigning his appointment in order to facilitate changes at the war office. He had been given the C.B. in 1880, and in Nov. 1887, after his father's death, he was made a baronet. He was a charity commissioner in 1891–2, and in 1898 was appointed a royal commissioner for the Paris Exhibition of 1900. He was also for a time chairman of the Associated Chambers of Commerce, and became well known and much trusted in business circles. In 1899 he was appointed to be governor of Bombay, and in Jan. 1900 he was raised to the peerage with the title of Baron Northcote of the city of Exeter, next month being made G.C.I.E.

On 17 Feb. 1900 Lord Northcote landed at Bombay, where he served as governor for three and a half years. His tenure of office was marked by 'a famine of unprecedented severity, incessant plague, an empty exchequer, and bad business years generally' (*Times of India*, 5 Sept. 1903). Famine did not completely disappear till 1902–3, and plague was still rife when Northcote left India. He faced the situation with self-denying energy. Immediately on arrival at Bombay he inspected the hospitals, including the plague hospitals, and within a month of his landing went to Gujarat, where the peasantry were in sore straits from the effects of the famine. The district of Gujarat depended largely upon its fine breed of cattle which was in danger of dying out from scarcity of fodder, and one great result of the governor's visit was the establishment, largely on his initiative, of the cattle farm at Charodi, known as the Northcote Gowshala, to preserve and improve the breed. His sympathy with and interest in the small cultivators of the Bombay Presidency were shown by what was perhaps the chief legislative measure of his government, the passing of the Bombay Land Revenue Code Amendment Act, which aroused much criticism on its introduction in 1901. The object of the act was to protect the cultivators in certain famine-stricken districts of the Presidency against the money-lenders, by wiping out the arrears of revenue due from the holder on condition of his holding being forfeited to the government, and then restored to him as occupier on an inalienable tenure. He took other steps in the direction of land revenue reform, doing much to bring the somewhat rigid traditional policy of the Bombay government into harmony with the views of the government of India. In municipal matters, too, he made improvements, though the most important municipal act passed in his time—the District Municipalities Act, by which local self-government in the Moffussil was much enlarged—was a legacy from his predecessor, Lord Sandhurst. Northcote travelled widely through the Bombay Presidency, and he paid a visit to Aden. He was a warm supporter of schools and hospitals, but his efforts were hampered by the impoverished state of the public finances. 'So far as he was able, Lord Northcote drew on his privy purse for money which the State should have furnished, and especially in the administration of relief and in the assistance of charitable undertakings was he able to take a more personally active part than any of his predecessors' (*Bombay Gazette Budget*, 29 Aug. 1903). He was present in 1903 at the Coronation Durbar which celebrated the accession of King Edward VII. When he left India on 5 Sept. 1903 the viceroy, Lord Curzon, expressed the general feeling, in the message 'Bombay and India are losing one of the most sympathetic and sagacious governors that they have known.'

On 29 Aug. 1903 Northcote had been appointed Governor-General of the commonwealth of Australia. On 21 Jan. 1904, when he was made a G.C.M.G., he was sworn in at Sydney, and he remained in Australia for nearly four years and eight months. Northcote's task in Australia was no easy one. The Commonwealth came into existence on 1 Jan. 1901, and Northcote had had two predecessors (Lords Hopetoun and Tennyson) in three years. He was thus the first to hold his office for an appreciable length of time, and it fell to him largely to establish the position, and to create traditions. Federation was in its infancy. A national feeling as apart from state interests hardly existed, and the difficulties of the governor-general consisted at the outset in the relations of the states to the Commonwealth with resulting friction and jealousies, and in the absence of two clearly defined parties in Australian politics. Mr. Alfred Deakin was prime minister when Northcote reached Australia, but in April (1904) he was succeeded by the labour prime minister of Australia, Mr. John Christian Watson. In the following August Mr. (now Sir) George Reid became prime minister, and in July 1905 Mr. Deakin once more came into office and held it for the rest of Lord Northcote's term. In India Northcote had learnt the difficulty of harmonising the views of the government of a province with those of the central government, and his Indian experience therefore stood him in good stead when called upon to reconcile the claims of Commonwealth and states in Australia, while his earlier foreign office and political training qualified him to deal with political life. In Australia, as in India, he travelled widely. He was determined, as the head of a self-governing Commonwealth, to identify himself with the people in all parts of Australia. During his term of office he travelled through the greater part of every state, visited most county towns, every mining centre, the great pastoral and agricultural districts; and succeeded in obtaining a grasp of the industrial work and life of the people. He averaged in travelling over 10,000 miles a year by land and sea. Especially he made a tour in the Northern Territory and called public attention to this little known and somewhat neglected part of the continent. In Sydney and Melbourne he visited every factory of importance, while in social life, and in the support of institutions and movements for the public good, he won respect and affection. He laid stress on the importance of defence and of encouraging immigration for the development of the land. Thus amid somewhat shifting politics, by his sincerity and straightforwardness, he attached to the office of governor-general a high standard of public usefulness. His speeches were dignified, enlivened by humour, and excellently delivered. His ample means enabled him to exercise a generous hospitality and a wide benevolence.

After his return from Australia in the autumn of 1908 Northcote took a considerable though not a very prominent part in public life up to the time of his death. He spoke on occasion in the House of Lords, and welcomed to his home visitors from the dominions beyond the seas. He had a singular power of attracting affection, and his good judgment, coupled with entire absence of self-interest, made him a man of many friends. In 1909 he was made a privy councillor, and at the Coronation of King George V he carried the banner of Australia. He died at Eastwell Park, Ashford, Kent, on 29 Sept. 1911, and was buried at Upton Pynes, near Exeter. He married on 2 Oct. 1873 Alice, the adopted daughter of Lord Mount Stephen. He had no issue and the peerage became extinct. A portrait of Northcote, painted by A. S. Cope, R.A., is in possession of Lady Northcote at 25 St. James's Place, London, S.W.

[The Times, 30 Sept. 1911; Foreign Office List; Lovat Fraser, India under Curzon and after, 1911; private sources.] C. P. L.

NORTHCOTE, JAMES SPENCER (1821-1907), president of Oscott College and archæologist, born at Feniton Court, Devonshire, on 26 May 1821, was second son of George Barons Northcote of Feniton Court and of Somerset Court, Somerset, by his wife Maria, daughter and coheir of Gabriel Stone of South Brent, Somerset. Educated at Ilmington grammar school (1830–7), he matriculated in 1837 as a scholar from Corpus Christi College, Oxford, where he readily yielded to Newman's influence. Graduating B.A. in 1841 with a first class in the final classical school, and marrying next year, he took holy orders in 1844, and proceeded M.A. Serving as curate in Ilfracombe, he there became intimate with Dr. Pusey, and his doubts of the Anglican position increased.

In 1845 his wife with three of her sisters joined the Roman communion. Thereupon Northcote resigned his curacy, and he followed their example next year. He was at once appointed master at Prior Park College, Bath, and explained his spiritual perplexities in 'The Fourfold Difficulty of Anglicanism' (Derby, 1846; reprinted 1891; French translation by J. Gordon, 1847). A three years' stay in Italy (1847–50), where Northcote became intimate with G. B. de Rossi, the historian of the catacombs, developed a warm interest in the archæology of Christian Rome.

The next three years were spent at Clifton, and were devoted mainly to literary work. From June 1852 to September 1854 he acted as editor of the 'Rambler,' to which he had contributed since its foundation by his lifelong friend, John Moore Capes, in January 1848, and he helped to edit the 'Clifton Tracts.' On the death of his wife in 1853 Northcote studied for the priesthood at the Oratory, Birmingham, in 1854 and later at the Collegio Pio, Rome, where he pursued his study of Christian antiquities. Ordained priest on 29 July 1855 at St. Dominic's, Stone, near Stafford, he spent the greater part of 1856 in theological studies in Rome, and on his return to England took charge in 1857 of the mission at Stoke-on-Trent. In 1860 he was made canon of St. Chad's Cathedral Church, canon theologian of the diocese of Birmingham in 1862, and on 2 March 1884 he was installed provost of the cathedral chapter of Birmingham. In January 1861 he received from Pope Pius IX the degree of D.D.

Meanwhile in January 1860 Northcote was appointed vice-president of St. Mary's College, Oscott, becoming president in July following. Through the early years of his presidency Oscott College prospered. Imbued with Oxford culture, and holding wise views of education, he remodelled the studies and the life on the lines of the chief English public schools. A swimming bath was provided in 1867, and a gymnasium erected in 1869; and a cricket ground and pavilion were added. In July 1863 he entertained at Oscott Cardinal Wiseman and Monsignor (afterwards Cardinal) Manning at the twenty-fifth anniversary of the college. But difficulties beset the later period of Northcote's career at Oscott. The competition of the Oratory School, Birmingham (opened in May 1859), two epidemics in 1862 and 1868, and the success of Fitzgerald, a dismissed student, in a lawsuit brought against Northcote in 1865 for technical assault, depressed the fortunes of the college. Northcote retired through ill-health in 1877, and from 1889 the institution was used as an ecclesiastical seminary. Northcote went back on leaving Oscott to his first mission at Stone, removing in 1881 to the mission at Stoke-on-Trent. After 1887 creeping paralysis withdrew him from active work, and he died at the Presbytery, Stoke-on-Trent, on 3 March 1907, being buried at Oscott cemetery, which he had opened in 1863. Northcote married on 10 Dec. 1842 his cousin Susannah Spencer (*d.* June 1853), daughter of Joseph Ruscombe Poole, solicitor, of Bridgwater, and had issue three sons and three daughters, all of whom predeceased him.

Northcote published much on the early Christian antiquities in Rome. Articles on the Catacombs in the 'Rambler' (Jan. and July 1860) gave rise to much discussion. His 'Roma Sotterranea; or an Account of the Roman Catacombs' (1869; 2nd edit. 1878) (with Bishop William Robert Brownlow) was compiled from G. B. de Rossi's Italian work 'Roma Sotterranea;' it remains the standard work in English on the subject. It was translated into German in 1873 (2nd edit. 1879) and into French. Other works by Northcote on the subject are: 1. 'The Roman Catacombs,' 1857; 2nd edit. 1859. 2. 'A Visit to the Roman Catacombs,' 1877; reprinted 1891. 3. 'Epitaphs of the Catacombs,' 1878. He also published: 4. 'A Pilgrimage to La Salette,' 1852. 5. 'Mary in the Gospels' (sermons and lectures), 1867; 2nd edit. 1885; new revised edit. 1906. 6. 'Celebrated Sanctuaries of the Madonna,' 1868 (articles reprinted from the 'Rambler,' 1850–2). 7. 'Sermons,' 1876. With Charles Meynell he published in 1863 'The "Colenso" Controversy from the Catholic Standpoint.' A portrait in oils, executed by J. R. Herbert, R.A., in 1873, hangs in the breakfast parlour at Oscott College. Northcote is commemorated by the 'Northcote Hall' at Oscott, which he inaugurated in 1866.

[The Times, Birmingham Daily Post, and Tablet, 9 March 1907; funeral sermon by William Barry, D.D., entitled The Lord my Light, 1907; The Oscotian (Northcote number), July 1907; Report of case Fitzgerald *v.* Northcote, 1866; Catholic Encyclopædia (s.vv. Northcote and Oscott); Cath. Univ. Bulletin, Washington, March–April 1909; Gasquet's Acton and his Circle, pp. xxi and 300–1.] W. B. O.

NORTON, first Baron. [See Adderley, Charles Bowyer (1814–1905), president of the board of trade.]

NORTON, JOHN (1823–1904), architect, born on 28 Sept. 1823 at Bristol, was son of John Norton by his wife Sarah Russell. After education at Bristol grammar school he entered as a pupil in 1846 the office in London of Benjamin Ferrey [q. v.] and attended classes of Prof. Thomas Leverton Donaldson [q. v.] at the University of London, where he received in 1848 the first prize from Lord Brougham.

Norton became an associate of the Royal Institute of British Architects in 1850 and fellow in 1857; he was for a time a member of its council, and became president of the Architectural Association for the session 1858–9. He was honorary secretary of the Arundel Society (for producing printed copies of paintings by old masters) throughout its existence (1848–98).

Norton quickly built up a large and lucrative architectural practice in both domestic and ecclesiastical buildings. He was fortunate in finding many patrons of distinction and wealth. For the Maharajah Duleep Singh he built Elveden Hall, Suffolk; for William Gibbs he rebuilt Tyntesfield, Somerset; and for Sir Alexander Acland-Hood, first Baron St. Audries, he designed a house at St. Audries in the same county, as well as a church there. Other works were Badgemore, Oxfordshire, for Richard Ovey; Ferney Hall, Shropshire, for W. Hurt-Sitwell; Horstead Hall, Norfolk, for Sir E. Birkbeck; Nutfield, Surrey, for H. E. Gurney; Monkhams, Essex, for H. Ford Barclay; Euston Hall, Suffolk, for the Duke of Grafton; public works and buildings of the new boulevard, Florence; International College, Isleworth; Winter Gardens, &c., at Great Yarmouth and Tynemouth; Langland Bay Hotel, South Wales; South Western Terminus Hotel, Southampton; Fickle Castle, Esthonia; Framlingham Hall, Norfolk; Brent Knoll, Somerset; Summers Place, Sussex; Chew Magna Manor House, Somerset; Town Hall and Constitutional Club, Neath; Training College for the diocese of Gloucester and Bristol.

Among his London designs were the Turf Club, Piccadilly; the Submarine Telegraph Co.'s office, Throgmorton Avenue; the Canada Government Buildings and Victoria Mansions, Westminster; residential mansions, Mandeville Place, W., with several hotels, business premises, and residential flats.

Though not working exclusively in the Gothic style, Norton designed much ecclesiastical work in the Gothic style of the mid-nineteenth century. He designed the churches of Stapleton, Stoke Bishop, and Frampton Cotterell in Gloucestershire; those at Bourton, High Bridge, and Congresbury in Somersetshire. At Bristol he was responsible for St. Luke's, St. Matthias, Emmanuel (Clifton), and the parish church of Bedminster; and in Wales and Monmouthshire for those at Pontypridd, Neath, Rheola, Ebbw Vale, Blaina, Abertillery, Ystrad Mynach, Penmaen, Llwyn Madoc, Dyffryn, Cwm, and Ysfra. Norton designed St. Matthew's, Brighton; Christ Church, Finchley; St. John's, Middlesbrough; churches at Croxley Green (since increased in size); Lundy Island; Powerscourt, Wicklow; Chevington, near Howick; Bagnères de Bigorre; and Bishop Hannington's Memorial Church, Frere Town, Africa. The C.M.S. Children's Home at Limpsfield, the Royal Normal College for the Blind at Norwood, the County Courts at Williton, Dunster, and Long Ashton in Somerset, and the High Cross at Bristol were also Norton's work.

Norton died on 10 Nov. 1904, and was buried at Bournemouth. He married in 1857 Helen Mary, only daughter of Peter Le Neve Aldous Arnold, by whom he had eight daughters and two sons. The younger son, Mr. C. Harrold Norton, succeeded to his father's practice.

[The Builder, lxxxvii. 526; R.I.B.A. Journal, vol. xii. 3rd series, p. 63; information by Mr. C. Harrold Norton.] P. W.

NOVELLO, CLARA ANASTASIA, COUNTESS GIGLIUCCI (1818–1908), oratorio and operatic prima donna, born in Oxford Street, London, on 10 June 1818, was fourth daughter of Vincent Novello [q. v.] by his wife Mary Sabilla Hehl. Mrs. Mary Victoria Cowden Clarke [q. v. Suppl. I] was her eldest sister. Clara was taken in childhood to York, and was placed under Miss Hill, the leading singer, and John Robinson, organist of the Roman catholic chapel there. Her talents were at once displayed; and on Easter Sunday, when Miss Hill was suddenly indisposed, Clara offered to sing all her solos from memory, and succeeded. In 1829 she became a pupil of Choron's academy in Paris. She always retained the strongest appreciation of her training there; Palestrina's music was much sung, and Clara ascribed her perfect sostenuto to having sung in his motets, and being obliged to hold the suspensions. The academy declined after the revolution of 1830, and Clara, who had had unpleasant experiences of the fighting, returned to England. On 22 Oct. 1832 she made her first public appearance, in a concert at Windsor, with full success; and in December she took the soprano part in Beethoven's 'Missa Solennis,' a remarkable feat for a girl of fourteen. She was soon among the first singers of the day, being engaged at the whole series of Ancient Concerts, at the Philharmonic Concerts, and the Three Choirs Festival. She sang in a sestet, Grisi leading, at the Handel commemoration in June 1834; Lord Mount-Edgcumbe (*Musical Reminiscences*, p. 278) describes her as 'a very young girl with a clear good voice.' Her father's friend, Charles Lamb, though quite unmusical, wrote the lines 'To Clara N.' published in the 'Athenæum,' 26 July 1834. She was left without a rival on the retirement of Catherine Stephens, afterwards countess of Essex [q. v.], in 1835, and took the leading soprano part at all important English concerts. Her voice was a pure clear soprano, extending to D in alt, perfectly trained, perfectly under control, and used with musical science as well as with feeling expression. Handel's music was particularly adapted to her style. Her appearance was attractive; she had exceptionally luxuriant hair, and to lessen the load she cut off half a yard. At the Manchester Festival in September 1836 she had much useful advice from the dying Malibran. Next year Mendelssohn invited her to the Gewandhaus Concerts, Leipzig, where she appeared on 2 Nov. 1837, and several times later. She was well received, and succeeded in making German audiences appreciate Handel's solos. Schumann declared that nothing for years past had given him so much pleasure as Miss Novello's voice, 'every note sharply defined as on the keyboard.' (*Neue Zeitschrift für Musik: Das Musikleben* . . . 1837–8). Mendelssohn wrote that Clara Novello and Mrs. Shaw (her successor next winter) 'are the best concert singers we have heard in Germany for a long time.' She sang also at Berlin, Dresden, Prague (KUHE, *My Musical Recollections*, p. 26), Vienna (SCHUMANN, *Letter to Fischhof*), and Munich. Then visiting Rossini at Bologna, she was advised to study opera for a year; she took lessons of Micheroux at Milan. In 1839 she once more made a concert tour, travelling down the Rhine to Düsseldorf, through North Germany to Berlin, and thence to St. Petersburg. Her first appearance on the stage was at Padua in Rossini's 'Semiramide,' on 6 July 1841. Unqualified successes in Rome, Genoa, and other large Italian cities followed; Rossini sent specially for her to take the soprano part in his just completed 'Stabat Mater.' Owing to the mismanagement of agents, she was announced to sing at two places—at Rome and Genoa—during the carnival of 1843; the Roman authorities refused a permit to leave the territory and detained her under arrest at Fermo. On her appealing as a British subject to Lord Aberdeen, then English foreign secretary, the matter was arranged by arbitration. Count Gigliucci, the governor of Fermo, fell in love with his prisoner; she agreed to marry him as soon as professional engagements permitted. At Clara Novello's last appearance in Rome she was recalled twenty-nine times; there was some disturbance at Genoa.

In March she returned to England, and appeared in English opera at Drury Lane; also in Handel's 'Acis and Galatea,' and at the Sacred Harmonic Society and other concerts. On 22 Nov. she was married to Count Gigliucci at Paddington parish church, and retired with him to Italy. During the troubles of 1848 their property was confiscated, and the countess resolved to resume her public appearances. In 1850 she sang in opera at Rome; then at Lisbon, and on 18 July 1851 re-appeared in London, singing in Handel's 'Messiah' at Exeter Hall. Her embellishments brought some disapprobation, though her voice was pronounced to have gained in strength, and to have lost nothing of its beauty. She took the place of leading English concert soprano, appearing only once again in England in opera, in 'I Puritani' at Drury Lane on 5 July 1853. At Milan she sang in opera during the carnivals from 1854–6. In England her singing was regarded as the embodiment of the best traditions of the Handelian style; like Mara and Catalani before, and Lemmens-Sherrington after, she was specially distinguished in her rendering of 'I know that my Redeemer liveth,' and she sang the opening phrase in one breath. On the opening of the Crystal Palace, on 10 June 1854, her singing, 'heard to remote corners of the building' (*Athenæum*, 17 June 1854), seemed grander than ever before; probably the finest revelation of her powers was at the Handel Festival there in June 1859. She then determined to retire. After singing in Handel's 'Messiah' at the Crystal Palace, she made her last appearance at a benefit concert at St. James's Hall on 21 Nov. 1860, the final strain being the National Anthem.

In her retirement she lived with her husband at Rome and Fermo. He died on 29 March 1893; she died in her ninetieth year, on 12 March 1908, at Rome, leaving a daughter, Valeria. Her portrait was twice painted, by her brother Edward Petre Novello, and by Edward Magnus of Berlin. These pictures were reproduced, with photographs, in Clayton's 'Queens of Song,' the memorial article by 'F. G. E.' in 'Musical Times,' April 1908, the Novello centenary number, June 1911, and in her volume of 'Reminiscences' (1910).

[Her posthumous Reminiscences (1910), compiled by her daughter Valeria; works and periodicals quoted.] H. D.

NUNBURNHOLME, first Baron. [See Wilson, Charles Henry (1833–1907), shipowner and politician.]

NUNN, JOSHUA ARTHUR (1853–1908), colonel, army veterinary service, born on 10 May 1853 at Hill Castle, co. Wexford, Ireland, was son of Edward W Nunn, J.P., D.L. He was educated at Wimbledon school, and served in the royal Monmouthshire engineer militia from 1871 to 1877. In 1874 he entered the Royal Veterinary College at Camden Town, and was admitted M.R.C.V.S. on 4 Jan. 1877, being elected F.R.C.V.S. on 29 April 1886. In 1877 he obtained a certificate in cattle pathology from the Royal Agricultural Society. He was gazetted veterinary surgeon on probation in the army veterinary service on 21 April 1877 and veterinary surgeon to the royal artillery on 24 April 1877, being the last officer to obtain a commission under the old regimental system.

Nunn proceeded to India at the end of 1877, and from September 1879 to August 1880 he took part in the Afghan war as the veterinary officer in charge of transport on the Khyber line of communication. Later, accompanying the expeditionary column in the Lughman valley, he was in charge of the transport base hospital at Gandamak. For these services he gained the war medal.

He was employed on special duty from 1880 to 1885 as a civil servant under the Punjab government, first in the suppression of glanders under the Glanders and Farcy Act, afterwards in connection with the agricultural department of the Punjab as the veterinary inspector. In this capacity he travelled widely to collect all manner of information and statistics about cattle, including folklore and disease. This he embodied in a series of valuable reports: 'Animal Diseases in Rohtak' (1882); 'Diseases in Sialkote and Hazara' (1883); 'Diseases in the Montgomery and Shapur Districts' (1884 and 1885). At the same time he lectured to native students at the

Lahore veterinary college. He left India in 1886, and the government of the Punjab recognised his valuable services in a special minute.

Immediately after leaving India he was ordered to South Africa to investigate 'horse sickness,' which was thought to be due to anthrax. After taking short courses of bacteriology at Cambridge and Paris, he reached South Africa in January 1887 and remained there until October 1888. He proved that the sickness was malarial in type. Engaging meanwhile in the campaign against the Zulus in 1888, he was at the surrender of the chief Somkali at St. Lucia Lagoon.

He returned to India in January 1889, and was appointed inspecting veterinary officer of the Chittagong column during the Chin Lushai expedition. He was mentioned in despatches and was decorated with the Distinguished Service Order, being the first member of the army veterinary service to receive this distinction. At the end of the Chin Lushai campaign he was appointed in 1890 principal of the Lahore veterinary school, where he laboured for six years and laid the foundations of the native veterinary service, being rewarded with the C.I.E. in 1895. Nunn did much to advance the cause of veterinary science in India. Of untiring energy, he was personally popular with varied classes of his comrades.

From December 1896 to August 1905 Nunn was in England, spending part of his time in studying law. He was called to the bar at Lincoln's Inn in November 1899, and was afterwards nominated an advocate of the supreme court of the Transvaal. Again in England, he was from 1901 to 1904 deputy director-general of the army veterinary department, and was principal veterinary officer (eastern command) in 1904–5. From August 1905 he filled a similar position in South Africa, but was transferred to India in June 1906 and was made a C.B. He served in spite of illness till 1907, when he was forced to return to England. He died at Oxford on 23 Feb. 1908. He married in 1907 Gertrude Ann, widow of W. Chamberlain and daughter of E. Kellner, C.I.E.

Nunn, who was joint editor of the 'Veterinary Journal' from 1893 to 1906, published, in addition to the reports noticed above: 1. 'Report on South African Horse Sickness,' 1888. 2. Notes on 'Stable Management in India,' 1896; 2nd edit. 1897. 3. 'Lectures on Saddlery and Harness,' 1902. 4. 'Veterinary First Aid in Cases of Accident or Sudden Illness,' 1903. 5. 'The Use of Molasses as a Feeding Material,' from the French of Édouard Curot, 1903. 6. 'Diseases of the Mammary Gland of the Domestic Animals,' from the French of P. Leblanc, 1904. 7. 'Veterinary Toxicology,' 1907.

[Veterinary Record, 7 March 1908, p. 649; Veterinary Journal, March 1908, p. 105 (with portrait).] D'A. P.

NUTT, ALFRED TRÜBNER (1856–1910), publisher, folklorist, and Celtic scholar, born in London on 22 Nov. 1856, was eldest and only surviving son of David Nutt (*d.* 1863), a foreign bookseller and publisher, by his wife Ellen, daughter of Robert Carter and grand-daughter of William Miller, publisher, of Albemarle Street, predecessor of John Murray II. His second name commemorated his father's partnership with Nicholas Trübner [q. v.]. He was educated first at University College School and afterwards at the College at Vitry le François in the Marne. Having served three years' business apprenticeship in Leipzig, Berlin, and Paris, he in 1878 took his place as head of his father's firm, which, founded in 1829 at 58 Fleet Street, was moved in 1848 to 270–271 Strand. The business, which had been mainly confined to foreign bookselling, soon benefited by young Nutt's energy and enterprise, especially in the publishing department, which he mainly devoted to folklore and antiquities. Among his chief publications were the collection of unedited Scottish Gaelic texts known as 'Waifs and Strays of Celtic Tradition,' the 'Northern Library' of old Norse texts, the 'Tudor Library' of rare sixteenth-century works, the Tudor translations (in sixteenth-century prose), the 'Grimm Library,' the 'Bibliothèque de Carabas,' a critical edition of 'Don Quixote' in Spanish, 'Nutt's Juvenile Library,' the works of W. E. Henley, and the collection of English, Celtic, and Indian fairy tales. He also produced a number of excellent school books. The business was carried on at 57–59 Long Acre, 'At the sign of the Phœnix,' from 1890 to 1912, when it was removed to Grape St., New Oxford St.

Besides possessing much business capacity Nutt was a lifelong student of folklore and of the Celtic languages, and showed scholarship and power of original research in a number of valuable contributions which he made to both studies. His name will be 'definitely associated with the plea for the insular, Celtic, and popular *provenance* of the Arthurian cycle' (*Folk-lore*, 1910, p. 513). He founded the 'Folk-lore Journal' (afterwards 'Folk-lore'), was one of the earliest members of the Folk-lore Society (1879), and was elected president in 1897 and 1898. Besides presidential addresses he contributed many valuable articles to the society's journal, the 'Folk-lore Record,' and in 1892 he edited a volume of 'Transactions' of the International Folk-lore Congress (1891). In 1886 he helped to establish the English Goethe Society. He was one of the founders of the movement which led in 1898 to the formation of the Irish Texts Society. His most important literary productions were: 'Studies on the Legend of the Holy Grail with Special Reference to the Hypothesis of its Celtic Origin' (1888, *Folk-lore Soc.* vol. 23), and two essays on The Irish Vision of the Happy Otherworld and The Celtic Doctrine of Rebirth, appended to 'The Voyage of Bran, son of Febal, to the Land of the Living, an Old Irish Saga now first edited with Translation by Kuno Meyer' (*Grimm Library*, vols. 4 and 6, 1895–7).

On 21 May 1910, while on a holiday at Melun on the Seine, he was out driving with an invalid son, who fell into the river; Nutt bravely plunged to the rescue but was unfortunately drowned. His wife, Mrs. M. L. Nutt, who had been his secretary for several years, succeeded him as head of the firm. Two sons survived him.

Nutt also wrote: 1. 'The Aryan Expulsion and Return Formula in the Folk and Hero Tales of the Celts' (*Folk-lore Record*, vol. iv. 1881). 2. 'Mabinogion Studies, I. The Mabinogi of Branwen, Daughter of Llyr' (*ib.* vol. v. 1882). 3. 'Celtic and Mediæval Romance,' 1899 (*Popular Studies*, no. 1). 4. 'Ossian and Ossianic Literature,' 1899 (*ib.* no. 3). 5. 'The Fairy Mythology of Shakespeare,' 1900 (*ib.* no. 6). 6. 'Cuchulainn, the Irish Achilles,' 1900 (*ib.* no. 8). 7. 'The Legends of the Holy Grail,' 1902 (*ib.* no. 14). He added notes to Douglas Hyde's 'Beside the Fire, a Collection of Irish Gaelic Folk Stories' (1890); introductions and notes to several volumes of Lord A. Campbell's 'Waifs and Strays of Celtic Tradition'; a preface to Jeremiah Curtin's 'Tales of the Fairies and of the Ghost World'; a chapter on Folk-lore to 'Field and Folk-lore,' by H. Lowerison (1899); introduction, notes, and appendix to Matthew Arnold's 'Study of Celtic Literature' (1910), and notes to Lady Charlotte Guest's 'Mabinogion' (1902; revised and enlarged 1904).

[Obituary notice by E. Clodd in Folk-lore, 30 Sept. 1910, pp. 335–7 (with lithograph portrait) and pp. 512–14; The Times, 24 May 1910; Athenæum, and Publishers' Circular, 28 May 1910; Bookseller, 27 May 1910; Who's Who, 1910.] H. R. T.

O

OAKELEY, Sir HERBERT STANLEY (1830–1903), musical composer, born at Ealing on 22 July 1830, was second son of Sir Herbert Oakeley, third baronet [q. v.]. Educated at Rugby and at Christ Church, Oxford, he graduated B.A. in 1853 and proceeded M.A. in 1856. Oakeley showed an early taste for music, studied harmony with Stephen Elvey while at Oxford, and later visited Leipzig, Dresden, and Bonn, having organ lessons from Johann Schneider, and theory and piano lessons from Moscheles, Plaidy, and others. In 1865 he was elected Reid professor of music in Edinburgh University. He did much to improve the position of the chair; converted the annual 'Reid concert' into a three days' festival; engaged the Hallé orchestra to take part in concerts; gave frequent organ recitals in the music class room; and organised and conducted a University Musical Society. He was also director of music at St. Paul's episcopal church, Edinburgh, and in 1876 he directed the music at the inauguration of the Scottish national monument to the Prince Consort. He was then knighted by Queen Victoria at Holyrood, and was appointed 'composer to the Queen in Scotland.' To Queen Victoria, who appreciated his work, he dedicated many of his compositions. He received numerous honorary degrees, Mus.Doc. (Oxford, Dublin, St. Andrews, Edinburgh and Adelaide) and LL.D. (Aberdeen, Edinburgh, and Glasgow). He retired from his professorship in 1891, and died unmarried at Eastbourne on 26 Oct. 1903.

Oakeley was an excellent organist, with a marked gift for improvisation. He gave frequent popular lectures on musical subjects, was musical critic to the 'Guardian' 1858–68, and contributed to other journals. He was a prolific composer of vocal and instrumental music. Twenty of his songs were published in a 'Jubilee Album' (1887) dedicated to Queen Victoria. He wrote also twelve part-songs for mixed choir, choruses for male voices and students' songs, and made choral arrangements of many Scottish national airs. Among his church works are a motet, a 'Morning and Evening Service,' some dozen anthems, a 'Jubilee Cantata' (1887), and several hymn tunes. It is by two of the latter, 'Edina' and 'Abends,' associated respectively with the words 'Saviour, blessed Saviour,' and 'Sun of my Soul, Thou Saviour dear,' that he is best known. 'Edina,' composed in 1862, appeared first in the Appendix to 'Hymns Ancient and Modern,' 1868; 'Abends, composed in 1871, in the Irish 'Church Hymnal,' edited by Sir R. P. Stewart, Dublin, 1874.

[Life by his brother, Mr. E. M. Oakeley (with portrait), 1904; Hole's Quasi Cursores, 1884 (with portrait); Musical Times, Dec. 1903; Brit. Musical Biog.; Grove's Dict. of Music; Love's Scottish Church Music; personal knowledge.] J. C. H.

O'BRIEN, CHARLOTTE GRACE (1845–1909), Irish author and social reformer, born on 23 Nov. 1845 at Cahirmoyle, co. Limerick, was younger daughter in a family of five sons and two daughters of William Smith O'Brien [q. v.], Irish nationalist, by his wife Lucy Caroline, eldest daughter of Joseph Gabbett, of High Park, co. Limerick. On her father's return in 1854 from the penal settlement in Tasmania, Grace rejoined him in Brussels, and stayed there until his removal to Cahirmoyle in 1856. On her mother's death in 1861 she removed with her father to Killiney, near Dublin, and was his constant companion till his death at Bangor in 1864. From 1864 she lived at Cahirmoyle with her brother Edward, tending his motherless children, until his remarriage in 1880. She then went to live at Foynes on the Shannon, and there devoted herself to literary pursuits. She had already published in 1878 (2 vols. Edinburgh) her first novel, 'Light and Shade,' a tale of the Fenian rising of 1869, the material for which had been gathered from Fenian leaders. 'A Tale of Venice,' a drama, and 'Lyrics' appeared in 1880.

From 1880–1 her interests and pen were absorbed in Irish political affairs, in which she shared her father's opinions. She contributed articles to the 'Nineteenth Century' on 'The Irish Poor Man' (December 1880) and 'Eighty Years' (March 1881). In the spring of 1881 the attitude of the liberal government towards Ireland led her to address many fiery letters to the 'Pall Mall Gazette,' then edited by Mr. John (afterwards Viscount) Morley. Another interest, however, soon absorbed her activities. The disastrous harvest in Ireland in 1879, combined with Irish political turmoil, led to much emigration to America. At Queenstown, the port of embarkation, female emigrants suffered much from overcrowded lodgings and robbery (see article by Miss O'Brien in *Pall Mall Gazette*, 6 May 1881). Miss O'Brien not only induced the board of trade to exercise greater vigilance but also founded in 1881 a large boarding-house at Queenstown for the reception and protection of girls on the point of emigrating. In order to improve the steamship accommodation for female emigrants, and to study their prospects in America, Miss O'Brien made several steerage passages to America (see her privately printed letter on *The separation of the sexes on emigrant vessels*, addressed to Mr. Joseph Chamberlain, president of the board of trade, 1881). She also established in New York a similar institution to that in Queenstown for the protection of girls. Many experiences during this period found expression in her 'Lyrics' (Dublin, 1886), a small volume of poems, which gives simple pictures of the emigrants and contains some stirring nationalist ballads.

On her retirement from active public work in 1886 Miss O'Brien returned to Ardanoir, Foynes, on the bank of the Shannon, devoting her leisure to writing and to study of plant life; she contributed much on the flora of the Shannon district to the 'Irish Naturalist.' She had joined the Roman communion in 1887. She died on 3 June 1909 at Foynes, and was buried at Knockpatrick. 'Selections from her Writings and Correspondence' was published at Dublin in 1909. Her verses have dignity and grace; her polemical essays are vigorous and direct, and her essays on nature charm by their simple style.

[Charlotte Grace O'Brien, selections from her writings and correspondence, ed. by her nephew, Stephen Gwynn, M.P., 1909 (with memoir and portraits); The Times, 5 and 26 June, 1909. Miss O'Brien's works are to be distinguished from those written from 1855 onwards by Mrs. Charlotte O'Brien, which are wrongly attributed in the Brit. Mus. Cat. to Charlotte Grace O'Brien.] W. B. O.

O'BRIEN, CORNELIUS (1843–1906), catholic archbishop of Halifax, Nova Scotia, born near New Glasgow, Prince Edward Island, on 4 May 1843, was seventh of the nine children of Terence O'Brien of Munster by his wife Catherine O'Driscoll of Cork. After school training he obtained, as a boy, mercantile employment, but at nineteen entered St. Dunstan's College, Charlottetown, to study for the priesthood. In 1864 he passed to the College of the Propaganda in Rome, and concluded his seven years' course in 1871 by winning the prize for general excellence in the whole college. While he was in Rome Garibaldi attacked the city, the Vatican Council was held, and the temporal power fell. O'Brien, who had literary ambition and a taste for verse, founded on these stirring events an historical novel which he published later under the title 'After Weary Years' (Baltimore, 1886). On his return to Canada he was appointed a professor in St. Dunstan's College and rector of the cathedral of Charlottetown, but failing health led to his transfer in 1874 to the country parish of Indian River. There he devoted his leisure to writing, issuing 'The Philosophy of the Bible vindicated' (Charlottetown, 1876); 'Early Stages of Christianity in England' (Charlottetown, 1880); and 'Mater Admirabilis,' in praise of the Virgin (Montreal, 1882). He twice revisited Rome, and in 1882 O'Brien, on the death of Archbishop Hannan, was appointed his successor in the see of Halifax. O'Brien administered the diocese with great energy, building churches and schools, founding religious and benevolent institutions, and taking an active part in public affairs whenever he considered the good of the community demanded it. His hope of seeing a catholic university in Halifax was not realised, but he established a French College for the Acadians at Church Point, and founded a collegiate school, St. Mary's College, in Halifax, which was to be the germ of the future university. He died suddenly in Halifax on 9 March 1906, and was buried in the cemetery of the Holy Cross. A painted portrait is in the archiepiscopal palace in Halifax.

O'Brien, who was elected president of the Royal Society of Canada in 1896, was a representative Irish-Canadian prelate, combining force of character with depth of sentiment and winning the esteem of his protestant fellow-subjects while insisting on what he believed to be the rights of the Roman catholic minority. Advocating home rule for Ireland, he was at the same time a staunch imperialist and a strong Canadian. In addition to the books named he wrote 'St. Agnes, Virgin and Martyr' (Halifax, 1887), his patroness; 'Aminta,' a modern life drama (1890), a metrical novel after the model of 'Aurora Leigh'; and 'Memoirs of Edmund Burke (1753–1820), the first Bishop of Halifax' (1894). The last work called forth a reply, 'Mémoires sur les Missions de la Nouvelle Ecosse' (Quebec, 1895).

[Archbishop O'Brien: Man and Churchman, by Katherine Hughes (his niece), Ottawa, 1906 (with portraits); Morgan, Canadian Men and Women of the Time, 1898; Toronto Globe, 10 March 1906.] D. R. K.

O'BRIEN, JAMES FRANCIS XAVIER (1828–1905), Irish politician, born in Dungarvan, co. Waterford, Ireland, on 16 October 1828, was son of Timothy O'Brien, a merchant there, who owned some vessels which traded between England and Ireland and South Wales. His mother, Catherine, also belonged to an O'Brien family. When Father Mathew, the total abstinence missionary, visited Dungarvan, O'Brien, then aged eight, took the pledge, which he kept till he was twenty-one. He was educated successively at a private school in Dungarvan and at St. John's College, Waterford. In boyhood he adopted Irish nationalist principles of an advanced type. During the disturbances of 1848 he took part in the abortive attack of James Finton Lalor [q. v.] upon the police barrack of Cappoquin. A warrant was issued for O'Brien's arrest, but he escaped to Wales in one of his father's vessels. On his return to Ireland he engaged, at first at Lismore and then at Clonmel, in the purchase of grain for the export business carried on by his father and family. After his father's death in 1853 he gave up this occupation in order to study medicine. In 1854 he gained a scholarship at the Queen's College, Galway, but soon left to accompany a political friend, John O'Leary [q. v. Suppl. II], to Paris, where he continued his medical studies. He attended lectures at the École de Médecine, and visited hospitals—La Pitié, La Charité, Hôtel Dieu. Among the acquaintances he formed in Paris were the artist James MacNeill Whistler [q. v. Suppl. II], John Martin [q. v.], and Kevin Izod O'Doherty [q. v. Suppl. II], members of the Young Ireland party. A failure of health broke off his medical studies. After returning to Ireland in 1856 he sailed for New Orleans, with the intention of seeking a new experience by taking part in William Walker's expedition to Nicaragua. Through the influence of Pierre Soule, then attorney-general for the state of Louisiana, O'Brien joined Walker's staff. He sailed with the expedition to San Juan and up that river to Fort San Carlos, but Walker made terms without fighting. Returning to New Orleans, O'Brien became a book-keeper there. In 1858 he met James Stephens [q. v. Suppl. II], one of the founders of the Fenian organisation, and Stephens led him to join the local branch. On the outbreak of the American civil war in 1861 he served as assistant-surgeon in a volunteer militia regiment, consisting mainly of Irishmen.

In 1862 he returned to Ireland, and joined the Fenian organisation in Cork, and here he met Stephens again in 1865. He deemed the Fenian rising in 1867 to be premature, but on the night of 3 March 1867 he loyally joined his comrades at the rendezvous on Prayer Hill outside Cork, and led an attack upon the Ballynockan police barracks, which surrendered. The party seized the arms there, and marched on towards Bottle Hill, but scattered on the approach of a body of infantry. O'Brien was arrested near Kilmallock, and taken to Limerick jail. He was subsequently taken to Cork county gaol, and in May tried for high treason. He was convicted, and was sentenced in accordance with the existing law to be hanged, drawn, and quartered. The sentence was commuted to penal servitude for life. O'Brien is said to have been the last survivor of those sentenced to the barbarous punishment provided by the old law of treason. By a new act of 1870, hanging or beheading was appointed to be the sole penalty of the extreme kind. From Mountjoy Prison, Dublin, O'Brien was soon taken with some twenty-nine other political prisoners, chained together in gangs, to Holyhead on a gunboat, whence he was removed to Millbank, where he was kept in solitary confinement for fourteen months. Next he was removed to Portland with others, chained in sets of six. In Portland he worked at stone-dressing. He was finally released on 4 March 1869. On visiting Waterford, and subsequently Cork, he received popular ovations.

Before his arrest O'Brien was manager of a wholesale tea and wine business at Cork. He resumed the post on his release, and was soon appointed a traveller for his firm. Having rejoined the Fenian organisation (finally becoming a member of the supreme council of that body) he combined throughout Ireland the work of Fenian missionary and commercial traveller until 1873. Subsequently he carried on the business of a tea and wine merchant in Dublin, and was at a later period secretary to the gas company at Cork.

Meanwhile he was gradually drawn into the parliamentary home rule movement under Parnell's leadership. In 1885 he became nationalist M.P. for South Mayo, and acted as one of the party treasurers till his death. In the schism of 1891 he seceded from Parnell. Afterwards he became general secretary of the United Irish League of Great Britain, an office which he held for life. He continued member for South Mayo till 1895, when he became member for Cork City and retained the seat till his death. He died at Clapham on 28 May 1905, and was buried in Glasnevin cemetery, Dublin. He was twice married: (1) in 1859 to Mary Louisa Cullimore (*d.* 1866), of Wexford; and (2) in 1870 to Mary Teresa O'Malley. By his first wife he had one son; by his second, three daughters and two sons. A portrait painted by an artist named Connolly belongs to the family.

[Private information; John O'Leary's Recollections, 2 vols. 1896.] R. B. O'B.

O'CALLAGHAN, Sir FRANCIS LANGFORD (1839–1909), civil engineer, born on 22 July 1839, was second son of James O'Callaghan, J.P., of Drisheen, co. Cork, by his wife Agnes, daughter of the Rev. Francis Langford. Educated at private schools and at Queen's College, Cork, he received practical engineering training under H. Conybeare between 1859 and 1862, when he was employed on railway construction in Ireland and in South Wales. He then entered the public works department of India by competitive examination, and was appointed probationary assistant engineer on 13 June 1862. He became an executive engineer on 1 April 1866, and reached the first grade of that rank in March 1871, becoming superintending engineer, third class, on 1 Jan. 1880, and first class in March 1886. On 9 May 1889 he was appointed chief engineer, first class, and consulting engineer to the government of India for state railways, and on 8 Aug. 1892 he was appointed secretary to the public works department, from which he retired in 1894.

In the course of his thirty-two years' service O'Callaghan was engaged on the Northern Road in the Central Provinces (including the Kanhan bridge); on surveys for the Chanda, Nagpur and Raipur, Nagpur and Chhattisgarh, Sind-Sagor, and Khwaja-Amran railways; and on the construction of the Tirhoot, Punjab Northern (Pindi-Peshawar section), Bolan, and Sind-Pishin railways. He was thanked by the government of India in May 1883 for his work on the Attock bridge across the Indus, on the completion of which he was made C.I.E. On four subsequent occasions the government tendered O'Callaghan its thanks, viz. for services connected with the question of frontier railways (Feb. 1886), for the construction of the Bolan railway (June 1886), for the erection of the Victoria bridge at Chak Nizam on the Sind-Sagor railway (special thanks, June 1887), and for the construction of the Khojak tunnel and extension of the railway to New Chaman. In 1887 he was commended by the secretary of state for work on the Sind-Sagor state railway. Next year, for the construction of the railway through the Bolan Pass to Quetta, he was made C.S.I. His technical abilities were linked with tact, judgment, and genial temper. On his retirement he returned to England, and was appointed in Sept. 1895 by the colonial office to be the managing member of the Uganda railway committee; and he held the position until the committee was dissolved on 30 Sept. 1903. In 1902 he received the recognition of K.C.M.G.

O'Callaghan was elected an associate of the Institution of Civil Engineers on 12 Jan. 1869, and became a full member on 23 April 1872. He was also a fellow of the Royal Geographical Society. He published in 1865 'Bidder's Earthwork Tables, intended and adapted for the Use of the Public Works Department in India.'

He died suddenly at his residence, Clonmeen, Epsom Road, Guildford, on 14 Nov. 1909, and was buried at Holy Trinity Church, Guildford. He married, on 22 Sept. 1875, Anna Maria Mary (*d.* 1911), second daughter of Lieut.-colonel Henry Claringbold Powell, of Banlahan, co. Cork, and left an only son, Francis Reginald Powell (1880–1910), captain R.E.

[History of Services of Officers of the Indian Public Works Department; Proc. Inst. Civ. Eng., clxxix. 364.] W. F. S.

O'CONNOR, CHARLES YELVERTON (1843–1902), civil engineer, son of John O'Connor of Ardlonan and Gravelmount, co. Meath, was born at Gravelmount on 14 Jan. 1843. He was educated at the Waterford endowed school, was articled at the age of seventeen to John Challoner Smith, and after three years' experience on railway work in Ireland emigrated to New Zealand in 1865. There he was employed as an assistant engineer on the construction of the coach road from Christchurch to the Hokitika goldfields. Gradually promoted, he was appointed in 1870 engineer of the western portion of the province of Canterbury. From 1874 to 1880 he was district engineer for the combined Westland and Nelson districts, and from 1880 to 1883 inspecting engineer for the whole of the Middle Island. In 1883 he was appointed under secretary for public works for New Zealand, and he held that position until May 1890, when he was made marine engineer for the colony.

In April 1891 O'Connor was appointed engineer-in-chief to the state of Western Australia; the office carried with it the acting general managership of the railways, but of this he was relieved at his own request in December 1896, in order that he might devote all his time to engineering work. He remained engineer-in-chief until his death, and in that capacity was responsible for all new railway work. He was a strong advocate of constructing railways quite cheaply in new countries.

The discovery of the Coolgardie goldfield in 1892 led to an extraordinary and rapid development of the state of Western Australia, and in that development O'Connor, as engineer-in-chief, played a part probably second only to that of the premier, Sir John Forrest. In the short period of eleven years he undertook two works of the utmost importance to the colony, namely Fremantle harbour and the Coolgardie water-supply, besides constructing all new railways. He also executed a large number of smaller works, such as bridges, harbours, and jetties, and improvements in the permanent way, alignment, and gradients of the railways.

The Fremantle harbour works, carried out from 1892 to 1902, at a cost of 1,459,000*l.*, made Fremantle, instead of Albany, the first or last calling-place in Australia for liners outward or homeward bound. A safe and commodious harbour, capable of receiving and berthing the largest ocean steamships at all states of the tide and in all weather, was formed by constructing north and south moles of limestone rock and rubble; while an inner harbour with wharves and jetties was provided by dredging the mouth of the Swan river. The Coolgardie water scheme, carried out between 1898 and 1903 at a cost of 2,660,000*l.*, was designed to afford a supply of water to the principal goldfields of the colony. The source is the Helena river, on which, about twenty-three miles from Perth, a reservoir was constructed whence five million gallons of water could be pumped daily through a steel main thirty inches in diameter to Coolgardie, a distance of 328 miles. O'Connor visited England in 1897 on business connected with this and other work for the colony, and while at home he was made a C.M.G.

The execution of works of this magnitude threw on O'Connor heavy labour and responsibility for which his professional ability and high principle well fitted him, but conflicting influences in the administration and polity of the new colony caused him at the same time anxieties and worries, which ultimately destroyed his mental balance. On 10 March 1902 he shot himself through the head on the beach at Robb's Jetty, Fremantle. He married in 1875 a daughter of William Ness of Christchurch, New Zealand. She survived him, with seven children.

O'Connor was elected a member of the Institution of Civil Engineers 6 April 1880. He wrote numerous reports on engineering matters in the colony, among which may be mentioned two on the Coolgardie water-supply scheme (Perth, 1896) and the projected Australian trans-continental railway (Perth, 1901). The Fremantle harbour works and the Coolgardie water-supply were described in the 'Proceedings of the Institution of Civil Engineers' (clxxxiv. 157 and clxii. 50) by O'Connor's successor, Mr. C. S. R. Palmer.

A bronze statue of O'Connor by Pietro Porcelli was erected at Fremantle in 1911.

[Minutes of Proceedings, Inst. Civ. Eng., cl. 444; Engineer, 18 April 1902.] W. F. S.

O'CONNOR, JAMES (1836–1910), Irish journalist and politician, was born on 10 Feb. 1836 in the Glen of Imaal, co. Wicklow, where his father, Patrick O'Connor, was a farmer. His mother's maiden surname was Kearney. After education at an Irish national school, he entered early on a commercial career. He was one of the first to join the Fenian organisation. and when its organ, the 'Irish People,' was established in 1863, he joined the staff as book-keeper. With John O'Leary [q. v. Suppl. II], Thomas Clarke Luby [q. v. Suppl. II], O'Donovan Rossa, and C. J. Kickham [q.v.], and the other officials and contributors, O'Connor was arrested on 15 Sept. 1865 at the time of the seizure and suppression of the paper. Convicted with his associates, he was sentenced to seven years' imprisonment. After five years, spent chiefly in Millbank and Portland prisons, he was released, and became sub-editor to the 'Irishman' and the 'Flag of Ireland,' advanced nationalist papers conducted by Richard Pigott [q. v.]. When Pigott sold these papers to Parnell and the Land League in 1880 and they were given up, O'Connor was made sub-editor of 'United Ireland,' which was founded in 1881. In December of that year O'Connor was imprisoned with Parnell and other political leaders in Kilmainham.

After the Parnellite split in 1887, 'United Ireland,' which opposed Parnell, was seized by the Irish leader and O'Connor left. He was shortly after appointed editor of the 'Weekly National Press,' a journal started in the interests of the anti-Parnellites. In 1892 he became nationalist M.P. for West Wicklow, and he retained the seat till his death at Kingstown on 12 March 1910.

Though an active journalist, O'Connor published little independently of his newspapers. A pamphlet, 'Recollections of Richard Pigott' (Dublin, 1889), supplies the most authentic account of Pigott's career.

O'Connor was married twice; his first wife with four children died in 1890 from eating poisonous mussels at Monkstown, co. Dublin. A public monument was erected over their grave in Glasnevin. By his second wife, whose maiden name was McBride, he had one daughter.

[Recollections of an Irish National Journalist, by Richard Pigott; Recollections of Pigott, by James O'Connor, 1889 New Ireland, by A. M. Sullivan, p. 263, 10th edition; Recollections of Fenians and Fenianism, by John O'Leary; Recollections, by William O'Brien; Freeman's Journal, Irish Independent, and The Times, 13 March 1910.] D. J. O'D.

O'CONOR, CHARLES OWEN, styled O'Conor Don (1838–1906), Irish politician, born on 7 May 1838 in Dublin, was eldest son of Denis O'Conor of Belanagore and Clonallis, co. Roscommon, by Mary, daughter of Major Blake of Towerhill, co. Mayo. His family was Roman catholic. A younger son, Denis Maurice O'Conor, LL.D. (1840–1883), was M.P. in the liberal and home rule interest for Sligo county (1868–83).

Charles Owen, after education at St. Gregory's College, Downside, near Bath, matriculated at London University in 1855, but did not graduate. He early entered public life, being elected M.P. for Roscommon county as a liberal at a bye-election in 1860. He sat for that constituency till the general election of 1880. In 1874 he was returned as a home ruler, but, refusing to take the party pledge exacted by Parnell, was ousted by a nationalist in 1880. In 1883 he was defeated by Mr. William Redmond in a contest for Wexford. An active member of parliament, he was an effective though not an eloquent speaker and a leading exponent of Roman catholic opinion. He frequently spoke on Irish education and land tenure. He criticised unfavourably the Queen's Colleges established in 1845 and the model schools, and advocated separate education for Roman catholics. In 1867 he introduced a measure to extend the Industrial Schools Act to Ireland, which became law next year. He opposed Gladstone's university bill of 1873, and in May 1879 brought forward a measure, which had the support of almost every section of Irish political opinion, for the creation of a new examining university, 'St. Patrick's,' with power to make grants based on the results of examination to students of denominational colleges affiliated to it. This was withdrawn on 23 July on the announcement of the government bill creating the Royal University of Ireland. Of the senate of that body he was for many years an active member, and received the honorary degree of LL.D. in 1892. He was also on the intermediate education board established in 1878.

O'Conor steadily urged a reform of the Irish land laws. During the discussion of the land bill of 1870 he advocated the extension of the Ulster tenant right to the other provinces. He sat on the select committee appointed in 1877 to inquire into the working of the purchase clauses of the Land Act of 1870.

On social and industrial questions he also spoke with authority. He was a member of the royal commissions on the Penal Servitude Acts (1863), and on factories and workshops (1875); and the passing of the Irish Sunday Closing Act of 1879 was principally due to his persevering activity. He seconded Lord Claud Hamilton's motion (29 April 1873) for the purchase by the state of Irish railways.

From 1872 onwards O'Conor professed his adherence to home rule and supported Butt in his motion for inquiry into the parliamentary relations of Great Britain and Ireland in 1874, though admitting that federal home rule would not satisfy nationalist aspirations. He also acted with the Irish leader in his endeavours to mitigate the severity of coercive legislation, though declaring himself not in all circumstances opposed to exceptional laws.

After his parliamentary career ceased in 1880 O'Conor was a member of the registration of deeds commission of 1880, and took an active part in the Bessborough land commission of the same year (see PONSONBY, FREDERICK GEORGE BRABAZON). He was a member of both the parliamentary committee of 1885 and the royal commission of 1894 on the financial relations between Great Britain and Ireland, and became chairman of the commission on the death of Hugh Culling Eardley Childers [q. v. Suppl. I], in 1896. O'Conor held that Ireland was unfairly treated under the existing arrangements. In local government he was also active. He had presided over parliamentary committees on Irish grand jury laws and land valuation in 1868 and 1869, and was elected to the first county council of Roscommon in 1898. He was lord-lieutenant of the county from 1888 till his death. He had been sworn of the Irish privy council in 1881.

O'Conor was much interested in antiquarian studies, and published in 1891 'The O'Conors of Connaught: an Historical Memoir compiled from a MS. of the late John O'Donovan, LL.D., with Additions from the State Papers and Public Records.' He was for many years president of the Antiquarian Society of Ireland, as well as of the Royal Irish Academy. He was president of the Irish Language Society, and procured the insertion of Irish into the curriculum of the intermediate education board.

O'Conor died at Clonallis, Castlerea, on 30 June 1906, and was buried in the new cemetery, Castlerea. He married (1) on 21 April 1868, Georgina Mary (*d.*1872), daughter of Thomas Aloysius Perry, of Bitham House, Warwickshire; and (2) in 1879, Ellen, third daughter of John Lewis More O'Ferrall of Lisard, Edgeworthstown, co. Longford. He had four sons by the first marriage.

[Burke's Landed Gentry of Ireland; Walford's County Families; Men of the Time, 1899; Who's Who, 1906; The Times, 2 and 5 July 1906; Roscommon Journal, 7 July (containing obituaries from Freeman's Journal, Irish Times, &c.); Hansard's Parl. Debates.] G. LE G. N.

O'CONOR, SIR NICHOLAS RODERICK (1843–1908), diplomatist, born at Dundermott, co. Roscommon, on 3 July 1843, was youngest of three sons of Patrick A. C. O'Conor of Dundermott by his wife Jane, second daughter of Christopher Ffrench of Frenchlawn, co. Roscommon. Educated at Stonyhurst College, and afterwards at Munich under Dr. Döllinger, he entered the diplomatic service in 1866, passed the necessary examination, and after some months of employment in the foreign office was appointed attaché at Berlin, where he attained in 1870 the rank of third secretary. After service at Washington and Madrid, he returned to Washington on promotion to be second secretary in 1874, and was transferred in 1875 to Brazil, where he was employed on special duty in the province of Rio Grande do Sul in November 1876. In October 1877 he was removed to Paris, where he had the advantage of serving for six years under Lord Lyons. In December 1883 he was appointed secretary of legation at Peking, and on the death of the minister, Sir Harry Parkes [q. v.], in March 1885, assumed charge of the legation for a period of fifteen months. He found himself almost immediately involved in somewhat awkward discussions with the Chinese and Korean governments in regard to the temporary occupation of Port Hamilton, a harbour formed by three islands at the entrance to the Gulf of Pechili, of which the British admiral had taken possession as a coaling station, in view of the apparent imminence of an outbreak of war between Great Britain and Russia. The Chinese and Korean governments were not unwilling to agree to the occupation for a pecuniary consideration on receiving assurances that no permanent acquisition was contemplated, but were threatened by Russia with similar occupations elsewhere if they gave their consent. The question was eventually settled, after the apprehension of war with Russia had disappeared, by the withdrawal of the British occupation in consideration of a guarantee by China that no part of Korean territory, including Port Hamilton, would be occupied by any foreign power. The annexation of Upper Burma to the British Indian empire, proclaimed by Lord Dufferin in 1886, gave rise to an equally embarrassing question. The Chinese government viewed the annexation with great jealousy. The new British possession was, along a great portion of the eastern frontier, conterminous with that of China, while on the north it abutted on the vassal state of Tibet. China claimed indeterminate and somewhat obsolete rights of suzerainty over the Burmese, which were still evidenced by a decennial mission from Burma charged with presents to the Emperor. The country contained a considerable and influential Chinese population, and China could easily create trouble by raids into the frontier districts. A friendly arrangement was almost imperative. After a tedious negotiation O'Conor succeeded in concluding an agreement on 24 July 1886, making provision for the delimitation of frontier by a joint commission, for as future convention to settle the conditions of frontier trade, and agreeing to the continuance of the decennial Burmese mission, in return for a waiver of any right of interference with British authority and rule. Though this agreement was only the preliminary to a series of long and toilsome negotiations, it placed the question in the way of friendly solution. On its conclusion O'Conor, who had been made C.M.G. in Feb. 1886, was created C.B.

After a brief tenure of the post of secretary of legation at Washington, he in Jan. 1887 succeeded (Sir) Frank Lascelles as agent and consul-general in Bulgaria. The principality was at the time in a critical situation. Prince Alexander, whose nerve had been shaken by his forcible abduction, having failed to obtain the Czar's approval of his resumption of power, had abdicated in September 1886, and the government was left in the hands of three regents, of whom the principal was the former prime minister, Stambuloff. For the next few months, in the face of manœuvres on the part of Russia to prolong the interregnum or procure the selection of a nominee who would be a mere vassal of Russia, vigorous endeavours were made by the regency to obtain a candidate of greater independence, and on 7 July 1887 Prince Ferdinand of Saxe-Coburg was elected, and Stambuloff again became prime minister. O'Conor, who united great shrewdness with a blunt directness of speech, which, although not generally regarded as a diplomatic trait, had the effect of inspiring confidence, exercised a steadying influence on the energetic premier. Excellent relations were maintained between them in the course of five years' residence. Among other results was the conclusion in 1889 of a provisional commercial agreement between Great Britain and Bulgaria.

In April 1892 O'Conor was again appointed to Peking, this time in the position of envoy to the Emperor of China, and to the King of Korea. A notable change in the etiquette towards foreign representatives was made by the court in his reception at Peking; he was formally received with the staff of the legation at the principal entrance by the court officials and conducted to a personal audience with the Emperor in the Cheng Kuan Tien Palace. In July 1894 the disputes between China and Japan as to the introduction of reforms in the administration of Korea led to open war between the two countries, and O'Conor's responsibilities were heavy. The Chinese forces were routed by land and sea, and in April 1895 the veteran statesman Li-Hung-Chang concluded the treaty of Shimonoseki, by which the Liao-Tung Peninsula, the island of Formosa, and the Pescadores group were ceded to Japan, China agreeing further to pay an indemnity of 200 millions of taels. Popular excitement in China ran high during these events. The Chinese government provided the foreign legations with guards of native soldiers, who, though perfectly well behaved, did not inspire complete confidence as efficient protectors. The British admiral gave the British legation the additional safeguard of a party of marines. Almost immediately after the ratification of the treaty of Shimonoseki a fresh complication occurred. The French, German, and Russian governments presented to Japan a collective note, urging the restoration to China of the Liao-Tung Peninsula on the ground that its possession, with Port Arthur, by a foreign power would be a permanent menace to the Chinese capital. The course pursued by the British government was not calculated to earn the gratitude of either of the parties principally interested. They declined to join in the representation of the three European powers, but they did not conceal from Japan their opinion that she might do wisely to give way. Japan with much wisdom assented to the retrocession in consideration of an additional indemnity of 30 millions of taels. In recognition of O'Conor's arduous labours he received the honour of K.C.B. in May 1895. Meanwhile the signature of peace was followed by anti-foreign outbreaks in several provinces of China, in one of which, at Ku-cheng, British missionaries were massacred. The Chinese government, as usual, while ready to pay compensation and to execute a number of men arrested as having taken part in the riot, interposed every kind of obstacle to investigation of the real origin of the outbreaks and to the condign punishment of the officials who secretly instigated or connived at them. In the end, after exhausting all other arguments, O'Conor plainly intimated to the Tseng-li-Yamen that unless his demands were conceded within two days the British admiral would be compelled to resort to naval measures, and a decree was issued censuring and degrading the ex-viceroy of Szechuen.

In Oct. 1895 O'Conor left China to become ambassador at St. Petersburg. In the following year he attended the coronation of the Emperor Nicholas II, who had succeeded to the throne in November 1894. He received the grand cross of St. Michael and St. George and was sworn a privy councillor in the same year. He was as popular at St. Petersburg as at his previous posts, but towards the close of his residence our relations with Russia were seriously complicated by the course taken by the Russian government in obtaining from China a lease of Port Arthur and the Liao-Tung Peninsula. The discussions, which at one time became somewhat acute, were carried on by O'Conor with his usual tact; but a disagreeable question arose between him and Count Muravieff, the Russian minister for foreign affairs, as to an assurance which the latter had given but subsequently withdrew that Port Arthur, as well as Talienwan, should be open to the commerce of all nations. This incident and the manner in which Count Muravieff endeavoured to explain it made it on the whole fortunate that in July 1898 an opportunity offered for O'Conor's transference to Constantinople. He had been promoted G.C.B. in 1897.

O'Conor's last ten years of life, which were passed in Constantinople, were very laborious. He worked under great difficulties for the policy of administrative reform, which was strenuously pressed whenever possible by the British government. He succeeded, however, in winning to a considerable extent the personal goodwill and confidence of the Sultan and of the ministers with whom he had to deal, and by persistent efforts cleared off a large number of long outstanding claims and subordinate questions which had been a permanent burden to his predecessors. Among more important questions which he succeeded in bringing to a settlement were those of the Turco-Egyptian boundary in the Sinai Peninsula, and of the British frontier in the hinterland of Aden. His health had never been strong since his residence in China, and in 1904 he came to England for advice, and underwent a serious operation. The strain of work on his return overtaxed his strength, and he died at his post on 19 March 1908. He was buried with every mark of affection and respect in the cemetery at Haidar Pasha, where a monument erected by his widow bears with the date the inscription 'Nicolaus Rodericus O'Conor, Britanniæ Regis apud Ottomanorum Imperatorem Legatus, pie obiit.' O'Conor succeeded in May 1877, on the death of his surviving elder brother, Patrick Hugh, to the family estate of Dundermott. He married on 13 April

1887 Minna, eldest daughter of James Robert Hope-Scott [q. v.], the celebrated parliamentary advocate, and of Lady Victoria Alexandrina, eldest daughter of Henry Granville Howard, 14th duke of Norfolk; by her O'Conor had three daughters.

[Burke's Landed Gentry; The Times, 20 March 1908; Foreign Office List, 1909, p. 403; Cambridge Modern History, vol. xii. p. 509; papers laid before Parliament; Annual Register, 1895.] S.

O'DOHERTY, KEVIN IZOD (1823–1905), Irish and Australian politician, born in Gloucester Street, Dublin, on 7 Sept. 1823, was son of William Izod O'Doherty, solicitor, by his wife Anne McEvoy. After a good preliminary education at Dr. Wall's school in Hume Street, Dublin, he entered the School of Medicine of the Catholic university there in 1843. While pursuing his medical studies he identified himself with the Young Ireland movement and contributed to its organ, the 'Nation,' and was one of the founders of the Students' and Polytechnic Clubs, which opposed the constitutional leaders under O'Connell. When John Mitchel [q. v.] seceded from the 'Nation,' and openly advocated revolution, O'Doherty leaned to his views, and when Mitchel's paper, the 'Weekly Irishman,' was suppressed and himself arrested, O'Doherty helped to carry on Mitchel's campaign, chiefly in the 'Irish Tribune,' which he started with Richard Dalton Williams, the first number appearing on 10 June 1848. After five weeks the paper was seized, and O'Doherty and his colleagues were arrested and charged with treason-felony. After two juries had disagreed as to their verdict, he was convicted by a third jury, and sentenced to transportation for ten years to Van Diemen's Land. He arrived in that colony on the Elphinstone with John Martin (1812–1875) [q. v.] in November 1849.

In 1854 O'Doherty received, with the other Young Irelanders, a pardon on condition that he did not return to the United Kingdom. He went to Paris to continue his medical studies, but managed to pay a flying visit to Ireland in 1855. In 1856 his pardon was made unconditional, and having taken his medical degrees in the Royal Colleges of Surgeons and Physicians of Ireland in 1857 and in 1859 he practised his profession for a while in his native city. In 1862 he emigrated to Sydney, New South Wales, soon proceeding to the new colony of Queensland, and settled in Brisbane. Here he long practised as a physician. He was elected a member of the Queensland Legislative Assembly. In 1877 he was made a member of the legislative council of the colony, but resigned in 1885, and returned to Europe. He was presented with the freedom of the city of Dublin in that year. At Parnell's invitation he was elected nationalist member for North Meath in 1885. But he had lost touch with home politics and in 1888 went back to Brisbane, where he failed to recover his extensive professional connection. His last years were clouded by pecuniary distress. He died on 15 July 1905, leaving his widow and daughter unprovided for. Four sons had predeceased him.

His wife, MARY ANNE KELLY (1826–1910), Irish poetess, daughter of a Galway gentleman farmer named Kelly by his wife, a Miss O'Flaherty of Galway, was born at Headford in that county in 1826. Early in the career of the 'Nation' newspaper she contributed powerful patriotic verses. Her earliest poem in the paper appeared on 28 Dec. 1844 under her original signature 'Fionnuala.' Subsequently she adopted the signature 'Eva.' Of the three chief poetesses of Irish nationality 'Mary' (Ellen Mary Patrick Downing), and 'Speranza' (Jane Elgee, afterwards Lady Wilde [q. v.]), being the other two), 'Eva' was the most gifted. She also wrote much verse, full of patriotism, feeling, and fancy, for the nationalist papers, 'Irish Tribune,' 'Irish Felon,' the 'Irishman,' and the 'Irish People.'

Before O'Doherty was convicted in 1849 he had become engaged to her, and she declined his offer to release her. In 1855 O'Doherty paid a surreptitious visit to Ireland and married her in Kingstown. After her husband's death in 1905 she was supported by a fund raised for her relief by Irish people. Mrs. O'Doherty died at Brisbane on 21 May 1910, and was buried there by the side of her husband. A monument was placed by public subscription over their graves.

'Poems by "Eva" of "The Nation"' appeared in San Francisco in 1877. A selection of her poems was issued for her benefit in Dublin in 1908, with a preface by Seumas MacManus and a memoir by Justin McCarthy.

[Poems by 'Eva,' Dublin, 1908; Heaton's Australian Book of Dates, 1879; Duffy's Young Ireland, and Four Years of Irish History; Queenslander, 22 July 1905 and 28 May 1910; A. M. Sullivan's New Ireland; O'Donoghue's Poets of Ireland; Rolleston's Treasury of Irish Poetry, 1905, page 153;

Cameron's Hist. of the Coll. of Surgeons in Ireland, 1880, p. 614; information kindly supplied by Mr. P. J. Dillon, formerly of Brisbane; private correspondence of 'Eva' with John O'Leary, in present writer's possession.]
D. J. O'D.

OGLE, JOHN WILLIAM (1824–1905), physician, born at Leeds on 30 July 1824, was only child of Samuel Ogle, who was engaged in business in that town, and Sarah Rathmell. His father, who was first cousin to Admiral Thomas Ogle and second cousin to James Adey Ogle [q. v.], regius professor of medicine at Oxford was a member of an old Staffordshire and Shropshire family which originally came from Northumberland. John was educated at Wakefield school, from which he passed in 1844 to Trinity College, Oxford, where he graduated B.A. in 1847, and developed sympathy with the tractarian movement. He entered the medical school in Kinnerton Street attached to St. George's Hospital, and became in 1850 a licentiate (equivalent of present member) and in 1855 a fellow of the Royal College of Physicians. At Oxford he proceeded M.A. and B.M. in 1851 and D.M. in 1857. At St. George's Hospital he worked much at morbid anatomy, and was for years curator of the museum with Henry Grey, after whose death in 1861 he became lecturer on pathology. In 1857 he was elected assistant physician, and in 1866 he became full physician, but resigned owing to mental depression in 1876. Cured shortly afterwards by an attack of enteric fever, he returned to active practice, but not to his work at St. George's Hospital, where, however, he was elected consulting physician in 1877.

He was censor (1873, 1874, 1884) and vice-president (1886) of the Royal College of Physicians, and an associate fellow of the College of Physicians of Philadelphia. Although he was an all-round scholarly physician, his main interest lay in nervous diseases. In a lecture on aphasia, or inability to translate thoughts into words, he made some interesting historical references to the cases of Dr. Johnson and Dean Swift. Always a strong churchman, he was on friendly terms with W. E. Gladstone, Newman, Church, Liddon, Temple, and Benson. He was elected F.S.A. on 7 March 1878.

After some years of increasing paralytic weakness, dating from 1899, he died at Highgate vicarage on 8 Aug. 1905, and was buried at Shelfanger near Diss in Norfolk. He married, on 31 May 1854, Elizabeth, daughter of Albert Smith of Ecclesall, near Sheffield, whose family subsequently took the name of Blakelock. He had five sons and one daughter.

Ogle was active in medical literature. Together with Timothy Holmes [q. v. Suppl. II] he founded the now extinct 'St. George's Hospital Reports' (1866–79) and edited seven out of the ten volumes. He was also editor of the 'British and Foreign Medico-Chirurgical Review.' He contributed widely to the medical papers and societies, making 160 communications to the 'Transactions of the Pathological Society of London' alone. His independently published works were the Harveian oration for 1880 at the Royal College of Physicians, which contains much scholarly information, and a small work 'On the Relief of Excessive and Dangerous Tympanites by Puncture of the Abdomen,' 1888.

[British Medical Journal, 1905, ii. 416; private information.] H. D. R.

O'HANLON, JOHN (1821–1905), Irish hagiographer and historical writer, born in Stradbally, Queen's Co., on 30 April 1821, was son of Edward and Honor Hanlon of that town. Destined by his parents for the priesthood, he passed at thirteen from a private school at Stradbally to an endowed school at Ballyroan, and in 1840 he entered the ecclesiastical college at Carlow. In May 1842 he emigrated with some relatives to Quebec, Lower Canada, and moved in the following August to the state of Missouri, U.S.A. In 1847 he was ordained by Peter Richard Kenrick, archbishop of St. Louis, and spent the next few years as a missionary priest among the Irish exiles of Missouri. His experiences in America are fully described in his 'Life and Scenery in Missouri' (Dublin, 1890). In Sept. 1853, owing to ill-health, he returned to Ireland. From 1854 to 1859 he was assistant-chaplain of the South Dublin Union, and from 1854 to 1880 curate of St. Michael's and St. John's, Dublin. On the nomination of Cardinal McCabe [q. v.] he became, in May 1880, parish priest of St. Mary's, Irishtown, where he remained till his death. In 1891 he revisited America in connection with the golden jubilee of Archbishop Kenrick. Archbishop Walsh conferred on him the rank of canon in 1886. He died at Irishtown on 15 May 1905.

O'Hanlon was devoted to researches in Irish ecclesiastical history, and especially to the lives of the Irish saints. While still a curate he travelled on the Continent in order to pursue his researches, and visited nearly all the important libraries of England and southern Europe. In 1856 he began to collect material for his great work, 'The Lives of the Irish Saints.' The first volume appeared in 1875, and before his death he issued nine complete volumes and portion of a tenth, besides collecting and arranging unpublished material. Apart from this storehouse of learning, with its wealth of notes and illustrations, O'Hanlon wrote incessantly in Irish reviews and newspapers, and published the following: 1. 'Abridgment of the History of Ireland from its Final Subjection to the Present Time,' Boston (Mass.), 1849. 2. 'The Irish Emigrant's Guide to the United States,' Boston, 1851; new edit. Dublin, 1890. 3. 'The Life of St. Laurence O'Toole, Archbishop of Dublin,' Dublin, 1857. 4. 'The Life of St. Malachy O'Morgair, Bishop of Down and Connor, Archbishop of Armagh,' Dublin, 1859. 5. 'The Life of St. Dympna, Virgin Martyr,' Dublin, 1863. 6. 'Catechism of Irish History from the Earliest Events to the Death of O'Connell,' Dublin, 1864. 7. 'Catechism of Greek Grammar,' Dublin, 1865. 8. 'Devotions for Confession and Holy Communion,' 1866. 9. 'The Life and Works of St. Oengus the Culdee, Bishop and Abbot,' Dublin, 1868. 10. 'The Life of St. David, Archbishop of Menevia, Chief Patron of Wales,' Dublin, 1869. 11. 'Legend Lays of Ireland,' in verse (by 'Lageniensis'), Dublin, 1870. 12. 'Irish Folk-Lore, Traditions and Superstitions of the Country, with Numerous Tales' (under the same pseudonym), Glasgow, 1870. 13. 'The Buried Lady, a Legend of Kilronan,' by 'Lageniensis,' Dublin, 1877. 14. 'The Life of St. Grellan, Patron of the O'Kellys,' Dublin, 1881. 15. 'Report of the O'Connell Centenary Committee,' Dublin, 1888. 16. 'The Poetical Works of Lageniensis,' Dublin, 1893. 17. 'Irish-American History of the United States,' Dublin, 1902. 18. 'History of the Queen's County,' vol. i. (completed by Rev. E. O'Leary), Dublin, 1907. He also edited Monck Mason's 'Essay on the Antiquity and Constitution of Parliaments of Ireland' (1891), Molyneux's 'Case of Ireland . . . stated' (1893), and 'Legends and Stories of John Keegan' (to which the present writer prefixed a memoir of Keegan), Dublin, 1908

[Autobiographical letters to present writer and personal knowledge; O'Donoghue's Poets of Ireland, p. 188; Freeman's Journal. 16 May 1905; Brit. Mus. Cat.; Life and Scenery in Missouri (as stated in text). Information from Rev. J. Delany, P.P. Stradbally.]

D. J. O'D.

OLDHAM, HENRY (1815–1902), obstetric physician, sixth son and ninth child of Adam Oldham (1781–1839) of Balham, solicitor, was born on 31 Jan. 1815. His father's family claimed kinship with Hugh Oldham [q. v.], bishop of Exeter, the founder of Corpus Christi College, Oxford, and of the Manchester grammar school. His mother, Ann Lane, was a daughter of William Stubbington Penny, whose father, Francis Penny (1714–1759), of a Hampshire family, once edited the 'Gentleman's Magazine.' Oldham's younger brother, James, was a surgeon at Brighton whose son, CHARLES JAMES OLDHAM (1843–1907), also a surgeon in that town, invented a refracting ophthalmoscope, and bequeathed 50,000*l*. to public institutions, including the Manchester grammar school, Corpus Christi College, Oxford, and the universities of both Oxford and Cambridge, for the foundation of Charles Oldham scholarships and prizes for classical and Shakespearean study.

Oldham, educated at Mr. Balaam's school at Clapham and at the London University, entered in 1834 the medical school of Guy's Hospital. In May 1837 he became M.R.C.S. England; in September following a licentiate of the Society of Apothecaries; in 1843 a licentiate (corresponding to the present member), and in 1857 fellow, of the Royal College of Physicians of London. He proceeded M.D. at St. Andrews in 1858. In 1849 he was appointed—with Dr. J. C. W. Lever—physician-accoucheur and lecturer on midwifery and diseases of women at Guy's Hospital. Before this appointment he had studied embryology in the developing chick by means of coloured injections and the microscope. After twenty years' service he became consulting obstetric physician. He was pre-eminent as a lecturer and made seventeen contributions to the 'Guy's Hospital Reports,' besides writing four papers in the 'Transactions of the Obstetrical Society of London,' of which he was one of the founders, an original trustee, and subsequently president (1863–5). He invented the term 'missed labour,' that is, when the child dies in the womb and labour fails to come on; but the specimen on which he based his view has been differently interpreted. His name is also associated with the hypothesis that menstruation is due to periodic excitation of the ovaries.

Oldham had an extensive and lucrative

practice in the City of London, first at 13 Devonshire Square, Bishopsgate Street, and then at 25 Finsbury Square; about 1870 he moved to 4 Cavendish Place, W., and in 1899 retired to Bournemouth, where he died on 19 Nov. 1902, being buried in the cemetery there. He was a great walker, an extremely simple eater, and for the last fifteen years of his life never ate meat, fish, or fowl.

He married in 1838 Sophia (*d.* 1885), eldest daughter of James Smith of Peckham, and had six children, four daughters and two sons, of whom one died in infancy and the other is Colonel Sir Henry Hugh Oldham, C.V.O., lieutenant of the honourable corps of gentlemen-at-arms.

[Obstet. Soc. Trans., 1903, xlv. 71; information from Colonel Sir Henry H. Oldham, C.V.O., and F. Taylor, M.D., F.R.C.P.]

H. D. R.

O'LEARY, JOHN (1830–1907), Fenian journalist and leader, born in Tipperary on 23 July 1830, was eldest son of John O'Leary, a shopkeeper of that city, by his wife Margaret Ryan. His sister Ellen is separately noticed. He inherited small house property in Tipperary. After education at the Erasmus Smith School in his native town, he proceeded to Carlow school. At seventeen he entered Trinity College, Dublin, intending to join the legal profession. While he was an undergraduate he was deeply influenced by the nationalist writings of Thomas Davis [q. v.], and he frequently attended the meetings of the Irish Confederation. He became acquainted with James Finton Lalor [q. v.] and the Rev. John Kenyon, two powerful advocates of the nationalist movement. He threw himself with ardour into the agitation of 1848, and taking part in an attack on the police known as the 'Wilderness affair,' near Clonmel, spent two or three weeks in Clonmel gaol. On discovering that he could not become a barrister without taking an oath of allegiance to the British crown, he turned to medicine, and entered Queen's College, Cork, in January 1850, as a medical student. In 1851 he left Cork and went to Queen's College, Galway, where he obtained a medical scholarship and distinguished himself in examinations. While he was in Galway he contributed occasionally to the 'Nation,' but he left the city in 1853 without passing his final examination. He spent the greater part of the following two years in Dublin, and was then in Paris for a year (1855–6).

Meanwhile O'Leary had fully identified himself with the advanced Irish section under John Mitchel [q. v.]. In Paris he made the acquaintance of John Martin [q. v.], Kevin Izod O'Doherty [q. v. Suppl. II], and other Irishmen of similar views. Returning to Dublin, he came to know the Fenian leaders James Stephens [q. v. Suppl. II] and Thomas Clarke Luby [q. v. Suppl. II], who formed the Fenian organisation called the Irish Republican Brotherhood on St. Patrick's Day, 17 March 1858 (*Recollections*, i. 82).

O'Leary was still irregularly studying medicine, and although he aided in the development of the Fenian movement, and was in sympathy with its aims, he was never a sworn member of the brotherhood. His younger brother Arthur, who died on 6 June 1861, however, took the oath. John frequently visited Stephens in France, and with some hesitation he went to America in 1859 on business of the organisation. In New York in April 1859 he met John O'Mahony [q. v.] and Colonel Michael Corcoran [q. v.], as well as John Mitchel and Thomas Francis Meagher [q. v.]. He contributed occasional articles to the 'Phœnix,' a small weekly paper published in New York, the first avowedly Fenian organ.

In 1860 O'Leary returned to London. The Fenian movement rapidly grew, although its receipts were, according to O'Leary, wildly exaggerated (*Recollections*, p. 135). During its first six years of existence (1858–64) only 1500*l.* was received; from 1864 to 1866, 31,000*l.*; and from first to last, a sum well under 100,000*l.* O'Leary watched the growth of the movement in London between 1861 and 1863.

In 1863 he was summoned to Dublin to become editor of the 'Irish People,' the newly founded weekly journal of Fenianism, which first appeared on 28 Nov. 1863. O'Leary's incisive style gave the paper its chief character. The other chief contributors were Thomas Clarke Luby and Charles Joseph Kickham [q. v.]. Cardinal Cullen [q. v.] and the catholic bishops warmly denounced the Fenian movement and its organ, and O'Leary and his colleagues replied to the prelates defiantly. Bishop Moriarty declared that 'Hell was not hot enough nor eternity long enough' to punish those who led the youth of the country astray by such teaching. After nearly two years the paper was seized on 14 Sept. 1865 by the government. O'Leary, Kickham, Luby, O'Donovan Rossa (the manager), and other leading Fenians were arrested. An informer named Pierce Nagle, who had been employed in the office of the paper, gave damaging evidence, and O'Leary and others were sentenced to twenty years' imprisonment. He was released after nine years, chiefly spent in Portland. A condition of the release was banishment from Ireland, and he retired to Paris. There he cultivated his literary tastes, and became acquainted with Whistler and other artists and literary men. In 1885 the Amnesty Act enabled him to settle again in Dublin, where his sister Ellen kept house for him till her death in 1889 and where his fine presence was very familiar. Mainly encouraged by his friends, he devoted himself to writing his reminiscences. The book was published in 1896 under the title of 'Recollections of Fenians and Fenianism.' The work proved unduly long and was a disappointment to his admirers. His critical treatment of his associates seemed to belittle the Fenian movement. To the end of his life he pungently criticised modern leaders, and especially various manifestations of the agrarian movement, while retaining his revolutionary sympathies. In the Irish literary societies of Dublin and London he played a prominent part, but chiefly occupied himself till his death in reading and book collecting.

He died at Dublin unmarried on 16 March 1907, and was buried in Glasnevin cemetery, where a Celtic cross has been placed over his grave. His books, papers, and pictures were bequeathed by him to the National Literary Society of Dublin, which transferred the first portrait of him by John B. Yeats, R.H.A., to the National Gallery of that city. He published, besides his 'Recollections,' the following pamphlets: 'Young Ireland, the Old and the New' (Dublin, 1885), and 'What Irishmen should Read, What Irishmen should Feel' (Dublin, 1886); and he also published a short introduction to 'The Writings of James Finton Lalor,' edited by the present writer in 1895. The article on John O'Mahony in this Dictionary was written by him.

[Recollections of O'Leary, 1896; Ireland under Coercion, by Hurlbert, 2 vols. 1888; O. Elton, Life of F. York Powell, 1906; Sullivan's New Ireland; Richard Pigott's Recollections of an Irish Journalist, 1882; Irish press and London Daily Telegraph, 18 March 1907; personal knowledge and private correspondence of O'Leary in present writer's possession.]

D. J. O'D.

OLIVER, SAMUEL PASFIELD (1838–1907), geographer and antiquary, born at Bovinger, Essex, on 30 Oct. 1838, was eldest and only surviving son of William Macjanley Oliver, rector of Bovinger, by his wife Jane Weldon. He entered Eton in 1853, and after passing through the Royal Military Academy, Woolwich, he received a commission in the royal artillery on 1 April 1859. In the following year he went out with his battery to China, where hostilities had been renewed owing to the attempt of the Chinese to prevent Sir Frederick Bruce [q. v.], the British envoy, from proceeding up the Pei-ho. Peace was however signed at Peking soon after Oliver's arrival (24 Oct. 1860), and his service was confined to garrison duty at Canton. On the establishment of a British embassy at Peking in 1861 he accompanied General Sir John Michel [q. v.] on a visit to the capital, and subsequently made a tour through Japan. In the following year he was transferred to Mauritius, and thence he proceeded with Major-general Johnstone on a mission to Madagascar to congratulate King Radama II on his accession. He spent some months exploring the island, and witnessed the king's coronation at Antananarivo (23 Sept.). A second brief visit to the island followed in June 1863, when Oliver, on receipt of the news of King Radama's assassination, was again despatched to Madagascar on board H.M.S. Rapid. The history and ethnology of the island interested him, and he devoted himself subsequently to a close study of them. On his return to Mauritius he studied with attention the flora and fauna of the Mascarene islands. In 1864 the volcanic eruption on the island of Réunion gave him the opportunity of recording some interesting geological phenomena. A curious drawing by Oliver of a stream of lava tumbling over a cliff was reproduced in Professor John Wesley Judd's 'Volcanoes, what they are and what they teach' (1881).

Oliver returned to England with his battery in 1865. But his love of adventure would not allow him to settle down to routine work. In 1867 he joined Captain Pym's exploring expedition to Central America. A route was cut and levelled across Nicaragua from Monkey Point to Port Realejo; and it was anticipated that this route might be more practicable than that projected by M. de Lesseps for the Panama canal. At a meeting of the British Association at Dundee on 5 Sept. 1867 Oliver read a paper in support of this view on 'Two Routes through Nicaragua.' His descriptive diary of this journey, 'Rambles of a Gunner through Nicaragua' (privately printed, 1879), was subsequently embodied in a larger volume of vivacious reminiscences, entitled 'On and Off Duty' (1881).

Archæology now seriously engaged Oliver's attention. From Guernsey, where he was appointed adjutant in 1868, he visited Brittany, and drew up a valuable report on the prehistoric remains at Carnac and other sites (*Proc. Ethnological Soc.* 1871). In 1872 a tour in the Mediterranean resulted in some first-hand archæological observations in Asia Minor, Greece, and Sardinia, published as 'Nuragghi Sardi, and other Non-Historic Stone Structures of the Mediterranean' (Dublin, 1875). Meanwhile Oliver, who had been promoted captain in 1871, was appointed superintendent of fortifications on the Cornish coast in 1873, and there devoted his leisure to elucidating the history of two Cornish castles, 'Pendennis and St. Mawes' (Truro, 1875). After serving on the staff of the intelligence branch of the quartermaster-general's department he was sent to St. Helena on garrison duty. There he resumed his botanical studies, and made a valuable collection of ferns, which he presented to the Royal Gardens, Kew. Impatience of professional routine induced Oliver to resign his commission in 1878. For a time he acted as special artist and correspondent of 'The Illustrated London News' in Cyprus and Syria. But his health had been seriously affected by his travels in malarial countries, and he soon settled down to literary pursuits at home, first at Gosport and later at Worthing. The value of Oliver's work both as explorer and as antiquary was generally recognised. He was elected F.R.G.S. in 1866, became fellow of the Ethnological Society in 1869, and F.S.A. in 1874. He died at Worthing on 31 July 1907, and was buried at Findon. He married on 10 Sept. 1863 at Port Louis, Mauritius, Clara Georgina, second daughter of Frederic Mylius Dick, by whom he had five sons and four daughters.

Oliver's versatile interests prevented him from achieving eminence in any one subject. But his sympathetic volumes descriptive of Malagasy life remain the standard English authority on the subject. In 1866 he published 'Madagascar and the Malagasy,' a diary of his first visit to the island, which he illustrated with some spirited sketches. This was followed by an ethnological study in French, 'Les Hovas et les autres tribus caractéristiques de Madagascar' (Guernsey, 1869). In 'The True Story of the French Dispute in Madagascar' (1885) Oliver passed adverse criticisms on the treatment of the Malagasy by the French colonial officials. Finally his two volumes, on 'Madagascar' (1886), based on authentic native and European sources, give a detailed and comprehensive account of the island, its history, and its inhabitants.

Oliver also edited: 1. 'Madagascar, or Robert Drury's Journal,' 1890. 2. 'The Voyage of François Leguat,' 1891 (Hakluyt Society). 3. 'The Memoirs and Travels of Mauritius Augustus Count de Benyowsky,' 1893. 4. 'The Voyages made by the Sieur Dubois,' 1897 (translation). In addition to these works he assisted in the preparation of 'The Life of Sir Charles MacGregor,' published by his widow in 1888, and from the notes and documents collected by Sir Charles MacGregor he compiled the abridged official account of 'The Second Afghan War, 1878–80' (posthumous, 1908). 'The Life of Philibert Commerson,' which appeared posthumously in 1909, was edited with a short memoir of Oliver by Mr. G. F. Scott Elliot. To this Dictionary he contributed the articles on François Leguat and Sir Charles MacGregor.

[Memoir of Capt. Oliver prefixed to the Life of Philibert Commerson, 1909; S. P. Oliver, On and Off Duty, 1881; Athenæum, 17 Aug. 1907; Worthing Gazette, 14 Aug. 1907; private information from Miss Oliver.]

G. S. W.

OLPHERTS, Sir WILLIAM (1822–1902), general, born on 8 March 1822 at Dartry near Armagh, was son of William Olpherts of Dartry House, co. Armagh. He was educated at Dungannon School, and in 1837 received a nomination to the East India Military College at Addiscombe. He passed out in the artillery, and joined the headquarters of the Bengal artillery at Dum Dum in Dec. 1839. On the outbreak of disturbances in the Tenasserim province of Burma, Olpherts was detached to Moulmein in Oct. 1841 with four guns. Returning at the end of nine months, he was again ordered on field service to quell an insurrection in the neighbourhood of Saugor, and was thanked in the despatch of the officer commanding the artillery for his conduct in action with the insurgents at Jhirna Ghaut on 12 Nov. 1842. Having passed as interpreter in the native languages, Olpherts was given the command of the 16th Bengal light field battery, and joined Sir Hugh Gough's expedition against Gwalior. Olpherts's battery was posted on the wing of the army commanded by General Grey, Lieutenant (Sir) Henry Tombs, V.C. [q. v.], being his subaltern. He was heavily engaged at Punniar on

29 December 1843, and was mentioned in despatches.

For his services in the Gwalior campaign Olpherts received the bronze decoration. Being specially selected by the governor-general, Lord Ellenborough, to raise and command a battery of horse artillery for the Bundelcund legion, he was at once detached with the newly raised battery to join Sir Charles Napier's army in Sind. His march across India, a distance of 1260 miles, elicited Napier's highest praise. In 1846 Olpherts took part in the operations at Kot Kangra during the first Sikh war, when his conduct attracted the attention of (Sir) Henry Lawrence [q. v.], and he was appointed to raise a battery of artillery from among the disbanded men of the Sikh army. He was then hurried off to the Deccan in command of a battery of artillery in the service of the Nizam of Hyderabad, but was soon recalled to a similar post in the Gwalior contingent. In 1851 Olpherts applied to be posted to a battery at Peshawur, where he was under the command of Sir Colin Campbell [q. v.] and took part in the expedition against the frontier tribes. For this service he afterwards received the Indian general service medal sanctioned in 1869 for frontier wars. In the following year (1852) Olpherts took furlough to England, and was appointed an orderly officer at the Military College of Addiscombe.

On the outbreak of the Russian war in 1854 Olpherts volunteered for service, and was selected to join (Sir) William Fenwick Williams [q. v.] at Kars. On his way thither he visited the Crimea. Crossing the Black Sea, he rode over the Zigana mountains in the deep snow; but soon after reaching Kars he was detached to command a Turkish force of 7000 men to guard against a possible advance of the Russians from Erivan by the Araxes river. Olpherts thus escaped being involved in the surrender of Kars. Recalled to the Crimea, he was nominated to the command of a brigade of bashi bazouks in the Turkish contingent. On the conclusion of peace in 1856 he returned to India, and received the command of a horse battery at Benares.

Olpherts served throughout the suppression of the Indian Mutiny (1857–9). He was with Brigadier James Neill [q. v.] when he defeated the mutineers at Benares on 4 June 1857, and accompanied Havelock during the relief of Lucknow. His conduct in the course of that operation was highly distinguished. On 25 Sept. 1857, after the troops entered the city of Lucknow, Olpherts charged on horseback with the 90th regiment when under Colonel Campbell two guns were captured in the face of a heavy fire of grape. Olpherts succeeded under a severe fire of musketry in bringing up the limbers and horses to carry off the captured ordnance (extract from *Field Force Orders* by General Havelock, 17 Oct. 1857). Olpherts almost surpassed this piece of bravery by another two days later. When the main body of Havelock's force penetrated to the Residency, the rearguard consisting of the 90th with some guns and ammunition was entirely cut off. However, Olpherts, with Colonel Robert (afterwards Lord) Napier [q. v.], sallied out with a small party, and by his cool determination brought in the wounded of the rearguard as well as the guns. Sir James Outram [q. v.], then in command of the Residency at Lucknow, wrote: 'My dear heroic Olpherts, bravery is a poor and insufficient epithet to apply to a valour such as yours.' Colonel Napier wrote in his despatch to the same effect. From the entry into Lucknow of Havelock's force until the relief by Sir Colin Campbell on 21 Nov. Olpherts acted as brigadier of artillery, and after the evacuation of the Residency by Sir Colin Campbell he shared in the defence of the advanced position at the Alumbagh under Sir James Outram. He took part in the siege and capture of the city by Sir Colin Campbell in March 1858, being again mentioned in despatches for conspicuous bravery. At the close of the campaign Olpherts received the brevets of major and lieutenant-colonel, as well as the Victoria cross, the Indian Mutiny medal with two clasps, and the companionship of the Bath.

In 1859–60 Olpherts served as a volunteer under Brigadier (Sir) Neville Chamberlain [q. v. Suppl. II] in an expedition against the Waziris on the north-west frontier of the Punjab, thus completing twenty years of continuous active service. Olpherts's dash and daring earned for him the sobriquet of 'Hell-fire Jack,' but he modestly gave all the credit for any action of his to the men under him. From 1861 to 1868 he commanded the artillery in the frontier stations of Peshawur or Rawal Pindi, and in that year he returned home on furlough, when he was presented with a sword of honour by the city and county of Armagh. Returning to India in 1872, he commanded successively the Gwalior, Ambala, and Lucknow brigades, but quitted the country in 1875 on attaining the rank of major-general. He was promoted lieutenant-general on 1 Oct. 1877, general on 31 March 1883, and in 1888 became colonel commandant of the royal artillery. Olpherts was raised to the dignity of K.C.B. in 1886 and of G.C.B. in 1900.

He died at his residence, Wood House, Norwood, on 30 April 1902, and was buried at Richmond, Surrey. Olpherts married in 1861 Alice, daughter of Major-general George Cautley of the Bengal cavalry, by whom he had one son, Major Olpherts, late of the Royal Scots, and three daughters.

[The Times, 1 May 1902; Broad Arrow, 3 May 1902; Army and Navy Gazette, 3 May 1902; H. M. Vibart, Addiscombe and its Heroes, 1894; Lord Roberts, Forty-one Years in India, 30th edit. 1898; W. H. Russell, My Diary in India; Sir James Outram's Life; A. M. Delavoye, History of the Ninetieth Light Infantry; Sir W. Lee-Warner, Memoirs of Sir Henry Norman, 1908, p. 90; J. S. O. Wilkinson, The Gemini Generals, 1896; Selections from State Papers in Military Department, 1857–8, ed. G. W. Forrest, 3 vols. 1902.] C. B. N.

OMMANNEY, Sir ERASMUS (1814–1904), admiral, born in London on 22 May 1814, was seventh son, in a family of eight sons and three daughters, of Sir Francis Molyneux Ommanney, well known as a navy agent and for many years M.P. for Barnstaple, by his wife Georgiana Frances, daughter of Joshua Hawkes. The Ommanneys had long distinguished themselves in the navy. Erasmus' grandfather was Rear-Admiral Cornthwaite Ommanney (*d.* 1801); Admiral Sir John Acworth Ommanney [q. v.] and Admiral Henry Manaton Ommanney were his uncles, and Major-general Edward Lacon Ommanney, R.E., was his eldest brother, while Prebendary George Druce Wynne Ommanney [q. v. Suppl. II] was a younger brother. Ommanney entered the navy in August 1826 under his uncle John, then captain of the Albion, of seventy-four guns, which in December convoyed to Lisbon the troops sent to protect Portugal against the Spanish invasion. The ship then went to the Mediterranean, and on 20 Oct. 1827 took part in the battle of Navarino [see Codrington, Sir Edward], for which Ommanney received the medal. The captured flag of the Turkish commander-in-chief was handed down by seniority among the surviving officers, and came eventually into the possession of Ommanney, who in 1890, being then the sole survivor, presented it to the King of Greece, from whom he received in return the grand cross of the order of the Saviour. In 1833 he passed his examination, after which he served for a short time as mate in the Symondite brig Pantaloon [see Symonds, Sir William], employed on packet service. On 10 Dec. 1835 he was promoted to lieutenant, and in the same month was appointed to the Cove, frigate, Captain (afterwards Sir James) Clark Ross [q. v.], which was ordered to Baffin's Bay to release a number of whalers caught in the ice. He received the special commendation of the Admiralty for his conduct during this dangerous service. In October 1836 he joined the Pique, frigate, Captain Henry John Rous [q. v.], an excellent school of seamanship; and a year later was appointed to the Donegal, of seventy-eight guns, as flag lieutenant to his uncle, Sir John, commander-in-chief on the Lisbon and Mediterranean stations. He was promoted to commander on 9 Oct. 1840, and from August 1841 to the end of 1844 served on board the Vesuvius, steam sloop, in the Mediterranean, being employed on the coast of Morocco for the protection of British subjects during the period of French hostilities, which included the bombardment of Tangier by the squadron under the Prince de Joinville. He was advanced to the rank of captain on 9 Nov. 1846, and in 1847–8 was employed under the government commission during the famine in Ireland, carrying into effect relief measures and the new poor law.

When Captain Horatio Austin was appointed to the Resolute for the command of the Franklin search expedition in February 1850 he chose Ommanney, whom he had known intimately in the Mediterranean, to be his second-in-command. The Resolute and Ommanney's ship, the Assistance, each had a steam tender, this being the first occasion on which steam was used for Arctic navigation. This expedition was also the first to organise an extensive system of sledge journeys, by means of which the coast of Prince of Wales Land was laid down. On 25 Aug. 1850 Ommanney discovered the first traces of the fate of Sir John Franklin; these on investigation proved that his ships had wintered at Beechey Island. On the return of the expedition to England in October 1851 Ommanney received the Arctic medal, and several years later, in 1868, he was elected a fellow of the Royal Society in recognition of his scientific work in the Arctic. In 1877 he was knighted for the same service. In December 1851 he was appointed deputy controller-general of the coast-guard, and held this post until 1854, when, on the outbreak of the Russian war, he commissioned the Eurydice as senior officer of a small squadron for the White Sea, where he blockaded Archangel, stopped the coasting trade, and destroyed government property at several points. In 1855 he was appointed to the Hawke, block ship, for the Baltic, and was employed chiefly as senior officer in the gulf of Riga, where the service was one of rigid blockade, varied by occasional skirmishes with the Russian gunboats and batteries. In October 1857 he was appointed to the Brunswick, of eighty guns, going out to the West Indies, and was senior officer at Colon when the filibuster William Walker attempted to invade Nicaragua. The Brunswick afterwards joined the Channel fleet, and in 1859 was sent as a reinforcement to the Mediterranean during the Franco-Italian war. Ommanney was not again afloat after paying off in 1860, but was senior officer at Gibraltar from 1862 until promoted to flag rank on 12 Nov. 1864. In March 1867 he was awarded the C.B.; on 14 July 1871 he was promoted to vice-admiral, and accepted the retirement on 1 Jan. 1875. He was advanced to admiral on the retired list on 1 Aug. 1877. To the end of his life Ommanney continued to take a great interest in geographical work and service subjects, being a constant attendant at the meetings of the Royal Geographical Society, of the Royal United Service Institution, of both of which bodies he was for many years a councillor, and of the British Association. He was also a J.P. for Hampshire and a member of the Thames conservancy. In June 1902 he was made K.C.B.

Ommanney died on 21 Dec. 1904 at his son's residence, St. Michael's vicarage, Portsmouth, and was buried in Mortlake cemetery. He was twice married: (1) on 27 Feb. 1844 to Emily Mary, daughter of Samuel Smith of H.M. dockyard, Malta; she died in 1857; and (2) in 1862 to Mary, daughter of Thomas A. Stone of Curzon Street, W.; she died on 1 Sept. 1906, aged eighty-one. His son, Erasmus Austin, entered the navy in 1863, retired with the rank of commander in 1879, took orders in 1883, and was vicar of St. Michael's, Portsmouth, from 1892 to 1911.

A portrait by Stephen Pearce is in the National Portrait Gallery.

[The Times, 22, 28, and 29 Dec. 1904; Geog. Journal, Feb. 1905; xxv. 221; Proc. Roy. Soc. lxxxv. 335; O'Byrne's Naval Biography; R. N. List.] L. G. C. L.

OMMANNEY, GEORGE DRUCE WYNNE (1819–1902), theologian, born in Norfolk Street, Strand, on 12 April 1819, was younger brother of Sir Erasmus Ommanney [see above]. After education at Harrow (1831–8), where in 1838 he won the Robert Peel gold medal and the Lyon scholarship, he matriculated as scholar from Trinity College, Cambridge, in 1838; graduated B.A. as senior optime and second class classic in 1842; and proceeded M.A. in 1845. Taking holy orders in 1842, he was curate of Edwinstone, Nottinghamshire (1843–9); of Cameley, Somerset (1849–52); of Oldbourne, Wilts (1852–3); of Woodborough, Wilts (1853–8); vicar of Queen Charlton, near Bristol (1858–62); curate in charge of Whitchurch, Somerset (1862–75); and vicar of Draycot, Somerset (1875–88). He was made prebendary of Whitchurch in Wells Cathedral in 1884. He died on 20 April 1902 at 29 Beaumont Street, Oxford, where he had lived in retirement since 1888, and was buried at St. Sepulchre's cemetery, Oxford. He married Ellen Ricketts of Brislington, Bristol, and had no issue.

Ommanney was a voluminous and lucid writer on the Athanasian creed, to which he devoted a large portion of his later life, studying Arabic and visiting the chief European libraries for purposes of research. He was a vigorous champion of the retention of the creed in the church of England services. He supported its claims to authenticity against the critics who ascribed its composition to the eighth and ninth centuries. His published works include: 1. 'The Athanasian Creed: Examination of Recent Theories respecting its Date and Origin,' 1875; new edit. 1880. 2. 'Early History of the Athanasian Creed,' 1880. 3. 'The S.P.C.K. and the Creed of St. Athanasius,' 1884. 4. 'Critical Dissertation on the Athanasian Creed, its Original Language, Date, Authorship, Titles, Text, Reception, and Use,' 1897.

[The Times, 22 April 1902; Guardian, 23 April 1902; Crockford's Clerical Directory, 1902; private information.] W. B. O.

ONSLOW, WILLIAM HILLIER, fourth Earl of Onslow (1853–1911), governor of New Zealand, born at Alresford, Hampshire, on 7 March 1853, was only son of George Augustus Cranley Onslow (*d.* 1855) of Alresford, Hampshire, who was great-grandson of George Onslow, first earl [q. v.], grandson of Thomas Onslow, second earl, and nephew of Arthur George Onslow, third earl. His mother was

Mary Harriet Ann, eldest daughter of Lieut.-general William Fraser Bentinck Loftus of Kilbride, co. Wicklow, Ireland. He succeeded his great-uncle as fourth earl in 1870. Educated at Eton, he entered Exeter College, Oxford, in Easter term 1871, and left after rather more than a year without sitting for the university examinations. A conservative in politics, he was a lord-in-waiting to Queen Victoria in Lord Beaconsfield's administration at the beginning of 1880, and he represented the local government board in the House of Lords; he was again a lord-in-waiting under Lord Salisbury in 1886–7. In February 1887 he was appointed by Lord Salisbury parliamentary under-secretary of state for the colonies, representing the colonial office in the House of Lords. Sir Henry Holland was then secretary of state for the colonies, and when in February 1888 he was raised to the House of Lords as Lord Knutsford, Lord Onslow was transferred as parliamentary secretary to the board of trade. While he was at the colonial office, in April 1887, the first colonial conference took place, of which he was a vice-president. He was also a delegate to the sugar bounties conference in 1887–8, and in 1887 he was made K.C.M.G.

Onslow was not long at the board of trade, for on 24 Nov. 1888 he was appointed governor of New Zealand, and assumed office on 2 May 1889, being made G.C.M.G. soon after. He held the office till the end of February 1892. He was a successful and popular governor, businesslike and straightforward; and the New Zealanders appreciated his frankness of character and his open-air tastes. He encouraged acclimatisation societies, and used his personal influence to establish island preserves for the native birds of New Zealand. There was one change of ministry during his term of office, the administration of Sir Harry Atkinson [q. v. Suppl. I] being at the beginning of 1891 succeeded by that of John Ballance [q. v. Suppl. I], and some appointments to the upper house which the governor made on the advice of the outgoing premier were the subject of criticism by the opposite party (see *H. of C. Return*, No. 198, May 1893). Otherwise his government was free from friction. In New Zealand his younger son was born (13 Nov. 1890), and he paid the Maoris the much appreciated compliment of giving to the child the Maori name of Huia, and presenting him for adoption into the Ngatihuia tribe in the North Island in September 1891.

In 1895, when the unionists were returned to power, he became parliamentary under-secretary of state for India, and remained at the India Office till 1900, when he went back to the colonial office in the same position, Mr. Joseph Chamberlain being secretary of state. He took part in the colonial conference of 1902, and he acted as secretary of state during Mr. Chamberlain's visit to South Africa. In 1903 he obtained cabinet rank as president of the board of agriculture, and was made a privy councillor. As head of an office he proved himself to be hard-working and shrewd. His appointment synchronised with the passing of the Board of Agriculture and Fisheries Act, 1903, which transferred the control of the fishery industry from the board of trade to the board of agriculture. Onslow took a strong personal interest in the new duties which devolved on the board. For the care of agriculture he was well fitted by his own private inclinations and pursuits, and he paid much attention to the question of railway rates so far as they affected farmers.

In 1905 he succeeded Albert Edmund Parker, third earl of Morley [q. v. Suppl. II], as chairman of committees in the House of Lords, and held that post till the Easter recess of 1911, when he retired on account of failing health. Unlike his immediate predecessor in the chairmanship he did not dissociate himself from party politics, but his politics were too genial to give offence, and in his official room there was no political atmosphere. He was rapid yet patient in the transaction of business, took great care in the selection of members and chairmen for committees on bills, and fully maintained the reputation of the House of Lords committees for justice and integrity. Onslow was chairman of the small holdings committee appointed by the board of agriculture in 1905; he was also chairman of the executive committee of the Central Land Association, and in 1905–6 he was president of the Royal Statistical Society. Onslow was an alderman of the London county council (1896–9) and for a time leader of the moderate party in the council; he was also an alderman of the city of Westminster (1900–3), and he had adequate sympathetic knowledge of municipal questions.

At Clandon, Surrey, the family home, Onslow was a good landlord and neighbour. He held the office of high steward of Guildford. He was a keen sportsman and a good whip, being a member of the Coaching and the Four in Hand Clubs, and in all respects a good representative of the country gentleman. He died on 23 Oct. 1911 at his son's house at Hampstead, and was buried at Merrow near Guildford, a memorial service being held at St. Margaret's, Westminster. He married on 3 Feb. 1875 Florence Coulston Gardner, elder daughter of Alan Legge, third Lord Gardner, and had two sons and two daughters.

His portrait, painted by the Hon. John Collier, is at 7 Richmond Terrace, and an engraving of it at Grillion's Club. A cartoon portrait by 'Spy' appeared in 'Vanity Fair' in 1883.

[The Times, 24 Oct. 1911; Gisborne's New Zealand Rulers, 1897 (portrait); Colonial Office List; Who's Who; Burke's Peerage; Walford's County Families; private sources.] C. P. L.

ORCHARDSON, Sir WILLIAM QUILLER (1832–1910), artist, born in Edinburgh on 27 March 1832, was only surviving son of Abram Orchardson, tailor, by his wife Elizabeth Quiller. The artist traced his father's family to a Highland sept named Urquhartson. His mother's family of Quiller was of Austrian origin.

On 1 Oct. 1845, when thirteen and a half, he entered the art school in Edinburgh known as the Trustees' Academy on the recommendation of John Sobieski Stuart [q. v.]. He enrolled himself as an 'artist.' The master of the Academy, Alexander Christie, A.R.S.A., taught ornament and design, and John Ballantyne, R.S.A., took the antique, life and colour classes. They were not inspiring teachers, but Orchardson made rapid progress. Erskine Nicol, Thomas Faed, James Archer, Robert Herdman and Alexander Fraser were amongst his fellow students, and gave him the stimulus of friendly rivalry. In February 1852 Robert Scott Lauder [q. v.] succeeded Christie as master, and Orchardson, whose name remained without a break on the roll until the close of the session 1854–5, enjoyed in his final years of pupilage the benefits of Lauder's fine taste and wide knowledge of art. The younger students who gathered about Lauder—Chalmers, McTaggart, Cameron, Pettie, MacWhirter, Tom and Peter Graham—while they influenced Orchardson's work, regarded him as their leader. At this period Orchardson was neither a very regular attendant nor a very hard worker. It is said that he seldom finished a life-study; but when he did it was masterly and complete, and it evoked the applause of his fellows. He took an active part in the sketch club founded by Lauder's early pupils, and formed enduring friendships with the members, more especially with Tom Graham [q. v. Suppl. II] and John Pettie [q. v.].

Orchardson began to exhibit at the Royal Scottish Academy as early as 1848, and his pictures showed great promise 'George Wishart's Last Communion' (exhibited in 1853) was a wonderful performance for a youth of less than twenty-one, yet his work failed to impress academicians. His temperament combined ambition with a certain aloofness; and after a short trial of residence in London, he settled there for good in 1862. Within a few months he was joined by his friend John Pettie, and from 1863 to 1865 these two, with Tom Graham who had also gone south, and Mr. C. E. Johnston, another Edinburgh friend, shared a house, 37 Fitzroy Square.

For some time the art of Orchardson and Pettie, while each possessed qualities of its own, was very similar in character. Both found their subjects in past history, with its picturesque costumes and accessories, and shared the technical qualities due to Scott Lauder's training. Their work soon attracted the attention of connoisseurs, Orchardson's 'Challenged' (1865) being his first popular triumph. Orchardson's pictures proved subtler and more distinguished than Pettie's, and in a greater degree he devoted himself to subjects directly suggested by literature. Shakespeare and Scott were favourite sources, and amongst his work of this kind were 'Hamlet and Ophelia' (1865), 'Christopher Sly' (1866), 'Talbot and the Countess of Auvergne' (1867), 'Poins, Falstaff and Prince Henry' (1868), and 'Ophelia' (1874). Like most of his early associates, Orchardson was no mere illustrator of his text. His pictures had always a true pictorial and æsthetic basis for the dramatic situations they embodied. In 1868 Orchardson was elected A.R.A., and in 1870 he paid a long visit to Venice—his only stay abroad of any duration. The result was a number of pictures, 'The Market Girl from the Lido' (1870), 'On the Grand Canal' (1871), and 'A Venetian Fruit-Seller' (1874), of a more realistic kind than any of his previous paintings. 'Toilers of the Sea' (1870) and 'Flotsam and Jetsam' (1876) showed a like character and suggested a growing independence of literary suggestion. To the Academy of 1877 he sent 'The Queen of the Swords,' which, while originating in a description in 'The Pirate,' belonged in conception and sentiment to the painter alone. In it his earlier style culminated and it inaugurated the work on which his reputation finally rested. Orchardson was at once made R.A. When the picture was exhibited in the Paris Exhibition next year, together with his

'Challenged' (1865), it evoked in the French art public an admiration which his later work made lasting.

Every year now added to Orchardson's reputation. His drawing, always constructive and real, attained a more incisive elegance; his sense of design grew thoroughly architectonic, especially in the use of blank spaces; his colour lost its tendency to greyness and became, in M. Chesneau's happy phrase, 'as harmonious as the wrong side of an old tapestry'; and his appreciation of character and dramatic situation acquired an absolute sureness. His technical equipment, if limited in certain directions, was eventually wellnigh perfect in its kind. Henceforth his subjects were divided into incidents in the comedy of manners (sometimes gay but more often grave, and usually touched with a delicate irony) and incidents from the careers of the great. The situation was always an epitomised expression of the interplay of character and circumstance rather than a rendering of a particular event, and the effect was highly dramatic. The first of his social pieces, 'The Social Eddy: Left by the Tide' (1878), was followed a year later by the intensely dramatic 'Hard Hit,' one of his most notable achievements. In 1880, 'Napoleon on board the Bellerophon'—purchased by the Chantrey Trustees—made a deep and enduring impression and became through engravings perhaps the most widely known of his works. Other themes from French manners or history were 'Voltaire' (1883), 'The Salon of Madame Récamier' (1885), 'The Young Duke' (1889), and 'St. Helena, 1816; Napoleon dictating the Account of his Campaigns' (1892). With these may be grouped the dramatically conceived and coloured 'Borgia' (1902), and some lighter pieces such as 'A Tender Chord' (1886), 'If Music be the Food of Love' (1890), and 'Rivalry' (1897), in which the actors wear the costume of the past. During this period the artist also presented with poignant feeling domestic drama in modern clothes and surroundings. Notable examples of such work are the 'Mariage de Convenance' series (1884 and 1886), 'The First Cloud' (1887), 'Her Mother's Voice' (1888), and 'Trouble' (1898).

At the same time Orchardson's insight into character, subtlety of draughtsmanship, and distinction of design made him a fascinating portrait painter. The more important of his portraits belong to the last three decades of his career, and during his latest years he painted little else. The charming portrait of Mrs. Orchardson (1875); the 'Master Baby'—the artist's wife and child (1886); the spirited rendering of himself standing before his easel, painted for the Uffizi in 1890; 'Sir Walter Gilbey' (1891); and 'H. B. Ferguson, Esq.' in the Dundee Gallery are splendid proofs of his skill in portraiture. Save 'Master Baby,' these were all three-quarter lengths; but the full lengths of 'Sir David Stewart' (1896), in his robes as lord provost of Aberdeen, and of 'Lord Peel' (1898), when speaker of the House of Commons, are hardly less effective. Later portraits like 'Sir Samuel Montagu' (1904) and 'Howard Coles, Esq.' (1905) were often only of the head and shoulders, but if rather weaker and thinner in handling than earlier efforts they revealed an even subtler apprehension of character.

After his marriage in 1873 Orchardson lived successively at Hyndford House, Brompton Road, at 1 Lansdowne Road, Notting Hill, and at 2 Spencer Street, Victoria, and in 1888 or 1889 he settled finally at 13 Portland Place, where he built a splendid studio. For some twenty years from 1877 he had also a country house, Ivyside, at Westgate-on-Sea, Kent, where he built another studio, in which some of his most famous pictures were painted. After 1897 he occupied Hawley House, Dartford, Kent.

Besides honorary membership of the Royal Scottish Academy, which was conferred on him in 1871, Orchardson received many honours from foreign art societies. He was made a D.C.L. of Oxford in 1890, and in 1907 he was knighted. He died at 13 Portland Place, London, on 13 April 1910. Only a fortnight before he had completed, with an effort, the portrait of Lord Blyth, which appeared in the Academy after his death. He was buried at Westgate-on-Sea.

Orchardson married on 8 April 1873, at St. Mary Abbots, Kensington, Ellen, daughter of Charles Moxon of London; she survived him with four sons and two daughters, and was granted a civil list pension of 80*l.* in 1912. The eldest son, Mr. C. M. Q. Orchardson, is an artist.

Of distinguished appearance, if of slight physique, Orchardson was very active and lithe. In early life he hunted, and at Westgate he became a devotee of tennis, for which he had an open court built. He was also a keen angler, especially with the dry fly, and latterly took to golf. Indoors he played billiards and talked with penetrating insight. Apart from the portrait of himself in the Uffizi, there are others by Tom

Graham (seated half length, in Lady Orchardson's possession), by J. H. Lorimer (in Scottish National Portrait Gallery), and by his son, as well as a bronze bust by E. Onslow Ford [q. v. Suppl. II], which belongs to Mrs. Joseph. A cartoon portrait by 'Spy' appeared in 'Vanity Fair' in 1898. By way of memorial, a reproduction of Ford's bust is to be placed by public subscription in the Tate Gallery and a plaque in the crypt of St. Paul's Cathedral.

Four of Orchardson's best pictures are in the Tate Gallery, London, and he is represented by characteristic examples in the permanent collections in Glasgow, Dundee, Aberdeen, and Edinburgh. The 'Voltaire' was included in Mr. Schwabe's gift to Hamburg and the larger version of 'The First Cloud' was acquired for the art gallery at Melbourne, Victoria. Sixty-eight pictures, illustrating every phase of his art, except the charcoal drawings and studies in which his draughtsmanship was often seen at its best, were brought together at the winter exhibition of the Royal Academy in 1911.

[Private information; Registers of the Trustees' Academy; Graves's Academy Exhibitors; Exhibition Catalogues; The Art of W. Q. Orchardson, by Sir W. Armstrong (Portfolio monograph, 1895); Art Annual, 1897, by Stanley Little; Scottish Painting, by J. L. Caw, 1908; Martin Hardie's John Pettie, 1908; The Times, 14 April 1910; Athenæum, 23 April 1910.] J. L. C.

ORD, WILLIAM MILLER (1834–1902), physician, born on 23 Sept. 1834 at Brixton Hill, was elder of the two sons of George Ord, F.R.C.S., of an old Border family, by his wife Harriet, daughter of Sir James Clark, a London merchant. After education at King's College school, where he distinguished himself in classics, he entered the medical school of St. Thomas's Hospital in 1852. There he soon came under the influence of (Sir) John Simon [q. v. Suppl. II], surgeon at the hospital and afterwards professor of pathology. They remained professional and personal friends to the end of their days. Ord graduated M.B. at London University in 1857. After being house surgeon, surgical registrar, and demonstrator of anatomy at St. Thomas' Hospital, he became lecturer on zoology and assistant physician and joint lecturer on physiology on 8 Sept. 1870; he was dean of the medical school (1876–87) and largely instrumental in its success. He was physician from 1877 until 1898, when he was elected consulting physician. In early life Ord had joined his father in general practice, but already in 1869, when he became M.R.C.P., had started as a consultant. In 1875 he became F.R.C.P., and proceeded M.D. of London in 1877.

Ord's name is intimately connected with the elucidation of the disease now known as myxœdema. In 1873 Sir William Gull [q. v.] described its symptoms in a paper 'on a cretinoid state supervening in adult life in women.' In 1877, in a contribution 'on myxœdema, a term proposed to be applied to an essential condition in the "cretinoid" affection occasionally observed in middle-aged women,' Ord showed that the essential cause of the disease was atrophy or fibrosis of the thyroid gland. The name myxœdema which has been adopted was based on the belief that there was an excess of mucin in the tissues; this, however, has been shown not to be constant throughout the disease. Ord was subsequently chairman of the committee of the Clinical Society of London appointed in 1883 to investigate the subject of myxœdema (report issued 1888), and gave the Bradshaw lecture at the Royal College of Physicians in 1898 'On Myxœdema and Allied Conditions.' He was a censor of the college in 1897–8.

Ord was a clinical teacher of the first rank, a busy consultant, and extremely active in medical life in London. He was secretary of the committee which prepared the second edition of the official 'Nomenclature of Diseases' issued by the Royal College of Physicians of London in 1880; in the following year he was secretary of the medical section of the International Medical Congress held in London, and in 1885 he was president of the Medical Society of London. He was also chairman of the committee of the Royal Medical and Chirurgical Society which drew up the 'Report on the Climates and Baths of Great Britain' (vol. i. 1895; vol. ii. 1902).

Failing health obliged him to give up practice and retire to the village of Hurstbourne Tarrant near Andover in 1900. He died at his son's house at Salisbury on 14 May 1902, and was buried there in the London Road cemetery.

Ord married (1) in 1859 Julia, daughter of Joseph Rainbow of Norwood; she died in 1864, leaving two daughters and one son; (2) Jane, daughter of Sir James Arndell Youl [q. v. Suppl. II]. There were two daughters by the second marriage.

Ord edited the collected works of Dr. Francis Sibson [q. v.]. He published 'Influence of Colloids upon Crystalline Forms and Cohesion' (1879) and 'On some Disorders of Nutrition related with Affections of the Nervous System' (1885), and made many contributions to current medical literature. He also took a keen interest in natural history, as may be seen in his oration to the Medical Society in 1894, entitled 'The Doctor's Holiday.'

[St. Thomas's Hosp. Rep. 1902, xxxi. 349; Lancet, 1902, i. 1494; information from his son, W. W. Ord, M.D.] H. D. R.

O'RELL, MAX (pseudonym). [See BLOUET, LÉON PAUL (1848–1903), humorous writer.]

ORMEROD, ELEANOR ANNE (1828–1901), economic entomologist, born at Sedbury Park, West Gloucestershire, on 11 May 1828, was youngest daughter of George Ormerod [q. v.] by his wife Sarah, daughter of John Latham, M.D. (1761–1843) [q. v.]. Three of her seven brothers, George Wareing, William Piers, and Edward Latham, are noticed separately. Of her two sisters, Georgiana enthusiastically co-operated in her work till her death on 19 Aug. 1896.

Eleanor Ormerod was educated at home in elementary subjects by her mother, who instilled in all her children strong religious feeling and artistic tastes. Latin and modern languages, in which she became an adept, Eleanor studied by herself. She early cherished a love of flowers, showed unusual powers of observation, and made free use of her father's library. With her sister Georgiana she studied painting under William Hunt, and both became efficient artists.

As a child Eleanor aided her brother William in his botanical work, and was soon expert in preparing specimens. But it was not, according to her own account, until 12 March 1852, when she obtained a copy of Stephens's 'Manual of British Beetles,' that she began the study of entomology, and laid the foundation for her researches into insect life. In 1868 she actively aided the Royal Horticultural Society in forming a collection illustrative of economic entomology, and for her services received in 1870 the silver Flora medal. To the International Polytechnic Exhibition at Moscow in 1872 she sent a collection of plaster models (prepared by herself) as well as electrotypes of plants, fruits, leaves, and reptiles, for which she was awarded silver medals and also received the gold medal of honour from Moscow University.

After the death of the father, on 9 Oct. 1873, the Ormerod family was broken up. Eleanor and her sister Georgiana lived together at Torquay, and then at Dunster Lodge, Spring Grove, Isleworth, where they were near Kew Gardens and in close touch with Sir Joseph and Lady Hooker. At Isleworth Miss Ormerod undertook a comprehensive series of meteorological observations. She was the first woman to be elected fellow of the Meteorological Society (1878). The sisters finally removed to Torrington House, St. Albans, in September 1887.

In the spring of 1877 Miss Ormerod issued the pamphlet, 'Notes for Observations of Injurious Insects,' which was the first of twenty-four 'Annual Reports of Observations of Injurious Insects' (1877–1900). With a view to the preparation of these reports she carried on till her death a large correspondence with observers all over the country and in foreign lands. Her reports, fully illustrated, were printed at her own expense and sent free to her correspondents and to all public bodies at home and abroad that were interested in the subject. A 'General Index of the Annual Reports' (1877–1898) was compiled by Mr. Robert Newstead, subsequently lecturer on medical entomology in Liverpool University. At the same time Miss Ormerod was generous in advice, notably on insect pests, to all correspondents who sought her counsel. Many of those from abroad she hospitably entertained on their visits to this country. She led an especially useful crusade against the ox-warble fly and the house sparrow or 'avian rat,' and she showed how these and other farm and forest, garden and orchard pests could best be resisted.

From 1882 to 1892 Miss Ormerod was consulting entomologist to the Royal Agricultural Society of England. On the day of her assuming the office (June 1882) she met with an accident at Waterloo railway station which resulted in permanent lameness. Her first official work was to prepare, with her sister, 'six diagrams illustrating some common injurious insects, with life histories and methods of prevention,' which were issued by the society.

Her work was incessant, and she declined the help of a coadjutor. She greatly valued the co-operation in her scientific efforts of Professor Westwood, life president of the Entomological Society, of Dr. C. V. Riley, entomologist of the department of agriculture, U.S.A., and of Professor Huxley. With Huxley she sat from 1882 to 1886 on the committee of economic entomology appointed by the education department, and gave important advice as to the improvement of the collections in the South Kensington and Bethnal Green Museums.

Miss Ormerod also lectured with success. From October 1881 to June 1884 she was special lecturer on economic entomology at the Royal Agricultural College, Cirencester, delivering six valuable lectures on insects. Ten lectures delivered at South Kensington Museum were published as 'Guide to the Methods of Insect Life' (1884). In 1889 she lectured at the Farmers' Club, of which she was elected an honorary member.

Miss Ormerod's activities did not lessen in her last years, although the death of her sister in 1896 greatly depressed her. Many honours were awarded her by agricultural societies in all parts of the world. On 14 April 1900 she was made hon. LL.D. of Edinburgh, being the first woman to receive the honour, and being greeted by the vice-chancellor, Sir Ludovic Grant, 'as the protectress of agriculture and the fruits of the earth, a beneficent Demeter of the nineteenth century.' Although so energetic in public work, Miss Ormerod had little sympathy with the agitation for woman's suffrage. She died at Torrington House, St. Albans, of malignant disease of the liver, on 19 July 1901, and was buried at St. Albans.

In addition to the 'Annual Reports' and 'The Cobham Journals,' abstracts and summaries of meteorological observations, made by Miss Caroline Molesworth, 1825–1850 (Stanford, 1880), she published 'A Manual of Remedies and Means of Prevention for the Attacks of Insects on Food Crops, Forest Trees, and Fruit' (1881; 2nd edit. 1890); 'Injurious Fruit and Farm Insects of South Africa' (1889); 'A Text Book of Agricultural Entomology, being a Plain Introduction to the Classification of Insects and Methods of Insect Life' (1892); 'Hand Book of Insects Injurious to Orchard and Bush Fruits' (1898); and several important papers on ox bot or warble fly, all being comprised in 'Flies Injurious to Stock' (i.e. sheep, horse, and ox) (1900) her latest work.

A lifelike oil painting of Miss Ormerod in academic costume (1900) hangs in Edinburgh University court room. To the university she presented a set of insect diagrams, hand-painted by her sister Georgiana, and a collection of insect cases furnished by herself, besides bequeathing unconditionally a sum of 5000*l*. This money has been applied to general purposes. An offer to the university by her executor of her fine working library, on condition that her bequest should be devoted to scientific objects, was refused.

[Eleanor Ormerod, LL.D., Economic Entomologist, Autobiography and Correspondence, edited by the present writer, with portrait and illustrations, 1904; The Times, 20 July 1901; Canadian Entomologist, vol. 33, Sept. 1901; Royal Agric. Soc. Journal, vol. 62, 1901; Men and Women of the Time, 1899.] R. W.

ORR, Mrs. ALEXANDRA SUTHERLAND (1828–1903), biographer of Browning, born on 23 Dec. 1828 at St. Petersburg, where her grandfather, (Sir) James Boniface Leighton, was court physician, was second daughter of Frederic Septimus Leighton (1800–1892), a doctor of medicine, by his wife Augusta Susan, daughter of George Augustus Nash of Edmonton. Frederic Leighton, Lord Leighton [q. v. Suppl. I], was her only brother. She was named Alexandra after her godmother the Empress of Russia. The family travelled much in Europe, and Alexandra was educated mostly abroad. Her health was always delicate. On account of her defective sight, most of her very considerable knowledge was acquired by listening to books read aloud to her. She married on 7 March 1857 Sutherland George Gordon Orr, commandant of the 3rd regiment of cavalry, Hyderabad contingent, and accompanied him to India. They were there during the Mutiny, and Mrs. Orr had a narrow escape from Aurungabad, her ultimate safety being due to the fidelity of Sheikh Baran Bukh. Orr died on 19 June 1858, worn out by the sufferings and privations endured in the Mutiny. He was gazetted captain and brevet major and C.B. on the day of his death. Mrs. Orr then rejoined her father, who, after sojourns in Bath and Scarborough, finally settled in London in 1869.

Mrs. Orr's main interests lay in art and literature, and in social intercourse with artists and men of letters. Already in the winter of 1855–6 she had met, in Paris, the poet Robert Browning, with whom her brother was on intimate terms from early manhood. The poet's acquaintance with Mrs. Orr was renewed at intervals until 1869, when, both having fixed their residence in London, they became close friends. For many years he read books to her twice a week. Shortly after its formation in 1881, Mrs. Orr joined the Browning Society, became a member of the committee wrote notes on various difficult points in Browning's poems, and was generous in money donations. The most important fruit of the connection was her illuminating

'Handbook to the Works of Robert Browning' (1885; 3rd edit. 1887); written at the request of some members of the society, and with the encouragement and help of the poet, the book is a kind of descriptive index, based partly on the historical order and partly on the natural classification of the various poems' (cf. Pref. 1885). The scheme of classification owed something to the suggestion of John Trivett Nettleship [q. v. Suppl. II]. The sixth edition (1892, often reprinted) embodied Mrs. Orr's final corrections.

In 1891 Mrs. Orr published her well-planned 'Life and Letters of Robert Browning,' largely based on material supplied by Browning's sister. Since 1891 new letters of the poet have come to light, but Mrs. Orr's biography retains the value due to personal knowledge and judgment. A new edition, revised and in part rewritten by (Sir) Frederic G. Kenyon, was published in 1908. Mrs. Orr's estimate of Browning's religious opinions gave rise to discussion, and she answered her critics in an article in the 'Contemporary Review' (Dec. 1891). To that and other periodicals Mrs. Orr contributed occasional articles on art and literature, as well as on 'Women's Suffrage,' of which she was a strong opponent.

After her father's death in 1892 Mrs. Orr continued to live in the house which he had occupied, 11 Kensington Park Gardens, until her death on 23 Aug. 1903. She was buried in Locksbrook cemetery, Bath, beside her parents.

Her portrait as a young widow was painted by her brother Frederic (Lord) Leighton in 1860. It was exhibited at the Royal Academy in 1861. Leighton wrote that it was more admired than anything else. It is now at Leighton House, Kensington. There is a reproduction in Mrs. Russell Barrington's 'Life and Letters of Frederic Leighton,' 1906, vol. ii. Another portrait, painted by Leighton about 1889, is in the possession of Mrs. Orr's sister, Mrs. Augusta Matthews. They are both fine pictures of a beautiful woman.

[The Times, 26 and 31 Aug. 1903; Mrs. Russell Barrington, Life, Letters and Work of Frederic Leighton, 2 vols. 1906; private information.]

E. L.

OSBORNE, WALTER FREDERICK (1859–1903), painter, was the son of William Osborne, R.H.A., a popular painter of animals, by Anne Woods, his wife. He was born in 1859 at 5 Castlewood Avenue, Rathmines, Dublin, which was his home for the whole of his life. His general education was acquired at Rathmines school, under the Rev. C. W. Benson. His first training in art was obtained in the schools of the Royal Hibernian Academy, where he won the Albert prize in 1880 with 'A Glade in the Phœnix Park.' In 1881, and again in 1882, he won the Taylor scholarship of 50*l.* per annum, given by the Royal Dublin Society, the chief reward open only to art students of Irish birth. With the help of this scholarship he proceeded to Antwerp, where he studied for two years under Verlat. On his return home he set himself to paint, in water-colour, pastel, and oil, the life of the English and Irish fields and streets. He spent his summers in the rural parts of England, in Sussex, Berkshire, Warwickshire, Norfolk, and other districts where subjects unspoiled by commerce, and farmhouses ready to accept a 'paying guest,' were to be found. These scenes he painted with sincerity, delicacy, and truth, and his pictures soon became widely popular, especially among artists. He painted, too, in Brittany, in the neighbourhood of Quimper, while his pictures of street life in Dublin helped to increase his reputation. He was a regular contributor to the exhibitions of the Royal Hibernian Academy and of the Royal Academy (1886–1903), his contributions to the latter being chiefly portraits. In 1895 he and the writer of this article made a tour in Spain, where he found subjects for several excellent drawings in water-colour and sketches in oil. A year later he travelled in Holland with the same companion and painted canal scenes in Amsterdam. During the last ten years of his life he was much sought after as a portrait painter, a form of art for which he showed a remarkable gift. Among his sitters were Lord Houghton, now marquess of Crewe, K.G., Lord Ashbourne, Lord Powerscourt, K.P., Sir Thomas Moffett, Serjeant Jellett, the duke of Abercorn, K.G.. Sir Frederick Falkiner, Sir Walter Armstrong, and many ladies. The portrait of the duke of Abercorn, a full length in a duke's parliamentary robes, was left unfinished at the painter's death. It is in the Masonic Hall, Dublin. In 1900 Osborne was offered knighthood in recognition of his distinction as a painter. He was elected an associate of the Royal Hibernian Academy in 1883, and a full member in 1886. He was delightful in every relation of life and enjoyed great popularity with all his friends. To his powers as an artist he added those which go with a vigorous, athletic body, and had fate made him a professional cricketer, he would probably have acquired fame as a bowler.

He died at 5 Castlewood Avenue, Rathmines, Dublin, on 24 April 1903, of double pneumonia, and was buried in Mount Jerome cemetery. He was unmarried, and left considerable savings behind him.

The National Gallery of Ireland owns four of his subject pictures in oil: 'The Lustre Jug,' a cottage interior with children; 'A Galway Cottage'; 'In County Dublin'; and 'A Cottage Garden'; also two water-colour drawings, 'The Dolls' School' and 'The House-builders'; as well as many pencil drawings. 'Life in the Streets: Hard Times' (R.A. 1902) was bought by the Chantrey bequest. His own portrait by himself hangs in the collection of Irish national portraits, with his portraits in chalk and pencil of Miss Margaret Stokes and Thomas Henry Burke [q.v.], the under-secretary to the lord-lieutenant.

[Personal knowledge.] W. A.

O'SHEA, JOHN AUGUSTUS (1839–1905), Irish journalist, born on 24 June 1839 at Nenagh, co. Tipperary, was son of John O'Shea, a well-known journalist in the south of Ireland, who was long connected with the 'Clonmel (afterwards Nenagh) Guardian,' and published a volume of poems entitled 'Nenagh Minstrelsy' (Nenagh, 1838). After receiving his elementary education in his native town, O'Shea was sent on 31 Oct. 1856 to the Catholic University then recently established in Dublin under the direction of John Henry (afterwards cardinal) Newman. In his 'Roundabout Recollections' O'Shea has given an account of his residence at the university, with sketches of its rector, professors, and fellow students. In 1859 O'Shea migrated to London, and sought work as a journalist. His love of adventure led him to become a special correspondent. In 1860 he represented an American journal at the siege of Ancona, defended by the papal troops, and he described part of the Austro-Prussian war. Settling in Paris, he acted for some time as a correspondent of the 'Irishman' newspaper, then conducted by Richard Pigott [q.v.]. For this paper, and for the 'Shamrock,' a small magazine owned by the same proprietor, O'Shea wrote many of his best stories and sketches, especially the 'Memoirs of a White Cravat' (1868). His usual signature was 'The Irish Bohemian.' In 1869 he joined the staff of the London 'Standard,' and for many years was one of its most active special correspondents. In his 'Iron-Bound City' (1886), perhaps the best of his books, he gives a graphic account of his adventures during the Franco-German war. He was in Paris through the siege. His subsequent services to the 'Standard' included reports of the Carlist war, of the coronation of the king of Norway, and of the famine in Bengal. Many of his articles were republished in independent books. He left the 'Standard' after twenty-five years association. Henceforth he wrote occasional articles in various English and Irish papers, including the 'Freeman's Journal' and 'Evening Telegraph' of Dublin. He was long a regular member of the staff of the 'Universe,' an Irish catholic paper published in London. Keenly interested in his native country he was a prominent member of Irish literary societies and a frequent lecturer. An attack of paralysis disabled him in his last years, and a fund was raised by the Irish Literary Society of London to relieve his wants. He died at his home in Jeffreys Road, Clapham, on 13 March 1905, and was buried in St. Mary's cemetery, Kensal Green. He was twice married, his second wife and a daughter surviving him.

O'Shea's admirable sense of style, his dash and wit, distinguish his writing and suggest a touch of Lever's spirit. He was a witty conversationalist and raconteur and an admirable public speaker. His chief publications are: 1. 'Leaves from the Life of a Special Correspondent,' 2 vols. 1885. 2. 'An Iron-Bound City, or Five Months of Peril and Privation,' 2 vols. 1886. 3. 'Romantic Spain: a Record of Personal Experience,' 2 vols. 1887. 4. 'Military Mosaics: a Set of Tales,' 1888. 5. 'Mated from the Morgue: a Tale of the Second Empire,' 1889. 6. 'Brave Men in Action' (in collaboration with S. J. McKenna), 1890; new edit. 1899. 7. 'Roundabout Recollections,' 2 vols. 1892.

[Men and Women of the Time, 1899; Freeman's Journal, and The Times, 14 March 1905; Brit. Mus. Cat.; Reg. of Catholic University, Dublin; O'Donoghue's Poets of Ireland; works mentioned in text; personal knowledge.] D. J. O'D.

O'SHEA, WILLIAM HENRY (1840–1905), Irish politician, born in 1840, was only son of Henry O'Shea of Dublin by his wife Catharine, daughter of Edward Craneach Quinlan of Rosana, co. Tipperary. His parents were Roman catholics. Educated at St. Mary's College, Oscott, and at Trinity College, Dublin, he entered the 18th hussars as cornet in 1858, retiring as captain in 1862. On 24 Jan. 1867 he married Katharine, sixth and youngest daughter of the Rev. Sir John Page Wood, second baronet, of Rivenhall Place, Essex, and sister of Sir Evelyn Wood. In 1880 O'Shea was introduced by The O'Gorman Mahon [q. v.] to Parnell, who shortly afterwards made the acquaintance of Mrs. O'Shea. Suspicions of an undesirable intimacy between them caused O'Shea in 1881 to challenge Parnell to a duel. His fears however were allayed by his wife. Meanwhile in April 1880 O'Shea had been elected M.P. for county Clare, professedly as a home ruler. But his friendly relations with prominent English liberals caused him to be distrusted as a 'whig' by more thorough-going nationalists. In Oct. 1881 the Irish Land League agitation reached a climax in the imprisonment of Parnell and others as 'suspects' in Kilmainham gaol, and in April 1882 O'Shea, at Parnell's request, interviewed, on his behalf, Gladstone, Mr. Joseph Chamberlain, and other leading members of the government, arranging what has since been called the 'Kilmainham Treaty.' The basis of the 'treaty' was an undertaking on Parnell's part, if and when released, to discourage lawlessness in Ireland in return for the promise of a government bill which would stop the eviction of Irish peasants for arrears of rent. This arrangement was opposed by William Edward Forster, the Irish secretary, who resigned in consequence, and it ultimately broke down. In 1884 O'Shea tried without success to arrange with Mr. Chamberlain a more workable compromise between the government and Parnell, with whom O'Shea's social relations remained close.

At the general election in Nov. 1885 O'Shea stood as a liberal without success for the Exchange division of Liverpool. Almost immediately afterwards, in Feb. 1886, he was nominated by Parnell for Galway, where a vacancy occurred through the retirement of Mr. T. P. O'Connor, who, having been elected for both Galway and the Scotland division of Liverpool, had decided to represent the latter constituency. O'Shea had not gained in popularity with advanced nationalists, and his nomination was strongly opposed by both J. G. Biggar and Mr. T. M. Healy, who hurried to Galway and nominated M. A. Lynch, a local man, in opposition. Biggar telegraphed to Parnell 'The O'Sheas will be your ruin,' and in speeches to the people did not conceal his belief that Mrs. O'Shea was Parnell's mistress. Parnell also went to Galway and he quickly re-established his authority. O'Shea's rejection, he declared, would be a blow at his own power, which would imperil the chances of home rule. O'Shea was elected by an overwhelming majority (942 to 54), but he gave no pledges on the home rule question. He did not vote on the second reading of Gladstone's first home rule bill on 7 June 1886, and next day announced his retirement from the representation of Galway. In 1889 he filed a petition for divorce on the ground of his wife's adultery with Parnell. The case was tried on 15 Nov. 1890. There was no defence, and a 'decree nisi' was granted on 17 Nov. On 25 June 1891 Parnell married Mrs. O'Shea. O'Shea lived during his latter years at Brighton, where he died on 22 April 1905. He had issue one son and two daughters.

[The Times, and the Irish Times, 25 April 1905; O'Brien's Life of Parnell, 1898; Annual Register 1882; Paul's Modern England, vol. v. 1904; Lucy, Diary of the Gladstone Parliament, 1880–5, 1886.] S. E. F.

OSLER, ABRAHAM FOLLETT (1808–1903), meteorologist, born on 22 March 1808 in Birmingham, where his father was a glass manufacturer, was eldest son of Thomas Osler by his wife Fanny Follett. From 1816 to 1824 he was at Hazelwood school, near Birmingham, which was kept by Thomas Wright Hill [q. v.]. On leaving school in 1824 Osler became assistant to his father. In 1831 the business came under his sole management, and through his energy and ability he greatly developed it.

Osler was early interested in meteorology. In 1835 the council of the Birmingham Philosophical Institute purchased a set of such meteorological instruments as were then in use. Osler perceived the need of appliances which should give continuous records of atmospheric changes. He therefore set himself to contrive a novel self-recording pressure-plate anemometer, and a self-recording rain-gauge. The first anemometer and rain-gauge was made by Osler in 1835, and erected at the Philosophical Institution, Cannon Street, Birmingham. A description of its work, illustrated with records obtained from it, was published in the annual report of the Institution for 1836. Osler's self-recording anemometer received the varying wind pressure on a plate of known area, supported on springs and kept at right angles to the direction of the wind by means of a vane. The degree to which this plate was pressed back upon the springs by each gust of wind was registered, in pounds avoirdupois per square foot, by a pencil on a sheet of paper graduated in hours and moved forward at a uniform rate by means of a clock. On the same sheet the direction of the wind was recorded. This was done by means of a vane, and its movements were conveyed, by an ingenious contrivance, to a pencil which moved transversely upon a scale of horizontal lines representing the points of the compass. The curve thus drawn gave a continuous record of the direction of the wind. The rainfall was also recorded on the same paper. The rain was collected in a funnel, the top of which had a known area, and flowed into a vessel supported on a bent lever with a counterbalancing weight; the accumulating water caused the vessel to descend, and this movement was registered by a pencil, which produced a line on a part of the paper that was ruled with a scale of fractions of an inch. When the limit of the capacity of the counterbalanced vessel was reached, it discharged its contents automatically, and the pencil returned to the zero line.

The importance to meteorological observation of Osler's invention was at once recognised, and his pressure-plate anemometer was soon installed at Greenwich observatory (1841), the Royal Exchange, London, at Plymouth, Inverness, and Liverpool. Osler read a paper in 1837 before the British Association describing his instruments. To Dr. Robinson's cup anemometer for measuring the horizontal motion of the air Osler subsequently applied his own self-recording methods, thus obtaining records of mean hourly velocities as well as total mileage of the wind. Later the curves of pressure, direction, velocity, and rainfall in connection with time were recorded on the same sheet of paper.

As he explained in papers read before the British Association at Birmingham in 1839 and at Glasgow in 1840, Osler at the request and expense of the association soon developed his graphic contrivances. His self-recording methods soon came into very general use.

By means of another series of monthly, quarterly, and annual and mean diurnal wind curves, he illustrated the average distribution of winds during each part of the day, and for the different seasons. Mean diurnal wind velocity curves were made to run parallel to the mean diurnal temperature curve, and on reducing the two maxima and minima to the same values they proved almost identical. Sir David Brewster [q. v.], who came independently to the same conclusion in 1840, paid high tribute to Osler's labours, and described his results respecting the phenomena and laws of the wind 'as more important than any which have been obtained since meteorology became one of the physical sciences.' Osler persistently urged a more scientific and methodical study of meteorology by the establishment of observatories in different latitudes. To the British Association at Birmingham in 1865 he described 'the horary and diurnal variations in the direction and motion of the air' in the light of a minute comparison of his observations at Wrottesley, Liverpool, and Birmingham. Osler in further researches showed the relation of atmospheric disturbances to the great trade winds, and the effect of the earth's rotation in inducing eastern and western velocities in the northerly and southerly winds. Many other papers on his anemometer and on his meteorological investigations were printed in the reports of the association. He communicated his last paper to the meeting at Birmingham in 1886, the subject being 'The Normal Form of Clouds.'

Other interests occupied Osler's energies. After delivering three lectures on chronometry and its history at the Birmingham Philosophical Institution (Jan. 1842) he collected funds and set up a standard clock for Birmingham in front of the Institution, and on the roof equipped a transit instrument and an astronomical clock. Subsequently he altered the clock from Birmingham to Greenwich time, to which the other public clocks in Birmingham were gradually adjusted. In 1883 he presented to Birmingham a clock and bells, of the same size and model as those at the Law Courts in London, to be placed in the clock tower of the newly built municipal buildings. Craniometry also attracted Osler's attention; he devised and constructed a complete and accurate instrument for brain measurements, which gave full-sized diagrams of the exact form of the skull.

Osler was made F.R.S. in 1855. He retired from business in 1876, devoting himself thenceforth entirely to scientific pursuits. Among many speculative papers was an attempt to account for the distribution of sea and land on the earth's surface by a theory that the earth had once two satellites, one of which returned to it within geological time. He generously supported scientific and literary institutions in Birmingham. His benefactions, always anonymous, included 7500*l.* to the Birmingham and Midland Institute and 10,000*l.* for the purposes of Birmingham University.

Osler died at South Bank, Edgbaston, on 26 April 1903, and was buried at Birmingham. He married in 1832 Mary, daughter of Thomas Clark, a Birmingham merchant and manufacturer, and had issue eight children, of whom three survived him. A daughter Fanny was married to William James Russell [q. v. Suppl. II]. A portrait painted in 1863 by W. T. Roden is in the possession of his son, H. F. Osler, of Burcot Grange, Bromsgrove.

[The Times, 28 April 1903; Proc. Roy. Soc. vol. 75, 1905; personal knowledge.]

P. E. D.

O'SULLIVAN, CORNELIUS (1841–1907), brewers' chemist, born at Bandon, co. Cork, on 20 Dec. 1841, was son of James O'Sullivan, a merchant of that town, by his wife Elizabeth Morgan. His only surviving brother, James O'Sullivan, became head of the chemical laboratory of Messrs. Bass, Ratcliff and Gretton, Burton-on-Trent.

Cornelius, after attending a private school in Bandon known as 'Denny Holland's' and the Cavendish school there, went to evening science classes in the town held under the auspices of the Science and Art Department, winning in September 1862 a scholarship at the Royal School of Mines, London. On the completion of the prescribed three years' course of study he joined the teaching staff of the Royal College of Chemistry, London, as a student assistant under Prof. A. W. von Hofmann, who recognised O'Sullivan's promise, and on becoming professor of chemistry at Berlin in 1865 made O'Sullivan his private assistant. A year later the professor's influence secured him the post of assistant brewer and chemist to Messrs. Bass & Co., Burton-on-Trent. In that capacity he applied his chemical knowledge and aptitude for original research to the scientific and practical issues of brewing. Ultimately he became head of the scientific and analytical staff of Messrs. Bass & Co., holding the appointment till his death.

Pasteur's researches on fermentative action gave O'Sullivan his cue in his earliest investigation. He embodied his contributions to the technology of brewing in a series of papers on physiological and applied chemistry communicated to the Chemical Society. Of these the chief are: 'On the Transformation Products of Starch' (1872 and 1879); 'On Maltose' (1876); 'On the Action of Malt Extract on Starch' (1876); 'Presence of Raffinose in Barley' (1886); 'Researches on the Gums of the Arabin Group' (1884 and 1891); Invertase: a Contribution to the History of an Enzyme' (with F. W. Tompson, 1890); and (with A. L. Stern) 'The Identity of Dextrose from Different Sources, with Special Reference to the Cupric Oxide Reducing Power' (1896). His name is especially associated with the delicate research which re-established and elucidated the distinct character of maltose, a sugar produced by the action of diastase on starch. O'Sullivan described in detail the properties of this substance, therein confirming earlier but practically forgotten observations (see *Encyclo. Brit.* 11th edit., art. Brewing). He was elected a fellow of the Chemical Society in 1876, served on the council 1882–5, and was awarded the Longstaff medal in 1884 for his researches on the chemistry of the carbohydrates (see remarks by W. H. PERKIN, F.R.S., Anniversary Address, *Chem. Soc. Trans.* vol. xlv.). In 1885 he was elected F.R.S. An original member of the Institute of Chemistry, the Society of Chemical Industry, and the Institute of Brewing, he served on the council of each.

He died at his residence, 148 High Street, Burton-on-Trent, on 8 Jan. 1907, and was buried near Bandon. He married in 1871 Edithe, daughter of Joseph Nadin of Barrow Hall, near Derby, and had issue three sons (one died in early youth) and one daughter.

[Journ. Inst. Brewing, vol. xiii.; Proc. Inst. Chemistry, 1907, part ii., and Presidential Address, ibid.; Memorial Lectures, Chem. Soc., p. 592; Nature, vol. lxxv.; Analyst, vol. xxxii.; Journ. Soc. Chem. Industry, vol. xxvi.; The Times, 9 Jan. 1907; private information.]

T. E. J.

OTTÉ, ELISE (1818–1903), scholar and historian, was born at Copenhagen on 30 September 1818, of a Danish father and an English mother. In 1820 her parents went to Santa Cruz, in the Danish West Indies, where her father died. Her mother returned to Copenhagen, where she met the English philologist, Benjamin Thorpe [q. v.], while he was studying Anglo-Saxon under Rask in Denmark, and married him. Elise accompanied her mother and step-father to England. From her step-father Elise Otté received an extraordinary education, and at a very tender age knew so much Anglo-Saxon and Icelandic as to be able to help Thorpe in his grammatical work. His tyranny, however, became more than she could bear, and in 1840 she went to Boston, U.S.A., to secure her independence. Here her mind turned from grammar to science, and she studied physiology at Harvard. Later on she travelled much in Europe, and then resumed her life with her step-father, whom she helped in his version of the 'Edda of Sæmund.' But the bondage was again found intolerable, and in 1849 Elise Otté escaped to St. Andrews, where she worked at scientific translations for the use of Dr. George Edward Day [q. v.], Chandos professor of anatomy and medicine. In 1863 she went to reside with Day and his wife at Torquay, and in 1872, after Day's death, made London her home. Here, for years, she carried on an active literary career, writing largely for scientific periodicals. In 1874 she published a 'History of Scandinavia,' which is her most durable work; she compiled grammars of Danish and of Swedish, and issued translations of standard works by De Quatrefages, R. Pauli, and others. Her translation of Pauli's 'Old England' (1861) was dedicated to her step-father, Thorpe. Miss Otté was one of the most learned women of her time, especially in philology and physical science, but she never acquired ease in literary expression. She lived wholly in the pursuit of knowledge, even in extreme old age, when rendered inactive and tortured by neuralgia. She died at Richmond on 20 Dec. 1903, in her eighty-sixth year.

[Personal knowledge; Athenæum, 2 Jan. (by the present writer) and 16 Jan. (by Miss Day), 1904.] E. G.

OUIDA (pseudonym). [See De la Ramée, Marie Louise (1839–1908), novelist.]

OVERTON, JOHN HENRY (1835–1903), canon of Peterborough and church historian, born at Louth, Lincolnshire, on 4 Jan. 1835, was only son of Francis Overton, surgeon, of Louth, a man of learning and of studious habits, by his wife Helen Martha, daughter of Major John Booth, of Louth. Educated first (1842–5) at the Louth grammar school, and next at a private school at Laleham, Middlesex, under the Rev. John Buckland, Overton went to Rugby in Feb. 1849, and thence obtained an open scholarship at Lincoln College, Oxford. He was placed in the first class in classical moderations in 1855 and in the third class in the final classical school in 1857, was captain of his college boat club, rowed stroke of its 'eight,' was a cricketer and throughout his life retained a keen interest in the game, and in his later years was addicted to golf. He graduated B.A. in 1858, and proceeded M.A. in 1860. In 1858 he was ordained to the curacy of Quedgeley, Gloucestershire, and in 1860 was presented by J. L. Fytche, a friend of his father, to the vicarage of Legbourne, Lincolnshire. While there he took pupils and studied English church history, specially during the eighteenth century. In 1878, in conjunction with his college friend, Charles John Abbey, rector of Checkendon, Oxfordshire, he published 'The English Church in the Eighteenth Century,' 2 vols., which was designed as a review of 'different features in the religion and church history of England' during that period rather than as 'a regular history' (*Preface to second edition*); it was well received and ranks high among English church histories; a second and abridged edition in one volume was published in 1887. Overton was collated to a prebend in Lincoln cathedral by Bishop Christopher Wordsworth [q. v.] in 1879, and in 1883, on Gladstone's recommendation, was presented by the crown to the rectory of Epworth, Lincolnshire, the birthplace of John Wesley [q. v.], in whose career he took a warm interest. While at Epworth he was rural dean of Axholme. In 1889 he was made hon. D.D. of Edinburgh University. From 1892 to 1898 he was proctor for the clergy in convocation, and took an active part in its proceedings, speaking with weight and judgment. In 1898 he was presented by the dean and chapter of Lincoln to the rectory of Gumley, near Market Harborough, and represented the chapter in convocation. He was a frequent and popular speaker at church congresses. In 1901 he was a select preacher at Oxford, and from 1902 Birkbeck lecturer at Trinity College, Cambridge. Early in 1903 Dr. Carr Glyn, the bishop of Peterborough, made him a residentiary canon of his cathedral; he was installed on 12 Feb., and as the canonry was of small value, he retained his rectory. He kept one period of residence at Peterborough, but did not live to inhabit his prebendal house, for he died at Gumley rectory on 17 Sept. of that year. He was buried in the churchyard of the parish church of Skidbrook near Louth, where many of his family had been interred. A high churchman and a member of the English Church Union, he appreciated the points of view of those who differed from him. He was an excellent parish priest, and was courteous, good-tempered, and humorous.

On 17 July 1862 Overton married

Marianne Ludlam, daughter of John Allott of Hague Hall, Yorkshire, and rector of Maltby, Lincolnshire; she survived him with one daughter. As memorials of Overton a brass tablet was placed in Epworth parish church by the parishioners, a stained glass window and a reredos in Skidbrook church, and a two-light window in the chapter-house of Lincoln Cathedral.

As an historian and biographer Overton showed much insight both into general tendencies and into personal character; was well-read, careful, fair in judgment, and pleasing in style. The arrangement of his historical work is not uniformly satisfactory; he was apt to injure his representation of a movement in thought or action by excess of biographical detail. Besides his share in the joint work with Abbey noticed above, he published: 1. 'William Law, Nonjuror and Mystic,' 1881. 2. 'Life in the English Church, 1660–1714,' 1885. 3. 'The Evangelical Revival in the Eighteenth Century' in Bp. Creighton's 'Epochs of Church History,' 1886. 4. 'Life of Christopher Wordsworth, Bp. of Lincoln,' with Miss Wordsworth, 1888, 1890. 5. 'John Hannah, a Clerical Study,' 1890. 6. 'John Wesley,' in 'Leaders of Religion' series, 1891. 7. 'The English Church in the Nineteenth Century,' 1894. 8. 'The Church in England,' 2 vols., in Ditchfield's 'National Churches,' 1897. 9. 'The Anglican Revival' in the 'Victorian Era' series, 1897. 10. An edition of Law's 'Serious Call' in the 'English Theological Library,' 1898. 11. 'The Nonjurors, their Lives, &c.,' 1902. 12. 'Some Post-Reformation Saints,' 1905, posthumous. 13. At his death he left unfinished 'A History of the English Church from the Accession of George I to the End of the Eighteenth Century,' a volume for the 'History of the English Church' edited by Dean Stephens [q. v. Suppl. II] and William Hunt; the book was edited and completed by the Rev. Frederic Relton in 1906. He contributed many memoirs of divines to this Dictionary, and wrote for the 'Dictionary of Hymnology,' the 'Church Quarterly Review,' and other periodicals.

[Private information; The Times, 19 Sept. 1903; Guardian, 23 Sept. 1903; obituary notices in Northampton Mercury, the Peterborough and other local papers.] W. H.

OVERTOUN, first Baron. [See White, John Campbell (1843–1908), Scottish philanthropist.]

OWEN, ROBERT (1820–1902), theologian, born at Dolgelly, Merionethshire, on 13 May 1820, was third son of David Owen, a surgeon of that town, by Ann, youngest daughter of Hugh Evans of Fronfelen and Esgairgeiliog, near Machynlleth. His brothers died unmarried in early manhood.

Educated at Ruthin grammar school, where he showed much precocity (Harriet Thomas, *Father and Son*, p. 60), he matriculated from Jesus College, Oxford, on 22 Nov. 1838; was scholar from 1839 to 1845; graduated B.A. in 1842 with a third class in classical finals, proceeding M.A. in 1845, and B.D. in 1852 (Foster, *Al. Oxon.*). He was fellow of his college from 1845 till 1864, and public examiner in law and modern history in 1859–60.

Though he was ordained by Dr. Bethell, bishop of Bangor, in 1843, and served a curacy till 1845 at Tremeirchion, he held no preferment. Coming under the influence of the Tractarians, he maintained an occasional correspondence with Newman long after the latter seceded to Rome. In 1847 Owen edited, for the Anglo-Catholic Library, John Johnson's work on 'The Unbloody Sacrifice,' which had been first issued in 1714. He reached the view that establishment and endowment were all but fatal to the 'catholic' character of the Church of England, and in 1893 he joined a few other Welsh clergymen in discussing such proposed legislation as would restore to the church her independent liberty in the appointment of bishops and secure some voice to the parochial laity.

In 1864, owing to an allegation of immorality, he was called upon to resign his fellowship. He was at that time probably the most learned scholar on the foundation. He shortly afterwards retired to Bronygraig, Barmouth, in which district he owned considerable property. There he died unmarried on 6 April 1902, and was buried at Llanaber.

Owen's original works were: 1. 'An Introduction to the Study of Dogmatic Theology,' 1858; 2nd edit. 1887. 2. 'The Pilgrimage to Rome: a Poem,' Oxford, 1863. 3. 'Sanctorale Catholicum, or Book of Saints,' 1880: 'a sort of Anglican canon of saints, especially strong in local British saints.' 4. 'An Essay on the Communion of Saints, together with an Examination of the Cultus Sanctorum,' 1881; nearly the whole issue perished in a fire at the publishers. 5. 'Institutes of Canon Law,' 1884, written at the instance of Dr. Walter Kerr Hamilton, bishop of Salisbury. 6. 'The Kymry: their Origin, History, and International Relations,' Carmarthen, 1891.

[The Times, 10 April 1902; T. R. Roberts, Dict. of Eminent Welshmen, 1907, p. 386; Brit. Mus. Cat.] D. Ll. T.

P

PAGE, H. A. (pseudonym). [See JAPP, ALEXANDER HAY (1837–1905), author.]

PAGET, FRANCIS (1851–1911), bishop of Oxford, second son of Sir James Paget, first baronet [q. v. Suppl. I], surgeon, was born on 20 March 1851 at St. Bartholomew's Hospital, E.C., in his father's official residence as warden (cf. STEPHEN PAGET, *Memoirs and Letters of Sir James Paget*, p. 127). His mother was Lydia, youngest daughter of the Rev. Henry North, and his brothers are Sir John Rahere Paget, K.C., Dr. Henry Luke Paget, bishop suffragan of Stepney, and Stephen Paget, F.R.C.S. He was educated first at St. Marylebone and All Souls' grammar school, and then at Shrewsbury under Benjamin Hall Kennedy [q. v.] and Henry Whitehead Moss, contributing elegant Latin verse to 'Sabrinæ Corolla.' He was elected to a junior studentship at Christ Church, Oxford, in 1869. He won the Hertford scholarship, the chancellor's prize for Latin verse, and a first class in classical moderations in 1871. He graduated B.A. with a first class in the final classical school in 1873, proceeding M.A. in 1876 and D.D. in 1885. He was elected senior student in 1873, tutor in 1876 and honorary student in 1901. Ordained deacon in 1875 and priest in 1877, he became a devoted follower of the great Tractarians of the time, Edward Bouverie Pusey [q.v.], who allowed him to read in the university pulpit a sermon of his which ill-health prevented him from delivering himself, Henry Parry Liddon [q. v.], Richard William Church [q. v. Suppl. I], whose eldest daughter he married, and James Russell Woodford [q. v.], bishop of Ely, whom he served as examining chaplain (1878–1885). But, being a witty and stimulating companion, he also established warm friendships with younger and less conservative men of the same school, while his influence over undergraduates grew as they became accustomed to a certain reserve in his manner.

In 1881 Paget was appointed Oxford preacher at the Chapel Royal, Whitehall, and in 1882 accepted the vicarage of Bromsgrove, but returned to Oxford in 1885, having been nominated by Gladstone to succeed Edward King [q.v. Suppl.II], bishop of Lincoln, as regius professor of pastoral theology and canon of Christ Church. Bromsgrove had given him a brief insight into parochial activities and had considerably widened the range of his sympathy (*Commonwealth*, September 1911, p. 276). Liddon's influence was counteracted by close association with younger men, and in the autumn of 1889 he joined Charles Gore, his successor in the see of Oxford, Henry Scott Holland, and others, in publishing the volume of essays called 'Lux Mundi.' Liddon, who was deeply distressed at parts of Gore's essay, regarded Paget's essay, on 'Sacraments,' as 'a real contribution to Christian theology' (J. O. JOHNSTON, *Life and Letters of H. P. Liddon*, 1904, p. 367; cf. p. 396).

In 1892, on the resignation of Henry George Liddell [q. v. Suppl. I], Paget was promoted by Lord Salisbury to the deanery of Christ Church. His task was difficult, and a certain tendency to extravagant rowdiness among the undergraduates had to be dealt with firmly. Estimates of his popularity vary, for 'he could only open out to a few,' and his 'elaborate courtesy' was apt 'to keep people back behind barriers of civility' (*Commonwealth*, September 1911, p. 277). But he was an anxious and capable administrator (cf. letter from 'Ex Æde Christi,' *The Times*, 7 Aug. 1911). The deanery was more accessible than heretofore. He was chaplain to William Stubbs [q. v. Suppl. II], bishop of Oxford, from 1889 until the bishop's death. Thus in 1901 the cathedral and the diocese were drawn closely together, and Paget learnt much of local episcopal problems.

In 1901, on the death of Bishop Stubbs, Dean Paget was promoted by Lord Salisbury to the bishopric of Oxford, and was consecrated on 29 June following. To the bishopric is attached the chancellorship of the Order of the Garter; Paget's most notable function in that capacity was the admission of Edward, Prince of Wales, to the order at Windsor on 10 June 1911. He was also chosen as 'supporter' bishop at their coronations by both Queen Alexandra in 1902 and Queen Mary in 1911. His administration of the diocese of Oxford was marked by the same anxious care which he had devoted to his college. He was eager to do everything himself; much of the episcopal correspondence was written in his own clear but characteristic handwriting; and it took some time for the people to feel that they knew him intimately, though his pastoral earnestness was keenly appreciated by humble folk in the rural villages. Early in 1903 he declined Mr. Balfour's offer of the see of Winchester. In 1904, by royal warrant dated 23 April, he became a member of the royal commission on ecclesiastical discipline, and signed its report on 21 June 1906. He was one of the three out of fourteen members who attended at each of the 118 sittings, and he exhibited 'a genius for fairness towards hostile witnesses' (*The Times*, 3 July 1906) and a remarkable gift for fusing opinions in the drafting of the report. His attitude to prevailing excesses in ritual was shown in the charge which he began to deliver to his diocese on 8 Oct. 1906, and by the action which he took against the Rev. Oliver Partridge Henly, vicar of Wolverton St. Mary, in respect of 'reservation' and 'benediction.' The case was taken to the court of arches (*The Times*, 20 and 21 July 1909); the vicar, who was deprived, obtained employment in another diocese, and afterwards joined the Roman church. Paget sought to provide for a sub-division of the diocese. For this purpose he made a vain endeavour to dispose of Cuddesdon Palace. In July 1910 he showed his active zeal for the wider work of the church by becoming chairman of the Archbishops' Western Canada fund.

To his intimate friends, and in particular to Archbishop Davidson, he was not only a wise counsellor but a delightful companion. He had a cultivated sense of beauty in nature, in music, and in words, and his tall, willowy figure and impressive, courtly bearing made him notable in any assembly. He was attacked by serious illness in the summer of 1910, and seemed to recover; but he died of a sudden recurrence of the malady in a nursing home in London on 2 Aug. 1911. He was interred in his wife's grave in the little burying ground to the south of Christ Church Cathedral, Oxford. He married on 28 March 1883 Helen Beatrice, eldest daughter of Richard William Church, dean of St. Paul's. Paget's career was permanently saddened by his wife's death at the deanery on 22 Nov. 1900, aged forty-two. She left four sons and two daughters; one of the latter, wife of the Rev. John Macleod Campbell Crum, predeceased Paget in 1910.

There is a portrait by Orchardson at Christ Church, and a memorial fund is being raised (November 1912) to provide a portrait for Cuddesdon Palace and an exhibition with a view to clerical service abroad, to be held at an English university. A cartoon portrait by 'Spy' appeared in 'Vanity Fair' in 1894.

As a theological scholar Paget is to be remembered chiefly for his 'Introduction to the Fifth Book of Hooker's Treatise of the Laws of Ecclesiastical Polity' (1899; 2nd edit. 1907); for his 'Lux Mundi' essay mentioned above; and for a masterly essay on *acedia* or accidie, written at Christ Church in 1890 (reprinted separately in 1912), and published with a collection of sermons entitled 'The Spirit of Discipline' in 1891 (7th edit. 1896). He also published 'Faculties and Difficulties for Belief and Disbelief' (1887; 3rd edit. 1894); and two other collections of sermons, entitled respectively 'Studies in Christian Character' (1895) and 'The Redemption of War' (1900).

[Memoir of Paget by Stephen Paget and the Rev. J. M. C. Crum, 1912; The Times, 3 Aug. 1911; Guardian, and Church Times, Aug. 1911; Crockford, 1911; Canon H. S. Holland in Commonwealth (brilliant character-sketch), Sept. 1911; Oxford Diocesan Mag., Sept. 1911; Stephen Paget, Memoirs and Letters of Sir James Paget, 1903; private information.] E. H. P.

PAGET, SIDNEY EDWARD (1860–1908), painter and illustrator, born on 4 Oct. 1860 at 60 Pentonville Road, London, N., was fourth son of Robert Paget, vestry clerk from 1856 to 1892 of Clerkenwell, by his wife Martha Clarke. At the Cowper Street school, London, Paget received his early education, and passing thence to Heatherley's school of art, entered the Royal Academy schools in 1881, where he was preceded by his brothers, Henry Marriott and Walter Stanley, both well-known artists and illustrators. At the Academy schools, among other prizes, he won in the Armitage competition second place in 1885, and first place and medal in 1886 for his 'Balaam blessing the Children of Israel.' Between 1879 and 1905 Paget contributed to the Royal Academy exhibitions eighteen miscellaneous paintings, of which nine were portraits. The best-known of his pictures, 'Lancelot and Elaine,' exhibited in 1891, was presented to the Bristol Art Gallery by Lord Winterstoke. In 1901 Paget exhibited a whole-length portrait of the donor, then Sir William Henry Wills, which is now at Mill Hill school, while a study is in the possession of Miss J. Stancomb-Wills. Among other portraits painted by him were Dr. Weymouth (R.A. 1887), headmaster of Mill Hill School, a three-quarter length in scarlet robes as D.Litt.; his father, and brother, Robert Ernest (his father's successor as vestry clerk), both in the town hall, Finsbury; and Sir John Aird, as mayor, in Paddington town hall.

It was as an illustrator that Paget won a wide reputation. His vigorous work as a black-and-white artist became well known not only in the United Kingdom but also in America and the colonies, by his drawings for the 'Pictorial World' (1882), the 'Sphere,' and for many of Cassell's publications. He also drew occasionally for the 'Graphic,' 'Illustrated London News,' and the 'Pall Mall Magazine.' Paget's spirited illustrations for Sir A. Conan Doyle's 'Sherlock Holmes' and 'Rodney Stone' in the 'Strand Magazine' greatly assisted to popularise those stories. The assertion that the artist's brother Walter, or any other person, served as model for the portrait of 'Sherlock Holmes' is incorrect.

A few years before his death Paget developed a painful chest complaint, to which he succumbed at Margate on 28 Jan. 1908. He was buried at the Marylebone cemetery, Finchley. He married in 1893 Edith Hounsfield, who survived him with six children.

[The Times, Telegraph, Morning Post and Daily Chronicle, 1 Feb. 1908, and Sphere, 8 Feb. (with portrait and reproductions of drawings); Who's Who, 1908; Graves's Royal Acad. Exhibitors; information from Mr. H. M. Paget, Royal Academy, and the headmaster of Mill Hill School.] J. D. M.

PAKENHAM, Sir FRANCIS JOHN (1832–1905), diplomatist, born on 29 Feb. 1832 in London, was seventh son of Thomas Pakenham, second earl of Longford, by his wife Emma Charlotte, daughter of William Lygon, first Earl Beauchamp. After private education he matriculated from Christ Church, Oxford, on 17 Oct. 1849. On leaving the university he was appointed attaché at Lisbon in 1852, and was promoted paid attaché at Mexico two years later. He was transferred in 1858 to Copenhagen, and in 1863 to Vienna. In June 1864 he was promoted to be secretary of legation at Buenos Ayres. During April, May, and June of the following year he was employed on special service in Paraguay on board of H.M.S. Dotterel, which had been sent up the River Plate and its tributaries for the protection of British subjects during the war between Paraguay, the Argentine Republic, and Brazil. He acquitted himself of this duty to the entire satisfaction of his superiors. In August of that year he was transferred to Rio de Janeiro, but remained in charge of the legation at Buenos Ayres till December 1865. In December 1866 he was employed on special service at Rio Grande do Sul in connection with an attempt which had been made on the life of the British consul, Mr. (afterwards Sir) R. de Courcy Perry from motives of personal revenge. He was transferred to Stockholm in March 1868, and later in the same year to Brussels, thence to Washington in 1870, and to Copenhagen in 1874. In March 1878 he was promoted to be minister resident and consul-general at Santiago, where he remained till 1885, serving in 1883 as British commissioner for claims arising out of the war between Chile and Bolivia and Peru. In February 1885 he was appointed British envoy at Buenos Ayres, with the additional office of minister plenipotentiary to Paraguay. In February 1896 he was transferred to Stockholm, where he remained till his retirement from the service in 1902. He was made K.C.M.G. in 1898.

While travelling for reasons of health he died at Alameda in California on 26 Jan. 1905. He married on 29 July 1879 Caroline Matilda, seventh daughter of the Hon. Henry Ward, rector of Killinchy, co. Down; she survived him, without issue. A portrait painted in 1900 by Count George de Rosen, member of the Royal Swedish Academy, is at Bernhurst House, Hurst Green, Sussex, the residence of his widow, which Pakenham inherited in 1858 by the will of Comte Pierre Coquet de Tresseilles.

Sir Francis was distinguished rather for the British qualities of phlegmatic calmness and sturdy good sense than for those which are generally attributed to the Irish race. His good nature and hospitality made him very popular with the British communities at the various posts in which he served, and he was successful in maintaining excellent personal relations with the governments to which he was accredited, even when, as in his South American posts, the questions to be discussed were of a nature to occasion some heat.

[The Times, 27 Jan. 1905; Foreign Office List, 1906, p. 300.] S.

PALGRAVE, Sir REGINALD FRANCIS DOUCE (1829–1904), clerk of the House of Commons, fourth son of Sir Francis Palgrave [q. v.], was born at Westminster on 28 June 1829. He entered Charterhouse school in 1841 and left in 1845. He was articled to Messrs. Bailey, Janson & Richardson, solicitors, of Basinghall Street, was admitted solicitor in May 1851, and entered the office of Messrs. Sharpe & Field. All his spare time he employed in sketching and sculpture. Through the influence of Sir Robert Harry Inglis [q. v.] and other friends of his father he was appointed to a clerkship in the House of Commons in 1853. From 1866 to 1868 he was examiner of petitions for private bills; he became second clerk assistant in 1868, clerk assistant in 1870, and from 1886 until his retirement in 1900 was clerk of the House of Commons. In 1887 he was made C.B., and in 1892 K.C.B. He was exact and careful in his official work, was thoroughly familiar with the practice and procedure of the House, and gave interesting evidence before various select committees, especially before that of 1894 on the vacating of a seat by accession to a peerage (Lord Coleridge's case). He was responsible for the 8th, 9th, 10th, and 11th (1886–96) editions of the 'Rules, Orders, and Forms of Procedure of the House of Commons,' first prepared by his predecessor in office, Sir Thomas Erskine May, Lord Farnborough [q. v.], and jointly with Mr. Alfred Bonham Carter for the 10th and much enlarged (1893) edition of May's 'Practical Treatise on the Law, &c., of Parliament.' Samuel Rawson Gardiner [q. v. Suppl. II], in the preface to his 'Fall of the Monarchy of Charles I,' speaks of Palgrave's 'great knowledge of the documents of the time' and of the valuable help which he gave him in revising that work. He was deeply interested in the local antiquities of Westminster and indicated some famous sites.

Palgrave, who before 1870 lived first at Reigate, and then for a short time at Hampstead, had from 1870 to 1900 an official residence in the Palace of Westminster; after his retirement he resided at East Mount, Salisbury. For many years after 1870 he spent his summer vacations at a house built for him at Swanage, Dorset. He had much artistic taste, inherited probably from his maternal grandfather, Dawson Turner [q. v.], and to the end of his life practised water-colour sketching, at which he was fairly proficient, and he was for an amateur an exceptionally skillful modeller in low relief. Officially neutral in politics, he was personally a strong conservative; he was a decided churchman and was churchwarden of St. Martin's, Salisbury; he was generally popular and was an excellent talker, especially on artistic subjects. He died at his residence, Salisbury, on 13 July 1904, and was buried in the cemetery there. He married in 1857 Grace, daughter of Richard Battley [q. v.], who died at East Mount, Salisbury, on 17 July 1905, and had one son, Augustin Gifford (*d.* 1910), an electrical engineer, and five daughters. A village cross at Swanage has been erected to the memory of Sir Reginald and Lady Palgrave by members of their family.

Palgrave published: 1. A 'Handbook to Reigate and the adjoining Parishes,' Dorking, 1860; out of print; an excellent little guide-book, especially as regards architecture, with engravings, some of them from his own drawings. 2. 'The House of Commons, Illustrations of its History and Practice,' 1869; revised edit. 1878. 3. 'The Chairman's Handbook, Suggestions and Rules for the Conduct of Chairmen of Public and other Meetings,' 1877; 13th edit. 1900. A most useful book, based on long experience at the table of the House of Commons. 4. 'Oliver Cromwell, the Protector,' 1890 (new edition 1903), a strange book, which represents Cromwell as the 'catspaw' of the major-generals, a discredited trickster, and the fomenter of plots which enabled him to crush his enemies by unjust executions. He wrote letters in the 'Athenæum,' 22 Jan. and 5 and 26 Feb. 1881, on the date of the warrant for the execution of Charles I, which S. R. Gardiner criticised adversely (*History of the Great Civil War*, iii. 584–5*n*).

[Private information; information received from and through Sir Courtenay P. Ilbert, K.C.B.] W. H.

PALMER, Sir ARTHUR POWER (1840–1904), general, born on 25 June 1840 at Kurubul, India, was son of Captain Nicholas Power Palmer of the 54th Bengal native infantry, by his wife, Rebecca Carter, daughter of Charles Barrett, of Dungarvan, co. Waterford. His father was killed on the retreat from Kabul in 1841, and his mother married secondly, in 1849, Morgan, son of Morgan Crofton, captain R.N., of co. Roscommon.

Educated at Cheltenham College (1852–6), he entered the Indian army on 20 Feb. 1857 as ensign in the 5th Bengal native infantry. He served throughout the Indian Mutiny campaign of 1857–9, raising a regiment of Sikhs 600 strong for service in Oude in March 1858. After receiving his commission as lieutenant on 30 April 1858, he joined Hodson's horse at Lucknow in the following June. At the action of Nawabgunge Barabunki his horse was killed under him, and he was present at minor affairs (during one of which he was wounded) in the Oude campaign until its conclusion on the Nepaul frontier. He was mentioned in despatches and received the medal.

In 1861 Palmer was transferred to the Bengal staff corps, and shared in the campaign on the north-west frontier in 1863–4, being present in the affair with the Momunds near Shubkudder and receiving the medal with clasp. He served as adjutant to the 10th Bengal lancers in the Abyssinian expedition of 1868, and his services were favourably noticed by Lord Napier of Magdala. Again he was awarded the medal.

Palmer acted as aide-de-camp to General Stafford in the Duffla expedition of 1874–5, and was mentioned in despatches. In 1876–7 he was on special duty with the Dutch troops in Achin, and fought in several actions in the Dutch conflict with the native forces. He was mentioned in despatches and received the Dutch cross with two clasps from the Netherland government. Meanwhile he was promoted captain in 1869, and his next service was in the Afghan war of 1878–80, when he acted as assistant adjutant and quartermaster-general to the Kuram field force. In the attack on the Peiwar Kotal (2 Dec. 1878) Palmer rendered good service by making a feint on the right of the Afghan position, and in January 1879 he accompanied the expedition into the Khost Valley. He was mentioned in despatches (*Lond. Gaz.* 4 Feb. 1879), and received the medal with clasp, and was given the brevet of lieutenant-colonel on 12 Nov. 1879. From 1880 to 1885 he was assistant adjutant general in Bengal, becoming colonel in 1883. Two years later he took part as commander of the 9th Bengal cavalry in the expedition to Suakin. He showed great dash and energy through the campaign. For his share in the raid on Thakul on 6 May 1885 he was mentioned in despatches (*Lond. Gaz.* 25 Aug. 1885). He received the medal with clasp, the bronze star, and the C.B. on 25 Aug. 1885.

During the campaign in Burma in 1892–3 Palmer was once more in action, commanding the force operating in the Northern Chin Hills. He received the thanks of the government of India; he was mentioned in despatches and government orders, and was nominated K.C.B. on 8 May 1894. Meanwhile he attained the rank of major-general in 1893 and of lieutenant-general in 1897. In 1897–8 he served in the Tirah campaign as general officer on the line of communications, and subsequently commanded the second division at the action of Chagru Kotal. He was awarded the medal with two clasps, and his services were acknowledged in government orders and in despatches (*Lond. Gaz.* 1 March, 25 April 1898). He commanded the Punjab frontier force from 1898 to 1900, being promoted general in 1899. On the death of Sir William Lockhart [q. v. Suppl I] he was appointed provisional commander-in-chief in India, and member of the viceroy's council (19 March 1900).

In selecting regiments and commanders for service in South Africa and China in 1900 Palmer showed high administrative capacity, and though owing to the uncertainty of his tenure of office he carried out no sweeping changes, he introduced many practical reforms in musketry. He held the post of commander-in-chief till 1902, when he was succeeded by Lord Kitchener.

He was nominated G.C.I.E. in 1901, and G.C.B. in 1903. He died on 28 Feb. 1904 in London, after an operation for appendicitis, and was buried at Brompton. He married (1) in 1867 Helen Aylmer (*d.* 1896), daughter of Aylmer Harris; and (2) in 1898 Constance Gabrielle (*d.* 1912), daughter of Godfrey Shaw and widow of Walter Milton Roberts, who survived him with two daughters.

An oil painting of Palmer by Herbert Brooks belongs to Palmer's step-sister, Mrs. Schneider.

[The Times, 29 Feb. 1904; Cheltenham Coll. Reg. 1911; The Cheltonian, March 1904; Lord Roberts's Forty-one Years in India, 30th edit. 1898, p. 362; S. P. Oliver, Second Afghan War, 1908; R. H. Vetch, Life of Sir Gerald Graham, 1901; H. D. Hutchinson, The Campaign in Tirah, 1898, p. 62; Hart's and official Army Lists.] H. M. V.

PALMER, Sir CHARLES MARK, first baronet (1822–1907), ship-owner and ironmaster, born at King's Street, South Shields, on 3 Nov. 1822, was fourth son in a family of seven sons and one daughter of George Palmer (1789–1866), a ship-owner and merchant engaged in the Greenland and Indian trades. His mother was Maria, daughter of Thomas Taylor of Hill House, Monkwearmouth. He was educated privately, first in South Shields and afterwards at Bruce's Academy, Percy Street, Newcastle, one of the leading private schools in the north of England. On leaving school he studied for a short time in France. At sixteen he entered his father's firm, Messrs. Palmer, Bechwith & Company, timber merchants; but a year later, at the early age of seventeen, he formed a partnership with Sir William Hutt, Nicholas Wood, and John Bowes in the manufacture of coke. The firm subsequently acquired collieries in the north. At that time the northern coalfield was practically shut out from the London markets, owing to the difficulties of conveying the coal by rail. Palmer solved the problem by building boats wherein to bring coal by sea to London, and thus laid the foundation of the extensive colliery services which now ply between northern ports and the metropolis. In 1851 he and his brother George established a shipyard near the pit village of Jarrow. The first iron vessel launched from this yard was a paddle tug, the Northumberland, and this was followed (in 1852) by the John Bowes, which was the first iron screw collier to be built, and had a coal capacity of 690 tons. The experiment was a complete success.

With the growth of the shipyard, the village of Jarrow, which at the outset contained only some thousand inhabitants, grew into a town with a population of nearly 40,000. To their original objects the firm added the construction of battleships. During the Crimean war the admiralty accepted Palmer's tender for the construction of a floating battery for the destruction of the forts at Kronstadt, and the Terror, an armoured battery, was constructed and launched within three months. He further revolutionised the industry by substituting rolled armour plate for forged armour plate, and at Jarrow the first armour plate mill was laid down for the manufacture of what were known as 'Palmer's rolled plates.' He was also one of the first to recognise the value of the Cleveland ironstone, which was smelted at the blast furnaces at Jarrow from 1860. Deeply interested in science, he was an original member of the Iron and Steel Institute, and at the first annual meeting in London, 1870, he read a paper on 'Iron as a Material for Shipbuilding.'

He introduced the co-operative principle for the benefit of his workmen, and zealously promoted the welfare of Jarrow. In 1875, when the town received its charter, he became its first mayor.

In 1868 Palmer unsuccessfully contested the representation in Parliament of South Shields in the liberal interest. In 1874 he and Sir Isaac Lowthian Bell [q.v. Suppl. II] were returned for North Durham after a severe contest, although they were subsequently unseated on a petition. Palmer was placed at the head of the poll at a new election in June 1874, Sir George Elliot, the conservative candidate, being returned with him, and Bell, the second liberal candidate, being defeated. A threatened petition against Palmer's return was withdrawn. When Jarrow was created a contituency, in 1885, he became its member till death. No conservative candidate ventured to oppose him, and although labour candidates contested the seat in 1885, 1892, and 1906, they were severely defeated. He was a deputy lieutenant for Durham and for the North Riding of Yorkshire. In 1886 he was created a baronet, while from the King of Italy he received the commandership of the order of St. Maurice and St. Lazarus. He founded in Jarrow the Mechanics' Institute and the Palmer Memorial Hospital. He was honorary colonel of the Newcastle-on-Tyne and Durham engineer volunteers.

Palmer acquired Easington and Hinderwell Manors and Grinkle Park and Seaton Hall estates, to which he devoted much attention. He died on 4 June 1907 at his residence, 37 Curzon Street, Mayfair, London, and was buried at Easington church, Yorkshire, the parish church on the estate. He was married three times: (1) on 29 July 1846 to Jane (*d.* 1865), daughter of Ebenezer Robson of Newcastle, by whom he had four sons, of whom the second, George Robson (1849–1910), became second baronet, and Alfred Molyneux (*b.* 1853), third baronet; (2) on 4 July 1867 to Augusta Mary (*d.* 1875), daughter of Alfred Lambert of Paris, by whom he had two sons; and (3) on 17 Feb. 1877 to Gertrude, daughter of James Montgomery of Cranford, Middlesex, by whom he had one son, Godfrey Mark (*b.* 1878), liberal M.P. for Jarrow since 1910, and a daughter.

A bronze statue by Albert Toft, subscribed for by friends and employees, is in the grounds of the memorial hospital at Jarrow. A marble bust, also by Toft, is in the Newcastle-on-Tyne Commercial Exchange. A cartoon portrait by 'Ape' appeared in 'Vanity Fair' in 1884.

[Pioneers of the Iron Trade, by J. S. Jeans, 1875; Journal Iron and Steel Institute, vol. lxxiii.; Men and Women of the Time, 1899; The Times, 5 June 1907.] L. P. S.

PALMER, Sir ELWIN MITFORD (1852–1906), finance officer in India and Egypt, born in London on 3 March 1852, was second son of Edward Palmer by his wife Caroline, daughter of Colonel Gunthorpe. Educated at Lancing College, he entered the financial department of the government of India in 1870, and being attached to the comptroller-general's office on 10 Nov. 1871, became assistant comptroller-general. Leaving India, Palmer on

16 Aug. 1885 succeeded Sir Gerald Fitzgerald as director-general of accounts in Egypt where he had already served from 31 December 1878 to 30 April 1879. To Fitzgerald and Palmer 'Egypt owes a system of accounts which can bear comparison with those of any other country in Europe' (MILNER, p. 253). He was created C.M.G. in 1888. Next year he succeeded Sir Edgar Vincent as financial adviser to the Khedive, and 'ably and prudently continued his predecessor's policy with 'brilliant results' (*ibid.* p. 251). He was largely instrumental in the conversion of the privileged, Daïra, and Domains loans, and had much to do with the contract for the construction of the Assouan reservoir (COLVIN, pp. 285–6). In 1898 the National Bank of Egypt was created by khedivial decree, and Palmer resigned his appointment as financial adviser in order to become its first governor at Cairo. In the same year he became chairman of the Cairo committee of the Daïra Sanieh Company, which had taken over from the government the Daira or private estates of Ismail Pasha. In 1902 he was made president of the Agricultural Bank of Egypt, which was an offshoot of the National Bank. Palmer was a shrewd, hard-working man, with long financial training and great knowledge of accounts; he was a specialist rather than a man of general administrative capacity, and his particular faculties were brought into play in developing industrial and commercial enterprises at the time when Egypt began to reap the benefit of administrative reform and engineering works. He was made K.C.M.G. in 1892, K.C.B. in 1897, and held the grand cordons of the orders of Osmanie and Medjidie. He died at Cairo on 28 January 1906. In 1881 he married Mary Augusta Lynch, daughter of Major Herbert M. Clogstoun, V.C., and left one son and two daughters.

[The Times, 29 Jan. 1906; England in Egypt by Alfred (Viscount) Milner, 3rd edit. 1893; Sir Auckland Colvin, The Making of Modern Egypt, 1906; the Earl of Cromer, Modern Egypt, 1908.] C. P. L.

PARISH, WILLIAM DOUGLAS (1833–1904), writer on dialect, was fifth son of Sir Woodbine Parish [q. v.] by his first wife Amelia Jane, daughter of Leonard Becher Morse. Of his seven brothers and five sisters, the eldest, Major-General Henry Woodbine Parish, C.B. (1821–1890), served with distinction in South Africa under Sir Harry Smith, and later in Abyssinia; the second, John Edward (1822–1894), became an admiral, and the third, Francis (1824–1906), was some time consul at Buenos Ayres, and later consul-general and state commissioner at Havana. His half-sister, Blanche Marion Parish, married in 1871 Sir Ughtred James Kay-Shuttleworth, first Baron Shuttleworth.

Born at 5 Gloucester Place, Portman Square, St. Marylebone, on 16 Dec. 1833, Parish was at Charterhouse School from 1848 to 1853. He matriculated at Trinity College, Oxford, in the latter year, graduating B.C.L. in 1858. Next year he was ordained to the curacy of Firle in Sussex, becoming vicar in 1863 of the adjoining parishes of Selmeston and Alciston. That benefice he held until his death. He endeared himself not only to his parishioners but also to gypsies and vagrants. From 1877 to 1900 he was chancellor of Chichester Cathedral. Parish died unmarried in Selmeston vicarage on 23 Sept. 1904, and was buried in Selmeston churchyard. There are a window and two brasses to his memory in the church.

Parish's principal work, 'A Dictionary of the Sussex Dialect and Collection of Provincialisms in use in the County of Sussex' (Lewes, 1875, 2 editions), is more than a contribution to etymology: it is the classic example of what a country parson with antiquarian tastes, a sense of humour, and a sympathetic affection for his peasant neighbours, can do to record for posterity not only the dialect but the domestic habits of the people of his time and place.

Parish's other publications were: 1. 'The Telegraphist's Easy Guide,' 1874, an explanation of the Morse system written primarily for the boys of his parish, to whom he taught signalling as a pastime. 2. 'School Attendance secured without Compulsion,' 1875 (5 editions), a pamphlet describing his successful system of giving back to parents their children's school payments as a reward for good attendances. 3. 'Domesday Book in Relation to the County of Sussex,' 1886 fol., for the Sussex Archæological Society, on the council of which he served for many years. 4. 'A Dictionary of the Kentish Dialect' (with the Rev. W. F. Shaw), 1887, on the lines of the Sussex book, but lacking evidence of intimate acquaintance with the Kentish people. Parish also edited a useful alphabetical 'List of Carthusians [Charterhouse schoolboys], 1800–79' (Lewes, 1879).

[A Life of Sir Woodbine Parish, 1910, pp. 419–425; The Times, 26 and 28 Sept. 1904; East Sussex News, 30 Sept. 1904; works mentioned; private information.] P. L.

PARKER, ALBERT EDMUND, third EARL OF MORLEY (1843–1905), Chairman of Committees of the House of Lords, born in London on 11 June 1843, was only son of Edward Parker, second earl (1810–1864), by his wife Harriet Sophia (*d.*1897), only daughter of Montagu Edmund Parker of Whiteway, Devonshire, and widow of William Coryton, of Pentillie Castle, Cornwall. Educated at Eton, where he subsequently became a fellow and governor, and at Balliol College, Oxford, he took a first class in literæ humaniores and graduated B.A. in 1865, having succeeded his father in the peerage in 1864. In the House of Lords he figured as a polished speaker of liberal principles. From 1868 to 1874 he was a lord-in-waiting to Queen Victoria during Gladstone's first administration. When Gladstone returned to office in 1880 Morley became under-secretary for war, serving first under Hugh Childers [q. v. Suppl. I] and then under Lord Hartington [q. v. Suppl. II]. He proved an efficient minister, notably in speeches upon recruiting (*Hansard*, cclxxx. cols. 1846–1859) and upon army organisation (*ibid.* cclxxxi. cols. 750–756); and he displayed a grasp of affairs during the debates on the suppression of the rebellion of Arabi Pasha in Egypt and the expedition to Khartoum. He quitted office with the ministry in 1885.

When the home rule question arose to divide the liberal party, Morley at first followed Gladstone; and from February to April 1886 was first commissioner of public works in that minister's third government. On 12 April he resigned, together with Mr. Edward (afterwards Lord) Heneage, chancellor of the duchy of Lancaster, after Gladstone had divulged the scope of his measure. He took little part in the ensuing political controversy, but his judicial temper was put to profitable use when, on 4 April 1889, he was chosen chairman of committees and deputy-speaker of the House of Lords on the proposal of Lord Granville by ninety-five votes to seventy-nine given to Lord Balfour of Burleigh, who was proposed by Lord Salisbury. He exercised his powers over private bill legislation with much discretion. For the guidance of promoters, 'a model bill' was annually devised by his standing counsel and himself, and by the beginning of every session the proposed measures, however numerous, had been passed under thorough review. Attacked by a lingering illness, he, to the general regret, sent in his resignation, which he intended to be temporary, in February 1904, Lord Balfour of Burleigh taking his place (*Hansard*, vol. cxxix. cols. 1139–1142). On 12 Feb. 1905 he finally resigned. Lord Lansdowne then said that, 'besides great diligence and ability, Lord Morley had shown great qualities of firmness, great powers of conciliation, and a sound and steady judgment, unswayed by considerations of personal popularity' (*ibid.* vol. cxli. col. 287). He died fourteen days later, on 26 Feb. 1905, at Saltram, Plympton St. Mary, and was buried in the parish churchyard. On the announcement of his death in the House of Lords further tributes to his memory were paid by Lord Spencer, Lord Halsbury, and Dr. Talbot, then bishop of Rochester.

The earl took an active interest in Devonshire affairs. He was a chairman of quarter sessions and vice-chairman of the Devon county council from 1889 to 1901, when he succeeded Lord Clinton as chairman. His speeches displayed a wide knowledge of local finance and requirements, and he held the appointment until 1904. In 1900, as one of the three deputy lords-lieutenant, he took an active part in the county in the equipment of imperial yeomanry and volunteers for the South African war. In succession to his father and grandfather he interested himself in the Plymouth chamber of commerce, became its president in 1864, and made its annual dinner the occasion for a speech on public affairs. He took pride in the fine collection of pictures at Saltram, and was an enthusiastic gardener.

He married in 1876 Margaret, daughter of Robert Stayner Holford of Dorchester House, London, and Weston Birt House, Tetbury, and had a daughter and three sons, of whom Edmund Robert, Viscount Boringdon, born on 19 April 1877, succeeded him as fourth earl. His portrait by Ellis Roberts is at 31 Prince's Gardens, London, S.W., and a copy of the head and shoulders, made after his death by the artist at the request of the Devon county council, is in the council's chamber at Exeter.

[The Times, and Western Morning News, 27 Feb. 1905; private information.]

L. C. S.

PARKER, CHARLES STUART (1829–1910), politician and author, born at Aigburth, Liverpool, on 1 June 1829, was the eldest son of Charles Stewart Parker of Fairlie, Ayrshire, a partner in the prosperous Liverpool firm of Sandbach, Tinne & Co., West India merchants. His mother was Anne, eldest daughter of Samuel Sandbach of Hafodunos, Denbighshire. Dr. Chalmers, a friend of his paternal grandparents, was one of

Parker's godfathers. He was through life influenced by the religious temper of his home training. On 13 Aug. 1838 his father's sister Anne married Edward (afterwards Viscount) Cardwell [q. v.], whose political views he came to share. Parker was at Eton from 1842 to 1847, and won in 1846 the Prince Consort's prize for German. On 10 June 1847 he matriculated from Brasenose College, Oxford, but gaining a scholarship at University College next year migrated thither. At University College, with which he was long closely associated, he formed intimacies with Arthur Penrhyn Stanley, Goldwin Smith, John Conington, Arthur Gray Butler, William Bright, and T. W. Jex-Blake, afterwards dean of Wells. Friends at other colleges included Arthur Peel, afterwards Speaker of the House of Commons, G. C. Brodrick, Thomas Hill Green [q. v.], George Joachim Goschen, W. H. Fremantle (Dean of Ripon), Mr. Frederic Harrison, and Grant Duff. In 1852 he joined Goschen, Brodrick, and others in starting the Oxford Essay Club, and he frequently attended the club dinners in later life at Goschen's house and elsewhere.

In Easter term 1852 Parker was placed in the first class in the final classical school, and in the second class of the mathematical school. He graduated B.A. and proceeded M.A. in 1855. He was elected fellow of his college in 1854, and retained the office till 1868. He resided at Oxford till 1864, throwing himself with vigour into the work of both college and university. He was college tutor from 1858 to 1865, and lectured in modern history. He was examiner in the final classical school in 1859, 1860, 1863, and 1868. He won the confidence of undergraduates, and introduced them to men of note from the outer world, whom from an early date he entertained at Oxford. He organised the university volunteer corps and did much while major of the battalion (1865–8) to improve its efficiency, especially in shooting. The main recreation of his university days was mountaineering. He preferred climbing without guides, and it was without guides that he with his brothers Sandbach and Alfred made the second and fourth attempts on the Matterhorn in 1860 and 1861 respectively (cf. WHYMPER'S *Scrambles amongst the Alps*). Subsequently Parker's companions in the Alps included William Henry Gladstone and Stephen Gladstone, sons of the statesman, who was an early friend of Parker and his family.

Like Brodrick, Goldwin Smith, and other brilliant Oxford men, Parker was a contributor to the early issues of the 'Saturday Review' in 1855, but he soon withdrew owing to his dislike of the cynical tone of the paper, and a characteristic impatience of its partisan spirit. He gradually concentrated his interest on a liberal reform of the university. He especially urged a prudent recognition of the claims of science, modern history, and modern languages in the academic curriculum, and the throwing open of scholarships to competition. He early declared for a national system of elementary education which should be efficient and compulsory, rather than voluntary. In 1867 he published two essays, one on 'Popular Education' in 'Questions for a Reformed Parliament,' and the other on 'Classical Education' in F. W. Farrar's 'Essays on a Liberal Education.'

In 1864 Parker, who inherited ample means, diversified his academic duties by becoming private secretary to Edward Cardwell, whose wife was his aunt. Cardwell was then colonial secretary, and Parker remained with him till he went out of office in 1866. At the wish of Gladstone, with whom his relations steadily became closer, he stood for Perthshire in 1868 in the liberal interest, gaining a startling victory over the former conservative member, Sir William Stirling Maxwell [q. v.]. He remained in the House of Commons throughout Gladstone's first administration, but was defeated by Stirling Maxwell in his old constituency at the general election of 1874. He was however re-elected for the city of Perth in 1878, and retained the seat till 1892, when he was defeated in a three-cornered contest. He failed to win a seat in West Perthshire in 1900. His refinement of manner and accent militated against his gaining the ear of the house, but his leaders respected him for his conscientious study of political issues and his judicial habit of mind. During his first parliament he was in constant touch with his old chief Cardwell, then secretary for war, and supported the abolition of purchase and Cardwell's other reforms of the army. He was often consulted by Gladstone, to whose measures and policy throughout his parliamentary career he gave a discriminating assent. At Gladstone's invitation he revised his speeches for the Midlothian campaign of 1878–80.

But it was on educational policy that Parker exerted his chief influence. Joining the public schools commission (1868–74), he proved one of its most active members, urging that the public school curriculum should be modernised in sympathy with a progressive policy at the universities. He also sat on the commission for military education in 1869, and advocated the linking up of the public schools with Sandhurst and Woolwich, so as to ensure a broad general culture before technical and professional training. Again, as a member of the Scotch educational endowments commission in 1872, he argued persistently that the benefits of endowments should go 'not to the most necessitous of those fairly fitted intellectually, but to the most fit among those who were fairly necessitous.' His views greatly stimulated the development of secondary education in Scotland. He wished the Scotch elementary schools to form a 'ladder' to the university, and he sought to protect them from the evil system of 'payment by results.' He was in 1887 chairman of a departmental committee on higher education in the elementary schools of Scotland, and the report which he drew up with Sir Henry Craik in 1888 gave practical effect to his wise proposals.

Parker, whose wide interests embraced a precise study of scientific hypotheses, engaged in his later years in biographical work of historical importance. In 1891 he brought out the first volume of a life of Sir Robert Peel 'from his private correspondence,' which was completed in 3 vols. in 1899. In 1907 there followed 'The Life and Letters of Sir James Graham' (2 vols.). He allowed the subjects of his biographies to tell their story in their own words as far as possible. Parker, who was elected honorary fellow of University College in 1899, was made hon. LL.D. of Glasgow and hon. D.C.L. of Oxford in 1908. In 1907 he was admitted to the privy council. His last public act was to attend the council in May 1910 on the death of King Edward VII and sign the proclamation of King George V.

Parker died unmarried at his London residence, 32 Old Queen Street, Westminster, on 18 June 1910, and was buried at Fairlie. His portrait was painted by Sir Hubert von Herkomer. He bequeathed 5000*l.* to University College, where two Parker scholarships for modern history have been established.

[The Times, 19 June, 29 Aug. (will) 1910; Eton School Lists; Foster's Alumni Oxon.; private information; personal knowledge.]

PARKER, JOSEPH (1830–1902), congregationalist divine, born at Hexham on 9 April 1830, was the only son of Teasdale Parker, a stonemason, and deacon of the congregational church, by his wife Elizabeth Dodd. His education at three local schools was interrupted at fourteen with a view to his following the building trade under his father; he soon went back to school, and became teacher of various subjects, including Latin and Greek. Though he taught in the congregational Sunday school, he joined the Wesleyan body, to which his parents had for a time seceded. This led to his becoming a local preacher; his first sermon was in June 1848. The family returned to congregationalism in 1852, and Parker, having obtained a preaching engagement from John Campbell (1794–1867) [q. v.], of the Moorfields Tabernacle, left for London on 8 April 1852. While in London, Campbell gave him nine months' sermon drill, and he attended the lectures of John Hoppus [q. v.] at University College. Soon becoming known as a preacher of original gifts, he was called to Banbury (salary 120*l.*), and ordained there on 8 Nov. 1853. His Banbury ministry of four years and eight months was marked by the building of a larger chapel, a public discussion on secularism with George Jacob Holyoake [q. v. Suppl. II], and the winning of the second prize (75*l.*) in a Glasgow prize essay competition on the 'Support of the Ordinances of the Gospel.' In 1858 he was called to Cavendish Chapel, Manchester, in succession to Robert Halley [q. v.]. He declined to leave Banbury till the debt (700*l.*) on his new chapel there was discharged. The Manchester congregation cleared off this, along with a debt (200*l.*) on their own chapel. Parker accepted their call in a letter (10 June 1858) stipulating for 'the most perfect freedom of action,' and maintaining that 'the office of deacon is purely secular.' He began his Manchester ministry on 25 July 1858, and for eleven years made himself as a preacher a power in that city, while exercising a wider influence through his literary labours.

In 1862 he received the degree of D.D. from Chicago University, but he first visited America in 1873. In 1867 he was made chairman of the Lancashire congregational union. Rejecting in 1868, he accepted in 1869, a call to the Poultry Chapel, London, in succession to James Spence, D.D. (1811–76). He rapidly filled an empty chapel, instituted the Thursday noon-day service, and conducted for three years an 'institute of homiletics' for the gratuitous instruction of young students in the art of preaching. He had come to London on condition of a removal of the congregation from the Poultry to a new site. After some delay a site on Holborn Viaduct was secured for 25,000*l.*, and the Poultry Chapel sold for 50,200*l.* Parker meanwhile carried on his ministry in Cannon Street hall (Sunday mornings), Exeter Hall (Sunday evenings), and Albion Chapel (Thursdays). His newly built chapel, called the City Temple, was opened on 19 May 1874, when the lord mayor attended in state; Dean Stanley spoke at the collation which followed.

To the end of his days Parker's popularity never waned, nor did his resources fail. At his Thursday services clergymen irrespective of denomination were constantly seen. William Henry Fremantle (dean of Ripon) and Hugh Reginald Haweis [q. v. Suppl. II] would have preached at these services but were inhibited; a notable address on preaching was given by Gladstone (22 March 1877) after Parker's discourse. In 1880 Parker came forward as parliamentary candidate for the City of London, with a programme which included disestablishment and the suppression of the liquor traffic; on the advice of nonconformist friends the candidature was withdrawn. In 1884, and again in 1901, he was chairman of the Congregational Union of England and Wales. Visiting Edinburgh in February 1887, he delivered an address on preaching, and preached in various churches, including St. Giles'. His fifth voyage to America was made in the following August, and on 4 Oct. he delivered at Brooklyn the panegyric of Henry Ward Beecher (*d.* 8 March 1887), whom he was thought to resemble in gifts, and whose place in America some expected him to fill. In July and August 1888 he conducted a 'rural mission' in Scotland; in May 1894 he addressed the general assembly of the Free Church in Edinburgh, against some phases of the 'higher criticism.' In the following November he protested against the reporting of sermons as a form of literary piracy. 'The Times' of 18 May 1896 contains his letter in favour of 'education, free, compulsory and secular.' In March 1902 he was made president of the National Free Church council. After a long illness in that year he resumed preaching in September. His letter to 'The Times,' 'A Generation in a City Pulpit,' appeared on 22 Sept.; his last sermon was preached on 28 Sept.; he died at Hampstead on 28 Nov. 1902, and was buried in the Hampstead cemetery.

At the City Temple his portrait, painted in 1894 by Robert Gibb, R.S.A., is in the vestry, as well as a bust by C. B. Birch, A.R.A. (1883), in the entrance. Another bust was executed by John Adams-Acton [q. v. Suppl. II]. A cartoon portrait by 'Ape' appeared in 'Vanity Fair' in 1884.

Parker married (1) on 15 Nov. 1851 Ann Nesbitt (*d.* 1863) of Horsley Hills; (2) on 22 Dec. 1864 Emma Jane (*d.* 26 Jan. 1899), daughter of Andrew Common, banker, of Sunderland. He had no issue.

Both by its strength and its freshness Parker's pulpit work impressed some of the best judges in his time. Holyoake, who commends his fairness in controversy, says he 'had a will of adamant and a soul of fire.' Further, he was a master in the arts of advertisement, and in the power of investing old themes with a novelty which startled and arrested. His writings, embodying much of his own experience, are racy in style and imbued with strong sense. He was a constant contributor to periodicals, beginning with the 'Homilist,' edited by David Thomas (1813–94) [q. v.]; he himself brought out various periodicals, the 'Congregational Economist' (1858), the 'Cavendish Church Pulpit,' 'Our Own,' the 'Pulpit Analyst' (1866–1870), the 'City Temple' (1869–73), the 'Fountain,' and the 'Christian Chronicle.'

His chief publication was 'The People's Bible,' 25 vols., 1885–1895. Other of his works were: 1. 'Six Chapters on Secularism,' 1854. 2. 'Helps to Truthseekers,' 1857; 3rd edit. 1858. 3. 'Questions of the Day,' 1860 (sermons). 4. 'John Stuart Mill on Liberty: a Critique,' 1865. 5. 'Wednesday Evenings at Cavendish Chapel,' 1865; 2 edits. 6. 'Ecce Deus . . . with Notes on "Ecce Homo,"' Edinburgh, 1867; 5th edit. 1875. 7. 'Springdale Abbey: Extracts from the Diaries and Letters of an English Preacher,' 1868 (fiction). 8. 'Ad Clerum: Advices to a Young Preacher,' 1870. 9. 'Tyne Chylde: My Life and Teaching,' 1880; 1886 (an autobiographical fiction). 10. 'The Inner Life of Christ,' 3 vols. 1881–2; 1884 (commentary). 11. 'Weaver Stephen,' 1886, (a novel). 12. 'Well Begun: Notes for those who have to Make their Way,' 1894. 13. 'Tyne Folk,' 1896. 14. 'Gambling in Various Aspects'; 5th edit. 1902. 15. 'Christian Profiles in a Pagan Mirror,' 1898. 16. 'Paterson's Parish: A Lifetime amongst the Dissenters,' 1898. 17. 'The City Temple Pulpit,' 1899. 18. 'A Preacher's Life,' 1899 (autobiography). 19. 'The Pulpit Bible,' 1901, 4to. 20. 'The Gospel of Jesus Christ,' 1903; new edit. 1908 (posthumous sermons).

[Marsh's Memorials of the City Temple, 1877; Men and Women of the Time, 1899; A Preacher's Life, 1899 (portrait); A. Dawson, Joseph Parker, D.D., Life and Ministry, 1901; W. Adamson, Life, 1902 (nine portraits); The Times, 29 Nov., 1 and 5 Dec. 1902; G. J. Holyoake, Two Great Preachers, 1903; J. Morgan Richards, Life of John Oliver Hobbes, 1911; G. Pike, Dr. Parker and his Friends, 1904.] A. G.

PARR, Mrs. LOUISA (*d.* 1903), novelist, born in London, was the only child of Matthew Taylor, R.N. Her early years were spent at Plymouth. In 1868 she published in 'Good Words,' under the pseudonym of 'Mrs. Olinthus Lobb,' a short story entitled 'How it all happened.' It attracted attention, and appeared in a French version as a *feuilleton* in the 'Journal des Débats,' the editor apologising for departing from his rule of never printing translations. At the request of the Queen of Württemberg it was translated into German, and it was issued in America in pamphlet form. The next year Miss Taylor married George Parr, a doctor living in Kensington and a collector of early editions of works on London. He predeceased her.

In 1871 Mrs. Parr published 'Dorothy Fox,' a novel of Quaker life, which was so much appreciated in America that a publisher there paid Mrs. Parr 300*l.* for the advance sheets of her next novel. Nothing of importance followed until 1880, when her best novel, 'Adam and Eve,' was published. It is an interesting story, told with artistic restraint, of Cornish smuggling life founded on incidents related in Jonathan Couch's 'History of Polperro' (1871). Six novels followed, none coming near to 'Adam and Eve' in merit, the last, 'Can This be Love?' appearing in 1893. The life of Miss Mulock (Mrs. Craik) in 'Women Novelists of Queen Victoria's Reign' (1897) is from her pen. She also contributed short stories to magazines. A sense of humour and a pleasing style are the main characteristics of her work. She was always at her best in dealing with the sea.

Mrs. Parr died on 2 Nov. 1903 at 18 Upper Phillimore Place, Kensington, London.

[Who's Who, 1902; Men and Women of the Time, 1899; Athenæum, 14 Nov. 1903; Helen C. Black, Pen, Pencil, Baton and Mask, 1896; The Times, 7 Nov. 1903 (a mere reference).] E. L.

PARRY, JOSEPH (1841–1903), musical composer, born on 21 May 1841 at Merthyr Tydfil, was son of Daniel Parry (*d.* 1867), an ironworker of that town, by his wife Mary. A brother (Henry) and two sisters (Jane and Elizabeth) gained some prominence as vocalists in the United States (*Y Cerddor Cymreig*, 1869, p. 15). Joseph started work at the puddling furnaces before he was ten. In 1853 his father emigrated to the United States, and the family followed in 1854, settling at Danville, Pennsylvania. Parry first studied music at about seventeen years of age, attending a class conducted by two of his Welsh fellow-workers at the iron-works. At an eisteddfod held at Danville at Christmas 1860 he won his first prize for composition, namely for a temperance march. Next year a subscription raised by the Welsh colony at Danville enabled Parry to study at a normal college at Genesee, New York. He returned after a short course to become organist at Danville. After winning many prizes at American eisteddfods, he sent several pieces for competition to the national eisteddfod held at Swansea in September 1863 and at Llandudno in August 1864, and at each gained prizes. In the summer of 1865 he attended the Aberystwyth eisteddfod, where the title 'Pencerdd America' was conferred on him. A glee, 'Ar dòn o flaen gwyntoedd,' published shortly afterwards at Wrexham, was widely popular in Wales, and appeared in New York in 'Y Gronfa Gerddorol' of Hugh J. Hughes (*Y Drych*, 19 March 1903). On his return to America, a fund was started to enable him to pursue his musical education. In aid of the fund Parry gave a series of concerts in Pennsylvania, Ohio, and New York, generally singing songs of his own composition (*Y Cerddor Cymreig*, 1870, p. 30). Meanwhile he was awarded prizes for his cantata 'The Prodigal Son' at Chester eisteddfod, September 1866 (still in MS., though the overture to it was played at the Royal Academy of Music in 1871), and for his glee 'Rhosyn yr Haf' (published in 1867) at Utica (January 1867).

In 1868 Parry and his family (he was already married) removed to London, and in September he entered the Royal Academy of Music, where he studied for three years, and won the bronze and silver medals. In 1871 he took the degree of Mus. Bac. at Cambridge. His exercise, a choral fugue in B minor, was performed at the Academy concert on 21 July. After going back to America to keep a music school at Danville (1871–3) he became professor of music at the newly founded University College of Wales at Aberystwyth. The appointment gave a great impetus to musical studies in Wales. He proceeded Mus.Doc. at Cambridge in 1878, his exercise, a cantata, 'Jerusalem,' being performed by a Welsh choir from Aberdare. When the Aberystwyth professorship was discontinued in 1879 (Davies and Jones, *University of Wales*, pp. 121, 133), Parry kept a private school of music, first at Aberystwyth and then (1881–8) at Swansea. In 1888 he was appointed lecturer, and subsequently professor of music, at the University College, Cardiff, which he held (together with the directorship of a private musical institute in the town) till his death at his residence, Cartref, Penarth, on 17 Feb. 1903. He was buried at St. Augustine's, Penarth.

Joseph Parry was a most prolific composer. One of his first published pieces was a song, 'My Childhood's Dreams,' issued from Scranton, Pennsylvania, in 1865 (*Cerddor Cymreig*, Sept. 1865, p. 69). His opera 'Blodwen,' with Welsh words by Richard Davies (Mynyddog), performed from MS. at Aberystwyth and Aberdare in 1878, and later at the Alexandra Palace, London, but not published till 1888 (Swansea), has been performed hundreds of times in Wales, most often, however, as a cantata. It was the first opera performed in the Welsh language. His other operas include 'Virginia,' written in 1882 but still in MS., based on incidents in the American civil war; 'Sylvia' (1889), the words by his son, David Mendelssohn; 'Ceridwen,' a one-act dramatic cantata, first performed at the Liverpool eisteddfod, 1900; and 'The Maid of Cefn Ydfa' (words by Joseph Bennett), first produced by the Moody Manners Co. at the Grand Theatre, Cardiff, on 14 Dec. 1902.

Parry was also the author of two oratorios, 'Emmanuel,' performed at St. James's Hall, London, in 1880, but not published till 1882 (Swansea), and 'Saul of Tarsus,' first performed at the Rhyl eisteddfod on 8 Sept. 1892 (published London, 1893); also the following cantatas, 'The Birds' (Wrexham, 1873); 'Nebuchadnezzar' (London, 1884); 'Cambria' (first performed at the Llandudno eisteddfod, 1896); 'Joseph' (Swansea, 1881). His contributions to sacred music include some 400 hymn tunes, the best known being 'Aberystwyth,' composed on 3 July 1877 for the second volume (1879) of the Welsh Congregationalists' Hymnal of Edward Stephen (Tanymarian) [q. v.] This and sixty-six other tunes and a number of short anthems were published by Parry in 1892 as a Welsh national tune-book. The copyright in these and in a Sunday-school tune-book ('Telyn yr Ysgol Sul,' first published in 1877) was acquired after Dr. Parry's death by the Welsh Congregational Union, to which connexion Parry belonged. The appearance of his anthems resulted in a great advance in Welsh sacred music, and his setting of 'The Lord is my Shepherd' is said to rival Schubert's.

He edited and harmonised the music of a 'National Collection of Welsh Songs,' entitled 'Cambrian Minstrelsie' (Edinburgh, 6 vols. 1893). He also brought out a collection of his own songs, 'Dr. Parry's Book of Songs' (in five parts with portrait of the author), and issued a Welsh handbook on theory, being part i. of an intended series on music ('Elfenau Cerddoriaeth,' Cardiff, 1888).

Parry married (at Danville) Jane daughter of Gomer Thomas, who survived him with one son, David Mendelssohn, and two daughters. Of two sons who predeceased him, William Sterndale (1872–1892) and Joseph Haydn Parry (1864–1894), the latter, who showed much musical promise, was appointed professor at the Guildhall school of music in 1890, and composed, among other works, 'Cigarette,' a comic opera (the libretto by his brother, David Mendelssohn Parry), produced on 15 Aug. 1892 at the Theatre Royal, Cardiff, and in September at the Lyric Theatre, London, and 'Miami,' a more ambitious work, set to an adaptation of 'The Green Bushes,' and produced 16 Oct. 1893 at the Princess's Theatre, London (Grove's *Dict. of Music and Musicians*, 1907, v. 499; *Western Mail*, 30 March 1894; *Annual Register*, 1894, p. 157; Mardy Rees, *Notable Welshmen*, 432).

[For his life to 1868 see contemporary references in the Welsh musical monthly, Y Cerddor Cymreig, between 1865 and 1871 (see especially that for 1871, pp. 65–7); articles by his pupil, Prof. David Jenkins, Mus.Bac. Aberystwyth, in Y Cerddor for March 1903 (p. 27), Feb. 1904 (p. 16), and April 1911, and by Mr. D. Emlyn Evans in the same magazine for December 1903, p. 130; the Welsh American weekly, Y Drych (Utica), for 26 Feb., 19 and 26 March 1903, and subsequent issues (not always trustworthy); The Times, and Western Mail (Cardiff), 18 Feb. 1903; T. R. Roberts's Eminent Welshmen, 1907, p. 403 (with photo.); Grove's Dict. of Music and Musicians (1907); Baker's Biog. Dict. of Music, 1900 (with portrait); and Y Geninen for 1903, p. 73, and for 1906, p. 237; Cymru, xxxii. 168.]

D. Ll. T.

PARSONS, Sir LAURENCE, fourth Earl of Rosse (1840–1908), astronomer, born at Birr Castle, Parsonstown, King's Co., Ireland, on 17 Nov. 1840, was eldest of four surviving sons of William Parsons, third earl of Rosse [q. v.], the astronomer. The youngest brother, Sir Charles Algernon Parsons, C.B., F.R.S. (*b.* 1854), is well known for his invention of the compound steam turbine, since applied to marine propulsion.

Known in youth by the courtesy title of Baron Oxmantown, co. Wexford, Laurence was educated at home, first under the tutorship of the Rev. T. T. Gray, M.A., of Trinity College, Dublin, and then of John Purser, LL.D., afterwards professor of mathematics in Queen's College, Belfast.

Subsequently he entered Trinity College, Dublin, graduating in 1864, but he was non-resident. He was early imbued with his father's spirit of inquiry. At his father's observatory at Birr he assisted in the workshops and met leading men of science. Succeeding in 1867 to the peerage on his father's death, Lord Rosse thenceforward divided his interests between the management of his estates and the pursuit of astro-physics. He was made sheriff of King's Co., Ireland, in 1867, and became a representative peer of Ireland in 1868. On 29 Aug. 1890 he was created a knight of the Order of St. Patrick. He was subsequently lord-lieutenant of King's Co. (1892–1908).

According to Dr. Otto Boeddicker (technical coadjutor at Birr Observatory), Rosse had 'an inherited genius for mechanical relations and contrivances, and endless were his ideas and designs, all of a most ingenious character.' His first scientific paper, 'Description of an Equatoreal Clock,' appeared in the 'Monthly Notices' of the Royal Astronomical Society (1866). This was followed by a classical memoir in practical astronomy, 'An Account of Observations of the Great Nebula in Orion, made at Birr Castle, with the three-feet and six-feet Telescopes, between 1848 and 1867,' published in the 'Philosophical Transactions' of the Royal Society. An elaborate drawing of the nebula (engraved by J. Basire) accompanied the paper, and was characterised by Dr. J. E. L. Dreyer (*Monthly Notices Roy. Astron. Soc.* Feb. 1909) as being 'always of value as a faithful representation of the appearance of the Orion nebula in the largest telescope of the nineteenth century.' This study completed, Rosse took up (1868–9) an investigation on the radiation of heat from the moon (see *Proc. Roy. Soc.* vols. xvii., xix), which formed the subject of the Royal Society's Bakerian lecture for 1873 (*Phil. Trans.* vol. clxiii.), and occupied his attention for the greater part of his life, despite somewhat scant notice from the scientific world. At the Royal Institution (1895) he gave a lecture, 'The Radiant Heat from the Moon during the Progress of an Eclipse' (*Proc. Roy. Inst.* vol. xiv.). Two days after Rosse's death, Sir Howard Grubb, F.R.S., exhibited at the Dublin meeting of the British Association Rosse's new development of apparatus for lunar heat observation. Other contributions comprised 'The Electric Resistance of Selenium' (*Phil. Mag.* 1874); 'On some Recent Improvements made in the Mountings of the Telescopes at Birr Castle' (*Phil. Trans.* 1881); 'On a Leaf-arrester, or Apparatus for removing Leaves, &c., from a Water Supply' (*Rept. Brit. Assoc.* 1901).

Lord Rosse was elected chancellor of Dublin University in 1885, succeeding Earl Cairns, and held office till his death. In 1903, in association with the provost and members of the university, he issued an appeal for funds (subscribing liberally himself) to secure the erection and equipment of science laboratories in Trinity College; the project had a successful issue.

The University of Oxford conferred the honorary degree of D.C.L. in 1870, and Dublin and Cambridge Universities that of LL.D. in 1879 and 1900 respectively. Elected a fellow of the Royal Society on 19 Dec. 1867, he served on the council (1871–2, 1887–8), and was vice-president for those years. On 13 Dec. 1867 he was elected a fellow of the Royal Astronomical Society, and served on the council (1876–8). Rosse was president of the Royal Dublin Society (1887–92) and of the Royal Irish Academy (1896–1901). He was made an honorary member of the Institution of Mechanical Engineers in 1888.

He died at Birr Castle on 30 Aug. 1908, and was buried in the old churchyard of Birr. He married on 1 Sept. 1870 Frances Cassandra Harvey, only child of Edward William Hawke, fourth baron Hawke of Towton, by his second wife, Frances, daughter of Walker Fetherstonhaugh. He had issue two sons and one daughter. The elder son, William Edward Parsons, succeeded to the title.

Lord Rosse was interested in the prosecution of magnetic observations at Valencia Observatory, Ireland, and collected a sum of money in furtherance of that object. After his death the capital was transferred to the trusteeship of the Royal Society, and is known as the 'Rosse Fund.' By his will he left 1000*l.* to the Science Schools Fund of Trinity College, Dublin, and the Rosse telescope and all his scientific instruments, apparatus, and papers to his sons in order of seniority, successively, whom failing, to the Royal Society. He left 2000*l.* upon trust for the upkeep of the telescope.

[Proc. Roy. Soc., vol. lxxxiii., A. and Catal. Sci. Papers; Monthly Notices Roy. Astron. Soc., vol. lxix.; Roy. Irish Acad. Minutes, session 1908–9, pp. 1, 8; Proc. Inst. Mechan. Eng. 1908; Roy. Soc. Arts Journ., vol. lvi.; The Observatory, Oct. 1908; Engineering, 4 Sept. 1908; Nature, vol. lxxxviii.; The Times, 31 Aug., 3 Sept., 17 Dec. 1908.] T. E. J.

PATON, JOHN BROWN (1830–1911), nonconformist divine and philanthropist, son of Alexander Paton by his wife Mary, daughter of Andrew Brown of Newmilns, Ayrshire, was born on 17 Dec. 1830 at Galston, Ayrshire. On his father's side he was descended from John (*not* James) Paton (*d.* 1684) [q. v.], the covenanter. Both his parents, who were brought up in distinct seceding bodies (burgher and anti-burgher), now belonged to the united secession church, Newmilns. The father ultimately joined the congregationalists. From Loudon parish school Paton passed in 1838 to the tuition of his maternal uncle, Andrew Morton Brown, D.D., congregational minister, then at Poole, Dorset. In 1844 Paton was at Kilmarnock, where he met Alexander Russel [q. v.], and came under the spell of James Morison (1816–1893) [q. v.]. Returning in 1844 to his uncle's care, now at Cheltenham, Paton's future career was determined by the influence of Henry Rogers (1806–1877) [q. v.]. Deciding to become a congregational minister, he entered in Jan. 1847 Spring Hill College, Birmingham (now Mansfield College, Oxford), in which Rogers held the chair of literature and philosophy. With his fellow-student, Robert William Dale [q. v. Suppl. I], he formed a close and lifelong friendship. He heard Emerson lecture on the 'Conduct of Life' in the Birmingham town hall, and attended (from 1850) the ministry of Robert Alfred Vaughan [q. v.], to whose 'intense spirituality' he owed much. During his college course he graduated B.A. at London University in 1849; gained the Hebrew and New Testament prize there (1850), and a divinity scholarship (1852) on the foundation of Daniel Williams (1643 ?–1716) [q. v.], and proceeded M.A. London in 1854, both in classics and in philosophy (with gold medal).

Leaving college in June 1854 he took charge of a mission in Wicker, a parish in the northern part of Sheffield. His ministry was eminently successful; the Wicker congregational church was built in 1855; in addition, the congregation in Garden Street chapel, Sheffield, was revived. In 1861 Cavendish College, Manchester, was started for the training of candidates for the congregational ministry; Paton went weekly from Sheffield to take part in its professorial work. In 1863 the institution was transferred to Nottingham as the Congregational Institute, with Paton as its first principal. Temporary premises were exchanged for a permanent building (1868), and the institute gained increasing reputation during the thirty-five years of Paton's headship. In his management of young men he was an ideal head; no feature of his teaching was more marked than the skill and judgment with which he conducted the work of sermon-making and delivery. In 1882 he was made D.D. of Glasgow University. On his retirement in 1898 his portrait by Arnesby Brown, promoted by a committee headed by the archbishop of Canterbury (Temple), was presented on 26 Oct. 1898 by the bishop of Hereford (Percival) to the city of Nottingham, and is now in the Castle Museum (a replica was given to Paton).

Paton's beneficent activity took other than denominational directions. A visit to Kaiserswerth had impressed him with the idea of the co-operation of all creeds to bring the influence of religion to the regeneration of society. In conjunction with Canon Morse, vicar of St. Mary's, Nottingham, he promoted a series of university lectures which led the way to the establishment of the Nottingham University College in 1880. It was due to Paton's suggestion that the bishop of Lincoln (Wordsworth) sent a letter of sympathy in 1872 to the Old Catholics (Marchant, p. 289). Greatly interested in the Inner Mission, founded in 1848 by Dr. Wichern of Hamburg, he took an active share in plans for the raising of social conditions, e.g. home colonisation with small land-holders, the co-operative banks movement, the social purity crusade. Among societies of which he was the founder were the 'National Home Reading Union' (1889), suggested by the account given by Sir Joshua Girling Fitch [q. v. Suppl. II] of 'The Chautauqua Reading Circle' in the 'Nineteenth Century,' Oct. 1888. He also instituted the 'Recreative Evening School

Associations' (1885) out of which sprang the 'continuation classes' of the State schools (1893); the 'Bible Reading and Prayer Union' (1892); the 'English Land Colonisation Society,' 1892 (now the 'Co-operative Small Holders Association'); a colony for unemployables and epileptic children at Lingfield (now at Wallingford), 1894; the 'Christian Social Service Union,' which undertook the care of the Lingfield and similar colonies (1894); the 'Social Institutes Union' (1896); the 'Scottish Christian Social Union' (1901); the Boys' (1900) and Girls' (1903) Life Brigades; the Young Men's and Young Women's Brigade of Service (1905); and the Boys' and Girls' League of Honour (1906). He was president of the Licensing Laws Information Bureau (1898–1902), and vice-president of the British Institute for Social Service (1904), and of the British and Foreign Bible Society (1907).

Paton, in conjunction with Dale, edited (1858–61) 'The Eclectic Review.' With F. S. Williams, his colleague, he edited a 'Home Mission and Tract Series' (1865). He was a consulting editor (1882–8) of the 'Contemporary Review,' to which, at his urgent request, Lightfoot previously contributed (1874–7) his articles on 'Supernatural Religion.' With Sir Percy William Bunting [q. v. Suppl. II], editor of the 'Contemporary Review,' and the Rev. Alfred Ernest Garvie, he edited a series of papers entitled 'Christ and Civilisation' (1910), his last work.

He died at Nottingham on 26 Jan. 1911, and was buried in the general cemetery, where the service at the graveside (after a nonconformist service in Castlegate chapel) was conducted by the bishop of Hereford (Percival) and the dean of Norwich (Wakefield), now bishop of Birmingham. He married Jessie, daughter of William P. Paton of Glasgow, and was survived by three sons and two daughters; his son, John Lewis, is high master of the Manchester grammar school.

Paton's publications include: 1. 'The Origin of the Priesthood in the Christian Church,' 1877. 2. 'Christianity and the Wellbeing of the People. The Inner Mission of Germany,' 1885; 2nd edit. 1900. 3. 'The Two-fold Alternative . . . Materialism or Religion . . . a Priestly Caste or a Christian Brotherhood,' 1889; 4th edit. 1909. 4. 'Criticisms and Essays,' 2 vols. 1895–7. 5. 'Christ's Miracle of To-day,' 1905. 6. 'Social Questions of the Day,' 6 vols. 1906. 7. 'The Life, Faith and Prayer of the Church,' 1909, 16mo (four sermons). 8. 'Present Remedies for Unemployment,' 1909.

[James Marchant, J. B. Paton, 1909 (two portraits, autobiographical fragments and full bibliography); London Univ. Gen. Reg., 1860; W. J. Addison, Roll of Graduates, Glasgow, 1898; Who's Who, 1911; The Times, 27 and 30 Jan. and 1 Feb. 1911; R. Cochrane's Beneficent and Useful Lives, 1890, pp. 146–159 (for account of the National Home Reading Union); Life and Letters, by John Lewis Paton, his son in preparation).]

A. G.

PATON, JOHN GIBSON (1824–1907), missionary to the New Hebrides, born on 24 May 1824 at Braehead, Kirkmahoe, Dumfriesshire, was eldest of the eleven children (five sons and six daughters) of James Paton, a peasant stocking-maker, by his wife Janet Jardine Rogerson. Both parents were of covenanting stock and rigid adherents of the 'Reformed Presbyterian Church of Scotland,' which still represented the faith of the covenanters. When Paton was five years old, the family removed to Torthorwold, a few miles from Dumfries, where his parents passed the remaining forty years of their lives. Here he attended the parish school, till, in his twelfth year, he was put to his father's trade of stocking-making. Paton soon freed himself from the family workshop, and began to support and educate himself. He put himself for six weeks—all he could afford—to Dumfries Academy; he served under the surveyors for the ordnance map of Dumfries; he hired himself at the fair as a farm labourer; he taught, when he could get opportunity, in schools, and even for a time set up a school for himself; but every spare moment was devoted to serious study. At last he settled down for ten years as a city missionary in a then very neglected part of Glasgow, where he created an excellent school and put the whole district in order.

The 'Reformed Church,' by which John Paton was ordained, had already a single missionary, the Rev. John Inglis, at Aneityum, the southernmost of the New Hebrides Islands in the South Seas; and the elders of the church were seeking somewhat vainly for volunteers to join in that hazardous enterprise. Paton offered himself, and was accepted. On 1 Dec. 1857 he was licensed as a preacher, in his thirty-third year, and on 23 March following he was ordained. With his newly married young wife, Mary Ann Robson, he reached the mission station at Aneityum on 30 Aug., and the pair were soon sent on to establish a new station in the island of Tanna, the natives of which were then entirely untouched by Western civilisation, except in so far as they had from time to time been irritated by aggression on the part of sandalwood traders. The young Scotchman and his wife, without any experience of the world outside the small body to which they belonged, were thus the first white residents in an island full of naked and painted wildmen, cannibals, utterly regardless of the value of even their own lives, and without any sense of mutual kindness and obligation. A few months later, in March 1859, a child was born to this strangely placed couple, and in a few days more wife and child were both dead.

Paton, alone but for another missionary on the other and almost inaccessible side of the island, was left for four years to persuade the Tannese to his own way of thinking. In May 1861 a Canadian missionary and his wife, on the neighbouring island of Erromango, were massacred; and the Tannese, encouraged by the example, redoubled their attacks on Paton, who, after many hairbreadth escapes, got safely away from Tanna, with the loss of all his property except his Bible and some translations which he had made into the island language during his four years' struggle.

From Tanna Paton reached New South Wales, where he knew no one, walked into a church, pleaded successfully for a few minutes' hearing, and spoke with such effect that from that moment he entered on the career of special work which was to occupy the remaining forty-five years of his long life. His main objects—in which he succeeded to a marvellous degree—were to provide missionaries for each of the New Hebridean islands, and to provide a ship for the missionary service. As the direct result of his extraordinary personality and power of persuasion, the 'John G. Paton Mission Fund' was established in 1890 to carry on the work permanently. Returning for the first time to Scotland (1863–4), he there married again, and with his new wife and certain missionaries whom he had persuaded to join in his work was back in the Pacific early in 1865. After placing the new missionaries in various islands, Paton himself settled on the small island of Aniwa, the headquarters whence from 1866 to 1881 he contrived to make his influence felt. After 1881 his 'frequent deputation pilgrimages among the churches in Great Britain and the colonies rendered his visits to Aniwa few and far between,' and his headquarters were at Melbourne.

In addition to his special work as missionary he took considerable part in moving the civil authorities—not merely British, but also those of the United States—to check the dangerous local traffic in strong drink and firearms. He also resisted the recruiting of native labour from the islands; and he lost no opportunity of protesting against the growth of non-British influence in the same places.

During a visit home in 1884, at the suggestion of his youngest brother, Dr. James Paton, the missionary somewhat reluctantly undertook to write his autobiography. James Paton (1843–1906), who had also passed from the ministry of the 'reformed' to that of the Free Church of Scotland, and had graduated D.D. of Glasgow University, shaped his brother's rough notes into a book which, first published in 1889, has played a great part in spreading Paton's influence.

His last years were mainly spent in Melbourne. He died there on 28 Jan. 1907, and was buried in Boroondara cemetery.

Paton's second wife, Margaret, whom he married at Edinburgh in 1864, was daughter of John Whitecross, author of books of scriptural anecdote, and was a woman of great piety and strong character. She showed literary ability in her 'Letters and Sketches from the New Hebrides' (1894), and remarkable power of organisation in her work for the Australian 'Presbyterian Women's Missionary Union.' She was of great assistance to her husband up to her death on 16 May 1905; in her memory a church was erected at Vila, now the centre of administration in the New Hebrides. By her Paton had two daughters and three sons. Two sons became missionaries in the New Hebrides; and one daughter married a missionary there.

[John G. Paton, Missionary to the New Hebrides: an Autobiography, edited by his brother, the Rev. James Paton, D.D., with portrait and map (2 pts. 1889); vol. i. 1891; 're-arranged and edited for young folks,' 1892 and 1893 (a penny edition); Letters and Sketches from the New Hebrides, by Mrs. John G. Paton, 1894; John G. Paton, Later Years and Farewell: a Sequel, by A. K. Langridge and (Paton's son) Frank H. L. Paton, 1910; The Triumph of the Gospel in the New Hebrides, by Frank H. L. Paton, 1903.] E. im T.

PATON, Sir JOSEPH NOËL (1821–1901), artist, born on 13 December 1821, at Dunfermline, was elder son of Joseph Neil Paton, designer of patterns for damask (the staple industry of the town), who was a collector of works of art and after many phases of religious development became a Swedenborgian. His mother, Catherine MacDiarmid, who claimed descent from

Malcolm Canmore, through the Robertsons of Struan, was an enthusiast for fairy-tales and the traditions and legends of the Highlands. His younger brother, Waller Hugh [q. v.], was the landscape-painter, and one of his two sisters, Amelia (1820–1904), who married David Octavius Hill [q. v.], modelled with skill and executed several public statues of merit. At an early age the boy Joseph, who read widely, was impressed by the designs, as well as the poetry, of William Blake. By the time he was fourteen he had made a series of illustrations to the Bible. After completing his general education at a local school, he in 1839 assisted his father in designing, and for the next three years (1840–42) held a situation as a designer for sewed muslins in Paisley. His leisure was devoted to art, and he commenced to paint in oils. In 1843 he entered the schools of the Royal Academy in London, where he began a lifelong friendship with (Sir) John Everett Millais [q. v. Suppl. I], but the Academy training proved uncongenial, and Paton soon went north again. Senior to the Pre-Raphaelites by a few years, Paton sympathised with their ideals, and anticipated some of their practice, but he did not share their ardour for reality, and his pictures, being more conventional both in subject and in style than theirs, more readily won popular approval. In the Westminster Hall competitions, held in connection with the decoration of the Houses of Parliament, Paton was awarded in 1845, when he was only twenty-four, one of the three 200*l.* premiums for his cartoon 'The Spirit of Religion or The Battle of the Soul,' and in 1847 the sum of 300*l.* for his oil-paintings of 'The Reconciliation of Oberon and Titania' and 'Christ bearing the Cross,' a colossal canvas. To 'The Reconciliation' (1847) Paton soon added a companion painting, 'The Quarrel of Oberon and Titania' (1849), the former being purchased by the Royal Scottish Academy, the latter by the Royal Association; both are now in the National Gallery of Scotland. They received enthusiastic welcome, and thenceforth Paton enjoyed an outstanding position, at any rate in Scotland. Elected an associate of the Royal Scottish Academy in 1847, he became an academician in 1850.

From 1856 to 1869 Paton exhibited fourteen pictures at the Royal Academy, and during that period fully maintained his popularity as painter of scenes from fairy tale or history. 'Home from the Crimea' (1856) was one of the few pictures in which the artist touched contemporary life. He showed technical accomplishment and intensity of feeling in 'Luther at Erfurt' (1861). 'The Fairy Raid' (1867) evinced abundant fancy. Other notable works of this time were 'Dante meditating the Episode of Francesca da Rimini' (1852); 'The Dead Lady' (1854); 'In Memoriam' (1857); 'Hesperus' (1858), now in the Glasgow Gallery; 'The Bluidie Tryste' (1858); 'The Dowie Dens of Yarrow' series (1860). 'The Pursuit of Pleasure' (1855) is the first work in which Paton's strong leaning to allegory was revealed. In 1865 Paton was made by Queen Victoria Her Majesty's Limner for Scotland, and he was knighted in 1867. Meantime, while not wholly abandoning fanciful or romantic subjects, he devoted his chief strength to religious themes. 'Mors Janua Vitæ,' shown in 1866 at the Royal Academy, marks the beginning of the series to which belong 'Faith and Reason' (1871); 'Satan watching the Sleep of Christ' (1874); 'Lux in Tenebris' (1879); 'In Die Malo' (1881); 'Vigilate et Orate' (1885), painted for Queen Victoria; 'The Choice' (1886); and 'Beati Mundo Corde' (1890). These large pictures were not shown in the usual exhibitions, but were sent on tour all over the country, with footlights and a lecturer; they proved highly popular, and long lists of subscribers for reproductions were secured. But their artistic value and interest were small, and Paton's reputation among connoisseurs declined.

Paton's gift was that of an illustrator. He valued intention more highly than execution, and set moral purpose above æsthetic charm. His work lacks the true effects of colour. Technically his strongest qualities were drawing, which was correct and was marked by a sense of suave beauty; the design, if wanting in simplicity and concentration, was usually learned and accomplished. His draughtsmanship is seen at its best perhaps in his drawings and studies in black and white, and in the outline compositions he made in illustration of Coleridge's 'Ancient Mariner' (issued by the Art Union of London in 1864) and other poems. This feeling for form and design also found an outlet in some graceful works in sculpture and in a few ambitious projects of a monumental kind.

Paton's interests were varied. Widely read, he published two volumes of verse, 'Poems by a Painter' (1861) and 'Spindrift' (1867), marked by considerable charm and originality, mainly dealing with themes similar to those of his pictures. The delightful song, 'With the Sunshine and the Swallows and the Flowers,' set to music by the Rev. Dr. John Park, is widely known. His fine collection of art-objects and of arms and armour, which was admirably arranged in his Edinburgh house, 33 George Square, was purchased after his death, largely by public subscription, and placed in the Royal Scottish Museum, Chambers Street, Edinburgh. Paton was made hon. LL.D. by Edinburgh University in 1876, and on two occasions, in 1876 and again in 1891, he was offered the presidentship of the Royal Scottish Academy. He died at Edinburgh on 26 Dec. 1901, and was buried in the Dean cemetery.

In 1858 Paton married Margaret (*d.* April 1900), daughter of Alexander Ferrier, Bloomhill, Dumbartonshire; by her he had issue seven sons and four daughters. The eldest son, Dr. Diarmid Noël Paton, is professor of physiology in Glasgow University.

In the Scottish National Portrait Gallery there is a marble bust of Paton by his sister, Mrs. Hill. Other portraits are a picture by his son Ranald, painter, and a bust by another son, who became a lawyer.

[Scotsman, and The Times, 27 Dec. 1901; Easter number, Art Journal, by A. T. Story, 1895; Scots Pictorial, 28 Aug. 1897; exhibition catalogues; Ruskin's Notes on the Royal Academy, 1856 and 1858; R.S.A. Report, 1902; catalogue, National Gallery of Scotland; J. L. Caw's Scottish painting, 1908; The English Pre-Raphaelites, by Percy Bate; private information.] J. L. C.

PAUL, CHARLES KEGAN (1828–1902), author and publisher, son of the Rev. Charles Paul (1802–1861), by his wife Frances Kegan Horne (1802–1848), was born on 8 March 1828 at White Lackington near Ilminster, Somersetshire, where his father was curate. He was educated first at Ilminster grammar school under the Rev. John Allen and afterwards at Eton, where he entered Dr. Hawtrey's house in 1841. He matriculated at Exeter College, Oxford, in January 1846, and in 1849 made the acquaintance of Charles Kingsley, whose contagious energy greatly impressed him. Tractarian theories did not appeal to him, and he showed a leaning towards broad church views in theology. Graduating B.A. in October 1849, he was ordained deacon in the Lent of 1851, and accepted the curacy of Tew, in the diocese of Oxford. Friendship with Kingsley brought him into association with F. D. Maurice, Tom Hughes, J. M. Ludlow, and other co-operative and Christian socialist leaders. He was now broadly high church in doctrine, given to ritualism, and a radical in politics. About this time he took up the practice of mesmerism. In 1852, when he was ordained priest, he became curate of Bloxham, near Banbury, travelled in Germany with pupils, and in November 1853 was given a 'conductship' or chaplaincy at Eton College. In 1853 appeared his first literary production, a sermon on 'The Communion of Saints.' He became a vegetarian and turned his attention to Positivism, and was appointed a 'Master in College' (*Memories*, p. 205) in 1854. Two years later he married Margaret Agnes Colvile (youngest sister of Sir James W. Colvile [q. v.]). He contributed to the 'Tracts for Priests and People,' brought out by Maurice and Tom Hughes, one on 'The Boundaries of the Church' (1861), in which he stated that the very minimum of dogma was required from lay members of the Church of England. These views brought down upon him the wrath of Bishop Wilberforce. He left Eton in 1862 to become vicar of an Eton living at Sturminster Marshall, Dorsetshire. As the endowment was small, he took pupils. In 1870 he joined a unitarian society called the Free Christian Union. In 1872 he associated himself with Joseph Arch's movement on behalf of the agricultural labourers in Dorset, and in 1873 he edited the new series of the 'New Quarterly Magazine.' He gradually found himself out of sympathy with the teaching of the Church of England, and in 1874 threw up his living and came to London. In 1876 appeared his most noteworthy production, 'William Godwin, his Friends and Contemporaries,' with portraits and illustrations, 2 vols. The work was undertaken at the request of Sir Percy Shelley, Godwin's grandson, who placed at Paul's disposal a mass of unpublished documents, which he used with judgment.

For some years Paul had acted as reader for Henry Samuel King, publisher, of Cornhill, who brought out several of his books; King in 1877 relinquished the publishing part of his business and Paul took it over, inaugurating the house of C. Kegan Paul and Co. at No. 1 Paternoster Square. Paul thus succeeded King as Tennyson's publisher. Among Paul's earliest publications were the 'Nineteenth Century,' the new monthly periodical (1877), the works of George William Cox [q. v. Suppl. II], the 'Parchment Library of English Classics,' Tennyson's works in one volume, the 'International Scientific' series (begun by H. S. King), some works of Thomas Hardy, George Meredith, and R. L. Stevenson, and Badger's English-Arabic Lexicon. One of his ventures was to give 5000 guineas for the 'Last Journals of General Gordon,' which cost the firm 7000*l.* before a single copy was ready. In 1881 Mr. Alfred Trench, son of the archbishop, joined the firm, now styled Kegan Paul, Trench & Co. After various vicissitudes, including a calamitous fire in 1883, Messrs. Trübner & Co. and George Redway joined the firm in 1889, and the amalgamation was converted into a limited company under the style of Kegan Paul, Trench, Trübner & Co., Ltd. They moved into large new premises, called Paternoster House, in Charing Cross Road, in 1891, and for some years the business was prosperous. In 1895 the profits of the publishing firm fell with alarming abruptness, the directors resigned, and the capital was reduced. Paul at the same time lost money as director of the Hansard Printing and Publishing Company, and other enterprises. Paul's publishing concern is now incorporated in that of Messrs. Routledge.

Meanwhile from 1888 Paul began to attend mass, and in 1890 during a visit to France he decided to enter the catholic church, and made his submission at the church of the Servites at Fulham on 12 Aug. 1890. His new views were displayed in tracts on 'Miracle' (1891), 'Abstinence and Moderation' (1891), and 'Celibacy' (1899), issued by the Catholic Truth Society, and an edition of 'The Temperance Speeches' of Cardinal Manning (1894). A volume of 'Memories' (1899), which is interesting for its stories of early school and Eton life, ends with his conversisn.

In 1895 Paul was run over in Kensington Road, and never recovered from the accident. He died in London on 19 July 1902, in his seventy-fifth year, and was buried at Kensal Green.

A portrait painted by Mrs. Anna Lea Merritt is in the possession of Miss R. M. Paul, his daughter.

Paul also wrote: 1. 'Reading Book for Evening Schools,' 1864. 2. 'Shelley Memorials, from Authentic Sources,' 3rd edition, 1874. 3. 'Mary Wollstonecraft [afterwards Mrs. Godwin], Letters to Imlay, with Prefatory Memoir,' 1879 (expanded from 'Godwin, his Friends, &c.'). 4. 'Biographical Sketches,' 1883 (Edward Irving, John Keble, Maria Hare, Rowland Williams, Charles Kingsley, George Eliot, John Henry Newman). 5. 'Faith and Unfaith and other Essays,' 1891 ('The Production and Life of Books' deals with the ethics and practice of publishing). 6. 'Maria Drummond, a Sketch,' 1891 (Mrs. Drummond of Fredley, near Dorking, widow of Thomas Drummond (1797-1840) [q. v.]). 7. 'Confessio Viatoris,' 1891 (religious development elaborated in 'Memories'). 8. 'On the Way Side, Verses and Translations,' 1899.

Paul also published several translations including 'Goethe's Faust, in Rime' (1873) (a careful piece of work in the metres of the original); 'Pascal's Thoughts' (1885, several reissues); 'De Imitatione' (1907); and he edited with a preface 'The Genius of Christianity unveiled, being Essays never before published; by William Godwin' (1873).

[Family information; Paul's Memories, 1899; Allibone, Dict. Eng. Lit. Suppl., 1891; Athenæum, 26 July 1902; The Publishers' Circular, 26 July 1902 (with a portrait after a photograph); Bookseller, 7 Aug. 1902; The Times, 21 July 1902; Who's Who, 1902.]

H. R. T.

PAUL, WILLIAM (1822–1905), horticulturist, born at Churchgate, Cheshunt, Hertfordshire, on 16 June 1822, was second son of Adam Paul, a nurseryman of Huguenot descent, who came to London from Aberdeenshire towards the close of the eighteenth century and purchased the Cheshunt nursery in 1806. After education at a private school at Waltham Cross, William joined his father's business. On Adam Paul's death in 1847 the business was carried on as A. Paul & Son by William and his elder brother George. In 1860 this partnership was dissolved. William Paul & Son carried on the Waltham Cross nursery, which he had founded a year before, while George established the firm of Paul & Son at Cheshunt.

John Claudius Loudon [q. v.] before his death in 1843 discovered Paul's literary abilities, and for him Paul did early literary work. He afterwards helped John Lindley [q. v.], for whom, in 1843, he wrote the articles in the 'Gardeners' Chronicle' on 'Roses in Pots,' which were issued separately in the same year, and reached a ninth edition in 1908. Paul's book, 'The Rose Garden,' which was first published in 1848, and reached its tenth edition in 1903, has enjoyed the unique fortune of maintaining a pre-eminent authority for sixty years. It is a practical treatise, to which Paul's wide reading gave a literary character. Coloured illustrations long rendered the book expensive;

later editions were issued in two forms, with and without these plates.

Paul served on the committee of the National Floricultural Society from 1851 until it was dissolved in 1858, when the floral committee of the Royal Horticultural Society was established. In July 1858 he joined the National Rose Society, which Samuel Reynolds Hole [q. v. Suppl. II] had just founded, and in 1866 he was one of the executive committee of twenty-one members for the great International Horticultural Exhibition. He also acted as a commissioner for the Paris Exhibition of 1867. Paul was elected a fellow of the Linnean Society in 1875, and received the Victoria medal of horticulture when it was first instituted in 1897.

Although best known as a rosarian, Paul from the outset of his career devoted attention to the improvement of other races of plants, such as hollyhocks, asters, hyacinths, phloxes, camellias, zonal pelargoniums, hollies, ivies, shrubs, fruit-trees, and Brussels sprouts. He dealt with these subjects in 'American Plants, their History and Culture' (1858), the 'Lecture on the Hyacinth' (1864), and papers on 'An Hour with the Hollyhock' (1851) and on 'Tree Scenery' (1870–2). He contributed papers on the varieties of yew and holly to the 'Proceedings' of the Royal Horticultural Society (1861, 1863). In addition to 'The Rose Annual,' which he issued from 1858 to 1881, Paul was associated with his friends Dr. Robert Hogg and Thomas Moore in the editorship of 'The Florist and Pomologist' from 1868 to 1874. The practical knowledge with which he wrote of varied types of plant life impressed Charles Darwin (cf. *Animals and Plants under Domestication*, vol. ii.). Clear and fluent as a speaker, he proved an acceptable lecturer. One of his best lectures, 'Improvements in Plants,' at Manchester in 1869, was included in his 'Contributions to Horticultural Literature, 1843–1892' (1892).

Paul died of a paralytic seizure on 31 March 1905, and was buried in the family vault at Cheshunt cemetery. His wife, Amelia Jane Harding, predeceased him. His business was carried on by his son, Arthur William Paul. The rich library of old gardening books and general literature, which he collected at his residence, Waltham House, was sold at Sotheby's after his death, but many volumes were bought by his son.

Besides the works mentioned, Paul was author of: 1. 'Villa Gardening,' 1855; 3rd revised edit. 1876. 2. A shilling brochure, 'Roses and Rose-Culture,' 1874; 11th edit. 1910. 3. 'The Future of Epping Forest,' 1880.

[Garden, lvii. (1900), 166; lxiii. (1903), preface with portrait; and lxvii. (1905), 213; Journal of Horticulture, l. (1905), 305 (with portrait); Gardeners' Chron. 1905, i. 216, 231; Proc. Linnean Soc. 1904–5, 46–7.]

G. S. B.

PAUNCEFOTE, Sir JULIAN, first Baron Pauncefote of Preston (1828–1902), lawyer and diplomatist, born at Munich on 13 Sept. 1828, was second son of Robert Pauncefote (formerly Smith) of Preston Court, Gloucestershire (1788–1843), by his wife Emma (*d.* 1853), daughter of R. Smith. His paternal grandfather, Thomas Smith, of Gedling, Nottinghamshire, and Foel Allt, Wales, was first cousin of Robert Smith, first baron Carrington. Educated partly at Marlborough College, partly at Paris and Geneva, Julian was called to the bar as a member of the Inner Temple on 4 May 1852. He was private secretary to Sir William Molesworth, eighth baronet [q. v.], during the latter's short term of office as secretary of state for the colonies in 1855. On Molesworth's death he returned to the bar and practised as a conveyancer. In 1862 he went to Hong Kong, where there was an opening for a barrister, and three years afterwards he received the appointment of attorney-general in that colony. This office he held for seven years, acting for the chief justice of the supreme court when the latter was absent on leave, and preparing 'The Hong Kong Code of Civil Procedure.'

In 1872 he was appointed chief justice of the Leeward Islands, which had recently been amalgamated in one colony. On quitting Hong Kong he was formally thanked for his services by the executive and legislative councils, and received the honour of knighthood. He took up his new appointment in 1874, opened the new federal court, and put the administration of justice into working order. Towards the end of the year he returned to England and succeeded Sir Henry Holland, now Viscount Knutsford, as legal assistant under-secretary in the colonial office. In 1876, on the recommendation of a committee of the House of Commons, a similar post was created at the foreign office, and was bestowed by Lord Derby, then foreign secretary, on Pauncefote, who was specially qualified for it by his knowledge of French. His services were recognised by the bestowal on him of the K.C.M.G. in Jan. 1880, and of the C.B. three months later. After doing much political work in addition to his normal duties, owing to the long illness of Charles Stuart Aubrey Abbott, third baron Tenterden [q. v.], the permanent under-secretary of state, and the infirm health of other members of the staff, Pauncefote, on Lord Tenterden's death in 1882, was appointed by Earl Granville, then foreign secretary, to the vacant place, while he continued to superintend the legal work. In 1885 he and Sir Charles Rivers Wilson took part in the international commission at Paris concerning the free navigation of the Suez Canal, and were largely concerned in the draft settlement on which was based the convention of Constantinople (29 Oct. 1888). He was created G.C.M.G. at the close of 1885, and K.C.B. in 1888.

On 2 April 1889 Pauncefote was appointed envoy extraordinary and minister plenipotentiary to the United States; Lord Salisbury had left the office vacant for some months after the abrupt dismissal of Lord Sackville [q. v. Suppl. II]. At Washington, Pauncefote by his personal influence contributed materially to the solution of the various differences, some of them sufficiently acute, which arose between the two countries, and rendered invaluable service in producing a more friendly feeling towards Great Britain in the United States. His patience, urbanity, and habits of complete and impartial study of complicated details combined with his legal training greatly to assist him in dealing with American politicians and officials, most of whom were lawyers. Among the most critical questions with which he had to deal were the claim of the United States to prevent pelagic sealing by Canadian vessels in the Behring Sea, a question which, after passing through some menacing phases, was eventually referred to the decision of an arbitral tribunal at Paris in February 1892; an arrangement was concluded for a *modus vivendi* pending the award. A second question, which concerned the boundary between Venezuela and British Guiana, was taken up by the United States government in 1895, and the unusual tenour and wording of President Cleveland's message to Congress on the subject, in December, threatened at one moment serious complications. The matter was referred in February 1897 to an arbitral tribunal at Paris, which in October 1899 decided substantially in favour of the British claim. In the discussions and negotiations which preceded the outbreak of war between the United States and Spain, in April 1898, Pauncefote tactfully sought with the representatives of the great European powers to secure a pacific arrangement without suggesting any indifference to freedom and good government in Cuba. Pauncefote's prudence throughout the period of the war did much to establish a lasting friendship between England and the United States.

In 1893, after it had been ascertained that such a step would be agreeable to the United States government, the British representative at Washington was raised from the rank of envoy to that of ambassador. Other great powers followed suit, and Pauncefote, as the senior ambassador, was of much service in settling various questions of precedence and etiquette consequent on the change.

In 1897, after prolonged negotiations, he concluded a convention with the United States for the settlement by arbitration of differences between the two countries. The convention, however, was not approved by the senate, and remained unratified.

In 1899 Pauncefote was appointed senior British delegate at the first Hague conference which met to devise means for the limitation of armaments and the pacific settlement of international differences. Pauncefote here rendered his most important service to the cause of peace. Insuperable obstacles were soon apparent to the general acceptance of any binding obligation to reduce armaments or to submit disputes to arbitration. Pauncefote, therefore, ably assisted the president, M. de Staal, in setting the conference to work, as the best alternative, on establishing a suitable permanent tribunal of arbitration, to which voluntary recourse could at any time be readily had, and which other powers might bind themselves to recommend to disputants. In framing the needful machinery Pauncefote gave unostentatious but most efficient assistance, and shared with the president the credit of the success attained. On his return to England, after the termination of the conference, he was raised to the peerage on 18 Aug. 1899. The remaining years of his life were spent as British ambassador in the United States. In February 1900 he signed with Mr. John Hay, the United States secretary of state, a convention designed to replace the provisions of the Clayton-Bulwer treaty of 19 April 1850 with regard to the construction of a canal across the Isthmus of Panama. The convention, however, failed to secure confirmation by the senate, and was not ratified. A second convention ('the

Hay-Pauncefote treaty') signed by him on 18 Nov. 1901 was more fortunate. By its provisions the ships of all nations passing through the canal were placed on an equal footing, and the United States government precluded itself from imposing preferential dues. Nevertheless, and in spite of the protests of the British government, the United States government passed in Aug. 1912 a law allowing free passage through the canal to American coasting vessels.

Growing years, the climate of Washington, the constant strain of work, and sedentary habits had by 1901 seriously impaired Pauncefote's naturally vigorous constitution, and he died at Washington, of a prolonged attack of gout, on 24 May 1902. He had been made Hon. LL.D. of Harvard and Columbia Universities in 1900. His death called forth unprecedented expressions of public regret in the United States; the funeral ceremony in Washington was attended by the president and by the leading authorities, and the United States government, with the assent of the British government, conveyed the body to England in a United States vessel of war. The burial took place at St. Oswald's Church, Stoke near Newark. A fine monument, executed in bronze by George Wade, has been placed at the head of the grave in the churchyard by his widow and daughters.

Pauncefote married on 14 Sept. 1859 Selina Fitzgerald, daughter of Major William Cubitt, of Catfield, Norfolk. By her he had one son, who died in infancy, and four daughters.

An excellent portrait by Benjamin Constant is in the possession of Lady Pauncefote, and a copy is at Marlborough College. A cartoon portrait appeared in 'Vanity Fair' in 1883.

[The Times, 26, 27, 30 May 1902; Foreign Office List, 1902, p. 194; Papers laid before Parliament.] S.

PAVY, FREDERICK WILLIAM (1829–1911), physician, born at Wroughton, Wiltshire, on 29 May 1829, was son of William Pavy, a maltster there, by Mary his wife. Educated at Merchant Taylors' School in Suffolk Lane, London, where he entered in Jan. 1840, he experienced a Spartan discipline under James Bellamy, the headmaster, father of Dr. James Bellamy [q. v. Suppl. II]. He proceeded to Guy's Hospital in 1848, and matriculated at the University of London. Here he gained honours at the intermediate examination in medicine in 1850, and the scholarship and medal in materia medica and pharmaceutical chemistry. In 1852 he graduated M.B. with honours in physiology and comparative anatomy, obstetric medicine and surgery, and the medal in medicine (the medal in surgery being gained by Joseph, afterwards Lord, Lister). Pavy then served as house surgeon and house physician at Guy's Hospital, and in 1853 he went to Paris and joined the English Medical Society of Paris, of which he became a vice-president. The society met in a room near the Luxembourg and owned a small library. It was the rendezvous of the English medical students, where they met weekly to read papers and to report interesting cases. In Paris Pavy came more especially under the influence of Claude Bernard, who was at this time giving a course of experimental lectures on the rôle and nature of glycogen and the phenomena of diabetes. Pavy made the study of diabetes the work of his life and imitated his master in the manner of his lectures.

On his return to England Pavy was appointed lecturer on comparative anatomy at Guy's Hospital in 1854, and from 1856 to 1878 he lectured there upon physiology and microscopical anatomy, and afterwards upon systematic medicine. He was elected assistant physician to the hospital in 1858, on the promotion of (Sir) William Gull [q. v.], and became full physician in 1871, when the number of physicians was increased from three to four. He was appointed consulting physician to the hospital in 1890, his tenure of office upon the full staff having been prolonged for an additional year.

At the Royal College of Physicians of London he was elected a fellow in 1860; he served as an examiner in 1872–3 and in 1878–9; he was a councillor from 1875 to 1877 and again from 1888 to 1890; a censor in 1882, 1883, and 1891. He delivered the Goulstonian lectures in 1862–3; the Croonian lectures in 1878 and 1894, and the Harveian oration in 1886. He was awarded the Baly medal in 1901.

He also did good work at the medical societies of London. In 1860 he delivered the Lettsomian lectures at the Medical Society 'On Certain Points connected with Diabetes.' He served as president of the Pathological Society from 1893 to 1895 and as president of the Royal Medical and Chirurgical Society from 1900 to 1902. He acted for some years as president of the Association for the Advancement of Medicine by Research, and from 1901 he served, after the death of Sir William MacCormac [q. v. Suppl. II], as president of the national committee for Great Britain and Ireland of the International Congress of Medicine. The permanent committee of this congress, meeting at the Hague in 1909, appointed him the first chairman.

Pavy was elected F.R.S. in 1863; the University of Glasgow conferred upon him the hon. degree of LL.D. in 1888, and in 1909 he was crowned Lauréat de l'Académie de Médecine de Paris and received the Prix Godard for his physiological researches. On 26 June 1909, at a meeting of the Physiological Society of Great Britain and Ireland held at Oxford, he was presented with a silver bowl bearing an expression 'of affection and admiration.'

Pavy died at his house, 35 Grosvenor Street, London, W., on 19 Sept. 1911, and was buried at Highgate cemetery.

He married in 1854 Julia, daughter of W. Oliver, by whom he had two daughters who predeceased him. The elder, Florence Julia (*d.* 1902), was married in 1881 to the Rev. Sir Borradaile Savory, second baronet, son of Sir William Scovell Savory, first baronet, F.R.S. [q. v.].

A sketch—a good likeness—made by W. Strang, A.R.A., hangs in the rooms of the Royal Society of Medicine.

Pavy was the last survivor of a line of distinguished physician-chemists who did much to lay the foundations and advance the study of metabolic disorders; at the same time he ranks as a pioneer amongst the chemical pathologists of the modern school. As a pupil of Claude Bernard he recognised that all advances in the study of disease must rest upon investigations into the normal processes of the body; but as his investigations proceeded, he found himself obliged to dissent from the views of his master and to adopt new working hypotheses which he put to the test of experiment and frequently varied. Some of his theories did not meet with the approval of those who were working along similar lines, and others never obtained general acceptance. He made the study of carbohydrate metabolism the work of his life, and he was the founder of the modern theory of diabetes. In this connection his name was associated with many practical improvements in clinical and practical medicine, and 'Pavy's Test' for sugar and his use of sugar tests and albumen tests in the solid form have made his name familiar to physicians and medical students throughout the world. As a practical physician, too, he was greatly interested in dietetics, and he wrote a well-known book upon the subject, 'A Treatise on Food and Dietetics physiologically and therapeutically considered' (1873; 2nd edit. 1875; Philadelphia, 1874; New York, 1881). Throughout life he remained a student, and even to the last week he was at work in the laboratory which he had built at the back of his consulting room in Grosvenor Street. Quiet in bearing, gentle and courteous in speech, and with a somewhat old-fashioned formality of manner, he was generous in his benefactions. At Guy's medical school he built a well-equipped gymnasium and presented it to the students' union in 1890.

Besides the works cited Pavy published: 1. 'Researches on the Nature and Treatment of Diabetes,' 1862; 2nd edit. 1869; translated into German by Dr. W. Langenbeck, Göttingen, 1864. 2. 'A Treatise on the Functions of Digestion, its Disorders and their Treatment,' 1867; 2nd edit. 1869. 3. 'The Croonian Lectures on Certain Points connected with Diabetes, delivered at the Royal College of Physicians,' 1878. 4. 'The Harveian Oration, delivered at the Royal College of Physicians,' 1886. 5. 'The Physiology of the Carbohydrates, their Application as Food and Relation to Diabetes,' 1894; translated into German by Karl Grube, Leipzig and Vienna, 1895. 6. 'On Carbohydrate Metabolism (a course of advanced lectures on Physiology delivered at the University of London, May 1905), with an appendix on the assimilation of carbohydrate into proteid and fat, followed by the fundamental principles and the treatment of Diabetes dialectically discussed,' 1906.

[The Lancet, 1911, ii. 976 (with portrait and bibliography of chief papers contributed to periodicals and societies); Brit. Med. Journal, 1911, ii. 777 (with portrait); The Guy's Hosp. Gaz. 1911, xxv. 393 (with bibliography); additional information kindly given by Sir William Borradaile Savory, Bart., his grandson, by H. L. Eason, Esq., M.S., dean of the medical school at Guy's Hospital, and by Dr. J. S. Edkins; personal knowledge.]

D'A. P.

PAYNE, EDWARD JOHN (1844–1904), historian, born at High Wycombe, Buckinghamshire, on 22 July 1844, was the son of Edward William Payne, who was in humble circumstances, by his wife Mary Welch. Payne owed his education largely to his own exertions. After receiving early training at the grammar school of High Wycombe, he was employed by a local architect and surveyor named Pontifex, and he studied architecture under William Burges [q. v.]. Interested in music from youth, he also acted as organist of the parish church. In 1867, at the age of twenty-three, he matriculated at Magdalen Hall, Oxford, whence he passed to Charsley's Hall. While an undergraduate he supported himself at first by pursuing his work as land surveyor and architect at Wycombe, where he designed the Easton Street almshouses, and afterwards by coaching in classics at Oxford. In 1871 Payne graduated B.A. with a first class in the final classical school, and in 1872 he was elected to an open fellowship in University College. He remained a fellow till his marriage in 1899, and was thereupon re-elected to a research fellowship. Although his life was mainly spent in London, he was keenly interested in the management of the affairs of his college, and during the years of serious agricultural depression his good counsel and business aptitude proved of great service.

On 17 Nov. 1874 he was called to the bar by Lincoln's Inn, and in 1883 was appointed honorary recorder of Wycombe, holding the office till his death. But Payne's mature years were mainly devoted to literary work. English colonial history and exploration were the main subjects of his study. In 1875 he contributed a well-informed 'History of European Colonies' to E. A. Freeman's 'Historical Course for Schools.' In 1883 he collaborated with Mr. J. S. Cotton in 'Colonies and Dependencies' for the 'English Citizen' series, and the section on 'Colonies' which fell to Payne he later developed into his 'Colonies and Colonial Federation' (1904). He also fully edited Burke's 'Select Works' (Oxford, 1876; new edit. 1912) and 'The Voyages of Elizabethan Seamen to America' (from Hakluyt, 1880; new edit. 1907). But these labours were preliminaries to a great design of a 'History of the New World called America.' The first and second volumes (published respectively in 1892 and 1899) supplied a preliminary sketch of the geographical knowledge and exploration of the Middle Ages, an account of the discovery of America, and the beginning of an exhaustive summing up of all available knowledge as to the ethnology, language, religion, social and economic condition of the native peoples. Nothing more was published, and an original plan to extend the survey to Australasia was untouched. Payne contributed the first two chapters on 'The Age of Discovery' and 'The New World' to the 'Cambridge Modern History' (vol. i. 1902).

At the same time Payne wrote much on music. He contributed largely to Grove's 'Dictionary of Music and Musicians.' His article on 'Stradivari' was recognised as an advance on all previous studies. The history of stringed instruments had a strong attraction for him, and he was himself an accomplished amateur performer on the violin and on various ancient instruments. He helped to found the Bar Musical Society, and was its first honorary secretary.

In his later years Payne lived at Wendover, and suffered from heart-weakness and fits of giddiness. On 26 Dec. 1904 he was found drowned in the Wendover canal, into which he had apparently fallen in a fit. On 5 April 1899 he married Emma Leonora Helena, daughter of Major Pertz and granddaughter of Georg Heinrich Pertz, editor of the 'Monumenta Germaniæ Historica.' She survived him with one son and two daughters, and was awarded a civil list pension of 120*l.* in 1905. A portrait by A. S. Zibleri is in her possession.

[Records of Buckinghamshire, vol. ix.; The Times, 28 Dec. 1904; Oxford Mag. 25 Jan. 1905; Musical Times, Feb. 1905; private information.] D. H.

PAYNE, JOSEPH FRANK (1840–1910), physician, son of Joseph Payne [q. v.], a schoolmaster, professor of education at the College of Preceptors, by his wife Eliza Dyer, also a teacher of great ability, was born in the parish of St. Giles, Camberwell, on 10 Jan. 1840. After school education under his father at Leatherhead, Surrey, he went to University College, London, and thence gained in 1858 a demyship at Magdalen College, Oxford. He graduated B.A. in 1862, taking a first class in natural science, and afterwards obtained the Burdett-Coutts scholarship in geology (1863), the Radcliffe travelling fellowship (1865), and a fellowship at Magdalen, which he vacated on his marriage in 1883, becoming an honorary fellow on 30 May 1906. He also took a B.Sc. degree in the University of London in 1865. He studied medicine at St. George's Hospital, London, and graduated M.B. at Oxford in 1867, and M.D. in 1880. He became a member of the College of Physicians in 1868, and was elected a fellow in 1873, being the junior chosen to deliver the Goulstonian lectures. His subject was 'The Origin and Relation of New Growths.' In accordance with the terms of Dr. Radcliffe's foundation he visited Paris, Berlin, and Vienna, and made good use of their pathological opportunities. He described his foreign experiences in three articles published in the

'British Medical Journal' in 1871. His first post at a medical school in London was that of demonstrator of morbid anatomy at St. Mary's Hospital in 1869, and he became assistant physician there as well as at the Hospital for Sick Children in Great Ormond Street. In 1871 he left St. Mary's on becoming assistant physician to St. Thomas's Hospital, an office which he held till appointed physician in 1887. In 1900 he had reached the age limit, and became consulting physician. He was also on the staff of the Hospital for Skin Diseases at Blackfriars, and was thus engaged in the active practice and teaching of his profession for over thirty years.

Pathology, epidemiology, dermatology, and the history of medicine were the subjects in which he took most interest, and he made considerable additions to knowledge in each. In September 1877 he was the chief medical witness for the defence at the sensational trial in London of Louis Staunton and others for the murder of his wife Harriet by starvation, and effectively argued that cerebral meningitis was the cause of death, a view which in spite of the prisoner's conviction was subsequently adopted (ATLAY's *Trial of the Stauntons*, 1911, pp. 176 *et passim*). He edited in 1875 Jones and Sieveking's 'Manual of Pathological Anatomy,' and in 1888 published a full and original 'Manual of General Pathology,' besides reading many papers before the Pathological Society, of which he became president in 1897. He delivered at the College of Physicians in 1891 the Lumleian lectures 'On Cancer, especially of the Internal Organs.' In 1879 he was sent to Russia by the British government with Surgeon-major Colvill to observe and report upon the epidemic of plague then existing at Vetlanka (*Trans. Epidemiological Soc.* vol. iv.). The Russian government did little to facilitate the inquiry, and a severe illness prevented Payne from accomplishing much, but he always retained a warm interest in epidemiology, and wrote articles on plague in the 'Encyclopædia Britannica' (9th edit.), 'St. Thomas's Hospital Reports,' 'Quarterly Review' (October 1901), and 'Allbutt's System of Medicine,' vol. 2, 1907. He took an active part on a committee of the College of Physicians in 1905 on the Indian epidemic of plague and was chosen as the spokesman of the committee to the secretary of state. He printed in 1894, with an introduction on the history of the plague, the 'Loimographia' of the apothecary William Boghurst, who witnessed the London plague of 1665, from the MS. in the Sloane collection. Payne also made numerous contributions to the 'Transactions' of the Epidemiological Society, of which he was president in 1892–3. In 1889 he published 'Observations on some Rare Diseases of the Skin,' and was president of the Dermatological Society (1892–3). Many papers by him are to be found in its 'Transactions.'

Payne's first important contribution to the history of medicine was a life of Linacre [q. v.] prefixed to a facsimile of the 1521 Cambridge edition of his Latin version of Galen, 'De Temperamentis' (Cambridge, 1881). In 1896 he delivered the Harveian oration at the College of Physicians on the relation of Harvey to Galen, and in 1900 wrote an excellent life of Thomas Sydenham [q. v.]. He had a great knowledge of bibliography and of the history of woodcuts, and read (21 Jan. 1901) a paper before the Bibliographical Society 'On the "Herbarius" and "Hortus Sanitatis."' In 1903 and 1904 he delivered the first FitzPatrick lectures on the history of medicine at the College of Physicians. The first course was on 'English Medicine in the Anglo-Saxon Times' (Oxford, 1904), the second on 'English Medicine in the Anglo-Norman Period.' The history of Gilbertus Anglicus and the contents of his 'Compendium Medicinæ' had never before been thoroughly set forth. Payne showed that Gilbert was a genuine observer of considerable ability. The lectures of 1904 which Payne was preparing for the press at the time of his death did much to elucidate the writings of Ricardus Anglicus and the anatomical teaching of the Middle Ages. Payne demonstrated that the 'Anatomy of the Body of Man,' printed in Tudor times and of which the editions extend into the middle of the seventeenth century, was not written by Thomas Vicary [q. v.], whose name appears on the title-page, but was a mere translation of a mediæval manuscript of unknown authorship. He wrote long and valuable articles on the history of medicine in the 'Encyclopædia Britannica,' and in Allbutt's 'System of Medicine' (vol. i. 1905), besides several lives in this Dictionary. During the spring of 1909 he delivered a course of lectures on Galen and Greek medicine at the request of the delegates of the Common University Fund at Oxford. His last historical work was entitled 'History of the College Club,' and was privately printed in 1909.

In 1899 he was elected Harveian librarian of the College of Physicians, a post for which his qualifications were exceptional.

He gave many valuable books to the library, and opened the stores of his mind to everyone who sought his knowledge. He was for eight years an examiner for the licence of the College of Physicians, was a censor in 1896–7, and senior censor in 1905. He discharged in 1896 the laborious duty of editor of the 'Nomenclature of Diseases,' and in addition to these public services sat on the royal commission on tuberculosis (1890), on the general medical council as representative of the University of Oxford (1899–1904), on the senate of the University of London (1899–1906), and on the committee of the London Library. He collected a fine library, the medical part of which, except five manuscripts and two books which he bequeathed to the College of Physicians, was sold to one purchaser for 2300*l*. He had a large collection of editions of Milton's works and a series of herbals. His conversation was both learned and pleasant, and though full of antique lore he was an earnest advocate of modern changes. He was below the middle height and had a curious jerky manner of expressing emphasis both in public speaking and in private conversation. Among the physicians of London there was no man of greater general popularity in his time. He lived at 78 Wimpole Street while engaged in practice, and after his retirement at New Barnet. Failing health interrupted the literary labours of his last year, and he died at Lyonsdown House, New Barnet, on 16 Nov. 1910, and was buried at Bell's Hill cemetery, Barnet. He married, on 1 Sept. 1882, Helen, daughter of the Hon. John Macpherson of Melbourne, Victoria, by whom he had one son and three daughters. A fine charcoal drawing of his head, made by Mr. J. S. Sargent shortly before his death, hangs in the dining-room of the College of Physicians.

[The Times, 18 Nov. 1910; Lancet, and Brit. Med. Journal, 26 Nov. 1910; Sir T. Barlow, Annual Address to Royal Coll. of Physicians; Macray, Reg. Fellows Magd. Coll. vi. 170–1 and vii.; Sotheby, Cat. of Library, 12 July 1911; personal knowledge.] N. M.

PEARCE, STEPHEN (1819–1904), portrait and equestrian painter, born on 16 Nov. 1819 at the King's Mews, Charing Cross, was only child of Stephen Pearce, clerk in the department of the master of horse, by his wife, Ann Whittington. He was trained at Sass's Academy in Charlotte Street, and at the Royal Academy schools, 1840, and in 1841 became a pupil of Sir Martin Archer Shee [q. v.]. From 1842 to 1846 he acted as amanuensis to Charles Lever [q. v.], and he afterwards visited Italy. Paintings by him of favourite horses in the royal mews (transferred in 1825 to Buckingham Palace) were exhibited at the Academy in 1839 and 1841, and from 1849, on his return from Italy, till 1885 he contributed numerous portraits and equestrian paintings to Burlington House.

Early friendship with Colonel John Barrow, keeper of the admiralty records, brought Pearce a commission to paint 'The Arctic Council discussing a plan of search for Sir John Franklin.' This work he completed in 1851; it contained portraits of Back, Beechey, Bird, Parry, Richardson, Ross, Sabine, and others; was exhibited at the Royal Academy in 1853, and was engraved by James Scott. Pearce's picture increased the public interest in Franklin's fate. Pearce also painted for Colonel Barrow half-lengths of Sir Robert McClure, Sir Leopold McClintock, Sir George Nares, and Captain Penny in their Arctic dress, and a series of small portraits of other arctic explorers. Lady Franklin also commissioned a similar series, which passed at her death to Miss Cracroft, her husband's niece. All these pictures are in the National Portrait Gallery, to which Colonel Barrow and Miss Cracroft respectively bequeathed them. Pearce's other sitters included Sir Francis Beaufort and Sir James Clark Ross (for Greenwich Hospital), Sir Edward Sabine and Sir John Barrow (for the Royal Society), and Sir George Gabriel Stokes, Charles Lever, Sims Reeves, Sir Erasmus Wilson (Hospital for Diseases of the Skin, Westgate-on-Sea, copied for the Royal College of Surgeons), and the seventh Duke of Bedford.

Pearce was also widely known as a painter of equestrian presentation portraits and groups, the most important of which is the large landscape 'Coursing at Ashdown Park,' completed in 1869, and presented by the coursers of the United Kingdom to the Earl of Craven. For this picture, which measures ten feet long and contains about sixty equestrian portraits, including the Earl and Countess of Craven and members of the family, the Earls of Bective and Sefton, Lord and Lady Grey de Wilton, the artist received 1000 guineas and 200 guineas for the copyright. Pearce painted equestrian portraits of many masters of foxhounds and harriers, as well as of the Earl of Coventry, Sir Richard and Lady Glyn, and of Mr. Burton on 'Kingsbridge' and Captain H. Coventry on 'Alcibiade,' winners of the Grand National.

Pearce retired from general practice in

1885 and from active work in 1888. He contributed ninety-nine subjects to the Academy exhibitions, and about thirty of his pictures were engraved by J. Scott, C. Mottram, and others. His portraits, almost entirely of men, are accurate likenesses, and his horses and dogs are well drawn. The earlier paintings are somewhat tight in execution, with a tendency to over-emphasis of shadow, but the later pictures are freer in style.

Pearce's somewhat naïve 'Memories of the Past,' published by him in 1903, contains nineteen reproductions from his paintings, a list of subjects painted, biographical and some technical notes. He died on 31 Jan. 1904 at Sussex Gardens, W., and was buried at the Old Town cemetery, Eastbourne. A portrait of himself he bequeathed to the National Portrait Gallery.

He married in 1858 Matilda Jane Cheswright, who survived him with five sons.

[Memories of the Past, 1903, by Stephen Pearce; Sporting Gaz., 2 Oct. 1869; Lists of the Printsellers' Association; Royal Acad. Catalogues; misc. pamphlets, letters, and official records, Nat. Port. Gall.; personal knowledge and private information.]

J. D. M.

PEARCE, Sir WILLIAM GEORGE, second baronet, of Carde (1861–1907), benefactor to Trinity College, Cambridge, born at Chatham on 23 July 1861, was only child of Sir William Pearce [q. v.] by his wife Dinah Elizabeth, daughter of Robert Sowter of Gravesend. Educated at Rugby (1876–1878), he matriculated in 1881 at Trinity College, Cambridge, and graduated B.A. and LL.B. in 1884, proceeding M.A. in 1888. He was called to the bar at the Inner Temple in 1885. On the death of his father in December 1888 he succeeded him in the chairmanship of the Fairfield Shipbuilding and Engineering Company of Glasgow, an undertaking the development of which had been the principal work of his father's life. Under Pearce's chairmanship, which lasted from 1888 until his death, the company maintained its high reputation [see Elgar, Francis, Suppl. II]. Pearce was returned to parliament in 1892 as conservative member for Plymouth along with Sir Edward Clarke, but did not seek re-election in 1895. He was honorary colonel of the 2nd Devon volunteers Royal Garrison Artillery. He was a keen sportsman, and his estate of Chilton Lodge, Hungerford, was noted for the excellence of its shooting. He died after a short illness on 2 Nov. 1907 at 2 Deanery Street, Park Lane, and was buried at Chilton Foliat near Hungerford.

He married on 18 March 1905 Caroline Eva, daughter of Robert Coote. There was no issue of the marriage. By his will he left the residue of his property, estimated at over 150,000*l.*, subject to his wife's life interest, to Trinity College, Cambridge, of which he had remained a member, although he had maintained no close association with the college after his life there as an undergraduate. Lady Pearce only survived her husband a few weeks. The college thus acquired probably the most valuable of the many accessions which have been made to its endowments since its foundation by Henry VIII.

[The Times, 4 and 8 Nov. 1907; History of the Fairfield Works.]

H. M'L. I.

PEARSON, Sir CHARLES JOHN, Lord Pearson (1843–1910), Scottish judge, born at Edinburgh on 6 Nov. 1843, was second son of Charles Pearson, chartered accountant, of Edinburgh, by his wife Margaret, daughter of John Dalziel, solicitor, of Earlston, Berwickshire. After attending Edinburgh Academy, he proceeded to the University of St. Andrews, and thence to Corpus Christi College, Oxford, where he distinguished himself in classics, winning the Gaisford Greek prizes for prose (1862) and verse (1863). He graduated B.A. with a first class in the final classical school in 1865. He afterwards attended law lectures in Edinburgh, and became a member of the Juridical Society, of which he was librarian in 1872–3, and of the Speculative Society (president 1869–71). He was called to the English bar (from the Inner Temple) on 10 June 1870, and on 19 July 1870 passed to the Scottish bar, where he rapidly obtained a large practice. Though not one of the crown counsel for Scotland, he was specially retained for the prosecution at the trial of the City of Glasgow Bank directors (Jan. 1879), became sheriff of chancery in 1885, and procurator and cashier for the Church of Scotland in 1886. In 1887 he was knighted, and was appointed sheriff of Renfrew and Bute in 1888, and of Perthshire in 1889. Pearson was a conservative, though not a keen politician, and in 1890 was appointed solicitor-general for Scotland in Lord Salisbury's second administration, and was elected (unopposed) as M.P. for Edinburgh and St. Andrews Universities. In the same year he became Q.C. In 1891 he succeeded James Patrick Bannerman Robertson, Lord Robertson [q. v. Suppl. II], as lord advocate, and was sworn of the privy council. At the general election of 1892 he was again returned unopposed for

Edinburgh and St. Andrews Universities. After the fall of Lord Salisbury's ministry in 1892 he ceased to be lord advocate, and was chosen dean of the Faculty of Advocates. He received the honorary degree of LL.D. from Edinburgh University in 1894, and on the return of the conservatives to power in the following year became again lord advocate, and resigned the deanship. In 1896, on the resignation of Andrew Rutherfurd Clark, Lord Rutherfurd Clark, he was raised to the bench, from which he retired, owing to bad health, in 1909. He died at Edinburgh on 15 Aug. 1910, and was buried in the Dean cemetery there.

Pearson married on 23 July 1873 Elizabeth, daughter of M. Grayhurst Hewat of St. Cuthbert's, Norwood, by whom he had three sons. A painting, by J. Irvine, belongs to his widow.

[Scotsman, and The Times, 16 Aug. 1910; Roll of the Faculty of Advocates; Hist. of the Speculative Soc., p. 156; Records of the Juridical Soc.; Acts of the General Assembly of the Church of Scotland, 1886; Foster, Men at the Bar.] G. W. T. O.

PEASE, Sir JOSEPH WHITWELL, first baronet (1828–1903), director of mercantile enterprise, born at Darlington on 23 June 1828, was elder son of Joseph Pease (1799–1872), by his wife Emma, daughter of Joseph Gurney of Norwich. Edward Pease [q. v.] was his grandfather. In January 1839 he went to the Friends' school, York, under John Ford (in January 1900 he laid the foundation stone of extensive new buildings at Bootham). Entering the Pease banking firm at Darlington in 1845, he became largely engaged in the woollen manufactures, collieries, and iron trade with which the firm was associated. He was soon either director or chairman of the Owners of the Middlesbrough Estate, Ltd., Robert Stephenson & Co., Ltd., Pease & Partners, Ltd., and J. & J. W. Pease, bankers. In 1894 he was elected chairman of the North Eastern railway, having been deputy chairman for many years. He also farmed extensively, and read a paper on the 'Meat Supply of Great Britain' at the South Durham and North Yorks Chamber of Agriculture, 26 Jan. 1878.

In 1865 Pease was returned liberal M.P. for South Durham, which he represented for twenty years. After the Redistribution Act of 1885 he sat for the Barnard Castle division of Durham county until his death. He strongly supported Gladstone on all questions, including Irish home rule, and rendered useful service to the House of Commons in matters of trade, particularly in regard to the coal and iron industries of the North of England. He was president of the Peace Society and of the Society for the Suppression of the Opium Traffic, and a champion of both interests in parliament. On 22 June 1881 he moved the second reading of a bill to abolish capital punishment, and his speech was separately printed. In 1882 Gladstone created him a baronet (18 May). No quaker had previously accepted such a distinction, although Sir John Rodes (1693–1743) inherited one.

At the end of 1902 the concerns with which Pease and his family were identified became involved in financial difficulties. Liabilities to the North Eastern railway amounted to 230,000*l*. Voluntary arrangements were made by various banking firms of quaker origin with whom the Peases had intimate connection, and the actual loss to the railway was reduced at least one-half. Heavy losses fell on the companies with which Pease was associated and on several London banks.

He died at Kerris Vean, his Falmouth residence, of heart failure, on 23 June 1903 and was buried at Darlington.

He married in 1854 Mary, daughter of Alfred Fox of Falmouth (she died on 3 Aug. 1892), and by her left two sons and six daughters. The elder son, Alfred Edward Pease, second baronet, M.P. for York (1885–92), and for the Cleveland division of Yorkshire (1897–1902), was resident magistrate in the Transvaal in 1903. The second son, Joseph Albert Pease, who sat as a liberal in the House of Commons from 1892, became president of the board of education in 1911.

A cartoon portrait by 'Spy' appeared in 'Vanity Fair' in 1887.

[The Times, 24 June 1903; Who's Who, 1902; Hansard; private information.] C. F. S.

PEEK, Sir CUTHBERT EDGAR, second baronet (1855–1901), amateur astronomer and meteorologist, born at Wimbledon on 30 Jan. 1855, was only child of Sir Henry William Peek, first baronet (created 1874), of Wimbledon House, Wimbledon, Surrey, a partner in the firm of Messrs. Peek Brothers & Co. (now Peek, Winch & Co.), colonial merchants, of East Cheap, and M.P. for East Surrey from 1868 to 1884. His mother was Margaret Maria, second daughter of William Edgar of Eagle House, Clapham Common. Cuthbert, after education at Eton, entered Pembroke College, Cambridge, in 1876 and graduated B.A. in 1880, proceeding M.A. in

1884. After leaving Cambridge he went through a course of astronomy and surveying, and put his knowledge to practical use in two journeys, made in 1881, into unfrequented parts of Iceland, where he took regular observations of latitude and longitude and dip of the magnetic needle (cf. his account, *Geograph. Soc. Journal*, 1882, pp. 129–40). On his return he set up a small observatory in the grounds of his father's house at Wimbledon, where he observed with a 3-inch equatorial. In 1882 Peek spent six weeks at his own expense at Jimbour, Queensland, for the purpose of observing the transit of Venus across the sun's disc in Dec. 1882. There, with his principal instrument, an equatorially mounted telescope of 6·4 inches, he observed, in days preceding the transit, double stars and star-clusters, paying special attention to the nebula round η Argus, one of the wonders of the Southern sky, which he described in a memoir. Observations of the transit were prevented by cloud. Peek made extensive travels in Australia and New Zealand, bringing back with him many curious objects to add to his father's collection at Rousdon near Lyme Regis.

In 1884 he established, on his father's estate at Rousdon, a meteorological station of the second order, and in the same year he set up there an astronomical observatory to contain the 6·4 inch Merz telescope and a transit instrument with other accessories. With the aid of his assistant, Mr. Charles Grover, he began a systematic observation of the variation of brightness of long period variable stars, by Argelander's method, and on a plan consistent with that of the Harvard College Observatory. Annual reports were sent to the Royal Astronomical Society, which Peek joined on 11 Jan. 1884, and short sets of observations were occasionally published in pamphlet form. The complete series of the observations of 22 stars extending over sixteen years were collected at Peek's request by Professor Herbert Hall Turner of Oxford and published by him after Peek's death in the 'Memoirs of the Royal Astronomical Society' (vol. lv.). The introduction to the volume contains a section written by Peek in 1896 explaining his astronomical methods. With similar system regular observations were made with his meteorological instruments, and these were collected and published in annual volumes.

Peek succeeded to the baronetcy and to the estates that his father had bought in Surrey and Devonshire on his father's death on 26 Aug. 1898. He was elected F.S.A. on 6 March 1890, was hon. secretary of the Anthropological Society, and often served on the council or as a vice-president of the Royal Meteorological Society between 1884 and his death. He endowed the Royal Geographical Society, of whose council he was a member, with a medal for the advancement of geographical knowledge. Interested in shooting, he presented a challenge cup and an annual prize to be shot for by members of the Cambridge University volunteer corps. He died at Brighton on 6 July 1901 of congestion of the brain, and was buried at Rousdon, Devonshire.

On 3 Jan. 1884 he married Augusta Louisa Brodrick, eldest daughter of William Brodrick, eighth Viscount Midleton, and sister of Mr. St. John Brodrick, ninth Viscount Midleton, sometime secretary of state for war. She survived him with two sons and four daughters. His elder son, Wilfrid (*b.* 9 Oct. 1884) succeeded to the baronetcy.

[Obituary notice by Charles Grover in the Observatory Magazine, August 1901; Monthly Notices of the Royal Astronomical Society, February 1902.] H. P. H.

PEEL, Sir FREDERICK (1823–1906), railway commissioner, born in Stanhope St., London, W., on 26 Oct. 1823, was second son of Sir Robert Peel, second baronet [q. v.], statesman, by his wife Julia, daughter of General Sir John Floyd, first baronet [q. v.]. His eldest brother was Sir Robert Peel, third baronet [q. v.]; his younger brothers were Sir William Peel [q. v.], naval captain, and Arthur Wellesley (afterwards first Viscount) Peel, who was speaker of the House of Commons (1884–95).

Frederick was educated at Harrow (1836–41), and thence he matriculated at Cambridge from Trinity College. He graduated B.A. in 1845 as a junior optime and as sixth classic in the classical tripos, and proceeded M.A. in 1849. On leaving Cambridge he became a student at the Inner Temple on 5 May 1845, and was called to the bar on 2 Feb. 1849. In the same month he entered the House of Commons, being returned unopposed as liberal member for Leominster. His promising maiden speech (11 May 1849) in favour of the removal of Jewish disabilities called forth general commendation (*Grevile Memoirs*, vi. 295). Peel was a staunch supporter of free trade and of the extension of the franchise, but being distrustful of secret voting he was not in favour of the ballot. His outspoken criticism of the liberal government's ecclesiastical titles bill (14 Feb. 1851) showed independent judgment, and Lord John Russell recognised his ability by appointing him under-secretary for the colonies. After the general election of 1852, when Peel successfully contested Bury, he resumed the post of under-secretary for the colonies in Lord Aberdeen's coalition ministry. On 15 Feb. 1853 he introduced the clergy reserves bill (Hansard, *Parliamentary Debates*, 3 S., cxxiv. col. 133), which was designed to give the government of Canada effective control over the churches there. The object of the measure was to repeal the clauses in the Canadian Constitutional Act of 1791, by which one-seventh of the lands of the colony was appropriated for the maintenance of the protestant clergy. Under Peel's auspices the bill passed the House of Commons, despite violent opposition from the conservatives, and received the royal assent on 9 May 1853. On the fall of the Aberdeen ministry in January 1855 Peel was nominated by Lord Palmerston under-secretary for war. In view of the popular outcry against the mismanagement of the Crimean war the post involved heavy responsibilities. Peel's chief, Lord Panmure [q. v.], sat in the House of Lords, and Peel was responsible minister in the House of Commons. He incurred severe censure for the misfortunes and failures incident to the war. In 1857 he lost his seat for Bury and resigned office. In recognition of his services he was made a privy councillor. He was once more returned for Bury in 1859 and was advanced by Lord Palmerston to the financial secretaryship of the treasury, a post which he held till 1865, when he was again defeated at Bury at the general election. After the death of Palmerston, Peel found himself ill-suited to the more democratic temper of parliamentary life. He unsuccessfully contested south-east Lancashire in 1868, and never re-entered the House of Commons. He was created K.C.M.G. in 1869, and thenceforth devoted himself to legal pursuits.

In 1873, on the passing of the Regulation of Railways Act, Peel was appointed a member of the railway and canal commission, on which he served till his death. The tribunal was constituted as a court of arbitration to settle disagreements between railways and their customers which lay beyond the scope of ordinary litigation. The commission rapidly developed in importance, and was reorganised by the Railway and Canal Act of 1888, a judge of the high court being added to its members. Peel and his colleagues rendered useful service to the farming and commercial interests by reducing preferential rates on many railways. In Ford & Co. *v.* London and South Western Railway they decided that the existence of a favoured list of passengers constituted an undue preference (*The Times*, 3 Nov. 1890). The decisions of the commissioners were seldom reversed on appeal. In the case of Sowerby & Co. *v.* Great Northern Railway, Peel dissented from the judgment of his colleagues, Mr. Justice Wills and Mr. Price, to the effect that the railway company was entitled to make charges in addition to the maximum in respect of station accommodation and expenses, but the view of the majority was upheld by the court of appeal (21 March 1891). As senior commissioner Peel became the most influential member of the tribunal. He had his father's judicial mind and cautious, equable temper, but his reticence and aloofness militated against his success in public life. He died in London on 6 June 1906, and was buried at Hampton-in-Arden, Warwickshire. He married (1) on 12 Aug. 1857, Elizabeth Emily (*d.* 1865), daughter of John Shelley of Avington House, Hampshire, and niece of Percy Bysshe Shelley [q. v.], the poet; and (2) on 3 Sept. 1879, Janet, daughter of Philip Pleydell-Bouverie of Brymore, Somersetshire, who survived him. He left no issue. A cartoon portrait by 'Spy' appeared in 'Vanity Fair' in 1903.

[The Times, and Morning Post, 7 June 1906; C. S. Parker, Sir Robert Peel, 3 vols., 1899; Harrow School Register, 1911; Burke's Peerage and Baronetage; Herbert Paul, History of Modern England, vol. i. 1904; Railway Commission Reports.] G. S. W.

PEEL, JAMES (1811–1906), landscape painter, born on 1 July 1811 in Westage Road, Newcastle-on-Tyne, was son of Thomas Peel, woollen draper (*d.* 24 April 1822), partner in the firm of Fenwick, Reid & Co. Educated at Bruce's school, he had as schoolfellows there Sir Charles Mark Palmer [q. v. Suppl. II] and John Collingwood Bruce, the antiquary. Edward Dalziel, father of the wood engravers the Dalziel Brothers [see Dalziel, Edward, Suppl. II], first taught him drawing, and in 1840 he came to London to paint portraits. Among his early work were full-sized copies of Wilkie's 'Blind Fiddler' and 'The Village Festival,' in the National Gallery, as well as portraits and miniatures. Eventually he confined himself wholly to landscape painting, in which he exhibited at the

Royal Academy from 1843 to 1888 and at the Royal Society of British Artists from 1845 onwards. His pictures made their mark by their sincere feeling for nature and their excellent drawing, especially of trees. Three of his pictures, 'A Lane in Berwickshire,' 'Cotherstone, Yorkshire,' and 'Pont-y-pant, Wales,' are in the Laing Art Gallery, Newcastle, where a loan exhibition of his works was held in 1907. Several were bought for other provincial galleries at Glasgow, Leeds, and Sunderland, and for clients in Newcastle. He resided at Darlington from 1848 to 1857, when he again settled in London.

In 1861 he was admitted a member of the Royal Society of British Artists, of which he became a leading supporter. In association with Madox Brown, William Bell Scott [q. v.], and other artists he was an active organiser of 'free' exhibitions like those of the Dudley Gallery and of the Portland Gallery, of which the latter ended disastrously. Working to the end with all the vigour of earlier years, he died at his residence, Elms Lodge, Oxford Road, Reading, on 28 Jan. 1906. Peel married at Darlington, on 30 May 1849, Sarah Martha, eldest daughter of Thomas Blyth, and left issue.

[The Times, 5 Feb. 1906; Newcastle Weekly Chron., 20 March 1897 (with photographic reproduction); Illustr. Cat. of Exhib. of Works by James Peel, Laing Art Gall., Newcastle, March 1907 (with portrait); private information.] F. W. G-N.

PEILE, Sir JAMES BRAITHWAITE (1833–1906), Indian administrator, born at Liverpool on 27 April 1833, was second son in a family of ten children of Thomas Williamson Peile [q. v.], by his wife Mary, daughter of James Braithwaite. Colonel John Peile, R.A., was a brother. In 1852 James proceeded from Repton School, of which his father was headmaster, with a scholarship to Oriel College, Oxford.

At Michaelmas term 1853 he won a first class in classical moderations and two years later a first class in the final classical school. Meanwhile in 1855 the civil service of India was thrown open to public competition, and Peile obtained one of the first twenty appointments, being placed tenth.

He travelled out to India to join the Bombay service in September 1856 by the paddle steamer Pekin, having as a fellow traveller William Brydon [q. v.], sole survivor of the Kabul retreat in 1842. Peile was at once nominated to district work. From the Thana district he was sent to Surat, and thence to Ahmedabad on 15 April 1857, where the belated news of the Meerut outbreak reached that station on 21 May 1857. Peile thus experienced some of the stern realities of the Mutiny, and he described them graphically in private letters to a friend who published them in 'The Times' on 3 Dec. 1857. In 1858 Peile was actively engaged in extending primary education and learning an inspector's duties under Sir Theodore Hope. On 4 May 1859 he was entrusted with the special inquiry into the claims made against the British government by the ruler of Bhavnagar, a native state in Kathiawar. His successful settlement of this difficulty brought him to the front and he was made under-secretary of the Bombay government.

Peile's observations in Bhavnagar had deeply impressed him with the impoverished condition of Girassias and Talukdars, depressed landowners descended from ruling chiefs, who were rapidly losing their proprietary rights. For the next five years (1861–6) he was chiefly absorbed in endeavours to remedy this state of affairs. He devised and carried out in Gujarat a scheme of summary settlement for the holders of 'alienated' estates (*i.e.* lands granted on favourable terms by government). There followed the enactment of Bombay Act, vi., 1862, for the relief of the Talukdars of Western Ahmedabad. Peile resigned the post of under-secretary to government in order that he might ensure the success of legislation inspired by himself. Many estates were measured and valued by him, complicated boundary disputes settled, and the rents due to government were fixed for a term of years. His reputation for overcoming difficulties was so established that, on the occurrence of a dispute in the Rajput state of Dharanpur which threatened civil disturbance, he was sent to compose it. His arrangements were satisfactory, and his thoroughness and efficiency greatly impressed Sir Bartle Frere. In April 1866 he was selected as commissioner for revising subordinate civil establishments throughout Bombay, and then, when a wave of speculation passed over the province, he became registrar-general of assurances, and took an active part in compelling companies to furnish accounts. Having thus established his claims to promotion, he took furlough to England from September 1867 to April 1869.

On his return to duty he became director of public instruction in succession to Sir Alexander Grant [q. v.], and held the post till 1873. He laid truly the foundations of primary education, in which Bombay has always taken the lead. He also compiled an outline of history to assist school teachers in giving their lessons. In 1872 the finances of the city of Bombay became embarrassed, and Peile was sent to settle them, acting as municipal commissioner. Subsequently he undertook for a short period the political charge of Kathiawar, to which he returned again in 1874, holding it until 1878. As political agent of Kathiawar Peile greatly added to his reputation. This important agency covered 23,000 square miles, the territorial sovereignty being divided among the Gaekwar of Baroda and 193 other chiefs, all equally jealous of their attributes of internal sovereignty. Peile found the province in disorder and its chiefs discontented, and he left it tranquil and grateful. In 1873 Waghirs and other outlaws terrorised the chiefs and oppressed their subjects. Capt. Herbert and La Touche had been murdered, and one morning as Peile reached his tent the famous leader Harising Ragji, who was under trial for seven murders and had just escaped from prison, appeared before him. Peile, who was alone, refused to guarantee to him more than justice, and the fugitive was rearrested, tried, and convicted. Gradually the chiefs were persuaded to co-operate in maintaining order, and a police force was organised. While the British officer asserted the rights of the paramount power, he did not ignore the rights of the chiefs, whose claims to revenue from salt and opium he vigorously asserted against the government of Bombay in later years, and he encouraged the chiefs to send their karbharis or ministers in order to discuss with him and each other their common interests. He lent Chester Macnaghten his powerful support and encouragement in establishing an efficient college at Rajkote for the sons and relatives of the ruling chiefs. Able to take up the records of a tangled suit or case and read them in the vernacular, he defeated intrigue and corruption, for which the public offices had gained a bad name, by mastering details and facts without the aid of a native clerk. By such means he won the confidence of the chiefs, and secured their active assistance. The Peile bridge, opened on 17 June 1877, over the Bhadar in Jetpur, and the consent won from the ruler of Bhavnagar in 1878 to the construction of a railway, are standing records of a policy of united effort which to-day covers the province with roads and railways. In 1877 the shadow of famine lay over the province, and Peile sought help from Sir Richard Temple [q. v. Suppl. II], who told him plainly that he 'could not spare a single rupee.' Peile's answer, 'I know then where I stand,' impressed Temple. He at once proceeded to organise self-help by local co-operation, and averted a grave catastrophe. Peile was a member of the famine commission (1878–80), and Temple in giving evidence before it declared that 'the condition of Kathiawar was a credit to British rule.'

Peile spent a few months in Sind in 1878, but declined an offer of the commissionership there. From 1879 to 1882 he was secretary and acting chief secretary to the Bombay government. During 1879 he accompanied the famine commission on its tour of inquiry, receiving in the course of it the honour of C.S.I. In October he proceeded to London to assist in writing the famous famine report remarkable 'for its detailed knowledge of varying conditions and grasp of general principles' (LORD HARTINGTON'S *Despatch*, No. 4, dated 14 March 1881). On his return to Bombay he was sent to Baroda to clear off appeals against the government of Baroda in respect of Girassia claims. He had hardly rejoined the secretariat when the governor-general recalled him to Simla to take part in a conference regarding the rights of certain Kathiawar states to manufacture salt. On 23 Dec. 1882 he became member of council at Bombay, and to him Lord Ripon [q. v. Suppl. II] looked with confidence to give effect to his self-government policy. Peile matured and carried through such important measures as the legislative councils Bombay Acts I and II, 1884, Local Boards, and District Municipalities Acts. These Acts did not go as far as Lord Ripon hoped in the elimination of official guidance from municipal and local board committees; but Peile knew that it was unsafe to go further, and the viceroy cordially acknowledged his services. In 1886 he carried an amendment of the Bombay Land Revenue Code, securing to the peasantry the benefit of agricultural improvements. His experience in educational matters was of great service. He had become vice-chancellor of the university in 1884, and in 1886 he dealt with technical education in his convocation address. In 1886 Peile left the Bombay council on his appointment by Lord Dufferin, Lord Ripon's successor on the supreme council. From 4 Oct. 1886 to 8 Oct. 1887, with a few days' interval, Peile served as a member of the supreme government. His presence greatly assisted the enactment of the Punjab Tenancy Act and the Land Revenue Bill, while Lady Dufferin found an active supporter and exponent at a public meeting of her benevolent scheme for female medical aid.

To the regret of Lord Dufferin, Peile left India on his nomination to the India council in London (12 Nov. 1887). In 1897 his ten years' term of office was extended for another five years. During these fifteen years he took a leading part at the India office in the government of India. He was one of the first to urge upon his colleagues the need for enlarging provincial councils and for increasing their powers. He was a jealous guardian of the finances of India, strenuously opposing the application of her revenues to the cost of sending troops in 1896 to Suakin as 'not being a direct interest of India.' He also objected to imposing on cotton exported to India a differential and preferential rate (3 per cent.) of import duties, when the general tariff fixed for revenue purposes was 5 per cent. While he advocated a progressive increase in the number of Indians admitted to the higher branches of the service, he firmly opposed the 'ill-considered resolution' of the House of Commons (2 June 1893), in favour of simultaneous examinations. He declined the offer of chairmanship of the second famine commission, but he served on the royal commission on the administration of the expenditure of India in 1895, and recorded the reservations with which he assented to their report dated 6 April 1900. He was made K.C.S.I. in 1888.

Throughout his career he had found recreation in sketching, and some of his productions in black and white won prizes at exhibitions in India. Retiring from public office on 11 Nov. 1902, he devoted himself to family affairs, and found leisure to record an account of his life for his children. He died suddenly on 25 April 1906 at 28 Campden House Court, London, W., and was buried at the Kensington cemetery, Hanwell.

Peile married in Bombay, on 7 Dec. 1859, Louisa Elisabeth Bruce, daughter of General Sackville Hamilton Berkeley. His wife survived him with two sons, James Hamilton Francis, archdeacon of Warwick, and Dr. W. H. Peile, M.D., and a daughter.

[The Times, 27 April 1906; Annals of the Peiles of Strathclyde, by the Rev. J. W. Peile (brother of Sir James); Famine Commissioners Reports; Legislative Proc. of Governments of India and Bombay; Kathiawar administration Reports; private papers lent by the archdeacon of Warwick.] W. L-W.

PEILE, JOHN (1837–1910), Master of Christ's College, Cambridge, and philologist, born at Whitehaven, Cumberland, on 24 April 1837, was only son of Williamson Peile, F.G.S., by his wife Elizabeth Hodgson. Sir James Braithwaite Peile [q. v. Suppl. II] was his first cousin. His father died when he was five years old, and in 1848 he was sent to Repton School, of which his uncle, Thomas Williamson Peile [q. v.], was then headmaster. At Repton he remained till his uncle's retirement in 1854. During the next two years he attended the school at St. Bees, and in 1856 was entered at Christ's College, Cambridge. In 1859 he won the Craven scholarship, and in 1860 was bracketed with two others as senior classic, and with one of these, Mr. Francis Cotterell Hodgson, as chancellor's medallist. He graduated B.A. in 1860 and proceeded M.A. in 1863. Having been elected a fellow of Christ's in 1860, and appointed assistant tutor and composition lecturer, he settled down to college and university work, which occupied him till near his death. He took up the study of Sanskrit and comparative philology, and in 1865, and again in 1866, spent some time working with Professor Benfey at Göttingen. Till the appointment of Professor Edward Byles Cowell [q. v. Suppl. II] in 1867, he was teacher of Sanskrit in the university, and when Sanskrit became a subject for a section of part 2 of the classical tripos, he published a volume of 'Notes on the Tale of Nala' (1881) to accompany Professor Jarrett's edition of the text. He also corrected Jarrett's edition, which in consequence of a difficult method of transliteration was very inaccurately printed. In 1869 appeared his book 'An Introduction to Greek and Latin Etymology.' The lecture form of the first edition was altered in the second, which was issued in 1871; a third appeared in 1875. Soon after the point of view of comparative philologists changed in some degree, and Peile, who by this time was becoming more immersed in college and university business, allowed the book to go out of print. A little primer of 'Philology' (1877) had for long a very wide circulation. To the ninth edition of the 'Encyclopædia Britannica' he contributed the article on the alphabet and also articles upon the individual letters. He was for many years a contributor to the 'Athenæum,' reviewing classical and philological publications. In 1904 he was elected a member of the British Academy.

Peile was tutor of his college from 1870 to 1884, when, on his appointment to the newly constituted post of university reader in comparative philology, which was not tenable with a college tutorship, he resigned, but remained a college lecturer. On the death of Dr. Swainson in 1887 he was elected Master of Christ's, but continued to lecture for the university till his election as vice-chancellor in 1891. His two years' tenure of the vice-chancellorship (1891–3) was eventful beyond the common. The most important incident was the passing of an act of parliament, whereby the perennial conflict of jurisdictions between 'town and gown' was brought to an end satisfactory to both parties, the university surrendering its jurisdiction over persons not belonging to its own body and receiving representation on the town council. The controversy had reached an acute stage over a case of proctorial discipline, and the new arrangement was mainly due to Peile's broadmindedness and statesmanship. His vigorous vice-chancellorship made him henceforward more than ever prominent in the affairs of the university. While he was vice-chancellor a new chancellor—Spencer Compton Cavendish, eighth duke of Devonshire [q. v. Suppl. II] —was installed, and Peile visited Dublin on the occasion of the tercentenary of Trinity College, which conferred upon him the honorary degree of Litt.D. (1892). He had been one of the early recipients of the degree of Litt.D. on the establishment of that degree at Cambridge in 1884.

In 1874 Peile had been elected a member of the council of the senate, a position which he held uninterruptedly for thirty-two years. Along with Prof. Henry Sidgwick [q. v. Suppl. I] and Coutts Trotter [q. v.] he represented in the university the liberalising movement then perhaps at the zenith of its influence. He was long an active supporter of women's education and a member of the council of Newnham College, and in the university controversy of 1897 on the question of 'Women's Degrees' he advocated the opening to women of university degrees. After the death of Prof. Arthur Cayley [q. v. Suppl. I] in 1895 he became president of the council, and a new block of college buildings at Newnham has been named after him. He was in favour of making Greek no longer compulsory on all candidates for admission to the university when the question was debated in 1891, and again in 1905 and 1906. He also took an active part in the university extension movement.

Though he never ceased to take an interest in comparative philology, and remained for many years an active and influential member of the special board for classics, most of his leisure, after he ceased to be vice-chancellor in 1893, was devoted to compiling a biographical register of the members of his college and of its forerunner, God's House, a work which entailed a great amount of research. In connection with this undertaking he wrote in 1900 a history of the college for Robinson's series of college histories. The first volume of his register (1448–1665) was completed before Peile's death, which took place at the college after a long illness on 9 Oct. 1910. He is buried in the churchyard of Trumpington, the parish in which he lived before becoming Master of Christ's College.

In 1866 he married Annette, daughter of William Cripps Kitchener, and had by her, besides two children who died in infancy, two sons, and a daughter, Hester Mary, who married, in 1890, John Augustine Kempthorne, since 1910 bishop-suffragan of Hull.

Peile was a man of moderate views who had the faculty of remaining on good terms with his most active opponents. He was an effective speaker and a good chairman. As a college officer he was very popular, and the college prospered under him. As a lecturer on classical subjects (most frequently on Theocritus, Homer, Plautus, and Lucretius), and on comparative philology, he was able to put his views clearly and interestingly, and, like Charles Lamb, he sometimes found the slight hesitation in his speech a help in emphasising a point. To him much more than to anyone else was due the successful study of comparative philology in Cambridge.

A portrait by Sir George Reid, P.R.S.A., is in the possession of the college; a replica presented to Mrs. Peile was given by her to Newnham College, and now hangs in Peile Hall.

[Information from Mrs. Peile, Dr. Shipley, Master of Christ's College, Prof. Henry Jackson, and the headmaster of Repton; Prof. W. W. Skeat in Proc. Brit. Acad. 1910; Dr. W. H. D. Rouse in Christ's Coll. Mag. 1910; personal knowledge since 1882.] P. G.

PELHAM, HENRY FRANCIS (1846–1907), Camden professor of ancient history, Oxford, was grandson of Thomas Pelham, second earl of Chichester [q. v.], and eldest of the five children of John Thomas Pelham, bishop of Norwich [q. v.], by his wife Henrietta, second daughter of Thomas William Tatton of Wythenshawe Hall, Cheshire. Of his three brothers, John Barrington became vicar of Thundridge in 1908, and Sidney archdeacon of Norfolk in 1901. Pelham was born on 19 Sept. 1846 at Bergh Apton, then his father's parish. Entering Harrow (Westcott's house) in May 1860, he moved rapidly up the school, and left in December 1864. Next year he won an open classical scholarship at Trinity College, Oxford (matriculating on 22 April 1865); he came into residence in October. At Oxford he took 'first classes' in honour classical moderations and in literæ humaniores, was elected a fellow of Exeter College in 1869, and graduated B.A. in the same year. In 1870 he won the chancellor's English essay prize with a dissertation on the reciprocal influence of national character and national language. He worked continuously as classical tutor and lecturer at Exeter College from 1870 till 1889. He was elected by his college proctor of the university in 1879. Losing his fellowship on his marriage in 1873, he was re-elected in 1882, under the statutes of the second university commission.

From school onwards his principal subject was ancient and more particularly Roman history. He soon began to publish articles on this theme (first in 'Journal of Philology,' 1876), while his lectures, which (under the system then growing up) were open to members of other colleges besides Exeter, attracted increasingly large audiences; he also planned, with the Clarendon Press, a detailed 'History of the Roman Empire,' which he was not destined to carry out. In 1887 he succeeded W. W. Capes as 'common fund reader' in ancient history, and in 1889 he became Camden professor of ancient history in succession to George Rawlinson [q. v. Suppl. II], a post to which a fellowship at Brazenose is attached. As professor he developed the lectures and teaching which he had been giving as college tutor and reader, and attracted even larger audiences. But his research work was stopped by an attack of cataract in both eyes (1890), and though a few specimen paragraphs of his projected 'History' were set up in type in 1888, he completed in manuscript only three and a half chapters, covering the years B.C. 35–15, and he never resumed the work after 1890; his other research, too, was hereafter limited to detached points in Roman imperial history. On the other hand, he joined actively in administrative work, for which his strong personality and his clear sense fitted him at least as well as for research; he served on many Oxford boards, was a member of the hebdomadal council from 1879 to 1905, aided semi-academic educational movements (for women, &c.), and in 1897 accepted the presidency of his old college, Trinity. He was elected honorary fellow of Exeter in 1895, was an original fellow of the British Academy in 1902 and received the hon. degree of LL.D. at Aberdeen in 1906. He became F.S.A. in 1890. He died in the president's lodgings at Trinity on 12 Feb. 1907, and was buried in St. Sepulchre's cemetery, Oxford. On 30 July 1873 he married Laura Priscilla, third daughter of Sir Edward North Buxton, second baronet, and granddaughter of Sir Thomas Fowell Buxton, first baronet [q. v.]; she survived him with two sons and a daughter.

Pelham was a somewhat unusual combination of the scholar and the practical man. An excellent teacher, lecturing at a time when Oxford was widening its outlook and Mommsen and his school were recreating Roman history, he helped to revolutionise the study of ancient history in Oxford, and by consequence in England. Still more, as one who combined practical organising genius with an understanding of the real needs of learning and the true character of scientific research, he did more than any other one man to develop his university as a place of learning, while conserving its value as a place of education. Thus, he was prominent in providing endowments for higher study and research, in introducing archæology and geography to the circle of Oxford historical work, and in founding the British Schools at Rome and Athens. In pursuit of his principles he helped actively to put natural science, English and foreign languages on a more adequate basis in Oxford, and to give women full opportunities of academic education at the university. After his death his friends founded in his memory a Pelham studentship at the British School at Rome, to be held by Oxford men (or by women students) pursuing higher studies at Rome.

Pelham wrote little. His chief publications were: 1. 'Outlines of Roman History,' London, 1893, enlarged from a monograph in the 'Encyclopædia Britannica,' 1887. 2. Scattered essays and articles on Roman history, of which the chief, with a fragment of the unfinished 'History,' have been collected in a posthumous volume of 'Essays,' Oxford, 1911. Both volumes exhibit very high historical powers, but Pelham's eyesight and perhaps his temperament turned him to other activities with more result.

A portrait by Sir Hubert von Herkomer hangs in the hall of Trinity College.

[Memoir by Prof. Haverfield, prefixed to Pelham's Essays, 1911; The Times, 13 Feb. 1907; Proc. Brit. Acad. 1907–8; private information.] F. J. H.

PELL, ALBERT (1820–1907), agriculturist, born in Montagu Place, Bloomsbury, London, on 12 March 1820, was eldest of three sons of Sir Albert Pell (1768–1832), serjeant-at-law in 1808, who retired from practice in 1825 in indignation at being passed over by Lord Eldon for judicial promotion, but in 1831 was persuaded by his friend Brougham, when he became lord chancellor, to accept a judgeship of the court of review in bankruptcy; he was at the same time knighted on 7 Dec. (cf. WOOLRYCH'S *Serjeants-at-Law* (1869), ii. 752–71). Pell's mother was Margaret Letitia Matilda (1786–1868), third daughter and co-heiress of Henry Beauchamp St. John, twelfth Lord St. John of Bletsoe.

Brought up at his father's houses at Pinner Hill and in Harley Street, Pell from 1832 to 1838 was at Rugby school under Arnold. Thence he passed in 1840 to Trinity College, Cambridge, where he describes himself as 'idle and unstudious.' He was, however, instrumental in introducing Rugby football to Cambridge. His parentage entitled him to take the honorary degree of M.A. in 1842, after two years' residence. Plans for reading for the bar were abandoned, owing to his liking for a country life. He at first took a farm in the Harrow Vale, twelve miles from London, and after his marriage in 1846 lived near Ely, finally settling for good in the spring of 1848 at Hazelbeach, mid-way between Northampton and Market Harborough, in a house which he rented from his wife's relative Sir Charles Isham. He found his farm at Hazelbeach to be 'dreadfully out of order, foul, wet and exhausted'; but he set to work on its improvement with characteristic energy. He became a regular attendant at the local markets, besides being 'churchwarden, overseer, surveyor of the highways, guardian of the poor, and justice of the peace' (*Reminiscences*, p. 165). The outbreak of cattle plague in 1865 bestirred him to a vehement campaign in his district in defence of the system of slaughter for stamping out the contagion; and he organised a great meeting of agriculturists in London on the subject. An indirect outcome of this gathering was the establishment of the central chamber of agriculture, of which Pell became in 1866 the first chairman. At a bye-election for South Leicestershire in 1867, Pell, owing to his exertions in exterminating the cattle plague, was chosen as conservative candidate, but was beaten by a small majority. In 1868 he was returned, and he represented the constituency until his retirement in 1885. Though nominally a conservative, he was, in the words of his friend, Mr. James Bryce, 'no more of a party man than his sense of party loyalty required. His political opinions might be described as half tory, half radical. The tory views and the radical views were not mixed to make what used to be called a liberal conservative, but remained distinct, leaving him a tory in some points, a radical in others' (*Reminiscences*, introd. p. xliv).

Pell was an authority on questions of poor law, of which he had a wide experience. He was guardian for his own parish of Hazelbeach as early as 1853. In 1873 he moved at his own board of guardians (Brixworth) for a committee to inquire into the mode of administration of outdoor relief in that and other unions, and as the outcome of the committee's report out-door relief was practically abolished in the Brixworth union, with remarkable results. In 1876 he carried an amendment on Lord Sandon's education bill, providing for the abolition of school boards in districts where there were only voluntary schools (H. PAUL, *Hist. of Modern England*, 1905, iii. 413–4). From 1876 to 1889 Pell had a seat as a nominated guardian for St. George's-in-the-East, London, in which parish he had property, and tried to enforce there his views on out-door relief. He failed in his endeavours to induce the House of Commons to consider his proposals (*Hansard*, ccxxx. 1515). But in 1884 he carried against the government by 208 votes to 197 a motion deprecating 'the postponement of further measures of relief acknowledged to be due to ratepayers in counties and boroughs in respect of local charges imposed on them for national services.' On this occasion he made his longest speech in the house, speaking for an hour and a half (*Hansard*, cclxxxvi. 1023). Pell was a prominent figure at poor law conferences, and was chairman of the central conference from 1877 to 1898. He was also an active member of the Northamptonshire county council from its establishment in 1889. Indeed, on all subjects connected with county government, social reform, local taxation, and agricultural improvement he was regarded as an authority both in and out of parliament. In June 1879 he and his friend Clare Sewell Read [q. v. Suppl. II] went, as assistant commissioners to the Duke of Richmond's royal commission on agriculture, to America and Canada to study agricultural questions there. Another inquiry which much interested him was that of the royal commission on the City guilds, of which he was appointed a member at the instance of his friend Sir William Harcourt, who said to Pell that 'he would give him something to keep him quiet for a year or two' (*Reminiscences*, p. 314). He sat also on the royal commissions as to the City parochial charities and the aged poor.

Shortly after his retirement from parliament in 1885 Pell became (30 June 1886) a member of the council of the Royal Agricultural Society, and did excellent work on its 'Journal,' and on its chemical and education committees. He contributed to its 'Journal' two articles on 'The Making of the Land in England' (1887 and 1889) and a biography of Arthur Young (1893), as well as other minor articles and notes. He was a member of the Farmers' Club, which he joined in February 1867, becoming a member of the committee in 1881, and chairman in 1888. He was one of the pioneers of the teaching of agriculture at his old university, and was made hon. LL.D. there when the Royal Agricultural Society met at Cambridge in 1894. In his later years he suffered much from deafness and from his lungs, and wintered at Torquay. There he died on 7 April 1907, and was buried at Hazelbeach.

In 1846 Pell married his cousin, Elizabeth Barbara, daughter of Sir Henry Halford, second baronet (1825–1894), being attired for the occasion 'in puce-coloured kerseymere trousers, straps, and Wellington boots, an embroidered satin waistcoat and a blue dress coat with brass buttons' (*Reminiscences*, p. 139).

He had no children; and on his death a nephew, Albert Julian Pell, succeeded to the family property at Wilburton Manor, Ely, where there hangs a portrait of Pell, painted in 1886 by Miss S. Stevens.

[Pell's Reminiscences (up to 1885), edited after his death by Thomas Mackay, 1908; article in Poor Law Conferences of 1899–1900, by W. Chance; personal knowledge.] E. C.

PEMBER, EDWARD HENRY (1833–1911), lawyer, eldest son of John Edward Rose Pember of Clapham Park, Surrey, by his wife Mary, daughter of Arthur Robson, was born at his father's house on 28 May 1833. He was educated at Harrow, and after reading for a short time with the Rev. T. Elwin, headmaster of Charterhouse School, a noted teacher, he matriculated on 23 May 1850 at Christ Church, Oxford, where he was elected a student in 1854. He took a first class in classical moderations in 1852, and in 1854 he was placed in the first class in literæ humaniores, and in the third class of the newly founded school of law and modern history. He entered as a student of Lincoln's Inn on 2 May 1855, reading in the chambers first of the conveyancer Joseph Burrell and then of George Markham Giffard, afterwards lord justice [q. v.]. Called to the bar on 26 Jan. 1858, he chose the Midland circuit, and laid himself out for common law practice; briefs were slow in coming when a fortunate accident introduced him to the parliamentary bar. For that class of work and tribunal Pember was admirably equipped. His fine presence, his command of flowing classical English, together with his quickness of comprehension and his readiness in repartee, soon made him a prime favourite with the committees of both houses. Edmund Beckett (afterwards Lord Grimthorpe) [q. v. Suppl. II] and George Stovin Venables [q.v.] were then the chiefs of the parliamentary bar, but Pember more than held his own with them, and after they were gone he disputed the lead at Westminster for over thirty years with such formidable rivals as Samuel Pope [q. v. Suppl. II] and (Sir) Ralph Littler [q. v. Suppl. II]. Perhaps the greatest achievement in his forensic career was his conduct of the bill for creating the Manchester Ship Canal, which was passed in July 1885 in the teeth of the most strenuous opposition; Pember's reply for the promoters, which was largely extemporary, was one of the most effective speeches ever delivered in a parliamentary committee room. His speeches as a rule were most carefully prepared, and were fine examples of literary style. His treatment of witnesses was not always adroit, and he was over-prone to argument with experts and men of science; but his straightforwardness gave him the full confidence of those before whom he practised. In April 1897 he appeared as counsel for Cecil Rhodes [q. v. Suppl. II] before the parliamentary committee appointed to investigate the origin and attendant circumstances of the Jameson raid. Pember took silk in 1874, was made a bencher of his Inn in 1876, and served the office of treasurer in 1906–7. He retired from practice in 1903 in full vigour of mind and body. He died after a short illness on 5 April 1911, at his Hampshire home, Vicar's Hill, Lymington, and was buried at Boldre Church, Brockenhurst.

Pember was throughout his life a prominent figure in the social and literary life of London. A brilliant talker, he was one of the most regular and welcome attendants at the dinners of 'The Club.' From 1896 to 1911 he acted as joint secretary of the Dilettanti Society, and in 1909 his portrait was painted for that body by Sir Edward Poynter, R.A. He was an accomplished musician, having studied singing under Perugini and possessing considerable technical theoretical knowledge. In 1910 Pember was elected perpetual secretary of the newly formed academic committee of the Royal Society of Literature. During the days of waiting at the bar he was a constant contributor to the weekly press, and he is generally credited with the famous epigram on Lord Westbury's judgment in the 'Essays and Reviews' case—'Hell dismissed with costs.' Some extracts from a mock Newdigate poem of his, 'On the Feast of Belshazzar' (the subject for 1852, when the prize was awarded to Edwin Arnold), were long current in Oxford. Widely read in general literature and highly critical in taste, he found relaxation and amusement in the making of *vers de société* and of translations and adaptations from the Greek and Latin, especially from Horace and the Greek dramatists. During the latter years of his life his leisure was largely occupied in the composition of classical plays in English, cast in the Attic mould, drawn from scriptural and mythological themes. He had a good dramatic sense and a correct and fastidious ear. He refrained from publication, and confined the circulation of his plays and poems to a fit and cultured audience.

Pember married on 28 August 1861 Fanny, only daughter of William Richardson of Sydney, New South Wales, who survived him. His eldest and only surviving son, Francis William, became fellow of All Souls in 1884 and bursar in 1911.

Besides the picture by Sir Edward Poynter, now in the rooms of the Dilettanti Society, there is a portrait of Pember by Frank Holl, R.A., in the possession of his widow.

Pember 'printed for private distribution': 1. 'Debita Flacco, Echoes of Ode and Epode,' 1891. 2. 'The Voyage of the Phocæans and other Poems, with Prometheus Bound done into English Verse,' 1895. 3. 'Adrastus of Phrygia and other Poems, with the Hippolytus of Euripides done into English Verse,' 1897. 4. 'The Death-Song of Thamyris and other Poems, with the Œdipus of Colonos done into English Verse,' 1899. 5. 'The Finding of Pheidippides and other Poems,' 1901. 6. 'Jephthah's Daughter and other Poems,' 1904. 7. 'Er of Pamphylia and other Poems,' 1908. He contributed also 'Lives of early Italian Musicians' to Sir George Grove's 'Dictionary of Music,' and a searching anonymous criticism of Lord Lovelace's Astarte' to Mr. John Murray's Detractors of Byron' (Roxburghe Club 1906).

[Memoir by W. J. Courthope in Proc. Acad. Committee Royal Soc. of Lit., 1911; The Times, 6 April 1911; Foster's Men at the Bar; Oxf. Univ. Cal.; private information.] J. B. A.

PEMBERTON, THOMAS EDGAR (1849–1905), biographer of the stage, born at Birmingham Heath on 1 July 1849, was eldest son of Thomas Pemberton, J.P., the head of an old-established firm of brass founders in Livery Street, Birmingham. Charles Reece Pemberton [q. v.] belonged to the same old Warwickshire family. Educated at the Edgbaston proprietary schools, Pemberton at nineteen entered his father's counting-house, and in due course gained control of the business of the firm, with which he was connected until 1900. Of literary taste from youth, Pemberton long divided his time between commerce and varied literary endeavours. His industry was unceasing. After the publication of two indifferent novels, 'Charles Lysaght: a Novel devoid of Novelty' (1873) and 'Under Pressure' (1874), he showed some aptitude for fiction in 'A Very Old Question' (3 vols. 1877). There followed 'Born to Blush Unseen' (1879) and an allegorical fairy tale, 'Fairbrass,' written for his children.

At his father's house he met in youth E. A. Sothern, Madge Robertson (Mrs. Kendal), and other players on visits to Birmingham, and he soon tried his hand at the drama. His comedietta 'Weeds,' the first of a long list of ephemeral pieces, mainly farcical, was written for the Kendals, and produced at the Prince of Wales's Theatre, Birmingham, on 16 Nov. 1874. His many plays were rarely seen outside provincial theatres. He came to know Bret Harte, and his best play, 'Sue,' was adapted with Bret Harte's collaboration from the latter's story 'The Judgment of Bolinas Plain.' Originally brought out in America, it was subsequently produced at the Garrick on 10 June 1898. The partnership was continued. 'Held Up,' a four-act play by Harte and Pemberton, was produced at the Worcester theatre on 24 Aug. 1903. One or two unproduced plays written by the two remain in manuscript. On Bret Harte's death in 1902 Pemberton wrote 'Bret Harte: a Treatise and a Tribute.'

In succession to his friend Sam Timmins, Pemberton was the dramatic critic of the

'Birmingham Daily Post' from 1882 until he retired to the country at Broadway in 1900. As a theatrical biographer, Pemberton made his widest reputation, writing memoirs of Edward Askew Sothern (1889); the Kendals (1891); T. W. Robertson (1892); John Hare (1895); Ellen Terry and her sisters (1902); and Sir Charles Wyndham (1905). He was personally familiar with most of his themes, but his biographic method had no literary distinction. An excellent amateur actor, Pemberton frequently lectured on theatrical subjects. In 1889 he was elected a governor of the Shakespeare Memorial theatre, Stratford-on-Avon, and showed much interest in its work. He died after a long illness at his residence, Pye Corner, Broadway, Worcestershire, on 28 Sept. 1905, and was buried in the churchyard there.

Pemberton married on 11 March 1873, in the 'Old Meeting House,' Birmingham, Mary Elizabeth, second daughter of Edward Richard Patie Townley of Edgbaston, who survived him, with two sons and three daughters.

Besides the works cited, Pemberton published 'Dickens's London' (1875), 'Charles Dickens and the Stage' (1888), and 'The Birmingham Theatres: a Local Retrospect' (1889).

[Edgbastonia, vol. xxv. No. 293; Birmingham and Moseley Society Journal, vol. vii. No. 75 (with portrait); Birmingham Daily Mail, 28 Sept. 1905; Birmingham Daily Post, 29 Sept. 1905; private information; personal knowledge and research.] W. J. L.

PENNANT, GEORGE SHOLTO GORDON DOUGLAS-, second Baron Penrhyn (1836–1907), colliery owner. [See Douglas-Pennant.]

PENRHYN, second Baron. [See Douglas-Pennant.]

PENROSE, FRANCIS CRANMER (1817–1903), architect, archæologist, and astronomer, born on 29 Oct. 1817 at Bracebridge near Lincoln, was youngest son of John Penrose, vicar of that place. Both his father and his mother, Elizabeth Penrose, writer for the young under the pseudonym of 'Mrs. Markham,' are noticed separately in this Dictionary. Penrose owed his second name to direct descent through his mother from the sister of Archbishop Cranmer. His aunt Mary Penrose became the wife of Dr. Thomas Arnold [q. v.] of Rugby.

Francis was the original of the 'Mary' in the 'History of England,' by his mother ('Mrs. Markham'). After a few years at Bedford grammar school (1825–9) he passed to the foundation at Winchester College. From early years he had shown a taste for drawing, and on leaving Winchester he went in 1835 to the office of the architect Edward Blore [q. v.], where he worked until 1839. Thereupon, instead of starting architectural practice, he entered Magdalene College, Cambridge, as an undergraduate, and came out tenth senior optime in 1842. With his artistic and mathematical bents he combined repute as an athlete. He thrice rowed in the race against Oxford, in 1840, 1841, and 1842. He was captain of his college boat, which he brought from a low place to nearly head of the river, and was the inventor of the system of charts still in use in both universities for registering the relative positions of crews in the bumping races. More than once he walked in the day from Cambridge to London, and skated from Ely to the Wash. Among his friends while an undergraduate were Charles Kingsley [q. v.], almost a contemporary at Magdalene, Charles Blachford Mansfield [q. v.], John Malcolm Ludlow [q. v. Suppl. II], and John Couch Adams [q. v. Suppl. I], who with George Peacock [q. v.] awakened an interest in astronomy. Through Kingsley he came to know Frederick Denison Maurice [q. v.], and as a young man he saw much of his first cousin Matthew Arnold [q. v. Suppl. I].

In 1842 Penrose was appointed travelling bachelor of the University of Cambridge, and at once set out on an important architectural tour (1842–5). To his skill as a draughtsman he had added command of the art of water-colour, in which he had taken lessons from Peter De Wint [q. v.]. He made his first prolonged halt at Paris, where he visited the observatory, as well as architectural scenes. At Paris, and subsequently at Chartres, Fontainebleau, Sens, Auxerre, Bourges, Avignon, Nismes, and Arles, he sketched and studied industriously. At Rome in 1843 his keen eye criticised the pitch of the pediment of the Pantheon as being 'steeper than I quite like,' a comment which subsequently received justification. Fifty-two years later M. Chedanne of Paris read a paper in London (at a meeting over which Penrose presided), and proved that the pitch of the pediment had been altered from the original design. Penrose stayed six months at Rome, and thence wrote the stipulated Latin letter as travelling bachelor to the University of Cambridge. He chose as his theme the Cathedral of Bourges.

Between June 1843 and the following spring Penrose visited the chief cities of Italy, and after a brief return to England started somewhat reluctantly for Greece. He describes Athens as 'by far the most miserable town of its size I have ever seen' (9 Jan. 1845). But he soon fell under the spell of the 'Pericleian Monuments,' to which his first enthusiasm for Gothic architecture quickly gave way. In August he made his way home through Switzerland, Augsburg, Munich, and Cologne.

Already Penrose realised the importance of exact mensuration to a critical study of Greek architecture. The pamphlet on the subject by John Pennethorne [q. v.] attracted his attention on its publication in 1844. On his arrival in England the Society of Dilettanti had determined to test thoroughly Pennethorne's theories as to the measurements of Greek classical buildings, and they commissioned Penrose to undertake the task in their behalf. In 1846 Penrose was again at Athens. His principal collaborator in the work of measurement there was Thomas Willson of Lincoln. They completed their labours in May 1847. Despite corrections in detail Penrose confirmed in essentials Pennethorne's theories. When in 1878 Pennethorne brought out his 'Geometry and Optics of Ancient Architecture' he adopted with due acknowledgment Penrose's mass of indisputable material.

'Anomalies in the Construction of the Parthenon,' which the Society of Dilettanti published in 1847, was the first result of Penrose's labours, but it was in 1851 that there appeared his monumental work, 'Principles of Athenian Architecture,' of which a more complete edition was issued in 1888. Penrose's exhaustive and minutely accurate measurements finally established that what is apparently parallel or straight in Greek architecture of the best period is generally neither straight nor parallel but curved or inclined. He solved the puzzle which all Vitruvius's commentators had found insoluble by identifying the 'scamilli impares' with those top and bottom blocks of the columns which, by virtue of the inclination of the column or the curvature of stylobate and architrave, are 'unequal' (i.e. they have their upper and lower faces out of parallel). Some important conclusions relating to the Roman temple of Jupiter Olympius at Athens Penrose laid before the Institute of British Architects in 1888.

In 1852 Dean Milman and the chapter appointed Penrose surveyor of St. Paul's Cathedral. The appointment was made with a view to the completion of the interior decoration in accordance with the intentions of Wren. Penrose deemed it necessary to allot, apart from the decorative scheme, 2000*l.* per annum to the maintenance of the fabric, and a public appeal in 1870 provided substantial financial support. Penrose took up the decorative scheme with enthusiasm, and he insisted on respecting his conception of Wren's generous intentions. In the result he soon found himself at variance with the chapter, who favoured a more restricted plan. Nor was he at one with them on the methods of completing the Wellington monument (see STEVENS, ALFRED). Counsels prevailed in which the surveyor was neither consulted nor concerned.

Like Wren himself Penrose found relief from the disappointment in astronomical study, which had already attracted him at Cambridge and in Paris. He was an adept at mechanical inventions, and an instrument for drawing spirals won him a prize at the Great Exhibition of 1851. A theodolite which he had bought in 1852 primarily for use in measurement of buildings, he applied at the suggestion of Dr. G. Boole to such astronomical purposes as accurate determination of orientation and time in connection, for example, with the fixing of sundials. In 1862 came the purchase of a small astronomical telescope which was soon superseded by a larger one with a 5½-inch object-glass (Steinheil), equatorially mounted by Troughton & Simms. In 1866 Penrose, finding the prediction of the time of an occultation of Saturn in the 'Nautical Almanac' inadequate for his purpose, endeavoured with success 'to obtain by graphical construction a more exact correspondence suited to the site' of the observer. He published his results in 1869 in 'The Prediction and Reduction of Occultations and Eclipses' (4to), and the work reached a second edition in 1902.

In 1870 he visited Jerez in the south of Spain to view the total eclipse of the sun with his smaller (2¾-inch) instrument. The observation was spoilt by a cloud, but Penrose made the acquaintance of Professor Charles A. Young of America, whom he met again at Denver in 1878. Penrose's observations on the eclipse of 29 July 1878 were published in the Washington observations (Appendix III). He afterwards extended to comets the graphical method of prediction which he had applied to the moon (cf. his paper before the Royal

Astronomical Society, December 1881, and chapter vi. in G. F. CHAMBERS'S *Handbook of Astronomy*, 4th edit. 3 vols. 1889).

His last astronomical work was a study of the orientation of temples, to which Sir Norman Lockyer directed his attention. Presuming that 'the object sought by the ancients in orienting their temples was to obtain from the stars at their rising or setting, as the case might be, a sufficient warning of the approach of dawn for preparation for the critical moment of sacrifice,' he perceived the importance of calculating the places of certain stars at distant epochs, and the possibility of estimating the age of certain temples by assuming an orientation and calculating the period of variation or apparent movement in the stars due to the precession of the equinoxes. Penrose applied his theory to certain Greek temples (see *Proceedings* and *Philosophic Transactions of Royal Society*), and with Lockyer he worked out a calculation on this basis in relation to Stonehenge (see also *Journal R.I.B.A.* 25 Jan. 1902). He joined the Royal Astronomical Society in 1867, and in 1894 his astronomical researches were recognised by his election as F.R.S.

Penrose's creative work as an architect was incommensurate in quantity with his obvious ability. He built at Cambridge the entrance gate at Magdalene, and a wing at St. John's; at Rugby School he erected the infirmary; at Wren's church, St. Stephen's, Walbrook, he designed the carved choir stalls. The vicarages at Harefield near Uxbridge and at Maids Moreton were his, as also were church restorations at Chilvers Coton and Long Stanton.

When in 1882 the foundation of the British School at Athens was projected, Penrose generously designed the building without fee. It was completed in 1886, when Penrose accepted the directorate for one season, 1886–7. He held the office again in 1890–1. At St. Paul's, where his chief architectural work was done, he designed the choir school, the choir seats and desks, the marble pulpit and stairs, carved oak lobbies at the western entrances of the north transept, the mosaic pavements in the crypt, the Wellington tomb in the crypt, the font and pavement in the south chapel, and the marble memorial to Lord Napier of Magdala. He was also responsible for the removal of the Wellington monument to a new position, the rearrangement of the steps at the west entrance, and the exposure of the remains of the ancient cathedral in the churchyard.

Penrose, whose fellowship of the Royal Institute of British Architects dated from 1848, received the royal gold medal of the institute in 1883 and was president in 1894–6. He became F.S.A. in 1898, when he was elected antiquary to the Royal Academy. He was made in 1884 one of the first honorary fellows of Magdalene College, Cambridge, and in 1898 he became a Litt.D. of his university as well as an hon. D.C.L. of Oxford. He was a knight of the order of the Saviour of Greece.

His own house, Colebyfield, Wimbledon (which had a small observatory), was designed by himself. There, where he resided for forty years, he died on 15 Feb. 1903. He was buried at Wimbledon. He married in 1856 Harriette, daughter of Francis Gibbes, surgeon, of Harewood, Yorkshire. His wife predeceased him by twelve days. He left a son, Dr. Francis G. Penrose, and four daughters, the eldest of whom, Emily, became successively principal of Bedford College, Holloway College, and Somerville College, Oxford.

Penrose's portrait at the Royal Institute of British Architects is one of the most characteristic works of J. S. Sargent, R.A. (a copy is at Magdalene College). A memorial tablet was placed in the crypt of St. Paul's Cathedral, chiefly by architectural friends.

[R.I.B.A. Journal, vol. x. 3rd series, 1903, p. 337, article by Mr. J. D. Crace, also pp. 213–4; Royal Society Obituary Notices, vol. i. pt. 3, 1904, p. 305; information from Dr. Francis G. Penrose.] P. W.

PERCY, HENRY ALGERNON GEORGE, EARL PERCY (1871–1909), politician and traveller, born at 25 (now 28) Grosvenor Square, London, on 21 Jan. 1871, was eldest son of Henry George Percy, Earl Percy, who became seventh duke of Northumberland in succession to his father in 1899. As Lord Warkworth he won at Eton the prize for English verse, and at Christ Church, Oxford, first class honours in classical moderations in 1891 and literæ humaniores in 1893, his class in the latter school being reputed one of the best of the year. He also obtained at Oxford in 1892 the Newdigate prize for English verse on the subject of St. Francis of Assisi, and his recitation of his poem in the Sheldonian Theatre was long remembered as one of the most impressive of these performances. In 1895 he contested Berwick-on-Tweed as a conservative without success against Sir Edward Grey, but later in the year was chosen at a bye-election for South Kensington, which he represented continuously till his death. Marked out from the first as a debater of ability, industry, and independence, he soon became conspicuous in a group of conservatives who sometimes adopted a critical attitude towards their leaders, and, in view of his future prospects, few felt surprise when, on Mr. Balfour becoming prime minister in July 1902, Earl Percy (as he had been styled since his father's succession to the dukedom in 1899) was appointed parliamentary under-secretary for India. Approving himself in this office by the immense pains which he took to master matters proper to his department, he passed to foreign affairs as under-secretary of state on the reconstruction of Mr. Balfour's cabinet in October 1903. Since his chief, Lord Lansdowne, was in the upper house, Lord Percy had occasion to appear prominently in the commons and to prove both his capacity and his independence, especially in dealing with Near Eastern matters, which had long engaged his interest, and had induced him once and again to visit Turkish soil.

Travel in the Near East divided his interests with politics. In 1895 he first visited the Ottoman dominions, when he returned with Lord Encombe from Persia though Baghdad and Damascus. He went back to Turkey in 1897 to make with Sir John Stirling Maxwell and Mr. Lionel Holland a journey through Asia Minor to Erzerum, Van, the Nestorian valleys, and the wilder parts of central Kurdistan. He returned by Mosul, Diarbekr, and Aleppo, and published his experiences in 'Notes of a Diary in Asiatic Turkey' (1898), a volume which showed strong but discriminating Turcophilism, sensitiveness to the scenic grandeur of the regions traversed, and growing interest in their history and archæology. True to the traditions of his family, he began to collect antiques, particularly cylinder seals; and subsequently extending his interest to Egypt, he applied himself to the study of hieroglyphics.

His most important tour in Turkey was undertaken in 1899. He then made his way with his cousin, Mr. Algernon Heber Percy, through Asia Minor and up the course of the southern source of the Euphrates to Bitlis and his Nestorian friends of Hakkiari. Thence he went on into the Alps of Jelu Dagh, traversing a little-known part of Kurdistan near the Turco-Persian border, and passed by Neri to Altin Keupri, whence he descended the Lesser Zab and Tigris on a raft to Baghdad. On his way out he had been received by Sultan Abdul Hamid. His second book, 'The Highlands of Asiatic Turkey' (1901), was inspired by his old sympathy for Turks, but also by a deepened sense of the evils of Hamidism, whose downfall he foresaw. Intolerant equally of Armenian and of Russian aspirations, he advocated agreement with Germany on Ottoman affairs.

He was in Macedonia in 1902, when appointed to office, and returned home through a wild part of North Albania, although not followed by the large Turkish escort which the solicitude of the Porte had prescribed for him. Thereafter parliamentary duties prevented him from making other than short recess tours, during one of which he took a motor-boat up the Nile, to practise for a projected cruise on the Euphrates, which he did not live to achieve. On Macedonian and indeed all Ottoman affairs his authority was acknowledged, although his views were not always welcome to the advocates of the *rayah* nationalists. An effective and thoughtful though not ambitious or frequent speaker, and a forceful but reserved personality, he had come to be regarded as a future leader in his party, when, to general sorrow, he died of pneumonia on 30 Dec. 1909, while passing through Paris on his way to Normandy. He was unmarried. He became a trustee of the National Portrait Gallery in 1901, and received in 1907 the degree of D.C.L. from the University of Durham.

[The Times, 31 Dec. 1909; private information.] D. G. H.

PERKIN, Sir WILLIAM HENRY (1838–1907), chemist, born on 12 March 1838 at King David's Lane, Shadwell, was youngest of three sons of George Fowler Perkin (1802–1865), a builder and contractor, by his wife Sarah Cuthbert. With his two brothers and three sisters he inherited a pronounced musical talent from his father. William Henry, after early education at a private school, was sent in 1851 to the City of London school, where his native aptitude for chemical study was effectively encouraged by his master, Thomas Hall. In 1853 he entered the Royal College of Chemistry as a student under Hofmann. By the end of his second year he had, under Hofmann's guidance, carried out his first piece of research, a study of the action of cyanogen chloride on naphthylamine, the results of which he announced in a paper read before the Chemical Society. In 1857 he was appointed an honorary assistant to his professor.

In 1854 he fitted up a laboratory in

his own home, where he prosecuted independent research. Here, in conjunction with Mr. (now Sir) A. H. Church, he soon discovered the first representative of the group of azo-dyes, namely, 'azodinaphthyldiamine' or, in modern nomenclature, 'aminoazonaphthalene.' This substance was patented at a later date (Eng. Pat. 893 of 1863) and had a limited use as a dyestuff. During the Easter vacation of 1856, with the idea of synthesising quinine, Perkin tried, with a negative result, the experiment of oxidising a salt of allyltoluidine with potassium dichromate. On repeating the experiment with aniline, however, he obtained a dark-coloured precipitate which proved to be a colouring matter possessed of dyeing properties, and was the first aniline dye to be discovered. Encouraged by the favourable report made on his new product by practical dyers and especially by Messrs. Pullar of Perth, Perkin resigned his position at the Royal College of Chemistry and entered on the career of an industrial chemist. Assisted by his father and his elder brother, Thomas D. Perkin, he opened a chemical factory at Greenford Green. The new dye was patented (Eng. Pat. 1984 of 1856), and at the end of 1858 it was first manufactured at Perkin's works under the name of 'Aniline Purple' or 'Tyrian Purple.' The name 'Mauve,' by which it was afterwards generally known, was at once given to it in France. Perkin straightway devoted himself to developing processes of manufacturing his raw material (aniline) and to improvements in the methods of silk dyeing, as well as of suitable mordants for enabling the dyestuff to be applied to the cotton fibre. To Perkin's discovery of the first of the aniline dyes was ultimately due the supersession of vegetable by chemical dye-stuffs. In recognition of his invention the 'Société Industrielle de Mulhouse' awarded him, in 1859, a silver medal, and afterwards a gold one.

In 1868 the German chemists Graebe and Liebermann showed that 'alizarin,' the 'Turkey red' dyestuff or colouring matter of the madder-root, was a derivative of the coal-tar product anthracene and not of naphthalene, as had hitherto been believed. They then patented in Germany and in Great Britain a process for the manufacture of 'alizarin' which was too costly to hold out much hope of successful competition with the madder plant, requiring, as it did, the use of bromine. With the object of cheapening this process, Perkin in 1869 introduced two new methods for the manufacture of artificial alizarin, one starting from dichloroanthracene and the other, which is still in use, from the sulphonic acid of anthraquinone. This branch of the coal-tar industry developed rapidly, and, in spite of some competing effort of German manufacturers, the English market was almost entirely held by Perkin until the end of 1873. Perkin delivered before the Society of Arts in 1879 two lectures, which were published under the title 'The history of alizarin and allied colouring matters, and their production from coal-tar.' Meanwhile, in 1873, when the increasing demand for artificial alizarin rendered imperative an enlarged plant at Perkin's Greenford Green works, he transferred the concern to the firm of Brooke, Simpson & Spiller, and, retiring after eighteen years from the industry, thenceforth devoted himself to pure chemical research.

Concurrently with his industrial work Perkin had maintained a strong interest in pure chemistry, and had already published many important papers in the 'Transactions of the Chemical Society,' where his contributions finally numbered ninety. In 1858, in conjunction with Duppa, he discovered that aminoacetic acid could be obtained by heating bromoacetic acid with ammonia, and in 1867 he published a description of his method of synthesising unsaturated organic acids, known as the 'Perkin synthesis.' Next year the synthesis of coumarin, the odorous substance contained in Tonka bean, etc., was announced, and the continuation of this work, after his retirement from the industry, led to his celebrated discovery of the synthesis of cinnamic acid from benzaldehyde. Scientific papers on the chemistry of 'Aniline Purple' or 'mauve' were also published in the 'Proceedings of the Royal Society' in 1863 and 1864 and in the 'Transactions of the Chemical Society' in 1879. In 1881 he first drew attention to the magnetic rotatory power of some of the compounds which he had prepared in his researches, and mainly to the study of this property as applied to the investigation of the constitution or structure of chemical molecules he devoted the rest of his life.

Perkin's services were widely recognised. Having joined the Chemical Society in 1856, he held the office of president from 1883 to 1885, and received the society's Longstaff medal in 1888. He was elected F.R.S. in 1866 and received from the Royal Society a royal medal in 1879, and the Davy medal in 1889. He was president of the Society of Chemical Industry in 1884–5, receiving the gold medal of the society in 1898, and at his death was president of the Society of Dyers and Colourists. The Society of Arts conferred on him the Albert medal in 1890, and the Institution of Gas Engineers the Birmingham medal in 1892. He also received honorary doctorates from the universities of Würzburg (1882), St. Andrews (1891), and Manchester (1904).

In July 1906 the jubilee was celebrated universally of Perkin's discovery of 'mauve,' the first aniline dye, which had created the important coal-tar dyeing industry and had revolutionised industrial processes in varied directions. Perkin was knighted and received honorary degrees of doctor from the universities of Oxford, Leeds, Heidelberg, Columbia (New York), Johns Hopkins (Baltimore), and Munich Technical High School. He was presented with the Hofmann medal by the German Chemical Society and the Lavoisier medal by the French Chemical Society. A sum of 2700*l.*, subscribed by chemists from all countries, was handed to the Chemical Society as the 'Perkin Memorial Fund,' to be applied to the encouragement of research in subjects relating to the coal-tar and allied industries. The 'Perkin medal' for distinguished services to chemical industry was instituted by the Society of Dyers and Colourists, and the American memorial committee founded a Perkin medal for American chemists.

Perkin died at Sudbury on 14 July 1907, and was buried at Christ Church graveyard, Harrow. He was twice married: (1) on 13 Sept. 1859 to Jemima Harriett, daughter of John Lisset; she died on 27 Nov. 1862; (2) on 8 Feb. 1866 to Alexandrine Caroline, daughter of Ivan Herman Mollwo; she survived him. He had three sons and four daughters. His eldest son, William Henry Perkin, Ph.D. (Würzburg), Hon. Sc.D. (Cantab.), Hon. LL.D. (Edin.), F.R.S., professor of organic chemistry at Manchester University; the second son, Arthur George Perkin, F.R.S.; and the youngest son, Frederick Mollwo Perkin, Ph.D., have all distinguished themselves in the same department of science as their father.

Perkin's portrait in his robe as LL.D. of the university of St. Andrews, painted by Henry Grant in 1898, is on the wall at the Leathersellers' Hall in St. Helen's Place, of which company he was master in 1896; another portrait by Arthur Stockdale Cope, R.A., presented to him on the jubilee celebration of 1906, is destined for the National Portrait Gallery. There is also an engraved portrait by Arthur J. Williams in the British Museum of Portraits, South Kensington collection, and a marble bust by F. W. Pomeroy, A.R.A., is in the rooms of the Chemical Society at Burlington House.

[Trans. Chemical Society, 1908, 93, 2214–2257, and Roy. Soc. Proc. 80A, 1908 (memoirs by R. Meldola); Jubilee of the Discovery of Mauve and of the Foundation of the Coal-tar Colour Industry by Sir W. H. Perkin, ed. by R. Meldola, A. G. Green and J. C. Cain, 1906.]

J. C. C.

PERKINS, Sir ÆNEAS (1834–1901), general, colonel commandant royal engineers (late Bengal), born at Lewisham, Kent, on 19 May 1834, was sixth son in a family of thirteen children of Charles Perkins, merchant, of London, by his wife Jane Homby, daughter of Charles William Barkley (*b.* 1759), after whom Barkley Sound and Island in the Pacific are named. His grandfather was John Perkins of Camberwell, a partner in Barclay & Perkins's Brewery. A brother George, in the Bengal artillery, was killed at the battle of the Hindun before Delhi in 1857.

Educated at Dr. Prendergast's school at Lewisham and at Stoton and Mayor's school at Wimbledon, where Frederick (afterwards Earl) Roberts, his lifelong friend, was his schoolfellow, Æneas entered the military seminary of the East India Company at Addiscombe on 1 Feb. 1850, in the same batch as Roberts. At Addiscombe he showed ability in mathematics, and was a leader in all sports. Obtaining a commission as second lieutenant in the Bengal engineers on 12 Dec. 1851, he, after professional instruction at Chatham, arrived at Fort William, Calcutta, on 16 Jan. 1854.

As assistant engineer in the public works department Perkins was soon employed on irrigation work on the Bari Doab Canal in the Punjab. Promoted first lieutenant on 17 Aug. 1856, he was transferred in November to the Ambala division, and in the following May, when the Mutiny began, joined the force under General George Anson [q. v.], commander-in-chief in India, which marched to the relief of Delhi. Perkins was present at the battle of Badli-ki-serai on 8 June, and at the subsequent seizure of the Delhi Ridge. He did much good work during the early part of the siege. On 11–12 June he was employed in the construction of a mortar battery, known as 'Perkins's Battery'; on the 17th he took part in the destruction of a rebel battery and the capture of its guns; and on 14 July in the repulse of the sortie; but, wounded a few days later near the walls of Delhi, he was sent to Ambala. Although he soon recovered from the actual wound, he was forced by broken health to remain there until March 1858, when he was invalided home. For his services in the Mutiny campaign he received the medal and clasp.

On returning to India in 1859, Perkins held various offices in Bengal, including those of assistant principal of the Civil Engineering College at Calcutta, assistant consulting engineer for the railways, and executive engineer of the Berhampur Division. On 12 March 1862 he was promoted second captain and in the autumn of 1864 took part as field engineer in the Bhutan Expedition, during which he was three times mentioned in despatches for gallant conduct, and was recommended for a brevet majority. Towards the end of the expedition he was appointed chief engineer of the force. A strong recommendation for the Victoria Cross for conspicuous gallantry in storming a stockade at the summit of the Baru Pass was rejected on account of the delay in sending it in. For his services in Bhutan, Perkins received the medal and a brevet majority on 30 June 1865.

Perkins was next stationed at Morshedabad as executive engineer, and in 1866 was transferred to the Darjeeling division in the same grade. Promoted first captain in his corps on 31 Oct. 1868, two years later he was sent to the North West provinces as superintending engineer, and in April 1872 he was transferred in the same grade to the military works branch. He became regimental major on 5 July 1872, brevet lieut.-colonel 29 Dec. 1874, and regimental lieut.-colonel on 1 Oct. 1877.

A year later Perkins was selected for active service in Afghanistan at the request of Major-general (afterwards Field-marshal Earl) Roberts, commanding the Kuram field force. He was appointed commanding royal engineer of that force. During the operations in front of the Peiwar Kotal he skilfully reconnoitred the enemy's position, and selected a site from which the mountain battery could shell the Afghan camp. The works carried on under his control in the Kuram Valley greatly facilitated the subsequent advance on Kabul. He was mentioned in despatches, and was created a C.B. in 1879. On the conclusion of peace with Sirdar Yakub Khan, Perkins remained in the Kuram Valley, laying out a cantonment proposed to be formed at Shalofzan, but on the news of the massacre of Sir Louis Cavagnari [q. v.] and his escort at Kabul an immediate advance was made by the Kuram column, and Perkins was present at the victory of Charasiab and the entry into Kabul on 8 Oct. 1879. He was again mentioned in despatches.

The work which then devolved upon the engineers was extremely heavy. The Sherpur cantonment and Bala Hissar had to be repaired, and a new line of communication with India viâ Jalalabad had to be opened out. The Sherpur cantonment was rendered defensible by the beginning of December and none too soon. A few days later the Afghans assembled in such overwhelming numbers that Sir Frederick Roberts had to assemble the whole of his force within the walls of Sherpur. Under Perkins's direction emplacements and abattis were rapidly constructed, blockhouses were built on the Bimaru heights, walls and villages dangerously near the cantonment were blown down and levelled, and a second line of defence within the enclosure was improvised. On 23 Dec. the enemy delivered their assault in great numbers. It was repulsed, and a counter attack dispersed the Afghans to their homes. Perkins was mentioned in despatches and promoted brevet colonel on 29 Dec. 1879.

Steps were now taken by Perkins to render the position at Kabul absolutely secure. A fort and blockhouse were erected on Siah Sang, the Bala Hissar and the Asmai Heights were fortified, Sherpur was converted into a strongly entrenched camp, bridges were thrown across the Kabul river, the main roads were made passable for artillery, and many new roads were laid out. The works completed during the next seven months, chiefly by means of unskilled Afghan labour, comprised ten forts, fifteen detached posts, three large and several small bridges, 4000 yards of loopholed parapet, 45 miles of road, and quarters for 8000 men. At the end of July 1880 the news of the Maiwand disaster reached Kabul, and Perkins accompanied Sir Frederick Roberts as commanding royal engineer with the picked force of 10,000 men in the famous march to Kandahar. He was present at the battle of Kandahar on 1 Sept. 1880 and soon afterwards returned to India. He received the medal with four clasps and bronze decoration, and was made an aide-de-camp to the Queen.

Rejoining the military works department, Perkins was appointed superintending engineer at Rawal Pindi, and from April to July 1881 he officiated as inspector-general of military works. After a furlough lasting two years, Perkins was appointed chief engineer of the Central Provinces, was transferred in the same capacity in April 1886 to the Punjab, and on 10 March 1887 was promoted major-general. In May 1889 he vacated his appointment in the military works department on attaining the age of fifty-five years, and in 1890 was selected by Lord Roberts, then commander-in-chief in India, to command the Oudh division; but this command was cut short by his promotion to lieutenant-general on 1 April 1891, and he returned to England. Promoted to be general on 1 April 1895, and made a colonel commandant of his corps on the same date, he was two years later created K.C.B. He died in London on 22 Dec. 1901, and was buried at Brookwood cemetery. Lord Roberts wrote of him with admiring affection, crediting him with 'quick perception, unflagging energy, sound judgment, tenacity of purpose and indomitable pluck.' Perkins figures in de Langé's picture of the march to Kandahar.

He married in 1863 Janette Wilhelmina (who survived him), daughter of Werner Cathray, formerly 13th light dragoons, by whom he left two sons—Major Arthur Ernest John Perkins, R.A., and Major Æneas Charles Perkins, 40th Pathans, and three daughters, two of whom are married.

[Royal Engineers' Records; obituary notice, The Times, 23 Dec. 1901; memoir in Royal Engineers' Journal, June 1903, by Field-marshal Earl Roberts; private information.]
R. H. V.

PEROWNE, EDWARD HENRY (1826–1906), Master of Corpus Christi College, Cambridge, younger brother of John James Stewart Perowne [q. v. Suppl. II], was born at Burdwan, Bengal, on 8 Jan. 1826. After private education he was admitted pensioner of Corpus Christi College, Cambridge, in 1846 and scholar in 1847; he was Porson prizeman in 1848, members' prizeman in 1849 and 1852, and senior classic in 1850. He graduated B.A. in 1850, proceeding M.A. in 1853, B.D. in 1860, D.D. in 1873. He was admitted *ad eundem* (M.A.) at Oxford in 1857. Ordained deacon in 1850 and priest in 1851, he was curate of Maddermarket, Norfolk (1850–1). Elected fellow and tutor of Corpus in 1858, he became Master in 1879. He was Whitehall preacher (1864–6); Hulsean lecturer in 1866, examining chaplain to the bishop of St. Asaph (1874–88); prebendary of St. Asaph (1877–90); vice-chancellor of Cambridge University (1879–81); hon. chaplain to Queen Victoria (1898–1900), and chaplain-in-ordinary (1900–1), examining chaplain to the bishop of Worcester (1891–1901). Devoted to his college and university, a sound disciplinarian, a man of many friendships and wide interests, Perowne refused high preferment and was long one of the most conspicuous figures in the academic and social life of Cambridge. He was a strong evangelical, and in politics a somewhat rigid conservative. He died unmarried at Cambridge, after a long illness, on 5 Feb. 1906, and was buried at Grantchester. A portrait of Perowne, painted in 1885 by Rudolf Lehmann, is at Corpus Christi College, Cambridge.

His principal works were: 1. 'The Christian's Daily Life, a Life of Faith,' 1860. 2. 'Corporate Responsibility,' 1862. 3. 'Counsel to Undergraduates on entering the University,' 1863. 4. 'The Godhead of Jesus,' 1867. 5. 'Commentary on Galatians' ('Cambridge Bible for Schools'), 1890. 6. 'Savonarola,' 1900.

[The Times, 6 Feb. 1906; Guardian, 7 Feb. 1906; Record, 9 Feb. 1906; Cambridge Review, 15 Feb. 1906 (by C. W. Moule); Crockford's Clerical Directory; Cambridge Univ. Calendar; cf. Charles Whibley's In Cap and Gown (1889), p. 326.] A. R. B.

PEROWNE, JOHN JAMES STEWART (1823–1904), bishop of Worcester, born at Burdwan, Bengal, on 13 March 1823, was eldest of three sons of the Rev. John Perowne, a missionary of the Church Missionary Society, by his wife, Eliza Scott of Heacham, Norfolk. His brothers were Edward Henry Perowne [q.v. Suppl. II] and Thomas Thomason Perowne, archdeacon of Norwich from 1898 to 1910. The family is of Huguenot origin. From Norwich grammar school Perowne won a scholarship at Corpus Christi College, Cambridge. He was Bell University scholar in 1842; members' prizeman in 1844, 1846, and 1847; Crosse scholar in 1845; Tyrwhitt scholar in 1848. He graduated B.A. in 1845, proceeding M.A. in 1848, B.D. in 1856, and D.D. in 1873. In 1845 he became assistant master at Cheam school; was ordained deacon in 1847 and priest in 1848; and served the curacy of Tunstead, Norfolk, 1847–9. In 1849 he became a master at King Edward's school, Birmingham; and in 1849 was elected to a fellowship at Corpus Christi College, Cambridge. For a time he served his college as assistant tutor, whilst also lecturing at King's College, London, and acting as assistant preacher at Lincoln's Inn. He examined for the classical tripos in 1851 and 1852, and was select preacher in 1853, an office he also filled in 1861, 1873, 1876, 1879, 1882, and 1897.

From 1862 till 1872 Perowne worked in Wales. He was vice-principal of St. David's College, Lampeter (1862–72); cursal prebendary of St. David's (1867–72); canon of Llandaff (1869–1878); and rector of Llandisilio, Montgomeryshire (1870–71). Meanwhile his commentary on the Psalms (1864) made his name as an Old Testament scholar, and in 1870 he was chosen one of the Old Testament revision company. In 1868 he had become Hulsean lecturer, and in 1872 he returned to Cambridge. From 1873 to 1875 he held a fellowship at Trinity; he was Lady Margaret preacher in 1874, and Whitehall preacher from 1874 to 1876; in 1875 he succeeded Joseph Barber Lightfoot [q. v.] as Hulsean professor, and held office until 1878. For the same period (1875–1878) he was one of the honorary chaplains to Queen Victoria.

In 1878 Perowne was appointed dean of Peterborough. He developed the cathedral services, carried on the restoration of the fabric, and cultivated friendly relations with nonconformists. In 1881 he was appointed to the Ecclesiastical Courts Commission, and was one of seven commissioners who signed a protest against the exercise by the bishop of an absolute veto on proceedings. In 1889 he aided in founding a body known as 'Churchmen in Council,' which aimed at uniting 'moderate' churchmen in a policy regarding ritual; he explained the aim of the society by issuing in the same year a proposal for authorising both the maximum and the minimum interpretation of the Ornaments Rubric, which was widely discussed but led to no results.

Perowne was consecrated bishop of Worcester in Westminster Abbey on 2 Feb. 1891. He obtained the appointment of a suffragan bishop, created a new archdeaconry, and summoned a diocesan conference. In 1892 he presided at some sessions of an informal conference on reunion of all English protestants held at Grindelwald, and at an English church service there administered the Holy Communion to nonconformists, an act which provoked much criticism. The church congress, hitherto excluded from the diocese, met at Birmingham in 1893, when the bishop announced his assent to the division of his diocese, and his willingness to contribute to the stipend of the new see 500*l.* a year from the income of Worcester. This was afterwards made contingent on his being allowed to give up Hartlebury Castle, to which the ecclesiastical commissioners refused consent. Attacked in the Birmingham press for his action in the matter in 1896, Perowne was presented with an address of approval by 60 beneficed clergy of three rural deaneries. He resigned the see in 1901, and retired to Southwick, near Tewkesbury, where he died on 6 Nov. 1904. The Worcester diocese was divided under Perowne's successor and the see of Birmingham founded in 1905.

Perowne married in 1862 Anna Maria, daughter of Humphrey William Woolrych, serjeant-at-law, by whom he had four sons and one daughter, all of whom survived him.

Though a life-long evangelical, Perowne took a line independent of his party in regard to Biblical criticism, home reunion, and proposals for meeting ritual difficulties. As a bishop he accepted a difficult see late in life, but showed himself an industrious, capable administrator. There is a portrait of the bishop by the Hon. John Collier in the hall of Corpus Christi College, Cambridge, and another by Weigall at Hartlebury Castle.

Perowne's main work was the translation of and commentary on the Psalms (1864), of which a sixth edition appeared in 1886. His Hulsean lectures on Immortality were published in 1868. In acting as general editor of the 'Cambridge Bible for Schools' (1877, &c.), he directed a work of much greater importance than its title suggests. He also edited Thomas Rogers on the 'Catholic Doctrine of the Church of England' (for the Parker Society, 1854); 'Remains of Connop Thirlwall, Bishop of St. David's' (1877); 'The Letters, Literary and Theological, of Connop Thirlwall' (1881); 'The Cambridge Greek Testament for Schools' (1881).

[The Times, 8 Nov. 1904; Record, 11 Nov. 1904; Lowndes, Bishops of the Day; Report of the Ecclesiastical Courts Commission, 1883; Report of the Birmingham Church Congress, 1893; private information.] A. R. B.

PERRY, WALTER COPLAND (1814–1911), schoolmaster and archæologist, born in Norwich on 24 July 1814, was second son of Isaac Perry (1777–1837), who was at first a congregational minister at Cherry Lane, Norwich (1802–14), then a unitarian minister, Ipswich (1814–25) and at Edinburgh (1828–30), and afterwards a schoolmaster at Liverpool. Walter's mother was Elizabeth, daughter of John Dawson Copland. He had his early education from his father, a fine scholar. In 1831 he was entered, as Walter Coupland Perry, at Manchester College, then at York (now at Oxford), remaining till 1836. He distinguished himself as a classical scholar, and on the advice of John Kenrick [q. v.], who had studied at Göttingen, he went thither in 1836, gaining (25 August 1837) the degree of Ph.D. with the highest honours. In his ninetieth year he received from this university, unsolicited, a document recording his services to letters (16 Nov. 1903). Returning to York, he supplied (1837–8) Kenrick's place as classical tutor. His first publication consisted of two letters on 'German Universities,' contributed to the 'Christian Reformer' (1837). From 1838 to 1844 he was minister at George's Meeting, Exeter, as colleague with Henry Acton [q. v.]. His pulpit services had more of a scholarly than a popular character. In 1844 he conformed to the Anglican church as a layman; his 'Prayer Bell' (1843) suggests that his views were more evangelical than was common in his previous denomination.

On 12 January 1844 he entered as a student at the Middle Temple, but was not called to the bar till 31 Jan. 1851. Settling as a schoolmaster at Bonn (end of 1844) he obtained great reputation as a teacher, in which capacity he was ably seconded by an admirable wife. On 17 Sept. 1860, Perry, along with nine other English residents at Bonn, was put on trial in the Bonn police court in consequence of their published protest against language used by the public prosecutor in presenting a charge against Captain Macdonald, arising out of a dispute at the railway station on 12 Sept. On 24 Sept. Perry, who stated during the trial that he 'had been in the habit of acting as the organ and representative of the English visitors at Bonn,' was sentenced to a fine of 100 thalers, or five weeks' imprisonment in default; the sentence was not carried out, owing to the general amnesty on the death of Frederick William IV (1 Jan. 1861). Among Perry's pupils were Edward Robert Bulwer, first earl of Lytton [q. v.], Sir Francis Bertie, British ambassador in Paris, and Sir Eric Barrington. The Crown Prince Frederick, who was, through the late Prince Consort, brought into connection with Perry in 1852, twice gave him his portrait, and at Buckingham Palace in 1887 produced the English Prayer Book which Perry had given him in 1867.

Returning to this country in 1875, Perry settled in London, where he was a member of the Athenæum Club, and employed his leisure in the production of works on classical and mediæval subjects. On 29 April 1876 his former pupils made a large presentation of plate to Dr. and Mrs. Perry. By his efforts, initiated at a meeting in Grosvenor House on 16 May 1877, followed by his paper 'On the Formation of a Gallery of Casts from the Antique in London' (1878), he succeeded in furnishing the country with a large collection of casts, installed at first in a special gallery at the South Kensington Museum. He strongly resented a rearrangement by which they were relegated to a badly lighted gallery, and welcomed their transference to the British Museum.

Perry, who had great charm of manner, was a mountaineer, an excellent horseman, a sportsman with rod and gun, and a good amateur actor. He retained his eyesight and hearing to the last. On 21 June 1904, anticipating his ninetieth birthday, he entertained at dinner a number of his pupils. He lived over seven years longer, dying at his residence, 25 Manchester Square, London, W., on 28 Dec. 1911; he was buried in Hendon parish churchyard. He married (1) on 23 June 1841 Hephzibah Elizabeth (*d.* 1880), second daughter of Samuel Shaen of Crix Hall, Hatfield Peverel, Essex, by whom he had five sons, who all survived him, and one daughter (*d.* 1898); (2) in 1889 Evelyn Emma, daughter of Robert Stopford, who survived him. His portrait was painted in water-colour and in oils; both are in the possession of his widow.

Perry's period of authorship covered no less than seventy-one years, his literary energy being maintained to the age of ninety-four. He published: 1. 'A Prayer Bell for the Universal Church . . . Reflections preparatory to . . . Prayer . . . Addresses . . . for . . . Holy Communion,' 1843, 16mo. 2. 'German University Education,' 1845, 12mo; 2nd edit. 1846, 12mo (expanded from letters (1837) in the 'Christian Reformer'). 3. 'The Franks . . . to the Death of King Pepin,' 1857. 4. 'Greek and Roman Sculpture: a Popular Introduction,' 1882 (illustrated). 5. 'A Descriptive Catalogue of . . . Casts from the Antique in the South Kensington Museum,' 1884, 1887. 6. 'Walter Stanhope,' 1888 (a novel published under the pseudonym 'John Copland'). 7. 'The Women of Homer,' 1898 (illustrated). 8. 'The Revolt of the Horses,' 1898 (a story, suggested by Swift's 'Houyhnhnms'). 9. 'The Boy's Odyssey,' 1901, 1906. 10. 'The Boy's Iliad,' 1902. 11. 'Sancta Paula: a Romance of the Fourth Century,' 1902. 12. 'Sicily in Fable, History, Art and Song,' 1908 (maps). He translated from the German H. C. L. von Sybel's 'History of the French Revolution,' 1867–9, 4 vols. Some works of fiction additional to the above were published without his name.

[The Times, 1 and 3 Jan. 1912; Christian Life, 6 Jan. 1912; Browne, Hist. Cong. Norf. and Suff., 1877, pp. 271, 392; Hist. Account, St. Mark's Chapel, Edinburgh, 1908; Roll of Students, Manchester College, 1868; Foster, Men at the Bar, 1885, p. 361 (needs correction); Trial of the English Residents at Bonn, 1861; information from Rev. T. L. Marshall, Exeter, Rev. J. Collins Odgers, Liverpool, and Col. Ottley Lane Perry.] A. G.

PETIT, Sir DINSHAW MANOCKJEE, first baronet (1823–1901), Parsi merchant and philanthropist, born at Bombay on 30 June 1823, was elder of two sons of Manockjee Nasarwanji Petit (1803–59), merchant, by his wife Bai Humabai (1809–51), daughter of J. D. Mooghna. In 1805 his grandfather, Nasarwanji Cowasjee Bomanjee, migrated from Surat to Bombay, where he acted as agent to French vessels and those of the East India Company. On account of his small stature his French clients gave him the cognomen of Petit, and, in accordance with Parsi custom, this became the family surname, though with Anglicised pronunciation. Dinshaw went at the age of nine to a school kept by a pensioned sergeant named Sykes, and later to a more ambitious seminary kept by Messrs. Mainwaring and Corbet. At the age of seventeen he obtained a clerkship on a monthly salary of Rs. 15 (then the equivalent of 1*l.* 10*s.*) in the mercantile office of Dirom, Richmond and Co., of which his father was native manager. Subsequently his father built up a large broker's business, in which Dinshaw and his younger brother, Nasarwanjee, became partners in 1852, carrying it on after their father's death in May 1859 till 1864, when they divided a fortune of about 25 lakhs of rupees and separated by mutual consent.

Meanwhile Dinshaw inaugurated the cotton manufacturing industry which has made Bombay the Manchester of India. A cotton mill was started for the first time in Bombay in 1854 by another Parsi, Cowasjee Nanabhai Davur, but it spun yarns only. In 1855 Dinshaw induced his father to erect a similar mill with additional machinery for weaving cloth. This mill commenced work as the Oriental Spinning and Weaving Mill, in 1857. In 1860 he and his brother started the Manockjee Petit mill, which they converted into a joint-stock company concern.

During the 'share mania' of 1861 and 1865, when the ruin of the cotton industry of Lancashire by the American civil war excited wild speculation in Bombay, Dinshaw Petit maintained his self-control and reaped colossal gains. Other mills were soon built by him, or came under his management, and he led the way in the manufacture of hosiery, damask, other fancy cloths, sewing thread, and also in machine dyeing on a large scale. Before his death he had the chief interest in six joint-stock mills aggregating nearly a quarter of a million spindles and 2340 looms, and employing some 10,000 persons. He is thus mainly responsible for the conversion of the town and island of Bombay into a great industrial centre.

Dinshaw Petit served on the board of the bank of Bombay; was a justice of the peace for the city, and for a short time a member of the municipal corporation; and was sheriff of the city (1886–7). He served on the legislative council of the governor-general (1886–8), and was the first Parsi to receive that honour. Having been knighted in February 1887, he was created a baronet of the United Kingdom on 1 Sept. 1890, with special limitation to his second son. Petit was the second Indian native to receive this hereditary title, the first being Sir Jamsetjee Jeejeebhoy [q. v.]. Like Sir Jamsetjee, Petit obtained special legislation requiring all successors to the title to assume his name in the event of not possessing it at their succession.

Throughout western India Dinshaw Petit showed public spirit in the disposal of his great wealth. He arranged for housing the technical institute at Bombay—a memorial of Queen Victoria's jubilee of 1887—in the manufacturing district of the city. He founded the Petit hospital for women and children; gave a lakh of rupees (nearly 7000*l.*) towards building a home for lepers; erected a hospital for animals as a memorial to his wife; and presented property both in Bombay and Poona for research laboratories. A devout Parsi, he was always attentive to the claims of his own community, and in various places where small colonies of them are to be found erected for their use fire temples and towers of silence (i.e. places for the disposal of the dead).

Petit died at his Bombay residence, Petit Hall, on 5 May 1901, and his remains were committed to the towers of silence, Malabar Hill, the same day. At the *oothumna*, or third day obsequies, charities were announced amounting to Rs. 638,551 (42,570*l.*).

Petit married on 27 Feb. 1837 Sakerbai, daughter of Framjee Bhikhajee Panday, of

Bombay; she died on 5 March 1890, having issue three sons and eight daughters. Petit's second son, Framjee Dinshaw, on whom the baronetcy had been entailed, predeceased his father on 8 Aug. 1895, and his eldest son, Jeejeebhoy Framjee (*b.* 7 June 1873), became second baronet under the name of Sir Dinshaw Manockjee Petit. A posthumous painting of the first baronet by Sir James Linton belongs to the present Sir Dinshaw of Petit Hall, Bombay, and a statue, to form the public memorial in Bombay, is being executed by Sir Thomas Brock, R.A.

[History of the Parsis, 1884, 2 vols.; Representative Men of India, Bombay, 1891; Sir W. Hunter's Bombay, 1885 to 1890, 1892; Imperial Gazetteer of India; Burke's Peerage; Times of India, 6 May 1901.] F. H. B.

PETRE, Sir GEORGE GLYNN (1822–1905), diplomatist, born on 4 Sept. 1822 at Twickenham, was great-grandson of Robert Edward Petre, ninth Baron Petre, and was second son of Henry William Petre of Dunkenhalgh, Clayton-le-Moors, by his first wife Elizabeth Anne, daughter of Edmund John Glynn, of Glynn, Cornwall. Educated at Stonyhurst College and Prior Park, Bath, he entered the diplomatic service in 1846 as attaché to the British legation at Frankfort, then the seat of the diet of the German confederation, and was there during the revolutionary movements which convulsed Germany in 1848. He was transferred to Hanover in 1852 and to Paris in 1853, and was appointed paid attaché at the Hague in 1855 and at Naples in March 1856. Owing to the neglect by the tyrannical government of the Two Sicilies of the joint remonstrance of the British and French governments in May, diplomatic relations were broken off in the summer. Sir William Temple, the British minister, was compelled by ill-health to leave Naples in July, and Petre assumed charge of the legation until it was withdrawn at the end of October. Petre performed his duties with judgment and ability; his reports laid before parliament give an interesting narrative of the course of events. In 1857 he was temporarily attached to the embassy at Paris, and in June 1859 he accompanied Sir Henry Elliot [q. v. Suppl. II] on his special mission to Naples, diplomatic relations having been resumed on the accession of Francis II to the throne. He then proceeded as secretary of legation to Hanover, and acted as chargé d'affaires there from December 1859 until February 1860; he was transferred in 1864 to Copenhagen (where, in the following year, he assisted at the investiture of King Christian IX with the order of the Garter), to Brussels in 1866, and was promoted to be secretary of embassy at Berlin in 1868. After four years of service at Berlin, covering the period of the Franco-German war, he became chargé d'affaires at Stuttgart in 1872, and in April 1881 he was appointed British envoy at Buenos Ayres. In 1882 he was also accredited to the republic of Paraguay as minister plenipotentiary. In January 1884 he was appointed British envoy at Lisbon, where he remained until his retirement on a pension (1 Jan. 1893).

During the latter years of his service in Portugal the obstacles offered by the Portuguese authorities to free communication with the British missions and settlements established on the Shiré river and the shores of Lake Nyassa, and the seizure of British vessels while passing through Portuguese waters on their way to the lake, led to a state of acute tension between the two governments. A convention for the settlement of these and cognate questions was signed by Lord Salisbury and the Portuguese minister in London on 20 Aug. 1890, but in consequence of popular and parliamentary opposition the Portuguese government resigned office without obtaining the authority of the Cortes to ratify it, and their successors found themselves equally unable to carry it through. The negotiations had therefore to be resumed *de novo*. A *modus vivendi* was agreed upon and signed by Lord Salisbury and the new Portuguese minister, Senhor Luiz de Soveral, on 14 Nov. 1890, by which Portugal granted free transit over the waterways of the Zambesi, Shiré and Pungwe rivers and a satisfactory settlement was finally placed on record in the convention signed by Petre and the Portuguese minister for foreign affairs on 11 June 1891. Petre's naturally calm and conciliatory disposition and the excellent personal relations which he succeeded in maintaining with the Portuguese ministers did much to keep the discussions on a friendly basis and to procure acceptance of the British demands. He was made C.B. in 1886 and K.C.M.G. in 1890. He died at Brighton on 17 May 1905, and was buried at Odiham, Hampshire.

A portrait in water-colours is in the possession of his widow at Hatchwoods, Winchfield, Hampshire. Another, in oils, painted when he was at Berlin, is at Dunkenhalgh.

Petre married on 10 April 1858 Emma Katharine Julia, fifth daughter of Major Ralph Henry Sneyd, and left six sons. One son and an only daughter predeceased him.

[The Times, 23 May 1905; Lord Augustus Loftus, Diplomatic Reminiscences, 2nd ser. i. 374; Foreign Office List, 1906, p. 399; Papers laid before Parliament; Burke's Peerage, s.v. Petre.] S.

PETRIE, WILLIAM (1821–1908), electrician, born at King's Langley, Hertfordshire, on 21 Jan. 1821, was eldest of four sons of William Petrie (*b.* 1784), a war office official. His mother, Margaret, was daughter and coheiress of Henry Mitton, banker, of the Chase, Enfield. In 1829 Petrie's father was sent to the Cape of Good Hope, where he acted until 1837 as deputy commissary-general, having as a near neighbour Sir John Herschel [q. v.], the astronomer. After home education in Cape Town, Petrie, with his brother Martin [q. v.], was entered at the South African College. He had early shown a liking for mechanics and chemistry, and his youthful studies were much influenced by Herschel's friendly encouragement.

In 1836 Petrie commenced studying for the medical profession, attending the Cape Town Hospital, but in the year following the family returned to London, and the curriculum was not pursued. He then attended King's College. Later (1840) he studied at Frankfort-on-Main, devoting himself to magnetism and electricity. His inquiries bore fruit in 'Results of some Experiments in Electricity and Magnetism,' published in the 'Philosophical Magazine' in 1841; and 'On the Results of an Extensive Series of Magnetic Investigations, including most of the known Varieties of Steel,' communicated at the British Association's Southampton meeting of 1846 (see also papers presented to the Association in 1850).

Petrie returned to England in 1841, when he took out a patent for a magneto-electric machine. From 1846 to 1853 he worked assiduously at electric lighting problems in collaboration with William Edwards Staite. To Petrie's acumen is due the invention (1847–8) of the first truly self-regulating arc lamp. The essential feature was 'to impart more surely such motions to one of the electrodes that the light may be preserved from going out, be kept more uniform, and be renewed by the action of the apparatus itself whenever it has been put out.' Petrie's working drawings (still preserved) were made in conformity with this automatic principle, and he superintended the manufacture of the new lamp at Holtzapffel's works in Long Acre. It was submitted to rigorous tests, and was found to yield a light of between 600 and 700 standard candle-power, with a consumption of $\frac{1}{3}$ lb. of zinc per 100 candle-power per hour. On 28 Nov. and 2 Dec. 1848 Petrie made displays with a lamp of 700 candle-power from the portico of the National Gallery, and on various nights in 1849 from the old Hungerford suspension bridge in London. The demonstrations were witnessed by Wheatstone and other prominent men of science. On 6 Feb. 1850, Petrie (with Staite) read a paper before the Society of Arts on 'Improvements in the Electric Light.'

Petrie and Staite's long and courageous efforts to promote electric illumination were financially disastrous, and their pioneering services escaped the recognition of those who perfected the applications of the illuminant. Subsequently Petrie turned his attention to electro-chemistry, and superintended large chemical works; he introduced into the processes many improvements which he patented. He also designed and equipped chemical works in France, Australia, and the United States. For many years he was adviser and designer with Johnson, Matthey & Co.

Petrie died on 16 March 1908 at Bromley, Kent, and was buried there. He married on 2 Aug. 1851 Anne, only child of Matthew Flinders [q. v.]. She was a competent linguist, and studied Egyptology. Under the pseudonym 'Philomathes' she published a work on the relation between mythology and scripture, and as 'X.Q.' contributed essays to periodical literature. Their son, the sole issue of the marriage, is William Matthew Flinders Petrie, F.R.S., professor of Egyptology in University College, London.

[Electrical Engineer, 29 Aug. 1902 and 6 Feb. 1903, articles by J. J. Fahie (portraits and diagrams); Roy. Soc. Catal. Sci. Papers; Patent Office Specifications; Illustrated London News, 9 Dec. 1848; private information.] T. E. J.

PETTIGREW, JAMES BELL (1834–1908), anatomist, born on 26 May 1834 at Roxhill, Lanarkshire, was son of Robert Pettigrew and Mary Bell. He was related on his father's side to Thomas Joseph Pettigrew [q. v.], and on his mother's side to Henry Bell [q. v.], the builder of the Comet steamship. Educated at the Free West Academy of Airdrie, he studied arts at the University of Glasgow from 1850 to 1855. He then migrated to Edinburgh, where he pursued medical studies. In 1858–9 he was awarded Professor John Goodsir's senior anatomy gold medal for the best treatise 'On the arrangement of the muscular fibres in the ventricles of the vertebrate heart' (*Phil. Trans.* 1864). This treatise procured him the appointment of Croonian lecturer at the Royal Society of London in 1860. He gained at Edinburgh in 1860 the annual gold medal in the class of medical jurisprudence with an essay 'On the presumption of survivorship' (*Brit. and For. Med. Chirurg. Rev.* Jan. 1865). He graduated M.D. at Edinburgh in 1861, obtaining the gold medal for his inaugural dissertation on 'the ganglia and nerves of the heart and their connection with the cerebro-spinal and sympathetic systems in mammalia' (*Proc. Royal Soc. Edin.* 1865). In 1861 he acted as house surgeon to Prof. James Syme [q. v.] at the Royal Infirmary, Edinburgh, and in 1862 he was appointed assistant in the Hunterian museum at the Royal College of Surgeons of England. Here he remained until 1867, adding dissections to the collection and writing papers on various anatomical subjects. In 1867 he contributed a paper to the 'Transactions of the Linnean Society' 'On the mechanical appliances by which flight is maintained in the animal kingdom,' and in the same year he left the Hunterian museum in order to spend two years in the south of Ireland so as to extend his knowledge of the flight of insects, birds and bats. He also experimented largely on the subject of artificial flight.

Elected F.R.S. in 1869, in the autumn of that year he became curator of the museum of the Royal College of Surgeons of Edinburgh and pathologist at the Royal Infirmary. He continued his anatomical, physical, and physiological researches, especially those on flight, and in 1870 he published a memoir 'On the physiology of wings, being an analysis of the movements by which flight is produced in the insect, bird and bat' (*Trans. Royal Soc. Edin.* vol. xxvi.).

At Edinburgh he was elected F.R.S. in 1872 and F.R.C.P. in 1873. He was appointed in the same year lecturer on physiology at the Royal College of Surgeons of Edinburgh. In 1874 he was awarded the Godard prize of the French Académie des Sciences for his anatomico-physiological researches and was made a laureate of the Institut de France. In 1875 he was appointed Chandos professor of medicine and anatomy and dean of the medical faculty in the university of St. Andrews. In 1875–6–7 he delivered special courses of lectures on physiology in Dundee, and University College, Dundee, owes its origin largely to his efforts. In 1877 he was elected by the Universities of Glasgow and St. Andrews to represent those bodies on the General Medical Council. He continued the dual representation until 1886, when a new medical act enabled each of the Scottish universities to return its own member. Pettigrew thenceforth represented St. Andrews on the council. In 1883 he received the hon. degree of LL.D. at Glasgow.

He died at his residence, the Swallowgate, St. Andrews, on 30 Jan. 1908. He married in 1890 Elsie, second daughter of Sir William Gray, of Greatham, Durham, but left no family. His portrait by W. W. Ouless was exhibited at the Royal Academy in 1902. A museum for the botanic gardens was erected in his memory by his widow as an adjunct to the Bute medical buildings of St. Andrews University.

Pettigrew was author of: 1. 'Animal Locomotion, or Walking, Swimming, and Flying, with a Dissertation on Aëronautics,' in International Scientific Series, 1873, translated into French (1874) and into German (1879). 2. 'The Physiology of Circulation in Plants, in the Lower Animals and in Man,' illustrated, 1874. 3. 'Design in Nature,' illustrated by spiral and other arrangements in the inorganic and organic kingdoms, 3 vols. 4to, 1908, published posthumously; this work occupied the last ten years of Pettigrew's life.

[Men and Women of the Time, 1899; Lancet, 1908, vol. i. p. 471; Brit. Med. Journal, 1908, vol. i. p. 357; information kindly given by Mrs. Bell Pettigrew.] D'A. P.

PHEAR, Sir JOHN BUDD (1825–1905), judge in India and author, born at Earl Stonham, Suffolk, on 9 Feb. 1825, was eldest of three sons of John Phear, thirteenth wrangler at Cambridge in 1815, fellow and tutor of Pembroke College, Cambridge, and rector of Earl Stonham from 1824 to 1881, by his wife Catherine Wreford, only daughter of Samuel Budd, medical practitioner, of North Tawton, Devon. Of his two brothers, Henry Carlyon Phear (1826–1880) was second wrangler and first Smith's prizeman in 1849, fellow of Caius College, Cambridge, and a chancery barrister of some eminence, and Samuel George Phear (*b.* 1829) was fourth wrangler in 1852, and fellow and from 1871 to 1895 Master of Emmanuel College, Cambridge. Educated privately by his father, John entered Pembroke College, Cambridge, on 29 March 1843, graduated B.A. as sixth wrangler in 1847 and proceeded M.A. in 1850. He was elected fellow of Clare College on 23 April 1847, mathematical lecturer in September following, and assistant tutor in 1854. He showed mathematical ability in two text-books, 'Elementary Mechanics' (Cambridge, 1850) and 'Elementary Hydrostatics with Numerous Examples' (Cambridge, 1852; 2nd edit. 1857). He left Cambridge in 1854, but retained his fellowship until his marriage in 1865. He was moderator of the mathematical tripos in 1856.

Entering as a student at the Inner Temple on 12 Nov. 1847, Phear was called to the bar on 26 Jan. 1854 and joined the western circuit, subsequently transferring himself to the Norfolk circuit. In 1864 he was appointed a judge of the High Court of Bengal and went out to Calcutta. He was in complete sympathy with the natives of India and they acknowledged his wise and impartial administration of justice. He displayed activity in other than judicial work, was president of the Asiatic Society of Bengal (1870–1), of the Bengal Social Science Association, and of the Bethune Society (for social purposes), and closely studied native social life. Leaving Calcutta in 1876, he was knighted on 4 Oct. 1877, and became in the same year chief justice of Ceylon. He revised the civil and criminal code for Ceylon, and the Ceylon bar presented a portrait of him (in oils) to his court in appreciation of his services.

On his return to England in 1879 Phear settled at Marpool Hall, Exmouth, Devonshire, and at once took active part in local public life. He was chairman of quarter sessions from 18 Oct. 1881 till 15 Oct. 1895, and an alderman of the Devon county council from 24 Jan. 1889 till death. An ardent liberal politician, he thrice contested unsuccessfully Devon county divisions in the liberal interest—Honiton in 1885, Tavistock in 1886, and Tiverton in 1892. He joined the Devonshire Association for the Advancement of Science, Literature, and Art in June 1881, contributed among other interesting papers one on manorial tenures, and was president in 1886. A keen sportsman, a good cricketer, and a life member of the London Skating Club, he was a fellow of the Geological Society from 1852.

Sir John died at Marpool Hall, Exmouth, on 7 April 1905, and was buried at Littleham. He married at Madras on 16 Oct. 1865 Emily, daughter of John Bolton of Burnley House, Stockwell. She was a member of the Exmouth school board, and died on 31 Dec. 1898, leaving two daughters and a son.

Phear's most important publication was 'The Aryan Village in India and Ceylon' (1880), which embodies the fruit of much intelligent observation. He had previously issued 'The Hindoo Joint Family' (Calcutta, 1867), a lecture at the Bethune Society, 18 March 1867. Phear's other works include 'A Treatise on Rights of Water, including Public and Private Rights to the Sea and Sea-shore' (1859), and 'Observations on the Present State of the Law affecting Title to Land and its Transfer' (1862).

[Private information; The Times, 8 April 1905; records of Pembroke and Clare Colleges and Inner Temple.] T. C. H.

PHILLIPS, WILLIAM (1822–1905), botanist and antiquary, born at Presteign, Radnorshire, on 4 May 1882, was fourth son in a family of ten children of Thomas Phillips and Elizabeth, daughter of James Cross, whose ancestors had been farmers of Hanwood and burgesses of Shrewsbury since 1634. After receiving a very rudimentary education at a school at Presteign, Phillips was apprenticed to his elder brother James, a tailor, in High Street, Shrewsbury, with whom and another brother, Edward, he went in due course into partnership. In 1859 he joined the Shrewsbury volunteers, and became a colour-sergeant and an excellent rifle-shot, winning the bronze medal of the National Rifle Association in 1860. After some early private study of astronomy and photography, he took up botany about 1861 at the suggestion of his friend William Allport Leighton [q. v.], the lichenologist. Beginning with flowering plants, Phillips turned to the fungi about 1869, first to the Hymenomycetes and afterwards mainly to the Discomycetes, though other groups of cryptogams were not neglected. Between 1873 and 1891, in conjunction with Dr. Plowright, he contributed a series of notes on 'New and rare British Fungi' to 'Grevillea,' and between 1874 and 1881 he issued a set of specimens entitled 'Elvellacei Britannici.' In 1878 he helped to found, and formed the council of, the Shropshire Archæological and Natural History Society, and in its 'Transactions' (vol. i.) appeared his paper on the ferns and fern-allies of Shropshire, which he had printed privately in 1877; many other papers followed in the subsequent 'Transactions.' In 1878 Phillips published a

'Guide to the Botany of Shrewsbury,' and before his death completed for the 'Victoria County History' an account of the botany of the county. After nearly twenty years' preparation Phillips in 1887 published his chief work, 'A Manual of the British Discomycetes,' in the International Scientific series (with twelve excellent plates drawn by himself).

Compelled with advancing years to discontinue microscopic work, Phillips engaged in archæological research of various kinds. He made special studies of the earthworks, castles, and moated houses of Shropshire. Many of his results were published in the 'Transactions of the Shropshire Archæological Society,' in 'Salopian Shreds and Patches,' in 'Bye-Gones,' and in 'Shropshire Notes and Queries,' which he edited, and to a great extent wrote, towards the close of his life. 'The Ottley Papers,' relating to the civil war, which he edited for the Shropshire Society between 1893 and 1898, form a complete county history for the period; and he carefully edited the first part of Blakeway's 'Topographical History of Shrewsbury.' He took a prominent part in the preservation of the remains of Uriconium; actively helped to arrange the borough records of Shrewsbury, and to prepare the calendar (1896); edited the 'Quarter Sessions Rolls' of Shropshire from 1652 to 1659, and transcribed the parish registers of Battlefield (2 vols. 1899–1900) and Stirchley (1905) for the Shropshire Parish Register Society. In 1896 Phillips, a methodist and at one time a local preacher, published 'Early Methodism in Shropshire.' The conversion of the Shrewsbury Free School buildings into a museum and free library (from 1882) owed much to Phillips, who became the curator of botany. Many manuscript volumes by him on antiquarian subjects are preserved there. His botanical manuscripts and drawings, including his large correspondence with botanists at home and abroad, were purchased at his death for the botanical department of the British Museum. Phillips was elected a fellow of the Linnean Society in 1875, and was F.S.A. He became a borough magistrate in 1886, and was presented with the freedom of the borough on 17 Aug. 1903. He died of heart-disease at his residence in Canonbury, Shrewsbury, on 23 Oct. 1905, and was buried in the general cemetery, Shrewsbury.

Phillips married in 1846 Sarah Ann, daughter of Thomas Hitchins of Shrewsbury, who died in 1895. Two sons and two daughters survived him.

Miles Joseph Berkeley [q.v.] dedicated to Phillips a genus of fungi under the name *Phillipsia.*

[Trans. Shropshire Archæol. Soc., series iii. vol. vi. 407–418 (with a portrait); Journal of Botany, xliii. (1905) pp. 361–2 (with a portrait); Gardeners' Chron. 1905, ii. 331 (with a portrait); Proc. Linnean Soc. 1905–6, pp. 44–5; Shrewsbury and Border Counties Advertiser, 28 October 1905 (with portrait).]

G. S. B.

PIATTI, ALFREDO CARLO (1822–1901), violoncellist and composer, was born on 8 Jan. 1822 at Bergamo, where his father, Antonio Piatti, was leader of the town orchestra. At five years old he began to learn the violoncello under his great-uncle Zanetti, and at seven played in the orchestra, next year succeeding to Zanetti's place. In 1832 he obtained a five years' scholarship at the Conservatorio of Milan. At the end of his course he played in public a concerto of his own composition, and was presented with the violoncello he had used, on 21 Sept. 1837. He then played in the Bergamo orchestra, taking trips with his father when there was a chance of playing solos. After a time he went into Austria and Hungary, but fell ill at Pesth, and was obliged to sell his prize violoncello. Rescued by a Bergamo friend he returned home by way of Munich, where he met Liszt, and played at his concert. Liszt publicly embraced him, and he was thrice recalled. After appearing at Paris and Ems, he reached London, where he played in the opera orchestra and at private parties, and made his debut as soloist at Mrs. Anderson's concert on 31 May 1844. The boy Joachim first appeared at the same concert. Piatti made several other appearances, and a provincial tour in the autumn; his success everywhere was immediate and complete, but he earned little, and was able to return home only by the assistance of the vocalist Mme. Castellan. In 1845 he toured in Russia. In 1846 he returned to England, where he at once became a principal figure in London musical life. His small figure and serious spectacled face were thenceforth familiar for half a century to all London concert-goers. Mendelssohn talked of writing a concerto for him, which however has not been found. Alike in execution, in tone, and in expression he was unsurpassed. Difficulties had no existence for him, and his delivery of a melody was a lesson to vocalists. He took composition lessons from Molique. After Lindley's retirement in 1851 Piatti had no rival, leading the violoncellos at the principal concerts, and taking part in chamber music, for which he was peculiarly fitted. Sterndale Bennett's sonata-duo (1852), Molique's concerto (1853), and Sullivan's concerto (1866) and Duo (1868) were all written for him and first performed by him. At the Monday Popular Concerts Piatti played from their establishment in 1859 till 1896. He lived at 15 Northwick Terrace, St. John's Wood, latterly spending the summer at an estate he had bought at Cadenabbia, Lake Como. He rarely played outside London; he appeared at Bergamo in 1875 and again in 1893, on the latter occasion receiving the order of the Crown of Italy from King Humbert. On 22 March 1894, to celebrate the jubilee of his and Joachim's first appearances in London, a testimonial to both was publicly presented to them at the Grafton Galleries.

In 1898 Piatti retired. His last few months were spent with his only surviving daughter, Countess Lochis, at Crocetta near Bergamo, where he died on 22 July 1901. He was buried in the castle chapel; four professors played his favourite movement, the variations on 'Der Tod und das Mädchen' in Schubert's D minor quartett, and agreed to play it annually at the graveside. Piatti married in 1856 Mary Ann Lucey Welsh, daughter of a singing master; but they separated. She died in Sept. 1901.

Piatti's compositions included six sonatas, three concertos, twelve caprices, and some slighter pieces for the violoncello, as well as some songs with violoncello obbligato, one of which, 'Awake, awake,' had a lasting success. He re-edited works by Boccherini, Locatelli, Veracini, Marcello, and Porpora, and Kummer's method. He arranged for the violoncello Ariosti's sonatas, melodies by Schubert and Mendelssohn, and variations from Christopher Sympson's 'Division-Violist' (1659).

A portrait by Frank Holl was exhibited at the Royal Academy in 1879.

[Morton Latham, Alfredo Piatti (with portraits); Grove's Dict. of Music; Musical Times (with portrait), Aug. 1901.] H. D.

PICKARD, BENJAMIN (1842–1904), trade union leader, born on 26 Feb. 1842 at Kippax, near Pontefract, in Yorkshire, was son of Thomas Pickard, a working miner, by his wife Elizabeth Firth. He was educated at the colliery school. At twelve he commenced to work in the mine with his father, and in due course went through the various grades of labour there. He early joined the miners' union, becoming lodge secretary in 1858, and in 1873, when the membership and work of the West Yorkshire Miners' Association greatly increased, he was elected its assistant secretary, succeeding to the secretaryship in 1876. He had also joined the Wesleyan body and became one of its local preachers. He foresaw that the next step in trade unionism was the amalgamation of local societies, and in 1881 he brought about the union of the south and west Yorkshire associations, under the title of the Yorkshire Miners' Association, and became its secretary; and when the Miners' Federation of Great Britain was formed in 1888 he was elected president. His policy was to protect members by restricting output and so check excessive driving. In 1885 the employers resolved to reduce wages. Pickard advised acceptance, but the men declined to follow his lead and a strike ensued which was unsuccessful, but events then gave Pickard his grip upon the miners which he never lost. Prosperous times followed, but he again found himself involved in the dispute of 1893, when the miners again resisted a reduction of 25 per cent. and refused arbitration on the ground that they were entitled to a living wage. It was another form of the opposition to a sliding scale for wages which the Miners' Federation had been formed to carry on. In this great dispute, which lasted sixteen weeks, Pickard played the leading part, and in the end received a testimonial of 750*l.* from the men. The result of this strike was the establishment of conciliation boards to settle all wages disputes. Things went smoothly until 1902 when reductions were again threatened, unrest was widespread, and the Denaby Main strike ensued. During the board of trade inquiry which followed this strike and at which he gave evidence, Pickard died in London on 3 Feb. 1904; he was buried in the Barnsley cemetery.

A liberal in politics, Pickard sat in parliament for the Normanton division of Yorkshire from 1885 till his death. In parliament he was the leader of the eight hours for miners agitation, and his interest in arbitration sent him in 1887 on a peace deputation to the president of the United States (Grover Cleveland). In 1897 he received a cheque for 500*l.* from liberal members of the House of Commons as a mark of respect. Before entering parliament he was a member of the Wakefield school board, and in 1889 was elected an alderman of the West Riding county council.

He married in 1864 the daughter of John Freeman of Kippax; she died in 1901.

[The Times, 4 Feb. 1904; Reports of Miners' Federation; Sidney Webb's History of Trades Unionism 1894, and his Industrial Democracy 1897; family information.] J. R. M.

PICTON, JAMES ALLANSON (1832–1910), politician and author, born at Liverpool on 8 Aug. 1832, was eldest son of Sir James Allanson Picton [q. v.] by his wife Sarah Pooley. After early education at the High School, then held at the Mechanics' Institute, he entered the office of his father, who was an architect, in his sixteenth year. In his nineteenth year he resolved to study for the ministry, and joined both the Lancashire Independent College and Owens College, Manchester. At Owens College he was first in classics in his final examination, and in 1855 he proceeded M.A. at London University. A first attempt in 1856 to enter the ministry failed owing to a suspicion of heterodoxy. Study of German philosophy dissatisfied him with conventional doctrine. Later in the year, however, he was appointed to Cheetham Hill congregational church, Manchester. There with the Rev. Arthur Mursell he undertook a course of popular lectures to the working classes. A sermon on the 'Christian law of progress' in 1862 led to a revival of the allegation of heresy. Removing to Leicester, he accepted the pastorate of Gallowtree Gate chapel, and there made a high reputation. In 1869 he became pastor of St Thomas's Square chapel, Hackney, remaining there till 1879. At Hackney, to the dismay of strict orthodoxy, he delivered to the working classes, on Sunday afternoons, popular lectures on secular themes such as English history and the principles of radical and conservative politics. He thus prepared the way for the Pleasant Sunday Afternoon movement. His growing tendency to rationalism inclined him to pantheism in later years.

Picton soon took an active part in public life as an uncompromising radical of an advanced type. A champion of secularism in education, he represented Hackney on the London school board from 1870 to 1879. For three years he was chairman of the school management committee. In 1883 he was accepted as a radical candidate for parliament for the Tower Hamlets, but withdrew in 1884, when in June he entered parliament as member for Leicester, succeeding Peter Alfred Taylor [q. v.], most of whose opinions he shared. He was re-elected for Leicester in 1885, 1886, and 1892, retiring from the House of Commons and from public life in 1894. Picton, who was very small in stature, possessed much oratorical power, but, never losing the manner of the pulpit, failed to win the ear of the House of Commons, where he was only known as a sincere advocate of extreme views.

Picton wrote much in the press and published many sermons, pamphlets, and volumes on religion and politics. From 1879 to 1884 he was a frequent leader writer in the 'Weekly Dispatch,' then an advanced radical organ, and contributed to the 'Christian World,' the 'Theological Review,' the 'Fortnightly Review,' the 'Contemporary Review,' 'Macmillan's Magazine,' the 'Examiner,' and other periodicals.

His books included: 1. 'A Catechism of the Gospels,' 1866. 2. 'New Theories and the Old Faith,' 1870. 3. 'The Mystery of Matter,' 1873. 4. 'The Religion of Jesus,' 1876. 5. 'Pulpit Discourses,' 1879. 6. 'Oliver Cromwell: the Man and his Mission,' 1882 (a popular eulogy). 7. 'Lessons from the English Commonwealth,' 1884. 8. 'The Conflict of Oligarchy and Democracy,' 1885. 9. 'Sir James A. Picton: a Biography,' 1891. 10. 'The Bible in School,' 1901. 11. 'The Religion of the Universe,' 1904. 12. 'Pantheism,' 1905. 13. 'Spinoza: a Handbook to the Ethics,' 1907. 14. 'Man and the Bible,' 1909. He died at Caerlyr, Penmaenmawr, North Wales, where he had lived since his withdrawal from parliament, on 4 Feb. 1910, and his remains were cremated at Liverpool.

He married (1) Margaret, daughter of John Beaumont of Manchester; and (2) Jessie Carr, daughter of Sydney Williams, publisher, of Hamburg and London. Of four sons one survives.

[Morrison Davidson, Eminent Radicals, 1880; Frederick Rogers, Biographical sketch, 1883; H. W. Lucy's Diary of the Salisbury Parliament, 1886–92; House of Commons Guides, 1884–94; Who's Who, 1910; Christian World, Literary Guide, and Leicester Daily Post and Liverpool Daily Post, Feb., March 1910.] F. R.

PIRBRIGHT, first Baron. [See De Worms, Henry (1840–1903), politician.]

PITMAN, Sir HENRY ALFRED (1808–1908), physician, born in London on 1 July 1808, was youngest of the seven children of Thomas Dix Pitman, a solicitor in Furnival's Inn, by his wife Ann Simmons, of a Worcester family. Educated privately, he entered Trinity College, Cambridge, in 1827, where he graduated B.A. in 1832.

After travelling abroad for a year he spent six months in the office of his brother-in-law, who was a solicitor, and thus obtained a training in business methods. He then turned to medicine, working first for a year at Cambridge and then at King's College and at St. George's Hospital; in 1835 he graduated M.B. at Cambridge, and after passing in 1838 the then necessary additional examination for the licence at that university, he proceeded M.D. in 1841. In 1840 he became a licentiate (equivalent to member), and in 1845 a fellow, of the Royal College of Physicians of London. In 1846 he was elected assistant physician, and in 1857 physician and lecturer on medicine at St. George's Hospital. He resigned in 1866 and was the first to be elected consulting physician there. After being censor in 1856–7, he was in 1858, in succession to Dr. Francis Hawkins [q. v.], elected registrar to the Royal College of Physicians.

Pitman, whose mental equipment was rather of the legal than of the medical order, had a gift for administration. He was long identified with the management of the Royal College of Physicians and the regulation and arrangement of the medical curriculum. The Medical Act of 1858 entailed numerous changes in the organisation of the college, which then surrendered the power to confer the exclusive right to practise in London. He was largely responsible for the translation of the old Latin statutes of the college into English bye-laws and regulations in harmony with the Medical Acts of 1858 and 1860. He took a prominent part in the construction of the first edition of the 'Nomenclature of Diseases,' which was prepared by the college for the government, being begun in 1859 and published in 1869. A fresh edition is issued decennially. He was largely responsible for the initiation and organisation of the conjoint examining board in England of the Royal College of Physicians and the Royal College of Surgeons, and it was in recognition of his work on the new diplomas (L.R.C.P., M.R.C.S.) that he was knighted in 1883. He also took an active part in the institution of a special examination and diploma in public health. From 1876 to 1886 he was the representative of the college on the general council of medical education and registration, and in 1881 chairman of the executive committee of the council. He resigned the registrarship of the College of Physicians in 1889, being then elected emeritus registrar.

Pitman died at the patriarchal age of 100 at Enfield on 6 Nov. 1908, and was buried in the Enfield cemetery. He married in 1852 Frances (*d.* 11 Nov. 1910), only daughter of Thomas Wildman of Eastbourne, and had issue three sons and four daughters.

A portrait by Ouless hangs in the reading-room of the Royal College of Physicians, to which it was presented on behalf of some of the fellows by Sir Risdon Bennett in 1886.

[Autobiography in Lancet, 1908, ii. 1418; Brit. Med. Journal, 1908, ii. 1528; presidential address at the Royal College of Physicians by Sir R. Douglas Powell, Bt., K.C.V.O., on 5 April 1909.] H. D. R.

PLATTS, JOHN THOMPSON (1830–1904), Persian scholar, born at Calcutta on 1 August 1830, was second son of Robert Platts of Calcutta, India, who left at his death a large family and a widow in straitened circumstances. John, after being educated at Bedford (apparently privately), returned to India in early manhood, and during 1858–9 was mathematical master at Benares College. He was in charge of Saugor School in the Central Provinces from 1859 to 1861, when he became mathematical professor and headmaster of Benares College. In 1864 Platts was transferred to the post of assistant inspector of schools, second circle, North-west Provinces, and in 1868 he became officiating inspector of schools, northern circle, Central Provinces. He retired on 17 March 1872, owing to ill-health. Platts then returned to England, and settling at Ealing occupied himself with teaching Hindustānī and Persian. He had closely studied both languages and had thoroughly mastered their grammars and vocabulary. On 2 June 1880 he was elected teacher of Persian in the University of Oxford. He matriculated from Balliol College on 1 Feb. 1881, and on 21 June of that year was made M.A. *honoris causâ*. On 19 March 1901 the degree of M.A. was conferred upon him by decree. He died suddenly in London on 21 Sept. 1904, and was buried at Wolvercote cemetery near Oxford.

Platts was twice married: (1) in 1856, at Lahore, India, to Alice Jane Kenyon (*d.* 1874), by whom he had three sons and four daughters; and (2) on 4 Oct. 1876 to Mary Elizabeth, only daughter of Thomas Dunn, architect and surveyor, of Melbourne, Australia, and widow of John Hayes, architect and surveyor, of Croydon; by her Platts had one son. His widow was awarded a civil list pension of 75*l.* in 1905.

Platts compiled: 1. 'A Grammar of the Hindustānī Language,' 1874. 2. 'A Hindustānī-English Dictionary,' 1881. 3. 'A Dictionary of Urdu, Classical Hindī, and English,' 1884. 4. 'A Grammar of the Persian Language, Part I, Accidence,' 1894. He also edited the text of 'Gulistān of Sa'dī' (1872), and published 'Sa'dī (Shaikh Muslihuddīn Shīrāzī)' photographed from MS. under his superintendence (1891). He translated the 'Ikhwānu-ṣ-Ṣafā' from the Hindustānī of Maulavi Ikrām Alī (1875), and the 'Gulistān of Sa'dī' (1876).

Platts' grammars of Persian and Hindustānī were a marked advance upon the work of any English predecessor, and still hold the field. His 'Hindustānī-English Dictionary' is a monument of erudition and research.

[Record Department, India Office; Oxford Times, 1 Oct. 1904.] G. S. A. R.

PLAYFAIR, WILLIAM SMOULT (1835–1903), obstetric physician, born at St. Andrews, where his family had long been prominent citizens, on 27 July 1835, was fourth of the five sons of George Playfair, inspector-general of hospitals in Bengal, by his wife Jessie Ross of Edinburgh. Lyon, first Lord Playfair [q. v. Suppl. I], and Sir Robert Lambert Playfair [q. v. Suppl. I] were two of his brothers.

After being educated at St. Andrews, he became a medical student at Edinburgh in 1852, graduating M.D. in 1856 and then working for some time in Paris. In 1857 he entered the Indian medical service, and was an assistant surgeon at Oude during the Mutiny. During 1859–60 he was professor of surgery at the Calcutta Medical College; but for reasons of health he retired, and after practising for six months in St. Petersburg, he returned in 1863 to London without definite plans, but was soon elected assistant physician for diseases of women and children at King's College Hospital. In 1872, on the retirement of Sir William Overend Priestley [q. v. Suppl. I], he was appointed professor of obstetric medicine in King's College and obstetric physician to King's College Hospital, posts which he vacated after twenty-five years' service in 1898, and was elected emeritus professor and consulting physician. In 1863 he became M.R.C.P., and in 1870 was elected F.R.C.P.

Playfair became one of the foremost obstetricians in this country, and was among the first to decline to hand over obstetric operations to general surgeons, and thus set obstetricians the example of operating on their own patients. He was a prolific writer with a clear and graceful style. He introduced into this country with much enthusiasm and success the Weir-Mitchell or 'rest-cure' treatment, which was soon widely adopted. In 1896 an action was brought against him by a patient for alleged breach of professional confidence which attracted much attention, and was notable for the enormous damages (12,000*l.*) given against him by the jury; this amount however was reduced by agreement to 9200*l.* on application for a new trial. Though opinion was much divided on the merits of the case, no stain was left on Playfair's professional character. He was physician accoucheur to the Duchess of Edinburgh and to the Duchess of Connaught, an hon. LL.D. of the Universities of Edinburgh (1898) and of St. Andrews (1885), an honorary fellow of the American and of the Boston Gynæcological Societies, and of the Obstetrical Society of Edinburgh. He was president of the Obstetrical Society of London (1879–80).

Playfair after an apoplectic stroke at Florence in 1903 died at St. Andrews, his native place, on 13 Aug. 1903, and was buried there in the new cemetery of St. Andrews, where his two distinguished brothers lie. A sum was collected to found a memorial to him in the new King's College Hospital at Denmark Hill, London. His portrait, painted by Fräulein von Nathusius, was presented by his widow to the Royal College of Physicians of London.

Playfair married on 26 April 1864 Emily, daughter of James Kitson of Leeds and sister of the first Lord Airedale; he had issue two sons and three daughters.

Playfair was author of: 1. 'Handbook of Obstetric Operations,' 1865. 2. 'Science and Practice of Midwifery,' 1876; 9th edit. 1898, translated into several languages. 3. 'Notes on the Systematic Treatment of Nerve Prostration and Hysteria connected with Uterine Disease,' 1881. He was joint editor with Sir Clifford Allbutt, K.C.B., of a 'System of Gynæcology' (1896; 2nd edit. revised by T. W. Eden, 1906). He contributed to Quain's 'Dictionary of Medicine' (1882) the article on 'Diseases of the Womb,' and to H. Tuke's 'Dictionary of Psychological Medicine' (1892) the article on 'Functional Neuroses,' and wrote much for medical periodicals, including forty-nine papers for the 'Transactions of the Obstetrical Society.'

[Obstetrical Trans., London, 1904, xlvi. 80–86; Brit. Med. Journal, 1903, ii. 439; the Families of Roger and Playfair, printed for private circulation, 1872; information from Hugh Playfair, M.D.] H. D. R.

PLUNKETT, Sir FRANCIS RICHARD (1835–1907), diplomatist, born at Corbalton Hall, co. Meath, on 3 Feb. 1835, was sixth son of Arthur James, ninth earl of Fingall, and Louise Emilia, only daughter of Elias Corbally of Corbalton Hall. Educated at the Roman catholic college, St. Mary's, Oscott, he was appointed attaché at Munich in January 1855, and transferred in July of that year to Naples, where he remained until diplomatic relations were broken off on 30 Oct. 1856. After a few months of service at the Hague he was transferred to Madrid, and in July 1859 was promoted to be paid attaché at St. Petersburg. In January 1863 he was transferred as second secretary to Copenhagen, where he served during the troubled times of the war of Austria and Prussia against Denmark. After service at Vienna, Berlin, Florence, and again at Berlin, he was promoted to be secretary of legation at Yedo in 1873, then at Washington in 1876, becoming secretary of embassy at St. Petersburg in 1877. He was transferred to Constantinople in 1881, but after a few months of service, during part of which he was in charge of the embassy in the absence of the ambassador, Lord Dufferin [q. v. Suppl. II], he was removed to Paris, with promotion to the titular rank of minister plenipotentiary. In July 1883 he was appointed British envoy at Tokio, and while there in 1886 he was made K.C.M.G. In 1886 and 1887 he took part as the senior British delegate in the conferences on the very difficult question of the revision of the treaties between Japan and the European powers, and the conditions on which the rights of extra-territorial jurisdiction enjoyed by those powers over their nationals resident in Japan should be abandoned. The conditions agreed upon at the conference were considered by the Japanese government to be too onerous, and it was not until 1894 that a definitive agreement was arrived at. In 1888 he was transferred to Stockholm, and in 1893 to Brussels, where in 1898 and 1899 he took part in the conferences for the abolition of bounties on the export of sugar and for the regulation of the liquor trade in Africa. In September 1900 he was appointed British ambassador at Vienna, and held that post till his retirement on pension in October 1905. He was made G.C.M.G. during his residence at Brussels in 1894, G.C.B. in 1901, and a G.C.V.O. in 1903, was sworn a privy councillor on his appointment as ambassador, and received from the Emperor Francis Joseph the grand cross of the order of Leopold on leaving Vienna, where his natural kindliness of disposition and urbanity of manner had made him universally popular. He died at Paris on 28 Feb. 1907 and was buried at Boulogne-sur-Seine.

He married on 22 Aug. 1870 May Tevis, daughter of Charles Waln Morgan, of Philadelphia, by whom he had two daughters.

[The Times, 1 and 2 March 1907; Foreign Office List, 1908, p. 401; papers laid before Parliament.] S.

PODMORE, FRANK (1855–1910), writer on psychical research, born at Elstree, Hertfordshire, on 5 Feb. 1855, was the third son of the Rev. Thompson Podmore, at one time headmaster of Eastbourne College, by his wife Georgina Elizabeth, daughter of George Gray Barton and Sarah Barton. Educated first at Elstree Hill school (1863–8), Frank won a scholarship at Haileybury, leaving in 1874 with a classical scholarship at Pembroke College, Oxford. At Oxford he obtained a second class in classical moderations (1875) and a first class in natural science (1877). In 1879 he was appointed to a higher division clerkship in the secretary's department of the post office. This position he held till 1907, when he retired without a pension.

Through life Podmore was keenly interested in psychical research. At Oxford he had studied spiritualistic phenomena, had contributed papers to 'Human Nature' (the spiritualist organ) in 1875 and 1876, and had placed unqualified confidence in a slate-writing performance of the medium Slade. In 1880 however he changed his attitude and announced to the National Association of Spiritualists that he had become sceptical about spiritualistic doctrine. He was a member of the council of the Society for Psychical Research from 17 March 1882 until his resignation in May 1909. In that capacity he argued for theories of psychological, as opposed to spiritualist, causality, and for a far-reaching application of the hypothesis of telepathy. He became 'sceptic-in-chief' concerning spirit agency, and the official *advocatus diaboli* when the society undertook to adjudicate on the claim to authenticity of spiritualistic phenomena. His hostility was criticised by F. C. S. Schiller (*Mind*, N.S. no. 29) and by Andrew Lang. Podmore helped in compiling the census of hallucinations which the society began in 1889 (*Report* in *Proceedings*, vol. x. 1894), and with Edmund Gurney and F. W. H. Myers [q. v. Suppl. I] he assisted in preparing 'Phantasms of the Living' (1886), an encyclopædic collection of tested evidence. In 'Modern Spiritualism' (1902) and 'The Newer Spiritualism' (posthumously issued, 1910) he critically studied the history of spiritualist manifestations from the seventeenth century onwards, and incidentally contested Myers' doctrine of the subliminal self in relation to human personality and its survival after death.

Podmore was one of the founders and members of the first executive committee of the Fabian Society, the title of which he apparently originated (4 Jan. 1884). He helped to prepare an early, and now rare, report on government organisation of unemployed labour, to which Sidney Webb also contributed. His rooms at 14 Dean's Yard, Westminster, were frequently the place of meeting. He wrote none of the 'Fabian Tracts,' and his interest in 'social reconstruction' bore its chief fruit in his full biography of Robert Owen the socialist and spiritualist in 1906.

In 1907 Podmore left London for Broughton near Kettering, a parish of which his brother, Claude Podmore, was rector. He died by drowning in the New Pool, Malvern, where he was making a short stay, on 14 Aug. 1910. The jury returned a verdict of 'found drowned.' He was buried at Malvern Wells cemetery.

Podmore married on 11 June 1891 Eleanore, daughter of Dr. Bramwell of Perth, and sister of Dr. Milne Bramwell, a well-known investigator of the therapeutic aspect of hypnotism. In his later years Podmore lived apart from his wife; there was no issue. A civil list pension of 60*l.* was granted his widow in 1912.

Podmore combined a good literary style with scientific method. Apart from the works cited he published: 1. 'Apparitions and Thought Transference,' 1894. 2. 'Studies in Psychical Research,' 1897. 3. 'Spiritualism (with Edw. Wake Cook, in 'Pro and Con' series, vol. 2), 1903. 4. 'The Naturalisation of the Supernatural,' 1908. 5. 'Mesmerism and Christian Science,' 1909. 6. 'Telepathic Hallucinations: the New View of Ghosts,' 1910.

His contributions to the 'Proceedings' of the Society for Psychical Research are very numerous, and he wrote articles on his special themes in the 'Encyclopædia Britannica' (11th edit.).

[The Times, 20 Aug. 1910; Malvern Gazette, 19 and 26 Aug. 1910; Proceedings of the Society for Psychical Research, lxii.; Minutes of the Fabian Society, 1884; Archibald Henderson, George Bernard Shaw, Pall Mall Mag. 1903 (with photographic reproduction); private information.]

E. S. H-R.

POLLEN, JOHN HUNGERFORD (1820–1902), artist and author, born at 6 New Burlington Street, London, W., on 19 Nov. 1820, was second son (in a family of three sons and three daughters) of Richard Pollen (1786–1838) of Rodbourne, Wiltshire, by his wife Anne, sister of Charles Robert Cockerell [q. v.], the architect. Sir John Walter Pollen (1784–1863), second baronet of Redenham, Hampshire, was his uncle. Educated at Durham House, Chelsea (1829–33), and at Eton (1833–8) under Edward Coleridge, Pollen matriculated at Christ Church, Oxford, in 1838; he graduated B.A. in 1842, and proceeded M.A. in 1844; he was fellow of Merton College (1842–52), and dean and bursar in 1844, and served as senior proctor of the university (1851–2).

Pollen fell early under the influence of the Oxford Movement, and read much patristic literature. Taking holy orders, he became curate of St. Peter-le-Bailey, Oxford; but the Tractarian upheaval of 1845 weakened Pollen's attachment to the Church of England, and he resigned his curacy in 1846. With Thomas William Allies [q. v. Suppl. II] he visited Paris in 1847, and studied the organisation of the French church. On his return he associated himself with Pusey, Charles Marriott [q. v.], and the leading ritualists, and became pro-vicar at St. Saviour's, Leeds, the church which Pusey had founded in 1842. During his stay there (1847–52) most of his colleagues seceded to Rome. In December 1852 he was inhibited by Charles Thomas Longley [q. v.], then bishop of Ripon, for his extreme sacramental views, and on 20 Oct. 1852 he was himself received into the Roman catholic church at Rouen. His elder brother Richard (afterwards third baronet) followed his example next year (see POLLEN'S *Narrative of Five Years at St. Saviour's, Leeds*, Oxford, 1851, and his *Letter to the Parishioners of St. Saviour's, Leeds*, Oxford, 1851). Visits to Rome at the end of 1852 and 1853 led to friendship with (Cardinal) Herbert Vaughan [q. v. Suppl. II] and with W. M. Thackeray.

Pollen, who remained a layman, thenceforth devoted himself professionally to art and architecture. He had already studied the subjects at home and on his foreign travel, and practised them as an amateur.

with the encouragement of his uncle, Charles Cockerell.

In 1842 he restored the aisle of Wells Cathedral, where another uncle Dr. Goodenough, was dean. While curate he designed and executed in 1844 the ceilings of St. Peter-le-Bailey, Oxford, and he was responsible for the fine ceiling of Merton College chapel in 1850. Early in 1855 he accepted the invitation of John Henry Newman [q. v.], the rector, to become professor of fine arts in the catholic university of Ireland in Dublin, and to build and decorate the university church. His lectures, which began in June 1855 (printed in 'Atlantis,' the official magazine of the university), dealt with general æsthetic principles rather than with technique, in which he had no adequate training. He also joined the staff of the 'Tablet' newspaper, where he showed independence and sagacity as an art critic, detecting the merits of Turner and Whistler long before their general recognition.

In the summer of 1857 Pollen finally settled in London, living first at Hampstead and from 1858 to 1878 at Bayswater. He had previously met at Oxford Turner and Millais, and through Millais grew intimate with other Pre-Raphaelites. With Rossetti, Burne-Jones, and William Morris he assisted in the fresco decoration of the hall of the Union Society at Oxford in the summer of 1858 (see HOLMAN HUNT'S *Story of the Paintings at the Oxford Union Society*, Oxford, 1906, fol.; ESTHER WOOD'S *Gabriel Rossetti and the Pre-Raphaelite Movement*, 1894, pp. 142–6; *Memorials of Sir E. Burne-Jones*, 1904, i. 158 seq.). He was one of the first to reintroduce fresco decoration into England. Meanwhile his admiration for Turner's work brought him Ruskin's acquaintance (1855), and in 1860, at Ruskin's request, he designed for the new Oxford Museum a scheme of decoration, which was not carried out; his drawing is in the Museum (see *The Times*, 11 Feb. 1909).

From 1860 onwards Pollen was busily engaged on private and public commissions. Chief among his works were the decoration of Blickling Hall, Aylsham, for the Marquis of Lothian in 1860, and the fresco decoration at Alton Towers, the seat of the Earl of Shrewsbury (1874–7). At Alton Towers he produced the effect of tapestry by skilfully and with archæological accuracy painting in oil on rough canvas incidents in the hundred years' war. A design in water-colours for one of the canvases, 'The Landing of Henry V at Harfleur,' was purchased after Pollen's death for South Kensington Museum. He was responsible for stained glass windows, furniture, and panels in the Jacobean style at another of Lord Shrewsbury's seats, Ingestre Hall, Stafford, from 1876 to 1891; he built a house in 1876 for Lord Lovelace on the Thames Embankment, and an ornamental cottage in 1894 at Chenies for the Duchess of Bedford. Among many ecclesiastical commissions was the building and decoration in 1863 of the church of St. Mary, Rhyl, and of the convent of the Sacred Heart at Wandsworth in 1870.

Meanwhile, Thackeray, for whose 'Denis Duval' Pollen made in 1863 an unfinished series of sketches, introduced him to Sir Henry Cole [q. v.], who appointed him in December 1863 official editor of the art and industrial departments of the South Kensington (now Victoria and Albert) Museum. He also served on the advisory committee for purchases until November 1876. Pollen devoted his energies to the South Kensington collections, and besides issuing official catalogues gave lectures on historical ornament and kindred subjects. He served on the jury for art at the international exhibition at South Kensington in 1862, at the Dublin exhibition in 1865, and at Paris in 1867. At the Society of Arts he lectured frequently on decorative art, delivering the Cantor lectures in 1885 on 'Carving and Furniture,' and winning the society's silver medal for a paper on 'Renaissance Woodwork' in 1898.

Resigning his South Kensington post in November 1876, Pollen became in December private secretary to the Marquis of Ripon [q. v. Suppl. II], and continued to conduct the marquis's correspondence in England after 1880, when Lord Ripon went to India as viceroy. In the autumn of 1884 Pollen visited India, and after a brief archæological tour returned home with the viceroy in December 1884. A privately printed pamphlet entitled 'An Indian Farewell to the Marquis of Ripon' (1885) described his Indian experience. He thenceforth avowed himself an advanced liberal in both Indian and Irish politics, supporting the efforts of Mr. Wilfrid Scawen Blunt in Ireland and forming an intimacy with Gladstone.

Artistic pursuits however remained to the end his chief interest, and his services as a decorator continued in demand. In 1886 and 1887 he exhibited drawings at the Royal Academy and at the Paris Salon, and he prepared in 1880 a series of designs for St. George's Hall, Liverpool, which were not executed. He supported the newly founded United Arts and Crafts Guild, and was an exhibitor at the Guild's Exhibition at the New Gallery in October 1889. He died suddenly at 11 Pembridge Crescent, North Kensington, on 2 Dec. 1902, and was buried in the family vault at Kensal Green cemetery. He married on 18 Sept. 1855 Maria Margaret, second daughter of John Charles La Primaudaye, of Huguenot descent, of St. John's College, Oxford, and Graffham Rectory, by Ellen, sister of John Gellibrand Hubbard, first Lord Addington [q. v.], and had issue seven sons and three daughters. His widow published 'Seven Centuries of Lace' in 1908.

Pollen did much to reform taste in domestic furniture and decoration at home and abroad. He was an ardent sportsman and a member of the artists' corps of volunteers, formed in 1860. He was always active in catholic philanthropy. His most important publication was the 'Universal Catalogue of Books on Art' (2 vols. 1870; supplementary vol. 1877, 4to), which he prepared for South Kensington. Other official compilations were: 1. 'Ancient and Modern Furniture and Woodwork,' 1873; 2nd edit. 1875; revised edit. completed by T. A. Lehfeldt, 1908. 2. 'Catalogue of the Special Loan Exhibition of Enamels on Metals,' 1874. 3. 'A Description of the Trajan Column,' 1874. 4. 'Description of the Architecture and Monumental Sculptures,' 1874. 5. 'Ancient and Modern Gold and Silversmith's Work,' 1878. 6. 'A Catalogue of a Special Loan Collection of English Furniture and Figured Silk' (Bethnal Green Branch), 1896. He also contributed chapters on furniture and woodwork to Stanford's series of 'British Manufacturing Industries' (1874; 2nd edit. 1877).

There is a pencil sketch of Pollen by Sir William Ross (1823), a painting in oils by Mrs. Carpenter (1838), and an etching by Alphonse Legros (1865), as well as a rough pen-and-ink sketch drawn by himself in 1862. Reproductions of these appear in the 'Life' (1912). A drawing of Mrs. Pollen was made by D. G. Rossetti in 1858.

[The Times, 5 Dec. 1902; Tablet, 6 Dec. 1902; John Hungerford Pollen, by Anne Pollen, 1912; Liddon's Life of Pusey, iii. 112–136, 355–368; Bryan's Dict. of Painters; Graves's Royal Acad. Exhibitors, 1906; private information from Sir George Birdwood.]

W. B. O.

POORE, GEORGE VIVIAN (1843–1904), physician and authority on sanitation, born at Andover on 23 Sept. 1843, was youngest of ten children of Commander John Poore, R.N., who had retired from the service on the reduction of the navy in 1815. His mother was Martha Midlane. In his early days he was destined for his father's profession, and after education at home was sent at the age of ten to the Royal Naval School at New Cross, where he stayed until he was nearly seventeen. Here he gained a medal for good conduct, but having determined to enter the medical profession declined a marine cadetship. He began his medical training by an apprenticeship at Broughton near Winchester under Dr. Luther Fox, father of Dr. William Tilbury Fox [q. v.]. On leaving Dr. Fox he matriculated at the University of London and entered as a student at University College Hospital, qualifying as M.R.C.S. England in 1866. During the same year he acted as surgeon to the Great Eastern while she was employed in the laying of the Atlantic cable.

In 1868 he graduated M.B. and B.S. at the University of London, proceeding to the doctorate in 1871. In 1870 he was admitted a member of the Royal College of Physicians of London, and in 1877 was elected a fellow. During 1870 and 1871 he travelled as medical attendant with Prince Leopold, Duke of Albany, and he remained in charge of his health until 1877. In 1872 he was selected by Queen Victoria to accompany Edward VII, when Prince of Wales, during his convalescence in the south of France after his severe attack of typhoid fever. In 1872, too, Poore became lecturer on medical jurisprudence at Charing Cross Hospital, and gave a course of lectures on the 'Medical Uses of Electricity,' a study which was then in its infancy. In 1876 he was elected assistant physician to University College Hospital and professor of medical jurisprudence and clinical medicine. Among his colleagues were Sir William Jenner, Sir John Russell Reynolds, Sir John Erichsen, Tilbury Fox, Grailly Hewett, and Sir Henry Thompson. In 1876 he also published his 'Text Book of Electricity in Medicine and Surgery,' at the time the most complete and useful English work on the subject.

Poore was a brilliant lecturer, his delivery being admirable, and his matter being always well arranged. His lectures on medical jurisprudence were published as 'A Treatise on Medical Jurisprudence' (1901; 2nd edit. 1902). In 1883 he was elected full physician to the hospital, and held this post with his professorship until May 1903, when failing health compelled his retirement to his country house at Andover. He died there on 23 Nov. 1904 from cardiac failure due to aortic disease. He was unmarried.

Outside his purely medical work Poore was well known both to the medical profession and to the public as an ardent sanitarian. In 1891 he was general secretary of the sanitary congress. In his garden at Andover he proved that living humus had a powerful disinfecting property. In his 'Essays on Rural Hygiene' (1893), chapter iv., entitled 'The Living Earth,' he set forth this opinion with characteristic charm of style and wealth of illustration. He dealt with sanitation and with the wastefulness of the water carriage of sewage in his Milroy lectures for 1899, 'The Earth in Relation to the Destruction and Preservation of Contagia' (1902, with appendix of public addresses), and in 'The Dwelling House' (2nd edit. 1898). His views were regarded by many sanitary authorities as heretical, but he proved their practical value as far as the country dwelling was concerned.

Poore also published, together with contributions to medical journals and orations upon dietetic and sanitary matters: 1. 'Physical Diagnosis of Diseases of the Throat, Mouth, and Nose,' 1881. 2. 'London Ancient and Modern from the Sanitary and Medical Point of View,' 1889. 3. 'Nervous Affections of the Hand,' 1897.

[Lancet, 10 Dec. 1904; British Medical Journal, 3 Dec. 1904; information from friends; personal knowledge.] H. P. C.

POPE, GEORGE UGLOW (1820–1908), missionary and Tamil scholar, was born on 24 April 1820 in Prince Edward Island, Nova Scotia. His father, John Pope, born at Padstow, Cornwall, emigrated to Prince Edward Island in 1818, and in 1820 removed to Nova Scotia, where giving up trade he became a missionary; returning in 1826 to Plymouth, he there resumed his business as merchant and shipowner, and took a prominent part in municipal affairs. George's mother was Catherine Uglow of Stratton, North Cornwall. Both parents were devout Wesleyans. William Burt Pope [q. v. Suppl. II] was his younger brother. Educated at Wesleyan institutions at Bury and Hoxton, George resolved in his fourteenth year to become a missionary to the Tamil-speaking population of Southern India. He landed at Madras in 1839, having learned Tamil from books during the voyage. In 1843 he was ordained in the Church of England, and henceforth was associated with the Society for the Propagation of the Gospel, which had recently taken over the native congregations founded by Christian Friedrich Schwartz [q. v.] and other German missionaries in the extreme south of India. During the first ten years his sphere of work was in Tinnevelly. Then came a visit to England (1849–51), mostly spent at Oxford, where he came into intimate relation with Cardinal Manning, Archbishop Trench, Bishop Samuel Wilberforce, Bishop Lonsdale, Dr. Pusey, and John Keble. On his return to India there followed another ten years of missionary labour in Tanjore, during which he felt himself compelled to protest against the practices of the Lutheran missionaries of Tranquebar in the toleration of caste and native customs. At this time he founded in Tinnevelly district the Sawyer-puram seminary for training native clergy, which has a Pope memorial hall and library; and also St. Peter's schools for boys (now a college) and for girls at Tanjore.

In 1859 he founded the grammar school at Ootacamund, on the Nilgiri Hills, of which he was the first headmaster; and in 1870 he was transferred to the principalship of Bishop Cotton's schools and college at Bangalore, in Mysore, where he left the reputation of severity with the cane. With both these appointments he combined clerical duty, and during this period published many educational manuals. In 1859 he became a fellow of the newly founded Madras University, for which he was a constant examiner. In 1864 the Lambeth degree of D.D. was conferred on him by Archbishop Longley. He left India finally in 1880, after forty years of active work. A short time was passed in Manchester, and then he settled at Oxford as diocesan secretary of the S.P.G. In 1884 he was appointed teacher of Tamil and Telugu in the university; in 1886 he was awarded the honorary degree of M.A.; and from 1888 he was chaplain at Balliol College, where he enjoyed the intimate friendship of two Masters, Jowett and Caird. In 1906 he received the gold medal of the Royal Asiatic Society, which is awarded every three years to an oriental scholar (cf. *Journ. Roy. Asiatic Soc.* 1906, pp. 767–790). He died at Oxford, after a brief illness, on 11 Feb. 1908, and was buried in St. Sepulchre's cemetery. His friends and pupils in India, the majority Hindus, placed by subscription a monument on his grave and founded a memorial prize for Tamil studies in the university of Madras;

a gymnasium called by his name has also been erected in Bishop Cotton's school at Bangalore.

Pope married (1) in 1841 Mary, daughter of the Rev. J. Carver; she died at Tuticorin in 1845; (2) in 1849, at Madras, Henrietta Page, daughter of G. Van Someren. She and her two daughters were awarded a joint civil list pension of 50*l.* in 1909. She died at Forest Hill, London, on 11 Sept. 1911, and is buried with her husband. Three sons won distinction in the service of the Indian government, viz. John Van Someren Pope, for seventeen years director of public instruction in Burma; Arthur William Uglow Pope, C.I.E. (1906), railway engineer and manager in India and China; and Lieut.-colonel Thomas Henry Pope, I.M.S., professor of ophthalmology at the Madras Medical College. A not very satisfactory portrait by Alfred Wolmark, painted by subscription among his Madras pupils, is in the Indian Institute at Oxford.

Pope ranks as the first of Tamil scholars, even when compared with Beschi, Francis Whyte Ellis [q. v.], and Bishop Caldwell, though he did not concern himself much with the cognate Dravidian languages. With him Tamil was the means to understand the history, religion, and sentiment of the people of Southern India. As early as 1842 he published (in Tamil) his 'First Catechism of Tamil Grammar,' which was re-issued in 1895, with an English translation, by the Clarendon Press. His educational books of this kind reached completion in the series entitled 'Handbook to the Ordinary Dialect of the Tamil Language,' which includes Tamil-English and English-Tamil dictionaries, as well as a prose reader and the seventh edition of his Tamil handbook (Oxford, 1904–6). But his reputation rests upon his critical editions of three classical works of old Tamil literature: the 'Kurral' of the pariah poet Tiruvalluvar, which has supplied a metrical catechism of morality to the people of Southern India for at least a thousand years (1886); the 'Nāladiyār,' or four hundred quatrains of similar didactic sayings, probably of yet earlier date and of equal popularity (1893); and the 'Tiruvaçagam,' or sacred utterances of Manikka-Vaçagar, to which is prefixed a summary of the life and legends of the author, with appendices illustrating the system of philosophy and religion in Southern India known as Saiva Siddhantam (1900). Of this last the preface is dated on the editor's eightieth birthday and the dedication is to the memory of Jowett. All these books contain translations into English, together with copious notes and a lexicon. Apart from their erudition, they reveal Pope's warm sympathy with the people and their literature. In addition to his published books, Pope left in MS. complete editions and English translations of at least three Tamil works, as well as a vast amount of material for a standard Tamil dictionary, which it is hoped will be utilised by a committee of native scholars that has been formed at Madras. He further began about 1890 a catalogue of the Tamil printed books in the British Museum, which was carried out by Dr. L. D. Barnett. Among numerous pamphlets and sermons, published chiefly in his early days, was 'An Alphabet for all India' (Madras, 1859), a plan for adapting the Roman alphabet to all the languages of India.

Pope, whose culture was wide, was an enthusiastic student of all great literature. His favourite poet was Browning, to whose loftiness of speculation he paid tribute in his 'St. John in the Desert' (1897; 2nd edit. 1904, an introduction and notes to Browning's 'A Death in the Desert). He knew Browning personally, and to him the poet gave the 'square old yellow book with crumpled vellum covers,' which formed the basis of 'The Ring and the Book,' and which Pope presented to the library of Balliol College. Keenly interested in all phases of philosophy and religion, he welcomed the development of modern Christian thought, but was always loyal to the Wesleyanism in which he had been brought up. His brilliant and picturesque talk bore witness to the variety of his intellectual interests and his catholicity of thought.

[Obituary by M. de Z. Wickremasinghe in Journal of Royal Asiatic Soc. 1908; personal reminiscences by Rev. A. L. Mayhew in Guardian, 26 Feb 1908.] J. S. C.

POPE, SAMUEL (1826–1901), barrister, born at Manchester on 11 Dec. 1826, was eldest son of Samuel Pope, a merchant of London and Manchester, by his wife Phebe, daughter of William Rushton, merchant, of Liverpool. After private education he was employed in business, and in his leisure cultivated in debating societies an aptitude for public speaking. Coming to London, he studied at London University, entered at the Middle Temple on 13 Nov. 1855, and was called to the bar on 7 June 1858. Deeply interested in politics, he unsuccessfully contested Stoke as a liberal in the following year. For a few years he practised with success in his native town, but removed to London in 1865. In the same year, and again in 1868, he unsucessfully contested Bolton. In 1869 he was however made recorder of the town and took silk. In London he soon devoted himself to parliamentary practice, for which his persuasive eloquence and commanding personality admirably fitted him. He presented complicated facts and figures simply and interestingly and in due perspective. At his death he was the leader of the parliamentary bar. He was chosen a bencher of his inn on 27 Jan. 1870, and was treasurer in 1888–9, when he made a valuable donation of books to the library.

A keen advocate of the temperance cause from youth, Pope was at his death an honorary secretary of the United Kingdom Alliance. He was a freemason, becoming senior grand deacon in grand lodge in 1886. He died at his residence, 74 Ashley Gardens, Westminster, on 22 July 1901, and was buried at Llanbedr in Merionethshire, of which county he was a J.P. and deputy lieutenant. Pope married Hannah, daughter of Thomas Bury of Timperley Lodge, Cheshire; she predeceased him without issue in 1880.

A portrait by Sir Hubert von Herkomer is in possession of the family. A loving cup with a bust of him in relief was presented to the Middle Temple in his memory by some friends (*Master Worsley's Book*, ed. A. R. Ingpen, K.C., p. 327). A cartoon portrait by 'Spy' appeared in 'Vanity Fair' in 1885.

[The Times, 24 July 1901; Foster, Men at the Bar; Men and Women of the Time, 1899; Hutchinson, Notable Middle Templars, 1902; private information.] C. E. A. B.

POPE, WILLIAM BURT (1822–1903), Wesleyan divine, born at Horton, Nova Scotia, on 19 Feb. 1822, was younger son of John Pope, and younger brother of George Uglow Pope [q. v. Suppl. II for full parentage]. After education at a village school at Hooe and at a secondary school at Saltash, near Plymouth, William spent a year in boyhood (1837–8) at Bedeque, Prince Edward Island, assisting an uncle, a shipbuilder and general merchant. Devoting his leisure to the study of Latin, Greek, French and German, he was accepted, in 1840, by the methodist synod of Cornwall as a candidate for the ministry, and entered the Methodist Theological Institution at Hoxton. There he added Hebrew and Arabic to his stock of languages. In 1842 he began his active ministry at Kingsbridge, Devonshire, and served for short periods at Liskeard, Jersey, Sandhurst, Dover and Halifax, and for longer periods at City Road, London, Hull, Manchester, Leeds, and Southport.

In 1867 he succeeded Dr. John Hannah the elder [q. v.] as tutor of systematic theology at Didsbury. He received the degree of D.D. from the Wesleyan University, U.S.A., in 1865 and from the University of Edinburgh in 1877. In 1876 he visited America with Dr. Rigg as delegate to the general conference of the methodist episcopal church at Baltimore. In 1877 he was president of the Wesleyan conference at Bristol. He resigned his position at Didsbury in 1886. He died, after much suffering from mental depression, on 5 July 1903, and was buried in Abney Park cemetery, London.

Pope's industry was unflagging. He began his day at 4 A.M., and made notable contributions to theological literature which were deemed authoritative by his own church, while he was actively engaged in the ministry and in teaching. His chief work was the 'Compendium of Christian Theology,' in three volumes (1875; 2nd edit. 1880). In the same year appeared his Fernley lecture on 'The Person of Christ,' which was translated into German. His published collections of sermons included 'The Prayers of St. Paul' (2nd edit. 1896), and his characteristic 'Sermons, Addresses and Charges,' delivered during the year of his presidency (1878). In 1860 he became editor, having as his co-editor (1883–6) James Harrison Rigg [q. v. Suppl. II], of the 'London Quarterly Review,' to which he was already a contributor. Pope translated from the German, in whole or part, three important books for Messrs. T. and T. Clark's 'Theological Library,' Stier on 'The Words of the Lord Jesus' (1855); Ebrard on the 'Epistles of St. John' (1860); and Haupt on the 'First Epistle of St. John' (1879), and he contributed to 'Schaff's Popular Commentary' expositions of Ezra, Nehemiah (1882) and the Epistles of St. John (1883).

A portrait, painted by Mr. A. T. Nowell, was presented to Didsbury College by old students and friends in 1892.

Pope married, in 1845, Ann Eliza Lethbridge, daughter of a yeoman farmer of Modbury, near Plymouth. By her he had six sons, two of whom died in early life, and four daughters.

[William Burt Pope: Theologian and Saint, by R. W. Moss, D.D., 1909; Telford's Life of Dr. J. H. Rigg, 1909.] C. H. I.

PORTAL, MELVILLE (1819-1904), politician, born on 31 July 1819 at his father's second seat of Freefolk Priors, Hampshire, was eldest surviving son of John Portal of Freefolk Priors and Laverstoke, Hampshire, the head of the Huguenot family of that name, by his second wife, Elizabeth, only daughter of Henry Drummond and Anne Dundas, daughter of Henry, first Viscount Melville [q. v.]. He was sent to Harrow school in 1832 to the house of Archdeacon Phelps, and left in 1837. He matriculated at Christ Church, Oxford, on 30 May 1838, graduated B.A. in 1842, and proceeded M.A. in 1844. He was treasurer in 1841 and president next year of the Union at Oxford, and was an admirer of John Henry Newman [q. v.], whom he venerated throughout life and who occasionally wrote to him (WARD, *Life of Newman*, i. 617), though Portal's convictions never advanced further towards Rome. With four other young Oxonians he provided the funds for the building of the church of Bussage, a neglected village in Gloucestershire. On 15 April 1842 he was entered a student of Lincoln's Inn, was called to the bar on 24 Nov. 1845, and went the western circuit. He succeeded to his father's estate in 1848, and on 6 April 1849 was elected M.P. for the northern division of Hampshire as a conservative with a majority of 331 over William Shaw. In July 1852 Portal was re-elected without opposition, and sat till the next general election in 1857, when he retired. His first speech in the House of Commons was on 25 March 1851, the seventh night of the debate on the ecclesiastical titles assumption bill. He described it as 'the hasty effusion of an off-handed premier' and voted against it. In 1855 he married a sister of the wife of the prime minister, Lord John Russell [q. v.], and became his friend. Portal resided constantly at Laverstoke, and from 1846, when he was appointed a county magistrate, took a prominent part in the judicial and administrative work of the county; in 1863 he was high sheriff. He was chairman of the judicial business (1865–89) and was chairman of quarter sessions (1879–1903), during which time he reformed the treatment of prisoners in the county goal and introduced arrangements since adopted throughout England. In 1871 Portal persuaded the quarter sessions to order the restoration of the great hall of the castle of Winchester, where the assizes were held, and the work was carried out under his supervision. He published in 1899 'The Great Hall of Winchester Castle,' a quarto containing the history and architectural description of the castle, which he had written and illustrated in memory of fifty years' familiar intercourse with friends within its walls. He died at Laverstoke on 24 Jan. 1904, and was buried in the mortuary chapel in Laverstoke park. His life was spent in laborious and disinterested public service. His portrait by Archibald Stuart Wortley was presented to the county by members of the court of quarter sessions on 13 Oct. 1890, and is in the great hall at Winchester. He married on 9 Oct. 1855 Lady Charlotte Mary, fourth daughter of Gilbert Elliot, second earl of Minto [q. v.]. She died on 3 June 1899. They had three sons, of whom the second was Sir Gerald Herbert Portal [q. v.], and three daughters.

[Hampshire Chronicle, 18 Oct. 1890, 4 July 1903, 30 Jan. 1904; Burke's Peerage and Baronetage; Foster, Alumni Oxonienses; Harrow School Register; P. M. Thornton, Harrow School; Hansard, Debates; information from Miss E. M. Portal.] N. M.

POTT, ALFRED (1822–1908), principal of Cuddesdon College, born on 30 Sept. 1822 at Norwood, was the second son of Charles Pott of Norwood, Surrey, and Anna, daughter of C. S. Cox, master in chancery. Educated at Eton under Edward Craven Hawtrey [q. v.], he matriculated at Balliol College, Oxford, on 16 Dec. 1840. Having been elected to a demyship at Magdalen College in 1843, he graduated B.A. in 1844 with a second class in literæ humaniores, and next year he won the Johnson theological scholarship. He proceeded M.A. in 1847, and B.D. in 1854. He was ordained deacon in 1845 and priest in the following year. He became curate of Cuddesdon, and in 1851 vicar on the nomination of Bishop Samuel Wilberforce [q. v.]. In 1853 he was elected a fellow of Magdalen College; and in 1854 he was appointed first principal of the new theological college at Cuddesdon. Here he laid down the lines upon which the college was subsequently carried on. But he was somewhat overshadowed by his vice-principal, Henry Parry Liddon [q. v.], and he resigned owing to ill-health shortly after Charles Pourtales Golightly [q. v.] had called attention to the extreme high church practices of the Cuddesdon system. In 1858 he accepted the living of East Hendred, Berkshire, becoming vicar of Abingdon in 1867. Bishop Wilberforce appointed Pott one of his examining chaplains, made him hon. canon of Christ Church in 1868, and in 1869 preferred him to the archdeaconry of Berkshire. Pott subsequently held the benefices of Clifton-Hampden (1874–82) and of Sonning (1882–99). He resigned the archdeaconry in 1903, but retained his hon. canonry. In convocation Pott was a recognised authority on ecclesiastical law; and as archdeacon he showed wisdom and judgment. Although a high churchman he enjoyed the friendship of men of widely divergent opinions. He died at Windlesham, Surrey, on 28 Feb. 1908, and was buried at Clifton-Hampden. In 1855 he married Emily Harriet (*d.* 1903), daughter of Joseph Gibbs, vicar of Clifton-Hampden.

Besides sermons and charges, Pott published: 1. 'Confirmation Lectures delivered to a Village Congregation,' 1852; 5th edit. 1886. 2. 'Village Lectures on the Sacraments and Occasional Services of the Church,' 1854.

[The Times, 29 Feb. 1908; Guardian, 4 March 1908; Life of Samuel Wilberforce, 1883, ii. 366, iii. 399; Johnston, Life and Letters of Henry Parry Liddon, 1904, pp. 30 seq.; Cuddesdon College (1854–1904), 1904; Bloxam, Register of St. Mary Magdalen College, Oxford, 1881, vii. 357; Foster, Alumni Oxon. 1888.]

G. S. W.

POWELL, FREDERICK YORK (1850–1904), regius professor of modern history at Oxford, born on 14 Jan. 1850 at 33 Woburn Place, Bloomsbury, was eldest child and only son of Frederick Powell, by his wife Mary (*d.* 1910), daughter of Dr. James York (*d.* 1882), 'a very clever and good physician and a pretty Spanish scholar and a handsome man.' His father, a commissariat merchant, who had an office in Mincing Lane, came of a south Wales family, and the son was proud to call himself a Welshman. Much of Powell's early life was spent at Sandgate, where he learned to love the sea and developed enduring friendships with the fisher folk. In the autumn of 1859 he was put to a preparatory school at Hastings (the Manor House, kept by Mr. Alexander Murray). In 1864 he entered Dr. Jex Blake's house at Rugby, but though he gained a name for 'uncanny stories and remote species of knowledge,' he never rose above the lower fifth and left, chiefly for reasons of health, in July 1866. The next two years were fruitfully spent in travel and self-education. There was a visit to Biarritz, and a tour in Sweden which gave Powell, who had read Dasent's story of 'Burnt Njal' at Rugby, occasion to learn and practise a Scandinavian tongue. At eighteen he was placed under the care of Mr. Henry Tull Rhoades at Bonchurch, and began to work at Old French, German, and Icelandic. He was already a strong socialist and agnostic, and had formed most of the tastes and prejudices which accompanied him through life—an interest in old armour, a special attraction for the art of William Blake, a passion for northern and medieval literature, and an aversion from philosophy, excepting always the work of Kant and Schopenhauer.

Powell went to Oxford in 1868, and after a year spent with the non-collegiate students was received into Christ Church, on the recommendation of Dr. George William Kitchin, censor of the non-collegiate body and formerly student and tutor of Christ Church. He gained a first class in the school of law and modern history in Trinity term 1872. After graduating B.A., Powell spent two years (1872–4) at his father's house in Lancaster Gate. He had entered at the Middle Temple on 8 Nov. 1870, and was called to the bar on 6 June 1874.

Powell's first academic appointment was to teach one of the few subjects in which he had no enthusiastic interest. In 1874 he was appointed to a lectureship in law at Christ Church, and save for a year's interlude as history lecturer at Trinity—an engagement terminated owing to the representation of some of his pupils who wished to be crammed for examinations—Powell's official teaching in Oxford was, until 1894, confined to the uncongenial subjects of law and political economy. He had however attracted the attention of Mandell Creighton [q. v. Suppl. I], one of his examiners in the schools, and was invited to contribute a volume on Early England to Longman's 'Epochs of English History,' of which Creighton was editor. The book, 'Early England to the Norman Conquest,' which was published in 1876, delighted Creighton, who pronounced it to be written 'in a charmingly simple, almost Biblical style.' Meanwhile, in 1869, Powell had met Gudbrandr Vigfusson [q. v.], who had come to Oxford in 1866 to edit the 'Icelandic-English Dictionary' for the Oxford Press. In 1877 Powell was already engaged with Vigfusson upon the Prolegomena to an edition of the 'Sturlunga Saga,' 'taking down across the table,' said Vigfusson, 'my thoughts and theories, so that though the substance and drift of the arguments are mine, the English with the exception of bits and phrases here and there is Mr. Powell's throughout.' An 'Icelandic Prose Reader,' the notes to which were mainly the work of Powell, followed in 1879, and two years later the 'Corpus Poeticum Boreale,' an edition of the whole of 'Ancient Northern Poetry,' with translations and a full commentary. The translations were provided by Powell and exhibited his easy command of a fresh, manly English style.

The first volume contains the old mythical and heroic poetry—the poems of the 'Elder Edda' and other pieces of like character. The second volume is a collection of the poems written, chiefly by Icelanders, in honour of successive kings of Norway and other important personages. It is here that Powell's work is most valuable in illustration of Scandinavian history. The poems are those which were used as authorities by the early historians of Norway (such as Snorre Sturluson); the introductions to the different sections, in the second volume of the 'Corpus,' containing biographical notices of the poets, form the only original work in English on this portion of Scandinavian history. It is hardly possible to describe the extraordinary variety of contents in the editorial part of the two volumes—essays on mythology and points of literary history, often venturesome and always full of life.

The 'Corpus Poeticum Boreale' at once made Powell's name as a northern scholar and was intended to be the prelude to an even more ambitious work. In August 1884 Powell spent a fortnight with Vigfusson in Copenhagen examining Icelandic manuscripts, with the view to an edition and translation of the best classics in the northern prose, a proposal for which had been submitted to the Clarendon Press. The work was steadily pushed on and most of the 'Origines Islandicæ' was already in proof when Vigfusson died in 1889. So long as Vigfusson was alive Powell was kept steadily working at his Scandinavian task, but with the removal of his friend and associate the passion for miscellaneous reading gained the ascendant, with the result that the work was never pushed to a conclusion and was only published in 1905 after Powell's death. Here, as before, the labour of the two fellow-workers is often indistinguishable. The text of the prose sagas is substantially the work of Vigfusson, 'the ordering, the English, and many of the literary criticisms, portraits, and parallels are Powell's' (Elton, i. 101). But though Vigfusson was the leading partner in these northern expeditions, Powell's assistance was substantive and essential, adding as it did to the fine technical scholarship of the Icelandic patriot a wide knowledge of medieval history and literature and a simple nervous English exactly adapted to its purpose.

Meanwhile, in 1884, through the good offices of Dean Liddell, Powell had been made a student of Christ Church. His official duties as law lecturer were to coach men for the law school, to look after Indian civil service candidates, and to lecture on pass political economy. His real and congenial avocations extended far beyond this narrow circuit. Besides his work on Scandinavian literature, he taught Old English, Old French, and even for a time Old German, for the Association for Education of Women in Oxford, took a leading share in founding the 'English Historical Review' (1885), and published a history of 'England from the Earliest Times to the Death of Henry VII' (1885), designed for 'the middle forms of schools,' which is remarkable for its fresh use of chronicles, ballads, and romances, and for its insight into the material fabric of medieval civilisation. Then a valuable series of little books, 'English History from Contemporary Writers,' began under his editorship in 1885.

Thus Powell built for himself a reputation as one of the most profound scholars in medieval history and literature in England, and, accordingly, no surprise was felt when upon the death of James Anthony Froude [q. v. Suppl. I] in 1894, and upon the refusal of Samuel Rawson Gardiner [q. v. Suppl. II] to come to Oxford, the regius professorship of modern history was conferred on Powell on the recommendation of Lord Rosebery (Dec. 1894). The post was accepted with misgivings. Powell had no gift either for public lecturing or for organisation. He was shy of an audience which he did not know, and although both in his inaugural lecture and upon subsequent occasions he pleaded for the scientific treatment of history, for the training of public archivists, for the divorce of history and ethics, his practice was consistently better or worse than his theory, and his numerous articles contributed to the press abound in the vigorous ethical judgments which were the necessity of his strong temperament.

As professor of history Powell disappointed some of his friends. He made no special contribution to the advance of historical science, and failed to make any general impression upon the undergraduates as a teacher. Indeed, from his fortieth year to the end of his life he published only two works, a translation of the 'Færeyinga Saga' (1896), dedicated jointly to Henry Liddell, dean of Christ Church, and Henry Stone, an old fisherman at Sandgate, and a rendering of some quatrains from 'Omar Khayyám' (1901). His services to knowledge cannot however, be measured by the ordinary tests. Powell was the most generous as well as the most unambitious of men. His time was his friends' time, and the hours which might have been spent upon his own work were freely lavished upon the assistance of others. Thus the edition of the mythical books of 'Saxo Grammaticus,' translated by Professor Elton, was due to his suggestion, and the bulk of the introduction was his work; and again as delegate of the Clarendon Press, an office which he held from 1885 till his death, Powell was able to render services to the advancement of learning which were none the less substantial because they were unadvertised. As professor he regularly lectured in his rooms at Christ Church on the sources of English history, and on every Thursday evening was at home to undergraduates, and here, as on any other informal occasion, he was an unfailing source of inspiration. In his pleasant rooms in the Meadow Buildings of Christ Church, with their stacks of books and Japanese prints, his shyness would disappear and he would discourse freely on any subject which came up, from boxing and fencing (of which he was an excellent judge) to the last Portuguese novel. His knowledge of foreign, especially of Romance, literature was singularly wide. He brought Verlaine to lecture in Oxford in 1891, and as a curator of the Taylorian Institute (from 1887) procured an invitation to Stéphane Mallarmé to give a lecture at the Taylorian on 28 Feb. 1894. The Belgian poet Verhaeren and the French sculptor Rodin were likewise at different times Powell's guests at Christ Church. He had also worked at Old Irish, and as one of the presidents of the Irish Texts Society urged in 1899 the importance of publishing the MS. Irish literature of the sixteenth, seventeenth and eighteenth centuries. On 7 April 1902 he lectured in Dublin to the Irish Literary Society on Irish influence in English literature, and in December of the same year went to Liverpool to speak for the endowment of Celtic studies in the university. Meanwhile, he was becoming a student of Persian, had dived into Maori and Gypsy, and had made a valuable collection of Japanese prints. Rumour asserted that he contributed to the 'Sporting Times,' and he was certainly as well acquainted with the boxing reports in the 'Licensed Victuallers' Gazette' as with the 'Kalevala' or 'Beowulf.' With all this he found time to write numerous reviews for the daily and weekly press, principally for the 'Academy,' and after 1890 for the 'Manchester Guardian' (see extracts in ELTON'S *Biography*). Another side of Powell's versatile nature is illustrated by the preface which he wrote to a penny garland of songs of labour, written by his friend William Hines (1893), chimney sweeper, herbalist, and radical agitator, of Oxford, and by the active share which he took in the foundation of Ruskin College, an institution devised to bring working men to Oxford. Powell, who had the genius for making friends among the poor, presided over the inaugural meeting at the town hall on 22 Feb. 1899, and acted from the first as a member of the council of the college. In religion Powell described himself as a 'decent heathen Aryan,' in politics as 'a socialist and a jingo.' He was a strong home ruler, an advocate of the Boer war, and the first president of the Oxford Tariff Reform League. He was made hon. LL.D. of Glasgow in 1901.

In 1874 Powell married Mrs. Batten, a widow with two young daughters. Mrs. Powell did not live in Oxford. It was Powell's habit for many years to spend the middle of the week during term time in Oxford and the week-end with his family in town. In January 1881 he moved his household from 6 Stamford Green West, Upper Clapton, where he had resided since his marriage, to Bedford Park, then 'an oasis of green gardens and red houses' and the resort of painters, players, poets, and journalists, where he resided till 1902. Here his only child, a daughter, Mariella, was born in 1884. Four years later Powell lost his wife. In the summer of 1894 he visited Ambleteuse on the coast of Normandy for the first time, and for the next ten years was 'a centre at the Hôtel Delpierre' during the summer season. Many of his graphic letters and poems refer to the delights of Ambleteuse, where he developed a taste for sketching. In December 1902 Powell gave up his London house and settled in North Oxford with his daughter. The next year came warnings of heart trouble. He died on 8 May 1904 at Staverton Grange, Woodstock Road, Oxford. He was buried at Wolvercote cemetery, without religious rites by his own desire. His daughter was granted a civil list pension of 70*l.* in 1905, and married Mr. F. H. Markoe in Christ Church cathedral, on 6 July 1912.

Oil-portraits by J. B. Yeats and J. Williamson are in the possession of his daughter. He also figures in a caricature by 'Spy' in 'Vanity Fair' (21 March 1895) and in William Rothenstein's 'Oxford Sketches.'

In appearance and dress Powell resembled a sea-captain. He was broad, burly and bearded, brusque in manner, with dark hair and eyes, and a deep rich laugh: in temperament an artist and a poet, in attainments a scholar, as a man simple, affectionate, observant, with rare powers of sensitive enjoyment, the delight of his friends, clerk and lay, rich and poor, and the centre of many clubs both in Oxford and London. In the sphere of learning he will chiefly be remembered for his published services to northern literature, and for the general stimulus which he gave to the study of medieval letters in Great Britain.

Besides the works mentioned, Powell published 'Old Stories from British History' (1882; 3rd edit. 1885; new impression 1903), and contributed with Vigfusson to the Grimm Centenary: 'Sigfred-Arminius and other Papers' (1886). He wrote several articles for this Dictionary, including a memoir of Vigfusson. Some chapters from his pen are included in W. G. Collingwood's 'Scandinavian Britain' (1908).

[Frederick York Powell: a Life and a Selection from his Letters and Occasional Writings, by Oliver Elton, 2 vols., Oxford, 1906, with full bibliography; Sette of Odd Volumes, Opusculum No. xxxviii., London, 1910, being a privately printed reprint of Powell's Some Words on Allegory in England, with biographical matter, by Dr. John Todhunter and Sir Ernest Clarke; Eng. Hist. Review, July 1904; Oxford Mag., 18 May 1904; The Times, 10 May 1904; Manchester Guardian, 10 May 1904; Monthly Review, June 1904; Morning Post, 10 May 1904; Folklore, June 1904; United Irishman, 16 July 1904; information from Prof. W. P. Ker; private knowledge.]

H. A. L. F.

PRATT, HODGSON (1824–1907), peace advocate, born at Bath on 10 Jan. 1824, was eldest of five sons of Samuel Peace Pratt by his wife Susanna Martha Hodgson (*d.* 1875). After education at Haileybury College (1844–6), where he won a prize for English essay in his first term, he matriculated at London University in 1844. In 1847 he joined the East India Company's service at Calcutta, subsequently becoming under-secretary to the government of Bengal and inspector of public instruction there.

While in India Pratt showed much sympathy with the natives, stimulating the educational and social development of the province of Bengal, and urging on the Bengalis closer relations with English life and thought. In 1851 he helped to found the 'Vernacular Literature Society' which published Bengali translations of standard English literature, including Macaulay's 'Life of Clive,' 'Robinson Crusoe,' Lamb's 'Tales from Shakespeare,' and selections from the 'Percy Anecdotes' (see *Reports of Transactions,* 1854–7). Pratt acted as secretary till 1856. He also started a school of industrial art. In 1857 Pratt was at home on leave and at the close of that year he contributed to the 'Economist' articles and letters dealing with Indian questions, social, political, educational, and religious, which were published collectively in a pamphlet. The spread of the Indian Mutiny recalled Pratt hurriedly to India, which he left finally in 1861.

Settling in England Pratt immediately threw himself into the industrial cooperative movement, in association with Vansittart Neale, Tom Hughes, and George Jacob Holyoake. He met Henry Solly in 1864 and became a member of the council of the Working Men's Club and Institute Union (founded by Solly in June 1862). In its interest he travelled up and down the country, encouraging struggling branches and forming new ones (see PRATT'S *Notes of a Tour among Clubs,* 1872). He was president from 1885 to 1902. With Solly he also started trade classes for workmen in St. Martin's Lane in 1874. In 1867 he was a vice-president with Auberon Herbert, W. E. Forster, George Joachim Goschen, and others of the Paris Excursion Committee, through whose efforts over 3000 British workmen visited the Paris Exhibition of that year (see PRATT'S preface to *Modern Industries: Reports by 12 British Workmen of the Paris Exhibition,* 1868).

At the same time Pratt, who had a perfect command of French, was an ardent champion of international arbitration. On the outbreak of the Franco-Prussian war of 1870 he pleaded for the peaceful settlement of the dispute. Two years later he joined in an appeal to M. Thiers, the French premier, for the release of Elisée Reclus, the geographer, who had thrown in his lot with the Commune, and had been taken prisoner (EUGENE OSWALD, *Reminiscences of a Busy Life,* pp. 518–21). In 1880 he joined William

Phillips and others in founding the International Arbitration and Peace Association, becoming first chairman of the executive committee. Four years later (1 July 1884) he founded, and for some time edited, the association's 'Journal' (still continued under the title of 'Concord'). In behalf of the association he visited nearly all the countries of Europe and helped largely in the formation of many kindred Continental societies—in Belgium, Italy, Germany, Austria, and Hungary. He took part in many international peace congresses at Paris and elsewhere from 1889 onwards. For the association Pratt translated Elie Ducommun's 'The Programme of the Peace Movement' (1896) and he summarised in English Descamps's 'The Organisation of International Arbitration' (1897). Pratt's persuasive advocacy of international arbitration and industrial co-operation bore good fruit, and his work was appreciated by governments and peoples at home and abroad. But his disinterested and retiring disposition withheld from him any general fame. On his friends' recommendation his claims to the Nobel Peace Prize were considered in Dec. 1906, when the award was made to Theodore Roosevelt. A few years before his death Pratt grew convinced that the only complete solution of industrial and social problems lay in socialism.

Pratt, who suffered much from defective eyesight, spent the last years of his life at Le Pecq, Seine et Oise, France, where he died on 26 Feb. 1907. He was buried in Highgate cemetery. He married (1) in 1849 Sarah Caroline Wetherall, daughter of an Irish squire; and (2) in 1892 Monica, daughter of the Rev. James Mangan, D.D., LL.D. She survived him with one daughter. A portrait in oils by Mr. Felix Moscheles hangs at the Club and Institute Union, Clerkenwell Road, London. The Annual Hodgson Pratt Memorial Lecture and travelling scholarship for working men, as well as prizes, were established in 1911.

[Concord, March 1907; The Times, 5 March and 14 Nov. 1907; Henry Solly, These Eighty Years, 1893, ii. 243–4, 434 seq.; B. T. Hall, Our Fifty Years (Jubilee History of the Working Men's Club), 1912; Frédéric Passy, Pour la paix, 1909, p. 113; Memorials of Old Haileybury College, 1894; information from Mr. J. F. Green and Mr. J. J. Dent.] W. B. O.

PRATT, JOSEPH BISHOP (1854–1910), engraver, son of Anthony Pratt, a printer of mezzotints, by his wife Ann Bishop, was born at 4 College Terrace, Camden New Town, London, N., on 1 Jan. 1854. In 1868 he was apprenticed to David Lucas, with whom he remained five years. The first plate for which he received a commission, 'Maternal Felicity,' after Samuel Carter, was published in Dec. 1873. For the firms of Agnew, Graves, Lefèvre, Leggatt, and Tooth he engraved many plates of animal subjects after Landseer, Briton Rivière, Peter Graham, Rosa Bonheur, whom he visited at Fontainebleau, and others; these were varied occasionally by figure subjects and landscapes after Constable and Cox. Pratt's early engravings were chiefly in the 'mixed' manner, a combination of etching, line work and mezzotint, but a second period in his career began in 1896, from which date he confined himself to pure mezzotint, and almost exclusively to subjects after the English painters of the Georgian era, who had then come into fashion. Plates commissioned in that year and published in 1897 by Messrs. Agnew after Raeburn's 'Mrs. Gregory' and Lawrence's 'Mrs. Cuthbert' met with great success, and Pratt was thenceforth much employed by the same firm in engraving pictures by Gainsborough, Reynolds, Romney, Hoppner, and their contemporaries. In doing so, he limited himself to subjects that had not been engraved before. He continued to engrave for Messrs. Tooth a series of subjects after Peter Graham, R.A., and he was selected by Sir Luke Fildes, R.A., to engrave the state portraits of Edward VII (1902) and Queen Alexandra (1906). One of his last important plates, 'The Countess of Warwick and her Children,' after Romney, was published by Messrs. P. and D. Colnaghi in 1909. Pratt purchased from the widow of Thomas Oldham Barlow [q. v. Suppl. I], their late possessor, the set of mezzotinter's tools that had been used by Samuel Cousins. Exhibitions of Pratt's engravings held by Messrs. Agnew at Manchester and Liverpool in 1902, and by Messrs. Vicars in Bond Street in 1904, proved him to be the foremost reproductive engraver of his time. A considerable, though incomplete, collection of his work is in the British Museum. Pratt long resided at Harpenden, Hertfordshire, but removed in 1907 to Brenchley, Kent. Pratt died in London, after an operation, on 23 Dec. 1910. He had six children by his marriage, on 26 August 1878, to Caroline Almader James, who survived him; his eldest son, Stanley Claude Pratt, born on 9 June 1882, an engraver, was pupil of his father; his first plate was published in 1904.

[The Times, 24 Dec. 1910; Daily Telegraph,

1 Jan. 1911; Exhibition Catalogues; lists of the Printsellers' Association; private information.] C. D.

PRICE, FREDERICK GEORGE HILTON (1842–1909), antiquary, born in London on 20 Aug. 1842, was son of Frederick William Price (for many years partner and eventually chief acting partner in the banking firm of Child & Co.), who died on 31 Jan. 1888. Educated at Crawford College, Maidenhead, he entered Child's Bank in 1860, where he succeeded his father as chief acting partner. Much of his early leisure was devoted to the history of Child's Bank, and in 1875 he published 'Temple Bar, or some Account of Ye Marygold, No. 1 Fleet Street' (2nd edit. 1902), where Child's Bank had been established in the seventeenth century. In 1877 he brought out a useful 'Handbook of London Bankers' (enlarged edit. 1890–1). He was a member of the Council of the Bankers' Institute and of the Central Bankers' Association.

Price's life was mainly devoted to archæology. Always keenly interested in the prehistoric as well as historic annals of London, he formed a fine collection of antiquities of the stone and bronze ages, of the Roman period, of Samian ware vessels imported during the first and second centuries from the south of France, English pottery ranging from the Norman times down to the last century, tiles, pewter vessels and plates, medieval ink-horns, coins, tokens (many from the burial pits on the site of Christ's Hospital), and so forth; the whole of his collection was secured to form in 1911 the nucleus of the London Museum at Kensington Palace (*The Times*, 25 March 1911).

Excavations at home and abroad had a great fascination for Price. He took a leading part in the excavation of the Roman villa at Brading in the Isle of Wight, the remains of which were by his exertions kept open to the public for some time, and on which, in conjunction with Mr. J. E. Price, he read a paper before the Royal Institute of British Architects on 13 Dec. 1880 (printed in the *Transactions* of that society, 1880–1, pp. 125 *seq.*). On the excavations at Silchester or Calleva Attrebatum (of the research fund of which he was treasurer) he read a paper at the Society of Antiquaries on 11 Feb. 1886 (printed in *Archæologia*, l. 263–280). At the same time he actively engaged in studying and collecting Egyptian antiquities. In 1886 he described a portion of his collection in the 'Proceedings of the Society of Biblical Archæology' (of which he was elected member in 1884, vice-president in 1901); a large selection from his collection was exhibited at the Burlington Fine Arts Club in 1895, and two years later he published an elaborate Catalogue of his Egyptian antiquities, which was followed in 1908 by a supplement. In 1905 he was elected president of the Egypt Exploration Fund (which he joined in 1885).

Price was deeply interested in the Society of Antiquaries, of which he became a member on 19 Jan. 1882. He was elected director on 23 April 1894, retaining the post till his death. A keen numismatist, he joined the Royal Numismatic Society in 1897. He was also elected fellow of the Geological Society in 1872. He was a voluminous contributor to the Transactions and Proceedings of most of the societies and institutions to which he belonged (cf. G. L. GOMME's *Index of Archæological Papers*, 1663–1890, pp. 617–8 and *Annual Indexes of Archæological Papers*, 1891 *et seq.*). A valuable series of illustrated papers on 'Signs of Old London' appeared in the succeeding issues of the 'London Topographical Record' (ii.-v.).

He died at Cannes on 14 March 1909, after an operation, and was buried at Finchley (in the next grave to his father). He bequeathed 100*l.* to the Society of Antiquaries for the Research Fund. His books, coins, old spoons, and miscellaneous objects of art and vertu fetched at auction (1909–1911) the sum of 2606*l.* 10*s.* 6*d.* His Egyptian collection realised 12,040*l.* 8*s.* 6*d.* at Sotheby's on 12–21 July 1911 (see *The Times*, 6 June 1911). The same firm sold his coins on 17–19 May 1909 and 7–8 April 1910, 575 lots realising 2309*l.* 9*s.* He married in 1867 Christina, daughter of William Bailey of Oaken, Staffordshire, who survived him, and by whom he had one son and one daughter.

In addition to works already mentioned Hilton Price edited 'Sketches of Life and Sport in S.E. Africa' (1870) and wrote 'The Signs of Old Lombard Street' (1887; revised edit. 1902) and 'Old Base Metal Spoons' (1908).

[Who's Who, 1909; The Times, 18 March 1909; Athenæum, 20 March 1909; Proc. Soc. of Antiquaries, second series, xxii. 444, 471–2; London Topographical Record, vi. 1909, pp. 107–8.] W. R.

PRICE, THOMAS (1852–1909), premier of South Australia, born at Brymbo near Wrexham, North Wales, on 19 Jan.

1852, was son of John Price by his wife Jane. Spending his childhood in Liverpool, he was educated at a penny school there, and then followed the trade of stonecutter, taking an interest in public matters and adopting the temperance cause as an ardent Rechabite. Ordered to Australia for his health in 1883, he landed at Adelaide at a time when there was much difficulty in getting employment. He was temporarily employed as clerk of works at the government locomotive shops at Islington. Returning to his old calling of stonecutter, he long worked on the new parliament buildings at Adelaide, then in course of erection, in which he afterwards sat as premier. In 1891 he became secretary of the Masons' and Bricklayers' Society in South Australia, and in 1893 he entered the House of Assembly of the colony as member for Starb in the labour interest. That constituency he represented until 1902, when he was elected for the re-formed district of Torrens. Of the labour party he became secretary in 1900 and parliamentary leader in 1901. In July 1905 he was chosen premier of South Australia, combining with it the duties of commissioner of public works and minister of education, and being the first labour premier of an Australian state, though the commonwealth had for four months in 1904 had a labour prime minister in Mr. Watson. Price held the office of premier until his death, nearly four years later. His cabinet was a coalition of liberal and labour members, and his capacity for leadership held it well together. Price was a man of the most kindly character: he had a strong sense of humour and an abundance of rugged eloquence. He was one of the few parliamentary speakers who are known to have changed votes and decided the fate of a measure by power of speech. During his premiership he was responsible for Acts relating to wages boards, municipalisation of the tramway system, which had previously been in the hands of seven companies, reduction of the franchise for the upper house, and the transfer of the northern territory to the commonwealth. The transfer of the territory, however, did not take place in his lifetime, as the commonwealth parliament only passed the necessary legislation for the purpose in the session of 1910. He died at the height of his popularity at his house at Hawthorn, near Adelaide, on 31 May 1909, and was buried in the West Terrace cemetery at Adelaide. He married on 14 April 1881 Anne Elizabeth, daughter of Edward Lloyd, timber merchant, of Liverpool, and had issue four sons and three daughters. A portrait in oils, painted by Mr. Johnstone, was presented to the Walker Art Gallery at Liverpool in 1908; a replica is in the Adelaide Art Gallery.

[Johns's Notable Australians; The Times, 1 June 1909; private sources.] C. P. L.

PRINSEP, VALENTINE CAMERON, known as VAL PRINSEP (1838–1904), artist, born at Calcutta on St. Valentine's Day, 14 Feb. 1838, was second son of Henry Thoby Prinsep [q. v.], Indian civil servant and patron of artists, by his wife Sara Monckton, daughter of James Pattle. His mother, who was of French descent, was, like her six sisters, singularly handsome.

At an early age Valentine was sent to England to be educated, and with a view to the Indian civil service went to Haileybury. But close intimacy in youth with George Frederick Watts [q. v. Suppl. II] who for five and twenty years lived with his parents at Little Holland House and painted portraits of all the members of the family, and contact at weekly gatherings there with many celebrated artists, encouraged in Prinsep a taste for art, and giving up a nomination for the civil service, he resolved to adopt the profession of an artist. He went out with Watts in 1856–7 to watch Sir Charles Newton's excavation of Halicarnassus. After studying under Watts he proceeded to Gleyre's atelier in Paris. There Whistler, Poynter, and du Maurier were among his fellow students, and he sat unconsciously as a model for Taffy in du Maurier's novel 'Trilby.' From Paris Prinsep passed to Italy. With Burne-Jones he visited Siena and there he made the acquaintance of Robert Browning, of whom he saw much in Rome during the winter of 1859–60.

Friendship with Dante Gabriel Rossetti at first inclined him to Pre-Raphaelitism, but he soon came under the influence of another friend, Sir Frederic (afterwards Lord) Leighton, with whose work his own had much affinity. In 1858 he was one of the eight painters who under the direction of Rossetti and William Morris decorated the new hall of the Union Society at Oxford. In 1862 he exhibited at the Royal Academy his first picture, 'How Bianca Capello sought to poison the Cardinal de Medici'; it was well placed. From that time to his death Prinsep was an annual exhibitor. Prinsep's chief paintings were 'Miriam watching the Infant Moses' (exhibited at the Royal

Academy in 1867), 'A Venetian Lover' (1868), 'Bacchus and Ariadne' (1869), 'News from Abroad' (1871), 'The Linen Gatherers' (1876), 'The Gleaners,' and 'A Minuet.'

In 1876 he received a commission from the Indian government to paint a picture of the historical durbar held by Lord Lytton for the proclamation of Queen Victoria as Empress of India. The result was one large canvas and a number of smaller works on Eastern subjects. The chief picture, called 'At the Golden Gate' (1882), is a good example of Prinsep's work; it is in the possession of the family.

Prinsep was elected A.R.A. in 1878 and R.A. in 1894. His diploma picture, 'La Révolution,' was exhibited in 1896.

He died at Holland Park on 11 Nov. 1904, and was buried at Brompton cemetery. He married in 1884 Florence, daughter of Frederick Robert Leyland of Wootten Hall, Liverpool. She survived him with three sons.

Prinsep possessed versatile accomplishments, social gifts, great physical strength, and after his marriage ample means. He was a major of the artists' volunteer corps. He published an account of his visit to India under the title 'Imperial India: an Artist's Journals' (1879). Two plays by him, 'Cousin Dick' and 'M. le Duc,' were produced respectively at the Court Theatre in 1879 and at the St. James's in 1880. He was also author of two novels, 'Virginie' (1890) and 'Abibal the Tsourian' (1893). His painting never had much passion or power. His interests were too dispersed to enable him to become a great artist.

His portrait, painted in 1872 by G. F. Watts, R.A., belongs to his family. A statuette by E. Roscoe Mullins was exhibited at the Royal Academy in 1880. A cartoon portrait by 'Spy' appeared in 'Vanity Fair' in 1877.

[Mag. of Art, 1883 (woodcut portrait by A. Legros) and 1905; The Times, 14 Nov. 1904; Graves's Royal Acad. Exhibitors, 1906; Mrs. Orr, Life of Robert Browning, 1908, pp. 224 seq.; private information.]

F. W. G-N.

PRIOR, MELTON (1845–1910), war artist, born in London on 12 Sept. 1845, was son of William Henry Prior (1812–1882), a draughtsman and landscape painter, by his wife Amelia. Educated at St. Clement Danes grammar school, London, where he attended art classes, and at Blériot College, Boulogne, he helped his father, and thus first developed his own artistic powers. He began working for the 'Illustrated London News' in 1868, and after spending five years in sketching for the paper in England, he first acted as war correspondent in 1873, when the proprietor, Sir William Ingram, sent him to Ashanti with Sir Garnet (afterwards Lord) Wolseley's expedition. Thenceforth for thirty years he was similarly engaged for the 'Illustrated London News' with little intermission. In 1874 he proceeded to Spain to sketch incidents in the Carlist rising, and in 1876 to the Balkan peninsula, where he campaigned with the Austrians in Bosnia, followed the fortunes of the Servians in their short war with Bulgaria, and went through the Turco-Russian war. Prior watched the long series of campaigns in South Africa (1877–1881), including the Kaffir, Basuto and Zulu wars, and the Boer campaign which culminated at Majuba Hill (27 Feb. 1881). On 14 Sept. 1882 he was present with the English army on its entry into Cairo, was with Baker Pasha's army at El Teb (29 Feb. 1884), accompanied Lord Wolseley's relief expedition up the Nile (1884–5), and was with Sir Gerald Graham [q. v. Suppl. I] in his campaign in the Soudan early in 1885. From the Soudan he passed to Burma, where (Sir) Frederick (afterwards Earl) Roberts was engaged in active warfare (1886–7). The successive revolutions in Brazil, Argentine and Venezuela kept him much in South America between 1889 and 1892. Trouble in the Transvaal recalled him to South Africa in 1896; he went through the Greco-Turkish war, and the north-west frontier war in India next year, and saw the Cretan rising in 1898. When the South African war opened in October 1899 Prior went out with the first batch of correspondents, and was with the British besieged force in Ladysmith (2 Nov. 1899–28 Feb. 1900). In 1903 he was with the Somaliland expedition. His last campaign was the Russo-Japanese war, when he accompanied General Oku's army into the Liao-tung Peninsula (July 1904). Prior's many journeys to illustrate great social ceremonials included a visit to Athens in 1875 in the suite of King Edward VII when Prince of Wales, to Canada with King George V when Prince of Wales in 1901, and to the Delhi Durbar of 1903.

He twice went round the world, and every part of America was familiar to him. During his active career he only spent the whole of one year (1883) at home. Besides his drawings for the 'Illustrated London News' he occasionally made illustrations for the 'Sketch,' a paper under the same control. Prior's art, if not of the highest order, was eminently graphic, and he had a keen eye for a dramatic situation. He worked almost entirely in black and white, with the pen or the pencil, and with extraordinary rapidity. He belonged to the adventurous school of war correspondents, of which Archibald Forbes [q. v. Suppl. I] was the leading spirit. In character he was genial, kind-hearted, and impulsive.

He died without issue on 2 Nov. 1910, at Carlyle Mansions, Chelsea, and was buried at Hither Green cemetery. He was twice married: (1) in 1873, to a daughter (*d.* 1907) of John Greeves, surgeon; (2) in 1908 to Georgina Catherine, daughter of George MacIntosh Douglas. A portrait of Prior, painted by Frederick Whiting, is at the Savage Club. A tablet to his memory in the crypt of St. Paul's Cathedral was unveiled by Sir Evelyn Wood on 22 Oct. 1912.

[Prior's Campaigns of a War Correspondent, ed. S. L. Bensusan, 1912; Mag. of Art, 1902; Art Journal, 1910; The Times, 3 Nov. 1910; private information.] F. W. G-N.

PRITCHARD, Sir CHARLES BRADLEY (1837–1903), Anglo-Indian administrator, born at Clapham on 5 May 1837, was eldest son of Prof. Charles Pritchard (1808–1893) [q. v.] by his first wife Emily, daughter of J. Newton. After early education by his father he entered Rugby in 1849, and was transferred to Sherborne in 1852. Obtaining a nomination to the Indian army, he went to Addiscombe in 1854, but securing a writership in the Indian civil service, he completed his education at Haileybury.

On his arrival at Bombay in Jan. 1858 Pritchard first served as assistant magistrate and collector at Belgaum, and did useful work in freeing the district of bandits. In 1865 he was put in charge of the Thana district, and carried on a successful crusade against a system of frauds on the forest department. Nominated to the province of Khandesh in 1867, he was active in checking the enslavement of the native Bhils by the moneylenders, and in organising relief measures during the famine of 1868. The trenchant manner in which he dealt with frauds in the public departments led to his appointment as first collector of salt revenue in the Bombay presidency. In this capacity Pritchard reformed the administration, suppressed smuggling, and established a large salt factory at Kharaghoda. Considerable opposition was excited by the system of private licences, which he introduced with a view to ensuring that the salt was properly weighed, but thanks to his persevering efforts the hostile movement gradually collapsed. The stability of the Bombay salt revenue was henceforth assured, and when in 1876 a commission was appointed to reform the abuses of the Madras salt revenue, Pritchard was nominated its president.

In 1877 he undertook the difficult task of reforming the system for the manufacture and sale of opium and native spirits in the Bombay presidency. Pritchard's policy was to confine the manufacture of opium and spirits to a few selected places, to raise the excise duty to the highest possible rate, to reduce the number of retail shops, and to levy high licence fees. Measures were also taken to bring under control the supply of raw material from which the spirit was manufactured, and to restrict to contractors of known probity the right to sell spirits. These regulations despite their unpopularity were steadily enforced, and in recognition of his services Pritchard was made commissioner of customs in 1881, and of salt and *abkari* (excise on spirits) in 1882. Under his capable administration the Bombay presidency derived a largely increased revenue, amounting between 1874 and 1888 to an advance of 145 per cent. Pritchard, who had been made C.S.I. in 1886, held the post of commissioner of Sind from 1887 to 1889, and there he did much to develop harbour works and railway communications. He revived the idea of the Jamrao canal, which was completed in 1901, and he set on foot the scheme for the construction of a line linking up Karachi with the railway system of Rajputana, which was carried out by his successor, Sir Arthur Trevor.

In Nov. 1890 Pritchard was promoted to be revenue member of the government of Bombay, and in 1891 was created K.C.I.E. In the following year he took his seat on the viceroy's legislative council as member for the public works department. During his tenure of office he frequently found himself at variance with Lord Elgin, the viceroy, and with the majority of his colleagues on questions of high policy. He disapproved of the 'forward' policy, and he joined Sir Antony (afterwards Lord) MacDonnell and Sir James Westland [q. v. Suppl. II] in protesting against the expenditure of blood and treasure on expeditions to Waziristan, Swat, Chitral, and Tira. In 1896 his health showed signs of failure, and he resigned his seat on the council. Returning home, he settled in London, where he died on 23 Nov. 1903. He was buried at Norwood.

He married in 1862 Emily Dorothea, daughter of Hamerton John Williams, by whom he had issue two surviving sons and two daughters, both deceased. His youngest daughter, Ethel, married in 1898 Sir Steyning Edgerley, K.C.V.O., and died in 1912.

A memorial tablet to Pritchard was placed in the crypt of St. Paul's Cathedral, London. A portrait by Sir George Reid is at Karachi, Sind, India.

[The Times, 25 Nov. 1903; Times of India, 29 Nov. 1896; National Review, Jan. 1904, art. by H. M. Birdwood; Ada Pritchard, Memoirs of Prof. Pritchard, 1897; C. E. Buckland, Dictionary of Indian Biography; private information from his daughter, Mrs. Ranken.] G. S. W.

PRITCHETT, ROBERT TAYLOR (1828–1907), gunmaker and draughtsman, born on 24 Feb. 1828, was son of Richard Ellis Pritchett, head of the firm of gunmakers at Enfield which supplied arms to the East India Company and to the board of ordnance. His mother was Ann Dumbleton. After leaving King's College school Robert was brought up to his father's trade, and made himself thoroughly familiar with the details of the business. By 1852 he had become intimate with William Ellis Metford [q. v.], 'the father of the modern rifle.' The 'Pritchett bullet,' with a hollow, unplugged base, which he and Metford invented in 1853, brought him fame and an award of 1000*l.* from the government on its adoption by the small-arms committee. As early as 1854 Pritchett was using his three-grooved rifle of his own invention.

The abolition of the East India Company in 1858 deprived Pritchett's firm of its principal customer, and he sought other interests; but for some years he kept in touch with military rifle matters (partly through the Victoria Rifles, which corps he joined at its foundation in 1853), and he lectured on gunlocks and rifles at the Working Men's College and elsewhere. He interested himself in 1854 in the foundation of that college, of which Frederick Denison Maurice [q. v.] and Charles Kingsley [q. v.] were among the pioneers. He remained a liveryman of the Gunmakers' Company till his death.

Art meanwhile became one of Pritchett's pursuits. He exhibited views of Belgium and Brittany at the Royal Academy as early as 1851 and 1852. He soon formed intimate friendships with John Leech [q. v.], Charles Keene [q. v.], and Birket Foster [q. v. Suppl. I]. Through (Sir) John Tenniel he joined the staff of 'Punch,' for which he executed some 26 drawings between 1863 and 1869. In 1865 he sketched in Skye and the Hebrides, and next year he executed 100 illustrations for Cassell, Petter & Galpin. In 1868, after a visit to Holland, he received a commission for work from Messrs. Agnew, who showed a collection of his pictures in their galleries in 1869. One picture was purchased by Queen Victoria, and he was soon employed on many water-colour drawings of royal functions from 'Thanksgiving Day' in 1872 to Queen Victoria's funeral in 1901. Meanwhile he returned to Holland, where he dined at Loo with King Leopold II. and came to know Josef Israels. In 1869 and 1871 he exhibited scenes at Scheveningen at the Royal Academy, and in the latter year he published 'Brush Notes in Holland' and made numerous sketches in Paris after the Commune. After a visit to Norway in 1874–5 he issued 'Gamle Norge' (1878). In 1880 he cruised round the world with Mr. and Mrs. Joseph Lambert in their yacht the Wanderer, and illustrated their book on 'The Voyage of the Wanderer' (1883). In 1883 and 1885 he joined as artist the tours of Thomas (afterwards Earl) and Lady Brassey in the Sunbeam yacht, and many of his drawings appeared in Lady Brassey's 'In the Trades, the Tropics and the Roaring Forties' (1885) and 'The Last Voyage of the Sunbeam' (1889).

Pritchett also drew illustrations for 'Good Words' in 1881 and 1882, and made drawings for H. R. Mills's 'General Geography' (1888) and the 1890 edition of Charles Darwin's 'Voyage of the Beagle.' Exhibitions of his work were repeated in London between 1884 and 1890, and he lectured on his travels. He was an enthusiastic yachtsman, and an expert on yachts and craft of all kinds. He illustrated the Badminton volumes on 'Yachting' (1894) and 'Sea Fishing' (1895), and wrote much of the text of the former. His 'Pen and Pencil Sketches of Shipping and Craft all round the World' first appeared in 1899. A collector of curios, he was an authority on ancient armour, and issued in 1890 an illustrated account of his collection of pipes in 'Smokiana (Pipes of All Nations).' He was more successful in black-and-white than in water-colour; his drawings of shipping are noteworthy for technical accuracy.

Pritchett, who was an ardent sportsman, a good churchman, and a clever raconteur, resided for many years at The Sands, Swindon, and subsequently at Burghfield, Berkshire, where he died on 16 June 1907;

he was buried in the parish churchyard. His wife, Louisa Kezia McRae (*d.* 1899), whom he married on 22 Oct. 1857, his son Ellis (*d.* 1905), and his daughter Marian predeceased him. With the exception of some *netsuké*, which he bequeathed to the Victoria and Albert Museum, and some silver badges of the Ligue des Gueux, which he left to the British Museum, most of his curios, together with some of his drawings, were sold by auction by Messrs. Haslam & Son at Reading on 30 and 31 Oct. 1907; some of his pipes were subsequently dispersed by sale in London. The Victoria and Albert Museum has magazine illustrations, landscapes, and other drawings by him. His portrait by Daniel Albert Wehrschmidt was exhibited at the Royal Academy in 1899.

[Preface by H. G. W. to catalogue of sale at Reading; M. H. Spielmann's History of Punch, 423, 520 (portrait), 521; Graves, Dict. of Artists and Roy. Acad. Exhibitors; Brit. Mus. Cat.; The Times, 20 June 1907; Encycl. Brit. 11th edit. (s. v. Rifle); E. H. Knight, Dict. of Mechanics, i. 401–2; Engl. Cycl. iv. 91; private information.] B. S. L.

PROBERT, LEWIS (1841–1908), Welsh divine, third son of Evan and Mary Probert, was born at Llanelly, Breconshire, on 22 Sept. 1841. He became a congregational church member in 1860, at a time of revival, began to preach in 1862, and, after a short preparatory course under Henry Oliver at Pontypridd, entered Brecon College in 1863. In July 1867 he was ordained to the congregational ministry at Bodringallt, in the Rhondda valley, where he was active in establishing new churches among a rapidly growing colliery population. From 1872 to 1874 he was pastor of Pentre Ystrad, in this district; in Oct. 1874 he moved to Portmadoc, Carnarvonshire, where he spent twelve years. In 1886 he returned to Pentre; he soon gained considerable repute through his theological writings, and upon the death in 1896 of Evan Herber Evans [q. v. Suppl. I] was chosen to succeed him as principal of the congregational college at Bangor. That position he held until his death on 29 Dec. 1908. In 1891 he received the degree of D.D. from Ohio University and was chairman of the Welsh Congregational Union for 1901. He was twice married: (1) in 1870 to Annie, daughter of Edward Watkins, of Blaina, Monmouthshire, who died in 1874; and (2) in 1886 to Martha, only daughter of Benjamin Probert of Builth.

In theology Probert had conservative views, but was highly esteemed for the breadth and solidity of his learning. He published the following: 1. A prize essay on the nonconformist ministry in Wales (Blaenau Festiniog, 1882). 2. A Welsh commentary upon Romans (Wrexham, 1890). 3. A companion volume upon Ephesians (Wrexham, 1892). 4. 'Crist a'r Saith Eglwys' (Rev. i.–iii.) (Merthyr 1894). 5. 'Nerth y Goruchaf,' a treatise on the work of the Spirit (Wrexham, 1906).

[Album Aberhonddu (1898); Congregational Year Book for 1910, pp. 185–6; Rees and Thomas, Hanes yr Eglwysi Annibynol, ii. 351, iv. 285, 467, 477.] J. E. L.

PROCTER, FRANCIS (1812–1905), divine, born at Hackney on 21 June 1812, was only son of Francis Procter, a warehouseman in Gracechurch St., Manchester, by Mary his wife. The son was of delicate health, and spent the early years of his life at Newland vicarage, Gloucestershire, under the care of an uncle, Payler Procter, who was vicar there. In 1825 he was sent to Shrewsbury school under Dr. Samuel Butler [q. v.], and thence passed in 1831 to St. Catharine's College, Cambridge, where another uncle, Dr. Joseph Procter, was Master. In 1835 he graduated B.A. as thirtieth wrangler and eleventh in the second class of the classical tripos. In the following year he was ordained deacon in the diocese of Lincoln, and in 1838 priest in the diocese of Ely. He served curacies at Streatley, Bedfordshire, from 1836 to 1840, and at Romsey from 1840 to 1842, when he gave up for the time parochial work in order to become fellow and assistant tutor of his college. In 1847 he left the university for the vicarage of Witton, Norfolk. There the rest of his long life was spent. After serving the cure for nearly sixty years, he died at Witton on 24 Aug. 1905, and was buried in the churchyard there. In 1848 he married Margaret, daughter of Thomas Meryon of Rye, Sussex, and had issue five sons and three daughters.

Procter was author of 'A History of the Book of Common Prayer, with a Rationale of its Offices,' which was originally published in 1855. In many fresh editions Procter kept the work abreast of the liturgical studies of the day. Further revised with Procter's concurrence in 1901, it still remains in use. Later he projected an edition of the 'Sarum Breviary,' for which he transcribed the text of the 'Great Breviary' printed at Paris in 1531. Procter published the first volume at Cambridge in 1879 with Christopher Wordsworth as joint-editor and with the co-operation of Henry Bradshaw, W. Chatterley Bishop, and others; the second volume followed in 1882, and the concluding one in 1886.

Procter's liturgical work was careful and scholarly; his text-book followed the lines of sound exposition laid down by Wheatley and his followers, and his edition of the 'Sarum Breviary' was the most notable achievement of an era which was first developing the scientific study of medieval service-books. A portrait painted by an amateur is in the possession of his son.

[Information from Miss Procter (daughter); Shrewsbury School Register; Records of St. Catharine's College; Crockford's Clerical Directory.] W. H. F.

PROCTOR, ROBERT GEORGE COLLIER (1868–1903), bibliographer, born at Budleigh Salterton, Devonshire, on 13 May 1868, was only child of Robert Proctor (1821–1880) by his wife Anne Tate. The father, a good classical scholar, was crippled from boyhood by rheumatic fever. Proctor's grandfather, Robert Proctor (1798–1875), who published in 1825 'A Narrative of a Journey across the Cordillera of the Andes and of a Residence in Lima and other Parts of Peru in 1823 and 1824,' married Mary, sister of John Payne Collier [q. v.], who was thus the bibliographer's grand-uncle. A sister of Proctor's father (Mariquita) was first wife of George Edmund Street [q. v.], the architect.

Proctor, who in childhood developed a precocious love of study, went from a preparatory school at Reading to Marlborough College at the age of ten. Owing to his father's death on 5 March 1880, he stayed at Marlborough only a year. Thereupon he and his mother, who was thenceforth his inseparable companion, settled at Bath. In January 1881 he entered Bath College, where his scholarly instincts rapidly matured. In 1886 he won an open classical scholarship at Corpus Christi College, Oxford, and he matriculated at the university in October. His mother lived at Oxford during his academic course. He won a first class in classical moderations in Hilary term, 1888, and a second in the final classical school in Trinity term 1890, when he graduated B.A. While an undergraduate Proctor engaged in antiquarian research outside the curriculum of the schools. A visit to Greece stimulated his archæological predilections. Already as a schoolboy he had collected books, and at Oxford he spent much time in his college library. A love of bibliographical study developed, and a catalogue which he prepared of the Corpus incunabula and printed books up to 1600 gave promise of unusual bibliographical aptitude.

He remained at Oxford after taking his degree in order to continue his study of early printed books. Between 23 Feb. 1891 and Sept. 1893 he catalogued some 3000 incunabula in the Bodleian library, in continuation of work begun by Mr. Gordon Duff, and he did similar work at New College and at Brasenose.

On 16 Oct. 1893 he competed successfully (after a first failure) for entry into the library of the British Museum, and he remained an assistant in the printed books department until his death. There he made indefatigable use of his opportunities and quickly constituted himself a chief expert on early typography and bibliography. He rearranged the incunabula at the Museum and revised the entries of them in the catalogue, in which he was also responsible for the heading 'Liturgies.' He soon set himself to describe every fount of type used in Europe up to 1520, and by way of preparation read through the whole of the British Museum catalogue. His reputation was finally established by his 'Index of Early Printed Books from the Invention of Printing to the Year MD,' which was issued in four parts in 1898, after four years' toil. He then worked on a similar index for the period 1501–20, but of four projected sections only one—the German—was completed in his lifetime (1903).

Proctor's earliest contribution to bibliographical literature was an article on John van Doesborgh, the fifteenth-century printer of Antwerp, which appeared in 'The Library' in 1892 and was expanded into a monograph for the Bibliographical Society in 1894. Proctor soon read many learned papers before that society, for which he also prepared 'A Classified Index to the Serapeum' (1897) and 'The Printing of Greek in the Fifteenth Century' (1900). He likewise printed for private circulation three 'tracts on early printing,' viz. 'Lists of the Founts of Type and Woodcut Devices used by the Printers of the Southern Netherlands in the Fifteenth Century' (1895); 'A Note on Abraham Frammolt of Basel, Printer' (1895); and 'Additions to Campbell's "Annales de la typographie néerlandaise au XV siècle"' (1897).

Proctor subsequently experimented in Greek printing, adapting a beautiful type from the sixteenth-century Spanish fount used in the New Testament of the Complutensian Polyglot Bible. With his new type Proctor caused to be printed at the Chiswick Press an edition of Æschylus's 'Oresteia,' which (Sir) Frederic Kenyon completed for publication in 1904. In the same type there subsequently appeared Homer's 'Odyssey' (1909).

Interest in the work of William Morris's Kelmscott Press led to a personal acquaintance with Morris, with whose socialistic views Proctor was in sympathy. On F. S. Ellis's death in 1901 Proctor became one of the trustees under Morris's will. Morris's influence developed in Proctor an enthusiasm for Icelandic literature. His first rendering of an Icelandic saga, 'A Tale of the Weapon Firthers,' was printed privately in 1902 as a wedding gift for his friend Mr. Francis Jenkinson, librarian at Cambridge University. He subsequently published a version of the Laxdæla saga (1903).

From boyhood Proctor was in the habit of making long walking tours, usually with his mother. The practice familiarised him not only with England and Scotland but with France, Switzerland, Belgium and Norway. On 29 Aug. 1903 he left London for a solitary walking tour in Tyrol. He reached the Taschach hut in the Pitzthal on 5 Sept. and left to cross a glacier pass without a guide. Nothing more was heard of him. He doubtless perished in a crevasse. At the end of the month, when his disappearance was realised in England, the weather had broken and no search was possible.

A memorial fund was formed for the purpose of issuing his scattered 'Bibliographical Essays,' including his privately printed tracts. The collection appeared in 1905, with a memoir by Mr. A. W. Pollard. The memorial fund also provided for the compilation and publication of the three remaining parts of Proctor's 'Index of Early Printed Books from 1501 to 1520.'

[Proctor's Bibliographical Essays (with memoir by A. W. Pollard and reproduction of a photograph taken at Oxford), 1905; Athenæum, 10 Oct. 1903; Brit. Mus. Cat.; private information.] S. L.

PROPERT, JOHN LUMSDEN (1834–1902), physician and art critic, born on 9 April 1834, was the son of John Propert (1792–1867), surgeon, by his wife Juliana Ross. His father founded in 1855 the Royal Medical Benevolent College, Epsom, of which he was long treasurer. Propert was educated at Marlborough College (Aug. 1843–Dec. 1847), and at King's College Hospital. He obtained the diploma of the Royal College of Surgeons of England and the licence of the Society of Apothecaries in 1855, and in 1857 he graduated M.B. with honours in medicine at the University of London. He then joined his father in general practice in New Cavendish Street, London, and became highly successful.

Propert was widely known in artistic circles as a good etcher and a connoisseur of art. His house, 112 Gloucester Place, Portman Square, was filled with beautiful specimens of Wedgwood, bronzes, and jewelled work. He was credited with being one of the first to revive the taste for miniature painting in England. His very fine collection of miniatures was dispersed by sale in 1897. He published in 1887 'A History of Miniature Art, Notes on Collectors and Collections,' and compiled in 1889, with introduction, the illustrated catalogue of the exhibition of portrait miniatures at the Burlington Fine Arts Club.

Propert died at his house in Gloucester Place on 7 March 1902, and was buried at Brookwood cemetery. He married in 1864 Mary Jessica, daughter of William Hughes of Worcester, and had three sons and three daughters, of whom a son and three daughters survived him.

[Lancet, 1902, vol. i. p. 782; the Brit. Med Journal, 1902, vol. i. p. 689; Marlborough Coll. Reg. i. p. 12; Connoisseur, 1902, iii. 48 (portrait); private information.] D'A. P.

PROUT, EBENEZER (1835–1909), musical composer, organist, and theorist, the son of a dissenting minister, was born at Oundle, Northamptonshire, on 1 March 1835, He studied at London University, graduating B.A. in 1854, and showing a gift for languages; but music was his passion from an early period. After acting as schoolmaster for some years he devoted himself to the musical profession, in spite of strong opposition from his father. Though he had some pianoforte lessons from Charles Kensington Salaman, he was almost entirely self-taught. He acted as organist in nonconformist chapels, and he contributed anthems to a volume (1872) for Dr. Allon's chapel at Islington, where he officiated (1861–73). In 1862 he won the first prize in a competition for a new string quartet, instituted by the Society of British Musicians, and in 1865 their prize for a pianofor e quartet; this work was occasionally played for several decades. A pianoforte quintet was still more successful. From 1861 to 1885 Prout was professor of the pianoforte at the Crystal Palace School of Art.

In 1871 the 'Monthly Musical Record'

was started by Augener and Co., and Prout was appointed editor. He at once introduced a new element into musical criticism, which he made the prominent feature of his journal. He wrote detailed analyses of the less known works of Schubert, of Schumann's symphonies, and some of the later music-dramas of Wagner, all of which were practically unknown here. Prout and his coadjutors, notably Dannreuther, quickly widened the outlook of the musical public, and led the way for the introduction of Wagner's operas. In 1875 he was compelled to resign the editorship of the 'Record,' and after serving as musical critic of the 'Academy,' acted in a like capacity for the 'Athenæum' from 1879 to 1889.

Inspired, no doubt, by the performance of one of Handel's organ concertos with the orchestral accompaniment (then a quasi-novelty) at the Handel Festival, in 1871, Prout composed an organ concerto in E minor for modern resources of solo and orchestra. Stainer performed it at a Crystal Palace concert with great success, and many other performances were given elsewhere. Another undeveloped resource, the combination of pianoforte and harmonium, was next treated by Prout, who composed a duet-sonata in A major; this also was long successful. Afterwards he turned into the beaten tracks of English musical composition, and produced the cantatas 'Hereward' (1878), 'Alfred' (1882), 'Freedom' (1885), 'Queen Aimée' (for female voices, 1885), 'Psalm 100' (1886), 'The Red-Cross Knight' (1887), 'Damon and Phintias' (for male voices, 1889), as well as three symphonies for orchestra, and overtures, 'Twelfth Night' and 'Rokeby.' A string quartet, a piano quartet, an organ concerto, and sonatas for piano, with flute (1882) and clarinet (1890), failed to obtain much recognition. Prout published many arrangements of classical pieces for the organ. In 1877 he contributed a valuable primer on instrumentation to Novello's series of music primers. After being converted to a belief in Dr. Day's theory of harmony, he began a series of text-books in 1889 with 'Harmony, its Theory and Practice,' which reached a 24th edition. There followed 'Counterpoint, Strict and Free' (1890; 9th edit. 1910), 'Double Counterpoint and Canon' (1891), 'Fugue' (1891), 'Musical Form' (1893), 'Applied Forms' (1895), and 'The Orchestra' (2 vols. 1897), besides volumes of illustrative exercises These, especially 'Fugue,' became standard text-books. In later life Prout abandoned the 'Day Theory,' and in consequence largely re-wrote the book on harmony (*Musical Herald*, October 1903).

From 1876 to 1890 Prout was conductor of the Borough of Hackney Choral Association, performing many important works new and old. At the establishment of the National Training School for Music in 1876 he became professor of harmony, migrating in 1879 to the Royal Academy of Music, where he taught till his death; he was also professor at the Guildhall School of Music in 1884.

The repute of his text-books secured him the professorship of music at Dublin University in succession to Sir Robert Prescott Stewart [q. v.] in 1894. The university granted him the honorary degree of Mus. Doc. Although he was non-resident in Dublin, he fulfilled his duties as lecturer and examiner with zeal and ability. He was an active member of the Incorporated Society of Musicians, and frequently lectured at the annual conferences.

In his later years Prout's interest was mainly concentrated in Bach. Large selections of airs from Handel's operas and Bach's cantatas, translated and edited by Prout, appeared in 1905–9. A modernised edition of Handel's 'Messiah' (1902) had little success.

He lived at 246 Richmond Road, Hackney, always spending the summer vacation at Vik, Norway. He died suddenly at his house in Hackney on 5 Dec. 1909, and was buried at Abney Park cemetery. Prout married Julia West, daughter of a dissenting minister, and had a son, Louis B. Prout, who follows his father's profession, and three daughters. His large and valuable library was acquired by Trinity College, Dublin.

His portrait, painted in 1904 by E. Bent Walker, at the cost of his pupils, was presented to the Incorporated Society of Musicians.

[Interview in Musical Times, April 1899, with full details of early life; obituaries in Musical Times, Musical Herald, Monthly Musical Record, Monthly Report of the Incorporated Society of Musicians, January 1910; personal knowledge. See also for long controversy between Prout and Joseph Bennett, the musical critic, over Robert Franz's edition of Handel's Messiah, Monthly Musical Record, April–July 1891; caricature in Musical Herald, June 1891, Feb. 1899 and Dec. 1902; Musical Times, 1891.] H. D.

PRYNNE, GEORGE RUNDLE (1818–1903), hymn-writer, born at West Looe, Cornwall, on 23 Aug. 1818, was younger son in a family of eight children of John Allen Prynn (a form of the surname abandoned later by his son) by his wife Susanna, daughter of John and Mary Rundle of Looe, Cornwall. The father, who claimed descent from William Prynne [q. v.] the puritan, was a native of Newlyn, Cornwall.

After education first at a school kept by his sister at Looe, then at the (private) Devonport Classical and Mathematical School, Prynne matriculated at St. John's College, Cambridge, in October 1836, but migrated to Catharine Hall (now St. Catharine's College), graduating B.A. on 18 Jan. 1840 (M.A. in 1861, and M.A. *ad eundem* at Oxford on 30 May 1861). Ordained deacon on 19 Sept. 1841, and priest on 25 Sept. 1842, he was licensed as curate first to the parish of Tywardreath in Cornwall, and on 18 Dec. 1843 to St. Andrew's, Clifton. At Clifton he first came in contact with Dr. Pusey [q.v.], whose views he adopted and publicly defended, but he declined Pusey's suggestion to join St. Saviour's, Leeds, on account of an implied obligation of celibacy. On the nomination of the prime minister, Sir Robert Peel, he became vicar of the parish of Par, Cornwall, newly formed out of that of Tywardreath, from October 1846 to August 1847, when he took by exchange the living of St. Levan and St. Sennen in the same county. From 16 Aug. 1848 until his death he was incumbent of the newly constituted parish of St. Peter's, formerly Eldad Chapel, Plymouth.

At Plymouth Prynne's strenuous advocacy of Anglican catholicism on Pusey's lines involved him in heated controversy. The conflict was largely fostered by John Hatchard, vicar of Plymouth. In 1850 Prynne brought a charge of criminal libel against Isaac Latimer, editor, publisher, and proprietor of the 'Plymouth and Devonport Weekly Journal,' for an article prompted by religious differences which seemed to reflect on his moral character (24 Jan. 1850). The trial took place at Exeter, before Mr. Justice Coleridge, on 6 and 7 Aug. 1850, and excited the bitterest feeling. The defendant alleged that the English Church Union was responsible for the prosecution and was supplying the necessary funds. The jury found the defendant not guilty (*Western Times*, Exeter, 10 Aug. 1850), and the heavy costs in which Prynne was mulcted gravely embarrassed him. In 1852 Prynne's support of Priscilla Lydia Sellon [q. v.] and her Devonport community of Sisters of Mercy, together with his advocacy of auricular confession and penance, provoked a pamphlet war with the Rev. James Spurrell and the Rev. Michael Hobart Seymour. An inquiry by Phillpotts, bishop of Exeter, on 22 Sept. 1852, into allegations against Prynne's doctrine and practice resulted in Prynne's favour, but a riot took place when Dr. Phillpotts held a confirmation at Prynne's church next month. In 1860 Prynne 'conditionally' baptised Joseph Leycester Lyne, 'Father Ignatius' [q. v. Suppl. II], and employed him as unpaid curate. He joined the Society of the Holy Cross in 1860 and the English Church Union in 1862, becoming vice-president of the latter body in 1901. Meanwhile opposition diminished. His church was rebuilt and the new building consecrated in 1882 without disturbance. Although Prynne remained a tractarian to the end, he was chosen with Prebendary Sadler proctor in convocation for the clergy of the Exeter diocese from 1885 to 1892, and despite their divergence of opinion he was on friendly terms with his diocesans, Temple and Bickersteth. Contrary to the views of many of his party, he submitted to the Lambeth judgment (1889), which condemned the liturgical use of incense.

Prynne died at his vicarage after a short illness on 25 March 1903, and was buried at Plympton St. Mary, near Plymouth. He married on 17 April 1849 Emily (*d.* 1901), daughter of Admiral Sir Thomas Fellowes, and had issue four sons and six daughters. The sons Edward A. Fellowes Prynne and George H. Fellowes Prynne were connected as artist and architect respectively with the plan and adornment of their father's church at Plymouth, and the Prynne memorial there, a mural painting, allegorically representing the Church Triumphant, is by the son Edward.

Of Prynne's published works the most important was 'The Eucharistic Manual,' 1865 (tenth and last edit. 1895); it was censured by the primate, Archbishop Longley [q. v.]. He was also author of 'Truth and Reality of the Eucharistic Sacrifice' (1894) and 'Devotional Instructions on the Eucharistic Office' (1903). Other prose works consisted of sermons and doctrinal or controversial tracts. As a writer of hymns Prynne enjoyed considerable reputation. 'A Hymnal' compiled by him in 1875 contains his well-known 'Jesu, meek and gentle,' written in 1856, and some translations of Latin hymns. He also took part in the revision of 'Hymns Ancient and Modern,' and published 'The Soldier's Dying Visions, and other Poems and Hymns' (1881) and 'Via Dolorosa' in prose, on the Stations of the Cross (1901).

An oil painting by his son Edward Prynne in 1885 and a chalk drawing by Talford about 1853 belong to members of the family. A lithograph from a photograph was published by Beynon & Co., Cheltenham.

[A. C. Kelway, George Rundle Prynne, 1905; Miss Sellon and the Sisters of Mercy, and A Rejoinder to the Reply of the Superior . . . by James Spurrell, 1852; Nunneries, a lecture, by M. Hobart Seymour, 1852; Life of Pusey, by H. P. Liddon (ed. J. O. Johnston, R. J. Wilson, and W. C. E. Newbolt), iii. 195–6–9, 369 (1893–97); Life of Father Ignatius, by Baroness de Bertouch, 1904; private information.] E. S. H-r.

PUDDICOMBE, Mrs. ANNE ADALISA, writing under the pseudonym of Allen Raine (1836–1908), novelist, born on 6 Oct. 1836 in Bridge Street, Newcastle-Emlyn, was the eldest child in the family of two sons and two daughters of Benjamin Evans, solicitor of that town, by his wife Letitia Grace, daughter of Thomas Morgan, surgeon of the same place. The father was a grandson of the Rev. David Davis (1745–1827) [q. v.] of Castell Howel, and the mother a granddaughter of Daniel Rowlands (1713–1790) [q. v.] (J. T. Jones, *Geiriadur Bywgraffyddol*, ii. 290). After attending a school at Carmarthen for a short time she was educated first (1849–51) at Cheltenham with the family of Henry Solly, unitarian minister, and from 1851 till 1856 (with her sister) at Southfields, near Wimbledon. She learnt French and Italian and excelled in music, though she was past forty when she learned the violin. At Cheltenham and Southfields she saw many literary people, including Dickens and George Eliot. The next sixteen years she spent mainly at home in Wales, where her colloquial knowledge of Welsh was sufficient to gain her the intimacy of the inhabitants, and she acquired a minute knowledge of botany. On 10 April 1872 she was married at Penbryn church, Cardiganshire, to Beynon Puddicombe, foreign correspondent at Smith Payne's Bank, London. For eight years they lived at Elgin Villas, Addiscombe, near Croydon, where Mrs. Puddicombe suffered almost continuous ill-health. They next resided at Winchmore Hill, Middlesex. Her husband became mentally afflicted in February 1900, and she removed with him to Bronmor, Traethsaith, in the parish of Penbryn, which had previously been their summer residence. Here he died on 29 May 1906, and here also she succumbed to cancer on 21 June 1908, being buried by the side of her husband in Penbryn churchyard. There was no issue of the marriage.

From youth Miss Evans showed a faculty for story-telling, and the influence of the Sollys and their circle helped to develop her literary instincts. At home a few sympathetic friends of like tastes joined her in bringing out a short-lived local periodical, 'Home Sunshine' (printed at Newcastle-Emlyn). It was not however till 1894 that she took seriously to writing fiction. At the National Eisteddfod held that year at Carnarvon she divided with another the prize for a serial story descriptive of Welsh life. Her story, 'Ynysoer,' dealing with the life of the fishing population of an imaginary island off the Cardiganshire coast, was published serially in the 'North Wales Observer,' but was not issued in book form. By June 1896 she completed a more ambitious work, which after being rejected (under the title of 'Mifanwy') by six publishing houses (see letter of Mr. A. M. Burghes in *Daily News*, 24 July 1908) was published by Messrs. Hutchinson & Co. in August 1897, under the title 'A Welsh Singer. By Allen Raine.' Her pseudonym was suggested to her in a dream. Like most of her subsequent works 'A Welsh Singer' is a simple love-story; the chief characters are peasants and seafaring folk of the primitive district around the fishing village of Traethsaith. Despite its crudities it caught the public ear. She dramatised the novel, but it was only acted for copyright purposes. Thenceforth Mrs. Puddicombe turned out book after book in rapid succession. Her haste left her no opportunity of improving her style or strengthening her power of characterisation, but she fully sustained her first popularity mainly owing to her idealisation of Welsh life, to the prim, simple and even child-like dialogue of characters in such faulty English as the uncritical might assume Cardiganshire fishermen to speak, and also to the imaginative or romantic element which she introduces into nearly all her stories. Her later works (all issued by the same publishers) were: 1. 'Torn Sails,' 1898. 2. 'By Berwen Banks,' 1899. 3. 'Garthowen,' 1900. 4. 'A Welsh Witch,' 1902. 5. 'On the Wings of the Wind,' 1903. 6. 'Hearts of Wales,' 1905, an historical romance dealing with the period of Glendower's rebellion (dramatised by Mr. and Mrs. Leon M. Leon). 7. 'Queen of the Rushes,' 1906, embodying incidents of the Welsh revival of 1904–5. After her death there appeared: 8. 'Neither Storehouse nor Barn,' 1908; published serially in the 'Cardiff Times,' 1906. 9. 'All in a Month,' 1908, treating of her husband's malady. 10. 'Where Billows Roll,' 1909. 11. 'Under the Thatch,' 1910, treating of her own disease.

All her works have been re-issued at sixpence, and their total sales (outside America), it is stated, exceed two million copies. An 'Allen Raine Birthday Book' appeared in 1907.

Mrs. Puddicombe wrote some short stories for magazines (cf. 'Home, Sweet Home' in the 'Quiver' of June 1907), and translated into English verse Ceiriog's poem 'Alun Mabon' (*Wales* for 1897, vol. iv.).

[Information from her brother, Mr. J. H. Evans, and from Mrs. Philip H. Wicksteed, Childrey, near Wantage (daughter of the Rev. Henry Solly); South Wales Daily News and Western Mail, 23 June 1908; The Rev. H. Elvet Lewis in the British Weekly for 25 June 1908; Review of Reviews, Aug. 1905; probably the most reliable notice of her is a Welsh one by her friend Mrs. K. Jones, of Gellifaharen, in Yr Ymofynydd for Sept. 1908. For a criticism of her work from a Welsh point of view, see Mr. Ernest Rhys in Manchester Guardian, 24 and 27 June 1908, and Mr. Beriah Evans in Wales, May 1911, p. 35.] D. Ll. T.

PULLEN, HENRY WILLIAM (1836–1903), pamphleteer and miscellaneous writer, born at Little Gidding, Huntingdonshire on 29 Feb. 1836, was elder son of the four children of William Pullen, rector of Little Gidding, by his wife Amelia, daughter of Henry Wright. From Feb. 1845 to Christmas 1848 Henry was at the then newly opened Marlborough College under its first headmaster, Matthew Wilkinson. In 1848 his father, who owing to failing health had then removed with his family to Babbacombe, Devonshire, caused to be published a volume of verses and rhymes by the boy, called 'Affection's Offering.' After an interval Pullen proceeded to Clare College, Cambridge, where he graduated B.A. in 1859, proceeding M.A. in 1862. In 1859 he was ordained deacon on appointment to an assistant-mastership at Bradfield College, and became priest next year. Deeply interested in music, he was elected vicar-choral of York minster in 1862, and was transferred in 1863 to a similar post at Salisbury cathedral. At Salisbury he passed the next twelve years of his life, and did there his chief literary work. Several pamphlets (1869–72) on reform of cathedral organisation and clerical unbelief bore witness to his pugnacious and somewhat unpractical temper.

Near the end of 1870, a month after the investment of Paris by the Germans, Pullen leapt into fame with a pamphlet 'The Fight at Dame Europa's School.' Here he effectively presented the European situation under a parable which all could understand, however they might differ from its moral. John, the head of the school, refuses to separate Louis and William, though he sees that Louis is beaten and that the prolongation of the fight is mere cruelty. John is reproached by Dame Europa for cowardice—is told that he has grown 'a sloven and a screw.' and is threatened with loss of his position.

The success of this squib is almost unexampled. The first edition of 500 copies was printed at Salisbury on 21 Oct. Twenty-nine thousand copies had been issued by 1 Feb. 1871. The Salisbury resources then becoming overstrained, Messrs. Spottiswoode of London printed 50,000 copies (1–9 Feb.). The 192nd thousand appeared on 18 April. The 193rd and final thousand was printed in April 1874. The pamphlet was translated into French, German, Italian, Danish, Dutch, Frisian, Swedish, Portuguese and Jersey-French. A dramatised version by George T. Ferneyhough was acted on 17 March 1871 by amateurs at Derby, in aid of a fund for French sufferers. 'The Fight,' which brought Pullen 3000*l*., evoked a host of replies, of which 'John Justified' is perhaps the most effective. In 1872 Pullen renewed his onslaught on Gladstone's administration in 'The Radical Member,' but neither then nor in 'Dr. Bull's Academy' (1886) did he repeat his success.

In 1875 Pullen retired from Salisbury. During 1875–6 he served in Sir George Nares's arctic expedition as chaplain on the Alert, receiving on his return the Arctic medal. Thenceforth for twelve years he travelled widely on the Continent, making Perugia his headquarters. The publisher John Murray, to whom he had sent useful notes of travel, appointed him editor of the well-known 'Handbooks.' An admirable linguist in five or six languages, he successively revised nearly the whole of the series, beginning with North Germany.

Re-settling in England in 1898, Pullen held successively the curacy of Rockbeare, Devon (1898–9) and several locum-tenencies. In May 1903 he became rector of Thorpe Mandeville, Northamptonshire, but died unmarried in a nursing-home at Birmingham seven months later, on 15 Dec. 1903.

He is buried at Birdingbury, Warwickshire. There is a brass tablet to his memory on the chancel wall at Thorpe Mandeville.

Pullen's pen was busied with controversy till near the end. In some stories of school life, 'Tom Pippin's Wedding' (1871), 'The Ground Ash' (1874), and 'Pueris Reverentia' (1892), he attacked defects in the country's educational system. Pullen also published apart from pamphlets: 1. 'Our Choral Services,' 1865. 2. 'The Psalms and Canticles Pointed for Chanting,' 1867. 3. 'The House that Baby built,' 1874. 4. 'Clerical Errors,' 1874. 5. 'A Handbook of Ancient Roman Marbles,' 1894. 6. 'Venus and Cupid,' 1896. Many of his books were published at his own expense and he lost heavily by them.

[The Rev. W. Pullen's preface to Affection's Offering, 1848; The Fight at Dame Europa's School and the literature connected with it, by F. Madan, 1882; Narrative of a Voyage to the Polar Sea, by Sir George Nares, 1878; The Times, 18 Dec. 1903; and private information.] H. C. M.

PYNE, Mrs. LOUISA FANNY BODDA (1832–1904), vocalist. [See Bodda Pyne.]

Q

QUARRIER, WILLIAM (1829–1903), founder of the 'Orphan Homes of Scotland,' the only son, and the second of three children, of a ship carpenter, was born in Greenock on 29 Sept. 1829. When the boy was only a few years old his father died of cholera at Quebec, and shortly afterwards the mother removed with her children to Glasgow, where she maintained herself by fine sewing, the boy and the elder sister assisting her. At the age of seven Quarrier entered a pin factory, where, for ten hours a day in working a hand machine, he received a shilling a week. In a few months, however, he was apprenticed to a boot and shoe maker, becoming a journeyman at the age of twelve. About his sixteenth year he obtained work in a shop in Argyle St., Glasgow, owned by a Mrs. Hunter, who induced him, for the first time, to attend church, and not long afterwards he was appointed church officer. At the age of twenty he started a bootshop, and seven years afterwards, on 2 Dec. 1856, he married Isabella, daughter of Mrs. Hunter. Business prospered with him and he soon had three shops; but his early life of hardship made him resolve to devote his profits towards the assistance of the children of the streets. In 1864 the distress of a boy whose stock of matches had been stolen from him led Quarrier, with the help of several others, to found the shoeblack brigade. This was followed by a news brigade and a parcels brigade, with headquarters for the three brigades in the Trongate, called the Industrial Brigade Home; but, from various causes, the brigades were not so successful as he anticipated, and in 1871 he turned his attention to the formation of an orphan home, which was opened in November in Renfrew Lane. In the same year a home for girls was opened in Renfield Street. From these homes a number of children were, through a lady's emigration scheme, sent each year to Canada, where there were receiving homes with facilities for getting the children placed in private families. In 1872 the home for boys was removed to Cessnock House, standing within its own grounds in the suburb of Govan, and shortly afterwards Elm Park, Govan Road, was rented for a girls' home. About the same time, a night refuge was established at Dovehill, with a mission hall attached to it. This was superseded in 1876 by a city orphan home, erected at a cost of 10,000*l.*, the building, which apart from the site cost 7000*l.*, being the gift of two ladies. There about 100 children are resident, the boys being at work at different trades in the city, and the girls being trained in home duties; the building also includes a hall for mission work. In 1876 a farm of forty acres near Bridge of Weir was purchased, where three separate cottages, or rather villas, and a central building, were opened in 1878, as the 'Orphan Homes of Scotland.' The homes, the gifts chiefly of individual friends, and erected at an average cost of about 1500*l.*, each provide accommodation for about thirty children, who are under the care of a 'father' and 'mother.' The homes now number over fifty; and the village also includes a church—protestant undenominational—a school, a training-ship on land, a poultry farm, extensive kitchen gardens, stores, bakehouses, etc. On additional ground the first of four consumptive sanatoriums was opened in September 1896; and there are now also homes for epileptics. The annual expenditure of the orphan homes, amounting to about 40,000*l.*, is met by subscriptions which are not directly solicited.

Quarrier died on 16 Oct. 1903 and Mrs. Quarrier on 22 June 1904. They were buried in the cemetery of the 'Orphan Homes.' They left a son and three daughters. The institution is now managed by the family with the counsel and help of influential trustees.

[John Clunie's William Quarrier, the Orphans' Friend; J. Urquhart, Life-Story of William Quarrier, 1900; The Yearly Narrative of Facts; information from Quarrier's daughter, Mrs. Bruges.] T. F. H.

QUILTER, HARRY (1851–1907), art critic, was the youngest of three sons of William Quilter (1808–1888), first president of the Institute of Accountants, and a well-known collector of water-colour drawings by British artists. Quilter's grandfather was a Suffolk farmer. His mother, his father's first wife, was Elizabeth Harriet, daughter of Thomas Cuthbert. His eldest brother, William Cuthbert, is noticed below. Born at Lower Norwood on 24 Jan. 1851, Harry was educated privately, and entered Trinity College, Cambridge, at Michaelmas 1870; he graduated B.A. in 1874 and proceeded M.A. in 1877. At Cambridge he played billiards and racquets, and read metaphysics, scraping through the moral sciences tripos of 1873 in the third class. He was intended for a business career, but on leaving the university travelled abroad, and devoted some time to desultory art study in Italy. He had entered himself as a student of the Inner Temple on 3 May 1872, and on returning to England he spent six months in studying for the bar, chiefly with Mr. (now Lord Justice) John Fletcher Moulton; he also attended the Slade school of art at University College and the Middlesex Hospital. He was called to the bar on 18 Nov. 1878. An attack of confluent small-pox injured his health, and the possession of a competence and a restless temperament disabled him from concentrating his energies. From 1876 to 1887 he was busily occupied as an art critic and journalist, writing chiefly for the 'Spectator.' In 1880–1 he was also for a time art critic for 'The Times' in succession to Tom Taylor, and in that capacity roused the anger of J. M. Whistler [q.v. Suppl. II.] by his frank criticism of the artist's Venetian etchings (cf. *The Gentle Art of Making Enemies*, p. 104). He also angered Whistler by his 'vandalism' in re-decorating Whistler's White House, Chelsea, which he purchased for 2700*l.* on 18 Sept. 1879 and occupied till 1888 (Pennell, *Life of Whistler*, i. 258). Whistler's antipathy to critics was concentrated upon Quilter, to whom he always referred as ''Arry' and whom he lashed unsparingly until his death (cf. *ibid.* i. 267–8; and Quilter's 'Memory and a Criticism' of Whistler in *Chambers's Journal*, 1903, reprinted in *Opinions*, pp. 134–151).

Besides writing on art Quilter was a collector and a practising artist. His work was regularly hung at the Institute of Painters in Oil Colours from 1884 to 1893. Between 1879 and 1887 he frequently lectured on art and literature in London and the provinces. In 1885 he studied landscape painting at Van Hove's studio at Bruges, and in 1886 was an unsuccessful candidate for the Slade professorship at Cambridge in succession to (Sir) Sidney Colvin (*Gentle Art*, pp. 118 *et seq.*). In January 1888, 'tired of being edited,' he started, without editorial experience, an ambitious periodical, the 'Universal Review,' of which the first number was published on 16 May 1888, and was heralded with a whole page advertisement in 'The Times'; it was elaborately illustrated, and contained articles by leading authorities in England and France (George Meredith contributed in 1889 his 'Jump to Glory Jane'). Its initial success was great, but the scheme failed pecuniarily and was abandoned with the issue for December 1890. He exhibited his paintings at the Dudley Gallery in January 1894, and a collection of his works in oils, sketches in wax, water-colours on vellum, chiefly of Cornish scenes, was shown at the New Dudley Gallery in February 1908. From 1894 to 1896 he conducted boarding schools at Mitcham and Liverpool on a 'rational' system which he had himself formulated, and on which he wrote an article, 'In the Days of her Youth,' in the 'Nineteenth Century' (June 1895). In 1902, after two years' continuous labour, he published 'What's What,' an entertaining miscellany of information (with photograph and reproductions of two of his pictures); of the 1182 pages he wrote about a third, containing 350,000 words.

Until the end he occupied himself with periodical writing, travelling, and collecting works of art. He died at 42 Queen's Gate Gardens on 10 July 1907, and was buried at Norwood. Most of his collections were sold at Christie's in April 1906, and fetched over 14,000*l.* He married in 1890 Mary Constance Hall, who survived him with two sons and four daughters.

Quilter's separate publications include: 1. A thin volume of light verse, 'Idle Hours,' by 'Shingawn' (a name taken from a sensational story in the *London Journal* of the time), 1872. 2. 'Giotto,' 1880; new edit. 1881. 3. 'The Academy: Notice of Pictures exhibited at the R.A. 1872–82,' 1883. 4. 'Sententiæ Artis: First Principles of Art,' 1886. 5. 'Preferences in Art, Life, and Literature,' 1892. 6. 'Opinions on Men, Women and Things,' 1909 (a collection of periodical essays made by his widow). He edited an edition of Meredith's 'Jump to Glory Jane' (1892), and illustrated one of Browning's 'Pied Piper of Hamelin' (1898).

[Quilter's Opinions, 1909; Who's Who, 1906; The Times, 13 July 1907; Morning Post, 12 July 1907; Mrs. C. W. Earle, Memoirs and Memories, 1911, pp. 291–8; information kindly supplied by Mrs. Harry Quilter (now Mrs. MacNalty) and his sister, Mrs. S. E. Muter.] W. R.

QUILTER, Sir WILLIAM CUTHBERT, first baronet (1841–1911), art collector and politician, born in London on 29 Jan. 1841, eldest brother of Harry Quilter [q. v. Suppl, II], was educated privately. After five years (1858–63) in his father's business he started on his own account with a partner as a stockbroker, and eventually founded the firm of Quilter, Balfour & Co. in 1885. He was one of the founders of the National Telephone Co. (registered on 10 March 1881), and was a director and large shareholder till his death. In 1883 he bought the Bawdsey estate near Felixstowe, extending to about 9000 acres, and spent large sums on sea defences, a spacious manor house, and an alpine garden (see *Gardeners' Chronicle*, 12 Dec. 1908). He showed enterprise as an agriculturist, particularly as a cattle-breeder (see *The Times*, 20 Nov. 1911). A keen yachtsman, he owned at various times several well-known boats, and was vice-commodore of the Royal Harwich Yacht Club (1875–1909). Quilter was elected as a liberal for the Sudbury division of Suffolk in Dec. 1885. Declining to accept Gladstone's home rule policy, he was re-elected unopposed as a liberal unionist in July 1886 and continued to represent the same constituency in parliament until the dissolution of Dec. 1905. Being returned after a contest in 1892, and unopposed in 1895 and 1900, he was defeated by 136 votes in Jan. 1906. He rarely spoke in the house. He was created a baronet on 13 Sept. 1897; and was a J.P. and D.L. for Suffolk, and an alderman of the West Suffolk county council. Inheriting his father's taste for pictures, he formed a collection on different lines, confining himself to no one period or school. He was generous in loans to public exhibitions. Nearly the whole of his collection was displayed at Lawrie's Galleries, 159 Bond Street, in Nov. 1902, in aid of King Edward's Hospital Fund (cf. description by F. G. Stephens in *Magazine of Art*, vols. 20 and 21, privately reprinted with numerous illustrations). He presented Sir Hubert von Herkomer's portrait of Spencer Compton Cavendish, eighth duke of Devonshire [q. v. Suppl. II], to the National Portrait Gallery in 1909 (*The Times*, 21 July 1909). The collection of his pictures at his London house, 28 South Street, Park Lane (120 lots), realised 87,780*l*. at Christie's on 9 July 1909 (*The Times*, 10 July 1909; *Connoisseur*, July 1909; Catalogue Raisonné of the collection, by M. W. Brockwell and W. Roberts, privately printed, 100 copies, 1909).

He died suddenly at Bawdsey on 18 Nov. 1911, and was buried in the parish churchyard. His estate was valued at 1,220,639*l*., with net personalty 1,035,974*l*. (*The Times*, 15 Jan. 1912). He married on 7 May 1867 Mary Ann, daughter of John Wheeley Bevington of Brighton. She survived him with five sons and two daughters.

His portrait by Sir Hubert von Herkomer was exhibited at the Royal Academy in 1890; a caricature by 'Lib' (Prosperi) appeared in 'Vanity Fair' on 9 Feb. 1889.

[The Times, 20 Nov. 1911; Burke's Peerage, 1911; Who's Who, 1909; personal knowledge; information kindly supplied by Mr. A. J. Grout, Sir Cuthbert's private secretary.]

W. R.

R

RADCLIFFE-CROCKER, HENRY (1845–1909), dermatologist, born at Brighton on 6 March 1845, was son of Henry Radcliffe Crocker. After attending a private school at Brighton, he was thrown on his own resources at the age of sixteen, and went as apprentice and assistant to a doctor at Silverdale, Staffordshire. Studying by himself amid the duties of his apprenticeship, he passed the matriculation and preliminary scientific examination for the M.B. London degree, and in 1870 entered University College Hospital medical school, eking out his narrow means by acting as dispenser to a doctor in Sloane Street. In 1873 he passed M.R.C.S., and next year L.R.C.P. In his later London University examinations he gained the gold medal in materia medica (1872) and the university scholarship and gold medal in forensic medicine, besides taking honours in medicine and obstetric medicine (1874). At the hospital he won the Fellowes gold medal in clinical medicine (1872). In 1874 he graduated B.S. (London) and next year M.D.

Meanwhile he was a resident obstetric physician and physician's assistant at University College Hospital; clinical assistant at the Hospital for Consumption and Diseases of the Chest, Brompton; and resident medical officer at Charing Cross Hospital (for six months). In 1875 he was appointed resident medical officer in University College Hospital, and next year assistant medical officer to the skin department, in succession to (Sir) John Tweedy.

In 1878 he was appointed assistant physician and pathologist to the East London Hospital for Children at Shadwell, and in 1884 honorary physician. He remained on the staff of the hospital until 1893. He became a member of the Royal College of Physicians in 1877, and a fellow in 1887, and he served on the council (1906–8). He was a member of the court of examiners of the Society of Apothecaries for many years (1880–8 and 1888–96).

Meanwhile Radcliffe-Crocker was specialising in diseases of the skin under the influence of William Tilbury Fox [q. v.], whom in 1879 he succeeded as physician and dermatologist at the University College Hospital. He was an original member of the Dermatological Society of London (1882; treasurer, 1900–5), and of the Dermatological Society of Great Britain and Ireland (1894; president, 1899). When these societies amalgamated with other London societies to form the Royal Society of Medicine (1907), he was first president of the dermatological section (1907–8). He also was president of his section at the annual meeting of the British Medical Association in London (1905). He was an honorary member of the American Dermatological Society, of the Wiener Dermatologische Gesellschaft, and of the Società Italiana di Dermatologia e Sifilografia, and corresponding member of the Société Française de Dermatologie, and of the Berliner Dermatologische Gesellschaft; and he delivered the Lettsomian lectures on inflammations of the skin before the Medical Society of London (1903).

He was a prominent and active member of the British Medical Association, serving on the council from 1890 to 1904, and as treasurer from 1905 to 1907, and being a good business man he was chiefly instrumental in bringing about, whilst treasurer, the rebuilding and enlargement of the headquarters of the association in the Strand, and in making important changes in the business conduct of 'The British Medical Journal,' the journal of the association.

During his later years ill-health interrupted his public work. He died suddenly from heart failure whilst on a holiday at Engelberg, Switzerland, on 22 Aug. 1909, and was buried there. He married in 1880 Constance Mary, only daughter of Edward Fussell of Brighton, physician to the Sussex County Hospital, who survived him. There were no children.

From 1898 he had a country residence at Bourne End, Buckinghamshire. His extensive library, consisting of dermatological works in English, French, German, and Italian, was given by Mrs. Radcliffe-Crocker to the medical school of University College, together with 1500*l.* in 1912 to found a dermatological travelling scholarship.

Radcliffe-Crocker's high position as a dermatologist was due to his general knowledge of medicine, his particular skill as a clinician, and his power of expressing himself in his writings clearly and attractively. He always was emphatic in insisting on the importance of treating the general condition or diathesis which might be the predisposing cause of a skin affection, as well as treating directly the local condition itself. He was always among the first to test the value of new remedies and means of treatment. He was a distinguished leprologist, and his papers on rare skin diseases were most illuminating.

Radcliffe-Crocker's chief work, which held standard rank in the medical literature of the world, was 'Diseases of the Skin: their Description, Pathology, Diagnosis and Treatment' (1888), with a companion volume of 'The Atlas of Diseases of the Skin,' issued in bi-monthly parts (1893–6; 2 vols. fol. 1896). A second edition of the treatise in 1893, which greatly improved on the first, was recognised as the most comprehensive manual of dermatology then published in England. In the third edition (2 vols. 1903), in which he was helped by Dr. George Pernet, 15,000 cases of skin diseases were analysed and classified, and more plates of the microscopical anatomy of the diseases were included. The 'Atlas' forms a complete and systematic pictorial guide to dermatology, each disease being represented by coloured plates of actual cases, which were accompanied by a short and clear descriptive text.

Radcliffe-Crocker wrote on psoriasis and drug eruptions in Quain's 'Dictionary of Medicine' (new edit. 1894); on leprosy, purpura, guineaworm, erythema, ichthyosis &c., in Heath's 'Dictionary of Surgery' (1886); on psoriasis and other squamous eruptions, and phlegmonous and ulcerative eruptions in 'Twentieth Century Medicine' (1896); on diseases of the hair in Clifford Allbutt's 'System of Medicine' (vol. viii. 1899). He was a regular contributor to the 'Lancet,' writing reviews and notices of contemporary dermatological work.

[Information from Mrs. Radcliffe-Crocker (widow); Lancet, 4 Sept. 1909; Brit. Med. Journal, 11 Sept. 1909; Index Cat. Surgeon-General's Office Washington.] E. M. B.

RAE, WILLIAM FRASER (1835–1905) author, born in Edinburgh on 3 March 1835, was elder son of George Rae and his wife, Catherine Fraser, both of Edinburgh. A younger brother, George Rae, settled early in Toronto, Canada, and became a successful lawyer there.

After education at Moffat Academy and at Heidelberg, where he became an excellent German scholar, Rae entered Lincoln's Inn as a student on 2 Nov. 1857, and on 30 April 1861 was called to the bar. But he soon abandoned pursuit of the law for the career of a journalist. He edited for a time about 1860 the periodical called the 'Reader,' and early joined the staff of the 'Daily News' as a special correspondent in Canada and the United States. With the liberal views of the paper he was in complete sympathy. On his newspaper articles he based the volume 'Westward by Rail' (1870; 3rd edit. 1874), which had a sequel in 'Columbia and Canada: Notes on the Great Republic and the New Dominion' (1877). There subsequently appeared 'Newfoundland to Manitoba' (1881; with maps) and 'Facts about Manitoba' (1882), which reprinted articles from 'The Times.'

Afterwards throat trouble led Rae to spend much time at Austrian health resorts, concerning which he contributed a series of articles to 'The Times.' These reappeared as 'Austrian Health Resorts, and the Bitter Waters of Hungary' (1888; 2nd edit. 1889). In 'The Business of Travel' (1891) he described the methods of Thomas Cook & Son, the travel agents, and a visit to Egypt produced next year 'Egypt to-day; the First to the Third Khedive.'

Rae meanwhile made much success as the translator of Edmond About's 'Handbook of Social Economy' (1872; 2nd edit. 1885) and Taine's 'Notes on England' (1873; 8th edit. 1885). But his interests were soon largely absorbed by English political history of the eighteenth century. In 1874 he brought out a political study entitled 'Wilkes, Sheridan, and Fox: or the Opposition under George III,' which echoed the style of Macaulay and showed some historical insight. Further study of the period induced him to tackle the question of the identity of 'Junius,' and he wrote constantly on the subject in the 'Athenæum' between 11 Aug. 1888 and 6 May 1899 and occasionally later. He justified with new research the traditional refusal of that journal, for which Charles Wentworth Dilke [q. v. Suppl. II] was responsible, to identify Junius with Sir Philip Francis. He believed himself to be on the road to the true solution, but his published results were only negative. Rae also made a careful inquiry into the career of Sheridan. With the aid of Lord Dufferin and other living representatives he collected much unpublished material and sought to relieve Sheridan's memory of discredit. His labour resulted in 'Sheridan, a Biography' (2 vols. 1896, with introduction by the Marquess of Dufferin and Ava). Rae succeeded in proving the falsity of many rumours, but failed in his purpose of whitewashing his hero. In 1902 he published from the original MSS. 'Sheridan's Plays, now printed as he wrote them,' as well as 'A Journey to Bath,' an unpublished comedy by Sheridan's mother.

Rae also made some halting incursions into fiction of the three-volume pattern. His 'Miss Bayle's Romance' (1887) was followed by 'A Modern Brigand' (1888), 'Maygrove' (1890), and 'An American Duchess' (1891).

In his last years he reviewed much for the 'Athenæum,' whose editor, Norman MacColl [q. v. Suppl. II], was a close friend. He spent his time chiefly at the Reform Club, which he joined in 1860, and where he was chairman of the library committee from 1873 till his death. He wrote the preface to C. W. Vincent's 'Catalogue of the Library of the Reform Club' (1883; 2nd and revised edit. 1894). To this Dictionary he was an occasional contributor. Chronic ill-health and the limited favour which the reading public extended to him tended somewhat to sour his last years. He died on 21 Jan. 1905 at 13 South Parade, Bath, and was buried at Bath.

Rae married, on 29 Aug. 1860, Sara Eliza, second daughter of James Fordati of the Isle of Man and London. She died at Franzensbad, where Rae and herself were frequent autumn visitors, on 29 Aug. 1902; she left two daughters.

Besides the works mentioned, Rae published anonymously in 1873 'Men of the Third Republic,' and translated 'English Portraits' from Sainte-Beuve in 1875.

[Who's Who, 1905; The Times, 25 Jan. 1905; Athenæum, 28 Jan. 1905; Foster's Men at the Bar; private information.] S. E. F.

RAGGI, MARIO (1821–1907), sculptor, born at Carrara, Italy, in 1821, studied art at the Royal Academy, Carrara, winning all available prizes at the age of seventeen. He then went to Rome, where he studied under Temerani. In 1850 he came to London, working at first under Monti, afterwards for many years under Matthew Noble [q. v.], and finally setting up his own studio about 1875. His principal works were memorial busts and statues. He executed the national memorial to Beaconsfield in Parliament Square, a Jubilee memorial of Queen Victoria for Hong Kong, with replicas for Kimberley and Toronto, and statues of Lord Swansea for Swansea, Dr. Tait for Edinburgh, Dr. Crowther for Hobart Town, Sir Arthur Kennedy for Hong Kong, and Gladstone for Manchester.

His first exhibit in the Royal Academy was a work entitled 'Innocence' in 1854. No further work was shown at the Academy till 1878, when he exhibited a marble bust of Admiral Rous, which he executed for the Jockey Club, Newmarket. He afterwards exhibited intermittently till 1895, among other works being busts of Cardinal Manning (1879), Cardinal Newman (1881), Lord John Manners, afterwards seventh Duke of Rutland (1884), and the duchess of Rutland (1895). Raggi died at the Mount, Roundstone, Farnham, Surrey, on 26 Nov. 1907.

[The Times, 29 Nov. 1907; Graves's Roy. Acad. Exhibitors, 1906.] S. E. F.

RAILTON, HERBERT (1858–1910), black-and-white draughtsman and illustrator, born on 21 Nov. 1858 at Pleasington, Lancashire, was eldest child (in a family of two sons and a daughter) of John Railton by his wife Eliza Ann Alexander. His parents were Roman catholics. After education at Malines, in Belgium, and at Ampleforth College, Yorkshire, he was trained as an architect in the office of W. S. Varley of Blackburn, and showed great skill as an architectural draughtsman, but he soon abandoned his profession for book-illustration, and came to London to practise that art in 1885. Some of his earliest work was contributed to the 'Portfolio' in that year. He first attracted attention by his illustrations in the Jubilee edition of the 'Pickwick Papers' (1887), and in the following year joined Mr. Hugh Thomson in illustrating 'Coaching Days and Coaching Ways,' by W. O. Tristram. Some of his best drawings appeared in the 'English Illustrated Magazine,' and among books which he illustrated may be mentioned 'The Peak of Derbyshire' by J. Leyland (1891), 'The Inns of Court and Chancery' by W. J. Loftie (1893), 'Hampton Court' by W. H. Hutton (1897), 'The Book of Glasgow Cathedral' by G. Eyre-Todd (1898), 'The Story of Bruges' by E. Gilliat-Smith (1901), and 'The Story of Chartres' by C. Headlam (1902). Railton was a delicate and careful draughtsman, and rendered the texture and detail of old buildings with particular charm. The crisp, broken line of his work lent his drawings an air of pleasant picturesqueness, though it was not without a mannerism which tended to become monotonous. His pen work was eminently suited for successful reproduction by process, and he exercised a wide influence on contemporary illustration.

Railton died in St. Mary's Hospital from pneumonia on 15 March 1910, and was buried at St. Mary's catholic cemetery, Kensal Green. He married on 19 Sept. 1891 Frances Janetta Edney, who survived him with one daughter.

[The Times, 18 March 1910; Pennell's Pen Drawing and Pen Draughtsmen, 1889; information from Miss Railton.] M. H.

RAINE, ALLEN (pseudonym). [See PUDDICOMBE, MRS. ANNE ADALISA (1836–1908), novelist.]

RAINES, SIR JULIUS AUGUSTUS ROBERT (1827–1909), general, born at Rome on 9 March 1827, was only son of Colonel Joseph Robert Raines of Cork, of the 77th, 82nd, 95th, and 48th regiments, who had served in the Peninsular war, by his wife Julia, daughter of Edward Jardine of Sevenoaks, Kent, banker. In boyhood he lived with his mother's family at Sevenoaks, and attended the school there. He received his military education at the Ecole Militaire in Brunswick (where an uncle by marriage, Baron von Girsewald, was master of horse to the duke). Thence he passed to the Royal Military College, Sandhurst. He entered the army as ensign 3rd Buffs on 28 Jan. 1842, and in the same year exchanged into the 95th regiment. He was promoted lieutenant on 5 April 1844, and captain on 13 April 1852.

He served throughout the Crimean war, 1854–5. For his services with the Turkish army in Silistria, prior to the invasion of the Crimea, he long after received the first-class gold medal of the Liākāt. After the affair at Bulganak he carried the Queen's colour at the battle of the Alma. He was at the battles of Inkerman and Tchernaya, and through the siege and fall of Sevastopol he served as an assistant engineer, being severely wounded in the trenches during the bombardment of 17 Oct. 1854, and being present in the trenches at the attack on the Redan on 18 June 1855. He received the medal with three clasps, and was mentioned in despatches 'as having served with zeal and distinction from the opening of the campaign.' The Sardinian and Turkish medals and fifth class Medjidie were also awarded him. A brevet of major was granted him on 24 April 1855, and he became major on 1 May 1857.

Raines commanded the 95th regiment throughout the Indian Mutiny campaign in 1857–9. He was present at the assault and capture of Rowa on 6 Jan. 1858, when he received the high commendation of the governor of Bombay and the commander-in-chief for 'gallantry displayed and ably conducting these operations.' He led the left wing of the 95th regiment at the siege and capture of Awah on 24 Jan., and at the siege and capture of Kotah on 30 March was in command of the third assaulting column. At the battle of Kotah-ke-Serai he was mentioned in despatches by Sir Hugh Rose 'for good service.' He was especially active during the capture of Gwalior on 19 June, when he was wounded by a musket ball in the left arm, after taking by assault two 18-pounders and helping to turn the captured guns on the enemy. For gallantry in minor engagements he was four times mentioned in despatches. The 95th regiment, while under his command in Central India, marched 3000 miles (*Lond. Gaz.* 11 June and 10 Oct. 1858, 24 March, 18 April, and 2 Sept. 1859). He received the medal with clasp, was promoted to lieut.-colonel on 17 Nov. 1857, received the brevet of colonel on 20 July 1858, and was made C.B. on 21 March 1859. Raines next saw active service at Aden, where he commanded an expedition into the interior of Arabia in 1865–6. The British troops captured and destroyed many towns and ports, including Ussalu, the Fudthlis capital, and seven cannon. Raines received the thanks of the commander-in-chief at Bombay. Subsequently Raines was promoted major-general on 6 March 1868, lieut.-general on 1 Oct. 1877, and general (retired) on 1 July 1881, and was nominated colonel-in-chief of the Buffs, the East Kent regiment, in 1882.

He was advanced to K.C.B. on 3 June 1893 and G.C.B. in 1906, and in the same year he received the grand cross of the Danish Order of the Dannebrog. He died on 11 April 1909 at his residence, 46 Sussex Gardens, Hyde Park, W., and was buried in the parish church, Sevenoaks. He married on 15 Nov. 1859 his cousin, Catherine Elizabeth, eldest daughter and co-heiress of John Nicholas Wrixon of Killetra, Mallow, co. Cork. He had no issue.

Raines published in 1900 'The 95th (Derbyshire) Regiment in Central India.'

[The Times, 13 April 1909; Dod's Knightage; Walford's County Families; Hart's and Official Army Lists; Raines, The 95th (Derbyshire) Regiment in Central India, 1900.] H. M. V.

RAINY, ROBERT (1826–1906), Scottish divine, elder son of Harry Rainy, M.D. (*d.* 6 Aug. 1876), professor of forensic medicine in Glasgow University, by his wife Barbara Gordon (*d.* July 1854), was born at 49 Montrose Street (now the Technical College), Glasgow, on 1 Jan.

1826. On 10 Oct. 1835 he entered the Glasgow High School, where Alexander Maclaren [q. v. Suppl. II] was his schoolfellow. In October 1838 he proceeded to Glasgow University, where he graduated M.A. in April 1844. His father designed him for the medical profession; he had been taken by his father's friend, Robert Buchanan (1802–1875) [q. v.], to the debates in the general assembly of 1841 leading to 'disruption,' and when 'disruption' came in 1843 he felt a vocation to the ministry of the Free Church; on his father's advice he gave a year (1843–4) to medical study. In 1844 he entered the divinity hall of the Free Church New College, Edinburgh, studying under Chalmers, David Welsh [q. v.], William Cunningham [q. v.], 'rabbi' John Duncan [q. v.], and Alexander Campbell Fraser. He was at this time a member of the famous 'speculative society' at the Edinburgh University. He was licensed on 7 Nov. 1849 by the Free Church presbytery of Glasgow, and for six months had charge of a mission at Inchinnan, near Renfrew. By Elizabeth, dowager duchess of Gordon [q. v.], he was made chaplain at Huntly Lodge; declining other calls, he became minister of Huntly Free Church, ordained there by Strathbogie presbytery on 12 Jan. 1851. His repute was such that in 1854 he was called to Free High Church, Edinburgh, in succession to Robert Gordon [q. v.]. As he wished to remain in Huntly, his presbytery declined (12 April 1854) to sustain the call; so did the synod; the general assembly (22 May 1854) transferred him to Edinburgh, henceforth his home. His pastorate lasted till 1862, when he was made professor of church history in the Free Church College, delivering his inaugural lecture on 7 Nov 1862. In 1863 he received the degree of D.D. Glasgow. He became principal of the college in 1874, and retained this dignity till death, resigning his chair in 1901.

Rainy's position soon became that of the ecclesiastical statesman of his church, of whose assembly he was moderator in 1887, in 1900, and in 1905. No one since William Carstares (1649–1715) [q. v.] (not even William Robertson (1721–1793) leader of the moderates) exercised so commanding an influence on the ecclesiastical life of Scotland. David Masson [q. v. Suppl. II] described him as a 'national functionary.' His three lectures (Jan. 1872) in reply to Dean Stanley's four lectures on the 'History of the Church of Scotland,' given in that month at the Edinburgh Philosophical Institution (first delivered at Oxford, 1870), were not only a remarkable effort of readiness but a striking vindication of the attitude of Scottish religion. The flaw in his statesmanship was his dealing with the case (1876–81) of William Robertson Smith [q. v.]; in this matter there was some justification for Smith's description of Rainy as 'a jesuit' (SIMPSON, i. 396*n*). Yet of the Assembly speech (1881) by Marcus Dods [q. v. Suppl. II], in opposition to his action, Rainy said 'The finest thing I ever heard in my life' (MACKINTOSH, p. 77). Rainy's advocacy of the 'voluntary' policy (simply, however, as expedient in the circumstances) began in 1872, when, in criticism of the abolition of patronage (effected in 1874), he declared 'that the only solution was disestablishment.' This opened the way for a union with the United Presbyterian Church (mooted as early as 1863); but while Rainy rightly interpreted the feeling of the majority of his own generation, the older men and the 'highland host,' led by James Begg [q. v.] and John Kennedy [q. v.], were unprepared to surrender the principle of a state church. In 1876, after long negotiation, Rainy achieved the union of the reformed presbyterian synod with the Free Church; the original secession synod had been incorporated with the Free Church in 1852. In 1881 Rainy was made convener of the 'highland committee' of his church, a post which he held till death. He was hampered by unacquaintance with Gaelic, but succeeded in winning over a section of the minority opposed to the policy of union. The opposition was not so much to disestablishment as to union with a body which imperfect knowledge led them to distrust (SIMPSON, i. 446). As convener, Rainy raised, between 1882 and 1893, 10,795*l.* for the endowment scheme promoted by his predecessor, Thomas McLauchlan [q. v.], and over 10,000*l.* for the erection of church buildings, mainly in the Outer Hebrides, and subsequently 7500*l.* for special agencies (*Highland Witness*, p. 1074 seq.). In 1890 he supported the motion for refusing any process of heresy against professors Marcus Dods and Alexander Balmain Bruce [q. v. Suppl. I], who were let off with a caution. The question at issue was the inerrancy of Scripture, which Rainy held 'under difficulties,' but would not press, if inspiration were admitted. In 1892 he succeeded in passing into law the Declaratory Act, which distinguished in the Confession of Faith between 'substance' and points open to 'diversity of opinion,' and disclaimed 'any principles inconsistent with liberty of conscience and the right of private judgment.' Union with the United Presbyterian Church was effected on 31 Oct. 1900, and Rainy was elected the first moderator of the united body. Within six weeks from the date of the union a court of session summons was served upon all the general trustees of the former Free Church and all the members of the union assembly, the pursuers contending that they alone represented the Free Church, and were entitled to all its property. While litigation was going on, a charge of heresy was brought against George Adam Smith, D.D., on the ground of his Old Testament criticism; Rainy carried a motion declining to institute any process, maintaining that it was 'a question about the respect due to facts,' and could not be 'settled ecclesiastically' (SIMPSON, ii. 272–3). Judgments in the courts of session were given (9 Aug. 1901; 4 July, 1902) in favour of the United Free Church. An appeal to the House of Lords was heard from 24 Nov. to 4 Dec. 1903, and reheard from 9 to 23 June 1904. Judgment was given on 1 Aug., when five peers (Halsbury, Davey, James, Robertson, and Alverstone) found there had been a breach of the Free Church constitution; two (Macnaghten and Lindley) held there had not; one (Halsbury) found definite doctrinal change on predestination; two (Davey and Robertson) held that the position of the confession had been illegally modified; two (Macnaghten and Lindley) held the contrary. The entire church property was handed over to the so-called 'Wee Frees,' the United Free Church raising an emergency fund of 150,000*l.*; its assembly in 1905 passed a declaration of spiritual independence. After a royal commission which reported that 'the Free Church are unable to carry out all the trusts of the property,' the Churches (Scotland) Act (11 Aug. 1905) appointed an executive commission for the allocation of the property between the two bodies. The 'Wee Frees' got a sufficient equipment; the United Free Church raised a further sum of 150,000*l.* to supplement the property recovered. Rainy did not live to re-enter the recovered college building. He had been operated upon for an internal disorder, and left Edinburgh on 24 Oct. 1906 for a recuperative voyage to Australia. His last sermon was at sea on 11 Nov. He reached Melbourne on 8 Dec., and died there of lymphadenoma on 22 Dec. 1906; on 7 March 1907 he was buried in the Dean cemetery, Edinburgh. He married on 2 Dec. 1857 Susan (*b.* 1835; *d.* 30 Sept. 1905), daughter of Adam Rolland of Gask, by whom he had four sons and three daughters. In 1894 his portrait by Sir George Reid was presented to the New College, and a replica to his wife.

His eldest son, ADAM ROLLAND RAINY (1862–1911), M.A., M.B., and C.M.Edin., studied at Berlin and Vienna, and practised (1887–1900) as a surgeon oculist in London. He travelled in Australia and New Zealand (1891), in the West Indies (1896), in Spain and Algiers (1899 and 1903). Entering on political work, he contested Kilmarnock Burghs in 1900 as a radical, gained the seat in 1906, and held it till his sudden death at North Berwick on 26 Aug. 1911. He married in 1887 Annabella, second daughter of Hugh Matheson, D.L. of Ross-shire, who survived him with a son and two daughters.

Robert Rainy was a man of fascinating personality and infinite tact, amounting to skilled diplomacy, being 'a rare manager of men,' regarded by his students with 'peculiar veneration and affection,' and, in spite of a certain aloofness, winning by his earnestness and goodwill the warm attachment of men in all parties. In general politics he took little part, but he followed Gladstone on the home rule question. His writings were not numerous but weighty. He published: 1. 'Three Lectures on the Church of Scotland,' Edinburgh 1872 (in reply to Dean Stanley). 2. 'The Delivery and Development of Christian Doctrine,' 1874 (Cunningham Lecture, delivered 1873). 3. 'The Bible and Criticism,' 1878 (four lectures to students of the Presbyterian Church of England). 4. 'The Epistle to the Philippians,' 1893 (in the 'Expositor's Bible'). 5. 'Presbyterianism as a Form of Church Life and Work,' Cambridge, 1894. 6. 'The Ancient Catholic Church from . . . Trajan to the Fourth . . . Council,' 1902. 7. 'Sojourning with God, and other Sermons,' 1902.

He edited 'The Presbyterian' (1868–71), and made contributions to many composite collections of theological literature, including W. Wilson's 'Memorials of R. S. Candlish' (1880), F. Hastings' 'The Atonement, a Clerical Symposium' (1883), and 'The Supernatural in Christianity' (1894).

The Times, 24 Dec. 1906; Highland Witness, February 1907 (memorial number; eight portraits); R. Mackintosh, Principal Rainy, a biographical study, 1907 (two portraits); P. C. Simpson, Life, 1909, 2 vols. (eight portraits).] A. G.

RAMÉ, MARIE LOUISE ('Ouida'). [See De la Ramée.]

RAMSAY, ALEXANDER (1822–1909), Scottish journalist, son of Alexander Ramsay, sheep farmer, was born in Glasgow on 22 May 1822. In 1824 his family removed to Edinburgh, where he was educated at Gillespie free school, and where, in 1836, he entered the printing office of Oliver and Boyd. The years 1843–44 he spent in London in the government printing office of T. and J. W. Harrison. Returning to Edinburgh in 1845, he engaged in literary work of different kinds until, in 1847, he was appointed editor of the 'Banffshire Journal,' a post which he filled for sixty-two years. He greatly raised the position of that newspaper, in which he gave prominence to the subject of the sea fisheries, and made a special feature of agriculture and the pure breeding of cattle. He was joint editor of vols. 2 (1872) and 3 (1875) of the 'Aberdeen-Angus Herd Book,' and sole editor of vols. 4 to 33 (1876–1905). Therein he performed a monumental work of a national kind, which was recognised in 1898 by a presentation from breeders of polled cattle throughout the United Kingdom and others; and later by the presentation of a cheque for 150*l*. by members of the Herd Book Society. He was elected provost of Banff in 1894, and next year received the hon. degree of LL.D. from Aberdeen University. He was twice married. He died at Earlhill, Banff, on 1 April 1909. A portrait, painted by Miss Evans, is in possession of the family. Many of his contributions to the 'Banffshire Journal' were reprinted as pamphlets. He also wrote a 'Life of Goldsmith,' privately circulated; and a 'History of the Highland and Agricultural Society of Scotland,' 1879.

[Obituary in Banffshire Journal, reprinted as a pamphlet (with portrait); information from the family; personal knowledge.] J. C. H.

RANDALL, RICHARD WILLIAM (1824–1906), dean of Chichester, born at Newbury, Berkshire, on 13 April 1824, was eldest son of James Randall, archdeacon of Berkshire, by his wife Rebe, only daughter of Richard Lowndes of Rose Hill, Dorking. A younger brother, James Leslie, was appointed suffragan bishop of Reading in 1889. Richard entered Winchester College in 1836, and matriculated at Christ Church, Oxford, on 12 May 1842. He graduated B.A. in 1846, with an hon. fourth class in classics, and proceeded M.A. in 1849 and D.D. in 1892. In 1847 he was ordained to the curacy of Binfield, Berkshire, and in 1851 was nominated to the rectory of Lavington-cum-Graffham, Sussex, in succession to Archdeacon (afterwards Cardinal) Manning [q. v.], who had just seceded to Rome. At Lavington Randall's innovations in high church doctrine and ritual excited some opposition. His name became widely known in high church circles, and he was frequently chosen by Bishop Samuel Wilberforce [q. v.] as preacher of Lenten sermons at Oxford.

In 1868 Randall was presented by the trustees to the new parish of All Saints, Clifton. Under his care All Saints became the centre of high church practice and teaching. Daily services as well as daily celebrations of the holy communion were instituted, and lectures, Bible classes, guilds, and confraternities were organised in the parish. Randall showed himself a capable administrator, and raised large sums in support of church work. Although a staunch ritualist and a supporter of the English Church Union, he avoided romanising excesses. In 1873, owing to complaints as to certain practices at All Saints, Charles John Ellicott [q. v. Suppl. II], bishop of Gloucester, refused to license curates to the church, but he declined to allow proceedings to be taken against Randall under the Public Worship Regulation Act. In 1889 the bishop resumed confirmations in the church, and in 1891 bestowed on Randall an honorary canonry in the cathedral, where he occupied the stall formerly held by his father.

In February 1892 Randall was appointed by Lord Salisbury dean of Chichester. For ten years he earnestly devoted himself to his duties, and he was select preacher at Oxford in 1893–4. Owing to ill-health he retired in 1902, and settled in London. He died at Bournemouth on 23 Dec. 1906, and was buried at Branksome. On 6 Nov. 1849 he married Wilhelmina, daughter of George Augustus Bruxner of the Manor House, Binfield, Berkshire, who survived him with three sons and three daughters.

Randall's published volumes, which were mainly devotional, included: 1. 'Public Catechising, the Church's Method of Training her Children,' two papers read at the Church Congress in 1873 and 1883 respectively; 2nd edit. 1888. 2. 'Life in the Catholic Church: its Blessings and

Responsibilities,' 1889. 3. 'Addresses and Meditations for a Retreat,' 1890.

[The Times, 24 Dec. 1906; Church Times, and Guardian, 27 Dec. 1906; Winchester College Register, 1907; A. R. Ashwell and R. G. Wilberforce, Life of Samuel Wilberforce, 1883, vols. ii. and iii.; Brit. Mus. Cat.] G. S. W.

RANDEGGER, ALBERTO (1832–1911), musician, born at Trieste on 13 April 1832, was son of a schoolmaster. The family name was derived from Randegg near Schaffhausen. His mother, a Tuscan lady, was an amateur musician, but the boy showed no musical taste till at the age of thirteen he played without preparation a tune with correct melody and harmonies. He was then placed under Tivoli, of Trieste Cathedral, and afterwards under Lafont, for pianoforte. He studied composition under Ricci. In 1852–4 he conducted at several theatres in Italy and Dalmatia, composed ballets, and collaborated in an opera buffa. His grand opera 'Bianca Capello' was produced at Brescia, with a success that brought him an offer to conduct it in America. On the way he was stopped by the news of the cholera outbreak at New York. On the invitation of his eldest brother he came to London for a visit in 1854, and decided to remain. He had never heard an oratorio, and the huge number of performers at an Exeter Hall performance daunted him, the strangeness of the style soon sending him to sleep. But on the advice of Sir Michael Costa he persevered, mastered the English language, and soon became known in London as a versatile musician equally capable as performer, conductor, and teacher. He took further lessons in composition in London from Bernhard Molique. In 1857 he conducted an opera season at St. James's Theatre. From 1859 to 1870 he was organist at St. Paul's, Regent's Park; on the Prince Consort's death he composed an anthem so impressive that the vicar preached no sermon, saying that any words would fail of their effect. Randegger was most successful as a teacher of singing, and in 1868 was appointed to the staff of the Royal Academy of Music. His compositions were distinguished by practical qualities, were always tasteful and externally effective, but had no deep originality, and soon fell into disuse. The principal were 'The Rival Beauties,' operetta (Leeds, 1864), and 'Fridolin,' cantata (Birmingham Festival, 1873); a trio, 'I Naviganti,' was much sung. For Novello's series of primers he wrote 'Singing,' which has had an exceptionally wide circulation. To the end of his life he remained an indefatigable worker, and attended the performance of new works, always taking a copy which he marked with all details of the rendering. He conducted the Carl Rosa company in English opera in 1880, and Italian opera for Sir Augustus Harris from 1887 to 1898, as well as many choral concerts. He introduced many important novelties, mainly English, at the Norwich Triennial Festivals, which he conducted from 1881 to 1905. He edited collections of classical airs, utilising his memoranda of Exeter Hall performances, thus continuing English musical traditions. Besides his extensive practice at the Royal Academy he also became in 1896 a teacher at the Royal College, sharing in the management of both institutions. He was much in request as an adjudicator in competitions, and would give his verdicts in well-chosen words, with practical advice that proved of value to the unsuccessful candidates. He was an honorary member of the Philharmonic Society of Madrid, and in 1892 the King of Italy raised him to the rank of Cavaliere.

He was still actively engaged, and a familiar figure at London musical functions, in 1911 when, after a short illness, he died at his residence, 5 Nottingham Place, W., on 18 Dec. A memorial service, attended by very many prominent musicians, was held at St. Pancras church by Canon Sheppard of the Chapel Royal on 21 Dec.; the remains were cremated at Golder's Green. He married in 1897 Louise Baldwin of Boston, U.S.A.

[Detailed account (with portrait) and many valuable reminiscences of older musicians in Musical Times, Oct. 1899; obituaries in Musical News, and Musical Standard, 23 Dec. 1911; Musical Times, and Musical Herald, Jan. 1912.] H. D.

RANDLES, MARSHALL (1826–1904), Wesleyan divine, born at Over-Darwen, Lancashire, on 7 April 1826, was son of John Randles of Derbyshire by his wife Mary Maguire. He was educated at a private school, and after engaging in business at Haslingden he was accepted as a candidate for the methodist ministry in 1850 and studied at Didsbury College. He commenced his ministry in 1853, and was stationed successively at Montrose, Clitheroe, Boston, Nottingham, Lincoln, Halifax, Cheetham Hill, Altrincham, Bolton and Leeds. In 1882 he was elected a member of the legal conference, and in

1886 succeeded Dr. William Burt Pope [q. v. Suppl. II] as tutor of systematic theology at Didsbury. For many years he was chairman of the Manchester district, and in 1896 was elected president of the conference. In 1891 he received the degree of D.D. from the Wesleyan Theological College, Montreal. He retired in 1902 from the active ministry, and died at Manchester on 4 July 1904, being buried in Cheetham Hill Wesleyan churchyard.

In August 1856 he married Sarah Dewhurst, second daughter of John Scurrah of Padiham; by her he had a son and daughter; the son, Sir John Scurrah Randles, is conservative M.P. for North West Manchester.

A strong advocate of total abstinence, he first dealt with the question in 'Britain's Bane and Antidote' (1864). But his pen was mainly devoted to theology on conservative lines. In his best-known work, 'For Ever, an Essay on Everlasting Punishment' (1871; 4th edit. 1895), he argued in favour of the eternity of future punishment. Of kindred character was his book 'After Death: is there a Post-Mortem Probation?' (1904), in which he discusses 'Man's Immortality' (1903), by Dr. Robert Percival Downes, a work which favoured an intermediate period of moral probation after death. The view that God is incapable of suffering he strongly maintained, against Baldwin Brown, Dr. A. M. Fairbairn, George Matheson, George Adam Smith, and others, in 'The Blessed God: Impassibility' (1900). His ablest criticism of modern scepticism is found in his 'First Principles of Faith' (1884), in which he deals with the views of Mill, Herbert Spencer, and Mansel. He also published 'Substitution: a Treatise on the Atonement' (1877), and 'The Design and Use of Holy Scripture' (Fernley lecture, 1892), in which he incidentally acknowledges the service of the higher criticism.

A portrait, painted by Arthur Nowell, is at Didsbury College.

[Private information; works as above; Methodist Recorder, 23 July 1896.] C. H. I.

RANDOLPH, FRANCIS CHARLES HINGESTON- (1833–1910). [See HINGESTON-RANDOLPH.]

RANDOLPH, SIR GEORGE GRANVILLE (1818–1907), admiral, born in London on 26 Jan. 1818, was son of Thomas Randolph, prebendary of St. Paul's Cathedral from 1812 till his death in 1875, chaplain-in-ordinary to Queen Victoria and rector of Hadham, Hertfordshire. Dr. John Randolph [q. v.], bishop of London, was his grandfather. George entered the navy as a first-class volunteer on 7 Dec. 1830. He passed his examination in 1837, and received his commission as lieutenant on 27 June 1838. In Sept. following he was appointed to the North Star, frigate, Captain Lord John Hay [q. v], commodore on the north coast of Spain, and next, from 1840 to 1844, served on board the Vernon in the Mediterranean, being first lieutenant during the latter part of the commission. In Oct. 1844 he became first lieutenant of the Daedalus, of 20 guns, on the East India station, and on 19 Aug. 1845 commanded her barge at the destruction of Malloodoo, a piratical stronghold in Borneo. The force landed on this occasion numbered 540 seamen and marines, under the command of Captain Charles Talbot of the Vestal; there was sharp fighting, and the British loss amounted to 21 killed and wounded. On 9 Nov. 1846 Randolph was promoted, and a year later was appointed to the Bellerophon, in which ship and in the Rodney he served for six years in the Mediterranean. He was present in the Rodney at the attack on Fort Constantine, Sevastopol, took part in other operations in the Black Sea, and received for his services the Crimean medal with clasp, the Turkish medal, and the fourth class of the Medjidie. He was also made a knight of the Legion of Honour, and promoted to captain on 18 Nov. 1854. In that rank he commanded the Cornwallis, coastguard ship in the Humber, and afterwards the Diadem and Orlando, screw frigates, on the North American station. The Orlando was transferred to the Mediterranean in 1863, and Randolph remained in her till May 1865, when he was appointed to the guardship at Sheerness. He was awarded a good service pension in March 1867, and from Sept. of that year till March 1869 was commodore at the Cape of Good Hope. He received the C.B. in June 1869, and was promoted to his flag on 24 April 1872. From Dec. 1873 to June 1875 he commanded the detached squadron, this being his last active employment. He was promoted to vice-admiral on 16 Sept. 1877, retired on 26 July 1881, and was advanced to the rank of admiral on 8 July 1884. At Queen Victoria's diamond jubilee of 1897 he was raised to the K.C.B.

Randolph published in 1867 a treatise on 'The Rule of the Road at Sea,' and in 1879 his 'Problems in Naval Tactics'; he was also a corresponding member of the Royal United Service Institution and a fellow of the Royal Geographical Society. He died on 16 May 1907 at Hove, Brighton, and was buried there.

Randolph married, in 1851, Eleanor Harriet, daughter of the Rev. Joseph Arkwright of Mark Hall, Essex. She died in April 1907.

[O'Byrne's Naval Biography; The Times, 18 May 1907.] L. G. C. L.

RANSOM, WILLIAM HENRY (1824–1907), physician and embryologist, born at Cromer, Norfolk, on 19 Nov. 1824, was elder son of Henry Ransom, a master mariner of that town, who died in 1832. His mother, Mary Jones, was daughter of a Welsh clergyman. Educated at a private school at Norwich, Ransom was apprenticed at sixteen to a medical practitioner at King's Lynn. In 1843 he proceeded to University College, London, where Huxley was a fellow student. Writing to Herbert Spencer on 1 June 1886, Huxley points out that at the examination in 1845 Ransom came out first, winning an exhibition, and he second, with momentous results to himself. 'If Ransom,' Huxley continues, 'had worked less hard I might have been first and he second, in which case I should have obtained the exhibition, should not have gone into the navy, and should have forsaken science for practice' (*Life and Letters of T. H. Huxley*, 1900, ii. 133). After holding residential posts at University College Hospital, Ransom studied in Paris and Germany, graduating M.D.London in 1850. Then settling at Nottingham, he was from 1854 to 1890 physician to the Nottingham General Hospital. He became F.R.C.P. London in 1869, and fellow, respectively, of the Royal Medical and Chirurgical Society and University College, London, in 1854 and 1896. He was elected F.R.S. on 2 June 1870 for his knowledge of physiology and original observations in ovology, his candidature being supported among others by Huxley, Paget, and Lister.

Ransom's chief contributions to pure science were made when he was comparatively young, his later activities being absorbed in professional work. He was author of nine papers of value on embryological subjects, of which the first, 'On the Impregnation of the Ovum in the Stickleback,' appeared in the 'Proceedings of the Royal Society' (vol. vii. 1854–5). Another, 'On the Ovum of Osseous Fishes,' was published in the 'Philosophical Transactions' for 1867. He was interested in geology and assisted in the exploration of Nottinghamshire and Derbyshire caves, reading at the first meeting of the British Association at Nottingham, in 1866, a paper 'On the Occurrence of *Felis Lynx* as a British Fossil.' In 1892, when the British Medical Association met there, Ransom was president of the section of medicine, his address dealing with various aspects of vegetable pathology.

In 1870 Ransom devised a disinfecting stove (gas-heated) for the sterilisation of infected clothing, which was used extensively till steam methods were adopted. A presidential address to the Nottingham Medico-Chirurgical Society, 'On Colds as a Cause of Disease,' delivered on 4 Nov. 1887, attracted attention. His only independent publication, 'The Inflammation Idea in General Pathology,' appeared in 1906 (*Nature*, 29 Nov. 1906; *Brit. Med. Journ.* 23 June 1906).

Through his long career at Nottingham Ransom identified himself with the welfare of the place. Zealous in support of the volunteer movement, he served for fifteen years in the 1st Notts rifle corps. Interested in educational questions, he helped in the establishment of University College, Nottingham, of the governing body of which he was a member. He died at his residence, Park Valley, Nottingham, on 16 April 1907.

In 1860 he married Elizabeth, daughter of Dr. John William Bramwell of North Shields, who predeceased him. They had issue four sons and one daughter. The eldest son, Dr. W. B. Ransom (*b.* 5 Sept. 1860), succeeded his father as physician to the General Hospital, Nottingham, dying in 1909.

[Brit. Med. Journ., 27 April 1907; Lancet, 27 April 1907; Medico-Chirurgical Trans. vol. xc.; Roy. Soc. Catal. Sci. Papers; Report Brit. Assoc. 1866.] T. E. J.

RASSAM, HORMUZD (1826–1910), Assyrian explorer, born at Mosul in Asiatic Turkey in 1826, was youngest son and eighth child of Anton Rassam, archdeacon in the Chaldean Christian community at Mosul, by his wife Theresa, granddaughter of Ishaak Halabee (of Aleppo). His father was a Nestorian or Chaldean Christian, and claimed to be of Chaldean race, but he was probably of Assyrian descent. The word 'Rassam' is Arabic for designer or engraver, and the family were originally designers of patterns for muslins, the staple product of Mosul. An elder brother, Christian, married

Matilda, sister of George Percy Badger [q. v. Suppl. I], the Arabic scholar, and became the first English consul at Mosul.

As an infant Hormuzd narrowly escaped death by the plague. In childhood he learned to write and speak both the Chaldean and Syrian language, which the native Christians used, and Arabic, the speech of the country. As a boy he was induced to serve as an acolyte in the Roman catholic church of St. Miskinta, but a project to send him to Rome to study the catholic faith came to nothing owing to his doubts of Roman doctrine. A brother Georges was excommunicated by the Roman church on that ground. Mrs. Badger, his brother's mother-in-law, finally converted him to protestantism and helped him in the study of English. In 1841 he accompanied an Austrian traveller on a scientific expedition to study the flora and fauna of the Assyrian and Kurdish mountains. Next year he became clerk to his brother Christian. In the summer Sir Austen Henry Layard [q. v. Suppl. I], who passed through Mosul on his way from Persia to Constantinople, lodged at Christian's house and made Hormuzd's acquaintance, with crucial effect on his career.

With Christian's permission Layard took Hormuzd with him in 1845, to make excavations in the mounds of Nimroud, the site of the Biblical Calah. Hormuzd won Layard's fullest confidence, and when Layard went to Bagdad to arrange for the transport of the antiquities to England, Hormuzd was left in charge, and all the accounts of the excavations passed through his hands. His services, however, were unpaid. After the discovery at Nimroud of the palaces of Aššur-nasir-âpli, Shalmaneser II, Tiglath-pileser IV, Sennacherib, and Esarhaddon, work was pursued from May 1847 with equal success at Kouyunjik (Nineveh).

In 1848 by Layard's advice Rassam came to England with a view to finishing his education at Magdalen College, Oxford. He came to know Pusey and the leaders of the Oxford Movement, but his sympathy with them was small. His stay in Oxford was short. While Charles Marriott [q. v.] was preparing him for matriculation, Layard recalled him to Assyria to assist in excavations at the expense of the trustees of the British Museum. He subsequently presented to Magdalen College a sculptured slab from Nineveh. Rassam had now a fixed salary, with an allowance for travelling. Arriving late in 1849 he pushed on vigorously with the work at Kouyunjik, and the excavations at Nimroud were reopened. Rassam accompanied his patron to the ruins in Babylonia and returned to England in 1851, when Layard brought back his discoveries.

Next year the trustees of the British Museum sent Rassam out alone—Layard's health compelling his withdrawal. He worked at Nimroud, Kouyunjik, and tried again the mounds representing Aššur, the old capital of Assyria, now called Qala'a-Shergat. In all these places antiquities were found, many of them of considerable importance. His great discovery on this occasion, however, was the palace of Aššur-bani-âpli at Kouyunjik—the North Palace—with a beautiful series of bas-reliefs, including the celebrated hunting-scenes. Among the numerous tablets were some supplying accounts of the Creation and Flood legends. A few of the slabs found in this edifice are now in the Louvre at Paris, but most of them are in the British Museum.

On returning to England, Rassam in 1854 accepted from the Indian government the post of political interpreter at Aden, leaving further excavating work to William Kennett Loftus [q. v.]. At Aden, where Rassam remained eight years, he soon served as postmaster as well as political interpreter. Later he became judge and magistrate without salary, and was given the rank of political resident and justice of the peace. Rassam's chief duty was to qualify the hostility of the neighbouring tribes to the British authorities and to one another. Forming a friendship with Seyyid Alaidrous, whose ancestor he described as the patron saint of Arabia Felix, he got into touch with the tribes of the interior with the best results. In 1861 he was sent by the Indian government to Zanzibar to represent British interests while the claim of the Sultan of Muscat to suzerainty over his brother, the Sultan of Zanzibar, was under investigation by the Indian government.

In 1864 an exciting episode in Rassam's career opened. Two years earlier Theodore, King of Abyssinia, had cast into prison at Magdala, Consul Charles Duncan Cameron [q. v.], Henry Aaron Stern [q. v.], and other British missionaries of the London Jews' Society. In 1864 Rassam was chosen for the perilous duty of delivering a friendly letter of protest to Theodore. Arriving at Massowah, he and two companions, Lieutenant Prideaux and Dr. Blanc, of the Indian army, were kept waiting there nearly a year before receiving permission to enter the country, which even then was only granted in response to Rassam's threat to return to Aden. Rassam met Theodore at Damot on 28 Jan. 1866. At first the mission was well treated; the captives were set at liberty and reached Rassam's camp, while a letter of apology from the king was drafted (12 March 1866). Suddenly the king's conduct changed; he imposed fresh conditions (12 April) and claimed an indemnity for the liberation of the captives. Having re-arrested the prisoners, Theodore now seized the three members of the British mission and threw all, loaded with chains, into the rock-fortress of Magdala.

Rassam, whose personal relations with Theodore were not unamiable, succeeded in communicating with the frontier, and a military expedition was despatched to Abyssinia to effect the release of the captives, under Sir Robert Napier (afterwards Lord Napier of Magdala). On 2 Dec. 1867 Theodore heard of its landing. An ultimatum from the commander-in-chief destined for the king was intercepted by Rassam, who believed its receipt would lead to the massacre of himself and of his fellow-captives. Recognising his peril, Theodore ordered Rassam's chains to be taken off on 18 March 1868, and he and the three captives were released on the arrival of the British force before Magdala on 11 April 1868. Until his death Rassam suffered physically from his long confinement. On the 14th the fortress was taken by storm, and Theodore died by his own hand next day. Rassam narrated his strange experiences in his 'British Mission to Theodore, King of Abyssinia, with Notices of the Country traversed from Massowah through the Soudan and the Amhara and back to Annesley Bay from Magdala' (2 vols. 1869).

Returning to England, Rassam during a year's leave of absence married an English wife, and resigning his appointment at Aden travelled widely in the United Kingdom and the Near East. He then settled first at Twickenham and afterwards at Isleworth. In 1877 he was again employed by the British government in Asiatic Turkey, where he inquired into the condition of the Christian communities and sects in Asia Minor, Armenia, and Kurdistan. He revisited his native town of Mosul on 16 Nov. 1877. He gave a detailed account of his observations on the journey in his 'Asshur and the Land of Nimrod' (Cincinnati and New York, 1897).

Meanwhile, in 1876, with the help of Layard, then British ambassador in Turkey, Rassam had obtained a firman from the Turkish government, on behalf of the trustees of the British Museum, for the continuation of the excavations in Assyria and Babylonia. He at once organised the work of exploration, and every year from 1876 until the end of 1882 he carried on excavations, not only at Kouyunjik (Nineveh) and Nimroud (Calah) but also at Balawat. In Babylonia the sites explored included the ruins of Babylon, Tel-Ibrahim (Cuthah), Dailem, and Abu-Habbah (Sippar). Among the more important finds were the bronze gates of the Assyrian king Shalmaneser II (Balawat), the beautiful Sungod-stone, the cylinder of Nabonidus giving his date for the early Babylonian kings Sargon of Agadé and his son Naram-Sin, and a valuable mace-head with the name of king Sargani. The inscriptions included additions to the Creation and Flood legends, the first tablet of a bilingual series prefaced by a new and important version of the Creation story in Sumerian and Semitic Babylonian, and numerous other documents; the fragments, large and small, amounted, it was estimated, to close upon 100,000, though many of these were small, and consequently of little value. Among the imperfect documents was the cylinder of Cyrus the Great, in which he refers to the capture of Babylon. Rassam's important discoveries attracted world-wide attention, and the Royal Academy of Sciences at Turin awarded him the Brazza prize of 12,000 fr. for the four years 1879–82. His discovery of the site of the city Sippara is especially noticed among the grounds of the award. An allegation that Rassam's kinsmen had withheld from the British Museum the best of Rassam's finds was successfully refuted in 1893 in an action at law in which Rassam was awarded 50*l.* damages for libel.

After 1882 Rassam lived mainly at Brighton, writing on Assyro-Babylonian exploration, on the Christian sects of the Nearer East, or on current religious controversy in England. Like most Oriental Christians, he was a man of strong religious convictions, and having adopted evangelical views became a bitter foe of the high church movement. He was fellow of the Royal Geographical Society, the Society of Biblical Archæology, and the Victoria Institute.

An autobiography which he compiled before his death remains in manuscript. He died at his residence at Hove, Brighton, on 16 Sept. 1910, and was buried in the cemetery there. By his wife Anne Eliza, daughter of Captain Spender Cosby Price, formerly of the 77th Highlanders, whom he married on 8 June 1869, he had issue a son and six daughters. The son, Anthony Hormuzd, born on 31 Dec. 1883, joined the British army, and is now captain in the New Zealand staff corps at Wellington.

[Rassam's published books and MS. autobiography; Clements Markham's Hist. of the Abyssinian Expedition, 1869; H. A. Stern's The Captive Missionary, 1868; Parliamentary Papers (Abyssinian), 1867–9; Lord A. Loftus's Reminiscences (2nd edit.), i. 206; Men of Mark, 1881 (with portrait); The Times, 17 Sept. 1910.] T. G. P.

RATHBONE, WILLIAM (1819-1902), philanthropist, born in Liverpool on 11 Feb. 1819, was eldest of six sons of William Rathbone (1787–1868) [see under WILLIAM RATHBONE (1757–1809)] by his wife Elizabeth Greg, and was the sixth William Rathbone in direct succession, merchants in Liverpool from 1730. After passing through schools at Gateacre, Cheam, and Everton, he was apprenticed (1835–8) to Nicol, Duckworth & Co., Bombay merchants in Liverpool. In October 1838 he went with Thomas Ashton (father of Baron Ashton of Hyde) for a semester at the University of Heidelberg, where he 'gained habits of steady work and study,' and acquired a knowledge of foreign politics. His high ideals of public duty were formed under the teaching of John Hamilton Thom [q. v.], who had married in 1838 his sister Hannah. From Heidelberg he made (in 1839) an Italian tour, and on his return obtained a clerkship in the London firm of Baring Brothers. In April 1841 the senior partner, Joshua Bates [q. v.], took him on a business tour to the United States; the impression of this visit, confirmed by two subsequent ones (his third visit, 1848, was with his first wife, whose parents were American by birth), made him an 'uncompromising free-trader.' At the end of 1841 he became a partner in his father's firm, Rathbone Brothers & Co. His philanthropic work began in 1849, when he acted as a visitor for the District Provident Society; in later life he said that in the House of Commons he was 'often far more tempted to take a low and sordid view of human nature than he had ever been in the slums.' His first experiment in district nursing was made in 1859, by the engagement for this work of Mary Robinson, who had attended his first wife in her fatal illness. He consulted Florence Nightingale [q. v. Suppl. II] about a supply of nurses, who suggested that Liverpool should form a school to train nurses for itself. Hence the establishment by Rathbone of the Liverpool Training School and Home for Nurses, which began work on 1 July 1862. By the end of 1865 Liverpool had been divided into eighteen districts, each provided with nursing under the superintendence of ladies, who made themselves responsible for the costs entailed; for about a year Rathbone himself took the place of one of the lady superintendents during her absence. Long after, a colleague remarked that Rathbone was 'the one male member of the committee who knew what the homes of the poor were actually like.' The reform of sick nursing in the workhouses was also achieved by Rathbone, who secured for this in 1865 the invaluable services of Agnes Elizabeth Jones (1832–68). For three years he bore the whole expenses. His nursing reforms were extended to Birmingham and Manchester, and to London in 1874, when the National Association for providing Trained Nurses was formed, with Rathbone as chairman of its sub-committee for organising district nursing. In 1888–9 he was honorary secretary and subsequently vice-president of Queen Victoria's Jubilee Institute for Nurses, to which the Queen had devoted 70,000*l*. out of the Women's Offering. Meanwhile, during the cotton famine of 1862–3, caused by the civil war in the United States, he did much, in conjunction with his cousin, Charles Melly, to raise to 100,000*l*. the Liverpool contribution to the relief fund, and brought wise counsel to its distribution.

His political action began locally in 1852, on the liberal side. He took a leading part in 1857 in procuring the Liverpool address upholding the findings of the commissariat commissions appointed after the Crimean war. Gladstone's election in 1865 for South Lancashire owed much to his energy. In November 1868 he was elected as one of the three members for Liverpool. Among other matters he took part in shaping the bankruptcy bill (1869). He was especially interested in measures for local government and in the licensing laws, opposing 'prohibition,' and demanding not more legislation but stricter administration. He commissioned in 1892 Mrs. Evelyn Leighton Fanshawe to report on temperance legislation in the United States and Canada (published 1893). For Liverpool he sat till 1880, when he contested south-west Lancashire, and was defeated, but was returned in the following November at a bye-election for Carnarvonshire, sitting for the county till 1885, and from 1885 for North Carnarvonshire. He followed Gladstone on the home rule question. In 1895 Rathbone retired from parliament. He was deputy-lieutenant for Lancashire.

In the foundation of the University College of Liverpool (opened in Jan. 1882) he was greatly interested; with his two brothers he founded a King Alfred chair of modern literature and English language; he was president of the college from 1892. He was also very active in the movement for establishing the University College of North Wales (opened Oct. 1884), of which he was president from 1891 He was actively concerned in the Welsh Intermediate Education Act of 1889. Liverpol gave him the freedom of the city on 21 Oct. 1891. In May 1895 he was made LL.D. by Victoria University.

Straightforwardness and pertinacity, with entire unselfishness, were leading features in Rathbone's character. With little of the bonhomie and none of the humour of his large-hearted father, seeming indeed to be a dry man, he had a tenderness of disposition which found expression rather in act than in word. Principled against indiscriminate giving, he was constantly liable to be overcome by personal appeal. A convinced unitarian in theology, he carried many traces of his Quaker antecedents. His manner of life was simple. He died at Greenbank, Liverpool, on 6 March 1902, and was buried in Toxteth cemetery. He married (1) on 6 Sept. 1847, Lucretia Wainwright (*d.* 27 May 1859), eldest daughter of Samuel Gair of Liverpool, by whom he had four sons, of whom two survived him, and one daughter; (2) in 1862, Emily Acheson (his second cousin), daughter of Acheson Lyle of Londonderry, who survived him with her two sons and two daughters.

Rathbone published: 1. 'Social Duties . . . Organisation of . . . Works of Benevolence and Public Utility,' 1867. 2. 'Local Government and Taxation,' 1875. 3. 'Local Government and Taxation,' 1883 (reprinted from the 'Nineteenth Century'). 4. 'Protection and Communism . . . Effects of the American Tariff on Wages,' 1884. 5 'Reform in Parliamentary Business,' 1884. 6. 'Sketch of the History and Progress of District Nursing,' 1890.

His bust, by Charles Allen, was presented to University College, Liverpool. Another bust, by Hargreaves Bond, was presented (1889) to the Liverpool Reform Club. A bronze statue by (Sir) George Frampton, R.A., was erected by public subscription in St. John's Gardens, Liverpool.

[The Times, 7 March 1902; Christian Life, 7, 12, and 29 March 1902; Memorials of Agnes E. Jones, 1871; Eleanor F. Rathbone's William Rathbone; a Memoir, 1905 (portrait); information from the Rev. J. Collins Odgers; personal recollection.] A. G.

RATTIGAN, Sir WILLIAM HENRY (1842–1904), Anglo-Indian jurist, born at Delhi on 4 Sept. 1842, was youngest son of Bartholomew Rattigan, who left his home, Athy, co. Kildare, at an early age and entered the ordnance department of the East India Company. Educated at the high school, Agra, he entered the 'uncovenanted' service of government in youth as extra assistant commissioner in the Punjab, acting for a short time as judge of the small causes court at Delhi. But being dissatisfied with his prospects he resigned, contrary to the wishes of his family, in order to study law. Enrolled as a pleader of the Punjab Chief Court on its establishment in 1866, he built up an extensive practice, first in partnership with Mr. Scarlett, and then on his own account.

Coming to England, he was admitted a student of Lincoln's Inn on 3 Nov. 1871, and was called to the bar there on 7 June 1873, also studying at King's College, London. Returning to Lahore, he speedily rose to be head of his profession there. He was for many years government advocate, and in 1880, 1881, 1882, and 1886, for varying short periods, he acted as a judge of the chief court. In Nov. 1886 he resigned his acting judgeship so as to continue his practice without further interruption. A linguist of unusual ability, Rattigan mastered in all five European languages, several Indian vernaculars, and Persian. German he studied assiduously, and he translated the second volume of Savigny's 'System of Roman Law—Jural Relations' (1883). In 1885 he took the degree of D.L., with first-class honours, at Göttingen.

In February 1887 Rattigan became vice-chancellor of the Punjab University, then on the verge of bankruptcy. He succeeded in regenerating the institution, and was reappointed biennially, retaining the vice-chancellorship till April 1895. He was made a D.L. of the university in Jan. 1896, and LL.D. of Glasgow in 1901. In 1891 he accepted the presidentship of the Khalsa College committee, and by his energy and influence overcame dissension among the Sikhs, with the result that an institution for their higher education on a religious basis was established at Amritsar in 1897. When he retired from India in April 1900 the Sikh council appointed him life president, and on his death a memorial hospital was erected at the college (opened in 1906). He was an additional member of the viceroy's legislative council in 1892–3 and of the Punjab legislative council in 1898–9.

A self-made man, without advantages of family influence, Rattigan made substantial contributions to legal literature amid his professional and public labours. He published 'Selected Cases in Hindu Law decided by the Privy Council and the Superior Indian Courts' (2 vols., Lahore, 1870–1), 'The Hindu Law of Adoption' (1873), 'De Jure Personarum' (1873), and he collaborated with Mr. Justice Charles Boulnois (1832–1912), of the Punjab chief court, in 'Notes on the Customary Law as administered in the Punjab' (1878). His most important book, 'A Digest of Civil and Customary Law of the Punjab' (Lahore, 1880), which reached a seventh edition (1909), was designed to classify material for a future codification, and rendered Rattigan a foremost authority upon customary law in Northern India. His other works were 'The Science of Jurisprudence' (Lahore, 1888), which, chiefly intended for Indian students, reached a third edition (1899); 'Private International Law' (1895); and a pamphlet on the international aspects of 'The Case of the Netherlands South African Railway' (1901). Rattigan was knighted in Jan. 1895, was made queen's counsel in May 1897, and was elected bencher of his inn in June 1903.

On settling in England in 1900 he practised before the privy council. At the general election of 1900 he unsuccessfully contested North East Lanark in the liberal-unionist interest; but at the bye-election on 26 Sept. 1901 he won the seat by a majority of 904. Speaking rarely, and chiefly on Indian matters, he was respected by all parties. He was killed in a motor-car accident near Biggleswade, on his way to Scotland, on 4 July 1904, and was buried in Kensal Green cemetery.

He married (1) on 21 Dec. 1861, at Delhi, Teresa Matilda (*d.* 9 Sept. 1876), daughter of Colonel A. C. B. Higgins, C.I.E., examiner of accounts, public works department; (2) at Melbourne, on 1 April 1878, her sister Evelyn, who survives. By his first marriage he had two daughters and four sons, and by his second marriage three sons.

There is a memorial window in Harrow Chapel, where Rattigan's sons were educated, and a tablet is in the cathedral at Lahore.

[Rattigan's legal works; the Punjab Magazine, Feb. 1895; Men of Merit, London, 1900; Glasgow Contemporaries at Dawn of XXth Century, Glasgow 1901; Punjab Civil Lists; The Times, 5, 6, 7, and 11 July 1904; The Biographer, Nov. 1901; Civil and Military Gazette, Lahore, 7, 9, and 22 July 1904; Pioneer, 7 July 1904; Law Times, 9 July 1904; family details kindly supplied by Lady Rattigan.] F. H. B.

RAVEN, JOHN JAMES (1833–1906), archæologist and campanologist, born on 25 June 1833 at Boston, Lincolnshire, was eldest son of eight children of John Hardy Raven, of Huguenot descent, rector of Worlington, Suffolk, by his wife Jane Augusta, daughter of John Richman, attorney, of Lymington, Hampshire. A younger brother, the Rev. John Hardy Raven (1842–1911), was headmaster of Beccles school. John, after early training at home, entered St. Catharine's College, Cambridge, on 18 Oct. 1853, and migrated on 17 Dec. following to Emmanuel College (where he was awarded first an Ash exhibition and subsequently a sizarship). He graduated B.A. as a senior optime in the mathematical tripos of 1857, proceeding M.A. in 1860 and D.D. in 1872. In 1857 he was appointed second master of Sevenoaks grammar school, and was ordained curate of the parish church there. In 1859 he became headmaster of Bungay grammar school, an office which was for nearly 300 years in the gift of Emmanuel College. He improved the working of the school and raised money for a new building, which was opened in 1863. A commemorative tablet testifies to his share of the work. From 1866 to 1885 he was headmaster of Yarmouth grammar school. He served for some time as curate of the parish church, Yarmouth, and was from 1881 to 1885 vicar of St. George's in that town. In 1885 he was presented by the Master of Emmanuel to the consolidated vicarage of Fressingfield and rectory of Withersdale in Suffolk, and was admitted on 23 March 1895 (under a dispensation from the archbishop of Canterbury) to the vicarage of Metfield in the same county. He was chosen honorary canon of Norwich in 1888, and rural dean of Hoxne in 1896, and a co-opted member of the County Education Committee on its formation in 1902.

While a youth Raven began his lifelong

archæological study by examining the bells of the churches near his home at Worlington and by contributing to Parker's 'Ecclesiastical History of Suffolk' in 1854. He served from 1881 till his death on the committee of the Norfolk and Norwich Archæological Society, which he joined in 1871, was a vice-president of the Suffolk Institute of Archæology, and was elected F.S.A. on 23 April 1891. The best English campanologist of his time, he was president of the Norwich Diocesan Association of Ringers, and published books on 'The Church Bells of Cambridgeshire' (Lowestoft, 1869; 2nd edit. Camb. Antiq. Soc. 1881), 'The Church Bells of Suffolk' (1890), and 'The Bells of England' (in the 'Antiquary's Books' series, 1906). He died at Fressingfield vicarage on 20 Sept. 1906, and was buried in the churchyard. A reredos was erected to his memory in the church. His pupils at Yarmouth presented him with his portrait by Alfred Lys Baldry (now belonging to his eldest son at Fressingfield), and a tower at Yarmouth school commemorated his successful headmastership. His fine library of county and bell literature was sold at Fressingfield in Nov. 1906.

He married on 19 March 1860, at Mildenhall parish church, Suffolk, Fanny, youngest daughter of Robert Homer Harris of Botesdale, and had, with two daughters, seven sons, of whom three took holy orders.

Besides the works already mentioned, separate sermons, and contributions to periodicals, including 'Emmanuel College Magazine,' Raven published 'The History of Suffolk' (in the 'Popular County Histories' series, 1895), and 'Mathematics made easy: Lectures on Geometry and Algebra' (1897). He also compiled the 'Early Man' section of the 'Victoria County History of Suffolk,' and projected a volume, 'Sidelights on the Revolution Period,' for which he transcribed Archbishop Sancroft's commonplace book.

[Athenæum, 29 Sept. 1906; Emmanuel Coll. Mag., vol. xvii. no. 1; private information.]

T. C. H.

RAVERTY, HENRY GEORGE (1825–1906), soldier and Oriental scholar, born at Falmouth on 31 May 1825, was the son of Peter Raverty of co. Tyrone, a surgeon in the navy. His mother belonged to the family of Drown of Falmouth. Educated at Falmouth and Penzance, at fifteen or sixteen he showed an inclination for the sea, but a short voyage as a passenger from Penzance disillusioned him, and he resolved to become a soldier. The interest of Sir Charles Lemon secured him a cadetship, and he sailed for India. Appointed to the Welsh fusiliers, he very soon (in 1843) exchanged into the 3rd Bombay native infantry. With his regiment he was present at the siege of Multan in 1848; served in Gujarat, and in the first frontier expedition in 1850 against tribes on the Suwāt border. For his services at Multan and Gujarat he received a medal with two clasps, and a medal with one clasp for the north-west frontier. Raverty held a civil appointment as assistant-commissioner in the Punjab from 1852 to 1859. He was promoted major in 1863 and retired from the army next year.

Settling in England, first near Ottery St. Mary, and afterwards at Grampound Road, Cornwall, Raverty pursued till the end of his long life various Oriental studies which he had begun in India. Although he lacked academic training, he was gifted with scholarly instincts, and devoted himself to linguistic, historical, geographical, and ethnological study on scientific lines. In India he first learned Hindustani, Persian, Gujarati, and Marathi, and for his knowledge of these languages gained the 'high proficiency' prize of 1000 rupees from his government. A 'Thesaurus of English Hindustani Technical Terms' (1859) proved his linguistic aptitude in Hindustani. His transference to the north-west frontier at Peshawar in 1849 had meanwhile directed his chief attention to the Pushtu or Afghan language, history, and ethnology. To the 'Transactions' of the Geographical Society of Bombay, Raverty contributed in 1851 'An Account of the City and Province of Peshawar,' illustrated with maps and sepia sketches. In order to acquire practical knowledge of the Pushtu tongue he had to collect, arrange, and systematise almost the whole of the needful grammatical and lexical material. Raverty thus became 'the father of the study of Afghan.' His first efforts proved comprehensive and final. In 1855 he published his 'Grammar of the Pushto or Language of the Afghans,' which Dr. Dorn, the eminent orientalist of St. Petersburg, warmly commended. In 1860, besides a second and improved edition of the Grammar (3rd edit. 1867), he published his monumental 'Dictionary of the Pushto or Afghan Language' (2nd edit. 1867), and his admirable anthology of Pushtu prose and poetry entitled 'Gulshan i Roh.' He was as well acquainted with the Pushtu literature as with the spoken language. In 1862 there followed 'Selections from the Poetry of the Afghans from the Sixteenth to the Nineteenth Century' in an English translation. After leaving India, in 1864, he published 'The Gospel of the Afghans, being a Critical Examination of a Small Portion of the New Testament in Pushtu'; in 1871 a translation of 'Æsop's Fables' into Pushtu, and in 1880 a 'Pushtu Manual.' Between 1881 and 1888 he issued in four instalments his ponderous work 'Notes on Afghanistan and Baluchistan,' in which he describes as many as three and twenty routes in those countries. Besides its geographical and topographical information, the book contains an important contribution to the ethnology of those regions, and much concerning the manners and customs of the tribes and clans. The 'Notes' were prepared at the request of the marquis of Salisbury when secretary of state for India in 1875–6.

Simultaneously Raverty was working at his translation of the 'Ṭabaḳāt i Nāṣirī,' which was published in 1881. It is a rendering from Persian into English of Minhāj ibn Sirāj's work on general history, with special reference to the Muhammadan dynasties of Asia, and particularly those of Ghūr, Ghaznah (now parts of Afghanistan), and Hindustan. By his critical remarks and copious illustrative notes derived from his wide reading of other native authors, Raverty vastly enhanced the historical value and completeness of Minhāj's work.

Other of Raverty's valuable studies appeared chiefly in the 'Journal of the Asiatic Society,' Bengal. Among these papers were 'Remarks on the Origin of the Afghan People' (1854); 'Notes on Kafiristan and the Siah-Posh Kafir Tribes' (1858); 'On the Language of the Siah-Posh Kafirs of Kafiristan' (1864); 'An Account of Upper Kashghar and Chitral' (1864); 'Memoir of the Author of the Tabakāt i Nāsirī' (1882); 'The Mihran of Sind and its Tributaries—a Geographical Study' (1892); and 'Tibbat three hundred and sixty-five Years ago' (1895). 'Muscovite Proceedings on the Afghan Frontier' was reprinted from the 'United Service Gazette' in 1885.

Raverty died at Grampound Road, Cornwall, on 20 Oct. 1906. He married in 1865 Fanny Vigurs, only daughter of Commander George Pooley, R.N. She survived him without issue.

Raverty, whose frankness in controversy cost him many friends, received small recognition in his lifetime from his fellow-countrymen, but his immense labours gave him a high reputation among foreign Oriental scholars. At his death Raverty had seven important works either completed in manuscript or in preparation, viz.: 1. 'A History of Herat and its Dependencies and the Annals of Khurāsān from the earliest down to modern Times,' based upon the works of native historians, which are treated with critical acumen; the six bulky quarto volumes of MS., the result of fifty years' research, are now at the India office. 2. 'A History of the Afghan People and their Country' (the whole material collected and the composition just commenced). 3. 'A brief History of the Rise of the Isma'iliah Sect in Africa.' 4. 'A History of the Mings and Hazarahs of Afghanistan and other Parts of Central Asia.' 5. 'A Translation of the Ta'rīkh i Alfi from the Persian.' 6. 'The Gospels in Pushtu' (completed). 7. 'An English-Pushto Dictionary' (not completed).

[The Times, 26 Oct. 1906; Buckland's Dict. of Indian Biog.; Journal of the Royal Asiatic Soc., 1907, pp. 251–3; papers kindly lent by Major Raverty's widow.] E. E.

RAWLINSON, GEORGE (1812–1902), canon of Canterbury, writer on ancient history, born on 23 Nov. 1812, at Chadlington, Oxfordshire, was third son of Abraham Tysack Rawlinson by his wife Eliza Eudocia Albinia, daughter of Henry Creswicke, of Morton, Worcester. Sir Henry Creswicke Rawlinson [q. v.], was his brother. Educated at Swansea grammar school and at Ealing school, he matriculated in 1834 at Trinity College, Oxford, as a commoner, and in 1838 took a first class in the final school of classics, graduating B.A. in that year and proceeding M.A. in 1841. He played for Oxford in the first cricket match with Cambridge in 1836 and was president of the Union in 1840. He was elected fellow of Exeter College in 1840 and tutor in 1841. In 1841 and 1842 he was ordained deacon and priest, and gained the Denyer prize for a theological essay twice—in 1842 and 1843. In 1846 he vacated his tutorship on his marriage, and for a short time (1846–7) was curate of Merton, Oxfordshire. But he soon found ways of renewing his activities and interests in Oxford. He served on the committee of the Tutors' Association, a body formed to consider the proposals of the University Commission of 1852, with Church, Marriott, Osborne Gordon, Mansel, and others. In 1853, with Dean Lake, he laid before Gladstone the views of the Tutors' Association, and thus had an important influence in shaping the Oxford University Act of 1854. Gladstone's interest in Rawlinson may be dated from this interview. In the newly organised examination of classical moderations Rawlinson was a moderator from 1852 to 1854, with Scott, Conington, Mansel, and others. He was an examiner in the final classical school in 1854, 1856, 1867; and in theology in 1874. In 1859 Rawlinson succeeded Mansel as Bampton lecturer, his subject being 'The Historical Evidences of the truth of the Scripture Records stated anew, with special reference to the doubts and discoveries of modern times' (1859; 2nd edit. 1860). In 1861 he was appointed Camden professor of ancient history. He held that post till 1889, and it left him leisure for writing and research. His interests in Oxford were not wholly academic. He was a pioneer in the attempt to establish friendly and useful connections between the university and the town. From 1860 to 1863 he was a guardian of the poor; he was a perpetual curator of the University Galleries, and an original member and first treasurer of the Oxford Political Economy Club. From 1859 to 1870 he held the office of classical examiner under the council of military education.

In 1872 the crown appointed him canon of Canterbury. Indistinctness of speech interfered with his efficiency as a speaker and preacher, so that Gladstone's choice must be taken as a recognition of his learning, broad-mindedness, and administrative capacity. His interest in Canterbury Cathedral was shown by valuable gifts and more particularly on the occasion of his golden wedding in 1896 by the presentation of a gold and jewelled paten and chalice. He was proctor in convocation for Canterbury from 1873 to 1898. In 1888, the year before he resigned the Camden professorship, he was preferred by the chapter of his cathedral to the rich rectory of All Hallows, Lombard Street.

Early in his career Rawlinson devoted himself to the preparation of an elaborate English edition of Herodotus. He arranged that his brother, Sir Henry Rawlinson, and Sir J. Gardner Wilkinson, should contribute special articles on historical, archæological and racial questions, while he himself prepared the translation with short notes and other adjuncts of scholarship. The edition was dedicated to Gladstone and superseded all other editions at Oxford for many years; it was entitled 'The History of Herodotus. A new English version, edited with copious notes and appendices. Embodying the chief results, historical and ethnographical, which have been obtained in the progress of Cuneiform and Hieroglyphical discovery. By G. Rawlinson . . . assisted by Sir H. Rawlinson and Sir J. G. Wilkinson' (4 vols. 1858–60; 2nd edit. 1862; 3rd edit. 1875). An abridgement in two volumes by A. T. Grant appeared in 1897, and the translation, edited by G. H. Blakeney, was reprinted in 'Everyman's Library' (2 vols.) in 1910. Pursuing his researches in this field, Rawlinson summarised for his generation in scholarly form the results of research and excavation in the East, in a series of works of considerable constructive ability which have hardly yet been superseded in English. The first was 'The Five Great Monarchies of the ancient Eastern World; or the history, geography, and antiquities of Chaldæa, Assyria, Babylonia, Media, and Persia. . . .' (4 vols. 1862–7; 2nd edit., 3 vols. 1871). This was followed by 'The Sixth Great Oriental Monarchy; or the geography, history, and antiquities of Parthia' (1873); to which was added 'The Seventh Great Oriental Monarchy; or the geography, history, and antiquities of the Sassanian or New Persian Empire' (1876). Supplementary to this series were 'The History of Ancient Egypt' (2 vols. 1881); and 'The History of Phœnicia' (1889).

Rawlinson was the champion of a learned orthodoxy which opposed the extremes of the literary higher critics by an appeal to the monuments and the evidence of archæology. In 1861 he contributed to 'Aids to Faith,' the volume of essays written to counteract 'Essays and Reviews,' a paper 'On the genuineness and authenticity of the Pentateuch,' and he published in the same year 'The Contrasts of Christianity with Heathen and Jewish Systems, or nine sermons preached before the University of Oxford.' In 1871, at the request of the Christian Evidence Society, he delivered a lecture on 'The Alleged Historical Difficulties of the Old and New Testaments,' which appeared in the volume entitled 'Modern Scepticism.' As a commentator and expositor Rawlinson wrote for the 'Speaker's Commentary' on Kings, Chronicles, Ezra, Nehemiah, Esther, and the two Books of the Maccabees; and for Ellicott's 'Old Testament Commentary for English Readers' on Exodus. His last work was the life of his brother, entitled 'A Memoir of Major-general Sir H. C. Rawlinson. . . . with an introduction by Field-Marshal Lord Roberts of Kandahar' (1898).

Rawlinson was a fellow of the Royal Geographical Society, a corresponding member of the Royal Academy of Turin and of the American Philosophical Society. His health failed two years before his death, which took place suddenly from syncope on 6 Oct. 1902. He was buried in Holywell cemetery at Oxford. A portrait by his son-in-law, Wilson Forster, was presented to Trinity College, Oxford, in 1899.

Rawlinson married in 1846 Louisa, second daughter of Sir Robert Alexander Chermside [q. v.], and had issue four sons and five daughters.

Besides the works already mentioned, large contributions to Dr. Smith's 'Dictionary of the Bible,' pamphlets among 'Present Day Tracts,' and numerous sermons, Rawlinson published: 1. 'A Manual of Ancient History from the earliest times to the Fall of the Western Empire,' 1869. 2. 'Historical Illustrations of the Old Testament,' 1871. 3 and 4 (for the R.T.S.): 'The Origin of Nations,' 1877; 'The Religions of the Ancient World,' 1882. 5. 'St. Paul in Damascus and Arabia,' 1877. 6. 'Egypt and Babylon from Scripture and profane sources,' 1885. 7, 8, 9 (for the 'Story of the Nations' series): 'Parthia,' 1885; 'Phœnicia,' 1885; 'Ancient Egypt,' 1887. 10. 'A Sketch of Universal History,' 1887. 11. 'Biblical Topography,' 1887. 12, 13, 14 (for the 'Men of the Bible' series): 'Moses, his Life and Times,' 1887; 'Kings of Israel and Judah,' 1890; 'Isaac and Jacob, their Lives and Times,' 1890. 15. Large contributions to the 'Pulpit Commentary.' 16. The article on 'Herodotus' in the 9th edition of the 'Encyclopædia Britannica.'

[The Times, 7 Oct. 1902; Athenæum, 11 Oct. 1902; Men and Women of the Time, 1899; Crockford's Clerical Directory.] R. B.

RAWSON, Sir HARRY HOLDSWORTH (1843–1910), admiral, second son of Christopher Rawson of Woolwich, J.P. for Surrey, was born at Walton-on-the-Hill, Lancashire, on 5 Nov. 1843. He was at Marlborough College from Feb. 1854 to Christmas 1855. Entering the navy on 9 April 1857, he was appointed to the Calcutta, flagship of Sir Michael Seymour [q. v.] on the China station. He served through the second Chinese war, being present in the Calcutta's launch at the capture of the Taku forts in 1858, and in 1860 was landed as aide-de-camp to Captain R. Dew of the Encounter, with whom he was present at the second capture of the Taku forts, at the battle of Palikao, and at the taking of Peking. He saw much further active service against the Chinese rebels; for the capture of Ning-po, which place he afterwards held for three months against the rebels with 1300 Chinese under his command, and for Fungwha, where he was severely wounded, he was mentioned in despatches. He also was thanked on the quarter-deck for jumping overboard at night in the Shanghai river to save life. On 9 April 1863 he was promoted to sub-lieutenant, and a month later to lieutenant. In the same year he was one of the officers who took out to Japan the gunboat Empress, a present from Queen Victoria to the Mikado and the first ship of the modern Japanese navy. Rawson then qualified as a gunnery lieutenant, and after serving a commission as first lieutenant of the Bellerophon in the Channel, was appointed in Jan. 1870 to the Royal yacht, whence on 7 Sept. 1871 he was promoted to commander. In Aug. 1871 he gained the silver medal of the Royal Humane Society for saving life at Antwerp. As commander he served two commissions in the Hercules, in the Channel and in the Mediterranean, and on 4 June 1877 was promoted to captain. In Nov. following he was appointed to the Minotaur as flag-captain to Lord John Hay, commanding the Channel squadron; and, going to the Mediterranean in 1878, he received the thanks of the Admiralty for a report on the capabilities of defence of the Suez Canal, hoisted the British flag at Nicosia, Cyprus, and was for a month commandant there. Following this service he was again flag-captain in the Channel squadron until March 1882, and then was appointed to the Thalia for the Egyptian campaign, during which he served as principal transport officer. He was awarded the medal, the Khedive's star, the third class of the Osmanieh, and the C.B. From Feb. 1883 to Sept. 1885 he was again flag-captain to Lord John Hay, then commander-in-chief in the Mediterranean, and in Oct. 1885 became captain of the steam reserve at Devonport, where he remained till 1889. He was a member of the signal committee of 1886, was captain of the battleship Benbow in the Mediterranean from 1889 to 1891, and was an aide-de-camp to Queen Victoria from Aug. 1890 until promoted to flag rank on 14 Feb. 1892.

Rawson was a member of the international code signals committee from 1892 to 1895, in 1893 was one of the umpires for the naval manœuvres, and in May 1895 was appointed commander-in-chief on the Cape of Good Hope and west coast of Africa station, with his flag in the St. George. He held this command until May 1898, and during it organised and carried out two expeditions. In Aug. 1895 he landed the brigade which captured M'weli, the stronghold of Mburuk, a rebellious Arab chief, for which service the general Africa medal with 'M'weli, 1895' engraved on the rim was awarded; in Aug. 1896 part of his squadron bombarded the palace at Zanzibar and deposed the pretender, Rawson receiving the brilliant star of Zanzibar, first class, in acknowledgment from the sultan; his action was officially approved, and he received the thanks of the admiralty. In Feb. 1897 he landed in command of the naval brigade of his squadron, with which, together with a force of Haussas, he advanced to and captured Benin city, in punishment for the recent massacre of British political officers. He received the K.C.B. for this service in May 1897, and the clasp for Benin. On 19 March 1898 he was promoted to vice-admiral.

Rawson commanded the Channel squadron from Dec. 1898 to April 1901, after which he was appointed president of the committee which investigated the structural strength of torpedo-boat destroyers. This was his last naval service. In Jan. 1902 he was appointed governor of New South Wales, 'a post for which his tact, kindliness, and good sense were sturdy qualifications.' Sir Harry was a successful and popular governor, and in 1908 his term of office was extended by one year to May 1909. He was promoted to admiral on 12 Aug. 1903, and retired on 3 Nov. 1908; in June 1906 he was made a G.C.B., and a G.C.M.G. in Nov. 1909. He died in London, following an operation for appendicitis, on 3 Nov. 1910, and was buried at Bracknell parish church, a memorial service being held at St. Margaret's, Westminster.

Rawson married on 19 Oct. 1871 Florence Alice Stewart, daughter of John Ralph Shaw of Arrowe Park, Cheshire, and had issue five children. Lady Rawson died in the Red Sea on 3 Dec. 1905, while on passage out to Australia.

A cartoon by 'Spy' appeared in 'Vanity Fair' in 1901.

[The Times, 4 Nov. 1910. An engraved portrait was published by Messrs. Walton of Shaftesbury Avenue. Royal Navy List.]

L. G. C. L.

READ, CLARE SEWELL (1826–1905), agriculturist, the eldest son of George Read of Barton Bendish Hall, Norfolk, by Sarah Ann, daughter of Clare Sewell, was born at Ketteringham on 6 Nov. 1826. His ancestors had been tenant-farmers in Norfolk since the end of the sixteenth century. He was educated privately at Lynn, and from the age of fifteen to twenty was learning practical agriculture upon his father's farm. Before he was of age he was managing the large farm of Kilpaison in Pembrokeshire, and was afterwards resident agent on the earl of Macclesfield's Oxfordshire estates. He returned to Norfolk in 1854 and took his father's farm at Plumstead, near Norwich, until 1865, when he succeeded a relative at Honingham Thorpe, and farmed about 800 acres there until Michaelmas 1896.

In July 1865 he was returned to parliament as conservative member for East Norfolk, which he continued to represent until the Reform Act of 1867, when Norfolk was divided into three constituencies. He sat for South Norfolk from 1868 to 1880, when he was defeated at the general election by one vote. He then declined to stand for North Lincolnshire and Cambridgeshire, but in Feb. 1884 was returned unopposed for West Norfolk, sitting until the dissolution of parliament in 1885, when he retired from the representation of the county. He unsuccessfully contested Norwich in July 1886.

In his first speech in parliament, in 1866, in support of Sir Fitzroy Kelly's motion for the repeal of the malt tax, he suggested, as an alternative, a beer tax of one penny per gallon upon all beer that was sold; that a licence should be paid by private brewers; and that all cottagers should be free to brew their own beer, a concession granted later. He strenuously supported and promoted all the acts of parliament passed for the suppression of cattle plague and all other imported diseases among live stock; advocated the inalienable right of the occupier of the land to destroy ground game; persistently contended for the compulsory payment of tenant farmers' improvements in the soil; argued that all property, and not land and buildings alone, should contribute to local as well as imperial burdens; and in 1876 carried a unanimous resolution in the House of Commons in favour of representative county boards.

In 1865 he served on the cattle plague commission, and for twenty years sat upon almost every agricultural committee of the House of Commons. In Feb. 1874 he was appointed by Disraeli parliamentary secretary to the local government board, but resigned in Jan. 1876, in consequence of the government refusing to extend to Ireland the Cattle Diseases Act which had been passed for Great Britain. This, however, soon afterwards became law. Upon his resigning his government appointment, he was presented by the farmers of England with a silver salver and a purse of 5500*l.* at a dinner given at the Cannon Street Hotel on 2 May 1876.

On the appointment in June 1879 of the duke of Richmond's royal commission on agriculture, Clare Sewell Read and Albert Pell [q. v. Suppl. II] were made assistant commissioners to visit the United States and Canada to inquire into and report on the conditions of agriculture there, particularly as related to the production and exportation of wheat to Europe. They were away six months, and travelled 16,000 miles.

In 1848 Read won the Royal Agricultural Society's prize essay on the farming of South Wales, and in 1854 and 1856 obtained the society's prizes for similar reports on Oxfordshire and Buckinghamshire. He contributed numerous other papers to the Royal Agricultural Society's 'Journal,' and acted frequently as judge at the Royal, Smithfield, Bath and West of England, and other agricultural shows.

He also wrote a valuable article on the Agriculture of Norfolk for the 4th edition of White's 'History, Gazetteer and Directory' of that county (1883).

In January 1866 he joined the Farmers' Club (originally founded in 1842), and was an active member till his death, frequently reading papers at meetings, serving on the committee, and acting as chairman for two separate years, in 1868 and again in 1892 (jubilee year). He was also a member of the council of the central chamber of agriculture (of which he was chairman in 1869) and of the Smithfield Club.

When his intention to give up farming in Norfolk was made known, a county committee organised a fund for presenting him with his portrait. This picture, painted by J. J. Shannon, R.A., now hangs in the castle at Norwich. In his later years Read lived in London at 91 Kensington Gardens Square, where he died on 21 Aug. 1905, but he was buried in his native soil at Barton Bendish. In 1859 he married Sarah Maria, the only daughter of J. Watson, and had by her four daughters.

[The Times, 23 and 28 Aug. 1905; Mark Lane Express, 18 Aug. 1905; personal knowledge.] E. C.

READ, WALTER WILLIAM (1855–1907), Surrey cricketer, was born at Reigate on 23 Nov. 1855. He was educated at the Reigate Priory school, which was managed by his father. Showing early aptitude for cricket, he joined the Reigate Priory Club, and at the age of thirteen scored 78 not out against Tonbridge and the bowling of Bob Lipscombe. In 1873 Read was introduced to Charles William Alcock, the secretary of the Surrey cricket club, and from that date to 1897 was a regular member of the Surrey team. He assisted his father at Reigate Priory school until 1881, when he became assistant secretary to the Surrey cricket club, and thenceforth he devoted all his time to cricket. From 1883 he helped George Lohmann [q. v. Suppl. II] to restore Surrey to a leading cricketing position among the counties. In 1885 he became partner in a City auctioneering and surveying business. In his last years he was coach to young players at the Oval.

During his twenty-five years' career in first-class cricket (1873–97) Read gained triumphal success as a batsman, scoring no fewer than 46 centuries. At his best from 1885 to 1888, he scored in successive matches in June 1887 for Surrey *v.* Lancashire and Cambridge University respectively 247 and 244 not out, and 338 in 1888 for Surrey *v.* Oxford University. Between 1877 and 1895 Read played in 23 matches for Gentlemen *v.* Players, his best score being 159 in July 1885, and in twelve test matches in England against the Australians between 1884 and 1893, his most memorable performance in Australian matches being at Kennington Oval in August 1884, when going in tenth he scored 117. In this match William Lloyd Murdoch [q. v. Suppl. II] scored 211 for the Australians. Read twice visited Australia: in 1882–3 with Ivo Bligh's team, and in 1887–8 with G. F. Vernon's team. In the second tour Read averaged over 65 runs per innings in eleven-a-side matches. He took a team in the winter of 1891–2 to South Africa. Of strong physique, Read was a determined hitter, and a very attractive batsman who brought 'pulling' to a fine art. A very safe field, he shone especially at point, and he was also a useful 'lob' bowler. As a captain he had few superiors.

Read, who published a useful record called 'Annals of Cricket' in 1896, died on 6 Jan. 1907 at Colworth Road, Addiscombe Park, Croydon, and was buried at Shirley. He married and had issue. A painted portrait depicting Read at the wicket, by G. H. Barrable and Mr. Staples, was exhibited at the Goupil Gallery in 1887; he also figures in 'Punch' (13 Aug. 1887) in 'Cricket at the Oval.'

[W. W. Read, Annals of Cricket, 1896; Daft, Kings of Cricket (with portrait, p. 195); Wisden's Cricketers' Almanack, 1907, clxxiv–vi; 1908, pp. 148–151; Haygarth's Cricket Scores and Biographies, xii. 894–5; xiv. xcv–xcvii; portraits in Cricket, 26 April 1888, 21 Aug. 1890; Cricket Field, 24 Sept. 1892; Wisden's Cricketers' Almanack, 1893; Sporting Sketches, 17 Sept. 1894; information from Mr. P. M. Thornton.] W. B. O.

READE, THOMAS MELLARD (1832–1909), geologist, born on 27 May 1832 in Mill Street, Toxteth Park, Liverpool, where his father William James Reade kept a small private school, was of common descent from Staffordshire yeomen with Joseph Bancroft Reade [q. v.] and Sir Thomas Reade, deputy adjutant-general at St. Helena during Napoleon's captivity. His mother, Mary Mellard, of Newcastle-under-Lyme, was aunt to Dinah Maria Mulock [q. v.]. After private schools he began work at the end of 1844 in the office of Eyes and Son, architects and surveyors, Liverpool. At the beginning of 1853 he entered the engineer's office of the London and North Western railway company at Warrington, where he rose to be principal draughtsman. In 1860 he started on his own account in Liverpool as architect and civil engineer and built up a good business, being architect to the Liverpool school board during its existence from 1870 to 1902, and laying out the Blundellsands estate in 1868, on which he resided from 1868 till death. He died at his house, Park Corner, Blundellsands, on 26 May 1909, and was buried at Sefton, Lancashire.

Always fond of natural history, Reade began serious work in geology when about thirty-five years old, and lost none of the opportunities for that study which his profession offered. In addition to two books, he wrote nearly 200 papers and addresses, of which many were communicated to the Liverpool Geological Society, others to the 'Geological Magazine' and the Geological Society of London. Of these one group deals with the glacial and post-glacial geology of Lancashire and the adjoining counties. They record many important facts disclosed in excavations, which would otherwise have been lost. A very practical result of his studies was that when the tunnel under the Mersey was projected in 1873 he predicted that it would encounter a buried river channel filled with drift; his prophecy was verified in 1885. He also made valuable collections of specimens from boulders and of marine shells from the glacial drifts. In the later years of his life, co-operating with Mr. Philip Holland, Reade studied the mineral structure and changes of sedimentary, and especially slaty, rocks, forming for this purpose a collection of rocks, slices, sands and sediments. These are now in the Sedgwick Museum, Cambridge, as the gift of his son, Mr. Aleyn Lyell Reade. A third group of his papers dealt with questions of geomorphology, with which also his two books are occupied. In the earlier, on the 'Origin of Mountain Ranges' (1886), he discussed among other hypotheses that which attributes them to a localised crumpling of the earth's crust, caused by a shortening of its radius while cooling. Reade maintained them to be the slow cumulative result of successive variations of temperature in this crust, largely produced by the removal of sediment (like the transference of a blanket) from one part to the other; pointing out the necessary existence in a cooling globe of a 'level of no strain.' His second book, on the 'Evolution of Earth Structure' (1903), further defined and illustrated the above view, arguing that while the relative proportion of sea and land had been fairly constant through geological time, regional changes of level were due to alterations in the bulk of the lithosphere, caused by expansion and contraction. Though the majority of geologists have not as yet accepted his opinions on this question, all must agree that, as was usual with him, they are ably argued and demand careful consideration.

Reade became a Fellow of the London Geological Society in 1872, and was awarded its Murchison medal in 1896. He was three times president of the Liverpool Geological Society, was a past president of the Liverpool Architectural Society, an associate member of the Institution of Civil Engineers, and an honorary member of other societies.

He married on 19 May 1886 Emma Eliza, widow of Alfred Taylor, C.E., who predeceased him, and by whom he had three sons and one daughter. Of the former, Mr. Aleyn Lyell Reade is author of 'The Reades of Blackwood Hill' and 'Dr. Johnson's Ancestry' (privately printed, 1906), and 'Johnsonian Gleanings,' part i. (1909).

[Geolog. Mag. 1909; Quarterly Journal Geolog. Soc. 1910; Liverpool Geolog. Soc. vol. xi. pt. i.; information from Mr. Aleyn Lyell Reade; personal knowledge.] T. G. B.

REDPATH, HENRY ADENEY (1848–1908), biblical scholar, born at Sydenham on 19 June 1848, was eldest son of Henry Syme Redpath, solicitor, of Sydenham, by his wife Harriet Adeney of Islington. In 1857 he entered Merchant Taylors' School, and won a scholarship at Queen's College, Oxford, in 1867, taking a second class in classical moderations in 1869 and a third class in literæ humaniores in 1871, graduating B.A. in 1871, and proceeding M.A. in 1874 and D.Litt. in 1901. Ordained deacon in 1872 and priest in 1874, Redpath, after being curate of Southam, near Rugby, and then of Luddesdown, near Gravesend, was successively vicar of Wolvercote, near Oxford (1880–3), rector of Holwell, Sherborne (1883–90), and vicar of Sparsholt, with Kingston Lisle, near Wantage (1890–8). In 1898, by an exchange, he became rector of St. Dunstan-in-the-East, City. Redpath was sub-warden of the Society of Sacred Study in the diocese of London, and examining chaplain to the Bishop of London (1905–8).

Redpath, who had learned Hebrew at Merchant Taylors' School, specialised, while a country parson, in the Greek of the Septuagint, completing and publishing the work which Edwin Hatch [q. v.] left unfinished: 'A Concordance to the Septuagint and other Greek Translations of the Old Testament' (Oxford, 1892–1906, 3 vols.). The value of his work was recognised both here and on the Continent (cf. Adolf Deissmann, *The Philology of the Greek Bible*, 1908, pp. 69–78). Redpath was Grinfield lecturer on the Septuagint at Oxford (1901–5), and shortly before his death designed a 'Dictionary of Patristic Greek.'

As a biblical scholar he was conservative. He expounded his opposition to the 'critical' view of the Old Testament in 'Modern Criticism and the Book of Genesis' (1905), published by the Society for Promoting Christian Knowledge. An abler and more constructive work was his painstaking 'Westminster Commentary' on Ezekiel, with introduction and notes (1907). He was also a contributor to Hastings's 'Dictionary of the Bible' (1904, 4 vols.) and to the 'Illustrated Bible Dictionary.'

Redpath died at Sydenham on 24 Sept. 1908, and was buried at Shottermill, Surrey. He married at Marsh Caundle, Dorsetshire, on 5 Oct. 1886, Catherine Helen, daughter of Henry Peter Auber of Marsh Court, Sherborne. She died at Shottermill, on 26 Aug. 1898, leaving one son.

[The Times, 25 Sept. 1908; Guardian, 30 Sept. and 7 Oct. 1908; C. J. Robinson, Merchant Taylors' School list; private information.]

E. H. P.

REED, Sir EDWARD JAMES (1830–1906), naval architect and chief constructor of the navy, son of John Reed of Sheerness, was born there on 20 Sept. 1830, and after serving an apprenticeship with a shipwright in Sheerness dockyard was chosen in 1849 to enter the school of mathematics and naval construction which had been established at Portsmouth in 1848 with Dr. John Woolley [q. v.] as its principal. After passing through the school he received in 1852 an appointment as supernumerary draughtsman in the mould loft at Sheerness, but finding his duties, which were of a routine nature and involved no responsibility, irksome, he left the admiralty service in the same year. Reed devoted his leisure at this time to writing poetry, and turned to technical journalism; in 1853 he was offered and accepted the editorship of the 'Mechanic's Magazine.' In 1854 he submitted to the admiralty a design for a fast armour-clad frigate, but the need of such a type was not yet admitted and the design was refused. At the end of 1859 John Scott Russell [q. v.] called together a small body of naval architects, of whom Reed was one, in order to attempt the foundation of a technical society. The effort was immediately successful, and the Institution of Naval Architects was established early in 1860, Reed, who had been organising secretary from the first, being permanently appointed to the secretaryship. In 1862 he submitted to the admiralty designs for the conversion of wooden men-of-war into armour-clads on the belt and battery system, and was encouraged to proceed. The conversion of three ships was put in hand and carried out under Reed's supervision, and before their completion he was offered and accepted, in 1863, the post of chief constructor of the navy. With this appointment a new epoch of naval construction began. The earliest ironclads were very long and unhandy ships, mounting all their guns on the broadside. Reed's object was to produce shorter ships of greater handiness, and to develop their end-on fire without sacrificing their weight of broadside. The battle between guns and armour had already begun, and the demand on the one part for heavier armour and on the other for larger guns was insistent. The Bellerophon, the first ship designed by Reed after he took office, was typical of many others that followed, and marked a great advance towards the realisation of the desired qualities. Launched in May 1865, she was a high freeboard ship, fully rigged as then seemed necessary to seamen; she was protected by a complete belt at the waterline, and amidships rose an armoured citadel enclosing the main battery and covering the vitals of the ship. An attempt to gain end-on fire was made by mounting a smaller battery behind armour in the bows, but in later ships this expedient was improved on by the introduction of recessed ports for the guns at the corners of the central battery. Structurally also the Bellerophon was an important ship, for in her Reed introduced a new system of framing, known as the longitudinal and bracket-frame system, which was better suited than the old method to the use of iron, which was still quite a novel material for the hulls of men-of-war.

At the same time an entirely different type of armoured ship was advancing in favour. This was the low freeboard monitor, with its heavy guns mounted in turrets, a type which had done well in the peculiar circumstances of the American civil war. Reed built several ships of this type, all of them in the main similar to the Glatton; but he fought strenuously against the idea of building large masted monitors as seagoing ships. He held, and indeed proved, that the low freeboard monitor would be dangerously lacking in stability under sail, and at the time when the Captain was building to the plans of Capt. Cowper Phipps Coles [q. v.], he put forward a design for a large seagoing monitor which should be entirely mastless. This was the Devastation, a ship whose design exercised a greater influence on the course of naval architecture perhaps than any other. Reed's plans for the ship, which was laid down in Nov. 1869, were modified in some, as he thought, important particulars, and, owing to a failure to agree with the admiralty on questions connected with the construction of turret ships, he resigned office in July 1870. The report of the committee on designs which sat after the loss of the Captain (7 Sept. 1870) was in many respects a justification of Reed's views, and directly reassured public opinion as to the safety of the Devastation. On resigning from the admiralty he joined Sir Joseph Whitworth [q. v.] at his ordnance works at Manchester; in 1871 he became chairman of Earl's Company, Hull, and in the same year began practice as a naval architect in London. He designed ships for several foreign navies, including those of Turkey, Japan, Germany, Chili, and Brazil, and of these three, the Neptune in 1877, and the sister ships Swiftsure and Triumph in 1903, were bought into the royal navy. In Oct. 1878 he visited Japan at the invitation of the imperial government. He was also consulting naval engineer to the Indian government and to the crown colonies. Reed was a keen advocate of technical education, and while at the admiralty used his influence in favour of the Royal School of Naval Architecture and Marine Engineering, which was established in 1864. It was also in great measure due to his appreciation of the value of the work, and to his recommendation of it, that the support of the admiralty was given to William Froude [q. v.] in his model-experiments on the resistance and propulsion of ships. In 1876 he was elected a fellow by the Royal Society; he had received the C.B. in 1868, and was advanced to the K.C.B. in 1880, besides which he held several foreign decorations. From 1865 to 1905 he was a vice-president of the Institution of Naval Architects, and in addition was an active member of other technical societies.

In 1873 Reed attempted unsuccessfully to enter parliament as liberal candidate for Hull, and in the following year was returned as member for the Pembroke boroughs. From the general election of 1880 until 1895, when he was defeated, he sat for Cardiff, and was a lord of the treasury in the short Gladstonian administration of 1886. In 1900 he was again returned for Cardiff, but did not seek re-election in 1905. He served on several important parliamentary committees, and was chairman of the load-line committee of 1884, and of the manning of ships committee of 1894. He was for many years a J.P. for Glamorgan.

Reed's contributions both to general and to technical literature were numerous. His published volumes include 'Corona, and other Poems' (12mo, 1857); 'Letters from Russia in 1875' (first printed in 'The Times' 1876); 'Japan, its History, Traditions, and Religions: with a Narrative of a Visit in 1879' (2 vols. 1880); and a further volume of 'Poems' (1902). In 1860 he became editor of the 'Transactions of the Institute of Naval Architects,' to which he continued to contribute to the end of his life, his papers in vols. iv. to x., issued while he was chief constructor, being of especial interest. In 1869 he wrote 'Our Ironclad Ships,' which was in great measure a vindication of his policy; and in the same year 'Shipbuilding in Iron and Steel,' for several years the standard treatise on the subject. In 1868 and 1871 he contributed papers on the construction of ironclad ships to the 'Philosophical Transactions'; and in 1871 wrote 'Our Naval Coast Defences.' In 1872 he founded a quarterly named 'Naval Science,' many articles in which were from his pen; he continued it till 1875. His 'Treatise on the Stability of Ships' was published in 1884, and 'Modern Ships of War,' in writing which he had Admiral E. Simpson as a collaborator, in 1888. He was in addition a frequent contributor to 'The Times' and other periodicals, and took an ardent part in many controversies on technical subjects. He died in London on 30 Nov. 1906, and was buried at Putney Vale cemetery.

Reed married in 1851 Rosetta, eldest daughter of Nathaniel Barnaby of Sheerness, and sister of Sir Nathaniel Barnaby, who succeeded him as chief constructor in 1870. Edward Tennyson Reed (*b.* 1860), for many years an artist on the staff of 'Punch,' is his only son.

A painted portrait by Miss Ethel Mortlock, exhibited at the Royal Academy in 1886, was presented by the engineer officers of the royal navy to Lady Reed. A cartoon portrait was published in 'Vanity Fair' for 1875, and a photogravure portrait is prefixed to the 'Transactions of the Institute of Naval Architects' for 1907.

[Trans. Inst. Nav. Architects, xlix. 313; Proc. Inst. of Civil Engineers, clxviii. pt. ii.; The Times, 1 Dec. 1906; Reed's own works.]

L. G. C. L.

REEVES, Sir WILLIAM CONRAD (1821–1902), chief justice of Barbados, born at Bridgetown, Barbados, in 1821 (the date is often given erroneously), was one of three sons of Thomas Phillipps Reeves, a medical man, by a negro slave Peggy Phyllis. Reeves, cared for by his father's sister, received some education at private schools and attracted the notice of Samuel Jackman Prescod, a journalist. The boy was fond of reading. Prescod gave him employment on his paper, the 'Liberal.' Reeves learned shorthand, and mastering the details of management, was soon able on occasion to edit and manage the paper. He joined the debating club at Bridgetown, and proved ready in debate.

Disappointed in the hope of obtaining an official appointment, Reeves by the kindness of friends went to England, and became a student at the Middle Temple in May 1860, being called to the bar on 6 Jan. 1863. While in London he acted as correspondent for the Barbados press. In 1864 he returned to Barbados to practise at the local bar. From May 1867 he acted for a short time as attorney-general of St. Vincent, an island which at that time was under the same governor as Barbados, and soon gained an assured position in Barbados.

In August 1874 Reeves entered the local house of assembly of Barbados as member for St. Joseph, and became solicitor-general. In April 1876, when the governor, Sir John Pope-Hennessy [q. v.], provoked a conflict between the crown (as represented by himself) and the legislature, Reeves resigned office and took up the cause of the old constitution of Barbados as against schemes of confederation and crown government. Reeves was acclaimed by all classes and colours as a Pym or Hampden. Equally in 1878 he opposed the proposal introduced by Sir George Strahan for the reform of the elective house of assembly by the introduction of crown nominees, He thus became the champion of the ancient Barbados constitution, and the general public marked their sense of his services by presenting him with an address and a purse of 1000 guineas.

In 1881, however, the next governor, Sir William Robinson, enlisted Reeves's cordial support in framing the executive committee bill. The enactment of this bill enabled the executive to secure a proper control in matters of finance and administration without interference with the traditions of the house of assembly. The governor acknowledged Reeves's support by appointing him attorney-general in Feb. 1882. Reeves was created K.C. in 1883. As attorney-general he helped in 1884 to carry out an extension of the franchise. Later in the year he went on long leave to recruit his health, returning to Barbados in 1885.

In 1886 Reeves became chief justice of Barbados. The promotion was a rare recognition of worth in a black man, and was well justified in the result. He was knighted in 1889. His judgments were clear and well worded. Several of them were collected in a volume by Sir William Herbert Greaves, a successor as chief justice, and Mr. Clark, attorney-general. Reeves died on 9 Jan. 1902, at his home, the Eyrie, St. Michael's, and was accorded a public funeral, with a service in the cathedral at Westbury cemetery.

Reeves married in 1868 Margaret, eldest daughter of T. P. R. Budder of Bushey Park, St. Thomas, Barbados. He left one daughter, who was married and resided in Europe.

[Memoir by Valence Gale reprinted locally in 1902; information furnished by Chief Justice Sir H. Greaves; Barbados Globe and Barbados Agricultural Reporter, 10 Jan. 1902; The Times, 31 Jan. 1902; Who's Who, 1901.] C. A. H.

REICH, EMIL (1854–1910), historian, son of Louis Reich, was born on 24 March 1854 at Eperjes in Hungary. After early education at Eperjes and Kassa he went to the universities of Prague, Budapest, and Vienna. Until his thirtieth year he 'studied almost exclusively in libraries.' Then 'finding books unsatisfactory for a real comprehension of history, he determined to travel extensively in order to complement the study of books with the study of realities.' In July 1884 Reich, with his parents, his brother, and two sisters, emigrated to America, where after much hardship he was engaged in 1887 by the Appleton firm of New York in preparing their encyclopædia. On his father's death, his mother and one sister settled in Budapest; the brother and other sister settled in Cincinnati, the one as a photo-engraver, the other as a public school teacher. In July 1889 Reich went to France. At the end of the year he visited England. In February and March 1890 he delivered at Oxford four lectures, subsequently published under the title of 'Græco-Roman Institutions' (Oxford, 1890; French translation, Paris, 1891), in which he attempted to 'disprove the applicableness of Darwinian concepts to the solution of sociological problems.' His theory of the hitherto unsuspected influence of *infamia* on Roman law at first aroused opposition, but later was developed in England and France. Reich spent his time mainly in France till 1893, when he settled in England for good. There as a writer, as a lecturer to popular and learned audiences in Oxford, Cambridge, and London, and as a coach at Wren's establishment for preparing candidates for the civil service, he displayed remarkable vigour, versatility, and self-confidence. His width of interests appealed to Lord Acton, who described him as 'a universal specialist.' His work, although full of stimulating suggestions, was inaccurate in detail, and omission of essential facts discredited his conclusions. A lover of paradox, and a severe censor of established historical and literary reputations, Reich made useful contributions to historical criticism in his lectures on 'Fundamental Principles of Evidence' and in his 'The Failure of the Higher Criticism of the Bible' (1905), in which he combated modern methods of biblical criticism. Of a 'General History of Western Nations,' the first part on 'Antiquity' was published in two volumes in 1908–9. There Reich waged war on the evolutionist theory of history; he attached little or no importance to race in national history, laid excessive stress on the geo-political and economic conditions, unduly subordinating the influences of heredity to that of environment. In this work (ii. 339, 340 footnote) Reich unjustifiably charged A. H. J. Greenidge [q. v. Suppl. II] with adopting without acknowledgment some researches of his own; the accusation called forth a stout defence from Greenidge's friends (see *The Times, Lit. Suppl.* 23 and 30 July, 13 and 20 Aug. 1908). His most successful published work was his 'Hungarian Literature' (1897; 2nd edit. 1906). In the dispute between British Guiana and Venezuela (1895–9) in regard to the Venezuelan boundary, Reich was engaged by the English government to help in the preparation of their case. A course of lectures on Plato at Claridge's Hotel, London, in 1906, which were attended by leading ladies of London society, brought him much public notoriety. He died after a three months' illness at his residence at Notting Hill on 11 Dec. 1910, and was buried at Kensal Green. He married in 1893 Céline Labulle of Paris, who, with a daughter, survived him. Reich was fond of music and was an accomplished pianist.

Reich's other published works were: 1. 'History of Civilization,' Cincinnati, 1887. 2. 'New Student's Atlas of English History,' 1903. 3. 'Foundations of Modern Europe,' 1904. 4. 'Success among Nations,' 1904 (translated into French, Italian, and Spanish). 5. 'Select Documents illustrating Mediæval and Modern History,' 1905. 6. 'Imperialism: its Prices; its Vocation,' 1905 (translated into Russian). 7. 'Plato as an Introduction to Modern Criticism of Life' (lectures delivered at Claridge's Hotel), 1906. 8. 'Success in Life,' 1906. 9. 'Germany's Swelled Head,' Walsall, 1907. 10. 'Atlas Antiquus,' 1908. 11. 'Handbook of Geography, Descriptive and Mathematical,' 2 vols. 1908. 12. 'Woman through the Ages,' 2 vols. 1908. 13. 'Nights with the Gods,' 1909 (a criticism of modern English society). Reich was editor of 'The New Classical Library,' and for that series compiled an alphabetical encyclopædia of institutions, persons, and events of ancient history in 1906; he published an abridgment of Dr. Seyffert's 'Dictionary of Classical Antiquities' (1908). He was also a contributor on Hungarian history to the 'Cambridge Modern History,' and on Hungarian literature to the 'Encyclopædia Britannica' (11th edition).

[The Times, 13 Dec. 1910; English Mail, 15 Dec. 1910; Bevándorló, New York, 16 Dec. 1910; information kindly supplied by Mr. Lewis L. Kropf.] W. B. O.

REID, ARCHIBALD DAVID (1844–1908), painter, born in Aberdeen on 8 June 1844, was fourth of five sons (in a family of thirteen children) of George Reid, manager of the Aberdeen Copper Company, by his wife Esther Tait. An elder son is Sir George Reid, president of the Royal Scottish Academy from 1891 to 1902, and the youngest son is Mr. Samuel Reid, R.S.W. At the age of ten Reid entered Robert Gordon's Hospital, now Gordon's College, Aberdeen, which he left at fourteen for a mercantile career. The friendly and cultivated influence of John F. White, LL.D., miller, in whose counting-house he was employed, and the example of his brother George, drew him to artistic pursuits. Modelling and painting engaged his leisure. There were then no studios in Aberdeen, and his earliest practical training in art was received at the old Mechanics' Institute.

Abandoning commerce at twenty-three, Reid went to Edinburgh to attend the classes of the Trustees' Academy, and, later, the life-class of the Royal Scottish Academy. He remained three years in Edinburgh. He first exhibited at the Scottish Academy in 1870, and his contributions to its exhibitions of 1873–4 were specially remarked for their predisposition to tone. A visit to Holland, which he paid in 1874, lastingly affected his art. Four years later he went to Paris, and for a short time worked in Julien's studio. Next, with a commission from Dr. White, he visited Spain. In 1892 he was elected A.R.S.A., and five years afterwards a member of the Royal Institute of Painters in Oils, from which body, however, he soon resigned. He was also a member of the Royal Scottish Society of Painters in Water-colours. His work was rarely exhibited in London galleries.

Reid travelled much, as the titles of his pictures show: 'On the Giudecca, Venice,' 'A Court in the Alhambra,' 'The Scotch House, Campvere,' 'Auxerre, France,' the last of which was well reproduced in colours in the 'Studio' ('Royal Scottish Academy Number,' 1907). He always, however, kept closely in touch with his native city, which he made his permanent home. At one time he had a studio in King Street there, but afterwards he used those at his brother's residence at St. Luke's, Kepplestone, which he occupied for some years before his death. Besides a natural predilection for Dutch art, he shared the friendship of many modern Dutch masters with his brother George, who had early in life studied under Josef Israels. Reid enjoyed also a long intimacy with George Paul Chalmers [q. v.], who painted many pictures in the Reids' studio.

Reid undertook a few commission portraits, the most masterly of them perhaps that of John Colvin, the sacrist at King's College, Aberdeen, where the picture now hangs; but landscapes and the scenery of his native shores were his main themes. Two of his sea-pieces are included in the Macdonald Bequest at Aberdeen. A large picture, 'A Lone Shore,' exhibited at the Royal Academy in 1875, was purchased for 300*l*. after his death by some friends and presented to the Aberdeen Art Gallery. Of his works in private collections may be mentioned a 'Harvest Scene' (Glasgow Loan Exhibition, 1878), 'Guessing the Catch,' and 'Before Service,' a view of the interior of King's College Chapel, Aberdeen, with figures of monks introduced. Towards the end of his life Reid produced many landscapes in charcoal. He etched a few plates, and some black-and-white illustrations by him are to be found in the files of 'Life and Work.'

An accomplished musician and possessed of a fine literary taste, Reid was a popular member of the Aberdeen club known as the 'New Deer Academy' (see *Memories Grave and Gay*, by John Kerr, LL.D., pp. 221–8). When out walking at Wareham, Dorsetshire, on 30 Aug. 1908, he died suddenly of heart failure, and was buried in St. Peter's cemetery, Aberdeen. He married in 1893 Margaret, daughter of George Sim, farmer, of Kintore, who survived him without issue.

A portrait painted by himself is in the Macdonald Bequest at Aberdeen.

[Private information; Aberdeen Free Press, 1 Sept. 1908.] D. S. M.

REID, Sir JOHN WATT (1823–1909), medical director-general of the navy, born in Edinburgh on 25 February 1823, was younger son of John Watt Reid, surgeon in the navy, by his wife Jane, daughter of James Henderson, an Edinburgh merchant. Educated at Edinburgh Academy, at the university there, and at the extra-mural medical school, he qualified L.R.C.S. Edinburgh in 1844. He entered the navy as an assistant surgeon on 6 Feb. 1845, and after serving a commission on board the Rodney in the Channel was appointed in March 1849 to the naval hospital, Plymouth, and received the approval of the Admiralty for his services there during the cholera epidemic of that year. In Jan. 1852 he was appointed as acting surgeon to the Inflexible, sloop, in the Mediterranean; on 12 Sept. 1854 he was promoted to surgeon, and in June 1855 appointed to the London, line-of-battle ship, on the same station. In these two ships he served in the Black Sea until the fall of Sevastopol, and received the Crimean and Turkish medals with the Sevastopol clasp, and was also thanked by the commander-in-chief [see DUNDAS, SIR JAMES WHITLEY DEANS] for his services to the crew of the flagship when stricken with cholera in 1854. In 1856 he took the degree of M.D. at Aberdeen; and, after serving for a short time in the flagship at Devonport, was appointed in April 1857 to the Belleisle, hospital ship, on board which he continued during the China war of 1857–9, for which he received the medal. In Jan. 1860 he was appointed to the Nile, of 90 guns, and served in her for four years on the North American station, after which he went to Haslar hospital until promoted to staff surgeon on 5 Sept. 1866. After a year's further service in the Mediterranean, he was in June 1870 placed in charge of the naval hospital at Haulbowline, where he remained till 1873. During the concluding months of the Ashanti war (see HEWETT, SIR WILLIAM] he served on board the Nebraska, hospital ship, at Cape Coast Castle, for which he was mentioned in despatches, received the medal and, on 31 March 1874, was promoted to deputy inspector-general. In that rank he had charge of the medical establishments at Bermuda from 1875 to 1878, when he was appointed to Haslar hospital. On 25 Feb. 1880 he was promoted to be inspector-general and was appointed medical director-general of the navy. This post he held till his retirement eight years later, when the board of admiralty recorded their high opinion of his zeal and efficiency. He became an honorary physician to Queen Victoria in Feb. 1881 and to King Edward VII in 1901, was awarded the K.C.B. (military) on 24 Nov. 1882, and had the honorary degree of LL.D. conferred upon him by Edinburgh University at its tercentenary in 1884. A medical good service pension was awarded him in July 1888.

Reid died in London on 24 Feb. 1909, and was buried at Bramshaw, Hampshire. He married, on 6 July 1863, Georgina, daughter of C. J. Hill of Halifax, Nova Scotia.

[The Times, 26 Feb. 1909; Men and Women of the Time, 1899; R.N. List.]

L. G. C. L.

REID, SIR ROBERT GILLESPIE (1842–1908), Canadian contractor and financier, born of Lowland parents at Coupar Angus, Perthshire, in 1842, received his early education there and was trained as a bridge-builder by an uncle. Entering into business on his own account, he made some successful contracts and with the proceeds emigrated to Australia in 1865. In Australia he engaged principally in gold mining and the construction of public works.

In 1871 Reid went to America, and ultimately settled at Montreal. He at once made a reputation by building the International Bridge across the Niagara river at Buffalo. He was subsequently entrusted with the construction of several bridges between Montreal and Ottawa on the line of the Montreal, Quebec, and Ottawa railway, which now forms part of the Canadian Pacific system. Another international bridge across the Rio Grande between Texas and Mexico greatly extended his fame. Other great bridges of his construction span the Colorado at Austin, Texas, the 'Soo' at Sault Ste. Marie, Ontario, and the Delaware at the famous Water Gap in Pennsylvania. In 1886 the directors of the Canadian Pacific railway, without inviting tenders, commissioned him to undertake the Lachine Bridge across the St. Lawrence above Montreal, three-quarters of a mile long. The work was completed in six months. The bridge across Grand Narrows, Cape Breton, was built for the Canadian government in connection with the railway in that island in 1889–90.

Reid was as active and efficient in the building of railways as in the construction of bridges. The difficult Jackfish Bay section of the Canadian Pacific railway on the rough and almost impassable northern coast of Lake Superior was his work.

Newfoundland, with which Reid's association began in 1890, was the scene of his most varied activities. He first contracted for the building of the Hall Bay railway (260 miles), which he undertook in 1890 and completed in 1893. He then contracted to build for the Newfoundland government the Western railway from Whitbourne Junction to Port-aux-Basques (500 miles). This was accomplished in 1897. The contract gave Reid the right to operate the whole road for ten years from Sept. 1893. Meanwhile his firm had secured a charter for constructing an electric street railway in the city of St. John's, and had leased coalfields from the government. Owing to the geographical difficulties in organising an efficient transport system of the island and the financial embarrassment of the time the Newfoundland government made, in 1898, a new contract with Reid on a gigantic scale, which Mr. Joseph Chamberlain described as 'without parallel in the history of any country.' An effort to arrange terms of confederation with the Dominion of Canada had just failed, owing to the amount of the Newfoundland debt ($16,000,000), and some heroic step was deemed necessary by the government. The agreement with Reid, dated 3 March 1898, and known as the 'Railway Operating Contract,' empowered him to work free of taxation all trunk and branch railway lines in the island for fifty years and gave him control of the telegraph system. Reid was to provide an improved mail service by eight steamboats plying in the bays and between the island and the mainland. For $1,000,000, to be paid within a year after the signing of the contract, Reid was further to obtain the reversion of the whole railway system at the end of fifty years. The agreement at the same time transferred to Reid, for a consideration, the St. John's dry dock, the largest at that time on the Atlantic coast of British North America, and it conceded to him some 4,500,000 acres of land, including 'mines, ores, precious metals, minerals, stones, and mineral oils of every kind therein and thereunder' (sec. 17). The government promised to impose a duty of not less than one dollar a ton upon imported coal so soon as the contractor was able to produce not less than 50,000 tons per annum from his mines, provided he supplied coal to wholesale dealers at prices agreed upon (sec. 45). The government also reserved the right of imposing royalties upon minerals raised from the contractor's lands.

The transfer to Reid of the 'whole realisable assets' of the island was ratified by the Assembly, but there was strong opposition among the people. An effort was made to prevent the royal assent being given to the bill on the ground that it would interfere with the interests of the holders of Newfoundland government bonds. But Mr. Chamberlain (*Colonial Office Despatch*, No. 70, 5 Dec. 1898) traversed this plea, maintaining (sec. 20) that 'the debts of the colony have been incurred solely on the credit of the colony,' and he could sanction 'no step which would transfer responsibility for them in the slightest degree to the imperial government.' The agitation continued. Sir James Spearman Winter [q. v. Suppl. II], whose government passed the contract, fell from power, and was replaced after a general election by a liberal government under (Sir) Robert Bond, who was supported by an overwhelming majority. On the accession of the new government to office Reid applied for permission to transfer all his interests under the contract to the Reid-Newfoundland limited liability company. Negotiations which lasted eighteen months followed between the new premier and Reid. By a new agreement, which was ratified by the House of Assembly in July 1901, Reid's former contract was materially revised. Reid surrendered the control of the telegraph, the reversion of the Newfoundland railway at the end of fifty years, and 1,500,000 acres of land. He received in exchange $2,025,000 cash, and a further claim was referred to arbitration. The Reid-Newfoundland Company was duly authorised by the legislature, and to it Reid made over the property and privileges of the old contract which the new arrangement left untouched.

Of the 'Reid-Newfoundland Company,' with a capital of $25,000,000, of which he held the largest share, Reid became the first president (9 Aug. 1901) and worked with his usual energy to ensure its financial success. If the terms of the contract justified to some extent the bestowal on Reid of the title 'Czar Reid,' he showed benevolence and beneficence in developing the resources of the colony. In 1907 he was knighted as a reward for his services to the island. Meanwhile Sir Robert kept up his residence in Montreal, where he retained large financial interests, being a director of the Canadian Pacific railway, of the Bank of Montreal, and the Royal Trust Company. His rugged constitution broke down under the strain of his labours in Newfoundland. He suffered from inflammatory rheumatism, and found no relief in the many health resorts to which he had recourse. He was in Egypt when his son, as his attorney, signed the contract of 1898. Keenly interested in his various enterprises to the last, he died of pneumonia at his home, 275 Drummond Street, Montreal, on 3 June 1908. His remains were cremated at the Mount Royal Crematorium. By a resolution of the Board of Trade of St. John's, Newfoundland, all stores and public places of business were closed during the funeral.

Reid's integrity was unquestioned, his judgment was sound, and his disposition generous. His relations with labour were invariably harmonious: he never had a strike and never employed a private secretary. He left large sums to charitable and educational institutions. In 1865 he married Harriet Duff, whom he met on his way out to Australia. She survived him with three sons and a daughter. The eldest son, William Duff Reid, succeeded his father as president of the Reid Company, and the second, Henry Duff Reid, became vice-president.

[Morgan, Canadian Men and Women of the Time, 1898, 2nd edit. 1912; Prowse, History of Newfoundland, pp. 619–29 (portrait); Canadian Mag. xvi. 329–34 (portrait); Montreal Gazette, 19 June 1908; Montreal Witness, 3 June 1908; Montreal Star, 3 and 8 June 1908; St. John's, Newfoundland, Royal Gazette, 21 Dec. 1898; Free Press, 24 July 1901; St. John's Daily News, 25–29 July 1901; St. John's Evening Herald, 23 July 1901; Toronto Mail, 19 Aug. 1901; Toronto Star, 4 June 1908; personal information.] D. R. K.

REID, Sir THOMAS WEMYSS (1842–1905), journalist and biographer, born in Elswick Row, Newcastle-on-Tyne, on 29 March 1842, was second son of Alexander Reid, congregational minister of that town from 1830 to 1880, by his second wife, Jessy Elizabeth, daughter of Thomas Wemyss (*d.* 1845) of Darlington, a Hebrew scholar and biblical critic of distinction. After a short stay at Madras College, St. Andrews, where he had brain fever, Reid was educated at Percy Street Academy, Newcastle, by John Collingwood Bruce [q. v. Suppl. I]. In 1856 he became a clerk in the 'W. B.' [i.e. Wentworth Beaumont] Lead office at Newcastle. Cherishing as a boy literary aspirations, at fifteen he sent papers on local topics to the 'Northern Daily Express.' These attracted the notice of the proprietor, who had him taught shorthand. Reid did occasional reporting work at seventeen; and a local cartoon, labelled 'The Press of Newcastle,' depicted him at the time as a boy in a short jacket perched on a stool taking down a speech. Another boyish exploit was the foundation near his father's chapel of 'The West End Literary Institute,' which included a penny bank. In July 1861 he gave up his clerkship for a journalistic career, becoming chief reporter on the 'Newcastle Journal.' His brilliant descriptive report of the Hartley colliery accident in January 1862 was issued as a pamphlet, and realised 40*l.* for the relief of the victims' families.

In 1863 Reid varied reporting with leader-writing and dramatic criticism. In June 1864 he was appointed editor of the bi-weekly 'Preston Guardian,' the leading journal in North Lancashire; and in January 1866 he moved to Leeds to become head of the reporting staff of the 'Leeds Mercury,' a daily paper founded and for more than a century owned by the Baines family. He maintained a connection with that journal for the rest of his life.

From the autumn of 1867 till the spring of 1870 Reid was London representative of the paper. In order to gain admission to the press gallery of the House of Commons he had to become an occasional reporter for the London 'Morning Star,' then edited by Justin McCarthy. He subsequently took a leading part in the movement which resulted in 1881 in the opening of the gallery to the provincial press. An acquaintance with William Edward Baxter [q. v. Suppl. I], secretary to the admiralty, placed at his disposal important political information which gave high interest to his articles.

Reid at this time lived on intimate terms with Sala, James Macdonell [q. v.], W. H. Mudford, and other leading journalists. Meanwhile he sent descriptive articles to 'Chambers's Journal' and formed a lifelong friendship with the editor, James Payn. To the 'St. James's Magazine,' edited by Mrs. Riddell, he sent sketches of statesmen which were republished as 'Cabinet Portraits,' his first book, in 1872.

On 15 May 1870 Reid returned to Leeds, to act as editor of the 'Leeds Mercury.' The paper rapidly developed under his alert control. In 1873 he opened on its behalf a London office, sharing it with the 'Glasgow Herald,' and arranged with the 'Standard' for the supply of foreign intelligence. His policy was that of moderate liberalism. A 'writing editor' with an extremely able pen, he was the first provincial editor to bring a newspaper published far from the capital into line with its London rivals alike in the collection of news of the first importance, and in political comments on the proceedings of parliament. He successfully challenged the views of 'The Times' as to the seaworthiness of the Captain, which was sunk with its designer, Captain Cowper Coles [q. v.], on 7 Sept. 1870; and he obtained early intelligence of Gladstone's intended dissolution of parliament in 1874. Reid upheld Forster's education bill against the radicals, and supported against the teetotallers Bruce's moderate licensing bill. In the 1880 election at his suggestion Gladstone was invited to contest Leeds as well as Midlothian. With W. E. Forster, Reid's relations were always close, and he vigorously championed his political action in Ireland during 1880–2. The 'Mercury' under his editorship continued to support Gladstone when he took up the cause of home rule. Whilst at Leeds, Reid was also on friendly terms with Richard Monckton Milnes, Lord Houghton, at whose house at Fryston he was a frequent guest.

Reid made many journeys abroad, chiefly in his journalistic capacity. In 1877 he visited Paris with letters of introduction from Lord Houghton to the Comte de Paris and M. Blowitz, and was introduced to Gambetta. A holiday trip in Germany, Hungary, and Roumania in 1878 he described in the 'Fortnightly Review.' He went to Tunis as special correspondent of the 'Standard' in 1881, and narrated his experiences in 'The Land of the Bey' (1882).

In 1887 Reid withdrew from the editorship of the 'Leeds Mercury,' to which he continued a weekly contribution till his death, in order to become manager of the publishing firm of Cassell and Co. London was thenceforth his permanent home, and his work there was incessant. In January 1890 he added to his publishing labours the editorship of the 'Speaker,' a new weekly paper which he founded and which combined literature with liberal politics. A keen politician, he enjoyed the confidence of Gladstone and his leading followers, but his zeal in their behalf at times provoked the hostility of the extreme radical wing of the party. Reid became a strong supporter and a personal friend of Lord Rosebery, whose views he mainly sought to expound in the 'Speaker.' He was knighted on Lord Rosebery's recommendation in 1894 in consideration of 'services to letters and politics.'

In Sept. 1899 Reid ceased to be editor of the 'Speaker,' which in spite of its literary merits was in the financial respect a qualified success. Subsequently he wrote a shrewd and well-informed survey of political affairs month by month for the 'Nineteenth Century,' as well as weekly contributions to the 'Leeds Mercury.' He was elected president of the Institute of Journalists for 1898–9. He had become in 1878 a member of the Reform Club on the proposition of Forster and Hugh Childers [q. v. Suppl. I], and he soon took a prominent part in its management, long acting as chairman of committee. He was elected an honorary member of the Eighty Club in 1892, at the instance of his friend Lord Russell of Killowen.

Meanwhile Reid, who received the degree of LL.D. from St. Andrews University in 1893, made a reputation in literature. During his first residence at Leeds he had visited Haworth and interested himself in the lives of the Brontës. Ellen Nussey, Charlotte Brontë's intimate friend and schoolfellow, entrusted to him the novelist's correspondence with herself and other material which had not been accessible to Mrs. Gaskell. With such aid Reid wrote some articles in 'Macmillan's Magazine' which he expanded into his 'Charlotte Brontë: a Monograph' (1877), which drew from Swinburne high appreciation. Reid showed admirable skill, too, as the biographer of W. E. Forster (2 vols. 1888) and of Richard Monckton Milnes, first Lord Houghton (2 vols. 1890). In both works he printed much valuable correspondence, and Gladstone helped him by reading the proofs. He also published memoirs of Lyon Playfair, first Lord Playfair of St. Andrews (1899); of John Deakin Heaton, M.D., of Leeds (1883); and a vivid monograph on his intimate friend William Black the novelist (1902). A 'Life of W. E. Gladstone,' which he edited in 1899, includes a general appreciation and an account of the statesman's last days from Reid's own pen. He further enjoyed success as a novelist. His 'Gladys Fane: a Story of Two Lives' (1884; 8th edit. 1902), and 'Mauleverer's Millions: a Yorkshire Romance' (1886), each had a wide circulation. He also left 'Memoirs' including much confidential matter of a political kind; portions were edited by his brother, Dr. Stuart Reid, in 1905.

Reid died, active to the last, and almost pen in hand, at his house, 26 Bramham Gardens, South Kensington, on 26 Feb. 1905, and was buried in Brompton cemetery. He was twice married: (1) on 5 Sept. 1867 to his cousin Kate (*d.* 4 Feb. 1870), daughter of the Rev. John Thornton of Stockport; and (2) on 26 March 1873 to Louisa, daughter of Benjamin Berry of Headingley, Leeds, who survived him. There was one son by the first marriage, and a son and a daughter by the second. A portrait in possession of the family was painted by Mr. Grenville Manton.

[Memoirs of Sir Wemyss Reid, 1842–1885 (with portrait), edited by Stuart J. Reid, D.C.L., 1905 (the remainder of the autobiography is at present unpublished); Men of the Time, 1899; The Times, 27 Feb., 3, 4 March 1905; Speaker, 4 March; Newcastle Weekly Chronicle (portrait), 4 March; Leeds Mercury,

27 Feb.; Lucy's Sixty Years in the Wilderness, pp. 67, 68, 84; Stead's Portraits and Autobiographies; Brit. Mus. Cat.; private information.] G. Le G. N.

RENDEL, GEORGE WIGHTWICK (1833–1902), civil engineer, was the second son in the family of four sons and three daughters of James Meadows Rendel [q. v.] by his wife Catherine Jane Harris. Born at Plymouth on 6 Feb. 1833, he was educated at Harrow. On leaving school he lived for three years with Sir William (afterwards Lord) Armstrong at Newcastle in order to study engineering. He subsequently received his final training as an engineer in his father's office. As an assistant to his father, he was engaged on the building of the superstructure of the large bridges on the East Indian railway across the Ganges and Jumna at Allahabad. Like his younger brothers Stuart (afterwards Lord Rendel, *d.* 4 June 1913) and Hamilton Owen (*d.* 1902), George became in 1858 a partner in the firm of Sir William Armstrong & Co. at Elswick, and for twenty-four years, in conjunction with Sir Andrew Noble, he directed the ordnance works there.

During his twenty-four years at Elswick Rendel took a prominent part in the development of the construction and armament of ships of war, especially in the design of gun-mountings. To him is due the hydraulic system of mounting and working heavy guns, which was first tried in the fore-turret of H.M.S. Thunderer when she was re-armed before her completion in 1877. The experiment proved very successful, and about the same time the Téméraire was fitted with a special type of barbette mounting designed by Rendel. Another type was used in the Admiral class of battleships; and, with various improvements suggested by experience, his hydraulic system has been used for all the later warships of the British navy, as well as in some foreign navies. Rendel was one of the first (if not the first) in England to apply forced draught to war-vessels other than torpedo-boats, namely, in two cruisers built for the Chinese and one for the Japanese government in 1879. In 1881–2 he designed for the Chilian and Chinese governments a series of 1350-ton unarmoured 16-knot cruisers, carrying comparatively powerful armaments, protection being afforded by light steel decks and by coal-bunkers. Immediately afterwards he built for the Chilian navy the unarmoured protected cruiser Esmeralda (displacement 3000 tons, speed 18 knots per hour). He thus is responsible for the introduction into the navies of the world of the cruiser class, intermediate between armour-clad men-of-war and the wholly unprotected war vessel. He further designed the twin-screw gunboats of the Staunch class, most of which were built at the Armstrong yard, and numerous similar gunboats for the Chinese navy.

In 1871 Rendel was appointed by the British government a member of the committee on designs of ships of war; and he was also a member of the committee appointed in Aug. 1877 to consider questions relating to the design of the Inflexible.

Rendel was elected a member of the Institution of Naval Architects in 1879, and became vice-president of that society in 1882. He was elected a member of the Institution of Civil Engineers in 1863, and in 1874 he contributed to its 'Proceedings' (xxxviii. 85) a paper on 'Gun-Carriages and Mechanical Appliances for working Heavy Ordnance,' for which he was awarded a Watt medal and Telford premium.

In March 1882 Rendel left the Armstrong firm to become an extra professional civil lord of the admiralty, while Lord Northbrook was first lord. The post was a new one, and the admission of 'a practical man of science' to the admiralty board was generally commended. Rendel resigned the office when Lord Northbrook retired in July 1885, owing to ill-health. In 1887 he rejoined the Armstrong firm. He and Admiral Count Albini became the managing directors in Italy of the Armstrong Pozzuoli Company, and Rendel took up his residence at Posilippo, near Naples. In the winter of 1887 he vainly offered his house there to the Emperor Frederick, who, then stricken by fatal illness, was recommended to try the air of South Italy. The recommendation, which came too late, brought Rendel the close friendship of the Empress, which lasted till her death. At Naples, too, Rendel formed a cordial intimacy with Lord Rosebery.

While he lacked the commercial instinct and had no great gift as an organiser, Rendel combined lucidity of intellect and general sagacity with an exceptionally fertile faculty of invention. He received the Spanish order of Carlos III in 1871, and the order of the Cross of Italy in 1876. He died at Sandown, Isle of Wight, on 9 Oct. 1902, and by his widow's wish, although he was not a member of the Roman catholic church, was buried at Kensal Green Roman catholic cemetery.

He was twice married: (1) on 13 Dec. 1859, at Brighton, to Harriet (1837–1877), third daughter of Joseph Simpson, British vice-consul at Cronstadt; by her he had five sons; (2) on 17 March 1880, at Rome, to Licinia, daughter of Giuseppe Pinelli of Rome, and had issue three sons and a daughter.

A portrait painted by H. Hudson and a bust by Mr. Alfred Gilbert are in the widow's possession. Lord Rendel owns a replica of the bust.

[Men of the Time, 1899; Minutes of Proc. Inst. Civ. Eng. cli. 421; Trans. Inst. Naval Arch. xlv. 332; Engineering, 17 Oct. 1902; information from Lord Rendel.] W. F. S.

RHODES, CECIL JOHN (1853–1902), imperialist and benefactor, born at Bishop Stortford in Hertfordshire on 5 July 1853, was fifth son of Francis William Rhodes (1806–1878), vicar of that parish, by his second wife, Louisa, daughter of Anthony Taylor Peacock, of South Kyme, Lincolnshire (*d.* 1 Nov. 1873). The family consisted of nine sons, four of whom joined the army, and of two daughters, both unmarried. There survive the three youngest sons, Major Elmhirst (*b.* 1858), formerly of the Berkshire regiment and director of army signalling in South Africa during the Boer war (1899–1901), Arthur Montagu (*b.* 1859), and Bernard (*b.* 1861), captain R.A., and the elder daughter Louisa (*b.* 1847). The eldest son, Herbert, was killed in Central Africa in 1879. The third and sixth sons, Basil and Frederick, died in infancy. The second son, Colonel Francis William, is noticed below. The fourth son, Ernest Frederick (*b.* 1852), captain R.E., died on 4 April 1907. The younger daughter, Edith Caroline (*b.* 1848), died on 8 Jan. 1905.

The father came of yeoman stock. The father's great-great-grandfather, William Rhodes (*d.* 1767), described as a prosperous grazier, left Cheshire about 1720, and purchased near London an estate, 'The Brill Farm,' which included the region now occupied by Mecklenburgh and Brunswick Squares and the Foundling Hospital, and was buried on 24 April 1767 in Old St. Pancras churchyard, where a monument of granite now stands bearing the inscription 'Erected to replace two decayed family tombs by C. J. R., 1890.' William Rhodes's only son, Thomas, churchwarden of St. Pancras in 1756 and 1757, married twice, and died in 1787, leaving a son, Samuel (1736–1794), of Hoxton, the possessor of brick and tile works marked 'Rhodes' Farm' in Carey's map of London (1819), in Islington parish, and the purchaser of the Dalston estate now held by the trustees of the Rhodes family. Samuel's third son, William (1774–1843), married Margaret, daughter of Francis Cooper of St. Michael's, Crooked Lane, London, by Lucy his wife, daughter of Joseph Yates of Stoke Newington, and he settled at Leyton Grange in Essex; their eldest son was Cecil Rhodes's father. The latter, born in 1806, graduated B.A. from Trinity College, Cambridge, in 1830 (M.A. 1833) and was perpetual curate of Brentwood in Essex from 1834 until 1843, and vicar of Bishop Stortford from 1849 to 1876; he died at Fairlight, Sussex, on 28 Feb. 1878.

Cecil, 'a slender, delicate-looking, but not delicate, boy, of a shy nature,' was sent to Bishop Stortford grammar school in 1861. He won a silver medal for reading aloud, and he showed efficiency in charge of a class in his father's Sunday school. In 1869, at sixteen, his health broke down, and since, to his father's disappointment, he had no vocation for the church, he was sent out to his eldest brother, Herbert, then settled in Natal, growing cotton. He landed at Durban on 1 Oct. 1870. 'Very quiet and a great reader' he appeared to friends with whom he stayed in Natal on his way to his brother's rough quarters at Umkomaas. Forty-five acres of bush had been cleared and planted with cotton before Cecil's arrival; a few months later a hundred acres were planted, and the brothers won a prize at an important agricultural show. Herbert Rhodes was often away, and Cecil mainly ran the plantation, discovering a sympathy with native labourers and a turn for managing them which never failed him. He found congenial company in the son of the local resident magistrate, a retired soldier. In their spare time the youths tried to 'keep up their classics'; both cherished a dream that they should one day return to England and enter at Oxford 'without outside assistance.'

By this time the discovery of diamonds in the Orange Free State had resulted in the rush for Colesberg Kopje (now the Kimberley mine), Du Toit's Pan (later the De Beers mine), and other points in what is now the Kimberley division. The Rhodes brothers were drawn with the rest, Herbert starting for the diamond fields in Jan. 1871, while Cecil stayed behind to dispose of the stock and wind up their joint affairs. In Oct. 1871 he started for Colesberg Kopje in a Scotch cart drawn by a team of oxen, carrying a pick, two spades, several volumes of the classics, and a Greek lexicon.

At Kimberley as in Natal he was thrown much upon his own resources, for at the end of November his brother left for England and handed over to him the working of his claim. Rhodes is described in 1872 as 'a tall, fair boy, blue-eyed and with somewhat aquiline features, sitting at table diamond-sorting and superintending his gang of Kafirs near the edge of the huge open chasm or quarry which then constituted the mine'; and again as 'pleasant-minded and clever, sometimes odd and abstracted and apt to fly off at a tangent.' The 'claim' modestly flourished, and was added to; the brothers found themselves with a certain amount of ready money, and in the bracing air of the high veld Cecil's health was re-established.

In October 1873 Rhodes returned to England to fulfil his ambition of 'sending himself' to Oxford. He had hoped to enter University College, but the Master, Dr. G. G. (afterwards Dean) Bradley, finding him unprepared to read for honours, refused him admission, but gave him an introduction to Edward Hawkins [q. v.], provost of Oriel, whom he impressed. At Oriel he matriculated on 13 Oct. 1873, keeping Michaelmas term to 17 December, and living at 18 High Street. In November 1873 his mother died, the only human being with whom he is known at any time to have regularly corresponded. Early in the new year he caught a chill while rowing; a specialist found both the heart and the lungs affected, and entered against his name in his case book 'Not six months to live.' His Oxford career was thus interrupted, but it was not closed. He returned to South Africa and Kimberley, where his lungs soon ceased to trouble him; henceforth, indeed, his heart caused him his only physical anxiety, and that was never cured. A growing absorption in South African affairs left unmodified his resolve to graduate in the university, and until this ambition was gratified he revisited Oxford from time to time at no long intervals. In 1876 and again in 1877 he kept each term of the academic year, spending only his long vacations in South Africa. On 16 May 1876, too, he entered himself as a student at the Inner Temple, and although he was not called to the bar his name remained on the books till it was withdrawn on 17 Dec. 1889, to be restored on 20 Feb. 1891. In 1878 he kept Lent, Easter, and Trinity terms at Oxford, living at 116 High Street. He was back again in Michaelmas term, 1881, when he at length by dogged effort passed the ordinary examination for B.A., and took that degree and proceeded M.A. on 17 Dec. He lodged at the time at 6 King Edward Street, where a tablet commemorates the fact. He retained his name on the college books, paying a composition fee. Though an indifferent horseman, he was master of the drag during his early sojourns at Oxford, and did a little rowing; otherwise he is remembered as making one in 'a set which lived a good deal apart from both games and work.' Although he was 'not a great reading man,' he was always a devourer of books, and his feeling for certain classical authors was strong. Marcus Aurelius was his constant companion, and at his South African home, Groote Schuur, there was (until 1902, when it disappeared) a copy of the 'Meditations' marked and annotated by his hand. He commissioned for his library new translations of the chief classical writers, which were sent him in typed script. Aristotle's 'Energeia the highest activity of the soul to be concentrated on the highest object' remained his perpetual watchword.

Meanwhile his South African career had made rapid progress. On his second advent in Kimberley in 1874 he took root there, and was soon counted with the more successful diggers. His brother Herbert early left the diamond fields to hunt and explore the interior; he was killed through the accidental firing of his hut in 1879, in what is now Nyassaland. In 1874, and for some years after, Rhodes was in partnership with Mr. Charles Dunell Rudd (*b.* 1844), who had been educated at Harrow and had after matriculating at Trinity College, Cambridge, in 1863 broken down through overtraining. Rudd and Rhodes gradually increased their holdings after the old regulation against the possession of more than one claim on the diamond fields was repealed. Rhodes specially concentrated his holdings in one of the two great mines of Kimberley, called after De Beers, the Dutch farmer, who originally owned the land. Rhodes was quickly recognised as one of the ablest speculators in the district, with one conspicuous rival or opponent in Barnett Isaacs, later known as Barney Barnato [q. v. Suppl. I], but from 1875 until his death he was greatly helped in all financial undertakings by Alfred Beit [q. v. Suppl. II]. Mr. Gardner Williams, afterwards general manager of the amalgamated industry (the De Beers corporation), describes Rhodes in these days as 'a tall, gaunt youth, roughly dressed, coated with dust, sitting moodily on a bucket, deaf to the clatter and rattle about him, his blue eyes fixed intently on his work or on some fabric in his brain.' It was a life of vicissitude. There was camp fever, and other forms of epidemic, and during 1874 the reef fell in both in Colesberg Kopje and in De Beers, covering many claims under tons of shale. Floods prevailed, mining board taxation was heavy, there was constant litigation between claim holders and miners and the Griqualand West legislative council. Banks refused advances and bankruptcy was common. Many diggers left the fields, but Rhodes and his partners held on. Towards the end of October 1874 they successfully completed an undertaking to pump out Kimberley mine, and in 1876 they drained of water De Beers and Du Toit's Pan. A contemporary recalls how at a meeting of a mining board in 1876, when the members were 'fractious and impatient,' Rhodes, 'still quite a youth, was able to control that body of angry men.' As regards the diamond industry he, like his rival Barnato, already recognised that so long as individual diggers produced and threw upon the uncertain markets all the diamonds they could find, no real progress was possible, and that the remedy lay in an amalgamation of interests and the regulation of supply. To that end, but with different motives and ambitions, each was steadily working, Rhodes with De Beers mine, Barnato with Kimberley mine, as his base and nucleus. On 1 April 1880 the Rhodes group had established themselves as the De Beers Mining Company, with a capital of 200,000*l.*, while in the same year the Barnato Mining Company was formed to work the richest claims in Kimberley mine.

But Rhodes's ambitions were from the first other than commercial. During 1875 he spent eight months in a solitary journey on foot or ox-wagon through Bechuanaland and the Transvaal. The experience helped to shape his aims. He found the country to be not merely of agricultural and of great mineral value, but also beautiful and healthy. The scattered Dutch farmers proved hospitable and he felt in sympathy with them. He aspired to work with the Dutch settlers and at the same time to secure the country for occupation by men of English blood and to make Great Britain the dominant influence in the governance of South Africa, and indeed of the world. In 1877 he had his first serious heart attack and made his first will, dated 19 Sept. 1877. The testator disposed of the fortune which he had not yet made to 'the establishment, promotion, and development of a Secret Society the aim and object whereof shall be the extension of British rule throughout the world, the perfecting of a system of emigration from the United Kingdom and of colonisation by British subjects of all lands where the means of livelihood are attainable by energy, labour, and enterprise, and especially the occupation by British settlers of the entire continent of Africa, the Holy Land, the valley of the Euphrates, the islands of Cyprus and Candia, the whole of South America, the islands of the Pacific not heretofore possessed by Great Britain, the whole of the Malay Archipelago, the sea-board of China and Japan, *the ultimate recovery of the United States of America* as an integral part of the British Empire, the inauguration of a system of colonial representation in the imperial Parliament, which may tend to weld together the disjointed members of the empire, and finally the foundation of so great a power as hereafter to render wars impossible and promote the best interests of humanity.' The form and substance of these aspirations are youthful, but they dominated Rhodes's life. A federation of South Africa under British rule, with Cape Dutch assent, was always before his eyes.

Just before leaving to graduate at Oxford in 1881 Rhodes had entered public life in South Africa. In 1880 the Act for absorbing Griqualand West in the Cape Colony created two electoral divisions at Kimberley and Barkly West. As one of two members for Barkly West, Rhodes was elected in 1880 and took his seat in the Cape legislature next year. (He retained the seat for life.) The battle of Majuba Hill on 27 Feb. 1881, with its sequel in the recognition anew of the independence of the Transvaal Republic, had just given an immense advantage to the Dutch claim to supremacy in the colony and had almost crushed the hope of a permanent British predominance. The foundation of the Afrikander Bond in 1882 was but one fruit of a Dutch national movement, in sympathy with the Boer republic, which looked forward to independence of the British Empire [see HOFMEYR, JAN HENDRIK, Suppl. II]. In such unpromising conditions Rhodes entered Cape politics. His aim from the first was to maintain the widest powers of local self-government and at the same time to organise, confirm, and extend the area and force of British settlement and British influence, not by invoking the imperial factor, but by rousing in the average Briton a sense of the responsibilities of race and empire. In his first session he took a friend aside and, placing his hand on a map of Africa, said 'That is my dream, all British.' But while he sought to bring home to Englishmen in South Africa the possibilities of new empire in South Africa, he desired to co-operate with the Dutch. In his second session he frankly remarked 'Members on the other side believe in a United States of South Africa, and so do I, but under the British flag.' Rhodes first spoke in the Cape Assembly on 19 April 1881. He championed the Basutos, his interest in whom led presently to a friendship with General Gordon, who invited him in 1884 to accompany him to Khartoum. On 25 June he spoke again, in opposition to the introduction of the Taal in the Cape parliament, for which he asserted that there was no real desire in the country. He impressed his hearers as 'a good type of English country gentleman'—nervous, ungainly, but of a most effective frankness. As a speaker he seemed to think, or rather dream, out loud. His vocabulary was poor, although he hit sometimes on a telling phrase; he had moments of a discursive obscurity. Yet men who had listened to the famous orators of the world found themselves strangely impressed by his speaking. A strong persuasiveness and candour, helped by his appearance, held any audience. But 'fundamental brain-work' had been done before he rose, and when trimmed of excrescences the ordered clearness of his sequences was perfect.

His political activities were soon concentrated on that northern expansion which formed a great part of his completed work. The Cape Colony was then bounded on the north by the Orange River, beyond which lay Bechuanaland, of vast extent and the only avenue to the coveted northern territories which were the objective alike of Rhodes and of the Transvaal Boers. By the Pretoria Convention of 1881 the westward expansion of the Transvaal was limited to a line east of the trade routes from Bechuanaland. This did not prevent a series of raids from the Transvaal by which, not by haphazard but by design, the republic sought to occupy Bechuanaland, and, if might be, the regions of the north, even of the west. Rhodes's first important step was to urge the appointment of a delimitation commission in 1881. On this he served. An offer was obtained in 1882 from Mankoroane of the whole of his territory, about half Bechuanaland, for the Cape government. To this proposal Rhodes secured the agreement of the chief men of Stellaland, a Boer raider's settlement consisting of 400 farms, 'with a raad and all the elements of a new republic,' seated at Vryburg. Prolonged correspondence and a long appeal to the Cape Assembly on 16 Aug. 1883 did not avail to procure the acceptance of this offer, and it seemed certain that the Stellalanders and another group of Dutch immigrants, with two Bechuanaland chiefs, the opponents of Mankoroane, would be annexed by the Transvaal. Rhodes turned to the imperial government, and, after endless appeals, the force of his personality having impressed the high commissioner, Sir Hercules Robinson, he procured the declaration in 1884 of an imperial protectorate, the British flag being carried to the twenty-second parallel. On 27 Feb. 1884 a second convention signed in London gave definite frontiers on the eastern border of Bechuanaland, behind which the Transvaal covenanted to abide.

A few days later Bechuanaland was raided afresh by President Kruger. The imperial government promptly proclaimed the formal annexation of Bechuanaland, and sent up as resident the Rev. John Mackenzie, a veteran missionary. On 16 July Rhodes appealed once more, and this time with success, to the Cape Assembly, reminding them that Bechuanaland was 'the neck of the bottle and commanded the route to the Zambesi . . . We must secure it, unless we are prepared to see the whole of the north pass out of our hands. . . . I want the Cape Colony to be able to deal with the question of confederation as the dominant state of South Africa.' While those definitely committed to supporting the Dutch republics were not won over, a majority of the house concurred with Rhodes. Voters may have been influenced by the fact that that year, and within six months after the second convention of London was signed, a new factor entered South Africa, and by the supineness alike of the imperial and colonial governments all Damaraland and Namaqualand between twenty-six degrees south and the Portuguese border, 320,000 square miles in all, was occupied by Germany. The significance of the fact, if lost on the imperial government, impressed Rhodes and one other man, Jan Hendrik Hofmeyr [q. v. Suppl. II], leader of the Afrikander Bond, who combined his Dutch sympathies with a deep antipathy to Germany. Despite the diversity between the two men's aims, Rhodes at once saw the wisdom of co-operation with a view to promoting northern expansion.

Towards the end of 1884 it was clear that Mackenzie, though loyal and upright, was scarcely the man for the time and place, proclaiming as he did all Boer farms in Bechuanaland to be the property of the British government, and otherwise making too much of the imperial authority. The resident was recalled by the high commissioner, nominally for the purpose of conference, and Rhodes replaced him, by the style of deputy-commissioner. Reaching Rooi-Grand in Goshen, the lesser of the two Boer centres, on 25 August, he found Generals Joubert and Delarey just arrived from the Transvaal, and armed burghers preparing that night to advance on Mafeking and on Montsoia the local chief. All Rhodes could do was to warn the Boers that, in view of the convention, they were making war, in effect. on the British government, and that done, to retire on the larger concentration in Stellaland. Arriving at Commando Drift on 1 September, he went straight to the house of the Boer commandant, Van Niekirk, who had refused to acknowledge Mackenzie as resident. He informed Rhodes that 'blood must flow.' Rhodes replied 'Give me my breakfast and let us see to that afterwards.' Having dismounted, he stayed with Van Niekirk six weeks, and became godfather to his child. By 8 September he had recognised the titles of individual Boer settlers and reported to the high commissioner that the armed burghers had dispersed and that Stellaland had accepted the flag. But the return of Joubert to Pretoria was followed by a proclamation of President Kruger on 16 September, annexing the Mafeking region and so cutting off Cape Colony from access northwards. The imperial government moved. Sir Charles Warren's expeditionary force was sent to patrol Bechuanaland and the Transvaal frontier, and by 14 Feb. 1885 President Kruger met the general and Rhodes at Fourteen Streams in peaceful conference. This was the first meeting between Rhodes and Kruger, who henceforth typified for Rhodes the force which his policy of expansion might yet encounter. Bechuanaland south of the Milopo, with the Kalahari, now became part of the Cape Colony, while the territory to the north was constituted a protectorate. The expansion was thus at once both imperial and colonial, or colonial under imperial sanction, the ideal alike of Rhodes and of Sir Hercules Robinson. The high commissioner's despatches (*Bechuanaland Blue Book* C. 4432) testify how much the intervention and influence of Rhodes in keeping the country quiet, and insisting that the title of Stellalanders should not be cancelled nor the susceptibilities of Kruger and his officers wounded by too much military parade, conduced to this result. The despatch of Lord Derby, the colonial secretary (No. 17 of September 1886), took the same view.

But Rhodes had no security that in the coveted hinterland itself the Transvaal and Germany might not combine against England. Germany's acquisition in the south-west had been followed by an attempt —frustrated by the governor of Natal— to occupy St. Lucia Bay in Zululand on the east. The Transvaal, while refusing customs and railway union with the Cape, on which Rhodes counted to smooth the way to federation, and seeking, though vainly, from President Brand an alliance defensive and offensive with the Orange Free State, had given German capitalists an exclusive right to construct railways within the republic, at a sensible cost to British prestige. The fear of such a conjunction was quickened by the discovery of gold on Witwatersrand in 1886, when the Transvaal leapt from beggary to wealth and importance. North of the twenty-second parallel meanwhile was the dominion of Lobengula, the able king of the warlike Matabele, and Boer and German emissaries were reported as coming and going about Gobulawayo, the king's kraal. Late in 1887 Kruger, in defiance of a convention signed at Pretoria on 11 June of that year, confirming the delimitation of Transvaal boundaries, sent up Piet Grobelaar with the title of consul to arrange terms with the Matabele king. Rhodes was apprised, and hurrying from Kimberley to Cape Town besought the high commissioner to proclaim a formal protectorate over the northern territories. The high commissioner declined this step on his own responsibility, but, acting on an alternative suggestion, sent the Rev. John Smith Moffat, assistant-commissioner of Bechuanaland, to Lobengula, and on 11 Feb. 1888 the king entered into a treaty which bound him to alienate no part of his country without the knowledge and sanction of the high commissioner. True to his principle, Rhodes looked first to the sinews of war, and while still hoping for annexation by the imperial government, sought to make sure of substantial assets in view of a possible alternative. Messrs. Rudd, James Rochfort Maguire, and Francis R. Thompson, to whom the north was well known, were advised to approach the king at Gobulawayo, and on the Unqusa river, on 30 Oct. 1888, Lobengula signed a concession, granting them mineral rights in all his territories and promising to grant no land concessions from that day. It was by this time clear that Lord Salisbury's government would not undertake a protectorate over the northern territories. Rhodes asked whether a chartered company, roughly modelled on the old East India Company, would be acceptable, and was told that it would, and after much manœuvring on the part of *soi-disant* claimants to concessions the charter incorporating the British South Africa Company was granted on 13 July 1889. The territory under the new company's control which the company was empowered to develop lay to the north of the Transvaal and Bechuanaland, and vaguely extended to the Zambesi. It was soon named Rhodesia after the projector of the great scheme.

Meanwhile Rhodes was developing his material interests in the south. By 1885 the De Beers Mining Company, after a period of pecuniary embarrassment, had grown by the absorption of additional claims to be an enterprise of importance with a capital of 84,000*l.*, while the Kimberley Mine, practically controlled by Barnato, represented an even larger and a rival amalgamation. But the permanence of the diamond industry was still regarded as doubtful. The assistance of the Cape government, confidently expected, had been refused to the mining board. Diamonds were sinking in value. Only a final amalgamation could save the industry, the question being whether the De Beers or the Barnato Company should be supreme. Barnato's financial position was the stronger, and his ability at least equal to Rhodes's. But he had failed to secure the important interests of the Compagnie Française in the Kimberley Mine. On 6 July 1887 Rhodes sailed for Europe, obtained the necessary financial support in London, and going to Paris bought the entire assets of the French company for 1,400,000*l.* Barnato challenged the right of purchase; there was bickering and imminent litigation, when Rhodes appeared to weaken. He offered the French company shares to Barnato at cost price, taking payment in Kimberley mining shares; Barnato believed the day to be his. But the holding in the Kimberley Mine thus acquired was used by Rhodes to obtain other shares, until at last he had secured a controlling interest in the mine; and on 13 March 1888 both companies were amalgamated by the style of De Beers Consolidated Mines, with Rhodes as its chairman and virtual ruler. The trust deed which defined the powers conferred on its holders was singular. Barnato had desired a trust deed limiting the activities of the company to diamond mining. Rhodes declared that the company should be legally capable of carrying out any business not in itself unlawful. There was a fresh encounter between the two men, who measured their wits against each other through a whole night, and Rhodes prevailed. The trust deed empowered De Beers Consolidated Mines to increase its capital as it could, to acquire what it could, and where it could. It could 'acquire tracts of country' in Africa or elsewhere together with any rights that might be granted by the valuers thereof, and spend thereon any sums deemed requisite for the maintenance and good government thereof. 'Since the time of the East India Company,' said Mr. (now Chief Justice Sir) James Rose-Innes during the litigation with shareholders which followed, 'no company has had such power as this. They are not confined to Africa; they are authorised to take any steps for the good government of any country. If they obtain a charter from the secretary of state, they could annex a portion of territory in Central Africa, raise and maintain a standing army, and undertake warlike operations.' Such was the corporation—the largest in the world—of which Rhodes found himself the master at thirty-six. At the same time Rhodes acquired large stakes in the gold mines of the Rand on the discovery of a reef there. His partner, Mr. Rudd, proceeded from Kimberley and obtained on their joint behalf interests in a gold-mining corporation which was soon known as the Consolidated Goldfields of South Africa.

Rhodes's energetic interest in the organisation of the Chartered Company was not diminished by his other activities. By arrangement with the Cape government the British South Africa Company undertook the construction of a railway line northwards from Kimberley to Fourteen Streams, then subsequently to the British Bechuanaland border and on to Vryburg. With a view to the occupation of the new territories a pioneer expedition was arranged in London with Mr. F. C. Selous, the famous hunter and explorer, while Dr. Leander Starr Jameson, relinquishing in 1890 a large medical practice at Kimberley which he had carried on since 1878, spent months of daring and adroit diplomacy in Lobengula's kraal, preparing the king for the establishment of Englishmen in Matabeleland and Mashonaland. On 11 Sept. 1890, after many hardships and perils, Dr. Jameson hoisted the Union Jack on the site of the present Salisbury, and he became the company's administrator.

In addition to a holding acquired on Lake Nyassa, the company's range of operations was rapidly extended beyond the Zambesi, to the southern end of Lake Tanganyika. It was Rhodes's hope to push farther and connect Africa under the British flag from the Cape to Cairo. But the Anglo-German treaty of 1890, which extended German East Africa to the Congo, made this impossible. In 1892, when the retention of Uganda by the imperial government seemed doubtful, Rhodes protested against its surrender, and wrote to Lord Salisbury, the foreign secretary, offering to carry the telegraph from Salisbury to Uganda at his own expense. The offer was declined, but Uganda was retained. In 1893 came war with the Matabele, who were oppressing the neighbouring tribe, the Mashonas. A stubborn fight was waged, largely under the direction of Rhodes but immediately by Dr. Jameson, who as administrator of the company at Fort Victoria took the field. The company's victory, despite heavy loss, was assured by the submission of the Matabele chiefs (14 Jan. 1894). After the death of the Matabele chief Lobengula (23 Jan.) Rhodes brought three of his sons to Cape Town to be educated at his cost. The war confirmed the British possession of 440,000 square miles of territory.

On 17 July 1890 Rhodes became prime minister of the Cape in succession to Sir John Gordon Sprigg. He was maintained in power by Dutch and English votes practically for more than five years, and for that period was virtually dictator of South Africa. He was at the outset head of a 'ministry of all the talents.' John Xavier Merriman was treasurer-general, J. W. Sauer colonial secretary, and Sir James Sivewright commissioner of crown lands. The propriety of his combining the dual position as head of the British South Africa Company and of the Cape ministry was questioned (22 June 1893); but he at once made clear his readiness at any time to resign the premiership. While the development of the north occupied much of his attention, no colonial premier did so much to raise and broaden Cape politics. He carried through important reforms, notably in local education and in native policy, and went far to unite to their own consciousness the interests of British and Dutch in South Africa. The formidable Dutch political organisation, the Afrikander Bond, which sought openly the dominance of the Dutch in Cape politics and furtively the establishment of a Dutch republic, with the Transvaal as basis, was coaxed into his service. It is said that of 25,000 Chartered Company shares reserved for him to dispose of at will, a large proportion were given to Dutch applicants. This is the nearest approach to anything like bribery which his career discloses. He admitted that he struck a bargain with Hofmeyr, the leader of the Bond, who pledged himself with some reluctance in the name of the Bond not to throw any obstacles in the way of northern expansion in return for Rhodes's support of a tariff to protect the agricultural interest of South Africa. He was entirely frank in his desire to identify Bondmen with the Chartered Company's work, and when seeking to create a local board of control in the colony, he offered its presidency to the most distinguished of living Dutchmen, the chief justice, now Lord De Villiers, whose sympathies were with the Boer republics. He attended a Bond banquet on Easter Monday 1891, to show that there was no longer anything antagonistic between the Bond and the mother country. He deprecated on the one hand too sentimental a regard for the Boer republics, and on the other any wish to interfere with the independence of neighbouring states, with which he counselled 'customs relations, railway communication, and free trade in products.' With equal candour he addressed the Bond by letter on 17 April 1891, defining his views about the settlement in the north.

In the early days of his ministry (Feb. 1891) Rhodes and the governor, Sir Henry (afterwards Lord) Loch [q. v. Suppl. I] had visited London to discuss South African affairs. He discouraged interference of the home government in local affairs, but he hoped for the realisation of an imperial federal scheme. That hope had led him in 1888 to subscribe a sum of 10,000*l.* to the funds of Parnell's followers. Rhodes admired Parnell's earnestness but stipulated that the Irish members should remain at Westminster. He made it clear that home rule was in his belief a step on the road to imperial federation. But he felt convinced that 'the future of England must be liberal' and gave to the funds of the English liberal party 5000*l.* (February 1891) on condition that the gift should be kept secret, and that Irish representation at Westminster should be preserved in any home rule bill. Misgivings of the liberal policy in Egypt caused him subsequent concern, but he was assured that there was no intention of abandoning English rule there.

After a second visit to England early in 1893 differences within the Cape ministry compelled its reconstruction. Rhodes resigned his post of prime minister on 3 May, to resume office next day with a reconstructed ministry, which included Sir Gordon Sprigg, W. P. Schreiner, and others, but excluded almost all his former colleagues. An Act was soon passed abolishing the secretaryship for native affairs and amalgamating the duties with those of the prime minister.

Rhodes's native policy was always courageous. Technical education and temperance he encouraged. He restricted by an Act of 1892 the franchise to men who could read and write and had the equivalent of a labourer's wage, without respect of colour, thus making an end of the raw Kafir vote and its abuses; while in his Glen Grey Act of 1894 he introduced into native territories village and district councils in which natives could discuss educational and other matters, levy rates, and thus train themselves in the principles of self-government.

Towards the end of 1893 Rhodes made a tour through Mashonaland and Matabeleland. The war had closed, and Rhodes brought back encouraging reports of the results of the victory. A budget surplus of 334,161*l.* (14 June 1894) attested the colony's prosperity under Rhodes's rule. In June 1895 the legislature formally pronounced the absorption of British Bechuanaland in Cape Colony.

In the early months of 1895 he was once more in England, and was well received. On 2 Feb. he was admitted to the privy council, and though he was blackballed at the Travellers' Club (Jan.), he was in March elected by the Committee to the Athenæum.

At the end of 1895 Rhodes while still premier entered on a course of action which prejudiced his reputation. His disposition hardly suffered him to weigh advice, and his heart trouble, which taught him that he was doomed to an early death, made him favour impulsively 'short cuts' to his goal of a South Africa under sole British sway. He had sought in vain President Kruger's co-operation in a system of federation which should leave the independence of the republics intact while establishing a customs union, equal railway rates, and a common court of appeal, and he distrusted the capacity of those who should come after him to grapple with a problem still unsolved. During 1895 the usage by the Boer government of the Uitlander population, to which that government owed most of its wealth and power, led to great tension between Briton and Boer. The episode which brought Rhodes's premiership to a disastrous close was the consequence, not the cause, of an intolerable situation. In December 1895 the mining population of Witwatersrand, including both Americans and English, at Johannesburg, resolved, in despair of a peaceful solution, to compass a reform of their status by recourse to arms. Rhodes was asked and agreed to give this irregular movement his support. As a large mine-owner, who was the practical head of the Consolidated Goldfields of the Rand, where his brother Francis William held joint local control, he was within his rights, but as prime minister of a neighbouring government he had no business to meddle in the matter. He did far more than become a party to the movement for reform. In the words of the finding of the subsequent Cape commission of inquiry: 'In his capacity of controller of three great joint-stock companies, the British South Africa Company, the De Beers Company, and the Consolidated Goldfields, he directed and controlled a combination which rendered a raid on President Kruger's territory possible.' On 23 September certain areas had been ceded to the British South Africa Company by native Bechuana chiefs near the frontier. Here, with Rhodes's approval, Dr. Jameson, who was acting as administrator of the South Africa Company, placed an armed force of 500 men. Meanwhile Rhodes gave money and arms and lent his influence to the movement within the Transvaal; Jameson hovering on the border was in close concert with the leaders of the reform party. The movement hung fire. The form of government which was to replace Kruger's rule was undetermined. On 27 December Jameson on his sole authority precipitated the crisis by crossing the Transvaal border with an armed force. In a conflict with the Boers near Krugersdorp (1 January) the raiders were captured. For the raid Rhodes had no responsibility, but he acknowledged his complicity in the preliminary movement and resigned his office of premier (6 Jan. 1896). Next month he arrived in London to interview Mr. Chamberlain, the colonial secretary.

The course of Rhodes's career was thenceforth changed. He returned to the Cape resolved to devote himself solely to the improvement of fruit and wine industries in Cape Colony and to the development of Rhodesia. He assumed the office of joint administrator with Lord Grey of the British South Africa Company, but resigned the directorship in May. In the interval most of his plans in the north had been defeated by the outbreak in March of a Matabele rebellion. Rhodes took command of one of the columns, and the fighting continued till August. Military operations had then driven the Matabele rebels to the Matoppo Hills, where they held an impregnable position. The prospect was one of a continued war, which might smoulder for years. Rhodes conceived the idea of ending the war by his own unarmed and unaided intervention. He moved his tent to the base of the Matoppo Hills, and lay there quietly surrounded by the rebels for six weeks. Word was sent to the natives that Rhodes was 'there, to have his throat cut, if necessary,' but as one trusting the Matabele, and anxious above all to 'have it out with them,' he was ready undefended to hear their side of the case. A council was held by the chiefs in the heart of the granite hills. Rhodes was told that he might attend it (21 August). Accompanied by Dr. Sauer and Johan Colenbrander, the scout and interpreter, he rode to the appointed place. There was a long discussion without result. A week later (28 August) another conference followed. Rhodes was accompanied by Colenbrander and his wife, by Mr. J. G. Macdonald and Mr. Grimmer, Rhodes's private secretary. At one point the young warriors got out of hand; Colenbrander thought that all was lost and bade the party mount and fly. But Rhodes stood his ground and shouted to the Matabele 'Go back, I tell you!' They fell back, and Rhodes asked the assembled chiefs 'Is it peace, or is it war?' They answered 'It is peace.' Riding home in silence, Rhodes said 'These are the things that make life worth while.' The rebellion came to an end after a final meeting with the chiefs (13 October). Next year Rhodes held an 'Indaba' of Matabele chiefs (23 June 1897) and the settlement was confirmed.

Meanwhile the Jameson raid and Rhodes's relation with it had roused both in South Africa and in England an embittered party controversy. The Cape parliament adopted a majority report of a select committee condemning Rhodes's action, while absolving him of any sordid motives (17 July 1896). On 11 Aug. 1896 a select committee of the British House of Commons was appointed to investigate the affairs of the British South Africa Company. Rhodes was examined at length (16 Feb.–5 March 1897), and the report of the committee on 15 July pronounced Rhodes guilty of grave breaches of duty both as prime minister of the Cape and as acting manager of the company.

During the few years which remained to him Rhodes's best work was given to developing Rhodesia and consolidating the loyal party at the Cape, where he kept to the end his seat in the House of Assembly. In Rhodesia he brought the railway from Vryburg to Bulawayo (opened 4 Nov. 1897), and made arrangements for carrying the line to Lake Tanganyika as part of his scheme for connecting the Cape through a British line of communication with Cairo. On 21 April 1898 he was re-elected director of the company. He revisited Europe early next year, and then arranged to carry the African telegraphic land line through to Egypt, discussing the project with the German Emperor in Berlin and forming a highly favourable impression of the Kaiser. In the Cape general election of the same year and in the succeeding session he made some fine speeches which were loudly applauded, but his own action had for the time shattered the scheme of a Federal Union of South Africa, which was always his great objective. At the encænia of 1899 the honorary degree of D.C.L. was conferred on him at Oxford. He had been offered the distinction at the encænia of 1892, but was unable to attend at that time. The bestowal of the degree in 1899 elicited an unavailing protest in the university from resident graduates who resented his share in the raid [see CAIRD, EDWARD, Suppl. II]. The honour was one which Rhodes warmly appreciated, and he acknowledged it generously in the terms of his will, which he signed soon after he received the degree. On returning to Cape Town (19 July) he was received with great enthusiasm.

The South African war broke out on 11 Oct. 1899. Rhodes was then at Cape Town, but he at once made his way to Kimberley. Feeling that it was but right for the chief employer of workmen there to share the dangers of his employees, and impelled by a feeling, which events justified, that the Boers in their desire to catch him might be delayed on their advance down the ill-defended Cape Colony, Rhodes reached Kimberley just in time to be besieged (15 October). He took a man's part in organising the defence, and directed some needed measures of sanitation. The place was relieved on 16 Feb. 1900. From this trial he emerged apparently well, but his health was broken and his days were numbered. On 20 July 1901 he arrived at Southampton on a last visit to Europe. He resided at Rannoch Lodge, in Perthshire, till 6 Oct., when he left for Italy and Egypt. On his return to London in Jan. 1902 he spent a day at Dalham, Suffolk, an estate which he had just bought in the belief that the air there was easier to breathe than elsewhere. Business called him back to Cape Town in Feb.; his malady grew critical, and moving from Groote Schuur to a cottage by the sea at Muizenberg, he died there after weeks of extreme suffering, courageously borne, on 26 March. He was forty-nine years and eight months old. By his direction he was buried in a hole cut in the solid granite of the Matoppos; he had chosen the spot during his negotiations with the Matabele chiefs in 1896.

Rhodes's work did not end with his death. His last will, his sixth, was dated 1 July 1899, with codicils of Jan. and 11 Oct. 1901 and 18 Jan. and 12 March 1902. By its provisions his beautiful residence, Groote Schuur, an old Dutch house, rebuilt on the slopes of Table Mountain, was left for the use of the premier of a federated South Africa. Dalham, the Suffolk estate, was bequeathed to his family, with a characteristic direction against any 'loafers' inheriting it. Save for minor personal bequests his entire fortune, amounting to 6,000,000*l.*, was given to the public service. Part of this money was left for the purpose of founding some 160 scholarships at Oxford, of the value of 300*l.* each, to be held by two students from every state or territory of the United States of America, and three from each of eighteen British colonies. Fifteen other scholarships of the value of 250*l.* were reserved for German students to be selected by the Emperor William II. The total scholarship endowment was 51,750*l.* a year. In selecting the scholars his trustees were enjoined to consider not only the scholastic attainments of candidates but their athletic capacity and moral force. One hundred thousand pounds was left to his old college, Oriel, and his land near Bulawayo and Salisbury was left to provide a university for the people of Rhodesia. Rhodes appointed among others as trustees for the execution of his will Lord Rosebery, lately prime minister of England, Lord Milner, then high commissioner of South Africa, Dr. Jameson, prime minister of the Cape, Alfred Beit, and Earl Grey, presently governor-general of the Dominion of Canada. Rhodes's last will embodied all that was practicable of the boyish ideals of his first will made at twenty-four. Its benefactions stirred people less than the revelation of his ideals; and those who had been foremost in detraction admitted the purity of his motives. The last word on behalf of the Dutch was spoken on 28 June 1910 by Lord De Villiers, chief justice of the supreme court of South Africa, who, unveiling a statue at Cape Town, erected by public subscription, pronounced Rhodes to be a patriotic Englishman, a friend to the Dutch, the forerunner of the Union of South Africa.

Rhodes's impetuosity and impatience in act and speech gave in his lifetime an impression of him which was misleading. Like all statesmen he accepted the conditions of life as he found them, having much to do and little time, as he knew from his malady, to do it in. By nature he had the shy sensitive kindness of a boy. But while his nameless benefactions were many, he affected brutality and hardness, making it his principle to subordinate friendships and all individual claims to his schemes. Yet he was not in truth a hard man. Except in finance, where he was out-distanced by Alfred Beit, his mere aptitudes were not remarkable; in conventional accomplishments he was not well equipped. He had few ideas, but these he had worked for, testing their value by his life's experience, and wore them, so to say, next his skin. The ideas and dexterities which most cultivated men of affairs have about them, as it were ready made, were not his. His temperament was unequal, almost incalculable, combining extreme naïveté and simplicity with strokes of amazing and unexpected shrewdness. His work in its entire detail seemed to be done by others. While he apparently dreamed they really and on their own initiative drafted letters, designed meetings and conjunctions, supported or opposed policies, and drew up as it were programmes, which in a little he roused himself to act upon. Yet there was no end to the qualities he held in reserve. He seemed to muse, yet was suddenly alert with the perception of clairvoyance, revealing a grasp of detail in subjects where he had been rashly supposed ignorant. He talked anyhow; yet his felicity of phrase after columns of confused commonplace was uncanny. The subordinates who did so much of his work, apparently without consulting him, were lost without him. He was there, and the rest followed; he was not there, and nothing was done. In a word he was 'dæmonic,' and the impression of greatness which he made on his subordinates is reflected in the view now taken of him by his countrymen. His life, however rightly or wrongly conducted in detail, is seen to have been steadily devoted to impersonal and public service and a cause which was really the greater friendliness of mankind.

Rhodes was over six feet high, enormously broad and deep chested, with a fair complexion, deep blue eyes, and light brown waving hair, which grew white in his later years. In his blood there was a Norse strain, and he had the look of a viking. His head was huge and the brow massive, and was compared erroneously to Napoleon's. The likeness was imperial but recalled rather the Roman empire than the French. Rhodes is best represented in sculpture in the statue by John Tweed at Bulawayo (unveiled 7 July 1904). A bust by Henry Pegram, A.R.A., is at Grahamstown (7 Nov. 1904), a statue by the same sculptor at Cape Town (1909), and a colossal equestrian statue by William Hamo Thornycroft, R.A., at Kimberley (1907). On 5 July 1912 Earl Grey dedicated to the public an elaborate monument to Rhodes outside Cape Town on the Groote Schuur slopes of Table Mountain, consisting of a columned Doric portico approached by a long flight of steps lined on each side by four lions of the Egyptian type from the chisel of John McAllan Swan; at the foot of the steps is the statue of 'Physical Energy' by George Frederick Watts, who originally presented it to Lord Grey for erection at Groote Schuur. An unfinished painting by Watts was presented to the National Portrait Gallery by the executors of the artist in 1905. Another portrait by Sir Hubert von Herkomer is in the Kimberley Club; a replica belongs to Lord Rosebery. A third by A. Tennyson Cole is in Oriel College Common room. A fourth by Sir Luke Fildes was left unfinished. Of several miniatures painted of him, none is so good as a photograph taken by Messrs. Downey in 1898, before the fine contour of his face was blunted by disease.

[No 'standard' or adequate biography of Rhodes has yet appeared. Sir Thomas Fuller's Cecil Rhodes: a Monograph and a Reminiscence (1910) is the most considerable study of the man and his career, and is a balanced and informed appreciation. The Life by Sir Lewis Michell, Rhodes's banker and one of his trustees (2 vols. 1910), though painstaking, does not exhaust the authorities accessible, and is not authorised by the Rhodes trustees. Cecil Rhodes's Private Life, by his private secretary, Philip Jourdan (1911), written by one of several young colonists—a Dutchman in this case—who acted for Rhodes in that capacity, abounds in intimate personal observation. Cecil Rhodes, his Political Life and Speeches, by Vindex, i.e. the Rev. F. Verschoyle (1900), is the chief account of Rhodes' s public career yet published, consisting largely of his speeches from 1881 to 1900 with an explanatory thread of narrative. Cecil Rhodes, by Imperialist (1897), is a popular account of his career up to the Jameson Raid, and has a chapter by Sir Starr (then Dr.) Jameson. Cecil Rhodes, by Howard Hensman (2 vols. 1911), is of a fugitive and popular type. See also With Rhodes in Mashonaland, by D. C. De Waal (Cape Town, Juta, 1895); article on Rhodes in The Empire and the Century, London, 1905, by Edmund Garrett, the best short impression; Lord Milner and South Africa, by E. B. Iwan Müller (Heinemann, 1902), also written from personal observation; Sir Percival Lawrence's On Circuit in Kaffirland; Rights and Wrongs of the Transvaal War, by E. T. Cook (1902); Sir Charles Dilke's Problems of Greater Britain (1890); English and South African papers of 27 March 1902 and of 16 and 17 April 1902; address at the grave in the Matoppos by the bishop of Mashonaland, and the archbishop of Cape Town's sermon, Cape Town Cathedral, 30 March 1902; Scholz and Hornbeck's Oxford and the Rhodes Scholarships, 1907. This article is further based on personal knowledge and association and on private information from Rhodes's brothers and sisters, from Sir Starr Jameson, and many other of Rhodes's associates.] C. W. B.

RHODES, FRANCIS WILLIAM (1851–1905), colonel, elder brother of Cecil John Rhodes [see above], born on 9 April 1851 at Bishop Stortford, entered Eton in 1865, where he was in the army class and in the cricket elevens of 1869 and 1870. After passing through Sandhurst he was gazetted lieutenant of the 1st royal dragoons in April 1873. He saw service in the Sudan as a member of the staff in 1884, and was present at the battles of El Teb and Tamai. He was mentioned in despatches, received the medal with clasp and bronze star, and was promoted captain in Oct. 1884. He accompanied the Nile expedition in 1884–5 for the relief of Khartoum as aide-de-camp to Sir Herbert Stewart [q. v.], and distinguished himself at the battles of Abu Klea and El Gubat, where his horse was shot under him. He was mentioned in despatches, and received two clasps and the brevet of major and lieutenant-colonel (Sept. 1885). Stewart described Rhodes as the best A.D.C. a general could have.

He next served in the Sudan expedition of 1888, and was present at the action of Gemaiza (20 Dec.); he was again mentioned in despatches, and received the clasp and the order of the Medjidie (3rd class). He was made colonel in Sept. 1889. From 1890 to 1893 he was military secretary to his schoolfellow, Lord Harris, governor of Bombay; he received the D.S.O. in 1891, and in 1893 accompanied as chief of staff the mission of Sir Gerald Herbert Portal [q.v.] to Uganda. On this perilous journey Rhodes nearly succumbed to blackwater fever.

On his recovery he went out in 1894 to the South African territory of Rhodesia, which, through his brother Cecil's exertions, had just been placed under the control of the newly incorporated British South Africa Company. He was made military member of the council of four in the new government of Matabeleland, of which Dr. L. S. Jameson was first administrator (18 July 1894). In Dr. Jameson's absence in Europe he acted as administrator that year. Next year he went to Johannesburg as representative of the Consolidated Goldfields, of which his brother was a director. In Sept. 1895 he was at Ramoutsa negotiating on behalf of his brother for the cession of native territory close to the Transvaal border, which soon came under the jurisdiction of the British South Africa Company (Sir Lewis Michell, *Life of Cecil Rhodes*, 1910, i. 197). As one of the members of the Johannesburg reform movement for the protection of the Uitlanders he was one of the five signatories of the undated letter (Nov. 1895) to Dr. Jameson which ostensibly led to the Jameson raid. On the failure of the raid, he was arrested by the Boer government, tried for high treason, and sentenced to death (April 1896). The sentence was soon commuted to fifteen years' imprisonment. After being in prison in Pretoria until June, Rhodes and his companions were released on payment of a fine of 25,000*l.* each and on promising to abstain from politics for fifteen years. This latter condition Rhodes alone of the ringleaders refused to accept, and he was banished from the Transvaal. For his encouragement of the Raid, Rhodes was placed on the army retired list. In July he joined his brother Cecil in the war in Matabeleland.

In 1898 he went with General Kitchener's Nile expedition as war correspondent to 'The Times,' and was wounded at the battle of Omdurman. For his services in that campaign his name was restored to the active list (Sept. 1898).

On the outbreak of the war in South Africa in 1899 Rhodes went thither and served in the early battles in Natal. He was besieged in Ladysmith, where by his optimism and geniality he helped to keep his companions in good spirits (L. S. Amery, *The War in South Africa*, iii. 175). In the fight on Wagon Hill (5–6 Jan. 1900) Rhodes displayed great courage, and took Lord Ava, who was mortally wounded, out of fire into cover (*ibid.* iii. 194). In May following he was intelligence officer with the flying column under Brigadier-general Bryan Thomas Mahon, which hurried to the relief of Mafeking (4–17 May 1900) (*ibid.* iv. 222). For his services in the war he was created a military C.B. In Jan. 1903 he was Lord Kitchener's guest at the Durbar at Delhi. In the same year he retired from the army, and was till his death managing director of the African transcontinental telegraph company.

Rhodes had a great knowledge of the continent of Africa, and aided with his experience of the Sudan Mr. Winston Spencer Churchill in preparing his 'The River War' (1899; new edit., by Rhodes, 1902). He also contributed an introduction and photographs to 'From the Cape to the Zambesi' (1905), by G. T. Hutchinson, whom he accompanied in that year to the Zambesi. The strain of this journey brought on the fatal illness of which he died, unmarried, at his brother's residence, Groote Schuur, Capetown, on 21 Sept. 1905. His body was brought to England for interment at Dalham, Suffolk. A memorial tablet was placed by his friends in Eton College chapel in October 1906, and prizes for geography have been founded at Eton in his memory.

[The Times, 22 Sept. 1905; Broad Arrow, 23 Sept. 1905; Anglo-African Who's Who, 1905; Official Army List; Amery, Hist. War in South Africa, esp. i. 163 seq. (portrait); Sir Lewis Michell, Life of Cecil J. Rhodes, 1910; Eton School Lists.] W. B. O.

RICHMOND AND GORDON, sixth Duke of. [See Gordon-Lennox, Charles Henry (1818–1903), lord president of the council.]

RIDDELL, CHARLES JAMES BUCHANAN (1817–1903), major-general R.A., meteorologist, born at Lilliesleaf, Roxburghshire, on 19 Nov. 1817, was third son of Sir John Buchanan Riddell, ninth baronet, by his wife Frances, eldest daughter of Charles Marsham, first earl of Romney. With the exception of a year at Eton, Riddell was educated at private schools. In 1832 he entered the Royal Military Academy, Woolwich, passing thence (1834) into the royal artillery as second lieutenant. The following year he was transferred to Quebec, receiving promotion as first lieutenant in 1837, after which he returned to England, and was ordered to Jamaica, being however invalided back a year later.

In 1839 Riddell became identified with scientific research. The Royal Society and the British Association were deeply interested in the prosecution of inquiries in terrestrial magnetism and in meteorology, and it was decided to establish stations in certain colonies for the advancement of these objects. Riddell was selected for the post of superintendent of a magnetical and meteorological observatory at Toronto, subject to the instructions of the ordnance department and under Major (afterwards General Sir Edward) Sabine, R.A. [q.v.]. At the end of a year Riddell was invalided home, but he had done excellent service. Soon after, at Sabine's instance, he was appointed assistant superintendent of Ordnance Magnetic Observatories at the Royal Military Repository, Woolwich. During his four years' tenure of this post he assisted Sabine in the reduction of magnetic data and the issue of results of observations made by the directors of the affiliated observatories (see *Toronto Observations*, vol. i. Introduction; and *Rept. Brit. Assoc.* 1841, p. 340, and p. 26, 'Sectional Transactions'). He was elected a fellow of the Royal Society on 13 Jan. 1842.

In 1844 the admiralty published Riddell's 'Magnetical Instructions for the Use of Portable Instruments adapted for Magnetical Surveys and Portable Observatories, and for the Use of a Set of Small Instruments for a Fixed Magnetic Observatory.'

Subsequently he was placed on the staff at Woolwich. During the Crimean war he was deputy assistant quartermaster-general, and of him General Palliser reported that 'To his untiring energy throughout the late war the successful embarcation of the artillery without casualty and the provision of all the necessary supplies are to be mainly attributed.' Riddell served in the Indian Mutiny in 1857–8, commanding the siege artillery of Outram's force at the siege and capture of Lucknow, and the artillery of Lugard's column at the engagement of the Tigree; he was three times mentioned in despatches, was made a C.B., and received the medal with clasps. He retired in 1866 with the rank of major-general. Afterwards he lived quietly at Chudleigh, Devonshire. There he owned a farm, which he managed, and also engaged in parochial and educational work. He died at his home, Oaklands, Chudleigh, on 25 Jan. 1903, and was buried at Chudleigh. He married on 11 Feb. 1847 Mary (*d.* 1900), daughter of Sir Hew Dalrymple Ross [q. v.], and had issue one daughter.

[Proc. Roy. Soc. lxxv.; Nature, 5 March 1903; The Times, 26 Jan. 1903; Burke's Baronetage.] T. E. J.

RIDDELL, Mrs. CHARLOTTE ELIZA LAWSON, known as Mrs. J. H. Riddell (1832–1906), novelist, born on 30 Sept. 1832 at the Barn, Carrickfergus, co. Antrim, was the youngest daughter of James Cowan of Carrickfergus, by his wife Ellen Kilshaw. After her father's death Charlotte lived with her mother at Dundonald, co. Down, the scene of her novel 'Berna Boyle' (1884), and then came to London. Her mother died in 1856, and in 1857 Miss Cowan married J. H. Riddell, a civil engineer, of Winson Green House, Staffordshire. Her husband soon lost his money, and Mrs. Riddell began to write for a livelihood.

Her first novel, 'The Moors and the Fens,' appeared in 1858 (3 vols.; 2nd edit. 1866). She issued it under the pseudonym of F. G. Trafford, which she only abandoned for her own name in 1864. Novels and tales followed in quick succession, and between 1858 and 1902 she issued thirty volumes. The most notable is perhaps 'George Geith of Fen Court, by F. G. Trafford' (1864; other editions 1865, 1886), for which Tinsley paid her 800*l.* It was dramatised in 1883 by Wybert Reeve, was produced at Scarborough, and was afterwards played in Australia. From 1867 Mrs. Riddell was co-proprietor and editor of the 'St. James's Magazine,' which had been started in 1861 under Mrs. S. C. Hall [q. v.]. She also edited a magazine called 'Home' in the sixties, and wrote short tales for the Society for the Promotion of Christian Knowledge and Routledge's Christmas annuals. Her short stories were less successful than her novels.

Her husband died in 1880. Despite harass and misfortune her twenty-three years of married life were happy. After 1886 she lived in seclusion at Upper Halliford, Middlesex. She was the first pensioner of the Society of Authors, receiving a pension of 60*l.* a year in May 1901. She died at Hounslow on 24 Sept. 1906. There were no children of the marriage.

Mrs. Riddell, by making commerce the theme of many of her novels, introduced a new element into English fiction, although Balzac had naturalised it in the French novel. She was intimately acquainted with the topography of the City of London, where the scenes of her novels were often laid. At the same time she possessed a rare power of describing places of which she had no first-hand knowledge. When she wrote 'The Moors and the Fens' she had never seen the district.

[The Times, 26 Sept. 1906; Helen C. Black, Notable Women Authors of the Day, 1893; W. Tinsley, Random Recollections of an Old Publisher, 1900, i. 93–6; Brit. Mus. Cat.]

E. L.

RIDDING, GEORGE (1828–1904), headmaster of Winchester and first bishop of Southwell, was born on 16 March 1828 in Winchester College, of which his father, Charles Henry Ridding (afterwards vicar of Andover), was then second master. His mother (*d.* 1832) was Charlotte Stonhouse, daughter of Timothy Stonhouse-Vigor, archdeacon of Gloucester, and grand-daughter of Sir James Stonhouse, eleventh baronet [q. v.]. Isaac Huntingford [q. v.], bishop of Gloucester and Hereford and warden of Winchester, was great-great-uncle and godfather. Ridding was a scholar of Winchester (1840–6), rising to be head of the school, while his three brothers won equal distinction as cricketers. In default of a vacancy at New College, he matriculated as a commoner at Balliol, where he rowed in the college boat and gained the Craven scholarship, a first class in classics and a second in mathematics, and a mathematical fellowship at Exeter College (all in 1851); he won the Latin essay and proceeded M.A. in 1853; and took the degree of D.D. in 1869. From 1853 to 1863 he was tutor of Exeter (of which college he was made an honorary fellow in 1890); there he took a considerable part on the liberal side in college and university politics.

On 14 Jan. 1863 Ridding was elected second master of Winchester; and on 27 Sept. 1866, when Dr. George Moberly [q. v.] resigned the headmastership, he was at once elected to succeed him. The time was ripe for reforms, educational and material, and Ridding was a wise and courageous reformer. Carrying on the policy initiated by Moberly, he established six additional boarding-houses, and transferred thither the 'commoners' (boys not on the foundation), who had hitherto been housed in an unsightly and insanitary block of buildings, which Ridding converted into much-needed class-rooms and a school library. Land was bought, drained, levelled, and presented to the school as additional playing-fields, since called Ridding Field. A racquet court, three fives courts, and a botanical garden were likewise given to the school. A new bathing-place and a gymnasium were provided. Wykeham's chapel was re-seated and rearranged, with results which though artistically unfortunate were held to be good for discipline; and 'Chantry,' a beautiful fifteenth-century building in the centre of the cloisters, was converted into a chapel for the smaller boys. The funds for carrying out his reforms were provided by Ridding out of his own salary and private property, to an extent estimated at 20,000*l.*, of which about half was eventually repaid to him. Educationally Ridding was a pioneer in the expansion of the curriculum of public schools. He was one of the founders of the headmasters' conference in 1870, and of the Oxford and Cambridge schools examination board in 1873; but he did not wait for the collaboration of other headmasters to carry out the reforms which he saw to be desirable. He more than doubled the staff of assistant masters. He greatly enlarged the scope of the mathematical teaching; he practically introduced the teaching of history, modern languages, and natural science, and made them, especially the first-named, vital elements in the education of the school. No separate 'modern side' was established; but opportunities were given in the upper part of the school for the development of special individual capacity. Ridding was himself a fine classical scholar and a stimulating teacher, and by a system of periodical inspection he kept the whole teaching of the school under his own eye. He had the gift of commanding both the respect and the affection of his pupils, and the perhaps rarer gift of carrying with him in a course of drastic reforms the co-operation and devotion of his assistant masters. His reforms were often viewed with disfavour by the fellows, who before 1871 constituted the governing body of the college, and were strenuously criticised by Wykehamists in general; but Ridding won his way, and the results justified him. The school rose in numbers from about 250 to over 400, and might have been much further enlarged but for Ridding's conviction that a school should not exceed the number with which a headmaster can keep in personal touch. The record of university successes was excellent; after his resignation he was entertained at dinner by sixteen fellows of Oxford colleges who were the product of the last eight years of his rule at Winchester. In 1872 occurred the 'tunding row,' arising out of a somewhat excessive punishment of a stalwart 'inferior' by a prefect. The incident was trivial, but the victim's father appealed to 'The Times,' and an animated, though in general ill-informed, correspondence followed (*The Times*, Nov. and Dec. 1872). Two members of the governing body resigned; but neither Winchester nor the prefectorial system was affected by it. A further valuable extension of the activities of the school was the foundation, after the example of Uppingham, of a School Mission, first in 1876 at Bromley in East London, and subsequently in 1882 at Landport in Portsmouth, where the mission came into more intimate connection with the life of the school.

In 1883 Ridding refused the offer of the deanery of Exeter (while at Oxford he had refused a colonial bishopric); but in 1884 he was appointed the first bishop of Southwell, and consecrated on 1 May. Southwell was a new diocese, formed by separating the counties of Derby and Nottingham from the dioceses of Lichfield and Lincoln respectively. The cathedral town was so inaccessible that Ridding firmly declined to live in it, and rented Thurgarton Priory as his residence in place of the ruined episcopal palace. In population the diocese was the fifth in England, but it had no chapter, no diocesan funds, no common organisation; the two counties had diverse traditions, and much of the patronage remained in the hands of external bishops and chapters. Ridding's work was to bring unity and a corporate spirit out of diversity and jealousy, to create all kinds of diocesan organisations, to raise the intellectual standard of the clergy, and to stimulate spiritual life in neglected districts. As at Winchester, he was not understood at first, and encountered some opposition; but his sincerity, genuineness, and liberality (the whole of his official income was spent on the diocese) ultimately gained the affection and loyalty of both clergy and laity. He was emphatic in upholding the national church, and very definite in his advocacy of church principles. His independence and originality of thought made him a valued adviser of two successive archbishops; with Temple in particular he was united by cordial friendship, based on considerable resemblances of character. This same independence, on the other hand, often separated him from the main parties of church thought. During the controversy of 1902 on religious education, he was not in accord with either the government or the opposition of the day, but strenuously advocated a universal system of state schools, accompanied by universal liberty of religious teaching.

With the exception of a long holiday (necessitated by overwork) in Egypt and Greece from December 1888 to April 1889, his work in his diocese was unbroken. In 1891 he refused translation to Lichfield. In 1893 occurred the great strike in the coal trade, lasting four months (July–Nov.), during which his efforts to restore peace were unceasing. In 1897 he presided at the Nottingham Church Congress. In 1902 repeated attacks of rheumatism and sciatica began to tell upon his health. In July 1904 he tendered his resignation; but before it had taken effect an acute crisis supervened, and on 30 Aug. he died at Thurgarton. He was buried just outside Southwell minster. Ridding was twice married: (1) on 20 July 1858 to Mary Louisa, third child of Dr. George Moberly [q. v.], then headmaster of Winchester; she died on the first anniversary of their marriage; and (2) on 26 Oct. 1876 to Laura Elizabeth, eldest daughter of Roundell Palmer, first earl of Selborne [q. v.].

Ridding published one volume of sermons, 'The Revel and the Battle' (1897); and after his death his 'Litany of Remembrance' (1905) and his visitation charges, 'The Church and Commonwealth' (1906), 'Church and State' (1912), were edited by his wife. His style, whether in writing or in speaking, was peculiar: full of thought, tersely and trenchantly expressed, but often difficult to follow from lack of connecting links and phrases. Nevertheless it was stimulating from its vigour and obvious sincerity, as well as from the unexpectedness which was a characteristic quality also of his teaching and conversation. His administrative powers are best shown by the results: as headmaster he earned the title (conferred on him by the conservative warden of New College, Dr. Sewell) of 'second founder of Winchester,' and as bishop he was the founder and organiser of the diocese of Southwell.

Ridding's portrait, painted by W. W. Ouless, R.A., in 1879, as a wedding gift from old Wykehamists, hangs in Moberly Library, Winchester; it was engraved by Paul Rajon. Another portrait by H. Harris Brown in 1896 belongs to Lady Laura Ridding. A full-length memorial brass by T. B. Carter was placed in Winchester College chapel by the warden and fellows in 1907; and a fine bronze statue, kneeling, by F. W. Pomeroy, A.R.A., was presented to Southwell Cathedral by the diocese and friends. There are engravings from photographs in 1897 and 1904. A cartoon portrait by 'Spy' appeared in 'Vanity Fair' in 1901.

[George Ridding, Schoolmaster and Bishop, by his wife, Lady Laura Ridding, with bibliography, 1908; Miss C. A. E. Moberly, Dulce Domum, 1911; articles in the Church Quarterly Rev., July 1905, and Cornhill Mag., Dec. 1904; personal knowledge.] F. G. K.

RIDLEY, Sir MATTHEW WHITE, fifth baronet and first Viscount Ridley (1842–1904), home secretary, born at Carlton House Terrace, London, on 25 July 1842, was elder son in a family of two sons and one daughter of Sir Matthew White Ridley, fourth baronet, of Blagdon, Northumberland (1807–1877), M.P. for North Northumberland. His mother was Cecilia Anne, eldest daughter of Sir James Parke, Baron Wensleydale [q. v.]. Edward, the younger brother (*b.* Aug. 1843), became a judge of the high court in 1897. The Ridleys were an old Border family, originally of Williemoteswick and Hardriding. On 18 Nov. 1742 Matthew Ridley of Heaton married Elizabeth, daughter of Matthew White, who had purchased of the Fenwicks the estate of Blagdon, and owned much other landed property. Her brother Matthew was created a baronet in 1756 with special remainder in the absence of issue of his own to his sister's son, Matthew White Ridley. The latter in 1763 succeeded as second baronet, and inherited Blagdon and other of Matthew White's estates.

Ridley was at Harrow from 1856 to 1861. There he was in the football and shooting elevens, and became captain of the school in 1860. In the same year he gained a classical scholarship at Balliol College, Oxford, and matriculated on 12 Oct. 1861. Taking a first class in classical moderations in 1863 and in the final classical school in 1865, he in the latter year graduated B.A., and was elected a fellow of All Souls, proceeding M.A. in 1867. He vacated his fellowship in 1874, after his marriage.

Destined for a political career, Ridley in 1868 succeeded his father in the conservative interest as member of parliament for North Northumberland; his colleague was Lord Percy, afterwards seventh duke of Northumberland; they were returned unopposed. In 1874 they were again returned without a contest. On his father's death on 21 Sept. 1877 he succeeded as fifth baronet and owner of the family estates. Next year under Lord Beaconsfield's administration he received his first official recognition, becoming under-secretary to the home office. At the general election of 1880 he was returned for the third time with Lord Percy, but now after a contest with a liberal opponent. The conservative government was defeated at the polls and went out of office. Ridley remained a private member until the summer of 1885, when in Lord Salisbury's first short administration he was made in September financial secretary to the treasury, retiring with his colleagues in Jan. 1886. Meanwhile the Redistribution Act of 1885 changed the Northumberland constituencies, and at the general election in Nov. 1885 Ridley stood for the Hexham division, where he was beaten by Miles MacInnes. At the next general election of July 1886 he stood for Newcastle-on-Tyne with Sir William Armstrong, but both seats were won by the liberal candidates, Mr. John Morley and James Craig. In the following August a bye-election at Blackpool gave Ridley an opportunity of returning to parliament, and he retained the seat until he was raised to the peerage in 1900. Lord Salisbury's second administration had been formed in the previous July. Ridley remained a private member until 1895. He was, however, created a privy councillor on the resignation of the conservative government in 1892.

Although Ridley took little part in the debates of the house, he won its respect, and early in 1895, when Arthur Wellesley (Viscount) Peel retired, was put forward on 10 April as the conservative candidate for the speakership, being proposed by Sir John Mowbray and seconded by John Lloyd Wharton, in opposition to the liberal candidate, William Court Gully (afterwards Viscount Selby [q. v. Suppl. II]. On a division Gully was elected by 285 votes against 274 for Ridley. It was asserted at the time that in the event of a change of government after the approaching general election, Sir Matthew would at once be placed in the chair. But when Lord Salisbury returned to office on 25 June, Gully was not disturbed, and Sir Matthew became home secretary in the new government. This post he filled until the dissolution of 1900.

Ridley's administration of the home office was thoroughly safe and consequently attracted little attention. In 1897, when he released from prison some men convicted of dynamite outrages, he defended himself with effect against an attack from his own side, led by Mr. (later Sir) Henry Howorth and James Lowther [q. v. Suppl. II], but he was not otherwise molested. When the government was reconstituted after the general election (Sept. 1900) Sir Matthew, who was left a widower a year earlier, retired from political life. His last years were mainly spent at Blagdon.

Ridley was always active in the administration of his property. Throughout the north of England, where his influence was great, he was known as an extremely capable man of business. He was long a director of the North Eastern railway, and on the resignation of Sir Joseph Pease in 1902 he became chairman. He especially devoted himself to the development of the town of Blyth, which, originally part of the estates of the Radcliffe family forfeited to the Crown after the rising of 1715, had descended to Ridley with the other estates of Matthew White. In the eighteenth century it was an important place of export for coal, and from 1854 was under the control of the Blyth Harbour and Dock Company; but owing to shallowness of entrance and increase in the size of ships, trade fell off, and in 1883 amounted to only 150,000 tons. Ridley, after succeeding to the baronetcy, carried a bill through parliament for the creation of a board of commissioners with powers to develop the place. As chairman of this board Ridley soon transformed the harbour and dock. Trade returned, and ultimately reached a yearly average output of four million tons of coal. As principal proprietor Ridley benefited largely, but he contrived that the inhabitants should share in the prosperity. He gave an open space for public recreation, which in the year of his death he opened as the Ridley Park. He had already given sites, either as a free gift or at a nominal rent, for a mechanics' institute, a church, and a hospital, and he was occupied until the end on a large scheme of planting trees in convenient places. Ridley was chairman of the Northumberland quarter sessions from 1873, and of the county council from 1889; but he resigned both offices in 1895, when he became home secretary. He was also president of the National Union of Conservative Associations, and was president of the Royal Agricultural Society in 1888, when the meeting was at Nottingham; he joined the society in 1869. He was D.L. and J.P. for Northumberland, Provincial Grand Master of Freemasons for Northumberland from 1885, and he commanded the Northumberland yeomanry from 1886 to 1895.

Ridley died at Blagdon on 28 Nov. 1904, and was buried there. He married on 10 Dec. 1873 Mary Georgiana, eldest daughter of Dudley Coutts Marjoribanks, first Lord Tweedmouth; she died on 14 March 1899, leaving two sons and two daughters. Ridley was succeeded as viscount by his elder son, Matthew (*b.* 1874), conservative M.P. for Stalybridge from 1900 to 1904.

A portrait of Ridley by Sir Hubert von Herkomer is at Blagdon. A cartoon by 'Ape' appeared in 'Vanity Fair' in 1881.

[The Times, and Daily Chronicle, 29 Nov. 1904; Foster's Alumni Oxon.; private information.] R. L.

RIEU, CHARLES PIERRE HENRI (1820–1902), orientalist, born at Geneva on 8 June 1820, was son of Jean Louis Rieu, first syndic of Geneva, whose memoirs he edited (Geneva, 1870). His mother was Marie Lasserre. On leaving school Charles entered the Académie de Genève in Nov. 1835, where he went through courses both in philosophy and science. At Geneva he first took up Oriental languages and became the pupil of Jean Humbert, who had studied under the French orientalist Sylvestre de Sacy. In 1840 Rieu proceeded to the university of Bonn, where he was inscribed in the philosophical faculty (30 Oct.). There he read Sanskrit with Lassen, and Arabic with Freytag and Gildermeister, and at the same time he acquired a thorough mastery of German. In 1843, on completing his studies, he received the degree of Ph.D. and published his thesis entitled 'De Abul-Alæ poetæ arabici vita et carminibus secundum codices Leidanos et Parisiensem commentatio' (Bonn, 1843). After a visit to Paris, where he was elected a member of the Société Asiatique on 8 Nov. 1844, he removed to St. Petersburg, and there in conjunction with Otto Boehtlingk he edited with German notes the text of 'Hemakandra's Abhidhânakíntâmani' or Sanskrit dictionary (St. Petersburg, 1847). While engaged on this work he visited Oxford for the purpose of transcribing the unique manuscript in the Bodleian library.

In 1847 Rieu settled in London, and thanks to his eminent qualifications as an Arabic and Sanskrit scholar he secured the post of assistant at the British Museum in the department of Oriental manuscripts. Henceforth he was engaged on the important task of cataloguing the museum collections. In 1867 he became first holder of the office of keeper of Oriental manuscripts, and in 1871 he completed the second part of the 'Catalogus codicum manuscriptorum orientalium,' of which the first portion had been published by William Cureton [q. v.] in 1846. Besides Arabic and Sanskrit, Rieu had an extensive knowledge of Persian and Turkish. At the British Museum he drew up the 'Catalogue of Persian Manuscripts' (4 vols. 1879–95) and the 'Catalogue of Turkish Manuscripts' (1888). These volumes constitute an invaluable storehouse of information concerning Mohammedan literary history, and show a high degree of critical scholarship.

Rieu, who was for many years professor of Arabic and Persian at University College, London, received a congratulatory address from the University of Bonn on the jubilee of his doctorate (6 Sept. 1893). In 1894, despite his advanced age, he was elected Adams professor of Arabic in the University of Cambridge in succession to William Robertson Smith [q. v.]. Of a gentle and retiring disposition, he resigned his post at the British Museum in 1895, and died at 28 Woburn Square, London, on 19 March 1902. He married in 1871 Agnes, daughter of Julius Heinrich Nisgen, by whom he had issue five sons and two daughters. A portrait (*c.* 1887) by his son, Charles Rieu, is in the possession of his widow.

[The Times, 21 March 1902; Athenæum, 29 March 1902; Journal of the Royal Asiatic Society, July 1902, obit. notice by Prof. E. G. Browne; congratulatory address from Bonn University in Brit. Mus., 1893; private information from Mrs. Rieu.] G. S. W.

RIGBY, Sir JOHN (1834–1903), judge, born at Runcorn, Cheshire, on 4 Jan. 1834, was second son of Thomas Rigby of that place by his wife Elizabeth, daughter of Joseph Kendall of Liverpool. He received his early education at the institution which afterwards became Liverpool College, and matriculating at Trinity College, Cambridge, in Michaelmas term 1852, he was elected to an open scholarship there in 1854. In 1856 he graduated as second wrangler and second Smith's prizeman, taking a second class in the classical tripos. He became fellow of his college in the same year, and proceeded M.A. in 1859. He entered as a student at Lincoln's Inn on 17 Oct. 1855, and was called to the bar on 26 Jan. 1860. Starting as 'devil' in the chambers of Richard Baggallay, Q.C. [q.v. Suppl. I], one of the leaders of the chancery bar, he rapidly acquired a large practice both in chambers and in court, and in 1875 Baggallay, who was then attorney-general, made him junior equity counsel to the treasury, a post which is held to confer the reversion of a judgeship. Rigby, however, was not content to wait; he took silk in 1880 and attached himself to the court of Mr. Justice Kay [q. v. Suppl. I], where he obtained a complete ascendancy both over his rivals and over the judge himself. Within a very few years he was in a position to confine his main practice to the court of appeal, the House of Lords, and the privy council, only going before the judges at first instance with a special fee. The rivals with whom he divided the work were Horace (afterwards Baron) Davey [q. v. Suppl. II], Edward (afterwards Lord) Macnaghten, and Montague Cookson (afterwards Crackanthorpe). In May 1884 he was made a bencher of his inn.

In December 1885 he entered parliament as the liberal member for the Wisbech division of Cambridgeshire, and in the split which arose out of the introduction of the home rule bill of 1886 he followed Gladstone, and made a powerful speech in support of the second reading (28 May 1886). At the general election of that year he lost his seat, and did not return to the House of Commons until July 1892, when he was elected for Forfarshire. So little had his fame penetrated beyond legal circles, that he was denounced in his new constituency as an English carpet-bagger on the look-out for a county court judgeship. He was appointed solicitor-general by Gladstone on 20 Aug. 1892, receiving the honour of knighthood, and on 3 May 1894 he became attorney-general in succession to Sir Charles (afterwards Lord) Russell (of Killowen); a few weeks later he took the place in the court of appeal vacated by his old rival Sir Horace Davey, then appointed to be a lord of appeal, and was admitted to the privy council.

Rigby owed his success at the bar to a complete mastery of the science of equity, to his ingenuity and pertinacity, and to his impressive and rugged personality. 'He had a natural gift for rhetoric,' says a writer in 'The Times,' 'in which his fervid utterance seemed to contend with an almost pedantic desire to measure his words and give weight to every syllable.' He had a rare faculty of being at his best in a bad case, and of never losing confidence either in the integrity of his client or in his ultimate success with the court. During his short term as law officer he gave invaluable assistance to Sir William Harcourt over the intricate details of the Finance Act of 1893. He was not so successful in his discharge of general parliamentary business. His unconventional ways, apparent lack of humour, and somewhat uncouth exterior at first provoked the ridicule of opponents. But the popularity which he enjoyed at the bar was ultimately assured him in the house. As solicitor-general he conducted at the central criminal court without success the prosecution of the directors of the Hansard Union. Rigby, who was entirely without experience of this branch of his profession, betrayed a bewilderment which was almost pathetic. The case, which lasted for twenty-four days, terminated on 26 April 1893 in the acquittal of all the defendants.

On the bench he did not altogether justify the high expectations that had been formed of him. He displayed his accustomed skill and ingenuity in the unravelling of complicated and contradictory statutes; he showed characteristic independence and individuality in coming to a conclusion, and his dissentient judgments were from time to time upheld by the House of Lords in preference to those of his colleagues. But his intellect, which was massive rather than flexible, failed to adapt itself to new demands. He resigned in October 1901, after showing signs of failing powers, the effect, as was believed, of a severe fall a year or two previously. He died on 26 July 1903 at Carlyle House, Chelsea, and was buried at Finchley. He was unmarried.

An oil painting by A. T. Nowell is in the possession of his family; cartoon portraits, by 'Stuff' and 'Spy' respectively, appeared in 'Vanity Fair' of 1893 and 1901.

[The Times, 27 July 1903; private information.] J. B. A.

RIGG, JAMES HARRISON (1821–1909), Wesleyan divine, born at Newcastle-on-Tyne on 16 Jan. 1821, was son of John Rigg, a methodist minister there, by his second wife Anne, daughter of James McMullen, Irish methodist missionary at Gibraltar. Brought up in straitened circumstances, the boy was for five years (1830–5) a pupil and for four years (1835–9) a junior teacher at the Kingswood school for preachers' sons near Bristol. In 1839 he became assistant in the Rev. Mr. Firth's Academy, Hartstead Moor, near Leeds, and having made an unsuccessful effort to conduct a school of his own at Islington, London, he became in 1843 classical and mathematical master at John Conquest's school at Biggleswade. In July 1845 he entered the methodist ministry as probationer, and being ordained on 1 Aug. 1849, served in successive circuits at Worcester, Guernsey, Brentford, Stockport, Manchester, Folkestone, and Tottenham.

From an early date Rigg read widely and wrote much on religious and theological themes. A vigorous and clear style gave his writings influence in his denomination. He was a chief contributor to the 'Biblical Review' (1846–9), and frequently wrote in the Wesleyan newspaper, the 'Watchman.' Contributing to the first number of the 'London Quarterly Review,' a Wesleyan methodist periodical, in September 1853, he soon joined its editorial staff (1868), was co-editor with Dr. William Burt Pope [q. v. Suppl. II] (1883–6), and ultimately sole editor (1886–98). Rigg explained his theological position in three suggestive volumes: 'Principles of Wesleyan Methodism' (1850; 2nd edit. 1851), 'Wesleyan Methodism and Congregationalism contrasted' (1852), and 'Modern Anglican Theology' (1857; 3rd edit. 1880). In the last, which showed a keen interest in the historical development of the Church of England, he ably criticised the broad-church teaching of Maurice, Kingsley, and Jowett, but his differences with Kingsley were so considerately expressed that Kingsley sought his acquaintance, and Rigg stayed with him at Eversley (cf. MRS. KINGSLEY'S *Life of Kingsley*, ii. 317–8). In 1866 he republished many periodical articles as 'Essays for the Times on Ecclesiastical and Social Subjects,' and in 1869 he issued 'Churchmanship of John Wesley' (new edit. 1879). His literary work was early valued in America. He acted as English correspondent of the 'New Orleans Christian Advocate' (1851) and of the 'New York Christian Advocate' (1857–76). In 1865 he received the degree of D.D. from Dickinson College, U.S.A.

In 1868 Rigg was appointed principal of the Westminster (Wesleyan) training college for day school teachers, and he held that post till 1903. In matters of education he acquired an expert knowledge and was an active controversialist. When the first elementary education act was passed in 1870, Rigg took the traditional Wesleyan view, opposing secularism and favouring denominational schools, although without sympathy for sectarian exclusiveness. From William Arthur [q. v. Suppl. II] and Hugh Price Hughes [q. v. Suppl. II], both of whom supported the transfer of Wesleyan schools to the school board as created in 1870, he differed profoundly. He pressed his views, in correspondence, on the attention of Gladstone and W. E. Forster, and the Wesleyan conference supported him. In 1870 he was elected a member for Westminster on the first London school board, and served in that capacity till 1876. With the help of Professor Huxley and W. H. Smith, M.P., he secured the provision of a syllabus of religious instruction. In 1873 he summarised his attitude in 'National Education in its Social Conditions and Aspects.' Subsequently he was a member of the royal commission on elementary education (1886–8), over which Sir Richard Cross presided and which reported in favour of the school board management as against the voluntary system.

In the general administration of Wesleyan affairs Rigg was recognised to be a statesmanlike leader of liberal-conservative temper. Elected chairman of the Kent district in 1865, he was made a member of the legal hundred in 1866. In 1878 he was elected president of the Wesleyan conference, and the unusual distinction was paid him of re-election in 1892. From 1877 until 1896, with two brief intervals, he was chairman of the second London district, and from 1881 to 1909 he was treasurer of the Wesleyan Missionary Society. In controversies concerning the internal organisation of the Wesleyan church Rigg took a middle course. He met the demand of the 'progressive' section under Hugh Price Hughes for an enlarged participation of the laity in the work of the conference, by proposing and carrying the 'Sandwich Compromise' in 1890, which 'sandwiched' a representative lay session between the two sittings of the pastoral session. The compromise lasted till 1901, when the liberal section prevailed and conference was opened by ministers and laymen together, though the pastoral session still retained the privilege of electing the president. Rigg's proposal of 1894, in which Hughes supported him (*Methodist Times*, 8 Feb. 1894), to exempt chairmen of districts from circuit duties and leave them free to exercise supervision over the district, was rejected by the conference from a suspicion that Rigg's 'separated chairmen' had a colour of episcopacy. Rigg's own position in the matter was defined in his 'Comparative View of Church Organisation, Primitive and Protestant' (1887; 3rd edit. 1896). With Hughes and the progressive party Rigg's relations were often strained. Writing privately to Cardinal Manning, a colleague on the education commission, on the education question, 17 Dec. 1888, he described Hughes as 'your intemperate temperance coadjutor, our methodist firebrand.' The unauthorised publication of the letter in Purcell's 'Life' of the cardinal (1895) led to reprisals by Hughes, who wrote in the 'Methodist Times' an article on 'The Self-Revelation of Dr. Rigg.' At Rigg's request the letter was withdrawn from later editions of Purcell's book, and Hughes and he were reconciled.

Rigg, whose somewhat rough manner caused even friendly admirers to liken him to Dr. Johnson, never abated his literary energies amid his varied activities. For many years he was a member of the committee of the London Library. The chief publications of his later life were: 'The Living Wesley' (1875; re-issued as 'The Centennial Life of Wesley' in 1891); 'Discourses and Addresses on Religion and Philosophy' (1880); 'Character and Life-work of Dr. Pusey' (1893); and 'Oxford High Anglicanism and its Chief Leaders' (1895; 2nd edit. 1899), an interesting study and the only attempt made by a nonconformist to write a history of the Oxford movement. Rigg was a severe critic of Newman. There followed 'Reminiscences sixty Years ago' (1904), and 'Jabez Bunting, a short Biography' (1905). Rigg also wrote the article on 'Methodism' in the 'Encyclopædia Britannica' (9th edit.). He died on 17 April 1909, at 79 Brixton Hill, where he had lived since 1889, and was buried in Norwood cemetery.

He married, on 17 June 1851, Caroline, daughter of John Smith, alderman of Worcester. She died on 17 Dec. 1889, leaving two daughters and a son. The elder daughter, Caroline Edith, is head-mistress of the Mary Datchelor School and Training College, Camberwell; and the son, James McMullen, barrister-at-law, has contributed many articles to this Dictionary.

A marble medallion portrait by Adams-Acton is in possession of his daughter, Mrs. Telford, and a marble bust by the same sculptor, exhibited at the Royal Academy in 1892, is in Westminster Training College.

[J. H. Rigg: Life by John Telford (his son-in-law), 1909; Miss Hughes's Life of Hugh Price Hughes, 1904; Purcell's Life of Cardinal Manning, 1895; Men and Women of the Time, 1899; Report of Royal Commission on Education, 1888.] C. H. I.

RINGER, SYDNEY (1835–1910), physician, born at Norwich in 1835, was second son of John M. Ringer, a Norwich tradesman, who died when his children were very young, by his wife Harriet. His two brothers became successful merchants in the East. Ringer, whose simple and retiring disposition always bore the impress of severely nonconformist training in youth, began his medical education as an apprentice in Norwich, and soon after entered the medical faculty of University College in 1854, graduating M.B.London in 1860 and M.D. in 1863. He became M.R.C.P. in 1863 and in 1870 F.R.C.P. After being resident medical officer for two years (1861–2) he was appointed assistant physician to University College Hospital in 1863, physician in 1865, and consulting physician in 1900. From 1864 to 1869 he was assistant physician to the Hospital for Sick Children. At University College he was successively professor of materia medica, pharmacology, and therapeutics (1862–78), professor of the principles and practice of medicine (1878–87), and Holme professor of clinical medicine (1887–1900).

Ringer was pre-eminent in two fields of work, namely clinical medicine and physiological research; at the outset of his career he confined his energies to medicine, but when his position as a physician was established his interest in physiological problems awakened, and for thirty years he worked incessantly at them both. He was an admirable clinical teacher and physician, but was more widely known as the author of 'A Handbook of Therapeutics' (1869), which reached its 13th edition in 1897. His experimental work covered a large area, some of the most important researches being into the influence of organic salts, especially calcium, on the circulation and beat of the heart; 'Ringer's solution' is widely known in connection with experiments on animals' hearts. He was also author of 'The Temperature of the Body as a Means of Diagnosis of Phthisis, Measles, and Tuberculosis' (1865; 2nd edit. 1873), of articles on parotitis, measles, and sudamina in Reynolds's 'System of Medicine' (vol. i. 1886), and of numerous papers in the 'Journal of Physiology.'

He was elected F.R.S. in 1885, and was an honorary member of the New York Medical Society and a corresponding member of the Academy of Medicine of Paris. He died of apoplexy on 14 Oct. 1910 at Lastingham, Yorkshire, and was buried there. He married Ann, daughter of Henry Darley of Aldby Park near York, and had issue two daughters.

[Brit. Med. Journ. 1910, ii. 1384; Proc. Roy. Soc. 84 A; private information.] H. D. R.

RIPON, first MARQUIS OF. [See ROBINSON, GEORGE FREDERICK SAMUEL (1827–1909), statesman.]

RISLEY, SIR HERBERT HOPE (1851–1911), Indian civil servant and anthropologist, was born on 4 Jan. 1851 at Akeley, Buckinghamshire, where his father, John Risley, was rector. His mother was Frances, daughter of John Hope, at one time residency surgeon of Gwalior. The Risley family for centuries held a high position in the county and in Oxfordshire. On 13 July 1863 he was elected in open competition a scholar of Winchester, a privilege which his ancestors had for many generations enjoyed by the mere right of founder's kin. He won there the Goddard scholarship and the Queen's gold medal, and on 30 July 1869 obtained a scholarship at New College, Oxford. He passed on 29 April 1871 the competitive examination for the Indian civil service, but he graduated B.A. in 1872 with a second class in law and modern history, before he joined the service on 3 June 1873. Posted to Midnapur as assistant collector he entered at once into the interests of district life, and until his death, despite the calls of duties in the secretariat, he cultivated an intimate knowledge of the peoples of India. At a 'domum' dinner at Winchester in 1910 he asserted that 'a knowledge of facts concerning the religions and habits of the peoples of India equips a civil servant with a passport to their affection.' His zeal for work and his literary power early attracted the attention of the government, and Sir William Wilson Hunter [q. v. Suppl. I], then engaged on the compilation of the 'Gazetteer of Bengal' as director-general of statistics, made Risley on 15 Feb. 1875 one of his assistants. The chapter on Chota Nagpur was written by him. Within five years of his arrival in India he rose from assistant secretary to be under-secretary in Bengal, and in 1879 was promoted to the imperial secretariat as under-secretary to the government of India in the home department. But despite this unusually rapid promotion his heart was still in the districts, and by his own wish he reverted to them, going to Govindpur in 1880, Hazaribagh, and then to Manbhum, where he superintended the survey of Ghatwali and other lands held on service tenure. In Jan. 1885 he was employed on the congenial task of compiling statistics relating to the castes and occupations of the people of Bengal. He thus acquired a wide acquaintance with scientific authorities in Europe, including Professor Popinard, whose system of anthropological research Risley applied to India. His work on 'Tribes and Castes of Bengal' (Calcutta, 1891–2) was well received by the public as well as the government, and he was made an officier d'académie by the French government in 1891. Next year he received the C.I.E. In 1898 he was acting financial secretary to the government of India. In 1899 he was appointed census commissioner, and chapter vi. on Ethnology and Caste in vol. i. of the 'Imperial Gazetteer of India' (1907) is an epitome of his monumental contribution to the 'Census Report,' 1901, on that subject. From the date of his report a new chapter was opened in Indian official literature, and the census volumes, until then regarded as dull, were at once read and reviewed in every country. In 1901 he became director of ethnography for India, and next year secretary to the government of India in the home department, acting for a short time as member of council. He had served as member and secretary to the police commission in 1890, and his special knowledge was of great value to Lord Curzon in many administrative matters, including the partition of Bengal. When the administrative reforms suggested by Lord Morley came under the consideration of Lord Minto in 1908–9, Risley proved an admirable instrument for the work in hand. With clear judgment and rare facility of expression Risley excavated from an enormous mass of official documents the main issues on reform, enlarged councils, and administrative changes (cf. *Blue Books*, 1909), and he submitted the needful points to Lord Minto's council. Although every provincial government held different views, Risley directed the members of council to conclusions and compromises, and finally put their orders into resolutions, regulations, and laws. He was created C.S.I. in 1904 and K.C.I.E. in 1907. In 1910 he returned to England to fill the post of secretary in the public and judicial department at the India office in London.

Despite the pressure of his secretariat labours Risley continued to pursue his study of ethnography and anthropometry. He became president of the Royal Anthropological Institute in Jan. 1910. On the processes by which non-Aryan tribes are admitted into Hinduism he was recognised to be the greatest living authority, and he established by anthropometric investigation the fact that the Kolarians south of Bengal are not to be distinguished from their Dravidian neighbours. He strongly advocated the addition of ethnology to the necessary training of civilians for work in India. His chief contributions to literature, besides those already cited, were, 'Anthropometric Data' (2 vols. Calcutta, 1891) and 'Ethnographical Glossary' (2 vols. Calcutta, 1892); the 'Gazetteer of Sikhim: Introductory Chapter' (Calcutta, 1894); and 'The People of India' (Calcutta, 1908). His work completely revolutionised the native Indian view of ethnological inquiry. 'Twenty years ago in his own province of Bengal inquiries into the origin of caste and custom by men of alien creed were resented. Ethnology is now one of the recognised objects of investigation of the Vangiya Sahitya Parisat' (Mr. J. D. Anderson in *Roy. Anthropol. Record*, Jan. 1912).

Risley died at Wimbledon on 30 Sept. 1911, pursuing almost to the last his favourite studies despite distressing illness. He was buried in the Wimbledon cemetery.

He married at Simla, on 17 June 1879, Elsie Julie, daughter of Friedrich Oppermann of Hanover, who survived him with a son, Crescent Gebhard, born in Oct. 1881, captain of the 18th King George's Own Lancers, Indian army, and a daughter, Sylvia.

[The Times, 3 Oct. 1911; Man, a monthly record of anthropological science, Jan. 1912; Buckland's Indian Biography; Parliamentary Blue Books, and official reports; Records of Buckinghamshire, vol. iii. no. 6.] W. L–W.

RITCHIE, CHARLES THOMSON, first Baron Ritchie of Dundee (1838–1906), statesman, born on 19 Nov. 1838 at Hawkhill, Dundee, was the fourth son in a family of six sons and two daughters of William Ritchie, a landed proprietor, of Rockhill, Broughty Ferry, Forfarshire, head of the firm of William Ritchie & Son of London and Dundee, East India merchants, jute spinners, and manufacturers. His mother was Elizabeth, daughter of James Thomson. The Ritchies had been connected with the burgh of Dundee for two centuries. The second son, James Thomson Ritchie (1835–1912), became an alderman of the City of London, served as sheriff in 1896–7, was lord mayor from 1903 to 1904, and was created a baronet on 15 Dec. 1903. The father designed his sons for a business life, and Charles, after education at the City of London School, which he entered in September 1849 and left in July 1853, passed immediately into the London office of his father's firm. In 1858, while still under twenty, he married Margaret, a daughter of Thomas Ower of Perth. For the next sixteen years (1858–74) Ritchie's time was almost wholly absorbed by the business of the firm, of which he soon became a partner. His offices lay in the

East End of London, and he thus enjoyed opportunities of studying conditions of life among the poorer classes. He interested himself in politics, adopting a toryism which was from the first of a 'progressive' type. In 1874 he was elected in the conservative interest member for the great working-class constituency of the Tower Hamlets amid the tory reaction which followed Gladstone's first administration. For the first time the constituency, which had two members, returned a tory. Ritchie headed the poll with 7228 votes—a majority of 1328 over the liberal, J. D'Aguilar Samuda, who was his colleague in the representation. The older tories regarded him with some suspicion, and he was termed a 'radical' when, in meeting his constituents after his first session, he described his work in the House of Commons (report of speech in *Observer*, 3 Oct. 1874). In his second session he increased his popularity with the working classes of East London by securing the passage of a bill extending the application of the Bank Holiday Act of 1871 to dockyard and customs house employees (24 Nov. 1875).

During the Disraeli government of 1874–1880 and later he devoted much of his parliamentary activity to the grievances of the English sugar refiners and the colonial growers of cane-sugar, notably in the West Indies, owing to the bounties paid in European countries upon the exportation of sugar beet. On 22 April 1879 he moved that a select committee should be appointed to 'consider the question and to report whether in their opinion any remedial measures could be devised by Parliament.' He suggested 'a countervailing duty equivalent to the bounty.' He defined free trade as 'the circulation of commodities at their natural value,' the natural value being what they would bring in free competition, but he deprecated the identification of his opinion either with protection or what is called reciprocity.' The proposed duty would be only 'an establishment of the principles of free trade, which had been practically destroyed by the bounties.' The motion was opposed by Mr. (now Lord) Courtney, but the committee was appointed, and Ritchie became chairman of it. The result was a recommendation in favour of the abolition of the continental bounties by means of an international agreement. The inquiry began a campaign against the economic system which was exemplified in the policy of sugar-bounties. Ritchie followed up the question in the next parliament, and found himself in conflict with Mr. Joseph Chamberlain, then president of the board of trade and an advocate of free imports. Many years later, in a speech at Tynemouth (21 Oct. 1903), when both Ritchie's and Mr. Chamberlain's views of free trade had undergone a reversal, Mr. Chamberlain recalled the curious 'chassé-croisé' which characterised their positions (*Imperial Union and Tariff Reform: Speeches by J. Chamberlain*, 1903, p. 109).

In the general election of March–April 1880 Ritchie was again chosen for the Tower Hamlets, no fewer than 11,720 votes being cast for him, but the first place at the poll was taken by a liberal, Mr. James Bryce, who obtained 12,020 votes. By vigorous criticism of the Gladstonian government, together with his work on the sugar bounty question, he acquired as a private member a reputation for business ability and a mastery of detail. After the Redistribution Act of 1885 Ritchie won the seat of St. George's-in-the-East. He was first elected on 20 Nov. 1885 and was re-elected on 6 July 1888.

In Lord Salisbury's first administration of June 1885 to Jan. 1886, Ritchie was first admitted to office, becoming financial secretary to the admiralty. During his seven months' tenure of this post he acted as chairman of a departmental committee to inquire into the general management and working of the dockyards and especially to investigate the causes of the slowness with which warships were turned out. The committee's recommendations resulted in a great acceleration in the process of shipbuilding and a considerable reduction in cost. Up to that time the construction and equipment of a first-class ironclad had taken on an average about seven years. The Royal Sovereign, a battleship of 14,000 tons, was built in two years and eight months (1888–91).

After the defeat of Gladstone's home rule government in July of 1886 and the return of the conservatives to power, Ritchie was appointed president of the local government board—at first without a seat in the cabinet. Mr. Henry Chaplin had been offered and had refused the post on the ground of its holder being excluded from the cabinet. But the conservatives had put the reform of local government among the first of the measures on their programme, and in April 1887, when the government decided to deal comprehensively with the subject, Ritchie received cabinet rank. For nearly a year he was occupied in the preparation of a voluminous measure dealing with the subject. On 19 March

1888 he introduced the local government bill (for England and Wales) into the House of Commons, in a speech which Gladstone called 'a very frank, a very lucid, and a very able statement.' It was a complicated measure, with its 162 clauses, its five schedules, and its eighty folio pages of amendments. The general aim almost amounted to a social revolution. In place of the nominated magistrates who in quarter sessions had hitherto managed the business of the county it established for administrative purposes councils elected by the ratepayers to be independent of any but parliamentary control. Their business was to include the levying of county rates, the maintenance of roads and hedges, lunatic asylums, industrial and reformatory schools, registration, weights and measures, and such matters as adulteration of food and drugs. The management of the county police, meanwhile, was transferred to a joint committee of quarter sessions and the county council, the appointment of chief constable remaining with quarter sessions. Together with the sanitary authorities already existing, the county councils were to enforce the provisions of the Rivers Pollution Act; and all such powers of the local government board as related to piers, harbours, electric lighting, gas and water, tramways, the administration of the Sale of Food and Drugs Acts, the settlement of boundary disputes, and so on, were to be transferred to them. They were also to have the power to promote emigration by making advances to emigrants, and their administration of funds raised by the imperial executive was further widened by the power to increase the contribution towards the cost of maintaining indoor paupers. The act further provided for the distribution of the 'county'—a geographical unit to be retained, as far as possible, as it existed—into equal electoral divisions, with one member for each, the number of divisions being fixed by the local government board, and the council being purely elective with co-opted aldermen.

London received separate treatment in the bill. Together with certain other large towns it was made a county in itself, and an elected council, with co-opted aldermen, superseded the Metropolitan Board of Works. The metropolitan police, however, were left under the control of the home office, as being a national and not a municipal force, and the City of London proper was to remain the same as a quarter sessions borough. While many of its administrative duties were transferred to the London county council the City Corporation was exempted from the general condemnation of all unreformed corporations.

As originally drafted Ritchie's bill provided for the creation of district councils and included a readjustment of the licensing laws, making the county councils the licensing authority and authorising them to refuse the renewal of licences, with compensation to the licence holder. These clauses, which embodied the principle of compensation for interference with public houses, and so recognised a legal vested interest on the part of the licence-holder, were warmly contested by the temperance party, and, after considerable discussion, they were dropped (June 12). The establishment of district councils was relinquished also; but under the Local Government Act of 1894 this part of Ritchie's work was completed six years later by the liberals.

Some extreme tories, particularly in the City of London, censured the bill, but its reception was generally favourable as being 'a great work of safe and moderate decentralisation' bound to 'reinvigorate the local energies of our people' (*The Times*, 20 March 1888). Ritchie's management of its complicated details in committee, his mastery of every point and phase of it, his good temper, and his clearness in explanation, constituted a parliamentary achievement of the first order, and when the bill was read a third time and passed on 27 July 1888, Sir William Harcourt, amid universal cheering, paid a warm tribute to the 'ability, the conciliatory temper, and the strong common-sense' he had displayed (*Hansard*, vol. 329, 3rd series). The bill received the royal assent on 13 Aug. 1888, and came into force next year. A similar bill for Scotland became law in Aug. 1889.

In addition to the Local Government Act, Ritchie was responsible, while at the local government board, for the Allotments Acts of 1887 and 1890; for the Infectious Diseases Notification Act of 1889; and for the Housing of the Working Classes Amendment and Consolidation Acts of July 1890. His power of mastering and classifying enormous masses of detail was again shown in his two Public Health Acts, involving the vast and complicated machinery which controls the sanitary condition of London. The first of these, introduced on 8 April 1891, was a consolidation bill which put in order the chaos of twenty-nine Acts already treating of the subject; the second and more important was the public health amendment bill for the metropolis, which was read for a third time on 27 June 1891, and, in its final form, represented the results of the best sanitary knowledge of the day. Ritchie's poor law administration showed the sympathetic spirit with which he always approached the study of the welfare of the poorest classes.

Ritchie's six years at the local government board fully established his reputation as an administrator who brought to political work the sound common-sense trained in years of business life. At the general election of 1892 he was defeated in the contest at St. George's-in-the-East. A liberal government returned to power, and Ritchie was out of parliament until 1895. At a bye-election on 24 May of that year he was chosen for Croydon without a contest. The liberal government resigned in the following June, and in Lord Salisbury's third administration Ritchie again accepted a seat in the cabinet, being made president of the board of trade. In that capacity Ritchie was responsible for much useful legislation, touching the railway, marine, commercial, labour, and statistical departments of the board.

His first important measure was the Conciliation Act of 1896, which established conciliation boards for the settlement of labour disputes. The board of trade was authorised to formulate regulations of procedure and thus first exercised the power of negotiating in trade disputes. Between the passing of the Act in 1896 and the end of Ritchie's presidency in 1900, the number of cases so dealt with was 113, seventy of which were settled under the Act (*Official Memorandum of the Board of Trade*). In Feb. 1898 his personal intervention put an end to an eight months' strike in the engineering trade. Another useful measure of the same year (1896) was the Light Railways Act, which embodied experience gained by Ritchie on visits to France and Belgium. The Act provides that light railways may be proposed by any local authority and, if their proposals are approved by the commissioners appointed to consider them, they may take the necessary land, after paying a fair valuation, by compulsion, and may proceed with the work without obtaining parliamentary sanction. In 1897 Ritchie appointed a very important departmental committee on commercial intelligence, which was required to consider the best means whereby British manufacturers might obtain information as to the most favourable markets for their goods in the colonies and in India. As a result of the committee's report, there was established in October 1899 a new intelligence branch of the commercial, labour, and statistical departments of the board of trade (*Board of Trade Memorandum*). A Merchant Shipping (Mercantile Marine Fund) Act which was passed by Ritchie in 1898 was based upon the recommendations of a committee appointed by Mr. James Bryce in 1894 and presided over by Mr. Leonard (now Lord Courtney). Its most important provision was an allowance to shipowners for carrying boys who enrol themselves in the royal naval reserve. The intention was to check the serious decline in the numbers of British-born merchant seamen, who were estimated to have decreased at the rate of more than a thousand annually during the past five years and were in regard to foreign sailors in the proportion of one to three. Under Ritchie's Act the British boy sailors in the reserve numbered 302 in 1899–1900, the first year of its operation, and 2230 on 31 March 1903.

The growth of fatal or serious accidents amongst railway servants (1896–8) led Ritchie to procure the appointment of a royal commission of inquiry, with the result that he passed in 1900 the Railway Employment (Prevention of Accidents) Act, which dealt fully with the means of increased protection. Ritchie's Companies Act of 26 June 1900, which was practically a bill passed by a select committee of the House of Commons appointed in 1894 (*Parliamentary Debates*, vol. 84, 4th series), endeavoured to strengthen the existing law against fraudulent and inflated companies.

At the general election of September 1900 Ritchie was returned for Croydon unopposed. The conservatives retained their majority, but in November 1900 Lord Salisbury made some changes in the ministry, and Ritchie was transferred from the board of trade to the home office in succession to Sir Matthew White Ridley [q. v. Suppl. II]. His administration of the board of trade, which had shown diligence, conciliatory spirit, and powers of clarifying confusion, had greatly improved the repute of the department.

As home secretary, one of Ritchie's earliest duties was to carry out the ancient ceremonies incident to the death, after a reign of sixty-three years, of Queen Victoria, with whom his personal relations were always cordial. Soon afterwards Ritchie undertook an elaborate and complicated

Factory and Workshop Act which, in its 163 clauses and seven schedules, consolidated and amended the whole of the Factory Acts since 1878. Another useful Act, the Youthful Offenders Act, provided that in some instances young offenders on remand should be committed to the charge of some responsible person, instead of being sent either to prison or to the workhouse; and also that when offences committed by children could be directly traced to the habitual and wilful negligence of parents or guardians, the latter should be liable to prosecution. On 30 Jan. 1902, also, he introduced a licensing bill, the first part of which strengthened the law against the individual drunkard, while the second authorised a summary refusal of licences of offending publicans on the annual applications for renewal. The bill also put all retail licences absolutely under the control of the justices and provided for the registration of all clubs (*Parliamentary Debates*, vol. 101, 4th series).

In August 1902 Lord Salisbury resigned the post of prime minister, and Mr. Balfour, his successor, reconstructed the cabinet. Ritchie accepted with reluctance the office of chancellor of the exchequer. In the first place, as he explained to Mr. Balfour, he unwillingly left a post which was very congenial; and secondly, he was apprehensive of the favour bestowed by the colonial secretary, Mr. Chamberlain, on colonial preference, with which he felt himself out of agreement, but in regard to which, as finance minister, he would have special responsibilities. His hope that the question would not soon arise in an acute form was disappointed. Mr. Chamberlain and a section of the cabinet argued for a reconsideration of the tariff system, with a measure of preference for the colonies, and the argument soon took a practical turn. Ritchie's predecessor, Sir Michael Hicks-Beach (afterwards Viscount St. Aldwyn), had in the budget of April 1902 imposed on corn an import duty of one shilling a quarter, which was estimated to bring in two and a half millions annually. Although it was regarded as little more than a registration duty, Mr. Chamberlain now desired to retain it as a first step towards granting preference to the colonies, and before leaving for South Africa in December he pressed the cabinet to continue it in this guise. Ritchie declined to commit himself to the imposition or remission of a particular tax so long before the end of the financial year. He declared in any case the shilling duty on corn to be a mere incident in the budget, and that he had no objection to retaining it provided that it was not to be treated as a differentiation or preferential duty or as an earnest of a new fiscal policy which could only be adopted after mature consideration as part of a specifically declared policy. The cabinet decided in favour of Mr. Chamberlain's arguments; Ritchie registered his dissent, and was assured that the matter would come on later for further consideration. During Mr. Chamberlain's absence in South Africa Ritchie several times informed the prime minister of his inability to act on the decision of the cabinet. That information was communicated to Mr. Chamberlain on his return. Mr. Chamberlain replied that if he could not secure the corn duty for preferential purposes, he did not care to have it at all. The cabinet thereupon accepted Ritchie's recommendation to remit the duty.

On 23 April 1903 Ritchie introduced his first and only budget. The war in South Africa was at an end. The financial situation, however, did not allow the chancellor to remit all the war taxes, but, on the basis of the existing taxation, he budgeted for a surplus of 10,816,000*l.*, and therewith he took fourpence off the income-tax. At the same time he dropped the shilling a quarter duty on corn.

The abolition of the corn tax was resented by the supporters of Mr. Chamberlain and by a large section of the unionist party. On 15 May 1903 Mr. Chaplin headed a deputation to Mr. Balfour asking that it should be retained. The prime minister made a moderate reply, with which Ritchie stated that he was in complete agreement; but on the same day Mr. Chamberlain at Birmingham, in an impassioned speech in favour of a policy of preference, 'initiated the acute stage of the fiscal controversy' (BALFOUR, *Fiscal Reform Speeches*, p. 16). During the debate on the finance bill on 9 and 10 June 1903 the differences within the cabinet were more clearly defined. Ritchie declared himself to be a freetrader. He declined to be (see *Parliamentary Debates*, 4th series, vol. 123) 'a party to a policy which, in my opinion, would be detrimental to both the country and the colonies.' Ritchie's budget received the royal assent without alteration on 30 June.

The breach in the cabinet thenceforth developed rapidly. Mr. Chamberlain came to the conclusion that he could best forward his views as to imperial preference from without. He sent his resignation to Mr. Balfour from Birmingham on 9 September, and it was accepted by the prime minister in a personal interview on 14 September. The cabinet met later in the day. As a result of its deliberations Ritchie and Lord George Hamilton resigned. They were without any knowledge of Mr. Chamberlain's earlier withdrawal, and were under the impression that he was committing the cabinet to a protective policy. Their resignations were published on 18 September with, to their astonishment, that also of Mr. Chamberlain. The duke of Devonshire alone of Mr. Balfour's free-trade colleagues had learned of Mr. Chamberlain's withdrawal before the cabinet meeting, and he remained for the time in the cabinet. Lord Balfour of Burleigh, the remaining free trade minister, resigned on the 21st. Much controversy ensued between Ritchie and his friends on the one hand and Mr. Balfour and the protectionists of the cabinet on the other. The prime minister, who in his endeavour to keep his party together had avoided any but indefinite pronouncements on the fiscal question, had yet in his 'Economic Notes on Insular Free Trade' (published September 1903, but circulated earlier as a cabinet memorandum) 'approached the subject from the free trade point of view.' Between him and Ritchie there was at the time no extreme divergence of view. It was solely the presence of Mr. Chamberlain in the cabinet that made Ritchie's retention of office impossible. Had Mr. Chamberlain's retirement been announced to Ritchie, the ground for his own resignation at the moment would have been removed. Mr. Balfour replied in later speeches that he and the majority of the cabinet inclined to some kind of change in the fiscal system, and that Ritchie and his free trade colleagues were in opposition on that point to the majority; that Mr. Chamberlain had already threatened resignation if preference were excluded from the official programme of the government, to which it was not admitted; and that Ritchie's dissent from views expressed by himself in a valedictory letter to Mr. Chamberlain (17 Sept. 1903) showed that he would have retired in any case a day or two after he actually did go (see BALFOUR, *Fiscal Reform Speeches*, p. 143). Ritchie and his friends retorted that Mr. Chamberlain's *verbal* announcements of resignation had been frequent in the heat of controversy and were not taken seriously. After the withdrawal of Ritchie and his friends the prime minister's pronouncements leant more decisively to the side of the tariff reformers, with the result that the duke of Devonshire parted from him on 2 October. On 19 Oct. 1903 at Croydon, on 18 November at Thornton Heath, and finally at Croydon on 2 December, Ritchie defended his attitude throughout the fiscal controversy. 'So far as Mr. Balfour's policy of retaliation is concerned he had never said . . . that he would not be prepared to adopt it.' 'What he had said was, that "we will be no parties to any arrangement with the colonies which shall impose upon us the necessity for putting a tax upon the food of the people"' (speech at Thornton Heath in *Daily Chronicle*, 19 Nov. 1903).

With his resignation and his public explanation Ritchie's public life ceased, though in the sessions of 1904 and 1905 he spoke more than once in the House of Commons in support of free trade principles. On 10 Feb. 1905 he suffered a severe blow in the death of his wife after forty-seven years of mutual attachment and happiness. It is doubtful if he recovered from the shock. The resignation of Mr. Balfour's government came on 17 Dec. 1905, and five days later Ritchie was raised to the peerage as Baron Ritchie of Dundee, of Welders, Chalfont St. Giles, co. Buckingham, his country residence. But he was not to enjoy the honour long. A few days before Christmas he went to Biarritz on a visit to Lord and Lady Dudley, and while there was stricken with paralysis. He died at Biarritz on 9 Jan. 1906, and was buried at Kensal Green. He left nine children—two sons and seven daughters. A first-born son, William, predeceased him. His elder surviving son, Charles Ritchie, succeeded him in the peerage.

Ritchie was tall and very dark, with something of a Southerner's swarthiness of complexion. His portrait by John Pettie, R.A., belongs to the present Lord Ritchie. A bust by E. Roscoe Mullins was exhibited at the Royal Academy in 1889. A cartoon portrait by 'Ape' appeared in 'Vanity Fair' in 1885.

Ritchie was never as well known to the public as might have been expected from the usefulness of his political work. He lacked the qualities which make for popularity. Clear and persuasive as a speaker in the House of Commons, he was not an effective platform speaker. In his own constituency of Croydon he was mercilessly interrupted and several times shouted down when defending his fiscal views. But his grasp of complicated detail and his shrewd common-sense gave him substantial influence in the inner circle of his party. An unconciliatory manner repelled many members of his own side, although his circle of personal friends was wide. He seldom entertained, and took scarcely any part in the social side of politics.

[Private information; personal knowledge; official memoranda and letters; The Times, and Daily Telegraph, 10 Jan. 1906; reports of speeches, &c., from the Dundee Advertiser and Croydon Advertiser; Hansard's Parliamentary Debates from 1874 to 1892 and from 1895 to 1906; The Times Parliamentary Debates, vol. vii. (speeches on introduction of local government bill); Annual Register for 1888, 1889, 1890, 1895–1900, 1903, and 1906; Debrett's Peerage; Our Conservative and Unionist Statesmen, vol. i. (with portrait from good photograph); articles Balfour, Chamberlain, and Duke of Devonshire in Encyclopædia Britannica, 11th edit.; Lucy's Diary of Two Parliaments, 1888; Imperial Union and Tariff Reform speeches by J. Chamberlain, 1903; Fiscal Reform Speeches by A. J. Balfour, 1906; Jenks's English Local Government, 2nd edit. 1907; L. Gomme's The London County Council: its Duties and Powers according to the Local Government Act of 1888; Arthur Elliot's Life of Lord Goschen, 1911; Holland's Life of Duke of Devonshire, 1911; Annals of our Time, by H. Hamilton Fyfe, 1887–1891; Herbert Paul's A History of Modern England, vol. v.; Sidney Low and L. C. Sanders, Political History of England; Speeches of Lord Randolph Churchill, ed. by L. J. Jennings, vol. ii.] R. J.

RITCHIE, DAVID GEORGE (1853–1903), philosopher, born at Jedburgh on 26 Oct. 1853, was only son of three children of George Ritchie, D.D., minister of the parish and a man of scholarship and culture, who was elected to the office of moderator of the general assembly of the Church of Scotland in 1870. His mother was Elizabeth Bradfute Dudgeon. The family was connected with the Carlyles, and in 1889 Ritchie edited a volume of 'Early Letters of Jane Welsh Carlyle.'

Ritchie received his early schooling at Jedburgh Academy. Not allowed to make friends with other boys of his own age, he never learned to play games, and lived a solitary life, concentrating his mind rather too early on purely intellectual subjects. He matriculated in 1869 at Edinburgh University, where he made a special study of classics under Professors W. Y. Sellar [q.v.] and J. S. Blackie [q.v. Suppl. I], while he began to study philosophy under Prof. Campbell Fraser, in whose class and in that of Prof. Henry Calderwood [q. v. Suppl. I] (on moral philosophy) he gained the highest prizes. After graduating M.A. at Edinburgh in 1875 with first-class honours in classics, Ritchie gained a classical exhibition at Balliol College, Oxford, and won a first-class both in classical moderations (Michaelmas 1875) and in the final classical school (Trinity term, 1878). In 1878 he became a fellow of Jesus College and in 1881 a tutor. From 1882 to 1886 he was also a tutor at Balliol College. At Oxford Ritchie came under the influence of Thomas Hill Green [q.v.] and Arnold Toynbee [q. v.], and it was during his early life there that the foundations were laid both of his interest in idealistic philosophy associated with the name of Hegel, and also of his strong bent towards practical politics; his political philosophy was dominated by the belief that practical action must be derived from principles.

In 1894 Ritchie left Oxford on being appointed professor of logic and metaphysics at St. Andrews University. At the time the university was in the midst of a turmoil of conflicting interests which involved litigation and much party feeling. In this conflict Ritchie supported the side of progress, which ultimately prevailed. He remained at St. Andrews until his death on 3 Feb. 1903, and was buried there.

Ritchie was made hon. LL.D. of Edinburgh in 1898, and was president of the Aristotelian Society in 1898–9.

Ritchie married twice: (1) in 1881 Flora Lindsay, daughter of Col. A. A. Macdonell of Lochgarry, and sister of Professor A. A. Macdonell of Oxford (she died in 1888); (2) in 1889 Ellen, sister of Professor J. B. Haycraft. He left a daughter by the first marriage and a son by the second.

Both at Oxford and at St. Andrews Ritchie wrote much on ethics and political philosophy. One of his earliest writings was an essay on 'The Rationality of History,' contributed to 'Essays in Philosophical Criticism,' written in 1883 by a number of young men influenced largely by Hegel and his interpreters, and edited by Professor Andrew Seth (afterwards Pringle-Pattison) and Mr. R. B. (afterwards Viscount) Haldane. In 1885 he translated with Professor Richard Lodge and Mr. P. E. Matheson, 'Bluntschli's Theory of the State,' and he published 'Darwinism and Politics' in 1889. In 1891 was published his 'Principles of State Interference,' and in 1893 his 'Darwin and Hegel.' After leaving Oxford Ritchie published 'Natural Rights' (1895); 'Studies in Political and Social Ethics,' and 'Plato' (both in 1902). He was also a contributor to 'Mind,' the 'Philosophical Review,' the 'International Journal of Ethics,' and kindred periodicals. After his death a collection of 'Philosophical Studies' was issued in 1905, edited with a memoir by Prof. Robert Latta of Glasgow.

Of an absolutely simple and unaffected nature, Ritchie pursued the truth he set himself to seek with an entire devotion. Despite his retiring manner, he had many friends. He held strongly that questions of ethics and politics must be regarded from the metaphysical point of view. For him the foundation of ethics necessarily rested on the ideal end of social well-being, and keeping this end in view, he proceeded to trace its history at different times, the manner in which it shapes itself in the mind of each individual, and the way in which it can be developed and realised. Ritchie was an advanced liberal with socialistic leanings. He considered that the ultimate value of religion depended on the ideal it set before mankind when represented in its highest form.

[Philosophical Studies, by D. G. Ritchie, with Memoir by Prof. Robert Latta, 1905; Prof. E. B. Poulton's Memoir of John Viriamu Jones, 1911.] E. S. H.

ROBERTS, ALEXANDER (1826–1901), classical and biblical scholar, born at Marykirk, Kincardineshire, on 12 May 1826, was son of Alexander Roberts, a flax-spinner. He was educated at the grammar school and King's College, Old Aberdeen, where he graduated M.A. in March 1847, being the Simpson Greek prizeman. He was presbyterian minister (1852–71) in Scotland and London. In 1864, being then minister at Carlton Hill, London, he was made D.D. of Edinburgh. He was also minister at St. John's Wood, and was a member of the New Testament revision company (1870–84). In 1872 he succeeded John Campbell Shairp [q. v.] in the chair of humanity at St. Andrews; he was made emeritus professor in 1899. He died at St. Andrews, Mitcham Park, Surrey, on 8 March 1901. He married on 2 Dec. 1852 Mary Anne Speid (*d.* 18 Jan. 1911), and had fourteen children, of whom four sons and eight daughters survived him.

Roberts co-operated with Sir James Donaldson as editor and part translator of the English versions of ecclesiastical writers published as the 'Ante-Nicene Christian Library' (1867–72, 24 vols.); he translated also the 'Works of Sulpitius Severus' (1895) in the 'Select Library of Nicene and Post-Nicene Fathers.' He is best known for the series of works in which he maintains that Greek was the habitual speech of our Lord, a conclusion which has not met with general favour, despite the ability with which Roberts managed his case.

He published: 1. 'The Threefold Life,' 1858, 12mo. 2. 'Inquiry into the Original Language of St. Matthew's Gospel,' 1859. 3. 'Discussions on the Gospels,' 2 pts. 1862; 2nd edit. 1864. 4. 'The Life and Work of St. Paul practically considered,' 1867. 5. 'The Words of the New Testament,' Edinburgh, 1873 (in conjunction with William Milligan [q. v. Suppl. I], a work of textual criticism). 6. 'Hints to Beginners in Latin Composition,' Edinburgh, 1873. 7. 'The Bible of Christ and His Apostles,' 1879. 8. 'Companion to the Revised Version of the English New Testament,' 1881; 3rd edit. 1885 (reprinted, New York, 1881, with supplement by an American reviser). 9. 'Old Testament Revision,' 1883. 10. 'Greek the Language of Christ and His Apostles,' 1888. 11. 'A Short Proof that Greek was the Language of Christ,' Paisley, 1893.

[Who's Who, 1901; The Times, 11 March 1901; Athenæum, 16 March 1901; P. J. Anderson's Officers and Graduates of King's College, Aberdeen, 1893, p. 299; Calendar of St. Andrews University, 1910, p. 676; Alphabetical List of Graduates, Edinb. Univ. (1859–1888), 1889, p. 114; information from Mr. J. Maitland Anderson.] A. G.

ROBERTS, ISAAC (1829–1904), amateur astronomer, son of William Roberts, a farmer of Groes, near Denbigh, North Wales, was born at that place on 27 Jan. 1829; though in childhood he left Wales with his family for Liverpool, he retained a knowledge of Welsh through life. In 1844 he was apprenticed for seven years to the firm of John Johnson & Son, afterwards Johnson & Robinson, builders and lime burners, of Liverpool. One of the partners, Robinson, died in 1855, and Roberts was made manager. In the next year the surviving partner died. Roberts, after winding up the concern, began business for himself in 1859 as a builder in Liverpool, and being joined in 1862 by Mr. J. J. Robinson, son of his former master, the firm traded for a quarter of a century under the name of Roberts & Robinson, undertaking many large and important contracts in Liverpool and its neighbourhood. In 1888 Roberts retired with means sufficient to allow him to devote himself to scientific research. Whilst still occupied in business, very many branches of science had engaged his attention. Geology was the first subject that he took up seriously. He became a fellow of the Geological Society in 1870, and at the British Association meeting of 1878 he read a paper on the filtration of water through triassic sandstone. Between 1882 and 1889 he made an elaborate series of experiments on the movement of underground water as affected by barometric and lunar changes. A paper on a different subject, 'the determination of the vertical and lateral pressures of granular substances,' which appeared in the 'Proceedings of the Royal Society' for 31 Jan. 1884, embodied the results of elaborate experiments made for the purpose of furnishing data to engineers and builders of storehouses.

Meanwhile his attention had been turned to astronomical observation. In 1878 he had a 7-inch refractor by Cooke at his home at Rock Ferry, Birkenhead, which he used for visual observation, but a few years later he applied himself with zeal to the advancing practice of stellar photography. In 1883, a year after his removal to Kennessee, Maghull, near Liverpool, he experimented in photographing stars with ordinary portrait lenses varying in aperture between three-eighths of an inch and five inches. After consideration of the results of these experiments and comparisons with the photograph of the nebula in Orion by Andrew Ainslie Common [q. v. Suppl. II], he ordered from Grubb of Dublin a 20-inch silver-on-glass reflector of 100 inches focal length, the photographs to be taken directly in the focus of the mirror to obviate any loss of light by a second reflection, and the photographic telescope to be mounted on the same declination axis as the 7-inch refractor, one being the counterpoise of the other (*Monthly Notices R.A.S.* xlvi. 99).

At the meeting of the Royal Astronomical Society of January 1886, Roberts, who was at the time the president of the local Astronomical Society at Liverpool, reported taking during the past year 200 photographs of stars which might be measured for position, as well as long exposure photographs of the Orion nebula, the Andromeda nebula, and the Pleiades. At the November meeting in the same year he presented a photograph of the Pleiades taken with his 20-inch reflector with exposure of three hours, which showed the stars Alcyone, Maia, Merope, and Electra surrounded by nebulosity extending in streamers and fleecy masses till it seemed almost to fill the spaces between the stars and extend far beyond them. This photograph was accepted as revealing structure about the group never before seen or suspected. A photograph of the great nebula in Andromeda presented at the meeting of December 1888, which suggested that the object is of the spiral type, evoked considerable interest because it was supposed to illustrate the main idea of the nebular hypothesis. Photographs of the great nebula in Orion, presented a few months later, were equally successful. Roberts persistently urged the superiority of the reflector over the refracting telescope, a view which has since received much confirmation. In the early years of his work Roberts designed an instrument, the pantograver, an example of which was made for him by Mr. Hilger, for transferring mechanically the images on a photographic negative to a copper plate, to be used for making reproductions (*Monthly Notices*, Nov. 1888).

Roberts attended by invitation the Conference of Astronomers at Paris in 1887 which initiated the international survey of the heavens by photography, but took no part in the scheme, which was entrusted to professional astronomers at national observatories with instruments of a uniform type. In order to continue his work on the nebulæ and star clusters in a clearer atmosphere than that of Liverpool, he finally settled in 1890 at Crowborough Hill, Sussex, in a house appropriately named Starfield. There Mr. W. S. Franks, an astronomer and skilful photographer, became his working assistant, and Roberts confined himself to organisation and supervision. Month by month for several years he exhibited at the Royal Astronomical Society splendid photographs of remarkable objects in the sky taken with his reflector. Two volumes of selections of Roberts's photographs of stars, star clusters, and nebulæ, 125 reproductions in all, appeared respectively in 1893 and 1899. In 1896 Roberts, following the example of Professor Barnard in America, added to the equipment of his observatory cameras with portrait lenses of different types, in order to compare their photographic results with those of the reflecting telescope (cf. a discussion on the relative efficiency of the two methods between Roberts and Professor Barnard in *R.A.S. Monthly Notices*, lvi. 372, lvii. 10, lviii. 392). Between 1896 and 1902 Roberts prepared photographs of fifty-two regions of the sky called 'nebulous' by Sir William Herschel, made with his reflector and with a portrait lens of 5 inches aperture made by Messrs. Cooke of York. No diffused nebulosity was shown on forty-eight of these plates, a result which was not confirmed by Dr. Max-Wolf of Heidelberg, who made special examination of several cases (*Monthly Notices*, lxiii. 303). Roberts's report of this research was presented in November 1902 (*Monthly Notices*, lxiii. 26).

Roberts joined the Royal Astronomical Society in 1882. In 1890 he was elected a fellow of the Royal Society, and in 1892 the honorary degree of D.Sc. was conferred on him by Trinity College, Dublin, on the occasion of its tercentenary. In 1895 the Royal Astronomical Society awarded the gold medal to Roberts for his photographs of star clusters and nebulæ, the award being announced and the address being delivered by Captain (now Sir William) Abney, the leading authority on photography, who congratulated him on his 'conclusion that a reflector is better for his purpose than a refractor.' Roberts went to Vadso, Norway, on the Norse King, to observe the total solar eclipse of 9 August 1896, but an overcast sky prevented observations.

Roberts, who was a zealous liberal, interested himself in legislation affecting education. He was one of the governors of the University of North Wales. He died suddenly at Crowborough on 17 July 1904, and his cremated remains were entombed four years later in a stone in Birkenhead cemetery, Flaybrick Hill, Birkenhead, on 21 July 1908. After providing for his widow and other relatives, he left the residue of his large estate for the foundation of scholarships in the University of Liverpool and the university colleges of Wales, Bangor, and Cardiff.

He married (1) in 1875 Ellen Anne, daughter of Anthony Cartmel; and (2) in 1901 Dorothea Klumpke of San Francisco, a member of the staff of the National Observatory, Paris, who had been a fellow voyager on the Norse King in 1896. He had no children.

A photograph is in the British Museum series of portraits at South Kensington.

[Proceedings of the Royal Society, vol. lxxv.; Royal Astronomical Society Monthly Notices, vol. lxvi and as quoted; private information.]

H. P. H.

ROBERTS, ROBERT DAVIES (1851–1911), educational administrator, born at Aberystwyth on 5 March 1851, was eldest son of Richard Roberts, timber merchant and shipowner of that town. His early training was sternly Calvinistic, but he quickly developed, with a studious temper, versatile human interests and a spirit of adventure. From a private school at Shrewsbury he proceeded to the Liverpool Institute, and thence to University College, London. Here he distinguished himself in geology; he graduated B.Sc. in the University of London with first-class honours and scholarship in that subject in 1870. In 1871 he entered Cambridge University as foundation scholar of Clare College, graduating B.A. in 1875 as second (bracketed) in the first class of the natural science tripos. He proceeded M.A. at Cambridge and D.Sc. at London in 1878; and was from 1884 to 1890 fellow of Clare College. He became fellow of University College, London, in 1888.

Meanwhile Roberts was lecturer in chemistry at University College, Aberystwyth, during 1877, and in 1884 was appointed university lecturer in geology at Cambridge. In geological study, especially on its palæontological side, Roberts showed originality and imaginative powers. His 'Earth's History: an Introduction to Modern Geology' (1893) was well received both at home and in the United States.

But Roberts was diverted from a pursuit in which he promised to achieve distinction by an ambition to organise and develop higher education among the classes that were at that time not touched by the universities. In 1881 he had become assistant and organising secretary to the syndicate at Cambridge which had been formed in 1873 to control the 'local lectures' or 'university extension' work. He was here engaged in association with Professor James Stuart and Professor G. F. Browne, afterwards bishop of Bristol. From 1885 to 1904 he was secretary to the London Society for the Extension of University Teaching, which, in the absence of a teaching university in London, had been founded as an independent organisation to direct the work in the metropolitan area. In 1891 he published his 'Eighteen Years of University Extension,' which contains an admirable account of the movement down to that date. In 1894 he returned to Cambridge to take full charge of the work under the Cambridge syndicate; and eight years later he became the first registrar of the Extension Board in the recently reconstituted University of London. This post he held till his death. The university extension movement owed much to Roberts's long service of more than thirty years. He sought to establish and maintain a high standard of 'extension' lecture, encouraging among the local committees continuous courses of study (often extending over three years).

Devoted to Wales, he actively interested

himself in the affairs of the principality. In the new Welsh University he served as junior deputy chancellor (1903–5) and as chairman (1910–11) of the executive committee of the court, on which he sat as one of the representatives of the college of his native town. He was J.P. for Cardiganshire, and high sheriff of that county (1902–3). To qualify himself for such public work he had become a student of the Middle Temple, and, though he was not called to the bar, he made a considerable study of law.

Long a lecturer for the Gilchrist Educational Trust, he acted as its secretary from 1899 till his death, bringing the organisation to a high state of efficiency and inaugurating valuable developments.

Roberts, who held many minor educational offices, showed exceptional skill and tact as an organiser, inspired others with his own enthusiasm, perseverance, and breadth of outlook, and devoted himself unsparingly to the improvement of the educational opportunities of all classes. While he was a fervent liberal in general politics, his wide sympathy made him equally at home among the Northumbrian miners and in Cambridge common-rooms.

In 1911 he was appointed secretary of the Congress of the Universities of the Empire which the University of London, with the co-operation of the other British universities, organised for the summer of 1912. In June 1911 he attended a preliminary conference of Canadian universities at Montreal, and was making active preparation at home when he suddenly died of calcification of the coronary arteries at his house at Kensington on 14 Nov. 1911. His body was cremated at Golder's Green, and was subsequently buried with public honours at Aberystwyth. In his memory two scholarships for the encouragement of university extension work were founded by public subscription, the administration of the fund being undertaken by the Gilchrist trustees.

Roberts married in 1888 Mary, eldest daughter of Philip S. King of Brighton. He left no children, and by his will he bequeathed the ultimate residue of his estate to Aberystwyth College to form the nucleus of a fund which should provide for its professors periodic terms of release from their duties.

[The University Extension Bulletin of the Oxford, Cambridge, and London Work—Dr. R. D. Roberts memorial number, January 1912 (with photograph); University records; private information; personal knowledge.]

P. M. W.

ROBERTS-AUSTEN, Sir WILLIAM CHANDLER (1843–1902), metallurgist, born at Kennington, Surrey, on 3 March 1843, was eldest son of George Roberts, of Welsh descent, who was in the service of the Hudson's Bay Company, by his wife Maria Louisa, daughter of William Chandler, M.D., of Canterbury, of an old Kentish family which had intermarried with the Hulses and Austens. In 1885 he assumed, by royal licence, at the request of his uncle, Major Nathaniel Lawrence Austen of Haffenden and Camborne, in Kent, the name of Austen. After education at private schools, where he early showed a taste for science, he entered the Royal School of Mines, South Kensington, at eighteen, with the view of qualifying as a mining engineer, and obtained the associateship there in 1865. The same year he joined Thomas Graham [q. v.], master of the mint, as private assistant. In 1870 (shortly after Graham's death) he was appointed to the new post of 'chemist of the mint,' and from 1882 to his death was 'chemist and assayer.' He filled temporarily the office of deputy master between the death of Sir Horace Seymour in June 1902 and the appointment of Mr. William Grey Ellison-Macartney next year. While assayer he was responsible for the standard fineness of about 150,000,000*l.* of gold coin, over 30,000,000*l.* of imperial silver coin, and about 10,000,000*l.* of bronze and colonial silver coin (T. K. Rose). On all scientific and technical operations of coinage he became the leading authority in all parts of the world. From 1880 to 1902 Roberts-Austen was also professor of metallurgy at the Royal School of Mines, having succeeded Dr. John Percy [q. v.]. He proved an illuminating teacher.

Roberts-Austen freely placed his special knowledge at the public disposal, taking part in numerous official scientific inquiries. In 1897 he served on the treasury committee (of which Lord Rayleigh was chairman) to consider the desirability of establishing a national physical laboratory, and was in 1899 an original member of the war office explosives committee.

Roberts-Austen's researches largely dealt with alloys. He delivered five series of Cantor lectures at the Society of Arts (1884–90) on investigations in alloys, which are printed in the society's 'Journal.' In 1891 he exhibited at the Royal Society's soirée a new alloy of gold and aluminium which he discovered; it contained 78·4 per cent. of gold and 21·6 of aluminium, and was remarkable for its intense purple colour. As the outcome of a research on the effects of admixture of impurities on the mechanical properties of pure metals, the alloys-research committee of the Institution of Mechanical Engineers was established (1889), Roberts-Austen becoming 'reporter' to the committee and supplying five reports, a sixth being under revision at his death. In the first (1891) he described his automatic recording pyrometer, 'by means of which the temperature of furnaces or masses of metal, and the exact time at which each change in temperature occurs, are recorded in the form of a curve on a moving photographic plate.' The work of alloys-research he thus initiated is now carried on at the National Physical Laboratory. The practical value of these labours led the council of the institution to enroll him an honorary life member (*Annual Report Inst. Mechan. Eng.* 1898, pp. 5, 30).

Roberts-Austen, who was elected a fellow of the Royal Society on 3 June 1875, served on the council (1890–2), and was Bakerian lecturer for 1896, his subject being the diffusion of metals (*Phil. Trans.* vol. 187 A.). An original member of the Physical Society in 1874, he was the first secretary, and he acted also as honorary general secretary of the British Association, 1897–1902. As president of the Iron and Steel Institute (1899–1901) he rendered signal services during his term of office. From his hand, on 18 July 1899, Queen Victoria accepted the institute's Bessemer gold medal in commemoration of the progress made in the metallurgy of steel during her reign. He was elected in 1901 an honorary member of the Institution of Civil Engineers (where he gave the Forrest lecture on 23 April 1902), was a vice-president of the Chemical Society and of the Society of Arts, and member of various foreign societies. The University of Durham conferred the honorary degree of D.C.L. in 1897, and Victoria University, Manchester, that of D.Sc. in 1901. In 1889 he was created a chevalier of the Légion d'Honneur, France, and was made C.B. in 1890 and K.C.B. in 1899.

At the Royal Institution, the British Association meetings, and at the Chemical and other societies, Roberts-Austen held a high reputation as lecturer and demonstrator. His attractive personality made him socially popular; he had a keen sense of humour and was an admirable mimic. He was an intimate friend of Ruskin, whose works influenced him greatly in early life. He died at the Royal Mint on 22 Nov. 1902, and was buried at Canterbury.

He married in 1876 Florence Maude, youngest daughter of Richard William Alldridge, of Old Charlton, Kent; he had no issue.

Roberts-Austen's chief independent publication was 'An Introduction to Metallurgy' (1891; 6th edit. revised, 1910), a work indispensable to researchers in metallurgy. He contributed the article 'Metallography' in the 'Encyclopædia Britannica,' 10th edition. The Royal Society's 'Catalogue of Scientific Papers' enumerates seventy-four papers by Roberts-Austen, a few jointly with other authors (1868–1900). They deal with the absorption of hydrogen by electro-deposited iron, the analysis of alloys by means of the spectroscope (with Sir Norman Lockyer), the action of the projectile and of the explosives on the tubes of steel guns, and memoirs on the physical properties of metals and alloys. Before the Society of Arts he read, in 1895, a paper with Mrs. Lea Merritt on 'Mural Painting by the Aid of Soluble Silicates and Metallic Oxides.'

[Roy. Soc. Proc., vol. lxxv., and Roy. Soc. Catal.; Iron and Steel Inst. Journ., vol. lxii.; Inst. Civil Eng. Proc. vol. cli.; Inst. Mech. Eng. Proc. 1902 (pts. 3–5); Chem. Soc. Trans., vol. lxxxiii. (part i.); Phys. Soc. Proc., vol. xviii., and presidential address, 1903; Annual Reports, Royal Mint; Nature, vol. lxvii.; The Times, 24 Nov. 1902; Engineering, 28 Nov. 1902; Athenæum, 29 Nov. 1902; private information.] T. E. J.

ROBERTSON, DOUGLAS MORAY COOPER LAMB ARGYLL (1837–1909), ophthalmic surgeon, born in Edinburgh in 1837, was son of Dr. John Argyll Robertson, surgeon and lecturer in the extra-academical school of medicine and president of the Royal College of Surgeons of Edinburgh in 1846. His father took a special interest in ophthalmic surgery and was one of the founders of the Edinburgh Eye Dispensary in 1822. Douglas was educated successively at the Edinburgh Institution, at Neuwied in Germany, and at the universities of Edinburgh and St. Andrews. He graduated M.D. at St. Andrews in 1857, and in the same year was appointed house surgeon at the Royal Infirmary, Edinburgh. He then went to Berlin to study ophthalmic surgery under von Graefe. On his return to Edinburgh he acted for several sessions as assistant to Prof. John Hughes Bennett [q. v.], and in that capacity conducted the first course of practical physiology held in the University of Edinburgh. He was succeeded by Prof. William Rutherford [q.v. Suppl. I]. In 1862 he was admitted F.R.C.S. Edinburgh, and published his observations on Calabar Bean in the 'Edinburgh Medical Journal.' He proved that its alkaloid, physostigmin, more commonly known as eserin, led to constriction of the pupil of the eye and thus provided a satisfactory myotic, the want of which had long been felt by oculists. This discovery attracted universal attention and made the young Edinburgh surgeon famous. In 1867 he was appointed assistant ophthalmic surgeon to the Royal Infirmary under Dr. William Walker, whose colleague he became in 1870. In 1882 Dr. Walker retired, and Argyll Robertson remained the sole ophthalmic surgeon to the Infirmary until 1897, when he was appointed consulting surgeon. He lectured on his subject for many years during each summer session. In 1869–70 he published in the 'Edinburgh Medical Journal' the records of the cases which showed that disease of the spinal cord is sometimes associated with loss of light reflex of the pupil, which still retains its movement on accommodation. This condition was christened by common accord 'the Argyll Robertson pupil,' and its value as an aid to diagnosis has steadily increased.

Robertson was president of the Royal College of Surgeons of Edinburgh for 1886–7. He was the first president (1893–5) of the Ophthalmological Society of Great Britain to be chosen from the ophthalmic surgeons who practised outside London; he presided over the International Ophthalmological Congress in Edinburgh in 1894, and over the Edinburgh Medico-Chirurgical Society in 1896. In 1896 the University of Edinburgh conferred upon him the honorary degree of LL.D. He was also surgeon oculist in Scotland to Queen Victoria and later to King Edward VII.

Argyll Robertson attained much repute as a golfer. He won the gold medal of the Royal and Ancient Club five times, and that of the Honourable Company of Edinburgh Golfers thrice. He was the first captain of the Royal Colleges Golf Club and presented to it a handsome scratch medal, which is known by his name and is awarded annually for the best scratch score. This medal he won himself on two occasions. He was also fond of shooting and was a member of the Royal Archers of the King's Body-Guard for Scotland, and he was a good curler and fisherman.

Robertson was one of the earliest in the United Kingdom to adopt ophthalmic surgery as an independent profession throughout his career; previously a surgeon adopted this branch of work after a longer or shorter experience of general surgery. As an operator he was neat, rapid, and resourceful, and he introduced into practice several new methods of procedure, especially that of trephining the sclerotic for the relief of glaucoma.

On retiring from practice in 1904 he settled at Mon Plaisir, St. Aubyn's, Jersey, where he took charge of the eldest daughter of the Thakur of Gondal, a former pupil at Edinburgh, and afterwards his friend. In 1892 and 1900 Robertson visited India and on a third visit in the winter of 1908–9 he died at Gondal, India, on 3 Jan. 1909; he was cremated on the banks of the river Gondli, the Thakur Sahib himself kindling the funeral pyre of his guru and friend.

He married in 1882 Carey, fourth daughter of William Nathaniel Fraser of Findrack and Tornaveen, Aberdeenshire, but had no family.

His portrait, painted by Sir George Reid, was presented to him by members of his profession before he retired from practice. A replica hangs in the Surgeons' Hall at Edinburgh.

[Edinburgh Med. Journal, 1909, N.S. ii. 159 (with portrait); Lancet, 1909, i. 208; Brit. Med. Journal, 1909, i. 191, 252 (with portrait); Hole's Quasi Cursores, 1884 (with portrait).] D'A. P.

ROBERTSON, JAMES PATRICK BANNERMAN, Baron Robertson of Forteviot (1845–1909), lord president of the Court of Session in Scotland, born in the manse of Forteviot on 10 Aug. 1845, was second son of Robert John Robertson, parish minister of Forteviot, Perthshire, by his wife Helen, daughter of James Bannerman, parish minister of Cargill, Perthshire. He was educated at the Royal High School, Edinburgh, of which he was 'dux,' or head boy, in 1860, and at Edinburgh University, where he specially distinguished himself as a political speaker in college debates, graduating M.A. in 1864. He became a member of the Juridical Society in 1866 (librarian 1868–9, president 1869–70), and passed to the Scottish bar on 16 July 1867. His progress was slow at first, but he gradually acquired a large practice. His interests were more in politics than law. 'Westminster seems to have been his real goal from the first' (*The Times*, 3 Feb. 1909). Early in life he lost sympathy with his presbyterian surroundings. At the disruption of the Scottish church (1843) his father had remained in the establishment, while his mother went out with those who formed the Free Church. Robertson himself, on attaining manhood, joined the Scottish episcopal communion. He was the best speaker of his day at the bar. An ardent admirer of Disraeli, he did much to promote a conservative revival in Scotland, and at the general election of 1880 contested Linlithgowshire against Peter Maclagan, the sitting member, but lost by a large majority. He became Q.C. in 1885, was appointed solicitor-general for Scotland in the short-lived Salisbury government of 1885, and was returned for Buteshire at the general election of that year, but lost office when the liberals came in, in Feb. 1886. On the defeat of Gladstone on home rule in June 1886 and the consequent dissolution of parliament, he was re-elected for Buteshire. In Salisbury's second administration he became again solicitor-general for Scotland.

Robertson made his mark in the House of Commons at once. On 13 April 1887 he spoke with effect in support of the criminal law amendment (Ireland) bill. His speech, a defence of the bill on the analogy of the Scottish criminal law, was published under the title of 'Scotland and the Crimes Bill.' In 1889 he was appointed lord advocate, succeeding John Hay Athole Macdonald, who was made lord justice clerk, and he was sworn of the privy council. As lord advocate he carried the Local Government (Scotland) Act, 1889 (52 & 53 Vict. c. 60), by which 250,000*l.*, derived from probate and license duties, was to be annually applied to the relief of fees in elementary public schools, thus establishing free education in Scotland. In 1890 he received the honorary degree of LL.D. from Edinburgh University, of which three years later he became lord rector.

In 1891 Robertson succeeded John Inglis [q. v.] as lord president of the Court of Session, and in 1899, on the death of William Watson, Baron Watson [q. v. Suppl. I], he became a life peer, as Baron Robertson of Forteviot (14 Nov.), with a seat on the judicial committee of the privy council. He was elected an honorary bencher of the Middle Temple (24 Nov. 1899–18 Jan. 1900). As a judge in Scotland, Robertson had often shown that he found his position there uncongenial; but on the broader ground of the two final courts of appeal—the House of Lords and the judicial committee of the privy council—his acute and penetrating intellect had wider scope. In the privy council he was not infrequently charged with the duty of delivering the judgment of the board, especially in appeals from those parts of the empire where Roman-Dutch law prevails (*The Times*, 3 Feb. 1909). In the House of Lords, on the appeal Walter *v.* Lane, he dissented (6 Aug. 1900) from Halsbury (Lord Chancellor) and other judges, and held that 'The Times' had no copyright in Lord Rosebery's speeches published by Lane in book-form from 'The Times' reports (*Law Reports*, Appeals, 1900, pp. 539–61). In 1904 he was one of the judges who heard the appeal by the minority of the Free Church of Scotland against the decision of the Court of Session in the litigation which followed the union (1900) of the Free Church and the United Presbyterians; and his judgment in favour of reversing the decision, and giving the property of the Free Church to the objecting minority, is a masterly statement of that side of the question (*Law Reports*, Appeals, 1904, pp. 515–764; see SHAND (afterwards BURNS), ALEXANDER, BARON SHAND, Suppl. II).

Robertson was chairman of the Irish University commission, and author of its report (1904), which, while recognising that the ideal system for Ireland would combine all creeds, recommended a virtually catholic university as the only practicable solution of the problem. He remained a keen politician to the last, but refused to follow Mr. Balfour on the fiscal question. He spoke in the House of Lords on the Duke of Devonshire's motion against Mr. Chamberlain's tariff proposals (22 July 1905). Describing himself as 'a loyal member of the tory party,' he attacked the Birmingham policy, which he predicted would ruin the party, and severely censured the tactics of Mr. Balfour, the conservative leader, whom he accused of mistaking 'cleverness' for statesmanship. As the tariff policy developed Robertson's hostility increased. He died suddenly at Cap Martin on 2 Feb. 1909, and was buried at Elmstead, Kent.

Robertson married on 10 April 1872 Philadelphia Mary Lucy, daughter of W. N. Fraser, of Tornaveen, Aberdeenshire (*d.* 27 Jan. 1907). By her he had two sons—Robert Bannerman Fraser (*b.* 14 Feb. 1873), barrister-at-law (Middle Temple), who served in the imperial yeomanry in South Africa, and entered the army (capt. 21st lancers); Hugh (*b.* 27 Sept. 1879), who entered the army (14th hussars), and died in South Africa on 1 Feb. 1900—and one daughter, Philadelphia Sybil. A small sketch in oils of Robertson, which represents him addressing the House of Commons, is in the possession of his son.

[Scotsman, and The Times, 3 Feb. 1909; Records of Juridical Society; Roll of Faculty of Advocates; Hansard, 3rd ser., vol. 150, pp. 847–63; 4th ser., vol. 150, pp. 500–11.]

G. W. T. O.

ROBINSON, FREDERICK WILLIAM (1830–1901), novelist, born in Spitalfields on 23 Dec. 1830, was second son of William Robinson of Acre Lane, Brixton, who owned much house property in London. His mother's surname was St. John. After education at Dr. Pinches' school at Clarendon House, Kennington, where (Sir) Henry Irving, (Sir) Edward Clarke, and J. L. Toole were also pupils, he acted for some time as his father's secretary. But he soon embarked upon a literary career, his first novel 'The House of Elmore,' begun before he was eighteen, being published in 1855. It met with success and was followed by upwards of fifty other efforts in fiction. 'Grandmother's Money' (1860; 2nd edit. 1862) secured a wide vogue, which was maintained in an anonymous series of semi-religious novels: 'High Church' (1860); 'No Church' (1861); 'Church and Chapel' (1863); 'Carry's Confession' (1865); 'Beyond the Church' (1866), and 'Christie's Faith' (1867). Meanwhile he was equally successful with two works of a different character: 'Female Life in Prison, by a Prison Matron' (1862) and 'Memoirs of Jane Cameron, Female Convict' (1863). These sketches and stories, based upon actual records, were so realistic in treatment as to be mistaken for literal history. Donations for prisoners reached Robinson, and his revelations led to improvement in the conditions of prison life. (These works are wrongly assigned by Halkett and Laing and by Cushing to Mary Carpenter [q. v.], the philanthropist.) Robinson was also a pioneer in novels of low life, which included 'Owen, a Waif' (1862; new edit. 1870); 'Mattie, a Stray' (1864; new edit. 1870); and 'Milly's Hero' (1865; 5th edit. 1869). Among his later works of fiction the best were 'Anne Judge, Spinster' (1867; last reissued in 1899), in which the dialogue is excellent; 'No Man's Friend' (1867; last edit. 1884); and 'The Courting of Mary Smith' (1886). 'Poor Humanity' (1868; last edit. 1884) was dramatised by the author and played with some success at the Surrey Theatre with Creswick in the chief rôle, a returned convict. Robinson's last complete novel, 'The Wrong that was done,' appeared in 1892, and a volume of short stories, 'All they went through,' in 1898. Robinson contributed to the 'Family Herald,' 'Cassell's Magazine' and other periodicals, and for some years wrote dramatic criticisms for the 'Daily News,' the 'Observer,' and other papers. His novels appeared in the three-volume form, and with the extinction of that mode of publication his popularity waned. A disciple of Defoe and Dickens, he wrote too rapidly to put such power as he possessed to the best purpose. Yet his work found constant readers in Dante Gabriel Rossetti and other men of note.

In 1884 Robinson brought out a weekly penny magazine, called 'Home Chimes,' which was heralded by a sonnet from Mr. Theodore Watts-Dunton, and contained contributions by Swinburne, Moy Thomas, and Phil Robinson. In February 1886 the paper was converted into a fourpenny monthly, and was carried on in that form till the end of 1893. Much early work by Mr. J. M. Barrie, Mr. J. K. Jerome, and Mr. I. Zangwill, in whom the editor inspired great attachment, appeared in it. Robinson's friends of an older generation included, besides Swinburne and Mr. Watts-Dunton, Ford Madox Brown, Philip Bourke Marston and his father, and Sir Henry Irving. Chess-playing was among his accomplishments. He died at Elmore House, St. James's Road, Brixton, on 6 Dec. 1901, and was buried in Norwood cemetery. His wife, whose maiden name was Stephens, survived him, with six sons and five daughters. A portrait painted by C. W. Pittard, in possession of the family, is not a satisfactory likeness.

[Private information; Mr. T. Watts-Dunton in Athenæum, 14 Dec. 1901; The Times, 9 Dec. 1901; Daily News, 9 Dec. 1901; Harper's Mag., June 1888 (with portrait); Black and White, 14 Dec. 1901 (portrait); Brixtonian, 13 Dec. 1901; Literature, 14 Dec. 1901; J. C. Francis's Notes by the Way, 1909, p. 306; E. A. Baker's Descriptive Guide to Modern Fiction; Allibone's Dict. Eng. Lit. vol. ii. and Suppl.; Halkett and Laing's Dict.; Cushing's Anonyms; Brit. Mus. Cat.]

G. Le G. N.

ROBINSON, GEORGE FREDERICK SAMUEL, first Marquis of Ripon (1827–1909), governor-general of India and statesman, was the second son but sole surviving child of Frederick John Robinson [q. v.], who was created Viscount Goderich on 28 April 1827, and Earl of Ripon on 13 April 1833. His father's elder brother was Thomas Philip Robinson, second Earl de Grey (1781–1859), lord-lieutenant of Ireland from 1841 to 1844. His mother was Lady Sarah Albinia Louisa (*d.* 1867), daughter of Robert Hobart, fourth earl of Buckinghamshire [q. v.].

Born on 24 Oct. 1827 at 10 Downing

Street, during the brief tenure of the office of prime minister by his father, George began life with every advantage that high position and political opportunity could offer. His parents anxiously devoted themselves to his care and education, and they preferred private tuition under their direct supervision to public school or university. From 1833 until he succeeded to his father's earldom in 1859 the boy was known by the courtesy title of Viscount Goderich. His father combined conservative instincts with growing liberal aspirations, and his son was to repeat many of his official experiences. As a boy Goderich discussed with his father the stirring political controversies of the day touching religious disabilities, freedom of speech and of meeting, protection, colonial relations, financial strictness, and franchise reform. Many years later, in Feb. 1886, he asserted 'I have always been in favour of the most advanced thing in the liberal programme' (Dasent's *Life of John Delane*).

In 1849 Goderich began a public career as attaché to the special mission—which proved brief and abortive—of Sir Henry Ellis (1777–1855) [q. v.] to Brussels to open negotiations for peace between Austria and Piedmont. For the next two years Goderich devoted himself to social and county work. As a young man he was greatly influenced by the Christian socialist movement which F. D. Maurice, Charles Kingsley, and Thomas Hughes initiated in 1849, and with Tom Hughes he formed a lifelong friendship. When the Christian socialists encouraged the strike of engineers in Lancashire and London early in 1852, Goderich showed his sympathy by sending the strikers 500*l*. In November of the same year the Christian socialists first gave effect to their endeavour to provide working men with opportunities of advanced education at the Hall of Association, in Castle Street East, Oxford Street. Goderich lectured on entomology (*Working Men's College*, ed. Llewelyn Davies, 1904, p. 16). During 1852, also, he wrote a plea for democracy entitled 'The Duty of the Age' which he submitted to Hughes, Charles Kingsley, and J. M. Ludlow, members of the Christian Socialist Publication Committee, and they passed the manuscript for press. When, however, Frederick Denison Maurice, chairman of the committee, read the tract after an edition was printed off, he condemned its extreme radical tendency and gave orders, which were carried out, for the suppression of the pamphlet (Maurice, *Life of F. D. Maurice*, ii. 125–30). At a later period Goderich took an active part in inaugurating the volunteer movement, becoming in 1860 honorary colonel of the first volunteer battalion Prince of Wales's own (West Yorkshire regiment) and subsequently receiving the volunteer decoration.

Goderich first engaged in active politics in July 1852, when he was returned with James Clay as liberal member for Hull. Both were however unseated on petition on grounds of treating. In the following April, at a bye-election at Huddersfield, Goderich successfully contested the seat against another liberal. He represented the constituency for four years, till the end of the parliament. On 29 Jan. 1855 he voted for John Arthur Roebuck's motion for an inquiry into the condition of the army and the conduct of the war in the Crimea, and on the fall of Lord Aberdeen's ministry of all the talents and Lord John Russell's failure to form a ministry, he gave his support to Palmerston until the dissolution of 1857 which followed Cobden's defeat of the ministers on Chinese affairs. On 30 March 1857 he was returned without opposition, but with a conservative colleague, Edmund B. Denison, for the West Riding of Yorkshire. His seat had just been vacated by Cobden. During the session he urged an extension of open competition by means of examination for posts in the civil service. His father's death in Jan. 1859 soon removed him to the upper house as Earl of Ripon, and in the following November his uncle's death made him also Earl de Grey.

From this time Earl de Grey and Ripon, whom Earl Granville in a letter (15 Aug. 1884) to Gladstone described depreciatively as 'a very persistent man with wealth,' rapidly advanced in public life (cf. Fitzmaurice, *Lord Granville*, ii. 364). He received his first recognition from his party by his appointment as under-secretary for war in June 1859, in Palmerston's second administration. For six months in 1861 (Jan. to July) he filled a similar position at the India office, but he returned to the war office and remained under-secretary until on the death of his chief, Sir George Cornewall Lewis, on 13 April 1863, he succeeded to the headship of the war office, with a seat in the cabinet. He was admitted at the same time to the privy council. On 16 Feb. 1866, shortly after Palmerston's death had made Lord Russell prime minister, Ripon succeeded Sir Charles Wood (afterwards Viscount Halifax) at the India office.

Ripon's position as one of the official leaders of the liberal party was thus assured, and when Gladstone formed his first ministry on 9 Dec. 1868, Ripon became lord president of the council, being appointed K.G. next year. On Lord Salisbury's installation as chancellor of Oxford in 1870 Ripon was made hon. D.C.L. During 1870, as president of the council, Ripon was technically responsible for the education bill which his deputy, W. E. Forster, carried with difficulty through the House of Commons. In 1871 a new and vaster responsibility was placed on him. The United States and the United Kingdom at length agreed to appoint a joint high commission for the settlement of American claims against Great Britain in regard to the depredations of the Alabama and other privateering vessels, which had sailed from English ports to aid the South in the late American civil war. Ripon was appointed chairman, to the disappointment of Lord Houghton and others. His colleagues were Sir Stafford Northcote, Sir Edward Thornton, British minister at Washington, Sir John Alexander Macdonald, representative of Canada, and Professor Mountague Bernard. On 8 March 1871 the American case was opened before the commission at Washington. The negotiations proceeded rapidly, and a satisfactory treaty, which among other things referred the American claims to an international tribunal, was signed at Washington on 8 May. Ripon had emphatically declined to discuss indirect losses (see LANG's *Sir Stafford Northcote*, ii. 9), and an ambiguous clause in the treaty led to subsequent controversy, but the end was a reaffirmation of Ripon's action. For his conduct of the negotiations nothing but praise was due. Northcote wrote enthusiastically of his 'excellent sense, tact, and temper' (MORLEY's *Life of Gladstone*, bk. vi. ch. ix.). His services were rewarded by promotion to a marquisate on 23 June 1871. On 19 March 1873 he was made lord-lieutenant of the North Riding.

In Aug. 1873 Ripon caused general surprise by resigning his cabinet office on the ground of 'urgent private affairs.' The 'private affairs' concerned his spiritual struggles, of which his intimate friends were kept in ignorance. Hitherto he had been a zealous freemason, and on 23 April 1870 had become Grand Master of the Freemasons of England. That office he resigned without explanation in Aug. 1874. Next month, on 7 Sept., he was received into the Roman catholic communion at the Brompton Oratory. The step, which caused widespread astonishment, was the fruit of anxious thought. During the conservative administration of 1874–80 Ripon lived much in retirement. But he was active in the affairs of the religious community which he had joined, and was thenceforth reckoned as authoritative a leader of the Roman catholic laity in England as the duke of Norfolk. Both men joined in 1878 in urging on Manning Newman's claims to the cardinalate (PURCELL's *Life of Manning*, ii. 554). John Hungerford Pollen [q. v. Suppl. II], who had gone through the same religious experiences, became Ripon's private secretary in 1876, and was on confidential terms with him.

On Gladstone's return to power in April 1880 Ripon fully re-entered public life and proved that his religious conversion had in no way impaired his devotion to public duty (cf. CARDINAL BOURNE, *The Times*, 12 July 1909). On 28 April he was appointed governor-general of India on the resignation of Lord Lytton. Ripon's health seemed hardly robust enough for the office, but he gained strength after settling in India. He took over charge at Simla on 8 June 1880.

A critical position in Afghanistan at once confronted him. Sir Donald Stewart, after recognising Wali Sher Ali as independent governor of Kandahar, had joined forces with General Roberts at Kabul, expecting to evacuate Afghanistan in the near future. The attitude of the Afghan nobles and people was one of sullen tranquillity, while Lepel Griffin [q. v. Suppl. II], chief political agent of the government of India, was waiting to complete negotiations with Abdur Rahman, who was secretly exciting the nobles to fresh hostilities and demanding assurances as to British intentions with regard both to Kandahar and to his own bearing towards his late allies the Russians. Lord Ripon acted with vigour. Under his orders Abdur Rahman was proclaimed Amir at Kabul on 22 July, after he had been informed (14 June) that he could have no political relations with any foreign power except the English, while if any such power interfered and 'such interference should lead to unprovoked aggression on the Kabul ruler,' he would receive aid in such a manner and at such a time as might be necessary to repel it, provided he followed British advice. This cautious intimation has stood the test of time, and was reaffirmed by Lord Curzon in the formal treaty of 21 March 1905, concluded with

Abdur Rahman's son and successor. Meanwhile the unexpected happened. Ayub Khan, Sher Ali's younger son, who had been holding Herat, took advantage of Stewart's absence, and defeated General Burrows at Maiwand on 27 July 1880. Lord Ripon again showed no wavering. He authorised the march of Roberts from Kabul to Kandahar. The Afghans were routed; Stewart in September withdrew his troops from Kabul; and before the year closed Kandahar was evacuated and in due course reunited to Kabul by the Amir. Each step in this policy was fiercely contested at home and in India, but the viceroy carried it out without faltering, and without incurring any of the predicted evil consequences.

The three other main episodes of Ripon's Indian administration—his dealings with the press, his development of schemes of self-government, and the Ilbert bill—call for a more qualified judgment than Ripon's triumphant policy in Afghanistan. The Vernacular Press Acts, ix. and xvi. of 1878, passed by Lord Lytton's government, were capable of amendment, but to Lord Ripon's strong liberalism they were wholly objectionable as conflicting with British traditions of the freedom of the press, and they were hastily repealed in 1882. Lord Ripon scarcely realised the differences between the conditions attaching to the press in the two countries. The vernacular press of India did not further discussion, but was used by political intriguers to spread false reports and create an attitude of hostility not against a party in the state but against the reign of law and order. None of the effective safeguards which the hostility of public opinion to untruth and extravagance provides in England are available in India. After nearly thirty years' experience, press restrictions 'for the better conduct of the press' were re-imposed by Viscount Morley, a liberal secretary of state for India, in 1910, and Lord Ripon's action in 1882 was proved so far to be too uncompromising.

Ripon's efforts to encourage the development of self-government in India were similarly marred by the tendency to judge India by British standards. The viceroy made clear his point of departure when he announced in the 'Gazette of India,' dated 4 Oct. 1882, that 'only by removing the pressure of direct official interference can the people be brought to take sufficient interest in local matters.' In the next few years the provincial governments passed laws entrusting local bodies with education, dispensaries, and the concern of other local requirements, but it was found impossible to expect or seek for self-government in rural or small urban areas without official guidance. The educated classes in India welcomed the reform. But although Ripon gave new force to the transfer of public duties to local boards, little progress was effected, as is shown by the report of the royal commission on decentralisation presided over in 1907 by Mr. C. E. Hobhouse, a sympathiser with Ripon's aims. Section 806 of the report puts the matter thus: 'Those who expected a complete revolution in existing methods in consequence of Lord Ripon's pronouncement were inevitably doomed to disappointment. The political education of any people must necessarily be slow, and local self-government of the British type could not at once take root in Indian soil.'

In the racial controversy over the 'Ilbert bill' which Ripon's action fanned he showed no better appreciation of Indian conditions. On 23 Feb. 1882 he declared in council that he would 'be very glad if it was possible to place the law in regard to every person not only on the same footing, but to embody it in the very same language whether it relates to Europeans or natives.' At the time the Criminal Procedure Code, which amended and consolidated the law based on Macaulay's famous Indian Law Commission, was being enacted. By chapter xxxiii. of this Act only magistrates who were justices of the peace, or judges who were European British subjects, or judges of the highest court of appeal, were empowered to try (with jurors or assessors) Europeans and Americans charged with criminal offences. Although there was no general demand for a change of law, on 30 Jan. 1883 Sir Courtenay Ilbert, then legal member, introduced into the council, in the spirit of Lord Ripon's declaration, a bill 'to remove from the Code at once and completely every judicial disqualification which is based merely on race distinctions.' Lord Ripon, in the course of subsequent debates in March 1883, added fuel to the fire by the imputation that the opposition to the bill was 'really opposition to the declared policy of parliament about the admission of natives to the covenanted civil service.' British planters and traders felt that justice and not privilege was at stake. They had no complaint whatever against the admission of Indians by competition. What they feared was trial by inexperienced Indian magistrates. During several months violent and unreasonable speeches and memorials on both sides agitated India. Eventually a compromise which would have been accepted at the outset was arrived at, and jurisdiction over Europeans was given to certain qualified native officials, while the right was reserved of the accused person to trial by a jury of which half should be Europeans. There was no further attempt to 'remove at once and completely every judicial disqualification.'

Apart from these errors of somewhat hasty language which, while gratifying native feeling, had the unfortunate effect of alienating the Anglo-Indian population, Ripon's administration was excellent. He was a good man of business, hard-working, of transparent honesty, and loyal to his colleagues in council and his subordinates. Ably served by Sir Evelyn Baring (afterwards Earl Cromer), he developed the system of provincial settlements introduced by Lord Mayo in 1871. Local governments were no longer limited to a fixed grant, they were encouraged to be careful in collection and economical in expenditure by being entrusted with the whole product of some sources of revenue and a share in other receipts. Although the Bengal Tenancy Act was not passed until 1885, that important measure was made ripe by Lord Ripon for legislation. In education important reforms were introduced as the result of the comprehensive report of the commission of 1882 which he appointed. He left India in December 1884, having prepared the ground for the reception of the Amir of Afghanistan at Rawalpindi in April 1885, by his successor, Lord Dufferin.

At home, tory opponents had attacked Ripon's 'policy of sentiment,' and on his return he spoke vigorously in defence of his Indian administration (cf. Ripon's speech at National Liberal Club on 25 Feb. 1885). He at once resumed his place among the liberal leaders. Gladstone's brief return to office, Feb. to Aug. 1886, brought him back to the cabinet as first lord of the admiralty. He supported Gladstone's home rule policy, and was rewarded by the bestowal on him of the freedom of the city of Dublin in 1898. Lord Morley received the distinction at the same time. In Gladstone's fourth ministry of 1892, and in that of Lord Rosebery of 1894, he took charge of the colonial office. His approval of the Matabele war of 1894 strained the allegiance of many of his own party. When the unionists resumed office in 1895, Ripon entered on a period of comparative inactivity. On Mr. Balfour's resignation and the formation of the ministry of Sir Henry Campbell-Bannerman, 5 Dec. 1905, Lord Ripon accepted the privy seal with the post of leader of the party in the lords, which the recent illness of Lord Spencer had left vacant. The task which devolved upon him at the advanced age of seventy-eight was no light one. Supporters of the liberal party in the house were few, while the opposition was powerfully represented. The liberal measures which had to be recommended to the chamber were peculiarly distasteful to the majority of its members. The House of Lords rejected the government's education bill of which Lord Crewe had charge in 1906, the licensing bill in 1908, and other measures. Lord Ripon faced his difficulties with characteristic tact and courage, and while he endeared himself by his geniality and good-humour to his small band of followers he commanded the respect of his foes. He seldom spoke at great length, but the clear and pithy sentences in which he wound up the debates, and embodied his long experience of business and the traditions of the upper house, carried weight. Within the cabinet his wide knowledge of foreign and colonial affairs was of value to his party on its resumption of power after long exclusion. The death of Lord Kimberley in 1902, the enforced withdrawal of Lord Spencer in the year 1905, and the retirement of Lord Rosebery from official life gave him exceptional prestige. On 9 Nov. 1906 he replied for the government, in the absence, through mourning, of Campbell-Bannerman, the prime minister, at the lord mayor's annual banquet. In 1908, when Mr. Asquith succeeded Campbell-Bannerman, Lord Ripon at length retired. He resigned the leadership of the upper house to Lord Crewe on 14 April 1908, and the office of lord privy seal on 8 Oct. At a lunch given to him at the Savoy Hotel by the Eighty Club on 24 Nov. 1908 he delivered his farewell address to his political friends. In reviewing his fifty-six years of public life he said 'I started at a high level of radicalism. I am a radical still.' On 9 July 1909 he died of heart failure at Studley Royal, Ripon. His body was placed in the vault beneath the church of St. Mary the Virgin in Studley park on 14 July, and a solemn requiem mass was sung at Westminster Cathedral in the presence of a large congregation.

On 8 April 1851 he married his cousin, Henrietta Anne Theodosia, eldest daughter of Henry Vyner of Gautby Hall, Horncastle, and granddaughter of Thomas Philip, second Earl de Grey. He was succeeded in the title by his only son, Frederick Oliver, Earl de Grey (*b.* 29 Jan. 1852).

Portraits were painted by Sir Edward Poynter, P.R.A., in 1886; by Sir Hubert von Herkomer (for presentation) in 1894; and by G. F. Watts, R.A., in 1896. Cartoon caricatures by 'Ape' and 'Spy' appeared in 'Vanity Fair' in 1869 and 1892 respectively.

[Obituary notice in The Times, 10 July 1909; Morley's Gladstone; A. Lang's Sir Stafford Northcote; Evelyn Ashley's Lord Palmerston; A. I. Dasent's John T. Delane; Herbert Paul's Hist. of Modern England; A. D. Elliot's Lord Goschen, 1911; Sketches and Snapshots, by G. W. E. Russell; The Gladstone Government, by A Templar, 1869; Moral and Material Progress Reports of India; Parliamentary Papers; Gazetteer of India; information from Lord Fitzmaurice. Lord Ripon's papers have been entrusted to Mr. Lucien Wolf for the purpose of writing his biography.] W. L-W.

ROBINSON, Sir JOHN (1839–1903), first prime minister of Natal, son of George Eyre Robinson, was born at Hull, Yorkshire, in 1839, and came out to Natal with his parents in 1850. Coming to a colony which was only seven years old, where there were as yet no secondary schools, he had little chance of education, apart from the stimulus of 'cultured parents.' Entering the office of the 'Natal Mercury,' which his father started, he cherished leanings towards the life of a missionary, and then towards the law; but he finally accepted the career of journalism, and by the time of his majority was able to take over the active management of the paper from his father, whose health had failed (31 March 1860). In September 1860 he entered into partnership with Mr. Richard Vause, afterwards a prominent mayor of Durban; but himself remained editor.

Arranging for the conduct of the 'Mercury' during his absence, in 1861 he journeyed to England by the east coast of Africa, Mauritius, and the Red Sea, whence he passed through Egypt, Palestine, Syria, certain of the Levant and Mediterranean ports to Athens, Rome, and Paris. He stayed some five months in the United Kingdom, where he studied the International Exhibition of 1862, and lectured on the colony; he also visited part of the Continent before setting out for Natal again. Six months after his return in 1863 he was elected to the council for Durban, thus becoming one of the twelve elected members of the old legislative council, with the work of which he had been familiar in the first instance as reporter.

But Robinson devoted himself chiefly to his newspaper and literary work. The 'Natal Mercury' passed from a weekly paper to three issues a week, and thence to a daily paper. He contributed to the neighbouring press at Capetown, and to home journals such as the 'Cornhill Magazine,' where his first article, 'A South African Watering Place,' appeared in 1868. He also found time to write a good novel, 'George Linton' (1876). He maintained a reputation as a lecturer, but this work became gradually merged in the more absorbing claims of the political platform.

After some fifteen years' experience of administration by the crown, Robinson formed a strong opinion in favour of responsible government for Natal. He had been impressed by the troubles of the Langalibalele affair in 1873; he was a delegate for Natal at the South African Conference in London in 1876, and then had to face the Zulu campaign in 1879. Convinced that it was his mission to obtain self-government for the colony, he was opposed by his friend Sir Harry Escombe [q. v. Suppl. I], and his policy was defeated in the elections of May 1882, when he lost his seat for Durban. He was nevertheless back in the council in 1884, and in 1887 was chosen as their representative at the Colonial Conference in London of that year. On the occasion of this visit to England he was received by Queen Victoria and presented the colony's loyal address. In 1888 he represented Natal in the South African Customs Conference which led to the formation of the Customs Union. He was created K.C.M.G. in 1889. But he always kept before him the ideal of a self-governed colony, and his writings and speeches gradually convinced his opponents; in 1892 he had the satisfaction of finding Escombe fighting by his side. He was one of the representatives who proceeded to England in that year to press the colonists' views.

Robinson's efforts proved successful, and on 4 July 1893, when the new *régime* began, he assumed office as the first prime minister of Natal, with the portfolios of colonial secretary and minister of education. The gradual organisation of a responsible administration was effected quietly, and Robinson's nearly four years of office were uneventful. In March 1897 he resigned on account of failing health, hastening his retirement so that his successor might accept the invitation to Queen

Victoria's Diamond Jubilee. He went to England that summer in a private capacity, and thence on to Rome, of which he was fond, and which he revisited in 1900.

In 1898 the legislature voted him a pension of 500*l.* a year. For the rest of his life he mainly lived in retirement at his home, the Gables, Bayside, Durban, where he died on 5 Nov. 1903. He was buried at the Durban cemetery; the staff of the 'Mercury' bore him to his grave.

Robinson's life was governed by the highest ideals and motives. As a journalist he aimed not only at style and lucidity but at justice and temperance of statement.

He married in 1865 Agnes, daughter of Dr. Benjamin Blaine of Verulam, Natal, who survived him; he had issue three sons and four daughters. A statue of him was erected in the Town Gardens of Durban, and some scholarships were also founded from the money subscribed.

In addition to the work cited, Robinson published: 1. 'The Colonies and the Century,' 1899. 2. 'A Lifetime in South Africa,' 1900.

[Natal Mercury, 6 and 7 Nov. 1903; Natal Witness, 6 Nov. 1903; South Africa, 7 Nov. 1903; Henderson's Durban, p. 217; Natal Blue Books, 1882 sqq.] C. A. H.

ROBINSON, SIR JOHN RICHARD (1828–1903), journalist, born on 2 Nov. 1828 at Witham, Essex, was second son of eight children of Richard Robinson, congregational minister, by his wife Sarah, daughter of John Dennant, also a congregational minister, of Halesworth, Suffolk. At eleven he entered the school for the sons of congregational ministers, then at Lewisham, but now at Caterham. Withdrawn from school on 26 June, 1843, he was apprenticed to a firm of booksellers at Shepton Mallet. His ambitions, however, were directed towards journalism, and his first effort was a descriptive account (in the 'Daily News,' 14 Feb. 1846) of a meeting of Wiltshire labourers to protest against the corn laws. After reporting for the 'Bedford Mercury,' he obtained a post on the 'Wiltshire Independent' at Devizes, and soon sent regular reports of the local markets to the 'Daily News.' In 1848 Robinson went to London. Having become a unitarian, he was made sub-editor of a unitarian journal, the 'Inquirer,' and did most of the work for John Lalor [q. v.], the editor. His next post was on the 'Weekly News and Chronicle,' under John Sheehan [q. v.], and in 1855 he became editor of the 'Express,' an evening paper in the same hands as the 'Daily News.' At the same time he was a prolific contributor elsewhere. He cherished a deep interest in movements for freedom throughout Europe. He had a profound reverence for Mazzini, who asked to make his acquaintance after reading an appreciation of himself from Robinson's pen. He also knew Kossuth, Garibaldi, and other revolutionary leaders.

In 1868, when the price of the 'Daily News' was reduced to one penny, Robinson was appointed manager. Under his direction the fortunes of the paper, which had been falling, quickly rose. He saw that the public demanded news not only quickly but in an attractive form. At the opening of the Franco-German war he instructed his correspondents to telegraph descriptive details and not merely bare facts, and after the war was well in progress he secured with exemplary promptitude the services of Archibald Forbes [q. v. Suppl. I], who long remained a valuable contributor. At the prompting of another correspondent, John Edwin Hilary Skinner [q. v.], he started the 'French Peasants Relief Fund,' which reached a total of 20,000*l.*

On 22 June 1876 Mr. (afterwards Sir) Edwin Pears of Constantinople contributed to the 'Daily News' the first of a series of letters describing Turkish atrocities in Bulgaria. Public indignation was roused, and Robinson sent out an American journalist, Januarius Aloysius MacGahan, who was accompanied by Mr. Eugene Schuyler, the American consul-general in Turkey, to make inquiries. Pears's charges were corroborated, and Robinson's services were warmly acknowledged by Bulgarians. In 1887 Robinson became titular editor, the actual night editing being carried on chiefly by Peter William Clayden [q. v. Suppl. II]. In 1893 he was knighted. The fortunes of the paper meanwhile declined. In 1896 (Sir) E. T. Cook became editor with undivided control of policy, and Robinson resumed his post of manager. During 1899 and 1900 the editor supported the South African war. The sympathies of Robinson were with the Boers. Early in 1901 the paper was sold to a new proprietor of pro-Boer sentiment, and the engagement of the editor, (Sir) E. T. Cook, was terminated. On different grounds Robinson's management then came to an end (Feb. 1901). At a dinner given him by the former proprietors he was presented with a service of plate and his portrait was painted by E. A. Ward (now owned by his son, Mr. O. R. Robinson).

Robinson was an habitué of the Reform Club, and formed one of the circle in which

James Payn, William Black, Sir Wemyss Reid, and George Augustus Sala were conspicuous. He was an excellent raconteur and mimic, a great reader, especially of modern French literature, and a regular 'first night' visitor to the leading theatres.

In 1854 Robinson became a professional member of the Guild of Literature and Art, a society which was founded by Charles Dickens and his friends for the benefit of authors and artists. The guild failed to fulfil the aims of its founders, and Robinson with Frederick Clifford [q. v. Suppl. II], as the last surviving trustees, arranged for its dissolution in 1897. In 1897 he was chairman of the Newspaper Press Fund dinner, and in 1898 of the Newspaper Society dinner; the former body represents journalists, and the latter proprietors. No other active journalist has filled the double office.

Robinson died in London on 30 Nov. 1903, and was buried in Highgate cemetery. He married on 14 July 1859 Jane Mapes (*d.* 1876), youngest daughter of William Granger of the Grange, Wickham Bishops, Essex; he had one son and one daughter.

[The Times, and Daily News, 2 Dec. 1903; F. Moy Thomas, Recollections of Sir J. R. Robinson, 1904; Memoirs of Sir Wemyss Reid, 1905, pp. 253–5; G. W. Smalley's Anglo-American Memories, 1911; private information; personal recollections.]

W. B. D.

ROBINSON, PHILIP STEWART, 'PHIL ROBINSON' (1847–1902), naturalist and author, born at Chunar, India, on 13 Oct. 1847, was eldest son in a family of three sons and three daughters of Julian Robinson, Indian army chaplain and editor of the 'Pioneer,' by his wife Harriet Woodcocke, daughter of Thomas Sharpe, D.D., vicar of Doncaster and canon of York. After education at Marlborough College (August 1860 to Midsummer 1865), he was from 1866 to 1868 librarian of the free library, Cardiff. He resigned this post to go to India, where he assisted his father in editing the 'Pioneer' in 1869; he was appointed editor of the 'Revenue Archives' of the Benares province in 1872, and became in 1873 professor of literature and of logic and metaphysics in Allahabad College. He was also censor of the vernacular press. Returning to England in 1877, he joined the staff of the 'Daily Telegraph' as leader writer.

In 1878 he was correspondent of the 'Daily Telegraph,' both in the second Afghan campaign and in the Zulu war. Between 1878 and 1893 he acted as publisher's reader for Messrs. Sampson Low and Co., and edited and prepared for the press Stanley's 'Through the Dark Continent' (1878). From 1881–2 he was special commissioner of the 'New York World' in Utah, and later in 1882 went to Egypt as war correspondent of the 'Daily Chronicle.' Subsequently he made lecturing tours through the United States and Australia, and in 1898 was correspondent at first of the 'Pall Mall Gazette' and then of the Associated Press in Cuba during the Spanish-American war. The hardships of the Cuban campaigns, including imprisonment and fever, undermined his health, and in his last year he wrote very little beyond occasional articles for the 'Contemporary Review' and for 'Good Words.' He died on 9 Dec. 1902. He married in 1877 Elizabeth King, by whom he had issue, a daughter and a son.

Robinson was one of the pioneers of Anglo-Indian literature, and was foremost in inaugurating the literature descriptive of animate nature in India. His essays on the common objects of Indian scenery abound in keen observation and whimsical humour and show literary skill and taste. His work, which found many imitators, anticipated Mr. Rudyard Kipling's early devotion to Indian themes. Robinson's published works include: 1. 'Nugæ Indicæ, or on Leave in my Compound,' Allahabad, 1871; subsequently published with additions and a preface by (Sir) Edwin Arnold, under the title of 'In my Indian Garden' (three editions, London, 1878; 8th edit. 1893). 2. 'Under the Punkah,' 1881; 3rd edit. 1891. 3. 'Noah's Ark, or Mornings at the Zoo,' 1881. 4. 'Under the Sun,' Boston, 1882. 5. 'The Poet's Birds,' 1883. 6. 'Sinners and Saints: a Tour across the States and round them,' 1883 (new edit. 1892). 7–9. The 'Indian Garden' series, which enjoyed the largest circulation of any of Robinson's books: 'Chasing a Fortune,' 18mo, 1884; 'Tigers at Large,' 18mo, 1884; and 'The Valley of Teetotum Trees,' 18mo, 1886. 10. 'The Poet's Beasts,' 1885. 11. 'Some Country Sights and Sounds,' 1893. 12. 'The Poets and Nature,' 1893. 13. 'Birds of the Wave and Woodland,' 1894. 14. 'In Garden, Orchard and Spinney,' 1897. 15. 'Bubble and Squeak,' 1902. 16. (With Edward Kay Robinson and Harry Perry Robinson) 'Tales by Three Brothers,' 1902.

[Allibone's Dict. of Eng. Lit.; Who's Who, 1902; Cardiff Free Libraries Annual Reports;

information from brother, Mr. Harry Perry Robinson, and Sampson Low, Marston & Co.]

W. B. O.

ROBINSON, VINCENT JOSEPH (1829–1910), connoisseur of oriental art, born in London on 5 March 1829, was eldest of three sons of Vincent Robinson, sailing ship-owner and merchant, by his wife Elizabeth Hannah. A younger brother, Henry, was president of the society of civil engineers and professor of civil engineering at King's College, London, from 1880 to 1902. Of his two sisters, Elizabeth Julia Robinson *d.* 1904) obtained repute as an etcher; a posthumous exhibition of her work being held at the Fine Art Gallery, Bond Street, in 1905.

After education at private schools at Kilburn and Finchley, Vincent studied at King's College, London. On his father's premature death he extricated his affairs from confusion, and soon built up a prosperous concern as a merchant and commission agent. Interesting himself in the industrial arts of India, Robinson dealt largely in oriental ware of fine character, and at the same time studied the problem of preserving the artistic handicrafts of India. Sir George (then Dr.) Birdwood, who on his return from Bombay entered the India office in 1871, gave Robinson much encouragement. At the Paris exhibition of 1878 Robinson showed some oriental carpets which attracted general attention, and he published in 1882, under the title of 'Eastern Carpets' (London, large 4to), reproductions of the patterns of these and other carpets from water-colour drawings by his sister; Sir George Birdwood supplied descriptive notices. The work preceded the more authoritative treatises of Wilhelm Bode (Leipzig, 1890) and Alois Riegl (Leipzig, 1891). Published originally at three guineas, the price soon rose to ten (cf. *Encycl. Brit.* 11th edit., v. 396–7, s.v. 'Carpets'). Robinson's example, in part at least, led the Austrian Commercial Museum to prepare and publish its monumental work on 'Oriental Carpets' (Vienna, 1892–6; English edition by Sir Caspar Purdon Clarke), to which Robinson was a contributor.

Robinson was director of the Indian section of the Paris Exhibition, 1889, and was made a knight of the Legion of Honour. He was elected F.S.A. the same year (6 June), and he was created C.I.E. in May 1891. About 1878 his business was turned into the limited liability company which, trading in Wigmore Street, still bears his name. He was at first managing director, but soon severed his direct connection with the firm. With his sister, Elizabeth Julia, his lifelong companion, he devoted himself to collecting treasures of decorative art in France, Spain, Italy, and Egypt. In 1894–5 he made a long tour in India.

His collections were first housed at Hopedene, a house near Dorking, built by Mr. Norman Shaw, R.A., but in October 1896 he purchased Parnham House, a fine old Tudor mansion near Beaminster, Dorsetshire, which he restored. There he classified his possessions, describing their main features in 'Ancient Furniture and other Objects of Art, illustrative of a Collection formed . . . at Parnham House, Dorset' (4to, 1902). On the death, on 16 Oct. 1904, of his sister, to whose memory he erected a market-cross at Beaminster, he built another residence, Netherbury Court, overlooking the village churchyard where she was buried. There he died unmarried on 21 Feb. 1910, and was buried by his sister's side. The artistic contents of Parnham were sold there by auction (2–9 Aug. 1910), realising 13,510*l.* Blunt and plain-spoken, Robinson helped to revive in Europe the taste for oriental art.

[Robinson's writings; The Times, 23 Feb. and 10 Aug. 1910; Times of India, 1 March 1910; Frank Archer's An Actor's Notebooks, 1912 (with photograph); Birdwood's Handbook to the British Indian Section 1878; papers lent by his nephew, Mr. Keith Robinson; personal knowledge.]

F. H. B.

ROGERS, EDMUND DAWSON (1823–1910), journalist and spiritualist, born at Holt, Norfolk, on 7 Aug. 1823, was only surviving child of John Rogers and Sarah Dawson his wife.

After education at the Sir Thomas Gresham grammar school in his native town, and working for six years as chemist's apprentice and then as a chemist on his own account, he went in 1845 as surgeon's dispenser to Wolverhampton. He soon afterwards joined the staff of the 'Staffordshire Mercury,' published at Hanley, and in 1848 went to Norwich to take charge of the 'Norfolk News,' a weekly periodical founded in 1845. On 10 Oct. 1870 he started for the proprietors of the 'Norfolk News' the first daily paper in the eastern counties, the 'Eastern Counties Daily Press,' which since May 1871 has been known as the 'Eastern Daily Press.' Removing early in 1873 to London, he established the National Press Agency in Shoe Lane (now in Tudor Street); this he managed until his retirement on a pension in 1894. In his early days in London Rogers helped to produce a weekly paper, 'The Circle'; later he produced on his own account 'The Tenant Farmer' and 'The Free Speaker' (1873–4).

Rogers, who had been brought up a strict Wesleyan, was introduced by Sir Isaac Pitman [q. v. Suppl. I] to Swedenborg's writings, which greatly influenced his religious views; later he was led to study mesmerism and mesmeric healing. He had also while living at Hanley made the acquaintance of Joseph Barker [q. v.]. Convincing himself of the genuineness of spiritualistic manifestations, he helped to form in 1873 the British National Association of Spiritualists. On 8 Jan. 1881 he founded a weekly journal, 'Light,' which became the leading organ of spiritualism and psychical research, and was its editor from 1894 till his death. In 1882 Rogers, Prof. W. F. Barrett, and others joined in establishing the Society for Psychical Research; among the original members were F. W. H. Myers [q. v. Suppl. I], Prof. Henry Sidgwick [q. v. Suppl. I], Edmund Gurney [q. v.], and William Stainton Moses [q. v.]. Rogers was a member of the council from 1882 to 1885. Although painstaking and cautious in psychical research, Rogers, to whom spiritualism was of vital importance, had little sympathy with what he considered the anti-spiritualistic bias of the Psychical Research Society, and resigned his membership in its early years, although he subsequently became an honorary member in 1894. In 1884 he was a founder of the London Spiritualist Alliance, of which he was president from 1892 to death.

On his eightieth birthday he was presented with an album consisting of an illuminated address signed by 1500 spiritualists from all parts of the world. In July 1907 his health failed, and he died at Finchley on 28 Sept. 1910. He was buried in the Marylebone cemetery, Finchley. His 'Life and Experiences,' an autobiography, came out in 1911. Rogers married, on 11 July 1843, Sophia Jane (*d.* 1892), daughter of Joseph and Ann Hawkes, and had issue two sons and four daughters. The younger surviving daughter, Alice, married in January 1908 Mr. Henry Withall, treasurer and vice-president of the London Spiritualist Alliance.

His portrait in oils, painted by James Archer, R.S.A. [q. v. Suppl. II], in 1901, was presented by the artist to the London Spiritualist Alliance.

[Light, 8 Oct. 1910 (obit. memoir), 15 Oct., and following issues (autobiography); published separately as Life and Experiences of Dawson Rogers, 1911 (portraits); Mystic Light Library Bulletin, Feb. 1912; Journ. Soc. Psych. Research, Oct. 1910, xiv. 372; Rogers's horoscope by John B. Shipley (Sarastro) in Modern Astrology, March 1911, pp. 106–109; J. S. Farmer's 'Twixt Two Worlds, pp. 147 seq.; F. Podmore, Modern Spiritualism, 1902, ii. 176–8; private information.] W. B. O.

ROGERS, JAMES GUINNESS (1822–1911), congregational divine, one of thirteen children of Thomas Rogers (1796–1854), of Cornish birth, by his wife Anna, daughter of Edwin Stanley, of Irish birth (connected, through her mother, with the Guinness family), was born on 29 December 1822 at Enniskillen, where his father (like his mother, originally an Anglican) was a preacher in the service of the Irish Evangelical Society (congregational). His father, a successful preacher, removed to Armagh, and in 1826 to Prescot, where he was 'on terms of close intimacy with the unitarian minister,' Gilbert William Elliott. His first schooling was at Silcoates, near Wakefield. Through the kindness of his relative, Arthur Guinness (1768–1855), grandfather of Baron Ardilaun and of Viscount Iveagh, he entered Trinity College, Dublin, where he was a contemporary of William Digby Seymour [q. v.], and latterly was engaged as teacher in an English school. After graduating B.A. in 1843 he entered the Lancashire Independent College, Manchester, where he had as contemporaries Robert Alfred Vaughan [q. v.] and Enoch Mellor; the latter appears to have influenced him most. Leaving in 1845, he was ordained on 15 April 1846, and became minister of St. James's chapel, Newcastle-on-Tyne, where he had to combat the rationalistic spirit engendered by Joseph Barker [q. v.] and came under the spell of Edward Miall [q. v.]. In 1851 he removed to the pastorate of Albion Chapel, Ashton-under-Lyne, then known as 'Cricketty,' from its situation off Crickets' Lane (a fine Gothic structure now takes its place). His ministry here was one of great power, and he was the means of erecting new school premises. In 1857 charges of heresy were brought against Samuel Davidson [q. v. Suppl. I], who as one of his tutors had taken part in the ordination of Rogers. The main point was an alleged impugning of the Mosaic authorship of the Pentateuch. Nothing contributed more to the expulsion of Davidson from his chair in the Lancashire Independent College than a bitter pamphlet,

'Dr. Davidson: His Heresies, Contradictions, and Plagiarisms. By Two Graduates' [namely, Mellor and Rogers] (1857). Long after, Rogers wrote of Davidson: 'The controversies of later years separated us, but they never led me to forget or underrate the benefit I derived from his patient, painstaking, and most valuable labours' (*Autobiog.* 1903, p. 70); this contradicts the tone of the pamphlet, but Rogers was a man who mellowed in many respects as time went on. In 1865 he was chairman of the Lancashire Congregational Union. In the same year he removed to the pastorate of Clapham (Gratton Square) congregational church. Here he ministered till 1900. His denomination honoured him by making him chairman of the Surrey Congregational Union (1868), of the London Congregational Union, and of the Congregational Union of England and Wales (1874). His influence extended beyond his own body, till he came to be regarded, almost as Calamy had been in the early eighteenth century, as the representative of sober yet convinced nonconformity, and was trusted as such by leading authorities in church and state. His friendship with Gladstone was not merely political, but rested on a common feeling of the necessary religious basis for public movements. Edinburgh University made him an honorary D.D. in 1895. He retained his interest in public affairs and his power of address almost to the last. After a short period of failing health he died at his residence, 109 North Side, Clapham Common, on 20 August 1911, and was buried at Morden cemetery, Raynes Park.

He married in 1846 Elizabeth (*d.* 1909), daughter of Thomas Greenall (1788–1851), minister of Bethesda Church, Burnley (1814–48). His three sons and one daughter survived him.

His publications include: 1. 'The Life of Christ,' 1849 (twelve lectures). 2. 'The Ritual Movement. A Reason for Disestablishment,' 1869. 3. 'Why ought not the State to give Religious Education?' 1872. 4. 'Nonconformity as a Spiritual Force,' 1874. 5. 'Facts and Fallacies relating to Disestablishment,' 1875. 6. 'Anglican Church Portraits,' 1876 (a book of merit). 7. 'The Church Systems of England in the Nineteenth Century,' 1881, 1891. 8. 'Friendly Disendowment,' 1881. 9. 'Clericalism and Congregationalism,' 1882 (Jubilee lecture, Congregational Union). 10. 'Present-day Religion and Theology; . . . Down-grade Controversy,' 1888. 11. 'The Forward Movement of the Christian Church,' 1893. 12. 'The Gospel in the Epistles,' 1897. 13. 'The Christian Ideal: a Study for the Times,' 1898. 14. 'An Autobiography,' 1903 (five portraits; vivid impressions, with lack of dates). 15. 'The Unchanging Faith,' 1907 (his best book; has a Quaker publisher). He also edited the 'Congregationalist' (1879–86) and the 'Congregational Review' (1887–91).

[Autobiography, 1903; The Times, 21 Aug. 1911; Who's Who, 1911; Congregational Year Book, 1912; B. Nightingale's Lancashire Nonconformity, 1891, ii. 159, iv. 161, 245.]

A. G.

ROLLS, CHARLES STEWART (1877–1910), engineer and aviator, born on 28 Aug. 1877 at 35 Hill Street, Berkeley Square, London, was third son of John Allan Rolls, first Baron Llangattock (1837–1912), of The Hendre, Monmouth, by his wife Georgiana Marcia, fourth daughter of Sir Charles FitzRoy Maclean, ninth baronet, of Morvaren.

After education at Eton from 1890 to 1893, where he specialised in practical electricity, he matriculated from Trinity College, Cambridge, in 1895, graduating B.A. in mechanical engineering and applied sciences in 1898, and proceeding M.A. in 1902. Rolls was a cyclist from boyhood, riding the high bicycle, and obtaining considerable reputation in the amateur racing field; he won his 'half-blue' for cycling at Cambridge in 1896, and was captain of the university racing team in 1897.

After leaving the university Rolls made a study of practical engineering; he spent some time at the L. & N. W. railway works at Crewe, obtained a third engineer's (marine) certificate and for a time was engineer on his father's yacht 'Ave Maria.' Already in his first year as an undergraduate Rolls had interested himself in the then recent French invention of the motor car. In Dec. 1895 he purchased and imported into England a $3\frac{3}{4}$ h.p. Peugeot car, then the most powerful made. Sir David Salomons, the Hon. Evelyn Ellis, and Mr. T. R. B. Elliot were the only Englishmen who previously owned automobiles. The traffic legislation at the time forbade self-propelled vehicles to travel faster than four miles an hour, and a man carrying a red flag had to precede them on highways. On procuring his car Rolls set out from Victoria station, London, for Cambridge, and was stopped by a policeman owing to the absence of a red flag. He made the journey to Cambridge in $11\frac{3}{4}$ hours—travelling at $4\frac{1}{2}$ miles an hour. In Aug. 1896 the Locomotives on Highways Act freed motor traffic of some of its restrictions. The maximum speed, which was then limited to twelve miles an hour, was raised to twenty by a new Act of 1903. Rolls was prominent among the Englishmen whose sedulous experiments in driving brought motor cars into general use in Great Britain. He met with many hairbreadth escapes, but his courage was indomitable. He tested with intelligent eagerness the numerous improvements in mechanism, with a view to increased speed, which the French pioneers devised. Joining the Self-propelled Traffic Association, he was soon a member of the Automobile Club of France, which was started in 1895, and in 1897 he became a member of the (Royal) Automobile Club in London, serving on the committee till 1908. He soon took part in the races and reliability trials organised by both these clubs. In 1900 he won on a 12 h.p. Panhard the gold medal of the English club for the best performance on the part of an amateur in the thousand miles motor trip between London and Edinburgh. In the next few years he competed in the French motor races between Paris and Madrid, Vienna, Berlin, Boulogne, and Ostend, and in 1905 he was the British representative in the race in France for the Gordon Bennett trophy.

Meanwhile he had formed in London a business, 'C. S. Rolls & Co.,' for the manufacture of motor cars in England, and was joint general manager with Mr. Claude Johnson. The two joined in March 1904 Mr. F. H. Royce, an electrical and mechanical engineer, who had greatly developed the efficiency of the vehicle, and they established the company of 'Rolls-Royce, Ltd.' Mr. Royce became engineer-in-chief, Rolls technical managing director, and Mr. Johnson managing director. Works were constructed in 1898 at Derby. The Rolls-Royce cars proved exceptionally powerful, and from 1906 onwards Rolls drove in racing competitions one of his own cars with great success. He broke the record in 1906 for the journey from Monte Carlo to London with a 20 h.p. Rolls-Royce car, driving 771 miles on end from Monte Carlo to Boulogne in 28 hours 14 minutes.

In 1903 he had become a captain in the motor volunteer corps, afterwards reconstituted as the army motor reserve. He was a delegate for the Royal Automobile Club and the Roads Improvement Association at the International Road Congress in 1908. Aeronautics meanwhile had caught Rolls's attention. In the course of 1901 he began making balloon ascents, which before his death reached a total of 170. He helped to found the Aero Club in England in 1903, and joined the Aero Club of France in 1906. On 1 Oct. of the last year, in the Gordon Bennett international balloon race, he was the British representative, and crossing the Channel from Paris was awarded the gold medal for the longest time spent in the air. At the end of 1908 he visited Le Mans in France to study Wilbur Wright's experiments with his newly invented aeroplane. He was one of the first to fly with Wright, and he published an account of the experience in 'Un vol en aéroplane Wright,' an article in 'La Conquête de l'Air,' Brussels (Nov. 1908).

Acquiring a Wright aeroplane for use in England, he was soon an expert aviator. In June 1910 he made a great reputation by a cross-Channel flight in a Wright aeroplane. He left Dover at 6.30 on the evening of 2 June, and arrived at Calais at 7 o'clock; a quarter of an hour later, after circling round the semaphore station at Sangatte, he started on the homeward journey without touching French soil, and reached Dover at five minutes past eight, at the point from which he set out. This record exploit attracted universal attention.

Next month he took part in a flying tournament at Bournemouth, and was killed on 12 July 1910 through the collapse of the tail-plane of his machine while he was making a steep gliding descent to the aerodrome. He was the first Englishman to be killed while flying on an aeroplane. He was buried at Llangattock-Vibon-Avel church, near Monmouth. A bronze statue over sixteen feet high, by Sir William Goscombe John, R.A., representing Rolls in the costume in which he flew across the Channel, was unveiled by Lord Raglan in Agincourt Square, Monmouth, on 19 Oct. 1911. Another statue by W. C. May was unveiled at Dover on 27 April 1912. A stained glass window in joint memory of Rolls and of Cecil A. Grace, who disappeared while flying on an aeroplane from Calais to Dover on 22 Nov. 1910, was unveiled at Eastchurch church, Kent, on 26 July 1912. Rolls, who was unmarried, was a fellow of the Royal Geographical Society and of the Royal Metallurgical Society as well as an associate member of the Institute of Mechanical Engineering.

He frequently lectured on motors and the history and development of mechanical road locomotion, and besides the publications mentioned contributed a chapter on 'The Caprices of Petrol Motors' in the

Badminton volume on 'Motors' (1902, pp. 164 seq.) and the article on pleasure motors to the eleventh edition of the 'Encyclopædia Britannica.' A paper read by Rolls at the Automobile Club of Great Britain and Ireland was privately printed in 1904. An article, 'My Voyage in the World's Greatest Airship,' was also privately reprinted from the 'London Magazine' (May 1908). Rolls was an accomplished amateur musician and actor, and a good football player.

[The Times, 13–18 July 1910; 20 Oct. 1911; Pearson's Mag., July 1904; M.A.P., art. by Rolls entitled In the Days of my Youth; Page's Engineering Biographies, 1908; Aeronaut. Journ., July 1910 (portrait); Motors, in Badminton Series, 1902; a life of Rolls by Lady Llangattock is in preparation.]

C. J.

ROOKWOOD, first Baron. [See Selwin-Ibbetson, Sir Henry John (1826–1902), politician.]

ROOPER, THOMAS GODOLPHIN (1847–1903), writer on education, born at Abbots Ripton, Huntingdonshire, on 26 Dec. 1847, was son of William Henry Rooper, rector of Abbots Ripton, by his third wife, Frances Catherine, younger daughter of John Heathcote of Conington Castle, Huntingdonshire. Rooper's father was a liberal high churchman. In 1862 Rooper was sent to Harrow into the boarding-house of Dr. H. M. Butler, recently appointed headmaster. In his essay 'Lyonesse' Rooper vividly describes his school days at Harrow (1862–1866), where he began his lifelong study of botany, being one of the founders of the school scientific society. In October 1866 he went to Balliol College, Oxford, taking a second class both in classical moderations in 1868 and in the final classical schools in 1870. To Benjamin Jowett [q. v. Suppl. I], T. H. Green [q. v.], and his college friend, Bernard Bosanquet, his chief intellectual debt was due. He felt that Green's teaching laid the foundation of the beliefs in which he lived and worked. As an undergraduate Rooper intended to take orders, but in 1872 conscientious difficulties deterred him, though he remained till death a communicant lay member of the Church of England. From 1871 to 1877 he was private tutor to Herbrand Russell (afterwards eleventh duke of Bedford), gaining experience in teaching, studying German education, and acquiring a knowledge of history, literature, and science. After teaching for a few months Dr. Butler's young children at Harrow, he was appointed in Nov. 1877 inspector of schools under the Education Department, and spent the rest of his life in the public service, successively in Northumberland, in the Bradford district, and in the Southampton district, including the Isle of Wight.

His influence upon the teachers, the inspectorate, public opinion, and the policy of the board of education grew steadily from year to year. The specific service which he rendered to English elementary education lay mainly (1) in his efforts for the improvement of the teaching of geography, (2) in his encouragement of manual training, (3) in his influence upon methods of teaching in infant schools, (4) in the reforms which he secured in the professional and general education of younger teachers, and (5) in the closer adaptation of the course of study in rural schools to the conditions of country life, especially by the practical encouragement of school gardens. To improve the teaching of geography he wrote two papers, organised a geographical exhibition at Bradford in 1887, and in 1897 founded a Geographical Society at Southampton. Manual training he regarded as a necessary part of general education. He prepared himself for the advocacy of this educational reform by studying Dr. Goetze's work in Leipzig, and by attending Slöjd classes at Nääs. His ideas on the subject were set forth in four important papers. He made a special study of the subject of drawing in infant schools, and of reforms in the methods of teaching children in the lower classes of the elementary schools. Both in the West Riding and in Southampton and the Isle of Wight he initiated classes for ex-pupil teachers, which met an urgent local need, and were subsequently taken over by the local education authorities. In the movement for the improvement of the curriculum of rural schools, Rooper played an unobtrusive but highly influential part. He was unsparing in his attendance at meetings held to advance the cause of rural education, and by the establishment of a school garden at Boscombe provided a model for imitation in other parts of England. His experiments in this field had influence upon the improvement of rural education in Canada. In all these activities Rooper was almost lavish in the financial aid which he privately gave to educational experiments at their critical stage. And in every case he mastered the practical technique of the improvements which he advocated, not only by visits to foreign countries, but by strenuous private study and by investigation in different parts of England. He constantly examined the house of education at Ambleside for his friend, Miss Mason, the founder of the Parents' National Educational Union, for the meetings of which many of his best addresses were prepared. And in the last years of his life he devoted much time and labour to the foundation of the Hartley University College at Southampton.

Rooper's official work began while the elementary schools were still cramped by the narrow traditions of formal training, and by the effects of the system of 'payment by results.' He was one of the inspectors who breathed a new spirit into the methods of English elementary education. Always exacting a high standard, he rose above formalism and routine. He threw himself into every movement likely to interest teachers in their profession and to humanise their work.

Rooper died unmarried at Southampton on 20 May 1903, from spinal tuberculosis, and was buried in the old cemetery there. A memorial tablet is at Hartley University College, Southampton; a memorial scholarship was founded at the same college, and a memorial prize for geography at the Bradford grammar school.

Rooper's chief publications were: 1. 'The Lines upon which Standards I. and II. should be taught under the Latest Code' (Hull and London), 1895. 2. 'School and Home Life' (Hull and London), 1896; new edit. 1907. 3. 'Reading and Recitation,' written in conjunction with Mr. F. B. Lott (Hull and London), 1898. 4. 'Educational Studies and Addresses,' 1902. 5. 'School Gardens in Germany' (in 'Board of Education's Special Reports on Educational Subjects, vol. 9), 1902. He also contributed papers to 'Hand and Eye,' a manual training magazine.

The 'Selected Writings of Thomas Godolphin Rooper,' edited by R. G. Tatton (1907), contains an excellent memoir and good portrait, and a selection of papers already published in Nos. (2) and (4) above, together with 'Handwork in Education,' 'Practical Instruction in Rural Schools,' and other essays.

[Memoir by R. G. Tatton in Rooper's Selected Writings, 1907; family information; personal knowledge.] M. E. S.

ROOSE, EDWARD CHARLES ROBSON (1848–1905), physician, born at 32 Hill Street, Knightsbridge, London, on 23 Nov. 1848, was grandson of Sir David Charles Roose, and was third son of Francis Finley Roose, solicitor, by his wife Eliza Burn. He entered at Trinity Hall, Cambridge, but left the university without a degree. He then went to Guy's Hospital, London, and afterwards spent some time in Paris. He obtained the licence of the Society of Apothecaries in 1870, and in the same year he was admitted L.R.C.P. and L.R.C.S. Edinburgh. In 1872 he became M.R.C.S. England; M.R.C.P. Edinburgh in 1875, and F.R.C.P. Edinburgh in 1877. He graduated M.D. at Brussels in 1877.

Roose first practised at 44 Regency Square, Brighton. In 1885 he migrated to 49 Hill Street, Berkeley Square, London. Here he built up a large and fashionable practice, which his medical attainments hardly justified. He owed his professional success to his social popularity. Later in life he became director of a company interested in Kent coal which involved him in litigation. He emerged from it honourably, but the anxiety led him to limit his professional work, and he retired to East Grinstead, Sussex, where he died on 12 Feb. 1905.

He married in 1870 Edith, daughter of Henry Huggins, D.L.; she died in 1901.

Roose published the following compilations, which, in spite of a wide circulation, had no genuine scientific value: 1. 'Remarks upon some Disease of the Nervous System,' Brighton, 1875. 2. 'Gout and its Relations to Diseases of the Liver and Kidneys,' 1885; 7th edit. 1894; translated into French from the third edition, Paris, 1887; and into German from the fourth edition, Vienna and Leipzig, 1887. 3. 'The Wear and Tear of London Life,' 1886. 4. 'Infection and Disinfection,' 1888. 5 'Nerve Prostration and other Functional Disorders of Daily Life,' 1888; 2nd edit. 1891. 6. 'Leprosy and its Prevention as illustrated by Norwegian Experience,' 1890. 7. 'Waste and Repair in Modern Life,' 1897.

[The Times, 13 Feb. 1905; Medical News, New York, 1905, vol. 86, p. 418.] D'A. P.

ROSS, Sir ALEXANDER GEORGE (1840–1910), lieutenant-general, born at Meerut in the East Indies on 9 Jan. 1840, was eldest of four sons of Alexander Ross of the Bengal civil service (1816–1899) by his wife Isabella, third daughter of Justin McCarty of Carrignavan, co. Cork, Ireland. The father was a descendant of the Rosses of Auchlossin, a branch of the ancient Nairnshire family of Kilravock; he retired from the Bengal civil service after serving as puisne judge of the high court of the

North-West Provinces. His grandfather, also Alexander Ross, went to India as a writer in 1795, and died in 1856 after holding the appointments of resident at Delhi, governor of the Agra presidency, president of the supreme council, and deputy-governor of Bengal. Of his three brothers, Justin Charles, lieutenant-colonel of the Royal 'Bengal' engineers, C.M.G., LL.D. of Edinburgh University, was some time inspector-general of irrigation in Egypt; William Gordon, lieutenant-colonel of the Royal 'Bengal' engineers, retired in 1889, and George Edward Aubert was a barrister-at-law practising at Allahabad.

Ross was brought to England in infancy, and after education at private schools in Edinburgh proceeded to the Edinburgh Academy, where he took many prizes and whence he passed to Edinburgh University. In 1857 his father, while at home on furlough at the outbreak of the Mutiny in India, procured a cadetship for his son, who accompanied him to Calcutta at the end of that year. On arriving in India Ross was attached to the 35th foot, and served with that corps at the attack on Arrah in 1858, receiving the Mutiny medal. On the formation of the Bengal staff corps in 1861 he was posted to the first Sikh infantry of the Punjab frontier force, and served in that regiment in every capacity until his death in 1910, when he was its colonel-in-chief.

In 1867 Ross, then a lieutenant, was selected to raise and equip a mule train for service in the Abyssinian expeditionary force under Sir Robert Napier, afterwards Lord Napier of Magdala [q. v.]. Ross was present at the capture of Magdala and was honourably mentioned in despatches, receiving the medal for the campaign. Ten years later he served throughout the Jowaki expedition on the north-west frontier of the Punjab, first as second-in-command of the 1st Sikhs, and when its commandant, Major Rice, was severely wounded, he assumed command of the regiment. Here again he was mentioned in despatches and received the medal with clasp. He commanded the 1st Sikhs in the Afghan war of 1878–9, including the capture of Ali Musjid, again being mentioned in despatches and receiving the Afghan medal with Ali Musjid clasp. In the campaign against the Mahsud Waziris in 1881 Ross was second-in-command of the 1st Sikhs, and in the Zhob valley expedition in 1890 he commanded the Punjab frontier force column; in both expeditions he was mentioned in despatches.

Ross, who was promoted lieutenant-general in 1897, was created C.B. in 1887 and K.C.B. in 1905. After his retirement he lived at 16 Hamilton Road, Ealing, where he died on 22 June 1910; he was buried in Ealing cemetery. He married on 1 Oct. 1870, at Simla, his father's first cousin, Emma Walwyn, daughter of Lieutenant-general George Edward Gowan, C.B., colonel commandant of the royal (Bengal) horse artillery. An only child, Alexander Edward, joined the Indian Forest Department.

[Holland and Hozier, Official History of the Abyssinian War; Official History of the Second Afghan War; Paget and Mason, Record of Expeditions against the North-West Frontier Tribes.] C. B. N.

ROSS, Sir JOHN (1829–1905), general, son of field-marshal Sir Hew Dalrymple Ross [q. v.] by his wife Elizabeth Margaret, daughter of Richard Graham of Stone House, near Brampton, Cumberland, was born at Stone House on 18 March 1829. He entered the army as second lieutenant of the rifle brigade on 14 April 1846. In 1847 he proceeded to Canada with his regiment, being promoted lieutenant on 29 Dec. 1848. Returning home in 1852, he was promoted captain on 29 Dec. 1854. He accompanied the rifle brigade to the Crimea in 1854; was present at the battles of Alma and Inkerman and siege of Sevastopol, and remained at the seat of war until Feb. 1855. He was mentioned in despatches and received the medal with three clasps, the brevet of major (6 June 1856), the Turkish medal and the fifth class of the Medjidie. He was nominated A.D.C. to Major-general Lawrence at Aldershot in 1856. Proceeding to India in July 1857, he served throughout the Mutiny. He took part in the action of Cawnpore, and the siege and capture of Lucknow, where he helped to raise the camel corps (10 April 1858), consisting of volunteers chiefly from the rifle brigade. Joining Sir Hugh Rose's force in central India, he commanded the corps at the actions of Gowlowlie and Calpi (23 May 1858), in the operations in Central India, and at Jugdespore (20 Oct.). The camel corps was finally disbanded at Agra in April 1860, after having marched over 3000 miles (cf. Despatches, *Lond. Gaz.* 25 May 1858, 22 Feb., 18 April, and 9 Sept. 1859). Ross was awarded the medal with two clasps, a brevet of lieut.-col. (20 July 1858), and the C.B. (28 Feb. 1861). In the campaign on the north-west frontier of India (1863–4) Ross served with the rifle brigade, and was in the action of Shubkuddar (2 Jan.

1864). He received the medal with clasp, and was promoted colonel on 3 April 1865. Subsequently he commanded the Laruf field force as brigadier-general during the operations in the Malay Peninsula in 1875–6, and took part in the capture of Kota-Lana (4 Jan. 1876). On bringing the operations to a successful issue he was mentioned in the general orders of the government of India (*Lond. Gaz.* 18 Feb. and 23 Feb. 1876), and was given the medal with clasp.

Ross held the command of the Saugor district at Jubbulpore in 1874, and of the Presidency district at Fort William (1875 and 1876–9). He became major-general on 1 Oct. 1877 (antedated in 'London Gazette,' 1 March 1870). The Indian expeditionary force which was sent to Malta by Lord Beaconsfield's orders in 1878 during the Eastern crisis was under Ross's command. During the Afghan war of 1878–80 he led the second division of the Kabul field force which defeated the enemy at Shekabad, and was accorded for the service the thanks of the governor-general in council and of the commander-in-chief in India. He accompanied Sir Frederick (afterwards Lord) Roberts in the march from Kabul to Kandahar in command of the infantry division, and was present at the battle of Kandahar (*Lond. Gaz.* 30 July and 3 Dec. 1880). He received the thanks of both houses of parliament, was nominated K.C.B. on 22 Feb. 1881, and was awarded the medal with clasp and bronze decoration. From 1881 to 1886 he held the command of the Poona division of the Bombay army, and in the latter year was promoted lieut.-general (12 Jan.). In 1888 he was appointed commander-in-chief in Canada, and in the following May served as administrator pending the arrival of the governor-general, Sir Frederick Stanley (afterwards sixteenth earl of Derby) [q. v. Suppl. II]. He was nominated G.C.B. on 30 May 1891. He was appointed colonel of the Leicestershire regiment on 6 Feb. 1895, and colonel commandant of the rifle brigade on 29 July 1903. He received the reward for distinguished service, and retired on 18 March 1896. He died on 5 Jan. 1905 at Kelloe, Berwickshire. He married in 1868 Mary Macleod, daughter of A. M. Hay, but obtained a divorce in 1881. He had issue one son and one daughter.

[The Times, 6 Jan. 1905; H. B. Hanna, The Second Afghan War, vol. iii. 1910; Dod's Knightage; Hart's and Official Army Lists; Pratt's People of the Period; Rifle Brigade Chronicle, 1905.] H. M. V.

ROSS, JOSEPH THORBURN (1849–1903), artist, born at Berwick-on-Tweed on 15 May 1849, was youngest child of two sons and two daughters of Robert Thorburn Ross, R.S.A. (1816–1876), by his wife Margaret Scott. The parents removed to Edinburgh for good when Joseph was a baby. Having been educated at the Military Academy, Hill Street, Edinburgh, he was engaged for a time in mercantile pursuits in Leith and Gloucester, but eventually, after a successful career as a student in the Edinburgh School of Art and the life school of the Royal Scottish Academy (1877–80), he devoted himself to painting as a profession. He first exhibited in 1872, but an unconventional strain in his work retarded its official recognition, and it was not till 1896 that he was elected an associate of the Royal Scottish Academy. Portraiture, incident (but not anecdote), fantasy, landscape, and the sea were all treated by him, and if at times decorative intention and realism were imperfectly harmonised, and the execution and draughtsmanship, though bold, lacked mastery, the colour was nearly always beautiful and the result novel and interesting. But it was in sketches made spontaneously for themselves or as studies for more ambitious pictures that he was at his best. He worked in both oil and water-colour and possessed instinctive feeling for the proper use of each medium. Ross was familiar with the best art on the Continent, travelling much in Italy, and he was a frequent exhibitor at some of the leading exhibitions abroad, his 'Serata Veneziana' winning a diploma of honour at Dresden in 1892. He was unmarried and resided at Edinburgh with his sisters. He died from the effects of a fall in his Edinburgh studio on 28 Sept. 1903.

Shortly afterwards, at a memorial exhibition of his work held in Edinburgh, his admirers purchased 'The Bass Rock,' one of his most important pictures, and presented it to the National Gallery of Scotland. One of his two sisters, Christina Paterson Ross, R.S.W. (1843–1906), was well known as a water-colour painter. His other sister, Miss Jessie Ross, Edinburgh, has three portraits of her brother, two when a child by his father, and one in oils painted by Mr. William Small in 1903.

[Scotsman, 29 Sept. 1903; Exhib. catalogues; R.S.A. Report, 1903; introd. to cat. Memorial Exhibition, 1904, by W. D. Mackay, R.S.A.; Scottish Painting, by J. L. Caw; private information.] J. L. C.

ROSS, WILLIAM STEWART, known by the pseudonym of 'SALADIN' (1844–1906), secularist, born at Kirkbean, Galloway, on 20 March 1844, was son of Joseph Ross, a farm servant and a presbyterian. In early life Ross developed a love for poetry and romance. After being educated at the parish school of New Abbey, Kirkcudbrightshire, and at Hutton Hall Academy, Caerlaverock, he became usher at Hutton Hall, and in 1861 was for a short time master at Glenesslin school, Dunscore. After two years as assistant at Hutton Hall Academy, during which he occasionally contributed to newspapers and periodicals, he went in 1864 to Glasgow University to prepare for the Scottish ministry. There he showed much promise as a debater at the Dialectical Society. Conscientious scruples prevented the completion of his theological course. While at the university he sent fugitive pieces in poetry and prose to the 'Dumfries-shire and Galloway Herald,' of which Thomas Aird [q. v.] was editor, and to the 'Dumfries and Galloway Standard,' edited by William M'Dowall [q. v.]. The favourable reception of a novel, 'Mildred Merlock,' which was published serially in the 'Glasgow Weekly Mail,' and brought him forty guineas, finally led him to seek a livelihood from his pen.

On the invitation of the publisher Thomas Laurie, Ross went to London to assist in the publishing of educational works. In 1872 he turned writer and publisher of educational works on his own account at 41 Farringdon Street, calling his firm William Stewart & Co. Many works on English history and literature came from his pen and press. He published books by John Daniel Morell [q. v.], John Miller Dow Meiklejohn [q. v. Suppl. II], and issued 'Stewart's Local Examination' series, and 'Stewart's Mathematical' series of handbooks, as well as four educational magazines, of one of which, the 'School Magazine,' he succeeded Dr. Morell as editor.

In London Ross entered with enthusiasm into the free-thought movement, assisting Charles Bradlaugh [q. v. Suppl. I] in the 'National Reformer' in his struggle for liberty of thought and speech. The publication by Bradlaugh and Mrs. Besant of Knowlton's neo-Malthusian pamphlet, 'The Fruits of Philosophy,' in 1877–8 alienated Ross's sympathies, and he subsequently contributed to the rival free-thought newspaper, the 'Secular Review.' This was amalgamated in June 1877 with the 'Secularist' under the joint editorship of Mr. Charles Watts and Mr. G. W. Foote, and in 1880 Ross became joint editor with Watts, and finally in August 1884 sole editor and proprietor. The name of the journal was changed in January 1889 to the 'Agnostic Journal and Secular Review.' Ross, who wrote for the paper under the pseudonym of 'Saladin,' raised the circulation of the journal by his literary energy and business ability. An outspoken writer on both theology and sociology, he embodied much pungent criticism in 'God and his Book' (1887; new edit. 1906), and in 'Woman, her Glory and her Shame' (2 vols. 1894; new edit. 1906).

Ross was also an enthusiastic writer of verse. His narrative poems, 'Lays of Romance and Chivalry' (1881, 12mo) and 'Isaure and other Poems' (1887), are full of fervour, and betray the influence of Sir Walter Scott. Ross won the medal for the best poem commemorating the unveiling by Lord Rosebery of the statue to Robert Burns at Dumfries in 1879, and also the gold medal for the best poem describing the visit of Kossuth to the grave of Burns.

Ross died of heart failure at Brixton on 30 Nov. 1906, and was buried at Woking cemetery. His wife (born Sherar), who was a teacher at Hutton Hall, survived him with three sons and a daughter.

[The Times, 25 Dec. 1906; Agnostic Journal, 8 Dec. 1906 (special memoir number), 15 Dec. 1906 (with portrait); Gordon G. Flaws, Sketch of the Life and Character of Saladin (W. Stewart Ross), 1883; Biograph, 1879, ii. 155; H. R. Hithersay and G. Ernest, Sketch of the Life of Saladin, 1872.] W. B. O.

ROSSE, fourth EARL OF. [See PARSONS, SIR LAURENCE (1840–1908).]

ROUSBY, WILLIAM WYBERT (1835–1907), actor and theatrical manager, born at Hull on 14 March 1835, was son of a London commercial man. He made his first appearance on the stage as a 'boy-prodigy,' at the Queen's Theatre, Hull, as Romeo, on 16 July 1849, under the management of Mr. Caple, who took a great interest in him and gave him a thorough theatrical training. Before he was sixteen Rousby appeared at Glasgow, Edinburgh, and Liverpool in such characters as Romeo, Hamlet, Othello, Macbeth, and Shylock.

After an engagement at Norwich he joined Samuel Phelps at Sadler's Wells Theatre, and there, as Malcolm in 'Macbeth,' made his first appearance on the London stage on 27 Aug. 1853. He at once achieved success, and while with Phelps he played Lucius in 'Virginius,' Laertes in 'Hamlet,'

Master Waller in 'The Love Chase,' Lysander in 'A Midsummer Night's Dream,' and the Dauphin in 'Henry V.' At the royal command performance at Windsor Castle on 10 Nov. 1853 he played the duke of Bedford in 'Henry V.'

Rousby was still under nineteen when he proceeded to the Theatre Royal, Jersey, to play leading parts there. He afterwards starred in the provinces, where he was likened to Edmund Kean. In 1860 he commenced a series of dramatic recitals, and he also impersonated at the principal provincial theatres leading characters in 'Richard III,' 'The Man in the Iron Mask,' 'The Lady of Lyons,' 'Still Waters Run Deep,' and 'Hamlet.'

At the Theatre Royal, Manchester, in Sept. 1862, he played Harry Kavanagh in Falconer's 'Peep o' Day,' and in 1864, at the same theatre, at the Shakespearean tercentenary anniversary festival, he played Romeo in 'Romeo and Juliet' with Henry Irving as Mercutio, Charles Calvert as Friar Laurence, and Mrs. Charles Calvert as Juliet.

In 1868 he married Clara Marion Jessie Dowse [see ROUSBY, CLARA MARION JESSIE]. On the introduction of William Powell Frith, R.A. [q. v. Suppl. II], who had seen them act in Jersey, Tom Taylor [q. v.], the dramatist, engaged them for the Queen's Theatre, Long Acre. They appeared on 20 Dec. 1869 as Bertuccio and Fiordelisa in 'The Fool's Revenge,' Taylor's adaptation of Hugo's 'Le Roi s'amuse.' Rousby's performance was well received, despite a tendency to over-elaboration. On 22 Jan. 1870 he played Courtenay, earl of Devon, in Tom Taylor's ''Twixt Axe and Crown,' in which his wife achieved a popular triumph. In February 1871 he played Orlando to his wife's Rosalind, and on 18 April 1871 Etienne de Vignolles in Taylor's 'Joan of Arc.' At Drury Lane, under Falconer and F. B. Chatterton's management, he acted King Lear to his wife's Cordelia (29 March 1873). At the Princess's Theatre, under Chatterton's management, he was Cosmo in Miss Braddon's 'Griselda' (13 Nov. 1873) and John Knox in W. G. Wills's 'Mary Queen of Scots' (23 Feb. 1874).

After the death of his wife in 1879 Rousby became proprietor and manager of the Theatre Royal, Jersey, where he reappeared from time to time in his old parts in such plays as 'Jane Shore,' 'Trapped,' and 'Ingomar.' He was also manager of St. Julian's Hall, Guernsey, and to the end of his life gave dramatic recitals in the island. Finally retiring from the stage in 1898, he died at Guernsey on 10 Sept. 1907, and was buried at the Mont-à-l'Abbé cemetery, Jersey. His second wife, Alice Emma Maud Morris, whom he married on 5 July 1880, survived him without issue. An oil portrait painted by Richard Goldie Crawford in 1896 belongs to the widow.

In his prime Rousby was a conscientious actor, with a good voice and a mastery of correct emphasis, but he gave an impression of stiffness and self-consciousness, which grew on him and prevented him from rising high in his profession.

[The Era, 1853–4; 14 Sept. 1907; Guernsey Gossip, 18 Sept. 1907; Pascoe's Dramatic List, 1879; Scott and Howard's Blanchard, 1891; see art. ROUSBY, CLARA MARION JESSIE.]

J. P.

ROUTH, EDWARD JOHN (1831–1907), mathematician, born at Quebec on 20 Jan. 1831, was son of Sir Randolph Isham Routh [q. v.], commissary-general in the army, by his second wife, Marie Louise, sister of Cardinal Elzéar Alexandre Taschereau [q. v.] and first cousin of Sir Henri Elzéar Taschereau [q. v. Suppl. II], chief justice of Canada. Martin Joseph Routh [q. v.], president of Magdalen College, Oxford, recognised a distant relationship by leaving Edward a bequest on his death in 1854.

When eleven years of age Routh was brought to England, and was educated first at University College school, and later at University College, London, where the influence of Augustus De Morgan led him to devote himself to mathematics. He matriculated at London University in 1847, winning an exhibition; he graduated B.A. as a scholar in 1849, and carried off the gold medal for mathematics and natural philosophy in the examination for M.A. in 1853.

Meanwhile he entered Peterhouse, Cambridge, as a 'pensioner' on 1 June 1850, and read with the great coach of that time, William Hopkins [q. v.]. James Clerk-Maxwell [q. v.] entered at Peterhouse in the same term with Routh, but migrated to Trinity at the end of his first term, from, it is said, an anticipation of future rivalry. In the mathematical tripos of 1854 Routh came out senior wrangler with Clerk Maxwell as second. In the examination for the Smith's prizes, the two, for the first time on record, divided the honours equally between them.

On graduating B.A. in January 1854 Routh commenced 'coaching' in mathematics, at first assisting William John Steele, a fellow of Peterhouse, who had a high reputation and a large connection. Routh was elected fellow of Peterhouse next year, and was appointed college lecturer in mathematics, a post which he retained till 1904. He was also assistant tutor from 1856 to 1868 and was at various times junior dean, junior bursar, and prælector of his college.

In 1857 he was invited to the Royal Observatory, Greenwich, with a view to a vacant post there as a first assistant. He did not take the appointment, but at Greenwich he met Hilda, eldest daughter of Sir George Biddell Airy [q. v. Suppl. I], the astronomer-royal, whom he married on 31 Aug. 1864.

For more than thirty years Routh's chief energies were spent at Cambridge in preparing private pupils for the mathematical tripos. On Steele's early death he became the chief mathematical coach in the university, and the successes of his pupils were unprecedented. In the tripos of 1856 Charles Baron Clarke, his first pupil [q. v. Suppl. II], was third wrangler. In 1858 two pupils, Slesser (Queens') and (Sir) Charles Abercrombie Smith, were respectively first and second wrangler and first and second Smith's prizemen. In the following years, pupils of his were senior wranglers twenty-seven times and Smith's prizemen forty-one times. In the tripos of 1862 fifteen of his nineteen pupils were in the list of thirty-two wranglers, seven among the first ten. From 1862 to 1882 inclusive he had an unbroken succession of twenty-two senior wranglers (two in 1882, one in January and one in June under new regulations), and he had four more in 1884, in 1885, in 1887 (when four seniors were bracketed), and in 1888, when he retired. His senior wranglers included Lord Justice Stirling (1861), Lord Justice Romer (1863), Lord Rayleigh (1865, chancellor of Cambridge University), Lord Moulton (1868), John Hopkinson (1871), (Sir) Donal McAlister (1877, principal of Glasgow University), (Sir) Joseph Larmor (1880, M.P. for Cambridge University); and of other wranglers may be mentioned (Sir) J. J. Thomson, O.M., (Sir) C. A. Parsons, Lord Justice Buckley, and (Sir) Richard Solomon. Of the 990 wranglers between 1862 and 1888, 480 were Routh's pupils. On Routh's retirement from his work as private coach in 1888 his old pupils presented Mrs. Routh with her husband's portrait by (Sir) Hubert von Herkomer (*The Times*, 5 Nov. 1888).

Apart from his personality, which inspired his pupils with implicit confidence in his powers, and his lucidity of exposition, Routh owed his success as a teacher to his perception of the relative proportions in which the many subjects of the tripos should be studied; to his capacity for showing his pupils how to learn and how to use their knowledge, and to his practice of continually testing their work by causing them to reproduce what they had been learning.

Despite his absorption in teaching Routh kept fully abreast of current advances in mathematical knowledge and made many original investigations. Elected fellow of the Cambridge Philosophical Society in 1854, an original member of the London Mathematical Society in 1865, a fellow of the Royal Astronomical Society in 1866, and of the Royal Society in 1872, he contributed to the 'Proceedings' of these societies as well as to the 'Mathematical Messenger' and the 'Quarterly Journal of Mathematics' numerous papers on varied topics in geometry, dynamics, physical astronomy, wave motion, vibrations, and harmonic analysis. As early as 1855 he had joined Lord Brougham in preparing a separate volume, 'An Analytical View of Newton's Principia,' and in 1860 he supplied an urgent want by issuing a masterly elementary treatise on 'Rigid Dynamics' (7th enlarged edit. 2 vols. 1905; German transl., Leipzig, 1898, with pref. by Prof. Klein of Göttingen). Other important contributions by Routh to mathematical literature were a treatise on 'Statics' (1891, 2 vols.; revised edit. 1896; enlarged edit. 1902) and 'Dynamics of a Particle' (1898). These three dynamical treatises constitute an encyclopædia and bibliography on the subject which have no equal either here or abroad. In 1877 Routh won the Adams prize with his 'Treatise on the Stability of a Given State of Motion, particularly Steady Motion,' which he wrote in a Christmas vacation. Since the publication of Hamilton's equations of motion and Sir William Thomson's (Lord Kelvin) theory of the 'ignoration of co-ordinates' no greater advance has probably been made in dynamics than by Routh's theorem of the 'Modified Lagrangian Function,' first given in this essay. A large part of the work on equations of motion in Thomson and Tait's 'Natural Philosophy' was rewritten for the second edition in the light of Routh's developments of the theme.

Routh took little part in academic business, but he served for four years (1888–92) on the council of the senate of Cambridge University, and also on the Board of Mathematical Studies. He examined in the mathematical triposes of 1860, 1861, 1888, 1889, 1893, and 1900, besides acting as examiner in London University from 1859 to 1864 and again from 1865 to 1870. To the last he actively opposed the changes in the Cambridge mathematical tripos which were effected in 1907.

In 1883 he and his friend, W. H. Besant, St. John's College, were the first to take the new Cambridge degree of Sc.D., and in the same year his college elected him one of its first honorary fellows under the new statutes. He was made hon. LL.D. of Glasgow in 1878, and hon. Sc.D. of Dublin in 1892. He was also a fellow of the Geological Society from 1864 and of London University.

Routh died at Cambridge on 7 June 1907, and was buried at Cherryhinton. His wife survived him. By her he had five sons and one daughter. The eldest son, Edward Airy, a lieutenant in the royal artillery, died in 1892 from the effects of service in Egypt; and the youngest, Rupert John, in the Indian civil service, died at the beginning of a promising career in September 1907. George Richard Randolph is an H.M. inspector of schools; Arthur Lionel, a lieutenant in the royal artillery; and Harold Victor, professor of Latin at Trinity University, Toronto.

A replica of the portrait by Sir Hubert von Herkomer was presented by Mrs. Routh to Peterhouse in 1890, and it hangs in the hall.

Besides the works cited, Routh published 'Solutions of Senate House Problems' with Henry William Watson [q. v. Suppl. II] (1860).

[Family information; personal knowledge; Proc. Roy. Soc., 84A; Proc. Royal Astron. Soc., and London Math. Soc.; The Times, 8 June 1907; Nature, 27 June 1907].

J. D. H. D.

ROWE, JOSHUA BROOKING (1837–1908), antiquary and naturalist, born at Plymouth on 12 June 1837, was only son of Joshua Brooking Rowe of Brixton, near Plymouth, printer and bookseller of Plymouth, by his second wife, Harriett Caroline, daughter of Captain Charles Patey, R.N. Samuel Rowe [q. v.], writer about Dartmoor, was his uncle. After education at a private school in Plymouth the younger Joshua was in 1860 admitted a solicitor, and practised for many years in Plymouth in partnership with Francis Bulteel, and latterly with W. L. Munday.

Through life he devoted his leisure to literary and scientific research. A paper on 'The Mammals, Birds, Reptiles, and Amphibians of Devon,' which he read before the Plymouth Institution in 1862, was issued separately next year. Subsequently he published much on archæological topics, and encouraged local archæological study. In 1862 he helped to form the Devon Association, of which he was president in 1882, and joint honorary secretary from 1901 till death. To the 'Transactions' of the association he contributed over fifty papers. In 1875 he was elected F.S.A., of which he was a local secretary. He was also a fellow of the Linnean Society, and a member of numerous antiquarian societies, being a founder of the Devon and Cornwall Record Society.

From 1882 he resided at Plympton St. Maurice, where he was active in local affairs. He transcribed the parish registers for publication in the 'Parish Magazine.' On 28 June 1908 he died at Plympton St. Maurice, and was buried in the churchyard there.

In December 1864 he married at St. Andrew's, Plymouth, Sara Foale, daughter of Henry Crews, of Plympton, by whom he had no issue.

A photograph hangs in the Exeter public library, to which he bequeathed his library of about 10,000 volumes, pamphlets and manuscripts, including an unpublished history of Plympton St. Mary.

Rowe revised Samuel Rowe's 'Perambulation of . . . Dartmoor' (Exeter, 1896), and also published: 1. 'The Cistercian Houses of Devon,' Plymouth, 1878. 2. 'The History of Plympton Erle,' Exeter, 1906. 3. 'The Ecclesiastical History of Plymouth,' 4 parts; Plymouth, 1873–4–5–6. He wrote for many local periodicals, and was joint editor of 'Devon Notes and Queries,' some of his contributions to which were reprinted separately. The article on the 'Mammals of Devon,' for the Devon volume of the 'Victoria County Histories,' is by him.

[Trans. of Devonshire Association, vol. 40, 1908; Devon and Cornwall Notes and Queries, 1908, v. 121; private information.]

H. T.-S.

ROWLANDS, DAVID, 'DEWI MON' (1836–1907), Welsh scholar and poet, son of John and Margaret Rowlands, was born on 4 March 1836 at Geufron, Rhosybol, Anglesey. Two years later, his father moved to the farm at Ty Cristion, Bodedern. After a village education he was apprenticed at thirteen, and spent some time in shops at Holyhead and Hatfield. But at the instance of the

Rev. W. Griffith, Holyhead, he became an independent preacher, and in 1853 entered Bala Congregational College. Thence he went in 1856 to New College, London; he returned to Bala in 1857 for a year as assistant-tutor, and in 1858 became a member of the Congregational College at Brecon, graduating B.A. at London University in 1860. His first pastorate was at Llanbrynmair (1861–6); he was then for four years (1866–70) minister of the English church at Welshpool, and for two (1870–2) of the English church at Carmarthen. From 1872 to 1897 he was one of the tutors of Brecon College, and from 1897 head of the institution. He died at Brecon on 7 Jan. 1907.

Rowlands, whose bardic name was 'Dewi Mon,' was of versatile gifts, an able preacher and teacher, a skilful writer of Welsh and English verse, and a conspicuous figure in Welsh literary and political life. In his later years the critical state of his health kept him somewhat in retirement. His chief works are: 1. 'Caniadau Serch' (Welsh lyrics), Bala, 1855, published when he was nineteen. 2. 'Sermons on Historical Subjects,' London, 1870. 3. 'Grammadeg Cymraeg,' Wrexham, 1877, a short Welsh grammar. 4. 'Gwersi mewn Grammadeg,' Dolgelly, 1882, a manual of lessons in grammar. 5. A Welsh version of the 'Alcestis' of Euripides, 1887, sent in for competition at the Aberdare eisteddfod of 1885; it divided the prize with another version and both were printed in one volume at the cost of the marquis of Bute. 6. 'Telyn Tudno,' Wrexham, 1897, containing the life and works of his brother-in-law, the poet Tudno (Thomas Tudno Jones). Rowlands worked much with the composer Joseph Parry, [q. v. Suppl. II], and supplied English words for the opera 'Blodwen' and the oratorios 'Emmanuel' and 'Joseph'; he was also literary editor of Parry's 'Cambrian Minstrelsie' (Edinburgh, 1893). He was one of the four editors of the hymns in 'Y Caniedydd Cynulleidfaol' (London, 1895), the hymn and tune book of the Welsh congregationalists, and in 1902 was chairman of the Congregational Union of Wales. He took a leading part in Breconshire politics and was a member of the committee which drafted the county scheme of intermediate education. He married (1) in 1864, Mary Elizabeth, daughter of William Roberts of Liverpool, by whom he left a son, Wilfred; (2) in 1897, Alice, step-daughter of J. Prothero, of Brecon.

[Who's Who, 1907; 'Album Aberhonddu' ed. T. Stephens, 1898, pp. 118–9; T. R. Roberts, Dict. of Eminent Welshmen; Brit. Weekly, 10 Jan. 1907; Geninen, March 1907; Congregational Yearbook, 1908, pp. 196–7.]

J. E. L.

ROWTON, Baron. [See Corry, Montagu William Lowry (1838–1903), politician and philanthropist.]

RUNDALL, FRANCIS HORNBLOW (1823–1908), inspector-general of Indian irrigation, born at Madras on 22 Dec. 1823, was youngest son of the seven children of Lieut.-colonel Charles Rundall, of the East India Company's service, judge advocate-general of the Madras army, by his wife Henrietta Wryghte. The second of his three brothers, Captain John William, Madras engineers, died on active service in the second Burmese war on 12 Nov. 1852.

Educated at Kensington grammar school and at the East India Company's military seminary at Addiscombe (1839–41), he was gazetted to the Madras engineers on 10 Dec. 1841, and after the usual course at Chatham reached India on 23 Dec. 1843. He was adjutant of the Madras sappers and miners for a few months, but in Sept. 1844 joined the public works department as assistant to General Sir Arthur Thomas Cotton [q. v. Suppl. I] in his surveys for the irrigation of the Godavery delta. After brief duty in Tanjore, to acquire knowledge of the great Cauvery works, he assisted Cotton in the construction of the Godavery works from 1845 to 1851. Warmly attached to his chief, he shared both his religious fervour and his enthusiastic belief in irrigation and navigable canals for India. He was appointed district engineer of Vizagapatam and Ganjam in 1851 (when also he was promoted captain) and district engineer of Rajamahendri in May 1855, a position which gave him charge of the further Godavery works then in progress.

In 1859 Rundall became superintending engineer of the northern circle and departmental secretary to the Madras government. He was soon serving in addition as consulting engineer to the government for the Madras Irrigation Company's works. In 1861 he was gazetted lieutenant-colonel and granted special leave to be chief engineer to the East India Irrigation and Canal Company, then constructing the Orissa canals on plans laid down by Cotton. Though water was supplied from 1865, the works were not sufficiently advanced to be effective in the terrible famine of the following year, but under Rundall they constituted an excellent form of relief labour. Cotton's sanguine estimates had to be largely exceeded; the cultivators were slow to avail themselves of the water supply; rates had to be lowered to an unremunerative figure; the company failed to raise further capital, and the canals were taken over by the government in 1869. Though no financial success, they are of great value in time of drought.

From July 1867 Rundall was chief irrigation engineer and joint secretary to the Bengal government, and the Son canals, which had also been projected by the East India Irrigation and Canal Company, for the service of the Shahabad, Gaya, and Patna districts, were commenced under his orders. By them more than half a million acres are annually watered, and they yield about 4 per cent. on the capital invested. From April 1872 he was inspector-general of irrigation and deputy secretary to the government of India, and was thus brought into close touch with the progress of irrigation throughout the country. He gained a reputation for enthusiasm, soundness of judgment, and accuracy in estimates. During his service, which terminated in April 1874, he had only once taken leave home.

Rundall, who had been promoted colonel in June 1868 and major-general in March 1869, was created a C.S.I. in Dec. 1875, and was made colonel commandant of the royal engineers in 1876. He became lieutenant-general at the end of 1878, and general in Nov. 1885, being placed on the unemployed supernumerary list in July 1881.

At the invitation of the Khedive Ismail, Rundall examined the delta of the Nile in 1876–7, and submitted plans and estimates for irrigation. His proposals, which included the construction of a mighty dam not far from the site of the present one at Assouan, were frustrated by the bankruptcy of the country. Rundall's services were engaged by a syndicate formed in 1883 to construct a Palestinian canal admitting of the passage of the largest vessels from the Mediterranean to the Red Sea, by way of the Jordan Valley and the Gulf of Akaba, but the project did not mature (cf. his 'The Highway of Egypt: Is it the Suez Canal or any other Route between the Mediterranean and the Red Sea?' London 1882). After retirement he lectured on Indian irrigation at the Chatham school of military engineering, and some of the lectures were privately printed (Chatham, 1876). He also wrote the following pamphlets, 'Notes on Report of Ganges Canal Committee' (Cuttack, 1866); 'Memo. on the Madras Irrigation Company's Works at Kurnool' (Dorking, undated); and a 'Review of Progress of Irrigation Schemes in relation to Famine Aspects,' placed before a Parliamentary select committee in 1878.

He died at Moffat, N.B., at the house of his son-in-law, the Rev. Francis Wingate Pearse, headmaster of St. Ninian's school, on 30 Sept. 1908, and was buried at Moffat cemetery. He married on 8 Dec. 1846 Fanny Ada, daughter of Captain W. G. Seton-Burn, 3rd light dragoons, and had three daughters and two sons, of whom the eldest is Colonel Frank Montagu Rundall, C.B., D.S.O., late 4th Gurkha rifles.

[Vibart's Addiscombe: its Heroes and Men of Note, 1894; Lady Hope's Life of General Arthur Cotton, 1900; India List, 1908; Imp. Gaz. of India, 1908, articles on Orissa and Son canals; Journ. of Royal Engineers, vol. viii. Dec. 1908; The Times, 1 Oct. 1908; information kindly supplied by Colonel F. M. Rundall.] F. H. B.

RUSDEN, GEORGE WILLIAM (1819–1903), historian of Australia and New Zealand, born at Leith Hill Place, Surrey, on 9 July 1819, was third son of the Rev. George Keylock Rusden and Anne, only daughter of the Rev. Thomas Townsend. While yet a lad he emigrated to New South Wales in 1834 with his father, who was appointed chaplain for the Maitland district.

Rusden first tried his hand at pastoral work, but he soon turned to politics; from 1841 onwards he wrote for the press and lectured. On 4 July 1849 he became under the New South Wales government agent for national schools at Port Phillip; later he was transferred to Moreton Bay. When in 1851 the new colony of Victoria was constituted, he was appointed (10 Oct.) chief clerk in the colonial secretary's office, and on 11 Oct. 1852 clerk to the executive council. On 18 Nov. 1856, when a full parliament of two chambers was established, he became clerk of parliaments. In 1853 he joined the national board of education for Victoria and the council of the Melbourne University. Always deeply interested in Shakespeare, he had much to do with the establishment of the Shakespeare scholarships at that university in 1864.

Having gradually formed the idea of writing a history of Australasia, Rusden visited England in 1874 with a view to finding support for the enterprise, and was much encouraged by Anthony Trollope; in the latter part of 1878 he visited New Zealand in connection with the history which he was writing of that part of the empire. In 1882, having retired on pension, he again visited New Zealand and then came on to England to take up his residence and see to the publication of his histories, both of which came out in 1883. Their publication produced an unfortunate episode: an action for libel was brought against Rusden by the Hon. John Bryce, a member of the New Zealand legislature, respecting whose action during the Maori wars the historian had used severe and unguarded criticism. The most eminent counsel at the bar were engaged, and the case lasted eight days during March 1886. A jury cast Rusden in 5000*l.* damages, afterwards reduced by consent to about half that amount on a new trial at which Rusden himself conducted his case with marked ability. At the second hearing Rusden retracted his statements. The press was on the whole unfavourable to Rusden, who was held to be guilty of serious indiscretion.

About 1893 Rusden returned to Melbourne to spend the rest of his life. He divided his time between his literary work and municipal affairs; but his health gradually failed, and he died at his house, Cotmandene, South Yarra, on 23 Dec. 1903. Rusden was of striking appearance and was a genial and interesting companion.

Rusden's chief works were his 'History of Australia' (3 vols. 1883) and 'History of New Zealand' (3 vols. 1883); revised editions of both were published at Melbourne in 1895–7. These works offer a broad survey of the growth of two great colonies, but Rusden's defect of critical faculty better adapts them to the use of the public man than of the student.

Rusden also published: 1. 'Moyarra, an Australian Legend,' a poem, Maitland, 1851. 2. 'National Education,' 1853. 3. 'Discovery, Survey, and Settlement of Port Phillip,' 1872. 4. 'Curiosities of Colonisation,' 1874. 5. 'William Shakespeare: his Life, Work and Teaching,' Melbourne, 1903. Among many pamphlets which he issued under his own name or the pseudonyms of 'Vindex' or 'Yittadavin' the most interesting are his 'Character of Falstaff' (1870) and a 'Letter to "The Times" on the Law of Libel' (1890).

[Melbourne Argus and Age, 24 Dec. 1903; Athenæum, 6 Feb. 1904; Mennell's Dict. of Australas. Biog.; Early Victorian Blue Books; his own evidence in Bryce *v.* Rusden (pp. 264 seq.); Brit. Mus. Cat.; personal knowledge.] C. A. H.

RUSSELL, HENRY CHAMBERLAINE (1836–1907), astronomer, born at West Maitland, New South Wales, on 17 March 1836, was son of the Hon. Bourne Russell. After education at the West Maitland grammar school and at Sydney University, where he graduated B.A. in 1858, he was appointed (1 Jan. 1859) an assistant at the Sydney observatory, and succeeded to the position of government astronomer in August 1870. The first years of his directorship were devoted to the enlargement and re-equipment of the observatory, and to the establishment throughout the colony of a very large number of meteorological stations, furnished in great part with instruments designed and made by him, and maintained by volunteer observers who were drawn into the work by Russell's enthusiasm. Throughout his life he devoted much time to the discussion of the great mass of observations furnished by these volunteers. His proof that the River Darling loses very much more water than can be accounted for by discharge and evaporation led to important gain in knowledge of the underground water systems of the country.

Russell's first great service to astronomy was the organisation of the Australian observations of the transit of Venus in 1874. He equipped four parties, and prepared the account of the whole work which appeared in 1892. He represented Australia at the congress summoned to meet in Paris in 1887 to consider the construction of a photographic chart of the sky. He promised the co-operation of the Sydney observatory, and at once ordered the necessary objective, but with characteristic resource decided to construct the mounting at his observatory. To Sydney the committee of the astrographic chart entrusted the zone of south declination 54° to 62°. The carrying forward of this work, very considerable for an observatory of modest resources, fully occupied the later years of Russell's directorship. He could not complete it, but he left it well established, and on the way to completion.

Russell took an active part in initiating technical education in New South Wales; he was a fellow of the University of Sydney, and vice-chancellor in 1891. He was four times president of the Royal Society of New South Wales, and first president of the Australasian Association for the Advancement of Science. He was elected F.R.S. in 1886, and was created C.M.G. in 1890.

His published works include: 'Climate of New South Wales: Descriptive, Historical, and Tabular' (Sydney, 1877); 'Photographs of the Milky Way and Nubeculæ taken at Sydney Observatory 1890' (fol. Sydney, 1891); 'Description of the Star Camera at the Sydney Observatory' (4to, Sydney, 1892); 'Observations of the Transit of Venus, 9 Dec. 1874; made at Stations in New South Wales' (4to, Sydney, 1892), with many volumes of astronomical and meteorological observations published from the Sydney observatory, and a great number of papers in the memoirs and monthly notices of the Royal Astronomical Society, the Royal Society of New South Wales, and other scientific societies.

Russell resigned the position of government astronomer in 1905, and died at Sydney on 22 Feb. 1907. He married Emily Jane, daughter of Ambrose Foss of Sydney, in 1861; she survived him with one son and four daughters.

[Proc. Roy. Soc., A. 80, 1908; Monthly Notices Roy. Astr. Soc. lxviii. 241, 1908.]

A. R. H.

RUSSELL, THOMAS O'NEILL (1828–1908), a founder of the Gaelic movement in Ireland, born at Lissanode, Moate, co. Westmeath, in 1828, was son of Joseph Russell, a gentleman farmer who belonged to the Society of Friends. After a sound elementary education at the national school he assisted in the management of his father's extensive farm. About 1850 he found employment in Dublin in a small business firm of W. R. Jacob, a Quaker, which subsequently developed into one of the greatest concerns in Ireland. Russell soon travelled for the firm, and subsequently he followed the same calling for other houses in Ireland, France, and America.

In 1858 he was an occasional contributor to the newly established 'Irishman,' an advanced nationalist organ. There he urged the revival of the ancient Irish tongue. This became the foremost aim of his career. He learned Irish and soon wrote it with facility. His association with the 'Irishman' during the Fenian activity exposed him to risk of arrest. Migrating to America, he remained in the United States for nearly thirty years. There he obtained employment as a commercial traveller, and in that capacity he visited every state of the Union. He regularly contributed to the 'Chicago Citizen' and corresponded with the Irish press, invariably writing on the Irish language. He also lectured on the same theme.

In 1895 he returned to Ireland with a moderate competence, and at once began to organise opinion in Dublin by means of essay and lecture in the interests of a Gaelic revival. To his efforts to arouse in Irishmen a sense of the value of their ancient language and music was largely due the inauguration of the Gaelic League in 1893 and of the Feis Ceoil (Irish musical festival) in 1897. He died on 15 June 1908 in Synge St., Dublin, and was buried in Mount Jerome cemetery. Russell was helped in his propaganda by his splendid physique, his fiery enthusiasm, and his command of forcible language.

Apart from his contributions to the press Russell published two novels, descriptive of Irish life, of which the first, 'Dick Massey' was issued at Glasgow in 1860 (under the pseudonym of 'Reginald Tierney') and has run through numerous editions. It is a homely story, not without serious faults of composition and construction, but it hit the popular taste. Russell's other works are: 1. 'True Hearts' Trials,' a novel, Glasgow 1873; new edit. Dublin 1907. 2. 'Speech of Robert Emmet translated into Irish,' New York, 1879. 3. 'Beauties and Antiquities of Ireland,' 1897. 4. 'Teanga Thíoramhuil na h-Eireann,' Dublin, 1897. 5. 'A Selection of Moore's Irish Melodies, translated by Archbishop McHale,' edited, with additions, Dublin, 1899. 6. 'Fíor Chláirsseach na h-Eireann, or the True Harp of Ireland,' edited by Russell, Dublin, 1900. 7. 'An Borama Laigean, or the Leinster Tribute, put into modern Irish,' Dublin, 1901. 8. 'The Last Irish King,' a drama in three acts, Dublin, 1904. 9. 'Red Hugh,' a drama in three acts, Dublin, 1905. 10. 'Is Ireland a Dying Nation?' Dublin, 1906.

[Literary Year Book, 1906; Journal of National Literary Society of Ireland, 1900–4, p. 128; Irish Independent, 1908; personal knowledge.]

D. J. O'D.

RUSSELL, WILLIAM CLARK (1844–1911), novelist, born at New York on 24 Feb. 1844, was son of Henry Russell [q. v. Suppl. I], vocalist and song composer, by his wife Isabella daughter of Charles Lloyd of Bingley Hall, Birmingham. From his mother, who was a relative of the poet William Wordsworth [q. v.], and herself a writer of verse, Clark Russell mainly inherited his taste for literature. After education at private schools at Winchester and Boulogne he joined the British merchant service in 1858, and served as an apprentice on board the sailing vessel Duncan Dunbar.

He made several voyages to India and Australia, and while off the coast of China in 1860 he witnessed the capture of the Taku forts by the combined British and French forces. His life on shipboard was marked by privations which seriously undermined his health. Nevertheless from these early experiences Clark Russell gathered the material which was to be his literary stock-in-trade.

In 1866 he retired from the merchant service, and after a few months in a commercial calling he adopted a literary career. He began by writing a tragedy in verse, which was produced at the Haymarket Theatre in 1866, but proved a failure. Subsequently he took up journalism. In 1868 he served as editor of 'The Leader,' and in 1871 he wrote for the 'Kent County News.' But he soon settled down to writing nautical tales of adventure, which was henceforth his main occupation. His first novel, 'John Holdsworth, Chief Mate' (1875), at once attracted attention, and the still more popular 'Wreck of the Grosvenor' (1877; new edit. 1900) established his reputation as a graphic writer of sea stories. While these early works brought him little profit owing to the sale of the copyright to the publishers, they served as useful advertisement. For thirty years a constant stream of more or less successful novels flowed from his fertile pen; in all he produced fifty-seven volumes.

Meanwhile Clark Russell continued to contribute articles on sea topics to the leading journals. In 1880 he received an invitation from Joseph Cowen [q. v. Suppl. I] to join the staff of the 'Newcastle Chronicle,' and later for a brief period he was editor of 'Mayfair.' In 1882 he accepted the offer of a post on the 'Daily Telegraph,' and for seven years he was a regular contributor to that paper under the pseudonym of 'A Seafarer.' The tragedies and comedies of the sea were his principal theme, and his masterly account of the wreck of the Indian Chief on the Long Sand (5 Jan. 1881) enhanced his growing reputation as a descriptive writer. Many of his fugitive articles in the 'Daily Telegraph' were reprinted in volume form under such titles as 'My Watch Below' (1882) and 'Round the Galley Fire' (1883).

A zealous champion in the press of the grievances of the merchant seamen, Clark Russell urged that the hardships of their life were practically unchanged since the repeal of the Navigation Acts in 1854, and that despite the Merchant Shipping Act of 1876 [see Plimsoll, Samuel, Suppl. I] ships were still sent to sea undermanned and overladen. In response to this agitation further acts of parliament to prevent unseaworthy vessels putting to sea were passed in 1880, 1883, 1889, and 1892. In 1885 Clark Russell protested against the seamen and firemen not being represented on the shipping commission, which was appointed by Mr. Chamberlain (*Contemporary Review*, March 1885). In 1896 the Duke of York (afterwards King George V) expressed his opinion that the great improvement in the conditions of the merchant service was due in no small degree to Clark Russell's writings (cf. preface to Clark Russell's *What Cheer!* 3rd edit. 1910).

Latterly severe attacks of rheumatoid arthritis considerably reduced his literary activity, and compelled him to retire first to Ramsgate and subsequently to Deal. His last years were spent at Bath. Although crippled by disease, he continued working up to the last. He died at Bath on 8 Nov. 1911. He married in 1868 Alexandrina, daughter of D. J. Henry of the Institute of Civil Engineers, younger brother of Sir Thomas Henry [q. v.], police magistrate. She survived him with one son, Mr. Herbert Russell, writer on naval subjects, and three daughters.

Sir Edwin Arnold [q. v. Suppl. II] wrote of Clark Russell as 'the prose Homer of the great ocean,' while Algernon Charles Swinburne [q. v. Suppl. II], with characteristic exaggeration, called him 'the greatest master of the sea, living or dead.' Clark Russell's novels rendered the same benefit to the merchant service that those of Captain Marryat [q. v.] did to the royal navy. They stimulated public interest in the conditions under which sailors lived, and thereby paved the way for the reform of many abuses. His descriptions of storms at sea and atmospheric effects were brilliant pieces of word painting, but his characterisation was often indifferent, and his plots were apt to become monotonous.

In addition to the works already mentioned the following are a few of his best-known novels: 1. 'The Frozen Pirate,' 1877. 2. 'A Sailor's Sweetheart,' 1880; 4th edit. 1881. 3. 'An Ocean Tragedy,' 1881. 4. 'The Death Ship,' 1888; new edit. 1901. 5. 'List, ye Landsmen,' 1894; 2nd edit. 1899. 6. 'Overdue,' 1903. He also published popular lives of 'Dampier' ('Men of Action' series, 1889), 'Nelson' ('Heroes of the Nations' series, 1890; new edit. 1905), and 'Collingwood' (1891), which was illustrated by Frank Brangwyn, A.R.A. His poems and naval ballads were collected into a volume entitled 'The Turnpike Sailor, or Rhymes on the Road' (1907), of which a third edition appeared in 1911 under the title of 'The Father of the Sea.'

[The Times and Daily Telegraph, 9 Nov. 1911; Athenæum, 11 Nov. 1911; Harper's Mag., June 1888; Idler, Aug. 1892; A National Asset, by Capt. W. J. Ward, prefixed to Clark Russell's Father of the Sea (portrait), 1911; private information.] G. S. W.

RUSSELL, Sir WILLIAM HOWARD (1820–1907), war-correspondent, was born at Lily Vale, in the parish of Tallaght, county Dublin, on 28 March 1820. His father, John Russell, came of a family which had been long settled in county Limerick, and was agent in Dublin for a Sheffield firm. His mother was Mary, daughter of John Kelly, a grazier, who owned a small property at Lily Vale. Near by the house in which Russell was born some ruins, known as Castle Kelly, suggested a family prosperity, which was already only a legend at the time of Russell's birth. John Russell was a protestant, and Mary Kelly a Roman catholic. In the early years of Russell's life misfortune broke up the business of his father, who migrated to Liverpool, where he tried more than one occupation. Young William Russell was brought up first by his grandfather Kelly, and then in Dublin by his grandfather William Russell. John Russell's wife and younger son, John Howard Russell, both died in Liverpool. William Howard Russell, after starting life as a Roman catholic, was converted to the protestant faith by his grandfather in Dublin. He was educated at Dr. E. J. Geoghegan's school in Hume Street, Dublin (1832–1837), and entered Trinity College, Dublin, in 1838. He left Trinity College in 1841 without a degree, yet he acquired a good knowledge of the classics and a real liking for them, which did not desert him through life. His tutor frequently spoke of the possibility of his taking a fellowship.

In 1841 he was invited to help in reporting the Irish general election for 'The Times.' He was ignorant of journalism, except for some slight work on the Dublin 'Evening Mail.' At Longford, being anxious to pick up information from both sides as to some events he had missed, he was led by his mother wit straight to the hospital. There he found all the information he desired, and more. At the end of the elections he went to London to read for the bar, and was for two terms junior mathematical master at Kensington grammar school. J. T. Delane, the editor of 'The Times,' next asked him to report the episodes of the repeal agitation in Ireland in 1843. Russell attended many of the 'monster meetings' and had some amusing encounters with O'Connell, who more than once good-humouredly denounced the 'Times' Server.' His vivacious work was so much appreciated by Delane that he became attached to 'The Times' regularly as a reporter. He reported O'Connell's trial and the 'railway mania,' and was engaged fairly frequently in the Press gallery of the House of Commons. In 1845 he joined the staff of the 'Morning Chronicle.' In the autumn of 1848 he rejoined 'The Times.' In June 1850 he was called to the bar at the Middle Temple, but he never applied himself seriously enough to the work to succeed, though it was some years before he ceased to take an occasional brief. In 1850 he accompanied the Schleswig-Holstein forces in their campaign against the Danes and was present at the decisive battle of Idstedt.

The great opportunity of his life came in 1854, when the Crimean war broke out. With this war his name will always be connected. He landed at Gallipoli on 5 April 1854, and within a few days predicted the sufferings of the Crimea, as he found the management of the commissariat and medical departments infamous. His letters from here and from Varna were resented by the headquarters' staff, and when the army reached the Crimea he was an outcast, not authorised to draw rations, and knowing that his irregular and indeed unprecedented position might be challenged at any moment and that he might be removed from the theatre of war. He had lost most of his clothes, and by a freak of irony wore a commissariat cap. If he had not had great personal charm, which made friends for him rapidly, he could scarcely have contrived to do his work in the early days of the campaign, when he was dependent for food and shelter on the liberality of chance acquaintances. His letters to 'The Times' from the Crimea were narratives of remarkable ease, never disdaining any subject as too small, yet always relevant and appropriate. In writing of the battle of Balaclava (25 Oct. 1854) he applied to the English infantry the phrase 'the thin red line' which has since passed into the language. But the letters which moved Englishmen to an intensity of indignation, not before or since produced by such a means, were those describing the sufferings of the British army in the winter of 1854–5. It was these which made the public aware of the true condition of the army, which largely inspired the heroic work of Florence Nightingale [q. v. Suppl. II] and others, and which caused a stream of 'comforts' to be despatched from home to the stricken troops. Russell's letters to 'The Times' were no doubt also the chief cause of the fall of the Aberdeen ministry (29 Jan. 1855). The question whether he was unjust to Lord Raglan, the commander-in-chief in the Crimea, may remain a matter of opinion. The blame for the sufferings of the troops of course belonged much more to the government which had made war without preparing for it than to Lord Raglan. Russell always denied, however, that he had attacked Lord Raglan, who was the first general to conduct a war under the eyes of newspaper correspondents. As to Russell's service to the army on the whole there are not now two opinions. Lord Raglan complained that his published letters, especially during the siege of Sevastopol, revealed much that was of advantage to the enemy. But in Sir Evelyn Wood's words Russell 'saved the remnant' of the army (KINGLAKE'S *Crimea*, 6th edit. 208–11, 226–7). On his return home he was created an honorary LL.D. of Trinity College, Dublin.

Russell's next experience of fighting was in India, where he accompanied Sir Colin Campbell (Lord Clyde) in the compaign of 1858 against the mutineers. Colin Campbell put all the information of headquarters at his disposal. Delane attributed the cessation of indiscriminate executions to Russell's first letter from Cawnpore.

In 1860 Russell founded the 'Army and Navy Gazette,' which he edited, and in which he owned the chief interest, to the end of his life. In spite of this occupation he was still able to work on important occasions for 'The Times.' In March 1861 he sailed for the United States to inquire into the dispute between North and South which culminated in the civil war. 'The Times' supported the Southern cause, but Russell had not been long in the country before he discovered that his sympathies were strongly with the North. A visit to the South made him dislike the 'peculiar institution' of slavery so intensely that he was unable to tolerate even the most indirect excuses for it. After his return to the North he watched the disorderly recoil of the federal troops at the first battle of Bull Run (21 July 1861). He wrote a faithful description of what he saw, and when his narrative was published in the United States such a storm of anger broke about his head that he doubted whether his life was safe. He was now as unpopular in the north as in the south, and it was no doubt difficult for him to pursue his work usefully. He returned to England without warning in April 1862, much to the displeasure of Delane. He received a pension of 300*l.* a year from 'The Times' in 1863, but he remained an occasional contributor to the paper till his death.

In 1866 he was present at the last phase of 'the seven weeks' war' between Austria and Prussia. He saw the battle of Königgrätz (3 July), and was impressed by the deadly effectiveness of the 'needle-gun,' the adoption of which he recommended with much earnestness. He took the field again in 1870, when he accompanied the army of the Crown Prince of Prussia (afterwards the Emperor Frederick III) in the Franco-German war. He was treated with such consideration that Matthew Arnold satirically imagined him in 'Friendship's Garland' as being hoisted into the saddle by the old King of Prussia, while Bismarck was at the horse's head and the Crown Prince held the stirrup. In this war Russell became conscious that all the conditions of his work had been changed by the telegraph since Crimean days. Speed in transmission now earned more praise than skilful writing or acute judgments. He was frequently beaten in the competition by Archibald Forbes [q. v. Suppl. I] and other correspondents. Russell's last campaign was with Sir Garnet (afterwards Lord) Wolseley, for the 'Daily Telegraph,' during the Zulu war in South Africa in 1879.

Meanwhile Russell unsuccessfully contested Chelsea in the conservative interest in 1869. He was one of the companions of King Edward VII when Prince of Wales in journeys through the Near East in 1869 and through India in 1875–6. Of both tours Russell published full narratives. With King Edward he remained on terms of intimacy till his death. He revisited Canada and the United States in 1881, was in Egypt through the rebellion of Arabi Pasha and the beginnings of the British occupation in 1882, and in 1889 travelled in South America.

Russell may be said to have invented the office of the modern special correspondent. He was distinguished throughout his career by great moral courage, but he was often reckless in his statements. He wrote at white heat, when his indignation or pity was moved. When he felt it his duty to speak out no thoughts of his own comfort or of friendship restrained him. His personal qualities carried him through many difficulties of his own making. He was matchless 'good company' and a renowned story-teller. His literary friends included Douglas Jerrold, Dickens, Thackeray, and Shirley Brooks. Thackeray used to say that he would pay a guinea any day to have Russell dining at his table at the Garrick Club.

Russell was knighted in 1895, and was created C.V.O. in 1902. He received orders from France, Prussia, Austria, Turkey, Greece, and Portugal. He died on 10 Feb. 1907 at 202 Cromwell Road, Kensington, W., and was buried at Brompton cemetery.

He was married twice, first on 16 Sept. 1846 to Mary Burrowes, a great-niece of Peter Burrowes [q. v.] the Irish judge. By this marriage he had two daughters and two sons. Mrs. Russell died on 24 Jan. 1867. Russell married his second wife, the Countess Antoinetta Malvezz, on 18 Feb. 1884. There were no children of this marriage. His widow, who survived him, received a civil list pension of 80*l.* in 1912.

Russell published the following works, which are mostly a reprint or recasting of his journalistic work: 1. 'The War from the Landing at Gallipoli to the Death of Lord Raglan,' 2 vols. 1855 and 1856. 2. 'The British Expedition to the Crimea,' 1858; new edit. 1877. 3. 'Rifle Clubs and Volunteer Corps,' 1859. 4. 'My Diary in India in the years 1858–9,' 2 vols. 1860; new edit. 1905. 5. 'The Battle of Bull Run,' New York, 1861. 6. 'A Memorial of the Marriage of Albert Edward Prince of Wales and Alexandra Princess of Denmark,' 1863. 7. 'My Diary North and South: Canada, its Defences, Conditions, and Resources,' 3 vols. 1863–5. 8. 'General Todleben's History of the Defence of Sebastopol: a Review,' 1865. 9. 'The Atlantic Telegraph,' 1866. 10. 'The Adventures of Dr. Brady,' 3 vols. 1868. 11. 'My Diary in the East, during the Tour of the Prince and Princess of Wales,' 1869 (2 editions). 12. 'My Diary during the Last Great War,' 1874. 13. 'The Prince of Wales's Tour; with some Account of Visits to the Courts of Greece, Egypt, Spain, and Portugal,' illustrations by S. P. Hall, 1877. 14. 'The Crimea 1854–5'; comments on Mr. Kinglake's 'Apologies for the Winter Troubles,' 1881. 15. 'Hesperothen. Notes from the West, being a Record of a Ramble in the United States and Canada,' 2 vols. 1882. 16. 'A Visit to Chile and the Nitrate Fields of Tarapaca,' 1890. 17. 'The Great War with Russia: the Invasion of the Crimea: A Personal Retrospect'; reprinted from the 'Army and Navy Gazette,' 1895.

On 9 Feb. 1909 a memorial bust of Russell by Mr. Bertram Mackennal was unveiled in the crypt of St. Paul's Cathedral. A cartoon portrait by 'Ape' appeared in 'Vanity Fair' in 1875.

[Russell's published works; his private diaries and correspondence; reminiscences of friends; The Life of Sir William Howard Russell, by the present writer (London, 2 vols. 1911); Herbert Paul's History of Modern England, i. 370–1; S. M. Mitra's Life of Sir John Hall, 1911.] J. B. A–s.

RUSSELL, WILLIAM JAMES (1830–1909), chemist, born at Gloucester on 20 May 1830, was son of Thomas Pougher Russell (1775–1851), a banker at Gloucester, and was grandson of Priestley's friend, William Russell (1740–1818) [q.v.]. His mother was Mary (1790–1877), fourth daughter of Col. James Skey. Educated at private schools at Bristol and Birmingham, he entered University College, London, in 1847, studying chemistry under Thomas Graham [q.v.] and Alexander Williamson [q. v. Suppl. II]. For two years a demonstrator at Owens College, Manchester, under Frankland (1851–3), he proceeded thence to Heidelberg University, becoming a pupil of Bunsen and graduating Ph.D. in 1855. In 1857 he became assistant to Prof. Williamson and carried out researches on the analysis of gases, the results of which were communicated to the Chemical Society. For Henry Watts's 'Dictionary of Chemistry' he wrote the article on 'Gas Analysis' (1868). Other investigations comprised the determination of the atomic weights of cobalt and nickel; memoirs on absorption spectra; and papers on the action of wood and other substances on a photographic plate in darkness (see *Philosophical Transactions, Royal Society*, vol. 197, B. 1905). From 1868 to 1870 he was lecturer in chemistry at the medical school, St. Mary's Hospital, London, and subsequently (1870–97) held a similar post at St. Bartholomew's. He was (1860–70) professor of natural philosophy at Bedford College, London, and in later life was chairman of the council.

Following a long period of honorary service at the Chemical Society, Russell became president, 1889–91. Elected F.R.S. on 6 June 1872, he was Bakerian lecturer in 1898. One of the founders of the Institute of Chemistry, he was president 1894–7. He died at Ringwood on 12 Nov. 1909. Russell married in 1862 Fanny, daughter of Abraham Follett Osler [q. v. Suppl. II], by whom he had issue one son and one daughter; the latter married Dr. Alexander Scott, F.R.S.

[Roy. Soc. Proc. lxxxiv. A; Chem. Soc. Jubilee vol. 1891, and Trans. presidential addresses; St. Bart.'s Hosp. Reports (with portrait), vol. xlv.; Nature, 25 Nov. 1909 (by Prof. G. Carey Foster); The Times, 13 Nov. 1909; S. H. Jeyes's Russells of Birmingham, 1911, p. 268 (with photograph).] T. E. J.

RUTHERFORD, WILLIAM GUNION (1853–1907), classical scholar, was born at Glasgow on 17 July 1853, the second son of Robert Rutherford, minister of the United Presbyterian church at Mountain Cross, in Peeblesshire, and his wife Agnes, daughter of William Gunion, a Glasgow merchant. A younger brother, John Gunion Rutherford, C.M.G. (*b.* 1857), has had a distinguished career in Canada as a veterinary surgeon in the service of the Dominion.

After receiving Latin lessons from a dominie William was sent to Glasgow High School, and thence to St. Andrews University, where Lewis Campbell [q. v. Suppl. II] was Greek professor. In April 1873 he went to Oxford as an exhibitioner of Balliol, and in 1874 was in the first class in classical moderations, but he chose natural science for his final school (in which he took a second class), reading at the same time much Greek on his own account. He graduated in Dec. 1876, and at once became a classical master at St. Paul's school.

In 1878 he published a 'First Greek Grammar,' which soon came into wide use. It owed something to Cobet's study of Attic forms, but much also to original research. In deference to convention some spurious forms were retained, but these disappeared from later editions. Working on the same lines, Rutherford produced in 1881 'The New Phrynichus,' the greatest contribution of English scholarship to the study of Attic usage in vocabulary and inflexions. This was followed in 1883 by an edition of 'Babrius' with critical dissertations and notes.

Rutherford's reputation as a scholar was now established, and in the same year he was elected fellow and tutor of University College, Oxford. Before he went into residence the headmastership of Westminster fell vacant, and at the instigation of Benjamin Jowett [q. v. Suppl. I] Rutherford became a candidate. He was elected and entered on office in September 1883.

Coming to the school as a reformer, Rutherford met with opposition from the sentiment of some Old Westminsters. Especial objection was taken to his abolition of 'water,' that is to say, rowing on the Thames. Though in this matter his judgment was at one with the Westminster staff, he took no shelter behind that fact. Nor did he waver in any of his more vital improvements, and the opposition gradually died away. In school he was a strong disciplinarian, a character which did not prevent him from becoming in the end extremely popular with the boys. He was a great teacher, always treating words as the vehicle of thought, using them with reverent precision, and in translation showing 'a horror of looseness, poverty of vocabulary, and English idiom all stuccoed over with a base convention' (J. S. Phillimore). Though he was not much given to the practice of verse composition, his prologues to the Westminster plays were marked by Terentian ease and grace. In 1884 St. Andrews gave him the honorary degree of LL.D. He had taken orders on going to Westminster, and in 1901 published under the title of 'The Key of Knowledge' some of his sermons preached at the school services in Westminster Abbey.

In 1889, in an edition of the fourth book of Thucydides, Rutherford exemplified a theory that the current texts of Greek authors are disfigured by ascripts imported from the margins. Some of his corrections have been accepted, but not all are necessary. Afterwards his view of the time at which the interpolations took place was modified in face of the evidence of the Egyptian papyri. His first recension of the newly discovered 'Mimiambi' of Herondas (1892) was a somewhat hasty piece of work which did not add to his reputation. In connexion with his work on Attic he had studied the scholia to Aristophanes, and he now visited Italy to examine the Ravenna manuscript. In 1896 he published a revised text of the scholia with a translation and notes, promising a third volume to deal with the conclusions which he had drawn. His health having begun to fail, early in 1899 he went with his wife on a voyage to New Zealand. The benefit was not lasting, and in July 1901 he gave up his headmastership and retired to Little Hallands, near Bishopstone, which had been for some years his country house.

The third volume on the Aristophanic scholia came out in 1905 under the title of 'A Chapter in the History of Annotation.' It supplied no formal proof of the theory of ascripts, but threw light on it by tracing the history of Greek studies from the earliest commentators to the fall of Constantinople, and was a vigorous protest against the spirit which ranks the annotation with the text.

Rutherford was profoundly dissatisfied with the revised version of the New Testament. His sense of Hellenistic Greek told him that the author of the Pauline epistles thought in one language and wrote in another. In 1900 he brought out a new translation of the Epistle to the Romans. He began a new translation of the Epistles to the Thessalonians and to the Corinthians. He completed the work as far as 2 Cor. viii. 24, when on 19 July 1907 he died somewhat suddenly at Little Hallands. He was buried in Bishopstone churchyard. His last work was published posthumously with a biographical sketch by his friend Spenser Wilkinson.

Rutherford, though an admirer of Cobet and Blass, had too independent a genius to be any man's disciple. His fame as a scholar rests chiefly on his studies of Attic, of Aristophanes, and of New Testament Greek. His translations of St. Paul have to contend against some theological prejudice, but he was more learned and acute than any of his critics.

Rutherford married, on 3 Jan. 1884, Constance Gordon, daughter of John Thomson Renton, of Bradston Brooke, Surrey. His wife with three daughters survives him.

A crayon portrait by J. Seymour Lucas, R.A., is in Ashburnham House, Westminster School. A portrait in oils by the same artist, for which Old Westminsters subscribed in 1901, is with Mrs. Rutherford for her life and will ultimately come to the school. The cartoon by 'Spy' in 'Vanity Fair,' 3 March 1898, is a remarkable likeness.

[Personal knowledge; Spenser Wilkinson's biog. sketch, noticed supra.] J. S.

RUTLAND, seventh DUKE OF. [See MANNERS, LORD JOHN JAMES ROBERT (1818–1906), politician.]

RYE, MARIA SUSAN (1829–1903), social reformer, born at 2 Lower James Street, Golden Square, London, on 31 March 1829, was eldest of the nine children of Edward Rye, solicitor and bibliophile of Golden Square, London, by his wife Maria Tuppen of Brighton. Edward Rye of Baconsthorpe, Norfolk, was her grandfather. Of her brothers, Edward Caldwell Rye [q. v.] was an accomplished entomologist, and Walter, solicitor, antiquary, and athlete, has published many works on Norfolk history and topography and was mayor of Norwich in 1908–9.

Miss Rye received her education at home and read for herself in the large library of her father. Coming under the influence of Charles Kingsley's father, then vicar of St. Luke's, Chelsea, she devoted herself at the age of sixteen to parochial work in Chelsea. She was early impressed by the disabilities of her sex, and by their lack of opportunity of employment outside the teaching profession. In succession to Mary Howitt [q. v.], she soon became secretary of the association for promoting the married women's property bill, which was brought forward by Sir Thomas Erskine Perry [q. v.] in 1856 but was not fully passed till 1882. She joined the Women's Employment Society on its foundation, but, disapproving of the women's franchise movement which the leading members supported, soon left it. In 1859 she undertook a private law-stationer's business at 12 Portugal Street, Lincoln's Inn, in order to give employment to middle class girls. At the same time she helped to establish the Victoria printing press in association with her business in 1860 (under the charge of Miss Emily Faithfull), and the registry office and telegraph school in Great Coram St., with Miss Isa Craig [q. v. Suppl. II] as secretary. The telegraph school anticipated the employment of girls as telegraph clerks.

Miss Rye's law-stationer's business prospered, but the applications for employment were far in excess of the demands of the concern. With Miss Jane Lewin, Miss Rye consequently raised a fund for assisting middle class girls to emigrate, and to the question of emigration she devoted the rest of her life. She founded in 1861 the Female Middle Class Emigration Society (absorbed since 1884 in the United British Women's Emigration Association; cf. her *Emigration of Educated Women*, 1861). Between 1860 and 1868 she was instrumental in sending girls of the middle class and domestic servants to Australia, New Zealand, and Canada, and she visited these colonies to form committees for the protection of the emigrants.

From 1868, when she handed over her law business to Miss Lewin, Miss Rye devoted herself exclusively to the emigration of pauper children, or, in a phrase which she herself coined, 'gutter children.' After visiting in New York the Little Wanderers' Home for the training of derelict children for emigrant life which Mr. Van Meter, a baptist minister from Ohio, had founded, she resolved to give the system a trial in London. Encouraged by the earl of Shaftesbury and 'The Times' newspaper and with the financial support of William Rathbone, M.P. [q. v. Suppl. II], she purchased in 1869 Avenue House, High Street, Peckham, and with her two younger sisters, in spite of public opposition and prejudice, took there from the streets or the workhouses waifs and strays from the ages of three to sixteen. Fifty girls from Kirkdale industrial school, Liverpool, were soon put under her care; they were trained in domestic economy and went through courses of general and religious instruction. At Niagara, Canada, Miss Rye also acquired a building which she called 'Our Western Home.' It was opened on 1 Dec. 1869. To this house Miss Rye drafted the children from Peckham, and after further training they were distributed in Canada as domestic servants among respectable families. The first party left England in October 1869. Poor law children were subsequently received at Peckham from St. George's, Hanover Square, Wolverhampton, Bristol, Reading, and other towns. By 1891 Miss Rye had found homes in Canada for some five hundred children. She personally accompanied each batch of emigrants, and constantly visited the children already settled there. The work was continued with great success for over a quarter of a century, and did much to diminish the vicious habits and the stigma of pauperism. Lord Shaftesbury remained a consistent supporter, and in 1884 the duke of Argyll, then governor-general of Canada, warmly commended the results of Miss Rye's pioneer system, which Dr. Barnardo [q. v. Suppl. II] and others subsequently adopted and extended.

In 1895, owing to the continuous strain, Miss Rye transferred the two institutions in Peckham and Niagara with their funds to the Church of England Waifs and Strays Society. That society, which was founded in 1891, still carries on her work. In her farewell report of 1895 she stated that 4000 English and Scottish children then in Canada had been sent out from her home in England. She retired with her sister Elizabeth to 'Baconsthorpe,' Hemel Hempstead, where she spent the remainder of her life. There she died, after four years' suffering, of intestinal cancer on 12 Nov. 1903, and was buried in the churchyard. Of powerful physique and resolute character, Miss Rye cherished strong religious convictions, and her dislike of Roman catholicism often led her into controversy. She received a civil list pension of 70*l.* in 1871.

[The Times, 17 Nov. 1903; 1862, passim; Guardian, 25 Nov. 1903; Yorkshire Post, 18 Nov. 1903; Christian World, 19 Nov. 1903; Norfolk Chronicle, 14 Nov. 1903; Our Waifs and Strays, Jan. 1904 (portrait), March and April 1910; Good Words, 1871, xii. 573–7 (art. by William Gilbert); Illustrated London News, 25 Aug. 1877; Englishwoman's Journal, 1858–63, passim; E. Hodder, Life of Seventh Earl of Shaftesbury, popular edit. 1892, p. 711; private information.] W. B. O.

RYE, WILLIAM BRENCHLEY (1818–1901), keeper of printed books in the British Museum, born at Rochester on 26 Jan. 1818, was the younger son of Arthur Rye, a medical practitioner in that city. He was educated at the Rochester and Chatham Classical and Mathematical School, but the death of his father in 1832 left him with slender means, and in 1834 he came to London and entered the office of a solicitor, where he met John Winter Jones [q. v.], afterwards principal librarian of the British Museum, who in 1838, soon after his own appointment, obtained for him a subordinate post in the library there. His diligence and efficiency gained for him the good opinion of Sir Anthony Panizzi, then keeper, who in 1839 secured his appointment as a supernumerary assistant, and in 1844 he was placed on the permanent staff. On the bequest to the nation in 1846 of the splendid library of Thomas Grenville, Rye was entrusted with its removal to the British Museum and afterwards with its arrangement there. At a later date he selected and arranged the library of reference in the new reading-room opened in 1857, and he devised the plan showing the placing of the books which is still in use. He became an assistant-keeper in the department of printed books in 1857, and succeeded Thomas Watts in the keepership in 1869, but failing health and eyesight compelled him to retire in July 1875. The Weigel sale of block-books and incunabula in 1872, at which some important purchases were made, was the chief event of his brief term of office.

Rye's tastes were antiquarian rather than literary, and he possessed a great store of information relating to old English literature and to mediæval architecture and antiquities. He also practised etching. He edited for the Hakluyt Society in 1851, with an introduction and notes, Richard Hakluyt's translation of Fernando de Soto's Portuguese narrative of the 'Discovery and Conquest of Terra Florida,' but his principal work was 'England as seen by Foreigners in the Days of Elizabeth and James the First' (1865), a collection of the narratives of foreign visitors, with a valuable introduction, and etchings by himself. He contributed to the early volumes of 'Notes and Queries,' and papers on 'A Memorial of the Priory of St. Andrew at Rochester' and 'Visits to Rochester and Chatham of Royal, Noble, and Distinguished Personages, English and Foreign, 1300–1783,' to the 'Archæologia Cantiana,' as well as others to the 'Antiquary,' in which that on 'Breuning's Mission to England, 1595,' appeared in 1903. The etchings which he contributed to the 'Publications of the Antiquarian Etching Club' (1849–1854) were brought together in a privately issued volume in 1859. His collections for a 'History of Rochester,' in three quarto volumes, are in the British Museum.

Rye, who in his last years was totally blind, died at West Norwood, from an attack of bronchitis, on 21 Dec. 1901, and was buried in Highgate cemetery. He married twice; secondly, on 13 Dec. 1866, Frances Wilhelmina, youngest daughter of William Barker of Camberwell, by whom he left two sons and one daughter. The elder son, William Brenchley Rye (1873–1906), became an assistant librarian in the John Rylands Library, Manchester; the younger, Reginald Arthur Rye, is Goldsmiths' Librarian of the University of London, and author of 'The Libraries of London' (2nd edit. 1910).

[Library Association Record, Jan. and Feb. 1902, by Dr. Richard Garnett, reprinted privately with corrections; Athenæum, 4 Jan. 1902; information from Mr. Reginald A. Rye.]

R. E. G.

S

SACKVILLE-WEST, Sir LIONEL SACKVILLE, second Baron Sackville of Knole (1827–1908), diplomatist, born at Bourn Hall, Cambridgeshire, on 19 July 1827, was fifth son of George John West, fifth Earl de la Warr, by his marriage with Lady Elizabeth, daughter and co-heiress of John Frederick Sackville, third duke of Dorset, and Baroness Buckhurst by creation in 1864. His elder brother Mortimer (1820–1888) was created Baron Sackville in 1876. Privately educated at home, Lionel served as assistant précis writer to the fourth earl of Aberdeen when secretary of state for foreign affairs in 1845, and after further employment in the foreign office was appointed attaché to the British legation at Lisbon in July 1847. He was transferred successively to Naples (1848), Stuttgart (1852), Berlin (1853), was promoted to be secretary of legation at Turin 1858, and was transferred to Madrid in 1864. In November 1867 he became secretary of embassy at Berlin, and in June 1868 was transferred to Paris in the same capacity with the titular rank of minister plenipotentiary. He served under Lord Lyons [q. v.] throughout the exciting incidents of the Franco-German war, following him to Tours when the capital was invested by the German forces, and returning with him to Paris on the conclusion of peace. He was left in charge of the British embassy during the first weeks of the Commune, when the ambassador had accompanied the French ministry to Versailles. In September 1872 he was promoted to be British envoy at Buenos Ayres, but remained in charge of the embassy at Paris until 7 November and did not arrive at his new post until September 1873. In January 1878 he was transferred to Madrid, where he served for over three years, acting as the plenipotentiary of Great Britain and also of Denmark in the conference which was held in 1880 to define the rights of protection exercised by foreign legations and consulates in Morocco. In June 1881, shortly after the assassination of President Garfield, he was appointed to succeed Sir Edward Thornton [q. v. Suppl. II] as British envoy at Washington, and then entered upon the most eventful and, as it turned out, the final stage of his diplomatic career. The feeling in the United States towards Great Britain had improved since the settlement of outstanding questions provided for by the Treaty of Washington in 1871, and the reception given to West was cordial. But he soon found that the influence in congress and in the press of the Irish Fenian party formed a serious bar to the satisfactory settlement of important questions. The measures taken by the British government for the protection of life and property in Ireland after the 'Phœnix Park murders' of 1882 caused intense excitement among sympathisers with the Fenian movement in the United States. The publication in the American press of incitements to murder and violence, and the arrests in the United Kingdom of Irishmen, naturalised citizens of the United States, on a suspicion of crime, involved West in disagreeabie correspondence between the two governments, and when some of those who had taken part in the Phœnix Park murders were traced and convicted, there were veiled threats against the British minister's life at the time of their execution. A trip in the president's yacht was deemed a wise precaution.

The discussion of various questions connected with Canada, especially the seizure by United States cruisers of Canadian vessels engaged in the pelagic seal fishery, and the measures taken by the Canadian government to protect their fishing rights in territorial waters against incursions by United States fishermen, occupied much of West's attention in succeeding years. In June 1885 he was made K.C.M.G. In 1887 he was called upon to discuss in conference with the United States secretary of state and the German minister the questions which had arisen in regard to the status of the Samoan Archipelago, but the negotiations did not result in an agreement, and the matter was left to be settled at Berlin in 1889. In October 1887 the English government decided to send out Mr. Joseph Chamberlain on a special mission for the purpose of negotiating jointly with West and Sir Charles Tupper (the Canadian high commissioner in England) a treaty for the settlement of the questions connected with the fishery rights in the seas adjacent to British North America and Newfoundland. A treaty was concluded on 15 Feb. 1888, but it failed to obtain confirmation by the United States Senate. It was however accompanied by a provisional arrangement for a *modus vivendi* under which United States fishing vessels were admitted for two years to fishing privileges in the waters of Canada and Newfoundland on payment of a moderate licence fee; thus the risk of serious friction was for the time removed.

During the seven years of his residence at Washington, West, who combined unfailing good temper and unaffected geniality of manner and disposition with a singular power of reserve and laconic speech, had enjoyed unqualified popularity, and had maintained excellent personal relations with the members of the United States government. Yet in the autumn of 1888 his mission was brought to an abrupt and unexpected close. In September of that year, six weeks before the presidential election, he received a letter from California purporting to be written by a British subject naturalised in the United States, expressing doubts whether the writer should vote for the re-election of President Cleveland on account of the hostile policy which the democratic president appeared to be bent on pursuing towards Canada, and asking for advice. West unguardedly answered that any political party which openly favoured Great Britain at that moment would lose in popularity, and that the democratic party in power were no doubt fully alive to that fact, but that he had no reason to doubt that President Cleveland if re-elected would maintain a spirit of conciliation. West was the victim of a political trick. The letter sent to him was an imposture, and on 22 Oct. his reply was published in the 'New York Tribune,' an organ of the republican party, for the purpose of discrediting the democratic president with the Irish party. For a foreign representative to advise a United States citizen as to his vote was obviously a technical breach of international conventions. At first the United States government showed no disposition to treat the matter otherwise than as one admitting of explanations and expressions of regret, which West freely tendered. The popular excitement, however, increased as the date of the election approached; copies of West's letter were distributed broadcast for the purpose of influencing votes against President Cleveland, and unfortunately West admitted the reporters of the 'New York Herald' and 'New York Tribune' to interviews. West disclaimed the statements attributed to him in the newspapers, but the United States government held them, in the absence of a published repudiation, to justify the immediate delivery to West of his passports. His mission consequently terminated on 30 Oct. 1888. Lord Salisbury, then foreign secretary, protested against the United States government's action in a note to the United States minister in London. 'There was nothing in Lord Sackville's conduct' (wrote Lord Salisbury) 'to justify so striking a departure from the circumspect and deliberate procedure by which in such cases it is the usage of friendly states to mark their consideration for each other.' To this the American secretary of state replied in a long despatch of justification, which, whatever may be thought of the technical arguments adduced, fails to remove the impression that West's abrupt dismissal was in reality an electoral device, adopted in the unavailing hope of averting the imminent defeat of the party in power.

Benjamin Harrison, the republican candidate, was elected.

West on the death (16 Oct. 1888) of his elder brother Mortimer, first Baron Sackville, had succeeded to the title by special remainder a fortnight previous to his departure from the United States, and had inherited the historic property of Knole Park near Sevenoaks, where he passed the rest of his life. He retired from the diplomatic service on pension in April 1889, was made G.C.M.G. in September following, and lived at Knole till his death there on 3 Sept. 1908. There is at Knole an excellent portrait of him in pastel by Mr. Philip Laszlo.

Lord Sackville was not married. While an attaché at Stuttgart in 1852 he had formed an attachment for a Spanish lady, whom he met during a visit to Paris, and who subsequently left the stage to live with him, but with whom, as she was a strict catholic and already married to a husband who survived her, he was unable to contract any legal union. He had by her two sons and three daughters. The daughters joined him at Washington, their mother having died some years previously, in 1871, and were received there and in English society as his family. The two sons were established on an estate in Natal. The younger, Ernest Henri Jean Baptiste Sackville-West, claimed on his father's death to be the legitimate heir to the peerage and estates, but his action, after long delays in collecting evidence on either side, was finally dismissed by the probate division of the high court in February 1910. The title and entailed property consequently descended to Lord Sackville's nephew, Lionel Edward (eldest son of Lieutenant-colonel the Hon. William Edward Sackville-West), who had married Lord Sackville's eldest daughter.

[The Times, 4 Sept. 1908; Lord Sackville's Mission, 1895; Lord Augustus Loftus, Diplomatic Reminiscences, 2 ser. i. 374; papers laid before Parliament; Foreign Office List, 1909, p. 404.] S.

ST. HELIER, Baron. [See Jeune, Francis Henry (1843–1905), judge.]

ST. JOHN, Sir SPENSER BUCKINGHAM (1825–1910), diplomatist and author, born in St. John's Wood, London, on 22 Dec. 1825, was third of the seven sons of James Augustus St. John [q. v.] by his wife Eliza Agar, daughter of George Agar Hansard of Bath. Percy Bolingbroke St. John [q. v.] and Bayle St. John [q. v.] were elder brothers, and Horace Stebbing Roscoe St. John [q. v.] and Vane Ireton St. John (see below) were younger brothers. After education in private schools, Spenser wrote 'innumerable articles' on Borneo, to which the adventures of Sir James Brooke [q. v.], rajah of Saráwak, were directing public attention, and he took up the study of the Malay language (St. John's *Life of Sir James Brooke*, p. 129). He was introduced to Sir James Brooke on his visit to England in 1847, and he accompanied Brooke as private secretary next year, when Brooke became British commissioner and governor of Labuan. Lord Palmerston, an acquaintance of St. John's father, allowed him 'in a roundabout way 200*l.* a year' (*ib.* p. 130). Thenceforth St. John and Brooke were closely associated. St. John was with Brooke during his final operations in 1849 against Malay pirates, and he accompanied Brooke to Brunei, the Sulu archipelago, and to Siam in 1850. Although St. John deemed some of his chief's dealings with the natives high-handed and ill-advised, he in a letter to Gladstone defended Brooke against humanitarian attack in the House of Commons. While the official inquiry into Brooke's conduct, which the home government appointed, was in progress at Singapore, St. John acted temporarily as commissioner for Brooke (1851–5), and visited the north-western coast of Borneo and the north-eastern shore, ascending the principal rivers. Appointed in 1856 British consul-general at Brunei, St. John explored the country round the capital, and penetrated farther into the interior than any previous traveller. He published his full and accurate journals, supplemented by other visitors' testimonies, in two well-written and beautifully illustrated volumes entitled 'Life in the Forests of the Far East' (1862; 2nd enlarged edit. 1863).

In November 1859 St. John revisited England with Brooke, and after returning to Borneo became chargé d'affaires in Hayti in January 1863. He remained in the West Indies twelve years. During his residence in Hayti the republic was distracted by civil strife, and by a war with the neighbouring state of Santo Domingo, and St. John frequently took violent measures against native disturbers of the public peace. On 28 June 1871 he became chargé d'affaires in the Dominican republic, and he was promoted on 12 Dec. 1872 to the post of resident minister in Hayti. His leisure was devoted to a descriptive history of the country, which was finally published in 1884 as 'Hayti;

or the Black Republic' (2nd edit. 1889; French translation 1884). St John gave an unfavourable but truthful account of the republic and its savage inhabitants (cf. A. Bowler, *Une Conférence sur Haïti*, Paris, 1888).

For nine years (from 14 Oct. 1874 till 1883) St. John was minister residentiary in Peru and consul-general at Lima. In 1875 he went on a special mission to Bolivia, and in 1880–1 witnessed the war between Peru and Chile. With the ambassadors of France and Salvador he negotiated an armistice in January 1881, and by his diplomatic firmness helped to protect Lima from destruction after the defeat of the Peruvians by Chile. He was created K.C.M.G. on 20 March 1881. In May 1883 St. John was sent to Mexico to negotiate the resumption of diplomatic relations with Great Britain. An agreement was signed at Mexico on 6 Aug. 1884, and was ratified, not without much opposition, mainly by his tact. He was appointed envoy extraordinary and minister plenipotentiary to Mexico on 23 Nov. 1884, and remained there till 1893. In 1886 a mixed commission was appointed to investigate British financial claims on the Mexican government, and in 1887 a long-standing dispute was equitably terminated under St. John's guidance. From 1 July 1893 to January 1896 St. John was at Stockholm as minister to Sweden. He was created G.C.M.G. in 1894. Retiring from the diplomatic service in 1896, St. John spent his last years in literary pursuits. He died on 2 Jan. 1910 at Pinewood Grange, Camberley, Surrey. He married, on 29 April 1899, Mary, daughter of Lieutenant-colonel Fred. Macnaghten Armstrong, C.B., of the Bengal staff corps, who survived him.

St. John's chief work, besides those mentioned above, was his authentic 'Life of Sir James Brooke, Rajah of Saráwak' (1879). He also wrote 'Rajah Brooke' (1899) for the 'Builders of Britain' series. St. John drew upon his early experiences in the Malay archipelago in two vivacious volumes, 'Adventures of a Naval Officer' (1905) and 'Earlier Adventures' (1906), both of which he attributed to a fictitious Captain Charles Hunter, R.N. A final publication was a collection of sympathetic but rather colourless 'Essays on Shakespeare and his Works' (1908), edited from the MSS. and notes of an unnamed deceased relative.

St. John bequeathed his portrait of Brooke by Sir Francis Grant (1847) to the National Portrait Gallery.

Vane Ireton Shaftesbury St. John (1839–1911), Sir Spenser's youngest and last surviving brother, pursued a literary and journalistic career. He was a pioneer of boys' journals, starting and editing the 'Boys of England' and similar periodicals. He was also the author of 'Undercurrents: a Story of our own Day' (3 vols. 1860) and of many story books for boys. He died at Peckham Rye in poor circumstances on 20 Dec. 1911. He was twice married, and had seventeen children.

[Burke's Peerage, &c.; Men of the Time, 1899; Who's Who, 1910; Haydn's Book of Dignities; Sir C. R. Markham's War between Chile and Peru, ch xvi.; Ann. Reg. (s.v. Mexico), 1884, &c.; The Times, and Morning Post, 4 Jan. 1910; Allibone's Dict. Engl. Lit. Suppl.; St. John's works.] G. Le G. N.

SALAMAN, CHARLES KENSINGTON (1814–1901), musical composer, born at 11 Charing Cross, London, on 3 March 1814, was the eldest son and one of the fourteen children of Simeon Kensington Salaman, a member of a Jewish family of German and Dutch origin, by his wife Alice Cowen, an amateur pianist. Mrs. Julia Goodman [q. v. Suppl. II] was his eldest sister. Another sister, Rachel, married Sir John Simon (1818–1897) [q .v.], while a third, Kate (1821–1856), attained some reputation as a miniature-painter, and exhibited at the Royal Academy. After being educated privately Charles gave early evidence of musical talent, and had his first lessons on the piano from his mother. In 1824 he was awarded second place in the competition for studentship at the new Royal Academy of Music, but preferred to study the pianoforte independently, first with Stephen Francis Rimbault and then (1826–1831) under Charles Neate, the friend of Beethoven. Meanwhile in 1828 he studied under Henri Herz in Paris, and to him and to Neate his earliest compositions were dedicated in the same year. As a boy he played duets with Liszt and came to know Clementi. His first public appearance was at Lanza's concert at Blackheath, in June 1828. He composed the ode (with words by Isaac Cowen, his uncle) for the Shakespeare Festival at Stratford-on-Avon, 30 April 1830. In 1831 he commenced his long career as a pianoforte teacher. In May 1833 he gave his first annual orchestral concert at the Hanover Square rooms, when Mendelssohn's Concerto in G Minor was first rendered in public by a player other than the composer. At his annual orchestral concerts he introduced many distinguished artists and classical novelties.

On 9 November 1835 he instituted, with Henry Blagrove and others, the 'Concerti da Camera,' a chamber music organisation. In 1838 he visited the Continent, played at Vienna, Munich, Homburg, and other places, and made the acquaintance of Schumann, of Mozart's widow and son, of Thalberg, and of Czerny. At Mainz he published his popular pianoforte romance, 'Cloelia.' From 1846 to 1848 he resided in Rome, conducting Beethoven's Symphony No. 2 for the first time there and composing his 'Saltarello' and several songs with Italian words. He was elected an honorary member of the Academy of St. Cecilia. Returning to London, he resumed his teaching, and founded the first Amateur Choral Society in 1849. In 1855 he began a series of musically illustrated lectures in London and the provinces, taking as his first topic 'The History of the Pianoforte and its Precursors.' At the Polytechnic Institution (10 May 1855) he gave this lecture before Queen Victoria, Prince Albert, and their children. In 1858 he founded the Musical Society of London, which lasted till 1868, and of which he was honorary secretary till 1865. In 1874 he was one of the founders of the Musical Association, and for three years its secretary and afterwards a vice-president. He gave his last concert in 1876 and soon retired from active work, but he maintained his vigour until near his death, in London, on 23 June 1901. He was buried in the Jewish cemetery at Golder's Green, Hendon. He married on 24 Dec. 1848 Frances Simon of Montego Bay, Jamaica, by whom he had three sons and two daughters. His eldest son, Malcolm Charles Salaman, is well known as a dramatic and art critic.

Salaman's compositions are numerous, including songs and orchestral and pianoforte pieces. In his later years he made an annual custom of publishing a song on his birthday, and he wrote close on one hundred songs. The most famous is his beautiful setting of Shelley's 'I arise from dreams of thee,' written at Bath in 1836, when he was twenty-two, and published in an album called 'Six Songs' (1838). Some of his songs were written for Hebrew, Greek, and Latin words. A deeply religious man, he composed and arranged in 1858 the choral and organ music for the psalms and service of the synagogue of the Reformed Congregation of British Jews; some of his settings of the psalms were used as anthems in cathedrals. His literary ability was favourably shown in 'Jews as they are' (1882), in his published lectures, and in many articles contributed to the musical journals.

Among portraits of Salaman are a three-quarter length (oils) by his sister, Mrs. Julia Goodman, 1834, in the possession of Mr. Malcolm C. Salaman; a sketch, seated at piano (oils), by S. Starr, 1890, in the possession of Brandon Thomas; a marble medallion in high relief, by Girometti, Rome, 1847; and a lithograph, by R. J. Lane, A.R.A., after S. A. Hart, R.A., published in 1834.

[J. D. Brown's Biographical Dictionary of Musicians, 1886; Grove's Dictionary of Musicians (ed. Fuller Maitland); Brown and Stratton's British Musical Biography, 1897; the Biograph, September 1880; Who's Who, 1901; Pianists of the Past. Personal Recollections by the late Charles Salaman, in Blackwood's Magazine, September 1901; Musical Times (obituary notice), August 1901 (with portrait and facsimiles); Jewish World, 28 June 1901; volumes of collected programmes, press notices, MS. correspondence, dating from 1828, in the possession of Malcolm C. Salaman; Musical Keepsake for 1834; Concordia, 1875–6.] J. C. H.

SALAMAN, JULIA. [See Goodman, Mrs. Julia (1812–1906), portrait painter.]

SALISBURY, third Marquis of. [See Cecil, Robert Arthur Talbot Gascoyne- (1830–1903), prime minister.]

SALMON, GEORGE (1819–1904), mathematician and divine, born at Cork on 25 Sept. 1819, was only son of Michael Salmon, linen merchant, by his wife Helen, daughter of the Rev. Edward Weekes. Of three sisters one, Eliza, married George Gresley Perry [q. v. Suppl. I], archdeacon of Stow. Salmon, after attending Mr. Porter's school in Cork, entered Trinity College, Dublin, in 1833, where he had a brilliant career, winning a classical scholarship in 1837 and graduating as first mathematical moderator in 1838. He attended some divinity lectures in 1839, as scholars of the house were bound to do, and was persuaded to sit for a fellowship, without much preparation, in 1840. He obtained Madden's prize, i.e. was next in merit to the successful candidate, and in 1841 was elected fellow of the college, under the old system of public examination, conducted *viva voce* and in Latin, his general scholarship gaining him success at an earlier age than was customary.

Salmon settled down at once to the work of a college don (M.A. 1844), and was ordained deacon in 1844, and priest in 1845. His work was mainly mathematical, but in

1845 he was appointed divinity lecturer as well, and his long life was devoted to these two diverse lines of study. For many years he was a college tutor ; from 1848 to 1866, the period during which his mathematical books were written, he was Donegal lecturer in mathematics.

Salmon's first mathematical paper, 'On the properties of surfaces of the second degree which correspond to the theorems of Pascal and Brianchon on Conic Sections,' was published in the 'Philosophical Magazine' in 1844. In 1847 there appeared his 'Conic Sections,' the work which made him known as a mathematician to a wide circle (6th edit. 1879). Admirably arranged, and constructed with an unerring sense of the distinction between important principles and mere details, it exhibited more fully than any other book of the time at once the power of the Cartesian coordinates and the beauty of geometrical method; and for half a century it was the leading text-book on its subject. It was followed in 1852 by a treatise on the 'Higher Plane Curves' (3rd edit. 1879), a subject of which little was then known, and which was introduced to the ordinary student by Salmon's labours. The investigations of Cayley and Sylvester into the invariants of quantics were beginning to attract attention ; and Salmon proceeded to apply their results to geometrical theory, the result being his 'Lessons Introductory to the Modern Higher Algebra' (1859; 4th edit. 1885), in which he incorporated much original matter. Finally in 1862 appeared the 'Geometry of Three Dimensions' (5th edit. 2 vols. 1912), in which the sections upon the general theory of surfaces are specially remarkable (the work was translated into French, German, and Spanish). Upon these four treatises his fame as a mathematician rests, while many minor papers by him appeared in the learned journals. Salmon's methods made little use of the calculus, or of the quaternion analysis invented by his contemporary, Sir W. R. Hamilton [q.v.]; nor, again, did he ever handle the non-Euclidean geometry. His strength lay in his complete mastery of geometric and algebraic processes, and this, coupled with his indefatigable industry as a calculator, enabled him to produce original work of permanent value. In later life, the theory of numbers fascinated him ; and he spent many odd half-hours in determining the number of figures in the recurring periods in the reciprocals of prime numbers. His last mathematical paper was upon this subject ('Messenger of Mathematics,' 1873), but he never published his latest results, and he used to speak of his calculations as a useless amusement.

Salmon's mathematical labours by no means exhausted his energies, and he took a large share in the work of the Divinity School of Trinity College from 1845 to 1888. He proceeded B.D. and D.D. in 1859, and from 1866 to 1888 he was regius professor of divinity. He played an active part in the reconstruction of the Irish Church after its disestablishment in 1870, and enjoyed a unique position in the General Synod and as a member of the Representative Church body, his skill as a debater and his ability in the management of the church's finance being equally remarkable.

Salmon's first publication on a theological subject was a sermon on Prayer (1849), the precursor of a long series of printed discourses. His preaching always commanded attention, but his sermons (of which five volumes were published) were better to read than to hear, for his voice was hardly effective in a large building. In 1852 Archbishop Whately made him an examining chaplain, and the archbishop's influence upon Salmon's theological opinions seems to have been considerable. Both men were strong Protestants, and viewed the rise of the Oxford movement with suspicion and dislike, Salmon co-operating with Whately and others in the issue of 'Cautions for the Times' (1853), intended as a counterblast to the famous 'Tracts.' He was also a frequent contributor to the 'Catholic Layman,' which dealt with the Roman catholic controversy, and he printed anonymously three short 'Popular Stories' (Dublin 1854) written in the same interest. This preparation bore fruit later on, when, as divinity professor, he lectured on the points at issue between Romanism and Anglicanism; and his lectures formed the material of 'The Infallibility of the Church' (1889; 2nd edit. 1890), a trenchant and brilliant polemic which exhibited his learning, his humour, and the vigour of his controversial methods. Salmon founded no school of theological thought, deeply as he was revered by his pupils, his genius being analytic and even destructive rather than constructive and synthetic ; but his tendency was towards a liberal evangelicalism, which distrusted (and more and more as years went on) the appeal to any authority other than that of the individual conscience.

The studies by which he became most widely known as a divine lay, however, outside the sphere of dogmatic theology, and his work as a New Testament critic attracted a larger audience. His numerous articles in the 'Dictionary of Christian Biography' (1877–87) show his grasp of the history of the second century; and his 'Introduction to the New Testament' (1885; 7th edit. 1894) was acclaimed on its publication as a powerful reply to the dissolvent speculations of German criticism. Conservative in tendency, the book is destructive of extravagant theories of Christian origins rather than a positive statement of the results which a sober scholarship is prepared to maintain. The same characteristic of the author's method was apparent in his criticisms of Hort's reconstruction of the Greek text of the New Testament, which appeared in 1897 ('Thoughts on the Textual Criticism of the New Testament'), criticisms of which the sagacity has since been widely recognised. During the last ten years of life, Salmon spent much time upon the Synoptic problem, and his illuminating notes were carefully edited after his death in 1907 by a former pupil, N. J. D. White, under the title 'The Human Element in the Gospels.'

In 1888 Salmon was appointed provost of Trinity College by Lord Salisbury, on the recommendation of the lord-lieutenant of Ireland (Lord Londonderry), with the unanimous approval of the fellows. In 1892 he presided with dignity over the tercentenary festival of Dublin University. A conservative in politics, he was also conservative of academic tradition, and as provost he rather opposed than promoted changes in the university system under which he had been trained. He was *de facto* as well as *de jure* master of the college. The admission of women to university degrees, which was carried in the last year of his life, was almost the only important reform, introduced into the academic system under his rule, which was distasteful to him.

Salmon received many academic honours, besides those which his own university bestowed. He was a member of the Royal Irish Academy (1843), which awarded him the Cunningham medal in 1858, besides being a foreign member of the Institute of France, and honorary member of the Royal Academies of Berlin, Göttingen, and Copenhagen. He was fellow of the Accademia dei Lincei of Rome (1885); was made hon. D.C.L. Oxford (1868), LL.D. Cambridge (1874) D.D. Edinburgh (1884), D.Math. Christiania (1902); was fellow of the Royal Society (1863), which awarded him the royal medal in 1868 and the Copley medal in 1889; became F.R.S.Edinburgh, and was on the original list of the fellows of the British Academy (1902). He was president of the Mathematical and Physical Section of the British Association in 1878. He was also chancellor of St. Patrick's Cathedral (1871), and was presented with the freedom of the city of Dublin in 1892.

Hospitable and kindly, Salmon had many friends and interests. In youth a competent musician and a chess player of remarkable powers, he cultivated both recreations until an advanced age. He was always an omnivorous reader (except in the two departments of metaphysics and poetry, for which he had no taste), and had a special affection for the older novelists, being accustomed to recommend the study of Jane Austen as a liberal education. The homely vigour and the delightful wit of the long letters which he was accustomed to write to his friends entitle him to rank as one of the best letter-writers of the last century.

Salmon died in the Provost's House on 22 Jan. 1904, and was buried in Mount Jerome cemetery.

Salmon married in 1844 Frances Anne, daughter of the Rev. J. L. Salvador of Staunton, Herefordshire (*d.* 1878); of his four sons and two daughters the eldest son (Edward William) and the younger daughter (Fanny Mary) survived him.

A striking portrait of Salmon, painted by Benjamin Constant, at the request of the fellows of the college, in 1897, is preserved in the Provost's House at Dublin; and an earlier portrait (by Miss Sara Purser in 1888) belongs to the common room at Trinity. A posthumous bas-relief of his head, in bronze (by A. Bruce-Joy), forms part of the memorial in St. Patrick's Cathedral; while a seated statue in marble executed by Mr. John Hughes for Trinity College was unveiled on 14 June 1911. The Salmon fund (for poor students), and the Salmon exhibitions for members of the Divinity School, were endowed by him at Trinity while he was provost, in addition to other benefactions to the college. A window is dedicated to his memory in the church at the Riffel Alp, where he had spent several vacations.

Among Salmon's works, in addition to those already described, and apart from pamphlets, occasional sermons, and articles in reviews or magazines, are the following: 1. 'Sermons preached in Trinity College Chapel,' 1861. 2. 'The Eternity of Future Punishment,' 1864. 3. 'The Reign of Law,' 1873. 4. 'Non-miraculous Christianity,' 1881; 2nd edit. 1887. 5. Commentary on

Ecclesiastes in Ellicott's Old Testament Commentary, 1884. 6. 'Gnosticism and Agnosticism,' 1887. 7. Introduction to 'Apocrypha' in the 'Speaker's Commentary,' 1888. 8. 'Cathedral and University Sermons,' 1900; 2nd edit. 1901.

[Memoirs by the present writer in The Times (23 Jan. 1904), The New Liberal Review (March 1904), and Proc. Brit. Acad. (1904); obit. notices of the Royal Society (1904, by C. J. Joly), of the London Math. Soc. (1904, by Sir R. S. Ball), and in Nature (4 Feb. 1904); funeral sermons by the present writer and Bishop Chadwick of Derry (Dublin, 1904); Celebrities at Home in The World (6 Dec. 1899), by F. St. J. Morrow; Review of the Churches, by G. T. Stokes (15 June 1892); Minutes of Royal Irish Academy (1903–1904); Reminiscences in Weekly Irish Times, by Canon Staveley (9 July 1904); Dublin University Calendars; personal knowledge.] John Ossory.

SALOMONS, Sir JULIAN EMANUEL (1835–1909), Australian lawyer and politician, born at Edgbaston, Birmingham, on 4 Nov. 1835, was only son of Emanuel Solomons, a Jewish merchant of that city. Emigrating to Australia in youth, he was at first employed in a book-selling establishment in Sydney, and was for some time secretary of the Great Synagogue there. The Jewish community of Sydney interested themselves in him and he returned with their aid to England to be trained for a barrister. He entered at Gray's Inn on 14 Oct. 1858, and was called to the bar on 26 Jan. 1861. He then returned to New South Wales, and after admission to the bar of the colony in the same year, practised with success before the supreme court and rose quickly in his profession, being counsel for the crown in many important cases. A brilliant lawyer and an analytical reasoner rather than an eloquent advocate, he showed to advantage in examination and cross-examination and was witty and prompt in repartee. His prosecution in 1866 of Louis John Bertrand, a dentist, for the murder of a bank clerk named Henry Kinder—a trial which caused vast excitement—laid the foundation of his reputation. But he chiefly devoted himself to civil business.

Salomons was nominated a member of the legislative council of New South Wales on 5 Aug. 1869, and resigned on 15 Feb. 1871. He was reappointed on 7 March 1887, and took a prominent part in the debates of the chamber till 21 Feb. 1899, when he again resigned. From 18 Dec. 1869 to 15 Dec. 1870 he was solicitor-general in the Robertson ministry which merged into that of (Sir) Charles Cowper, and was representative of the government in the upper house with a seat in the cabinet from 11 Aug. to 5 Dec. 1870. From 7 March 1887 to 16 Jan. 1889 he was vice-president of the executive council and representative of (Sir) Henry Parkes's ministry in the legislative council and held the like office in (Sir) George Dibbs's ministry from 23 Oct. 1891 to 26 Jan. 1893.

On 16 Aug. 1881 he was appointed a royal commissioner to inquire into the Milburn Creek Copper Mining Company scandal. In 1886 he was nominated chief justice on the death of Sir James Martin; but owing to the hostile attitude of some members of the supreme court bench he gave up the office without being sworn in. He took a prominent part in the federation campaign, but opposed the commonwealth enabling bill. He acted as agent-general for the colony in London from 25 March 1899 to 13 May 1900, and on his return to Australia he retired from public and professional life, but was appointed in 1903 standing counsel to the commonwealth government in New South Wales. He died at his residence at Woollahra on 6 April 1909, and was buried in the Hebrew portion of the Rookwood general cemetery.

On 13 July 1891 Salomons was knighted by patent. He was a Q.C. of New South Wales, and from 1899 till death a bencher of Gray's Inn. He was a trustee of the Sydney National Art Gallery and the National Park of New South Wales.

Salomons married on 17 Dec. 1862 Louisa, fourth daughter of Maurice Salomons of Lower Edmonton, Middlesex; she survived him with two daughters. A half-length oil portrait by Mr. Percy Bigland belongs to his daughter, Mrs. J. T. Wilson, in Sydney.

[The Times, Sydney Morning Herald, and Sydney Mail, 7 April 1909; Sydney Daily Telegraph, 7 and 9 April 1909; Johns's Notable Australians, 1908; Year Book of Australia, 1898–1903; Mennell's Dict. of Australas. Biogr. 1892; Foster, Men at the Bar; Colonial Office Records.] C. A.

SALTING, GEORGE (1835–1909), art collector and benefactor, was elder son of Severin Kanute Salting and Louise Fiellerup, both of Danish origin. The father was born at Copenhagen on 3 Oct. 1805, and died at Chertsey on 14 Sept. 1865. The son George was born on 15 Aug. 1835 at Sydney, New South Wales, where the father had become a partner in the firm of Flower, Salting, Challis & Co., merchants.

They lived in Macquarie Street. George, with his younger brother, William Severin (*b.* 18 Jan. 1837, *d.* 23 June 1905), at first went to a school in Sydney until 1848, when George was sent home to Eton. His parents followed him to England two years later. He seems to have left no impression on his contemporaries at Eton save that of 'a pale, lean, tall, eccentric person,' although a contemporary portrait shows him as a handsome youth. Shooting was the only form of sport for which he cared. The whole family returned to Sydney in 1853, on account of George's health, contrary to the wishes of his Eton tutor, who saw in him the making of a good classical scholar. The brother William was at the same time withdrawn from Brighton College. A tutor was brought out for the two boys, and he complained of George's dreamy poetic temperament, which hindered continuous application. In the Lent term of 1854 Salting entered the newly founded University of Sydney with a scholarship for general proficiency. After a career in which he especially distinguished himself in classics, he graduated B.A. in 1857. When George and his brother left the university their father acknowledged their debt to its training by founding 'The Salting Exhibition,' tenable for three years by any pupil of the Sydney grammar school.

The Saltings returned to England in 1857, and settled in Rutland Gate. In October 1857 George matriculated from Balliol College, Oxford, but left after one term, owing apparently to his mother's death and its effect upon his father. The father gave up his London house and spent the autumn of 1858 in Rome. This sojourn moulded George's future career. While in Rome he devoted his whole time to the galleries, churches, and architectural monuments or to available books on the artistic and archæological treasures of the city. To other modes of study he added photography, then a serious undertaking, which involved his wheeling on a truck about the streets the apparatus together with a kind of tent, in which to develop his plates. Early in 1859 the party went to Naples and then to Florence. After a short visit to Australia they settled at a house named Silverlands, near Chertsey, where the father died (14 Sept. 1865). Thereupon George took for himself a suite of rooms over the Thatched House Club at the bottom of St. James's Street. There he remained unmarried and living with the utmost simplicity until death.

On his father's death Salting inherited a fortune generously estimated at 30,000*l.* a year. Thenceforth he devoted himself exclusively to collecting works of art, to which he brought a rare judgment and an unfaltering zeal. His severe training in Rome had prepared him for the vocation, which he was encouraged to pursue by the example of his friend Louis Huth, of Charles Drury Edward Fortnum [q. v. Suppl. I], and of (Sir) Augustus Wollaston Franks [q. v. Suppl. I], who had lately given a new seriousness to the study of medieval and renaissance art. But Salting was unique among the collectors of his time in consecrating the whole of his time and money to the pursuit, to the exclusion of every other interest.

For more than forty years Salting when in London spent each afternoon on a pilgrimage from one dealer to another, examining their wares with the greatest deliberation. When an object was selected as a desirable purchase, the price involved tedious negotiation, which Salting seems purposely to have prolonged so as to give him continuous occupation. Where he felt uncertain of his own judgment, he would walk to one or other of the museums or to a fellow collector, to obtain an opinion. At times he bought objects that on examination did not prove to be of good enough quality for his taste, and he would cause dealers embarrassment by offering these, which he called 'marbles' in allusion to schoolboy usage, in part payment for something of higher quality.

In the early days of his occupation of the Thatched House Club his purchases went there, but when the limited space proved inadequate even as storage, he lent his main collection of oriental porcelain to South Kensington (Victoria and Albert Museum), and subsequently many purchases went thither direct from the dealer.

Chinese porcelain was Salting's first serious interest, probably owing to the influence of Louis Huth. Here he formed what is without doubt one of the great collections of the world. It is especially valuable and important as presenting, perhaps more satisfactorily than any other, a complete series of the strictly artistic productions of the Chinese in this material. He cared but little for the historical interest of the wares or for tracing their history; in his taste Chinese porcelain was confined to what he considered beautiful, without regard either to antiquity or to the evolution of the manufacture. To a limited extent he collected Japanese art products, but never with the same enthusiasm. His eclectic mind and sensitive eye evidently failed to find in them the same satisfaction. In the province of Western art he was fairly catholic: Italian and Spanish majolica, small sculptures in all materials, enamels, jewellery, bronze statuettes and medals, and all the varied productions of the artist craftsmen of the Middle Ages and Renaissance—these he collected with persistency and unfailing enthusiasm, and in many of the classes his collection is unrivalled. Pictures and drawings had less attraction for him, though he bought both, and he developed in his later years a passion for pictures by Corot, paying the inflated prices of the day. Another phase of collecting more in keeping with his normal tastes was that of English miniature portraits. Of these he had a superb series, many of them of high historical interest, and by the great artists from Tudor times to the eighteenth century. In addition he had also a few admirable antiques, bronzes, terra cottas, and the like. No matter what new style of collecting he took up, he sought only the finest specimens of their kind.

Although Salting was a familiar figure at Christie's sale rooms, and was well known to the great foreign collectors and dealers, his reputation hardly became a continental one until the Spitzer sale in 1893. To attend this sale he spent some time in Paris, where he endeavoured to lead the same simple life as at home, while bidding for himself in the sale room and spending there some 40,000*l.* on fine works of art.

Salting died in his rooms at the Thatched House Club on 12 Dec. 1909, and was buried at Brompton cemetery. Though he was not generally suspected of possessing any genius for finance, he left a fortune of 1,287,900*l.* net, a sum vastly greater than that inherited from his father. Despite his procrastinating and undecided character, which led intimate friends to foretell that he would die intestate, he made a will dated 11 Oct. 1889. There were small bequests of money to the London hospitals, and to relatives and friends, the residuary legatee of his pecuniary estate being his niece, Lady Binning, daughter of his late brother. But he divided his collections among the National Gallery, the British Museum, and the Victoria and Albert Museum (at South Kensington), the main portion going to the last. The trustees of the first two had the power to select such of his pictures and prints and drawings as they thought fit. The bequest to the Victoria and Albert Museum was conditional on the objects being 'not distributed over the various sections, but kept all together according to the various specialities of my exhibits.' This reasonable condition serves the double purpose of providing the most appropriate monument of a munificent benefactor, and enables the public to measure the importance of the gift, which would have been impossible if the collection had been distributed over the whole museum. Further, such an arrangement provides in the future the means of judging of the standard of taste prevailing in the nineteenth century. The Salting collection was first opened to the public at South Kensington on 22 March 1911.

[Eton College Register; Sydney University Register; The Times, 14, 15, 17, 23, 25, 28, 31 Dec. 1909; 26 and 28 Jan. 1910, and 23 March 1911; private information from relatives and friends; personal knowledge; there is a good portrait from a photograph in The Salting Collection (V. & A. Museum), 1911.] C. H. R.

SALVIN, FRANCIS HENRY (1817–1904), writer on falconry and cormorant-fishing, born at Croxdale Hall on 4 April 1817, was fifth and youngest son of William Thomas Salvin, of Croxdale Hall, Durham, by his wife Anna Maria, daughter of John Webbe-Weston, of Sutton Place, Surrey. Educated at Ampleforth, a Roman catholic school in Yorkshire, he served for several years in the militia, joining the 3rd battalion of the York and Lancaster regiment in 1839 and retiring with the rank of captain in 1864. In 1857 he inherited from his uncle, Thomas Monnington Webbe-Weston, the fine old Tudor mansion Sutton Place, near Guildford, but he usually lived at Whitmoor House, another residence on the estate. An early love of hawking was stimulated by an acquaintance with John Tong, assistant falconer to Col. Thomas Thornton (1757–1823) [q. v.].

In 1843 Salvin made a highly successful hawking tour with John Pells (employed by the hereditary grand falconer of England) through the north of England; and when quartered with his regiment at remote places in Ireland he used to fly falcons at rooks and magpies. Near Fermoy in 1857 he killed in four months eighty-four of these birds. He also for some years kept goshawks and made successful flights with them at mountain hares, rabbits and water-hens. He invented a portable bow-perch for these birds. He was a prominent member from 1870 of the old Hawking Club which met on the Wiltshire downs.

Salvin was also the first to revive successfully in England the old sport of fishing with cormorants. In 1849 he took with four birds in twenty-eight days some 1200 large fish at Driffield, Kilney, and other places in the north of England. His famous cormorant, 'Izaak Walton,' brought from Rotterdam, was stuffed in 1847 by John Hancock and is now in the Newcastle-on-Tyne Museum. Another, 'Sub-Inspector,' the first known instance of a cormorant bred in confinement (*Field*, 27 May 1882), was exhibited at the Fisheries Exhibition, South Kensington, in 1883, and was sent to the Zoological Gardens after Salvin's death, surviving till 1911. This bird and its master are depicted in a drawing by F. W. Frohawk (reproduced in the *Field*, 18 Oct. 1890) now in the possession of Mr. Charles Sibeth.

Salvin had great power over animals. He tamed two young otters to follow him like dogs and sleep in his lap, and at one time kept a wild boar with collar and bell. He was active in field sports when past seventy.

He died unmarried on 2 Oct. 1904, at the Manor House, Sutton Park, Guildford, and was buried in St. Edward's cemetery, Sutton Park.

Salvin, who was a frequent contributor to the 'Field,' collaborated in two works on falconry. The first, 'Falconry in the British Isles' (1855; 2nd edit. 1873), written in conjunction with William Brodrick of Chudleigh, has been pronounced the best modern English work on the subject. The figures of hawks, drawn by Brodrick, are said to bear comparison with the work of Josef Wolf [q. v.] the animal painter. The text of the second edition is to be preferred, but the illustrations are inferior to those of the original (*Quarterly Review*, July 1875).

Salvin also assisted Gage Earle Freeman [q. v. Suppl. II] in 'Falconry: its Claims, History, and Practice' (1859); the 'Remarks on training the Otter and Cormorant' appended to it being wholly his. Both books are now out of print and much sought after. A portrait of Salvin by Mr. Hinks of Farnham is in the possession of Mr. Charles Sibeth of Lexham Gardens, Kensington. He is also represented in J. C. Hook's 'Fishing by Proxy,' exhibited at the Royal Academy in 1873.

[Burke's Landed Gentry (s.v. Salvin and Witham); Field, 8 Oct. 1904; The Times, 4 Oct. 1904; Ibis, Jan. 1905; Harting's Bibliotheca Accipitraria; Harding Cox and Hon. G. Lascelles, Coursing and Falconry (Badminton Library); Michell's Art and Practice of Hawking; Major Chas. Hawkins Fisher's Reminiscences of a Falconer (with portrait showing Salvin with hawk on fist); F. Harrison's Annals of an Old Manor House; private information.] G. Le G. N.

SAMBOURNE, EDWARD LINLEY (1844–1910), artist in black and white, born at 15 Lloyd Square, Pentonville, London, on 4 Jan. 1844, was only surviving child of Edward Mott Sambourne, by his wife Frances Linley, of Norton, Derbyshire, a member of the well-known family to which Elizabeth Anne Linley, wife of Richard Brinsley Sheridan [q.v.] belonged [see Linley, Thomas, the elder]. His father's father had left England for the United States and had been naturalised an American citizen. His father, born at Easton, Pennsylvania, in 1802, eventually carried on a wholesale furrier's business in St. Paul's Churchyard, London.

Sambourne was educated at the City of London school (September 1855 to Easter 1856) and afterwards at Chester Training College school (1857–60). At the age of sixteen he entered as an apprentice the marine engine works of Messrs. John Penn & Son, Greenwich. He had already shown a talent for drawing, which was encouraged by his father's sister, Mrs. Barr, herself an accomplished artist; and at Greenwich he continued to amuse himself and his friends by drawing caricatures and fanciful sketches. In 1867 one of these drawings was shown by Sambourne's fellow apprentice, Alfred Reed, to his father, German Reed, who in turn submitted it to his friend Mark Lemon, the editor of 'Punch.' Mark Lemon found promise in it and offered the young artist work on 'Punch.' Sambourne's first drawing appeared in 'Punch,' 27 April 1867 (lii. 159). Retiring from Penn's works, he soon became a regular contributor, and was in 1871 made a full member of the staff. In the meantime he studied technique and had attended the School of Art at South Kensington, although only for a fortnight. In 'Punch' he was soon set to illustrate the 'Essence of Parliament,' and this work gradually developed in his hands into a second weekly cartoon. On Sir John Tenniel's retirement towards the end of 1900 Sambourne succeeded him as cartoonist-in-chief.

Sambourne also made his mark as an illustrator of books. He illustrated Sir Francis Burnand's 'New Sandford and Merton' (1872); James Lynam Molloy's 'Our Autumn Holiday on French Rivers' (1874), and the 1885 edition of Charles Kingsley's 'Water Babies,' which contains

Sambourne's best work in this line. In 1883 he designed and executed for the Fisheries Exhibition a diploma card which earned the enthusiastic praise of Tenniel (Spielmann, *Hist. of Punch*, p. 534). In 1900 he was one of the royal commissioners and sole juror for Great Britain in class 7 of the fine arts at the Paris exhibition.

In the autumn of 1909 Sambourne fell ill, and on 3 Nov. of that year his last cartoon appeared in 'Punch' (cxxxvii. 317). Two previously executed full-page drawings appeared in the 'Punch' almanack for 1910. He died at his home, 18 Stafford Terrace, Kensington, on 3 Aug. 1910, and his remains were buried, after cremation, in the graveyard of St. Peter's church, near Broadstairs.

Sambourne is entitled to a very high place among 'black-and-white' artists. His career as a contributor to 'Punch' extended over nearly forty-three years, and the marked growth of his powers may be studied in the pages of that journal. His youthful contributions show ingenuity and a certain grotesque humour, but little artistic merit. In his middle period the grotesqueness and the humour increased, with the addition of a great, but somewhat mechanical, vigour of execution. Only in his later period, fortunately a prolonged one, did he achieve that combination of artistic grace and dignity with an extraordinary firmness and delicacy of line which is the mark of his best work. He did not aim at Tenniel's massive simplicity, nor did his strength lie in the portrayal of living persons by way of caricature; but in imaginative designs, especially where his subject permitted him to introduce classically draped female figures, or where his ingenious and fertile fancy could invent and harmonise in a large and balanced composition a great variety of details, he was without a rival. So sure and accurate were his hand and eye that he could accomplish Giotto's feat of drawing a perfect circle. Fond of sport and outdoor exercise, Sambourne was a delightful companion noted for his *bonhomie* and good stories.

Sambourne married on 20 Oct. 1874 Marion, eldest daughter of Spencer Herapath, F.R.S., of Westwood, Thanet; by her he had a son, Mawdley Herapath, and a daughter, Maud Frances (Mrs. L. C. R. Messel), who has contributed sketches to 'Punch.' A portrait of Sambourne (1884), by Sir George Reid, R.S.A., is in the possession of the city of Aberdeen. A caricature portrait of him by Leslie Ward ('Spy') in 1882 is in the 'Punch' room.

[Punch, vols. lii.–cxxxviii.; Spielmann's History of Punch, 1895; Who's Who, 1910; The Times, 4 Aug. 1910; baptismal register, St. Philip's church, Clerkenwell.] R. C. L.

SAMUELSON, Sir BERNHARD, first baronet (1820–1905), ironmaster and promoter of technical education, born at Hamburg, where his mother was on a visit, on 22 Nov. 1820, was eldest of the six sons of Samuel Henry Samuelson (1789–1863), merchant, by his wife Sarah Hertz (*d.* 1875). Bernhard's grandfather, Henry Samuelson (1764–1813), was a merchant of London. In his infancy his father settled at Hull. Educated at a private school at Skirlaugh, Yorkshire, he showed mathematical aptitude, but he left at fourteen to enter his father's office. At home he developed a love of music and a command of modern languages. He was soon apprenticed to Rudolph Zwilchenhart & Co., a Swiss firm of merchants, at Liverpool. There he spent six years. In 1837 he was sent to Warrington by his masters to purchase locomotive engines for export to Prussia. The experience led him to seek expert knowledge of engineering, and it suggested to him the possibility of expanding greatly the business of exporting English machinery to the Continent. In 1842 he was made manager of the export business of Messrs. Sharp, Stewart & Co., engineers, of Manchester. In this capacity he was much abroad, but owing to the railway boom at home in 1845, the firm gave up the continental trade. Next year Samuelson went to Tours and established railway works of his own, which he carried on with success till the revolution of 1848 drove him back to England.

In 1848 Samuelson purchased a small factory of agricultural implements at Banbury, which the death of the founder, James Gardner, brought into the market. Samuelson developed the industry with rare energy, and the works, which in 1872 produced no less than 8000 reaping-machines, rapidly became one of the largest of its kind. A branch was established at Orleans. The business, which was turned into a limited liability company in 1887, helped to convert Banbury from an agricultural town into an industrial centre. Meanwhile Samuelson in 1853 undertook a different sort of venture elsewhere. At the Cleveland Agricultural Show he met John Vaughan, who had discovered in 1851 the seam of Cleveland ironstone, and now convinced Samuelson of the certain future of the Cleveland iron trade. Samuelson erected blast-furnaces at South Bank, near Middlesbrough, within a mile of the works of Bolckow & Vaughan at Eston. These he worked until 1863, when they were sold, and more extensive premises were built in the neighbourhood of Newport. Samuelson, whose interest in practical applications of science grew keen, studied for himself the construction of blast-furnaces and resolved to enlarge their cubical capacity at the expense of their height. By 1870 eight furnaces were at work, most of them of greater capacity than any others in the district. In 1872 between 2500 and 3000 tons of pig-iron were produced weekly. In 1871 a description of the Newport ironworks which he presented to the Institution of Civil Engineers won him a Telford medal.

In 1887 the iron-working firm of Sir B. Samuelson & Co., Ltd., was formed with a nominal capital of 275,000*l.* Sir Bernhard was chairman of the company until 1895, when he handed over the chairmanship to his second son, Francis. The blast furnaces were in 1905 producing about 300,000 tons of pig iron annually, and the by-products from the coke ovens started in 1896 averaged about 270,000 tons of coke, 12,000 tons of tar, 3500 of sulphate of ammonia, and 150,000 gallons of crude naphtha.

An important extension of Samuelson's commercial energies took place in July 1870. He then built the Britannia ironworks at Middlesbrough, his third manufacturing enterprise (which subsequently became part of the property of Messrs. Doman Long & Co.). The site was twenty acres of marsh land, which was only adaptable to its purpose after being covered with slag. In the Britannia works there was installed the largest plant at that date put into operation at one time, and their output of iron, tar, and by-products was soon gigantic. One of Samuelson's endeavours which bore tribute to his mechanical ambition came to nothing. He was anxious to make steel from Cleveland ore—an effort in which no success had yet been achieved. He learned on the Continent of the Siemens-Martin process, and now spent some 300,00*l.* in experimenting with it. In 1869 he leased for the purpose the North Yorkshire ironworks at South Stockton; but the attempt proved unsuccessful, though the trial taught some useful lessons to ironmasters.

Samuelson, who was a considerate employer of labour, took part in developing Middlesbrough and the Cleveland district, identifying himself with local institutions and effort. But his home was at Banbury, and he was prominent there in public affairs. Seeking a parliamentary career, he represented the place and district in parliament for more than thirty years. He was a zealous upholder of liberal principles, was loyal to his party, and a staunch supporter of Gladstone. He was first elected for Banbury by a majority of one vote in Feb. 1859, but he was defeated at the general election two months later. In 1865 however he was again elected, and an allegation that he was not of English birth and therefore ineligible was examined and confuted by a committee of the House of Commons. He retained the seat in 1868, 1874, and 1880. In 1885, when the borough was merged in the North Oxfordshire division, he was returned for that constituency, and he sat for it until 1895, when he retired and was made a privy councillor. Although he supported home rule, he lost sympathy with the ultra-radical sentiment which increased in the party during his last years. Through life Samuelson cherished free-trade convictions, yet in his last years he reached the conclusion that 'a departure from free trade' was 'admissible with a view to widening the area of taxation.' In a paper read before the Political Economy Club in London on 5 July 1901, the chief conclusions of which he summarised in a letter to 'The Times' (6 Nov.), he urged a 'tariff for revenue,' and sketched out the cardinal points of the tariff reform movement before they had been formulated by Mr. Joseph Chamberlain.

In the House of Commons Samuelson, who gave expert advice on all industrial questions, was best known by his strenuous advocacy of technical instruction. His chief public services were identified with that subject. He thoroughly believed in the need among Englishmen of every rank of a strict scientific training. In 1867 he investigated personally and with great thoroughness the conditions of technical education in the chief industrial centres of Europe and made a valuable report (*Parl. Papers*, 1867). He was in 1868 chairman of a committee of the House of Commons to inquire into the provisions for instruction in theoretical and applied science to the industrial classes; and he was a member of the duke of Devonshire's royal commission on scientific instruction (1870), being responsible for that part of the report which dealt with the Science and Art Department. In 1881 he had full opportunity of using his special study to the public advantage on being made chairman of the royal commission on technical instruction. He was also a member of Viscount Cross's royal commission on elementary education in 1887, and next year of the parliamentary committee for inquiring into the working of the education acts.

His activity in other industrial inquiries was attested by a series of reports which he prepared in 1867 for the foreign office, on the iron trade between England and France, when renewal of the commercial treaty between the two countries was under consideration. He was chairman of parliamentary committees on the patent laws (1871–2) and on railways (1873). He was a member of the royal commission for the Paris exhibition of 1878, and received in that year the cross of the Legion of Honour. In 1886 he was chairman of the Associated Chambers of Commerce of the United Kingdom.

His scientific attainments were acknowledged by his election as a fellow of the Royal Society in 1881. He was a member of the council in 1887–8. He joined the Institution of Mechanical Engineers in 1865, and the Institution of Civil Engineers in 1869. He was one of the founders of the Iron and Steel Institute in the latter year, and was president of that body in 1883–5.

In 1884 Samuelson presented to Banbury a technical institute, which was opened by A. J. Mundella on 2 July 1884. Mundella then announced that a baronetcy had been conferred on Samuelson for his services to the education of the people. The benefactor's portrait by Sir Hubert von Herkomer, of which a replica hangs in the reading room, was presented to him on the same occasion.

Samuelson, who was long an enthusiastic yachtsman, died of pneumonia at his residence, 56 Princes Gate, S.W., on 10 May 1905, and was buried at Torre cemetery, Torquay. He was succeeded in the baronetcy by his eldest son, Henry Bernhard, formerly M.P. for Frome. Samuelson married (1) in 1844 Caroline (*d.* 1886), daughter of Henry Blundell, J.P., of Hull, by whom he had four sons and four daughters; and (2) in 1889 Lelia Mathilda, daughter of the Chevalier Leon Serena and widow of William Denny of Dumbarton.

Samuelson published at Gladstone's request a memoir on Irish land tenure (1869), and a report on the railway goods tariffs of Germany, Belgium, and Holland, presented to the Associated Chambers of Commerce Birmingham, 1885). Besides his presidential address (1883), he contributed to the 'Journal of the Iron and Steel Institute' papers on the Terni steelworks (1887, pt. i. p. 31) and on the construction and cost of blast-furnaces in the Cleveland district (*ib.* p. 91).

An oil painting by Gelli of Florence belongs to the eldest son, and a bronze bust by Fantachiotti of Florence, of which there are terra-cotta replicas, belongs to the second son, Francis. Sir Bernhard's eldest son added to the Queen Victoria Memorial Hospital at Mont Boron, Nice, the 'Sir Bernhard Samuelson memorial annexe' for infectious cases, with twenty beds; a replica of Fantachiotti's bust is on the façade. An addition was also made in Sir Bernhard's memory to the Middlesbrough infirmary. A memorial painted window has been placed in Over Compton church, Sherborne, Dorsetshire, by Sir Bernhard's eldest daughter, Caroline, wife of Colonel Goodden.

[Banbury Guardian, Yorkshire Post, and The Times, 11 May 1905; Journal of the Iron and Steel Institute, 1905, pt. i. p. 504; Engineer, and Engineering, 12 May 1905; Burke's Peerage and Baronetage; private information.] W. F. S.

SANDBERG, SAMUEL LOUIS GRAHAM (1851–1905), Tibetan scholar, born on 9 Dec. 1851 at Oughtibridge in Yorkshire, was fifth child in a family of five sons and two daughters of Paul Louis Sandberg (*d.* 1878), then vicar of Oughtibridge, by his wife Maria (1815–1903), daughter of James Graham of the diplomatic service and grand-daughter of Dr. James Graham (1745–1794) [q. v.], a London doctor. Both parents were distinguished by linguistic talents. The father, whose ancestors came to England from Sweden, had won the Tyrwhitt Hebrew scholarship and other successes at Cambridge, and was conversationally acquainted with as many as thirteen languages, including Arabic, Syriac, and Hindustani. He was in India as a missionary from 1843 to 1849, becoming principal of Jai Nārāyan's College at Benares. From 1874 till his death in 1878 he was rector of Northrepps in Norfolk. His widow, a writer of devotional works and a philanthropist, who died in April 1903, aged eighty-eight, received the exceptional title of honorary life member of the Church Missionary Society. She was acquainted with seven languages, including Hindustani (*The Times*, 27 April 1903).

Young Sandberg, after attending Liverpool College (1861–3) and Enfield School, Birkenhead (1863–7), graduated B.A. of Dublin University at nineteen in 1870. His tastes were linguistic and mathematical, with a leaning towards Asiatic languages, such as Chinese and Japanese. He developed an aversion for the medical profession, for which he was originally destined, and on leaving Dublin University was admitted a student at the Inner Temple on 9 June 1871, and was called to the bar on 30 April 1874, and joined the northern circuit. His practice was insignificant, and he mainly divided his time between journalism, the preparation of an elaborate treatise entitled 'The Shipmaster's Legal Handbook,' which he failed to publish, and private tuition. A year's prostration by Maltese fever (1877–8), contracted while travelling with a pupil, was followed in 1879 by his ordination as a clergyman. He was curate of St. Clement's, Sandwich, from 1879 to 1882, and chaplain of the Seckford Hospital, Woolbridge, from 1882 to 1884. In 1885 he went to India as chaplain on the Bengal establishment, and held charges at Kidderpur (1886), Dinapur (1886–7), Calcutta (1887 and 1892–4), Dacca (1887–8), Jhansi (1888–9), Muradabad (1890), Roorkee (1890), Howrah (1890–1), Cuttack (1891–2), Sabathu (1894–6), Nowgong (1897–8), Barrackpore (1898–9), St. John's, Calcutta (1899–1901), Darjeeling (1901–2), Calcutta (1903), and Cuttack (1903–4). When on a holiday at Darjeeling he made his first acquaintance with the Tibetan language, and in 1888 he published at Calcutta a 'Manual of the Sikkim-Bhutia Dialect' (2nd edit. enlarged, Westminster, 1895). He learned much of the secret explorations of Tibet in progress during the next seventeen years, and wrote in the press and the magazines about the topography of Tibet and routes through the country. In 1901 he issued at Calcutta 'An Itinerary of the Route from Sikkim to Lhasa, together with a Plan of the Capital of Tibet.' On the eve of the British expedition in 1904 he published a systematic treatise, 'The Exploration of Tibet: its History and Particulars from 1623 to 1904' (Calcutta and London). Sandberg drafted the letter from Lord Curzon, the viceroy, to the Grand Lama, the rejection of which precipitated the expedition of 1904.

To Tibetan philology Sandberg's contributions were equally notable. In 1894 there appeared at Calcutta his 'Manual of Colloquial Tibetan,' a practical work embodying much useful information. His most important philological work was his share in 'A Tibetan-English Dictionary' (Calcutta, 1902), which he was commissioned in 1899 by the Bengal government to prepare in conjunction with the Rev. A. W. Heyde from the materials collected by Sarat Chandra Das. The work was not final or faultless, but it was far more complete than any other.

His writings relating to Tibet also included the following magazine articles: 'The City of Lhasa' (*Nineteenth Century*, 1889); 'A Journey to the Capital of Tibet' (*Contemporary Review*, 1890); 'Philosophical Buddhism in Tibet' (*ibid.*); 'Monks and Monasteries in Tibet' (*Calcutta Review*, 1890); 'The Great Lama of Tibet' (*Murray's Magazine*, October 1891); 'The Exploration of Tibet' (*Calcutta Review*, 1894); 'The Great River of Tibet: its Course from Source to Outfall' (*ibid.* 1896); 'Note to Gait's Paper on Ahom Coins' (*Proc. Asiat. Soc. of Bengal*, 1896, pp. 88 sq.); 'Monasteries in Tibet' (*Calcutta Review*, 1896); and 'A Tibetan Poet and Mystic,' i.e. Milaraspa' (*Nineteenth Century*, 1899).

Sandberg at the same time proved the width of his interests in 'A Neglected Classical Language (Armenian)' (in *Calcutta Review*, 1891), and in 'Bhotan, the Unknown Indian State' (*ibid.* 1898). He was especially concerned in the condition of the Eurasians, whose cause he espoused in 'Our Outcast Cousins in India' (*Contemp. Rev.* 1892). His modesty and reticence concealed the extent of his attainments, which included a thorough knowledge of the Italian language and literature.

In the August of 1904 Sandberg was attacked by tubercular laryngitis, and was invalided home. He died at Bournemouth on 2 March of the following year. He married in 1884 Mary Grey, who died without issue in 1910.

[Ecclesiastical and Official records of services; The Times, 6 March 1905; The Homeward Mail, 11 March 1905; see also notices of father in the Liverpool Albion, 1878, and mother in The Times for 27 April 1903; private information.] F. W. T.

SANDERSON, Sir JOHN SCOTT BURDON-, first baronet (1828–1905), regius professor of medicine at Oxford. [See Burdon-Sanderson.]

SANDERSON, EDGAR (1838–1907), historical writer, born at Nottingham on 25 Jan. 1838, was son of Edgar Sanderson by his wife Eliza Rumsey. The father, who was a direct descendant of Bishop Robert Sanderson [q. v.], had at first a lace-factory at Nottingham, but afterwards kept private schools at Stockwell and Streatham Common. The younger Sanderson was educated at the City of London School and at Clare College, Cambridge, where he won a scholarship. He graduated in 1860 as fourth in the 2nd class of the classical tripos, proceeding M.A. in 1865. After holding a mastership in King's Lynn grammar school he was ordained deacon in 1862 and priest in 1863. At first curate of St. Dunstan's, Stepney, and second master of Stepney grammar school, he held successively curacies at Burcombe-cum-Broadway, Dorsetshire (with a mastership at Weymouth school), and at Chieveley, Berkshire. From 1870 to 1873 Sanderson was headmaster of Stockwell grammar school; from 1873 to 1877 of Macclesfield; and from 1877 to 1881 of Huntingdon grammar school. Thenceforth he lived at Streatham Common, and occupied himself in writing educational manuals and popular historical works. He died at 23 Barrow Road, Streatham Common, on 31 Dec. 1907, and was buried at Norwood cemetery. He married in 1864 Laetitia Jane, elder daughter of Matthew Denycloe, surgeon, of Bridport. She died in October 1894, leaving two sons and four daughters.

Sanderson had a retentive memory and a faculty for lucid exposition. His chief works, all of which were on a comprehensive scale and enjoyed a large circulation, were: 1. 'History of the British Empire,' 1882; 20th edit. 1906: a well-arranged handbook. 2. 'Outlines of the World's History, Ancient, Mediæval and Modern,' 1885, issued both in four parts and in one volume; revised edit. 1910. 3. 'History of the World from the Earliest Historical Time to 1898,' 1898. 4. 'The British Empire in the 19th Century: its Progress and Expansion at Home and Abroad,' 6 vols. 1898–9 (with engravings and maps); reissued in 1901 as 'The British Empire at Home and Abroad.'

[Private information; The Times, 1 Jan. 1908; Guardian, 8 Jan. 1908; Crockford's Clerical Directory; Introduction by Mr. Roger Ingpen to Sanderson's abridgment of Carlyle's Frederick; note in Mrs. Valentine's Cameos of Engl. Literature, 1894; Sanderson's works.]

G. Le G. N.

SANDHAM, HENRY (1842–1910), painter and illustrator, born in Montreal on 24 May 1842, was son of John Sandham by his wife, Elizabeth Tait. The father had emigrated from England to Canada as a house decorator.

Sandham taught himself art in youth, with some aid from Vogt, Way, Jacobi, and other Canadian painters. He early entered the photographic studio, in Montreal, of W. Notman, whose partner he became. Here he executed his first public artistic work for the 'Century Magazine' of New York. Recognising his ability, Mr. Notman recommended him to the notice of J. A. Fraser, R.C.A., under whose tuition Sandham quickly came to the front. He then travelled in Europe to study the classical works and settled in Boston on his return in 1880. In this year the Royal Canadian Academy was founded by the Marquis of Lorne and Princess Louise, and Sandham was chosen as a charter member.

In the United States Sandham had great success as a painter of battle and historical scenes. He also painted many portraits of distinguished persons, and continued to work at illustrations. His best-known pictures are 'The March of Time,' to commemorate the grand army of the republic, now in the National Gallery, Washington; 'The Dawn of Liberty,' in the town hall, Lexington, U.S.; portrait of Sir John A. Macdonald, in the Parliament Buildings, Ottawa. Others are hung in the Parliament Buildings, Halifax, N.S., in the Smithsonian Institute, Washington, and the State House, Boston. 'Some of his figure groups are most skilfully handled. He was an excellent draughtsman' (Edmund Morris). His greatest success was in the medium of water colours. He excelled also in colour work for book and magazine illustrations, often contributing to the 'Century,' 'Scribner's,' and 'Harper's' magazines. Besides the various American galleries, he exhibited at the Royal Canadian Academy and the Salon of Paris, and was awarded medals at the Philadelphia centennial exhibition, 1876, and at the Indian colonial exhibition, South Kensington, London, 1886.

He died in London on 21 June 1910, and was buried in Kensal Green. A memorial exhibition of his chief paintings was held in the Imperial Institute, London, in June 1911.

Sandham married on 23 May 1865 Agnes, daughter of John Fraser, a Canadian journalist. Mrs. Sandham was a contributor to the various American magazines. Of six children, two reached maturity—

Arthur, a wood-engraver, and Gwendoline.

[Art in Canada: the Early Painters, by Edmund Morris, Canada, July 1910 (an illustrated article); Morgan, Canadian Men and Women of the Time; Cat. Exhibition of Sandham's work in London, 1911; information from his daughter.] W. S. J.

SANDYS, FREDERICK (1829–1904), Pre-Raphaelite painter, whose full name was originally ANTHONY FREDERICK AUGUSTUS SANDS, was born at 7 St. Giles's Hill, Norwich, on 1 May, probably in 1829. No baptismal entry or other record exists to attest the year. In the Norfolk and Norwich Art Union catalogue of 1839 a note to a drawing (No. 278) entitled 'Minerva, by A. F. A. Sands,' states that the artist was 'aged ten,' and thus makes him born in 1829, but in later years, when he was in the habit of giving friends somewhat varied and inconsistent details of his career, he represented 1832 as the year of his birth. His father, Anthony Sands, originally a dyer by profession, became a drawing-master in Norwich and subsequently a portrait and subject painter; examples of his work are in the Norwich Museum (No. 50) and in Mr. Russell Colman's collection at Norwich; he died in 1883. The mother's maiden name was Mary Anne Negus. An only sister, Emma, who was also a painter and exhibited at the Royal Academy, died in 1877. The spelling of the family name was changed from Sands to Sandys to suggest, it is said, a not well authenticated connection with the family of Lord Sandys. The grandfather was a shoemaker in Upper Westwick Street, Norwich.

Sandys was educated at the Norwich grammar school. His artistic training was presumably superintended by his father, for he acknowledged no other master. But George Richmond [q. v.] was an old friend of his family and a constant visitor to Norwich, and although Sandys repudiated any suggestion of Richmond's influence, analogies in the portraiture of both artists cannot be entirely dismissed. Sandys's first commissions were for illustrations to local handbooks such as 'Birds of Norfolk' and Bulmer's 'Antiquities of Norwich.' He exhibited at local exhibitions until 1852. His first work seen at the Royal Academy was a crayon drawing of Lord Henry Loftus in 1851, when he was living in London at 21 Wigmore Street.

In 1857 he published anonymously in London a lithographic print entitled 'A Nightmare,' which was a caricature of 'Sir Isumbras at the Ford,' Millais's well-known Pre-Raphaelite picture in the Academy of that year. The faces of Rossetti, Millais, and Holman Hunt were substituted for those of the girl, the knight, and the boy respectively; the horse of the original being transformed into a donkey labelled J. R., i.e. John Ruskin. The verses at the bottom of the print were by Tom Taylor, who was also the author of the mock mediæval lines printed in the Royal Academy catalogue for the original picture. The print measures 13⅜ inches by 19¼; a reduced facsimile is reproduced in Fisher's 'Catalogue of Engravings' (1879).

Dante Gabriel Rossetti [q. v.], on whom Sandys had called in order to obtain a likeness for the skit, was delighted. Sandys became an intimate and constant visitor at Rossetti's house, 16 Cheyne Walk. From this time (1857), Sandys associated with the artists, poets, and writers of the Pre-Raphaelite group, which then included Whistler. His painting and drawing grew definitely Pre-Raphaelite in character and handling, and he became an interesting link between the great school of his native place and the Pre-Raphaelites. He always resisted the imputation that he had seen Menzel's work, to which his own has been compared. There was perhaps a common origin in Dürer, or Rethel, whose prints were popular in England.

Sandys soon concentrated much of his energy on wood block designs in black and white, which appeared in 'Cornhill,' 'Once a Week,' 'Good Words,' and other publications between 1860 and 1866. Their technical accomplishment is unsurpassed by that of any contemporaries. They called forth from Millais the compliment that Sandys was 'worth two Academicians rolled into one'; while Rossetti with some exaggeration pronounced his friend the 'greatest living draughtsman.' On a drawing by Sandys of Cleopatra, Swinburne wrote a poem called 'Cleopatra,' which appeared with the woodcut after Sandys's drawing in 'Cornhill Magazine' in September 1866. (The poem was published in a separate volume the same year, but was never reprinted; cf. NICOLL and WISE, *Lit. Anecdotes of Nineteenth Century*, ii. 314–6.) Sandys illustrated poems by George Meredith [q. v. Suppl. II] ('The Chartist'), Christina Rossetti [q. v.] ('Amor Mundi'), and others in current periodicals.

Meanwhile Sandys contributed a few notable subject pictures to the Academy. These included 'Oriana' (1861), 'Vivien' and 'La Belle Ysonde' (1863), 'Morgan le Fay' (1864), one of the finest, and 'Cassandra' (1868). Two oil portraits, those of Mrs. Anderson Rose (1862) and Mrs. Jane Lewis (in the Academy of 1864), deserve a place among the great achievements of English painting. The two magnificent versions of 'Autumn,' of which the larger belongs to Mr. Russell Colman of Norwich and the smaller is in the Birmingham Art Gallery, are among other of the too rare examples of the artist's achievements in oil. In 1868 'Medea,' an oil painting generally regarded as one of Sandys's masterpieces, though accepted by the hanging committee, was crowded out from the Academy. The violent protests in the press, among which Swinburne's was pitched in his characteristic key, resulted in the picture being hung on the line in the following year, 1869. He continued to contribute to the Academy until 1886; and after 1877 to the Grosvenor Gallery, where he showed altogether nine works. But after 'Medea' Sandys practically abandoned the medium of oil except for a few portraits.

From an early period Sandys had achieved a high repute among patrons and critics by his crayon heads, of which one of the best is 'Mrs. George Meredith' (1864). In 1880 he received a commission from Messrs. Macmillan & Co. for a series of literary portraits, which include Robert Browning, Matthew Arnold, Tennyson, J. R. Green, and J. H. Shorthouse. They are hard and unsympathetic in treatment, though Sandys retained his old correctness and precision. In his last year he executed a series of crayon portraits of members of the Colman family in Norwich, representing five generations. In other works of his late period he succumbed to a sentimental and barren idealism.

Intemperate and bohemian modes of life seem to have atrophied his powers. He was a constant borrower and a difficult if delightful friend. His relations with most of his associates were chequered. In 1866 he accompanied Rossetti on a trip through Kent (ROSSETTI, *Letters*, ii. 189), but a quarrel followed. Rossetti considered that too many of his pictorial ideas were being appropriated by Sandys (W. M. ROSSETTI, *Reminiscences*, p. 320). The breach, which was healed in 1875, prejudicially affected the qualities of Sandys's imagination and technique. A friendship with Meredith lasted longer. Sandys often stayed with the novelist, who mentions him in a letter as a guest at Copseham Cottage in 1864. He was then painting the background of 'Gentle Spring,' shown in the Academy of 1865. At one time Sandys consorted a good deal with gipsies, one of whom, Kaomi, was a favourite model. She appears in Rossetti's 'Beloved,' and is the original of Kiomi in Meredith's Harry Richmond.' Sandys was a great 'bruiser' and the hero, by his own account, of a good many brawls.

In 1898 Sandys was elected an original member of the newly formed International Society of Sculptors, Painters and Gravers, and through Mr. Pennell renewed his acquaintance with Whistler. In the intervals of long disappearances he was sometimes seen at the Café Royal in Regent Street, London, in company with Aubrey Beardsley and younger artists.

In appearance Sandys was tall and distinguished: in later life not unlike Don Quixote. He was always neatly dressed, whatever his circumstances, a spotless white waistcoat and patent leather boots being features of his toilet. Personal charm and the lively gift of the raconteur to the end reconciled friends to his embarrassing habit of borrowing. He died at 5 Hogarth Road, Kensington, on 25 June 1904, and was buried at Old Brompton cemetery. No tombstone marks the grave. The cemetery register records his age as seventy-two.

The earliest oil painting by Sandys was a portrait of himself, painted in 1848. This was offered for purchase to the trustees of the National Portrait Gallery and rejected by them. Mr. Fairfax Murray owns a miniature of him (aged six) by his father, Anthony Sands. Most of his pictures and drawings are in private collections in London and Norwich or in America. There is no example of Sandys's work at the Tate Gallery. At the Birmingham Art Gallery, besides the small version of 'Autumn,' are superb examples of his black and white drawings from the Fairfax-Murray collection. Five drawings are in the Print Room of the British Museum; two are in the Norwich Museum (Nos. 354, 377); a portrait of Mr. Louis John Tillett, M.P., hangs in St. Andrew's Hall, Norwich. Some of his works, chiefly drawings, were collected at the Leicester Galleries in London in March 1904, and after his death there was another exhibition at Burlington House in the winter of 1905.

[The fullest and best account, in which Sandys assisted, is A Consideration of the Art of Frederick Sandys, by Esther Wood, with admirable reproductions, in a special winter number of The Artist (a defunct periodical),

1896. Mrs. Wood challenges the accuracy of certain statements in Mr. J. M. Gray's critical appreciation in the Art Journal, March 1884, in the Hobby Horse, 1888, vol. iii. and 1892 vol. vii., and in Mr. Pennell's articles in Pan (German publication, 1895), in the Quarto, 1896, vol. i., and in the Savoy, January 1896. See also Family Letters of D. G. Rossetti, 1895, i. 210, 242, 256, ii. 184, 189, 190, 192, 193; Ford Madox Hueffer, Life of Ford Madox Brown, 1896, p. 182; Life and Letters of Millais, by his son, 1899, i. 51, 312; Reminiscences of W. M. Rossetti, 1906, p. 320; Pennell's Life of Whistler, 1911, new edit., pp. 79, 83, 359, 366; Norvicensian, Midsummer 1904, reprint of an obituary from the Eastern Daily Express; Percy H. Bate's English Pre-Raphaelite Painters, 1899; Some Pictures of 1868, by A. C. Swinburne, reprinted in Essays and Studies, 1876; Gleeson White, English Illustration, 1897, with complete eikonography of published black and white drawings; George Meredith's Letters, 1912; Catalogue of Burlington House Winter Exhibition, 1905; A Great Illustrator, Pall Mall Magazine, November 1898; Bryan's Dictionary of Painters and Engravers, 1905 (article by Dr. G. C. Williamson); information kindly supplied by Mr. James Reeve of Norwich and Miss Colman; personal knowledge.] R. R.

SANFORD, GEORGE EDWARD LANGHAM SOMERSET (1840–1901), lieut.-general, born on 19 June 1840, was son of George Charles Sanford.

After education at the Royal Military College, Woolwich, he entered the royal engineers as lieutenant on 18 Oct. 1856, when little over sixteen. As a subaltern he saw much service in China, where he arrived in 1858. He took part in the occupation of Canton, in the expedition to Pei-ho, and in the demolition of forts at the mouth of the river and advance to Tientsin. Subsequently he was engaged in the campaign in the north of China in 1860, and received the medal with clasp. In 1862 Sanford joined Charles George Gordon [q. v.] in the operations against the Taipings, and played a useful part in the capture of the stockades of Nanksiang, and in the escalade of the walled cities of Kahding, Singpoo, and Cholin, and of the fortified town of Najow. He did useful survey work during the campaign, and assisted Gordon in drafting a 'Military Plan of the District round Shanghai under the Protection of the Allied Forces' (London, 1864; Shanghai, 1872). Gordon described him as the best officer he had ever met. He was promoted second captain on 8 Feb. 1866 and captain on 5 July 1872.

Returning to England, Sanford served in the ordnance survey in England until 1872. Next year he proceeded to India as executive engineer in the public works department there, becoming major 10 Dec. 1873. In 1878 he served in the Afridi expedition as assistant quartermaster-general Peshawar district (medal with clasp). Later in 1878–9 he took part in the Afghan war, and was present at the capture of Ali Masjid. He was mentioned in despatches (*Lond. Gaz.* 7 Nov. 1879) and received the medal with clasp and brevet of lieut.-colonel (22 Nov. 1879). Sir Frederick (afterwards Earl) Roberts rewarded his efficiency by appointment as assistant quartermaster-general of 1st division in the Peshawar Valley field force. Thenceforth his work lay long in the quartermaster-general's department. In 1880 he was deputy quartermaster-general of the newly formed Indian intelligence department, and during the absence of Sir Charles Macgregor [q. v.] he officiated for a year (1882–3) as quartermaster-general in India. He showed great ability in despatching the Indian contingent to Egypt in 1882, becoming lieutenant-colonel on 26 April of that year. Sanford had previously prepared excellent intelligence reports on Egypt as a possible theatre of war, and the success of the transport arrangement was largely due to him.

On completion of his term as deputy quartermaster-general at headquarters in Dec. 1885, Sanford, who was promoted colonel on 22 Nov. 1883, saw service as commanding royal engineer in the Burmese expedition of 1885–6, and received the thanks of the government of India, being mentioned in despatches (*Lond. Gazette*, 22 June 1886). He was rewarded with the clasp and was made C.B. on 25 Nov. 1886.

From March 1886 till 1893 he was director-general of military works in India, and held office during a period of great activity in connection with frontier defences. On 1 Jan. 1890 he was nominated C.S.I. On leaving the military works department he was in command of the Meerut district in India till 1898. He had been made major-general on 1 Jan. 1895, and became lieut.-general on 1 April 1898. He was mentioned in 1898 for the Bombay command, when it fell to Lieut.-general Sir Robert C. Low [q. v. Suppl. II]. A first-rate soldier and an accomplished man, he died, while still on the active list, at Bedford on 27 April 1901.

He married in 1867 Maria Hamilton (*d.* 1898), daughter of R. Hesketh of Southampton.

[The Times, 11 May 1901; Hart's and Official Army Lists; S. Mossman, General Gordon's Private Diary, 1885, p. 209.] H. M. V.

SANGER, GEORGE, known as 'LORD GEORGE SANGER' (1825–1911), circus proprietor and showman, born at Newbury, Berkshire, on 23 Dec. 1825, was sixth child of ten children of James Sanger (*d.* 1850), a naval pensioner who served on board the Victory at Trafalgar and was afterwards a showman. His mother, a native of Bedminster, was named Elliott. John Sanger [q. v.] was his elder brother. George, who was born to the showman's business and to caravan life, made his first appearance as a performer on the day of Queen Victoria's coronation, 28 June 1838. In 1845 he joined his brother John in a conjuring exhibition at the Onion Fair, Birmingham, and in 1848 he and his brothers William and John started an independent show at Stepney Fair; here George was the first to introduce the naphtha lamp to London. In 1853 George and John Sanger inaugurated on a very modest scale a travelling show and circus, which first appeared at King's Lynn in February 1854. Their equipment steadily increased, and Sanger's circus gradually outstripped its American and English competitors. In 1860 a 'world's fair' was established at the Hoe, Plymouth, with about one hundred separate shows—waxworks, monstrosities, balloon ascents, circuses, and the like. The Agricultural Hall at Islington was soon leased for winter exhibitions; circuses were built in many of the chief towns of Great Britain, a hall was purchased at Ramsgate, and the headquarters of the enterprise was fixed at the Hall by the Sea at Margate. In November 1871 Astley's Amphitheatre in Westminster Bridge Road was bought for 11,000*l.* Soon afterwards the brothers dissolved partnership, George, who outdistanced John in enterprise and public repute, taking over Astley's and the Agricultural Hall and retaining some interest in the Margate centre. Astley's flourished under his management till its demolition in 1893. His shows there were staged on a lavish and generous scale. In 1886 he exhibited the spectacle of 'The Fall of Khartoum and Death of General Gordon' at 280 consecutive performances, in which 300 men of the guards, 400 supers, 100 camels, 200 real Arab horses, the fifes and drums of the grenadiers, and the pipers of the Scots guards were brought on to the stage. Even more ambitious was his pantomime of 'Gulliver's Travels'; the performers in which included three elephants, nine camels, and 52 horses, as well as ostriches, emus, pelicans, deer, kangaroos, Indian buffaloes, Brahmin bulls, and living lions.

Meanwhile Sanger paid some eleven annual visits to the Continent, making summer tours through France, Germany, Austria, Bohemia, Spain, Switzerland, Denmark, and Holland. On leaving Astley's in 1893 he toured continuously through England and Scotland. On 19 June 1898 he appeared before Queen Victoria at Balmoral, and he repeated the experience at Windsor next year (17 July 1899).

Sanger was in later life hampered by the rivalry of American travelling circus proprietors. In 1887 he took the title of 'Lord' George Sanger by way of challenge to 'the Hon.' William Cody ('Buffalo Bill'), who was touring England with his 'Wild West' show. Universally regarded as the British head of his profession, Sanger owed his success mainly to his gift for patter and pompous phraseology in advertisement, and to his influence over animals, which he tamed by kindness, forbidding his subordinates to employ the harsh methods in vogue elsewhere. He was a tireless worker, a considerate employer, and a generous friend of circus folk. In 1887 he established the Showman's Guild, of which he was president for eighteen years, making generous contributions to its funds. He was one of the last of a calling which decayed in his closing years before the rising popularity of music-halls, football matches, and cinematograph exhibitions, innovations which seemed to Sanger to be symptomatic of degeneracy.

Sanger disposed of his circus in October 1905, and retired to Park Farm, East End Road, Finchley. He published his autobiography, 'Seventy Years a Showman,' in 1910. He was shot dead at Park Farm by one of his employees, to whom he had shown much kindness, on 28 Nov. 1911. The murderer committed suicide. Sanger was buried with municipal honours by the side of his wife at Margate.

He married in November 1850, at St. Peter's church, Sheffield, Ellen Chapman (*d.* 30 April 1899), an accomplished lion tamer, who till her marriage performed at Wombwell's menagerie as Madame Pauline de Vere; they had issue a son (who predeceased Sanger) and a daughter, Harriett, wife of Mr. Arthur Reeve of Asplins Farm, Park Lane, Tottenham. To his daughter he left his property, which was valued for probate at 29,348*l.*

[Seventy Years a Showman, by 'Lord'

George Sanger, 1910 (with photographic reproductions); J. O'Shea, Roundabout Recollections, 1892, i. 267 seq.; Charles Frost, Circus Life, 1875; The Times, 30 Nov. 1911; Era, 2 and 9 Dec. 1911 (photograph); Cassell's Mag., vol. xxii. 1896.] W. B. O.

SANKEY, Sir RICHARD HIERAM (1829–1908), lieutenant-general, royal (Madras) engineers, born at Rockwell Castle, co. Tipperary, on 22 March 1829, was fourth son of Matthew Sankey, barrister, of Bawnmore, co. Cork, and Modeshil, co. Tipperary, by his wife Eleanor, daughter of Colonel Henry O'Hara, J.P., of O'Hara Brook, co. Antrim. Educated at the Rev. D. Flynn's school in Harcourt Street, Dublin, he entered the East India Company's military seminary at Addiscombe in February 1845. Sankey showed considerable talent as an artist, and won a silver medal at an exhibition of the Dublin Society in 1845 and the prize for painting on leaving Addiscombe at the end of 1846. Commissioned as second lieutenant in the Madras engineers on 11 Dec. 1846, he arrived in Madras after the usual instruction at Chatham in Nov. 1848.

After serving with the Madras sappers at Mercatur he officiated in 1850 as superintending engineer, Nagpore subsidiary force; but owing to ill-health he was at home for three years (1853–6). Promoted lieutenant on 1 Aug. 1854, he was appointed, on returning to Madras in 1856, superintendent of the east coast canal. In May 1857 Sankey was called to Calcutta as under-secretary of the public works department under Colonel (afterwards General Sir) William Erskine Baker [q. v.].

On the outbreak of the Mutiny Sankey was commissioned as captain of the Calcutta cavalry volunteers, but in September was despatched to Allahabad for field duty. Besides completing the defensive works along the Jumna, he levelled the whole of the Allygunge quarter of the city, employing some 6000 workmen to clear the front of the entrenchments of obstructions and to construct a causeway across the muddy bed of the Ganges. He established a bridge of boats, and having to provide shelter for the advancing troops all along the grand trunk road in the North-west Provinces, he arrived at Cawnpore, in the course of this duty, the day before it was attacked by the Gwalior force under Tantia Topi. He acted as assistant field engineer under Lieutenant-colonel McLeod, the commanding engineer of General Windham's force, and when that force fell back on the entrenchments was employed in strengthening the defences; noticing that the whole area as far as an outpost some 600 yards away was swept by the enemy's fire, he effectively connected the outpost with the entrenchment by a simple screen of mats fixed during one night.

After the rebels were defeated by Sir Colin Campbell on 6 Dec., Sankey was transferred as field engineer to the Gurkha force under Jung Bahadur. He organised an engineer park at Gorakpur and procured material for bridging the Gogra and Gumti rivers for the march to Lucknow. Alone he reconnoitred the Gogra, which was crossed on 19 Feb. 1858, when the fort Mowrani on the other side of the river was seized. Next day he took part in the action of Phulpur, where he constructed a bridge of boats 320 yards long in two days and a half, and made three miles of road. The Gurkha army, 20,000 strong of all arms, then crossed into Oude, and Sankey received the thanks of his commander and of the government of India for 'his great and successful exertions.' While on the march on 26 Feb., Sankey's conspicuous gallantry in forcing an entry into a small fort at Jumalpur occupied by the rebels was highly commended by the commander in his despatch, and he was unsuccessfully recommended for the Victoria Cross.

Sankey was at the action of Kanduah Nulla on 4 March, and was mentioned in despatches. He constructed the bridge to pass the troops over the river to Sultanpur and received the thanks of government. At Lucknow the Gurkha army was posted in a suburb south-east of the Charbagh, which it attacked on the 14th. Next day Sankey was with the Gurkhas when they carried all before them to the gate of the Kaisar Bagh, which General Thomas Franks [q. v.] had captured. Sankey was also engaged with the enemy on the 15th, 18th, and 19th, and on the final capture of the city made arrangements for establishing the bridge over the canal near the Charbagh.

Soon after the fall of Lucknow Sankey returned to Calcutta in ill-health, and was sent to the Neilgherries to recruit. For his services in the mutiny campaign he received the medal with clasp, was promoted second captain on 27 August 1858, and brevet major the next day. During 1859 he was executive engineer, and also superintendent of the convict gaol at Moulmein in Burma, and received the thanks of the government of India for his management of the prison. In 1860–1 he was garrison engineer at Fort William, Calcutta.

Promoted first captain in his corps on 29 June 1861, and appointed assistant to the chief engineer, Mysore, he held the post with credit until 1864. In 1864 he succeeded as chief engineer and secretary to the chief commissioner, Mysore, and during the next thirteen years managed the public works of that province. He originated an irrigation department to deal scientifically with the old native works; the catchment area of each valley was surveyed, the area draining into each reservoir determined, and the sizes and number of reservoirs regulated accordingly. He also improved the old roads and opened up new ones in all directions. Government offices were built, and the park around them laid out at Bangalore.

In 1870 Sankey spent seven months on special duty at Melbourne, at the request of the Victorian government, to arbitrate on a question of works for supplying water to wash down the gold-bearing alluvium of certain valleys. He was promoted brevet lieutenant-colonel on 14 June 1869, regimental lieutenant-colonel on 15 Oct. 1870, and brevet colonel on 15 Oct. 1875.

In 1877 he was transferred to Simla as under-secretary to the government of India, and in September 1878, when war with the Amir of Afghanistan was imminent owing to the rebuff to the Chamberlain mission, was appointed commanding royal engineer of the Kandahar field force under Lieutenant-general, afterwards Field-marshal, Sir Donald Stewart [q. v. Suppl. I]. Sankey arrived with the rest of his staff at Quetta on 12 Dec., and being sent forward to reconnoitre recommended an advance by the Khawga Pass, leaving the Khojak for the second division under Major-general (afterwards Sir) Michael Biddulph [q. v. Suppl. II]. On 30 Dec. 1878 he was promoted regimental colonel. On 4 Jan. 1879 Sankey was with the advanced body of cavalry under Major-general Palliser when a cavalry combat took place at Takt-i-pul. Stewart's force occupied Kandahar, and advanced as far as Kalat-i-Ghilzai, when the flight of the Amir Shere Ali put an end, for a brief period, to the war. While Sankey was preparing winter quarters for the force at Kandahar he was recalled to Madras to become secretary in the public works department. For his share in the Kandahar expedition he was mentioned in despatches, created a C.B., and given the medal.

During five years at Madras Sankey became member of the legislative council, and was elected a fellow of the Madras University. He helped to form the Marina and to beautify the botanical gardens and Government House grounds. On 4 June 1883 he was promoted major-general. He retired from the army on 11 Jan. 1884, with the honorary rank of lieutenant-general. He had previously received the distinguished service reward in India.

On his return to England in 1883 Sankey was appointed chairman of the Irish board of works. In 1892 he was gazetted K.C.B. After his retirement in 1896 he resided in London, but his activity was unabated. He visited Mexico and had much correspondence with the president Diaz. He died suddenly at his residence, 32 Grosvenor Place, on 11 Nov. 1908, and was buried at Hove, Sussex. Sankey was twice married: (1) in 1858, at Ootacamund, to Sophia Mary (*d.* 1882), daughter of W. H. Benson, Indian civil service; (2) in 1890, at Dublin, to Henrietta, widow of Edward Browne, J.P., and daughter of Pierce Creagh; she survived him. By his first wife he had two daughters, one of whom married his nephew, Colonel A. R. M. Sankey, R.E.

[India Office Records; Vibart's Addiscombe; The Times, 12 Nov. 1908; memoir with portrait in Royal Engineers' Journal, June 1909.] R. H. V.

SAUMAREZ, THOMAS (1827–1903), admiral, born at Sutton, Surrey, on 31 March 1827, was grandnephew of James, first Baron de Saumarez, and was son of Captain (afterwards Admiral) Richard Saumarez. After a few years at the Western Grammar School, Brompton, he entered the navy in 1841, and was actively employed during the whole of his junior time on the east coast of South America, at Buenos Ayres, Monte Video, and in Parana. He was made a lieutenant in March 1848. As a lieutenant he served principally on the west coast of Africa, where on 31 March 1851 he saved a man from drowning and received the Royal Humane Society's silver medal. Later in the year he commanded a division of gunboats at Lagos and was severely wounded; in September 1854 he was promoted to commander. In May 1858 he had command of the Cormorant, and served with rare distinction at the capture of the Taku forts, where the Cormorant led the attack, broke through a really formidable boom, and with her first broadside, fired at the same moment, dismounted the largest of the enemy's guns. He afterwards took part in the operations in the river Peiho and in the occupation of Tientsin, and on the coast of

China. His promotion to the rank of captain was dated 27 July 1858. He had no further active service, but his brilliant advance on 20 May 1858 is worthy to be held in remembrance. On 12 April 1870 he was retired, and was nominated a C.B. in 1873. He became by seniority a rear-admiral in 1876, vice-admiral in 1881, and admiral in 1886. He died at his residence, 2 Morpeth Mansions, Westminster, on 22 Jan. 1903. He married (1) in 1854 a daughter (*d.* 1866) of S. R. Block of Greenhill, Barnet; and (2) in 1868, Eleanor, daughter of B. Scott Riley, of Liverpool. He left no issue.

[Royal Navy List; Debrett's Peerage; Who's Who, 1902; The Times, 23 Jan. 1903; Clowes, The Royal Navy, vol. vii.; personal knowledge.] J. K. L.

SAUNDERS, EDWARD (1848–1910), entomologist, born at East Hill, Wandsworth, on 22 March 1848, was youngest of seven children (four sons and three daughters) of William Wilson Saunders, F.R.S. [q. v.]. His elder brother, George Sharp Saunders, F.L.S. (*d.* 1910), also an entomologist, was editor of the 'Journal of the Royal Horticultural Society' from 1906 to 1908. The youngest sister married the Rev. T. R. R. Stebbing, F.R.S.

Saunders, who was educated entirely at home, was the author (from 1867) of many papers on entomology, relating chiefly to the Buprestidæ, Hemiptera Heteroptera, and Aculeata Hymenoptera. These he contributed to the 'Entomologist's Monthly Magazine,' the 'Transactions of the Entomological Society,' the 'Journal of the Linnean Society,' and other serials. His independent publications comprised 'The Hemiptera Heteroptera of the British Isles' (1892); 'The Hymenoptera Aculeata of the British Isles' (1896); and a popular work (with illustrations by his daughter) 'Wild Bees, Wasps, and Ants, and other Stinging Insects' (1907).

On 5 June 1902 he was elected F.R.S. He died at Bognor on 6 Feb. 1910, and was buried in Brookwood cemetery. He married in 1872 Mary Agnes, daughter of Edward Brown (*d.* 1866), of East Hill, Wandsworth, East India merchant, and had issue eight sons and four daughters.

[Proc. Linn. Soc. 1910; Entomol. Month. Mag., March 1910 (portrait); Proc. Entomol. Soc. 1910, Presidential Address; Entomologist's Record, March 1910; Roy. Soc. Catal. Sci. Papers; Nature, 3 March 1910.] T. E. J.

SAUNDERS, Sir EDWIN (1814–1901), dentist, born in London on 12 March 1814, was son of Simon Saunders, senior partner in the firm of Saunders & Ottley, publishers, in Brook Street, London. From an early age he showed aptitude for mechanical contrivances, and from the age of twelve to fourteen he experimented in methods of superseding steam by hydraulic power for the propulsion of vessels. He also invented a sweeping machine for use in city streets, not unlike those now in use. A native bent for civil engineering was not encouraged owing to the uncertain prospects of the profession. The mechanical opportunities which dentistry affords attracted him, and he was articled as a pupil to Mr. Lemaile, a dentist in the Borough. At the end of three years he was thoroughly grounded in dental mechanics, and gave a course of lectures on elementary mechanics and anatomy at a mechanics' institute. Frederick Tyrrell [q. v.], surgeon to St. Thomas's Hospital, who happened to be present at one lecture, was so impressed that, after consultation with his colleagues, he invited Saunders to lecture at St. Thomas's Hospital. Saunders appears to have lectured here unofficially from 1837, but having obtained the diploma of the Royal College of Surgeons in 1839 he was in that year appointed dental surgeon and lecturer on dental surgery to St. Thomas's Hospital, a post he occupied until 1854. In 1855 he was elected F.R.C.S. He was also dentist from 1834 to the Blenheim Street Infirmary and Free Dispensary, and in 1840 he started, in conjunction with Mr. Harrison and Mr. Snell, a small institution for the treatment of the teeth of the poor. It was the first charity of its kind, and lasted about twelve years.

Whilst working at the subject of cleft palate, Saunders came to know Alexander Nasmyth, who had a large dental practice in London, and after 1846, when Nasmyth was incapacitated by an attack of paralysis, Saunders bought Nasmyth's practice, which he carried on at Nasmyth's house, 13a George Street, Hanover Square, until he retired to Wimbledon. He succeeded Nasmyth in 1846 as dentist to Queen Victoria, the Prince Consort, and the other members of the Royal family.

Saunders held that dentistry was a part of medicine. A good organiser and a man of considerable scientific attainments, he was amongst the first to attempt the formation into a compact profession of the heterogeneous collection of men who practised dentistry. In 1856 he, with others, petitioned the Royal College of Surgeons of England to grant a diploma in dental surgery, but it was not until after many negotiations that the college obtained powers, on 8 Sept. 1859, to examine candidates and grant a diploma in dentistry. The Odontological Society was founded at Saunders's house in 1857 to unite those who practised dental surgery. Saunders was the first treasurer, and was president in 1864 and 1879. Saunders was trustee of the first dental hospital and school established in London, in Soho Square in 1859. The institution prospered, and in 1874 the Dental Hospital in Leicester Square was opened, being handed over to the managing committee free of debt. Saunders rendered to the new hospital important services, which his colleagues and friends commemorated by founding in the school the Saunders scholarship. Saunders was president of the dental section at the meeting of the International Medical Congress which met in London in 1881, and in the same year was president of the metropolitan counties branch of the British Medical Association. In 1883 he was knighted, being the first dentist to receive that honour. In 1886 he was president of the British Dental Association. He died at Fairlawn, Wimbledon Common, on 15 March 1901, and was buried at the Putney cemetery. In 1848 he married Marian, eldest daughter of Edmund William Burgess, with whom he celebrated his golden wedding in 1898.

Saunders was author of: 1. 'Advice on the Care of the Teeth,' 1837. 2. 'The Teeth as a Test of Age considered in reference to the Factory Children. Addressed to the Members of both Houses of Parliament,' 1837; this work was adopted by the inspectors of factories and led to the detection of much fraud.

[Journal of Brit. Dental Assoc., vol. xxii. new ser., 1901, p. 200; Medico-Chirurgical Trans., vol. lxxxv. 1902, p. cii; private information.] D'A. P.

SAUNDERS, HOWARD (1835–1907), ornithologist and traveller, born in London on 16 Sept. 1835, was son of Alexander Saunders by his wife Elizabeth, daughter of Joseph Laundy. Educated at private schools at Leatherhead and Rottingdean, he subsequently entered the firm of Anthony Gibbs & Sons, South American merchants and bankers in the City of London, and in 1855, when twenty years old, left England to take up a post at Callao, in Peru. His love of natural history and archæology and liking for adventurous travel led him, however, to relinquish business pursuits. Leaving Peru in 1860, he crossed the Andes and explored the headwaters of the Amazon river, descending thence to Pará. The perilous journey provided novel and rich material for scientific study.

After his return in 1862 Saunders devoted himself to ornithological research. His first memoir, which appeared in 1866 in the 'Ibis,' the organ of the British Ornithological Union, gave an account of the albatrosses observed whilst on his voyage from Cape Horn to Peru. Turning his attention to the avifauna of Spain, he next wrote papers on the birds of Spain (*Ibis*, 1869–78) and the birds of the Pyrenees and Switzerland (*Ibis*, 1883–97). He had become an accomplished Spanish scholar and often travelled to Spain, contributing 'Ornithological Rambles in Spain and Majorca' to the 'Field' newspaper in 1874. Saunders was joint-editor with Dr. P. L. Sclater of the 'Ibis' (1883–8 and 1894–1900); and from 1901 till his death was secretary and treasurer of the British Ornithological Union, which he had joined in 1870. He was the recorder of *Aves* for the 'Zoological Record' (1876–81).

From 1880 to 1885 Saunders was honorary secretary of Section D (zoology) of the British Association. A fellow of the Zoological and Linnean Societies, he served on the councils of each, and wrote for their 'Proceedings' and 'Journal' memoirs, many of which dealt more especially with the *Laridæ* (gulls and terns). He was a fellow of the Royal Geographical Society, and deeply interested in all branches of geographical research.

Saunders's chief independent publication was 'An Illustrated Manual of British Birds' (1889; 2nd edit. 1899). He also edited 'Yarrell's British Birds' (4th edit. 1882–5, vols. iii. and iv.) in succession to Prof. Alfred Newton [q. v. Suppl. II], and he wrote the monograph on terns, gulls, and skuas (vol. xxv. 1896) for the 'Catalogue of the Birds in the British Museum.' He revised and annotated Mitchell's 'Birds of Lancashire' (2nd edit. 1892).

He died at his residence, 7 Radnor Place, W., on 20 Oct. 1907, and was buried in Kensal Green cemetery. He married in 1868 Emily, youngest daughter of William Minshull Bigg, of Stratford Place, W., and had issue two daughters.

Saunders was a frequent writer in the 'Field' and 'Athenæum.' In addition to those cited he wrote memoirs on the eggs collected on the transit of Venus expeditions, 1874–5 (*Phil. Trans.* vol. 168, 1879); on the birds (*Laridæ*) collected during the voyage of H.M.S. Challenger (*Report, Zoology*, vol. ii.), and the article 'Birds' in the 'Antarctic Manual' (National Antarctic Expedition, 1901).

[Proc. Linn. Soc., 1908; The Ibis, ser. ix., vol. 2, Jubilee Suppl. (with portrait); Trans. Norfolk and Norwich Nat. Soc., vol. viii.; Roy. Soc. Catal. Papers; Zoologist, ser. iv. vol. ii. (with portrait); Field, 26 Oct. 1907; Nature, 24 Oct. 1907; Athenæum, 26 Oct. 1907; The Times, 22 Oct. 1907.] T. E. J.

SAUNDERSON, EDWARD JAMES (1837–1906), Irish politician, born on 1 Oct. 1837 at Castle Saunderson, was fourth son of Colonel Alexander Saunderson (1783–1857) of Castle Saunderson, Belturbet, co. Cavan, by his wife Sarah Juliana (*d.* 1870), elder daughter of the Rev. Henry Maxwell, sixth Baron Farnham. The Saundersons trace their lineage to a family called de Bedic, settled in co. Durham in the fourteenth century, of which one branch after a settlement in Scotland removed to Ireland in the seventeenth century.

Before Saunderson was ten his father shut up his house and chose to live abroad. Saunderson and his brothers were educated chiefly at Nice, by private tutors. He learnt to talk French fluently, but his attention was largely devoted to the designing, building, and sailing of boats, always his favourite recreations. One or two of his foreign tutors were Jesuits, but Saunderson and his brothers grew up in earnest attachment to protestant principles. Through life Saunderson was an ardent protestant and Orangeman, and, although he was not careful of dogmas and formularies, he cherished an absolute faith in divine guidance, was an earnest and eloquent preacher, and was in the habit until death of conducting the services in the church at Castle Saunderson.

His father died in Dec. 1857 and left Castle Saunderson to his younger son, Edward, to come into possession of it on reaching the age of twenty-five in 1862. Settling accordingly in Ireland, Saunderson was high sheriff of Cavan in 1859, and soon joined the Cavan militia, of which he later was colonel commanding (1891–3). At first he spent most of his time in hunting or sailing on Lough Erne. In politics he was a liberal of the whig type, and an admirer of Lord Palmerston. At the general election of 1865 he was returned unopposed for his county (Cavan), his colleague being a conservative, Hugh Annesley, afterwards earl of Annesley. The two were re-elected without opposition at the election of 1868. Saunderson opposed the disestablishment of the Irish church in 1869, but otherwise gave little sign of political interest or activity. In 1874 he stood for Cavan for a third time, again with Annesley, and both were defeated by home rulers, one of them Joseph Gillis Biggar [q. v. Suppl. I]. For the next ten years Saunderson pursued the uneventful life of a country gentleman at home, with occasional visits abroad. But the advance of the home rule movement under Parnell's leadership, which he regarded as dangerous and disloyal, drew him into the fighting line. In July 1882 he appeared at Ballykilbeg on a platform as an Orangeman. Although he never ceased to call himself a whig, he was in London in 1884 eagerly assisting his conservative friends in their opposition to the franchise bill, which (he foresaw) promised a serious advantage to the followers of Parnell in Ireland. In a pamphlet, 'Two Irelands, or Loyalty versus Treason' (1884), he explained his hostility to the nationalist agitation. At the general election in Nov. 1885 he was elected for North Armagh as a conservative in contest with a liberal, and he represented the constituency until his death, twenty-one years later. He defeated a nationalist at the general election of July 1886, and an independent conservative at that of Oct. 1900; in July 1892, July 1895, and Jan. 1906 he was returned unopposed.

Saunderson rapidly became the most conspicuous member of the Irish unionist party in the House of Commons. He was never a good debater and made little pretence of mastering details, but he had an imposing presence, a fine voice, great fluency, abundant humour, and a zest for personal controversy with opponents. During the passage of Gladstone's second home rule bill through the House of Commons in 1893 he was indefatigable in protest and frequently evoked disturbances by his attacks on the nationalists. He declared the nationalist members to be eighty-five reasons for not passing the bill. On 2 Feb. 1893 he raised a storm by describing an Irish priest named Macfadden as a 'murderous ruffian,' words which he afterwards changed to 'excited politician.' On 27 July 1893, while the home rule bill was in committee, he engaged in a free fight with his Irish foes on the floor of the chamber. Although he supported the conservative party in their main policy, he showed independence on occasions, and criticised adversely the conservative land bill of 1896, and joined the nationalists in 1897 in denouncing the financial relations between England and Ireland as unjust to the smaller country. In regard to South African policy he was in sympathy with Mr. Joseph Chamberlain. In 1897–8 he visited South Africa, with other members of Parliament, to attend the opening of the Bechuanaland railway, and made several stirring speeches from the English point of view upon the vexed questions which were then disturbing the South African colonies and were leading towards war. On the political platform outside the House of Commons both in England and Ireland Saunderson proved a formidable champion of the Irish union. On 31 May 1894 he took part in an adjourned debate on home rule at the Oxford Union, answering a speech by Mr. John Dillon of the week before. The proposal in favour of home rule was defeated by 344 to 182. He threw himself with enthusiasm into the work of the Orange lodges and was grand master at Belfast from 1901 to 1903.

Saunderson was made a privy councillor in 1898 and lord-lieutenant of Cavan in 1900. In private life his ardent spiritual aspirations never diminished his natural humour nor his love of recreation. He was a capable artist and caricaturist, and many spirited sketches of his parliamentary associates are of historic value. He continued to the last to design and build boats which held their own with the best yachts on Lough Erne. He shot and played billiards and latterly golf. A serious illness in 1904 impaired his health. He died at Castle Saunderson on 21 Oct. 1906, and was buried in the churchyard in his park. He married on 22 June 1865 Helena Emily, youngest daughter of Thomas de Moleyns, third Lord Ventry. He left four sons and one daughter, of whom the eldest son Somerset (late captain, king's royal rifles) succeeded to the property. In 1907 three of his religious addresses were published under the title 'Present and Everlasting Salvation,' with a preface by J. B. Crozier, then bishop of Ossory. A portrait by Edwin Long, R.A., painted in 1890, belongs to Mr. Burdett-Coutts, together with a crayon drawing by R. Ponsonby Staples dated 1899. Another portrait by H. Harris Brown is at Castle Saunderson. A statue by (Sir) William Goscombe John, subscribed for by the public, was unveiled at Portadown in 1910.

[Reginald Lucas's Colonel Saunderson: a Memoir, 1908; The Times, 22 Oct. 1906; H. W. Lucy's Home Rule Parliament, 1892–5, and The Salisbury Parliament, 1895–1900.]

R. L.

SAVAGE-ARMSTRONG, GEORGE FRANCIS (1845–1906), poet, born at Rathfarnham, co. Dublin, on 5 May 1845, was the third son of Edmund John Armstrong of Wicklow and Dublin and Jane, daughter of the Rev. Henry Savage of Glastry, co. Down, of the family of the Savages of the Ards. Edmund John Armstrong, the poet [q. v.], was his elder brother. After some early education in Jersey, he made a pedestrian tour in France with his brother Edmund in 1862, and in later years he tramped through many other continental countries. He matriculated at Trinity College, Dublin, in 1862, won the vice-chancellor's prize for an English poem on Circassia, and graduated B.A. in 1869. In 1869 he published his first volume of verse, 'Poems Lyrical and Dramatic' (2nd edit. 1872), and in the following year 'Ugone: a Tragedy' (2nd edit. 1872), a work largely written in Italy. In 1870 he was appointed professor of history and English literature in Queen's College, Cork. The hon. degree of M.A. was conferred upon him by Trinity College in 1872, and in the same year he issued 'King Saul,' the first part of his 'Tragedy of Israel.' 'King David' and 'King Solomon,' the second and third parts of his trilogy, followed in 1874 and 1876, and in 1877 he brought out an edition of his brother's 'Poems,' following it up with a collection of that writer's 'Essays' and 'Life and Letters.' A journey to Greece and Italy in 1881 led to the publication of his verses entitled 'Garland from Greece' (1882). He was made a fellow of the Royal University (1881), and in 1891 received the honorary degree of D.Litt. from the Queen's University. In 1892 the board of Trinity College commissioned him to write the tercentenary ode, which was set to music by Sir Robert Prescott Stewart [q. v.] and performed with success during the tercentenary celebrations of the summer of 1892.

In 1891, on the death of a maternal aunt, Armstrong assumed the additional surname of Savage. He continued his duties as professor at Cork and as examiner at the Royal University in Dublin until 1905. He died on 24 July 1906 at Strangford House, Strangford, co. Down.

Savage-Armstrong, who in fertility stands almost alone among Irish poets, continued publishing verse till near his death. His latest work was for the most part his best. He wrote of nature with fresh enthusiasm if in stately diction, and also showed philosophic faculty with command of passion. He has none of the Celtic mysticism of the later Irish school. His mature power is seen to special advantage in his 'Stories of Wicklow' (1886), 'One in the Infinite,' a philosophical sequence in verse (1892), and 'Ballads of Down' (1901). His other works were: 1. 'Victoria Regina et Imperatrix: a Jubilee Song from Ireland,' 1887. 2. 'Mephistopheles in Broadcloth: a Satire in Verse,' 1888. 3. 'Queen-Empress and Empire,' 1897, a loyal tribute in alliterative verse. 4. 'The Crowning of the King,' 1902. A laborious genealogical work, 'The Noble Family of the Savages of the Ards,' appeared in 1888.

He married in 1879 Marie Elizabeth, daughter of John Wrixon, M.A., vicar of Malone, co. Antrim, who survived him, and by whom he had two sons and a daughter.

[Dublin Evening Mail, 25 July 1906; Athenæum, 28 July 1906; Savages of the Ards (as above); Stopford Brooke's and Rolleston's Treasury of Irish Poetry, pp. 534–9; D. J. O'Donoghue, Poets of Ireland, 1912; Brit. Mus. Cat.; personal knowledge and private correspondence.] D. J. O'D.

SAVILL, THOMAS DIXON (1855–1910), physician, born on 7 Sept. 1855 at Kensington, was only son of T. C. Savill, member of a firm of printers and publishers, by his wife, Eliza Clarissa Dixon. He received his early education at the Stockwell grammar school, and, having chosen the profession of medicine, entered St. Thomas's Hospital with a scholarship in natural science. Here he had a distinguished career, gaining the William Tite scholarship and many prizes. He continued his medical studies at St. Mary's Hospital, at the Salpêtrière in Paris, at Hamburg, and at Vienna. In 1881 he graduated M.B. of the University of London, proceeding M.D. in the following year, and being admitted a member of the Royal College of Physicians of London. In rapid succession he became registrar, pathologist, and assistant physician to the West London Hospital, and early showed a bent towards neurology by translating in 1889 the lectures of Professor Charcot on 'Diseases of the Nervous System.'

In 1885 he was appointed medical superintendent of the Paddington Infirmary, then just opened, a post which gave him an intimate knowledge of the working of the poor law hospitals. He was also president of the Infirmary Medical Superintendents' Society, and was recognised as an authority on many of the questions raised in both the majority and minority reports of the Poor Law Commission in 1909. Much of his medical experience as medical superintendent was embodied in his chief work, 'A System of Clinical Medicine' (2 vols. 1903–5), in which he approached the subject from a symptomatological point of view. Each of the chief systems of the body is discussed seriatim, and under each section descriptions are grouped of prominent symptoms pointing to disease in any particular system. In the section on arterial diseases he gave an account of the condition of the tunica media, which he studied at the Paddington Infirmary, and called arterial hypermyotrophy. This condition Savill, after a large number of investigations both macro- and micro-scopic, concluded to be a genuine hypertrophy of the muscular coat of the arteries.

At the same time Savill made a reputation as a dermatologist, and was appointed in 1897 physician to St. John's Hospital for Diseases of the Skin. Meanwhile he had retired in 1892 from Paddington Infirmary to become a consulting physician, mainly with a view to pursuing his study of neurology. He was soon appointed physician to the West End Hospital for Diseases of the Nervous System. In 1899 he brought out a course of clinical lectures upon Neurasthenia (originally delivered at the Paddington Infirmary and the West End Hospital). The book showed Savill to be an original thinker and clear expositor. Instead of separating the special symptomatic varieties of the neurasthenic condition, such as cardiac, gastric, or pulmonary, he devoted his main thesis to a discussion of its essential nature, suggesting an etiological classification in some ways more satisfactory than had yet been advanced. He embodied further observations in lectures on hysteria and the allied vaso-motor conditions, which were published in 1909. There he defended with a wealth of clinical illustration the thesis that the majority of hysterical phenomena are due to a vascular disturbance affecting especially the central nervous system, and occurring in individuals with an inborn instability of the vaso-motor centres. He admitted, however, that his hypothesis would not explain 'all the various symptoms of this protean and strange disorder' of hysteria.

Savill died at Algiers on 10 Jan. 1910 from a fracture of the base of the skull caused by a fall from his horse.

He married in 1901 Dr. Agnes Forbes Blackadder, then assistant and later full physician to St. John's Hospital for Diseases of the Skin. She aided her husband in his book on 'Clinical Medicine.'

Besides the works mentioned, Savill contributed, mainly to 'The Lancet' (1888–1909), many papers upon neurological and dermatological subjects. Another valuable piece of work was the 'Report on the Warrington Small-Pox Outbreak, 1892–3.'

[Personal knowledge; The Times, 14 Jan. 1910; The Lancet, 15 Jan. 1910; private information.] H. P. C.

SAXE-WEIMAR, Prince EDWARD of (1823–1902), field-marshal. [See Edward of Saxe-Weimar.]

SCHUNCK, HENRY EDWARD (1820–1903), chemist, born in Manchester on 16 Aug. 1820, was youngest son of Martin Schunck (*d.* 1872), a leading export shipping merchant of that city, who became a naturalised Englishman. His mother was daughter of Johann Jacob Mylius, senator of Frankfort on the Main. His grandfather, Carl Schunck, an officer in the army of the Elector of Hesse, had taken part in the American war of independence on the British side. The father settled in Manchester in 1808, on removal from Malta, and founded the firm of Schunck, Mylius & Co., subsequently Schunck, Souchay & Co. After education at a private school in Manchester Schunck studied chemistry abroad. From Berlin, where Heinrich Rose and Heinrich Gustav Magnus were among his teachers, he proceeded to Giessen University, where he worked under Liebig, and graduated Ph.D. On returning from Germany he entered his father's calico-printing works in Rochdale, but after a few years relinquished business with a view to original research in chemistry, particularly in regard to the colouring matters of vegetable substances. To this unexplored field of inquiry he mainly devoted his career. In 1841 Schunck published in Liebig's 'Annalen' his first paper on a research conducted in the Giessen laboratory on the action of nitric acid on aloes. Next year he presented to the Chemical Society of London (*Memoirs*, vol. i.) an investigation made at Liebig's suggestion 'On some of the Substances contained in the Lichens employed for the Preparation of Archil and Cudbear.' This inquiry he pursued in the paper 'On the Substances contained in the *Roccella tinctoria*' (*ib.* vol. iii. 1846). He isolated and determined the formula of the crystalline substance *lecanorin*.

From 1846 to 1855 he made new and exhaustive researches on the colouring matter of the madder plant (*Rubia tinctorum*), communicating the results to the British Association in 1846, 1847, and 1848. In the 'Philosophical Transactions' for 1851, 1853, and 1855 he gave further account of his investigation in his classical memoir 'On Rubian and its Products of Decomposition,' and described the peculiar bitter substance which he had isolated and named 'rubian.' Schunck's analyses first showed the chemical nature of alizarin, the colouring matter obtained from madder root by Colin and Robiquet in 1826, and of the other constituents of the root. He thus paved the way for the researches of Graebe and Liebermann, who synthesised alizarin. Subsequently Sir William Henry Perkin [q. v. Suppl. II] by further investigation made alizarin a commercial product (see Schunck's later communications in *Manchester Lit. and Phil. Soc. Memoirs*, 1871, 1873, and 1876). Hermann Roemer collaborated with him from 1875, and with his help Schunck published a series of eighteen papers in the 'Berichte' of the German Chemical Society and elsewhere on the chemistry of colouring matters (1875–80).

Schunck made researches on indigo which had much practical importance. In 1853 he extracted from the plant 'Isatis tinctoria' an unstable syrupy glucoside which he named *indican* (cf. *Manchester Lit. and Phil. Soc. Memoirs*, 1855, 1856, 1857, and 1865). He also published in 1901 a monograph, illustrated with coloured plates, 'The Action of Reagents on the Leaves of Polygonum tinctorium.' Study of the constitution and derivatives of chlorophyll, the green colouring matter of plants, occupied Schunck's later years. The initial results appeared in the 'Proceedings of the Royal Society' for 1884 and were subsequently continued with Marchlewski. A crystalline substance, 'phylloporphyrin,' chemically and spectroscopically resembling hæmatoporphyrin,' as obtained from the hæmoglobin of the blood, was prepared. Schunck suggested that the chlorophyll in the plant performed a function similar to that of hæmoglobin in the animal, the former being a carrier of carbon dioxide in the same way as the latter acts as a carrier of oxygen. Schunck wrote on 'Chlorophyll' (1890) in Watts's 'Dictionary of Chemistry.'

Schunck joined the Chemical Society in

1841, the year of its foundation. He was elected a fellow of the Royal Society on 6 June 1850 (on the same day as James Prescott Joule [q.v.]), and he was Davy gold medallist for 1899. Elected into the Manchester Literary and Philosophical Society on 25 Jan. 1842, he was secretary (1855–60), and president (1866–7, 1874–5, 1890–1, 1896–7), receiving in 1898 the society's Dalton bronze medal (struck in 1864 but not previously awarded). An original member of the Society of Chemical Industry, he was chairman of its Manchester section in 1888–9, president in 1896–7, and gold medallist in 1900 on the ground of his conspicuous services in applied chemistry. In 1887 Schunck was president of the chemical section of the British Association at the Manchester meeting. Victoria University, Manchester, conferred on him the honorary degree of D.Sc. in 1899. With R. Angus Smith and Henry Roscoe he had already communicated to the British Association (Manchester meeting, 1861) a comprehensive report, 'On the Recent Progress and Present Condition of Manufacturing Chemistry in the South Lancashire District.'

Schunck carried on his investigations in a private laboratory which he had built near his residence at Kersal, and housed there a fine library and large collections. He was deeply interested in travel, literature and art, and in works of philanthropy connected with his native city. He died at his home, Oaklands, Kersal, Manchester, on 13 Jan. 1903, and was buried in St. Paul's churchyard, Kersal. He married in 1851 Judith Howard, daughter of John Brooke, M.R.C.S., of Stockport, and had issue five sons and two daughters. His wife and three sons and a daughter survived him.

In 1895 Schunck presented 20,000*l.* to Owens College, Manchester, of which he was a governor, for the endowment of chemical research. By his will he bequeathed to Owens College, in trust, the contents of his laboratory (together with the building), which constitutes, with the previous endowment, the 'Schunck research laboratory' at the Victoria University of Manchester.

[Proc. Roy. Soc., vol. lxxv.; Journ. Soc. Chem. Industry, vol. xxii.; Memoir No. 6, Lit. Phil. Soc. Manch., vol. xlvii., and Report of Council, *ib.*; Ency. Brit., vol. vi. (11th edit.), p. 736; Roy. Soc. Catal. Sci. Papers; Poggendorff's Handwörterbuch, Bd. iii. (1898); Proc. Roy. Inst., vol. ix.; Nature, 22 Jan. 1903; The Times, 14 Jan. 1903, 6 March (will); Manchester Courier, 19 Jan. 1903; Men of the Time, 1899.] T. E. J.

SCOTT, ARCHIBALD (1837–1909), Scottish divine and leader of the general assembly of the Church of Scotland, born at Bogton, in the parish of Cadder, Lanarkshire, on 18 Sept. 1837, was sixth and youngest son of James Scott, farmer, by his wife Margaret Brown. From the parish school he passed to the High School of Glasgow, where Mr. James Bryce was a schoolfellow. Proceeding to the University of Glasgow, he graduated B.A. on 25 April 1856, and after taking the prescribed divinity course was licensed as a probationer of the Church of Scotland by the presbytery of Glasgow on 8 June 1859. Having served as assistant in St. Matthew's parish, Glasgow, and at Clackmannan, he was ordained by the presbytery of Perth, to East church, Perth, in Jan. 1860. In 1862 he was translated to Abernethy in the same county. In 1865 he was selected as first minister of a newly constituted charge, Maxwell church, Glasgow, where his vigorous work brought him into note throughout the west of Scotland. In 1867 he joined the Church Service Society, formed in 1865 for the better regulation of public worship. His next move was to Linlithgow in 1869, and thence in 1871 to Greenside, Edinburgh. In 1873 when James Baird [q. v.] made over 500,000*l.* for the benefit of the Church of Scotland he chose Scott, as a conspicuous example of the 'active and evangelical minister,' to be the clerical member of the governing trustees. Scott thereupon resigned his membership in the Church Service Society, but neither his doctrine, which inclined to be high, nor his form of service underwent any modification. In the controversy which was closed by the Scottish Education Act of 1872, and in the agitation for the abolition of patronage, Scott opposed the more conservative party, headed by Dr. John Cook of Haddington (1807–1874) [q.v.], believing that the Scottish people could be trusted to maintain religious instruction according to 'use and wont'—i.e. the Bible and Shorter Catechism—in the public schools. He sat on the first Edinburgh school board, and acted as chairman from 1878 to 1882. In 1876 the University of Glasgow conferred on him the degree of D.D. In 1890 he was made incumbent of St. George's church in the New Town of Edinburgh. There he held office till his death, working with exemplary fidelity and success.

Although no popular preacher, Scott

exerted great influence in the church courts and especially in the general assembly. For a time convener of the assembly's committee on foreign missions, he was appointed in 1887 convener of the general assembly's joint committee and business committee, positions which carried with them the leadership of the general assembly. He remained leader for twenty-one years, to the end of his life. His power was helped to some extent by his position on the Baird Trust, but it was mainly due to the vigour of his personality, his great capacity for business, his wide knowledge of the church, his magnanimity towards opponents, and good humour in debate. Among the main matters with which he dealt effectually, although he did not always escape charges of opportunism, were the enlargement of the membership of the general assembly, church reform, a case of heresy (the Kilmun case), changes in the educational system, and the agitation for amending the formula of clerical subscription to the Westminster confession. In 1896 he was elected moderator of the general assembly; and in 1902 he visited South Africa as one of a delegation to the presbyterian churches there, which was sent out jointly by the Church of Scotland and the United Free Church. The visit confirmed Scott's older desire for the reunion of Scottish presbyterians. From the larger movement inaugurated, or revived, by Bishop Wilkinson of St. Andrews [q. v. Suppl. II] for a reunion which should embrace the episcopalians also, he kept aloof. Scott was the author of the proposal that the Church of Scotland should confer with the general assembly of the United Free Church (24 May 1907). But before the negotiations began Scott's health suddenly gave way, and he died at North Berwick on 18 April 1909, being buried in the Dean cemetery, Edinburgh.

Scott published: 1. 'Endowed Territorial Work: the Means of Meeting Spiritual Destitution in Edinburgh,' Edinburgh, 1873. 2. 'Buddhism and Christianity: a Parallel and Contrast,' the Croall lecture, 1889–90, Edinburgh, 1890. 3. 'Sacrifice: its Prophecy and Fulfilment,' the Baird lecture, 1892–93, Edinburgh, 1894. 4. 'Our Opportunities and Responsibilities,' the moderator's closing address to the general assembly of the Church of Scotland, Edinburgh, 1896. 5. 'Lectures on Pastoral Theology.'

Scott was twice married: (1) to Isabella, daughter of Robert Greig, merchant, Perth; by her he had six children, of whom two survive, a daughter and a son, R. G. Scott, Writer to the Signet, Edinburgh; and (2) in 1883 to Marion Elizabeth, daughter of John Rankine, D.D., minister of Sorn, moderator of the general assembly 1883.

A portrait by Sir George Reid, P.R.S.A., painted in 1902, hangs in the offices of the Church of Scotland, 22 Queen Street, Edinburgh; a replica was presented to Scott at the same time. A bronze bust of him, the work of Pittendrigh Macgillivray, R.S.A., was placed in the vestibule of St. George's church by the kirk session and congregation, 1907.

[Private information; Scotsman, 19 April 1909; Layman's Book of the General Assembly, Edinburgh, 1907.] J. C.

SCOTT, CLEMENT WILLIAM (1841–1904), dramatic critic, born at Christ Church vicarage, Hoxton, on 6 Oct. 1841, was son of William Scott (1813–1872) [q. v.], then perpetual curate of Christ Christ, Hoxton, by his wife Margaret, daughter of William Beloe [q. v.]. After attending a private day-school at Islington, Scott was at Marlborough College from August 1852 until December 1859. On the nomination of Sidney Herbert, Lord Herbert of Lea [q. v.], a friend of his father, he entered the war office in May 1860 as a temporary clerk; was appointed a junior clerk on the establishment in January 1862, and retired on a pension in April 1879, without receiving any promotion during his service. Devoted to athletics in youth and middle age, he in 1874 played at Prince's Grounds, Hans Place, London, in the first game of lawn-tennis, together with Major Wingfield, the inventor, Alfred Thompson, and Alfred Lubbock.

From boyhood Scott had been interested in light literature and the drama. On the introduction of Thomas Hood the younger [q. v.], a colleague at the war office, he while very young assisted Frederick Ledger, editor of the 'Era.' In 1863 he became dramatic writer for the 'Sunday Times,' but retired after two years owing to the frankness of his pen, being succeeded by Joseph Knight (1829–1907) [q. v. Suppl. II]. He then wrote for the 'Weekly Dispatch' and for the comic weekly paper 'Fun,' of which his friend Hood became editor in 1865; his colleagues included H. J. Byron, (Sir) Frank Burnand, and (Sir) William Schwenck Gilbert, with all of whom he grew intimate. In 1870 he joined the staff of the 'London Figaro,' contributing caustic criticism of the drama over the signature of Almaviva.

Scott began in 1871 a long connection with the 'Daily Telegraph.' He then became assistant to the dramatic critic, Edward Laman Blanchard [q. v. Suppl. I], whom he shortly afterwards succeeded. With the 'Daily Telegraph' he was associated till 1898, becoming the best known dramatic critic of his day, and largely leading popular opinion in theatrical matters. For a time in 1893 he was also dramatic critic for the 'Observer,' and later of the 'Illustrated London News.' From 1880 to 1889 he edited the monthly periodical called 'The Theatre.'

Scott also tried his hand at the drama. On 1 April 1871 John Hollingshead produced anonymously at the Gaiety Theatre his 'Off the Line,' a popular farce from the French. In March 1877 he adapted at (Sir) Squire Bancroft's suggestion, for the Prince of Wales's Theatre, Octave Feuillet's 'Le Village' under the title of 'The Vicarage.' But his chief dramatic successes were won in the adaptation of comedies of Victorien Sardou, also for the Bancroft management. With B. C. Stephenson, Scott based 'Peril' on Sardou's 'Nos Intimes' (October 1876) and 'Diplomacy' on Sardou's 'Dora' (January 1878). The joint adapters called themselves 'Bolton Rowe and Saville Rowe.' 'Diplomacy' was parodied by Burnand at the Strand Theatre in 'Diplunacy.' In 1882, when the Bancrofts had removed to the Haymarket Theatre, Scott anonymously produced 'Odette,' a third adaptation of Sardou.

Lightly written accounts of holiday tours which Scott contributed serially to the 'Daily Telegraph' and other newspapers he collected into volumes under such titles as 'Round about the Islands' (1873), and 'Poppy Land,' a description of scenery of the east coast (1885; often reissued). An account of a journey round the world, which he made in 1893, was similarly issued as 'Pictures round the World' (1894). He also showed fluency as a versifier. After his friend (Sir) Frank Burnand became editor of 'Punch' in 1880, he occasionally contributed effective verse of sentimental flavour to that periodical, some of which he collected in 'Lays of a Londoner' (1882), 'Poems for Recitation' (1884), and 'Lays and Lyrics' (1888).

After his withdrawal from the 'Daily Telegraph' in 1898, Scott founded in 1901 a penny weekly paper, the 'Free Lance,' which obtained no recognised position. He died in London, after a long illness, on 25 June 1904, and was buried in the chapel of the Sisters of Nazareth at Southend. He married (1) on 30 April 1868, at Brompton Oratory, Isabel Busson du Maurier, sister of the artist, by whom he had four sons (two dying in infancy) and two daughters; she died on 26 Nov. 1890; and (2) in April 1893 Constance Margarite, daughter of Horatio Brandon, a London solicitor. A portrait by Mordecai belongs to his widow.

Despite the popular influence of his dramatic criticism, Scott's habit of mind was neither impartial nor judicial. Against modern schools of acting and of realistic drama of the Ibsen type he nursed a prejudice which involved him latterly in frequent controversy. In the van when he began to criticise, he never moved beyond the ideals of Robertson and Sardou. Yet he was a pioneer in the picturesque style of dramatic criticism in the daily press, which superseded the earlier method of bare reporting and owed something to the example of his fellow writer on the 'Daily Telegraph,' George Augustus Sala [q. v.].

Besides the books mentioned, Scott published numerous volumes chiefly collecting his newspaper criticisms of the drama; these include: 1. 'Thirty Years at the Play,' 1892. 2. 'From "The Bells" to "King Arthur": a critical record of the productions at the Lyceum Theatre from 1871 to 1895,' 1896. 3. 'The Drama of Yesterday and To-day,' 1899. 4. 'Ellen Terry: an Appreciation,' 1900. 5. 'Some Notable Hamlets of the Present Time,' 1900; 2nd edit. 1905.

[The Times, and Daily Telegraph, 26 June 1904; Marlborough Coll. Reg.; War Office Records; The Bancrofts: Recollections of Sixty Years, 1909, passim; Joseph Knight, Theatrical Notes, 1893, pp. 156, 198; Sir F. C. Burnand, Records and Reminiscences, 1904, 2 vols.; Hollingshead, My Lifetime, 1895, and Gaiety Chronicles, 1898; Scott, The Drama of Yesterday and To-day, 1899; Spielmann's History of Punch, 1895, pp. 388–9; Cat. Max Beerbohm's Caricatures, May 1911, No. 25 (caricature of Scott).] L. M.

SCOTT, Lord CHARLES THOMAS MONTAGU-DOUGLAS- (1839–1911), admiral, born at Montagu House, Whitehall, on 20 Oct. 1839, was fourth son of Walter Francis Scott, fifth duke of Buccleuch [q. v.], by his wife Charlotte Ann Le Thynne (*d.* 1895), youngest daughter of Thomas, second marquess of Bath. After beginning his education at Radley, he entered the navy on 1 May 1853 as a cadet on board the St. Jean d'Acre, then newly commissioned by Captain Keppel [see Keppel, Sir Henry, Suppl. II]. In her Scott took part in the Baltic campaign of 1854 being present at the capture of Bomarsund, and in 1855 saw further active service in the Black Sea. He received the Baltic, Crimean, and Turkish medals. In Nov. 1856 he followed Keppel into the Raleigh, going out to the China station, and after the wreck of the ship in April 1857 served in the tenders to which the officers and crew were transferred. He was thus present at the engagements at Escape Creek, Fatshan Creek, and other boat actions in the Canton River in June and July 1857, for which he received the China medal with Fatshan clasp. In July he was appointed to the Pearl, Capt. Sotheby [see SOTHEBY, SIR EDWARD SOUTHWELL, Suppl. II], which with the Shannon was ordered from Hong Kong to Calcutta on the outbreak of the Indian Mutiny. Scott landed with the Pearl's naval brigade in Sept. 1857, and served ashore with it till the end of the following year, the brigade forming part of the Goruckpore field force during the operations in Oudh. Lord Charles was twice specially mentioned in despatches, for gallant conduct at Chanderpore on 17 Feb. 1858, and again for having, with three others, captured and turned upon the enemy one of their own guns at the battle of Belwa on 5 March. He received the Indian medal and, having passed his examination on 21 May 1859, was specially promoted to lieutenant on 19 July following. In that rank he served on board the Forte, Keppel's flagship, on the Cape of Good Hope and south-east coast of America stations, and in June 1861 was appointed to the frigate Emerald, attached to the Channel Squadron. From Nov. 1863 until he was promoted to commander on 12 Sept. 1865 he was a lieutenant of the royal yacht. Early in 1868 he went out to the China station to take command of the sloop Icarus, and in Nov. of that year served as second in command of the naval brigade under Capt. Algernon Heneage landed for the protection of British subjects at Yangchow; in December he commanded a flotilla of boats which, in co-operation with a naval brigade under Commodore Oliver Jones, destroyed three piratical villages near Swatow. He returned home in 1871, and was promoted to captain on 6 Feb. 1872.

From 1875 to 1877 Lord Charles commanded the Narcissus, flagship of the detached squadron, and in July 1879 commissioned the Bacchante, in which ship he had the immediate charge of the royal cadets, Albert Victor, duke of Clarence and Avondale, and his younger brother George (subsequently King George V), who made their first cruise in her. The Bacchante went first to the Mediterranean, and to the West Indies and back; then, after cruising for a short time with the Channel squadron, she joined the flag of Rear-admiral the earl of Clanwilliam [see MEADE, RICHARD JAMES, fourth EARL OF CLANWILLIAM, Suppl. II], commanding the detached squadron. The squadron, after touching at Monte Video and the Falkland Islands, went to Simon's Bay, Australia, Japan, and China, and returned home by way of Singapore and the Mediterranean in 1882. For this service Scott was awarded the C.B. (civil). In 1885 and 1886 he commanded the Agincourt in the Channel, and in Jan. 1887 became captain of the dockyard at Chatham. He was an aide-de-camp to Queen Victoria from June 1886 until promoted to his flag on 3 April 1888. For three years from Sept. 1889 Lord Charles was commander-in-chief on the Australian station; on 10 March 1894 he was promoted to vice-admiral, and in May 1898 he was made a K.C.B. (military). On 30 June 1899 he reached the rank of admiral, and in March 1900 was appointed commander-in-chief at Plymouth, where he remained for the customary three years. He was advanced to the G.C.B. on 9 Nov. 1902, and retired on 20 Oct. 1904. He died, after a long illness, on 21 Aug. 1911 at Boughton House, near Kettering.

Lord Charles married on 23 Feb. 1883 Ada Mary, daughter of Charles Ryan of Derriweit Heights, Macedon, Victoria, Australia, by whom he had issue two sons.

[The Times, 23 Aug. 1911; R. N. List, Burke's Peerage; Dalton's Cruise of H.M.S. Bacchante, 1886.] L. G. C. L.

SCOTT, HUGH STOWELL (1862–1903), novelist, who wrote under the pseudonym of HENRY SETON MERRIMAN, born at Newcastle-on-Tyne on 9 May 1862, was son of Henry Scott, a shipowner, of Newcastle-on-Tyne, by his wife Mary Sweet, daughter of James Wilson Carmichael [q. v.], marine painter. Hugh was educated at Loretto school, Musselburgh, and afterwards at Vevey and Wiesbaden. At eighteen he was placed by his father in an underwriter's office at Lloyd's in London. The routine of commerce proved distasteful. He cherished an ardent desire to travel abroad and to study foreign nationalities, and was thus impelled to try his hand at romance. His first experiment was 'Young Mistley,' which he submitted to Bentley and published anonymously in 1888 (2 vols.).

In his next book, 'The Phantom Future' (1889, 2 vols.), he adopted the pseudonym of Henry Seton Merriman in order to evade the disapproval of his family, and he used the same disguise to the end. 'The Phantom Future' was followed by two other stories equally immature, 'Suspense' (1890, 3 vols.) and 'Prisoners and Captives' (1891, 3 vols.). Scott subsequently suppressed these three novels in England, but he failed to prevent their continued circulation in America. In 1892 he succeeded in interesting James Payn, then editor of 'Cornhill,' in a well-constructed story of French and English life, 'The Slave of the Lamp,' which after running through the magazine was well received on its separate issue. Its successor, 'From One Generation to Another' (1892), was welcomed so warmly as to justify Scott, whose means were always ample, in abandoning the City and in adopting exclusively the profession of novelist. In 1894 his West African story, 'With Edged Tools,' caught the fancy of the public and gave him a prominent position among popular romancists of his day. There quickly followed 'The Grey Lady' (1895), which dealt with seafaring life; some of its scenes were drawn from a visit to the Balearic Islands. Henceforth Merriman, as he was invariably called by the critics, lived a comparatively secluded life in the country, varied by foreign travel.

In conjunction with Stanley J. Weyman, a literary comrade who achieved a success parallel to his own, he studied the methods of Dumas and devoted all the time and money he could spare to the detailed *mise en scène* of a series of novels of modern nationalities. His most ambitious and on the whole most successful performance was the exciting Russian story which appeared in 1896 entitled 'The Sowers,' went through thirty editions in England alone, and was included in the Tauchnitz collection. It was followed at intervals of nearly eighteen months each by 'Flotsam,' a story of Delhi in Mutiny days (1896); 'In Kedar's Tents,' a tale of Spanish Carlist intrigue (1897); 'Roden's Corner,' an Anglo-Dutch story embodying an attack on unprincipled company promoting (1898); 'Dross' (Toronto, 1899), which was not issued in volume form in Great Britain; 'The Isle of Unrest,' a story of Corsican vendetta somewhat in the Mérimée vein (1900); 'The Velvet Glove' (1901), in which, following the lead of 'In Kedar's Tents,' he depicted a Spanish gentleman and put some of his best work; 'Barlasch of the Guard' (1902), a story of Dantzig in 1812 and of Borodino and after, one of his most successful attempts at historical presentation; 'The Vultures' (1902), dealing with the abortive rising in Poland after the assassination of the Czar Alexander in 1881; and 'The Last Hope' (1904), a curious story of 1849 in which strands of Bourbon and Louis Napoleon romance are ingeniously mixed. The last work was issued posthumously. At his death Scott was one of the most effective and widely read novelists of his day. His success under a pseudonym had led several impostors to represent themselves as authors of his most widely circulated books. More than most novelists he worked by a strenuous method, which involved rigid concentration and omission, close personal study of his backgrounds, and much rewriting of dialogue. His faults were a growing tendency to a moralising and sententious cynicism, a stereotyped repertory of characters—strong silent gentlemen, reserved and romance-loving maidens, and inflexibly trusty servants, and a progressive heightening of human faculties and idiosyncrasies at the expense of verisimilitude. His method did not suit either the short story or the essay, and his attempts in these directions, 'Tomaso's Fortune and other Stories' (1904), remained deservedly obscure. Scott's success was exclusively literary, for he avoided all self-advertisement.

Of singularly equable and genial temper, with a bent towards stoicism and the simple life, he had a gipsy-like love of 'the open road,' and watched with keen absorption the life about him, especially in foreign towns. He died prematurely, after an attack of appendicitis, on 19 Nov. 1903, at Long Spring, Melton, near Woodbridge, and was buried at Eltham, Kent. He married on 19 June 1889 Ethel Frances Hall, who survived him without issue and became in August 1912 wife of the Rev. George Augustus Cobbold, perpetual curate of St. Bartholomew's, Ipswich.

In two volumes of short stories, 'From Wisdom Court' (1893) and 'The Money Spinner' (1896), Scott collaborated with his wife's sister, Miss E. Beatrice Hall, who writes under the pseudonym of S. G. Tallentyre. A memorial collected edition of fourteen of Scott's novels in as many volumes appeared in 1909-10.

[The Times, 20 Nov. 1903; preface to Memorial Edition, 1909, by E. F. S[cott] and S. G. T., i.e. Miss E. Beatrice Hall; private information.] T. S.

SCOTT, Sir JOHN (1841–1904), judicial adviser to the Khedive, born at Wigan on 4 June 1841, was one of the family of three sons and a daughter of Edward Scott, solicitor of Wigan, by his first wife, Annie Glover. His father's second wife was Laura, sister of George Birkbeck Hill [q. v. Suppl. II], who married a daughter of Scott by his first wife. There were two sons and two daughters of the second marriage.

From 1852 to 1860 John was educated at Bruce Castle School, Tottenham, of which Birkbeck Hill's father was headmaster; matriculating at Pembroke College, Oxford, he graduated B.A. in 1864 and proceeded M.A. in 1869. A fast left-hand bowler, he was captain of his college eleven, and in 1863 he played for Oxford against Cambridge.

Called to the bar by the Inner Temple on 17 Nov. 1865, he joined the northern circuit. He wrote on legal questions for 'The Times,' the 'Law Quarterly,' and other periodicals, and his 'Bills of Exchange' (1869) became a widely read text-book. Heart affection hampered him through life, and drove him to the Riviera for many months in 1871–2. There he mastered French and Italian and the French legal system. On medical advice he went to Alexandria, at the close of 1872, to pursue his profession there, and found his knowledge of French and Italian of essential service. In 1874, on the formation of a court of international appeal from the courts for foreign and native litigants, Scott was made, on the recommendation of the British agent and consul-general, the English judge. He won a high reputation in this post, and in Feb. 1881 was made vice-president of the court. George Joachim (afterwards Lord) Goschen [q. v. Suppl. II], on his mission to Egypt in 1876, nominated Scott English commissioner of the public debt, but the Khedive, Ismail Pasha, declined to deprive the appeal court of his services, and the appointment went to Lord Cromer (then Major Baring). From 1873 onwards Scott regularly contributed to 'The Times' from Alexandria, and his letters form a useful record of Egyptian history of the period. He interested himself keenly in the condition of the fellaheen, and persistently used his influence to suppress slavery. In the Alexandria riots of June 1882 he narrowly escaped massacre, but remained at the court house day and night to assist in protecting the records.

In Oct. 1882, when the Khedive conferred on him the order of the Osmanie, he was appointed as puisne judge of the high court at Bombay. He quickly mastered the complex customs and usages of India. One of his judgments settled the law of partition among Hindus, and another defined the extent of Portuguese ecclesiastical jurisdiction over the Roman catholics of Western India. Scott continued to write for the local and London press, frequently noticing Egyptian affairs. A letter of his to the 'Times of India' (26 Dec. 1884), signed 'S,' foreshadowed later political transitions in India. For a year from April 1890 his services were lent by the government of India to Egypt in order that he might examine the whole system of native jurisprudence in Egypt, and make proposals for its amendment. Despite the opposition of the Egyptian premier, Riaz Pasha, Lord Cromer induced the Khedive to accept Scott's recommendations and to appoint him judicial adviser to the Khedive. Thereupon Riaz Pasha resigned (May 1891) on the plea of ill-health.

Scott's impartiality and manifest goodwill towards the Egyptian people, combined with a constructive genius which enabled him to remould, instead of destroying, existing material and institutions, helped him to create in Egypt a sound judicial system (Cromer's *Modern Egypt*, chap. xl.; Milner's *England in Egypt*, 1892). In place of only three centres of justice, circuits were established, comprising forty stations. The procedure of the courts was simplified and accelerated; a system of inspection and control was carefully organised; incompetent judges were replaced by men of better education and higher moral character; and for the supply of judges, barristers, and court officials an excellent school of law was established. Scott did much of the inspection himself, travelling all over the country, and his annual reports from 1892 to 1898 are of profound interest. Even the critics of the British occupation have nothing but commendation for Scott's work (cf. H. R. Fox Bourne's *Admn. of Justice in Egypt: Notes on Egyptian Affairs*, pamph. No. 6, 1909).

Scott, who was made K.C.M.G. in March 1894, retired in May 1898 from considerations of health and other reasons. The Khedive conferred on him the order of the Mejidie of the highest class. In June 1898 Oxford bestowed the hon. D.C.L., and he became an honorary fellow of his old college, Pembroke. He was elected a member of the Athenæum under Rule II. Wigan, his native town, conferred upon him its freedom early in 1893. He was a vice-president of the International Law Association.

At the close of 1898 he was appointed deputy judge advocate-general of the army, an ordinarily light post which the South African war rendered onerous. With other ex-judges of India he joined in a memorial advocating the separation of judicial and executive functions in India, dated 1 July 1899. He died after long illness at his residence at Norwood on 1 March 1904. He was buried in St. John's churchyard, Hampstead.

He married on 16 Feb. 1867 Edgeworth Leonora—named after Maria Edgeworth [q. v.]—daughter of Frederic Hill (1803–1896), inspector of prisons for Scotland, a brother of Sir Rowland Hill [q. v.] (cf. FREDERIC HILL'S *Autobiography*, 1893). Of four sons and four daughters, Leslie Frederic, K.C., became conservative M.P. for the Exchange division of Liverpool in Dec. 1910.

A portrait by Mr. J. H. Lorimer, R.S.A., presented by the courts in Egypt, is in Lady Scott's possession, and a portrait in chalks, showing him in judge's robes in India, by his sister-in-law, Miss E. G. Hill, is in the senior common room of Pembroke College.

[Works of Lord Cromer and Lord Milner; Sir A. Colvin's Making of Modern Egypt; Scott's reports as judicial adviser from 1892 to 1898; Encycl. Brit., 11th ed., art. Egypt; Oxford Mag., 9 March 1904; Indian Mag. and Rev., April 1904; The Times, 5 March 1894, 11 May 1898, 3 March 1904, and other dates; Wigan Observer, 7 Sept. 1892; Admn. of Justice in Egypt, pamphlet by H. R. Fox Bourne, London, 1909; information kindly given by Lady Scott.] F. H. B.

SCOTT, JOHN (1830–1903), shipbuilder and engineer, born at Greenock on 5 Sept. 1830, was eldest son in the family of five sons and six daughters of Charles Cuningham Scott of Halkshill, Largs, Ayrshire, by his wife Helen, daughter of John Rankin. His father was member of Messrs. Scott & Co., a leading firm of shipbuilders on the Clyde, which was founded by an ancestor in 1710. After education at Edinburgh Academy and Glasgow University, John served an apprenticeship to his father, and, on attaining his majority, was admitted to partnership in the firm. In 1868 he became its responsible head, in association with his brother, Robert Sinclair Scott, and directed its affairs for thirty-five years. The ships constructed in the Scott yard during his charge of it included many notable vessels for the mercantile marine as well as for the British navy; others, such as the battleships Canopus and Prince of Wales, were engined there.

Scott was closely connected with the development of the marine steam-engine. At an early date he recognised the economy likely to result from the use of higher steam-pressures, and about 1857 he built the Thetis, of 650 tons, which was fitted with a two-cylinder engine of his own design and with water-tube boilers of the Rowan type, the working-pressure being 125 lbs. per square inch. The result was satisfactory so far as economy of fuel was concerned, though internal corrosion of the tubes rendered it necessary to withdraw the boilers after a short time. A little later, with the assent of M. Dupuy de Lôme, then head of the French navy department, Scott introduced the water-tube boiler into a corvette which his firm built for the French navy—the first French warship fitted with compound engines. Similar boilers and engines were proposed by him and accepted for a corvette for the British navy, but owing to the impossibility of complying with the requirement that the tops of the boilers should be at least one foot below the load-line, the adoption of the water-tube boiler was deferred. Further pursuit of the question of higher steam-pressures brought him the acquaintance of Samson Fox [q. v. Suppl. II.], with whom he was associated for many years in the development of the corrugated flue. He became chairman of the Leeds Forge Company, and carried out in conjunction with Fox the first effective tests of the strength of circular furnaces.

Although his business claimed the greater part of his attention, Scott had several other interests. He made three unsuccessful attempts to enter Parliament as conservative candidate for Greenock—in 1880, 1884, and 1885. For many years he was deputy chairman of the Greenock Harbour Trust, and for twenty-five years chairman of the local marine board. He was a lover of books and formed one of the finest private libraries in Scotland, containing some rare first editions and early manuscripts as well as literature relating to his own profession. An ardent yachtsman, he was a member of many Scottish yacht clubs, and commodore of the Royal Clyde Yacht Club.

Scott also took an active interest in the volunteer movement, and in 1859 he raised two battalions of artillery volunteers. From 1862 to 1894 he was lieutenant-colonel of the Renfrew and Dumbarton artillery brigades, and on relinquishing active duty in the latter year he was made honorary colonel. For his services in connection with the movement he was made C.B. in 1887.

He was one of the original members of the Institution of Naval Architects, established in 1860, and became a member of council in 1886, and a vice-president in 1903. In 1889 he contributed to the Society's 'Transactions' a paper, 'Experiments on endeavouring to burst a Boiler Shell made to Admiralty Scantlings,' which was the outcome of some tests made by him with boilers for the gunboats Sparrow and Thrush built by his firm for the British navy. He was elected a member of the Institution of Civil Engineers in 1888, and was also a member of the Institution of Engineers and Shipbuilders in Scotland, F.R.S. of Edinburgh and F.S.A. Scotland.

He died at Halkshill on 19 May 1903, and was buried at Largs. He married in Sept. 1864 Annie, eldest daughter of Robert Spalding of Kingston, Jamaica, and had by her two sons and a daughter.

Scott's library, which was rich in works connected with Scotland and the Stuarts as well as in naval and shipbuilding literature, was sold at Sotheby's (27 March–3 April 1905).

Scott's portrait in oils, painted by (Sir) George Reid in 1885, was presented to Scott by the conservatives of Greenock, and is now at Halkshill.

[Engineering, 22 May 1903; Trans. Inst. Naval Architects, xlv. 335 (portrait); The Engineer, 22 May 1903; Athenæum, 25 March 1905.] W. F. S.

SCOTT, LEADER, pseudonym. [See **Baxter, Mrs. Lucy** (1837–1902), writer on art.]

SEALE-HAYNE, CHARLES HAYNE (1833–1903), liberal politician, born at Brighton on 22 Oct. 1833, was only son of Charles Hayne Seale-Hayne of Fuge House, Dartmouth (1808–1842), by his wife Louisa, daughter of Richard Jennings, of Portland Place, London. His father was second son of Sir John Henry Seale (1785–1844), first baronet and M.P. for Dartmouth, whose family was connected since the seventeenth century with Devonshire, where they were large landowners and held many public offices. Charles was educated at Eton, and called to the bar at Lincoln's Inn on 30 April 1857. In that year and in 1860 he unsuccessfully contested Dartmouth in the liberal interest. In 1885 he was elected M.P. for the Mid or Ashburton division of Devonshire, and retained the seat for the liberals to the day of his death. He was assiduous in his attendance at Westminster, and became in 1892 paymaster-general in Gladstone's fourth administration, being also made privy councillor. He held office until the defeat of the liberal government in 1895. He was treasurer of the Cobden Club, and took an active part in the local affairs of Devonshire. For many years he held the rank of lieutenant-colonel in the South Devon militia, and afterwards the same rank in the 2nd Devon volunteer artillery. He died, unmarried, in London on 22 Nov. 1903, and was buried at Kensal Green cemetery. By his will, dated 17 Jan. 1889, Seale-Hayne directed that, after paying certain legacies, the residue of his property should form a trust to establish and endow a college, to be erected in the neighbourhood of Newton Abbot, Devonshire, for the technical education of artisans and others, without distinction of creed, and for the special encouragement of the industries, manufactures, and products of the county of Devon. The trustees acordingly received the sum of over 90,000*l.*, from which a farm of 225 acres has been purchased two and a half miles outside Newton Abbot. A college is to be erected in the centre of the property. Seale-Hayne's publications include 'Annals of the Militia: being the Records of the South Devon Regiment' (Plymouth, 1873) and 'Politics for Working Men, Farmers and Landlords.'

[The Times, and Western Times, 23 Nov. 1903; Western Mag. and Portfolio, Jan. 1904; personal information.] H. T.-S.

SEDDON, RICHARD JOHN (1845–1906), premier of New Zealand, born at Eccleston Hill, St. Helens, Lancashire, on 22 June 1845, was second child in the family of four sons and three daughters of Thomas Seddon, headmaster of Eccleston Hill grammar school, by his wife Jane Lindsay of Annan, Dumfriesshire, headmistress of the denominational school in the same place. The father afterwards became an official of the board of guardians at Prescott, and later a greengrocer in the Liverpool Road, St. Helens. After attendance at his father's school, where he proved refractory and showed no aptitude for anything save mechanical drawing, he was sent at twelve to his grandfather at Barrownook Farm, Bickerstaffe, and then at fourteen was apprenticed to the firm of Dagiish & Co., engineers and ironfounders, of St. Helens. After five years at St. Helens he entered the Vauxhall Iron Foundry at Liverpool, and obtained his board of trade engineer's certificate.

Dissatisfied with his prospects in England he worked his way out to Victoria in the Star of England in 1863, and made for the goldfields of Bendigo. There his efforts were unsuccessful. From 1864 he was employed as a journeyman fitter in the railway workshops of the Victoria government at Williamstown. But in 1866 he was persuaded by an uncle, who had settled on the west coast of New Zealand, to try his luck anew at the old Six Mile diggings at Waimea. He joined several mates in washing a claim on the Waimea Creek without result. His knowledge of engineering however proved useful, and through his uncle's influence he did some work for the Band of Hope water race. He pressed for the construction of water races to bring water from higher levels to sluice the claims, and zealously pushed the miners' interests against sluggish or hostile authorities. Abandoning the diggings, he soon opened a store at Big Dam, and it prospered. In 1869 he was made chairman of the Arahura road board, where he showed himself a strong administrator. He unsuccessfully contested a seat for the Westland county council; but the affairs of his road board brought him to Stafford town, where he became a member of the school committee.

In 1874 Seddon moved his store to the new goldfields at Kumara, and there he at once played a prominent part in local affairs. At his persuasion the goldfields warden laid the place out as a township under the Mining Act; the citizens named one of their streets after him and elected him the first mayor. A member of the board of education, he supported the secular against the denominational system. As member for Arahura on the Westland provincial council, he was appointed chairman of committees. From 1876, when Westland became a county, he was chairman of the county council until 1891. From 1869 Seddon combined management of his store with practice as miners' advocate in the goldfields warden's court, for which his fighting instincts, cheery, voluble power of speech, and legal ability well fitted him. His public influence grew steadily. Although in 1876 he failed to win the parliamentary constituency of Hokitika as a supporter of Sir George Grey, he was in 1879 returned as second member. In 1881 he was elected for Kumara (which was renamed Westland in 1890). That constituency he represented till death.

When Seddon entered parliament the conservative party was in power on sufferance under Sir John Hall [q. v. Suppl. II]. The liberal opposition was split into two sections, the smaller of which followed the late prime minister, Sir George Grey, and the larger was without a leader. Seddon joined the latter section, known as the Young New Zealand reform party. The conservative government could retain office only by introducing liberal bills. Seddon carefully studied parliamentary procedure, and his readiness of speech enabled him to practise obstruction on a formidable scale. From 1884, when a liberal government was formed under Sir Robert Stout, Seddon introduced many private bills which he succeeded in passing at a later period. The most important of these were his bill for licensing auctioneers and regulating sales and one to abolish the gold duty, a tax which pressed heavily on the miners, whose interests he always furthered. In 1888, during the period of economic disturbance and labour unrest which attended Atkinson's conservative administration (1889–90), Seddon with his liberal colleagues accepted John Ballance [q. v. Suppl. I] as their party's leader, and a policy of social reform was adopted. In 1890 Seddon succeeded in reducing the audit office vote. In the course of the same year he spoke in support of the great shipping strike, and advocated principles of state ownership and state interference, urging the government to end the strike by taking over the steamships. At the general election in December 1890 the liberal party secured a large majority, and in January 1891 Seddon joined Ballance's cabinet as minister for mines, public works, and defence.

In office Seddon at once distinguished himself. He stopped the sub-letting of government contracts, and introduced a system of letting government work in small sections to co-operative parties of workmen, a system which proved successful and was adopted in other colonies. In the country he strengthened his position by constant speaking in different places.

The ministry meanwhile was busy with land legislation of great importance and with its programme of social reform. Economic conditions were improving, and general confidence in the government was strong. On 6 Sept. 1891 Ballance fell ill, and owing to Seddon's mastery of parliamentary procedure he became acting premier in the premier's brief absence. On 3 June 1892 he became minister for marine, and on 1 May 1893, on Ballance's death, he became premier, retaining at the same time the portfolios of public works, mines, and defence. On 6 Sept. he exchanged the department of mines for that of native affairs. Pledged to carry out his predecessor's policy, he accepted and carried the measure for conferring the parliamentary vote on women, although he personally disapproved of women's entry into the political sphere (19 Sept.). Other important acts passed by his government during this year were one simplifying and consolidating the criminal code, and another creating a form of local option to control the liquor traffic. At the general election of November 1893 Seddon's party was returned with a majority of thirty-four in a house which contained seventy white members.

In 1894 Seddon prevented a financial crisis by bringing government aid to the Bank of New Zealand, with which the government dealt, when the bank was on the point of failure. During this and the next two years Seddon and his colleagues carried an immense amount of progressive legislation, including a bill in 1896 to allow local authorities to levy their rates on the unimproved value of the land. The country was prosperous, and Seddon's personal popularity increased.

Although at the general election of 1896 the government's majority fell to twelve, Seddon's influence was unimpaired. All departments of government were more or less under his control. He gave up his posts as minister of public works and defence early in 1896, but he had become minister for labour on 11 Jan. 1896. Till his death he retained that office with the premiership, the colonial treasurership, on which he first entered on 16 June 1896, and the ministry of defence, which he resumed in 1899. He also held from the latter date the commissionerships of customs and electric telegraphs (till 21 Dec. 1899) and the commissionership of trade (till 29 Oct. 1900), in addition to the ministry of native affairs which he had held since 1893, and only gave up in December 1899. He attended Queen Victoria's diamond jubilee in London in 1897, when he was made a privy councillor and hon. LL.D. of Cambridge, but his democratic principles would not allow him to accept a knighthood. At the colonial conference of that year he proposed a consultative council of colonial representatives to advise the English government. The proposal was not carried. Brought much into touch with Mr. Joseph Chamberlain, the colonial secretary, he was attracted by his imperialistic views, and developed a strong sympathy with imperial federation and a preferential tariff. After his return to New Zealand, Seddon in 1898 passed the most important measure for which he was personally responsible, an old age pensions bill. In 1899 the pensioners numbered 7000, but in 1900 he enlarged the scope of the act by increasing the amount of the pension and lowering the age limit, and in 1906, the year of his death, over 12,000 persons were in receipt of pensions.

At the end of 1899 Seddon set the colonies an example of patriotism by despatching the first of nine contingents to help Great Britain in the South African war; 6700 officers and men and 6620 horses were despatched in the aggregate. After the general election (December 1899), Seddon had a majority of thirty-six in the new parliament. He again added to his other responsibilities the ministry of defence. On 8 October 1900 the Cook Islands were included within the boundaries of New Zealand. In 1901 his government arranged for a universal penny postage, and made coal mines and fire insurance concerns of the state.

Alike in the colony and in the empire at large Seddon was now a highly popular and imposing figure. In May 1902 he again set out for England to attend the coronation of King Edward VII, receiving before he left a congratulatory address and a testimonial which took the form of a purse of money (8 April). On his way he visited South Africa at the invitation of Lord Kitchener, and was warmly welcomed at Johannesburg and Pretoria, as well as at Cape Town. In London he was greeted with enthusiasm. At the colonial conference he urged a double policy of preferential tariffs within the Empire and a scheme for imperial defence, and during his stay he was granted the freedom of the cities of Edinburgh, of Annan, and of St. Helens, and was made hon. LL.D. of Edinburgh University.

On 25 Oct. 1902 he was back in New Zealand. On 26 Nov. a new election gave him a majority of twenty, and he added the ministries of immigration and education to his other offices. Next year, while speaking repeatedly on the prosperity of the colony, he flung himself into ardent support of Mr. Chamberlain's scheme of imperial tariff reform. Naval defence also found in him a strong champion, and in the autumn of 1903 he passed a naval defence bill which laid an annual charge of 40,000*l.* on New Zealand for the Australian squadron. At the same time he passed a Preferential and Reciprocal Trade Act, which favoured British imports at the expense of imports from foreign countries. In a series of enactments having what he termed a 'humanistic' basis, of which the chief was an act for the erection of state-owned workmen's dwellings, he sought to improve the health and comfort of the working-classes, particularly of mothers and young children.

In September 1904 he warmly declared against the introduction of Chinese labour into South Africa without the sanction of the votes of the white population. Troops, he said, would not have been sent to the war, if he could have foreseen the use to which the English victory would be put.

On 13 Dec. 1905 he fought his last general election, and his fifth as premier, securing, in a house of seventy-six white members, a majority of thirty-six. He remained minister of defence, labour, education, and immigration, and colonial treasurer, as well as premier. Later in the year he recommended a larger contribution to naval defence, forbade the admission of Japanese to the colony, promised to reduce indirect taxation and to increase the graduated land tax, and announced a larger surplus than had been known before.

Next year his health began to fail. On 12 May he left Wellington for Australia, to arrange for an international exhibition at Christchurch later in the year. He started from Sydney on his return voyage in the Oswestry Grange on 9 June 1906, and died at sea on the following day. He was buried at Wellington City cemetery on Cemetery Hill, and a monument in the form of a pillar was subsequently erected there by public and private subscription. On receipt of news of his death King Edward VII and the English government sent messages of sympathy. A memorial service was held in St. Paul's Cathedral, London, on 19 June. The New Zealand parliament granted Mrs. Seddon 6000*l.* on 28 Sept. 1906.

The social policy which Seddon helped to carry out was enlightened and commanded public sympathy, but his personal popularity was only partly due to his political principles. Frank and genial in manner and abounding in self-confidence, constantly moving about the country, he divined what the people of New Zealand wanted, and sought to satisfy their needs. His sympathy with democratic aspirations was combined with an imperialist fervour which notably won the hearts of the English people on his visits to Great Britain in 1897 and 1902. As an administrator he was energetic, industrious, and courageous. As a speaker he greatly improved in delivery with his years, and he was always liberal in information. He introduced over 550 bills into the lower house, and 180 of them became law.

New choir stalls were presented by Mrs. Seddon in his memory to the parish church of Eccleston, St. Helens, in February 1908. A bust with memorial tablet was unveiled in the crypt of St. Paul's Cathedral, London, on 10 Feb. 1910 (cf. *The Times*, 11 Feb. 1910). A cartoon portrait of Seddon appeared in 'Vanity Fair' in 1902.

Seddon married at Melbourne in 1869 Lousia Jane, daughter of Captain John Spotswood, of Melbourne. She survived him with six daughters and three sons. His eldest son, Captain R. J. S. Seddon, fought with the New Zealand troops in the South African war, and was afterwards appointed military secretary to the defence minister. The second son, Mr. T. E. Y. Seddon, is a member of the house of representatives.

[J. Drummond's The Life and Work of R. J. Seddon, 1907; J. E. le Rossignol and W. D. Stewart, State Socialism in New Zealand; Gisborne, New Zealand Rulers, 1897 (with portrait); The Times, 11 and 12 June 1906; private information.]

A. B. W.

SEE, Sir JOHN (1844–1907), premier of New South Wales, born at Yelling, Huntingdonshire, on 14 Nov. 1844, was son of Joseph See, formerly of that place. In 1853 he accompanied his parents to New South Wales. The family settled first at Hinton on the Hunter river, where See obtained his education and was employed upon a farm until he was sixteen. Accompanied by a brother, he then settled on the Clarence river and engaged in farming. Dissatisfied with his prospects, he soon went to Sydney and entered the produce trade, and by strenuous application and unremitting toil built up the flourishing concern of John See & Company, of which he was the head. At the same time he became a partner in the small coastal shipping house of Nipper & See, which ultimately developed into the North Coast

Steam Navigation Company, of which he was managing director.

See's first association with political life began in November 1880, when he was returned to the legislative assembly of New South Wales as member for Grafton. That constituency he represented continuously until 1904, being re-elected eleven times. In 1885 he joined Mr. (afterwards Sir George) Dibbs's first ministry, in which he was postmaster-general from 7 Oct. to 22 Dec., being sworn a member of the executive council. As treasurer in the third Dibbs administration (23 Oct. 1891–2 Aug. 1894) he introduced and piloted through parliament the protectionist tariff of the government. On 12 Sept. 1899 See joined the government of Mr. (afterwards Sir William) Lyne as chief secretary and minister for defence, and arranged for the despatch of troops to South Africa during the Boer war. He succeeded Sir William Lyne, who took office in the federal government as premier on 27 March 1901, and thus became the first premier of New South Wales as a state in the federation. During his term of office he received King George V and Queen Mary when, as duke and duchess of Cornwall and York, they visited Australia in 1901. On 15 June 1904 he resigned office on private grounds, and retired from the legislative assembly, but accepted a seat in the legislative council, which he held till his death. He was mayor of Randwick for three years and president of the Royal Agricultural Society of New South Wales, and was director of numerous insurance and other business concerns. He was created K.C.M.G. on 26 June 1902. See died at his residence, 'Urara,' Randwick, on 31 Jan. 1907, and was buried in the Long Bay cemetery.

He married on 15 March 1876, at Randwick, Charlotte Mary, daughter of Samuel Matthews, of Devonshire, and had four sons and three daughters.

[The Times, Sydney Daily Telegraph, and Sydney Morning Herald, 1 Feb. 1907; Sydney Mail, 6 Feb. 1907; Year Book of Australia, 1905; Johns's Notable Australians, 1908; Burke's Peerage, 1907; Colonial Office Records, 1908.] C. A.

SEELEY, HARRY GOVIER (1839–1909), geologist and palæontologist, born in London on 18 Feb. 1839, was second son of Richard Hovill Seeley, goldsmith, by his second wife, Mary Govier, who was of Huguenot descent. Sir John Richard Seeley [q. v.], the historian, was his cousin. Privately educated, he as a youth became interested in natural history, attended lectures by Sir Andrew Crombie Ramsay [q. v.] and Edward Forbes [q. v.] at the Royal School of Mines, read Lyell's 'Principles of Geology,' began to collect fossils, and received help and encouragement from Samuel Pickworth Woodward [q. v.], in the geological department of the British Museum. He described two new species of chalk starfishes in 1858 (*Ann. Mag. Nat. Hist.*). In 1859 he was invited by Adam Sedgwick, professor of geology at Cambridge, to assist in the arrangement of the rocks and fossils in the Woodwardian Museum. Sedgwick found that Seeley 'could not only be trusted to arrange and increase the collection, but could occasionally take his place in the lecture-room' (CLARK and HUGHES, *Life and Letters of Sedgwick*, ii. 356). Seeley entered Sidney Sussex College, there continuing his general education, but he never graduated. His interests were concentrated on his geological work, devoting himself zealously to the local geology, to the invertebrate fossils of the Cambridge greensand or basement chalk, the Hunstanton red rock, familiarly known as the red chalk, and the lower greensand. He also studied the great fen clay formation, separating the Ampthill clay (as he termed it) and associated rock-beds of Corallian age from the Kimmeridge clay above and the Oxford clay below. He accompanied Sedgwick on excursions to the Isle of Wight, Weymouth, and the Kentish coast in 1864–5, and remained his assistant until 1871.

His first paper on vertebrata, published in 1864, dealt with the pterodactyle, and fossil reptilia thenceforth engrossed much of his attention. In 1869 he published the important 'Index to the Fossil Remains of Aves, Ornithosauria, and Reptilia' in the Woodwardian Museum. Questions in ancient physical geography also interested him. In 1865 he wrote 'On the Significance of the Sequence of Rocks and Fossils' (*Geol. Mag.*), while he discussed the relationship between pterodactyles and birds. In 1870 he founded the genus Ornithopsis on remains from the Wealden of 'a gigantic animal of the pterodactyle kind,' which, however, was afterwards proved to be dinosaurian.

In 1872 Seeley settled in London, devoting himself to literary work and lecturing. In 1876 he was appointed professor of geography and lecturer on geology in King's College, London, and also professor of geography and geology in Queen's College, London, where he became dean in 1881. In 1896 he succeeded to the chair of geology and mineralogy at King's College. In 1885 he formed the London Geological Field Class, conducting summer excursions in and around the metropolis. During 1880–90 he lectured for the London Society for the Extension of University Teaching; and in 1890 he became lecturer and a year later professor of geology and mineralogy in the Royal Indian Engineering College at Cooper's Hill, a post he occupied until 1905. As a speaker he was deliberate and monotonous in articulation, but he taught clearly the methods as well as the results of research.

This educational work left time for much original research. During vacations he visited all the principal public museums in Europe for the special study of fossil reptilia, and he contributed descriptions of new points of structure and of new species of amphibians, reptiles, birds, and other vertebrata to scientific societies and magazines. Thus in 1874 he described a new ichthyosaurian genus from the Oxford clay under the name Ophthalmosaurus; in 1880 he called attention to evidence that the Ichthyosaurus was viviparous, and in 1887 he pointed out that the young of some plesiosaurs were similarly developed. Aided by a grant from the Royal Society, he devoted himself to a study of the structure of the anomodont reptilia, to which Sir Richard Owen [q. v.] had already given special attention. These fossil reptiles supply links, as he showed, between the older types of amphibia and the later reptilia and mammalia. He journeyed to Cape Colony and investigated the geological horizons whence anomodonts had been obtained, and was fortunate in finding in the Karroo a practically complete skeleton of Pareiasaurus, as well as many other interesting remains. He delivered in 1887 the Royal Society's Croonian lecture 'On Pareiasaurus bombidens (Owen) and the Significance of its Affinities to Amphibians, Reptiles, and Mammals,' and in 1888 he commenced the publication in the 'Philosophical Transactions' of 'Researches on the structure, organisation, and classification of the Fossil Reptilia.' In succeeding parts of this, his most important contribution to palæontology (10 parts, 1888–96), he dealt specially with the results of his South African work.

Seeley, who was a member of numerous scientific societies, was elected F.R.S. in 1879; he was awarded the Lyell medal in 1885 by the Geological Society, and became a fellow of King's College, London, in 1905. He died in Kensington, London, on 8 Jan. 1909, and was buried at Brookwood cemetery. Seeley married in 1872 Eleonora Jane, only daughter of William Mitchell, of Bath. His wife, who received a civil list pension of 70*l.* in July 1910, assisted him in his scientific work. Their family consisted of four daughters, the eldest of whom, Maud, was married in 1894 to Dr. Arthur Smith Woodward, F.R.S., now keeper of the geological department of the British Museum (natural history).

Seeley's published works include: 1. 'The Ornithosauria,' 1870. 2. 'Physical Geology and Palæontology,' being part i. of a second edition (entirely rewritten) of John Phillips' 'Manual of Geology,' 1885 (issued 1884). 3. 'The Freshwater Fishes of Europe,' 1886. 4. 'Factors in Life. Three Lectures on Health, Food, Education' (delivered 1884), 1887. 5. 'Handbook of the London Geological Field Class,' 1891. 6. 'Story of the Earth in Past Ages,' 1895. 7. 'Dragons of the Air: an account of Extinct Flying Reptiles,' 1901.

[Geol. Mag. 1907, p. 241 (with portrait and bibliography); Men and Women of the Time, 1899; Quart. Journ. Geol. Soc. lxv. 1909, p. lxx; Proc. Roy. Soc. lxxxiii. B. p. xv. 1911 (memoir by Dr. A. S. Woodward).]

H. B. W.

SELBY, VISCOUNT. [See GULLY, WILLIAM COURT (1835–1909), speaker of the House of Commons.]

SELBY, THOMAS GUNN (1846–1910), Wesleyan missionary in China, born at New Radford near Nottingham on 5 June 1846, was the son of William Selby, engaged in the lace trade, by his wife Mary Gunn. He was educated at private schools at Nottingham and Derby. At the age of sixteen he preached his first sermon, and in 1865 became a student at the Wesleyan College, Richmond. In 1867 he entered the Wesleyan ministry, and left England in the following year to become a missionary in China. He remained there for the greater part of fifteen years. He was in charge of the Wesleyan mission at Fatshan (Canton province) until 1876, and after eighteen months in England started in 1878 the North River Mission at Shiu Chau Foo, also in the province of Canton. He made long and perilous pioneer journeys into the interior of the province. He spent a month in the island of Hainan disguised as a Chinaman. He also travelled in India, Palestine, and Egypt. He made a close study of the Chinese language and wrote a 'Life of Christ' (about 1890) in Chinese, which is still used as a text-book in native missionary colleges.

Returning to England in 1882, Selby was pastor in various circuits: at Liverpool (1883), Hull (1886), Greenock (1889), Liverpool (1892), and Dulwich (1895–8). He was a successful preacher and sermon-writer. 'The Holy Writ and Christian Privilege,' written in 1894, was accorded in many circles the rank of a Christian classic. He also published in 1895 some translations of Chinese stories entitled 'The Chinaman in his own Stories.' His work was recognised in the Wesleyan ministry by his election to the 'Legal Hundred' in 1891 and his appointment as Fernley lecturer in 1896.

In 1898 Selby became a 'minister without pastoral charge.' Residing at Bromley in Kent, he devoted himself to preaching and writing, and in his 'Chinamen at Home' (1900) and 'As the Chinese see us' (1901) showed much insight and local knowledge. He was for twenty-five years a member of the Anti-Opium Society and a zealous advocate of the temperance cause. He died at his residence, Basil House, Oaklands Road, Bromley, Kent, on 12 Dec. 1910.

Selby married, in 1885, Catharine, youngest daughter of William Lawson, of Otley in Wharfedale. He had one son and five daughters.

Besides the works cited Selby published numerous volumes of collected sermons and many expositions of Scripture. 'The Commonwealth of the Redeemed' was published posthumously in 1911.

[Who's Who, 1910; The Times, 15 Dec. 1910; obituary notice presented to the Wesleyan Methodist Conference at Cardiff, July 1911; private information from Mrs. Selby.] S. E. F.

SELWIN-IBBETSON, Sir HENRY JOHN, first Baron Rookwood (1826–1902), politician, born in London on 26 Sept. 1826, was only son of Sir John Thomas Ibbetson-Selwin, sixth baronet, by his wife Elizabeth, daughter of General John Leveson Gower, of Bill Hill, Berkshire. His father had assumed the surname of Selwin on inheriting in 1825 the Selwin estates at Harlow, Essex. After education at home Henry was admitted a fellow-commoner at St. John's College, Cambridge, on 2 July 1845. He graduated B.A. in 1849, and proceeded M.A. in 1852. After leaving Cambridge, he travelled widely, and was present in the Crimea at the declaration of peace in 1856. In the same year he embarked, as a conservative, upon his political career. After twice suffering defeat at Ipswich, in March 1857 and in April 1859, he headed the poll for South Essex in July 1865. On a new division of the Essex constituencies (due to Disraeli's reform bill), he was returned without contest for the western division in 1868, again in 1874, and by a large majority in 1880. Subsequently (after the reform bill of 1884) he sat for the Epping division till his elevation to the peerage in 1892. Selwin took from the first a useful part in parliamentary discussion, cautiously supporting moderate reforms. In 1867 he resumed the old family name of Ibbetson in addition to that of Selwin, and in 1869 he succeeded his father in the baronetcy. In the same year, being then in opposition, he introduced and contrived to pass into law a bill which aimed at diminishing the number of beer-houses by placing all drink-shops under the same licensing authority and by leaving none under the control of the excise. He showed a commendable freedom from party ties in the support he gave in 1870 to the Elementary Education Act of William Edward Forster [q. v.].

In 1874 the conservatives were returned to power, and Selwin-Ibbetson became under-secretary to the home office after declining the chairmanship of ways and means. He proved a laborious and efficient administrator, but was perhaps too prone to deal with details which might have been left to subordinates. During his tenure of office acts were passed for the improvement of working-class dwellings in 1875, for the amendment of the labour laws so as to relax the stringency of the law of conspiracy, and for the provision of agricultural holdings, a measure which was largely based on information he had himself collected. In 1878 he became parliamentary secretary to the treasury, and piloted through the house the bill which made Epping Forest a public recreation ground, as well as the cattle diseases bill. As early as 1871 he had championed in the house public rights in Epping Forest.

In 1879 he declined the governorship of New South Wales. In Oct., while in Ireland with the chancellor of the exchequer, Sir Stafford Northcote [q. v.], he sanctioned a scheme for improving the navigation of the Shannon and planned a reconstruction of the Irish board of works which never became law but led to changes in the personnel of the board. In 1880 Ibbetson retired from office on the defeat at the polls of the conservative government. He acted as second church estates commissioner from 7 July

1885 to 2 March 1886, and again from 8 Sept. 1886 to 20 June 1892. At the general election of 1892 he was raised to the peerage by Lord Salisbury as Baron Rookwood, the title being taken from an old mansion in Yorkshire long in the possession of the Ibbetson family.

Through life Lord Rookwood devoted himself to county business, frequently presiding at quarter sessions with efficiency and impartiality. He also did much work for hospitals and charities. A keen sportsman, he was master of the Essex hounds from 1879 to 1886. In March 1893 Essex men of all parties presented him with his portrait by (Sir) W. Q. Orchardson, R.A., which is now at Down Hall, Harlow, Essex; it was engraved.

He died at Down Hall on 15 Jan. 1902, and was buried at Harlow, Essex. He was married thrice: (1) in 1850 to Sarah Elizabeth Copley, eldest daughter and co-heiress of Lord Lyndhurst [q. v.]; she died in 1865; (2) in 1867 to his cousin Eden, daughter of George Thackrah and widow of Sir Charles Ibbetson, Bart., of Denton Park, Yorkshire; she died on 1 April 1899; (3) in Sept. 1900 to Sophia Harriet, daughter of Major Digby Lawrell; she survived him. Lord Rookwood left no issue, and the barony became extinct at his death.

[Hansard, passim; The Times, 16 Jan. 1902; Essex County Chron. 17 Jan. 1902, with a letter from Colonel Lockwood, M.P.; Lord Eversley, Commons, Forests, and Footpaths, 1910; Report of Select Committee on Police Superannuation Funds, 13 April 1877; Ball and Gilbey, The Essex Foxhounds, 1896; Yerburgh, Leaves from a Hunting Diary, 1900, 2 vols.; Irish Times, 13 Oct. 1879; Report of the Commissioners of Public Works in Ireland, 1879–1880, p. 28.] W. B. D.

SELWYN, ALFRED RICHARD CECIL (1824–1902), geologist, born at Kilmington, Somersetshire, on 28 July 1824, was son of Townshend Selwyn, rector of Kilmington, vicar of Milton Clevedon, and a canon of Gloucester; his mother was Charlotte Sophia, daughter of Lord George Murray [q. v.], bishop of St. David's, and granddaughter of John Murray, third duke of Atholl [q. v.]. First educated at home by private tutors, and afterwards in Switzerland, where he developed great interest in geology, he was in 1845 appointed an assistant geologist on the geological survey of Great Britain, and for seven years was actively engaged in the difficult mountainous districts of North Wales. He personally surveyed areas about Snowdon, Festiniog, Cader Idris, in the Lleyn promontory, and Anglesey, as well as portions of Shropshire. In 1850 he recognised evidence of unconformity in Anglesey between the Cambrian and an older series of schists, now admitted to be pre-Cambrian. The results of Selwyn's work in North Wales were embodied in the geological survey memoir by Sir Andrew Crombie Ramsay [q.v.] on 'The Geology of North Wales' (1866; 2nd edit. 1881); and the geological maps and sections which he prepared in conjunction with Ramsay and Joseph Beete Jukes [q. v.] were models of careful detailed work.

In July 1852 Selwyn was appointed director of the geological survey of Victoria, Australia. His work in Australia extended over sixteen years (1853–1869). Areas of special economic importance claimed his attention, and he himself gave much time to field-work. Studying the distribution of the gold-bearing 'drifts' or placer-deposits, he found that certain of the tertiary strata derived from the waste of the older rocks contained little or no gold, while other and later deposits were rich. The former proved to be of miocene age, and Selwyn concluded that the quartz-veins formed prior to that period were barren, whereas auriferous quartz-veins of later date furnished material for the rich gold-bearing gravels of Ballarat and Bendigo (*Geol. Mag.* 1866, p. 457). In addition to his official reports on the geology of Victoria, he prepared special reports on some of the coal-bearing strata and goldfields of Tasmania and South Australia. In 1869 Selwyn resigned his directorship owing to the refusal of the colonial legislature of Victoria to grant the funds necessary to carry on the survey in a satisfactory way. Thereupon from Dec. 1869 until 1894 he was, in succession to Sir William Edmond Logan [q. v.], director of the geological survey of Canada, where his work increased as various provinces and territories in British North America were added to the Dominion. His aim was to make the department of growing practical use to parliament and the public. Special attention was given to the goldfields and other mineral areas, to the building materials, soils, agriculture and sylviculture, and to water-supply. As in Australia so in Canada Selwyn personally engaged in field-work. He was an enthusiastic sportsman and often had to use gun and rod for a living when camping out.

Apart from his many official reports dealing with the progress of the survey and with the economic products, he published in 1881 an important paper in the 'Canadian Naturalist' on 'The Stratigraphy of the Quebec Group and the Older Crystalline Rocks of Canada.' He also rendered valuable services to the Canadian commissioners at the Philadelphia Centennial Exhibition of 1876, the Paris Universal Exhibition of 1878, and the Colonial and Indian Exhibition, London, 1886.

Selwyn was elected F.R.S. in 1874, was made LL.D. in 1881 by the McGill University, Montreal, and was appointed C.M.G. in 1886. An original fellow of the Royal Society of Canada (founded in 1882), he was president in 1896. The Murchison medal was awarded to him by the Geological Society of London in 1876, and the Clarke gold medal by the Royal Society of New South Wales in 1884.

Selwyn died at Vancouver, B.C., on 19 Oct. 1902. He married in 1852 Matilda Charlotte, daughter of Edward Selwyn, rector of Hemingford Abbots in Huntingdonshire; three sons and a daughter survived him, one son, Percy H. Selwyn, being secretary of the Geological Survey of Canada.

Selwyn's few published works, apart from official reports, articles on Canada and Newfoundland in Stanford's 'Compendium of Geography and Travel' (1883), include: 1. 'Notes on the Physical Geography, Geology, and Mineralogy of Victoria' (with G. H. F. Ulrich), Melbourne, 1866. 2. 'Descriptive Catalogue of a Collection of the Economic Minerals of Canada, and Notes on a Stratigraphical Collection of Rocks,' Montreal, 1876 (for the Philadelphia Exhibition).

[Memoirs by Dr. H. Woodward, with portrait, in Geol. Mag. 1899, p. 49; by Dr. H. M. Ami in Trans. Roy. Soc. Canada, x. 1904, p. 173 (with portrait); by W. Whitaker in Proc. Roy. Soc. lxxv. 1905, p. 325; cf. Letters, &c., of J. Beete Jukes, 1871, and Sir A. Geikie, Memoir of Sir A. C. Ramsay, 1895.] H. B. W.

SENDALL, Sir WALTER JOSEPH (1832–1904), colonial governor, born on 24 Dec. 1832 at Langham Hall, Suffolk, was youngest son of S. Sendall, afterwards vicar of Rillington, Yorkshire, by his wife Alice Wilkinson. A delicate boy, he attended the grammar school at Bury St. Edmund's, and in 1854 proceeded to Christ's College, Cambridge, where he was a contemporary and friend of (Sir) Walter Besant, John Peile, afterwards Master, and above all Charles Stuart Calverley, whose sister he married later. He graduated B.A. in 1858 as junior optime and first classman in classics (M.A. in 1867).

In 1859 Sendall joined the educational branch of the civil service in Ceylon, and next year became inspector of schools there. In 1870 he rose to be director of education; but the climate and work told on his health, and in 1872, when on leave in England, he resigned.

In 1873 Sendall became assistant poor law inspector in the Oxfordshire district, but during 1875 these appointments were abolished and for six months he was out of employment and devoted himself to studying and reporting on the Dutch poor laws. Then in 1876 he became a poor law inspector in Yorkshire under the local government board; in 1878 he was appointed an assistant secretary of the board. Ambitious to follow the career of a colonial administrator, he in 1882 accepted an offer of the lieutenant-governorship of Natal. But the politicians of that colony declined to approve the choice of one so little known, and the nomination was withdrawn.

In 1885 Sendall became the first governor in chief of the Windward Islands on their separation from Barbados. Here he organised the new administration, living at the charming little government house of Grenada, which became the chief island of the group. In 1889 he was transferred to Barbados, and in 1892 became high commissioner of Cyprus, with the progress of which he closely identified himself. At the end of his term in 1898 he was transferred to British Guiana, where he arrived on 23 March. With the question of the boundary of the dependency with Venezuela, which was the subject of arbitration during his governorship, he had nothing directly to do. He left the colony on retirement on 1 Aug. 1901. Next year he represented the West Indian colonies at the coronation of King Edward VII.

Sendall appeared to lack quickness of sympathy and personal geniality, but his sound judgment and high character won him unqualified esteem and confidence in his capacity of governor. He was made C.M.G. in 1887, K.C.M.G. in 1889, and G.C.M.G. in 1899. He received the honorary LL.D. degree from Edinburgh. In his retirement he found recreation in literary work, as well as in the microscope, mechanics, and the lathe. He was a fellow of the Linnean, Royal Microscopical, and other scientific societies, as well as of the Hellenic Society. He was also chairman of the Charity Organisation Society. He edited the 'Literary Remains of C. S. Calverley,' with a memoir, in 1885.

Sendall died at Kensington on 16 March

1904. His remains were cremated and interred at Golder's Green. He married in 1870 Elizabeth Sophia, daughter of Henry Calverley, vicar of South Stoke, and prebendary of Wells. He left no issue. A bust was executed by Edward Lantéri. A memorial bronze has been placed in the chapel of St. Michael and St. George in St. Paul's Cathedral.

[Who's Who, 1903; C. O. List, 1903; The Times, 17 March 1904; private information; personal knowledge.] C. A. H.

SERGEANT, ADELINE (1851–1904), novelist, whose full Christian names were Emily Frances Adeline, born at Ashbourne, Derbyshire, on 4 July 1851, was second daughter of Richard Sergeant by his wife Jane, daughter of Thomas Hall, a Wesleyan minister. The father came of a Lincolnshire family, long settled at Melton Ross, which in the eighteenth century revival embraced dissent of a pronounced and political type. He began lay preaching as a lad, was accepted as a candidate for the Wesleyan ministry at seventeen, and sent to the Hoxton Institution under Dr. Jabez Bunting [q. v.]. He spent six years in Jamaica, married in 1840, abandoned missionary work and became a travelling preacher. He issued 'Letters from Jamaica' (1843), and with the Rev. R. Williams, a 'Compendium of the History and Polity of Methodism,' with other Wesleyan tracts and sermons. His wife, under the name 'Adeline,' wrote many evangelical lays and stories as well as 'Scenes in the West Indies and Other Poems' (1843; 2nd edit. 1849) and 'Stray Leaves' (1855).

Adeline Sergeant was thus brought up amid much literary and spiritual activity. At first educated by her mother, she was sent at thirteen to a school at Weston-super-Mare. At fifteen a volume of her poems was published (1866) with an introduction by 'Adeline'; it was noticed favourably in Wesleyan periodicals. From 'Laleham,' the nonconformist school at Clapham, the girl went to Queen's College, London, with a presentation from the Governesses' Benevolent Institution, and she won a scholarship there.

On her father's death in 1870 she joined the Church of England, and for the greater part of ten years was governess in the family of Canon Burn-Murdoch at Riverhead, Kent. After some minor literary experiments she in 1882 won a prize of 100*l.*, offered by the 'People's Friend' of Dundee, with a novel, 'Jacobi's Wife,' which she wrote while she was visiting Egypt with her friends, Professor and Mrs. Sheldon Amos. The work appeared serially in the paper and was published in London in 1887. By agreement with the proprietors of the 'People's Friend,' John Leng & Co., she was a regular contributor until her death, and gave the firm for a time exclusive serial rights in her stories. She wrote at great speed and two or three novels ran serially every year through the Dundee newspaper. For two years (1885–7) she lived in Dundee.

From 1887 to 1901 her home was in Bloomsbury, where, while busily engaged on fiction, she took an active part in humanitarian efforts, such as rescue work and girls' clubs; she also joined the Fabian Society and travelled much abroad, spending the spring of 1899 in Palestine. Her religious opinions underwent various developments. Her best novel, 'No Saint' (1886), reflects a phase of agnosticism. From 1893 she associated herself with the extreme ritualists at St. Alban's, Holborn, and on 23 Oct. 1899 was received into the Roman catholic church. The processes of thought she described in 'Roads to Rome, being Personal Records of some . . . Converts,' with an introduction by Cardinal Vaughan (1901). She removed to Bournemouth in 1901, and died there on 4 Dec. 1904.

Miss Sergeant wrote over ninety novels and tales. Her fertility, which prejudiced such literary power as she possessed, grew with her years (cf. *Punch*, 11 Nov. 1903, p. 338). Six novels appeared annually from 1901 to 1903, and eight in her last year. After her death fourteen volumes, seven in 1905, four in 1906, two in 1907, and one in 1908, presented work which had not been previously published. She often made an income of over 1000*l.* a year, but her generous and unbusinesslike temperament kept her poor.

Miss Sergeant, who was most successful in drawing the middle-class provincial nonconformist home, is seen to advantage in 'Esther Denison' (1889) (partly autobiographical), in 'The Story of a Penitent Soul' (anon. 1892), and in 'The Idol Maker' (1897). Other of her works are: 1. 'Beyond Recall,' 1882; 2nd edit. 1883. 2. 'Under False Pretences,' 1892; 2nd edit. 1899. 3. 'The Surrender of Margaret Bellarmine,' 1894. 4. 'The Story of Phil Enderby,' 1898, 1903. 5. 'In Vallombrosa,' dedicated to Leader Scott, 1897. 6. 'This Body of Death,' 1901. 7. 'A Soul Apart,' her one catholic novel, 1902. 8. 'Anthea's Way,' 1903. 9 'Beneath the Veil,' 1903, 1905. She contributed to 'Women Novelists of the Nineteenth Century' (1897), and was one of twenty-four authors who wrote without collusion 'The Fate of Fenella,' which appeared serially in the 'Gentlewoman' and was published in 1892.

[Life, by Winifred Stephens, 1905; Roads to Rome, 1901; works and personal knowledge; Athenæum, 10 Dec. 1904.] C. F. S.

SERGEANT, LEWIS (1841–1902), journalist and author, son of John Sergeant, who was at one time a schoolmaster at Cheltenham, by his wife Mary Anne, daughter of George Lewis, was born at Barrow-on-Humber, Lincolnshire, on 10 Nov. 1841. Adeline Sergeant [q. v. Suppl. II.] was Lewis's first cousin, being daughter of Richard Sergeant, his father's brother.

Lewis, after education under a private tutor, matriculated at St. Catharine's College, Cambridge, in 1861, graduating B.A. with mathematical honours in 1865. At the union he distinguished himself as an ardent liberal and supporter of Mr. Gladstone. On leaving college, after a period as assistant master under Dr. Hayman at Cheltenham grammar school, he took to journalism, becoming editor, in succession, of 'An anti-Game Law Journal,' of the 'Examiner,' and of the 'Hereford Times.' He was afterwards long connected with the 'Athenæum' and with the London 'Daily Chronicle' as leader writer. He became meanwhile a recognised authority on education, was elected to the council of the College of Preceptors, and edited the 'Educational Times' from 1895 to 1902.

Deeply interested in modern Greece, he worked zealously in Greek interests. From 1878 onwards he acted as hon. secretary of the Greek committee in London. He published 'New Greece' in the same year (republished 1879), and 'Greece' in 1880. There followed 'Greece in the Nineteenth Century: a Record of Hellenic Emancipation and Progress, 1821–1897,' with illustrations, in 1897. King George of Greece bestowed on him the Order of the Redeemer in October 1878.

Sergeant's historical writings covered a wide ground, and include: 1. 'England's Policy: its Traditions and Problems,' Edinburgh, 1881. 2. 'William Pitt,' in 'English Political Leaders' series, 1882. 3. 'John Wyclif,' in 'Heroes of the Nations' series, 1893. 4. 'The Franks' in 'Story of the Nations' series, 1898. He also wrote a volume of verse; a novel, 'The Caprice of Julia' (1898); and other fiction pseudonymously. Sergeant died at Bournemouth on 3 Feb. 1902. He married on 12 April 1871 Emma Louisa, daughter of James Robertson of Cheltenham, and left, with other children, an elder son, Philip Walsingham Sergeant, author of historical biographies.

[The Times, 4 Feb. 1902; Athenæum, 8 Feb. 1902; Sphere (with portrait), 8 Feb. 1902; Who's Who, 1901; Hatton's Journalistic London, 1882; private information.] C. F. S.

SETON, GEORGE (1822–1908), Scottish genealogist, herald, and legal writer, only son of George Seton of the East India Company's service, and Margaret, daughter of James Hunter of Seaside, was born at Perth on 25 June 1822. He was the representative of the Setons of Cariston, senior coheir of Sir Thomas Seton of Olivestob and heir of a line of Mary Seton, one of 'the Four Maries' of the Queen of Scots. He was brought up by his widowed mother, and after attending the High School and University of Edinburgh, entered on 11 Nov. 1841 Exeter College, Oxford (B.A. 1845 and M.A. 1848). He was called to the Scottish bar in 1846, but did not persevere in seeking to obtain a practice. In 1854 he was appointed secretary to the registrar-general for Scotland in Edinburgh, and in 1862 superintendent of the civil service examinations in Scotland; he held both offices till 1889. He was one of the founders of the St. Andrews Boat Club (Edinburgh) in 1846, the first vice-chairman of the Society for Improving the Condition of the Poor, a fellow of the Royal Society of Edinburgh and of the Society of Antiquaries of Scotland. Keenly interested in the characteristics of different nations and peoples, he spent much of his time in travelling, visiting Russia, Canada, and South Africa. Over six feet five inches in height, he was also of fine athletic build and lithe and active to an advanced age. Owing to his great height he occupied the position of right-hand man in the royal bodyguard of Scottish archers. He raised in 1859 a company of forty volunteer grenadier artillerymen (Midlothian coast artillery), all over six feet high. He died in Edinburgh on 14 Nov. 1908. By Sarah Elizabeth (*d.* 1883), second daughter of James Hunter of Thurston, whom he married in 1849, he had a surviving son, George, engaged in Indian tea-planting industry at first in Calcutta and then in London, and three daughters, of whom two predeceased him.

Seton's two principal works are 'The

Law and Practice of Heraldry in Scotland' (Edinburgh, 1863), a standard work, and the minutely learned and sumptuous 'Memoirs of an Ancient House: a History of the Family of Seton during Eight Centuries' (2 vols., privately printed, Edinburgh, 1896). Two other privately printed books are 'The Life of Alexander Seton, Earl of Dumfermline, Lord Chancellor of Scotland' (Edinburgh, 1882) and 'The House of Moncrieff' for Sir Alexander Moncrieff, K.C.B. (Edinburgh, 1890). His other works include: 1. 'Genealogical Tables of the Kings of England and Scotland,' 1845. 2. 'Treatment of Social Evils,' 1853. 3. 'Sketch of the History and Imperfect Condition of the Parochial Records of Scotland,' 1854. 4. 'Practical Analysis of the Acts relating to the Registration of Births, Deaths and Marriages,' 1854; 5th edit. 1861. 5. 'Cakes, Leeks, Puddings, and Potatoes' (a lecture on the national characteristics of the United Kingdom), 1864; 2nd edit. 1865. 6. 'Gossip about Letters and Letter Writers,' 1870. 7. 'The Convent of St. Catherine of Sienna near Edinburgh,' 1871. 8. 'The Social Pyramid,' 1878. 9. 'St. Kilda, Past and Present,' 1878. 10. 'Amusements for the People,' 1880. 11. 'Budget of Anecdotes relating to the Current Century,' 1886; 3rd edit. 1903. He also contributed various papers to the 'Transactions' of the Edinburgh Royal Society and the Scottish Society of Antiquaries.

[Who's Who; The Times, 16 Nov. 1908; Scotsman, 16 Nov. 1908; Seton's History of the House of Seton, which includes a biography of himself; Foster's Alumni Oxonienses.] T. F. H.

SEVERN, WALTER (1830–1904), water-colour artist, born at Frascati, near Rome, on 12 Oct. 1830, was eldest son of Joseph Severn [q.v.] by his wife Elizabeth, daughter of Archibald, Lord Montgomerie. His brother Arthur became a distinguished landscape painter, and his sister Mary, who married Sir Charles Newton [q. v. Suppl. I], was a clever figure painter. Walter was sent in 1843 with his brother Arthur to Westminster School, and from an early age showed a fondness for art. In 1852 he entered the civil service, and was for thirty-three years an officer in the education department. Meanwhile he took a lively interest in varied branches of art. In 1857, with his friend Charles Eastlake [q. v. Suppl. II], he started the making of art furniture. In 1865 he made a vigorous effort to resuscitate the almost forgotten craft of art needlework and embroidery, for skill in which he earned medals in South Kensington and much encouragement from Ruskin. But his leisure was chiefly devoted to landscape painting in water-colours. Fifty of his water-colours were exhibited in 1874 at Agnew's Gallery in Bond Street. The most popular of his works, 'Our Boys,' circulated widely in an engraving. He also made illustrations for Lord Houghton's poem 'Good Night and Good Morning' in 1859. In 1861 he published an illustrated Prayer Book, and in 1865 an illustrated calendar. In 1865 Severn instituted the Dudley Gallery Art Society. The Old Water-colour Society had lately rejected his brother Arthur when he applied for membership. The Institute of Painters in Water-colours also seemed to Severn too exclusive. He accordingly called a meeting of fifty artists at his brother's house, when Tom Taylor [q. v.], art critic of 'The Times,' took the chair, and the Dudley Gallery Art Society was the outcome. Exhibitions were held annually at the Egyptian Hall in Piccadilly until its demolition in 1909, when they were continued in the new building erected on the site of the hall. The artists who sent pictures included Albert and Henry Moore, George Leslie, Burne-Jones, and Watts. The merit of the Dudley Society's exhibitions led the Institute of Painters in Water-colours in 1883 to elect several of its members 'en bloc,' including Severn's brother Arthur, but not himself. Severn was elected president of the Dudley Society in 1883, and held office till his death on 22 Sept. 1904 at Earl's Court Square.

Examples of Severn's work are at the National Galleries of Melbourne, Sydney, and Adelaide. There is a portrait of him painted by C. Perugini.

He married on 28 Dec. 1866 Mary Dalrymple, daughter of Sir Charles Dalrymple Fergusson, fifth baronet, by whom he had five sons and one daughter.

[William Sharp's Life and Letters of Joseph Severn; Gordon's Life of Dean Buckland; The Times, 23 Sept. 1904; private information.] F. W. G-N.

SEWELL, ELIZABETH MISSING (1815–1906), author, born at High Street, Newport, Isle of Wight, on 19 Feb. 1815, was third daughter in a family of seven sons and five daughters of Thomas Sewell (1775–1842), solicitor, of Newport, and his wife Jane Edwards (1773–1848). She was sister of Henry Sewell [q. v.], of James Edwards Sewell [q. v. Suppl. II], warden of New College, Oxford, of Richard Clarke Sewell [q. v.], and of William Sewell (1804-

1874) [q. v.]. Elizabeth was educated first at Miss Crooke's school at Newport, and afterwards at the Misses Aldridge's school, Bath. At the age of fifteen she went home, and joined her sister Ellen, two years her senior, in teaching her younger sisters.

About 1840 her brother William introduced her to some of the leaders of the Oxford movement, among others, Keble, Newman, and Henry Wilberforce. Influenced by the religious stir of the period, she published in 1840, in 'The Cottage Monthly,' 'Stories illustrative of the Lord's Prayer,' which appeared in book form in 1843. Like all her early works these 'stories' were represented to have been edited by her brother William.

The family experienced money difficulties through the failure of two local banks, and the father died in 1842 deep in debt. Elizabeth and the other children undertook to pay off the creditors, and set aside each year, from her literary earnings, a certain sum until all was liquidated. Until 1844 the family lived at Pidford or Ventnor, but in that year Mrs. Sewell and her daughters settled at Sea View, Bonchurch. Elizabeth bought the house, enlarged it in 1854, and later changed the name to Ashcliff.

In 1844 Miss Sewell published 'Amy Herbert,' a well written tale for girls, embodying Anglican views. It has been many times reprinted and has enjoyed great success both in England and in America. In 1846 there followed two of the three parts of 'Laneton Parsonage,' a tale for children on the practical use of a portion of the Church Catechism. She interrupted her work on this book to publish 'Margaret Perceval' (1847), in which at the suggestion of her brother William she urged on young people, in view of the current secessions to Rome, the claims of the English church. The third part of 'Laneton Parsonage' appeared in 1848.

Her mother died in 1847, and in 1849 Miss Sewell made an expedition to the Lakes with her Bonchurch neighbours Captain and Lady Jane Swinburne and their son Algernon, the poet, then a boy of twelve. They visited Wordsworth at Rydal Mount. In 1852 she published 'The Experience of Life,' a novel largely based on her own experience and observations; her most notable literary production.

Miss Sewell had now assumed responsibility for the financial affairs of the family, and finding that her writing was not sufficiently lucrative, she and her sister Ellen (1813–1905) decided to take pupils. They never regarded their venture as a school, but as a 'family home,' which they conducted till 1891. They began with six girls, including their nieces. Seven was the customary number. Miss Sewell defined her methods of education in her 'Principles of Education, drawn from Nature and Revelation, and applied to Female Education in the Upper Classes' (1865). Good accounts of the life at Ashcliff are given in Miss Whitehead's 'Recollections of Miss Elizabeth Sewell and her Sisters' (1910, pp. 15–26 and pp. 33–42) and in Mrs. Hugh Fraser's 'A Diplomatist's Life in Many Lands' (1910, pp. 220–32); both the writers were pupils. Miss Sewell defied the demands of examinations, and made her pupils read widely, and take an interest in the questions of the day (cf. her article 'The Reign of Pedantry in Girls' Schools' in *Nineteenth Century*, 1888). She herself gave admirable lessons in general history. The holidays were often passed abroad, and in 1860 Miss Sewell spent five months in Italy and Germany, the outcome of which was a volume entitled 'Impressions of Rome, Florence, and Turin' (1862). She was in Germany again at the outbreak of the war of 1870 (cf. *Autobiography*, pp. 185–9). On visits to London and Oxford she met among others Miss Yonge, Dean Stanley, and Robert Browning. She had made Tennyson's acquaintance in the Isle of Wight in 1857.

In 1866 Miss Sewell, convinced of the need of better education for girls of the middle class, founded at Ventnor St. Boniface School, which came to have a building of its own and to be known as St. Boniface Diocesan School. Its many years' prosperity was gradually checked by the High Schools which came into being in 1872. The death of her sister Emma in 1897 caused deep depression, and her brain became gradually clouded. She died at Ashcliff, Bonchurch, on 17 Aug. 1906, and was buried in the churchyard there. A prayer desk was put up in memory of her by pupils and friends in Bonchurch church, where there is also a tablet commemorating Miss Sewell and her two sisters.

Miss Sewell's influence over young people was helped by her dry humour. Despite her firm Anglican convictions, she won the ear of those who held other views. She was an accomplished letter writer. Of small stature, with well-marked features, and fine brown eyes, she was painted by Miss Porter in 1890. That portrait and some sketches of her by her sister Ellen are in possession of Miss Eleanor Sewell at Ashcliff.

Between 1847 and 1868 Miss Sewell published, besides those already mentioned, seven tales, of which 'Ursula' (1858) is the most important. She wrote also many devotional works and schoolbooks. Of the former 'Thoughts for Holy Week' (1857) and 'Preparation for the Holy Communion' (1864) have been often reprinted, as late as 1907 and 1910 respectively. Her schoolbooks chiefly deal with history, and two volumes of 'Historical Selections' (1868) were written in collaboration with Miss Yonge. Miss Sewell contributed to the 'Monthly Packet.' Her autobiography appeared in 1907.

[The Times, 18 Aug. 1906; Autobiography of Elizabeth M. Sewell, ed. Eleanor L. Sewell, 1907; C. M. W[hitehead]'s Recollections of Miss Elizabeth Sewell and her Sisters, 1910; Mountague Charles Owen's The Sewells of the Isle of Wight; Brit. Mus. Cat.; private information.] E. L.

SEWELL, JAMES EDWARDS (1810–1903), warden of New College, Oxford, born at Newport, Isle of Wight, on 25 Dec. 1810, was seventh child and sixth son of Thomas Sewell, solicitor, of Newport, by his wife Jane, daughter of Rev. John Edwards, curate of Newport. He was one of a family of twelve, which included Richard Clarke Sewell, legal writer [q. v.], William Sewell, divine [q. v.], Henry Sewell, first premier of New Zealand [q. v.], and Elizabeth Missing Sewell [q. v. Suppl. II], authoress. Admitted a scholar of Winchester College in 1821, James became a probationary fellow of New College, Oxford, in 1827, and a full fellow in 1829. He graduated B.A. in 1832, proceeding M.A. in 1835, B.D. and D.D. in 1860, and was ordained deacon in 1834 and priest in 1836. Except for a few months in 1834–5, when he was curate to Archdeacon Heathcote [q. v.] at Hursley, he resided in New College from 1827 to his death in 1903. He filled successively every office in the college, and in 1860 was elected warden. He took a large part in university affairs, was the first secretary of the Oxford local examinations delegacy, and from 1874 to 1878 was vice-chancellor. He actively aided in the preservation and arrangement of the MS. records in the library of the college. The chief share in the growth of New College during his long wardenship is to be attributed to his colleagues, but Sewell loyally accepted changes which did not commend themselves to his own judgment. It was largely owing to him that there was no break in the continuity of college tradition and feeling, and that older generations of Wykehamists were reconciled to the reforms made by successive commissions and by the college itself. Sewell died unmarried in the warden's lodgings, New College, on 29 January 1903, and was buried in the cloisters of the college. A portrait by Sir Hubert von Herkomer (which has been engraved) hangs in the hall of New College. A cartoon portrait by 'Spy' appeared in 'Vanity Fair' in 1894. Sewell compiled a list of the wardens and fellows of New College, with notes on their careers; the MS. is preserved in the college library.

[The Sewells of the Isle of Wight, by Mountague Charles Owen (privately printed); Rashdall and Rait's New College (Oxford College Histories); New College, 1856–1906, by Hereford B. George, 1906.] R. S. R.

SHAND (afterwards BURNS), ALEXANDER, BARON SHAND OF WOODHOUSE (1828–1904), Scottish judge and lord of appeal, born at Aberdeen on 13 Dec. 1828, was son of Alexander Shand, merchant in Aberdeen, by his wife Louisa, daughter of John Whyte, M.D., of Banff. His grandfather, John Shand, was parish minister of Kintore. Losing his father in early boyhood, he was taken to Glasgow by his mother, who there married William Burns, writer, in whose office her son worked as a clerk while attending lectures at Glasgow University (1842–8). He assumed the surname of Burns, and was a law student at Edinburgh University (1848–52), spending during the period a short time at Heidelberg University. He became a member of the Scots Law Society and of the Juridical Society (17 March 1852), and passed to the Scottish bar on 26 Nov. 1853. His progress was rapid, and he was soon in full practice. In 1860 he was appointed advocate depute, in 1862 sheriff of Kincardine, and in 1869 of Haddington and Berwick. In 1872 he was raised to the bench. After serving with great distinction as a judge for eighteen years, he retired, and settled in London in 1890.

On 21 Oct. 1890 he was sworn of the privy council, and on 11 November following took his seat at the board of the judicial committee (under the Appellate Jurisdictions Act, 1887, 50 & 51 Vict. c. 70, sect. 3) as a privy councillor who had held 'a high judicial position.' He was elected an honorary bencher of Gray's Inn on 23 March 1892. On 20 August of that year he was raised to the peerage as Baron Shand of Woodhouse, Dumfriesshire, and for twelve years sat in the House of Lords as a lord of appeal. Of these, one of the last, and by far the most important, was the appeal by the minority of the Free Church of Scotland against the judgment of the Court of Session which rejected the minority's claim to the whole property of the Free Church on union with the United Presbyterians. Six lords of appeal heard the arguments, which finished on 7 Dec. 1903. Judgment was reserved. Shand and two other lords were believed to uphold the judgment of the Court of Session; but on 6 March 1904 Shand died in London, and was buried at Kintore, Aberdeenshire. In consequence of his death the appeal was re-heard by seven judges, who, on 1 August 1904, by a majority of five to two, reversed the judgment under review, and gave the whole property of the Free Church to the small minority which had opposed the union. The unfortunate effects of this decision were afterwards partially remedied by a commission, appointed in 1905, under Mr. Balfour's administration, which distributed the property on an equitable basis (5 Edw. VII, c. 12).

In politics Shand was a liberal, but never prominent. He took a useful share in public business, was president of the Watt Institute and School of Arts at Edinburgh, an active member of the Educational Endowments Commission of 1882, and in Jan. 1894 was nominated by the speaker of the House of Commons chairman of the coal industry conciliation board. He wrote letters to 'The Times' on law reform, and frequently delivered lectures to public bodies on that subject, publishing addresses in favour of the appointment of a minister of justice for Great Britain (before the Scots Law Society, 1874); on 'the liability of employers: a system of insurance by the mutual contributions of masters and workmen the best provision for accidents' (before the Glasgow Juridical Society, 1879); and on technical education (before the Watt Institute and School of Arts, 1882). He was made honorary LL.D. of Glasgow in 1873, and D.C.L. of Oxford in 1895.

Shand married in 1857 Emily Merelina (*d.* 1911), daughter of John Clarke Meymott, but had no family. He was of unusually small stature. A portrait of him, by Sir George Reid, hangs in one of the committee rooms at Gray's Inn. A caricature by 'Spy' appeared in 'Vanity Fair' in 1903.

[Scotsman, and The Times, 7 March 1904; Records of the Juridical Society; Roll of Faculty of Advocates; Law Reports, Appeals, 1904, pp. 515–764.] G. W. T. O.

SHAND, ALEXANDER INNES (1832–1907), journalist and critic, born at Fettercairn, Kincardineshire, on 2 July 1832, was only child of William Shand of Arnhalt, Fettercairn, by his second wife, Christina (*d.* 1855) daughter of Alexander Innes of Pitmedden, Aberdeenshire. His father possessed a considerable estate in Demerara, but his income was greatly reduced on the abolition of slavery. The family then moved to Aberdeen, where Alexander, after being educated at Blair Lodge school, entered the university, graduating M.A. in 1852.

Declining an offer of a commission in the 12th Bengal cavalry, owing to his widowed mother's objection to his going abroad, he turned to the law. But in 1855, on his mother's death, he began a series of prolonged and systematic European tours. When at home he engaged in sport and natural history on the estate of Major John Ramsay, a cousin, at Straloch in Aberdeenshire. In 1865 he was admitted to the Scottish bar and, marrying, settled in Edinburgh. Owing to his wife's health he soon migrated to Sydenham, and while there he discovered his true vocation. After contributing papers on 'Turkey,' 'America,' and other subjects during 1867 to the 'Imperial Review,' a short-lived conservative paper under the editorship of Henry Cecil Raikes [q. v.], he began writing for 'The Times' and for 'Blackwood's Magazine,' and also joined the brilliant staff of John Douglas Cook [q. v.], editor of the 'Saturday Review.' To these three publications he remained a prolific contributor for life, although at the same time he wrote much elsewhere. 'He fluked himself,' he wrote, 'into a literary income' (*Days of the Past*). But although he wrote too rapidly and fluently to be concise or always accurate, his habit of constant travel, wide reading, good memory, and powers of observation made him a first-rate journalist. To 'The Times' he contributed biographies of, among others, Tennyson, Lord Beaconsfield, and Napoleon III (cf. SHAND'S 'Memories of The Times,' *Cornhill Mag.* April 1904), as well as descriptive articles from abroad, from the west of Ireland and the highlands of Scotland, several series of which were collected for separate issue. He was also an occasional correspondent for the newspaper during the Franco-German war (1870), republishing his articles as 'On the Trail of the War.'

Shand at the same time wrote novels which enjoyed some success, but he showed to greater advantage in biography. In 1895 he published a life of his intimate friend, Sir Edward Hamley [q. v. Suppl. I], which reached a second edition. 'Old World Travel' (1903) and 'Days of the Past' (1905), consisting mainly of later sketches in the 'Saturday Review,' give a charming picture of Shand's character, of his capacity for making friends with 'poachers, gamekeepers, railway guards, coach drivers, railway porters, and Swiss guides,' and of his experience of London clubs, where he was at home in all circles. A tory of the old school, he united strong personal convictions with large-hearted tolerance. Among his friends were George Meredith, Laurence Oliphant, and George Smith the publisher. He was devoted to children and all animals, especially dogs, was a fine rider, good shot, and expert angler. He knew how to cook the game he killed, and wrote well on culinary matters.

In 1893 he was British commissioner with Sir Philip Cunliffe Owen at the Paris Exhibition. He was busily engaged in writing till his death, which took place on 20 Sept. 1907 at Edenbridge, Kent. He was buried in the churchyard of Crookham Hill. He married on 25 July 1865 Elizabeth Blanche, daughter of William Champion Streatfeild, of Chart's Edge, Westerham, Kent. She died on 6 June 1882, leaving no children.

Shand published, besides the works mentioned: 1. 'Against Time,' a novel, 1870. 2. 'Shooting the Rapids,' a novel, 1872. 3. 'Letters from the Highlands,' 1884. 4. 'Letters from the West of Ireland,' 1885. 5. 'Fortune's Wheel,' a novel, 1886. 6. 'Half a Century,' 1887. 7. 'Kilcurra,' a novel, 1891. 8. 'Mountain, Stream and Covert,' 1897. 9. 'The Lady Grange,' a novel, 1897. 10. 'The War in the Peninsula,' 1898. 11. 'Shooting' (in 'Haddon Hall Library'), in collaboration, 1899. 12. 'Life of General John Jacob,' 1900. 13. 'Wellington's Lieutenants,' 1902. 14. 'The Gun Room,' 1903. 15. 'Dogs' (in 'Young England Library'), 1903. There came out posthumously: 16. 'Soldiers of Fortune,' 1907. 17. 'Memories of Gardens' (his last sketches in the 'Saturday Review'), 1908.

Shand also contributed chapters on 'Cookery' to 8 vols. of the 'Fur, Fin, and Feather' series (1898–1905), and prefixed a memoir to Kinglake's 'Eothen' (1890 edition).

[Sir Rowland Blennerhassett's memoir prefixed to Memories of Gardens, 1908; The Times, 23 Sept. 1907; Shand's works, especially Old World Travel and Days of the Past; private information.] W. B. D.

SHARP, WILLIAM, writing also under the pseudonym of FIONA MACLEOD (1855–1905), romanticist, born at Paisley, on 12 Sept. 1855, was eldest son of David Galbraith Sharp, partner in a mercantile house, by his wife Katherine, eldest daughter of William Brooks, Swedish vice-consul at Glasgow. The Sharp family came originally from near Dunblane. His mother was partly of Celtic descent, but he owed his peculiar Celtic predilections either to the stories and songs of his Highland nurse or to visits three or four months each year to the shores of the western highlands. After receiving his early education at home he went to Blair Lodge school, from which with some companions he ran away thrice, the last time in a vain attempt to get to sea as stowaways at Grangemouth. In his twelfth year the family removed to Glasgow, and he went as day scholar to the Glasgow Academy. At the University of Glasgow, which he entered in 1871, he showed ability in the class of English literature; but it was mainly through access to the library that he found the university of advantage.

After spending a month or two with a band of gypsies, he was placed by his father, in 1874, in a lawyer's office in Glasgow, mainly with a view to discipline. While faithful to his office duties, he devoted himself to reading, the theatres, and similar diversions, allowing himself but four hours' sleep. After the death of his father in 1876 consumption threatened, and he went on a sailing voyage to Australia. Although he enjoyed a tour in the interior, the colonist's rough life was uncongenial, and he returned to Scotland resolved to 'be a poet and write about Mother Nature and her inner mysteries.' Without means or prospects, he was about to join the Turkish army against Russia in 1878 when a friend procured him a clerkship in London at the City of Melbourne Bank. Meanwhile he began to contribute verses to periodicals, and in 1881 he had the 'extraordinary good fortune' of obtaining from Sir Noel Paton an introduction to Dante Gabriel Rossetti, who encouraged him with kindly criticism and advice. Through Rossetti he obtained access to many 'literary houses' (see *Life*, p. 53). Failing to satisfy the requirements of the bank, he obtained a temporary post in the Fine Art Society's gallery in Bond Street; but soon depending wholly on his pen for a livelihood, he often ran risk of starvation.

At the end of 1882 Sharp wrote a short life of Rossetti (who died in April 1882). In 1882, too, appeared a volume of poems, 'The Human Inheritance,' which obtained some recognition and led to an invitation from the editor of 'Harper's Magazine' for other poems, which brought him 40*l.* A cheque for 200*l.* sent him by an unknown friend enabled him to study art in Italy for five months (1883–4). He contributed a series of articles on Etruscan cities to the 'Glasgow Herald,' and was appointed art critic to the paper. In 1884 he married his cousin and published a second volume of verse, 'Earth's Voices,' vividly impressionist, but somewhat diffuse. In 1884 he became editor of the 'Canterbury Poets,' contributing himself editions of Shakespeare's Sonnets (1885), English Sonnets (1886), American Sonnets (1889), and Great Odes (1890). For a series of 'Biographies of Great Writers' he wrote on Shelley (1887), Heine (1888), and Browning (1890). He also published 'The Sport of Chance' (1888), a sensational story, for the 'People's Friend'; contributed boys' stories to 'Young Folks,' which he edited in 1887; and published 'Romantic Ballads and Poems of Phantasy' (1888; 2nd edit. 1889), fluently fanciful but lacking in finish, and 'The Children of To-morrow' (1889), a romantic tale, in which he voiced his impatience of conventionality.

A visit in the autumn of 1889 to the United States and Canada reawakened his desire to wander. After a stay of some months in the summer of 1890 in Scotland and a tour through Germany, he went in the late autumn to Rome, where he wrote a series of impressionist unrhymed poems in irregular metre, 'Sospiri di Roma,' printed for private circulation in 1891. In the spring of that year he left Italy for Provence on the way to London, where he completed the 'Life and Letters of Joseph Severn' (published in 1892). Subsequently at Stuttgart he collaborated with the American novelist, Blanche Willis Howard, in a novel, 'A Fellowe and his Wife' (published in 1892). In the winter of 1891–2 he was again in America, when through an introduction from his friend, the American poet, E. C. Stedman, he had an interview with Walt Whitman. He also arranged for the publication in America of his 'Romantic Ballads' and 'Sospiri di Roma' in one volume, under the title 'Flower o' the Vine' (New York, 1892). The spring of 1892 was spent in Paris and the summer in London; and in the autumn he rented Phenice Croft, a cottage in Sussex, where, probably under the impulse of the Whitman visit and in a fit of irresponsible high spirits, he projected the 'Pagan Review,' edited by himself as W. H. Brooks and wholly written by himself under various pseudonyms. Only one number appeared; and, owing to his wife's unsatisfactory health, he set himself to the completion of two stories for 'Young Folks,' in order to obtain money to spend the winter in North Africa. Returning to England in the spring of 1893, he, while busy with articles and stories for the magazines, prepared a series of dramatic interludes, entitled 'Vistas'—'vistas of the inner life of the human soul, psychic episodes' (published 1894).

At Rome in 1890 he began a friendship with a lady who, 'because of her beauty, her strong sense of life and of the joy of life,' stood as 'a symbol of the heroic women of Greek and Celtic days, . . . unlocked new doors' within him, and put him 'in touch with ancestral memories' (*Life*, p. 223). Sharp thenceforth devoted himself to a new kind of literary work, penning much mystical prose and verse under the pseudonym of 'Fiona Macleod,' whose identity with himself he carefully concealed. Although in this phase of his literary production there was no collaboration with the lady of his idealism, he yet believed 'that without her there would have been no Fiona Macleod.' Much of the 'Fiona' literature was written under the influence of a kind of mesmeric or spiritual trance, or was the record of such trances.

The first of the books which Sharp wrote under the pseudonym of 'Fiona Macleod' was begun at Phenice Croft in 1893. It appeared in 1894 as 'Pharais: a Romance of the Isles,' and Sharp declared it to have been written 'with the pen dipped in the very ichor of my life.' The 'Fiona' series was continued in 1895 in 'The Mountain Lovers,' 'more elemental still' (1895), and 'The Sin Eater,' consisting of Celtic tales and myths 'recaptured in dreams' (1895). The latter volume was published by Patrick Geddes and Colleagues, a firm established in Edinburgh by Professor Geddes, with Sharp as literary adviser, for the publication of Celtic literature and works on science. There quickly succeeded 'The Washer of the Ford' (1896), a collection of tales and legendary moralities; 'Green Fire,' a Breton romance (1896), a portion of which, entitled 'The Herdsman,' was included in the 'Dominion of Dreams' (1899; revised American edit.

1901; German trans. Leipzig, 1905); 'From the Hills of Dream,' poems and 'prose rhythms' (Edinb. 1896; new edit. Lond. 1907); 'The Laughter of Peterkin,' a Christmas book of Celtic tales for children (1897); and 'The Divine Adventure; Iona; By Sundown Shores' (1900), a series of essays. A Celtic play, by 'Fiona,' 'The House of Usna,' was performed by the Stage Society at the Globe Theatre on 29 April 1900; and after its appearance in the 'National Review' on 1 July was issued in book form in America in 1903. Another drama, 'The Immortal Hour,' was printed in the 'Fortnightly Review' (Nov. 1900; reissued posthumously in America in 1907 and in London in 1908). 'Fiona' was also a contributor of articles to periodicals, many of which were collected, as 'The Winged Destiny' (1904) and 'Where the Forest murmurs' (1906). Selections of 'Fiona' tales appeared in the Tauchnitz series as 'Wind and Wave' (Leipzig, 1902; German trans. Leipzig, 1905; Danish trans. Stockholm, 1910), and as 'The Sunset of Old Tales' (1905). A uniform edition of 'Fiona's' works was published in England in 1910.

The secret of Sharp's responsibilities for the 'Fiona' literature was well kept in his lifetime. He sedulously encouraged the popular assumption that 'Fiona Macleod' was a young lady endowed with 'the dreamy Celtic genius.' Sharp contributed to 'Who's Who' a fictitious memoir of 'Fiona Macleod,' describing her favourite recreations as 'boating, hill-climbing, and listening,' and he corresponded with her admiring readers through the hand of his sister. Educated Highland Celts detected in the books the imperfection of the supposed lady's Celtic equipment. While her work reflected the influence of old Celtic paganism, it was chiefly coloured by a rapturous worship of nature and mirrored the insistent vividness and weirdness of dreams.

Meanwhile Sharp, under his own name, found it needful, both for pecuniary reasons and for the preservation of the 'Fiona' mystery, to be as productive as before. Fiction mainly occupied him. Of two volumes of short stories, one, 'The Gypsy Christ,' published in America in 1895, was reissued in 1896 in England as 'Madge o' the Pool,' and the other, 'Ecce Puella,' appeared in London in 1896. Later works of fiction were 'Wives in Exile,' a comedy in romance (Boston, Mass. 1896; London 1898) and 'Silence Farm,' a tale of the Lowlands (1899). With Mrs. Sharp he edited in 1896 'Lyra Celtica,' an anthology of Celtic poetry, with introduction and notes; and there followed 'The Progress of Art in the Century' (1902; 2nd edit. 1906) and 'Literary Geography' (from the 'Pall Mall Magazine') (1904; 2nd edit. 1907). In 1896–7 he was also editor of a quarterly periodical, the 'Evergreen,' issued by the Geddes firm. Two volumes of papers, critical and reminiscent, containing some of the best work of William Sharp, are included in a reissue of some of his writings (1912).

The 'Fiona' development, implying the 'continual play of the two forces in him, or of the two sides of his nature,' produced 'a tremendous strain on his physical and mental resources, and at one time, 1897–8, threatened him with a complete nervous collapse' (*Life*, p. 223). He found relief in travel and change of scene: the Highlands, America, Rome, Sicily, Greece, were all included in a constantly recurring itinerary. But his restless energy gradually undermined his constitution. After a cold caught during a drive in the Alcantara valley in Sicily he died at Castle Maniace, the home of his friend, the Duke of Brontë, to the west of Mount Etna, on 14 Dec. 1905. He was buried in a woodland cemetery on the hillside, where an Iona cross, carved in marble, has been erected. He left a letter, to be communicated to his friends, explaining why he found it necessary not to disclose his identity with 'Fiona.'

On 31 Oct. 1884 Sharp married Elizabeth, daughter of his father's elder brother, Thomas Sharp, by Agnes, daughter of Robert Farquharson of Breda and Allargue; he became secretly pledged to her in September 1875. There were no children of the marriage.

Sharp was tall, handsome, fair-haired, and blue-eyed. A painted portrait of him by Daniel Wehrschmidt and a pastel by Charles Ross are in the possession of his widow. There are also etchings by William Strang and Sir Charles Holroyd.

[Memoir by his wife, Elizabeth A. Sharp, 1910; Fiona Macleod, by Mr. Ernest Rhys, in Century Mag., May 1907; Academy, 16 Dec. 1905; Dublin Review, Oct. 1911; information from Mrs. Sharp.] T. F. H.

SHARPE, RICHARD BOWDLER (1847–1909), ornithologist, was born on 22 Nov. 1847, at 1 Skinner Street, Snow Hill, London, where his father, Thomas Bowdler Sharpe, edited and published 'Sharpe's London Magazine.' His grandfather, Lancelot Sharpe, was rector of All Hallows Staining, and headmaster of St. Saviour's grammar school, Southwark. From the age of six till nine Sharpe was under the care of an aunt, Mrs. Magdalen Wallace, widow of the headmaster of Sevenoaks grammar school, and herself a good classical scholar, who kept a preparatory school at Brighton. He afterwards gained a King's scholarship at Peterborough grammar school, where his cousin, the Rev. James Wallace, was master, and he became a choir-boy in the cathedral; but subsequently he migrated to Loughborough grammar school when his cousin was appointed master there.

From 1863 to 1865 Sharpe was a clerk with Messrs, W. H. Smith and Son. From 1865 to 1866 he was in the employment of Bernard Quaritch, the bookseller, where he had access to the finest books about birds; and from 1866 to 1872 he was the first librarian to the Zoological Society.

Meanwhile he was from boyhood devoted to the study of birds, carefully observing them, and enjoying a day's shooting. When about sixteen, he began the 'Monograph of Kingfishers,' which was issued in quarterly parts (1868–71). Prof. Alfred Newton declared the work of the youthful author, 'though still incomplete as regards their anatomy,' to be 'certainly one of the best of its class.' One hundred and twenty-five species were described, and nearly all were 'beautifully figured by Keulemans.'

Sharpe then began a comprehensive 'History of the Birds of Europe,' in collaboration with Mr. H. E. Dresser; but after fifteen parts were issued he abandoned the project on his appointment, in 1872, at the recommendation of Dr. John Edward Gray [q. v.], keeper of zoology in the British Museum, to the post of senior assistant in Gray's own department, to take charge of the birds. In 1895, on the recommendation of Sir William Flower, the director of the museum, a new post, that of assistant keeper of vertebrates, was created, and Sharpe was appointed to it. The sphere of his responsibilities was thus widened; but his own work remained exclusively ornithological. This position he retained till his death. Sharpe was elected a fellow of the Linnean Society in 1870, an honorary fellow of the Zoological Society in 1875, and became LL.D. of Aberdeen in 1891.

To Sharpe was entrusted the preparation of the British Museum Catalogue of Birds. Sharpe wrote no fewer than eleven of the twenty-seven volumes, with parts of two others, comprising more than 5000 species, fully described with bibliography and geographical distribution; a volume by him appeared approximately every two years from 1874 to 1898. His second important official publication was 'A Hand-list of the Genera and Species of Birds' (5 vols. 1899–1909); the last volume was published just before his death. Largely owing to Sharpe's zeal, the ornithological collection under his control at the museum increased from 35,000 specimens to over half a million, four or five times the number in any other museum. The confidence of donors in the use to which Sharpe would put their gifts stimulated their generosity, as was admitted by Mr. Allen Hume, who gave his Indian collection, and by the marquess of Tweeddale, who gave his Asiatic series. In 1886, at Mr. Hume's request, Sharpe went to Simla to pack and bring home his collection of 82,000 specimens.

After the death of John Gould [q. v.] in 1881, Sharpe completed the series of illustrated works on ornithology which Gould left unfinished, including 'The Birds of Asia,' 'The Birds of New Guinea,' and monographs on the trogons and humming birds. The publication extended from 1875 to 1888. Sharpe completed the work in 1893 with an index and memoir. Similarly he issued a revised and augmented edition of E. L. Layard's 'Birds of South Africa' (1875–84); and after the death of Henry Seebohm [q. v.] in 1895, he edited and completed his 'Eggs of British Birds' (1896) and 'Monograph of the Thrushes' (1898–1902).

Sharpe edited Allen's 'Naturalists' Library' in sixteen volumes, the first four volumes, on 'The Birds of Great Britain' (1894–7), being his own writing. More important original contributions to systematic ornithology were his monographs of the swallows, in collaboration with C. W. Wyatt (1885–94), and of the birds of paradise (1891–8). He illustrated the fulness of his scientific knowledge in his catalogue of the osteological specimens in the College of Surgeons Museum (1891), and in the address on the classification of birds at the second International Ornithological Congress at Buda-Pest (1891), when the Emperor of Austria conferred upon him the gold medal for art and science. Sharpe was long a popular lecturer on ornithological topics, showing some exquisite lantern-slides. He issued the substance of some of his lectures as 'Wonders of the Bird World' in 1898.

In 1892 Sharpe founded the British Ornithologists' Club, which organised research, especially with regard to migration; and in 1905 he presided over the

International Ornithological Congress in London, giving a presidential address on the history of the British Museum collection. This he also described in an official volume containing biographies of the various collectors (1906).

A vice-president of the Selborne Society, Sharpe laboriously edited White's 'Natural History' (1900, 2 vols.; for the fancy portraits of White, Sharpe repudiated responsibility, cf. *Nature Notes*, 1902, p. 135). While preparing this edition, Sharpe lived much at Selborne, and thoroughly studied the architecture and records of the district. At his death he had printed part of a work on 'Gilbert White's Country,' and was engaged on a history of the siege of Basing House. He died of pneumonia, at his home in Chiswick, on Christmas Day 1909. Sharpe married in 1867 Emily, daughter of James Walter Burrows of Cookham, who survived him with ten daughters. In 1910 his widow and three daughters were awarded a civil list pension of 90*l*.

In addition to the literary work already mentioned, Sharpe supplied the ornithological portion of the 'Zoological Record' between 1870 and 1908, and he described the birds in the 'Zoology of the Voyage of H.M.S. Erebus and Terror' (1875), in Frank Oates' 'Matabele Land' (1881), in the 'Voyage of H.M.S. Alert' (1884), in J. S. Jameson's 'Emin Pasha Relief Expedition' (1890), in the 'Second Yarkand Mission' (1891), and in the 'Voyage of the Southern Cross' (1902). He was also an extensive contributor to Cassell's 'New Natural History,' edited by Prof. Martin Duncan (1882), the 'Royal Natural History' (1896), and the volume on natural history in the 'Concise Knowledge Library' (1897).

[British Birds, 1910, iii. 273–288 (with a bibliography and photogravure portrait); Selborne Mag. 1910, xxi. 7, 127.] G. S. B.

SHAW, ALFRED (1842–1907), cricketer, born of humble parents at Burton Joyce, a village five miles north of Nottingham, on 29 Aug. 1842, was the youngest of thirteen children. Two of his brothers, William (*b*. 5 Aug. 1827) and Arthur (1834–1874), played in Nottinghamshire cricket. On his mother's death in 1852 Alfred left school to work as a farm servant. At eighteen he was apprenticed to a hand frame knitter. Early developing an aptitude for cricket, in 1862 he succeeded his brother Arthur as professional to the Grantham cricket club. Playing for the Notts Colts against the county eleven in 1863, he first displayed his great power as a bowler by taking 7 wickets, and helping to dismiss the county for 41 runs. In 1864, on his first appearance at Lord's for the Colts of England *v*. M.C.C., Shaw took 7 wickets for 24 runs and 6 for 39. Straightway appointed to the ground staff at Lord's, he held the post (with a brief interval in 1868 and 1869 when he was a member of George Parr's All-England eleven) until 1882. For several seasons he was the club's leading bowler.

Shaw played regularly for Notts from 1865 to 1887, and to his bowling was largely due the high position of the county during that period. His best bowling performances were for the M.C.C. *v*. the North of England, in June 1874, when he took all 10 wickets for 73 runs, and for Notts *v*. M.C.C., in June 1875, when in the second innings he dismissed seven of his opponents (including Dr. W. G. Grace, Lord Harris, and I. D. Walker) for 7 runs. In 1884, in Notts *v*. Gloucester, Shaw performed the 'hat trick' (i.e. obtained three wickets with successive balls) in each innings.

Shaw first appeared for the Players *v*. Gentlemen in 1865, and during his career played in twenty-eight of the matches. In the match at the Oval in 1880 he dismissed seven of the Gentlemen for 17 runs, and in 1881, at Brighton, six for 19. In 6–8 Sept. 1880 he played for England *v*. Australia in the first test match in this country.

Shaw paid two visits to America—in 1868 with Edgar Willsher's team, and again with that of Richard Daft [q. v. Suppl. I] in 1879, when he made the marvellous record of 178 wickets for 426 runs. He visited Australia five times: as a member of James Lillywhite's team in 1876–7; as captain and joint-manager of the English team in 1881–2, 1884–5, 1886–7; and as manager to Lord Sheffield's team in the autumn of 1891. [See Holroyd, Henry North, third earl of Sheffield, Suppl. II.]

From 1883 to 1894 Shaw had a private cricketing engagement with the earl of Sheffield in Sussex; during that period he coached many rising players for Sussex, and during 1894–5 he played for that county. He accompanied Lord Sheffield on a tour to Norway in August 1894, and took part in a match on board the Lusitania by the light of the midnight sun at Spitzbergen, on 12 Aug. 1894. Next year (Oct.–Nov.) he was with Lord Sheffield in the Crimea. After his retirement in 1895 Shaw acted as umpire in first-class matches.

Shaw, called by Daft 'The Emperor of Bowlers,' was a slow medium bowler, with a very short run, and with his arm almost level with the shoulder. Untiring and most accurate in attack, he was unplayable on 'sticky' wickets. He was a fair batsman, and a first-class fieldsman at 'shortslip.'

Along with professional cricket Shaw pursued some other occupation. From 1869 till 1878 he was landlord of the Lord Nelson inn in his native village, whence he went to Kilburn in November 1878 to take charge of the Prince of Wales' inn; while there he joined Arthur Shrewsbury [q. v. Suppl. II] in an athletic outfitter's business in Nottingham, and in 1881 left Kilburn to become landlord of the Belvoir inn, Nottingham.

He died on 16 Jan. 1907, after a long illness, at Gedling, near Nottingham, where he was buried.

[Daft's Kings of Cricket (portrait, p. 123); A. W. Pullin's Alfred Shaw, Cricketer, 1902; Wisden's Cricketers' Almanack, 1908 (pp. 130–2); The Times, 17 and 21 Jan. 1907; M.C.C. Cricket Scores and Biographies, 1877, viii. pp. 302–3; W. G. Grace's Cricketing Reminiscences, 1899, pp. 376–7 (picture of Shaw bowling, p. 212); information from Mr. P. M. Thornton.] W. B. O.

SHAW, Sir EYRE MASSEY (1830–1908), head of the London Metropolitan Fire Brigade, born at Ballymore, co. Cork, on 17 Jan. 1830, was third son of Bernard Robert Shaw of Monkstown Castle, co. Cork, by his first wife, Rebecca, daughter of Edward Hoare Reeves of Castle Kelvin and Ballyglissane, co. Cork. After attending Dr. Coghlan's school at Dublin he passed into Trinity College and graduated B.A. in 1848, proceeding M.A. in 1854. He was destined for holy orders, but doubting his fitness at the last moment he took ship for America, and after many weeks found himself on the western side of the Atlantic. His family intervened and obtained a commission for him in the army in 1854; he remained six years in the army and became captain in the North Cork rifles (militia), retiring in 1860. In 1859 he obtained the post of chief constable or superintendent of the borough forces of Belfast. His duties included control of the Belfast fire service, which he succeeded in reorganising. With characteristic vigour he suppressed disturbances and party fights in the town, which at that time were frequent, and his impartiality was recognised by both Orange and Catholic factions. His repute travelled outside the limits of Ulster. On the death of James Braidwood [q. v.], superintendent of the London fire brigade, at the great fire in Tooley Street in 1861, Shaw was chosen to fill his place. For the next thirty years he retained the office, and during that period by his personal efforts perfected the organisation of the metropolitan system, which it was his ambition to render the best in the world. He never spared himself. During the first six years of his command he was absent from duty only sixteen days. He was always astir at 3 A.M. to drill and train his men. He paid frequent visits to foreign countries to study any novel arrangements. While he was head of the brigade the number of fire-engine stations grew from 13 to 59, the number of firemen from 113 to 706, and the length of hose from 4 to 33 miles. He dealt with a total of 55,004 fires, an average of five a day, and 2796 men in all passed through his hands. He was more than once injured while directing operations—twice severely.

The instruction, discipline, and finance of the brigade were all under Shaw's control, and he gave important evidence before select parliamentary committees in the Houses of Lords and Commons. He also wrote on his special subject many treatises, which were reckoned of standard authority. Among these were 'Records of the Late London Fire Brigade Establishment' (1870); 'Fire Surveys: a Summary of the Principles to be observed in estimating the Risks of Buildings' (1872); 'Fires in Theatres' (1876; 2nd edit. 1889); 'Fire Protection' (1876); and 'A Complete Manual of the Organisation, Machinery, Discipline and General Working of the Fire Brigade of London' (1876; revised edit. 1890). In 1879 he was nominated C.B., and in 1884 he received the good service medal. When he retired on a pension in 1891, he was nominated K.C.B. (civil). He received the freedom of the Coachmakers' Company in the same year, and the freedom of the City of London in 1892. On his retirement the fire insurance companies showed their appreciation of his admirable work by the presentation of a splendid silver service. He was subsequently managing director of the Palatine Insurance Company, chairman of the Metropolitan Electric Supply Company, and a D.L. for Middlesex.

Shaw was a sportsman, engaging in early life in hunting and shooting, and subsequently in yachting. Some years before his death he suffered, despite his exuberant vitality, amputation of a diseased leg, and the remaining limb was removed at a later date. He met his physical disabilities in old age with courage. He died at Folkestone on 25 Aug. 1908, and was buried at Highgate.

In 1855 he married Anna (*d.* 1897),

daughter of Señor Murto Dove of Lisbon and Fuzeta, Portugal, and by her he had several daughters. A caricature by 'Ape' appeared in 'Vanity Fair' in 1871.

[The Times, 26 and 31 Aug. 1908; Daily Telegraph, 26 Aug. 1908; Dod's Knightage; Walford's County Families; private information.] H. M. V.

SHAW, JAMES JOHNSTON (1845–1910), county court judge, born at Kirkcubbin, co. Down, on 4 Jan. 1845, was second son of seven children of John Maxwell Shaw (*d.* 1852), a merchant and farmer at Kirkcubbin, by his wife Anne, daughter of Adam Johnston. Shaw was first taught in a local national school, and later by James Rowan, presbyterian minister of Kirkcubbin. In 1858 he was sent to the Belfast Academy, where he became a favourite pupil of the principal, Rev. Reuben John Bryce, LL.D. (uncle of Mr. James Bryce). In 1861 he entered Queen's College, Belfast, gaining the highest entrance scholarship in classics, the first of many honours. Diverging to the study of mental science and political economy, he graduated B.A. in 1865 and M.A. in 1866 in the Queen's University of Ireland with first-class honours in those subjects. In 1882 he received the honorary degree of LL.D. from his university.

After studying theology in the general assembly's college, Belfast, and at the University of Edinburgh, he was licensed to preach in 1869 by the presbytery of Ards, and was appointed in the same year by the general assembly professor of metaphysics and ethics in Magee College, Londonderry. In 1878 he resigned this chair and was called to the Irish bar, where he rapidly attained success. Meanwhile in 1876 he was elected Whately professor of political economy in Trinity College, Dublin. Several papers on economic subjects which he read before the Statistical and Social Inquiry Society of Ireland, the British Association, the Social Science Congress, and elsewhere, were published and attracted attention. He became president of the Statistical Society in 1901. In 1886 he was made a member of the senate of the Royal University of Ireland, and in 1891 a commissioner of national education. In the last year, however, he became county court judge of Kerry. The work of the new office proved congenial and afforded leisure to apply to other work. In 1902 he joined the council of trustees of the National Library of Ireland, and in 1908 was chairman of a viceregal commission of inquiry into the mysterious disappearance of the crown jewels from Dublin castle. When the Queen's University of Belfast was founded by royal charter in 1908 he was appointed by the crown chairman of the commission charged with the framing of the statutes, and the duties of this office he discharged with marked ability. He was also a member of the governing body of the University, and in 1909 pro-chancellor in succession to Sir Donald Currie [q. v. Suppl. II]. In 1909 he was created recorder of Belfast, and county court judge of Antrim. A singularly clear thinker and writer, and a high-principled administrator, Shaw died in Dublin on 27 April 1910, and was buried in the Mount Jerome cemetery there. In 1911 his portrait by Sydney Rowley was placed in the hall of the Queen's University of Belfast, together with a memorial brass; a Shaw prize in economics was also founded in his memory.

Shaw married in 1870 Mary Elizabeth (*d.* 1908), daughter of William Maxwell of Ballyherley, co. Down, by whom he had one daughter, Margaret (who married Robert H. Woods, president of the Royal College of Surgeons in Ireland, 1910–11), and two sons.

Shaw translated the 'Enchiridion' in 1873, for an edition of the works of Augustine edited by Dr. Marcus Dods. After his death his daughter, Mrs. Woods, collected and edited, with a biographical sketch, a number of his papers on economic and other subjects under the title 'Occasional Papers' (Dublin, 1910).

[Personal knowledge; address by Right Hon. Christopher Palles at unveiling of memorial tablet in Belfast University, 1911; biographical sketch by Mrs. Woods, *ut supra*.] T. H.

SHEFFIELD, third Earl of. [See Holroyd, Henry North (1832–1909), sportsman.]

SHELFORD, Sir WILLIAM (1834–1905), civil engineer, born at Lavenham, Suffolk, on 11 April 1834, was eldest son of William Heard Shelford (*d.*1856), fellow of Emmanuel College, Cambridge, and rector of Preston St. Mary, Suffolk. His grandfather and great-grandfather were also clergymen of the same name. His mother was Emily Frost, eldest daughter of Richard Snape, rector of Brent Eleigh. Of his brothers, Thomas became a member of the legislative council of the Straits Settlements, and was made C.M.G., while Leonard Edmund was appointed prebendary of St. Paul's

Cathedral in 1889 and vicar of St. Martin's-in-the-Fields, London, in 1903.

In Feb. 1850 Shelford went to Marlborough College, leaving at midsummer 1852 to become an engineer. He was first apprenticed to a mechanical engineer in Scotland, but in 1854 he became a pupil of William Gale, waterworks engineer, of Glasgow. During his two years' term of service he attended lectures at Glasgow University. In 1856, being thrown on his own resources by his father's death, he left Glasgow to seek his fortune in London, and in December of that year he entered the office of (Sir) John Fowler [q. v. Suppl. I] as an assistant engineer, remaining in his service until 1860. He was engaged upon the Nene river navigation and improvement works, of which he was in due course placed in charge, until 1859, when he was transferred to London and was engaged on the laying-out and construction of the first section of the Metropolitan railway. Leaving Fowler's service in the autumn of 1860, Shelford became an assistant to F. T. Turner, joint engineer with Joseph Cubitt of the London, Chatham and Dover railway. After employment on various surveys he was appointed resident engineer on the high-level railway to the Crystal Palace, an act of parliament for which was obtained in 1862. With the exception of the ornamentation of the stations, he designed and superintended all the engineering works of that line. In 1862–5 he was also engaged, under Turner, as resident engineer on the eastern section of the London, Chatham and Dover railway, to Blackheath Hill. In 1865 he started practice on his own account in partnership with Henry Robinson, who was afterwards professor of engineering at King's College, London. The work carried out by the firm during the next ten years included the railways, waterworks, sewage-works and pumping- and winding-engines, shafts, &c., for collieries and mines at home and abroad. In 1869 he visited Sicily and installed machinery and plant for working sulphur mines there, which had previously been worked by very primitive methods. For his services he was made a chevalier of the Order of the Crown of Italy.

The partnership was terminated in 1875, and thenceforward Shelford practised at 35A Great George Street, Westminster, taking his third son, Frederic, into partnership in 1899, and relinquishing work in 1904. His practice during these twenty-nine years covered an unusually wide field. In 1881 Shelford was appointed engineer of the Hull, Barnsley and West Riding Junction railway, which was designed to connect a new (Alexandra) dock at Hull with the Barnsley and West Riding districts. The Hull and Barnsley railway, which involved much difficult engineering work, was Shelford's most important piece of railway construction at home. The line authorised by the original act of parliament, which was sixty-six miles in length, was opened in June 1885, and extensions to Huddersfield and Halifax were made subsequently.

Shelford, who was in much request as an engineering witness, was consulting engineer to the corporation of Edinburgh in connection with the enlargement of Waverley Station and the attempt of the Caledonian Railway Company to carry its line into Edinburgh. Other work in Scotland included the Brechin and Edzell railway, which he carried out in 1893–5.

He reported on many railway schemes abroad, visiting for the purpose Canada in 1885, Italy in 1889, and the Argentine in 1890. With Sir Frederick Bramwell [q. v. Suppl. II] he was consulting engineer to the Winnipeg and Hudson's Bay railway, and under their direction forty miles of this line from Winnipeg were completed in Jan. 1887. His chief work abroad and the main work of his later years was the construction of railways in West Africa, in which he acted as consulting engineer to the crown agents for the colonies. After preliminary surveys, begun in 1893, a line of 2 ft. 6 in. gauge from Freetown, Sierra Leone, to Songo Town was commenced in March 1896 and opened in 1899. This line was gradually extended until, in Aug. 1905, shortly before Shelford's death, it had reached Baiima, 220 miles from Freetown. In the Gold Coast Colony a line of 3 ft. 6 in. gauge from Sekondi to Tarkwa was begun in 1898 and completed in May 1901. By October 1903 the line had been extended as far as Kumasi, 168 miles from Sekondi. In the colony of Lagos a line from Lagos to Ibadan (123 miles) was completed in March 1901. A short railway, six miles in length, from Sierra Leone to the heights above Freetown, was opened in 1904, and road-bridges were built to connect the island of Lagos with the mainland. On Shelford's retirement in 1904 Sir William MacGregor, formerly governor of Lagos, acknowledged Shelford's services to the colony, and how by his skill and perseverance he had overcome the formidable obstacles of the unhealthy climate, the density of the tropical forests which the lines traversed, and the difficulties of landing railway material.

From an early period Shelford interested himself in the engineering works of rivers and estuaries, with which his principal contributions to the literature of his profession dealt. In 1869 he presented to the Institution of Civil Engineers a paper 'On the Outfall of the River Humber,' for which he received a Telford medal and premium. In 1879 he examined the River Tiber and reported upon a modification of a scheme proposed by Garibaldi for the diversion of the floods of that river. For his paper presented in 1885 to the institution, 'On Rivers flowing into Tideless Seas, illustrated by the River Tiber,' he was awarded a Telford premium.

Shelford's colonial services were recognised by the honour of the C.M.G. in 1901 and the K.C.M.G. in 1904. He was elected a member of the Institution of Civil Engineers on 10 April 1866, and from 1887 to 1897 and from 1901 till death was a member of the council. In 1888 he was a vice-president of the mechanical science section of the British Association, before which he read two papers, in 1887 on 'The Improvement of the Access to the Mersey Ports,' and in 1885 on 'Some Points for the Consideration of English Engineers with Reference to the Design of Girder Bridges.' He was a fellow of the Royal Geographical and other societies, and served upon the engineering standards committee as a representative of the crown agents for the colonies.

After his retirement from practice he resided at 49 Argyll Road, Kensington, where he died on 3 Oct. 1905. He was buried at Brompton cemetery. He married in 1863 Anna, daughter of Thomas Sopwith, F.R.S. [q. v.], who survived him; by her he had eight children.

A portrait by Seymour Lucas, which was subscribed for by his staff for presentation to him but was not finished at his death, belongs to his widow.

[Life of Sir William Shelford, by Anna E. Shelford (his second daughter), printed for private circulation, 1909; Minutes of Proc. Inst. Civ. Eng. clxiii. 384; The Engineer, 6 Oct. 1905.] W. F. S.

SHENSTONE, WILLIAM ASHWELL (1850–1908), writer on chemistry, born at Wells-next-the-Sea, Norfolk, on 1 Dec. 1850, was eldest son of James Burt Byron Shenstone, pharmaceutical chemist of Colchester, by his wife Jemima, daughter of James Chapman, of Wells-next-the-Sea, Norfolk. Through his grandfather, Joseph Shenstone (*b.* at Halesowen), he traced collateral connection with William Shenstone the poet.

Educated at Colchester grammar school, Shenstone afterwards entered his father's business. He qualified as a chemist in the school of the Pharmaceutical Society of Great Britain, securing there a Bell scholarship (1871), and was awarded in 1872 the Pereira medal. For two years he was demonstrator of practical chemistry in that school under Professor J. Attfield, leaving to become assistant to Dr. (afterwards Sir) W. A. Tilden, chief science master at Clifton College. In 1875 he was appointed science master at Taunton School, and in 1877 science master at Exeter grammar school, where he built a laboratory (see *Nature*, 26 July 1878). He returned to Clifton in 1880, succeeding Dr. Tilden as science master and holding this post until his death.

While assistant to Tilden at Clifton, Shenstone collaborated with him in an investigation on the terpenes, the results appearing in the paper 'Isomeric Nitrosoterpenes' (*Trans. Chem. Soc.* 1877). Jointly with Tilden he published also the memoir 'On the Solubility of Salts in Water at High Temperatures' (*Phil. Trans. Roy. Soc.* 1884), and 'On the Solubility of Calcium Sulphate in Water in the Presence of Chlorides' (*Proc. Roy. Soc.* 1885). Other important papers, published in the Transactions of the Chemical Society, comprised 'Ozone from Pure Oxygen: its Production and its Action on Mercury' (1887, jointly with J. T. Cundall); 'Studies on the Formation of Ozone from Oxygen' (1893, jointly with M. Priest); 'Observations on the Properties of some Highly Purified Substances' (1897); and 'Observations on the Influence of the Silent Discharge on Atmospheric Air' (1898, jointly with W. T. Evans).

Shenstone was admitted a fellow of the Chemical Society in 1876, and was member of the council 1893–5; he was a fellow of the Institute of Chemistry from 1878, serving on the council 1905–6. He was an original member of the Society of Chemical Industry, and was elected F.R.S. on 9 June 1898.

He died on 3 Feb. 1908, at Polurrian, Mullion, Cornwall, and was buried there. He married in 1883 Jane Mildred, eldest daughter of Reginald N. Durrant, rector of Wootton, near Canterbury, and had issue one son and one daughter. Devoted to his profession, Shenstone was highly successful as a teacher in physical science, and generally influenced the introduction of improved methods of science teaching in schools.

Shenstone's chief independent publications were: 1. 'A Practical Introduction to Chemistry,' 1886; 3rd edit. 1892. 2. 'The Methods of Glass Blowing,' 1886; 3rd edit. 1894; a German translation was published at Leipzig, 1887. 3. 'Justus von Liebig: his Life and Work,' 1895. 4. 'The Elements of Inorganic Chemistry,' 1900. 5. 'The New Physics and Chemistry,' 1906, a reprint of a series of essays contributed to the 'Cornhill Magazine.' On 8 March 1901 he gave a lecture at the Royal Institution on 'Vitrified Quartz,' detailing important practical applications of the material for laboratory apparatus. For Henry Watts's 'Dictionary of Chemistry' he wrote the article 'Ozone.'

[Proc. Roy. Soc., vol. lxxxii. A; Journ. Soc. Chem. Industry, vol. xxvii.; Proc. Chem. Soc., vol. xxiv. No. 336; Trans. Chem. Soc., vol. xcv.; Proc. Inst. Chemistry, 1908, Pt. 2; Pharmaceut. Journ., 8 Feb. 1908; Poggendorff's Handwörterbuch, 1904; Roy. Soc. Catal. Sci. Papers; Nature, 13 Feb. 1908; The Times, 7 Feb. 1908.] T. E. J.

SHERRINGTON, MADAME HELEN LEMMENS- (1834–1906), soprano vocalist. [See LEMMENS-SHERRINGTON.]

SHIELDS, FREDERIC JAMES (1833–1911), painter and decorative artist, born at Hartlepool on 14 March 1833, was the third of the six children of John Shields, a bookbinder and printer, by his wife Georgiana Storey, daughter of an Alnwick farmer. His brothers and sisters all died in infancy. His father, after fighting as a volunteer in Spain for Queen Isabella (1835–6), removed to Clare Market in London, where the boy's mother opened a dressmaker's shop.

Frederic attended the charity school of the parish of St. Clement Danes until the age of fourteen. Having shown an early talent for drawing, he worked from the antique at the British Museum for a few months after leaving school, and on 4 Oct. 1847 was apprenticed to Maclure, Macdonald & Macgregor, a firm of lithographers. His indenture was for a term of three years, but after about a year he was sent for by his father, who had obtained work at Newton-le-Willows, although he was unable to provide for his family. He helped Frederic to find employment at 5*s.* a week with a firm of mercantile lithographers in Manchester.

An ingrained piety, a love of literature, and a passion for sketching enabled Shields to face stoically nine years of grinding poverty and of uncongenial drudgery at commercial lithography. In 1856 he obtained a better engagement in the like trade at Halifax at 50*s.* a week. There the first opportunity of book illustration was offered him, and he prepared fourteen illustrations for a comic volume called 'A Rachde Felley's Visit to the Grayt Eggshibishun.' The proceeds of this work enabled him to give up lithography, and he accepted the offer of C. H. Mitchell, a landscape painter at Manchester, to put figures and animals into his pictures. He was much influenced by the Pre-Raphaelite works which he saw at the great Manchester Exhibition of 1857. On a sketching tour in Devonshire with Mitchell he executed many successful water-colour drawings, for which he found purchasers, while his commissions for drawings on wood grew. In 1860 he received an important though badly paid commission for a series of drawings illustrating the 'Pilgrim's Progress,' some plates for which he sent to Ruskin in 1861, and they evoked the art critic's enthusiastic praise. To Ruskin's teaching, he wrote later, he owed 'a debt of inexpressible and reverential gratitude' (*Bookman*, Oct. 1908, p. 30). He also corresponded with Charles Kingsley, who encouraged him. After spending some time on water-colour work at Porlock and occasionally engraving for 'Once a Week,' Shields established his fame as an illustrator by his designs for Defoe's 'Journal of the Plague Year,' which were engraved in 1863. A water-colour version of his illustration of Solomon Eagle for this work is in the Manchester Art Gallery. In 1865 he was elected associate of the Royal Society of Painters in Water Colours. From 1864 onwards he spent some time each year in London, and there met Dante Rossetti and Madox Brown, as well as Ruskin, Holman Hunt, and Burne-Jones. With Rossetti and Brown his relations grew very close. He was with Rossetti through his fatal illness at Birchington in 1882, and designed the memorial window in the church there. But from 1867 to 1875 Shields's headquarters were lonely houses at Manchester, until 1871 at Cornbrook Park, and then at Ordsall Hall. After some time at Blackpool, he made a tour in Italy early in 1876, and on his return settled in London. For the next twenty years he resided at Lodge Place, St. John's Wood, whence he moved in 1896 to Wimbledon.

In later life Shields neglected that illustrative work for which his gifts eminently fitted him, and devoted himself to more ambitious decorative designs and oil-painting, in which he followed the lead of the Pre-Raphaelites without showing a trace of their romanticism. He was not a great colourist but a sound draughtsman. His later work is cold, formal, didactic and out of touch with actual life, though it is not lacking in loftiness of aim and nobility of design. Between 1875 and 1880 he designed the stained-glass windows for Sir William Houldsworth's private chapel at Coodham, Kilmarnock a work which was followed by the stained-glass and mosaic decoration for the duke of Westminster's chapel at Eaton. Shields also executed in 1887 the symbolic decoration for St. Luke's church, Camberwell (cf. HUGH CHAPMAN'S *Sermons in Symbols*, 1888). His most important work, which kept him busy for about twenty years from 1889, and was finished only a few months before his death, was the pictorial decoration of the walls in the Chapel of the Ascension, Bayswater Road, which was designed by Mr. Herbert P. Horne. The commission came from Mrs. Russell Gurney, to whom Lady Mount Temple had introduced Shields in 1889, and the work was executed in 'spirit-fresco.' Before beginning the work, Shields visited Italy for suggestions.

Shields, whose piety was a constant feature of his life, died at Morayfield, Wimbledon, on 26 Feb. 1911, and was buried at Merton churchyard. He was married at Manchester on 15 Aug. 1874 to Matilda Booth, a girl of sixteen, who was frequently his model; but they had no children, and husband and wife lived much apart. His features are recorded in the head of 'Wicklyffe' in Ford Madox Brown's fresco at Manchester town hall. An exhibition of his works was held at the Brazenose Club, Manchester, in May 1889, and there was a memorial exhibition at the Alpine Club Gallery in October 1911.

Nearly the whole of his substantial fortune was bequeathed to foreign missionary societies. The cartoons for the windows at Eaton were presented by his executors to the Young Men's Christian Association for their new London headquarters in Tottenham Court Road. A portfolio of Shields's studies for his 'Pilgrim's Progress' designs was purchased for the Victoria and Albert Museum in 1912.

[Mrs. Ernestine Mills's Life and Letters of Frederic Shields, 1912; Catalogue of the Memorial Exhibition of the works of Frederic J. Shields, 1911; The Times, 29 Sept. 1911; The Observer, 1 Oct. 1911; Ruskin's Works, ed. Cook and Wedderburn, vols. xiv. xvii. xviii. xxxvii.–viii.; M. H. Spielmann's History of Punch, 527–30; Charles Rowley, Fifty Years of Work without Wages, 1911, pp. 81–91; Ford M. Hueffer, Ford Madox Brown, 1896; Gleeson White, English Illustration: The Sixties, 1906; W. M. Rossetti, D. G. Rossetti's Letters and Memoirs, passim; private information.] P. G. K.

SHIPPARD, SIR SIDNEY GODOLPHIN ALEXANDER (1837–1902), colonial official, born at Brussels on 29 May 1837 and sprung of a naval family, was eldest son of Captain William Henry Shippard of the 29th regiment (son of Rear-Admiral Alexander Shippard [q. v.]) by his wife Elizabeth Lydia, daughter of Captain Joseph Peters. Educated at King's College School, London, he obtained an exhibition at Oriel College, Oxford, in 1856, but next year migrated to Hertford College on winning a scholarship. He graduated B.A. in law and modern history in 1863, and became B.C.L. and M.A. in 1864. Studying for the bar, he was called of the Inner Temple on 26 Jan. 1867, and soon afterwards he went out to South Africa. He was admitted to practise as an advocate of the supreme court of the Cape Colony in 1868.

On 25 Jan. 1873 Shippard was appointed acting attorney-general of Griqualand West, which had some two years previously been proclaimed a part of the British dominions, and had been attached to the Cape Colony, but under a practically separate administration. Shippard was formally appointed attorney-general on 17 Aug. 1875. In 1877 he acted as recorder of the high court of Griqualand West. Coming into collision with Sir Bartle Frere [q. v.] and Sir Owen Lanyon, he resigned his post. In 1878 he was in England, and took his D.C.L. degree at Oxford. On 20 April 1880 he was appointed a puisne judge of the supreme court of the Cape Colony.

From February to September 1885 Shippard served as British representative on the joint commission which sat at Capetown to determine the Anglo-German claims in respect of property acquired before the declaration of the German protectorate over Angra Pequena and the West Coast (see *Blue Book* C. 5180/87).

On 30 Sept. 1885, when a protectorate was formally proclaimed over Bechuanaland, Shippard was appointed administrator and chief magistrate of British Bechuanaland, and president of the land commission which was charged with determining the complicated claims to lands between the natives and concessionaires;

the result of his labours is embodied in a Blue Book (C. 4889 86). This position he held for ten years; and amongst the more interesting episodes of his administration were his expedition with a small escort in 1888 to visit Lobengula, whose attitude he changed from hostility to compliance, and discussions with the chief Khama on the liquor question. By the former he paved the way in some measure for the Charter of the British South Africa Company. He retired on pension on 16 Nov. 1895, when British Bechuanaland was annexed to Cape Colony. On his way home he was at Johannesburg just after the Jameson raid, and threw all his influence on the side of peace.

Shippard, who was made C.M.G. in 1886, and K.C.M.G. in 1887, became on 21 April 1898 a director of the British South Africa Company, and rendered the board wise and loyal service at a time when the development of the company's territories was at an anxious and critical stage. He died on 29 March 1902 at his residence, 15 West Halkin Street, London. He was buried at Nynehead, Somerset.

Shippard married, first, in 1864, Maria Susanna, daughter of Sir Andries Stockenström of Cape Colony (she died in 1870, leaving three children); secondly, on 18 Dec. 1894, Rosalind, daughter of W. A. Sanford of Nynehead Court, who with four children survived him.

Shippard, a man of culture and refinement, with a taste for music, acquired a high reputation as a Roman-Dutch lawyer. He published 'Dissertatio de vindicatione rei emptæ et traditione' (thesis for D.C.L. 1868), 'Report of Case of Bishop of Grahamstown (*v.* Merriman)' (1879), and several legal judgments in 'Buchanan's (Cape) Reports' (1880–5).

[The Times, 31 March 1902; South Africa, 5 April 1902; C.O. lists, 1875–1895; official blue books; Who's Who, 1901; Anglo African Who's Who, 1905; information from Lady Shippard.] C. A. H.

SHIRREFF. [See Grey, Mrs. Maria Georgina (1816–1906), promoter of women's education.]

SHORE, THOMAS WILLIAM (1840–1905), geologist and antiquary, born on 5 April 1840 at Wantage, was son of William Shore, architect, by his wife Susannah Carter. Brought up at Wantage, he became (about 1864) organising secretary to the East Lancashire Union of Institutions at Burnley. In 1867 he was sent (with others) by the science and art department at South Kensington to the Paris Exhibition to report on scientific and technical education, and gave evidence on the subject before a select committee of the House of Commons in 1868. In 1873 he was appointed secretary to the Hartley Institution (now the Hartley University College) at Southampton and curator of the museum, and later became executive officer of the institution. Shore was the founder of the Hampshire Field Club and Archæological Society, and remained its honorary secretary until his death. He contributed many papers to the society's 'Transactions,' including 'Ancient Hampshire Forests' (1888), 'The Clays of Hampshire and their Economic Uses' (1890), and 'Hampshire Valleys and Waterways' (1895). In 1882 he was secretary of the geological section of the Southampton meeting of the British Association. He was elected fellow of the Geological Society on 3 April 1878. Both as a geologist and an antiquary he was an authority of high repute upon Hampshire. In 1896 Shore moved to London and founded the Balham Antiquarian Society. Shortly before 1901 he became joint honorary secretary of the London and Middlesex Archæological Society, and contributed to its 'Transactions' a series of papers on 'Anglo-Saxon London and Middlesex.' He died suddenly at his residence, 157 Bedford Hill, Balham, on 15 Jan. 1905, and was buried at the cemetery of St. Mary Extra, Woolston, Southampton.

On 24 Jan. 1861 he married Amelia Lewis of Gloucester, who died on 31 May 1891; they had two sons, Thomas William Shore, M.D., dean of the medical school of St. Bartholomew's Hospital, and Lewis Erle Shore, lecturer on physiology at Cambridge, and three daughters.

Shore published: 1. 'Guide to Southampton and Neighbourhood,' 1882. 2. Letterpress description to 'Vestiges of Old Southampton,' by Frank McFadden, 1891. 3. 'A History of Hampshire, including the Isle of Wight' (Popular County Histories), 1892. At his death he was engaged on 'Origin of the Anglo-Saxon Race,' which was edited posthumously by his sons. A 'Shore Memorial Volume' (pt. i. 1908, ed. G. W. Minns), undertaken by the Hampshire Field Club and Archæological Society, contains his contributions to the society and other papers.

[Quarterly Journal Geol. Soc. 61, lviii–lix; private information.] C. W.

SHORTHOUSE, JOSEPH HENRY (1834–1903), author of 'John Inglesant,' eldest son of Joseph Shorthouse (*d.* Oct. 1880) and his wife Mary Ann, daughter of John Hawker, was born on 9 Sept. 1834 in Great Charles Street, Birmingham, where his father inherited some chemical works from his great-grandfather. Both parents belonged to the Society of Friends. At ten Shorthouse went to a quakers' school near his new home in Edgbaston, and at fifteen to Tottenham College, his studies being interrupted by a bad nervous stammer—a defect which developed powers of mental concentration. At sixteen he went into the family business, but he remained an intensive reader, being attracted by Hawthorne and Michelet and repelled by Macaulay. He was trained in writing by a Friends' Essay Society, to which he contributed papers much debated and commended by his associates. Through this meeting he came to know Sarah, eldest daughter of John and Elizabeth Scott of Edgbaston, to whom he was married at the Meeting house, Warwick, before he was three-and-twenty (19 Aug. 1857). Powerfully affected by Ruskin and Pre-Raphaelitism, Shorthouse discovered a strong sentimental sympathy for the Anglicanism of the seventeenth century as he conceived it; in Aug. 1861 he and his wife were baptised at St. John's, Ladywood, by his friend Canon Morse, to whom he afterwards dedicated 'Sir Percival' (1886). In 1862 he had an attack of epilepsy which made him more or less of an invalid. From 1862 to 1876 he lived in Beaufort Road, within a stone's throw of Newman at the Oratory; there he started a Greek Testament Society in 1873.

There too a psychological and historical romance, 'John Inglesant,' grew in its author's mind by a process of incrustation and was slowly committed to writing, beginning about 1866. Every free evening he was in the habit of reading a paragraph or two to his wife and to no one else. In 1876 the book was finished at Llandudno; but the publishers were shy of it, and great expense being involved in moving at this period from Beaufort Road to a beautiful house in spacious grounds, known as Lansdowne, Edgbaston, the manuscript remained undisturbed for five years in the drawer of a cabinet. Early in 1880 a notion of private issue was resumed; it was printed handsomely in a thick octavo of 577 pages with a vellum binding, and dedicated to Rawdon Levett, 17 June 1880. Private readers of this edition, commencing with the author's father, were greatly impressed; but James Payn [q. v. Suppl. I], reader of Messrs. Smith, Elder & Co., who read it with a view to its publication by his firm, gave an unfavourable verdict (cf. PAYN'S *Literary Recollections*). The 'Guardian' however took a more complacent view. Mrs. Humphry Ward was struck by the book, a copy of which with the author's consent she forwarded to Alexander Macmillan; and on 18 Feb. 1881 Macmillan wrote to Shorthouse to say that he would feel it an honour to publish the book. That a man whose paths had not lain among scholars and libraries and who had never travelled two hundred miles from his home should have written such a book as 'Inglesant,' with its marvellous atmospheric delineation of Italy, struck the world of English letters with amazement. That a mystic should arise from the ranks of the Birmingham manufacturers stimulated their curiosity. Though called a romance, wrote Macmillan, '"John Inglesant" is full of thought and power.' It attracted the interest of a remarkable variety of people—Gladstone, Huxley, Miss Yonge, and Cardinal Manning, and the writer was much lionised in London. He and his wife spent a week with his publisher at Tooting, where Huxley and others met him. At a reception at Gladstone's, where the Prince of Wales and many persons of distinction were assembled, Shorthouse was a centre of attraction. Nearly nine thousand copies were sold in the year. The success was partly due to fashion, for 'Inglesant,' which lacked the qualities of good continuous narrative, greatly overaccentuated the value of the Romanising movement of the time, was full of vague sermonising, and was destitute of humour. Some of the episodes (the Little Gidding ones prominently) exhibit beauty and pathos, which the author's fidelity to his period enabled him to clothe in an idiom of singular purity and charm, and the book fitted in admirably with a wave of catholic and historical feeling which was passing over the country. Few new books have had a more ardent cult than 'John Inglesant.'

Shorthouse rapidly extended his acquaintance, his new friends including Canon Ainger, Professor Knight, Mr. Gosse, and Bishop Talbot. Although he was incited to new effort he was essentially *homo unius libri*. His prefaces to Herbert's 'Temple' (1882) and the 'Golden Thoughts' of Molinos (1883), his essays on 'The Platonism of Wordsworth' (1882) and 'The Royal Supremacy' (1899), and his minor novels, chief among them 'Sir Percival' (1886), corroborate the idea of a choice but limited talent. The reviewers, who criticised them with blunted weapons, were unimpressed by Shorthouse's long and self-complacent Platonic disquisitions.

In life, as in scholarship, Shorthouse was an eclectic and a conservative. The constant foe of excess, eccentricity, over-emphasis, self-advertisement, he stood notably for cultured Anglicanism. His health began to fail in 1900, and muscular rheumatism compelled his abandonment of business; reading and devotion were his solace to the end. He died at his residence, Lansdowne, Edgbaston, on 4 March 1903, and was buried in Old Edgbaston churchyard. There also was buried his widow, who died on 9 May 1909. He left no issue. His library was sold at Sotheby's on 20 Dec. 1909.

In addition to the novels already mentioned, Shorthouse published: 1. 'The Little Schoolmaster Mark,' 1883. 2. 'The Countess Eve,' 1888. 3. 'A Teacher of the Violin, and other Tales,' 1888. 4. 'Blanche Lady Falaise,' 1891.

[Life and Letters of J. H. Shorthouse, edited by his wife, 2 vols. 1905 (portraits); Life and Letters of Alexander Macmillan, 1910; Miss Sichel's Life of Ainger, chap. xi.; The Times, 6 and 11 March 1903; Guardian, 25 March 1903; Spectator, 14 March 1903; Observer, 7 May 1905; Dublin Review, xc. 395; Blackwood, cxxxi. 365; Temple Bar, June 1903; Gosse's Portraits and Sketches, 1912. For the verdicts of Acton and Gardiner (Fraser, cv. 599) upon Shorthouse's historical point of view and his endeavours to reply, see Acton's Letters to Mary Gladstone.] T. S.

SHREWSBURY, ARTHUR (1856–1903), Nottinghamshire cricketer, fourth son of seven children of William Shrewsbury and Elizabeth Ann Wragg, was born in Kyle Street, New Lenton, Nottinghamshire, on 11 April 1856. His father, a designer, draughtsman, and lace manufacturer, was also proprietor of the Queen's Hotel, Nottingham. His elder brother William (*b.* 30 April 1854), who succeeded his father as proprietor of the Queen's Hotel in 1885 and emigrated to Canada in 1891, played cricket for Notts county in 1876, and was for a time cricket coach at Eton. After education at the People's College, Nottingham, Shrewsbury became a draughtsman. Showing promise in local cricket, as well as in football, he turned professional cricketer, and modelling his style on that of Richard Daft [q. v. Suppl. I], first appeared at Lord's for the Colts of England *v.* M.C.C. in May 1873. Ill-health prevented him from playing in 1874, but next year he played regularly for the Notts team, and in June 1876 he scored his first century (118 *v.* Yorkshire) in first-class cricket. In 1880 he established an athletic outfitter's business in Queen Street, Nottingham, with Alfred Shaw [q. v. Suppl. II].

The turning-point in Shrewsbury's career was his visit, in the winter of 1881, to Australia as joint manager of Alfred Shaw's team; the climate improved his health and strength. Shrewsbury thrice subsequently (in 1884–5, 1886–7, 1887–8) visited Australia as manager with Shaw. The fourth tour proved financially disastrous. But Shrewsbury remained in the colony after its close and managed, again at financial loss, a Rugby football tour, which he and Shaw organised, to Australia and New Zealand. On his return to England at the end of 1888 he received a testimonial from Nottingham, and played regularly (except in 1894 owing to ill-health) for the county until 1902.

Shrewsbury's most successful seasons were from 1882 to 1893, during which he headed the English batting averages on five occasions (in 1885, 1887, 1890, 1891, 1892); his chief scores were 207 for Notts *v.* Surrey at the Oval in August 1882, and 164 for England *v.* Australia at Lord's in July 1886, when he played the famous Australian bowlers with ease and confidence. In 1887 his success was unparalleled; he played eight three-figure innings (including 267 *v.* Middlesex), scored 1653 runs, and had the remarkable average of 78. Later noteworthy scores were 206 *v.* All Australia during his fourth visit to Australia in 1887–8, and 108 and 81 for England *v.* Australia at Lord's in July 1893 on a difficult wicket. In May 1890 he with William Gunn created a fresh record by putting on 398 runs for the second wicket for Notts *v.* Sussex. In his last season (of 1902) he scored in July two separate centuries (101 and 127 not out) in the match *v.* Gloucester at Trent Bridge. During his career he scored sixty centuries in first-class cricket.

The main features of Shrewsbury's batting were, like those of his model, Richard Daft, his strong back play and his perfect timing; his strong defence, caution, and unwearying patience made him excellent on treacherous wickets. He was short, and his body worked like clockwork together with the bat. He did much to popularise leg play. His fielding was first-class, especially close in to the wickets.

In 1903 an internal complaint, which

Shrewsbury believed to be incurable, unhinged his mind, and he shot himself at his sister's residence, The Limes, Gedling, on 19 May 1903, being buried in the churchyard there.

[The Times, 20 May 1903; Haygarth's Scores and Biographies, xii. 658, xiv. 89–90; Wisden's Cricketers' Almanack, 1904, 71–2; W. F. Grundy, Memento of Arthur Shrewsbury's last match, Nottingham, 1904; Daft's Kings of Cricket (portrait on p. 149); W. Caffyn's Seventy-one not out, 1889; A. W. Pullin's Alfred Shaw, Cricketer, 1902 (passim); W. G. Grace's Cricketing Reminiscences, 1899, pp. 379–80; A. T. Lilley, Twenty-five Years of Cricket, 1912; notes kindly supplied by Mr. P. M. Thornton. Portraits appeared in Sporting Mirror for July 1883; Cricket, 28 July and 29 Dec. 1892; Baily's Magazine, June 1894.] W. B. O.

SHUCKBURGH, EVELYN SHIRLEY (1843–1906), classical scholar, born at Aldborough on 12 July 1843, was third and eldest surviving son (in a family of twelve children) of Robert Shuckburgh, rector of Aldborough in Norfolk, by his wife Elizabeth (*d.* 1876), daughter of Dr. Lyford, Winchester. Evelyn was educated for some time at a preparatory school kept at Winchester by the Rev. E. Huntingford, D.C.L. Thence he proceeded to Ipswich grammar school, under Dr. Hubert Ashton Holden [q. v. Suppl. I], the editor of Aristophanes, of whose teaching Shuckburgh always talked with enthusiasm. His father died in 1860, and in 1862 Shuckburgh entered Emmanuel College as an exhibitioner. He was shortsighted, which probably prevented his taking an active part in athletics, but he took the lead in the intellectual life of the college, and as a speaker at the Union Debating Society became widely known in the university. He was president of the Union in 1865, and graduated as thirteenth classic in the classical tripos of 1866. From 1866 to 1874 he was a fellow and assistant tutor of Emmanuel College. In the latter year, having vacated his fellowship by his marriage with Frances Mary, daughter of the Rev. Joseph Pullen, formerly fellow and tutor of Corpus Christi College, Cambridge, and Gresham professor of astronomy, he accepted an assistant mastership at Eton. There he remained for ten years, when he returned to Cambridge. He was soon appointed librarian of Emmanuel College, and devoted himself, apart from his comparatively light duties in this capacity, to teaching and writing. He wrote with great facility, and immediately after his degree had published anonymously various translations of classical works for university examinations. He now undertook the editing of many volumes of elementary school classics, chiefly for Messrs. Macmillan and the Cambridge University Press. These books were for the most part compilations, but the notes are clear and to the point, and it is noticeable that, instead of being spoilt as a scholar by work of this kind, he showed greater accuracy, width of knowledge, and scholarship in his later books than in his earlier. For his skill in such work he was selected by Sir Richard Jebb [q.v. Suppl. II] to adapt his edition of Sophocles for use in schools. Shuckburgh however lived only to publish the 'Œdipus Coloneus,' 'Antigone,' and Philoctetes.' In 1889 he executed a complete translation of Polybius, the first and, in some respects, the most arduous of his labours in this field, though in point of length it was surpassed by his translation of the whole of Cicero's letters in Messrs. Bell's series (1889–1900). With his edition of Suetonius's 'Life of Augustus' (Cambridge University Press, 1896), Shuckburgh broke ground long untilled in England. This work obtained for him the degree of Litt.D. from the university in 1902. 'The Life of Augustus' (1903) was a natural corollary to the life by Suetonius, and gives Shuckburgh's own views of Augustus and his age. 'A General History of Rome to the Battle of Actium' had appeared in 1894. In 1901 Shuckburgh produced for the University Press 'A Short History of the Greeks from the Earliest Times to B.C. 146,' and in 1905, for the 'Story of the Nations' series, 'Greece from the Coming of the Hellenes to A.D. 14.' He devoted some attention also to earlier English literature, editing in 1889 with an introduction 'The A.B.C. both in Latyn and Englishe, being a facsimile reprint of the earliest extant English Reading Book,' and in 1891 Sidney's 'Apologie for Poetrie' from the text of 1595. To his college he was devotedly attached, and made many contributions to college history, including the account (anonymously published) of the 'Commemoration of the Three Hundredth Anniversary of Emmanuel College' (1884); 'Lawrence Chaderton (First Master of Emmanuel College), translated from a Latin Memoir of Dr. Dillingham and Richard Farmer (Master of Emmanuel 1775–1797). An Essay' (1884); 'Two Biographies of William Bedell, Bishop of Kilmore, with a Selection of his Letters and an unpublished Treatise' (1902); and the

'History of Emmanuel College' in Robinson's series of 'College Histories' (1904). He also published from a MS. in the library of Emmanuel College in 1894 'The Soul and the Body, a Mediæval Greek Poem.'

Shuckburgh also contributed essays and occasional verses to literary journals. He wrote for the 'Edinburgh Review' on the correspondence of Cicero (January 1901), and prepared several memoirs for this Dictionary.

Shuckburgh was an excellent conversationalist and a man of wide reading. His literary work was too voluminous and produced too rapidly to be all of first-class merit, but it was never slipshod, though he was an ineffectual corrector of proof. No small part of his time was devoted to examining in his own and other universities and in the public schools. In 1901 he was appointed by the Intermediate Education Board for Ireland to report on secondary education in Irish schools. He died suddenly on 10 July 1906, in the train between Berwick and Edinburgh, while on his way to examine at St. Leonard's School, St. Andrews, and was buried at Grantchester, where for some years he had lived. He left a family of two sons and three daughters.

Shuckburgh was tall and in countenance resembled Cardinal Newman. A good photograph hangs in the parlour of Emmanuel College, and in the library there is a bronze relief by Mr. E. Gillick.

[Information from the family; a Memoir by Dr. J. Adam in the Emmanuel College Magazine, 1906; personal knowledge.]

P. G.

SIEVEKING, Sir EDWARD HENRY (1816–1904), physician, born on 24 Aug. 1816 at 1 St. Helen's Place, Bishopsgate Street Within, London, was eldest son of Edward Henry Sieveking (1790–1868), a merchant who removed from Hamburg to London in 1809, by his wife Emerentia Luise, daughter of Senator J. V. Meyer (1745–1811) of Hamburg. The Sievekings long held a foremost position in Hamburg in commerce and municipal affairs. The father returned to Germany and served in the Hanseatic legion throughout the war of liberation (1813–14); he was a linguist, speaking five languages fluently and two fairly well (cf. H. Crabb Robinson's *Diary*, ii. 196). A life of Sir Edward's aunt, Amelia Wilhelmina Sieveking (1794–1859), a pioneer in philanthropic work in Hamburg, and the friend of Queen Caroline of Denmark and of Mrs. Elizabeth Fry, was translated from the German by Catherine Winkworth [q. v.] in 1863.

After early education in England Sieveking went in 1830 to the gymnasiums at Ratzeburg and at Berlin; in 1837 he entered the University of Berlin and studied anatomy and physiology, the latter under Johann Müller. During 1838 he worked at surgery at Bonn, and returning to England devoted two years to medicine at University College and graduated M.D. at Edinburgh in 1841, with a thesis on erysipelas. After a further year abroad, spent in visiting the hospitals of Paris, Vienna, Würzburg, and Berlin, he settled down in 1843 to practise among the English colony in Hamburg, and was associated with his aunt in founding a children's hospital there. Returning to London in 1847, Sieveking became a licentiate (corresponding to member) of the Royal College of Physicians, and while settling in practice, first in Brook Street and then in Bentinck Street, took an active part in advocating the nursing of the sick poor. In 1851 he became assistant physician to St. Mary's Hospital, being one of the original staff and the writer of the first prescription in that institution, where in due course he lectured on materia medica for sixteen years and was physician (1866–1887) and consulting physician. In 1855 he assisted John Propert in founding Epsom College, a school for the sons of medical men. He was also physician to the London Lock Hospital (1864–89) and to the National Hospital for the paralysed and epileptic (1864–7). He became a fellow of the Royal College of Physicians in 1852, and in 1858 he took a prominent part in bringing about the first reform at the college for 336 years, which gave to the general body of the fellows powers formerly enjoyed only by 'the eight elect.' He held numerous offices there, being censor in 1869, 1870, 1879, 1881, and vice-president in 1888; he delivered the Croonian lectures (1866) 'On the localisation of disease' and the Harveian oration (1877), containing a description of the MS. of Harvey's lectures, which had just been rediscovered. His reputation as a consulting physician was recognised by his election as president of the Harveian Society (1861), and of the Royal Medical and Chirurgical Society (1888), and as first honorary president of the British Balneological and Climatological Society (1895). He was a staunch supporter of the British Medical Association, and served on its council. He was also appointed in 1863 physician in ordinary to Edward VII when Prince of Wales; in 1873 physician extraordinary, and in 1888 physician in ordinary to Queen Victoria, and physician extraordinary to Edward VII in 1902. He was made hon. LL.D. of Edinburgh in 1884 at the tercentenary of the University. Together with Sir David Brewster and Dr. Charles Murchison he founded the Edinburgh University Club in London in 1864. He was knighted in 1886.

Sieveking, who invented in 1858 an æsthesiometer, an instrument for testing the sensation of the skin, was author of: 'A Treatise on Ventilation' (in German, Hamburg, 1846); 'The Training Institutions for Nurses and the Workhouses' (1849); 'Manual of Pathological Anatomy' (1854, with C. Handfield Jones, the illustrations reproducing excellent water-colours by Sieveking; 2nd edit. 1875, ed. by J. F. Payne); 'On Epilepsy and Epileptiform Seizures' (1858; 2nd edit. 1861); 'Practical Remarks on Laryngeal Disease as illustrated by the Laryngoscope' (1862); 'The Medical Adviser in Life Assurance' (1873; 2nd edit. 1882). He translated Rokitansky's 'Pathological Anatomy' (vol. ii. 1849) and Romberg's 'Nervous Diseases' (2 vols. 1853) for the Sydenham Society. He also edited the 'British and Foreign Medico-Chirurgical Review' from 1855, and contributed largely to medical periodicals, especially on nervous diseases, climatology, and nursing.

Sieveking died at his house, 17 Manchester Square, W., on 24 Feb. 1904, and was buried in the family grave at Abney Park cemetery, Stoke Newington. A portrait painted in 1866 by W. S. Herrick and a pastel picture by Carl Hartmann done in 1847 are in the possession of his family. A posthumous portrait is at the Royal Academy of Medicine. There is a brass tablet to his memory in the ancient chapel of the crypt beneath St. John's church, Clerkenwell, on which he is described as 'an ardent worker for the ambulance department of the Order (of St. John of Jerusalem) since 1878.' He had been gazetted a Knight of Grace in 1896.

Sieveking married, on 5 Sept. 1849, Jane, daughter of John Ray, J.P., of Finchley, and had issue eight sons and three daughters, the eldest of whom, Florence Amelia, married firstly Dr. L. Wooldridge and secondly Prof. E. H. Starling, F.R.S., and has translated some of Metchnikoff's works. A son, Mr. A. Forbes Sieveking, F.S.A., is well known as a writer on gardens and fencing.

[Lancet, 1904, i. 680; Med.-Chir. Trans., 1905, lxxxviii. p. cviii; Presidential Address to the Royal College of Physicians by Sir W. S. Church, 23 March 1904; information from his son, Herbert Sieveking, M.R.C.S.]

H. D. R.

SIMMONS, Sir JOHN LINTORN ARABIN (1821–1903), field marshal and colonel commandant royal engineers, born at Langford, Somersetshire, on 12 Feb. 1821, was fifth son of twelve children of Captain Thomas Simmons (*d.* 1842), royal artillery, of Langford, by his wife Mary, daughter of John Perry, of Montego Bay, for many years judge of the supreme court of Jamaica. His father was author of the treatise 'On the Constitution and Practice of Courts Martial,' which was long an authorised textbook. Six out of his eight brothers were officers in the army.

Educated at Elizabeth College, Guernsey, and at the Royal Military Academy at Woolwich, Simmons received his first commission in the royal engineers on 14 Dec. 1837, and after professional instruction at Chatham embarked for Canada in June 1839. He was promoted first lieutenant on 15 Oct. following. While in Canada he was employed for three years in the then disputed territory on the north-east frontier of the United States of America, constructing works of defence, and making military explorations.

Returning to England in March 1845, Simmons was stationed in the London district for a year, was then an instructor in fortification at the Royal Military Academy at Woolwich, and being promoted second captain on 9 Nov. 1846, was appointed next month inspector of railways under the railway commissioners. In 1850 he became secretary to the railway commissioners, and when the commission was absorbed by the board of trade on 11 Oct. 1851, secretary of the new railway department of the board.

In Oct. 1853 Simmons travelled on leave in Eastern Europe, where war had been declared between Turkey and Russia. After his arrival at Constantinople, he was of service to the British ambassador, Lord Stratford de Redcliffe [q. v.], in reporting on the defences of the Turkish Danube frontier and of the Bosphorus, and he also visited with Sir Edmund Lyons's squadron the Black Sea ports.

Promoted first captain on 17 Feb. 1854, he was preparing to leave for England when on 20 March the British ambassador sent him to warn Omar Pasha, the Turkish commander on the Danube, of the intention of the Russians to cross the Lower Danube near Galatz. With great promptitude and energy he found Omar at Tertuchan, and the hasty retreat of the Turkish army prevented catastrophe. Meanwhile in reply to a summons from the board of trade to return home at once or resign his appointment, Simmons, who had outstayed his leave, sent in his resignation, which was accepted on 30 June 1854. When at the end of March the Western powers allied themselves with Turkey against Russia, Simmons was formally attached to Omar Pasha's army on the Danube as British commissioner. He gave advice and help in the defence of Silistria, which he left during the siege on 18 June to join Omar Pasha and the allied generals at Varna. Five days later the siege of Silistria was raised, and the generals at Varna decided that Omar Pasha should take advantage of this success to cross the river and attack the Russian army at Giurgevo.

On 7 July Simmons was in command of 20,000 men of all arms at the passage of the Danube and the battle of Giurgevo. He threw up the lines of Slobodzie and Giurgevo in presence of the enemy, who tried to prevent him, while a Russian army of 70,000 men lay within seven miles. For his services with the Turkish army and his share in the defence of Silistria and the battle of Giurgevo, when the Russians were routed, Simmons was promoted brevet major on 14 July 1854, and given the local rank of lieutenant-colonel (a brevet lieutenant-colonelcy following, 12 Dec.). During the retreat of the Russians and the occupation of Wallachia by the Turks, Simmons was frequently in charge of reconnaissances upon the enemy's rear until they had evacuated the principality.

In the meantime the allies had invaded the Crimea, the battles of the Alma, Balaclava, and Inkerman had been fought, and the siege of Sevastopol was in progress. Simmons opposed Napoleon III's proposal that the Turks should advance on the Pruth so as to act on the Russian line of communications with the Crimea. Realising the weakened condition of the allies after Inkerman and that there were no reserves nearer than England and France, he urged that the Turkish army should reinforce the allies in the Crimea. After much discussion the advanced guard of the Turkish army in Jan. 1855 occupied Eupatoria, which Simmons at once placed in a state of defence, in time to repulse a determined attack by the Russians on 17 Feb. The Russians were 40,000 strong, while the Turkish garrison was small. After this action the remainder of the Turkish army arrived from Varna, and Simmons laid out and constructed an entrenched camp. From April to September 1855 he was with Omar Pasha's army before Sevastopol, taking part in the siege until the place fell. He was created C.B. on 13 Oct.

When after the fall of Sevastopol Omar Pasha took his army to Armorica to operate against the Russians south of the Caucasus, and thus relieve the pressure on the fortress of Kars invested by the Russians, Simmons continued with him as the British commissioner. Omar, advancing into Mingrelia with 10,000 men, encountered 12,000 Russians on the river Ingur on 6 Nov. 1855. Simmons commanded a division which, crossing the river by the ford of Ruki and turning the Russian position, captured his works and guns and compelled the enemy to retreat. The casualties were small, so sudden and unexpected was their turning movement, the Russians losing 400 and the Turks 300 in killed and wounded. Omar Pasha in his despatch attributed the success mainly to Simmons. Unfortunately the campaign began too late to enable the relief of Kars to be effected. It capitulated on 26 Nov.

Early in 1856 Omar Pasha sent Simmons to London to explain his views for the next campaign in Asia Minor against Russia, but, by the time he arrived in England, peace negotiations were in progress, and the treaty of Paris was signed on 30 March. For his services Simmons received the British war medal with clasp for Sevastopol; the Turkish gold medal for Danubian campaign, and the Turkish medal for Silistria; the third class of the order of the Mejidie (the second class was sent by the Sultan, but the British government refused permission for him to accept it on account of his rank); the Turkish Crimean medal; the French legion of honour, fourth class; and the Sultan of Turkey presented him with a sword of honour and made him a major-general in the Turkish army. In his service with the Turkish army Simmons had shown a knowledge of strategy and a power of command which should have led to further command in the field, but did not.

In March 1857 he was nominated British commissioner for the delimitation of the new boundary under the treaty of Paris between Turkey and Russia in Asia Major-general Charles George Gordon [q. v.] was one of three engineer officers who accompanied him as assistant commissioners. The whole frontier from Ararat to the Black Sea was traversed and questions of principle were settled by the commission; the actual marking of the boundary line was carried out by their expert assistants in the following year.

There were no carriage roads, and everything had to be carried on pack animals, while the altitudes over which they marched varied from 3000 to 7500 feet. Simmons returned home in Dec. 1857, and was promoted to a brevet colonelcy.

For two years (20 Feb. 1858–60) Simmons was British consul at Warsaw, where he gained the friendship of the viceroy, Prince Gortschakoff, and the esteem of both the Polish and the Russian communities. Promoted a regimental lieutenant-colonel on 31 Jan. 1860, Simmons was for the next five years commanding royal engineer at Aldershot. He received the reward for distinguished service on 3 Aug. 1862. Among several important committees of which he was a member during his command was one in 1865, on the Royal Engineers establishment at Chatham, presided over by the quartermaster-general, Sir Richard Airey [q. v.]. In September of the same year Simmons became director of the Royal Engineers establishment (now the School of Military Engineering) at Chatham with a view to carrying out the recommendations of the committee.

In Oct. 1868 he relinquished this appointment after his promotion as major-general (6 March), and in March 1869 he was made lieutenant-governor of the Royal Military Academy at Woolwich, becoming K.C.B. on 2 June. Hitherto the commander-in-chief was nominally governor of the Royal Military Academy, but in 1870 Simmons became governor with full responsibility. On 27 Aug. 1872 he was promoted lieutenant-general and was made a colonel commandant of royal engineers. The French Prince Imperial became a cadet at Woolwich in December, and thenceforth the Empress Eugénie regarded Sir Lintorn as a personal friend. While governor at Woolwich Simmons was a member of the royal commission on railway accidents in 1874 and 1875. After a highly successful reign of over six years he left Woolwich on his appointment as inspector-general of fortifications at the war office (1 Aug. 1875). In that office, which he held till 1880, he was the trusted adviser of the government on all questions connected with the defence of the empire. As chief technical military delegate with the British plenipotentiaries, Lord Beaconsfield and Lord Salisbury, at the Berlin Congress of 1878, he rendered valuable service. He had been promoted to be general on 1 Oct. 1877, and on 29 July 1878 was awarded the G.C.B. His services were again utilised by the foreign office at the international conference of Berlin, in June 1880, on the Greek frontier question, when he was chief technical military delegate with the British plenipotentiary, Lord Odo Russell [q. v.].

After leaving the war office in the summer of 1880 Sir Lintorn served on Lord Carnarvon's royal commission on the defence of British possessions and commerce abroad, until it reported in 1882. He was also a member of Lord Airey's committee on army reorganisation; he had published a pamphlet on the subject, 'The Military Forces of Great Britain,' in 1871.

Appointed governor of Malta in April 1884, Simmons satisfactorily inaugurated a change in the constitution whereby the number of elected members, which had been the same as the number of official members of council, was more than doubled. He did much to improve the condition of the island, especially as regards drainage, water supply, and coinage. On 24 May 1887 he was awarded the G.C.M.G. He remained at Malta until his retirement on 28 Sept. 1888. On 29 Oct. 1889 Sir Lintorn was appointed envoy extraordinary and minister plenipotentiary to Pope Leo XIII on a special mission with reference to questions of jurisdiction under the royal proclamation providing for the existing establishment of religion in Malta. With the assistance of Sir Giuseppe Carbone, the chief justice of Malta, he brought to a successful issue protracted negotiations respecting the marriage laws.

On 14 March 1890 the Sultan of Turkey conferred on Sir Lintorn the first class of the order of the Mejidie, and on 21 May of the same year Queen Victoria made him a field-marshal. As a devoted friend of General Gordon, Simmons was chairman of the Gordon Boys' Home, established in Gordon's memory. He spent the last years of his life with his son-in-law and daughter, Major and Mrs. Orman, at Hawley House, near Blackwater, Hampshire, where he died on 14 Feb. 1903; he was buried by his own wish at Churchill, Somersetshire, beside his wife. A military funeral service was held by command of King Edward VII at Hawley church. A memorial to the field-marshal's memory has been erected by his brother officers in the crypt of St. Paul's Cathedral, London, and at the Gordon Boys' Home at Woking.

Simmons was elected an associate of the Institution of Civil Engineers in 1847. He was also a member of the Royal United Service Institution, the Society of Arts, the Colonial Institute, and the Institute of Electrical Engineers.

His portrait in oils as a general was painted by Frank Holl, R.A., in 1883 for the corps of royal engineers, and hangs in the mess at Chatham. Another portrait in oils as a field-marshal, about 1890, was painted by H. Heute, a German artist, and is in Mrs. Orman's possession.

Simmons was married twice: (1) at Keynsham, near Bristol, Somersetshire, on 16 April 1846, to his cousin Ellen Lintorn Simmons, who died on 3 Oct. 1851, leaving a daughter, Eleanor Julia (*d.* unmarried in 1901); (2) in London, on 20 Nov. 1856, to Blanche (*d.* Feb. 1898), only daughter of Samuel Charles Weston, by whom he had one daughter, Blanche, wife of Major Charles Edward Orman, late Essex regiment.

[War Office Records; Royal Engineers' Records; Porter's History of the Royal Engineers, 1889; The Times, 16 Feb. 1903; Royal Engineers' Journal, Sept. 1903.]

R. H. V.

SIMON, Sir JOHN (1816–1904), sanitary reformer and pathologist, born in the City of London on 10 Oct. 1816, was sixth of the fourteen children of Louis Michael Simon (1782–1879), a member of the Stock Exchange, who served on the committee from 1837 till his retirement in 1868. His grandfathers were both Frenchmen, but having emigrated to England, each had there married an Englishwoman. Both his parents were very long lived, his father dying within three months of completing his ninety-eighth year, and his mother, Matilde Nonnet (1787–1882), within five days of completing her ninety-fifth year.

After three or four years at a preparatory school at Pentonville, John Simon spent seven and a half years at a private school at Greenwich kept by the Rev. Dr. Charles Parr Burney, son of Dr. Charles Burney [q. v.]. He then went to Rhenish Prussia to study with a German pfarrer for a year. The familiarity with the German language which he thus acquired was of great advantage to him later. He was intended for the medical profession, and on his return from Germany he was in the autumn of 1833 apprenticed for six years to Joseph Henry Green [q. v.], surgeon at St. Thomas's and professor of surgery at King's College, his father paying a fee of 500 guineas. In 1838 he became M.R.C.S. and in 1844 was made hon. F.R.C.S. In 1840, when King's College developed a hospital of its own, he was appointed its senior assistant surgeon. He held this post till 1847, when he was made lecturer on pathology at 200*l.* a year. He eventually became surgeon at St. Thomas's Hospital, his 'old and more familiar home,' where with progressive changes of title he remained officer for life (cf. *Personal Recollections*, privately printed, 1903). He became a great leader and teacher in pathology. In 1862–3 Simon was one of those who successfully urged the removal of the hospital from the Borough to the Albert Embankment. In 1876 he retired from the post of surgeon and was made consulting surgeon and governor of the hospital.

Ambitious of eventually becoming a consulting surgeon, Simon did not at first devote himself to his professional work with undue rigour. He spent his spare time on non-professional pursuits—on metaphysical reading, on Oriental languages, on study in the print-room of the British Museum. Such distribution of interest left the impress of literary ability and culture on his future writings and tastes (Dr. J. F. Payne in *Lancet,* ii. 1904). As early as 1842 he had written a pamphlet on medical education, and contributed the article 'Neck' to the 'Cyclopædia of Anatomy.' In 1844 he gained the first Astley-Cooper prize by an essay on the thymus gland (published with additions in the following year), and wrote for the Royal Society a paper on the thyroid gland (*Phil. Trans.* vol. 134), the value of which that society promptly recognised by electing him a fellow in January 1845, at the early age of twenty-nine. (As to the importance of these two researches in comparative anatomy, see Sir John Burdon Sanderson's Memoir in *Proc. Roy. Soc.* 1905, lxxv. 341.)

The current of Simon's thoughts and activities was wholly changed by his appointment in October 1848 as first medical officer of health for the City of London at a salary of 500*l.* a year (eventually 800*l.*). Liverpool was the first town in England to appoint a medical officer of health; London was the second. Simon, whose continued study of pathology at St. Thomas's Hospital gave him great advantage as a health officer, set to work at once with characteristic thoroughness, and presented a series of annual and other reports to the City commissioners of sewers which attracted great attention at the time, and may still be read with profit. They were unofficially reprinted in 1854, with a preface in which Simon spoke strongly of 'the national prevalence of sanitary neglect,' and demonstrated the urgent need of control of the public health by a responsible minister of state.

These views Simon kept steadily before him throughout his official career.

The general board of health had been created by government in 1848. It was reconstituted in 1854, and by a further act of 1855 the board was empowered to appoint a medical officer. Simon accepted the post in October 1855. The board was subject to successive annual renewals of its powers, and the new office was one of undefined purpose and doubtful stability (see a consolatory letter from Ruskin to Simon dated Turin, 20 July 1858, in vol. xxxvi. of RUSKIN'S *Complete Works*, p. 286). In 1858 the board was abolished, its duties being taken over by the lords of the council under the Public Health Act (1858), which to disarm opponents was framed to last for a single year. Simon thus became medical officer of the privy council. The act of 1858 was only made permanent in 1859 in face of strong opposition. Simon always held in grateful remembrance Robert Lowe [q.v.], then vice-president of the council for education, whose promptitude and vigour saved the bill (see his *English Sanitary Institutions*, chap. xii. p. 277 seq.; and for his appreciations of Lowe, PATCHETT MARTIN'S *Life*, ii. 185–98, 501–14).

Simon made to the general board of health several valuable and comprehensive reports: on the relation of cholera to London water supply (1856), on vaccination (1857), on the sanitary state of the people of England (1858), and on the constitution of the medical profession (1858). These are reprinted in full in his 'Public Health Reports' (vol. i. 1887). As medical officer of the privy council he instituted in 1858 annual reports on the working of his department, treating each year special subjects with broad outlook and in terse and graphic phrase. The most important parts were reprinted in 'Public Health Reports' (vol. ii. 1887). During this period (1858–71) Simon was implicitly trusted by his official superiors, was allowed a free hand, and rallied to his assistance a band of devoted fellow-workers, who helped to make the medical department a real power for good.

In August 1871, in accordance with the report of the royal sanitary commission which was appointed in April 1869 to consider means of co-ordinating the various public health authorities, the old poor law board, the local government act office (of the home office), and the medical department of the privy council were amalgamated to form one new department, the local government board. Simon became chief medical officer of the new board in the belief that his independent powers would be extended rather than diminished. But neither (Sir) James Stansfeld [q. v. Suppl. I], president of the board, nor (Sir) John Lambert [q.v.], organising secretary, took his view of his right of initiative and administrative independence. Simon protested in vigorous minutes and appeals, which were renewed when George Sclater-Booth [q.v.] became president in 1874. In the result, after a fierce battle with the treasury, his office was 'abolished,' and Simon retired in May 1876 on a special annual allowance of 1333*l.* 6*s.* 8*d.* He was less than sixty years old, and his energies were undecayed, so that the cause of sanitary progress was prejudiced by his retirement.

Simon received the inadequate reward of C.B., and was also made a crown member of the medical council, on which he did much good work until his resignation in 1895. In 1881 he was president of the state medicine section of the International Medical Congress held in London. With his friend, J. A. Kingdon, F.R.C.S., he was mainly responsible for the establishment by the Grocers' Company of scholarships for the promotion of sanitary science.

Simon took an active part in the affairs of the Royal College of Surgeons; from 1868 to 1880 he was one of the college council, from 1876 to 1878 was vice-president, and during 1878–9 acted as president. He filled also various honorary offices in professional societies. In 1887, on the occasion of Queen Victoria's first jubilee, he was promoted K.C.B. At the end of his career he received the first award of two medals which had been founded for the purpose of recognising eminence in sanitary science—the Harben medal of the Royal Institute of Public Health (1896) and the Buchanan medal of the Royal Society (November 1897). He was made hon. D.C.L. Oxford (1868), Med. Chir. Doctor Munich (1872), LL.D. Cambridge (1880), LL.D. Edinburgh (1882), and M.D. Dublin (1887).

In addition to professional and official acquaintances, Simon had many literary and artistic friends, including Alfred Elmore, R.A., Sir George Bowyer, George Henry Lewes, Mowbray Morris, (Sir) Edwin Chadwick, Thomas Woolner, R.A., Tom Taylor, Arthur Helps, and in particular John Ruskin [q. v. Suppl. I]. Simon first became acquainted with Ruskin and his parents through a chance meeting in Savoy in 1856, and the acquaintance ripened into a very warm friendship. Simon became in Ruskin's vocabulary, from the identity of Christian name, Ruskin's 'dear brother John' (*Works of Ruskin*, xxxv. 433; see especially *Sesame and Lilies*, xviii. 105, and *Time and Tide*, § 162, xvii. 450). Simon gave Ruskin sound advice as to his health, which Ruskin did not always adopt (see Sir E. T. COOK's *Life of Ruskin*, 1911, i. 392, and Ruskin's correspondence with Simon and his wife in *Ruskin's Works*, ed. COOK and WEDDERBURN, xxxvi.–vii. passim). To Ruskin the Simons owed their friendship with Sir Edward Burne-Jones and Lady Burne-Jones.

In March 1898, being then in failing health, Simon prepared for private circulation some 'Personal Recollections,' which were revised on 2 Dec. 1903, 'in blindness and infirmity.' He died at his house. 40 Kensington Square (where he had lived since 1867), on 23 July 1904, and was buried at Lewisham cemetery, Ladywell. By his will the ultimate residue of his estate was bequeathed to St. Thomas's Hospital. A bust by Thomas Woolner, R.A., executed in 1876, is at the Royal College of Surgeons.

On 22 July 1848 he married Jane (1816–1901) daughter of Matthew Delaval O'Meara, deputy commissary-general in the Peninsular war. He had no issue. Lady Simon was as close a friend of Ruskin as was her husband, and Ruskin familiarly named her his 'dear P.R.S.' (Pre-Raphaelite sister and Sibyl), or more shortly 'S.' (cf. LADY BURNE-JONES, *Memorials of Sir Edward Burne-Jones*, i. 257).

Sir Richard Douglas Powell, in his presidential address to the Royal Medico-Chirurgical Society in 1905 (vol. lxxxviii. p. cxv), said of Simon that he 'was a man gifted with true genius, and inspired with the love of his kind. He will ever remain a noble figure in the medicine of the nineteenth century, and will live in history as the apostle of sanitation.' The most important feature of Simon's work was his insistence that practice should be based on scientific knowledge, and his recognition of the large field for investigation without reference to immediate practical results. He was confident that such research (to use his own words) 'would lead to more precise and intimate knowledge of the causes and processes of important diseases, and thus augment, more and more, the vital resources of preventive medicine.'

Simon's chief reports and writings on sanitary subjects were issued collectively by subscription by the Sanitary Institute of Great Britain (2 vols. 1887). In 1890 he brought out 'English Sanitary Institutions, reviewed in their Course of Development, and in some of their Political and Social Relations' (2nd edit. 1897), a masterly survey which contains an elaborate vindication of his official career. Besides addresses to medical bodies, Simon wrote in 1878 a comprehensive article on Contagion for the 'Dictionary of Medicine' edited by Sir Richard Quain [q. v. Suppl. I].

[Personal Recollections of Sir John Simon, K.C.B. (privately printed in 1898, and revised in 1903); Public Health Reports (ed. Dr. E. Seaton), 2 vols. 1887 (with two portraits from photographs in 1848 and in 1876); English Sanitary Institutions, 1890; The Times, 25 July 1904; Lancet, vol. ii. 1904 (by Dr. J. F. Payne), pp. 308 et seq.; Brit. Med. Journal, vol. ii. 1904, pp. 265–356; Journal of Hygiene, vol. v. 1905, pp. 1–6; Proc. Roy. Soc., vol. lxxv. 1905 (by Sir John Burdon Sanderson); personal knowledge; private information.] E. C.

SIMONDS, JAMES BEART (1810–1904), veterinary surgeon, born at Lowestoft, Suffolk, on 18 Feb. 1810, was son of James Simonds (*d.* Oct. 1810) by his wife, a daughter of Robert Beart of Rickenhall, Suffolk, an agriculturist and horse-breeder. The father was grandson of James Simonds (born in 1717), who early left the original family home at Redenhall, Norfolk, for Halesworth, Suffolk. Of his five sons born there, Samuel (born in 1754), the fourth, who resided at Bungay in Suffolk, had four sons, the eldest (Samuel) and youngest (John) entering the veterinary profession; the second son, James, was father of the subject of this notice.

James Beart, brought up by his grandparents at Bungay, was educated at the Bungay grammar school, and entered the Veterinary College in London as a student on 7 Jan. 1828. He received his diploma to practise in March 1829, and succeeded to his uncle Samuel's business as a veterinary surgeon at Bungay. In 1836 he migrated to Twickenham, and shortly after took a share in organising the scientific work connected with the animals of the farm of the then newly established English Agricultural Society, of which he became an ordinary member on 25 July 1838 (honorary member, 3 April 1849; foundation life governor, 5 March 1890). In 1842 he was appointed to a new professorship of cattle pathology at the Veterinary College in Camden Town, and was made consulting veterinary surgeon to the Royal Agricultural Society (a position he held for sixty-two years until his death). Settling in London, and disposing of his practice at Twickenham, he was active in the movement for obtaining the charter which was granted on 8 March 1844 to the Royal College of Veterinary Surgeons, of which in due course (1862–3), he became president. He took a prominent part in the efforts of the Royal Agricultural Society to popularise information amongst farmers as to the diseases of animals, and he investigated their causes and means of prevention. In 1857 he carried out an inquiry on the Continent into the cattle plague, which was then committing great ravages, and made a report of eighty-three pages thereon. His information proved useful on a sudden outbreak of the same disease in London in June 1865. The privy council office, owing to doubt of its legal powers, delayed the issue of an order for the slaughtering and burial in quicklime of all diseased animals, until the infection had spread over a great part of England. A veterinary department was improvised at the privy council office to deal with the matter. Simonds was appointed chief inspector and professional adviser, and amongst his helpers was Professor (afterwards Sir) George Thomas Brown [q. v. Suppl. II]. After the stamping out of the outbreak of cattle plague, which was estimated to have cost five millions sterling in money loss alone, it was decided to continue the veterinary department as a permanent branch of the council office, and Simonds remained at its head until November 1871, when he resigned in order to become principal of the Royal Veterinary College in succession to Professor Charles Spooner [q. v.]. Owing to failing health, he retired in June 1881 on a pension, removing to the Isle of Wight. He remained senior consulting veterinary surgeon to the Royal Agricultural Society until his death, at the age of ninety-four years, on 5 July 1904.

He was twice married, his first wife being his cousin, Martha Beart (*d.* 22 Aug. 1851), by whom he was father of James Sexton Simonds, for some time chief of the metropolitan fire brigade, and of two daughters. His second wife survived him.

[Autobiography, reprinted with portrait from the Veterinarian, vol. lxvii. (1894), and privately issued in 1894; Veterinary Record, 9 July 1904; personal knowledge.] E. C.

SIMPSON, MAXWELL (1815–1902), chemist, was youngest son of Thomas Simpson, Beach Hill, co. Armagh, where he was born on 15 March 1815. His mother's maiden surname was Browne. After attending Dr. Henderson's school at Newry he entered Trinity College, Dublin, in 1832. Here he made the acquaintance of Charles Lever, by whose advice he began to study medicine. He graduated B.A. in 1837, but left Dublin without a medical degree. On a visit to Paris he heard a lecture by the chemist Jean Baptiste André Dumas on chemistry, which induced him to study that subject seriously. For two years he worked under Thomas Graham [q.v.] at University College, London. On his marriage in 1845 he returned to Dublin, and in 1847 he became lecturer on chemistry in the Park Street Medical School, Dublin, and proceeded M.B. In 1849, on the closure of the Park Street School, he became a lecturer on chemistry in the Peter Street or 'Original' School of Medicine. In 1851 he was granted three years' leave of absence. He studied in Germany under Adolph Kolbe in Marburg and Robert Bunsen in Heidelberg, and accomplished his first original work. In 1854 he resumed his duties at Dublin, but in 1857 resigned his lecturership and again went to the Continent, working chiefly with Wurtz in Paris till 1859. In 1860 Simpson took a house in Dublin and fitted up a small laboratory in the back kitchen. There he pursued with ardour and success chemical investigations which placed him among the first chemists of his time. One of his earliest results was the discovery of a method of determining the nitrogen in organic compounds difficult to burn. He obtained synthetically for the first time succinic and certain other di- and tri-basic acids (*Phil. Trans.* 1860, p. 61; *Proc. Roy. Soc.* 1863, pp. 12, 236), while not a year passed without his publishing one or two papers of the first importance. In 1867 he revisited Wurtz's laboratory in Paris, and for a few subsequent years he lived in London. He acted as examiner at Woolwich, at Coopers Hill for the Indian Civil Service, and in the Queen's University of Ireland. In 1872 he was appointed professor of chemistry in Queen's College, Cork, and held the post till 1891, devoting himself to teaching, to the practical exclusion of research.

In 1862 Simpson was elected a fellow of the Royal Society, and he was a fellow of the Royal University of Ireland from 1882 to 1891. From Dublin he received the honorary degrees of M.D. in 1864 and LL.D. in 1878, and from the Queen's University of Ireland the honorary degree of D.Sc. in 1882. In 1868 he was elected an honorary fellow of the

King's and Queen's College of Physicians. He became a fellow of the Chemical Society in 1857, and was vice-president from 1872 to 1874. He was president of the chemical section of the British Association at its Dublin meeting in 1878.

After his retirement in 1891 from the chair of chemistry at Cork, he resided in London, and died at 7 Darnley Road, Holland Park Avenue, London, on 26 Feb. 1902. He was buried in Fulham cemetery.

He married in 1845 Mary (*d.* 1900), daughter of Samuel Martin of Longhorne, co. Down, and sister of John Martin, M.P., the Irish politician [q. v.]. She was enthusiastically interested in her husband's work. There were six children of the marriage, of whom two survived him. Simpson was a man of wide culture, lively humour, and kindly personality.

[Obituary Notices in Year-Book of the Royal Society, 1903; Transactions of the Chemical Society (by Prof. A. Senier), June 1902; The Times, 8 March 1902; Cameron's History of the Royal College of Surgeons in Ireland; Todd's Catalogue of Graduates in the University of Dublin; MS. Entrance Book of Trinity College, Dublin.] R. J. R.

SIMPSON, WILFRED. [See HUDLESTON, WILFRED HUDLESTON, F.R.S. (1828–1909), geologist.]

SINGLETON, MRS. MARY. [See CURRIE, MARY MONTGOMERIE, LADY CURRIE (1843–1905), author under the pseudonym of 'VIOLET FANE.']

SKIPSEY, JOSEPH (1832–1903), the collier poet, born on 17 March 1832 at Percy, a parish in the borough of Tynemouth, Northumberland, was youngest of the eight children of Cuthbert Skipsey, a miner, by his wife Isabella Bell. In his infancy his father was shot in a collision between pitmen and special constables during some labour disturbances. Skipsey, who worked in the coal pits from the age of seven, had no schooling, but he soon taught himself to read and write. Until he was fifteen the Bible was the only book to which he had access. After that age he managed to study Milton, Shakespeare, Burns, and some translations from Latin, Greek, and German, particularly the poems of Heine and Goethe's 'Faust.' In 1852 he walked most of the way to London; and after finding employment connected with railway construction, and marrying his landlady, returned to work first at Coatbridge in Scotland for six months, then at the Pembroke Collieries near Sunderland, and subsequently at Choppington. In 1859 he published a volume of 'Poems,' no copy of which seems extant (cf. pref. to *Miscellaneous Lyrics*, 1878). The book attracted the attention of James Clephan, editor of the 'Gateshead Observer,' who obtained for him the post of under storekeeper at the Gateshead works of Hawks, Crawshay, and Sons. In 1863, after a fatal accident to one of his children in the works, he removed to Newcastle-on-Tyne, to become assistant librarian to the Newcastle Literary and Philosophical Society. The duties proved uncongenial, and he returned in 1864 to mines near Newcastle, remaining at work for various coal firms until 1882. Subsequently he obtained lighter employment. From 1882 to 1885 he and his wife were caretakers of the Bentinck board schools in Mill Lane, Newcastle. From September 1888 to June 1889 he was janitor at the Armstrong College (Durham University College of Science).

Meanwhile his poetic and intellectual faculty steadily developed, and his literary ambitions were encouraged by his friend Thomas Dixon, the working-man of Sunderland to whom Ruskin addressed the twenty-five letters published as 'Time and Tide by Weare and Tyne.' Skipsey published 'Poems, Songs, and Ballads' (1862); 'The Collier Lad, and other Lyrics' (1864); 'Poems' (1871); and 'A Book of Miscellaneous Lyrics' (1878, re-issued with additions and omissions as 'A Book of Lyrics,' 1881). There followed 'Carols from the Coalfields' (1886); and 'Songs and Lyrics' (1892). Skipsey's published work soon received praise from critics of insight. D. G. Rossetti commended his poems of mining life. 'A Book of Miscellaneous Lyrics' was appreciatively reviewed in the 'Athenæum' (16 Nov. 1878) by Theodore Watts-Dunton. Oscar Wilde likened his 'Carols from the Coalfields' to the work of William Blake. In 1884–5 Skipsey acted as first general editor of the 'Canterbury Poets' (published by Walter Scott of Newcastle), and wrote rhetorical and discursive but suggestive prefaces to the reprints of the poetry of Burns (two essays), Shelley, Coleridge, Blake, and Poe. A lecture, 'The Poet as Seer and Singer,' was delivered before the Newcastle-on-Tyne Literary and Philosophical Society in 1883, and was published in 1890.

Meanwhile in 1880 Dixon brought Skipsey to London and introduced him to Burne-Jones, to whose efforts the grant of a civil list pension of 10*l.* (raised in 1886 to 25*l.*, with a donation of 50*l.* from the Royal Bounty Fund) was largely due. On 24 June 1889 Skipsey and his wife were appointed custodians of Shakespeare's birthplace at Stratford-on-Avon on the recommendation of Browning, Tennyson, Burne-Jones, John Morley, Dante Gabriel Rossetti, William Morris, and other literary men of eminence. But he soon grew impatient of the drudgery of acting as cicerone to miscellaneous tourists, and he resigned the post on 31 Oct. 1891 (cf. HENRY JAMES's story, 'The Birthplace,' in *The Better Sort*, 1903, which was suggested by a vague report of Skipsey's psychological experience at Stratford-on-Avon). Thenceforth Skipsey and his wife subsisted in the north on his pension and the assistance of his children, with whom they lived in turns. Visits to the English Lakes and to Norway (with Newcastle friends, Dr. and Mrs. Spence Watson) varied the seclusion of his last years. He died at Gateshead, in the house of his son Cuthbert, on 3 Sept. 1903, and was buried in Gateshead cemetery. In 1854 he married Sara Ann (daughter of Benjamin and Susan Hendley), the proprietress of the boarding-house at which he was staying in London. His wife died in August 1902. Two out of five sons and the eldest of three daughters survived him.

Skipsey's poems were mainly lyrical, although he occasionally attempted more sustained flights, and they show the influence of Burns and Heine. He is at his best in the verse which was prompted by his own experience as a pitman. He acquired the habit of carefully revising his work, but he failed to conquer a native ruggedness of diction. De Chatelain translated his 'Fairies' Parting Song' and other shorter poems in his 'Beautés de la poésie anglaise,' vol. iii. A projected 'History of Æstheticism' proved beyond his powers. For a time he put faith in spiritualism, conceiving himself to be a clairvoyant, and he left some unpublished writings on the subject.

A portrait of Skipsey was painted by a German artist for Wigham Richardson, a member of a firm of shipbuilders of Walker-on-Tyne, and hangs in the Mechanics' Institute there.

[Joseph Skipsey, by R. Spence Watson, 1909; Autobiographical preface to A Book of Miscellaneous Lyrics, 1878; W. Bell Scott's Autobiographical Notes, 1892; A. H. Miles's Poets and Poetry of the Century, vol. 5; Athenæum, 16 Nov. 1878 and 12 Sept. 1903; Lady Burne-Jones's Memorials of Edward Burne-Jones, ii. 107-8; Shakespeare's Birthplace records; private information.]

E. S. H-R.

SLANEY, WILLIAM SLANEY KENYON- (1847-1908), colonel and politician. [See KENYON-SLANEY.]

SMEATON, DONALD MACKENZIE (1846-1910), Anglo-Indian official, born at St. Andrews on 9 Sept. 1846, was eldest of the twelve children of David James Smeaton, schoolmaster of Letham House, Fife, and Abbey Park, St. Andrews, by his wife Elizabeth, daughter of Capt. Donald Mackenzie of the 42nd Black Watch, who fought through the Peninsular war and at Waterloo. His ancestors included Thomas Smeton [q. v.], the first principal of Glasgow University, and John Smeaton, the engineer [q. v.]. His next brother, Robert Mackenzie (1847-1910), was his colleague in the civil service of the North-West provinces of India and a member of the local legislative council.

Smeaton was educated at his father's efficient school, Abbey Park, St. Andrews, and at the university there, where he graduated M.A. He passed second in the Indian civil service examination of 1865, and arriving in India in November 1867, served in the North-West provinces as assistant magistrate and collector, and from May 1870 in the settlement department. He won a medal and 100*l.* for proficiency in oriental languages. In 1873 he published an annotated edition of the revenue act of the provinces, and in 1877 a useful monograph on Indian currency. In April 1879 he was sent to Burma to organise the land revenue administration there, and in May 1882 he was appointed secretary in that department and director of agriculture.

After serving as director of agriculture and commerce in the North-West provinces from May 1886, he returned in April 1887 to Burma, on the annexation of the upper province, as officiating chief secretary to the chief commissioner, Sir Charles Bernard [q. v. Suppl. II]. In Upper Burma he closely studied the hill races of the new province, and he embodied his inquiries in 'Loyal Karens of Burma' (1887), which is the standard work on its theme. In May 1888 he became commissioner of the central division of Upper Burma, and his vigorous work in suppressing dacoits gained him the Burma medal with two clasps. Smeaton's interest in the people and mastery of their vernaculars established his influence over both the Burmans and the semi-civilised hill tribes. In March 1891 he was appointed financial commissioner of Burma, and helped to develop the mining industries, while rigidly abstaining from any private investments. Acting chief commissioner in May 1892, and also from 25 April to 9 Aug. 1896, he officially represented Burma on the supreme legislative council from 1898 to 1902. In the council he showed characteristic independence. He advocated an amendment of the Lower Burma chief courts bill, which the government of India opposed, and he boldly criticised Indian land revenue policy in March 1902. Selected by Lord Curzon to be secretary of the famine relief committee of 1900, he showed an energy which was acknowledged by the award of the Kaisar-i-Hind medal of the first class on its institution in May 1900. Disappointed of the lieutenant-governorship of Burma in succession to Sir Frederick Fryer, he retired from the service in 1902.

Settling for five years at Winchfield, Hampshire, Smeaton interested himself in local affairs and in the cause of the liberal party. He subsequently removed to Gomshall, Surrey. On platforms in London and in Scotland he urged reform of the government of India (cf. *A Future for India*, a reprint from *India*, 12 Feb. 1904), but he did not identify himself with the extreme section of Indian agitators. At the general election of 1906 he was elected liberal M.P. for Stirlingshire. In parliament he supported the strong measures taken by the Indian government against disorder in 1907 and 1908, and in the debates on the Indian Councils Act, 1909, embodying Lord Morley's reforms, he acknowledged the importance of maintaining the essentials of British authority. He worked hard in committee of the House of Commons, and followed Scottish questions with assiduity, speaking briefly and to the point, and obeying the party 'Whip' with conscientious discrimination. Failing health disabled him from offering himself for reelection on the dissolution in January 1910. He died on 19 April 1910 at his residence, Lawbrook, Gomshall, Surrey, and was buried at Peaslake, Surrey. An oil painting by Mr. H. J. C. Bryce belongs to his widow. He married twice: (1) on 2 Feb. 1873 Annette Louise, daughter of Sir Henry Lushington, fourth baronet; she died on 17 Jan. 1880; by her he had a son, Arthur Lushington, lieutenant in the 18th Tiwana lancers, who was killed at polo in July 1903, and a daughter; and (2) on 12 Nov. 1894 Marion, daughter of Major Ansell of the 4th (K.O.) regiment; she survived him with one daughter.

[India List, 1910; Ind. Finan. Statement and Discussion thereon for 1902–3; Parly. Debates, 1906 to 1909; Rangoon Gaz. and Rangoon Times of various dates; Pioneer, 5 and 20 Feb. 1902; The Times, 21 April 1910; personal knowledge; information kindly supplied by Mrs. Smeaton.] F. H. B.

SMILES, SAMUEL (1812–1904), author and social reformer, born at Haddington on 23 Dec. 1812, was one of eleven children of Samuel Smiles, at first a paper maker and afterwards a general merchant, who died of cholera early in 1832. His mother was Janet, daughter of Robert Wilson of Dalkeith. His paternal grandfather was an elder and field-preacher of the Cameronians, the sect which suffered persecution in Charles II's reign.

After education at Haddington grammar school, Smiles was bound apprentice for five years on 6 Nov. 1826 to a firm of medical practitioners in the town. Dr. Lewins, one of the partners, moved to Leith in 1829 and took Smiles with him. The lad matriculated at Edinburgh University in Nov. 1829 and attended the medical classes there. John Brown [q. v.], author of 'Rab and his Friends,' was a fellow student. On the expiration of his apprenticeship he took lodgings in Edinburgh and, pursuing his medical education, obtained his medical diploma on 6 Nov. 1832. Thereupon he settled as a general practitioner at Haddington, but his ambitions travelled beyond the routine of his profession, and he soon supplemented his narrow income by popular lectures on chemistry, physiology, and the conditions of health, as well as by contributions to the 'Edinburgh Weekly Chronicle.' In 1837 he published at Edinburgh. at his own expense, 750 copies of 'Physical Education, or the Nurture and Management of Children' (2nd edit. 1868). The work was generally commended. A new edition with additions by Sir Hugh Beevor, bart., appeared in 1905.

Discontented with the prospects of his Haddington practice and anxious to widen his experience, Smiles, in May 1838, sold such property as he possessed and left Haddington for Hull, with a view to a foreign tour. From Rotterdam he went to Leyden, where he submitted himself to examination for a degree. A pedestrian tour followed through Holland and up the Rhine. In Sept. 1838 he paid a first visit to London, lodging in the same boarding house (in Poland Street, Oxford Street) as Mazzini, and presenting introductions to (Sir) Rowland Hill. On his way north he visited Ebenezer Elliott at Sheffield. Thence in answer to a newspaper advertisement, he passed to Leeds to fulfil an engagement on the 'Leeds Times,' an organ of advanced radicalism, from the editorship of which Robert Nicoll [q. v.] had just retired. In Nov. 1838 Smiles became editor at a salary of 200*l.* a year.

At Leeds Smiles combined with his editorial duties an active share in political agitation in the advanced liberal cause. He was the first secretary of the Leeds 'Household Suffrage Association' for the redistribution and extension of the franchise. At public meetings in the city and its neighbourhood he advocated the anti-corn law movement. He corresponded with Cobden and enthusiastically supported Joseph Hume's abortive candidature for the representation of Leeds at the general election of 1841. While he opposed chartism, he urged the social and intellectual amelioration of the working classes, and interested himself in industrial organisation and the progress of mechanical science. In 1842 he resigned the editorship of the 'Leeds Times.' Devoting himself to popular lecturing and literary hack work, he prepared guides to America and the colonies, and brought out in 1843, in monthly numbers, 'A History of Ireland and the Irish People under the Government of England,' which was published collectively in 1844.

In June 1840 Smiles had attended the opening of the North Midland railway from Leeds to Derby, and met for the first time George Stephenson. When, at the end of 1845, the Leeds and Thirsk railway was projected, Smiles was appointed assistant secretary. He was closely associated with railway enterprise for the next twenty-one years. The new Thirsk line was opened on 9 July 1849. In the same year Smiles published an essay on 'Railway Property, its Conditions and Prospects,' which ran through two editions. Smiles also acted as secretary of the board which managed the new Leeds central station, into which many companies ran their trains. He was prominent in the negotiations for the amalgamation of the Leeds and Thirsk railway with the North Eastern, which was effected in 1854 and abolished his own office. Thereupon he left Leeds for London on being appointed secretary to the South Eastern railway (11 Nov.). He held the post for twelve years, in the course of which he successfully arranged for the extension of the line from Charing Cross to Cannon Street (1858–9).

Smiles's railway work had not blunted his energies as an advocate, in the press and on the lecture platform, of political and social reform, in agreement with the principles of the Manchester school. In the 'Constitutional,' a Glasgow paper, he urged the transference of private bills to local legislatures. He wrote much in behalf of workmen's benefit societies in the 'Leeds Mercury' and elsewhere, and for a time edited the 'Oddfellows' Magazine.' He championed state education. The formation of public libraries was one of his strenuous interests, and he gave evidence in their favour before a House of Commons committee in 1849, welcoming the permissive Library and Museums Act of the following year. From 1855 Smiles wrote occasionally on industrial subjects to the 'Quarterly Review'; an article on 'Workmen's Earnings, Strikes, and Savings' was reissued as a pamphlet in 1861. A speech at Huddersfield on the 'Industrial education of foreign and English workmen' was published in 1867.

Smiles was drawn to the study and writing of biography, in which he made his chief reputation, by the sanguine belief that concrete examples of men who had achieved great results by their own efforts best indicated the true direction and goal of social and industrial progress. On the death in 1848 of George Stephenson, with whom he had come into occasional contact at Leeds, he wrote a memoir in 'Eliza Cook's Journal' in 1849, and afterwards persuaded Stephenson's son Robert to allow him to write a full life. The book appeared in June 1857, and was received with enthusiasm; 2500 copies were sold before September, 7500 within a year. An American reprint appeared at Boston in 1858. An 18th thousand was reached in 1864, and an abridgment came out in 1859. The biography fully maintained its popularity in subsequent years. Fresh work on the same lines soon followed. In 1861–2 he produced 'Lives of the Engineers' (3 vols.); in 1863 'Industrial Biography: Iron Workers and Tool Makers'; and in 1865 'Lives of Boulton and Watt.' A new edition of the 'Life of George Stephenson' in 1868 contained an account of the son, Robert Stephenson. All these volumes were reissued under the single title of the 'Lives of the Engineers' in 1874 in 5 vols. (popular edit. 1904). Smiles had full access to manuscript sources, and the books are standard contributions to English biographical literature. A French translation of all the volumes came out in 1868. A supplemental compilation, 'Men of Invention and Industry,' appeared in 1884.

As early as March 1845 Smiles had delivered, at a small mutual improvement society at Leeds, an address on the education of the working classes, in which he showed how many poor men had created for themselves, with beneficial effect on their careers, opportunities of knowledge and culture. The lecture, which owed something to George Lillie Craik's 'Knowledge pursued under Difficulties' (1830–1), was constantly repeated with expansion, and was received with great applause in many parts of the country. By degrees Smiles enlarged the lecture into a substantial treatise under the title of 'Self-Help, with Illustrations of Character and Conduct.' The MS. was refused in 1855 by the publisher Routledge, but in July 1859 John Murray, who published Smiles's 'George Stephenson' and the other engineering biographies, undertook the publication on commission. An immense success was the result: 20,000 copies were sold in the first year; 55,000 by 1864; 150,000 by 1889, and 120,000 copies since. The book impressed the public to whom it was especially addressed, and Smiles was in constant receipt of assurances of the practical encouragement which he had given artisans in all parts of the world. 'Self-Help' was translated into almost all foreign languages—including Dutch, German, Danish, Swedish, Spanish, Italian, Turkish, Arabic, Japanese, and the native tongues of India. In succeeding volumes, 'Character' (1871), 'Thrift' (1875), 'Duty' (1880), and 'Life and Labour' (1887), Smiles pursued his useful scheme of collecting biographical facts and coordinating them so as to stimulate good endeavour. Repetition in these volumes was inevitable, and the triumph of 'Self-Help' did not recur. 'Character' approached but failed to reach the great sales of its predecessor. Yet all but the latest of these books achieved exceptional circulations in English-speaking countries as well as in foreign translations. In 1875 Smiles successfully brought an action against a Canadian publisher named Belford for smuggling into the United States pirated copies of 'Thrift.'

On 30 Aug. 1866 he left the South Eastern railway, receiving a service of plate from the directors and staff with a pass over the company's lines. He thereupon became president of the National Provident Institution, and in that capacity travelled much about the country. A lecture on a fresh topic, 'The Huguenots in England and Ireland,' which he delivered at Dublin to the Young Men's Christian Association, while on a business journey, was developed into a volume on 'The Huguenots: their Settlements, Churches and Industries in England and Ireland' (published Nov. 1867); 10,000 copies were rapidly sold.

A sharp stroke of paralysis, the result of overwork, in Nov. 1871 disabled Smiles for a year, and he retired from the National Provident Institution. But he made a good recovery, and thenceforth divided his time between literature on much the same lines as before, and travel during which he amused himself by close observation of racial characteristics. Besides tours in Ireland and Scotland, he visited the Huguenot country in the south of France, and embodied new researches in 'The Huguenots in France after the Revocation of the Edict of Nantes; with a Visit to the Vaudois' (1874). He returned to the south of France in 1881 to study the Basque people and language, and in the Gascon country during 1888 he collected details of the biography of the barber-poet of Agen, Jacques Jasmin (1798–1864), whose career illustrated his favourite text and of whom he published a memoir in 1891. In 1871 and 1881 he made a tour in Friesland and neighbouring lands, and in 1884 through the west coast of Norway. He thrice visited Italy, where his works enjoyed a wide circulation, and on his second visit in the spring of 1879 he was accorded a great reception in Rome, where he visited Garibaldi and Queen Margherita. Next year he received the Italian order of St. Maurice and St. Lazarus. On visits to Scotland he found fresh biographical materials of the kind which specially appealed to him, and he brought out lives of the self-taught Scotch naturalist, Thomas Edward of Banff, in 1876, and of Robert Dick, a baker of Thurso, who was also a botanist and geologist, in 1878.

Smiles lived at Blackheath until 1874, when he settled in Kensington. In 1878 he received the hon. degree of LL.D. from Edinburgh, and in the same year he issued a life of the philanthropist, George Moore, a task which he undertook reluctantly, but which was more popular than any of his later publications. He printed for the first time James Nasmyth's autobiography in 1883, but the edition had a scanty sale. Subsequently, for his friend and publisher John Murray, Smiles produced in 1891

'A Publisher and his Friends: Memoir and Correspondence of the late John Murray, with an Account of the Origin and Progress of the House, 1768–1843' (2 vols.; abridged edit. 1911). In 1894 there followed 'Josiah Wedgwood, F.R.S., his Personal History.' His last years were mainly spent on an unpretentious autobiography, bringing his career to 1890; it was edited for posthumous issue in 1905 by his friend Thomas Mackay. Smiles's powers slowly failed, and he died at his residence at Kensington on 16 April 1904, being buried at Brompton Cemetery.

Smiles married at Leeds, on 7 Dec. 1843, Sarah Ann Holmes (*d.* 1900), daughter of a Leeds contractor, and had issue three daughters and two sons. He edited in 1871 'A Boy's Voyage round the World in 1868–9,' by his younger son.

A portrait painted by Sir George Reid is in the National Portrait Gallery; it was etched by Paul Rajon. A sketch of Smiles was made at Rome by Guglielmo de Sancto in March 1889. Rossetti, an Italian sculptor, also executed a bust at Rome in 1879.

[Smiles's Autobiography, ed. Thomas Mackay, 1905; The Times, 17 April 1904; T. Bowden Green's Samuel Smiles, his Life and Work, with pref. by Mrs. Alec Tweedie, 1904 (a slight pamphlet with portraits); Sarah Tytler's Three Generations, 1911.] S. L.

SMITH, Sir ARCHIBALD LEVIN (1836–1901), judge, born at Salt Hill near Chichester on 27 Aug. 1836, was only son of Francis Smith of that place, by his wife Mary Ann, only daughter of Zadik Levin. After attending Eton, and receiving private tuition at home and at Chichester, he completed his education at Trinity College, Cambridge, where he graduated B.A. in 1858. Like several of his contemporaries on the judicial bench, he rowed in the university eight in the Oxford and Cambridge boat-race three years running (1857, 1858, 1859). On the last occasion the race was rowed in a gale of wind, and the Cambridge boat filled and sank between Barnes Bridge and the finish. According to tradition, Smith alone of the Cambridge oarsmen could not swim, and sat stolidly rowing until, when the water was up to his neck, he was rescued not without difficulty. Smith was also through life a good cricketer, playing frequently for the Gentlemen of Sussex. He had entered as a student of the Inner Temple on 27 May 1856, and was called on 17 Nov. 1860, when he joined the home circuit. He rapidly acquired a good and increasing junior practice, being largely employed in commercial cases and in election petitions, and having a full pupil-room. In 1879, on the appointment of Charles (afterwards Lord) Bowen [q. v. Suppl. I] to a judgeship, he was nominated by Sir John Holker [q. v.], attorney-general, to be standing junior counsel to the treasury, and after an unusually short tenure of that office he was made a judge of the Queen's Bench Division in 1883. He was elected a bencher of his inn on 12 April, and was knighted on 20 April of that year.

Smith, big and strong physically, was devoted to sport, and was in an exceptional degree 'a good fellow.' To these advantages he added cheerful and unremitting industry and great natural acuteness. Consequently it mattered very little that his voice was weak, or that he had no gift of eloquence, his language being to the end of his life confined to the homeliest vernacular. He was extremely fond of shooting and fishing; he was (in 1899) president of the M.C.C., and the university boatrace and cricket-match aroused his never-failing interest. He was, in the best sense of the words, a man of the world, and his honesty, vigour, and good sense were everywhere recognised.

In 1888 Smith was appointed a special commissioner with Sir James Hannen [q. v.] and Mr. Justice Day to inquire into allegations published by 'The Times' affecting C. S. Parnell and other Irish nationalists. During the sitting of this tribunal the commissioners adopted a practice of silence. On one occasion, when the president, Hannen, who had a gift for saying much in the fewest words, observed that he had not thought or imputed something of which some of those appearing before the commission had complained, Smith said 'Nor I,' and Day made an inarticulate sound of concurrence; but it was believed that, with this exception, neither of the junior judges said a word during the prolonged proceedings. Smith tried, while he was in the Queen's Bench Division, the first case heard under the Foreign Enlistment Act, 1870, when a Colonel Sandoval was convicted of fitting out a hostile expedition against Venezuela, and was sentenced to three months' imprisonment.

In 1892 Smith was promoted, with general approval, to the Court of Appeal, his original colleagues there being Esher, Master of the Rolls, Lindley, Bowen, Fry, and Kay. Esher had much in common with Smith; the others were all more learned lawyers. Smith's modesty, force of character, and great intelligence enabled him however to hold his own so effectively that he was appointed in October 1900 without any sign of dissatisfaction to succeed Lord Alverstone as Master of the Rolls. His health and strength soon began to fail. In August 1901 his wife, who had suffered from a long and distressing illness, was drowned in the Spey, near Aberlour, almost in his presence. Smith never recovered from the shock, and died at Wester-Elchies House, Aberlour, Morayshire, the residence of his son-in-law, Mr. Grant, on 20 Oct. 1901, a few days after resigning the mastership of the rolls. He was buried at Knockando, Morayshire. Smith married in 1867 Isobel, daughter of John Charles Fletcher, and left two sons and three daughters.

Smith contributed to 'The Walkers of Southgate' (1900) a chapter entitled 'Reminiscences by an old friend.'

[Foster's Men at the Bar; The Times, 21 Oct. 1901; Haygarth's Cricket Scores and Biographies, viii. 319; Wisden's Cricketers' Almanack for 1902, p. lxx.] H. S.

SMITH, Sir CHARLES BEAN EUAN- (1842–1910), diplomatist. [See Euan-Smith.]

SMITH, Sir FRANCIS, afterwards Sir Francis Villeneuve (1819–1909), chief Justice of Tasmania, born at Lindfield, Sussex, on 13 Feb. 1819, was elder son of Francis Smith, then of that place, and a merchant of London, by his wife Marie Josephine, daughter of Jean Villeneuve. At an early age Smith accompanied his father to Van Diemen's Land (now Tasmania), where the latter purchased an estate called Campania, near Richmond, in that colony. Returning to England for his education, he attended University College, London, and London University, where he graduated B.A. in 1840 and took a first prize in international law. He was called to the bar by the Middle Temple on 27 May 1842, and was a bencher of his Inn from 1890 to 1898. In October 1844 he was admitted to the bar of Van Diemen's Land.

During 1848 he acted as solicitor-general of the colony in the absence on leave of A. C. Stonor. On 1 Jan. 1849 he was appointed crown solicitor and clerk of the peace, and again acted as solicitor-general from 15 Dec. 1851 to 1 Aug. 1854, when he was appointed attorney-general, taking office only on the condition of being at liberty to oppose the influx of convicts into the colony. He retained the post until the change in the constitution in 1856, when his office was abolished and he was granted 4500*l*. as compensation. On 15 Dec. 1851 he was nominated a member of the legislative council.

Although opposed to the introduction of responsible government on the ground that the colony did not possess a leisured class from which suitable ministers could be drawn, and that the system would involve constant changes of administration, yet Smith was returned as one of the representatives of Hobart in the first House of Assembly, and accepted the portfolio of attorney-general in the first responsible ministry, which was formed by W. T. Champ on 1 Nov. 1856; he was also sworn a member of the executive council. Champ's administration fell by an adverse vote in the house on 26 Feb. 1857, but Smith returned to office on 25 April as attorney-general in W. P. Weston's government. On 12 May 1857 he took over the duties of premier in addition to those of attorney-general, and the reconstructed ministry remained in office for three years and a half. During that time much legislation of a useful character was passed, including the settlement of the long-pending 'Abbott claim,' the establishment of scholarships, the liberalising of the land laws, and the amendment of the Constitution Act.

On 1 Nov. 1860 Smith was made a puisne judge of the supreme court, and on 5 Feb. 1870 he was appointed chief justice in succession to Sir Valentine Fleming. In that position his legal knowledge and ability, combined with his high character, won for him every confidence. Twice he administered the government of the colony in the absence of the governor, viz. from 30 Nov. 1874 to 13 Jan. 1875, and again from 6 April to 21 Oct. 1880. He was knighted by patent on 18 July 1862, and retired on a pension 31 March 1884. He spent his remaining years in England, and died on 17 Jan. 1909 at his residence, Heathside, Tunbridge Wells. His remains were cremated at Golder's Green.

Smith married on 4 May 1851 Sarah (*d.* 29 July 1909), only child of the Rev. George Giles, D.D., and left one son and two daughters. In 1884 he assumed the additional name of Villeneuve.

[The Times, and Tasmanian Examiner, 20 Jan. 1909; Tunbridge Wells Advertiser, 22 Jan. 1909; Burke's Peerage, 1909; Johns's Notable Australians, 1908; Mennell's Dict. of Australas. Biog. 1892; Tasmanian Official Record, 1890; Fenton's History of Tasmania, 1884; Colonial Office Records; private information.] C. A.

SMITH, GEORGE (1824–1901), publisher, the founder and proprietor of the Dictionary. [See Memoir prefixed to the First Supplement.]

SMITH, GEORGE BARNETT (1841–1909), author and journalist, born at Ovenden, Yorkshire, on 17 May 1841, was son of Titus and Mary Smith. Educated at the British Lancastrian school, Halifax, he came in youth to London, and there worked actively as a journalist. From 1865 to 1868 he was on the editorial staff of the 'Globe,' and from 1868 to 1876 on that of the 'Echo.' He was subsequently a contributor to the 'Times.' With literary tastes and poetical ambition, Smith managed to become a contributor to the chief magazines, among them the 'Edinburgh Review,' the 'Fortnightly Review,' and the 'Cornhill Magazine.' Although he lacked scholarly training, he was an appreciative critic. A memoir of Elizabeth Barrett Browning in the ninth edition of the 'Encyclopædia Britannica' (1876) satisfied Robert Browning, with whom Smith came into intimate relations. It was the poet's custom to send Smith proofsheets of his later volumes in advance, to enable him to write early reviews.

An industrious compiler, Smith gained the ear of the general public by a long series of biographies, the first of which dealt with Shelley (1877). A strong liberal in politics, he was more successful in his 'Life of W. E. Gladstone' (1879; 14th edit. 1898), and in his 'Life and Speeches of John Bright' (1881). There followed popular lives of Victor Hugo (1885), Queen Victoria (1886; new edit. 1901), and the German Emperor William I (1887). His most ambitious publication, 'History of the English Parliament' (2 vols. 1892), occupied him five years, and claimed to be 'the first full and consecutive history of Parliament as a legislative institution from the earliest times to the present day'; but Smith's historical faculty was hardly adequate to his task.

Interested in art, Smith in his leisure practised etching with success. Several specimens of his work were included in 'English Etchings' (1884–7). An etching by him of Carlyle was purchased by Edward VII when Prince of Wales.

In 1889 lung-trouble forced Smith to leave London for Bournemouth, and for the rest of his life he was an invalid. A conservative government granted him a civil list pension of 80*l.* in 1891, and a liberal government increased it by 70*l.* in 1906. Writing to the last, he died at Bournemouth on 2 Jan. 1909, and was buried in the cemetery there. Smith was twice married: (1) to Annie Hodson (*d.* 1868); (2) in 1871, to Julia Timmis, who survived him. He had four daughters, of whom two survived him. An etching of him by Mortimer Menpes and an oil-painting by Rosa Corder are in the possession of his widow.

Smith published under the pseudonym of Guy Roslyn three volumes of verse and 'George Eliot in Derbyshire' (1876). He was an occasional contributor to the early volumes of this Dictionary. Among works not already noticed are the following: 1. 'Poets and Novelists,' 1875. 2. 'English Political Leaders,' 1881. 3. Women of Renown,' 1893. 4. 'Noble Womanhood,' 1894. 5. 'The United States,' 1897. 6. 'Canada,' 1898. 7. 'Heroes of the Nineteenth Century,' 3 vols. 1899–1901. 8. 'The Romance of the South Pole,' 1900.

[Letters of Robert Browning, privately printed by T. J. Wise, 1895; Brit. Mus. Cat.; The Times, 4 Jan. 1909; private information.]

SMITH, GEORGE VANCE (1816?–1902), unitarian biblical scholar, son of George Smith of Willington, near Newcastle-on-Tyne, was born in October, probably 1816 (he himself was not sure of the exact year), at Portarlington, King's and Queen's Cos., where his mother (Anne Vance) was on a visit. Brought up at Willington, he was employed at Leeds, where his preparation for a college course was undertaken by Charles Wicksteed (1810–1885), then minister of Mill Hill chapel. In 1836 he entered Manchester College (then at York) as a divinity student under Charles Wellbeloved [q. v.], John Kenrick [q. v.], and William Hincks [see HINCKS, THOMAS DIX]. In 1839–40 he was assistant tutor in mathematics. Removing with the college to Manchester in 1840, he pursued his studies under Robert Wallace [q. v.], James Martineau [q. v. Suppl. I], and F. W. Newman [q. v. Suppl. I], and graduated B.A. in 1841 at the London University, to which the college was affiliated. His first ministry was at Chapel Lane, Bradford, West Riding, where he was ordained on 22 Sept. 1841. He removed to King Edward Street chapel, Macclesfield, in 1843, remaining till 1846, when he was appointed vice-principal, and professor of theology and Hebrew, in Manchester College. On Kenrick's retirement in 1850 from the principalship Smith was appointed his successor. In 1853, on the removal of the college to London, John

James Taylor was made principal, and Smith professor of critical and exegetical theology, evidences of religion, Hebrew, and Syriac. He resigned in 1857, went abroad, and obtained at Tübingen the degrees of M.A. and Ph.D. In 1858 he became Wellbeloved's assistant and successor at St. Saviourgate chapel, York.

In 1870, after Kenrick had declined to serve on the score of age, Smith accepted Dean Stanley's invitation to join the New Testament revision company. His participation in the celebration of the eucharist in Henry VII's chapel, Westminster Abbey, on the morning of the first meeting of the company (June 1870) led to much criticism. The upper house of the Canterbury convocation, on the motion of Samuel Wilberforce [q. v.], passed a resolution condemning the appointment to either company of any person 'who denies the Godhead of our Lord,' and affirming that any such one should cease to act; a similar resolution was rejected by the lower house (Feb. 1871). Smith bore all this with an inflexible and irritating calmness. His work as a reviser was diligent and conscientious, though he was often in a minority of one. In 1873 the university of Jena made him D.D.

In July 1875 Smith left York for the ministry of Upper chapel, Sheffield, but in September 1876 he was promoted to the principalship of the Presbyterian College, Carmarthen, an office which he held till 1888, combining with it from 1877 the charge of Park-y-velvet chapel, Carmarthen, Retiring from the active ministry, he resided first at Bath, and latterly at Bowdon, Cheshire. Among unitarians his position was that of a mild conservatism; hence he was more at home in Carmarthen College than he had been in the atmosphere of the Manchester College. He died at Cranwells, Bowdon, on 28 Feb. 1902, and was buried at Hale, Cheshire, on 4 March. He married (1) in 1843 Agnes Jane, second daughter of John Fletcher of Liverpool, by whom he had three sons and one daughter; and (2) in 1894 Elizabeth Anne, daughter of Edward Todd of Tadcaster, who survived him.

Besides sermons and lectures, singly and in collections, his chief works are: 1. 'The Priesthood of Christ,' 1843 (Letters to John Pye Smith, D.D.; two series). 2. 'English Orthodoxy, as it is and as it might be,' 1863. 3. 'Eternal Punishment,' 1865, 12mo; 4th edit. 1875 (reprinted in 'The Religion and Theology of Unitarians,' 1906). 4. 'The Bible and Popular Theology,' 1871 (3rd edit. 1872); revised as 'The Bible and its Theology as popularly taught,' 1892, 1901. 5. 'The Spirit and the Word of Christ,' 1874; 2nd edit. 1875. 6. 'The Prophets and their Interpreters,' 1878. 7. 'Texts and Margins of the Revised New Testament affecting Theological Doctrine,' 1881. 8. 'Chapters on Job for Young Readers,' 1887. 9. 'Confession of Christ what it is not, and what it is,' 1890. He translated in an abridged form Tholuck's 'The Credibility of the Evangelic History Illustrated,' 1844; 'The Prophecies relating to Nineveh and the Assyrians, translated . . . with Introduction and Notes,' 1857; and in 'The Holy Scriptures of the Old Covenant,' 1857–62 (a continuation of Wellbeloved's work), I and II Samuel, Ezra, Nehemiah, Esther, Isaiah, Jeremiah, and Lamentations. To J. R. Beard's 'Voices of the Church' (1845) he contributed 'The Fallacy of the Mythical Theory of Dr. Strauss.'

[The Times, 4 March 1902; Services at Chapel Lane, Bradford, 1841; Manning, Hist. of Upper Chapel, Sheffield, 1900 (portrait); memoir (by present writer) in Christian Life, March 1902; information from Rev. G. Hamilton Vance.] A. G.

SMITH, GOLDWIN (1823–1910), controversialist, was born on 13 Aug. 1823 at 15 Friar Street, Reading, where a tablet now records the fact. His father, Richard Prichard Smith (1795–1867), a native of Castle Bromwich, Warwickshire, was son of Richard Smith (1758–1820), rector of Long Marston, Yorkshire; he was educated at Repton and at Caius College, Cambridge, where he graduated M.B. in 1817 and M.D. in 1825; was elected F.R.C.P. in 1826; practised with great success for many years at Reading; helped to promote the Great Western railway, of which he became a director, and ultimately retired to a large country house, Mortimer House, eight miles from Reading. Goldwin Smith was his son by his first wife, Elizabeth, one of the ten children of Peter Breton, of Huguenot descent. She died at Reading on 19 Nov. 1833, and was buried in St. Lawrence's churchyard, having borne her husband three sons and two daughters, of whom only Goldwin survived youth. In 1839 Goldwin's father married a second wife, Katherine, daughter of Sir Nathaniel Dukinfield, fifth baronet, and sister of Sir Henry Dukinfield, sixth and last baronet, rector of St. Giles's, Reading; with his stepmother Goldwin's relations were always distant. Goldwin was named after his mother's uncle, Thomas Goldwin (*d.* 1809) of Vicars Hill, Lymington, Hampshire, formerly a Jamaica planter, who distributed by will (proved 16 Nov. 1809) a part of a large fortune among his many nephews and nieces of the Breton family. He owned at his death 'slaves and stock' in Jamaica.

At eight the boy went to a private preparatory school at Monkton Farleigh, near Bath, and from 1836 to 1841 was a colleger at Eton. He boarded in the house of Edward Coleridge, whose nephew John Duke, afterwards Lord Coleridge, was a life-long friend. Henry Fitzmaurice Hallam, son of the historian, was another close companion at school. Goldwin abstained from games and was reckoned reserved and solitary. According to his own account he did not work hard. He only studied classics and chiefly Latin composition. Proceeding to Oxford, he matriculated at Christ Church on 26 May 1841, and benefited little, he said in after life, by the tuition of William Linwood [q. v.]. Next year he was elected demy of Magdalen College, where Martin Routh [q. v.] was president. At Magdalen there were few undergraduates besides the thirty demies. Among these John Conington was the 'star,' and Goldwin was his chief satellite. Roundell Palmer, recently elected a fellow, showed him kindly attention, and their affectionate relations continued through later years. For Magdalen College he always cherished a warm regard. Although he attended Buckland's lectures on geology, his main energies were absorbed by the classics, for which he showed unusual aptitude. He read privately with Richard Congreve [q. v. Suppl. I], and made a record as a winner of classical prizes in the university. The Hertford scholarship fell to him in 1842, and the Ireland in 1845, together with the chancellor's Latin verse prize for a poem on 'Numa Pompilius,' the Latinity of which his friend Conington highly commended. In the same year, too, he won a first class in literæ humaniores, and graduated B.A., proceeding M.A. in 1848. In 1846 he carried off the chancellor's prize for the Latin essay on 'The Position of Women in Ancient Greece,' and in 1847 the chancellor's prize for the English essay on 'The Political and Social Benefits of the Reformation in England.' Thus three years running he recited prize compositions at the encænia in the Sheldonian theatre. Meanwhile he had contributed Latin verse to the 'Anthologia Oxoniensis' of 1846, some of which was reproduced in the 'Nova Anthologia Oxoniensis' (ed. A. D. Godley and Robinson Ellis, 1899). Although Smith shone in the society of congenial undergraduates, he was (he wrote) 'unoratoric' and he did not join in the union debates (E. H. COLERIDGE's *Lord Coleridge*, 1904). His views on religious and political questions were from the first pronouncedly liberal. While he admired Newman's style, he was impatient of the Oxford movement and was scornful of all clerical influences. He characterised the pending religious controversy as 'barren.'

When Queen's College, with what was then rare liberality, threw open a fellowship to general competition, Smith's candidature failed, owing as he thought to his anti-clerical views (cf. MEYRICK's *Memories of Oxford*, 1905, whose accuracy Smith disputed). In 1846 however he was elected Stowell law fellow of University College; and his career was intimately associated with that college till 1867. But for his first four years there he resided intermittently. With a view to making the law his profession, he had entered as a student at Lincoln's Inn on 2 Nov. 1842, and after taking his degree spent most of his time in London. He saw much of Roundell Palmer, and through his Eton friends came to know Henry Hallam and Sir John Taylor Coleridge. He went on circuit as judge's marshal with the latter, and afterwards with Sir James Parke and Sir Edward Vaughan Williams. But although he was duly called to the bar on 11 June 1850, the law proved uncongenial. He would rather (he wrote to his friend Roundell Palmer) seek fame through 'a decent index to Shakespeare than the chancellorship.' The autumn of 1847 was devoted to a foreign tour with Conington and other Oxford friends. Conington and he were contemplating an elaborate joint edition of Virgil, on which a little later they set seriously to work. Some progress was made with the Eclogues and the Georgics. But the task was ultimately accomplished by Conington alone, who in dedicating the first volume to Smith in 1858 generously acknowledged his initial co-operation. The tour of 1847 extended to France, Italy, Switzerland, and Tirol, and Goldwin visited Guizot at Val Richer. His faith in liberal principles was confirmed by his social experience in London, where his Eton master introduced him to the duke of Newcastle, and he came to know the leading Peelites. But he hoped for progress without revolution, and in 1848 he acted as a special constable during the Chartist scare.

Meanwhile Oxford was stirring his reforming zeal. Already in 1848 he described himself as 'rouge' in university politics (SELBORNE, ii. 195). In 1850 his relations with Oxford became closer on his accepting an ordinary fellowship and tutorship at University in succession to Arthur Penrhyn Stanley [q. v.]. He held the tutorship for four years and the fellowship for seventeen. The current agitation for academic reform attracted him more than normal educational duties. He threw in his lot with those who were attacking clerical ascendancy and were endeavouring to dissipate the prevailing torpor. With Jowett and William Charles Lake [q. v. Suppl. I] he drafted a memorial to the prime minister, Lord John Russell, urging the grant of a royal commission of inquiry into the administration of the university. His hand, too, appears in the vigorously phrased letters in support of the same cause published soon afterwards in 'The Times' above the signature 'Oxoniensis' (*Life of A. C. Tait*, i. 158–9). A royal commission was appointed on 31 Aug. 1850, and Stanley and Smith were made joint secretaries. The report, which was issued on 27 April 1852, approved the relaxation of religious tests, the abrogation of restrictive medieval statutes, the free opening of fellowships to merit, and the creation of a teaching professorate. The government introduced a bill to give moderate and tentative effect to these findings, and Gladstone, who during 1854 piloted the measure through the House of Commons, frequently invited Smith's assistance. On the passing of the Oxford University Reform Act an executive commission was appointed to frame the necessary regulations for the university and the colleges. Of this body Smith again became joint secretary with the Rev. Samuel Wayte, and he was busily occupied with the task for nearly two years until it was completed in 1857. It fell to him to draw the statute which instituted the order of non-collegiate students. The general result fell far below his hopes, but he looked forward to a future advance, now that the ice was broken.

The business of the commission kept Smith much in London, where he widened his intercourse with men of affairs. With A. C. Tait, one of the original commissioners, with Edward Cardwell, and with Sidney Herbert he grew intimate, and he was a frequent guest of Lord Ashburton at the Grange near Alresford, where he met Carlyle and Tennyson.

His leisure in London Smith devoted to journalism of the best literary type. As early as 1850 he had begun writing for the 'Morning Chronicle,' the Peelite organ, and when the editor of that journal, Douglas Cook, started the 'Saturday Review' in 1855 Goldwin Smith joined his staff. To the first number, 3 Nov. 1855, he contributed an article 'On the War Passages in Tennyson's "Maud,"' in which he betrayed that horror of militarism which became a lasting obsession. He wrote regularly in the 'Saturday' for three years, chiefly on literary themes, for he was out of sympathy with the political and religious tone of the paper. Cook, the editor, described him as his 'most effective pen.' He also occasionally acted as literary critic for 'The Times,' reviewing sympathetically Matthew Arnold's 'Poems, by A' in 1854. His pen was likewise busy in the service of Oxford. To the 'Oxford Essays' he contributed in 1856 an essay on 'The Roman Empire of the West' by his old tutor Congreve, and another on 'Oxford University Reform' in 1858.

In the last year Smith's usefulness and ability were conspicuously acknowledged by an invitation to become a full member of another royal commission of great importance—that on national education, under the chairmanship of the duke of Newcastle. The section of the report issued in 1862 on the proper application of charitable endowments was from his pen. Smith deprecated the suggestion that his services should be recognised by office in a public department. But greatly to his satisfaction, on the nomination of Lord Derby, the conservative prime minister, he was appointed in 1858, without making any application, regius professor of modern history at Oxford. His predecessor was Henry Halford Vaughan [q. v.], and both Richard William Church [q. v. Suppl. I] and Edward Augustus Freeman [q. v. Suppl. I] were candidates for the vacancy. Smith's new post was, he asserted, 'the highest object of his ambition,' but he lacked the qualification of historical training. Abandoning for the moment his journalistic work in London, he settled down at Oxford, as it seemed, for life. Always of delicate health, he built for himself a house to the north of the city, beyond The Parks, in what was then the open country. For many years the house stood alone, but it subsequently became the centre of a populous suburb. The building, which was greatly enlarged after he ceased to occupy it, has since been known as 7 Norham Gardens, and was long tenanted by Prof. Max Müller.

Goldwin Smith delivered his inaugural

lecture as regius professor early in 1859. It was an eloquent and temperate plea for widening the old curriculum. Here, as in nearly all his subsequent public professorial lectures, his aim was to stimulate the thought and ethical sense of his hearers rather than to teach history in any formal way. His elevated intellectual temper broadened his pupils' outlook while his political fervour won adherents to his opinions. In private classes he was suggestive in comment, but he failed to encourage research, for which he had small liking or faculty. Controversy was for him inevitable, and he did not confine his controversial energy to the domain of history. In an early public lecture on the 'Study of History' he somewhat ironically imputed an agnostic tendency to H. L. Mansel's metaphysical Bampton lectures of 1858. Mansel complained of misrepresentation, and Smith retorted, with a thinly veiled sceptical intention, in 'Rational Religion and the Rationalistic Objections of the Bampton Lecturer of 1858.' With Bishop Wilberforce he was even in smaller sympathy than with Mansel. In 'The Suppression of Doubt is not Faith, by a Layman' (Oxford, 1861) he attacked some of the bishop's sermons and pleaded openly for the rights of scepticism. In a second tract, 'Concerning Doubt' (Oxford, 1861), he defended his position against the published censure of 'A Clergyman.'

In 1861 Smith collected into a volume five lectures on modern history. The fourth, 'On some Supposed Consequences of the Doctrine of Historical Progress,' was a suggestive contribution to political philosophy, and the fifth, 'On the Foundation of the American Colonies,' approached nearer than any other to the historical sphere and gave him an opportunity of proclaiming his democratic ardour. In Michaelmas term 1859 King Edward VII (then Prince of Wales) matriculated at Oxford, and Goldwin Smith gave him private lectures in modern history at the prince's residence at Frewen Hall. Goldwin Smith expressed a fear that he bored his royal pupil, but he was impressed by the prince's admirable courtesy, and the prince always treated him with consideration in later life (THOMPSON'S *Life of Liddell*). An invitation to accompany the prince on his Canadian tour of 1860 was declined, on the ground of Smith's duties at Oxford. In general university politics he continued to act with the advanced party, and warmly pleaded for a fuller secularisation of endowments. In regard to national politics he proved in the university an effective radical missionary. He supported Gladstone through the period of his liberal development. 'Young Oxford,' he wrote to the statesman (June 1859), 'is all with you; but old Oxford takes a long time in dying' (MORLEY'S *Gladstone*, ii. 630). His 'wonderful epigrammatic power' won him respect. 'With all his bitterness,' wrote J. B Mozley to his sister, 'he is something of a prophet, a judge who tells the truth though savagely.' Prof. George Rolleston, Prof. H. J. S. Smith, and Prof. J. E. Thorold Rogers were his closest friends among resident graduates of his own way of thinking, but he maintained good relations with some leaders in the opposite camp. With (Canon) William Bright [q. v. Suppl. II], who was a fellow of University during Smith's residence there, he formed, despite their divergences of opinion, a close intimacy.

Public affairs distracted Smith's attention from the work of his chair, and he soon flung himself with eager enthusiasm into the political agitation of the day. From the Peelites he had transferred his allegiance to Cobden, Bright, and the leaders of the Manchester school. With a persistence which never diminished he preached the school's doctrines of universal peace and freedom, and the duty of refusing responsibilities which condoned war or persecution. His admirable style, his power of clear and eloquent expression, and his passionate devotion to what he deemed to be righteous causes fitted him for a great pamphleteer, and he developed some capacity for carefully premeditated public speaking. The imperialistic trend of public opinion, which he identified with a spirit of wanton aggression, and the Irish discontent first brought him prominently into the political arena. In 1862–3 he contributed to the 'Daily News' a series of letters on 'The Empire' which were collected with some additions in a volume in 1863. He argued for what he called 'colonial emancipation'—for the conversion of the self-governing colonies into independent states. He advocated the abandonment of Gibraltar to Spain, declared his belief that India would be best governed as an independent empire under an English emperor, and described the Indian empire in its existing guise as 'a splendid curse' (letter to John Bright). Smith hailed the cession by Lord Palmerston's government of the Ionian Isles to Greece in 1862–3 as a step in support of his own principles. His views, which attracted much attention, offended a large section of the public. The colonial press, especially in Australia, hotly repudiated them (cf. Sir G. F. Bowen, *Thirty Years of Colonial Government*, 1889, i. 209; letter from Bowen to Gladstone, 18 Aug. 1862). Disraeli in the House of Commons ridiculed 'the wild opinions' of all professors, rhetoricians, prigs and pedants (*Hansard*, 5 Feb. 1863), and thenceforth he habitually imputed a mischievous tendency to Smith's political propaganda.

In 1862 Smith visited at Dublin his friend Cardwell, who was chief secretary for Ireland, and in the same year issued 'Irish History and Irish Character.' He divided the blame for the miseries of Ireland between English misgovernment, which disestablishment of the Irish church and revision of the land laws might correct, and defects of Irish character, which were irremediable.

But Smith's interests were soon absorbed by the civil war in America. His antipathy to war at first led him to doubt the adequacy of the federal cause, and to favour the claim of the South to the right of secession. But the eloquence of John Bright, which always powerfully influenced him, convinced him that the main principle at stake in the conflict was the liberation of the slave, and before long he engaged with fiery zeal in the agitation in England on behalf of the federal government. He first appeared on a political platform at the Free Trade Hall, Manchester, on 6 April 1863, at a meeting of the Manchester Union and Emancipation Society, which Thomas Bayley Potter [q. v.] had formed in the federal interest and was supporting at his own cost. Smith protested with sombre earnestness 'against the building and equipping of piratical ships in support of the Southern slaveholders' confederacy' (J. F. Rhodes, *Hist. of the Civil War*, iii. 470). Soon afterwards, at the Manchester Athenæum, he lectured on 'Does the Bible sanction American Slavery?' and answered the question in the negative. In the same year he published a pamphlet attesting 'the morality of the emancipation proclamation.'

Next year he resolved to visit America to carry to the North a message of sympathy from England. He landed on 5 Sept. 1864 at New York and saw much of the country during some three months' stay. At Washington, where he was the guest of Seward, the secretary of state, he was received with characteristic absence of ceremony by President Lincoln, whose precise and minute information impressed him (A. T. Rice, *Reminiscences of Lincoln*, 1886). He visited the federal camp before Richmond on the Potomac and conversed with General Butler. At Cambridge, Massachusetts, he met C. E. Norton and Lowell, and at Boston, where he witnessed the presidential election (9 Nov.), he saw Emerson and the historian Bancroft. At Providence, Brown University conferred on him the degree of LL.D. Chicago and Baltimore also came within the limits of his tour (*Proc. Mass. Hist. Soc.* Oct. 1910, account of Smith's visit, pp. 3–13). In letters to the London 'Daily News' he described some of his experiences, and commended the steady purpose of the North and its grim determination to make the South submit. The confederate press abused him roundly, but he was enthusiastically received by the federals, and before he left America the Union League Club entertained him at New York (12 Nov. 1864), when he expressed abounding sympathy with the American people.

Until the final triumph of the North, Smith continued its defence among his countrymen. A pamphlet 'England and America' (1865) effectively sought to bring the sentiments of the two countries into accord. At the meeting which saw the disbandment of the Manchester Union and Emancipation Society in Jan. 1866 he spoke with optimistic eloquence of America's future. 'Slavery,' he said, 'is dead everywhere and for ever.' 'By war no such delivery was ever wrought for humanity as this.'

Next year he engaged with wonted heat in another agitation. In 1867 he joined the Jamaica committee which was formed to bring to punishment Governor Eyre for alleged cruelties in suppressing a rebellion of negroes. J. S. Mill was the moving spirit of the committee, and with him Smith grew intimate. An opposing committee in Eyre's favour, of which Carlyle, Kingsley, Tennyson, and Ruskin were members, drew from Smith much wrathful denunciation; Ruskin's championship of what Smith viewed as cruelty excited his especial scorn, and a rancorous controversy followed later between the two men. In the interests of the funds of the Jamaica committee, Smith went about the country delivering a series of four 'Lectures on three English Statesmen'—one each on Pym and Cromwell and two on Pitt. These he published in 1867 with a dedication to Potter. His powers of historical exposition are here seen to advantage, but an irrepressible partisan fervour keeps the effort within the category of brilliant pamphleteering. With other philosophical radicals he co-operated in 'Essays on Reform' (1867), writing on 'Experience of the American Commonwealth.' Robert Lowe taxed Smith with an extravagant faith in democracy when he criticised the volume in the 'Quarterly Review' (July 1867).

Private anxieties unsettled Smith's plans. His father during 1866 had been injured in a railway accident; his mind was permanently affected, and he found relief only in his son's society. Smith was constantly at Mortimer House, and the frequency of his enforced absences from Oxford led him to resign his professorship in the summer of 1866. While he was away from home during the autumn of 1867 his father died by his own hand (7 Oct. 1867). Goldwin and his step-mother were executors of the will, which was proved on 30 Oct. by Goldwin for under 30,000*l*. and gave him a moderate competence. The shock powerfully affected Smith's nerves. The increase of private fortune again changed his position at Oxford; it disqualified him for his fellowship at University College, which was only tenable by men of smaller means. At Easter 1867 he had been chosen honorary fellow of Oriel —the college which, under the new statutes of 1857, had contributed 250*l*. a year to his professional salary—but no closer tie with the university remained.

Uncertain as to his prospects, Smith determined to revisit America. A rumour that he was leaving England for good quickly spread. Dean Church communicated it to Asa Gray on 17 Jan. 1868 (*Life of Church*, p. 24). In a letter to the 'New York Tribune' of the same date Smith explained that he had resolved on 'a prolonged residence in America in order to study American history.' His place of settlement was as yet undetermined. He had no intention of becoming an American citizen (cf. reprint in *The Times*, 11 Feb. 1868). In the spring of 1868 Andrew Dickson White, who had been appointed president of the newly projected Cornell University in Ithaca, New York State, arrived in England with a view to securing the aid of English teachers in the new venture. Smith had met Ezra Cornell, the founder of the institution, in 1864, and he strongly approved Cornell's design of endowing a university for comparatively poor men which should be free of all religious restrictions. Dickson's offer to Smith of a chair on the new foundation was accepted. Smith agreed to become first professor of English and constitutional history at Cornell University. As he desired to be wholly untrammelled by conditions of service, he declined remuneration. His political friends who had urged him to enter the House of Commons at the imminent general election lamented his decision. Chelsea was vainly pressed on him as a safe seat. There was talk of his candidature for the city of Oxford, where he had lately helped to found an Oxford Reform League (17 July 1866). He promised to stay in England and help the party till the coming general election was over. At the Manchester Reform Club he made (10 April 1868) a long speech on current political questions, which drew the censure of a leader writer in 'The Times' (13 April). He declared he would remain a good Englishman wherever he was. To Samuel Morley [q. v.], an organiser of the party, who again pressed him to stay at home, he replied that 'a student's duty' called him elsewhere. Later in the year he actively promoted the candidature of A. J. Mundella at Sheffield.

Smith's resolve of exile, to which many motives contributed, was doubtless influenced to some extent by disappointment at the slow advance of the cause of reform in the university. Amid other political distractions he had always found time for an active share in the current agitation for the complete abolition of tests at both universities. At an influential meeting in support of legislation on the subject held in the Freemasons' Tavern in Great Queen Street, London, on 10 June 1864 he was a chief speaker, and he published a powerful pamphlet on the question in the same year. There he seems for the first time to have applied the term 'the Free churches' to the dissenting persuasions. No legislation for the abolition of tests was passed till 1871 (L. CAMPBELL, *On the Nationalisation of the Old English Universities*, 1901).

Goldwin Smith's farewell to Oxford took the form of a pamphlet on the 'Reorganisation of the University' (1868). After regretting the limited character of the reforms of 1854, he pleaded for university extension, for the raising of the standard of pass examinations, for the separation of prize and teaching fellowships, for the marriage of fellows, and for various changes of administration. He dissociated him self from the cry for the endowment of research. But he privately urged on the University Press the preparation of a standard English Dictionary, and he recommended that new provincial universities, the creation of which he foresaw, should undertake technical instruction in some kind of affiliation with Oxford and Cambridge, while the two old universities should still confine their efforts to the humanities. He sought to preserve Oxford from discordant features of industrial progress, and in 1865 had by speech and pen actively resisted the choice of the city as the site of the Great Western railway's factories and workshops. He had, too, encouraged the volunteering movement of 1859, and had joined the university corps, but he deprecated the increasing zeal for athletic sports, and he always regarded the college rowing races as largely misapplied energy.

Smith left England for Cornell University on 25 Oct. 1868, and although his life was prolonged for another forty-one years and he paid frequent visits to his native country, his place of permanent residence thenceforth lay across the Atlantic. He reached Ithaca in November 1868, a month after Cornell University opened and long before the university buildings were erected. He entered with energy on the duties of his chair. Residence was not compulsory, but he took lodgings at first in an hotel, and then at 'Cascadilla,' a new boarding-house for the professors. The two years and more during which he watched at close quarters and with fatherly devotion the growth of the new institution were, he always declared, save for the time spent at Magdalen, the 'happiest of his life.' He cheerfully faced the discomforts of the rough accommodation and always cherished pleasant memories of his intercourse with his nine colleagues, who included Alexander Agassiz the naturalist, George William Curtis, Bayard Taylor, and Lowell, whom he had already met at Cambridge. He sent for his library from Oxford and subsequently presented it to the university with a small endowment fund ($14,000). He wrote to his friend Auberon Herbert to send out English stonemasons and carvers to work on the new university structures. In the 'campus' he placed a stone seat inscribed with the words 'Above all nations is humanity.' To John Bright he wrote (from Ithaca, 6 Sept. 1869) of his kind reception, and that only a little more health and strength was needed to make him 'altogether prosperous and happy.'

While at Cornell, intercourse with friends in England was uninterrupted, and he exchanged free comment with them on the public affairs of the two countries. Amid his academic work, he was soon disquieted by the course of current politics in America. During 1869 a popular outbreak of bitter hostility to England sprang out of the negotiations concerning the Alabama's depredations and the old disputes over Canadian boundaries and fisheries. Smith's first publication on American soil was a pamphlet called 'Relations between England and America' (Ithaca, May 1869), in which, at the beginning of the storm, he defended England's political aims and morality from the severe strictures of the American statesman and orator, Charles Sumner. The effort proved of small avail, and 'hatred of England' grew. On 7 Dec. 1869 he wrote from Ithaca to his friend T. B. Potter, 'The feeling is still very bad, especially in New England, and everything we say and do, however friendly, turns sour, as it were, in the minds of these people.' Among the people at large he was, however, hopeful of a better tone, but 'the politicians one and all' he denounced as 'hopeless'—as 'a vile crew quite unworthy of the people.' His perturbation was the greater because the principle of protection was making rapid headway, and the doctrine of free trade which he sought to propagate in the United States was repudiated as a piece of British chicanery, devised for the ruin of American manufacturers. The political and economic situation in America continued to occasion him grave concern through the early months of 1870. Nor was it lessened by an unwelcome reminder from home of his recent political activity there. Disraeli on the platform had already sneered at him as an 'itinerant spouter of stale sedition' and as a 'wild man of the cloister going about the country maligning men and things.' In 1870 the statesman published his 'Lothair,' and there he rancorously introduced an unnamed Oxford professor 'of advanced opinions on all subjects, religious, social and political, of a restless vanity and overflowing conceit, gifted with a great command of words and talent for sarcasm, who was not satisfied with his home career but was about to settle in the New World. Like sedentary men of extreme opinions he was a social parasite.' The attack stung Smith, and he injudiciously replied in a letter to 'The Times' (9 June 1870) in which he branded Disraeli's malignity as 'the stingless insults of a coward.' Smith's retort bore witness to an extreme sensitiveness linked with his reckless aggressiveness. Thenceforth he lost almost all self-control in his references to Disraeli, and with an illogical defiance of liberal principle seized every opportunity of assailing Disraeli's race. The 'tribal' character of the Jews and their unfitness for civic responsibilities in Christian states was a constant theme of his pen in middle life. On such grounds he went near justifying the persecution of the Jews in Russia and other countries of Eastern Europe.

In the autumn of 1870 Tom Hughes, Prof. A. V. Dicey, and Mr. James Bryce visited Smith at Cornell and saw him at his work. In the same year he made a tour in Canada, going as far as what was then the village of Winnipeg. This experience combined with a certain disillusionment in his views of American politics led him to alter his plans. Several cousins were settled at Toronto, and early in 1871 he left his comfortless quarters at Ithaca for the residence at Toronto of his relatives Mr. and Mrs. Colley Foster. It was thus that Toronto became his home for life, and his professorial labours at Cornell came gradually to an end. He paid frequent visits to the university till the end of 1872, when he formally resigned his resident professorship. He was thereupon appointed non-resident professor, and in 1875 he was also made lecturer in English history, but thenceforth he gave only occasional lectures. He ceased to be professor in 1881, but retained the lectureship till 1894, when he received the title of emeritus professor. He never ceased to speak with satisfaction of the part he played in the inauguration of Cornell University. Till his death he deeply interested himself in its welfare.

On 3 Sept. 1875 he married at St. Peter's, Toronto, a lady of wealth, Harriet, daughter of Thomas Dixon and widow of Henry Boulton of The Grange, Toronto. That old-fashioned house had been built by Boulton's father in 1817. There Smith lived in affluence from his marriage till his death. His wife, who was born at Boston in 1825, was his junior by two years. He spent many vacations in Europe, travelling in Italy on his latest visit in 1889; he also twice crossed Canada to the Pacific coast, and was always a frequent visitor to the United States. But he grew attached to The Grange, and disliked the notion of living elsewhere.

As soon as he settled in Toronto Smith zealously studied colonial life, and sought his main occupation in journalism. Although he wrote much on current literature, on religious speculation, and on the public affairs of the European continent, he applied his pen chiefly to the politics of Canada, England, and the United States. He adhered with tenacity and independence to the principles which he had upheld in England, and maintained warfare with undiminished vehemence on militarism, imperialism, and clericalism. In Canadian politics he always described himself as an onlooker or a disinterested critic. His favourite signature in the Canadian press was that of 'A Bystander,' a fit title he declared for 'a Canadian standing outside Canadian parties.' But his genuine ambition was to mould public opinion; he contemplated in 1874 finding a seat in the Ontario legislature and never shrank from close quarters with the political conflict.

On arriving in Toronto in 1871 he became a regular contributor to the 'Toronto Globe,' an advanced radical organ owned and edited by George Brown [q. v. Suppl. I]. A laudatory review by Smith of George Eliot's 'Middlemarch,' which offended the religious and moral susceptibilities of many readers, led to his withdrawal from the paper. The consequent quarrel with Brown moved Smith to aid others in the establishment of the 'Toronto Evening Telegram,' of which he was a staunch supporter, and to start a series of short-lived weekly or monthly journals of his own, in which he expounded his political and religious creed without restriction. His first venture, 'The Nation,' ran for two years (1874–6). 'The Bystander,' the whole of which came from his own pen, was a miscellany notable for its variety of topic and lucidity of expression; it was first a monthly and then a quarterly (1880–3). The 'Leader' and the 'Liberal' enjoyed briefer careers. The 'Week,' to which he contributed a weekly article signed 'A Bystander,' lasted from 1883 to 1886. At the same time his pen was active in a newly founded magazine, at first called 'The Canadian Monthly,' and afterwards 'The Canadian Magazine'; there he regularly wrote both literary and political essays from 1872 to 1897. He was subsequently the contributor of a weekly article on current events, again signed 'A Bystander,' to a weekly paper known at first as 'The Farmers' Sun' and afterwards as 'The Weekly Sun.' There was indeed scarcely any newspaper in Canada to which he failed to address plainly worded letters, and the lucid force of his style did much, despite the unpopularity of his opinions, to raise the standard of writing in Canadian journalism. At the same time in the United States he found in the New York 'Nation' and in the 'New York Sun' further outlets for his journalistic activity. Nor did he neglect the periodical press of England. Throughout his Canadian career he supplied comments on urgent political issues to 'The Times,' the 'Daily News,' the 'Manchester Guardian,' the 'Pall Mall Gazette,' the 'St. James's Gazette' among daily papers; to the 'Spectator' among weekly papers; and to 'Macmillan's Magazine,' the 'Contemporary Review,' the 'Fortnightly Review,' and the 'Nineteenth Century' among monthly magazines.

Smith's political propaganda in Canada aimed consistently at the emancipation of the colony from the British connection. The Dominion during his early settlement was passing through a period of depression which contrasted greatly with the growing prosperity of the United States, and Smith prophesied disaster unless the existing constitution underwent a thorough change. At first he urged complete independence, and he engaged in a movement started in 1871 by a Toronto barrister, named William Alexander Foster, which was known as 'Canada First,' and sought to create a self-sufficing sentiment of Canadian nationality. He joined the Canadian National Association and became president of the National Club; both institutions were formed in 1874 to promote the new cause independently of the recognised political parties. In 1890 Smith wrote an appreciative introduction to 'Canada First,' a volume issued to commemorate the founder of the movement.

But the cry of 'Canada First' made little headway, and Smith next flung himself into the movement for a commercial union with the United States. He had come to the new conclusion that annexation with the United States was the destiny appointed to Canada by nature, and that the removal of the tariff barrier was the first step to that amalgamation of the two countries, which could alone be safely effected by peaceful means. In spite of his free trade principles, he condoned the tariff against the mother country and Europe, when it appeared to him to be of twofold use, as a unifying instrument within the continent, and as a valuable source of revenue. In 1888 he published an introduction to 'Commercial Union'—a collection of papers in favour of unrestricted reciprocity with the United States. Over the policy of commercial union he came into conflict with almost all the political chieftains, including Sir John Macdonald and Edward Blake, the liberal leader, much of whose policy he had approved. But he was undaunted by opposition, and denounced every measure which seemed to imperil the prospects of continental union. He bitterly attacked the formation of the Canadian Pacific railway as a 'politico-military' project. As the imperialist spirit spread in the dominion, his persistence in his separatist argument exposed him to storms of abuse from the Canadian press and public. He was denounced as a 'champion of annexation, republicanism and treason.' A motion for his expulsion from the St. George's Society, a social organisation of Englishmen in Toronto, in March 1893, was narrowly defeated, and a proposal on the part of the University of Toronto to grant him the hon. LL.D. in 1896 was so stoutly opposed that he announced that he would not accept it, if it were offered him. For a time he was subjected to a social boycott. His political following in Canada steadily declined in numbers and influence. But to the end his position knew no change. Of the colonial conferences in London which aimed in his later years at solidifying the British empire he wrote and spoke with bitter scorn. Meanwhile in America his plea for a complete union 'of the English-speaking race on this continent' could always reckon on sympathetic hearing. Writing at the end of his life to the editor of the 'New York Sun' (4 March 1909), Smith recapitulated his faith in the coming fulfilment of his hopes.

Smith kept alive his interest in English affairs not only by correspondence with his friends there and by his controversies in the English press but by active intervention in public movements on his visits to the country. In 1874 he aided his friend G. C. Brodrick when standing for Woodstock against Lord Randolph Churchill. A speech on England's material prosperity which he delivered when opening an institute to promote intellectual recreation at his native town of Reading (June 1877) brought on him the censure of Ruskin; in 'Fors Clavigera' Ruskin ridiculed him as 'a goose' who identified wealth with progress (*Ruskin's Works*, ed. Cook and Wedderburn, xvii. 479; xxix. passim). Smith retorted in kind, and Ruskin was provoked into condemning Smith's 'bad English' and 'blunder in thought' (*ibid.* xxv. 429). In Oct. 1881 Smith presided over the economic section of the Social Science Congress at Dublin and delivered an address on 'Economy and Trade' (published independently as 'Economical Questions and Events in America'); there he attacked protection. In 1884 he was the chief speaker at the dinner of the Palmerston Club at Oxford.

There was always a strong wish among his English friends and political allies that he should abandon his Canadian domicile. But he was deaf to all entreaty, owing partly to a wish to watch the development of Canada and partly to his wife's reluctance to leave the American continent. Matthew Arnold often argued in vain that the national welfare required his presence in the House of Commons. In 1873 he was vainly invited to become a liberal candidate for Manchester. In 1878 he was sounded without result, by some liberals of Leeds, whether he would stand for the party at the next general election. In 1881 he was invited to become Master of his old college (University) at Oxford. Next year he was gratified by the bestowal on him of the honorary degree of D.C.L. by his university, but neither academic nor political baits could alter his purpose of Canadian residence.

The course of politics in England in subsequent years caused Smith many misgivings. To Gladstone's support of home rule in 1886 he offered a strenuous opposition. His attitude was that of John Bright, to whom he always acknowledged discipleship. With the Irish race he had no sympathy, and although he admired Gladstone's exalted faith in liberal institutions he credited him with an excess of party spirit and ambition and a strain of casuistry and a vanity which ruined his moral fibre. During the summer of 1886 he took as a liberal unionist an active part in the general election in England, and he wrote a pamphlet, 'Dismemberment no Remedy,' which had a wide circulation, and was translated into Welsh. In Toronto he soon became president of the Canadian branch of the loyal and patriotic union, which was formed to fan the agitation against home rule. To his views on the Irish union he was faithful to the end. He repeated them in 'Irish History and the Irish Question' as late as 1906. He complacently ignored the apparent discrepancy between his Irish convictions and his hopes of Canadian 'emancipation.'

The subsequent predominance in Great Britain of the unionist party between 1886 and 1906 greatly encouraged the imperial sentiment, and Smith's disquietude consequently grew. On Mr. Joseph Chamberlain, who became colonial secretary in 1895 and whom he regarded as the chief promoter of the imperial spirit, he bestowed in his latest years all his gift of vituperation. The South African war he regarded as an inhuman crime, and he defended the cause of the Boers with vigour in the American as well as in the Canadian press. In a volume entitled 'In the Court of History, the South African War' (1902) he pushed to the utmost the pacificist argument against the war. He saw almost a satanic influence in Cecil Rhodes, and he viewed with suspicion Rhodes's benefaction to Oxford. Nor in the development of American politics did he find much consolation. The success of the policy of protection, the war with Spain and the annexation of the Philippine Islands (1900) profoundly dissatisfied him. In 'Commonwealth and Empire' (New York, 1902) he raised his voice once more against the moral perils of imperialism as exemplified in the recent history of the United States.

Smith welcomed the liberal triumph in England at the polls in 1906, and he was until the close indefatigable in English political controversy. On the reconstitution of the House of Lords, the last great question which engaged public attention in England in his lifetime, he urged in letters to the 'Spectator' the need of a strong upper chamber on wholly elective principles. To a single chamber he was strongly opposed. The socialistic trend of English political opinion found no favour with him. Although as a courtesy to J. S. Mill he signed in 1867 the first petition to the House of Commons for woman's suffrage, he came to regard the movement as a menace to the state.

But amid his political exertions, which had small effect beyond stirring ill-feeling, Smith was active in many causes which either excited no angry passion or invited general sympathy. He never forsook his historical or literary studies. In monographs on 'Cowper' ('English Men of Letters' series, 1880) and 'A Life of Jane Austen' ('Great Writers' series, 1892) he showed his gentler intellectual affinities, if to no great literary advantage. In 'Bay Leaves,' translations from the Latin poets (1892), and in 'Specimens of Greek Tragedy,' translations from Æschylus, Sophocles, and Euripides (2 vols. 1893), he proved the permanence of his classical predilections, although the clumsiness of his English renderings hardly fulfilled his early promise as a classical scholar. But in 'A Trip to England' (reprinted from the 'Week,' Toronto, 1888, reissued in 1895) he gave a pleasant description of the country for Transatlantic visitors, and in 'Oxford and her Colleges' (1894) he sketched attractively the history of the university for the same class of readers.

Many slight pamphlets of his later years embodied reminiscences of earlier days. 'My Memory of Gladstone' (1904; new edit. 1909) gives a brief appreciation from personal observation of Gladstone's character and career. More ambitious were his historical treatises: 'The United States: an Outline of Political History, 1492–1871' (published in 1893; 4th edit. 1899), and 'The United Kingdom: a Political History' (2 vols. 1899). Both works are mere sketches of history slenderly authenticated. But they present the main facts agreeably, and although Smith's prejudices are unconcealed they are not displayed obtrusively. In 'The United Kingdom' he claimed to have written 'in the light of recent research and discussion.' The record ends with the accession of Queen Victoria; a few concluding remarks on the Empire—the history of Canada, India, and the West Indies—are on the familiar anti-imperialist lines.

In a number of small speculative treatises he explained his reasons for rejecting faith in supernatural religion. Such were 'Guesses at the Riddle of Existence' (New York, 1897); 'The Founder of Christendom' (Toronto, 1903); 'Lines of Religious Inquiry' (1904); 'In Quest of Light' (1906); and 'No Refuge but in Truth' (Toronto, 1908). Smith declared the Old Testament to be 'Christianity's millstone,' and there was much in his agnostic argument to scandalise the orthodox. Yet his attitude was reverent, and it was his habit at Toronto to attend church.

While Smith's political theories continued to offend Canadian opinion, his labours in other than the political sphere, his obvious sincerity, his intellectual eminence, and his growing years ultimately won him almost universal respect in Toronto and indeed throughout Canada. In matters of education, social reform, and public benevolence the value of his work, despite occasional friction with colleagues, could not be seriously questioned. In 1874 he was elected by the teachers of Ontario their representative on the council of public instruction, and he was afterwards president of the Provincial Teachers' Association. He never lost an opportunity of pleading with effect for higher education. He was a senator of the University of Toronto at an early date, and powerfully urged the federation of local sectarian colleges with the university. In 1908 he was a useful member of a royal commission appointed for the reorganisation of Toronto University, and he was granted at length the degree of LL.D. In the controversies over the place of religion in state education, and the claims of the Roman Catholics to control the state system, Smith consistently opposed the sectarian claim without aggravating religious animosities. The purity of political and municipal administration was another cause which evoked his enthusiasm to the satisfaction of the general public, and he became chairman of a citizen's committee at Toronto which made war on municipal corruption. He was also in sympathy with youthful effort. He actively helped in 1892 to organise the Toronto Athletic Club, to which he contributed $12,000, and although the club failed financially and was closed in 1896, its formation under Smith's direct auspices bore witness to his faith in well-regulated physical exercise. In 1895 he intervened in the discussions over the Canada copyright bill, which was designed in the interests of foreign authors. Smith sought to eliminate 'the manufacturing clause' which restricted foreign writers' copyright to books actually printed in Canada. This protective condition was rejected by the legislature, but the bill did not become law. Smith was liberal in private charity. He urged on the city council of Toronto the appointment of a relief officer to receive applications from persons in distress, to make inquiries about them, and to supply information as to suitable philanthropic agencies. The city council rejected his proposal: whereupon he appointed a charity officer at his own expense, with such good results that after two years the council adopted his plan.

Many attentions which pleased him were paid him in his last years. In Nov. 1903, in recognition of his eightieth birthday, surviving friends in Oxford sent him a congratulatory address. The fifteen signatures were headed by that of the vice-chancellor, D. B. Monro. In America, too, he received many honours. The University of Princeton made him LL.D. in 1892, and he was chosen president of the American Historical Association in 1904. On 19 Oct. 1904 he accepted the invitation to lay at Cornell University the corner stone of a new hall, 'the home of the humanities,' which was named after him 'Goldwin Smith Hall.' A copy of his 'United States' was placed in the box deposited in the stone. The imposing building, which cost 71,000*l.*, was dedicated on 19 June 1906. At the ceremonies of both 1904 and 1906 he gave addresses, and he placed in 'Goldwin Smith Hall' a copy of Bacon's bust of Alfred the Great, which adorned the common room of University College, Oxford.

Goldwin Smith's wife died at The Grange on 9 Sept. 1909. He continued writing letters to the press on current politics, but a mellowing tolerance for opponents seemed to be at length accompanied by some diminution of vigour. In March 1910 he accidentally broke his thigh, and after some three months of enforced inactivity he died at The Grange on 7 June 1910. He was buried in St. James's cemetery, Toronto.

Smith held The Grange, his wife's residence, for life under her will; in accordance with her direction it passed on his death to the city of Toronto to form an art museum there. Smith inherited none of his wife's property, which mainly consisted of real estate in the United States, stocks, and valuable mortgages, and was all distributed among members of her own family. But by prudent investments in Canada and the United States Smith greatly increased his comparatively small inheritance of some 20,000*l.* from his father, and he left an estate valued at $832,859, of which he disposed by a will dated 5 May 1910. His pictures and statuary went to the art museum at Toronto; $5000 was left to a nursing mission in the city, and $1000 each to the labour temple and a baptist church, in both of which he had been interested in his lifetime. Although Toronto University only inherited under the will Smith's library, the succession duty, amounting to $83,285, passed to the university by the law of the state. Save for modest sums to members of his household and to a few relatives and friends, the residue of Smith's fortune, amounting to $689,074, passed to Cornell University. The money was to be applied at Cornell to the promotion of liberal studies, languages ancient and modern, literature, philosophy, history, and political science. The bequest marked (Smith wrote) his devotion to the university in the foundation of which he took part, his respect for Ezra Cornell's memory, and his 'attachment as an Englishman to the union of the two branches of our race on this continent with each other and with their common mother' (*Ann. Report of the President and Treasurer, Cornell Univ.*, 1909–10, pp. 43–5. For full text of wills of both Smith and his wife see the *Evening Telegram*, Toronto, 13 Sept. 1910).

Smith's tracts and pamphlets, some privately printed, are very numerous. The chief of his scattered writings are collected in the volumes 'Lectures and Essays' (New York, 1881), and in 'Essays on Questions of the Day: Political and Social' (New York, 1893). There he embodied his dominant convictions.

Smith was a masterly interpreter of the liberal principles of the Manchester school and of the philosophical radicalism which embodied what seemed to him to be the highest political enlightenment of his youth. His views never developed. He claimed with pride in his latest years to be 'the very last survivor of the Manchester school and circle.' The evils of slavery, of war, and of clerical domination were the main articles of his creed through life, and he looked to a free growth of democracy for their lasting cure. The spread, despite his warnings, of the imperialist sentiment in his later years, not only in Great Britain but in Canada and the United States, was a bitter disappointment. But he stood by his doctrine without flinching, and faced with indifference the unpopularity in which it involved him. A burning hatred of injustice and cruelty lay at the root of his faith, and he followed stoically wherever it led. With his keen intellect there went a puritanic fervour and exaltation of spirit which tended to fanaticism and to the fostering of some unreasoning and ungenerous prejudices. But his intellectual strength combined with his moral earnestness gave a telling force to all expression of his views. His incisive style, which Conington in undergraduate days likened to that of Burke, owed, according to his own account, much to David Hume. The depth of his convictions and his melancholy and sensitive temper made controversy habitual to him, and as a disputant he had in his day few rivals. He devoted most of his energies to polemics, and poured forth with amazing rapidity controversial pamphlets of rare distinction. That detachment of mind which is essential to great history or philosophy was denied him. His historical work is little more than first-rate pamphleteering. For original research he had no aptitude, and he failed to make any addition to historical knowledge. The abandonment of his English career in the full tide of its prosperity, which is the most striking feature of his biography, is very partially explained by the change in his private circumstances due to his father's illness and death. Although he shared his progressive views with many Englishmen of his generation, he was exasperated by the strength of the reactionary forces in his native land, and believed that his aspirations had no genuine chance of being realised save in a new world. His hope was far from verified. His cry for Canada's annexation to America misinterpreted Canadian feeling. His prophecy that Canada's persistence in the British connection would stunt her growth was falsified. To all appearance the sentiment of empire, his main abhorrence, flourished at his death as vigorously in the new world as in the old. But Smith stubbornly declined to acknowledge defeat and never abated his enthusiasm for what his conscience taught him to be right.

A portrait by E. Wylie Grier, R.C.A., at the Bodleian Library, was presented by Oxford friends in 1894. Another portrait by the same artist is in the office of the 'Evening Telegram' at Toronto. At The Grange, Toronto, there is a bust executed at Oxford in 1866 by Alexander Munro, together with a portrait by another Canadian artist, J. W. L. Forster, who also painted portraits for the Toronto Art Museum and for Cornell University. A final portrait, painted in 1907 at Toronto by John Russell, R.C.A., remains in the artist's studio at Paris, but a replica was presented to the corporation of Reading on 1 Feb. 1912 by Dr. Jameson B. Hurry. A crayon sketch by Frederick Sandys was exhibited at the Royal Academy in 1882.

[Valuable assistance has been rendered in the preparation of this article by Mr. Arnold Haultain, who was for eighteen years Goldwin Smith's private secretary. In the last fifteen years of his life Goldwin Smith wrote out his reminiscences, but did not live to revise the manuscript. They were prepared for the press by Mr. Arnold Haultain in 1911. In spite of disjointed repetitions and inequalities the book offers useful material for biography. Mr. Arnold Haultain has also in preparation 'Goldwin Smith as I knew him' (chiefly records of conversations), together with a collection of Goldwin Smith's letters, and an edition in 10 vols. of the chief pamphlets and publications which are now out of print. Mr. Charles Hersey has supplied genealogical particulars in which he has made exhaustive research. The sons of John Bright and Thomas Bayley Potter have kindly lent the letters of Goldwin Smith in their possession, and Dr. T. H. Warren, the president of Magdalen College, Oxford, has generously placed at the writer's disposed the letters which Goldwin Smith addressed to him. A bibliography of Goldwin Smith's writings, including more than 1500 titles, by Waterman Thomas Hewett, M.A., P.L.D., of Cornell University, is in preparation. See Goldwin Smith's Early Days of Cornell, 1904; J. J. Cooper, Goldwin Smith: a Brief Account of his Life and Writings, Reading, 1912; The Times, 8 June 1910; The Nation, 9 July 1910; Oxford Magazine, 16 June 1910; The News, Toronto, 7 June 1910 (memoir by Martin J. Griffin); Lord Selborne's Memorials, two series; Frederic Harrison's Autobiographic Memoirs; Lives of Jowett, Stanley, Lord Coleridge, and E. A. Freeman; Lewis Campbell's Nationalisation of the Older Universities.] S. L.

SMITH, HENRY SPENCER (1812–1901), surgeon, born in London on 12 Sept. 1812, was younger son of George Spencer Smith, an estate agent, by Martha his wife. After education at Enfield he entered St. Bartholomew's Hospital in 1832, being apprenticed to Frederick Carpenter Skey [q. v.], with whom he lived, and whose house surgeon he afterwards became. He was admitted M.R.C.S. in 1837, and in 1843 he was chosen one of the 150 persons upon whom the newly established degree of F.R.C.S.England, was conferred without examination; of this band he was the last survivor.

He proceeded to Paris in 1837, studying medicine there for six months, and from 1839–41 he studied science in Berlin. On his return to England he was appointed surgeon to the Royal General Dispensary in Aldersgate Street, and he also lectured on surgery at Samuel Lane's school of medicine in Grosvenor Place. When St. Mary's Hospital was founded in 1851 Spencer Smith became senior assistant surgeon. Three years later, when the medical school of St. Mary's Hospital was instituted, he was chosen dean, and filled the office until 1860; for seventeen years he lectured on systematic surgery. He received from both colleagues and students valuable presentations on his resignation. He was member of the council of the Royal College of Surgeons of England (1867–75), and of the court of examiners (1872–7). He was secretary of the Royal Medical and Chirurgical Society of London (1855–88).

Caring little for private practice, Smith gave both time and thought to the welfare of the newly founded St. Mary's Hospital and its medical school. He died at his house, 92 Oxford Terrace, W., on 29 Nov. 1901. His library, rich in medical works of the sixteenth and seventeenth centuries as well as in editions of Thomas à Kempis and of Walton's 'Angler,' was sold by Messrs. Sotheby, Wilkinson, and Hodge on 14, 15, and 16 Nov. 1878, and on 17 and 18 June 1897. He married (1) Elizabeth Mortlock, daughter of John Sturges, by whom he had a son and a daughter; and

(2) Louisa Theophila, daughter of the Rev. Gibson Lucas.

Smith translated from the German, for the Sydenham Society, Dr. H. Schwann's 'Microscopical Researches into the Accordance in the Structure and Growth of Animals and Plants' (1847) and Dr. M. J. Schleiden's 'Contributions to Phytogenesis' (in the same volume). These translations gave an impetus in this country to the microscopic study of the tissues.

[Lancet, 1901, ii. 1383; Brit. Med. Journal, 1901, ii. 1445; private information.]

D'A. P.

SMITH, JAMES HAMBLIN (1829–1901), mathematician, born on 2 Dec. 1829 at Rickinghall, Suffolk, was only surviving child of James Hamblin Smith by his wife Mary Finch. He was cousin of Barnard Smith, fellow of Peterhouse, Cambridge (B.A. 1839, M.A. 1842), rector of Glaston, Rutland, and a writer of popular mathematical text-books. After school education at Botesdale, Suffolk, he entered as a 'pensioner' at Gonville and Caius College, Cambridge, in July 1846. On Lady Day 1847 he was elected to a scholarship. At the quincentenary of the foundation of the college, in 1848, he was selected to write the 'Latin Commemoration Ode,' a copy of which is preserved in the 'University Registry' (lxxxvi. 27). In 1850 he graduated B.A. as thirty-second wrangler in the mathematical tripos and in the second class of the classical tripos. He proceeded M.A. in 1853. After graduating, Hamblin Smith became a private tutor at Cambridge in mathematics, classics and theology. He was lecturer in classics at Peterhouse from 1868 to 1872. The career of private 'coach' he pursued with success till near his death. He had the power of simplifying mathematical reasoning, and produced to that end the unitary method in arithmetic and a simple and ingenious plan for the conversion into *l.s.d.* of money expressed in decimals, a development of which simplifies the process of long division in a large class of cases (*Brit. Assoc. Report*, 1902, p. 529; *Caius College Magazine*, Michs. Term, 1902).

He published many handbooks for his pupils' use in preparing for examination in mathematics, classics and theology. He also published 'Rudiments of English Grammar' (1876; 2nd edit. 1882), as well as a Latin and a Greek grammar. His elementary mathematical treatises enjoyed a wide circulation.

Hamblin Smith found time for public work at Cambridge, in which his strong yet conciliatory personality gave him much influence. He was one of the Cambridge improvement commissioners from 1875 until the Local Government Act abolished that body in 1889. He was a member of the council of the senate from 1876 to 1880, and for many years chairman of the Board of Examinations (Cambridge). He was one of the earliest members of the London Mathematical Society.

He died at Cambridge on 10 July 1901, and was buried at Mill Road cemetery. He married on 16 April 1857 Ellen Hales (*d.* June 1912), daughter of Samuel Chilton Gross of Alderton, Suffolk, and sister of Edward John Gross, M.A., Cambridge secretary of the Oxford and Cambridge schools examinations board. Three sons and one daughter (wife of John Clay, M.A., of the Cambridge University Press) survived him. A process portrait hangs in the combination room of Gonville and Caius College, Cambridge.

Hamblin Smith's mathematical handbooks are: 1. 'Elementary Statics,' 1868; 10th edit. 1890. 2. 'Elementary Hydrostatics,' 1868; new edit. 1887. 3. 'Elementary Trigonometry,' 1868; 8th edit. 1890. 4. 'Elementary Algebra,' part i. 1869; 13th edit. 1894 (pt. ii. by E. J. Gross). 5. 'Elements of Geometry,' 1872; 7th edit. 1890. 6. 'A Treatise on Arithmetic,' 1872; 15th edit. 1898; adapted to Canadian schools by William Scott and R. Fletcher, revised edit. 1907. 7. 'An Introduction to the Study of Heat,' 4th edit. 1877; 9th edit. 1890. 8. 'An Introduction to the Study of Geometrical Conic Sections,' 1887; 2nd edit. 1889.

[Private information.] J. D. H. D.

SMITH, LUCY TOULMIN (1838–1911), scholar, born at Boston, Massachusetts, U.S.A., on 21 Nov. 1838, was eldest child of a family of two sons and three daughters of Joshua Toulmin Smith (1816–1869) [q. v.] by his wife Martha, daughter of William Jones Kendall. About 1842 her parents returned to England and settled at Highgate, London, where she resided for more than fifty years. Lucy was educated at home, and early became her father's amanuensis, actively aiding him in the compilation of his periodical, the 'Parliamentary Remembrancer' (1857–65). In 1870 she began original research, completing for the Early English Text Society the volume on 'English Gilds' begun by her father and left unfinished at his death. In 1872 she edited for the Camden Society 'The Maire of Bristoweis Kalendar,' by R. Ricart, and for the New Shakspere Society, in 1879, C. M. Ingleby's 'Shakespeare's Centurie of Prayse,' to which she made many additions.

Miss Toulmin Smith's most important contributions to research and scholarship were her editions of the 'York Plays' (1885); of the 'Expeditions to Prussia and the Holy Land by Henry, Earl of Derby (afterwards Henry IV) in 1390–1 and 1392–3,' issued by the Camden Society in 1894, a mine of information upon continental travel in the fourteenth century; and of Leland's 'Itinerary,' the preparation of which occupied her leisure for many years. The 'Itinerary in Wales' was issued in 1906, and the 'Itinerary in England' in 4 vols. 1907–10.

In November 1894 Miss Toulmin Smith left Highgate on being elected librarian of Manchester College, Oxford; she was the first woman in England to be appointed head of a public library, and held the post until her death. Her house at Oxford became the meeting-place of British and foreign scholars, at whose disposal she always placed her aid and advice and even her labour. At the same time she was an accomplished gardener and housewife. She died at 1 Park Terrace, Oxford, on 18 Dec. 1911, and was buried in Wolvercote cemetery. A memorial is to be placed in the library of Manchester College.

Besides the works already mentioned Miss Toulmin Smith edited 'Gorboduc' for Vollmoeller's 'Englische Sprach- und Literaturdenkmale' (1883) and 'A Commonplace Book of the Fifteenth Century' (1886). She translated Jusserand's 'La Vie Nomade et les routes d'Angleterre' under the title of 'English Wayfaring Life' (1889). Her 'Manual of the English Grammar and Language for Self-help' (1886) is a clear and practical work on historical lines. She assisted Paul Meyer in editing 'Les Contes moralisés de Nicole Bozon' for the Société des anciens Textes français (1889), and took some part in the editing of the medieval chronicle 'Cursor Mundi' (1893) and of the Registers of the Knights Hospitaller of Malta, which she examined during a six months' visit to Malta (1880–1).

[The Times, 21 Dec. 1911; The Inquirer, 23 Dec. 1911 (notice by C. H. Herford); Brit. Mus. Cat.; private information.]

E. L.

SMITH, REGINALD BOSWORTH (1839–1908), schoolmaster and author, born on 28 June 1839 at West Stafford Rectory, was second son in the family of four sons and six daughters of Reginald Southwell Smith (1809–1896), who graduated M.A. from Balliol College, Oxford, in 1834, was rector of West Stafford, Dorset, from 1836, and canon of Salisbury from 1875. His grandfather was Sir John Wyldbore Smith (1770–1852), second baronet, of Sydling and the Down House, Blandford, Dorset. His mother was Emily Geneviève, daughter of Henry Hanson Simpson of Bitterne Manor House, Hampshire, and 12 Camden Place, Bath. From Milton Abbas school, Blandford, Bosworth Smith passed in August 1855 to Marlborough College, where he was head boy under two headmasters—George Edward Lynch Cotton [q. v.], afterwards bishop of Calcutta, and George Granville Bradley [q. v. Suppl. II], subsequently dean of Westminster. At Michaelmas 1858 he matriculated at Oxford, with an open classical scholarship at Corpus Christi College, and he graduated B.A. in 1862 with first-class honours both in classical moderations and in the final classical school. In the same year he was president of the union. In 1863 he was elected to a classical fellowship at Trinity College, Oxford, and was appointed tutor of that college, and lecturer both there and at Corpus Christi. In the same year he published 'Birds of Marlborough,' a first testimony to his native love of birds, which he cherished from boyhood. He proceeded M.A. in 1865.

On 16 Sept. 1864 he began work as a classical master at Harrow School, on the nomination of the headmaster, Dr. H. Montagu Butler. He married next year, and in 1870 he opened a new 'Large House,' The Knoll, which he built at his own expense, and where he designed an attractive garden. For more than thirty years Bosworth Smith mainly devoted his life to his duties at Harrow. His house was always one of the most distinguished in the school. His firm, but tolerant, government, his enthusiasm and simplicity, his wide interests, and his ready sympathy bound his pupils to him in ties of affection, which lasted long after they had left school. In his form teaching, which never lost its early freshness, he qualified the classical tradition by diverting much of his energy to history, scripture, geography, and English literature, especially Milton.

Bosworth Smith, who travelled frequently in his vacations and was keenly alive to the historical associations of foreign scenes, cherished many interests outside his school work, and was soon widely known as an author. In 1874 he delivered before the Royal Institution in London four lectures on Mohammed and Mohammedanism, originally prepared for an essay society at Harrow. They were published in the same year (3rd edit. 1889). While maintaining the infinite superiority of Christianity as a religion, Bosworth Smith ably defended the character and teaching of the Prophet. The book excited controversy, but its fairness was acknowledged by Asiatic scholars, and the volume ranks with the best accounts of Islam in English. It was translated into Arabic, and its author was for many years prayed for in the mosques of Western Africa.

'Carthage and the Carthaginians' (abridged edit. 1881, 'Rome and Carthage'), which followed in 1878, collected seven lectures also delivered before the Royal Institution. Here Bosworth Smith gave a graphic description of Carthage as 'Queen of the Mediterranean,' and defended the character of Hannibal. In 1879 he accepted the invitation of the family of the first Lord Lawrence [q. v.] to write his life. He had met Lord Lawrence, and in two letters in 'The Times' in 1878 had defended his Afghan policy. Three years were spent on the accumulated documents and in intercourse with Indian authorities, and the book was published in two volumes on 12 Feb. 1883. Its reception was enthusiastic. Within five days the first edition of 1000 copies (at a high price) was exhausted; a fourth edition was called for in April, and a sixth in 1885 (7th edit. 1901). The American government placed a copy in every great public library and on every ship in the U.S. navy. It was also translated into Urdu, and widely read among the natives of India. Although Bosworth Smith never visited India, critics were agreed as to both the accuracy of his portraiture and the charm of his style. The assertion of his own views on disputed questions like the Afghan frontier, and his condemnation of Hodson of Hodson's horse provoked remonstrance, but the book took a high place among English biographies. Owing to fear of the strain on his health, Bosworth Smith declined other work of similar kind, such as biographies of the first Earl Russell, of the seventh earl of Shaftesbury, of Lord Stratford de Redcliffe, and the duke of Wellington. At the same time Bosworth Smith constantly and effectively intervened in current political, religious, and educational controversies, chiefly through letters to 'The Times' or articles in the reviews. During the Turco-Russian conflict (1876–8) he defended the Turkish character, and insisted on the danger to India of Russia's aggressive policy (*The Times*, 21 July 1877; *Contemp. Review*, December 1876, 'Turkey and Russia'). In 1885 he urged the permanent occupation of the Soudan by England (*The Times*, 13 Feb. 1885), and in 1892 he protested against the threat of evacuating Uganda which was not carried out (*ib.* 18, 25 Oct. 13 Dec. 1892; cf. also *Contemp. Rev.* January 1891, 'Englishmen in Africa'). On 20 Oct. 1892, speaking on the subject for a deputation of the British and Foreign Anti-Slavery Society to Lord Rosebery, then secretary of state for foreign affairs, he pleaded for 'the continuity of the moral policy of England.' His letters were reprinted as a pamphlet and had a wide circulation. In the autumn of 1885 he in like manner defended the Church of England against Gladstone's and Mr. Chamberlain's menaces of disestablishment (*The Times*, 13, 20, 31 Oct.). To an early evangelical training he added a wide tolerance, but his loyalty to the church was intense. Gladstone vaguely replied to his appeal for some reassuring message to liberal churchmen (*ibid.* 31 Oct. 1885). Smith's letters were published by the Church Defence Institution as a pamphlet entitled 'Reasons of a Layman and a Liberal for opposing Disestablishment' (cf. also arts. by Bosworth Smith, *Nineteenth Century*, 1889, 'The Crisis in the Church'; *National Review*, July 1907, 'Sunday').

In 1895 Bosworth Smith purchased an old manor house at Bingham's Melcombe, Dorset, and there he resided on his retirement from Harrow in 1901.

He was J.P. for Dorsetshire, a member of the education committee of the county council, vice-president of the Dorset Field Club, to which he lectured more than once, a member of the Salisbury Diocesan Synod, and a member of the house of laymen in the representative church council at Westminster. At Harrow he had steadily pursued his lifelong study of birds, making annual expeditions with chosen pupils to neighbouring woods, and occasionally to the Norfolk Broads and other places, to observe, but not to rob, birds' nests. In his holidays, too, he had been a keen but humane sportsman. At Bingham's Melcombe he enjoyed full scope for his predilections. To the 'Nineteenth Century' (November 1902–February 1904) he contributed six articles on birds, which were published with other chapters descriptive of Dorset life, as 'Bird Life and Bird Lore,' in 1905 (new edit. 1909). After many months' illness he died at Bingham's Melcombe on 18 Oct. 1908, and was buried beside his parents and brothers in the churchyard of West Stafford, his birthplace.

On 9 Aug. 1865 he married Flora, fourth daughter of the Rev. Edward Dawe Wickham, rector of Holmwood, Surrey (1851–1893), whose fifth daughter, Alice Bertha, was wife of Bosworth's elder brother, Henry John (1838–1879). Bosworth Smith's own handwriting was all but illegible, and his wife, who fully shared all his interests, copied and recopied every line he wrote for publication and most of his important private letters. She survived him with five sons and four daughters; the second son, Alan Wyldbore Bosworth, lieutenant R.N , lost his life at sea when in command of H.M.S. Cobra (18 Sept. 1901).

A portrait of Bosworth Smith, painted by Hugh G. Riviere, presented by old pupils at Harrow and engraved by the Fine Arts Society, is now in the possession of his widow at Bingham's Melcombe. He is commemorated by tablets in Harrow school chapel and in the church at Bingham's Melcombe, and in his memory were erected a portion of the reredos in the church at West Stafford and (by friends and pupils) a stone balustrade in the terrace gardens at Harrow.

[Reginald Bosworth Smith, a Memoir, by his eldest daughter, Ellinor Flora, wife of Major Sir Edward Ian Grogan, 2nd bart., 1909; Harrovian, 27 July 1901 and 14 Nov. 1908; The Times, 20 Oct. 1908; Salisbury Gazette, Nov. 1908; Marlburian, Dec. 1908; Dorset County Chronicle, 22 Oct. 1908.]

E. G–M.

SMITH, SAMUEL (1836–1906), politician and philanthropist, born on 11 Jan. 1836 at Roberton, in the parish of Borgue, Kirkcudbrightshire, was eldest of the seven children of James Smith, a large farmer of Borgue, who also farmed land of his own in South Carleton and other places. His grandfather and an uncle, both named Samuel Smith, were each parish minister of Borgue. The former (*d.* 1816) wrote 'A General View of the Agriculture of Galloway' (1806); the latter seceded at the disruption of the Scottish church in 1843.

Smith, after being educated at the Borgue parish school and at Kirkcudbright, entered Edinburgh University before he was sixteen, and spent three sessions there. In spite of his literary tastes, he was apprenticed to a cotton-broker in Liverpool in 1853. There he spent his leisure in study, frequenting the Liverpool literary societies and speaking at the Philomathic Society, of which he became president, and forming close friendships with (Sir) Donald Currie [q. v. Suppl. II], W. B. Barbour, and William Sproston Caine [q. v. Suppl. II]. In 1857 Smith became manager of the cotton saleroom and began to write with authority on the cotton market in the 'Liverpool Daily Post,' under the signature 'Mercator' (cf. THOMAS ELLISON, *The Cotton Trade of Great Britain*). In 1860 he visited New Orleans and the cotton-growing districts of North America, of which he published a description. On his return, having made a tour of the leading Lancashire manufacturing centres, he started in business as a cotton-broker in Chapel Street, Liverpool, and he established the first monthly cotton circular, conducting it till his entrance into parliament. In the winter of 1862–3 he went to India on behalf of the Manchester Chamber of Commerce to test the cotton-growing possibilities of the country, in view of the depletion of the English market owing to the American civil war. In a communication to the 'Times of India' (embodied in a pamphlet published in England) Smith questioned India's fitness to grow cotton. The visit generated in him a lifelong interest in India and its people. He travelled back slowly by way of the Levant, Constantinople, and the Danube, and greatly improved his business prospects. Toward the close of his career he recommended the growing of cotton in British Africa, Egypt, the Soudan, and Scinde. On 1 Jan. 1864 the firm of Smith, Edwards & Co., cotton-brokers, was launched, and three months later Samuel Smith also became head of the Liverpool branch of James Finlay & Co. of Glasgow and Bombay. Cotton-spinning and manufacturing were subsequently added to his activities by the purchase of Millbrook mills, Stalybridge.

From an early period Smith was active as a philanthropist. At Liverpool he interested himself in efforts for prevention of cruelty to children, for establishing scholarships to connect primary and secondary schools (1874), and for improving public-houses; he entered the town council in 1879 as an ardent temperance reformer. A zealous presbyterian of liberal views, he joined in inviting Messrs. Moody and Sankey to Liverpool in 1875; presided at a meeting of 4000 held at Hengler's Circus in aid of 'General' Booth's 'Darkest England' scheme in 1890; and received 14,000 American delegates of the Christian Endeavour Society in 1897. In 1876 Smith became president of the Liverpool chamber of commerce.

At a bye-election at Liverpool in Dec. 1882, caused by Lord Sandon's succession to his father's earldom of Harrowby, Smith was elected in the liberal interest by a majority of 309, winning a seat for his party in what was regarded as a conservative stronghold. In 1885 he was defeated in the Abercromby division of Liverpool, but in March 1886 was returned for Flintshire during his absence in India. That seat he retained till 1905. Gladstone's residence, Hawarden Castle, was in his constituency, and Smith was often there, exchanging views with the statesman. Smith, who seconded the address to the crown at the opening of the session of 1884, constantly spoke in the House of Commons on moral, social, religious, currency, and Indian questions. Critics likened him to Jeremiah, but he was sincere and well-informed. He pressed untiringly for compulsory evening continuation schools for children leaving school at thirteen, and for the abrogation of payment by results and of overstrain in elementary schools. He zealously promoted the Criminal Law Amendment Act of 1885, and by his efforts made legal the evidence of young children. The Prevention of Cruelty to Children Act of 1889 embodied reforms which he had advocated in Liverpool. He lamented that his attacks on the opium trade between India and China were not very effectual.

Gradually adopting bimetallic views, on which he gave addresses in many parts of the country, he several times raised the question in parliament. On 18 April 1890 he initiated a parliamentary debate in which Mr. Balfour, Sir Edward Clarke, and Sir Richard Webster supported, and Sir W. Harcourt and Mr. W. H. Smith opposed his resolution (which was lost by 183 to 87). Smith contributed 'Three Letters on the Silver Question' to H. Cernuschi's 'Nomisma' (1877), and published 'The Bimetallic Question' (1887).

Smith revisited India in 1886, and his subsequent articles in the 'Contemporary Review' (reprinted as 'India Revisited; the Social and Political Problem,' 1886) were answered by Sir Mountstuart Grant Duff [q. v. Suppl. II], governor of Madras. Thenceforth the grievances of India were a main theme of his in the House of Commons. On 30 April 1889 Smith carried by a majority of ten against the government a motion condemning the liquor policy of the Indian government. The result was a reduction of licences in India. In 1894 Smith's motion for a parliamentary inquiry into the condition of the Indian people was followed by a royal commission which recommended a reduction by 250,000*l.* of Indian liabilities. He encouraged the native claim to a larger share in the government. Other native races found in Smith a warm champion. In 1892–3 he called attention to the abuses of the Kanaka labour traffic from the New Hebrides to Queensland, and in March 1896 the motion of sympathy with the Armenians in consequence of the recent massacres was carried unanimously.

Religious questions chiefly occupied his closing years. He urged in parliament disestablishment both in Wales and England, and denounced ritualistic offences with sustained vehemence, publishing pamphlets on the subject which reached a circulation of a million. In the summer of 1901 his health failed, but he retained his seat in parliament till the end of 1905, when he was named a privy councillor on his retirement.

Smith, who was again in India in 1904–5, returned thither with Mr. William Jones, M.P., at the end of 1906 in apparently improved health, arriving on 25 Dec.; but after attending some sittings of the Indian National Congress he died rather suddenly on 28 Dec. at Calcutta. He was buried in the Scottish cemetery there. He bequeathed upwards of 50,000*l.* to various Liverpool institutions.

Smith married on 20 July 1864 Melville (*d.* 1893), daughter of the Rev. John Christison, D.D., of Biggar, Lanarkshire. In memory of a son, James Gordon Smith (1870–1900), who predeceased him, the Gordon Smith Institute for Seamen, in Paradise Street, Liverpool, was founded in 1900 and carried on by his father.

Smith was constantly engaged in controversy in the press. He met Henry George in debate at the National Liberal Club, each making four speeches (printed in the appendix to his 'My Life Work,' 1902).

His many publications include, besides those mentioned, 'The Credibility of the Christian Religion' (1872; last edit. 1889) and 'India and its Problems: Letters written from India in 1904–5' (1905). His 'Cotton Trade of India' (1863) was translated into French by F. Emion.

[Smith's My Life Work, 1902 (with portrait), contains, besides the narrative, copious extracts from his letters written in India and America and excerpts from speeches; The Times, and Daily News, 31 Dec. 1906; Liverpool Daily Post, 31 Dec. 1906 and 1 Jan.

1907 (with portrait); Hansard's Parl. Debates; Lucy's Diary of the Unionist Parlt. 1901, pp. 262–4; John Newton's W. S. Caine, 1907; Who's Who, 1906; Brit. Mus. Cat.]

G. Le G. N.

SMITH, SARAH, writing under the pseudonym of 'Hesba Stretton' (1832–1911), author, born on 27 July 1832, in New Street, Wellington, Shropshire, was third daughter and fourth child (in a family of eight) of Benjamin Smith, a bookseller and publisher, by his wife Ann Bakewell, a woman of strong evangelical views, who died when Sarah was eight years old. Sarah attended a large girls' day school at the Old Hall, Watling Street, Wellington, conducted by Mrs. Cranage. The school was continued by her son, Dr. Cranage, as a boys' school, and became well known. But Sarah's education was chiefly gained by reading the books in her father's shop. She early began to write little tales without thought of publication. In 1859, however, her sister Elizabeth (1830–1911), her life-long companion, sent, unknown to Sarah, one of these stories, 'The Lucky Leg,' to Charles Dickens, then editor of 'Household Words.' He accepted it, sending a cheque for 5*l.*, and published it on 19 March 1859, intimating he would be glad of further contributions. A friendship sprang up between Dickens and the young author, who contributed to nearly every Christmas number of 'All the Year Round' until 1866. Her most notable tale in that connection was 'The Travelling Post Office' in 'Mugby Junction,' Dec. 1866. Feeling that her name lacked distinction, she adopted in 1858 the pseudonym 'Hesba Stretton.' Hesba represented the initial letters of the names of her brothers and sisters then living in order of age, and 'Stretton' was taken from All Stretton (near Church Stretton, Shropshire), where by the bequest of an uncle her younger sister Ann (*b.* 1837) had property. Hesba, who adopted her new name in all relations of life, visited the place annually till near her death.

At the end of 1863 Hesba Stretton and her sister left Shropshire, and lived for some years in Manchester, and after a short sojourn abroad settled in 1870 in Bayswater, London. Her work attracted little notice until the appearance in the 'Sunday at Home' in 1866 of 'Jessica's First Prayer,' a touching story, simply written, of a girl waif's awakening to the meaning of religion. Issued in book form in 1867, it won an immediate and lasting popularity. Over a million and a half copies have been sold, and it has been translated into every European language and into most Asiatic and African tongues. The tale shows accurate knowledge of the life of destitute children in large cities, and embodies personal investigations of slum conditions. The story was commended by the earl of Shaftesbury [q. v.]. The Tsar Alexander II ordered it to be placed in all Russian schools, but the decree was revoked by his successor, who had all the copies burnt. Similar stories followed, of which the most popular were 'Little Meg's Children' (1868) and 'Alone in London' (1869), which reached a combined circulation of three-quarters of a million copies. Between 1866 and 1906 Hesba Stretton published in all fifty volumes, mostly short religious and moral tales issued by the Religious Tract Society; a few, however, like 'The Clives of Burcot' (1866), 'David Lloyd's Last Will' (1869), and 'The Doctor's Dilemma' (1872) are long novels.

A woman of wide and varied sympathies, Hesba Stretton did not confine her energies to writing. She became acquainted with the Baroness Burdett-Coutts [q. v. Suppl. II] and assisted her in her works of charity. Hesba Stretton took a prominent part in the founding of the London Society for the Prevention of Cruelty to Children. She had for some years been associated with Benjamin Waugh [q. v. Suppl. II] in the 'Sunday Magazine,' and in consultation with him she published a letter in 'The Times' in Jan. 1884, directing attention to the need for such a society. She attended a meeting of twenty persons, including the Baroness Burdett-Coutts and the earl of Shaftesbury, at the Mansion House on 11 July 1884, when the foundations of the society were laid. A report which she drew up for an organising sub-committee was printed and circulated. Hesba Stretton continued an active member of the executive committee until 15 Dec. 1894, when she resigned. The Baroness Burdett-Coutts had resigned just before because she disapproved on financial grounds of the development of the London society into a national society.

During the Russian famine of 1892 Hesba Stretton collected 1000*l.* for the relief of the peasants, and took much trouble to ensure its proper distribution.

About 1890 Miss Stretton settled at Ivy Croft, Ham, near Richmond, where she died on 8 Oct. 1911, after having been confined to her room for four years. She was buried in the churchyard, Ham Common, Surrey.

Hesba Stretton, who led a retired, simple,

and hardworking life, and avoided publicity, wholly depended for her livelihood on her pen. She never went to a theatre, cared nothing for dress, and owned no jewellery. She found recreation in foreign travel and in the society of children and of friends, who included foreigners of distinction like J. H. Merle D'Aubigné, the French protestant historian, and Franz Delitzsch, the German theologian. The latter translated many of her stories into German.

[The Times, 10 Oct. 1911; Seed Time and Harvest, Dec. 1911; Sunday at Home, Dec. 1911; Brit. Mus. Cat.; private information.]

E. L.

SMITH, THOMAS (1817–1906), missionary and mathematician, born at Symington manse on 8 July 1817, was eldest son in a family of ten children of John Smith, parish minister of Symington, Lanarkshire, by his wife Jean Stodart. After attending the parish school, he matriculated at thirteen at Edinburgh University, where he took the highest honours in mathematics and physics. Entering the divinity hall in 1834, he studied under Thomas Chalmers [q. v.], and in 1839 was licensed to preach. Coming under the influence of Dr. Alexander Duff [q. v.], he was ordained to the Scottish mission in Calcutta (7 March 1839). At the Church of Scotland's headquarters at Calcutta he quickly distinguished himself both as an intellectual preacher and as a teacher of mathematics and physical science. In 1843, on the disruption of the Church of Scotland, Smith and his colleagues in India joined the Free Church.

Thenceforth Smith was busily engaged in building up the Indian mission of the Free Church. Besides exercising much influence among the natives, he furthered the cause of education; was an active contributor to missionary literature and to Indian journalism, was a chief writer in the 'Calcutta Review' from its foundation, and was editor from 1851 to 1859.

When he went to India, it was impossible for male missionaries to reach the women, all of whom above the very lowest class were shut off from the society of men. Smith's proposal in the 'Christian Observer' in 1840 to send lady missionaries and governesses, both European and Indian, into the zenana bore fruit in the first Zenana mission, which was started in 1854 and was the crowning achievement of Smith's Indian career. On the outbreak of the Indian Mutiny in 1857 Smith acted as chaplain of the 42nd Highlanders (Black Watch) at Calcutta, and he accompanied the regiment on active service up country.

Smith finally returned to Scotland in 1859, and from that date until 1879 conducted a home mission charge in one of the poorest districts of Edinburgh. In 1880 he succeeded his friend, Alexander Duff [q. v.], in the chair of evangelistic theology in New College, Edinburgh, retiring in 1893 with the rank of emeritus professor and a seat in the senatus. In 1891 he was moderator of the general assembly of the Free Church of Scotland, and in March 1899 he celebrated his ministerial diamond jubilee.

In ecclesiastical politics Smith was a conservative, usually co-operating with Dr. James Begg [q. v.], whose biography he wrote (1885–8). He strongly opposed the first proposals for the union of the Free and United Presbyterian Churches (1863–73), but reluctantly accepted the change at the close of his life. From Edinburgh University Smith received three honorary degrees, M.A. in 1858, D.D. in 1867, and LL.D. in 1900.

Smith was also a brilliant mathematician, scholar, and linguist. Lord Kelvin said: 'Had [he] devoted himself to mathematical science . . . he would unquestionably have risen to the very highest eminence in that science. As it was, *teste* his logarithmic calculations (which were not completed), he was one of the foremost mathematical scholars of his day.' In 1857 Smith published 'An Elementary Treatise on Plane Geometry according to the Method of Rectilineal Co-ordinates,' and in 1902 'The Life of Euclid' in Oliphant Smeaton's series of 'World's Epoch-Makers.' Smith edited a noteworthy edition of the puritan divines (1860–6), and learned French in order to translate Vinet's 'Studies in Pascal,' and German to prepare English versions of Warneck's missionary writings. Besides publishing a short biography of Dr. Alexander Duff [q. v.] for the 'Men Worth Remembering' series (1883), and 'Mediæval Missions' ('Duff Missionary Lectures,' 1880), he edited the 'Letters of Samuel Rutherford' (1881).

Smith died at Edinburgh on 26 May 1906, and was buried in the Grange cemetery. A presentation portrait, painted by J. H. Lorimer, R.S.A., in 1903, is now in the custody of the senatus of New College, Edinburgh. In 1839 Smith married Grace, daughter of D. K. Whyte, paymaster, R.N.; she died in 1886. His third son, the Rev. William Whyte Smith, B.D., minister of Newington Free Church, Edinburgh, predeceased him. His only surviving son, David Whyte Ewart Smith, is a justice of the peace and honorary sheriff substitute for Haddingtonshire.

[Scotsman, 27 May 1906; Scottish Review, 31 May 1906 (memorial notice by George Smith, LL.D., C.I.E.); private information.]

W. F. G.

SMITH, Sir THOMAS, first baronet (1833–1909), surgeon, born at Blackheath on 23 March 1833, was sixth son of Benjamin Smith, a London goldsmith, by his wife Susannah, daughter of Apsley Pellatt, whose ancestor Thomas Pellatt was president of the Royal College of Physicians of London (1735–9). Two brothers became canons of Canterbury, and a third, Stephen, was prime warden in the Goldsmiths' Company in 1885–6.

Tom Smith was educated at Tonbridge school, which he entered in Lent term, 1844. His father, having suffered reverses in business, apprenticed his son to Sir James Paget [q. v. Suppl. I] in 1847. Smith was thus the last of the 'hospital apprentices' at St. Bartholomew's Hospital. He was admitted M.R.C.S. in 1854, and in August became house surgeon at the Children's Hospital in Great Ormond Street. This post he resigned from ill-health on 7 Dec., receiving a special minute of commendation from the committee of management. Taking rooms in Bedford Row, he coached pupils for examinations and at the same time assisted Paget in his private and hospital practice. From 1857 onwards for several years it was his custom to take a class of students to Paris in the Easter vacation, where, with the help of Brown-Séquard [q. v. Suppl. I], he taught them operative surgery. The outcome of this work was a 'Manual of Operative Surgery on the Dead Body,' published in 1859 (2nd edit. 1876). In 1858 he was admitted F.R.C.S.England, and in 1859 was appointed, jointly with George W. Callender, demonstrator of anatomy and operative surgery at St. Bartholomew's Hospital. He was elected assistant surgeon on 24 Feb. 1864 on the resignation of Frederick Carpenter Skey [q. v.], and for a time had charge of the aural department. He was appointed surgeon in 1873. In the medical school attached to the hospital he lectured on anatomy jointly with Callender from 1871. On resigning his hospital appointments on 10 March 1898 at the retiring age of sixty-five he was appointed a consulting surgeon.

From 1858 to 1861 Smith was assistant surgeon at the Great Northern Hospital, then recently established in York Road, King's Cross. In September 1861 he was elected assistant surgeon at the Children's Hospital in Great Ormond Street, where he was surgeon from June 1868 to November 1883 and afterwards consulting surgeon. He was also surgeon to the Alexandra Hospital for hip disease in Queen Square.

Smith was surgical secretary of the Royal Medical and Chirurgical Society (1870–2), and he contributed to the 'Transactions' of this body (vol. 51, p. 79) his paper 'On the Cure of Cleft Palate by Operation in Children, with a Description of an Instrument for Facilitating the Operation.' The method recommended in this paper governed the technique of the operation for many years. He also took an important part in the commission appointed to report upon the administration of remedies by hypodermic injection.

At the Royal College of Surgeons of England Smith was elected a member of the council in 1880. He acted as a vice-president in 1887–8, and again in 1890–1, but he refused nomination for the office of president. He was chosen a trustee of the Hunterian collection in 1900. He was gazetted surgeon-extraordinary to Queen Victoria in 1895, in succession to Sir William Savory [q. v.], and was created a baronet in 1897. He actively aided the Misses Keyser in founding their home for officers wounded in the South African war, and was created K.C.V.O. in 1901. Becoming an honorary serjeant-surgeon to King Edward VII on his accession in 1901, he was in attendance when Sir Frederick Treves operated on the King on the day appointed for the Coronation (24 June 1902).

He lived at 7 Montagu Street, Russell Square, until 1868, when he removed to 5 Stratford Place, Oxford Street, where he died on 1 Oct. 1909. He was buried in the Finchley cemetery.

He married on 27 Aug. 1862 Ann Eliza, second daughter of Frederick Parbury, an Australian by birth. She died on 9 Feb. 1879, shortly after the birth of her ninth child, and in 1880 he instituted in her memory the Samaritan Maternity Fund at St. Bartholomew's Hospital. Through life Smith trusted more to his own observation and experience than to knowledge acquired from others. A dexterous operator, a sure guide in difficult questions of diagnosis, and a first-rate clinical teacher of surgery, he was popular with students, who appreciated his wit and humour.

A three-quarter length in oils—a good likeness—painted by the Hon. John Collier, hangs in the great hall of St. Bartholomew's Hospital. It was presented by his colleagues and old pupils with a replica for himself on his retirement from the hospital in 1898.

[St. Bartholomew's Hosp. Reports, vol. xl. 1909; Lancet, 1909, ii. 1108; personal knowledge.] D'A. P.

SMITH, THOMAS ROGER (1830–1903), architect, born at Sheffield on 14 July 1830, was only son of the Rev. Thomas Smith of Sheffield by his wife Louisa Thomas of Chelsea. After private education he entered the office of Philip Hardwick [q. v.] and spent a year and a half in travel before beginning independent practice in 1855. Mr. A. S. Gale was in partnership with him until 1891, and from 1888 his son, Mr. Ravenscroft Elsey Smith, who co-operated in all his subsequent works.

Having been selected to prepare the design for the exhibition buildings in Bombay, Smith proceeded thither in 1864. The erection was abandoned after the contract was signed owing to the cotton famine, but several important buildings were erected in India from his designs, including the post office and British Hospital at Bombay, and the residency at Gunersh Kind. In England his work included the Technical Schools (and Baths) of the Carpenters' Company at Stratford; the Ben Jonson schools at Stepney (1872), as well as other schools for the London school board; Emmanuel church and vicarage, South Croydon; the Sanatorium at Reedham (1883); the North London Hospital for Consumption at Hampstead (built 1880, enlarged 1892, completed 1903); laboratories at University College (opened 1892), forming part of an uncompleted scheme for the Gower Street front of the large quadrangle; many City warehouses; and, besides other domestic work, Armathwaite Hall, Cumberland; Brambletye House, East Grinstead; a house at Taplow for Mr. G. Hanbury, and Beechy Lees at Otford, Kent.

Smith, who devoted much of his energies to lecturing on architecture and to official duties external to actual professional practice, became in 1851 a member of the Architectural Association, a body to which he delivered an extensive series of lectures; he was president in 1860–1 and again in 1863–4. At the Royal Institute of British Architects he was elected an associate in 1856 and in 1863 a fellow. He took a prominent part in its debates and committees, was for several sessions a member of its council, and became chairman in 1899 of the statutory board of examiners (under the London Building Acts) which the institute appoints. In 1874 he was made district surveyor under the Metropolitan Board of Works for Southwark and North Lambeth, and was transferred in 1882 to the more important district of West Wandsworth. Smith's other official appointments were numerous. At the Carpenters' Company, for which he acted as examiner in carpentry, &c., as a frequent lecturer, and as surveyor, he attained in 1901 the office of master. He was an examiner in architecture to the Science and Art Department, South Kensington, as well as to the City and Guilds Institute, and surveyor to the licensing justices of Wimbledon and Wandsworth; but the most important of his posts was the professorship of architecture at University College, London, which he held from 1880 to his death. His wide practical experience in questions of rights of light brought him frequent engagements as an expert and arbitrator, and in 1900 he served (as chairman) on a joint committee of the Royal Institute of British Architects and the Surveyors' Institution appointed to discuss the amendment of the law of ancient lights. Smith was often an architectural assessor in competitions.

Smith prepared many papers on professional and artistic subjects, but his only published books were the manual on 'Acoustics' in Weale's series (1861), and two handbooks, one on 'Architecture, Classic and Early Christian' (1882; new edit. 1898); the other on 'Gothic and Renaissance Architecture' (1888, 'Illustrated Handbooks of Art History'), of which Mr. John Slater was joint author. Though afflicted with serious lameness for many years, Smith continued his professional labours till within three months of his death on 11 March 1903 at his residence, Gordon Street, Gordon Square, London. His office was at Temple Chambers, Temple Avenue, E.C.

He married in 1858 Catherine, daughter of Joseph Elsey of Highgate, and was survived by his widow, one daughter, and three sons, one of whom, his partner, Mr. Ravenscroft Elsey Smith, became in 1899 professor of architecture at King's College, London.

[R.I.B.A. Journal, 3rd series, x. 276; The Builder, 1903, lxxxiv. 289; Building News, 1903, lxxxiv. 369; information from Professor R. Elsey Smith.] P. W.

SMITH, WALTER CHALMERS (1824–1908), poet and preacher, son of Walter Smith, builder, by his wife Barbara Milne, was born in Aberdeen on 5 Dec. 1824. He was educated at the grammar school, Aberdeen, and at Marischal College, which he entered at the age of thirteen, graduating M.A. in 1841. His original intention was to adopt law as his professsion, but under the influence of Dr. Chalmers he entered the New College, Edinburgh, to study for the ministry of the Free Church of Scotland. In 1850 he was ordained pastor of the Free (Scottish) Church in Chadwell Street, Pentonville, London. The small congregation did not become larger under his ministry. In 1853 he resigned and was appointed to Milnathort, in the parish of Orwell, Kinross-shire; and in 1857 he removed to Roxburgh Free Church, Edinburgh. In 1862 he was chosen to succeed the Free Church leader, Dr. Robert Buchanan (1802–1875) [q. v.], in the Free Tron Church, Glasgow. Smith was a thoughtful preacher, catholic in his sympathies, and of rather advanced opinions for the Free Church of his time, though in the end his influence was felt in broadening its outlook. Two 'Discourses' that he published in 1866, advocating more liberal views in regard to Sunday observance than those then prevailing in Scotland, came under the ban of his Presbytery, and he was 'affectionately admonished' by the General Assembly in June 1867. In 1876 he was translated to the Free High Church, Edinburgh. During the prosecution of Professor Robertson Smith [see SMITH, WILLIAM ROBERTSON] his strong sympathy with the professor gave some offence to the orthodox church leaders; but in 1893 he had so won the confidence of the church that he was chosen moderator of the general assembly. The following year he retired from his charge, when he was presented with his portrait painted by Sir George Reid. He received the degrees of D.D. from the University of Glasgow (1869), and LL.D. from the universities of Aberdeen (1876) and Edinburgh (1893). He died on 20 Sept. 1908. He married Agnes Monteith and left a son and three daughters.

Under the pseudonym of 'Orwell,' Smith published, in 1861, a book of poems with the title 'The Bishop's Walk'; and in 1872, under the pseudonym of 'Hermann Knott,' 'Olrig Grange,' which reached in 1888 a fourth edition. His other volumes of verse are: 1. 'Borland Hall,' 1874. 2. 'Hilda amongst the Broken Gods,' 1878. 3. 'Raban or Life Splinters,' 1880. 4. 'North Country Folk,' 1883. 5. 'Kildrostan, a dramatic Poem,' 1884. 6. 'Thoughts and Fancies for Sunday Evening,' 1887. 7. 'A Heretic,' 1890. A selection of his poems appeared in 1890, and a complete edition in 1902; a volume of sermons was published posthumously in 1909. Smith's verse is smooth and pleasant, touched with humour and full of sympathy, simple and unpretending in style. Several of his pieces are merely tales or character sketches in verse, shrewdly humorous, but rather too colloquial in manner to be termed poetry.

[Who's Who, 1908; Scotsman, and Glasgow Herald, 20 Sept. 1908; Miles's Poets and Poetry of the Nineteenth Century, xii. 109 seq.; information from his daughter, Mrs. Carlyle.] T. F. H.

SMITH, WILLIAM SAUMAREZ (1836–1909), archbishop of Sydney, born at St. Helier's, Jersey, on 14 Jan. 1836, was son of Richard Snowden Smith, prebendary of Chichester, by his wife Anne, daughter of Thomas Robin of Jersey. He entered Marlborough College in 1846, and obtained a scholarship at Trinity College, Cambridge, in 1855. In 1857 he won the Carus Greek Testament (undergraduate's) prize; in 1858 he graduated B.A. (first class, classical tripos); in 1859 was placed in the first class (middle bachelors) of the theological examination, won the Scholefield prize, the Carus Greek Testament (bachelor's) prize, and Crosse scholarship. In 1860 he won the Tyrwhitt Hebrew scholarship and was elected fellow of his college. He proceeded M.A. in 1862, and won the Seatonian prize for an English sacred poem in 1864 and 1866.

Ordained deacon in 1859, priest in 1860, he was curate of St. Paul's, Cambridge (1859–61). In 1861 he went out to India as chaplain to Frederick Gell, bishop of Madras, and remained there till 1865, learning Tamil, and associating himself with missionary work. Returning to Cambridge as curate of Trumpington (1866), he became vicar there in 1867, and was awarded the Maitland prize for an essay on 'Obstacles to Missionary Success.' In 1869 he accepted the principalship of St. Aidan's, Birkenhead, a theological college then at a low ebb. He raised it to prosperity, wiping out a heavy debt and creating an endowment fund. He also served from 1869 to 1890 as examining chaplain to the bishop of Norwich, and in 1880 was made hon. canon of Chester.

In 1889, on the retirement of Bishop Alfred Barry [q. v. Suppl. II] from the see of Sydney, Smith was elected his successor by the Australian bishops when nomination had been declined by Handley Carr Glyn Moule, afterwards bishop of Durham. He was consecrated at St. Paul's Cathedral on 24 June 1890. He was made D.D. at Cambridge in that year and at Oxford in 1897. As metropolitan of New South Wales and primate of Australia, Smith, with the approval of the Lambeth conference, assumed in 1897 the title of archbishop. His Australian rule was useful rather than eventful. An evangelical of wide sympathies, a hard worker, and a firm though kind administrator, he died at Sydney on 18 April 1909.

Smith married in 1870 Florence, daughter of Lewis Deedes, rector of Braintfield, Hertfordshire; she died in 1890, leaving one son and seven daughters.

Smith was a contributor of biblical articles to the 'Encyclopædia Britannica' (8th edit.) and published: 1. 'Obstacles to Missionary Success' (Maitland prize essay), 1868. 2. 'Christian Faith: Five Sermons preached before the University of Cambridge,' 1869. 3. 'Lessons on the Book of Genesis,' 1879. 4. 'The Blood of the Covenant,' 1889. A posthumous volume, 'Capernaum and other Poems,' appeared in 1911.

[Record, 23 and 30 April 1909; Guardian, 21 April 1909; Cambridge University Calendar; personal knowledge.] A. R. B.

SMYLY, Sir PHILIP CRAMPTON (1838–1904), surgeon and laryngologist, born at 8 Ely Place, Dublin, on 17 June 1838, was eldest son in a family of four sons and eight daughters of Josiah Smyly, M.D. (*d.* 1864), a Dublin surgeon of good position, by his wife Ellen (*d.* 1901), daughter of Matthew Franks, of Jerpoint Hill, Thomastown, co. Kilkenny. His mother devoted herself to philanthropic work in Dublin, founding and maintaining many schools for poor children. His grandfather, John Smyly, K.C., a member of the Irish bar, came of a family settled in the north of Ireland from the sixteenth century. Sir Philip Crampton [q. v.] was his grand-uncle. A younger brother, Sir William Josiah Smyly, is an obstetrician and gynæcologist of distinction in Dublin. A sister, Louisa Katharine, married Robert Stewart, a missionary to Hwa-Sang, China, where they were both murdered in 1892.

Philip after education at home was apprenticed at fifteen to his grand-uncle Sir Philip Crampton, and after the latter's death in 1858 to William Henry Porter [q. v.]. During his apprenticeship he attended lectures in the schools of Trinity College, Dublin, and of the Royal College of Surgeons, and at the Meath Hospital. In 1854 he entered Trinity College, and in 1859 he graduated B.A., winning a junior moderatorship and silver medal in experimental and natural science. Next year he proceeded M.B., and obtained the licence of the Irish College of Physicians. After some months' study in Berlin he returned home, and in 1863 he proceeded M.D., and was admitted fellow of the Royal College of Surgeons of Ireland. In 1861 he succeeded Porter, his former master, as surgeon to the Meath Hospital, his father being one of his colleagues. This post he retained till his death. He was a member of the viceregal staff during successive viceroyalties from 1869 to 1892. He was president of the Royal College of Surgeons in Ireland in 1878–9, and from 1898 to 1900 he represented that college on the General Medical Council. In 1895 he was appointed surgeon-in-ordinary to Queen Victoria in Ireland, and in 1901, on her death, honorary surgeon to King Edward. He was president of the Laryngological Association of Great Britain in 1889, of the Irish Medical Association in 1900, and of the Irish Medical Schools and Graduates' Association in 1902. He was consulting surgeon to the Hospital for Diseases of the Throat and Ear, the Children's Hospital, Harcourt Street, and the Rotunda Hospital, all in Dublin.

Smyly, though he always practised general surgery, was specially interested in laryngology, a field almost untouched in his younger days. His example familiarised the profession in Ireland with the use of the laryngoscope, which he introduced to Ireland in 1860. He also took special interest in abdominal and urethral surgery. He published little except occasional lectures to his pupils, and notes read before surgical societies. His observations on the use of tobacco juice as an antidote in strychnin poisoning are of interest, and he was one of the first to make practical application of Professor Haughton's study of the chemistry of strychnin and nicotin (*Dublin Journal of Medical Science*, vol. 34).

Smyly enjoyed a large practice for many years and was knighted in 1892. Of courteous manners and striking appearance, he was generous in charitable gifts. He devoted his leisure to music, and was no mean violinist. At the time of his death he was president of the Hibernian Catch Club. He obtained high rank in freemasonry. He died suddenly from cerebral hæmorrhage on 8 April 1904, at 4 Merrion Square, Dublin, and was buried in Mount Jerome Cemetery, Dublin. He married on 1 Feb. 1864 Selina Maria, sixth daughter of John Span Plunket, third Baron Plunket, sister of William Conyngham, fourth baron, archbishop of Dublin, and of David, first Baron Rathmore; by her he had three sons and six daughters. His eldest son, Sir Philip Crampton (knighted in 1905), became chief justice of Sierra Leone, and his second son, Gilbert Josiah, is professor of Latin in Trinity College, Dublin.

A portrait painted by Sir T. Jones, P.R.H.A., was presented to his wife by Smyly's brother freemasons in 1876; it is in her possession at 4 Merrion Square, Dublin.

[Brit. Med. Journal, 16 April 1904; Cameron's History of the Royal College of Surgeons in Ireland; Ormsby's Medical History of the Meath Hospital; Dublin Univ. Calendars; private information.] R. J. R.

SMYTH, SIR HENRY AUGUSTUS (1825–1906), general and colonel commandant royal artillery, born at St. James's Street, London, on 25 Nov. 1825, was third son in the family of three sons and six daughters of Admiral William Henry Smyth (1788–1865) [q. v.] by his wife Annarella, only daughter of Thomas Warington, British consul at Naples. His elder brothers were Sir Warington Wilkinson Smyth (1817–1890) [q. v.] and Charles Piazzi Smyth (1819–1900) [q. v. Suppl. I]. Of his six sisters, Henrietta married Prof. Baden-Powell [q. v.], and Rosetta married Sir William Henry Flower [q. v. Suppl. I].

Educated at Bedford grammar school from 1834 to 1840, Smyth entered the Royal Military Academy at Woolwich on 1 Feb. 1841. Receiving a commission as second lieutenant in the royal artillery on 20 Dec. 1843, and being promoted lieutenant on 5 April 1845, he was on foreign service in Bermuda from 1847 to 1851. Promoted second captain on 11 Aug. 1851, he was quartered at Halifax, Nova Scotia, till 1854, and at Corfu from February 1855. On becoming first captain on 1 April, he was sent in May to the Crimea to command a field battery of the second division of the army which supported the right attack on Sevastopol. Smyth and his battery did arduous work with the siege train in the trenches. He took part in the third bombardment, was present at the fall of Sevastopol, and remained in the Crimea until July 1856. For his services he received the British war medal with clasp for Sevastopol and the Turkish medal.

After he had spent over five years at home stations, principally at Shorncliffe, hostilities threatened with the United States over the Trent affair, and Smyth took his field battery of the Crimea out to New Brunswick in December 1861, landing his horses fit for service after an exceptionally tempestuous voyage. While still in Canada Smyth obtained a brevet majority on 12 Feb. 1863, and on promotion to a regimental lieutenant-colonelcy on 31 Aug. 1865 he returned home. While on ordinary leave of absence in Canada he visited the scenes of the American civil war, saw the capture of Richmond, and was the only foreigner present in the subsequent pursuit of the southern army. At a later period he attended, while on leave from India, some of the operations of the Franco-German war. His observations in both cases were commended by the authorities and partly published in the 'Proceedings of the Royal Artillery Institution.'

From 1867 to 1874 Smyth served in India. He became a brevet colonel on 31 Aug. 1870. In 1872 he presided over a committee at Calcutta which condemned the bronze rifled guns then proposed for adoption for field service and conducted valuable researches into the explosive force of Indian gunpowders. His services were eulogised by the governor-general in council in May 1874. On 16 Jan. 1875 Smyth succeeded to a regimental colonelcy and was deputed to attend the German army manœuvres in the autumn. He commanded the artillery at Sheerness in 1876, and from 1877 to 1880 the artillery in the southern district. He served on various professional inquiries, such as the revision of siege operations in view of the adoption of more powerful rifled guns and howitzers. In 1876 and 1887 he was awarded the gold medal of the Royal Artillery Institution for essays respectively on 'Field Artillery Tactics' and 'Training of Field Artillery.'

From 1881 to 1883 Smyth served on the ordnance committee at Woolwich. During that time steel was introduced into the service on the recommendation of the committee as the material for rifled guns. Promoted major-general on 1 Nov. 1882, Smyth was commandant of the Woolwich garrison and military district from 1882 to 1886. He became lieutenant-general on 1 Nov. 1886, and went out the next year to command the troops in South Africa.

Soon after his arrival at the Cape he rapidly crushed a rising in Zululand, which had been formally annexed in May 1887. The Zulus fled into the territories of the South African republic, where they dispersed. Dinizulu and his chiefs ultimately surrendered to the British, and were banished to St. Helena. For some eight months in 1889–90 Smyth acted as governor of Cape Colony between the departure of Sir Hercules Robinson, afterwards Lord Rosmead [q. v. Suppl. I], and the arrival of Sir Henry Brougham Loch, afterwards Lord Loch [q. v. Suppl. I]. Smyth was created C.M.G. in January 1889, and K.C.M.G. in 1890, when he was appointed governor of Malta. He was promoted general on 19 May 1891, and on 20 Dec. 1893 his jubilee in the Royal Artillery service was celebrated at Malta. He left the island at the end of the year on retirement, and settled at his father's house, which he had inherited, St. John's Lodge, Stone, Aylesbury, Buckinghamshire.

Smyth became a colonel commandant of the royal artillery on 17 Oct. 1894. He was honorary colonel of the royal Malta militia, a J.P. for Buckinghamshire, and fellow both of the Society of Antiquaries and of the Royal Geographical Society. He died on 18 Sept. 1906 at his own house, and was buried in Stone churchyard. He married at Lillington, near Leamington in Warwickshire, on 14 April 1874, Helen Constance, daughter of John Whitehead Greaves, of Berecote, near Leamington. His widow survives him without issue. A portrait painted by Lowes Dickinson is in Lady Smyth's possession. Memorial tablets have been erected in the garrison church at Woolwich and in the church at Stone.

[Royal Artillery Records; private information; The Times, 20 Sept. 1906; the Biographer.] R. H. V.

SNELUS, GEORGE JAMES (1837–1906), metallurgist, born on 25 June 1837 in Camden Town, London, N., was son of James and Susannah Snelus; his father, a master builder, died when George was about seven. He was trained at the St. John's College, Battersea, for the profession of a school teacher, but subsequently, whilst teaching in a school at Macclesfield, he attended lectures on science at the Owens College, Manchester (now the Victoria University, Manchester), where he came under the influence of Sir Henry Roscoe. In 1864, on winning a Royal Albert scholarship, he entered on a three years' course at the Royal School of Mines, gaining at its conclusion the associateship in metallurgy and mining together with the De la Beche medal for mining. On the recommendation of Dr. John Percy [q. v.] he was appointed chemist to the Dowlais Ironworks, and he held the post for four years. In 1871 he was commissioned by the Iron and Steel Institute to proceed to the United States to investigate the chemistry of the Danks's rotary puddling process, and the report which he subsequently presented on the subject proved of the utmost value (*Journal of the Iron and Steel Institute*, vol. i. 1872).

It was during this investigation that Snelus conceived the possibility of completely eliminating phosphorus from molten pig iron by oxidation in a basic lined enclosure. In 1872 he took out a British patent for such a process, afterwards proving by actual trial the soundness of the underlying idea. In a Bessemer converter, lined with overburnt lime, he succeeded in almost entirely eliminating phosphorus from 3 to 4 ton charges of molten phosphoric pig iron; in these trials he made the first specimens of 'basic' steel by the pneumatic process. But certain practical difficulties attendant upon the prescribed use of lime he never fully overcame, and it was not until the 'basic' process was finally developed in 1879 by Messrs. Thomas and Gilchrist [see THOMAS, SIDNEY GILCHRIST] that it became commercially practicable. For the conspicuous part which he had played in regard to this invention he was awarded a gold medal at the Paris Exhibition of 1878, and the Iron and Steel Institute awarded him, jointly with Thomas, the Bessemer gold medal. He was elected a fellow of the Royal Society in 1887. Another conspicuous contribution to metallurgical chemistry was his proof of the true practical value of the molybdate method for the determination of phosphorus in steel, a process which is now universally employed in steel-works laboratories.

In 1872 he was appointed works manager (and subsequently general manager) of the West Cumberland Iron and Steel Company, Workington, where he remained until 1900. He also became director of several mining concerns in Cumberland. In 1902 he took out a patent for the manufacture of iron and steel in a basic lined rotary furnace, experiments upon which were being carried out at the time of his death by the Distington Iron Company, but were afterwards discontinued.

Snelus was an original member of the Iron and Steel Institute in 1869, and from 1889 onwards until his death he was a vice-president. His most important contributions to the 'Journal' of the Institute were those on 'The Removal of Phosphorus and Sulphur in Steel Manufacture' (1879) and on 'The Chemical Composition of Steel Rails' (1882).

He was an enthusiastic member of the volunteer force from 1859 till 1891, when he retired with the rank of hon. major and with the officer's long service medal. He was one of the best rifle shots in the country, being for twelve successive years, from 1866, a member of the English Twenty, and during that period gained a greater aggregate than any other member of the team. He carried off the first all-comers' small-bore prize at Wimbledon in 1868. He was also a keen horticulturist.

Snelus died at his residence, Ennerdale Hall, Frizington, Cumberland, on 18 June 1906, and was buried at the parish church, Arlecdon, Cumberland.

In 1867 he married Lavinia Whitfield, daughter of David Woodward, a silk manufacturer of Macclesfield, and had three sons and three daughters. Two of his sons (George James and John Ernest) became mining engineers, whilst the third (Percy Woodward) is an electrical engineer.

[Proceedings of the Royal Society, 1907, 78 A., and Journal of the Iron and Steel Institute, 1906, i. 273.] W. A. B.

SNOW. [See Kynaston (formerly Snow), Herbert (1835–1910), canon of Durham and classical scholar.]

SOLOMON, SIMEON (1840–1905), painter and draughtsman, born at 3 Sandys Street, Bishopsgate Without, on 9 Oct. 1840, was the youngest son of Michael Solomon, a Leghorn hat manufacturer, by his wife Kate Levy. His father was a prominent member of the Jewish community in the City of London. His elder brother, Abraham Solomon [q. v.], and his elder sister, Rebecca (*d.* 1886), both made art their profession. The sister, who subsequently developed like Simeon an errant nature and came to disaster, schooled him in Hebraic history and ritual. After steady education he, while still a boy, was admitted to the Gower Street studio of his elder brother, Abraham Solomon, and there his talents quickly asserted themselves.

Before he was fifteen he entered the Royal Academy schools, and in 1858 he exhibited at the Academy 'Isaac offered.' This was followed in 1860 by 'The Finding of Moses,' and by the 'Musician in the Temple' in 1861, 'The Child Jeremiah' in 1862, 'Juliett' and 'Isaac and Rebecca' in 1863, and 'A Deacon' in 1864. To the same period belong ten early drawings of Jewish festival ceremonies which prove the artist's devotion to his own faith and people. Eight designs for the 'Song of Solomon' and the same number for 'The Book of Ruth' (reproduced, like most of his work, by Mr. Hollyer) well attest his capacity and sentiment. Solomon also tried his hand at illustration for books and magazines. An etching in a 'Portfolio of Illustrations of Thomas Hood' (1858) and work in 'Once a Week' (1862) and for Dalziel's 'Bible Gallery' (1881) have importance.

Solomon's scriptural painting, which was marked by Pre-Raphaelite sincerity, poetic feeling, and beauty of colour and design, attracted attention. Thackeray credited the 'finely drawn and composed "Moses" with a great intention' (*Roundabout Papers,* 1860, 'Thorns in the Cushion'). The leaders of the Pre-Raphaelite school acknowledged his promise, and he early came to know D. G. Rossetti and Burne-Jones. The latter prophesied that his genius would soon prevail (cf. *Life of Burne-Jones,* i. 260). A charming humour, of which his art shows no sign, gave him abundant social fascination. Another early associate was Algernon Charles Swinburne, who became one of his warmest admirers and constant companions. Through Swinburne he made the acquaintance of Lord Houghton, and visited Fryston. Under such influences Solomon abandoned Hebraic themes for classical subjects, such as his 'Habet,' which was exhibited at the Royal Academy in 1865, and his 'Damon and Aglae,' in 1866. His delightful 'Bacchus' (exhibited in 1867, now in Lady Lewis's collection) brought enthusiastic laudations from Walter Pater. Other work of his evoked poetic elucidation. Swinburne's poems 'Erotion' and 'The End of the Month' were both inspired by Solomon's drawings, and three sonnets of John Payne owed their origin to the like source. His classical tastes were reinforced by visits to Italy. He was at Florence in 1866 and at Rome in 1869 with Mr. Oscar Browning. On the second occasion he wrote a mystical effusion, 'A Vision of Love revealed in Sleep' (privately printed, 1871; enlarged and published later in the same year). To the 'Dark Blue' in July 1871 Swinburne contributed 'Notes' of extreme praise (never reprinted) on Solomon's 'Vision,' crediting the artist with exceptional spiritual insight. At the same time the artist was steadily adding to his fame, not only by his oil-pictures at the Academy—'Toilet of Roman Lady' (1869), 'Youth relating Tales to Ladies' (1870), and 'Love Bound and Wounded' (1870)—but by his pencil studies and water-colours, which were shown chiefly at the Dudley Gallery. In an article in the 'Portfolio' (March 1870) (Sir) Sidney Colvin, while praising Solomon's artistic gifts, protested against signs of sentimental weakness, which excess of eulogy was tending to aggravate. The warning had a tragic sequel. After sending 'Judith and her Attendant' to the Academy in 1872 Solomon ceased exhibiting, and his career collapsed. Through alcohol and other vicious indulgence he became 'famous for his falls.' Efforts of kinsmen and friends to help him proved of no avail. A waif of the streets, he refused commissions when they were offered him, though in an occasional drawing such as 'The Mystery of Faith,' akin to an earlier 'Rosa Mystica,' he showed that he still preserved some of his skill and cherished some of his earlier mystical predilections. To the 'Hobbyhorse' (1893) he contributed 'The Study of a Medusa Head stung by its own Snakes,' a favourite theme, with the legend—apt for his own case—'Corruptio optimi pessima.' He found some brief consolation in visits to the Carmelite church at Kensington, and painted a number of subjects connected with the Roman rite. His main source of income in the long years of his ruin were the occasional few shillings earned by hasty drawings of a futile but, in reproductions, popular sentimentality. He tried his hand without success as a pavement artist in Bayswater. At length he became an almost habitual inmate of St. Giles's workhouse. Found insensible in Great Turnstile in May 1905, he was carried to King's College Hospital and thence to the workhouse, where he died suddenly of heart failure in the dining hall on 14 Aug. following. He was buried in the Jewish cemetery at Willesden. He was unmarried.

Many of his more important paintings in oil and water-colour were exhibited at Burlington House in Jan.–Feb. 1906. The pictures included 'Love in Winter' (Florence, 1866); 'The Mother of Moses' (1860); 'Hosanna!' (1861); 'A Prelude by Bach' (1868); 'The Bride' and 'The Bridegroom' (1872). Solomon's work is chiefly in private collections, including those of Miss Colman at Norwich, Mrs. Coltart, Mr. Fairfax Murray, Lady Battersea, and Mr. W. G. Rawlinson. In public collections he is represented by 'A Greek Acolyte' (1867–8) in the Birmingham Art Gallery; by several paintings in the Dublin Gallery of Modern Art; by a water-colour drawing, 'In the Temple of Venus' (1865), at the Victoria and Albert Museum, South Kensington; by 'Love dreaming by the Sea' at Aberystwyth, and by a beautiful drawing of a girl (1868) in the British Museum.

A portrait drawing by Solomon of himself (1859) is in the More-Adey collection.

[Mr. Robert Ross's essay in Masques and Phases, 1909; Millais's Life of Millais, ii. 440; Mrs. Ernestine Mills's Frederic John Shields, 1912; Mrs. Julia Ellsworth Ford's Simeon Solomon, an Appreciation, New York, 1908; Mr. Oscar Browning's Memories of Sixty Years, 1910; Grave's Roy. Academy Exhibitors; private information.] E. M-L.

SORBY, HENRY CLIFTON (1826–1908), geologist, was born on 10 May 1826 at Woodbourne near Sheffield. With cutlery, the staple industry of that town, his family had been connected since the sixteenth century. One ancestor, who died in 1620, was the first master cutler, and Sorby's grandfather filled the same office. His father, Henry Sorby, was a partner in the firm of John and Henry Sorby, edge-tool makers, and his mother, Amelia Lambert, a woman of much force of character, was a Londoner. Sorby received his early education at a private school in Harrogate and at the collegiate school, Sheffield. After leaving school he read mathematics at home with a tutor, who fostered his love of natural science. He also practised drawing in water-colour, of which in later life he made much use. Sorby, of independent means, determined to devote himself to a career of original investigation. Sheffield was always his home, and he lived with his widowed mother until her death in 1872. After that he purchased a small yacht, the Glimpse, on board which, for many years, he spent the summer in dredging and in making biological and physical investigations in the estuaries and inland waters of the east of England. The winter was passed in Sheffield, where he did much to stimulate the intellectual life of the place, taking an active part in its societies, helping to found Firth College, of which he was one of the vice-presidents, aiding the development of the college into a university, and bequeathing to the latter ultimately his valuable collections and money to found a chair in geology. His health failed in the autumn of 1903, but he continued to write and work up his great stock of accumulated observations till within a few days of his death on 9 March 1908. He was unmarried.

Sorby's scientific work is distinguished by versatility and originality. His greatest advances were in geology, but 'scarcely any branch of knowledge or question of scientific interest escaped his attention: the use of the spectroscope in connection with the microscope; the nature of the colouring matter in blood, hair, foliage, flowers, birds' eggs, and minerals; meteorological problems of all kinds; improvements in blowpipe analysis and in the methods of detecting poisons.' Later, he collected marine plants and animals, preparing catalogues to show their distribution, devising methods for preserving them with their natural colours and exhibiting them as transparent objects, in which he was remarkably successful. But in addition to these he took up archæological studies: the churches of East Anglia; the evolution of mythical forms of animals in ancient ecclesiastical architecture; Roman, Saxon, and Norman structures, and the characteristics of the materials employed in them; while as amusements he collected ancient books and maps, and studied Egyptian hieroglyphics.

To geology his contributions were as valuable as they were varied. He discussed the origins of slaty cleavage, demonstrating by experiment that Daniel Sharpe [q. v.] was right in attributing it to pressure, of cone-in-cone structure, of impressed pebbles, of the magnesian limestone, and of the Cleveland ironstone. He also dealt with the nature of coccoliths in the chalk, questions of rock denudation and deposition, the formation of river terraces; besides water supply, and the contamination of rivers by sewage. In working at the latter he spent about seven months in studying the lower Thames in connection with the royal commission on the drainage of London, and laid before that body a large amount of important evidence. But Sorby's most memorable work was in the field of petrology. William Crawford Williamson [q. v.] had already improved a process originated by William Nicol (the inventor of the Nicol polarising prism) of making thin slices of fossil wood for microscopic examination, and he applied it to some other organisms. Sorby visited Williamson in Manchester prior to 1849 and learnt the art. It occurred to him to try it on rocks, and in that year he made his first thin slice. The first result of this method of investigation was a paper, published by the Geological Society in 1851, on the 'Calcareous Grit of Scarborough.' It however excited little attention, and one on 'Slaty Cleavage' (1853) met with such a chilling reception that he published it elsewhere. Even his great paper 'On the Microscopic Structure of Crystals, &c.,' published in 1858, was ridiculed by many In another decade he had gathered a small but enthusiastic band of disciples, both in England and on the Continent, and before he died was justly hailed as the father of microscopic petrology. He published several other important papers on the microscopic structure of rocks, notably his presidential addresses in 1879 and 1880 to the Geological Society on the structure of stratified rocks; only three months before his death he communicated to that society a paper dealing with the quantitative study of rocks; and last, but not least, he studied the microscopic structure of irons and steels, with results of great industrial value. This study was begun to illustrate meteorites, and it proved the latter to be a mixture when molten which became a compound on cooling. He had a Yorkshireman's shrewdness, but his willingness to help fellow workers and freedom from all self-seeking won him many friends. He was elected F.G.S. in 1850, received the Wollaston medal in 1869 and was president in 1878–80. He was president of the geological section of the British Association in 1880, and also filled that office in the Microscopical and the Mineralogical Societies. He was elected F.R.S. in 1857, and was awarded a royal medal in 1874. He was an honorary member of many foreign societies, receiving from Holland the Boerhaave medal. In 1879 the University of Cambridge made him an honorary LL.D. In 1898 his fellow-townsmen presented him with his portrait (now in Sheffield university, together with a marble bust), and the Geological Society at its centenary in 1907 sent an address to 'The Father of Microscopical Petrology.'

[Journal Geol. Soc. 1909 (Professor Sollas); Proc. Roy. Soc. 1908, vol. lxxx. (Sir A. Geikie); Geol. Mag. 1908 (with portrait) (Professor Judd); Nature, lxxvii. 465; Proc. Yorks. Geol. Soc. vol. xvi. 1909; Fifty Years of Scientific Research, Proc. Sheffield Lit. and Phil. Soc. 1897 (by Sorby himself); list of papers in Naturalist, 1906.] T. G. B.

SOTHEBY, Sir EDWARD SOUTHWELL (1813–1902), admiral, born at Clifton on 14 May 1813, was second son in a family of two sons and three daughters of Admiral Thomas Sotheby (1759–1831) by his second wife, Lady Mary Anne (*d.* 1830), fourth daughter of Joseph Deane Bourke, third earl of Mayo and archbishop of Tuam. William Sotheby [q. v.] was his uncle. After going through the course at the Royal Naval College, Portsmouth, Edward went to sea in 1828. He passed his examination in 1832, was promoted to lieutenant on 3 Oct. 1835, and in Dec. was appointed to the Caledonia, of 120 guns, flagship in the Mediterranean. In April 1837 he joined the Dido, corvette, as first lieutenant, and in her served during the war on the coast of Syria in 1840, for which he received the medal and, on 30 Oct. 1841, his promotion to commander. In June 1846 he was appointed to command the sloop Racehorse, in which he took part in the later operations of the first New Zealand war and served in China till 1848. He commissioned the Sealark for the west coast of Africa in June 1850, and was employed cruising for the suppression of the slave trade. On 6 Sept. 1852 Sotheby was promoted to captain, and in Dec. 1855 was appointed to the Pearl, corvette, which he commanded on the East Indies and China station until 1858. In July 1857 the Pearl, with the frigate Shannon, Capt. William Peel [q. v.], was sent from Hong Kong to Calcutta on the receipt of news of the outbreak of the Indian Mutiny. Sotheby himself took command of the Pearl's brigade, which was landed on 12 Sept., and for the following fifteen months formed part of the Goruckpore field force during the operations in Oudh. Sotheby and his brigade were thirteen times mentioned in despatches, and received the thanks of both houses of parliament, of the governor-general of India, of the admiralty, and of the naval and military commander in India (cf. Forrest's *Hist. of Indian Mutiny*, ii. 262). In addition to the medal Sotheby was made a C.B. and an extra aide-de-camp to Queen Victoria (1858–67). In 1863 he commanded the Portland coastguard division, after which he was not again actively employed. He reached flag rank on 1 Sept. 1867, and retired on 1 April 1870. He was advanced to vice-admiral on the retired list on 25 Aug. 1873, was awarded the K.C.B. in 1875, and became admiral on 15 June 1879. After leaving the sea Sotheby devoted himself to philanthropic work; in 1886 he was a commissioner for investigating and reporting on the condition of the blind, and was for many years chairman of the Blind Institute in Tottenham Court Road.

Sotheby died at 26 Green Street, London, W., on 6 Jan. 1902, and was buried at Ecton, Northamptonshire. He married in 1864 Lucy Elizabeth, daughter of Henry John Adeane, of Babraham, Cambridgeshire, and granddaughter of John Thomas, first Baron Stanley of Alderley, by whom he had issue three sons.

[O'Byrne's Naval Biogr. Dict.; The Times, 8 Jan. 1902; R.N. List; Burke's Landed Gentry; Sir J. W. Kaye, Sepoy War in India; G. B. Malleson, Hist. of Indian Mutiny.]

L. G. C. L.

SOUTAR, Mrs. ROBERT. [See Farren, Ellen (1848–1904), actress.]

SOUTHESK, ninth Earl of. [See Carnegie, James (1827–1905), author.]

SOUTHEY, Sir RICHARD (1808–1901), Cape of Good Hope official, born at Culmstock, Devonshire, on 25 April 1808, was second son of George Southey of that place by his wife Joan, only daughter of J. Baker of Culmstock. Richard's grandfather was a distant cousin of Robert Southey, the poet.

After being educated at Uffculme grammar school till the age of twelve, he went in 1820 with his father to South Africa. The family settled at Round Hill, between Bathurst and Grahamstown, and Richard joined in pioneer farming. In 1824 he was sent to Grahamstown as a clerk in the mercantile house of Heugh and Fleming; but the life being distasteful to him he went in his twenty-first year on a trading and hunting expedition, which was not financially a success. On his return he married and settled down to farming and cattle dealing.

Already in 1828 he had responded to the call for volunteers to take charge of the military outposts of the frontier while the regular troops went on special service into Kafirland, and in the Kafir war of 1834–5, after acting as guide to the headquarters column, he was directed by Colonel (afterwards Sir) Harry Smith [q. v.] to form a corps of guides, of which he was appointed captain, and was frequently commended in general orders. At the close of the war he was appointed resident agent with certain of the Kafir tribes, and served until Sir Benjamin D'Urban's frontier policy was reversed by the home government at the close of 1836, when his office was abolished. He then removed with his brothers to

Graaffreinet, and from 1836 to 1846 was engaged in mercantile and farming pursuits.

On the return of Sir Harry Smith to South Africa in 1847 he made Southey, of whom he had formed a high opinion, secretary to the high commissioner. He accompanied his chief in the operations against the emigrant Boers, and was present at the hard-fought victory of Boomplaats. On the withdrawal of the troops Southey was left at Bloemfontein to collect the fines levied on the Boers who had been in arms against the government, which he did tactfully and with success. He remained in Bloemfontein until the country had quieted down and Major Warden was installed as British resident.

At the end of 1849 he was appointed civil commissioner and resident magistrate of Swellendam, one of the oldest and most important divisions of the colony, and although at times political feelings ran high he won the confidence of the inhabitants as well as the approbation of the government. During the Kafir war of this period he was active in enrolling and forwarding native levies, and on the termination of hostilities he received the thanks of the government for his services.

Southey was acting secretary to the Cape government from 1 May 1852 to 26 May 1854. A dispute with Lieutenant-Governor Darling led to his temporary suspension from office, to which however by order of the home authorities he was honourably restored. On 8 March 1858 he became secretary to the lieutenant-governor at Grahamstown (Lieut.-Gen. James Jackson). From January to April 1859 he was auditor-general of the colony, and on 22 Aug. 1860 he became acting colonial secretary. In the latter capacity he gave great satisfaction by his budget speech in the first session. The governor (Sir George Grey) in a despatch to the Duke of Newcastle, 14 Aug. 1861, warmly commended his tactful conduct of government business.

Southey was appointed treasurer and accountant-general on 6 Dec. 1861, and at the same time was made a member of the executive council, with a seat in both houses of the legislature. He was colonial secretary of the colony from 22 July 1864 until the advent of responsible government on 30 Nov. 1872, when he retired on a pension.

Southey was a consistent opponent of the grant of responsible government to the Cape, and on 26 April 1871 he, with three other members of the executive council, signed a minute adducing grave reasons against its introduction into the colony at that moment. In October 1872 he declined the proposal of the governor (Sir Henry Barkly) that he should obtain a seat in parliament and form a responsible ministry.

In 1871 the long-standing dispute with the Orange Free State respecting the ownership of the diamond fields was terminated by their annexation to the Cape, and Southey at Sir Henry Barkly's request undertook the difficult task of administration. On 7 Feb. 1873 the territory was erected by letters patent into a province under the name of Griqualand West, and Southey received the Queen's commission as lieutenant-governor (29 March 1873). The difficulty of carrying on the government was great, and the opposition of a section of the diggers grew so formidable that troops were summoned from the Cape to preserve order. The secretary of state (Lord Carnarvon) decided that Southey's continuance in office was impossible, and that the financial condition of the province required a less expensive form of administration. Southey resigned in August 1875.

On 4 Dec. 1876 he was returned to the house of assembly as one of the members for Grahamstown, and joined the opposition to the Molteno ministry. He did not seek re-election on the dissolution in Sept. 1878, and took no further part in public affairs. Southey died at his residence, Southfields, Plumstead, on 22 July 1901, and was buried in St. John's cemetery, Wynberg.

He was created C.M.G. on 30 Nov. 1872, and K.C.M.G. on 30 May 1891.

He married twice: (1) in 1830 Isabella, daughter of John Shaw of Rockwood Vale, Albany, by whom he had six sons; (2) Susan Maria Hendrika, daughter of Anthony Krynauw of Cape Town, a member of one of the oldest Dutch families of the Cape of Good Hope; she died in 1890, leaving one son and one daughter.

A half-length portrait in oils of Southey by F. Wolf, a German artist, is in the Civil Service Club at Cape Town.

[Theal's History of South Africa since 1795, 5 vols. 1908; Wilmot's Life and Times of Sir Richard Southey, 1904; Autobiography of Lieut.-Gen. Sir Harry Smith, vol. ii. 1902; Burke's Peerage, 1901; The Times, 23 July 1901; Cape Argus, 23 July 1901; Cape Times, 24 July 1901; Wilmot's History of Our Own Times in South Africa, vol. i. 1897; Pratt's People of the Period; Cunynghame's My Command in South Africa, 1874–1878, 1879; Colonial Office Records.] C. A.

SOUTHWARD, JOHN (1840–1902), writer on typography, born on 28 April 1840, was son of Jackson Southward, printer, of Liverpool, a native of Corney, Cumberland, by Margaret Proud of Enniscorthy, county Wexford. After education at the Liverpool Collegiate Institution (now Liverpool College), he gained a thorough practical knowledge of printing in his father's office, Pitt Street, Liverpool. At seventeen he became co-editor with the Rev. A. S. Hume of the 'Liverpool Philosophical Magazine,' and from November 1857 till its discontinuance in 1865 he conducted the 'Liverpool Observer,' the first penny weekly issued in the town, which was printed in Jackson Southward's office. On the failure of the paper John Southward came to London to increase his typographical knowledge, and was reader successively for Cox & Wyman (until 1868) and for Eyre & Spottiswoode.

In 1868 Southward travelled in Spain for a firm of English watchmakers, traversing all parts of the country, visiting every newspaper office, and securing copies of all serial publications. He embodied his experiences in four articles in the 'Printers' Register' in 1869. Many further contributions followed, and from February 1886 till June 1890 he edited the paper. He also contributed to other trade organs, and in 1891 took over from Mr. Andrew Tuer the 'Paper and Printing Trades Journal.' This he relinquished in 1893.

Southward soon became recognised as the leading authority on the history and processes of printing. His 'Dictionary of Typography and its Accessory Arts,' after being issued as monthly supplements to the 'Printers' Register,' was published in book form in 1872. It was printed simultaneously in the Philadelphia 'Printers' Circular,' and formed the basis of Ringwalt's American 'Encyclopædia of Printing.' A revised edition appeared in 1875.

'Practical Printing: a Handbook of the Art of Typography,' a much larger work, which also first appeared in the 'Printers' Register,' was first published independently in 1882, and became a standard text-book. Southward prepared revised editions in 1884 and 1887. The fourth and fifth editions (1892 and 1900) were edited by Mr. Arthur Powell. Southward's 'Progress in Printing and the Graphic Arts during the Victorian Era' (illustrated) appeared in 1897. 'Modern Printing,' which Southward edited in four profusely illustrated sections between 1898 and 1900, was designed to be at once a reference book for the printing-office and a manual of instruction for class and home reading. The work, in which leading experts cooperated, was adopted as a text-book in the chief technological institutions. Among Southward's minor publications were: 'Authorship and Publication,' a technical guide for authors (1881), and 'Artistic Printing' (1892). He contributed the article 'Modern Typography' to the ninth edition of the 'Encyclopædia Britannica,' and also wrote technical articles for 'Chambers's Encyclopædia.' The 'Bibliography of Printing,' issued under the names of Edward Clements Bigmore and C. W. H. Wyman (3 vols. 1880–6), was to a large extent his work.

Southward was much interested in philanthropic work, and in 1888 founded and edited for a short time a monthly paper called 'Charity.' During his later years he resided at Streatham, but died in St. Thomas's Hospital, Westminster, after an operation, on 9 July 1902. He was buried in Norwood cemetery. Southward was twice married. His first wife, Rachel Clayton of Huddersfield, by whom he had three sons and four daughters, died in 1892. His second wife, Alice, widow of J. King, whom he married in 1894, survived him. An engraved portrait is in 'Modern Printing,' section 1.

[Private information; Printers' Register, 6 Aug. 1902 (with portrait); The Times, 11, 12, 17 July 1902; Streatham News, 19 July 1902; Southward's Works.] G. Le G. N.

SOUTHWELL, THOMAS (1831–1909), naturalist, born at King's Lynn on 15 June 1831, was son of Charles Elmer Southwell, chief cashier at the Lynn branch of Gurney's bank (now Barclay's), by his wife Jane Castell. After private education at Lynn, Southwell entered the service of Gurney & Co. there (14 Sept. 1846). In 1852 he was transferred to Fakenham, and in November 1867 to the headquarters of the bank at Norwich, from which he retired in 1896 after fifty years' service.

Almost all his life was spent in Norfolk and all his leisure was devoted to the natural history of the county. He was also an authority on the topography and archæology of the fen district adjacent to his birthplace. When the Norfolk and Norwich Naturalists' Society was founded in 1869 Southwell became an active member; he was president both in 1879 and 1893, and his contributions to the 'Transactions,' over one hundred in all, covered a wide range, and are mostly of permanent value. From his earliest years he showed a keen interest in birds. 'I have myself,' he wrote, 'talked with men who have taken the eggs of the avocet and black-tailed godwit, and who have seen the bustard at large in its last stronghold. The bittern was so common in Feltwell Fen that a keeper there has shot five in one day, and his father used to have one roasted for dinner every Sunday. I have found the eggs of Montagu's harrier, and know those who remember the time when the hen harrier and short-eared owl bred regularly in Roydon Fen, and who have taken the eggs of the water-rail in what was once Whittlesea Mere.' He devoted much attention to the preservation of birds. For the educational series of the Society for the Protection of Birds he wrote papers on the swallow (No. 4), and the terns (No. 12). His most useful achievement was the completion of the 'Birds of Norfolk,' by Henry Stevenson, F.L.S., of which the earlier volumes had been published (1866–1870). Stevenson died on 18 Aug. 1888, and in 1890 Southwell brought out the third volume, thus completing 'a model county ornithology,' from letters and manuscripts left by the author, but largely supplemented by information supplied by himself.

In 1881 Southwell published 'The Seals and Whales of the British Seas' (sm. 4to), papers reprinted from 'Science Gossip.' From 1884 onwards he contributed annually to the 'Zoologist' a lucid report with authentic statistics on the seal and whale fisheries. He had been elected a fellow of the Zoological Society on 22 Feb. 1872, his proposer being Professor Alfred Newton [q. v. Supp. II]. He closely identified himself with the work of the Norwich museum, serving on the committee from 1893, when the old museum was transferred to Norwich castle. He compiled an admirable official guide in 1896, and contributed an article entitled 'An Eighteenth Century Museum' to the 'Museum Journal' in 1908.

Southwell died at 10 The Crescent, Norwich, on 5 Sept. 1909. He married, on 15 June 1868, Margaret Fyson of Great Yarmouth (*d.* 10 July 1903), and by her had two daughters, who survived him.

Besides the works mentioned and many other contributions to periodicals, Southwell published a revised edition of the Rev. Richard Lubbock's 'Fauna of Norfolk' (1879; first published in 1845), and 'Notes and Letters on the Natural History of Norfolk, more especially on the Birds and Fishes' (1902), from Sir Thomas Browne's MSS. in the British Museum and the Bodleian Library.

[Eastern Daily Press, 6 Sept. 1909; Field, 11 Sept. 1909; Trans. Norfolk and Norwich Naturalists' Soc., ix. 134 (with portrait); Annals of an East Anglian Bank, 1900, p. 347; Ibis, 1910, p. 191; private information.] J. H.

SPENCER, HERBERT (1820–1903), philosopher, was born in Derby on 27 April 1820. The Spencer family had been settled for several centuries in the parish of Kirk Ireton in Derbyshire. All Spencer's four grandparents were among the early followers of John Wesley. His paternal grandfather, Matthew Spencer, settled in Derby as a schoolmaster; he had six sons, and on his death left his property in Kirk Ireton, consisting of a few cottages and two fields, to his eldest son, William George Spencer [q. v.], the father of Herbert Spencer. George Spencer, as he was commonly called to distinguish him from his youngest brother, who was also William, was a man of extremely strong individuality and advanced social and religious views. In 1819 he married Harriet Holmes, the only daughter of a plumber and glazier in Derby. On her mother's side a dash of Huguenot and Hussite blood was traceable. Of this, however, she showed little trace in her character, which was patient, gentle, and conforming. Neither in intellect nor in force of character was she able to cope with her somewhat overbearing husband, and the marriage was not a happy one. Herbert was eldest and only surviving child. Four brothers and four sisters succeeded him (DUNCAN), but all died within a few days of their birth, with the exception of one sister, Louisa, who lived for nearly three years. His father's energies were taken up with teaching, and Herbert's early education was somewhat neglected. Until the age of thirteen he lived at Derby, with an interlude of three years in the neighbourhood of Nottingham; he attended a day school, but was particularly backward in Latin, Greek, and the other usual subjects of instruction. On the other hand, in natural history, in physics, and in miscellaneous information of all kinds he was advanced for his age. He acquired some knowledge of science from the literature circulated by the Derby Philosophical Society, of which his father was honorary secretary. His father did everything to encourage him in the cultivation of his natural tastes for science and observation of nature. At thirteen he was sent to Hinton Charterhouse, near Bath, to live with his uncle, Thomas Spencer [q. v.], who was an advanced radical and a leader of various social movements, such as temperance reform. From his strict régime the lad quickly ran away, walking to Derby in three days (48 miles the first day, 47 the next, and about 20 the third day), with little food and no sleep. He was sent back to his uncle, however, and for three years his education was carried on at Hinton Charterhouse with greater success.

At sixteen he returned to Derby, with his education completed. A year later he commenced his career as assistant to a schoolmaster at Derby. After some three months, however, his uncle William obtained for him a post under (Sir) Charles Fox [q. v.], resident engineer of part of the London and Birmingham railway. He was thus definitely launched in 1837 on the career of civil engineer, a profession which was recognised as well suited to him. Fox soon perceived his capacities, and in less than a year he was promoted to a better post on the Birmingham and Gloucester railway (now absorbed by the Midland railway), with headquarters at Worcester. Capt. Moorsom, the engineer-in-chief, appointed him his private secretary for a few months. Spencer continued to work on the construction of the line till its completion in 1841, when his services were no longer required and he was discharged. 'Got the sack—very glad' was the entry in his diary; and he refused a permanent appointment in the locomotive service, without asking what it was. During this period of a little over three years' engineering his interest had centred largely on geometrical problems, which fill his letters to his father. He also published a few short articles in a technical newspaper, and made one or two inventions of considerable ingenuity, such as a velocimeter for determining velocities in the trials of engines. Good-looking in appearance, but with brusque and unpolished manners, he was on the whole liked by his companions; but was probably somewhat hampered in promotion by his excessive self-assertiveness and tendency to argue with his chiefs.

After his discharge Spencer returned to Derby, and a period of miscellaneous speculation and activity commenced: natural history, mechanical inventions, phrenology, modelling all occupied his attention. The following year his first serious literary attempt took the form of a series of letters to the Nonconformist,' an organ of the advanced dissenters. There he urged the limitations of the functions of the State and displayed the extreme individualism which characterised the whole of his social writings in after life. The same year he plunged into active politics, becoming associated with the 'complete suffrage movement,' which was closely connected with the chartist agitation, and was honorary secretary of the Derby branch. In 1843 he was sanguine enough to republish his letters to the 'Nonconformist' as a pamphlet entitled 'The Proper Sphere of Government'; but it attracted no attention, beyond a polite acknowledgment from Carlyle of a presentation copy. One or two articles sent to reviews were refused; but at last, in 1844, Spencer was selected as sub-editor to a newspaper called the 'Pilot,' which was at that time being established in Birmingham as organ of the complete suffrage movement. In the anti-corn-law agitation, the anti-slavery agitation, and that for the separation of church and state he took an active part, and was described by one of his friends as 'radical all over.'

The insecurity of the 'Pilot' and some of its promoters' dislike of his anti-religious views, which were becoming manifest, made him welcome an opportunity of returning to his old profession. For the next two years Spencer was engaged in one capacity or other in the work of railway construction. The railway mania was at its height. He continued to improve his position with his colleagues; but with the failure of some of his chief's schemes his appointment was again brought to an end —this time permanently—through no fault of his own. In 1846–7 he was occupied with various mechanical inventions and projects, including one for a sort of flying machine; but only on one of them did he succeed in making a little money—a binding-pin for binding together loose sheets of music or printed periodicals. At last the nomadic period of his life came to an end, when in 1848 he was appointed sub-editor of the 'Economist' at a salary of 100 guineas a year, with free lodgings and attendance. The 'Economist' was the property of James Wilson, M.P. (1805–60) [q. v.], who had under his own editorship brought it to a high degree of prosperity.

The years during which Spencer was at the 'Economist' were fruitful in laying the foundations of many of the friendships which profoundly affected his later life. John Chapman [q. v. Suppl. I] carried on a publishing business just opposite the

'Economist' office in the Strand, and through Chapman's soirées Spencer made many acquaintances. Among these was George Henry Lewes [q. v.], first met in the spring of 1850, who afterwards became one of his most intimate friends. Among them also was Miss Mary Ann or Marian Evans, then chiefly known as the translator of Strauss, and afterwards famous as 'George Eliot.' By Lewes, Spencer was introduced to Carlyle; but their temperaments were too much opposed to permit the acquaintanceship to endure. With 'George Eliot' Spencer's relations were so intimate as to excite gossip about the likelihood of their marriage. Though in the abstract he was very desirous of marrying, and regarded 'George Eliot' 'as the most admirable woman, mentally, I ever met,' yet he did not embark upon a suit which, in all probability, would have been successful. Apparently the absence of personal beauty restrained the growth of his affection (*Autobiog.* ii. 445). Another acquaintance, made in 1852, was that of Huxley, still quite unknown. By Huxley he was introduced the following year to Tyndall, the physicist; and with both Huxley and Tyndall there commenced friendships which ripened into close intimacy.

The comparative liberty which Spencer's duties at the 'Economist' office afforded gave him an opportunity of writing his first book, 'Social Statics: or the Conditions Essential to Human Happiness specified, and the first of them developed.' The main object of this work, which appeared at the beginning of 1851, was to set forth the doctrine that 'every man has freedom to do all that he wills, provided he infringes not the equal freedom of any other man.' From this general principle he deduced the public claims to freedom of speech, to property, &c. He went so far as to assert the right of the citizen to refuse to pay taxes, if he surrendered the advantages of protection by the state. The functions of the state were limited solely to the performance of police duties at home, and to protection against foreign aggression by the maintenance of an army and navy. National education, poor laws, sanitary supervision are all explicitly condemned, as well as every other branch of state activity that is not included in the above formula.

'Social Statics' was unexpectedly successful. The extreme individualism which characterised it fitted in well with the views of the philosophical radicals and the Manchester school, then reaching the height of their influence. He was asked by Lewes, who was literary editor of a radical paper called the 'Leader,' to contribute articles; and wrote several anonymously which have since been republished in his essays. Most important of these was that on the 'Development Hypothesis' in March 1852, in which the theory of organic evolution was defended (seven years prior to the publication of the 'Origin of Species'). For the 'Westminster Review,' now in the hands of Chapman, he elaborated a 'Theory of Population' which adumbrated one of the doctrines subsequently embodied in 'The Principles of Biology.' Relations were also established with the 'British Quarterly Review' and the 'North British Review.' In 1853 his uncle Thomas Spencer died, leaving Herbert Spencer a little over 500*l.* With this sum in hand, and the literary connections he had formed, he felt he could safely sever his connection with the 'Economist,' and in July of that year he brought his engagement to an end.

Increased freedom enabled Spencer to cultivate friends, already made, who lived in the country. Mr. and Mrs. Richard Potter, of Standish House, on the Cotswold Hills, and Mr. Octavius Smith, of Ardtornish in Argyllshire, where Spencer paid a long series of visits, thenceforth furnished him with his chief pleasures and holidays. A visit to Switzerland at this time, involving physical over-exertion, produced cardiac disturbances of disastrous effect hereafter. Further articles were written for reviews on diverse subjects before Spencer again gathered his energies for another book—'The Principles of Psychology,' published in 1855. To this work Spencer gave astonishingly little preparation. He was never a large reader, and rarely read through a serious book. He had read one or two books, like Lewes's 'Biographical History of Philosophy,' which chanced to come his way; but neither then nor afterwards did he ever read the philosophical classics; and he was fond of relating how he had always thrown down Kant with disgust on finding he disagreed with the first two or three pages. 'The Principles of Psychology' exhibits the results of this habit; for it had little connection with previous psychological results, but was an independent excursion into an almost new line of inquiry. Later editions of this book formed an integral portion of Spencer's 'Philosophy,' which is described below. Naturally the sale was small. Richard Holt Hutton [q. v. Suppl. I] attacked it in an article entitled

'Modern Atheism' in the 'National Review,' a quarterly organ of the unitarians, and the anti-religious tone of the book caused much adverse criticism.

During the writing of 'The Principles of Psychology' Spencer's health finally gave way. While engaged upon it, he stayed at various country places, and the continuous hard work, unrelieved by society, caused a nervous breakdown from which he never afterwards recovered. The disorder took the form of a peculiar sensation in the head, which came on when he tried to think, as a result of cerebral congestion, and led to inveterate insomnia. For eighteen months he travelled in various country places, avoiding all kinds of work and excitement, spending some of his time in fishing. At length it became necessary for him to earn money; and, though little improved, he returned to London at the end of 1856, and wrote the article on 'Progress: its Law and Cause' for the 'Westminster Review,' foreshadowing one of the doctrines of 'First Principles.' Other articles followed: and although his health remained disorganised, he was able with frequent breaks to carry on a certain amount of work.

It was in 1857 that the idea of writing a system of philosophy first occurred to Spencer. In that year he was engaged in revising his essays to be re-published in a single volume; and the successive reading of the scattered ideas embodied in them revealed to him a marked unity of principle. They all adopted a naturalistic interpretation of phenomena, they were nearly all founded upon the doctrine of evolution. In the early days of 1858 he drew up a plan for a system of philosophy in which these fundamental principles were to be set forth, and their applications traced. To obtain the necessary leisure, he endeavoured to obtain various official posts, with the help of strong testimonials from John Stuart Mill and others; but finding his efforts fruitless, he at length hit upon the plan of issuing the work by subscription. In 1860 the programme of the 'Philosophy' was published, and subscriptions invited at the rate of 10*s.* a year for four quarterly instalments. With the help of friends a strong backing of weighty names was secured, and over 400 subscribers were registered in England; while in America Professor E. L. Youmans helped to obtain about 200 more. With this arrangement Spencer commenced to write 'First Principles'; but he soon found difficulties in his way. A nervous break-down involved a delay of a month or two in the issue of the first instalment. Repetition of these attacks before long caused him to abandon all attempt to keep regular intervals between the issues. Subscribers moreover did not pay up as well as was hoped; but the death of his uncle William Spencer, bringing a legacy, saved the situation. The book was at last completed in 1862. It was received with little attention; the few notices were mainly devoted to adverse criticism of the metaphysical portion. During the writing of 'First Principles' Spencer collected together four essays written for reviews, to form the four chapters of his book on 'Education,' of which the first edition appeared in 1861. This famous work, now translated into all the chief languages of the world and into many of the minor languages such as Arabic and Mohawk, strongly urged the claims of science, both as intrinsically the most useful knowledge, and as the best mental discipline. The method of education advocated resembles that of Pestalozzi in aiming at a natural development of the intelligence, and creating pleasurable interest. The child is to be trained, not by the commands and prohibitions of its parents, enforced by punishments, but by giving it the greatest possible amount of freedom, and allowing the natural consequences of wrong actions to be felt by it, without parental interference. The 'Education' has had an enormous influence, and is still recognised as a leading text-book.

The two years following the publication of 'First Principles' were devoted to the first volume of 'The Principles of Biology,' published in 1864. Since Spencer had not a specialist's knowledge of biology, he arranged with his friends Huxley and Sir Joseph Hooker [q. v. Suppl. II] to read the proofs. The publication evoked little notice: a fate which likewise befell a second series of 'Essays,' which he re-published the previous year. Other occupations of 1864 were the essay on the 'Classification of the Sciences,' published as a separate *brochure*, to which was appended 'Reasons for dissenting from the Philosophy of M. Comte.' Spencer's branched classification undoubtedly represents a great advance on the linear classification of the older philosopher. The second volume of the 'Biology' was commenced immediately on the conclusion of the first, and published in 1867. But before it was completed, Spencer's financial position obliged him to give subscribers notice of cessation. The diminution in the number of subscribers, and the difficulty of collecting their subscriptions, together with the fact that he had now to give support to his aged father, rendered the continuance of the issues impossible. In vain did John Stuart Mill offer to indemnify his publishers against possible future losses. A movement was set on foot by Mill, Huxley, Tyndall, Busk, and Lubbock (now Lord Avebury) for obtaining subscribers for a large number of extra copies; but the death of his father in 1866 greatly improved his position, and enabled him to continue the issues without the help of friends. Already, however, his vehement adherent Youmans had been active in America, with the result that Spencer's admirers in that continent presented him with a valuable gold watch, and invested 7000 dollars in his name in public securities, so as to deprive him of the option of refusal. The second volume of 'The Principles of Biology' was not sent round to the critical journals, and was therefore ignored by the press. But Spencer's name was by this time widely known. He was a member of the celebrated *x* club, to which Huxley, Tyndall and other of his friends belonged. In 1866 he was, in common with most of the other leading evolutionists, an active member of the Jamaica committee for the prosecution of Governor Eyre [q. v. Suppl. II]. The death of his father revived his inventive faculties; and he invented a new kind of invalid bed which obtained the approval of medical men. In 1866, for the first time, he fixed upon a settled abode at a boarding-house in Queen's Gardens, Lancaster Gate, with a room in the vicinity to serve as a study.

Henceforward Spencer's life becomes a mere record of the publication of his books. He was elected a member of the Athenæum Club by the committee in 1868, and went there regularly in the afternoons to play billiards and see his friends. Ill-health negatived any extended social relationships, as well as every other mode of activity beyond that of completing the 'Synthetic Philosophy.' Every autumn there was a visit to Scotland. Once he made a tour in Italy, once in Switzerland, once in the Riviera, once in Egypt. Signs of public appreciation were soon manifest; the first in 1871 when he was offered the lord rectorship of St. Andrews University. But neither this nor any other honour could he be induced to accept. His works, which had hitherto been a dead loss, began to pay; and since he had adopted the principle of publishing on commission, he obtained the full benefit of their sale.

Spencer's first business on concluding the 'Biology' was to re-cast 'First Principles,' in the first edition of which he now recognised sundry imperfections. He then turned his attention to 'The Principles of Psychology,' the next portion of the 'Philosophy.' By adding various divisions he brought his previously published work on 'Psychology' into line with the plan of the rest of the 'philosophy.' The first volume was published in 1870, and the second in 1872. The next step was to deal with 'The Principles of Sociology.' As early as 1867 Spencer had recognised that it would be necessary for him to collect large masses of facts on which to found his sociological generalisations. Accordingly, he secured the services of Mr. David Duncan (afterwards his biographer) to read books of travel and accounts of primitive peoples, selecting all statements of sociological significance, and classifying them according to a plan drawn up by Spencer. Two other gentlemen, Mr. James Collier and Dr. Richard Scheppig, were subsequently engaged for the same purpose; and Spencer, thinking the collections of facts might be useful to other social inquirers besides himself, decided to publish them. Financially the scheme was a complete failure; but he persisted, in spite of heavy losses, and by 1881 the 'Descriptive Sociology' had reached eight volumes, when its issue was suspended, not to be revived till after Spencer's death. One other work published in 1873 was the 'Study of Sociology.' Spencer had assisted his friend Youmans to found the 'International Scientific Series,' and found himself now compelled to yield to Youmans' pressure to contribute a volume to it himself. The 'Study of Sociology' was devoted to setting forth the difficulties, objective and subjective, that confront the student of the social science. The many varieties of bias which are likely to perturb his judgment were discussed in full. The book, being of a comparatively popular character, was immensely successful; and the preliminary publication of its chapters in the 'Contemporary Review' in England and the 'Popular Science Monthly' in America did much to assist the sale of Spencer's works. Spencer's next task was the preparation of the first volume of 'The Principles of Sociology,' published in 1877. Hitherto the serial method of publication had been adhered to, but with the conclusion of this volume Spencer sent to subscribers a notice of discontinuance, determining in future to publish the volumes as they were completed. He began the second volume of 'The Principles of Sociology,' but finding his health still very precarious abandoned it to write 'The Data of Ethics.' Any form of continuous application brought on symptoms due to cerebral congestion, and many expedients were tried to prevent them. He would dictate to his secretary while rowing on the Serpentine or playing games of racquets. Dictating for twenty minutes or so at a time, he then broke off to row or play vigorously and relieve the brain. When able to do nothing else he would dictate his autobiography; and the bulkiness of that work is a concrete result of Spencer's efforts to kill time. 'The Data of Ethics,' which subsequently formed part I of 'The Principles of Ethics,' was published in 1879; and 'Ceremonial Institutions,' the first instalment of the second volume of 'The Principles of Sociology,' was published shortly afterwards. Having set forth the foundations of his views on ethics, Spencer felt at liberty to revert to the original order of his philosophy, and conclude the second volume of the 'Sociology'; and 'Political Institutions' was published in 1882. The foundation in the same year, in conjunction with Mr. Frederic Harrison, Mr. John Morley, and others less known, of an Anti-aggression League, in opposition to aggressive war, greatly over-taxed Spencer's energies. In 1882 he paid a visit to America, resisting the numerous attempts to fête him, save in one instance where a dinner in his honour was given in New York. Thenceforward the decline in health proceeded steadily. In 1884 appeared four articles from the 'Contemporary Review,' now bound together to form 'The Man versus The State.' Spencer had been watching with alarm the gradual encroachment of the state upon the liberty of the individual, and its ever-widening sphere of activity. The purpose of these essays was to propose a new creed for liberals—the limitation of state-functions to protection against foreign aggression and the maintenance of justice at home. He refused an invitation to become parliamentary candidate for Leicester in 1884. 'Ecclesiastical Institutions,' with which the third volume of 'The Principles of Sociology' opens, was published in 1885. Thereafter Spencer once again turned to 'The Principles of Ethics,' in order to elaborate his final beliefs on the functions of government in 'Justice.' From 'Justice' he passed on to the other divisions of 'The Principles of Ethics,' and published the whole of that work before reverting to the final volume of the 'Sociology.'

In 1889 he took a house in Avenue Road, St. John's Wood, in conjunction with two maiden ladies. For a few years the arrangement worked well; but, after a time, disputes arose; and in 1898 he moved to 5 Percival Terrace, Brighton, where he remained till his death. In 1896 the last volume of 'The Principles of Sociology' was published, and with it the 'Synthetic Philosophy' was completed. Congratulations poured in from all quarters; among others an influentially signed document, asking permission to employ an artist to take his portrait for presentation to one of the national collections. The portrait was ultimately painted by Sir Hubert von Herkomer. But Spencer could not rest, now that his work was completed. Two further books, entitled 'Various Fragments' and 'Facts and Comments' were issued before his death, each consisting of short essays on a great variety of subjects. The latter work attracted special attention on account of the vehement language with which Spencer denounced the policy of the Boer war. The increasing militarism which he believed he saw everywhere around him largely embittered his later years. Both this and the tendency to increase the functions of government were in close conflict with the social doctrines of his philosophy, which constituted Spencer's strongest sentiments. The chronicle of the last years of his life shows that his nervous system was shattered beyond repair. Everywhere he was trying to correct misrepresentations of his views, or to maintain his priority in some theory or idea. Death at Brighton at the age of eighty-three on 8 Dec. 1903 was a welcome relief from his sufferings. He was cremated at Golder's Green, an address by Mr. Leonard (afterwards Lord) Courtney taking the place of a religious ceremony. The ashes were subsequently buried in Highgate cemetery. In his will he left the bulk of his property in trust for carrying on the publication of the 'Descriptive Sociology.'

Several portraits of Spencer are in existence. That by Sir Hubert von Herkomer, painted when Spencer was seventy-seven and had just completed the 'Synthetic Philosophy,' is at Edinburgh in the Scottish National Portrait Gallery. The portrait by J. B. Burgess, painted in 1872, hangs in the National Portrait Gallery in London, while the copy of it made by J. Hanson Walker is in the Public Library of Derby. In the Derby Museum there is a plaster cast of his hands, and several relics. The marble bust made by Sir Edgar Boehm in 1884 is in the National Portrait Gallery. A bronze bust by E. Onslow Ford was exhibited at the Royal Academy in 1897. Mrs. Meinertzhagen owns a portrait painted by Miss Alice Grant in the last year of Spencer's life, mainly from photographs taken in 1898. A cartoon portrait by 'C. G.' appeared in 'Vanity Fair' in 1879.

In appearance Spencer betokened nothing of his years of invalidism. He was 5 ft. 10 in. in height, of almost ruddy complexion, but thin and spare. His face with unwrinkled forehead showed no effects of his long life of thought, and his walk and general bearing were vigorous. Naturally of a robust constitution, he never lost a tooth, and his eyes were so strong throughout life that he never had to wear spectacles for reading. The damage to his nervous system was displayed by his irritability in later life, his morbid fear of misrepresentation, and various eccentricities which gave rise to many false and exaggerated stories. Among the peculiarities which nervous invalidism wrought in him was the use of ear-stoppers, with which he closed his ears when an exciting conversation to which he was listening threatened him with a sleepless night. The extreme originality of mind and contempt of authority, the habit of driving principles to their minutest applications, naturally gave rise to eccentricities, but these toned down in later life.

Although predominantly intellectual, he showed an emotional side, especially in his strong affection for his father. Throughout the greater part of his life he was obsessed by the execution of the 'Synthetic Philosophy,' which absorbed the main intellectual and emotional powers of his mind. One of his least pleasant traits was the tendency to assert his own priority in scientific and philosophic ideas. The claim was never made unjustly, but the animosity with which he defended it showed, as in the case of Newton, that the mere advancement of knowledge was not his sole end. He persistently declined all honours, academic or otherwise. The list of those offered is detailed in Duncan's 'Life' (App. D), but it would undoubtedly have been much longer had not his rule of refusing them become generally known.

Spencer's place in the history of thought must be ranked high. His influence in the latter half of the nineteenth century was immense: indeed it has so woven itself into our modern methods of thinking that its driving and revolutionary energy is nearly spent, and there is little likelihood of its being hereafter renewed. It was the best synthesis of the knowledge of his times; and by that very fact was from the beginning destined to be replaced and to lose much of its utility when new branches of knowledge were opened up. The central doctrines of the philosophy were, in its social side, individualism and opposition to war; on its scientific side, evolution and the explanation of phenomena from the materialistic standpoint. It has been said that the advancement of knowledge depends mainly on interrogating nature in the right way. Spencer may be said to have nearly always *asked nature the right questions*; but not infrequently his answers to the questions were wrong. He concentrated the attention of mankind on the problems of fundamental importance. The main deficiency of his reasoning was a too free use of the deductive method, more especially in his biological and sociological writings, where this method is always attended by grave dangers. Huxley correctly singled out Spencer's weakness when he laughingly said that Spencer's definition of a tragedy was the spectacle of a deduction killed by a fact.

Spencer's fame extended far throughout the world. In France, Russia, and other European nations he was widely studied. In America his books had a very large circulation, and his fame was certainly not less than in England. During the awakening of Japan, he was one of the authors most studied by the young Japanese; and probably his opinion was held in higher esteem than that of any other foreign writer whatever. His works were also held in high esteem by the Indian nationalists; and, shortly after his death, one of them, Mr. Shyamaji Krishnavarma, founded a 'Herbert Spencer Lectureship' at Oxford University, by which a sum of not less than 20*l*. a year was to be paid to the annually appointed lecturer.

The following is a summary of his philosophical works:—

'First Principles' is divided into two parts, of which the first, or metaphysical part, is an attempt at a reconciliation between science and religion by postulating a belief in the 'Unknowable,' as the cause and origin of all phenomenal existence. The doctrine has found scarcely more favour on the side of science than it has on the side of religion, and may be regarded as the least important part of the philosophy. Part ii. sets forth the fundamental principles of the 'Synthetic Philosophy,' as Spencer has named his system. Defining the business of philosophy as the formulation of truths which hold good for *all* orders of phenomena, as distinct from those of the special sciences, which hold good only for limited departments, he founds his system upon the physical principles of the indestructibility of matter, and the continuity of motion, unified under the general heading of the Persistence of Force. From this is deduced the Uniformity of Law. Spencer then proceeds, in his attempt at the unification of knowledge, to seek for a law of the continuous redistribution of matter and motion, as comprising every department of the 'Knowable.' He finally reaches his famous law:—*Evolution is an integration of matter and concomitant dissipation of motion; during which the matter passes from a relatively indefinite, incoherent homogeneity to a relatively definite, coherent heterogeneity; and during which the contained motion undergoes a parallel transformation.* Evolution is supplemented by the reverse process of Dissolution; and these formulas express the law of the entire cycle of changes passed through by every existence and at every instant, with no limitations of time or space. Evolution, however, tends ultimately to equilibrium, in which the incessant changes come to an end.

In 'The Principles of Biology' Spencer applied the law of evolution to animate existence. He defined life in the same manner as in his 'Principles of Psychology.' As factors of evolution he not only named natural selection, or (to use Spencer's own term) *survival of the fittest*, but he argued strongly in favour of the direct modification of organisms by the environmental action, and also in favour of the inheritance of functionally-produced modifications. In this latter belief he is at variance with the best, though not the unanimous, opinion of modern biologists. In the second volume he promulgated the interesting theory that the shapes of animals and plants are an expression of the environmental forces which act upon them. He sets forth also his well-known law of the antagonism between individuation and reproduction. His attempt to facilitate the comprehension of heredity by supposing the existence of 'constitutional units' (first named physiological units) has attracted wide attention, and is probably not very remote from the truth.

'The Principles of Psychology' was materialistic in its general point of view; for, although Spencer emphatically affirmed the existence of mind and its total distinction from matter, yet his efforts were devoted to interpreting mental manifestations by reference to physical and chemical laws. He defined life as 'the continuous adjustment of internal relations to external relations' and argued that the degree of life was proportional to the degree of correspondence between these two sets of relations. The development of memory, instinct, &c., was explained on the very questionable hypothesis that the results upon an organism of the direct action of the environment could be transmitted to its descendants. But although this attempted explanation cannot stand, it is remarkable that an evolutionary basis is given to the whole work, of which the first edition had appeared four years before Darwin published his great book. In the analytical portions he attributes all acts of intelligence to the variously compounded consciousnesses of relations of likeness and unlikeness. Finally he sets forth his famous 'Universal Postulate' to the effect that the criterion of the truth of a proposition is the inconceivability of its negation. Opinion still differs as to the merits of many parts of this work. Doubtless much of the detail and some of the principles are erroneous; but much has become generally accepted; and in view of the state of knowledge at the time when it was written, it must be considered a masterpiece.

'The Principles of Sociology' begins by an exposition of the so-called 'Ghost Theory,' in which Spencer regards all primitive mythological beliefs as modified forms of ancestor-worship. In the part dealing with 'The Inductions of Sociology' he minutely draws the analogy between the social and physical organism. The remaining volumes of the work deal with ceremonial institutions, political institutions, ecclesiastical institutions, professional institutions, industrial institutions. The general result is to distinguish between two main types of society, the militant resting on a basis of *status*, and the industrial resting on a basis of *contract*.

'The Principles of Ethics' was considered by Spencer as the flower of the whole philosophy. His system is hedonistic, in so far as it regards happiness as the object to be attained; it is evolutionary, in so far as it represents that evolution is carrying us to a state in which happiness will far exceed what we now experience. The utilitarians are attacked on the ground that, in their enthusiasm for altruism, they attach insufficient importance to a rational egoism. In the second volume, part iv., 'Justice,' is Spencer's final and most philosophic statement of the duties of the state. As in his earliest book, he limits state-functions to the maintenance of justice at home, and the repelling of aggression abroad. His formula of justice is stated by him in the words: 'Every man is free to do that which he wills, provided he infringes not the equal freedom of any other man.' Two further divisions indicate the duties of men towards one another, which are not, however, to be enforced by law.

The following is a list of the volumes published by Spencer: 1. 'Social Statics,' 1850; abridged and revised edition (together with 'The Man versus The State'), 1892. 2. 'The Principles of Psychology,' 1 vol. 1855; 2nd edit. vol. i. 1870, vol. ii. 1872; 4th edit. 1899. 3. 'Essays,' 1st series, 1857; 2nd series, 1863; 3rd series, 1874; American reprints of the first two series; final edit. (in three volumes) 1891. 4. 'Education,' 1861; cheap reprint, 1878. 5. 'First Principles,' 1862; 6th edit. 1900; 3rd impression, 1910. 'The Principles of Biology,' vol. i. 1864, vol. ii. 1867; revised and enlarged edit. vol. i. 1898, vol. ii. 1899. 7. 'The Study of Sociology ('International Scientific Series'), 1873; library edit. 1880. 8. 'The Principles of Sociology,' vol. i. 1876; 3rd edit. 1885; part iv. 'Ceremonial Institutions,' 1879; part v. 'Political Institutions,' 1882; parts iv. and v. were subsequently bound together to form vol. ii. of 'The Principles of Sociology,' 1882; part vi. 'Ecclesiastical Institutions,' 1885; part vi. was subsequently bound up with two further divisions and issued as vol iii. of 'The Principles of Sociology' in 1896. 9. 'The Principles of Ethics': part i. 'The Data of Ethics,' 1879; new edit. 1906; part i. was afterwards bound up with two more divisions to form vol. i. of 'The Principles of Ethics,' 1892; part iv. 'Justice,' 1891; part iv. was similarly bound up subsequently with two more divisions and issued as vol. ii. of 'The Principles of Ethics' in 1893. 10. 'The Man versus The State,' 1884; 2nd edit. (bound together with 'Social Statics') 1892. 11. 'The Nature and Reality of Religion,' 1885. This work, published in America, embodied a controversy on the Positivist religion that had taken place between Spencer and Mr. Frederic Harrison. Owing to copyright difficulties raised by Mr. Harrison, Spencer suppressed the book soon after its publication. It was however reissued the same year without his knowledge under the title 'The Insuppressible Book.' 12. 'Various Fragments,' 1897; enlarged edit. 1900. One of these 'fragments,' entitled 'Against the Metric System' (1896), was reissued separately in 1904 with additions, under a provision in Spencer's will. 13. 'Facts and Comments,' 1902. 14. 'Autobiography,' 1904. Portions of various of these works are on sale separately. 'Education,' 'Man versus the State,' 'Social Statics,' and 'Selected Essays' have been issued in sixpenny editions by the Rationalist Press Association, while the trustees contemplate the issue of a complete popular edition of Spencer's 'Philosophy,' and have already published shilling editions of 'First Principles,' 2 vols., 'Education,' and 'The Data of Ethics.' In addition to the above list of works, Spencer issued during his lifetime eight instalments of the 'Descriptive Sociology,' viz.: No. 1, 'English,' 1873; No. 2, 'Ancient Mexicans, Central Americans, Chibchas, and Ancient Peruvians,' 1874; No. 3, 'Types of Lowest Races, Negritto Races, and Malayo-Polynesian Races,' 1874; No. 4, 'African Races,' 1875; No. 5, 'Asiatic Races,' 1876; No. 6, 'American Races,' 1878; No. 7, 'Hebrews and Phœnicians,' 1880; No. 8, 'French,' 1881. Since Spencer's death further instalments have been issued, and No. 9, 'Chinese,' and No. 10, 'Greeks: Hellenic Era,' appeared in 1910. The series is now in regular progress, the intention being to bring the number to some 24 parts.

Spencer reissued his father's 'Inventional Geometry' with a preface in 1892; and he also published his father's 'System of Lucid Shorthand' in 1893.

[Autobiography, 1904; Life and Letters, by D. Duncan, 1908 (with full bibliography); Personal Reminiscences, by Grant Allen, published in the Forum for April–June 1904; A Character Study, by W. H. Hudson (at one time Spencer's private secretary), in Fortnightly Review, January 1904; Herbert Spencer, in Edinburgh Review, July 1908; Josiah Royce, Herbert Spencer (with an interesting chapter of personal reminiscences by James Collier), New York, 1904; Home Life with Herbert Spencer, by Two, 1906, 1910; Hector Macpherson, Herbert Spencer, the Man and his Work, 1900; W. H. Hudson, Herbert Spencer, 1908; W. H. Hudson, An Introduction to the Philosophy of Herbert Spencer (containing a biographical sketch), 1895, 1897, 1904; J. Arthur Thomson, Herbert Spencer, 1906; Life and Letters of Charles Darwin, ii. 188, iii. 55, 120, 141, 165, 193; Life and Letters of T. H. Huxley, passim. There are innumerable less important works on Spencer or his philosophy. Among the latter, the most read (besides those already enumerated) are J. Fiske, Outlines of Cosmic Philosophy, 1874; H. Sidgwick, Lectures on the Ethics of T. H. Green, Mr. Herbert Spencer, and J. Martineau, 1902; H. Sidgwick, The Philosophy of Kant and other Lectures, 1905; W. R. Sorley, The Ethics of Naturalism, 1904. The annual Herbert Spencer lectures are for the most part concerned very indirectly with Spencer's life: the 1910 lecture by Professor Raphael Meldola should be mentioned, however. A volume of Aphorisms from the Writings of Herbert Spencer was published by Miss J. R. Gingell in 1894. An Epitome of the Synthetic Philosophy, by F. Howard Collins (5th edit. 1901), is an excellent summary in one volume. Its formality and necessary brevity, however, render it unsuitable for reading, and its chief use is as an elaborate index to the Philosophy.]

H. S. R. E.

SPENCER, JOHN POYNTZ, fifth Earl Spencer (1835–1910), statesman and viceroy of Ireland, was only son, in a family of three children by his first wife, of Frederick, the fourth earl (1798–1857). His mother was Elizabeth Georgiana (*d.* 1851), second daughter of William Stephen Poyntz of Cowdray, Sussex. His father, who as a naval officer had commanded the Talbot at the battle of Navarino, was the third son of George John Spencer [q. v.], second earl, at one time first lord of the admiralty. John Charles [q. v.], third earl, best known in political history as Viscount Althorp, was the latter's eldest son and uncle of the fifth earl.

The fifth earl, born on 27 Oct. 1835, at Spencer House, St. James's, the town mansion of the family, was known in youth as Viscount Althorp. In June 1848 he entered Harrow school, and stayed there six years. He was in later life an active and influential governor of the school. In Michaelmas term 1854 he matriculated from Trinity College, Cambridge, and graduated M.A. (as a nobleman's son) in 1857. He received the honorary degree of LL.D. in 1864. He achieved no academical distinction. On 6 April 1857 he was elected to the House of Commons, in the liberal interest, as one of the two members for South Northamptonshire—a family seat. But the death of his father on 27 December following called him to the House of Lords.

A wealthy nobleman of manly character, commanding presence, and engaging manners, Spencer was soon a prominent and popular figure in society. At Spencer House in London and at Althorp Park, his Northamptonshire seat, he soon exercised magnificent hospitality. Devoted to sport, he was an admirable horseman. Through life he rode about London on business or social errands, and he was thrice master of the Pytchley hounds. In shooting, too, he always took a lively interest, largely with an eye to national needs. In 1860 he was chairman of the committee which met at Spencer House to form the National Rifle Association, and with that body he was closely connected till death. For nearly fifty years he was a member of the council, of which he was chairman in 1867–8. He gave the Spencer cup to be competed for at the annual meetings by boys at the public schools, and frequently shot in the Lords' team in the Lords and Commons match. A large canvas by H. T. Wells, R.A., depicting Spencer and others at the camp at Wimbledon in 1868, belongs to the present Earl Spencer, and Spencer presented in 1909 a portrait of himself by the same artist to the council of the Rifle Association.

Spencer's first public employment was at court. He was appointed groom of the stole to the Prince Consort in 1859, and held that office until the prince's death on 14 Dec. 1861. In the following year he was appointed to the same position in the newly constituted household of the Prince of Wales, afterwards King Edward VII. He retained the office until 1867. But Spencer was ambitious of political service. On 14 Jan. 1865 Lord Palmerston had nominated him K.G., and the liberal party welcomed his co-operation. On 11 Dec. 1868, when Gladstone formed his first administration, Spencer became lord-lieutenant of Ireland, but without a seat in the cabinet. Chichester Fortescue, afterwards Lord Carlingford [q. v. Suppl. I], was made chief secretary for Ireland with a seat in the cabinet.

With the measures of conciliation for Ireland—the disestablishment of the Church of Ireland and the reform of the land laws—to which the government was pledged, Spencer was in full sympathy, but he had no direct responsibility for them. In regard to the third remedial measure of the government—the Irish University education bill of 1873, which the House of Commons ultimately rejected—Spencer sought in vain to win the support of Cardinal Cullen (25 Feb. 1873). His duties were executive and administrative rather than legislative. While he preferred keeping order by ordinary methods of peaceful suasion, he had no compunction in meeting persistent defiance of the law by 'coercion.' On his entry into office 'Fenianism' proper had been crushed, and he found himself justified in releasing forty political prisoners. But within a year organised crime, chiefly in agrarian districts, developed anew. An increase of the military forces proved of little avail. Consequently early in 1870 Spencer obtained a Peace Preservation Act, with special clauses directed against sedition in the press. The Act received the royal assent on 4 April. The Land Act followed, and the consequent improvement in the country's tranquillity enabled Spencer at the end of the year to release the remaining Fenian prisoners subject to their banishment from the United Kingdom for life. A recrudescence of terrorism among the riband societies of Westmeath and neighbouring counties in 1871 called in Spencer's judgment for another coercive measure—the 'Westmeath Act' (16 June). He believed his task was greatly facilitated by that Act. In August 1871, when he entertained the Prince of Wales in Dublin, a riot in Phœnix Park showed continued need of vigilance. On the overthrow of Gladstone's government in 1874 Spencer left Ireland with a reputation for combining a firm with a conciliatory temper.

During the next six years, while his party was in opposition, he for the most part occupied himself privately. He had become lord-lieutenant of Northamptonshire (11 Aug. 1872), and was always attentive to county business. When Gladstone formed his second administration in 1880 Spencer joined the liberal cabinet as lord president of the council. The office constituted its occupant the chief of the education department. Spencer discharged his varied duties with discretion until the spring of 1882. Then he was suddenly reappointed to his former position in Dublin (3 May 1882). A grave crisis had arisen in Ireland, where at the instigation of the Land League disorder had raged for more than two years and coercive measures failed in their purpose. Gladstone and his government were now seeking some accommodation with the revolutionary leaders. But the Irish viceroy, Lord Cowper [q. v. Suppl. II], and the Irish secretary, W. E. Forster [q. v.], deprecated any reversal of policy, and both resigned. Spencer became viceroy, retaining his seat in the cabinet, and Lord Frederick Cavendish [q. v.] joined him as chief secretary. Their appointment was designed as a step towards conciliation. 'Suspects' imprisoned without trial were to be released. A new land bill was to be prepared. At the same time the cabinet felt that some exceptional powers were still needed by the Irish executive, and a measure for conferring them was ready for drafting before Spencer and Cavendish left for Dublin on 5 May (Lady Frederick Cavendish in *The Times*, 18 Aug. 1910).

On the morning of 6 May Spencer was sworn in as lord-lieutenant at Dublin Castle and Cavendish as a member of the Irish privy council. At a council in the afternoon the provisions of the proposed 'coercion' measure were discussed. At the close of the meeting Spencer rode to the Viceregal Lodge in the Phœnix Park. Cavendish soon followed on foot, and was joined by the under-secretary, Thomas Henry Burke [q. v.]. A terrible outrage followed. Cavendish and Burke were murdered by a gang of ruffians known as the 'Invincibles' in the Phœnix Park in full view of Spencer's windows. The outrage completely changed for the time the character of Spencer's mission. Sir George Trevelyan succeeded Lord Frederick as chief secretary, and together they sought to bring the conspirators to justice. The crimes bill, which was already sanctioned in principle by the cabinet, received the royal assent (12 July) and was rigorously enforced. The murderers were discovered and punished, and disorder was gradually suppressed.

The resolution with which Spencer and Sir George Trevelyan faced the situation exposed them to 'daily even hourly danger of their lives' (*ibid.*) and to floods of obloquy and calumny from the mass of the Irish people. Spencer was credited with a 'cruel, narrow, and dogged nature,' and was popularly christened the 'Red Earl.' The colour of his long and bushy beard had long before suggested that sobriquet as a friendly nickname, but the words were now freely employed to imply his delight in blood. By the law-abiding population he was hailed as a saviour of society. Trinity College conferred on him the honorary degree of LL.D. in 1883 amid immense applause.

In the spring of 1885, when the Crimes Act was about to expire, acute differences arose in the cabinet both as to its renewal and as to the general Irish policy of the party. Spencer with the support of the whig element in the cabinet desired that certain provisions in the old Coercion Act should be renewed, and he suggested that a new land purchase bill should accompany the new Coercion Act. The radical leaders, Mr. Chamberlain and Sir Charles Dilke [q. v. Suppl. II], dissented, unless Spencer accepted in place of the land bill a large measure of local government. Before the dispute went further, the government were defeated in the Commons on a different issue in regard to the budget, and Spencer with his colleagues resigned (8 June).

The new conservative administration, which enjoyed nationalist favour, not only declared against an immediate renewal of the Crimes Act but disclaimed 're-sponsibility for its practice in the past' (MORLEY, *Life of Gladstone*, iii. 213). When Parnell and his friends imputed to Spencer a wilful miscarriage of justice in the trial and conviction of persons charged with murder at Maamtrasna, the conservative leader of the house, Sir Michael Hicks-Beach (afterwards Lord St. Aldwyn), spoke with hesitating approval of Spencer's past action and promised inquiry (17 July). Spencer's friends held that the conservatives who had denounced him as being too lenient now threw him overboard as having been too severe. The debate brought home to many on both sides of the house the varied perils and temptations springing from a coercive policy. On 23 July 1885 Spencer was entertained at dinner at the Westminster Palace Hotel by 200 liberal members of parliament under the chairmanship of Lord Hartington, and he defended with spirit his administration of the Crimes Act.

When at the end of 1885 Gladstone adopted the policy of home rule, Spencer supported him. The change of view was partly due to Gladstone's commanding personal influence over him and to his sense of party loyalty. But another cause doubtless lay in his conviction that coercion was impracticable in view on the one hand of the impatience with it manifested by an important section of his own party, and on the other hand of the cynical readiness with which the tories had rejected the principle to gain a party advantage. In Spencer's belief the only alternative to effective repression was effective concession.

On 1 Feb. 1886 Gladstone resumed office, having committed himself to a measure of home rule as yet undefined. Spencer joined him as lord president of the council, and took an active part in the framing of the first home rule bill. The measure was rejected on the second reading by a majority of thirty owing to the opposition of the liberal unionists, who combined with the tories (7 June). Gladstone dissolved parliament at once, and was heavily defeated at the polls. During the six years of opposition which followed Spencer took from time to time a conspicuous share in the agitation for home rule. He met on the same platform many Irish members of parliament who had previously been prominent in scurrilous denunciation of him. At the general election of 1892 Gladstone secured a small majority, and in his fourth and last administration Spencer accepted the office of first lord of the admiralty. His grandfather had held the post from 1794 to 1800.

Spencer administered the navy with great energy and efficiency and with a single-minded regard to the national security on the seas. He was the first to set the precedent, which has since been consistently followed, of retaining in office the professional members of the board who had been appointed by his predecessor (SIR WILLIAM WHITE in *The Times*, 20 Aug. 1910). The large ship-building programme embodied in the Naval Defence Act of 1889 was in course of prosecution, and continuity of administration was therefore of primary importance. Spencer handled firmly and judiciously the critical questions, personal, administrative, and constructive, which were raised in 1893, when the Victoria was rammed and sunk by the Camperdown with great loss of life. The ship-building policy included the introduction of the 'torpedo-boat destroyer,' a new and valuable type of warship. Above all he made with his professional colleagues an historic stand against the indifference of some members of the cabinet to the requirements of national security. In this regard he came into conflict with both Sir William Harcourt [q. v. Suppl. II] and Gladstone. At the end of 1893, when Lord George Hamilton, Spencer's predecessor at the admiralty, moved a resolution declaring the necessity for an immediate and considerable increase in the navy and called on the government to make a statement of their intentions, Sir William Harcourt, then chancellor of the exchequer, professing to represent the opinion of the sea lords, asserted that in their opinion as well as his own the existing condition of things in respect to the navy was satisfactory. Spencer at once privately protested that Harcourt's statement was unjustified, and Spencer's colleagues at the admiralty threatened resignation if it were not corrected. The correction was made. Then followed the 'Spencer programme' of shipbuilding, extending over several years. Gladstone's final resignation in March 1894 was determined by the increased expenditure which Spencer's navy estimates involved (see MORLEY, *Life of Gladstone*, iii. 507–8). There is excellent authority for recording that when these estimates were presented to the cabinet, Gladstone exclaimed in an aside 'Bedlam ought to be enlarged at once.'

But Gladstone's high opinion of Spencer was not affected by such differences. On 2 March 1894, after Gladstone had forwarded his resignation to Queen Victoria, he remarked that should the queen consult him as to the selection of his successor he should advise her to send for Spencer. But his advice was not asked, and the queen chose Lord Rosebery, under whom Spencer agreed to continue at the admiralty. He steadily pursued his previous policy until Lord Rosebery's government fell in 1895.

Spencer did not return to office. But until his health failed he took a leading part in the counsels of the liberal party. In the House of Lords he acted as the lieutenant of the liberal leader, Lord Kimberley [q. v. Suppl. II], when the latter fell ill in 1901, and he succeeded him in the leadership on his death in 1902. Amid the anxieties caused to the party by the successive withdrawals of Lord Rosebery and Sir William Harcourt from its leadership and by the accession of Sir Henry Campbell-Bannerman to the leadership in the House of Commons, Spencer loyally did what was possible to preserve unity. Public opinion early in the twentieth century pointed to him as the probable prime minister when the liberals should return to power. But his withdrawal from public life was at hand. The death of his wife on 31 Oct. 1903, which greatly shook him, was followed in 1904 by a severe cardiac illness. Although he recovered and continued to lead his party in the House of Lords until the close of the session of 1905, a cerebral seizure in the autumn, while he was shooting on his estate in Norfolk, led to a gradual failure of his powers. In the new liberal government which was formed in December 1905 he could take no place. He resigned the lord-lieutenancy of Northamptonshire in 1908. He died at Althorp on 14 Aug. 1910, and was buried there beside his wife.

On 8 July 1858 Spencer married Charlotte Frances Frederica, fourth daughter of Frederick Charles William Seymour, a grandson of Francis, first marquis of Hertford. Lady Spencer was a woman of rare beauty and charm, and was known while she presided at Dublin Castle by the affectionate sobriquet of 'Spencer's Faery Queen.' She had no issue. Spencer was succeeded in the title by his half-brother, Charles Robert Spencer, who was created Viscount Althorp in 1905.

Spencer, whose family estates comprised some 26,000 acres in the Midlands, was a considerate landlord and was interested in the progress of agriculture. In 1860 he joined the Royal Agricultural Society, of which his uncle was a founder and first president, and was himself president in 1898, when the annual show was held at Four Oaks Park, Sutton Coldfield. Spencer's income suffered much from the agricultural depression of 1879 and the following years. In 1892 he sold for 250,000*l.*, to Mrs. John Rylands, the great library of Althorp, which now forms a main part of the John Rylands library at Manchester. He afterwards disposed of his Oriental MSS. to the earl of Crawford. Spencer was chancellor of the Victoria University, Manchester, from 1892 until 1907. He was from 1889 chairman of the Northamptonshire county council. In 1901 he became keeper of the privy seal of the duchy of Cornwall.

Spencer's lofty character, grace and dignity of manner, transparent sincerity, wide experience of affairs, and imperturbable fortitude in the midst of perils, lent weight to his utterances and opinions, but he was a hesitating and awkward speaker, and it is doubtful if his capacities were quite equal to the post of prime minister, for which at one time he seemed destined.

Besides the portraits already mentioned there are at Althorp portraits of Earl Spencer by Henry Tanworth Wells, R.A. (1867), and by Frank Holl (1888); the latter is admirable in every way. A third painting by Weigall is at Spencer House in London. A small statuette was done by Melilli in 1905. There is a good sketch, executed by Wells for Grillion's Club in 1881. Two cartoons appeared in 'Vanity Fair,' respectively by 'Ape' in 1870 and by 'Spy' in 1892.

[Personal reminiscences and private information; The Times, 15 Aug. 1910; Lord Morley's Life of Gladstone; B. Holland's The Duke of Devonshire; Lord Fitzmaurice's Lord Granville.] J. R. T.

SPRENGEL, HERMANN JOHANN PHILIPP (1834–1906), chemist, born at Schillerslage, near Hanover, on 29 Aug. 1834, was the second son of Georg Sprengel, a landed proprietor, of Schillerslage.

After early education at home and at a school in Hanover, he attended the universities of Göttingen and of Heidelberg, where he graduated Ph.D. in 1858. Next year he came to England and acted as an assistant in the chemical laboratory of Oxford University. Three years later he removed to London to engage in research at the Royal College of Chemistry, and at Guy's and St. Bartholomew's hospitals. From 1865 to 1870 Sprengel held a post at the chemical works of Messrs. Thomas Farmer, Kennington, becoming a naturalised Englishman.

Sprengel was the first who described and patented in England a number of substances called safety explosives. They were of two kinds, liquid and solid. The liquid ones were, in general, solutions of nitrated hydrocarbons—chiefly nitrobenzene or picric acid in nitric acid, mixtures that could be exploded with considerable effect by a detonator. Sprengel allowed his patents to lapse, deriving no pecuniary benefit. Patents subsequently taken out by Hellhoff for the explosive 'Hellhoffite' and by Turpin for 'Panclastite' were essentially the mixtures suggested by Sprengel (O. GUTTMANN). In a paper read before the Chemical Society, 'On a New Class of Explosives which are Non-explosive during their Manufacture, Storage, and Transport' (*Journal Chem. Soc.* 1873), Sprengel described these substances and gave a list of combustible agents. The mixtures were to be exploded by fulminate detonators wrapped in dry guncotton, a method called by Sprengel 'cumulative detonation' (see *Presidential Address*, SIR F. ABEL, Soc. Chem. Industry, 1883).

Sprengel's most notable achievement was his invention of a mercurial air-pump for the production of vacua of high tenuity by the fall of water or mercury in narrow tubes. This he described in his paper on 'Researches on the Vacuum' before the Chemical Society in 1865. The invention proved of immense service. In the hands of Bunsen, Graham, and Crookes the apparatus opened up departments of physical research of supreme interest; in those of Swan and Edison an era in regard to the incandescent electric light. 'It would be difficult indeed to enumerate the investigations which have owed their success to the invention of the Sprengel mercury pump' (LORD RAYLEIGH, *Presidential Address*, Royal Society, 1906); for details of its practical applications, see *Chemical News*, 1870; *The Times*, 29 Dec. 1879 and 2 Jan. 1880; and S. P. THOMPSON'S *The Development of the Mercurial Air-Pump*, 1888).

Sprengel described to the Chemical Society other researches of practical bearing in 'On the Detection of Nitric Acid' (*Journal*, 1863); 'A Method of Determining the Specific Gravity of Liquids with Ease and Great Exactness' (1873); 'An Air-bath of Constant Temperature between 100° and 200° C.' (1873). To the 'Chemical News' he contributed the papers on 'Use of the Atomiser or Spray-producer in the Manufacture of Sulphuric Acid' (1875); 'Use of Exhaust Steam in the Production of Sulphuric Acid' (1887); and 'An Improvement in the Production of Sulphuric Acid' (1887).

Sprengel was elected a fellow of the Chemical Society in 1864, and served on the council (1871–5). He became F.R.S. on 6 June 1878. In 1893 the German emperor conferred on Sprengel the honorary title of royal Prussian professor.

At the latter part of his life Sprengel alleged that his rights of priority with regard to certain inventions and discoveries had been infringed, and his caustic letters to the public press detailing his grievances were reprinted in book form, with notes, as: 'The Hell-Gate Explosion in New York and so-called "Rackarock," with a few words on so-called Panclastite' (1886); 'Origin of Melinite and Lyddite' (1890); and 'The Discovery of Picric Acid (Melinite, Lyddite) as a Powerful Explosive, and of Cumulative Detonation, with its Bearing on Wet Guncotton' (1902; 2nd edit. 1903).

Sprengel died unmarried at 54 Denbigh Street, London, S.W., on 14 Jan. 1906, and was buried in Brompton cemetery.

[Chem. Soc. Trans., vol. xci.; Journal Soc. Chem. Industry, vol. xxv.; Engineering, vol. lxxxi.; VIIth International Congress of Applied Chemistry (explosives section: Rise and Progress of the British Explosives Industry—portrait); O. Guttmann's Manufacture of Explosives, 1895; Roy. Soc. Catal. Sci. Papers; Poggendorff's Handwörterbuch, Bd. III, 1898; Ency. Brit. vol. xxii. (11th edit.); Nature, 25 Jan. 1906; The Times, 17 Jan. 1906; Men of the Time, 1899.] T. E. J.

SPROTT, GEORGE WASHINGTON (1829–1909), Scottish divine and liturgical scholar, born at Musquodoboit, Nova Scotia, on 6 March 1829, was eldest of five children of John Sprott, presbyterian minister there, by his third wife, Jane Neilson. Both his parents came from Wigtownshire. After early education in the colony Sprott entered Glasgow College in 1845 (see his *John Macleod Memorial Lecture*, Edinburgh 1902). One of his fellow students was (Sir) Henry Campbell-Bannerman [q. v. Suppl. II], who consulted him about studying for the ministry. Sprott, besides taking a good place in his classes, and graduating B.A.

in 1849, was prominent in the students' societies. He had introductions to the families of Dr. Norman Macleod the younger [q. v.], Dr. A. K. H. Boyd [q.v. Suppl. I], and Dr. Laurence Lockhart, brother of Scott's biographer. Both in Glasgow and in Galloway, where he spent his vacations, he gathered large stores of historical and genealogical information. His father, who had been born in the Church of Scotland, approved of his son's resolve to join that church. Ordained in 1852 by the presbytery of Dunoon, Sprott returned to his native colony to act as assistant at St. Matthew's, Halifax, Nova Scotia. There he served also as chaplain to the 72nd Highlanders, whom he was prevented from accompanying to the Crimea. After visits to Newfoundland and the United States, he returned to Scotland in 1856, and having served short periods as assistant minister at Greenock and Dumfries, he was gazetted to a chaplaincy to the Scottish troops at Kandy. He went out to Ceylon in 1857, and laboured there for seven years among the troops and coffee-planters, and to some extent among the natives. He studied Buddhism; he wrote a pamphlet on the Dutch Church in the island; he vigorously asserted the rights and defended the orders of the Church of Scotland as against Anglican claims, and he sought to stem the current drift of Scottish church people to episcopacy, which he attributed partly to the strifes of the disruption period, and partly to the slovenliness of her services. He kept in close touch, accordingly, with the movements beginning in Scotland to mend such defects. In a pamphlet which he wrote in Ceylon on 'The Worship, Rites and Ceremonies of the Church of Scotland,' he propounded the idea which resulted in the formation of the Church Service Society (1865).

In 1865 he left Ceylon and acted for a time as chaplain to the Scots troops at Portsmouth. Next year he was presented to the parish of Chapel of Garioch, Aberdeenshire. There he pursued his liturgical and historical studies, and soon became the most influential member of the editorial committee of the Church Service Society. In 1868 he published a critical edition of the 'Book of Common Order,' commonly called 'John Knox's Liturgy.' In 1871 there appeared Sprott's most learned and original work, 'Scottish Liturgies of James VI.'

Meanwhile Sprott, who opposed the movement for the abolition of patronage in the established church, carried through the Synod of Aberdeen an overture to the general assembly in favour of that celebration of holy communion during the sitting of that body which has since been an established practice. Through a committee of assembly on aids to devotion he was able, with the help of Thomas Leishman [q. v. Suppl. II], to procure a recommendation to use the Apostles' Creed in baptism. As moderator of the Synod in 1873 he preached at its April meeting a sermon on 'The Necessity of a Valid Ordination,' which exercised a powerful influence on the Scottish clergy.

After an unsuccessful application for the chair of church history in Edinburgh University, Sprott, early in 1873, was presented to the parish of North Berwick. He was soon prominent in his new office in presbytery, synod, and assembly. In 1884 he was successful in procuring the erection of a new parish church after a nine years' struggle. In the summer of 1879 the assembly sent him to visit the presbyterian churches of Canada, and also appointed him to a lectureship in pastoral theology. In this capacity he delivered at the four Scottish universities a series of important prelections which appeared as 'Worship and Offices of the Church of Scotland' (1882). In recognition of the merit of those lectures the University of Glasgow conferred on him in 1880 the degree of D.D. But he was disappointed in two further applications for professorships of church history—at Glasgow in 1886 and at Aberdeen in 1889. At the assembly of 1882 Sprott successfully joined Dr. Leishman in the protest against the admission of congregational ministers without presbyterian ordination. He joined on its formation, in 1886, the Aberdeen (now the Scottish) Ecclesiological Society, and showed interest in its work till his death. In 1892 Sprott took a leading part in founding and conducting the Scottish Church Society for the assertion and defence of orthodox doctrine and sound church principles. Another useful society, the Church Law Society, owns him as its founder. Through life an advocate of Church reunion, he cordially welcomed the efforts both of Bishop Charles Wordsworth [q. v.] and Bishop George Howard Wilkinson [q. v. Suppl. II]; of the Scottish Christian Unity Association founded by the latter he became an active member. In 1902 he celebrated his ministerial jubilee, but owing to heart weakness he petitioned the presbytery next year for the appointment of an assistant and successor, and he retired to Edinburgh, where he was able to engage in literary and ecclesiastical work. To this period of his life belong several notable literary productions—his John Macleod Memorial Lecture, 'The Doctrine of Schism in the Church of Scotland' (Edinburgh, 1902), a new edition of 'John Knox's Liturgy' (1901), an edition (1905) of 'The Liturgy of Compromise used in the English Congregation at Frankfort, 1557,' bound up with Mr. H. J. Wotherspoon's 'Second Prayer Book of Edward VI,' and a new edition (1905) of 'Euchologion, a Book of Common Order,' with historical introduction of great value to the student of Scottish worship—all issued by the Church Service Society. He also wrote a delightful account of his father and of Nova Scotian life 'Memorials of the Rev. John Sprott' (Edinburgh, 1906). Sprott died at Edinburgh of heart disease on 27 Oct. 1909, and was buried at North Berwick.

Sprott married in 1856 Mary (*d.* 1874), daughter of Charles Hill of Halifax, Nova Scotia. Four sons also predeceased their father; a son, Harold, a lawyer in Edinburgh, and four married daughters survived.

Stern in aspect, Sprott was full of warm and deeply religious feeling, and had much wit and humour. Memorials were erected to him in North Berwick church and in St. Oswald's parish church, Edinburgh, where he worshipped in his later years.

In addition to the works mentioned Sprott contributed many notices of Scottish divines to this Dictionary.

[Sprott's diaries and letters; private information from his son and daughters; personal knowledge; notices of his life in his own works; Scotsman, 28 Oct. 1909, and in The Gallovidian (Dumfries, Summer, 1911), written by his son (with portrait); a memoir by the present writer is in preparation.] J. C.

STABLES, WILLIAM [GORDON] (1840–1910), writer for boys, son of William Stables, vintner, of Marnock, and afterwards of Inverurie, was born at Aberchirder, Marnoch, Banffshire, on 21 May 1840. He was educated at a school at Marnock and at Aberdeen grammar school. In 1854 he entered Aberdeen University, and was a member of the arts class until 1857. Refusing a commission in the army, he studied medicine, and took the degrees of M.D. and C.M. on 26 April 1862 (*Aberdeen University Calendar*, 1863, pp. 30, 33). While still a student, at the age of nineteen, he made a first voyage to the Arctic on a small Greenland whaler of 300 tons, an experience he subsequently repeated in a larger vessel. On 19 Jan. 1863 he obtained a commission as assistant surgeon in the Royal Navy, and on 2 Feb. was appointed to H.M.S. Narcissus on the Cape of Good Hope station. Later his vessel, the Penguin, was sent in pursuit of slavers off the Mozambique coast (*Medical Life in the Navy*, 1868, by W. STABLES, pp. 67–9). On his return home he was commissioned, on 18 Feb. 1864, to the Princess Royal, at Devonport, and in the following year to the Meeanee, on the Mediterranean station. Stables was appointed to the Pembroke at Sheerness on 18 March 1870, and in the following year, after serving in the Wizard on the Mediterranean station, he retired on half-pay owing to ill-health. Subsequently Stables was for two years in the merchant service, cruising all round America to Africa, India, and the South Seas.

About 1875 Stables settled at Twyford, and henceforth occupied himself in writing boys' books, assuming the name of Gordon Stables. Personal experience formed the basis of his tales of adventure and exploration. His best-known volumes are: 'Wild Adventures in Wild Places' (1881); 'Wild Adventures round the Pole' (1883); 'The Hermit Hunter of the Wilds' (1889); 'Westward with Columbus' (1894); 'Kidnapped by Cannibals' (1899); 'In Regions of Perpetual Snow' (1904). Stables also wrote many historical novels, dealing mainly with naval history; these included: ''Twixt Daydawn and Light,' a tale of the times of Alfred the Great (1898), and 'On War's Red Tide,' a tale of the Boer War (1900). His literary output averaged over four books a year for thirty years, and his writings occupy seven pages of the British Museum catalogue. His stories, which inculcated manliness and self-reliance, were popular with more than one generation of boys.

In 1886 Stables started caravanning as a pastime, being one of the earliest pioneers. He described his first tour in the 'Cruise of the Land Yacht Wanderer' (1886), and thenceforth he made annual caravan expeditions. On the formation of the Caravan Club in 1907 he was elected vice-president. A lover of animals and an active supporter of the Sea Birds Protection Society and the Humanitarian League, he illustrated his devotion to domestic pets in 'Friends in Fur' (1877) and 'Our Friend the Dog' (1884). He was known as an expert authority on dogs, cats, and rabbits, both in England and America, frequently acting as judge at shows, and compiling some popular treatises on the medical treatment of children and dogs. He died at his house, the Jungle, Twyford, on 10 May 1910.

In 1874 Stables married Theresa Elizabeth Williams, elder daughter of Captain Alexander McCormack of Solva, Pembrokeshire, and left four sons and two daughters.

[Records of the arts class, 1854–8, Marischal College, p. 51 (photograph, p. 48); Navy List, 1864–5, 1870–72; The Times, 12 May 1910; the World, 3 Dec. 1907 (report of interview); private information.] G. S. W.

STACPOOLE, FREDERICK (1813–1907), engraver, born in 1813, was apparently son of Edmund Stackpoole, lieutenant R.N., whose death was reported in the 'Navy List' of January 1816, and whose widow subsequently married a naval captain named Jefferies. He received his general education in Ghent, and later became a student at the Academy schools, gaining two silver medals in 1839 for a drawing from the antique, and in 1841 for the best copy made in the painting school. Circumstances induced him to give up his original intention of becoming a portrait painter in favour of engraving, and he devoted the best part of his life to this art. Most of his plates are executed in a mixed mezzotint (i.e. mezzotint in conjunction with line and stipple). His work was exclusively reproductive, including a large number of prints after Briton Rivière (chiefly published by Messrs. Agnew), Thomas Faed (chiefly published by Messrs. H. Graves), and C. Burton Barber. He also engraved pictures by Lady Butler, G. D. Leslie, Reynolds, Holman Hunt, Richard Ansdell, Sir Francis Grant, Sir J. W. Gordon, Landseer, Thomas Brooks, Frederick Goodall, Robert Collinson, Jerry Barrett, Alice Havers, Frederick Tayler, A. Bouvier, Philip R. Morris, and J. Sant. One of his most successful engravings is the 'Shadow of Death,' after Holman Hunt (1877). It is stronger and less mechanical in its style than the majority of his plates. 'Pot Pourri: Rose Leaves and Lavender,' after G. D. Leslie (1881), may also be singled out for the simplicity and breadth of its treatment. Among his most popular subjects were the 'Palm Offering,' after Frederick Goodall (1868), and the 'Roll Call,' after Lady Butler (1874).

He was a regular exhibitor at the Royal Academy from 1842 to 1899. He was elected an associate in 1880, retiring from active membership in 1892 (being the last engraver made associate until the election of Frank Short and William Strang in 1906). His first Royal Academy exhibit (1842) was an oil portrait, and he exhibited six other paintings (portrait, subject, and landscape) at the Academy between 1843 and 1869, but from 1858 to 1893 his regular contributions were engravings. He also exhibited paintings at the Society of British Artists between 1841 and 1845. Two of his earliest published engravings are after Sir Edwin Landseer, and both are done in collaboration with other engravers, i.e. 'Peace' with T. L. Atkinson (1848), and the 'Hunted Stag' (engraved under the title of the 'Mountain Torrent') with Thomas Landseer (1850) (both after pictures from the Vernon collection, now in the National Gallery of British Art). During the last ten years of his life he again took up painting, sending five small subject pictures to the Royal Academy between 1894 and 1899. He died in London on 19 Dec. 1907, and was buried in Brompton cemetery. In 1844 he married Susannah Atkinson, and had issue four daughters and one son.

[The Times, 21 Dec. 1907; Lists of the Printsellers' Association; A. Graves, Dict. of Artists, 1895, and Royal Acad. Exhibitors; Cat. of Soc. of Brit. Artists; information supplied by his daughter, Mrs. Arthur Bentley.] A. M. H.

STAFFORD, Sir EDWARD WILLIAM (1819–1901), prime minister of New Zealand, born on 23 April 1819 at Edinburgh, was eldest son of Berkeley Buckingham Stafford of Maine, co. Louth, and of Anne, third daughter of Lieutenant-colonel Duff Tytler. His mother's cousin was Patrick Fraser Tytler [q. v.], and on early visits to Edinburgh he joined a cultured circle which widened for life his intellectual interests. Educated at Trinity College, Dublin, he emigrated in January 1843 to Nelson, New Zealand, where he at once took part in public affairs. In 1853, when provincial councils were called into existence by Sir George Grey [q. v. Suppl. I], Stafford was chosen to be superintendent of Nelson. While he was on the council he carried through an education ordinance which was afterwards made the basis of an Education Act applying to the whole colony, and a road board ordinance. He retired from the council in 1856.

In the general election of 1855 he was elected to the House of Representatives, and on 2 June 1856 he formed, after the granting of representative institutions, the first government which was able to hold office for any length of time. On 4 Nov. he also assumed the office of colonial secretary. During his premiership, which was distinguished by a resolve to respect the best parliamentary traditions of the mother country, he created three new provinces, Hawke's Bay in 1858, Marlborough in 1859, and Southland in 1861, though a few years later Southland, by its own wish, was reunited to its parent colony of Otago. He transferred the land revenue and part of the customs revenue to the provincial councils by Act of Parliament, and since the home government had refused to allow a bill to this effect, he made arrangements by which the councils were virtually placed in control of their own land. He also passed several bills permitting the provinces to raise loans. In 1858 he secured a bill allowing the governor to formulate bye-laws for native districts based on the expressed wishes of tribal assemblies, a second bill establishing itinerant courts of justice and native juries, and a third bill providing grants for Maori schools.

In 1859 he visited England in order to discuss plans for a Panama mail service and for establishing military settlements in the north island. He was unsuccessful in the latter project, but an agreement which he concluded for a Panama postal service was approved by the New Zealand government. When he returned in 1860, he found that his party had plunged the country into war with the Maoris. Although if he had been on the spot he might have prevented a conflict, he considered himself committed to the policy of his colleagues, and continued to support the continuance of the war until 1870, when peace was finally assured. In July 1861 Sir William Fox defeated the Stafford ministry by one vote on a general vote of confidence, and at the same time Governor Gore Browne was replaced by Sir George Grey. When Fox resigned in 1862 Stafford refused to form a ministry, and he remained out of office until 1865. On 16 Oct. of that year he defeated the Weld government, although Weld's followers had as a rule belonged to his old party. Himself a centralist, Stafford came into office at the head of the provincialists. In 1866 he reconstructed his cabinet, replacing the provincialists by those members of the Weld government with whom he was really in sympathy. Meanwhile he was holding the office of colonial secretary (16 Oct. 1865–28 June 1869), colonial treasurer (18 Oct. 1865–12 June 1866), and postmaster-general (31 Oct. 1865–8 May 1866, and 6 Feb.–28 June 1869). He remained in office for three years. In 1867 he took over the provincial loans at par, and in the same year special representation was given to the native race.

In 1869 McLean and Fox together carried a vote of want of confidence in native affairs against him. An impression prevailed that he was inclined to press the war in circumstances where forbearance and compromise were more to the interests of the colonists. On 10 Sept. 1872 he again became premier on a motion condemning the administration of the Fox-Vogel public works policy, but his tenure of office only lasted for a month, and he resigned on 11 Oct. upon a no-confidence motion carried by Vogel.

In 1874 he returned to England, where he lived for the rest of his life. At various times he was offered but refused the governorship of Queensland and that of Madras. In 1886 he was commissioner for the colonial and Indian exhibition. He was created K.C.M.G. in 1879 and G.C.M.G. in 1887. He died at 27 Chester Square, London, W., on 14 Feb. 1901. He married (1) on 24 Sept. 1846 Emily Charlotte (*d.* 18 April 1857), only child of Colonel William Wakefield and Emily Elizabeth, daughter of Sir John Shelley Sidney, first baronet; (2) on 5 Dec. 1859 Mary, third daughter of Thomas Houghton Bartley, speaker of the legislative council, New Zealand. By her he had three sons and three daughters.

[The Times, 15 Feb. 1901; Mennell's Dict. of Australas. Biog.; Gisborne's New Zealand Rulers and Statesmen; Rusden's Hist. of New Zealand; Reeves's The Long White Cloud; New Zealand Herald, 2 March 1901; Canterbury Press, 2 March 1901; Christchurch Press; Lyttelton Times; Auckland Star; private information from Mr. E. Howard Stafford.] A. B. W.

STAINER, Sir JOHN (1840–1901), organist and composer, born on 6 June 1840, at 2 Broadway, Southwark, was younger son (in a family of six children) of William Stainer, schoolmaster of the parish school at St. Thomas's, Southwark, by his wife Ann Collier, who was descended from an old Huguenot family settled in Spitalfields. The father was much devoted to music, and possessed amongst other musical instruments a chamber organ. The elder son, Dr. William Stainer, died in 1898, after a life devoted to the care of the deaf and dumb. The eldest daughter, Anne Stainer (*b.* 1825), who was unmarried and is still living (1912), held from 1849 to 1899 the post of organist of the Magdalen Hospital Chapel, Streatham, and during all the fifty years she never missed a single service.

John was indebted to his father for his first music lessons, and for his bias towards the organ. Although he was deprived of the sight of the left eye by an accident when he was five years old, his progress was unimpeded. At the age of seven he could play Bach's Fugue in E major. Early in 1848 he became a probationer in the choir of St. Paul's Cathedral, and on 24 June 1849 he was formally admitted as a full chorister. Under William Bayley, the choirmaster, he studied harmony from the book written by the cathedral organist, (Sir) John Goss [q. v.]. He sang at the funeral of J. M. W. Turner (1851) and of the Duke of Wellington (1852). He possessed a beautiful voice and exceptional ability as a singer, while his manner and personality endeared him to his associates.

In 1854 he was appointed organist of St. Benedict and St. Peter, Paul's Wharf. He had a remarkable facility in extemporising on the organ, in the manner of Bach. About this time he had lessons in organ playing from George Cooper, at St. Sepulchre's church. In 1856 Sir Frederick Gore Ouseley [q. v.] came to an afternoon service at St. Paul's and found Stainer deputising at the organ. He was so struck with the youth's ability that he offered him the post of organist at St. Michael's, Tenbury, then, as now, a centre for the study of ecclesiastical music. In 1857 Stainer was settled at Tenbury. He used to ascribe much of his ultimate success as a church musician to his two years' experience here under Ouseley.

Matriculating at Christ Church, Oxford, on 26 May 1859, he proceeded B.Mus. there on 10 June following, whilst he was still at Tenbury. In July 1860 he was appointed organist of Magdalen College, Oxford, and next year became organist to the university. He then went into residence at St. Edmund Hall, in order to read for an arts degree, and he graduated B.A. in 1864. On 9 Nov. 1865 he passed his examination for the degree of doctor of music, the oratorio 'Gideon' being his degree exercise. In 1866 he proceeded M.A., and was appointed a university examiner in music. In this capacity he examined (Sir) Hubert Parry for his bachelor of music degree. He founded the Oxford Philharmonic Society, and conducted its first concert on 8 June 1866.

The supreme opportunity of his life occurred when in 1872 he became organist at St. Paul's Cathedral. At this period the service music at St. Paul's had drifted into an unsatisfactory condition. Stainer brought to its reform great tact in administration and exceptional musical ability, and the cathedral soon acquired a worldwide reputation for the beauty and reverence of its service music, and for Stainer's masterly organ playing. During his career at St. Paul's he found time for music composition and other exacting work. He was organist to the Royal Choral Society from 1873 until 1888. He was one of the chief founders of the Musical Association, which was established in 1874. In 1876 he became professor of the organ at the new National Training School for Music, and in 1881 he succeeded (Sir) Arthur Sullivan [q. v. Suppl. I] as principal. He was a juror at the Paris Exhibition of 1878, and for his services was created a chevalier of the Legion of Honour in France. In 1882 he was appointed government inspector of music in the training colleges for elementary school teachers in Great Britain. In spite of the blindness of one eye, his sight long bore the strain of music reading and writing without any sign of weakness. But in 1888 he was warned that it was in danger, and he resigned the organistship of St. Paul's and other professional appointments. On 10 July he was knighted by Queen Victoria. In 1889 he succeeded Sir Frederick Ouseley as professor of music in the University of Oxford, and he retained this post until 1899. The last important position he occupied in the musical world was the mastership of the Musicians' Company, which he accepted in 1900.

Among Stainer's other distinctions were honorary fellowships of Magdalen College, Oxford, and of St. Michael's College, Tenbury. At Durham he was made hon. Mus.D. (1858) and hon. D.C.L. (1895). He was also member or officer of the chief musical societies, being vice-president of the Royal College of Organists; president of the Plain Song and Mediæval Music Society; president of the London Gregorian Association; president of the Musical Association.

He died suddenly at Verona on 31 March 1901, and was buried at Holywell cemetery, Oxford.

On 27 Dec. 1865 he married Eliza Cecil, only daughter of Alderman Randall of Oxford. She survived him with four sons and two daughters. His elder daughter, Miss E. C. Stainer, published a 'Dictionary of Violin Makers' in 1896, and she greatly assisted her father in his historical inquiries.

His chief compositions were the following oratorios and sacred cantatas: 'Gideon' (his exercise for the degree of doctor of music), 1865; 'The Daughter of Jairus' (Worcester Festival, 1878); 'St. Mary Magdalen' (Gloucester Festival, 1887); 'Crucifixion' (first performed at St. Marylebone church, 24 Feb. 1887); 'The Story of the Cross' (1893), and about forty anthems, the best known of which are: 'I am Alpha and Omega'; 'Lead, kindly Light'; 'What are these arrayed in white robes'; 'Ye shall dwell in the land'; 'Sing a song of praise'; 'O clap your hands.' Stainer himself considered 'I saw the Lord' (eight parts) his most important effort in this form.

Other contributions to ecclesiastical music were services: No. 1 in E flat, No. 2 in A and D, and No. 3 in B flat. A sevenfold Amen has been in constant use throughout the world in the service of the Church. It was used at the coronation of King Edward VII and King George V.

He composed over 150 hymn tunes, many of which were contributed to 'Hymns, Ancient and Modern,' and to other hymnals. The whole collection was published in one volume in 1900 (Novello & Co.). Compositions for the organ are contained in 'Twelve Pieces' (two books), a 'Jubilant March,' 'The Village Organist' (of which he was for some time joint editor), and five numbers of organ arrangements.

His chief works in the category of secular music were a few madrigals and part songs, a book of seven songs, and another book of six Italian songs.

Of his twenty-nine Oxford professorial lectures only one, 'Music in relation to the Intellect and Emotions,' was published (1892). He edited with Rev. H. R. Bramley 'Christmas Carols, New and Old' (1884), and he wrote numerous articles for the 'Dictionary of Musical Terms,' which he compiled with W. A. Barrett (1876). Six essays read before the Musical Association are published in their 'Proceedings' (1874–1901), the first 'On the Principles of Musical Notation,' and the last 'On the Musical Introductions found in Certain Musical Psalters.'

'A Theory of Harmony' (1871) attracted much attention, from the boldness and unconventionality of its treatment. 'Music of the Bible,' a book displaying much knowledge and research, was published in 1879.

His most important contribution to musical history is the volume entitled 'Dufay and his Contemporaries' (1899), in which the evolution of harmony and counterpoint during a somewhat obscure period (the fifteenth century) is traced with great erudition. Another work devoted to early musical history was that on 'Early Bodleian Music' (2 vols. 1902). This was completed just before his death.

He was the first editor of Novello's 'Music Primers,' and for this series he wrote his primers on the 'Organ' and 'Harmony,' which have had an immense sale, and others on 'Counterpoint,' and 'Choral Society Vocalisation.' He also edited the 'Church Hymnary' for the united Scotch churches.

Stainer gathered a unique collection of old song books, especially of those published during the eighteenth century. In 1891 a catalogue enumerating about 750 volumes of this portion of his library was printed for private circulation. The whole collection of books is now (1912) in the possession of his eldest son.

A portrait of Stainer was painted by Sir Hubert von Herkomer, and is now in the possession of Lady Stainer, at her residence in Oxford. A replica is in the Music School, Oxford. A memorial window was placed in Holywell church in 1902 (reproduced in *Musical Times*, May 1902). A memorial marble panel was placed in St. Paul's Cathedral on the eastern wall of the north transept in December 1903. A mural tablet of brass is placed on the west wall of the ante-chapel of Magdalen College, Oxford, and another at St. Michael's, Tenbury.

Stainer's sacred music has enjoyed great vogue, greater probably than that of any other English church musician. It is distinguished by melodiousness, and the harmonic texture is rich, and it is often deeply expressive. Stainer began his career as a composer at a period when the influence of Mendelssohn was great, and that of Spohr only less so. The style of both composers can be traced in the idiom adopted by Stainer, but there was also much that was individual. His knowledge of Bach's music, and his intimate acquaintance with that of the early English school of cathedral composers and the madrigal writers, were also formative influences.

[Personal knowledge; Musical Times, May 1901; Grove's Dictionary; private information.] W. G. McN.

STAMER, Sir LOVELACE TOMLINSON, third baronet (1829–1908), bishop-suffragan of Shrewsbury, born at Ingram's Lodgings in the city of York on

18 Oct. 1829, was elder son of Sir Lovelace Stamer, second baronet, a captain in the 4th dragoon guards, by his wife Caroline, only daughter of John Tomlinson, solicitor, of Cliffville, Stoke-upon-Trent. His grandfather Sir William Stamer, sheriff, alderman, and twice lord mayor of Dublin, commanded a regiment of Dublin yeomanry during the rebellion of 1798, and was created a baronet, while lord mayor of the city, on 15 Dec. 1809, the year of King George III's jubilee.

After attending Mr. Fleming's school at Sea View, Bootle, and H. Lovell's English institution at Mannheim, Stamer was at Rugby, under Dr. Tait, from August 1843 to December 1848, his contemporaries including Lord Goschen, Sir Godfrey Lushington, and Edward Parry, suffragan-bishop of Dover. In 1849 he entered Trinity College, Cambridge. He rowed in the first Trinity boat. In 1853 he graduated B.A. with a second class in the classical tripos; he proceeded M.A. in 1856, and D.D. in 1888.

Ordained deacon by the bishop of Lichfield in 1853, he served the curacies of Clay Cross in Derbyshire (1853–4) and of Turvey in Bedfordshire (1854–5). After his ordination as priest by the bishop of Ely in 1855, he was curate-in-charge of Long Melford, Suffolk (1855–7). He succeeded his uncle, John Wickes Tomlinson, as rector of Stoke-upon-Trent in January 1858 on the nomination of his grandfather's trustees, who were patrons. The living was of great value, and Stamer held it for thirty-four years. He became third baronet on the death of his father on 5 March 1860.

Stamer's work at Stoke-upon-Trent showed untiring zeal and an extraordinary capacity for work, coupled with great administrative powers and common-sense views on social questions. He found at Stoke a population of 8000, with one church and one block of schools. When he left Stoke in 1892, there were four churches and five school or mission churches manned by a staff of nine clergy, and five schools with twelve separate departments. Stoke owed an immense debt to him in regard to education. Long before the conscience clause was incorporated in any education acts, he laid it down as a rule in his church schools that any parents might withdraw their children from religious instruction. In 1863 he started night schools, and used his utmost endeavours to induce lads and young men to continue their education after leaving school. He was chairman of the Stoke school board from its formation in 1871 until 1888, and took an active interest in schemes for building groups of new schools to meet the rapid increase of population. He also took keen interest in the training of young men and women for the teaching profession, and freely admitted nonconformists as pupil teachers in his schools. He heartily aided, too, in all philanthropic movements. By the joint exertions of himself and Sir Smith Child nearly 17,000*l.* was raised for the relief of the widows and orphans of the colliers killed in the terrible explosion which occurred on 13 Dec. 1866 at the Talk o' the Hill colliery in North Staffordshire. With a view to future contingencies of the kind, Stamer originated in 1870 the North Staffordshire Coal and Ironstone Workers' Permanent Relief Society, a contributory society of which Stamer was chairman of the committee for thirty-eight years. Its membership in 1897 exceeded 9500—nearly two-thirds of the miners in the district—and by its agency more than 103,000*l.* has been paid to disabled miners and their families. In 1872 he founded the Staffordshire Institution for Nurses, an organisation which employs 130 trained nurses, and through his instrumentality the nurses' home was erected at Stoke in 1876. He was a warm supporter of the North Staffordshire Discharged Prisoners' Aid Society, and on his initiative there was founded in 1879 an industrial home for discharged female prisoners and friendless women, of which he acted many years as chairman of the management committee. In 1867 he served the office of chief bailiff of Stoke.

Stamer was appointed rural dean of Stoke in 1858, prebendary of Longdon in Lichfield Cathedral in 1875, and archdeacon of Stoke-upon-Trent in 1877. As archdeacon he was an unfailing helper and adviser of the clergy. In 1877 he supported the government's burial bill, which enabled nonconformists to have their own funeral services in the churchyards of parishes where there was no nonconformist burial-ground. In 1888 he was appointed suffragan-bishop of Shrewsbury, and was consecrated at St. Paul's Cathedral on 24 Feb. 1888. At the same time he resigned his offices of rural dean and archdeacon, retaining his prebendal stall and his rectory.

In 1889, through Stamer's instrumentality and with a noble disregard of his private family interests, the Stoke Rectory Act was passed, which conveyed the patronage and endowment of the rectory of Stoke-upon-Trent from the trustees who represented

Stamer's mother's family to the bishops of Lichfield, and provided for the material increase of the incomes of six neighbouring parishes.

Stamer resigned the rectory of Stoke in 1892, and from that year to 1896 he was vicar of St. Chad's, Shrewsbury. At Shrewsbury he set the schools on a sound basis, starting a club-house for boys, and obtaining a new scheme for the parochial charities. He was for a time a member of the Shrewsbury school board. As chaplain to the corporation of Shrewsbury, he denounced the bribery and corruption which were prevalent in the town, and the insanitary condition of the slums. In 1896 Stamer became rector of Edgmond, the patron of which had conveyed it to trustees as an endowment for the assistant or suffragan bishop for the time being. Here he built new schools, obtained a water supply at his own expense, and provided a working men's club and reading-room. Owing to illness he resigned the rectory of Edgmond and his suffragan bishopric in September 1905, and removed to Halingdene, a house at Penkridge, Staffordshire, where he died on 29 Oct. 1908. He was buried at Hartshill cemetery, Stoke-upon-Trent. He was married at Hunsingore, Yorkshire, on 16 April 1857 to Ellen Isabel, only daughter of Joseph Dent of Ribston Hall, Yorkshire. His wife, five sons, and three daughters survived him. A portrait of the bishop in his robes, painted by the Hon. John Collier, was presented to him in April 1893 by North Staffordshire friends.

Besides several single sermons and articles in the 'Church Sunday School Institute Magazine,' Stamer published: 1. 'Charges to the Clergy of the Archdeaconry of Stoke-upon-Trent,' 1887–8. 2. 'The Holy Communion considered as generally necessary to Salvation,' 1858.

[F. D. How's Memoir of Bishop Sir Lovelace Tomlinson Stamer, Baronet, D.D., 1910; Burke's Peerage and Baronetage; Foster's Baronetage; Cambridge Book of Matriculations and Degrees, 1851–1900; Plarr's Men and Women of the Time, 1899, p. 1024; The Times, 31 Oct. 1908; The Guardian, 4 Nov. 1908; Shrewsbury Chronicle, 6 Nov. 1908; Staffordshire Advertiser, 31 Oct. and 7 Nov. 1908; Birmingham Daily Post, 31 Oct. 1908; Stoke-upon-Trent Parish Magazine, Dec. 1908; The Evangelist Monthly, March 1906, pp. 52–6; Rupert Simms' Bibliotheca Staffordiensis, p. 433; Lichfield Diocesan Magazine, Dec. 1908; two volumes of newspaper cuttings, belonging to Lady Stamer, 1866–1908; and private information.]

W. G. D. F.

STANLEY, Sir FREDERICK ARTHUR, sixteenth Earl of Derby (1841–1908), governor-general of Canada, born in London on 15 Jan. 1841, was second son in the family of three children of Edward Geoffrey Stanley, fourteenth earl of Derby [q. v.], three times prime minister, by his wife Emma Caroline, daughter of Edward Bootle Wilbraham, first Baron Skelmersdale (created 1828), and aunt of Edward Bootle Wilbraham, first earl of Lathom (created 1880). Stanley's elder brother was Edward Henry Stanley, fifteenth earl [q. v.].

Frederick Stanley, after education at Eton, joined the grenadier guards in 1858. In 1865 he retired from the army as lieutenant and captain. He was subsequently honorary colonel of the third and fourth battalions of the King's own royal Lancashire regiment, and of the first volunteer battalion of the Liverpool regiment. On leaving the army Stanley was returned to the House of Commons unopposed as one of the conservative members for Preston, near which the family estates lay (11 July 1865). When his father resigned in Feb. 1868 and Disraeli became prime minister, he received his first official appointment, as a civil lord of the admiralty. At the general election in November he successfully contested North Lancashire jointly with Colonel Wilson-Patten (afterwards Lord Winmarleigh), displacing Lord Hartington, who had sat for the constituency as a liberal since 1857. Stanley represented this constituency until 1885, being returned unopposed at the general election in 1874 and at two bye-elections (on taking office on 8 April 1878 and 1 July 1885), and after a contest at the general election in 1880. After the Redistribution Act of 1885 he sat for the Blackpool division until he was raised to the peerage in 1886, being unopposed at the general elections of Nov. 1885 and July 1886.

Stanley, following in the steps of his father and brother, held a long succession of political offices. In Feb. 1874 he was appointed financial secretary to the war office in Disraeli's second administration. Although he was ineffective as a speaker, his capacity for business was acknowledged by his chief the secretary of state for war, Gathorne-Hardy, who deplored his transfer in August 1877 to the financial secretaryship to the treasury (*Life of Gathorne-Hardy*, ii. 29). Some months later (April 1878) he returned to the war office as secretary of state, was admitted to the privy council, and joined the cabinet.

His brother and Lord Carnarvon had left the government owing to differences with their colleagues on their anti-Russian policy in Eastern Europe; and Gathorne-Hardy (created Viscount Cranbrook) left the war office vacant on his transference to the India office. Stanley's appointment was popular in the army. The duke of Cambridge wrote to Gathorne-Hardy: 'No one that I could think of in political life would be equally acceptable to me' (*ibid.* ii. 60).

The crisis with Russia which had caused the schism in the cabinet soon ended, and Stanley's two years of office were not eventful. Like his predecessor, he was content to carry on the policy of Cardwell (1868–74) without introducing any novel schemes of reform. In the autumn of 1878 he and W. H. Smith, first lord of the admiralty, paid an official visit to Cyprus, which Turkey had recently ceded to Great Britain. After the defeat of the tory government at the general election of April 1880, Stanley resigned office with his colleagues and was created a G.C.B. During Lord Salisbury's short first administration of 1885–6 Stanley was again in high office, becoming secretary of state for the colonies. The recall of Sir Charles Warren from Bechuanaland was the chief fruit of his brief tenure of the post. In Feb. 1886 he retired on the change of ministry. In August he left the House of Commons on being created Baron Stanley of Preston, and joined Lord Salisbury's new (second) administration as president of the board of trade.

On 1 May 1888 Lord Stanley was nominated to succeed Lord Lansdowne as governor-general of Canada. He was well fitted for the post. Of retiring disposition, and without any pretensions to oratory, there lay behind his natural modesty a firm mind and strong common sense. His patrician lineage gave him an instinctive habit of command, and his manner had a peculiar charm. In Canada Stanley won much popularity; he encouraged the imperial sentiment in the dominion, and although the course of affairs was unexciting, he had full scope for the exercise of his judgment and tact. When he retired, the secretary of state (Lord Ripon) wrote in a despatch: 'In dealing with the many difficult and delicate questions which have arisen in connection with Canada during your term of office, it has been the greatest satisfaction to Her Majesty's government to have the services of a statesman of your lordship's experience and attainments' (22 June 1893).

On 21 April 1893 Stanley succeeded, on the death of his brother, to the earldom and the family estates. The heavy domestic responsibilities compelled him to resign his post in Canada. Thenceforward he held no official post, although he did not neglect politics. In Jan. 1895 he presided over a demonstration at St. Helens in honour of the duke of Devonshire, whom as Lord Hartington he had opposed in North Lancashire in 1868. He fully recognised the value of the alliance of liberal unionists with conservatives in Lord Salisbury's third administration of 1895. He consistently urged the strengthening of the ties between England and the colonies and in 1904 he succeeded the duke of Devonshire as president of the British Empire League. At the Mansion House on 15 March 1904 he spoke of the desirability of bringing representative colonial opinion into efficient touch with the mother country.

Derby performed with dignity and zeal the local civil and social duties attaching to his position. In Liverpool he was a prominent and active figure. In 1895–6 he was first lord mayor of greater Liverpool, and the freedom of the city was conferred on him in 1904. He was chancellor of Liverpool University from its foundation in 1903. In 1902 he was guild mayor of Preston. He entertained largely at his chief country seat at Knowsley, where King Edward VII was regularly among his later guests. He had on his father's death in 1869 inherited a property at Witherslack in Westmorland; he built a country residence there, and gave his neighbours a public hall in 1886. In 1897 he became lord-lieutenant of Lancashire. On succeeding to the title in 1893 he resumed the connection with racing for which his father had been famous. He joined the Jockey Club in the same year. His two greatest successes were in 1893 and 1906, when he won the Oaks with Canterbury Pilgrim and Keystone II respectively. In the latter year he won altogether forty-four races. He was a prominent figure at all Liverpool race meetings.

Derby, who was made K.G. in 1897 and G.C.V.O. in 1905, was active in London in both social and philanthropic affairs. He was a vice-president and benefactor of the Middlesex Hospital, and was president of the Franco-British Exhibition of 1907 at Shepherd's Bush. Early in 1908 Lord Derby's health gave cause for uneasiness, and he died on 14 June at his house, Holwood in Kent. He was buried at Knowsley.

He married, on 31 May 1864, Lady Constance, eldest daughter of George William Frederick Villiers, fourth earl of Clarendon [q. v.], the liberal statesman. His widow survived him with seven sons and one daughter. The eldest son, Edward George Villiers Stanley, seventeenth earl (*b.* 1865), who served in the South African war, was postmaster-general in Mr. Balfour's cabinet (1903–5).

A portrait by Sir Hubert von Herkomer is in the possession of the dowager countess of Derby. A marble statue by F. W. Pomeroy, A.R.A., was unveiled by Lord Halsbury in St. George's Hall, Liverpool, on 3 Nov. 1911. There is a bust by Sir William Goscombe John in Preston town hall.

[The Times, 15 June 1908; H. W. Lucy's Disraeli Parliament; private information.]

R. L.

STANLEY, HENRY EDWARD JOHN, third BARON STANLEY OF ALDERLEY (1827–1903), diplomatist and orientalist, born at Alderley Park, Cheshire, on 11 July 1827, was eldest son of Edward John, second Baron Stanley of Alderley [q. v.], by Henrietta Maria [q. v.], daughter of the thirteenth Viscount Dillon. Of his three brothers, Edward Lyulph became fourth Baron Stanley of Alderley, and fourth Baron Sheffield of Roscommon, and Algernon Charles became Roman catholic bishop of Emmaus in 1903. Of his six sisters, Katharine Louisa married in 1864 John Russell, Viscount Amberley [q. v.]; and Rosalind Frances, in the same year, George James Howard, ninth earl of Carlisle [q. v. Suppl. II]. Henry Edward entered Eton in 1841, but owing to illness was removed in the following year, and placed under the care of Henry Alford [q. v.], afterwards dean of Canterbury, at that time vicar of Wymeswold, Leicestershire. He proceeded to Cambridge in 1846 as a pensioner of Trinity College, and during his stay at the university showed his early predilection for Oriental subjects by devoting himself to the study of Arabic.

Stanley left Cambridge in December 1847 to enter the foreign office with the object of qualifying himself for the diplomatic service. He was appointed précis writer to Lord Palmerston, then foreign secretary. In 1851 he was sent as an attaché to Constantinople, where Lord Stratford de Redcliffe was ambassador. He had charge of the consulate of Varna from June to August 1853, and was appointed secretary of legation at Athens in 1854, holding that position during the critical period of the Crimean war. From July 1856 till May 1858 he was attached as secretary to Sir Henry Bulwer's special commission to the Danubian provinces, when the free navigation of the river was secured and the new Russo-Turkish frontier delimited by an international commission appointed at the Congress of Paris. He resigned his post at Athens on 27 Feb. 1859.

During his diplomatic career Stanley acquired most of the European, as well as the Arabic, Turkish, Persian, and Chinese tongues. Of the last-named language he published a manual in 1854. He now began extensive travels in the East, stimulated by the example of his intimate friend, Sir Richard Burton [q. v. Suppl. I]. He visited Tartary, Persia, Kurdistan, Ceylon, the Malay Peninsula, Siam, and Java, everywhere studying the languages, customs, and religions of the countries. The East appealed to his imagination and sympathies; and he came to appreciate the Eastern character, value Eastern customs, and accept the Moslem religion for his faith. He was awarded the collar and star of the Turkish order of Osmanieh. He became a prominent member of the Asiatic and Hakluyt Societies, for the latter of which he translated and edited several volumes.

Succeeding to the peerage on the death of his father on 16 June 1869, Stanley settled down to the life of a country gentleman, devoting much care to the improvement of his Cheshire and Anglesey estates, which were largely augmented on the death of his uncle, William Owen Stanley, in 1884. He gave close personal attention to his property, kept his farm buildings in excellent order, and made a hobby of improved dairy accommodation. On the Penrhôs estate he adorned a farm-dairy with scenes from an Indian epic. In spite of a somewhat imperious manner he was esteemed by his tenants.

Though he was a Mussulman, he was an ardent supporter of the Church of England especially in Wales. In the diocese of Bangor in general, and the island of Anglesey in particular, he rebuilt or restored many churches. He also worked energetically to increase the endowments of poor parishes, himself contributing largely to this object.

In the House of Lords, although a frequent questioner and speaker, he was handicapped by deafness, a weak voice, and hurried articulation. Despite conservative predilections he sat on the cross benches, declining to identify himself with either political party.

Stanley took an active interest in the welfare of the native races of India. His knowledge of Indian life and institutions was wide, and he maintained a constant correspondence with educated Indians and regularly studied Indian newspapers. He was always ready to bring Indian grievances before the party leaders, the press, or parliament. He was a warm supporter of the National Congress movement, and would often quote the Arabic proverb that 'a child that does not cry gets no milk.' To Indians resident in England he was a friend and frequent host. He was a keen sportsman and a strict total abstainer, closing three inns on his Alderley estate. Stanley died at Alderley from pneumonia on 10 Dec. 1903. He was buried, by his own desire, in Alderley Park with Moslem rites, the Imam of the Turkish embassy officiating. His death was announced to the Indian National Congress, which was meeting at the time, and the assembly, numbering 1800 persons, rose as a mark of respect.

He married in August 1862 Fabia, daughter of Don Santiago Federico San Roman of Seville, by whom he left no children. Lady Stanley survived her husband till 15 May 1905. His eldest surviving brother, Edward Lyulph, succeeded him in the peerage.

Besides the works mentioned Stanley edited: 1. 'Rouman Anthology,' 1856. 2. 'Essays on East and West,' 1865. He translated for the Hakluyt Society: 'Barbosa's Description of the Coasts of E. Africa and Malabar in the 16th Century,' from the Spanish (1865); 'The Philippine Islands, Moluccas, etc.,' from the Spanish (1868); 'Vasco da Gama's Three Voyages,' from the Portuguese (1869); 'Barbaro and Contarini's Travels to Tana and Persia,' from the Italian (1873); 'Magellan's First Voyage round the World' (1874); 'Alvarez' Narrative of the Portuguese Embassy to Abyssinia, 1520–1527,' from the Portuguese (1881). He also translated Lamennais's 'Essay on Religious Indifference' (1895), and wrote introductions to Hockley's 'Tales of the Zenana' (1874) and Plumer-Ward's 'Rights and Duties of Belligerents and Neutrals' (1875). He was a contributor to the 'Nineteenth Century' and a constant writer of letters to the 'Morning Post.'

[G. E. C[okayne]'s Peerage; Burke's Peerage; Reis and Rayyet, 9 Jan. 1904; family information; personal knowledge.] F. S.

STANLEY, Sir HENRY MORTON (1841–1904), explorer, administrator, author and journalist, was born at Denbigh on 29 June 1841. He was the son of John Rowlands of Llŷs, near Denbigh, and of Elizabeth Parry, the daughter of a small butcher and grazier of that town. The boy was baptised at Tremeirchion church in the name of John Rowlands. His father died in 1843; his paternal grandfather, a well-to-do farmer, declined to have anything to do with him, and he was left to the care of his mother's relatives.

His boyhood was hard and loveless. His mother, who had gone to service in London and afterwards married again, he seldom saw; and he was boarded out with an old couple who lived within the precincts of Denbigh Castle, his maternal uncles paying half-a-crown a week for his maintenance. In 1847 the weekly subsidy was withdrawn, and he was taken to St. Asaph workhouse. Here he spent nine years, exposed to the brutal tyranny of the workhouse schoolmaster, John Francis, a savage ruffian who ended his career in a lunatic asylum. He seems, however, to have taught his victims something. Young Rowlands read the Bible and the religious biographies and romances in the school library; and he also learnt a little geography, arithmetic, drawing, and singing, as well as gardening, tailoring, and joiner's work. His energy of character developed early. In May 1856 the boy wrested a rod from the hands of the brutal schoolmaster, and thrashed him soundly. Then he ran away from the workhouse, and took refuge with his Denbigh relatives. One of his cousins, the master of the National school at Brynford, employed him as a pupil teacher, and taught him some mathematics, Latin, and English grammar. Nine months later he was helping an aunt who kept a farm and inn near Tremeirchion, whence he passed to some other relatives, working-people in Liverpool. He got a place in a haberdasher's shop, and then at a butcher's till he shipped as a cabin-boy in the winter of 1859 on board an American packet bound for New Orleans.

He received no wages for the voyage, and stepped ashore, friendless and penniless. Walking along the streets of New Orleans in search of work, he attracted the notice of a kindly cotton-broker named Henry Stanley, who obtained a situation for him in a store. Mr. Stanley took to the boy from the first, made him free of his house, and eventually adopted him as his son, intending to prepare him for a mercantile career. John Rowlands, thenceforward and for the remainder of his life known by his benefactor's name, spent two happy years travelling among the Mississippi towns with this kindly and cultivated man, and educating himself by sedulous reading. In September 1860 he was sent up to Cyprus Bend, Arkansas, where he was to serve a sort of apprenticeship in a country store, while his adopted father went on a trip to settle some business in Havana. They never saw one another again. The elder Stanley died suddenly in the spring of 1861, without having made any provision for his adopted son.

Meanwhile the state of Arkansas was seething with excitement over the approaching civil war. The young Welshman's friends and neighbours were ardent secessionists, and all the young men were eager to put on uniform for 'Dixie.' Stanley was carried away in the stream, and in July 1861 he entered the service of the Confederate States as a volunteer in the 6th Arkansas regiment. In later life he regarded this step as 'a grave blunder,' for his sympathies, if he had considered the matter, would have been with the north. He served with the Confederates nearly ten months, and had some rough experiences in camp and on the march in the winter of 1861–2. On 6 April in the latter year his regiment was in the thick of the fighting at the battle of Shiloh. Stanley seems to have borne himself bravely, and advancing beyond the firing line when his company retired he was taken prisoner. He was confined at Camp Douglas, Chicago, with some hundreds of other captured Confederates in a state of utter wretchedness and squalor. He endured the miseries of this situation, with disease and death all round him, for some two months. On 4 June he obtained his release by enlisting in the United States artillery. For this transaction he was often reproached afterwards, but in all the circumstances it was excusable enough. He had, however, no opportunity of taking part in the operations of the Federal armies. He was attacked by dysentery and low fever within a few days of his enrolment, taken to hospital, and a fortnight later discharged from the service at Harper's Ferry, without a penny in his pocket, and almost too weak to walk, in a condition 'as low as it would be possible to reduce a human being to, outside of an American prison.'

A kindly farmer took pity on him, and gave him shelter for several weeks until his health was restored by good food and fresh air. He left this harbourage in August 1862, and for the next two years was engaged in an arduous, and at first unpromising, struggle for a livelihood, taking such employment as he could obtain. In the late autumn of 1862 he shipped on board a vessel bound for Liverpool and made his way to his mother's house at Denbigh, very poor, in bad health, and shabbily dressed. He was told that he had disgraced his family and was 'desired to leave as speedily as possible.' He returned to America and the life of the sea. During 1863 and the earlier part of 1864 he made various voyages, sailing to the West Indies, Italy, and Spain. He was wrecked off Barcelona and swam ashore naked, the only survivor of the ship's company. In August 1864 he enlisted in the United States navy, and served as a ship's writer on vessels which took part in the two expeditions against Fort Fisher in North Carolina. A daring exploit commonly credited to him was that of swimming under the fire of the batteries in order to fix a rope to a captured Confederate steamer. Some accounts of these stirring events he sent to the newspapers, and so made his entry into journalism. When he left the navy at the close of the war in April 1865 he had already established a sufficient connection with the press to enable him to wander about the western states as a more or less accredited correspondent of the newspapers. With his budget of adventures, his keen observation, and the graphic descriptive style he was already beginning to acquire, his journalistic progress was rapid. He was well paid for his contributions, and by July 1866 his resources and his connections were sufficient to enable him with a companion to take a trip to Asia Minor. The two young men left Smyrna in search of adventures, and found them, as Stanley usually did. They were attacked by a body of Turkoman brigands, robbed of their money, insulted, beaten, and threatened with death. Escaping with some difficulty, they made their way to Constantinople, where the American minister took up their cause, and obtained compensation for them from the Turkish government. Later in this year, on his way back to America, Stanley revisited his Welsh birthplace, where some of his relatives were now by no means unwilling to recognise the clever and rising young man of the world.

The following year he was sent by the 'Missouri Democrat' as special correspondent with General Hancock on his expedition against the Comanche, Sioux, and Kiowa Indians. His picturesque letters were afterwards republished by himself in the first volume of the book called 'My Early

Travels and Adventures in America and Asia' (London, 1895). Through his contributions to the 'Democrat' and other newspapers, he was able to make ninety dollars a week in addition to his expenses; and 'by economy and hard work' he had saved at the beginning of 1868 six hundred pounds. Hearing of the British expedition to Abyssinia, he threw up his engagement with the Missouri journal, went to New York, and offered his services to the 'Herald,' which gave him a commission as its correspondent for the campaign. He accompanied Sir Robert (Lord) Napier's column in the long and difficult march to Magdala, and described the operations and the entry of the British troops into King Theodore's capital in animated despatches. The campaign established his reputation as a graphic writer and an exceptionally able and energetic journalist. By a smart piece of enterprise he outpaced all his competitors as well as the official despatch-writers, so that London first heard the news of the fall of Magdala through the telegrams of the 'New York Herald.' Stanley was now a man of mark, and was recognised as one of the foremost newspaper correspondents of the time.

His ambition rose to higher things. 'I was not sent into the world,' he wrote long afterwards in his autobiography, 'to be happy or to search for happiness. I was sent for a special work.' He had a premonition that the work was concerned with travel and exploration in Asia or Africa, and he was preparing himself for it by the study of history and geographical literature. His Abyssinian letters are those of the student as well as the adventurer. He had further opportunities of enlarging his knowledge and experience. After the Abyssinian war he wandered about the Mediterranean islands, sending interesting letters from Crete and elsewhere to the 'Herald.' Then he went to Spain, where he saw more fighting, and described the flight of Queen Isabella, and the republican rising of 1869.

It was in October of that year that his great opportunity came. Dr. David Livingstone [q. v.], the famous Scottish missionary and explorer, was lost somewhere in the Lake Tanganyika region, and England and America were interested in his fate. In November 1868 Stanley had been requested by Mr. Gordon Bennett, the proprietor of the 'New York Herald,' to interrupt his Spanish tour in order to go to Egypt and meet Livingstone, who was supposed to be returning down the Nile. He went to Aden and spent ten weeks there, corresponding with the consul at Zanzibar; but no tidings could be gathered of the missionary, and Stanley was sent back to Spain. He was at Madrid in the autumn of the following year when he received a hasty summons to Paris to meet Bennett, who gave him instructions to 'find Livingstone,' wherever he might be. Stanley was to make such arrangements as he thought fit and to be supplied with all the funds he would require. The commission was accepted without a moment's hesitation, and Stanley set to work to carry it out the next day, 17 Oct. 1869. But Mr. Bennett required him to undertake a number of other important missions before entering upon the search for Livingstone. The first was to describe the series of imposing fêtes and ceremonies with which the opening of the Suez Canal was celebrated. Afterwards he went up the Nile and wrote of the scenery and antiquities of Egypt with a growing breadth of knowledge and outlook. Then he was at Jerusalem looking on at Sir Charles Warren's explorations of the underground passages and conduits, and writing with enthusiasm and interest of Biblical topography. From Palestine he passed to Constantinople and began a long journey to the Caucasus, Batoum, Tiflis, Baku, and Resht, and over the Persian table-land through Teheran and Shiraz to Bushire, where he took ship for Bombay. Thus it was not till 6 Jan. 1871 that he reached Zanzibar and was able to begin organising his expedition into the interior of Africa.

He left Bagamoyo on 21 March with a 'compact little force' of three whites, thirty-one armed Zanzibaris, 153 porters, and twenty-nine pack-animals and riding horses. The objective of the journey was Lake Tanganyika, as it was understood that Livingstone was somewhere near the borders of that inland sea. The march was long and arduous. Passing through the Unyamwezi country, Stanley came to the Arab colony of Unyanyembe, where he imprudently took part in the war between the Arabs and the powerful chief Mirambo and suffered considerable losses both of men and stores. He was compelled to turn southward, and at one time was reduced to so much distress through the disorganisation of his caravan and the exactions of native chiefs that he had thoughts of returning to the coast. News of a white man on the lake shore encouraged him to go forward, and on 10 Nov. 1871 he arrived at Ujiji. Livingstone had reached this place only ten days earlier on his return from his long journey west of the lake to trace the course of the Lualaba and ascertain whether it flowed into the Nile. The missionary was 'reduced to the lowest ebb in fortune,' in very bad health, 'a mere ruckle of bones,' almost without followers and provisions. He was, however, still determined to pursue his discoveries, and declined Stanley's offer to escort him back to Zanzibar. The two explorers spent some weeks together on the lake, examined its northern shore, and arrived at Unyanyembe on 18 Feb. 1872. On 14 March Stanley began his journey to the coast, reaching Zanzibar fifty-four days afterwards. A fortnight later he was able to despatch to Unyanyembe a well-equipped caravan with which Livingstone set out on what proved to be the last of his explorations.

Stanley returned to find himself famous. England and America rang with the story of his African adventures, which he proceeded to describe in detail in his book 'How I found Livingstone' (1872). But there was a good deal of jealousy of the young explorer, and a tendency among the high-priests of geographical orthodoxy to sneer at his enterprise as a piece of advertising journalism promoted by a newspaper which had become notorious for its sensationalism. Sir Henry Rawlinson [q.v.], president of the Royal Geographical Society, said that it was not Stanley who had discovered Livingstone, but Livingstone who had discovered Stanley; and some of the newspapers threw doubts upon the authenticity of the whole story of the expedition, and found 'something mysterious and inexplicable' in its leader's narrative. Stanley's own bearing did little to soften the prejudices of those who were determined to dislike him. He was quick of speech and temper, and he answered the aspersions cast upon him and his work with passionate directness. At the meeting of the geographical section of the British Association at Brighton he gave an account of his travels to a large and distinguished audience. In the discussion which followed Francis Galton [q. v. Suppl. II] and other eminent men of science showed little respect for either Stanley or Livingstone as geographical experts, and pointed out the weakness of the missionary's theory that the Lualaba was the source of the Nile. It was reserved for Stanley himself at a later period to demonstrate the erroneousness of this belief. But the attacks upon his friend as well as himself nettled him, and at this meeting and at other gatherings he hit back with a vigour that was sometimes indiscreet, and gave fresh opportunities for hostile criticism. These episodes created a prejudice against him in certain sections of the English press and London society which left traces for years. 'All the actions of my life,' he wrote long afterwards, 'and I may say all my thoughts since 1872, have been strongly coloured by the storm of abuse and the wholly unjustifiable reports circulated about me then. So numerous were my enemies that my friends became dumb.' But the authenticity of the journals he had brought home was certified by Livingstone's family; and in spite of the sneers of the geographers, Stanley received many gratifying proofs of recognition. He was entertained by the duke of Sutherland at Dunrobin Castle, and there presented to Queen Victoria, who sent him a gold snuff-box set with brilliants. His book was widely read and was a great pecuniary success, and so were the lectures which he delivered during the next few months to large audiences, first in England and then in America.

In 1873 the 'New York Herald' commissioned him to accompany the British expedition against the Ashantis under Sir Garnet Wolseley. Stanley won the approval of the English officers by his conduct during the march to Kumassi. Lord Wolseley was struck by his courage. 'I had been,' he wrote (in his *Story of a Soldier's Life*, ii. 342) 'previously somewhat prejudiced against him, but all such feelings were slain and buried at Amoaful. Ever since I have been proud to reckon him amongst the bravest of my brave comrades; and I hope he will not be offended if I add him amongst my best friends also.' Stanley embodied his account of this, and the other British campaign which he had witnessed, in the vivacious pages of his book, 'Coomassie and Magdala,' published in 1874.

On 25 Feb. of this year, on his way back from West Africa, he heard the news of Livingstone's death. 'May I be selected to succeed him,' he wrote in his diary, 'in opening up Africa to the shining light of Christianity!' He was anxious also to settle the great geographical problems left unsolved by Livingstone and by Speke, Burton, Grant, and Baker—that of the Lualaba and of the outlets and extent of the Great Lakes. It was to clear up some of these mysteries that Stanley undertook his next great expedition to equatorial Africa under a joint commission from the 'New York Herald' and the London 'Daily Telegraph.'

In the autumn of 1874, after elaborate and expensive preparations in London and Zanzibar, he was able to begin his march from the coast. He was in his thirty-fourth year, with a store of invaluable experience, and a fund of dauntless energy. The expedition he commanded was probably the best equipped which had ever accompanied white traveller into the interior of Africa, and it did more to open up the heart of the continent and to elucidate its geography than any other before or since. Stanley with two white companions, Francis and Edward Pocock, a white servant, and 356 native followers, left Zanzibar on 11 Nov. It was nearly three years before he emerged upon the shores of the Atlantic, having in the interval crossed Africa from ocean to ocean, determined the limits, area, and northern river connections of Lakes Nyanza and Tanganyika, examined the interesting kingdom of Uganda, and laid the foundations for its conversion to Christianity by his conversations with King Mtesa, and his communications to the Church Missionary Society. From the lake region he struck west for the Lualaba, worked down it till he reached its confluence with the Congo, and then traced the course of that river along its immense curve to the sea. The difficulties of this amazing march through lands unknown even to the Arab traders and slave-hunters were prodigious. Stanley triumphed over them by the exercise of that indomitable resolution, invincible patience, and sagacious judgment which entitle him to a place in the very front rank of the world's greatest explorers. This journey of 1874–7 left an enduring impress upon history: for out of it grew the Congo State and the Anglo-Egyptian dominion on the Upper Nile; and its direct result was to embark the nations of the West upon that 'scramble for Africa' which created new dominions, protectorates, and spheres of influence in the dark continent, and new rivalries and alliances in Europe. Incidentally Stanley solved a geographical problem of the first importance, and revealed the estuary of the Congo as the entrance to one of the mightiest rivers of the earth.

It was on 9 Aug. 1877 that Stanley's wearied column staggered into Boma. His three white companions were dead; he himself had suffered severely from the strain and solitude of the prolonged marches. With that solicitude for his native followers which he always exhibited, in spite of stories to the contrary effect, his first care was to convey them to their homes on the shores of the Indian ocean. He took them round to Zanzibar by sea, and thence made his own way back to England. The full account of his expedition was published in 'Through the Dark Continent' (1878), and the book was read with avidity in every civilised country. Its author threw himself into the task of bringing commercial enterprise and civilised government into the vast regions he had disclosed to the world. He lectured to interested audiences in the great manufacturing and trading centres, corresponded with merchants and financiers, and approached the British government; but he met with no effective support in England for his project of bridging the rapids of the Lower Congo by a road and railway from the sea to the navigable portion of the river. He was reluctantly compelled to obtain assistance from another quarter. King Leopold II of Belgium, a monarch of many faults, but with some large and imaginative ideas, was alive to the possibilities of equatorial Africa. In August 1878 Stanley met King Leopold's commissioners in Paris, and in November he was the king's guest at Brussels, and assisted in the formation of the 'Comité d'Études du Haut Congo,' which was intended to prove the capabilities of the Congo territory, and to lay the basis for its systematic exploitation. And it was as the representative of this committee, which afterwards changed its name to that of 'Association Internationale du Congo,' and with funds supplied by its subscribers, that Stanley again set out for Central Africa.

As before he recruited his immediate followers in Zanzibar, taking some of his old faithful retainers who had served with him through the great trans-continental march. He brought them by sea to the mouth of the Congo, where he arrived on 15 Aug. 1879, just two years after he had reached it on his descent of the great river. He remained in the Congo region for nearly five years, and they were years of arduous and fruitful labour. Their story is told in 'The Congo and the Founding of its Free State,' which Stanley published in 1885. The explorer and adventurer had now to act as pioneer, town-builder, road-maker, administrator, and diplomatist. M. de Brazza, a French traveller who had heard of Stanley's projects, made a rapid dash for the Upper Congo, and just forestalled its discoverer in obtaining from the native chiefs the cession of a long strip of territory on the north bank of the river. Thus was Stanley indirectly responsible for endowing France with a great tropical dominion. He secured for the Association Internationale the whole south bank of the river and the north and west shores as well beyond the confluence with the Mobangi. Then he began the work of establishing a chain of trading stations and administrative stations along the course of the Congo, making treaties with the native chiefs, buying land, building fortified block-houses and warehouses, choosing sites for quays, river-harbours, streets, European settlements, even gardens and promenades. The work was all done under his personal superintendence, and some of it with his own hand; for he often toiled in the midst of his assistants with axe and hammer under the blazing African sun, and his energy in road-making through the boulder-strewn valley of the Lower Congo caused the natives to call him Bula Matari, the Breaker of Rocks, a name which appealed to his imagination and was recalled by him with satisfaction to the end of his life. He was frequently prostrated by fever, and in 1882 he was compelled to make a trip to Europe. He returned after a few weeks' absence and went on steadily with his political and pioneering work along the thousand miles of the navigable Congo from Stanley Pool to Stanley Falls, laying the foundations of that vast administrative system, extending from the Atlantic to the great lakes, and from the Sudan to Barotseland, which became the Congo State. By the summer of 1884 he felt that the initial stage in the establishment of the State was finished, and it only remained for him to hand over his functions to a competent successor.

He returned to Europe, having given to the huge tract of the dark continent which he had opened to the light, definite boundaries, and the elements of what he hoped might develop into an organised system of government under European direction. He had shown high administrative talent, and on the whole a just and liberal conception of the principles by which European rule over Africans should be inspired. If his counsels had been followed, the abuses which overtook the Congo administration some years later would have been avoided. For these scandals of the Belgian régime Stanley was in no way responsible, and they caused him much chagrin and vexation, which he sometimes revealed in private, though his loyalty to his former employer, the king of the Belgians, restrained him from any public expression of opinion on the subject. The king frequently invited him to return to the Congo; but he declined, having no desire (so he wrote in 1896) 'to see mistakes consummated, to be tortured daily by seeing the effects of an ignorant and erring policy,' or to be tempted to 'disturb a moral malaria injurious to the re-organiser.'

But for some time after his return to Europe in 1884 he continued to be closely interested in Congo affairs. He attended the Berlin Conference, in which he gave his services to the American delegation as an expert adviser on geographical and technical questions. He lectured in Germany on the commercial possibilities of the newly discovered region, and did much to rouse German interest in Central African trade and exploitation. In England, by lectures and by personal communication with influential groups of financiers and merchants, he endeavoured to promote enterprise in the equatorial regions, and he tried hard to get his scheme for a Congo railway carried out by English capitalists. He regretted that England had allowed the first-fruits of the harvest he had sown to be reaped by others; but he was anxious that she should still obtain the advantage of being the pioneer in that portion of the African continent which was still unappropriated. It was in pursuance of these ideas that he undertook his next and final mission to the lands of the equator.

The expedition was indirectly due to the catastrophe of 26 Jan. 1885, when Khartoum fell into the hands of the Mahdists and Gordon was killed. The Sudan was submerged by the dervish hordes and the only organised Egyptian force left was that under Emin Pasha in Wadelai on the left bank of the Nile, about 25° north of Lake Nyanza. Emin, a German naturalist whose real name was Eduard Schnitzer, had been appointed by Gordon to the governorship of the equatorial province, and was understood to be in a very precarious situation. His difficulties aroused much sympathy in England; Sir William Mackinnon [q. v. Suppl. I], chairman of the British India Steam Navigation Company, raised a fund for his relief, and received a grant for the same purpose from the Egyptian government. To Stanley was entrusted the organisation and leadership of the rescue expedition. Sufficient funds were in the hands of Mackinnon's committee by the end of 1886; and in December of that year Stanley, who had gone to America on a lecturing tour, was recalled to England by cable to begin his preparations for the adventure.

It proved in some respects the least successful of his greater enterprises. From the outset it was hampered by divided aims and inconsistent purposes. It had other objects besides that of relieving Emin Pasha. Mackinnon and his Glasgow and Manchester friends desired to establish a British sphere of influence and trade in the region between Lake Victoria and the Indian Ocean, and they believed that this project might be carried out in connection with the advance to Wadelai. Stanley, fully concurring in this scheme, was also anxious to do what he could for the Congo State and its proprietors. The expedition had been intended to start from Zanzibar and to march westward through Uganda to Lake Albert. But the route was changed almost at the last moment, and it was decided to work from the east coast and march across the whole extent of the Congo state to the Nile. The north-eastern portion of the state would thus be explored, and it was hoped that Stanley would be able to make suitable arrangements with the local chiefs and Arab slave-traders who had not yet acknowledged the authority of the new government. The decision, as it turned out, led to difficulties and misfortunes of many kinds. There were other adverse circumstances. Stanley was not a man who worked easily with others; his personality was too strong and dominating to allow him to give his complete confidence to his lieutenants. On this occasion a good deal of pressure was brought to bear to induce him to accept the services of some of the young men of spirit and social standing who were eager to accompany him. Among those selected were Major E. M. Barttelot and three other officers of the British army, and Mr. Jameson, a wealthy sportsman and naturalist. These young gentlemen, though brave and adventurous, had no specific knowledge of African exploration, and they did not always carry out their leader's instructions with the unquestioning obedience he expected from those under his command.

He recruited his native followers as usual in Zanzibar, and early in 1887 took them by sea to the mouth of the Congo. The expedition arrived at Stanley Pool on 21 March 1887. Stanley had made an agreement with Tippu Tib, a great Arab trading chief, whereby that powerful personage was appointed governor of the Eastern Congo district, and in return undertook to supply the caravan with provisions, guides, and porters. The party worked its way up the Congo to its junction with the Aruwimi, and then at the end of May turned eastward to march direct to the Albert Nyanza. A fortnight later Yambuya was reached, and at this place Stanley divided his force. Major Barttelot and Jameson were left in command of a strong rear-guard which was to remain at Yambuya and advance when required with the reserve stores and baggage. Stanley himself, with five Europeans and three hundred and eighty-four natives, pushed on, believing Emin to be in such desperate straits that it was essential to lose no time in going to his assistance. The march lay through five hundred and forty miles of absolutely unknown country, much of it dense tropical forest, through which a path had to be cleared with axe, cutlass, and billhook. For five months the party were hidden under this 'solemn and foodless forest,' scarcely ever seeing the open sky, or a patch of clearing, 'with ooze frequently a cubit deep, the soil often as treacherous as ice to the barefooted carrier, creek-beds strewn with sharp-edged oyster shells, streams choked with snags, chilling mist and icy rain, thunder-clatter and sleepless nights, and a score of other horrors.' The Manyuema raiders had scared away such natives as might have supplied food, privation and fever worked havoc in the column, and half the coloured followers had perished before the Albert Nyanza was reached on 13 Dec. Here Stanley expected to find Emin and the steamers he was known to have at his disposal.

The Pasha, however, was not there nor were his vessels. The governor, as it turned out, was by no means anxious to be rescued in the sense intended by his English friends. Relief, in his view, did not include being relieved of his governorship or coming away as a fugitive. He exercised a show of authority in the province, his Egyptian officers, though insubordinate and unruly, yielded him a nominal obedience, and he had made terms with some of the powerful local chiefs. He remained at Wadelai, and for nearly three months the relief column awaited him in vain. At length Stanley sent up one of his assistants, Arthur Jermy Mounteney Jephson [q. v. Suppl. II,] to get into touch with the German Pasha, who was with much difficulty induced to come down the lake in his steamer, with a Sudanese guard, an Italian, and several Egyptian officers, and a welcome and much-needed supply of provisions. Twenty-five days were spent by Stanley in camp with Emin, who continued to exhibit the greatest reluctance to be taken away without his 'people,' the soldiers and civilians who had come with him from Egypt and their native dependants. He was still undecided when Stanley left him to retrace his steps through the forest and look for his rear-guard.

Of that force nothing had been heard, and Stanley's anxiety on its account was fully justified. The rear-column had met with terrible disaster. Tippu Tib had broken faith, and failed to supply food and proper transport; and Major Barttelot had been compelled to linger for ten months at Yambuya before setting out on Stanley's traces with a body of disorderly Manyuema savages, whom Tippu Tib had sent as carriers. With these Barttelot advanced ninety miles to a place called Banalya. A month before Stanley's arrival the Manyuema broke out into mutiny and Barttelot was shot through the heart. Jameson, who had been sent up the Congo to collect fresh carriers, soon afterwards died of fever, two other officers had gone down to the coast, and only one European was left; three-quarters of the native followers were dead or dying. The remnants Stanley re-organised with his own column, and once more made a march through the Aruwimi forest. Many perished during this toilsome and painful journey; but by the first month of 1889 the whole force (reduced, however, to a third of its original number) was collected on the shores of Lake Albert. Emin, whose troops had revolted during Stanley's absence, was at length induced to join the party, with several hundred of his people, Egyptian officers, clerks, native servants, women, and children. The march to the coast occupied the summer and autumn of 1889; and in the course of the journey Stanley discovered the great snow-capped range of Ruwenzori, the Mountains of the Moon, besides a new lake which he named the Albert Edward Nyanza, and a large south-western extension of Lake Victoria. On the morning of 4 Dec. 1889 the expedition reached the ocean at Bagamoyo. Friction again occurred with Emin, who ultimately transferred himself to the German service, leaving Stanley to come home without him. Thus the expedition had failed to achieve its primary object. It had, however, accomplished great things, it had made notable additions to African geography and ethnology, and it had come upon the pigmy tribes who had inhabited the great African forest since prehistoric times. On his way down to the coast Stanley had concluded treaties with various native chiefs which he transferred to Sir William Mackinnon's company and so laid the foundation of the British East African Protectorate. In the short space of fifteen years a single private individual, unsupported by a great armed force or the authority of a government, had been the means of incorporating over two million square miles of the earth's surface with the political system of the civilised world.

Before he returned to Europe Stanley stayed for some weeks in Egypt to rest after the fatigue and privations of a journey which shortened the lives of his younger companions and left his own health shattered. After his arrival in England he had to encounter much hostile comment upon the miscarriage of the Emin Pasha 'rescue' project; and an embittered controversy arose over the tragedy of the rear-guard. But the value of Stanley's work and the magnitude of his achievements were recognised by those best capable of understanding them and by the public at large. If he cannot be cleared of all responsibility for some of the misfortunes incurred in the expedition, his gifts of character were never more conspicuously displayed than in the courage and tenacity by which he redeemed the failures, saved his broken columns from utter ruin, and rendered the enterprise fruitful, and, in its ultimate consequences, epoch-making. Only a man of his iron resolution and invincible resource could have carried through the awful marches and counter-marches in the tropical forests and along the banks of the Aruwimi. The journey from the lakes to the coast, with his own weak and exhausted column escorting Emin's mob of a thousand men, women, and children, a worn, diseased multitude, ill-supplied with food, in itself called for the highest qualities of leadership. Sir George Grey, the veteran pro-consul, wrote from Auckland to congratulate Stanley on his exploit. 'I have thought over all history, but I cannot call to mind a greater task than you have performed. It is not an exploration alone you have accomplished; it is also a great military movement.' Honours and distinctions were conferred upon Stanley by universities and learned societies at home and abroad. Ten thousand people attended the reception given by the Royal Geographical Society at the Albert Hall to hear him lecture on his discoveries; and the vote of thanks to the lecturer was moved by the Prince of Wales. The press controversy only increased the demand for the book, 'In Darkest Africa' (1890), in which he wrote an account of his journey. It was published simultaneously in English, French, German, Italian, Spanish, and Dutch, and in its English form alone it had a sale of a hundred and fifty thousand copies.

On 12 July 1890 Stanley was married in Westminster Abbey to Miss Dorothy Tennant, a lady with many accomplishments and many friends, a painter of distinguished talent, the second daughter of Charles Tennant of Cadoxton, Glamorgan, sometime M.P. for St. Albans. After a restful honeymoon in the south of France and the Engadine, Stanley went with his bride to the United States, where he gave lectures, and had a great reception everywhere. The following year he started with Mrs. Stanley on a prolonged lecturing tour in Australasia, and returned to settle down in England. The king of the Belgians offered him another mission to the Congo; but his health was no longer equal to the strain of any journey more arduous than a holiday trip. Other activities, however, still lay before him. He abandoned his American citizenship and was re-naturalised as a British subject; and in June 1892 he endeavoured, or was induced to endeavour, to enter parliament. Only a fortnight before the polling day he came forward as liberal unionist candidate for North Lambeth, declaring in his election address that his 'one mastering desire' was for 'the maintenance, the spread, the dignity, the usefulness of the British Empire.' He was defeated by a majority of a hundred and thirty votes; and though he heartily detested everything connected with electioneering he consented to stand again. In July 1895, more by his wife's exertions than his own, he was returned as member for North Lambeth with a majority of four hundred and five.

In the House of Commons his career was inconspicuous. He spoke occasionally on African affairs and strongly urged the construction of the Uganda railway. But he made no parliamentary reputation and soon tired of his legislative duties. He had no real interest in party politics, and he disliked the bad air, the late hours, and the dilatory methods of the House of Commons. At the general election of 1900 he did not seek re-election. In October 1897 he paid a visit to South Africa at the invitation of the British South Africa Company and the citizens of Bulawayo, to take part in the opening of the railway connecting that town with the Cape. After a trip through Rhodesia to the Victoria Falls he made a tour in the Transvaal, the Orange Free State, and Natal, conversed with Boers and Uitlanders at Johannesburg, and had an interview with President Kruger, whose conduct and character he felt convinced would eventually lead to a rupture with the imperial government. His estimate of the military as well as the political situation was singularly acute, and in a letter written just two years before the outbreak of the Boer war he pointed out the strategic weakness of the English position in Natal. With the account of his tour published under the title of 'Through South Africa' (1898) his literary activity came to an end.

His health made a country life essential. In the autumn of 1898 he bought the estate of Furze Hill, Pirbright, Surrey; and there he passed most of his time, residing in London occasionally at the house of his wife's mother, 2 Richmond Terrace, Whitehall. In 1899 his services to geographical science and the British empire were tardily recognised by the grand cross of the Bath. The king of the Belgians had already conferred upon him in 1885 the grand cordon of the order of Leopold. His life at Furze Hill was peaceful and happy. He drained, built, and planted, and devoted himself to the improvement of his Surrey estate with the same systematic method and forethought which he had bestowed on greater enterprises. Time and matured experience had toned down his former nervous, self-assertive vitality. He was a man essentially of a kindly and humane disposition, with strong religious convictions; and there was never any warrant for the allegation that he treated the African natives with brutality or callousness, though no doubt in his earlier expeditions he was sometimes hasty and violent in his methods. His views on the subject are expressed in a letter he sent to 'The Times' in December 1890, during the discussion over the Emin relief expedition.

'I have learnt' (he then wrote) 'by actual stress of imminent danger, in the first place, that self-control is more indispensable than gunpowder, and, in the second place, that persistent self-control under the provocation of African travel is impossible without real, heartfelt sympathy for the natives with whom one has to deal.' The natives should be regarded not as 'mere brutes' but 'as children, who require, indeed, different methods of rule from English or American citizens, but who must be ruled in precisely the same spirit, with the same absence of caprice and anger, the same essential respect to our fellow-men.'

His constitution had never completely

recovered from the effects of his equatorial expeditions, particularly the last. On 15 April 1903 he was stricken with paralysis; and after a year of suffering, borne with characteristic fortitude, he died at Richmond Terrace on 10 May 1904. It was his wish to be buried in Westminster Abbey, beside Livingstone. But the requisite permission was not granted; and the traveller who had done more than Livingstone, or any other explorer, to solve the mysteries of African geography, and open up the interior of the dark continent to European trade, settlement, and administration, was buried in the village churchyard of Pirbright. A granite monolith above his grave bears only the inscription 'Henry Morton Stanley, 1841–1904,' with his African name 'Bula Matari,' and by way of epitaph the one word 'Africa.' Lady Stanley was married in 1907 to Mr. Henry Curtis, F.R.C.S.

There is a good portrait of Stanley in Windsor Castle, painted for Queen Victoria by von Angeli in 1890. It is an excellent likeness and a favourable example of the painter's work. Another portrait, also of considerable artistic merit, was painted by Lady Stanley in 1895. A portrait by Sir Hubert von Herkomer was exhibited at the Royal Academy in 1887; and a sculptured bust by Henry Stormont Leifchild in 1873.

[Personal knowledge and private information; The Autobiography of Sir Henry Morton Stanley, edited by his wife, Dorothy Stanley, London, 1909, which contains Stanley's absorbing account of his boyhood and experiences in America up to the time he quitted the Federal army, with many extracts from his later diaries and correspondence and a connecting narrative; Stanley's own My Early Travels and Adventures in America and Asia, 2 vols. 1895; Henry M. Stanley, the Story of his Life, London, n.d., written by a relative, Cadwalader Rowlands, about 1872, gives some information about Stanley's early years and his family, but is inaccurate and untrustworthy. The record of the great African adventures must be read in the vivid pages of the explorer's travel-books, the titles of which are given above; and they may be supplemented by two lighter works, My Kalulu, Prince, King, and Slave, 1873, and My Dark Companions and their Strange Stories, 1893. For the Emin relief expedition and the controversies that arose in connection with it, see H. Brode's Tippoo Tib, 1907; G. Schweitzer's Emin Pasha, his Life and Work, 2 vols. 1898; Major G. Casati's Ten Years in Equatoria and the Return with Emin Pasha, 1891; A. J. Mounteney-Jephson's Emin Pasha and the Rebellion at the Equator, 1890. The books compiled by those who had a close personal interest in the disasters of the rear column, J. R. Troup's With Stanley's Rear Column, 1890; Herbert Ward's With Stanley's Rear Guard, 1891; Mrs. J. S. Jameson's The Story of the Rear Column, 1890; and W. G. Barttelot's Life of Edmund Musgrave Barttelot, 1890, must be read with caution, especially the last, which is written in a spirit of virulent animosity against Stanley. See also for general summaries of Stanley's career and achievements, The Times, and The Standard, 11 May 1904; and an article by the present writer in the Cornhill Magazine for July 1904.] S. J. L.

STANLEY, WILLIAM FORD ROBINSON (1829–1909), scientific instrument maker and author, born at Buntingford, Hertfordshire, on 2 Feb. 1829, was son of John Stanley (1804–1865), a mechanical engineer, inventor, and builder, by his wife Selina Hickman (1809–1881). After scanty education at private schools at Buckland, Hertfordshire, Stanley as a boy successively worked in his father's unsuccessful building business (1843), obtained employment as a plumber and joiner in London through the good offices of his uncle and godfather, William Ford Hickman, who enabled him to attend classes in technical drawing and modelling at the Birkbeck Institution; he then joined his father in 1849 at an engineering works at Whitechapel, where he first substituted for the wooden wheel and spokes of the tricycle, the steel-wired spider wheel which has since become universal. For five subsequent years he was in partnership with a builder at Buntingford, where he commenced studies in architecture, astronomy, geology, and chemistry which he continued through life.

In 1854 Stanley left Buntingford, and with 100*l.* capital rented a shop and parlour at 3 Great Turnstile, Holborn (now rebuilt), and at his father's suggestion started business for himself as a metal and ivory worker and maker of mathematical and drawing instruments, at first in wood but afterwards in metal. A cousin, Henry Robinson, soon joined him with a capital of 150*l.*, but died in 1859. In 1855 his 'Panoptic Stereoscope,' a simplified and cheapened form of stereoscope, brought financial profit, and he started a metal drawing instrument branch, taking an additional shop at Holborn Bars and a skilled assistant. In December 1861 he patented the application of aluminium to the manufacture of mathematical instruments, and next year made a straight line dividing machine for which he was awarded the only medal for mathematical instrument work at the International Exhibition of 1862. This success brought him much work at home and abroad and laid the foundation of his later fortunes. He greatly improved the elegance and stability of surveying instruments, especially the theodolite. In 1866 he published 'A Descriptive Treatise on Mathematical Drawing Instruments,' which became the standard authority (7th edit. 1900). The rapid growth of the business led to the opening of branches at Lincoln's Inn, at London Bridge, and at Norwood, and in 1900 the firm became a limited company, with a capital of 120,000*l.*, under the title of W. F. Stanley & Co.

Stanley's scientific inventions, besides improvements in cameras, lenses, and surveying instruments, included a meteorometer, for recording wind direction, pressure, temperature, moisture, and rainfall (patented in 1867), an integrating anemometer (1883; described in *Quarterly Journal Roy. Meteor. Soc.* ix. 208 seq.), a machine for measuring the height of human beings automatically—one of the first modern 'penny in the slot' machines (1886; cf. caricatures in *Moonshine*, 6 Oct. 1888, and *Scraps*, 8 Dec. 1888), and spirometers, a machine for testing lung capacity (1887; cf. caricature by H. Furniss in *Yorkshire Evening Post*, 6 Sept. 1890).

Stanley's versatile interests embraced geology, astronomy, anthropology, phrenology, painting, music, the drama, photography, and wood-carving. In the intervals of business he lectured and wrote on scientific subjects for learned societies. He became a member of the Physical Society of London in 1882, a fellow of the Geological Society in 1884, and of the Royal Astronomical Society in 1894. An accomplished musician, artist, and architect, he was the composer of part songs; exhibited three oil paintings at the Marlborough Gallery in 1891; and designed his own residence at Norwood. He was fond of foreign travel, and visited Palestine and Egypt in 1889, and Switzerland in 1893.

To Norwood, whither Stanley retired in later life, and where he took a prominent part in philanthropic and municipal affairs, Stanley was a generous benefactor. There he designed and on 2 Feb. 1903 opened to the public the Stanley Public Hall and Gallery at a cost of 13,000*l.* for the purpose of lectures, concerts, and entertainments. A clock tower and hall were added in 1904. A further benefaction was a technical school, which was opened in 1907, for the education of boys as skilled scientific mechanics. The school met with instant success, and Stanley subsequently presented the buildings to the public with an endowment valued at 50,000*l.* In 1907 Stanley was made an honorary freeman of Croydon, and a clock tower was unveiled in South Norwood to commemorate his golden wedding.

Stanley died at his residence, Cumberlow, South Norwood, on 14 Aug. 1909, and was buried at Crystal Palace cemetery. He married on 22 Feb. 1857 Eliza Ann Savoury (*d.* April 1913) but had no issue. Many Croydon and Norwood hospitals, charities, and technical schools benefited under his will.

Besides the work already mentioned Stanley published: 1. 'Proposals for a New Reform Bill,' 1867. 2. 'Photography Made Easy,' 1872. 3. 'Stanley's Pretty Figure Book Arithmetic,' fol. 1875. 4. 'Experimental Researches into the Properties and Motions of Fluids,' 1881. (this work, which embodies the results of much study and research, was commended by Darwin and Tyndall; a supplementary work on sound motions in fluids was unfinished, and remains in manuscript). 5. 'Surveying and Levelling Instruments, theoretically and practically described,' 1890; 3rd edit. 1901. 6. 'Notes on the Nebular Theory,' 1895. 7. 'Joe Smith and his Waxworks,' 1896. 8. 'The Case of the Fox: a Political Utopia,' 1903.

[William Ford Stanley, his Life and Work, mainly autobiographical, by Richard Inwards, 1911; The Times, 16 Aug. 1909; Croydon Times, 18 Aug. 1909; Engineer, 20 Aug. 1909; Engineering, 28 Sept. 1909 (an account of his inventions); Norwood News, 28 Aug. 1909; Quarterly Journal Geol. Soc. 1910, vol. lxvi. p. lii.; Astron. Soc. Monthly Notices, 1910, lxx. 300.] W. B. O.

STANNARD, Mrs. HENRIETTA ELIZA VAUGHAN, writing under the pseudonym of 'John Strange Winter' (1856–1911), novelist, born on 13 Jan. 1856 in Trinity Lane, York, was only daughter of Henry Vaughan Palmer, rector of St. Margaret's, York, by his wife Emily Catherine Cowling. Her father had been an officer in the Royal Artillery before taking orders, and came of several generations of soldiers. Her great-great-great-grandmother was Hannah Pritchard [q. v.] the actress. Henrietta was educated at Bootham House School, York. In 1874 she began her career as a novelist by writing under the pseudonym of 'Violet Whyte' for the 'Family Herald.' Her connection with that journal lasted for ten years, and she contributed to it 42 short stories issued as supplements, besides many long serials. In 1881 appeared 'Cavalry Life,' a collection of regimental sketches, and in 1883 'Regimental Legends.' Both bore the name of 'John Strange Winter,' a character in one of the tales in the former volume. The publisher refused to bring out the books under a feminine pseudonym. The public assumed the author to be a cavalry officer. She retained the name for literary and business purposes through life.

Miss Palmer married at Fulford, York, on 26 Feb. 1884, Arthur Stannard, A.M.I.C.E. (*d.* 1912) and had issue one son and three daughters. She settled in London and continued her literary labours. In 1885 'Bootles' Baby: a story of the Scarlet Lancers,' the tale that assured her popularity, appeared in the 'Graphic.' Two million copies were sold within ten years of its first publication. Tales of a similar character, with military life for their setting, followed in rapid succession until her death. There are 112 entries to her name in the British Museum Catalogue. She found an admirer of her work in Ruskin, whom she visited at Sandgate in 1888. Ruskin wrote of 'John Strange Winter' as 'the author to whom we owe the most finished and faithful rendering ever yet given of the character of the British soldier' (*Daily Telegraph*, 17 Jan. 1888; cf. also RUSKIN'S *Letters*, 1909, ii. 592–3). For some time Ruskin and John Strange Winter constantly corresponded.

In 1891 she started a penny weekly magazine, 'Golden Gates'; in 1892 the title was altered to 'Winter's Weekly,' and so continued until 1895. In 1896 the health of her husband and of her youngest daughter made residence at the seaside imperative, and Dieppe became her home until 1901, when she returned to London, retaining a house at Dieppe for summer residence until 1909. She wrote enthusiastic articles about Dieppe which greatly increased its popularity. The municipality presented her with a diamond ring in recognition of her services to the town.

Mrs. Stannard wrote vivaciously, and sketched with lightness of touch the personality of the British officer as he was at the end of the purchase system. Well known in journalistic circles, she was first president of the Writers' Club (1892), and was president of the Society of Women Journalists (1901–3). She was intensely fond of animals. Interesting herself in matters concerning women's dress and personal appearance, she towards the end of her life compounded and sold a number of toilet preparations for the hair and complexion which found wide acceptance.

Mrs. Stannard died, from complications following an accident, on 13 Dec. 1911 at York House, Hurlingham, Putney. She was cremated and the ashes interred at Woking crematorium. Notwithstanding her many activities she left only 547*l.*

A crayon drawing by Lionel Smythe (1887) and an etched portrait by Batley (1889) were in possession of Mr. Arthur Stannard; a pastel portrait (1891) by Mrs. Jopling is owned by the artist.

[The Times, 15 Dec. 1911; Daily Chronicle, 15 Dec. 1911; Helen C. Black's Notable Women Authors of the Day, 1893; Men and Women of the Time, 1899; Allibone, Suppl. II, 1891; private information.] E. L.

STANNUS, HUGH HUTTON (1840–1908), architect, author, and lecturer, born at Sheffield on 21 March 1840, was son of the Rev. Bartholomew Stannus, member of an old Irish family, by his wife Jane, daughter of the Rev. William Hutton of Belfast. His first artistic training was gained in Sheffield under H. D. Lomas at the local School of Art, after which he was articled to the firm of H. E. Hoole & Co. in that town, whose foundry was then engaged in producing work from the designs of Alfred Stevens [q. v.]. From this apprenticeship resulted a close acquaintance with the details of artistic metal casting. Some designs by Stannus for foundry work were selected for the Exhibition of 1862, and an 'Essay on the History of Founding in Brass, Copper, and Bronze' won him in 1881 the freedom and livery of the Founders' Company, of which he became in 1907 sub-warden. A more important consequence of the employment at Hoole's was the personal acquaintance with Stevens. Stannus became his pupil, his assistant, his devoted friend, and afterwards his biographer. With Stevens he worked at the production of the Wellington monument for St. Paul's Cathedral, and the long story of the delays which beset that production may be read in 'Alfred Stevens and his Work' (1891), an important folio in which Stannus commemorated his master.

Some years before the death of Stevens in 1875 Stannus appears to have decided to make his training more definitely architectural, and in 1872 he was studying architecture at the Royal Academy Schools. In 1873 he passed the voluntary examination of the Royal Institute of British

Architects with such distinction as to be awarded the Ashpitel Prize. In 1877 he won at the same institute the silver medal for essays with a paper on 'The Decorative Treatment of Constructive Ironwork' (printed Jan. 1882). He was elected an associate of the institute in 1880 and a fellow in 1887, taking till the year of his death an active part in its meetings and committee work. His independent practice dated from 1879, but was never extensive, and he never established an office. After bringing to a close Stevens's work on the Wellington monument, he was engaged simultaneously with (Lord) Leighton [q. v. Suppl. I] and (Sir) Edward J. Poynter in the preparation of a design for the decoration of the cupola of St. Paul's, which was not carried out. Stannus's executed work consisted chiefly of structural or decorative alterations to existing buildings such as the Cutlers' Hall, the gas offices, the unitarian church, and the Channing Hall at Sheffield, the residences of Sir Edwin Durning Lawrence at Ascot and at Carlton House Terrace, the Phœnix brewery at Bedford, a house for Mr. Faber, M.P., at Beckenham, and Norman Macleod's church in Edinburgh. He designed the Sunday School centenary memorial at Essex church (unitarian), Notting Hill, and his own house, The Cottage, Hindhead, Surrey. He also carried out some work in the picture gallery at Kew designed by James Fergusson [q. v.]. When in 1903 it was decided further to complete the Wellington monument by the addition of the equestrian statue of the duke, Stannus, whose forethought had preserved Stevens's plaster model for the figure, was able to lay before the authorities several important drawings and other evidences of the original designer's intentions.

Stannus had great powers of architectural composition. A scheme which he submitted in the competition for the University of California was considered exceptionally skilful. But his energies were mainly absorbed from the age of forty to sixty in the work of a teacher and lecturer, to which he brought exceptional powers of analysis and great lucidity of expression. From 1881 to 1900 he taught modelling at the Royal Academy, and he held appointments as lecturer at University College, London, and at the Royal College of Art, South Kensington. For two years (1900–1902) he was director of architectural studies at the Manchester School of Art, and subsequently (1905–1907) he lectured at the evening school of the Architectural Association. In 1890 and 1898 he was Cantor lecturer to the Society of Arts, and twice received the Society's silver medal. In 1891 he delivered for the same society a course of lectures on Romanesque Architecture in North Italy.

Stannus belonged to the Hellenic and Japan Societies, to the St. Paul's Ecclesiological Society, to the Society of Arts and Crafts, and to that for the Preservation of Ancient Buildings. He had great knowledge of all periods of art, being a continual student and a frequent traveller. His collection of examples, sketches, and photographic lantern-slides was exceptional. He was a good linguist, a great reader, a musician, and in a measure a poet. His writing, always carefully studied, shows certain idiosyncrasies of punctuation and style. He died at Hindhead on 18 Aug. 1908.

In 1872 he married Ann, daughter of John Anderson, B.A. London, who with two daughters and a son (Dr. Hugh S. Stannus) survived him.

Apart from the work on Stevens, Stannus's publications, which were largely based on his lectures, were: 1. 'Decorative Treatment of Natural Foliage,' 1891. 2. 'Decorative Treatment of Artificial Foliage,' 1895. 3. 'Theory of Storiation in Applied Art,' 1898. 4. 'Some Principles of Form Design in Applied Art,' 1898. 2. 'Some Examples of Romanesque Architecture in North Italy,' 1901. He also revised for the 3rd (English) edition Meyer's 'Handbook of Ornament,' and assisted James Fergusson in some of the illustrations for his books. He left materials for a work on the classic orders, a subject upon which he had some original ideas.

[Athenæum, 29 Aug. 1908; R.I.B.A. Journal, 3rd Series, 1908, xv. 587, 588 (by R. Phené Spiers) and 621; personal knowledge and information from Mrs. Stannus.] P. W.

STARK, ARTHUR JAMES (1831–1902), painter, born in Beaufort Street, Chelsea, on 6 Oct. 1831, was the only son of James Stark [q. v.], the landscape painter, by his wife Elizabeth Young Dinmore. An artistic aptitude was early fostered by lessons from his father. Between 1839 and 1849, when the family was residing at Windsor, young Stark studied animal painting under Edmund Bristow [q. v.], an intimate friend of the family, and acquired a love of the Thames valley, where he found the subjects of many of his pictures. As early as 1848 he exhibited at the Royal Academy and the British Institution, his first picture at the Academy being hung on the line between works by Landseer and Sir Francis Grant. In 1849 the elder Stark removed to London for the sake of the education of his son, who entered the Royal Academy schools in the same year. For some time young Stark used to paint in the stables of Messrs. Chaplin & Horne, the carriers, and at a later period he rented for three years at Tattersall's a studio where he perfected his painting of horses. His ability became known, and in 1874, from a fear of hampering his progress, he declined a private offer of the post vacated by the death of Frederick William Keyl [q. v.], of animal painter to Queen Victoria. For many years he taught art in London as well as painted. In 1886 he retired to Nutfield, Surrey, where he devoted the remainder of his life exclusively to painting.

Stark was one of the last artists of the Norwich school (of which his father was a chief disciple), and probably the only one to acquire a reputation for animal painting. The minute touch of his earlier work shows the strong influence of his father, but his later pictures display a more marked individuality and abandon many of the traditions of his father's school. He was fond of depicting homely English scenes, such as haymaking, harvesting, and the farmyard; his landscapes were largely derived from the Thames valley (especially the neighbourhood of Sonning), Surrey, and Norfolk. He painted both in oil and water-colour.

Between 1848 and 1887 he exhibited thirty-six pictures at the Royal Academy, thirty-three at the British Institution, fifty-one at the Society of British Artists, three at the Institute of Painters in Water Colours, and fifty-seven at other galleries. Among his works were 'A Water Mill' (1848), 'Forest Scene' (1850), 'Interior of a Stable' (1853), 'A Quiet Nook' (1857), 'A Shady Pool' (1861), 'In Moor Park, Rickmansworth' (1865), 'Timber Carting' (1874), 'A Farmyard' (1875), and 'Dartmoor Drift' (1877)—the last-named was one of his best paintings.

A water-colour drawing of 'Calves' is at the Victoria and Albert Museum; three water-colours, 'Interior of a Windmill (on Reigate Heath) fitted up as a Chapel,' 'Windmill and Cottage,' and 'Heath Scene,' are at the British Museum, and an oil painting of 'Dartmoor Ponies' is in the Norwich Castle Museum. Exhibitions of works by him were held at the Dudley Galleries, 169 Piccadilly, in Oct. 1907 and Oct. 1911.

Stark, who was a man of culture and high principle, and of simple and genial manner, was at work till within a few days of his death at Thornbank, South Nutfield, Surrey, on 29 Oct. 1902. He was cremated at Woking, and a tablet was placed to his memory in Nutfield old church. His portrait in miniature by H. B. Love (1837); in oil, as a child, by Charles Hancock, and in water-colour by his wife (1883) are in the possession of his widow.

He married on 20 Nov. 1878, at Ascot, Rose Isabella youngest daughter of Thomas Fassett Kent, counsel to the chairman of committees in the House of Lords, by whom he had a daughter (*b.* 1879) and a son (*b.* 1881), both of whom survived him.

[Information kindly supplied by Mrs. Stark; The Times, 30 Oct. 1902; Eastern Daily Press, 10 Oct. 1911; A. P. Nicholson in The Nineteenth Century and After, April 1907; Graves's Dict. of Artists, Roy. Acad. and British Institution.] B. S. L.

STEGGALL, CHARLES (1826–1905), organist and composer, son of Robert William Steggall, was born in London on 3 June 1826. He was educated at the Royal Academy of Music, principally under Sir William Sterndale Bennett. In 1848, while still a student, he was appointed organist of Christ Chapel, Maida Vale, and in 1849 was consulted by Bennett as to the inauguration of the Bach Society, of which he was honorary secretary till its dissolution in 1870. He was appointed a professor of the organ at the Royal Academy of Music in 1851; and next year graduated Mus.Bac. and Mus.Doc. at Cambridge. In 1855 he was chosen the first organist of Christ Church, Lancaster Gate, being at the same time organist of Clapham grammar school, and in 1864 he became organist of Lincoln's Inn Chapel, where he remained till his death, though for the later years his son, William Reginald Steggall, usually discharged the duties. Between 1850 and 1870 he frequently lectured on musical subjects in London and the provinces. He was one of the founders of the Royal College of Organists in 1864, gave the inaugural lecture, and, with John Hullah and Edward John Hopkins, conducted the first examination in July 1866. In 1884 he joined the board of directors of the Royal Academy of Music; and when Principal Macfarren died, in 1887, he took his place until the election of a successor. He resigned his professorship at the Academy in 1903, after fifty-two years' service. He died in London on 7 June 1905. As a composer he is best known by his church music—hymn tunes, anthems, services, carols, chants, organ compositions and arrangements. He wrote an 'Instruction Book for the Organ' (1875) edited 'Church Psalmody' (1848) and six motets of Bach, and succeeded Dr. W. H. Monk as musical editor of 'Hymns Ancient and Modern' (1889).

[Musical Times, July 1905; Musical Herald, July 1905, with portrait; Grove's Dictionary of Music; personal knowledge.] J. C. H.

STEPHEN, Sir ALEXANDER CONDIE (1850–1908), diplomatist, born at Dudley, Worcestershire, on 20 July 1850, was third and youngest son of Oscar Leslie Stephen (1819–1898) by his wife Isabella, daughter of William Birkmyre. Oscar Leslie Stephen was a director of the London and North Western and chairman of the North London railways, and by his descent from James Stephen of Ardenbraught was third cousin of Sir James Stephen, (1789–1859) [q. v.]. Stephen was at Rugby for rather more than a year (1865–6). Subsequently in 1876 he entered the diplomatic service, and in 1877 was sent as attaché to St. Petersburg. His aptitude in foreign languages, especially Russian, assisted his rapid promotion, and having been appointed third secretary at Constantinople in 1879, he was in 1880 put in charge of the consulate-general at Philippopolis, and thus became the official representative of Great Britain in Eastern Rumelia, the southern province of Bulgaria which had obtained 'autonomy' under that name by the provisions of the treaty of Berlin. At the end of 1881 Stephen, who had been made C.M.G. that year, was promoted second secretary and transferred to Teheran, being then in receipt of special allowances in respect of his knowledge of Russian, Turkish, and Persian. In 1882–3 he was employed on special service in Khorassan, the north-east province of Persia, at that time of critical importance as the neighbour both of Afghanistan and of that part of Central Asia over which the Russian power was extending. In 1884 Stephen was made C.B., and in 1885 was appointed assistant commissioner to Sir Peter Lumsden in the Anglo-Russian Commission for the demarcation of the north-west boundary of Afghanistan. In this capacity he was present at the affray between Russian and Afghan troops at Penjdeh, which involved the danger of war between England and Russia, and he was sent home with the official despatch describing that event. He rode in six days from the Afghan frontier to Astrabad on the Caspian Sea, and delivered his despatch sooner than had been thought possible, but peace had been practically secured by telegraphic communications before his arrival in England. Stephen's next appointment was at Sofia, and he held it when in 1886 Prince Alexander of Bulgaria was kidnapped. It is said that his presence of mind saved the Prince's private papers from falling into the hands of the conspirators. In the following year Stephen was second secretary, first at Vienna and then at Paris. It is probable that had he exerted himself to that end he might have filled the highest positions in his service, but in 1893 he accepted the office of chargé d'affaires at Coburg, and in 1897 was appointed minister resident both to Saxony and Coburg, his services being acknowledged by his creation in 1894 as K.C.M.G., and in 1900 as K.C.V.O. The discharge of his duties at Coburg involved close and constant personal relations with King Edward VII, when Prince of Wales, and various members of the English and the related royal families. In 1901, after the accession of King Edward VII, Stephen retired from the diplomatic service, and became a groom-in-waiting to the king, an appointment which he held until his death. In that situation he made good use of his exceptional acquirements and experience.

He died at 124 Knightsbridge, London, after an operation for appendicitis on 10 May 1908. He was unmarried. He wrote in French a short 'Comédie vaudeville' (1872), and published 'The Demon,' a translation of a Russian poem by Mikhail Yar'evich Lermontov (1875; 2nd edit. 1881), and a volume of stories adapted from Persian originals called 'Fairy Tales of a Parrot' (1892).

A cartoon portrait by 'Spy' appeared in 'Vanity Fair' in 1902.

[The Times, 11 May 1908; private information; Lodge's Peerage.] H. S.

STEPHEN, Sir LESLIE (1832–1904), first editor of this Dictionary, man of letters and philosopher, was born at a house in Kensington Gore, now 42 Hyde Park Gate, on 28 Nov. 1832. His grandfather, James Stephen, his father, Sir James Stephen, and his elder brother, Sir James Fitzjames Stephen, are already noticed separately. His father's sister, Annie

Mary, married Thomas Edward Dicey and was mother of Edward James Stephen Dicey [q. v. Suppl. II] and of Prof. Albert Venn Dicey. His mother, whom Leslie credited with 'strength absolutely free from harshness,' was Jane Catherine, daughter of John Venn, the evangelical rector of Clapham. Her children numbered three sons and two daughters. The eldest son, Herbert Venn, died in 1846 aged twenty-four, and the elder daughter, Frances Wilberforce, in infancy in 1824. The surviving daughter, Caroline Emelia, the youngest of the family, is noticed at the close of this article.

In the autumn of 1840 Leslie's parents removed to Brighton for the sake of his health, which suffered from a precociously active brain. There he attended a day school, but on 15 April 1842 he and his brother James Fitzjames entered Eton College as town boys. His parents took a house at Windsor so that their sons might live at home. Leslie made little progress, and was removed by his father at Christmas 1846. After a short experience of a small day school at Wimbledon during 1847, he was sent to King's College, London, on 15 March 1848. There he attended F. D. Maurice's lectures in English literature and history, but they failed to rouse in him any enthusiasm, although his literary sympathies were pronounced from childhood. His health was still uncertain. At Easter 1850 he left King's College. After some coaching at Cambridge from Llewelyn Davies he entered Trinity Hall at Michaelmas 1850. At the end of his first year he won a scholarship in mathematics.

To the university Stephen owed an immense debt. His health rapidly improved and became robust, while he quickly assimilated the prevalent atmosphere of dry common-sense. Although mathematics was his chief study, he developed his youthful taste for literature, tried his hand at sketching, and taught himself shorthand, which he practised in correspondence with his sister till the end of his life. He spoke occasionally at the Union Society on the liberal side, and joined the library committee. He was spontaneously drawn to athletics, to which he was previously almost a stranger, and soon distinguished himself as a long-distance runner, a walker of unusual endurance, and 'a fanatical oarsman.' His chief undergraduate friend was Henry Fawcett, who migrated to Trinity Hall in 1853. In Jan. 1854 Stephen was twentieth wrangler in the mathematical tripos. He continued to reside at Cambridge in the hope of gaining a fellowship. In the following long vacation he went to Heidelberg to improve his German.

On 23 Sept. 1854 Stephen was appointed to a Goodbehere fellowship at his college. It was a small post bringing only 100*l.* a year. Its holder was bound to give some assistance to the two college tutors and to take holy orders within a year. The clerical condition presented no difficulty to Stephen. He had been reared by his parents in orthodox beliefs and had taken them on trust. Accordingly on 21 Dec. 1855 he was ordained deacon by the archbishop of York, and became priest on Trinity Sunday 1859. He pleased his father by entering the church, and the step provided him with a modest livelihood. Meanwhile on 29 April 1856 he was admitted to the junior tutorship which then fell vacant at Trinity Hall, and was only tenable by a clergyman. He occasionally preached in the college chapel and at St. Edward's church in the town, and he taught mathematics to the more promising undergraduates. But his chief energies were absorbed by the social welfare of the college and its athletic prestige, by private study of current literature and philosophy, and by intercourse with the manliest and most enlightened of resident graduates.

Stephen's athletic prowess brought him his first fame. For the college boat, which he coached for many years, he cherished an especial affection (cf. Sir G. O. Trevelyan in *Macmillan's Magazine*, May 1860). His staying power grew as a runner and walker. He walked from Cambridge to dine in London—fifty miles—in twelve hours. In 1860 he won the mile race (5 mins. 4 sec.) at the university athletic games, which he helped to start, and he encouraged the inauguration of the inter-university sports which began in 1864. But it was as a mountaineer that his athletic zeal showed to best advantage. In 1855 he had tramped through the Bavarian highlands in Tyrol, and in 1857, during a holiday spent at Courmayeur, he made, with Francis Galton, his first Swiss ascent—the Col du Géant. Next year, after climbing Monte Rosa, he joined the Alpine Club, of which he remained a member till death. Thenceforth he was an ardent Alpinist and distinguished himself by many new ascents. In 1860 he described the 'Ascent of the Allalinhorn' in Francis Galton's 'Vacation Tourists' (1861). In 1861 he first vanquished the Schreckhorn in the Oberland and made the passage of the Eiger Joch, writing of these exploits in

'Peaks, Passes, and Glaciers' (vol. ii. 1862). In the same year (1861) he achieved the first complete ascent of Mont Blanc from St. Gervais. In 1862 he added to his conquests the Jungfrau Joch, the Viescher Joch, and the Monte della Disgrazia. In 1864 he scaled the Lyskamm, Zinal Rothhorn, and the Jungfrau. The summer of 1866 was spent in the eastern Carpathians with Mr. James Bryce.

After his first marriage in 1867 his mountaineering activity gradually diminished (cf. his *Regrets of a Mountaineer*, Nov. 1867). But he explored the Dolomites in 1869 and was in Switzerland again in 1871, in 1873, and 1875. In later life he only visited the Alpine country in the winter. The last visit was paid in 1894, when he stayed at Chamonix with his friend of early mountaineering days, M. Gabriel Loppé, the French Alpine artist.

Stephen became a master of mountain craft, fleet of foot, but circumspect and cautious. His merit was acknowledged by his election as president of the Alpine Club (1865–8). From 1868 to 1871 he served, too, as editor of the 'Alpine Journal.' But mountaineering appealed to Stephen not only as a sport but also as an incentive to good-fellowship. Many of his closest friendships were formed in the Alps. With his guide Melchior Anderegg, whom he regularly employed from his first season in 1858, he was always on the best of terms. Anderegg was Stephen's guest in London in 1861 and 1888. Stephen felt deeply the beauty of the mountains, and it was his Alpine experiences which led him to become an author. His first book was a modest translation from the German of H. Berlepsch's 'The Alps: or Sketches of Life and Nature in the Mountains.' But he was soon contributing accounts of his Alpine ascents to the 'Alpine Journal' and elsewhere. These papers he collected in 1871 as 'The Playground of Europe,' with a frontispiece by his fellow-mountaineer Edward Whymper [q. v. Suppl. II] (2nd edit. revised, 1894, reissued in Longmans' 'Silver Library,' 1899). In the literature of mountaineering, Stephen's papers inaugurated a new style. It was vivid, direct, and unpretendingly picturesque, at the same time as it was serious and reflective.

The years which Stephen spent at Cambridge as a college don were probably the happiest of his life. But his position underwent an important change in the summer of 1862. His reading in Mill, Comte, and Kant, and his independent thought had led him to reject the historical evidences of Christianity. He declined to take part in the chapel services. Thereupon at the Master's request he resigned his tutorship. Owing apparently to the influence of his friend Fawcett, he was allowed to retain his fellowship and some minor offices. He had never taken the clerical vocation very seriously. He had not examined closely the religious convictions in which he was bred, and he abandoned them with relief and without mental perturbation. He did not, he said, lose his faith, he merely discovered that he never had any. Stephen's scepticism steadily grew thenceforth, and on 25 March 1875 he took advantage of the Act of 1870, and relinquished his orders.

When he was freed from tutorial and clerical duties, Stephen's interests took a wider range. He naturally sympathised with the views of the philosophical radicals of whom Mill was high priest. In university politics he was on the side of reform and desired to see the efficiency of the university increased. In 1863 he published a tract, 'The Poll Degree from the Third Point of View,' in which he urged the need of making the pass examination more adaptable to students' needs and abilities. But he was not greatly excited by university controversies. He was more stirred by the political ambitions of his college friend Henry Fawcett, professor of political economy in the university, who had become blind in 1859. Resolved to enter the House of Commons in the radical interest, Fawcett early in 1863 vainly contested the town of Cambridge with Stephen's active help. Next year Fawcett stood, again unsuccessfully, for Brighton; Stephen was his ablest electioneering lieutenant, and, by way of advocating his friend's candidature, ran a daily paper which he wrote himself and called 'The Brighton Election Reporter.'

One political issue of the day moved Stephen's especial ardour. He was a staunch adherent of the cause of the North in the American civil war, and an enthusiastic champion of slavery emancipation. In the summer of 1863, armed with some introductions from his first cousin, Edward Dicey, he went to America to study the question at first hand. At Boston he met J. R. Lowell, who was soon an intimate friend, and he made the acquaintance of Garrison and Wendell Phillips. His itinerary took him from New York to Chicago, down the Mississippi to St. Louis, and thence by Cincinnati to Philadelphia and Washington. After seeing Abraham Lincoln at the White House he visited the seat of war in Virginia and inspected General Mead's army. He came home more convinced than before of the righteousness of the northern plea. Subsequently he published 'The Times on the American War, by L. S.' (1865), in which he sought to refute the English arguments in favour of the South.

At the end of 1864 Stephen left Cambridge for London in order to embark on a literary career. He retained his fellowship till 1867, when it lapsed on his marriage. At times he thought of attempting other than literary occupation. He was for a brief period secretary of the newly formed Commons Preservation Society in 1865, and on 27 May 1867 he was admitted a student of the Inner Temple, in spite of some doubt as to his eligibility owing to his clerical orders; but he was not called to the bar, and removed his name from the books of the Inn in 1875. Sufficient literary work was quickly offered him to make it needless for him to seek employment elsewhere. His brother, James Fitzjames Stephen, was between 1860 and 1870 dividing his practice at the bar with a vigorous pursuit of journalism. He was acquainted with Carlyle, Froude, and other literary leaders, and to his recommendations Leslie owed a promising start in the literary world. Leslie was soon invited to write for the 'Saturday Review,' and for many years he contributed two articles a week—a review and a 'middle.' There he attacked every subject from popular metaphysics to the university boatrace, but avoided politics and religion, on which the paper pursued conservative lines. But more important to his future literary career was his brother's early introduction of him to George Smith, who during 1864 was laying the foundation of a new evening paper, the 'Pall Mall Gazette.' The editor, Frederick Greenwood, welcomed Stephen's co-operation, and from the second number on 8 Feb. 1865 he was a regular contributor of miscellaneous literary matter for six years, and was an occasional contributor at later dates, notably in 1880, when Mr. John Morley suddenly succeeded Greenwood as editor. To the 'Pall Mall' he contributed at the outset a series of frankly humorous and occasionally flippant 'Sketches from Cambridge, by a Don' (1865). From October 1866 to August 1873 he wrote, too, a fortnightly article on English affairs for the weekly 'Nation' of New York, of which the editor was Edwin Lawrence Godkin [q. v. Suppl. II]. Here Stephen dealt with the political situation at Westminster and occasionally attended for the purpose the sittings of the House of Commons, which wearied him.

At the same time he formed important connections with the chief monthly magazines. In 1866 he began writing for the 'Cornhill Magazine,' another of George Smith's literary ventures. At first he wrote there on social themes under the signature of 'A Cynic' (not reprinted), but he soon confined himself in the 'Cornhill' to literary criticism, which, according to the practice of the magazine, was anonymous. His literary essays from 1871 onwards bore the general heading 'Hours in a Library,' and were collected from time to time in separate volumes (1st ser. 1874; 2nd ser. 1876; 3rd ser. 1879). His position as an independent and sagacious literary critic was thereby established. His relations with the 'Cornhill' had meanwhile grown in importance. In February 1871 George Smith appointed him editor, and he held the post for more than eleven years. He was thus enabled to abandon much of his journalism, but he remained faithful to the 'Saturday.' In the 'Cornhill' magazine he sought to uphold a high standard of theme and style. He encouraged young writers, many of whom afterwards became famous, and with whom he formed cordial and enduring personal relations. Robert Louis Stevenson, Thomas Hardy, James Sully, W. E. Henley, Henry James, and Edmund Gosse were among the contributors in whose work Stephen took especial pride. When visiting Edinburgh to lecture on the Alps in February 1875 he sought out in the infirmary there W. E. Henley, who had offered the magazine his 'In Hospital' series of poems; a day or two later Stephen introduced R. L. Stevenson to the sick-room, with the result that an interesting literary friendship was formed. Matthew Arnold's 'Literature and Dogma' ran through the 'Cornhill' under Stephen's auspices; but it was in purely literary work that the magazine won its reputation during Stephen's editorship.

Not that literature was by any means the editor's sole personal interest. Religious and philosophical speculation engaged much of his attention, and he presented his results elsewhere than in the 'Cornhill.' J. A. Froude, who was editor of 'Fraser's Magazine,' and Mr. John Morley, who was editor of the 'Fortnightly Review,' gave him every opportunity of defining his position in the pages of those periodicals. A collection of religious and philosophic essays, which he fittingly entitled 'Essays on Free Thinking and Plain Speaking,' came out in

1873. The book constituted him a leader of the agnostic school, and a chief challenger of the popular religion, which he charged with inability to satisfy genuine spiritual needs. But Stephen was not content to dissipate his energy in journalism or periodical writing. His leisure was devoted to an ambitious 'History of English Thought in the Eighteenth Century' (1876, 2 vols.), in which he explained the arguments of the old English deists and the scepticism of Hume. In June 1876 his article called 'An Agnostic's Apology,' in the 'Fortnightly Review,' further revealed his private convictions and went far to familiarise the public with the term 'agnostic,' which had been invented in 1870 by Huxley, but had not yet enjoyed much vogue.

In spite of his unpopular opinions, Stephen's critical powers were generally acknowledged, and although somewhat distant and shy in manner he was an honoured figure in the best intellectual society. He had married in 1867 the younger daughter of Thackeray, and settled with his wife and her sister (now Lady Richmond Ritchie) at 16 Onslow Gardens, South Kensington; thence he moved in 1872 to a newly built residence at 8 Southwell Gardens, and in 1876 to 11 (now 22) Hyde Park Gate, where he remained till death. A second visit to America in 1868 (with his wife) greatly extended his American acquaintance and confirmed his sympathies with the country and its people. He there met Emerson, 'a virtuous old saint,' who was never one of his heroes, but Charles Eliot Norton and Oliver Wendell Holmes the younger were, like Lowell, thenceforth reckoned for life among his dearest friends and most faithful correspondents. In England he came to be on affectionate terms with George Meredith, whom he first met by chance at Vienna in 1866 on a holiday tour, and with Mr. John Morley. Carlyle, whom he often visited, equally repelled and attracted him, and he usually felt dazed and speechless in his presence. In 1877 the committee elected Stephen to the Athenæum under Rule II. In 1879 he formed among his literary friends a society of Sunday walkers which he called 'The Tramps'; he remained its 'leader' till 1891, making his last tramp in 1894, when the society dissolved. 'The Tramps,' with Stephen at their head, were from time to time entertained on their Sunday expeditions by Darwin at Down, by Tyndall at Hindhead, and by George Meredith at Box Hill.

Stephen's literary fertility was exceptional, and seemed little affected by the domestic crises of his career, his first wife's sudden death in 1875 and his second marriage in 1878. During 1876–1877 he wrote fourteen articles for the 'Cornhill' and four for the 'Fortnightly.' On 7 Aug. 1877 Mr. John Morley invited him to inaugurate with a volume on Johnson the projected series of monographs called 'English Men of Letters.' The manuscript was delivered on 4 Feb. 1878 and was soon published. It was, Stephen wrote, 'the cause of more compliments than anything he had done before.' The book satisfied the highest requirements of brief literary biography. To the same series Stephen subsequently contributed with little less success memoirs of Pope (1880) and Swift (1882), and towards the close of his life for a new series of 'English Men of Letters' he wrote on 'George Eliot' (1902) and on Hobbes (1904). But again his deepest thought was absorbed by philosophical questions. He had joined in 1878 the Metaphysical Society on the eve of its dissolution, and read two papers at its meetings, but he spoke with impatience of the society's debates. In 1882 he produced his 'Science of Ethics,' in which he summed up, in the light of his study of Mill, Darwin, and Herbert Spencer, his final conclusions on the dominant problems of life.

In the summer of 1881 George Smith broached to Leslie Stephen a project, which he then first contemplated, of a great Dictionary of Biography. The discussion continued through great part of the next year (1882) and ended in the evolution of the plan of this 'Dictionary of National Biography.' Stephen urged that the scheme should be national rather than universal, the scope which was originally suggested. George Smith entrusted Stephen with the editorship, and he entered on its duties in November 1882. At the same time he resigned the editorship of the 'Cornhill,' which had failed pecuniarily of late years, and was succeeded there by his friend, James Payn [q. v. Suppl. I].

Stephen possessed obvious qualifications for the control of George Smith's great literary design. His wide reading, his catholic interests in literary effort, his tolerant spirit, his sanity of judgment, and his sense of fairness, admirably fitted him for the direction of an enterprise in which many conflicting points of view are entitled to find expression. On the other hand, though familiar with the general trend of history, he was not a trained historical student, and was prone to impatience with mere antiquarian research. But he recognised that archæological details within reasonably liberal limits were of primary importance to the Dictionary, and he refused mercy to contributors who offered him vague conjecture or sentimental eulogy instead of unembroidered fact. To the selection of contributors, to the revision of manuscripts, to the heavy correspondence, to the clerical organisation, he gave at the outset anxious atention. But he never quite reconciled himself to office routine, and his steady application soon developed a nervous depression. The first volume of the Dictionary appeared under his editorship in January 1885, and the stipulated issue of the succeeding volumes at quarterly intervals was never interrupted. But Stephen's health soon rendered periodic rests necessary. At the end of 1886 he spent the Christmas vacation in Switzerland, and he revisited the Alps in the winters of 1888, 1889, and 1890. In 1889 a serious breakdown compelled a year's retirement from the editorship, in the course of which he paid a third visit to America and received the degree of LL.D. from Harvard. A recurrence of illness led to his resignation of his editorial office in April 1891, after more than eight years' tenure. He was succeeded by the present writer, who had become his assistant in March 1883, and was joint editor from the beginning of 1890. The twenty-sixth volume of the original issue of the Dictionary is the last bearing Stephen's name on the title-page. But Stephen had been from the outset a chief contributor to the work as well as editor, and re-established health enabled him to write important articles for the Dictionary until the close of the first supplement in 1901. To the substantive work he contributed 378 articles, covering 1000 pages, and dealing with such names as Addison, Burns, Byron, Carlyle, Coleridge, Defoe, Dickens, Dryden, Goldsmith, Hume, Landor, Macaulay, the Mills, Milton, Pope, Scott, Swift, Thackeray, and Wordsworth. Although in letters to friends Stephen repeatedly complained of the 'drudgery' of his editorial task, and frequently avowed regret at his enforced withdrawal from speculative inquiry, he expressed every satisfaction in living to see the work completed.

While Stephen was actively engaged in editorial labours he yet found time for other literary work. In 1883 he was chosen the first Clark lecturer at Trinity College, Cambridge, and delivered a course of lectures on eighteenth-century literature, but he resigned the post at the end of the year. In 1885 he wrote a sympathetic biography of Henry Fawcett, his intimate friend from Cambridge days, who had died on 6 Nov. 1884. On his retirement from the editorship of the Dictionary in 1891 he reverted to a plan which had long occupied his mind—of extending to the nineteenth century his 'History of English Thought in the Eighteenth Century.' But his scheme underwent many vicissitudes, and after long delay the work took the limited shape of an account of 'The English Utilitarians,' which was published in three volumes in 1900. Although somewhat discursive, the work abounds in happy characterisation of movements and men.

Stephen, although little of a propagandist, was never indifferent to the growth in the number of adherents to his ethical and religious views. The movement for forming ethical societies with Sunday services in various parts of London found in him an active supporter. He became president of the Ethical Societies of London, and in that capacity he delivered many lectures, which he collected in two volumes, entitled 'Social Rights and Duties' (1896). At the same time he continued to write on biography, criticism, and philosophy in the magazines with all his old zest and point, and as was his wont he collected these efforts from time to time. A volume named 'An Agnostic's Apology,' after the opening paper, which was reprinted from the 'Fortnightly' of June 1876, came out in 1893, and 'Studies of a Biographer,' in two series, each in two volumes, in 1899 and 1902.

Loss of friends and kinsfolk deeply tried Stephen's affectionate nature towards the end of his life. With James Russell Lowell, while he was United States ambassador in London, Stephen's relations grew very close (1880–7), and after Lowell's death on 12 Aug. 1891 Stephen organised with his wife's aid the presentation of a stained glass memorial window to the chapter-house at Westminster. The death of George Croom Robertson [q. v.] in 1892 and of James Dykes Campbell [q. v. Suppl. I] in 1895 removed two very congenial associates. Of his friends Henry Sidgwick and James Payn he wrote in the first supplement of this Dictionary. But a severer blow was the death on 11 March 1894 of his elder brother, Sir James Fitzjames Stephen [q. v.], of whom he prepared with great rapidity a full memoir between November 1894 and January 1895. The death, on 5 May 1895, of his second wife, to whose devotion he owed much, caused him poignant grief, from which he recovered slowly. Yet in spite of private sorrows and of the growing infirmity of deafness which hampered his social intercourse in his last years he wrote, shortly before his death, that 'not only had he had times of exceeding happiness,' but that he had been 'continuously happy except for certain periods.'

Stephen received in later life many marks of distinction. He was chosen president of the London Library in 1892 in succession to Lord Tennyson, and keenly interested himself until his death in its welfare. He was made hon. LL.D. of Edinburgh in 1885, and of Harvard in 1890; hon. Litt.D. of Cambridge in June 1892, and D.Litt. of Oxford in December 1901. He was elected hon. fellow of Trinity Hall on 13 June 1891, and a corresponding member of the Massachusetts Historical Society in December 1895. In June 1902, on the occasion of King Edward VII's coronation, he was made K.C.B. He was also appointed in 1902 an original fellow of the British Academy, and he was for a year a trustee of the National Portrait Gallery.

In 1901 Stephen edited 'The Letters of J. R. Green,' and in 1903 he contributed to the 'National Review' four autobiographical articles called 'Early Impressions,' which showed no decline of vivacity (not reprinted). His latest books were the monograph on Hobbes (posthumously published, 1904), and 'English Literature and Society in the Eighteenth Century' (published on the day of his death), a course of lectures prepared in his capacity of Ford lecturer in English History at Oxford for 1903; illness compelled him to entrust to another the delivery of these lectures.

Stephen's health broke down in the spring of 1902, when internal cancer manifested itself. The disease progressed slowly. An operation in December 1902 gave temporary relief, but he thenceforth lived the life of an invalid. He was able to pursue some literary work till near the end. He died at his residence, 22 Hyde Park Gate, on 22 Feb. 1904. He was cremated at Golder's Green, and his ashes were buried in Highgate cemetery.

Stephen's work, alike in literary criticism and philosophy, was characterised by a frank sincerity which is vivified by a humorous irony. His intellectual clarity bred an impatience of conventional religious beliefs and many strenuous endeavours to prove their hollowness. The champions of the broad church excited his particular disdain, because to his mind they were muddle-headed, and therefore futile. He put no trust in halfway houses. At the same time both in his philosophical and especially in his literary judgments there was an equability of temper which preserved him from excesses of condemnation or eulogy. Reserved and melancholy in manner, he enjoyed the affectionate admiration of his most enlightened contemporaries. His friend George Meredith sketched him in the 'Egoist' (1879) as Vernon Whitford, 'a Phœbus Apollo turned fasting friar'; Meredith admitted that the portrait did not do Stephen 'full justice, though the strokes within and without are correct' (MEREDITH's *Letters*, ii. 331). There was something of the Spartan in Stephen's constitution. But there was no harshness about his manly tenderness, his unselfishness, and his modesty. To younger associates he was always generous in encouragement and sympathy. His native magnanimity abhorred all the pettiness of temper which often characterises the profession of letters. It is supererogatory to dwell here on the services which he rendered to this Dictionary, alike as first editor and as chief contributor.

Stephen married (1) on 19 June 1867, Harriet Marian, younger daughter of Thackeray the novelist (she died in London suddenly on 28 Nov. 1875); (2) on 26 March 1878, Julia Prinsep, widow of Herbert Duckworth and youngest daughter of Dr. John Jackson, long a physician at Calcutta, by his wife Maria Pattle; she was a woman of singular beauty and refinement of mind, and died after a short illness on 5 May 1895. She was a close friend of G. F. Watts, who painted her portrait, of James Russell Lowell, and of George Meredith. She published in 1883 'Notes from Sick Rooms,' and wrote for this Dictionary a memoir of her aunt, Julia Margaret Cameron. By his first wife Stephen left a daughter, Laura; and by his second wife two sons and two daughters. The elder son, Julius Thoby Stephen (1880–1906), was at one time scholar of Trinity College, Cambridge.

A portrait by G. F. Watts, painted in 1878, belongs to his surviving son, Adrian. His 'Collected Essays' (10 vols., with introd. by Mr. James Bryce and Mr. Herbert Paul) came out in 1907.

Stephen's friends founded in 1905 the Leslie Stephen lectureship in Cambridge, for the biennial delivery of a public lecture 'on some literary subject, including therein criticism, biography, and ethics.' The subscribers also presented an engraving of Stephen's portrait by Watts to the Athenæum, the London Library, Trinity Hall, Cambridge, the Working Men's College, London, and Harvard University, institutions with which he had been associated.

Caroline Emelia Stephen (1834–1909), Sir Leslie Stephen's only surviving sister, and youngest of the family, was born at Kensington on 8 Dec. 1834. Educated at home in a literary atmosphere, she became an occasional contributor at an early age to the 'Saturday Review' and the 'Spectator.' Always religiously inclined, she occupied herself with philanthropic work, and in 1871 published a sympathetic tractate on 'The Service of the Poor.' Acquaintance with Robert Fox and his family at Falmouth interested her in the Society of Friends. After attending several Friends' meetings she joined the society in 1879, being almost the only convert to Quakerism of her generation. She explained the grounds of her conversion in 'Quaker Strongholds' (1891). She remained till her death a loyal and zealous member of the society. Establishing herself in Chelsea after her mother's death in 1875, she continued in spite of feeble health her philanthropic activities. She was on friendly terms with Octavia Hill (1838–1912), and under her influence built in Chelsea a block of tenements which she called Hereford Buildings, and collected the rents herself. She subsequently moved to Westcott, near Dorking, and in 1882 to West Malvern. In 1885 she settled at Cambridge, where she remained till her death. Her niece, Miss Katharine Stephen, was principal of Newnham College, and Miss Stephen occasionally gave addresses there and at Girton. Some of these were published in the 'Hibbert Journal.' A collected volume of addresses and essays, chiefly on religious subjects, appeared in 1908 as 'Light Arising.' In 1908 she privately printed a selection of her father's correspondence under the title 'The First Sir James Stephen.' Until deafness disabled her she served on the committee of management of the convalescent home attached to Addenbrooke's hospital. She died at The Porch, Cambridge, on 7 April 1909, and was buried there. After her death was published 'The Vision of Faith and other Essays' (1911), with a memoir by her niece, Katharine Stephen, and notice of her relation with the Society of Friends by Dr. Thomas Hodgkin.

[F. W. Maitland, Life and Letters of Leslie Stephen, 1906; The Times, 23 Feb. 1904 (by the present writer); the present writer's Principles of Biography, the Leslie Stephen Lecture, Cambridge, 1911; Life and Letters of J. R. Lowell; George Meredith's Letters, 1912; Alpine Journal, vol. xxii., May 1904 (by James Bryce); Cornhill Mag., April 1904 (art. by Frederic Harrison); A. W. Benn, History of English Rationalism, in the Nineteenth Century, 1906, ii. 384 seq.] S. L.

STEPHENS, FREDERIC GEORGE (1828–1907), art critic, born on 10 Oct. 1828, was the son of Septimus Stephens and his wife, who were for a time during Frederic's youth master and mistress of the Strand Union Workhouse in Cleveland Street. He was lamed for life through an accident at the age of nine. He entered as a student in the Royal Academy on 13 Jan. 1844, on the nomination of Sir William Ross [q. v.], who lived in Fitzroy Square hard by. Here he made the acquaintance of Holman Hunt, of Millais, and subsequently of Rossetti and of Madox Brown. When in process of time the Pre-Raphaelite Brotherhood was founded in 1848 by Millais and Holman Hunt, Stephens was nominated a member by the latter. In 1849 he made some progress with a picture of King Arthur and Sir Bedivere, and in 1850 acted as an assistant to Holman Hunt in the restoration of Rigaud's ceiling decoration at Trinity House. He painted small whole-length portraits of his father and mother, both of which were exhibited at the Royal Academy, the latter in 1852 and the former in 1854. But it soon became evident that Stephens had mistaken his vocation, and he became an art-critic. He contributed some papers on Italian painting to 'The Germ,' the Pre-Raphaelite organ. He was soon writing notices for the 'Critic,' the 'London Review,' 'Dublin University Magazine,' 'Macmillan's Magazine,' 'Weldon's Register,' and for some American and French periodicals. In 1861 he was introduced by David Masson [q. v. Suppl. II] to Hepworth Dixon, the editor of the 'Athenæum,' and from that time till January 1901 he was the art-critic of that periodical, contributing to every number but two for forty years. His series of articles on 'The Private Collections of England,' correcting and supplementing van Waagen, were invaluable at the time, and are even now often the sole sources of the information they supply. As a critic he was industrious, learned, and careful, accumulating and testing facts most laboriously and conscientiously; but he was out of sympathy with modern developments of his art. He was for many years teacher of art at University College School, where he taught with much seriousness drawing from the antique. He was also secretary of the Hogarth Club. Besides his contributions to periodicals Stephens was a voluminous writer of books. His best-known works are the unfinished 'Catalogue of Prints and Drawings (Personal and Political Satire) in the British Museum' (4 vols. 1870–83), a massive collection of minute detail, and his 'Portfolio' sketch of the work and life of D. G. Rossetti (1894; new edit. 1908), which, though not free from inaccuracies, is of great value as written from personal knowledge. Stephens's anonymous pamphlet, 'William Holman Hunt and his Work' (1860) (on Holman Hunt's 'Christ in the Temple') gives a good idea of the inspiration and methods of the Pre-Raphaelites, and he remained for many years a personal friend of Holman Hunt. But he was more in sympathy with the aims and teaching of Rossetti, whose champion he constituted himself, than with those of the Pre-Raphaelite school. A rupture between him and Holman Hunt took place in their old age, and after the publication of Holman Hunt's 'Pre-Raphaelitism' in 1905 some controversy took place in the press between them over the respective parts that Holman Hunt and Rossetti played in the initiation of the Pre-Raphaelite movement. Stephens contended that Rossetti was the moving spirit and Holman Hunt the disciple (cf. *The Times*, 16 Feb. 1906).

Other of Stephens's more important publications were: 1. 'Masterpieces of Mulready,' 1867, much of which appeared in 'Memorials of William Mulready' in 'Great Artists' series, 1890. 2. 'The Early Works of Sir Edwin Landseer, R.A.,' anon. 1869; re-issued as 'Memoirs of Landseer,' 1874; revised in a volume in 'Great Artists' series, 1880. 3. 'A Memoir of George Cruikshank' (including an essay by W. M. Thackeray), 1891. He also wrote two works on Norman and Flemish art (1865). He contributed letterpress to illustrations of Reynolds (1866), J. C. Hook (1884), and Alma Tadema (1895), and notes to the catalogues of exhibitions at the Grosvenor Gallery of the works of Reynolds (1884), Gainsborough (1885), Millais (1886), and Van Dyck (1887). He also penned a prefatory essay to Ernest Rhys's 'Sir Frederic Leighton' (folio, 1895).

In the course of his career Stephens brought together a large collection of prints and drawings at his house in Hammersmith Terrace, where he died of heart disease on 9 March 1907. He married early in 1866. His widow survives with one son, Holman Stephens, a civil engineer, born on 31 Oct. 1868.

Stephens was in his youth remarkably handsome. He was the model for the head of Christ in Ford Madox Brown's 'Christ washing Peter's Feet,' the Ferdinand in Millais's 'Ferdinand and Ariel,' and the servant in the same artist's 'Lorenzo and Isabella.'

[Athenæum, 16 March 1907; Letters of Dante Gabriel Rossetti, passim; W. M. Rossetti, P.R.B. Journal; Esther Wood, Dante Rossetti and the Pre-Raphaelite Movement, 1894; Letters to William Allingham, 1911; Francis, Notes by the Way, xxxiii–iv; MS. note supplied by Mr. Denis Eden, a pupil at University College School; private information.] R. S.

STEPHENS, JAMES (1825–1901), organiser of the Fenian conspiracy, the son of an auctioneer's clerk, was born in the city of Kilkenny either in 1824 (*Pall Mall Mag.* xxiv. 331) or, more probably, in 1825. Displaying as a boy considerable talent for mathematics, he received a fairly good education with a view to becoming a civil engineer, and at the age of twenty he obtained an appointment on the Limerick and Waterford railway, then in course of construction. He was a protestant, and like many of his class and creed he fell under the influence of the Young Ireland propaganda, but unlike the majority his interests were rather of an active than of a literary sort, and he took a chief part in organising the military clubs which were intended to secure the success of the revolutionary movement. He joined William Smith O'Brien [q. v.] shortly before the Killenaule affair, and acted as a sort of aide-de-camp to him both before and during the affray at Ballingarry on 29 July 1848. He was slightly wounded on that occasion, but by shamming death he managed to elude detection and effect his escape. While wandering about the country from one hiding-place to another he fell in with Michael Doheny of the 'Felon's Track,' and with him planned a daring scheme for kidnapping the prime minister, Lord John Russell, who was at the time visiting Ireland. The plot miscarried, and after several hairbreadth escapes Stephens managed on 24 Sept. to slip out of the country in disguise and eventually to reach Paris.

Here he seems for some years to have earned a scanty livelihood by giving lessons in English; but he was a born plotter, and the atmosphere of conspiracy hung at the time thickly over Europe (cf. O'Leary, *Fenians and Fenianism*, i. 70, note). A scheme of a plot for effecting the freedom of Ireland was broached to him by John O'Mahony [q. v.], and while O'Mahony and Doheny proceeded to America to see what could be done in that quarter, Stephens, accompanied by Thomas Clarke Luby [q. v. Suppl. II], made a tour of inspection through Ireland. After travelling up and down the country for nearly a year and mixing with all classes and conditions of the population, Stephens was convinced of the feasibility of a fresh movement in the form of a secret conspiracy, with himself as its chief organiser.

Thus the Irish Republican Brotherhood, as it was afterwards called, came into being. The society was based on military principles, the unit being the 'circle' or regiment. For the purposes of organisation the country was divided into provinces, and to each province (Dublin being reserved by Stephens for himself as a separate province) was assigned an organiser whose business it was, wherever he thought fit, to select some individual as a 'centre' or colonel, who in his turn was to choose nine captains, each captain nine sergeants, and each sergeant nine men to form the rank and file of the 'circle.' In this way a 'circle' would consist of 820 men. The scheme appealed to the military instincts of the Irish, and before long Leinster and Munster and even parts of Ulster were dotted with 'circles.' The main drawback was the lack of funds to provide arms. To remedy this defect Stephens visited America towards the close of 1858. During the five months he spent there his enthusiasm and ability as an organiser gave life to the Fenian Brotherhood, which was simultaneously planned on the same lines and with the same aims as the Irish Republican Brotherhood, established there by O'Mahony, and when he returned to Europe in March 1859 he was richer by some 700*l.* His success stimulated the movement in Ireland, and in 1861, by way of demonstrating the strength of his organisation, he exerted himself, after some hesitation, to give as imposing a character as possible to the public funeral in Glasnevin cemetery, Dublin, of Terence Bellew MacManus [q. v.], a rather insignificant member of the Young Ireland party. After that event there was no question as to the strength of Fenianism in Ireland. But neither the arms nor the opportunity of using them seemed to be forthcoming, and as time went on Fenian opinion in both Ireland and America grew restive. Stephens encouraged the belief that O'Mahony was to blame for the inaction. The result was that under the impression that O'Mahony was acting as a drag on the movement a party of action sprang into existence in America which in the end wrecked the conspiracy.

Meanwhile Stephens had been employing his leisure time in drawing up a scheme for the future government of Ireland in the event of the success of the conspiracy, which he published as a pamphlet entitled 'On the Future of Ireland, and on its Capacity to exist as an Independent State. By a Silent Politician' (Dublin, 1862). If his plan had been realised, it would have conferred almost unlimited power on him as the probable president of the proposed republic (cf. RUTHERFORD, *Secret Hist. of the Fenian Conspiracy*, i. 288–95). In the autumn of 1863 Stephens founded a newspaper for the propagation of his ideas. Under the editorship of Luby, Kickham, and O'Leary the 'Irish People' proved a great success both financially and as an organ of the party. In America, on the other hand, the agitation, owing to the quarrel between O'Mahony and the party of action, was stagnating, and in March 1864 Stephens recrossed the Atlantic. Though his intervention was at first resented by O'Mahony he was on the whole well received, and during his five months' visit he did much to restore order and to extend the organisation. He announced that in the case of England being drawn into war, as seemed probable at the time, over the Schleswig-Holstein business, he would at once raise Ireland, and that war or no war a rising should take place in 1865 or the association be dissolved. His pronouncement stimulated the flow of subscriptions.

On returning to Ireland in August, Stephens found things there in a very forward state. But England did not go to war, and when the summer of 1865 arrived the situation was unchanged except for the fact that the clamour for an immediate rising or dissolution, fed by American intrigues, had grown practically irresistible. Unable to go back on his promise, Stephens finally fixed as the day for the rising the anniversary of Robert Emmet's execution, 20 Sept. But before that day arrived government had obtained information of what was intended, and on 15 Sept. the offices of the 'Irish People' were raided and the principal conspirators arrested. Stephens represented that the loss of some papers by an American envoy put the police on the track. On the other hand

Rutherford hints that Stephens himself, seeing the game was up, betrayed the plot. The fact seems to be that while there was no direct treachery there was a good deal of culpable negligence. Stephens was not arrested at the time, a point which is considered to weigh heavily against him, but neither were Kickham, Brophy and others, and there is no reason to doubt that, had he liked, Stephens could easily have slipped out of the country. He remained at his post, hoping against hope that the expected money to purchase arms would arrive from America in time. The money miscarried, and on 11 Nov. Stephens, under the name of Herbert, was arrested at Fairfield House, Sandymount, and confined in Richmond prison. He had boasted that his organisation was so perfect that no gaol in Ireland was strong enough to hold him. His confidence proved well founded. With the connivance of his warder and the assistance of his friends outside he managed to escape on 24 Nov. A large reward was offered for his capture, but Stephens seemed to lead a charmed life. No assistance arrived from America, and he easily escaped to Paris on 11 March 1866. Some weeks later he sailed for New York. His efforts to close up the Fenian ranks there proved fruitless. As a last desperate throw he announced amid applause, at a monster meeting on 28 Oct., his intention of immediately returning to Ireland and unfurling the flag of rebellion. But when in the succeeding weeks Stephens showed no sign of action he was denounced as a traitor on 20 Dec. at a meeting at which he was present. Next day he was formally deposed as 'a rogue, an impostor, and a traitor.' After lingering for some time in New York in constant fear of his life, Stephens made his way back to Paris, where he eked out a scanty livelihood by journalism and by giving lessons in English. In 1885 he was wrongly suspected of being concerned in the American dynamite plots and his expulsion from France was demanded, but the mistake being admitted he was allowed to return to Ireland, where his friends organised a national subscription on his behalf. He was thereby enabled to live in comparative comfort at Blackrock, where he died on 29 April 1901.

Stephens was the creator of an organisation which, if it failed in its immediate object, exercised an enormous influence not only on Irish opinion the wide world over but on the relations between England and Ireland for many years. Believing that it was only by open force—by meeting England on the field of battle—that the freedom of Ireland could be won, he had no sympathy with the methods of the dynamite conspirators, and even less with the parliamentary methods of Butt and Parnell. He was a difficult man to deal with—vain, arrogant, and not scrupulously truthful. On the accessible evidence he may be pronounced not guilty of treachery to his fellow-conspirators. At any rate the charge is not proven.

Stephens is described as a broad-shouldered, stoutly built man of medium height, with small, furtive-looking eyes. A photographic likeness of him forms the frontispiece to vol. ii. of O'Leary's 'Fenians and Fenianism,' and there is another by Lafayette, Ltd., in the article in the 'Pall Mall Magazine.' Stephens married the sister of his friend George Hopper, whose father was a small tradesman in Dublin.

[O'Leary's Recollections of Fenians and Fenianism; James Stephens, by one who knew him, in Pall Mall Mag. xxiv. 331–7; Rutherford's Secret Hist. of the Fenian Conspiracy; Doheny's Felon's Track; Pigott's Personal Recollections of an Irish Journalist; Le Caron's Twenty-five Years of Secret Service; Eye-Witness's Arrest and Escape of James Stephens; J. Stephens, Chief Organiser of the Irish Republic, N.Y., 1866; and authorities mentioned in the text. An examination of Stephens's unpublished papers, lately in the possession of a personal friend of Michael Davitt (cf. Davitt's Fall of Feudalism in Ireland, ch. vii.), is needed to reveal the full truth.]

R. D.

STEPHENS, JAMES BRUNTON (1835–1902), Queensland poet, born at George Place, Borrowstounness in Linlithgowshire, on the Firth of Forth, on 17 June 1835, was son of a schoolmaster there in poor circumstances. When he was still quite young, his family moved to Edinburgh, and he was educated at Edinburgh University (1852–4), paying his college fees, it is said, by teaching in the evening and in the vacations. He had a successful university career, although he took no degree, and on leaving college became a travelling tutor for three years, spending a year in Paris, six or seven months in Italy, and visiting Egypt, Palestine, Turkey, the Levant, and Sicily. Subsequently he was for six years a schoolmaster at Greenock, and did some writing in a small way. In 1866, on account of health, he emigrated to Queensland, and landed in the colony about the end of April. For a short time he lived with a cousin at Kangaroo Point on the outskirts of Brisbane. He engaged in tutorial work there, and afterwards at a bush station, where he wrote the first and most important of his poems, 'Convict Once.' This was published in London in 1871. In 1873 he was appointed a teacher in the department of public instruction under the government of Queensland, and became headmaster successively of schools at Stanthorpe on the Darling Downs and at Ashgrove in the Brisbane suburbs. In 1883 he was appointed by Sir Thomas McIlwraith correspondence clerk in the colonial secretary's office. He proved a capable and hard-working official, and was chief clerk and acting under-secretary, when he died at Brisbane on 29 June 1902. He was buried in the South Brisbane cemetery. In 1876 he married Rosalie, eldest daughter of Thomas Willet Donaldson, of Danescourt, co. Meath, Ireland, and left one son and four daughters.

Stephens, who stands in the forefront of Australian poets, long contributed both verse and prose to Australian newspapers and reviews. A blank verse poem, 'Mute Discourse,' was first published in the 'Melbourne Review,' and 'A Hundred Pounds,' a novelette, appeared in the 'Queenslander,' being republished in 1876. His first separately issued poem, 'Convict Once' (London, 1871; Melbourne, 1885, 1888), written in English hexameters, alternately rhymed, showed a rare wealth of imagination and diction called forth by the Australian bush. Other volumes which prove his whimsical humour and metrical facility, as well as serious sentiment, were 'The Godolphin Arabian,' written in 1872 (Brisbane, 1873; new edit. 1894), and 'The Black Gin and other Poems' (Melbourne, 1873); 'Mute Discourse' (Brisbane, 1878); 'Marsupial Bill' (Brisbane, 1879); 'Miscellaneous Poems' (London and Brisbane, 1880); and 'Fayette or Bush Revels' (Brisbane, 1892). A collection of his poetical works was published at Sydney in 1902. Although he did not confine himself to Australian subjects, and some of his inspiration came from books and travel, yet his work bears the impress of Australia, especially of Queensland, where he spent his Australian life. He was a central figure in the literary circle at Brisbane which developed into the Johnsonian Club, of which he was at one time president, and which gave occasion to one of his lighter pieces, 'A Johnsonian Address.'

[Queenslander, 5 July 1902; Melbourne Review, Oct. 1884, by Alexander Sutherland; Mennell's Dict. of Australas. Biog. 1892; Johns's Notable Australians and Who's Who in Australia (Notable Dead of Australasia), 1908; Bertram Stevens's An Anthology of Australian Verse, 1907; A. H. Miles, Poets and Poetry of the Nineteenth Century, x. 469 seq.]

C. P. L.

STEPHENS, WILLIAM RICHARD WOOD (1839–1902), dean of Winchester, born on 5 Oct. 1839 at Haywards Field, Stonehouse, Gloucestershire, where his father carried on a wool or cloth business before he became partner in a Reading bank, was younger son of Charles Stephens and Catharine, daughter of Sir Matthew Wood [q.v.] and sister of William Page Wood, baron Hatherley [q. v.]. Being delicate in boyhood, Stephens was educated at home until he went to Balliol College, Oxford, where he obtained a second class in moderations and a first in the final classical school, and graduated B.A. in 1862, proceeding M.A. in 1865, B.D. in 1895, and D.D. in 1901. After leaving Oxford he lived at home or travelled on the continent in company with his college friend John Addington Symonds (1840–1893) [q. v.] until 1864, when he was ordained to the curacy of Staines, Middlesex. In 1866 he became curate of Purley, Berkshire, and in 1870, on the recommendation of Walter Farquhar Hook [q. v.], dean of Chichester, the duke of Richmond presented him to the vicarage of Mid Lavant, Sussex; he was lecturer at Chichester Theological College (1872–5), and examining chaplain to the bishop of Chichester 1875–94. In 1875 he was preferred to the prebend of Whitring or Wittering, then an office of emolument and carrying with it the post of theological lecturer in Chichester Cathedral. He was presented to the rectory of Woolbeding, Sussex, in 1876, and was proctor of the clergy in convocation 1880–6. In 1894 he was appointed by the crown to the deanery of Winchester, and was installed on 4 Feb. 1895. In the same year he was elected F.S.A. After an illness of about six weeks he died at the deanery of typhoid fever on 22 Dec. 1902, and was buried in the graveyard of the cathedral. He married, on 31 Aug. 1869, Charlotte Jane, youngest daughter of Dean Hook; she survived him with one son and three daughters.

Stephens was wealthier than most clergy, and spent his money liberally; he restored the church at Mid Lavant and practically rebuilt the chancel at Woolbeding. At Winchester he contributed largely to the repair of the roof of the cathedral, which was carried out while he was dean, mainly through his exertions in raising money, at a cost of 12,600*l.* Other improvements in the fabric and the character and order of the services were due to his authority or influence; he spared no trouble and no expense in fulfilling his desire to make the cathedral services 'a pattern of devout worship.' The chapter benefited by his capacity for business. He devoted much time to conducting working people and colonial and foreign visitors over the cathedral and instructing them in its history and architecture; he took part in many local endeavours for religious and social reforms, and was active in the cause of temperance. He was a liberal in politics, and although a high churchman, cordially co-operated with nonconformists in social and philanthropic work.

Throughout life he read and wrote much ecclesiastical history and biography. His historical work is scholarly, careful, and attractively presented. He was a sympathetic biographer, and able to depict personality. He published: 1. 'St. Chrysostom: his Life and Times,' 1872, 1880. 2. 'Memorials of the South Saxon See and the Cathedral Church of Chichester,' 1876. 3. 'Christianity and Islam, the Bible and the Koran, Four Lectures,' 1877. 4. Two pamphlets on the 'Burials Question' and 'Cathedral Chapters considered as Diocesan Councils,' 1877. 5. 'The Life and Letters of Walter Farquhar Hook, D.D.,' 2 vols. 1878, a biography of high merit which met with much success (condensed edition, 1880). 6. 'The Relations between Culture and Religion, Three Lectures,' 1881. 7. 'The South Saxon Diocese, Selsey, Chichester,' in 'Diocesan Histories,' 1881. 'Memoir of the Right Hon. William Page Wood, Baron Hatherley,' 2 vols. 1883. 9. 'Hildebrand and his Times,' in Bp. Creighton's 'Epochs of Church History,' 1886. 10. A translation from St. Chrysostom, 'On the Christian Priesthood,' in Schaff's 'Nicene and Post-Nicene Fathers,' xii. 1889. 11. 'Life and Letters of E. A. Freeman,' 2 vols. 1895, too long a record of the uneventful life of a scholar. 12. Completion of Dean Kitchin's pamphlet on 'The Great Screen in Winchester Cathedral,' 1899. 13. 'Memoir of Richard Durnford, D.D., Bishop of Chichester,' 1899. 14. 'Helps to the Study of the Book of Common Prayer,' 2nd edit. 1901. 15. 'A History of the English Church from the Norman Conquest to the Accession of Edward I,' 1901, the second volume of 'A History of the English Church,' edited by him and W. Hunt, complete in 9 vols., of which he only lived to see four published. 16. 'The Bishops of Winchester,' with the Rev. Canon W. W. Capes, reprinted from the 'Winchester Diocesan Chronicle,' 1907, 4to. He also in 1887, in conjunction with the Rev. Walter Hook, produced a revised edition of Dean Hook's 'Church Dictionary,' and he contributed several articles, including that on St. Anselm, to this Dictionary.

A portrait in oils by Mr. Frederic Calderon is in the possession of his widow.

[Private information; personal knowledge; the Guardian, 31 Dec. 1902; Memoir reprinted, with reproduction of a photograph, from the Hampshire Observer, 27 Dec. 1902 and 3 Jan. 1903.] W. H.

STEPHENSON, Sir FREDERICK CHARLES ARTHUR (1821–1911), general, born in London on 17 July 1821, was son of Sir Benjamin Charles Stephenson, K.C.H., surveyor-general of the board of works by his wife Maria, daughter of the Rev. Sir Peter Rivers, sixth baronet. He was present as a page of honour at the coronation of William IV on 8 Sept. 1831, and thereby became entitled to a commission in the army. He joined the Scots Guards as a lieutenant on 25 July 1837, and was promoted captain on 13 Jan. 1843. He was appointed brigade major in April 1854, and attained the rank of lieut.-colonel on 20 June following. He served throughout the Crimean war with his regiment. He was engaged at the battles of Alma and Inkerman, and during the siege of Sevastopol he acted as military secretary to General Sir James Simpson [q. v.], who succeeded to the command of the British troops in the Crimea on 28 June 1855. For his services Stephenson received the medal with four clasps, the legion of honour, and the fourth class of the order of the Mejidie. In 1857 he sailed for China, and was wrecked in the transport vessel Transit off the straits of Banca. Although some of the troops under his charge were diverted to India, where the Mutiny had just broken out, Stephenson himself proceeded to China, where he was nominated assistant adjutant-general to the force under Sir Charles Van Straubenzee [q. v.]. He took part in the capture of Canton (5 Jan. 1858), and after the conclusion of peace at Tientsin he remained with the army of occupation. He was gazetted C.B., and was twice mentioned in despatches (*Lond. Gaz.* 5 Mar., 15 Oct. 1858). On the renewal of hostilities in 1860 he shared in Sir Hope Grant's expedition and was present at the storming of the Taku forts (21 Aug.) and the capture of Pekin (15 Oct.). Stephenson was awarded the Chinese medal with three clasps, and on his return home he was promoted colonel on 15 Feb. 1861. In 1868 he was given the command of the Scots fusiliers, and was advanced to major-general. From 1876 to 1879 he commanded the brigade of guards, and meanwhile he attained the rank of lieut.-general on 23 Feb. 1878.

In May 1883 Stephenson succeeded Sir Archibald Alison [q. v. Suppl. II] as commander of the army of occupation in Egypt. After the defeat of Valentine Baker [q. v. Suppl. I] at El Teb on 4 Feb. 1884 he organised the expedition under Sir Gerald Graham [q. v. Suppl. I] for the relief of Tokar and the defence of Suakin. In the following May, when the British government was contemplating the despatch of an expedition to the relief of Charles George Gordon [q. v.], Stephenson made urgent representations to Lord Hartington [q. v. Suppl. II] in favour of an advance on Khartoum by the Suakin-Berber route. His scheme, however, was rejected by the cabinet, and the Nile expedition proposed by Lord Wolseley was carried out in opposition to Stephenson's advice. He was nominated K.C.B. in 1884, and after the evacuation of the Sudan he took command of the frontier field force. On 30 Dec. 1885 he inflicted a severe defeat on the main body of the Mahdists at Giniss. For his services he received the thanks of parliament, the G.C.B., and the grand cross of the order of Mejidie. He resigned his command in 1887 and returned to England. In 1889 he became colonel of the Lancashire and Yorkshire regiment, and in 1892 he succeeded to the colonelcy of the Coldstream guards. He was made constable of the Tower of London in 1898. He died unmarried in London on 10 March 1911, and was buried at Brompton cemetery. A cartoon portrait by 'Spy' appeared in 'Vanity Fair' in 1887.

[The Times, 11 March 1911; Daily Telegraph, 13 March 1911; Official Army List; Lord Wolseley, Story of a Soldier's Life, 1903, i. 231; R. H. Vetch, Life, Letters, and Diaries of Lieut.-general Sir Gerald Graham, 1905; Sir Charles Watson, Life of Major-general Sir Charles Wilson, 1909; H. E. Colvile, History of the Sudan Campaign, 2 parts, 1889; Ross of Bladensburg, History of the Coldstream Guards, 1896.] G. S. W.

STEPHENSON, GEORGE ROBERT (1819–1905), civil engineer, born at Newcastle-on-Tyne on 20 Oct. 1819, was only son of Robert Stephenson, brother of George Stephenson of railway fame [q. v.]. He was thus a first cousin of Robert Stephenson [q. v.]. At the age of twelve he was sent to work with underground viewers and surveyors at the Pendleton collieries, near Manchester, where his father was chief engineer. He was then trained for two years in the colliery workshops and was given charge of one of the engines used for drawing wagons up an incline. Owing to his father's improved circumstances a better education was then designed for him, and he was sent to King William's College, Isle of Man. In 1837 his father died, and he was obliged to set to work again. Thereupon his uncle George employed him in the drawing-office of the Manchester and Leeds railway, where he remained until 1843, when he was appointed engineer to the Tapton collieries. Shortly afterwards his cousin Robert made him resident engineer on the new lines of the South Eastern railway, of which Robert was engineer-in-chief. He superintended the construction of the Maidstone and the Minster and Deal branches; the surveys and construction of the North Kent line; the conversion into a railway of the long canal tunnel between Strood and Higham, and the completion of the line to Gravesend; the laying out and partial construction of the Ashford, Rye and Hastings line, and the design of the iron swing-bridge at Rye, one of the earliest of its kind for railway purposes; the laying out of the line from Red Hill to Dorking, and other work. He remained with the South Eastern Railway Company until his cousin Robert's resignation. His activities were not confined to the South Eastern system. In 1845 he laid out an abortive line between Manchester and Southampton, and he constructed the Waterloo and Southport railway near Liverpool. He was engineer-in-chief of the Ambergate, Matlock and Rowsley, the Grantham, Sleaford and Boston, and the Northampton and Market Harborough railways (the last opened in 1855). He was a persistent advocate of a line from the north to London for the sole purpose of mineral traffic. With George Parker Bidder [q. v.] he constructed railways for the Danish government in Schleswig-Holstein and laid out lines in Jutland; and in 1860, as consulting engineer to the provincial government of Canterbury, New Zealand, he built the line from Lyttelton to Christchurch, and designed breakwaters for Lyttleton harbour, which were executed in accordance with his plans. In 1864 he was joint engineer-in-chief with (Sir) John Hawkshaw [q. v. Suppl. I] for the East London railway.

Stephenson was associated with his

cousin Robert in the design and construction of the Victoria tubular bridge across the St. Lawrence, completed in 1859, and he built the large railway bridge across the Nile at Kafr Zayat and many smaller fixed and swing bridges at home and abroad. With Robert Stephenson and Bidder he wrote a joint report (London, 1862) to the corporation of Wisbech on improvement of the River Nene; he reported with Sir John Rennie [q. v.] on the River Ouse from Lynn to the Middle Level sluice; and was responsible for the diversion of the river from Lynn to the sea, through Vinegar Middle Sand. For Said Pasha he built at Alexandria a huge bathing palace of iron and glass, the materials alone costing 70,000*l.*

In 1859, owing to the death of his cousin, he became proprietor of the locomotive-works at Newcastle-on-Tyne, with extensive collieries at Snibston and Tapton. He thereupon gradually relinquished his private practice and personally controlled these works until 1886, when the firm (Robert Stephenson & Co.) was registered as a private limited liability company. Later it was formed into a joint-stock company, of which Stephenson was a director until 1899.

He was elected a member of the Institution of Civil Engineers on 24 May 1853, became a member of the council in 1859, and was president in 1875–7. His presidential address (xliv. 2) was his only contribution to its 'Proceedings,' apart from his share in debates; but he actively fostered the welfare of the institution and helped the extension of its premises in Great George Street in 1868 by presenting his interest in premises at the rear of No. 24.

Stephenson was an enthusiastic yachtsman, and a member of the Royal Yacht Squadron. By giving prizes and in other ways he endeavoured to improve the design of the rowing and sailing vessels in use in the Kyles of Bute. His efforts for the general welfare of the district were acknowledged by the freedom of the royal burgh of Rothesay, which was conferred upon him in 1869. Keenly interested in the volunteer movement, he was a lieutenant-colonel of the engineer volunteer staff corps.

He wrote, in addition to the presidential address and the reports already mentioned, a pamphlet in the form of a letter to the president of the board of trade on 'High Speeds' (London, 1861), a protest against what he considered excessive speeds on railways. Jointly with J. F. Tone he issued a pamphlet, 'The Firth of Forth Bridge' (London, 1862), in which the bridging of the Forth about 4 miles above Queensferry was advocated.

He died on 26 Oct. 1905 at his home, Hetton Lawn, Charlton Kings, Cheltenham.

He married (1) in 1846 Jane (1822–1884), daughter of T. Brown of Whickham, co. Durham; and (2) in 1885 Sarah (*d.* 1893), younger daughter of Edward Harrison, of co. Durham. He had a family of six children. A life-size portrait in oils by J. Lucas, as well as a three-quarter length portrait, belongs to his son, Mr. F. St. L. Stephenson.

[Proc. Inst. Civ. Eng. clxiii. 386; Engineer, and Engineering, 3 Nov. 1905; The Times, 31 Oct. 1905; private information.] W. F. S.

STERLING, ANTOINETTE, Mrs. John MacKinlay (1843–1904), contralto singer, was born at Sterlingville, New York State, U.S.A., on 23 Jan. 1843. Her father, James Sterling, owned large blasting furnaces, and she claimed descent from William Bradford [q. v.], a pilgrim father. In childhood she imbibed anti-British prejudices, and her patriotic sympathies were so stirred in childhood by the story of the destruction of tea cargoes in Boston harbour, that she resolved never to drink tea, and kept the resolution all her life. She already possessed a beautiful voice of great compass and volume, and took a few singing lessons at the age of eleven from Signor Abella in New York. When she was sixteen her father was ruined by the reduction in 1857 of the import duties in the protective tariff, and died; she went to the state of Mississippi as a teacher, and after a time gave singing lessons. When the civil war broke out her position became very unpleasant, and with another northern girl she fled by night during the summer of 1862, and was guided north by friendly negroes. Afterwards she became a church singer and was engaged in Henry Ward Beecher's church at Brooklyn, where a special throne-like seat was erected for her. In 1868 she came to Europe for further training; she sang at Darlington in Handel's 'Messiah' on 17 Dec., and elsewhere, taking some lessons under W. H. Cummings in London before proceeding to Germany. There she studied under Madame Marchesi and Pauline Viardot-Garcia, and finally under Manuel Garcia in London. In 1871 she returned to America and became a prominent concert singer. Her voice had settled into a true contralto of exceptional power and richness. She came back to England at the beginning of 1873, but almost immediately returned to America, and toured with Theodore Thomas's orchestra; on 13 May she gave a farewell concert at Boston. Her first engagement in London was at the promenade concert of 5 Nov. 1873; the programmes were then distinctly popular, with a tendency towards vulgarity; she insisted, in spite of all expostulations, in singing the 'Slumber Song' from Bach's 'Christmas Oratorio' and some classical Lieder. She obtained great popular success, and enthusiastic receptions on her appearance at the Crystal Palace, the Albert Hall, Exeter Hall, and St. James's Hall quickly followed. In Feb. 1874 she sang in Mendelssohn's 'Elijah' on two consecutive nights at Exeter Hall and Royal Albert Hall. Her repertory was entirely oratorio music or German Lieder. Dissentient voices were not lacking; 'her style is wanting in sensibility and refinement. Excellence of voice is not all that is required in the art of vocalisation' (*Athenæum*, 14 March). Her popularity was undeniable, and she was engaged for the three choirs festival at Hereford. On Easter Sunday 1875 she was married at the Savoy Chapel to John MacKinlay, a Scotch American; they settled in Stanhope Place, London.

She did not improve in musicianship; her time was quite untrustworthy. Engagements for high-class concerts gradually ceased, but she still for some years sang in oratorio, and her taste remained faithful to the German school, including Wagner. In 1877 she found her vocation. Sullivan's 'Lost Chord' exactly suited her, and attained unprecedented popularity. She became more and more restricted to simple sentimental ballads, especially those with semi-religious or moralising words, which she declaimed with perfect distinctness and intense fervour. She invested 'Caller Herrin'' with singular significance. In her later years she favoured Tennyson's 'Crossing the Bar' in Behrend's setting.

She had always leant to eccentricity, refusing to wear a low-necked dress, and getting permission to dispense with one at a command performance before Queen Victoria. She never wore a corset. After belonging to various sects, she at last became an ardent believer in 'christian science.' In 1893 she made an Australian tour, during which her husband died at Adelaide. In 1895 she revisited America, but did not feel at home there, and soon returned to London.

In the winter of 1902–3 her farewell tour was announced. Her last appearance was at East Ham on 15 Oct. 1903, and the last song which she sang was 'Crossing the Bar.' She died at her residence in Hampstead on 10 Jan. 1904, and was cremated at Golder's Green. She was survived by a son and a daughter, both now popular vocalists.

A full-length portrait by James Doyle Penrose, exhibited at the Royal Academy in 1891, now belongs to her son.

[Her son, M. Sterling MacKinlay's Antoinette Sterling and other Celebrities (with two portraits), 1906; the same writer's Garcia the Centenarian and his Times, 1908; Illustrated London News, 24 April 1875 (with portrait); Musical Herald, Feb., March, and Nov. 1904; Musical Times, Feb. 1904; Grove's Dict. (with inaccurate date of birth); personal reminiscences from March 1874.] H. D.

STEVENSON, DAVID WATSON (1842–1904), Scottish sculptor, born at Ratho, Midlothian, on 25 March 1842, was son of William Stevenson, builder. Educated at the village school, Ratho, he was for eight years (1860–8) in Edinburgh as pupil of the sculptor William Brodie [q. v.]. During that time he attended the School of Art and the Life School of the Royal Scottish Academy. In 1868 he took a studio at Edinburgh and commenced work as a sculptor on his own account. Subsequently, in 1876, he pursued his studies in Rome, and later interest in modern French sculpture took him frequently to Paris. Elected an associate of the Royal Scottish Academy in 1877, he gradually added to his reputation, and in 1886 he was chosen academician. As early as 1868 he undertook the groups of 'Labour' and 'Learning' for the Prince Consort memorial, Edinburgh, and amongst later commissions of a monumental kind were the Platt memorial, Oldham, the colossal figure of Wallace for the national monument on the Abbey Craig, and statues of Tannahill at Paisley, 'Highland Mary' at Dunoon, and Burns at Leith. Of his ideal works, 'Nymph at the Stream,' 'Echo,' 'Galatea,' and 'The Pompeian Mother' may be named. He also executed many portrait busts. While his earlier work was pseudo-classic in manner, his later shows a certain sensitiveness to modern developments in which realism, individuality, and style are combined. After a few years of failing health, he died unmarried in Edinburgh on 18 March 1904. His younger brother, Mr. W. G. Stevenson, R.S.A., is a sculptor, and his sister, Mrs. Drew, is an accomplished embroiderer.

[Private information; R.S.A. catalogues

and report, 1904; Scotsman, 19 March 1904.] J. L. C.

STEVENSON, JOHN JAMES (1831–1908), architect, born in Glasgow on 24 Aug. 1831, was third son of James Stevenson by his wife Jane, daughter of Alexander Shannan. His education, begun in the High School of Glasgow, was continued in the university, where he graduated M.A. Being intended for the Scottish ministry, he took the theological course at Edinburgh, followed by a summer at Tübingen.

But a strong personal bent towards architecture, strengthened by a visit to Italy, induced him in 1856 to enter the office of David Bryce [q. v.] of Edinburgh, whence in 1858 he proceeded to London for further training under Sir George Gilbert Scott [q. v.]. With R. J. Johnson, a fellow student at Scott's, he made an architectural tour in France and began practice about 1860 as a partner with Campbell Douglas in Glasgow. Nine years later he spent a winter studying in Paris, and in 1870 joined E. R. Robson, a fellow pupil under Scott, who had just been appointed architect to the London school board. With him Stevenson evolved a simple type of brick design sufficiently in sympathy with early eighteenth-century architecture to be styled 'Queen Anne,' and at about the same date he built for himself 'The Red House,' Bayswater Hill, which became the meeting-place of friends prominent in literature and art, such as Alfred Ainger [q. v. Suppl. II], George MacDonald [q. v. Suppl. II], Sir W. Q. Orchardson [q. v. Suppl. II], J. H. Middleton [q. v. Suppl. I], William Morris [q. v. Suppl. I], and Prof. Robertson Smith [q.v.]. In association with Morris he became one of the original members of the committee of the Society for the Protection of Ancient Buildings. Besides the board schools, Stevenson's work comprised many designs of an ecclesiastical and domestic nature. Among the former were churches at Monzie (1868), Crieff (1881), Perth (1883), the first modern example of a crowned tower, Fairlie, an enlargement (1894), Stirling (1900), and Glasgow (1900). His country house designs include two at Westoe, South Shields (1868 and 1874); Ken Hill, Norfolk (1888); Oatlands Mere, Weybridge (1893); several in the neighbourhood of Camberley, and at Oxford and Cambridge.

His London houses were numerous, among them being groups in Palace Gate and Lowther Gardens (1878), a house, with studio, for Colin Hunter in Melbury Road (1878), others in South Street (1879), Kensington Court (1881), the south side of Cadogan Square (1881), and Buckingham Palace Road (1892). He designed a school at Fairlie (1880), the offices of the Tyne Commissioners at Newcastle (1882), and some shipping offices in Fenchurch Avenue.

At Oxford Stevenson carried out restorations or repairs at St. John's College (1889) and Oriel (1899), besides designing the University Morphological Laboratory (1899). At Cambridge he was responsible for the university chemical laboratory (1889), new buildings at Christ's College (1886 and 1906), and made designs for the Sedgwick Memorial Museum and additions to Sidney Sussex and Clare Colleges, none of which were however carried out.

For the Orient Company he designed the interior decoration of several vessels, being the first architect to undertake such work. In 1896 Stevenson took into partnership Mr. Harry Redfern, and all works carried out after that date may be assigned to their joint authorship.

Among papers read by Stevenson to societies, many were concerned with the preservation of ancient buildings; some had an archæological trend; he especially interested himself in the attempt to recover the design of the Mausoleum at Halicarnassus. In 1880 he published an illustrated work in two volumes, entitled 'House Architecture.'

Stevenson was elected F.S.A. in 1884 and fellow of the Royal Institute of British Architects in 1879.

Stevenson died at 4 Porchester Gardens on 5 May 1908. He married in 1861 Jane, daughter of Robert Omond, M.D. F.R.C.S.England, and was survived by her and two sons and four daughters.

[Journal of the Royal Institute of British Architects, 3rd series, vol. xv. 1908, p. 482; the Builder, vol. xciv. 1908, p. 551; information from Mr. Harry Redfern.] P. W.

STEVENSON, Sir THOMAS (1838–1908), scientific analyst and toxicologist, born on 14 April 1838 at Rainton in Yorkshire, was second son and fourth of the six children of Peter Stevenson, a pioneer in scientific farming. Thomas, a first cousin of the father, was an author and publisher, whose business at Cambridge was acquired in 1846, a year after his death, by Daniel and Alexander Macmillan, the founders of the publishing firm of Macmillan. His mother was Hannah, daughter of Robert Williamson, a banker and coachmaker of Ripon.

Stevenson, educated privately and at Nesbit's school of chemistry and agriculture, studied scientific farming for a year with his father and then in 1857 became a medical pupil under Mr. Steel of Bradford. In 1859 he entered the medical school of Guy's Hospital, graduating M.B. in 1863 and M.D. at London in 1864. In the earlier examinations he gained the scholarship and gold medal in organic chemistry (1861), in forensic medicine, and in obstetric medicine (1863). In 1864 he became M.R.C.P. and in 1871 F.R.C.P.London. In 1863 he started private practice in Bradford, but after a year returned to Guy's Hospital, where he became successively demonstrator of practical chemistry (1864–70), lecturer on chemistry (1870–98), and lecturer on forensic medicine (1878–1908), succeeding in both lectureships Alfred Swaine Taylor [q. v.]. He was analyst to the home office from 1872 to 1881, when he was appointed senior scientific analyst. That office he held till death. He was also analyst to the counties of Surrey and Bedfordshire and the boroughs of St. Pancras and Shoreditch, and medical officer of health to St. Pancras. He served as president of the Society of Medical Officers of Health, of the Society of Public Analysts, and of the Institute of Chemistry.

Pre-eminent as a scientific toxicologist, Stevenson was best known to the public as an expert witness in poisoning cases, especially in the well-known cases of Dr. G. H. Lamson (aconitine) in 1882; Mrs. Maybrick (arsenic) in 1889; Dr. Thomas Neill or Cream (strychnine) in 1892; George Chapman (antimony) in 1903; Miss Hickman (morphine) in 1903; Arthur Devereux (morphine) in 1905. He was an admirable witness, his evidence being so accurately and carefully prepared that cross-examination strengthened rather than weakened its effect. He was knighted in 1904.

Stevenson died on 27 July 1908, and was buried at Norwood cemetery. He married in 1867 Agnes, daughter of George Maberly, a solicitor of London, and had issue two sons and five daughters. His portrait was painted and is in possession of his family. A cartoon portrait appeared in 'Vanity Fair' in 1899.

Stevenson edited and greatly enlarged the 3rd edition of A. Swaine Taylor's 'Principles and Practice of Medical Jurisprudence' (1883), and together with Sir Shirley Murphy edited a treatise on 'Hygiene and Public Health' (1894). He made eighteen contributions to the 'Guy's Hospital Reports.'

[Brit. Med. Journ. 1908, ii. 361; information from son, C. M. Stevenson, M.D., G. A. Macmillan, and F. Taylor, M.D., F.R.C.P.]

H. D. R.

STEWART, CHARLES (1840–1907), comparative anatomist, born in Princess Square, Plymouth, on 18 May 1840, was son of Thomas Anthony Stewart of Princess Square, Plymouth, M.D. of Leyden and surgeon to the Plymouth public dispensary, by his wife Harriet Howard. Charles was educated at St. Bartholomew's Hospital, and was admitted M.R.C.S.England in 1862. After practising for four years at Plymouth, he was appointed in 1866 curator of the museum at St. Thomas's Hospital, then situated in the Surrey Gardens. In 1871, shortly after the removal of the hospital to the Albert Embankment, he was appointed lecturer on comparative anatomy in the medical school, and in 1881 he became lecturer on physiology jointly with Dr. John Harley. He was also professor of biology and physiology at the Bedford College for Women from 1882–4. He left St. Thomas's Hospital in 1884 on his appointment as conservator of the Hunterian museum at the Royal College of Surgeons in succession to Sir William Henry Flower [q. v. Suppl. I]. In 1886 he became Hunterian professor of comparative anatomy and physiology at the college, and gave an annual course of lectures until 1902. Stewart fully maintained at the college the Hunterian tradition. Abreast of the current knowledge of anatomy, physiology, and bacteriology, which together make up modern pathology, he was able to utilise to the best advantage the stores of specimens collected by John Hunter. His dissections enabled him to correlate many facts for the first time, and his results were set forth in his lectures. In 1885 he lectured on the structure and life history of the hydrozoa; in 1886 and 1887 on the organs of hearing; in 1889 and again in 1896 on the integumental system; in 1890 on phosphorescent organs and colour; in 1891 on secondary sexual characters; in 1895 on the endoskeleton; in 1897 on joints, and on the protection and nourishment of the young; in 1899 on the alternation of generations. He spoke without notes and drew admirably on the blackboard, illustrating his remarks from the stores of the museum. But unhappily the lectures were neither published nor reported, and only remain in the memories of his auditors or in their scanty notes. His valuable work survives alone in the catalogues of the Hunterian museum.

In spite of ill-health Stewart was active outside the College of Surgeons. From 1894 to 1897 he was Fullerian professor of physiology at the Royal Institution, where on two occasions he delivered the 'Friday evening' discourse. In 1866 he was elected a fellow of the Linnean Society, and served as its president (1890–4). He also took an active part in founding the Anatomical Society of Great Britain and Ireland, of which he was the original treasurer (1887–1892). He also served as secretary of the Royal Microscopical Society from 1879 to 1883. He was deeply interested in the welfare of the Marine Biological Association which was established at Plymouth, his native place. He was admitted F.R.S. in 1896, and in 1899 he received the honorary degree of LL.D. from Aberdeen. He died in London on 27 Sept. 1907, and was buried at Highgate cemetery. He married in 1867 Emily Browne, and left three sons and two daughters.

[Lancet, 1907, ii. 1061; Brit. Med. Journal, 1907, ii. 1023; Proc. Royal Soc. 1908, vol. lxxx. p. lxxxii; Field, 5 Oct. 1907; personal knowledge.] D'A. P.

STEWART, ISLA (1855–1910), hospital matron, born at Slodahill, Dumfriesshire, on 25 Aug. 1855, was second daughter of John Hope Johnstone Stewart by Jessie Murray his wife. Her father, a journalist who had served as an officer of irregular cavalry in the earlier South African campaigns, was a fellow of the Scottish Society of Antiquaries and published 'The Stewarts of Appin' in conjunction with Lieut.-colonel Duncan Stewart (Edinburgh, 1880, 4to).

Miss Stewart received her early education at home, and entered St. Thomas's Hospital, London, as a special probationer on 29 Sept. 1879. Here she made rapid progress and was entrusted with the charge of a ward sixteen months later. She left St. Thomas's Hospital in 1885 on her appointment as matron of a smallpox hospital at Darenth, in Kent, and in 1886 she became matron of the Homerton Fever Hospital. She was elected matron and superintendent of nursing at St. Bartholomew's Hospital in 1887 in succession to Miss Ethel Manson (Mrs. Bedford Fenwick). As matron she founded the League of St. Bartholomew's Hospital Nurses, the first organisation of its kind in England, though it had been foreshadowed by the American Nursing Alumnæ. She remained president of the league until 1908. In 1894 Miss Stewart was one of the founders of the Matrons' Council for Great Britain and Ireland, and she remained its president until her death. From this body came the National and the International Councils of Nurses and the Society for the State Registration of Trained Nurses, in all of which Miss Stewart was keenly interested. She was a member of the Nursing Board of Queen Alexandra's Imperial Military Nursing Service, and Principal Matron of No. 1 (City of London Hospital) of the territorial nursing service. She was also an honorary member of the Irish Nurses' Association, the German Nurses' Association, and the American Federation of Nurses. During 1907 she gave much good advice and active assistance in furthering the professional training of French nurses on the lines which had been found successful in England. For these services she was on 27 June 1908 publicly presented with a medal specially struck in her honour by the Assistance Publique, the official department which controls the hospitals at Paris.

Miss Stewart was one of the hospital matrons who by powers of organisation, foresight, and ability finally raised nursing of the sick by women from a business to a profession. In the large nursing school at St. Bartholomew's Hospital she introduced the methods of the English public schools and ruled by inculcating an *esprit de corps* which made her nurses proud to serve under her. She died at Chilworth, in Surrey, during a week-end holiday, on 6 March 1910, and was buried at Moffat, N.B. There is a bronze tablet to her memory in the church of St. Bartholomew-the-Less. A memorial to her took the form of an annual 'oration' on subjects connected with nursing; the first oration was delivered on 24 Nov. 1911.

Miss Stewart published 'Practical Nursing' in conjunction with Dr. Hubert Cuff (London and Edinburgh, vol. i. 1899; vol. ii. 1903; 11th edit. 1910).

[Brit. Journal of Nursing, vol. xliv. 1910, p. 202; St. Bartholomew's Hospital Journal, 1910, p. 104; The first Isla Stewart Oration, by Miss Rachel Cox-Davies, 1911; information from Miss Janet Stewart and Miss Hay-Borthwick; personal knowledge.] D'A. P.

STEWART, JAMES (1831–1905), African missionary and explorer, born at 5 South Charlotte Street, Edinburgh, on 14 Feb. 1831, was son of James Stewart, at one time a prosperous cab proprietor in Edinburgh, who lost his means as tenant (1842–7) of the farm of Pictstonhill, between Perth and Scone. His mother was

Jane Dudgeon, of Liberty Hall, near Gladsmuir, in Haddingtonshire. After attending successively a preparatory school, Edinburgh High School, and Perth Academy, James worked as a boy on his father's farm. When the farm was abandoned, he was put to business for a time in Edinburgh. From 1850 to 1852 and 1854 to 1856 he was at Edinburgh University, spending the intervening two years (1852–4) at St. Andrews. He took the arts course, but mainly interested himself in science. His study of botany yielded two short treatises: 'A Synopsis of Structural and Physiological Botany, presenting an Outline of the Forms and Functions of Vegetable Life' (n.d.), and 'Botanical Diagrams' (1857), both of which were long in use as school and college text-books.

From 1855 to 1859 Stewart studied theology at New College, Edinburgh. The summer session of 1858 was passed at the University of Erlangen, and at the close he made a tour through Europe, including Greece and Turkey. Later, he visited North America, crossing to the Pacific coast. In 1859 he began the study of medicine at Edinburgh University.

Meanwhile in 1857 Stewart came under the spell of David Livingstone [q. v.], who was then revisiting Scotland. In 1860 he announced to the foreign missions committee of the Free Church of Scotland his intention of establishing a mission in Central Africa. He was told that a separate fund, independently administered, was needful. Accordingly he formed an influential committee, at whose request he went to Central Africa to make inquiries. With Mrs. Livingstone, who was rejoining her husband, he sailed from Southampton on 6 July 1861, and reaching Cape Town on 13 Aug., he arrived on 9 March 1862 at Livingstone's headquarters at Shupanga. There for four busy months he often acted as both doctor and chaplain. Deciding to push into the interior, he, with only one white man, a member of the Universities' Mission, explored on foot the highland lake region on both sides of the Shiré and the district now covered by the Blantyre Mission. He returned, after many perilous adventures, to Shupanga on 25 Sept. 1862, and, a fortnight later, started to explore the Zambesi. Reaching Shupanga again on New Year's Day 1863, he was in Scotland in the autumn. The special mission committee in Edinburgh, on receiving his report in November, declined immediate action. The Royal Geographical Society, which elected him (1866) an honorary fellow, acknowledged that his travels had helped to extend British territory and to undermine the slave traffic.

Stewart's interrupted medical studies were resumed at Glasgow University in 1864 and completed in 1866, when he received the degrees of M.B. and C.M., with special distinction in surgery, materia medica, and forensic medicine. At the end of 1866 he returned to Africa, reaching, on 2 Jan. 1867, Lovedale, near the eastern boundary of Cape Colony, 700 miles north-east of Cape Town. In 1870 Stewart became principal of the Lovedale Missionary Institute, which was founded in 1841 by the Glasgow Missionary Society for the training of native evangelists. Under Stewart's supervision the institute greatly extended its operations. Though supported financially by the Free Church of Scotland (now the United Free Church), Lovedale, under Stewart's rule, became a non-sectarian centre of religious, educational, industrial, and medical activity. Lovedale, owing to Stewart's efforts, is now recognised as one of the foremost educational missions in the world, and its methods have been widely adopted.

In 1870 Stewart co-operated in the establishment of a mission at Umsinga in Natal as a memorial to the Hon. James Gordon, brother of the seventh earl of Aberdeen, and in 1875 he founded the Blythswood Mission Institute, Transkei, which was opened in July 1877 with accommodation for 120 native and thirty European boarders, and quickly proved a powerful civilising agency.

On 18 April 1874, while at home for the purpose of raising money for Lovedale and Blythswood, he attended Livingstone's burial in Westminster Abbey, and soon reopened the question of establishing a mission in that part of Africa associated with Livingstone's name. In May he brought his proposal before the general assembly of the Free Church of Scotland, urging the foundation of a mission town to be called Livingstonia. 10,000*l.* was soon raised, a small steamer, the Ilala, was built, and an advance party which made its way to Lake Nyasa in 1875 founded Livingstonia near Cape Maclear at the southern end of Lake Nyasa. Next year, on 21 Oct., Stewart arrived and chose a new site at Bandawe, 200 miles farther north, on the western side of the lake. He spent fifteen months in organising the settlement. Meanwhile he and Dr. Robert Laws explored Lake Nyasa, which they found to be 350 miles long, with a breadth varying from sixteen to fifty miles. They were the first white men to set foot on its northern shores. The natives were the most uncivilised they had seen. Stewart soon arranged to start a store for the benefit of the natives. The African Lakes Corporation, Ltd., 'the first of all the trading companies in that region, was formed, and did excellent civilising service' (STEWART'S *Dawn in the Dark Continent*, p. 219). The corporation acquired a capital of 150,000*l.*, and proved of immense service in fighting the slave traffic. Stewart, who returned to Lovedale at the end of 1877, left Livingstonia, which he modelled on Lovedale, to the guidance of Dr. Laws. Its prosperity grew quickly. The mission now consists of a network of stations stretching for many miles along the western shore of Lake Nyasa as well as inland, while Livingstonia itself has become a city of modern type.

From 1878 to 1890 Stewart chiefly devoted his energies to the consolidation and expansion of Lovedale, alike on its missionary and its educational sides. Sir George Grey [q. v.] obtained for him a government grant of 3000*l.* for industrial training there. He erected technical workshops, initiated a mission farm of 2000 acres, and founded a mission hospital, the first in South Africa, where native nurses and hospital assistants might be trained, and a medical school begun.

Stewart became a leading authority on all native questions, and was frequently consulted by Sir Bartle Frere [q. v.], General Gordon [q. v.], Cecil Rhodes [q. v. Suppl. II], and Lord Milner. In 1888 he helped to draft a bill codifying the native criminal law, and did much to ensure the adoption by Cape Colony of the principle that legally the native has equal rights with the white man. In 1904 he gave evidence before the Native Affairs Commission, stoutly opposing the creed of Ethiopianism, which aimed at setting up in Africa a self-supporting and self-governing native church.

In September 1891 Stewart, amid many difficulties and dangers, established a new mission on the model of Lovedale, within the territories of the Imperial British East Africa Company, now the East African Protectorate, about 200 miles from Mombasa. This East African mission is now large and flourishing.

Returning to Scotland, Stewart in the winter of 1892–3 gave a course of lectures on evangelistic theology to the divinity students of the Free Church of Scotland in Edinburgh, Glasgow, and Aberdeen; in 1892 he received from Glasgow University the honorary degree of D.D., and in 1899 he was moderator of the general assembly of the Free Church of Scotland. Later in 1899, at the seventh general council of the Alliance of Reformed Churches at Washington, U.S.A., he pleaded for a union of all presbyterian churches in the mission field, in an address entitled 'Yesterday and To-day in Africa.'

Stewart defended British action in the Boer war (1899–1901) on the ground that the Transvaal government was incurably corrupt and injurious to the interests of the natives and the country. In 1902 he delivered the Duff missionary lectures in Edinburgh, which, published as 'Dawn in the Dark Continent' (1903), gave a popular account of what missionary societies have accomplished in Africa, and is used as a text-book in mission circles in Great Britain and America. He revisited America in 1903 to examine new methods in negro colleges. Returning to Lovedale in April 1904, he presided over the first General Missionary Conference at Johannesburg (June). In November 1904 and January 1905 he was at Cape Town with a view to furthering native education. He died at Lovedale on 21 Dec. 1905, and was buried on Christmas Day on Sandili's Kop, a rocky eminence about a mile and a half east of Lovedale. At the funeral all races and denominations in South Africa were represented.

A presentation portrait, painted by John Bowie, A.R.S.A., Edinburgh, now hangs in the United Free Church Assembly Hall of Edinburgh.

In November 1866 he married Mina, youngest daughter of Alexander Stephen, shipbuilder, of Glasgow. She survived him, having borne him one son and eight daughters.

As the founder of Livingstonia, Stewart played no mean part as an empire-builder. Lord Milner described him as 'the biggest human in South Africa.' Besides the works cited, Stewart was author of: 1. 'Lovedale, Past and Present,' 1884. 2. 'Lovedale Illustrated,' 1894. 3. 'Livingstonia, its Origin,' 1894. 4. 'Kafir Phrase Book and Vocabulary,' 1898. 5. 'Outlines of Kafir Grammar,' 1902. He was also a contributor to religious and geographical periodicals, and founded and edited the newspapers, 'Lovedale News' and the 'Christian Express,' both of which are published at Lovedale and have well served the mission cause.

[Life of James Stewart, D.D., M.D., by James Wells, D.D. (n.d.); Robert Young, F.R.G.S., African Wastes Reclaimed, illustrated in the Story of the Lovedale Mission, 1902; J. W. Jack, Daybreak in Livingstonia, 1901; W. A. Elmslie, Among the Wild Ngoni, Edinburgh, 1899; reprint, 1901.] W. F. G.

STEWART, Sir WILLIAM HOUSTON (1822–1901), admiral, third son of Admiral of the Fleet Sir Houston Stewart [q. v.] by his wife Martha, daughter of Sir William Miller, first baronet, was born at Kirkmichael House, Ayrshire, on 7 Sept. 1822. He entered the navy on 29 April 1835, and as a midshipman of the Tweed served on shore in the Carlist war of 1836–7, being present at the different actions in which the royal marine battalion under Col. Owen co-operated with the British legion under Sir George de Lacy Evans [q. v.] and with the Spanish army. He served as a midshipman of the Carysfort during the Syrian war of 1840, was mentioned in despatches for gallant conduct at Tortosa, and was present at the bombardment of St. Jean d'Acre. He received the Syrian medal, with clasp, and the Turkish medal. He passed his examination in April 1841, and as mate served in the Illustrious, flagship on the North America station. On 29 June 1842 he was promoted to lieutenant and moved into the Volage, from which ship he returned, in March following, to the flagship. In 1844 he was first lieutenant of the sloop Ringdove, on the coast of Africa, and next, after a short spell of service as flag lieutenant to Sir E. Durnford King, commander-in-chief at the Nore, was appointed in Nov. 1845 to the Grampus in the Pacific. On his return home in 1847 he passed in steam at Woolwich, a thing which few officers then did, and on 19 May 1848 he was promoted to commander. In August 1851 Stewart was appointed to the paddle sloop Virago, which he commanded in the Pacific till 1853. He retook the revolted Chilian colony of Punta Arenas in the Straits of Magellan, released an American barque and an English vessel with a freight of treasure which had been illegally captured, and received the thanks of the French, American, and Chilian governments for these services. He was promoted to captain on 9 July 1854.

Stewart commanded the steam sloop Firebrand in the Black Sea in 1854, and was specially mentioned for his services at the bombardment of Sevastopol on 17 Oct., when he was wounded. He received the Crimean and Turkish medals, with the clasp for Sevastopol, the fourth class of the Mejidie, and was nominated for the Legion of Honour. In the campaign of 1855 he commanded the Dragon, paddle frigate, in the Baltic and saw much active service. At the bombardment of Sveaborg he had command of a division of the gunboats and mortar vessels; he was again mentioned in despatches and received the medal. For three years from May 1857 he was flag captain to the commander-in-chief at Devonport, and in May 1860 joined the Marlborough, of 131 guns, as flag captain to Sir William Fanshawe Martin [q. v. Suppl. I], commander-in-chief in the Mediterranean, where he remained for three years. The rest of his service was in administrative appointments. From Nov. 1863 to Nov. 1868 he was captain-superintendent of Chatham dockyard. On 1 April 1870 he was promoted to flag rank, and from July of that year was admiral-superintendent of Devonport dockyard until Nov. 1871, when he was appointed in the same capacity to Portsmouth dockyard. There he remained until he was chosen to be controller in April 1872. He held that post till 1881, but by the arrangement published in the Order in Council of 19 March 1872 was without a seat at the board. He was promoted to vice-admiral on 12 Nov. 1876, and was awarded the K.C.B. in June 1877. On 23 Nov. 1881 he reached the rank of admiral, and in Dec. was chosen as commander-in-chief at Devonport, where he remained for the full period of three years. On 31 March 1885 he accepted retirement; at Queen Victoria's Jubilee of 1887 he was made an additional G.C.B., and in 1894 he was awarded a flag officer's good service pension. He was a fellow of the Royal Geographical Society, served on the council of the Royal United Service Institution, and took part in the work of several naval benevolent societies. He occasionally published his views, contributing to the newspaper controversies which led to the passing of the Naval Defence Act of 1889 and to subsequent programmes for the strengthening of the navy. He died at 51 Hans Road, Chelsea, on 13 Nov. 1901, and was buried at Brompton.

Stewart was twice married: (1) on 20 Feb. 1850 to Catherine Elizabeth (*d.* 23 Nov. 1867), only daughter of Eyre Coote of West Park, Hampshire; (2) on 11 Jan. 1872 to Blanche Caroline, third daughter of Admiral the Hon. Keith Stewart, C.B., and granddaughter of George, eighth earl of Galloway. He left issue two sons and three daughters by his first marriage, and one daughter by the second.

[The Times, 14 and 18 Nov. 1901; O'Byrne's Naval Biogr. Dict.; R.N. List; an engraved portrait was published by Messrs. Walton of Shaftesbury Avenue.] L. G. C. L.

STIRLING, JAMES HUTCHISON (1820–1909), Scottish philosopher, born in Glasgow on 22 June 1820, was youngest of the six children of William Stirling, a Glasgow manufacturer, who was a man of intellectual ability, a student more especially of mathematics. His mother, Elizabeth Christie, died while he was still a child. Three brothers died young. James Stirling was educated first at Young's Academy, Glasgow, and then for nine successive sessions (1833–42) at Glasgow University, where he attended the classes in the faculties of arts and medicine, and took a high place in mathematics and classics. He became M.R.C.S.Edinburgh in July 1842, and F.R.C.S. in 1860. In 1843 he was appointed assistant to a medical practitioner at Pontypool in Monmouthshire, and in 1846 he was made surgeon to the Hirwain iron-works. Meanwhile he nterested himself in literature, and as early as 1845 contributed to 'Douglas Jerrold's Magazine.' After his father's death in 1851 Stirling gave up medical practice, and, inheriting a competency, took no other professional post. He travelled in France and Germany, devoting himself mainly to the study of German philosophy. Stirling's first and most important book was 'The Secret of Hegel, being the Hegelian System in Origin, Principle, Form and Matter' (2 vols. 1865; 2nd edit. 1898). The book may be said to have revealed for the first time to the English public the significance and import of Hegel's idealistic philosophy. Stirling's style of writing, trenchant and forceful as that of Carlyle, from whom he learned much, emphasised the lessons he set himself to teach. Few philosophical books have exerted an equal influence on the trend of thought in younger students, and to it and Stirling's succeeding works may be ascribed in great measure the rise of the school of idealism which has flourished of late years, more especially in the Scottish universities. The 'Secret' was succeeded in 1865 by an 'Analysis of Sir William Hamilton's Philosophy,' a forcible attack on Hamilton's philosophy of perception; but the point of view differs from that of Mill's famous onslaught. In 1867 was published Stirling's translation with annotations of Schwegler' 'History of Philosophy,' which has gone through fourteen editions and still holds its place as a standard text-book. The next of Stirling's works, 'As Regards Protoplasm' (1869; new edit. 1872), was a refutation, by means of reasoning based on physiological considerations, of Huxley's theory 'that there is one kind of matter' named Protoplasm 'common to all living beings.' Then came 'Lectures on the Philosophy of Law,' delivered in Edinburgh in 1871 and afterwards republished, which contain an exposition of Hegelianism in short form; and finally, in 1881, his 'Text-book to Kant,' a scholarly exposition and faithful reproduction of the 'Critique of Pure Reason' (which is translated), and of Kantian doctrines generally, with a biographical sketch of Kant. A masterpiece of criticism and interpretation, Stirling's 'Text-book' resolves many difficulties which seemed to former critics well-nigh insoluble, and shows how Hegel's philosophy originates in the Kantian system, from which it was a natural and necessary development, and how the English philosopher Hume, who had propounded the questions Kant set himself to answer, stands in relationship to German philosophy.

Stirling was appointed Gifford lecturer at Edinburgh (1889–90), and his lectures 'Philosophy and Theology' were published there in 1890. He was made hon. LL.D. of the University of Edinburgh in 1867 and of Glasgow in 1901; he was elected a foreign member of the Philosophical Society of Berlin in 1871. In 1889 he was granted a civil list pension of 50*l.* Meanwhile he wrote much in the 'Fortnightly Review,' 'Macmillan's Magazine,' and 'Mind,' as well as in American periodicals. His themes included materialism, philosophy in the poets, and nationalisation of the land; in 'Community of Property' (1885) he sought to refute the views of Henry George.

Stirling lived the ideal life of a philosopher, devoting all his time and talents to special studies. He died at Edinburgh on 19 March 1909, and was buried at Warriston cemetery there. He married in 1847 Jane Hunter Mair, and had two sons and five daughters. His daughter Amelia has written several historical books and was joint translator of 'Spinoza's Ethic' with Mr. Hale White; another, Florence, was for three successive years the Scottish lady chess champion.

Besides the books already cited, Stirling also published: 1. 'Jerrold, Tennyson and Macaulay, with other Critical Essays,' Edinburgh, 1868. 2. 'Burns in Drama, together with Saved Leaves,' Edinburgh, 1878, a collection of literary writings. 3. 'Darwinianism: Workmen and Work,' Edinburgh, 1894, an acute criticism of the Darwinian theory of evolution. 4. 'What is Thought?' Edinburgh, 1900. 5. 'The Categories,' Edinburgh, 1903; 2nd edit. 1907; an appendix to the former book, both further elucidating the Hegelian position.

A painted portrait by Stirling's daughter Florence is in the possession of the family. There is also a black-and-white drawing, of which a replica is in the philosophy classroom of St. Andrews University.

[A biography of Stirling, by his daughter Amelia, is in course of publication.]

E. S. H.

STOKES, Sir GEORGE GABRIEL, first baronet (1819–1903), mathematician and physicist, born at Skreen, co. Sligo, 13 Aug. 1819, was youngest son of Gabriel Stokes, rector of Skreen, by his wife Elizabeth, daughter of John Haughton, rector of Kilrea, co. Derry. First educated at Dr. Wall's school in Dublin from 1831, he proceeded in 1835 to Bristol college under Dr. Jerrard, the mathematician, and entered Pembroke College, Cambridge, in 1837, becoming senior wrangler, first Smith's prizeman, and fellow of his college in 1841.

In his early Cambridge years he established a close scientific friendship with William Thomson (afterwards Lord Kelvin) [q. v. Suppl. II], which gathered force throughout their long lives. Both were impelled by the keenest interest in the advance of scientific discovery, but their endowments were in some respects complementary. Stokes remained a student throughout his life, closely pondering over mathematical questions and the causes of natural phenomena, perhaps over-cautious in drawing conclusions and in publication of his work, remarkable for his silence and abstraction even in crowded assemblies, but an excellent man of affairs, inspiring universal confidence for directness and impartiality in such administration as came to him. Thomson, during all his career, took Stokes as his mentor in the problems of pure science which he could not find leisure to probe fully for himself; and, though their opinions sometimes clashed, yet in the main no authority was with him more decisive or more venerated than that of his friend. In 1845, at the end of his undergraduate course, Thomson took over the editorship of the 'Cambridge Mathematical Journal' from Robert Leslie Ellis [q. v.], and for the following ten years his own contributions and those which he obtained from Stokes made that journal a classic. In 1849 Stokes was appointed Lucasian professor of mathematics at Cambridge, and he held the post till his death.

In his early years of residence as a graduate Stokes promoted most conspicuously the development of advanced mathematical knowledge at Cambridge. His own earliest work was mainly on the science of the motion of fluids, which he found in the preliminary stage in which it had been left by Lagrange, notwithstanding some sporadic work done by George Green [q.v.], then resident at Cambridge; in a few years he developed it into an ordered mathematical and experimental theory. To this end, in addition to a very complete discussion of the phenomena of waves on water, he created, in two great memoirs of dates 1845 and 1850, the modern theory of the motion of viscous fluids, a subject in which some beginnings had been made by Navier. In the later of these memoirs the practical applications, especially to the important subject of the correction of standard pendulum observations for aerial friction, led him into refined extensions of mathematical procedure, necessary for the discussion of fluid motion around spheres and cylinders; these, though now included under wider developments in pure analysis, have remained models for physical discussion, and have been since extensively applied to acoustics and other branches of physical science.

In the science of optics he had already in 1849 published two memoirs on Newton's coloured rings, treated always with dynamical implications; one appeared in 1851 establishing on a firm physical basis the explanation of Newton's colours of thick plates; and he had elucidated the principles of interference and polarisation in many directions. In 1849 a new path was opened in the great memoir on 'The Dynamical Theory of Diffraction,' which deals with the general problem of propagation of disturbances spreading from vibrating centres through an elastic æther, and in which mathematical expressions were developed wide enough to include the Hertzian theory of electrical vibrations and other more recent extensions of the theory of radiation. A side problem was the experimental investigation of the displacement of the plane of polarisation of light by diffraction, in order, by comparison with the theory, to ascertain the relation of the plane of its vibration to that of its polarisation. Such a determination, though fundamental for a purely dynamical view, is not essential to the construction of an adequate formal account of the phenomena of radiation, and the workers in the modern electric theory have been content in the main to stop short of it.

The calculations relating to corrections for pendulums had led him into pure analysis connected with Bessel functions and other harmonic expansions; in various subsequent memoirs he established and justified the semi-convergent series necessary to their arithmetical use over the whole range of the argument, thus making practical advances that were assimilated only in later years into general analysis. Likewise the discrepancies which he encountered in practical applications of Fourier's theory led him as early as 1847 to a reasoned exposition of doctrines, now fundamental, relating to complete and limited convergence in infinite series. Here and elsewhere, however, his work developed rather along the path of advance of physical science than on the lines of formal pure analysis; and the recognition of its mathematical completeness was in consequence delayed.

In 1859 great interest was excited by the announcement of the discovery and development of spectrum analysis by Kirchhoff and Bunsen, and its promised revelations regarding the sun and stars by means of the Fraunhofer lines, an advance which was introduced to English readers by Stokes's translation of their earlier papers. It was soon claimed by William Thomson (Lord Kelvin) that he had been familiar with the scientific possibilities in this direction since before 1852, having been taught by Stokes the dynamical connection between the opacity of a substance to special radiation and its own power of emitting radiation of the same type. The theoretical insight thus displayed, on the basis of the interpretation of isolated observations, was, of course, no detraction from the merit of the practical establishment of the great modern science of spectrum analysis by the former workers: yet the feeling in some circles, that such a claim for Stokes was not quite warranted, was only set at rest by the posthumous discovery, among his papers, of a detailed correspondence with Lord Kelvin on this subject, mainly of date 1854, which is now printed in vol. iv. of his 'Collected Papers' (cf. pp. 126–36 and 367–76).

But in fact it was hardly necessary to wait for this evidence: for the same general considerations had already entered essentially into Stokes's discussion of one of his most refined and significant experimental discoveries. Shortly after he entered on the study of optics as a subject for his activity in the Lucasian chair at Cambridge, his attention was attracted to the blue shimmer exhibited by quinine in strong illumination, which had been investigated by Sir John Herschel [q. v.] in 1845. He soon found (1852) that the phenomenon was at variance with the Newtonian principle of the definite prismatic analysis of light, as the blue colour appeared when it was not a constituent of the exciting radiation. He discovered that this emission of light, called by him fluorescence from its occurrence in fluor-spar, was provoked mainly by rays beyond the violet end of the visible spectrum; and as a bye-product he thus discovered and explored the great range of the invisible ultra-violet spectrum, having found that quartz prisms could be used for its examination, though glass was opaque. Discussion of the exceptional nature of this illumination, created by immersion of the substance in radiation of a different kind, necessarily led him into close scrutiny of the dynamics of ordinary absorption and radiation; and the idea of a medium absorbing specially the same vibrations which it could itself spontaneously emit was thus fully before him (cf. § 237 of the memoir).

Another mathematical memoir (1878), suggested by the feeble communication of sound from a bell to hydrogen gas, elucidated the circumstances which regulate the closeness of the grip that a vibrating body gets with the atmosphere; and its ideas have also wider application, to the facility for emission and absorption of radiations of all kinds from and into the vibrating bodies which are their sources.

In two memoirs of date 1849 (*Papers*, ii. 104–121), on the variation of gravity over the earth's surface, he became virtually the founder of the modern and more precise science of geodesy. The fundamental proposition was there established, as the foundation of the subject, that the form of the ocean level determines by itself the distribution of the earth's attraction everywhere outside it, without requiring any reference to the internal constitution of the earth, which in this regard must remain entirely unknown.

His earlier scientific work, with that of Helmholtz and Lord Kelvin, may be said to mark the breaking away of physical science from the *à priori* method depending on laws of attraction, which was inherited from the astronomers; for this there was substituted a combination of the powerful analysis by partial differentials, already cultivated by Laplace and Fourier, with close attention to the improvement of physical ideas and modes of expression of natural phenomena. The way was thereby prepared for Clerk Maxwell's interpretation of Faraday, and for the modern wide expansion of ideas.

The copious early output of Stokes's own original investigation slackened towards middle life. In 1851 he had been elected F.R.S., and next year was awarded the Rumford medal for his discovery of the nature of fluorescence. In 1854 he became secretary of the Royal Society, and the thirty-one years of his tenure of this office (1854–85) were devoted largely to the advancement of science in England and the improvement of the publications of the Royal Society. There were few of the memoirs on physical science that passed to press through his hands that did not include valuable extensions and improvements arising from his suggestions. When the Indian geodetic survey was established, he was for many years its informal but laborious scientific adviser and guide. The observatory for solar physics, which was founded in 1878, was indebted to him in a similar manner. His scientific initiative as a member of the meteorological council, who managed from 1871 the British weather service, was a dominant feature of their activity. During these years the imperfect endowment of his chair at Cambridge made it necessary for him to supplement his income from other sources: thus he was for some time lecturer at the School of Mines, and a secretary of the Cambridge University Commission of 1877–81. He had vacated his fellowship at Pembroke on his marriage in 1857, but was re-elected under a new statute in 1869.

In 1883 Stokes was appointed, under a new scheme, Burnett lecturer at Aberdeen, and delivered three courses of lectures on 'Light' (1883–5), which were published in three small volumes (1884–7). In 1891 he became Gifford lecturer at Edinburgh, and delivered other three courses on the same general subject (1891–3). The theme in all these courses was treated from the point of view of natural theology, as the terms of the foundations required. His interests as a churchman and theologian were strong through life, and found occasional expression in print. He often took part in the proceedings of the Victoria Institute in London, which was founded for inquiry into Christian evidences.

Stokes received in his later years nearly all the honours that are open to men of science. He was president of the British Association at the Exeter meeting in 1869. In 1885 he succeeded Professor Huxley as president of the Royal Society, holding the office till 1890, when he was himself succeeded by his friend Lord Kelvin; he remained on the council as vice-president two years longer, and on his retirement he was immediately awarded in 1893 the society's Copley medal. On the death of Beresford-Hope in 1887, he was elected without opposition, in the conservative interest, one of the members of parliament for Cambridge University, and he sat in the House of Commons till 1891. He was a royal commissioner for the reform of the University of London (1888–9). In 1889 he was created a baronet (6 July). In 1899 the jubilee of his tenure of the Lucasian chair was celebrated at Cambridge by a notable international assembly. Through the friendship of Hofmann, Helmholtz, Cornu, Becquerel, and other distinguished men, he became in his later years widely known abroad; and the Prussian order *pour le mérite* and the foreign associateship of the Institute of France were conferred on him. At his jubilee celebration the Institute of France sent him the special Arago medal; and he was one of the early recipients of the Helmholtz medal from Berlin. He received honorary doctor's degrees from Edinburgh. Dublin, Glasgow, and Aberdeen, as well as from Oxford and Cambridge. In October 1902 his colleagues of Pembroke College, of which he had long been fellow and of late years president, elected him Master. He died at Cambridge on 1 Feb. 1903, and was buried there at the Mill Road cemetery.

Stokes married on 4 July 1857 Mary (*d.* 30 Dec. 1899), daughter of Thomas Romney Robinson, the astronomer [q. v.], and left issue two sons and one daughter. His elder son, Arthur Romney Stokes succeeded him as second baronet.

Stokes's writings have been collected into five volumes of 'Mathematical and Physical Papers' (Cambridge, 1880–1905) of which the first three were carefully edited by himself, and the other two were prepared posthumously by Sir Joseph Larmor, his successor in the Lucasian chair. Two volumes of his very important 'Scientific Correspondence' were published in 1907 under the same editorship, and include a biographical memoir (pp. 1–90) prepared mainly by his daughter, Mrs. Laurence Humphry.

There is a portrait by G. Lowes Dickinson in Pembroke College, and one by Sir Hubert von Herkomer at the Royal Society; marble busts by Hamo Thornycroft were presented to the Fitzwilliam Museum and to Pembroke College on the celebration of his jubilee as Lucasian professor in 1899, and a memorial medallion bust by the same sculptor is in Westminster Abbey.

[Mrs. Humphry's memoir mentioned above; notice by Lord Rayleigh in Proc. Royal Soc. 1903, and reprinted in Papers, vol. v. pp. ix-xxv; cf. also Silvanus Thompson's Life of Lord Kelvin, 1910.] J. L.

STOKES, Sir JOHN (1825–1902), lieutenant-general, royal engineers, born at Cobham, Kent, on 17 June 1825, was second son in a family of three sons and three daughters of John Stokes (1773–1859), vicar of Cobham, Kent, by his wife Elizabeth Arabella Franks (1792–1868). Educated first at a private school at Ramsgate, then at the Rochester Proprietary School, Stokes passed into the Royal Military Academy at the head of the list in the summer of 1841. On leaving he was awarded the sword of honour and received a commission as second lieutenant in the royal engineers on 20 Dec. 1843. After professional instruction at Chatham, he was posted in February 1845 to the 9th company of royal sappers and miners at Woolwich, with which he proceeded in June to Grahamstown, South Africa. He was promoted lieutenant on 1 April 1846.

In Cape Colony he spent five adventurous years, taking part in the Kaffir wars of 1846–7 and of 1850–1. In the first war he was deputy assistant quartermaster-general on the staff of Colonel Somerset commanding a column of the field force in Kaffraria. He was particularly thanked by the commander-in-chief, General Sir Peregrine Maitland [q. v.], for his conduct in the action of the Gwanga on 8 June 1846, and on 25 July following, when he opened communications through the heart of the enemy's country. In the war of 1850–1 he was again on the staff as a deputy assistant quartermaster-general to the 2nd division of the field force; he was in all the operations of the division from February to July 1851, and helped to organise and train some 3000 Hottentot levies. He was repeatedly mentioned in general orders, and was thanked by the commander-in-chief, Sir Harry Smith [q. v.].

Returning home from the Cape in October 1851, Stokes became instructor in surveying at the Royal Military Academy at Woolwich. He was promoted captain on 17 Feb. 1854, and in March 1855 was appointed to the Turkish contingent, a force of 20,000 men raised for service in the war with Russia and commanded by Sir Robert John Hussey Vivian [q. v.]. Stokes sailed at the end of July after raising and organising a nucleus for the contingent's corps of engineers, to be supplemented by Turks on the spot. He was given the command of the corps, and arriving in the Crimea in advance, witnessed the final assault on Sevastopol on 8 Sept. 1855. The Turkish contingent was sent to Kertch, where Stokes employed his corps in fortifying the place and in building huts for the troops during winter. When peace was concluded in March 1856 Stokes was made British commissioner for arranging the disbandment of the contingent. For this work he received the thanks of the government, and for his services in the Crimea a brevet-majority on 6 June 1856, the fourth class of the Mejidie, and the Turkish medal.

In July 1856 Stokes was nominated British commissioner on the European commission of the Danube, constituted under the treaty of Paris to improve the mouths and navigation of the Lower Danube. The commission, at first appointed for two years, became a permanent body, with headquarters at Galatz. Stokes's colleagues were often changed, but he held office for fifteen years, and thus came to exert a commanding influence on the commission's labours. By Stokes's advice (Sir) Charles Hartley was appointed engineer and the Sulina mouth of the Danube was selected for experimental treatment. The waterway was straightened and narrowed so as to confine and accelerate the current and thus concentrate its force to scour away the bar. In 1861 it was decided to replace the temporary constructions by permanent piers which should extend into the deeper water of the Black Sea. In order to obtain the necessary funds small loans were raised on the shipping dues, but these proved insufficient for the larger scheme. Stokes devoted himself to the finances and at the same time suppressed disorders on the river, and regulated the navigation and pilotage. The fixing of a new scale of dues involved a thorough investigation into the mode of measuring ships, as to which all nations then differed. In 1865 the 'Public Act' was promulgated, embodying the decision of the commission and establishing the 'Danube Rule' of measurement, which was a modification of the English rule.

On 6 July 1867 Stokes was promoted to be a regimental lieutenant-colonel and paid one of his periodical visits home. He prevailed on Lord Stanley, then foreign secretary, to provide needful financial help for the moment and to arrange with the powers concerned to guarantee a loan, which was sanctioned next year by an international convention, Russia alone standing out. Great Britain gave effect to the convention in the 'Danube Loan Act.' When in the autumn of 1870 Russia repudiated the Black Sea articles of the treaty of Paris, Stokes urged the British government to secure in perpetuity European control over the mouths of the Danube by means of the commission. During the congress in London in 1871 he acted as the intermediary of Lord Granville, foreign secretary, with the foreign ambassadors and plenipotentiaries on questions affecting the Danube. He arranged the terms with them and drafted the articles on the Danube in the treaty of London of March 1871. For his services he was created a C.B., civil division.

The works at the Sulina branch of the Danube were now approaching completion; the channel had been increased from eight or nine to twenty feet at low water, and was available for large ships for a hundred miles above its mouth; the new tariff gave a yearly increasing income for the maintenance of the navigation, the river was well lighted, and the pilotage satisfactorily arranged (see Stokes's paper on the mouths of the Danube in *Roy. Eng. Establishment Papers*, 1865, and 'The Danube and its Trade' in *Soc. of Arts Journal*, 1890). Accordingly, when the war office summoned Stokes to return to corps duties, if he wished to remain on the effective list, he resigned the commissionership. In 1872 he was appointed commanding royal engineer of the South Wales military district, and on 4 June 1873 received a brevet colonelcy.

But international diplomacy continued to be his main occupation. Stokes served at Constantinople as British commissioner (Oct.–Dec. 1873) on the international commission to settle a difficulty that had arisen over the Suez Canal dues, which, hitherto calculated by the canal company on net tonnage, had recently been charged on gross tonnage. The view of the majority of the commissioners in favour of the charge on net tonnage was resisted on behalf of the canal company by the representatives of France and some other powers. The difference was settled by a compromise, which Stokes proposed, to the effect that in addition to the ten francs a ton on net tonnage, the company should be empowered to levy a surtax of three and a half francs a ton, to be reduced in certain defined proportions as the traffic through the canal increased. The sultan marked his satisfaction by promoting Stokes to the second class of the order of the Mejidie in 1874. After reporting for the foreign office on the condition of the canal, Stokes in the spring resumed his duties at Pembroke Dock. M. Ferdinand de Lesseps, however, objected to the arrangements made at Constantinople, and Stokes was in frequent attendance at the foreign office. Early in 1875 he was made commanding royal engineer of the Chatham district, to be more within reach.

On 1 Nov. 1875 he was appointed commandant of the School of Military Engineering at Chatham. Later in the month his opinion was invited as to the purchase, which he advised, of the Khedive's shares in the Suez Canal, and subsequently at the Khedive's request the British government sent Mr. Cave of the paymaster-general's department and Colonel Stokes to Egypt for four months to examine and report on the Khedive's financial embarrassments. In pursuit of separate instructions he concluded a convention settling outstanding difficulties with M. de Lesseps and the Suez Canal Company under the Constantinople agreement of 1873. The terms included representation of the British government on the board of directors, and Stokes was nominated to the board in June 1876. Next year he was created a K.C.B., civil division. During 1879–80 he served on an international commission, with headquarters at Paris, to examine the works at the port of Alexandria in Egypt, and decide what dues should be levied on the shipping. In Nov. 1880 he joined the royal commission on tonnage measurement, which reported in 1881. Appointed deputy adjutant-general for royal engineers at the war office on 1 April 1881, Stokes was a member of the Channel tunnel committee, and opposed its construction in 1882. The Egyptian expedition of that year exposed him to some friction with French colleagues on the Suez Canal board, who objected to the use made of the canal by the British authorities, but his tact overcame all objections, and he received the personal thanks of Gladstone, the prime minister, for his good service. In March 1885 Stokes was given the temporary rank of major-general, succeeding to the establishment on 6 May following. His services as deputy adjutant-general were retained for three months over the usual five years, and he left the war office on 30 June 1886, retiring from the service with the honorary rank of lieutenant-general on 29 Jan. 1887.

On leaving the war office he resided first at Haywards Heath and afterwards at Ewell. The Suez Canal board, of which he became vice-president in 1887, frequently called him to Paris, and he undertook the administration of the 'Lady Strangford Hospital' at Port Said after her death in 1887. In the same year he was appointed a visitor of the Royal Military College at Sandhurst. In 1894 he attended de Lesseps's funeral in Paris, and delivered a set oration in French. He paid his last visit to Egypt in 1899 to be present at the unveiling of de Lesseps's statue at the entrance to the canal at Port Said. Stokes, who was also director in later life of several public companies, died suddenly of apoplexy at Ewell on 17 Nov. 1902. He was elected an associate member of the Institution of Civil Engineers on 13 Jan. 1875.

He married at Grahamstown, Cape Colony, on 6 Feb. 1849, Henrietta Georgina de Villiers (*d.* 1893), second daughter of Charles Maynard, of Grahamstown. By her he had three sons and three daughters. The second son, Arthur Stokes, is a brevet colonel in the royal artillery and a D.S.O.

[War Office Records; Royal Engineers' Records; private information; Porter's History of the Royal Engineers, 1889; Royal Engineers' Journal, 1903; Leading Men of London, 1894; Men and Women of the Time, 1899; Proc. Inst. Civ. Eng. 1902; The Times, 18 Nov. 1902.] R. H. V.

STOKES, WHITLEY (1830–1909), Celtic scholar, eldest son of William Stokes, M.D. [q. v.], by his wife Mary Black, was born in Dublin on 28 Feb. 1830. His family tree does not contain a single native Irish name. He entered St. Columba's College at Rathfarnham, co. Dublin, on 8 Oct. 1845, and left on 16 Dec. in the same year. Denis Coffey, a Munster man, was the Irish teacher there, and his 'Primer of the Irish Language,' which had just appeared, was probably the first Irish book placed in the hands of Stokes. The next was undoubtedly the 'Grammar of the Irish Language' of John O'Donovan, published in 1845 at the expense of St. Columba's College. His first guide to the vocabulary of Irish was the Irish dictionary of Edward O'Reilly, as is shown by Stokes's interleaved, annotated, and marked copy of the book. He entered Trinity College, Dublin, in 1847, and graduated B.A. in 1851. In his father's house he became acquainted with George Petrie [q. v.], deep in Irish architecture and music, with John O'Donovan [q. v.], the best Irish scholar of the time and the greatest of all Irish topographers, and with Eugene O'Curry [q. v.], the most accomplished modern representative of the ancient Irish scribes. Stokes thus had the opportunity of laying a broad foundation for every part of Irish learning. He elected early to devote himself to the study of the words and forms of the Irish language, and regarded Irish literature as chiefly interesting in so far as it furnished material for comparative philology. Rudolf Thomas Siegfried, a philologist from Tübingen, first assistant librarian of Trinity College and afterwards professor there of Sanscrit and comparative philology, a man of much learning and great enthusiasm, became his friend and influenced his studies, and the vast field for philological research opened by the publication of the 'Grammatica Celtica' of John Caspar Zeuss in 1853 decided the direction of the studies which Stokes pursued with unremitting industry till death. He took some lessons in Irish from John O'Donovan, but never acquired its pronunciation, and used always to read Irish exactly as English schoolboys once read Latin, according to the English powers of the letters, and he never sounded the 'r,' nor had he any idea of quantity.

Stokes became a student of the Inner Temple on 9 Oct. 1851, and was called to the bar on 17 Nov. 1855. He was a pupil of Cayley, Cairns, and Chitty, and practised in London for six years till 1862, when he went to Madras and afterwards to Calcutta. In India he formed a friendship with Sir Henry Sumner Maine [q. v.], and partly through his influence, after being secretary to the governor-general's legislative council, was made secretary to the legislative department in 1865, and was from 1877 to 1882 law member of the council of the governor-general. In 1879 he was appointed president of the Indian law commission. He had published in London 'A Treatise on the Liens of Legal Practitioners' in 1860, and one on 'Powers of Attorney' in 1861. He drafted many Indian consolidation acts and the bulk of the codes of procedure, and published 'Hindu Law Books' at Madras in 1865, the Anglo-Indian codes (two volumes) in 1887–8, with supplements 1889–91, and three other books on the statutes of India. He was made C.S.I. in 1877 and C.I.E. in 1879. In 1882 he left India, and for the rest of his life resided for a time in Oxford and at Camberley in Surrey, but chiefly in Kensington.

Meanwhile Stokes continued his Irish studies without intermission alike in England and in India. In 1859 he published as a paper in the 'Transactions of the Philological Society of London,' 'Irish Glosses from a MS. in Trinity College, Dublin.' His first book was 'A Mediæval Tract on Latin Declension, with Examples explained in Latin and the Lorica of Gildas, with the Gloss thereon and Glosses from the Book of Armagh'; it was printed in 1860 in Dublin by the Irish Archæological and Celtic Society, and he received for it the gold medal of the Royal Irish Academy. In 1862 he published in London three Irish glossaries. The first was that of Cormac MacCuillenain, the second that of Domnall O'Dubhdhaboirenn, written in 1569, and the third that occurring in the 'Calendar of Oengus Cele Dé.' These are accompanied by a long introduction and verbal indexes, but are not translated. In 1868 Stokes published at Calcutta an edition of John O'Donovan's manuscript translation of Cormac's glossary, with notes and sixteen separate verbal indexes, as well as three of matters, authors, and persons. Throughout his writings he retained the practice of having many indexes to each book. He published 'Goidelica,' a collection of Old and Early-middle Irish glosses, at Calcutta in 1866, (2nd edit. London, 1872), as well as many smaller collections of glosses, Irish, Welsh, and Breton, and in 1901 and 1903, with John Strachan [q.v. Suppl. II], a 'Thesaurus Palæohibernicus' of more than twelve hundred pages of old Irish glosses from manuscripts anterior to the eleventh century. The Italian government had spent large sums in the publication of the Milan glosses and thought part of the work an unjust invasion of their property, and a reflection upon it. An apologetic statement was in consequence inserted in the second volume by the editors. The book rendered the mass of Old Irish glosses on the Continent and in Ireland easily accessible for the first time, All this glossarial study rendered Stokes in the highest degree competent to write the 'Urkeltischer Sprachschatz' in 1894, with Professor Bezzenberger. He also prepared many papers on grammatical subjects, of which one of the chief is an elaborate investigation of 'Celtic Declension' issued by the Philological Society in 1885–6. He published texts and translations with notes, and generally with glossaries, of a great many pieces of Irish literature, of which the earliest was the 'Fis Adamnain,' the account of the journey of Adamnan, grandson of Tinne, to Paradise and to Hell, from a manuscript of 1106. This was printed at Simla in 1870. At Calcutta in 1877 he published Irish lives of Patrick, Brigit, and Columba from a fifteenth-century manuscript, and at the same place in 1882 the 'Togail Troi,' a tale of the destruction of Troy in part based on Dares Phrygius. In 1890 he published at Oxford, in the 'Anecdota Oxoniensia,' 'Lives of Saints from the Book of Lismore,' a manuscript of about 1450. The 'Felire' of Angus, a sort of metrical calendar of saints, he first edited in 1871, in the publications of the Royal Irish Academy, and again from ten manuscripts in 1905, in a volume of the Henry Bradshaw Society. The same society published in 1895 his edition of the 'Felire' of O'Gorman, another metrical calendar. He edited in the Rolls series in 1887, 'The Tripartite Life of St. Patrick,' in two volumes. Besides all these and many more Irish works he edited and translated the Cornish mystery, 'Gwreansan Bys' (Creation of the World), in 1864, 'The Life of St. Meriasek' in 1872, and a volume of 'Middle Breton Hours' in 1876 (Calcutta). Another part of his writings consists of controversial attacks, generally on the interpretation of texts, on O'Beirne Crowe, O'Curry, Sullivan, Prof. Robert Atkinson [q. v. Suppl. II], S. H. O'Grady, and others. Nemesis is always on the watch in such controversies, and Stokes himself fell into many errors of the kind he censured in others. No man could have edited so many difficult texts for the first time without making some mistakes. Stokes often came to perceive his own, and altered them quietly in a fresh edition. The severity of his studies sometimes broke down his health, and produced conditions of extreme irritability or of depression, which explain the violence of his language. His last Irish work was an edition of the Irish prose version of Lucan's 'Pharsalia' known as 'Cath Catharda,' which Professor Ernst Windisch of Leipzig printed after his death. Windisch and Stokes together brought out a series of 'Irische Texte,' at Leipzig, 1884–1909, of which this was the last.

Stokes died at 15 Grenville Place

Kensington, after a short illness, on 13 April 1909. He was an original fellow of the British Academy, a foreign associate of the Institute of France, and an honorary fellow of Jesus College, Oxford. He was a kindly and hospitable entertainer and was fond of laughter in his conversation and of relating anecdotes, but did not pour out in talk the extensive knowledge he possessed, nor often take part in fruitful discussion. He wished to pursue his subject with paper, ink, and books at hand, doggedly progressing from point to point, and was unwilling to commit himself by word of mouth. His whole life was one of unflagging industry in Celtic studies.

Stokes married: (1) in 1865 Mary, daughter of Colonel Bazely of the Bengal artillery, by whom he had two sons and two daughters; (2) on 18 Oct. 1884 Elizabeth (*d.* 1901), third daughter of William Temple.

His daughters presented, in Dec. 1910, his library of Celtic printed books to University College, London. Its most important feature is a collection of all his own works, which is scarcely to be found anywhere else. It was his habit to paste letters and printed scraps into books to which they referred. Many of his books bear the marks of his study and criticism.

[Works; personal knowledge; Kuno Meyer in Proc. Brit. Acad., vol. iv.; full bibliography by Prof. R. I. Best in Zeitschrift für celtische Philologie, viii. 351-406, 1911; Letters of William Allingham, 1911; information from Rev. W. Blackburn of St. Columba's College.] N. M.

STONEY, BINDON BLOOD (1828–1909), civil engineer, born at Oakley Park, King's Co., Ireland, on 13 June 1828, was younger brother of George Johnstone Stoney [see below]. Bindon was educated at Trinity College, Dublin, where he graduated B.A. with distinction in 1850, proceeding M.A. and M.A.I. in 1870. In 1850–2 he served as assistant to the earl of Rosse [q. v.] in the Parsonstown observatory. There he made more accurate delineations of nebulæ than had been obtained previously, and ascertained, before the days of astronomical photography, the spiral character of the great nebula in Andromeda.

His first work as an engineer was on railway surveys in Spain in 1852–3. In 1854–5 he was resident engineer on the construction of the Boyne Viaduct under James Barton. This viaduct was probably the earliest instance of the use of metal girders of any considerable span in which latticed bars were substituted for a continuous plate web, and the cross sections of the web members as well as of the flanges were proportioned to the stresses imposed by the rolling load. In Barton's account of the viaduct (*Proc. Inst. Civ. Eng.* xiv. 452) Stoney's assistance on an important point in connection with the design of this type of structure is acknowledged. His work on this viaduct led him to that thorough study of stresses in girders which bore fruit in his elaborate treatise 'The Theory of Strains in Girders and Similar Structures' (2 vols. 1866; 2nd edit. 1873; 1 vol.; 3rd edit. 1886, entitled 'The Theory of Stresses in Girders, &c.').

Meanwhile Stoney in 1856 became assistant engineer to the port authority of Dublin; three years later, owing to the ill-health of the chief engineer, George Halpin, junior, he acted as executive engineer, and in 1862 he succeeded Halpin as chief engineer. He held that post until his retirement in 1898. As engineer to the port and docks board he improved the channel between Dublin Bay and the city, designing for the purpose powerful dredging plant. He also rebuilt about 1½ mile of quay-walls, providing deep-water berths for oversea vessels, extended the northern quays to the east, and began the Alexandra basin. In the construction of the northern quays he employed concrete monoliths of the then unprecedented weight of 350 tons, and designed the appliances necessary for handling and setting the huge blocks. He also rebuilt the Grattan and O'Connell bridges, and built the Butt bridge across the Liffey.

Stoney was elected F.R.S. in 1881, and in the same year was made hon. LL.D. by Trinity College, Dublin. He was elected an associate of the Institution of Civil Engineers on 12 Jan. 1858, became a full member on 17 Nov. 1863, and was a member of the council from 1896 to 1898. Of the Institution of Civil Engineers of Ireland he was elected a member in 1857, served as joint honorary secretary (1862–70), and was president in 1871 and 1872. He was also a member of the Royal Irish Academy, of the Royal Dublin Society, and of the Institution of Naval Architects. The Institution of Civil Engineers awarded him in 1874 a Telford medal and premium for a paper on his work on the Dublin northern quays (*Proc.* xxxvii. 332; cf. other papers, *ibid.* xx. 300 and lviii. 285). To the Institution of Civil Engineers of Ireland he contributed eight papers between 1858 and 1903, including his presidential address (1872) and a paper on 'Strength and Proportions of Riveted Joints' which was re-published in book form (1885). To the publications of the Royal Irish Academy he contributed four papers dealing with the theory of structures (*Proc.* vii. 165; viii. 191; *Trans.* xxiv. 189; xxv. 451).

He died in Dublin on 5 May 1909, and was buried in Mount Jerome cemetery. He married, in 1879, Susannah Frances, daughter of John Francis Walker, Q.C., by whom he had one son and three daughters.

[Proc. Roy. Soc. vol. 85; Minutes of Proc. Inst. Civ. Eng. clxxvii. 287; Who's Who, 1907.] W. F. S.

STONEY, GEORGE JOHNSTONE (1826–1911), mathematical physicist, born at Oakley Park, King's Co., Ireland, on 15 Feb. 1826, was elder son of George Stoney of Oakley Park by his wife Anne, second daughter of Bindon Blood of Cranagher and Rockforest, co. Clare. Bindon Blood Stoney [q. v. Suppl. II] was his only brother. His sister, who married her cousin, William FitzGerald, afterwards bishop of Cork and subsequently of Killaloe, was mother of George Francis FitzGerald [q. v. Suppl. II]. Sir Bindon Blood, general R.E., G.C.B., and Sir Frederic Burton [q. v. Suppl. I] were also his cousins. Three members of the family besides himself—his brother Bindon, his eldest son, George, and his nephew, George Francis FitzGerald—were fellows of the Royal Society.

Stoney, whose father's Irish property had greatly depreciated in value after the Napoleonic wars, and had to be sold at the time of the Irish famine (1846–8), was sent with his brother to Trinity College, Dublin, where he paid his expenses by 'coaching.' There he had a distinguished career, and obtained in 1847 the second senior moderatorship in mathematics and physics. He graduated B.A. in 1848, proceeding M.A. in 1852. On leaving Trinity College, he was in 1848 appointed by Lord Rosse the first astronomical assistant at the Parsonstown Observatory, a post which he held till 1852. His interest in astronomy continued through life, and he contributed occasional papers on astronomical subjects to the scientific societies' journals, several of them being instigated by the expected appearance of a profuse shower of Leonid meteors in 1899 (*Proc. Roy. Soc.* lxiv. 403; *Monthly Notices*, vols. lvi.–lix). The present use of the cælostat in astronomical observation is largely due to his efforts in reviving a forgotten principle, and papers by him on improvements in the Foucault-Sidenstat as well as on the phenomena of shadow bands in eclipses will be found in the 'Monthly Notices.' While he was with Lord Rosse he unsuccessfully competed in 1852 for the fellowship at Trinity, winning the second place and the Madden prize. The same year he became through Lord Rosse's influence professor of natural philosophy at Queen's College, Galway, one of his unsuccessful rivals being Professor Tyndall. After five years' work in Galway he returned to Dublin in 1857 as secretary of the Queen's University, with an office in Dublin Castle, and till the dissolution of the university in 1882 he devoted himself wholeheartedly to his duties, which involved the organisation of the scattered colleges constituting the university. The excellence of Stoney's report and minutes on educational matters led the Irish under-secretary, Sir Thomas Aiskew Larcom [q. v.], to recommend Stoney as his successor on his own retirement in 1868. But Stoney approved of Gladstone's disestablishment policy, and declined the post, although the conservative Irish secretary, Lord Mayo, urged its acceptance. At the request of the civil service commissioners, Stoney soon after became superintendent of civil service examinations in Ireland, a post which he held till he left Dublin in 1893. He did much for Irish education. He was a member of the royal commission on the Queen's Colleges, 1885. He was an able advocate of higher education for women, and mainly through his exertions women obtained legal medical qualifications in Ireland before they were available in England or Scotland. His many essays in reviews on educational subjects include 'On the Demand for a Catholic University' (*Nineteenth Century*, Feb. 1902). At the same time he was frequently consulted by the Irish government, not only on education, but (in virtue of his connection with the Royal Dublin Society) on questions of agriculture, fisheries, light railways, and the like. The death of his wife in 1872, and other family trouble, followed by two severe illnesses—small-pox in 1875 and typhoid in 1877—enfeebled his health. These misfortunes, combined with his manifold official duties, greatly hampered his scientific research, which was the main interest of his life.

Physical optics was a subject to which Stoney gave much attention, and he treated it on somewhat original lines. One of his first papers explained by geometrical reasoning the conditions of the propagation of undulations of plane waves in media (*Trans. Roy. Irish Acad.* vol. 24, 1861). Late in life he pursued the subject in his 'Monograph on Microscopic Vision' (*Phil. Mag.* Oct.–Dec. 1896), in which he analysed and proved the fundamental proposition—first enunciated by Sir George Stokes in 1845—that 'the light which emanates from the objective field may be resolved into undulations, each of which consists of uniform plane waves,' suffering no change as they advance. This theme was pursued after the close of his official life in several papers and memoirs in the 'Philosophical Magazine,' the last being a monograph on 'Telescopic Vision' (Aug.–Dec. 1908), in which he discussed among other matters the possibility of seeing very small markings on the planet Mars.

Valuable as these optical researches are, Stoney's work in molecular physics and the kinetic theory of gases proved more important. An early paper on Boyle's law (*Proc. Roy. Irish Acad.* vol. vii. 1858) was followed ten years later (in *Phil. Mag.* Aug. 1868) by his paper 'On the Internal Motions of Gases compared with the Motions of Waves of Light,' in which he estimated the number of molecules in a gas at standard pressure and temperature.

There followed inquiries into the conditions limiting planetary atmospheres. As early as 1868 he published a long paper 'On the Physical Constitution of the Sun and Stars' (*Proc. Roy. Soc.* 1868), in which he first suggested limits of atmospheres. Stoney considered this paper one of his chief achievements. In a very valuable contribution, 'On Atmospheres of Planets and Satellites' (*Trans. Roy. Soc.* Dublin, 1897, vi. 305), Stoney afterwards explained from inductive reasoning the absence of hydrogen and helium from the atmosphere of the earth, and the absence of an atmosphere from the moon and from the satellites and minor planets of the solar system. This paper was reprinted in the 'Astrophysical Journal' (vii. 25), and gave rise to controversy, but Stoney's position was unshaken. His investigations as to helium are of great importance in view of recent inquiries into the length of geological epochs, and into the past history of the radio-activity of the materials of the earth's crust.

To Stoney was due the introduction of the word 'electron' into the scientific vocabulary. In a paper 'On the physical units of nature,' which he read before the British Association at Belfast in 1874 (printed in *Phil. Mag.* May 1881), he pointed out that 'an absolute unit of quantity of electricity exists in that amount of it which attends each chemical bond or valency.' He proposed that this quantity should be made the unit of electricity, and for it subsequently suggested the name 'electron' in place of the old name 'corpuscle' proposed by Prof. J. J. Thomson (cf. *Phil. Mag.* Oct. 1894). Stoney worked with admirable results on the periodic motion of the atom and its connection with the spectrum (*Proc. Roy. Irish Acad.* Jan. 1876; *Trans. Roy. Soc. Dublin*, May 1891). To the units of physical science and their nomenclature Stoney devoted much of his attention. He served on the committee of the British Association for the selection and nomenclature of dynamical and electrical units in 1873, which adopted the C[entimetre] G[ramme] S[econd] system of units in England. He did much work in physical mensuration, and strove to facilitate the introduction of the metric system into England.

In 1888 Stoney entered upon a study of the numerical relations of the atomic weights (see *Proc. Roy. Soc.* April 1888). His versatility was also illustrated by papers on 'The Magnetic Effect of the Sun or Moon on Instruments at the Earth's Surface' (*Phil. Mag.* Oct. 1861); 'On the Energy expended in driving a Bicycle' (*Trans. Roy. Dublin Soc.* 1883, with his son); 'On the Relation between Natural Science and Ontology' (*Proc. Roy. Dublin Soc.* 1890), and many papers on abstract physics. In bacteriology he suggested that the source of the life energy in bacteria was to be found in their bombardment by the faster moving molecules surrounding them, whose velocity is great enough to drive them well into the organism, and carry in energy, of which they can avail themselves (*Phil. Mag.* April 1890).

Music also claimed his attention, and he wrote papers on musical shorthand and on echoes (*Proc. Roy. Dublin Soc.* 1882), and did much for the advance of musical culture in Dublin by inducing the council of the Royal Dublin Society to inaugurate chamber music concerts by leading European musicians.

During the twenty years that he was hon. secretary of the Royal Dublin Society he zealously fulfilled the duties of the office at a period when the affairs of the society demanded much attention. He was afterwards vice-president till 1893, and to its

'Transactions' he communicated most of the earlier results of his researches. He received the society's first Boyle medal in 1899. He also became hon. D.Sc. of Queen's University in Ireland in 1879, and hon. Sc.D. of the University of Trinity College, Dublin, in 1902. Stoney's work received recognition from learned societies at home and abroad. He was a foreign member of the Academy of Science at Washington, and of the Philosophical Society of America and a corresponding member of the Accademia di scienze, lettere ed arti di Benevento. He regularly attended the meetings of the British Association, served on several committees, and acted as president of section A at the meeting at Sheffield in 1879. Elected F.R.S. in 1861, he was vice-president of the society in 1898–9, and he was a member of the council (1898–1900). He was a visitor of the Royal Observatory at Greenwich and of the Royal Institution. He was also a member of the joint permanent eclipse committee of the Royal Society and the Royal Astronomical Society, and of several international committees for scientific objects.

In 1893 Stoney left Dublin for London, in order to give his daughters the opportunity, denied them at that time in Dublin, of university education. He settled first at Hornsey and afterwards at Notting Hill, engaging in physical experiments, principally optical, and in writing scientific papers. Stoney, who was always ready to help younger scientific men, died on 5 July 1911 at his residence, 30 Chepstow Crescent, Notting Hill Gate, W. After cremation his ashes were buried in Dundrum, co. Dublin. Stoney married in Jan. 1863 his cousin, Margaret Sophia (*d.* 1872), second daughter of Robert Johnstone Stoney of Parsonstown, sister of Canon Stoney, and left issue two sons and three daughters. His elder son, George Gerald, F.R.S., holds a Watt medal of the Institute of Electrical Engineers, and was till 1912 manager of the turbine works of the Hon. Sir Charles Parsons, F.R.S. Of the daughters Edith Anne (equal to seventeenth wrangler in the mathematical tripos at Cambridge in 1893, and M.A. Trinity College, Dublin) is lecturer in physics at the London School of Medicine for Women; the second, Florence Ada, M.D., B.S. London, is in practice in London, and is head of the electrical department, New Hospital for Women, London.

A collection of Stoney's scientific writings is being prepared for publication by his eldest daughter.

Of four portraits in oils, one painted in 1883 by Sir Thomas Jones, P.R.H.A., for the old students of the Queen's University on its dissolution, was presented by them to the Royal Dublin Society, in whose council room in Leinster House, Kildare Street, Dublin, it now hangs; a second portrait by the same artist (1883), presented to Stoney, as well as two other portraits (1896)—one in oils and one in chalk—by his third daughter, Gertrude, are in the possession of his elder daughters at 20 Reynolds' Close, Hampstead.

[Proc. Roy. Soc., 86A, 1912 (with portrait; art. by Prof. J. Joly); Abstract of Mins. Roy. Irish Acad. 1911–12; The Observatory, Aug. 1911 (notice by Sir Robert Ball, F.R.S.); Nature, 12 July 1911 (art. by Prof. F. T. Tronton, F.R.S.); The Times, and Daily Express (Dublin), 6 July 1911; E. E. Fournier d'Albé, The Electron Theory, with preface by and frontispiece portrait of Stoney, 1907; and Contemporary Chemistry, 1911; notes from Mr. H. P. Hollis; information from son and from daughter, Edith A. Stoney.] W. B. O.

STORY, ROBERT HERBERT, D.D. (1835–1907), principal of Glasgow University, born at Roseneath manse, Dumbartonshire, on 28 Jan. 1835, was only surviving son of Robert Story (1790–1859) [q.v.], parish minister of Rosneath, by his wife Helen Boyle Dunlop. After home teaching from his father and learning mathematics and other subjects at the parish school, he studied arts at Edinburgh University (1849–54), gaining distinction in literature and philosophy. He spent a semester in 1853 at Heidelberg. He won prizes for poetry, and Professor Aytoun urged him to discipline his gift for verse; he wrote later much occasional poetry, including some excellent hymns. He studied divinity at Edinburgh and St. Andrews Universities (1854–7), and after the first of many continental trips was licensed a preacher by the presbytery of Dumbarton on 2 Nov. 1858.

Story was assistant in St. Andrew's church, Montreal, from 12 March to 20 Nov. 1859, when he left to become assistant to his father at Rosneath. Before he reached home his father died and the patron, the Duke of Argyll, presented him to the parish into which he was inducted on 23 Feb. 1860. In general accord with Dr. Robert Lee [q. v.] he sought to systematise the form of service and to modify the old observances at the celebration of the communion. With two others he founded, on 31 Jan. 1865, the Church Service Society, which in the course of years efficiently transformed ancient usages.

Both Lee, who died in 1868, and himself persevered in spite of opposition, and Story had the satisfaction of seeing their views prevail. In 1884 a lectureship was founded in memory of Lee, and Story delivered the first lecture in St. Giles's Cathedral, Edinburgh, in April 1886, his subject being 'The Reformed Ritual in Scotland.'

Story, who meanwhile proved himself an ideal country parson, gradually became a leader in the church courts. From 1863 to 1875 he attended the general assembly of the church in accordance with ordinary regulations, but through special provisions he was a regular member from 1877 onwards. He became one of the ablest debaters in the house, advocating useful measures and sensible reforms. His name is conspicuously associated with discussions on Sabbath observance, on the abolition of patronage, on the Free Education Act, on the adaptability of the Confession of Faith to modern conditions, and, notably, on the movement for disestablishment before and after 1885. In May 1886 he was appointed junior clerk to the general assembly and in 1894 he was moderator, closing the meetings with a lucid and stirring address on 'The Church of Scotland, its Present and its Future.' Next year he became senior clerk of the assembly, holding the position for the rest of his life. From 1885 to 1889 he edited a magazine—first called 'The Scottish Church' and then 'The Scots Magazine'—primarily designed for support of the principles he upheld. He had grave doubts as to the wisdom of the Free Education Act, but resolved to make the best of it when it had passed, and he was chairman of Rosneath school board from its first meeting in March 1873 till he left the parish. In 1886 he succeeded John Caird [q. v. Suppl. I] as chaplain-in-ordinary to Queen Victoria, and the appointment was renewed in 1901 by King Edward VII.

On 9 Nov. 1886 Story became professor of church history in Glasgow University. While zealously performing his special work he readily responded to the numerous calls which the city made upon him. In 1895 he was one of several Scottish ministers who discussed presbyterian reunion at a conference held at Grindelwald. In 1897 he was the Baird lecturer and took for his theme 'The Apostolic Ministry in the Scottish Church.' He was one of the representative divines who convened at Iona, on 9 June 1897—the anniversary of the death of Columba, 597—to offer 'thanksgiving for the introduction of the Gospel into our land.' Meanwhile he actively interested himself in the position of the church in the Highlands and in India, and in the Layman's League and home missions.

In 1898 Story was appointed principal of Glasgow University in succession to Dr. John Caird [q. v. Suppl. I]. In 1901 the ninth jubilee of the university was celebrated under his presidency. To his exertions was largely due the provision of new university buildings, mainly for medical and scientific purposes. At the same time he was a convinced champion of 'the humanities,' and his tenure of office was not free from friction with students. With the Carnegie Trust for the benefit of the Scottish Universities he was not in full sympathy, partly because of the exclusion of literary studies from its scope, but chiefly owing to its haphazard scheme for the payment of fees; but he fully recognised its value as a means of encouraging post-graduate research. After a period of gradually declining strength he died on 13 Jan. 1907, and was interred in the family burying-ground at Roseneath.

Story was made hon. D.D. of Edinburgh in 1874; hon. LL.D. of Michigan University, U.S.A. in 1887; hon. LL.D. of St. Andrews in 1900. He was also a fellow of the Scottish Society of Antiquaries, and he reached high degree as a freemason.

Story's chief publications were: 1. 'Memoir of [his father] the Rev. Robert Story,' Cambridge, 1862, an admirable contribution to ecclesiastical biography. 2. 'The Life and Remains of Robert Lee, D.D.,' 1870. 3. 'William Carstares: a Character and Career of the Revolutionary Epoch (1649–1715),' 1874, a survey of church and state in a time of transition. 4. 'The Apostolic Ministry of the Scottish Church' (Baird lecture), Glasgow, 1897. Other works were 'Christ the Consoler, or Scripture Hymns and Prayers for Times of Trouble and Sorrow' (Edinburgh, 1865); 'Creed and Conduct,' a collection of sermons (Glasgow, 1878; new edit. 1883); 'Saint Modan of Rosneath: a Fragment of Scottish Hagiology' (1878); and 'Health Haunts of the Riviera and South-West of France' (1881), the fruit of a continental holiday. Story edited a 'History of the Church of Scotland' (4 vols. 1890–91).

A portrait, presented by friends and painted in 1890 by Sir Philip Burne-Jones, and a study by John Bowie, A.R.S.A., for a group of Queen's chaplains, belong to the family. Two portraits in oil, by Sir George Reid, P.R.S.A., were prepared respectively for the Church of Scotland (now at 22 Queen

Street, Edinburgh, the offices of the church) and for Glasgow University (in the Hunterian Museum, Glasgow University). Of the latter there is a good photogravure. There is a fine drawing by William Strang A.R.A. A memorial window was unveiled in Rosneath Church on 24 Sept. 1908, and another, by Douglas Strachan, was placed in the Bute Hall, Glasgow University, on 21 Oct. 1909.

On 31 Oct. 1863 Story married Janet Leith, daughter of Captain Philip Maughan, H.E.I.C. Mrs. Story was author of three well-constructed novels, 'Charley Nugent,' 'The Co-heiress,' and 'The St. Aubyns of St. Aubyn,' and of 'Kitty Fisher,' a children's story. In 1911 she published deeply interesting 'Early Reminiscences,' Two surviving children, Elma and Helen Constance Herbert, jointly wrote a memoir of their father.

[Memoir of Robert Herbert Story, D.D., LL.D., by his daughters; Mrs. Oliphant, Memoir of Principal Tulloch, 1888, and Autobiography 1899; Twenty-five Years of St. Andrews, by Dr. A. K. H. Boyd, 1896; Life of Dr. Robert Wallace, by Sheriff Campbell Smith; Scotsman, and Glasgow Herald, 14 Jan. 1907; information from Miss Story; personal knowledge.] T. B.

STORY-MASKELYNE, MERVYN HERBERT NEVIL (1823–1911), mineralogist, born at Basset Down House, near Wroughton, Wiltshire, on 3 Sept. 1823, was eldest son in the family of two sons and four daughters of Anthony Mervyn Reeve Story, F.R.S. (1791–1879), by his wife Margaret, only child and ultimate heiress of Nevil Maskelyne [q. v.], astronomer royal. The father acquired through his wife the Maskelyne estates in Wiltshire, and in 1845 adopted the surname of Story-Maskelyne. One of the mineralogist's sisters, Antonia, married Sir Warington Wilkinson Smyth [q. v.].

After spending ten years at Bruton grammar school in Somerset, Story-Maskelyne was admitted to Wadham College, Oxford, as a commoner on 19 Nov. 1840, and graduated B.A. with a second class in mathematics in Easter term 1845. He proceeded M.A. on 7 June 1849. On leaving Oxford he studied for the bar, but he had, almost from boyhood, taken a keen interest in natural science, and his early studies in photography led to a friendship with William Henry Fox Talbot [q. v.]. He was persuaded to abandon the law for science in 1847 by Benjamin Brodie the younger [q. v.], and in 1850 was invited to deliver lectures on mineralogy at Oxford. He accepted this invitation on condition that a laboratory should be assigned to him, where he could teach mineralogical analysis and chemistry in general. Chemical manipulation had not been taught previously in the University of Oxford, and great interest was excited by the opportunity of learning what sort of thing chemistry might be. A suite of rooms under the Ashmolean Museum was allotted Story-Maskelyne, and there he lived and worked from 1851 to 1857. His first student was William Thomson [q. v.], afterwards archbishop of York.

Story-Maskelyne was an early advocate of the due recognition of natural science in the Oxford curriculum, and was examiner in the new school of natural science in 1855 and 1856. He was active in the struggle which lasted from 1847 to 1857 over the proposal to erect a museum in Oxford. The foundation stone of the museum was laid in 1855 and it was opened in 1861 (cf. ATLAY'S *Henry Acland: a Memoir*, 1903, pp. 197 seq.). Story-Maskelyne became professor of mineralogy in 1856 in succession to Dean William Buckland [q. v.], and was duly allotted as professor a laboratory in the new museum. The chair had been founded by George IV in 1813, but it was very inadequately remunerated till 1877, when it was reconstituted as the Waynflete professorship of mineralogy.

In 1857 Story-Maskelyne was appointed to the newly created post of keeper of the minerals at the British Museum and, although he retained his Oxford professorship, he settled in London. It became his practice to invite the most promising of his Oxford pupils, who included Professor W. J. Lewis, Dr. L. Fletcher, and Sir Henry A. Miers, to work with him at the British Museum. He thus extended the usefulness of both his London and Oxford offices, and trained many distinguished members of the next generation of British mineralogists.

Since 1851 no one at the British Museum had taken any special interest in mineralogy. Story-Maskelyne undertook the re-arrangement of all the minerals under his charge according to the crystallochemical system of Rose. He also maintained and developed the collections so that they became the largest and best arranged series of minerals and meteorites in existence. During his tenure of the keepership no fewer than 43,000 specimens were added to the collection. He published a catalogue of minerals at the museum in 1863 (new edit. 1881) and a 'Guide to the Collection' in 1868.

Story-Maskelyne was always much interested in meteorites, which he was one of the first to study by means of thin sections for the microscope. He published the results of his numerous researches, of which the most important are those on the nature and constitution of the Parnallee, Nellore, Breitenbach, Manegaum, Busti, Shalka, and Rowton meteorites. Chief among his mineral researches were those upon Langite, Melaconite, Tenorite, Andrewsite, Connellite, Chalkosiderite, and Ludlamite. New minerals described by him were Andrewsite, Langite, Liskeardite, and Waringtonite. Asmanite, Oldhamite, and Osbornite, constituents of meteoric stones, were first isolated and determined by him, though the first named, described by him in 1871, is now generally regarded as identical with the mineral tridymite. He was also the first to recognise the presence of enstatite in meteorites.

Deeply interested in the history of the diamond, he wrote on the Koh-i-noor stone (*Chemical News*, 1860, i. 229; *Nature*, 1891, xliv. 555; xlv. 5). In 1880 he proved that the supposed diamonds manufactured by Mactear were in reality a crystallised silicate. The mode of occurrence of the diamond in South Africa also occupied his attention, and he described the enstatite rock which is associated with it in that part of the world (*Philosophical Magazine*, 1879, vii. 135).

Story-Maskelyne gave some notable courses of lectures on crystallography both in London and Oxford. In a course delivered in 1869 he announced an important proof of the number and mutual inclinations of the symmetry planes possible in a crystalloid system. His general views were stated in a series of lectures before the Chemical Society in 1874. On his lectures he largely based his well-known text book, 'The Morphology of Crystals,' which was published in 1895. In his mathematical as well as in his purely scientific treatment of his theme his writing was characterised by distinction and charm of style.

Story-Maskelyne's scientific attainments were widely recognised. Elected a fellow of the Royal Society in 1870, he was vice-president from 1897 to 1899. He received in 1893 the Wollaston medal of the Geological Society, of which he became a fellow in 1854, was chosen an honorary fellow of Wadham College in 1873, and was made hon. D.Sc. in 1903. He was corresponding or honorary member of the Imperial Mineralogical Society of St. Petersburg, of the Society of Natural History of Boston, of the Royal Academy of Bavaria, and of the Academy of Natural Sciences in Philadelphia.

On the death of his father in 1879 Story-Maskelyne succeeded to the Basset Down estates, and thenceforward became an active country gentleman. He resigned his post at the British Museum next year, but he continued to hold the professorship of mineralogy at Oxford till 1895. By that time funds were obtained for securing the whole time of a resident professor, and he was succeeded by (Sir) Henry A. Miers.

Story-Maskelyne entered the House of Commons in 1880, when he was elected in the liberal interest as member for the borough of Cricklade. He was re-elected for the Cricklade division of North Wiltshire in 1885 and 1886, but he refused to follow Gladstone in his home rule policy in 1886, and thenceforth sat in parliament as a liberal-unionist until his defeat in July 1892. He took no prominent part in the debates, but introduced in 1885 the Thames preservation bill, and was chairman of the committee to which the bill's consideration was referred. The bill was passed on 14 Aug. 1885. He was a member of the Wiltshire county council from its foundation in 1889 till 1904, when he was over eighty years of age, and was for many years chairman of the agricultural committee. He was an active member of the Bath and West of England Agricultural Society, and it was at his suggestion that the first itinerant dairy school was established. He was a good scholar and was one of the few scientific men who read Homer till late in life. He formed a valuable private collection of antique engraved gems, and he privately printed a catalogue of the intaglios and cameos known as the Marlborough Gems.

Story-Maskelyne died at Basset Down on 20 May 1911, after a prolonged illness, and was buried at Purton, Wiltshire.

He married on 29 June 1858, after settling in London, Thereza Mary, eldest daughter of John Dillwyn Llewellyn, F.R.S., and granddaughter of Lewis Weston Dillwyn [q. v.], the botanist. He was survived by his wife and three daughters, of whom the second, Mary Lucy, married Hugh Oakeley Arnold-Forster [q. v. Suppl. II], some time secretary of state for war, and the third, Thereza Charlotte, became wife of Sir Arthur Rücker, F.R.S., in 1892.

His portrait by the Hon. John Collier,

subscribed for by friends in 1895, is now a Basset Down House, Swindon.

[Burke's Landed Gentry; Gardiner's Reg. Wadham College, p. 401; The Times, 21 May 1911; Proc. Roy. Soc.] H. A. M. A. W. R.

STRACHAN, JOHN (1862–1907), classical and Celtic scholar, born at the farm of Brae near Keith, Banffshire, on 31 Jan. 1862, was only son of James Strachan, farmer of Brae, by his wife Ann Kerr. He was educated at the grammar school of Keith under Dr. James Grant till he entered the University of Aberdeen in 1877 at the age of fifteen. Strachan proved an excellent all-round scholar, but especially distinguished himself in classics and philosophy. In 1880 he spent the summer at Göttingen working with Professor Benfey. In 1881, having completed the course at Aberdeen with first-class honours in classics, he entered Pembroke College, Cambridge, where another Aberdonian, Robert Alexander Neil [q. v. Suppl. II], was the principal classical lecturer. In 1882 he won the Ferguson scholarship, which is open to the four Scottish universities. In 1883 he won at Cambridge the Porson university scholarship, and having taken the first part of the classical tripos with the highest distinction, proceeded to Jena, where he worked at Sanskrit with Professor Delbrück and at Celtic with Professor Thurneysen. The following year he spent the whole summer at Jena in the same pursuits, and in 1885 graduated at Cambridge with special distinction in classics and comparative philology. He was also second chancellor's medallist. In the summer of the same year he was elected professor of Greek at Owens College, Manchester, and in 1889, by a re-arrangement of work with Augustus Samuel Wilkins [q.v. Suppl. II], the professor of Latin, he added to Greek the teaching of comparative philology.

In his first years at Manchester, Strachan busied himself especially with work upon Herodotus, the fruit of which was an excellent school edition of book vi. (1891), containing an account of the Ionic dialect superior to anything preceding it. At his death he left in manuscript a large Greek grammar treated on philological principles, which is not yet published. He gradually devoted himself, however, more and more to Celtic studies, and during the last few years of his life his distinction in this department was recognised by the university, which appointed him to a newly founded and unpaid lectureship in Celtic; in order to give him time for this work he was granted an additional assistant in Greek. His publications on Celtic were numerous and important; the greatest of them was the 'Thesaurus Palæo-Hibernicus,' which he undertook in conjunction with Dr. Whitley Stokes [q. v. Suppl. II]; it appeared in two large volumes in 1901 and 1903. At the time of his death he was making arrangements for compiling the Dictionary to the texts thus published.

The increasing interest in Irish studies was fostered by the School of Irish Learning established in 1903 by Professor Kuno Meyer in Dublin, in which during several long vacations Strachan taught Old Irish with much enthusiasm. For his pupils he produced several little books containing the grammar and selections from the Old Irish texts. In the 'Transactions of the Philological Society' he published a long series of valuable memoirs upon the 'History of Irish,' the most important perhaps being 'The Compensatory Lengthening of Vowels in Irish' (1893), 'The Deponent Verb in Irish' (1894), 'The Particle "ro" in Irish' (1896), 'The Subjunctive Mood in Irish' (1897), 'The Sigmatic Future and Subjunctive in Irish' and 'Action and Time in the Irish Verb' (both in 1900). Shorter papers appeared in the 'Zeitschrift für celtische Philologie,' and other journals at home and abroad. In 1906 and 1907 he took up the study of early Welsh, and began preparing for the press 'An Introduction to Early Welsh.' This was published posthumously in 1909 by the Manchester University Press after a satisfactory settlement of a lawsuit brought against the publishers by the Welsh scholar Dr. John Gwenogvryn Evans, who thought that inadequate acknowledgment of Strachan's debt to his own published Welsh texts had been made by the editor. In September 1907 Strachan went for a few days to Wales in order to collate at Peniarth the texts of some of the early manuscripts which he wished to publish. While at Peniarth he caught a chill which on his return to Manchester developed into pneumonia. On 25 Sept. he died at Hilton Park, Prestwich, where he had lived for some years.

Besides his work on Greek, comparative philology, and Celtic, Strachan also taught Sanskrit at Manchester. In 1900 Aberdeen University conferred upon him the honorary degree of LL.D. No good portrait of Strachan exists, and the bronze bust in the possession of Manchester University only faintly resembles him. His Celtic books were purchased by Manchester University. In 1886 he married Mina, eldest daughter of Dr. James Grant, his old schoolmaster, and by her had issue two sons and six daughters. A pension of 80*l.* from the civil list was granted to his widow in 1909.

[Information from Mrs. Strachan; personal knowledge from 1880.] P. G.

STRACHEY, Sir EDWARD, third baronet (1812–1901), author, born at Sutton Court, Chew Magna, Somerset, on 12 Aug. 1812, was eldest of the six sons of Edward Strachey by his wife Julia Woodburn, third daughter of Major-general William Kirkpatrick [q. v.], 'a singular pearl of a woman' (Carlyle, *Reminiscences*, i. 128). His five brothers, all long-lived, were Sir Henry Strachey (1816–1912), lieutenant-colonel of the Bengal army; Sir Richard Strachey [q. v. Suppl. II]; William Strachey (1819–1904), of the colonial office; Sir John Strachey [q. v. Suppl. II], and George (1828–1912), minister at the court of Saxony.

His father, Edward (1774–1832), second son of Sir Henry Strachey [q. v. Suppl. I], first baronet, was educated at Westminster and St. Andrews, went to Bengal as a writer in 1793, became a judge, was employed in diplomacy, and was one of the dearest friends of Mountstuart Elphinstone [q. v.], who said that in his early years he owed much to Strachey's advice and example, and depended on his friendship (*Life*, ii. 309). He married in 1808, returned to England in 1811, and retired from the Bengal service in 1815. He resided at Sutton Court until 1820, when, having been appointed an examiner at the India House, he moved to London, and there became a friend of Thomas Carlyle, who was often at Strachey's house in Fitzroy Square, and visited him at his summer residence at Shooters Hill. He was a student of English literature, and a good Persian scholar: he published 'Bija Ganita' (1813, 4to), a translation from the Persian of a Hindu treatise on algebra, originally written in Sanskrit.

Edward Strachey was destined for the East India Company's service, and was educated at Haileybury, but when about to sail for India he was attacked by inflammation of the knee-joint, which destroyed his hope of an Indian career, and forced him to use crutches for more than twenty years. He was eventually cured when past forty by the waters of Ischia when on a visit to Naples, but his knee always remained stiff. In 1836, having been attracted by 'Subscription no Bondage,' by F. D. Maurice [q. v.], he obtained an introduction to him through John Sterling [q. v.], a friend of his mother, and asked to be allowed to read with him with a view to entering a university. This intention an increase of his malady forced him to abandon. However, he spent the second half of that year with Maurice at Guy's Hospital, and from that time an intimate friendship existed between them; Maurice became his spiritual adviser and exercised a lasting influence on his mind.

In 1858 he succeeded to the title and the Somersetshire estates of his uncle, Sir Henry Strachey, the second baronet, who died unmarried. He took a warm interest in the welfare of his tenants, specially those of the labouring class, was an active magistrate and a deputy-lieutenant, and in 1864 was high sheriff of Somerset; he was a poor-law guardian and was a member of the first Somerset county council. A keen politician, and a liberal of a somewhat idealistic type, he was an admirer of Gladstone and in 1870 wrote a series of articles in the 'Daily News' on the proposed Irish Land bill, for which materials were supplied him by his friend and neighbour, Chichester Fortescue, afterwards Lord Carlingford [q. v. Suppl. I]. His life was largely that of a man of letters; he followed up his early studies in Oriental languages, especially in Persian, occasionally making translations from Persian poems, and was well versed in English literature. Besides his books he wrote articles in the 'Spectator,' 'Blackwood's Magazine,' and other periodicals. His interests were wide and his mind alert. As a disciple of Maurice he was firmly attached to the Church of England, but was strongly opposed to high church doctrines and practices, and respected the opinions of his nonconformist neighbours. He was deeply religious, although his religious opinions in his early days were in advance of contemporary standards of orthodoxy. Biblical criticism, especially on its historical side, was one of his favourite studies, and he learnt Hebrew in order to pursue it. He died at Sutton Court on 24 Sept. 1901, and was buried in Chew Magna churchyard.

He married (1) on 27 Aug. 1844, Elizabeth, eldest daughter of the Rev. W. Wilkieson, of Woodbury Hall, Bedfordshire; she died without issue on 11 April 1855; and (2) on 3 Nov. 1857, Mary Isabella, second daughter of John Addington Symonds (1807–1871) [q. v.]; she died on 5 Oct. 1883, leaving three sons: Edward, who was created Baron Strachie of Sutton Court on

3 Nov. 1911; John St. Loe, editor of the 'Spectator'; Henry, an artist, and one daughter, all now (1912) living.

There are three painted portraits of Strachey at Sutton Court, one by Samuel Laurence [q. v.] and two by his son, Mr. Henry Strachey.

Strachey published: 1. 'A Commentary on the Marriage Service,' 1843, 24mo. 2. 'Shakespeare's Hamlet: an Attempt to find a Key to a great Moral Problem,' 1848. 3. 'Hebrew Politics in the Time of Sargon and Sennacherib: an Inquiry into the Meaning of the Prophecies of Isaiah,' 1853, revised and enlarged as 'Jewish History and Politics,' 1874, bringing the prophecies into connection with what is known from other sources as to the Jewish kingdom, and discussing the questions of their unity, arrangement, authorship, &c. 4. 'Miracles and Science,' 1854. 5. 'Politics Ancient and Modern,' with F. D. Maurice, in 'Tracts for Priests,' 1861. 6. 'Talk at a Country House,' 1895, originally published in the 'Atlantic Monthly,' largely autobiographical in thought though not in circumstance, the 'Squire' being the author and his interlocutor 'Forster,' Sir Edward used to say, representing his ideas in his younger days. He also edited Malory's 'Morte d'Arthur' (1868, 1891) for the Globe edition; contributed to Richard Garnett's edition of Peacock's works, vol. x., 'Recollections' of the author, Peacock having been a colleague of Strachey's father at the India House, and wrote an introduction to Edward Lear's 'Nonsense Songs' (1895, 4to).

[Private information; Sir F. Maurice's Life of F. D. Maurice, 1884. For Sir Edward's father see Carlyle's Reminiscences, ed. Froude, 1881; Sir E. Colebrooke's Life of Mountstuart Elphinstone, 1884.] W. H.

STRACHEY, Sir JOHN (1823–1907), Anglo-Indian administrator, born in London on 5 June 1823, was fifth son of Edward Strachey by his wife Julia, youngest daughter of Major-General William Kirkpatrick [q. v.]. Sir Edward Strachey [q. v. Suppl. II] and Sir Richard Strachey [q. v. Suppl. II] were elder brothers.

After being educated at a private school at Totteridge, John entered Haileybury in 1840, among his contemporaries being Sir E. Clive Bayley, Sir George Campbell [q. v. Suppl. I]. Sir Alexander Arbuthnot [q. v. Suppl. II], W. S. Seton-Karr, and Robert Needham Cust [q. v. Suppl. II]. He was one of the editors of the 'Haileybury Observer,' to which he contributed a vindication of Shakespeare, described as 'displaying a considerable mastery of Coleridge's writings.' He passed out second on the list for Bengal in 1842, having won prizes for classics and English and also the medal for history and political economy. Literature and art were always among his interests.

Appointed to the North West Provinces, he divided his first years of service between the plains of Rohilkhand and the neighbouring hills of Kumaon. At the outbreak of the Mutiny he was absent on furlough in England. Hitherto he had served as an ordinary district officer, without any of the chances that are open to those at headquarters. But after his return to India he was selected for a series of special appointments. Lord Canning nominated him in 1861 president of a commission to inquire into a great epidemic of cholera; and Lord Lawrence made him in 1864 president of the permanent sanitary commission then formed as a result of the report of a royal commission on the health of the army in India. Meanwhile, in 1862, he had been judicial commissioner, or chief judge, in the newly constituted Central Provinces. Lord Lawrence formed so high an opinion of him as to appoint him in 1866 to be chief commissioner of Oudh, at a time when the question of tenant-right there was rousing heated controversy. Strachey succeeded in persuading the taluqdars or landlords to accept a compromise, afterwards enacted by the legislative council, though his private views would have granted much larger privileges to the tenant class. In 1868 he became a member of the governor-general's council, and held office throughout Lord Mayo's viceroyalty. When the news of Lord Mayo's assassination first reached Calcutta in Feb. 1872, he acted for a fortnight as governor-general. With the legal member of the council, Sir James Fitzjames Stephen, he formed an enduring friendship (cf. Leslie Stephen, *Life of Sir J. F. Stephen*, pp. 245 seq.). In 1874 Strachey was appointed lieutenant-governor of the North West Provinces; but he vacated the post in 1876, when Lord Lytton persuaded him to enter the governor-general's council for a second time as finance member.

His lieutenant-governorship of the North West Provinces was too brief to leave a permanent mark, but the measures associated with his name include the creation of a department of agriculture and commerce; a new system of village accounts, by which the record is written up annually instead of only on the occasion of a thirty years' settlement; the extension of the survey to permanently settled districts; the attempt to construct railways from provincial resources. It was also his pride that he took the first active steps to secure the conservation of the historic Mogul buildings at Agra.

As finance minister Strachey shares with his brother Sir Richard, whose work in India was closely connected with his own, the credit of extending the decentralisation of provincial finance, started under Lord Mayo in 1871, and of abolishing the customs line across the peninsula, which permitted the equalisation and ultimate reduction of the salt duty. To Strachey and his brother were due too the recognition of a light income tax as a permanent part of the system of taxation; the creation of a famine insurance fund of incalculable benefit, amounting to a million and a half sterling annually; and the application of free trade principles to the customs tariff so far as circumstances permitted. Another of Strachey's reforms, which has not been carried out, was the passing of a statute authorising the introduction of the metric standard of weights and measures. Unhappily, Strachey's term of office as finance minister closed prematurely under a cloud. The cost of the war in Afghanistan, owing mainly to a defective system of military accounts, was found to have been under-estimated by no less than twelve millions sterling [see LYTTON, EDWARD ROBERT BULWER, first EARL OF LYTTON]. Strachey, upon whom the responsibility was fixed by the home government, thought it his duty to retire twelve months before his full time. He finally left India at the close of 1880, after thirty-eight years' service. He had been knighted in 1872 and made G.C.S.I. in 1878.

After India, Italy appealed to his sympathies. An ardent supporter of the movement for national unity and liberation, he used to regret that he could not have enlisted under Garibaldi. On his retirement from India he occupied for some time a villa at Florence, where he studied art and architecture. Subsequently he spent the winter there or on the Italian lakes. He was familiar with the language and literature, and Italians were among his intimate friends. Part of this period of rest he devoted to literary work. As early as 1881 he collaborated with his brother, Sir Richard, in a record of what the two had helped to accomplish in India, under the title of 'The Finances and Public Works of India' (1882), which is a mine of historical information. Again, after settling in England, he in 1884 gave before the University of Cambridge a course of lectures on India, which were published under the title 'India' in 1888, and reached a fourth edition in 1911, being revised by Sir T. W. Holderness after the author's death. In 1885 Strachey was nominated by Lord Randolph Churchill to be a member of the secretary of state's council of India, an office which then lasted for ten years. While actively engaged on the council he found time to follow the example of his friend, Sir James Fitzjames Stephen, and to attempt in 'Hastings and the Rohilla War' (1892), to clear the memory of Warren Hastings from the charges arising from the Rohilla war of 1774.

Strachey, who on the occasion of Lord Curzon's inauguration as chancellor at Oxford, in June 1907, received the honorary degree of D.C.L., died at his house in Cornwall Gardens, South Kensington, on 19 Dec. 1907, and was buried at Send, near Woking. On 8 Oct. 1856 Strachey married Katherine Jane, daughter of George H. M. Batten, of the Bengal civil service; she received the imperial order of the Crown of India on its institution in 1878. Of their sons, the eldest, Colonel John Strachey, M.V.O., was controller of the household to Lord Curzon when viceroy of India; Sir Arthur is mentioned below; and Charles is principal clerk in the colonial office. A bronze tablet in Send church commemorates him and his wife, who predeceased him by a few months. There is also a tablet in the church of Chew Magna, Somerset, the burial-place of the family. In India the Strachey Hall of the Muhammadan Anglo-Oriental College at Aligarh is named after him as a memorial; and a tablet in the fort at Agra records that he cleared and restored the Diwan-i-Am, or hall of public audience of the Mogul emperors, in 1876.

Strachey holds an almost unique position in Anglo-Indian administration as minister to no fewer than three viceroys, and as the literary expositor of their domestic and financial policy. With his brother, Sir Richard [q. v. Suppl. II], he exerted the dominant influence in consolidating the new system of government gradually adopted after the catastrophe of the Mutiny. By inheritance and education they belonged to the school of philosophical radicalism represented in John Stuart Mill; and their best work, much of which came to fruition after the brothers had left India, was accomplished under two viceroys (Mayo and Lytton) who rank as conservatives at home but as active reformers in India. Strachey's valuable literary work in connection with India shows throughout the mind of a strong man and the pen of a ready writer.

Sir Arthur Strachey (1858–1901), second son of Sir John, was born on 5 Dec. 1858. Educated first at Uppingham and afterwards at Charterhouse, he proceeded to Trinity Hall, Cambridge, where he graduated in 1880 with a second class in the law tripos, taking later the degree of LL.B. Among his chief friends at the university were James Kenneth Stephen and Theodore Beck. Called to the bar from the Inner Temple in 1883, he went out almost at once to India, to practise before the high court at Allahabad. In 1892 he became public prosecutor and standing counsel to the provincial government. In 1895 he was appointed judge of the high court at Bombay, in which capacity it fell to him to preside at the first trial for sedition of Bal Gangadhar Tilak in 1897. An unfortunate phrase in his charge to the jury, that 'disaffection means simply the absence of affection,' attracted much censure, but the general purport of his language on this point was approved on appeal to a full bench. In 1899 he was promoted to be chief justice of the high court at Allahabad, and knighted. He died at Simla on 14 May 1901. His remains were cremated in Hindu fashion, and the ashes brought home and deposited in the churchyard of Send, near Woking. A bronze tablet to his memory has been placed in the church of Trent, near Yeovil, where much of his boyhood was passed. On 22 Oct. 1885 he married Ellen, daughter of John Conolly, who survived him. There was no issue of the marriage.

[The Times, 20 Dec. 1907; R. Bosworth Smith, Life of Lord Lawrence (1883); Sir William Hunter, Life of Lord Mayo, 1875; Sir Richard Temple, Men and Events of my Time in India (1882); Herbert Paul, Hist. of Modern England, iv. passim; Lady Betty Balfour, Memoir of Lord Lytton.] J. S. C.

STRACHEY, Sir RICHARD (1817–1908), lieutenant-general, royal (Bengal) engineers, younger brother of Sir Edward Strachey [q. v. Suppl. II for parentage] and elder brother of Sir John Strachey [q. v. Suppl. II], was born on 24 July 1817 at Sutton Court, Somerset, the seat of his uncle, Sir Henry Strachey (1772–1858), second baronet.

Educated at a private school at Totteridge, Richard entered the East India Company's military seminary at Addiscombe in 1834, and left it as the head of his term with a commission as second lieutenant in the Bombay engineers on 10 June 1836. After professional instruction at Chatham, Strachey went to India, and did duty first at Poona and then at Kandeish. On the augmentation of the Bengal engineers in 1839 he was transferred to that corps, and posted to the irrigation works of the public works department on the Jumna Canal, under (Sir) William Erskine Baker [q. v.]. Promoted lieutenant on 24 Feb. 1841, he was appointed in 1843 executive engineer on the Ganges Canal under (Sir) Proby Thomas Cautley [q. v.], and began the construction of the head works at Hurdwar.

In December 1845 Strachey was hurried off with all the other engineer officers within reach of the Sikh frontier to serve in the Sutlej campaign. He was appointed to Major-general Sir Harry Smith's staff, was present at the affair of Badiwal, at the battle of Aliwal on 28 Jan. 1846, where he had a horse shot under him, and at the victory of Sobraon on 10 Feb. After the battle he assisted in the construction of the bridge over the Sutlej, by which the army crossed into the Punjab. Sir Harry Smith, in his despatch after the battle of Aliwal, dated 30 Jan. 1846, highly commended the ready help of Strachey and of Richard Baird Smith [q. v.], also describing them as 'two most promising and gallant officers.' Strachey drew the plan of the battle to illustrate the despatch, and he was also employed on the survey of the Sobraon field of battle. For his services he received the medal with clasp, and, the day after his promotion to the rank of captain on 15 Feb. 1854, a brevet majority.

At the end of the campaign Strachey returned to the Ganges Canal, but frequent attacks of fever compelled him in 1847 to go to Nani Tal in the Kumaon Himalayas for his health. There he made the acquaintance of Major E. Madden, under whose guidance he studied botany and geology, making explorations into the Himalaya ranges west of Nepal for scientific purposes. In 1848 he accompanied Mr. J. E. Winterbottom, F.L.S., botanist, into Tibet, penetrating as far as lakes Rakas-tal and Manasarowar, previously visited by his elder brother, Captain Henry Strachey, in 1846. Starting from the plain of Rohilkhand at an elevation of about 1000 feet above sea level, a north-easterly route was taken across the snowy ranges terminating on the Tibetan plateau at an altitude of between fourteen and fifteen thousand feet, on the upper course of the river Sutlej. Strachey's detailed account of this journey, entitled 'Narrative of a Journey to Lakes Rakas-tal and Manasarowar in Western Tibet,' appeared in the 'Geographical Journal' (1900), vol. xv. (see also Mr. W. B. HEMSLEY's paper on the 'Flora of Tibet or High Asia' published in the *Journal of the Linnean Society*, vol. xxv. 1902). Over 2000 botanical species (including cryptogams) were collected, and of these thirty-two new species and varieties bear Strachey's name. The result of his geological observations was to establish the fact, which had been doubted by Humboldt, that in Kumaon there were glaciers in all respects similar to those of the European Alps, as shown, among other things, by the direct measurements of their rates of motion; he also settled another disputed point—the true position of the snow line. Travelling over the mountains, he observed the existence of a great series of paleozoic beds along the line of passes into Tibet with jurassic and tertiary deposits overlying them. These fruits of his journey were given in a paper on 'The Physical Geography of the Provinces of Kumaon and Garhwal,' published in the 'Geographical Journal' in 1851.

Strachey returned to England in 1850, and remained at home for nearly five years, occupied, among other things, in arranging and classifying his Kumaon collection. A provisionally named catalogue was prepared by him and printed; it was afterwards revised, and appeared in 1882 in Atkinson's 'Gazetteer of the Himalayan Districts of the North-West Provinces and Oude.' Another revised edition was prepared at Strachey's request by Mr. J. F. Duthie, and published in 1906. In 1854 Strachey was elected a fellow of the Royal Society. He returned to India in the following year, and for a short time had charge of irrigation works in Bundelkhand.

His first connection with the secretariat of the public works department was in 1856, when he was acting under-secretary in the absence of (Sir) Henry Yule [q. v.]. At Calcutta he was brought into contact with (Sir) John Peter Grant [q. v. Suppl. I], a member of the supreme council. When the Mutiny broke out, John Russell Colvin [q. v.], lieutenant-governor of the North West Provinces in Agra, was cut off by the mutineers from all communications with a portion of his territory; that portion was temporarily constituted a separate government, called the Central Provinces, under Grant as lieutenant-governor, and he appointed Strachey secretary in all departments under him.

Grant and Strachey went to Benares in July 1857, accompanied so far by Sir James Outram [q. v.] and Colonel Robert Napier, afterwards Lord Napier of Magdala [q. v.], who were on their way to Lucknow. After the fall of that place, Grant and Strachey moved to Allahabad, and when Grant was nominated president in council, Strachey remained behind to lay out the new railway station of Allahabad, the mutineers having almost destroyed the old one. He returned to Calcutta in 1858 on his appointment as consulting engineer to government in the railway department. He obtained acceptance of the principle so abundantly justified by its results—that for the construction of irrigation works and for railway development it was right to supply by loan the funds which could not otherwise be provided. His great constructive ability was shown in his reorganisation of the public works department, and in the initiation of an adequate forest service; he was appointed secretary and head of the public works department in 1862.

From this time until he left India for good Richard Strachey was a power in the country, and was, perhaps, the most remarkable man of a family which, for four generations, extending over more than a century, served the Indian government. A strong man with a determined will and a somewhat peppery temperament, he generally carried his way with beneficial results, though he sometimes took the wrong side in a controversy, as in the battle of the railway gauges. Strachey remained secretary to government for the public works department until 1865. Meanwhile he had been promoted lieut.-colonel on 2 July 1860, and colonel on 31 Dec. 1862. He was created a C.S.I. in 1866 for his services and appointed inspector-general of irrigation, and in 1869 acting secretary of the public works department, with a seat in the legislative council. On leaving India on promotion to major-general on 24 March 1871 (antedated to 16 March 1868), he received the thanks of government for his valuable services during a period of thirty-three years.

Soon after reaching England, Strachey was appointed by Lord Salisbury inspector of railway stores at the India office, and after retirement from the army on 23 Feb. 1875, with the honorary rank of lieutenant-general, a member of the council of India.

In 1877 Strachey was sent to India to arrange with the Indian government the terms for the purchase of the East Indian railway, the first of the guaranteed railways to be taken over by the government on the termination of the original thirty years' lease, and he initiated the policy of and drew up the contract for the continued working of the railway by the company under government control. While in India he presided with great ability over a commission to inquire into the causes of the terrible famine and to suggest possible remedies. He also filled the post of financial member of council during the absence of his brother John, and was thus associated with the Indian government in the negotiations which led to the rupture with Shere Ali and war with Afghanistan.

On his return home in 1879 Strachey was re-appointed to a seat in the council of India; he was one of the British commissioners at the Prime Meridian Conference held at Washington, U.S.A., in 1884, and was elected one of the secretaries; in 1887 he was chosen president of the Royal Geographical Society and held the post for two years; he was also an honorary member of the geographical societies of Berlin and of Italy. He resigned his seat on the India council in 1889 to become chairman of the East India Railway Company, and his beneficial rule is commemorated by the 'Strachey' bridge over the river Jumna, opened shortly before his death. He was also chairman of the Assam Bengal Railway Company, and only resigned these positions when nearly ninety years of age, in consequence of increasing deafness. Under his management the East India railway became the most prosperous trunk line in the world.

In 1892 Strachey was one of the delegates to represent India at the international monetary conference at Brussels, and the same year he was a member of the committee on silver currency presided over by Lord Herschell, when there was adopted a far-reaching reform which he had proposed when finance minister in India in 1878, viz. to close the Indian mint to the free coinage of silver. In June 1892 he received from the University of Cambridge the honorary degree of LL.D.

Strachey did much good work for the Royal Society, served on its council four times, from 1872 to 1874, 1880 to 1881, 1884 to 1886, and 1890 to 1891, and was twice a vice-president; he was a member of its meteorological committee (which controlled the meteorological office) in 1867, and he was a member of the council which replaced the committee in 1876, and from 1883 to 1895 was its chairman. From 1873 he was on the committee of the Royal Society for managing the Kew observatory. The royal medal of the society was bestowed upon him in 1897 for his researches in physical and botanical geography and in meteorology, and the Royal Meteorological Society awarded him the Symons medal in 1906. His most important scientific contributions to knowledge were made in meteorology. He laid the foundations of the scientific study of Indian meteorology, organising a department whose labours have been of use in assisting to forecast droughts and consequent scarcity and of no little advantage to meteorologists generally. For years he served on the committee of solar physics. A sound mathematician, Strachey delighted in mechanical inventions and especially in designing instruments to give graphic expression to formulas he had devised for working out meteorological problems. In 1884 he designed an instrument called the 'sine curve developer' to show in a graphic form the results obtained by applying to hourly readings of barograms and thermograms his formula for the calculation of harmonic coefficients. In 1888 and 1890 he designed two 'slide rules,' one to facilitate the computation of the amplitude and time of maximum of harmonic constants from values obtained by applying his formula to hourly readings of barograms and thermograms; the other to obtain the height of clouds from measurements of two photographs taken simultaneously with cameras placed at the ends of a base line half a mile in length. A further invention was a portable and very simple instrument, called a 'nephoscope,' for observing the direction of motion of high cirrus clouds, whose movement is generally too slow to allow of its direction being determined by the unaided eye.

Strachey had been granted a distinguished service pension and created C.S.I. in 1866, after thirty years' service. Subsequently he declined the offer of K.C.S.I. But on the diamond jubilee of Queen Victoria in 1897 he was gazetted G.C.S.I. After leaving India he lived at Stowey House on Clapham Common; later he moved to Lancaster Gate, and only a few months before his death to Hampstead. He died at 67 Belsize Park Gardens on 12 Feb. 1908, and was cremated at Golder's Green.

On his return from India in 1879 Richard Strachey collaborated with his brother John in writing 'The Finances and Public Works of India' (1882), a record of their joint achievements from 1869 to 1881. In the preface to the fourth edition (1911) of Sir John Strachey's 'India: its Administration and Progress,' a development of the original work by the two brothers, Sir Thomas W. Holderness says: 'It describes a system of government which they, more than any other public servants of their day, had helped to fashion. It narrates the concrete results of this system, with intimate first-hand knowledge of its working and of the country and the populations which it affected, with an honourable pride in its pacific triumphs and in the benefits which it had conferred on their fellow Indian subjects.' Strachey wrote the articles on 'Asia' and 'Himalaya' in the ninth edition of the 'Encyclopædia Britannica' and contributed many more papers than those already cited to scientific journals.

Sir Richard was twice married: (1) on 19 Jan. 1854 to Caroline Anne (*d.* 1855), daughter of the Rev. George Downing Bowles; (2) on 4 Jan. 1859 to Jane Maria, daughter of Sir John Peter Grant [q. v. Suppl. I.] of Rothiemurchus, N.B., his chief in the Mutiny days. She survived him with five sons and five daughters.

A portrait in oils (1889), by Lowes Dickinson [q. v. Suppl. II]; another in water-colours by Miss Jessie MacGregor; a third in pastel (1902), by Simon Bussy; and a medallion in bronze (1898), by Mr. Alfred Gilbert, R.A., are in possession of the family.

[Vibart's Addiscombe: its Heroes and Men of Note, 1898; Royal Engineers' Journal, 1908; Proceedings of the Royal Society, vol. lxxxi. 1908; Geographical Journal, March 1908; The Times, 13 Feb. 1908; Nature, 27 Feb. 1908; Spectator, 22 Feb. 1908; Engineering, 21 Feb. 1908; private information.]

R. H. V.

STRETTON, HESBA, pseudonym. [See SMITH, SARAH (1832–1911), authoress.]

STRONG, SIR SAMUEL HENRY (1825–1909), chief justice of Canada, born at Poole, Dorsetshire, on 13 Aug. 1825, was son of Samuel S. Strong, D.D., LL.D., by his wife Jane Elizabeth Gosse of that town, sister of Philip Henry Gosse [q. v.]. In his eleventh year he accompanied to Canada his father, who became chaplain of the forces in Quebec and rector of Bytown (now Ottawa) and rural dean. Educated in the Quebec High School and privately, the son began to study law in Bytown, and was called to the bar in Toronto in 1849. He entered into partnership with H. Eccles (afterwards librarian of Osgoode Hall) and later with Sir Thomas W. Taylor (subsequently chief justice of Manitoba) and (Sir) James David Edgar (who became speaker of the Canadian House of Commons). Strong rapidly secured a reputation in the courts of equity, and was appointed in 1856 a member of the commission for the consolidation of the statutes of Canada and of Upper Canada. He was elected a bencher of the Law Society of Upper Canada in 1860 and took silk in 1863. Six years later he was raised to the bench as one of the vice-chancellors of Ontario. He served on the commission of inquiry into a union of the law and equity courts in 1871. In 1874 he was transferred to the Court of Error and Appeal of Ontario, then the highest of the provincial tribunals.

In 1875 Strong was advanced to the newly constituted Supreme Court of Canada as a puisne judge, and on the death in Dec. 1892 of Sir William Johnstone Ritchie [q. v.], he became chief justice. He was knighted next year. His appointment as a member of the judicial committee of the privy council followed in Jan. 1897. He resigned the chief-justiceship in 1902 in order to become chief of a commission for the consolidation of the statutes of Canada. He died at Ottawa on 21 Aug. 1909.

One of the ablest jurists of Canada, Strong was distinguished by his powerful memory for cases, by a scientific knowledge of the principles of both law and equity, and by a power of incisive comment that added much to the force of his *obiter dicta*. He married in 1850 Elizabeth Charlotte Cane, by whom he had two children.

A portrait in oils hangs in the Supreme Court at Ottawa.

[Rose, Cyclopedia of Canadian Biography, 1886; Morgan's Canadian Men and Women of the Time, 1898; Canadian Law Times, xxix. 1044.]

D. R. K.

STRONG, SANDFORD ARTHUR (1863–1904), orientalist and historian of art, born in London on 10 April 1863, was second son of Thomas Strong of the war office. His eldest brother, Thomas Banks Strong, is dean of Christ Church, Oxford. In 1877 he entered St. Paul's School as a foundation scholar, but remained there for little more than a year. His next two years were passed as a clerk at Lloyd's, though during this time he also attended classes at King's College. In 1881 he matriculated at Cambridge, with a Hutchinson studentship at St. John's College. He graduated in 1884, with a third class in Part I of the classical tripos, being placed in the second class in Part II the following year. He proceeded M.A. in 1890. Even in his undergraduate days the bent of his mind had been towards oriental studies, and on the recommendation of Professor Edward Byles Cowell [q. v. Suppl. II] he worked at Sanskrit with Cecil Bendall [q. v. Suppl. II]. But receiving little encouragement at Cambridge, he migrated to Oxford towards the end of 1885. There he found occupation as subkeeper and librarian of the Indian Institute, and also friends in Max Müller, Professor Sayce, and Adolf Neubauer [q. v. Suppl. II]. Neubauer advised him to visit the continent, and gave him letters of introduction to Renan and James Darmesteter at Paris. Both were deeply impressed with his attainments, and he also studied with Schrader at Berlin. Renan wrote of him: 'L'étendue et la sagacité de son intelligence me frappèrent. Ses connaissances littéraires et scientifiques sont vastes et sûres. C'est certainement un des esprits les plus distingués que j'ai recontrés.' Darmesteter spoke no less confidently of his 'exactitude and precision' as a specialist, and his width of views and interest. Despite the qualifications thus attested, Strong on his return to England found recognition or remunerative employment slow in coming. To Sanskrit he added Pali, to Arabic he added Persian and Assyrian, and he made some progress in hieroglyphics and Chinese. On all these he wrote in learned publications, and he also contributed reviews to the 'Athenæum' and the 'Academy.' But he failed in his candidature for the chair of Arabic at Cambridge vacant by the death of Robertson Smith in 1894, nor was it a consolation to be appointed in 1895 professor of Arabic at University College, London, though he held that almost nominal office until his death.

But at the darkest hour a new career suddenly opened before him. (Sir) Sidney Colvin introduced him to the duke of Devonshire, who was then in need of a librarian to succeed Sir James Lacaita. Installed at Chatsworth in 1895, he was as much interested in the historic collection of pictures and other works of art there as in the books in the library. He now showed what the scientific training of a scholar could accomplish in a novel field, which was indeed the return to an old love. As a boy he had been taught drawing by Albert Varley, who gave him a copy of Pilkington's 'Dictionary of Painters,' and he had made himself acquainted with the style of the different masters in the National Gallery. The discoveries he made at Chatsworth, and no doubt also his personal charm, opened to him other collections—the Duke of Portland's at Welbeck, where he also acted for a time as librarian, the Earl of Pembroke's at Wilton, and Lord Wantage's at Lockinge. Between 1900 and 1904 he published descriptions of these treasures, artistic and literary. In 1897 he was appointed librarian at the House of Lords, where he compiled two catalogues, one of the general library and one of the law books. This appointment, while it did not interrupt his studies, nor his tenure of office at Chatsworth, introduced him to another sphere of interest, where he made himself equally at home. He became absorbed in politics and even dreamed that his ideal occupation would be to govern orientals. But his health was never robust, and he had strained the measure of physical vigour that he possessed. After a lingering illness, he died in London on 18 Jan. 1904, and was buried in Brompton cemetery. In 1897 Strong married Eugénie Sellers, the well-known classical archæologist. His wife survived him, but there were no children of the marriage. Two portraits by Legros and one by Sir Charles Holroyd are in the possession of his widow. A bust by the Countess Feodora Gleichen (1894) was presented by a group of his friends to the 'Arthur Strong Oriental Library' at University College, London, the nucleus of which is formed by his books given in his memory by his widow.

Of special importance among Strong's oriental publications are his editions of the 'Maha-Bodhi-Vamsa' for the Pali Text Society (1891), and of the 'Futah al-Habashah' or 'Conquest of Abyssinia' (1894) for the Royal Asiatic Society's monographs. At his death he was engaged on the Arabic text of Ibn Arabshah's 'History of Yakmak, Sultan of Egypt,' the first part of which appeared in the 'Journal of the Royal Asiatic Society' for 1904.

Among his art publications the principal are: 1 'Reproductions of Drawings by the Old Masters in the Collection of the Earl of Pembroke and Montgomery at Wilton House,' 1900. 2. Preface to Messrs

Hanfstaengl's 'Plates of National Gallery Pictures,' 1901. 3. 'Masterpieces of the Duke of Devonshire's Collection of Pictures,' 1901. 4. 'Reproductions of Drawings by the Old Masters at Chatsworth,' 1902. 5. 'Catalogue of Letters and other Historical Documents in the Library of Welbeck,' 1903.

[Memoir by Lord Balcarres, prefixed to 'Critical Studies and Fragments' by S. Arthur Strong, with reproductions of portraits and full bibliography, 1905; The Times, 19 Jan. 1904; éloge by Lord Reay, Journal Royal Asiatic Society, 1904; and A Distinguished Librarian, by M. E. Lowndes, June 1905.] J. S. C.

STUBBS, WILLIAM (1825–1901), historian and bishop successively of Chester and Oxford, was the eldest son of William Morley Stubbs, solicitor, of Knaresborough, and Mary Ann, daughter of William Henlock. He came of such solid yeoman stock that he could amuse himself in later life by working out his line of ancestors among the crown tenants of the forest of Knaresborough as far back as the fourteenth century. He was born on 21 June 1825 in High Street, Knaresborough. In 1832 he went to a school at Knaresborough kept by an old man named Cartwright, and thence in 1839 to Ripon grammar school, where he attracted the attention of Charles Thomas Longley [q. v.], afterwards archbishop of Canterbury, then bishop of Ripon. In 1842 his father died, leaving the widow (who survived till 1884) to face a severe struggle against poverty with her six young children. Shortly afterwards Longley's influence obtained from Dean Gaisford his nomination to a servitorship at Christ Church, Oxford, where he went into residence in April 1844, and took his degree in 1848 with a first in classics and a third in mathematics. At Christ Church he was 'kept at arms length as a servitor,' and is described as 'timid, grateful, feeling his isolation, and possessed of an amazing memory.' His father had taught him to read old charters and deeds, and he now laid the foundations of his historical learning in the college library, where he attracted 'the amused and approving surprise' of the dean by his devotion to such strange studies. Though official good-will refused to break through the tradition which forbade the election of a servitor as a student, he ever remained a 'loyal son of the House.' However, within a few weeks of his degree he was elected to a fellowship at Trinity College, where he resided till 1850. Stubbs had come to Oxford a tory and an evangelical, but tractarian influence soon made him a lifelong high churchman (*Visitation Charges*, pp. 347–8). In 1848 he was ordained deacon and in 1850 priest by Bishop Wilberforce, and on 27 May 1850 he was presented to the college living of Navestock, near Ongar, in Essex, thereby vacating his fellowship. He remained vicar of Navestock until 1866, performing diligently the work of a country parson, and winning the affection of his flock by his kindliness and geniality. 'I suppose,' he said in later years, 'I knew every toe on every baby in the parish' (HUTTON, p. 259). In June 1859 he married Catherine, daughter of John Dellar of Navestock, who survived him. She had been mistress of the village school. He had a family of five sons and one daughter.

Stubbs utilised his leisure while a village parson in acquiring such a knowledge of the sources for mediæval English history as made him the foremost scholar of his generation. He published nothing before 1858, when he issued his 'Registrum Sacrum Anglicanum,' which exhibited in a series of tables the course of episcopal succession in England. Its genesis is described in the autobiographical postscript (ix–xi) to the preface of the second edition (1897). Modest as was its scope, it had kept him busy for ten years. He now began to write more freely. In 1861 came his first edition of a mediæval document, 'De inventione Sanctæ Crucis,' and in the same year began his contributions to the 'Archæological Journal' and other occasional papers. Increasing practical duties as a guardian of the poor and a diocesan inspector of schools did not drive him from study. He sometimes had private pupils, among them Henry Parry Liddon [q. v.] and Algernon Charles Swinburne [q. v. Suppl. II]. His appointment by Archbishop Longley in Oct. 1862 as Lambeth librarian gave him access to a great library, hampered by but few routine duties. His learning was known to a few discerning friends, such as Edward Augustus Freeman [q. v. Suppl. I] and later John Richard Green [q. v.]. Public recognition, however, came very slowly. He was anxious to be employed as an editor for the Rolls Series, which had been projected in 1857, but it was not until 1863 that official 'polite obstructiveness' was overcome and the new series obtained its most distinguished editor. In 1862 he was a candidate for the Chichele professorship of modern history at Oxford, but the electors preferred Montagu Burrows [q. v. Suppl. II]. In 1863 he was a candidate for the professorship of ecclesiastical history, when Walter Waddington Shirley [q. v.] was chosen. In 1866 he sought to become principal librarian of the British Museum, but the trustees appointed John Winter Jones [q. v.]. Though sometimes rather restive, he continued steadily at his work. In 1864–5 the two volumes of the 'Chronicles and Memorials of Richard I,' edited for the Master of the Rolls, showed that he was a consummate editor and a true historian. Yet when Goldwin Smith [q. v. Suppl. II] resigned the regius professorship of history at Oxford, he was too discouraged to avow himself a candidate. 'I am not,' he wrote to Freeman, 'going to stand for any more things. If I am not worth looking up, I am not ambitious enough to like to be beaten!' (Hutton, p. 102). However, Lord Derby ascertained from Longley that Stubbs would accept the post, and made him an offer on 2 Aug. 1866, which was joyfully accepted. Before the end of the year Stubbs left Navestock for Oxford, which remained his home until 1884. After 1870 he lived at Kettel Hall, a roomy and interesting old house in Broad Street, which belonged to Trinity College, and is now part of the college buildings. He was the first regius professor to be an ex-officio fellow of Oriel College.

On 7 Feb. 1867 Stubbs introduced himself in his inaugural lecture, 'not as a philosopher, nor as a politician, but as a worker at history,' and anticipated 'the prospect of being instrumental, and able to assist in the founding of an historical school in England.' He soon, however, found that there were great difficulties in his path in Oxford itself. He took immense pains in preparing his lectures. He not only set before his pupils a great deal of the best that he afterwards published in his books, but put together elaborate courses on mediæval German history and foreign history from the Reformation to the Treaty of Westphalia. In later years he sometimes took his 'Select Charters' as a text-book, and made them the starting-point of illuminative, informal talks on mediæval constitutional history. He was compelled by statute to produce, as he said, 'something twice a year which might attract an idle audience without seeming to trifle with a deeply loved study.' This was the only side of his professorial work that he actively disliked, yet the only lectures which he himself thought fit to publish were some of these popular discourses contained in the 'Seventeen lectures on the study of mediæval and modern history and kindred subjects' which he issued in 1886 (3rd edit., with additions, 1900), soon after he resigned the professorship. After his death four volumes of his more formal lectures were published. These were 'Lectures on European History' (1904), 'Lectures on Early English History' (1906), 'Germany in the Early Middle Ages, 476–1250' (1908), 'Germany in the Later Middle Ages, 1250–1500' (1908). The editing of these volumes is perfunctory, and the attempt made in the English volume to weave together lectures delivered at various times and to various audiences is not successful.

Stubbs's lectures never attracted a large audience. During his professorship the number of undergraduates who read for honours in the school of modern history enormously increased, but his hearers, if anything, diminished in numbers. Between 1869 and 1874 arose an organised system of 'combined lectures,' largely the work of his friend Mandell Creighton [q. v. Suppl. I], which satisfied the wants of those who read history for examinations, and there were few who required what he had to give. Even Creighton 'convinced himself that the only real function which remains for professors to accomplish is that of research' (*Life of Mandell Creighton*, i. 62). This doctrine Stubbs could not accept. In after years he described rather bitterly how he 'revolted against the treatment which he had to undergo,' and that after 1874 he had 'scarcely a good class or any of the better men,' and that 'the historical teaching of history has been practically left out in favour of the class-getting system of training' (Hutton, pp. 264, 270). In the end he renounced the idea, if he had ever entertained it, of organising a school of history such as had been set up by his colleagues in Germany. He refused to impose on others the fetters of an organisation which he himself resented. Closely associated with the strongest school of conservatism in all other matters, he had no fellow-workers in carrying out ideals that would have involved a radical recasting of the prevailing methods of historical teaching. He disliked controversy, and always remained friendly with the tutors.

Despite the limitations imposed upon him, there were few earnest students of history at Oxford who were not indebted to him for advice, encouragement, sympathy, and direction.

The restrictions under which he chafed allowed Stubbs to concentrate himself upon his personal work. Society and academic business did not appeal to him. He disliked dinner-parties, smoking, late hours, and committees. He conscientiously discharged every duty that lay straight before him, but he did not spend too much time in doing so. His real life, however, was in his study, and in the libraries where he sought material. His literary output was prodigious. The history of scholarship would have to be ransacked to afford parallels of a work so distinguished both in quantity and quality within the seventeen years of his professorship. He worked with extraordinary rapidity, accuracy, and sureness. Of many large literary schemes, perhaps the only one which he did not complete was his projected reproduction 'in accordance with the present state of our knowledge and materials' of all that part of Wilkins's 'Concilia' antecedent to the Reformation. Leaving the Welsh, Scottish, and Irish sections to his colleague, Arthur West Haddan [q. v.], Stubbs undertook the Anglo-Saxon period, and published in 1878 vol. iii. of 'Councils and Ecclesiastical Documents covering the History of the Anglo-Saxon Church,' but the plan never went any further. A by-product of this was the long series of lives of Anglo-Saxon bishops, saints, kings, and writers, from Stubbs's pen, which were published in the four volumes of the 'Dictionary of Christian Biography' between 1877 and 1887. He also contributed to the two volumes of the 'Dictionary of Christian Antiquities' (1875-80), and had a share in the editing of that work (*Preface* to vol. i. p. xi).

The most characteristic work done by Stubbs in these fruitful years is to be found in the editions of chronicles which he contributed to the Rolls Series. The two volumes of the 'Chronicles and Memorials of Richard I,' issued in 1864–5, were followed by the two volumes of the 'Gesta regis Henrici II' attributed to Benedict of Peterborough (1867), the four volumes of Roger Howden or Hoveden's 'Chronica' (1868–71), the two volumes of the 'Memoriale or historical collections of Walter of Coventry' (1872–3), the one volume of the 'Memorials of Saint Dunstan' (1874), the two volumes of 'The Historical Works of Ralph Diceto' (1878), the two volumes of 'The Historical Works of Gervase of Canterbury' (1879–80), and the two volumes of the 'Chronicles of the Reigns of Edward I and Edward II' (1882–3). While professor Stubbs published for the Rolls Series fifteen large volumes. There were also the two published before, and the two volumes of William of Malmesbury issued later. This monumental series won a very high reputation for a collection which, apart from Stubbs's contributions to it, contains some bad and more indifferent work. They are in every respect models of what the 'editio princeps' of an original authority should be. The text is impeccable, and based upon the careful collation of the available manuscripts. Every help is given in the way of introductions, notes, and elaborate indexes to lighten the labours of those using the texts. They are much more than ideal examples of editorial workmanship. A liberal construction of the directions given to the Rolls editors allowed Stubbs to write 'excellent history on a large scale' in every one of his introductions which revealed him as an historical narrator of the first order, equally at home in painting a large gallery of historical portraits, and in working out the subtlest of problems. The shy student, who had been thought a mere antiquary, proved to be a constructive historian of real power and eloquence. The range of his historical vision was enormous. Here he vindicated the claims of Dunstan to be a pioneer of English political unity and of mediæval intellectual life. There he threw new light on the reign of Edward I, and for the first time analysed fully the causes of the fall of Edward II. Yet while all periods were treated with wonderful grasp, a special mastery was shown of the age of Henry II. It was unfortunate for Stubbs's wider fame that the form in which the historical part of these introductions appeared made them inaccessible to general readers. An attempt to collect them in a detached form, made after his death (*Historical Introductions to the Rolls Series*, 1902), was too carelessly performed to be entirely successful.

Side by side with his other tasks, Stubbs devoted himself to writing on a large scale the constitutional history of mediæval England. As a forerunner to this great work, he issued in 1870 the most widely used of all his publications. This was 'Select Charters, and other Illustrations of English Constitutional History from the Earliest Times to the Reign of Edward I,' with a luminous tightly packed 'introductory sketch.' No single book has done so much to put the higher study of English mediæval history on the sound basis of the study of original texts. 'Select Charters' was followed in 1873 by the first volume of the 'Constitutional History of England,' which covers the ground from the origins to the Great Charter. Next came in 1875 vol. ii., which went to 1399, and in 1878 vol. iii., which took the story down to 1485, and completed the work. It is by this massive work of historic synthesis that Stubbs's position among historians has generally been estimated, and not unjustly, if we recognise that the immense ground covered made pioneer work such as illuminated his contributions to the Rolls Series impossible, and that his limitation to the history of institutions gave few opportunities for the remarkable narrative and pictorial gifts there displayed. Rapidly as the book was executed, it shows extraordinary mastery of the mass of material which had to be dealt with. Stubbs evenly distributes his attention over the whole corpus of printed chronicles, printed charters, laws, rolls, and documents; he has at his fingers' ends the monumental compilations of the great seventeenth-century scholars, and he uses to the full (perhaps too fully) the modern investigations of his German masters such as Maurer and Waitz. He moves easily under all this mass of learning and uses it with accuracy, precision, and insight. By the happy device of dividing his book into analytic and descriptive chapters alternating with annalistic narratives, he furnished the best skeleton of our mediæval political history that has been written, and gave width and human interest to his pages. Though necessarily dealing with great masses of detail, general principles are wisely and impressively emphasised; though constantly concerned with abstractions and tendencies, it has rightly been pronounced to be 'marvellously concrete.' Self-suppression, impartiality, accuracy, sympathy, sobriety of judgment, and sense of proportion stand out in every part of the great book.

No work of erudition can altogether stand the test of time, but 'Stubbs's Constitutional History' still remains unsuperseded nearly forty years after its publication. It gave a new direction to the study of mediæval English history, and its influence for good is as lively now as when it first issued from the press. The austerity which sometimes repels the beginner has been mitigated by a whole literature of easy introductions to its doctrines, some good, more indifferent, none original, nearly all useful. By-ways which Stubbs was not able to explore have been pursued by critical disciples, among whom we may place Frederic William Maitland [q. v. Suppl. II], Mary Bateson [q. v. Suppl. II], Prof. Vinogradoff, and Dr. J. Horace Round. It is inevitable, under such circumstances, that many of Stubbs's conclusions have to be reviewed. This is especially the case since absorbing occupations and, perhaps, an increasingly conservative temper of mind prevented Stubbs from adequately revising what he had written. The 'Germanist' school of which he was the soberest and most reasonable exponent in England is no longer in universal favour, and it is plain that large portions of the 'Constitutional History,' notably the Anglo-Saxon and Norman parts, will have, to some extent, to be re-written. Problems of 'origins' did not appeal to him, and he only moved easily when texts were abundant. As regards Anglo-Saxon history Stubbs confessed himself an 'agnostic' as compared with his friends Freeman and Green. Yet the passages in which his conclusions least meet the views of modern scholars are those in which he looked into the facts with the eyes of his German guides. In later parts of the book there is little to alter, though there is much to supplement. After the Norman reigns he seldom goes astray save when unconsciously influenced by general theories of tendency, or when dealing with subjects like the royal revenue in the fourteenth century, which could not be blocked out even in outline in the light of the printed materials then available. In 1907 the first volume of a French translation, 'Histoire constitutionnelle de l'Angleterre par W. Stubbs. Traduction de G. Lefebvre,' was published with notes and elucidations by Professor C. Petit-Dutaillis, wherein an effort was made to summarise the more generally accepted criticisms and amplifications of the early part of Stubbs's history. These criticisms have been translated by Mr. W. E. Rhodes in 1908 as 'Studies and Notes supplementary to Stubbs's "Constitutional History," down to the Great Charter.'

Stubbs never forgot that he was a clergyman. Pusey was his 'master,' and he was intimate with Liddon and the other high church leaders in Oxford, and strenuously supported their ecclesiastical and academic programme. In 1868 he would gladly have changed his professorship for that of ecclesiastical history. In 1869 he spent much labour in preparing for the press Cardinal J. de Torquemada's treatise on the 'Immaculate Conception,' a fifteenth-century treatise reissued at Pusey's instigation to influence the Vatican council. Between 1875 and 1879 he was rector of the Oriel living of Cholderton on Salisbury Plain, and spent his summers there until his resignation in 1879. After 1876 he acted as chaplain to Balliol College, and in 1878 he was sorely tempted by the offer of the living of the university church of St. Mary's. In April 1879 he accepted a canonry at St. Paul's Cathedral, London, vacated by the promotion of Joseph Barber Lightfoot [q. v.] to the bishopric of Durham. He appreciated this preferment very much; it was the first tangible recognition in his own country of his great work; it gave him an ecclesiastical position in which he could urge his opinions with authority, a residence in London which was helpful to his historical work, and emoluments which put him in easy circumstances. His friendship with the dean, Richard William Church [q. v. Suppl. I], and other members of the chapter made his personal relations pleasant. During his periods of residence he worked on the muniments and chronicles of St. Paul's, and took immense pains with his Sunday afternoon sermons, though he humorously quoted the newspapers which said 'the sermons in the morning and evening were preached by Mr. A. and Mr. B., in the afternoon *the pulpit was occupied by* the canon in residence' (Hutton, p. 131). In fact his sermons became exceedingly weighty, valuable, and strong, though he made too great demands on the attention of his hearers ever to attract the immense congregations which flocked to hear Liddon.

In 1881 Stubbs was appointed a member of the royal commission on ecclesiastical courts, and was present at every one of the seventy-five sessions which that body held between May 1881 and July 1883. Church called him 'the hero of the commission' (Church's *Life*, p. 312). He took a leading part in its debates, waged fierce war against 'lawyers' and the 'Erastians' among his colleagues, and presented suggestions for a final court of appeal which left to ecclesiastical tribunals the sole determination of points of ritual and doctrine. He drew up five historical appendices to the report in which he discussed the nature of the courts which exercised ecclesiastical jurisdiction in England at various times, the trials for heresy up to 1533, the acts by which the clergy recognised the royal supremacy, and some aspects of the power and functions of convocation. There can be no doubt of the permanent value of the great bulk of the very careful and detailed research contained in these appendices. Nevertheless some of the main positions maintained by Stubbs were subjected to damaging criticism from Professor Frederic William Maitland [q. v. Suppl. II], in articles published in the 'English Historical Review' of 1896 and 1897, and soon afterwards in book form as 'Roman Canon Law in the Church of England' (1898). It may be recognised that Stubbs minimised unduly the authority of the Pope as 'universal ordinary' and suggested the unhistorical view that the English church might, and did, accept or reject canonical legislation emanating from the Papacy, and that without such acceptance Roman canon law was not held to be binding in the English ecclesiastical courts. Stubbs himself never dealt with Maitland's arguments, but contented himself with affirming that his appendices contained 'true history and the result of hard work' (preface to third edit. of *Seventeen Lectures*).

In Feb. 1884 Stubbs was offered by Gladstone the bishopric of Chester. Accepting the post he was consecrated on 25 April in York Minster by Archbishop Thomson. Bidding adieu to the university on 8 May in the characteristic last statutory public lecture (published in his 'Seventeen Lectures,' 1886), he was enthroned in Chester Cathedral on 24 June. For a time he cherished the hope of carrying on his historical work, but his edition for the Rolls Series of the 'Gesta regum Anglorum' and the 'Historia novella' of William of Malmesbury, published in two volumes in 1887 and 1889, mark the practical conclusion of his historical labours. He maintained to the last his interest in his subject, and was never weary in aiding his friends and disciples with advice and substantial assistance. He kept up with the best work done in his subject in England and Germany, though somewhat blind to the new school of mediæval historians growing up in France. He had, however, little sympathy now for historical novelties. The conservative note sounded in the new preface to the last edition of the 'Select Charters' published in his lifetime is characteristic of his later attitude (preface to eighth edit. 1895).

As bishop, Stubbs was at his best when

dealing with big issues, and somewhat less successful when tackling the petty details of administration and correspondence. His friend Liddon warned him to be on his guard against 'looking at persons and events from the critical and humorous side,' and of the danger of killing zeal. Though no man approached the episcopal office in a more earnest spirit, it cannot be said that he was always mindful of his friend's advice. As he became known his clergy better understood the seriousness that underlay his humorous modes of expression, and appreciated his simplicity of life, his unostentatious friendliness, his liberality, shrewd insight into men, and wise counsels. He made an energetic and successful attempt to build new churches, and increase the number of the clergy in the densely peopled district that ranges from Stockport to Stalybridge. He was unwearied in visiting the parishes of his diocese, and in preaching in them. 'I am engaged,' he wrote, 'in a regularly organised attempt to prove to the clergy of the diocese that I am not a good preacher. I think I shall succeed' (HUTTON, p. 262). He urged on his clergy the necessity of 'constructive not controversial' teaching in church history. He interested himself in educational and historical work in his neighbourhood; he welcomed the Archæological Institute to Chester in 1886; he became vice-president, and ultimately president, of the Chetham Society; he was a member of the court of the newly founded Victoria University, and championed, unsuccessfully for the moment, the establishment of a theological faculty in it. He was much consulted on matters of general ecclesiastical policy. His brother prelates heard his opinions with extreme respect. In 1886 he drew up at the request of E. W. Benson, archbishop of Canterbury, an historical paper on the possibility of establishing a national synod in England; he took a prominent part in the Lambeth conference of 1888, and a large part of the encyclical letter drawn up by it was written out in his own clear hand. It was composed by Stubbs and two other bishops, who sat up all night in the Lollards' tower at Lambeth Palace.

In July 1888 Stubbs accepted from Lord Salisbury an offer of translation from Chester to the bishopric of Oxford. But the resignation of his predecessor, John Fielder Mackarness [q. v.], did not take legal effect till November, and it was not until 24 Dec. 1888 that he was elected bishop. He began his work in the spring of 1889. A strong reason which weighed with Stubbs in accepting translation was the prospect of returning to his old surroundings. However, he disliked a large and remote country house like Cuddesdon. He strongly urged the ecclesiastical commissioners to sell Cuddesdon, and buy for the see a house in Oxford. Though the prime minister supported him, the ecclesiastical commissioners refused his request, perhaps through the influence of Archbishop Benson, who believed that bishops should maintain high state. Stubbs never reconciled himself to Cuddesdon, and vented his spleen in humorous verses, wherein lurks just a trace of bitterness. He found it very difficult to work a diocese of three counties from a village remote from railway stations. Age soon began to tell upon him, and he found his routine work increasingly irksome and laborious, and his clergy did not appreciate his attempts to distinguish between his strictly episcopal functions, which he rigidly discharged, and the conventional duties which modern bishops are expected to fulfil, and for which he did not conceal his distaste. He was greatly helped by his chaplain, Canon E. E. Holmes, and before the end of 1889 the consecration of J. L. Randall as a suffragan bishop of Reading lessened the travelling and administrative work. In all essential matters, however, he remained to the end the model of the careful, judicious, and sympathetic diocesan, and the wise and courageous advocate of the older high church tradition. Perhaps the most permanent records of his episcopate are to be found in his public utterances, the most important of which were published by Canon Holmes after his death. These were: (1) 'Ordination Addresses by William Stubbs, late bishop of Oxford' (1901), and (2) 'Visitation Charges delivered to the Clergy and Churchwardens of the Dioceses of Chester and Oxford' (1904). In all these addresses can be seen his ardent faith, his strong sense of personal religion, his kindly tolerance, his strenuous maintenance of the ancient ways in all matters of dogma and church usage, and his increasing dislike of all ecclesiastical innovations. Very noteworthy are the luminous surveys of the history and actual position of the English church, which give permanent value to his visitation charges.

Stubbs's intellectual interests remained unabated, though he constantly complained that he had no time for study. He managed, however, to bring out a new edition of the 'Registrum Sacrum Anglicanum' in 1897, and revised editions of 'Select Charters,' 'Constitutional History,' and the 'Seventeen Lectures.' To the last he amused himself with pedigrees, writing prefaces, reading proof sheets, and helping his historical friends. He renewed his interest in the University of Oxford, and again became a curator of the Bodleian, a delegate of the university press, and a member of the board of modern history. Even more than at Chester he was constantly consulted on general matters of ecclesiastical politics. In 1889 he unwillingly yielded to the strong pressure of Archbishop Benson to act as one of his assessors in the trial of Edward King [q. v. Suppl. II], bishop of Lincoln, for ritualistic practices. His personal affection for the archbishop was his main reason for undertaking this unwelcome task. He was convinced that the archbishop was no 'Canterbury pope,' with a right to sit alone in judgment on his suffragans. Stubbs, too, was little interested in questions of vestments and ceremonies, though he strongly shared Bishop King's theological convictions, and regarded him as the victim of persecution. Between 12 Feb. 1889 and 21 Nov. 1890 Stubbs regularly attended the archbishop's court in the Lambeth library. He felt compromised by being there, and was bored by the lengthy arguments. He vented his displeasure in jest and verse. 'It is a sheer waste of time,' he cried, 'and the court has not a shadow of real authority.' 'We are discussing forms and ceremonies. Oh! the wearing weariness of it all!' (HUTTON, pp. 326–8). He expressed, however, his hearty approval 'of all and every part' of the primate's judgment. (*Visitation Charges*, pp. 154–166, expounds in full his point of view. Benson's is seen in A. C. BENSON's *Life of E. W. Benson*, ii. 348–81.) For the rest of his life he scrupulously adhered to it, and forbade his clergy to practise any of the ceremonies which Benson had declared illegal.

Early in 1898 Stubbs's health began to fail. Though he rallied somewhat he was again ill in 1900. Early in 1901 he wrote 'I can do all my hand and head work, but am weak in moving about.' He felt deeply the deaths of Bishop Creighton and Queen Victoria. Ordered by King Edward VII to preach the sermon in St. George's chapel the day after Queen Victoria's funeral, he disobeyed his physicians, and went. For the next two months he struggled against increasing weakness, but at the end of March he was told that he must resign his bishopric. He began his preparations to move from Cuddesdon, when he had a serious relapse, and died on 22 April 1901. He was buried in Cuddesdon churchyard. A portrait in oils by Sir Hubert von Herkomer (1885) is in the picture gallery of the Bodleian Library; another, by Charles Wellington Furse (1892), is at Cuddesdon.

Among the public honours Stubbs received may be mentioned membership of the Berlin, Munich, and Copenhagen academies, corresponding membership of the Académie des sciences morales et politiques of the French Institut, honorary doctorates of Heidelberg, Edinburgh, Cambridge, Dublin, and Oxford, and the rarely conferred Prussian order *pour le mérite* (1897). Perhaps no recognition pleased Stubbs better than that of his old Oxford contemporaries and brother historians, the friendship of such German scholars as Pauli, Maurer, Waitz, and Liebermann, and his honorary studentship of Christ Church.

Stubbs's more important writings have already been enumerated. He seldom contributed to periodical writings after the early years of his literary activity, and he boasted that he wrote only one review, which apparently has not been identified. Yet besides those mentioned above there were many books which he edited and prefaces which he wrote. The list of these occasional and minor writings can be found in the bibliography of his historical works, edited for the Royal Historical Society by Dr. W. A. Shaw (pp. 17–23, 1903), and in the bibliography in Archdeacon Hutton's 'Letters of William Stubbs' (pp. 409–15, 1904).

[The most copious materials for Stubbs's biography are to be found in The Letters of William Stubbs, Bishop of Oxford, edited by W. H. Hutton, 1904. Of special value are the autobiographical fragments that Stubbs was fond of inserting in some of his later utterances, as for instance Seventeen Lectures, 3rd edit., pp. vi–xii, 432–3, 474–8; Visitation Charges, pp. 347–8; postscript to preface to Registrum Sacrum Anglicanum, 1897. Some further details can be gleamed from Mrs. Creighton's Life and Letters of Mandell Creighton (1904), W. R. W. Stephens's Life and Letters of E. A. Freeman (1895), and Leslie Stephen's Letters of J. R. Green (1901). To these may be added particulars derived from the various obituary notices, and from personal knowledge and private information. Among the most noteworthy appreciation of Stubbs's historical work may be mentioned that by F. W. Maitland in the English Historical Review, xvi. 417–26 (1901), reprinted in The Collected Papers of F. W. Maitland, iii. 495–511 (1911). Others appear in Quarterly

Review, ccii. 1–34 (1905); Revue Historique, lxxvi. 463–6 (1901, by Charles Bémont); Church Quart. Rev. lii. 280–99.] T. F. T.

STURGIS, JULIAN RUSSELL (1848–1904), novelist, born at Boston, Massachusetts, U.S.A., on 21 Oct. 1848, was fourth son of Russell Sturgis of Boston, U.S.A., by his wife Juliet Overing Boit, also of Boston. When seven months old, the boy was brought to England, and he resided there for the rest of his life. Educated at Eton (in Dame Evans's house) from 1862 to 1867, he matriculated at Balliol College, Oxford, on 27 Jan. 1868, and graduated B.A. in 1872, taking a second class in the final classical school; he proceeded M.A. in 1875. His intellectual interest at the university lay chiefly in history and political economy. He was also a notable athlete in school and college days, being captain of the school football eleven and rowing in his college boat. In 1876 he was called to the bar of the Inner Temple. He became a naturalised British subject in Jan. 1877. In 1878 he travelled in the Levant, visiting the Turkish and Russian armies before Constantinople, and in 1880 he made a tour in the west of America. He was more attracted by life and character than by art and archæology, and he wove descriptions of his travels into his novels (cf. *John Maidment*, 1885, and *Stephen Calinari*, 1901).

His first work, a novel entitled 'John-a-Dreams,' appeared in 1878. It was followed by 'An Accomplished Gentleman' in 1879, and by 'Little Comedies,' dialogues in dramatic form, containing some of his most delicate and characteristic writing, in 1880. 'Comedies New and Old' and 'Dick's Wandering' appeared in 1882.

Sturgis married on 8 Nov. 1883, at St. Patrick's Cathedral, Armagh, Ireland, Mary Maud, daughter of Colonel Marcus de La Poer Beresford. There were three sons of the marriage. Possessed of ample means, Sturgis after his marriage divided his time between London and the country, first at Elvington near Dover, and then at Compton near Guildford, where he built a house. He continued writing, issuing the novels 'My Friends and I' in 1884, 'John Maidment' in 1885, 'Thraldom' in 1887, 'The Comedy of a Country House' in 1889, 'After Twenty Years' in 1892, 'A Master of Fortune' in 1896, 'The Folly of Pen Harrington' in 1897, and 'Stephen Calinari,' his last and best novel, in 1901. He also attempted verse in 'Count Julian: a Spanish Tragedy' (1893) and 'A Book of Song' (1894), and wrote the librettos for Goring Thomas's 'Nadeshda' (1885), for Sir Arthur Sullivan's 'Ivanhoe' (1891), and for Sir Charles Villiers Stanford's 'Much Ado about Nothing' (1901).

Sturgis died on 13 April 1904 at 16 Hans Road, London, S.W., and after cremation at Woking was buried in the Compton burial ground.

Sturgis was a man of singular charm of character, the reticence which distinguishes his writings being laid aside in his intercourse with his friends. His novels show a peculiar and sympathetic insight into the immature mind of masculine youth. His style, clear, delicate, and expressive of the writer's refinement and culture, is at times allusive and elliptical, and bears witness to the influence of Pater and Meredith; of the latter Sturgis was a great admirer and a personal friend.

[The Times, 14 and 18 April 1904; Who's Who, 1903; Monthly Review, No. 46, July 1904 (article by P. Lubbock and A. C. Benson); private information.] E. L.

STURT, HENRY GERARD, first Baron Alington (1825–1904), sportsman, born on 16 May 1825, was eldest son of Henry Charles Sturt (1795–1866) of Crichel, Dorset, sometime M.P., by his wife Charlotte Penelope, third daughter of Robert Brudenell, sixth earl of Cardigan. From Eton he went to Christ Church, Oxford, where he graduated B.A. in 1845, proceeding M.A. in 1848. From 1847 to 1856 he was conservative M.P. for Dorchester, and from 1856 to 1876 for the county of Dorset. He was raised to the peerage on 15 Jan. 1876, as Baron Alington, a title borne by maternal ancestors in both the English and Irish peerages which had become extinct.

Sturt's name first appeared in 1849 in the list of winning owners on the turf, and he was elected to the Jockey Club next year. The colours he registered were 'light blue, white cap,' which were those formerly belonging to Lord George Bentinck. Almost throughout his career on the turf Lord Alington had a racing partner. His first confederate was Mr. H. Curzon, with whom he owned a filly called Kate. Thinking she was of no account, they sold her as a two-year-old, and the following year, 1852, had the mortification of seeing her win the One Thousand Guineas. For some years Sturt's horses were trained by John Day at Danebury, but when in 1868 he entered into a racing partnership with Sir Frederic Johnstone—a partnership which was dissolved only by the death of Lord Alington—the horses were next transferred to William Day at Woodyates. The colours adopted by the 'confederates' were those of Sir Frederic Johnstone, 'chocolate, yellow sleeves.' The new partnership, which in after years came to be known as 'the old firm,' speedily scored a notable success, for in 1869 Brigantine, bought as a yearling for a small sum, won the Oaks and the Ascot Cup. In 1871 a reverse was experienced. As the result of bad jockeyship, Allbrook was beaten by a head by Sabinus for the Cambridgeshire Stakes. Sturt stood to win a sum variously stated as 30,000*l.* to 50,000*l.* on Allbrook.

In 1881 the partners transferred their horses to John Porter at Kingsclere, and a series of important successes followed. In 1883 the partners won the Derby with St. Blaise; in 1891 Common won the Two Thousand Guineas, the Derby, and the St. Leger; in 1894 Matchbox ran second to Ladas in the Derby, and Throstle won the St. Leger, beating Ladas and Matchbox. Matchbox had been sold for 16,000*l.* to Baron Hirsch, who after the St. Leger parted with it to the Austrian government. St. Blaise was sold to Mr. Belmont, an American sportsman, after whose death the horse was sold at auction in New York for 20,000*l.* Sir Blundell Maple bought Common for 15,000*l.* the day after he won the St. Leger. Among the partners' many other victories was that of Friar's Balsam in all his races as a two-year-old in 1887. Meeting with an accident to his jaw, the horse failed next year to win 'classic' honours.

At his home, Crichel, Lord Alington dispensed a liberal hospitality. He was a delightful host, a considerate landlord, and magnificently generous. He died of heart failure at Crichel on 17 Feb. 1904, after a lingering illness, and was buried there. A full-length portrait by Graves is in the staircase hall at Crichel.

Alington married (1) on 10 Sept. 1853 Augusta (*d.* 1888), eldest daughter of George Charles Bingham, third earl of Lucan; by her he had one son and five daughters; (2) on 10 Feb. 1892 Evelyn Henrietta, daughter of Henry Blundell Leigh; she survived him without issue. He was succeeded by his son, Humphrey Napier Sturt, M.P. for East Dorset (1891–1904).

[Sportsman, and The Times, 19 Feb. 1904; The Field, 20 Feb.; Truth, 24 Feb.; William Day's The Race Horse in Training, 1880, and Reminiscences of 'Woodyates,' 1886; Burke's Peerage; Ruff's Guide to the Turf.]

E. M.

SUTHERLAND, ALEXANDER (1852–1902), Australian journalist, born at Wellcroft Place, Glasgow, on 26 March 1852, was eldest son of George Sutherland, artist, by his wife Jane, daughter of William Smith, of Galston, Ayrshire. Two brothers, George and William, distinguished themselves, the former as a journalist and inventor and the latter as a mathematician and an original scientific inquirer. Alexander was educated in Glasgow until 1864, when the state of his father's health led to the whole family emigrating to Sydney, Australia. At the age of fourteen he became a pupil teacher in the education department of New South Wales and studied for the arts course at Sydney University. In 1870 the family removed to Melbourne, where he taught at the Hawthorn grammar school during the day and worked at night for the arts course at Melbourne University. He entered that university in the first term of 1871 and graduated B.A. with distinction in 1874, proceeding M.A. in 1876.

On leaving the university he was mathematical master in the Scotch College, Melbourne (1875–7) and principal of Carlton College, Melbourne (1877–92). In 1892 he retired, chiefly with a view to devoting himself to a work on the 'Origin and Growth of the Moral Instinct' (published in London in 1898). The financial crisis of 1893, however, compelled him to take up journalism, and he contributed largely to the 'Melbourne Review,' 'Argus,' 'Australasian,' and other papers and periodicals. He made two vain attempts to enter politics. In 1897 he contested Williamstown in the Victorian legislature, and in 1901 stood for South Melbourne in the federal parliament. At the close of 1898 he came to London as representative of the 'South Australian Register,' and reported the sittings of the Peace Conference at the Hague. On his return to Australia he was appointed in 1901 registrar of Melbourne University, and after the death of Professor Morris continued his lectures on English literature. The double duty overtaxed him, and he died suddenly on 9 Aug. 1902, and was buried in Kew cemetery, Melbourne. A tablet was placed to his memory in Carlton College by his old pupils.

Sutherland married Elizabeth Jane, the second daughter of Robert Dundas Ballantyne (who was controller-general of the convict settlement at Port Arthur, Van Diemen's Land), and had two sons (the elder of whom predeceased him) and three daughters.

Sutherland was in the front rank of Australian men of letters. A stimulating teacher, he was equally successful in the preparation of school books. His 'History of Australia from 1606 to 1876' (Melbourne, 1897) (in which his brother George collaborated) had a very large circulation. He was a poet of taste and a scientific investigator, acting for some years as secretary of the Royal Society of Victoria. His published books include, besides the works noticed: 1. 'A New Geography,' Melbourne, 1885. 2. 'Victoria and its Metropolis,' 2 vols. Melbourne, 1888. 3. 'Thirty Short Poems,' Melbourne, 1890, 4. 'Geography of British Colonies,' London, 1892. 5. 'A Class Book of Geography,' London, 1894. 6. 'History of Australia and New Zealand, 1606–1890,' London, 1894. 7. Lives of Kendall and Gordon in the 'Development of Australian Literature,' Melbourne, 1898. 8. 'Origin and Growth of the Moral Instinct,' London, 1898. 9. 'The Praise of Poetry in English Literature,' Melbourne, 1901.

An India-ink sketch of Sutherland at the age of twenty-two, drawn by his father, is in the possession of his sister, Miss Sutherland, of 4 Highfield Grove, Kew, Melbourne. A photographic copy is in the library of the colonial office, London.

[Alexander Sutherland, M.A.: his Life and Work, by Henry Gyles Turner, 1908; Johns's Notable Australians, 1908; Melbourne Argus, 11 Aug. 1902; The Times, 16 Sept. 1902; Athenæum, 11 Oct. 1902; Nature, 23 Nov. 1911; Mennell's Dictionary of Australasian Biography, 1892; information from Mr. Henry Gyles Turner.] C. A.

SUTTON, HENRY SEPTIMUS (1825–1901), author, born at Nottingham on 10 Feb. 1825, was seventh child in a family of seven sons and three daughters of Richard Sutton (1789–1856) of Nottingham, bookseller, printer and proprietor of the 'Nottingham Review,' by his wife Sarah, daughter of Thomas Salt, farmer, of Stanton by Dale, Derbyshire. A sister, Mrs. Eliza S. Oldham, was author of 'The Haunted House' (1863) and 'By the Trent' (1864). From childhood he spent his time among the books in his father's shop, and early acquired literary tastes. He was educated at a private school in Nottingham and at Leicester grammar school. A study of medicine was soon abandoned for literature and journalism. Among early literary friends were his fellow townsman, Philip James Bailey [q. v. Suppl. II], and Coventry Patmore, with whom an intimacy was formed soon after the publication of Patmore's first volume of poems in 1844, and continued till Patmore's death in 1896. The two friends long corresponded on literary and religious subjects (see BASIL CHAMPNEYS, *Coventry Patmore*, vol. ii. ch. lx. pp. 142–65).

Sutton, who was through life a vegetarian and total abstainer, developed a strong vein of mysticism with an active interest in social and religious problems. Emerson's writings greatly influenced his early thought and style. His first book in prose, 'The Evangel of Love' (1847), which closely echoed Emerson, was welcomed by Patmore with friendly encouragement, while his master Emerson, to whom the book had been shown by J. Neuberg, Carlyle's friend and admirer, declared it to be 'worthy of George Herbert.' When Emerson visited Manchester in 1847 he invited Sutton from Nottingham to meet him, and a lifelong friendship was begun. Emerson visited Sutton at Nottingham next year; they met again in Manchester in 1872. In 1849, on Emerson's recommendation, Alexander Ireland [q. v.] found for Sutton, who became an expert shorthand writer, journalistic employment in Manchester, and in 1853 he became chief of the 'Manchester Examiner and Times' reporting staff. Soon after he met George MacDonald [q. v. Suppl. II] in Manchester; they became lifelong friends, and mutually influenced each other's spiritual development (*Letters to William Allingham*, 1911, pp. 44–8).

In 1848 his first poetical work, a tiny volume of mystical tone entitled 'Clifton Grove Garland,' came out at Nottingham. In 1854 there appeared his 'Quinquenergia: Proposals for a New Practical Theology,' including a series of simply phrased but subtly argued poems, 'Rose's Diary,' on which his poetic fame rests. The volume was enthusiastically received. Emerson's friend, Bronson Alcott, writing on 15 Oct. 1854, detected in Sutton's 'profound religious genius' a union of 'the remarkable sense of William Law with the subtlety of Behmen and the piety of Pascal' (F. G. SANBORN and WILLIAM T. HARRIS, *A. Bronson Alcott*, 1893, ii. 484–5). The book became Frances Power Cobbe's constant companion. James Martineau rated it very highly. Francis Turner Palgrave included 'How beautiful it is to be alive' from 'Rose's Diary' and two other of Sutton's poems in his 'Golden Treasury of Sacred Poetry.' Carlyle, however, scornfully wondered that 'a lad in a provincial town' should have presumed to handle such themes (F. Espinasse, *Literary Recollections*, p. 160). To a collected edition of his poems (1886) Sutton added, among other new poems, 'A Preacher's Soliloquy and Sermon,' which reveals a genuine affinity with Herbert. 'Rose's Diary' with other poems was reprinted in the 'Broadbent' booklets as 'A Sutton Treasury' (Manchester, 1899; seventeenth thousand, 1909).

Meanwhile Sutton was pursuing his journalistic work on very congenial lines. He had joined the United Kingdom Alliance on its foundation at Manchester in 1853, and was editor of its weekly journal, the 'Alliance News,' from its inception in 1854 until 1898, contributing leading articles till his death. He was also editor from 1859 to 1869 of 'Meliora,' a quarterly journal devoted to social and temperance reform. His religious mysticism at the same time deepened. In 1857 he joined the Peter Street Society of Swedenborgians. He took an active part in Swedenborgian church and Sunday school work, was popular as a lay preacher, and zealously expounded Swedenborg's writings on somewhat original lines in 'Outlines of the Doctrine of the Mind according to Emanuel Swedenborg' (1889), in 'Five Essays for Students of the Divine Philosophy of Swedenborg' (1895), with a sixth essay, 'Our Saviour's Triple Crown' (1898), and a seventh and a last essay, 'The Golden Age: pt. i. Man's Creation and Fall; pt. ii. Swedenborgian Phrenology' (Manchester, 1900).

Sutton, who was of retiring but most genial and affectionate disposition, died at 18 Yarburgh St., Moss Side, Manchester, on 2 May 1901, and was buried at Worsley. He was twice married: (1) in January 1850 to Sarah Prickard (*d.* June 1868), by whom he had a son, Arthur James, a promising scholar of Balliol College, Oxford, who predeceased him in 1880, and a daughter who survived him; (2) in May 1870 to Mary Sophia Ewen, who survived him without issue till April 1910. A painted portrait by his sister Eliza belongs to the family.

[The Times, 6 May 1901; New Church Mag., June 1901, 271–86; Alliance News, 9 May 1901 (with portrait); Manchester Guardian, 3 May 1901; Manchester City News, 20 and 27 May 1899 (Sutton's Reminiscences of Emerson's Visit to Manchester); Francis Espinasse, Literary Recollections and Sketches, 1893; A. H. Miles, Poets of the Nineteenth Century, xii. 151 seq.; works cited; private information from brother, Mr. R. C. Sutton.] W. B. O.

SWAIN, JOSEPH (1820–1909), wood-engraver, born at Oxford on 29 Feb. 1820, was second son of Ebenezer Swain by his wife Harriet James. Joseph Swain, pastor of East Street baptist church, Walworth, was his grandfather. He was educated at private schools, first at Oxford, and afterwards in London, whither the family removed in 1829.

In 1834 he was apprenticed by his father (who was a printer of the firm of Wertheimer & Co.) to the wood-engraver Nathaniel Whittock, and was transferred in 1837 to Thomas Williams. In 1843 he was appointed manager of the engraving department of 'Punch,' but in the following year set up in business for himself, retaining the whole of the engraving for 'Punch' from 1844 until 1900. His name is best known from his wood-engravings of 'Punch' cartoons by Sir John Tenniel. Nearly all the illustrations in the 'Cornhill Magazine' were engraved by him, and he also worked largely for other periodicals such as 'Once a Week,' 'Good Words,' the 'Argosy,' and for the publications of the Religious Tract Society and the Baptist Missionary Society. He was one of the most prolific wood-engravers of the nineteenth century, engraving very largely after Fred Walker, J. E. Millais, Frederick Sandys, Richard Doyle, R. Ansdell, F. Barnard, and practically all famous illustrators from 1860 onwards. His own work is not always signed, and the signature 'Swain sc.' must be taken to include the engraving of assistants working for the firm. In the latter part of the nineteenth century his wood-engravings were more generally printed from electrotypes, but those done for 'Punch' were invariably printed from the original wood-blocks. He died at Ealing on 25 Feb. 1909.

In 1843 he married Martha Cooper, and had issue three daughters and a son, Joseph Blomeley Swain, who carries on his printing and engraving establishment.

A series of articles on Fred Walker, C. H. Bennett, G. J. Pinwell, and F. Eltze, which he wrote for 'Good Words' (1888–9), were incorporated in 'Toilers in Art,' edited by H. C. Ewart (1891).

[The Times, 4 March 1909; M. H. Spielmann, Hist. of Punch, 1895; Gleeson White, English Illustration: The Sixties, 1897; Thackeray, Harry Furniss Centenary edition, artist's preface to the Virginians, 1911; information supplied by Mr. J. B. Swain.]

A. M. H.

SWAN, JOHN MACALLAN (1847–1910), painter and sculptor, was the son of Robert Wemyss Swan, a civil engineer, by his wife Elisabeth MacAllan. He was born at Old Brentford on 9 Dec. 1847, both parents being Scots. Swan began his study of art in the schools at Worcester and Lambeth and in those of the Royal Academy. He afterwards worked in Paris, under Gérôme and Frémiet. His chief school after his return to London was the Zoological Gardens, where his friends were almost as likely to find him as in his own house.

In 1878 he began to exhibit, sending pictures to both the Royal Academy and the Grosvenor Gallery. At first he confined himself to animals, but he soon began to introduce the human figure, choosing subjects of a more or less idyllic character, which lent themselves to the use of the nude. Commencing chiefly as a painter, he gradually devoted himself more and more to modelling, until at last he divided his time pretty equally between the two forms of art. Among his best, and best-known, pictures are 'The Prodigal Son' (bought for the Chantrey bequest in 1888) in the Tate Gallery; 'Maternity' (a lioness suckling her cubs) in the Rijksmuseum, Amsterdam; 'A Lioness defending her Cubs' in Mr. J. C. Williams's collection; and 'Leopards' in the Bradford gallery.

Among his works in sculpture the following may be named: 'The Walking Leopard' at Manchester; 'Orpheus,' in silver, in Mrs. Joseph's collection; a larger and slightly different group of the same in bronze in Mrs. Coutts Michie's collection; 'Indian Leopard and Tortoise,' silver, in Mr. Ernest Sichel's collection, and the same in bronze in Mrs. Swan's possession; 'Leopard running' in Lady Shand's collection; a bronze bust of Cecil Rhodes [q. v. Suppl. II] and the eight colossal lions for Rhodes's monument at Groote Schuur, Capetown; and a 'Lioness drinking' in the Luxembourg.

Swan was elected an associate of the Royal Academy in 1894, and a full member in 1905. He was elected a member of the Royal Water Colour Society in 1899. He was also an hon. LL.D. of Aberdeen. He was one of the few English artists who won a wide acceptance abroad at the outset of their career. In 1885 he became a member of the Dutch Water Colour society. He won a silver medal at Paris in 1889, a gold medal at Munich in 1893, the grand medal at Munich in 1897, two gold medals at the Chicago World's Fair, and three gold medals at the Paris exhibition of 1900. He was a member of the 'Secessions' of Vienna and Munich, and in 1911, after his death, his work was awarded a memorial gold medal at Barcelona.

Swan early gained a reputation among the more discriminating collectors in this country, and from about 1880 until the time of his death the only things which debarred him from a wide popularity were his own fastidiousness and consequent slowness of production. Few artists have lavished so much care on their work before allowing it to leave their studios. Consequently he left a vast number of unfinished pictures and works of sculpture, as well as preparatory drawings. His studies, of which a special exhibition was held by the Fine Art Society in 1897, are among the finest ever made; a special fund was raised after his death, chiefly through the exertions of Mr. J. C. Drucker, to acquire as many as possible for the nation, so that the British Museum, the National Galleries of England, Scotland, and Ireland, the Guildhall Gallery, and many provincial museums are rich in his drawings. These are characterised by an almost unrivalled combination of artistic with scientific qualities. Even in his most fragmentary studies the structure and movement of his favourite models, the great cats, are at once given with extraordinary truth and vivacity and organised into æsthetic unity. As a painter his chief qualities were a touch of poetry in his imagination; good, sometimes fine, colour, which was in a key of his own; tone; and great power of modelling.

Swan died in London on 14 Feb. 1910, He married in 1884 Mary, eldest daughter of Hamilton Rankin of Carndonagh, co. Donegal, by whom he had two children, a son and a daughter. The latter follows her father's profession. Swan's appearance was remarkable. He was tall, dark, and burly, with a large head, like a Roman emperor's. His best portraits are a bust by Sir William Goscombe John, R.A., a bronze relief by H. Pegram, A.R.A., and paintings by Mr. McClure Hamilton and Mrs. Swan. He figures in Herkomer's 'Council of the Royal Academy' (1907) at the Tate Gallery.

Swan was the author of a 'Treatise on Metal Work,' read before the R.I.B.A. in 1906, and of papers on technical artistic questions, some of which were printed in the 'Proceedings of the Japanese Society.'

A memorial exhibition of his works, nearly a hundred items, was held at the Royal Academy in the winter of 1911.

[Personal knowledge and private information; Drawings of J. M. Swan, by A. L.

Baldry, 1905; Introduction to Fine Art Society's Catalogue of Exhibition of Wild Beasts, by Cosmo Monkhouse.] W. A.

SWAYNE, JOSEPH GRIFFITHS (1819–1903), obstetric physician, born on 18 Oct. 1819 at Bristol, was second son of John Champeny Swayne, lecturer on midwifery in the Bristol medical school, whose father was for nearly sixty years vicar of Pucklechurch, Gloucestershire. His mother was eldest daughter of Dr. Thomas Griffiths, a medical practitioner in Bristol. After education at the now extinct proprietary Bristol college, where one of his teachers was Francis William Newman [q. v. Suppl. I], Swayne was apprenticed to his father and at the same time studied at the Bristol medical school and the royal infirmary. Later he went to Guy's Hospital and became M.R.C.S. and a licentiate of the Society of Apothecaries in 1841. He also studied in Paris, and in 1842 graduated M.B. of the University of London, obtaining the gold medal in obstetric medicine and being bracketed with Sir Alfred Baring Garrod [q. v. Suppl. II] for the gold medal in medicine. In 1845 he proceeded M.D. at London and joined his father as lecturer on midwifery in the Bristol medical school; he was sole lecturer from 1850 until 1895, when he was appointed emeritus professor. In 1853 he was elected physician accoucheur to the Bristol general hospital, one of the first appointments of the kind out of London; he held this post until 1875, when he became consulting obstetric physician. Greatly esteemed as a consultant, he had a large practice in the west of England. He attached an importance in advance of his time to asepsis, and deprecated long hair or beards for those who practise surgery or midwifery. As early as 1843 he investigated cholera, and described a micro-organism which some have suggested was the comma bacillus which Koch proved to be the cause of the disease in 1884. Swayne died suddenly on 1 Aug. 1903, and was buried at Arno's Vale cemetery, Bristol. He married Georgina (*d.* 1865), daughter of the Rev. G. Gunning, and had issue one son and one daughter.

Swayne possessed much artistic and literary ability. He published, in addition to many papers in medical journals, 'Obstetric Aphorisms for the Use of Students' (1856; 10th edit. 1893), which was translated into eight languages, including Japanese and Hindustani.

[Bristol Med. Chir. Journal, 1903, xxi. 193–202 (with photograph and bibliography); Brit. Med. Journal, 1903, ii. 338.] H. D. R.

SWAYTHLING, first Baron. [See Montagu, Sir Samuel (1832–1911).]

SWINBURNE, ALGERNON CHARLES (1837–1909), poet, born in Chester Street, Grosvenor Place, London, on 5 April 1837, was eldest child of Admiral Charles Henry Swinburne (1797–1877), by his wife Lady Jane Henrietta (1809–1896), daughter of George Ashburnham, third earl of Ashburnham. His father was second son of Sir John Edward Swinburne (1762–1860), sixth baronet of Capheaton, in Northumberland. This baronet, who exercised a strong influence over his grandson, the poet, had been born and brought up in France, and cultivated the memory of Mirabeau. In habits, dress, and modes of thought he was like a French nobleman of the *ancien régime*. From his father, a cut and dried unimaginative old 'salt,' the poet inherited little but a certain identity of colour and expression; his features and something of his mental character were his mother's. Lady Jane was a woman of exquisite accomplishment, and widely read in foreign literature. From his earliest years Algernon was trained, by his grandfather and by his mother, in the French and Italian languages. He was brought up, with the exception of long visits to Northumberland, in the Isle of Wight, his grandparents residing at The Orchard, Niton, Ventnor, and his parents at East Dene, Bonchurch.

He had been born all but dead and was not expected to live an hour; but though he was always nervous and slight, his childhood, spent mainly in the open air, was active and healthy. His parents were high-church and he was brought up as 'a quasi-catholic.' He recollected in after years the enthusiasm with which he welcomed the process of confirmation, and his 'ecstasies of adoration when receiving the Sacrament.' He early developed a love for climbing, riding, and swimming, and never cared, through life, for any other sports. His father, the admiral, taught him to plunge in the sea when he was still almost an infant, and he was always a fearless and, in relation to his physique, a powerful swimmer. 'He could swim and walk for ever' (Lord Redesdale). He was prepared for Eton by Collingwood Forster Fenwick, rector of Brook, near Newport, Isle of Wight, who expressed his surprise at finding the child so deeply read in certain directions; Algernon having, from a very early age, been 'privileged to have a book at meals' (Mrs. Disney Leith).

He came to Eton at Easter 1849, arriving, 'a queer little elf, who carried about with him a Bowdlerised Shakespeare, adorned with a blue silk book-marker, with a Tunbridge-ware button at the end of it' (Lord Redesdale). This volume had been given to him by his mother when he was six years of age. Up to the time of his going to Eton he had never been allowed to read a novel, but he immediately plunged into the study of Dickens, as well as of Shakespeare (released from Bowdler), of the old dramatists, of every species of lyrical poetry. The embargo being now raised, he soon began to read everything. It is difficult to say what, by the time he left Eton, 'Swinburne did not know, and, what is more, appreciate, of English literature' (Sir George Young). He devoured even that dull *gradus* the 'Poetæ Græci,' a book which he long afterwards said 'had played a large part in fostering the love of poetry in his mind' (A. G. C. Liddell). In 1850 his mother gave him Dyce's Marlowe, and he soon knew Ford and Webster. He began, before he was fourteen, to collect rare editions of the dramatists. Any day he could be found in a bay-window of the college library, the sunlight in his hair, and his legs always crossed tailor-wise, with a folio as big as himself spread open upon his knees. The librarian, 'Grub' Brown, used to point him out, thus, to strangers as one of the curiosities of Eton. He boarded at Joynes's, who was his tutor; Hawtrey was headmaster.

It has been falsely said that Swinburne was bullied at Eton. On the contrary, there was 'something a little formidable about him' (Sir George Young), considerable tact (Lord Redesdale), and a great, even audacious, courage, which kept other boys at a distance. He did not dislike Eton, but he cultivated few friendships; he did not desire school-honours, he never attempted any game or athletics, and he was looked upon as odd and unaccountable, and so left alone to his omnivorous reading. He was a kind of fairy, a privileged creature. Lord Redesdale recalls his taking 'long walks in Windsor Forest, always with a single friend, Swinburne dancing as he went, and reciting from his inexhaustible memory the works which he had been studying in his favourite sunlighted window.' Sir George Young has described him vividly: 'his hands and feet all going' while he talked; 'his little white face, and great aureole of hair, and green eyes,' the hair standing out in a bush of 'three different colours and textures, orange-red, dark red, and bright pure gold.' Charles Dickens, at Bonchurch in 1849, was struck with 'the golden-haired lad of the Swinburnes' whom his own boys used to play with, and when he went to congratulate the poet on 'Atalanta' in 1865, he reminded him of this earlier meeting. In 1851 Algernon 'passed' in swimming, and at this time, in the holidays, caused some anxiety by his recklessness in riding and climbing; he swarmed up the Culver Cliff, hitherto held to be impregnable: a feat of which he was proud to the end of his life. Immediately on his arrival at Eton he had attacked the poetry of Wordsworth. In September 1849 he was taken by his parents to visit that poet in the Lakes; Wordsworth, who was very gracious, said in parting that he did not think that Algernon 'would forget' him, whereupon the little boy burst into tears (Miss Sewell's *Autobiography*). Earlier in the year Lady Jane had taken her son to visit Rogers in London; the old man laid his hand on Algernon's head in parting, and said 'I think that you will be a poet, too!' He was, in fact, now writing verses, but none of these were ever printed, and in 1855 he burnt 'every scrap of MS. he had in the world.' (Some verse appearing in 'Fraser's Magazine' in 1848 and following years under the initials A. C. S. and subsequently assigned in error to Swinburne was by Sir Anthony Coningham Sterling [q. v.].) At the age of fourteen many of his lifelong partialities and prejudices were formed; in the course of 1851 we find him immersed in Landor, Shelley and Keats, in the 'Orlando Furioso,' and in the tragedies of Corneille, and valuing them as he did throughout his life; while, on the other hand, already hating Euripides, insensible to Horace, and injurious to Racine. In the catholicity of his poetic taste there was one odd exception: he had promised his mother, whom he adored, not to read Byron, and in fact did not open that poet till he went to Oxford. In 1852, reading much French with Tarver, 'Notre Dame de Paris' introduced him to Victor Hugo. He now won the second Prince Consort's prize for French and Italian, and in 1853 the first prizes for French and Italian. His Greek elegiacs were greatly admired. He was, however, making no real progress at school, and was chafing against the discipline; in the summer of 1853 he had trouble with Joynes, of a rebellious kind, and did not return to Eton, 'although nothing had been said during the half about his leaving' (YOUNG). When he left he was within a few places of the headmaster's division.

In 1854 there was some talk of his being trained for the army, which he greatly desired; but this was abandoned on account of the slightness and shortness of his figure. All his life he continued to regret the military profession. He was prepared for Oxford, in a desultory way, by John Wilkinson, perpetual curate of Cambo in Northumberland, who said that he 'was too clever and would never study.' He now spent a few weeks in Germany with his uncle, General the Hon. Thomas Ashburnham. On 24 Jan. 1856 Swinburne matriculated at Balliol College, Oxford, and he kept terms regularly through the years 1856, 1857, and 1858. After the first year his high-church proclivities fell from him and he became a nihilist in religion and a republican. He had portraits of Mazzini in his rooms, and declaimed verses to them (LORD SHEFFIELD); in the spring of 1857 he wrote an 'Ode to Mazzini,' not yet published, which is his earliest work of any maturity. In this year, while at Capheaton, he formed the friendship of Lady Trevelyan and Miss Capel Lofft, and was for the next four years a member of their cultivated circle at Wallington. Here Ruskin met him, and formed a very high opinion of his imaginative capacities. In the autumn Edwin Hatch [q.v.] introduced him to D. G. Rossetti, who was painting in the Union, and in December the earliest of Swinburne's contributions to 'Undergraduate Papers' appeared. To this time belong his friendships with John Nichol, Edward Burne-Jones, William Morris, and Spencer Stanhope. Early in 1858 he was writing his tragedy of 'Rosamond,' a poem on 'Tristram,' and planning a drama on 'The Albigenses.' In March 1858 Swinburne dined at Farringford with Tennyson, who thought him 'a very modest and intelligent young fellow' and read 'Maud' to him, urging upon him a special devotion to Virgil. In April the last of the 'Undergraduate Papers' appeared. In the Easter term Swinburne took a second in moderations, and won the Taylorian scholarship for French and Italian. He now accompanied his parents to France for a long visit. The attempt of Orsini, in January 1858, to murder Napoleon III had found an enthusiastic admirer in Algernon, who decorated his rooms at Oxford with Orsini's portrait, and proved an embarrassing fellow-traveller in Paris to his parents. He kept the Lent and Easter terms of 1859 at Balliol, and when the Austrian war broke out in May, he spoke at the Union, 'reading excitedly but ineffectively a long tirade against Napoleon and in favour of Orsini and Mazzini' (LORD SHEFFIELD). He began to be looked upon as 'dangerous,' and Jowett, who was much interested in him, expressed an extreme dread that the college might send him down and so 'make Balliol as ridiculous as University had made itself about Shelley.' At this time Swinburne had become what he continued to be for the rest of his life, a high tory republican. He cultivated few friends except those who immediately interested him poetically and politically. But he was a member of the club called the Old Mortality, in which he was associated with Nichol, Dicey, Luke (who was drowned in 1861), T. H. Green, Caird, and Pater, besides Mr. Bryce and Mr. Bywater.

Jowett thought it well that Swinburne should leave Oxford for a while at the end of Easter term, 1859, and sent him to read modern history with William Stubbs [q. v. Suppl. II] at Navestock. Here Swinburne recited to his host and hostess a tragedy he had just completed (probably 'The Queen Mother'). In consequence of some strictures made by Stubbs, Swinburne destroyed the only draft of the play, but was able to write it all out again from memory. He was back at the university from 14 Oct. to 21 Nov., when he was principally occupied in writing a three-act comedy in verse in the manner of Fletcher, now lost; it was called 'Laugh and Lie Down.' He had lodgings in Broad Street, where the landlady made complaints of his late hours and general irregularities. Jowett was convinced that he was doing no good at Oxford, and he left without taking a degree. His father was greatly displeased with him, but Algernon withdrew to Capheaton, until, in the spring of 1860, he came to London, and took rooms near Russell Place to be close to the Burne-Joneses. He had now a very small allowance from his father, and gave up the idea of preparing for any profession. Capheaton was still his summer home, but when Sir John Swinburne died (26 Sept. 1860) Algernon went to the William Bell Scotts' in Newcastle for some time. His first book, 'The Queen Mother and Rosamond,' was published before Christmas; it fell dead from the press.

When Algernon returned to London early in 1861 his friendship with D. G. Rossetti became intimate; for the next ten years they 'lived on terms of affectionate intimacy; shaped and coloured, on his side, by cordial kindness and exuberant generosity, on mine by gratitude as loyal and admiration as fervent as ever strove and ever failed to express all the sweet and sudden passion of youth towards greatness in its elder' (from an unpublished statement, written by Swinburne in 1882). This was by far the most notable experience in Swinburne's career. Rossetti developed, restrained, and guided, with marvellous skill, the genius of 'my little Northumbrian friend,' as he used to call him. Under his persuasion Swinburne was now writing some of his finest early lyrics, and was starting a cycle of prose tales, to be called 'The Triameron'; this was to consist of some twenty stories. Of these 'Dead Love' alone was printed in his lifetime; but several others exist unpublished, the most interesting being 'The Marriage of Mona Lisa,' 'A Portrait,' and 'Queen Fredegonde.' In the summer of 1861 he was introduced to Monckton Milnes, who actively interested himself in Swinburne's career. Early in 1862 Henry Adams, the American writer, then acting as Monckton Milnes's secretary, met Swinburne at Fryston on an occasion which he has described in his privately printed diary. The company also included Stirling of Keir (afterwards Sir W. Stirling-Maxwell) and Laurence Oliphant, and all Milnes's guests made Swinburne's acquaintance for the first time. He reminded Adams of 'a tropical bird,' 'a crimson macaw among owls'; and it was on this occasion that Stirling, in a phrase often misquoted, likened him to 'the Devil entered into the Duke of Argyll.' All the party, though prepared by Milnes's report, were astounded at the flow, the volume and the character of the young man's conversation; 'Voltaire's seemed to approach nearest to the pattern'; 'in a long experience, before or after, no one ever approached it.' The men present were brilliant and accomplished, but they 'could not believe in Swinburne's incredible memory and knowledge of literature, classic, mediæval and modern, nor know what to make of his rhetorical recitation of his own unpublished lyrics, "Faustine," "The Four Boards of the Coffin Lid" [a poem published as "After Death"], "The Ballad of Burdens," which he declaimed as though they were books of the "Iliad."' These parties at Fryston were probably the beginning of the social 'legend' of Swinburne, which preceded and encouraged the reception of his works a few years later. It was at Milnes's house that he met and formed an instant friendship with Richard Burton. The relationship which ensued was not altogether fortunate. Burton was a giant and an athlete, one of the few men who could fire an old-fashioned elephant-gun from his shoulder, and drink a bottle of brandy without feeling any effect from it. Swinburne, on the contrary, was a weakling. He tried to compete with the 'hero' in Dr. Johnson's sense, and he failed.

He was being painted by Rossetti in February 1862 when the wife of the latter died so tragically; Swinburne gave evidence at the inquest (12 Feb.). In the spring of that year he joined his family in the Pyrenees, and saw the Lac de Gaube, in which he insisted on swimming, to the horror of the natives. He was now intimate with George Meredith, who printed, shortly before his death, an account of the overwhelming effect of FitzGerald's 'Rubáiyát' upon Swinburne, and the consequent composition of 'Laus Veneris,' probably in the spring of 1862. In this year Swinburne began to write, in prose as well as in verse, for the 'Spectator,' which printed 'Faustine' and six other important poems, and (6 Sept.) a very long essay on Baudelaire's 'Fleurs du Mal,' written 'in a Turkish bath in Paris.' A review of one of Victor Hugo's books, forwarded to the French poet, opened his personal relations with that chief of Swinburne's literary heroes. He now finished 'Chastelard,' on which he had long been engaged, and in October his prose story, 'Dead Love,' was printed in 'Once a Week' (this appeared in book form in 1864). Swinburne joined Meredith and the Rossettis (24 Oct. 1862) in the occupation of Tudor House, 16 Cheyne Walk, Chelsea. Rossetti believed that it would be good for Swinburne to be living in the household of friends who would look after him without seeming to control him, since life in London lodgings was proving rather disastrous. Swinburne's extremely nervous organisation laid him open to great dangers, and he was peculiarly unfitted for dissipation. Moreover, about this time he began to be afflicted with what is considered to have been a form of epilepsy, which made it highly undesirable that he should be alone.

In Paris, during a visit in March 1863, he had made the acquaintance of Whistler, whom he now introduced to Rossetti. Swinburne became intimate with Whistler's family, and after a fit in the summer of 1863 in the American painter's studio, he was nursed through the subsequent illness by the mother of Whistler. On his convalescence he was persuaded, in October, to go down to his father's house at East Dene, near Bonchurch, where he remained for five months and entirely recovered his health and spirits. He brought with him the opening of 'Atalanta in Calydon,' which he completed at East Dene. For a story called 'The Children of the Chapel,' which was being written by his cousin, Mrs. Disney Leith, he wrote at the same time a morality, 'The Pilgrimage of Pleasure,' which appeared, without his name, in March 1864. From the Isle of Wight, at the close of February 1864, Swinburne went abroad for what was to remain the longest foreign tour in his life. He passed through Paris, where he saw Fantin-Latour, and proceeded to Hyères, where Milnes had a villa, and so to Italy. From Rossetti he had received an introduction to Seymour Kirkup [q. v.], then the centre of a literary circle in Florence, and Milnes added letters to Landor and to Mrs. Gaskell. Swinburne found Landor in his house in Via della Chiesa, close to the church of the Carmine, on 31 March, and he visited the art-galleries of Florence in the company of Mrs. Gaskell. In a garden at Fiesole he wrote 'Itylus' and 'Dolores.' Before returning he made a tour through other parts of Italy. Two autumn months of this year (1864) were spent in Cornwall, at Tintagel (in company with Jowett), at Kynance Cove, and at St. Michael's Mount. On his return to London he went into lodgings at 22A Dorset Street, where he remained for several years.

'Atalanta in Calydon,' in a cream-coloured binding with mystical ornaments by D. G. Rossetti, was published by Edward Moxon [q. v.] in April 1865. At this time Swinburne, although now entering his twenty-ninth year, was entirely unknown outside a small and dazzled circle of friends, but the success of 'Atalanta' was instant and overwhelming. Ruskin welcomed it as 'the grandest thing ever done by a youth—though he is a Demoniac youth' (E. T. Cook's *Life of Ruskin*). In consequence of its popularity, the earlier tragedy of 'Chastelard' was now brought forward and published in December of the same year. This also was warmly received by the critics, but there were murmurs heard as to its supposed sensuality. This was the beginning of the outcry against Swinburne's literary morals, and even 'Atalanta' was now searched for evidences of atheism and indelicacy.

He met, on the other hand, with many assurances of eager support, and in particular, in November 1865, he received a letter from a young Welsh squire, George E. J. Powell of Nant-Eôs (1842–82), who soon became, and for several years remained, the most intimate of Swinburne's friends. The collection of lyrical poems, written during the last eight years, which was now almost ready, was felt by Swinburne's circle to be still more dangerous than anything which he had yet published; early in 1866 (probably in January) the long ode called 'Laus Veneris' was printed in pamphlet form, as the author afterwards stated, 'more as an experiment to ascertain the public taste—and forbearance!—than anything else. Moxon, I well remember, was terribly nervous in those days, and it was only the wishes of mutual good friends, coupled with his own liking for the ballads, that finally induced him to publish the book at all.' The text of this herald edition of 'Laus Veneris' differs in many points from that included in the volume of 'Poems and Ballads' which eventually appeared at the end of April 1866. The critics in the press denounced many of the pieces with a heat which did little credit to their judgment. Moxon shrank before the storm, and in July withdrew the volume from circulation. Another publisher was found in John Camden Hotten [q. v.], to whom Swinburne now transferred all his other books. There had been no such literary scandal since the days of 'Don Juan,' but an attempt at prosecution fell through, and Ruskin, who had been requested to expostulate with the young poet, indignantly replied 'He is infinitely above me in all knowledge and power, and I should no more think of advising or criticising him than of venturing to do it to Turner if he were alive again.'

Swinburne now found himself the most talked-of man in England, but all this violent notoriety was unfortunate for him, morally and physically. He had a success of curiosity at the annual dinner of the Royal Literary Fund (2 May 1866), where, Lord Houghton being in the chair, Swinburne delivered the only public speech of his life; it was a short critical essay on 'The Imaginative Literature of England' committed to memory. In the autumn he spent some time with Powell at Aberystwyth. His name was constantly before the public in the latter part of 1866, when his portraits filled the London shop-windows and the newspapers outdid one another in legendary tales of his eccentricity. He had published in the summer a selection from Byron, with an introduction of extreme eulogy, and in October he answered his critics in 'Notes on Poems and Reviews'; William Michael Rossetti also published a volume in defence.

The winter was spent at Holmwood, near Henley-on-Thames, which his father bought in 1865, and where his family was now settled; here in November he finished a large book on Blake, which had occupied him for some time, and in February 1867 completed 'A Song of Italy,' which was published in September. His friends now included Simeon Solomon [q. v. Suppl. II], whose genius he extolled in the 'Dark Blue' magazine (July 1871) and elsewhere. In April 1867, on a false report of the death of Charles Baudelaire (who survived until September of that year), Swinburne wrote 'Ave atque Vale.' This was a period of wild extravagance and of the least agreeable episodes of his life; his excesses told upon his health, which had already suffered, and there were several recurrences of his malady. In June, while staying with Lord Houghton at Fryston, he had a fit which left him seriously ill. In August, to recuperate, he spent some time with Lord Lytton at Knebworth, where he made the acquaintance of John Forster. In November he published the pamphlet of political verse called 'An Appeal to England.' The Reform League invited him to stand for parliament; Swinburne appealed to Mazzini, to whom he had been introduced, in March 1867, by Karl Blind [q.v. Suppl. II]. Mazzini strongly discouraged the idea, advising him to confine himself to the cause of Italian freedom, and he declined. Swinburne now became intimate with Adah Isaacs Menken [q. v.], who had left her fourth and last husband, James Barclay. It has often been repeated that the poems of this actress, published as 'Infelicia' early in 1868, were partly written by Swinburne, but this is not the case; and the verses, printed in 1883, as addressed by him to Adah Menken, were not composed by him. She went to Paris in the summer of 1868 and died there on 10 Aug.; the shock to Swinburne of the news caused an illness which lasted several days, for he was sincerely attached to her. He was very busily engaged on political poetry during this year. In February 1868 he wrote 'The Hymn of Man,' and in April 'Tiresias'; in June he published, in pamphlet form, 'Siena.' Two prose works belong to this year: 'William Blake' and 'Notes on the Royal Academy,' but most of his energy was concentrated on the transcendental celebration of the Republic in verse. At the height of the scandal about 'Poems and Ballads' there had been a meeting between Jowett and Mazzini at the house of George Howard (afterwards ninth earl of Carlisle) [q. v. Suppl. II], to discuss 'what can be done *with* and *for* Algernon.' Mazzini had instructed Karl Blind to bring the poet to visit him, and had said 'There must be no more of this love-frenzy; you must dedicate your glorious powers to the service of the Republic.' Swinburne's reply had been to sit at Mazzini's feet and to pour forth from memory the whole of 'A Song of Italy.' For the next three years he carried out Mazzini's mission, in the composition of 'Songs before Sunrise.'

His health was still unsatisfactory; he had a fit in the reading-room of the British Museum (10 July), and was ill for a month after it. He was taken down to Holmwood, and when sufficiently recovered started (September) for Étretat, where he and Powell hired a small villa which they named the Chaumière de Dolmancé. Here Offenbach visited them. The sea-bathing was beneficial, but on his return to London Swinburne's illnesses, fostered by his own obstinate imprudence, visibly increased in severity; in April 1869 he complained of 'ill-health hardly intermittent through weeks and months.' From the end of July to September he spent some weeks at Vichy with Richard Burton, Leighton, and Mrs. Sartoris. He went to Holmwood for the winter and composed 'Diræ' in December. In the summer of 1870 he and Powell settled again at Étretat; during this visit Swinburne, who was bathing alone, was carried out to sea on the tide and nearly drowned, but was picked up by a smack, which carried him in to Yport. At this time, too, the youthful Guy de Maupassant paid the friends a visit, of which he has given an entertaining account. When the Germans invaded France, Swinburne and Powell returned to England. In September Swinburne published the 'Ode on the Proclamation of the French Republic.' He now reappeared, more or less, in London artistic society, and was much seen at the houses of Westland Marston and Madox Brown. 'Songs before Sunrise,' with its prolonged glorification of the republican ideal, appeared early in 1871. In July and August of this year Swinburne stayed with Jowett in the little hotel at the foot of Loch Tummel. Here he made the acquaintance of Browning, who was writing 'Hohenstiel-Schwangau.' Browning was staying near by, and often joined the party. Swinburne, much recovered in health, was in delightful spirits; like Jowett, he was ardently on the side of France. In September he went off for a prolonged walking-tour through the highlands of Scotland, and returned in splendid condition. The life of London, however, was always bad for him, and in October he was seriously ill again; in November he visited George Meredith at Kingston. He was now mixed up in much violent polemic with Robert Buchanan and others; early in 1872 he published the most effective of all his satirical writings, the pungent 'Under the Microscope' [see under BUCHANAN, ROBERT WILLIAMS, Suppl. II]. He had written the first act of 'Bothwell,' which F. Locker-Lampson set up in type for him; this play, however, was not finished for several years. His intercourse with D. G. Rossetti had now ceased; his acquaintance with Mr. Theodore Watts (afterwards Watts-Dunton) began. In July and August of this year he was again staying at Tummel Bridge with Jowett, and once more he was the life and soul of the party, enlivening the evenings with paradoxes and hyperboles and recitations of Mrs. Gamp. Jowett here persuaded Swinburne to join him in revising the 'Children's Bible' of J. D. Rogers, which was published the following summer. In May 1873 the violence of Swinburne's attacks on Napoleon III (who was now dead) led to a remarkable controversy in the 'Examiner' and the 'Spectator.' Swinburne had given up his rooms in Dorset Street, and lodged for a short time at 12 North Crescent, Alfred Place, whence he moved, in September 1873, to rooms at 3 Great James Street, where he continued to reside until he left London for good. Meanwhile he spent some autumn weeks with Jowett at Grantown, Elginshire. During this year he was busily engaged in writing 'Bothwell,' to which he put the finishing touches in February 1874, and published some months later.

The greater part of January 1874 he spent with Jowett at the Land's End. Between March and September he was in the country, first at Holmwood, afterwards at Niton in the Isle of Wight. In April 1874 he was put, without his consent, and to his great indignation, on the Byron Memorial Committee. He was at this time chiefly devoting himself to the Elizabethan dramatists; an edition, with critical introduction, of Cyril Tourneur had been projected at the end of 1872, but had been abandoned; but the volume on 'George Chapman' was issued, in two forms, in December 1874. This winter was spent at Holmwood, whence in February 1875 Swinburne issued his introduction to the reprint of Wells's 'Joseph and his Brethren.' From early in June until late in October he was out of London—at Holmwood; visiting Jowett at West Malvern, where he sketched the first outline of 'Erechtheus'; and in apartments, Middle Cliff, Wangford, near Southwold, in Suffolk. His monograph on 'Auguste Vacquerie,' in French, was published in Paris in November 1875; the English version appeared in the 'Miscellanies' of 1886. Two volumes of reprinted matter belong to this year, 1875: in prose 'Essays and Studies,' in verse 'Songs of Two Nations'; and a pseudonymous pamphlet, attacking Buchanan, entitled 'The Devil's Due.' Most of 1876 was spent at Holmwood, with brief and often untoward visits to London. In July he was poisoned by lilies with which a too-enthusiastic hostess had filled his bedroom, and he did not completely recover until November. In the winter of this year appeared 'Erechtheus' and 'A Note on the Muscovite Crusade,' and in December was written 'The Ballad of Bulgarie,' first printed as a pamphlet in 1893. Admiral Swinburne, his father, died on 4 March 1877. The poet sent his 'Charlotte Brontë' to press in June, and then left town for the rest of the year, which he spent at Holmwood and again at Wangford, where he occupied himself in translating the poems of François Villon. He also issued, in a weekly periodical, his unique novel entitled 'A Year's Letters,' which he did not republish until 1905, when it appeared as 'Love's Cross-Currents.' In April 1878 Victor Hugo talked of addressing a poem of invitation to Swinburne, and a committee invited the latter to Paris in May to be present as the representative of English poetry at the centenary of the death of Voltaire; but the condition of his health, which was deplorable during this year and the next, forbade his acceptance. In 1878 his chief publication was 'Poems and Ballads (Second Series).'

Swinburne's state became so alarming that in September 1879 Mr. Theodore Watts, with the consent of Lady Jane Swinburne, removed him from 3 Great James Street to his own house, The Pines, Putney, where the remaining thirty years of his life were spent, in great retirement but with health slowly and completely restored. Under the guardianship of his devoted companion, he pursued with extreme regularity a monotonous course of life, which was rarely diversified by even a visit to London, although it lay so near. Swinburne had, since about 1875, been afflicted with increasing deafness, which now (from 1879 onwards) made general society impossible for him. In 1880 he published three important volumes of poetry, 'Studies in Song,' 'Heptalogia' (an anonymous collection of seven parodies), and 'Songs of the Springtides'; and a volume of prose criticism, 'A Study of Shakespeare.' In April 1881 he finished the long ode entitled 'Athens,' and began 'Tristram of Lyonesse'; 'Mary Stuart' was published in this year. In February 1882 he made the acquaintance of J. R. Lowell, who had bitterly attacked his early poems. Lowell was now 'very pleasant' and the old feud was healed. In April, as he was writing the last canto of 'Tristram,' he was surprised by the news of D. G. Rossetti's death, and he wrote his (still unpublished) 'Record of Friendship.' In August Mr. Watts took him for some weeks to Guernsey and Sark. In September, as he 'wanted something big to do,' Swinburne started a 'Life and Death of Cæsar Borgia,' of which the only fragment that remains was published in 1908 as 'The Duke of Gandia.' The friends proceeded to Paris for the dinner to Victor Hugo (22 Nov.) and the resuscitation of 'Le Roi s'amuse' at the Théâtre Français. Swinburne was introduced for the first time to Hugo and to Leconte de Lisle, but he could not hear a line of the play, and on his return to Putney he refused to go to Cambridge to listen to the 'Ajax,' his infirmity now excluding him finally from public appearances. To 1883 belongs 'A Century of Roundels,' which made Tennyson say 'Swinburne is a reed through which all things blow into music.' In June of that year Swinburne visited Jowett at Emerald Bank, Newlands, Keswick. His history now dwindles to a mere enumeration of his publications. 'A Midsummer Holiday' appeared in 1884, 'Marino Faliero' in 1885, 'A Study of Victor Hugo' and 'Miscellanies' in 1886, 'Locrine' and a group of pamphlets of verse ('A Word for the Navy,' 'The Question,' 'The Jubilee,' and 'Gathered Songs') in 1887.

In June 1888 his public rupture with an old friend, Whistler, attracted notice; it was the latest ebullition of his fierce temper, which was now becoming wonderfully placid. His daily walk over Putney Heath, in the course of which he would waylay perambulators for the purpose of baby-worship, made him a figure familiar to the suburban public. Swinburne's summer holidays, usually spent at the sea-side with his inseparable friend, were the sources of much lyrical verse. In 1888 he wrote two of the most remarkable of his later poems: 'The Armada' and 'Pan and Thalassius.' In 1889 he published 'A Study of Ben Jonson' and 'Poems and Ballads (Third Series).' His marvellous fecundity was now at length beginning to slacken; for some years he made but slight appearances. His latest publications were: 'The Sisters' (1892); 'Studies in Prose and Poetry' (1894); 'Astrophel' (1894); 'The Tale of Balen' (1896); 'Rosamund, Queen of the Lombards' (1899); 'A Channel Passage' (1904); and 'Love's Cross-Currents'—a reprint of the novel 'A Year's Letters' of 1877—in 1905. In that year he wrote a little book about 'Shakespeare,' which was published posthumously in 1909. In November 1896 Lady Jane Swinburne died, in her eighty-eighth year, and was mourned by her son in the beautiful double elegy called 'The High Oaks: Barking Hall.'

Swinburne's last years were spent in great placidity, always under the care of his faithful companion. In November 1903 he caught a chill, which developed into double pneumonia, of which he very nearly died. Although, under great care, he wholly recovered, his lungs remained delicate. In April 1909, just before the poet's seventy-second birthday, the entire household of Mr. Watts-Dunton was prostrated by influenza. In the case of Swinburne, who suffered most severely, it developed into pneumonia, and in spite of the resistance of his constitution the poet died on the morning of 10 April 1909. He was buried on 15 April at Bonchurch, among the graves of his family. He left only one near relation behind him, his youngest sister, Miss Isabel Swinburne.

The physical characteristics of Algernon Swinburne were so remarkable as to make him almost unique. His large head was out of all proportion with his narrow and sloping shoulders; his slight body, and small, slim extremities, were agitated by a restlessness that was often, but not correctly, taken for an indication of disease. Alternately he danced as if on wires or sat in an absolute immobility. The quick vibrating motion of his hands began in very early youth, and was a sign of excitement; it was accompanied, even when he was a child, by 'a radiant expression of his face, very striking indeed' (Miss Isabel Swinburne). His puny frame required little sleep, seemed impervious to fatigue, was heedless of the ordinary incentives of physical life; he inherited a marvellous constitution, which he impaired in early years, but which served his old age well. His character was no less strange than his physique. He was profoundly original, and yet he took the colour of his surroundings like a chameleon. He was violent, arrogant, even vindictive, and yet no one could be more affectionate, more courteous, more loyal. He was fierce in the defence of his prejudices, and yet dowered with an exquisite modesty. He loved everything that was pure and of good report, and yet the extravagance of his language was often beyond the reach of apology. His passionate love for very little children was entirely genuine and instinctive, and yet the forms of it seemed modelled on the expressions of Victor Hugo. It is a very remarkable circumstance, which must be omitted in no outline of his intellectual life, that his opinions, on politics, on literature, on art, on life itself, were formed in boyhood, and that though he expanded he scarcely advanced in any single direction after he was twenty. If growth had continued as it began, he must have been the prodigy of the world, but his development was arrested, and he elaborated during fifty years the ideas, the convictions, the enthusiasms which he possessed when he left college. Even his art was at its height when he was five and twenty, and it was the volume and not the vigour that increased. As a magician of verbal melody he impressed his early contemporaries to the neglect of his merit as a thinker, but posterity will regard him as a philosopher who gave melodious utterance to ideas of high originality and value. This side of his genius, exemplified by such poems as 'Hertha' and 'Tiresias,' was that which showed most evidence of development, yet his masterpieces in this kind also were mainly written before he was thirty-five.

No complete collection of Swinburne's works has appeared, but his poems were published in six volumes in 1904, and his tragedies in five in 1905–6.

The authentic portraits of Swinburne are not very numerous. D. G. Rossetti made a pencil drawing in 1860, and in 1862 a water-colour painting, an excellent portrait, now in the Fitzwilliam Museum, Cambridge; the bust in oils, by G. F. Watts, May 1867, is now in the National Portrait Gallery; as a likeness this is very unsatisfactory. A water-colour drawing (*circa* 1863) by Simeon Solomon has disappeared. Miss E. M. Sewell made a small drawing in 1868, lately in the possession of Mrs. F. G. Waugh; a water-colour, by W. B. Scott (*circa* 1860), is now in the possession of Mr. T. W. Jackson; a large pastel, taken in old age (Jan. 1900), by R. Ponsonby Staples, is in the possession of Mr. Edmund Gosse. A full-length portrait in water-colour was painted by A. Pellegrini ('Ape') for reproduction in 'Vanity Fair' in the summer of 1874; this drawing, which belonged to Lord Redesdale, was given by him to Mr. Gosse. Although avowedly a caricature, this is in many ways the best surviving record of Swinburne's general aspect and attitude.

[Personal recollections, extending in the case of the present writer over more than forty years; information about childhood kindly supplied by Miss Isabel Swinburne; the memories of contemporaries at school and college, particularly those kindly contributed by Sir George Young, by the poet's cousin Lord Redesdale, and by Lord Sheffield; the bibliographical investigations of Mr. Thomas J. Wise, principally embodied in A Contribution to the Bibliography of Swinburne (published in Robertson Nicoll & Wise's Lit. Anecdotes of the Nineteenth Century, 1896, ii. 291–364, and more fully in his privately printed Bibliography of Swinburne, 1897); and the examination of a very large unpublished correspondence are the chief sources of information. To these must be added the valuable notes on The Boyhood of Algernon Swinburne, published in the Contemporary Review for April 1910 by another cousin, Mrs. Disney Leith. The Life of Jowett has some notes, unfortunately very slight, of the Master of Balliol's lifelong salutary influence over the poet, who had been and never ceased to be his pupil, and something is guardedly reported in the Life of Lord Houghton. Mr. Lionel Tollemache contributed to the Spectator and to the Guardian in 1909 some pleasant recollections. The Life of Edmund Clarence Stedman, by his granddaughter (New York, 1911), contains some very important autobiographical letters, and there are mentions in the Autobiography of William Bell Scott, and the privately printed Diary of Henry Adams (quoted above). The name of Swinburne, with an occasional anecdote, occurs in many recent biographies, such as The Autobiography of Elizabeth M. Sewell, the Recollections of Mr. A. G. C. Liddell, the lives of D. G. Rossetti, Edward Burne-Jones, Richard Burton, Whistler, John Churton Collins, and Ruskin. R. H. Shepherd's Bibliography of Swinburne (1887) possesses little value. Swinburne left behind him a considerable number of short MSS., principally in verse. The prose tales have been recorded above, and certain of the verse; his posthumous poems, none of which have yet been published, also include a series of fine Northumbrian ballads.]

E. G.

SYME, DAVID (1827–1908), Australian newspaper proprietor and economist, born on 2 Oct. 1827 at North Berwick, Haddingtonshire, Scotland, was youngest of five sons and two daughters of George Syme, parish schoolmaster of North Berwick, by his wife Jean Mitchell of Forfarshire. Of his brothers two died in early manhood and two, George and Ebenezer, reached middle age. The elder of these, George (M.A., Aberdeen), was successively a free-church minister in Dumfriesshire and a baptist pastor in Nottingham, while the younger, Ebenezer, who was educated at St. Andrews, also joined the baptist ministry, which he abandoned in 1850 to become sub-editor of the 'Westminster Review.' Both the brothers, George and Ebenezer, joined David in Melbourne, and died within a few years of their settlement there.

After education by his father, who died when David was sixteen, he visited his eldest brother, James, who was practising as a surgeon at Bathgate, Linlithgowshire. Accepting the doctrine of universal salvation promulgated by James Morison [q. v.] of Kilmarnock, he next studied theology with him, but in 1849 he went to Germany and to Vienna, and a year's study of philosophy in Heidelberg destroyed his faith in Christianity. On his return to Scotland he procured a situation as reader on a Glasgow newspaper, but hopeless of advancement he sailed at the end of 1851 for San Francisco, and went from Sacramento to the goldfields, where he had no luck and disliked his companions. The report of the discovery of gold in Australia brought him to Melbourne in 1852, after a perilous voyage in an unseaworthy ship. In the Australian goldfields he was no more prosperous than in California, although on one occasion his claim included what was afterwards the famous Mt. Egerton mine, but it was jumped, and Syme could obtain no redress from the government. Meanwhile David's brother Ebenezer, whose literary abilities were high, followed in his footsteps and settled in Melbourne. On 17 Oct. 1854 a newspaper, 'The Age,' was founded there by two local merchants, John and Henry Cooke, and Ebenezer was appointed one of the editors. The editors supported the cause of the miners at the time of the Ballarat riots, to the disgust of the proprietors, who gave the paper up; the editors thereupon ran it for themselves, and in eighteen months the concern was nearly bankrupt. In 1856, on his brother's advice, David bought 'The Age' for 2000*l.*, which he had earned on the goldfields. In 1857, after eighteen months' trial, the paper proved unable to support both brothers, and David left it to Ebenezer's sole care, and turned with some success to road-contracting. Ebenezer, who was elected member for Mandurang in the first legislative assembly of the colony, but retired at the end of his term owing to inability to reconcile journalistic independence with party obligation, died of consumption in March 1860. David then took control of 'The Age,' mainly in the interest of his brother's wife and family, and for ten years worked it single-handed on independent lines which championed protection in the working-class interests, and vigorously challenged capitalist predominance. He attacked the distribution of 60,000,000 acres of land in Victoria among a thousand squatters, who paid a rent of 20*l.* apiece, and he denounced the monopoly of the importers, which made local industries impossible and denied work to skilled artisan immigrants. The diminution in the output of gold threatened in these circumstances to drive from the colony the poorer population. Syme in his paper boldly urged a programme which included the opening of the land to small farmers and a system of protective duties on imports, a policy which none in Australia suggested before him. Syme, through 'The Age,' soon became the admitted leader of the liberal party, but it was necessary to secure manhood suffrage and a diminution of the powers of the upper house before legal effect could be given to his proposals. A land act embodying Syme's policy was passed in 1869, and until his death he never ceased to urge drastic measures for the prevention of large estates. At the same time 'The Age' also demanded, and finally obtained, in addition to land and protective legislation, disestablishment, payment of members, and free compulsory secular education. Syme's enemies, the landowners and importers, ceased to advertise in 'The Age,' and in 1862 they persuaded the premier, (Sir) John O'Shanassy [q. v.], to withdraw the advertisements of the government. The price of the paper had been reduced in 1861 from 6*d.* to 3*d.* Now in 1862 Syme reduced it further to 2*d.*, and his attacks on the government redoubled. Meanwhile the circulation increased. Popular anger prevented the premier, O'Shanassy, from carrying a libel bill designed in April 1863 to gag Syme, and in August 1864 a protectionist house was returned, with the result that a first tariff bill was passed in March 1866 by the ministry of (Sir) James M'Culloch. In 1868 the importers, despite Syme's resolute adherence to his policy, renewed their advertisements in 'The Age'; he thereupon brought out the paper at 1*d.*, and its circulation more than doubled in a week. In 1869 Syme went to England on his only holiday since 1860, and a fresh endeavour by the importers to boycott his paper in his absence failed.

Syme subsequently continued his campaign both on land and tariff questions with unabated vigour. His insistence on still higher duties led to a long conflict between the two houses in which supply was more than once refused. In critical situations Syme's advice was solicited and adopted by the governor and premier, and after 1881, when Syme forced (Sir) Graham Berry [q. v. Suppl. II], the premier, to withdraw the tariff measure which he had announced to the house the day before, but of which Syme disapproved, Syme claimed with justice to exercise until his death the deciding voice in the appointment of every Victorian premier and cabinet minister. In 1887, during a period of great prosperity, parliament, mainly yielding to the appeals of landjobbers and speculators, accepted a scheme for covering the whole colony with a network of non-paying railways under the direction of official railway commissioners. Syme attacked the movement in a series of articles which ultimately in 1892 forced the government to abandon its railway scheme and dismiss the commissioners. The chief commissioner, Mr. Richard Speight, claimed 25,000*l.* damages from Syme for libel. The litigation lasted from March 1890 to September 1894, and although Syme won, Speight's bankruptcy made him liable for his own costs, which amounted to 50,000*l.* The paper's prosperity was confirmed, and it became the fountain-head of all progressive legislation. To its suggestion the colony owed anti-sweating and factory acts, and it initiated the movement which issued in the levy of an income-tax. Syme sent Mr. J. L. Dow to America and Mr. Alfred Deakin to India at his own cost in order to study systems of irrigation. He supported Australian federation and first adopted the policy of conscription and the formation of an Australian navy. Towards the end of his life he realised that protection, while it had destroyed the monopoly of the importers, was enriching the manufacturers at the expense of the workers. He thereupon advocated a 'new protection' system and persuaded parliament to pass measures to protect industry against rings and trusts.

Syme, who declined the offer of a knighthood, died of heart disease at Blythewoode, Kew, near Melbourne, on 14 Feb. 1908, and was buried at Melbourne. On his deathbed he dictated an account of his career which was edited by Mr. Ambrose Pratt and published in 1908. By his will he left the sum of 50,000*l.* to various Victorian charities. In 1904 he had endowed an annual prize of 100*l.* for original Australian research in biology at Melbourne University.

On 17 August 1858 he married Annabella, daughter of John William Johnson of Yorkshire and Melbourne. He left five sons and two daughters.

Syme prepared interesting expositions of his economic, political, and philosophical principles. In 1877 he published 'Outlines of an Industrial Science,' an exposition of protection which has since become a text-book, and in 1882 'Representative Government in England,' a discussion of cabinet government and the party system, in which he advocates elective ministries and a system under which constituents should be able to dismiss their members without waiting for an election. At the end of his life he published two books on philosophy. The first, 'On the Modification of Organisms' (1890; 2nd edit. 1892), was an attack on Darwin's theory of natural selection. The second, 'The Soul: a Study and an Argument' (1903), continuing the earlier theme, attacked both materialism and the current argument for design, and described Syme's own belief as a kind of pantheistic teleology. Syme was also a contributor to the 'Westminster,' the 'Edinburgh,' and the 'Fortnightly' Reviews.

[Meynell's Dict. of Australas. Biog.; David Syme, by Ambrose Pratt (with several photographic reproductions); West Australian, Argus, Age, Herald, Adelaide Advertiser, and Adelaide Register, 15 Feb. 1908.] A. B. W.

SYMES-THOMPSON, EDMUND (1837–1906), physician, born in London on 16 Nov. 1837, was son of Theophilus Thompson [q. v.] by his wife Anna Maria, daughter of Nathaniel Walker of Stroud. The name Symes was adopted by his father on inheriting property from the Rev. Richard

Symes, the last surviving member of the Somerset branch of the Sydenhams, who were descended from Dr. Thomas Sydenham [q. v.]. Edmund received his early education at St. Paul's School, and in 1857 entered King's College. There he gained a gold medal and the Leathes and Warneford prizes for divinity, and prizes for general proficiency. His medical education was pursued at King's College Hospital, and whilst a student he took an active part in physiological investigations with Lionel Smith Beale [q. v. Suppl. II]. He graduated M.B. in 1859, gaining the scholarship in medicine, a gold medal and honours in surgery, botany, and midwifery; in 1860 he proceeded M.D.

In 1860 he was elected honorary assistant physician to King's College Hospital, and in 1863 to a similar post at the Hospital for Consumption, Brompton, to which his father had also been attached for many years. Having made up his mind to devote himself specially to consumption, he resigned his post at King's College Hospital in 1865. In 1869 he became honorary physician, and in 1889 honorary consulting physician to the Brompton Hospital. He was also honorary physician to the Royal Hospital for Consumption, Ventnor, and to the Artists' Benevolent and Artists' Annual funds. In 1867 he was elected professor of physic at Gresham College, and lectured regularly and with increasing efficiency to the end of his life. With his brother professors at the college, especially Benjamin Morgan Cowie, dean of Exeter [q. v. Suppl. I], and John William Burgon, dean of Chichester [q. v. Suppl. I], professor of geometry, he helped to develop the scheme of this old foundation and to popularise the lectures.

He became a member of the Royal College of Physicians in 1862, and a fellow in 1868. He was a fellow of the Royal Medical and Chirurgical and Medical societies, and a member of the Clinical and Harveian societies of London, acting as president in 1883 of the last society.

Symes-Thompson was specially interested in the value of climate and spa treatment for the relief of diseases, especially of the lungs, and travelled widely on the Continent, besides visiting Egypt, Algeria, and South Africa. He was one of the founders of the British Balneological and Climatological Society, and was president in 1903. It was largely through his influence and his pamphlet on 'Winter Health Resorts in the Alps' (1888) that Davos and St. Moritz became popular health resorts, and he was an active mover in the establishment of the invalids' home at Davos (1895), and of the Queen Alexandra Sanatorium, which was opened there (1909) after his death. His most important contributions to medical literature were 'Lectures on Pulmonary Tuberculosis' (1863) and 'On Influenza: an Historical Survey' (1890), both being in part revision of books by his father. He was also closely concerned in the publication by the Royal Medical and Chirurgical Society of the book entitled 'The Climates and Baths of Great Britain and Ireland' (1895), besides contributing himself to its pages.

Life insurance also interested him greatly, and besides holding a prominent position amongst assurance medical officers in London as physician to the Equity and Law Life Assurance Society, he contributed an article on the subject to the two editions of Sir Clifford Allbutt's 'System of Medicine' (1896 and 1905).

Symes-Thompson, who had a large consulting practice amongst members of the church of England, cherished deep religious convictions, and he took active interest in many church institutions. He was a prominent worker in the guild of St. Luke, of which he was provost from 1893 to 1902, and he also assisted in establishing (1896) the annual medical service at St. Paul's Cathedral and the Medical Missionary College (1905). Both service and college were under the ægis of the guild of St. Luke. He was interested in the oral training for the deaf and dumb, writing a pamphlet on the subject, and being chairman for many years of the training college for teachers of the deaf and dumb at Ealing.

He lived first at 3 Upper George Street, and from 1878 to his death at 33 Cavendish Square. In 1899 he bought Finmere House, Oxfordshire, where he spent much of his leisure and gratified an early love for botany and a country life.

He died on 24 Nov. 1906 at his house in Cavendish Square, London, and was buried in the parish churchyard at Finmere. There is an oil portrait in possession of the family by Mr. A. Tennyson Cole, and crayon portraits in Gresham College and the Royal Society of Medicine. His coat of arms is on one of the windows of St. Paul's School. He married on 25 July 1872 Elizabeth, daughter of Henry George Watkins, vicar of Potter's Bar, who survived him with four sons and two daughters.

[Memories of Edward Symes-Thompson, M.D., F.R.C.P., 1908; information from Dr.

Henry Symes-Thompson (son); Journal of Balneology and Climatology, Jan. 1907 (with portrait from photograph); Brit. Med. Journal and Lancet, 1 Dec. 1906.] E. M. B.

SYMONS, WILLIAM CHRISTIAN (1845–1911), decorative designer, painter in oil and water-colours, was the elder son of William Martyn Symons by his wife Elizabeth White. The father, who came originally from Trevice, St. Columb, Cornwall, carried on a printing business in Bridge Street, Vauxhall, where Christian, his second child, was born on 28 Nov. 1845. There was one other son and two daughters, of whom the elder, Annie, survives. Symons was educated at a private school in Penzance until he was sent at an early age to the Lambeth Art School, then under the direction of a teacher of repute named Sparkes. In 1866 he entered the Royal Academy as a student for a short while, gaining that year a silver medal in the antique school. In 1869 for the first time one of his works (a portrait of his sister) was hung at the Academy Exhibition, to which he was an intermittent contributor until the year of his death, when he was represented by an 'Interior of Downside Abbey.' His easel pictures were also shown at the New English Art Club, the Institute of Painters in Oil, and various other galleries. In 1870 he was received into the Roman catholic church, and began his long connection with the firm of Lavers, Barraud and Westlake, for whom he designed a number of stained windows. He became a member of the Royal Society of British Artists in 1881, but seceded with James McNeill Whistler [q.v. Suppl. II] in 1888. He only came personally before the public in 1899, when he acted as secretary to the celebrated dinner organised in honour of Whistler on 1 May (cf. PENNELL, *Life of Whistler*, 2nd edit. p. 277). In 1899 he began the execution of his commission for certain mosaic decorations at Westminster Cathedral, the work by which he was chiefly known until the posthumous exhibition of his paintings and water-colours at the Goupil Gallery in 1912. He worked at Newlyn in Cornwall for some time, and though never a member of the school associated with that locality he contributed an account of it to the 'Art Journal' in April 1890. In later life he lived almost entirely in Sussex. He died at Udimore, near Rye, where he is buried, on 4 Sept. 1911.

He married at Hampstead in 1885 Cecilia, daughter of J. L. Davenport of Wildemlow, Derby. He left nine children, two daughters and seven sons, all of whom survive him. The eldest, Mark Lancelot, a painter of portraits and subject pieces, exhibits occasionally at the New English Art Club.

Symons was better known to a limited circle as a decorator and designer than as a painter. His varied talents, though recognised by fellow artists, with all of whom he was personally very popular, were insufficiently appreciated by the public during his lifetime. A retiring, over-modest nature accounted in some measure for his ill-success. His mosaic work at Westminster Cathedral consists of the chapel of the Holy Souls, the altar-piece of 'St. Edmund blessing London' in the crypt, and the panel of the 'Veronica' in the chapel of the Sacred Heart, and that of 'The Blessed Joan of Arc' in the north transept. The unpleasant technique (*opus sectile*) employed for some of these, in accordance with Bentley's instructions, has hardly done justice to their fine design and courageous colour. They have been criticised for an over-emphasis of pictorial illusion, to which the medium of mosaic is unsuited. The defect was probably due to misapprehension, common among all modern ecclesiastical authorities, with regard to the functions of mosaic decoration. Another characteristic example of the artist's powers may be seen in the spandrels at St. Botolph's, Bishopsgate. One of his best oil pictures, 'The Convalescent Connoisseur,' is in the Dublin Municipal Gallery of Modern Art. In the Mappin Art Gallery at Sheffield are 'In Hora Mortis' and 'Home from the War.' 'The Squaw' belongs to the Contemporary Art Society. The British Museum, the Manchester City Art Gallery, and the Brighton Art Gallery possess characteristic examples of his water colours. His flower pieces are of particular excellence. Mr. Le Brasseur of Hampstead possesses the largest collection of his paintings. Symons was obviously influenced by Sargent and Brabazon, but preserved his own individuality and did not allow his art to be affected by his friendship for Whistler.

[Private information from the family; Mr. William Marchant: Catalogue of Posthumous Exhibition at the Goupil Gallery in 1912; Pennell's Life of James McNeill Whistler, 2nd edit.; Tablet, 16 Sept. 1911.] R. R.

SYNGE, JOHN MILLINGTON (1871–1909), Irish dramatist, born at Newtown Little, near Rathfarnham (a suburban village adjoining Dublin), on 16 April 1871 was youngest child (in a family of one

daughter and four sons) of John Hatch Synge, barrister-at-law, by his wife Kathleen, daughter of the Rev. Robert Traill, D.D. (*d.* 1847), of Schull, county Cork, translator of Josephus.

His father dying when he was a year old, his mother moved nearer Dublin to Orwell Park, Rathgar, which was his home until 1890, when he removed with his mother and brother to 31 Crosthwaite Park, Kingstown, which was his family home until shortly before his death.

After attending private schools, first in Dublin and then at Bray, he studied with a tutor between the ages of fourteen and seventeen. The main interest of his boyhood was an intimate study of nature. 'He knew the note and plumage of every bird, and when and where they were to be found.' In youth he joined the Dublin Naturalists Field Club, and later took up music, becoming a proficient player of the piano, the flute, and the violin. His summer vacations were spent at Annamoe, co. Wicklow, among the strange people of the glens.

On 18 June 1888 he entered Trinity College, Dublin, as a pensioner, his college tutor being Dr. Traill (now provost). He passed his little go in Michaelmas term, 1890 (3rd class), obtained prizes in Hebrew and in Irish in Trinity term, 1892, and graduated B.A. with a second class in the pass-examination in December 1892. His name went off the college books six months later (3 June 1893).

While at Trinity he studied music at the Royal Irish Academy of Music, where he obtained a scholarship in harmony and counterpoint in 1891. On leaving college he thought of music as a profession, and went to Germany to study that art and to learn the German language. He first visited Coblentz, and (in the spring of 1894) Würzburg. Before the end of 1894 he altered his plans, and, deciding to devote himself to literary work, settled by way of preparation as a student in Paris in January 1895. For the next few years his time was generally divided between France and Ireland, but in 1896 he stayed in Italy long enough to learn Italian. He had a natural gift for languages, and during these years he read much. From 1897 he wrote much tentative work, both prose and verse, in French and English, and contemplated writing a critical study of Racine and a translation from the Italian (either the 'Little Flowers,' or the 'Companions of St. Francis of Assisi'). In May 1898 he first visited the Aran Islands.

In 1899, when he was living at the Hôtel Corneille (Rue Corneille), near the Odéon theatre, in Paris, Synge was introduced to Mr. W. B. Yeats, one of the founders and the chief inspiration of the Irish Literary Movement. Mr. Yeats suggested that Synge should give up writing criticism either in French or English and go again to the Aran Islands off Galway, or some other primitive place, to study and write about a way of life not yet expressed in literature. But for this meeting it is likely that Synge would never have discovered a form in which he could express himself; his mind would have continued to brood without vitality upon questions of literary criticism. As a result of this meeting, Synge went again to the Aran Islands (September 1899); the visit was repeated in the autumns of 1900, 1901, and 1902. He lived among the islanders as one of themselves, and was much loved by them; his natural genius for companionship made him always a welcome guest. He took with him his fiddle, his conjuring tricks, his camera and penny whistle, and feared that 'they would get tired of him, if he brought them nothing new.'

During his second stay he began a book on the Aran Islands, which was slowly completed in France, Ireland, and London, and published in April 1907, with illustrations by Mr. Jack B. Yeats.

Meanwhile he wrote two plays, 'The Shadow of the Glen' and the 'Riders to the Sea,' both founded on stories heard in Aran, and both finished, but for slight changes, by the winter of 1902–3. 'The Shadow of the Glen' was performed at the Molesworth Hall, Dublin, on 8 Oct. 1903. 'Riders to the Sea' was performed at the same place on 25 Feb. 1904. They were published in a single volume in May 1905. 'Riders to the Sea' is the deepest and the tenderest of his plays. 'The Shadow of the Glen' is the first example of the kind of tragically hearted farce which is Synge's main contribution to the theatre. Of two other tragic farces of the same period, 'The Tinker's Wedding' (the first drama conceived by him), was begun in 1902, but not finished till 1906, and only published late in 1907; the more beautiful and moving 'The Well of the Saints' was written in 1903–4. 'The Tinker's Wedding,' the only play by Synge not publicly acted in Ireland, was produced after his death at His Majesty's Theatre, by the Afternoon Theatre, on 11 Nov. 1909.

In the winter of 1902–3 Synge lived for a few months in London (4 Handel Street,

W.C.). Afterwards he gave up his lodging in Paris (90 Rue d'Assas), and thenceforth passed much time either in or near Dublin, or in the wilds of Wicklow and Kerry, the Blasket Islands, and the lonely places by Dingle Bay. There he found the material for the occasional papers 'In Wicklow' and 'In West Kerry,' published partly, from time to time, in the 'Manchester Guardian' and the 'Shanachie,' and reprinted in the fourth volume of the 'Works.' From 3 June till 2 July 1905 he made a tour with Mr. Jack B. Yeats through the congested districts of Connemara. Some descriptions of the journey, with illustrations by Mr. Jack B. Yeats, were contributed to the 'Manchester Guardian.' Twelve of the papers are reprinted in the fourth volume of the 'Works.'

The Abbey Theatre was opened in Dublin 27 Dec. 1904, and Synge became one of its three literary advisers, helping to direct its destinies until his death. There on 4 Feb. 1905 was first performed 'The Well of the Saints' (published in December following). There, too, was first acted (26 Jan. 1907) 'The Playboy of the Western World,' written in 1905–6. This piece excited the uproar and confusion with which the new thing is usually received, but was subsequently greeted with tumultuous applause both in Dublin and by the most cultured audience in England.

During his last years Synge lived almost wholly in Ireland, mostly in Dublin. His health, never very robust, was beginning to trouble him. His last months of life, 1908–9, were spent in writing and rewriting the unfinished three-act play 'Deirdre of the Sorrows,' which was posthumously published at Miss Yeats's Cuala Press, on 5 July 1910, and was acted at the Abbey Theatre on 13 Jan. 1910. He also worked at translations from Villon and Petrarch, wrote some of the strange ironical poems, so like the man speaking, which were published by the Cuala Press just after his death, and finished the study 'Under Ether,' published in the fourth volume of the 'Works.' He died unmarried at a private nursing home in Dublin on 24 March 1909. He was buried in a family tomb at the protestant Mount Jerome general graveyard at Harold's Cross, Dublin. His 'Poems and Translations'—the poems written at odd times between 1891 and 1908, but most of them towards the end of his life—was published on 5 June 1909 by the Cuala Press.

Synge stood about five feet eight or nine inches high. He was neither weakly nor robustly made. He was dark (not black-haired), with heavy moustache, and small goatee on lower lip, otherwise clean-shaven. His hair was worn rather long; his face was pale, drawn, seamed, and old-looking. The eyes were at once smoky and kindling; the mouth had a great play of humour on it. His voice was very guttural and quick, and lively with a strange vitality. His manner was generally reserved, grave, courteous; he talked little; but had a bright malice of fun always ready. He gave little in conversation; for much of his talk, though often wise with the criticism seen in his prefaces, was only a reflection of things he had seen, and of phrases, striking and full of colour, overheard by him at sea or on shore; but there was a charm about him which all felt.

He brought into Irish literature the gifts of detachment from topic and a wild vitality of tragedy. The ironical laughter of his comedy is always most mocking when it covers a tragic intention. He died when his powers were only beginning to show themselves. As revelations of himself, his poems and one or two of the sketches are his best works; as ironic visions of himself, 'The Playboy,' 'The Shadow of the Glen,' and 'The Tinker's Wedding' are his best; but in 'The Well of the Saints,' in 'Riders to the Sea,' in the book on Aran, in the heart-breaking lyric about the birds, and in the play of Deirdre, he touches with a rare sensitiveness on something elemental. Like all men of genius he awakened animosity in those anxious to preserve old standards or fearful of setting up new ones.

Among the most important portraits (other than photographs) are: 1. An oil painting by Mr. J. B. Yeats, R.H.A., now in the Municipal Gallery in Dublin. 2. A drawing by Mr. J. B. Yeats, R.H.A. (the best likeness), reproduced in the 'Samhain' for December 1904. 3. A drawing by Mr. J. B. Yeats, R.H.A., 'Synge at Rehearsal,' reproduced as a frontispiece to 'The Playboy of the Western World,' and to the 'Works,' vol. ii. 4. A drawing by Mr. James Paterson (the frontispiece to the 'Works,' vol. iv.).

'The Works of John M. Synge' (4 vols. 1910), with four portraits (two from photographs), contain all the published books and plays, and all the miscellaneous papers which his literary executors thought worthy of inclusion. Much unpublished material remains in their hands, and a few papers contributed to the 'Speaker' during 1904–5 and to the 'Manchester Guardian' during 1905–6–7–8, and an early article in

'L'Européen' (Paris, 15 March 1902) on 'La Vieille Littérature Irlandaise,' have not been reprinted.

[Personal memories; private sources; Mr. W. B. Yeats's Collected Works, viii. 173; Contemp. Rev., April 1911, p. 470; art. by Mr. Jack B. Yeats in New York Sun, July 1909; Manchester Guardian, 25 March 1909; J. M. Synge: a Critical Study, by P. P. Howe, 1912; notes kindly supplied from M. Maurice Bourgeois's forthcoming study of the man and his writings; information from Mr. J. L. Hammond.] J. M.

T

TAIT, PETER GUTHRIE (1831–1901), mathematician and physicist, born on 28 April 1831 at Dalkeith, was only son in a family of three children of John Tait, secretary to Walter Francis Scott, fifth duke of Buccleuch [q. v.], by his wife Mary Ronaldson. John Ronaldson, an uncle, who was a banker at Edinburgh and an amateur student of astronomy, geology, and the recently invented photography, first interested Peter in science. At six his father died, and he removed with his mother to Edinburgh. From the grammar school of Dalkeith he passed to a private school (now defunct) in Circus Place, and thence at ten (in 1841) to Edinburgh Academy. Lewis Campbell [q. v. Suppl. II] and James Clerk Maxwell [q. v.] were his seniors there by a year. Fleeming Jenkin [q. v.] was one of his own contemporaries. During his first four years he showed promise in classics, of which he retained a good knowledge through life. But his mathematical bent soon declared itself. He was 'dux' of his class in each of his six years at the academy (1841–7). At sixteen, in 1847, he entered Edinburgh University, and joined the senior classes in mathematics and natural philosophy. Next year he left Edinburgh for Peterhouse, Cambridge, where William Hopkins [q. v.] coached him for the mathematical tripos. In January 1852 he graduated B.A. as senior wrangler—the youngest on record. He was also first Smith's prizeman. A friend and fellow countryman of his, William John Steele, also of Peterhouse, was second wrangler. The only previous Scottish senior wrangler was Archibald Smith [q. v.] of Jordanhill in 1836. In Edinburgh Tait's success evoked boundless enthusiasm. Obtaining a fellowship at Peterhouse immediately afterwards, he began 'coaching,' and at the same time with his friend Steele commenced a treatise on 'Dynamics of a Particle.' Steele died before the book had progressed far, and it was completed by Tait, who chivalrously published it in 1856 as the joint work of 'Tait and Steele' (MS. presented by Mrs. Tait, in Peterhouse library). A second and improved edition appeared in 1865, and a seventh edition, with further revision, in 1900. The book, which still holds its own, helped to re-establish Newton's proper position in the science of dynamics, from which the brilliant work of the French mathematicians half a century earlier had apparently displaced him.

Meanwhile Tait had removed to Belfast (September 1854) to become professor of mathematics in Queen's College. Here he remained six years, and made lasting and important friendships. These friends included his fellow professor, Thomas Andrews [q. v. Suppl. I], (Sir) Wyville Thomson, James Thomson (Lord Kelvin's brother), James McCosh (afterwards president of Princeton, U.S.A.) and above all Sir William Rowan Hamilton [q. v.], the inventor of quaternions. Tait had been fascinated by Hamilton's work on 'Quaternions' while he was an undergraduate, and he soon, to the delight of Hamilton, made great and fundamental additions to the theory, subsequently producing an 'Elementary Treatise on Quaternions' (1867; 2nd edit. 1873; 3rd edit. 1890). Still later he joined with Philip Kelland [q. v.] in a more formal 'Introduction' (1873; 2nd edit. 1881; 3rd edit. 1904). To the end of his life Tait returned, when he could find the leisure, to this early study. With his colleague Andrews, Tait meanwhile made researches on the density of ozone and the action of the electric discharge on oxygen and other gases, and published the results in several papers. At Belfast he married on 13 Oct. 1857 Margaret Archer, daughter of the Rev. James Porter. Two of her brothers were among Tait's friends at Peterhouse, and one of these, James, was master from 1876 to 1901.

In 1860 Tait was elected professor of natural philosophy at Edinburgh in succession to James David Forbes [q. v.]. The candidates included Clerk Maxwell and Edward John Routh [q. v. Suppl. II]. Tait's proclivity lay towards physical rather than purely mathematical work. On his arrival in Edinburgh he was elected a fellow of the Royal Society, and four years later became one of its secretaries. Henceforth his spare time was divided between literary work and criticism, and experimental research of exceptional note in the university laboratory, the results of which were presented to the Royal Society of Edinburgh or published in Journals of other societies. Unusual thoroughness characterised all his scientific work, whether expository or experimental. He was a good linguist, French, German, and Italian being equally at command, and he was quickly conversant with the scientific work of the continent. He contributed to British scientific journals translations of valuable foreign papers, including Helmholtz's famous papers on 'Vortex Motion' (*Phil. Mag.* 1867) and F. Mohr's 'Views on the Nature of Heat' (*ibid.* 1876).

Tait early came into contact with (Sir) William Thomson (afterwards Lord Kelvin) [q. v. Suppl. II], who had become fellow of Peterhouse in 1845, but had left Cambridge next year to become professor of natural philosophy at Glasgow. In that capacity Thomson first made Tait's acquaintance. In 1861 Tait was engaged on a book on mathematical physics, and had nearly completed arrangements for publication with the Cambridge firm of Macmillan, 'when Thomson to my great delight offered to join.' The result was Thomson and Tait's 'Natural Philosophy.' Two books were at first intended: a handbook for students and another, 'Principia Mathematica,' which Tait referred to as 'quite unique in mathematical physics,' and 'our great work'; but Thomson's other engagements threw the bulk of the writing on Tait, and only a single 'first' volume came to birth late in 1867. The earlier portion was written by Tait. Thomson's hand is more apparent in the later portion. The work was epoch-marking, and created a revolution in scientific development. For the first time 'T & T,' as the authors called themselves, traced to Newton (*Principia*, Lex iii., Scholium) the concept of the 'conservation of energy' which was just then obtaining recognition among physicists, and they showed once for all that 'energy' was the fundamental physical entity and that its 'conservation' was its predominating and all-controlling property. In Tait's words, 'Thomson and he had rediscovered Newton for the world.' Their treatise takes rank with the 'Principia,' Laplace's 'Mécanique Céleste,' and Clerk Maxwell's 'Electricity and Magnetism.'

A second edition of 'Thomson and Tait' appeared in two parts, issued respectively in 1879 and 1883. No further opportunity of collaboration offered. The material which Tait had collected for the second section of the joint original design he worked up independently into volumes for students on 'Heat' (1884; new edit. 1892), 'Light' (1884; last edit. 1900), and 'Properties of Matter' (1885; 5th edit. 1907). In these educational handbooks Tait presented each subject as a connected whole, avoiding all examination methods of presentation, carrying on the student logically by experiment and general reasoning to the main truths, and only introducing mathematics when really necessary or useful to shorten some process of reasoning. 'Heat' and 'Properties of Matter' were soon translated into German.

Tait was a strenuous controversialist, especially where his friends were concerned. He actively defended his predecessor, James David Forbes, in his struggle with Tyndall, who asserted his priority to Forbes in his theory of the motion of glaciers. In Tait's second important work, 'Thermodynamics' (1868; 2nd edit. 1877), which still enjoys authority, he established against Julius Robert Mayer, the German physicist, the claim of James Prescott Joule [q. v.] to have first determined strictly the relationship between heat and work. Tait similarly defended Thomson (Lord Kelvin) against Clausius's claim in 1854 to prior discovery, both theoretically and experimentally, of the fact that Carnot's function was inversely proportional to the temperature as measured on the absolute dynamic scale (KNOTT'S *Life of Tait*, p. 223).

In the spring of 1874 Tait lectured before the Edinburgh Evening Club, a gathering of congenial friends, on 'Recent Advances in Physical Science.' Tait spoke from notes, but a shorthand transcript was published in 1876 (3rd edit. 1885). The book, which holds a high place in scientific literature, was translated into French, German, and Italian. Subsequently Tait, whose religious sentiment was always strong, joined his colleague Balfour Stewart [q. v.] in an endeavour 'to overthrow materialism by a purely scientific argument.' The result, 'The Unseen Universe, or Physical Speculation on a Future State,' appeared anonymously in 1875 and greatly stirred public opinion. The fourth edition, which appeared within twelve months of the first, acknowledged the authorship. The tenth edition was translated into French (1883). In order to make clearer points which readers missed, the two authors produced in 1878 a sequel entitled 'Paradoxical Philosophy.' For the 'Encyclopædia Britannica' (9th edit. 1883) Tait wrote many articles, including one, 'Mechanics,' which he afterwards developed into an advanced treatise on 'Dynamics' (1895). Here, as he wrote to Cayley, he evolved a system, which he believed to be new, 'from general principles such as conservation and transformation of energy, least action, &c., without introducing either force, momentum, or impulse.' A small book on 'Newton's Laws of Motion' followed in 1899.

Tait's laboratory work was at the same time of a rarely equalled magnitude and importance. To his students his manner was always that of an elder brother. Although his laboratory was not a formal institution definitely housed in College buildings till 1868, nevertheless, following the example of his predecessors, he until then used for laboratory purposes his class-room and private room in college. At first he leaned to the chemical side. He continued his investigations on the properties of ozone, which he had begun with Andrews at Belfast, and in 1862 worked with James Alfred Wanklyn [q. v. Suppl. II] on the production of electricity by evaporation and during effervescence. In 1865 he dealt with the curious motion of iron filings on a vibrating plate in a magnetic field. In 1866 he began with Balfour Stewart [q. v.] the experimental investigation of the heating of a rapidly rotating disc in vacuo, a work extending continuously through two years, being resumed after three years and again six years later. Between 1870 and 1874 he worked out and verified with his students Thomson's (Lord Kelvin's) discovery of the 'latent heat of electricity,' and his theory of thermo-electricity, and he produced the first, and still the practical, working thermo-electric diagram on Thomson's lines. When he delivered the Rede lecture before the University of Cambridge in 1873 he chose thermo-electricity for his subject. His next great work was on knots, a theme which presented itself to him as the outcome of the simple proposition that two closed plane curves which intersect each other must do so an even number of times. Begun in 1876, this research occupied him, when time allowed, till 1885, and resulted in a remarkable series of masterly papers. In 1881 he dealt with the physical side of the 'Challenger' reports, especially with the effect of pressure on the readings of thermometers used in deep-sea soundings, and on the compressibility of water and alcohol. In 1886, on the suggestion of Lord Kelvin, he undertook a searching investigation into the foundations of the kinetic theory of gases, on which he was continuously engaged for five years (it still occupied his attention in 1896). His results were published in more than twenty papers, which form collectively a 'classic' contribution to the literature of the subject.

During the same period, Tait, who was an ardent votary of golf, closely studied the flight of a golf ball ('the path of a rotating spherical projectile'), which he saw was not that of a smooth heavy sphere through a resisting medium. After an endless series of experiments with the laws of impact and cognate points, he discovered the principle of the 'underspin' which gave a new development to the art of the game (cf. his paper in *Badminton Magazine*, 1896). Sir J. J. Thomson, in a Friday-evening discourse at the Royal Institution (18 March 1910), showed to his audience an ingenious experimental verification of Tait's general conclusions.

Tait's alertness of mind and versatile interests led to careful and abstract inquiry in every possible direction, often apparently playful, and constantly alien to his special studies. As director of the Scottish Provident Institution, he was drawn to investigate problems of life assurance. Although he had no sympathy with easy efforts to popularise science, he sought to bring true science home to the unlearned, either in articles in popular magazines like 'Good Words,' to which he contributed with Thomson a paper on 'Energy' and a series of articles on 'Cosmical Astronomy,' or in lectures to a general audience on 'Force,' 'Sensation and Science,' 'Thunderstorms,' 'Religion and Science,' 'Does Humanity require a New Revelation ?' Tait's scientific papers were collected in 2 vols. (Cambridge, 1898–1900).

Tait's eminence was widely recognised. Although he was never a fellow of the Royal Society of England, he received a Royal medal from the society in 1886. He was made hon. LL.D. of Glasgow in 1901, and hon. Sc.D. of the University of Ireland in 1875. He twice received the Keith prize from the Royal Society of

Edinburgh as well as the Gunning Victoria Jubilee prize. He was fellow or member of the Danish, Dutch, Swedish, and Irish scientific academies. He was made hon. fellow of Peterhouse in 1885. Resigning his professorship early in 1901, Tait died at Edinburgh on 4 July 1901, and was buried there.

Sir George Reid painted three portraits of Tait: one is the property of the family; another, which has been engraved, hangs in the rooms of the Royal Society of Edinburgh, and the third is in the hall of his college, Peterhouse, Cambridge.

Two scholarships in scientific research were founded in Tait's memory at Edinburgh university, and a sum of money contributed to improve the apparatus in the natural philosophy department. A second ('Tait') chair in that department is also in process of foundation.

Of Tait's four sons the eldest, John Guthrie, is principal of the Government Central College at Mysore. The third son, FREDERICK GUTHRIE (1870–1900), born at Edinburgh on 11 Jan. 1870, after being educated at Edinburgh Academy and Sedbergh, entered Sandhurst as an Edinburgh University candidate. In 1890 he was gazetted to the Leinster regiment, and in 1894 was transferred to the Black Watch. In 1899 he volunteered for active service in South Africa. At Magersfontein (19 Dec. 1899) young Tait, 'in front of the front company,' was shot in the leg. After a few weeks in hospital he rejoined his company, and on the same day, 7 Feb. 1900, at Koodoosberg, leading a rush on the Boers' position, he was shot through the heart, and died instantly. Lieutenant Tait, known everywhere as 'Freddie Tait,' was from 1893 until he sailed for South Africa probably the most brilliant amateur golfer. He was champion golfer both in 1896 and in 1898 (Low's *F. G. Tait, a Record*, 1902, with characteristic portrait).

[Dr. Knott's Life and Scientific Work of P. G. Tait, Cambridge, 1911, with four portraits and bibliography enumerating some 365 papers, besides 22 vols.; family records and personal recollections.] J. D. H. D.

TALLACK, WILLIAM (1831–1908), prison reformer, born at St. Austell, Cornwall, on 15 June 1831, was son of Thomas Tallack (1801–65) by his wife Hannah (1800–76), daughter of Samuel Bowden, members of the Society of Friends. He was educated at the Friends' school, Sidcot (1842–5), and the Founders' College, Yorkshire (1852–4). He was engaged in teaching (1845–52 and 1855–8). An early friendship with the Quaker philanthropist Peter Bedford (1780–1864) determined his career. In 1863 he became secretary to the Society for the Abolition of Capital Punishment, exchanging this in 1866 for the secretariate of the Howard Association, which he held till 31 Dec. 1901. In pursuit of his duties as an agent in the cause of penal reform he visited not only the Continent, but Egypt, Australia, Tasmania, Canada, and the United States. His advocacy of the same cause found expression in numerous tracts, addresses, flyleaves, and articles in periodicals. He wrote much in the 'Friends' Quarterly Examiner'; 'The Times' in an obituary notice speaks of him as 'at one time a frequent contributor,' and justly characterises his writing as 'discursive and somewhat confused,' but emphasising 'wholesome principles,' keeping 'a grip on facts,' and exhibiting 'courtesy and tact.' His 'Penological and Preventive Principles' (1888, 2nd edit. 1896) may be considered a standard work on the subject. His religious writings and correspondence present a liberal type of evangelical religion in conjunction with broad sympathies.

He died at 61 Clapton Common on 25 Sept. 1908, and was buried in the Friends' cemetery, Winchmore Hill, Middlesex. He married on 18 July 1867, at Stoke Newington, Augusta Mary (*b.* 28 Dec. 1844; *d.* 21 Jan. 1904), daughter of John Hallam Catlin, and had by her several children.

A nearly complete bibliography of his writings to 1882 (including magazine articles) will be found in 'Bibliotheca Cornubiensis' (1874–82). The following may be specially noted: 1. 'Malta under the Phenicians, Knights and English,' 1861. 2. 'Friendly Sketches in America,' 1861 (noticed in John Paget's 'Paradoxes and Puzzles,' 1874, 405–7). 3. 'Peter Bedford, the Spitalfields Philanthropist,' 1865; 2nd edit. 1892. 4. 'A Common Sense Course for Diminishing the Evils of War,' 1867. 5. 'Thomas Shillitoe, the Quaker Missionary and Temperance Pioneer,' 1867. 6. 'George Fox, the Friends and the Early Baptists,' 1868. 7. 'Humanity and Humanitarianism. . . . Prison Systems,' 1871. 8. 'Defects of the Criminal System and Penal Legislation,' 1872 (circulated by the Howard Association). 9. 'Christ's Deity and Beneficent Reserve,' 1873. 10. 'India, its Peace and Progress,' 1877. 11. 'Howard Letters and Memories,' 1905 (autobiographical).

[The Times, 28 Sept. and 1 Oct. 1908; Annual Register, 1908; Howard Letters and Memories, 1905 (two portraits); Stuart J. Reid, Sir

Richard Tangye, 1908; Joseph Smith's Cat. of Friends' Books, 1867, ii. 690 seq.; 1893, p. 18; Boase and Courtney's Bibliotheca Cornubiensis, 1878, ii. 700 seq.; 1882, p. 1342.] A. G.

TANGYE, Sir RICHARD (1833–1906), engineer, born at Broad Lane, Illogan, Cornwall, on 24 Nov. 1833, was fifth son in a family of six sons and three daughters of Joseph Tangye, a quaker Cornish miner of Redruth, who afterwards became a small shopkeeper and farmer there, by Anne (*d.* 1851), daughter of Edward Bullock, a small farmer and engine driver. After attending the British school at Illogan, and helping his father on his farm, he was at the age of eight disabled for manual labour through fracturing his right arm, and spent three years (1844–7) at a school at Redruth kept by William Lamb Bellows, father of John Bellows [q. v. Suppl. II]; thence he went in February 1847 to the Friends' School, Sidcot, Somerset, where he formed a lifelong friendship with William Tallack [q. v. Suppl. II]. He remained there as pupil teacher and assistant until 1851; in that year he visited with his brother James the Great Exhibition in London.

Finding the teaching profession uncongenial, Tangye at the end of 1852, in reply to an advertisement, went to Birmingham and entered the office of Thomas Worsdell, a quaker engineer, as clerk at 50*l.* a year. His younger brother George soon joined him as junior clerk; they were followed by two other brothers, James and Joseph, mechanical experts who had worked under Brunel for Mr. Brunton, engineer to the West Cornwall railway, and had made a hydraulic press which favourably impressed Brunel.

At Birmingham Tangye soon obtained a complete grasp of the commercial details of the engineering business, and he proved his interest in the welfare of the workmen by obtaining the firm's assent to a half-holiday on Saturdays, a concession to labour which was subsequently adopted in England universally. In 1855, owing to a difference with his employer, Richard left the firm. Soon he and three brothers, including Joseph, who had made himself an expert lathemaker, began to manufacture tools and machinery on their own account, renting a room at 40 Mount Street, Birmingham, for 4*s.* a week. The brothers prospered, and took a large workshop for 10*s.* a week, bought an engine and boiler to supply their own motive power, and took one workman into their employ. In 1856 Brunel, mindful of James and Joseph's earlier efforts, commissioned the brothers at Birmingham to supply him with hydraulic lifting jacks to launch the 'Great Eastern' steamship. The successful performance of this commission proved the first step in the firm's prosperity. In 1858 the brothers bought the sole right to manufacture differential pulley blocks, recently invented by Mr. J. A. Weston; but rival claims to the patent rights involved them in 1858 in a long and costly though successful lawsuit.

A fifth brother, Edward, joined them that year. The firm now devoted itself solely to the manufacture of machinery and every kind of power machine. The growth of the industry led to their removal in 1859 to new premises in Clement Street, Birmingham; three years later the firm acquired three acres of land at Soho, three miles from Birmingham, and built there the 'Cornwall Works.' Ultimately this factory through Richard's skill, energy, and business acumen absorbed thirty acres of surrounding land and gave employment to 3000 hands. Works in Belgium were established under Edward's management in 1863; a London warehouse was added in 1868, and branches were subsequently formed at Newcastle, Manchester, Glasgow, Sydney, Melbourne, and Johannesburg. One of the engineering successes of the firm was the use of their hydraulic jacks in placing Cleopatra's Needle (weighing over 186 tons) on its present site on the Thames Embankment on 12 Sept. 1878. The firm became a limited liability company, 'Tangyes Limited,' on 1 Jan. 1882.

The brothers were considerate employers. In 1872, in which year the three elder brothers, James, Joseph, and Edward, retired from the business, Richard permanently instituted the Saturday half-holiday which he had pressed on his first employer twenty years earlier, and he averted a strike by granting unasked a nine hours day. In 1876 Tangye instituted at the works a large dining-hall, educational classes, concerts, and lectures, with which his friend, Dr. J. A. Langford [q. v. Suppl. II], was closely associated.

In the religious, municipal, and political life of Birmingham Tangye took an active share. In his early days there he helped Joseph Sturge [q. v.] at the Friends' Sunday schools. A staunch liberal in politics, he supported John Bright in every election at Birmingham, but refused many invitations to stand for parliament himself. He was a firm free trader, and remained loyal to Gladstone after the home rule split of 1886, keeping alive the principles of liberalism in the 'Daily Argus,' which he founded in association with Sir Hugh Gilzean Reid in 1891. He was knighted in 1894 on Lord Rosebery's recommendation. A member of the Birmingham town council from 1878 to 1882 and of the Smethwick school board, Tangye and his brothers were generous benefactors to the town. To the municipal art gallery (founded in 1867) the firm in 1880 gave 10,000*l.* for new buildings (opened by King Edward VII, then Prince of Wales, in 1885), as well as for the acquisition of objects of art; later they presented Albert Moore's 'The Dreamers'; Tangye also loaned his fine collection of Wedgwood ware, of which a handbook was published in 1885. The School of Art (founded in 1843), to which the Tangyes in 1881 contributed 12,000*l.*, was rebuilt in 1884.

Tangye cherished literary interests. His admiration for Oliver Cromwell led him from 1875 to collect literature and relics relating to the Protector, and in 1889 he bought the fine Cromwellian collection of J. de Kewer Williams, congregational minister, to which he made many additions. He embodied the results of his study of the period of the protectorate in 'The Two Protectors, Oliver and Richard Cromwell' (1899). A catalogue of his Cromwellian collection of MSS., miniatures, and medals, by W. Downing, was published in 1905.

Between 1876 (when Langford was his companion) and 1904 Tangye made eight extended voyages, visiting Australia, America, South Africa (where his firm had business branches), and Egypt. Tangye recounted his experiences in 'Reminiscences of Travel in Australia, America, and Egypt' (1883), and 'Notes on my Fourth Voyage to the Australian Colonies, 1886' (Birmingham, 1886).

On a short record of his early career contributed in 1889 to a series of biographies of self-made men in the 'British Workman' Tangye based his full autobiography 'One and All' (1890), which, reaching its twentieth thousand in 1905, was reissued in a revised form under the title of 'The Rise of a Great Industry.' Tangye also published 'Tales of a Grandfather' (Birmingham, 1897).

Tangye resided at Birmingham till 1894, spending his summers from 1882 at Glendorgal, a house which he had purchased near Newquay. In 1894 he removed to Kingston-on-Thames. He died at Coombe Bank, Kingston Hill, on 14 Oct. 1906, and was buried in Putney Vale cemetery. He married on 24 Jan. 1859 Caroline, daughter of Thomas Jesper, corn merchant, of Birmingham. She survived him with three sons, of whom two, Harold Lincoln and Wilfrid, joined the business, and two married daughters. The son Harold, who was created a baronet in June 1912, is author of 'In New South Africa' (1896) and 'In the Torrid Sudan' (1910).

A portrait in oils, by E. R. Taylor, hangs in the Birmingham School of Art. A bronze memorial plate erected by public subscription, with relief portraits of Richard and George Tangye, is in the Birmingham Art Gallery.

[Stuart J. Reid, Sir Richard Tangye, 1908; Tangye, The Rise of a Great Industry, 1905; The Times, 15 Oct. 1906; Biograph, 1879, ii. 266.] W. B. O.

TARTE, JOSEPH ISRAEL (1848–1907), Canadian statesman and journalist, born on 11 Jan. 1848 at Lanoraie, Berthier county, Quebec, was son of Joseph Tarte, habitant farmer, by his wife Louise Robillard. Educated at L'Assomption College, he qualified himself as a notary in 1871, and settled in Quebec, but after two years drifted into journalism. He quickly made his mark as a journalist. He early edited 'Les Laurentides' (St. Lin), and subsequently accepted the editorship of 'Le Canadien' and 'L'Événement' of Quebec. He conducted 'L'Événement' for over twenty years, and represented 'Le Canadien' in the press galleries of Quebec and Ottawa. In 1891 he moved to Montreal, where he published for a time 'Le Cultivateur,' the weekly edition of 'Le Canadien.' In 1896 he transferred this paper to his sons, L. J. and E. Tarte, who in 1897 acquired 'La Patrie,' which presented Tarte's political views.

Tarte sat in the Quebec assembly for Bonaventure from 1877 until its dissolution in 1881. He belonged to the party of the 'bleus' or tories. In 1891 he was elected to the federal parliament at Ottawa in the conservative interest, and was closely associated with Sir Hector Langevin [q. v. Suppl. II]. But his part in politics, which was that of a 'stormy petrel,' contributed not a little to the wreck of the conservative party. Becoming cognisant of gross irregularities in the public administration in Quebec, he formulated his charges upon the floor of the house in 1891, and the conservative premier, Sir John Abbott, granted a committee of investigation. The charges were fully proved. The member for Quebec centre, Thomas

McGreevy, was expelled from parliament, and Sir Hector Langevin resigned his portfolio as minister of public works. The conservative party, which warmly resented these damaging exposures, grew thoroughly demoralised, and Tarte went over to Laurier and the liberal opposition. Unseated on petition in 1892, he remained out of parliament until 5 Jan. 1893, when he was returned for L'Islet at a bye-election. In the critical Manitoba education question, on which Sir Charles Tupper committed the conservatives to a policy of coercing the Manitoba legislature into granting special privileges to Roman catholic schools, Laurier was said to be wavering until Tarte persuaded him to declare for conciliation between the rival interests in Manitoba rather than for coercion in favour of the catholics. Tarte's organising ability proved to the liberal party a most valuable asset, especially in Quebec; the party came into power in 1896 and remained in office till 1911. Tarte was rewarded with the office of minister of public works in the Laurier administration (13 July 1896). Although he was defeated in the general election in Beauharnois, he was soon returned for St. John and Iberville. His administration of his department was most effective. Through his efforts the port of Montreal was equipped, and the St. Lawrence widened and deepened for twenty-five miles between Quebec and Montreal.

Unlike his liberal colleagues, Tarte was a strong protectionist. While he was the first leading French-Canadian openly to espouse the imperial federation cause, his policy of 'Canada for the Canadians' was hardly imperialistic, and he is said to have opposed the sending of Canadian contingents to take part in the South African war. In 1902 his public advocacy of higher tariffs for Canada compelled his retirement from the government. Thereupon he at once assumed the editorship of 'La Patrie.' He died in Montreal on 18 Dec. 1907, and was buried in the Côte des Neiges cemetery.

Tarte was twice married: (1) to Georgiana Sylvestre, by whom he had three sons and three daughters, who survive; and (2) to Emma Laurencelle, by whom he had one daughter.

[The Times, 19 and 23 Dec. 1907; Morgan, Canadian Men of the Time.] P. E.

TASCHEREAU, Sir HENRI ELZEAR (1836–1911), chief justice of Canada, born at St. Mary's in Beauce county, province of Quebec, on 7 Oct. 1836, was eldest son of Pierre Elzéar Taschereau, a member of the Canadian Legislative Assembly, and Catherine Hénédine, daughter of the Hon. Amable Dionne, a member of the legislative council. The Taschereau family came from Touraine to Canada in the seventeenth century, and Taschereau was a co-proprietor of the Quebec seigniory of Ste. Marie de la Beauce, which had been ceded to his great-grandfather in 1746. The Taschereaus had been for two generations distinguished in the judicial and ecclesiastical life of Canada. Cardinal Elzéar Alexander Taschereau [q.v.] was Sir Henri's uncle.

Henri Elzéar was educated at the Quebec Seminary, was called to the Quebec bar in 1857, and practised in the city of Quebec. He became a Q.C. in 1867, and in 1868 was appointed clerk of the peace for the district of Quebec, but soon resigned. From 1861 to 1867 he represented Beauce county as a conservative in the Canadian Legislative Assembly, and supported Sir John Alexander Macdonald [q. v.] and Sir George Cartier [q. v.] on the question of federation. On 12 Jan. 1871 he became a puisne judge of the superior court of the province of Quebec, on 7 Oct. 1878 a judge of the supreme court of Canada, and in 1902 chief justice of Canada in succession to Sir Samuel Henry Strong [q.v. Suppl. II]. Knighted in 1902, he became in 1904 a member of the judicial committee of the privy council. In 1906 he resigned the chief justiceship, and was succeeded by Sir Charles Fitzpatrick. Twice in that capacity he administered the government as deputy to the governor-general.

Taschereau was a LL.D. both of Ottawa and of Laval universities. When a law faculty was established at Ottawa University he was appointed to a chair, and in 1895 became dean of the faculty in succession to Sir John Sparrow Thompson [q. v.].

Taschereau's extensive knowledge of Roman and French civil law, as well as of the English statute and common law, enabled him to render important service to Canadian jurisprudence. As a legal writer he made a reputation by publishing the 'Criminal Law Consolidation and Amendment Acts of 1869 for the Dominion of Canada with Notes, Commentaries, etc.' (vol. i. Montreal, 1874; vol. ii. Toronto, 1875, with later editions), and 'Le Code de Procédure Civile du Bas-Canada' (Quebec, 1876). He further published in 1896 a 'Notice Généalogique sur la Famille

Taschereau.' Tall in stature, he was a refined scholar and a cultured gentleman. He died at Ottawa on 14 April 1911. He married twice: (1) on 1 May 1857 Marie Antoinette (*d.* June 1896), daughter of R. U. Harwood, member of the legislative council of Quebec; by her he had five sons and three daughters; (2) in March 1897 Marie Louise, daughter of Charles Panet of Ottawa; she survived him.

Sir Henri Thomas Taschereau (1841–1909), Canadian judge, first cousin of the chief justice, born in Quebec on 6 Oct. 1841, was son of Jean Thomas Taschereau, judge of the supreme court of Canada, by his first wife, Louise Adèle, daughter of the hon. Amable Dionne, a member of the legislative council. After education at the Quebec Seminary and at Laval University, where he graduated B.L. in 1861 and B.C.L. in 1862, and received the hon. degree of LL.D. in 1890, he was called to the Quebec bar in 1863 and practised there. While an undergraduate he edited in 1862 a journal, 'Les Débats,' in which he first reported verbatim in French the parliamentary debates. He was also one of the editors in 1863 of the liberal journal 'La Tribune.' In 1870 Taschereau was elected to the city council of Quebec, serving for some time as alderman, and he represented Quebec on the north shore railway board for four years. As a liberal he sat in the dominion parliament for Montmagny from 1872 to 1878, and actively supported Sir Antoine Aimé Dorion [q. v. Suppl. I] and Alexander Mackenzie [q. v.]. On 7 Oct. 1878 he was appointed a puisne judge of the superior court of the province of Quebec. On 29 Jan. 1907, on the resignation of Sir Alexander Lacoste, he was made chief justice of the king's bench for Quebec, and next year (on 26 June) he was knighted. Taschereau left Canada in May 1909 for a tour in England and France; he died suddenly at the residence of his daughter, Mrs. J. N. Lyon, at Montmorency, near Paris, on 11 Oct. 1909. Taschereau was twice married, and had four sons and five daughters (*Canadian Law Times*, 1909, xxix. 1045–6; *Quebec Daily Telegraph*, 12 Oct. 1909).

[The Times and Montreal Daily Star, 15 April 1911; G. M. Rose's Cyclopædia of Canadian Biography, 1888; Morgan's Canadian Men and Women of the Time, 1898; Canadian Mag. xx. 291 (with portrait); Canadian Law Journ. xlvii. 284–5; Canadian Law Rev. v. 273–4; Canadian Who's Who, 1910; notes from Prof. D. R. Keys.] C. P. L.

TATA, JAMSETJI NASARWANJI (1839–1904), pioneer of Indian industries, born on 3 March 1839 at Naosari, in Gujerat, was only son of five children of Nasarwanji Ratanji Tata, a Parsi of priestly family, by his wife (and cousin) Jiverbai Cowasjee Tata. When he was thirteen his father started business in Bombay, and after sending him to the Elphinstone College from 1855 to 1858, put him in his office. In 1859 the youth visited China and laid the foundations of the large export business in which, after some vicissitudes, the firm of Tata & Co. (later Tata & Sons) successfully engaged on an immense scale, forming branches in Japan, China, Paris, and New York, and agencies in London and elsewhere. Returning from China in 1863, Tata paid the first of many visits to England, mainly with a view to the establishment of an Indian bank in London. That scheme was frustrated by the financial crisis following the 'share mania' in Bombay. Tata's firm, which was brought to bankruptcy, was rehabilitated by contracts for army supplies in the Abyssinian war.

Turning his attention to the nascent cotton manufacturing industry in Bombay, Tata returned to England in 1872 to study the work and conditions of the Lancashire mills. Subsequently he fixed upon Nagpur as a site for a model mill, and his Empress mills were opened there on 1 Jan. 1877, the day of Queen Victoria's proclamation as Empress. He afterwards founded at Coorla, near Bombay, the Swadeshi ('own country') mills. These concerns were soon recognised to be the best managed of Indian-owned factories. Improvements were adopted to protect and advance the interests of operatives and to reduce the cost of production. At first Indian mills confined themselves almost entirely to coarse goods which the deteriorated country staple was alone capable of producing. Tata, resolved to spin finer 'counts,' not only initiated the importation of longer-stapled cotton, but perseveringly sought to acclimatise Egyptian cotton in spite of the discouragement of agricultural advisers of government. In 1896 Tata published a convincing pamphlet on 'Growth of Egyptian Cotton in India,' which was republished in 1903. Another pamphlet (1893) discussed methods of increasing the supply of skilled labour. In order to reduce the heavy freight charges between Bombay and the Far East, Tata helped to promote in 1893 the Nippon Yusen Kaisha (Japanese Steam Navigation Company) so as to break down the monopoly of three allied steamship companies—the P. and O., the Austrian-Lloyd, and the Rubattino. The three companies met the new service with a war of freights. In a widely circulated pamphlet Tata protested against the employment by the P. and O. Company of its mail subsidy from Indian revenues in maintaining a monopoly injurious to Indian trade. After spending more than two lakhs of rupees in the fight, he in June 1896 aided in reaching an agreement for a permanent reduction of freights on a reasonable competitive basis. He vigorously opposed the imposition of excise duty on the products of Indian mills to countervail the cotton import duties in 1894 and 1896, and directed an elaborate statistical inquiry into the hampering effects of the duty on the industry (V. CHIROL'S *Indian Unrest*, p. 277).

Tata's greatest service to the cause of Indian economic development was the inauguration of a scheme whereby Indian iron ore, after numerous unsuccessful efforts from 1825 onwards, might be manufactured on a large capitalistic basis. Apart from the comparatively small works of the Bengal Iron and Steel Company at Barrakur [see MARTIN, SIR THOMAS ACQUIN, Suppl. II], iron had been manufactured only on a very small scale by peasant families of smelters. In 1901 Tata thoroughly investigated the problem; his expert English and American advisers prospected large tracts of country and made exhaustive experiments, a preliminary outlay of some 36,000*l.* being incurred. Good progress was made at the time of his death, and under the control of his two sons the Tata Iron and Steel Company was registered in Bombay on 26 Aug. 1907 with a rupee capital equivalent to 1,545,000*l.*, by far the largest amount raised by Indians for a commercial undertaking. The works since constructed have created a large industrial centre at Sakchi, in the Singhbum district, 153 miles west of Calcutta, 45 miles from the principal ore supplies in the Mhorbunj State, Orissa, and 130 miles from the collieries on the Jherria field. Connecting railways have been built, and there are two blast furnaces for an annual production of about 120,000 tons of pig-iron, and steel furnaces for an output of 70,000 tons. This great enterprise, which marks a new era in Indian economic development, will support 60,000 workers and dependants (see *Quinquennial Review of Mineral Production in India*, 1904–8 in *Recds. of Geol. Surv.*, vol. 39, 1910). The manufacture was commenced at the end of 1911.

Another of Tata's great schemes was the utilisation of the heavy monsoon rainfall of the Western Ghauts for electric power in Bombay factories. On 8 Feb. 1911 the Governor of Bombay laid the foundation stone of the works at Lanouli in the hills, 43 miles from Bombay, and the completion of the project is expected in 1913. Whole valleys are being dammed up to hold the water, creating lakes 2521 acres in extent. The capital of about $1\frac{1}{4}$ millions sterling was subscribed by Indians.

Tata rendered many other services to Bombay. He built the fine Taj Mahal hotel, the best appointed hotel in Asia, at a cost of a quarter of a million. He did much to improve the architectural amenities of Bombay, and to provide healthy suburban homes. In these and other enterprises, such as the introduction of Japanese silk culture into Mysore, he showed 'first, broad imagination and keen insight, next a scientific and calculating study of the project and all that it involved, and finally a high capacity for organisation.' His personal tastes were of the simplest kind, and he scorned publicity or self-advertisement (L. FRASER'S *India under Curzon and After*, p. 322).

He endowed scholarships, originally confined to Parsis, but thrown open in 1894, to enable promising young Indians to study in Europe. He was a fellow of the Bombay University. His offer to government on 28 Sept. 1898 of real property worth 200,000*l.* (since increased in value) to found a post-graduate institute for scientific research, resulted in the establishment by Tata's sons, in accordance with his plans, of the Indian Institute of Science at Bangalore, which teaches, examines, and confers diplomas. Its aims include the fuller application of science to Indian arts and industries.

Taken seriously ill while in Germany in the spring of 1904, he died at Nauheim on 19 May 1904, and was buried in the Parsi cemetery, Brookwood, Woking. He married in 1855 a girl of ten—early marriages then being general among the Parsis—named Berabai (*d.* March 1904), daughter of Kharsetji Daboo, and they had issue a daughter who died at the age of twelve and two sons, Sir Dorabji Jamsetji (knighted 1910) and Ratan Jamsetji, of York House, Twickenham, and Bombay, upon whom the business of the firm has devolved. A three-quarter length painting by M. F. Pithawalla, a Bombay artist (1902), is in the Parsi

Gymkhana, Bombay ; three copies are in the Elphinstone club there, in the Empress mills and the Parsi fire-temple, Nagpur, and a fourth belongs to R. J. Tata. An earlier portrait by E. Ward belongs to Sir Dorabji. A bronze statue by W. R. Colton, A.R.A., publicly subscribed, was unveiled on 11 April 1912 near the municipal office, Bombay.

[The character sketch in India under Curzon and After (1911), by Lovat Fraser, who is preparing a biography ; Ind. Textile Journ., 15 Aug. 1901 ; Tata's pamphlets ; personal knowledge ; personal correspondence with Tata ; Sir T. Raleigh's Lord Curzon in India, 1906 ; lect. by Sir Thos. Holland, F.R.S., Soc. of Arts, 27 April 1911 ; Quin. Rept. Edcn. in India, 1902–7 ; Times of India, 21 May 1904, 1 Oct. 1907, 2 and 10 Feb. and 11 Oct. 1911 ; ditto Illus. Weekly, 28 April 1909 ; Bombay Gaz., weekly summary, 21 and 28 May 1904 ; Pioneer Mail, 22 Aug. 1902 ; The Times, 24 May 1904 and 28 Oct. 1907.]

F. H. B.

TAUNTON, ETHELRED LUKE (1857–1907), ecclesiastical historian, born at Rugeley, Staffordshire, on 17 Oct. 1857, was youngest son of Thomas Taunton of Rugeley, by his wife Mary, daughter of Colonel Clarke. His parents were Roman catholics, and from the age of eleven to fourteen he was at St. Gregory's school, Downside, near Bath. Ill-health, which pursued him through life, precluded his admission to the Benedictine order. After a musical training at Lichfield, he joined the community of St. Andrew's, founded by Father Bampfield at Barnet, and remained there six years as professor of music. In 1880 he joined the oblates of St. Charles, Bayswater ; and was ordained priest there on 17 Feb. 1883. In 1886 he was placed by Cardinal Manning in charge of the newly formed Stoke Newington mission. A church was opened in January 1888, and a congregation formed ; but a few weeks later, Taunton's frail physique was permanently injured by the accidental fall upon him of a ladder in the church. During a two years' convalescence at Bruges he engaged in literary work, contributing articles to the 'Irish Ecclesiastical Record' and to other Roman catholic publications, and conducting a periodical called 'St. Luke's.' On returning to England he devoted himself, in spite of physical weakness and scanty means, to historical research, ecclesiastical study, musical composition, and devotional writing. On liturgiology, church music, and ecclesiastical history he became a recognised authority. He died suddenly from heart failure in London while on his way to a hospital in a police ambulance on 9 May 1907, and was buried at Kensal Green.

Taunton's chief works are : 1. 'The English Black Monks of St. Benedict,' 2 vols. 1898, which embodied much original research for the last three centuries, depending for the early periods on the MS. collections of Mr. Edmund Bishop and those of Dom Allanson at Ampleforth. 2. 'The History of the Jesuits,' 1901, presenting an independent outlook, which provoked some controversy. 3. 'Thomas Wolsey, Legate and Reformer,' 1902, a favourable estimate of Wolsey. 4. 'The Little Office of Our Lady : a treatise, theoretical, practical, and exegetical,' 1903, a compilation of much learning. 5. 'Law of the Church, a Cyclopædia of Canon Law for English-speaking Countries,' 1906. Taunton left unfinished a 'Life of Cardinal Pole' and a 'History of the English Catholic Clergy since the Reformation.' A popular 'History of the Growth of Church Music' (1887), which originally appeared in a catholic paper, the 'Weekly Register,' shows scholarly discrimination. Taunton himself composed motets and other pieces, besides musical settings to church hymns, some of which were printed. He was a finished organist.

[Tablet, 18 May 1907 ; Downside Review, July 1907 ; The Times, 20 May 1907 (gives Christian name wrongly); Taunton's works; Brit. Mus. Cat. ; private information.]

G. Le G. N.

TAYLOR, CHARLES (1840–1908), Master of St. John's College, Cambridge, born in London on 27 May 1840, was son of William Taylor, tea-dealer, by Catherine his wife. The family had formerly been settled near Woburn in Bedfordshire. His grandfather, a man of energy and foresight, had come to London, where he acquired considerable property in Regent Street, then in course of construction. He is said to have been the first job-master in London. Charles Taylor lost his father at the age of five, when his mother, with her three young sons, went to live near Hampstead. He attended the grammar school of St. Marylebone and All Souls (in union with King's College), and, afterwards, King's College School itself, winning prizes at both schools. It was at King's College School that he began his lifelong friendship with Ingram Bywater, afterwards regius professor of Greek in the University of Oxford.

In October 1858 Taylor entered St. John's College, Cambridge, where at first he devoted himself mainly to mathematics.

In 1860 he was elected to one of the new foundation scholarships, and in 1862, a year in which St. John's had six wranglers out of the first ten, he was ninth wrangler. In the same year he was placed in the second class of the classical tripos; in 1863 he obtained a first class in the theological examination; and in 1864 the Crosse scholarship and the first Tyrwhitt scholarship, while in his college he vacated the Naden divinity studentship for a fellowship. On the river he was fond of sculling, and he also rowed in the college boat-races from 1863 to 1866. He was always a great walker.

In 1863 he published 'Geometrical Conics, including Anharmonic Ratio and Projection.' This was followed, in 1872, by a text-book entitled 'The Elementary Geometry of Conics,' which passed through several editions, and, in 1881, by a larger treatise, 'An Introduction to the Ancient and Modern Geometry of Conics,' including a brief but masterly sketch of the early history of geometry. He here lays special stress on the principle of geometrical continuity, usually associated with the name of Poncelet, and traces this principle back to Kepler. He returned to the subject in the memoir on 'The Geometry of Kepler and Newton,' which he contributed to the volume of the 'Transactions of the Cambridge Philosophical Society' published in honour of Sir George Gabriel Stokes's jubilee, and in the article on 'Geometrical Continuity' printed in the 'Encyclopædia Britannica' in 1902, and reprinted in 1910. He was one of the founders of the 'Oxford, Cambridge, and Dublin Messenger of Mathematics,' and continued to be an editor from 1862 to 1884. He joined the London Mathematical Society in 1872, and was president of the Mathematical Association in 1892. His mathematical writings include some thirty or forty papers, mostly on geometry, published in the 'Messenger,' the 'Quarterly Journal of Pure and Applied Mathematics,' and the 'Proceedings of the Cambridge Philosophical Society.' All of them are 'marked by elegance, conciseness, a rare knowledge of the history of the subject, and a veneration for the great geometers of the past' (Prof. A. E. H. LOVE in *Proceedings of the London Mathematical Society*, 1909).

He was ordained deacon in 1866 and priest in 1867, the year in which he obtained the Kaye University prize for an essay published in an expanded form under the title of 'The Gospel in the Law.' He had given a course of sermons on the subject as one of the curates at St. Andrew's the Great. In 1873 he was appointed college lecturer in theology. He soon made his mark as a Hebrew scholar. In 1874 he issued 'The Dirge of Coheleth in Ecclesiastes xii. Discussed and Literally Interpreted.' This was followed in 1877 by his edition of the 'Sayings of the Jewish Fathers, in Hebrew and English, with Critical and Illustrative Notes' (2nd edit. 1897; appendix, 1900). This work was authoritatively pronounced to be 'the most important contribution to these studies made by any Christian scholar since the time of Buxtorf' (J. H. A. HART, in the *Eagle*, xxx. 71).

From 1870 to 1878 he was an energetic and indefatigable mountaineer, in spite of his bulky physique. He wrote for the 'Alpine Journal' (vi. 232–43) a record of a notable ascent of Monte Rosa from Macugnaga in 1872 (see also T. G. BONNEY, in the *Eagle*, xxx. 73–77). He was a member of the Alpine Club from 1873 till death.

In 1877–8, during the Cambridge University commission, Taylor took an active part in the discussions on the revision of the statutes of the college. In 1879 he was chosen, with the Master (Dr. Bateson) and Mr. Bonney, one of three commissioners to represent the college in conferring with the university commission. Before the new statutes came into force the Master (Bateson) died, on 27 March 1881, and on 12 April Taylor was chosen as his successor. On 14 June he was presented by the public orator for the complete degree of D.D. *jure dignitatis* (J. E. SANDYS' *Orationes et Epistolæ Academicæ*, p. 31). As Master, Taylor left details of administration to others, but he was not inactive. His college sermons, delivered in a quiet, level tone, with no rhetorical display, were marked by a solid grasp of fact and a patient elaboration of detail. His commemoration sermons of 1903 and 1907 mainly dealt with three college worthies, William Gilbert, Thomas Clarkson, and William Wilberforce (the *Eagle*, xxiv. 352 f.; xxviii. 279 f.).

While Master, Taylor published: 'The Teaching of the Twelve Apostles' (1886); 'An Essay on the Theology of the Didache' (1889); 'The Witness of Hermas to the Four Gospels' (1892); and 'The Oxyrhynchus Logia, and the Apocryphal Gospels' (1899).

Since November 1880 he had been a member of the council of the university. In the four years from 1885 to 1888 he presented the university with 200*l.* in each year, to be applied to the increase of the stipend of the reader in Talmudic. In 1886, as vice-chancellor elect, he represented the university at the commemoration of the 250th anniversary of the founding of Harvard, Cambridge, U.S.A., where he received an honorary degree on 8 Nov. From New Year's Day, 1887, to the corresponding date in 1889 he filled with dignity the office of vice-chancellor. On 18 July 1888 (*Orationes et Epistolæ Academicæ*, pp. 72–75) the vice-chancellor invited more than eighty bishops attending the Lambeth Conference, and nearly seventy other guests, to a memorable banquet in the hall of St. John's. At the end of the year he presented to the university his official stipend of 400*l.* as vice-chancellor for the year, and the money was spent in providing the nine statues which adorn the new buildings of the university library. Taylor was one of the two university aldermen first chosen in 1889 as members of the borough council; he held the office till 1895.

Among further proofs of his generous temper was his gift to the university library of the Taylor-Schechter collection of Hebrew MSS., which, by the energy of Dr. Schechter, the university reader in Talmudic, and by the generosity of Dr. Taylor, had been obtained from the Genizah of Old Cairo, with the consent of the heads of the local Jewish community (letters of thanks in *Orationes et Epistolæ Academicæ*, pp. 250 f.). Taylor and Dr. Schechter published in 1899, under the title of 'The Wisdom of Ben Sira,' portions of Ecclesiasticus from Hebrew MSS. in this collection. In 1907 Taylor presented to the library a fine copy of the 'Kandjur,' which 'at once secured for Cambridge a first place among the repositories of Buddhist texts.' In his own college, the Lady Margaret mission in Walworth, the first of the Cambridge College missions in south London, found in him a generous supporter; he provided the Lady Margaret Club with the site for its boat-house, and sent the boat to Henley; while his gifts to the general funds of the college were constant and lavish.

'He had an intense church feeling, without the slightest appearance of ecclesiasticism, . . . and his moderation, which was no part of a policy, but was natural to the man, was an invaluable quality in the head of a large college containing many varieties of religious opinion.' Though reserved and stiff in manner, he was endeared to his friends by 'his practical wisdom, sense of humour, detachment of view, and absolute freedom from petty enmities' (the *Eagle*, xxx. 78).

He died suddenly on 12 Aug. 1908, at the Goldner Adler, Nuremberg, while on a foreign tour. After a funeral service in the chapel of St. John's College his body was buried in St. Giles's cemetery on the Huntingdon Road, near Cambridge. He married on 19 Oct. 1907, at St. Luke's church, Chelsea, Margaret, daughter of the Hon. Conrad Dillon.

He is commemorated by a stained-glass window placed in the college chapel by his widow. A portrait by Charles Brock of Cambridge belongs to his widow. A bronze medallion by Miss Florence Newman was exhibited at the Royal Academy in 1909.

[Obit. notices in the Guardian, 20 Aug. 1908; and Cambridge Review, Oct. 1908; the Eagle, xxx. (1909), 34–85, 196–204 (with photographic portraits); Alpine Journal, Nov. 1908.] J. E. S.

TAYLOR, CHARLES BELL (1829–1909), ophthalmic surgeon, born at Nottingham on 2 Sept. 1829, was son of Charles Taylor by his wife Elizabeth Ann Galloway. His father and brother were veterinary surgeons in the town. After brief employment in the lace warehouse of his uncle, William Galloway, he apprenticed himself to Thomas Godfrey, a surgeon at Mansfield. He was admitted M.R.C.S.England in 1852, and a licentiate of the Society of Apothecaries in 1855. He graduated M.D. at the University of Edinburgh in 1854, and in 1867 he obtained the diploma of F.R.C.S.Edinburgh. In 1854 Taylor was pursuing his medical studies in Paris. He acted for some time as medical superintendent at the Walton Lodge Asylum, Liverpool, but in 1859 he returned to Nottingham, where he lived during the remainder of his life. In that year he joined the staff of the newly established Nottingham and Midland Eye Infirmary, and his attention was thus directed to a branch of the profession in which he gained renown.

A consummate and imperturbable operator, especially in cases of cataract, he soon enjoyed a practice that extended beyond Great Britain. He always operated by artificial light, held chloroform in abhorrence, never employed a qualified assistant, and had no high opinion of trained nurses.

Taylor died, unmarried, at Beechwood Hall, near Nottingham, on 14 April 1909, and was buried at the Nottingham general cemetery.

An uncompromising individualist, Taylor took a prominent, and professionally unpopular, part in securing the repeal of the Contagious Diseases Act; he was a determined opponent of vivisection and of compulsory vaccination. He held strong views on diet, was an abstainer not merely from alcohol and tobacco but even from tea and coffee, and took only two meals a day. Most of his estate of 160,000*l.* was distributed by will among the British Union for the Abolition of Vivisection; the London Anti-Vivisection Society; the British committee of the International Federation for the Abolition of the State Regulation of Vice; the National Anti-Vaccination League; and the Royal Society for the Prevention of Cruelty to Animals.

[Brit. Med. Journal, 1909, i. 1033; Ophthalmoscope, vol. ix. 1909, p. 376 (with portrait); Ophthalmic Review, xxviii. 133; The Times, 1 July 1909 some of his eccentricities are well described by Col. Anstruther Thomas, Master of the Pytchley, in his Eighty Years' Reminiscences; additional information kindly obtained by Mr. Charles Taylor, M.R.C.V.S., of Nottingham, his nephew.] D'A. P.

TAYLOR, HELEN (1831–1907), advocate of women's rights, born at Kent Terrace, London, on 27 July 1831, was only daughter and youngest of three children of John Taylor, wholesale druggist of Mark Lane, and his wife Harriet, daughter of Thomas Hardy of Birksgate, near Kirkburton, Yorkshire, where the family had been lords of the manor for centuries. Taylor, a man of education, early inspired his daughter with a lifelong love for history and strong filial affection. Helen's education was pursued desultorily and privately. She was the constant companion of her mother, who, owing to poor health, was continually travelling. Mrs. Taylor's letters to her daughter, shortly to be published, testify to deep sympathy between the two.

The father died in July 1849, and in April 1851 Helen's mother married John Stuart Mill [q. v.]. Mrs. Mill died on 3 Nov. 1858 at the Hôtel de l'Europe, Avignon, when on the way with her husband to the south of France. In order to be near his wife's grave Mill bought a house at Avignon, which subsequently passed to Miss Taylor. Miss Taylor now devoted herself entirely to Mill, and became his 'chief comfort.' She not only took entire charge of practical matters and of his heavy correspondence, answering many of his letters herself, but also co-operated in his literary work, especially in 'The Subjection of Women' (1869), much of which had already been suggested by her mother. Mill used to say of all his later work that it was the result not of one intelligence, but of three, of himself, his wife, and his step-daughter. Mill died in 1873. Miss Taylor, who had edited in 1872, with a biographical notice, the miscellaneous and posthumous works of H. T. Buckle, a devoted adherent of Mill's school of thought, edited in 1873 Mill's 'Autobiography'; and in 1874 she issued, with an introduction, his essays, 'Nature, The Utility of Religion, Theism.'

Mill's death left Miss Taylor free to enter public life and so further the social and political reforms in which her step-father had stirred her interest. Possessed of ample means, which she generously employed in public causes, she made her home in London, while spending her holidays at the house at Avignon which Mill left her. On all subjects her opinions were advancedly radical. Her principles were at once democratic and strongly individualist, but she favoured what she deemed practicable in the socialist programme. A fine speaker in public, she fought hard for the redress of poverty and injustice. Mill had refused, in 1870, through lack of time, the invitation of the Southwark Radical Association to become its candidate for the newly established London School Board. In 1876 Miss Taylor accepted a like request, and was returned at the head of the poll after a fierce conflict. Although a section of liberals opposed her on account of her advanced opinions, her eloquence and magnetic personality won the support of all shades of religious and political faith. She was again returned at the head of the poll both in 1879 and 1882. She retired in 1884 owing to ill-health. During her nine years' service she scarcely missed a meeting. Her educational programme included the abolition of school fees, the provision of food and shoes and stockings to necessitous children, the abolition of corporal punishment, smaller classes, and a larger expenditure on all things essential to the development of the child and the health of the teacher. While she was a member of the board, she provided at her own expense, through the teachers and small local committees, a midday meal and a pair of serviceable boots to necessitous children in Southwark. She was a prominent member of the endowment committee of the board, and was successful in inducing the charity commissioners to restore some educational endowments to their original purposes. A zealous advocate of the reform of the industrial schools, she brought to public notice in 1882 certain scandals imputed to St. Paul's Industrial School. The home secretary instituted an inquiry, and the school was ordered to be closed. In June 1882 Thomas Scrutton, a member of the school board and chairman of its industrial schools sub-committee, brought an action for libel against Miss Taylor. Sir Henry Hawkins was the judge, (Sir) Edward Clarke was Miss Taylor's counsel, (Sir) Charles Russell, afterwards Lord Russell of Killowen, was for the plaintiff. On the fourth day, 30 June, Miss Taylor's case broke down on the plea of justification, and Miss Taylor paid the plaintiff 1000*l*. by consent. The judge acknowledged Miss Taylor's public spirit and exonerated her from any personal malice (cf. *The Times*, 28, 29, 30 June, 1, 4 July 1882). Her action brought about a drastic reform of the London industrial schools.

At the same time Miss Taylor threw herself with equal energy into political agitation. She was active in opposition to the Irish coercion policy of the liberal government of 1880–5, and was one of the most energetic supporters of the English branch of the Irish Ladies' Land League, frequently presiding at its meetings both in England and Ireland. Anna Parnell was often her guest. The causes of land nationalisation and the taxation of land values powerfully appealed to her. She was a leading member of the Land Reform Union, and of the League for Taxing Land Values, addressing in their behalf large audiences, chiefly of working men, both in England and Ireland. Her enthusiasm for land nationalisation brought her the acquaintance of Henry George, the American promoter of the policy. He stayed at her house in South Kensington in 1882. In his opinion she was 'one of the most intelligent women I ever met, if not the most intelligent' (cf. HENRY GEORGE, JUNIOR *Life of Henry George*, 1900).

In 1881 Miss Helen Taylor's faith in the practicability of certain socialist proposals led her to take part in the preliminary meetings for the establishment of the Democratic Federation, the forerunner of the Social Democratic Federation. She joined the first executive committee. Already, in anticipation of the federation's aims, she had given practical support to labour candidates for parliament. She personally attended on George Odger [q. v.], the first labour candidate, during his last illness in 1877. Miss Taylor consistently advocated female suffrage, believing that it would improve the morals of the people. But on 15 Aug. 1878, writing from Avignon, she positively denied a rumour that she intended to seek nomination as a parliamentary candidate for Southwark. In 1885, however, special circumstances led her to essay a parliamentary candidature. Mr. W. A. Coote, the secretary of the Vigilance Association, with the objects of which Miss Taylor closely associated herself, sought nomination as liberal candidate for North Camberwell, but was finally set aside by the party organisers. By way of protest Miss Taylor took Mr. Coote's place. Her programme included just and better laws for women, the prevention of war, and 'less work and better pay' for the working classes. A letter of support from Henry George advocating her candidature was widely circulated during her campaign. George Jacob Holyoake [q. v. Suppl. II] was an active worker for her. She carried on her campaign amid much turbulence until the nomination day, when the returning officer refused to receive either the nomination papers or the cash deposit for his expenses. In her electoral contest Miss Taylor attempted what no woman had done before.

Soon afterwards she relinquished public work, owing to age and failing health, and retired for some nineteen years to her house at Avignon, where she had invariably spent her holidays and where she endeared herself to the people by her generous benefactions. Stress of work told on her appearance as well as on her health. Although she had been beautiful as a girl, she acquired in middle life an aspect of sternness. But in old age some of her youthful beauty reappeared. At the end of 1904 she returned to England, and under the care of her niece, Miss Mary Taylor, settled at Torquay. She died there on 29 Jan. 1907, and was buried in the Torquay cemetery.

The laconic words on her tombstone, 'She fought for the people,' well sum up her work. Outspoken in criticism, and an untiring fighter, she never spared her opponents, but her earnestness and sincerity gained her friends not only among liberals and radicals, but among tories and even clericals, though she was hostile to the church. The Irish Roman catholics who formed the larger part of her Southwark constituents regarded her with affection. She was an admirable popular speaker, was generous to all around her, and subscribed largely to the associations in which she was interested. At the instance of Lord Morley of Blackburn, Miss Taylor, in 1904, presented Mill's library to Somerville College, Oxford.

[The Times, 31 Jan. 1907; Justice, 2 Feb. 1907; Le Mistral, 6 Feb. 1907; J. S. Mill, Autobiography, 1873; Note on Mill's private life by Mary Taylor in Letters of J. S. Mill, ed. Hugh S. R. Elliot, 1910; private information.] E. L.

TAYLOR, ISAAC (1829–1901), archæologist and philologist, born on 2 May 1829 at Stanford Rivers, Essex, was eldest son and second child in the family of eight daughters and three sons of Isaac Taylor (1787–1865) [q. v.] by his wife Elizabeth (1804–1861), daughter of James Medland of Newington. His grandfather and great-grandfather were also named Isaac Taylor and were well known for literary or artistic talent [see Taylor, Isaac (1730–1807), and Taylor, Isaac (1759–1829)]. His aunts Ann and Jane Taylor and uncle Jefferys Taylor, writers for children, are likewise noticed in this Dictionary.

Isaac, brought up in an atmosphere of plain living and high thinking, was early accustomed to help his father in minor literary tasks. He was educated at private schools, and was from 1847 to 1849 at King's College, London. In 1849 he passed to Trinity College, Cambridge, where he carried off many college prizes, including the silver oration cup. He graduated B.A. in 1853 as nineteenth wrangler. On leaving Cambridge, he went as a master to Cheam school until 1857, when he proceeded M.A. and was ordained to the curacy of Trotterscliffe, Kent. He was curate of St. Mary Abbots, Kensington, in 1860–1, and of St. Mark's, North Audley Street, from 1861 to 1865, when he became vicar of St. Matthias, Bethnal Green.

The difficulties of serving a parish of 7000 people of the poorest class without funds or helpers were intensified by the outbreak of cholera in 1866. In 1867, at Highgate, Taylor preached a sermon on behalf of East London charities. It was published at the expense of one who heard it, under the title of 'The Burden of the Poor,' and made a deep impression throughout the country. The vivid account which Taylor gave of the conditions of the Spitalfields silk-weavers and child workers in and about his parish brought him subscriptions to the amount of over 4000*l*. But the strain of administration was severe, and an attack of typhoid fever finally compelled his retirement. In 1869 Bishop Jackson nominated him vicar of Holy Trinity, Twickenham, and in 1875 he was presented by Earl Brownlow to the living of Settrington, Yorkshire, which he held until his death. In 1885 he was made canon of York and prebend of Kirk Fenton.

Taylor's family tradition, which combined puritan piety with philosophic thought, drew him to the broad church party. A lover of controversy and of paradoxical statement through life, he roused much opposition in 1860 by a pamphlet, 'The Liturgy and the Dissenters,' in which he advocated the revision of the Prayer Book 'as an act of justice to the Dissenters.' In 1887 a paper on Islam, at the Wolverhampton Church Congress, in which he pleaded for a more tolerant comprehension of 'the second greatest religion in history,' excited indignation. He developed his views on Islam in 'Leaves from an Egyptian Note-book' (1888), and he did not conciliate his opponents by his stringent criticisms in the 'Fortnightly Review' (Nov. and Dec. 1888) on the methods of missionary societies. He was a member of the Curates' Clerical Club, or 'C.C.C.,' and counted among his friends in London F. D. Maurice, Dean Stanley, Farrar, Stopford Brooke (a fellow curate at Kensington), Haweis, and J. R. Green.

Taylor's chief interest lay in philological research, his pursuit of which gave him a wide reputation. In 1854 he produced an edition of Becker's 'Charicles.' In 1864 there followed 'Words and Places,' which went through several editions, and was adopted as a text-book for the Cambridge higher examination for women. The book was practically the first attempt in English to apply the results of German scientific philology to the derivation of local names. It was followed in 1867 by 'The Family Pen, Memorials of the Taylor Family of Ongar,' 2 vols. Later, a winter in Italy led him to study the remains of ancient Etruria, and in 1874 he published 'Etruscan Researches,' in which he propounded the now accepted theory that the Etruscan language was not Aryan, but was probably akin to the Altaic or agglutinative family of speech.

The problem of the origin of letters had always attracted him, and he recalled how, when learning the alphabet, he used to wonder why certain shapes should represent certain sounds. About 1875 he took up the subject in earnest, and in 1883 he published 'The Alphabet' (2 vols.; 2nd edit. 1899). He was one of the first to apply the principle of selection—in this case he called it the Law of Least Effort—to the evolution of written symbols, a discovery which led a critic to call him 'the Darwin of philology.' His scientific reputation rests mainly on this book, which, though now partially superseded by subsequent researches, remains a scholarly and exhaustive inquiry, set forth in admirably lucid English.

His studies of the alphabet led Taylor to the problem of the Runes, and his conclusion that they were derived from Greek sources he embodied in a separate volume, 'Greeks and Goths' (1879). In 1889 he wrote 'The Origin of the Aryans' for the 'Contemporary Science' series. It assailed the hitherto accepted theory of Max Müller as to a Central Asian cradle of the Aryans, and maintained that kinship of race cannot be postulated from kinship of speech. A French translation was published at Paris in 1895. Taylor took a prominent part in the Domesday celebration of 1886, and contributed three essays to the memorial volume (1888). Notes for a revised and enlarged version of 'Words and Places,' which his health disabled him from completing, appeared as an alphabetically arranged handbook of historical geography—'Names and their Histories' (1896; 2nd edit. 1897). He wrote many articles for the new edition of 'Chambers's Encyclopædia,' and was a frequent contributor to the 'Academy,' the 'Athenæum,' and 'Notes and Queries.' In 1879 the University of Edinburgh conferred on him the honorary degree of LL.D., and in 1885 he was made doctor of letters by his own University of Cambridge.

Taylor's versatile interests embraced the practice of photography and the study of botany, entomology, geology, and archæology. He was an original member of the Alpine Club, joining in 1858; he retired in 1891. He died on 18 Oct. 1901 at Settrington, Yorkshire, and was buried there. He married, on 31 July 1865, Georgiana Anne, daughter of Henry Cockayne Cust, canon of Windsor. His only child, Elizabeth Eleanor, married in 1903 Mr. Ernest Davies.

[Personal knowledge; The Biograph and Review, April 1881; Athenæum and Literature, 26 Oct. 1901; York Diocesan Mag., Dec. 1901.]

TAYLOR, JOHN EDWARD (1830–1905), art collector and newspaper proprietor, second son of John Edward Taylor [q. v.], founder of the 'Manchester Guardian,' was born at Woodland Terrace, Higher Broughton, on 2 Feb. 1830. He received a desultory education under Dr. Beard, the unitarian minister, at Higher Broughton, Dr. Heldermayer at Worksop, and Daniel Davies at Whitby, and at the University College School, London. In 1848–9 he went through some journalistic routine at Manchester and was for some months a student at the university of Bonn. He entered the Inner Temple on 25 Jan. 1850, and was called to the bar on 6 June 1853 (Foster, *Men at the Bar*, p. 459). His father's death in 1844, and that of his elder brother, Russell Scott Taylor, B.A., a young man of great promise, on 16 Sept. 1848, left him sole proprietor of the 'Manchester Guardian,' which in 1855 he transformed from a bi-weekly to a daily, and which he reduced in price from twopence to one penny. In the interval he made an effort—at first unsuccessful—to obtain independent reports of parliamentary proceedings, the provincial press being then and for some years afterwards entirely dependent on the often inadequate and inaccurate reports supplied by news agencies. After an agitation which lasted some years, and in which Taylor took a very prominent part, the Press Association was started in 1868 and obtained a footing in the gallery of the House of Commons (W. Hunt, *Then and Now*, pp. 11–12, 129, 132).

In 1868 he acquired the 'Manchester Evening News,' which had been started by Mitchell Henry [q. v. Suppl. II]; in 1874 he was, with Peter Rylands, an unsuccessful candidate in the liberal interest for S.E. Lancashire. An early supporter of Owens College, he was appointed one of its trustees in 1864, and a life governor in 1874. From 1854 till death he was a trustee of Manchester College, a unitarian college, which had been transferred to London in 1853, and thence to Oxford in 1889. He became a member of the Manchester Literary and Philosophical Society on 22 Jan. 1856. An ardent educationalist, he helped to found in 1863 the Manchester Education Aid Society. He advocated temperance and free trade, and was deeply interested in the British and Foreign Bible Society. A liberal contributor to party funds, he refused a baronetcy offered him by Lord Rosebery in 1895. At the time of his death he was head of the firm of Taylor, Garnett & Co., newspaper proprietors, senior partner of W. Evans & Co., proprietors of the 'Manchester Evening News,' and a director of the Buenos Ayres Great Southern Railway Co.

Taylor was best known to the public as a connoisseur. He was one of the guarantors of the Manchester Art Treasures Exhibition in 1857. For many years he collected pictures and objects of art, some few of which he lent to the Manchester Exhibition of 1887, to the old masters at Burlington House, and to the Burlington Fine Arts Club (of which he was a member). The sale of his collection in 1545 lots occupied twelve days at Christie's in July 1912, and realised 358,499*l.* 11*s.* 3*d.* (works of art, 231,937*l.* 13*s.*; pictures, 103,891*l.* 8*s.* 6*d.*; silver, 15,418*l.* 17*s.* 3*d.*; and engravings and books, 7251*l.* 12*s.* 6*d.*), a total only exceeded in this country by the Hamilton Palace sale in 1882 (*The Times*, 17 July; *Nineteenth Century*, August 1912).

Taylor presented a large number of pictures and drawings by modern English artists, notably twenty-four drawings by Turner, to the Manchester Whitworth Institute (official catalogue, 1909); in 1893 he was largely instrumental in raising funds for the purchase of a magnificent carpet from the mosque at Ardebil in Persia, for the Victoria and Albert Museum; and he gave a complete set of Turner's 'Liber Studiorum' to the British Museum.

Taylor lived for some time at Platt Cottage, Rusholme, and built The Towers, Didsbury, but never lived there. A few years after his marriage in 1861 he removed to London, and resided at 20 Kensington Palace Gardens. He died at Eastbourne on 5 Oct. 1905, and was buried at Kensal Green. The net value of his estate was provisionally sworn at 354,130*l.* He married in 1861 Martha Elizabeth, youngest daughter of R. W. Warner of Thetford. She continued to occupy Taylor's London house till her death on 10 May 1912. Many of Taylor's legacies then became payable, including 20,000*l.* to Owens College.

[Manchester Guardian, 6 Oct. 1905 and 24 July 1912; Manchester Courier, Westminster Gazette, and The Times, 6 Oct. 1905; Sell's Dictionary of the World's Press, 1906, pp. 58-60.] W. R.

TAYLOR, LOUISA (*d.* 1903), novelist. [See PARR, MRS. LOUISA.]

TAYLOR, WALTER ROSS (1838–1907), Scottish ecclesiastic, born 11 April 1838 in the manse of Thurso, was only son in a family of five children of Walter Ross Taylor, D.D., minister of the parish who at the disruption of the Church of Scotland in 1843 joined the Free Church and became moderator of its general assembly in 1884. Taylor's mother was Isabella, daughter of William Murray of Geannes, Ross-shire. Educated at the Free Church school at Thurso, he in 1853 entered Edinburgh University, where he won prizes in Greek and natural philosophy, the medal in moral philosophy, and the Stratton scholarship. Leaving without a degree, he entered the ministry of the Free Church, studying theology at New College, Edinburgh. In 1861 he was licensed to preach by the presbytery of Caithness. In the following year he became minister of the Free Church at East Kilbride, and in 1868 was translated to Kelvinside Free Church, Glasgow, where he ministered until his death.

Taylor played a leading part in denominational affairs. As convener of the sustentation fund (1890–1900) and joint-convener of the sustentation and augmentation funds (1900–7), he sought to raise ministerial stipends within his church to a minimum of 200*l.* A powerful advocate and practical organiser of the union of the Free and United Presbyterian Churches of 1900, he was elected, May 1900, moderator of the last general assembly of the Free Church, and in October he constituted the first general assembly of the United Free Church.

Taylor steadily favoured a conciliatory attitude towards those who were opposed to the union, and with Robert Rainy [q. v. Suppl. II] he shared the burden of the work connected with the crisis of 1904, when a judgment of the House of Lords handed over the whole property of the undivided Free Church to a small minority who resisted the union. At meetings throughout the country he eloquently defended the amalgamation, and was largely responsible for the passing of the Act of Parliament of 1905, which aimed at an equitable division of the property of the Free Church between the majority and the dissentient minority.

Taylor was made hon. D.D. of Glasgow University in 1891. He died, after a protracted illness, at his residence in Glasgow, on 6 Dec. 1907, and was buried in Glasgow necropolis three days later. In 1876 he married Margaret, daughter of Dr. Joshua Paterson, Glasgow, who survived him with three sons and two daughters. A full-length portrait of Taylor hangs in the United Free Church assembly buildings in Edinburgh. He published a volume of addresses, 'Religious Thought and Scottish Church Life in the Nineteenth Century' (Edinburgh, 1900).

[Glasgow Herald, 7 Dec. 1907; Scottish Review, 12 Dec. 1907; British Monthly, July 1904; Life of Principal Rainy, by P. C. Simpson, M.A., 1909, vol. ii.; private information.] W. F. G.

TEARLE, OSMOND (1852–1901), actor, whose full name was GEORGE OSMOND TEARLE, born at Plymouth on 8 March 1852, was son of George Tearle, colour-sergeant in the royal marines. After serving in the Crimean and China wars his father retired on pension to Liverpool. Educated there at St. Francis Xavier's College, Tearle took part in amateur theatricals, and in 1868 in 'penny readings' with Mr. T. Hall Caine. Inspired by Barry Sullivan's acting, he took to the stage, making his debut at the Adelphi Theatre, Liverpool, on 26 March 1869, as Guildenstern to Miss Adelaide Ross's Hamlet. In 1870, on Sullivan's recommendation, he became leading man at the Theatre Royal, Aberdeen. At Warrington in 1871 he appeared for the first time as Hamlet, a character which he played in all some 800 times. Early in 1874 he was a prominent and popular member of the Belfast stock company. After six years' stern provincial probation he made his first appearance in London at the Gaiety on 27 March 1875 as George de Buissy in Campbell Clarke's unsuccessful adaptation of 'Rose Michel,' subsequently playing there Charles Courtly in 'London Assurance.' Beginning on 17 May following, he acted 'Hamlet' at the Rotunda Theatre, Liverpool, for eighteen successive nights. Afterwards he toured with Mrs. John Wood's old comedy company as Charles Surface and Young Marlow.

At Darlington in 1877 Tearle started with his own travelling company. On 30 Sept. 1880 he made his American debut at Wallack's Theatre, New York, as Jaques in 'As You Like It,' and he remained there as leading actor of the stock company. After spending the summer of 1882 in England, he reappeared on 31 April 1883 at the Star Theatre, New York, as Hamlet, and subsequently toured in the United States as Wilfred Denver in 'The Silver King.' In 1888 he returned to England and organised his Shakespearean touring company. In 1889, and again in 1890, he conducted the festival performances at Stratford-on-Avon, producing in the first year 'Julius Cæsar' and 'King Henry VI,' pt. i. (in which he acted Talbot), and in the second year 'King John' and 'The Two Gentlemen of Verona.' His travelling company changed its bill nightly, and had a repertory of thirteen plays. It was deemed an excellent training ground for the stage novice. Tearle last appeared in London at Terry's Theatre on 4 July 1898 as Charles Surface to Kate Vaughan's Lady Teazle. His last appearance on the stage was at Carlisle on 30 Aug. 1901, as Richelieu. He died on 7 Sept. following at Byker, Newcastle-on-Tyne, and was buried beside his second wife at Whitley Bay, Northumberland.

As a Shakespearean actor Tearle combined the incisive elocution of the old school and the naturalness of the new. A man of commanding physique and dignified presence, he was well equipped for heroic parts. In later life he subdued his declamatory vigour, and played Othello and King Lear with power and restraint. He gained no foothold in London, but in America and the English provinces he won a high reputation.

Tearle was twice married: (1) to Mary Alice Rowe, an actress, who divorced him; and (2) in 1883 to Marianne Levy, widow and actress, daughter of F. B. Conway, the New York manager, and granddaughter of William Augustus Conway, the tragedian [q. v.]. His second wife died on 9 Oct. 1896. His three sons, one by his first wife and two by his second, took to the stage. An only daughter by his first wife did not join the profession.

[Pascoe's Dramatic List; R. M. Sillard's Barry Sullivan and his Contemporaries; R. J. Broadbent's Annals of the Liverpool Stage; Col. T. Allston Brown's History of the New York Theatres; J. A. Hammerton's The Actor's Art; The Stage, 12 Sept. 1901; The Era, 14 Sept. 1901; private information.] W. J. L.

TEMPLE, FREDERICK (1821–1902), archbishop of Canterbury, born 30 Nov. 1821, at Santa Maura, was son of Octavius Temple (*d.* 1834), major in 4th foot, subinspector of militia in the Ionian Islands, and resident at Santa Maura. William Johnstone Temple [q. v.] was his grandfather. Archbishop Temple claimed to belong to the Stowe branch of the Temple family, of which Richard Grenville, third duke of Buckingham and Chandos [q. v.], was the head. Temple's mother was Dorcas, daughter of Richard Carveth, of Probus, Cornwall, who traced his descent through the Le Despensers to Guy de Beauchamp, second earl of Warwick.

Temple was thirteenth and youngest survivor of fifteen children, seven of whom died young. On the death of his father, on 13 Aug. 1834, at Sierra Leone, where he was made governor the year before, the mother resided with her eight children at Culmstock, Devonshire. In narrow circumstances, she herself educated her boys until the time of their going to school, and thus exercised an unusual influence over all her children, especially the youngest, who never forgot his debt to her for his early training, and as soon as he had a home to offer, he shared it with her until her death at Rugby, 8 May 1866. On 29 Jan. 1834 he entered Blundell's School, Tiverton, and remained there till 5 March 1839. From the first he gave proof of great ability and industry. In half a year he passed through the lower to the upper school, two years being the usual period required. In 1838 he won the Blundell scholarship, and entered Balliol College, Oxford, 9 April 1839, an anonymous gift of 50*l.* enabling him to avail himself of the scholarship. Throughout his undergraduate days he practised of necessity the strictest economy. He came up to Oxford a first-rate mathematician, but during the three years following he so much improved his smaller stock of classics that he was 'proxime accessit' for the Ireland university scholarship in March 1842. In May 1842 he obtained without the help of any private tuition (owing to the kindness of his tutors) a double first class in classics and mathematics. He had the great advantage of having as his tutors men of real distinction, such as Scott, joint author with Liddell of the Greek lexicon; Tait, afterwards archbishop of Canterbury, to whose friendship and wisdom he owed much; Jowett, who was only four years his senior, and became one of his most intimate friends; and W. G. Ward, who was his mathematical tutor. Among his friends and contemporaries were A. H. Clough, A. P. Stanley, J. D. (afterwards Lord) Coleridge, Matthew Arnold, and Lingen (afterwards Lord Lingen). He was much attracted by the deep religious tone of Newman and Pusey, and though naturally much interested in the theological discussions arising out of the publication of the 'Tracts for the Times' and the 'Ideal of a Christian Church,' he was never carried away by them. He came up to Oxford a tory, and so remained while he was an undergraduate. But Oxford enlarged his outlook, and his views gradually settled into the liberalism which characterised him through life. When W. G. Ward's case came before convocation at Oxford, Temple voted in the minority against the censure and also against his degradation; and later, in 1847, he gave his name to the memorial against Bishop Hampden's condemnation. In November 1842 he was appointed lecturer, and was afterwards elected fellow of Balliol, and in 1845 junior dean of his college. He was ordained deacon in 1846, and in 1847 priest, by Bishop Wilberforce of Oxford.

When Tait left Balliol for Rugby in 1842, he had vainly offered Temple a mastership there. Temple then felt that his first duty was to his college, but in the spring of 1848 he left Oxford to undertake work under the committee of education, first as examiner in the education office at Whitehall to the end of 1849, then as principal of Kneller Hall, Twickenham, a training college for workhouse schoolmasters. In 1855, when Kneller Hall was closed, Temple was made inspector of training colleges for men. For some years previously he had been looked upon as an authority on educational matters. He was invited by the Oxford University Commission of 1850 to give evidence in writing, and he proposed several reforms, which were afterwards carried into effect. To 'Oxford Essays' of 1856 he contributed an essay on 'National Education,' and in 1857, in conjunction with (Sir) Thomas Dyke Acland [q. v. Suppl. I], he was mainly instrumental in persuading the University of Oxford to institute the associate-in-arts examination, which later developed into the Oxford and Cambridge local examinations.

On 12 Nov. 1857 he was appointed headmaster of Rugby School. His success there was undoubted. He exercised influence both on masters and boys, as a stimulating intellectual teacher, and as an earnest religious man. Some necessary reforms, which he introduced, were to increase the staff, to enlarge and systematise the teaching of history, to make the English language and literature a 'form' subject throughout the school, and to introduce natural science, music, and drawing into the regular curriculum. Before he left, he had obtained money for the building of a new quadrangle, containing a music school and drawing school, two science lecture-rooms, and six good classical class-rooms. The chapel was also enlarged to meet the increased numbers. While headmaster of Rugby, he gave evidence, in 1860, before the Popular Education Commission, of which the duke of Newcastle was chairman, and when a new commission was appointed in December 1864 to inquire into the schools which had not been the subject of inquiry under either the Popular

Education Commission, or the Public Schools Commission, Temple became a member of it, and was a leading spirit. Their report was issued in 1868; chapter ii. on the kinds of education desirable, and chapter vii., containing the recommendations of the commissioners, were written by him. These chapters, together with his Oxford essay, give Temple's mature views on secondary education.

In July 1869 Gladstone offered him the deanery of Durham. This was refused, but in September of the same year he was offered the see of Exeter, which he accepted. His appointment raised a storm of opposition on the ground that he had been a contributor to the notorious 'Essays and Reviews' (1860; 12th edit. 1865). His contribution, 'The Education of the World,' was little open to exception, but he had associated himself with writers two of whom were tried and condemned, the one, Rowland Williams [q. v.], for denying the inspiration of scripture, the other, Henry Bristow Wilson [q. v.], for denying the doctrine of the eternity of punishment; both sentences, however, were on appeal reversed by the privy council. The book had also been censured by the convocation of Canterbury. The earl of Shaftesbury and Dr. Pusey united to oppose his consecration, and it was doubtful beforehand whether the dean and chapter of Exeter would act on the *congé d'élire*. Ultimately, of the twenty-three members entitled to vote, thirteen were in favour, six against, and four were absent. When the confirmation took place in Bow church, two of the beneficed clergy of the diocese appeared in opposition. Urged on many sides by friends and opponents to make some declaration as to his orthodoxy, he refused, with characteristic firmness, to break silence till after his consecration, which took place on St. Thomas' Day in Westminster Abbey. The consecrating bishops were the bishops of London (Jackson), acting for Archbishop Tait, who was ill, St. David's (Thirlwall), and Ely (Browne). After his consecration he withdrew his essay from future editions of 'Essays and Reviews.' To quote the words of Lightfoot, 'he was courageous in refusing to withdraw his name when it was clamorously demanded, and not less courageous in withdrawing it when the withdrawal would expose him to the criticism of his advanced friends.'

In his change from youthful toryism to liberalism two main ideas possessed his mind: first, the need of raising the condition of the working classes, and secondly, the conviction that their amelioration could only be effected by enabling them to help themselves. A strong advocate of educational reform, he was also a social reformer, as evidenced, among other things, by his strong and persistent advocacy of temperance; but all his experience strengthened his conviction that neither education nor temperance could have its perfect work apart from religion. As bishop of Exeter he had an early opportunity of putting his views into practice.

Forster's Education Act was passed in 1870. It was necessary for church people to improve and add to their schools, and at a meeting at Exeter, by his words and his example in subscribing 500*l*., he induced the diocese to raise a large sum for the purpose. It was also necessary to deal with schools of higher rank in the diocese of Exeter. His letter to the mayor on the endowed schools commissioners' proposals carried such weight that the main points for which he contended were eventually adopted. They embodied a system of exhibitions, furnishing a ladder by which the poorest child might rise from the elementary to the highest class of school and so to the university, and the establishment of two good schools for the secondary education of girls. In short, as stated by a member of a subsequent royal commission thirty years later, 'there are more boys and girls per thousand of population receiving secondary education in Exeter than in any other city in this country, due in no small measure to the improvements carried out largely under Dr. Temple.' The same might be said in its degree of Plymouth, where he was instrumental in founding secondary schools.

At Rugby he had already taken part in the temperance movement, which had come into prominence partly owing to the report of the committee of convocation of Canterbury in 1869. When as bishop he took the chair in Exeter in 1872 at a meeting of the United Kingdom Alliance, the proceedings were so unruly as to require the intervention of the police, and a bag of flour aimed at the bishop struck him full in the chest. In a short time, however, he was always enthusiastically received, whenever he addressed public meetings (as he frequently did) on the subject. 'He was so much impressed,' he once said, 'with the importance of the movement, that he felt at times he could wish to divest himself of other duties and devote himself entirely to it.'

Notwithstanding the huge extent of a

diocese comprising Devon and Cornwall, he visited most of the parishes, in many of which a bishop had not been seen for long, but he early felt the need of the division of the diocese. The donation by Lady Rolle in 1875 of 40,000*l*. gave a great impetus to the scheme, and in 1876 a bill to create the diocese of Truro was passed [see BENSON, EDWARD WHITE, Suppl. I].

In 1874 he was petitioned by the chancellor of the diocese to inquire into the legality of the erection of a new reredos in the cathedral. As visitor and ordinary he gave sentence for its removal. The dean of arches reversed this judgment, but the privy council on appeal reversed the judgment of the court of arches, in so far as it limited the bishop's visitatorial jurisdiction over the cathedral, but maintained it on two points, viz. the non-requirement of a faculty and the legality of the figures. When a similar question was raised in regard to the reredos in St. Paul's, April 1888, by the Church Association, circumstances had changed. The privy council had ruled there was nothing illegal in the figures, and the legislature had granted to the bishops discretionary power to stop proceedings. Accordingly, as bishop of London he refused to allow the case to proceed. His speeches while bishop of Exeter, in the House of Lords on the university tests bill (1870) and the bill for opening churchyards to nonconformists (1880), showed him true to his liberal principles. While bishop of Exeter he became a member of the governing body of Rugby School, and for the last ten years of his life was its chairman. He was also governor of Sherborne School. In 1884 he delivered at Oxford the Bampton lectures, on 'the relation between religion and science.' Among his hearers on one occasion were Matthew Arnold and Robert Browning; many younger men who heard him never forgot the impression which he made, partly by his vigorous arguments and still more by his native strength, simplicity, and sincerity.

On 25 Feb. 1885 he was called to the see of London. A public meeting in the Guildhall at Exeter and the testimonials that emanated from it proved how entirely the bishop had won his way. The clergy of the diocese, who had protested against his election in 1869, almost unanimously signed a memorial of regret at his departure. He was enthroned in St. Paul's in April 1885. He threw himself with his accustomed vigour into the work of the diocese and into all the great social questions of the day. In accordance with his views on self-government he introduced the plan of allowing the clergy to elect their own rural deans. Besides delivering his episcopal charges, he gave addresses in turn at the several ruridecanal chapters. He took such subjects as 'relation of the church to the poor in London,' 'the growth of scepticism and indifference,' and in 1892 he dealt with the archbishop's judgment in the bishop of Lincoln's case. On this case, with four other bishops, he had been assessor to Archbishop Benson [q. v. Suppl. I]. In 1887 it was mainly due to his energy and advocacy that the church's memorial of Queen Victoria's jubilee took the permanent form of the Church House now in Dean's Yard, Westminster. The Pluralities Act amendment bill was carried through the House of Lords by the bishop, and became an Act of Parliament in 1885. The Clergy Discipline Act passed in 1892 owed much to his efforts. In 1888 he was a member of the royal commission on education presided over by Lord Cross, and never missed a sitting. In the summer of 1889 he tendered evidence of great value before a commission presided over by Lord Selborne with reference to a teaching university for London, and before the secondary education commission of 1894, of which Mr. James Bryce was chairman. While bishop of London, he gave land to enlarge Bishop's Park, Fulham, which was opened by the chairman of the London county council on 2 Dec. 1893. Later, when archbishop of Canterbury, he handed over a field adjoining Lambeth Palace for a recreation ground. This was put in order by the London county council and opened on 24 Oct. 1901.

At the time of the dockers' strike in the autumn of 1889 the bishop of London's return to town from his holiday led the lord mayor to intervene and form the conciliation committee by means of which an arrangement was ultimately reached.

At the request of senator G. F. Hall of Massachusetts, backed by the principal Antiquarian Societies of America, the bishop had agreed to hand over to U.S.A. the 'Bradford MS.,' incorrectly termed the 'Log of the Mayflower,' then in the library of Fulham Palace. Bishop Creighton carried out the wish of his predecessor by delivering the MS. to the American ambassador on 29 May 1897.

In October 1896 he was nominated by Lord Salisbury to the archbishopric of Canterbury. A meeting took place at the Guildhall on 18 Jan. 1897 to commemorate his London episcopate, when the lord mayor and corporation of the City of London attended in state and at least 1500 persons were present, and many presentations were made to the archbishop. The 'Morning Post' stated that 'the history of church work in London since Dr. Temple entered upon the diocese has scarcely a parallel in the history of church work during the century.' He was enthroned in Canterbury Cathedral in 1897. With the consent of the ecclesiastical commissioners he sold Addington Park, the country residence of the archbishops since its purchase by Archbishop Manners Sutton, and with part of the proceeds of the sale he bought a house in the precincts at Canterbury known as the Old Palace, which he converted into a suitable residence. On 21 June 1897 the archbishop attended in state the great service in St. Paul's to commemorate the sixtieth year of Queen Victoria's reign, and on the following Tuesday he was the principal figure on the steps of St. Paul's, when Her Majesty made her progress through the city. Immediately after he presided at the fourth Lambeth Conference of bishops of the Anglican communion. On 3 July he received in Canterbury Cathedral the members of the conference at an inaugural service, and delivered an address from the chair of Augustine. The summary of the resolutions arrived at by the conference, called the encyclical letter, was drafted in the course of a night entirely by himself, and with but slight exceptions it was adopted by the conference and published. In 1898, at the invitation of Dr. James Paton, convener of the committee on temperance of the Church of Scotland, the archbishop paid a visit to the general assembly, and delivered an address chiefly on temperance. He visited Scotland a second time in 1902 at the request of Bishop Wilkinson for the dedication of the chapter house added to St. Ninian's Cathedral, Perth, in memory of Bishop Charles Wordsworth. During the six years of his archbishopric he made two visitations of his diocese. In his first charge in 1898 he dealt with the questions of 'the doctrine of the eucharist,' 'improper objects of worship,' and 'prayers for the dead.' The second charge was entirely devoted to the education bill of 1902.

In 1899 the lawfulness of the use of incense and of processional lights was referred to the archbishops of the two provinces for judgment. The 'hearing' took place at Lambeth on 8, 9, and 10 May, and their decision was delivered by Temple at Lambeth, 31 July 1899. They decided that the two practices were neither enjoined nor permitted by the law of the Church of England. A third question, viz. the reservation of the Blessed Sacrament, referring only to the southern province, was brought before the archbishop of Canterbury alone, and he decided that the Church of England does not at present allow reservation in any form.

Temple, who had been made hon. LL.D. of Cambridge on 20 Jan. 1897, received the honorary freedom of the city of Exeter on 22 Jan. 1897, and of the borough of Tiverton on 3 Oct. 1900. In January 1901 he officiated at the funeral of Queen Victoria in St. George's Chapel, Windsor. He crowned King Edward VII in Westminster Abbey on 9 Aug. 1902, and received the collar of the Victorian order.

He spoke for the last time in the House of Lords on 4 Dec. 1902, when Mr. Balfour's education bill came up for the second reading. Earl Spencer, as the leader of the opposition, spoke against the bill, and the archbishop followed in its favour, but before he had completed his speech he was seized with illness and had to leave the house.

He died at Lambeth Palace on 22 Dec. 1902, and was buried in the cloister of Canterbury Cathedral.

Great as was the work which Archbishop Temple was able to accomplish owing to his unusual vigour of mind and body, the man was greater even than his work. He had a rugged force of character and a simplicity which distinguished him from his most able contemporaries. No one ever less 'beat about the bush': he went straight to his point with a directness which sometimes earned for him the reputation of brusqueness, or even of want of consideration for other people's feelings. This, however, was a superficial view of his character, as those who worked with him and knew him well soon came to acknowledge. With his strength he combined a tenderness of feeling and warmth of affection which not unfrequently were noticeable, in spite of himself, in his public utterances. His devotion to his mother, who lived with him till the day of her death, and to whose opinion he always reverently deferred, was a marked trait in his character. As a preacher, he was not eloquent in the usual sense of the word; any tricks of oratory were utterly alien to his nature, but his sermons in Rugby School chapel (of which three volumes were published) are eloquent from their force and terseness, their earnestness and genuine feeling. The effect of them on the boys was, by the testimony of many men of mark, both masters and pupils, far-reaching and abiding. As a speaker he carried weight by his evident sincerity as well as by his vigorous language. In the latter part of his life he spoke most frequently on foreign missions, temperance, and the education controversy. On these subjects the fire of his younger days never died away,

He married, on 24 Aug. 1876, Beatrice Blanche, fifth daughter of William Saunders Sebright Lascelles and Lady Caroline Georgiana Howard, daughter of George sixth Earl of Carlisle. He had two sons, Frederick Charles, born in 1879, appointed in 1908 district engineer under Indian government; William, born in 1881, fellow and tutor of Queen's College, Oxford, 1908–1910, headmaster of Repton School, 1910.

A portrait by G. F. Watts is at Rugby, another by Prynne is in the Palace at Exeter, a third by Sir Hubert von Herkomer, R.A., is at Fulham Palace; of the last, replicas are at Lambeth Palace and in possession of Mrs. Temple, and the picture was engraved by the artist. A bust by Woolner is at Rugby in the Temple reading-room; a medallion by Brock in the chapel, Rugby; and a bust by Frampton at Sherborne School, with a replica in bronze in the Temple speech-room, Rugby. A monument by F. W. Pomeroy was erected in St. Paul's Cathedral in 1903. The new speech-room at Rugby, mainly a memorial to Archbishop Temple, was opened by King Edward VII in 1909. Cartoon portraits appeared in 'Vanity Fair' in 1869 and 1902 (by 'Spy').

Temple's chief published works were: 1. 'Sermons preached in Rugby School Chapel,' three series, the first 'in 1858–9–60' (1861; 3rd ed. 1870); the second 'in 1862–7' (1871; reprinted 1872, 1876); the third 'in 1867–9' (1871; reprinted 1873, 1886). 2. 'Quiet Growth, a Sermon preached in Clifton College Chapel, Sunday, 16 June 1867.' 3. 'The Three Spiritual Revelations, a Sermon preached in the Cathedral Church of Exeter on Wednesday, 29 Dec. 1869, by Frederick, Lord Bishop of the Diocese, on that Day enthroned,' 1870. 4. 'Episcopal Charges, Exeter,' 1883, 1884. 5. 'The Relations between Religion and Science,' eight Bampton lectures, 1884; reprinted 1885, 1903. 6. Charge delivered at his First Visitation, Canterbury, 1898. 7. 'On the Reservation of the Sacrament, Lambeth Palace, 1 May 1900.' 8. 'Five of the Latest Utterances of Frederick Temple, Archbishop of Canterbury,' 1903.

[Memoirs of Archbishop Temple by Seven Friends, edited by E. G. Sandford, Archbishop of Exeter, 2 vols. 1906; A. C. Benson, Life of Edward White Benson, 1899; Mrs. Creighton, Life of Mandell Creighton, 1904; L. Campbell and E. Abbott, Life of Benjamin Jowett, 1897.] H. M. S.

TEMPLE, Sir RICHARD, first baronet (1826–1902), Anglo-Indian administrator, born at Kempsey, near Worcester, on 8 March 1826, was elder son of the six children of Richard Temple (1800–1874) of the Nash, Worcestershire, a country squire, by his first wife Louisa (*d.* 1837), youngest daughter of James Rivett Carnac, governor of Bombay, and sister of Sir James Rivett Carnac [q. v.]. From a private school at Wick near his home Temple proceeded to Rugby under Thomas Arnold in August 1839. His contemporaries included the headmaster's son, William Delafield Arnold [q. v.] (1828–1859), Lord Stanley, afterwards the fifteenth earl of Derby [q. v.], M. W. D. Waddington, subsequently prime minister of France, and John Conington [q. v.]. In 1844 his education at Rugby was cut short by the offer and acceptance of a writership in the East India Co.'s service. Passing out head of Haileybury College, he reached Calcutta in January 1847.

Transferred to the North West Provinces, he was sent to Muttra and thence to Allahabad, where he gained some experience of settlement work, and came under the favourable notice of the lieutenant-governor, James Thomason [q. v.]. On 27 Dec. 1849 he married the sister-in-law of his collector, Charlotte Frances, daughter of Benjamin Martindale. History was then in the making in the adjoining province of the Punjab, and he secured in 1851 a second transfer to that newly annexed province in which, under the immediate eye of Lord Dalhousie [q. v.], the board, including the brothers Henry and John Lawrence [q. v.], was reducing chaos to order and establishing a settled government. From 1851 Temple laboured as the disciple, the assistant, and the official reporter of the views and work of John Lawrence, who was appointed chief commissioner in February 1853, unfettered by any colleagues. At first Temple was entrusted with settlement work, and at the close of the period he had executive charge of a division as commissioner. But the appointments which enabled him to assimilate the unrivalled experiences of Lawrence, and win his patronage, were those of special assistant to the board

(1852–3), and then secretary to the chief commissioner from July 1854. The historic reports on Punjab administration were penned by him, and Lord Dalhousie so appreciated his strenuous activities that, when it was proposed in 1853 to take Temple into the government of India's secretariat from Lahore, he remarked that 'it would be setting an elephant to draw a wheelbarrow.' So Temple worked on, until the death of his first wife in 1855 and the strain of public duties compelled him to take furlough in the following year. Everything seemed quiet, and there was 'not the faintest sound of warning, not the slightest breath of suspicion regarding the storm about to burst' (TEMPLE'S *Story of My Life*, i. 78). When he returned at the end of 1857, it was the 'White mutiny,' and not the rebel Sepoys, with which he was confronted as commissioner.

Soon after his return to duty an unexpected opportunity of gaining a new experience presented itself. In November 1859, when James Wilson [q. v.], the finance minister, was sent out to inaugurate a new system of financial administration, Temple accepted Wilson's invitation to aid him, and remained with him until Wilson's untimely death, 11 Aug. 1860. The assistant not only profited by his master's experience, but by this appointment he became known to Lord Canning [q.v.], who deputed Temple to visit and confer with the authorities in Burma and Hyderabad. On 25 April 1862 he was promoted to act as chief commissioner of the central provinces, in which post with some brief interludes he remained until April 1867. This was Temple's first independent essay in the responsibilities of high administration. Everything was new to him in the province, but by persistent inquiry and verification he acquired local knowledge, and visited every part of his large charge. He poured out a stream of comprehensive reports, which attracted notice at Calcutta, and indulged to his heart's content his favourite relaxation of sketching and painting in water-colours. The district entrusted to him had only lately, 11 Dec. 1861, been constituted into a chief commissioner's province, and the foundation of its future administration had to be laid. The American civil war, fortunately for all parties, created a brisk demand for cotton and other agricultural produce, which benefited the rural population. An education department was organised, and more than a thousand schools brought under it. From 1863 the cadastral survey of village lands was pushed on, and long-term settlements of revenue for thirty years in thirteen of the districts were introduced. Lease-holding tenants were converted into freehold proprietors. A municipality was established in Nagpur in 1864, leading the way for smaller bodies elsewhere. District local boards were created, but in all cases under the fostering and necessary care of officials. Eighteen dispensaries broke the ground for the hospitals which his successors were to build. His Punjab experience had taught him the value of picked subordinates, and no chief commissioner was ever served by better assistants than Alfred Lyall, Charles Elliott, and Charles Bernard. The connection at length established with Bombay by the Great Indian Peninsula railway system in 1867 enabled Temple to leave Nagpur in full confidence to his successor, upon whom frowning times of famine were to fall. The belated honour of C.S.I. was conferred upon him in 1866, and he was made K.C.S.I. next year.

A brief interval was filled up by short appointments as resident at Hyderabad, 5 April 1867, where the relations between the Nizam and his able minister, Sir Salar Jung, were strained, and then as foreign secretary to the government of India. In April 1868, on the resignation of William Nathaniel Massey [q. v.], Temple became financial member of council and undertook the financial business of the supreme government. From 1868 to 1874 he thus served first as a colleague of his old chief, Sir John Lawrence, then throughout the administration of Lord Mayo, 1869–72, and for a time with Lord Northbrook. The shock given by the Mutiny to the credit of India had not been spent, and the needs of administrative progress were increasing. Naturally, therefore, the period was one of experiment, sometimes premature, and of recourse to unpopular measures to maintain solvency. In 1867 a tax on profits from professional trades and offices had been imposed, being followed in 1868 by the certificate tax, assessed at a lower rate but more productive. In 1869 came the income tax with a duty of one per cent. on companies and a sliding scale on private incomes. In November the rates were increased, and the zeal of collectors stimulated. Much indignation was expressed, and for the next two years the rates were restored to a point below that of 1869, the limit of exemption being also raised. Temple showed firmness in a critical time, and preserved the direct tax, while in the management of provincial assignments and in discussions about a gold standard and state insurance he left valuable suggestions for his successors. During his tenure of the office of financial member he married on 28 Jan. 1871 his second wife, Mary Augusta, daughter of Charles R. Lindsay of the chief court in the Punjab, a lady of great personal attractions and intellectual gifts.

From charge of the finances of India, Temple was sent in January 1874 to conduct the campaign against famine in Behar which embarrassed and almost overtaxed the powers of the government of Bengal. He averted a catastrophe by his personal energy in providing transport and supplying food for the famished, but his expenditure was on too liberal a scale—a mistake which he avoided in later years. Having performed this task, he was lieutenant-governor of Bengal from 9 April 1874 to 8 Jan. 1877. His term of office was uneventful, but his literary and administrative activity was proved by the minutes which he penned and printed. He was made a baronet in 1876, and at the close of the year, owing to the grave anxiety felt by Lord Lytton [q. v.] in regard to the severe famine prevailing in southern India, he was appointed special commissioner to inspect and suggest measures of relief to the governments concerned. Although the scale of expenditure was less lavish than in Bengal, the operations entailed an expenditure and a remission of taxes aggregating eleven millions sterling. Having completed his task, Temple proceeded to Bombay and took over charge of the government from Sir Philip Wodehouse [q. v. Suppl. I] on 30 April 1877. He was promoted G.C.S.I., and was created C.I.E. when that order was instituted on 1 Jan. 1878.

At Bombay he was assisted in the government by a council of three members, and, as he admitted, he found a progressive administration in excellent order. But there was work to be done for which a single head was needed, and Temple provided the driving power. The despatch of Indian troops to Malta in 1878, and the Afghan war which followed, 1878–80, involving the employment of 65,000 British and 135,000 native troops, required strenuous exertions. Sailing ships had to be adapted for the work of transports, and stores despatched in the former case, while in the latter the Kandahar force was supplied from Bombay, and the railway aligned and constructed after careful inspection of various routes. Temple was equal to the occasion, and received the thanks of government. On the civil administration he left his mark not only by improving the port of Bombay but also by extensive, indeed almost excessive, additions to the forest area. His frequent tours and conferences with the local officials soon made him familiar with the special conditions of the presidency. But his thoughts had constantly of late been turned towards England, and calculating on the probable fall of Lord Beaconsfield's government he, without awaiting the arrival of his successor, Sir James Fergusson [q. v.], hurried home on 13 March 1880, to stand for parliament. Disappointment awaited him. Contesting East Worcestershire in the conservative interest, he was defeated. Thereupon he took to literature, producing 'India in 1880,' of which a third edition was published in 1881, 'a vivid picture of the condition of India as he left it' (*Quarterly Review*, No. 303). This was followed by 'Men and Events of My Time' (1882) and several contributions to reviews and magazines, some of which were republished in 'Oriental Experience' (1883) and others as 'Cosmopolitan Essays' (1886). He gratified his insatiable desire for travel and his taste for painting by the publication of 'Palestine Illustrated' (1888), and performed a pious duty to his three chief patrons by writing monographs on 'James Thomason' (1893) for the Clarendon press series of Rulers of India, and 'John, Lord Lawrence' (1889) for Macmillan's 'English Men of Action,' and by delivering a panegyric on 'Bartle Frere' at the Mansion House (1884). The universities conferred upon him the hon. degrees of D.C.L., 1880 (Oxford), LL.D., 1883 (Cambridge), and LL.D., 1884 (M'Gill University, Montreal), when he visited Canada as president of the section of economic science and statistics of the British Association. But he longed for a more active part in affairs, and in 1884 he joined the London school board, of which he remained a member till 1894, serving as vice-chairman for four years and for many years as chairman of its finance committee. In 1885 he was returned as conservative member for Evesham, in which division of Worcestershire his own property lay. He sat for the constituency until 1892, when he was elected for the Kingston division of Surrey, which he represented until 1895. Although he knew more about India than any other member, he was heard with impatience by the House of Commons, and did not take there the place to which his abilities entitled him. On retiring from parliament he was sworn a member of the privy council on 8 Feb. 1896, an honour which led to his election in March following as a fellow of the Royal Society.

In 1896 he published 'The Story of My Life.' 'Character Sketches from the House of Commons 1886–7' appeared posthumously in 1912. He died at Heath Brow, Hampstead Heath, on 15 March 1902, and was buried at Kempsey on 19 March. His second wife, Lady Temple, C.I., survived him, with two sons by his first marriage, Colonel Richard Carnac Temple, C.I.E., formerly chief commissioner Andamans, who succeeded him in the baronetcy, and Colonel H. M. Temple, consul-general at Meshed, and one son by his second marriage. Temple's personal appearance was ungraceful and lent itself to caricature, which he accepted with characteristic good temper. A cartoon portrait by 'Spy' appeared in 'Vanity Fair' in 1881.

A statue of him, executed by Sir Thomas Brock was erected in Bombay, shortly after he left that presidency.

[Temple, Story of My Life, 1896, and his other books mentioned above; Proceedings of Royal Society, 1902, p. 115; Times, 18 March 1902; Official Administration Reports of India, Bengal, and Bombay; Sir Henry Cotton, Indian and Home Memories, 1911; Bosworth Smith, Life of Lord Lawrence, 1883, 2 vols.; Lee-Warner, Life of Marquis of Dalhousie, 1904; H. W. Lucy, Salisbury Parliament, 1892, and Balfourian Parliament, 1906.]

W. L-W.

TENNANT, Sir CHARLES, first baronet (1823–1906), merchant and art patron, born in Glasgow on 4 Nov. 1823, was elder of the two sons of John Tennant of St. Rollox, Glasgow. The family settled as tenant-farmers near Ayr in the fifteenth century, and descends in unbroken line from John Tennant of Blairston Mill, Maybole, who was born in 1635 (see Rogers's *Book of Robert Burns*, ii. 265). A later John Tennant (1725–1810) was appointed factor of the Ochiltree estate, belonging to the Countess of Glencairn, in 1769, when he settled at Glenconner in the parish of Ochiltree. He was the intimate friend of the father of Robert Burns, and was one of the first to recognise the poet's genius. In his 'Epistle to James Tennant,' second son of this John, the poet refers in detail to all the members of that family. Charles (1768–1838) [q.v.], fourth son of John (referred to by Burns as 'Wabster Charlie'), was the grandfather of Sir Charles, and was the founder of the chemical works at St. Rollox. His elder son, John Tennant (1796–1878), Sir Charles's father, succeeded to these works and developed the business extensively.

Charles Tennant was educated at the High School, Glasgow, and was trained commercially at St. Rollox works, after a brief experience at Liverpool. In 1846 he was admitted as a partner in the concern, and was soon known as an exceptionally enterprising and farseeing man of business. In 1900 the St. Rollox chemical works were combined with many similar works throughout the kingdom to form the United Alkali Co., of which Sir Charles became chairman. At the same time he resigned his control of St. Rollox to his two sons. From the outset Tennant also interested himself in other of his father's ventures, which included the Tharsis Sulphur and Copper Co. and the Steel Company of Scotland. He succeeded in transforming the Tharsis Co. into the British Metal Extracting Co. Subsequently he became chairman of the Union Bank of Scotland, and engaged in many further mercantile ventures of great importance. He was concerned in several of the most extensive gold-mining companies in India; he was director of the Assam Oil Co. and of the Assam Railways and Trading Co.; and he acquired interests in the Chicago Great Western Railway Co., Nobel's Explosives Co., and the British South Africa Explosives Co. His keen business instinct, which enabled him to accumulate vast wealth, helped to rescue some of these companies from impending disaster and to set them on the road to prosperity.

In 1854 Tennant purchased the mansion and estate of The Glen, in Traquair parish, Peeblesshire. Here he found ample scope for his taste for landscape-gardening, and he lived to witness the fruition of his arboricultural plans. He also developed artistic tastes, and gradually acquired a collection of notable pictures. He bought Millais's portrait of Gladstone (presented to the

National Portrait Gallery in 1898); a group of portraits by Sir Joshua Reynolds, including 'Lady Crosbie,' 'Collina' (Lady Gertrude Fitzpatrick), 'Sylvia' (Lady Anne Fitzpatrick), and 'The Fortune-teller' (portraits of Lord Henry and Lady Charlotte Spencer-Churchill); and he owned masterpieces of portraiture by Gainsborough and Romney. In 1894 Sir Charles was made a trustee of the National Gallery. His private collection, which descended to his eldest son, now known as the Tennant gallery, is housed at 34 Queen Anne's Gate, London, S.W., and is open to the public on Wednesdays and Saturdays.

Tennant was till near the close of his life a liberal in politics. He was elected for Glasgow at a bye-election in 1879, and at the general election in 1880 won Peebles and Selkirk from the conservative member, Sir Graham Graham Montgomery, by 32 votes. He retained the seat till 1886, when he was defeated by the liberal-unionist, Mr. Walter Thorburn, by 50 votes. In 1890 he unsuccessfully contested the Partick division of Lanarkshire against Mr. Parker Smith, and made no further attempt to enter the House of Commons, in which he played no prominent part. In July 1885, on Gladstone's recommendation, he was created a baronet. By 1904 his economic views had undergone a change, and he became in that year a member of Mr. Chamberlain's tariff reform commission. He died at Broad Oaks, Byfleet, Surrey, on 4 June 1906, and was buried in Traquair churchyard.

Tennant married twice: firstly, on 1 Aug. 1849, Emma (*d.* 1895), daughter of Richard Winsloe of Mount Nebo, Taunton, Somerset, by whom he had six sons and six daughters; his eldest surviving son, Edward Priaulx Tennant (*b.* 31 May 1859), succeeded to the baronetcy in 1906, and was raised to the peerage in 1911 as Baron Glenconner; the youngest son, Harold John Tennant, was elected M.P. for Berwickshire in 1895, and served in minor posts in the liberal administrations of Sir Henry Campbell-Bannerman and Mr. Asquith; Emma Alice Margaret, the youngest daughter, became in 1894 second wife of Mr. Asquith, prime minister from 1909. Sir Charles married secondly, in Nov. 1898, Marguerite, youngest daughter of Colonel Charles W. Miles of Burton Hill, Malmesbury, by whom he had four daughters.

A portrait in oils, painted by W. W. Ouless in 1900, and a bust by McAllum in 1870 are in the possession of Lord Glenconner at The Glen, Traquair.

[Scotsman, Glasgow Herald, and Dundee Advertiser, 5 June 1906; Blair's Sketches of Glasgow Necropolis, 1857; A Hundred Glasgow Men, 1886; Who's Who, 1905; Catalogue of Pictures in Tennant Gallery; private information.] A. H. M.

TENNANT, Sir DAVID (1829–1905), speaker of the House of Assembly of the Cape of Good Hope, born at Cape Town on 10 Jan. 1829, was the eldest son of Hercules Tennant, sometime civil commissioner and resident magistrate of Uitenhage and author of 'Tennant's Notary's Manual for the Cape of Good Hope,' by his first wife Aletta Jacoba, daughter of Johannes Hendricus Brand, member of the court of justice at the Cape, and sister of Sir Christoffel Brand, first speaker of the Cape House of Assembly. His grandfather, Alexander Tennant, who belonged to an Ayrshire family, landed on his way to India at the Cape, where he eventually decided to settle.

After being educated at a private school in Cape Town young Tennant was admitted on 12 April 1849 attorney at law of the supreme court, and practised also as a notary public and conveyancer and in the vice-admiralty court of the colony, with much success. For many years he was registrar of the diocese of Cape Town and legal adviser to the bishop; during his tenure of office there took place the prolonged litigation concerning Bishop Colenso.

In May 1866 he was returned to the House of Assembly of the Cape of Good Hope as member for the electoral division of Piquetberg, which he continued to represent until his retirement in 1896. On 18 June 1874 he was unanimously elected speaker of the House of Assembly in succession to his uncle, Sir Christoffel Brand, and was re-elected unopposed in 1879, 1884, 1889, and 1894, holding the position for nearly twenty-two years. During this long period his rulings were seldom questioned and his personal influence in the house was very great. At the close of the session of 1893, when he was accorded a special vote of thanks for his services in the chair, the prime minister, Cecil Rhodes, bore witness to 'the firmness and impartiality with which he had maintained the dignity and rights of the house' (*Debates of the House of Assembly*, 1893, p. 368). He retired on a pension on 26 Feb. 1896, when he again received the thanks of the house for his services in the chair.

Tennant was closely identified with the educational life of the colony, and for some years was a member of the council of the university of the Cape and chairman of the South African College Council. He was justice of the peace for Cape Town, Wynberg, and Simon's Town, and served on several government commissions. He was knighted by patent on 4 Oct. 1877, and was created K.C.M.G. on 25 May 1892. On his retirement from the speakership he acted for five years as agent-general for the colony in London. But his previous career had given him small opportunity of acquiring the requisite business aptitude for the position. He resigned on 31 Dec. 1901. He died on 29 March 1905 at 39 Hyde Park Gardens, London, and was buried in Brompton cemetery.

In 1856 he published a second and revised edition of his father's 'Notary's Manual for the Cape of Good Hope.'

Tennant was twice married: (1) on 3 May 1849 to Josina Hendrina Arnoldina, daughter of Jacobus François du Toit of Stellenbosch, a descendant of one of the French refugee families who settled at the Cape after the Revocation of the Edict of Nantes in 1685 (she died on 19 April 1877, leaving two sons and one daughter); (2) on 8 Oct. 1885, in London, to Amye Venour, elder daughter of Lieutenant-general Sir William Bellairs, K.C.M.G., C.B., of Strawberry Hill, Twickenham, by whom he had no issue.

A portrait of Tennant in oils, three-quarter length, by W. Gretor, a Danish artist, is in the possession of his widow.

[The Times, 31 March and 3 April 1905; Cape Argus, 30 March 1905; Cape Times, 31 March 1905; Burke's Peerage, 1905; Cape Argus Annual, 1896; Colonial Office Records; information supplied by relatives.] C. A.

THESIGER, FREDERIC AUGUSTUS, second BARON CHELMSFORD (1827–1905), general, born on 31 May 1827, was eldest son of Frederick Thesiger, first baron [q. v.], by Anna Maria, youngest daughter of William Tinling. Educated at Eton, he was commissioned as second-lieutenant in the rifle brigade on 31 Dec. 1844, and exchanged to the grenadier guards as ensign and lieutenant on 28 Nov. 1845. He was promoted lieutenant and captain on 27 Dec. 1850. He went to Ireland in February 1852 as A.D.C. to the lord-lieutenant (the earl of Eglinton), and from January 1853 to August 1854 he was A.D.C. to Sir Edward Blakeney, commanding the forces there. He joined his battalion in the Crimea on 31 May 1855, and served there till the end of the war, being A.D.C. to General Markham, commanding second division, from 18 July to 29 Sept. 1855, and deputy assistant quartermaster-general from 8 Nov. 1855 to 24 June 1856. He was made brevet-major (2 Nov. 1855) and received the medal with clasp, the Sardinian and Turkish medals, and the Mejidie (5th class).

He was promoted captain and lieutenant-colonel on 28 Aug. 1857, and exchanged into the 95th (Derbyshire) regiment on 30 April 1858, to take part in the suppression of the Indian Mutiny. He joined the regiment in November, and was present at the last action in which it was engaged, the capture of Man Singh's camp at Koondrye, where he commanded the infantry of Michael Smith's brigade of the Rajputana field force. He received the medal. From 13 July 1861 to 31 Dec. 1862 he was deputy adjutant-general of the British troops in the Bombay presidency. He became brevet-colonel on 30 April 1863. He was employed in the Abyssinian expedition of 1868 as deputy adjutant-general, and Lord Napier spoke of his 'great ability and untiring energy' in his despatch (*Lond. Gaz.* 30 June 1868). He received the medal, and was made C.B. and A.D.C. to the queen.

Thesiger was adjutant-general in the East Indies from 17 March 1869 to 15 March 1874. In a lecture at Calcutta in 1873 on the tactical formation of British infantry he maintained that much less change was needed than most people supposed, and that the two-deep line still met the case (*Journal of the United Service Institution*, xvii. 411–23). Having returned to England, he commanded the troops at Shorncliffe as colonel on the staff from 1 Oct. 1874 to 31 Dec. 1876, and then a brigade at Aldershot. He received a reward for distinguished service on 22 May 1876, and was promoted major-general on 15 March 1877. In February 1878 he went to South Africa, to command the troops, with the local rank of lieutenant-general. He took over the command from Sir Arthur Cunynghame [q. v.] at King William's Town on 4 March. A Kaffir war was in progress in that neighbourhood, the Gaikas having invaded Cape Colony and established themselves in the Perie bush. On 12 June Thesiger was able to report that this war had been brought to an end, thanks mainly to Colonel (Sir) Evelyn Wood and Major (Sir) Redvers Buller (*Lond. Gaz.* 15 July 1878). But there was a general ferment among the natives of South Africa, and he went to Natal in August to make arrangements for an expedition against Sekukuni, who had been giving trouble in the north-east part of the newly annexed Transvaal. The expedition, under Colonel Rowlands, V.C., reached Fort Burgers, on Steelpoort river, at the end of September, but owing to want of water operations had to be suspended, to be resumed a year later.

A more serious business claimed attention. The Zulu king, Cetywayo, had an army of 40,000 men, well trained, well armed, and eager to 'wash their spears.' He was a standing menace to Natal and the Transvaal, as Sir Garnet (now Lord) Wolseley had pointed out three years before. It was difficult to guard a frontier of 200 miles against so mobile an enemy, and the high commissioner, Sir Bartle Frere [q. v.], thought it best to bring matters to a head by presenting an ultimatum, in which Cetywayo was called upon to break up his military system. On 11 Jan. 1879, the term allowed for acceptance having expired, the invasion of Zululand began. Lord Chelmsford, as Thesiger had become by his father's death on 5 Oct. 1878, had over 5000 European troops available and nearly 8000 armed natives. He decided to operate in three columns of nearly equal strength. The centre column (which he accompanied) crossed the Buffalo at Rorke's drift; the right, under Colonel Pearson, crossed the Tugela near its mouth, eighty miles to the south-east; the left, under Colonel (Sir) Evelyn Wood, had already crossed the Blood river, thirty-five miles to the north of Rorke's drift. All three were to converge on Ulundi, the king's kraal, fifty to sixty miles off.

On 22 Jan. came the disaster of Isandhlwana. The centre column had encamped under the hill so named, and Chelmsford, learning that his scouting troops, ten miles ahead, were in need of support, joined them on that morning with more than half his force, leaving six companies of the 24th with two guns and some native troops to guard the camp. The cavalry vedettes were to be far advanced, but the infantry outposts to be drawn in closer, and the force was to act on the defensive if attacked. At mid-day this camp-guard was suddenly attacked, enveloped and annihilated by a body of 10,000 Zulus. Of the six companies only three men escaped; the total number of Europeans killed was 860. Chelmsford had been warned by Kruger and others that laagers should be formed, but that precaution was not taken; and the troops, relying on the effect of their fire, fought in too open formation. 'We have certainly been seriously underrating the power of the Zulu army,' was Chelmsford's own confession (Verner, ii. 148).

In addition to the loss of men and the moral effect of such a blow, the transport and camp equipment of the column were lost and the natives deserted in large numbers. The invasion of Zululand was brought to a standstill; the right column entrenched itself at Etshowe, the left at Kambula, and the remains of the centre column recrossed the Buffalo at Rorke's drift. The successful defence of the post there, held by one company of the 24th against 3000 Zulus on the night of the 22nd, discouraged the Zulus from pushing on into Natal. Reinforcements, which had been refused in the autumn of 1878, were now sent out from England to the number of 10,000 men, but took some months to arrive. On 3 April Chelmsford relieved Colonel Pearson's force at Etshowe, having on the previous day beaten off 10,000 Zulus, who attacked his laager at Gingihlovo. Wood had won a similar victory at Kambula on 29 March.

In June Chelmsford resumed the convergent advance on Ulundi, which had failed in January. The first division, under General Crealock, marched near the coast to Port Durnford, and established a new base there. The second division, under General Newdigate, was joined by Wood's flying column, and by 1 July they reached the White Umvolosi near Ulundi, Chelmsford being with them. They met with little resistance on their march, but there was one deplorable incident: the death of the Prince Imperial on 1 June. He had been allowed to join headquarters as a spectator, and was put in charge of a small scouting party, which was surprised by a few Zulus. Five of the party rode off, but four, including the prince, were killed. On 4 July Chelmsford crossed the Umvolosi with 4166 white and 958 native troops, twelve guns and two gatlings. Formed in a hollow rectangle, they marched on Ulundi. The Zulu army, estimated at 20,000, attacked in its usual enveloping fashion, but was soon driven off and suffered severely from the cavalry in its flight. The Zulu power was broken, Cetywayo's kraal was burnt, and he became a fugitive (*Lond. Gaz.* 19 Aug. 1879).

Before this battle was fought Chelmsford had ceased to be the commander of the forces in South Africa. Isandhlwana had caused much murmuring in England, and the government had been blamed for 'replacing the able Thesiger by the incompetent Chelmsford.' There had been friction between him and Sir Henry Bulwer, the lieutenant-governor of Natal, as to the raising and employment of native levies; and the government decided to send out Sir Garnet Wolseley to supersede them both. Wolseley landed at Durban on 28 June, and joined the first division at Port Durnford on 7 July. He disapproved of the plan of operating with two widely separated forces. Chelmsford accordingly moved southward to St. Paul's mission station, and met Wolseley there on 15 July. On the 27th he left Durban for England. He was mentioned in Wolseley's despatch (*Lond. Gaz.* 10 Oct. 1879) as entitled to all the merit of the victory of Ulundi. He had been made K.C.B. on 11 Nov. 1878, and received the G.C.B. on 19 Aug. 1879, also the medal with clasp.

He became lieutenant-general on 1 April 1882, and general on 16 Dec. 1888. From 4 June 1884 to 29 March 1889 he was lieutenant of the Tower of London. On 7 June 1893 he was placed on the retired list. He had been made colonel of the 4th (West London) volunteer battalion of the king's royal rifle corps on 27 Aug. 1887. He was given the colonelcy of his old regiment (the Derbyshire) on 30 Jan. 1889, and was transferred to the 2nd life guards on 27 Sept. 1900. He was made G.C.V.O. in 1902. He died on 9 April 1905, at the United Service Club, having had a sudden seizure while playing billiards there. He was buried with military honours at Brompton cemetery, his grave being next to his father's. He was well described by the duke of Cambridge in 1879 as 'a gallant, estimable and high-principled man, generous to others, unsparing of himself, and modest withal.' (Verner, ii. 165.)

A portrait of him by Harris Brown is in the mess of the 2nd life guards, and another by the same artist is in the possession of his widow. A cartoon portrait appeared in 'Vanity Fair' in 1881.

He married on 1 Jan. 1867 Adria Fanny, eldest daughter of Major-general John Heath of the Bombay army. She survived him, and he left four sons, of whom the eldest, Frederick John Napier, third Baron Chelmsford, was governor of Queensland (1905–9) and afterwards of New South Wales.

[The Times, 10 April 1905; Official Narrative of the Zulu War, 1881; Further Correspondence on the affairs of South Africa, presented to parliament, 1878 (5 parts), 1879 (12 parts); John Martineau, Life of Sir Bartle Frere, 1895; Willoughby C. Verner, Life of the Duke of Cambridge, 1905; Sir Evelyn Wood, From Midshipman to Field-Marshal, 1906.]

E. M. L.

THOMAS, WILLIAM MOY (1828–1910), novelist and journalist, born in Hackney, Middlesex, on 3 Jan. 1828, was younger son of Moy Thomas, a solicitor. William's uncle, J. H. Thomas, co-author with the boy's father, of 'Synopsis of the Law of Bills of Exchange and Promissory Notes' (1814), and also editor of 'Coke upon Littleton' (3 vols. 1818), took charge of the boy's education. But William soon left the study of the law to follow literature as a profession. He became private secretary to Charles Wentworth Dilke [q. v.], proprietor of the 'Athenæum.' In 1850 he was introduced by Sir Thomas Noon Talfourd [q. v.] to Charles Dickens, who engaged him next year as a writer on 'Household Words,' to which he contributed down to 1858. He commenced to write criticisms in political philosophy for the 'Athenæum' in 1855, and contributed on literary history and political economy to 'Chambers's Journal,' the 'North British Review,' the 'Economist,' and other journals. His first book was an edition of the 'Poetical Works of William Collins' (1858), with notes and a useful biography. In the same year a series of able papers by him in 'Notes and Queries' established the facts about the biography of Richard Savage [q. v.]. In 1861 appeared his valuable edition of 'The Letters and Works of Lady Mary Wortley Montagu, edited by Lord Wharncliffe; third edition, with additions and corrections derived from the original MSS., illustrative notes and a new memoir' (2 vols.; reprinted in Bohn's Series, 1887, 2 vols., and in 1893). In 1866–7 he was London correspondent of the New York 'Round Table' under the signature of 'Q,' and in 1868 he joined the staff of the 'Daily News,' writing the weekly article 'In the Recess' and the dramatic criticisms. He also wrote leading articles, reviews, and descriptive sketches for that newspaper down to 1901. He was the first editor of 'Cassell's Magazine,' in which appeared 'A Fight for Life' (3 vols. 1868), an excellent novel, which was dramatised. He was honorary secretary of the Authors' Protection Society (1873), and was instrumental in procuring the royal commission on copyright which reported in 1878 (John Hollingshead, *My Lifetime*, 1895, ii. 54–56). He was dramatic critic for the 'Academy' from 1875 to 1879, and for the 'Graphic' from 1870 until his active journalistic career closed some nine years before his death. He died after a long illness at Eastbourne on 21 July 1910.

He married Sara Maria, daughter of Commander Francis Higginson, R.N., who survived him, and by whom he had eight children, of whom two married daughters and one son, Frederick Moy Thomas, are living.

He also wrote: 1. 'When the Snow falls,' 2 vols. 1859 (1861 and other editions; stories republished from 'Household Words'). 2. 'Pictures in a Mirror,' 1861 (tales). 3. 'Golden Precepts, or the Opinions and Maxims of Prince Albert,' 1862. 4. 'Toilers of the Sea,' by Victor Hugo, authorised English translation, 1866, 3 vols.

[Allibone's Dict. of Engl. Lit.; Men of the Time, 1899; Who's Who, 1909; Athenæum, 30 July 1910; Morning Post, 29 July 1910; Daily News, 22 July 1910; Bookseller, 29 July 1910; John Hollingshead, My Lifetime, 1895, 2 vols. passim; Thomas Cooper's Life, 1873, p. 320; Sir John Robinson's Fifty Years of Fleet Street, ed. by F. Moy Thomas, 1904.]
H. R. T.

THOMPSON, D'ARCY WENTWORTH (1829–1902), Greek scholar, elder son of John Skelton Thompson, shipmaster, by his wife Mary Mitchell, both of Maryport, Cumberland, was born at sea on board his father's barque Georgiana, off Van Diemen's Land, on 18 April 1829. Nearly all his male relatives for generations had followed the sea. D'Arcy Thompson, after twelve years (1835–47) at Christ's Hospital, London, matriculated from Trinity College, Cambridge, at Michaelmas 1848, afterwards migrating to Pembroke College. At Cambridge he read chiefly with Augustus Arthur Vansittart and with Joseph Barber (afterwards Bishop) Lightfoot, both of Trinity; his closest friends were James Lemprière Hammond of Trinity and Peter Guthrie Tait [q. v. Suppl. II] of Peterhouse. Thompson gained a medal for Latin verse in 1849 with an ode 'Maurorum in Hispania Imperium,' and was placed sixth in the first class in the classical tripos of 1852, being bracketed with William Jackson Brodribb [q. v. Suppl. II]. After graduating B.A. in 1852 he became classical master in the Edinburgh Academy, where R. L. Stevenson was, in 1861–2, one of his pupils, a fact recorded by Stevenson in his song called 'Their Laureate to an Academy Class Dinner Club' and beginning 'Dear Thompson Class.' In 1863, after twelve years' service, he left the school for the chair of Greek in Queen's College, Galway. In 1867 he delivered the Lowell lectures at Boston. He died at Galway on 25 Jan. 1902, a few hours after lecturing on Thucydides.

He married twice: (1) in Edinburgh, in 1859, Fanny (*d.* 1860), daughter of Joseph Gamgee and sister of Joseph Sampson Gamgee [q. v.], by whom he had one son, D'Arcy Wentworth; and (2) in Dublin, in 1866, Amy, daughter of William B. Drury, of Boden Park, co. Dublin, by whom he had two sons and four daughters.

D'Arcy Thompson's reputation mainly rests on his 'Day Dreams of a Schoolmaster' (Edinburgh, 1864, 1865), a pathetic and humorous record of his schooldays at 'St. Edward's,' and of his teaching years at the 'Schola Nova' of 'dear Dunedin.' Interwoven with a thread of autobiography, the book is a plea for the sympathetic teaching of the ancient languages, a protest against the then narrow education of women, and a passionate defence of the dignity of the schoolmaster's calling. Some skilful translations, chiefly of Tennyson, are included.

In 1865 followed three sets of little essays, 'Wayside Thoughts of an Asophophilosopher,' the first part containing 'Rainy Weather, or the Philosophy of Sorrow,' 'Goose-skin, or the Philosophy of Horror,' and 'Te Deum Laudamus, or the Philosophy of Joy.' In 1867 he published his Lowell lectures under his old title of 'Wayside Thoughts'; they dealt, after the manner of the 'Day Dreams,' with school and college memories and with the practice and philosophy of education.

D'Arcy Thompson, whose classical scholarship was literary and poetic, possessed a rare power of easy and eloquent translation. Many of his renderings from the Greek appeared in the 'Museum'; others in a volume called 'Ancient Leaves' (1862), which also comprises some 'paraphrases,' or original poems on classical models. 'Sales Attici' (1867) collects 'the maxims, witty and wise, of the Athenian Tragic Drama.'

For his eldest son in childhood D'Arcy Thompson wrote 'Nursery Nonsense, or Rhymes without Reason' (1863–4), and 'Fun and Earnest, or Rhymes with Reason' (1865). These books, admirably illustrated by Charles H. Bennett, and now scarce, were the delight of a past generation of children. Of a third volume, cancelled before publication, 'Rhymes Witty and Whymsical' (Edinburgh, 1865), a copy was sold in Sir T. D. Brodie's sale at Sotheby's in 1904.

Thompson also contributed, chiefly to the 'Scotsman' and to 'Macmillan's Magazine,' a few essays and fugitive poems.

[Autobiographical details in Thompson's works; family information; Galway Express, 1 Feb. 1902; T. P. O'Connor, M.P. (Thompson's pupil at Galway) in M.A.P., 8 Feb. 1902, and in T.P.'s Weekly, 17 June 1904.]

D. W. T.

THOMPSON, EDMUND SYMES- (1837–1906), physician. [See Symes-Thompson.]

THOMPSON, FRANCIS (1859–1907), poet and prose-writer, was born on 18 Dec. 1859 at 7 Winckley Street, Preston. His father, Charles Thompson (1824–1896), a native of Oakham, Rutland, practised homœopathy at Preston and Ashton-under-Lyne, and married Mary Morton. Francis's uncles, Edward Healy Thompson (*b.* 1813) and John Costall Thompson, were both authors. Edward, who was professor of English literature at the catholic university in Dublin (1853–4) and sub-edited the 'Dublin Review' (1862–4), wrote devotional works, which were widely circulated; John published a volume of poems, 'The Vision of Liberty,' which won the approval of Sir Henry Taylor and of Gladstone. Like these uncles, Francis's father and mother were converts to the Roman catholic church. Francis was their second child, but the elder son died in infancy. Three sisters were born later.

Francis, who was brought up in the catholic faith, was sent in 1870 to Ushaw College, there to receive a fair classical education and to be prepared, if he and his mentors saw fit, for the priesthood. A frail and timid child of studious tastes, Thompson nurtured at Ushaw his life-long allegiance to the doctrines and liturgy of the church. At seventeen he left to study medicine by his father's wish at Owens College, Manchester. Medical study was repugnant to him, and after six years' trial, in the course of which he thrice failed in examination for a degree, he attempted in a helpless fashion humble means of livelihood. He made no plea in favour of a literary career, but he had read with ardent sympathy the works of Æschylus and Blake, while the gift from his mother of De Quincey's 'Confessions of an Opium Eater' gave his thought a perilous direction. His father's reproaches at his failure to earn a livelihood led him suddenly in Nov. 1885 to seek his fortune in London. There he filled for a time some small posts, among them that of a publisher's 'collector.' But, tormented by neuralgia and other ills, he fell a prey to opium, and soon passed through every phase of destitution, sleeping in the open, and seeking a few pence by selling matches or newspapers. During this period a Leicester Square bootmaker, accosting him in the street, gave him for a time light employment in his shop, and—what proved a more enduring gift—old account books for scribbling paper. Sustained through his sufferings by opium, he developed poetical powers, and at the end of two years of outcast life he copied out on ragged scraps of paper in the spring of 1888 two poems, 'The Passion of Mary' and 'Dream Tryst,' and a prose essay, 'Paganism Old and New.' These compositions he sent, giving Charing Cross Post Office as his address, to 'Merry England,' where the work of his uncle, Edward Healy Thompson, had already appeared. They were accepted by the editor, Mr. Wilfrid Meynell, and were duly published in the numbers for April, May, and June respectively. Browning read them shortly before his death, and pronounced their author to be a poet capable of achieving whatever his ambition might suggest. At the time opium eating and privation had ruined Thompson's health. Having been traced with difficulty, he was induced to enter a hospital, and afterwards to recruit at Storrington, Sussex. His recovery largely depended on the breaking of the opium habit. During this painful process his literary sense gathered fresh strength, and he wrote the 'Ode to the Setting Sun' and other verse and the 'Essay on Shelley.'

In 1893 he published his first volume of 'Poems,' chiefly written at Storrington. Coventry Patmore was among the earliest and most enthusiastic admirers of the book. The chief poem, 'The Hound of Heaven,' found wide popularity despite its somewhat recondite theme, which treated in the spirit of the strictest catholic dogma of conflict between human and divine love (cf. Burne-Jones's *Life*, ii. 240). Of the first section of the poems called 'Love in Dian's Lap' Patmore wrote that these were 'poems of of which Laura might have been proud' (*Fortnightly Review*, lxi.). There followed in 1895 'Sister Songs' (new edit. 1908), dedicated to Monica and Madeline Meynell, children of his friend and protector. There he described with subtlety and ingenuous calmness the days of his outcast experience, but the profuse imagery and visionary obscurity of his style rendered a cool reception for the moment inevitable.

From 1893 till 1897 Thompson lived, with short intervals, near the Franciscan monastery in Pantasaph, North Wales. There he wrote nearly all the 'New Poems,' which he published in 1897, and dedicated to Coventry Patmore, whose death spoilt the pleasures of publication. The book shows the powerful influence of older mystical poets, but the 'Mistress of Vision,' of which he himself said that it contained as much science as mysticism, takes with the 'Anthem of Earth' a place in the forefront of English verse.

In prose Thompson also gave proof of notable power. To the 'Academy,' under Mr. C. L. Hind's editorship, and, during the last years of his life, to the 'Athenæum,' he contributed a large body of literary criticism. In 1905 he issued 'Health and Holiness: a Study of the Relations between Brother Ass the Body and his Rider the Soul' (with a preface by Father George Tyrrell). There were published posthumously the 'Life of St. Ignatius Loyola' (1909), 'The Life of John Baptist de la Galle' (1911), and the 'Essay on Shelley' (1909), with a preface by Mr. George Wyndham, who pronounced it 'the most important contribution to pure letters written in English during the last twenty years.'

Despite his ascetic temper and his mystical prepossessions, Thompson found recreation in watching cricket matches, and wrote odds and ends of verse in honour of the game. During his last months he lodged in London and also paid a visit to an admirer, Mr. Wilfrid Scawen Blunt, at Newbuildings Place near Horsham. There Mr. Neville Lytton painted his portrait. In the summer of 1907 he was prevailed upon to enter the Hospital of St. Elizabeth and St. John, St. John's Wood, where he died from consumption on 13 Nov. 1907, fortified by the rites of the catholic church. He was buried in the catholic cemetery, Kensal Green, where his tomb is inscribed with his own words 'Look for me in the nurseries of Heaven.'

[The Athenæum, obit. by Mr. Wilfrid Meynell, since reprinted in Thompson's Selected Poems, 1908; Wilfrid Blunt in the Academy, 23 Nov. 1907; the Dublin Review, cxlii., art. by Alice Meynell; A Rhapsodist at Lord's (Francis Thompson's cricketing poems) in E. V. Lucas's One Day and Another, 1909, p. 199; Le Poète Francis Thompson, by Floris Delattre, in Revue Germanique, July–Aug. 1909; La Phalange, 20 June 1909, translations by Valéry Larbaud; Francis Thompson, par K. Rooker, Bruges, 1912; Francis Thompson, by G. A. Beacock, Marburg, 1912; Thompson's papers in the hands of his literary executor, Mr. Wilfrid Meynell; private information.] E. M-L.

THOMPSON, Sir HENRY, first baronet (1820–1904), surgeon, born at Framlingham, Suffolk, 6 Aug. 1820, was only son of Henry Thompson, a general dealer, by his wife Susannah, daughter of Samuel Medley [q. v.], the artist. Thompson was educated under Mr. Fison, a nonconformist minister at Wrentham. He early engaged in mercantile pursuits, as his parents, who were uncompromising baptists, disliked the idea of a profession. Coming to London, he was, however, apprenticed to George Bottomley, a medical practitioner at Croydon, in January 1844, and in October he entered University College, London, as a medical student. He obtained the gold medal in anatomy at the intermediate examination at the London University in 1849, and the gold medal for surgery at the final M.B. examination in 1851. From June 1850 he acted as house surgeon at University College Hospital to (Sir) John Erichsen [q. v. Suppl. I], who was newly appointed surgeon. Joseph Lister, afterwards Lord Lister, was one of his first dressers, and on his advice Lister went to Edinburgh to work under James Syme [q. v.]. In January 1851 Thompson entered into partnership at Croydon with Bottomley, his former master, but after a few months he returned to London, and took the house 35 Wimpole Street where he lived during the rest of his life.

At the Royal College of Surgeons of England Thompson was admitted a member in 1850 and a fellow in 1853. He gained the Jacksonian prize in 1852 for his dissertation 'On the Pathology and Treatment of Stricture of the Urethra,' and he had the unusual distinction of obtaining the prize a second time in 1860 with his essay 'On the Healthy and Morbid Conditions of the Prostate Gland.' In 1883 he was appointed Hunterian professor of surgery and pathology.

Thompson acted for a short time as surgeon to the St. Marylebone Infirmary, but in 1853 he was appointed assistant surgeon to University College Hospital, becoming full surgeon in 1863, professor of clinical surgery in 1866, consulting surgeon and emeritus professor of clinical surgery in 1874.

Thompson early showed his predilection for the surgery of the urinary organs, and in July 1858 he visited Paris to study the subject still further under Jean Civiale

(1792–1867), who first removed a stone from the bladder by the operation of crushing. Beginning life as a pupil of Civiale, Thompson at first crushed stones in the bladder at repeated intervals, leaving it to nature to remove the fragments. When Henry Jacob Bigelow (1818-1890) recommended crushing at a single sitting and removal of the fragments by operative measures, Thompson improved the technique of the operation. Later, about 1886, when the discredited operation of suprapubic cystotomy was revived, Thompson became its advocate.

Thompson's successful crushing operations at University College soon attracted attention, and in 1863 he operated at Brussels upon Leopold I, King of the Belgians, completing the work which had been begun by Civiale eighteen months previously. In July and December 1872 Thompson treated Napoleon III, Emperor of the French, at Camden Place, Chislehurst. He performed the operation of lithotrity under chloroform on 2 Jan. 1873, and again on 7 Jan. A third sitting was arranged for noon on 9 Jan., but the emperor died of sudden collapse an hour before.

Thompson's attainments and interests were exceptionally versatile. He not merely came to be facile princeps in his own branch of surgery; his zeal for hygiene made him a pioneer of cremation; he was at the same time an authority on diet, a devoted student of astronomy, an excellent artist, a collector of china, and a man of letters.

To the subject of cremation Thompson first drew attention in England by an article in the 'Contemporary Review' in 1874. Experiments had been recently made in Italy, but a cremation society, the first of its kind in Europe, was founded in London, chiefly by Thompson's energy, in 1874. From that time onwards he acted as the president, and did all in his power to promote the practice both in England and on the Continent. A crematorium was built at Woking in 1879. Its use was forbidden by the home secretary, and it was not employed until March 1885, after the government had brought a test case against a man who had cremated his child in Wales, and Sir James Stephen had decided that the practice was not illegal if effected without causing a nuisance. Thompson also took a leading part in 1902 in the formation of the company which erected the crematorium at Golder's Green, near London, and the rules laid down for the guidance of that company have proved a model for cremation societies throughout the world. The introduction of cremation drew Thompson's attention incidentally to the unsatisfactory nature of the law in regard to death certification. The Cremation Act of 1902 (2 Ed. VII. c. 8) was an attempt to remedy some of the evils to which Thompson directed attention.

Astronomy occupied much of Thompson's leisure. He long worked at an observatory of his own, which he erected at his country house at Molesey. But his chief services to the science were his gifts to Greenwich observatory of some magnificent instruments, including a fine photo-heliograph of 9-inch aperture, a 30-inch reflecting telescope, and a large photographic telescope of 26-inch aperture and 2½ feet focal length; the last telescope, twice the size of any previously at Greenwich, was offered in March 1894, and being manufactured by Sir Howard Grubb of Dublin, was erected in April 1897.

Thompson doubtless inherited artistic power from his maternal grandfather, Samuel Medley. His original talent was improved by study under Edward Elmore, R.A., and Sir Lawrence Alma Tadema, R.A. Paintings by him were exhibited at the Royal Academy in 1865, 1870, annually from 1872 to 1878, and again in 1881, 1883, and 1885. Two of these pictures were afterwards shown in the Paris salon, and to this exhibition he contributed a landscape in 1891. Thompson was also an eminent collector of china. He acquired many fine specimens of old white and blue Nankin. A catalogue illustrated by the owner and James McNeill Whistler [q. v. Suppl. II] was issued in 1878. The collection was sold at Christie's on 1 June 1880.

Besides numerous articles in magazines, Thompson wrote two novels under the name of 'Pen Oliver.' 'Charlie Kingston's Aunt,' published in 1885, presents the life of a medical student some fifty years before. 'All But: a Chronicle of Laxenford Life' (1886), is illustrated by twenty full-page drawings by the author, in one of which he portrayed himself as he was in 1885.

Cultured society had great attractions for Thompson. As a host he was famous for his 'octaves,' which were dinners of eight courses for eight people at eight o'clock. They were commenced in 1872, and the last, which was the 301st, was given shortly before his death. The company was always as carefully selected as the food, and for a quarter of a century the most famous persons in the worlds of art, letters, science, politics, diplomacy, and fashion met at his table in Wimpole Street. King George V, when Prince of Wales, attended Thompson's 300th 'octave.'

Thompson, who was knighted in 1867, was created a baronet on 20 Feb. 1899. He died at 35 Wimpole Street on 18 April 1904, and was cremated at Golder's Green. He married, on 16 Dec. 1861, Kate Fanny, daughter of George Loder of Bath. His wife, a well-known pianist, long suffered from paralysis, but survived her husband, dying on 30 Aug. 1904, leaving issue a son, Henry Francis Herbert, who became second baronet, and two daughters.

A three-quarter length portrait, painted by Sir J. E. Millais, R.A., in 1881, hangs in the National Gallery. There is also a bust by F. W. Pomeroy, A.R.A., at Golder's Green. A cartoon portrait by 'Ape' appeared in 'Vanity Fair' in 1874.

Thompson's chief works are: 1. 'The Pathology and Treatment of Stricture of the Urethra both in the Male and Female,' 1854; 4th edit., London and Philadelphia, 1885; translated into German, München, 1888. 2. 'The Enlarged Prostate, its Pathology and Treatment,' 1858; 6th edit. London and Philadelphia, 1886; translated into German, Erlangen, 1867. 3. 'Practical Lithotomy and Lithotrity,' 1863; 3rd edit. 1880; translated into German, Kassel und Berlin, 1882. 4. 'Clinical Lectures on Diseases of the Urinary Organs,' 1868; 8th edit. 1888; also American editions; translated into French, 1874 and again in 1889; translated into German, Berlin, 1877. 5. 'The Preventive Treatment of Calculous Disease,' 1873; 3rd edit. 1888. 6. 'Cremation,' 1874; 4th edit. 1901. 7. 'Food and Feeding,' 1880; 12th edit. enlarged, 1910. 8. 'On Tumours of the Bladder,' 1884. 9. 'Lectures on some Important Points connected with the Surgery of the Urinary Organs,' 1884. 10. 'Diet in Relation to Age and Activity,' 1886, 12mo; 4th edit. 1903; revised edit. 1910. 11. 'On the Suprapubic Operation of opening the Bladder for the Stone and for Tumours,' 1886. 12. 'Modern Cremation, its History and Practice,' 1889; 4th edit. 1901.

Thompson was also part author of the article on cremation in the 11th edition of the 'Encyclopædia Britannica.' 'Traité pratique des maladies des voies urinaires,' a collected edition of Thompson's surgical works, was published at Paris in 1880.

[Lancet, 1904, i. 1167 (with portrait); Brit. Med. Journal, 1904, i. 1191 (with portrait); private information.] D'A. P.

THOMPSON, LYDIA (1836–1908), actress, was born in London on 19 Feb. 1836. Her father died during her childhood, her mother remarried, and she was compelled early to earn her living. Having a taste for dancing, she took to the stage, and was joined there by her younger sister, Clara. In 1852 Lydia made her début in the ballet at Her Majesty's Theatre. In the Christmas of 1853 she was engaged to play Little Silverhair at the Haymarket in the pantomime of 'Little Silverhair, or Harlequin and the Three Bears.' Her performance won the praise of Professor Henry Morley in the 'Examiner.' In 1854 she danced delightfully for sixty nights at the same house in Planché's Easter extravaganza, 'Mr. Buckstone's Voyage round the Globe,' and appeared on 18 Oct. at the St. James's in the burlesque of 'The Spanish Dancers,' in which she mimicked Señora Perea Nana. At Christmas she returned to the Haymarket, in the leading character of 'Little Bopeep who lost her Sheep,' and was again highly praised by Morley. At the close of 1856 it was announced that she was dancing her way through the theatres of Germany with pleasant success. In the winter season of 1859–60 she made a hit at the St. James's by her dancing in a succession of light pieces. At the Lyceum on 9 April 1861 she acted in the Savage Club burlesque of 'The Forty Thieves,' and played, among other rôles, Norah in the first production of Falconer's comedy of 'Woman, or Love against the World' (19 Aug. 1861).

By this period she had begun to make excursions into the country, where she long maintained her popularity. On 31 Oct. 1864, at the opening of the new Theatre Royal, Birkenhead, by Alexander Henderson (whose second wife she subsequently became), she sustained the title character in Burnand's 'Ixion,' the first modern burlesque in more than one act. Afterwards she fulfilled several engagements under Henderson at the Prince of Wales's, Liverpool. Here, in Dec. 1864, she played Mary in 'Used up' to the Sir Charles Coldstream of Sothern and the Ironbrace of Mr. (now Sir) Squire Bancroft. Here, also, on Whit Monday 1866 she was seen as the title character in the burlesque of 'Paris,' to the Œnone of (Sir) Henry Irving. Meanwhile, early in 1865, she had fulfilled a successful engagement at Drury Lane.

On 15 Sept. 1866 Lydia Thompson made her first appearance at the new Prince of Wales's Theatre, Tottenham Court Road, in the afterpiece of the 'Pas de Fascination,' and on 10 Oct. played with acceptance the chief character in Byron's poor burlesque of 'Der Freischütz.' In 1868, after performing at the Strand Theatre in William Brough's extravaganza 'The Field of the Cloth of Gold,' she sailed for America, where she was the pioneer of latter-day English burlesque and was the first 'star' to bring a fully organised company across the Atlantic. She was out of England six years. Her New York début at Wood's Museum (28 Sept.) in 'Ixion,' which ran 102 nights, was encouraging. A tour of the leading American cities in 1870 included a successful visit to the Californian Theatre, San Francisco. At New York, during the winter season of 1870–1, began Lydia's association with Willie Edouin [q. v. Suppl. II]. Her troupe subsequently voyaged to Australia and India.

Lydia Thompson reappeared in London on 19 Sept. 1874 at the Charing Cross Theatre under the management of W. R. Field. Farnie's famous burlesque of 'Blue Beard,' already performed 470 times in America, formed the opening bill. Thanks to the acting of Lydia Thompson, Willie Edouin, and Lionel Brough, this poor piece proved a remarkable success alike in London and the provinces.

In 1877 Lydia Thompson and her husband took another burlesque company to America, opening 20 Aug. at Wallack's Theatre, New York, in 'Blue Beard.' The engagement terminated on 12 Jan. 1878. Lydia Thompson reappeared at the Gaiety, London, on 13 Feb. as Morgiana in the famous amateur pantomime of 'The Forty Thieves.' On 25 Jan. 1879 she played Carmen at the Folly in Reece's new burlesque of 'Carmen, or Sold for a Song.' After some two years in retirement, she reappeared at the Royalty on 12 Nov. 1881 as Mrs. Kingfisher in the farcical comedy of 'Dust.'

On 1 Feb. 1886 Alexander Henderson, her husband, died at Caen. (For details of his managerial career see *Dramatic Notes*, 1887, p. 15.) On 17 May following she began a new engagement at the Fourteenth Street Theatre, New York, and was seen again in New York in the winter seasons of 1888–9 and 1891. Meanwhile, on 21 Sept. 1886, she opened the Strand Theatre, under her own management, with 'The Sultan of Mocha,' then first given in London, and on 26 Jan. 1888 was heartily welcomed on making her reappearance there as Antonio the page in the comic opera 'Barbette.' Thenceforth her vivacity showed signs of decay. In the autumn of 1896 she was touring in England as Rebecca Forrester in Appleton's farcical comedy 'The Co-respondent.' In May 1899 a testimonial performance of 'London Assurance' was given at the Lyceum on her behalf. Her last appearance on the stage was at the Imperial in December 1904 as the Duchess of Albuquerque in John Davidson's adaptation of 'A Queen's Romance.' She died on 17 Nov. 1908, at 48 Westminster Mansions, London, and was buried in Kensal Green cemetery, leaving a daughter, Mrs. L. D. Woodthrope, professionally known as Zeffie Tilbury. Portraits of her, in character, are reproduced in Laurence Hutton's 'Curiosities of the American Stage' and in the 'Theatre' (Jan. 1886).

[Pascoe's Dramatic List; Prof. Henry Morley's Journal of a London Playgoer; Broadbent's Annals of the Liverpool Stage; The Bancroft Memoirs; H. P. Phelps's Players of a Century; Col. T. Allston Brown's History of the New York Theatres; John Hollingshead's Gaiety Chronicles; New York Dramatic Mirror for 28 Feb. 1891; Daily Telegraph, 20 Nov. 1908; Green Room Book, 1909.] W. J. L.

THOMPSON, WILLIAM MARCUS (1857–1907), journalist, born at Londonderry, Ireland, on 24 April 1857, was second son in a family of four sons and four daughters of Moses Thompson, a customs official, by his wife Elizabeth Smith. His family was of intensely Orange and anti-nationalist sympathies. After education at a private school, Thompson was for a time clerk in the office of James Hayden, solicitor. At the age of sixteen he contributed verses to the 'Derry Journal' and developed an aptitude for journalism. He found employment on the 'Belfast Morning News,' and then in 1877, at the age of twenty, through the influence of Sir Charles Lewis, baronet, M.P. for Derry, he joined the staff of the conservative 'Standard' in London, writing chiefly on non-political themes. In 1884 he became parliamentary reporter to the paper, which he served till 1890. Meanwhile he had outgrown his inherited political principles, and developed a sturdy radicalism and an aggressive sympathy with the Irish nationalists.

Thompson had entered as a student at the Middle Temple on 6 April 1877, and was called to the bar on 26 Jan. 1880. He formed a practice as the leading professional advocate of trade societies and of persons of advanced opinions charged with political offences. As a member from 1886 of the democratic club in Chancery Lane he became intimate with leading democrats, including Mr. John Burns, Mr. Robert Bontine Cunninghame Graham, and Mr. Bennet Burleigh. On 3 March 1886 he successfully defended Mr. Burns at the Old Bailey on the charge of inciting the mob to violence at Trafalgar Square in February of that year. In Jan. 1888 he again defended Mr. Burns, for similar conduct in November 1887; the latter was then sentenced to six weeks' imprisonment. Thompson also appeared for the defence in the Walsall conspiracy case (March–April 1892). He represented many trade unions in the arbitration over the prolonged Grimsby fishing dispute (November 1901). During the same period he contributed to the 'Radical' newspaper (started in 1880), and on its death to 'Reynolds's Newspaper,' the weekly Sunday paper, for which he wrote most of the leading articles as well as general contributions under the pseudonym of 'Dodo.' He succeeded Edward Reynolds as editor of the paper in February 1894, and held the post until his death. The uncompromising warfare on privilege and rank, which had always characterised 'Reynolds,' lost nothing of its force at Thompson's hand.

Thompson, who was a powerful platform speaker, was elected to the London county council as radical member for West Newington in 1895, but was defeated in his attempt to enter parliament for the Limehouse division of Tower Hamlets in July of that year. To his initiative was due the establishment in 1900 of the National Democratic League, of which he was first president. He was original member and promoter of the National Liberal Club (1882).

Thompson died of bronchitis and pneumonia on 28 Dec. 1907 at his residence, 14 Tavistock Square, London, and was buried at Kensal Green cemetery. He married on 3 April 1888, Mary, only daughter of Thomas Crosbie, editor and afterwards proprietor of the 'Cork Examiner.' She survived him with one daughter. A portrait of Thompson, painted by J. B. Yeats (father of W. B. Yeats), belongs to the widow.

[The Times, 29 Dec. 1907; Reynolds's Newspaper, 30 Dec. 1907; Derry Journal, 30 Dec. 1907; Foster's Men at the Bar; Joseph Burgess, Life of John Burns, 1911; H. M. Hyndman, Record of an Adventurous Life, 1911; information from Mrs. Thompson and Mr. William Roddy, editor of the Derry Journal.] W. B. O.

THOMSON, JOCELYN HOME (1859–1908), chief inspector of explosives, born at Oxford on 31 Aug. 1859, was the second of four sons of William Thomson, provost of Queen's College, Oxford, afterwards archbishop of York [q. v.]. Educated at Eton and the Royal Academy, Woolwich, Thomson entered the royal artillery in 1878, and engaged the following year in the Zulu war. Subsequently he was transferred to India, and thence he proceeded to Egypt, where he served in the royal horse artillery.

From an early age he was an earnest student of astronomy, and when twenty-three years of age he was nominated by the Royal Society an observer of the transit of Venus in the island of Barbados, receiving commendation for his accurate and painstaking work. From 1887 to 1892 he served on the staff of the Department of Artillery and Stores, and from 1892 to 1893 was second assistant to the director-general of ordnance factories. Meanwhile in 1888 he acted as secretary to the war office explosives committee, of which Sir Frederick Abel [q. v. Suppl. II] was president. The smokeless powder 'cordite,' recommended to the government in 1890 for adoption, received its name from Thomson. His comprehensive grasp of the characteristics of explosive substances enabled him to render conspicuous services to the committee. In 1891 he went to Canada to conduct tests on cordite when exposed to the influence of a cold climate.

Thomson was appointed an inspector of explosives under Sir Vivian Majendie in 1893, and in 1899 he succeeded Majendie as chief inspector.

In 1901 the Belgian government conferred upon him the Order of Leopold. He was made C.B. in 1907.

From 1900 to 1902 Thomson by official leave acted as consulting engineer in connection with the undertaking for transmitting electrical power from the Cauvery Falls to the Mysore gold fields. Afterwards he acted in a similar capacity to the Jhelum Valley electrical transmission scheme. In each his efforts met with signal success.

Thomson displayed versatile gifts in mechanical invention. Among useful apparatus which he devised were a mercury vacuum pump, a petroleum testing appliance, and a 'position-' or 'range-finder.' For the last named he received a grant of 500*l.* from the war department.

Suffering from nervous breakdown, Thomson shot himself on 13 Feb. 1908 at his residence in Draycott Place, Chelsea. He was buried in Brompton cemetery. He married in 1886 Mabel Sophia, fourth daughter of Thomas Bradley Paget, of Chipping Norton, Oxfordshire vicar of

Welton, East Yorkshire. He had no issue.

He was the author of a useful compendium, 'Guide to the Explosives Act, 1875,' and wrote many valuable official reports. He collaborated with Sir Boverton Redwood in 'Handbook on Petroleum; with Suggestions on the Construction and Use of Mineral Oil Lamps' (1901; 2nd edit. 1906); and 'The Petroleum Lamp, its Choice and Use' (1902).

[Private information; 32nd Annual Report, H.M. Inspectors of Explosives; Rise and Progress of the British Explosives Industry, 1909; Arms and Explosives, March 1908; Annual Register, 1908; The Times, 15 and 18 Feb. 1908.] T. E. J.

THOMSON, Sir WILLIAM, first Baron Kelvin of Largs (1824–1907), man of science and inventor, born on 26 June 1824 in College Square East, Belfast, was second son and fourth child of James Thomson (1786–1849) [q. v.], professor of mathematics in the Royal Academical Institution of Belfast, by his wife Margaret, eldest daughter of William Gardiner of Glasgow. The elder brother, James (1822–1892) [q. v.], was professor of engineering, first in Belfast, then in Glasgow. When William was six years old his mother died, and the father himself taught the boys, who never went to school. In 1832, when William was eight, his father moved to Glasgow as professor of mathematics in the university there. In 1834, in his eleventh year, William matriculated in the University of Glasgow. He loved in later life to talk of his student days and of his teachers, William Ramsay, Lushington, Thomas Thomson, Meikleham, and John Pringle Nichol. He early made his mark in mathematics and physical science; and in 1840 won the university medal for a remarkable essay, 'On the Figure of the Earth.' During his fifth year as a student at Glasgow (1839–40) he received a notable impulse toward physics from the lectures of Nichol and of David Thomson, who temporarily took the classes in natural philosophy during the illness of Meikleham. At the same time he systematically studied the 'Mécanique Analytique' of Lagrange, and the 'Mécanique Céleste' of Laplace, and made the acquaintance—a notable event in his career—of Fourier's 'Théorie Analytique de la Chaleur,' reading it through in a fortnight, and studying it during a three months' visit to Germany. The effect of reading Fourier dominated his whole career. During his last year at Glasgow (1840–1) he communicated to the 'Cambridge Mathematical Journal' (ii. May 1841), under the signature 'P.Q.R.,' an original paper 'On Fourier's Expansions of Functions in Trigonometrical Series,' which was a defence of Fourier's deductions against some strictures of Professor Kelland. The paper is headed 'Frankfort, July 1840, and Glasgow, April 1841.'

He left Glasgow after six years without taking his degree; and on 6 April 1841 entered as a student at Peterhouse, Cambridge, where he speedily made his mark. An undergraduate of seventeen, he handled methods of difficult integration readily and with mastery, and proved his power in a paper entitled 'The Uniform Motion of Heat in Homogeneous Solid Bodies, and its Connection with the Mathematical Theory of Electricity,' published in the 'Cambridge Mathematical Journal,' vol. iii. 1842. In other papers he announced various important theorems, in some of which he found, however, that he had been anticipated by Sturm, Gauss, and George Green [q. v.], all of them master minds in mathematics. At Cambridge he rowed in the college races of 1844, and won the Colquhoun silver sculls. He also helped to found the Cambridge University Musical Society, and in its first concert, and afterwards in others, played the French horn. His love of good music he retained to the end of his life. He read mathematics with William Hopkins [q. v.]. In January 1845 he came out second wrangler in the mathematical tripos, but he beat the senior wrangler, Stephen Parkinson [q. v.], in the severer test of the competition for Smith's prize.

On leaving Cambridge he visited Faraday's laboratory at the Royal Institution in London. Faraday and Fourier were the chief heroes of his youthful enthusiasm. Then he went to Paris University to work in the laboratory of Regnault with a view to acquiring experimental skill. There he spent four months, and there also he made the acquaintance of Biot, Liouville, Sturm, and Foucault. Returning to Cambridge, he was elected fellow of his college in the autumn of 1845, and became a junior mathematical lecturer and editor of the 'Cambridge Mathematical Journal.'

Thomson at twenty-one years had gained experience in three universities—Glasgow, Cambridge, and Paris—had published a dozen original papers, and had thus established for himself a reputation in mathematical physics. In 1846, at twenty-two, he became professor of natural philosophy in Glasgow on the death of Meikleham. The subject of his inaugural dissertation (3 Nov. 1846) was 'De Motu Caloris per Terræ Corpus.' He held this professorship till 1899. Admittedly a bad expositor, he proved himself to be a most inspiring teacher and a leader in research. With the slenderest material resources and most inadequate room, he created a laboratory of physics, the first of its kind in Great Britain, where he worked incessantly, gathering around him a band of enthusiastic students to collaborate in pioneering researches in electric measurement and in the investigation of the electrodynamic and thermoelectric properties of matter. In the lecture theatre his enthusiasm won for him the love and respect of all students, even those who were unable to follow his frequent flights into the more abstruse realms of mathematical physics. Over the earnest students of natural philosophy he exercised an influence little short of inspiration, which extended gradually far beyond the bounds of his own university.

From his first days as professor Thomson worked strenuously with fruitful results. By the end of four years (1850), when he was twenty-six, he had published no fewer than fifty original papers, most of them highly mathematical in character, and several of them in French. Amongst these researches there is a remarkable group which originated in his attendance in 1847 at the meeting at Oxford of the British Association, where he read a paper on electric images. But a more important event of that meeting was the commencement of his friendship with James Prescott Joule [q. v.] of Manchester, who had for several years been pursuing his researches on the relations between heat, electricity, and mechanical work. Joule's epoch-making paper, which he presented on this occasion, on the mechanical equivalent of heat, would not have been discussed at all but for Thomson's observations. Thomson had at first some difficulty in grasping the significance of the matter, but soon threw himself heart and soul into the new doctrine that heat and work were mutually convertible. For the next six or eight years, partly in cooperation with Joule, partly independently, he set himself to unravel those mutual relations.

Thomson was never satisfied with any phenomenon until it should have been brought into the stage where numerical accuracy could be determined. He must measure, he must weigh, in order that he might go on to calculate. 'The first step,' he wrote, 'toward numerical reckoning of properties of matter . . . is the discovery of a continuously varying action of some kind, and the means of observing it definitely, and measuring it in terms of some arbitrary unit or scale division. But more is necessary to complete the science of measurement in any department, and that is the fixing on something *absolutely* definite as the unit of reckoning.' It was in this spirit that Thomson approached the subject of the transformation of heat.

Sadi Carnot in 1824 had anticipated Joule in his study of the problem in his 'Réflexions sur la Puissance Motrice du Feu,' where was discussed the proportion in which heat is convertible into work, and William John Macquorn Rankine [q. v.] had carried the inquiry a stage farther in 1849; while Helmholtz in 'Die Erhaltung der Kraft' (1847)—'On the Conservation of Force' (meaning what we now term Energy)—denied the possibility of perpetual motion, and sought to establish that in all the transformations of energy the sum total of the energies in the universe remains constant. Thomson in June 1848 communicated to the Cambridge Philosophical Society a paper 'On an Absolute Thermometric Scale founded on Carnot's Theory of the Motive Power of Heat, and calculated from Regnault's Observations.' There he set himself to answer the question: Is there any principle on which an absolute thermometric scale can be founded? He arrived at the answer that such a scale is obtained in terms of Carnot's theory, each degree being determined by the performance of equal quantities of work in causing one unit of heat to be transformed while being let down through that difference of temperature. This indicates as the absolute zero of temperature the point which would be marked as − 273° on the air thermometer scale. In 1849 he elaborated this matter in a further paper on 'Carnot's Theory,' and tabulated the values of 'Carnot's function' from 1° C. to 231° C. Joule, writing to Thomson in December 1848, suggested that probably the values of 'Carnot's function' would turn out to be the reciprocal of the absolute temperatures as measured on a perfect gas thermometer, a conclusion independently enunciated by Clausius in February 1850.

Thomson zealously continued his investigation. He experimented on the heat developed by compression of air. He verified the prediction of his brother, Professor James Thomson, of the lowering by pressure of the melting-point of ice. He gave a thermodynamic explanation of the non-scalding property of steam issuing from a high-pressure boiler. He formulated between 1851 and 1854, with scientific precision, in a long communication to the Royal Society of Edinburgh, the two great laws of thermodynamics—(1) the law of equivalence discovered by Joule, and (2) the law of transformation, which he generously attributed to Carnot and Clausius. Clausius, indeed, had done little more than put into mathematical language the equation of the Carnot cycle, corrected by the arbitrary substitution of the reciprocal of the absolute temperature; but Thomson was never grudging of the fame of independent discoverers. 'Questions of personal priority,' he wrote, 'however interesting they may be to the persons concerned, sink into insignificance in the prospect of any gain of deeper insight into the secrets of nature.' He gave a demonstration of the second law, founding it upon the axiom that *it is impossible by means of inanimate material agency to derive mechanical effect from any portion of matter by cooling it below the temperature of the coldest of the surrounding objects*. Further, by a most ingenious use of the integrating factor to solve the differential equation for the quantity of heat needed to alter the volume and temperature of unit mass of the working substance, he gave precise mathematical proof of the theorem that the efficiency of the perfect engine working between given temperatures is inversely proportional to the absolute temperature. In collaboration with Joule, he worked at the 'Thermal Effects of Fluids in Motion,' the results appearing between 1852 and 1862 in a series of four papers in the 'Philosophical Transactions,' and four others in the 'Proceedings of the Royal Society.' Thus were the foundations of thermodynamics laid. In later years he rounded off his thermodynamic work by enunciating the doctrine of available energy.

This brilliant development and generalisation of the subject did not content Thomson. He inquired into its applications to human needs and to the cosmic consequences it involved. Thus he not only suggested the process of refrigeration by the sudden expansion of compressed cooled air, but propounded the doctrine of the dissipation of energy. If the availability of the energy in a hot body be proportional to its absolute temperature, it follows that as the earth and the sun—indeed, the whole solar system itself—cool down towards one uniform level of temperature, all life must perish and all energy become unavailable. This far-reaching conclusion once more suggested the question of a beginning of the Cosmos, a question which had arisen in the consideration of the Fourier doctrine of the flow of heat. His note-books of this time show that he had also been applying Fourier's equations to a number of outlying problems capable of similar mathematical treatment, such as the diffusion of fluids and the transmission of electric signals through long cables.

In 1852 Thomson married his second cousin Margaret, daughter of Walter Crum, F.R.S., and resigned his Cambridge fellowship. His wife's precarious health necessitated residence abroad at various times. In the summer of 1855, while they stayed at Kreuznach, Thomson sent to Helmholtz, whose acquaintance he desired to make, an invitation to come to England in September to attend the British Association meeting at Glasgow. On 29 July Helmholtz arrived at Kreuznach to make Thomson's acquaintance before his journey to England. On 6 August Helmholtz wrote to his wife of the deep impression that Thomson, 'one of the first mathematical physicists of Europe,' made on him. 'He far exceeds all the great men of science with whom I have made personal acquaintance, in intelligence, and lucidity, and mobility of thought, so that I felt quite wooden beside him sometimes.' A year later Helmholtz again met Thomson at Schwalbach and described him as 'certainly one of the first mathematical physicists of the day, with powers of rapid invention such as I have seen in no other man.' Subsequently Helmholtz visited Thomson in Scotland many times, and his admiration grew steadily.

The utilisation of science for practical ends was Thomson's ambition through life. 'There cannot,' he said in a lecture to the Institution of Civil Engineers in May 1883, 'be a greater mistake than that of looking superciliously upon practical applications of science. The life and soul of science is its practical application; and just as the great advances in mathematics have been made through the desire of discovering the solution of problems which were of a highly practical kind in mathematical science, so in physical science many of the greatest advances that have been made from the beginning of the world to the present time have been made in the earnest desire to turn the knowledge of the properties of matter to some purpose useful to mankind' (see *Popular Lectures and Addresses*, i. 79).

Hitherto Thomson's work had lain mainly in pure science; but while still engaged on his thermodynamic studies, he was drawn toward the first of those practical applications that made him famous. Early in 1853 he had communicated to the Glasgow Philosophical Society a paper 'On Transient Electric Currents,' in which he investigated mathematically the discharge of a Leyden jar through circuits possessing self-induction as well as resistance. He founded his solution on the equation of energy, ingeniously building up the differential equation and then finding the integral. The result was remarkable. He discovered that a critical relation occurred if the capacity in the circuit was equal to four times the coefficient of self-induction divided by the square of the resistance. If the capacity was less than this the discharge was oscillatory, passing through a series of alternate maxima and minima before dying out. If the capacity was greater than this the discharge was non-oscillatory, the charge dying out without reversing. This beautiful bit of mathematical analysis passed almost unnoticed at the time, but it laid the foundation of the theory of electric oscillations subsequently studied by Oberbeck, Schiller, Hertz, and Lodge, and forming the basis of wireless telegraphy. Feddersen in 1859 succeeded in photographing these oscillatory sparks, and sent photographs to Thomson, who with great delight gave an account of them to the Glasgow Philosophical Society.

At the Edinburgh meeting of the British Association in 1854 Thomson read a paper 'On Mechanical Antecedents of Motion, Heat, and Light.' Here, after touching on the source of the sun's heat and the energy of the solar system, Thomson reverted to his favourite argument from Fourier according to which, if traced backwards, there must have been a beginning to which there was no antecedent.

In the same year, in the 'Proceedings of the Royal Society,' appeared the result of Thomson's investigation of cables under the title 'On the Theory of the Electric Telegraph.' Faraday had predicted that there would be retardation of signals in cables owing to the coating of gutta-percha acting like the glass of a Leyden jar. Forming the required differential equation, and applying Fourier's integration of it, Thomson drew the conclusion that the time required for the current at the distant end to reach a stated fraction of its steady value would be proportional both to the resistance and to the capacity; and as both of these are proportional to the length of the cable, the retardation would be proportional to the square of the length. This famous law of squares provoked much controversy. It was followed by a further research, 'On Peristaltic Induction of Electric Currents,' communicated to the British Association in 1855, and afterward in more complete mathematical form to the Royal Society.

Submarine telegraphy was now becoming a practical problem of the day [see BRIGHT, SIR CHARLES TILSTON, Suppl. I]. Sea cables were laid in 1851 between England and France, in 1853 between Holyhead and Howth, and in 1856 across the Gulf of St. Lawrence. In the last year the Atlantic Telegraph Company was formed, with capital mostly subscribed in England, with a view to joining Ireland to Newfoundland. Bright was engineer; Whitehouse (a retired medical practitioner) was electrician; Thomson (of 2 The College, Glasgow) was included in the list of the directors. In a pamphlet issued by the company in July 1857 it was stated that 'the scientific world is particularly indebted to Professor W. Thomson, of Glasgow, for the attention he has given to the theoretical investigation of the conditions under which electrical currents move in long insulated wires, and Mr. Whitehouse has had the advantage of this gentleman's presence at his experiments, and counsel, upon several occasions.' As a matter of fact Whitehouse had previously questioned Thomson's 'law of squares' at the British Association meeting of 1856, declaring that if it was true Atlantic telegraphy was hopeless. He professed to refute it by experiments. Thomson effectively replied in two letters in the 'Athenæum.' He pointed out that success lay primarily in the adequate section of the conductor, and hinted at a remedy (deduced from Fourier's equations) which he later embodied in the curb signal transmitter. Thomson steadily tested his theories in practice. In December 1856 he described to the Royal Society his device for receiving messages, namely a sort of tangent galvanometer, with copper damper to the suspended needle, the deflections being observed by watching through a reading telescope the image of a scale reflected from the polished side of the magnet or from a small mirror carried by it. Subsequently he abandoned this subjective method for the objective plan in which a spot of light from a lamp is reflected by the mirror upon a scale. It is probably true that the idea of thus using the mirror arose from noticing the reflection of light from the monocle which Thomson, being short-sighted, wore round his neck on a ribbon.

The first attempt to lay the Atlantic cable was made in 1857 and failed, and in subsequent endeavours Thomson played a more active part. His discovery that the conductivity of copper was greatly affected —to an extent of 30 or 40 per cent.—by its purity led him to organise a system of testing conductivity at the factory where the additional lengths were being made, and he was in charge of the test-room on board the Agamemnon, which in 1858 was employed in cable-laying in the Atlantic. Whitehouse was unable to join the expedition, and Thomson, at the request of the directors, also undertook the post of electrician without any recompense, though the tax on his time and energies was great.

After various mishaps, success crowned the promoters' efforts. Throughout the voyage Thomson's mirror galvanometer was used for the continuity tests and for signalling to shore, with a battery of seventy-five Daniell's cells. The continuity was reported perfect, and the insulation improved on submersion. On 5 Aug. the cable was handed over to Whitehouse and reported to be in perfect condition. Clear messages were interchanged, but the insulation was soon found to be giving way, and on 20 Oct., after 732 messages had been conveyed, the cable spoke no more. The cause of the collapse was the mistaken use in defiance of Thomson's tested conclusions, by Whitehouse, of induction coils working at high voltage. Thomson's self-abnegation and forbearance throughout this unfortunate affair are almost beyond belief. He would not suffer any personal slight to interfere with his devotion to a scientific enterprise.

During the next eight years Thomson sought to redeem the defeat. Throughout the preparations for the cables of 1865 and 1866, the preliminary trials, the interrupted voyage of 1865 when 1000 miles were lost, the successful voyage of 1866, when the new cable was laid and the lost one recovered and completed, Thomson was the ruling spirit, and his advice was sought and followed. On his return from the triumphant expedition he was knighted. He had in the meantime made further improvements in conjunction with Cromwell Fleetwood Varley [q. v.]. In 1867 he patented the siphon recorder, and, in conjunction with Fleeming Jenkin [q. v.], the curb-transmitter. He was consulted on practically every submarine cable project from that time forth. In 1874 Thomson was elected president of the Society of Telegraph Engineers, of which, in 1871, he had been a foundation member and vice-president. In 1876 he visited America, bringing back with him a pair of Graham Bell's earliest experimental telephones. He was president of the mathematical and physical section of the British Association of that year at Glasgow.

In the winter of 1860–1 Thomson had met with a severe accident. He fell on the ice when curling at Largs, and broke his thigh. The accident left him with a slight limp for the rest of his life.

Meanwhile much beside the submarine cable occupied Thomson's fertile mind, and his researches were incessant. In 1859–60 he was studying atmospheric electricity. For this end he invented the water-dropping collector, and vastly improved the electrometer, which he subsequently developed into the elaborate forms of the quadrant instrument and other types. He also measured electrostatically the electromotive force of a Daniell's cell, and investigated the potentials required to give sparks of different lengths in the air. At the same time he urged the application of improved systems of electric measurement and the adoption of rational units. In 1861 he cordially supported the proposal of Bright and Clark to give the names of ohm, volt, and farad to the practical units based on the centimetre-gramme-second absolute system, and on his initiative was formed the Committee of Electrical Standards of the British Association, which afterwards went far in perfecting the standards and the methods of electrical measurement. He was largely responsible for the international adoption of the system of units by his advocacy of them at the Paris Congress in 1881. He was an uncompromising advocate of the metric system, and lost no opportunity of denouncing the 'absurd, ridiculous, time-wasting, brain-destroying British system of weights and measures.'

A long research on the electrodynamic qualities of metals, thermoelectric, thermoelastic, and thermomagnetic, formed the subject of his Bakerian lecture of 1856, which occupies 118 pages of the reprinted 'Mathematical and Physical Papers.' He worked long also at the mathematical theory of magnetism in continuation of Faraday's labours in diamagnetism. Thomson set himself to investigate Faraday's conclusions mathematically. As early as 1849 and 1850, with all the elegance of a mathematical disciple of Poisson and Laplace, he had discussed magnetic distributions by aid of the hydrodynamic equation of continuity. To Thomson are due the now familiar terms 'permeability' and 'susceptibility' in the consideration of the magnetic properties of iron and steel. In these years Thomson was also writing on the secular cooling of the earth, and investigating the changes of form during rotation of elastic spherical shells. At the same time he embarked with his friend Professor Peter Guthrie Tait [q. v. Suppl. II] on the preparation of a text-book of natural philosophy. Though the bulk of the writing was done by Tait, the framework of it thought and its most original parts are due to Thomson. The first part of the first volume of Thomson and Tait's 'Treatise on Natural Philosophy' was published in 1867, the second part only in 1874. No more was published, though the second edition of the first part was considerably enlarged. The book had the effect of revolutionising the teaching of natural philosophy.

Thomson's contributions to the theory of elasticity are no less important than those he made to other branches of physics. In 1867 he communicated to the Royal Society of Edinburgh a masterly paper 'On Vortex Atoms'; seizing on Helmholtz's proof that closed vortices could not be produced in a liquid perfectly devoid of internal friction, Thomson showed that if no such vortex could be artificially produced, then if such existed it could not be destroyed, but that being in motion and having the inertia of rotation, it would have elastic and other properties. He showed that vortex rings (like smoke-rings in air) in a perfect medium are stable, and that in many respects they possess qualities essential to the properties of material atoms—permanence, elasticity, and power to act on one another through the medium at a distance. The different kinds of atoms known to the chemist as elements were to be regarded as vortices of different degrees of complexity. The vortex-atom theory was linked to his other important researches on gyrostatic problems. Though he came to doubt whether the vortex-atom hypothesis was adequate to explain all the properties of matter, the conception bears witness to his great mental power.

In 1870 Lady Thomson, whose health had been failing for several years, died. In the same year the University of Glasgow was removed to the new buildings on Gilmore Hill, overlooking the Kelvin River. Thomson had a house here in the terrace assigned for the residences of the professors, adjoining his laboratory and lecture-room.

On 17 June 1874 he married Frances Anna, daughter of Charles F. Blandy of Madeira, whom he had met on cable-laying expeditions. In 1875 he built at Netherhall, near Largs, a mansion in the Scottish baronial style; and in his later life, though he had a London house in Eaton Place, Netherhall was his chief home. From his youth he had been fond of the sea, and had early owned boats on the Clyde. For many years his sailing yacht the Lalla Rookh was conspicuous, and he was an accomplished navigator. His experiences at sea in cable-laying had taught him much, and in return he was now to teach science in navigation. Between 1873 and 1878 he reformed the mariners' compass, on which he undertook to write a series of articles in 'Good Words' in 1873; he lightened the moving parts of the compass to avoid protracted oscillations, and to facilitate the correction of the quadrantal and other errors arising from the magnetism of the ship's hull. At first the Admiralty would have none of it. Even the astronomer royal condemned it. 'So much for the astronomer royal's opinion,' he ejaculated. But the compass won its way; and until recently was all but universally adopted both in the navy and in the mercantile marine (see, for Thomson's contributions to navigation, his *Popular Lectures*, vol. iii., and the Kelvin Lecture (1910) of Sir J. A. Ewing).

Dissatisfied with the clumsy appliances used in sounding, when the ship had to be stopped before the sounding line could be let down, Thomson devised in 1872 the well-known apparatus for taking flying soundings by using a line of steel piano wire. He had great faith in navigating by use of sounding line, and delighted to narrate how, in 1877, in a time of continuous fog, he navigated his yacht all the way across the Bay of Biscay into the Solent trusting to soundings only. He also published a set of Tables for facilitating the use of Sumner's method at sea. He was much occupied with the question of the tides, not merely as a sailor, but because of the interest attending their mathematical treatment in connection with the problems of the rotation of spheroids, the harmonic analysis of their complicated periods by Fourier's methods, and their relation to hydrodynamic problems generally. He invented a tide-predicting machine, which will predict for any given port the rise and fall of the tides, which it gives in the form of a continuous curve recorded on paper; the entire curves for a whole year being inscribed by the machine automatically in about four hours. Further than this, adopting a mechanical integrator, the device of his ingenious brother, James Thomson, he invented a harmonic analyser —the first of its kind—capable not only of analysing any given periodic curve such as the tidal records and exhibiting the values of the coefficients of the various terms of the Fourier series, but also of solving differential equations of any order.

Wave problems always had a fascination for Thomson, and he was familiar with the work of the mathematicians Poisson and Cauchy on the propagation of wave-motion. In 1871 Helmholtz went with him on the yacht Lalla Rookh to the races at Inverary, and on some longer excursions to the Hebrides. Together they studied the theory of waves, 'which he loved,' says Helmholtz, 'to treat as a race between us.' On calm days he and Helmholtz experimented on the rate at which the smallest ripples on the surface of the water were propagated. Almost the last publications of Lord Kelvin were a series of papers on 'Deep Sea Ship Waves,' communicated between 1904 and 1907 to the Royal Society of Edinburgh. He also gave much attention to the problems of gyrostatics, and devised many forms of gyrostat to elucidate the problems of kinetic stability. He held that elasticity was explicable on the assumption that the molecules were the seat of gyrostatic motions. A special opportunity of practically applying such theories was offered him by his appointment as a member of the admiralty committee of 1871 on the designs of ships of war, and of that of 1904–5 which resulted in the design of the Dreadnought type of battleship.

In 1871 he was president of the British Association at its meeting in Edinburgh. His presidential address ranged luminously over many branches of science and propounded the suggestion that the germs of life might have been brought to the earth by some meteorite. With regard to the age of the earth he had already from three independent lines of argument inferred that it could not be infinite, and that the time demanded by the geologists and biologists for the development of life must be finite. He himself estimated it at about a hundred million of years at the most. The naturalists, headed by Huxley, protested against Thomson's conclusion, and a prolonged controversy ensued. He adhered to his propositions with unrelaxing tenacity but unwavering courtesy. 'Gentler knight there never broke a lance,' was Huxley's dictum of his opponent. His position was never really shaken, though the later researches of John Perry, and the discovery by R. J. Strutt of the degree to which the constituent rocks of the earth contain radioactive matter, the disgregation of which generates internal heat, may so far modify the estimate as somewhat to increase the figure which he assigned. In his presidential address to the mathematical and physical section of the British Association at York in 1881 he spoke of the possibility of utilising the powers of Niagara in generating electricity. He also read two papers, in one of which he showed mathematically that in a shunt dynamo best economy of working was attained when the resistance of the outer circuit was a geometric mean between the resistances of the armature and of the shunt. In the other he laid down the famous law of the economy of copper lines for the transmission of power.

Thomson's lively interest in the practical —indeed the commercial—application of science, led him to study closely the first experiments in electric lighting. Such details as fuses and the suspension pulleys with differential gearing by which incandescent lamps can be raised or lowered absorbed some of his attention. He gave evidence before the parliamentary committee on electric lighting of 1879, and discussed the theory of the electric transmission of power, pointing out the advantage of high voltages. The introduction into England in 1881 of the Faure battery accumulator by which electricity could be economically stored excited him greatly. Thomson's various inventions—electrometers, galvanometers, siphon-recorders, and his compasses were at first made by James White, an optician of Glasgow. In White's firm, which became Kelvin & White, Limited, he was soon a partner, taking the keenest commercial interest in its operations, and frequenting the factory daily to superintend the construction. To meet demands for new measuring instruments he devised from time to time potential galvanometers, ampere gauges, and a whole series of standard electric balances for electrical engineers. His patented inventions thus grew very numerous. Up to 1900 they numbered fifty-six. Of these eleven related to telegraphy, eleven to compasses and navigation apparatus, six to dynamo machines or electric lamps, twenty-five to electric measuring instruments, one to the electrolytic production of alkali, and two to valves for fluids. Helmholtz, visiting Thomson in 1884, found him absorbed in regulators and measuring apparatus for electric lighting and electric railways. 'On the whole,' Helmholtz wrote, 'I have an impression that Sir William might do better than apply his eminent sagacity to industrial undertakings; his instruments appear to me too subtle to be put into the hands of uninstructed workmen and officials. . . . He is simultaneously revolving deep theoretical projects in his mind, but has no leisure to work them out quietly.' But he shortly added 'I did Thomson an injustice in supposing him to be wholly immersed in technical work; he was full of speculations as to the original properties of bodies, some of which were very difficult to follow; and, as you know, he will not stop for meals or any other consideration.'

Thomson's teaching was always characterised by a peculiar fondness for illustrating recondite notions by models. The habit was possibly derived from Faraday; but he developed it beyond precedent. 'I never satisfy myself,' he wrote, 'until I can make a mechanical model of a thing. If I can make a mechanical model, I can understand it. As long as I cannot make a mechanical model all the way through I cannot understand it.' He built up chains of spinning gyrostats to show how the rigidity derived from the inertia of rotation might illustrate the property of elasticity. The vortex-atom presented a dynamical picture of an ideal material system. He strung together little balls and beads with sticks and elastic bands to demonstrate crystalline dynamics. Throughout all his mathematical speculation his grip of the physical reality never left him, and he associated every mathematical process with a physical significance.

In 1893 Lord Kelvin astonished the audience at the Royal Institution by a discourse on 'Isoperimetrical Problems,' endeavouring to give a popular account of the mathematical process of determining a maximum or minimum, which he illustrated by Dido's task of cutting an ox-hide into strips so as to enclose the largest piece of ground; by Horatius Cocles' prize of the largest plot that a team of oxen could plough in a day; and by the problem of running the shortest railway line between two given points over uneven country. On another occasion he entertained the Royal Society with a discourse on the 'Homogeneous Partitioning of Space,' in which the fundamental packing of atoms was geometrically treated, and he incidentally propounded the theory of the designing of wall-paper patterns.

In 1884 Thomson delivered at Baltimore twenty lectures 'On Molecular Dynamics and the Wave Theory of Light.' His hearers, mostly accomplished teachers and professors, numbered twenty-six. The lectures, reported verbatim at the time, were issued with many revisions and additions in 1904. They show Thomson's speculative genius in full energy and brilliance. Ranging from the most recondite problems of optics to speculations on crystal rigidity, the tactics of molecules and the size of atoms, they almost embody a new conception of the ultimate dynamics of physical nature. Thomson accepted little external guidance. He never accepted Maxwell's classical generalisation that the waves of light were essentially electromagnetic displacements in the ether, although in 1888 he gave a nominal adhesion to the theory, and in his preface in 1893 to Hertz's 'Electric Waves,' he used the phrase 'the electromagnetic theory of light, or the undulatory theory of magnetic disturbance.' But later he withdrew his adhesion, preferring to think of things in his own way. Yet to the last he took an intense interest in the most recent discoveries. He discussed the new conception of electrons—or 'electrions,' as he called them—and read again and again Mr. Ernest Rutherford's book on 'Radioactivity' (1904). He objected, however, *in toto* to the notion that the atom was capable of division or disintegration. In 1903, in a paper called 'Æpinus Atomized,' he reconsidered the views of Æpinus and Father Boscovich from the newest standpoint, modifying the theory of Æpinus to suit the notion of 'electrions.'

Honours fell thickly on Thomson in his later life. He was thrice offered and thrice declined the Cavendish professorship of physics at Cambridge. He had been made a fellow of the Royal Society in 1851, and in 1883 had been awarded the Copley medal. He was president from 1890 to 1894. He was raised to the peerage in 1892 under the style and title of Baron Kelvin of Largs in the county of Ayr. On 15–17 June 1896 the jubilee of his Glasgow professorship was impressively celebrated by both the town and university in the presence of guests who included the chief men of science of the world. He resigned his professorship in 1899. He was one of the original members of the Order of Merit founded in 1902, was a grand officer of the Legion of Honour, and held the Prussian Order Pour le Mérite. In 1902 he was named a privy councillor. In 1904 he was elected chancellor of the University of Glasgow and published his installation address. He was a member of every foreign academy, and held honorary degrees from almost every university.

After taking part in the British Association meeting of 1907 at Leicester, where he lectured on the electronic theory of matter and joined with keenness in discussions of radioactivity and kindred questions, he went to Aix-les-Bains for change. He had barely reached his home at Largs in September when Lady Kelvin was struck down with a paralytic seizure. Lord Kelvin's misery at her helpless condition was intense, and his vitality was greatly diminished. He had himself suffered for fifteen years from recurrent attacks of facial neuralgia, and a year before underwent a severe operation. A chill now seized him, and after a fortnight's prostration he died on 17 Dec. He was buried in Westminster Abbey on 23 Dec. 1907. Lady Kelvin survived him.

In politics he was, up to 1885, a broad liberal; but as an Ulsterman he became an ardent unionist on the introduction of the home rule bill in 1886, and spoke at many political meetings in the West of Scotland in the years which followed. In religion Kelvin was an Anglican—at least from his Cambridge days—but when at Largs attended the Presbyterian Free Church. A simple, unobtrusive, but essential piety was never clouded. He had a deep detestation of ritualism and sacerdotalism, and he denounced spiritualism as a loathsome and vile superstition. But his studies led him again and again to contemplate a beginning to the order of things, and he more than once publicly professed his belief in creative design. Kindly hearted and exceptionally modest, he carried through life intense love of truth and insatiable desire for the advancement of natural knowledge. His high ideals led him to underrate his achievements. 'I know,' he said at his jubilee, 'no more of electric and magnetic force, or of the relation between ether, electricity, and ponderable matter, or of chemical affinity, than I knew and tried to teach to my students in my first session.' He strove whole-heartedly through life to reach a great comprehensive theory of matter. If he failed to find in the equations of dynamics an adequate and necessary foundation for the theories of electricity and magnetism, or to assign a dynamical constitution to the luminiferous ether, it is because the physical nature of electricity and of ether is probably more fundamental than that of matter itself. But he never allowed his intellectual grasp of physical matters to be clouded by metaphysical cobwebs, and insistently strove for precision of language.

Lord Kelvin's portrait was painted by Lowes Dickinson in 1869 for Peterhouse. Another portrait by (Sir) Hubert von Herkomer, R.A., was presented to Glasgow University in 1892. A third portrait by Sir W. Q. Orchardson was presented to the Royal Society by the fellows in 1899. A fourth portrait, by Mr. W. W. Ouless, R.A., was exhibited at the Royal Academy in 1902. A statue was erected in Belfast in 1910. A Kelvin lectureship in his memory was founded in 1908 at the Institution of Electrical Engineers, and lectures have been given by S. P. Thompson (1908), Sir J. A. Ewing (1910), and H. G. J. Du Bois (1912).

To scientific societies' proceedings or journals Kelvin contributed 661 papers between 1841 and 1908. In 1874 he collected his papers in 'Electrostatics and Magnetism.' In 1882 he began to collect and revise his scattered mathematical and physical papers. Three volumes were issued before his death, and the collection was completed in five volumes (1882–1911) under the editorship of Sir Joseph Larmor. Thomson also wrote for the 'Encyclopædia Britannica' of 1879 the long and important articles on Elasticity and on Heat.

[Silvanus P. Thompson, Life of William Thomson, Baron Kelvin of Largs, 2 vols. 1910, with full bibliography; Lord Kelvin's Early Home, being the recollections of his sister, the late Mrs. Elizabeth King, edited by Elizabeth Thomson King; William Thomson, Lord Kelvin, his way of teaching Natural Philosophy, by David Wilson, 1910; Lord Kelvin, by (Sir) Joseph Larmor, in Proc. Roy. Soc. London, 1908; Record of the Royal Soc., 3rd edit. 1912, pp. 205, 247 (with portrait); Lord Kelvin, by John Munro (Bijou Biographies), 1902; Lord Kelvin, his Life and Work, by Alexander Russell, 1912 (The People's Books); Lord Kelvin: an Account of his Scientific Life and Work, by Andrew Gray, 1908; Lord Kelvin: an Oration, by Andrew Gray, 1908; Lord Kelvin's Patents, by Magnus Maclean, Philosophical Society of Glasgow, 1897–8; Lord Kelvin's Contributions to Geology, by J. W. Gregory, Geological Society of Glasgow, 1908; Lord Kelvin: a Biographical Sketch, by J. D. Cormack, Cassier's Magazine, May and June, 1899; Charles Bright's Life Story of Sir Charles Tilston Bright, and his Story of the Atlantic Cable; L. Koenigsberger's H. von Helmholtz, transl. by F. A. Welby; On Certain Aspects of the Work of Lord Kelvin by Sir Oliver Lodge, Faraday Society, 1908; Kelvin in the Sixties, by W. E. Ayrton, Popular Science Monthly, New York, March 1900; Lord Kelvin: a Recollection and an Impression, by John Ferguson, Glasgow University Magazine, 1909.] S. P. T.

THOMSON, Sir WILLIAM (1843-1909), surgeon, born at Downpatrick, Ireland, on 29 June 1843, was youngest son (in a family of three sons and two daughters) of William Thomson of Lanark, Scotland, by his wife Margaret, daughter of Thomas Patterson of Monklands, Lanarkshire. His father died in Thomson's infancy, and his mother married Mr. McDougal, proprietor of the 'Galway Express' newspaper. While a lad he worked in the editorial office of this paper, and in 1864, without giving up his journalistic work, he entered as a student of Queen's College, Galway, then a constituent college of the Queen's University. He graduated B.A. in 1867. Having obtained a post on the Dublin 'Daily Express,' Thomson began to attend lectures at the Carmichael School of Medicine, and in 1872 he graduated M.D. and M.Ch. of the Queen's University, receiving the hon. M.A. in 1881, and in 1874 he became F.R.C.S.Ireland.

On obtaining his medical degrees he became house surgeon to the Richmond Hospital, Dublin, and demonstrator of anatomy in the Carmichael School. Next year he was elected visiting surgeon to the Richmond Hospital, a post he held to his death. In 1873 he was also appointed lecturer in anatomy in the Carmichael School. In 1882 he became the first general secretary of the newly formed Royal Academy of Medicine in Ireland, his principal duty being to edit its 'Transactions.' From 1896 to 1906 he was direct representative of the Irish medical profession on the General Medical Council. From 1896 to 1898 he was president of the Royal College of Surgeons in Ireland, and in 1897 was knighted. In December 1899 he was invited by Lord Iveagh to organise a field hospital for service in South Africa. In February 1900 he set out and accompanied Lord Roberts in his march to Pretoria. He proved his powers of rapid organisation by establishing, immediately on entering that capital, a hospital of 600 beds in the Palace of Justice, and it was in great part due to him and his colleagues that Pretoria escaped the outbreak of enteric fever which proved disastrous elsewhere. Lord Roberts mentioned his services in despatches. He returned home in November 1900, and he and his colleagues were entertained at a public banquet at the Royal College of Surgeons, Dublin (24 Nov.).

While in South Africa he was appointed surgeon in ordinary to Queen Victoria in Ireland, and in 1901 he became honorary surgeon to King Edward VII. For his services in the South African war he was mentioned in despatches and received the Queen's medal with three clasps. He was also made C.B. From 1895 to 1902 he was surgeon to the lord-lieutenant, Earl Cadogan. He was from 1906 to his death inspector of anatomy for Ireland.

Thomson was a surgeon of considerable ability. In 1882 he ligatured the innominate artery, and published an important paper on the subject. In later years he devoted attention to the surgery of the genito-urinary organs, and was the first among Dublin surgeons to remove an enlarged prostate. He wrote clearly and well, and edited several books, notably the third edition of Power's 'Surgical Anatomy of the Arteries' (1881), and Fleming's 'Diseases of the Genito-Urinary Organs' (1877), as well as the 'Transactions of the Royal Academy of Medicine in Ireland' from 1882 to 1896. For several years he acted as Dublin correspondent to the 'British Medical Journal.' In 1901 he delivered the address in surgery at the annual meeting of the British Medical Association held at Cheltenham, choosing as his subject 'Some Surgical Lessons from the South African Campaign' (*British Medical Journal*, 1901, vol. ii.). His most notable publication was an exhaustive and judicial report on the poor law medical service of Ireland, undertaken in 1891 at the request of Ernest Hart, editor of the 'British Medical Journal.' The report must form the basis of any inquiry into, or reform of, the poor law medical service. As an organiser, Thomson was at his best. He had a large share in the reorganisation of the school of the Royal College of Surgeons of Ireland during 1880–90, and in the organisation of the Royal Academy of Medicine in Ireland, formed in 1882 by the amalgamation of several old societies, whose interests and aims were not always concordant.

Thomson, who was a polished speaker and ready debater, died at his residence, 54 St. Stephen's Green, Dublin, on 13 Nov.

1909. He was buried at Mount Jerome cemetery, Dublin. A mural tablet has been erected in the Richmond Hospital, to commemorate his thirty-six years' services as surgeon, and his share in the rebuilding of the hospital in 1899. He married on 27 June 1878 Margaret Dalrymple, younger daughter of Abraham Stoker, chief clerk in the office of the chief secretary, Dublin Castle, and sister of Sir William Thornley Stoker, first baronet (1845–1912), surgeon, and of Bram Stoker (1848–1912), novelist. He left a son and daughter.

[Daily Express (Dublin), 15 Nov. 1909; Lancet and Brit. Med. Journal, 20 Nov. 1909; Cameron's History of the Royal College of Surgeons in Ireland; private information.]

R. J. R.

THORNTON, Sir EDWARD (1817–1906), diplomatist, born in London on 13 July 1817, was only surviving son of Sir Edward Thornton, G.C.B. [q. v.]. Educated at King's College, London, and at Pembroke College, Cambridge, he graduated B.A. among the senior optimes in 1840, proceeding M.A. in 1877. He was appointed attaché at Turin, April 1842, paid attaché at Mexico in February 1845, and secretary of legation there December 1853. He witnessed the occupation of Mexico by the United States forces in 1847, and rendered some secretarial assistance in the peace negotiations. He served as secretary to Sir Charles Hotham's special mission to the River Plate (1852–3), which resulted in the conclusion of a convention for the free navigation of the Parana and Uruguay rivers. He was appointed chargé d'affaires and consul-general at Monte Video in 1854, and minister plenipotentiary at Buenos Ayres in 1859. He was made C.B. in 1863 and was accredited to the republic of Paraguay in the same year. In July 1865 he was sent on a special mission to Brazil for the renewal of diplomatic relations (which had been broken off by the Brazilian government in 1863), and received shortly afterwards the definitive appointment of British envoy at Rio de Janeiro. In September 1867 he was nominated British envoy at Lisbon, but within a few days was selected for the difficult post of minister at Washington on the death of Sir Frederick W. A. Bruce [q. v.]. Thornton remained at Washington for over thirteen years. During the earlier period a state of tension existed between the two countries which at times almost threatened an open rupture. The American public resented the recognition by Great Britain of the southern states as belligerents. English sympathy for the South and the depredations of the Alabama and other confederate cruisers, which had escaped from or been received in British ports, increased the soreness of feeling. Other causes of dispute included questions of boundary between the United States and Canada, especially in the Straits of San Juan de Fuca to the south of Vancouver Island, and the exclusion of United States citizens from fishing privileges in the coastal waters of Canada which had been secured to them by the Reciprocity Treaty of 1814, but had been withdrawn in consequence of the denunciation of that treaty by the United States in 1865. Thornton brought to his work much patience and the spirit of calm, fair-minded moderation. But although some of the difficulties were settled, others persisted, and the irritation in the United States tended rather to augment than to diminish. Eventually a joint commission was instituted at Washington in February 1871 for the discussion and settlement of existing differences. Thornton's British colleagues were Earl de Grey (afterwards marquess of Ripon), Sir Stafford H. Northcote (subsequently earl of Iddesleigh), Sir John Alexander Macdonald [q. v.], prime minister of Canada, and Dr. Mountague Bernard [q. v.]. The result was the conclusion of the celebrated Treaty of Washington of 8 May 1871, by which the various outstanding questions and claims were referred to arbitration under specified conditions. Thornton, who was made K.C.B. in 1870, was created a privy councillor in August 1871. Further serious misunderstandings threatened during the progress of the arbitrations, but these were removed, and the eventual settlement did much to lead to more cordial feelings on the part of the United States towards this country. The United States government fully recognised that Thornton had effectively contributed to this result, and paid a tribute to his impartiality and judgment by selecting him in 1870 to act as arbitrator on the claim made on the Brazilian government for compensation on account of the loss of the American merchant vessel Canada on the coast of Brazil, and again from 1873 to 1876 on claims of United States and Mexican citizens. He was warmly thanked for these services, but declined offers of remuneration.

On 26 May 1881 Thornton succeeded Lord Dufferin [q.v. Suppl. II] as British ambassador at St. Petersburg. Here he again found himself faced by a situation of increasing gravity. England had watched with growing anxiety the rapid advance of Russia on the east of the Caspian Sea towards the northern frontiers of Persia and Afghanistan. In February 1884 Merv was annexed, notwithstanding repeated assurances given in 1881 that Russia had no such intention and without any previous notice of a change of policy. Thereupon Thornton, in accordance with his instructions, arranged for the delimitation of the northern frontier of Afghanistan by a joint commission. Before the boundary commissioners got to work a Russian and an Afghan force found themselves face to face at Penjdeh, a debatable point on the frontier, and on 30 March 1885, notwithstanding the assurances of the Russian foreign minister, General Komaroff drove the Afghan troops off with considerable loss. A period of extreme tension followed. But in the end an agreement was arrived at by the two governments, a protocol as to the general line of the frontier being signed by Lord Salisbury (who had succeeded Lord Granville as foreign secretary) and by the Russian ambassador, M. de Staal, on 10 Sept. 1885. Thornton had been appointed on 1 Dec. 1884 to succeed Lord Dufferin at Constantinople, but he remained at St. Petersburg during the whole of this trying episode, his place at Constantinople being temporarily filled by Sir William White [q. v.].

Thornton's arrival at Constantinople was delayed until February 1886, in order to leave in White's hands the negotiations consequent on the revolution in Eastern Roumelia, which broke out in September 1885, and the subsequent war between Servia and Bulgaria. A settlement was arrived at, but a fresh serious crisis was created by the abduction and abdication of Prince Alexander in August and September 1886. The cabinet were desirous that White, who had a unique knowledge of Balkan questions, should resume charge of the embassy. Thornton, despite some feeling of mortification, procured the Sultan's acceptance of White's appointment, placed his own resignation in the hands of the government, receiving their thanks for his public spirit, and returned to England. As no embassy was vacant to which he could be appointed, he retired on pension in January 1887. He declined the government's offer of a baronetcy. He had been promoted in 1883 to be G.C.B. He received honorary degrees of D.C.L. and LL.D. respectively from the universities of Oxford and Harvard, U.S.A., and was made hon. fellow of Pembroke. He had inherited on the death of his father in 1852 the title of Count de Cassilhas, which had been conferred on his father by King John VI of Portugal for three lives.

On his return to England Thornton took a considerable part in various commercial undertakings, and was also a member of the council of foreign bondholders, where his experience of South America was of much service. He died at his residence in Chelsea on 26 Jan. 1906.

He married on 15 Aug. 1854 Mary, daughter of John Maitland, and widow of Andrew Melville, by whom he had a son and two daughters. His widow died on 6 Jan. 1907. The son, Edward Thornton (1856–1904), a young diplomatist of great promise, graduated B.A. from Trinity College, Cambridge, in 1878, and after serving in Eastern Europe rose to be British minister in Central America, where he succumbed to the climate.

A cartoon portrait of Thornton by 'Ape' appeared in 'Vanity Fair' in 1886.

[The Times, 27 Jan., 6 Feb. 1906; Foreign Office List, 1907, p. 401; Papers laid before Parliament.] S.

THRING, GODFREY (1823–1903), hymnologist, born at Alford, Somerset, on 25 March 1823, was third son of John Gale Dalton Thring, rector and squire of Alford, by his wife Sarah, daughter of John Jenkyns, vicar of Evercreech, and sister of Richard Jenkyns [q. v.], Master of Balliol. Henry Thring, Lord Thring [q. v. Suppl. II], and Edward Thring [q. v.], headmaster of Uppingham, were elder brothers. Educated at Shrewsbury school, he matriculated at Balliol College, Oxford, in 1841, graduating B.A. in 1845. After his ordination in 1846 he held successively the curacies of Stratfield-Turgis (1846–50), of Strathfieldsaye (1850–3), of Euston, Norfolk (1856), and of Arborfield, Berkshire (1857), and in 1858 succeeded his father as rector of Alford, becoming in 1876 prebendary of Wells. He resigned his living in 1893, and died at Shamley Green, Surrey, on 13 September 1903. Thring published 'Hymns and other Verses' (1866); 'Hymns, Congregational and Others' (1866); and 'Hymns and Sacred Lyrics' (1874). He also edited in 1880 'A Church of England Hymn Book, adapted to the Daily Services of the Church throughout the Year' (a revised edition appeared in 1882; 3rd edit. 1891)

The literary standard of this collection is very high, but its practical use has been limited. Thring wrote many hymns which have attained popularity. Among them are 'The radiant morn hath passed away'; 'Fierce raged the tempest'; 'Saviour, blessed Saviour'; and 'Thou, to whom the sick and dying.' He produced what is generally admitted to be the best translation for singing of Luther's 'Ein' feste Burg,' 'A Fortress sure is God our King'; this is No. 245 in 'Church of England Hymn Book' (1882).

[Julian's Dictionary of Hymnology; W. Garrett Horder's The Hymn Lover; Duncan Campbell's Hymns and Hymn Writers, with particulars supplied by the author.]

J. C. H.

THRING, Sir HENRY, first Baron Thring (1818–1907), parliamentary draftsman, born at Alford, Somerset, on 3 Nov. 1818, was second son of the Rev. John Gale Dalton Thring by Sarah, daughter of John Jenkyns, vicar of Evercreech, Somerset. His father was both squire and rector of Alford; his mother was a sister of Richard Jenkyns [q. v.], Master of Balliol College, Oxford. He came of a long-lived stock. His father died at the age of ninety, his mother lived to be 101. Of his younger brothers Edward Thring [q. v.] was headmaster of Uppingham school, and Godfrey Thring [q. v. Suppl. II] acquired reputation as a writer of hymns.

Henry Thring was educated at Shrewsbury school under Benjamin Hall Kennedy [q. v.], to whose teaching, and that of his brother George, Thring used in after years to attribute that nice sense of the exact meaning of words which he rightly considered essential to the work of a good draftsman. From Shrewsbury Thring went to Magdalene College, Cambridge, was in 1841 third classic in the classical tripos, and was subsequently elected to a fellowship at his college. He occasionally examined for the classical tripos, but does not seem to have taken any other part in university or college work. He went to London, studied law, and on 31 Jan. 1845 was called to the bar as a member of the Inner Temple. He worked at conveyancing, 'the driest of all earthly studies,' as he describes it in the autobiographical introduction to his little book on 'Practical Legislation.' Having much leisure, and finding that the task of a conveyancer was neither profitable nor attractive, he passed to the study of the statute law, and there found the work of his future life. He read the English statute book critically from its earliest pages downwards, extolled Stephen Langton as 'the prince of all draftsmen,' and contrasted the draftsman of Magna Charta favourably with his wordy successors. He convinced himself that a radical departure ought to be made from the conveyancing models then followed by the draftsmen of Acts of parliament. He sought for better principles and a better type of drafting in Coode's book on legal expression (1845) and in the American codes, especially those of David Dudley Field, which then enjoyed a high reputation. In 1850 he tried his hand as an amateur in framing for Sir William Molesworth [q. v.] a colonial bill in which he endeavoured to simplify and shorten the expression of legal enactments. In 1851 he published portions of this bill as an appendix to a pamphlet which he entitled 'The Supremacy of Great Britain not inconsistent with Self-Government of the Colonies.' In this pamphlet he carefully enumerated and analysed the powers exercisable by the home government and the colonial government respectively, and distributed them on lines which foreshadowed the lines of the Irish home rule bill drawn at the end of his official life. Sir William Molesworth's bill did not become law, but drew attention to its draftsman, who soon obtained employment from the government on the lines in which he had specialised. Thring drew the Succession Act of 1853 which formed part of Gladstone's great budget of that year. At the same time he was engaged on a more comprehensive piece of legislative work. Edward (afterwards Lord) Cardwell [q. v.] was then president of the board of trade, and desired to recast the body of merchant shipping law administered by his department. Accordingly, under Cardwell's instructions, and in co-operation with Thomas Henry (afterwards Lord) Farrer [q. v. Suppl. I], Thring drew the great Merchant Shipping Act of 1854 which for forty years was the code of British merchant shipping law. In the preparation of this measure he found an opportunity for putting into practice those principles of draftsmanship which he afterwards expounded in his 'Instructions to Draftsmen.' He divided the bill into parts, divided the parts under separate titles, arranged the clauses in a logical order, and constructed each clause in accordance with fixed rules based on an analysis of sentences. From merchant shipping law Thring passed to another branch of law with which the board of trade is intimately concerned, that relating to joint-stock companies, and drew the series of bills which culminated in the Companies Act of 1862. His treatise on this Act went through three editions. Thring's work on these measures began when he was still in private practice at the bar, but in 1860 he was appointed to the important office of home office counsel. This office had been created in 1837, when, as a consequence of the Reform Act of 1832, the responsibility of the government for current legislation had been largely increased, and had devolved mainly on the home secretary. John Elliot Drinkwater Bethune [q. v.] was the first holder of the post, and, on his appointment in 1845 to the governor-general's council at Calcutta, his successor, Walter Coulson [q. v.], was entrusted with the wider duties of preparing under the direction of the home secretary bills originating from any department of the government, and of revising and reporting on any other bills referred to him by the home office. These were the duties taken over by Thring, and in his performance of them he appears to have drawn all the most important cabinet measures of the time. In his introduction to 'Practical Legislation' (1902) he described how he drew for Lord Derby's government the famous 'ten minutes' bill, the bill which, after radical alterations in parliament, became law as the Representation of the People Act, 1867. The story illustrates the conditions in which the work of drafting parliamentary bills is sometimes performed. On 3 March 1867 (November in Thring's account is an obvious slip) Spencer Walpole [q. v.], the home secretary, sent for Thring and asked him to read a bill which had been prepared by (Sir) Philip Rose, a parliamentary agent who acted for Disraeli in election matters. Thring expressed to Walpole, and on the following day to Lord Derby, an unfavourable opinion on the draft. He was asked to put himself in communication with the draftsman, and was engaged in doing so when he received from Disraeli, through his private secretary Montagu Corry (afterwards Lord Rowton), a message saying that the bill was to be entirely redrafted on different lines, and must be ready on Saturday the 17th. On Friday 16 March Thring took the bill in hand, and, working with two shorthand writers from ten to six, completed it. It was printed during the night, laid before the cabinet on Saturday, considered by Disraeli on Monday, and circulated to the House of Commons on Tuesday. This *tour de force* in draftsmanship could not, as Thring explains, have been accomplished if he had not been saturated with his subject. He had drawn for the government the franchise bill of 1866, which did not become law, and had prepared in connection with it a series of memoranda and notes which bore fruit in the following year.

At the end of 1868 Disraeli was succeeded as prime minister by Gladstone, with Lowe as chancellor of the exchequer. One of Lowe's first steps was to improve the machinery for the preparation of government bills. The most important of them were, at that time, prepared by the home office counsel, but some departments continued to employ independent counsel to draw their bills, and other bills were drawn by departmental officers without legal aid. The result of this system, or absence of system, was unsatisfactory. The cost was great, for counsel charged fees on the parliamentary scale. There was no security for uniformity of language, style, or arrangement in laws which were intended to find their places in a common statute book. There was no security for uniformity of principle in measures for which the government was collectively responsible. And, lastly, there was no check on the financial consequences of legislation, nothing to prevent a minister from introducing a bill which would impose a heavy charge on the exchequer and upset the budget calculations for the year. The remedy which Lowe devised was the establishment of an office which should be responsible for the preparation of all government bills, and which should be subordinate to the treasury, and thus brought into immediate relation, not only with the chancellor of the exchequer, but with the first lord of the treasury, who was usually prime minister. The office was constituted by a treasury minute dated 8 Feb. 1869. The head of the office was to be styled parliamentary counsel to the treasury, and was given a permanent assistant, and a treasury allowance for office expenses and for such outside legal assistance as he might require. The whole of the time of the parliamentary counsel and his assistant was to be given to the public, and they were not to engage in private practice. The parliamentary counsel was to settle all such departmental bills and draw all such other government bills (except Scotch and Irish bills) as he might be required by the treasury to settle and draw. The instructions for the preparation of every bill were to be in writing or sent by the head of the department concerned to the parliamentary counsel though the treasury, to which latter department he was to be considered responsible. On the requisition of the treasury he was to advise on all cases arising on bills or Acts drawn by him and to report in special cases referred to him by the treasury on bills brought by private members. Thring was appointed head of the office, and was given as his assistant (Sir) Henry Jenkyns, who succeeded to the office on Thring's retirement.

Thring held the office of parliamentary counsel during Gladstone's first ministry of 1868 to 1874, during Disraeli's ministry of 1874 to 1880, and until the close of Gladstone's third brief ministry of 1886.

This period was one of great legislative activity. The first important measure prepared by him as parliamentary counsel was the Irish Church Act of 1869; the last was Gladstone's Irish home rule bill of 1886. In the interval, among a host of other bills which did or did not find their way to the statute book, but which absorbed the time of the parliamentary counsel and his office, were the Irish Church Act of 1869, the Irish Land Act of 1871, and the Army Act of 1871, which was based on instructions given to Thring by Cardwell in 1867, and the labours on which, as its draftsman has remarked, lasted longer than the siege of Troy. The preparation of many bills relating to Ireland, which strictly lay outside the scope of his office, is accounted for by the circumstance that Irish bills always involve finance, and in practice the work of preparing them is apt to fall mainly on the office which works immediately under the treasury. It may be added that Thring's experience of Irish legislation made him a convinced home ruler.

Thring will be remembered as a great parliamentary draftsman. He broke away from the old conveyancing traditions, and introduced a new style, expounded and illustrated in the 'Instructions to Draftsmen,' which were used for many years by those working for and under him, and were eventually embodied in his little book on 'Practical Legislation' (1902, with an interesting autobiographical introduction). His drafting was criticised by the bench and elsewhere, often without regard for the difficulties inherent in parliamentary legislation, but the value of the improvements which he introduced into the style of drafting was emphatically recognised by the select committee on Acts of parliament which sat in 1875.

Thring was not merely a skilful draftsman. He was also 'a great legislator, so far as his duties and functions allowed, in the constructive sense. The quickness of his mind and the force of his imagination, controlled and restrained as they were by his rare technical skill, his vast knowledge of administrative law, and his instinctive insight into the nature, ways, and habits of both houses of parliament, enabled him at once to give effect to the views and wishes of the ministers who instructed him in a form best adapted to find the line of least parliamentary resistance' (*The Times*, 6 Feb. 1907). He thought in bills and clauses, and knew by instinct whether suggestions presented to him were capable of legislative expression, and if so how they should be expressed and arranged.

Improvement of the statute law was the object to which Thring persistently devoted the energies of his long and active life. He endeavoured to effect this object, not merely by introducing a better style of drafting new laws, but by throwing light upon the contents, diminishing the bulk, and reducing to more orderly arrangement the vast and chaotic mass of existing statute law. He was an original member of the statute law committee which was first appointed by Lord Cairns [q. v.] in 1868; he was for many years, and until his death, chairman of that committee and the last survivor of its original members. The work done by this committee fell under four heads:—(1) indexing; (2) expurgation; (3) republication; (4) consolidation. The chronological table of and index to the statutes, now annually published, were prepared in accordance with a plan and in pursuance of detailed instructions carefully framed by Thring. The contents of the statute book having been thus ascertained, the next step was to purge it of dead matter. This has been done by a long succession of statute law revision bills, most of which were framed under the directions of the statute law committee at a time when Thring was its most active member. Then came the republication of the living matter under the title of the statutes revised. The first edition of these statutes substituted eighteen volumes for 118 volumes of the statutes at large, the second comprised in five volumes the pre-Victorian statutes which had formerly occupied seventy-seven volumes. In the process of consolidation, although a great deal still remains to be done, much was done in Thring's time and under his guidance, and his name takes the first place in the history of this important task.

It was to Thring's initiative that was due the valuable publication of state trials from 1820, when Howell's series ended, to 1858. Its preparation arose out of a memorandum which he wrote in 1885, while he was parliamentary counsel, and he was an unfailing attendant at the meetings of the committee which supervised the publication.

Thring was made a K.C.B. in 1873, and was created a peer in 1886, on his retirement. In 1893 he seconded the address to the crown, but he was not a frequent speaker in the House of Lords, though, when he did speak, he could express himself clearly, cogently, and incisively. His quick mind and constructive intellect made him a valuable member of many public bodies, especially after his retirement from office in 1886. He had a country house at Englefield Green, in Surrey, and discharged his local duties by active membership of the Surrey county council and of the governing body of Holloway College. He also took a large part in the work of the council of the Imperial Institute and of the Athenæum club, where he was a well-known and popular figure.

Thring was a keen, vivacious little man, with a sharp tongue, which was often outspoken in its criticism of those whom he efficiently and loyally served. Robert Lowe seems to be responsible for the story that Cardwell said one day, at the outset of a cabinet committee, 'Now, Thring, let us begin by assuming that we are all d—d fools, and then get to business.'

Thring's published writings arose out of his professional or official work. Besides those mentioned he contributed an article to the 'Quarterly Review' of January 1874 which was republished in 1875 as a pamphlet under the title 'Simplification of the Law.' He superintended the compilation of the first edition of the war office 'Manual of Military Law,' and contributed to it four chapters, one of which, on the laws and customs of war on land, was made by Sir Henry Maine [q. v.] the text of some lectures on international law.

Thring died in London on 4 Feb. 1907, and was buried at Virginia Water. He married on 14 Aug. 1856 Elizabeth (*d.* 1897), daughter of John Cardwell of Liverpool and sister of Lord Cardwell. He left one daughter, but no son, and the peerage became extinct on his death.

A cartoon portrait by 'Spy' appeared in 'Vanity Fair' in 1893.

[Practical Legislation introd.; The Times, 6 Feb. 1907; personal knowledge.]

C. P. I.

THRUPP, GEORGE ATHELSTANE (1822–1905), author of 'History of the Art of Coachbuilding,' born in Somerset Street, Portman Square, on 16 July 1822, was second son of Charles Joseph Thrupp, coachbuilder, by his wife Harriet Styan [see THRUPP, FREDERICK, and THRUPP, JOHN]. A younger brother was Admiral Arthur Thomas Thrupp (1828–1889). Educated privately at Clapham, George entered at an early age the family coachmaking business in Oxford Street, which his great-grandfather had founded, and on the death of his father in 1866 he carried on the business with George Henry Maberly, who joined the firm in 1858 and died in December 1901. As a coachmaker Thrupp enjoyed a high reputation both in this country and on the continent, and did much to promote the general welfare of the trade. He was one of the founders in 1881 of the Institute of British Carriage Manufacturers, and of the Coach Makers' Benevolent Institution in 1856; he also took a leading part in establishing the technical schools for coach artisans in George Street (now Balderton Street), which were in 1884 taken over by the Regent Street Polytechnic. He became a liveryman of the Coachmakers' Company in 1865, a member of the court of assistants in 1879, and served as master in 1883.

In 1876 Thrupp delivered a series of lectures on coachbuilding before the Society of Arts. Published in 1877 as a 'History of the Art of Coachbuilding,' the volume became a standard work. He also published with William Farr a volume on 'Coach Trimming' (1888), and edited in the same year (2nd edit. 1894) William Simpson's 'Hand Book for Coach Painters.' Thrupp retired from business about 1889, and residing at Maida Vale divided his interests between local affairs and foreign travel. He died at his residence in Maida Vale on 1 Sept. 1905, and was buried in Paddington cemetery, Willesden Lane.

He married in August 1858 Elizabeth, daughter of Thomas Massey, by whom he had an only child, George Herbert Thrupp, who is now sole member of the firm of Thrupp & Maberly.

[City Press, 9 Sept. 1905, p. 5; Journ. Soc. Arts, 1904–5, vol. 53, pp. 1038, 1144; private information.]

C. W.

THUILLIER, SIR HENRY EDWARD LANDOR (1813–1906), surveyor-general of India, born at Bath on 10 July 1813, was youngest of eleven children (five sons and six daughters) of John Pierre Thuillier, merchant, of Cadiz and Bath, by his wife Julia, daughter of James Burrow of Exeter. An elder sister, Julia, married Walter Savage Landor [q. v.] in 1811. He descended from Huguenots who, on the revocation of the Edict of Nantes in 1685, first settled in Geneva. Educated at the East India Company's military academy, Addiscombe, Thuillier was gazetted to the Bengal artillery on 14 Dec. 1832, and was stationed at the headquarters, Dum Dum. Transferred to the survey department in Dec. 1836, he first served with parties in Ganjam and Orissa, and later was in charge of the revenue surveys in the Bengal districts of Cachar, Sylhet, Cuttack, and Patna. In Jan. 1847, ten months before receiving his captaincy, he was appointed deputy surveyor-general and superintendent of revenue surveys. That post he held for seventeen years, in the course of which he much improved the survey system and rendered the results more readily accessible to the public. He 'followed in the track of the different trigonometrical series, and thus had the advantage of fixed stations on which to base his detailed surveys' (*Memoir on Ind. Surveys*, 1878). In 1854 he prepared in his office in Calcutta the postage stamps first used in India, receiving the special thanks of government. He was joint author with Captain R. Smythe of 'The Manual of Surveying in India' (Calcutta, 1851; 3rd edit. 1885). There he discussed the difficult question of Indian orthography, which was officially standardised while he had charge of the department.

Succeeding Sir Andrew Scott Waugh [q. v.] as surveyor-general on 13 March 1861, he was promoted lieutenant-colonel in the same year, colonel on 20 Sept. 1865, and major-general on 26 March 1870. The survey of the more settled parts of India had been completed, and many of the surveys under Thuillier were over mountainous and forest-clad regions or sandy deserts, and frequently in parts never before visited by Europeans. In every branch he showed organising and administrative talent. In 1868 he transferred the preparation of the Atlas of India from England to Calcutta, selecting a staff of engravers there for the purpose, and encouraging John Bobanau Nicklerlieu Hennessey [q. v. Suppl. II] to introduce the photo-zincographic process. Under Thuillier's superintendence 796,928 square miles, or more than half the dependency, were dealt with. He was elected a fellow of the Royal Society in 1869, made a C.S.I. in May 1870, and knighted in May 1879. In July 1876 he was awarded a good service pension. He retired on 1 Jan. 1878, and the secretary of state, in a despatch dated 18 July 1878, highly commended the energy and perseverance of his forty-one years' service, and congratulated him on the results. He was gazetted lieutenant-general on 10 July 1879, general on 1 July 1881, and (a rare distinction for an officer with little actual military service) colonel commandant of the royal artillery on 1 Jan. 1883. Settling at Richmond, he was long a useful member of the Royal Geographical Society's council, and came to be looked upon as the father of the East India Company's service. Of fine presence and genial temper, he retained his faculties till his death on 6 May 1906 at Richmond, where he was buried.

He married (1) in 1836 Susanne Elizabeth (*d.* 1844), daughter of the Rev. Haydon Cardew of Curry Malet, Somerset, by whom he had a son (Colonel Sir Henry Ravenshaw Thuillier, K.C.I.E., also Indian surveyor-general 1887–95), and a daughter; and (2) in 1847 Annie Charlotte, daughter of George Gordon Macpherson, Bengal medical service, by whom he had six sons (three of them became officers in the Indian army) and two daughters.

There are three portraits in oils: (1) by Mr. Beetham (1846), belonging to Sir Henry Thuillier; (2) by Mr. G. G. Palmer (1885), now in the surveyor-general's office, Calcutta; and (3) by Mrs. Rowley (1896), presented by her to his eldest daughter, Mrs. Westmoreland.

[Markham's Memoir on Indian Surveys, London, 1878; official papers and survey reports; India List, 1906; Times, 8 May 1906; Army and Navy Gaz., 12 May 1906; Geographical Journ., June 1906; information kindly supplied by Sir Henry Thuillier.]

F. H. B.

THURSTON, Mrs. **KATHERINE CECIL** (1875–1911), novelist, born at Wood's Gift, Cork, on 18 April 1875, was only child of Paul Madden, banker, of Wood's Gift by his wife Catherine Barry. The father was chairman and director of the Ulster and Leinster bank and an intimate friend of Charles Stewart Parnell [q. v.]. He was elected mayor of Cork and took a leading part in local politics on the nationalist side. Katherine's early life was passed at her father's house, where she was privately educated. Of a vivacious temperament, she became devoted to riding and swimming. But it was not till after her marriage in 1901 to Ernest Charles Temple

Thurston, the novelist, that she evinced literary ability.

Her career as a writer began with 'The Circle' (1903), which, if less sensational than her subsequent novels, showed originality. In 1904 she acquired wide fame through the publication of 'John Chilcote, M.P.,' which appeared simultaneously in America under the title of 'The Masquerader.' Mrs. Thurston handled an improbable story of impersonation and mistaken identity with much skill and force. None of her subsequent works attained the same degree of popularity. 'The Gambler' (1906), a brightly written study of Irish life and scenery, was followed by 'The Mystics' (1907) and 'The Fly on the Wheel' (1908), novels of a more conventional type. In 'Max' (1910) Mrs. Thurston repeated with less success a story of impersonation. In all her work a genuine gift for story-telling is combined with a fluent style and signs of intellectual insight.

Meanwhile domestic disagreements arose with her husband, and on 7 April 1910 she obtained a decree nisi. Mrs. Thurston, who was of delicate health, suffered periodically from fainting fits. She died from asphyxia during a seizure at Moore's Hotel, Cork, on 5 Sept. 1911. She was buried in the family grave at Cork. The bulk of her property passed to her executor, A. T. Bulkeley Gavin, M.D.

[The Times, 8 April 1910 and 7 Sept. 1911; Athenæum, 9 Sept. 1911; private information.] G. S. W.

TINSLEY, WILLIAM (1831–1902), publisher, born in 1831, was the son of a Hertfordshire gamekeeper. He was educated at a dame's school, and as a child worked in the fields. He came to London in 1852 and obtained employment at Notting Hill. He joined his younger brother Edward in the publishing business of Tinsley Brothers in Holywell Street, Strand, in 1854. They afterwards moved to Catherine Street, Strand. After issuing some small volumes of essays by W. B. Jerrold and J. E. Ritchie, their first serious venture was G. A. Sala's novel 'The Seven Sons of Mammon' (1861). The next success of the firm was with Miss Braddon's (Mrs. Maxwell) 'Lady Audley's Secret' (1862) and 'Aurora Floyd' (1863). They published 'The New Quarterly Review' (1854–9), but lost money in supporting 'The Library Company,' founded to rival Messrs. Mudie's and Messrs. W. H. Smith & Son's circulating libraries. Edward Tinsley died at a little over the age of thirty in 1866 (*Athenæum*, 22 Sept. 1866). In 1868 Tinsley started 'Tinsley's Magazine,' which was for some time edited by Edmund Yates and afterwards by the publisher himself; it continued till 1881. For many years the firm was the chief producer of novels and light literature in London. Among the authors whose works were issued by the Tinsleys were Ouida (Louise de la Ramée), William Black, Thomas Hardy, Sir W. H. Russell, J. S. Le Fanu, Joseph Hatton, Tom Hood, Blanchard Jerrold, Justin McCarthy, Andrew Halliday, Mrs. Cashel Hoey, Sir Walter Besant, Viscount Morley, Benjamin Leopold Farjeon, George Meredith, G. A. Lawrence (Guy Livingstone), Mrs. Henry Wood, Edmund Yates, Henry Kingsley, Mrs. Lynn Linton, Mrs. Riddell, Rhoda Broughton, Jean Ingelow, Mrs. Oliphant, Florence Marryat, Anthony Trollope, Mortimer Collins, Wilkie Collins, James Payn, Sir Richard Burton, George MacDonald, Captain Mayne Reid, W. Harrison Ainsworth, Amelia B. Edwards, George A. Henty, G. Manville Fenn, and Alfred Austin.

In 1878 Tinsley failed, with liabilities amounting to about 33,000*l.* He published in 1900 his reminiscences of the authors and actors he had known, under the title of 'Random Recollections of an Old Publisher,' 2 vols., with a photogravure after a photograph. He died at Wood Green, Middlesex, on 1 May 1902.

[The Bookseller, 8 May 1902; The Times, 3 May 1902; The Publishers' Circular, 10 May 1902; H. Sutherland Edwards, Personal Recollections, 1900, pp. 134–42 (doubtful accuracy); G. A. Sala, Life, 1895, i. 425; E. Yates, Recollections, 1884, ii. 87–88; S. M. Ellis, W. H. Ainsworth and his Friends, 1911, passim.] H. R. T.

TODD, Sir CHARLES (1826–1910), government astronomer and postmaster-general of the colony of South Australia, born at Islington, London, on 7 July 1826, was elder son of George Todd, a grocer at Greenwich. Charles in 1841, at the age of fifteen, obtained employment in the Royal Observatory as a supernumerary computer under Sir George Airy, the astronomer royal. He held the post, except for a few months' interval, until the end of 1847. Early next year he became assistant astronomer at the Cambridge University observatory, where, being in charge of the large telescope, the Northumberland equatorial, he was one of the earliest observers of the planet Neptune discovered in 1846), and with the same instrument took a daguerreotype picture of the moon, this being one of the first attempts in astronomical photography. The electric telegraph was then first being applied to astronomic observation, and Todd whilst at the University Observatory helped in the operations of determining telegraphically the difference of longitude between Cambridge and Greenwich. In 1854 he was recalled to the Royal Observatory to take charge of the electro-galvanic apparatus which had just been introduced for the transmission of time signals, and in the following year Airy recommended him to the colonial office for the post of superintendent of the telegraphs to be established in South Australia, and director of the Adelaide observatory, which it was just decided to create. Todd landed in Australia on 5 Nov. 1855. He remained in charge of the colonial observatory at Adelaide until 31 Dec. 1906. The varied calls of official work prevented him from personally undertaking any extensive research. But in 1868 he co-operated with the government astronomers of Victoria and New South Wales in the determination of a more accurate position of the 141st meridian, which was to be adopted as the common boundary of South Australia and New South Wales. In 1874, during the transit of Venus, a large number of micrometric measures of the planet were made at the observatory. On the occasion of the transit in 1882 Todd journeyed to Wentworth for its observations. Long series of observations of the phenomena of Jupiter's satellites, most of them made by Todd himself, with notes on the physical appearance of the planet, were published in the 'Royal Astronomical Society's Monthly Notices,' vols. xxxvii., xxxix. and xl. He observed the Great Southern Comet of 1880 and other comets, and under his direction his assistants effected a considerable amount of observation with the transit-circle which was provided by the government of South Australia at Todd's instigation about 1880. The routine meteorological work of the observatory he directed with characteristic thoroughness, and he organised an extensive meteorological service, extending over the whole state.

But his chief energies were absorbed as soon as he reached Australia in 1855 with designs for a great telegraphic system on the Australian continent. Private enterprise had made a first effort in telegraphy in South Australia with a short line from the city of Adelaide to the port. But immediately on his arrival Todd set up a government line over the same route, which was opened on 21 Feb. 1856. Its success was immediate and the private line was bought up and dismantled. In the same year Todd proposed to the South Australian government the establishment of an intercolonial telegraph line joining Adelaide and Melbourne, and after negotiation with the government of Victoria he brought the service between the two capitals into use in July 1858. The telegraph systems in the adjoining states, New South Wales and Queensland, had been developing contemporaneously with that in South Australia. In proposals for connecting Brisbane and Sydney with Melbourne and Adelaide Todd effectively co-operated. The line between Sydney and Melbourne was opened in 1858, and was extended to Brisbane in 1861.

Before he left England Todd had recognised the desirability of bringing Australia into closer connection with the mother country by means of the telegraph. As early as 1859 Todd submitted to Sir Richard MacDonnell [q. v.], governor of South Australia, a scheme for a line to cross the continent from Adelaide to Port Darwin, in the extreme north. This proposal, which he embodied in a despatch to the colonial secretary, was greatly helped by the exploration in the interior of John McDouall Stuart [q. v.]. Meanwhile an English company (afterwards the Eastern Extension Company) were planning a cable from Singapore via Java to Port Darwin, where a connection could be made with an Australian land line and the Australian continent could be thus united telegraphically with the rest of the world. Todd pressed his scheme with pertinacity in official quarters, and the internal line was authorised in 1870. In 1869 the telegraph and postal departments of South Australia had been amalgamated, and Todd became postmaster-general next year. The colony bore the whole charge of constructing the internal telegraph line, which was nearly two thousand miles long, mostly across unknown country. Todd supervised the difficult work, and in August 1872, being at Mount Stuart, in the centre of the Australian continent, he had the satisfaction of telegraphing by means of a portable instrument in both directions to Port Darwin and to Adelaide. The cable from Port Darwin to Singapore was in working order a little later, and complete communication was established between Adelaide and England on 21 Oct. Three weeks later banquets were held in London, Adelaide, and Sydney to celebrate the event, and Todd was made C.M.G. The subsequent construction of the telegraph line under Todd's direction, joining West Australia to the Eastern colonies, practically completed the system for the continent, which finally extended over 5000 miles. The whole came into being in less than forty years after Todd had landed in Australia.

Todd, who was made K.C.M.G. in 1893, retained his offices till June 1905, although the Commonwealth Act of 1901 introduced slight changes into his duties and title. So long as he remained in the public service the state parliament declined to pass an Act for the compulsory retirement of septuagenarians. He joined the Royal Astronomical Society on 8 April 1864, and was elected F.R.S. in 1889. The University of Cambridge conferred on him the honorary degree of M.A. in 1886. He was a fellow of the Royal Meteorological Society and of the Society of Electrical Engineers. He died at Adelaide on 29 Jan. 1910, and was buried there.

He married on 5 April 1855 Alice Gillam (*d.* 1898), daughter of Edward Bell of Cambridge, and left one son, Dr. C. E. Todd, and four daughters.

[Adelaide journals: The Advertiser and The Register, 30 Jan. 1910; Monthly Notices R.A.S., Feb. 1911; Heaton's Australian Dict. of Dates; Burke's Colonial Gentry; private information.] H. P. H.

TOMSON, ARTHUR (1859–1905), landscape painter, born at Chelmsford, Essex, on 5 March 1859, was sixth child of Whitbread Tomson by his wife Elizabeth Maria. From a preparatory school at Ingatestone in Essex he went to Uppingham. As a lad he showed an artistic bent, and on leaving school he studied art at Düsseldorf. Returning to England in 1882, he settled down to landscape painting, working chiefly in Sussex and Dorset. His landscapes were poetic, and rather similar in sentiment to the art of George Mason and Edward Stott. Although he was at his best in landscape, cats were favourite subjects of study, and he occasionally painted other animals. At the New English Art Club, of which he was an early member and in whose affairs he took warm interest, he was a regular exhibitor, but he also showed at the Royal Academy from 1883 to 1892 and at the New Gallery. An excellent and characteristic example of his refined art is the canvas called 'The Chalk Pit,' which was presented by his widow to the Victoria and Albert Museum. He was also an interesting writer on art, and his book on 'Jean-François Millet and the Barbizon School' (1903; reissued in 1905) is sympathetic and discriminating. For some years he was art critic for the 'Morning Leader,' under the pseudonym of Verind, and he contributed to the 'Art Journal' descriptions of places in the southern counties, illustrated by his own drawings. He illustrated 'Concerning Cats,' poems selected by his first wife 'Graham R. Tomson' (1892).

He died on 14 June 1905 at Robertsbridge, and was buried in Steeple churchyard, near Wareham, in Dorset.

Tomson married in 1887 his first wife Rosamund (1863–1911), writer of poetry, youngest child of Benjamin Williams Ball, whom he divorced in 1896, and who afterwards married Mr. H. B. Marriott Watson. Tomson married secondly in 1898 Miss Hastings, a descendant of Warren Hastings, who survived him with a son.

[Art Journal, 1905; Grave's Roy. Acad. Exhibitors, 1906; private information.] F. W. G–N.

TOOLE, JOHN LAWRENCE (1830–1906), actor and theatrical manager, born at 50 St. Mary Axe, London, on 12 March 1830, and baptised in the church of St. Andrew Undershaft on 25 July, was younger son of James Toole by his wife Elizabeth (*Parish Reg.*). His father at the time was an India House messenger, but afterwards combined the offices of City toast master and usher in the Central Criminal Court at the Old Bailey. As toast master he enjoyed an extended fame. 'An Ode to Toast-Master Toole' appeared in 'Punch' on 11 Nov. 1843. In 1846 Dickens wrote of him as 'the renowned Mr. Toole, the most emphatic, vigorous, attentive, and stentorian toast master in the Queen's dominions.' Thackeray, in his 'Roundabout Paper' on 'Thorns in the Cushion,' describes 'Mr. Toole' bawling behind the lord mayor's chair. Educated at the City of London School, young Toole began life as a wine merchant's clerk, and while so employed became a member of the City Histrionic Club, which gave performances in the Sussex Hall, Leadenhall Street, making his first appearance as Jacob Earwig in 'Boots at the Swan.' Encouraged by Dickens, who saw him in a monologue entertainment at the Walworth Literary Institute in 1852, Toole made one or two experimental appearances that year for benefits in town and country, notably at the Haymarket on 22 July, when he played Simmons in 'The Spitalfields Weaver' at the end of a long programme, terminating at two o'clock A.M. Finally, on 8 Oct., he made his professional début in the same character at the Queen's Theatre, Dublin, where he was engaged by Charles Dillon as stock low comedian at a salary of 2*l.* per week, and, becoming an immediate favourite, remained six months. Here, for his benefit on 30 Nov., he played his popular rôle of Paul Pry for the first time. On 9 July 1853, tempted by a better offer, he transferred his services to the Theatre Royal, Edinburgh, making his first appearance as Hector Timid in 'A Dead Shot.' At Edinburgh, where he delighted his audiences by imitations of popular actors, he appeared for the first time on 7 March 1854 in his droll embodiment of the Artful Dodger in 'Oliver Twist,' singing 'The Dodger's Lament,' specially written for him by Hill, a member of the company. Returning to London for Passion Week, he gave his entertainment 'Toole at Home, or a Touch at the Times,' at the Southwark, Hackney, Walworth, and Beaumont Institutions. On 18 May 1854 he had a farewell benefit at Edinburgh, playing, *inter alia*, young Master Willikind in Hill's new burlesque 'The Loves of Willikind and his Dinah.'

On 2 Oct. Toole began his first professional engagement in London by originating at the St. James's Theatre the poorly drawn character of Samuel Pepys in Taylor and Reade's ineffective comedy, 'The King's Rival,' and the more congenial rôle of Weazle, the disguised sheriff's officer, in Selby's farce, 'My Friend the Major.' But the engagement proved disquieting, and on 26 March 1855 he returned with relief to the Edinburgh stock company. On 2 Oct. he was seen as Lord Sands in an elaborate revival of 'King Henry VIII,' and on 3 Dec. as Bottom in 'A Midsummer-Night's Dream.' For his benefit on 15 April 1856 he played Felix Rosemary in 'Toole's Appeal to the Public,' and on 29 August following concluded his Edinburgh engagement. Transferring his services for two seasons to the Lyceum in London under Charles Dillon, he first appeared there on 15 Sept. as Fanfaronade in Webb's adaptation of 'Belphegor the Mountebank,' to the Belphegor of Dillon and the Henri of Marie Wilton (Lady Bancroft), who then made her metropolitan début. The afterpiece was Brough's new burlesque 'Perdita, or the Royal Milkmaid,' in which Toole was the Autolycus. In the succeeding summer he started provincial starring with a small company of his own, a custom he followed annually, with great pecuniary advantage, till his retirement. During a three months' sojourn at Edinburgh in the summer of 1857 he made the acquaintance of Henry Irving, playing Adolphus Spanker to his Dazzle in 'London Assurance.' A warm and lifelong friendship between the two followed.

At the Lyceum in London he was seen for the first time on 10 March 1858 in his long popular characterisation of Tom Cranky in Hollingshead's sketch 'The Birthplace of Podgers.'

Engaged by Benjamin Webster [q. v.] of the New Adelphi on the strength of a warm recommendation from Charles Dickens, Toole made his first appearance at that house on 27 Dec. 1858, and remained there nine years. At the Adelphi he succeeded Edward Richard Wright [q. v.] in many of his parts, and inherited much of Wright's fame. On 9 May he was the original Spriggins in T. J. Williams's farce, 'Ici on parle Français,' an eccentric embodiment that maintained perpetual vogue. The revival of 'The Willow Copse' in September was notable for Toole's rendering of Augustus de Rosherville, a character formerly deemed the vehicle for the broadest kind of humour, but now rationalised by the genius of the actor. Toole created leading parts in many ephemeral farces, and was also the first Brutus Toupet in Watts Phillips's 'The Dead Heart' (10 Nov. 1859). At Christmas he made an effective Bob Cratchit in 'The Christmas Carol.' He did justice to Enoch Flicker, a powerfully drawn semi-serious character in Phillips's spectacular 'A Story of '45' (12 Nov. 1860), which Webster produced at Drury Lane; and was Wapshot in the first performance in England of Boucicault's 'The Life of an Actress' (Adelphi, 1 March 1862). On 14 April following Toole showed his full power in his delicate embodiment of old Caleb Plummer, the toymaker, in 'Dot' (Boucicault's version of 'The Cricket on the Hearth'), an impersonation in which he combined irresistibly humour and pathos. Toole's Caleb Plummer undoubtedly ranks among the histrionic masterpieces of his century. Among succeeding triumphs in drama or burlesque are to be noted his rendering of Azucena in Byron's burlesque 'Ill-treated Il Trovatore' (21 May), and of Mr. Tetterby in 'The Haunted Man' at the Adelphi (27 June 1863).

Toole had now attained a salary of 35*l.*

per week. On 7 March 1864 he was the original policeman in Brough and Halliday's farce 'The Area Belle' to the soldier of his ally Paul Bedford. In this he first sang E. L. Blanchard's ditty 'A Norrible Tale.' For his annual benefit on 14 Sept. he produced Oxenford's adaptation of 'Le Père Goriot' entitled 'Stephen Digges,' which had been written specially to suit his capacity for serio-comic acting of the Robsonian order. After seeing this masterly performance Dickens wrote to Forster that Toole had shown 'a power of passion very unusual indeed in a comic actor, as such things go, and of a quite remarkable kind.' But the play proved unattractive and was not revived. On 26 June 1865 he originated with acceptance another semi-serious plebeian character, Joe Bright, in Walter Gordon's comedy-drama 'Through Fire and Water,' and surprised his audience in the opening act by a grimly realistic exhibition of drunken savagery. In the summer of 1866 he went on tour with Henry Irving.

On 25 Nov. 1867, after Toole's association with the Adelphi ended, he produced at the Alexandra, Liverpool, Byron's comedy 'Dearer than Life,' in which the character of Michael Garner had been specially designed for his serio-comic capabilities. On its production in London at the Queen's Theatre, Long Acre, on 8 Jan. 1868, Toole was supported by a new cast, comprising Charles Wyndham, Henry Irving, Lionel Brough, and Henrietta Hodson, and the harmony of the acting concealed the defective construction of the play. Toole's mingled exhibition of grief, passion, and humour as the brave old man who could endure starvation with a pleasant face raised him higher in critical estimation. In association with Henry Irving, he subsequently fulfilled an engagement of seven weeks at the Standard Theatre. After his usual autumn tour he returned to the Queen's, Long Acre, on 26 Dec., and on 13 Feb. 1869 originated Jack Snipe in Watts Phillips's drama 'Not Guilty.'

On 13 Dec. 1869 Toole began his long and varied association with the Gaiety under John Hollingshead [q. v. Suppl. II], by producing there Byron's drama 'Uncle Dick's Darling,' in which his half-pathetic, half-comic acting as Dick Dolland, the Cheap Jack, delighted Dickens. Seven nights later Toole played the title-character in Sala's new burlesque 'Wat Tyler, M.P.,' and was well supported by Nellie Farren [q. v. Suppl. II] and Marie Litton. In his autumn tours of 1869 and 1870 Toole was accompanied by Henry Irving, the two playing, *inter alia*, Jacques Strop and Robert Macaire, characters in which they were afterwards seen at the Lyceum on 15 June 1883. For some time from 16 April 1870 Toole had the Grimaldian experience of acting nightly at two theatres. After appearing in 'Uncle Dick's Darling' at the Standard he finished the evening as Cabriolo in Offenbach's opera-bouffe 'The Princess of Trebizonde,' at the Gaiety. At the latter house in the following Christmas he contributed materially to the success of Alfred Thompson's opera-bouffe 'Aladdin II,' by his whimsicality as Ko-Kli-Ko. There also on 24 Jan. 1871 he appeared as Sergeant Buzfuz in Hollingshead's sketch 'Bardell *v.* Pickwick,' for the benefit of the Royal Dramatic College Fund. At Christmas he performed acceptably as Thespis in Gilbert and Sullivan's first extravaganza, 'Thespis, or the Gods Grown Old.' In September 1872 he revelled in the title-character of Reece's burlesque 'Ali Baba.' Burlesque chiefly occupied him at the Gaiety, but he was seen there in Liston's character of Billy Lackaday in 'Sweethearts and Wives' (3 April 1873), as Mawworm in 'The Hypocrite' to Phelps's Doctor Cantwell (15 Dec.), as Dennis Brulgruddery in 'John Bull' to Charles Mathews's Hon. Tom Shuffleton (21 Dec.), and as Bob Acres in association with Phelps and Mathews (14 Feb. 1874). His salary at the Gaiety at this period was 100*l.* per week.

On 6 April 1874 Toole opened the Globe Theatre for ten weeks, first producing there Albery's new domestic drama 'Wig and Gown,' in which he originated the extravagant character of Hammond Coote the barrister. After being banqueted at Willis's Rooms by a distinguished gathering under the presidency of Lord Rosebery on 24 June, Toole sailed for a first and last visit to America, accompanied by his wife and family and four supporting players. On 17 August he made his first appearance at Wallack's Theatre, New York, acting in 'Wig and Gown' and 'The Spitalfields Weaver.' The American public gave him a lukewarm reception, and condemned his humour as Cockneyfied. Returning to London after a year's absence, he reappeared at the Gaiety on 8 Nov. 1875, and on 3 Dec. was seen there in Reece's absurdity 'Toole at Sea.' He subsequently originated the title-character in Byron's comic drama of 'Tottles,' and created Professor Muddle in Reece's 'A Spelling Bee, or the Battle of the Dictionaries,' in which he sang 'The Two Obadiahs.' The last new production of importance in which he appeared at the Gaiety was Burnand's farcical comedy 'Artful Cards' (24 Feb. 1877), in which, as Mr. Spicer Rumford, his humour had full scope.

Taking the Globe for a season, Toole produced there on 17 Dec. 1877 his own farcical sketch 'Trying a Magistrate,' and exactly a month later he originated the congenial rôle of Charles Liquorpond, the retired footman, in Byron's successful comedy 'A Fool and his Money.' At the end of 1879 Toole leased for a term ultimately extending to sixteen years the Folly (formerly the Charing Cross) Theatre, a little house in King William Street, Strand. He inaugurated his management on 17 Nov. 1879 with 'A Fool and his Money' and 'Ici on parle Français.' At the Folly, where he maintained a small permanent stock company, some members of which, such as John Billington and Eliza Johnstone, remained with him for years, he mainly relied on farcical comedies or burlesques by Byron or Reece. His production of Byron's comedy 'The Upper Crust' on 31 March 1880, with himself as Barnaby Doublechick, the soap-boiler, proved remarkably successful. Early in 1882 he took the Folly on a long lease, and re-opened it as Toole's Theatre on 16 Feb., when he was seen as Paul Pry. After producing Law and Grossmith's musical farce 'Mr. Guffin's Elopement,' at the Alexandra, Liverpool, on 29 Sept., with himself as Benjamin Guffin, he transferred it to Toole's on 7 Oct., and was very successful in his singing of 'The Speaker's Eye.' At the close of the month he originated Solomon Protheroe, the village cobbler-pedagogue in Pinero's unconventional comedy 'Girls and Boys'; but the play was puzzling and proved a failure. Subsequently he brought out from time to time several travesties of popular plays by Burnand, himself amusingly caricaturing Charles Coghlan as Loris Ipanoff in 'Stage Dora' (26 May 1883), Wilson Barrett as Claudian in 'Paw Clawdian' (14 Feb. 1884), and Irving as Mephistopheles in 'Faust and Loose' (4 Feb. 1886).

On 24 Nov. 1886 Toole produced at the Theatre Royal, Manchester, Mr. and Mrs. Herman Merivale's domestic comedy 'The Butler,' in which he was admirably fitted as David Trot. On its transference to Toole's on 6 Dec. the new piece proved very successful. Of equal popularity was the same authors' comedy 'The Don,' as produced at the King William Street house on 7 March 1888, with Toole as Mr. Milliken, M.A.

Domestic distress caused his retirement during 1888 and 1889. In Feb. 1890, shortly after his return to the stage, he accepted an offer to visit Australia, where he was warmly welcomed and remained longer than he had intended. He reappeared at Toole's on 23 April 1891 in 'The Upper Crust.' On 30 May he appeared as Ibsen, wonderfully made up, in J. M. Barrie's sketch 'Ibsen's Ghost; or Toole up to Date.' The most noteworthy production of his declining years was Barrie's comedy 'Walker, London,' brought out at Toole's on 25 Feb. 1892 with himself as Jasper Phipps, the fugitive bridegroom and barber. Gout now began to make serious inroads on his health, and from this time onwards his acting became a painful spectacle. On 28 Sept. 1895 his lease of the theatre expired and his London career ended. The theatre was pulled down at the end of the year to afford extension to Charing Cross Hospital. For a few months Toole lagged superfluous on the provincial stage, making his last appearance at the Theatre Royal, Rochdale, on 19 Dec. 1896, when he was seen as Caleb Plummer and Tom Cranky. Degeneration of the spinal cord soon rendered Toole a helpless invalid. Retiring to Brighton, he died there on 30 July 1906. He was buried in Kensal Green cemetery beside his wife and children, who all predeceased him. Toole's later life was marked by severe domestic distresses. He married in 1854 Susan Kaslake, a young widow unconnected with the stage, with whom he lived very happily, and who almost invariably accompanied him while on tour. By her he had a son and a daughter. On 4 Dec. 1879 the son, Frank Lawrence Toole, died, aged 23. The daughter, Florence, died on 5 Nov. 1888, and his wife a few months later.

He left a fortune of 79,964*l.* By his will he made numerous legacies to friends and to charities. In 1889 there was published his 'Reminiscences,' which were compiled by Joseph Hatton [q.v. Suppl. II].

Toole's eccentric drollery was the outward expression of a frolicsome, boyish, sunny nature, which otherwise manifested itself in ebullitions of practical joking, wholly void of offence. Simple in his tastes and domestic in his habits, he was entirely lovable, never making an enemy or losing a friend. Although he was fundamentally an artist, with high personative qualities and considerable gifts of pathos, the preponderance of his work was of the laughter-making order. But his Caleb Plummer and Michael Garner showed a capacity for higher things. As a low comedian he was a disciple of the school of Liston and Wright, a school that believed in establishing so complete an understanding with the public that liberties might be taken with it. Where the author failed, the comedian made fun on his own account. Toole had all Wright's propensities for 'gagging,' and (especially in the provinces) gratified them to the full. If his humour was neither so rich nor so spontaneous as Wright's, it at least lacked his coarseness and lubricity. The last great low comedian of the old school, Toole was certainly the cleanest. A portrait of him by the Hon. John Collier, presented in 1895 by Sir Henry Irving, hangs in the Garrick Club (No. 340). Several other portraits of the comedian in character were sold at the auction of his effects at Sotheby's on 8 Nov. 1906. A cartoon portrait by 'Spy' appeared in 'Vanity Fair' in 1876.

[Joseph Hatton's Reminiscences of J. L. Toole; W. Clark Russell's Representative Actors; Forster's Life of Charles Dickens; J. C. Dibdin's Annals of the Edinburgh Stage; Theatrical Journal for 1852–5; The Bancroft Memoirs; Recollections of Edmund Yates; Pascoe's Dramatic List; Era Almanack for 1877; W. Davenport Adams's Dict. of the Drama; T. Edgar Pemberton's Dickens and the Stage; Dramatic Notes, 1879–88; Col. T. Allston Brown's History of the New York Theatres; William Archer's The Theatrical World for 1894–5; Dutton Cook's Nights at the Play; Pemberton's The Birmingham Theatres; John Hollingshead's Gaiety Chronicles; The Lady of the House (Dublin) for 15 Aug. 1906; Idler Mag., April 1893; Daily Telegraph, Dublin Evening Herald, and Dublin Evening Mail, 31 July 1906; personal knowledge and research.]

W. J. L.

TORRANCE, GEORGE WILLIAM (1835–1907), musician and divine, born at Rathmines, Dublin, in 1835, was eldest son of George Torrance, merchant tailor, and was a chorister in Christ Church Cathedral from 1847 to 1851, under Sir Robert Prescott Stewart [q. v.]. He was organist for a short time at Blackrock, and then at St. Andrew's in 1852 and at St. Ann's in 1854. A 'Te Deum' and 'Jubilate' which he composed in early youth showed promise, and in 1854 he composed an oratorio, 'Abraham,' which was performed—with Sir Robert Stewart at the organ—at the Antient Concert Rooms, Dublin, next year. In order to complete his musical studies he went to Leipzig in 1856, returning to Dublin in 1858. A second oratorio, 'The Captivity' (words by Goldsmith), was given at the Antient Concert Rooms on 19 December 1864. Meanwhile drawn towards the ministry, he entered Trinity College in 1859, and graduated B.A. in 1864, proceeding M.A. in 1867. Ordained deacon in 1865 and priest in 1866, he was curate of St. Michael's, Shrewsbury (1865–7), and of St. Ann's, Dublin (1867–9).

In 1869 Torrance went in search of health to Australia, holding successively the curacies of Christ Church, Melbourne (1870–1); St. John's, Melbourne (1871–7); and the incumbencies of All Saints, Geelong (1877–8); Holy Trinity, Balaclava (1878–94); and St. John's, Melbourne (1894–7). In 1879 he received the degree of Mus.D. from Dublin University, and in 1880 Melbourne University conferred on him a similar honour. His third oratorio, 'The Revelation,' was produced at Melbourne in June 1882.

In 1897 Torrance returned to Ireland, and was appointed chaplain to the bishop of Ossory, being made in 1899 bishop's vicar choral and librarian of St. Canice's Cathedral library, and in 1900 prebendary of Killamery and canon of St. Canice's. He was also registrar for the united dioceses of Ossory, Ferns, and Leighlin. He continued to compose much sacred and secular music. In January 1902 he won the prize of ten guineas offered by the 'School Music Review' for the best coronation song for school singing, namely, 'Come, raise we now our voices,' published as No. 676 of Novello's 'School Songs.' In 1903 his madrigal 'Dry be that tear' obtained the Molyneux prize and the society's medal, offered by the Madrigal Society (London). Two of his anthems, 'Who shall roll us away' and 'I will pray the Father,' were published in Novello's 'Octavo Anthems,' and ten of his hymns are included in the 'Church Hymnal' (Ireland)—'Euroclydon' being still a favourite. He died on 20 Aug. 1907. He was married, and his wife died two days before him.

[Grove's Dict. of Music, 1910; private information; personal knowledge.]

W. H. G. F.

TOWNSEND, MEREDITH WHITE (1831–1911), editor of the 'Friend of India' and the 'Spectator,' born in London on 1 April 1831, was the only son (in the family of three children) of William Townsend, one of the sixteen children of Charles Townsend of Ferriers, Bures St. Mary, on the borders of Essex and Suffolk. The family had been long settled in North Essex, both at Coggeshall and Bures, and

William Townsend inherited a few hundred acres, which he farmed himself. His wife Alicia was daughter of John Sparrowe of 'The Ancient House' or 'Sparrowe House,' Ipswich. On the death in early middle age of William Townsend, who was unsuccessful in business, his widow returned to Ipswich with her three children.

Meredith Townsend was educated at Queen Elizabeth's grammar school, Ipswich, where he had for schoolfellow Edward Byles Cowell [q. v. Suppl. II], the orientalist, and distinguished himself greatly in classics, but left at sixteen in 1847 to become assistant in a school in Scotland. From this work, on which he looked back with something like horror, he was speedily rescued by an invitation from a friend of the family, John Clark Marshman [q. v], to come out and assist him in the editing of the 'Friend of India' (founded in 1835) at Serampore, near Calcutta. Townsend left the Scotch school on the day on which he received the message, and sailed in 1848 for India. He lived with the Marshmans at Serampore, and sent home the whole of his first year's salary to his mother. From the first he threw himself into his work with such energy and ability that at twenty-one he was already editor of the 'Friend of India' and in 1853 he became proprietor. His knowledge of native affairs was largely derived from an old pundit who taught him Bengali. Amongst others who contributed to the 'Friend' was Dr. George Smith, but it was essentially a one-man paper in Townsend's time. In later years he used to say that he often wrote the whole paper 'except the advertisements.' The influence he exerted and the value of his support were attested by Lord Dalhousie and Lord Canning. The former, whose policy Townsend stoutly defended, writing on the eve of his departure, 3 March 1856, thanked Townsend for the fairness 'with which you have always set your judgment of my public acts before the community whose opinions are largely subject to your influence,' and again on 28 Dec. 1857 for standing by him 'at a time when, literally fettered and gagged, I am deprived of all power of defending myself.' Lord Canning, in a letter dated 2 April 1857, expressed his special satisfaction with the service Townsend had rendered to the army and the state by an article on the officers of native regiments. Besides his work on the 'Friend,' Townsend also undertook temporarily the editorship of 'The Calcutta Quarterly Review' and the 'Annals of Indian Administration.' He further edited a vernacular journal, 'Satya Pradip' formerly 'Sumachar Durpun' (or 'Mirror of News') and acted as correspondent of 'The Times.' Returning to England to recruit his health, he was summoned back to India by the outbreak of the Mutiny. Townsend remained at his post at Serampore throughout this trying period, in which the influence of the 'Friend of India' reached its zenith, but his health broke down under the strain, which was aggravated by domestic trouble. In 1859 he was peremptorily ordered home by the doctors. Dr. George Smith succeeded him as editor.

Rapidly regaining his health on his return to England, Townsend bought the 'Spectator' in 1860 from Mr. Scott, the successor of Robert Stephen Rintoul [q. v.], and a few months later took into partnership Richard Holt Hutton, to whom he had been introduced by Walter Bagehot. The terms of the agreement made them joint-editors and co-proprietors, but the ultimate control rested with Townsend. Their relations were defined by Townsend in the 'Spectator' (11 Sept. 1897) after Hutton's death as 'an unbroken friendship of thirty-six years and a literary alliance which at once in its duration and completeness is probably without a precedent.' During the first few years of their alliance the 'Spectator,' which had declined in prestige after Rintoul's death, was worked at a loss. The editors ran counter to the opinion of the well-to-do classes in England by their unflinching support of the unpopular side in the American civil war. They upheld and prophesied victory for the North all along; their excellent military critic, George Hooper, was quick to seize the immense significance of Sherman's famous 'March to the Sea'; and as the tide of war turned, so also did the fortunes of the paper.

Townsend, though he contributed freely to all departments of the paper, wrote chiefly on foreign politics and always on India. He brought to bear on his special subject an immense store of illustrative information, not invariably accurate, for he was an omnivorous reader, and had a picturesque and even romantic outlook on the future. He wrote with the utmost ease and unfailing zest in a clear, vigorous, natural style and never qualified his statements. He dogmatised freely, but was never pedantic. His habitual indulgence in prophecy occasionally led him astray. Thus his accurate prediction of the danger to Cavagnari's mission to Kabul in 1879 was neutralised by his unfounded pessimism—

which he frankly owned afterwards—in regard to the expedition of Lord Roberts.

The peculiar quality of the 'Spectator' under the Townsend and Hutton *régime* was due to the fact that it was written mainly by two men of remarkable ability, whose equipments were supplementary to each other, and who devoted their entire energies to the paper. They enlisted, however, the occasional assistance of many able men, among them Walter Bagehot, Charles Henry Pearson, afterwards minister of education in Victoria, Sir Robert Giffen, Mr. H. H. Asquith, and Mr. W. F. Monypenny, the biographer of Lord Beaconsfield. Townsend's journalistic activity extended over a period of exactly sixty years, during which time he must have written close on 10,000 articles. Besides his work on the 'Spectator,' for many years he contributed the political article in the 'Economist.' In 1898 Townsend resigned his editorial control of the paper on its sale to Mr. St. Loe Strachey, who had been assistant-editor since 1886, but he continued to contribute to its columns with little abatement of his powers though in diminished volume for another ten years. His last article appeared in the issue of 16 May 1908, and bore the characteristic title 'The Unrest of Asia.' In 1909 his health failed rapidly, and after a long illness he died on 21 Oct. 1911 at the Manor House, Little Bookham, in Surrey. He had removed thither in 1899 from the house in Harley Street which he had occupied since 1864. He was buried in Little Bookham churchyard.

Townsend was married thrice: (1) in 1853, to his cousin, Miss Colchester, who died in the same year; (2) in 1857, to Isabel Collingwood, who died shortly after the birth of a son in 1858; and (3) shortly after his final return to England, in January 1861, to Ellen Frances, daughter of John Francis Snell of Wentford House, Clare, Suffolk; she survived him till May 1913 with a son and two daughters.

Townsend wrote little except for the press. But he collaborated with his friend John Langton Sanford [q. v.] in 'The Great Governing Families of England' (2 vols. 1865), which gives in a condensed but animated form 'the leading ascertained facts in the history of our great families.' In August 1901 he republished a number of articles contributed to various reviews besides the 'Spectator' under the title 'Asia and Europe.' The volume, which contains an interesting study of Mahomet, is somewhat pessimistic in tone. Townsend expresses the view that the Indian peoples will almost certainly become Mohammedan, and the general drift of his conclusions is summed up in the sentence 'The fusion of the continents has never occurred, and in the author's best judgment will never occur.' His only non-political essay outside the 'Spectator' was an appreciative study in the 'Cornhill' of the novels of Mrs. Oliphant, whom he attached to the 'Spectator,' and who for some time wrote for it 'A Commentary from an Easy Chair.'

Townsend went little into society, and never belonged to a club, but received his friends regularly at Harley Street on Mondays. In private life he was remarkable for his genial old-fashioned courtesy and brilliant paradoxical talk. He was generous beyond ordinary experience; no master of his craft was kinder or more helpful to the raw apprentice.

[Obituary notices in The Times, Manchester Guardian, and Glasgow Herald, 24 Oct. 1911, and in British Weekly; personal knowledge; information supplied by the family.]

C. L. G.

TRACEY, Sir RICHARD EDWARD (1837–1907), admiral, son of Commander Tracey of the royal navy, was born on 24 Jan. 1837, and entered the navy in 1852. He served during the Baltic campaign of 1854 as a midshipman of the Boscawen, and received the medal; he passed his examination in Jan. 1858 while serving in the Harrier, sloop, on the south-east coast of America, and was promoted to lieutenant on 28 June 1859. After studying on board the Excellent he was appointed in July 1860 to the Conqueror in the Channel squadron, and two years later received a supernumerary appointment to the Euryalus, flagship of Sir Augustus Leopold Kuper [q. v.] on the East Indies and China station. While in her he took part in the active operations in Japan, especially the engagement with the forts at Kagosima in Aug. 1863, and the attack on the batteries in the Straits of Simonoseki in Sept. 1864. For these services he was mentioned in despatches, and on 21 Nov. 1864 was promoted to commander. The Japanese government under the Tokugawa Shōgurata having asked that English naval officers might be lent for training purposes to their newly formed modern navy, the request was granted and Tracey placed in charge of the mission. He and his companions set about organising and superintending the naval school at Tsukiji during 1867–8, and while thus employed he was borne on the books of the flagship. But a new Japanese administration interrupted Tracey's work, which was not resumed till 1873, when Commander (Sir) Archibald Douglas took out to Japan a second naval mission. Tracey, however, for a short time rendered similar services to the Chinese navy, for which he was decorated by the emperor with the order of the Double Dragon, and in Nov. 1869 was appointed to command the gun-vessel Avon, in which he remained on the China station until his promotion to captain on 29 Nov. 1871. In July 1876 he was appointed to the Spartan, corvette, which he commanded for four years on the East Indies station, and particularly on the east coast of Africa, where he cruised for the suppression of the slave trade. In Jan. 1881 he became flag captain in the Iron Duke to Sir George Ommanney Willes [q. v. Suppl. II], commander-in-chief on the China station, and returning home early in 1884 was appointed to the Sultan, which he commanded for a year in the Channel squadron. In April 1885 Tracey became an aide-de-camp to Queen Victoria, and in July was appointed to Portsmouth dockyard. He reached flag rank on 1 Jan. 1888.

Tracey first hoisted his flag as second-in-command of the fleet under Sir George Tryon [q. v.] in the manœuvres of 1889, and in Sept. of that year was appointed in the same capacity to the Channel Squadron. In Jan. 1892 he was made admiral superintendent at Malta, and on 23 June 1893 was promoted to vice-admiral. In 1896 he was an umpire for the naval manœuvres, and for three years from Oct. 1897 was president of the Royal Naval College at Greenwich. He was awarded the K.C.B. in May 1898, was promoted to admiral on 29 Nov. following, and retired on 24 Jan. 1901. He died in London on 7 March 1907, and was buried at Kensal Green.

Tracey was twice married: (1) in 1865 to Janet (*d.* 1875), daughter of the Rev. W. Wingate; (2) on 30 Nov. 1887 to Adelaide Constance Rohesia, only daughter of John Constantine de Courcy, 29th Baron Kingsale in the Irish peerage.

[The Times, 9 and 12 March 1907; R.N. List; an engraved portrait was published by Messrs. Walton of Shaftesbury Avenue.]

L. G. C. L.

TRAFFORD, F. G. (pseudonym). [See Riddell, Mrs. Charlotte Eliza Lawson (1832–1906), novelist.]

TRAILL-BURROUGHS, Sir FREDERICK WILLIAM (1831–1905), lieutenant-general. [See Burroughs.]

TREVOR, WILLIAM SPOTTISWOODE (1831–1907), major-general, royal (Bengal) engineers, born in India on 9 Oct. 1831, was second son of Captain Robert Salusbury Trevor, 3rd Bengal cavalry, by his wife Mary, youngest daughter of William Spottiswoode, laird of Glenfernate, Perthshire, N.B. His father was one of the party of three murdered with Sir William Macnaghten [q. v.] at Kabul in 1841. The widow and children were detained in captivity by Akbar Khan for nine months in Afghanistan. After their release and return to England William was educated at the Edinburgh Academy and at the East India Company's military seminary at Addiscombe. He obtained a commission as second-lieutenant in the Bengal engineers on 11 Dec. 1849. While under professional instruction at Chatham, he was for some months on special duty at the Great Exhibition of 1851. He arrived in India in 1852 in time to take part in the Burmese war; was severely wounded in the escalade and capture of the White House Picquet stockade in the operations before Rangoon on 12 April 1852, and was mentioned in despatches. In the autumn he had sufficiently recovered to join the force under Sir John Cheape [q. v.] in the Donabew district, and was present in several actions, ending with the attack on the entrenched position at Kym Kazim on 19 March 1853. For his conduct on this occasion, when he was again wounded, Trevor received the thanks of government in a 'notification' dated 22 April 1853 and the medal with clasp. He was promoted lieutenant on 1 August 1854.

After the conclusion of the Burmese war he was employed on the Pegu survey, and later on the Bassein river in Burma, with a view to constructing a sanatorium at the mouth of the river. The country was in an unsettled state and Trevor's position most insecure. Transferred in October 1857 to Bengal, he accompanied the Darjeeling field force, to intercept the mutineers of the 75th native infantry from Dacca, and engaged them at Cherabandar on the Bhutan frontier. Promoted captain on 27 Aug. 1858, Trevor was employed in the construction of the Ganges and Darjeeling road. In 1861 he was appointed garrison engineer at Fort William, Calcutta, and converted a tract of waste land on the bank of the Hooghly into the pleasure resort known as the Eden Gardens. In Feb. 1862 he officiated as superintending engineer of the northern circle, and completed the Ganges and Darjeeling road to the foot of the mountains. In May 1863 he was appointed controller of accounts, and improved the method of keeping them.

In Feb. 1865 Trevor joined the Bhutan field force as field engineer under Major-general (Sir) Henry Tombs [q. v.]. At the attack on Dewan-Giri on 30 April following, Trevor and a brother officer, James Dundas [q. v.], greatly distinguished themselves in forcing their way alone ahead of their Sikh soldiers into a barely accessible blockhouse, the key of the enemy's position, in which some 180 to 200 of the enemy had barricaded themselves after the rest of the position had been carried. His gallantry was rewarded by the V.C. He was suffering from illness at the time, and was five times wounded in the desperate encounter. After being treated at Gauhâti he went on long leave of absence, and on his return became superintending engineer at the Bengal Presidency. He was made brevet major on 15 May 1866, and received the medal and clasp for his services in the campaign.

Promoted lieut.-colonel on 19 Aug. 1874, Trevor was appointed special chief engineer for the famine relief works north of the Ganges. He received the thanks of the government for his work. After serving as inspector-general of military works he was transferred as chief engineer to Central India, and in Dec. 1875 was appointed chief engineer of British Burma. In this post, which he held for five years, he helped to draft a scheme for the reorganisation of the engineer establishment, for which he was again thanked by the government. He attained the rank of brevet colonel on 19 Aug. 1879. From Feb. 1882 to Feb. 1887 Trevor was secretary to the government of India in the public works department. He retired with the honorary rank of major-general on 20 Feb. 1887. He was a steady shot with a revolver, to which on several occasions he owed his life, an expert swordsman, and a daring rider. He died on 2 Nov. 1907 at 58 Victoria Street, London, and was buried at Kensal Green.

He married on 19 June 1858, at Darjeeling, India, Eliza Ann, daughter of the Rev. H. Fisher, Indian chaplain. She died in 1863, leaving two daughters, the elder of whom died in 1878. The younger daughter, Florence Mary, married in 1882 Colonel Maule Campbell Brackenbury, C.S.I., royal engineers.

A painting by Miss G. Brackenbury (1901) belongs to his daughter.

[Royal Engineers' Records; Royal Engineers' Journal, 1908; The Times, 4 and 7 Nov. 1907; Vibart's Addiscombe; India Office Records; private information.]

R. H. V.

TRISTRAM, HENRY BAKER (1822–1906), divine and naturalist, born at Eglingham, Northumberland, on 11 May 1822, was eldest son of Henry Baker Tristram, vicar of Eglingham, by Charlotte, daughter of Thomas Smith. A younger brother, Thomas Hutchinson (*b.* 25 Sept. 1825), an ecclesiastical lawyer, became chancellor of London and many other dioceses, and died on 8 March 1912.

Educated first at Durham school, Henry matriculated on 9 Nov. 1839 as a scholar of Lincoln College, Oxford, and graduated B.A. with a second class in classics in 1844, proceeding M.A. in 1846. He was ordained deacon in 1845 and priest in 1846, and was curate of Morchard Bishop (1845–6). Threatened with lung trouble, he went to Bermuda, where he was secretary to Sir William Henry Elliott [q. v.], the governor, acting also as naval and military chaplain, 1847–9. There he took up the study of birds and shells. In 1849 he became rector of Castle Eden, co. Durham, and held the living till 1860; but ill-health drove him to Algeria for the winters of 1855–6, 1856–7. He penetrated far into the desert, made an ornithological collection. and gathered material for his first book, 'The Great Sahara' (1860). The following winter he visited Palestine and Egypt, and, on returning, became master of Greatham Hospital and vicar of Greatham, co. Durham. Revisiting Palestine in 1863–4, he produced on his return the first of his books on the Holy Land. In 1868 he received from Edinburgh University the hon. degree of LL.D., and was elected F.R.S. In 1870 Tristram was made hon. canon of Durham and canon residentiary in 1874, when he left Greatham.

In 1879 Tristram declined Lord Beaconsfield's offer of the Anglican bishopric in Jerusalem, although he visited Palestine again in 1880–1, in 1894, and in 1897. During 1891 he travelled in Japan, China, and North-West America. In ritual controversy at home, while his convictions were strongly protestant, he associated himself with the moderate evangelicals. But his chief interest lay in the work for the Church Missionary Society, and he acted for forty years as its representative in the county of Durham. An enthusiastic freemason, Tristram was in 1884 appointed grand chaplain of England, and in 1885 deputy provincial grand master for Durham. In 1891 he visited Japan, where a daughter was a missionary. In 1893 he presided over the biological section of the British Association at Nottingham. He retained his vigour of mind and body till his death at Durham on 8 March 1906. Tristram married in 1850 Eleanor Mary, daughter of Captain P. Bowlby, 4th King's Own (*d.* 1903), by whom he had one son and seven daughters.

As a traveller and a naturalist, Tristram was a close observer and diligent collector. His knowledge of the geology, topography, and natural history of Palestine was unrivalled. His study of the larks and chats of North Africa led him, before the issue of the 'Origin of Species' in Nov. 1859, to support (*The Ibis,* 1859, p. 429) 'the views set forth by Messrs. Darwin and Wallace in their communication to the Linnæan Society' (1 July 1858), though he afterwards modified his language. His collection of 20,000 birds, of which he published a catalogue (Durham, 1889), he sold to the public museum of Liverpool; his collection of birds' eggs ultimately passed to the Natural History Museum.

Tristram's scientific accuracy and picturesque style rendered his writings at once valuable and popular. In addition to contributions to periodical literature and much work in Smith's 'Dictionary of the Bible,' he published: 1. 'The Land of Israel: a Journal of Travel with Reference to its Physical History,' 1865; 3rd ed. 1876. 2. 'The Natural History of the Bible,' 1867. 3. 'The Topography of the Holy Land,' 1872—later entitled 'Bible Places, or the Topography of the Holy Land,' 5th ed. 1897. 4. 'The Land of Moab: Travels and Discoveries on the East Side of the Dead Sea and the Jordan,' 1873. 5. 'Pathways of Palestine: a Descriptive Tour through the Holy Land,' 1881–2. 6. 'The Fauna and Flora of Palestine,' 1884. 7. 'Eastern Customs in Bible Lands,' 1894. 8. 'Rambles in Japan,' 1895.

[Proc. Roy. Soc., B. vol. lxxx.; Field, 17 March 1906; Record, 16 March 1906; Church Missionary Intelligencer, April 1906; private information.] A. R. B.

TRUMAN, EDWIN THOMAS (1818–1905), dentist and inventor, born on 20 Dec. 1818, was the son of Thomas Truman, a descendant of Sir Benjamin Truman, the founder of the firm of brewers, Truman, Hanbury and Buxton. He was educated at King's College School, London, and King's College Hospital. On 28 Feb. 1855 he was appointed dentist to the royal household, holding this appointment until his death, a period of fifty years. He became M.R.C.S.England in 1859. His dental work led him to study the varied properties and uses of gutta-percha. His chief claim to notice is his invention of an improved method of preparing gutta-percha as the protective covering for the Atlantic cable. The failure of the first cable of 1858 and those subsequently laid was due to imperfect insulation, which a committee of inquiry appointed by the privy council attributed to the improper preparation of the gutta-percha employed. Truman discovered that gutta-percha could be purified in any quantity by mechanical means without injury, and after his discovery had been satisfactorily tested by the committee, the invention was patented, on 25 Aug. 1860, the rights were sold to the Gutta-Percha Company, and all subsequent cables which were laid were covered with gutta-percha prepared by Truman's process. In 1860 he invented a machine for the preparation of crude gutta-percha, and established a factory at Vauxhall Cross, and between that year and 1889 took out many patents for perfecting processes connected with the use of gutta-percha. He pursued his investigations with a view to expediting the making of the insulating material and to reducing its porosity and cost; after thirty years of experiment he succeeded in producing a perfectly insulated conductor possessing, according to Lord Kelvin, ten times the insulation of the French Atlantic cable. The general post office adopted Truman's process, and he received until shortly before his death a minimum annual royalty of 500*l.* In his profession as a dentist he acquired a wide repute by his success in correcting cleft palate. He was the inventor of gutta-percha stoppings for dental work, receiving royalty from every dentist making use of his patent.

From the age of fifteen he was an enthusiastic collector of books and prints, and an habitué of Sotheby's sale rooms. The intimate friend of George Cruikshank, he made a special hobby of collecting Cruikshank's satirical prints and caricatures as well as books illustrated by him, eventually forming the largest collection known. This collection, with his general library and historical and other portraits, was dispersed by Messrs. Sotheby in 1906, the sale occupying twenty-one days and realising nearly 15,000*l.* Truman also busied himself with religious and social questions, on which he wrote with sense and conviction. He died at Home Field, Putney, on 8 April 1905.

Truman married in 1845 Mary Ann, daughter of Robert Cooper of Eastbourne, and at his death was succeeded as dentist to the royal household by his only son, Charles Edwin Truman.

Truman was author of: 1. 'On the Construction of Artificial Teeth with Gutta-Percha,' 1848. 2. 'The Necessity of Plasticity in Mechanical Dentistry,' 1861. 3. 'The Strength and Beauty of Mineral Teeth,' 1862. He also contributed to the 'Archives of Dentistry,' of which he was editor, 'On the Importance of Dental Knowledge to the Medical Profession,' and 'Papers on Mechanical Dentistry.'

[Information supplied by Mr. Charles Edwin Truman; The Times, 18 April 1881 and 10 April 1905; Lancet, 22 April 1905; Sotheby's Sale Catalogues of the Truman Collections; personal knowledge.] H. W. B.

TUCKER, HENRY WILLIAM (1830–1902), secretary of the Society for the Propagation of the Gospel, born at Exeter on 17 Aug. 1830, was only son of William Tucker of Exeter, barrister-at-law, by Sophia, daughter of Colonel Cole of Pedmore, Worcestershire. He entered Exeter grammar school on 1 Feb. 1841, and matriculated at Magdalen Hall, Oxford, in Dec. 1850. He graduated B.A. in 1854 and M.A. in 1859. Ordained deacon in 1854 and priest in 1855, he was successively curate of Chantry, Somerset (1854–6), West Buckland, Devonshire (1856–60), and Devoran, Cornwall (1860–5). At Chantry he came under the notice of Richard William Church [q. v. Suppl. I], then rector of Whatley, Somerset, and afterwards dean of St. Paul's. In 1865 Tucker was appointed an assistant secretary of the Society for the Propagation of the Gospel. He brought to his work zeal, industry, a remarkable memory and a strong will. In 1875 he undertook additional work in the secretaryship to the associates of Dr. Bray, an organisation allied in origin to the S.P.G. In 1879 he succeeded W. T. Bullock as principal secretary of the S.P.G., becoming also hon. secretary of the colonial bishoprics fund. In 1881 the bishop of London (Jackson) made him a prebendary of St. Paul's.

Tucker well served the S.P.G. for thirty-six years, notably promoting the colonial and missionary work of the society. When he joined the society's staff there were only forty-seven colonial and missionary sees; when he resigned there were 103. He was consulted by successive primates as to the church's work abroad (cf. A. C. BENSON's *Edward White Benson*, ii. 450–2). Archbishop Benson described Tucker as one of two persons 'for whom I have as much respect as I have for any people in this world' (*Report of the Missionary Conference of the Anglican Communion*, 1894, p. 15). Tucker's methods, often autocratic, created resentment, especially in his later years. He resigned in July 1901, when the society acknowledged his 'invaluable assistance and unexampled services.' He declined the deanery of Salisbury, and died at Florence on 3 Jan. 1902, being buried in the English cemetery there. He married in 1860 his second cousin, Jeannetta, daughter of William Tucker of Exeter, and left one daughter.

Tucker published: 1. 'Under His Banner,' 1872. 2. 'Memoirs of the Life and Episcopate of Edward Field, D.D., Bishop of Newfoundland, 1844–1876,' 1877. 3. 'Memoir of the Life and Episcopate of G. A. Selwyn, Bishop of New Zealand, 1867–1878,' 1879. 4. 'The English Church in Other Lands,' 1886. He also edited 'A Classified Digest of the Records of the S.P.G.,' 1893.

[The Times, 7 Jan. 1902; Guardian, 8 and 15 Jan. 1902; Mission Field, Nov. 1901; Foster's Alumni Oxonienses; private information.] A. R. B.

TUPPER, SIR CHARLES LEWIS (1848–1910), Anglo-Indian official and author, born in London on 16 May 1848, was elder son of Capt. Charles William Tupper, 7th fusiliers, by his wife Frances Letitia, sister of Sir Charles F. D. Wheeler-Cuffe, 2nd bart. Rear-Admiral R. G. O. Tupper, C.V.O., is his younger brother. He went to Harrow in the midsummer term 1861, was in the football eleven of 1865, and passed out in the following year as Neeld scholar. He became a scholar of Corpus Christi College, Oxford, graduating B.A. in 1870. He took fourth place in the Indian civil service examination of 1869, and arrived in India on 1 Nov. 1871.

Posted to the Punjab, he, after serving as assistant commissioner and assistant settlement officer, was appointed under-secretary to the local government in April 1877. He was under-secretary in the revenue department of the government of India from September 1878; junior secretary to the Punjab government from March 1882; secretary from November 1888; and chief secretary from March 1890.

Tupper brought to his official work an

aptitude for minute literary research. In 1880 he compiled, with great care under official authority, 'The Customary Law of the Punjab' (3 vols.), while in 'Our Indian Protectorate' (1893) he laboriously classified and co-ordinated for the first time the rich store of materials concerning the relations between the British government and its Indian feudatories. Somewhat discursive and at times conjectural, the latter volume proved of administrative service and remains of value, though for practical purposes it has been superseded by Sir William Lee-Warner's more compact 'Protected Princes' (1894, revised as 'The Native States of India,' 1910). Owing to his historical knowledge, Tupper was placed on special duty in the foreign department of the government of India in 1893–4, and from April 1895 he was engaged in drawing up for confidential official use a body of leading cases, illustrating the political relationship of the paramount power to the native states. Therein he fully maintained his reputation as an historian.

Tupper reached the grade of commissioner and superintendent in September 1895, and in November 1899 he was appointed financial commissioner of the Punjab. In 1900 he served on both the provincial and the supreme legislatures, and from April to October 1905, and again from April to September 1906, acted as a member of the governor-general's executive council. He had been made a C.S.I. in January 1897, and was created K.C.I.E. in January 1903. His last service in India was to preside over the telegraph committee which devised the scheme whereby the department was reorganised so as to meet expanding needs. Tupper helped to create the Punjab university in Oct. 1882, and was vice-chancellor in 1900–1. His addresses to the students dealt elaborately with questions of constitutional law and jurisprudence. He also was one of the founders of the Punjab Law Society in 1903, and gave the inaugural address as first president. A warm love of justice distinguished his relations with the Indian people and with his subordinates.

After retirement from India in 1907, Tupper settled in East Molesey, and devoted himself to literature and to local and national affairs. He was a strong advocate of imperial federation from the first inception of the movement, and of the National Service League. He died at his residence, East Molesey, on 20 July 1910, and was buried in West Molesey cemetery. A bust of Tupper by Henry Bain Smith was exhibited at the Royal Academy in 1892. Tupper married on 2 Oct. 1875 Jessie Catherine, daughter of Major-general Henry Campbell Johnstone, C.B., by whom he had two sons and a daughter.

[Tupper's writings; India List; Indian Financial Statement for 1908–9; Civil and Military Gazette, Lahore, 24 July 1910; Pioneer, Allahabad, 25 July 1910; The Times, 22 July 1910; Surrey Advertiser, 23 July 1910; The Harrovian, Nov. 1910; information kindly supplied by Lady Tupper; personal knowledge.] F. H. B.

TURNER, CHARLES EDWARD (1831–1903), Russian scholar, second son of John Alderson Turner of the legacy office, was born at King's Lynn on 21 Sept. 1831. He entered St. Paul's School on 9 Feb. 1843, and remained till August 1850. On 29 March 1854 he was admitted commoner at Lincoln College, Oxford. Although shy and reserved until he was drawn out in congenial company, he took a prominent part in his College Debating Society, where he showed an exceptional knowledge of European politics. On leaving Oxford without graduating he worked for three years as a schoolmaster. In 1859 he went to Russia, and in 1862 was elected, after competitive examination, professor of English literature at the Imperial Alexander Lyceum in St. Petersburg. In 1864 he was, again by competitive examination, appointed lector of the English language in the Imperial University of St. Petersburg. That post he held for life. On occasional visits to England he frequently lectured on Russian literature. He was highly respected both by the British colony in St. Petersburg and by Russian friends and colleagues. He died at St. Petersburg on 14 Aug. 1903, and was buried in the Smolensk cemetery, St. Petersburg. A monument to his memory, raised by public subscription, was unveiled by his successor, Mr. William Sharpe Wilson, in 1905. He was married, but had no issue.

Turner became intimately acquainted with Russian life and literature, and in his writings on Russian literature showed sound critical judgment and a grasp of its history. In 1881 he lectured at the Royal Institution in London on 'Famous Russian Authors,' which he published in 1882 in amplified form as 'Studies in Russian Literature.' Other courses of lectures at the same place treated of 'Russian Life' (in 1883) and of 'Count Tolstoi as Novelist and Thinker' (in 1888). The latter course was published in amplified form in the same year. In 1889 he lectured at the Taylorian Institute in Oxford on 'The Modern Novelists of Russia,' which he amplified for publication in 1890. In 1893 he issued a translation of C. A. Behrs' 'Recollections of Count Leo Tolstoy,' and in 1899, simultaneously in London and St. Petersburg, a volume of excellent 'Translations from Pushkin in Memory of the Hundredth Anniversary of the Poet's Birthday.' Besides these works he published in St. Petersburg: 1. 'Our Great Writers, a Course of Lectures on English Literature,' two volumes, 1865. 2. 'Lessons in English Literature,' two parts, 1870. 3. 'Principal Rules of English Grammar,' 1879. 4. 'English Reading Book,' 1891. 5. 'Robert Burns,' 1896. 6. 'English Writers of the Nineteenth Century: Wordsworth, Byron, Shelley, Coleridge, Keats, Moore, Crabbe,' 1897. 7. 'Robert Browning's "Sordello,"' 1897. The three last appeared only in Russian translations from Turner's English MSS. A translation of Turgénev's 'On the Eve' appeared in 1871.

[Athenæum, 29 Aug. 1903; Foster's Alumni Oxon.; Lincoln College Register; private information.] N. F.

TURNER, JAMES SMITH (1832–1904), dentist, born at Edinburgh on 27 May 1832, was son of Joseph Turner and Catherine Smith, his wife. His father, a hatter, was well known as a political speaker against the corn laws. At the age of fourteen Turner was apprenticed as a mechanic to a dentist named Mien of Edinburgh. He came to London in 1853, just after the failure of an appeal to the Royal College of Surgeons of England to give dentists a professional status. In 1857 Turner became a member of the college of dentists, and in August 1863 he was admitted M.R.C.S. of England and a licentiate in dental surgery of this body, the first examination for the L.D.S. having been held in May 1860.

He was appointed assistant dental surgeon to the Middlesex Hospital 19 July 1864; dental surgeon 16 April 1874; lecturer on dental surgery 2 Feb. 1881, and consulting dental surgeon 22 Feb. 1883. In succession to Robert Hepburn he was lecturer on dental surgery mechanics at the Royal Dental Hospital from 1871 until 1880, becoming consulting dental surgeon in 1896. He was an examiner on the dental board of the Royal College of Surgeons of England 1886–8.

In association with (Sir) John Tomes [q. v.] and a few other public-spirited men Turner succeeded in converting the trade of dentistry into an organised profession. In 1872 he visited the United States to study the conditions of dental practice there, and in 1875 he began work as secretary of the executive council of the dental reform committee. The object of the committee was to obtain an act of parliament to regulate dental practice and to provide for a dentists' register, admittance to and removal from which should be under the supervision of the general medical council. Much opposition was experienced, but was overcome largely by Turner's untiring energy. The Dentists Act was passed by the help of Sir John Lubbock (Lord Avebury), and received the royal assent on 22 July 1878. On 15 August the dental register was opened, (Sir) John Tomes's name being the first to be inscribed. The British Dental Association was founded early in 1879, and Smith Turner was for many years the president of its representative board. He also held office at the Odontological Society of Great Britain from 1873 until 1884, when he was chosen president.

He died at Ealing, 22 Feb. 1904, and was buried at St. George's cemetery, Ealing.

A scholarship in practical dental mechanics was established in his memory. It is awarded by the British Dental Association and is tenable at any school.

Turner married (1) in Nov. 1866 Annie, daughter of Richard Whitbourn of Godalming, by whom he left five sons and three daughters; (2) in Dec. 1900 Agnes, daughter of the Rev. Henry Ward, M.A.

A portrait—a good likeness—was painted by Sidney Hodges in 1890 for the British Dental Association, and a replica by the same artist was presented to Turner during the annual meeting of the British Dental Association at Exeter in 1891.

[British Dental Journal, vol. xxv. 1904, p. 153 (with two portraits); Lancet, 1904, i. 519; private information.] D'A. P.

TURPIN, EDMUND HART (1835–1907), organist and musical composer, eldest son of James Turpin, lace manufacturer, of Nottingham, was born there 4 May 1835. The Turpins were descended from an Huguenot family. Edmund's father, an amateur musician, gave him his first lessons, after which he took up organ study with Charles Noble, at St. Mary's church, Nottingham, studying later with John Hullah and Ernst Pauer. In 1847, before he was twelve, he was appointed organist of Friar Lane congregational church, Nottingham. In 1850, at the age of fifteen, he became organist of St. Barnabas Roman catholic cathedral, Nottingham and retaining that post for fifteen years, brought the music to a degree of excellence hitherto unknown in the Midlands. He was also bandmaster of the Nottingham corps of volunteers known as the 'Robin Hood Rifles.' Meanwhile he was drawn to London, where he gave an organ recital at the Great Exhibition of 1851; though only sixteen, he created a notable impression. Six years later he settled in London, though still maintaining his professional connection with Nottingham. In 1860 he was appointed organist and choir director of the Catholic Apostolic church in Gordon Square, Bloomsbury, a post which he practically, by himself or by deputy, retained till his death. In 1869 he went to St. George's, Bloomsbury, where he remained until his last appointment at St. Bride's, Fleet Street, in 1888.

Turpin was honorary secretary of the Royal College of Organists from 1875 onwards, and rendered splendid service as an administrator and examiner. The college commemorates him by a prize fund instituted in 1911. He received the degree of Mus. Doc. from the archbishop of Canterbury in 1889, and in 1892 was appointed warden of Trinity College of Music, London. Turpin died in London on 25 October 1907. He married (1) in 1857 Sarah Anne, daughter of Robert Watson of Whitemoor, Nottinghamshire, by whom he had a daughter; (2) in 1905 Miss Sarah Hobbs.

Turpin was widely known as an organist, and inaugurated many new organs; he was also a good pianist, and could play most of the orchestral instruments. He was a successful lecturer on musical subjects, and was intimately associated with London musical journalism, editing the 'Musical Standard' from 1880 to 1886, and again from 1889 to 1890. For some years he was co-editor of 'Musical News,' and he had connections also with the 'Musical World' and the 'Academic Gazette.' He edited the 'Student's Edition' of classical pianoforte music (Weekes), with marginal analyses; completed Mr. W. T. Best's edition of Bach's organ works (Augener), and prepared numerous organ arrangements and voluntaries. His own compositions include a Stabat Mater, two oratorios, two cantatas, a symphony, various concert overtures, church music of different kinds, pianoforte music, and about twenty organ pieces.

[Biographical Sketch of Edmund Hart Turpin, by Charles W. Pearce, with bibliography, 1911; Musical Herald, Dec. 1907 (with portrait); Brit. Musical Biog.; Grove's Dict. of Music, 1906, v. 188.] J. C. H.

TWEEDMOUTH, second Baron. [See Marjoribanks, Edward (1849–1909), politician.]

TYABJI, BADRUDDIN (1844–1906), Indian judge and reformer, born at Bombay on 10 Oct. 1844, was fifth of the six sons of Tyabji Bhaimai, a Sulimani Bhora, by his wife Aminabibhi. (The Bhoras are Gujerati Musalmans converted from various Hindu castes, and the Sulimanis seceded from the general body in the sixteenth century.) Tyabji's father, a native of Cambay, was the first of his family to settle in Bombay, and, building up a large business there, he became both the secular and religious head of his community. At a time when the Indian Mahomedans held aloof from Western influence, he sent all his sons to be trained in Europe. The third son, Camruddin, the first Indian to come to England for a professional education, was the first Indian to be admitted a solicitor in England (25 Nov. 1858), and established a lucrative business in Bombay.

Badruddin received his early education at the Elphinstone Institution (now College), Bombay, and in April 1860 came to England and studied at the Newbury Park high school. He entered the Middle Temple as a student 27 April 1863, and matriculated at the London University in the same year. Returning to India in October 1864, owing to eye-trouble, he was not called to the English bar till 30 April 1867; he was the first Indian to attain that honour.

Settling in Bombay, he became the first native barrister of an Indian high court, and soon built up a prosperous practice. About 1879 he first engaged in public affairs outside his professional work. At a town meeting in May 1879 he urged a memorial to parliament against the abolition of the import duties on Manchester goods. In 1882 he was nominated by government to the Bombay legislative council, and served for the customary period of two years. In December 1885 he associated himself with the first Indian National Congress, which met at Bombay, and he was president of the third annual session held in Madras in December 1887. His presidential speech was moderate and sensible. Unlike Syed (afterwards Sir) Ahmed Khan, who largely influenced Mahomedan feeling, he deprecated the aloofness of Mahomedans from the movement. A warm supporter of the Syed in establishing the Mahomedan and Anglo-Oriental College at Aligarh, Tyabji took a keen interest in the annual Mahomedan educational conferences, presiding over the session held in Bombay in 1903. He was an ardent advocate of higher education for Indian women, and gave three of his daughters advanced training—one in England and two in Bombay. A fellow of the Bombay University, he took a prominent part in debates of the senate. He was a founder of the most progressive Moslem institution of Western India, the Anjaman-i-Islam (Islamic Society), serving first as hon. secretary and from 1890 till death as president.

In June 1895 Tyabji was made a judge of the Bombay high court, being the first Indian Moslem and the third Indian of any race to reach this dignity. He sat chiefly on the 'original' (as distinct from the appellate) side. His courtesy was notable, but he proved a strong judge, who was more of a practical than a scientific lawyer (*Times of India Weekly*, 1 Sept. 1906). In 1903 he acted for some months as chief justice. Unlike many educated Indians, he did not Anglicise his attire. He reprobated the extreme nationalism in Indian politics of his closing years.

He died suddenly in London of heart failure on 19 Aug. 1906, and was buried in the Sulimani Bhora cemetery at Bombay on 10 Oct. 1906. Memorial meetings were held in London and Bombay. In January 1907 the governor of Bombay, Lord Lamington, presided at a large public meeting at the town hall to promote a permanent memorial, the form of which has not been decided. A painting of Tyabji, by Mr. Haite, subscribed for by the Bombay bar, hangs in the Bombay high court.

Tyabji married in 1865 Rahat Unnafs, daughter of Sharafali Shujatali of Cambay. She took a prominent part in the ladies' branch of the National Indian Association, Bombay, and similar movements for the advancement of Indian women and for the relaxation of the purdah restrictions. There were five sons, of whom one, the eldest, joined the Indian Civil Service, and two the legal profession, and seven daughters.

[Times, 21 August 1906; Foster's Men at the Bar, p. 476; Eminent Indians, Bombay, 1892; Indian Nat. Congress, Madras, 1909; booklet biog. published by Natesan, Madras; Indian Mag. and Review, September 1906; Bombay Law Reporter, September 1906; Times of India, weekly edit. 25 Aug. and 1 Sept. 1906; information kindly supplied by Mr. C. Abdul Latif; personal knowledge.]

F. H. B.

TYLER, THOMAS (1826–1902), Shakespearean scholar, was born in London in 1826. An evening student (1857–8) at King's College, London, he there distinguished himself in scripture and classics. Matriculating at London University in 1857, he graduated B.A. in classics in 1859 and M.A. in 1871, obtaining prizes for Hebrew and for New Testament Greek. He soon engaged in biblical research. An article contributed to the 'Journal of Sacred Literature' in January 1854 was expanded in 1861 into a volume called 'Jehovah the Redeemer God: the Scriptural Interpretation of the Divine name "Jehovah."' The New Testament interpretation of the name was discussed in a second volume, 'Christ the Lord, the Revealer of God, and the Fulfilment of the Prophetic Name "Jehovah."' In 1872 he joined the newly formed Society of Biblical Archæology, and in a small pamphlet, 'Some New Evidence as to the Date of Ecclesiastes' (1872), he first indicated exclusively from the literary point of view (as Zirkel had urged in 1792 on philological grounds) the influence of Greek, especially Stoic, philosophy on the teaching of the author, and assigned the composition of the work to the second century B.C. Tyler developed his view in his exhaustive 'Ecclesiastes, a Contribution to its Interpretation; with Introduction, Exegesis, and Translations with Notes' (1874; 2nd edit. 1879; new revised edit. 1899). Professor Ewald praised the work, but questioned Tyler's conclusions as to the date (*Göttingische gelehrte Anzeiger*, 23 Oct. 1872). Tyler was also a student of Hittite antiquities, on which he lectured at the British Museum, and his lectures and writings helped to stimulate in England the study of the Hittite language.

Tyler made many suggestive contributions to Shakespearean study. He published in 1874 'The Philosophy of "Hamlet,"' and took part in the proceedings of the New Shakspere Society from its foundation in 1874. In the introduction to the facsimile edition of 'Shakespeare's Sonnets, the first quarto, 1609,' which Tyler edited in 1886, he with the assistance of the Rev. W. A. Harrison, vicar of St. Anne's, Lambeth, first propounded the theory that Mary Fitton [q. v.] was the 'dark lady' of the sonnets. He elaborated his argument in his interesting edition of 'Shakespeare's Sonnets' (1890). By way of confutation Lady Newdigate-Newdegate in 'Gossip from a Muniment Room' (1897; 2nd edit. 1898) showed from extant portraits at Arbury that Mary Fitton was of fair complexion, and (Sir) Sidney Lee contested Tyler's view in his 'Life of Shakespeare' (1898). Tyler answered his critics in 'The Herbert-Fitton Theory: a Reply' (1898), disputing the authenticity of the Arbury portraits. He also edited in 1891 the facsimile issue of 'The True Tragedy. The First Quarto, 1595.'

Tyler, who suffered from birth from a goitrous disfigurement, was for nearly half a century an habitual frequenter of the British Museum reading-room. He died in London, unmarried and in straitened circumstances, on 27 Feb. 1902.

[The Times, 6 March 1902; Athenæum, 26 July 1890 and 1 March 1902; Standard, 27 Oct. 1897; Lady Newdigate-Newdegate's Gossip from a Muniment Room, 2nd edit. 1898, Appendix A.] W. B. O.

TYLOR, JOSEPH JOHN (1851–1901), engineer and Egyptologist, born at Stoke Newington on 1 Feb. 1851, was eldest child (of two sons and four daughters) of Alfred Tylor [q. v.], brass founder and geologist, and Isabella Harris (both of the Society of Friends). Sir Edward Burnett Tylor, the anthropologist, was his uncle. Joseph, after being educated at the Friends' school, Grove House, Tottenham, matriculated at London University in June 1868, and then turning to engineering, studied at the Polytechnic School at Stuttgart, 1868–70. On returning home he entered the Bowling ironworks in Yorkshire. In February 1872 he became partner in the family firm of J. Tylor & Sons, brass founders, 2 Newgate Street, E.C., which had been founded by his grandfather, John Tylor; on his father's death in 1884 he became senior partner. He was elected A.M.I.C.E. on 1 May 1877, and patented many successful inventions, particularly in connection with hydraulic meters. A liberal in politics, he was associated with his brother-in-law, William Leatham Bright, and with Arthur Williams in founding the National Liberal Club in 1882.

In 1891 failing health prevented him from following his profession, and he turned to Egypt and Egyptology in search of health and occupation. Here he experimented with the pictorial reproduction of the ancient sculptures and paintings of tombs and temples. His method was to divide up a wall (often irregular in form and surface) into equal spaces with stretched threads, and having photographed these without distortion to enlarge the negatives and print them faintly. The essential outlines were then strengthened with pencil, the injuries, dirt-marks, &c., on the original eliminated, and the result rephotographed for publication. In conjunction with Mr. Somers Clarke, Tylor selected El Kab in Upper Egypt as a field for his labours, and began a series of monographs under the general title of 'Wall Drawings and Monuments of El Kab.' The separate monographs were: 'The Tomb of Pakeri' (1895); 'The Tomb of Sebeknekht' (1896); 'The Temple of Amenketep III' (1898); and 'The Tomb of Renni' (1900). He died at his winter residence, Villa la Guerite, La Turbie, Alpes-Maritimes, on 5 April 1901, and was buried at Beaulieu. He married on 15 Sept. 1887 Marion (*d.* 1889), third daughter of George, Lord Young [q. v. Suppl. II], and had two sons, Alfred and George Cunnyngham.

His portrait as a boy of thirteen by W. Hay, and an oil portrait by Charles Vigor, 1894, are in possession of his son, Alfred Tylor, 34 Palace Gardens Terrace, London, W.

[The Times, 12 April 1901; private information.] F. Ll. G.

TYRRELL, GEORGE (1861–1909), modernist, born at 91 Dorset Street, Dublin, on 6 Feb. 1861, was younger and posthumous son of William Henry Tyrrell, a Dublin journalist of some repute, by his second wife, Mary Chamney. Dr. Robert Yelverton Tyrrell of Trinity College, Dublin, was his first cousin. At Rathmines School, George, unlike his brother William, whose brilliant career as a scholar was cut short by death, gave no promise of future distinction. His religious training was of the evangelical type, but from his brother he early imbibed sceptical ideas. In 1875, however, he came under the influence of Dr. Maturin of Grangegorman, whose moderate and devout high churchmanship sowed in him a seed that was afterwards quickened by Father Robert Dolling [q. v. Suppl. II]. Dolling did not oppose Tyrrell's eventual predilection for the Roman communion. He was received into that church on 18 May 1879, and forthwith became a postulant for admission into the Society of Jesus. After a year's probation in their college at Malta, he entered the novitiate at Manresa House, Roehampton, in September 1880, and in 1882 took the first vows. After a course of scholastic philosophy at Stonyhurst

College, he emerged in 1885 an ardent Thomist, and returned to the college at Malta, where he was employed as a schoolmaster. Then followed, at St. Beuno's College, North Wales, the usual four years' theological course; which ended, he was ordained priest on 20 Sept. 1891, and served his tertianship at Manresa House in 1891–2. The next two years he spent in mission work at Oxford, Preston, and St. Helens; after which he lectured on philosophy at St. Mary's Hall, Stonyhurst, until his transference in 1896 to the literary staff at Farm Street, London. During his residence in London he produced three works of unimpeachable orthodoxy, viz. 'Nova et Vetera: Informal Meditations' (1897; 3rd edit. 1900); 'Hard Sayings: a Selection of Meditations and Studies' (1898); and 'External Religion: its Use and Abuse' (1899). His views, no doubt, had been gradually broadening, but an article on Hell, entitled 'A Perverted Devotion,' which he contributed to the 'Weekly Register,' 16 December 1899, was the first unmistakable indication of the change. It raised a storm which compelled his retirement to the Mission House of his order at Richmond, Yorkshire, where he continued to reside in great seclusion so long as he remained a Jesuit. There he completed 'Oil and Wine' (1902; new edit. 1907) and 'Lex Orandi' (1903), the latter, the last of his works that bears the *imprimatur*, being an expansion of a pamphlet written under the pseudonym Dr. Ernest Engels and entitled 'Religion as a Factor of Life.' A sequel, 'Lex Credendi,' also appeared in 1906. In these two volumes the influence of the pragmatic school of philosophy is apparent, though Tyrrell resented being classed with the Pragmatists. 'The Church and the Future,' a translation privately printed about this time of an essay of a strongly liberal character, which he had written in French under the pseudonym Hilaire Bourdon, retained its pseudonymity until after Tyrrell's death; but the wide circulation incautiously given to a privately printed 'Letter to a Professor of Anthropology,' in which he dealt with the relations between faith and culture, brought about the final crisis in Tyrrell's relations with his order. Some passages from the 'Letter,' not altogether accurate but substantially authentic, were printed in the 'Corriere della Sera' of Milan, 1 Jan. 1906. The authorship of the 'Letter' was imputed to Tyrrell, and as the passages in question amounted to an acknowledgment of the total untenability of the position of conservative catholicism, and Tyrrell was unable to disavow them, he was dismissed from the Society of Jesus (February 1906). The subsequent publication of the peccant opuscule under the title 'A much abused Letter' (1906), with copious annotations by Tyrrell, completed his estrangement from the church. Unable to obtain episcopal recognition, he thenceforth resided chiefly at Storrington, Sussex, immersed in literary work. In 1907 the Vatican fulminated against modernism in the decree 'Lamentabili' (2 July) and the encyclical 'Pascendi' (8 Sept.), to which Tyrrell replied in two powerful and pungent letters to 'The Times' (30 Sept., 1 Oct.). This temerity brought upon him the minor excommunication, with reservation of his case to Rome. Meanwhile he recorded the development of his religious opinions in 'Through Scylla and Charybdis; or the Old Theology and the New' (1907), a work which thus corresponds to Newman's 'Apologia.' In 1908 Cardinal Mercier, archbishop of Malines, made modernism and Tyrrell as its protagonist the subject of an attack in his Lenten pastoral, which Tyrrell repelled with great animation in a volume entitled 'Medievalism' (1908). This work was followed by 'Christianity at the Cross-Roads' (1909), in which he essayed to vindicate his essential fidelity to the 'idea' of catholicism. It was hardly finished, when he was disabled by a severe illness, which terminated in his death at Storrington on 15 July 1909. As his case was reserved to Rome, and he had made no sign of retractation, the bishop of Southwark prohibited his interment with catholic rites. The funeral therefore took place on 21 July at the parish cemetery, Storrington, where his friend, Abbé Brémond, officiated, paid an eloquent tribute to his great qualities of mind and character, and blessed his grave.

The cardinal principle of Tyrrell's modernism is the strict delimitation of the contiguous provinces of revelation and theology. By revelation he means the evolution of religious experience as such. In his view that evolution, initiated by the deeper self-reflection commonly called mysticism, by man's recognition of himself as a being transcending space and time, and by his consequent inability to 'rest but in a conscious relation to the Universal and Eternal,' reached its final consummation in the spiritual life which Christ communicated to His apostles, and which in a lesser degree has been and still is shared by all the saints. The truth of revelation being thus 'not the truth of theological statement, but that of fact and experience,' it is, in Tyrrell's view, 'a patent fallacy to speak of a "development" of revelation as though it were a body of statements or theological propositions,' and the sole legitimate function of theology is 'the protection and preservation of revelation in its original form and purity.' Even to the dogmatic decisions of councils he therefore allows only a 'protective' value, as reassertive, by no means as ampliative. of revelation (*Through Scylla and Charybdis*, pp. 200 seq., 273–4. 291–3 seq.).

The actual doctrinal system of the church he regards as a 'pseudo-science' begotten of the 'dogmatic fallacy' by which the 'figurative,' 'artless,' 'symbolic' and rather 'pragmatical' than 'speculative' utterances of revelation are tortured into a spurious logical exactitude and then employed as premisses of deductive reasoning. This system, 'full blown in all its hybrid enormity,' he dubs theologism (*ib.* pp. 204, 210–12, 231, 234 et seq.). Nor does he shrink from affirming that in regard to the mysteries of the Trinity in unity, the Incarnation and the Real Presence, the refinements of scholastic metaphysics are even further from the truth than the simple faith of the peasant (*ib.* pp. 97–103).

But after all Tyrrell finds himself unable to dispense with development. Some measure of doctrinal development he admits, but it is determined not by the subtle speculations of the schools, but by 'the spirit of Holiness' (*Lex Orandi*, pp. 209–13; *Lex Credendi*, pp. 1–3, 9–10). He also recognises a development, not dialectical but morphological, of the Christian idea as distinguished from the Christian revelation; and thereby, in common with Newman and M. Loisy, he maintains the essential identity of the modern catholic church with the church of the apostles; while as against the liberal protestant view of Jesus as merely the ideally just man, and of the Kingdom of Heaven as merely the reign of righteousness in men's hearts, he insists on the predominance of the 'otherworldly' over the ethical elements in the gospel. Neither in his ethics nor in his 'otherworldliness' was Christ, indeed, original. The ethics were common to 'the prophets, psalmists, and saints of the Jewish people, not to speak of the pagan moralists and saints,' the 'otherworldliness' was but 'the religious idea in a certain stage of development along a particular line,' i.e. the line of Jewish apocalyptic eschatology, e.g. the Book of Enoch (*Christianity at the Cross-Roads*, pp. 30–51, 65 et seq., 91). It is the emphasis that Jesus laid on the otherworldly idea, and his sense of oneness with God that effectually distinguish Him from all other religious teachers (*ib.* pp. 66, 80, 81). Moreover, the Christian idea, as conceived by Tyrrell, has in it the potentiality not only of indefinite development but inexhaustible symbolism, for he contends that 'its meaning' is to be 'rendered by each age in its own terms' (*ib.* pp. 137, 214). And in such 'rendering' he makes some rather startling experiments. Thus the Messiahship of Christ is symbolic of certain spiritual experiences of Jesus and His followers, 'transcendent realities' that defy theological definition. Hence it follows that the atonement is a corollary of the communion of saints (*ib.* pp. 178–184 et seq., 199 et seq.). And again, though the belief in the physical resurrection and ascension of Christ was founded only on certain phenomena of the subjective order which the apostles in accordance with their apocalyptic prepossessions misconstrued and 'intercalated into those of the physical series,' yet the subjective phenomena thus fallaciously objectified were 'signs and symbols of Christ's spiritual transformation, of the fulness of His eternal and transcendent life,' and by consequence 'of the eternity and plenary expansion of that super-individual life that lies hid in the depths of our being' (*ib.* pp. 145–6, 150–3).

As to the character of the future life Tyrrell is in the main faithful to the idea in its traditional form. He prefers 'the conception of eternal life as a super-moral life, as a state of rest after labour, of ecstatic contemplation of the face of God' to the Tennysonian 'glory of going on,' and regards even 'the bric-à-brac, rococo Heaven of the Apocalypse of St. John' as 'a truer symbol of man's spiritual aspirations than the cold constructions of intellectualism' (*ib.* pp. 78, 150, 207).

'The compendium of all heresies' was the pope's sorrowful verdict on modernism; and the apophthegm is no less just than felicitous; for, as frankly avowed by Tyrrell himself, modernism is but the critical spirit of the age in the specific form in which it has tardily manifested itself within the Roman church (*ib.* p. 10).

By Tyrrell's untimely death, modernism suffered a serious if not irreparable loss. He was unquestionably the leader of the movement, and a leader not readily to be replaced; for, much as he owed to Newman's inspiration, in learning, critical acumen, and mystical depth the disciple far surpassed the master.

Besides the works mentioned above Tyrrell was author of 'Versions and Perversions of Heine and others' (1909); and joint author with Miss Maude D. Petre of 'The Soul's Orbit' (1904). A reprint of 'The Church and the Future' appeared in 1910.

The more important of Tyrrell's contributions to periodical literature are collected in 'The Faith of the Millions' (1901–2, 2 vols.) and 'Through Scylla and Charybdis' (1907). Many others appeared in 'The Month' between Feb. 1886 and Dec. 1903; in the 'Weekly Register,' 1899; the Catholic Truth Soc. Publ. ser. 1 and 2, 1905–6; 'Quarterly Review,' 1909: 'The Mystical Element of Religion' (posthumous); 'Contemporary Review,' 1909; 'The Quest,' 1909; 'Grande Revue,' 1909; 'Hibbert Journal,' 1908–9; 'Il Rinnovamento' (Milan), 1907; 'Home and Foreign Review,' 1908–9; 'Nova et Vetera' (Rome), 1906–8; 'Harvard Theological Review,' 1908.

[Autobiography and Life of George Tyrrell, by Maude D. Petre, 1912; private information from Miss Petre; Memorials by Baron F. von Hügel and Reminiscences by the Rev. Charles E. Osborne in Hibbert Journal, January 1910, pp. 233–52 and 252–63; R. Gout, L'Affaire Tyrrell, 1910; The Times, 16, 17, 22 July, 5 Aug. 1909; Hakluyt Egerton (pseud.), 'Father Tyrrell's Modernism,' 1909; Tablet, 28 Sept. 1907, 24, 31 July, 7, 14 Aug. 1909.] J. M. R.

U

UNDERHILL, EDWARD BEAN (1813–1901), missionary advocate, born at St. Aldate's, Oxford, on 4 Oct. 1813, was one of seven children of Michael Underhill, a grocer of Oxford, by his wife Eleanor Scrivener. After education at the school in Oxford of John Howard Hinton [q. v.], baptist minister, Underhill engaged in business as a grocer in Beaumont Street, Oxford, from 1828 until 1843. Owing to the ill-health of his wife he then removed to Avening, near Stroud, Gloucestershire, where he devoted himself to the study of ecclesiastical history from the baptist point of view. In 1845 he founded the Hanserd Knollys Society for the publication of works by early baptist writers. Of the ten volumes which appeared Underhill edited seven, two with elaborate introductions on the Tudor history of the sect. In 1848 he became proprietor and editor of the 'Baptist Record,' to which he contributed historical papers. After the cessation of the magazine in June 1849 Underhill became joint secretary of the Baptist Missionary Society (July 1849). He was sole secretary from 1869 to 1876, and honorary secretary from 1876 until death. The society's work grew rapidly under his guidance. He visited the missionary centres of the society, and during a long stay in India and Ceylon from October 1854 to February 1857 acquired a full knowledge of Indian problems, which he placed at the disposal of the committee of the House of Commons on the affairs of India in 1859.

After visiting the West Indies, Trinidad, and Jamaica in 1859, Underhill published 'The West Indies: their Social and Religious Condition' (1862). Subsequently he took part in the violent controversy over the treatment of the native population in Jamaica. Under the title of 'The Exposition of Abuses in Jamaica' he published in 1865 a letter, exposing the cruelty of the planters, which he had addressed to Edward Cardwell, the colonial secretary (5 Jan. 1865). A rising of the natives followed in October. The governor, Edward John Eyre [q. v. Suppl. II], denounced Underhill's pamphlet as an incitement to sedition, and with his champions vehemently impugned Underhill's accuracy.

In 1869 Underhill went to the Cameroons, and settled differences among the baptist missionaries. On his return he devoted himself to missionary organisation and literary work, writing, besides magazine articles and accounts of baptist missions, biographies of J. M. Phillippo (1881), Alfred Saker (1884), and J. Wenger, D.D. (1886).

In 1873 he became president of the Baptist Union; in 1876 he was made treasurer of the Bible Translation Society, and in 1880 treasurer of the Regent's Park Baptist College, of the committee of which he had been a member since 1857; in 1886 he was president of the London Baptist Association. In 1870 the honorary degree of LL.D. was conferred on him by the Rochester University, U.S.A. He died at Hampstead on 11 May 1901, and was buried at Hampstead cemetery. He married thrice: (1) in 1836 Sophia Ann, daughter of Samuel Collingwood, printer to Oxford University, by whom he had three daughters; she died on 25 Oct. 1850; (2) on 17 Nov. 1852 Emily, eldest daughter of John Lee Benham of London; she died in the Cameroons on 22 Dec. 1869; (3) on 17 July 1872 Mary, daughter of Alfred Pigeon, distiller, of London. She survived Underhill till 2 Dec. 1908.

The works which Underhill edited for the Hanserd Knollys Society were: 1. 'Tracts on Liberty of Conscience and Persecution, 1614–1661,' 1846. 2. 'The Records of a Church of Christ meeting in Broadmead, Bristol, 1640–1687,' 1847. 3. 'The Bloudy Tenent of Persecution discussed: by Roger Williams [1644],' 1848. 4. 'A Martyrology of the Baptists during the Era of the Reformation: translated from the Dutch of T. J. Van Braght [1660], 2 vols. 1850. 5. 'Records of the Churches of Christ gathered at Fenstanton, Warboys, and Hexham, 1644–1720,' 1854. 6. 'Confessions of faith and other Public Documents illustrative of the History of the Baptist Churches of England in the Seventeenth Century,' 1854. Other works include 'Distinctive Features of the Baptist Denomination' (1851) and 'The Divine Legation of Paul the Apostle' (1889). He also contributed an article on Bible translation to the Baptist Missionary Society's centenary volume, 1892.

[The Times, 14 May 1901; In Memoriam volume with appreciation by Rev. D. J. East (with portrait); Baptist Magazine, November 1886 (with portrait); J. S. Dennis, Christian Missions and Social Progress, 3 vols. 1897-9; private information.] W. B. O.

URWICK, WILLIAM (1826–1905), nonconformist divine and chronicler, born at Sligo on 8 March 1826, was second son of William Urwick [q. v.], nonconformist divine, by his wife Sarah (1791–1852), daughter of Thomas Cooke of Shrewsbury. His early education was under his father. He graduated at Trinity College, Dublin, B.A. in 1848, M.A. in 1851. From Dublin he proceeded to the Lancashire Independent College, Manchester, where he studied (1848–51) under Robert Vaughan [q. v.] and Samuel Davidson [q. v. Suppl. I]. On 19 June 1851 he was ordained minister at Hatherlow, Cheshire, where he remained for twenty-three years, doing good work as pastor, as district secretary (later, president) of the Cheshire Congregational Union, and as a translator of German theological works. Here, too, he began the series of his contributions to nonconformist annals. Removing to London, he filled (1874–7) the chair of Hebrew and Old Testament exegesis at New College. Still living in London, he became in 1880 minister of Spicer Street chapel, St. Albans, where he rebuilt the Sunday schools, improved the church premises, and took an active part in temperance and other social works, resigning in 1895. On a visit to his sisters in the old home at Dublin, he died there on 20 Aug. 1905. He married on 1 June 1859 Sophia (1832–1897), daughter of Thomas Hunter of Manchester, by whom he had four sons and five daughters.

Urwick's account of Cheshire nonconformity in 1864, an unequal medley of papers by local ministers and laymen, is not his best work. His own workmanship in it is sharply criticised by H. D. Roberts in 'Matthew Henry and his Chapel' (1901). His book on Hertfordshire nonconformity (1884) is distinctly the best, so far, of the nonconformist county histories. Good in its way is his book on Worcester nonconformity (1897); still better is his very valuable little book on the early annals of Trinity College, Dublin (1892). He is, however, essentially an annalist, with no historical breadth of view.

He published, besides the works cited: 1. 'Historical Sketches of Nonconformity in the County Palatine of Chester,' 1864. 2. 'Life and Letters of William Urwick, D.D.' (his father), 1870. 3. 'Ecumenical Councils,' 6 pts. 1870. 4. 'Errors of Ritualism,' Manchester, 1872 (lectures). 5. 'The Nonconformists and the Education Act,' 1872. 6. 'The Papacy and the Bible,' Manchester, 1874 (in controversy with Kenelm Vaughan). 7. 'The Servant of Jehovah,' 1877 (commentary on Isaiah lii. 13–liii. 12). 8. 'Indian Pictures,' 1881. 9. 'Bible Truths and Church Errors,' 1888 (embodies argument to prove Bunyan not a baptist). He translated from the German: H. Martensen's 'Christian Dogmatics' (1886); J. Müller's 'Christian Doctrine of Sin' (1868, 2 vols.); F. Bleek's 'Introduction to the New Testament' (1869–70, 2 vols.); H. Cremer's 'Biblico-theological Lexicon of New Testament Greek (1872). He edited his father's 'Biographic Sketches of J. D. Latouche' (1868), and T. A. Urwick's 'Records of the Family of . . . Urwick' (1893).

[The Times, 28 Aug. 1905; Lancashire Independent College Report, 1905; Congregational Year Book, 1906 (portrait); Records of the Family of Urwick, 1893; Cat. of Graduates, Univ. Dublin, 1869.] A. G.

V

VALLANCE, WILLIAM FLEMING (1827–1904), marine painter, born at Paisley, on 13 Feb. 1827, was youngest son in the family of six sons and one daughter of David Vallance, tobacco manufacturer, by his wife Margaret Warden. William, whose father died in William's childhood, was sent at a very early age to work in a weaver's shop; but on the family's subsequent removal to Edinburgh he was apprenticed in 1841 as a carver and gilder to Messrs. Aitken Dott. During his apprenticeship he began to paint, and made a little money by drawing chalk-portraits; but he was twenty-three before he received any proper instruction. He then worked for a short time in the Trustees' Academy under E. Dallas, and later, from 1855, studied under R. S. Lauder [q. v.]. Vallance commenced to exhibit at the Royal Scottish Academy in 1849, but it was not until 1857 that he took up art as a profession. His earlier work had been chiefly portraiture and genre. After 1870 he painted, principally in Wicklow, Connemara, and Galway, a series of pictures of Irish life and character, humorous in figure and incident, and fresh in landscape setting. But a year or two spent in Leith in childhood had left its impress on his mind, and it was as a painter of the sea and shipping that he was eventually best known. His first pictures of this kind hovered between the Dutch convention and the freer and higher pitched art of his own contemporaries and countrymen. Gradually the influence of the latter prevailed, and in such pictures as 'Reading the War News' (1871), 'The Busy Clyde' (1880), and 'Knocking on the Harbour Walls' (1884) he attained a certain charm of silvery lighting, painting with considerable, if somewhat flimsy, dexterity. Probably, however, his feeling for nature found its most vital expression in the water-colours, often in body-colour, which he painted out-of-doors. Vallance was elected associate of the Royal Scottish Academy in 1875, and became academician in 1881. He died in Edinburgh on 30 Aug. 1904. On 2 Jan. 1856 he married in Edinburgh Elizabeth Mackie, daughter of James Bell, and by her had issue two sons and six daughters. His widow possesses a chalk portrait of him as a young man by John Pettie, R.A.

[Private information; Glasgow Evening News, 1888; catalogues and reports of R.S.A.; Scotsman, 1 Sept. 1904.] J. L. C.

VANDAM, ALBERT DRESDEN (1843–1903), publicist and journalist, born in London in March 1843, was son of Mark Vandam, of Jewish descent, district commissioner for the Netherlands state lottery. Before he was thirteen he was sent to Paris, where he was privately educated and remained fifteen years. According to his own story, he was looked after in boyhood by two maternal great-uncles, who had been surgeons in Napoleon's army, had set up after Waterloo in private practice at Paris, enjoyed the *entrée* to the court of the second empire, and entertained at their house the leaders of Parisian artistic society. Vandam claimed that his youth was passed among French people of importance, and that he, at the same time, made the acquaintance of the theatrical and Bohemian worlds of the French capital (VANDAM, *My Paris Note-Book*, pp. 1–3). He began his career as a journalist during the Prusso-Austrian war of 1866, writing for English papers, and he was correspondent for American papers during the Franco-Prussian war of 1870–71. Settling in London in 1871, he engaged in translation from the French and Dutch and other literary work, occasionally going abroad on special missions for newspapers. From 1882 to 1887 Vandam was again in Paris as correspondent for the 'Globe,' subsequently making his home anew in London.

Vandam's 'An Englishman in Paris,' which was published anonymously in 1892 (2 vols.), excited general curiosity. It collected gossip of the courts of Louis Philippe and the second empire of apparently a very intimate kind. Vandam wrote again on French life and history, often depreciatingly, in 'My Paris Note-Book' (1894), 'French Men and French Manners' (1895), 'Undercurrents of the Second Empire' (1897), and 'Men and Manners of the Second Empire' (1904), but he did not repeat the success of his first effort.

He translated for the first time into English, under the title of 'Social Germany in Luther's Time,' the interesting autobiography of the sixteenth-century Pomeranian notary, Bartholomew Sastrow, which he published in 1902 (with introduction by H. A. L. Fisher). He died in London on 25 Oct. 1903. He married Maria, daughter of Lewin Moseley, a London dentist.

Other of Vandam's works, apart from translations, included: 1. 'Amours of Great Men' (2 vols.), 1878. 2. 'We Two at Monte Carlo,' 1890, a novel. 3. 'Masterpieces of Crime,' 1892. 4. 'The Mystery of the Patrician Club,' 1894. 5. 'A Court Tragedy,' 1900.

[The Times, 27 Oct. 1903; Who's Who, 1903; Vandam's My Paris Note-Book and French Men and French Manners, 1894; private information.] L. M.

VANSITTART, EDWARD WESTBY (1818–1904), vice-admiral, born at Bisham Abbey, Berkshire, on 20 July 1818, was third son (in a family of five children) of Vice-admiral Henry Vansittart [q. v.] of Eastwood, Canada, by his wife Mary Charity, daughter of the Rev. John Pennefather. He entered the navy as a first-class volunteer in June 1831, and passed through the course at the Royal Naval College, Portsmouth. As a midshipman of the Jaseur he served on the east coast of Spain during the Carlist war of 1834–6, and having passed his examination on 2 Aug. 1837, served as mate in the Wellesley, flagship on the East Indies station, being present at the reduction of Karachi in Feb. 1839 and at other operations in the Persian Gulf. In Dec. 1841 he was appointed to the Cornwallis, flagship of Sir William Parker [q. v.] on the East Indies and China station, and in her took part in the operations in the Yangtsekiang, including the capture of the Woosung batteries on 16 June 1842. He received the medal, was mentioned in despatches, and was promoted to lieutenant on 16 Sept. 1842. In Feb. 1843 he was appointed to the sloop Serpent, and remained in her in the East Indies for three years, and, after a short period of service on board the Gladiator in the Channel, joined in Dec. 1846 the Hibernia, flagship of Sir William Parker in the Mediterranean. During the Portuguese rebellion of 1846–7 he acted as aide-de-camp to Sir William Parker, and was present at the surrender of the Portuguese rebel fleet off Oporto. On 1 Jan. 1849 he was appointed first lieutenant of the royal yacht, and on 23 Oct. of that year was promoted to commander.

In August 1852 Vansittart commissioned the Bittern, sloop, for the China station, where he was constantly employed in the suppression of piracy, for which he was mentioned in despatches. During the Russian war the Bittern was attached to the squadron blockading De Castries Bay in the Gulf of Tartary. In Sept. and Oct. 1855 Vansittart destroyed a large number of piratical junks and the pirate stronghold of Sheipoo, and rescued a party of English ladies from the hands of the pirates. For these services he was thanked by the Chinese authorities, and received a testimonial and presentation from the English and foreign merchants. On 9 Jan. 1856 he was promoted to captain. In Nov. 1859 he was appointed to the Ariadne, frigate, which in 1860 went out to Canada and back as escort to the line of battleship Hero, in which the Prince of Wales (afterwards King Edward VII) visited the North American colonies (see T. BUNBURY GOUGH, *Boyish Reminiscences* of the visit, *passim*). The Ariadne then returned to the American station for a full commission. In Sept. 1864 Vansittart was appointed to the Achilles in the Channel squadron, and remained in command of her for four years. He was made a C.B. in March 1867, and awarded a good service pension in Nov. 1869. In September 1871 he commissioned the Sultan for the Channel squadron, in which he was senior captain, and continued in her until retired for age on 20 July 1873. In the Sultan he saluted at Havre in 1872 M. Thiers, president of the new French republic. He was promoted to rear-admiral, retired, on 19 Jan. 1874, and to vice-admiral on 1 Feb. 1879. He died at Worthing on 19 Oct. 1904.

[O'Byrne's Nav. Biog. Dict.; The Times, 20 Oct. 1904; R.N. List.] L. G. C. L.

VAUGHAN, DAVID JAMES (1825–1905), honorary canon of Peterborough, and social reformer, born at St. Martin's vicarage, Leicester, on 2 Aug. 1825, was sixth and youngest son of Edward Thomas vaughan, fellow of Trinity College, Cambridge, and vicar of St. Martin's, Leicester, by his second wife Agnes, daughter of John Pares of The Newarke, Leicester. Charles John Vaughan [q. v.], master of the Temple, and General Sir John Luther Vaughan, G.C.B., were elder brothers. James Vaughan, a physician of Leicester and one of the founders of the Leicester Infirmary, was his grandfather, and his uncles included Sir Henry (who took the name of Halford) [q. v.], physician; Sir John Vaughan [q. v.], baron of the exchequer and father of Henry Halford Vaughan [q. v.]; and Sir Charles Richard Vaughan [q. v.], diplomatist.

David James was educated first at the

Leicester Collegiate School, under W. H. Thompson, afterwards Master of Trinity College, Cambridge, and in August 1840 he went to Rugby, first under Arnold and then under Tait. In 1844 he won a scholarship at Trinity College, Cambridge, and next year the Bell university scholarship, along with John Llewelyn Davies. In 1847 he was Browne medallist for Latin ode and epigrams; and in 1847 and 1848 he obtained the members' prize for a Latin essay. In 1848 he was bracketed fifth classic with his friend Llewelyn Davies, and he was twenty-fourth senior optime. He graduated B.A. in 1848, proceeded M.A. in 1851, and was a fellow of Trinity College from 1850 to 1858.

Vaughan, Davies, and Brooke Foss Westcott [q. v. Suppl. II], all fellows of Trinity, formed at Cambridge a lifelong friendship. The three were amongst the earliest members of the Cambridge Philological Society. In 1852 Vaughan and Llewelyn Davies brought out together a translation of Plato's 'Republic,' with introduction, analysis, and notes. Davies undertook the first five books, and Vaughan the last five, each author submitting to the other his work for correction or amendment. The analysis was the work of Vaughan, whilst Davies was responsible for the introduction. In 1858 a second edition was issued, and in 1860 a new edition, without the introduction, in the 'Golden Treasury' series. This was stereotyped, and has since been frequently reprinted. An edition de luxe in two quarto volumes appeared in 1898. The translators sold their copyright for 60*l.* (information from J. L. Davies). The translation is exact and scholarly. Despite the superiority of Jowett's translation in respect alike of English style and of the presentation of Plato's general conceptions, Davies and Vaughan's rendering excels Jowett's in philological insight, and indicates with far greater fidelity the construction of difficult passages.

In 1853 Vaughan was ordained deacon, and began his pastoral work in Leicester, living on his fellowship, and serving as honorary curate, first to his eldest brother at St. Martin's, and then at St. John's church. In 1854 he was ordained priest, and in 1856 he succeeded his friend Llewelyn Davies as incumbent of St. Mark's, Whitechapel. In 1860 he was appointed vicar of St. Martin's, Leicester, and master of Wyggeston's Hospital. The living was then in the gift of the crown, and had been held by his father and two of his brothers continuously since 1802, save for a short interval of twelve years. In the case of each of the three sons the appointment was made at the urgent request of the parishioners. Vaughan refused all subsequent offers of preferment, including a residentiary canonry at Peterborough and the lucrative living of Battersea, which Earl Spencer offered him in 1872. He accepted an honorary canonry of Peterborough in 1872, and he was rural dean of Leicester from 1875 to 1884 and from 1888 to 1891. In June 1894 he was made hon. D.D. of Durham University.

In early life Vaughan was influenced by the liberal theology of John Macleod Campbell [q. v.], and while in London he, like his friend Llewelyn Davies, came under the influence of Frederick Denison Maurice [q. v.]. Maurice's example as social and educational reformer largely moulded his career. His teaching on the atonement and inspiration was at the outset called in question, but Vaughan soon concentrated his interests in social questions, to which he brought a broad public spirit and sympathy. His efforts to elevate the working classes by means of education were no less earnest and successful than those of Maurice and his colleagues in London. In 1862 he started in Leicester, on the lines of the Working Men's College founded by Maurice in London in 1854, a working men's reading-room and institute in one of the parish schools. He arranged for classes and lectures, and the numbers attending them grew steadily, the teachers being all volunteers. In 1868 there were four hundred adults under instruction, and the name of the institute was changed to 'college' as being in Vaughan's words 'not only a school of sound learning, but also a home for Christian intercourse and brotherly love.' At one time the Leicester Working Men's College was educating 2300 students. In addition to Sunday morning and evening classes, night classes, and advanced classes, there were established a provident society, sick benefit society, and book club. Some of the students became leading manufacturers in Leicester, and several have filled the office of mayor. The college still holds an important place among the educational institutions of the town.

On Sunday afternoons, Vaughan gave in St. Martin's church addresses on social and industrial as well as religious themes to working men, including members of the great friendly societies in Leicester, and students of the college. The first was delivered on 13 Feb. 1870, on 'The Christian Aspect and Use of Politics.' Some of his Sunday afternoon addresses were published in 1894 as 'Questions of the Day.'

Vaughan was chairman of the first Leicester school board in 1871, and exercised a moderating influence over stormy deliberations. During an epidemic of small-pox in 1871, he constantly visited the patients in the improvised hospital, and from that time to near the end of his life he regularly ministered to the staff and patients of the borough isolation hospital.

In 1893 failing health compelled him to resign his parish, and he retired to the Wyggeston Hospital on the outskirts of the town. He continued to act as chairman of the Institution of District Nurses, president of the Working Men's College, and honorary chaplain to the isolation hospital. He died at the master's house at Wyggeston's Hospital on 30 July 1905, and was buried at the Welford Road cemetery, Leicester. He married, on 11 Jan. 1859, Margaret, daughter of John Greg of Escowbeck, Lancaster; she died on 21 Feb. 1911 and was buried beside her husband.

To commemorate Vaughan's work at St. Martin's, as well as that of his father and two brothers, all former vicars, a new south porch was erected at St. Martin's church in 1896-7 at the cost of 3000*l.* After his death, a new Vaughan Working Men's College, situate in Great Central Street and Holy Bones, Leicester, was erected as a memorial to him at the cost of 8000*l.* The building was formally opened by Sir Oliver Lodge on 12 Oct. 1908.

Besides the works already mentioned, Vaughan published: 1. 'Sermons preached in St. John's Church, Leicester,' 1856. 2. 'Three Sermons on the Atonement,' 1859. 3. 'Christian Evidences and the Bible,' 1864; 2nd edit. 1865. 4. 'Thoughts on the Irish Church Question,' 1868. 5. 'Sermons on the Resurrection,' 1869. 6. 'The Present Trial of Faith,' 1878.

[Cambridge Matriculations and Degrees, 1851–1900; The Times, 31 July 1905; The Guardian, 9 Aug. 1905; Leicester Advertiser, 5 Aug. 1905; Leicester Chronicle and Mercury, 12 May 1877 and 17 Oct. 1908; Leicester Daily Post, 31 July and 3 Aug. 1905; Midland Free Press, 5 Aug. 1905; The Wyvern, 7 July 1893; Peterborough Diocesan Magazine, Sept. 1905; Macmillan's Bibliographical Catalogue, 1891; Arthur Westcott's Life of Brooke Foss Westcott, 2 vols. 1903; Fletcher's Leicestershire Pedigrees and Royal Descents, pp. 132–8; Burke's Peerage and Baronetage; Foster's Baronetage; private information and personal knowledge.]

W. G. D. F.

VAUGHAN, HERBERT ALFRED (1832–1903), cardinal, born in Gloucester on 15 April 1832, was eldest son of Colonel John Francis Vaughan (1808–1880) of Courtfield, by his first wife, Louisa Elizabeth, third daughter of John Rolls of the Hendre. His mother's nephew was John Allan Rolls, first Lord Llangattock (1837–1912). Always royalists and catholics, the Vaughans of Courtfield suffered for generations in fines and imprisonment and double land tax. The cardinal's uncle, William Vaughan (1814–1902), was catholic bishop of Plymouth. His mother, a convert from Anglicanism, used to pray every day that all her children should become priests or nuns. Of her eight sons, six became priests—three of them bishops—and all her five daughters entered convents. The cardinal's next brother, Roger William Bede Vaughan, catholic archbishop of Sydney, is already noticed in the Dictionary. His third brother, Kenelm (1840–1909), was for a time private secretary to Cardinal Manning and was a missionary in South America.

Herbert was educated at Stonyhurst from 1841 to 1846. Thence he went for three years to a Jesuit school at Brugelette in Belgium. Later, after a year with the Benedictines at Downside, he passed to Rome in the autumn of 1851 to study for the priesthood. His school career was undistinguished. His natural tastes were those of an ordinary country gentleman, and he has left it on record that when, at the age of sixteen, he definitely made up his mind to give himself to the church he chiefly regretted dissociation from the gun and the saddle.

During his stay in Rome his work was constantly hindered by ill-health. It was thought that he could not live to be ordained. A special rescript was obtained from Pius IX to enable him to receive priest's orders eighteen months before he was of the canonical age. He was ordained at Lucca on 28 Oct. 1854. The following year he went to St. Edmund's, Ware, as vice-president of the seminary; in 1857 he joined the congregation of the Oblates, then introduced into England by Manning; and he left St. Edmund's when the Oblates were withdrawn as the result of litigation in Rome between Cardinal Wiseman and his chapter in 1861. During the two following years of doubt and indecision a desire to do something for the conversion of the heathen world became almost an obsession. Under the influence of an old Spanish Jesuit he finally resolved to found in England a college for foreign missions and to find the means by begging in foreign countries. Having obtained at Rome the blessing of the pope, he sailed at the end of 1863 for the Caribbean Sea.

Landing at Colon, he crossed the isthmus to Panama, then part of the republic of New Granada. The town was suffering from small-pox, and the dead were counted in hundreds. At the same time, owing to the refusal of the clergy to accept a new constitution requiring what was regarded as an acknowledgment of the civil power in spiritual matters, all the churches had been closed, and priests were forbidden to say mass or administer the sacraments. Vaughan spent his days among the sufferers, saying mass, hearing confessions, and consoling the dying. He was summoned before the president of the republic and warned to desist. He had promised to say mass in the room of a woman sick of the small-pox, and he did so. Taken before the prefect of the city and committed for trial, he escaped by boarding a ship bound for San Francisco. After spending five months travelling up and down California with varying success he determined to try his fortune in South America. His plan was to beg his way through Peru and Chili, and then to ride across the Andes into Brazil, and to sail from Rio, either for Australia or home. This plan he carried out except that instead of riding across the Andes he sailed round the Horn in H.M.S. Charybdis. These wanderings, during which his begging exposed him to varied risks, lasted nearly two years.

The work was suddenly cut short by a letter of recall from Manning. Vaughan reached England in the last week of July 1865, bringing with him 11,000*l.* in cash and holding promises for a considerably larger sum. Friends now came to his help, and a house and land were purchased at Mill Hill without his having to touch the money collected in the Americas. That was to be assigned to the maintenance of the students. The college, called St. Joseph's College, was opened in a very humble way on 1 March 1866. The most rigid economy was practised in all household arrangements. The progress was rapid; additional accommodation became necessary, the foundations of the present college were laid, and in March 1871 the new buildings opened, free from debt, with a community of thirty-four. In the autumn Vaughan saw the first fruits of his labours when the Holy See assigned to St. Joseph's missionaries the task of working among the coloured population of the United States. In November he sailed with the first four missioners, and after settling them in Baltimore started on a journey of discovery and inquiry through the southern states, in the course of which he visited St. Louis, New Orleans, Mobile, Savannah, Memphis, Vicksburg, Natchez, and Charleston. All his life he continued to take the deepest interest in the development of the Mill Hill college, and he remained president of St. Joseph's Missionary Society till his death. The college which he had built has now three affiliated seminaries. His missionaries are at work in the Philippines, in Uganda, in Madras, in New Zealand, in Borneo, in Labuan, in the basin of the Congo, in Kashmir, and Kafiristan. In 1911 they gave baptism to nearly 15,391 pagans.

Vaughan's first visit to America convinced him of the power of the press. In November 1868 he bought 'The Tablet,' which was founded by Frederick Lucas [q. v.] in 1840, and for nearly three years he was its acting editor. It was the time of the controversy about the papal infallibility. A disciple of Manning and W. G. Ward, Vaughan advocated uncompromisingly in 'The Tablet' the Ultramontane cause.

After the death of Dr. Turner, bishop of Salford, in July 1872, Vaughan, largely through Manning's influence, was chosen as his successor. He was consecrated at St. John's Cathedral, Salford, on 26 Oct. 1872. The catholic diocese of Salford, although geographically small, was estimated to contain 196,000 souls and was rapidly increasing. The new bishop was soon in love with Lancashire and its people, and, wrote of Salford as 'the grandest place in England for popular energy and devotion.' After his first survey of the wants of his diocese the bishop saw the need of a pastoral seminary, where newly ordained priests might spend together their first year. A sum of 18,000*l.* was collected, and the Pastoral Seminary was opened within three years. The bishop's second project was St. Bede's College, a catholic school of his own in Manchester, mainly for commercial education. Two houses facing Alexandra Park were purchased close to the Manchester Aquarium, which had hitherto been associated with high scientific and philanthropic ideals. The news that the Aquarium Company was near to bankruptcy and might be converted into a music hall, led the bishop to secure it summarily for 6800*l.* With the support of the leading catholics of Manchester the old Aquarium was in the summer of 1877 absorbed in the new buildings of St. Bede's college which were opened in 1880; a central block was completed in 1884. More than two thousand boys have since passed through the school, and in 1910 one hundred and eighty boys were taught within its walls.

The diocese was comparatively well equipped in regard to elementary schools, but in other respects the diocesan organisation was deficient. Vaughan soon placed the whole administration on a thoroughly business footing. The diocesan synods which had been held every seven years were made annual. The system of administering the affairs of the diocese through deaneries was developed. Each dean was made responsible for the proper management of all the missions within his deanery. A board of temporal administration was appointed annually at the synod to advise the bishop on matters of finance, and to control schemes for new expenditure. The bishop was insistent that earnest efforts should be made to reduce the indebtedness of the missions and diocese. When he left Salford after fourteen years, the general debt had been reduced by 64,478*l*.

As a result of a census of the catholics of Manchester and Salford and a thorough inquiry into the various dangers menacing catholic children the bishop issued in November 1886 a pamphlet, 'The Loss of our Children,' in which he announced and justified the formation of the 'Rescue and Protection Society.' Ten thousand catholic children were declared to be in peril of their faith. It was shown that eighty per cent. of the catholic children who left the workhouses of Manchester were lost to the catholic church. The bishop resolved on a crusade of rescue. Much money and many workers were needed. He gave at once 1000*l*., together with the whole of the episcopal *mensa*, or official income, each year until he went to Westminster. 'Rescue Saturday' was established to make collections throughout the diocese every week on 'wages night.' Within three years litigation had removed all catholic children from protestant philanthropic homes, and a sufficiency of certified poor law schools for catholic children was soon established. The report of the Rescue Society for 1890 showed that seven homes, including two certified poor law schools, had been bought or built, and that in them 536 destitute children were maintained. In the same year 1515 cases were dealt with by a central committee, which met every Thursday at the bishop's house, and 8385 by district committees in various parts of the diocese. In the same period 234 children were adopted by catholic families in Canada. The cost was 159*l*. a week; 2000 people were taking an active part in the rescuing and protecting of the children.

Vaughan identified himself with the resistance of the English catholic bishops to certain claims put forward on behalf of the regular clergy in regard to the right to open schools without the authority of the diocesan, to the division of missions and the attendance at synods. In 1879 Vaughan joined in Rome the bishop of Clifton, the Hon. W. Clifford, who was the principal agent of the English bishops there, and a decision was substantially given in their favour in the bull 'Romanos Pontifices' on 14 May 1881.

In the general position of denominational schools in England, Vaughan took early a strong stand from which he never departed. In 1883 he had convinced himself that without the help of parliament the catholic, like all denominational schools, must perish. He therefore began a campaign in favour of financial equality between the voluntary and the board schools, starting the voluntary schools association. Branches sprang up over the country, while its programme received the sanction of Manning and the hierarchy. Its demands were formulated in February 1884. The agitation was thenceforth carried on with immense vigour, especially in Lancashire.

The bishop mixed freely with men of all denominations in Manchester. He was a frequent speaker at public meetings on temperance, sanitation, and the better housing of the poor. He advocated the establishment by the local authority of covered recreation grounds for public use, urging that amusements should tend to unite and not divide the family group. He was the founder of the Manchester Geographical Society, and he frequently attended the discussions before the Chamber of Commerce, where, on occasion, his missioners from Mill Hill were invited to give an account of the countries they were helping to open up.

On the death of his father in December 1880 Vaughan succeeded to a life interest in the entailed estate at Courtfield. He arranged to receive 1000*l*. a year; and, subject to that annuity, he renounced his interest in the property. Of his seven brothers, six, including the eldest four, were priests at their father's death.

Besides Herbert, the next brothers, Roger, Kenelm, and Joseph, were ready in their turn each to give up his contingent right. Courtfield consequently passed at once, in the lifetime of all of them, to the fifth son, Colonel Francis Baynham Vaughan.

Vaughan was appointed archbishop of Westminster in succession to Manning on 29 March 1892 on the unanimous recommendation of the English bishops. He himself protested that his lack of learning unfitted him for the high office. On leaving Lancashire a marble bust was placed by public subscription in Manchester town hall. He was enthroned very quietly in the Pro-Cathedral, Kensington, on 8 May, and received the pallium from the hands of the apostolic delegate, the Hon. and Rt. Rev. Mgr. Stonor, archbishop of Trebizond, on 16 August in the Church of the Oratory. On 19 Jan. 1893 he became cardinal, receiving the red hat from the hands of Leo XIII, with the title of SS. Andrea and Gregorio on the Cœlian. His long intimacy with Manning and frequent visits to Archbishop's House had made him quite familiar with the main problems which awaited him. But his efforts at solution often differed from those of his predecessor.

Vaughan embarked without delay on a large scheme of concentration in catholic ecclesiastical education throughout the country. He closed St. Thomas's Seminary at Hammersmith. On 15 July 1897 St. Mary's College, Oscott, was constituted *de jure* and *de facto* the common seminary for a group of dioceses, Westminster, Birmingham, Clifton, Newport, Portsmouth, Northampton, and what was then the vicariate of Wales. In the interest of concentration and efficiency the cardinal accepted a policy of complete self-effacement both for himself and his diocese. The supreme control of the central seminary was vested in a board of co-interested bishops. The cardinal provided as much money for the new endowment of the seminary as the other bishops together, and Westminster sent more students than any other diocese. But he claimed for himself and Westminster only one-seventh share in the government of the seminary, and no greater part in its management than was conceded to a bishop who had perhaps only a couple of students there. This policy was a mistake; and before his death he realised that in founding the Central Seminary on such lines he had largely parted with the power to control the training of his own students. The arrangement was brought to an end shortly after his death.

Although Vaughan had previously opposed, like Manning and Ward, the education of catholic youths at the national universities, he changed his mind on coming to London, and at a meeting of the bishops on 4 Jan. 1895 he induced a majority to join him in urging that the Holy See should be asked to withdraw on certain conditions its former admonition against catholic attendance at Oxford and Cambridge. A resident chaplain should be provided with courses of lectures on catholic philosophy and church history. The resolutions of the bishops were finally approved by Leo XIII on 2 April 1895, and before his death Vaughan reported the success of the new policy.

From the first Vaughan meant to build Westminster Cathedral. In July 1894 he issued a private circular on the subject, suggesting a church after the style of Constantine's Church of St. Peter. The scheme met at the outset with little encouragement, but appeal was made for funds, and 45,000*l.* was received when John Francis Bentley [q. v. Suppl. II] was selected as architect. In the final design the idea of a Roman basilica was combined with the constructive improvements introduced by the Byzantine architects. On 29 June 1895 the foundation stone was laid. The building fund then stood at 75,000*l.*, and it rose in May 1897 to 100,848*l.* Some 64,000*l.* was added before the cardinal's death, and his funeral service on 25 June 1903 was the cathedral's opening; there was no other.

Between 1894 and 1897 Vaughan played an official part in the controversy over the validity of Anglican orders which was raised by Anglican advocates of corporate reunion. Vaughan held that corporate reunion could come only by a process of corporate submission. Even as providing a point of contact and an opportunity for an exchange of views he thought the question of the validity of Anglican orders was unfortunately chosen. It was mainly a question of fact. But he urged the appointment in March 1896 of the international commission to report upon the question in all its bearings. The result was a declaration from Rome that Anglican orders were null and void (16 July 1896) and the issue of the bull *Apostolicæ Curæ* (13 September).

In the cause of denominational schools Vaughan laboured with even greater persistency in London than in Manchester. He was anxious to work in harmony with the leaders of the Church of England. In

1895 both anonymously in 'The Tablet' and over his own name in 'The Times' (30 Sept. 1895) he repudiated the term 'voluntary school' and declared for the cessation of voluntary subscriptions for the support of the public elementary schools. Dr. E. W. Benson, archbishop of Canterbury, inclined to more temporising courses (29 November). But Vaughan was resolute, and his steadfastness was rewarded by the education bill of 1902, which recognised his fundamental principle that all the schools are the common care of the state. In spite of illness he followed the debates of 1902 with unfailing interest. He discussed every clause and amendment with the special emergency committee of the catholic education council which had been appointed to watch the bill.

During his last five years the cardinal's health gradually failed. Periods of rest became necessary and frequent. In June 1902 he was ordered to Bad Nauheim. On 25 March 1903 he left Archbishop's House, Westminster, for St. Joseph's College, Mill Hill, where he died on 19 June 1903. He was buried in the garden there. There is a recumbent figure of him in a chantry chapel in Westminster Cathedral.

The leading notes of the cardinal's character were its directness, impulsiveness, and perfect candour. His mind was not subtle or speculative; he loved plain dealing and plain speech. His sympathies were wide and generous; there was an element of romance in his nature to which large and bold enterprises easily appealed. On the other hand he was apt to be impatient of details. His life was coloured and governed by an internal faith. It was his custom to spend an hour every night in prayer before the blessed sacrament. His manner in public was sometimes thought to be haughty and unsympathetic, and notes in his diary show a consciousness of hardness which he tried hard to dispel. An iron bracelet with sharp points made of piano wire was cut off his arm after death.

Tall in stature, he was strikingly handsome. He was never painted by any artist of repute. A caricature portrait by 'Spy' appeared in 'Vanity Fair' in 1893.

Vaughan published many popular manuals of devotion and religious instruction which owed their success to his simplicity of style and directness of thought.

[Snead-Cox's Life of Cardinal Vaughan, 1910; Ward's Life of Wiseman; Purcell's Life of Manning; private information.]

J. G. S.-C.

VAUGHAN, KATE (1852?–1903), actress and dancer, whose real name was Catherine Candelon, born in London, was elder daughter of a musician who played in the orchestra of the Grecian Theatre, City Road. After receiving some preliminary training in the dancing academy conducted by old Mrs. Conquest of that theatre, she took finishing lessons from John D'Auban, and, in association with her sister Susie, made her debut of dancer as one of the Sisters Vaughan at the Metropolitan music-hall in 1870. Early in 1872 she sustained a small part at the Royal Court Theatre in 'In Re Becca,' a travesty of Andrew Halliday's recent Drury Lane drama. In Dec. 1874 she danced the bolero delightfully at Drury Lane in Matthison's opera bouffe, 'Ten of 'em.' At the same house, in the Christmas of 1875, she sustained the leading character of Zemira in Blanchard's pantomime of 'Beauty and the Beast,' displaying abilities as a burlesque actress of an arch and refined type.

A notable seven years' association with the Gaiety began on 26 Aug. 1876, when she appeared as Maritana in Byron's extravaganza 'Little Don Cæsar.' Thenceforth she formed, with Nellie Farren [q. v. Suppl. II], Edward Terry, and E. W. Royce, one of a quartette which delighted the town in a long succession of merry burlesques by Byron, Burnand and Reece. Her last performance at the Gaiety was as Lili in Burnand's burlesque drama, 'Blue Beard' (12 March 1883). In the summer of 1885 she danced at Her Majesty's in the spectacular ballet 'Excelsior,' and, although only appearing for two minutes nightly, proved a great attraction. Subsequently from reasons of health she abandoned dancing for old comedy, in which she showed unsuspected capacity. At the Gaiety on John Parry's farewell benefit (7 Feb. 1877) she had already appeared as First Niece in 'The Critic.' In 1886 she organised the Vaughan-Conway comedy company in conjunction with H. B. Conway, and made a successful tour of the provinces. Dissolving the partnership in 1887, she began a season of management at the Opera Comique on 5 Feb., appearing there as Lydia Languish in 'The Rivals,' and subsequently as Miss Hardcastle to the Young Marlow of Mr. Forbes Robertson, and as Peg Woffington in 'Masks and Faces' to the Triplet of James Fernandez. The chief success of the season (which terminated on 29 April) was the revival of 'The School for Scandal,' in which she made an admirable Lady Teazle. In a later provincial tour she delighted country playgoers by her rendering of Peggy in 'The Country Girl,' and of the title-character in Hermann Vezin's 'The Little Viscount.' At Terry's Theatre on 30 April 1894 she returned to burlesque as Kitty Seabrook in Branscombe's extravaganza, 'King Kodak,' but her old magic had departed. In 1896, after a testimonial performance at the Gaiety, she went to Australia for her health. In the summer of 1898 she had a short season at Terry's Theatre in her old-comedy characterisations. In 1902 failing health necessitated a visit to South Africa, but a theatrical tour which she opened at Cape Town proved unsuccessful. She died at Johannesburg on 21 Feb. 1903.

Miss Vaughan married on 3 June 1884, as his second wife, Colonel the Hon. Frederick Arthur Wellesley, third son of the first Earl Cowley. Her husband divorced her in 1897. A water-colour drawing of her as Morgiana in 'The Forty Thieves,' by Jack, was shown at the Victorian Era Exhibition in 1897.

In point of grace, magnetism, and spirituality, Kate Vaughan was the greatest English dancer of her century. She owed little to early training and much to innate refinement and an exquisite sense of rhythm. Ignoring the conventions of stage traditions, she inaugurated the new school of skirt-dancing. A woman of varied accomplishments, she was a capable actress in old comedy.

[John Hollingshead's Gaiety Chronicles (portrait), 1898; The Theatre Mag., May 1881 (portrait); Dramatic Notes, 1887–8; Dramatic Peerage, 1891; Era, 21 April 1894; Gaston Vuillier and Joseph Grego's History of Dancing, 1908; Daily Telegraph, 24 Feb. 1903.]

W. J. L.

VEITCH, JAMES HERBERT (1868–1907), horticulturist, born at Chelsea on 1 May 1868, was elder son (by his wife Jane Hodge) of John Gould Veitch, the senior member of a family distinguished as nurserymen for a century. James Herbert's great-great-grandfather, John Veitch (1752–1839), came from Jedburgh to be land-steward to Sir Thomas Acland, and held nursery-ground at Killerton, near Exeter, in 1808. John Veitch's son James (1772–1863), James Herbert Veitch's great-grandfather, founded the Exeter nursery in 1832, employed the celebrated plant-collectors William and Thomas Lobb as gardeners there, and, in conjunction with his sons, purchased, in 1853, the business of Messrs. Knight and Perry at Chelsea. In 1864 the two gardens were separated, that at Chelsea being carried on by James Herbert's grandfather, James Veitch (1815–1869), and that at Exeter by the latter's younger brother Robert. In 1865 James Veitch took into partnership at Chelsea his sons, John Gould Veitch (1839–1870), James Herbert's father, and Harry James Veitch, James Herbert's uncle.

Veitch was educated at Crawford College, Maidenhead, and in technical subjects in Germany and France, beginning work at the Chelsea nursery in 1885. He was elected fellow of the Linnean Society in 1889 and was also fellow of the Horticultural Society. From 1891 to 1893 he made a tour round the world, going by way of Rome and Naples to Ceylon, thence overland from Cape Tuticorin to Lahore, thence to Calcutta, the Straits Settlements, Buitenzorg, Japan, Corea, Australia and New Zealand. Among the results of his journey was the introduction of the large winter-cherry, *Physalis Francheti*. A series of letters on the gardens visited during the journey was printed in the 'Gardener's Chronicle' (March 1892–Dec. 1894), and privately printed collectively as 'A Traveller's Notes' in 1896.

In 1898 the firm of James Veitch & Sons was formed into a limited company, of which Veitch became managing director. One of the first steps taken by the company, in accordance with the firm's earlier practice, was to send out Mr. E. H. Wilson to China and Tibet to collect plants. In 1906 Veitch prepared for private distribution, under the title of 'Hortus Veitchii,' a sumptuous history of the firm and its collectors, illustrated with portraits. The botanical nomenclature was revised by George Nicholson [q. v. Suppl. II]. Shortly afterwards Veitch retired from business, owing to failing health, his uncle, Mr. Harry James Veitch, resuming work in his place. He died of paralysis at Exeter on 13 Nov. 1907, and was buried there. Veitch married in 1898 Lucy Elizabeth Wood, who survived him without issue.

[Hortus Veitchii, pp. 89–91; Athenæum, 20 Nov. 1907; Proc. Linnean Soc. 1907–8, pp. 65–6; information supplied by the family.]

G. S. B.

VERNON-HARCOURT, LEVESON FRANCIS (1839–1907), civil engineer, born in London on 25 Jan. 1839, was second son of Admiral Frederick Edward Vernon-Harcourt and grandson of Edward Harcourt, archbishop of York [q. v.]. He was thus a first cousin of Sir William

Harcourt [q. v. Suppl. II]. His mother was Marcia, daughter of Admiral John Richard Delap Tollemache, and sister of John Tollemache, first Lord Tollemache. His elder brother, Augustus George, F.R.S., is one of the metropolitan gas referees. Educated at Harrow and at Balliol College, Oxford, he obtained a first-class in mathematical moderations in Michaelmas term, 1861, and graduated with a first class in the natural science school in Easter term 1862. From 1862 to 1865 he was a pupil of (Sir) John Hawkshaw [q. v. Suppl. I] and was employed on the Penarth and Hull docks. After serving in the office as an assistant, he was appointed in 1866 resident engineer on the new works at the East and West India Docks (cf. his paper, *Proc. Inst. Civ. Eng.* xxxiv. 157). On their completion early in 1870 he gained, in open competition, the county surveyorship of Westmeath, but within a few months he resigned and took up the duties of resident engineer at Alderney harbour (cf. *Proc. Inst. Civ. Eng.* xxxvii. 60). From 1872 to 1874 he was resident engineer on the Rosslare harbour works and the railway to Wexford. He then returned to London, and in 1877 made a survey of the Upper Thames Valley, on behalf of Hawkshaw.

In 1882 he commenced practice as a consulting engineer in Westminster, and in the same year became professor of civil engineering at University College, London. He filled the chair with great success till 1905, being appointed emeritus professor next year. He chiefly devoted himself to the engineering of harbours and docks, rivers and canals, and water-supply, and in this branch of engineering he became an acknowledged authority, pursuing the study of it with enthusiasm in all parts of the world. In text-books and papers as well as in evidence before parliamentary inquiries he showed to advantage a practical training combined with literary and scientific aptitudes. His chief text-books are 'Rivers and Canals' (2 vols. Oxford, 1882; 2nd edit. 1896); 'Harbours and Docks' (Oxford, 1885); 'Civil Engineering as applied in Construction' (1902); 'Sanitary Engineering' (1907). In 1891 he published a popular work, 'Achievements in Engineering during the last Half-century.'

Vernon-Harcourt's fluent command of French enabled him to take an active part in the proceedings and organisation of navigation congresses. He attended on behalf of the Institution of Civil Engineers the Navigation Congresses held at Brussels in 1898 (cf. *Proc. Inst. Civ. Eng.* cxxxvi. 282), at Paris in 1900 (*ib.* cxlv. 298), and at Düsseldorf in 1902 (*ib.* clii. 196). At the Milan congress in 1905 he was also delegate of the British government (*ib.* clxvi. 346). In 1906 he was a member of the International Consultative Commission for the Suez Canal works. He also served on an international jury in Vienna to consider schemes for large canal-lifts, and was created in 1904 a commander of the Imperial Franz-Josef Order of Austria-Hungary. In 1896 he reported to the Commissioners of the Port of Calcutta upon the navigation of the river Hooghly (cf. his paper in *Proc. Inst. Civ. Eng.* clx. 1905, p. 100). Other engineering reports relate to the rivers Usk, Ribble, Mersey (Crossens Channel), Orwell, and Dee, the Aire and Calder navigation, the Ouse navigation, and the harbours of Poole in Dorsetshire, Sligo and Newcastle in Ireland, and Newport, Monmouthshire. An essay written in 1881 'On the Means of Improving Harbours established on Low and Sandy Coasts, like those of Belgium' (MS. at the Institution Civ. Eng.) was placed second at the first quadrennial international competition instituted by the King of the Belgians. He was held in high repute among continental engineers as well as in his own country. At his death he was the oldest member of council of the Permanent International Association of Navigation Congresses.

Elected an associate of the Institution of Civil Engineers on 5 Dec. 1865, and transferred to membership on 19 Dec. 1871, he contributed eighteen papers in all to its 'Proceedings,' for which he was awarded the Telford and George Stephenson medals, six Telford premiums, and a Manby premium. These papers include, besides those already mentioned, 'Fixed and Movable Weirs' (lx. 24); 'Harbours and Estuaries on Sandy Coasts' (lxx. 1); 'The River Seine' (lxxxiv. 210); 'The Training of Rivers' (cxviii. 1). He also contributed to the 'Proceedings' of the Royal Society, the Society of Arts, and the Institution of Mining Engineers, and in 1905 he was president of the mechanical science section of the British Association at Cape Town. He wrote on 'River Engineering' and 'Water Supply' in the 'Encyclopædia Britannica' (9th edit.).

He died at Swanage on 14 Sept. 1907, and was buried at Brookwood cemetery. To the Institution of Civil Engineers he bequeathed 1000*l*. for the provision of biennial lectures on his special subjects. He married, on 2 Aug. 1870, Alice, younger daughter of Lieut.-colonel Henry Rowland

Brandreth, R.E., F.R.S., and left a son (*d.* 1891) and two daughters.

[Proc. Inst. Civ. Eng. clxxi. 421; Catalogue of the Library Inst. Civ. Eng.; Engineering, 20 Sept. 1907 Burke's Peerage.] W. F. S.

VEZIN, HERMANN (1829–1910), actor, born at Philadelphia, Pennsylvania, U.S.A., on 2 March 1829, was son of Charles Henri Vezin, merchant, of French origin, by his wife Emilie Kalisky. His great-great-grandfather, Pierre de Vezin, married in the seventeenth century Marie Charlotte de Châteauneuf, an actress at the French theatre at Hanover; Rouget de Lisle, composer of the 'Marseillaise,' was one of the great-grandsons of this union. Hermann Vezin was educated in Philadelphia, entering Pennsylvania University in 1845. Intended for the law, he graduated B.A. in 1847, proceeding M.A. in 1850. In 1848–9 he underwent in Berlin successful treatment for threatened eye-trouble.

In 1850 he came to England, and an introduction from Charles Kean secured him an engagement with John Langford Pritchard at the Theatre Royal, York. There he made his first appearance on the stage in the autumn of 1850, and played many minor Shakespearean parts in support of Mr. and Mrs. Charles Kean, William Creswick, and G. V. Brooke. In the following year he fulfilled engagements at Southampton, Ryde, Guildford, Reading, and at the Theatre Royal, Edinburgh, where his rôles included Young Norval in Home's 'Douglas,' Claude Melnotte in 'The Lady of Lyons,' and Richelieu.

In 1852 Charles Kean engaged him for the Princess's Theatre in London, and he made his first appearance on the London stage on 14 April 1852, as the Earl of Pembroke in 'King John.' Minor parts in Shakespearean and modern plays followed. In royal command performances at Windsor Castle, Vezin appeared as Snare in the second part of 'King Henry IV' (7 Jan. 1853) and as the wounded officer in 'Macbeth' (4 Feb. 1853).

On the termination of his engagement at the Princess's in 1853 he returned for some four years to the provinces to play leading parts like Fazio in Milman's tragedy of that name, Lesurques and Dubosc in 'The Courier of Lyons' (which he repeated at the Gaiety on 4 July 1870), and Sir Giles Overreach in 'A New Way to Pay Old Debts.' In 1857 he crossed to America, where he remained two years. Returning to England in 1859, he undertook the management of the Surrey theatre for six weeks, opening there on 13 June 1859, as Macbeth. He improved his reputation in important parts like Hamlet, Richard III, Louis XI, Shylock, Othello, and King John.

After a further tour in the provinces he was engaged by Samuel Phelps for Sadler's Wells Theatre, where he opened, on 8 Sept. 1860, as Orlando in 'As You Like It.' He soon made there a great impression as Aufidius in 'Coriolanus,' and in various Shakespearean rôles, including Bassanio, Mark Antony, and Romeo. At Windsor Castle, on 24 Jan. 1861, he played De Mauprat in Lytton's 'Richelieu,' in a command performance. He was Laertes (a favourite part) to the Hamlet of Charles Fechter [q. v.] at the Princess's Theatre on 1 April 1861, but he again supported Phelps at Sadler's Wells in June.

Vezin was now widely recognised as an actor of talent in both high tragedy and comedy. Engaged by Edmund Falconer for the Lyceum Theatre, he made a great success as Harry Kavanagh in Falconer's 'Peep o' Day' (9 Nov. 1861), playing the part for over 300 nights.

On 21 Feb. 1863, at St. Peter's church, Eaton Square, he was married to Mrs. Charles Young [see VEZIN, MRS. JANE ELIZABETH, Suppl. II], a member of Phelps's company. After a 'starring' tour with his wife in the provinces he played at the Princess's Theatre on 2 Jan. 1864, Don Cæsar in 'Donna Diana,' specially adapted for Vezin and his wife by Dr. Westland Marston from Moreto's Spanish play, 'Desden con el Desden.' He then rejoined Fechter, this time at the Lyceum. Undertaking a three months' management of the Princess's Theatre, which proved an artistic success, he opened on 20 July 1867 as James Harebell in W. G. Wills's 'The Man o' Airlie.' The fine impersonation, which he repeated at the Haymarket in May 1876, placed him in the first rank of English actors.

For the next twenty years Vezin played almost continuously leading parts at the chief London theatres in new or old pieces of literary aims. At the recently opened Gaiety Theatre he, with Phelps, Charles Mathews, and John L. Toole, played Peregrine in the revival of George Colman's 'John Bull' on 22 Dec. 1873; supported Phelps during 1874 in a series of revivals of old comedies; was Jaques in 'As You Like It,' on 6 Feb. 1875, and Benedick in 'Much Ado about Nothing' on 26 April. His Jaques proved a singularly fine performance, full of subtle irony, humour, and poetry. Subsequently it largely contributed to the success of Marie Litton's revival of 'As You Like It' for a hundred nights at the Imperial Theatre (25 Feb. 1880), and Vezin repeated his triumph when the comedy was revived by Messrs. Hare and Kendal at the St. James's Theatre on 24 June 1885.

Meanwhile, under Chatterton's management of Drury Lane, he played Macbeth to the Lady Macbeth of Miss Geneviève Ward (4 Feb. 1876). At the Crystal Palace, on 13 Jan. 1876, he took the part of Œdipus in a translation of Sophocles' 'Œdipus at Colonos,' in which his declamatory powers showed to advantage. At the Haymarket Theatre on 11 Sept. 1876, he won further success by his creation of the title rôle of W. S. Gilbert's play, 'Dan'l Druce, Blacksmith' (revived at the Court in March 1884). At the opening of the Court Theatre, on 25 Jan. 1871, he had created Buckthorpe in Gilbert's comedy 'Randall's Thumb,' and returning to that theatre, under John Hare, on 30 March 1878, he gave a pathetic impersonation of Dr. Primrose in W. G. Wills's 'Olivia,' which he repeated at the Lyceum Theatre in Jan. 1897. At the Adelphi Theatre he supported Adelaide Neilson in 'The Crimson Cross' (27 Feb. 1879). At Sadler's Wells Theatre, late in 1880, he was seen as Iago in 'Othello' and as Sir Peter Teazle in 'The School for Scandal,' subsequently alternating the parts of Macduff and Macbeth with Charles Warner [q. v. Suppl. II].

At Drury Lane Theatre on 14 May 1881 he played Iago to the Othello of the American tragedian, John McCullough. At the Globe Theatre he created on 11 Nov. 1882 Edgar in Tennyson's 'The Promise of May.' At the Grand Theatre, Islington, on 7 May 1886 he played for the Shelley Society Count Francesco Cenci in a single private performance of Shelley's tragedy, 'The Cenci,' for which the Lord Chamberlain had refused his license (cf. *Frederick James Furnivall, a Record,* 1911, pp. lxxiii–v ; *Pall Mall Gazette,* 1886). He joined Henry Irving at the Lyceum Theatre on 23 May 1888 as Coranto in the revival of A. C. Calmour's 'The Amber Heart.' At the same theatre, on 17 Jan. 1889, owing to Irving's illness, he filled that actor's place as Macbeth with marked success.

From this time onward Vezin's appearances in London were few. Much time was spent in touring the provinces, and he gave occasional dramatic recitals at the St. James's, St. George's, and Steinway Halls. He mainly devoted himself to teaching elocution. Among his latest appearances in London he played at the Opera Comique in 'Cousin Jack' and 'Mrs. M.P.,' two adaptations by himself of German farces (12 Nov. and 1 Dec. 1891); at Drury Lane Theatre, from September to December 1896, he was the Warden of Coolgardie in Eustace Leigh and Cyril Dare's 'The Duchess of Coolgardie,' and Robespierre in George Grant and James Lisle's 'The Kiss of Delilah'; and at the Strand Theatre on 2 May 1900, he was Fergus Crampton in Bernard Shaw's 'You Never Can Tell.' His final engagement was with Sir Herbert Tree at His Majesty's Theatre, 7 April 1909, when he appeared as Rowley in 'The School for Scandal.' His health was then rapidly failing, and he relinquished his part before the 'run' was over. After a career extending over nearly sixty years, he died at his residence, 10 Lancaster Place, Strand, on 12 June 1910; in accordance with his instructions his body was cremated at Golder's Green and his ashes scattered to the winds.

A distinguished elocutionist, Vezin was probably the most scholarly and intellectual actor of his generation, although he never reached the first place in the profession. He had a fine intellectual face, a firm mouth, and sharp, clear-cut features which he used expressively. His defect lay in a lack of emotional warmth and of personal magnetism and in the smallness of his stature (he was only five feet five and a half inches in height). He was an admirable instructor in elocution and acting, and many of his pupils attained prominence in their calling. A good engraved portrait appeared in the 'Theatre' for July 1883.

[Personal recollections; The Times, 14 June 1910; Athenæum, Jan. 1859, 18 June 1910; Henry Morley's The Journal of a London Playgoer, 1866; new edit. 1891; Dramatic List, 1879; Dramatic Year Book, 1892; Joseph Knight's Theatrical Notes, 1893; Hollingshead's Gaiety Chronicles, 1898 (with portrait); Pratt's People of the Period, 1897; Green Room Book, 1909.] J. P.

VEZIN, Mrs. JANE ELIZABETH, formerly Mrs. Charles Young (1827–1902), actress, born while her mother was on tour in England in 1827, was daughter of George Thomson, merchant, by his wife Peggy Cook, an actress, whose aunt, Mrs. W. West [q. v.], enjoyed a high position on the stage. At an early age she accompanied her parents to Australia, and at eight, as a child singer and dancer, earned the reputation of a prodigy. In 1845 she was playing at the Victoria Theatre, Melbourne, and in June 1846, at

Trinity Church, Launceston, Tasmania, she was married to Charles Frederick Young, a comedian. She supported G. V. Brooke, the well-known actor, during his Australian tour of 1855, appearing with him as Beatrice in 'Much Ado About Nothing,' Emilia in 'Othello,' Pauline in 'The Lady of Lyons,' and Lady Macbeth.

As Mrs. Charles Young she made her first appearance on the London stage under the management of Samuel Phelps, at Sadler's Wells Theatre, on 15 Sept. 1857, playing Julia in 'The Hunchback.' She was welcomed with enthusiasm as an accomplished interpreter of the poetic and romantic drama. During the seasons of 1857 and 1858 she played most of the leading parts in Phelps's productions, making striking successes as the Princess of France in 'Love's Labour's Lost,' Rosalind in 'As You Like It,' Clara Douglas in 'Money,' Portia, Desdemona, Fanny Stirling in 'The Clandestine Marriage,' Imogen, Cordelia, Mrs. Haller in 'The Stranger,' Mistress Ford in 'The Merry Wives of Windsor,' Lydia Languish in 'The Rivals,' Lady Mabel Lynterne in Westland Marston's 'Patrician's Daughter,' Pauline in 'The Lady of Lyons,' Virginia in 'Virginius,' Mrs. Oakley in George Colman's 'The Jealous Wife,' Lady Townley in Vanbrugh and Cibber's 'The Provoked Husband,' Viola in 'Twelfth Night,' Constance in 'King John,' and Juliet.

During the summer vacation of 1858 she had appeared at the Haymarket and Lyceum theatres, playing at the former house the Widow Belmour in Murphy's 'The Way to Keep Him,' on 10 July, the last night of Buckstone's five years continuous 'season.'

In March 1859 she appeared at the Lyceum under Benjamin Webster and Edmund Falconer. At the opening of the Princess's Theatre under the management of Augustus Harris, senior (24 Sept.), she rendered Amoret in 'Ivy Hall,' adapted by John Oxenford from 'Le Roman d'un Jeune Homme Pauvre'; Henry Irving made his first appearance on the London stage on this occasion. When Phelps reopened Sadler's Wells Theatre, under his sole management, on 8 Sept. 1860, Mrs. Young appeared as Rosalind, acting for the first time with Hermann Vezin [q. v. Suppl. II], who appeared as Orlando. She remained with Phelps through the season of 1860–61, adding the parts of Miranda in 'The Tempest,' and Donna Violante in 'The Wonder' to her repertory. Her chief engagement during 1861 was at the Haymarket Theatre, where on 30 Sept. she played Portia to the Shylock of the American actor Edwin Booth, who then made his first appearance in London.

In May 1862 she obtained a divorce from her husband, Young, and on 21 Feb. 1863, at St. Peter's church, Eaton Square, she was married to Hermann Vezin [q. v. Suppl. II], whom she at once accompanied on a theatrical tour in the provinces. Afterwards she played with him in Westland Marston's 'Donna Diana,' at the Princess's theatre on 2 Jan. 1864. On the tercentenary celebration of Shakespeare's birthday at Stratford-on-Avon, in April 1864, she acted Rosalind. There followed a long engagement at Drury Lane Theatre, under F. B. Chatterton and Edmund Falconer. There she first appeared on 8 Oct. 1864 as Desdemona, in a powerful cast which included Phelps as Othello and William Creswick as Iago. She repeated many of the chief parts she had already played at Sadler's Wells, adding to them the Lady in Milton's 'Comus' (17 April 1865), Marguerite in Bayle Bernard's 'Faust' (20 Oct. 1866), in which she made a great hit; Helen in 'The Hunchback,' with Helen Faucit as Julia (November 1866); and Lady Teazle in 'The School for Scandal' (4 March 1867). At the Princess's Theatre, on 22 August 1867, she gave a very beautiful performance of the part of Peg Woffington in Charles Reade's 'Masks and Faces.' Again with Phelps at Drury Lane, during the season of 1867–8, she played Lady Macbeth (14 Oct. 1867); Angiolina in 'The Doge of Venice' (2 Nov.); and Charlotte in 'The Hypocrite' (1 Feb. 1868).

Less important London engagements followed. At the St. James's Theatre, on 15 Oct. 1870, she was highly successful as Clotilde in 'Fernande,' adapted from the French by H. Sutherland Edwards, and on 4 March 1871 as Mrs. Arthur Minton in James Albery's comedy, 'Two Thorns.'

During March 1874 she toured in the chief provincial cities with her own company, playing parts of no great interest. At Drury Lane Theatre she reappeared under F. B. Chatterton as Lady Elizabeth in 'Richard III' (Cibber's version) (23 Sept. 1876), as Lady Macbeth (22 Nov.), as Paulina in 'The Winter's Tale,' with Charles Dillon (28 Sept. 1878), and later in the season as Emilia in 'Othello,' and Mrs. Oakley in 'The Jealous Wife.' She subsequently joined the company at the Prince of Wales's Theatre in Tottenham Court Road, under the management of the

Bancrofts, appearing on 27 Sept. 1879 as Lady Deene in James Albery's 'Duty,' an adaptation from Sardou's 'Les Bourgeois de Pont Arcy.' She again supported Edwin Booth at the Princess's Theatre on 6 Nov. 1880, as the Queen in 'Hamlet'; on 27 Dec. as Francesca Bentivoglio in 'The Fool's Revenge'; and on 17 Jan. 1881 as Emilia in 'Othello.'

After playing at the Adelphi Theatre, Olga Strogoff in H. J. Byron's 'Michael Strogoff' (14 Mar. 1881), she fulfilled her last professional engagement at the St. James's Theatre, under the management of Messrs. Hare and Kendal on 20 Oct. 1883, when she effectively acted Mrs. Rogers in William Gillette and Mrs. Hodgson Burnett's 'Young Folks' Ways.'

Mrs. Vezin was a graceful and earnest actress, of agreeable presence, with a sweet and sympathetic voice, a great command of unaffected pathos, and an admirable elocution. Comedy as well as tragedy lay within her compass, and from about 1858 to 1875 she had few rivals on the English stage in Shakespearean and poetical drama.

The death of an only daughter (by her first marriage) in 1901 unhinged her mind. At Margate, on 17 April 1902, she eluded the vigilance of her nurses, and flung herself from her bedroom window, with fatal result. She was buried at Highgate cemetery.

[Era, May 1862 and 26 April 1902; Henry Morley's Journal of a London Playgoer, 1866; Pascoe's Dramatic List, 1879; Dutton Cook's Nights at the Play, 1883; Pascoe's Dramatic Notes, 1883; May Phelps and Forbes Robertson's Life of Samuel Phelps, 1886; Scott and Howard's Blanchard, 1891; Joseph Knight's Theatrical Notes, 1893; Athenæum, 26 April 1902.] J. P.

VICTORIA ADELAIDE MARY LOUISE (1840–1901), Princess Royal of Great Britain and German Empress, born at Buckingham Palace at 1.50 p.m. on 21 Nov. 1840, was eldest child of Queen Victoria and Prince Albert. The princess was baptised at Buckingham Palace on 10 Feb. 1841. Lord Melbourne, the prime minister, remarked 'how she looked about her, conscious that the stir was all about herself' (Martin, *Life of Prince Consort*, i. 100). Her English sponsors were Adelaide, the queen dowager, the duchess of Gloucester, the duchess of Kent, and the duke of Sussex. Leopold I, king of the Belgians, who was also a godfather, attended the ceremony in person, while the duke of Wellington represented the duke of Saxe-Coburg-Gotha.

Queen Victoria and Prince Albert bestowed unremitting care on the education of the princess. From infancy she was placed in the charge of a French governess, Mme. Charlier, and she early showed signs of intellectual alertness. At the age of three she spoke both English and French with fluency (*Letters of Queen Victoria*, ii. 3), while she habitually talked German with her parents. By Baron Stockmar she was considered 'extraordinarily gifted, even to the point of genius' (Stockmar, *Denkwürdigkeiten*, p. 43), and both in music and painting she soon acquired a proficiency beyond her years. Yet she remained perfectly natural and justified her father's judgment: 'she has a man's head and a child's heart.' (Cf. Lady Lyttelton's Letters, 1912, *passim*.)

Childhood and girlhood were passed at Windsor and Buckingham Palace, with occasional sojourns at Osborne House, which was acquired in 1845, and at Balmoral, to which the royal family paid an annual visit from 1848. In August 1849 the princess accompanied her parents on their visit to Ireland, and on 30 Oct. following she was present with her father and eldest brother at the opening of the new Coal Exchange in London. Strong ties of affection bound her closely to her brothers and sisters, and to her eldest brother, the Prince of Wales, afterwards King Edward VII [q. v. Suppl. II], she was devotedly attached. She shared his taste for the drama, and in the theatricals which the royal children organised for their parents' entertainment (Jan. 1853) she played the title rôle in Racine's 'Athalie' to the Prince of Wales's Abner. She joined her brothers in many of their studies, and impressed their tutors with her superior quickness of wit.

At the age of eleven the princess royal first met her future husband, Prince Frederick William, who came to London with his father, Prince William of Prussia, for the Great Exhibition of 1851. On Prince Frederick William she made an impression which proved lasting. In 1853, when the prince's father again visited England, a matrimonial alliance with the princess was suggested. But the prince's uncle, Frederick William IV, king of Prussia, whose assent was needful and who was mainly influenced by Russophil advisers, was at first disinclined to entertain the proposal, and the outbreak of the Crimean war in 1854 quickened his Russian sympathies.

The Crimean war was responsible, too, for the princess's first trip abroad. In Aug. 1855 she accompanied her parents and the Prince of Wales on a visit at the Tuileries to Napoleon III, England's ally in the Russian war. She was delighted with her reception and completely enchanted by the Empress Eugénie. Paris had throughout life the same fascination for her as for her brother King Edward VII. In later life, however, national animosities debarred her from visiting the French capital save under the strictest incognito.

At length in 1855 King Frederick William IV yielded to sentimental rather than to political argument and sanctioned his nephew's offer of marriage. On 14 Sept. of the same year the young prince arrived at Balmoral. A few days later Queen Victoria and Prince Albert accepted his proposal for the hand of the princess. She was fifteen and he was twenty-four, although young for his age. The parents at first desired that the child princess should know nothing of the plan until after her confirmation (*Letters of Queen Victoria*, iii. 186). But an excursion with the princess on 29 Sept. to Craig-na-Ben gave the prince his opportunity. 'He picked a white piece of heather (the emblem of good luck), which he gave to the princess, and this enabled him to make an allusion to his hopes and wishes' (*Journal of our Life in the Highlands*, p. 154). On 1 Oct. the prince left Balmoral; it was understood that the marriage should take place after the girl's seventeenth birthday. Henceforth her education was pursued with a special eye to her future position. The prince consort himself devoted an hour a day to her instruction. He discussed with her current social and political questions and fostered liberal and enlightened sympathies. At his suggestion she translated into English Johann Gustav Droysen's 'Karl August und die Deutsche Politik' (Weimar, 1857), a plea for a liberal national policy in Germany. The princess now first took part in social functions. On 8 May 1856 she made her début at a court ball at Buckingham Palace. On 20 March the same year she was confirmed by John Bird Sumner [q. v.], archbishop of Canterbury, in the private chapel of Windsor Castle.

The betrothal was not publicly announced until 29 April 1856, on the conclusion of the Crimean war by the treaty of Paris. But the secret had leaked out already, and the news was received coolly in both countries. 'The Times' (3 Oct. 1855) poured contempt on Prussia and its king. On 19 May 1857 Parliament voted a dowry of 40,000*l.*, with an annuity of 4000*l.* In June Prince Frederick, accompanied by Count Moltke, came to England, and made his first public appearance with the princess at the Manchester Art Exhibition (29 June). The marriage negotiations were not concluded with the Prussian court without a hitch. Queen Victoria refused the Prussian proposal that the marriage should take place at Berlin. 'Whatever may be the practice of Prussian princes,' she wrote to Lord Clarendon [q. v.], secretary for foreign affairs, 'it is not every day that one marries the daughter of the Queen of England' (*Letters of Queen Victoria*, iii. 321). Accordingly the marriage was fixed to take place in London early in 1858. The bridegroom arrived in London on 23 Jan. and the marriage was celebrated in the chapel royal, St. James's Palace, on the 25th. The honeymoon was spent at Windsor. The public was at length moved to enthusiasm. Richard Cobden hailed the bride as 'England's daughter' (*ib.* iii. 334). On 2 Feb. she and her husband embarked at Gravesend for Germany.

In Germany the princess was well received. Her childish beauty and charm of manner won the sympathy of all classes on her formal entry into Berlin (8 Feb. 1858). After her reception by King Frederick William IV her husband telegraphed to Prince Albert 'The whole royal family is enchanted with my wife.' Princess Hohenlohe gave Queen Victoria an equally glowing account of the favourable impression which the princess created at Berlin (Martin, *Life of the Prince Consort*, iv. 172). 'I feel very happy,' she told a guest at a court reception on 27 March, 'and am proud to belong to this country' (Bernhardi, *Aus meinem Leben*, iii. 17).

During the early years of her married life the princess made a tour of the smaller German courts, but she lived much in retirement in Berlin, at first in the gloomy old Schloss. Her first summer in Germany was spent at the castle of Babelsberg, where her father visited her in June 1858, and both he and her mother in August. On 20 Nov. following she and her husband moved into the Neue Palais on the Unter den Linden, which was henceforth her residence in Berlin. There on 27 Jan. 1859 she gave birth to her eldest son, William, afterwards German Emperor.

From the first, many of the conditions of the princess's new life proved irksome. The tone of the Prussian court in matters of religion and politics was narrower than that in England. The etiquette was more constrained and the standard of comfort was lower. The princess chafed somewhat under her mother-in-law's strict surveillance, and few sympathised with her unshakeable faith in the beneficence of constitutional government as it was practised in England. She could not conceal her liberal convictions or hold aloof from political discussion. She steadily continued the historical and literary studies to which her father had accustomed her, and she wrote to him a weekly letter, asking his advice on political questions, and enclosing essays on historical subjects. His influence over her was unimpaired till his death. In Oct. 1858 her father-in-law, Prince William, assumed the regency, and his summons of a moderate liberal ministry evoked an expression of her satisfaction which irritated the conservative party at court. In December 1860 she delighted her father with an exhaustive memorandum, whereby she thought to allay the apprehensions of the Prussian court, on the advantages of ministerial responsibility (MARTIN, *Life of the Prince Consort*, v. 259). She was outspoken in all her criticism of her environment, and her active interests in art and philanthropy as well as in politics ran counter to Prussian ideas and traditions. She was constantly comparing her life in Germany with the amenities of her English home (BERNHARDI, *Aus meinem Leben*, vi. 116), and she wounded Prussian susceptibilities by pointing out England's social advantages. Over her husband she rapidly acquired a strong influence which increased distrust of her in court circles. Her energy and independence undoubtedly conquered any defect of resolution in him, but his liberal sentiments were deeply rooted. Meanwhile the English press was constantly denouncing the illiberality of Prussian rule, and the unpopularity of the princess, who was freely identified with such attacks, increased. 'This attitude of the English newspapers,' wrote Lord Clarendon in 1861, 'preys upon the princess royal's spirits, and materially affects her position in Prussia' (*Memoirs and Letters of Sir Robert Morier*, i. 295).

In Jan. 1861, when King William I succeeded his brother Frederick William IV on the throne of Prussia, the princess and her husband became crown princess and crown prince. On 18 Oct. she attended the coronation of her father-in-law at Königsberg. Before the close of the year she suffered the shock of her father's premature death (14 Dec. 1861). Her husband represented her at the funeral, which her delicate health prevented her from attending. In her father the princess lost a valued friend and counsellor, while the Prussian king was deprived of an adviser, whose circumspect advice had helped him to reconcile opposing forces in Prussian politics.

In March 1862 a breach between the king of Prussia and both the moderate and advanced liberals led him to summon to his aid Bismarck and the conservative (Junker) party. To the new minister constitutional principles had no meaning, and the crown prince and princess made open declaration of hostility. The crown prince absented himself from cabinet meetings, which he had attended since the king's accession, and he and his wife withdrew from court (BERNHARDI, *Aus meinem Leben*, v. 8). In October 1862 they left Berlin, and subsequently joined the Prince of Wales, a frequent visitor at his sister's German home, on a cruise in the Mediterranean. Early in 1863 the crown princess with her son and consort was in England, where she filled the place of her widowed mother, Queen Victoria, at a drawing-room at Buckingham Palace (28 Feb.). On 10 March she was present at the Prince of Wales's wedding at Windsor.

The steady growth under Bismarck's ascendancy of absolutist principles of government in Prussia intensified the resentment of the crown princess and her husband. In June 1863 the crown prince made an open protest in a speech at Dantzig. The princess, with characteristic want of discretion, frankly told President Eichmann that her opinions were those of the liberal press (WHITMAN, *Emperor Frederick*, p. 162). Bismarck imputed to her a resolve 'to bring her consort more into prominence and to acquaint public opinion with the crown prince's way of thinking' (BUSCH'S *Bismarck*, iii. 238). The king demanded of the crown prince a recantation of the Dantzig speech. The request was refused, but the prince offered to retire with his family to some place where he could not meddle with politics. In the result Bismarck imposed vexatious restrictions on the heir-apparent's freedom of action. Spies in the guise of aides-de-camp and chamberlains were set over him and his wife at Berlin, and by 1864 the whole of their retinue consisted of Bismarck's followers (*Memoirs of Sir Robert Morier*, i. 343, 410). The vituperative conservative press assigned the heir-apparent's obduracy to his wife's influence.

The princess met Queen Victoria at Rosenau near Coburg in August 1863, and in her mother she had a firm sympathiser. The queen contemplated active intervention at Berlin on her daughter's behalf, and was only dissuaded by (Sir) Robert Morier [q. v.]. From September to December following the crown prince and his wife made a prolonged visit to the English court, and on their return to Berlin held aloof for a season from political discussion (BISMARCK, *Neue Tischgespräche und Interviews*, ii. 33).

The reopening of the Schleswig-Holstein question by the death of King Frederick VIII of Denmark (15 Nov. 1863) widened the breach with Bismarck. The crown princess and her husband warmly espoused the claims to the duchies of Duke Frederick of Augustenburg. The controversy divided the English royal family. The rival claim of Denmark had strong adherents there. While staying at Osborne the princess engaged in warm discussion with her sister-in-law, the Princess of Wales, the king of Denmark's daughter (BERNHARDI, *Aus meinem Leben*, v. 282). Bismarck's cynical resolve to annex the duchies to Germany thoroughly roused the anger of the crown princess. Bismarck complained that she was involving herself, with her husband, her uncle (the duke of Coburg), and her mother, in a conspiracy against Prussian interests. When she and the minister met, bitter words passed, and she ironically asked Bismarck whether his ambition was to become king or president of a republic (HORST KOHL, *Bismarck: Anhang*, i. 150).

The Austro-Prussian conflict of 1866 was abhorrent to the princess, and it accentuated the strife between her and the minister. On the outbreak of war (18 June) the crown prince took command of the second division of the Silesian army operating in Bohemia. Dislike of the conflict and its causes did not affect the princess's anxiety to relieve its suffering, and she now showed conspicuously for the first time that philanthropic energy and organising capacity which chiefly rendered her career memorable. She organised hospitals and raised money for the care of the wounded. It was mainly due to her efforts that the national fund for disabled soldiers (Nationalinvalidenstiftung) was inaugurated at the close of the war. The Prussian victory involved, to the princess's sorrow, the deposition of Austria's allies among the princely families of Germany. With George V, the dispossessed king of Hanover, the princess avowed very lively sympathy.

The crown prince's exclusion from business of state continued, to his wife's unconcealed irritation. Bismarck declared that her devotion to English as opposed to Prussian interests rendered the situation inevitable. On occasion, however, the crown prince was suffered to represent his father on visits to foreign sovereigns. Delicate health and the cares of a growing family did not always allow the crown princess to accompany him. But in May 1867 she went with him to Paris for the opening of the International Exhibition, and there she made the acquaintance of Renan. Subsequently in April 1873 she was the guest of the Emperor Francis Joseph at Schönbrunn on the occasion of the International Exhibition at Vienna. In Jan. 1874 she attended at St. Petersburg the wedding of her brother Alfred, duke of Edinburgh, with the grand duchess Maria Alexandrovna. But foreign travel in less formal conditions was more congenial to her, and she lost no opportunity of journeying incognito through the chief countries of Europe.

The Franco-German war of 1870–1 plunged the crown princess in fresh controversy. The impression generally prevailed in Germany that England was on the side of France. She sought to convince Bismarck of the genuineness of England's professions of neutrality, but only provoked an incredulous smile. 'The English,' she wrote to Queen Victoria on 9 Aug. 1870, 'are more hated at this moment than the French. Of course *cela a rejailli* on my poor innocent head. I have fought many a battle about Lord Granville, indignant at hearing my old friend so attacked, but all parties make him out French' (FITZMAURICE, *Life of Lord Granville*, ii. 38). At the same time the crown princess bestirred herself in the interest of the German armies in the field. She appealed for funds on behalf of the soldiers' families (19 July 1870). In September she joined her sister, Princess Alice of Hesse-Darmstadt, at Homburg, and was indefatigable in organising hospitals for the wounded, in recruiting volunteer corps of lady nurses, and in distributing comforts to the troops on the way to the front. Yet compassionate kindness to French prisoners exposed her to suspicion. The threatened bombardment of Paris after the investment horrified her, and she appealed to her father-in-law to forbid it. The step was ineffectual, and excited the bitter sarcasm of Bismarck. Undeterred by failure, she started a scheme to collect supplies in

Belgium for the rapid provisioning of Paris after the capitulation. The British government and other neutral powers were approached, but Bismarck stepped in to foil the plan (*Memoirs and Letters of Sir Robert Morier*, ii. 211).

The crown princess welcomed the proclamation of the German Emperor at Versailles on 18 Jan. 1871, and took part in the festivities at Berlin on the return of the victorious German army. In Sept. 1871 she and her husband visited London, and were received with cordiality by Queen Victoria and the Prince of Wales. Their reception did much to dissipate the atmosphere of tension which had prejudiced the relations of England and Germany during the war.

The princess's public interests extended far beyond politics, and embraced philanthropy, education, art, and literature. Indeed enlightened progress in all branches of effort powerfully appealed to her. She cultivated the society of leaders of thought, art, and science. As a hostess she ignored the conventions of etiquette which restricted her guests to members of the aristocracy. Her receptions were invariably attended by the historians Mommsen and Dove, by Zeller the philosopher, by the scientist Virchow, and by Gustav Freytag the writer, who dedicated to her 'Die Ahnen' (six parts, 1872–80). With especial eagerness the princess encouraged intercourse with German painters and sculptors. Art was one of her main recreations. Elected a member of the Berlin Academy in 1860, she studied in her leisure hours sculpture under Begas and painting under Prof. Hagen. She drew correctly, but showed little power of imagination (for examples of her work cf. *Magazine of Art*, May and Sept. 1886). Her favourite artists were Werner and von Angeli, and with the latter she was long on intimate terms.

Prussia was almost the last state in Germany to assimilate the artistic development of the nineteenth century, and it was the crown princess who gave a first impulse towards the improvement of applied art. She carefully followed the progress of industrial art in England, and in 1865 she commissioned Dr. Schwabe to draw up a report, entitled 'Die Forderung der Kunst-Industrie in England and der Stand dieser Frage in Deutschland.' Her efforts to stimulate the interest of the Prussian government bore fruit. Schools of applied art were established in Prussia, and on 15 Sept. 1872 she had the satisfaction of witnessing the opening of an industrial art exhibition at Berlin. Subsequently she and her husband set to work to form a permanent public collection of 'objets d'art,' and the Berlin Industrial Art Museum (Kunst-Gewerbe Museum); which was opened on 20 Nov. 1881, was mainly due to her personal initiative. In the structural evolution of the modern city of Berlin the princess's interest was always keen and her active influence consistently supported the civic effort to give the new city artistic dignity.

Her early endeavours in philanthropy were mainly confined to hospitals. The experiences of the wars of 1866 and 1870 had shown the inadequacy of existing hospital organisations in Germany. A more scientific training for nurses was a first necessity. The crown princess was well acquainted with the reforms effected in England by Florence Nightingale [q. v. Suppl. II], and in 1872 she drafted an exhaustive report on hospital organisation. At her instigation the Victoria House and Nursing School (Viktoria-Haus für Krankenpflege), which was named after her, was established at Berlin in 1881, and soon the Victoria sisters, mainly women of education, undertook the nursing in the municipal hospital at Friedrichshain. Out of the public gift to her and her husband on their silver wedding in 1883 she applied 118,000 marks to the endowment of the Victoria House. The success of the school led to the establishment of similar institutions throughout Germany. The value of her work for hospitals was recognised beyond Germany. In 1876 she received a gold medal at the Brussels exhibition for her designs for a barrack hospital, and on 26 May 1883 she was awarded the Royal Red Cross by Queen Victoria on the institution of that order.

From hospitals the crown princess soon passed to schemes for ameliorating the social conditions of the working classes. On her initiative the society for the promotion of health in the home (Gesellschaft für häusliche Gesundheit) was started in 1875; it undertook regular house to house visits for the purposes of sanitary inspection. Both at Bornstedt, her husband's country seat, and later at Cronberg, whither she retired after his death, she founded hospitals, workhouses, schools, and libraries.

The cause of popular education, especially for women, was meanwhile one of her chief concerns. In the development in Germany of women's higher education, the crown princess was a pioneer whose labour had far-reaching results. Her untiring work for her own sex brought about a general improvement in the social position of German women. In 1868 at her instance Miss Georgina Archer [see ARCHER, JAMES, Suppl. II] was invited to Berlin and started the Victoria Lyceum, the first institution in Germany for the higher education of women. Two educational institutions, the Lette Verein (1871), a school for the technical training of soldiers' orphans; and the Heimathaus für Töchter hoherer Stände, or home for girls of the higher middle classes, were mainly set on foot by her exertions, while her interest in modern educational methods was apparent in her patronage of the Pestalozzi-Fröbel Haus (1881). No less than forty-two educational and philanthropic institutions flourished under her auspices, and the impulse she gave to women's education throughout Germany swept away most of the old reactionary prejudices against opening to women the intellectual opportunities which men enjoyed.

Despite the public services of the princess, the value of which the German people acknowledged, the humiliating political position of her husband and herself underwent no change. Knowledge of political business was still denied them (GONTAUT-BIRON, *Dernières Années de l'ambassade*, p. 298). In June 1878 the Emperor William was wounded by an assassin (Nobiling), and the crown prince was appointed regent. But Bismarck contrived that his office should not carry with it any genuine authority. The prompt recovery of his father fully restored the old situation. At the end of 1879 the crown princess withdrew from Berlin on the ground of ill-health, and she spent several months with her husband and family at Pegli near Genoa. During the following years her appearances in public were few. In May 1883 she visited Paris incognito, and on 24 May 1884 she laid the foundation stone of St. George's (English) church at Berlin.

The health of the old emperor was now declining, and the crown prince's accession to the throne was clearly approaching. Bismarck showed some signs of readiness to cultivate better relations with the heir apparent and his family. On 21 Nov. 1884 he attended a soirée given by the crown princess in honour of her birthday (BISMARCK, *Neue Tischgespräche und Interviews*, ii. 127).

But the crown princess's long-deferred hopes of a happy change of estate were doomed to a cruel disappointment. In the autumn of 1886 the crown prince contracted on the Italian Riviera an affection of the throat, which gradually sapped his strength. For nearly two years her husband's illness was the princess's main preoccupation, and she undertook with great efficiency the chief responsibilities of nursing. In May 1887, when the Berlin physicians diagnosed cancerous symptoms, an English physician, (Sir) Morell Mackenzie [q. v.], was called into consultation with the princess's assent, and his optimism initiated an unedifying controversy with his German colleagues, which involved the princess's name. She treated the English specialist with a confidence which the German specialists thought that she withheld from them. Both prince and princess took part in the celebration of Queen Victoria's jubilee (21 June 1887). After a visit to Toblach in Tyrol they moved in November to the Villa Zirio, San Remo, where the fatal progress of the malady no longer admitted of doubt. On 9 March 1888 the old emperor William died at Berlin, and the crown prince, a dying man, succeeded to the throne as Frederick III.

The Emperor Frederick and his consort immediately left San Remo for Charlottenburg, and in a rescript addressed to the chancellor, Prince Bismarck, the new sovereign announced his intention of devoting the remainder of his life to the moral and economic elevation of the nation. He was no longer able to speak, and all communications had to be made to him in writing. The empress undertook to prepare her husband for necessary business (H. BLUM, *Lebenserinnerungen*, ii. 220), and Bismarck's jealousy of her influence was aroused. A family quarrel embittered the difficult situation. Already in 1885 the princess had encouraged a plan for the marriage of her second daughter, Princess Victoria, to Alexander of Battenberg, Prince of Bulgaria. But the scheme had then been rejected. It was now revived, and the old quarrel between the empress and Bismarck found in the proposed match new fuel. The chancellor threatened to resign. He declared the marriage to be not only a breach of caste etiquette owing to Prince Alexander's inferior social rank, but to be an insult to Russia, which had declared its hostility to the Bulgarian ruler. The empress, who regarded her daughter's happiness as the highest consideration, ignored Bismarck's arguments. The chancellor prompted an unscrupulous press campaign which brought public opinion to his side. The dying emperor yielded to the combined pressure of Bismarck and public opinion, and on 4 April 1888 he agreed to a postponement of the announcement of the marriage. The empress remained obdurate. But Queen Victoria visited Berlin (24 April) and was convinced by Bismarck of the fatal consequences of further resistance. The empress out of deference to her mother's wishes acquiesced in the situation. Crown Prince William sided with Bismarck throughout the dispute, but Queen Victoria reconciled him to his mother.

On 1 June 1888 the court moved from Charlottenburg to the new palace (Friedrichskron) at Potsdam, and there on 15 June the emperor died in the presence of his wife and family.

One of the last acts of the dying monarch was to place Bismarck's hand in that of the empress as a symbol of reconciliation. But the chancellor did not spare her humiliation in the first days of her widowhood. After her husband's death a cordon of soldiers was drawn round the palace at Potsdam to prevent the removal of any compromising documents; when the empress requested Bismarck to visit her, he replied that he had no time and must go to her son the emperor, his master (Hohenlohe, ii. 419). Bismarck had taken timely precautions against the adoption by the new emperor of the liberal views of his parents; he had instilled into the young man his own political principles. Mother and son were as a consequence for a time estranged. Even the memory of the Emperor Frederick became involved in acute controversy. Extracts from the late emperor's diary were published by Dr. Friedrich Heinrich Geffcken in the 'Deutsche Rundschau' (Sept. 1888). They were intended as a reply to his traducers and as proof of the part that he had played while crown prince in the achievement of German unity. The suppression of the offending review by Bismarck's orders and the imprisonment of Dr. Geffcken (who was not convicted) on the charge of high treason excited the empress's deepest indignation. Bismarck's triumph, however, was short-lived. The new emperor dismissed him from office in March 1890. With curious inconsistency the fallen minister invited the empress's sympathy (Hohenlohe, ii. 419), and in the presence of a witness she reminded him that his own past treatment of her had deprived her of any power of helping him now.

In 1891 a political rôle was assigned to her by the emperor. He was anxious to test the attitude of the French people towards his family. Under strict incognito she accordingly made a week's stay (19–27 Feb.) at the German embassy in Paris. Queen Victoria was anxious that the English ambassador should arrange a meeting between her and the French president. The empress met in Paris French artists and visited the studios of Bonnat, Détaille, and Carolus Duran. But an indiscreet excursion to Versailles and St. Cloud, where memories of the German occupation of 1870 were still well alive, brought the experiment to an unhappy end. The French nationalist party protested against her presence, threatened a hostile demonstration, and cut short her sojourn (Gaston Routier, *Voyage de l'impératrice Frédéric à Paris en* 1891).

After the death of her husband the Empress Frederick settled at Cronberg, where she purchased an estate on the slopes of the Taunus hills. With a legacy left her by the duchess of Galliera she built there a palatial country seat, which she named Friedrichshof. There she still followed the current course of politics, literature, and art, and entertained her relatives. During the last few months of her life she initiated the Empress Frederick Institute for the higher scientific education of members of the medical profession; this was opened at Berlin on 1 March 1906 after her death. Her relations with her son improved on the removal of Bismarck, and she was touched by the many tributes he paid to his father's memory. During her last years she repeatedly visited England, and on 22 June 1897 she took part in Queen Victoria's Diamond Jubilee procession. In the autumn of 1898 a fall from her horse, while out riding at Cronberg, brought on the first symptoms of cancer. She bore her sufferings with the same heroic patience as her husband had borne his. She outlived her mother six months, and died at Friedrichshof on 5 Aug. 1901. She was buried beside her husband in the Friedenskirche at Potsdam.

The empress's interests and accomplishments were of exceptional versatility and variety, and if there was a touch of dilettanteism about her discursive intellectual aptitudes, her devotion to intellectual and artistic pursuits was genuine. She was a clever artist, and an experienced connoisseur in music, though her skill as a performer was inferior to that of Queen Victoria. To philosophy and science she cherished a lifelong devotion, and followed their notable developments in her own time with eagerness. Although she retained her attachment to the Church of England, her religion was undogmatic, and she sympathised with the broad views of Strauss, Renan, Schopenhauer, and Huxley. An ardent champion of religious toleration, she severely condemned anti-semitism. In politics she was steadfast to the creed of civil liberty in which her father had trained her, and she declined to reconcile herself to the despotic traditions of the Prussian court. She made little effort to adapt herself to her German environment, which was uncongenial to her. She often acted unwisely on the impulse of the moment; she was no good judge of character and was outspoken in her dislikes of persons, which she frequently conceived at first sight. Her unflinching resistance to Bismarck proves her courage, and her persistent support of social, artistic, and philanthropic reform in Prussia bears permanent testimony to the practical quality of her enlightenment. Her wise benevolence earned the gratitude of the German people, but she failed to win their affection.

Of her eight children she was survived by her two eldest sons (the Emperor William II and Prince Henry) and four daughters. Her third son, Sigismund, died as an infant on 19 June 1866, and she lost her youngest son, Waldemar, on 27 March 1879, at the age of eleven. She lived to see the marriages of all her remaining children. The Emperor William married, on 27 Feb. 1881, Princess Augusta Victoria of Schleswig-Holstein, and Prince Henry married on 24 May 1888 Princess Irene of Hesse-Alt. Her four daughters, Princesses Charlotte, Victoria, Sophie, and Margarete, wedded respectively Prince Bernard of Saxe-Meiningen (on 18 Feb. 1878), Prince Adolph of Schaumburg-Lippe (on 19 Nov. 1890), Constantine, Duke of Sparta (on 27 Oct. 1889), and Prince Frederick Charles of Hesse (on 25 Jan. 1893). All her children, except Princess Victoria of Schaumburg-Lippe, had issue, and her grandchildren numbered seventeen at the time of her death. Her grandchild Féodora (*b.* 1879), daughter of Princess Charlotte of Saxe-Meiningen, married on 24 Sept. 1898 Prince Henry XXX of Reuss.

As princess royal of England from her infancy and then as crown princess of Germany the Empress Frederick was frequently drawn, painted, and sculptured. The earliest portrait, perhaps, is that in 'The Christening of the Princess Royal,' painted by Charles Robert Leslie, R.A., now at Buckingham Palace. As a child the princess was painted more than once by Sir William Ross, R.A., in miniature, and by Sir Edwin Landseer, R.A., with a pony, and again with Eos, her father's favourite greyhound. In the series of small statuettes in marble, by Mary Thornycroft [q. v.], now at Osborne House, the princess royal appears as 'Summer.' Another bust was made by Emil Wolff in 1851. The princess appears in the large family group of Queen Victoria and Prince Albert, by Winterhalter in 1846, and she was painted by the same artist at different stages of her life—as a girl, on her first début in society, at her marriage, and as princess of Prussia. 'The Marriage of the Princess Royal and Prince Frederick William of Prussia' (1858), painted by John Phillip, R.A., is now at Buckingham Palace. Among other English artists who drew portraits of the princess were Thomas Musgrave Joy and Edward Matthew Ward, R.A. After her marriage portraits were painted by A. Graefle, F. Hartmann, Ernst Hildebrand, and other leading German artists. Most of these remain in the private possession of her family in England and Germany. Many of them became well known in England in engravings. The picture by Hildebrand is in the Hohenzollern Museum at Berlin. In 1874 an important drawing was made by von Lenbach, as well as a portrait in oils in the costume of the Italian Renaissance by Heinrich von Angeli of Vienna, who then succeeded Winterhalter as favourite painter of Queen Victoria and her family. A half-length by the same artist (1882) is in the Wallace Collection in London, and another (1885) is in the Museum at Breslau. In 1894 Angeli painted a noble and pathetic portrait of the widowed empress, seated, at full-length, one version of which is at Buckingham Palace; it has been mezzotinted by Borner. The crown princess is conspicuous in the large painting by Anton von Werner of 'The Emperor William I receiving the Congratulations of his Family on his Birthday,' which was presented to Queen Victoria at the Jubilee of 1887 by the British colony at Berlin (information kindly supplied by Mr. Lionel Cust). Among other German artists who portrayed her, Begas executed a very life-like bust (1883) and also the sarcophagus over her tomb in the Friedenskirche, Potsdam. A cartoon by 'Nemo' appeared in 'Vanity Fair' in 1884. Memorial tablets were placed in the English church at Homburg (1903) and in the St. Johanniskirche, Cronberg (1906). A bust by Uphues was erected in 1902 on the Kaiser Friedrich promenade at Homburg. A striking statue of the empress in coronation robes, executed by Fritz Gerth, was unveiled by the Emperor William II on 18 Oct. 1903, opposite the statue of her husband in the open space outside the Brandenburg gate at Berlin.

[No complete biography has been published. A summary of her life appeared in The Times, and Daily Telegraph, 6 Aug. 1901, and in a memoir by Karl Schrader in the Biographisches Jahrbuch und Deutscher Nekrolog (Berlin, 1905, vii. 451). Her early years may be followed in Sir Theodore Martin's Life of the Prince Consort (1874–80); Letters of Sarah Lady Lyttelton, 1912; in Sir Sidney Lee's Queen Victoria (1904), and Edward VII, Suppl. II; Queen Victoria's Letters, 1837–61 (1907). For her career in Germany see especially Martin Philippson's Friedrich III als Kronprinz und Kaiser (Wiesbaden, 2nd edit. 1908) and Margarete von Poschinger's Life of the Emperor Frederick (trans. by Sidney Whitman, 1901). Other biographies of her husband by H. Hengst (Berlin, 1883), V. Böhmert (Leipzig, 1888), E. Simon (Paris, 1888), Sir Rennell Rod (London, 1888), and H. Müller-Bohn (Berlin, 2nd edit. 1904) are also useful. Hints as to the princess's relations with German politicians may be gleaned from the Memoirs of Duke Ernest of Saxe-Coburg-Gotha (trans. 4 vols. 1888–70); T. von Bernhardi's Aus meinem Leben, vols. ii., v., and vi. (Berlin, 1893–1901); R. Haym's Das Leben Max Dunckers (Berlin, 1891); Memoirs of Prince Chlodwig of Hohenlohe-Schillingsfürst (trans. 2 vols. 1906); Moritz Busch's Bismarck, some secret Pages of his History (trans. 3 vols. 1898); Bismarck, His Reflections and Reminiscences (trans. 2 vols. 1898); untranslated supplement ('Anhang') to latter work edited by H. Kohl in 2 vols. entitled respectively Kaiser Wilhelm und Bismarck and Aus Bismarck's Briefwechsel (Stuttgart, 1901); Gustav zu Putlitz, Ein Lebensbild (Berlin, 1894); H. Abeken's Ein Schlichtes Leben in bewegter Zeit, 1898, and H. Oncken's Rudolf von Bennigsen (2 vols. Stuttgart, 1910). The empress's artistic and philanthropic work are mainly described in L. Morgenstern's Viktoria, Kronprinzessin des Deutschen Reichs (Berlin, 1883); D. Roberts's The Crown Prince and Princess of Germany (1887); B. von der Lage's Kaiserin Friedrich (Berlin, 1888); and J. Jessen's Die Kaiserin Friedrich (1907). References of varying interest may be found in Lady Bloomfield's Reminiscences of Court and Diplomatic Life (2 vols. 1883); Princess Alice's Letters to Queen Victoria, 1885; Sir C. Kinloch-Cooke's Mary Adelaide, Duchess of Teck (1900); le Vicomte de Gontaut-Biron's Mon Ambassade en Allemagne, 1872–3 (Paris, 1906), and Dernières Années de l'ambassade en Allemagne (Paris, 1907); Memoirs and Letters of Sir Robert Morier, 1826–76 (2 vols. 1911); G. W. Smalley's Anglo-American Memoirs, 1911; W. Boyd Carpenter's Some Pages of my Life, 1911; T. Teignmouth Shore's Some Recollections, 1911; and Walburga Lady Paget's Scenes and Memories, 1912. Lady Blennerhassett has kindly supplied some unpublished notes. A character sketch by Max Harden in Köpfe (pt. ii. Berlin, 1910) represents the extreme German point of view. Some account of her latter years may be gathered from H. Delbrück's Kaiser Friedrich und sein Haus (Berlin, 1888); E. Lavisse's Trois Empereurs d'Allemagne (Paris, 1888; Sir Morell Mackenzie's Frederick the Noble, 1888; and G. A. Leinhaas, Erinnerungen an Kaiserin Friedrich (Mainz, 1902); see also Fortnightly Review and Deutsche Revue, September 1901; Quarterly Review and Deutsche Rundschau, October 1901 for general appreciations.]

G. S. W.

VINCENT, Sir CHARLES EDWARD HOWARD, generally known as Sir Howard Vincent (1849–1908), politician, born at Slinfold, Sussex, on 31 May 1849, was second and eldest surviving son of the five sons of Sir Frederick Vincent (1798–1883), eleventh baronet, sometime rector of Slinfold, Sussex, and prebendary of Chichester Cathedral, by his second wife, Maria Copley, daughter of Robert Young of Auchenskeoch. His father was succeeded in the baronetcy by William, his elder son by his first wife. Of Vincent's younger brothers, Claude (1853–1907) was under-secretary of the public works department in India, and Sir Edgar, K.C.M.G., was M.P. for Exeter from 1899 to 1906.

Howard Vincent, one of whose godfathers was Cardinal Manning, then archdeacon of Chichester, was an extremely delicate child, although in manhood his activity and vitality were exceptional. At Westminster school he made no progress, but being sent to travel in France and Germany he acquired an interest in foreign languages. At Dresden in 1866 he caught a glimpse of the Seven Weeks' war. In November of the same year he passed into Sandhurst, and in 1868 obtained a commission in the royal Welsh fusiliers. In 1870 he was refused permission to go out as a correspondent to the Franco-German war; but next year, as a special correspondent of the 'Daily Telegraph,' he succeeded in getting to Berlin. After carrying despatches for Lord Bloomfield [q. v.], the British ambassador, to Copenhagen and Vienna, he went on to Russia to study the language and the military organisation of the country. He published in 1872 a translation of Baron Stöffel's 'Reports upon the Military Forces of Prussia,' addressed to the French minister of war (1868-70), and in the same year 'Elementary Military Geography, Reconnoitring and Sketching.' Although only a subaltern of two and twenty, he was also soon writing in service magazines and was delivering lectures at the Royal United Service Institution. He next visited Italy to learn the language. In 1872 he was sent to Ireland in command of a detachment of his regiment. There much of his time was devoted to hunting, to private theatricals, and to addressing political meetings in which he expressed broadly liberal views on the Irish question. Next year he resigned as lieutenant his commission in the army. On 3 May 1873 he entered himself a student at the Inner Temple. Excursions to Russia and to Turkey in the course of 1873 and 1874 extended his range of languages and knowledge of the politics of the Near East. He issued in 1873 'Russia's Advance Eastward,' a translation from the German of Lieutenant Hugo Sturman, as well as an Anglo-Russian-Turkish conversation manual for use in the event of war in the East.

Vincent, who was called to the bar on 20 Jan. 1876, and joined the south-eastern circuit, was sufficiently interested in his new profession to publish immediately 'The Law of Criticism and Libel' (1876); but he never devoted himself to practice. He illustrated his versatility by publishing for 1874 and 1875 'The Year Book of Facts in Science and the Arts' (2 vols. 1875-6). On the outbreak of the Russian-Turkish war in 1876 he joined, as a representative of the 'Daily Telegraph,' the Russian army, but suspicion of intimacy with the Turks prejudiced his position. During 1874-5 he was captain of the Berkshire militia, and from 1875 to 1878 lieut.-colonel of the Central London rangers. While filling the last office he studied volunteer organisation, and promoted a series of conferences for the purpose of securing more generous treatment from government. In 1878 he published a volume on 'Improvements in the Volunteer Force.' From 1884 to 1904 he was colonel commandant of Queen's Westminster volunteers, and he brought the regiment to a high state of efficiency.

Questions of law and police meanwhile absorbed Vincent's interest. In 1877 he entered himself at Paris as a student of the faculté de droit, and after completing a close examination of the Paris police system he extended his researches to Brussels, Berlin, and Vienna. The experience fitted him for appointment in 1878 to the newly created post of director of criminal investigation at Scotland Yard. With infinite energy he reorganised the detective department of the London police system, and for three years he never left London for a day. His current duties were soon rendered arduous by Fenian outrages and threats. At the same time he formed plans for the reform of criminals and the aid of discharged prisoners. From 1880 to 1883 he was chairman of the Metropolitan and City Police Orphanage. In 1880 he published a French 'Procedure d'Extradition,' and in 1882 'A Police Code and Manual of Criminal Law,' which became a standard text-book. From 1883 he edited the 'Police Gazette.' His interest in his detective work was abiding, and he bequeathed a hundred guineas for an annual prize, the 'Howard Vincent cup,' for the most meritorious piece of work in connection with the detection of crime.

In 1884 Vincent resigned his association with Scotland Yard, and turned his attention to politics. A tour round the world led him to repudiate the liberalism towards which he had hitherto inclined, and developed an ardent faith in imperialism and protection. He was soon adopted as conservative candidate for Central Sheffield; and at the general election in Nov. 1885 he defeated Samuel Plimsoll [q. v. Suppl. I] by 1149 votes. This constituency he represented until his death, being re-elected five times, thrice after a contest in July 1886, July 1892, and January 1906, and twice unopposed in 1895 and 1900. Soon after entering parliament he joined the first London county council, on which he served from 1889 to 1896. Into politics Vincent carried the industry and persistency which had characterised his earlier work. He was soon a prominent organiser of the party, becoming in 1895 chairman of the National Union of Conservative Associations, in 1896 chairman of the publication committee of the conservative party, and in 1901 vice-chairman of the grand council of the Primrose League. Inside the House of Commons he was indefatigable as a private member, and although he was never invited to join an administration he had remarkable success in converting into statutes private measures of his own or of his friends' devising. To his persistence were mainly due the Acts dealing with the probation of first offenders (1887), saving life at sea, merchandise marks (1887), alien immigration (1905), and the appointment of a public trustee (1906). To the last measure Vincent devoted many years' labour and met with many rebuffs; he regarded its passage as his chief political achievement. He long urged the prohibition of the importation of prison-made goods from foreign countries. Vincent was best known in the House of Commons by his unwavering advocacy of protection, when tariff reform was no part of the official conservative policy. Between 1888 and 1891 he agitated for the denunciation of British commercial treaties and the adoption of the principle of colonial preference. In the same cause he founded in 1891 the United Empire Trade League, and acted thenceforth as its honorary secretary, visiting Canada and the West Indies to gather information and evoke colonial sympathy. Under the League's auspices 'the Howard Vincent Map of the British Empire' was published in 1887, and reached a 19th edition in 1912.

Vincent, who was made C.B. in 1885, was knighted in 1896. In 1898 he attended as British delegate the Conference at Rome on the treatment of anarchists, and was made K.C.M.G. for his services. When the South African war broke out in 1899 Vincent busily helped to form and equip volunteer contingents. His selection for the command of the infantry of the C[ity] I[mperial]V[olunteers] in South Africa was, to his disappointment, cancelled owing to a heart affection. But he went to South Africa as a private observer. In 1901 he served as chairman of a departmental inquiry on the Irish constabulary and Dublin police. He died suddenly at Mentone on 7 April 1908, and was buried at Cannes. He was aide-de-camp to King Edward VII, and received decorations from France, Germany, and Italy.

A bronze tablet was placed in 1908 in his memory in the chapel of St. Michael and St. George in St. Paul's Cathedral. A cartoon by 'Spy' was issued in 'Vanity Fair' in 1883. Vincent married on 20 May 1882 Ethel Gwendoline, daughter and coheiress of George Moffatt, M.P., of Goodrich Court, Herefordshire, and he left issue one daughter.

[Life by S. H. Jeyes and F. D. How, 1912; The Times, 8 and 11 April 1908; H. W. Lucy's Unionist Parliament, p. 42, and Balfourian Parliament, p. 330 (caricatures by E. T. Reed); private sources.] R. L.

VINCENT, JAMES EDMUND (1857–1909), journalist and author, born on 17 Nov. 1857 at St. Anne's, Bethesda, was eldest son of James Crawley Vincent, then incumbent there, by his wife Grace, daughter of William Johnson, rector of Llanfaethu, Anglesey. His grandfather, James Vincent Vincent, was dean of Bangor (1862–76). The father's devoted service as vicar of Carnarvon during the cholera epidemic of 1867 caused his death. James Edmund was elected to scholarships both at Eton and Winchester, 1870, but went to Winchester. In 1876 he won a junior studentship at Christchurch, Oxford, matriculating on 13 Oct. He gained a second class in classical moderations in 1878 and a third class in the final classical school in 1880, when he graduated B.A. Entering at the Inner Temple on 13 April 1881, he was called to the bar on 26 Jan. 1884. He went the North Wales circuit, and was also a reporter for the 'Law Times' in the bankruptcy department of the queen's bench division from 1884 to 1889. In 1890 he was appointed chancellor of the diocese of Bangor.

But Vincent had already begun to devote more attention to journalism than law. He joined the staff of 'The Times' in 1886, and for the greater part of his life was the principal descriptive reporter of the paper. In 1901, as special correspondent, he accompanied King George V, then duke of Cornwall and York, on his colonial tour; and later wrote on motoring. From 1894 to 1897 he edited the 'National Observer,' after W. E. Henley's retirement, and from 1897 to 1901 'Country Life.'

Vincent did much work outside newspapers. He contributed occasionally to the 'Quarterly Review' and the 'Cornhill.' In 1885 he collaborated with Mr. Montague Shearman in a volume on 'Football' in the 'Historical Sporting' series; in 1887 he published 'Tenancy in Wales'; and in 1896, in 'The Land Question in North Wales,' defined the landowners' point of view. But his best literary work was in biography and topography. His 'Life of the Duke of Clarence,' 1893, was written by authority. 'From Cradle to Crown' (1902) was a profusely illustrated popular account of the life of King Edward VII; it was reissued in 1910 as 'The Life of Edward the Seventh.' Other biographical studies were 'John Nixon, Pioneer of the Steam Coal Trade in South Wales' (1900); and 'The Memories of Sir Llewelyn Turner' (1903), his father's friend and co-worker in North Wales. Vincent bought Lime Close, Drayton, a house near Abingdon, and became interested in the district. In 1906 he wrote 'Highways and Byways in Berkshire,' as well as the historical surveys in W. T. Pike's 'Berks, Bucks, and Bedfordshire in the Twentieth Century' (1907) and 'Hertfordshire in the Twentieth Century' (1908). He was at work upon his 'Story of the Thames' (1909) at his death. 'Through East Anglia in a Motor-Car' (1907) was a vivacious record of travel. Vincent died of pleurisy at a nursing home in London on 18 July 1909, and was buried in Brookwood cemetery. A brass memorial tablet, with Latin inscription, was placed in Bangor Cathedral on St. Thomas's Day, 1910.

Vincent married on 12 Aug. 1884 Mary Alexandra, second daughter of Silas Kemball Cook, governor of the Seamen's Hospital, Greenwich, who survived him with two daughters.

[The Times, 19, 22 July, 23 Aug. 1909; N. Wales Chron. 23 July 1909, 23 Dec. 1900; Wainewright's Winchester Reg.; Foster's Alumni Oxon.; Brit. Mus. Cat.; private information; Cornhill, Sept. 1909 (Winchester in the Seventies, by J. E. Vincent), and Wykehamist, 21 Dec. 1909.]

G. Le G. N.

W

WADE, SIR WILLOUGHBY FRANCIS (1827–1906), physician, born at Bray, co. Wicklow, on 31 Aug. 1827, was eldest son of Edward Michael Wade (*d.* 1867), vicar of Holy Trinity, Derby, by his wife, the daughter of Mr. Justice Fox of the Irish bench. Wade counted Field-Marshal George Wade [q. v.], the military engineer, as a member of his family, and Sir Thomas Francis Wade [q. v.], ambassador to Pekin, was his cousin. After early education at Brighton, Wade entered Rugby school on 13 Aug. 1842, and passed to Trinity College, Dublin, in 1845. There he graduated B.A. in 1849 and M.B. in 1851, after being apprenticed to Douglas Fox, F.R.C.S. England, of Derby (brother of Sir Charles Fox [q. v.], the engineer). He was admitted M.R.C.S., England, and a licentiate in midwifery of Dublin in 1851 and M.R.C.P., London, in 1859, becoming F.R.C.P. in 1871. Soon after graduating in medicine, Wade was appointed resident physician and medical tutor at the Birmingham general hospital, and he filled this post until 1855, when he settled in practice in the town. In 1857 he was appointed physician to the Birmingham general dispensary, and in 1860 to the Queen's Hospital, Birmingham, soon becoming senior physician to the hospital and professor of the practice of physic and clinical medicine at Queen's College. In 1865 he was elected physician to the general Birmingham hospital, and remained upon its staff until April 1892. He was elected consulting physician on his retirement. He long enjoyed a large consulting practice in and around Birmingham. He became J.P. for Warwickshire, and in 1896 was knighted and was made hon. M.D. of Dublin. He retired from practice in 1898 and went to Florence, where he lived at Villa Monforte, Maiano, until 1905 He then removed to Rome, where he died on 28 May 1906.

He married in 1880 his cousin Augusta Frances, daughter of Sir John Power, second baronet, of Kilfane, but had no children.

Wade was more interested in the problems of general pathology than in clinical medicine. But he was the first to draw attention to the presence of albuminuria in diphtheria, showing that the disease was more than a local affection of the throat and nose. His chief claim to remembrance lies in his active control of the British Medical Association when that body still had its central offices in the midlands. He was elected to the council by the Birmingham branch in 1865; he succeeded George Callender as chairman of the scientific grants committee in 1880; he served as treasurer from 1882 to 1885, and as president at the Birmingham meeting in 1890, when in an address on medical education, he pointed out the insufficiency of the scientific knowledge required of medical students. He saw the members grow from 2500 to 20,000, with central offices in London, and on his initiative the association endowed the research scholarships which have proved a valuable help to the progress of medicine.

Besides contributions to scientific journals Wade was author of: 1. 'Notes on Clinical Medicine': No. 1. On diphtheria; No. 2. On a case of aortic aneurism, Birmingham, 1863; No. 3. On rheumatic fever, Birmingham, 1864. 2. 'On Gout as a Peripheral Neurosis,' 12mo., London and Birmingham, 1893.

[Brit. Med. Journal, 1906, i. 1379 (with portrait).]

D'A. P.

WAKLEY, THOMAS (1851–1909). [See under WAKLEY, THOMAS HENRY.]

WAKLEY, THOMAS HENRY (1821 1907), surgeon and journalist, eldest son of Thomas Wakley [q. v.], was born in London on 21 March 1821. With a view to taking holy orders, he was educated, preparatory to matriculation at Oxford, by a private tutor, the Rev. James Basnett Mills, a son of a partner in the printing firm Mills & Jowett, who printed the 'Lancet' in its early days. Wakley resided in Oxford for a short time without matriculating as the son of a prominent radical, he probably found the atmosphere uncongenial. Then entering the University of London, he took up medicine at University College. Among his teachers were Samuel Cooper, Liston, Richard Quain, and Erasmus Wilson; the last named coached him privately. Continuing his medical studies in Paris, he there not only attended surgical lectures and clinics, but also devoted much time to music and singing under Garcia and Ronconi. In 1845 he became M.R.C.S., and in 1848 was elected assistant surgeon to the Royal Free Hospital. Taking a house in Guilford Street near the hospital, he filled the position of an informal casualty surgeon. As a young untried man, nearly all of whose studies had been pursued abroad, he incurred the hostility of his father's enemies, who held his appointment to be a breach of principles of hospital administration which his father's newspaper, the 'Lancet,' was vigorously upholding against abuses. Wakley was accused of malpraxis in treating a child for fracture complicated with scarlet fever, and an action was brought against him. In spite of the mental strain, he passed the examination for the fellowship of the College of Surgeons on 6 Dec. 1849, four days before the trial came on. The jury found a verdict for Wakley without leaving the box. Wakley soon moved to No. 7 Arlington Street, where for many years he practised as a consulting surgeon. As a surgeon his name is chiefly associated with the invention of a form of urethral dilator and with the use of glycerine in the treatment of affections of the external auditory canal (cf. *Clinical Reports on the Use of Glycerine*, ed. W. T. Robertson, 1851).

In 1857 his father made him and his youngest brother, James Goodchild Wakley, part proprietors of the 'Lancet,' with a share in the management. In 1862 the father died. The youngest son, James, became editor, while Thomas maintained an active interest in its conduct. Until 1882, when he retired from practice, he pursued the double occupation of consulting surgeon and journalist. Upon the death of James Wakley in 1886 he assumed the editorship in association with his son Thomas. Thenceforth, until near his death, he devoted himself to his journalistic duties. Although he lacked the training of a journalist, he was a practical and shrewd editor, and maintained the position of the paper. The active management devolved in course of time on his son, but Wakley always kept in his own hands the 'Lancet' relief fund to meet accidental distresses of medical practitioners and their families, which he and his son founded and financed from 1889. To the last he helped to direct the Hospital Sunday Fund, which had been virtually founded by his brother. He manifested his interest in Epsom College for the sons of medical men by a donation in 1902 of 1000*l.* in the name of the proprietors of the 'Lancet.'

Wakley's energy was unbounded. When young he was a fine runner; he hunted until late in life, was a good shot, and fond of fishing. He died on 5 April 1907 of cardiac failure and senile decay, his last illness being practically his first. Wakley married in 1850 Harriette Anne, third daughter of Francis Radford Blake of Rickmansworth. She survived him, with a son, Thomas [see *infra*], and a daughter, Amy Florence.

Wakley wrote little. An article on diseases of the joints in Samuel Cooper's 'Dictionary of Practical Surgery' (new ed. revised by S. A. Lane, 1872) is the most important of his publications.

Wakley's only son, THOMAS WAKLEY (1851–1909), born in London on 10 July 1851, was educated at Westminster School and at Trinity College, Cambridge, where he studied medicine but took no degree. After he left Cambridge a serious bicycle accident interrupted his medical studies for some six years, but having entered St. Thomas's Hospital he became L.R.C.P. in 1883. Thenceforth he worked in the 'Lancet' office, first as assistant to his uncle, James Wakley, then as editor, later on his uncle's death in 1886 as joint-editor with his father, and finally as sole editor in succession to his father. A good amateur actor, a prominent freemason, and a numismatist, he died on 5 March 1909 of a gradually progressive hepatitis. He married in 1903 Gladys Muriel, daughter of Mr. Norman Barron, by whom he left one son, Thomas.

[Lancet, 13 April 1907 and 13 March 1909; personal knowledge.] H. P. C.

WALKER, Sir FREDERICK WILLIAM EDWARD FORESTIER- (1844–1910), general. [See Forestier-Walker.]

WALKER, FREDERICK WILLIAM (1830–1910), schoolmaster, was born in Bermondsey on 7 July 1830. He was the only son of Thomas Walker of Tullamore in Ireland, hat manufacturer, who claimed to be descended from George Walker [q. v.], the defender of Londonderry in 1689. His mother was Elizabeth Elkington, of a Warwickshire family. He was sent in 1841 to St. Saviour's grammar school, Southwark, but during his early boyhood his parents went to live at Rugby, and he was entered as a day boy at Rugby school under Tait. Among his contemporaries was George Joachim Goschen [q. v. Suppl. II]. The two boys are said to have been coerced to fight for the amusement of their schoolfellows and to have displayed 'cumbrous ineptitude' (Elliot, *Life of G. J. Goschen*, 1911, i. 10). His father had suffered financial loss, and while at Rugby worked for some years in a hatter's shop, a fact which gave rise to a legend identifying him with Nixon, the school hatter mentioned in 'Tom Brown's School Days.'

In 1849 Walker won an open scholarship at Corpus Christi College, Oxford, after declining a Bible clerkship at Wadham. He took a first class in moderations in classics and a second in mathematics; in 1853 he won a first class in the final classical school, followed by a second in the final mathematical school; in 1854 he gained the Boden (Sanskrit) and the Vinerian (law) and Tancred (law) scholarships. He graduated B.A. in 1853, and proceeded M.A. in 1856. In 1854 he was entitled in due course to a fellowship at Corpus, but there was no vacancy for him to fill until 1859; he was appointed philosophical tutor, and in that capacity earned from Mark Pattison [q. v.] the title of 'malleus philosophorum.' About this time he spent six months in Dresden learning German with a special view to grammatical and philological study. He did miscellaneous educational work in England, acting as examiner of Grantham school for his college, as assistant master for a short time at Brighton College, and as private tutor in the family of the Bullers of Crediton, where Redvers Buller [q. v. Suppl. II] was his pupil. As a young man he was attracted by the high church doctrine, and his former headmaster, Dr. Tait, when bishop of London, urged him to take holy orders with a view to becoming his examining chaplain. On 26 Jan. 1858 he was called to the bar at Lincoln's Inn, and joined the western circuit; but in 1859 the high mastership of Manchester grammar school, which was in the gift of the president of Corpus (see Oldham, Hugh), fell vacant; the post was offered to Walker, who reluctantly accepted it, mainly owing to the persuasions of Prof. John Matthias Wilson [q. v.].

Manchester grammar school was in 1859 a free school, with no power to charge fees, and with a decaying revenue derived partly from fishing rights in the Irk and partly from a monopoly in grinding corn, attached to a soke mill belonging to the school. The governing body was confined to members of the Church of England; the buildings were old and unsuitable; the scholars numbered barely 200; the educational system was obsolete. During Walker's tenure of office the school was completely reorganised in every direction; a change in the constitution of the governing body enlisted the help of the wealthy and able nonconformists of Manchester; the admission of fee-paying scholars, vehemently opposed by those who clung to the idea of a free school, put the finances of the school upon a secure basis; bequests and gifts to the amount of about 150,000*l.* provided new buildings and scholarships. By the time that Walker left, the numbers of the school were second only to those of Eton; in intellectual distinction it was scarcely surpassed.

In 1876 Walker was elected high master of St. Paul's school, which at that time was situated at the east end of St. Paul's Churchyard; and he continued in that post until his retirement from active work in July 1905. St. Paul's in 1876—the only other school in England whose head bears the title of high master—was in some respects not unlike what Manchester grammar school had been in 1859; but its constitution had just been remodelled by the charity commissioners, and it possessed ample and increasing revenues. One hundred and fifty-three foundation scholars [see Colet, John] and a few paying pupils were educated at the school; the foundationers were generally chosen by patronage, and the traditions were not favourable to educational efficiency. The removal of the school from the City was contemplated, but its destination was uncertain. Walker at once set himself to organise the teaching and to revive the discipline; and in the eight years during which the school still remained in St. Paul's Churchyard he greatly increased its reputation. In 1884 the school was removed to Hammersmith; a real expansion became possible, and the effect of Walker's organisation was seen in the rapid increase of numbers, and still more in the long series of notable successes gained by his pupils. The numbers rose from 211 in 1884 to 573 in 1888 and eventually to 650; in 1886 the first classical scholarship at Balliol was won by Richard Johnson Walker, the high master's only son, and for twenty years the success of his pupils at the universities and in every kind of open examination was one of the conspicuous facts in educational history. At Oxford the Ireland scholarship was won six times, the Craven eleven times, the Hertford eight times, the Derby five times; at Cambridge four Paulines were senior wranglers, six were Smith's prizemen; at the two universities twenty-one were elected to fellowships. From 1890 until the beginning of 1899 the high master and the governors of St. Paul's were engaged in a tedious struggle with the charity commissioners, whose proposals threatened to cripple the resources and to alter the character of the school chiefly by lowering the standard of the foundation scholarships. Walker's persistence and ingenuity were largely responsible for the issue, which was only reached after an appeal to the judicial committee of the privy council. The appeal came on for hearing in June 1896, but the judicial committee was spared the need of giving judgment. The commissioners gave way and on 25 Feb. 1899 they consented to frame a scheme in accordance with the wishes of the governors.

Walker took little or no part in general educational movements either in Manchester or in London; but in 1868 and 1869 he was public examiner at Oxford for the honours school of literæ humaniores, and in 1900 he sat with Dr. Warre of Eton on the commission for the education of officers in the army. In 1894 he was made an honorary fellow of Corpus; in 1899 he received the degree of Litt.D. from Victoria University. Walker, who had in 1869 declined the Corpus professorship of Latin at Oxford in succession to John Conington [q. v.], had a high reputation for accurate scholarship, and though he published nothing except occasional papers in the 'Classical Review,' he gave both direction and impulse to the philological work of Dr. W. G. Rutherford, J. E. King, C. Cookson, and other scholars of eminence, and also to the literary activities of Paul Blouët ('Max O'Rell'), another member of his staff at St. Paul's.

He became a freeman and liveryman of the Fishmongers' Company in April 1878, and was elected a member of the court in 1897; he was consequently appointed on the Gresham school committee and later became a governor of that school, in the reorganisation of which he took a prominent part.

He resigned the high mastership of St. Paul's in July 1905, and for the rest of his life resided at 7 Holland Villas Road, Kensington, within a mile of the school, which he never revisited. He died at his residence on 13 Dec. 1910, and was buried in the Kensington cemetery at Hanwell after a service in St. Paul's Cathedral.

By his devotion to accurate and vigorous teaching (though for many years he never himself taught a class) and by the remarkable success of his methods Walker did much to raise the standard of public-school education throughout the country. He was a man of great force of character, formidable in opposition alike by his determination and his judgment, but generous and sympathetic as a friend and adviser. From his Oxford days he was on terms of friendship with the leaders of the positivist movement—Congreve, E. S. Beesly, Cotter Morison, and Mr. Frederic Harrison; for Congreve in particular he had an unbounded admiration. He was the lifelong friend of Jowett, to whose influence he believed himself to owe much.

He married in 1867 Maria, daughter of Richard Johnson, of Fallowfield, near Manchester, who brought him a considerable fortune; she died in 1869. His only son, the Rev. Richard Johnson Walker, entered Balliol College, Oxford, in October 1887, and won the Hertford, Ireland, and Craven scholarships; he was for a time an assistant master at St. Paul's under his father, but resigned with him in 1905. He has since been mayor of Hammersmith.

A marble bust of Walker was executed by Mr. H. R. Hope Pinker in 1889 and exhibited in the Royal Academy of 1890; it stands in the library of St. Paul's School. On his retirement his portrait was painted by Mr. Will Rothenstein and hangs in the board room. A characteristic sketch of him by Leslie Ward ('Spy') appeared in 'Vanity Fair' on 27 June 1901

[The Times, 14 and 15 Dec. 1910; the Manchester Guardian, and the Guardian;

Res Paulinæ (a series of papers written for the four hundredth anniversary of the foundation of St. Paul's School and published at the school in 1910); the Pauline (school magazine); Foster's Alumni Oxon.; Spectator, 7 Jan. 1911; private information and personal knowledge.] R. F. C.

WALKER, Sir MARK (1827–1902), general, born at Gore Port on 24 Nov. 1827, was eldest of three sons of Captain Alexander Walker of Gore Port, Finea, Westmeath, by Elizabeth, daughter of William Elliott, of Ratherogue, co. Carlow. The father, of the West Kent (97th) regiment, served at the battles of Vimiero, Salamanca, Talavera, Busaco, and Albuera, and at Talavera saved the colours of his regiment, which he carried, by tearing them off the pole and tying them round his waist. Sir Samuel Walker [q. v. Suppl. II] and Alexander Walker, captain 38th South Staffordshire regiment, who died unmarried at Aden of cholera in 1867, were younger brothers. Educated at Arlington House, Portarlington, under the Rev. John Ambrose Wall, he entered the army on 25 Sept. 1846, in the 30th foot, without purchase, on account of his father's services. In 1851 the regiment embarked for Cephalonia, and was detached in the Ionian Islands.

Walker was appointed adjutant to the company depot, under command of Major Hoey, which remained at Walmer until the following year, when it moved to Dover, and in 1853 to Fermoy. In October 1853 he proceeded with a draft to Cork, and embarked for Gibraltar, where the regiment was then stationed. On 4 Feb. 1854 he was promoted lieutenant and appointed adjutant. On 1 May 1854 the regiment embarked for Turkey; it was encamped at Scutari, and formed part of the 1st brigade under Brig.-General Pennefather, and of the 2nd division under Sir De Lacy Evans. In July Walker was with his regiment at Varna, and in September embarked for the Crimea. At the battle of the Alma (20 Sept.) Walker had his horse shot under him and was wounded in the chest by a spent grape shot. But he made the forced march to Balaklava and was present at its capture. On the following day the advance was resumed to the Inkerman Heights, and next day the 30th regiment took up its position on the right of the army. He was present when the Russians made a strong sortie on 26 Oct., and at the battle of Inkerman on 5 Nov. showed a resourceful gallantry which won him the Victoria Cross (date of notification of Victoria Cross, 2 June 1858).

He was present with the regiment during the severe winter of 1854, serving continually in the trenches. On the night of 21 April, when on trench duty, he volunteered and led a party which took and destroyed a Russian rifle-pit, for which he was mentioned in despatches and promoted into the 'Buffs' (cf. Kinglake's *Crimea*, viii. 214). He joined that regiment, and on the night of 9 June in the trenches was severely wounded by a piece of howitzer shell and had his right arm amputated the same night. He received the Crimean medal with three clasps, the Turkish medal and 5th class of the Mejidie (Despatches, *London Gazette*, 7 May 1855). On 7 July 1855 he was sent home, and six months after joined the depot at Winchester. Early in 1856 the depot of the Buffs went to the Curragh, and on 6 June he was promoted brevet-major for his services in the Crimea. After serving two years in Ireland, he joined the Buffs in the Ionian Islands in July 1858, and early in November the regiment was concentrated at Corfu, where he was presented with the Victoria Cross by General Sir George Buller at a parade of all the troops. The same month he went with the Buffs to India, and was stationed at Dum-Dum, and on 22 Nov. 1859 proceeded with a wing of the regiment to Canton. Serving through the China campaign, he was on 30 March 1860 appointed brigade major of the 4th brigade, which was in the 2nd division, commanded by Sir Robert Napier, the commander-in-chief being Sir James Hope Grant [q. v.]. He was present at the capture of Chusan, at the battle of Sinho, at the assault of the Taku forts, at the surrender of Pekin, and at the signing of the treaty of peace by Lord Elgin. He received the medal with two clasps for Taku forts and Pekin and the brevet of lieutenant-colonel on 15 Feb. 1861. He embarked with the regiment for England on 27 Oct., arriving on 15 April 1862, and was quartered successively at Dover, Tower of London, Aldershot, Sheffield, and the Curragh. In July 1867, when the Buffs proceeded to India, Walker remained in command of the company depot at home, and after two years exchanged into the 2nd battalion at Aldershot. He was promoted brevet-colonel on 15 Feb. 1869, and on 3 Aug. 1870 was advanced to a regimental majority in the 1st battalion, then quartered at Sitapur in Oude. He joined them in Jan. 1871, and served at Benares, Lucknow, and Calcutta. On 10 Dec. 1873 he was appointed to the command of the 45th regiment (Sherwood Foresters), then at Rangoon, and on leaving the Buffs at Calcutta was given a rousing farewell by officers and men. In March 1875 he took the 45th regiment (Sherwood Foresters) to Bangalore, and on 24 May (Queen Victoria's birthday) was gazetted C.B. In August that year he was appointed a brigadier-general to command the Nagpore force, with headquarters at Ramptee. He vacated this command on 4 Nov. 1879, owing to promotion to major-general (11 Nov. 1878). On 22 Nov. 1879 he proceeded to England. In October 1882 he received the reward for distinguished service, and on 1 April 1883 was appointed to the command of the 1st brigade at Aldershot. From 1 April 1884 to 1 April 1888 he was in command of the infantry at Gibraltar. On 16 Dec. 1888 he became lieut.-general, and general on 15 Feb. 1893. He retired 1 April 1893, and on 3 June following was appointed K.C.B. On 27 Sept. 1900 he was nominated to the command of the 45th Sherwood Foresters.

Walker died at Arlington Rectory, near Barnstaple, on 18 July 1902, and was buried at Folkestone. He married on 6 June 1881 Catharine, daughter of Robert Bruce Chichester, barrister-at-law, of Arlington, Devon, brother of Sir John Palmer Bruce Chichester, first baronet, of Arlington (cr. 1840); she survived him. An oil painting, painted in Rome in 1891 (by Signor Giove, 300 Via del Corso), was bequeathed to the Buffs, subject to Lady Walker's life interest. A small oil painting is in the library of the United Service Club in Pall Mall. A memorial tablet is in the nave of Canterbury Cathedral.

[Dod's Knightage; Burke's Landed Gentry; Hart's and Official Army Lists; G. S. Creasy, The British Empire; Carter's Medals of the British Army, Crimea, p. 181; The XXX, the paper of the 1st battalion East Lancashire regiment; History of 45th Regiment, by General Hearn, private information.]

H. M. V.

WALKER, Sir SAMUEL, first baronet (1832–1911), lord chancellor of Ireland, born at Gore Port, Finea, co. Westmeath, on 19 June 1832, was second of the three sons of Captain Alexander Walker of Gore Port. His eldest brother was General Sir Mark Walker [q. v. Suppl. II for fuller family details]. Walker was educated at Arlington House, Portarlington, a celebrated school whose headmaster, the Rev. John Ambrose Wall, anticipated for him a brilliant university career. Walker matriculated in Trinity College, Dublin, in 1849, and was throughout the best man of his year in the classical schools, winning a scholarship in 1851, a year before the usual time, and graduating B.A. in 1854 as first senior moderator in classics and the large gold medallist. He was called to the Irish bar in Trinity term 1855.

Walker quickly attained a large practice both in equity and at the common law side, and went the home circuit. He was neither a fluent nor an attractive speaker, but his profound knowledge of law and penetration of motive, combined with his shrewd common sense, rendered him invaluable in consultation. An efficient cross-examiner, he impressed juries by his grasp of the salient points of a case, and was more successful as a verdict-getter than more brilliant advocates. He took silk on 6 July 1872. At the inner bar Walker increased his reputation, and rapidly came to the very front rank of the leaders. He attained the zenith of his fame at the bar in the state trial of Parnell in 1881, when, owing to the illness of his leader, Francis MacDonagh, Q.C., who had been counsel for O'Connell in 1844, the responsibility for the defence mainly devolved on Walker. The trial ended in a disagreement of the jury and a virtual triumph for the traversers.

In Trinity term 1881 Walker was appointed a bencher of the King's Inns. He was made solicitor-general for Ireland on 19 Dec. 1883, when Andrew Porter, the attorney-general, was made master of the rolls. Walker had always been a liberal in politics, and he now (Jan. 1884) entered the House of Commons unopposed as one of the members for the county of Londonderry—to fill the seat vacated by Porter. He had been an enthusiastic upholder of the tenants' side in the land controversy, which had reached an acute stage. Entering the House of Commons as a law officer of the crown, and sitting by virtue of his office on the treasury bench, Walker was somewhat embarrassed by the abrupt change from the law courts of Dublin to the prominent parliamentary position in which his ministerial office at once placed him. But his knowledge of the world came to his aid. He spoke only when compelled to do so, and then briefly and to the point. His dry humour rendered him quite equal to the ordeal of parliamentary interrogation. When Sir George Trevelyan, who was chief secretary to the lord lieutenant, broke down in health in 1884 owing to the strain of the Irish office, Walker as solicitor-general

—the attorney-general John Naish not being a member of the House of Commons —was the acting Irish secretary till the appointment of Sir Henry Campbell-Bannerman [q. v. Suppl. II] to the chief secretaryship in 1884. In May 1885 Walker became attorney-general for Ireland, and was sworn of the Irish privy council, but within a few weeks the Gladstone administration resigned on a defeat in the House of Commons (8 June 1885). Walker for the remainder of the session was as assiduous in his attendance as when in office.

At the general election of 1885, the county of Londonderry being divided under the Redistribution Act into two divisions, each returning one member, Walker sought election for North Londonderry; but he was defeated by Henry Lyle Mulholland (second Lord Dunleath) on 1 Dec. 1885. A month earlier, at a banquet in the Ulster Hall, Belfast, at which the Marquis of Hartington (Duke of Devonshire [q. v. Suppl. II]) was present, and at which the term liberal unionist was invented, Walker was present and said: 'The liberals of Ireland will not permit the union to be tampered with, and any attempt in that direction, no matter by what party, will not be tolerated.' But when Gladstone's adoption of home rule split the liberal party, Walker cast in his lot with the Gladstonian liberals. On the appointment of Gladstone as prime minister on 6 Feb. 1886, Walker, though without a seat in the House of Commons, again filled the office of attorney-general for Ireland, and he held the post till the fall of Gladstone's third administration on 3 Aug. 1886. While the liberal party was in opposition (1886–92) Walker pursued with distinction his practice at the Irish bar, and took a prominent part in the meetings of the liberal party held in Dublin. He was defeated in his candidature for South Londonderry in July 1892. On the formation of Gladstone's fourth administration in August 1892, Walker was appointed to the lord chancellorship of Ireland. At a complimentary dinner of the members of his old circuit, Walker was designated by Mr. Justice Gibson as the greatest lawyer of the Irish bar. He fully sustained on the bench his reputation as a lawyer. His judgments were masterpieces in their application of legal principles controlled by common sense. A good example of his work is presented by his judgment in Clancarty *v.* Clancarty (31 L.R.J. 530), dealing with precatory trusts. He retired from the chancellorship on the fall of the liberal administration, on 8 July 1895. As lord chancellor he presided over the court of appeal in Ireland, and still remained as a lord justice of appeal a member of that court, though no longer its president. Although he received no salary, he was as unremitting in his judicial duties as any other member of that tribunal. He also went on several occasions on circuit as a commissioner of assize, with great satisfaction to the bar and the public. He was appointed in 1897 by Earl Cadogan, the unionist lord-lieutenant, to preside over the commission on the Irish fisheries. On the formation of Sir Henry Campbell - Bannerman's administration, Walker was reappointed lord chancellor of Ireland on 14 Dec. 1905. He was then in his seventy-fourth year, but he held the great seal till his death on 13 Aug. 1911. He was created a baronet on 12 July 1906. He died in Dublin somewhat suddenly, and is buried in Mount Jerome cemetery.

Walker was below rather than above the medium height. He had finely chiselled features and clear grey eyes of great lustre. His memory was encyclopædic; and he recalled particulars of cases on the instant without apparent effort. In conversation he was entertaining, and his mots were often remarkable for their caustic wit and insight. Although devoted to legal studies, Walker enjoyed to the full the generous amusements of life. In his younger days he was an admirable shot, and all through life was an enthusiastic angler. His long vacations were generally spent in fishing in the lakes of Connemara, and he employed the same boatman for six-and-forty years.

Walker was twice married: (1) on 9 Oct. 1855 to Cecilia Charlotte (*d.* 18 June 1880), daughter of Arthur Greene, and niece of Richard Wilson Greene, baron of the Irish Court of Exchequer, by whom he had two sons and four daughters; (2) on 17 Aug. 1881 to Eleanor, daughter of the Rev. Alexander MacLaughlin, by whom he had a son and daughter. His eldest son, Sir Alexander Arthur Walker, second baronet, is secretary of the Local Marine Board, Dublin.

A photograph of Walker in his judicial robes, by Walton & Co., has been finely engraved.

[The Times, Freeman's Journal, and Irish Times, 14 Aug. 1911; private information; personal knowledge.] J. G. S. M.

WALKER, VYELL EDWARD (1837–1906), cricketer, born at Southgate House, Southgate, on 20 April 1837, was fifth of seven sons of Isaac Walker of Southgate, member of the prosperous brewing firm, Taylor, Walker & Co. of Limehouse, by his wife Sarah Sophia Taylor, of Palmer's Green, Middlesex. John Walker, of Arnos Grove, Southgate, was his grandfather. An uncle, Henry Walker, twice played for the Gentlemen of England *v.* Players. All Vyell's brothers—John, the eldest (1826–1885), Alfred (1827–1870), Frederick (1829–1880), Arthur Henry (1833–1878,, Isaac Donnithorne (1844–1898), and Russell Donnithorne (*b.* 1842), who alone survives—distinguished themselves in the cricket field. Of these Isaac Donnithorne and Russell Donnithorne proved themselves, like Vyell, cricketers of the first class. From 1868 to 1874 'The "Walker Combination," formed of these three brothers (when V. E. was bowling and fielding his own bowling at short mid-on, with I. D. and R. D., like two terriers watching a rat-hole, in the field), was nearly, if not quite, as fatal as the three Graces very often; . . . there is no instance within the memory of living cricketers when the strategy of the game was better displayed than when three Graces or three Walkers were on the out side' (F. Gale in *Lillywhite*, 1880).

Educated at Stanmore, where Vyell learned cricket under Mr. A. Woodmass, and at Bayford, Hertfordshire, he was at Harrow school from 1850 to 1854, and played in the cricket matches against both Eton and Winchester in 1853 and 1854. On leaving school he, like his brothers, mainly devoted himself to cricket, although some twenty years later he joined the family brewing firm. In 1856, at nineteen, he appeared at Lord's for the Gentlemen of England against the Players. With three brothers, John, Frederick, and Arthur, he played for the Gentlemen next year, when the match with the Players was first contested at Kennington Oval. He regularly played for the Gentlemen until 1869, captaining the team on ten occasions. By 1859 he was considered the best all-round cricketer in the world. In July of that year he scored 108 for England *v.* Surrey at the Oval, and took all ten Surrey wickets in the first innings for 74 runs—still an unparalleled feat in first-class cricket. He twice subsequently—in 1864 and 1865—repeated the exploit of taking all ten wickets in an innings.

Vyell Walker's eldest brother, John, founded in 1858, on his own land, the Southgate club, which became a chief centre of local cricket and a notable scene of activity for Walker and his brothers up to July 1877, when the club ceased to be their private property. There in 1859 John Walker invited the Kent eleven to play a Middlesex eleven which included five members of his family. John Walker and his brothers were mainly responsible for the creation of the Middlesex cricket club, which was definitely formed in 1864, and after many wanderings found a permanent home at Lord's in 1877. Vyell was secretary of the club from 1864 to 1870, joint-captain with his eldest brother, John, 1864–5, and sole captain (1866–72); he was succeeded in the captaincy (1873–84) by his youngest brother, Isaac Donnithorne, he was vice-president (1887–97), treasurer in 1895, president and trustee in 1898. In 1891 he served as president of the Marylebone cricket club.

As a batsman Walker played in an orthodox style; he was a powerful hitter, but had a safe defence. As a slow 'lob' bowler he was second only to William Clarke; he threw the ball higher than was customary, rendering its flight more deceptive; in the field he was exceptionally quick, especially in backing up his own crafty bowling. As a captain he had the gift of getting the best out of his men; his captaincy permanently raised Middlesex cricket to a foremost position.

On his brother Frederick's death in 1889 Walker succeeded to the family mansion and estate of Arnos Grove, Southgate, and in 1890 he presented to the new Southgate local board fifteen acres of land (valued at 5000*l.*) for use as a public recreation ground, and gave a further sum of 1000*l.* in 1894 to complete the laying out (*Standard*, 15 Nov. 1894). He became in 1891 J.P. and in 1899 D.L. for Middlesex, and was an active magistrate. He died at Southgate, unmarried, on 3 Jan. 1906. By his will he left Arnos Grove to his only surviving brother, Russell Donnithorne, and made bequests (amounting to 24,500*l.*) to London hospitals, societies, churches, and to the Cricketers' Fund Society (*The Times*, 23 March 1906). A chapel built at his expense in Southgate church was completed, a month after his death, in February 1906.

[W. A. Bettesworth's The Walkers of Southgate, 1900 (with various portraits of Walker and his brothers); Daft, Kings of Cricket, pp. 236–8 (portrait); Wisden's Cricketers' Almanack, 1907, pp. ci–civ; W. J. Ford, Middlesex County C.C. (1864–1899), 1900 (portrait of V. E. Walker as frontispiece); information kindly supplied by Mr. R. D. Walker and Mr. P. M. Thornton.]

W. B. O.

WALLACE, WILLIAM ARTHUR JAMES (1842–1902), colonel, royal engineers, born at Kingstown, co. Dublin, on 4 Jan. 1842, was son of William James Wallace, J.P., of co. Wexford. Educated at private schools and at the Royal Military Academy at Woolwich, he was commissioned as lieutenant in the royal engineers on 19 Dec. 1860. After two years' instruction at Chatham and two years' service at home stations, Wallace in 1864 joined the railway branch of the public works department in India. He became executive engineer in 1871, then deputy consulting engineer for guaranteed railways administered from Calcutta. Promoted captain on 25 August 1873, and appointed officiating consulting engineer to the government of India at Lucknow in 1877, he went to Europe in 1878 in connection with the railway exhibits to the Paris Exhibition, and on his return to India in the autumn was appointed secretary to the railway conference at Calcutta. He worked out the details of a policy, advocated at the conference, of vigorous railway construction in India, a result of experience gained in the recent famine.

At the end of 1878 Wallace received the thanks of the commander-in-chief, Sir Frederick Haines [q. v. Suppl. II], for conducting the transport of General Sir Donald Stewart's division over 300 miles of new railway on the Indus Valley line between Multan and Sakkar, on its march to Kandahar. Serving under Sir Frederick (afterwards Earl) Roberts as field engineer to the Kuram Valley column in the Afghan campaign of 1879, Wallace was mentioned in despatches, and commended for his work on road-making and for his energy and skill in the management of the Ahmed Khel Jagis. He received the medal.

Returning from active service to railway work in August, he was appointed engineer-in-chief and manager of the northern Bengal railway at Saidpur, was promoted major on 1 July, and arrived home on furlough in June 1882. On the recommendation of Major-general Sir Andrew Clarke [q. v. Suppl. II], inspector-general of fortifications, Wallace was made director of a new railway corps, formed of the 8th company of royal engineers, to work the Egyptian railways in the coming Egyptian war. The railway corps contributed largely to the success of the operations in Egypt. The advance from Ismailia was mainly dependent on the transport by railway of supplies, which amounted to 100 tons daily, while another 100 tons had to be stored at the advanced depots at Kassassin and Mahuta (see *Report, Professional Papers of the Royal Engineers*, vol. ix.). Wallace's improvised corps proved how essential in war such an organisation was, and led to its establishment in the service in an expanded form and on a more permanent basis. Wallace was present at the battle of Tel-el-Kebir on 13 September 1882, and for his services in the campaign was mentioned in despatches, received a brevet lieut.-colonelcy on 18 November 1882, medal with clasp, the 4th class of the Osmanieh, and the Khedive's bronze star.

Returning to India in October 1884, Wallace was appointed acting chief engineer to the government of India for guaranteed railways at Lahore. In the spring of the following year, when the Penjdeh incident in Central Asia caused great preparations to be made for war with Russia, Wallace was appointed controller at Lahore of military troops and stores traffic for the frontier. The Afghanistan boundary question was settled in September 1885, but Wallace remained at Lahore as chief engineer for guaranteed railways until his transference to Agra in April 1886. A brevet colonelcy was given to him on 18 Nov., and in the following year he returned to Lahore as chief engineer of the north-western railway.

In 1888 Wallace reported for the government of India on the Abt system of railways in Switzerland. On 1 Jan. 1890 he was made C.I.E. He retired from the service on 19 Dec. 1892. He died unmarried at Elm Park Gardens, London, on 6 Feb. 1902.

[War Office Records; Royal Engineers Records; W. Porter, History of the Corps of Royal Engineers, 2 vols. 1889; R. H. Vetch, Life of Lieutenant-general Sir Andrew Clarke, 1905; Susan, Countess of Malmesbury, Life of Major-general Sir John Ardagh, 1909; The Times, 11 Feb. 1902.] R. H. V.

WALLER, CHARLES HENRY (1840–1910), theologian, born at Ettingshall on 23 Nov. 1840, was eldest son of Stephen R. Waller, vicar of Ettingshall, Staffordshire. His grandfather, the Rev. Harry Waller of Hall Barn, Beaconsfield, was descended from Edmund Waller the poet. His mother was eldest daughter of the Rev. Charles Richard Cameron by his wife Lucy Lyttelton Cameron [q. v.], writer of religious tales for children, whose elder sister was Mary Martha Sherwood [q. v.], the authoress.

Educated at Bromsgrove School, he

matriculated on 4 June 1859 at University College, Oxford, and held a scholarship there (1859–64). He took a first class in classical and a second in mathematical moderations in 1861, and a second in lit. hum., and a third in mathematical finals in 1863, graduating B.A. in 1863; M.A. in 1867; B.D. and D.D. in 1891. He also won the Denyer and Johnson theological scholarship on its first award in 1866. Ordained deacon in 1864, and priest in 1865, he became curate of St. Jude, Mildmay Park, under William Pennefather [q. v.]. In 1865, on the recommendation of Canon A. M. W. Christopher of Oxford, he began his long service to the theological college, St. John's Hall, Highbury, as tutor under Dr. T. P. Boultbee [q. v.]. He served in addition as reader or curate on Sundays at Christ Church, Down Street (1865–9), and at Curzon Chapel, Mayfair, in 1869, under A. W. Thorold [q. v.]; and was minister of St. John's Chapel, Hampstead (1870–4). He became McNeile professor of biblical exegesis at St. John's Hall in 1882, and principal from 1884, on Boultbee's death, till his retirement on a pension in 1898. Of some 700 of his pupils at St. John's Hall, the majority entered the ministry of the Church of England.

A pronounced evangelical, he acted as examining chaplain to Bishop J. C. Ryle [q. v.]. At Oxford he had come under the influence of John William Burgon [q. v. Suppl. I], and through life his main interest lay in the conservative study and interpretation of the Scriptures, on which he wrote much. He died on 9 May 1910 at Little Coxwell, Faringdon, Berkshire, and was buried there. He married, at Heckington, Lincolnshire, on 22 July 1865, Anna Maria, daughter of the Rev. James Stubbs, by whom he left four sons (three in holy orders) and three daughters (one a C.M.S. missionary at Sigra, Benares).

Waller's published works include: 1. 'The Names on the Gates of Pearl, and other Studies,' 1875; 3rd edit. 1904. 2. 'A Grammar and Analytical Vocabulary of the Words in the Greek Testament,' 2 parts, 1877–8. 3. 'Deuteronomy' and 'Joshua' in Ellicott's 'Commentary,' 1882. 4. 'The Authoritative Inspiration of Holy Scripture, as distinct from the Inspiration of its Human Authors,' 1887. 5. 'A Handbook to the Epistles of St. Paul,' 1887. 6. 'Apostolical Succession tested by Holy Scripture,' 1895. 7. 'The Word of God and the Testimony of Jesus Christ,' 1903. 8. 'Moses and the Prophets, a Plea for the Authority of Moses in Holy Scripture,' 1907; a reply to the Rev. Canon Driver.

[Foster's Alumni Oxon.; Crockford, 1910; The Times, 11 May 1910; Record, 13 May 1910; Johnian (St. John's College, Highbury), Sept. 1910; private information.] E. H. P.

WALLER, SAMUEL EDMUND (1850–1903), painter of genre pictures, born at the Spa, Gloucester, on 18 June 1850, was son of Frederick Sandham Waller by his wife Anne Elizabeth Hitch. The father, an architect practising in Gloucester, ably restored considerable portions of Gloucester Cathedral in perfect harmony with the original design. Young Waller was educated at Cheltenham College with a view to the army, but showing artistic inclinations was sent to the Gloucester School of Art, and went through a course of architectural studies in his father's office. The training proved of service to him, for many of his pictures have architectural backgrounds. At eighteen he entered the Royal Academy Schools, and three years later (1871) he exhibited his first pictures at Burlington House entitled 'A Winter's Tale' and 'The Illustrious Stranger.' In 1872 he went to Ireland, and published an illustrated account of his travels entitled 'Six Weeks in the Saddle.' In 1873 he joined the staff of the 'Graphic.' Next year he appeared at the Royal Academy with a work called 'Soldiers of Fortune,' and henceforward was a steady exhibitor there until 1902. His chief and best-known pictures were 'Jealous' (1875), now in National Gallery, Melbourne; 'The Way of the World' (1876); 'Home?' (1877), now in National Gallery, Sydney; 'The Empty Saddle' (1879), with an architectural setting taken from Burford Priory, Oxfordshire; 'Success!' (1881) and 'Sweethearts and Wives' (1882), both in the Tate Gallery. Later works are 'The Day of Reckoning' (1883), 'Peril' (1886), 'The Morning of Agincourt' (1888), 'In his Father's Footsteps' (1889), 'Dawn' (1890), 'One-and-Twenty' (1891), 'The Ruined Sanctuary' (1892), 'Alone!' (1896), 'Safe' (1898), 'My Hero' (1902).

Old English country life strongly attracted his imagination, and furnished him with the romantic incidents which formed the subjects of his most notable pictures, and their backgrounds were frequently taken from Elizabethan houses in his native county or elsewhere in England. Many of his pictures are well known by reproductions and engravings throughout the English-speaking world. The originals are in many cases in private ownership in America and Australia as well as in England. Waller's great knowledge of horses and his skill in representing them gave his work much vogue among sportsmen. He took great pains in studying animals, and related some of his experiences in articles contributed to the 'Art Journal' (1893–6). His pictures usually tell a story effectively and dramatically, but he was more of an illustrator than a genuine artist.

He died at his studio, Haverstock Hill, London, N., on 14 June 1903, after a long illness, and was buried at Golder's Green. He married in 1874 Mary Lemon, daughter of the Rev. Hugh Fowler of Burnwood, Gloucestershire. His widow, a well-known artist, who exhibited at the Royal Academy from 1877 to 1904, survived him with a son.

A very fine oil portrait of Waller—a head—by John Pettie, R.A., belongs to the family.

[The Times, 15 June 1903; Art Journal, 1893, 1896, and 1903; Graves's Royal Acad. Exhibitors, 1906; private information.]

F. W. G-n.

WALPOLE, Sir SPENCER (1839–1907), historian and civil servant, born in Serle Street, Lincoln's Inn Fields, on 6 Feb. 1839, was elder son of Spencer Horatio Walpole [q. v.] by his wife Isabella, fourth daughter of Spencer Perceval, the prime minister. His younger brother, Sir Horatio George Walpole, was assistant under-secretary for India from 1883 to 1907.

Walpole's health in childhood was delicate, and it was chiefly on his account that his father, when the boy was six years old, moved with his family from London to Ealing for the sake of purer air. In the autumn of 1852 he was sent to Eton, where he became a favourite pupil of the Rev. William Gifford Cookesley [q. v.]. In 1854, when Cookesley left Eton, he changed to the pupil-room of William Johnson (afterwards Cory) [q. v. Suppl. I]. At Eton Walpole gained health and strength through rowing—becoming captain of a boat; to the effects of that exercise he attributed the excellent constitution which he enjoyed through life after an ailing childhood. Acceptance of office as home secretary in the short-lived administration of 1852 involved for Walpole's father the loss of a good practice at the bar, and for this reason the son, instead of being sent to a university on leaving Eton in 1857, became at the age of nineteen a clerk in the war office, achieving his first success in life by winning the first place in the preliminary examination. Though Walpole always regretted that he missed a university career, the loss allowed him, when his father again became home secretary in 1858, to gain an early insight into public life as his private secretary. He continued to hold the same position under Sotheran Estcourt, home secretary after the elder Walpole resigned in Jan. 1859. Estcourt on his retirement in the following June wrote to the head of the war office that almost his only regret in quitting office was that he lost Walpole as a companion of his work. Walpole resumed his duties at the war office until, on his father's return to the home office in 1866, he once more became his private secretary. Those were the years of the volunteer movement—the origin and significance of which Walpole afterwards described in his history. He entered with characteristic energy into the movement, taking his full share of the work of organisation at the war office, and himself joining the Ealing division.

In March 1867 Walpole was appointed, on his father's recommendation, one of two inspectors of fisheries for England and Wales with a salary of 700*l*. a year. The income enabled him to marry, while the work with its promise of 'many a pleasant wandering by river, lake and sea-shore' was most congenial. His great practical ability gave every assurance of success in the performance of his duties. He was fortunate, too, in his colleague, Frank Buckland, the naturalist, whose energy and kindliness rivalled his own. Nevertheless these were difficult years. After his marriage he lived, when in London, in a small house in Coleshill Street, where he supplemented his official income by hard work for the press. Frederick Greenwood [q. v. Suppl. II], to whose suggestions he owed something in the formation of his literary style, had recently become editor of the newly founded 'Pall Mall Gazette,' and Walpole contributed, often in hours stolen from sleep, the financial articles. His domestic expenses were increasing, and there had been loss of money through failure of an investment. Happily, in the intervals of official work and journalism he made time to write the life of his grandfather, Spencer Perceval. This book, published in 1874, so pleased Lord Egmont, the head of the Perceval family, that he bequeathed 10,000*l*. to the author, and his speedy death brought Walpole into possession of this bequest. This turn of fortune enabled him to relinquish journalism and to devote himself to the chief achievement of his life—the 'History of England from 1815'

—the first two volumes of which, appearing in 1878, quickly gave him rank as an historian.

Dislike of Beaconsfield's foreign policy, and whig sympathies derived from his historical studies, caused Walpole to recognise his true political convictions and to leave the Carlton Club. In April 1882 he was appointed by Gladstone governor of the Isle of Man. That post he held for nearly twelve years. His literary activity, though it was such as would have left to most men of letters little time for other occupation, was in no way checked by administrative duties efficiently discharged. In 1889 he published the official life of Lord John Russell—one of the best of political biographies. The history of England to 1856 appeared in its final form in 1890, when the last of the six volumes was published; in 1893 there followed a slim volume called 'The Land of Home Rule'—an essay on the history and constitution of the Isle of Man; and he contributed many articles to the 'Edinburgh Review.'

In 1893 Walpole left the Isle of Man on his appointment as secretary to the post office—a post which gave new opportunities to his aptitude for organisation and enabled him during his five years' tenure to effect lasting improvements in the British postal system. In 1897 he went as British delegate to the Postal Congress which met at Washington in that year, and was greatly interested by all that he heard and saw in America. A mutual attraction and respect marked his relations with Americans and led to the formation of friendships which he valued.

At the beginning of 1898, 'in recognition of his valuable public services,' Walpole was promoted to the rank of K.C.B.—an honour unduly delayed in the opinion of his friends. In Feb. 1899, to the regret of colleagues and subordinates, he left the post office, and early in the following year bought Hartfield Grove, a small property in Sussex pleasantly situated on the edge of Ashdown Forest.

In London, where he was very popular, Walpole had been warmly welcomed when he returned in 1893. Of versatile human interests, he won confidence and regard by his candour, modesty, consideration for others, and freedom from self-consciousness. Honours and compliments fell to him in abundance. In 1894 he had been elected president of the Literary Society—an office which his father had held for nearly thirty years, and he had been for some years a member of The Club when he was elected to Grillion's in May 1902. In 1904 he was given the honorary degree of D.Litt. at Oxford on Lord Goschen's installation as chancellor, and he was made a fellow of the British Academy. He was appointed chairman of the Pacific Cable Board in 1901 and chosen a director of the London and Brighton Railway Company in 1902. He was a valuable member of the committee of the London Library. A continuation of his history under the title of 'A History of Twenty-five Years (1856–1880)' appeared in 1904, and there were contributions from his pen in the 'Encyclopædia Britannica' and the 'Cambridge Modern History,' as well as in the 'Edinburgh Review.' At his country home he was made a magistrate, took much interest in his stock, and played golf. It was in the midst of these various activities that he was stricken down by cerebral hemorrhage and died at Hartfield Grove on 7 July 1907.

It is by his 'History of England from 1815,' brought down to 1880 in the four vols. of the 'History of Twenty-five Years,' that Walpole's name will be remembered. A knowledge derived from experience of the world which he describes, a high integrity of mind, the spirit of detachment, a just sense of proportion, an aptitude for the handling of statistics, with a perception of the right deductions to be drawn from them, and scrupulous accuracy, are high qualifications for the historian of recent events, and Walpole possessed them all. Like Macaulay he is at times too much inclined to accentuate his observations by the use of antithesis, and his generalisations, though interesting, are not always invulnerable when subjected to analysis, but, in the words of his friend, Sir Alfred Lyall, he has, in a style clear, level, and straightforward, 'filled up, with distinguished merit and ability, large vacant spaces in the history of our country.' Though educated in a conservative atmosphere, he ultimately accepted a political philosophy which was more nearly that of Manchester than of other schools of thought. A believer in *laissez faire*, he was equally distrustful of toryism and of socialism. Walpole's chief publications were: 1. 'The Life of Spencer Perceval,' 1874. 2. 'The History of England from the Conclusion of the Great War in 1815 to 1856,' 6 vols. 1876–90. 3. 'The Life of Lord John Russell,' 2 vols. 1889. 4. 'The Land of Home Rule,' 1893. 5. 'The History of Twenty-five Years (1856–1880),' of which the first two volumes appeared in 1904, and the last two, incomplete, under the supervision of Sir Alfred Lyall in 1908. 6. 'Studies in Biography,' 1907. 7. 'Essays Political and Biographical,' with a short memoir by his daughter, posthumously in 1908. Besides these works he wrote two volumes for the 'English Citizen' series, viz. 'The Electorate and the Legislature' (1881) and 'Foreign Relations' (1882).

Walpole married on 12 Nov. 1867 Marion Jane, youngest daughter of Sir John Digby Murray, tenth baronet of Blackbarony, who survived him till 9 May 1912. He left an only daughter, married to Mr. Francis C. Holland.

An excellent portrait of Walpole, painted in later life by Mr. Hugh Riviere, is in the possession of his daughter.

[Private information; Proc. Brit. Acad. (by Sir Alfred C. Lyall), 1907–8, pp. 373–8; memoir prefixed to Essays Political and Biographical, 1908.] F. C. H.

WALSH, WILLIAM PAKENHAM (1820–1902), bishop of Ossory, Ferns, and Leighlin, born at Mote Park, Roscommon, 4 May 1820, was eldest son of Thomas Walsh of St. Helena Lodge, co. Roscommon, by Mary, daughter of Robert Pakenham of Athlone. He entered Trinity College, Dublin, on 14 Oct. 1836, where he won the vice-chancellor's, the Biblical Greek, and the divinity prizes, with the Theological Society's gold medal. He graduated B.A. in 1841, proceeding M.A. in 1853, B.D. and D.D. in 1873. Ordained deacon in 1843, he was licensed to the curacy of Ovoca, co. Wicklow, and ordained priest the next year. From 1845 to 1858 he was curate of Rathdrum, co. Wicklow, where in the famine years 1846–7 his zeal and charity made him known far beyond his parish. From 1858 to 1873 he was chaplain of Sandford church, Ranelagh, Dublin.

As Donnellan lecturer of Trinity College he in 1860 chose as his theme Christian missions. He was long association secretary for Ireland of the Church Missionary Society. From 1873 to 1878 Walsh was dean of Cashel, and busily devoted his leisure there to literary work. In 1878 he was elected to the united sees of Ossory, Ferns, and Leighlin, being consecrated in Christ Church cathedral, Dublin, in September 1878.

As a bishop, Walsh was known by his gentle piety and wide sympathies. Zealous for foreign missions, he preached the annual sermon of the Church Missionary Society in 1882. A far-reaching movement for the increase of the society's funds was the result of his appeal. Although a decided evangelical, Walsh avoided ecclesiastical controversy. His influence was of great value in building up the disestablished church. Failure of health led to his resignation in October 1897. He died at Shankill, co. Dublin, on 30 July 1902. Walsh was twice married: (1) in 1861 to Clara, daughter of Samuel Ridley, of Muswell Hill, four sons and three daughters of whom survived him; and (2) in 1879 to Annie Frances, daughter of John Winthorpe Hackett, incumbent of St. James's, Bray, co. Dublin, who, with two sons, survived him.

His chief publications were: 1. 'Christian Missions,' Donnellan Lectures, 1862. 2. 'The Moabite Stone,' 1872. 3. 'The Forty Days of the Bible,' 1874. 4. 'The Angel of the Lord,' 1876. 5. 'Daily Readings for Holy Seasons,' 1876. 6. 'Ancient Monuments and Holy Writ,' 1878. 7. 'Heroes of the Mission Fields,' 1879. 8. 'Modern Heroes of the Mission Fields,' 1882. 9. 'The Decalogue of Charity,' 1882. 10. 'Echoes of Bible History,' 1887. 11. 'Voices of the Psalms,' 1890.

[Guardian, 6 Aug. 1902; Record, 8 Aug. 1902; Lowndes, Bishops of the Day; E. Stock, History of the C.M.S., 1899, ii. 37; iii. 265; private information.] A. R. B.

WALSHAM, Sir JOHN, second baronet (1830–1905), diplomatist, born at Cheltenham on 29 Oct. 1830, was eldest of four sons of Sir John James Walsham, first baronet, of Knill Court, Herefordshire, high sheriff of Radnorshire in 1870, by Sarah Frances, second daughter of Matthew Bell of Woolsington House, Northumberland. The father's family, of Norfolk origin, migrated to Radnorshire in the sixteenth century, and acquired by marriage the estates of the Knill family. The baronetcy conferred on a direct ancestor, General Sir Thomas Morgan [q. v.], on 1 Feb. 1661, became extinct in 1768, and was revived in 1831 in favour of Sir John's father.

After education at Bury St. Edmund's grammar school and at Trinity College, Cambridge, where he graduated B.A. in 1854 and M.A. in 1857, Walsham entered the audit office in March 1854. In October of the same year he was appointed a clerk in the foreign office, and was temporarily attached to the British legation at Mexico 30 Dec. 1857. He was appointed paid attaché there in 1860, and remained there till 1866, when he was transferred as second secretary to Madrid. The British legation was at that time engaged in correspondence arising out of the practice persisted in by the Spanish authorities of firing upon merchant vessels passing by the Spanish forts in the Straits of Gibraltar if they failed to display their national flags. This practice was abandoned in pursuance of an agreement signed in March 1865, but claims for losses occasioned by it still remained unsettled. Among these was one preferred by the owners of the schooner Mermaid of Dartmouth, alleged to have been sunk by a shot fired from the batteries at Ceuta. After much controversy it was referred by agreement to the arbitration of a joint commission, and Walsham, who had thoroughly mastered the details of this and other cases, was appointed to be one of the British commissioners. In 1870, after working for some time at the foreign office during the pressure of business occasioned by the outbreak of the Franco-German war, he proceeded to the Hague, and in 1873 was nominated as secretary of legation at Peking, but did not take up the appointment, withdrawing from the service shortly before his father's death on 10 Aug. 1874, when he succeeded as second baronet. In January 1875 he rejoined the service, being appointed secretary of legation at Madrid and remaining there till May 1878, when he was promoted to be secretary of embassy at Berlin. In 1883 he was transferred to Paris, receiving promotion to the titular rank of minister plenipotentiary, and on 24 Nov. 1885 was made British envoy at Peking. This onerous post he held for seven years, until his health was seriously affected by the combined strain of work and climate. On 31 March 1890 he obtained from the Chinese government the signature of an additional article to the Chefoo agreement of 1875, formally declaring Chungking on the Yang-tsze river to be open to trade on the same footing as other treaty ports. In 1891 a succession of outbreaks occurred in different parts of China, in which missionary establishments were plundered and destroyed and several British subjects lost their lives. Walsham pressed with vigour for adequate measures to ensure punishment of those responsible and better protection in the future, and his efforts, supported by the home government, were attended with considerable success. In April 1892 he was transferred to Bucharest, and retired on a pension in September 1894. He was made K.C.M.G. in Febuary 1895.

Walsham was a hardworking and meritorious public servant, whose unselfishness and kindness of heart earned for him great popularity, but whose work, partly on account of his naturally retiring disposition, partly in consequence of physical breakdown from over-exertion, scarcely received full public recognition. He died in Gloucestershire on 10 Dec. 1905, and was buried at the ancestral home of the family, Knill Court. He married on 5 March 1867 Florence, only daughter of the Hon. Peter Campbell Scarlett, by whom he left two sons.

[The Times, 12 Dec. 1905; Foreign Office List, 1906, p. 401; Burke's Peerage; Papers laid before Parliament.] S.

WALSHAM, WILLIAM JOHNSON (1847–1903), surgeon, born in London on 27 June 1847, was elder son of William Walker Walsham by his wife Louisa Johnson. Educated privately at Highbury, he early showed a mechanical bent, and was apprenticed to the engineering firm of Messrs. Maudslay. Soon turning to chemistry and then to medicine, he entered St. Bartholomew's Hospital in May 1867, and obtained the chief school prizes in his first and second years of studentship. In 1869 he gained the gold medal given by the Society of Apothecaries for proficiency in materia medica and pharmaceutical chemistry, and in 1870 was admitted a licentiate of the Society of Apothecaries. He then proceeded to Aberdeen, where he graduated M.B. and C.M. in 1871 with the highest honours. Returning to London, he was admitted M.R.C.S.England on 17 Nov. 1871. He served the offices of house physician and of house surgeon at St. Bartholomew's Hospital; in 1872–3 was assistant demonstrator of anatomy in the medical school; full demonstrator 1873–80; demonstrator of practical surgery 1880–9; lecturer on anatomy 1889–97, and lecturer on surgery from 1897. Walsham was appointed assistant surgeon at St. Bartholomew's Hospital on 10 March 1881, and took charge of the orthopædic department. He became full surgeon in 1897.

At the Metropolitan Hospital he was elected surgeon in 1876, taking charge of the department for diseases of the nose and throat. He became consulting surgeon in 1896. He also served as surgeon to the Hospital for Diseases of the Chest from 1876 to 1884. At the Royal College of Surgeons Walsham was elected a fellow on 10 June 1875, was an examiner in anatomy on the conjoint board in 1892, and in surgery from 1897 to 1902.

Walsham was a first-rate teacher of

medical students. As a pupil of Sir John Struthers [q. v.] at Aberdeen, he early turned his attention to dissection, and many of his preparations are still preserved at St. Bartholomew's Hospital. As surgical dresser to Sir James Paget he soon learned that pathology is the foundation of modern surgery, and of this fact he never lost sight. Physically delicate, he was unequal to the largest operations in surgery, but he excelled in those which required delicacy of touch, perfect anatomical knowledge, and perseverance, like the plastic operations of harelip and cleft palate and the tedious manipulations of orthopædic surgery.

He died at 77 Harley Street, London, on 5 Oct. 1903, and was buried at the Highgate cemetery. He married in 1876 Edith, the elder daughter of Joseph Huntley Spencer, but left no issue.

Walsham published: 1. 'Surgery: its Theory and Practice,' 1887; 8th edit. 1903; a widely circulated textbook for students. 2. 'A Manual of Operative Surgery on the Dead Body,' conjointly with Sir Thomas Smith [q. v. Supp. II]; 2nd edit. 1876. 3. 'A Handbook of Surgical Pathology for the use of Students in the Museum of St. Bartholomew's Hospital,' 1878; 2nd edit., with Mr. D'Arcy Power, 1890. 4. 'The Deformities of the Human Foot with their Treatment,' 1895. 5. 'Nasal Obstruction: the diagnosis of the various conditions causing it and their treatment,' 1898. Walsham edited the 'St. Bartholomew's Hospital Reports,' 1887–97, and contributed various articles to Heath's 'Dictionary of Surgery,' Treves's 'System of Surgery,' and to Morris's 'Treatise on Anatomy.'

[St. Bartholomew's Hosp. Reports, vol. xxxix. 1904 (with portrait); St. Bartholomew's Hosp. Journal, vol. xl. 1903, p. 17 (with portrait); Medico-Chirurgical Trans. vol. lxxxvii. 1904, pp. cxxxv–cxliii; private information; personal knowledge.] D'A. P.

WALTER, Sir EDWARD (1823–1904), founder of the Corps of Commissionaires, born in London 9 Dec. 1823, was third son of John Walter (1776–1847) [q.v.], proprietor of 'The Times,' by his wife Mary, daughter of Henry Smithe of Eastling, Kent. He was educated at Eton and at Exeter College, Oxford. He entered the army in 1843 as ensign of the 44th regiment; he exchanged as captain into the 8th hussars in 1848, and retired in 1853.

Early in 1859 he founded the Corps of Commissionaires for the purpose of finding employment for discharged soldiers and sailors of good character. The neglected position of the discharged soldier had long been a general reproach. Walter was the first to seek a remedy. Limiting his efforts at first to wounded men only, he obtained by personal canvassing situations in London for eight, each of whom had lost a limb. On 13 February 1859 Walter took seven crippled men to Westminster Abbey to return thanks for employment. Two days later he organised twenty-seven veterans of the army and navy into a society that should be self-supporting and entirely dependent on the exertions and earnings of its members. He provided the men with uniforms, and took offices in Exchange Court, where he carried on his work single-handed. At first he was handicapped by numerous failures of his men to retain their situations. But he had no lack of patience or confidence. For five years he was assisted only by members of his family, but in 1864, when the corps numbered 250, he appealed to the public for the purpose of creating an officers' endowment fund to enable him to engage a staff of officers to assist.

The appeal met with a generous response, and branches of the corps were opened in some provincial cities. The progress of the corps was steady. In 1874 the strength was a little under 500. By 1886 it reached 1200; in 1904 about 3000; in 1909, 3740; and on 11 June 1911, 4152. Of these 2541 men are stationed in London, while the remaining 1611 are distributed in ten other large cities, Belfast, Birmingham, Bristol, Edinburgh, Glasgow, Leeds, Liverpool, Manchester, Newcastle-on-Tyne, and Nottingham. The corps is wholly self-supporting, with its own pension and insurance fund and sick fund. King Edward VII, who inspected the corps at Buckingham Palace on 16 June 1907, described it as one of the best regulated and most useful institutions in the country. In 1884 Walter received a testimonial from officers of the navy and army. For his services as founder and captain of the corps Walter was knighted in 1885, and was nominated K.C.B. (civil) in 1887.

For the last years of his life he resided at Perran Lodge, Branksome, Bournemouth, where he died after a long illness on 26 Feb. 1904. He was buried at Bearwood, and a granite obelisk was erected by the corps to his memory in Brookwood cemetery. He was succeeded in the command of the corps by his nephew, Major Frederick Edward Walter (second son of John Walter of Bearwood). He married in 1853 Mary

Anne Eliza (*d.* 1880), eldest daughter of John Carver Athorpe of Dinnington Hall, Rotherham, Yorkshire.

A portrait in oils, by Mrs. Wey, is in possession of Lady Walter at Perran Lodge, Branksome, Bournemouth.

[Official information from the commandant of the corps; Burke's Landed Gentry; Dod's Knightage; Kelly's Handbook.] H. M. V.

WALTON, Sir JOHN LAWSON (1852–1908), lawyer, born on 4 Aug. 1852, was son of John Walton, Wesleyan minister in Ceylon and at Grahamstown, South Africa, who became president of the Wesleyan conference in 1887 and died on 5 June 1904, aged 80. After receiving his early education at Merchant Taylors' School, Great Crosby, in Lancashire, John Walton matriculated in 1872 at London University, but did not graduate, and entering the Inner Temple as a student on 2 Nov. 1874, he was called to the bar on 13 June 1877. Joining the north-eastern circuit, he rose rapidly in the profession, taking silk in 1890, only thirteen years after his call. He was helped at starting by a strong connection among the Wesleyans, especially in the West Riding towns. A born advocate, persuasive, tactful, and adroit, Walton acquired as large a practice in London as on circuit. He first came into public notice in March 1896 by his victory over Sir Frank Lockwood [q. v. Suppl. I] in the action brought against Dr. William Smoult Playfair [q. v. Suppl. II] for libel and slander; the damages, 12,000*l.*, were the largest that, up to that date, had been awarded by an English jury. His services were much in request on behalf of the trade unions, and he appeared for the respondents in the House of Lords in the case of Allen *v.* Flood (*Law Reports,* 1898, A.C. 1).

Walton was from his earliest years a keen politician, and in 1891 was chosen as the liberal candidate for Battersea; but rather than divide the party he withdrew his candidature in deference to the strong local claims of Mr. John Burns. At the general election of 1892 he contested Central Leeds unsuccessfully: at the bye-election, however, which followed the elevation of Sir Lyon Playfair [q. v. Suppl. I] to the peerage in the same year, he was returned for South Leeds, a seat which he held against all comers down to his death. During the ten years of unionist administration between 1895 and 1905 he played a prominent part in opposition; and though he carried his forensic style with him into parliament, his pleasant voice and carefully chosen language always procured him a ready hearing. A strong radical in domestic politics, especially where the House of Lords and the established church were concerned, he followed Mr. Asquith and Sir Edward Grey during the Boer War, and was a member of the short-lived liberal imperial party under Lord Rosebery. Though not himself a member of the Church of England, he took a lively interest in her affairs, and was a witness before the royal commission appointed in 1904 to inquire into ecclesiastical disorders; there he advocated a more effective procedure against clergy charged with breaking the law. On the formation of Sir Henry Campbell-Bannerman's government in December 1905 he was made attorney-general, and was knighted. The appointment was a result of Mr. (afterwards Viscount) Haldane's choice of the war office in preference to legal preferment. Though personally popular on all sides, Walton seemed never quite at home in his office. His attainments as a lawyer were neither deep nor varied, and ill-health interfered with his regular attendance in the House of Commons. One of his first duties as law officer was to introduce the trades disputes bill into the House of Commons; that measure, as originally drafted, made trade unions or their executive committees responsible for breaches of the law committed by their members. Walton's defence of this clause on 28 March 1906 caused much dissatisfaction in the ranks of the labour party, and on the second reading a month later, 25 April, the solicitor-general, Sir William Robson, announced that the clause would be abandoned in committee. This surrender on the part of the government did not tend to strengthen the attorney-general's position.

Walton died after a short illness at his house in Great Cumberland Place on 18 Jan. 1908. He was buried at Ellesborough, near Wendover in Buckinghamshire. He married on 21 Aug. 1882 Joanna M'Neilage, only daughter of Robert Hedderwick of Glasgow, by whom he had a family of one daughter and two sons. A caricature portrait by 'Spy' appeared in 'Vanity Fair' in 1902.

[The Times, 20 Jan. 1908 and 23 March et seq. 1896; Hansard, 4th series, cliv. 1295, clv. 1482.] J. B. A.

WALTON, Sir JOSEPH (1845–1910), judge, born in Liverpool on 25 Sept. 1845, was eldest son of Joseph Walton of Fazakerley, Lancashire, by his wife Winifred Cowley. His parents were Roman catholics. After being educated at St. Francis Xavier's College, Salisbury Street, and the Jesuit College at Stonyhurst, he passed to London University, and graduated in 1865 with first-class honours in mental and moral science. In the same year he entered Lincoln's Inn, where he was called to the bar on 17 Nov. 1868, and was made a bencher in 1896. Walton, who joined the northern circuit, entered the chambers of Charles (afterwards Lord) Russell [q. v. Suppl. I], then one of the leading juniors, and practised for several years as a 'local' at Liverpool. His chief work was in commercial and shipping cases, but his name is also associated with other important actions. A Roman catholic as well as a distinguished advocate, Walton was retained in the actions brought successfully in the interest of Roman catholic children against Thomas John Barnardo [q. v. Suppl. II]. Walton took a leading part in two cases which attracted considerable public interest. Having succeeded Sir Charles Russell as leading counsel to the Jockey Club, he appeared in Powell *v.* Kempton Park Racecourse Company ([1899] Appeal Court 143), which defined a 'place' within the meaning of the Betting Act, 1853, and in the copyright case of Walter *v.* Lane ([1900] Appeal Court 539), arising out of the republication of reports from 'The Times' of speeches by Lord Rosebery which decided that there is copyright in the report of a speech.

Walton's advancement in the profession was slow. He took silk in 1892, and became recorder of Wigan in 1895; but the general esteem in which he was held was shown by his election in 1899 to be chairman of the general council of the bar. Upon the appointment in 1901 of Sir James Mathew [q. v. Suppl. II] to be a lord justice, Walton succeeded him as a judge of the king's bench, and was knighted. His wide experience of commercial matters was of service to the commercial court, but on the whole his work as a judge did not fulfil expectation, though in judicial demeanour he was above criticism. He was interested in the work of the Medico-Legal Society, of which he became second president in 1905. He died suddenly at his country residence at Shinglestreet, near Woodbridge, on 12 Aug. 1910, having taken, in the previous week, an active part in the proceedings of the International Law Association in London. He was buried in the Roman catholic cemetery, Kensal Green.

In all that concerned the social and educational movements of the church of which he was a member Walton took an active part, and for a time was a member of the Liverpool school board. Much of his leisure was spent in yachting, and he was a frequent prize-winner at the Oxford and Aldeburgh regattas. He wrote a small work on the 'Practice and Procedure of the Court of Common Pleas at Lancaster' (1870), and was one of the editors of the 'Annual Practice of the Supreme Court' for 1884–5 and 1885–6.

He married on 12 Sept. 1871 Teresa, fourth daughter of Nicholas D'Arcy of Ballyforan, co. Roscommon, by whom he had eight sons and one daughter. A younger son, Louis Alban, second lieutenant, royal Lancaster regiment, died of enteric fever at Naauwpoort on 19 May 1901, aged twenty.

His portrait by Hudson was presented to him by old school friends, and is in the possession of Lady Walton. A caricature portrait by 'Spy' appeared in 'Vanity Fair' in 1902.

[The Times, 15 and 18 Aug. 1910; Foster Men at the Bar; Law Journal, 20 Aug. 1910; Trans. Medico-Legal Soc. vol. vii.; private information.] C. E. A. B.

WANKLYN, JAMES ALFRED (1834–1906), analytical chemist, born at Ashton-under-Lyne on 18 Feb. 1834, was son of Thomas Wanklyn of Ashton-under-Lyne. His mother's maiden name was Ann Dakeyne.

After studying at Owens College, Manchester, he qualified for the medical profession, becoming M.R.C.S. in 1856, but did not practise. He devoted himself in the first instance to chemical research, and afterwards to the science of public health.

In 1856 he acted as assistant to Prof. (Sir) Edward Frankland [q. v. Suppl. I]. Next, he studied chemistry at Heidelberg under Bunsen. In 1859 he was appointed demonstrator of chemistry in the University of Edinburgh, when Lyon (afterwards Lord) Playfair [q. v. Suppl. I] was professor. Migrating to London, Wanklyn was from 1863 to 1870 professor of chemistry at the London Institution, and from 1877 to 1880 lecturer in chemistry and physics at St. George's Hospital. At various periods he was public analyst for the boroughs of Buckingham, Peterborough, Shrewsbury, and High Wycombe. The latter part of his life was passed at New

Malden, Surrey, where he had a laboratory and practised as an analytical and consulting chemist. He died unmarried at 6 Derby villas, New Malden, on 19 July 1906 from heart failure, and was buried at New Malden cemetery.

Wanklyn was elected a corresponding member of the Royal Bavarian Academy of Sciences in 1869. Beyond honorary membership of the Edinburgh Chemical Society he was not allied with any British scientific society.

Wanklyn's first scientific paper, 'On Cadmium-ethyl,' was published by the Chemical Society (*Journal*, vol. ix. 1857). Next year he gave an account in Liebig's 'Annalen' of his preparation of propionic acid, and read a paper on the subject before the Chemical Society, 'On a New Method of preparing Propionic Acid: viz. by the Action of Carbonic Acid upon an Ethyl-compound' (*Journal*, vol. xi. 1859). The research afforded the first example of the artificial production of an organic substance directly from carbonic acid (see also *Journal*, vol. iv. (ser. 2), 1866). He contributed to the 'Proceedings of the Royal Society' the subjoined memoirs: 'On Some New Ethyl-compounds containing the Alkali Metals' (vol. ix. 1857–9); 'On the Action of Carbonic Oxide on Sodium-alcohol' (*ib.*); 'On the Synthesis of Acetic Acid' (vol. x.), and 'On the Distillation of Mixtures: a Contribution to the Theory of Fractional Distillation' (vol. xii.).

Several important papers were published in collaboration with others; with Lyon Playfair, 'On a Mode of taking the Density of Vapour of Volatile Liquids at Temperatures below the Boiling Point' (*Trans. Roy. Soc. Edin.* 1861); with Peter Guthrie Tait [q. v. Suppl. II], 'Note on the Electricity developed during Evaporation and during Effervescence from Chemical Action' (*Proc. Roy. Soc. Edin.* 1862); with Emil Erlenmeyer 'Sur la Constitution de la Mannite' (*Répertoire de Chimie Pure*, 1862); with Arthur Gamgee [q. v. Suppl. II] 'On the Action of Permanganate of Potash on Urea, Ammonia, and Acetamide in strongly Alkaline Solutions' (*Journ. Chem. Soc.* 1868); with J. S. W. Thudichum, 'Researches on the Constitution and Reactions of Tyrosine' (*ib.* 1869).

In 1871 Wanklyn gave much attention to milk-analysis, making for the 'Milk Journal' many hundreds of analyses of milk purchased in different parts of London, and investigating for the government the milk supplied to the metropolitan workhouses. But the Wanklyn method of estimation of the total solids of milk after evaporation of water was ultimately entirely superseded (see *Chemical News*, January 1886 and H. D. Richmond's *Dairy Chemistry*, 1899).

From 1865 to 1895 Wanklyn published many papers on the chemistry of public health in the 'Reports of the British Association,' the 'Chemical News,' and other scientific periodicals. His ammonia process of water analysis was first announced to a royal commission on 20 June 1867, and a paper on the subject was read the same day before the Chemical Society (*Journal*, 1867). With W. J. Cooper he made, for five years, for the local government board, monthly analyses by this process of the London water supply. Much controversy was aroused by his work, but Wanklyn was insistent on the value of the process (see his *Water-Analysis*.)

Wanklyn's independent publications were: 1. 'Milk Analysis: a Practical Treatise on the Examination of Milk and its Derivatives, Cream, Butter, and Cheese,' 1873; 2nd edit. 1886. 2. 'Tea, Coffee and Cocoa: a Practical Treatise on the Analysis of Tea, Coffee, Cocoa, Chocolate, Maté (Paraguay tea), &c.,' 1874. 3. 'The Gas Engineer's Chemical Manual,' 1886. 4. 'Arsenic,' 1901. He contributed several important articles to Watts's 'Dictionary of Chemistry' (see vol. iv. suppl. i. 1872). He collaborated with E. T. Chapman in 'Water-Analysis: a Practical Treatise on the Examination of Potable Water' (1868; 3rd edit. 1874, after Chapman's death; 10th edit. 1896—of this French and German translations appeared; 11th edit. 1907, with memoir and portrait of Wanklyn). He was joint author with W. J. Cooper of 'Bread Analysis: a Practical Treatise on the Examination of Flour and Bread' (1881; new edit. 1886); 'Air Analysis, with an Appendix on Illuminating Gas' (1890); and 'Sewage Analysis' (1899; 2nd edit. 1905). With W. H. Corfield [q. v. Suppl. II] and W. H. Michael, he collaborated in 'A Manual of Public Health' (1874).

[Private information; Journ. of Gas Lighting, 24 July 1906; Nature, 26 July 1906; Brit. Med. Journ. 4 Aug. 1906; Roy. Soc. Catal. Sci. Papers; Poggendorff's Handwörterbuch, Bd. iii. (1898); Men of the Time, 1899; Ency. Brit. 11th edit. i. 136.]

T. E. J.

WANTAGE, first Baron. [See Lindsay, afterwards Loyd-Lindsay, Robert James (1832–1901), soldier and politician.]

WARD, HARRY LEIGH DOUGLAS (1825–1906), writer on mediæval romances, born on 18 Feb. 1825, was fourth son of John Giffard Ward, successively rector of Chelmsford (1817) and St. James's, Piccadilly (1825), and dean of Lincoln (1845–1860). He was educated at Winchester and University College, Oxford (B.A. 1847), and in 1849 became an assistant in the department of manuscripts at the British Museum, where he remained until his superannuation at the end of 1893.

In his early official years he made a catalogue of the Icelandic manuscripts in the British Museum; this was never printed, but is preserved among the books of reference in the students' room. His attention was thus directed, by way of the Norse sagas, to the study of mediæval romantic literature in general, which became henceforth the engrossing interest of his life, and in which, through his wide reading, retentive memory, and sound critical instinct, he acquired exceptional proficiency. This bore fruit first in a comprehensive and admirable article on 'Romance, Mediæval,' which he wrote for Knight's 'English Cyclopædia' in 1873; and more fully afterwards in his monumental, though unfinished, 'Catalogue of Romances in the British Museum,' of which vol i. appeared in 1883, vol. ii. in 1893, and vol. iii., based largely on his notes, in 1910 (after his death). Vol. i. is the largest and also perhaps the most interesting to students of literature generally, comprising the great Arthurian and Charlemagne cycles, besides many other important groups of romances, such as those of Troy, Alexander, and Guillaume d'Orange, and a host of miscellaneous romances in prose or verse. It became at once a standard textbook, being no mere catalogue, but rather a collection of monographs, combining a succinct account of the conclusions of specialists with additions (often of considerable value) based on Ward's own independent studies. Vol. ii. includes the 'Beowulf' epic, but deals mainly with collections of shorter tales: Icelandic sagas, Æsopic fables, miracles of the Virgin, etc. Vol. iii. is entirely occupied with the 'exempla' used by preachers and moralists, and so appeals mainly to the professed mediævalist. The university of Halle conferred on him the honorary degree of Ph.D. in recognition of his work on the romances.

Ward's other published work was scanty, consisting merely (apart from reviews) of some translations of Andersen's 'Fairy Tales and Sketches' (1870); 'The Vision of Thurkill' (in 'Journal Brit. Archæol. Assoc.' xxxi. 420, 1875); and 'Lailoken (or Merlin Silvester)' (in 'Romania,' xxii. 504, 1893).

Ward's actual output in print by no means measures the full extent of his services to learning. During his long career at the British Museum he was continually consulted by students of various nationalities; and it was always a delight to him to place his rich stores of knowledge at their disposal, without any care for his own claims to priority of publication.

Ward died at Hampstead on 28 Jan. 1906. On 28 April 1866 he married Mary Elizabeth, daughter of Samuel George Fox, and had by her four sons and three daughters; one of the daughters predeceased him.

[The Times, 1 Feb. 1906; Gent. Mag. Feb. 1906, p. 106; private information.]

J. A. H.

WARD, HARRY MARSHALL (1854–1906), botanist, born at Hereford in 1854, was eldest son of Francis Marshall Ward, musician. He was educated first at the cathedral school at Lincoln, and then at a private school at Nottingham. After attending lectures by Huxley (in 1874–5) and by Prof. (now Sir William) Thiselton-Dyer, assisted by Professor Vines, in 1875, at the Normal School of Science, South Kensington, where he showed exceptional promise as a manipulator and draughtsman, he entered Owens College, Manchester, in 1875, and distinguished himself in chemistry, physiology, and botany, under Professors Roscoe, Gamgee, and Williamson. In 1876 he obtained an open science scholarship at Christ's College, Cambridge. There Ward attended the lectures of Sir Michael Foster on physiology, of Francis Maitland Balfour on embryology, and of Professor Vines on botany. In 1879 Ward graduated B.A. with first-class honours in the science tripos. He had already lectured at Newnham College and acted as demonstrator at South Kensington. During 1880 he visited the laboratory of Julius Sachs at Wurzburg. Here he began his first research work, on the development of the embryo-sac, which he continued at the Jodrell laboratory at Kew, the results being published in the Linnean Society's 'Journal' and in the 'Quarterly Journal of Microscopical Science' for 1880. Meanwhile he was appointed by the colonial office to investigate in Ceylon the coffee-leaf disease. Ward pursued the inquiry, which had been begun by (Sir) Daniel Morris, with characteristic thoroughness, although no effective prevention proved practicable. He communicated two valuable reports to the Ceylon government. While in Ceylon he made detailed observations on other tropical fungal parasites; and on his return to England in 1882 botanists recognised that the mycological side of botanical research had secured a valuable recruit.

After working for a short time under Anton de Bary at Strasburg, he was, through the influence of Sir Henry Roscoe, appointed to a Berkeley research fellowship at Owens College. In 1883 he was made fellow of Christ's College and assistant lecturer to Professor Williamson at Manchester, where he remained three years. An unsuccessful candidate for the chair of botany at Glasgow in 1885, Ward became in the same year professor of botany in the Royal Indian Engineering College, Coopers Hill, and proceeded M.A. at Cambridge in 1883. He was made Sc.D. there in 1892 and hon. D.Sc. of Victoria in 1902. He was elected a fellow of the Linnean Society in 1886, and served on its council from 1887 to 1889, and was elected to the Royal Society in 1888, receiving the royal medal in 1893.

The ten years (1885–95) that Ward held his chair at Coopers Hill proved the most productive period of his career of research. In 1887 he published his edition of Sachs's 'Vorlesungen über Pflanzenphysiologie' ('Lectures on the Physiology of Plants'), which was followed in 1889 by two smaller original volumes adapted to the need of students, 'Timber and some of its Diseases' (in the 'Nature' series), and 'Diseases of Plants' (in the 'Romance of Sciences' series); by 'The Oak: a Popular Introduction to Forest-Botany' (1892), a study recalling the method of his master Huxley's 'Crayfish'; and by an edition of Thomas Laslett's 'Timber and Timber-trees' (1894). The results of his original researches he communicated in papers to the Royal Society or to the 'Annals of Botany,' which was the organ of 'the new botany,' and of which, in 1887, he was one of the founders. The more important of these papers fall into four groups: (1) on the root-tubercles of the bean and the sources of nitrogen in the plant (1887–8); (2) on ferment-action, as exemplified in the colouring-matter of Persian berries (a research carried on with John Dunlop) and in the piercing of cell-walls by fungal hyphæ; (3) on symbiosis, or the relations between the host and the parasite, the subject of his Croonian lecture in 1890, also illustrated by his study of the ginger-beer plant in 1892; and (4) on the bacteriology of water, 1892–9. In the last research, undertaken with Professor Percy Frankland, at the request of the Royal Society, Ward identified eighty species of bacteria in the water of the Thames, but the bulk of the manuscript and drawings was so great as to render publication *in extenso* impossible. His conclusion as to the destructive effects of light upon bacteria (*Phil. Trans.* 1894) attracted public attention, owing to its hygienic implications.

On the death of Charles Babington, professor of botany at Cambridge, in 1895, Ward succeeded him, becoming at the same time professorial fellow of Sidney Sussex College. At Cambridge Ward worked with great vigour, infusing his own energy into university syndicates, colleagues, and students. Mainly through his effort the new botany schools were opened in 1904. They proved the best equipped laboratories in the kingdom.

As a teacher at Cambridge he took an elementary class besides advanced courses. Clear in speech, lucid and vivid in exposition, and a rapid draughtsman, he was prone to overcrowd his lectures with excess of matter. His text-book on 'Grasses' (1901), and that on 'Trees' (1904–5), which was completed after his death by Professor Groom for the Cambridge series of 'Natural Science Manuals,' showed that he recognised the claims upon him of every side of botanical study. Always alive to the practical side of botanical work, he devoted his last original research to the rusts affecting the brome grasses. He communicated his results to the Cambridge Philosophical Society, of which he was president, in 1902, and therein he incidentally refuted the mycoplasm theory of Professor Eriksson of Stockholm (cf. *British Association, Botany Section*, Debate, Cambridge, 1904). Ward was a regular attendant at the meetings of the British Association, and at Toronto in 1897 was president of section K, delivering an address on 'The Economic Significance of Fungi.'

Ward died at Babbacombe, Torquay, on 26 Aug. 1906, and was buried in the Huntingdon Road cemetery, Cambridge. He married in 1883 Linda, daughter of Francis Kingdon of Exeter, who, with a son and a daughter, survived him.

[Annals of Botany, xxi. pp. ix–xiii (with photogravure portrait) and bibliography; Nature, lxxiv. and Botanisches Centralblatt, cii., all by Prof. Vines; New Phytologist, vi. 1, by Sir W. Thiselton-Dyer; Proc.

Linnean Soc. 1906–7, by Dr. B. Daydon Jackson; Journal of Botany, xliv., by Prof. Bower; Kew Bulletin, 1906, pp. 281–2, by L. A. Boodle; Memoirs and Proc. of Manchester Lit. and Philosoph. Soc. li., by Prof. Weiss, Gardeners' Chron. xl.]

G. S. B.

WARD, HENRY SNOWDEN (1865–1911), photographer and author, born at Great Horton, Bradford, on 27 Feb. 1865, was eldest of five sons of William Ward, stuff manufacturer, by his wife Mary, only daughter of Henry Snowden, manufacturer.

After education at Great Horton national school, at Bradford grammar school (1876–9), and at Bradford Technical College, Ward entered in 1880 his father's business. He then with Herbert James Riley established the periodical 'The Practical Naturalist' (afterwards amalgamated with 'The Naturalist's World'), and founded the Practical Naturalists' Society. In 1885 he joined the printing and publishing firm of Percy Lund & Co. of Bradford, for whom in 1890 he founded and edited the monthly periodical, the 'Practical Photographer.' He soon became a recognised authority on photography and kindred technical subjects. He left Bradford for London in 1891, and paid his first visit to America in 1892. After his marriage there in 1893 he and his wife, an accomplished photographer, edited in London such photographic periodicals as the 'Photogram' (1894–1905), continued from 1906 as the 'Photographic Monthly'; 'The Process Photogram' (1895–1905), continued from 1906 as the 'Process Engravers' Monthly,' as well as 'Photograms of the Year' (from 1896) and 'The Photographic Annual' (from 1908). He also compiled many technical handbooks, of which the chief were 'Practical Radiography' (with A. W. Isenthal, 1896; new edits. 1897, 1898, and 1901, the first handbook in English on the Röntgen rays); 'The Figures, Facts, and Formulæ of Photography' (3 editions, 1903); 'Photography for the Press' (1905; 3rd edit. 1909); and 'Finishing the Negative' (1907). For the photographic firm of Dawbarn & Ward (in existence from 1894 to 1911), of which he was a joint director, he edited the 'Useful Arts Series' (1899), the 'Home Workers' Series,' and 'Rural Handbooks' (1902).

Becoming a member of the Royal Photographic Society in 1892 and a fellow in 1895, he did good service on the council. He was one of the first members in 1897 of the Röntgen Society, and was president in July 1909 of the Canterbury meeting of the photographic convention founded in 1886 to promote photographic research.

Literature and topography also attracted Ward, and he and his wife wrote and copiously illustrated with photographs taken by themselves: 'Shakespeare's Town and Times' (4to, 1896; 3rd enlarged edit. 1908); 'The Shakespearean Guide to Stratford-on-Avon' (1897); 'The Real Dickens Land' (4to, 1903); 'The Canterbury Pilgrimages' (1904). Ward also edited, with notes and introduction, an edition, elaborately illustrated by his wife, of R. D. Blackmore's 'Lorna Doone' in 1908.

Ward was an ardent traveller, and made many lecturing tours in Great Britain, Canada, and the United States. His topics were both technical and literary. An enthusiastic admirer of Dickens, he was an original member of the Dickens Fellowship, was chairman of council (1907–8), and was mainly responsible for the acquisition for the Guildhall Library of Frederick George Kitton's collection of Dickensiana in 1908. As commissioner of the Dickens Fellowship he went in October 1911 to America on a six months' lecture tour to stimulate American interest in the Dickens centenary; but he died suddenly in New York from mastoiditis-meningitis on 7 Dec. 1911, and was buried at Albany, New York State. He married on 15 July 1893 Catharine Weed, daughter of William Barnes of Albany, New York, and granddaughter of Thurlow Weed (1797–1822), a prominent New York journalist and politician. She became member of the Royal Photographic Society in 1893, and fellow in 1895, and collaborated with her husband in most of his literary work. They lived for many years at Golden Green, Hadlow, Kent.

[The Times, 8 Dec. 1911; Who's Who, 1911; Photogr. Soc. Journal, Dec. 1911; The Dickensian, Jan. 1912 (with portrait); information from Mrs. Ward.] W. B. O.

WARDLE, Sir THOMAS (1831–1909), promoter of the silk industry, born at Macclesfield on 26 Jan. 1831, was eldest son of Joshua Wardle, founder of the silk-dyeing industry at Leek, Staffordshire. Educated at a private school at Macclesfield and at the Leek grammar school, he entered his father's business at Leek-brook at an early age, and after his father's death he established in 1882 the silk and cotton-printing business of Wardle & Co. at Hencroft, Leek, and later the Churnet works there. He was also one of the founders and original directors of the Leek Spun Silk Manufacturing Company. An intimate friendship with William Morris [q. v. Suppl. I] began in 1875, when Morris paid the first of many visits to Leek and worked with Wardle at the lost art of indigo-dyeing. Together they succeeded in restoring vegetable dyeing to the position of an important industry (cf. MACKAIL's *Life of William Morris,* 1899). The friendship stimulated artistic workmanship at Wardle's factories, and he produced the earliest prints on cretonnes and silks from Morris's designs.

To Wardle was mainly due the commercial utilisation of Indian *tasar* or wild silk, to the possible manufacturing value of which Dr. (now Sir) George Birdwood had drawn the attention of the Bombay government in 1860. After much experimenting at Dr. Birdwood's instigation, Wardle in 1867 succeeded in bleaching the brown fibre and dyeing it so as to make it serviceable for manufacture. In 1872 he had a piece of this product woven in Crefield, and thenceforth *tasar* silk was utilised by the Yorkshire manufacturers, the waste being converted into 'seal-cloth' or plush—an imitation of seal-skin. Wardle exhibited his results at the British section of the Paris exhibition of 1878 (cf. BIRDWOOD's *Handbook* to the section), and was appointed a Chevalier of the Legion of Honour and an Officier d'Académie. Owing chiefly to Wardle's researches, *tasar* silk from China as well as from India became a generally important article of commerce.

By direction of the India office Wardle in 1885–6 visited Bengal to collect silk textiles and native embroideries for the Colonial and Indian exhibition at South Kensington, and to investigate the state of sericulture. His report, which showed that 60 per cent. of the silk-worms died of preventible diseases and that the reeling from the cocoons in the filatures was very imperfect, led to reform, and consequently to a revival of the almost lost trade in Bengal silk in England and France. On the same visit, in 1886, Wardle investigated the causes of the decay in the ancient silk productivity of Kashmir, and after his return to England long pressed a scientific scheme for its revival on the government. At length in 1897 he officially made large purchases in Europe of silk-worm eggs and cocoon-reeling machinery for the Kashmir Durbar, and under his advice a disappearing industry was placed on a footing of great prosperity. On a visit to Kashmir in 1903 he suggested the addition of silk weaving to silk production, with the result that Kashmir now produces silk of a quality comparable to that of Italy (*Imperial Gaz. of India,* vol. xv.). Wardle narrated the story of his efforts in 'Kashmir and its new Silk Industry' (1904). In Cyprus, too, Wardle reorganised silk production. Universally recognised as the chief authority on matters connected with silk, he had a principal share in founding, in 1887, the Silk Association of Great Britain and Ireland, of which he remained president to his death. Knighted in 1897, he was admitted to the honorary freedom of the Weavers' Company on 3 Feb. 1903.

Wardle was remarkable for his intellectual activity and versatility. To John Sleigh's 'History of Leek' (1862) he contributed a chapter on the geology of the neighbourhood which earned him the fellowship of the Geological Society. He also wrote on the geology of mid-England, of Roches, of Shuttinslowe, and of Cromer. He made a good collection of carboniferous limestone fossils, which he presented to the Nicholson Institute at Leek, and he wrote three monographs on fossils. He was on the council of the Palæontographical Society, and a fellow of the Chemical and Statistical Societies. An earnest churchman, and one of the originators of the Lichfield diocesan choral festival, Wardle composed a set of chants for the canticles and psalms for congregational singing, music for the marriage service, and also songs and Christmas carols. He took part in local affairs, serving as J.P. from 1898. He died at Leek on 3 Jan. 1909, and was buried in the Cheddleton churchyard. There is a memorial window in Warslow church, where a new chancel had been erected by Sir Thomas shortly before his death. He married in 1857 Elizabeth, daughter of Hugh Wardle of Leek (to whom he was not lineally related); her brother, George Wardle, was William Morris's manager at the Queen Square works. An expert in embroidery, she, with her husband, founded the Leek School of Embroidery, where tasteful and original work in both design and colour was done under her direction. An excellent copy in cloth of the Bayeux tapestry made there is now in the Reading Art Gallery. Lady Wardle died on 8 Sept. 1902, leaving five sons and four daughters.

Wardle wrote many monographs on silk. These include a report on the silk industry in England for the Royal Commission on Technical Instruction, 1884 (2nd report, vol. iii.); 'The Wild Silks of India,' a South Kensington handbook (1885); 'The Depression in the English Silk Trade and its Causes' (1886), a strong plea for a protective import tariff; 'On Silk, its Entomology, Uses, and Manufacture' (1888); 'On the Adulteration of Silk by Chemical Weighting' (1897); and 'The Divisibility of Silk Fibre' (1908). To 'Chambers's Encyclopædia' he contributed in 1888 an article on 'Silk.'

[Wardle's books and pamphlets; Mackail's Life of William Morris, 1899; Sir W. Lawrence's Valley of Kashmir, 1895; Imp. Gaz. of India, vol. xv.; Col. T. H. Hendley's Memoir, Jnl. of Indian Art and Industry, Oct. 1909; The Times, 5 Jan. 1909; Macclesfield Courier and Herald, Leek Post, and Textile Mercury, all of 9 Jan. 1909; Trans. North Staffs. Field Club, xliii. (1909); personal knowledge.] F. H. B.

WARING, ANNA LETITIA (1823–1910), hymn writer, born at Plas-y-Velin, Neath, Glamorganshire, on 19 April 1823, was the second daughter of Elijah and Deborah Waring, members of the Society of Friends. Her uncle, Samuel Miller Waring (1792–1827), a hymn writer, author of 'Sacred Melodies' (1826), had left the Friends for the Anglican communion; a desire for sacraments led his niece to follow his example; she was baptised on 15 May 1842 at St. Martin's, Winnall, Winchester. She early wrote hymns (her 'Father, I know that all my life' was written in 1846); her verse writing, continued to near the close of life, never lost its freshness, and exhibits at its best a real poetic vein, with a delicate purity of feeling and a ringing melody of diction. James Martineau writes of 'long-standing spiritual obligations' to her (Talbot, p. 27). She had learned Hebrew for the study of the poetry of the Old Testament, and daily read the Hebrew psalter. Her kindly nature was shown in her love of animals, her philanthropy in her constant visits to the Bristol prisons and her interest in the Discharged Prisoners Aid Society. Her friendships were few and deep. With an habitually grave demeanour she combined a 'merry, quiet humour.' She died unmarried on 10 May 1910 at Clifton, Bristol.

She published: 1. 'Hymns and Meditations,' 1850, 16mo; 17th edit. 1896; several American reprints. 2. 'Additional Hymns,' 1858, 12mo (included in subsequent editions of No. 1). 3. 'Days of Remembrance,' 1886 (calendar of Bible texts).

[The Times, 24 May 1910; Julian, Dict. of Hymnology, 1907, pp. 1233 sq., 1723; M. S. Talbot, In Remembrance of A. L. Waring, 1911 (portrait, additional hymns, and other verses); Joseph Smith, Cat. of Friends' Books, 1867, ii. 856.] A. G.

WARINGTON, ROBERT (1838–1907), agricultural chemist, eldest son and second child of Robert Warington [q. v.], one of the founders of the Chemical Society, was born at 22 Princes Street, Spitalfields, on 22 Aug. 1838. In 1842 his father was appointed chemical operator and resident director to the Society of Apothecaries, and the family took up their residence on 29 Sept. 1842 at Apothecaries' Hall. The son's constitution was naturally feeble, and life in the heart of the city did not strengthen it. Whilst still quite young, he studied chemistry in his father's laboratory and attended lectures by Faraday, Brande, and Hofmann. His father, being desirous of securing the youth employment in the country, obtained in Jan. 1859, from Sir John Bennet Lawes [q. v. Suppl. I], an engagement for his son at the Rothamsted Laboratory as unpaid assistant. He remained there for a year, devoting all his time to ash analyses, and then returned to London as research assistant to (Sir) Edward Frankland [q. v. Suppl. I]. In Oct. 1862 a further break-down in health forced him again to seek a country life, and he went as assistant to the Royal Agricultural College at Cirencester, where he remained till June 1867. During his stay at Cirencester his earliest papers on scientific subjects under his own name were published in the 'Journal of the Chemical Society.'

His first original work of importance was an investigation into the part played by ferric oxide and alumina in decomposing soluble phosphates and other salts, and retaining them in the soil. The results of this investigation (embodied in a series of four papers read before the Chemical Society) show careful work and close reasoning. In 1864 he commenced lecturing at Cirencester on the Rothamsted experiments, and it was proposed that Warington should publish a book on the subject. But Dr. Sir Joseph Henry Gilbert [q. v. Suppl. II], Lawes's collaborator, objected; the book remained in manuscript, and Gilbert and Warington were estranged for life.

Leaving Cirencester in June 1867, Warington was given by Lawes the post of chemist to his manure and tartaric and citric acid works at Barking and Millwall. His engagement terminated in 1874, but he remained in the Millwall laboratory for two years longer, working on citric and tartaric acids, and ultimately publishing his results in a paper of 70 pages in the 'Journal of the Chemical Society' (1875). In 1876 he returned to Rothamsted, under an agreement for one year only, to work simply as Lawes's private assistant. Before settling at Harpenden, he made in the autumn of 1876 a short tour of the German experimental stations. He was still associated with the Rothamsted investigations in 1889 when Sir John Lawes resigned to the present committee of management his active control over the experiments. It was then evident that the work of the station could no longer be carried on in its painful state of tension between Gilbert and Warington, and, all attempts at accommodation having failed, the committee reluctantly decided in June 1890 to terminate Warington's work at the end of that year. Warington had then reached a very interesting stage in an important research he had long been pursuing (since early in 1877) on the nitrification of the soil, and he was allowed to remain on his own petition without remuneration till June 1891. Before that date he had brought the work he had on hand to a successful termination. He was, however, denied the reward of seeing his work carried to its fullest natural conclusion, for though he obtained cultures which converted ammonia into nitrites, and others which produced the further conversion of nitrites into nitrates, and thus showed that nitrification was the work of two different organisms, it was left to Winogradski to isolate the organisms themselves.

Although Warington's original work in agricultural chemistry ended with his severance from Rothamsted, he was appointed by the committee lecturer in America under the Lawes trust. He gave six lectures, delivered 12–18 Aug. 1891, whilst in the United States, dealing chiefly with the subject of nitrification as illustrated by his own work at Rothamsted. These lectures were published by the U.S. department of agriculture in 'Expt. Station Bulletin,' No. 8, 1892. On his return to England Lawes entrusted him with an investigation at his Millwall factory into the contamination of tartaric acid and citric acid by the vessels used in their preparation; and he found a method for overcoming the evil. In 1894 he was appointed one of the examiners in agriculture for the science and art department, and (for three years) Sibthorpian professor of agriculture at the University of Oxford. Thereafter he retired into private life at Harpenden, busying himself with writings and in charitable and religious work.

His published writings mostly appeared in the 'Journal of the Chemical Society' and other scientific publications. They are clear in expression and precise in argument. Amongst other literary work, he contributed the article 'Manure' to Mackenzie's 'Chemistry as applied to the Arts and Manufactures,' various articles to Watts' 'Dictionary of Chemistry,' and the four articles on 'Cereals,' 'Citric Acid,' 'Artificial Manure,' and 'Nitrification' to Thorpe's 'Dictionary of Applied Chemistry' (1895). Warington wrote the greater part of the four articles on 'Rain and Drainage Waters at Rothamsted' which appeared in the 'Journal of the Royal Agricultural Society' under the joint names of Lawes, Gilbert, and Warington in 1881–83.

His greatest success was with a practical handbook entitled 'Chemistry of the Farm,' which he contributed to the Farm Series of Vinton & Co. This was first published in 1881, and was translated into several foreign languages; it reached its 19th English edition during his lifetime. Dr. J. A. Voelcker says of it that 'it is a model of what such a book should be. Whilst retaining its small compass, it is literally packed with sound information set out in concentrated form and with scientific method.' He was elected a fellow of the Chemical Society in 1863, subsequently becoming a vice-president, and he was admitted a fellow of the Royal Society in 1886.

He died at Harpenden on 20 March 1907, and was buried there.

He was twice married: (1) in 1884 to Helen Louisa (*d.* 1898), daughter of G. H. Makins, M.R.C.S., formerly chief assayer to the Bank of England, by whom he had five daughters; (2) in 1902 to Rosa Jane, daughter of F. R. Spackman, M.D., of Harpenden.

[Obituary by Spencer U. Pickering, F.R.S., in Journal of Chemical Society, No. dliv., Dec. 1908, pp. 2258–69 (also printed with some omissions in Proc. Royal Society, 80B, xv.–xxiv.); Cyclopædia of Modern Agriculture, 1911, xii. 79–80 (by Dr. J. A. Voelcker); personal knowledge and private information.]

E. C.

WARNE, FREDERICK (1825–1901), publisher, sixth and youngest son of the twelve children of Edmund Warne, builder, and of Matilda, daughter of R. A. Stannard, was born at Westminster on 13 Oct. 1825. Educated privately at Soho, he joined, at the age of fourteen, his brother, William Henry Warne (*d.* 1859), and his brother-in-law, George Routledge [q. v.], in the retail bookselling business which Routledge had founded in Ryder's Court, Leicester Square, in 1836. Routledge started a publishing business in 1843, and in 1851 Warne became a partner in the firm, which was then styled Routledge & Co.; the name was changed to Routledge, Warne & Routledge in 1858 on Routledge's son, Robert Warne Routledge, becoming a partner. From 1851 till 1865 Warne was largely identified with the success of the firm. In 1865, on the advice of the publisher George Smith, of Smith, Elder & Co., Warne began an independent publishing career at 15 Bedford Street, Strand (now Chandos House). There he was joined by Edward James Dodd (a lifelong friend and colleague at Routledge's), and by A. W. Duret, who left the firm of the Dalziel brothers to join him. An American branch was established in New York in 1881.

Warne effectively emulated Routledge's ambition to popularise good literature. In 1868 he inaugurated the 'Chandos Classics,' in which issue an edition of Shakespeare ultimately numbered 340,000 copies. Of the 154 volumes in the series, five million copies were sold. 'Nuttall's Dictionary,' which was originally published by Routledge, Warne & Routledge in 1863, was first issued by Warne in January 1867, when 668,000 copies were soon disposed of. In 1886 a fully revised edition appeared, of which the circulation approached by 1911 one million copies.

Warne was active in the publication of coloured picture books for children [see Evans, Edmund, Suppl. II]. He inaugurated a new era between 1870 and 1880 by his issue of the 'Aunt Louisa toy books,' which were followed by new editions of Edward Lear's 'Book of Nonsense,' by the children's books (1878–1885) of Randolph Caldecott [q. v.], and later by the works of Kate Greenaway [q. v. Suppl. II] and Mr. Walter Crane. In the field of fiction Warne issued Disraeli's novels before their transfer to Messrs. Longman in 1870 and published in London nearly all Mrs. Frances Hodgson Burnett's novels, including 'Little Lord Fauntleroy' (1886). He also first introduced to the English reading public the three American magazines, the 'Century,' 'St. Nicholas,' and 'Scribner's.'

In 1895 Warne, with his partner Dodd, left the business (Duret had retired in 1879), and he was succeeded by his three surviving sons, Harold Edmund, William Fruing, and Norman (*d.* 1905). Throughout his career Warne combined enterprise and business capacity with a keen interest in good literature. He died at his residence, 8 Bedford Square, on 7 Nov. 1901, and was buried at Highgate. He married on 6 July 1852, Louisa Jane, daughter of William Fruing of St. Helier's, Jersey, and had issue seven sons and three daughters. Three sons and two daughters survived him. A portrait in oils of Warne, painted by Henry Stannard, R.I., is in the possession of a daughter, Miss Amelia Louisa Warne, at 19 Eton Villas, Haverstock Hill, N.W.

[The Times, 15 Nov. 1901; Publishers' Circular (with portrait), Literature, Athenæum, 16 Nov. 1901; information kindly supplied by Mr. W. Fruing Warne.] W. B. O.

WARNER, CHARLES, whose real name was Charles John Lickfold (1846–1909), actor, born in Kensington, London, on 10 Oct. 1846, was son of James Lickfold, actor, by his wife Hannah. He was educated at Westbury College, Highgate, and was intended for the profession of an architect, to which a brother of his father belonged. His father was a member of Samuel Phelps's company at Sadler's Wells, and Charles made his first appearance on the stage on 24 Jan. 1861 at Windsor Castle, as a page in Lytton's 'Richelieu,' at a command performance by Phelps's company. Subsequently he entered the office of his uncle, the architect, but within a few months, despite his parents' objections, he ran away and obtained an engagement, under James Rodgers, at the Theatre Royal, Hanley. There he made his first appearance in February 1862, as Bras Rouge in Charles Dillon's 'The Mysteries of Paris,' appearing on the same evening as Muley Sahib in M. G. Lewis's tragedy 'The Castle Spectre.' He spent a short period with Rodgers at Hanley, Lichfield, and Worcester, and the following year joined H. Nye Chart's company at the Theatre Royal, Brighton.

He made his first appearance on the London stage, under George Vining's management, at the Princess's Theatre, 25 April 1864, when he played Benvolio in 'Romeo and Juliet' with Stella Colas. After a short season at Liverpool he was engaged by Edmund Falconer and F. B. Chatterton for three autumn and winter seasons at Drury Lane Theatre. He first appeared with Phelps there on 23 Sept. 1865 in a minor part in 'Macbeth,' and from September 1866 to March 1868 he supported Phelps and others in a round of Shakespearean and other plays. In the summer of 1866 he acted at the Sadler's Wells and Haymarket Theatres; his parts included Ned Plummer in 'Dot,' Careless in 'The School for Scandal,' and Modus in 'The Hunchback.'

Engaged by W. H. Liston for the Olympic Theatre, he opened there on 9 Oct. 1869 as Steerforth in 'Little Em'ly,' and subsequently played there a series of parts, in one of which, Charley Burridge in H. J. Byron's 'Daisy Farm,' he made his first pronounced success in London (1 May 1871). From the Olympic he went to the Lyceum Theatre under H. L. Bateman [q. v.]. There on 26 Dec. 1871 he succeeded Irving as Alfred Jingle in Albery's play of 'Pickwick.' In September 1872, at the Prince's Theatre, Manchester, he supported Adelaide Neilson as Romeo, Claude Melnotte, and Orlando, and in the following year he appeared with her in Paris at the Athénée Theatre.

On his return to London he was engaged by David James and Thomas Thorne for the Vaudeville, and 'opened' there on 20 Sept. 1873 as Charles Surface in 'The School for Scandal.' On the first performance there of H. J. Byron's comedy, 'Our Boys,' 16 Jan. 1875, he created the part of Charles Middlewick.

From the Vaudeville he passed to the Haymarket Theatre, where his rôles included Claudio in 'Measure for Measure,' in support of Adelaide Neilson (1 April 1876). Subsequently he returned to the Vaudeville to play his original part in 'Our Boys.' He was next seen at the St. James's Theatre under Mrs. John Wood, and as Vladimir in 'The Danischeffs' on 6 Jan. 1877 he made a great impression. At the Aquarium Theatre, 24 May, he made a further success in his impersonation of Young Mirabel in Farquhar's old comedy, 'The Inconstant.' At the Globe Theatre matinée performance, 2 Feb. 1878, he played Romeo for the first time in London.

Subsequently at the Princess's Theatre he achieved his chief reputation in melodrama. His performance of Tom Robinson in a revival of Charles Reade's drama, 'It's Never Too Late to Mend' (26 Dec. 1878), proved a popular triumph. On 2 June 1879 his rendering at the same theatre of Coupeau in Charles Reade's version of Emile Zola's 'L'Assommoir,' entitled 'Drink,' placed him among the most popular actors of his day. His presentation of the drunkard, who dies of delirium tremens, was as realistic and intense as any performance of which there is record. Francisque Sarcey, the French critic, declared it to be infinitely superior to that of Gil Naza, the French actor, who created the part in Paris.

On 20 Sept. 1880 he commenced an engagement at Sadler's Wells Theatre, when he appeared with effect as Othello. This was followed by William Tell, Claude Melnotte, and Ingomar, and he alternated the parts of Macbeth and Macduff with Hermann Vezin. A five years' engagement with the Gatti Brothers at the Adelphi Theatre began on 14 March 1881. He appeared as Michael Strogoff in a drama of that name, adapted from the French by H. J. Byron. Warner illustrated his strength of passion and will at this performance when, in a grim duel between himself as hero and James Fernandez as the villain, he impulsively caught at his antagonist's unhappily unblunted dagger, and dangerously wounded his hand; he ended the play and took his call, but fainted as soon as the curtain fell, and for several hours his life seemed in jeopardy. The joint of his middle finger was permanently stiffened. While at the Adelphi he confined himself to melodrama, playing Walter Lee in Henry Pettitt's drama, 'Taken from Life' (31 Dec. 1881), which ran for twelve months; Christian in Robert Buchanan's 'Stormbeaten' (14 March 1883); and Ned Drayton in Sims and Pettitt's drama, 'In the Ranks' (6 Oct.), which ran for eighteen months.

On 9 Dec. 1887 Warner was given a great complimentary 'benefit' performance at Drury Lane Theatre, prior to his departure on an Australian tour. His daughter Grace then made her first appearance on the stage, playing Juliet to her father's Romeo in the balcony scene. Originally intended to last a few weeks, his tour in Australia proved so successful that he remained there two and a half years. His repertory included many of his old parts, including those in 'Drink,' 'The Road to Ruin,' 'The School for Scandal,' 'It's Never Too Late to Mend,' and 'Dora,' also by Charles Reade. In addition he played many new parts, including Hamlet and Pygmalion in 'Pygmalion and Galatea.' On his return to England he continued his successes in melodrama. He acted for Augustus Harris at Drury Lane Theatre (6 Sept. 1890), and reappeared at the Princess's Theatre (16 April 1892). At the end of 1894 he toured as D'Artagnan in 'The Three Musketeers,' and in many ephemeral melodramas. At the Princess's on 27 Dec. 1897, he played Jack Ferrers in 'How London Lives'; and he gave a vivid performance of the part of a paralytic, Jan Perrott, in 'Ragged Robin,' on 23 June 1898, at Her Majesty's Theatre, under (Sir) H. Beerbohm Tree. At Wyndham's Theatre on 1 March

1902, he gave another remarkable performance as André Marex in 'Heard at the Telephone,' and also on the same evening as Raymond de Gourgiran in 'Cæsar's Wife.' At Drury Lane on 14 July 1903, he played Antonio in the 'all star' cast of 'The Merchant of Venice' at a performance in aid of the Actors' Benevolent Fund; and in the following year he went to America, playing in 'Drink' and 'The Two Orphans.'

On his return to London he was at the Savoy Theatre with Mrs. Brown-Potter, on 6 Dec. 1904, as Canio in a dramatic version of 'I Pagliacci.' At the New Theatre on 2 May 1905, he gave a powerful performance of the part of Kleschna in 'Leah Kleschna,' and at His Majesty's Theatre on 1 Sept. 1906 he appeared as Leontes in Tree's revival of 'The Winter's Tale,' with Ellen Terry as Hermione. This was his last appearance on the regular stage in England. In 1907 he returned to America, and played at the leading 'vaudeville' theatres in 'At the Telephone,' 'Devil Montague,' and a condensed version of 'Drink.' He committed suicide by hanging, whilst insane, at the Hotel Seymour, West 45th Street, New York, on 11 Feb. 1909, and was buried at Woodlawn cemetery, New York, on 13 Feb. 1909.

Warner was an effective actor in melodramatic parts which admitted of great nervous tension, but his high-strung nerves often found vent in a violence which proved alarming to his colleagues on the stage, and impaired his artistic control of voice and gesture. In old comedy he checked his emotional impulses with good results, and proved himself a sound and sympathetic interpreter. In private life he was of warm-hearted, generous, and buoyant temperament. He married in 1872, at Hampstead, Frances Elizabeth Hards, who was unconnected with the theatre. Of his two surviving children, both the son, H(enry) B(yron) Warner, and the daughter, Grace, are well known on the stage. The latter married a promising actor, Franklin McLeay, a Canadian by birth, who died prematurely in 1900 at the age of thirty-three.

[Personal recollections; private correspondence; Dramatic List, 1879; Clement Scott's Theatre, April 1881, Feb. 1891 (with portrait); Drama of Yesterday and To-day, 1899; Green Room Book, 1909; The Times, Daily Telegraph, and Era, 13 Feb. 1909 (with portrait).] J. P.

WATERHOUSE, ALFRED (1830–1905), architect, born in Liverpool on 19 July 1830, was eldest son of Alfred Waterhouse of Whiteknights, Reading, and previously of Liverpool, by his wife Mary, daughter of Paul Bevan. Both parents belonged to the Society of Friends. Educated at Grove House school, Tottenham, Waterhouse inclined, when his schooldays were over, to the career of a painter. He was articled, however, to Richard Lane, architect, of Manchester, with whom he served his time; and after completing his studies in France, Italy, and Germany, started in practice on his own account in Manchester in 1853. There he stopped till 1865, and in those twelve years succeeded in laying the foundations of a large practice in the north. Removal to London brought him a great increase of work in the south, but his connection with Liverpool and Manchester remained unbroken to the end.

In Manchester came his first opportunity, when in 1859 he won the competition for the assize courts, a building the planning of which offered him the sort of problem with which he was well qualified to deal. A clear thinker, he was capable of much useful innovation. The public entrance to the courts was made independent of the official part of the building: a new feature which no future designer could afford to ignore. With the power to grasp the principles by which a building might be made most suitable for its purpose went in Waterhouse the ability to see almost intuitively yet accurately the inherent possibilities of a site, and the proper disposition of the building to be placed on it.

After the Manchester assize courts there followed the more important commission of the Manchester town hall, this being also won in competition. The town hall, which was opened in 1877, is a well-planned building of a fine and picturesque massing placed on an irregular triangle. With such difficulties of site, Waterhouse found himself called upon to deal somewhat frequently, and did so with invariable success. The town hall shows to best advantage that individual type of Gothic which in Waterhouse's own work, and in that of many who followed in his footsteps, came to be generally associated with public and quasi-public buildings. Waterhouse was committed to the picturesque rather than the formal type of architectural design. A few of his buildings, such as the City and Guilds Institute in Exhibition Road (1881), were laid out on lines more severe and with real appreciation of the demands of formal treatment, but they were insignificant in number and probably dictated by special circumstances.

Other important works in Manchester were Owens College (1870), which, after later additions including the Christie Library and the Whitworth Hall, became the Victoria University, the Salford gaol (1863), the National Provincial Bank of England (1888), St. Mary's Hospital (1899), and the Refuge Assurance offices (1891), the southern half of which with the tower were added by his son. Waterhouse's work in Liverpool, which was little less important, included University College and engineering laboratories (1884), the Royal Infirmary (1887), the London and North-Western hotel (1868), the Turner memorial (1882), the Pearl Life Assurance (1896), and the Seaman's Orphanage (1871), while in the neighbouring county the Yorkshire College of Science, Leeds (1878), was a prominent example of his work.

Meanwhile Waterhouse was in 1866 one of the selected competitors for the new law courts in London, and he came near securing the first place, which, after much delay, was awarded to George Edmund Street [q. v.]. Before the final decision was announced, Waterhouse was entrusted with the construction of the new Natural History Museum in South Kensington (1868), which was regarded as a sort of solatium for his failure to obtain the larger commission. His useful suggestion that there should be a corridor for students at the back of the bays of the great hall, which should give them private means of access to the cases, and a freedom of examination which could not be permitted to the general public, the architect was not allowed to carry into effect. The work was completed in 1880. The plan is broad and simple; yet the architecture is marked by great richness. Adhering to his habitual picturesque treatment of outline, Waterhouse here allowed himself an unwonted exuberance of detail; the result is a building very distinctive and original, but in striking contrast to the studiously restrained treatment of the neighbouring City and Guilds Institute, which he designed in 1881.

In 1876 the first portion of the head London office of the Prudential Assurance was built in Holborn. This was twice enlarged till in its complete state it formed the chief architectural feature of the street, and the offices of the society which Waterhouse planned rapidly became conspicuous objects in the larger provincial towns. In 1881 a commencement was made with St. Paul's School, at West Kensington. In this building, as in others of the period, terra cotta was largely employed. His demands for this material were so large and continuous, and led to so general a use of it by others, that he may almost be said to have created a great industry. Possessing the courage of his opinions, he was always ready to give a trial to new materials and new methods of construction if, after examination, they commended themselves to him. He was thus one of the first architects to make a free use of constructional ironwork. Waterhouse worked seldom in stone, and on the rare occasions of his employment of it he seemed to lean to new forms of expression. The new University Club, St. James's Street (1866), is a Gothic effort, but in the National Provincial Bank, Piccadilly branch (1892), and again in the National Liberal Club (1884), the design is Renaissance in character. In the case of the last building he turned to good use an awkward site, the quiet and dignified edifice being graced by an angle tower which strikes a pleasant note of refinement.

Waterhouse did comparatively little ecclesiastical work or restoration, but he laid a tender hand on the ancient fabric of Staple Inn in Holborn (1887). St. Elisabeth, Reddish (1880), which he built for Sir W. Houldsworth, is his most successful church; others are St. Mary, Twyford (1876), St. Bartholomew, Reading, with a chancel added by Bodley, and St. John's, Brooklands, Manchester (1865). He also built the King's Weigh House chapel, in South Audley Street, London, and the Lyndhurst Road congregational church, Hampstead (1883), and at Yattendon, where he acquired a house and estate in 1887, he restored the fabric of the church partly at his own expense.

Of collegiate work he had his share. At Cambridge he made additions to Gonville and Caius College, commencing in 1868; he built a new court at Trinity Hall (1872), a block of undergraduates' rooms at Jesus (1869); the master's lodge, hall, library, and lecture rooms at Pembroke (1871), and the Union, begun in 1866 and finished later. At Oxford he was responsible for the south front and, afterwards, the hall at Balliol (1867), the interior of the latter having been since altered by his son, and for the debating hall of the Union (1878). His largest domestic works were the reconstruction of Eaton Hall (1870), Iwerne Minster, Dorset (1877), Heythrop Hall (1871), rebuilt after destruction by fire in a severe classical style, Hutton Hall, Guisborough (1865) and Blackmoor, Hampshire (1866), for the first Lord Selborne, with many surrounding buildings; he also built Abinger Hall (1871) for Lord Farrer; Buckhold, Berkshire (1884); and Allerton Priory, Liverpool (1867). Three times he built for himself, Barcombe Cottage, Fallowfield, Manchester (1864); Fox Hill in Whiteknights Park, Reading (1868); and lastly Yattendon Court (1877), where the village became a visible testimony to his sense of the obligations of a landlord.

In 1891 he took his eldest son, Paul, into partnership; works of note about this period were the National Provincial Bank, Piccadilly; the dining-hall and chapel, Girton (1872); additions to the Yorkshire College, Leeds (1878), a block of shops and offices, St. Andrews Square, Edinburgh (1895); medical school buildings for Liverpool University College, Liverpool Royal Infirmary, and a wing of the Nottingham General Hospital (1899). The Hôtel Métropole, Brighton (1888), followed a little later, as well as improvements in the Grand Hotel, Charing Cross (1898), extensive alterations to the Grosvenor Hotel (1900), the Surveyors' Institution and University College Hospital (1897), the last-named being completed by Mr. Paul Waterhouse. Other works carried out from time to time which deserve mention are New Court, Carey Street, Lincoln's Inn (1875), Reading grammar school (1870), Hove town hall (1880), Foster's Bank, Cambridge (1891), Brown's Bank (now Lloyds), Leeds (1895), St. Margaret's School, Bushey (1894), and Rhyl Hospital, first block (1898); the last two buildings in partnership with his son.

Waterhouse's productive capacity was combined with critical insight. His services as assessor in competitions were widely sought, and there a clearness of perception and a power of rapidly grasping a scheme as a whole enabled him to arrive rapidly at decisions authoritatively founded on reasoned data. He was a member of the international jury for the competition for the new west front to Milan cathedral; was on the committee of selection for the Imperial Institute, acted as assessor for the Birmingham law courts, of which he made a sketch plan for the competitors' guidance. Among the last competitions in which he took part himself was the first (inconclusive) competition for the admiralty and war office in 1882. Thenceforth his work came to him unsolicited.

Waterhouse's early liking for colour never deserted him; he was probably the most accomplished sketcher in water colours in the profession, and on various occasions exhibited in the water-colour room at the Royal Academy.

At the height of his career Waterhouse was regarded as the chief figure in the profession by a large majority of his fellow architects, and his eminence was recognised at home and abroad. He became a fellow of the Royal Institute of British Architects in 1861, was for many years a member of council, member and afterwards chairman of the art standing committee, president of the institute 1888–1891, and gold medallist in 1878, when the president described him as a 'great mason,' a phrase which expressed tersely the belief of architects generally that he knew precisely what his materials were capable of, and the best way to turn them to account. He was elected A.R.A. on 16 Jan. 1878, and R.A. on 4 June 1885, becoming treasurer in 1898, and proving of great service to the institution in that capacity. He gave up active membership of the R.A. in 1903. In June 1895 he received the LL.D. degree at Manchester, that being the first honorary degree conferred by the Victoria University. In 1893 he was made a corresponding member of the Institute of France. He held diplomas from Vienna, (1869), Brussels (1886), Antwerp (1887), Milan (1888), Berlin (1889); the 'grand prix' was awarded him at the Paris International Exhibition of 1867.

Waterhouse was treasurer of the Artists' General Benevolent Institution till 1901. He joined in founding and was president till 1901 of the 'Society for checking the Abuses of Public Advertising,' a form of vulgarisation of the scenery of town or country which was particularly odious to him.

In 1901 Waterhouse's health broke down and he retired from active work. His last years were spent at Yattendon, where he died on 22 Aug. 1905. He was buried in the churchyard there. He married in 1860 Elizabeth, daughter of John Hodgkin, and sister of Thomas Hodgkin the historian, by whom he had three sons and two daughters. His eldest son is Paul, his partner and successor; his elder daughter, Mary Monica, married Robert Bridges, the poet.

Besides official addresses, Waterhouse wrote an essay on architects in 'The Unwritten Laws and Ideals of Active Careers' (ed. Miss Pitcairn, 1889).

There is a good portrait of him by Sir William Quiller Orchardson, which hangs with those of other presidents in the galleries of the institute. Another portrait by Sir Lawrence Alma Tadema (1892) is in possession of the family. Both are in oil colour.

[The Builder, leading article and obit. notice, 26 Aug. 1905; Builders' Journal, 30 Aug. 1905; Building News, 25 Aug. 1905; private information from Mr. Paul Waterhouse, supplemented by personal recollections.]

WATERLOW, SIR SYDNEY HEDLEY, first baronet (1822–1906), lord mayor of London and philanthropist, born in Crown Street, Finsbury, on 1 Nov. 1822, was fourth of the five sons of James Waterlow (*b.* 19 April 1790, *d.* 11 July 1876) of Huntington Lodge, Peckham Road, Surrey, by his wife Mary, daughter of William Crakell. The family was of French Walloon descent, and the father, who was a member of the Stationers' Company and a common councilman for Cornhill ward, started in 1811 a small stationer's business in Birchin Lane, where in 1836 he was joined by his eldest son, Alfred James, and between 1840 and 1844 by other sons.

Brought up by his grandmother at Mile End till the age of seven, Sydney went first to a dame's school in Worship Street, then to a boarding school at Brighton, and lastly to St. Saviour's grammar school in Southwark, living at that time with his father in Gloucester Terrace, Hoxton. His father was a member of the unitarian congregation at South Place chapel, Finsbury, under the ministry of William Johnson Fox [q. v.], whose teaching greatly influenced young Waterlow. In Nov. 1836 he was apprenticed through the Stationers' Company to his uncle, Thomas Harrison, the government printer, with whom he lived at Pimlico and afterwards at Sloane Square. His diligence procured him in the fourth year of his apprenticeship the sole charge of the foreign office printing, with full responsibility for its secrecy. On the expiration of his indentures in Nov. 1843 he went to Paris, and was employed during the winter in printing for the publisher Galignani a catalogue of his library.

In Easter 1844 he joined his brothers Alfred, Walter, and Albert in adding a printing branch to the stationery business in Birchin Lane, the modest capital of 120*l.* being furnished by their father. They began by printing the 'Bankers' Magazine,' of which the first number appeared in April. Success at once followed, largely through the great share which the firm secured in railway printing and stationery. Additional premises were taken at 49 Parliament Street (1846), London Wall (1851), Carpenters' Hall (1854), Great Winchester Street (1866), Castle Street, Finsbury (1872), Little Chart Mills, Ashford, Kent (1875), and Paris in 1883 (*London Directories*). The firm was converted into a limited company in February 1876, under the style of Waterlow and Sons, Limited, and in February 1877 the company sold the Birchin Lane portion of their business to Waterlow Brothers and Layton. From this date until 1895, when he retired, Sydney was managing director of the company. The company was reconstructed in 1879, and again in 1897; its present capital is 1,350,000*l.*

Waterlow joined the city corporation in 1857, when he was elected a common councilman for the ward of Broad Street, and on 3 April 1862 received a special vote of thanks from the corporation for devising and establishing a system of over-house telegraphs for the City police stations (*Minutes of the Common Council*, 3 April 1862). He was elected alderman of Langbourn ward on 30 Jan. 1863, and served the office of sheriff in 1866–7. The year was notable for a banquet given to the Viceroy of Egypt at the Mansion House and the costly reception of the Sultan Abdul Aziz by the corporation at Guildhall. Waterlow and his brother sheriff were knighted on 3 Aug. 1867. On Michaelmas Day 1872 he was elected lord mayor. Among the more important events of his mayoralty were the establishment of the Hospital Sunday Fund (21 Nov.); the opening to the public of the newly built Guildhall Library (10 March 1873); and the entertainment of the Shah of Persia at Guildhall (20 June). On 29 July 1873 he was made a baronet. He was for ten years (from 29 May 1873) governor of the Irish Society, was treasurer of St. Bartholomew's Hospital from 1874 to 20 June 1892, and was chairman of the United Westminster Schools from 1873 to 1893. He resigned his alderman's gown on 18 Sept. 1883.

Waterlow had long been known in the metropolis for his practical philanthropy. He long laboured to secure for the poor of London decent housing and pure water. In 1862 he built at his own expense in Mark Street, Finsbury, a block of working-class dwellings, with accommodation for eighty families; these tenements, though built for comfort and let at moderate rents, produced a good return for the outlay. In 1863 he originated the Improved Industrial Dwellings Company, Limited, of which he was chairman till his death, when the company possessed 6000 tenements, which housed 30,000 persons. The company now has a capital of 1,000,000*l.*

Waterlow was returned as liberal member for Dumfriesshire in 1868, but was unseated in 1869 on technical grounds, his firm having taken a government contract of which he had no personal knowledge. After an unsuccessful contest for the same seat in 1869 and for Southwark in 1870, he was returned for Maidstone in 1874, and sat for that borough until 1880, when he was defeated. He was shortly afterwards elected for Gravesend, and retained that seat until 1885, when he unsuccessfully fought the Medway division of Kent. A stalwart liberal, he spoke in parliament in favour of a reform of the London Corporation. In 1870 he was appointed on the royal commission for inquiry into friendly and benefit societies (report presented 1874), in September 1877 on the royal judicature commission (which reported in 1881), and in July 1880 on the Livery Companies Commission (report presented 1884).

In 1872, a few months before his mayoralty, he presented Lauderdale House at Highgate, with its grounds, to St. Bartholomew's Hospital, for use as a convalescent home. The building was adapted and furnished at his expense, and was opened on 8 July 1872 by King Edward VII and Queen Alexandra, then Prince and Princess of Wales, but it was disused for hospital purposes in 1880. In 1889 Waterlow presented the house with a surrounding estate of twenty-nine acres to the London County Council. The fine grounds have since been known as Waterlow Park, where a statue of Waterlow was erected by public subscription in 1900.

Waterlow joined the livery of the Stationers' Company in 1847, serving as Master in 1872–3, the year of his mayoralty. He also became by redemption a freeman and liveryman of the Clothworkers' Company on 30 July 1873, and the same day passed (by election and fine) through the offices of assistant, warden, and master. He was a juror for Great Britain at the International Exhibitions of Paris (1867) and Philadelphia (1876), one of the royal commissioners of the 1851 exhibition, chairman of the city of London income tax commissioners, and treasurer of the City and Guilds of London Institute from 1879 (the year after its inception) to 1891. He was also a director of the Union Bank of London, vice-chairman of the London, Chatham and Dover Railway, and vice-president and chairman of the distribution committee of the Hospital Sunday Fund. In 1902 he was made a K.C.V.O.

Waterlow died, after a brief illness, on 3 August 1906, at his country residence, Trosley Towers, Wrotham, Kent, and was buried at Stansted, Kent. His estate was sworn for probate at 89,948*l.* 19*s.* 8*d.* gross; the residue after payment of various legacies was left to his wife, the testator having made in his lifetime what he considered an adequate provision for each member of his family.

He was twice married: (1) on 7 May 1845 to Anna Maria (*d.* 1880), youngest daughter of William Hickson of Fairseat, Wrotham, Kent, by whom he had five sons and three daughters; (2) in 1882 to Margaret, daughter of William Hamilton of Napa, California, U.S.A., who survived him. His eldest son, Philip Hickson, succeeded to the baronetcy. A subscription portrait by (Sir) Hubert von Herkomer (1892) is in the hall of St. Bartholomew's Hospital. A cartoon portrait appeared in 'Vanity Fair' in 1872.

[Authorities above cited; Life (with portrait) by George Smalley, 1909; Under Six Reigns; the house of Waterlows of Birchin Lane from 1811 to 1911 (portrait of James Waterlow); London Directories, 1822–44; Pratt, People of the Period; Whitaker, Red Book of Commerce, 1910, p. 925; Printers' Register, 6 Sept. 1906; Burke's Peerage and Baronetage; City Press, 11 Aug. 1906; The Times, 4 Aug., 29 Nov. 1906; Men of the Time, 1899; Ritchie, Famous City Men, p. 71; private information.] C. W.

WATKIN, Sir EDWARD WILLIAM (1819–1901), railway promoter, born in Ravald Street, Salford, on 26 Sept. 1819, was son of Absolom Watkin, a cotton merchant and prominent citizen of Manchester, by his wife Elizabeth, daughter of William Makinson of Bolton. Of two brothers, John (1821–1870) took holy orders and was vicar of Stixwold, Lincolnshire, and Alfred (1825–1875), a merchant, was mayor of Manchester in 1873–4.

Watkin, after education at a private school, entered the office of his father. Interesting himself from youth in public movements, he became when about twenty-one a director of the Manchester Athenæum, and helped to organise the great literary soirées in 1843–4. With some other members of the Athenæum he started the Saturday half-holiday movement in Manchester. In 1845 he wrote 'A Plea for Public Parks,' and acted as one of the secretaries of a committee which raised money for the opening of three public parks in Manchester and Salford. In the same year he joined in founding the 'Manchester Examiner.'

Watkin soon became partner in his father's business, but in 1845 he abandoned the cotton trade to take up the secretaryship of the Trent Valley railway, which line was afterwards sold at a profit of 438,000*l*. to the London and North Western Railway Company. Watkin, who had ably negotiated the transfer, then entered the service of the latter company. On recovering from a breakdown in health he paid his first visit to America in 1851, and in the following year published an account of it entitled 'A Trip to the United States and Canada.' In 1853 he was appointed general manager of the Manchester, Sheffield, and Lincolnshire railway, and entered on an intricate series of negotiations with the Great Northern, the London and North Western, and Midland railways, three lines whose hostile competition threatened disaster to his own company. At the desire of the Duke of Newcastle, secretary of state for the colonies, he undertook, in 1861, a mission to Canada in order to investigate the means of confederating the five British provinces into a dominion of Canada, and to consider the feasibility of transferring the Hudson Bay territory to the control of the government; the last was accomplished in 1869. Another object was that of planning railways designed to bring Quebec within easier reach of other parts of Canada and of the Atlantic.

On returning home Watkin resigned his appointment as manager of the Manchester, Sheffield, and Lincolnshire Company, through disagreement with his directors, who had come to terms in his absence with the Midland railway, and he became president of the Grand Trunk railway of Canada. Within two years, however, he resumed, in 1863, his connection with the Manchester company, first as director and from January 1864 as chairman. In that position, which he retained till May 1894, he did his chief work. With this office he combined the chairmanship of the South Eastern company from 1866–1894, and of the Metropolitan companies from 1872–94. For a short time he was a director of the Great Eastern (1867) and Great Western (1866) companies. Other enterprises also occupied him. He carried out a scheme for a new railway between Manchester and Liverpool, that of the Cheshire lines committee, which was opened in 1877, and he was actively interested in making the Athens and Piræus railway. He projected the practical union of the Welsh railway system by linking up a number of small lines with the object of forming a through route from Cardiff to Liverpool, thus bringing South and North Wales into direct railway communication with Lancashire by means of the Mersey Tunnel, opened in 1886. To this end a swing bridge over the river Dee at Connah's Quay was built (1887–90) and lines to Birkenhead completed.

Despite these varied calls on his attention, it was to the three railways of which he was chairman that Watkin long devoted his main energies. As chairman of the Manchester, Sheffield, and Lincolnshire railway, now the Great Central, he met with great difficulties by the competition of both the Great Northern and Midland companies, but he greatly improved its affairs. His chief aim was to form a through route under a single management from Manchester and the north to Dover. With that end in view, he projected the new and independent line from Sheffield to Marylebone, London. At the time the Manchester company's trains ran over the Great Northern line from Retford. The proposed Great Central line was strongly resisted by Watkin's competitors, but he had his way after a long struggle, and the line was opened for through traffic to London on 8 March 1899.

It was from a desire to extend his scheme of through traffic that Watkin long and ardently advocated a channel tunnel railway between Dover and Calais. This proposal was first made in 1869. A channel tunnel company was formed in 1872, and under Watkin's direction excavations were begun in 1881 beneath the seashore between Folkestone and Dover. At the instance of the board of trade the court of chancery at once issued an injunction forbidding Watkin to proceed, on the ground of his infringement of the crown's foreshore rights. Next session Watkin, who long sat in the House of Commons, introduced a private bill authorising his project; after consideration by a joint committee of the two houses, which pronounced against it by a majority of sixty-four, the bill was withdrawn. Subsequently in 1888, and again in 1890, Watkin reintroduced a bill authorising his experimental works without result, and it was finally withdrawn in 1893. In 1886 Watkin, on receiving a report from Professor Boyd

Dawkins, began boring for coal in the neighbourhood of Dover, and the work was continued until 1891, at the expense of the Channel Tunnel Company. Sufficient evidence was obtained to justify the sinking of a trial shaft and the formation of companies for further exploration. Watkin also proposed a railway tunnel between Scotland and Ireland and a ship canal in Ireland between Dublin and Galway. His passion for enterprise further led him to become chairman in 1889 of a company to erect at Wembley Park, Middlesex, a 'Watkin' tower on the model of the Eiffel tower in Paris. Owing to lack of funds only a single stage was completed; this was opened to the public in 1896, and was demolished in 1907.

Watkin was returned to Parliament as liberal member for Great Yarmouth in 1857, but was unseated on petition. He sat as member for Stockport from 1864 to 1868, when he was defeated. In 1869 he unsuccessfully contested East Cheshire, but was member for Hythe from 1874 to 1895. His political views remained liberal until 1885, when he became a unionist, but he often acted independently of any party. He was a member of the Manchester City Council from 1859 to 1862 and high sheriff of Cheshire in 1874. He was knighted in 1868 and created a baronet in 1880.

He died at Rose Hill, Northenden, Cheshire, on 13 April 1901, and was buried at Northenden parish church.

Watkin married in 1845 Mary Briggs (*d.* 8 March 1887), daughter of Jonathan Mellor of Oldham, by whom he had a son, Alfred Mellor Watkin, M.P. for Grimsby (1877–80), and his successor in the baronetcy, and a daughter Harriette, wife of H. W. Worsley-Taylor, K.C., of Moreton Hall, Whalley. His second wife, whom he married in 1893, when she was eighty-one years old, was Ann (*d.* 26 May 1896), daughter of William Little, and widow of Herbert Ingram, M.P., founder of the 'Illustrated London News.' A portrait of Watkin by (Sir) Hubert von Herkomer was exhibited at the Royal Academy in 1887. A cartoon portrait by 'Ape' (i.e. Carlo Pellegrini [q. v.], who also painted his portrait in oils) appeared in 'Vanity Fair' in 1875.

Besides the works named above he wrote: 1. 'Absolom Watkin. Fragment No. 1,' 1874 (a sketch of his father, with some of his writings). 2. 'Canada and the States: Recollections, 1851 to 1886,' 1887. 3. 'India: a Few Pages about it,' 1889 (on the public works policy of the Indian government). 4. 'Alderman Cobden of Manchester,' 1891 (letters and reminiscences of Richard Cobden).

[Manchester Guardian, 15 April 1901; Manchester Faces and Places, vols. 2 and 12 (portraits); Men and Women of the Time, 1899; Vanity Fair, 1875 (portrait), Lodge's Peerage, 1901; Paul, History of Modern England, 1905, iv. 308; Lucy, Diary of the Gladstone Parliament, 1886, p. 266, and Diary of the Salisbury Parliament, 1892, p. 81; C. H. Grinling's History of the Great Northern Railway, 3rd edit. 1903, passim; F. S. Williams's Midland Railway, 1875, pp. 157, 275; C. E. Stretton, Midland Railway, 1907, p. 222; J. Pendleton's Our Railways, 1894, vol. i. passim; W. B. Dawkins's paper in Trans. Manchester Geological Soc. 1897; Contemporary Rev. April 1890.] C. W. S.

WATSON, ALBERT (1828–1904), principal of Brasenose College, Oxford, and classical scholar, born at Kidderminster on 4 Dec. 1828, was fifth son of Richard Watson of that town. Educated at Rugby (1843–7), he entered Wadham College, Oxford, on 21 April 1847 as a commoner. In Easter term 1851 he obtained a first class in literæ humaniores (B.A. 1851), proceeding M.A. in 1853, and for a few months in 1854 was a master at Marlborough College. On 12 March 1852 he had been elected fellow of Brasenose College, Oxford, and took holy orders in 1853, becoming priest in 1856, but never holding any benefice. Settling down to educational work in Oxford he was tutor of his college (1854–67) and lecturer (1868–73). He was also librarian 1868–77 and senior bursar 1870–81, and during the three years 1886–9 served the office of principal. He was again fellow from 1890 till his death. His chief extra-collegiate positions were those of librarian of the Union Society 1852–3, examiner 1859, 1860, 1864, and 1866, and curator of the University Galleries. He died suddenly from heart failure at Oxford on 21 Nov. 1904. He was unmarried.

A posthumous portrait, based on photographs, is in Brasenose College common room.

Watson's only published work was an edition of 'Select Letters of Cicero,' with notes (Oxford, 1870; 4th edit., 1891; text only, 1874, 1875), a task suggested to him, it is believed, by John Conington, and carried out with conspicuous acumen and industry. 'Watson's Letters' was for many years a household word at Oxford.

He also translated part of Ranke's 'History of England' (Clarendon Press, 1875).

With wide reading in all branches of standard literature, but especially historical and political, and with a retentive memory, Watson combined a rare power of co-ordinating what he knew. The characteristics of decision and determination which his features suggested were quite overborne by his gentleness and benevolence. Reserved and retiring to an unusual degree, he yet in social converse put his stores of wit and learning at the free disposal of his guests. Throughout his life he was a convinced liberal, and a considerable force in Oxford politics.

[Brasenose Coll. Reg. 1909; Foster's Alumni Oxonienses; Oxford Mag. 30 Nov. 1904; C. B. Heberden, Address in Brasenose College Chapel, 27 Nov. 1904, privately printed.] F. M.

WATSON, GEORGE LENNOX (1851–1904), naval architect, born at Glasgow on 30 Oct. 1851, was eldest son of Thomas Watson, M.D., by his wife Ellen, daughter of Timothy Burstall, an engineer. Educated at the High School and then at the Collegiate School, Glasgow, he was apprenticed in 1867 to Robert Napier & Sons, shipbuilders and marine engineers of Govan. In 1871 he found employment with A. and J. Inglis, shipbuilders, of Pointhouse, near Glasgow, making with a member of the firm experiments in yacht-designing, and in 1872 he started business in Glasgow as a naval architect. Exact methods of yacht-modelling were only then being introduced, and Watson was the first to apply to the designing of yachts the laws governing the resistance of bodies moving in water which William John Macquorn Rankine [q. v.] and William Froude [q. v.] had formulated. During a career of over thirty years he designed many of the most successful yachts that have sailed in British waters.

Early successes were the 5-ton cutter Clotilde (1873), which beat Fife's Pearl; the 10-ton cutter Madge (1875), which had great success in American waters; the Vril (1876); the 68-ton cutter Marjorie (1883); and the Vanduara (1880), which was the fastest vessel of her class, beating the Formosa, the property of Edward VII, then Prince of Wales, on several occasions. When Dixon Kemp's new rule of measurement for racing purposes in 1887 required the building of a broader and lighter type of vessel, Watson was equally successful. The Yarana (1888), the Creole (1890), and the Queen Mab (1892) were all notable prize-winners, and a record success was achieved by the Britannia, which Watson built for King Edward VII, then Prince of Wales, in 1893. Between 1893–7 it won 147 prizes, 122 of them first prizes, out of 219 starts, the total value of the prizes amounting to 9973*l*. The Bona (1900), the Kariad (1900, at first named The Distant Shore), and the Sybarita (1901) were large vessels notable for their seaworthiness; a race between the two latter in the Clyde in 1901 during a storm which compelled the accompanying steam yachts to put back proved one of the most remarkable yachting contests on record.

Between 1887 and 1901 Watson was prominently before the public as the designer of the British challenger's yacht in the contest in American waters between Great Britain and America. Watson designed J. Bell & Brothers' Thistle (1887), Lord Dunraven's Valkyrie II (1893), and Valkyrie III (1895), and Sir Thomas Lipton's Shamrock II (1901). Though these vessels failed to regain the cup for Great Britain they were yachts of the highest class. The American yachts which defeated them had little success whenever they visited British waters.

Watson, in addition to racing craft, also designed passenger, cargo, and mail steamers, and many of the largest steam yachts of the day. Amongst the latter were the Lysistrata (2089 tons), built for James Gordon Bennett; the Atmah (1746 tons), built for Baron Edmond de Rothschild; the Alberta (1322 tons), built for the King of the Belgians; the Zarnitza (1086 tons), built for the Tsar of Russia, and other yachts built for foreign owners.

Watson contributed to 'Yachting' (2 vols. 1895, Badminton Library) and published in 1881 a series of lectures, 'Progress in Yachting and Yacht-building,' delivered at the Glasgow naval and marine engineering exhibition (1880–1). In 1882 he was elected a member of the Institute of Naval Architects, before which he read a paper on a new form of steering-gear. He was also for nearly twenty years consulting naval architect to the National Lifeboat Institution. He died at Glasgow on 12 Nov. 1904. Watson married in 1903 Marie, the daughter of Edward Lovibond of Greenwich. He had no issue.

[Trans. of Inst. of Nav. Architects, 1905; Who's Who, 1905; The Times, 14 Nov. 1904; Yachting, 1895; art. on Yachting in Encyc. Brit., 11th ed.; A. E. T. Watson, King

Edward VII as a Sportsman, 1911; Yacht Racing Calendar and Rev. 1904.] S. E. F.

WATSON, HENRY WILLIAM (1827–1903), mathematician, born at Marylebone on 25 Feb. 1827, was son of Thomas Watson, R.N., by his wife Eleanor Mary Kingston.

Educated at King's College, London, he won the first mathematical scholarship instituted there, proceeding in 1846 to Trinity College, Cambridge, where he was scholar. He graduated as second wrangler and Smith's prizeman in 1850, Dr. W. H. Besant being senior wrangler. He became fellow in 1851, and from 1851 to 1853 was assistant tutor. With James Fitzjames Stephen, who entered Trinity in 1847, Watson formed a close friendship (see Leslie Stephen's *Life of Sir J. F. Stephen*). Both were 'Apostles,' and (Sir) William Harcourt, (Sir) Henry Sumner Maine, and E. H. Stanley (afterwards fifteenth Earl of Derby) belonged to their coterie. After a short stay in London, studying law (with Stephen as fellow-student), Watson became mathematical master in the City of London School (1854), and was afterwards (1857) mathematical lecturer at King's College, London. Ordained deacon in 1856, he took priest's orders in 1858. From 1857 to 1865 he was a mathematical master at Harrow School, retiring on presentation to the benefice of Berkswell, near Coventry. One of the original founders of the Alpine Club in 1857, he delighted in mountaineering, but left the Club in 1862.

Watson was moderator and examiner during 1860–1 in the Cambridge mathematical tripos, and an additional examiner in 1877. From 1893 to 1896 he was examiner in mathematics at London University. One of the founders of the Birmingham Philosophical Society, he was president 1880–1. He was elected F.R.S. on 2 June 1881. Cambridge University conferred the Sc.D. degree in 1884.

Watson's independent publications were 'The Elements of Plane and Solid Geometry' (1871) and 'Treatise on the Kinetic Theory of Gases' (1876; 2nd edit. 1893, which embodied criticisms given in correspondence by Clerk Maxwell). In collaboration with Samuel Hawksley Burbury [q. v. Suppl. II] there appeared 'A Treatise on Generalised Co-ordinates applied to the Kinetics of a Material System' (1879), a work on abstract dynamics; and 'The Mathematical Theory of Electricity and Magnetism,' vol. i. 'Electrostatics' (1885), vol. ii. 'Magnetism and Electrodynamics' (1889). The article 'Molecule' in the 'Encyclopædia Britannica,' 9th edition, was also written jointly with Burbury.

Watson's contributions to serial scientific literature include 'Direct Investigation of Lagrange's and Monge's Methods of Solution of Partial Differential Equations,' in the 'Quarterly Journal of Mathematics' (1863); 'The Kinetic Theory of Gases' and 'On the Progress of Science, its Conditions and Limitations,' read at the Birmingham Philosophical Society (1877, 1891); and, jointly with Sir Francis Galton [q. v. Suppl. II], 'On the Probability of the Extinction of Families' (*Journ. Anthrop. Inst.* vol. iv.).

He died at Brighton on 11 Jan. 1903, five months after his resignation of Berkswell. He married in 1856 Emily, daughter of Henry Rowe, of Cambridge; his wife's sister married Robert Baldwin Hayward [q. v. Suppl. II]. He had issue one son and two daughters.

[Proc. Roy. Soc. vol. lxxv.; Roy. Soc. Catal. Sci. Papers; Nature, 22 Jan. 1903; Men of the Time, 1899; The Times, 13 Jan. 1903.] T. E. J.

WATSON, JOHN, who wrote under the pseudonym of Ian Maclaren (1850–1907), presbyterian divine and author, born at Manningtree, Essex, on 3 Nov. 1850, was only child of John Watson (*d.* 1 Jan. 1879), a clerk in the civil service, who subsequently became receiver-general of taxes in Scotland, by his wife Isabella Maclaren. He came of pure Highland stock. His father was born at Braemar, while his mother belonged to the Loch Tay district and spoke Gaelic. Her ancestors were Roman catholics. Watson's parents, however, belonged to the Free Church of Scotland.

When Watson was about four the family removed to Perth. After attending the grammar school of that city, he was sent to the high school of Stirling, where his companions included Henry Drummond [q. v. Suppl. I]. In 1866 he entered Edinburgh University. His career there was somewhat disappointing, but he showed some promise in philosophy and became president of the University Philosophical Society. He graduated M.A. in 1870.

Reluctantly, at his father's wish, he studied for the ministry of the Free Church of Scotland at New College, Edinburgh (1870–4); his teachers included Andrew Bruce Davidson [q. v. Suppl. II] and Robert Rainy [q. v. Suppl. II]. His course was undistinguished; at its close he passed a semester at Tübingen University, studying under Beck and Weizsäcker.

In the autumn of 1874 he became assistant to the Rev. Dr. J. H. Wilson, Barclay church, Edinburgh. There he had misgivings as to his ministerial fitness, and thought of studying for the bar. Early in 1875 he was inducted minister of the Free church at Logiealmond, Perthshire; his uncle, Hiram Watson, had been minister there from 1841 to 1853, leaving the Church of Scotland at the Disruption. In Logiealmond, the 'Drumtochty' of 'Beside the Bonnie Brier Bush,' Watson spent some three of his happiest years, making himself popular with the people and winning some repute as a preacher. In 1877 he became colleague and successor to the Rev. Dr. Samuel Miller of Free St. Matthew's church, Glasgow, a wealthy congregation and a centre of spiritual influence. His Glasgow ministry, which was less harmonious and successful than that at Logiealmond, lasted barely three years.

The main work of Watson's life began in 1880, when he accepted an invitation to form a new presbyterian charge in the Sefton Park district of Liverpool. There he remained exactly twenty-five years, and established a congregation which for wealth, culture, and influence became one of the foremost in the Presbyterian Church of England. His attractive personality and public spirit drew to him all sorts and conditions of people. His preaching, while resting on a basis of broad evangelicalism, was essentially modern, catholic, oratorical, and cultured. Matthew Arnold [q. v. Suppl. I] on the day he died (15 April 1888) heard Watson preach at Sefton Park church, and remarked that he had rarely been so affected by any preacher (W. Robertson Nicoll's *Life*, p. 130). Watson's congregation raised, while he was minister, nearly 150,000*l.*, and erected a church whose elegance and size has earned for it the title of 'the presbyterian cathedral of England,' as well as two large branch churches and a social institute. Watson's influence on the civic life of the community was considerable, no fewer than six members of his congregation becoming lord mayors of Liverpool, while others were prominent in the city council. He took a leading part in the creation of the University of Liverpool, and had a seat on its council (1903–6).

In 1894 Watson achieved a new and a wider reputation. In that year he published, under the pseudonym of 'Ian Maclaren,' a number of sketches of Scottish rural life entitled 'Beside the Bonnie Brier Bush.' The book at once made Watson one of the most popular authors in Great Britain and America. 'Ian Maclaren' knew little of the novelist's art, but out of simple elements he produced pictures of Scots character which, if not wholly free from sentimentalism, are artistic delineations of the Scottish peasant's nobility of sentiment and religious emotion. Watson was aware of 'the reverse side of the shield' which George Douglas Brown [q. v. Suppl. II] apotheosised in 'The House with the Green Shutters,' but his interpretation was admirably effective. In Great Britain more than a quarter of a million copies have been sold; in America the sale has amounted to about half a million, exclusive of an incomplete pirated edition which was circulated in large numbers at a low price. The work has also been translated into several European tongues, and has been popular in Germany. In 1895 there followed in the same vein 'The Days of Auld Langsyne,' hardly inferior in execution and popularity. There was some falling off in workmanship in 'Kate Carnegie and those Ministers' (1897), in spite of its geniality and easy command of the Scots vernacular. 'Afterwards, and Other Stories' (1898) shows the author's command of pathos; 'Young Barbarians' (1901) is a delightful boy's book; 'His Majesty Baby and some Common People' appeared in 1902; 'St. Jude's' (posthumously, 1907) contained sketches of Glasgow life. 'Graham of Claverhouse' (posthumously, 1908) was 'Ian Maclaren's' only serious attempt at novel writing, and proved a failure.

From 12 Oct. to 16 Dec. 1896 Watson, taking advantage of the popularity of his books, made his first American lecture tour under the management of Major J. B. Pond, and was welcomed with immense enthusiasm (Pond, *Eccentricities of Genius*, p. 405). At Yale University he was made hon. D.D. after delivering there the Lyman Beecher lectures on preaching, which he published in the same year under the title of 'The Cure of Souls.' Watson repeated his success in a second American lecture tour, also under Pond's direction (19 Feb.–10 May 1899).

Meanwhile Watson had engaged, under his own name, in theological literature. In 1896 he issued 'The Mind of the Master,' an able interpretation of the person and teaching of Christ, which brought him in 1897 under a passing suspicion of heresy (W. Robertson Nicoll's *Life*, p. 214).

The most notable of his theological works was 'The Doctrines of Grace' (1900). 'The Life of the Master' (1901) illustrated Watson's breadth of view.

Watson worked strenuously to arouse interest in the theological college of his denomination. As convener of the synod's college committee he took a leading part in the removal of the college from London to Cambridge. Mainly owing to his energy and eloquence a sum of 16,000*l.* was raised in five weeks, which enabled Westminster College, Cambridge, to be opened free of debt in October 1899. Watson in 1897 declined a call to St. John's presbyterian church, Kensington, and in April 1900 was elected moderator of synod. On the outbreak of the Boer war (Oct. 1899) he supported the British government, and alienated many nonconformists by preaching sermons justifying the war. He also encouraged the young men of Liverpool to volunteer for active service in South Africa. In 1901 ill-health led him to pass the winter in Egypt. On his return he delivered a short course of lectures at the Royal Institution, London, entitled 'The Scot of the Eighteenth Century: his Religion and his Life.' The lectures were repeated at Cambridge, and were published posthumously in 1907.

In February 1905 Watson celebrated the conclusion of twenty-five years' ministry at Sefton Park, and in October he resigned owing to ill-health and pressure of other work. A sum of 2600*l.* was then privately presented to him. He continued to reside in Liverpool. In January 1907 he accepted, on what proved to be the eve of his death, the presidency of the National Free Church Council, and was nominated for the principalship of Westminster College, Cambridge, in succession to Dr. Oswald Dykes.

On 30 Jan. 1907 he sailed for New York to undertake a third lecturing tour in America. His popularity showed no sign of abatement, but he suffered from fatigue and from the cold. At Haverford College, Philadelphia, he delivered a course of lectures on 'The Religious Condition of Scotland in the Eighteenth Century.' In 'God's Message to the Human Soul: the Use of the Bible in the Light of the New Knowledge' (Cole Lectures of Vanderbilt University at Nashville, 1907) he maintained that the authority of the Bible was indestructible, while he welcomed reverent biblical criticism. Towards the end of March he passed to Canada. He lectured and preached at Valley City, North Dakota, on 21 April. Two days later he arrived at Mount Pleasant, Iowa, where he fell ill and died on 6 May 1907 in the Brazelton hotel. His remains were accorded a public funeral on 27 May in Smithdown cemetery, Liverpool.

Watson, whose sense of humour was keen and patriotism intense, earnestly sought as a preacher to combine the spirit of faith with that of culture. The twofold character of his work as secular and religious writer led to some depreciating criticism of both results of his labours. But theology and literature equally appealed to him.

Besides the works cited, Watson was also the author, in his own name, of: 1. 'The Order of Service for Young People,' 1895. 2. 'The Upper Room' ('Little Books on Religion' series), 1896. 3. 'The Potter's Wheel,' 1898. 4. 'Companions of the Sorrowful Way,' 1898. 5. 'Homely Virtues,' 1903. 6. 'The Inspiration of our Faith, and Other Sermons,' 1905. 7. 'Respectable Sins,' a volume of sermons for young men, edited by his son, Frederick W. Watson, and published posthumously in 1909.

Watson married on 6 June 1878 Jane Burnie, daughter of Francis John Ferguson, of Glasgow, and a near relative of Sir Samuel Ferguson [q. v.]. She survived him with four sons.

A portrait, painted by Robert Morrison of Liverpool, hangs in the Guild Room of Sefton Park church, Liverpool.

['Ian Maclaren,' Life of Rev. John Watson, D.D., by W. Robertson Nicoll, 1908; Major J. B. Pond, Eccentricities of Genius, 1901, pp. 405–51; David Christie Murray, My Contemporaries in Fiction, 1897, pp. 110–11; George Adam Smith, Life of Henry Drummond, 7th edit. 1904; Liverpool Post and Mercury, 7 May 1907; Scotsman, 7 May 1907; British Weekly, 16 May 1907; Scottish Review (weekly), 9 May 1907; private information.]

W. F. G.

WATSON, Sir PATRICK HERON (1832–1907), surgeon, born at Edinburgh on 5 Jan. 1832, was third of four surviving sons of Charles Watson, D.D., minister of Burntisland, Fife, and Isabella Boog his wife. His three brothers all attained distinction, two (Charles and Robert Boog) in the church, and the third (David Matthew) in business.

Patrick Watson was educated at the Edinburgh Academy and at the University, where he graduated M.D. in 1853.

Admitted L.R.C.S.Edinburgh in 1853, he was elected F.R.C.S. in 1855. After a year's residence at the Royal Infirmary, Edinburgh, Watson volunteered for service at the opening of the Crimean war. He was appointed a staff assistant surgeon, but his operative skill and his teaching powers were so obvious that he was retained at Woolwich to instruct other volunteer surgeons. He went to the Crimea some months later, and was attached to the royal artillery; but an attack of enteric followed by dysentery caused him to be invalided home in 1856. He received the Crimean, Turkish, and Sardinian medals. As soon as his health was restored, Watson began to teach surgery at the High School Yards, Edinburgh, and became lecturer on systematic and clinical surgery at the Royal College of Surgeons there. Watson afterwards acted as private assistant to Prof. James Miller, whose eldest daughter he afterwards married. He declined an offer of a similar post under Professor James Syme [q. v.]. In 1860 he was chosen assistant surgeon to the Royal Infirmary, and full surgeon in 1863. On the expiration of his term of office in 1878, the managers appointed him an extra surgeon for five years.

Watson, who endeared himself to his patients, was as an operator unrivalled in Edinburgh for brilliancy of execution and rapidity of manipulation. He devised and carried out many of the operations which only became general in a succeeding generation. Before the introduction of Listerian methods he had removed the whole larynx, extirpated the spleen, performed ovariotomy with success, and popularised excision of the joints. As a lecturer he was eloquent, clear, and impressive; as a hospital surgeon and clinical teacher he was effective and popular.

In 1878 Watson accompanied the third Earl of Rosslyn on the special embassy sent to Spain on King Alfonso XII's marriage, and was decorated caballero of the order of Carlos III of Spain.

At the Royal College of Surgeons of Edinburgh, Watson was president in 1878 and again in 1905, at the quatercentenary festival. From 1882 to 1906 he represented the college on the General Medical Council. He was one of the honorary surgeons in Scotland to Queen Victoria and to King Edward VII. He was made hon. LL.D. of Edinburgh in 1884 and hon. F.R.C.S. Ireland in 1887. He was knighted in 1903. Through life he was a keen volunteer. He joined the Queen's Edinburgh brigade as a surgeon and retired with the rank of brigade surgeon lieutenant-colonel, V.D. He died at his residence in Charlotte Square, Edinburgh, on 21 Dec. 1907. Watson married in 1861 Elizabeth Gordon, the eldest daughter of Prof. James Miller, and left two sons and two daughters.

A portrait painted by Sir George Reid belongs to Watson's son, Charles Heron Watson, F.R.C.S.Edin.

Watson's works, all published at Edinburgh, are: 1. 'The Modern Pathology and Treatment of Venereal Disease,' 1861. 2. 'Excision of the Knee Joint,' 1867. 3. 'Amputation of the Scapula along with Two-thirds of the Clavicle and the Remains of the Arm,' 1869; 4. 'Excision of the Thyroid Gland,' 1873.

[Scottish Medical and Surgical Journal, vol. xxii. 1908, p. 66 (with portrait); Lancet, 1908, i. 69; Brit. Med. Journal, 1908, i. 62; private information.]

D'A. P.

WATSON, ROBERT SPENCE (1837–1911), politician, social and educational reformer, born at 10 Claremont Place, Gateshead-on-Tyne, on 8 June 1837, was the eldest son in a family of five sons and seven daughters of Joseph Watson of Bensham Grove, Gateshead-on-Tyne, by his wife Sarah, daughter of Robert Spence of North Shields. Like both his parents Spence Watson was a Quaker. His father was a solicitor of literary attainments. In 1846 Robert became a pupil of Dr. Collingwood Bruce, proceeding to the Friends' school at York in October 1848. In 1853 he entered University College, London, and tied for the English literature prize that year. He was articled to his father on leaving college, and after admission as a solicitor in 1860, he entered into partnership with him. Through life he was actively engaged in his profession.

From youth Watson played an energetic part in public life, interesting himself in political, social, philanthropic and educational movements. For nearly half a century he consequently held a position of much influence in his native place and the north of England. He bestowed especially close attention on means of improving and disseminating popular culture. In 1862 he became honorary secretary of the Literary and Philosophical Institution, Newcastle-upon-Tyne, founded in 1793. He held the office for thirty-one years when he became a vice-president of the society. In 1900 he succeeded Lord Armstrong as president. Between 1868 and 1883 he delivered seventy-five lectures to the society, mainly on the history and development of the English language.

In 1871 Watson helped to found the Durham College of Science, now known as Armstrong College, Newcastle-upon-Tyne, in the university of Durham. For forty years he took a leading part in its government, becoming its first president in 1910, and one of its representatives on the senate of Durham University, which conferred on him the honorary degree of D.C.L. in 1906.

Spence Watson was also elected a member of the first Newcastle school board in 1871, and he continued to sit on the board for twenty-three years. He was a pioneer of university extension in the north of England and of the Newcastle Free Public Library. From 1885 to 1911 he was president of the Tyneside Sunday Lecture Society, and became chairman of the Newcastle-upon-Tyne grammar school in 1911.

Nor were Watson's interests confined to affairs at home. He was from an early age an ardent traveller and mountaineer, joining the Alpine Club in 1862. His recreations included angling as well as mountaineering. In 1870, at the invitation of the Society of Friends, he went to Alsace-Lorraine as one of the commissioners of the War Victims Fund for the distribution of relief to the non-combatants in the Franco-German war. In January 1871 he revisited France to superintend similar work in the department of the Seine. In 1873 the French government, through the duc de Broglie, offered him the legion of honour, but he declined to accept the distinction. He was, however, presented with a gold medal which was specially struck in acknowledgment of his services. In 1879 he visited Wazan, the sacred city of Morocco, which no Christian European had entered before. With the assistance of Sir John Drummond Hay, the British minister at Tangier, he obtained an introduction to the great cherif of Wazan and his English wife. In 1880 he published an account of his journey in 'A Visit to Wazan, the Sacred City of Morocco.'

Spence Watson was an enthusiastic politician and a lifelong adherent of the liberal party. In 1874 he founded the Newcastle Liberal Association on a representative basis of ward elections, and was its president from 1874 to 1897. From 1890 to 1902 he was president of the National Liberal Federation. During that period he was probably the chief liberal leader outside parliament, influencing the policy of the party by force of character. His political friends included Joseph Cowen, John Morley, John Bright, Lord Ripon, and Earl Grey. Personally he had no desire to enter the House of Commons, and refused all invitations to become a parliamentary candidate. On 27 Feb. 1893 the National Liberal Federation presented him with his portrait by Sir George Reid, P.R.S.A. This he gave to the National Liberal Club, a replica by the artist being presented to Mrs. Spence Watson. In 1907 he was made a privy councillor on the nomination of Sir Henry Campbell-Bannerman, then prime minister.

His political principles embraced zeal for the cause of international peace and for the welfare of native races under British rule, especially in India. He was president of the Peace Society for several years previous to his death, and he took an active part in the Indian National Congress movement. The development of free institutions in Russia was another of his aspirations. He co-operated with Stepniak, and other Russian political exiles in England, in the attempt to disseminate information among Englishmen of existing methods of governing Russia. He was from 1890 to 1911 president of the Society of Friends of Russian Freedom.

Spence Watson was a pioneer in the settlement of trade disputes by arbitration. He first acted as umpire in 1864, and he was sole umpire on forty-seven occasions between 1884 and 1894 in disputes in the leading industries in the north of England. Such services, which ultimately numbered nearly 100, were always rendered voluntarily.

Spence Watson was made hon. LL.D. of St. Andrews in 1881. One of the earliest in England to interest himself in the adaptation of electrical power to industrial purposes, he helped the Newcastle-upon-Tyne Electric Supply Company, Limited, on Tyneside to acquire parliamentary powers in 1890. He died on 2 March 1911 at his residence, Bensham Grove, Gateshead, which he had inherited from his father, and was buried at Jesmond old cemetery, Newcastle-upon-Tyne. He married on 9 June 1863 Elizabeth, daughter of Edward and Jane Richardson of Newcastle-upon-Tyne. He had one son and five daughters.

Besides the book mentioned, Spence Watson published: 1. 'Cædmon the First English Poet,' 1890. 2. 'The History of the Literary and Philosophical Society of Newcastle-upon-Tyne,' 1897. 3. 'The History of the National Liberal Federation,' 1906. 4. 'Joseph Skipsey, his Life and Work,' 1909. Among his numerous pamphlets dealing with industrial, educational and political subjects, 'The History of English Rule and Policy in South Africa' (1897) had a circulation of nearly 250,000 copies, including translations into French and Dutch.

Painted portraits of Spence Watson are numerous. In addition to that by Sir George Reid at the National Liberal Club, one by Miss Lilian Etherington was given to the Newcastle Liberal Club in 1890. Another by Ralph Hedley, R.B.A., was presented to him in 1898 (now at Bensham Grove). A replica by H. Macbeth Raeburn, A.R.E., of Sir George Reid's portrait, presented by subscription to the Literary and Philosophical Institution, Newcastle-upon-Tyne, was unveiled by Mr. Thomas Burt, M.P., on 24 Sept. 1912. A portrait by Percy Bigland is in the John Bright Library, Friends' school, York, and a replica by the artist at Armstrong College, Newcastle-upon-Tyne. A bust by Christian Neuper is in the Free Library, Newcastle-upon-Tyne.

The 'Spence Watson' prize in English literature was founded in Armstrong College, Newcastle-upon-Tyne, out of funds which he bequeathed to the college. A fund to establish at the college a Spence Watson lectureship in English literature is in process of formation by members of the Literary and Philosophical Institution, Newcastle-upon-Tyne.

[Northumberland County History, vols. iii. and iv.; A Historical Sketch of the Society of Friends ('in scorn called Quakers') in Newcastle-upon-Tyne and Gateshead, 1653–1898, by John William Steel, with contributions from other Friends, 1899; Hist. of Literary and Philosophical Institution, Newcastle-upon-Tyne; Hist. of the National Liberal Federation; Who's Who, 1911; unpublished Reminiscences by Robert Spence Watson; and three unpublished volumes of collected speeches and personal records.] P. C.

WATTS, GEORGE FREDERIC (1817–1904), painter and sculptor, was the eldest child of the second marriage of George Watts, a musical-instrument maker (born 1774), who came to London from Hereford about 1800. Some Welsh names in the family of George Watts's mother indicate that he may have been partly of Welsh descent. (This is the only ground for the statement often confidently made that the artist was a 'Celt.') By his first marriage George Watts had a son and two daughters, who were nearly grown up when in 1816 he took for second wife a widow whose maiden name had been Harriet Smith. Their son, George Frederic, was born in Queen Street, Bryanston Square, on 23 Feb. 1817. Three more sons followed, who all died in infancy or early childhood. George Watts, besides being a piano maker and tuner, was much occupied with unsuccessful schemes for the invention and manufacture of new musical instruments. The second Mrs. Watts fell into a consumption and died in 1826. The boy George Frederic grew up as the ailing and cherished son of a refined, ineffectual father in straitened circumstances, his two half-sisters by the first marriage managing the household as best they might. He suffered much from giddiness and sick headache, and had no regular schooling, but devoured the books, few but good, that were in the house, especially the 'Iliad' and Scott's novels. He learned his Bible, and despite painful recollections of the gloom and depression of puritan Sundays, loved it in after life, not indeed as revelation, but as the highest ethical and traditional poetry and symbolism. From childhood he was devoted to drawing, and there are still extant minutely accurate copies of engravings made by him with a chalk point in his twelfth year. His father, who had some taste in art, encouraged this bent. The opportunity, not for regular teaching but for study of a kind perhaps more fruitful, came to him through acquaintance with the family of Behnes. The elder Behnes was a piano-maker from Hanover with whom George Watts was in some way associated. In the same house with him lived a French *émigré* practising as a sculptor, and this man's example moved two of Behnes's sons, Henry and William, to follow the profession of art. William and a crippled third brother, Charles, occupied first a studio in Dean Street, Soho, and afterwards one in Osnaburgh Street. Of these studios Watts in boyhood had the run, and learned all that could be learned there. William Behnes was a fine draughtsman and something of a painter as well as a sculptor; he taught the boy early to feel and understand the supreme qualities of the Parthenon marbles. A friend of Charles, a miniature painter, gave young Watts his first chance and first lesson in oil-painting by setting him to make a copy from Lely and prescribing the colours to be used. Soon we hear of the lad taking in William Behnes with a sham Vandyck which, for a jest, he had himself painted and smoked to make it look old. George Watts showed some of his son's drawings to Sir Martin Archer Shee.

whose verdict was not encouraging. The boy got more favourable notice from Haydon, who stopped him one day as he was carrying a bundle of drawings in the street. He drew continually, both copies and originals, and by the time he was sixteen had begun to earn a livelihood by small commissions for portraits in pencil or chalks at five shillings each. At eighteen he entered the Royal Academy schools, where he found the teaching slack and unhelpful. From Hilton, the keeper, he received praise and encouragement, but failed to win the medal which Hilton thought he deserved. In his twentieth year (1837) he had a studio of his own in Clipstone Street, and painted the fine study of a wounded heron, now in the memorial gallery at Limnerslease, from a bird he had bought in a poulterer's shop. At the Royal Academy he exhibited this picture and two portraits of ladies. Portraits of himself and of his father done in these years show already a frank and skilful handling of the oil medium.

By this time young Watts had made the acquaintance of Nicolas Wanostrocht [q. v.], an Englishman of Belgian extraction, who kept a successful school inherited from his father at Blackheath, and who was at the same time a professional cricketer and writer on cricket under the name of Nicholas Felix. At the Blackheath school Watts spent many of his evenings, studying music, French, Italian, and to some extent Greek, and acquiring from his new friend both a fresh zest for life and a wider range of reading. As a commission from him Watts drew and lithographed seven positions in the game of cricket, several of the figures being portraits of the famous cricketers of the day. These lithographs are now rare: five of the original drawings are preserved in the Marylebone cricket club. Life was however still a struggle to the young man. The failure of his father's undertakings weighed upon him, and he was subject to alternate moods of confident hope and acute physical and mental depression. In his twenty-first or twenty-second year he had the good fortune to be introduced to Mr. Constantine Ionides, a member of a leading family in the Greek colony in London and father of the well-known art collector of the same name. Mr. Ionides ordered from young Watts a copy of a portrait of his father by Lane, preferred the copy to the original when it was done, and gave him a commission for a family group. The connection was renewed later, and as many as twenty portraits of various members of the Ionides family, dating from almost all periods of his working life, are extant. Distinguished persons from other circles soon began to figure among his sitters, including members of the Noel and of the Spring Rice families. He had a commission to paint a portrait of Roebuck, and one of Jeremy Bentham from the wax effigy which the philosopher had ordered to be constructed over his bones. But in his own mind he from the first regarded portraiture as an inferior branch of art, and set his whole soul's ambition on imaginative and creative design.

In April 1842 was issued the official notice inviting cartoons in competition for a design from English history, Spenser, Shakespeare, or Milton, in commemoration of the rebuilding of Westminster Palace, just completed. Watts went ardently to work, and sent in, with no expectation of success, a cartoon of Caractacus led in triumph through Rome. To his extreme surprise he won one of the three premiums (300*l.*), the other winners being Edward Armitage [q. v. Suppl. I] and C. W. Cope [q. v. Suppl. I]. The cartoons were acquired by a speculator and sent on exhibition round the country; that by Watts fell into the hands of a dealer who cut it up; such fragments as have survived are now preserved in the collection of Lord Northbourne at Betteshanger Park. With the sum thus earned Watts determined to start on a journey to Italy. He travelled by diligence, then by water down the Saône and Rhône, and by steamboat from Marseilles to Leghorn, making good friends by the way; and so by Pisa to Florence, where he had promised himself a stay of two months. Absorbed in the enthusiasm of study, he had almost reached the end of his time when he was reminded of an introduction he had brought but neglected to deliver to Lord Holland, then British minister at the court of Tuscany. He called and was welcomed. The rare natural dignity, simplicity, and charm of presence and person which at all times distinguished him won him the warm regard and affection both of Lord and Lady Holland almost from his first visit. They invited him to stay with them for a few days in the house tenanted by the legation, the Casa Feroni (now Palazzo Amerighi) in the Via dei Serragli, Borgo San Frediano. In the result he lived as their guest for the next four years, partly at the Casa Feroni, partly at the old Medicean villa of Careggi without the walls. Studios in both houses—at the Villa Careggi a vast one—were arranged for him. Nothing was more characteristic of the man than his quietly ascetic way of living in the midst of luxury and the unshaken industry which never let itself be seduced by social attention or flattery. He worked hard during these Florence years, always with high ambitions though always with a modest estimate of himself. He began with portraits of Lord and Lady Holland, of which the former was afterwards nearly destroyed by fire. He also painted the grand duke of Lucca, Countess Walewska, and Princess Mathilde Bonaparte. In the evenings he drew pencil portraits of many interesting guests and friends. He decorated the courtyard of the Casa Feroni with frescoes, which have since disappeared under whitewash. At the Villa Careggi there is still preserved a fresco painted by him of the scene following the death of Lorenzo de' Medici. In the great studio at the villa he designed and began to execute many vast canvases inspired by Italian literature and legend. Among these was the subject from Boccaccio's tale of 'Anastasio degl' Onesti,' afterwards carried out on a huge scale in his studio in Charles Street; Dante's 'Paolo and Francesca,' in its final form perhaps the noblest extant rendering of the theme in painting; the Fata Morgana from Boiardo; and the scene of Buondelmonti riding under the portico on the day that saw the beginning of the great feud. He practised modelling also, and an alabaster Medusa of the time is still preserved. He paid visits with Lord and Lady Holland to their villa at Naples and to Rome, where he learned to prize the Sistine ceiling of Michelangelo as the highest achievement of human art after the marbles of the Parthenon. After 1845 the Hollands (no longer at the legation) lived much at Naples, Watts staying on by himself at Careggi, and receiving sympathetic attentions, such as at all times he needed and attracted, from Lady Duff Gordon and her two daughters, Georgiana and Alice, who remained his staunch friends to the end. In 1847 the Westminster Palace commissioners invited a new competition for an historical painting, and Watts began to prepare with immense pains preliminary studies for a great design of Alfred urging his countrymen to fight the Danes by sea.

In April of this year he sailed from Leghorn to London, and brought with him several huge canvases, intending to finish them in England and then return to Italy. But destiny decided otherwise, and the remainder of his life, except for an occasional trip abroad of a few weeks or months, was spent in England. The princely amateur Mr. R. S. Holford, whose acquaintance he had made shortly before leaving Careggi, offered him a vacant room in Dorchester House as a temporary studio. While working here he lodged at 48 Cambridge Street. In the Westminster Hall competition he won one of the three first premiums of 500*l.*, Frederick Richard Pickersgill [q. v. Suppl. I] and Edward Armitage [q. v. Suppl. I] carrying off the others. The commissioners desiring to purchase Watts's work, he offered it for the nominal price of 200*l.*, and it was placed in one of the committee rooms of the House of Commons. At Dorchester House Watts painted 'Life's Illusions' and 'Time and Oblivion,' the two of his allegorical designs with which to the end he remained least dissatisfied. John Ruskin, with whom Watts had made friends after his return from Italy, for a while had 'Time and Oblivion' in his house, but presently found in it not enough minute imitation of natural detail. He afterwards bought a picture by Watts of 'Saint Michael contending with Satan for the body of Moses.' For the Duff Gordon ladies Watts at this time painted a portrait of Louisa, Marchioness of Waterford, for whose gifts of mind and person and powers as an amateur artist he conceived the strongest admiration. Lord and Lady Holland having by this time (1847–8) come back to England, Watts resumed his intimacy with them, and painted decorations on some of the ceilings at Holland House, as well as a new full-length portrait of the lady. About the same time he painted portraits of Guizot and Panizzi. Pencil designs of nearly the same date were 'The Temptation of Eve' and 'Satan calling up his Legions.' Meanwhile he was cherishing a great dream, which has been aptly called 'the ambition of half his life and the regret of the other half.' This was for a vast comprehensive sequence of emblematic and decorative paintings illustrating the cosmic evolution of the world and of human civilisation. 'The House of Life' was the name which, looking back on the scheme in retrospect, he would have given it. But much as his enthusiastic projects for monumental works of painting impressed the circle of his immediate friends, they left cold the public powers who dispose of funds and wall-spaces, and scope and opportunity for their realisation were seldom granted him. Of this particular scheme only a few detached episodes were destined later to come into being, painted as separate pictures and on a different scale from his first conception. London life, the London climate, and the difficulty of even earning a livelihood by the kind of work he longed to do, depressed his never robust health. He planned a travel in Greece with Mr. Ionides in 1848, but gave it up in consequence of the disturbed state of Europe. By this time he had moved to a large studio at 30 Charles Street, Berkeley Square. Here he became a member of the distinguished circle, including Robert Morier, Chichester Fortescue, James Spedding, John Ruskin, Henry Layard, and William Harcourt, which met twice a week for evening conversation at Morier's rooms, 49 New Bond Street, and formed the nucleus of the Cosmopolitan Club. When in September 1853 Morier went abroad, and about the same time Watts gave up the Charles Street studio, the club established itself there, and with one short interruption held its meetings in the same place, with the great Boccaccio picture still hanging on the walls, until 1902, when the house was vacated and the picture removed to the great hall at the Tate Gallery.

A new friend of Watts about 1850–1 was the poet Aubrey de Vere [q. v. Suppl. II], a cousin of his early friends the Spring Rices and brother of Sir Vere de Vere, to whom the painter about this date paid a visit at Curragh Chase. He had always been interested in Ireland, and had previously painted from imagination a picture of an Irish eviction. Flying visits of this nature often proved tonic for his health, which in all these years was very frail. It was about this time that he conceived the scheme of a series of portraits of the distinguished men of his time to be ultimately presented to the nation, and began with Lord John Russell. Additions were made to the series at intervals until almost the year of his death, and the greater part of them have now found their home in the National Portrait Gallery. About the same time he was induced to admit a young gentleman from Yorkshire, Roddam Spencer Stanhope, to work in his studio; but he did not believe in the direct teaching of art to a pupil by a master, only in the exercise of a general stimulus and example. A fresh acquaintance which in 1850 had a decisive influence on his life was that with Miss Virginia Pattle, soon afterwards to become Lady Somers, the most beautiful and fascinating of the seven remarkable daughters of James Pattle, of the East India Company's service. She was then living with her brother-in-law and sister, Mr. and Mrs. Henry Thoby Prinsep [q. v.]. The whole family became his devoted and admiring friends; their features are commemorated in very many paintings and drawings by his hand. The Prinseps were looking for a new home, and Watts found them one in Little Holland House, Kensington, a rather romantic, rambling combination of two old houses in a spacious garden, and with much of a country aspect, in the south-west corner of Holland Park. In this home they invited Watts to join them, and he was domesticated there for the next five-and-twenty years; retaining also for the first year or two the studio in Charles Street. In this circle he first received the name 'Signor,' by which his nearer friends always afterwards spoke of and to him, as something less formal than a surname and less familiar than a Christian name. Meantime he was low in health and spirits; and the mood found its expression in pictures such as 'Found Drowned,' 'Under a Dry Arch,' 'The Seamstress.' In 1850 he exhibited a picture of 'The Good Samaritan.' Through his friend Lord Elcho he asked for leave to decorate the great hall of Euston Station with monumental paintings, if the company would pay for scaffolding and colours. The offer was declined. He accepted, under protest as to the conditions, an official commission, consequent on his success in the 1847 competition, to paint one of a series of twelve wall-paintings by different hands in a cramped corridor of Westminster Palace, and chose for his subject the 'Triumph of the Red Cross Knight' from Spenser. These paintings are now dilapidated and covered up. In 1853 he went for a month's trip to Venice with R. S. Stanhope, and, making his first intimate acquaintance with Venetian art, thought he found in the work of Titian and his contemporaries a pictorial expression of exactly those qualities in flesh and drapery the rendering of which in marble had from the first appealed to him above all things in the sculptures of the Parthenon. His life-long technical preoccupation was the attainment of something like these same Phidiac and Titianic qualities in his own work. In the same year he obtained the best chance of his life for a large decorative work of the kind he loved. For the north wall of the newly finished hall of Lincoln's Inn he offered to paint in fresco a great subject which he called 'Justice—a Hemicycle of Lawgivers.' The offer was accepted. The work, which could only be done during law vacations, took him six years to finish, after many delays due to weak health and absences abroad. Paralysing attacks of nervous headache and prostration continued to be frequent. It may be doubted if the physical atmosphere of Little Holland House was good for him. But its social atmosphere—largely of his own creation—was entirely congenial. He lived the life of a recluse so far as concerned outside society, and never broke his ascetic habits of early rising and day-long industry. But everything that was gifted, amiable, or admirable in the life of Victorian England seemed naturally drawn towards him, and came to seek him in the Kensington studio and garden. His chief time for receiving friends and visitors other than sitters (and these included practically all the distinguished men and beautiful women of his day) was on Sunday afternoons and evenings. A new and inspiring friend and sitter at this time was Mrs. Nassau Senior, of whom he painted one of his best portraits, exhibiting it by way of experiment under a pseudonym. He spent some months of the winter 1855–6 in Paris, where he had sittings from Thiers, Prince Jerome Buonaparte, and Princess Lieven among others. About this time he also undertook fresco work for Lord Somers at 7 Carlton House Terrace.

In 1856–7 Watts ventured upon a more extended travel than usual. His old friend (Sir) Charles Newton [q. v. Suppl. I], the archæologist, had for some years been British consul at Mitylene and had often pressed him to go out there for a visit. Now at length, in the autumn of 1856, when the Crimean war was over and Lord Stratford de Redcliffe had obtained the firmans enabling Newton to begin his long-desired task of excavation at Budrum, the site of the ancient Halicarnassus, Watts could not resist his friend's summons. He went out on H.M.S. Gorgon, accompanied by Valentine Prinsep [q. v. Suppl. II], the youngest son of his friends at Little Holland House, and stayed seven months, partly watching the excavations with Newton, partly on a visit to Lord Stratford de Redcliffe at Constantinople, where he painted the portrait of the ambassador now in the National Portrait Gallery. His brush was never idle, and he took in impressions of landscape of which the picture 'The Island of Cos' was a chief result. Returning in June 1857, he resumed work on the Lincoln's Inn fresco. During this summer Tennyson was a visitor at Little Holland House, and Watts painted the first of several portraits of him. In this year also Rossetti, with whom Watts was already on friendly terms, brought to him for the first time his young disciple Burne-Jones, whose genius the elder master with characteristic generosity recognised and with whom he maintained to the end a cordial friendship. In 1859 he painted the portrait of Gladstone now in the National Portrait Gallery. In the same year the Lincoln's Inn fresco was completed amidst general congratulations. Watts had in the meanwhile continued his fresco work for Lord Somers in London, and had undertaken new work of the same kind for Lord Lansdowne at Bowood, where his subjects were 'Coriolanus' and 'Achilles parted from Briseis.' Among his well-known pictures begun in these years were 'The Genius of Greek Poetry,' 'Time, Death, and Judgment,' 'Esau,' 'Chaos' (from the original 'House of Life' scheme), and 'Sir Galahad.'

To escape the fogs and glooms of London, Watts spent several winters before and after 1860 at Sandown House, Esher, the home of a sister of Thoby Prinsep. Here he lived in the intimacy of the Orleans princes, then at Claremont, and of Sir Alexander and Lady (Lucy) Duff Gordon and their circle, including George Meredith [q. v. Suppl. II]. He was a skilled rider, and gained health hunting with the Old Surrey foxhounds and the Duc d'Aumale's harriers on his favourite thoroughbred mare Undine. He took an eager interest and such share as his strength enabled him in the volunteer movement of the time. In the following years he formed a new and affectionate intimacy with Frederic Leighton, who in 1866 built the well-known house and studio in Holland Road, almost adjoining the Little Holland House garden. Another valued addition to the circle was Joachim the musician; and yet another, Sir John Herschel the astronomer: Watts's portraits of these friends are among his best work. John Lothrop Motley, then American minister in England, was a welcome sitter about this time. Through the initiative of Dean Milman, Watts was chosen to design figures of St. Matthew and St. John to be done in mosaic in St. Paul's: the dean's further wish that he should be charged with a whole scheme of interior decoration for the cathedral failed to take effect. Portraits of Lord Shrewsbury,

Lord Lothian, and the three Talbot sisters (of whom one was Lady Lothian) led to visits at Blickling and Ingestre. The incurable illness under which Lord Lothian was suffering suggested the motive of the painter's 'Love and Death,' the most popular and perhaps the finest of his symbolic designs. Of this subject, as of so many others, Watts painted in the ensuing years several versions varying in scale and handling. New sitters, who soon became admiring friends and buyers, continued to come about him: among them Sir William Bowman the oculist in 1863, and Mr. Charles Rickards of Manchester in 1865. The intelligent sympathy with his aims and enthusiasm for his work shown by the last-named friend was to the end of his life one of the artist's most valued encouragements. Meantime a change, sudden and of brief duration, had passed over his life. Miss Ellen Terry, then in the radiance of her early girlhood, was brought into the circle. A marriage, foredoomed to failure, was arranged between her and the recluse, half-invalid painter nearly thirty years her senior. This was in February 1864; in June of the next year they parted by consent, and in 1877 Watts sought and obtained a divorce.

To give a fixed date to any work of Watts is apt to be misleading, since it was his habit to paint upon a single picture, or upon variations and replicas of a single design, through many successive years. The decade 1860–70 saw the inception of most, and the completion of some, of the works in painting and sculpture by which he remains best known to the world. Such were in painting 'The Court of Death'; a series of three pictures on the story of Eve, and another of three on the story of Cain, each charged with a weight of brooding ethical and symbolic suggestion; 'The Return of the Dove'; the landscape 'Carrara Mountains'; with the classical subjects of 'Ariadne in Naxos,' 'The Childhood of Zeus,' 'The Judgment of Paris,' 'Daphne,' 'Thetis,' 'Diana and Endymion,' 'Orpheus and Eurydice,' and the so-called 'Wife of Pygmalion,' which was the interpretation in paint of a Greek bust in the Chantrey collection at Oxford. To these years also belong some of his finest female portraits, e.g. those of Lady Margaret Beaumont, Lady Bath, Mrs. Percy Wyndham, and Miss Edith Villiers, afterwards Countess of Lytton. From the same or the next following period date many of his portraits of celebrities now in the National Portrait Gallery, including those of Rossetti, Swinburne, Burne-Jones, Robert Lowe, Lord Aberdare, Lord Lawrence, Thomas Carlyle, and John Stuart Mill—the latter painted just before the philosopher's death in 1873. From this time also dates the devotion of a large part of the artist's time to works of sculpture. First came the mythological bust of Clytie struggling out of her flower-calyx; then an effigy of Mr. Thomas Owen for Condover church; then one of Bishop Lonsdale for Lichfield Cathedral; and later again a monument to Lord Lothian for Blickling. For his work as a sculptor Watts built himself a new studio in the Little Holland House garden. Finding that the Prinseps' lease of the place would expire in 1871, he tried unsuccessfully to secure a ten years' extension. Lord Holland had died in 1869, and his widow was now urged to sell this corner of the estate for the benefit of the rest. The tenancy was thenceforth only from year to year, and Watts foresaw with dismay that he would have to change his home and place of work. He bought some acres in the Isle of Wight adjoining Tennyson's property of Farringford, with intent to build there a house that should be for the Prinseps a permanent and for himself an occasional home. To provide the means for this and also for his own accommodation in London he forced himself to the distasteful task of miscellaneous portrait-painting. At the same time he continued to labour at the Condover and Blickling monuments and also at the statue of the first Lord Holland, done in conjunction with Edgar Boehm, which now stands behind the fountain facing the street from Holland Park. In 1870 the idea of a great equestrian statue for the Duke of Westminster of his ancestor Hugh Lupus, Warden of the Marches, was first mooted and the sketch begun. In the same year he painted a version of the 'Denunciation of Cain,' the second subject of the symbolic trilogy above mentioned, as his diploma picture for the Royal Academy. Without submitting his name as a candidate he had been elected an associate of that body in 1867 and a full member immediately afterwards. Four years earlier, as a witness before the parliamentary commission of 1863, he had made extremely candid comments on what he thought the Academy's errors and shortcomings: so that the honour now done him was an act of some generosity.

In 1872 Watts began to build The Briary at Freshwater, and in London two years later a new Little Holland House in Melbury Road, not two hundred yards from the old. The Prinseps occupied The Briary in the spring of 1874, Watts remaining at the old Little Holland House till August 1875. In the meantime he had painted one of his best allegorical pictures, 'The Spirit of Christianity,' as well as an official portrait of the Prince of Wales. After spending most of the winter at Freshwater he achieved the trying labour of shifting the accumulations of his life's work from one house to the other, and got settled in Melbury road by February 1876. Here he received in the following years many friendly services from his neighbours Mr. and Mrs. Russell Barrington: services which the lady has fully recorded in the volume cited at foot of this article. In 1877 he suffered a great loss by the death of Mrs. Nassau Senior. In the same year his public reputation was much enhanced by the first exhibition at the newly opened Grosvenor Gallery, to which he sent a large version of 'Love and Death' and three of his finest portraits. In this and subsequent exhibitions at the same place, and afterwards at the New Gallery, his contributions were more effectively seen than on the walls of the Royal Academy, where work of more popular aim seemed to crowd them out of sight. Every year confirmed his conviction that art should have a mission beyond the pleasure of the eye, and that the artist should strive to benefit and uplift his fellow-men by appealing through their visual sense to their hearts and consciences. Pictures of symbolic and ethical significance became more and more the main effort of his life, his purpose being in the end to offer what he thought the best of them to the nation. At the same time portraits, principally of sitters chosen by himself with the same object, continued to occupy him. He also gave much of his time and strength to a colossal equestrian statue which he called 'Physical Energy.' This was a variation upon his design of the original Hugh Lupus monument for the Duke of Westminster, so carried out as to gain a more abstract and universal significance.

In 1878 Thoby Prinsep died, and his widow moved to a house at Brighton, where a studio was arranged for Watts's occasional use, The Briary being given up. In 1880 Mr. Rickards's entire collection of pictures by Watts, fifty-six in number, was exhibited at the Manchester Institution, and made a great impression. In 1881 he was persuaded to publish some of his thoughts on art in the 'Nineteenth Century,' to which he continued afterwards to be an occasional contributor. Other friends, particularly Lady Marian Alford [q. v. Suppl. I] and her circle, engaged his active interest in the work of the School of Needlework: an interest which was afterwards extended to the Home Arts and Industries Association and the Arts and Crafts Guild. To the working studios which formed part of the new Little Holland House a separate exhibition studio was in 1881 attached, to which the public were admitted on Saturday and Sunday afternoons. A winter exhibition of two hundred of his pictures at the Grosvenor Gallery (1881–2) further increased his reputation with the general public. The Universities of Oxford and Cambridge having each proposed to confer upon him its honorary degree, he at first wished to decline these honours, but was ultimately persuaded to accept them (1882). The exhibition of some of his pictures at Paris moved to enthusiasm a young American lady, Miss Mead (afterwards Mrs. Edwin Abbey), whose energy organised in 1885 a display of his work in New York, thus spreading his fame to the western hemisphere. In 1885 he was offered a baronetcy by Gladstone, but declined it. His perfectly sincere diffidence as to the ultimate value of his work (though not as to the rightness of his aims) made him at all times shrink from official honours or public praise lest posterity should think they had been ill bestowed. In 1886 he learned officially that his proposal ultimately to present to the nation both a series of symbolic pictures and a series of contemporary portraits would be warmly welcomed. But despite these evidences of recognition, and despite the general honour and affection which surrounded him, the loneliness of his home and the weakness of his health, together with his ever-present sense of the gulf between his ideals and his achievement, caused him frequent depression.

In 1886 a new happiness came into his life through his marriage with a friend and disciple of some years' standing, Miss Mary Fraser Tytler. Helped by her wise tendance and devoted companionship, he lived on to a patriarchal age, through eighteen years more of fruitful industry, only interrupted by occasional illness and only darkened by the successive deaths of nearly all the friends of his early and middle life. The summers were spent regularly at the new Little Holland House; the first winter and spring in Egypt, with rests at Malta, Constantinople, and Athens; the next (1887–8) at Malta, where his work was interrupted by illness, and at Mentone; the third (1890–1) at Monkshatch on the Hog's Back, the home of his friends Mr. and Mrs. Andrew Hichens. The climate here specially suiting him, he decided to acquire and build on a picturesque wooded site near by. The house, called Limnerslease, was finished in the summer of 1891. Thenceforward his winters were regularly spent there, and as time went on a great part of his summers also. In 1894 he declined a second offer of a baronetcy from Gladstone. In 1895, as the new building for the National Portrait Gallery was approaching completion, he arranged to present to it fifteen paintings and two drawings of distinguished contemporaries; the number of his works there has since doubled. In 1897 his eightieth birthday was celebrated by an exhibition of his collected works at the New Gallery and the presentation of a widely signed address of congratulation. In the same year he made to the National Gallery of British Art a gift of some twenty of his chief symbolic and allegoric paintings. He published a proposal to commemorate the jubilee of Queen Victoria by a monument to the obscure and quickly forgotten doers of heroic deeds in daily civic life. The project hung fire, but he himself did something towards realising it by presenting to the public, in what is known as the Postmen's Park at St. Botolph's, Aldersgate, a shelter or covered corridor where inscriptions recording such deeds should be put up: this was completed and opened in 1900. He was much interested in the character and career of Cecil Rhodes [q. v. Suppl. II], and in 1897 began a portrait of him which remains unfinished. In 1898 he began at Limnerslease a labour of love in the shape of a monumental statue of Tennyson for Lincoln. A strong new interest in his life was the school of decorative terra-cotta work successfully started by Mrs. Watts in the village of Compton, close beside their home. In 1899 he made a summer trip to Inverness-shire—his first visit to Scotland—and brought back pictures of Scottish landscape marked by the same qualities of style, breadth, and grave splendour of colour and atmospheric effect as his earlier impressions of Asia Minor or the Bay of Naples or the Carrara Mountains or the Riviera. In 1902 the Order of Merit was instituted by King Edward VII. Watts was named one of the original twelve members, and accepted without demur the proffered honour, the only one he had so accepted in his life. In the same year he consented to a suggestion of Lord Grey that his equestrian statue of 'Physical Energy,' at which he had laboured for many years but which was not yet finished to his mind, should be cast in bronze for South Africa as a memorial to Rhodes's achievement as a pioneer of empire. Another cast has since the artist's death been placed in Lancaster Walk, Kensington Gardens. In 1903 he decided to give up Little Holland House and make Limnerslease his only home, and as a preliminary step built a gallery there a furlong from his house, to receive the pictures remaining on his hands; this was opened to the public in April 1904, and has since been much extended and enriched.

All this while there had been no falling-off in Watts's industry as a painter, and little in his power of hand. To the last fifteen or twenty years of his life belong such symbolic paintings as 'Sic transit,' 'Love Triumphant,' 'For he had Great Possessions,' 'Industry and Greed,' 'Faith, Hope and Charity,' 'The Slumber of the Ages,' 'The Sower of the Systems,' and such portraits as those of George Meredith, Lord Roberts, Mr. Gerald Balfour, Mr. Walter Crane, and Mr. Charles Booth, with others of himself and of Tennyson. The last portrait of himself, an experiment in the tempera medium, was painted in March 1904. During this spring he had several attacks of illness, but none that seemed alarming, till one day in early June he caught a chill working in the London garden studio in an east wind; he lacked strength for resistance, and died three weeks later, on 1 July 1904, in his eighty-eighth year. He was buried at Compton, near the mortuary chapel built there from his wife's designs.

The number of paintings left by Watts is computed at something like eight hundred, so that not a tithe of them has been mentioned above. Besides the twenty-five which are in the Tate Gallery, the thirty-six in the National Portrait Gallery, and a large number at Limnerslease, others have through the generosity of the artist found homes in most of the important public galleries of the United Kingdom and the colonies; the rest remain scattered in private hands.

To his contemporaries Watts set a great

example by unremitting industry and lofty purpose, by sweetness, dignity, and generosity of mind and character, and by the absolute devotion of all his powers to the benefit of his race and country as he conceived it. Other English artists before him who had thought nobly of their art and its mission, such as James Barry [q. v.] and Benjamin Robert Haydon [q. v.], had been deluded by pride and vanity into crediting themselves with gifts and aptitudes which they did not possess. Watts was beyond measure both generous in his estimate of other men's work and modest in his estimate of his own. A sense of failure pursued him always, yet never embittered him nor deterred him from striving after what he conceived to be the highest. 'I would have liked,' he said, 'to do for modern thought what Michelangelo did for theological thought.' But even to the genius of Michelangelo his achievement was possible only because of the great and unbroken collective traditions, both technical and spiritual, which he inherited. In the modern world no such tradition exists, and Watts was compelled to embody, by technical methods of his own devising, not the consenting thoughts of whole generations, but only his own private thoughts, on human life and destiny. His conceptions were as a rule so sane, so simple, so broad and general in their significance, that the painted symbols in which they are expressed present no ambiguity and can be read without an effort, appealing happily and harmoniously to the visual emotions before making their further appeal to the moral emotions and human sympathies. They vary greatly in power of vision and presentment, but hardly ever lack rhythmical flow and beauty, as well as originality, of composition, or richness of inventive and suggestive colour. The best of them, such as 'Love and Death,' 'Love and Life,' 'Love Triumphant,' 'The Spirit of Christianity,' and the Eve trilogy, seem never likely to be regarded as other than masterpieces of the painter's art. The same is true of many of his purely poetic compositions, whether from the classics or from later romantic literature, such as 'Diana and Endymion,' 'Orpheus and Eurydice' (especially in the first version), and 'Fata Morgana.' Where various versions of the same subject on different scales exist, it is generally the smaller rather than the larger or monumental version which is technically the most satisfying and the most directly handled. Watts might easily have been a master of brilliant and showily effective technique had he chosen. Some of his earlier work shows a remarkable aptitude that way; but he deliberately checked it, and laboured all his life, humbly and experimentally, to emulate the higher and subtler qualities which roused him to enthusiasm in Attic sculpture and Venetian painting. The result is generally a certain reticent and tentative method of handling, which does not, however, exclude either splendour of colouring or richness and vitality of surface. Something of the same reticence and tentativeness, the same undemonstrative brushwork, with an earnest and often highly successful imaginative endeavour to bring to the surface the inward and spiritual character of his sitters, marks the whole range of his portraits; at least of his male portraits; sometimes in those of women, as of Mrs. Cavendish Bentinck and her children, Lady Margaret Beaumont, Mrs. Nassau Senior, Mrs. Percy Wyndham, he let himself go, and produced effects of splendid opulence and power. The Victorian age was fortunate in having an artist of so fine a strain to interpret and record the beauty and graciousness of its best women and the breeding and intellect and distinction of its best men.

In person Watts was of middle height and rather slenderly made, the frame in later life somewhat bowed, but to the end suggesting the power of tenacious activity. The face was long, the features finely cut, the expression thoughtful and benign. His hair was brown, with a full moustache drooping into the beard; in later years it turned grey almost to whiteness and the beard was worn shorter. In and after middle age, with a small velvet skull-cap worn on the back of his head, he bore a remarkable resemblance to the portraits of Titian. There are many portraits of him, mostly by his own hand: one of the best is that which he painted in middle life for Sir William Bowman and is now in the Tate Gallery. He had a leisurely fulness and pensiveness in his way of speaking, and a beautiful simple courtesy and geniality of manner.

[Life of Watts by his widow (3 vols. 1912), kindly communicated in MS.; personal knowledge; The Times, 2 July 1904; Julia Cartwright, Life and Work of G. F. Watts (Art Journal Easter Annual, 1896); Watts, by R. E. D. Sketchley; G. F. Watts, by G. K. Chesterton; George Frederic Watts, by J. E. Phythian; G. F. Watts, Reminiscences, by Mrs. Russell Barrington; George Frederic

Watts, by O. van Schleinitz, in Knackfuss' Künstler-Monographien; art. by M. H. Spielmann in Bryan's Dict. of Painters, last edit.]

S. C.

WATTS, HENRY EDWARD (1826–1904), author, born at Calcutta on 15 Oct. 1826, was son of Henry Cecil Watts, head clerk in the police office at Calcutta, by his wife Emily Weldon. He was educated at a private school at Greenwich, and later at Exeter grammar school, where he became head-boy. Plans of proceeding to Exeter College, Oxford, or of training for the Honourable East India Company's Service came to nothing. At the age of twenty Watts returned to Calcutta, whence, after working as a journalist for some years, he went to Australia in search of an elder brother who had gone to the gold-diggings and was never heard of again. After an unsuccessful venture in mining, Watts joined the staff of the 'Melbourne Argus,' of which paper he became editor in 1859. On his return to England he was attached to a short-lived liberal newspaper at York, where he contracted small-pox, a disease of which he bore marked traces in after-life. Later he removed to London, and about 1868 joined the 'Standard,' acting as leader-writer and sub-editor in the colonial and literary departments. At this period he was also home correspondent for the 'Melbourne Argus.' He occupied rooms in Pall Mall before settling at 52 Bedford Gardens, Campden Hill, where he died of cancer on 7 Nov. 1904. He was unmarried. A contributor to the 'Westminster Review,' the 'Encyclopædia Britannica,' 'Blackwood's,' 'Fraser's,' the 'Saturday Review,' and the 'St. James's Gazette,' he is best remembered for his translation of 'Don Quixote' (1888; revised edit. 1895), originally begun in collaboration with A. J. Duffield [q. v. Suppl. I]. The first edition contained 'a new life of Cervantes,' which was corrected, enlarged, and issued separately in 1895. Watts also wrote a biographical sketch of Cervantes for the 'Great Writers' series in 1891, an essay on Quevedo for an English edition of 'Pablo de Segovia' (1892), illustrated by Daniel Vierge, and 'Spain' (1893) for the 'Story of the Nations' series.

Watts had no linguistic gifts, and only once travelled in Spain, when he went with his friend, Carlisle Macartney, for the purpose of visiting places associated with Cervantes or with 'Don Quixote'; yet his workmanlike knowledge of Spanish, his literary taste, and fluent English style enabled him to produce a well-annotated translation and to make a marked advance on the eighteenth-century versions which he condemned. His life of Cervantes is less satisfactory: apart from recent crucial discoveries, of which he was ignorant, Watts's work is disfigured by an extravagant hero-worship. A man of violent prejudices, Watts allowed his personal likings and antipathies to disturb his literary judgments. Though harsh in speech and brusque in manner, he was not unpopular at the Savile Club, London, of which he was an original member and an habitual frequenter.

[Private information.] J. F.-K.

WATTS, JOHN (1861–1902), jockey, born at Stockbridge, Hampshire, on 9 May 1861, one of a family of ten, was son of Thomas Watts. In due course he was apprenticed to Tom Cannon, then training at Houghton, near Stockbridge. In May 1876, when he weighed 6 stone, he rode at Salisbury his first winner, a horse called Aristocrat, belonging to his master, which dead-heated with Sir George Chetwynd's Sugarcane. The boy put on weight rapidly, and his riding opportunities while he held a jockey's licence were in consequence restricted. His abilities developed slowly, although he rode two other winners in 1876, eight in 1877, thirteen in 1878, eight in 1879, and nineteen in 1880.

In 1879 there began an association with Richard Marsh, then training at Lordship Farm, Newmarket, who became trainer for Edward VII when Prince of Wales. Marsh made Watts first jockey to the prince. Watts's first important success was gained in 1881, when he won the Cambridgeshire on the American horse Foxhall. Two years later he won the Oaks with Lord Rosebery's Bonny Jean, the first of four successes in that race.

After the death of Fred Archer in 1886 and the retirement of Tom Cannon, Watts was regarded as the leader of his profession, although, owing to the difficulty he experienced in keeping his weight down and his failure to obtain as many mounts as his chief rivals, he never occupied the first place in the list of winning jockeys. He was, however, second one year and third another. He rode nineteen classic winners. In the Derby he won on Merry Hampton (1887), on Sainfoin (1890), on Ladas (1894), and on the Prince of Wales's Persimmon (1896). The last-named horse defeated by a neck, after a prolonged tussle amid intense excitement, Mr. Leopold de Rothschild's St. Frusquin. In the Two Thousand Guineas

Watts won on Ladas (1894), and on Kirkconnel (1895); in the One Thousand on Miss Jummy (1886), Semolina (1889), Thais (1896), and Chelandry (1897); in the Oaks on Bonny Jean (1883), Miss Jummy (1886), Memoir (1890), and Mrs. Butterwick (1893); in the St. Leger on Ossian (1883), the Lambkin (1884), Memoir (1890), La Flêche (1892), and Persimmon (1896); and in the Ascot Cup on Morion, La Flêche, and Persimmon. His last winning mount in a 'classic' race was Lord Rosebery's Chelandry, who won the One Thousand Guineas in 1897. Watts gave up his jockey's licence in 1899, when his career in the saddle had extended over twenty-four years, and his winners numbered in all 1412. His most successful years were 1887, when he had 110 winning mounts, 1888 with 105 winners, 1891 with 114, and 1892 with 106 winners.

Watts, who acquired much of his skill from Tom Cannon, modelled his style on the 'old school' of which Fordham and Tom Cannon were masters. Nature had endowed Watts with the best of 'hands.' Perhaps he was seen to chief advantage on an inexperienced two-year-old, employing gentle persuasion with admirable effect, although he was equal to strenuous measures at need.

In 1900 Watts began to train racehorses at Newmarket. That season he only saddled one winner of a 100*l.* plate; but in 1901 he turned out seven winners of fifteen races worth 5557*l.*, and in 1902 four winners of five races valued at 1327*l.*, between March and July. On 19 July of that year he had a seizure at Sandown Park, and on the 29th of the same month died in the hospital on the course. He was buried in Newmarket cemetery. He was twice married: (1) in 1885 to Annie, daughter of Mrs. Lancaster of the Black Bear Hotel, Newmarket; and (2) in 1901 to Lutetia Annie, daughter of Francis Hammond of Portland House, Newmarket. His widow in 1911 married Kempton, son of Tom Cannon, formerly a successful jockey. Two of Watts's sons adopted their father's profession, and the eldest afterwards became a trainer at Newmarket.

A painting by Miss M. D. Hardy of Watts winning the Derby on Persimmon in 1896, and a photogravure of Watts on the same horse, with portraits of the King and Richard Marsh, are reproduced in A. E. T. Watson's 'King Edward VII as a Sportsman,' pp. 160–4. A caricature portrait by 'Lib' appeared in 'Vanity Fair' in 1887.

[Sportsman, 30 July 1902; Ruff's Guide to the Turf; Notes supplied by Mr. J. E. Watts; King Edward VII as a Sportsman, ed. A. E. T. Watson, 1911.] E. M.

WAUGH, BENJAMIN (1839–1908), philanthropist, born at Settle, Yorkshire, on 20 Feb. 1839, was the eldest son of James Waugh, by his wife Mary, daughter of John Harrison of Skipton. After education at a private school he went to business at fourteen. But in 1862 he entered Airedale College, Bradford, to be trained for the congregational ministry. He was congregational minister at Newbury from 1865 to 1866, at Greenwich from 1866 till 1885, and at New Southgate from 1885 till 1887, when he retired, to devote himself exclusively to philanthropic labours.

At Greenwich Waugh began to work in behalf of neglected and ill-treated children. In conjunction with John Macgregor ('Rob Roy') he founded a day institution for the care of vagrant boys, which they called the Wastepaper and Blacking Brigade; they arranged with two smack owners to employ the boys in deep-sea fisheries. The local magistrates acknowledged the usefulness of their plan and handed over to them first offenders instead of sending them to prison. Public appreciation of Waugh's work was shown by his election in 1870 for Greenwich to the London school board; he was re-elected in 1873, retiring on account of bad health in 1876, when he received a letter of regret from the education department and an illuminated address and a purse of 500 guineas from his fellow-members. He did good work on the board as first chairman of the books committee and as a champion of the cause of neglected children.

From 1874 to 1896 Waugh was editor of the 'Sunday Magazine,' having succeeded Dr. Thomas Guthrie [q. v.]. In 1873 he published a plea for the abolition of juvenile imprisonment, 'The Gaol-Cradle: who rocks it?'

After recovering his health in 1880 Waugh resumed his beneficent work, and in 1884 he assisted Miss Sarah Smith ('Hesba Stretton') [q. v. Suppl. II] in the establishment of the London Society for the Prevention of Cruelty to Children. In 1885 he collaborated with Cardinal Manning in an article in the 'Contemporary Review' entitled 'The Child of the English Savage,' describing the evils to be combated by his society. The society gradually gained support, and in 1888 was established by

Waugh's efforts upon a national non-sectarian basis, with a constitution approved by Manning, the Bishop of Bedford, and the chief rabbi. It was incorporated by royal charter in 1895 as the National Society for the Prevention of Cruelty to Children. Up to this date Waugh received no remuneration save a small salary for editing the society's organ, the 'Child's Guardian,' but from 1895 till 1905 he acted as paid director. His organising capacity, courage, and energy triumphed over obstacles. He was an admirable platform advocate, and his enthusiasm was tempered by candour and fairness. On legislation affecting children Waugh exerted much influence, chiefly with the aid of Samuel Smith, M.P. [q. v. Suppl. II]. He supported the agitation of William Thomas Stead in 1885, and caused to be inserted in the Criminal Law Amendment Act of that year a provision enabling young children's evidence to be taken in courts of law although they were too young to be sworn. To his effort was almost entirely due the important Act of 1889 for the prevention of cruelty to and better protection of children, which allowed a child to be taken from parents who grossly abused their power and to be entrusted to other relatives or friends or to an institution, whilst the parents were obliged to contribute to its maintenance. The Act recognised a civil right on the part of children to be fed, clothed, and properly treated. In accordance with Waugh's views, more stringent Acts followed in 1894, in 1904, and 1908, and all greatly improved the legal position of uncared-for and misused children.

Waugh's society worked in co-operation with the police by a system of local aid committees directed from the headquarters. Offending parents received warning before prosecution. Waugh was careful not to interfere unnecessarily with parental authority. Until 1891 his operations were hampered by want of funds, but subsequently the finances of the society prospered. In 1897 its administration was attacked in the press, but Waugh was amply vindicated by a commission of inquiry, consisting of Lord Herschell, Mr. Francis Buxton, and Mr. Victor Williamson. His disinterestedness was proved, and thenceforth the society's progress was unimpeded. Waugh resigned the active direction of the society in 1905, owing to failing health. He died at Westcliff-on-sea on 11 March 1908, and was buried in the Southend borough cemetery. He married in 1865 Lilian, daughter of Samuel Boothroyd of Southport. She survived him with three sons and five daughters. His widow was granted a civil service pension of 70*l.* in 1909.

Besides the work mentioned, Waugh published: 1. 'The Children's Sunday Hour,' 1884; new edit. 1887. 2. 'W. T. Stead: a Life for the People,' 1885. 3. 'Hymns for Children,' 1892. 4. 'The Child of Nazareth,' 1906. He was a leading member of a well-known literary dining club, the Eclectic, which met monthly in the Cathedral Hotel, St. Paul's Churchyard.

A memorial of Waugh with medallion portrait is affixed to the wall of the offices of the N.S.P.C.C. in Leicester Square.

[The Life of Benjamin Waugh, by Rosa Waugh and Ernest Betham, 1912; information from Mr. E. Betham. See also Review of Reviews, Nov. 1891 (with portrait); The Times, 13, 14, 17 March 1908; Who's Who, 1908; Brit. Mus. Cat.; Encycl. Brit., 10th ed.; Sunday Mag., vol. 34, pp. 661-5, art. 'The Champion of the Child,' by Hinchcliffe Higgins (with portrait); Benjamin Waugh: an Appreciation, by Robert J. Parr (Waugh's successor as director to the R.S.P.C.C.), 1909 (portrait), who has kindly revised this article.]

G. Le G. N.

WAUGH, JAMES (1831–1905), trainer of racehorses, born at Jedburgh on 13 Dec. 1831, was son of Richard Waugh, a farmer there. Brought up on his father's farm, he became in 1851 private trainer of steeplechasers at Cessford Moor to a banker named Grainger. He frequently rode the horses in races. In 1855 he went to Jedburgh to train for Sir David Baird and Sir J. Boswell, and four years later succeeded Matthew Dawson [q. v. Suppl. I] in the training establishment at Gullane. Thence he soon removed to Ilsley, in Berkshire, where he became private trainer to Mr. Robinson, an Australian, for whom he won the Royal Hunt Cup at Ascot with Gratitude. In 1866, on Robinson's retirement from the turf, Waugh succeeded Matthew Dawson at Russley, on the Berks-Wilts border, where he was a successful private trainer for James Merry. He saddled Marksman, who ran second to Hermit in the Derby of 1867; Belladrum, second to Pretender in the Two Thousand Guineas in 1869; and Macgregor, who, in 1870, won the Two Thousand Guineas.

At the close of the season of 1870 Waugh left Russley for Kentford, Newmarket, whence he soon migrated to Naclo, on the Polish frontier, to train for Count Henckel. After two years at Naclo he spent seven years at Carlburg, in Hungary, where he trained winners of every big race in Austria-Hungary. In some of the events successes were scored several times. His horses also won many important prizes in Germany. Returning to Newmarket in 1880, he settled first at Middleton Cottage and then at Meynell House for the rest of his life. Several continental owners sent horses to be trained by him, among them Prince Tassilo Festetics, for whom he won the Grand Prize at Baden Baden, the German Derby, and other important races. From 1885 to 1890 he took charge of Mr. John Hammond's horses, including St. Gatien, who in 1884 dead-heated with Harvester in the Derby, and won the Cesarewitch, carrying 8st. 10lb., and Florence, winner of the Cambridgeshire (1884). For Mr. Hammond, Waugh won the Ascot Cup in 1885 with St. Gatien, the Ascot Stakes with Eurasian in 1887, and the Cambridgeshire with Laureate in 1889. Other patrons were the Chevalier Scheibler, Count Lehndorff, Count Kinsky, and Messrs. A. B. Carr, Deacon, J. S. Baird-Hay, Sir R. W. Jardine, Dobell, James Russel, D. J. Jardine, and Inglis, and Miss Graham. He trained The Rush to win the Chester Cup in 1896, and the Ascot Gold Vase in 1898; Piety the Manchester Cup in 1897; and Refractor the Royal Hunt Cup at Ascot in 1899.

A skilful and conscientious trainer, Waugh achieved some success as a breeder of race horses, and when at Newmarket bought and sold thoroughbreds for continental patrons and foreign governments. He was an excellent judge of a horse. In all his dealings he was the soul of honour. He was noted for his geniality and hospitality, and took an interest in cross-country sport.

He died at Newmarket, after some years of failing health, on 23 Oct. 1905, and was buried in the cemetery there. He married in 1854 Isabella (*d.* 1881), daughter of William Scott of Tomshielhaugh, Southdean. Of his large family, six sons adopted the father's calling.

[Notes supplied by Waugh's daughter, Janet, wife of Joseph Butters, the trainer; Sportsman, 24 Oct. 1905; From Gladiateur to Persimmon (H. Sydenham Dixon), p. 47; Ruff's Guide to the Turf.] E. M.

WEBB, ALFRED JOHN (1834–1908), Irish biographer, born in Dublin on 10 June 1834, was eldest son of Richard Davis Webb, a printer in Abbey Street, by his wife Hannah Waring of Waterford. He was of Quaker family, and his father was a zealous worker in the anti-slavery movement and for social reform generally. In youth Alfred started a fund for the victims of the Irish famine of 1846–7. He was first sent to a day school kept by Quakers in Dublin, and later to Dr. Hodgson's High School, Manchester. On leaving this place he was apprenticed to his father's trade. About twenty he was sent to Australia, partly to benefit his health by change of climate, and partly for purposes of business. The business came to nothing, and he went off to the gold-fields. Recalled to England, he worked his passage home as a deck hand on a sailing vessel, although he had ample money for his journey (*Freeman's Journal*, 1 Aug. 1908). On his return to Ireland he resumed work in his father's printing office, becoming manager and proprietor. Interesting himself in Irish affairs, he was one of the earliest advocates of the home rule movement, which Isaac Butt [q. v.] inaugurated in 1870. He was a supporter of the united Irish party under Parnell, but left that leader in 1887. In 1890 he was returned as anti-Parnellite M.P. for West Waterford, and remained its representative until 1895. For many years he was one of the treasurers of the party funds. He died on 30 July 1908 near Hillswick in the Shetland Isles, while on a holiday. He was buried at the Quaker burial ground at Temple Hill, Blackwick, co. Dublin. He married Elizabeth, daughter of one of the Shackletons of Ballitore. She predeceased him in 1906. He had no children.

Webb was an enthusiastic traveller. Indian politics occupied his attention, and he visited that country more than once—the last time in 1898, when he was president of the Indian National Congress. Much of his leisure was devoted to literature. His chief work was 'A Compendium of Irish Biography,' Dublin, 1877, which, inadequate as it is, is so far the best separate work of its kind in existence. He was a frequent contributor of travel sketches and political and general articles to the 'Freeman's Journal,' the 'Irish Monthly,' and the New York 'Nation,' and also published 'The Opinions of some Protestants regarding their Irish Catholic Fellow-Countrymen' (3rd edit. 1886); 'The Alleged Massacre of 1641' (1887); and 'Thoughts in Retirement.'

[Freeman's Journal, 1 Aug. 1908; The Times, 1 Aug. 1908; Annual Register, 1908, p. 132; Brit. Mus. Cat.; information from his sister, Miss Deborah Webb.]

D. J. O'D.

WEBB, ALLAN BECHER (1839–1907), dean of Salisbury and bishop in South Africa, born on 6 Oct. 1839, at Calcutta, was eldest son of Allan Webb, M.D., surgeon to the governor-general of India and professor of descriptive and surgical anatomy at the Calcutta Medical College. His mother was Emma, daughter of John Aubrey Danby.

Admitted to Rugby under Edward Meyrick Goulburn [q. v. Suppl. I] in October 1855, Webb in 1858 won a scholarship at Corpus Christi College, Oxford, and in 1860 obtained a first class in classical moderations. He graduated B.A. in 1862 with a second class in literæ humaniores, and proceeded M.A. in 1864 and D.D. in 1871. In 1863 he was elected to a fellowship at University College, and was ordained deacon, serving the curacy of St. Peter-in-the-East, Oxford. From 1864 to 1865 he was vice-principal of Cuddesdon College, under Edward King [q.v. Suppl. II]. He resigned his fellowship on his marriage in 1867, and accepted the rectory of Avon Dasset, near Leamington.

In 1870 he was nominated to succeed Dr. Twells as bishop of Bloemfontein, Orange Free State. His consecration gave rise to some controversy. Webb, supported by Robert Gray [q. v.], bishop of Cape Town, declined to take the oath of allegiance to the English primate, on the ground that it was opposed to the canons of the South African synod, but offered to take the oath of obedience to his metropolitan, the bishop of Cape Town. Archibald Campbell Tait [q. v.], archbishop of Canterbury, however, held such procedure to infringe the Jerusalem Act of 1841 (5 Vict. c. 6), which regulated the appointment to bishoprics within the British dominions (*Guardian*, 23 Nov. 1870). The act was not, however, in force in Scotland, and the primate finally allowed Webb to take the oath of canonical obedience to Bishop Gray and his successors in Inverness cathedral on 30 November 1870. Webb was in full accord with the high church views generally prevalent in the South African province; and he was active in promoting the work of sisterhoods, whether missionary, educational, or medical. His diocese extended over the Orange Free State, Basutoland, and Bechuanaland; and his youth and vigour stood him in good stead. In 1883 he succeeded Nathaniel James Merriman [q. v.] as bishop of Graham's Town. Here, too, he actively engaged in developing mission and educational work both for natives and Europeans, and in fostering diocesan institutions like the college of St. Andrew and the sisterhood of the Resurrection. The chancel of the cathedral at Graham's Town, which was consecrated in 1893, stands as a permanent memorial of his episcopate, during which he did much to heal the schism that had rent the South African province since the Colenso controversy.

In 1898 Webb left South Africa after twenty-eight years' work. On his return home he was appointed provost of Inverness cathedral, and he also acted as assistant bishop in the diocese of Moray and Brechin. In 1901 he became dean of Salisbury in succession to George David Boyle [q. v. Suppl. II]. Webb was devoted to stately worship, and though never a fluent speaker was an impressive preacher at missions and retreats. He died on 12 June 1907 at the deanery, Salisbury, and was buried in the cathedral cloisters. In 1867 Webb married Eliza, daughter of Robert Barr Bourne, rector and patron of Donhead, St. Andrew. She survived him, with two sons.

There are in the possession of his son, Mr. A. Cyprian Bourne Webb, chancellor of the diocese of Salisbury, a crayon drawing by Frank Miles, done in 1878, and a portrait in oils, painted by Miss Agnes Walker in 1902; neither is a striking likeness. In his memory stained glass was placed in the great north window, and the screen was erected in the morning chapel at Salisbury cathedral.

In addition to sermons, Webb published the following devotional works: 1. 'The Priesthood of the Laity in the Body of Christ,' 1889. 2. 'The Life of Service before the Throne,' 1895. 3. 'The Unveiling of the Eternal Word,' 1897. 4. 'With Christ in Paradise,' 2nd edit. 1898.

[The Times, 13, 18 June 1907; Church Times, 14 June 1907; Guardian, 19 June 1907; Pelican Record, June 1907; Rugby School Register (1842–74), 1902; Farrer, Life of Robert Gray, 1876, ii. 509; Cuddesdon College (1854–1904), 1904; private information.] G. S. W.

WEBB, FRANCIS WILLIAM (1836–1906), civil engineer, born at Tixall rectory, Staffordshire, on 21 May 1836, was second son of William Webb, rector of Tixall. Showing at an early age a liking for mechanical pursuits, he became at fifteen a pupil of Francis Trevithick, then locomotive superintendent of the London and North Western railway. With that railway he was, save for an interval of five years, associated for life. When his pupilage ended he was engaged in the drawing-office;

in Feb. 1859 he became chief draughtsman, and from 1861 to 1866 he was works manager. After serving as manager of the Bolton Iron and Steel Company's works from 1866 to 1871, he became on 1 Oct. 1871 chief mechanical engineer and locomotive superintendent of the London and North Western railway. The post carried heavy responsibility. Not only is the company's system exceptionally extensive, but the locomotive superintendent had charge, in addition to his normal duties, of departments dealing with signals, permanent way, cranes, water-supply, and electrical work. For more than thirty years, during which the population of Crewe increased from 18,000 to 42,000, Webb, who was exceptionally energetic, self-reliant, and resourceful, was the autocratic ruler of the industrial colony there.

He was a prolific inventor and took out many patents for improvements in the design and construction of locomotives and other machinery, but his name is chiefly associated with the compound locomotive, the steel sleeper, the electric train-staff for working single-line railways, and the electrical working of points and signals.

Webb began work on the compound locomotive in 1878, by converting to the compound principle an old locomotive. This was worked for several years on the Ashby and Nuneaton branch, and in 1882 he put into service a three-cylinder compound engine of an entirely new type, named 'Experiment,' in which he used two outside high-pressure and one inside low-pressure cylinders, the high-pressure and low-pressure cylinders driving on separate axles. In 1884 he brought out the 'Dreadnought' class, with larger cylinders, and in 1889 the 'Teutonic' class, with cylinders of the same size as the 'Dreadnoughts' but larger driving-wheels and simplified low-pressure valve-gear. The 'Greater Britain' class of 1891 had still larger cylinders, and in 1897 Webb brought out the 'Black Prince' or 'Diamond Jubilee' class of compounds, which had two high-pressure and two low-pressure cylinders, all driving on one axle. He was a strong advocate of compounding, and he satisfied himself that by means of it he obtained, with substantial economy, the greater power called for by the steady increase in the weight of trains. The subject excited much controversy among engineers, and the question of the relative merits of simple and compound locomotives is not yet settled.

The town of Crewe owes much to his public spirit. The Mechanics' Institution, of which he was president for many years, was an object of his special solicitude. The Cottage Hospital is due to his initiative, and of it he was a generous supporter. With Sir Richard Moon he prevailed upon the directors of the railway company to present to the town a public park. He served on the governing body of the town, and was elected mayor in Nov. 1886, being re-elected for a second term in the following year. During the first term of his mayoralty the 4000th locomotive was completed at Crewe, and the occasion was signalised by the presentation to him of the freedom of the borough. He was also created in 1886 an alderman of the borough; and was for some time magistrate for the county and an alderman of the county council. To him was due the formation of the engineer volunteer corps at Crewe, a reserve of the royal engineers, which rendered valuable service in the South African war.

He was elected an associate of the Institution of Civil Engineers on 23 May 1865. and became a member on 3 Dec. 1872. He was elected to the council of that society in May 1889, and became a vice-president in Nov. 1900. At the time of his retirement from the council in 1905 he was the senior vice-president. He bequeathed to the institution money for a prize for papers on railway machinery, and made a generous legacy to the benevolent fund of the society.

His contributions to its 'Proceedings' were four papers dealing with a 'Standard Engine-Shed' (lxxx. 258); 'Steel Permanent Way' (lxxxi. 299); 'Locomotive Fire-box Stays' (cl. 89), and 'Copper Locomotive-Boiler Tubes' (clv. 401). He was also a member of council of the Iron and Steel Institute, to which he presented a paper 'On the Endurance of Steel Rails' (*Journal*, 1886, 148). He was a life member of the Société des Ingénieurs civils de France.

He retired from the London and North Western railway in Dec. 1902, when the directors recorded their appreciation of his 'devoted and exceptional services.' After his retirement his health failed, and on 4 June 1906 he died at Bournemouth, where he was buried. He was unmarried.

By his will Webb left 10,000*l.* to found a nursing institution at Crewe, and the residue of his estate, amounting to 50,000*l.*, to found an orphanage for children of deceased employees of the London and North Western Railway Company. The orphanage, which accommodates twenty boys and twenty girls, was opened on 18 Dec. 1911.

A bust of Webb, being a replica of a model made from life by Sir Henry B. Robertson of Corwen, is in the Cottage Hospital at Crewe. A second replica, as well as a portrait in oils by Hall Neale, is in the orphanage. Another portrait in oils, by Mr. Charles H. Charnock, a blacksmith employed at the Crewe works, is also in the Cottage Hospital.

[Minutes of Proc. Inst. Civ. Eng., clxvii. 373; The Times, 6 June 1906; Chronicle (Crewe), 29 Dec. 1902; Railway Mag., Feb. 1900; private information.] W. F. S.

WEBB, THOMAS EBENEZER (1821–1903), lawyer and man of letters, born at Portscatho, Cornwall, on 8 May 1821, was eldest of the twelve children of the Rev. Thomas Webb, who owned a small estate in Cornwall, by his wife Amelia, daughter of James Ryall, of an Irish family. After education at Kingswood College, Sheffield, where he was afterwards for a time an assistant master, he won a classical scholarship at Trinity College, Dublin, in 1845. He was moderator in metaphysics there in 1848, obtained vice-chancellor's prizes for English, Greek, and Latin verse composition, and distinguished himself at the college historical society. He was always a brilliant talker and an eloquent speaker. Well read in English literature, he from an early age contributed verse and prose to the press and to 'Kottabos' and other magazines. In 1857 he took the degree of LL.D. at Dublin, was elected professor of moral philosophy at the university, and published 'The Intellectualism of Locke,' a brilliant but paradoxical attempt to show that Locke anticipated Kant's recognition of synthetic *a priori* propositions. His literary gifts were greater than his philosophical powers. But he was re-elected to his professorship in 1862, and next year was chosen fellow of Trinity College—a post which he enjoyed for the next eight years.

Meanwhile Webb was called to the Irish bar in 1861, and took silk in 1874. He was regius professor of laws at Trinity College from 1867 to 1887, and was also public orator from 1879 to 1887. In 1887 he withdrew from academic office to become county court judge for Donegal. He filled that position till his death. He was elected bencher of the King's Inns in 1899.

Apart from his professional duties Webb was keenly interested through life in politics and literature. In 1868 he stood without success in the whig interest for the University of Dublin. But in 1880 he abandoned his old party, and was thenceforth a rigorous critic of liberal policy in Ireland. In a pamphlet on the Irish land question (1880) he denounced proposed concessions to the tenants as ruinous to freedom of contract, though he approved legislation enabling tenants to purchase their holdings. He was hostile to Gladstone's home rule scheme of 1886 (see his pamphlets 'Ipse Dixit on the Gladstonian Settlement of Ireland,' and 'The Irish Question: a Reply to Mr. Gladstone,' 1886). He regarded home rule as a step towards separation.

In 1880 Webb produced a verse translation of Goethe's 'Faust,' which is more faithful and poetical than the versions of his many rivals. In 1885 there followed 'The Veil of Isis,' essays on idealism which failed to establish his position as a philosopher. His latest years were largely devoted to formulating doubts of the received Shakespearean tradition. With characteristic love of paradox he claimed in 'The Mystery of William Shakespeare: a Summary of Evidence' (1902), to deprive Shakespeare of the authorship of his plays and poems. He was well acquainted with Shakespeare's text, but had small knowledge of Elizabethan literature and history.

Webb's favourite recreation was hunting, and he long followed the Ward and Kildare hounds. He died at his residence in Dublin, 5 Mount Street Crescent, on 10 Nov. 1903, and was buried in Mount Jerome cemetery. He married in 1849 Susan, daughter of Robert Gilbert of Barringlen, co. Wicklow; she survived him with three sons and a daughter.

[Private information; personal knowledge; The Irish Times, 11 Nov. 1903; The Times, 12 Nov. 1903; Athenæum, 14 Nov. 1903; Who's Who, 1903.] R. Y. T.

WEBBER, CHARLES EDMUND (1838–1904), major-general, royal engineers, born in Dublin on 5 Sept. 1838, was son of the Rev. T. Webber of Leekfield, co. Sligo. After education at private schools and at the Royal Military Academy at Woolwich, he was commissioned as lieutenant in the royal engineers on 20 April 1855. The exigencies of the Crimean war cut short his professional instruction at Chatham, and he was sent to the Belfast military district, being employed principally on the defences of Lough Swilly.

In September 1857 Webber was posted

to the 21st company of royal engineers at Chatham, which was ordered to join in India, during the Indian Mutiny campaign, the Central India field force, commanded by Major-general Sir Hugh Rose, afterwards Lord Strathnairn [q. v.]. Brigadier C. S. Stuart's brigade, to which Webber's company was attached, marched on Jhansi, which Sir Hugh Rose's brigade reached by another route. Webber was mentioned in despatches for his services on this march. He took part in the battle of the Betwa on 1 April and in the assault of Jhansi on the 3rd, when he led the ladder party at the Black Tower on the left up a loopholed wall twenty-seven feet high. Webber saved the life of Lieutenant Dartnell of the 86th regiment, who, severely wounded, was first to enter the place with him. Although Sir Hugh Rose recommended both officers for brevet promotion, only Dartnell was rewarded. Webber took part in the operations attending the capture of Kunch (7 May), of Kalpi (23 May), and of Gwalior (19 June). A detachment of his company in his charge joined a flying column under Captain McMahon, 14th light dragoons, in Central India against Tantia Topi, Man Singh, and Firozshah, and he was mentioned in despatches. He continued in the field until April 1859. When the mutiny was suppressed he was employed in the public works department, first at Gwalior and afterwards at Allahabad, until he returned to England in May 1860. For his services in the Indian Mutiny campaign he received the medal with clasp for Central India.

After service in the Brighton subdistrict until Oct. 1861 he was until 1866 assistant instructor in military surveying at Woolwich. He was promoted captain on 1 April 1862. During the latter part of the seven weeks' war in 1866 he was attached to the Prussian army in the field to report on the engineering operations and military telegraphs. Minor services on special missions abroad followed, with duty at the Curragh Camp in Ireland (1867–9). The 22nd company of royal engineers, of which he was in command at Chatham, was as a temporary expedient lent to the post office from 1869 to 1871 to assist in constructing and organising the telegraph service. In May 1870 Webber took the headquarters of the company to London, the rest being distributed about the country. In 1871 the 34th company was added to Webber's command and stationed at Inverness in Scotland. The total strength of the royal engineers at that time employed under the post office was six officers and 153 non-commissioned officers and men. The mileage both over and under ground constructed and rebuilt in 1871 was over 1000 line miles and over 3200 wire miles.

Webber, who was promoted major on 5 July 1872, was director of telegraphs with the southern army in the autumn manœuvres of that year. The headquarters of the 34th company were then moved to Ipswich as the centre of the eastern division (lying east of a line between Lynn and Beachy Head) of the postal telegraphs. In 1874, at Webber's suggestion, the south of England was permanently assigned for the training and exercise of military telegraphists, five officers and 160 non-commissioned officers and men being employed by the post office there. The scheme proved of great value both to the army organisation and the general post office. While employed under the post office he with Colonel Sir Francis Bolton [q. v. Suppl. I] founded in 1871 the Society of Telegraph Engineers (now the Institution of Telegraph Engineers); he was treasurer and a member of council, and in 1882 was president.

Webber's reputation as an expert in all matters affecting military telegraphy was well established when in May 1879 he resumed active military service in the field. Accompanying Sir Garnet Wolseley to South Africa for the Zulu war, he became assistant adjutant and quartermaster-general on the staff of the inspector-general of the lines of communication of the Zulu field force. He was stationed at Landmann's Drift. He afterwards took part in the operations against Sekukuni in the Transvaal. He was mentioned in despatches for his services (27 Dec. 1879), and received the South African medal and clasp.

Promoted regimental lieutenant-colonel on 24 Jan. 1880, Webber on his return home was successively commanding royal engineer of the Cork district in Ireland (July 1880–Feb. 1881), of the Gosport subdistrict of the Portsmouth command (Feb. 1881–July 1883), and of the home district (July 1883–Sept. 1884). Meanwhile he was at Paris in 1881 as British commissioner at the electrical exhibition, and as member of the International Electrical Congress.

In 1882 he accompanied Sir Garnet Wolseley as assistant adjutant and quartermaster-general in the Egyptian campaign, and was in charge of telegraphs. He was present at the battle of Tel-el-Kebir, and was mentioned in despatches, being created a C.B., and receiving the Egyptian medal with clasp, the Khedive's bronze star, and the third class of the Mejidie. Webber, who was promoted to a brevet colonelcy on 24 Jan. 1884, went again to Egypt in September, and served throughout the Nile expedition under Lord Wolseley as assistant adjutant and quartermaster-general for telegraphs. He received another clasp to his Egyptian medal. Coming home in 1885, he retired with the honorary rank of major-general. Thenceforth Webber engaged in electrical pursuits in London. He was at first managing director, and later consulting electric adviser of the Anglo-American Brush Electric Light Corporation, and was thus associated with the early application of electric lighting in London and elsewhere. He was also consulting electric engineer of the City of London Pioneer Company and of the Chelsea Electric Supply Company. He died suddenly at Margate of angina pectoris on 23 Sept. 1904, and was buried at St. Margaret's, Lee, Kent.

Webber was a member of the Royal United Service Institution, of the Institution of Civil Engineers, an original member of the Société Internationale des Electriciens, and a fellow of the Society of Arts. Among many papers, chiefly on military and electrical subjects, were those on 'The Organisation of the Nation for Defence' (United Service Institution, 1903); 'Telegraph Tariffs' (Society of Arts, May 1884); and 'Telegraphs in the Nile Expedition' (Society of Telegraph Engineers).

Webber married: (1) at Brighton, on 28 May 1861, Alice Augusta Gertrude Hanbury Tracy (*d.* 25 Feb. 1877), daughter of Thomas Charles, second Lord Sudeley; (2) at Neuchâtel, Switzerland, on 23 Aug. 1877, Mrs. Sarah Elizabeth Stainbank, born Gunn (*d.* 1907). By his first wife he had three sons, and a daughter who died young. The eldest son, Major Raymond Sudeley Webber, was in the royal Welsh fusiliers.

[War Office Records; Royal Engineers' Records; Electrician, Engineering, and the Royal Engineers' Journal, 1904; The Times, 24 Sept. 1904; Porter's History of the Royal Engineers, 1891.] R. H. V.

WEBSTER, WENTWORTH (1829–1907), Basque scholar and folklorist, born at Uxbridge, Middlesex, in 1829, was eldest son of Charles Webster. Owing to delicate health he had no regular schooling, but he was a diligent boy with a retentive memory, and was a well-informed student when he was admitted commoner of Lincoln College on 15 March 1849. He graduated B.A. in 1852, proceeding M.A. in 1855, and was ordained deacon in 1854 and priest in 1861. After serving as curate at Cloford, Somerset, 1854–8, he was ordered by his medical advisers to settle in the south of France. He lived for some time at Bagnères-de-Bigorre, Hautes-Pyrénées, and at Biarritz, Basses-Pyrénées, taking pupils, among them Henry Butler Clarke [q. v. Suppl. II]. An indefatigable walker, he became familiar with the Basque provinces on both sides of the Pyrénées, and with the Basques themselves, their language, traditions, and poetry. At the same time he grew well versed in French and Spanish, and in all the Pyrenean dialects.

From 1869 to 1881 he was Anglican chaplain at St. Jean-de-Luz, Basses-Pyrénées. In 1881 he settled at Sare, in a house which overlooked the valley of La Rhune. There he mainly devoted himself to study, writing on the Basques and also on church history. He contributed much on Basque and Spanish philology and antiquities to 'Bulletin de la Société des Sciences et des Arts de Bayonne,' 'Bulletin de la Société Ramond de Bagnères-de-Bigorre,' 'Revue de Linguistique,' and 'Bulletin de la Real Academia de la Historia de Madrid.' He was a corresponding member of the Royal Historical Society of Madrid. With all serious students of Basque, whether French, Spanish, English, or German, he corresponded and was generous in the distribution of his stores of information. He wrote many papers on church history and theology in the 'Anglican Church Magazine.' Gladstone awarded him a pension of 150*l.* from the civil list on 16 Jan. 1894. He died at Sare on 2 April 1907, in his seventy-ninth year, and was buried at St. Jean-de-Luz. He married on 17 Oct. 1866, at Camberwell, Surrey, Laura Thekla Knipping, a native of Cleve in Germany. There were four daughters and one son, Erwin Wentworth, fellow of Wadham College, Oxford.

Webster published: 1. 'Basque Legends, collected chiefly in the Labourd,' 1878; reprinted 1879; probably his best and most characteristic work; many of the legends were taken down in Basque from the recitation of people who knew no other language. 2. 'Spain,' London, 1882, a survey of the geography, ethnology, literature, and commerce of the country, founded mainly on information supplied by

Spanish friends of high position. 3. 'De Quelques Travaux sur le basque faits par des étrangers pendant les années 1892–4,' Bayonne, 1894. 4. 'Le Dictionnaire Latin-basque de Pierre d'Urte,' Bayonne, 1895. 5. 'Les Pastorales basques,' Paris, 1899. 6. 'Grammaire Cantabrique-basque de Pierre d'Urte,' 1901. 7. 'Les Loisirs d'un étranger au pays basque,' Châlons-sur-Saône, 1901, a selection from his miscellaneous papers in journals of foreign learned societies. 8. 'Gleanings in Church History, chiefly in Spain and France,' 1903.

[Crockford's Clerical Directory; private information; The Times, 9 April 1907; Guardian, 10 April 1907.] A. C.

WEIR, HARRISON WILLIAM (1824–1906), animal painter and author, born at Lewes, Sussex, on 5 May 1824, was second son of John Weir, successively manager of a Lewes bank and administration clerk in the legacy duty office, Somerset House, by his wife Elizabeth Jenner. A brother, John Jenner Weir, an ornithologist and entomologist, was controller-general of the customs. Weir was sent to school at Albany Academy, Camberwell, but showing an aptitude for drawing, he was withdrawn in 1837, in his fourteenth year, and articled for seven years to George Baxter (1804–1867), the colour-printer. Baxter, also a native of Lewes, had originally started as a designer and engraver on wood there, but he subsequently removed to London, and obtained a patent for his invention of printing in colour in 1835. Baxter employed Weir in every branch of his business, his chief work being that of printing off the plates. Weir soon found his duties uncongenial, and he remained unwillingly to complete his engagement in 1844. While with Baxter he learnt to engrave and draw on wood. His spare time was devoted to drawing and painting, his subjects being chiefly birds and animals. These unaided efforts promised well. In 1842 Herbert Ingram [q. v.] founded the 'Illustrated London News,' and Weir was employed as a draughtsman on wood and an engraver from the first number; he long worked on the paper, and at his death was the last surviving member of the original staff. His painting of a robin, to which he gave the name of 'The Christmas Carol Singer,' was purchased for 150*l.* by Ingram; issued in his paper as a coloured plate, it proved (it is said) the precursor of the modern Christmas supplement. About this time Weir became acquainted with the family of the animal painter, John Frederick Herring [q. v.], whose eldest daughter, Anne, he married, when just of age, in 1845. In this year he exhibited his first picture, 'The Dead Shot,' an oil painting of a wild duck, at the British Institution, and henceforth he was an occasional exhibitor at the Royal Academy, the Suffolk Street, and other galleries. On being elected in 1849 a member of the New Water-colour Society—now the Royal Institute—he exhibited chiefly with that society, showing altogether 100 pictures there.

Meanwhile Weir mainly confined his energy to illustrations for periodicals and books. He worked not only for the 'Illustrated London News' but for the 'Pictorial Times,' the 'Field,' and many other illustrated papers. As a book illustrator few artists were more prolific or popular. Gaining admission to literary society, his intimate friends included Douglas Jerrold, Henry Mayhew, Albert Smith, and Tom Hood the younger, and he was well acquainted with Thackeray and other men of letters.

Weir's drawings of landscape have the finish and smoothness common to contemporary woodcuts, but his animals and birds show a distinctive and individual treatment. Many of his best pictures of animals were designed for the Rev. J. G. Wood's 'Illustrated Natural History' (1853), and he furnished admirable illustrations for 'Three Hundred Æsop's Fables' (1867). In some cases Weir compiled the books which he illustrated. 'The Poetry of Nature' (1867) was an anthology of his own choosing. He was both author and illustrator of 'Every Day in the Country' (1883) and 'Animal Stories, Old and New' (1885). He persistently endeavoured to improve books for children and the poorer classes, and prepared drawing copy-books which were widely used. He did all he could to disseminate his own love of animals. He originated the first cat show in 1872, became a judge of cats, and later wrote and illustrated 'Our Cats and all about them' (1889). Among domestic animals he devoted especially close attention to the care of poultry. As early as 1853 he designed some coloured plates for 'The Poultry Book,' by W. Wingfield and G. W. Johnson, and when that work was re-issued in 1856 he contributed the descriptive text on pigeons and rabbits. An experienced poultry breeder, he for thirty years acted as a judge at the principal poultry and pigeon shows. An exhaustive work from his pen, entitled 'Our Poultry and all about them,' issued in 1903, had occupied him many years, and was illustrated throughout with his own paintings and drawings. His account there of old English game fowl is probably the most valuable extant; but the rest of the work is for the modern expert of greater historic than of practical interest.

Weir was at the same time a practical horticulturist, being much interested in the cultivation of fruit trees, and for many years contributing articles and drawings to gardening periodicals. He was engaged by Messrs. Garrard & Co. to design the cups for Goodwood, Ascot, and other race-meetings for over thirty years. In 1891 he was granted a civil list pension of 100*l*.

Weir's unceasing industry left him no time for travel. He was apparently only once out of England, on a short visit to Andalusia, in Spain. His leisure was divided between his garden and his clubs. After long residence at Lyndhurst Road, Peckham, he built himself a house at Sevenoaks. His latest years were passed at Poplar Hall, Appledore, Kent. There he died on 3 Jan. 1906, and was buried at Sevenoaks. Weir was thrice married: (1) to Anne, eldest daughter of J. F. Herring, in 1845; (2) to Alice, youngest daughter of T. Upjohn, M.R.C.S. (*d.* 1898); and (3) to Eva, daughter of George Gobell of Worthing, Sussex, who survives him. He had two sons, Arthur Herring Weir (1847–1902) and John Gilbert Weir, and two daughters.

[Daily Chronicle, 6 May 1904, 5 Jan. 1906; The Times, 5 Jan. 1906; Nature, 11 Jan. 1906; Field, 6 Jan. 1906; Royal Calendar, Who's Who, 1906; Brit. Mus. Cat.; Men and Women of the Time, 1899; George Baxter (Colour Printer), his Life and Work, by C. T. Courtney Lewis, 1908; personal knowledge; private information.] R. I.

WELDON, WALTER FRANK RAPHAEL (1860–1906), zoologist, born at Highgate, London, on 15 March 1860, was elder son and second of the three children of Walter Weldon [q. v.], journalist and chemist, by his wife Anne Cotton. His father frequently changed his place of residence and the sons received desultory education until 1873, when Weldon went as a boarder to Mr. Watson's school at Caversham near Reading. After spending nearly three years there he matriculated at London University in 1876, and in the autumn of the same year entered University College, London, with the intention of qualifying for a medical career. After a year's study at University College he was transferred to King's College, London, and on 6 April 1878 entered St. John's College, Cambridge, as a commoner, subsequently becoming an exhibitioner in 1879 and a scholar in 1881. At Cambridge Weldon came under the influence of Francis Maitland Balfour [q.v.] and abandoned medical studies for zoology. Though his undergraduate studies were interrupted by ill-health and by the sudden death of his brother Dante in 1881, he succeeded in gaining a first-class in the natural sciences tripos in that year, and in the autumn proceeded for a year's research work to the zoological station at Naples. Returning to Cambridge in Sept. 1882, he became successively demonstrator in zoology (1882–4), fellow of St. John's College (3 Nov. 1884), and university lecturer in invertebrate morphology (1884–91). After his marriage in 1883 he and his wife spent their vacations at such resorts as offered the best opportunities for the study of marine zoology. The most important of their expeditions was to the Bahamas in the autumn of 1886. As soon as the laboratory of the Marine Biological Association at Plymouth was sufficiently advanced, Weldon transferred his vacation work thither, and from 1888 to 1891 he was only in Cambridge for the statutory purposes of keeping residence and fulfilling his duties as university lecturer.

At Plymouth he began the series of original researches which established his reputation. Until 1888 he was engaged on the morphological and embryological studies which seemed to contemporary zoologists to afford the best hope of elucidating the problems of animal evolution. But the more he became acquainted with animals living in their natural environment the more he became convinced that the current methods of laboratory research were incapable of giving an answer to the questions of variation, inheritance, and natural selection that forced themselves on his attention. In 1889, when Galton's recently published work on natural inheritance came into his hands, he perceived that the statistical methods explained and recommended in that book might be extended to the study of animals. He soon undertook a statistical study of the variation of the common shrimp, and after a year's hard work published his results in the 47th volume of the 'Proceedings of the Royal Society,' showing that a number of selected measurements made on several races of shrimps collected from different localities gave frequency distributions closely following the normal or Gaussian curve. In a second paper, 'On Certain Correlated Variations in *Crangon vulgaris*,' published two years later, he calculated the numerical measures of the degree of inter-relation between two organs or characters in the same individual and tabled them for four local races of shrimps. These two papers were the foundation of that branch of zoological study afterwards known by the name of 'biometrics.'

Meanwhile Weldon had been elected a fellow of the Royal Society in May 1890, and at the end of the year succeeded Prof. (Sir) E. Ray Lankester as Jodrell professor of zoology at University College, London. The tenure of the Jodrell chair (1891–9) was a period of intense activity. A brilliant lecturer and endowed with the power of exciting enthusiasm, Weldon soon attracted a large class, and his association with Professor Karl Pearson, who had been independently drawn towards biometrical studies by Galton's work, led to increased energy in the special line of research which he had initiated. In 1894 Weldon became the secretary of a committee of the Royal Society 'for conducting statistical inquiries into the measurable characteristics of plants and animals,' the other members of the committee being F. Galton (chairman), F. Darwin, A. Macalister, R. Meldola, and E. B. Poulton. The committee undertook an ambitious programme which was not fully realised; its most important result was the investigation, undertaken by Weldon and presented to the Royal Society in Nov. 1894 under the title 'An Attempt to measure the Death Rate due to the Selective Destruction of *Carcinus mœnas*.' To this were appended 'Some Remarks on Variation in Animals and Plants,' in which Weldon stated that 'the questions raised by the Darwinian hypothesis are purely statistical, and the statistical method is the only one at present obvious by which that hypothesis can be experimentally checked.' The report showed that an apparently purposeless character in the shore-crabs of Plymouth Sound is correlated with a selective death rate, and it evoked a storm of criticism, which led Weldon to continue his experiments, with the result that he demonstrated that the character in question was connected with the efficient filtration of the water entering the gill-chamber, a matter of great importance in Plymouth Sound, whose waters are rendered turbid by china clay and the sewage discharged into the harbour. These experiments, which were conducted on a large scale and were extremely laborious, formed the subject of Weldon's presidential address to the zoological section of the British Association in 1898.

In addition to these and other exacting lines of research and the ordinary duties of his chair, Weldon took a leading part in the work of the association for promoting a professorial university for London, and his friends, fearing that he was over-straining his energies, hailed with relief his election to the Linacre professorship of comparative anatomy at Oxford in February 1899. But though Oxford afforded opportunities for greater intellectual leisure, Weldon disdained to make use of them. He had on hand numerous exacting projects, and he tried to deal with them all at once. His leisure hours at Oxford were spent in long bicycle rides, during which he studied the fauna of the neighbourhood; his vacations were spent in journeys to various parts of the continent, where he worked at his statistical calculations and collected material for fresh lines of research. He added to his labours by undertaking the co-editorship of 'Biometrika,' a new scientific journal devoted to his special branch of study, and contributed to it twelve separate original and critical papers between 1901 and 1906.

The rediscovery of Mendel's memoirs on plant hybridisation in 1900 drew Weldon into an active controversy which culminated at the meeting of the British Association at Cambridge in 1904. Though Weldon was always critical of what appeared to him to be loose or insufficiently grounded inferences on the part of the Mendelian school, he was by no means unappreciative of the significance of Mendel's work. He would not admit its universal applicability, and even before the meeting at Cambridge he had planned and was engaged on a book (never finished) which was to set forth a determinal theory of inheritance, with a simple Mendelism at one end of the range and blended inheritance at the other. At the close of 1905 his attention was diverted by a paper presented to the Royal Society by Captain C. C. Hurst, on the inheritance of coat colour in horses. Disagreeing with the author's conclusions, Weldon made a minute study of the 'General Studbook' in the autumn of 1905, and in Jan. 1906 he published 'A Note on the Offspring of Thoroughbred Chestnut Mares.' This was his last scientific publication. In the Lent term he was still engaged on the 'Studbook,' and had collected material for a much more copious memoir on inheritance in horses. In the Easter vacation, while he was staying with his wife at an inn at Woolstone, he was attacked by influenza, which on his return to London on 11 April developed into acute pneumonia. He died in a nursing home on 13 April 1906. He was buried at Holywell, Oxford. In addition to the book on inheritance he left behind him a mass of unfinished work which other hands have only partially completed. For this Dictionary he wrote the article on Huxley in the first supplement.

A Weldon memorial prize for the most noteworthy contribution to biometric science was founded at Oxford in 1907, and was first awarded in 1912 to Prof. Karl Pearson, who declined it on the ground that the prize was intended for the encouragement of younger men. The prize was then awarded to Dr. David Heron. A posthumous bust was placed in the Oxford museum.

Weldon married on 13 March 1883 Florence, eldest daughter of William Tebb of Rede Hall, Burstow, Surrey. His wife was his constant companion on his travels, and gave no inconsiderable help to his later scientific researches.

[Obituary notices in Biometrika, vol. v., by Prof. Karl Pearson; in the Proceedings of the Royal Society of London, vol. xxiv., by A. E. Shipley; in the Proceedings of the Linnean Society, 1906, by G. C. Bourne; personal recollections; information supplied by Mrs. Weldon.] G. C. B.

WELLESLEY, Sir GEORGE GREVILLE (1814–1901), admiral, born on 2 Aug. 1814, was third and youngest son of Gerald Valerian Wellesley, D.D. (1770–1848), prebendary of Durham (the youngest brother of the duke of Wellington), by his wife Lady Emily Mary, eldest daughter of Charles Sloane Cadogan, first Earl Cadogan. He entered the navy in 1828, taking the course at the Royal Naval College, Portsmouth. He passed his examination in 1834, and received his commission as lieutenant on 28 April 1838. In Jan. 1839 he was appointed to the flagship in the Mediterranean for disposal, and on 30 March was sent from her to the Castor frigate, in which he served for over two years, ending the commission as first lieutenant. In her he took part in the operations of 1840 on the coast of Syria, including the attacks on Caiffa, Jaffa, Tsour, and St. Jean d'Acre; he was twice gazetted and received the Syrian and Turkish medals with clasp. In November 1841 he was appointed to the Thalia, frigate, going out to the East Indies, and from her was, on 16 April 1842, promoted to commander and appointed to the Childers, brig, which he paid off two years later. On 2 Dec. 1844 he was promoted to captain, and in that rank was first employed in the Daedalus, which he commanded in the Pacific from 1849 to 1853. In February 1855 he was appointed to the Cornwallis, screw 60 gun ship, for the Baltic, and commanded a squadron of the fleet at the bombardment of Sveaborg. He received the Baltic medal, and in February 1856 the C.B. The Cornwallis then went for a year to the North America station, after which Wellesley was for five years in command of the Indian navy. He was promoted to rear-admiral on 3 April 1863, and in June 1865 was appointed admiral superintendent at Portsmouth, and held the post for four years. On resigning it he was appointed, on 30 June 1869, commander-in-chief on the North America and West Indies station, and on 26 July following became vice-admiral. He returned home in September 1870, and from October 1870 to September 1871 was in command of the Channel squadron. In September 1873 he again became commander-in-chief on the North America station, where he remained till his promotion to admiral on 11 Dec. 1875. From November 1877 to August 1879 he was first sea lord in W. H. Smith's board of admiralty. In June 1879 he was awarded a good service pension, and retired on 2 August of the same year. He was raised to the K.C.B. in April 1880, and to the G.C.B. at the Jubilee of 1887. In 1888 be became a commissioner of the Patriotic Fund. He died in London on 6 April 1901.

Wellesley married on 25 Jan. 1853 Elizabeth Doughty, youngest daughter of Robert Lukin. She died on 9 Jan. 1906, leaving a daughter, Olivia Georgiana, wife of Lieut.-col. Sir Henry Trotter, K.C.M.G.

[O'Byrne's Nav. Biog. Dict.; The Times, 8 and 12 April 1901; R.N. List; Burke's Peerage; a photographic portrait was published in Illus. London News, 1901.] L. G. C. L.

WELLS, HENRY TANWORTH (1828–1903), portrait-painter in oils and miniature, born on 12 Dec. 1828 in Marylebone, was only son of Henry Tanworth Wells, merchant, by his wife Charlotte Henman. One sister, Augusta, was an exhibitor at the Royal Academy, and another sister, Sarah, married Henry Hugh Armstead [q. v. Suppl. II]. Educated at Lancing, Wells was apprenticed in 1843 as a lithographic draughtsman to Messrs. Dickinson, with whom he soon, however, began work as a miniature-painter. His studies were continued in the evening at Leigh's school. In 1850 he spent six months at Couture's atelier in Paris. He also joined a society which met every evening in Clipstone Street for drawing and criticism. D. G. Rossetti, C. Keene, J. R. Clayton, F. Smallfield, the brothers E. and G. Dalziel, and G. P. Boyce were fellow members. From his youth Wells devoted himself to portraiture. At first he practised exclusively as a miniature painter, much in the manner of Sir W. Ross, with whom and Robert Thorburn he shared the practice of the time. Between 1846 and 1860 Wells contributed over seventy miniatures, principally of ladies and children, all of which are now in private hands, to the Royal Academy exhibitions. Among these the most noticeable are the Princess Mary of Cambridge, painted in 1853 by command for Queen Victoria, and whole-lengths of the Duchess of Sutherland (as Lady Stafford), Countess Waldegrave, and Mrs. Popham (1860).

Wells's sympathies were mildly attached in the early days of his career to the Pre-Raphaelites, and he counted among his friends many of the fraternity, though his own work remained uninfluenced by them. In December 1857, when in Rome, he married Joanna Mary Boyce, herself a gifted painter and writer for the 'Saturday Review,' and sister of George P. Boyce, the water-colour artist. Her 'Elgiva,' exhibited in the Academy in 1855, was pronounced by Madox Brown to be the work of 'the best hand in the rooms,' and after her premature death in 1861 William Rossetti pronounced her to have been 'the best painter that ever handled a brush with the female hand.' A charming miniature group painted by Wells in 1859–60 of himself standing beside her, riding a donkey, on a single piece of ivory 21 x 15½ inches (now owned by his daughter, Mrs. Hadley), is a fine example of his latest miniature work and perhaps his largest. Another group of himself, his wife, George Boyce, and John Clayton (owned by his elder daughter, Mrs. Street), painted in oils (1861), is the best example of his early work in this medium.

From 1861 Wells, fearing the strain upon his eyesight, abandoned miniature painting, and in that year contributed to Burlington House his first large work in oils, a portrait of Lord Ranelagh, lieutenant-colonel of the south Middlesex volunteers, now at the headquarters of the corps. Within the next decade he painted numerous other volunteers' portraits singly and in groups. Of the latter two are well known: the earlier group, 'Volunteers at the Firing Point,' a large canvas painted in 1866, the year of his election as associate of the Royal Academy, was engraved in mezzotint by Atkinson. This picture, now in the Diploma Gallery, was exchanged for another work 'News and Letters at the Loch Side' (1868), which formerly hung there and now belongs to Mrs. Nicholson at Arisaig House. The later group, 'Earl and Countess Spencer at Wimbledon,' with Lords Ducie, Grosvenor, and Elcho and others, was exhibited in 1868 (now the property of Earl Spencer). These and 'The Queen and her Judges at the Opening of the Royal Courts of Justice' (1887), are among the best of his larger works. In 1870 Wells was elected a full member of the Royal Academy.

Among the many presentation portraits painted by Wells are Hon. Robert Marsham, Warden, for Merton College (1866), the duke of Devonshire for the Iron and Steel Institute (1872), Sir S. J. Gibbons (1873), Lord Mayor, for the Salters' Company, Lord Chancellor Selborne (1874), for the Mercers' Company, Samuel Morley (1874), for the Congregational Memorial Hall, Rt. Hon. W. E. Forster (1875), Sir Lowthian Bell, F.R.S. (1895), for Newcastle-on-Tyne (photogravure by R. Paulussen), and Sir W. Macpherson (1901), for the Calcutta Turf Club. Other celebrities painted were Earl Spencer, K.G. (1867), engraved by S. Cousins, General Sir R. Buller (1889), Sir M. Hicks Beach (1896) the Bishop of Ripon (1897), and the Earl of Pembroke (1898); and among ladies who sat to him were the three daughters of Sir I. Lowthian Bell, exhibited in 1865 as 'Tableau Vivant,' Lady Coleridge, painted in miniature (1891), Miss Ethel Davis (1896), Mrs. Thewlis Johnson (1890), the Hon. Mrs. Sydney Smith (1903), Lady Wyllie (1890), and his daughter, Mrs. Street (1883).

The most popular of Wells's works was, however, a painting of Queen Victoria, as princess, receiving the news of her accession from the archbishop of Canterbury and the Marquess Conyngham, exhibited in 1880 as 'Victoria Regina.' This painting was presented by the artist's daughters to the National Gallery of British Art, and a second version is at Buckingham Palace.

In 1870 Wells succeeded George Richmond, R.A., as limner to Grillion's Club, and in this capacity drew crayon portraits of some fifty of its distinguished members, chiefly political, during the following thirty years. Many of these drawings were exhibited; a few were etched by C. W. Sherborn, and the rest were either engraved by C. Holl, J. Brown, J. Stodart, and W. Roffe, or reproduced by autotype. As a man of business and a strenuous supporter of the constitutional rights and privileges of the Academy, Wells was a valued member of the council, and in the agitation for reform, initiated in August and September 1886 in 'The Times' by Holman Hunt, he was the most vigorous defender of the existing order of affairs. He was nominated by Lord Leighton to act as his deputy on certain occasions during the president's absence abroad through ill-health in 1895. In 1879, at the time of the royal commission, and again in connection with the bill in 1900, he worked hard for the cause of artistic copyright.

Wells contributed, between 1846 and 1903, 287 works to the Royal Academy exhibitions, and, in addition to those already mentioned as being engraved, about forty-five were reproduced in Cassell's 'Royal Academy Pictures' (1891–1903). His portraits are usually signed with his monogram and dated.

Wells died at his residence, Thorpe Lodge, Campden Hill, on 16 Jan. 1903, and was buried at Kensal Green cemetery. He was survived by his two daughters, Alice Joanna (Mrs. A. E. Street) and Joanna Margaret (Mrs. W. Hadley). His son Sidney Boyce died in 1869. His portrait, painted by himself in 1897, and a bust by Sir J. E. Boehm (1888), belong to his elder daughter.

[The Times, 19 Jan. 1903, and other press notices; Athenæum, 24 Jan. 1903; Who's Who, 1903; Men of Mark, 1878; Royal Acad. Catalogues; A. Graves, Royal Acad. Exhibitors, 1906; Royal Acad. Pictures, Cassell and Co., 1891–1903; W. M. Rossetti, Pre-Raphaelite Letters and Diaries, 1900; Grillion's Club portraits; information from Wells's daughters and Mr. A. E. Street.] J. D. M.

WEST, EDWARD WILLIAM (1824–1905), Oriental scholar, born at Pentonville, London, on 2 May 1824, was eldest of twelve children (six sons and six daughters) of William West by his wife Margaret Anderson. His ancestors on the paternal side for three generations had been architects and engineers, or 'builders and mechanics,' as they were called in the eighteenth century. Owing to ill-health he was at first educated at home by his mother, but from his eleventh till his fifteenth year he attended a day school at Pentonville, and in Oct. 1839 entered the engineering department of King's College, London, where he won high honours in 1842. A year later, after a severe illness, he spent a twelvemonth in a locomotive shop at Bromsgrove, in Worcestershire.

His parents had lived in India for some years before their marriage, the father at Bombay, the mother in Calcutta. In 1844 West went out to Bombay, where he arrived on 6 June, to superintend a large establishment of cotton presses there. He retained the post for five years. Before leaving England he studied Hindustani for a few weeks under Professor Duncan Forbes of King's College, London, and learned to read the Perso-Arabic characters as well as the Nāgarī script, in which the Sanskrit language of India is commonly written. Otherwise his knowledge of Oriental languages was self-taught. His method was to study direct from grammars, dictionaries, texts, and manuscripts, supplemented by occasional conversations with native Indians. He soon interested himself in Indian religions, especially that of the Parsis, the ancient faith of Zoroaster. A visit to the Indian cave-temples at Elephanta, near Bombay, in March 1846, drew his attention to Hindu antiquities; and a vacation tour made in the following year, March 1847, with the Rev. John Wilson and a party, including Arthur West, his brother, to the Island of Salsette, north of Bombay, enabled him to visit the Kanheri caves, and inspired him with a wish to copy the inscriptions carved there in Pālī, the sacred Buddhist language. In January 1850 West, after resigning his office of superintendent of the cotton presses, revisited the Kanheri caves; but he spent the next year in England, and it was not until 1852 that he had opportunities of frequent inspection. In that year he became civil engineer, and later was chief engineer, of the Great Indian Peninsula railway, which ran through Bombay presidency.

Early in 1860 West laid before the Bombay Asiatic Society his copies of the Buddhist cave-records of Kanheri, and the results were published in 1861 in the society's 'Journal.' Copies of the inscriptions of the Nasik caves were made in a similar manner, and were published in 1862; these were followed later by transcripts of the Kura cave inscriptions and of other Buddhist sculptured records. As early as 1851 he had begun from the Buddhist scriptural text, the 'Mahāwānso,' a glossary of the Pālī language in which all the cave records were written; but he afterwards gave up this lexicographical design and ultimately withdrew from Pālī study, in the development of which he did yeoman service.

West's lasting renown rests upon his Iranian labours. Almost as soon as he reached India, occasional conversations with the Parsi manager of the cotton presses drew his attention to the Zoroastrian religion. But Martin Haug's 'Essays on the Sacred Language, Writings, and Religion of the Parsis' (Bombay, 1862) chiefly stimulated his interest, which was confirmed by a personal acquaintance with the author which he made at Poona in 1866. West began work on a copy of the Avesta, or the scriptures of Zoroaster, with a Gujarātī translation of the Avesta and Dhanjibhai Framji's 'Pahlavi Grammar' (1855). The rest of his life was devoted in co-operation with Haug to the study of Pahlavi, the difficult language and literature of Sasanian Persia. Both he and Haug returned to Europe in 1866, when Haug was appointed in 1867 to the professorship of Sanskrit and comparative philology at the University of Munich. West went to Munich for six years (1867–73) spending his time on the publication with translation of the Pahlavi texts of Zoroastrianism. On 17 June 1871 the University of Munich bestowed upon him the honorary degree of doctor of philosophy. After a year in England (1873–4) West revisited India (1874–6) in order to procure manuscripts of the important Pahlavi books 'Dēnkarṭ' and 'Dāṭistan-i Dēnīk'; he paid a last visit to the Kanheri caves on 6 Feb. 1875.

In 1876 he resumed residence in Munich, but soon settled finally in England, first at Maidenhead and afterwards at Watford. His main occupation was a translation of a series of Pahlavi texts for Max Müller's 'Sacred Books of the East.' His services to Oriental scholarship, especially in Pahlavi, were widely recognised. The Bavarian Academy of Sciences made him in 1887 a corresponding member. From 1884 to 1901 he was a member of the Royal Asiatic Society of Great Britain and Ireland; and on 6 July 1901 he was presented with the society's gold medal, personally handed to him with an address by the Prince of Wales (afterwards King Edward VII). The American Oriental Society also conferred upon him honorary membership (16 April 1899). West was ready in personal aid to scholars who corresponded with him. With characteristic modesty he acknowledged, shortly before his death, that 'although his studies and researches had always been undertaken for the sake of amusement and curiosity, they could hardly be considered as mere waste of time.'

He died in his eighty-first year at Watford, on 4 Feb. 1905. He was survived by his wife Sarah Margaret Barclay, and by an only son, Max, an artist.

West's principal publications relating to Pahlavi are: 1. 'Book of the Mainyō-i Khard, Pāzand, Sanskrit, and English, with a Glossary,' Stuttgart and London, 1871. 2. 'Book of Ardā-Vīrāf, Pahlavi and English' (edited and translated in collaboration with Hoshangji and Haug), Bombay and London, 1872. 3. 'Glossary and Index to the same' (with Haug), Bombay and London, 1872. 4. 'Shikand-gūmānīk Vijār' (with Hoshangji), Bombay, 1887. 5. Five volumes of translations from Pahlavi texts, in Max Müller's 'Sacred Books of the East,' v. xviii. xxiv. xxxvii. xlvii., Oxford, 1880–1897. 6. A valuable monograph, 'Pahlavi Literature,' in Geiger and Kuhn's 'Grundriss der iranischen Philologie,' Strassburg, 1897.

Besides the papers already cited West read a technical paper on 'Ten-ton Cranes' before the Bombay Mechanics' Institute in March 1857, and contributed numerous articles, reviews, and communications on Oriental subjects to the 'Journal of the Royal Asiatic Society of Great Britain and Ireland' (1869–1900); to the 'Academy' (1874–1900); to the 'Indian Antiquary' (1880–2); to 'Le Muséon' (1882–7); to 'Sitzungsberichte d. Akad. Wiss. zu München' (1888, p. 399 seq.); and to 'Epigraphia Indica' (iv. no. 21, p. 174 seq.).

[Correspondence and personal memoranda received during West's lifetime; a notice by L. C. Casartelli, Roman catholic bishop of Salford, in the Manchester Guardian, 13 March 1905.] A. V. W. J.

WEST, Sir LIONEL SACKVILLE-, second Baron Sackville (1827–1908), diplomatist. [See Sackville-West.]

WESTALL, WILLIAM [BURY] (1834–1903), novelist and journalist, born on 7 Feb. 1834 at White Ash, near Blackburn, in Lancashire, was eldest son of John Westall, a cotton spinner of White Ash, by his wife Ann, daughter of James Bury Entwistle. Richard Westall the painter [q. v.] belonged to the same stock. After being educated at the Liverpool high school, Westall engaged in his father's cotton-spinning business. But about 1870 he retired, lived much abroad, and devoted himself to journalism. While at Dresden he sent articles to 'The Times' and 'Spectator,' and moving to Geneva in 1874 acted as foreign correspondent both to 'The Times' and the 'Daily News,' besides editing the 'Swiss Times,' of which he became part proprietor. His first book, 'Tales and Traditions of Saxony and Lusatia,' appeared in 1877, but his earliest success in fiction, 'The Old Factory,' a story of Lancashire life with strong local colouring, was issued in 1881. His later novel, 'Her Two Millions' (1897), amusingly depicts the conditions of Anglo-continental journalism in Geneva, where Westall became acquainted with Russian revolutionaries, particularly with Prince Kropotkin and with S. Stepniak (i.e. Sergyei Mikhailowitch Kravchinsky). He persuaded the latter to settle in London, and collaborated with him in translations of contemporary Russian literature, and of Stepniak's book on the aims of reform, 'Russia under the Czars' (1885). Westall was long a prolific writer of novels, drawing freely on his experiences alike in Lancashire and on the continent and further afield. He extended his travels to North and South America and to the West Indies, but finally returned to England, making his residence in Worthing.

He died at Heathfield, Sussex, on 9 Sept. 1903, and was buried there. He had just completed his latest novel, 'Dr. Wynne's Revenge.'

Westall was married twice: (1) on 13 March 1855 to Ellen Ann, second daughter of Christopher Wood of Silverdale, Lancashire, by whom he had two sons and one daughter; and (2) at Neuchâtel on 2 Aug. 1863, to her elder sister Alicia, by whom he had two sons and two daughters.

A portrait—a bad likeness—belongs to Westall's daughter, Mrs. Chadwick, Clyde House, Heaton Chapel. A large photograph hangs in the Whitefriars Club.

Westall's numerous novels, which are of old-fashioned type, mainly dependent on incident and description, comprise, besides those mentioned: 1. 'Larry Lohengrin,' 1881 (another edition, 'John Brown and Larry Lohengrin,' 1889). 2. 'The Phantom City,' 1886. 3. 'A Fair Crusader,' 1888. 4. 'Roy of Roy's Court,' 1892. 5. 'The Witch's Curse,' 1893. 6. 'As a Man sows,' 1894. 7. 'Sons of Belial,' 1895. 8. 'With the Red Eagle,' 1897. 9. 'Don or Devil,' 1901. 10. 'The Old Bank,' 1902.

[The Times, 12 Sept. 1903; T. P.'s Weekly, 18 Sept. 1903; Who's Who, 1903; Brit. Mus. Cat.; private information.]

E. S. H-r.

WESTCOTT, BROOKE FOSS (1825–1901), bishop of Durham, born at Birmingham on 12 Jan. 1825, was the only surviving son of Frederick Brooke Westcott, lecturer on botany at Sydenham College Medical School, Birmingham, and hon. sec. of the Birmingham Horticultural Society, by his wife Sarah, daughter of W. Armitage, a Birmingham manufacturer. His paternal great-grandfather, whose Christian names he bore, was a member of the East India Company's Madras establishment and was employed by the company on some important missions. From 1837 to 1844, while residing at home, the future bishop attended King Edward VI's School in Birmingham under James Prince Lee [q. v.], who, while he insisted on accuracy of scholarship and the precise value of words, used the classics to stimulate broad historical and human interests and love of literature, and gave suggestive theological teaching. From boyhood Westcott showed keenness in the pursuit of knowledge, aptitude for classical studies, a religious and thoughtful disposition, interest in current social industrial movements, and a predilection for drawing and music. Music he did not cultivate to any great extent in after-years, but through life he found a resource in sketching.

In October 1844 he went up to Trinity College, Cambridge. During his undergraduate career his mind and character developed on the same lines as at school. In 1846 he obtained the Battie University scholarship, and was awarded the medal for a Greek ode in that and the following year, and the members' prize for a Latin essay in 1847. At the same time he read widely. In his walks he studied botany and geology, as well as the architecture of village churches. His closest friends were scholars of Trinity of his year, all of whom, like himself, became fellows; they included C. B. Scott, afterwards headmaster of Westminster school, John Llewelyn Davies, and D. J. Vaughan [q. v. Suppl. II]; another companion was Alfred Barry [q. v. Suppl. II], afterwards bishop of Sydney. Two other friends of the same year were J. E. B. Mayor [q. v. Suppl. II] of St. John's, afterwards professor of Latin, and George Howson (*d.* 1852) of Christ's (younger brother of J. S. Howson [q. v.], afterwards dean of Chester). The young men discussed varied topics, literary, artistic, philosophical, and theological, including the Oxford Movement, which reached a crisis in 1845 through the secession of J. H. Newman to Rome. Westcott liked Keble's poetry, and was attracted by the insistence of the Tractarians on the idea of the corporate life of the church and on the importance of self-discipline, but he was repelled by their dogmatism. In many respects he felt more in sympathy with the views of Arnold, Hampden, and Stanley.

He graduated B.A. as 24th wrangler in January 1848, his friend C. B. Scott being two places above him. He then went in for the classical tripos, in which he was bracketed with Scott as first in the first class. In the competition for the chancellor's medals Scott was first and Westcott second. Both were elected fellows of Trinity in 1849. For the three and a half years after his tripos examinations Westcott took private pupils, and threw himself into this work with great zeal. Among his pupils, with many of whom he formed close friendships, were J. B. Lightfoot [q. v.] and E. W. Benson [q. v. Suppl. I], who had come up to Trinity subsequently to himself from King Edward VI's School, Birmingham, and F. J. A. Hort [q. v. Suppl. I]. Outside his teaching work he interested himself in forming with friends a society for investigating alleged supernatural appearances and effects — an anticipation of the 'Psychical Society.' But he soon seems to have concluded that such investigations could lead to no satisfactory or useful result. He found time for some theological reading, and in 1850 obtained the Norrisian prize for an essay 'On the Alleged Historical Contradictions of the Gospels,' and published it in 1851, under the title 'The Elements of the Gospel Harmony.' He was ordained deacon on Trinity Sunday 1851, his fellowship being taken as a title, and priest on the 21st of the following December, in both cases by his old headmaster, Prince Lee, who had now become bishop of Manchester. He had already decided to leave Cambridge, and in Jan. 1852 accepted a post at Harrow. In December of the same year he married. His work at Harrow was to assist Dr. Vaughan, the headmaster, in correcting the sixth-form composition, and occasionally to take the form for him. For some time, too, he had charge of a small boarding-house, and along with it a pupil-room of boys drawn mainly from the headmaster's house and the home-boarders. At the end of 1863 he succeeded to a large boarding-house. For the work of an ordinary form-master he was not well fitted. He did not understand the ordinary boy, and he had some difficulty in maintaining discipline. But on individual boys, of minds and characters more or less responsive to his, he made a deep impression. Happily both in his small house and his large house there were an unusual number of boys of promise. Meanwhile the school —masters and boys alike—increasingly, as time went on, looked up to him as a man of great and varied learning.

By using every spare hour during the school terms and the greater part of the holidays for study and writing, Westcott succeeded in producing, while at Harrow, some of his best-known books and making a wide reputation as a biblical critic and theologian. In 1855 appeared his 'General Survey of the History of the Canon of the New Testament during the First Four Centuries'; in 1859 a course of four sermons preached before the University of Cambridge on 'Characteristics of the Gospel Miracles'; in 1860 his 'Introduction to the Study of the Gospels,' an enlargement of his early essay entitled 'The Elements of the Gospel Harmony'; in 1864 'The Bible in the Church,' a popular account of the reception of the Old Testament in the Jewish, and of both Old and New in the Christian, Church; in 1866 the 'Gospel of the Resurrection,' an essay in which he gave expression to some of his most characteristic thoughts on the Christian faith and its relation to reason and human life; in 1868, 'A General View of the History of the English Bible,' in which he threw light on many points which had commonly been misunderstood (3rd edit. revised by W. Aldis Wright, 1905). He also wrote many articles for 'Smith's Dictionary of the Bible,' of which the first volume appeared in 1860 and the second and third in 1863, and he was beginning to work at the Johannine writings and to collaborate with Hort in the preparation of a critical text of the New Testament In 1866 and 1867 he published three articles in the 'Contemporary Review' on 'The Myths of Plato,' 'The Dramatist as Prophet: Æschylus,' and 'Euripides as a Religious Teacher.' These were republished many years later in his 'Essays in the History of Religious Thought in the West' (1891). Further during his last two or three years at Harrow he gave a good deal of time to the study of Robert Browning's poems, and of the works of Comte, and in 1867 published an article in the 'Contemporary Review' on 'Aspects of Positivism in Relation to Christianity,' which was republished as an Appendix to the 3rd edit. of his 'Gospel of the Resurrection.'

In the autumn of 1868, Dr. Magee, who

had just been consecrated to the see of Peterborough, made Westcott one of his examining chaplains, and in 1869 appointed him to a residentiary canonry. The resignation of his mastership and large house at Harrow involved pecuniary sacrifice, but for two or three years past he had found school-work very wearing, and the canonry promised more leisure for literary work. Soon after leaving Harrow, however, Cambridge rather than Peterborough became his headquarters. In September 1870 the regius professorship of divinity at Cambridge became vacant through the resignation of Dr. Jeremie [q. v.]. Lightfoot, then Hulsean professor, refused to stand, and prevailed upon Westcott to do so, and used his great influence to secure the latter's election, which took place on 1 Nov. He retained his canonry till May 1883, but he resided at Peterborough only for three months in each long vacation.

At Peterborough Westcott taught himself so to use his naturally weak voice as to make himself audible in a large building. In the architecture and history of the cathedral he took deep interest. Like his friend Benson, he cherished the hope that ancient ideals might be so adapted to modern conditions as to make the cathedrals of England a more potent influence for good in the life of the church and nation than they had long been. He wrote two articles on the subject in 'Macmillan's Magazine'; and an essay in the volume on Cathedrals edited by Dean Howson. He strove in various ways to increase the usefulness of his own cathedral both to the city and diocese. He gave courses of expositions and addresses at other than the usual times of service. He also took an active interest both in the regular choir and in the formation of a voluntary choir to assist at special services in the nave; and he arranged the Paragraph Psalter with a view to the rendering of the Psalms in a manner that would better bring out their meaning. During his summers at Peterborough some able young Oxford graduates came to read theology under his guidance; one of them was Henry Scott Holland.

When Westcott resumed as professor his connection with Cambridge, active change was in progress in the university. The abolition of tests finally passed in 1871 was a challenge to earnest churchmen to strive to guard in new ways the religious influences which they felt to be most precious. In his 'Religious Office of the Universities,' a volume of sermons and papers published in 1873, Westcott showed what a source of far-reaching influence the university ought in his view to be, notwithstanding its changed relation to the church.

The arrangements for the encouragement of theological studies stood in great need of improvement, and in the movement for reform Westcott, as regius professor, took the lead. From time to time the lectures of particular professors had excited interest. But there was no concerted action among the professors or the colleges—in which indeed few theological lectures of much value were given—with a view to covering different branches of the subject. At the beginning of the Michaelmas term of 1871 the divinity professors for the first time issued a joint programme of their lectures. In 1871 it fell to the new regius professor to have a hand in framing fresh regulations for the B.D. and D.D. degrees, and the principal share in carrying them into effect and in raising the standard of attainment. He also bore a considerable part in drawing up the scheme for an honours examination in theology, held for the first time in 1874, by which the B.A. degree could be obtained and which was of wider scope than the existing theological examination, designed chiefly for candidates for orders. Again, he succeeded in establishing in 1873 the preliminary examination for holy orders, although it was not an examination under the management of the university.

Far more important than any administrative measures was the influence of his teaching and his character. His full courses for the first three years were on periods of, or topics chosen from, early church history. In that subject he was personally interested, and there was as yet no professor of ecclesiastical history in the university, and no prominent lecturer engaged in teaching it in any of the colleges. From 1874–9 his principal courses were on Christian doctrine; subsequent themes were a book, or selected passages, of the New Testament. He also held once a week from the first a more informal evening class, in which for many years he commented on the Johannine writings. Somewhat excessive condensation in expression made him at times difficult to follow. He dwelt by preference on the widest aspects of truth, which are the most difficult to grasp. But his lectures gave evidence of painstaking inquiry after facts, careful analysis, and thoroughness in investigating the significations of words. Above all he succeeded in communicating to many hearers somewhat of his own sense of the deep spiritual meaning of the scriptures, and his broad sympathy with various forms of Christian faith and hope, and with the best endeavours of pre-Christian times.

His counsel was often privately asked on questions of belief, or on the choice of a sphere of work. Younger members of the university turned to him for aid in various religious efforts. To his inspiration and guidance was largely due the inception of the Cambridge Mission to Delhi, which continues to bear the impress of his aims and spirit. So, too, with a view that men who were looking forward to be parochial clergy should receive more help at the university in preparing for their future work, the Cambridge Clergy Training School was founded, with Westcott as president; he delivered courses of devotional addresses to the members, and they regularly attended his classes on Christian doctrine. The school's subsequent position largely reflects Westcott's early interest in it. Its present home has received the name of Westcott House.

At public meetings in Cambridge he advocated foreign missions and other religious or social objects with inspiring eloquence. In general university business he was also active. From 1872 to 1876 and 1878 to 1882 he was a member of the council of the senate, the chief administrative body in the university, and he served on important syndicates. Like Lightfoot he urged on the senate the plan of university extension originated by (Prof.) James Stuart, for establishing, under the management of a university syndicate, systematic courses of lectures and classes in populous centres.

In May 1883 he resigned his examining chaplaincy at Peterborough. To his surprise Bishop Magee thereupon requested him to resign his canonry. Next month (June) he became examining chaplain to his old friend, Dr. Benson, newly appointed archbishop of Canterbury; and in October he received through Gladstone a canonry at Westminster. Gladstone had already sounded him as to his willingness to accept the deanery of Exeter, and in 1885 the liberal prime minister offered that of Lincoln, while in 1889 Lord Salisbury offered him that of Norwich. But he felt that so long as his strength was equal to his work at Cambridge he ought not to give it up for such a post.

He felt deeply the responsibility of preaching in the Abbey; and its historic associations powerfully appealed to him. He looked forward to settling altogether at Westminster on retiring from his professorship. During his months of residence there he took part in several public movements, and joined in an influential protest by members of various Christian bodies against the immense expenditure of the nations of Europe on armaments, and in a plea for the settlement of international differences by arbitration.

Though no considerable work appeared from his pen during the first ten years of the tenure of his professorship, he published various sermons, essays, and addresses and the articles on the Alexandrian teachers, 'Clement,' 'Demetrius,' and 'Dionysius,' in the 'Dictionary of Christian Biography' (vol. i. 1877). His literary energy was mainly absorbed by the preparation, in conjunction with Hort, of a critical text of the New Testament in Greek. This, the fruit of twenty-eight years' toil, was published in May 1881 (2 vols.; new edit. 1885). In 1870 he had been appointed a member of the committee for the revision of the English translation of the New Testament. The revised version was published in 1881, a few days after Westcott and Hort's Greek text. He was besides still at work upon the Johannine writings. His commentary upon the 'Gospel according to St. John' appeared in the 'Speaker's Commentary' in 1882, that on the 'Epistles of St. John' in 1883. Thereupon he devoted himself to the 'Epistle to the Hebrews,' and published his Commentary upon it in 1889.

Origen and his place in the history of Christian thought was a subject which peculiarly attracted him. He delivered two lectures on it at Edinburgh in 1877, wrote in the 'Contemporary Review' in 1878 on 'Origen and the Beginnings of Religious Philosophy' (see *Religious Thought in the West*, 1891), and contributed a masterly article on Origen to the 'Dictionary of Christian Biography' (vol. iv. 1889). Another favourite theme was 'Benjamin Whichcote,' 'father of the Cambridge Platonists' (see *Religious Thought* and BARRY'S *Masters of English Theology*). In 1881 he was appointed a member of the ecclesiastical courts commission, for which he did historical work of another kind. Sermons and addresses also continued to appear singly or in volumes, among them 'Christus Consummator' (1886) and 'Social Aspects of Christianity' (1887), two volumes of sermons preached at Westminster. The latter was his earliest treatment with some fulness of a subject in which he always took the deepest interest. In 'The Victory of the Cross,' sermons preached in Hereford Cathedral in 1888, he defined his views on the doctrine of the Atonement.

On 21 May 1882 Westcott was elected fellow of King's College, Cambridge. The degree of D.C.L. was conferred on him at Oxford in 1881; and that of D.D. (honorary) at the Tercentenary of Edinburgh University in 1884. He was made hon. D.D. of Dublin in 1888. Three months after the death of his friend Lightfoot the bishopric of Durham was offered to Westcott, on 6 March 1890. He was in his sixty-sixth year; he was wanting in some of the practical qualities that were conspicuous in Lightfoot; but it was certain that he would form a great conception of what he ought to attempt to do, and would strive to fulfil it with an enthusiasm which age had not abated. For himself, when his duty to accept the post became clear, he saw an unique opportunity for labouring, 'at the end of life,' more effectively than before for objects about which he had always felt deep concern, especially the fulfilment by the Church of her mission in relation to human society. He was consecrated in Westminster Abbey on 1 May 1890. On leaving Cambridge he was elected honorary fellow of both King's and Trinity Colleges, and the University of Durham made him hon. D.D. on settling in his diocese.

In a first letter to his clergy of the diocese, which he addressed to them as soon as he had been duly elected, he undertook 'to face in the light of the Christian faith some of the gravest problems of social and national life.' Very soon, with a view to furthering the solution of difficult social and economic problems and the removal of class-prejudices, he brought together for conferences at Auckland Castle employers of labour, secretaries of trade-unions, leading co-operators, men who had taken a prominent part in the administration of the poor laws or in municipal life. In the choice of the representatives Westcott found in Canon W. M. Ede, rector of Gateshead (now dean of Worcester), a valuable adviser. The men met at dinner in the evening for friendly intercourse, and after spending the night under the Bishop's roof, engaged the next morning in a formal discussion of some appointed question, when the bishop presided and opened the proceedings with a short and pertinent address. These conferences prepared the way for the part which the bishop was able to play in the settlement of the great strike which took place in the Durham coal trade and lasted from 9 March to 1 June 1892. For many weeks Westcott watched anxiously for a moment at which he could prudently intervene. Then he addressed an invitation to the representatives of the miners and of the owners to meet at Auckland Castle, which was accepted by both sides. The owners finally consented to reopen the pits without insisting on the full reduction that they had declared to be necessary, stating that they did so in consequence of the appeal which the Bishop had made to them 'not on the ground of any judgment on his part of the reasonableness or otherwise of their claim, but solely on the ground of consideration and of the impoverished condition of the men and of the generally prevailing distress.' The bishop also assisted in procuring the establishment of boards of conciliation in the county for dealing with industrial differences. At the same time he warmly supported movements for providing homes for aged miners, and better dwellings for the miners. He frequently addressed large bodies of workpeople, not merely at services specially arranged for them, such as an annual miners' service in Durham Cathedral, but at their own meetings. At various times he spoke to the members of co-operative societies, and in 1894 he addressed the great concourse at the Northumberland Miners' Gala. In many previous years this gathering had been addressed by eminent politicians, as well as by labour-leaders, but the invitation to a church dignitary was something new, and was a remarkable proof of the place that Westcott had won in the esteem of the pitmen. Before such audiences he held up high ideals of duty and human brotherhood; though he never condescended to partisan advocacy of their cause, they felt his enthusiasm and his strong sympathy. He used on these occasions few notes, and spoke with a greater eloquence and effect than in delivering sermons and addresses which were carefully written but were sometimes difficult to follow. The bishop's influence in labour matters is in some respects unique in the history of the English episcopate. (For Westcott's treatment of labour problems and for the impression which he made upon the miners, see especially the very interesting appreciation by Mr. Thomas Burt, M.P., in the *Life*, ii. 733 seq.)

In his more normal episcopal work his relations with his younger clergy were especially noteworthy. He continued Lightfoot's plan of having six or eight candidates for orders to read for a year or so at Auckland Castle. Once a week he lectured to them; for another hour also in each week he presided when one of the students read a short paper, which was then discussed. These 'sons of the house,' as they were called, present and past, including those who had been there in Lightfoot's time, assembled once a year at the Castle. Many of the junior clergy placed themselves in Westcott's hands to decide for them individually as their bishop what their work should be, whether in the church at home or abroad. His old interest in foreign missions never diminished, and thirty-six men in orders went from the diocese during his episcopate 'with the bishop's direct mission or glad approval' to foreign or colonial service.

In his charges, addresses at diocesan conferences, and the like the bishop did not dwell on controversial questions, but on fundamental truths and their application to the common life of the church. He did not collect large sums of money for church-building or church-work; he was satisfied with the organisation of the diocese as he found it. He was preoccupied with ideas which were not always congenial to business men, and he was not invariably a good judge of men's capabilities and characters. Yet the diocese acknowledged the influence of his saintliness, of his devotion to duty, and to some extent of his teaching.

While unassuming in demeanour and in the conduct of his household, he had a keen sense of the respect due to his office. He delighted in the historic associations of Auckland Castle, where he constantly entertained workpeople and church-workers. He was chary of undertaking work outside his diocese, but he presided at short notice at the Church Congress at Hull, owing to the illness of W. D. Maclagan, archbishop of York, and read a paper on 'Socialism.' In 1893 he was a chief speaker at the demonstration in the Albert Hall against the Welsh Church suspensory bill; and preached before the British Medical Association at Newcastle, and the Church Congress at Birmingham. In 1895 he delivered the annual sermon in London before the Church Missionary Society, and in 1901 the sermon before the York convocation. Of the Christian Social Union, which was formed in 1889 mainly under Oxford auspices, he was first president, and he held the office till his death, giving an address at each annual meeting. He continued to aid the cause of peace and international arbitration. Yet he supported the Boer war when it had become evident that the Boers were striving for supremacy in South Africa.

His literary work, although limited by the calls of his episcopate, did not cease. In the first two years he put into shape the notes of his Cambridge lectures on Christian doctrine, and published them under the title 'The Gospel of Life' (1892). During his summer holidays also up to the end he worked at a commentary on the Epistle to the Ephesians, and the portion of it that he left was edited and published after his death. For the rest, he composed little save sermons and addresses; but these cost him no small effort, for he never had a facile pen. Many of them he collected and published in such volumes as 'The Incarnation and Common Life' (1893), 'Christian Aspects of Life' (1897), and 'Lessons from Work' (1901). In 1898, when dedicating a memorial to Christina Rossetti in Christ Church, Woburn Square, he gave a careful and sympathetic appreciation of her character and poetry.

On 28 May 1901 his wife died; but in the weeks following this bereavement the bishop fulfilled his public engagements. He preached with great apparent vigour at the miners' service in Durham Cathedral on Saturday, 20 July. But his strength was giving way, and he died on 27 July. He was buried beside his wife in the chapel of Auckland Castle. It was his express wish that there should be no subscription for a memorial to him.

A lifelike portrait of Westcott, painted in 1889 by Sir W. B. Richmond, is now in the Fitzwilliam Museum, Cambridge. The artist wrote of his 'countenance so mobile, so flashing, so tender and yet so strong.' His old friend Llewelyn Davies recalled that as an undergraduate 'he had the intensity which was always noticed in him, rather feminine than robust, ready at any moment to lighten into vivid looks and utterance.' His figure was spare and rather below middle height; his movements were rapid and energetic.

Westcott married in 1852 Sarah Louisa Mary, elder daughter of Thomas Whithard of Kingsdown, Bristol, the sister of an old schoolfellow. He had seven sons and three daughters. The eldest son, Frederick Brooke, senior classic in 1881, is archdeacon of Norwich. Five other sons were ordained, four of whom became missionaries to India. The youngest of these died there; two (Foss and George Herbert) are now bishops of Nagpur and Lucknow respectively.

Westcott's life is remarkable for its many-sided activity and the extraordinary amount of achievement. On several of the subjects of biblical criticism and religious thought on which Westcott wrote inquiry and debate have since continued in Germany, and have become more or less active in England, and the position of some of the questions has consequently changed. Notably is this the case with the problems of the origin of the synoptic gospels and of the authorship of the fourth gospel; the former is discussed by Westcott in his 'Introduction to the Study of the Gospels,' and the latter both in that work and in the 'Prolegomena' to his 'Commentary on St. John's Gospel.' On the other hand, in his work on the 'Canon of the New Testament' he contends in the main for views which have now come to be widely accepted, and this work is probably still for English students the most serviceable 'survey of the history' of the reception of the books of the New Testament in the Church. His treatment of all these subjects represented in England a great advance at the time when he wrote both in knowledge and in the candid examination of opinions opposed to the traditional ones.

In the field of textual criticism the appearance of 'Westcott and Hort's Greek Testament' was admitted, on the Continent as well as in England, to have been epoch-making. But Westcott has perhaps hardly had his due share of the credit owing to the fact that the exposition of the principles on which the text had been made was left to Hort, probably because the latter had fewer engagements. But these principles and the determination thereby of each individual reading were arrived at through the independent investigations of the two scholars, followed by discussion between them. Anyone knowing the two men would hesitate to say that the contribution of either of them to the result thus obtained was greater than that of the other.

The value of Westcott's work as a commentator lies especially in the aid he affords towards an understanding of the profound teaching of the Johannine writings, and of the Epistle to the Hebrews (1889; 3rd edit. 1903). It may be held that he is sometimes too subtle in his interpretations; but through spiritual sympathy and deep meditation he has often penetrated far into the real meaning of the text. His commentaries also contain many careful discussions of the usages of important words or phrases. With his 'Commentary on the Epistles of St. John' (1883) he published three important essays on 'The Church and the World' (an examination of the relations of Christianity and the Roman Empire), 'The Gospel of Creation,' and 'The Relation of Christianity to Art.' The last is included in 'Religious Thought in the West' (1891). Westcott's leading ideas on the final problems of existence may be best gathered from his 'Gospel of the Resurrection' (1866; 7th edit. 1891) and 'Gospel of Life' (1892). He was perhaps too apt to enunciate propositions of wide import, which in his view corresponded with the constitution of man's being, without discussing with sufficient fulness the means of their verification. But no one can fail to be impressed by his conception of the task of theology and his conviction that it is the duty of the Christian theologian to take account of knowledge of all kinds and of all the religious aspirations of mankind. A strong resemblance has often been noticed between his teaching and that of F. D. Maurice. Westcott, however, though younger by twenty years, had thought out his own position independently, and in order that he might do so had for the most part refrained, as he more than once said, from reading Maurice's works. In 1884, after reading the latter's 'Life and Letters,' he wrote to Llewelyn Davies, 'I never knew before how deep my sympathy is with most of his characteristic thoughts.' Westcott by his writings certainly helped no little to extend the influence of these thoughts, which were characteristic of them both.

[Arthur Westcott's Life and Letters of the bishop, his father, 1903, 2 vols., where a complete bibliography will be found; Hort's Life of F. J. A. Hort; A. C. Benson's Life of Archbishop Benson, 1899; A. C. Benson's The Leaves of the Tree, 1901, pp. 21–8; H. Scott Holland's B. F. Westcott, 1910; The Times, 29 July 1901; Guardian, 7 Aug. 1901 (Bishop Westcott as a Diocesan); In Memoriam in Cambridge Review, 17 Oct. 1901; personal knowledge and inquiry.] V. H. S.

WESTLAND, Sir JAMES (1842–1903), Anglo-Indian financier, eldest of eight children of James Westland, manager of Aberdeen Town and County Bank, Dundee, by his wife Agnes Monro, was born in Dundee on 14 Nov. 1842. The second of his four brothers, William, also had a financial career in India, becoming deputy secretary and treasurer of the Bank of Bengal. James was educated in Aberdeen, at first privately under Dr. Tulloch (1847–53), then at the grammar school

(1853–6), and at the gymnasium (1856–7). In 1857 he entered Marischal College, and after some study at a school at Wimbledon passed first into Woolwich in January 1861. But he abandoned the army, and in July 1861 he headed the competitive examination for the Indian civil service, the second place being taken by (Sir) Alexander Mackenzie [q. v. Suppl. II].

Arriving in Calcutta in October 1862, he was assistant magistrate and collector in various Bengal districts until July 1866, when he served as collector, first of Nuddea and afterwards of Jessore. Of Jessore he compiled a valuable survey, officially published in 1874. He went to the Bengal secretariat in July 1869 as junior secretary. Of strong mathematical bent, he was soon transferred to the financial department of the government of India, being made under-secretary from June 1870. Here he revised the civil pension and leave codes, and examined actuarially the various presidency civil funds, embodying his results in a long series of notes and pamphlets. He was appointed officiating accountant-general of Bengal in March 1873, and in the following December went to the central provinces as substantive accountant-general, returning to Bengal at the end of 1876. After serving from November 1877 as inspector of local offices of account, he was appointed accountant and comptroller-general to the government of India in July 1878. In this capacity he reorganised and simplified Indian accountancy work, reducing to codified form the numerous departmental circulars, over which rules for account and treasury officers were dispersed.

After a few months in Egypt (March to June 1885) as head of the Egyptian accounts department in succession to (Sir) Gerald FitzGerald (LORD CROMER'S *Modern Egypt*, vol. i.), Westland returned to India; he was a member of Sir Charles Elliott's Indian expenditure commission in February 1886, acted as secretary of the financial department from September 1886, and was temporary finance member of government (August 1887 to November 1888). He was created C.S.I. in June 1888, and K.C.S.I. in January 1895, was elected a fellow of Calcutta University in January 1887, and was made honorary LL.D. Aberdeen in March 1890.

In July 1889 Westland went to Assam as chief commissioner; but in the following October, on grounds of health, he resigned the service, and turned to sheep-farming in New Zealand. On 27 Nov. 1893, however, he succeeded Sir David Barbour as finance member of the viceroy's council.

Indian finance was then in a critical condition, and Westland had to face a period of deficits. Preparatory to his first budget, he, in March 1894, renewed, at the general rate of 5 per cent., the import duties abandoned in 1882 by Sir Evelyn Baring (now Lord Cromer). But Henry Fowler, afterwards Viscount Wolverhampton [q. v. Suppl. II], secretary of state for India, owing to pressure from Lancashire manufacturers, declined to sanction the inclusion of cotton fabrics and yarns within Westland's schedule, as desired by Indian opinion, until the following December, when a countervailing excise was put on cotton fabrics manufactured at power mills in India. In February 1896 the duties were again revised. Imported yarns were then freed from duty, and cotton fabrics were charged 3½ instead of the general 5 per cent., with a corresponding excise on 'competing "counts"'—i.e. the finer fabrics—of Indian mills. Commercial opinion in India, with which Westland personally sympathised, remained dissatisfied, and Westland bore the brunt of the discontent.

Westland was more successful in converting the great bulk of the rupee debt, more than ninety crores, from 4 to 3½ per cent. in 1895–6, thereby saving the public exchequer nearly fifty lakhs of rupees in annual interest charges. A vigilant guardian of the public purse, he opposed the heavy additions to capital liabilities involved by the large programmes of railway construction which the viceroy, Lord Elgin, supported, although in respect to the great frontier campaigns of 1897–8 and other additions to military demands, Westland betrayed few economic scruples. In spite of the pressure of deficit at the time, he resisted proposals for a grant from the British exchequer towards the cost of the great 1897–8 famine, on the ground that the financial independence of the government of India would thereby be impaired.

The solution of the currency problem, which was the crucial point of the situation, had been prepared by his predecessor, Sir David Barbour, and Westland pursued the path marked out for him, if with less confidence than was desirable. He saw, however, the gold standard finally established during his rule and the sterling value of the rupee attain the fixed rate of 1*s.* 4*d.* In 1894–5 the rate averaged only 13·1*d.*; but from 1895 it rose steadily each year.

Westland remained in office to introduce in March 1899 the first budget of Lord Curzon's government. The 1*s.* 4*d.* rate had then been reached, and a few months later the gold standard became a reality, sovereigns and half-sovereigns being made legal tender. Westland found the government poor and left it rich; the lean years of deficit, the strain of which he bore patiently, were followed by years of large surplus and expanding revenue.

On returning to England Westland was nominated to the India council on 2 Aug. 1899. An indefatigable worker, he rather chafed under the comparative leisure of a consultative post. He was not a good platform speaker, and his efforts to inform the public on Indian affairs were failures. He found recreation in the study of astronomy and in chess, and was a great reader of German and French.

He died at his home at Weybridge on 9 May 1903, and was buried at Brookwood cemetery. He married on 23 April 1874 Janet Mildred, daughter of Surgeon-major C. J. Jackson, of the Indian medical service, and was survived by two sons and two daughters.

[Bengal Civil List; India List; Imp. Gazt. of India, vol. iv.; The Times, 16 May 1903; Pioneer (Allahabad), 29 and 31 March 1899; Englishman (Calcutta), 24 March 1899; official papers and private correspondence kindly lent by Lady Westland; personal knowledge.] F. H. B.

WEYMOUTH, RICHARD FRANCIS (1822–1902), philologist, and New Testament scholar, born at Stoke Damerel, Devonport (then called Plymouth Dock), on 26 Oct. 1822, was the only son of Commander Richard Weymouth, R.N., by his wife Ann Sprague, also of a Devonshire family. After education at a private school he went to France for two years. He matriculated at University College, London, in 1843, and graduated in classics—B.A. in 1846, M.A. in 1849. After acting as an assistant to Joseph Payne [q. v.], the educational expert, at the Mansion House School, Leatherhead, he conducted a successful private school, Portland grammar school, at Plymouth. In 1868 Weymouth was the first to receive the degree of doctor of literature at London University, after a severe examination in Anglo-Saxon, Icelandic, and French and English language and literature. The degree was not conferred again till 1879.

In 1869 also, Weymouth, who was elected fellow of University College, London, was appointed headmaster of Mill Hill School, which had been founded by nonconformists and was now first reorganised on the lines of a public school. A zealous baptist, Weymouth was long a deacon of the George St. baptist chapel, Plymouth, and subsequently a member of the committee of the Essex Baptist Union. At Mill Hill he proved a successful teacher and organiser and a strict disciplinarian, and the numbers increased. Among his assistants was (Sir) James A. H. Murray, editor of the 'New English Dictionary.' Weymouth retired with a pension in July 1886, when the school showed temporary signs of decline. Thenceforth he chiefly devoted himself to biblical study. As early as 1851 he had joined the Philological Society, and long sat on its council. He edited for the society in 1864 Bishop Grosseteste's 'Castell of Loue,' and contributed many papers to its 'Transactions,' one of which (on the Homeric epithet ὄβριμος) was commended by Gladstone in the 'Nineteenth Century.' Later contributions to philology comprised 'Early English Pronunciation, with Especial Reference to Chaucer' (1874), the views propounded being now generally accepted; a literal translation of Cynewulf's 'Elene' into modern English (1888); besides various papers in the 'Journal of Classical and Sacred Philology' and the 'Cambridge Journal of Philology.' In 1885, as president of the Devonshire Association, Weymouth read an address on 'The Devonshire Dialect: a Study in Comparative Grammar,' an early attempt to treat English dialect in the light of modern philology. In 1891 he was awarded a civil service pension of 100*l.*

On textual criticism of the Greek Testament Weymouth spent many years' study. The latest results of critical research he codified in 'Resultant Greek Testament, exhibiting the text in which the majority of modern editors are agreed,' 1886. Then followed a tract, 'The Rendering into English of the Greek Aorist and Perfect, with appendices on the New Testament Use of γὰρ and οὖν' (1894; new edit. 1901).

Weymouth's last work, which was issued after his death and proved widely popular, was 'The New Testament in Modern Speech' (1903; 3rd edit. 1909). Based upon the text of 'The Resultant Greek Testament,' it was partly revised by Mr. Ernest Hampden-Cook.

Since 1892 Weymouth lived at Collaton House, Brentwood, where he died on 27 Dec. 1902, being buried in the new cemetery.

A portrait, an excellent likeness, by

Sidney Paget [q. v. Suppl. II], was hung in the hall of Mill Hill school; and a memorial window is in the chapel.

Weymouth was twice married: (1) in 1852 to Louisa Sarah (*d.* 1891), daughter of Robert Marten, sometime secretary of the Vauxhall Bridge Company, of Denmark Hill; and (2) on 26 Oct. 1892 to Louisa, daughter of Samuel Salter of Watford, who survived him with three sons and three daughters, children of the first marriage.

[Private information; London University Register; Norman Brett James's History of Mill Hill School; The Times, 30 Dec. 1902; Weymouth's Works.] G. Le G. N.

WHARTON, Sir WILLIAM JAMES LLOYD (1843–1905), rear-admiral and hydrographer of the navy, born in London on 2 March 1843, was second son in a family of three sons and four daughters of Robert Wharton, county court judge of York, by his wife Katherine Mary, third daughter of Robert Croft, canon residentiary of York. After receiving his early education at Woodcote, Gloucestershire, and at the Royal Naval Academy, Gosport, Wharton entered the navy in August 1857. On passing his examination in 1865 he was awarded the Beaufort prize for mathematics, astronomy, and navigation [see Beaufort, Sir Francis]. As sub-lieutenant he served in the Jason, corvette, on the North America and West Indies station, and on 15 March 1865 he received his commission as lieutenant. In July 1865 he was appointed to the Gannet, surveying vessel, and in her served for another three years on the North America station. In February 1869 Sir James Hope [q. v.], commander-in-chief at Portsmouth, on the recommendation of Prof. Thomas John Main [q. v.] of the Royal Naval College there, offered Wharton the appointment as his flag-lieutenant. Wharton was inclined to refuse, wishing to enter the surveying branch of the service, but accepted on the advice of Main, who thought that the three years ashore would be to his advantage. On 2 March 1872 he received his promotion to commander, and in April was appointed to command the Shearwater, in which during the next four years he made surveys in the Mediterranean and on the east coast of Africa. 'In the Mediterranean his work was especially distinguished, and his examination of the surface and under-currents in the Bosphorus, the account of which was officially published, not only solved a curious problem in physical geography, but may be considered as prescribing the method for similar inquiries.' In May 1876 he was appointed to the Fawn, and continued his surveys on the same stations till 1880. On 29 Jan. 1880 he was promoted to captain, and in February 1882 was appointed to the Sylvia, in which he conducted surveys on the coast of South America, and especially in the Straits of Magellan. In 1882 he published his 'Hydrographical Surveying: a Description of the Methods employed in constructing Marine Charts,' a work which at once took its place as the standard textbook of the subject. In August 1884 he was appointed hydrographer to the navy in succession to Sir Frederick Evans [q. v.], and continued to hold this post, with increasing credit, until August 1904, when the state of his health compelled him to resign it. Wharton was a fellow of the Royal Society and of the Royal Astronomical and Royal Geographical Societies. He was perhaps most devoted to the last-named of these, as a vice-president, and as a member of numerous committees on which he did much important work. He was retired for non-service on 2 Aug. 1891, and was promoted to rear-admiral on the retired list on 1 Jan. 1895. He was made a C.B., civil, in 1895, and was raised to the K.C.B., civil, at the jubilee of 1897. In 1899 he took a prominent part in the work of the joint Antarctic Committee of the Royal and Royal Geographical Societies.

The chief of Wharton's publications were his 'Hydrographical Surveying,' already mentioned, of which new editions continue to appear; 'A Short History of H.M.S. Victory,' written while he was flag-lieutenant at Portsmouth, and re-issued in 1888; 'Hints to Travellers,' an edition of which he edited for the Royal Geographical Society in 1893; and the 'Journal of Captain Cook's First Voyage,' which he edited with notes in 1893.

In July 1905 Wharton left England for Capetown to act as president of the geographical section of the British Association, which was holding its annual meeting in South Africa. He attended all the meetings of the association, and subsequently visited the Victoria Falls of the Zambesi. There he fell ill of enteric fever. He was removed to the Observatory, Capetown, where he was the guest of Sir David Gill. He died there on 29 Sept. 1905, and was buried with full naval honours in the naval cemetery at Simonstown. He married on 31 Jan. 1880 Lucy Georgina, daughter of Edward Holland of Dumbleton, Woodcote, Gloucestershire, by whom he had three sons and two daughters.

After his death 'The Wharton Testimonial Fund' was formed wherewith an addition was made to the value of the existing Beaufort prize for naval officers, the double award being entitled 'The Beaufort Testimonial and the Wharton Memorial,' and including a gold medal, bearing on its obverse Wharton's bust. Two posthumous portraits were also presented in 1908, one of which was accepted by the Trustees of the National Portrait Gallery and hung there immediately; and the other was placed in the Painted Hall at Greenwich.

[The Times, 30 Sept. 1905; R. N. List; Geog. Journal, xxvi. 684.] L. G. C. L.

WHEELHOUSE, CLAUDIUS GALEN (1826–1909), surgeon, born at Snaith in Yorkshire on 29 Dec. 1826, was second son of James Wheelhouse, surgeon. At seven he left the grammar school at Snaith for Christ's Hospital preparatory school at Hertford, and entered Christ's Hospital in London in 1836. He was apprenticed at sixteen to R. C. Ward of Ollerton, Newark, and always strongly advocated the system of apprenticeship. He entered the Leeds school of medicine in October 1846, and was admitted M.R.C.S.England on 25 March 1849, and a licentiate of the Society of Apothecaries in 1850. He then went to the Mediterranean on a yachting cruise as surgeon to Lord Lincoln, afterwards fifth duke of Newcastle and secretary of state for war. He took with him one of the first photographic cameras which left England, and obtained many good photographs in spite of the cumbrous processes.

Wheelhouse returned to England in 1851, and entered into partnership with Joseph Prince Garlick of Park Row, Leeds, the senior surgeon to the dispensary and lecturer on surgery at the Leeds school of medicine. In the same year he was elected surgeon to the public dispensary and demonstrator of anatomy in the medical school, where he was successively lecturer on anatomy, physiology, and surgery. He was twice president of the school, and when the new university of Leeds was inaugurated in October 1904 Wheelhouse was made hon. D.Sc. He was surgeon to the Leeds infirmary from March 1884.

Elected F.R.C.S.England on 9 June 1864, he served on the college council from 1876 to 1881. President of the council of the British Medical Association 1881–4, he presided at the Leeds meeting in 1889. In 1897, when the association held its annual meeting at Montreal, McGill College made him hon. LL.D., and he received the gold medal of the association.

In 1886, when the Medical Act brought direct representatives of the profession on the general medical council, Wheelhouse headed the poll in England and Wales. Re-elected in 1891 at the end of his term. he did not seek re-election in 1897. From 1870 to 1895 he was first secretary and afterwards treasurer of the West Riding Medical Charity, and in 1902 he was presented by his fellow members with an address of thanks and testimonial.

On retiring from practice at Leeds in 1891 he settled at Filey, where he was active in local affairs. He died at Filey on 9 April 1909, and was buried there. He married in 1860 Agnes Caroline, daughter of Joseph Cowell, vicar of Todmorden, and had issue three daughters.

Wheelhouse filled the unusual position of a general practitioner who made a name in pure surgery. An admirable teacher, he did much to convert the Leeds medical school into a worthy integral part of the university. In 1876 he advocated that form of external urethrotomy for impermeable strictures to which his name is given; it has displaced all rival methods. The operation was first described in the 'British Medical Journal,' 1876, i. 779, in a paper entitled 'Perineal section as performed at Leeds.'

[Brit. Med. Journal, 1909, i. 983 (with portrait); Lancet, 1909, i. 1145.] D'A. P.

WHISTLER, JAMES ABBOTT McNEILL (1834–1903), painter, was eldest son (in a family of seven sons and one daughter) of George Washington Whistler, an American artillery officer whose life was mostly spent as a civil engineer, by his second wife, Anna Mathilda McNeill of Wilmington, North Carolina, who was connected with the Winans family of Baltimore. His half-sister, Dasha Delano; married in 1847 (Sir) Francis Seymour Haden [q. v. Suppl. II]. He was born on 10 July 1834 at Lowell, Massachusetts, in a house which is now a Whistler Memorial Museum. Christened James Abbott, he afterwards added to his Christian names his mother's maiden surname of 'McNeill,' and finally was in the habit of signing himself 'James McNeill Whistler,' or 'J. M. N. Whistler,' except in official documents. His paternal descent was from an old English family which had branches in Sussex, Oxfordshire, and Ireland. He sprang from the Irish branch. Maternally, he threw back to the

McNeills of Skye, many of whom emigrated to North Carolina after the Jacobite rising of 1745. In 1842 Major Whistler, the boy's father, was appointed engineer to the railway then about to be built from St. Petersburg to Moscow, and in the following year summoned his wife and family to Russia, where they settled in St. Petersburg. In 1846 Whistler was put to a school kept by one Jourdan, but in 1849 he left Russia for good. Major Whistler died in the spring of that year, and his widow, with her boys, returned to America. There she settled in Pomfret, Connecticut, and sent her son to a school kept by an alumnus of West Point who had turned parson. In 1851, after two years at this school, Whistler entered the Military Academy at West Point, where he remained for three years. He distinguished himself in drawing, but failed in other subjects and had to leave.

His next occupation was on the United States coast and geodetic survey, which gave him a useful training in accurate drawing and the technique of etching. After a year of the survey, he finally adopted art for his career. In the summer of 1855 he went to Paris, provided with a yearly income of 350 dollars. He entered the studio presided over by Charles Gleyre, to whom Paul Delaroche had bequeathed his pupils when he ceased to teach. In Paris he lived the regulation life of a student on a small income, living well one week, put to all sorts of shifts the next. To his companions, who included du Maurier, Poynter, Thomas Armstrong, and Val Prinsep, he appeared to be the reverse of industrious. He soaked in knowledge and skill, nevertheless, and became a fine draughtsman, a painter who could produce the results he aimed at, and a master of etching. His life in Paris was varied by excursions into other parts of France, during which he was never idle. In 1858 he published a set of thirteen etchings known as 'The French Set,' the material for which had been mostly gleaned in eastern France the year before, or in 1856. At this time he was influenced by the principles of Courbet and Lecoq de Boisbaudran, by the practice of Rembrandt, Hals, and Velazquez, and, no doubt, by the companionship of more young French painters whom he found sympathetic: Fantin-Latour and Legros chief among them. He copied many pictures in the Louvre, mostly in fulfilment of commissions from American friends. The first original picture done in Paris was 'Mère Gerard' (now owned by the executors of A. C. Swinburne), which was soon followed by 'The Piano Picture' or 'At the Piano.' The latter was rejected by the Salon jury of 1859, and this may have had something to do with the nibblings at London by which it was immediately followed. He spent some months in the English capital in 1859, renewing friendships made abroad and making new ones, and laying the foundations of a notoriety which was in time to blossom into fame. He stayed with his half-sister, Mrs. Francis Seymour Haden, and practised etching with his brother-in-law, the two exerting a mutual influence one upon the other. Whistler first exhibited at the Royal Academy in 1859, sending two 'etchings from nature.' In 1860 his 'At the Piano' was accepted at the Royal Academy and bought by an academician, John Phillip [q. v.]; it now belongs to Mr. Edmund Davis. In the same exhibitions were shown two dry-point portraits and three etchings. This modest success probably confirmed him in the intention to settle in London, which was practically his domicile from 1860 till his death.

During his first twelve months in London he was chiefly occupied with a series of sixteen etchings of the scenery and life of the Thames, including 'The Pool,' 'Thames Police,' and 'Black Lion Wharf.' He was much at Wapping, and etched the life of the neighbourhood and its framing. The chief pictures of the same period were 'The White Girl,' 'The Thames in Ice,' and 'The Music Room.' In 1861 he visited France again, painting on the coast of Brittany. A year later he travelled as far as Fuentarrabia on a journey to Madrid which was never completed. In 1863 he took his first London house, 7 Lindsey Row, now 101 Cheyne Walk, Chelsea. There he was joined by his mother, who had left America on the outbreak of the civil war. During these years he sent regularly to the Royal Academy, where his pictures met with quite as good a reception as a man of original genius, who was opening up a new walk in art, had any right to expect. Chief among them were 'On the Thames,' 'Alone with the Tide,' and 'The Last of Old Westminster.' During these years he also drew for some of the illustrated periodicals, contributing two drawings to 'Good Words' in 1862, and four to 'Once a Week' in the same year. It was about this time that Whistler became strongly affected by the example of the Japanese. For years his work bore much the same relation to Japanese art as all fine painting does to nature. He took from Japanese ideals the beauties he admired, and re-created them as expressions of his own personality. The 'Lange Leizen,' 'The Gold Screen,' 'The Balcony,' the 'Princesse du Pays de la Porcelaine,' are in no sense Japanese pictures, but they are full of Japanese material. Probably the finest æsthetic spark struck out by his contact with Japan is the exquisite picture variously known as 'The Little White Girl' and 'Symphony in White, No. II.' It was at the Royal Academy in 1865, with 'The Gold Screen' and 'Old Battersea Bridge,' and is now the property of Mr. Arthur Studd. In this year Whistler revisited eastern France and western Germany, and spent part of the autumn at Trouville, with Courbet for companion. In 1866 he made a sudden expedition to Chili, where he seems to have been implicated in some rather absurd war making, but found time to paint five pictures of Valparaiso, some of which are among his greater successes. At the close of this year he moved to a new house, now 96 Cheyne Row, where he remained longer than in any other of his numerous domiciles.

The years between 1866 and 1872 were busy. He exhibited more often than before or after. The chief pictures of this period were a 'Valparaiso,' 'Sea and Rain,' 'The Balcony,' and the famous 'Portrait of my Mother.' Whistler's uncomfortable relations with the Royal Academy began with the exhibition of this last-named picture. Rejected at first, it was only hung through the insistence of one member of the council. After 1872 Whistler exhibited no picture at Burlington House. Nothing of his was thenceforth seen there save an etching of 'Old Putney Bridge' in 1879. No doubt Whistler's irritation was deepened by the fact that, although his name remained for years on the candidates' book, he never came near to being elected into the Academy. These years about 1870 saw the production of most of his 'Nocturnes,' studies of tone, colour, and atmosphere to which the history of art then afforded no parallel; also the portraits of Carlyle and the fine 'Miss Alexander' (now belonging to Mr. W. C. Alexander). In these pictures Whistler first worked his initials into a fantastic shape resembling a butterfly, which soon became his accustomed signature.

In 1874 Whistler opened a show of his own work at 48 Pall Mall, the first of those occasions on which he appealed to the public almost as much by the setting of his pictures as by the works themselves. At this time he was also painting the famous peacock room, for Frederick Robert Leyland, in Prince's Gate: it is now at Mr. C. L. Freer's residence in Detroit. In 1877 he was represented by eight pictures, mostly loans, at the first exhibition of the Grosvenor Gallery. To the same gallery he sent in 1879 a portrait of Miss Connie Gilchrist [now Countess of Orkney], 'The Gold Girl: a Harmony in Yellow and Gold,' which was acquired by the Metropolitan Museum of New York in 1911.

One of his first exhibits at the Grosvenor Gallery, 'The Falling Rocket, a nocturne in Black and Gold,' was the nail on which Ruskin hung strong abuse of the artist in 'Fors Clavigera,' where Whistler was described as a 'coxcomb' asking 'two hundred guineas for throwing a pot of paint in the public's face.' Whistler brought an action for libel against the critic, which was heard before Baron Huddleston on 25 Nov. 1878. Burne-Jones and Frith were among Ruskin's witnesses. Whistler won his verdict, with a farthing damages, but had to pay his own costs. He set forth his view of the litigation in a shilling pamphlet, 'Whistler *v.* Ruskin: Art and Art Critics (1879, 12mo). For years before he had been ordering his life with extreme carelessness in financial matters, keeping open house, never hesitating over the cost of anything he thought necessary to his art or to his conception of his needs. All this, added to the costs of the trial and the loss of the money-making power which it involved, brought about his bankruptcy in 1879. He had left Cheyne Row at the end of 1878, and moved to the 'White House' in Tite Street, built for him by Edward William Godwin [q. v.], but this had to be sold with the rest of his effects in 1879. At the end of this year he went to Venice, where he spent the winter in producing a number of etchings and pastels on the commission of the Fine Art Society. They excited great interest and some controversy when shown on his return; and they sold well. From this time onward he worked much in pastel, producing those dainty notes from the model, nude and semi-nude, which were soon much sought after. He came back to London early in 1880. In 1881 his mother died at Hastings. In the same year he settled at No. 13 Tite Street, where he painted many of the best pictures of his later years. Among these were the portrait of Lady Meux, 'M. Duret,' 'The Blue Girl,' and the 'Yellow Buskin' (Lady Archibald Campbell), which is in the Memorial

Hall, Philadelphia. In 1884 Whistler sent twenty-five of his pictures to Ireland, where they were exhibited by the Dublin Sketching Club. In 1885 he moved from Tite Street to No. 454 Fulham Road; he made a tour in Belgium and Holland with Mr. W. M. Chase, the American painter; and he first gave the lecture which has become famous, the 'Ten o'clock.' In 1884 he had joined the Society of British Artists, which elected him its president in June 1886. His presidency was not of long duration, being determined in June 1888. His ways were too autocratic and his aims too free of the commercial spirit for the majority of his colleagues. In 1887 he travelled in Belgium with his brother, Dr. Whistler, and etched in Brussels. In 1888 Whistler married a pupil of his own, Beatrix Godwin, the widow of E. W. Godwin, and the daughter of John Birnie Philip [q. v.]. He had left Fulham Road for the Tower House, in Tite Street, but the early months after his marriage were spent in France, where he etched many plates in Touraine and its neighbourhood. The following year he worked in Holland, etching in the neighbourhood of Amsterdam and Dordrecht. In 1889 he exhibited at the Paris International Exhibition, in the British section. The next year saw yet another change of abode, to 21 Cheyne Walk, but its chief event was the publication of 'The Gentle Art of Making Enemies,' in which Whistler built up a sort of declaration of his artistic faith by reprinting, with comments, his letters to his 'enemies,' the Ruskin trial, his 'Ten o'clock,' &c. In 1891 his 'Carlyle' was bought for Glasgow and his 'Mother' for the Luxembourg, the former for 1000*l.*, the latter for 160*l.* The 'Luxembourg' also soon acquired his 'Old Man Smoking.' These purchases marked the beginning of the general acceptance of Whistler as a great painter, which was confirmed by the success of an exhibition held at Goupil's in Bond Street in the following year, and by that of his appearance at the Chicago Exhibition. In 1892 he moved to Paris, to a house in the Rue du Bac, where he painted several of the best portraits of his later years, and also busied himself much with lithography and a little with etching. In 1895 he was defendant in an action brought against him in the Paris court by Sir William Eden for refusing to deliver his portrait of Lady Eden, for which he had been paid. Whistler was allowed to keep the picture, but was amerced in costs, and the trial established, so far as France was concerned, an artist's right in his own work. In 1899 he published 'The Baronet and the Butterfly' [i.e. Whistler's monogram], a report of the litigation.

During 1895 Whistler was for a time at Lyme Regis, and his picture 'The Master-Smith of Lyme Regis' is at the Boston Museum: he also had a studio at No. 8 Fitzroy Street, and afterwards a cottage at Hampstead. There Mrs. Whistler died on 10 May 1896. After her death, by which he was profoundly affected, he stayed with Mr. William Heinemann, in Whitehall Court, for nearly three years. In 1898 he was elected president of the newly founded International Society of Sculptors, Painters, and Engravers. It was a post for which he was peculiarly fitted in one way, at least, for he had excelled in all the forms of art practised by his colleagues, with the exception of sculpture. He had painted in water-colour as well as oil, he had mastered dry-point as well as etching, he had lithographed, and he had proved himself a decorator of genius. He held this dignity till his death, and to the society's affairs he devoted much of his energy during his last years. In the same year he had been concerned in founding an atelier for students in Paris, partly for the benefit of a former model, Madame Carmen Rossi, after whom it was subsequently called the 'Académie Carmen.' This he visited as master during the three years of its existence. In 1900 he received a grand prix for painting and another for engraving at the Paris Exhibition du Centenaire, exhibiting this time in the American section. In 1900 he made a short stay in Ireland, in a house called Craigie, at Sutton, near Dublin, and at the end of the same year made an expedition to Tangier, Algiers, the South of France, and Corsica, in search of health. In May 1901 he returned to England, which he never left again except for a short visit to Holland in 1902. He died on Friday, 17 July 1903, at 74 Cheyne Walk, and was buried in Chiswick churchyard, by the side of his wife and not far from the grave of Hogarth. An elaborately sculptured tomb by Mr. Edward Godwin was erected in 1912. Whistler had no issue.

Whistler was an officer of the Legion of Honour, a member of the Société Nationale des Artistes Francais, commander of the Order of the Crown of Italy, chevalier of the Order of St. Michael, honorary member of the Academy of St. Luke, Rome, and of the Royal Academies of Bavaria and Dresden, and LL.D. of Glasgow University.

Few painters have exercised a deeper or wider influence over their contemporaries than Whistler. All that is good in real impressionism sprang originally from his teaching and example, and even now no one has equalled the unity and repose of his best works, 'The Little White Girl,' the 'Mother,' 'Miss Alexander,' 'Carlyle,' 'Duret,' 'Sarasate,' or even the little picture—nocturne blue and gold—'Old Battersea Bridge,' at the Tate Gallery, which, first exhibited in 1877, was presented by the National Art Collections Fund in 1905 and is, so far, his only representative in the London collections. The 'Sarasate' is at the Carnegie Institute, Pittsburg. But a tragic element was brought into his life by the conflicting strains in his own character. A love of pose, which found vent in eccentricities of dress, in extravagant paradox and biting epigram, gave him social notoriety. More exclusively an artist, perhaps, in his work than any painter since the days of Rembrandt, he yet thirsted after the worldly honours and acclamations which are only to be won by men whose productions can appeal to those who are not artists. He was at once capable of the deepest affection and so thin-skinned that he would allow a slight to cancel a long-standing friendship. He had an abnormally keen eye for provocation. He was eager to propagate true ideas about art, but he resented their existence in anyone but himself. Speaking broadly, his ambition was to be acknowledged as a sort of æsthetic dictator. Nothing would have satisfied him short of being accepted as both the greatest painter and the official figurehead of art, in his time, while his character unfitted him to take even the initial steps towards such a consummation. As a painter, he lacked something on the sensuous side. He was fond of asserting the partial truth that art is science. In distilling from a natural scene such constituents as can be fused into a simple, sternly concentrated, æsthetic unity Whistler has never been surpassed. It is only when we seek the touch of excess, the hint at some personal, irresponsible preference, through which genius so often speaks, that we feel a slight stirring of disappointment. As an etcher he ranks with Rembrandt, in command of the *métier*, and in contentment with what it can do without any kind of forcing. As a man Whistler was one of the most remarkable social units of his time. His epigrammatic wit and power of repartee inspired a curious mixture of dread and admiration, which was deepened by the inability of the slower minds about him to foresee when they would tread upon his toes and bring out his lightning.

A memorial exhibition of Whistler's work was held by the International Society at Knightsbridge in 1905, and a loan collection was brought together at the Tate Gallery in the summer of 1912. Six of his finest pictures are in the art collection of Mr. Charles Lang Freer, of Detroit, which has been presented to the Smithsonian Institution at Washington.

Portraits of Whistler are numerous, from an early miniature reproduced in Mrs. Pennell's 'Life,' and a head painted when the sitter was fourteen by Sir William Boxall, to the various portraits of himself drawn and painted throughout his active years. At one time he is said to have made some sort of a portrait of himself every day. Most of these were destroyed by himself. Self-portraits in oil survive in the McCulloch collection, in the possession of Mr. Douglas Freshfield, and in the Municipal Art Gallery at Dublin; a drawing in black chalk belongs to Mr. Thomas Way, and there are three etchings. The portrait known as 'Whistler with a large hat' belongs to Mr. Freer, who also owns a portrait by Fantin-Latour which was cut out from a large group, the rest of which was destroyed. He was also painted by Boldini and by W. M. Chase. There is a lithograph by Paul Rajon, dry-points by Helleu and Percy Thomas, a caricature in 'Vanity Fair' by 'Spy' in 1878, and a bust by Sir Edgar Boehm, R.A.

[E. R. and J. Pennell's Life of James McNeill Whistler, London, 2 vols. 1908, and revised edit. in 1 vol., 1911, is the indispensable authority. See also T. R. Way and G. R. Dennis's The Art of James McNeill Whistler, 1903; T. R. Way's Cat. of Lithographs, 1905, and his Memoirs of Whistler, 1912; Graves' Roy. Acad. Exhibitors; Duret, Histoire de J. McNeill Whistler et son œuvre, 1904; Mortimer Menpes's Whistler as I knew him, 1904; Howard Mansfield's Cat., 1909; E. G. Kennedy, The Etched Work of Whistler, issued by Grolier Club of New York, 6 vols., 1910; The Times, 18 July 1903; Writings by and about Whistler, by Don C. Seitz, Edinburgh, 1910; private information and personal knowledge.] W. A.

WHITE, JOHN CAMPBELL, first BARON OVERTOUN (1843–1908), Scottish churchman and philanthropist, born at Hayfield, near Rutherglen, on 21 Nov. 1843, was only son in a family of seven children of James White of Overtoun (*d.* 1884), one of the partners of the extensive chemical manufacturing firm of John and James White, Shawfield, near Rutherglen. His mother, Fanny (*d.* 1891), was a daughter of Alexander Campbell, sheriff of Renfrewshire. In 1851 he went to a preparatory school in Glasgow, and in 1859 he entered Glasgow University, where he took prizes in logic and natural philosophy. For a session he worked in the laboratory of Professor William Thomson, afterwards Lord Kelvin [q. v. Suppl. II], who was impressed by his abilities. He graduated M.A. in 1864, and after receiving a good business training joined in 1867 his father's firm, of which he ultimately became principal partner.

From an early period he devoted much time to religious and philanthropic work. Like his parents, he was a staunch supporter of the Free Church of Scotland, took a prominent part in its affairs, and was a munificent contributor to its funds. He supported the movement which in 1900 led to the union of the Free and United Presbyterian churches, and he was the principal defender in the consequent litigation, which temporarily deprived, by the judgment of the House of Lords of 1 Aug. 1904, the United Free Church of its property. White headed an emergency fund with a subscription of 10,000*l.*, and, later, gave a like sum to aid the dispossessed ministers and congregations in the Scottish highlands and islands.

From 1884 to his death he was in succession to his father convener of the Livingstonia Mission of the United Free Church of Scotland, which, with headquarters in Glasgow, supports missionaries in British Central Africa and Northern Rhodesia. He gave the mission no less than 50,000*l.* His zeal for home mission work was no less pronounced. Coming under the influence of the evangelical revival of 1859–60, he identified himself with the Scottish mission conducted by Moody and Sankey in 1874. Of the Glasgow United Evangelistic Association, an undenominational organisation carrying on extensive social and religious work in Glasgow, which was one of the outcomes of Moody and Sankey's visit, he was the energetic president, and the palatial buildings in Bothwell Street, Glasgow, where are housed the Christian Institute, the Bible Training Institute, and the Young Men's Christian Association (with all of which he was connected), bear witness to his liberality. He was himself a successful religious teacher. For thirty-seven years he conducted a Bible class at Dumbarton, which at his death numbered about five hundred members. White supported the liberal party in Scotland, and in 1893, on Gladstone's recommendation, on account of his philanthropy and political services, was raised to the peerage of the United Kingdom as Baron Overtoun, his title being taken from the finely wooded estate in Dumbartonshire which his father purchased in 1859. He became lord-lieutenant of Dumbartonshire in 1907. He died at Overtoun House on 15 Feb. 1908, and was buried in the family vault in Dumbarton cemetery. He married in 1867 Grace, daughter of James H. McClure, solicitor, Glasgow, who survived him without issue. A presentation portrait by Mr. Fiddes Watt (1909) hangs in the assembly buildings in Edinburgh.

[Glasgow Herald, 17 Feb. 1908; British Monthly, May 1903; Scottish Review, February 1908; Life of Principal Rainy by P. C. Simpson (2 vols. 1909); Free Church of Scotland Appeals, 1903–4, edited by Robert L. Orr, 1904.] W. F. G.

WHITEHEAD, ROBERT (1823–1905), inventor, born at Mount Pleasant, Bolton-le-Moors, Lancashire, on 3 Jan. 1823, was one of a family of four sons and four daughters of James Whitehead (1788–1872), the owner of a cotton-bleaching business at Bolton-le-Moors, by his wife Ellen, daughter of William Swift of Bolton. Educated chiefly at the local grammar school, he was apprenticed, when fourteen, to Richard Ormond & Son, engineers, Aytoun Street, Manchester. His uncle, William Smith, was manager of the works, where Whitehead was thoroughly grounded in practical engineering. He also acquired unusual skill as a draughtsman by attendance at the evening classes of the Mechanics' Institute, Cooper Street, Manchester. Meanwhile his uncle became manager of the works of Philip Taylor & Sons, Marseilles, and in 1844 Whitehead, on the conclusion of his apprenticeship, joined him in that employ. Three years later he commenced business on his own account at Milan, where he effected improvements in silk-weaving machinery, and also designed machinery for the drainage of some of the Lombardy marshes. His patents, however, as granted by the Austrian government, were annulled by the Italian revolutionary government of 1848. Whitehead then went to Trieste, where he served the Austrian Lloyd Company for two years; from 1850 to 1856 he was manager there of the works of Messrs. Strudhoff. In 1856 he started for local capitalists, at the neighbouring naval port of Fiume, the Stabilimento Tecnico Fiumano.

At Fiume, Whitehead designed and built engines for several Austrian warships, and the high quality of his work led to an invitation in 1864 to co-operate in perfecting a 'fireship' or floating torpedo designed by Captain Lupuis of the Austrian navy. The officer's proposals were dismissed by Whitehead as too crude for further development. At the same time he carried out with the utmost secrecy, in conjunction with his son John and one mechanic, a series of original experiments which culminated in 1866 in the invention of the Whitehead torpedo.

The superiority of the new torpedo over all predecessors was quickly established. But it lacked precision, its utmost speed and range were seven knots for seven hundred yards, and there was difficulty in maintaining it at a uniform depth when once in motion. The last defect Whitehead remedied in 1868 by an ingenious yet simple contrivance called the 'balance chamber,' the mechanism of which was long guarded as the 'torpedo's secret.' In the same year, after trials from the gunboat Gemse, the right, though not exclusive right, of construction was bought by the Austrian government, and a similar right, as the result of trials off Sheerness in 1870, was bought by the British government in 1871. France followed suit in 1872, Germany and Italy in 1873, and by 1900 the right of construction had been acquired by almost every country in Europe, the United States, China, Japan, and some South American republics. Meanwhile Whitehead in 1872 had in conjunction with his son-in-law, Count Georg Hoyos, bought the Stabilimento Tecnico Fiumano, devoting the works solely to the construction of torpedoes and accessory appliances. His son John subsequently became a third partner. In 1890 a branch was established at Portland Harbour, under Captain Payne-Gallwey, an ex-naval officer, and in 1898 the original works at Fiume were rebuilt on a larger scale.

Repeated improvements were made upon the original invention, many of them being by Whitehead and his son John. In 1876 by his invention of the 'servo-motor,' which was attached to the steering gear, a truer path through the water was obtained. In the same year he designed torpedoes with a speed of eighteen knots for six hundred yards, while further changes gave a speed in 1884 of twenty-four knots, and in 1889 of twenty-nine knots for one thousand yards. Means were also devised by which the torpedo could be fired from either above or below the surface of the water and with accuracy from the fastest ships, no matter what the speed or bearing of the enemy. Each individual torpedo, however, continued to show idiosyncrasies which required constant watching and correction, and absolute confidence in the weapon was not established till the invention in 1896, by Mr. Obry, at one time of the Austrian navy, of a small weighted wheel, or gyroscope, which acted on the 'servo-motor' by means of a pair of vertical rudders and steered a deflected torpedo back to its original course. The invention, which disarmed the torpedo's severest critics, was acquired and considerably improved by Whitehead. In its present form the Whitehead torpedo is a weapon of precision, its capabilities entirely eclipsing those of the gun and ram. Any doubts as to its usefulness in war were definitely dispelled by the ease with which on 9 Feb. 1904 a few Japanese destroyers reduced the Russian fleet outside Port Arthur to impotence.

Whitehead received many marks of favour and decorations from various courts. He was presented by the Austrian Emperor with a diamond and enamel ring for having designed and built the engines of the ironclad Ferdinand Max, which rammed the Re d'Italia at the battle of Lissa. On 4 May 1868 he was decorated with the Austrian Order of Francis Joseph in recognition of the excellence of his engineering exhibits at the Paris Exhibition in 1867. He also received Orders from Prussia, Denmark, Portugal, Italy, Greece, France (Legion of Honour, 30 July 1884), and Turkey. Whitehead did not apply for Queen Victoria's permission to wear his foreign decorations.

Whitehead for some years owned a large estate at Worth, Sussex, where he farmed on a large scale. He died at Beckett, Shrivenham, Berkshire, on 14 Nov. 1905, and was buried at Worth, Sussex.

Whitehead married in 1845 Frances Maria (*d.* 1883), daughter of James Johnson of Darlington, by whom he had three sons and two daughters. His eldest son, John (*d.* 1902), assisted him at Fiume and made valuable improvements in the torpedo. The second daughter, Alice (*b.* 1851), married in 1869 Count Georg Hoyos. A portrait of Robert Whitehead by the Venetian artist, Cherubino Kirchmayr, belongs to his grandson, John Whitehead (son of John Whitehead). The original sketch in oils of a second portrait by the same artist is owned by Sir James

Beethom Whitehead, K.C.M.G. (the second son), British minister at Belgrade since 1906; the finished portrait belongs to Robert Bovill Whitehead (the third son).

[G. E. Armstrong's Torpedoes and Torpedo Vessels, 1901, and art. in Cornhill Magazine, April 1904; The Times, 15 Nov. 1905; Burke's Peerage; Engineering, 20 Sept. 1901 (with illustrations of the works at Fiume and portrait) and 18 Nov. 1905; The Engineer, 18 Nov. 1905; private information.] S. E. F.

WHITELEY, WILLIAM (1831–1907), 'universal provider,' a younger son of William Whiteley, a corn factor in a small way of business at Agbrigg near Wakefield, by his wife Elizabeth, daughter of Thomas Rowland, was born at Agbrigg on 29 Sept. 1831, and spent several years with his brothers on his uncle's farm near Wakefield. In June 1848, however, he was apprenticed as a draper's assistant to Messrs. Harnew and Glover, of Wakefield, and in 1851 he paid a visit to the Great Exhibition in London. The idea of London as the centre of the world's commerce stimulated him in a remarkable manner, and in 1852 he obtained a position in The Fore Street Warehouse Company, in the City of London. His capital then was 10*l.*; in ten years he had amassed 700*l.*, and with its aid he opened a small shop with two female assistants as a fancy draper at 31 Westbourne Grove (11 March 1863). His ideas were laughed at as extravagant and his choice of a site ridiculed. Westbourne Grove was then known in the drapery trade as 'Bankruptcy Row.' But the attention he paid to window dressing, to marking in plain figures, and to dealing with orders by post soon distinguished his business from its competitors. In 1870 and succeeding years he accumulated shops side by side; in 1876 he had fifteen shops and two thousand employees. At the time of his death he had twenty-one shops, fourteen in Westbourne Grove (which he had adapted from pre-existing buildings), and seven of spacious dimensions in the adjoining Queen's Road which were wholly new erections. Meanwhile six serious fires which gutted the premises on each occasion threatened the progress of the business. On 17 Nov. 1882 some thirteen shops, 43–55 Westbourne Grove, were burned down, of an estimated value of 100,000*l.*; on 26 Dec. 1882 some stabling and outhouses valued at 20,000*l.* were destroyed; on 26 April 1884 the new premises suffered to the extent of 150,000*l.*; on 17 June 1885 four large shops valued at 100,000*l.* were ruined, and on 6–9 Aug. 1887 damage was done to the extent of 500,000*l.*; three lives were lost. The hand of an incendiary was suspected, and on the last occasion a reward of 3000*l.* was offered for discovery of the criminal. But 'Whiteley's' rose each time more splendid from the flames.

The field of operations had been gradually extended; in 1866 the owner added general to fancy drapery, and within ten years he undertook to provide every kind of goods, including food, drink, and furniture. He adopted the insignia of the two hemispheres and the style of 'universal provider.' Stories were widely current of Whiteley supplying a white elephant and a second-hand (or misfit) coffin. He set the example of professing to sell any commodity that was procurable. Whiteley's method of taking and dismissing assistants without references was peculiar, but in other respects his mode of organisation was soon adopted or paralleled by many other firms in London and the provinces. Whiteley's success was effected without sensational cutting of prices or extravagant disbursement in advertising. In 1899 the turnover exceeded a million sterling and the business was converted into a limited company (2 June); but the bulk of the shares was held in the family, and it was not until 1909 that the shares were publicly subscribed. The share capital amounted to 900,000*l.* with four-per-cent. first mortgage irredeemable debenture stock of 900,000*l.* Whiteley continued to live unpretentiously in close proximity to his business at 31 Porchester Terrace. Every day to the last he was in the shop. There on 24 Jan. 1907 he was visited by Horace George Rayner, a young man who falsely claimed to be an illegitimate son. Whiteley treated him as a blackmailer, and was about to summon a constable when Rayner shot him dead. Whiteley was buried with an imposing ceremonial at Kensal Green on 30 Jan. 1907. His assailant, who tried and failed to commit suicide, was sentenced to death at the Central Criminal Court on 22 March 1907, but the home secretary (Mr. Herbert Gladstone), yielding to public opinion, which detected extenuating circumstances in the crime, commuted the sentence to imprisonment for life.

By his wife Harriet Sarah Hill, who survived him, Whiteley left two sons, William and Frank, and two daughters, Ada and Clara. His estate was valued at 1,452,829*l.* Apart from a generous provision for his family by a will dated 20 May 1904, he left a million pounds in the hands of trustees to be devoted to the construction and maintenance of Whiteley Homes for the Aged Poor. For this purpose a garden city of over 200 acres, Whiteley Park, Burr Hill, Surrey, is in course of construction. The business was considerably enlarged by his sons in 1909–1910, and an immense building in the Queen's Road, costing over 250,000*l.* and covering nearly twenty acres, was opened in Oct. 1911.

A portrait in oils by Haymes Williams (1889) and a bust by Adams-Acton belong to his sons.

[Biograph, 1881, p. 421; The Times, Jan., Feb., March 1907, passim; Annual Reg. 1907; Whiteley's Diary and Almanac, 1877 and successive years; private information.]

T. S.

WHITEWAY, Sir **WILLIAM VALLANCE** (1828–1908), premier of Newfoundland, was younger son of Thomas Whiteway, a yeoman farmer of Buckyett House at Little Hempston, a village near Totnes, where he was born on 1 April 1828. Perpetuating the old-time connection between Devonshire and Newfoundland, he was presented at the time of the diamond jubilee of 1897 with the freedom of the borough of Totnes. Educated at Totnes grammar school and at the school of Mr. Phillips, M.A., at Newton Abbot, he went out to Newfoundland to be articled to his brother-in-law, R. R. Wakeham, a prominent lawyer in the colony, in 1843, when he was only fifteen years old. He qualified as a solicitor in December 1849, was called to the Newfoundland bar in 1852, and became Q.C. in 1862. In 1858 he entered the legislature. From 1865 to 1869 he was speaker of the House of Assembly. In 1869 he went with Sir Frederick Carter, then premier of Newfoundland, and Sir Ambrose Shea to Ottawa to negotiate terms of confederation with the then newly formed dominion of Canada. The terms were decisively rejected in the same year by the Newfoundland electorate. When Sir Frederick Carter returned to power in 1873, Whiteway became solicitor-general in his administration, with a seat in the cabinet; and when Carter took a seat on the judges' bench, Whiteway succeeded him in 1878 as premier and attorney-general. In the previous year, 1877, he had been appointed counsel for Newfoundland at the Halifax fisheries commission. This commission met, under the terms of the treaty of Washington of 1871, to assess the value of the difference between the privileges accorded to Great Britain and those acquired by the United States under the treaty. The commissioners awarded to Great Britain money compensation to the amount of 5½ million dollars, of which sum Newfoundland subsequently received one million dollars. For his services Whiteway received the thanks of both houses of the Newfoundland legislature. He was made K.C.M.G. in 1880. In 1885 his government made way for the Thorburn administration. He returned to power as premier and attorney-general in 1889, and held office till 1894. After the general election in 1893 petitions were filed in the supreme court against Whiteway and many of his colleagues and supporters on the ground of corrupt practices. As a result, Whiteway was, in 1894, unseated and disqualified under section 17 of the Elections Act of 1889. His government resigned on 11 April 1894; but critical times followed. In December a great bank crisis took place. On 27 Jan. 1895 an Act was passed by the legislature removing the disabilities of members who had been unseated by the decision of the supreme court. On 31 Jan. 1895 Whiteway again became premier, and held office until 1897, when he resigned, and practically ended his public career. He made an effort to re-enter public life in 1904, largely as a protest against the Reid contract of 1901 [see Reid, Sir Robert Gillespie, Suppl. II], but was unsuccessful, partly because he was supposed to favour confederation with Canada. In 1897 he represented Newfoundland, as premier, at the diamond jubilee and the colonial conference of that year, and was made a privy councillor, being the first Newfoundland minister to attain that honour. He was also made a D.C.L. of Oxford.

Whiteway played a prominent part in the negotiations respecting the Newfoundland fisheries and French shore questions, and went to England four times as a delegate from the colony to the imperial government. In 1891 he was heard at the bar of the House of Lords, when the French fishery treaty bill was before that house. The net result was that, as an alternative to imperial legislation, the Newfoundland legislature passed temporary measures for the purpose of carrying out the treaty obligations of Great Britain to France in respect of Newfoundland. Whiteway, too, was premier when the abortive Bond-Blaine convention was, in 1890, negotiated with the United States.

It is as a promoter of railways in Newfoundland that his name will be principally remembered (PROWSE'S *History of Newfoundland*, 1895, p. 495 note). In 1880 he carried the first railway bill through the island legislature for the construction of a light railway from St. John's to Hall's Bay, and though he was personally in favour of construction by the government, the work was entrusted to an American syndicate with unsatisfactory results. When he returned to power in 1889 he took up again with vigour the policy of developing the colony by railways, and during his second administration he concluded the earlier contracts with Robert Gillespie Reid of Montreal under which the railway was subsequently constructed via the Exploits river to Port aux Basques in the south-west of the island, the nearest point to Cape Breton Island and Nova Scotia. The later Reid contracts of 1898 and 1901 were not in accordance with his views.

A leading member of the Church of England in Newfoundland, and district grand master of the Freemasons, Whiteway died at St. John's on 24 June 1908, the natal day of Newfoundland, and was buried in the Church of England cemetery at St. John's.

He married (1) in 1862 Mary (*d.* 1868), daughter of J. Lightbourne, rector of Trinity Church in Bermuda; (2) in 1872 Catherine Anne, daughter of W. H. Davies of Nova Scotia. One son and two daughters survived him.

[The Daily News, St. John's, Newfoundland, 25 June 1908; The Times, 26 June 1908; Blue Books; D. W. Prowse's History of Newfoundland, 1895; 2nd edit. 1896; Colonial Office List; Who's Who.] C. P. L.

WHITMAN, ALFRED CHARLES (1860–1910), writer on engravings, youngest son of Edwin Whitman, a grocer, by his wife Fanny, was born at Hammersmith on 12 October 1860, and was educated at St. Mark's College School, Chelsea. On leaving school he was employed by the firm of Henry Dawson & Sons, typo-etching company, of Farringdon Street and Chiswick, with whom he remained till he was appointed on 21 Dec. 1885 an attendant in the department of prints and drawings in the British Museum. For some years he served in his spare time as amanuensis to Lady Charlotte Schreiber [q. v.] and assisted her in the arrangement and cataloguing of her collections of fans and playing-cards. He was promoted to the office of departmental clerk in the print department on 20 May 1903. His tact, patience, and courtesy, combined with an exceptional knowledge of the English prints in the collection, made his aid invaluable to visitors who consulted it, and he acquired, in particular, a well-deserved reputation as an authority on British mezzotint engraving. His earlier books, 'The Masters of Mezzotint' (1898) and 'The Print Collector's Handbook' (1901; new and enlarged edit. 1912), were of a popular character, and have less permanent value than the catalogues of eminent engravers' works, which were the outcome of notes methodically compiled during many years, not only in the British Museum, but in private collections and sale-rooms. 'Valentine Green,' published in 1902 as part of a series, 'British Mezzotinters,' to which other writers contributed under his direction, is less satisfactory than 'Samuel William Reynolds,' published in 1903 as the first volume in a series of 'Nineteenth Century Mezzotinters.' It was followed by 'Samuel Cousins' (1904) and 'Charles Turner' (1907). These two books rank among the best catalogues of an engraver's work produced in England. Whitman's health began to fail in the autumn of 1908, and he died in London after a long illness, on 2 Feb. 1910. His annotated copy of J. Chaloner Smith's 'British Mezzotint Portraits' was sold at Christie's on 6 June 1910 for 430*l.* 10*s.* On 12 August 1885 he married, at Hammersmith, Helena Mary Bing.

[The Athenæum, 12 Feb. 1910; private information.] C. D.

WHITMORE, SIR GEORGE STODDART (1830–1903), major-general, commandant of forces in New Zealand, born at Malta on 1 May 1830, was son of Major George St. Vincent Whitmore, R.E., and grandson of General Sir George Whitmore (1775–1862), K.C.H., colonel-commandant R.E. His mother was Isabella, daughter of Sir John Stoddart [q. v.], chief justice of Malta. Educated at Edinburgh Academy and at the Staff College, he achieved some success, and entered the army in 1847 as ensign in the Cape mounted rifles. He became lieutenant in May 1850, captain in July 1854, and brevet-major in June 1856. He distinguished himself in the Kaffir wars of 1847 and 1851–3, and was present at the defeat of the Boers at Boem Plaats in 1848. In 1855–6 he served with distinction in the Crimea, receiving the fourth class of the Mejidie. In 1861 he went to New Zealand as military secretary to Sir Duncan Alexander Cameron [q. v. Suppl. I], then in command of the English forces engaged in the Maori war. In the succeeding year he resigned his position in the army in order to buy and farm a run in Hawke's Bay. During 1865 the natives were in active revolt in this district. Whitmore, who complied with a request to take command of the Hawke's Bay militia on the east coast, decisively defeated the Maoris at Omaranui (October 1866), and thus secured peace for eighteen months. In June 1868 the war started again on the west coast, and in July Whitmore was sent in pursuit of an active minor chief called Te Kooti, at the head of the volunteers and a detachment of armed constabulary. He overtook the enemy at Ruakiture on 8 Aug., and an indecisive engagement followed. Te Kooti, although wounded in the foot, escaped, and Whitmore was obliged to fall back in order to procure supplies.

Shortly afterwards, on the west coast, Whitmore served under Colonel McDonnell, an officer who was his junior, in order to restore his prestige after defeat. On McDonnell's withdrawal on leave of absence, Whitmore assumed the command, and on 5 Nov. 1868 was defeated by Titokowaru at Moturoa. Summoned straightway to the east coast to oppose Te Kooti, who, after some fresh successes, had fortified himself in a pa on the crest of a hill called Ngatapa, Whitmore joined forces with the friendly natives and invested the pa, which after five days' siege fell on 3 January 1869; 136 Hau-Haus were killed, but Te Kooti escaped. This was the last important engagement fought in New Zealand. Whitmore left Ropata, the leader of the friendly Maoris, to deal with Te Kooti, and returned to Wanganui to pursue Titokowaru. He succeeded in chasing the enemy northwards out of the disputed territories until they took refuge in the interior, where, as they were now powerless, he left them alone. Then, sent against Te Kooti, who had started another insurrection in the Uriwera district, he seemed on the point of victory when the Stafford ministry fell, and the new premier, Fox, removed him from his command. Whitmore published an account of 'The Last Maori War in New Zealand' (1902); he stated that he retired through illness.

From 1863 Whitmore sat on the legislative council, where he supported Sir Edward William Stafford [q. v. Suppl. II] and the war policy. In 1870 he protested against the immigration and public works bill. From 18 October 1877 to October 1879 he was colonial secretary and defence minister under Sir George Grey. In 1879 he went to Taranaki with Grey and the governor to deal with the disturbance created by Te Whiti. On 16 Aug. 1874 he became a member of the Stout-Vogel cabinet without a portfolio, but, owing to jealousy between the provinces of Auckland and Canterbury, the government was defeated at the end of a fortnight. On 5 Sept. Stout and Vogel returned to power and Whitmore was created commandant of the colonial forces and commissioner of the armed constabulary, with the rank of major-general. This was the first time the honour had been conferred in New Zealand on an officer of the colonial troops. He was created C.M.G. in 1869, K.C.M.G. in 1882. He visited England in 1902 in order to publish his book on the Maori war. He returned to New Zealand in February 1903. He died at The Blue Cottage, Napier, Hawke's Bay, New Zealand, on 16 March 1903, and was buried in Napier Cemetery. In 1865 he married Isabella, daughter of William Smith of Roxeth, near Rugby, England. He left no issue.

[W. Pember Reeves's The Long White Cloud; Rusden's New Zealand; Mennell's Australas. Biog.; Gisborne, New Zealand Rulers, 1887 (with portrait); Whitmore, Last Maori War; New Zealand Times, Wellington Evening Post, and Christchurch Press, 17 March 1903.] A. B. W.

WHITWORTH, WILLIAM ALLEN (1840–1905), mathematical and religious writer, born at Bank House, Runcorn, on 1 Feb. 1840, was the eldest son in the family of four sons and two daughters of William Whitworth, at one time schoolmaster at Runcorn and incumbent of Little Leigh, Cheshire, and of Widnes, Lancashire. His mother was Susanna, daughter of George Coyne of Kilbeggan, co. Westmeath, and first cousin to Joseph Stirling Coyne [q. v.].

After education at Sandicroft School, Northwich (1851–7), Whitworth proceeded to St. John's College, Cambridge, in October 1858, and in 1861 was elected a scholar. In 1862 he graduated B.A. as 16th wrangler, proceeding M.A. in 1865; he was fellow of his college from 1867 to 1884. He was successively chief mathematical master at Portarlington School and Rossall School and professor of mathematics at Queen's College, Liverpool (1862–4).

From early youth Whitworth showed a mathematical promise and originality to which his place in the tripos scarcely did justice. While an undergraduate he was principal editor with Charles Taylor [q. v. Suppl. II] and others of the 'Oxford, Cambridge, and Dublin Messenger of Mathematics,' started at Cambridge in November 1861. The publication was continued as 'The Messenger of Mathematics'; Whitworth remained one of the editors till 1880, and was a frequent contributor. His earliest article on 'The Equiangular Spiral, its Chief Properties proved Geometrically' (i. 5–13), was translated into French in the 'Nouvelles Annales de Mathématiques' (1869). An important treatise on 'Trilinear Co-ordinates and other Methods of Modern Analytical Geometry of Two Dimensions' was issued at Cambridge in 1866. Whitworth's best-known mathematical work, entitled 'Choice and Chance, an Elementary Treatise on Permutations, Combinations and Probability' (Cambridge, 1867), was elaborated from lectures delivered to ladies at Queen's College, Liverpool, in 1866. A model of clear and simple exposition, it presents a very ample collection of problems on probability and kindred subjects, solutions to which were provided in 'DCC Exercises' (1897). Numerous additions to the problems were made in subsequent editions (5th edit. 1901).

Meanwhile Whitworth was ordained deacon in 1865 and priest in 1866, and won a high repute in a clerical career. He was curate at St. Anne's, Birkenhead (1865), and of St. Luke's, Liverpool (1866–70), and perpetual curate of Christ Church, Liverpool (1870–5). His success with parochial missions in Liverpool led to preferments in London. He was vicar of St. John the Evangelist, Hammersmith (1875–86), and vicar of All Saints', Margaret Street, Marylebone, from November 1886 till his death. He also held from 1885 the sinecure college living of Aberdaron with Llanfaebrhys in the diocese of Bangor (1885), and was from 1891 to 1892 commissary of the South African diocese of Blomfontein. Whitworth was select preacher at Cambridge in 1872, 1878, 1884, 1894, and 1900, Hulsean lecturer there (1903–4), and was made a prebendary of St. Paul's Cathedral in 1900.

Whitworth, who had been brought up as an evangelical, was influenced at Cambridge by the scholarship of Lightfoot and Westcott, and he studied later the German rationalising school of theology. As a preacher he showed critical insight and learning. His sympathies lay mainly with the high church party, and in 1875 he joined the English Church Union. In the ritual controversy of 1898–9 he showed moderation, and differed from the union in its opposition to the archbishops' condemnation of the use of incense. He contended that the obsolete canon law should not be allowed 'to supersede the canonical utterance of the living voice of the Church of England.' His ecclesiastical position may be deduced from his publications: 'Quam Dilecta,' a description of All Saints' Church, Margaret St., 1891; 'The Real Presence, with Other Essays,' 1893, and 'Worship in the Christian Church,' 1899. Two volumes of sermons were published posthumously: 'Christian Thought on Present Day Questions' (1906) and 'The Sanctuary of God' (1908). He also published 'The Churchman's Almanac for Eight Centuries,' a mathematical calculation of the date of every Sunday (1882).

Whitworth died on 12 March 1905 at Fitzroy House Nursing Home after a serious operation (28 February) and was buried at Brookwood in ground belonging to St. Alban's, Holborn. There is a slab to his memory in the floor of All Saints' Church, Margaret Street. He married on 10 June 1885 Sarah Louisa, only daughter of Timms Hervey Elwes, and had issue four sons, all graduates of Trinity College, Cambridge.

[Guardian, 15 and 22 March 1905; Church Times, 17 March 1905; The Times, 13 March 1905; Eagle, June 1905, xxvi. 396–9; information from brother, Mr. G. C. Whitworth, and Professor W. H. H. Hudson.] D. J. O.

WHYMPER, EDWARD (1840–1911), wood-engraver and mountain climber, born at Lambeth Terrace, Kennington Road, on 27 April 1840, was the second son of Josiah Wood Whymper [q. v. Suppl. II] by his first wife, Elizabeth Whitworth Claridge. He was privately educated. While still a youth he entered his father's business in Lambeth as a wood-engraver and in time succeeded to its control. For many years he maintained its reputation for the production of the highest class of book illustration, until towards the close of the last century the improvement in cheap photographic processes destroyed the demand for such work. His woodcuts may be found in his own works, the 'Alpine Journal,' and many books of travel between 1865 and 1895; among his more important productions were Josef Wolf's 'Wild Animals' (1874) and Cassell's 'Picturesque Europe' (1876–1879).

Edward, though he seldom exhibited, was,

like his father, a water-colour artist of considerable ability, and it was to this gift that he owed a commission that proved a turning-point in his life. In 1860 William Longman, of the firm of publishers, an early president of the Alpine Club, needed illustrations of the then little known mountains of Dauphiné for the second series of 'Peaks, Passes, and Glaciers' (1862) and young Whymper was sent out to make the sketches. He states (*Alpine Journal*, v. 161) that he saw in the chance of going to the Alps a step towards training himself for employment in Arctic exploration, an object of his early ambition. In the following year he showed his ability as a mountaineer by climbing Mont Pelvoux (*Peaks, Passes, and Glaciers*, 2nd series). In the seasons of 1862–5, by a series of brilliant climbs on peaks and passes, he made himself one of the leading figures in the conquest of the Alps. In 1864 he took part in the first ascent of the highest mountain in Dauphiné, the Pointe des Écrins, and of several peaks in the chain of Mont Blanc. In 1865 he climbed the western peak of the Grandes Jorasses and the Aiguille Verte.

Whymper's fixed ambition, however, during this period was to conquer the reputedly inaccessible Matterhorn. In this he had formidable rivals in Prof. Tyndall and the famous Italian guides, the Carrels of Val Tournanche. He made no fewer than seven attempts on the mountain from the Italian side, which were all foiled by the continuous difficulties of the climb or by bad weather. In one of them, while climbing alone, he met with a serious accident. At last, in July 1865, the plan of trying the Zermatt ridge was adopted, and success was gained at the first attempt. But the sequel was a tragedy rarely paralleled in the history of mountaineering. The party, from no fault of Whymper's, was too large and was ill constituted for such an adventure. It consisted of seven persons, Lord Francis Douglas, Charles Hudson, vicar of Skillington, Lincolnshire, his young friend D. Hadow, and Whymper, with the experienced guides Michel Croz of Chamonix and Peter Taugwalder of Zermatt, with the latter's son as porter. Hadow, the youngest member of the party, a lad inexperienced in rock-climbing, fell on the descent, and dragged down with him Douglas, Hudson, and the guide Croz. The rope broke, and Whymper was left, with the Zermatt men, clinging to the mountain side, while his companions disappeared over the precipice. Investigation showed that the rope that broke was a spare piece of inferior quality, which had been improperly used.

This terrible catastrophe gave Whymper a European reputation in connection with the Matterhorn, which was extended and maintained by the volume 'Scrambles amongst the Alps' (1871; 2nd edit. same year; 3rd edit. condensed as 'Ascent of the Matterhorn,' 1879; 4th edit. 1893, reissued in Nelson's shilling library, 1905), in which he told the story with dramatic skill and emphasis. The Matterhorn disaster terminated Whymper's active career as an Alpine climber, though he often subsequently visited the Alps, and for literary purposes repeated his ascent of the Matterhorn. In 1867 he turned his attention to Greenland with the idea of ascertaining the nature of the interior, and if possible of crossing it. But a second preliminary trip in 1872 convinced him that the task was too great for his private resources. The literary and scientific results of these journeys were recorded in three entertaining papers in the 'Alpine Journal' (vols. v. and vi.), a lecture to the British Association (*39th Report*, 1869), and a paper by Prof. Heer (*Philosophical Transactions*, 1869, p. 445) on the fossils, trees, and shrubs collected. The chief practical result was to show that the interior of Greenland was a snowy plateau which could be traversed by sledges, provided the start was made sufficiently early in the year, and thus to pave the way for Nansen's success in 1888.

In 1888 Whymper turned his attention to the Andes of Ecuador. At that date the still unsettled problem of the power of resistance, or adaptation, of the human frame to the atmosphere of high altitudes was being vigorously discussed. Whymper proposed as his main object to make experiments at heights about and over 20,000 feet. The results he obtained, if they did not settle a question complicated by many physical, local, and personal variations, served to advance our knowledge, and have been in important respects confirmed by the experiences of Dr. Longstaff, the Duke of the Abruzzi, and others at still higher elevations between 20,000 and 25,000 feet. For example, it is now admitted that long sojourn under low pressures diminishes the climbers' physical powers rather than trains them, and it is also agreed that Whymper was right in contesting the conclusion of Paul Bert that inhalation of oxygen would prove a convenient remedy, or palliative, in cases of 'mountain sickness.'

From a climber's point of view the expedition was completely successful. The summits of Chimborazo (20,498 feet) and six other mountains of between 15,000 and 20,000 feet were reached for the first time. A night was spent on the top of Cotopaxi (19,613 feet), and the features of that great volcano were thoroughly studied. From the wider points of view of the geographer, the geologist and the general traveller, Whymper brought home much valuable material, which was carefully condensed and embodied in the volume 'Travels among the Great Andes of the Equator' (1892). Its value was recognised by the council of the Royal Geographical Society, which in 1892 conferred on Whymper one of their Royal Medals in recognition of the fact that, apart from his mountaineering exploits, 'he had largely corrected and added to our geographical and physical knowledge of the mountain systems of Ecuador, fixed the position of all the great Ecuadorian mountains, produced a map constructed from original theodolite observations extending over 250 miles, and ascertained seventy altitudes by means of three mercurial barometers.' The Society also made a grant to the family of his leading guide, J. A. Carrel of Val Tournanche. The collection of rock specimens and volcanic dusts brought home by Whymper from this journey was described by Dr. Bonney in five papers in the 'Proceedings of the Royal Society' (Nos. 229–234). He also collected many natural history specimens, which were described in the supplementary volume of his 'Travels' (1892). For these explorations Whymper devised a form of tent which bears his name and is still in general use with mountain explorers. He also suggested improvements in aneroid barometers.

In 1901 and several subsequent summers Whymper visited the Canadian Rocky Mountains, but did not publish any account of his wanderings.

Finding his craft of wood engraving practically brought to an end, Whymper employed his leisure in his later years mainly in compiling and keeping up to date two local handbooks to Chamonix (1896) and Zermatt (1897). Well illustrated, and not devoid of personal and picturesque touches, these attained high popularity and passed in his lifetime through fifteen editions.

He died at Chamonix on 16 Sept. 1911 while on a visit to the Alps, and was buried in the churchyard of the English church at Chamonix.

With strangers Whymper's manner was apt to be reserved and at times self-assertive. But amongst acquaintances and persons interested in the same topics with himself his talk was shrewd, instructive, and entertaining. He was by instinct both a craftsman and an artist. With these gifts he coupled great physical endurance and intellectual patience and perseverance, qualities which he displayed both on the mountains and in his business. In everything he aimed at thoroughness. He would never if he could help it put up with inferior material or indifferent workmanship. To his own volumes he devoted years of careful preparation. 'Whymper,' writes Dr. Bonney, 'always laid hold of what was characteristic and useful, and his remarks upon what he had seen were shrewd and suggestive.' 'All his life long he was a modest, steady, and efficient worker in the things he undertook to do. He enjoyed the reputation of a serious writer, explorer, and a man of iron will and nerve, who has worthily accomplished not merely feats of valour, but explorations and studies which have yielded valuable additions to human knowledge' (Sir Martin Conway in *Fry's Mag.* June 1910).

Whymper served from 1872 to 1874 as a vice-president of the Alpine Club. In 1872 he was created a knight of the Italian order of St. Maurice and St. Lazarus. He was an honorary member of the French Geographical Society and of most of the principal mountaineering clubs of Europe and North America. He married in 1906 Edith Mary Lewin, and left by her one daughter, Ethel Rose. Photographs of him taken in 1865 and 1910 are given in the 'Alpine Journal' (vol. xxvi. pp. 55 and 58), Feb. 1912.

Besides the works cited Whymper published 'How to Use the Aneroid Barometer' (1891).

A portrait in oils by Lance Calkin was exhibited at the Royal Academy in 1894.

[Personal knowledge; family information; own works; Alpine Journal, Feb. 1912, art. by Dr. T. G. Bonney; Fry's Mag., June 1910, art. by Sir M. Conway; Strand Mag., June 1912, art. by Coulson Kernahan; Scribner's Mag., June 1903; Dr. H. Dübi, 'Zur Erinnerung an Edward Whymper' in Jahrbuch des Schweizer Alpen Club, 1911–12 (portrait).]

D. W. F.

WHYMPER, JOSIAH WOOD (1813–1903), wood-engraver, born in Ipswich on 24 April 1813, was second son of Nathaniel Whimper, a brewer, and for some time town councillor of Ipswich, by his wife Elizabeth Orris. The Whymper (or Whimper) family has been honourably known in Suffolk since the seventeenth century, one branch (including J. W. Whymper's great grandfather, Thomas Thurston) having been owners of the Glevering Hall estate (near Wickham Market) for several generations. After 1840 J. W. Whymper adopted what he considered the original spelling of his family name, Whymper; many of his early woodcuts are signed Whimper. He received his early education in private schools in his native town, and wishing to become a sculptor was apprenticed at his own desire to a stone-mason, but an accident in the mason's yard terminated his apprenticeship, and all but ended his life before he was sixteen. On his mother's death in 1829 he went to London with the hope of finding entrance to some sculptor's studio, but he was dissuaded from taking up that branch of art by John C. F. Rossi, R.A., to whom he had an introduction. Determined not to ask support from home, he turned to wood-engraving, teaching himself, and beginning by executing orders for shop-bills and the like. This led to some commissions for the 'Penny Magazine.' His prosperity started with the successful sale of an etching of New London Bridge at the time of its opening (1831), which realised 30*l*. profit. He lived for many years in Lambeth (20 Canterbury Place), doing much wood-engraving for John Murray, the S.P.C.K., and the Religious Tract Society. Among his best engravings are those in Scott's 'Poetical Works' (Black, 1857); 'Picturesque Europe' (Cassell, 1876–9); Byron's 'Childe Harold' (Murray); E. Whymper's 'Scrambles in the Alps' (Murray); and in Murray's editions of Schliemann's works. He had many pupils, the most distinguished being Fred Walker and Charles Keene. He engraved a very large number of illustrations by Sir John Gilbert, who was his intimate friend and a constant travelling companion for water-colour sketching. He had taken up water-colour after 1840, having a few lessons from Collingwood Smith. He commenced to exhibit in 1844, and became a member of the New Water-colour Society (now the Royal Institute of Painters in Water-colours) in 1854. From 1859 he had a country house at Haslemere, but did not finally retire from his work in London until 1884. He died at Town House, Haslemere, on 7 April 1903, and was buried in Haslemere churchyard.

He married twice: (1) in 1837 Elizabeth Whitworth Claridge (1819–1859), by whom he had nine sons and two daughters, including Edward [q. v. Suppl. II], the Alpine traveller and wood-engraver, and Charles, an animal painter; (2) in 1866 Emily Hepburn (*d*. 1886) (a talented water-colour painter, who exhibited at the Royal Academy 1877–8, and Royal Institute 1883–5).

A portrait by Lance Calkin was exhibited in the Royal Academy in 1889.

[D. E. Davy, Pedigrees of the Families of Suffolk, British Museum, MSS.; The Times, 8 April 1903; Catalogues of the New Water-colour Society (later the Royal Institute of Painters in Water-colours); information supplied by his daughter, Miss Annette Whymper.] A. M. H.

WICKHAM, EDWARD CHARLES (1834–1910), dean of Lincoln, eldest son of Edward Wickham, at one time vicar of Preston Candover, Hampshire, by his wife Christiana St. Barbe, daughter of C. H. White, rector of Shalden, Hampshire, was born on 7 Dec. 1834 at Eagle House, Brook Green, Hammersmith, where his father then kept a private school of high reputation. Here he received his early education, entering Winchester as a commoner in January 1848. On 8 July 1850 he was admitted to a place in college, was senior in school November 1851, and in January 1852 he succeeded to a fellowship at New College, Oxford, beginning his undergraduate career at the age of seventeen. In December 1854 he took a first class in classical moderations, and a second class in literæ humaniores in July 1856, winning the chancellor's prize for Latin verse in the same year, and the Latin essay in 1857. He graduated B.A. in 1857, and proceeded to the degrees of M.A. in 1859, and of B.D. and D.D. in 1894.

He was ordained deacon in 1857 and priest in 1858, and after a two years' experience in teaching Sixth Book at Winchester he was recalled to Oxford, where he still retained his fellowship, by the offer of a tutorship. Here he took a leading part in the series of reforms which threw New College open to scholars and commoners who had not been educated at Winchester, and he helped to amend the statutes so as to allow tutors and other college officers to retain their fellowships after marriage. In conjunction with his friend, Edwin Palmer of Balliol, he initiated the system of intercollegiate lectures. Wickham's fine scholarship, his influence with the undergraduates, and his power of preaching made him one of the most successful tutors of his time, and he gradually acquired an important position in the general management of university affairs. In September 1873 he succeeded Edward White Benson [q. v. Suppl. I] as headmaster of Wellington College, a post which he filled for twenty years. Though he possessed many of the qualifications of a successful schoolmaster, and won the affection of those masters and boys who were brought in close contact with him, his cold manner and unimpressive physique stood in the way of anything like general popularity. In spite of vicissitudes, however, he guided the college safely through some perilous crises and left it better equipped and organised than he found it. His scanty leisure was devoted to an elaborate edition of 'Horace' (vol. i. 1874; vol. ii. 1893), which bore tribute to his fine scholarship. He resigned Wellington in the summer of 1893, and in January 1894 was appointed dean of Lincoln in succession to William John Butler [q. v. Suppl. I]. Here he did excellent work, both in his official capacity in the cathedral and in the city at large. His sermons, exquisitely delivered and given in fastidiously chosen language, had been widely appreciated both at New College and Wellington, and he was chosen select preacher before the University of Oxford for four different years. Wickham also took a prominent share in the debates of convocation and devoted himself to the better organisation both of primary and secondary education in the diocese of Lincoln. He was one of the leading spirits on the education settlement committee formed in 1907 to bring nonconformists and churchmen together. In general politics he was a strong liberal, and his marriage to the daughter of Gladstone placed him in close relations with the liberal party; he followed his father-in-law with absolute faith and devotion. He died on 18 Aug. 1910 at Sierre in Switzerland, whither he had gone with his family for a holiday, and there he was buried, Dr. Randall Davidson, archbishop of Canterbury, performing the service.

He was married on 27 Dec. 1873 to Agnes, eldest daughter of William Ewart Gladstone, by whom he had a family of two sons and three daughters; she survived him. An oil painting of Wickham by Sir William Richmond hangs in the hall at New College.

Besides the edition of 'Horace' already referred to, his published works include: 1. 'Notes and Questions on the Church Catechism,' 1892. 2. 'The Prayer-Book,' 1895, intended for the middle form in public schools. 3. 'Wellington College Sermons,' 1897. 4. 'Horace for English Readers,' in the form of a prose translation, 1903. 5. 'The Epistle to the Hebrews,' in English, with introduction and notes, 1910. 6. 'Revision of Rubrics, its Purpose and Principles,' in the 'Prayer-Book Revision' series, 1910.

[A Memoir of Edward Charles Wickham, by the Rev. Lonsdale Ragg, B.D., 1911; The Times, 19 Aug. 1910; Spectator, 30 Dec. 1911; personal knowledge.] J. B. A.

WIGGINS, JOSEPH (1832–1905), explorer of the sea-route to Siberia, born at Norwich on 3 Sept. 1832, was son of Joseph Wiggins (*d.* 1843) by his wife Anne Petty (*d.* 1847). The father, a driver and later proprietor of coaches serving the London - Bury - St. Edmunds - Norwich Road, established himself in 1838–9 at Bury, where he combined inn-keeping with his coaching business, then beginning to suffer from railway competition. At his death in 1843 his widow, left with small means, returned with her family of six sons and three daughters to Norwich, where Joseph was sent to Farnell's school. At the age of fourteen he went to Sunderland as an apprentice to his uncle, Joseph Potts, a shipowner. He rose rapidly, being master of a ship at twenty-one and subsequently owning cargo-vessels. In 1868 he temporarily left the sea and became a board of trade examiner in navigation and seamanship at Sunderland. He was now first attracted by the ruling interest of his life—the possibility of establishing a trade route between western Europe and Asiatic Russia (Siberia), by way of the Arctic seas and the great rivers which drain into them from the land. The overland route (by sledge and caravan) was slow, erratic, and expensive, and the resources of Siberia, largely on that account, were little developed. The sea route was held, as the result of a Russian survey, to be impracticable owing to ice and fog. Wiggins argued that a branch of the warm Atlantic drift ought for a certain period of the year to open up the western entrances to the Kara Sea and (in conjunction with the outflow of the great rivers) a route through the sea itself. After full inquiry he chartered and fitted at his own charges a steamer of 103 tons and sailed from Dundee on 3 June 1874. (Sir) Henry Morton Stanley [q. v. Suppl. II] was anxious but unable to accompany him. On June 28 his ship entered upon her struggle with the ice; it was not until 5 Aug. that he rounded

White Island off the Yalmal Peninsula, and after reaching the mouth of the Ob, he was compelled to return owing to lack of provisions, expense, and the attitude of most of his crew. He reached Hammerfest on 7 Sept. and Dundee on 25 Sept. Though his route was already used by Norwegian fishermen and had been followed by the boats of Russian traders as early as the sixteenth century, his voyage called general attention to the possibility of establishing a new commercial route with large vessels. Wiggins expounded his results and opinions in lectures which won him a wide fame and thenceforth occupied him when on shore.

In 1875 he received private financial support and fitted out a sloop of twenty-seven tons for his next voyage. In her he reached Vardö on 27 July 1875, where he met the Russian admiral, Glassenov, and others interested in his work. He accompanied Glassenov, who promised to use his interest with the Russian government and merchants, to Archangel, where he obtained maps, rejoined his sloop, and worked her nearly to Kolguev Island, but thence turned back, the season being spent. Private munificence, partly British and partly Russian, rendered possible his third Siberian journey, in a steamer of 120 tons carrying an auxiliary launch. Sailing in July 1876, Wiggins inspected the Kara river late in August, and by 26 Sept., having found the Ob inaccessible owing to winds and current, was in the estuary of the Yenisei. On 18 Oct. his ship reached the Kureika (a right-bank tributary of the Yenisei, which it joins close to the Arctic circle), and was there laid up for the winter. Wiggins came home by way of St. Petersburg, where he was received with honour without obtaining material help, went on to England, and next year started for Siberia (overland) accompanied by Henry Seebohm [q. v.] the ornithologist. At the Kureika his ship was with difficulty released from the ice, and sailed down stream on 30 June 1877; but she was in ill condition and was wrecked three days later. In 1878 O. J. Cattley, a merchant in St. Petersburg, sent Wiggins in command of a trading steamer to the Ob, whence a cargo of wheat and other produce was successfully brought back. Other vessels performed the like feat. But in 1879–80 the failure of some British and Russian trading expeditions, with which Wiggins declined to be connected, owing to the unsuitability of the vessels, checked public confidence in his design, and from 1880 to 1887 he carried on the ordinary vocations of a master mariner in other seas. In 1887–8 a small company, named after its ship, the Phœnix (273 tons), and backed by Sir Robert Morier [q. v.], British ambassador at St. Petersburg, sent Wiggins in command of the vessel on perhaps his most brilliant voyage from the point of view of navigation. He took her up the river to Yeniseisk, far above what was supposed to be the head of navigation for so large a ship, and left his brother Robert, who was his chief officer, on the river as agent. Another ship followed in 1888, but this voyage and the company failed. In 1890 there was carried through, although Wiggins was not in command, the first successful trans-shipment of goods at the river mouth between a river steamer and a sea-going vessel. In 1893 Wiggins, by arrangement with the Russian government, took command of the Orestes, a larger vessel than any which had hitherto reached the mouth of the Yenisei, and safely delivered a cargo of rails for the Trans-Siberian railway. She convoyed at the same time the yacht Blencathra, belonging to Mr. F. W. Leybourne-Popham, who planned a voyage to the Kara sea to combine pleasure and trade. Acquiring an interest in the Siberian route, Mr. Leybourne-Popham helped in financing Wiggins's subsequent voyages. For this voyage of 1893 Wiggins was rewarded by the Russian government. Next year, after convoying two Russian steamers to the Yenisei, Wiggins was shipwrecked near Yugor Strait, and, with his companions, made a difficult land-journey home, when the Royal Geographical Society awarded him the Murchison medal. In 1895 he made his last voyage to Yeniseisk. Next year he failed to get beyond Vardö, and the failure involved him in some undeserved censure. In 1897–9 he was voyaging in other seas, and as late as 1903 he navigated a small yacht to Australia for the use of an expedition to New Guinea. In 1905 the Russo-Japanese war had begun and famine was rife in Siberia. The Russian government planned a large relief expedition by sea, and invited Wiggins to organise and lead it. In the organisation he took as active a part as failing health permitted, but when the ships sailed he was too ill to accompany them. He died at Harrogate on 13 Sept. 1905, and was buried at Bishopwearmouth. In 1868 he married his first cousin, Annie, daughter of Joseph Potts of Sunderland; she died without issue in 1904.

[Life and Voyages of Joseph Wiggins, by H. Johnson (London, 1907); private information. See also H. Seebohm's The Birds of Siberia for incidents of the journey on which he accompanied Wiggins, and Miss Peel's Polar Gleams (1894) for the voyage of the Blencathra. An interesting speech of Wiggins on Nansen's project for his drift across the polar area in the Fram is reported in the Geographical Journal, i. 26. See also Journ. Soc. of Arts, xliii. 499, and (for a report of one of Wiggins' lectures) Journ. Tyneside Geog. Soc. iii. 123.]

O. J. R. H.

WIGHAM, JOHN RICHARDSON (1829–1906), inventor, born at 5 South Gray Street, Edinburgh, on 15 Jan. 1829, was youngest son in the family of four sons and three daughters of John Wigham, shawl manufacturer, of Edinburgh, and member of the Society of Friends, by his wife Jane Richardson (*d.* 1830).

After slender schooling at Edinburgh, he removed at fourteen to Dublin, where he privately continued his studies, while serving as apprentice in the hardware and manufacturing business of his brother-in-law, Joshua Edmundson. The business, subsequently known as 'Joshua Edmundson & Co.,' passed, on Edmundson's death, under Wigham's control. It grew rapidly, a branch being opened in London which was eventually taken over by a separate company as 'Edmundson's Electricity Corporation,' with Wigham as chairman. In Dublin the firm devoted itself largely to experiments in gas-lighting, Wigham being particularly successful in designing small gas-works suitable for private houses and public institutions. In addition to his private business he held various engineering posts, and as engineer to the Commercial Gas Company of Ireland designed the gas-works at Kingstown. In the commercial life of Dublin he soon played a prominent part. He was from 1866 till his death a director of the Alliance and Dublin Consumers' Gas Company, director and vice-chairman of the Dublin United Tramways Company from 1881 to his death, and member of council (1879), secretary (1881–93), and eventually president (1894–6) of the Dublin Chamber of Commerce.

Wigham is mainly memorable as the inventor of important applications of gas to lighthouse illumination. In 1863 he was granted a small sum for experiments by the board of Irish lights, and in 1865 a system invented by him was installed at the Howth lighthouse near Dublin, the gas being manufactured on the spot. Its main advantages were that it dispensed with the lamp glass essential to the 4-wick Fresnel oil lamp of 240 candle-power then in universal use, while the power of the light could be increased or decreased at will, a 28-jet flame, which gave sufficient light for clear weather, being increased successively to a 48-jet, 68-jet, 88-jet, and 108-jet flame of 2923 candle-power on foggy nights. Though highly valued in Ireland, the system was condemned on trial by Thomas Stevenson [q. v.], engineer to the Scottish board of lights. It was made more effective, however, in 1868 by Wigham's invention of the powerful 'composite burner,' and in 1869 its further employment in Ireland was strongly advocated by John Tyndall [q. v.] in his capacity of scientific adviser to Trinity House and the board of trade. Wigham's ingenuity also acted as a powerful stimulant to rival patentees, leading to various improvements in oil apparatus by Sir James Nicholas Douglass [q. v. Suppl. I] and others.

In 1871 Wigham invented the first of the many group-flashing arrangements since of service in enabling seamen to distinguish between different lighthouses. His arrangement was adopted at Galley Head, Mew Head, and Tory Island off the Irish coast. In 1872 a triform light of his invention was installed experimentally at the High Lighthouse, Haisbro', Norfolk; but its further adoption in English lighthouses was discouraged by a committee of Trinity House in 1874. The board of Irish lights, however, continued to favour Wigham's system, and in 1878 they installed at Galley Head a powerful quadriform light of his with four tiers of superposed lenses and a 68-jet burner in the focus of each tier. In 1883 the board of trade appointed a lighthouse illuminants committee to consider the relative merits of gas, oil, and electric light. For some years Tyndall had felt that Sir James Douglass had used his influence as engineer to Trinity House for the furtherance of his own patents and to the disadvantage of Wigham's system. He now protested that, as rival patentees, Douglass and Wigham ought both to be members of the lighthouse illuminants committee or ought both to be excluded. His objection was overruled, and consequently he resigned his position of scientific adviser to the board of trade in March 1883. A bitter controversy followed in the press between Tyndall and Mr. Joseph Chamberlain, president of the board of trade. On Tyndall's resignation the lighthouse illuminants committee collapsed. A new committee, of which Douglass was a member, was appointed by Trinity House, and declared after extensive experiments at South Foreland for oil and electric light in preference to gas. Wigham protested against his lack of opportunity of demonstrating the advantages of his system, and claimed that his rival Douglass, who had condemned in official reports Wigham's invention of superposed lenses, afterwards employed them for the improvement of his own oil apparatus. Wigham eventually received 2500*l.* from the board of trade as compensation for the infringement of his patent. Among other of Wigham's inventions were fog-signals and gas-driven sirens, a 'sky-flashing arrangement,' and a 'continuous pulsating light' in connection with his system of gas-illumination for lighthouses, and a 'lighted buoy' or 'beacon' in which, using oil as the illuminant, he obtained, by imparting motion to the wick, a continuous light needing attention only once in thirty days.

Wigham was a member of the Dublin Society and of the Royal Irish Academy, an associate member of the Institute of Civil Engineers, and fellow of the Institution of Mechanical Engineers. He read papers on 'Gas as a Lighthouse Illuminant' and kindred subjects before the Society of Arts, the British Association, the Dublin Society, and the Shipmasters' Society. In politics he was a unionist and spoke at public meetings in opposition to home rule. He was also a zealous advocate of temperance. As a member of the Society of Friends he twice refused knighthood in 1887. He died on 16 Nov. 1906 after some four years' illness at his residence, Albany House, Monkstown, co. Dublin, and was buried in the Friends' burial ground, Temple Hill, Blackrock, co. Dublin. He married on 4 Aug. 1858 Mary, daughter of Jonathan Pim of Dublin, M.P. for Dublin city from 1865 to 1874, and had issue six sons and four daughters, of whom three sons and three daughters survived him. An enlarged photograph is in the council room of the Dublin Chamber of Commerce.

[The Irish Times, 17 Nov. 1906; Journal of Gas Lighting, 20 Nov. 1906; W. T. Jeans, Lives of the Electricians, 1887; Nineteenth Century, July 1888; Fortnightly Review, Dec. 1888 and Feb. 1889; Letters to The Times by Prof. Tyndall and others on lighthouse illuminants, 1885; paper by Wigham read before the Shipmasters' Society on 15 March 1895; T. Williams, Life of Sir James N. Douglass; Journal of Society of Arts, 1885–6; The Nautical Magazine, 1883 and 1884; art. on Lighthouses in Encyc. Brit. 11th edit.] S. E. F.

WIGRAM, WOOLMORE (1831–1907), campanologist, the fifth son of ten children of Money Wigram (1790–1873), director of the Bank of England, of Manor Place, Much Hadham, Hertfordshire, and Mary, daughter of Charles Hampden Turner, of Rooks Nest, Godstone, Surrey, was born on 29 Oct. 1831 at Devonshire Place, London. His father was elder brother of Sir James Wigram [q. v.], of Joseph Cotton Wigram [q. v.], and of George Vicesimus Wigram [q. v.]. Of his brothers, Charles Hampden (1826–1903) was knighted in 1902, and Clifford (1828–1898) was director of the bank of England. Wigram entered Rugby school in August 1844, and matriculated at Trinity College, Cambridge, in 1850, graduating B.A. in 1854 and proceeding M.A. in 1858. Among his intimate friends at Cambridge was John Gott, afterwards bishop of Truro [q. v. Suppl. II]. Taking holy orders in 1855, he was curate of Hampstead (1855–64), vicar of Brent Pelham with Furneaux Pelham, Hertfordshire (1864–76), and rector of St. Andrew's with St. Nicholas and St. Mary's, Hertford (1876–97). From 1877 to 1897 he was rural dean of Hertford, and in 1886 was made hon. canon of St. Albans, where he lived from 1898 till his death, and was an active member of the chapter. A high churchman, Wigram was long a member of the English Church Union.

Wigram was an enthusiastic campanologist, and became an authority on the subject. A series of articles in 'Church Bells' were published collectively in 1871 under the title of 'Change-ringing Disentangled and Management of Towers' (2nd edit. 1880).

In his earlier days Wigram was an enthusiastic Alpine climber. He was a member of the Alpine Club from 1858 to 1868. His most memorable feat was the first successful ascent, in the company of Thomas Stewart Kennedy (with Jean Baptiste Croz and Josef Marie Krönig as guides), of La Dent Blanche on 18 July 1862 (see his own account in *Memoirs*, 1908, pp. 81–95; T. S. Kennedy in *Alpine Journal*, 1864, i. 33–9: cf. Whymper's *Scrambles amongst the Alps*, chap. xiv.).

Wigram died from the effects of influenza at his residence in Watling Street, St. Albans, on 19 Jan. 1907, and was buried in St. Stephen's churchyard there. He married on 23 July 1863 Harriet Mary, daughter of the Rev. Thomas Ainger of Hampstead, and had issue four sons and three daughters.

[The Times, 22 Jan. 1907; Memoirs of Woolmore Wigram, 1831–1907, by his wife (with portrait), 1908.] W. B. O.

WILBERFORCE, ERNEST ROLAND (1840–1907), bishop successively of Newcastle and Chichester, the third son of the Right Rev. Samuel Wilberforce [q. v.] by his wife Emily Sargent, was born on 22 Jan. 1840 at his father's rectory at Brighstone in the Isle of Wight. He was educated at Harrow and at Exeter College, Oxford, graduating B.A. in 1864 and proceeding M.A. in 1867 and B.D. and D.D. in 1882. In December 1864 he was ordained deacon by his father, and priest in the following year. After serving the curacy of Cuddesdon and for a short time that of Lea in Lincolnshire, he was presented in 1868 to the living of Middleton Stoney, near Bicester, which he resigned in 1870 on account of his wife's health. In the same year he became domestic chaplain to his father, now bishop of Winchester, and in 1871 was made subalmoner to Queen Victoria by the dean of Windsor, Gerald Wellesley [q. v.]. On his father's death, 13 July 1873, he accepted from Gladstone the living of Seaforth, then a riverside suburb of Liverpool, but long since absorbed in the industrial quarter. Placed among a congregation of the old-fashioned evangelical type, he introduced a higher standard of churchmanship without causing offence, whilst making himself personally acceptable alike to the working classes and to the Liverpool merchants. Here he began that strong advocacy of temperance principles which henceforth became one of the main interests of his life. In October 1878 he was appointed by bishop Harold Browne [q. v. Suppl. I], his father's successor in the see of Winchester, to a residentiary canonry in that city, together with the wardenship of the Wilberforce Mission, formed and endowed as a memorial to his father. Owing to a readjustment of the diocesan boundaries, the court of chancery decided that the funds raised for the Wilberforce Mission must be devoted to the diocese of Rochester. Wilberforce retained his canonry and devoted himself with conspicuous success to mission work in Portsmouth and Aldershot. In 1882 he was appointed, on the recommendation of Gladstone, to the newly created see of Newcastle, of which he was consecrated the first bishop on 25 July in Durham cathedral. The occasion required exceptional energy and physical vigour, and Wilberforce, then in his forty-third year, devoted his great powers of work and organisation to recovering to the Church of England a territory which had been well-nigh lost to it. He made his way into the most remote Northumbrian parishes, confirming or otherwise officiating in every parish in his diocese, and inspiring with his own zeal a clergy by whom, in the past, the presence and authority of a bishop had been little felt. The 'Bishop of Newcastle's Fund,' inaugurated by him in 1882 was the means of raising, in a very short space of time, upwards of a quarter of a million of money for church purposes in the diocese. Though meeting at first with opposition from the more militant nonconformists, he gradually won the confidence of all classes, and found generous support from the wealthy laymen of the north, irrespective of creed. In November 1895 he was translated by Lord Salisbury to the see of Chichester, vacant by the death of Richard Durnford [q. v. Suppl. I], and he was enthroned in the cathedral on 28 Jan. 1896. The population of his new diocese was mainly agricultural, but the watering places on the south coast contained several churches in which the ritual was of a very 'advanced' description. Wilberforce was by temperament and conviction a high churchman of the old school, uniting a dislike for ritual with pronounced sacramentarian views. A vehement agitation against the excesses of some of his clergy was on foot, while the Lambeth 'opinions' of archbishops Temple and Maclagan had comprehensively condemned the use of incense and portable lights and the reservation of the sacrament. Wilberforce strove hard to bring the whole body of his clergy into acceptance of these decisions, endorsed as they were by the entire English episcopate, and he was successful in all but a handful of churches. He steadily refused to institute prosecutions against recalcitrant incumbents, but he declined to exercise his veto in their favour; and he refused to avail himself of the right, which he retained owing to the peculiar form of the patent to his chancellor, of personally hearing ritual cases in his own consistorial court. At the same time he deeply resented any interference with his episcopal authority, and he was brought into sharp contact with the Church Association.

His evidence before the royal commission appointed in 1905 to inquire into ecclesiastical disorders contained a vigorous defence of the clergy in his diocese. The success which crowned his policy was largely due to the exercise of what was practically a dispensing power.

These troubles were not allowed to interfere with the general administration of his diocese, and his exertions in setting on foot a regular system of Easter offerings as a means of increasing the stipends of the parochial clergy resulted in the annual collection of a sum which in the last year of his episcopate only just fell short of 10,000*l*. In 1896 he was elected chairman of the Church of England Temperance Society, and in 1904 he made one of a party of English clergy who visited South Africa on 'a mission of help.' Rhodesia and the northern Transvaal were allotted to him, and there his unaffected manners and downright speech proved highly attractive. He died after a short illness on 9 Sept. 1907 at Bembridge in the Isle of Wight, and he was buried at West Hampnett, near Chichester.

In many respects, and especially in speech and intonation, Ernest Wilberforce bore a marked resemblance to his father, from whom he inherited an eloquence which found a freer vent on the platform than in the pulpit. A somewhat chilling manner rendered him a formidable personality to those who had not the opportunity of penetrating beneath the reserve which covered a highly sympathetic and affectionate nature. Devoted to every form of exercise and sport, he spent part of his annual holidays on a salmon river in Norway. Endowed with extraordinary physical strength, he was a type of the muscular Christianity celebrated by Charles Kingsley and Tom Hughes. An oil painting by S. Goldsborough Anderson is in the possession of Mrs. Wilberforce; a replica hangs in the Palace at Chichester.

Wilberforce was twice married: (1) in 1863 to Frances Mary, third daughter of Sir Charles Anderson, Bart., who died in October 1870 at San Remo without issue; (2) on 14 Oct. 1874 to Emily, only daughter of George Connor, afterwards dean of Windsor [q. v.], who survived him, together with a family of three sons and three daughters.

[Ernest Roland Wilberforce, a Memoir by J. B. Atlay, 1912; Life of Samuel Wilberforce, by Canon Ashwell and Reginald Wilberforce; Chronicle of Convocation, Feb. 1908; Church Times, 13 Sept. 1907; Guardian, 11 Sept. 1907; the Temperance Chronicle, 13 Sept. 1907; Minutes of Evidence taken before the Royal Commission on Ecclesiastical Disorders, questions 18953–19154.] J. B. A.

WILKINS, AUGUSTUS SAMUEL (1843–1905), classical scholar, born in Enfield Road, Kingsland, London, N., on 20 Aug. 1843, was son of Samuel J. Wilkins, schoolmaster in Brixton, by his wife Mary Haslam of Thaxted, Essex. His parents were congregationalists. Educated at Bishop Stortford collegiate school, he then attended the lectures of Henry Malden [q. v.], professor of Greek, and of F. W. Newman [q. v. Suppl. I], professor of Latin, at University College, London. Entering St. John's College, Cambridge, with an open exhibition in October 1864, he became a foundation scholar in 1866, and won college prizes for English essays in 1865 and 1866, and the moral philosophy prize in 1868. He distinguished himself as a fluent speaker at the Union, and was president for Lent term, 1868. In the same year he graduated B.A. as fifth in the first class of the classical tripos. Both as an undergraduate and as a bachelor of arts he won the members' prize for the Latin essay, while his skill as a writer of English was attested by his three university prize essays—the Hulsean for 1868, the Burney for 1870, and the Hare for 1873, the respective subjects being 'Christian and Pagan Ethics,' 'Phœnicia and Israel,' and 'National Education in Greece.' All three were published: the first, which appeared in 1869 under the title of 'The Light of the World,' and quickly reached a second edition, was dedicated to James Baldwin Brown the younger [q. v.], congregational minister. The second prize essay (1871) was dedicated to James Fraser, bishop of Manchester, and the third (1873) to Connop Thirlwall, bishop of St. David's.

As a nonconformist, Wilkins was legally disqualified for a fellowship. When the religious disability was cancelled by the Tests Act of 1871, Wilkins was disqualified by marriage, nor was he helped by the removal of the second disability under the statutes of 1882, which rendered no one eligible who had taken his first degree more than ten years before.

In 1868 he took the M.A. degree in the University of London, receiving the gold medal for classics, and in the same year was appointed Latin lecturer at Owens College, Manchester, where he was promoted in the following year to the Latin professorship. For eight years he also lectured on comparative philology, and for many more he undertook the classes in Greek Testament criticism. In the University of London he was examiner in classics in 1884–6, and in Latin in 1887–90, and in 1894–9. He was highly successful as a popular lecturer on literary subjects in Manchester and in other large towns of Lancashire. He was of much service to education in Manchester outside Owens College, particularly as chairman of the Manchester Independent College, and of the council of the High School for Girls.

As professor, Wilkins proved a highly effective teacher and a valuable and stimulating member of the staff. 'Within the college he was the unwearied champion of the claims of women to equal educational rights with men,' and 'an even more vigorous champion of the establishment of a theological department in the university,' both of which causes were crowned with success. In 1903, after thirty-four years' tenure of the Latin professorship in Manchester, a weakness of the heart compelled him to resign, but he was appointed to the new and lighter office of professor of classical literature.

On 26 July 1905 he died at the seaside village of Llandrillo-yn-Rhos, in North Wales, and was buried in the cemetery of Colwyn Bay. In 1870 he married Charlotte, the second daughter of W. Field of Bishop Stortford; she survived him with a daughter and three sons. His portrait, painted by the Hon. John Collier, was presented to the University of Manchester by his friends in 1904.

As a writer Wilkins did good service by editing Cicero's rhetorical works and by introducing to English readers the results of German investigations in scholarship, philology, and ancient history. In 1868 he translated Piderit's German notes on 'Cicero De Oratore,' lib. i., and with E. B. England, G. Curtius's 'Principles of Greek Etymology' and his 'Greek Verb.' Wilkins's chief independent work was his full edition of 'Cicero De Oratore,' lib. i.–iii. (Oxford, 1879–1892). A critical edition of the text of the whole of Cicero's rhetorical works followed in 1903. He also issued compact and lucid commentaries on Cicero's 'Speeches against Catiline' (1871), and the speech 'De Imperio Gnæi Pompeii' (1879), and on Horace's 'Epistles' (1885); he contributed to Postgate's 'Corpus Poëtarum Latinorum' a critical text of the 'Thebais' and 'Achilleis' of Statius (1904); and he produced compendious primers of 'Roman Antiquities' (1877) and 'Roman Literature' (1890), the first of which was translated into French, as well as a book on Roman education (Cambridge, 1905). In the 'Encyclopædia Britannica,' 9th edit., he wrote on the Greek and Latin languages; in Smith's 'Dictionary of Antiquities,' 3rd edit., on Roman antiquities, and in 'Companion to Greek Studies' (Cambridge, 1904) on Greek education. He joined H. J. Roby in preparing an Elementary Latin Grammar in 1893.

Wilkins dedicated his edition of the 'De Oratore' to the University of St. Andrews, which conferred on him an honorary degree in 1882; he received the same distinction at Dublin in 1892, and took the degree of Litt.D. at Cambridge in 1885.

[Obituary notice (with complete bibliography) by the present writer, with full extracts from other notices, in The Eagle, xxvii. (1905), 69–84; see also Miss Sara A. Burstall's The Story of the Manchester High School for Girls, 1871–1911 (1911), pp. 148 seq.] J. E. S.

WILKINS, WILLIAM HENRY (1860–1905), biographer, born at Compton Martin, Somerset, on 23 Dec. 1860, was son of Charles Wilkins, farmer, of Gurney Court, Somerset, and afterwards of Mann's farm, Mortimer, Berkshire, where Wilkins passed much of his youth. His mother was Mary Ann Keel. After private education, he was employed in a bank at Brighton; entering Clare College, Cambridge, in 1884 with a view to taking holy orders, he graduated B.A. in 1887, and proceeded M.A. in 1899. At the university he developed literary tastes and interested himself in politics. An ardent conservative, he spoke frequently at the Union, of which he was vice-president in 1886. After leaving Cambridge he settled down to a literary career in London. For a time he acted as private secretary to the earl of Dunraven, whose proposals for restricting the immigration of undesirable foreigners Wilkins embodied in 'The Alien Invasion' (1892), with introduction by Dr. R. C. Billing, Bishop of Bedford. The Aliens Act of 1905 followed many recommendations of Wilkins's book. In the same year (1892) he edited, in conjunction with Hubert Crackanthorpe, whose acquaintance he had made at Cambridge, a shortlived monthly periodical called the 'Albemarle' (9 nos.). He next published four novels (two alone and two in collaboration) under the pseudonym of De Winton. 'St. Michael's Eve' (1892; 2nd edit. 1894) was a serious society novel. Then followed 'The Forbidden Sacrifice' (1893); 'John Ellicombe's Temptation,' 1894 (with the Hon. Julia Chetwynd), and 'The Holy Estate: a study in morals' (with Capt. Francis Alexander Thatcher). With another Cambridge friend, Mr. Herbert Vivian, he wrote under his own name 'The Green Bay Tree' (1894), which boldly satirised current Cambridge and political life and passed through five editions.

Wilkins's best literary work was done in biography. He came to know intimately the widow of Sir Richard Burton [q. v. Suppl. I], and after her death wrote 'The Romance of Isabel, Lady Burton' (1897), a sympathetic memoir founded mainly upon Lady Burton's letters and autobiography. Wilkins also edited in 1898, by Lady Burton's direction, a revised and abbreviated version of Lady Burton's 'Life of Sir Richard Burton,' and her 'The Passion Play at Ober-Ammergau' (1900), as well as Burton's unpublished 'The Jew, the Gypsy, and El Islam' (with preface and brief notes) (1898), and 'Wanderings in Three Continents' (1901).

Ill-health did not deter Wilkins from original work in historical biography which involved foreign travel. Patient industry, an easy style, and good judgment atoned for a limited range of historical knowledge. At Lund university in Sweden he discovered in 1897 the unpublished correspondence between Sophie Dorothea, the consort of George I, and her lover, Count Philip Christopher Königsmarck, and on that foundation, supported by research in the archives of Hanover and elsewhere he based 'The Love of an Uncrowned Queen, Queen Sophie Dorothea, Consort of George I,' which appeared in 2 vols. in 1900 and was well received (revised edit. 1903). Wilkins's 'Caroline the Illustrious, Queen Consort of George II' (2 vols. 1901; new edit. 1904), had little claim to originality. 'A Queen of Tears' (2 vols. 1904), a biography of Caroline Matilda, Queen of Denmark and sister of George III of England, embodied researches at Copenhagen and superseded the previous biography by Sir Frederic Charles Lascelles Wraxall [q. v.]. For his last work, 'Mrs. Fitzherbert and George IV' (1905, 2 vols.), Wilkins had access, by King Edward VII's permission, for the first time to the Fitzherbert papers at Windsor Castle, besides papers belonging to Mrs. Fitzherbert's family. Wilkins conclusively proved the marriage with George IV. In 1901 he edited 'South Africa a Century ago,' valuable letters of Lady Anne Barnard [q. v.], written (1797–1801) whilst with her husband at the Cape of Good Hope. Wilkins also published 'Our King and Queen [Edward VII and Queen Alexandra], the Story of their Life,' (1903, 2 vols.), a popular book, copiously illustrated, and he wrote occasionally for periodicals. He died unmarried on 22 Dec. 1905 at 3 Queen Street, Mayfair, and was buried in Kensal Green cemetery.

[Private information; personal knowledge; The Times, 23 Dec. 1905; Brit. Mus. Cat. and Engl. Cat.; Edinb. Rev. Jan. 1901, and supplement to Allgemeine Zeitung, 1902, N. 77 (by Dr. Robert Gerds).] G. Le G. N.

WILKINSON, GEORGE HOWARD (1833–1907), successively bishop of Truro and of St. Andrews, born at Durham on 12 May 1833, was eldest son of George Wilkinson, of Oswald House, Durham, by his wife Mary, youngest child of John Howard of Ripon. The father's family had long held an honourable position in Durham and Northumberland (cf. pedigree; Surtees, *History and Antiquities of the County of Durham*, i. 81). Educated at Durham grammar school, he went into residence at Brasenose College, Oxford, in Oct. 1851, and in November was elected to a scholarship at Oriel. He graduated B.A. with a second class in the final classical school in 1854, proceeded M.A. in 1859 and D.D. in 1883. After a year spent in travel, he was ordained deacon (1857) and priest (1858) and licensed to the curacy of St. Mary Abbots, Kensington. His fervour and industry gave him wide influence from the first. In 1859 Lady Londonderry, widow of the third marquess, presented him to the living of Seaham Harbour, co. Durham; and in 1863 the bishop of Durham, C. T. Baring [q. v.], collated him to the vicarage of Bishop Auckland. Wilkinson, although he was untouched at Oxford by the Tractarian movement, had been drawn towards it through the influence of Thomas Thellusson Carter [q. v. Suppl. II]. Difficulties followed with the bishop, who was an evangelical. Wilkinson's health suffered from the strain, and in 1867 he accepted the incumbency of St. Peter's, Great Windmill Street, London. In this poor parish he instituted open-air preaching, then a novelty. One of the earliest to take up parochial missions, he helped to organise the first general mission in London in 1869. During its progress he accepted the offer by the bishop of London, John Jackson, of St. Peter's, Eaton Square, and in January 1870 began there an incumbency of rare distinction.

Active in church affairs generally, he spoke at church congresses; sought in the years of ritual trouble, 1870–80, to act as an interpreter between the bishops and the ritualists; and zealously advocated foreign missions, the day of intercession for which owed its establishment to him. In 1877 the bishop of Truro, E. W. Benson [q. v. Suppl. I], made him an examining chaplain. In 1878 he declined an invitation to be nominated suffragan bishop for London. He was select preacher at Oxford 1879–81. In 1880 he was elected a proctor in convocation, and gave evidence before the royal commission of 1881 on ecclesiastical courts. In 1882 he declined an invitation from the bishop of Durham, J. B. Lightfoot, to become canon missioner.

In 1883, on the translation of Dr. Benson to Canterbury, Wilkinson succeeded him at Truro. He was consecrated at St. Paul's on 25 April 1883. At Truro he pressed forward the building of the cathedral; saw it consecrated on 3 Nov. 1887; founded a sisterhood, the community of the Epiphany; and did much for the clergy of poorer benefices. In 1885 he declined the see of Manchester; in 1888 he took part in the Lambeth conference; and in April 1891, after nearly two years of failing health, announced his resignation. Restored by a visit to South Africa, Wilkinson was on 9 Feb. 1893 elected to succeed Charles Wordsworth [q. v.] as bishop of St. Andrews, Dunkeld, and Dunblane, and was enthroned in St. Ninian's Cathedral, Perth, on 27 April. In 1904 the bishops of the Scottish episcopal church elected him primus. He created a bishop of St. Andrews fund for church extension; raised 14,000*l.* for building a chapter-house for St. Ninian's Cathedral, Perth; fostered interest in foreign missions, more especially in South Africa, which he again visited; and sought to promote closer relations between the episcopal and the presbyterian churches. He died suddenly at Edinburgh, on 11 Dec. 1907, and was buried in Brompton cemetery, London. There is a memorial (the bishop's figure by Sir George Frampton, R.A.) in St. Ninian's Cathedral. A cartoon portrait by 'Spy' appeared in 'Vanity Fair' in 1885.

Wilkinson combined deep spirituality with practical sagacity, courage in dealing with others and intense humility. He exercised his ministry through conversation as seriously as in pulpit work (cf. How's *Walsham How: a Memoir*, pp. 178–9). He abandoned his early evangelicalism, and his anglicanism grew more definite with years. He married on 14 July 1857 Caroline Charlotte, daughter of lieutenant-colonel Benfield Des Vœux, fourth son of Charles Des Vœux, first baronet; she died on 6 Sept. 1877; by her he had three sons and five daughters.

Wilkinson published many minor devotional works, of which the most widely circulated were: 1. 'Instructions in the Devotional Life,' 1871. 2. 'Instructions in the Way of Salvation,' 1872. 3. 'Lent Lectures,' 1873.

[A. J. Mason, Memoir of George Howard Wilkinson, 1909; A. C. Benson's Leaves of the Tree (character sketch of Wilkinson), 1911, and his The Life of Edward White Benson, 1899, 2 vols.; H. S. Holland, George Howard Wilkinson, 1909; Guardian, 18 Dec. 1907; Record, 8 July 1904; Daily Telegraph, 3 May 1911.] A. R. B.

WILKS, Sir SAMUEL, baronet (1824–1911), physician, born at Camberwell, on 2 June 1824, was second son of Joseph Barber Wilks, treasurer at the East India House, by his wife Susannah Edwards, daughter of William Bennett of Southborough, Kent. He went to Aldenham grammar school in 1836, and spent three years there, followed by a year at University College school in London. He was then apprenticed to Richard Prior, a general practitioner in Newington, and in 1842 entered as a student at Guy's Hospital; in 1847 he became a member of the Royal College of Surgeons. His natural turn was for medicine, and he graduated M.B. at the University of London in 1848 and M.D. in 1850, and was admitted a member of the Royal College of Physicians in 1851 and elected a fellow of that college in 1856, in which year he was appointed assistant physician to Guy's Hospital. He became physician in 1866, and held office till 1885. He was also successively curator of the museum, lecturer on pathology, and lecturer on medicine there, and attained a great reputation by his researches and teaching in the post mortem room and the wards. He published in 1859 'Lectures on Pathological Anatomy,' one of the most important works on the anatomy of disease since the appearance of the 'Morbid Anatomy' of Dr. Matthew Baillie [q. v.] in 1795. A second edition in which Dr. Walter Moxon [q. v.] took part appeared in 1875, and a third thoroughly revised by Wilks in 1887. The fame of Guy's Hospital from 1836 to the present day has been largely increased by its annual volumes of 'Reports,' and Wilks from 1854 to 1865 became editor and contributed numerous important papers to them. In 1874 he published 'Lectures on the Specific Fevers and on Diseases of the Chest,' and in 1878 'Lectures on Diseases of the Nervous System,' of which a second edition appeared in 1883. He was always anxious to increase the fame of other discoverers, and this quality appears in his edition of the works of Thomas Addison [q.v.], published in 1868, and in his insistence on the use of the term 'Hodgkin's disease' for a glandular enlargement to the knowledge of which he himself contributed, though its original description was found in the observations of Thomas Hodgkin [q. v.], a fact first demonstrated by Wilks. He was an accurate student of the history of medicine, and in 1892 wrote with G. T. Bettany 'A Biographical History of Guy's Hospital.' In this, as in his obituary notices of deceased fellows at the College of Physicians, Wilks, while never unkind, showed a rigid respect for truth, resembling that of Johnson's 'Life of Savage,' and never gave way to the adulatory style of biography applied equally to the just and the unjust. Wilks's last work was a memoir on the new discoveries or new observations made during the time he was a teacher at Guy's Hospital, published in 1911. It contains *inter alia* a bibliography of his writings.

He delivered the Harveian oration at the College of Physicians on 29 June 1879, and was elected president from 1896 to 1899. In 1897 he was created a baronet and appointed physician extraordinary to Queen Victoria. He was president of the Pathological Society 1881–3, was a member of the senate of the University of London in 1885, and sat on the general medical council as representative of that university from 29 Oct. 1887 to 22 April 1896.

He first lived at 11 St. Thomas's Street, near Guy's Hospital, and later in Grosvenor Street till 1901, when he retired to Hampstead. Severe illnesses in 1904 and 1907 and two consequent operations did not cloud his understanding, and he continued to take active interest in science and literature to the end of his life. He died at Hampstead on 8 Nov. 1911, and his body, after cremation, was buried there. He married on 25 July 1854 Elizabeth Ann, daughter of Henry Mockett, of Seaford, Sussex, widow of Richard Prior, M.R.C.S., of Newington, Surrey; she predeceased Wilks without issue.

Wilks was profoundly respected by the physicians of his time. His pupils were struck by the vast amount of information on morbid anatomy and clinical medicine which he could at any moment pour out. His conversation was delightful and filled with acute remarks on men as well as with learning of many kinds. His portrait by Percy Ryland hangs in the dining-room of the Royal College of Physicians.

[Works; The Times, 9 Nov. 1911; obituary notice in British Medical Journal, 18 Nov. 1911, with additional notes by his friends Dr. Frederick Taylor, Sir George Savage, Sir Bryan Donkin, and Dr. Jessop of Hampstead; personal knowledge.] N. M.

WILL, JOHN SHIRESS (1840–1910), legal writer, born in Dundee in 1840, only son of John Will, merchant, of Dundee, but described at the date of his son's admission to the Middle Temple —30 Oct. 1861—as 'of the parish of Hanover, co. Cornwall, Jamaica,' by his wife Mary, daughter of John Chambers. Educated first at Brechin grammar school, and afterwards at University College and King's College, London, Will was called to the bar by the Middle Temple on 6 June 1864, and obtained a large parliamentary practice, taking silk in 1883 and being made a bencher of his inn on 24 Jan. 1888. He discontinued his parliamentary practice in 1885 upon his election as liberal member for Montrose burghs, for which he was re-elected in 1886, in 1892, and in August 1895. He resigned the seat early in 1896, when Mr. John (afterwards Viscount) Morley, who had been recently defeated at Newcastle, was elected in his stead. Will then resumed his practice, becoming the principal authority on the law relating to lighting either by gas or electricity. He received tardy recognition of his ability and services by appointment in September 1906 as judge of the county court district (No. 7) of Liverpool. He died at Liverpool on 24 May 1910. He married in 1873 Mary Anne (*d.* 1912), daughter of William Shiress, solicitor, of Brechin, Forfarshire.

Will was author of: 1. 'The Practice of the Referees Courts in Parliament in regard to Engineering Details . . . and Estimates and Water and Gas Bills,' 1866. 2. 'Changes in the Jurisdiction and Practice of the County Courts and Superior Courts effected by the County Courts Act, 1867, with notes,' 1868. 3. 'The Law relating to Electric Lighting,' 1898; 3rd edit. 1903. He was joint author with W. H. Michael, a brother bencher of the Middle Temple, of a treatise on the law relating to gas and water, 1872, 5th edit. 1901, and was solely responsible for the later editions. He was also responsible for the fifth and sixth editions of 'Wharton's Law Lexicon' (1872, 1876).

[The Times, 25 May 1910, 16 Feb. 1912; Who's Who, 1909; Foster, Men at the Bar; Dod's Parl. Companion, 1895, N.P.; Law List, 1908; Brit. Mus. Cat.] C. E. A. B.

WILLES, Sir GEORGE OMMANNEY (1823–1901), admiral, son of Capt. George Wickens Willes, R.N., by Anne Elizabeth, second daughter of Sir Edmund Lacon, first baronet, M.P., was born at Hythe, Hampshire, on 19 June 1823, was entered at the R.N. College, Portsmouth, in Feb. 1836, and went to sea in 1838. He passed his examination in Sept. 1842, and as mate served first in the Cornwallis, flagship of Sir William Parker [q. v.], and afterwards in the Childers, brig, on the East Indies and China station. He received his commission as lieutenant on 11 Dec. 1844, and in March following was appointed to the Hibernia, again with Sir William Parker, then commander-in-chief in the Mediterranean. Three years later he was given the command of the Spitfire, steamer, on the same station. In August 1850 he was appointed first lieutenant of the Retribution, paddle frigate, in the Mediterranean, and was still in her at the bombardment of Odessa on 22 April 1854. Shortly afterwards he received his promotion to commander, dated 17 April, and on 1 June was moved into the flagship Britannia, in which he served during the remainder of the campaign, and especially at the bombardment of Fort Constantine, Sevastopol, on 17 Oct. He received the Crimean and Turkish medals, the clasp for Sevastopol, and the 5th class of the Mejidie, and was made a knight of the Legion of Honour. In the Baltic campaign of 1855 he served on board the flagship Duke of Wellington, and received the medal. He was promoted to captain on 10 May 1856.

In Feb. 1859 he was appointed to the Chesapeake as flag-captain to Rear-admiral James Hope [q. v.], commander-in-chief on the East Indies and China station, and in May 1861 followed his chief into the Impérieuse. Willes saw much active service during this commission. On 24 June 1859 he was in charge of the party sent to cut the boom across the Peiho river at the time of the unsuccessful attack, and in August 1860 he was in command of the rocket boats at the attack on the Peiho forts. For these services he received the China medal with the Taku clasp, and in July 1861 was awarded the C.B. In 1862 he was employed in investigating the creeks preliminary to operations against the Taiping, near Shanghai, and in July of that year was relieved and came home. He was next appointed, in Jan. 1864, to command the Prince Consort, ironclad, in the Channel squadron, and on leaving her in April 1866 became captain of the reserve at Devonport, where he remained until called to the Admiralty in Jan. 1869. The duties there assigned to him were similar to those afterwards discharged by the admiral superintendent of naval reserves, and he was confirmed in his appointment in Oct. 1870 with the title of chief of the staff. There was at this date no second sea lord, and the duties of the chief of the staff included a large share in the business of manning the fleet; he also commanded the reserve squadron on its annual cruise (see Sir Vesey Hamilton, *Naval Administration*, pp. 102–3). Willes remained at Whitehall for three years, and on 11 June 1874 reached flag rank. From April 1870 until his promotion he was an aide-de-camp to Queen Victoria.

In May 1876 he became admiral superintendent at Devonport, and on 1 Feb. 1879 was advanced to vice-admiral. For three years from Jan. 1881 he was commander-in-chief in China with his flag in the Iron Duke, and in May 1884 was awarded the K.C.B. He was promoted to admiral on 27 March 1885, and in November following was appointed commander-in-chief at Portsmouth, and was thus in command of the fleet at Spithead on the occasion of the Jubilee review of 1887. He struck his flag on retirement on 19 June 1888. In 1892 he was raised to the G.C.B. He was nominated a J.P. for Middlesex in 1884, and for many years, as a member of its council, took an active part in the affairs of the Royal United Service Institution. He died in Cadogan Square, London, on 18 Feb. 1901.

Willes married, on 16 May 1855, Matilda Georgiana Josephine, daughter of William Joseph Lockwood of Dews Hall, Essex. Admiral Sir George Lambart Atkinson, his nephew, took the additional surname of Willes in 1901 under the terms of his will.

[The Times, 19 Feb. 1901; R.N. List; an engraved portrait was published by Messrs. Walton of Shaftesbury Avenue.]

L. G. C. L.

WILLIAMS, ALFRED (1832–1905), Alpine painter, born at Newark-on-Trent on 4 May 1832, was youngest of the three sons of Charles Williams [q. v.], a congregational minister, by his wife Mary Smeeton. Frederick Smeeton Williams [q. v.] was a brother. Alfred was educated firstly at a private school and subsequently at University College School, London. He learnt drawing at a private academy and landscape painting of William Bennett (1811–1871), water-colour artist. As a young man he supported himself by drawing on wood for book illustrations. From 1849 to 1856 he illustrated publications of the Religious Tract Society and of Messrs. Cassell & Company, as well as his brother Frederick's 'Our Iron Roads' (1852); he also for a time was assistant to Sir John Gilbert [q. v. Suppl. I].

From 1854, when he made an extended walking tour in Northern Italy and Switzerland, his interest in painting centred in mountain scenery. In 1861 he settled at Salisbury, and founding there the maltster's business afterwards known as Williams Brothers, was engaged in trade until his retirement in 1886. Meanwhile, during the summer months he travelled, chiefly in Switzerland, pursuing his art, which occupied him wholly after his retirement. In 1878 he was elected a member of the Alpine Club. His subjects were chiefly drawn from the Alps and the mountains of Scotland, but in 1900–1 he spent twelve months in India. At the Alpine Club, exhibitions of his water-colour drawings were held in March 1889, of his Indian paintings in 1902, and again of water-colours from 5 to 23 Dec. 1905. Between 1880 and 1890 he exhibited four works at the Royal Academy, one at the Royal Society of British Artists, and one at the New Gallery. He was skilful in rendering the effect of sunlight on distant snow and in giving an impression of the size of great mountains. One of his water-colour drawings, 'Monte Rosa at Sunrise from above Alagna,' is in the Victoria and Albert Museum; another belongs to the corporation of Salisbury, and two to the Alpine Club.

He died at the Grand Hôtel, Ste. Maxime-sur-Mer, Var, France, on 19 March 1905, and was buried at Ste. Maxime. He married twice: (1) in 1863 Sarah, daughter of George Gregory of Salisbury, by whom he had no issue; and (2) in 1866 Eliza (*d.* 1892), daughter of William Walker of Northampton, by whom he had one son and one daughter.

[Information from Mr. Sidney S. Williams; pref. to cat. of Exhibition at Alpine Club in 1905; Graves, Dict. of Artists; Cat. of Water-colours, Victoria and Albert Museum.]

B. S. L.

WILLIAMS, CHARLES (1838–1904), war correspondent, was born at Coleraine on 4 May 1838. On his father's side he was descended from Worcestershire yeomen (of Tenbury and Mamble), on his mother's from Scottish settlers in Ulster. Educated at Belfast Academy under Reuben Bryce and at a private school in Greenwich, he went for his health to the southern states of America, where he took part in a filibustering expedition to Nicaragua, saw some hard fighting, and won the reputation of a daring blockade-runner. On his return to England he became a zealous volunteer, and was engaged as leader-writer for the London 'Evening Herald.' In October 1859 he began a connection with the 'Standard,' which lasted till 1884. He conducted the 'Evening Standard' as its first editor for three years, and he was first editor of the 'Evening News' from 1881 to 1884.

Williams did his best work as war correspondent. For the 'Standard' he accompanied the headquarters of the French army of the Loire at the beginning of the second phase of the Franco-German war (1870), and was one of the first two correspondents in Strasburg after its fall. In the summer and autumn of 1877 he was correspondent on the staff of Ahmed Mukhtar Pasha, commanding the Turkish forces in Armenia. Williams remained almost constantly at the front, and his letters were the only continuous series which reached England. He published them in a revised and somewhat extended form in 1878 as 'The Armenian Campaign.' Though written from a pro-Turkish standpoint, the narrative was a faithful record of events. Williams followed Mukhtar to European Turkey, and described his defence of the lines of Constantinople against the Russians. He was with the headquarters of Skobeleff when the treaty of San Stefano was signed; and he subsequently recorded the phases of the Berlin Congress of 1878. At the end of that year he was in Afghanistan, and in 1879 published 'Notes on the Operations in Lower Afghanistan, 1878–9, with Special Reference to Transport.' Williams accompanied the Nile expedition for the relief of General Gordon [q. v.] in the autumn of 1884. In an article in the 'Fortnightly Review,' May 1885 ('How we lost Gordon'), he ascribed to Sir Charles Wilson's delay and want of nerve the failure to relieve Gordon.

After leaving the 'Standard' in 1884, Williams was for some time connected with the 'Morning Advertiser,' but soon became war correspondent of the 'Daily Chronicle.' He was the only English correspondent with the Bulgarian army in the brief war with Servia in 1885. In the Greco-Turkish war of 1897 he was attached to the Greek army in Thessaly. In a contribution to the 'Fortnightly,' June 1897, he attributed the defeat of the Greeks to the disastrous influence of politics. Williams's last service in the field was in Kitchener's Soudanese campaign of 1898. He accompanied General Gatacre [q. v. Suppl. II] up the Nile on his way to join the British brigade in January, and supplied the 'Daily Chronicle' with a vivid account of the battle of Omdurman and the recapture of Khartoum in Sept. 1898. The state of his health did not permit of his going to South Africa, but he wrote in London a diary of the Boer War for the 'Morning Leader.' He published in 1902 a vigorous pamphlet entitled 'Hushed Up,' protesting against the limited scope of the official inquiry into the management of the Boer war.

Williams was a strong adherent of Lord Wolseley's military views and policy, and had an intimate knowledge of military detail. On these subjects he wrote much in the 'United Service Magazine,' the 'National Review,' and other periodicals. In 1892 he published a somewhat controversial 'Life of Sir H. Evelyn Wood,' independently vindicating Sir Evelyn's action after Majuba Hill in 1881 (cf. Sir H. E. Wood, *From Midshipman to Field-Marshal*, ch. 37). Williams also tried his hand at fiction, and wrote some 'Songs for Soldiers.' He was a zealous churchman, and presented to Bishop Creighton [q. v. Suppl. I] as a thank-offering for his safe return from Khartoum an ivory and gold mitre designed by himself. Williams vainly contested West Leeds in the conservative interest in 1886, against Mr. Herbert (now Viscount) Gladstone. Although of irascible temper, he was chairman of the London district of the Institute of Journalists in 1893–4, and was president in 1896–7 of the Press Club, of which he was founder. He died at lodgings in Brixton on 9 Feb. 1904.

[Men of the Time, 1899; Daily Chronicle, 10 Feb. 1904 (with portrait and memoir by Mr. H. W. Nevinson); The Times, and Standard, 10 Feb.; United Service Gazette, and Athenæum, 13 Feb.; Brit. Mus. Cat.; Allibone's Dict. Suppl.] G. Le G. N.

WILLIAMS, CHARLES HANSON GREVILLE (1829–1910), chemist, born at Cheltenham on 22 Sept. 1829, was only son of S. Hanson Williams, solicitor, of Cheltenham. His mother was Sophia, daughter of Thomas Billings, solicitor, of Cheltenham. After private education he obtained his first scientific employment as a consulting and analytical chemist (1852–3) in Oxford Court, Cannon Street, London, E.C. He then spent three years as assistant to Prof. Thomas Anderson at Glasgow University, and left to undertake work at Edinburgh University under Lyon (afterwards Lord) Playfair [q.v. Suppl. I]. Subsequently he was successively lecturer on chemistry in the Normal College, Swansea (1857–8); chemist to George Miller & Co., manufacturing chemists, at Glasgow; assistant to (Sir) William Henry Perkin [q. v. Suppl. II] at Greenford Green (1863–8); partner with Edward Thomas and John Dower at the Star Chemical Works, Brentford (1868–77); and chemist and photometric supervisor to the Gas Light and Coke Company, London (1877–1901).

Greville Williams's special studies were the volatile bases produced by the destructive distillation of certain shales, cinchonine, and one or two groups of hydrocarbons. He discovered cyanine or quinoline-blue (*Trans. Roy. Soc. Edin.* 1857), the first of the quinoline dye-stuffs. To him is due the isolation of the hydrocarbon isoprene (*Phil. Trans.* 1860).

To the 'Journal of Gas Lighting' he contributed many papers on the chemistry of coal-gas. In 1890 that journal described a method he had devised for producing artificial emeralds from the refuse of gas-retorts. To the Royal Society he sent in 1873 and 1877 two papers: 'Researches on Emeralds and Beryls'; part i.: 'On the Colouring-matter of the Emerald' (*Roy. Soc. Proc.* vol. xxi.); and (part ii.) 'On some of the Processes employed in the Analysis of Emeralds and Beryls' (*ib.* vol. xxvi.). He showed that emeralds lost about 9 per cent. of their weight on fusion, the specific gravity being reduced to about 2·4. At a meeting of the British Association of Gas Managers (1890) he delivered a lecture on 'The Past, Present, and Future of Coal Tar.' Two years later he contributed to the Gas Institute a paper on 'The Determination of the Specific Gravity of Gas.'

Greville Williams's independent publications were: 'A Handbook of Chemical Manipulation' (1857; Supplement, 1879) and 'Manual of Chemical Analysis for Schools' (1858). For King's 'Treatise on Coal Gas' he wrote the article 'Tar and Tar Products,' and he was a contributor to Watts' 'Dictionary of Chemistry' and other technical compilations.

Williams was admitted to the Chemical Society on 16 Jan. 1862, and was made F.R.S. on 5 June 1862. A versatile conversationalist, he possessed literary and artistic tastes, and in the intervals of chemical research gave much attention to Egyptian hieroglyphics.

He died at his home, Bay Cottage, Smallfields, Horley, on 15 June 1910, and was buried at Streatham. He married on 25 Nov. 1852 Henrietta, daughter of Henry Bosher of Taunton (she predeceased him), and had issue four sons and four daughters.

[Proc. Roy. Soc. vol. lxxxv. A; Journ. of Gas Lighting, cx., cxi.; Journ. Soc. Chem. Industry, vol. xxix.; Athenæum, 25 June 1910; Poggendorff's Handwörterbuch, Bd. iii. (1898); Roy. Soc. Catal. Sci. Papers; Nature, 7 July 1910.] T. E. J.

WILLIAMS, Sir EDWARD LEADER (1828–1910), engineer of the Manchester Ship Canal, born at Worcester on 28 April 1828, was eldest of the eleven children of Edward Leader Williams. Benjamin Williams Leader, R.A., is a brother. In 1842 his father was appointed chief engineer to the Severn navigation commissioners, and his improvements transformed that river into an important waterway for many years. Williams was educated privately, and being apprenticed at sixteen to his father, worked until 1846 on the Severn between Stourport and Gloucester. During the next three years he was engaged as assistant engineer under Joseph Cubitt [q. v.] in Lincolnshire on the Great Northern railway. He was resident engineer on the extensive works of Shoreham harbour from 1849 to 1852, and engineer to the contractors for the Admiralty pier at Dover from 1852 to 1855. In 1856 he became engineer to the River Weaver Trust, and thenceforth devoted himself entirely to works for inland navigation. He placed the river Weaver in the front rank of English waterways, deepening and widening it, enlarging the locks, and introducing steam traction; thus practically the whole of the salt traffic from Northwich and Winsford to Liverpool was secured. In order to establish through traffic with the Trent and Mersey canal, which the Weaver crosses at Anderton, Leader Williams designed, with Edwin Clark, an hydraulic lift for raising or lowering canal-boats from one to the other (see *Proc. Inst. of Civil Eng.* xlv. 107). In 1872, before the lift was completed, Williams became engineer to the Bridgewater Navigation Company. Here he enlarged the locks at Runcorn, deepened the canal from 4 ft. 6 ins. to 6 ft., and introduced steam propulsion, which he facilitated by building an almost vertical wall on one side of the canal for about thirty miles.

In 1882 Leader Williams became, jointly with Hamilton N. Fulton, engineer to the provisional committee which was considering the formation of a ship canal to Manchester. Fulton had previously put forward a project for a tidal canal. Each engineer submitted a proposal. The committee adopted Williams's proposal to use the tidal channel of the Mersey as far as practicable, and then to cut a canal with four huge locks for raising ships gradually to the level of Manchester. He was thereupon appointed chief engineer. Parliament refused the necessary powers in 1883 and 1884, but granted them in 1885. The three years' contest occupied 175 days, and cost 250,000*l.* The failure of the first two applications was due largely to the opposition of the Mersey docks and harbour board, who feared that the proposed training and deepening of the tidal channel through the Mersey would affect the navigation of the estuary. Leader Williams thereupon modified his proposals in regard to the lower portion of the projected waterway. In 1887 a contract for the construction of the canal was entered into with T. A. Walker, at a cost of 5,750,000*l.*, and the first sod was cut at Eastham by Lord Egerton of Tatton on 11 Nov. 1887. In 1889, however, Walker died, and the work was ultimately let in sections to several contractors. The lower portion of the canal was first used for traffic in Sept. 1891, and the whole canal on 1 Jan. 1894; the canal was formally opened by Queen Victoria on 21 May 1894 (for technical description of the work see four papers in the *Proc. Inst. Civil Eng.* cxxxi., two by Williams, 'The Manchester Ship-Canal' and 'The Manchester Ship-Canal: Mersey Estuary Embankments and other Works—Runcorn Division,' and two by (Sir) Whately Eliot and Mr. Meade-King, on the Eastham and Irlam divisions respectively; *Engineering*, 26 Jan. 1894, with illustrations; Sir Bosdin Leech, *History of the Manchester Ship Canal*, &c., 2 vols. 1907). The canal is 35½ miles in length from the entrance locks at Eastham to the Manchester docks, and has a minimum width of 120 feet at the bottom. It crosses five lines of railway and the Bridgewater canal at Barton, where Williams employed a device suggested by the Anderton canal lift. The docks at Manchester and Salford have an area of 104 acres and five miles of quay frontage. The total expenditure of the Canal Company, up to 1 Jan. 1897, was about 15,170,000*l.*, in which are included, however, nearly three millions for the purchase of the Bridgwater canals and the Mersey and Irwell navigation and for interest on capital during construction. Leader Williams, who was knighted on 2 July 1894, took charge of the canal until 1905; he then became its consulting engineer, and practised privately until a few years before his death.

He was elected a member of the Institution of Civil Engineers on 7 Feb. 1860, and served on the council from 1895 until his retirement in 1907—the last two years as a vice-president. He became a member of the Institution of Mechanical Engineers in 1883. In 1895 he was president of the Manchester Association of Engineers. He died at Altrincham on 1 Jan. 1910.

Leader Williams, who was of commanding presence, with a genial manner and abundant energy, courage, and patience, married (1) in 1852 Ellen Maria (*d.* 1860), daughter of Thomas Popplewell of Gainsborough, and (2) in 1862 Catherine Louisa, daughter of Richard Clinch of Northwich, who survived him. He had five sons and five daughters.

In addition to the two papers already mentioned, Leader Williams contributed to the 'Proceedings of the Institution of Civil Engineers' (lxx. 378) in 1882 a paper 'On the Recent Landslips in the Salt Districts of Cheshire,' and he wrote the larger portion of the article on 'Canals and Inland Navigation' in the supplement to the ninth edition of the 'Encyclopædia Britannica.'

[Engineering, 7 Jan. 1910; Minutes of Proc. Inst. Civ. Eng. clxxx. 341; The Times, and Manchester Guardian, 3 Jan. 1910; Altrincham Guardian, 8 Jan. 1910.]

W. F. S.

WILLIAMS, Sir GEORGE (1821–1905), founder of the Young Men's Christian Association, born at Ashway Farm, Dulverton, on 11 Oct. 1821, was youngest of the seven sons of Amos Williams, farmer, by his wife, Elizabeth. After being educated at a dame's school in Dulverton and then at Gloyn's grammar school, Tiverton, he was apprenticed in 1836 to one Holmes, a draper at Bridgwater. His parents were church people, but he came under religious impressions at the congregational chapel in Bridgwater, of which he became a member on 14 Feb. 1838. He took the 'teetotal pledge' in the Friends' meeting-house at Bridgwater in 1839, and was thenceforth an earnest temperance advocate, and a vigorous opponent of gambling and tobacco.

In 1841 he entered the employ of Messrs. Hitchcock & Rogers, drapers, then of Ludgate Hill, and afterwards of St. Paul's Churchyard, and was subsequently made 'buyer' in the drapery department. He soon became the most prominent employé in the house and was made a partner—the firm being thenceforth known as Hitchcock, Williams & Co. In 1853 he married Helen, daughter of the head of the firm, George Hitchcock.

From his arrival in London he devoted his leisure to evangelistic and temperance work. He was influenced by the severely puritanical preaching of an American evangelist, Charles G. Finney, but his views were soon modified by the more generous teaching of Thomas Binney (1798–1874) [q. v.], of the old Weigh House chapel in the City of London, where he became Sunday school secretary. He took part, too, in ragged-school work and open-air preaching. A small prayer-meeting which he early formed among his fellow-employés developed into a great organisation. At the end of 1842, when the members numbered nearly thirty, his master George Hitchcock joined Williams in establishing in the house a mutual improvement society and a young men's missionary society (1842). On 6 June 1844 twelve men, all but one being employés of Hitchcock, met in Williams's bedroom and established the Young Men's Christian Association, with the idea of extending the work to drapery houses throughout the metropolis. In October a room was taken at Radley's Hotel, Bridge Street, for the weekly meetings. Early in 1845 the first paid secretary, T. H. Tarlton, was appointed, and by Hitchcock's help premises were taken in Serjeant's Inn.

A similar institution had been started by David Nasmith [q. v.] in Glasgow as early as 1824, and branches had been opened in London, France, and America. But Williams worked independently of his predecessor's example, and his association grew on a wholly unprecedented scale. It attracted, at an early stage, men ready to work on inter-denominational lines, such as Thomas Binney [q. v.], Baptist W. Noel [q. v.], and Samuel Morley [q. v.]. In order to emphasise the 'mutual improvement' side of the work, popular lectures (1845), which afterwards became known from their place of delivery as the 'Exeter Hall lectures,' were arranged. They were published and had an annual sale of 36,000 copies. Lord Shaftesbury [see COOPER, ANTHONY ASHLEY, seventh EARL OF SHAFTESBURY], with whom Williams became closely associated, accepted the presidency in 1851. The work spread to the continent and the colonies, and in 1855 Williams was present at the first international conference of Young Men's Christian Associations held in Paris, where representatives of similar organisations in Europe and America agreed on the terms of the 'Paris basis,' on which a world-wide society was built up.

Up to 1864 its undenominational constitution and its sometimes narrow views about recreation and amusements hampered the association's development. But Williams's directness of purpose gradually overcame all difficulties. In 1880 he contrived the purchase of the lease of Exeter Hall, where the Association had often met, for the headquarters of the association, when there was danger of the hall becoming a place of amusement. Within forty-eight hours he raised 25,000*l.* giving 5000*l.* himself and securing four other gifts of like amount; he afterwards raised a further 20,000*l.* for the equipment of the building. Exeter Hall remained the association's headquarters till its demolition in 1907. During 1909–11 an enormous block of buildings was erected as a memorial to Williams for the offices of the association in Tottenham Court Road; the edifice was opened in 1912.

On Lord Shaftesbury's death, Williams was elected president (18 April 1886). In June 1894 the jubilee of the Y.M.C.A. institution was celebrated in London, when Queen Victoria knighted Williams on the recommendation of the prime minister, Lord Rosebery, and the freedom of the City of London was conferred on him. By that period there were some four hundred branches of the association in England, Ireland, and Wales, and over two hundred in Scotland, with a total membership of nearly 150,000. In America the institution struck even deeper roots. There the association had nearly 2000 branches with a membership exceeding 450,000. In Germany there were over 2000 branches with a membership of 120,000. Apart from the association's flourishing development in all the British dominions and in almost all the countries of Europe, branches had been formed in Japan, China, and Korea.

In April 1905 Williams was present at the jubilee of the world's alliance of Y.M.C.A.s in Paris. He died at Torquay, on 6 Nov. 1905, being buried in the crypt of St. Paul's, where there is a memorial.

Among numerous societies in which Williams was interested and which he generously aided with money were, apart from the Young Men's Christian Association, the Bible Society, the London City Mission, the Religious Tract Society, the Early Closing Association, and the Commercial Travellers' Christian Association.

By his marriage on 9 June 1853, with Helen Hitchcock, who survived him, he had five sons, and one daughter, who died aged nineteen. His son Mr. Howard Williams inherited his father's philanthropic and religious interests, and is treasurer of Dr. Barnardo's Homes.

A portrait of Williams by the Hon. John Collier was presented to Mrs. Williams in 1887 by the staff of Hitchcock, Williams & Co., to commemorate the firm's jubilee

[J. E. Hodder Williams, The Life of Sir George Williams, 1906 (several good portraits); The Times, 7 Nov. 1905; private information.]

E. H. P.

WILLIAMS, HUGH (1843–1911), ecclesiastical historian, son of Hugh Williams (*d.* 1905, aged ninety-two), carrier and small freeholder, of Menai Bridge, Anglesey, by his wife Jane, was born at Porthaethwy in Anglesey on 17 Sept. 1843. He got his schooling in his native village and at Bangor, and for some years worked as a mason, at the same time continuing his studies. In 1864 he entered at the Calvinistic Methodist College, Bala, where he acted (1867–9) as one of the tutors. He graduated B.A. London in 1870 (first in second class honours in classics); M.A. London in 1871 (second in philosophy honours). He then conducted a grammar school at Menai Bridge, at the same time ministering to calvinistic methodists in Anglesey, and was ordained without charge (1873) in the presbyterian church of Wales. Appointed professor of Greek and mathematics at Bala in August 1873, he entered on his duties in the following year. In the vacation of 1874 he visited Germany for the study of the language. When the Bala College became purely theological (1891), he was appointed professor of church history. In 1903 he was moderator of the North Wales assembly of the presbyterian church. On 19 April 1904 he received the degree of D.D. in Glasgow University. His 'high-pitched industry' told upon his health; he was for some time troubled with a form of laryngitis. In addition to his other work he preached every Sunday, though not reckoned a popular preacher, and conducted a weekly bible class. He was a member of the theological board and court of the University of Wales; also of the council of the Bangor College. After suffering for nearly two years from arterial disease, he died at Bala on 11 May 1911, and was buried in the churchyard of Llanycil, Merionethshire, the parish in which Bala is situated. On 31 Dec. 1884 he married Mary, eldest daughter of Urias Bromley, Old Hall, Chester, who survives him without issue.

Williams made his mark by his edition of 'Gildas, with English translation and notes,' pt. i. 1899; pt. ii. 1901 (*Cymrodorion Record* series). Various magazine articles and separate papers, *e.g.* 'Some Aspects of the Christian Church in Wales in the Fifth and Sixth Centuries' (1895); 'The Four Disciples of Illtud' (1897); the article on the Welsh church in the new edition (1889–96) of the 'Encyclopædia Cambrensis' ('Gwyddoniadur Cymreig'); a review of Heinrich Zimmer's 'Keltische Kirche' (1901) and 'Pelagius in Irland' (1901) in the 'Zeitschrift für Celtische Philologie' (1903); the article 'Church (British)' in Hastings's 'Encyclopædia of Religion and Ethics' (1910) prepared the way for his magnum opus, 'Christianity in Early Britain,' which was issued by the Clarendon press in February 1912. He had generally indicated his results in the Davies lecture, delivered at Birkenhead on 8 June 1905. During his last illness, Williams was engaged on a second revision of the proofs of his work, and left it to his colleagues, the Revs. D. Phillips and J. O. Thomas, to see through the press. As an historian of Celtic Christendom, Williams easily took first rank, not merely by his new and careful research into primary sources, but by his absolute freedom from sectarian bias, his excellent judgment, and his application to history, despite the Germans, of the Newtonian principle *hypotheses non fingo*; his work forms a basis on which all later research must build.

In addition to the above, he published, *inter alia*, in Welsh: 1. 'Yr Epistol at y Colossiaid,' &c., Bala, 1886. 2. 'Yr Epistol at y Galatiaid: cyfiethiad newydd [together with that of 1620] . . . a nodiadau. Gyda map,' Bala, 1892 (this and the preceding were new and annotated versions for Sunday school use). 3. 'Y Sacramentau: anerchiad agoriadol,' &c., Bala, 1894. 4. 'De Imitatione Christi . . Rhagdraeth,' &c., Bala, 1907 (the introduction by Williams, the translation by another hand). He also edited Lewis Edwards's 'Holiadau Athrawiaethol,' Bala, 1897.

[Who's Who, 1911; The Times, 13 May 1911; Univ. of London, Gen. Register, 1872; Cylchgrawn Myfyrwyr y Bala (Bala Students' Mag.), 1911, pp. 148 sq.; Blwyddiadur y Methodistiaid Calfinaidd (Calvinistic Methodist Year Book), 1912; information from Mrs. Williams; Mr. W. I. Addison, Registrar, Glasgow University; Principal Edwards, Bala; and the Rev. Rees Jenkin Jones, Aberdare.] A. G.

WILLIAMS, JOHN CARVELL (1821–1907), nonconformist politician, born at Stepney on 20 Sept. 1821, was the son of John Allen Williams by his wife Mary, daughter of John Carvell of Lambeth, and was brought up in connection with the old Stepney meeting, though his first membership was at Claremont chapel, Pentonville. From a private school he entered the office of a firm of proctors in Doctors' Commons. His life-work began on his appointment in 1847 as secretary to the British Anti-State Church Association, founded in 1844 by Edward Miall [q. v.]. Its change of name to the Society for the Liberation of Religion from State Patronage and Control was due to a suggestion by Williams. He remained secretary till 1877, when he was made chairman of the society's parliamentary committee, a post which he held till 1898, when he was made chairman of the executive committee; resigning this post in 1903 through failing eyesight, he was made vice-president. For over half a century Williams proved himself 'the chief strategist of the nonconformist force, in its steady advance upon the privileged position of the Church of England.' Williams occasionally preached, and to him was largely due the formation of a congregational church and the erection of its building in 1887 at Stroud Green. In 1900 he was chairman of the Congregational Union of England and Wales.

He entered parliament as liberal member for South Nottinghamshire in 1885, when his friends presented him with 1000*l.* In 1886 he was defeated, but he was returned in 1892 for the Mansfield division of Nottinghamshire, and retained that seat till 1900, retiring then on account of growing deafness. He was a chief promoter of the Burials Act in 1880 and of the Marriage Acts of 1886 (extending the hours for marriage from twelve to three o'clock; of this Act he was sole author) and 1898 (allowing nonconformist congregations to appoint their own registrars). In 1897 his friends presented him with 1000*l.* to mark the jubilee of his connection with the Liberation Society.

On this occasion Gladstone credited him with 'consistency, devotion, unselfishness, ability,' qualities not rendered less effective by his suave demeanour, his practical judgment of men, and his imperturbable temper. He was an effective speaker and in private life a genial companion. On his retirement from active work he was entertained at a public dinner (16 July 1906). He died at 26 Crouch Hall Road, Crouch End, on 8 Oct. 1907, and was buried in Abney Park cemetery. He married on 14 Aug. 1849 Anne, daughter of Richard Goodman of Hornsey, who predeceased him; of their five children, a son, Sidney Williams, alone survived him.

Williams, an admirable draughtsman of circulars and appeals, wielded also a busy pen, both on Miall's paper, the weekly 'Nonconformist' (started 1841), and on the 'Liberator,' a monthly founded by himself in 1853, and still in progress. His separate publications include the following: 1. 'A Plea for a Free Churchyard,' 1870. 2. 'The New Position of the Burials Question,' 1878; 2nd edit. 1879 (with 'Present' for 'New' in title). 3. 'Disestablishment' (in S. C. Buxton's 'The Imperial Parliament'), 1885. 4. 'Progress from Toleration to Religious Equality,' 1889 (Congregational Union bicentenary lecture). 5. 'Nonconformity in the Nineteenth Century,' 1900 (address as chairman of the Congregational Union).

[The Times, 9 and 14 Oct. 1907; Evangelical Magazine, January 1900 (portrait); Liberator, August and September 1906, November 1907; private information personal recollection.] A. G.

WILLIAMS, ROWLAND, 'Hwfa Môn' (1823–1905), archdruid of Wales, was born in March 1823, at Penygraig, near Pentraeth, Anglesey. In 1828 his parents moved to Rhos Trehwfa, near Llangefni, and it was from this place he took his bardic name of 'Hwfa Môn.' At an early age he was apprenticed to a carpenter and worked at Llangefni, Bangor, Ebenezer, and Port Dinorwic. He commenced to preach as a member of the independent church at Llangefni and in 1847 entered Bala Congregational College. In 1851 he was ordained minister of the Flint and Bagillt churches; on 12 May 1853 he married his predecessor's widow, Mary Evans. His next pastorate was at Brymbo (1855–62), and for a time he took charge of the Welsh church at Wrexham also. After a short but strenuous ministry at Bethesda, Carnarvonshire, he accepted a call in 1867 to the Welsh church meeting in Fetter Lane, London, where he remained until 1881. Two country pastorates, viz. Llanerchymedd (1881–7) and Llangollen (1887–93), closed his ministerial career; from 1893 he lived in retirement at Rhyl until his death on 10 Nov. 1905. He was buried in Rhyl new cemetery on the 14th. He left no issue.

Hwfa Môn was throughout his career a preacher of great descriptive and dramatic power. He was known to his countrymen as a poet rich in language and with much feeling for natural beauty. But his widest repute was won as the picturesque and arresting central figure in the annual pageant of the national eisteddfod. The first eisteddfod he attended was that of Aberffraw in 1849, when he was admitted to the 'gorsedd,' or bardic guild, and won a minor poetic prize. He won his first bardic chair in 1855 at Llanfair Talhaiarn, Denbighshire, for an ode on 'The Exit of Israel from Egypt,' and in the same year carried off a second chair at Llanfachreth, Anglesey, for an ode on 'The Poet.' The highest bardic distinction, the chair of the national eisteddfod, first fell to him in 1862, when his ode on 'The Year' was successful at Carnarvon. It was reckoned a special distinction that he defeated on this occasion the veteran Ebenezer Thomas (Eben Fardd). He was a competitor for this honour on several later occasions and was twice successful, winning the Mold chair in 1873 ('Caractacus in Rome') and the Birkenhead chair in 1878 ('Providence'). In 1867 he had won the eisteddfodic crown (given for verse in the 'free' metres) at Carmarthen, his subject being Owen Glendower. Henceforward, his part in these competitions was more often that of judge than competitor; from 1875 to 1892 he was constantly employed as chief bardic adjudicator in the great national festival.

As leader of the movement which gave the bardic Gorsedd its prominent and dignified position in the modern eisteddfod, he, on the death of Clwydfardd in 1894, naturally stepped into his place as archdruid. His personality and faith in the institution gave the Gorsedd and its ceremonies an entirely new importance, which was heightened by the artistic reforms introduced by Sir Hubert von Herkomer.

Collected editions of the works of Hwfa Môn are: 1. 'Gwaith Barddonol Hwfa Môn' (with portrait), Llanerchymedd, 1883. 2. 'Gwaith Barddonol Hwfa Môn, Ail Gyfrol' (with photograph), Bala, 1903.

Some of his poems have been separately printed, and there is much of his work in Parry's memoir (see below). Paintings of him in his official robes by Sir Hubert von Herkomer and by Christopher Williams are the property of the artists.

[Cofiant Hwfa Môn, ed. W. J. Parry, Manchester, 1907 (illustrated), is a memorial volume, biographical and critical, with some of the later pieces; see also The Times, 11 Nov. 1905, and T. R. Roberts, Eminent Welshmen.] J. E. L.

WILLIAMS, WATKIN HEZEKIAH (1844–1905), Welsh schoolmaster and poet, born on 7 March 1844 at his mother's home at Ddolgam, in the Llynfell valley, Carmarthenshire, was son of Hezekiah and Ann Williams his wife. He was brought up, the second of a family of ten, on his father's farm of Cwmgarw Ganol, near Brynaman. At an early age he found employment in the coal mines then being opened up in the district, and he worked, chiefly as a collier, with occasional periods of attendance at various local schools, until the age of twenty-seven. In 1870 he married Mary Jones of Trap, Carreg Cennen; the death of his wife in less than a year led him to quit his home and occupation, and in Jan. 1872 he entered the school of his relative, Evan Williams of Merthyr. His progress was rapid, and he was soon able to give assistance in teaching to Evan Williams and his successor, J. J. Copeland. In 1874 he resolved to qualify for the independent ministry; he returned home, began to preach at Gibea Chapel, and, after a little preliminary training, was admitted to the Presbyterian College at Carmarthen in 1875. On the conclusion of his course in 1879 he married Anne Davies of Carmarthen and accepted, instead of a pastorate, a post as teacher of a private school at Llangadock. Differences among the staff led to his moving, with the Rev. D. E. Williams, to Amanford in 1880, where the two friends founded the 'Hope Academy.' In 1884 Watkin took sole charge, and in 1888 he adapted for school purposes a building to which he gave the name of 'Gwynfryn.' Thenceforth until his death he conducted the institution as a preparatory school for those about to enter the dissenting ministry or other professions. He was ordained an independent minister in 1894, but held no pastoral charge. He died on 19 Nov. 1905, and was buried at Amanford.

'Watcyn Wyn,' as he was generally known, was an inspiring and original teacher, whose vivacity and wit endeared him to his pupils and whose early struggles made him a sympathetic guide of young men athirst for learning. He had also a wide reputation as a Welsh poet, dating from 1875, when he divided a prize with Islwyn [see Thomas, William, 1832–1878] at Pwllheli. Both the silver crown and the bardic chair, the two chief poetic prizes of the eisteddfod, were won by him, the former at Merthyr in 1881 for a poem in free metre on 'Life,' and the latter at Aberdare in 1885 for an ode in the strict metres on the subject 'The Truth against the World.' He was also the winner of the crown at the World's Fair eisteddfod of 1893 at Chicago, the subject being 'George Washington.' These longer productions are not so likely, however, to preserve his memory as the lyrical and humorous poems which came so easily from his pen. He published: 1. 'Caneuon Watcyn Wyn,' Wrexham, n.d.; second edit. 1873. 2. 'Hwyr Ddifyrion,' Swansea, 1883. 3. 'Llenyddiaeth Gymreig' (a survey of Welsh literature), Wrexham, 1900. 4. 'Storiau Cymru' (versified folk-tales), Wrexham, 1907, and other minor works. His autobiography ('Adgofion Watcyn Wyn'), edited by J. Jenkins ('Gwili'), appeared (with portrait) in 1907 (Merthyr).

[Album Caerfyrddin, 1909; Congregational Year Book for 1907; Adgofion Watcyn Wyn; Geninen, April 1906; information supplied by Mr. G. O. Williams, B.A.] J. E. L.

WILLIAMSON, ALEXANDER WILLIAM (1824–1904), chemist, born at Wandsworth on 1 May 1824, was second of three children of Alexander Williamson, originally of Elgin, who settled in London, and became a clerk in the East India House. His mother, Antonia (married 1820), was daughter of William McAndrew, merchant, of London. About 1830 the elder Williamson removed from Camberwell to Wright's Lane, Kensington, hard by the home of James Mill (father of John Stuart Mill), and Williamson's colleague in official work. The two families were on terms of friendship.

In early life young Williamson had delicate health, and took no part in the usual games of boyhood. A low vitality led, from various causes, to loss of sight in his right eye, and to chronic, though partial, disablement of the left arm. Though thus handicapped, he became eventually of robust constitution. After education at home and at Kensington grammar school Williamson went abroad with his parents, on his father's retirement from the India House. For some time he had private tuition at Dijon with his sister Antonia (*b.* 1822). In 1840 he entered Heidelberg University with a view to a medical career. He attended Friedrich Tiedemann's lectures in physiology and those of Leopold Gmelin in chemistry. Finally he decided to give up medicine for chemical research. Four years later he left to study chemistry under Liebig at Giessen University, going into residence with Prof. Hillebrand. He also joined Bischoff's classes in physiology. Williamson was of the opinion that the Giessen laboratory was the most efficient organisation for the promotion of chemistry that had ever existed (see *Brit. Assoc. address*, 1873). He graduated Ph.D. in 1846.

Williamson spent the next three years in Paris, studying mathematics with Auguste Comte. To his father he wrote, 'If my experience of Comte's superior powers were insufficient to convince you that his lessons were worth their price, John Stuart Mill's saying that he "would prefer him to any man in Europe to finish a scientific education," ought to carry the point and to induce you to consent to my continuing as I have begun.'

In 1849 he was appointed professor of practical chemistry in University College, London, succeeding George Fownes [q. v.]. In 1855 this post was joined with the professorship of general chemistry, vacant by the resignation of his friend Thomas Graham [q. v.]. Williamson occupied the chair for thirty-eight years, earning distinction as a teacher and instigator of research. In 1887 he retired and was made emeritus professor of chemistry (see *Life and Experiences of Sir H. E. Roscoe*, 1906; portrait of Williamson, and reminiscences). He delivered a farewell address on 14 June 1887, when Sir William Ramsay presided (*Chemical News*, 8 July 1887).

Owing to Williamson's scientific influence, force of character, and cosmopolitan outlook, he was chosen guardian of a small group of young Japanese noblemen, who came to England in 1863 with a view to familiarising themselves and their countrymen with European culture. Of five who first reached London three took up residence in Williamson's own house. Subsequently the Prince of Satsuma sent over sixteen more youths. The Marquis Ito, Count Inouye, and Viscount Yamao were among those who owed their early training to Williamson.

Williamson's published researches were comparatively few in number, but some of them were of such a character that they influenced profoundly the progress of chemical knowledge and philosophy. His chief chemical investigations were made between 1844 and 1859. While at Giessen he published three papers, which, though written for Liebig's 'Annalen,' appeared originally in the 'Memoirs of the Chemical Society of London' (1844–6). They were: 'On the Decomposition of Oxides and Salts by Chlorine'; 'Some Experiments on Ozone'; and 'On the Blue Compounds of Cyanogen and Iron.'

About 1849 he began his classical research on the theory of etherification, in which he laid the foundations of chemical dynamics, of the theory of ionisation, and of the theory of catalytic action. Embodied firstly in a communication to the British Association (Edinburgh meeting), 3 Aug. 1850, 'Results of a Research on Etherification,' the extended paper appeared in the 'Philosophical Magazine' for Nov. 1850 (see, in reference to priority, *Chemical News*, 8 July 1904). A chief ultimate fruit of the research was Williamson's theory of the constitution of salts, from which emerged the doctrine of valency and the linkage of radicles (see obit. notice by Sir T. E. Thorpe, *Proc. Roy. Soc.*). He cleared up, wrote Sir James Dewar, one of the most intricate and recondite of chemical reactions, and in so doing struck at the very root of the chemical problems connected with atomic and molecular weights. The subject was further elucidated in the memoirs 'On the Constitution of Salts' (*Journ. Chem. Soc.* vol. iv. 1852); 'On Gerhardt's Discovery of Anhydrous Organic Acids' (*Proc. Roy. Inst.* vol. i.); and 'Note on the Decomposition of Sulphuric Acid by Pentachloride of Phosphorus' (*Proc. Roy. Soc.* vol. vii.). His papers on Etherification and on the Constitution of Salts were issued as an Alembic Club reprint (Edinburgh, 1902). At the Royal Institution he delivered a lecture, 6 June 1851, 'Suggestions for the Dynamics of Chemistry, derived from the Theory of Etherification.'

Subsequent papers by Williamson of a miscellaneous nature comprised 'On the Dynamics of the Galvanic Battery' (*Phil. Mag.* 1863–4); 'On the Composition of the Gases evolved by the Bath Spring called King's Bath' (*Rept. Brit. Assoc.* 1865; see paper by Hon. R. J. Strutt, *Proc. Roy. Soc.* vol. lxxiii. (1904), p. 191); and 'On Fermentation' (*Pharmaceut. Journ.* 1871). Jointly with Dr. W. J. Russell [q. v. Suppl. II] he published 'Note on the Measurement of Gases in Analysis' (*Proc. Roy. Soc.* vol. ix. 1857–9); and 'On a New Method of Gas Analysis' (*Jour. Chem. Soc.* vol. ii. 1864).

Williamson was admitted into the Chemical Society on 15 May 1848, served on the council (1850–3, 1858–60), and was president (1863–5, and 1869–71). He was responsible for the introduction into the society's 'Journal' of abstracts of chemical memoirs of British and foreign authorship (see *Journal*, vol. xxiii. p. 290). He was president of the British Association in 1873 at the Bradford meeting, when he gave an address on the intellectual value of chemical studies and the duties of the government in relation to education; he presided over section B in 1863 (Newcastle) and in 1881 (York). At the latter, the jubilee meeting, he gave an address on 'The Growth of the Atomic Theory.' He succeeded William Spottiswoode as general treasurer in 1874, holding office until 1891.

Elected a fellow of the Royal Society on 7 June 1855, he served on the council (1859–61, 1869–71); from 1873 to 1889 he was foreign secretary. He received a royal medal in 1862 for his researches on the compound ethers and subsequent communications in organic chemistry (see *Proc. Roy. Soc.* xii. 279).

Many foreign bodies conferred distinctions on him; he became a corresponding member of the French Academy of Sciences, the Berlin Academy, and R. Accademia dei Lincei, Rome, respectively in 1873, 1875 and 1883. The Royal Society of Edinburgh made him an honorary fellow (1883); he was an honorary member of the Royal Irish Academy (1885), of the Manchester Literary and Philosophical Society (1889), and of the Society of Public Analysts (1875). He was also a foundation member (1872) of the Society of Telegraph Engineers (afterwards Institution of Electrical Engineers), and of the Society of Chemical Industry (1881). From Dublin and Edinburgh Universities he received the honorary degree of LL.D. respectively in 1878 and 1881; from Durham University that of D.C.L. in 1889.

Williamson was for some years examiner in chemistry in the University of London, and from 1874 a member of the senate. He took a prominent part in the introduction there of degrees of science, and was deeply interested in the formation of a teaching university for London. He was a member of the first electrical standards committee, inaugurated by the association in 1861. From 1876 to 1901 he was chief gas examiner under the board of trade, having succeeded Henry Letheby [q. v.].

Williamson, who wrote articles for Watts's 'Dictionary of Chemistry' (1863–6), was author of a text-book, 'Chemistry for Students' (1865; 3rd edit. 1873). Conjointly with T. H. Key he published the pamphlet 'Invasion invited by the Defenceless State of England' (1858). On 11 Nov. 1898 Williamson was one of six guests at a banquet given in London by the Chemical Society to those of its past presidents who had been fellows for half a century (see *Proc. Chem. Soc.* no. 199, speech by Williamson).

Williamson died on 6 May 1904 at his home, High Pitfold, Shottermill, Haslemere, and was buried at Brookwood cemetery, Surrey. He married in 1855 Emma Catherine, third daughter of Thomas Hewitt Key, F.R.S., headmaster of University College School, and had issue a son and a daughter, who, with his wife, survived him.

A subscription portrait of Williamson, painted by the Hon. John Collier, hangs in the council room of University College (see *Nature*, 20 Dec. 1888, speeches by Sir H. E. Roscoe and Williamson at presentation ceremony); another, executed in 1894–5 by Mr. W. Biscombe Gardner, was presented to the chemical department. An autotype portrait hangs in the council room of the Chemical Society in the series of past presidents.

[Proc. Roy. Soc. (with portrait), vol. lxxviii. A, and Presidential Address Roy. Soc. (Sir W. Huggins) in Year Book, 1905; Trans. Chem. Soc., vol. lxxxvii. (pt. i.); Jubilee Record Chem. Soc. 1896; Proc. Roy. Soc. Edin., vol. xxvi.; Memoirs Lit. Phil. Soc. Manch., vol. xlix. (ser. 4); Chemical News, 13 May 1904; Analyst, June 1904; Journ. Soc. Chem. Industry, vol. xxiii.; Journ. of Gas Lighting, 10 May 1904; English Mechanic, 13 May 1904; Roy. Soc. Catal. Sci. Papers; Poggendorff's Handwörterbuch, Bd. iii. (1898), Bd. iv. (1904); Encycl. Brit. (11th edit.) vol. xxviii.; Nature, 12 May 1904; The Times, 7 and 14 May 1904; Men of the Time, 1899.] T. E. J.

WILLIS, HENRY (1821–1901), organbuilder, born in London on 27 April 1821, was eldest of four sons of Henry Willis, a builder, who was a member of the choir of the old Surrey Chapel, Blackfriars Road, and of the Cecilian Society, where he played tympani and bass-drum. Of the organ builder's brothers, George became a celebrated voicer of organ reeds and Edwin was employed in organ building.

As a boy Henry taught himself to play

the organ, practising it in rivalry with a playmate, George Cooper [q. v.], and from a very early age began experimenting on the mechanism of the instrument. In 1835 he was articled for seven years to John Gray (afterwards Gray & Davison), organ builders, of London, and soon afterwards became organist of Christ Church, Hoxton, where Clement William Scott [q. v. Suppl. II], son of the vicar, was his solo-boy.

Subsequently he filled similar posts at Hampstead parish church, and was for some thirty years (*c.* 1860–1891) organist of Islington chapel-of-ease. He was an apt extemporiser in a diatonic and classic manner. He also was an efficient player on the double-bass, performing at many festivals, including the Gloucester festival of 1847 and the Handel festivals of 1871 and 1874.

Willis spent three years (1842–5) as assistant to W. E. Evans, a music-warehouseman, at Cheltenham, where he assisted in the construction of a new instrument of the 'Seraphina' class. In 1845 he started organ building in Manchester Street, Gray's Inn Road, London, W.C., removing in 1851 to Albany Street, Regent's Park, and in 1865 to King Street, Camden Town, finally settling in 1866 at Rotunda Works, Rochester Place, Camden Town. In 1847 he achieved his first success by rebuilding Gloucester Cathedral organ, which brought him 400*l*.

In 1851 he built the great organ in the west end gallery of the Great Exhibition, which he claimed to be entirely his own in conception, design and 'every detail.' It was afterwards erected in Winchester Cathedral, and, renovated in 1891, is still in use. In 1855 Willis won the competition for building the organ at St. George's Hall, Liverpool (rebuilt 1898). Another organ built for the exhibition of 1862 was equally notable; it was transferred to the Alexandra Palace, and when that building was burned in 1873 Willis replaced the destroyed organ by another instrument. His largest organ was that in the Albert Hall, London (opened 1871). Willis contracted to have a new organ ready at St. Paul's Cathedral by April 1872, but he was warned before that date that the instrument was required for the thanksgiving service (on 27 Feb.) on the recovery of Edward VII, then Prince of Wales, from serious illness. The pneumatic action for the pedals was not ready, but Willis made a temporary pedal-board and music desk by the pedal pipes, on which he played, while George Cooper played on the manuals. No discrepancy was noticeable. Willis was directly concerned in the building, or rebuilding, of over a thousand organs, including those, in addition to the places named, at the cathedrals of Canterbury, Carlisle, Durham, Hereford, Oxford, Salisbury, Truro, Wells, St. David's, Edinburgh, and Glasgow, at Windsor Castle and the Dome, Brighton. In 1878 Willis took his two sons into partnership—the firm assuming the style of Henry Willis & Sons, but he remained in active superintendence till his death. A special gold medal was awarded the firm at the Inventions Exhibition of 1885.

Willis took out numerous patents for important inventions in organ building. He practically extended the range of the pedal-board from G to C. He insisted on a high pitch. In 1877 he began with Alexander John Ellis [q. v. Suppl. I] some interesting experiments at the Rotunda Works, with reference to the temperament question; but Ellis and Willis disagreed in their conclusions.

Some critics have occasionally complained that Willis voiced the reed stops on so heavy a wind pressure that the flue stops could not contend with them, so that the full power appeared to consist of reed stops only. But Willis's work was always marked by scrupulous conscientiousness and artistic insight. He could make every part of an organ from his own drawings. The workmanship and material of his instruments were admirable, down to the smallest detail, and he may justly be regarded as the greatest organ-builder of his time.

His rectitude, enthusiasm, and artistic spirit won him the regard of many well-known musicians, including Best, Costa, Elvey, Goss, Hopkins, Monk, Ouseley, Henry Smart, Stainer, Walmisley, and S. S. Wesley, with whom he came into professional relations.

Of small physique, 'Father' Willis, as he came to be known, abounded in breezy energy. His chief recreation was yachting, to constant indulgence in which he attributed his excellent health. In his yacht Opal he circumnavigated Great Britain.

Busy to the end, he died in Bartholomew Road, Camden Town, London, on 11 Feb. 1901, and was buried at Highgate cemetery, where there is a monument to his memory.

In 1847 he married Esther Maria, daughter of Randall Chatterton, a London silversmith, by whom he had two sons, Vincent and Henry (his partners from 1878), and three daughters. After his death his firm removed in 1905 to High Street, Homerton.

[Notes supplied by Mr. Henry Davey; Grove's Dict. of Music; Musical Times, 1 May 1898 (personal interview, with two portraits), March 1901 (with portrait as skipper of yacht Opal); Musical Herald, March 1901; information from Sir George C. Martin, St. Paul's Cathedral, Henry Willis (son) and Henry Willis (grandson).] C. M.

WILLIS, WILLIAM (1835–1911), lawyer, born at Dunstable, Bedfordshire, on 29 April 1835, was eldest son and third child in the family of eight sons and six daughters of William Willis, a straw-hat manufacturer at Luton, by his wife Esther Kentish, daughter of Johnson Masters, of a Norfolk family, who carried on a straw-hat business at Dunstable. He received his early education at the free grammar school, Dunstable, then at schools at Hockcliffe, Bedfordshire, and at Hatfield, and lastly at Huddersfield College. He subsequently matriculated at London University, graduating B.A. in 1859, and LL.D., with gold medal, in 1865. After a short experience of business life in a drapery establishment in St. Paul's Churchyard Willis entered as a student at the Inner Temple on 21 April 1888, winning the studentship given by the Inns of Court; he was called to the bar on 6 June 1861. His success from the first was rapid; he had a sound and complete knowledge of the common law in all its branches, and he was endowed with a style of advocacy which rendered him singularly effective with juries. He took silk on 13 Feb. 1877, and was made a bencher of his Inn, 28 Jan. 1880. For the next twenty years he was one of the most conspicuous figures and determined fighters in the courts of law at Westminster and in the Strand. Of a fervid temperament and very voluble in speech, he would identify himself absolutely with the interests of his client, and assail his opponents with as much zeal and indignation as if his own honour and property were at stake. He came into frequent collision with both the bar and the bench, but nothing could daunt him. His services were greatly in demand in cases which required violent appeals to sentiment and emotion, and he could be forcible and convincing where the issue turned on points of law. Out of court his flow of conversation and his fondness for improving the occasion were the source of endless amusement to his brethren at the bar. A baptist by religion and a radical in politics, he advocated his principles in all companies. In 1903 he was chosen president of the baptist conference, a distinction rarely conferred upon a layman. In the general electon of 1880 he was returned second on the poll as liberal member for Colchester, defeating the conservative candidate by a single vote. He took frequent part in the proceedings of the house, and on 31 March 1884 he succeeded in carrying a motion for the exclusion of the bishops from the House of Lords by a majority of eleven votes in spite of the opposition of Sir William Harcourt [q. v. Suppl. II] on behalf of the government. In the general election of Nov. 1885, Colchester having been deprived of its second member, he stood for Peckham, but was defeated, and had no better success there in July of the following year. In March 1897 he was given a county court judgeship by Lord Halsbury; in the discharge of his judicial duties he was easily led away by his feelings, which inclined towards the servant as against the mistress, the employee against the employer. He was at constant war with counsel, and the 'scenes' which were chronicled in the press left a poor impression of his sense of official decorum.

Though largely a self-educated man, Willis had a wide knowledge of English literature and especially of the classic writers of the sixteenth and seventeenth centuries. He lectured on Milton and Bunyan with real eloquence. On 29 May 1902 he read publicly in the hall of the Inner Temple an imaginary 'report of the trial of an issue in Westminster Hall, 20 June 1627,' dealing with the Shakespeare-Bacon controversy; here he ably exposed the fallacies to which several learned lawyers had lent themselves on the Baconian side. In spite of his peculiarities Willis enjoyed much popularity at the bar; his closest friend being Sir John Day [q. v. Suppl. II], as much his opposite in character and manner as he was in personal appearance.

Willis died at his residence at Blackheath on 22 Aug. 1911, after a prolonged illness, and was buried in Lee cemetery. He was twice married: (1) on 21 March 1866 to Annie, eldest daughter of John Outhwaite of Clapham, by whom he had issue four sons and five daughters; and (2) on 2 Sept. 1897 to Marie Elizabeth, daughter of Thomas Moody, of Lewisham, who survived him.

Willis's works included: 1. 'Milton's Sonnets,' a lecture, privately printed, 1887. 2. 'Sir George Jessel,' a lecture, 1893.

3. 'The Law of Negotiable Securities,' six lectures delivered at the request of the Council of Legal Education, 1896. 4. 'The Society and Fellowship of the Inner Temple,' an address delivered in the Inner Temple Hall, 1897. 5. 'Law relating to Contract of Sale of Goods,' six lectures, 1902. 6. 'The Shakespeare-Bacon Controversy: a report of the trial of an issue in Westminster Hall, 20 June 1627,' read in the Inner Temple Hall, 29 May 1902. 7. 'The Baconian Mint: its Claims examined,' 1903. 8. 'The Baconian Mint: a Further Examination of its Claims,' 1908. 9. 'Recollections of Sir John C. F. Day, for Nineteen Years a Judge of the High Court,' 1908. 10. 'Cowper and his Connection with the Law,' privately printed, Norwich, 1910.

[The Times, 23 Aug. 1911; Hansard, 3rd series, cclxxxvi. 502; personal knowledge and private information.] J. B. A.

WILLOCK, HENRY DAVIS (1830–1903), Indian civilian, born on Christmas Day 1830, at Oujoun, Persia, was one of four sons of Sir Henry Willock (1790–1858), Madras cavalry, who accompanied Sir Harford Jones-Brydges [q. v.] on his mission to Persia as interpreter, was afterwards resident at the court of Teheran (1815–26), and later director of the East India Company, and in 1846–7 chairman. His mother was Eliza, eighth child of Samuel Davis, F.R.S., Bengal civil service, celebrated for his heroic defence of his house in Benares on 14 Jan. 1799, against the attack of Wazir Ali, the deposed Nawab of Oudh; she was sister to Sir John Francis Davis [q.v. Suppl. I], British plenipotentiary in China.

Willock was educated at Kensington and at the East India College, Haileybury (March 1850–December 1851). Appointed to the civil service, he arrived in India in 1852, and was posted to the North-West Provinces. Joint magistrate of Allahabad on the outbreak of the Mutiny, he commanded a company of volunteers, and served under General James G. S. Neill [q. v.] at the storming and capture of Kydgunj. As civil officer he volunteered with Major Renan's force for the relief of the Cawnpore garrison (which fell before its arrival), and served with the force subsequently commanded by Havelock. He was in the actions of Fatehpur, Pandu Nudi, Maharajpur, and Cawnpore, being one of the first persons to enter the Beebeegarh in which the British women and children had been slaughtered by order of the Nana Sahib.

Willock accompanied Havelock on his two unsuccessful advances to Lucknow; was with Outram and Havelock in their subsequent relief of the residency, and served as a member of the garrison until the final relief by Sir Colin Campbell (Lord Clyde) in November 1857 (cf. his letter to his parents, in *The Times* of 1 Feb. 1858, headed 'Lucknow Garrison, 19 Oct. 1857 to 18 Dec. at Allahabad'). Returning to Cawnpore, then besieged by the Gwalior contingent, he was appointed civil officer of Maxwell's movable column watching the banks of the Jumna in the Cawnpore and Etawah districts. He was at the capture of Kalpi by Sir Hugh Rose's central India force in May 1858, and at many minor engagements. In June he was appointed civil officer with the field force watching the southern borders of Oudh, being present at the capture of the Tirhol and Dehaen forts. General Sir Mowbray Thomson, the last survivor of the Cawnpore entrenchment, wrote that Willock's 'feats of arms were patent to all the force, who asserted that he had mistaken his profession and ought without doubt to have been a soldier' (*The Story of Cawnpore*, 1859, p. 253). He thus participated in the suppression of the Mutiny from first to last, and he was the only civilian to receive the medal with the three clasps for relief of Lucknow, Lucknow 1858, and Central India. Queen Victoria sent him a letter of thanks.

He subsequently served at Shahjehanpur, Bareilly, and Bulundshahar as magistrate and collector, and as judge of Benares, and finally, from 1876 to his retirement in April 1884, as judge of Azimgarh. He was for some years a major in the Ghazipore volunteer rifles, raised by Colonel J. H. Rivett-Carnac, C.I.E. (cf. his *Many Memories*, Edin. and Lond. 1910).

After his retirement Willock lived at Brighton and subsequently in London. He died on 26 April 1903 at Tunbridge Wells, and was buried at Little Bookham, Surrey. He married on 27 Oct. 1859, at Barnes, Surrey, his cousin Mary Elizabeth, only child of Major Charles L. Boileau, late rifle brigade, brother of Sir John Peter Boileau [q. v.]. He had two sons and two daughters. The elder son, Henry Court, took in 1906 the additional surname of Pollen on succeeding to the manor of Little Bookham.

[Homeward Mail, 4 May 1903; Dict. of Ind. Biog. 1906; Memorials of Old Haileybury College, 1894; J. W. Shorer's Daily Life during the Indian Mutiny, 1898 (later edit., Havelock's March on Cawnpore, 1910); information kindly supplied by Mr. H. C. Willock-Pollen.] F. H. B.

WILLOUGHBY, DIGBY (1845–1901), soldier adventurer, born in 1845, left England for South Africa in 1871 to seek his fortune. In the Zulu campaign of 1879 Willoughby was with the Natal native contingent, and was in command of the native mounted corps. He then for a time acted as auctioneer's assistant, subsequently becoming partner in the firm of Willoughby & Scoones at Maritzburg, where he resided. After a brief period with a theatrical company, he raised and commanded a troop of irregular horse, 'Willoughby's Horse,' which saw service in the Basuto war in 1880. In January 1884 he went to Madagascar, where, gaining the confidence of the Queen of Madagascar and her husband, who was prime minister, he was appointed general commander of the Hovas or Madagascar forces (18 May). On the outbreak of the Franco-Malagasy war next year he got together a well-drilled army of 20,000 soldiers. The Hovas, however, suffered from want of serviceable ammunition, and were severely defeated. At the close of the war in December 1885 he helped in negotiations with the French government, and went to London charged as minister plenipotentiary with a special mission on behalf of the Malagasy government. Although he was cordially received in England, the imperial authorities found it impossible to recognise him as an envoy, as he was still a British subject.

Wearing the uniform of a British field-marshal, he conducted a military spectacle at the Chicago Exhibition of 1893. In Oct. of the same year, after the outbreak of the first Matabele war, he proceeded to Rhodesia. The war was almost over, but he went up country by way of Kimberley, Vryburg and Palapye. On the journey he conferred with Cecil Rhodes, and reached Bulawayo just before the end of the campaign. On the declaration of peace he helped in the administration of Rhodesia. Next year (1894) he was again in London, lecturing on the Matabele war. On the outbreak of the second Matabele war in March 1896, he formed one of a council of defence at Bulawayo, under the acting administrator of Rhodesia. He revisited South Africa on the outbreak of the war there in 1899, but took no part in the fighting, and soon returned to England. Willoughby, who had made a wealthy second marriage, was then ruined in health, and had lost an eye. He died at Goring-on-Thames on 3 June 1901. His courage and soldiership were unquestioned, but love of spectacular adventure was his most salient characteristic. He was a vivid raconteur of his varied experiences.

[The Times, 5 June 1901; South Africa, 8 June 1901; see also issue of 14 July 1894 (interview); S. P. Oliver, Madagascar, 1886, vol. ii.; Howard Hensman, History of Rhodesia, 1900, p. 171.]

WILLS, Sir WILLIAM HENRY, first baronet, and first Baron Winterstoke (1830–1911), benefactor to Bristol, born at Bristol on 1 Sept. 1830, was second son and only surviving child of William Day Wills, a manufacturer of tobacco and snuff (*b.* 6 June 1797, *d.* 13 May 1865), by his wife Mary, third daughter of Robert Steven of Glasgow, and Camberwell, Surrey.

His grandfather, the first Henry Overton Wills (1761–1826), who was the earliest of the family to settle in Bristol, married Anne, eldest daughter of William Day of that place, on 24 June 1790; he joined his father-in-law in the tobacco trade and obtained a predominant interest in the firm, which his sons and grandsons greatly developed, all making immense fortunes. His second son, also Henry Overton Wills (1800–1871), Lord Winterstoke's uncle, was father, with other issue, of the third Henry Overton Wills (*d.* 1911), who left a fortune exceeding 2,000,000*l.*, having in 1909 bestowed 100,000*l.* on the projected Bristol University; of Sir Edward Payson Wills (1834–1910) of Hazelwood, Stoke Bishop, who gave the Jubilee Convalescent Home to Bristol and was created a baronet on 19 Aug. 1904; and of Sir Frederick Wills (1838–1909) of Northmoor, near Dulverton, who was unionist M.P. for North Bristol from 1900 to 1906, and was likewise created a baronet on 15 Feb. 1897.

The Wills family were congregationalists, and young Wills, after early training at home, went to the nonconformist public school at Mill Hill, which he left as head of the sixth form and captain. Illness prevented him from completing his studies for a London university degree, or going to the bar. When about eighteen he entered the family tobacco and snuff business at Bristol, then known as Wills, Ditchett, Day & Wills, his father being the junior partner. Acquiring a thorough knowledge of the trade, and of the growth and treatment of tobacco, he, with his first cousins Henry Overton Wills, jun., and Edward Payson Wills, was in 1858 taken into partnership, and the firm was styled W. D. and H. O. Wills. The concern was afterwards converted into a limited liability company and William Henry became chairman of the board of directors.

Wills's technical knowledge and sagacity largely promoted the success of the firm, and helped to meet such difficulties as the failures of the tobacco-leaf crop and the stoppage of supplies during the American war. He became the recognised head of the tobacco trade in Great Britain. In 1878 he was unanimously elected chairman of the committee organised to resist a threatened increase of duty on tobacco. In 1900–1 Wills took a leading part in the 'combine' promoted by British tobacco manufacturers to combat the contemplated American 'trust,' serving as chairman until his death of the Imperial Tobacco Company, which acquired in 1901 at a cost of 11,957,000*l.* the business of thirteen tobacco manufacturing concerns in the United Kingdom.

Wills was a prominent member of the liberal party in Bristol and was president of the Anchor Society in 1866. He entered parliament in 1880 as a member for Coventry, representing that borough until 1885, when it lost one of its members. After contesting South-East Essex twice unsuccessfully, first in 1885 and then as an advocate of home rule in 1886, he also failed in South Bristol in 1892, but he was returned at a bye-election in March 1895 for East Bristol, and he represented that constituency until his retirement in 1900. He was created a baronet on 12 Aug. 1893, being the first of his family to receive a titular honour, although baronetcies were also soon bestowed on two first cousins and business colleagues.

Closely identifying himself with local interests, Wills was for some years on the council of the Bristol Chamber of Commerce and in 1863 became its chairman. From 1862 to 1880 he served on the municipal council, was chosen one of the charity trustees in 1865, and was high sheriff of the city in 1877–8. To the public institutions of Bristol he was a notable benefactor. He provided organs for Colston Hall and Bristol grammar school. The Bristol Art Gallery and the St. George branch of the Bristol public libraries were built at his expense; and he erected on St. Augustine's Parade a statue of Burke, which was unveiled by Lord Rosebery on 30 Oct. 1894. Like other members of his family he was interested in the university of Bristol, which was incorporated in 1909, and his gifts to it amounted to 35,000*l.* He was appointed pro-chancellor. On 5 July 1904 he was made an honorary freeman of Bristol. In London, where he had a residence in Hyde Park Gardens, he was well known as a director of the Great Western railway and of the Phœnix Assurance companies and was chairman of the Provincial Companies Association.

A zealous nonconformist by personal conviction as well as by family tradition, he actively engaged in the affairs of the free churches. He joined the board of the dissenting deputies, was a trustee of the Memorial Hall in London, and took a practical interest in the refoundation of Mansfield College at Oxford in 1886. To the new chapel of Mill Hill School, opened in June 1898, he gave an organ and other substantial help; his portrait, subscribed for by the governors, is at the school.

On 1 Feb. 1906 Wills was raised to the peerage on Campbell-Bannerman's nomination as Baron Winterstoke of Blagdon, co. Somerset. His country seat Coombe Lodge was at Blagdon. There he took a deep interest in agriculture and was a well-known exhibitor of shire horses and shorthorn cattle. He was D.L. of Somerset, and high sheriff of the county in 1905–6.

Winterstoke died suddenly at his residence at Blagdon on 29 Jan. 1911, and was buried in the churchyard there. He married on 11 Jan. 1853 Elizabeth (*d.* 10 Feb. 1896), daughter of John Stancombe of Trowbridge, Wiltshire. Leaving no issue, the peerage became extinct at his death. He left a fortune exceeding 1,000,000*l.* Two adopted daughters, Miss Janet Stancombe Wilson and Mrs. Richardson, largely benefited under his will. The former presented 10,000*l.* to Bristol grammar school in Winterstoke's memory. Among the other property which he bequeathed to her was his collection of pictures, and he expressed a wish that she should leave twenty-four of these at her death to the Bristol Art Gallery which he had built.

A portrait by Mr. Hugh Riviere was presented to Winterstoke by his fellow-citizens of Bristol in October 1907, and was placed at his request in the Bristol Art Gallery.

[Lodge's Peerage, 1912; The Times, 30 Jan., 18 and 25 Feb. 1911; Western Daily Press, 30 Jan. 1911.] C. W.

WILSON, CHARLES HENRY, **first** BARON NUNBURNHOLME (1833–1907), shipowner, born at Hull on 22 April 1833, was eldest son of Thomas Wilson (*d.* 1869) of

Hull and Cottingham by his wife Susannah, daughter of John West of Hull. In 1835 the father joined others in forming at Hull a ship-owning firm, of which he soon acquired the chief control. A regular line of sailing boats to Swedish ports was established; the importation of iron from Russia and Sweden was developed; a service to Dunkirk was added; and with the substitution of steamships for sailing ships Thomas Wilson's firm was assured a permanent place in the shipping world.

Charles, who was educated at Kingston College, Hull, early joined with his brothers his father's firm, which was re-christened Thomas Wilson, Sons and Company. Charles and his brother Arthur [see below] became in 1867 joint managers, and to their energy the firm's rapid development was mainly due. The Norwegian and Baltic service for cargo and passengers was greatly extended; Adriatic and Sicilian, Indian and American and home coasting services were inaugurated from time to time after 1870. In 1891 the concern was turned into a private limited company, with a capital of two and a half millions and a fleet of over 100 vessels, and it is now the largest private ship-owning firm in the world. In 1903 the fleet of Messrs. Bailey and Leetham of Hull was absorbed, and in 1908 that of the North Eastern Railway Company. Charles was also chairman of Earle's Shipbuilding and Engineering Company, Limited, and of the United Shipping Company, and vice-chairman of the Hull Steam Fishing and Ice Company, Limited.

Wilson played a prominent part in public affairs outside his business. He was sheriff of Hull. In 1873 he actively promoted the Hull and South Western Junction Railway bill. In 1874 he entered Parliament for Hull as a liberal, and sat continuously till 1905, representing West Hull from 1885. As an ardent liberal he was a pronounced free-trader and an advocate of temperance reform. An opponent of the South African war of 1899–1901, he yet showed public spirit by placing at the disposal of the government the Ariosto, one of his firm's vessels, for the purpose of transporting the newly raised City Imperial Volunteers to the Cape.

In 1899 he received the freedom of his native town, and in 1905 he was made a peer under the title of Lord Nunburnholme.

He died at his residence, Warter Priory, Pocklington, Yorkshire, on 27 Oct. 1907. On 5 Oct. 1871 he married Florence Jane Helen, the eldest daughter of Colonel William Henry Charles Wellesley, nephew of the first Duke of Wellington. He had issue three sons and four daughters; the eldest son, Charles Henry Wellesley Wilson (*b.* 1875), succeeded to the peerage.

The first Lord Nunburnholme's youngest brother, ARTHUR WILSON (1836–1909), born on 14 Dec. 1836 at Hull, was educated like him at Kingston College; he was associated with him in the ship-owning firm, and on the death of Lord Nunburnholme became its head. To his foresight was largely due the firm's development of the Norwegian timber trade and the foundation of the Baltic Exchange. A director of the North Eastern Railway Company and chairman of the shipping committee of the Hull chamber of commerce, he served in 1891 as high sheriff of Yorkshire. For many years a warm supporter of the liberal interest in Yorkshire, he objected to Gladstone's home rule proposal of 1886, joined the liberal unionists, and finally in 1909 supported tariff reform. He was a generous benefactor to Hull, and among the institutions in which he was specially interested was the Victoria Children's Hospital, of which he was chairman. Arthur Wilson was an ardent sportsman, and was for twenty-five years master of the Holderness hunt, the members of which in January 1904 presented him with his portrait by A. S. Cope, R.A.; it is now at his home at Tranby Croft. Of genial disposition, he dispensed a lavish hospitality. While Edward VII (when Prince of Wales) was his guest at Tranby Croft, in Sept. 1890, an allegation of cheating at baccarat was made against Sir William Gordon-Cumming, Bart., who was also staying at the house. In the prolonged trial of an unsuccessful action of libel which Sir William brought against Wilson's son-in-law and daughter Mr. and Mrs. Lycett Green, the Prince of Wales was a witness. The affair attracted worldwide attention and involved Wilson in undeserved obloquy which clouded the remaining years of his life. He died on 21 Oct. 1909 at Tranby Croft, after a long illness, and was buried at Kirkella. He married on 1 July 1862 Mary Emma, daughter of Mr. E. J. Smith, postmaster of Leeds, and had three sons and three daughters. The eldest son, Arthur Stanley, has been unionist M.P. for the Holderness division of Yorkshire since 1900.

[The Times, and Hull Times, 23 Oct. 1909; Burke's Peerage and Landed Gentry; The Times, and Hull Daily Mail, 28 Oct.

1907; private information; Handbook of Thomas Wilson, Sons & Co., Ltd.]

L. P. S.

WILSON, CHARLES ROBERT (1863–1904), historian of British India, born at Old Charlton, Kent, on 27 March 1863, was only son of Charles Wilson, army tutor, by his wife Charlotte Woodthorpe Childs. Educated at the City of London School, where he gained the Carpenter scholarship on leaving, he was elected to a scholarship at Wadham College, Oxford, in 1881. He graduated B.A. in 1887, having been placed in the first class in mathematical moderations in 1883 and in the final classical school in 1886. On leaving Oxford he entered the Indian educational service in Bengal, being successively professor at Dacca and at the Presidency College, Calcutta, principal of the Bankipur College, Patna, and inspector of schools. In 1900 he was appointed officer in charge of the records of the government of India, an appointment which carries with it that of assistant secretary in the home department. Soon afterwards his health broke down, and he died unmarried at Clapham on 24 July 1904 and was buried in Streatham cemetery.

Wilson was a devoted student of the early history of the English in Bengal, ransacking the documentary evidence in India, at the India Office, at the British Museum, and wherever else it might be found. He was admitted to the degree of D.Litt. at Oxford in 1902. Apart from several articles in the 'Journal' of the Asiatic Society of Bengal, dealing chiefly with the tragedy of the Black Hole, his published works are: 1. 'List of Inscriptions on Tombs or Monuments in Bengal possessing Historical Interest,' Calcutta, 1896. 2. 'Descriptive Catalogue of the Paintings, etc., in the Rooms of the Asiatic Society of Bengal,' Calcutta, 1897. 3. 'The Early Annals of the English in Bengal,' being the Bengal public consultations for the first half of the eighteenth century, vol. i. 1895; vol. ii. pt. i. 1900, and pt. ii. 1911, posthumous. 4. 'Old Fort William in Bengal,' a selection of official documents dealing with its history, 2 vols. 1906, posthumous.

[Memoir by W. Irvine prefixed to vol. ii. pt. ii. of Early Annals.]

J. S. C.

WILSON, Sir CHARLES WILLIAM (1836–1905), major-general royal engineers, born at Liverpool on 14 March 1836, was second son of Edward Wilson by his wife Frances, daughter of Thomas Stokes, of Hean Castle, Pembrokeshire, a property which Edward Wilson bought from his wife's brother. Sir Charles's grandfather, also Edward Wilson (*d.* 1843), of a West Yorkshire family, owned property in America, where one of his sons, Thomas Bellerby Wilson, Sir Charles's uncle and godfather, lived, devoting himself to science; he founded the Entomological Society of Philadelphia and proved a munificent benefactor to that society and to the Academy of Natural Science in the same city.

Charles spent seven years at Liverpool College, and two years at Cheltenham College, which he left head of the modern side in June 1854. He then passed a year at Bonn University. In a special open competitive army examination held in Aug. 1855, Wilson, youngest of forty-six candidates, passed second, (Sir) Robert Murdoch Smith [q. v. Suppl. I] gaining the first place. The two obtained the only commissions given in the royal engineers, Wilson becoming lieutenant on 24 Sept. 1855.

After instruction at Chatham Wilson was posted to a company at Shorncliffe Camp in April 1857, and soon after was employed on the defences at Gosport. In February 1858 he was made secretary of the commission to delimitate the boundary between British Columbia and the United States of America, from the Lake of the Woods westward to the Pacific Ocean. With Captain (afterwards General Sir) J. S. Hawkins, R.E., the British commissioner, Wilson arrived at Esquimalt, by way of Colon and Panama, on 12 July. For the next four years Wilson was engaged in marking a straight boundary from the Pacific, through prairie and primeval forests, over mountains 7000 feet high, and in a climate of extreme temperatures, almost uninhabited and unknown. Astronomical stations were formed at suitable points. The outdoor work was finished at the end of 1861 in the hardest winter known, the thermometer down to 30° below zero at night. The commission returned to England on 14 July 1862 to draw up the report.

After eighteen months' employment on the defences of the Thames and Medway, and being promoted captain on 20 June 1864, Wilson volunteered for the duty of surveying Jerusalem. The secretary for war had agreed to appoint an engineer officer for the service, without paying his expenses. Wilson reached Jerusalem with a few sappers from the ordnance survey early in October 1864, and the work progressed steadily. At the request of Colonel Sir Henry James [q. v.], director of the ordnance survey, he ran a line of levels by way of Jericho to Jerusalem and thence by El Jeb and Lydda to Jaffa to ascertain the difference of level between the Mediterranean and the Dead Sea, and showed that in the month of March the Dead Sea was 1292 feet below the Mediterranean Sea, and in summer about six feet more. Wilson returned home in July 1865. The results of the survey were published, and included plans with photographs of Jerusalem and the vicinity. This survey led to the formation of the Palestine Exploration Fund, and Wilson undertook the preliminary work, starting for Palestine on 5 Nov. 1865. A general reconnaissance which he made of the country between Beirut and Hebron showed how little was known of the antiquities of Palestine, and the need of a thorough investigation. Elected a member of the executive committee of the fund on his return in June 1866, Wilson was one of its most energetic supporters for life, becoming chairman in 1901.

From October 1866 to October 1868 Wilson was at Inverness in charge of the ordnance survey in Scotland, being also employed, in the summer of 1867, as an assistant commissioner under the parliamentary boundary commission for part of the west midland districts of England. Between October 1868 and May 1869 he was surveying the Sinaitic peninsula, with, among others, Professor E. H. Palmer [q. v.]. Appointed on 16 May 1869 executive officer of the topographical branch of the ordnance survey in London under Sir Henry James, Wilson became on 1 April 1870 first director of the topographical department at the war office, when the other departments of the ordnance survey were transferred to the office of works; at his suggestion this department was reconstructed in 1873 as a branch of an intelligence department for war, and his title was changed to that of an assistant quartermaster general in the intelligence department. From 1876 Wilson was in charge of the ordnance survey in Ireland. Promoted major on 23 May 1873, he was created C.B., civil division, in 1877. In 1874 he was elected F.R.S.

The autumn of 1878 Wilson spent in Servia as British commissioner of the international commission for the demarcation of the new frontier under the treaty of Berlin, and in February 1879 he was appointed British military consul-general in Anatolia, Asia Minor. Wilson was promoted brevet lieutenant-colonel for his services in Servia (19 April 1879). Fixing his headquarters at Sivas, Wilson divided Anatolia into four consulates, with a British military vice-consul in each. One of the vice-consuls was Lieutenant (now Field-marshal Viscount) Kitchener. Wilson travelled much about Anatolia, learning the ways of the people and of the Turkish authorities, exerting a highly humane influence, and reporting to the foreign office through the British ambassador at Constantinople. Many of his notes on the geography, history, and archæology of the country he embodied in 'Handbooks for Asia Minor and Constantinople,' which he edited for John Murray in 1892 and 1895. In the summer of 1880, by direction of G. J. (afterwards Viscount) Goschen [q. v. Suppl. II], then special ambassador to the Porte, Wilson inquired into the state of affairs in Eastern Roumelia, Bulgaria, and Macedonia (see *Parl. Paper, Turkey*, No. 19, 1880). He returned to his duties in Anatolia in November. In 1881 he was created a K.C.M.G.

In Oct. 1882 Wilson was summoned to Egypt to serve under Sir Edward Malet, the British consul-general. He arrived at Alexandria on 3 Sept. 1882, when an English army was in the field against Arabi Pasha. Nominated British commissioner with an expected Turkish force, which, owing to the prompt success of the British arms, was not sent, he was next appointed military attaché to the British agency in Egypt, and took charge of the Egyptian prisoners of war, including Arabi and Toulba Pashas. Sir Charles watched for the British government the trial of Arabi and his companions, and later arranged for sending the exiles and their families to Ceylon. Resuming his duties on 1 April 1883 at the head of the ordnance survey in Ireland, Wilson was promoted brevet colonel on the 19th, and was made hon. D.C.L. of Oxford in June.

Appointed chief of the intelligence department (with the grade of deputy adjutant-general) in Lord Wolseley's Nile expedition to Khartoum for the rescue of Gordon in September 1884, Wilson reached Dongola on 11 Oct. and on 15 Dec. accompanied Lord Wolseley and the rest of the staff to Korti, going on with Sir Herbert Stewart across the desert on 30 Dec. He left Korti the second time on 8 Jan. 1885, and failing to reach Khartoum by steamer in time to save Gordon, he returned to Korti a month later. He published his journal of the experience in 'From Korti to Khar toum' (1885; 4th edit. 1886). An attempt was made to saddle Wilson with the responsibility for the failure of the expedition. Charles Williams [q. v. Suppl. II] and other critics urged that he might have been in time to save Gordon, had he not lost three days at Gubat on his way. A complete justification of the delay is given in an anonymous publication, 'Why Gordon Perished' (1896), by a war correspondent. Sir Lintorn Simmons [q. v. Suppl. II], governor of Malta, wrote on 18 June 1885: 'The true fault lies with those who planned the expedition and started it too late, and, when they did start it, did not take proper measures to facilitate its operations and ensure its success.' For his services Wilson was created K.C.B., military division, and when a vote of thanks was passed to the officers and men of the Nile expedition, in the House of Commons on 12 Aug. 1885, Lord Hartington refuted the charge against Wilson of unnecessary delay. Afterwards Queen Victoria summoned him to tell her his story. In the spring of 1886 he was made hon. LL.D. of Edinburgh University, and in the autumn addressed the British Association at Birmingham on the 'History and Anthropology of the Tribes of the Soudan.'

Wilson resumed his ordnance survey work in Ireland on 1 July 1885. In November 1886 he was appointed director-general of the ordnance survey in the United Kingdom, and until 1893 was on that service at Southampton. He was president of the geographical section of the British Association at Bath in 1888. The survey was transferred from the office of works to the board of agriculture in 1890, and in 1891 Wilson received the silver medal from the Society of Arts after an address on the survey's methods and needs. In 1893 he was awarded by Dublin University the honorary degree of master in engineering, and was given the temporary rank, receiving next year the permanent rank, of major-general. From the end of 1892 to 14 March 1898 Sir Charles was director-general of military education at the war office.

In 1899, and again in 1903, Wilson revisited Palestine and devoted much time to the controversy over the sites of Golgotha and the Holy Sepulchre. He rather inclined to conservative tradition. His arguments appeared in the 'Quarterly Statements of the Palestine Exploration Fund' (1902 to 1904), and were collected in 1906 as 'Golgotha and the Holy Sepulchre.' He died after an operation at Tunbridge Wells, on 25 Oct. 1905, and was buried there.

In addition to works already cited Wilson was author of: 1. 'Report on the Survey of Jerusalem,' 1866. 2. 'Report on the Survey of Sinai,' 1869. 3. 'Lord Clive,' 1890, in the 'Men of Action' series. He also contributed to the 'Encyclopædia Britannica,' 9th edit., to 'Smith's Dictionary of the Bible,' to the Palestine Pilgrims Text Society, to the 'Quarterly Review,' and to 'Blackwood's Magazine.'

Wilson married in London on 22 Jan. 1867, Olivia, daughter of Colonel Adam Duffin of the 2nd Bengal cavalry. She was granted a civil list pension of 100*l.* in 1905, and died on 19 May 1911. By her he had four sons and a daughter.

[War Office Records: Royal Engineers Records; Porter's History of the Royal Engineers; Life (1909) by Colonel Sir C. M. Watson; Proc. Roy. Soc., 78 A.] R. H. V.

WILSON, GEORGE FERGUSSON (1822–1902), inventor, born at Wandsworth Common on 25 March 1822, was the sixth son in a family of thirteen children of William Wilson, at one time a merchant in Russia and subsequently founder at Battersea of the candle-making firm known as 'E. Price & Son.' His mother was Margaret Nimmo Dickson of Kilbucho and Cultur in Scotland.

After education at Wandsworth, and a short time in a solicitor's office, Wilson in 1840 entered his father's business. Though without training as a chemist, he showed keen interest in the firm's experimental work, and in 1842 patented, in conjunction with W. C. Jones, a process by which cheap malodorous fats could be utilised in the place of tallow for candle-making. The original features of the process were the use of sulphuric acid as a decoloriser and deodoriser of strongly-smelling fats, and their subsequent distillation, when acidified, by the aid of super-heated steam. The invention added materially to the firm's profits, and in 1847, in the midst of a commercial panic, the business was sold for 250,000*l.*

A new concern, called Price's Patent Candle Company, with a capital of 500,000*l.*, was then formed, George Wilson and an elder brother, James, being appointed managing directors. Both engaged continually in research work which effected repeated changes in the firm's processes of manufacture. George in 1853 introduced moulded coco-stearin lights as 'New Patent Night Lights,' and the two together made improvements on a French patent which led to the wide adoption by English manufacturers of the company's 'oleine' or 'cloth oil.' In 1854 George made a discovery of first-class importance, namely a process of manufacturing pure glycerine, the glycerine being first separated from fats and oils at high temperature and then purified in an atmosphere of steam. Previously even glycerine sold at a high price was so impure as to be comparatively useless for most purposes. He retired from the position of managing director in 1863.

In 1845 Wilson was made a member of the Society of Arts. He contributed frequently to its 'Journal,' read a paper before it in 1852 on 'Stearic Candle Manufacture,' was a member of its council from 1854 to 1859 and again from 1864 to 1867, and its treasurer from 1861 to 1863. In 1854 he read before the Royal Society a paper on 'The Value of Steam in the Decomposition of Neutral Fatty Bodies,' and was elected a fellow in 1855. In that year, too, he was elected a fellow of the Chemical Society, and read at the meeting of the British Association at Glasgow a paper on 'A New Mode of obtaining Pure Glycerine.'

In later life Wilson lived at Wisley, Surrey, where he devoted himself to experimental gardening on a wide scale. The garden formed by him at Wisley now belongs to the Royal Horticultural Society. He was particularly successful as a cultivator of lilies, gaining between 1867 and 1883 twenty-five first-class certificates for species exhibited. Elected a fellow of the Horticultural Society, he served on various of its committees, and was at one time vice-president. At his suggestion the society introduced guinea subscriptions, and in 1876 he published a pamphlet entitled 'The Royal Horticultural Society: as it is and as it might be.' He was Victorian Medallist of Horticulture in 1897. In 1875 he was elected a fellow of the Linnean Society. He died at Weybridge Heath on 28 March 1902.

Wilson married on 13 Aug. 1862 Ellen, eldest daughter of R. W. Barchard, of East Hill, Wandsworth, who survived him with two sons and a daughter. The elder son, Scott Barchard, was author of 'Aves Hawaiienses: the Birds of the Sandwich Islands,' a handsomely illustrated work, which was issued in eight parts (large 4to, 1890–9).

[Proc. Roy. Soc., vol. lxxv.; Who's Who, 1902; Men and Women of the Time, 1899; Soc. of Arts Journal, 1902; The Garden, 1 Jan. 1900 (portrait) and 5 April 1902; Journal of Horticulture, 5 and 10 April 1902; Gardeners' Chronicle, 5 April 1902; Price's Patent Candle Company's Calendar, 1908; Pamphlets by Price's Patent Candle Company, 1853.] S. E. F.

WILSON, HENRY SCHÜTZ (1824–1902), author, born in London on 15 Sept. 1824, was son of Effingham Wilson (1783–1868) by his wife, a daughter of Thomas James of The Brownings, Chigwell, Essex. The father, a native of Kirby Ravensworth, Yorkshire, after serving an apprenticeship to his uncle, Dr. Hutchinson, a medical practitioner of Knaresborough, founded at the Royal Exchange, London, a publishing business chiefly of commercial manuals, which is still continued; a zealous politician of radical views, he died in London in July 1868.

After education at a private school at Highgate, Schütz Wilson was for ten years in a commercial house in London and thoroughly mastered French, German, and Italian. Subsequently assistant secretary of the electric telegraph company, he retired on a pension when the business was taken over by the post office in 1870. He edited the 'Journal of the Society of Telegraph Engineers' from 1872.

Wilson divided his leisure between foreign travel or mountaineering and study or criticism of foreign literature and history. A profound admirer of Goethe's work, he published 'Count Egmont as depicted in Fancy, Poetry, and History' in 1863. In later years he wrote frequently in London magazines, and reissued his articles in 'Studies and Romances' (1873), 'Studies in History, Legend, and Literature' (1884), and 'History and Criticism' (1886). He was an early admirer of Edward FitzGerald's long-neglected translations from the Persian, and FitzGerald welcomed Wilson's encouragement (*Letters*, ed. Aldis Wright, 1859, i. 481).

Wilson, who was a member of the Alpine Club from 1871 to 1898, ascended the Matterhorn on 26–7 Aug. 1875 with Frederic Morshead and A. D. Prickard, and on 15 Aug. 1876 with Morshead. Melchior Anderegg was one of Wilson's guides, and he wrote on 'Anderegg as a Sculptor' in the 'Alpine Journal' (November 1873). He collected pleasant descriptions of his experiences in 'Alpine Ascents and Adventures' (1878).

Interested in both the English and the German stage, he was popular in literary and artistic society. He was a capable fencer and a zealous volunteer, becoming captain in the artists' corps. He died unmarried at the house of his nephew, Dr. J. Schütz Sharman, 2 Avenue Gate, Norwood, on 7 May 1902. His body was cremated, and the ashes placed in the Sharman vault in Norwood cemetery. His portrait by James Archer, R.S.A., was exhibited at the Royal Academy in 1898.

Wilson's three novels, 'The Three Paths,' 'The Voyage of the Lady' (1860), and 'Philip Mannington' (1874), were translated into German.

[Private information; The Times, 19 May 1902; Ann. Register, 1902; Morning Post, 9 May; Works; Brit. Mus. Cat. (Wilson's works incomplete); Allibone's Dict. Engl. Lit. vol. iii. and Suppl.] G. Le G. N.

WILSON, Sir JACOB (1836–1905), agriculturist, born at Crackenthorpe Hall, Westmorland, on 16 Nov. 1836, was the elder son in a family of two sons and three daughters of Joseph Wilson, farmer, by Ann, daughter of Joseph Bowstead, of Beck Bank, Cumberland. He was educated at Long Marton, Westmorland, under the Rev. W. Shepherd, and was afterwards in London for a short time studying land agency under T. Walton. In 1854 he went to the Royal Agricultural College at Cirencester, and after eighteen months' tuition there obtained its diploma. He remained at Cirencester six months longer as honorary farm bailiff, and then went to Switzerland to assist in laying out on the English system an estate in that country. He returned home in 1857 to help his father in the management of a large farm at Woodhorn Manor, near Newbiggin, Northumberland, devoting much time to the study of agricultural mechanics, especially steam cultivation. In 1859 he won the first agricultural diploma awarded by the Highland and Agricultural Society of Scotland.

Adopting the profession of land agent, he in 1866 was appointed by the earl of Tankerville agent for his Chillingham estates. Subsequently he undertook the management of other estates and properties in different parts of England, and also took pupils in farming and land agency. His services were much in request as witness or arbitrator in valuation cases, and he was long an official umpire for the board of trade.

On 5 Dec. 1860 Wilson was elected an ordinary member of the Royal Agricultural Society of England. In the administration of the society he speedily made his mark after his election as a member of council on 22 May 1865—at a far earlier age than precedent sanctioned. As steward he was prominent in the management of the large annual provincial shows of the society from 1869 to 1874, and from 1875 to 1892 he was hon. director in succession to Sir Brandreth Gibbs. At the conclusion of the society's fiftieth show, held in Windsor Great Park under the presidency of Queen Victoria, Wilson was knighted by the Queen after dinner at the Castle on 29 June 1889. Until his death he remained a member of the society's council, and he resumed the honorary directorship, to the injury of his health, for the last show held in London in June 1905 on the society's showyard at Park Royal.

Wilson actively urged legislation for repressing the contagious diseases of animals, and the passing of the Animals Acts of 1878 and 1884 owed much to his energy. These services were acknowledged by a gift of silver plate and a purse of 3000 guineas (given by 1300 subscribers) at a public dinner on 8 Dec. 1884, with Charles Henry Gordon-Lennox, sixth duke of Richmond and Gordon [q. v. Suppl. II], in the chair. In April 1888 he presided over a departmental committee appointed to inquire into pleuro-pneumonia, and an Act of 1890 carried out most of its recommendations.

In 1881 he removed from Woodhorn Manor to a farm at Chillingham Barns, Northumberland, on the estate of Lord Tankerville. Here he maintained a herd of shorthorns of the 'Booth' blood, and as a county councillor and magistrate for Northumberland was active in county matters. From 1892 to 1902 he was agricultural adviser to the board of agriculture in succession to Sir James Caird [q. v. Suppl. I].

At the conclusion of the Royal Agricultural Society's show of 1905, of which Wilson was honorary director, King Edward VII conferred on him the distinction of K.C.V.O. A few days later he was seized with illness which terminated fatally from heart failure on 11 July 1905. He was buried at Chillingham. A memorial service was held at St. George's, Hanover Square.

Wilson was tall and handsome, with ingratiating manners. His skill in administration and tactful dealing with men made him a power in the agricultural world.

He married in 1874 Margaret, daughter of Thomas Hedley of Cox Lodge Hall, Newcastle-on-Tyne, by whom he had two sons, Albert Edward Jacob (godchild of King Edward VII) and Gordon Jacob (godchild of the duke of Richmond and Gordon), and two daughters, Beatrice and Mildred. His wife and all his children survived him.

[Memoir (by G. G. Rea) in Journ. Roy. Agric. Soc., vol. 66, 1905 (with engr. portrait from photograph); The Times, 30 June, 12 and 15 July 1905; Field, 15 July 1905; Trans. Surveyors' Inst., vol. xxxviii. 578; Estates Gaz., 15 July 1905, p. 117; private information; personal knowledge.] E. C.

WILSON, JOHN DOVE (1833–1908), Scottish legal writer, born at Linton, Roxburghshire, on 21 July 1833, was son of Charles Wilson, M.D., of Kelso (afterwards of Edinburgh). Educated at the grammar school, Kelso, and Edinburgh University, he studied law at Edinburgh, and spent a session at Berlin University. Called to the Scottish bar in 1857, he in 1861, through the influence of George (afterwards Lord) Young [q. v. Suppl. II], was appointed sheriff-substitute of Kincardineshire, taking up his residence at Stonehaven. In 1870 he was transferred to Aberdeen as colleague to Sheriff Comrie Thomson. This position he held with distinction for twenty years, establishing his reputation as an able lawyer and a conscientious judge.

Wilson, who wrote much in legal periodicals, had a profound knowledge of jurisprudence, and was an enthusiastic advocate of legal reform, especially in the matter of codification and the simplification of procedure. In 1865 he issued a new annotated edition of Robert Thomson's 'Treatise on the Law of Bills of Exchange' (1865). The work soon acquired standard rank. A 'Handbook of Practice in Civil Causes in the Sheriff Courts of Scotland' (Edinburgh, 1869; 2nd edit. 1883) constituted him the chief authority on sheriff court practice. On his handbook was based 'The Practice of the Sheriff Courts of Scotland in Civil Causes' (1875; 4th edit. 1891), which was characterised as 'one of the most accurate books in existence,' and remained the chief authority until superseded by later legislation in 1907, as well as 'The Law of Process under the Sheriff Courts (Scotland) Act, 1876, with Notes on Proposed Extensions of Jurisdiction' (Edinburgh, 1876). Some of the reforms proposed by Wilson were realised at a later date.

Wilson gave evidence before parliamentary committees on bills of sale and civil imprisonment, and aided various lord-advocates in the drafting of bills, particularly the Sheriff Court Act of 1876 and the Bills of Exchange Act of 1882, He took a prominent part in the movement for the codification of commercial law which began in April 1884 (see his address to the Aberdeen Chamber of Commerce in *Journal of Jurisprudence*, July 1884). A report by him of the proceedings of the congress on commercial law at Antwerp in 1885, where he represented the Aberdeen Chamber of Commerce, was translated into Italian. In 1884 Wilson received the degree of LL.D. from Aberdeen University.

On resigning his office as sheriff-substitute in Feb. 1890 Wilson was from the autumn of 1891 to 1901 professor of law at Aberdeen. After studying Roman law for a season at Leipzig he revived the study at Aberdeen. He induced the university to institute the B.L. degree; and he helped to found a lectureship on conveyancing, and to form a law library. In 1895–6 he served as Storr's lecturer on municipal law at Yale University, Newhaven, U.S.A., and published one of his lectures there, 'On the Reception of Roman Law in Scotland.'

Wilson had a wide acquaintance with French, German, and Italian, and published some graceful verse translations. He was active in philanthropic work at Aberdeen, was president of the Aberdeen Philosophical Society, and became D.L. of Aberdeenshire in 1886. Wilson died at San Remo on 24 Jan. 1908, and was buried at Allenvale cemetery, Aberdeen. An enlarged photograph is in the Advocates' Library, Aberdeen.

In 1863 Wilson married Anna (*d.* 1901), daughter of John Carnegie of Redhall, and left two sons and one daughter.

[Aberdeen Journal, 25 Jan. 1908; Scotsman, same date; Scottish Law Review and Sheriff Court Reporter, xxiv. 44 (1908); private information.] A. H. M.

WILSON, WILLIAM EDWARD (1851–1908), astronomer and physicist, born at Belfast on 19 July 1851, was only son of John Wilson, of Daramona, Streete, co. Westmeath, by his wife Frances Patience, daughter of the Rev. Edward Nangle. He was educated privately, and showed great interest in astronomy while still a boy. In 1870 he joined the British party under Huggins which went to Oran in Algeria to observe the total eclipse of the sun in that year, and on his return he set up a private observatory on his father's estate at Daramona, equipped with a twelve-inch refractor by Grubb. In 1881 he built a new observatory with a twenty-four inch silver on glass reflector, also by Grubb, and soon after added a physical laboratory.

Thus equipped, he began in 1886 the investigations on the temperature of the sun and the radiation from sunspots, which were remarkable pioneer work. In 1894 he published, with Philip Leman Gray, his 'Experimental Investigation on the Effective Temperature of the Sun' (*Phil. Trans.* 185A, p. 361), in which he arrived at the result 6590° C. This, with other important papers, published in the *Phil. Trans.* and *Monthly Notices* of the Royal Astronomical Society, and a selection of his admirable celestial photographs were collected in a volume, 'Astronomical and Physical Researches made at Mr. Wilson's Observatory, Daramona, Westmeath,' printed privately in 1900. Subsequent work included an examination of the effect of pressure on radio-activity, and an expedition to Plasencia to observe the solar eclipse of 1900. He was elected F.R.S. in 1896, and was made hon. D.S. of Dublin University in 1901.

Wilson, who mainly lived on his estate, was high sheriff of co. Westmeath in 1901.

He died at Daramona on 6 March 1908, and was buried in the family burying ground attached to the parish church of Streete, the village adjoining his demesne. There is a portrait in oils at Daramona, painted in 1886 by E. Marshall.

He married on 10 Nov. 1886, Caroline Ada, third daughter of Captain R. C. Granville of Grand Pré, Biarritz, and left one son, John Granville, and two daughters.

[Royal Soc. Proc., 83 A., 1910; Monthly Notices Roy. Astron. Soc., lxix. Feb. 1909.]

A. R. H.

WIMSHURST, JAMES (1832–1903), engineer, born at Poplar on 13 April 1832, was the second son of Henry Wimshurst, designer and builder of the Archimedes and Iris, the first two screw-propelled ships. After education at Steabonheath House, a private school in London, he was apprenticed at the Thames Ironworks to James Mare. In 1853, on the completion of his apprenticeship, he obtained an appointment in London as a surveyor of Lloyds. He was subsequently transferred to Liverpool, where in 1865 he was made chief of the Liverpool Underwriters' Registry, then a rival establishment to Lloyds, but since incorporated with it. In 1874 he joined the board of trade as chief shipwright surveyor in the consultative department. He attended as its representative the international conference at Washington in 1890, and retired on reaching the age limit in 1899.

Through life Wimshurst devoted his leisure to experimental work, erecting at his house in Clapham large workshops, which he fitted up with various engineering appliances and where he also built electric-lighting machinery. About 1880 he became interested in electrical-influence machines, and built several of the then current types, including machines of the Holtz and Carré patterns. In the former he made many modifications, the result being a plate machine remarkably independent of atmospheric conditions. This was followed by a compound machine of the same type in which there were twelve plates revolving between twenty-four rectangular glass inductor plates, and which had a miniature friction plate machine for producing the initial charge. The result, however, did not satisfy Wimshurst, and shortly afterwards he invented what he called the 'duplex machine,' but what is generally known simply as the 'Wimshurst machine.' It had two circular plates rotating in opposite directions with metallic sectors on the outer surface of each. This machine displaced all previous generators of static electricity, being self-exciting under any atmospheric condition. It has never been improved upon. In all Wimshurst constructed more than ninety electrical-influence machines, including the gigantic two-plate machine in the Science Collection at South Kensington. Many of his machines he presented to scientific friends. Some had cylindrical plates, and one was designed with two ribbons which travelled past each other in opposite directions. He took out no patents for his improvements, and was consequently precluded from exercising control over the design or construction of inferior machines put upon the market in his name.

In 1896 Wimshurst found his machines to be an admirable means of exciting the 'Röntgen rays,' and showed that for screen observation, where a steady illumination is desired, the steady discharge from one of his eight-plate influence machines was preferable to the intermittent discharge of the usual induction coil. His machines are also used in hospitals for the production of powerful brush discharges, efficacious in the treatment of lupus and cancer.

Wimshurst also invented an improved vacuum pump, an improved method for electrically connecting light-ships with the shore station, and an instrument for ascertaining the stability of vessels. He was elected F.R.S. in 1898. He was also a member of the Institute of Electrical Engineers, the Physical Society, the

Röntgen Society, and the Institute of Naval Architects. He was a member of the board of managers of the Royal Institution. He died at Clapham on 3 Jan. 1903.

Wimshurst married in 1864 Clara Tubb, and had issue two sons and one daughter.

Besides descriptions of his electrical machines, he published 'A Book of Rules for the Construction of Steam Vessels' (1898).

[Engineering, 9 Jan. 1903; Nature, 15 Jan. 1903; Proc. Roy. Soc. vol. 75, 1905; Institute of Elec. Eng. Journal, xxxii. 1157; Who's Who, 1903; art. on Electricity in Encyc. Brit. 11th edit.; private information.]

S. E F.

WINDUS, WILLIAM LINDSAY (1822–1907), artist, born in Liverpool on 8 July 1822, was grandson of William Windus, curate-in-charge of Halsall near Ormskirk from 1765 to 1785, and son of John Windus by his wife Agnes Meek, a Scotswoman. He received his early education at Mr. MacMorran's private school in Liverpool. At the age of sixteen he first showed an artistic bent while watching William Daniels, the Liverpool portrait painter, paint a portrait of his stepfather. A chalk drawing which he then made of another member of the family arrested the attention of Daniels, who gave him some instruction. He next studied at the Liverpool Academy, and attended a life class kept by a brother of J. R. Herbert, R.A. This was all his art training. His earliest picture appears to have been 'The Black Boy,' painted in 1844. His first exhibited work, 'Falstaff acting King Henry IV,' was shown at the Liverpool Academy in 1845. In 1847 at the same place there appeared 'Cranmer endeavouring to obtain a Confession from Queen Catherine' (now the property of Mr. Andrew Bain of Hunter's Quay). In the same year he was elected an associate of the Liverpool Academy, and in 1848 a full member. At the suggestion of John Miller, an art patron, he visited London in 1850, and was deeply influenced by Millais's 'Christ at the Home of His Parents' in the Royal Academy. Accepting Pre-Raphaelite principles, he painted in 1852 'Darnley signing the Bond before the Murder of Rizzio.' In 1856 he exhibited at the Royal Academy 'Burd Helen.' The work, though badly hung, attracted the attention of Dante Rossetti, who instantly took Ruskin to see it. Ruskin had overlooked it, but in a postscript to his academy notes of 1856 he wrote of 'Burd Helen' that its aim was higher, and its reserve strength greater, than any other work in the exhibition except the 'Autumn Leaves' by Millais. A photogravure of the picture, now belonging to Mr. Frederic Dawson Leyland, The Vyne, Basingstoke, is in Ruskin's works, library edit. xiv. p. 83. There followed in 1859 Windus's 'Too Late,' now the property of Mr. Andrew Bain, by which he is best known, and which he himself regarded as his masterpiece; but Ruskin condemned it 'as the product of sickness, temper, and dimmed sight,' a criticism which so pained Windus that he never sent to the Academy again. In 1861 he sent 'The Outlaw' to the Liverpool Academy.

Windus married in 1858 a sister of Robert Tonge, a fellow artist; she died on 2 Aug. 1862, after a long illness, leaving a fifteen months' daughter, and her death so shook Windus's health and nerves that he gave up the serious pursuit of painting. Possessed of a competence, he resided quietly at Walton-le-Dale near Preston, and although he often painted he generally destroyed in the evening what he had accomplished in the daytime. In 1880 he left Lancashire for London, and then destroyed most of his sketches and studies.

In London he first lived in a pleasant old house at Highgate and then at Denmark Hill, where he died on 9 Oct. 1907. Of self-portraits in oils, one at the age of twenty-two belongs to his daughter, Mrs. Teed; another belongs to the Rev. James Hamilton of Liverpool. Millais, whom he somewhat resembled, also painted a portrait.

After his retirement in 1862, Windus, an artist of extreme enthusiasm and sensitiveness, was practically forgotten until the spring exhibition of the New English Art Club of 1896, when three water-colours by him entitled 'The Flight of Henry VI from Towton,' 'The Second Duchess,' and 'A Patrician, Anno Domini 60,' were lent by their owners. They excited great interest amongst artists and connoisseurs. His work, which is scarce in quantity, is greatly valued as that of the most poetical and imaginative figure painter whom Liverpool has produced. In the early part of his career amateurs both in London and Liverpool eagerly bought anything he produced. Forty-five of his pictures were exhibited at the Historical Exhibition of Liverpool Art, in the Walker Art Gallery, Liverpool, May–July 1908.

[The Liverpool School of Painters, by H. C. Marillier; The Pre-Raphaelite School of

Painters, by Percy Bate; art. on Windus by E. R. Dibdin in Mag. of Art, 1900; Art Journal, 1907; The Times, 11 Oct. 1907; Ruskin's Works, libr. edit. xiv. (Academy Notes), 85, 233, 330–1; Harry Quilter's Preferences in Art, p. 72; information kindly supplied by Mr. E. Rimbault Dibdin.]

F. W. G–N.

WINTER, Sir JAMES SPEARMAN (1845–1911), premier of Newfoundland, born at Lamaline, Newfoundland, on 1 Jan. 1845, was son of James Winter, of the customs service at St. John's, Newfoundland. Educated at St. John's at the General Protestant and Church of England Academies, James went at the age of fourteen into a merchant's office, where he remained for two years, and at the age of sixteen was articled to (Sir) Hugh Hoyles, afterwards chief justice of Newfoundland. He was enrolled as a solicitor in 1866, was called to the bar in 1867, became Q.C. in 1880, and at his death was the senior member of the Newfoundland bar and president of the Newfoundland Law Society.

He entered the legislature as member for the Burin district in 1874, when he was twenty-nine years of age. In 1877–8 he was speaker of the House of Assembly. He was solicitor-general from 1882 to 1885 in Sir William Whiteway's first administration and attorney-general from 1885 to 1889 in the Thorburn administration. In 1893 he was appointed a judge of the supreme court of Newfoundland, but resigned the office in 1896, returned to politics as leader of the opposition, and in 1897 became premier of Newfoundland. He held the premiership, combining with it the post of attorney-general and later that of minister of justice, till 1900, when he practically retired from political life. His term of office as premier is chiefly noteworthy for the conclusion of the warmly discussed Reid contract of 1898 [see Reid, Sir Robert Gillespie, Suppl. II.]

Winter represented Newfoundland at the fisheries conference at Washington in 1887–8, when Mr. Chamberlain and Mr. Boyard negotiated a treaty which the senate of the United States failed to ratify; for his services he was made a K.C.M.G. In 1890 he went to London as one of the unofficial representatives of the Patriotic Association in connection with the French fishery question; in 1898, when premier, he visited London again on the same errand, and in the same year represented Newfoundland at the Anglo-American conference at Quebec. In 1910 he was one of the counsel on the British side before the Hague tribunal on the occasion of the North Atlantic fisheries arbitration between Great Britain and the United States.

He died at Toronto, while on a visit to a married daughter, at midnight on 6–7 Oct. 1911. Winter married in 1881 Emily Julia, daughter of Captain William J. Coen, governor of the Newfoundland penitentiary. She predeceased him in 1908, leaving four sons and four daughters.

[Evening Telegram, St. John's, Newfoundland, 7 Oct. 1911; The Daily News, St. John's, Newfoundland, and The Times, 9 Oct. 1911; Colonial Office List.]

C. P. L.

WINTER, JOHN STRANGE (pseudonym). [See Stannard, Mrs. Henrietta Eliza Vaughan (1856–1911), novelist.]

WINTERSTOKE, first Baron. [See Wills, Sir William Henry (1830–1911), benefactor.]

WINTON, Sir Francis Walter De (1835–1901), major-general. [See De Winton.]

WITTEWRONGE, Sir CHARLES BENNET LAWES- (1843–1911), sculptor and athlete. [See Lawes-Wittewronge.]

WODEHOUSE, JOHN, first Earl of Kimberley (1826–1902), secretary of state for foreign affairs, born at Wymondham, Norfolk, on 29 May 1826, was eldest son of the Hon. Henry Wodehouse (1799–1834) by his wife Anne, only daughter of Theophilus Thornhagh Gurdon of Letton, Norfolk. The father, eldest surviving son of John Wodehouse, second Baron Wodehouse, died in his own father's lifetime. Educated at Eton, where he was 'one of the cleverest boys' (Sir A. Lyall's *Dufferin*, i. 22), and at Christ Church, Oxford, John Wodehouse took a first class in the final classical school and graduated B.A. in 1847. Meanwhile he succeeded to the barony on the death of his grandfather on 29 May 1846. Showing political aptitude and adopting the whig politics of his family, Lord Wodehouse served as under-secretary of state for foreign affairs in the coalition government of Lord Aberdeen and afterwards in Lord Palmerston's first government (1852–1856). On 4 May 1856 he was appointed British minister at St. Petersburg, shortly after the close of the war with Russia. He accepted the post with some hesitation, telling Lord Clarendon that the foreign office was his object in life (Fitzmaurice's *Granville* i. 180), but he 'held his own with them all, including the Emperor.' He resisted attempts to play him off against Lord Granville, who had been sent over as ambassador extraordinary to the Tsar Alexander II on his coronation (*ibid.* 186–216). Gortschakoff complained however of his want of experience (*Letters of Sir Robert Morier,* i. 399). Wodehouse left St. Petersburg on 31 March 1858, and in the following year returned to the foreign office as under-secretary (June 1859 to Aug. 1861) in Lord Palmerston's second administration. On 9 Dec. 1863 he was sent on a special mission, nominally to congratulate King Christian IX of Denmark on his accession to the throne, but really to settle the Schleswig-Holstein dispute in concert with the representatives of Russia and France. He failed where success was probably impossible, but his knowledge of the questions at issue seems to have been limited (SPENCER WALPOLE'S *Lord John Russell,* ii. 386–387; *Letters of Sir Robert Morier,* i. 399).

After serving as under-secretary for India for a few months in 1864, while Palmerston was still prime minister, Wodehouse, on 1 Nov. became lord lieutenant of Ireland in succession to Lord Carlisle [see HOWARD, GEORGE WILLIAM FREDERICK]; he held the appointment until the fall of the liberal government in June 1866. He found the Fenian movement, an agitation partly agrarian and partly revolutionary, in full activity. Wodehouse displayed resolution in dealing with his difficulties. On 14 Sept. 1865 the office of the 'Irish People' was raided and the paper suppressed; and though James Stephens [q. v. Suppl. II], the 'head centre,' escaped from Rutland prison, the other leaders were sentenced to various terms of imprisonment (JOHN O'LEARY'S *Recollections of Fenians and Fenianism,* esp. vol. ii. chs. 28 and 29). Wodehouse, however, was under no illusions, and on 27 Nov. wrote to Lord Clarendon: 'The heart of the people is against us, and I see no prospect of any improvement within any time that can be calculated' (FITZMAURICE'S *Granville,* ii. 515). Still the country became quieter, and before his retirement from office, Wodehouse was created Earl of Kimberley, Norfolk, by letters patent (1 June 1866).

In Dec. 1868 Kimberley became lord privy seal in Gladstone's first administration and entered the cabinet for the first time, but in July 1870, when Granville became foreign secretary, Kimberley succeeded Granville at the colonial office. His administration witnessed the annexation of Griqualand West (27 Oct. 1871), after the energy of the high commissioner, Sir Henry Barkly [q. v. Suppl. I] had thwarted the Free State Boers. On 17 Nov. the British flag was hoisted in the diamond fields, and the township was called Kimberley, after the colonial secretary. In the following year, full responsible government was granted to Cape Colony. On 8 March, on a motion for the production of papers, Kimberley made an explanatory statement in which he declared that the colony could not advance unless it had free institutions, and hinted that ultimately 'he would not be astonished if the Orange Free State and Transvaal Republic found it more to their advantage to unite with those already under the British crown' (*Hansard,* vol. ccix., cols. 1626–1631; see also vol. ccxiii., cols. 29–33). Trouble having arisen on the Gold Coast owing to the bellicose temper of the Ashantis, Kimberley authorised an expedition which, commanded by Sir Garnet (afterwards Viscount) Wolseley, captured Kumassi (4 Feb. 1874) and imposed peace (SIR R. BIDDULPH'S *Lord Cardwell at the War Office,* 221–225). In Canada Rupert's Land was formed into a province named Manitoba (August 1870), after an amnesty had been granted at the instigation of the Canadian government for all offences committed during the Riel rebellion, excepting the murder of Thomas Scott; and British Columbia after some demur joined the dominion (June 1872). During the session of 1872 Kimberley introduced into the House of Lords and carried the government's much controverted licensing bill. Of his introductory speech, Henry Bruce (afterwards Lord Aberdare), the home secretary and author of the measure, wrote that it was 'a good and clear statement' prepared at brief notice, 'but,' Bruce added, 'Kimberley is not impressive, although extremely able and efficient.' On the defeat of his party at the polls in Feb. 1874 Kimberley resigned office.

Kimberley, in whom the Palmerstonian tradition was strong, dissented from the anti-Turkish attitude assumed by Gladstone and the duke of Argyll on the outbreak of the Russo-Turkish war in 1877, but he remained loyal to his party. When Gladstone formed his second administration, Kimberley again became colonial secretary on 28 April 1880. His tenure of the office proved in many ways unfortunate. Contrary to expectation, Sir Bartle Frere [q. v.] was at first retained at the Cape as High Commissioner, but, in obedience to liberal remonstrances, Kimberley abruptly recalled him by telegram (1 Aug.) on the plea that South African federation was no longer possible (JOHN MARTINEAU'S *Frere*, ii. 390–395). Irresolution also marked his treatment of the Transvaal Boers, who, encouraged by liberal election declarations, were chafing against annexation. The Queen's speech pronounced that British supremacy must be maintained in the Transvaal, and Kimberley defended that resolve on the ground that 'it was impossible to say what calamities our receding might not cause to the native population.' In his subsequent attitude to the crisis, Kimberley was freely credited with want of resolution and of clear purpose. The Boers took up arms; on 16 Dec. the South African Republic was proclaimed, and on 27 Feb. 1881 Sir George Colley [q. v.] was defeated and slain on Majuba Hill. Kimberley, meanwhile, had opposed in the cabinet on 30 Dec. the suggestion made by members of the Cape legislature that a special commissioner should be sent out (MORLEY'S *Gladstone*, iii. 33). But, early in January, on the prompting of President Brand of the Orange Free State, he set on foot three different sets of negotiations, while stipulating that armed resistance must cease before terms of peace could be discussed. Through the Free State agent in London he placed himself in communication with President Brand, who handed on his views to the Boer leaders, President Kruger and General Joubert; he also communicated with President Brand through Sir Hercules Robinson [q. v. Suppl. I], the new governor of Cape Colony, and with President Kruger through Sir George Colley (SIR WILLIAM BUTLER'S *Colley*, 322–352) and, after Colley's death, through Sir Evelyn Wood. Despite Colley's fatal reverse (27 Feb.), an eight days' armistice was arranged on 16 March; it was extended, and on the 22nd Gladstone announced the terms of peace, viz. the grant of complete self-government to the Boers on the acceptance of British suzerainty, native interests and questions of frontier to be settled by a royal commission. Kimberley had written to Colley on 24 Feb.: 'My great fear has been lest the Free State should take part against us, or even some movement take place in the Cape Colony' (MORLEY'S *Gladstone*, iii. 40). On 31 March Kimberley in the House of Lords defended the ministerial policy against the trenchant attacks of Lords Cairns and Salisbury. He maintained that if we conquered the Transvaal we could not hold it, and—taking up a phrase of Cairns's—that the real humiliation would have been if, 'for a mere point of honour,' we had stood in the way of practical terms (*Hansard*, vol. cclx. cols. 278 to 292). Kimberley tried to get the district of Zoutpansberg set aside as a native reserve, but the commissioners were unable to accept the suggestion, and the plan formed no part of the convention of Pretoria (8 Aug. 1881). [For Kimberley's despatches see *Parl. Papers*, vols. l. and li., and 1881, vols. lxvi. and lxvii.; for an apology for the government, MORLEY'S *Gladstone*, iii. 27–46.] In May 1881 Kimberley directed Sir Robert Morier, British minister at Lisbon, to drop the treaty he was negotiating with the Portuguese government, by which a passage was to be granted both to the Boers and to the British troops through Lourenço Marques; such an arrangement might have prevented the South African war of 1899–1902 (*Letters of Sir Robert Morier*, i. 400).

On 16 Dec. 1882 Kimberley was transferred to the India office in place of Lord Hartington, and held the appointment until the fall of the liberal government in June 1885. He cordially supported the viceroy, Lord Dufferin, in coming to an understanding with Abdur Rahman, Amir of Afghanistan, at the Rawal Pindi durbar (LYALL'S *Dufferin*, ii. 96); and on 21 May 1885 made a declaration in the House of Lords to the effect that Afghanistan must be regarded as outside the Russian sphere of influence, and inside the British (*Hansard*, vol. ccxcviii. cols. 1009–1011). During those years he was generally active in debate; he took charge of the franchise bill of 1884 and the redistribution bill of 1885 in the House of Lords, and spoke frequently on Egyptian and Soudanese affairs. He believed that if he had been in London he could have stopped the mission of Gordon to Khartoum, as he could have shown him to be unfit for the work (FITZMAURICE'S *Granville*, ii. 401). On 27 Feb. 1885 he defended the government against the vote of censure moved by Lord Salisbury, but was defeated by 159 votes to 68. He was made K.G. and retired with the fall of the administration in June.

Kimberley found no difficulty in supporting Gladstone's policy of home rule, which was announced in the winter of 1885–6, and returned to the India office during Gladstone's short-lived home rule administration of 1886 (February to August). In April 1891 he succeeded

Granville as leader of the liberal party in the House of Lords, after he had lamented his old associate in feeling terms (*Hansard,* vol. cclii. cols. 464–5). He became secretary for India once more in Gladstone's fourth administration, formed in 1892, serving at the same time as lord president of the council. Kimberley reluctantly accepted the policy of the Indian government in closing the mints and restricting the sale of council bills with the object of checking the depreciation of silver. At the last cabinet council which Gladstone attended (1 March 1894), Kimberley and Harcourt spoke on the ministers' behalf words 'of acknowledgment and farewell.' In Lord Rosebery's ministry (3 March 1894) he realised his early ambition, and became foreign secretary, while surrendering the leadership in the House of Lords to the new prime minister. Kimberley's tenure of the foreign office was undistinguished. He was unable to prevent the revision of the treaty of peace between China and Japan under pressure of Russia, Germany, and France, by which the Japanese, in consideration of an addition to their indemnity, evacuated the Liaotung peninsula. On 3 May 1894 he concluded an unhappy agreement with the Congo Free State, which met with strong opposition from Germany; and on 22 June the third article, which granted to Great Britain on lease a strip of Congolese territory along the frontier of German East Africa, had to be withdrawn (*Parl. Papers,* 1894, vols. lxii. and xcvi.). But he refused to be hurried into diplomatic crusades by emotional outbursts against the iniquities of Abdul Hamid, Sultan of Turkey.

Relegated to opposition by the general election, Kimberley resumed the leadership of the liberals in the upper house, after Lord Rosebery's abandonment of party politics in October 1896. Though his following was small, he led it with spirit, and was a sober and effective critic of unionist measures. On 8 June 1899 he seconded the resolution for making a provision for Lord Kitchener after the overthrow of the Khalifa at Omdurman. During the South African war, unlike some of his party, he never swerved from support of the military operations; he declined to take any advantage of the ignorance of ministers as to the Boer preparations; and while justly dwelling on the miscalculations involved in the recrudescence of the war after it had been declared to be at an end, he urged that no means or money should be spared in sending out adequate reinforcements. His last appearance was on 14 Feb. 1901, when, though ill and distressed, he spoke on the address to King Edward VII, after the death of Queen Victoria. During the rest of his life Lord Spencer acted as deputy-leader of the liberals in the lords.

Kimberley died at his London residence, 35 Lowndes Square, on 8 April 1902, and was buried at Wymondham, Norfolk. When the lords reassembled, effective tributes were paid to his memory (*Hansard,* vol. cvi. cols. 259–266), Lord Salisbury eulogising his freedom from party bias, Lord Spencer his grasp of detail, and Lord Ripon his private worth. He earned the reputation of thoroughness in administration if he sometimes showed lack of foresight and resolve in dealing with large questions of policy. The House of Lords generally held him in high esteem, but he was little known to the general public and was unrecognised by popular opinion. 'He is,' wrote Lord Dufferin, 'one of the ablest of our public men, but being utterly destitute of vanity, he has never cared to captivate public attention, and consequently has been never duly appreciated' (LYALL'S *Dufferin,* i. 22). He spoke fluently but not eloquently, and never used notes. Though he generally kept his temper under strict control, he was naturally impulsive, and to that failing, apart from the vacillation of his colleagues, may possibly be traced his nervous handling of affairs during the first Boer war. He took much interest in local business; was a deputy-lieutenant, county councillor and J.P. of Norfolk, and high steward of Norwich cathedral in succession to his father. He was a generous but critical landlord; and while in his youth a vigorous rider to hounds, he remained until late in life a capital shot. Kimberley was made hon. D.C.L., Oxford, in 1894, and chancellor of the University of London in 1899.

He married, on 16 Aug. 1847, Lady Florence (*d.* 4 May 1895), eldest daughter of Richard Fitzgibbon, third and last earl of Clare, and had three sons and two daughters. His successor, John, Baron Wodehouse, was born on 10 Dec. 1848; the third son, Armine (1860–1901), married in 1889 Eleanor Mary Caroline, daughter of Matthew Arnold; she re-married in 1909 the second Baron Sandhurst.

An excellent drawing by George Richmond was executed for Grillion's Club, and an oil painting (1866) by S. Catterson Smith is at Dublin Castle; replicas of both are at Kimberley. A cartoon portrait by 'Ape' appeared in 'Vanity Fair' in 1869.

[The Times, 9 April 1902; authorities cited; Paul's History of Modern England, 5 vols. 1904–6; J. Martineau, Life of Sir Bartle Frere, 2 vols. 1895; Lucy's Balfourian Parliament, 1906; Grant Duff, Notes from a Diary, 1888–91.] L. C. S.

WOLFF, Sir HENRY DRUMMOND CHARLES (1830–1908), politician and diplomatist, born in Malta 12 Oct. 1830, was only child of the rev. Joseph Wolff [q. v.] by his wife Lady Georgiana, daughter of Horatio Walpole, second earl of Orford. He was named Drummond after Henry Drummond [q. v.], a founder, with his father, of the Irvingite church. After education at Rugby, under Tait, he spent some time abroad in the study of foreign languages. At the age of sixteen he entered the foreign office as a supernumerary clerk, and became a member of the permanent staff in 1849. In June 1852 he was attached to the British legation at Florence, and was left in charge during the autumn of 1852 in the absence of the minister, Sir Henry Bulwer (afterwards Lord Dalling). He returned to the foreign office in 1853, and in 1856 he was attached to Lord Westmoreland's special mission to congratulate Leopold I, King of the Belgians, on the twenty-fifth anniversary of his accession. When the conservatives took office in February 1858, Wolff became assistant private secretary to the foreign secretary the earl of Malmesbury, and in October private secretary to the secretary for the colonies, Sir Edward Bulwer Lytton (afterwards Lord Lytton). Having been made C.M.G. and king of arms of the order in April 1859, he was secretary to Sir Henry Storks [q. v.], high commissioner of the Ionian Islands, from June 1859 till the transfer of the islands to Greece in June 1864. Throughout this period Wolff took an active part in various commissions of inquiry set on foot to redress grievances and to promote the material welfare of the islanders. In 1860 he acted as delegate for the islands to the international statistical congress in London; in 1861 he was vice-president of a commission to arrange for Ionian exhibits in the London international exhibition of 1862, and helped in the establishment of an Ionian Institute for the promotion of trade and education. In Oct. 1862 he became K.C.M.G., and subsequently arranged the details of the transfer of the islands to Greece, which was effected in June 1864. On relinquishing his office he received a pension from the Greek government.

For the next few years he travelled much, and was mainly engaged in promoting various financial undertakings, a kind of work for which his wide popularity and his astuteness and fertility of resource gave him great advantages. In 1864 he assisted at Constantinople in arranging for the conversion of the internal debt of Turkey into a foreign loan. In 1866 he laid a project for a ferry across the English Channel before the emperor of the French. Subsequently he aided in the liquidation of a large undertaking entitled the International Land Credit Company, which had come to disaster. In 1870, during the war between France and Germany, he made three expeditions from Spa, where he was staying, into the theatre of the campaign. At the beginning of September, with two English companions, he visited the battlefield of Sedan a day or two after the surrender of the French army, meeting on his return journey the emperor of the French on his way to Germany. A fortnight later Wolff and Henry James (afterwards Lord James of Hereford) visited the battlefields of Gravelotte and Saarbrücken and the environs of Strasburg while invested by the German forces, and came under the fire of the French artillery. Early in Oct. 1870 he proceeded from Spa to Baden, and thence to Strasburg, which had then surrendered, and on to Nancy and Toul. He narrated his experiences in the 'Morning Post,' and the narrative was privately printed in 1892 as 'Some Notes of the Past.'

Meanwhile he was actively interested in party politics. He was one of the select company of contributors to 'The Owl,' a short-lived but popular satirical journal, which was started in 1864 by Algernon Borthwick (afterwards Lord Glenesk [q. v. Suppl. II]) but abandoned in 1870 in consequence of the pressure of other work. In 1865 he stood as a conservative for Dorchester, with 'the most disastrous results.' Afterwards he purchased from Lord Malmesbury a small building property at Boscombe, near Bournemouth, which he set to work to develop, and at the general election in 1874 he was elected conservative M.P. for Christchurch. He took at once an active part in the House of Commons. He spoke often on foreign policy, especially in connection with the Eastern question. He was prominent in defending the purchase by the British government of the Khedive's shares in the Suez Canal Company. In 1875 he was appointed a member of the copyright commission, and signed the

Report presented in 1878, only dissenting on some points of detail. In 1876 he accompanied George Joachim (afterwards Lord) Goschen [q. v. Suppl. II] on a mission of inquiry into Egyptian finance to Egypt, in behalf of the Egyptian bondholders. During the Easter recess in 1878, when the revision of the treaty of San Stefano by a European congress was still in suspense. Wolff visited Paris, Vienna, and Berlin to ascertain the general feeling of European statesmen. In August 1878 he returned to employment under the foreign office, and was made G.C.M.G. Lord Salisbury selected him to be the British member of the international commission for the organisation of the province of Eastern Roumelia. After a preliminary discussion at Constantinople the commission established itself at Philippopolis in October. The Russian and British delegates were often at diplomatic odds, the former being openly hostile to the separation of the newly formed province from Bulgaria and seeking to give to it a fuller freedom from Turkish sovereignty than the treaty of Berlin sanctioned. Wolff appealed to the higher Russian authorities with considerable success. In April 1879 the organic statute was settled and signed. After assisting at the installation of the new governor-general, Aleko Pasha, Wolff returned to his parliamentary duties in England, and in September was created K.C.B. The Eastern Roumelian commission was further directed to draw up schemes for the administration of other European provinces of the Turkish empire, but before this task was approached, Gladstone's second administration began in England, and Wolff resigned (April 1880), being succeeded by Lord Edmond (now Lord) Fitzmaurice.

At the general election in the spring of 1880 Wolff was elected for Portsmouth. At the opening of the new parliament he took a leading part in opposing the claim of Charles Bradlaugh [q. v. Suppl. I] to take the oath, receiving the active support of Lord Randolph Churchill and Mr. (afterwards Sir John) Gorst. In the result these three members formed the combination, subsequently joined by Mr. Arthur Balfour and known under the title of the Fourth Party, which, during the next five years, did much to enliven the proceedings of the House of Commons and to make uneasy the positions both of the prime minister, Mr. Gladstone, and of the leader of the opposition, Sir Stafford Northcote, afterwards earl of Iddesleigh [see Churchill, Lord Randolph, Suppl. I]. Wolff was an active and efficient colleague, taking his full share in parliamentary discussions and being especially useful in reconciling his companions' differences. He was personally responsible for the passing of a bill, which he had introduced in the previous parliament, enabling the inhabitants of seaside resorts to let their houses for short periods without losing their qualification to vote at elections. But his attention was mainly devoted to party warfare. On 19 April 1883, after the unveiling of the statue of Lord Beaconsfield in Parliament Square, he first suggested to Lord Randolph Churchill the formation of a 'Primrose League,' to be so named after what was reputed to be the deceased statesman's favourite flower. In the course of the following autumn the league was set on foot. The statutes of the new association were drawn up by Wolff and revised by a small committee. They prescribed a form of declaration by which members undertook 'to devote their best ability to the maintenance of religion, of the estates of the realm, and of the imperial ascendancy of the British empire,' and they ministered to the weaker side of human nature by providing a regular gradation of rank with quaint titles and picturesque badges. The league, though at first somewhat scoffed at by the conservative leaders, was soon found to be a most efficient party instrument. In the dissension caused in the conservative party by Lord Randolph Churchill's advocacy of a frankly democratic policy, Wolff sided with his colleague, but he was too astute a politician to favour internal divisions, and was instrumental in procuring the reconciliation, which was effected in the summer of 1884. On Lord Salisbury's return to office in June 1885 Wolff was made a privy councillor, and in August was despatched on a special mission to Constantinople to discuss with the Turkish government the future of Egypt, which since 1882 had been in the military occupation of Great Britain. The British occupation, though accepted as a practical necessity, had not received formal recognition or sanction either from the Sultan or any of the powers. Wolff was instructed to arrange with the Porte the conditions on which the Sultan's authority should in future be exercised in Egypt and the methods for assuring the stability of the Khedive's government. After some months Wolff concluded with the Turkish government in Oct. 1885 a convention providing that the two governments should each send a special commissioner to Egypt who should in concert with the Khedive reorganise the Egyptian army, examine and reform all branches of the Egyptian administration, and consider the best means for tranquillising the Soudan by pacific methods. When these ends were accomplished, the two governments would consider terms for the withdrawal of the British troops from Egypt within a convenient period. Wolff went to Egypt as British commissioner under this convention. Moukhtar Pasha was the Turkish commissioner. At the end of twelve months Wolff returned to England in order to discuss the terms of a further arrangement with Turkey. In Jan. 1887 he proceeded to Constantinople, and there negotiated a second convention, signed on 22 May, which stipulated for the withdrawal of the British forces from Egypt at the end of three years, with the proviso that the evacuation should be postponed in the event of any external or internal danger at that time; that for two years after the evacuation Great Britain was to watch exclusively over the safety of the country; and that subsequently both the Sultan and the British government were each to have the right, if necessary, of sending a force to Egypt either for its defence or for the maintenance of order. In a separate note it was stated that the refusal of one of the Mediterranean great powers to accept the convention would be regarded by the British government as an external danger justifying the postponement of the evacuation. The governments of Austria, Germany, and Italy were favourably inclined to this arrangement, but the French government, which determinedly opposed it, intimated together with the Russian government that if it were ratified they would feel justified in occupying other portions of Turkish territory. The Sultan consequently refused to ratify it.

Wolff returned to England in July 1887. Lord Salisbury in a final despatch observed that the negotiations had defined formally the character of the English occupation and the conditions necessary to bring it to a close. The convention of Oct. 1885 remained in force as a recognition by the Porte of the occupation, and the continued presence of the Turkish commissioner in Egypt, though possibly not in all respects convenient, implied acquiescence in the situation.

Wolff's parliamentary career had been brought to a close by his defeat at Portsmouth in the general election of November 1885, while he was absent in Egypt. For the future his work was entirely in the diplomatic profession. In Dec. 1887 he was appointed British envoy in Persia, and proceeded to Teheran early in the following year. Here his versatile energy found ample occupation in watching the progress and development of Russian policy on the northern frontier, in devising plans for harmonious action by the two powers in lieu of the traditional rivalry between their legations, in promoting schemes for the development of British commercial enterprise, and in encouraging the Persian government in efforts for administrative and financial reform. Among the measures, which he was instrumental in promoting were the issue of a decree in May 1888 for the protection of property from arbitrary acts of the executive and the opening of the Karun river to steam navigation in October following. A concession obtained by Baron Reuter on the occasion of the Shah's visit to England in 1872, which was worded in such vague and comprehensive terms as to seem incapable of practical development, took, under Wolff's guidance, a business-like and beneficial shape in the establishment of the Imperial Bank of Persia. Some other schemes were less successful. A carefully considered project for the construction of a railway from Ahwaz on the Karun river in the direction of Ispahan failed to obtain sufficient financial support, and the concession of the tobacco régie to a group of English financiers, which seemed to promise considerable advantages to the Persian exchequer, excited such fanatical opposition that it was in the end abandoned some time after Wolff's departure from Persia. Wolff received the grand cross of the Bath in Jan. 1889, and was summoned home later in the year to attend the Shah on his visit to England. He accompanied the Persian sovereign during his tour in England and Scotland. On his way back to Teheran in Aug. 1889 Wolff passed through St. Petersburg, where he had an audience of the Emperor of Russia, and urged the importance of an agreement between the two countries on the policy to be pursued in Persia, obtaining an assurance that the new Russian minister at Teheran would be authorised to discuss any proposals, which he might be empowered to put forward for this object. He had intended in 1890 to visit India, but before his departure from Teheran he was struck down by a serious illness, during which his life was at one time despaired of. He recovered sufficiently to be brought to England, where he gradually regained strength, but his health was clearly unequal to a return to the arduous duties and trying climate of Teheran. In July 1891, somewhat against his will, he was transferred to Bucharest, and six months afterwards was appointed ambassador at Madrid. That post he held for eight years, till his retirement on pension in Oct. 1900. In June 1893 he effected a provisional commercial agreement with the Spanish government, pending the conclusion of a permanent treaty, and this arrangement was further confirmed by an exchange of notes in Dec. 1894. British relations with Spain gave no cause for anxiety, and Wolff's natural geniality and hospitable instincts secured him a general popularity, which was unimpaired by the war between Spain and the United States, when English public opinion pronounced itself somewhat clearly on the American side. After his retirement he lived for reasons of health quietly in England. He retained, however, his keen, restless interest in public affairs, his gift of amusing conversation, and his apparently inexhaustible fund of anecdote. Through life his good temper was imperturbable, and he delighted in mischievous humour, which was free from malice or vindictiveness. He professed in casual conversation a lower standard of conduct than he really acted upon, and despite his avowed cynicism he was by nature and instinct kind-hearted and always ready to assist distress. He became very infirm in the last few months of his life, and died at Brighton on 11 Oct. 1908.

He married at the British Consulate, Leghorn, on 22 Jan. 1853, Adeline, daughter of Walter Sholto Douglas, by whom he had two sons and a daughter. His widow was awarded a civil list pension of 100*l.* in 1909. His daughter, Adeline Georgiana Isabel, wife of Col. Howard Kingscote, was a prolific novelist, writing under the pseudonym of 'Lucas Cleeve.' Her chief works, which show an easy style and vivid imagination, include 'The Real Christian' (1901), 'Blue Lilies' (1902), 'Eileen' (1903), 'The Secret Church' (1906), 'Her Father's Soul' (1907). She was a great traveller and an accomplished linguist. She predeceased her father on 13 Sept. 1908 at Château d'Œx, Switzerland. A cartoon portrait of Wolff by 'Spy' appeared in 'Vanity Fair' in 1881.

[Sir H. D. Wolff published in 1908 two volumes, entitled Rambling Recollections, which give a very entertaining though somewhat discursive account of his varied experiences. Other authorities are The Times, 12 Oct. 1908; Foreign Office List, 1909, p 405; Winston Churchill's Life of Lord Randolph Churchill, 2 vols. 1906; Harold Gorst's The Fourth Party; art. on the Primrose League in Encycl. Brit. 11th ed.] S.

WOLVERHAMPTON, first Viscount. [See Fowler, Sir Henry Hartley (1830–1911), statesman.]

WOODALL, WILLIAM (1832–1901), politician, elder son of William Woodall of Shrewsbury, by his wife Martha Basson, was born there on 15 March 1832 and educated at the Crescent Schools, Liverpool. He entered the business at Burslem of James Macintyre, china manufacturer whose daughter Evelyn, he married in 1862, and at Macintyre's death in 1870 became senior partner. He was also chairman of the Sneyd Colliery Co.

Woodall was active in local affairs, devoting himself especially to the cause of technical education. He was chairman of the Burslem school board (1870–80), of the Wedgwood Institute there, and of the North Staffordshire Society for Promotion of the Welfare of the Deaf and Dumb. He sat on royal commissions on technical education (1881–4) and the care of the blind and deaf mutes (1886–9). In September 1897 he accompanied Sir Philip Magnus and others to Germany to study technical instruction methods there (Magnus, *Educational Aims and Efforts*, 1910, pp. 92, 94, 120).

Woodall was liberal M.P. for the borough of Stoke-on-Trent 1880–6, and was first representative of Hanley from 1885 to 1900. He was a warm supporter of home rule, disestablishment, and local veto, as well as of the extension of the franchise.

In 1884 he succeeded Hugh Mason (M.P. for Ashton-under-Lyne) in the leadership of the woman suffrage party in the house, and introduced (10 June) an amendment to the Representation of the People Act then before the house, providing that 'words having reference to the right of voting at parliamentary elections, importing the masculine gender, include women.' As chairman of the Central Committee for Women's Suffrage (established in 1872), he headed a memorial from 110 members to Gladstone but the prime minister resisted the amendment as likely to imperil the bill. The division was taken on 12 June, when

135 voted with Woodall and 271 against. In obedience to a strong party whip, 104 liberal supporters of the women's cause voted with the majority: had they voted according to their convictions the amendment would have been carried by 72 votes instead of being lost by 136. On 19 Nov. Woodall brought in a bill granting the vote to single women on the same terms as men, but the second reading was four times adjourned and never reached a division. Under Gladstone's short third administration of 1886 Woodall became surveyor-general of ordnance Feb. to June. He resumed charge of the women's suffrage bill in July 1887, and after further delays he reintroduced it in April 1889 and again in 1891. He accepted office as financial secretary to the war office (August 1892–June 1895) under Gladstone's fourth government.

To Burslem he presented a large wing to the Wedgwood institute and free library, besides founding the Woodall liberal club there and bequeathing a collection of valuable pictures to the art gallery. He died at the house of his nephew-in-law, Dr. Woodhouse of Llandudno, on 8 April 1901. The Woodall memorial congregational chapel at Burslem was built in 1906. There is a portrait in oils by W. M. Palin at the Wedgwood institute. A cartoon portrait by 'Spy' appeared in 'Vanity Fair' in 1896.

Woodall devoted some of his leisure to writing for magazines and reviews, and republished from 'Once a Week' in 1872 'Paris after Two Sieges, Notes of Visits during the Armistice and immediately after the Suppression of the Commune.' He was a chevalier of the Légion d'Honneur.

By his wife Evelyn Macintyre, who died in 1870, he had no children.

[The Times, 9 April 1901; Who's Who, 1900; Dod's Parl. Companion, 1899; Hansard's Parl. Debates; Helen Blackburn's Women's Suffrage, 1902, passim; Women's Suffrage Journal, 1880–1890; private information.] C. F. S.

WOODS, Sir ALBERT WILLIAM (1816–1904), Garter King of arms, born at Hampstead on 16 April 1816, was son of Sir William Woods, Garter King of arms from 1838 till his death in 1842. After private education he was appointed Fitzalan pursuivant of arms extraordinary in 1837, and entered the College of Arms as Portcullis Pursuivant in ordinary, on 3 Aug. 1838. On 28 Oct. 1841 he was appointed Norfolk Herald extraordinary, and was advanced on 9 Nov. following to the office of Lancaster Herald. In that capacity he was attached to the Garter missions for investing the Kings of Denmark (1865) and Belgium (1866) and the Emperor of Austria (1867). On 25 Oct. 1869 he succeeded Sir Charles George Young [q. v.] as Garter Principal King of arms, and was knighted on 11 Nov. in the same year. He retained that office until his death, and filled it with tact and rare courtliness of manner. As Garter he was joint plenipotentiary for investing respectively the Kings of Italy (1878), Spain (1881), and Saxony (1882) with the ensigns of the order of the Garter. He was appointed C.B. (civil division) in 1887, K.C.M.G. (1890), and K.C.B. (civil division) (1897), and was created G.C.V.O. on the occasion of King Edward VII's coronation in 1902. He was also a knight of grace and director-general of ceremonies of the order of St. John of Jerusalem in England. Woods held many other offices connected with various orders of knighthood. Appointed first, in 1841, Usher of the Scarlet Rod and Brunswick Herald, he eventually became registrar and secretary of the order of the Bath, registrar of the order of the Star of India on its establishment in 1861, registrar of the order of the Indian Empire on its foundation in 1878, King of arms of the order of St. Michael and St. George, registrar of the order of Victoria and Albert, and inspector of regimental colours. All these appointments he held at his death. He died at 69 St. George's Road, S.W., on. 7 Jan. 1904, and was buried at Norwood cemetery.

Woods became a freemason in 1849, and held for an exceptionally long period high office in the craft. He was advanced to the position of a grand officer and assistant grand director of ceremonies in 1858, and was from 1860 to his death grand director of ceremonies, an office in grand lodge which his father had held before him. He received in 1875 the dignity of past grand warden. On 25 March 1847 he was elected F.S.A.

On 1 Dec. 1838 he married Caroline, eldest daughter of Robert Cole of Rotherfield, Sussex (a lady of grace of the order of St. John of Jerusalem in England), who died at 69 St. George's Road, on 19 Nov. 1911, at the age of ninety-five, and was buried with her husband. Woods had two children, a son and a daughter. The former, William Woods, died in 1869, leaving two children, an only son, Albert William Woods, who was appointed Rouge Dragon Pursuivant of arms in 1886, and died in

1893 without issue, and a surviving daughter, Frances. Sir Albert's only daughter, Caroline Marianne, married on 6 Sept. 1873 the present writer, and the only child of this marriage, Mr. Gerald Woods Wollaston (*b.* 2 June 1874), maintains the long connection of the family with the College of Arms, being (1912) Bluemantle Pursuivant of arms.

[The Times, 8 Jan. 1904; private information.]

A. N. W.

WOODS, EDWARD (1814–1903), civil engineer, born in London on 28 April 1814, was son of Samuel Woods, a merchant. After education at private schools, and some training at Bristol, he became in 1834 an assistant to John Dixon, recently appointed chief engineer of the Liverpool and Manchester railway. Woods was placed in charge of the section, 15 miles in length, between Liverpool and Newton-le-Willows, including the tunnel, then under construction, between Lime Street and Edge Hill stations; and in 1836 he succeeded Dixon as chief engineer, taking also charge of the mechanical department. The Liverpool and Manchester railway was amalgamated with the Grand Junction railway in 1845. Woods remained until the end of 1852 in charge of the works appertaining to the Liverpool and Manchester section, including the construction of the Victoria tunnel (completed 1848) between Edge Hill station and the docks, a large goods station adjoining the Waterloo dock, and a line between Patricroft and Clifton, opened in 1850. In 1853 he established himself in London as a consulting engineer.

During his eighteen years' work on the Liverpool and Manchester line Woods took a prominent part in various early experimental investigations into the working of railways. In 1836 he made observations on the waste of fuel due to condensation in the long pipes conveying steam about ½ mile to the winding-engines used for hauling trains through the Edge Hill tunnel, the gradient of which was then considered too steep for locomotives. He was a member of a committee appointed by the British Association in 1837 to report on the resistance of railway trains, and presented a separate report (*British Assoc. Report*, 1841, p. 247) apart from two reports made by Dr. Dionysius Lardner [q. v.]. In 1838 he presented to the Institution of Civil Engineers a paper (*Transactions*, ii. 137), 'On Certain Forms of Locomotive Engines,' which contains some of the earliest accurate details of the working of locomotives, and for which he was awarded a Telford medal. The consumption of fuel in locomotives was the subject of a paper presented by him to the Liverpool Polytechnic Society in 1843 (published in 1844), and of a contribution to a new edition of Tredgold's 'Steam Engine' in 1850.

In 1853 Woods carried out, with W. P. Marshall, some experiments on the locomotives of the London and North Western railway, between London and Rugby, and three joint reports were made to the general locomotive committee of the railway, recommending certain weights and dimensions for various classes of engines. These were followed, in 1854, by a joint report on the use of coal as a substitute for coke, which had been used hitherto.

From that date onwards his practice was chiefly connected with the railways of South America, including the Central Argentine railway, the Copiapo extension, Santiago and Valparaiso, and Coquimbo railways in Chile, and the Mollenda-Arequipa and Callao-Oroya lines in Peru. He was responsible not only for surveys and construction, but also for the design of rolling stock to meet the somewhat special conditions. Other engineering work included a wrought-iron pier, 2400 feet long, built in 1851 on screw piles at Pisco on the coast of Peru, and a quay-wall built at Bilbao in 1877.

In the 'battle of the gauges' he favoured the Irish gauge (5 feet 3 inches) or the Indian gauge (5 feet 6 inches). He regarded break of gauge as a mistake.

In 1877, as president of the mechanical science section of the British Association, he delivered an address on 'Adequate Brake Power for Railway Trains.' Elected a member of the Institution of Civil Engineers on 7 April 1846, he became a member of its council in December 1869, and was president in 1886–7. His presidential address (*Proc. Inst. Civ. Eng.* lxxxvii. 1) contains much information as to the early history of railways. In 1884 he was president of the Smeatonian Society of Civil Engineers.

He died at his residence, 45 Onslow Gardens, London, on 14 June 1903, and was buried at Chenies, Buckinghamshire. His portrait in oils, by Miss Porter, is in the possession of the Institution of Civil Engineers.

He married in 1840 Mary, daughter of Thomas Goodman of Birmingham, by whom he had three sons and two daughters.

[Proc. Inst. Civ. Eng. cliii. 342; The Engineer, 19 June 1903; The Times, 16 June 1903.]

W. F. S.

WOODWARD, HERBERT HALL (1847–1909), musical composer, born 13 Jan. 1847, near Liverpool, was fifth and youngest son of Robert Woodward (1801–1882), by his wife Mary, youngest daughter of William Hall, of Ryall's Court, Ripple, Worcestershire. The father, a Liverpool merchant, purchased, in 1852, the Arley Castle estate, near Bewdley. Both the father's and mother's families had been long settled in Worcestershire. Herbert, after being educated at Radley College, matriculated at Corpus Christi College, Oxford, in 1862. At Radley he chiefly studied music under Dr. E. G. Monk and at Oxford under Dr. Leighton Hayne, and graduated Mus.B. in 1866 and B.A. in 1867. He spent eighteen months at Cuddesdon Theological College, and, being ordained deacon in 1870 and priest in 1871 in the diocese of Oxford, became curate and precentor of Wantage. There he remained for eleven years, working as assistant priest under William John Butler [q. v. Suppl. I], afterwards Dean of Lincoln. In 1881 he was appointed a minor canon of Worcester Cathedral, and became precentor in 1890. Here he formed a successful preparatory boarding school for the choir boys, of which he was warden for twenty-eight years (1881–1909). His devotional character had a great influence on the services at the cathedral, where he raised the standard of worship to a high level. A bachelor, and possessed of private means, he was widely known for his generous philanthropy. He died in London, after an operation, on 25 May 1909. At Worcester he is commemorated by the 'Woodward Memorial Wing' of the choir school buildings. As a composer he is best known by his church music. His anthem 'The Radiant Morn,' written in 1881, is probably the most generally popular of its kind; and 'The Souls of the Righteous,' 'Behold the days come,' 'Crossing the Bar,' 'Comes at times a Stillness as of Even,' and the Communion Service in E flat are also familiar.

[Brit. Musical Biog.; Musical Times, Nov. 1905 (with portrait); Burke's Landed Gentry; Clergy List, 1909; private information.] J. C. H.

WOOLGAR, SARAH JANE (1824–1909), actress. [See MELLON, MRS.]

WORDSWORTH, JOHN (1843–1911), bishop of Salisbury, was elder son of Christopher Wordsworth [q. v.], bishop of Lincoln, by his wife Susanna Hatley, daughter of George Frere. His brother is Christopher Wordsworth, master of St. Nicholas' Hospital, Salisbury, and formerly fellow of Peterhouse, Cambridge. Among his five sisters were Elizabeth, first principal of Lady Margaret Hall, Oxford, and Susan (*d.* 1912), first head of the Southwark Diocesan Society of Grey Ladies. He was born on 21 Sept. 1843 at Harrow, his father being headmaster of the school, and was educated as a pensioner at Winchester and as a scholar at New College, Oxford, from which he matriculated in 1861. In 1863 he was placed in the first class in classical moderations, and in 1865 in the second class in literæ humaniores. He graduated B.A. in 1865, proceeding M.A. in 1868. He won the Latin essay prize in 1866, and the Craven scholarship in 1867. After a year as assistant master at Wellington College under Edward White Benson, afterwards archbishop of Canterbury, he was elected in 1867 to a fellowship at Brasenose, and was ordained deacon and priest by Bishop Wilberforce of Oxford in 1867 and 1869. He served Brasenose College as chaplain. In 1870 he was appointed examining chaplain and was collated to a prebend in Lincoln Cathedral by his father, just consecrated to that see. Though he was from the first interested in divinity, his college work and his studies were chiefly classical. Beside writings of less importance, he published in 1874 'Fragments and Specimens of Early Latin,' still a standard work, though its philology is that of its date. It gave an ample and judicious collection of examples, with a sound and learned commentary, and proved Wordsworth to be one of the best Latin scholars in Oxford. Thenceforth he applied his Latin scholarship to biblical study. In 1878 the University Press accepted a proposal from him for the publication of a critical edition of the Vulgate text of the New Testament, which should reproduce, so far as possible, the exact words of St. Jerome. The enterprise was in progress the rest of his life. Wordsworth at once began to collect his material. MSS. were collated, principally by himself, in all the countries of Western Europe; earlier collations, such as those of Bentley and John Walker [q. v.] were examined; unused material of Tischendorf was purchased; the patristic writers were searched for quotations; readings of importance from one or another point of view were brought together from a multitude of printed editions. Fully a hundred sources were drawn upon for the text of the Gospels. Wordsworth met satisfactorily all the requirements of palæographical, grammatical, historical, and exegetical knowledge, and his notes and indices became mines of varied erudition. As a preliminary to the substantive publication, certain important MSS. were from 1883 onwards printed in full in 'Old Latin Biblical Texts'; in this task Wordsworth enlisted the aid of Dr. Sanday and other scholars. Subsequently he associated with himself in his work the Rev. Henry Julian White, now professor of New Testament exegesis in King's College, London. At length in 1889 St. Matthew was published, in 1891 St. Mark, in 1892 St. Luke, in 1895 St. John. An 'Epilogus' of discussions and results followed in 1898, the whole forming a quarto volume of over 800 pages. The Acts appeared in 1905; the work is still in progress under the care of Dr. White with the assistance of the Rev. George Mallows Youngman. Before his death the bishop passed through the press a minor edition of the whole Vulgate New Testament, which appeared in 1912. Owing to other occupations Wordsworth in his later years took no large share in the actual shaping of the work, but the materials were mostly of his collection, and he retained a full knowledge of every detail, and in doubtful questions gave the final decision.

Meanwhile Wordsworth had gained high office at Oxford and in the church. In 1877 J. B. Mozley [q. v.], regius professor of divinity, chose him as his deputy, and he served that office for two years. On his lectures as deputy professor he based the Bampton lectures of 1881. Entitled 'The One Religion,' they were a development of the 'testimonium animæ naturaliter Christianæ,' and a comparison of Christianity with other great religions. Wordsworth was no orientalist, and this is the only book in which he used second-hand knowledge. Nor did Wordsworth venture elsewhere upon the field of philosophy, which as in the case of his uncle Charles was alien to his mode of thought. At the same time the Bampton lectures illustrate his strong interest in missions. He was among the founders of the Oxford Missionary Association of Graduates, and of St. Stephen's House, which was designed to prepare members of the university for mission life. In 1883 Wordsworth's theological learning was recognised by his election to the Oriel professorship of the interpretation of scripture. The Oriel professorship was newly founded, and he was the first occupant; it carried with it a canonry of Rochester, where Wordsworth threw himself heartily into the work of church and cathedral. Two years later Wordsworth was nominated to the see of Salisbury in succession to George Moberly [q. v.]. He was consecrated on 28 Oct. 1885, and was made D.D. at Oxford. Thenceforth his literary work, apart from the Vulgate, was incidental to his new duties. Succeeding to a well-administered diocese, without the problem of an increasing population, he was able to devote much of his time to the general policy of the church. Possessed of a strong will and unfailing memory, combined with a genuine interest in the work of his clergy and an ample generosity, he fully exerted his authority. He made himself an efficient ecclesiastical lawyer, and was fearless in risking litigation, from which in fact his boldness protected him. He was the first to exercise the power under the Pluralities Act Amendment Act (1898), by which a bishop can appoint a curate, at the expense of an incompetent incumbent, to a neglected parish. He also revived the canonical right of examining and rejecting, on the score of insufficient learning, the presentee to a benefice. The diocesan work for which he found widest scope was that of education. Not only did he make great, and often successful, efforts to maintain elementary church schools, but he also concerned himself with higher instruction. He founded and endowed the Bishop's School at Salisbury for the secondary co-education of boys and girls.

In the central counsels of his church, Wordsworth's influence was especially powerful. He was on terms of close intimacy with Archbishop Benson, and his assistance proved indispensable to Benson's successors. He was one of the assessors in the bishop of Lincoln's case in 1889–90, and laboriously studied the relevant law and history.

Wordsworth cherished hopes of reunion of Christendom, and the aspiration stirred his best energies. But he inherited much of his father's strong feeling against Rome; and though he frankly expressed his admiration for its more scholarly representatives, he was always ready to state, in Latin or English, the points of difference and the claims of his own church to antiquity or authority. He was always interested in symptoms of internal revolt in the Roman communion, and watched such growth as might be found among the Old Catholics, especially of Austria. In fact, his range of interest covered the whole area of Christendom where bishops existed. In the general recognition of episcopacy he saw the one hope of unity. The common feature of episcopacy drew Wordsworth to remote Eastern churches of whose orthodoxy he was willing to take the most favourable view, and towards Swedes and Moravians, episcopal brethren, though other sides of their system might seem to rank them with those who care little for the historic ministry, and though their link with the past might, as in the last case, be very dubious. He grudged no effort to remove obstacles and in the negotiation of terms of possible association. His last work, the Hale lectures, delivered at Chicago in 1910, and published in England in 1911, on the national church of Sweden, was inspired by this motive. It was composed in ill-health, but is a substantial and original contribution to history. It has been translated into Swedish, and is a recognised text-book in the Swedish colleges. In his 'De successione Episcoporum in Ecclesia Anglicana' (1890) and 'De validitate ordinum Anglicanorum' (1894) he laboriously attempted to refute the scruples of the so-called Jansenist Church of Holland. The correspondence was kept up through his life, though his hopes were never fully realised. He also made some efforts to continue the attempts of his uncle Charles to draw together the episcopal and presbyterian churches of Scotland. His elaborate history of the episcopate of Charles Wordsworth (1899), like his later researches, as in his 'Ordination Problems' (1909) and 'Unity and Fellowship' (1910), was largely devoted to precedents for the absorption of religious societies with some defect in their title into others whose pedigree was unblemished.

Wordsworth found in history an authoritative clue to present duty. His two most important practical works, 'Holy Communion,' originally a series of visitation addresses in 1891 (3rd edit. 1910), and his 'Ministry of Grace,' charges of 1901 (2nd edit. 1902) are laboriously historical in method. The last is a history of the Christian ministry which contains substantial additions to knowledge. If history revealed institutions to be accepted as authoritative, scripture was equally a succession of oracles to be interpreted, not to be criticised. Though in his later years Wordsworth ceased to share such fears as Liddon's, he was to the last very conservative in regard to criticism of the Bible.

In his preaching Wordsworth showed himself equally sure of his ground, scriptural and historical, and spoke impressively and often with originality, although he sometimes forgot that his audience did not share his interests and his knowledge. Outside his own lines of reading, the literature that interested him was such as dealt with practical questions. His appetite for information was keen; the local and natural history of his diocese, for instance, became thoroughly familiar to him, and on most concrete topics he had something to impart. Though he was an accomplished critic and writer of Latin, style in English literature did not greatly interest him; in poetry he was chiefly attracted by the grave morality of his great-uncle, William Wordsworth. He is memorable chiefly for his efforts for the reunion of Christendom, which compare with those of Archbishop Wake, and for the scholarly work which places him among the masters in historical theology. He was made hon. LL.D. of Dublin in 1890, of Cambridge in 1908, and hon. D.D. of Berne in 1892. In 1905 he was chosen a fellow of the British Academy. He wrote in this Dictionary on Charles Wordsworth [q. v.] and on John Walker [q. v. Suppl. I].

The bishop died suddenly at his palace at Salisbury on 16 Aug. 1911, and was buried at Britford, near Salisbury. He married (1) in 1870, Susan Esther (*d.* 1894), daughter of Henry Octavius Coxe [q. v.]; (2) in 1896, Mary, daughter of Colonel Robert Williams, M.P., of Bridehead, Dorset, by whom he left four sons and two daughters.

Two portraits of him were painted in 1905 by Sir George Reid and presented to him by the diocese. One picture is in the Palace, Salisbury, the other belongs to the family. One of them has been engraved. He is to be commemorated by a recumbent statue and by the erection of choir-stalls in Salisbury cathedral.

[Personal knowledge; The Times, 17 and 21 Aug. 1911; Salisbury Diocesan Gazette, Sept. to Dec. 1911 (articles by the Archbishop of Canterbury, the Principal of Brasenose, Miss E. Wordsworth, and others); Dr. H. J. White in Journal of Theolog. Studies, Jan. 1912, xiii. 201; Dr. W. Sanday in Proc. Brit. Academy, 1912; a biography by the present writer is in preparation.] E. W. W.

WORMS, HENRY DE, first BARON PIRBRIGHT (1840–1903), politician. [See DE WORMS.]

WRIGHT, CHARLES HENRY HAMILTON (1836–1909), Hebraist and theologian, born at Dublin on 9 March 1836, was second son in a family of ten children of Edward Wright, LL.D., barrister, of Floraville,

Donnybrook, co. Dublin, by his wife Charlotte, daughter of Joseph Wright of Beech Hill, Donnybrook. Edward Perceval Wright [q. v. Suppl. II] was his eldest brother. Charles was privately educated, and entered Trinity College, Dublin, on 1 July 1852. While still an undergraduate he actively engaged in religious controversy and propaganda on the protestant side, and in 1853 he wrote his first work, 'Coming Events; or, Glimpses of the Future,' as well as an anonymous attack on Roman catholicism, 'The Pope the Antichrist.' For a time Celtic philology occupied his attention. His early work in a field which was then little explored was seen to advantage in 'A Grammar of the Modern Irish Language' (1855; 2nd ed. 1860). But he soon turned to theology and oriental languages, which formed his main study through life. In 1856 he won the primate's Hebrew premium, graduating B.A. with a first class in the examination for the divinity testimonium in 1857. He was awarded the Arabic prize in 1859, proceeding M.A. in the same year, B.D. in 1873, and D.D. in 1879. He also took the degree of Ph.D. at Leipzig in 1875.

Meanwhile Wright had been ordained in 1859 to the curacy of Middleton-Tyas, Yorkshire; but though an earnest preacher he was unsuited to ordinary parochial work. Appointed in 1863 to the English chaplaincy at Dresden, he made the acquaintance of the leading German theologians, such as Delitzsch and Lechler. His protestant zeal gained him many adherents among the English residents, but offended the high church party, who successfully petitioned A. C. Tait, bishop of London, to appoint an additional chaplain. In 1868 Wright undertook the chaplaincy at Boulogne-sur-mer, where he ministered not only to British seamen but to the German prisoners during the Franco-Prussian war of 1870–1. Thanks to his efforts the English church was repaired, and a house was erected, which combined a sailors' institute with a chaplain's residence. Returning to Ireland, Wright served successively as incumbent of St. Mary's, Belfast (1874–85), and of Bethesda Church, Dublin (1885–91). In 1891 he accepted the benefice of St. John's, Liverpool, retiring in 1898, when the church was pulled down to make way for city improvements.

Meanwhile Wright's activities were by no means limited to clerical duty. Incorporated M.A. at Exeter College, Oxford, on 5 July 1862, he was elected Bampton lecturer for 1878, and chose as his subject 'Zechariah and his Prophecies' (published in 1879). At Dublin he delivered the Donellan lectures (1880–1), in which he expounded 'The Book of Ecclesiastes in Relation to Modern Criticism' (1883). In 1893 he renewed his connection with Oxford on his appointment as Grinfield lecturer on the Septuagint, and was re-elected to that office in 1895 for a further term of two years. He also frequently acted as examiner in Hebrew in the Universities of Oxford, London, Manchester, and Wales.

One of the last great militant protestants, Wright devoted himself with conspicuous ability to the cause of the Protestant Reformation Society, of which he was clerical superintendent (1898–1907). From his prolific pen there flowed a steady stream of pamphlets denunciatory of Roman catholicism; these included 'The Church of Rome and Mariolatry' (1893), 'Roman Catholicism' (1896; 4th edit. 1909), and some trenchant articles in 'A Protestant Dictionary' (1904), of which he was joint editor. Wright's scholarship and acumen as a controversialist were acknowledged even by his opponents. But he lacked the gifts that make for popularity and public recognition. He died at his house on Wandsworth Common on 22 March 1909. He married on 23 June 1859 Ebba, daughter of Professor Nils Wilhelm Almroth, governor of the Royal Mint, Stockholm. He left five sons, of whom Sir Almroth, the pathologist, Charles Theodore Hagberg, LL.D., the librarian of the London Library, and Eric Blackwood, chief justice of the Seychelles since 1905, have attained distinction.

Wright's numerous theological works, though never enjoying a wide circulation, were valued by conservative critics. At the same time he reserved his independence of judgment as to the historical value of certain portions of the Old Testament, including 'Jonah,' which he regarded as allegorical. He published, with critical notes, the Hebrew text of the books of Genesis (1859) and Ruth (1864), and translations of 'The Pentateuch' (1869). Other exegetical works were 'Biblical Essays . . . Studies on the Books of Job and Jonah' (1886); 'An Introduction to the Old Testament' (Theological Educator, 1890; 4th edit. 1898); 'Daniel and his Prophecies' (1906), and 'Light from Egyptian Papyri on Jewish History before Christ' (1908). He also translated 'The Writings of St. Patrick' (1887), in collaboration with George Thomas Stokes [q. v. Suppl. I].

[The Times, 24 March 1909; Guardian, 31 March 1909; Mrs. C. H. H. [Ebba] Wright, Sunbeams on my Path, 2nd edit. 1900; private information from Dr. Hagberg Wright.]

G. S. W.

WRIGHT, EDWARD PERCEVAL (1834–1910), naturalist, born in Dublin on 27 Dec. 1834, was eldest son of Edward Wright, LL.D., barrister, of Floraville, Donnybrook, by his wife Charlotte, daughter of Joseph Wright of Beech Hill, Donnybrook. Charles Henry Hamilton Wright [q. v. Suppl. II] was a younger brother. Edward was educated at home, and began the study of natural history under Prof. George James Allman [q. v. Suppl. I] before he entered Trinity College, Dublin, at the end of 1852. In 1854 he commenced the publication of the quarterly 'Natural History Review,' which he continued to edit until 1866. His earliest papers contributed to this journal are of a varied character, dealing with rare Irish birds, fungi parasitic upon insects, the collecting of mollusca, and a disease of the minnow. Between 1856 and 1859 he also contributed a series of papers to the Dublin Natural History Society on the British filmy ferns. In 1857 he visited the Mitchelstown caves, where his discovery of blind springtails first showed the interest attaching to the living cave-fauna of Ireland. In the same year he graduated B.A., was made director of the university museum, and became a member of the Royal Irish Academy. In 1858 he was appointed lecturer in zoology in Trinity College, a post which he held for ten years, and was made lecturer in botany in the medical school of Dr. Steevens's Hospital. He was also elected secretary to the Royal Geological Society of Ireland. Wright had taken part in the meeting of the British Association in Dublin in 1857, and at the association's next meeting, at Leeds in 1858, he, in conjunction with Joseph Reay Greene, presented a 'Report on the Marine Fauna of the Irish coast'; he acted as secretary to Section D for that and succeeding years. To the 'Proceedings' of the Dublin University Zoological and Botanical Association, of which he was secretary, he contributed in 1859 papers on Irish Actinidæ and Irish Nudibranchs.

Meanwhile Wright, who had proceeded M.A. in 1859, taking an *ad eundem* at Oxford, continued his medical studies, and graduated M.D. in 1862. Determining to practise as an oculist, he visited for special study the medical schools of Berlin, Vienna, and Paris, publishing in 1864, from the German of F. C. Donders, 'The Pathogeny of Squint,' and a paper in 1865 on 'A Modification of Liebreich's Ophthalmoscope.' On his appointment as locum tenens for William Henry Harvey [q. v.], professor of botany at Trinity College (1865), he abandoned ophthalmic surgery for science (1866). He described the flora of the Aran Islands in Galway Bay after a visit in 1865 (see *Journ. Bot.* 1867; *Proc. Dublin Nat. Hist. Soc.* 1869), and in conjunction with Huxley the fossils of the Barrow colliery in Kilkenny (*Geol. Mag.* vol. iii. 1865; *Trans. Royal Irish Acad.* vol. xxiv. 1871).

In 1867 Wright paid a six months' visit to the Seychelles; and, although his collecting apparatus was lost by shipwreck on the way out, he brought back an important collection of plants and animals (see *Annals and Mag. Nat. Hist.*; *Trans. Roy. Irish Acad.*). He spent the spring of 1868 in Sicily and the autumn of the same year in dredging off the coast of Portugal, describing his results in attractive papers.

In 1869 Wright was appointed professor of botany and keeper of the herbarium at Trinity College. As a teacher he was fluent, energetic, and thorough; but he bestowed his chief care upon the arrangement of the herbarium. His continued interest in zoology was shown by his 'Notes on Sponges,' especially those of Ireland (*Proc. Roy. Irish Acad.*; *Quarterly Journal of Microscop. Science*); in his revision of Figuier's 'Ocean World' for Messrs. Cassell in 1872; in his adaptation of the same author's 'Mammalia' in 1875; in the 'Concise Natural History' of 1885; and, above all, in his report, in conjunction with Dr. T. L. Studer, on the Alcyonaria of the Challenger expedition (vol. xxxi. 1880).

Elected to the council of the Royal Irish Academy in 1870, he acted as secretary from 1874 to 1877, and from 1883 to 1899, carefully supervising the publications. In 1883 he was awarded the Cunningham gold medal [see CUNNINGHAM, TIMOTHY].

Besides his professional studies Wright took a keen interest in archæology, and from 1900 to 1902 he was president of the Royal Society of Antiquaries of Ireland. He spent many vacations on the continent of Europe, and was lamed for life in a carriage accident in Switzerland. In politics he was a strong radical. Owing to heart weakness, he resigned his chair in 1904, but continued to superintend the herbarium, living in his rooms in Trinity

College and maintaining his interest in his varied studies. He died of bronchitis at Trinity College, Dublin, on 2 March 1910, and was buried at Mount Jerome, Dublin. He married in 1872 Emily, second daughter of Colonel Ponsonby Shaw; she died without issue in 1886.

[The Irish Naturalist, xix. (1910), 61–63 (with portrait); Royal Irish Academy, Abstracts of Minutes, 1909–10, 16 March; Mrs. Janet Ross's The Fourth Generation, 1912.]

G. S. B.

WRIGHT, Sir ROBERT SAMUEL (1839–1904), judge, born at Litton rectory on 20 Jan. 1839, was eldest son of Henry Edward Wright, rector of Litton, Somerset, by his wife, a daughter of the Rev. Edward Edgell. Educated at King's School, Bruton, Somerset, he matriculated as a commoner at Balliol College, Oxford, on 6 June 1856, at the early age of seventeen, and in 1857 was elected a scholar. Benjamin Jowett was his tutor, and he became one of Jowett's favourite pupils, continuing his intimate friend until Jowett's death, which took place at Wright's house, Hadley Park, in 1893. In the Easter term, 1859, Wright was placed in the first class in classical moderations, and in Michaelmas term, 1860, in the first class in the final classical school. He obtained university prizes for Latin verse in 1859 and for the English essay in 1861, and the Arnold essay, his subject being 'The Danube as connected with the Civilisation of Central Europe,' in 1862. He was Craven scholar in 1861, and in the same year was elected to a fellowship at Oriel College. This he held until 1880. He graduated B.A. in 1861, proceeding B.C.L. in 1863, and M.A. in 1864. He remained at Oxford until 1865, occupying himself in private tuition and classical studies. During this period he published the 'Golden Treasury of Ancient Greek Poetry' (1866), subsequently revised (in 1889) by Evelyn Abbott [q. v. Suppl. II], and in collaboration with J. E. L. Shadwell, Christ Church, the 'Golden Treasury of Ancient Greek Prose' (1870). In 1882 he was elected honorary fellow of Oriel. Wright had become a student of the Inner Temple on 20 Nov. 1861, and was called to the bar on 9 June 1865. Removing to London, he speedily obtained a considerable junior practice both in London and on the northern circuit. In 1873 he published a short volume on the 'Law of Conspiracies and Agreements,' and in 1884, together with Henry Hobhouse, an 'Outline of Local Government and Taxation in England.' Subsequently he had occasion to study the thorny subject of possession in connection with the criminal law, and as Sir Frederick Pollock, then Corpus professor at Oxford, was doing the same thing in preparation for his standard work on the law of tort, they jointly produced a volume entitled 'An Essay on Possession in the Common Law' (Oxford, 1888). It is 'a composite not a joint work.' Wright's share, part iii., which is nearly half of the whole, relates to possession in respect of criminal offences against property. The subject is one of extreme complexity and much difficulty. Wright treats it with abundant learning and ingenuity, and though his essay is not sufficiently lucid or complete to take a place among the greatest legal treatises of the century, it may be said that there was not previously, and has not been since, any work containing a fuller or more accurate statement of this particular part of the law. In 1883 the attorney-general Henry (afterwards Lord) James [q. v. Suppl. II] appointed Wright junior counsel to the treasury ('attorney-general's devil') in succession to (Sir) Archibald Levin Smith [q. v. Suppl. II]. In that capacity he appeared as one of the counsel for the crown in some of the prosecutions of Fenian conspirators for treason-felony in connection with the dynamite explosions of 1883 and 1884, but the bulk of his labours was little known to the general public. Wright stood without success as a liberal candidate for parliament in 1884 for Norwich and in 1886 for Stepney. In Dec. 1890 Lord Halsbury appointed him a judge of the queen's bench division in succession to Baron Huddleston. His simple tastes and radical opinions made him unwilling to accept the honour of knighthood, but it was conferred in April 1891. In June 1891 Wright became a bencher of the Inner Temple.

Wright's great learning and his swift and keen intelligence were well fitted for a court of appeal. For real success in a court of first instance he lacked patience, stolidity, and willingness to listen without open disagreement to contentions which appeared to him to be groundless. He always thought quickly and often spoke hastily, not infrequently committing himself thereby to blunders which a man of less ability but more equable temper would easily have avoided. Both in criminal work and at *nisi prius* these weaknesses considerably impaired his efficiency. On the other hand he had not many superiors in the decision of a difficult question of law involving the examination and comparison of a great mass of authorities. His judgment in The British South Africa Company *v.* Companhia de Moçambique, which was reversed by the court of appeal, and restored, with strong expressions of approval, by the House of Lords, is an example of his judicial power at its best. He was one of the judges requested by the House of Lords to give their opinions in the great case of Allen *v.* Flood in 1897. He and Mr. Justice Mathew differed from their brethren in holding that the trade combination in question was not made unlawful by the fact that it was intended to injure and did injure another person for the benefit of those who combined. The House of Lords upheld this view.

Wright's ability and possibly his limitations led to his frequent selection to sit as an extra chancery judge, as judge in bankruptcy, and as the judicial member of the railway commission. It was in the first-named of these capacities that he decided in Jan. 1893 the important case of Samuel Hope and Arnold Morley *v.* William H. Loughnan and his brothers, in which, with the approval of the profession and the public, he set aside gifts amounting to nearly 150,000*l.*

During the later years of his life Wright lived at Headley Park, Hampshire, where he carried on the affairs of his home farm in the form of a small republic with himself as permanent president. Seated under a tree, he would invite the opinions of his labourers, and decide upon the course to be pursued in greater or less accordance with the sentiments of the meeting. He had the tastes of a sportsman, and being fond of shooting it was his habit to sue poachers in the county court for nominal damages and an injunction—the breach of which would lead to the imprisonment which he considered too harsh a penalty to be indiscriminately enforced.

After an operation in May 1904 Wright sent his resignation to the lord chancellor, but in the hope of his recovery it was not accepted. He was not, however, able to resume his labours, and died at Headley on 13 Aug. 1904, and was buried there. He married in 1891 Merriel Mabel Emily, daughter of the Rev. Richard Seymour Chermside, prebendary of Salisbury, and had two sons, of whom the younger, Michael Robert (*b.* 1901), survives.

A caricature appeared in 'Vanity Fair' in 1891.

[The Times, and Manchester Guardian, 15 Aug. 1904; Foster's Alumni Oxon.; Abbott and Campbell's Life of Jowett; personal knowledge.] H. S.

WRIGHT, WHITAKER (1845–1904), company promoter, was born in the north of England on 9 Feb. 1845, and at the age of twenty-one, equipped with some knowledge of inorganic chemistry and assaying, started as an assayer in the United States, and invested in a few mining shares in the west. He next bought a claim for 500 dollars, and by the sale of a half share in it covered all his outlay and provided working capital. The mine proved successful, and was the foundation of his fortune; to use his own words, 'after the first 10,000 dollars was made, the rest was easy.' He was one of the pioneers of the mining boom in 1879 at Leadville, where he made and lost two fortunes. Leaving Leadville, he acquired the Lake Valley mine in New Mexico, and built a branch railway to it. After these western adventures he came east and settled in Philadelphia, was for many years a member of the American Institute of Mining Engineers, and became chairman of the Philadelphia Mining Exchange; he was also a member of the Consolidated Stock Exchange of New York. At the age of thirty-one he was more than a millionaire. He had now resolved to retire from business, but his American career ended disastrously, owing to the failure of the Gunnison Iron and Coal Company, in which he was largely involved, and the great depreciation in other securities.

Returning to England in 1889, he brought out the Abaris Mining Corporation in 1891, but this enterprise gained little market or public attention, and was wound up in 1899. He became better known as a company promoter in 1894, when he floated the West Australian Exploring and Finance Corporation, a promoting concern. Next year he brought out a like venture, the London and Globe Finance Corporation. Both companies had for a time very prosperous careers. Wright's profits from these two undertakings were 238,436*l.* The times were favourable to Wright's special qualifications. He had personal knowledge of mining camps, could talk of them plausibly, and from his experience in Philadelphia knew the weak points of the average speculator. During 1896 the Lake View Consols was floated by the London and Globe with a capital of 250,000*l.* Other companies were formed for opening up mines in Western Australia, the most notable being Mainland Consols, Paddington Consols, and Wealth of Nations.

Early in 1897 he acquired the assets of the two companies, the London and Globe and the West Australian, and floated a new combination as the London and Globe Finance Corporation, of which he became the managing director. The new company had a capital of 2,000,000*l.* in 1*l.* shares, of which Wright received 605,000*l.* The names of the Marquis of Dufferin as chairman and of Lord Loch as a director were substantial assets; the shares went up to 2*l.*, and the promotion work of the new company was very profitable. It acquired the Ivanhoe mine at Kalgoorlie from a small colonial company with a capital of 50,000*l.* and refloated it in London with a capital of 1,000,000*l.* in 5*l.* shares, the issue being a great success. Meanwhile (in October 1897) Wright started the British America Corporation with a capital of 1,500,000*l.* to acquire mining interests in British Columbia and the Yukon region. This company and the Globe became jointly interested in floating the East and West Le Roy companies, the Rossland Great Western, Kootenay, Caledonia Copper, Nickel Corporation, Loddon Valley, and other companies, the shares of each reaching substantial premiums. Wright's personal gain from these operations was 50,000*l.*, apart from the profit obtained by his companies. In Feb. 1898 he started the Standard Exploration Company to take over the Paddington Consols, Wealth of Nations, and several other companies floated by the original undertakings, which had become unsuccessful.

Nearly all these undertakings were worked by one office (43 Lothbury), with a single staff of clerks, and were under Wright's direct control. The shares of the new London and Globe proved a popular instrument of speculation. The company constantly engaged in large market operations in shares of the companies under Wright's control, particularly the Lake View Consols. Alarming reports were occasionally spread as to the company's financial position; the Baker Street and Waterloo Railway Company, which was one of its promotions, was known to be a severe drag upon its resources. In spite, however, of evil reports, the Globe continued to pay small dividends at intervals until October 1899. During that year Lake View shares rose from 9*l.* to 28*l.* through the discovery of a rich patch of ore, the Globe making large profits in the shares. A sharp reaction soon set in, based on the knowledge that the rich find was exhausted. Wright, apparently misled as to the condition of the mine, made strenuous efforts to support the market. The results were disastrous to himself and to the company, which lost three-quarters of a million in Lake View shares in 1899. The crisis was reached on 28 Dec. 1900, when the Globe company announced its insolvency, and the Standard Exploration Company which was involved in the commitments of the Globe went also into liquidation. The disaster involved the failure of many members of the Stock Exchange, the liquidation of many subsidiary companies, including the British America Corporation, and the ruin of numerous small investors. The reports of the official receiver showed that the companies had long been on a false financial basis, the accounts having been manipulated in such a way as to conceal deficits, and the dividends paid by the Globe not having been earned but provided by means of loans from Wright and the other companies. The resources of practically all the undertakings under his control had been employed in his recent Stock Exchange operations.

In 1902 his fellow directors of the London and Globe Finance Corporation brought an action against the promoters of the Lake View syndicate for the recovery of 1,000,000*l.*, of which they had been deprived by misrepresentation. The case was heard before Lord Alverstone, lord chief justice, in June 1902. Wright was a chief witness for the plaintiffs. After a nine days' trial, a verdict was given for the defendants.

Meanwhile Wright had been examined before the official receiver in the London and Globe liquidation, but the public prosecutor refused to institute criminal proceedings. Public indignation was aroused, and on 19 Feb. 1902 an amendment to the address was moved in the House of Commons by Mr. George Lambert expressing regret that no prosecution had been instituted against the directors. The law officers stated that in the present state of the law a prosecution could not be confidently undertaken, but Sir Edward Carson, the solicitor-general, expressed his belief that a false balance-sheet had been issued. Mr. Balfour, the leader of the House of Commons, admitted the existence of 'deep and profound indignation' among the public, and promised that the law should be amended. Finally, Mr. John Flower, a creditor, obtained from Mr. Justice Buckley on 11 March 1903 an order for the official receiver to prosecute, and a warrant for the arrest of Wright was issued. Wright had sailed four days before from Havre to New York, where he was arrested by warrant on

15 March and imprisoned. After resisting extradition for some months by every legal artifice, he suddenly resolved on 6 July voluntarily to return to England, where he arrived on 5 August.

Protracted proceedings at the Guildhall ended in his committal for trial. The trial, which began on 11 Jan. 1904, was held for greater convenience at the law courts instead of at the Old Bailey. The prosecution was not under any of the Joint Stock Companies Acts, but under the Larceny Act of 1861. The issues were directed to the questions whether the balance-sheets and reports of the London and Globe Company for the years 1899 and 1900 were false in material particulars; whether they were false to the knowledge of Whitaker Wright; and if so, whether these false accounts and false reports were published for the purpose of deceiving shareholders or defrauding creditors or inducing other persons to become shareholders. The judge was Mr. Justice Bigham, afterwards Baron Mersey. (Sir) Rufus Isaacs, K.C., conducted the prosecution, and Wright was brilliantly defended by (Sir) John Lawson Walton [q. v. Suppl. II]. The prosecuting counsel alleged that 5,000,000*l.* capital had been lost in two years, not a penny of which had been returned to the shareholders, whilst debts of about 3,000,000*l.* had been contracted besides. On 26 Jan. Wright was convicted on all counts and sentenced to the maximum penalty of seven years' penal servitude. After receiving sentence he was talking with his legal adviser Sir George Henry Lewis [q. v. Suppl. II] in the consultation room, when he suddenly died. At the inquest on 28 Jan. it was shown that he poisoned himself with cyanide of potassium. He was buried at Witley, and left a widow, a son, and two daughters.

Wright acquired for his country residence a large estate at Lea Park, Witley, Surrey, four miles from Godalming. There he surrounded himself with extravagant luxuries, erecting a well-equipped observatory and a private theatre. He constantly devised new effects in architecture and landscape gardening; hills which obstructed views were levelled, and armies of labourers employed to fill up old lakes and dig new ones. He was fond of billiards, which he played in a saloon constructed of glass beneath one of the wide sheets of water in his grounds. After Wright's death the property was acquired by Lord Pirrie. Wright had also a palatial residence in Park Lane, filled with art treasures. As a yachtsman he gained great notoriety by his yawl Sybarita. Wright's persuasive manners and his abilities as a public speaker were turned to good account at shareholders' meetings, and inspired confidence in his most disastrous undertakings. He bequeathed his estate valued at 148,200*l.* to his wife Anna Edith, whom he made sole executrix.

[Annual Register, 1903, p. 24; 1904, p. 17; Saturday Review, xcvii. 133; Illustr. London News, 30 Jan. 1904; The Times, 20–27 Jan. 1904; Financial Times, 27 Jan. 1904; Star, 27 Jan. 1904; Blackwood's Magazine, clxxv, 397.]

WROTH, WARWICK WILLIAM (1858–1911), numismatist, born at Clerkenwell, London, on 24 Aug. 1858, was eldest son in the family of four sons and four daughters of Warwick Reed Wroth (1824–1867), vicar from 1854 to his death of St. Philip's, Clerkenwell (see preface to WROTH's *Sermons, chiefly Mystical*, edited by J. E. Vaux, 1869). His mother was Sophia, youngest daughter of Thomas Brooks, of Ealing, Middlesex.

After education at the King's School, Canterbury, where he had a sound classical training, Wroth joined the staff of the British Museum as an assistant in the medal room on 22 July 1878, and held the post for life. He mainly devoted his energies to a study of Greek coins, and made a high reputation by his continuation of the catalogues of Greek coins at the museum which his predecessors, S. L. Poole, Mr. Barclay Head, and Mr. Percy Gardner, had begun. Wroth's catalogues, in six volumes all illustrated with many plates, dealt with coins of Eastern Greece beginning with those of 'Crete and the Ægean Islands' (1886), and proceeding with those of 'Pontus, Paphlagonia, Bithynia and the Kingdom of Bosporus' (1889); of 'Mysia' (1892); of 'Galatia, Cappadocia and Syria' (1899); of 'Troas, Æolis and Lesbos' (1894); and finally of 'Parthia' (1903). Subsequently he prepared catalogues, which also took standard rank, of 'Imperial Byzantine Coins' (2 vols. 1908) and of the coins of the 'Vandals, Ostrogoths and Lombards' (1911). Before his death he returned to Greek coinage, and was preparing to catalogue that of Philip II and Alexander III, and the later kings of Macedon.

Outside his numismatic work at the museum, Wroth made between 1882 and 1907 valuable contributions to the 'Journal of Hellenic Studies' and the 'Numismatic Chronicle.' To the 'Journal' he contributed in 1882 'A Statue of the Youthful

Asklepios' (pp. 46–52) and 'Telesphoros at Dionysopolis' (pp. 282–300). For the 'Numismatic Chronicle' he wrote also in 1882 on 'Asklepios and the Coins of Pergamon' (pp. 1–51); on 'Cretan Coins' in 1884 (pp. 1–58), and several papers on 'Greek Coins acquired by the British Museum, 1887–1902' (1888–1904). He also co-operated with Mr. Barclay Head in 1911 in a new edition of Head's 'Historia Numorum' (1887). Wroth was a regular contributor of memoirs, chiefly of medallists, to this Dictionary from its inception in 1885 until his death.

Wroth's interests were not confined to numismatics. He was an eager student of English literature, especially of the eighteenth century; he had a wide knowledge of the history of London, of which he owned a good collection of prints. With his brother, Arthur Edgar Wroth, he published in 1896 'The London Pleasure Gardens of the Eighteenth Century,' a scholarly and pleasantly written embodiment of many years' research. This was supplemented by a paper on 'Tickets of Vauxhall Gardens' (*Numismatic Chron.* 1898, pp. 73–92) and by 'Cremorne and the Later London Gardens' (1907). He was elected F.S.A. on 7 March 1889.

Wroth died unmarried at his residence at West Kensington after an operation for peritonitis on 26 Sept. 1911.

[The Times, 28 and 29 Sept. 1911; Brit. Mus. Cat.; private information; Athenæum, 30 Sept. 1911; Numismatic Chron. 1912, 107 seq. (memoir by G. F. Hill with bibliography by J. Allan).] W. B. O.

WROTTESLEY, GEORGE (1827–1909), soldier and antiquary, born at 5 Powys Place, London, on 15 June 1827, was third son of John, second baron Wrottesley [q. v.], by Sophia Elizabeth, third daughter of Thomas Giffard of Chillington. He was educated at the Blackheath Proprietary School. Entering the Royal Military Academy, Woolwich, in 1842, he obtained a commission in the royal engineers in 1845. He was ordered almost immediately to Ireland in connection with the famine relief works, and thence in 1847 to Gibraltar, where he remained till 1849. In 1852 he joined the ordnance survey. He took part in the Crimean war, sailing for the Dardanelles on survey work in January 1854. With Sir John Fox Burgoyne [q. v.] he went on the mission to Omar Pàscha at Shumla. He afterwards became A.D.C. to General Tylden, officer commanding royal engineers in Turkey, and in this capacity he accompanied Lord Raglan to Varna. He was engaged at Varna on plans and reports on the Turkish lines of retreat from the Danube, when he was struck down by dysentery, which ultimately caused complete deafness. In October 1854 he was invalided home and promoted to captain. On Sir John Burgoyne's return from the Crimea to the war office in 1855 as inspector-general of fortifications, Captain Wrottesley was appointed his A.D.C., and he stayed with the field marshal, acting continually as his secretary on commissions and confidential adviser till Burgoyne's retirement in 1868. Wrottesley accompanied Burgoyne to Paris in 1855, when he presented to Napoleon III the funeral car of Napoleon I from St. Helena. He was secretary of the defence committee of the war office, 1856–60; of the committee on the influence of rifled artillery on works of defence, 1859; and of the committee on the storage of powder in magazines, 1865. In 1863, being then a major, he presided over the committee on army signalling which introduced the use of the Morse system. He was made lieutenant-colonel in 1868, and on Burgoyne's retirement took over the command of the engineers at Shorncliffe. In 1872 he commanded at Greenwich, and in 1875 became officer commanding R.E. at Woolwich, retiring from the army in 1881 with the rank of major-general.

Wrottesley collected and edited 'The Military Opinions of Gen. Sir J. F. Burgoyne' in 1859; and published 'Life and Correspondence of Field Marshal Sir J. F. Burgoyne' (2 vols.) in 1873. But his principal literary interest lay in genealogy. In 1879 he founded with Robert William Eyton [q. v.] the William Salt Society, of which he was honorary secretary from 1879 till his death. His abundant genealogical labour is embodied in the thirty-four volumes of the 'Staffordshire Collections' of the society. His most important contributions were those on the 'Liber Niger' (1880), his 'Pleas of the Forest' (1884), the 'Military Service of Knights in the 13th and 14th centuries, Crecy and Calais' (1897). The last, together with 'Pedigrees from the Plea Rolls,' 'The Giffards from the Conquest' (1902), 'The Wrottesleys of Wrottesley' (1903), 'The Okeovers of Okeover' (1904), and 'The Bagots of Bagots Bromley' (1908), were republished separately. These four family histories are so contrived as to form national histories in miniature. Wrottesley shares with Eyton the credit of initiating the modern method of genealogy. In comparing the two Mr. J. Horace Round says: 'Wrottesley's own critical sense was, I think, more developed . . . for no genealogist, perhaps, could claim with better reason that he placed truth foremost.' He had, too, that other virtue of the new school, the power of tacking on private history to public events in such a way as to give to the narration its reality and significance. He died on 4 March 1909, and is buried in the Wrottesley vault in Tettenhall church. He married (1) on 7 Jan. 1854 Margaret Anne, daughter of Sir John Fox Burgoyne; she died on 3 May 1883; and (2) on 21 Feb. 1889 Nina Margaret, daughter of John William Philips of Heybridge, Staffordshire, who survived him. He had no issue by either marriage.

[Salt Society, vols. i.–xviii. and i.–xii. n.s.; Genealogist, n.s. xxvi. 1909; Burgoyne's Life, 1873; J. H. Round, Staff. Cols. vol. 1910.]

J. C. W.

WYLLIE, Sir WILLIAM HUTT CURZON (1848–1909), lieutenant-colonel in the Indian army and of the government of India foreign department, born at Cheltenham on 5 Oct. 1848, was third and youngest son of the five children of General Sir William Wyllie, G.C.B. [q. v.], by Amelia, daughter of Richards Hutt of Appley, Isle of Wight, and niece of Captain John Hutt, R.N. [q. v.]. Both his brothers served in India—John William Shaw Wyllie [q. v.] and Francis Robert Shaw Wyllie, some time under-secretary to the government of Bombay.

Educated at Marlborough and Sandhurst, he entered the army in Oct. 1866 as ensign 106th foot (the Durham light infantry). Arriving in India Feb. 1867, he joined the Indian staff corps in 1869, and was posted to the 2nd Gurkha regt. (the Sirmoor rifles), now the 2nd King Edward's own Gurkhas. He was specially selected for civil and political employment in 1870, when he was appointed to the Oudh commission and served under General Barrow and Sir George Couper [q. v. Suppl. II].

In Jan. 1879 he was transferred to the foreign department, serving successively as cantonment magistrate of Nasirabad, assistant-commissioner in Ajmer-Merwara, and assistant to the governor-general's agent in Baluchistan, Sir Robert Groves Sandeman [q. v.]. He went through the Afghan campaign of 1878–80, including the march on Kandahar, with Major-general Sir Robert Phayre. He received the medal and was mentioned in the viceroy's despatches. After the war he was military secretary to his brother-in-law, William Patrick Adam, governor of Madras [q. v.], from Dec. 1880 until Adam's death in the following May, and until Nov. 1881 he was private secretary to Mr. William Hudleston (acting governor).

He married on 29 December 1881 Katharine Georgiana, second daughter of David Fremantle Carmichael, I.C.S., then member of the council, Madras, who survives him.

Wyllie had charge of Mulhar Rao, the ex-Gaekwar of Baroda, from Dec. 1881 to Nov. 1882. He then became assistant resident at Haiderabad. Subsequently he was assistant commissioner, Ajmer-Merwara, 1883; first assistant in Rajputana, 1884; additional political agent, Kotah, April 1885; boundary settlement officer, Meywar-Marwar border, Nov. 1886; political agent, Kotah, Jan. 1889; officiating commissioner of Ajmer, July 1891; officiating political agent, Jhallawar, in addition to Kotah, 1891–2; resident western states of Rajputana (Jodhpur), 1892–3; resident in Meywar (Udaipur), Nov. 1893 to Feb. 1898, when he officiated as resident in Nepal. Later in 1898 he attained one of the highest appointments in the service, viz. that of agent to the governor-general in central India. In May 1900 he was transferred in the same capacity to Rajputana, where he remained during the rest of his service in India. He was made C.I.E. in 1881, and he attained his lieutenant-colonelcy in 1892.

Throughout his long and varied services in the native states of India, and more especially in Rajputana, where seventeen of the most strenuous years of his life were spent, he gained by his unfailing courtesy, his charm of manner, and above all by his high character and strength of purpose, the most remarkable influence over the chiefs and officials of the principalities under his administrative charge. In addition Wyllie had the reputation, so dear to all Rajputs, of a keen sportsman and a skilful and daring rider, who held as a trophy the blue riband of Indian sportsmen, the Hog-hunters' Ganges cup, which he won in Oudh in April 1875.

His example stimulated all who served under him, and it was owing to his energy and to the confidence placed in him by the princes and people of Rajputana that the calamity of famine during the years 1899–1900 was successfully overcome by the measures of relief which he organised.

In March 1901 he came home on being selected by Lord George Hamilton for the post of political aide-de-camp to the secretary of state for India. His knowledge of India and long association with the ruling chiefs and their courts admirably fitted him for the important and often delicate duties of the office, which included that of advising the secretary of state for India on political questions relating to the native states. Arrangements for the reception of Indian magnates at the English court were in his charge, and heavy work devolved upon him at King Edward VII's coronation in 1902, in which year he received the decorations of K.C.I.E. and M.V.O. He became C.V.O. in June 1907.

His official position brought him into close contact with Indian students, in whose welfare he was always deeply interested. He also took an active part in the work of associations and charities for the benefit of Indians. To these objects he devoted himself unsparingly.

It was while attending, with Lady Wyllie, an entertainment given to Indians by the National Indian Association at the Imperial Institute, London, on the night of 1 July 1909, that Wyllie was assassinated, almost under the eyes of his wife, by Madho Lal Dhingra, a Punjabi student, who suddenly fired at him with a revolver, killing him instantly. This insane outrage upon an innocent and true friend of Indians was the precursor of similar crimes committed in India. Dr. Cawas Lalcaca, a Parsi physician of Shanghai, who bravely interposed to save Wyllie, was also mortally wounded. Dhingra was convicted of the double crime at the Central Criminal Court on 23 July, and was hanged at Pentonville prison on 17 August.

Wyllie's tragic death was felt as deeply in India as at home. Flags were put at half-mast, and public offices were closed throughout Rajputana and central India on reception of the news; and on the day of Wyllie's funeral (in Richmond cemetery) a salute of thirteen guns was fired from the palace fortresses of Rajputana. Viscount Morley, the secretary of state in council, recorded 'his high appreciation of Wyllie's admirable services,' and his 'profound sense of the personal loss' sustained by himself and his colleagues 'by the blind, atrocious crime.' He also granted a special pension of 500*l.* to Lady Wyllie 'in recognition of her husband's long and excellent service to the state, and in view of the circumstances in which he met his death.' Memorial funds were raised both in England and in India. From the English fund a marble tablet erected in the crypt of St. Paul's Cathedral was unveiled by Earl Roberts on 19 Oct. 1910, in the presence, among others, of the three successive secretaries of state (Lord George Hamilton, Viscounts Midleton and Morley) whom Wyllie had served at the India office. An inscription beneath a portrait medallion was written by Lord Curzon of Kedleston. The balance, 2551*l.*, the 'Curzon Wyllie memorial fund,' was entrusted to the Strangers' Home for Asiatics, Limehouse, on the governing body of which he had served. A brass tablet was also placed in the central hall of the home. At Marlborough College there was founded a Curzon Wyllie memorial medal to be given annually to the most efficient member of the officers' training corps. In India the Curzon Wyllie Central Memorial Fund committee have erected at a cost of 2000*l.* a marble *aramgarh* (place of rest) in Ajmer, Rajputana, to provide shade and rest and water for men and animals. A portrait by Mr. Herbert A. Olivier, exhibited at the Royal Academy of 1910, was presented to Lady Wyllie by the same committee; a replica has been placed in the Mayo college for chiefs at Ajmer. Local memorials have also been instituted in many of the states of Rajputana and central India.

[India List, 1909; Indian Magazine and Review, August 1909; The Times, 3, 4, 5, 7, 24 July and 18 Aug. 1909; 20 Oct. 1910; 13 March 1911, and other dates; Annual Reports, Strangers' Home for Asiatics, 1909 and 1910; Homeward Mail, 3 July 1911; personal knowledge.] F. H. B.

WYON, ALLAN (1843–1907), medallist and seal-engraver, born in 1843, was the son of Benjamin Wyon [q. v.], chief engraver of the royal seals, and the younger brother of Joseph Shepherd Wyon [q. v.] and Alfred Benjamin Wyon [q. v.]. He was early taught the arts hereditary in his family, and for a time aided his brother Joseph in his medal-work. From 1884 till his death he carried on in London the business of the Wyon firm of medallists and engravers founded by his grandfather, Thomas Wyon the elder [q. v.]. From 1884 to 1901 he held the post of engraver of the royal seals, a post that had been successively held by his father and his two elder brothers. He made the episcopal seals for the archbishops of Canterbury and York; the seal for the secretary of Scotland in 1889, and the great seal of Ireland in 1890. The great seal of Queen Victoria of 1899 was the work of George William De Saulles [q. v. Suppl. II]. Among Wyon's medals may be mentioned: Sir Joseph Whitworth (commemorating the Whitworth scholarships founded 1868); the Royal Jubilee medal of 1887; Charles Darwin (Royal

Society medal, first awarded 1890); Professor Max Müller, *circ.* 1902. He signed in full 'Allan Wyon.'

Wyon was a fellow of the Society of Antiquaries (elected 1889) and of the Numismatic Society of London (elected 1885), and was at one time treasurer and vice-president of the British Archæological Association. He compiled and published 'The Great Seals of England' (1887, with 55 plates), a work begun by his brother Alfred. Wyon died at Hampstead on 25 Jan. 1907. He married in 1880 Harriet, daughter of G. W. Gairdner of Hampstead, and had three daughters and two sons; the elder son is Mr. Allan G. Wyon, the medallist, seal-engraver, and sculptor.

[Numismatic Chronicle, 1907, p. 32; Proc. Soc. Antiquaries, April 1907, p. 439; Manchester Courier, 26 Jan. 1907; Hocking, Catal. of Coins, etc., in Royal Mint, vol. ii.; information from Mr. Allan G. Wyon.] W. W.

Y

YEO, GERALD FRANCIS (1845–1909), physiologist, born in Dublin on 19 January 1845, was second son of Henry Yeo of Ceanchor, Howth, J.P., clerk of the rules, court of exchequer, by his wife Jane, daughter of Captain Ferns. Yeo was educated at the royal school, Dungannon, and at Trinity College, Dublin, where he graduated moderator in natural science in 1866, proceeding M.B. and M.Ch. in 1867. In 1868 he gained the gold medal of the Dublin Pathological Society for an essay on renal disease. After studying abroad for three years, a year each in Paris, Berlin, and Vienna, he proceeded M.D. at Dublin in 1871, and became next year M.R.C.P. and M.R.C.S.Ireland. For two years he taught physiology in the Carmichael school of medicine in Dublin. He was appointed professor of physiology in King's College, London, in 1875, and in 1877 assistant surgeon to King's College Hospital, becoming F.R.C.S.England in 1878. He delivered for the College of Surgeons the Arris and Gale lectures on anatomy and physiology in 1880–2. Yeo did much good work with (Sir) David Ferrier, a fellow professor of neuro-pathology at King's College, on the cerebral localisation in monkeys, but he was best known from 1875 as the first secretary of the Physiological Society, which was originally a dining club of the working physiologists of Great Britain. Yeo conducted the society's affairs with tact and energy until his resignation in 1889, when he was presented with a valuable souvenir of plate. In conjunction with Professor Krönecker of Berne, Yeo inaugurated the international physiological congresses which are held triennially; the first met at Basle in 1891.

Yeo was elected F.R.S. in 1889. He resigned his chair of physiology at King's College in 1890 and received the title of emeritus professor. He then retired to Totnes, Devonshire, and later to Fowey, where he devoted himself to yachting, fishing, and gardening. He died at Austin's Close, Harbertonford, Devonshire, on 1 May 1909. Yeo married (1) in 1873 Charlotte, only daughter of Isaac Kitchin of Rockferry, Cheshire (she died without issue in 1884); (2) in 1886 Augusta Frances, second daughter of Edward Hunt of Thomastown, co. Kilkenny, by whom he had one son.

Yeo, who was a fluent speaker with a rich brogue, was good-natured, generous, and full of common sense.

His 'Manual of Physiology for the Use of Students of Medicine' (1884; 6th edit. 1894) was a useful and popular textbook. He contributed numerous scientific papers to the 'Proceedings and Transactions of the Royal Society' and to the 'Journal of Physiology.'

[Cameron's History of the Royal College of Surgeons of Ireland, Dublin, 1886, p. 682; Brit. Med. Journal, 1909, i. 1158; Dublin Journal of Medical Science, vol. cxxvii. 1909 ad fin.; personal knowledge.] D'A. P.

YONGE, CHARLOTTE MARY (1823–1901), novelist, and story-teller for children, born at Otterbourne, near Winchester, on 11 Aug., 1823, was daughter of William Crawley Yonge, J.P.(1795–1854), by his wife Frances Mary (*d.* 1868), daughter of Thomas Bargus, vicar of Barkway, Hertfordshire. The only other child was a son, Julian Bargus (*b.* 31 Jan. 1831). Her father's family was of old standing in Devonshire, and through an intermarriage in 1746 with Elizabeth, daughter of George Duke of Otterton, was allied with the large families of Coleridge and Patteson, both of whom descended from Frances (*d.* 1831), wife of James Coleridge and daughter and co-heiress of Robert Duke, of Otterton.

The father was fifth son of Duke Yonge, vicar of Cornwood, near Dartmoor; he left the army (52nd regt.) at twenty-seven, after serving in the Peninsular war and at Waterloo, in order to marry Miss Bargus, whose mother refused to allow her daughter to be the wife of a soldier. Charlotte was brought up on her parents' little estate at Otterbourne, where her father, an earnest churchman and a magistrate, interested himself in the church and the parochial schools, then a new feature in English villages. An only girl, she paid yearly visits to her many Yonge cousins in Devonshire. According to her own account, she was born clumsy, inaccurate, inattentive, and at no time of her life could she keep accounts. Most of her education was derived from her father, who believed in higher education for women but deprecated any liberty for them. He instructed her in mathematics, Latin, and Greek, while tutors taught her modern languages, including Spanish. She was also well versed in conchology and botany. Following her father's example of devotion to the church, she began at seven to teach in the village Sunday school, and continued the practice without intermission for seventy-one years. The earliest of her stories, 'The Château de Melville,' originally written as an exercise in French and printed when she was fifteen, was sold for the benefit of the village school.

In 1835, Keble's appointment to the living of Hursley (to which the parish of Otterbourne was then joined) brought into Charlotte's life a dominant influence. Keble imbued her with his enthusiasm for the Oxford movement. During 1837–9 she saw much of him and his wife, while her father was in constant communication with him over the building of Otterbourne church. Keble quickly discovered Miss Yonge's gifts and urged her to bring home to the uneducated, no less than to the educated, the tenets of his faith in the form of fiction. An older friend, Marianne Dyson, aided her in her first experiments, the manuscripts of which were rigorously revised by Keble. He allowed no allusion to drunkenness or insanity, and when a character in Miss Yonge's story of 'Heartsease' referred to the heart as 'a machine for pumping blood' he erased it as 'coarse'; while Mrs. Keble substituted 'jackanapes' for 'coxcomb,' as a fitter term of insult in the 'Heir of Redclyffe.' Before the publication of her first book, a family conclave decided that it would be wrong for her, a woman, to become a professed author, unless her earnings were devoted to the support of some good object.

The first of the tales which, in such conditions, was issued to the public was 'Abbey Church, or Self-Control and Self-Conceit' (1844), but 'Henrietta's Wish, or Domineering,' and 'Kenneth, or the Rear-guard of the Grand Army' (both 1850) secured a wider public, although the three volumes appeared anonymously. It was in 1853 that the appearance of 'The Heir of Redclyffe' brought her a genuine popular success; she gave her profits to Bishop Selwyn to provide a schooner, The Southern Cross, for the Melanesian mission. 'The fear that the book should be felt to be too daring' was not realised; it perfectly satisfied the religious fervour of the period, and its tendency to self-analysis. A twenty-second edition was reached in 1876, and it was reprinted numberless times. Thenceforth she described herself on her title-pages as 'author of "The Heir of Redclyffe."' There followed 'Heartsease' (1854) and 'The Daisy Chain' (1856), which were welcomed with especial warmth; 2000*l.* of the profits of 'The Daisy Chain' were devoted to a missionary college at Auckland, in New Zealand. Stories cast in the like mould were 'Dynevor Terrace' (1857); 'The Trial; more Links of the Daisy Chain' (1864); 'The Clever Woman of the Family' (1865); 'The Pillars of the House' (1873); 'Magnum Bonum' (1879). From an early date she wove historic legends into many of her stories, and her earliest historical romances included 'The Little Duke, or Richard the Fearless' (1854); 'The Lances of Lynwood' (1855); 'The Pigeon Pie: a Tale of Roundhead Times' (1860); 'The Prince and the Page: a Story of the Last Crusade' (1865); 'The Dove in the Eagle's Nest' (1866); and 'The Caged Lion' (1870). Through her sure command of character and her grasp of the details of domestic life Miss Yonge's fiction appealed to varied circles of readers. 'The Heir of Redclyffe' was eagerly read by officers in the Crimea. Charles Kingsley wept over 'Heartsease'; Lord Raglan, Guizot, Ampère, William Morris, D. G. Rossetti, were among her earlier, and Henry Sidgwick among her later admirers.

In 1851 Miss Yonge became the editor of a new periodical, the 'Monthly Packet,' which was designed to imbue young people, especially young women, with the principles of the Oxford movement. She edited the periodical without assistance for over thirty-eight years, and for nine years longer in partnership with Miss Christabel Coleridge. Later she also became the editor of 'Mothers in Council.' With fiction she soon combined serious work in history; and many novels, often in historical settings, as well as a long series of historical essays, appeared in the 'Monthly Packet.' Some among the eight series of her 'Cameos from English History' were collected respectively in 1868, 1871, 1876, 1879, 1883, 1887, 1890, 1896, and brought English history from the time of Rollo down to the end of the Stuarts. She provided serial lessons in history for younger students in 'Aunt Charlotte's Stories' of Bible, Greek, Roman, English, French, and German history, which came out between 1873 and 1878. To her interest in missions, which never diminished, she bore witness in 'Pioneers and Founders' (1871), and in a full life of Bishop Patteson in 1873.

Miss Yonge's literary work and religious worship formed her life. She taught Scripture daily in the village school, and attended service morning and evening in Otterbourne Church. She lived and died untroubled by religious doubts and ignored books of sceptical tendency. Workmen's institutes she condemned in one of her stories because the geological lectures given there imperilled religion. She only once travelled out of England, in 1869, when she visited Guizot and his daughter Madame de Witt, at Val Richer, near Lisieux in Normandy. Besides her kinsfolk, her dearest and lifelong friends were the members of the family of George Moberly [q. v.], headmaster of Winchester until 1866, and subsequently bishop of Salisbury; and in later days she became intimate with Miss Wordsworth, the Principal of Lady Margaret Hall, Oxford, and with some among the members of a little circle of young women which she had formed as early as 1859 for purposes of self-cultivation. This circle included Miss Christabel Coleridge, Miss Peard, and, for a short time, Mrs. Humphry Ward.

In 1854 her father had died, and in 1858, when her brother married, she and her mother moved from the larger house, which was his property, to a smaller home in the village of Elderfield. The death of her mother in 1868 and of her brother in 1892 deprived her of her nearest relatives. She lived much alone. Always very shy, she paid few visits and seldom called upon the villagers. But she overcame this timidity sufficiently to entertain occasional guests and to become a member of the diocesan council at Winchester. On her seventieth birthday, in 1893, subscribers to the 'Monthly Packet' presented her with 200*l.*, which she spent upon a lych-gate for the church at Otterbourne, and in 1899 a subscription was raised at Winchester High School to found in her honour a scholarship at Oxford or Cambridge. In her last and weakest story, 'Modern Broods' (1900), she tried to mirror the newer generation, with which she felt herself to be out of sympathy. Early in 1901 she contracted pleurisy, and died on 24 March. She was buried in Otterbourne churchyard at the foot of the memorial cross to Keble.

The many editions of Miss Yonge's historical tales, as well as of 'The Heir of Redclyffe' and 'The Daisy Chain,' testify to her permanence as a schoolroom classic. She published 160 separate books. Besides those works cited, mention may be made of: 1. 'Kings of England: a History for Young Children,' 1848. 2. 'Landmarks of History, Ancient, Medieval and Modern,' 3 pts. 1852–3–7. 3. 'History of Christian Names,' 2 vols. 1863. 4. 'The Book of Golden Deeds' ('Golden Treasury' series), 1864. 5. 'Eighteen Centuries of Beginnings of Church History,' 2 vols. 1876. 6. 'History of France' (in E. A. Freeman's 'Historical Course'), 1879. 7. 'Hannah More' ('Eminent Women' series), 1888. Miss Yonge also edited numerous translations from the French.

A portrait of Miss Yonge at the age of 20, by George Richmond, is in the possession of her niece, Miss Helen Yonge, at Eastleigh.

[Christabel Coleridge, Charlotte Mary Yonge, her Life and Letters (including a few chapters of Miss Yonge's Autobiography), 1903; Ethel Romanes, Charlotte Mary Yonge, an Appreciation; John Taylor Coleridge, Life of Keble; C. A. E. Moberly, Dulce Domum, 1911; Burke's Landed Gentry; articles in Church Quarterly, lvii. 1903–4, 337, and in National Review, Jan. and April 1861, p. 211; obituary notices in The Times, 26 March 1901, in Monthly Review, May 1901, and in Monthly Packet, May 1901.]

E. S.

YORKE, ALBERT EDWARD PHILIP HENRY, sixth Earl of Hardwicke (1867–1904), under-secretary of state for war, the only son of Charles Philip, fifth earl, by his wife Lady Sophia Wellesley, daughter of the first Earl Cowley, was born on 14 March 1867. The Prince of Wales, afterwards King Edward VII, was his godfather. Educated at Eton, he served as hon. attaché to the British embassy at Vienna from 1886 to 1891. In the following year he became a member of the London Stock Exchange, and, in 1897, a partner in the firm of Basil Montgomery & Co. In the same year he succeeded his father in the earldom. On

8 Feb. 1898 Hardwicke moved the address in the House of Lords, and his graceful speech favourably impressed Lord Salisbury. In that year he became an active member of the London County Council, representing West Marylebone as a moderate. In June 1900 he carried a motion condemning the erection of the statue of Cromwell in the precincts of the house (LUCY, *Diary of the Unionist Parliament*, pp. 366, seq.). In November 1900 he was offered by Lord Salisbury the under-secretaryship for India. Hardwicke accepted the appointment on condition that he should not take up his duties until the following year, by which time arrangements could be made for his becoming a sleeping partner in his firm. In the debate on the address, however, Lord Rosebery, wishing to assert a public principle, while styling Hardwicke 'the most promising member for his age in the House of Lords,' animadverted on his connection with the Stock Exchange (4 Dec.). Eight days afterwards Hardwicke gave a manly and spirited explanation, setting forth the facts of the case and stating that immediately after Lord Rosebery's attack he had placed his resignation in Lord Salisbury's hands, who declined to accept it (*Hansard*, 4th series, vol. lxxxviii. cols. 804–806). From the India office he was transferred to the war office as under-secretary in August 1902, and he moved the second reading of the militia and yeomanry bill for creating reserves for those forces. Returning to the India office, again as under-secretary, in the following year, he moved in a lucid speech in 1904 the second reading of the Indian councils bill, setting up a department of commerce and industry (*ibid.* vol. cxl. cols. 498–502). Those best qualified to form an opinion thought highly of his abilities.

In early life he was a bold rider in steeplechases. In 1898 he became principal proprietor of the 'Saturday Review.'

Hardwicke, who was a man of much personal charm, died suddenly at his house, 8 York Terrace, Regent's Park, on 29 Nov. 1904. A cartoon portrait by 'Spy' appeared in 'Vanity Fair' in 1901. He was unmarried, and was succeeded as seventh earl by his uncle, John Manners Yorke, formerly captain R.N., who had served in the Baltic and Crimean expeditions, and who died on 13 March 1909. The present and eighth earl is the eldest son of the seventh earl.

[The Times, 30 Nov. 1904; private information.] L. C. S.

YOUL, SIR JAMES ARNDELL (1811–1904), Tasmanian colonist, born at Cadi, New South Wales, on 28 Dec. 1811, was the son of John Youl, a Church of England clergyman, by his wife Jane Loder. As a child he accompanied his parents to Van Diemen's Land (now Tasmania), his father having been appointed in 1819 military chaplain at Port Dalrymple and first incumbent of St. John's, Launceston, in that colony. James Youl was sent to England to be educated at a private school near Romford, Essex, and returning to Van Diemen's Land took up his residence at Symmons Plains, a property he inherited on the death of his father in March 1827. There he became a successful agriculturist and county magistrate.

In 1854 he returned to England to reside permanently, and interested himself in Tasmanian and Australian affairs. From 1861 to 1863 he was agent in London for Tasmania, and for seven years was honorary secretary and treasurer of the Australian Association. In that capacity he was instrumental in inducing the imperial government to establish a mail service to Australia via the Red Sea, and in getting the Australian sovereign made legal tender throughout the British Dominions. He was acting agent-general for Tasmania from Feb. to Oct. 1888, and was one of the founders in 1868 of the Royal Colonial Institute, taking an active part in its management until his death.

But it is with the introduction of salmon and trout into the rivers of Tasmania and New Zealand that Youl's name is mainly associated. After patient and prolonged experiments and many failures he at length discovered the proper method of packing the ova for transmission on a long sea voyage, by placing them on charcoal and living moss with the roots attached, in perforated wooden boxes under blocks of ice, thus preserving the ova in a state of healthy vitality for more than 100 days.

In 1864 the first successful shipment to Tasmania was made. After some difficulty in obtaining ova and proper accommodation in a suitable vessel Messrs. Money Wigram & Sons placed 50 tons of space on the clipper ship Norfolk at Youl's disposal, and he was enabled to ship 100,000 salmon and 3000 trout ova in that vessel. The Norfolk arrived at Melbourne after a favourable voyage of 84 days. Some 4000 salmon ova were retained there, the remainder being transhipped to the government sloop Victoria and taken to Hobart. They were placed in the breeding ponds in the river Plenty on the ninety-first day after embarkation, and a fair proportion hatched out satisfactorily.

For several years afterwards Youl was engaged with others in sending out successful shipments of ova to Tasmania. He was also responsible for the first shipment of ova to Otago, New Zealand, in Jan. 1868, for which he received the thanks of the government of that colony and the special thanks and a piece of plate from the provincial council of Otago. In 1866 he was awarded the gold medal of the Société d'Acclimatation and in 1868 the medal of the Acclimatisation Society of Victoria.

In 1874 he was made C.M.G. and K.C.M.G. in 1891. He died on 5 June 1904 at his residence, Waratah House, Clapham Park, and was buried in Norwood cemetery.

Youl married twice: (1) on 9 July 1839, at Clarendon, Tasmania, Eliza, daughter of William Cox, who served in the Peninsular war and went afterwards with the 46th regiment to Australia and settled at Hobartville, New South Wales; she died on 4 Jan. 1881, leaving four sons and eight daughters; (2) on 30 Sept. 1882, Charlotte, widow of William Robinson of Caldecott House, Clapham Park, and younger daughter of Richard Williams of Philipville, Belgium.

[Burke's Colonial Gentry, vol. ii. 1895; The Times, 7 and 9 June 1904; Launceston (Tasmania) Examiner, 8 June 1904; Proceedings of the Royal Colonial Institute, vol. 35, 1903–4; Fenton's History of Tasmania, 1884; Nicols's Acclimatisation of the Salmonidæ at the Antipodes, 1882; Sir S. Wilson's Salmon at the Antipodes, 1879; Cannon's Historical Record of the Forty-sixth Regiment, 1851; information supplied by his daughter, Miss A. Youl.] C. A.

YOUNG, Mrs. CHARLES. [See Vezin, Mrs. Jane Elizabeth (1827–1902), actress.]

YOUNG, GEORGE, Lord Young (1819–1907), Scottish judge, born at Dumfries on 2 July 1819, was son of Alexander Young of Rosefield, Kirkcudbrightshire, procurator fiscal of Dumfriesshire, by his wife Marian, daughter of William Corsan of Dalwhat, Kirkcudbrightshire. After education at Dumfries Academy, he studied at Edinburgh University (where he was made LL.D. in 1871), joined the Scots Law Society on 21 Nov. 1838 (president 1842–3), and passed to the Scottish bar on 2 Dec. 1840. Successful from the first, he was soon one of the busiest juniors in the Parliament House. Appointed advocate depute in 1849, he became sheriff of Inverness in 1853. At the celebrated trial of Madeleine Smith for the murder of Emile L'Angelier (30 June–8 July 1857) he was junior counsel to John Inglis [q. v.], afterwards lord president, and the accused is said to have owed her acquittal largely to his skill in preparing the defence. In 1860 he was made sheriff of Haddington and Berwick, and in 1862 he succeeded Edward Maitland (raised to the bench as Lord Barcaple) as solicitor-general for Scotland in Lord Palmerston's government. His practice had now become enormous. He was retained as senior in almost every important case, frequently with James Moncreiff, first Baron Moncreiff [q. v. Suppl. I], as his opponent. He particularly excelled in the severe cross-examination of hostile witnesses, and in addressing juries his cool logic was often more than a match for the eloquence of Moncreiff.

In politics Young was a liberal, and continued solicitor-general in Lord Russell's government which came in after the death of Palmerston (October 1865). At the general election of 1865 he was returned for the Wigtown district. Out of office in 1867 and 1868, during the governments of Lord Derby and Disraeli, he became again solicitor-general on the formation of the Gladstone administration of December 1868. In the following year he succeeded James Moncreiff (when he was made lord justice clerk) as lord advocate. He was called to the English bar on 24 Nov. 1869 by special resolution of the Middle Temple, of which he was elected an honorary bencher on 17 Nov. 1871. In 1872 he was sworn of the privy council.

Young's management, as lord advocate, of Scottish business in parliament has been described as 'autocratic and masterful' (*Scotsman*, 23 May 1907). He was as severe with deputations as with witnesses in cross-examination, and alarmed the legal profession in Scotland by far-reaching schemes of law reform. He prepared a bill for the abolition of feudal tenure, and it was rumoured that he contemplated the abolition of the Court of Session. Nevertheless his legislative work was useful. He was the author of a Public Health Act for Scotland passed in 1871 (34 & 35 Vict. c. 38). He carried through parliament, in spite of considerable opposition from a party in Scotland which accused him of wishing to destroy religious teaching in elementary schools, the Scottish Education Act of 1872, which closed a long controversy by establishing elected school boards, and leaving it to each board to settle the religious question according to the wishes of the electors (35 & 36 Vict. c. 62). In 1873 his Law Agents Act set up a uniform standard of training for law agents in Scotland, and abolished exclusive privileges of practising in particular courts (36 & 37 Vict. c. 63).

At the general election of 1874, owing, it was thought, to resentment at his treatment of Henry Glassford Bell, sheriff of Lanarkshire [q. v.], over differences which had arisen between them, Young lost his election for the Wigtown district by two votes. Mark John Stewart (afterwards Sir M. J. Mactaggart Stewart) was declared successful. A scrutiny was demanded, and the election judges awarded the seat to Young, by one vote, on 29 May 1874. But he had already accepted a judgeship, and taken his seat with the title of Lord Young on the bench of the Court of Session (3 March 1874). On the return of the liberals to power in 1880 it was understood that he had offered to resign his judgeship, and become again lord advocate. John McLaren, Lord McLaren [q. v. Suppl. II], was appointed, and Young remained on the bench. Having been a judge for thirty-one years, he retired owing to failing health in April 1905. After a short illness, caused by a fall while walking in the Temple, he died in London on 21 May 1907, and was buried in St. John's episcopal churchyard at Edinburgh.

In his old age Lord Young was almost the last survivor of a generation which had walked the floor of the Parliament House when Alison was consulting authorities for his 'History of Europe' in the Advocates' Library below, and when Jeffrey and Cockburn were on the bench. He had come to the bar in the days of Lord Melbourne and Sir Robert Peel, and held office under Lord Russell and Lord Palmerston. It is believed that at the time of his death he was the oldest bencher of the Middle Temple. For many years he was a prominent figure in the social life of Edinburgh. He told good stories, and was famous for witty sayings. As a judge his powers were great; but his quickness of apprehension often made him impatient both with counsel and with his colleagues. He was too fond of taking the management of a case into his own hands; and it was largely owing to this defect that he was not conspicuously successful on the bench, though he fully retained his high reputation as a lawyer.

Young, who married in 1847 Janet (*d.* 1901), daughter of George Graham Bell of Crurie, Dumfriesshire, had a large family, of whom four sons, all in the legal profession, and six daughters survived him. Two portraits of him, by Sir George Reid and Lutyens respectively, are in the possession of his daughters, and a bust by Mrs. Wallace is in the Parliament House.

[Scotsman, 19 Feb. 1874, 12 and 23 May 1907; The Times, 23 May 1907; Records of Scots Law Society; Roll of the Faculty of Advocates; Notable Scottish Trials, Madeleine Smith, p. 286; Memoirs of Dr. Guthrie, ii. 294–305; Galloway Gazette, 13 Jan. 1872; Hansard, 3rd series, vol. 209, p. 250; Sir M. E. Grant-Duff's Notes from a Diary, ii. 181 *et passim.*]

G. W. T. O.

INDEX 1901-1911

A—E

INDEX 1901-1911

F—M

INDEX 1901–1911

N—Z